# Table

## Consonants

| Symbol | Keyword |
|---|---|
| p | **p**en |
| b | **b**ack |
| t | **t**en |
| d | **d**ay |
| k | **k**ey |
| g | **g**et |
| f | **f**at |
| v | **v**iew |
| θ | **th**ing |
| ð | **th**en |
| s | **s**oon |
| z | **z**ero |
| ʃ | **sh**ip |
| ʒ | plea**s**ure |
| h | **h**ot |
| x | lo**ch** |
| tʃ | **ch**eer |
| dʒ | **j**ump |
| m | su**m** |
| n | su**n** |
| ŋ | su**ng** |
| w | **w**et |
| l | **l**et |
| r | **r**ed |
| j | **y**et |

## Vowels

| | Symbol | Keyword |
|---|---|---|
| **short** | ɪ | b**i**t |
| | e | b**e**d |
| | æ | c**a**t |
| | ɒ | d**o**g *(BrE)* |
| | ʌ | b**u**t |
| | ʊ | p**u**t |
| | ə | **a**bout |
| | i | happ**y** |
| | u | act**u**ality |
| **long** | iː | sh**ee**p |
| | ɑː | f**a**ther |
| | ɒː | d**o**g *(AmE)* |
| | ɔː | f**our** |
| | uː | b**oo**t |
| | ɜː | b**ir**d |
| **diphthongs** | eɪ | m**a**ke |
| | aɪ | l**ie** |
| | ɔɪ | b**oy** |
| | əʊ | n**o**te *(BrE)* |
| | oʊ | n**o**te *(AmE)* |
| | aʊ | n**ow** |
| | ɪə | r**ea**l |
| | eə | h**air** *(BrE)* |
| | ʊə | s**ure** *(BrE)* |
| | uə | act**ua**l |
| | iə | pecul**ia**r |

## Special signs

| | |
|---|---|
| ‖ | separates British and American pronunciations, British on the left, American on the right |
| /ˈ/ | shows main stress |
| /ˌ/ | shows secondary stress |
| /◄/ | shows stress shift |
| /ᵻ/ | means that some speakers use /ɪ/ and some use /ə/ |
| /ᵿ/ | means that some speakers use /ʊ/ and some use /ə/ |
| /ə/ | means that /ə/ may or may not be used |

For more information on pronunciation see page xx

# LONGMAN

# DICTIONARY OF

# CONTEMPORARY

# ENGLISH

María Paula

Dell'Anerlina

Ríos

1998

The publishers and editorial team wish to thank the many people who have contributed advice to the making of the dictionary, in particular the Linglex Dictionary and Corpus Advisory Committee:

Lord Quirk (Chair)

Professor Douglas Biber, Rod Bolitho, Professor Gillian Brown, Professor David Crystal, Professor Geoffrey Leech, Dr Paul Meara, Philip Scholfield, Professor Peter Trudgill, Katie Wales, Professor John Wells

and also to Professor Yoshihiko Ikegami and the many teachers and students throughout the world who have given us feedback and advice, and helped in the piloting of the dictionary.

*Director*
Della Summers

*Editorial Director*
Adam Gadsby

*Associate Lexicographer*
Sue Engineer

*Usage Notes*
Phil Scholfield, Ingrid Freebairn

*Senior Editor (American English)*
Wendalyn Nichols

*Lexicographers (American English)*
Karen Cleveland Marwick, Elaine McGregor, Karen Stern

*Corpus development and computational analysis*
Steve Crowdy, Denise Denney, Keith Mardell, Duncan Pettigrew

*Frequency analysis and graphs*
Nick Ham, Brigitta Mittmann, Sylvia Shaw, Dewayne Crawford, Adrienne Gavin

*Computational Linguist*
Adam Kilgarriff

*Project Manager*
Alan Savill

*Production*
Clive McKeough

*Production Editors*
Sarah Gumbrell, Alison Steadman, Benjamin White

*Administrative Assistants*
Brenda Francis, Helen Spencer, Jane Whittle

*Managing Editor*
Michael Rundell

*Developmental Lexicographer*
Nick Ham

*Senior Editors (British English)*
Chris Fox, Patrick Gillard, Ted Jackson, Stella O'Shea

*Lexicographers (British English)*
Peter Blanchard, Pat Bulhosen, Emma Campbell, Jane Hansell, Lucy Hollingworth, Jill Leatherbarrow, Joanna Leigh, Sophie Leighton, Helen McClelland, Glennis Pye, Sylvia Shaw, Laura Wedgeworth and Evadne Adrian-Vallance, Andrew Delahunty, Sheila Dignen, Gilian Lazar, Fiona McIntosh, Carole Owen, Elaine Pollard, Valerie Smith, Penny Stock

*Pronunciation Editor*
Dinah Jackson

*Defining Vocabulary Research*
Patrick Snellings

*Design*
Jenny Fleet, Martin Raynor, Kathy Baxendale, Ken Brooks

*Illustrators*
Dave Bowyer, Colin Brown, David Browne, Andrew Clark, Bob Corley, Paul B Davies, Diane Fawsett, Sian Francis, Bob Harvey, Jason Horley, Bill Le Fever, Andrew Riley, Andy Walker, Ross Watton, Kevin White

*Keyboarders*
Pauline Savill, Michelle Kemp

# LONGMAN DICTIONARY OF CONTEMPORARY ENGLISH

**THIRD EDITION**

**Longman Group Ltd**
*Longman House, Burnt Mill, Harlow*
*Essex CM20 2JE, England*
*and Associated Companies throughout the World*



First published 1978
Second edition 1987
This edition 1995
5 7 9 10 8 6

British Library Cataloguing-in-Publication Data
a catalogue record for this book is
available from the British Library

ISBN
0 582 23751 3 (Cased edition)
0 582 23748 3 (Flexicover edition)
0 582 23750 5 (Paperback edition)
0 582 23749 1 (Low-priced edition)*
0 582 23747 5 (Handy edition)*
* available in certain markets only



The British National Corpus is a collaborative initiative carried out by Oxford University Press, Longman, Chambers Harrap, Oxford University Computing Services, Lancaster University's Unit for Computer Research in the English Language, and the British Library. The project received funding from the UK Department of Trade and Industry and the Science and Engineering Research Council and was supported by additional research grants from the British Academy and the British Library.

Set in Linotype Nimrod
By MFK Information Services Limited,
Hitchin, Herts.

Printed in Great Britain by Clays Ltd,
Bungay, Suffolk

**A bird in the hand is worth two in the bush.**
Más vale pájaro en mano que ciento volando.

**A cat in gloves catches no mice.**
Gato con guantes no caza ratones.

**A stitch in time saves nine.**
Más vale prevenir que curar.

**A word is enough to the wise.**
A buen entendedor, pocas palabras bastan.

**Absence makes the heart grow fonder.**
La ausencia alimenta al corazón.

**Actions speak louder than words.**
Los hechos valen más que las palabras.

**All cats are grey in the dark.**
Por la noche todos los gatos son pardos.

**All roads lead to Rome.**
Todos los caminos conducen a Roma.

**All that glitters is not gold.**
No es oro todo lo que reluce.

**All work and no play makes Jack a dull boy.**
Hay que divertirse y dejar de lado el trabajo por un rato.

**An apple a day keeps the doctor away.**
Más vale prevenir que curar.
**Appearances are deceptive.**
Las apariencias engañan.

**Barking dogs never bite.**
Perro ladrador, poco mordedor. / Perro que ladra no muerde.

**Better late than never.**
Más vale tarde que nunca.

**Better the devil you know than the devil you don't know.**
Más vale malo conocido que bueno por conocer.

**Birds of a feather flock together.**
Dios los cría y ellos se juntan.

**Blood is thicker than water.**
Los lazos familiares son más fuertes.

**Do what is right, come what may.**
Haz siempre lo correcto.

**Don't look a gift-horse in the mouth.**
A caballo regalado no le mires los dientes.

**Don't put all your eggs in one basket.**
No te lo juegues todo a una sola carta.

**Early to bed, early to rise,**
**makes the man healthy, wealthy and wise.**
A quien madruga, Dios lo ayuda.

**Every cloud has a silver lining.**
No hay mal que por bien no venga.

**Every law has its loophole.**
Hecha la ley, hecha la trampa.

**Every time the sheep bleats, it loses a mouthful.**
Oveja que bala, bocado pierde.

**Experience is the mother of knowledge.**
La experiencia es la madre de la ciencia.
**Give a dog a bad name and hang it.**
Hazte fama y échate a dormir. / Un perro maté y mataperros me llamaron.

**God tempers the wind to the shorn lamb.**
Dios aprieta pero no ahoga.

**Half a loaf is better than none.**
Algo es algo, peor es nada.

**You can't have your cake and eat it too.**
No se puede tener todo en la vida. / No puedes estar en misa y repicando.

**You have to take the rough with the smooth.**
Hay que tomar la vida como es. / Hay que estar a las duras y a las maduras.

**You scratch my back, I'll scratch yours.**
Hoy por ti, mañana por mí.

# Contents

**Hunt with cats and you catch only rats.**
Dime con quién andas y te diré quién eres.

**It never rains, but it pours.**
Las desgracias nunca vienen solas.

**It's good fishing in troubled waters.**
A río revuelto, ganancia de pescadores.

**It's no good crying over spilt milk.**
A lo hecho, pecho. / No hay que llorar sobre la leche derramada.

**It's the last straw that breaks the camel's back.**
Es la gota que colma el vaso.

**Let bygones be bygones.**
Lo pasado, pisado.

**Many hands make light work.**
Muchas manos hacen el trabajo ligero.
**Money is the root of all evil.**
El dinero es el camino de la perdición.

**More haste, less speed.**
Vísteme despacio que tengo prisa.

**Nothing ventured, nothing gained.**
Quien no arriesga, no gana. / Quien no se arriesga, no cruza la mar.

**One man's meat is another man's poison.**
Sobre gustos no hay nada escrito. / Para gustos, los colores.

**People who live in glass houses shouldn't throw stones.**
No hagas a los demás lo que no quieres que te hagan a ti.

**Politeness costs nothing.**
Lo cortés no quita lo valiente.

**Rome wasn't built in a day.**
Roma no se hizo en un día.

**Take care of the pennies/pence, and the pounds will take care of themselves.**
Ahorra la calderilla y tendrás dinero.

**The apple doesn't fall far from the tree.**
De tal palo, tal astilla.

**The die is cast.**
La suerte está echada.

**The early bird catches the worm.**
A quien madruga, Dios lo ayuda.

**The grass is always greener on the other side of the fence.**
Lo mejor siempre lo tiene el otro.

**The shoemaker's son goes always barefoot.**
En casa de herrero, cuchara de palo.

**To call a spade, a spade.**
Al pan, pan y al vino, vino.

**Too many cooks spoil the broth.**
Demasiados cocineros estropean el caldo. / Muchas manos en un plato hacen mucho garabato.

**Two in distress makes sorrow less.**
Las penas compartidas saben a menos.

**When in Rome, do as the Romans do.**
Donde fueres haz lo que vieres.

**When there's a will, there's a way.**
Querer es poder.

**While the cat's away, the mice will play.**
Cuando el gato no está, los ratones bailan.

# Preface

s of which its
red:

that the words
and that such
l from a wide
dealing with a
must embrace
re, and social
printed record
ubiquitous oral

hieve a greatly
ers has been in
exploiting such
ners has been
nglish Corpus
me in this new
*ry English*. In
DOCE is about

At the heart of
s ensuring that
porary use has
rgeon's scalpel.
he user of the
ithin the justly
ner refined and
vocabulary of
earners – even
h – can readily
f headwords in

ucratic phrase
used on official

CE users. It is
elves, obliging
enabling them
less left vague

to satisfy the
the forefront of
dictionary are
with a myriad
. These needs
mple of *marital*
tion shows the
cials – and they
uire about the

This same example illustrates another notable feature of the new LDOCE. It will not do to regard language as comprising simply a host of separate items called 'words'. Rather, a word tends to team up with one or more other words to constitute a *lexical unit*, and it is this lexical unit that assumes meaning. One such unit that shows "meaning" itself meaning something rather different from the way I have been using it in this Preface is "What's the meaning of *this*?" We should notice that, when used as a lexical unit, this question carries certain presuppositions: one, that it is not written but spoken (and usually spoken in indignation); two, that the referent of *this* will not be an unfamiliar word but an unacceptable situation.

A Preface is not of course the place to specify the whole range of features that mark a book, and I must reluctantly pass over many another of the learner needs addressed so splendidly by LDOCE. Among these is the grammatical information, for example, making the dictionary a tool not only for "decoding" (explaining what users have found obscure in material they have heard or read) but also for *encoding*. Thus learners are guided on how they can themselves organise the modal and aspectual items that cluster round the verb *to like* in the sentence: "I would have liked to have this dictionary when I was a student."

RANDOLPH QUIRK
(Professor the Lord Quirk, FBA)

Welcome to the third, completely new, edition of the Longman Dictionary of Contemporary English! In this dictionary, we have tried to provide new solutions to some problems that face teachers of English and students at intermediate to advanced level.

**Fast Access** – Students should not have to wade through a lot of irrelevant meanings, so all the definitions are in frequency order with the most common meanings first. Our new 'signposts', words or short phrases that distinguish the meanings of longer entries, act as a visual index to help the user access the meaning they want as quickly as possible.

**Spoken English** – Studying the spoken variety of English, with American English now joining our British spoken corpus, has been one of the most fascinating and enlightening aspects of the new Longman Dictionary of Contemporary English. All the recordings used are of natural speech, not radio or TV programmes or language that is in any way scripted. This has had a profound effect on the coverage of some frequent words such as *mean* and *better*, but definitions throughout the book that are particularly frequent in the spoken corpora are marked with the label *spoken*.

**Frequency** – Students are interested in frequency so that they can know which words are usual and which are unusual. We have been building the corpora that make up the Longman Corpus Network for nearly 10 years now, always with the intention that it would represent the broad span of the language and be reliable as a source of such frequency information. The frequency graphs in the dictionary show users which are the most common constructions of complex words, like *decide*, and just how much more common *let* is than *permit*, except in the formal varieties of English. We have also been able to mark the 3000 most frequent words in both spoken and written English, again relying on our authentic data from American as well as British English.

**Phrases and collocations** – English is expressed through fixed combinations of words, but it is difficult for students to predict what the words are, so collocations (*grim determination*), specific objects (*invade someone's privacy*) and phrases from spoken English (*bear with me a moment and been there, done that*) are given full treatment throughout the book.

All people involved in the creation of this new dictionary hope that you find it useful and informative, and we welcome any comments from users.

Della Summers
Director of Dictionaries
E-mail: 100441,2246@compuserve.com

# Explanatory Chart

| | |
|---|---|
| **ar·du·ous** /ˈɑːdjuəs‖ˈɑːrdʒuəs/ *adj* involving a lot of strength and effort: *an arduous journey through the mountains* —**arduously** *adv* —**arduousness** *n* [U] | Pronunciation is shown in the International Phonetic Alphabet. British and American pronunciations are shown. |
| **am·ber** /ˈæmbə‖-ər/ *n* [U] **1** a yellowish brown colour **2** a yellowish brown substance used to make jewellery —**amber** *adj* | Word class – verb, noun, adjective, preposition, etc. – is shown in italics. |
| **a·bode**[1] /əˈbəʊd‖əˈboʊd/ *n* [C] *formal or humorous* someone's home: *Welcome to my humble abode.* \| **of no fixed abode** (=having no permanent home)<br>**abode**[2] the past tense of ABIDE | Words that are spelled the same but belong to different word clases are treated as homographs and have separate entries. |
| **an·nu·al**[1] /ˈænjuəl/ *adj* **1** happening once a year: *an annual conference* **2** based on or calculated over a period of one year: *Steel output reached an annual figure of one million tons.* —**annually** *adv* | If a word has more than one meaning, each meaning is shown by a number in dark type. |
| **ar·dour** *BrE*, **ardor** *AmE* /ˈɑːdə‖ˈɑːr‖-ər/ *n* [U] **1** very strong positive feelings: *They sang with real ardour.* **2** *literary* strong feelings of love | If a word can be spelled in two different ways, both spellings are shown. |
| **a·bra·sive**[1] /əˈbreɪsɪv/ *adj* **1** seeming rude or unkind in the way you behave towards people because you say what you think very directly: *a rather abrasive manner* | Meanings are explained in clear, simple language, using the 2,000 word Longman Defining Vocabulary. |
| **ar·cher** /ˈɑːtʃə‖ˈɑːrtʃər/ *n* [C] someone who shoots ARROWS (1) from a BOW[3] (1) | Words that are not in the Defining Voacabulary are shown in small capital letters. |
| **an·noy·ing** /əˈnɔɪ-ɪŋ/ *adj* making you feel slightly angry: *an annoying habit of interrupting* \| *The annoying thing is he's usually right.* \| **it's annoying that** *It's annoying that we didn't know about this before.* —**annoyingly** *adv* \| *annoyingly small portions* | Useful natural examples, all based on information from the Longman Corpus Network. |
| **am·biv·a·lent** /æmˈbɪvələnt/ *adj* not sure whether you want or like something or not: *Her feelings about getting married are distinctly ambivalent.* —**ambivalence** *n* [U] —**ambivalently** *adv* | Derived words, that can be understood if you know the word they are derived from, are shown after it. |
| **ad·here** /ədˈhɪə‖-ˈhɪr/ *v formal* [I + **to**] to stick firmly to something<br>**adhere to** sth *phr v* [T] *formal* to continue to behave according to a particular rule, agreement, or belief: *adhere to your principles* \| *adhere to the regulations* | Phrasal verbs are listed directly after the entry for their main verb. |
| **after ef·fect** /ˈ·· ·,·/ *n* [C usually plural] an unpleasant effect that remains for a long time after the condition or event that caused it: *the after-effects of his illness* | Compound words are shown as headwords and their stress patterns are shown. |
| **au·ber·gine** /ˈəʊbəʒiːn‖ˈoʊbər-/ *n* [C,U] *BrE* a large dark purple vegetable; EGGPLANT *AmE* —see picture on page 494 | Both British and American English words are shown. |

**at·trib·u·ta·ble** /ə'trɪbjɡ̈təbəl/ *adj* [not before noun] likely to be caused by something: **[+ to]** *Death was attributable to gunshot wounds.*

Grammatical information is shown in square brackets, or in dark type before an example.

**ab·hor** /əb'hɔː‖-əb'hɔːr, æb-/ *v* **abhorred, abhorring** [T not in progressive] *formal* to hate a kind of behaviour or way of thinking, especially because you think it is morally wrong: *Some genuinely abhorred slavery, others were simply convinced by the economic arguments against it.*

**an·noyed** /ə'nɔɪd/ *adj* slightly angry: *I'll be annoyed if we don't finish by eight.* | **[+ with]** *She was annoyed with Duncan for forgetting to phone.* | **[+ about/by]** *He was annoyed by her apparent indifference.* | **be annoyed that** *Mr Davies was annoyed that the books were missing.*

**abandon²** *n* [U] **with gay/wild abandon** in a careless or uncontrolled way without thinking or caring about what you are doing: *The kids hurled pieces of wood on the fire with gay abandon.*

Phrases and idioms are shown and their meaning is given.

**ar·gu·ment** /'ɑːgjɡ̈mənt‖'ɑːr-/ *n* **1** [C] a situation in which two or more people disagree, often angrily: [+ **with**] *an argument with my husband* | [+ **about/over**] *The argument seemed to be about who was going to take the cat to the vet.* | **have an argument** *They were having an argument about the children.* | **get into an argument** *I got into an argument with the other driver.* | **win/lose an argument** *He lost his argument with the doctor.* | **heated argument** (=very angry argument)

Words that are often used together are shown in dark type, and followed by an example or an explanation.

**ab·sorb** /əb'sɔːb, əb'zɔːb‖-ɔːrb/ *v* [T]
**1 ▶ LIQUID ◀** if something absorbs a liquid, it takes the liquid into itself from the surface or space around it: *Plants absorb nutrients from the soil.*
**2 ▶ INFORMATION ◀** to read or hear a large amount of new information and understand it: *I haven't really had time to absorb everything that he said.*
**3 ▶ INTEREST ◀** to interest someone very much: **be absorbed in** *Judith lay on the settee, absorbed in her book.* | **absorb sb's attention** *The video was totally absorbing the children's attention.*

Signposts in longer entries help you to find the meaning that you need.

**ap·pend** /ə'pend/ *v* [T + to] *formal* to add something to a piece of writing

Information on what situations a word is used in, or where it comes from, is shown in italics.

**ante-** /æntɪ/ *prefix* before: *to antedate* (=be earlier than something) | *ante-natal* (=before birth) —compare ANTI-, POST-, PRE-

**an·te¹** /'ænti/ *n* **up/raise the ante** to increase your demands or try to get more things from a situation, even though this involves more risks —see also PENNY ANTE

References to other words and phrases, and to pictures and usage notes, are given.

**a·rise** /ə'raɪz/ *v past tense* **arose** /ə'rəʊz‖ə'roʊz/ *past participle* **arisen** /ə'rɪzən/ [I]

Irregular verb forms, and irregular plurals of nouns are shown.

# Guide to the Dictionary

## Contents



## 1 How to find the word you are looking for

Words are listed in this dictionary in alphabetical order.

### 1.1 Compound words

Compound words are groups of two or more words with a fixed form and a special meaning, such as **front man** and **front line**. Most of these are shown as full headwords (but see section 1.6 Phrases and idioms). They are treated like ordinary words in the alphabetical order; the space or hyphen between the two parts is ignored.

**front·al**
**frontal sys·tem**
**front-and-center**
**front bench**
**front·bench·er**
**front door**
**fron·tier**

### 1.2 Phrasal verbs

Multi-word verbs, like **give up** or **put off**, are listed in alphabetical order directly after the entry for their main verb. For example:

**face**[2] *v* [T]
**face** sb ↔ **down**
**face up to**
**face** sb **with**
**face card**

### 1.3 Derived words without definition

Some words do not need a definition, because they are derived from a headword by adding a suffix. For example **gracefully** and **gracefulness** are derived from **graceful**, and their meaning is simply that of the main word plus the meaning of the suffix. These words are shown at the end of the entry for the word that they are derived from.

**grace·ful** /ˈgreɪsfəl/ *adj* **1** moving in a smooth and attractive way, or having an attractive shape: *a slim graceful figure* **2** behaving in a polite and pleasant way: *a graceful apology* —**gracefully** *adv*: *When I am no longer needed, I shall retire gracefully.* —**gracefulness** *n* [U]

In this case, **gracefully** just means 'in a graceful way,' and **gracefulness** just means 'the quality of being graceful.'

## 1.4 Homographs

Homographs are words that have the same spelling but are different from each other in some other way, and are listed as separate entries in a dictionary. In this dictionary, words of different word classes are treated as homographs.

**face**[1] /feɪs/ *n* [C]
**1 ▶ FRONT OF YOUR HEAD ◀** the front part of the head from the chin to the forehead: *She has such a pretty face.* | *Bob's face was covered in cuts and bruises.* | **a sea of faces** (=a lot of faces seen together) *The Principal looked down from the platform at the sea of faces below* —see picture at HEAD[1].

**face**[2] *v* [T]
**1 ▶ DIFFICULT SITUATION ◀** if you face a difficult situation or if it faces you, you must deal with it: *The President faces the difficult task of putting the economy back on its feet.* | *McManus is facing the biggest challenge of his career.* | **be faced with/by** *I was faced with the awful job of breaking the news to the girl's family.*

The order of the homographs depends on how common they are. **Face** is used more often as a noun than as a verb, so the noun entry is shown first.

Words of the same word class and spelling that are pronounced differently, are separate headwords. For example, the nouns **row** (=a line) and **row** (=an argument) are separate headwords, because they are pronounced differently.

If two words are spelled the same, but one starts with a capital letter and has a completely different meaning, for example the adjectives **catholic** and **Catholic**, they are separate headwords.

If a word is a plural form of a noun, but has a separate meaning, it is usually shown as one of the meanings of that noun:

**blue**[2] *n* **1** [C,U] the colour that is blue: *the rich greens and blues of the tapestry* | *She nearly always dresses in blue.* **2 blues** [plural] a slow sad style of music that came from the southern US: *a blues singer* —see also RHYTHM AND BLUES **3 the blues** [plural] *informal* feelings of sadness: *Don't be surprised if you get the blues for a while after your baby is born.*

But if the plural form of the word is more important than the singular, and has several meanings, it is a separate headword. So **goods** has its own entry, separate from the noun **good**.

## 1.5 Other types of headwords

Abbreviations are headwords, and so are prefixes like **dis-** or suffixes like **-able**.

Different spellings are shown at the headword, and also have their own entry as headwords, directing you to the main entry.

**in·quire, enquire** /ɪn'kwaɪə‖-ər/ *v* [I,T] **1** to ask someone for information: *"Are you getting married?" the television interviewer inquired.*
**en·quire** /ɪn'kwaɪə‖-'kwaɪr/ *v* [I,T] *especially BrE* another spelling of INQUIRE

Irregular inflections of words are shown at the main form, and also as separate headwords, directing you to the main entry.

**have**[1] /v, əv, həv; *strong* hæv/ *auxiliary verb past tense* **had** /d, əd, həd; *strong* hæd/ *third person singular present tense* **has** /z, əz, həz; *strong* hæz/ *negative short forms* **haven't** /'hævənt/, **hadn't** /'hædnt/, **hasn't** /'hæzənt/
**had** /d, əd, həd; *strong* hæd/ **1** the past tense and past participle of HAVE

## 1.6 Phrases and idioms

Some words are often used in particular phrases, and an important feature of this dictionary is that we treat them as separate meanings. For example:

**face**[1] /feɪs/ *n* [C]
**17 sb's face doesn't fit** used to say that someone is not the right kind of person for a particular group, organization etc
**18 put a brave face (on)** to make an effort to behave in a happy cheerful way when you are upset or disappointed: *He was shattered, though he put on a brave face.*
**19 set your face against** *especially BrE* to be very determined that something should not happen

Some compound words are treated in this way, because they are idiomatic phrases. For example, **big deal** is given as a sense of **big**.

Phrases and idioms are usually listed under the first main word in a phrase (that is, not at words like *the*, *to*, *something*, or *be*), so the definition of **have egg on your face** is at **egg**, not at **face**. If you look for this phrase at **face**, you will find a cross-reference note at the end of the entry, telling you where to find it.

**face**[1] /feɪs/ *n* [C]
—see also **have egg on your face** (EGG[1] (4)), **fly in the face of** (FLY[1] (28)),

# 2 Understanding meaning

## 2.1 Words with more than one meaning.

Where a word has more than one meaning, each meaning is given a separate number, and the most frequent meaning, according to analysis of our spoken and written copora, is shown first.

**a·chieve·ment** /ə'tʃiːvmənt/ *n* **1** [C] something important that you succeed in doing by your own efforts: *Winning three gold medals is a remarkable achievement.* |

**no mean achievement/quite an achievement** (=a very impressive achievement) **2** [U] the act of achieving something: *the achievement of economic stability*| **sense of achievement** (=a feeling of pride when you succeed in doing something difficult) *You get a wonderful sense of achievement when you reach the top.*

This dictionary is based on analysis of large corpora of spoken and written English, which shows how often a word or phrase is used, and how often it is used in each meaning.

A phrase that contains the word and has its own distinct meaning is shown as a separate sense and listed in frequency order. For example:

**look·out** /'lʊk-aʊt/ *n*
**1 be on the lookout for** to watch a place or situation continuously in order to find something you want or to be ready for problems or opportunities: *Police were on the lookout for anyone behaving suspiciously.*| *We're always on the lookout for new business opportunities.*
**2 keep a lookout** to keep watching carefully for something or someone, especially for danger: **keep a sharp/special lookout** *When you're driving keep a sharp lookout for cyclists.*
**3** ▶ **PERSON** ◀ [C] someone whose duty is to watch carefully for something, especially danger: *A lookout reported an enemy plane approaching.*
**4** ▶ **PLACE** ◀ [C] a place for a lookout to watch from: *a coastguard lookout on the clifftop*
**5 it's your/their own lookout** *BrE spoken* used to say that what someone has chosen to do is their own problem or risk, and no one else's: *If he wants to ruin his health with all these drugs, that's his own lookout.*
**6 be a poor/bad lookout for sb** *BrE spoken* used to say that something bad or unsatisfactory is likely to happen: *It'll be a poor lookout for James if she finds that letter.*

This shows that the most common use of **lookout** is in the phrase **be on the lookout for**.

## 2.2 Definitions

All the definitions in this dictionary are written in clear and simple language, using the Longman Defining Vocabulary of about 2000 common words. The list of the words in the definitions is shown at the end of the dictionary after section 7 which explains exactly how the words are used.

## 2.3 Examples

Most definitions in this dictionary are followed by examples that show how the word is used.

The examples may be in short phrases or whole sentences, and they are written in *italic letters*:

*clear instructions*| *You must never do that again. Is that clear?*|

All the examples in this dictionary are based on what we find in the spoken and written corpus material in the Longman Corpus Network. Some examples are taken direct from the corpus; some have been changed slightly from the corpus to remove difficult words; and some have been written specially for the entry. In each case, the examples are carefully chosen to help show the ways in which a word or phrase is normally used.

Examples also exemplify the grammar of the word, and the way in which it is often used with other words (collocation).

**be clear on** *The rules are quite clear on the point.*| **clear to sb** *Is all this clear to you?*

## 2.4 Collocations

An important aim of this dictionary is to show very clearly the collocation of a word: the other words that are frequently and typically used with it. Collocations are shown in dark type, and are followed by a short definition in brackets, or an example, or both.

**make yourself clear** (=express something well) *To make yourself clear without using facial expressions can be very difficult.*| **get sth clear** *Let's get one thing clear; you have my whole-hearted support.*

These collocations are shown in frequency order, with the most important collocations coming first.

## 2.5 Finding the meaning you want – Signposts

In entries with many definitions, we have included "Signposts" to help you find the right definition quickly. These are shown in capital letters, before the definition, and are written using only the words in the Longman Defining Vocabulary.

**bridge**[1] /brɪdʒ/ *n* [C]
**1** ▶ **OVER A RIVER/ROAD ETC** ◀ a structure built over a river, road etc, that allows people or vehicles to cross from one side to the other
**2** ▶ **CONNECTION** ◀ something that provides a connection between two things; LINK[2] (1): *The training programme is seen as a bridge between school and work.*
**3** ▶ **SHIP** ◀ the raised part of a ship from which the officers control it
**4** ▶ **CARD GAME** ◀ [U] a card game for four players who play in pairs
**5 the bridge of your nose** the bony upper part of your nose between your eyes
**6** ▶ **PAIR OF GLASSES** ◀ the part of a pair of glasses that rests on the bridge of your nose —see picture at GLASS[1]
**7** ▶ **MUSICAL INSTRUMENT** ◀ a small piece of wood under the strings of a VIOLIN or GUITAR, used to keep them in position
**8** ▶ **FOR TEETH** ◀ a small piece of metal for keeping false teeth in place —see also **build bridges** (BUILD[1] (7)),

**burn your bridges** (BURN[1] (22)), **cross that bridge when you come to it** (CROSS[1] (7)), **be (all) water under the bridge** (WATER[1] (7))

A signpost is a word or short phrase that guides you to the right meaning. It may be a synonym, a short definition, or the typical subject or object of a verb.

## 2.6 Long entries with menus

In some of the longer entries, meanings that are closely related to each other are grouped together in 'paragraphs', or sections in the entry. A menu at the beginning of the entry tells you the paragraph headings, so that you can easily find the section that contains the sense that you want. All these senses begin on new lines, and they have signposts where these are helpful. Look at the words **run** and **way** for examples of the use of paragraphs.

## 2.7 Showing words with similar and opposite meanings

Sometimes it is useful to show a synonym, a word that has the same meaning, or almost the same meaning, as the word that is being defined. These are shown after the definition, like this:

**im·ma·te·ri·al** /ˌɪmə'tɪəriəl◂‖-'tɪr-/ *adj* **1** not important in a particular situation; IRRELEVANT: *The causes of the problem are immaterial now – we need solutions.* **2** *formal* not having a real physical form

Words with similar meanings or similar forms are shown with a 'compare' note, and useful opposites are also shown.

**i·ma·gi·na·ry** /ɪ'mædʒə̇nəri‖-neri/ *adj* not real, but produced from pictures or ideas in your mind: *All the characters in this book are imaginary.* —compare IMAGINATIVE

**im·mod·est** /ɪ'mɒdʒə̇st‖ɪ'mɑː-/ *adj* **1** having a very high opinion of yourself and your abilities, and not embarrassed about telling people how clever you are etc —opposite MODEST (1) **2** *old-fashioned* behaviour or clothes that are immodest may embarrass or offend people because they do not follow the usual social rules concerning sexual behaviour —**immodestly** *adv* —**immodesty** *n* [U]

# 3 Frequency

You have seen that this dictionary is organized on the basis of frequency. The most frequent meanings of a word are shown first, and homographs are shown in frequency order. At each sense of a word, the examples that show grammar, and those that show collocation, are each arranged in frequency order. All our judgments about frequency are made by analysis of corpus material. This principle of organization gives important information about the English language, and is helpful to the student.

At some important words, graphs give further information on frequency. Some show that a word is used much more frequently in spoken English than in written, and some compare words with the same meaning, showing which is more frequent in written English, and which in spoken. Some graphs show how often a word is used in each of its most frequent collocations or grammar patterns, and others highlight differences between British and American English.

The dictionary also shows which are the most frequently used words, according to the computer-based analysis of all corpus material available to Longman. The symbols S1, S2, and S3 show that a word is one of the thousand most frequently used words in spoken English, one of the next thousand most frequent, or one of the third thousand, in the list of three thousand words most often used in speech. The symbols W1, W2, and W3 give the same information for written English. Whether a word is S1, S2, or W1, W2 and so on depends on its overall frequency in American and British English combined.

# 4 Grammar

The dictionary contains a great deal of information about the grammar of words. It tells you the word class that a headword belongs to – whether it is a noun, a verb, an adjective or some other type of word. It also gives information about the inflections of words – how their form changes when they are used in the past tense, the plural, the comparative, or in some other way. And it gives a full explanation of the word's syntax - the various patterns in which the word combines with other words to form sentences.

## 4.1 Word classes

The word class, or 'part of speech' is shown like this:

**il·lo·gi·cal** /ɪ'lɒdʒɪkəl‖ɪ'lɑː-/ *adj* **1** not sensible or reasonable: *erratic and illogical behaviour* —opposite LOGICAL (1) **2** not based on the principles of LOGIC: *an illogical conclusion* —**illogically** /-kli/ *adv* —**illogicality** /ɪˌlɒdʒə̇'kæləti‖ɪˌlɑː-/ *n* [U]

This means that **illogical** is an adjective. Derived forms are also given a word class label: **illogically** is an adverb, and **illogicality** is a noun.

The word classes used in this dictionary are:

| **word class** | **example** |
|---|---|
| *adj* (adjective) | a **fast** *car,* **straight** *lines,* **amazing** *speed,* **frequent** *trains* |
| *adv* (adverb) | smiling **happily**, put it **away**, **frankly**, I'm not bothered |
| *auxiliary verb* | be, have |
| *conjunction* | and, but |
| *determiner* | this, which |
| *interjection* | damn, wow |
| *modal verb* | must, can, should |
| *n* (noun) | car, rabbit, president, dignity, excuse |
| *number* | five, ninth |
| *phr v* (phrasal verb) | put off, shut up, take over |
| *predeterminer* | all, both |
| *prefix* | dis-, centi- |
| *prep* (preposition) | in, after, to |
| *pron* (pronoun) | he, theirs, us |
| *quantifier* | many, several |
| *suffix* | -ity, –ness |
| *v* (verb) | go, send, indicate |

## 4.2 Inflections

Inflections are the changes that are made in the form of a word according to its function in a sentence. Most words form their inflections according to regular rules. For example, most nouns add *-s* or *-es* to form the plural, and most verbs add *-ed* to form the past tense. These 'regular inflections' are not shown in the dictionary, except where there is a possibility of confusion or if the regular inflection has a difficult pronunciation.

'Irregular inflections' are always shown. They come directly after the word class, and they are written in dark type, like this:

**cri·sis** /ˈkraɪsɪ̥s/ *n plural* **crises** /-siːz/ [C,U]
**eat** /iːt/ *v past tense* **ate** /et, eɪt‖eɪt/ *past participle* **eaten** /ˈiːtn/
**good¹** /gʊd/ *adj comparative* **better** /ˈbetə‖-ər/ *superlative* **best** /best/

Irregular inflections are also shown at their own place as headwords, referring you to the main word:

**ate** /et, eɪt‖eɪt/ the past tense of EAT

Inflections are also shown for:

verbs which have a double letter in the past and -ing forms:

**hug¹** /hʌg/ *v* **hugged, hugging** [T]

verbs which end in -y:

**car·ry¹** /ˈkæri/ *v* **carried, carrying**

adjectives which end in -y:

**dirt·y¹** /ˈdɜːti‖ˈdɜːr-/ *adj* **dirtier, dirtiest**

There is a full list of verbs with irregular inflections at the back of the book, starting on page B7.

## 4.3 Syntax – verbs

Basic information about the way a verb behaves is given in square brackets.

The codes [I] (intransitive) and [T] (transitive) show whether a verb has or does not have an object.

**hard·en** /ˈhɑːdn‖ˈhɑːrdn/ *v* **1** [I,T] to become firm or stiff, or to make something firm or stiff: *Make sure you give the paint enough time to dry and harden.* **2** [I] to become more strict and determined and less sympathetic: *Opposition to the military regime has hardened since the massacres.*|*a hardening of attitudes*|*His face hardened.* —compare SOFTEN (4) **3** [T] if an experience hardens someone, it makes them stronger and more able to deal with difficult or unpleasant situations

The code [linking verb] means that a verb shows that one thing is the same as another, or that something is true about a thing.

**look¹** /lʊk/ *v*
**3 ▶ SEEM ◀** [linking verb] to seem to be something, especially by having a particular appearance: *How do I look in this dress?*|**look like** *The intruder was holding what looked like a shotgun.*|**look as if** *You look as if you haven't slept all night.*

**be²** *v* **1** [linking verb] used to show that someone or something is the same as the subject: *It's me.*|*Lack of money is our biggest problem.*|*If I were you, I shouldn't do it.*

Square brackets may also contain restrictions on the way a verb can be used, including [not in progressive]

**pre·fer** /prɪˈfɜː‖-ˈfɜːr/ *v* **preferred, preferring** [T not in progressive] **1** to like someone or something more than someone or something else

[I always + adv / prep]:

**am·ble** /ˈæmbəl/ *v* [I always + adv/prep] to walk in a slow relaxed way: [+ **along/across etc**] *The old man came out and ambled over for a chat.* —**amble** *n* [singular]

You cannot simply say 'he ambled' without adding something like 'along' or 'towards me'.

**[usually in passive]:**

**carpet²** *v* [T] **1** [usually in passive] to cover a floor with carpet: *a carpeted corridor* **2** *informal especially BrE* to blame someone for something they have done;

REPRIMAND **3 carpeted with grass/flowers etc** *literary* covered with a thick layer of grass etc

**[not in passive]**

**concern**[2] *v* [T] **1** if an activity, situation, rule etc concerns you, it affects you or involves you: *The tax changes will concern large corporations rather than small businesses.* **2** [not in passive] to make someone feel worried or upset: *The fact that she spends so much time on her own really concerns me.* **3** [not in passive] if a story, book, report etc concerns someone or something, it is about them: *This article concerns a man who was wrongly imprisoned.* **4 concern yourself with/about sth** to become involved in something because you are interested in it or because it worries you: *More and more people are concerning themselves with environmental problems.* **5 to whom it may concern** an expression written at the beginning of a formal letter when you do not know the name of the person you want to communicate with —see also CONCERNED

If this basic information is true whenever a word is used, you will find it after the headword. If it is true for a particular sense of the word, you will find it after the number that marks that sense.

## 4.4 Phrasal verbs

For a phrasal verb, it is important to show whether the preposition can come both before and after the object or whether it is restricted to one of these positions. This is shown in this dictionary by a double arrow.

**hand**[2] *v* [T]
**hand** sth ↔ **out** *phr v* [T] **1** to give something to each member of a group of people; DISTRIBUTE: *Could you start handing these books out.* **2 hand out advice** to give advice, even if people do not want to hear it —see also HANDOUT

This entry shows that you can say 'hand the books out', or 'hand out the books', but it would not be correct to say 'hammer an agreement out'.

Other information about how a verb behaves is shown in the examples. A typical construction is shown in dark type before the example that illustrates it.

**4 decide in favour of/decide against a)** to choose or not choose someone or something: *After long discussion they decided in favour of the younger candidate.* **b)** if a judge or JURY (1) decides in favour of someone or against someone, they say in court that someone is guilty or not guilty: *The jury decided in favour of the plaintiff.*

These examples are shown in frequency order, with the most frequently used construction first.

## 4.5 Syntax – nouns

Grammatical information enclosed in square brackets shows whether a noun, or a particular sense of a noun, is countable (a pen, three pens), or uncountable (honour, daylight).

**hab·i·ta·tion** /ˌhæbɪ̈ˈteɪʃən/ *n formal* **1 unfit for human habitation** a building that is unfit for human habitation is not safe or healthy for people to live in **2** [U] the act of living in a place: *There was no sign of habitation as far as the eye could see.* **3** [C] a house or place to live in

**hes·i·ta·tion** /ˌhezɪ̈ˈteɪʃən/ *n* [C,U] the action of hesitating: *After some hesitation one of them began to speak.* | **have no hesitation in** *I would have no hesitation in declining the post.* | **after/without a moment's hesitation** *Without a moment's hesitation she kissed him.*

If a noun, or a particular sense of one, is always singular or always plural, this is also shown in a square bracket.

**hard right** /ˌ· ˈ·◂/ *n* [singular] the part of a political party that believes strongly in RIGHT WING political ideas

**high heels** /ˌ· ˈ·/ *n* [plural] women's shoes with high heels —**high-heeled** *adj* —see picture on page 840

If a noun is typically followed by a preposition or prepositions, this is shown in dark type before the example that illustrates it. A construction that typically follows a noun is also shown in dark type before an example.

**hope**[2] *n* [U]
**5 ▶CHANCE◀** [C,U] a chance of succeeding or of something good happening: **[+ of]** *there was no hope of escape* | **hope that** *There is some hope that we'll find a solution to our problems.*

## 4.6 Syntax – adjectives and adverbs

Information about how an adjective or adverb behaves is shown in a square bracket, and includes:

**[only before noun]**

**ac·tu·al** /ˈæktʃuəl/ *adj* [only before noun] **1** real, especially as compared with what is believed, expected or intended: *a big difference between the opinion polls and the actual election results* | *I'm not joking. Those were his actual words.* | **in actual fact** (=really) *In actual fact, there is not much evidence to support these allegations.*

**[only after noun]**

**ga·lore** /gəˈlɔː‖-ˈlɔːr/ *adj* [only after noun] in large amounts or numbers: *There are bargains galore in the sales this year.*

**[not before noun]**

**ad·vi·sab·le** /ədˈvaɪzəbəl/ *adj* [not before noun] something that is advisable should be done in order to avoid problems or risks: *For heavy smokers, regular medical checks are advisable.* | **it is advisable to do sth** *It is advisable to disconnect the computer before you open it up.* —**advisability** /ədˌvaɪzəˈbɪlɪ̈ti/ *n* [U]

[no comparative]

**ef·fec·tive** /ɪˈfektɪv/ *adj* **1** producing the result that was wanted or intended: *The ads were simple, but remarkably effective.* **2** impressive or interesting enough to be noticed: *an effective use of colour* **3** [no comparative] if a law, agreement, or system becomes effective, it officially starts: *The cut in interest rates is effective from Monday.* **4** [no comparative] real rather than what is officially intended or generally believed: *The rebels are in effective control of the city.* —**effectiveness** *n* [U]

[+adj/adv]

**in·creas·ing·ly** /ɪnˈkriːsɪŋli/ *adv* more and more all the time [+ adj/adv]: *The classes at the college have become increasingly full over the past five years.* [sentence adverb]: *Increasingly, it is the industrial power of Japan and South East Asia that dominates world markets.*

[sentence adverb]

**hap·pi·ly** /ˈhæpɪ̣li/ *adv* **1** in a happy way: *a happily married couple* **2** [sentence adverb] fortunately: *Happily, his injuries were not serious.* **3** very willingly: *I'd happily go for you.*

The grammar information [sentence adverb] indicates that in this sense **happily** is used to modify a whole sentence.

The prepositions or construction that follow an adjective are shown in dark type before an example.

**hope·ful**[1] /ˈhəʊpfəl‖ˈhoʊp-/ *adj* **1** believing that what you hope for is likely to happen: [+ **about**] *Everyone's feeling pretty hopeful about the future.*| **hopeful that** *We're hopeful that the team will be fit for next Saturday's game.*| **be hopeful of doing sth** *BrE*: *The police are hopeful of finding more clues to the murder.*

### 4.7 Very infrequent words

Very infrequent words, that a student is not likely to need to use, are given a shorter treatment, without examples, giving just the basic grammatical information.

## 5 Information on register and usage

### 5.1 Indicating register

Some words and senses have information on what type of situation they are likely to be used in. This is shown in italic after the headword, or after the sense number.

**clobber**[2] *n* [U] *informal especially BrE* someone's possessions, especially their clothes: *Don't forget all your clobber if you're staying the night.*| **fishing/swimming/football clobber etc** (=clothes and equipment needed for a particular activity)

**ab·ne·ga·tion** /ˌæbnɪ̣ˈgeɪʃən/ *n* [U] *formal* the act of not allowing yourself to have or do something that you want

**a·blu·tions** /əˈbluːʃənz/ [plural] *n formal or humorous* the things that you do to make yourself clean, such as washing yourself, cleaning your teeth etc

*Slang* or *taboo*, but especially *taboo*, show that you should be careful about using a word, even in an informal situation.

*Literary, poetic, technical, old use* or *old-fashioned* indicate a word that people do not normally use in speech or writing.

### 5.2 Spoken words and phrases

The label *spoken* indicates a phrase that is typically used in speech, rather than in writing.

**24 that's life** *spoken* used when you are disappointed or upset that something has happened but realize that you must accept it: *Oh well, that's life!*

Because we have spoken as well as written material on the Longman Corpus network, we were able to give a lot of attention to providing information of this kind. Some important words have graphs to show how much more frequently they occur in spoken than in written English. Some of these words, such as **mean**, have special 'spoken phrases' boxes or paragraphs.

### 5.3 Usage notes

Notes on particular points of English usage are included in the dictionary. Each note follows the entry for the main word that it treats. Other words dealt with in that Note have cross-references from their own places of entry.

## 6 Pronunciation

Each word is followed by its pronunciation, given in the International Phonetic Alphabet. The symbols used are shown in the table at the beginning of this Introduction. Alternative pronunciations are shown after a comma. If only part of the pronunciation is different, this part is given, and its place in the word shown by a hyphen.

**a·ber·rant** /ˈæbərənt, əˈberənt/ *adj formal* not usual or normal: *aberrant behaviour*

**ab·duct** /əbˈdʌkt, æb-/ *v* [T] to take someone away by force; KIDNAP: *Police suspect she was abducted late last night.* —**abductor** *n* [C] —**abduction** /əbˈdʌkʃən/ *n* [C,U]

Where a word is pronounced differently in British English and in American English, these different pronunciations are both shown, and separated by two vertical parallel lines. The British version is shown first, on the left of these lines, and the American is shown on the right.

**an·swer¹** /ˈɑːnsə‖ˈænsər/ *n*

Most words that are derived from another word in a regular way, and are shown after it without a definition, are simply pronounced as the main word plus the suffix. In these cases, no pronunciation is shown. In all other cases the pronunciation of a derived word is shown.

## 6.1 Compound words

Compound words that consist of two words with a separating space or hyphen are not usually given a full pronunciation. This is because each of the words has its own entry, where the pronunciation is given. Instead a stress pattern of the compound word is shown, with a dot representing each syllable, and the marks above and below that show main and secondary stress. Where British and American stress patterns are different, both are shown, in the same way that full pronunciations are.

**aircraft car·ri·er** /ˈ·· ˌ···/ *n* [C] a type of ship that has a large flat surface that planes fly from

Some compound words, such as **plate glass**, and a few single words, such as **independent**, have only one main stress (in the first place in the stress pattern) if they are used directly before a noun, such as in the phrase 'plate glass window' or 'independent observer'. This is shown by the stress shift mark /◂/ which is given after the stress pattern of the compound word

**plate glass** /ˌ· ˈ·◂/ *n* [U] big pieces of glass made in large thick sheets for use especially in shop windows

and after the pronunication of the simple word

**in·de·pen·dent** /ˌɪndɪ̣ˈpendənt◂/ *adj*

# 7 British and American English

Both British and American lexicographers have worked on this dictionary, so that it gives good coverage of both British and American English. The definition text is written in British English, with both British and American shown in the examples. Differences in pronunciation and spelling between the British and American forms of a word are shown. Words, senses of words, grammatical constructions, phrases, and collocations, that only occur in British English are marked *BrE*, and those that exist only in American English are marked *AmE*. Those that are much more frequent in one form of English than in the other are marked *especially BrE* or *especially AmE*.

## 7.1 Pronunciation and spelling differences

British and American pronunciations are separated by two vertical parallel lines, with the British on the left and the American on the right. An example of this is shown at the beginning of section 5.

If words are spelt differently in British and American English, both spellings are shown and marked.

**cen·tre¹** *BrE*, **center** *AmE* /ˈsentə‖-ər/ *n*
**1 ▶MIDDLE◀** [C] the middle of a space, area, or object, especially the exact middle: *Draw a line through the centre of the circle.* | *Tony only likes chocolates with soft centres.* | **[+ of]** *There was an enormous oak table in the center of the room.*

**cen·ter** /ˈsentə‖-ər/ *n v* the American spelling of CENTRE

If the word sometimes has a different spelling from the main one, in either British or American English, that spelling is shown after "also".

**jail¹** also **gaol** *BrE* /dʒeɪl/ *n* [C,U] a place where criminals are kept as part of their punishment, or where people who have been charged with a crime are kept before they are judged in a law court; PRISON (1)

Some verbs have a double letter in the past and -ing forms in British English, but not in American English. Both forms are shown and marked:

**label²** *v* **labelled, labelling** *BrE* **labeled, labeling** *AmE* [T]

## 7.2 Words and meanings – British and American differences

Sometimes, British and American English use quite different words to mean exactly the same thing. In these cases, the entry for the British word shows the American synonym, directly after the definition, and vice versa.

**el·e·va·tor** /ˈelɪ̣veɪtə‖-ər/ *n* [C] **1** *AmE* a machine that takes people and goods from one level to another in a building; LIFT² (1) *BrE* **2** a machine with a moving belt and containers, used for lifting grain and liquids, or for taking things off ships

In other cases, a word that is British or American does not have an exact equivalent in the other form of English, or it has an equivalent that is rarely used. Words like this are simply labelled *BrE* or *AmE*:

**airing cup·board** /ˈ·· ˌ··/ *n* [C] *BrE* a warm cupboard in a house where sheets and clean clothes are kept

**air·head** /ˈeəhed‖ˈer-/ *n* [C] *slang especially AmE* someone who is stupid

If a particular meaning of a word only exists in British or in American English, it is marked in this way after its sense number:

**home·ly** /ˈhəʊmli‖ˈhoʊm-/ *adj* **1** *BrE* simple and ordinary in a way that makes you feel comfortable: *The cottage had a warm, homely feel.* **2** *AmE* people or faces that are homely are unattractive or ugly: *I've never seen such a homely dog in my life!*

## 7.3 Differences in grammar

Some words are followed by a particular preposition or construction only in British or American English, and these differences are marked.

One difference is that group nouns, like **government** or **class**, can take a plural verb in British but not in American English. For important words of this type, this difference is shown and marked:

**gov·ern·ment** /ˈgʌvəmənt, ˈgʌvənmənt‖ˈgʌvərn-/ *n* **1** also **Government** [C] the group of people who govern a country or state: *The new military government does not have popular support.*|[also + plural verb *BrE*] *The Government are planning further cuts in public spending.*

## 7.4 Differences in phrases and collocations

An important difference between British and American English is that each has its own rich store of idiomatic phrases. Some words also have typical collocations in one of these forms of English, but not in the other. Phrases and collocations that occur only in British or only in American English are marked.

**jack**[2] *v*

**jack** sb **around** *phr v* [T] *AmE slang* to waste someone's time by deliberately making things difficult for them: *Stop jacking me around and make up your mind!*

**jack** sth ↔ **in** *phr v* [T] *BrE informal* to stop doing something: *I'd love to jack in my job and go live in the Bahamas.*

**A, a** /eɪ/ *plural* **A's, a's** *n* [C] the first letter of the English alphabet

S1 W1 **a** /ə/ also **an** /eɪ/ *strong indefinite article, determiner* **1** used before a noun that names something or someone that has not been mentioned before, or that the person you are talking to does not know about: *Do you have a car?|There's a spider in the bath.* —compare THE **2 a)** used before a noun that is one of a particular group or class of people or things: *I want to train to be a teacher.* **b)** used before someone's family name to show that they belong to that family: *Only a Peterson would drive a car like that!* **3 a)** one: *a thousand pounds|a dozen eggs* **b) a lot/a few/a little/a great deal etc** used before certain words that express an amount of something: *There were a lot of people at the party.|A few weeks from now I'll be in Venice.* **4 twice a week/£5 a day etc** two times each week, £5 each day etc; per: *I get paid once a month.|The eggs cost $2 a dozen.* **5** used before a noun to mean all things of that type: *A square has four sides.* (=all squares have four sides) **6** used before two nouns that are mentioned together so often that they are thought of as one thing: *a cup and saucer|Does everyone have a knife and fork?* **7 a)** used before singular nouns, especially words for actions, meaning one example of that action: *Take a look at this.|It needs a good clean.* **b)** used before the -ing form of verbs when they are used as nouns: *a crashing of gears* **c)** used before an UNCOUNTABLE noun when other information about the noun is added by an adjective or phrase: *Candidates must have a good knowledge of chemistry.|a beauty that became legendary* **8** used before an UNCOUNTABLE noun to mean a type of it: *a particularly fine Stilton cheese* **9** used before the name of a painter or artist etc meaning a particular painting, sculpture etc by that person: *an early Rembrandt* **10** used before a name to mean having the same qualities as that person or thing: *She was hailed as a new Marilyn Monroe.* **11 a)** used before someone's name when you do not know who they are: *There is a Mr Tom Wilkins on the phone for you.|***a certain** *A certain Lisa Blair wishes to speak to you.* **b)** used before names of days, events in the year etc to mean a particular one: *I can't remember a Christmas like it.* **12** used after such, what, rather and (formal) many to emphasize what you are saying: *What a day! I was late for work and my car broke down.|She had spent many a night* (=many nights) *waiting for him to come home.*

**A¹** /eɪ/ *n* **1** also **a** [C,U] the sixth note in the musical SCALE¹ (8) of C major or the musical KEY¹ (4) based on this note **2** [C] the highest mark that a student can get in an examination or for a piece of work: *I got an A in French.* **3 an A student** *AmE* someone who regularly gets the best marks possible for their work in school or college **4 from A to B** from one place to another: *Hiring a car was the best way to get us from A to B.* **5 from A to Z** describing, including, or knowing everything about a subject: *the history of 20th century art from A to Z* **6 A3/A4** standard sizes of paper in the European Union **7** [U] a common type of blood

**A²** the written abbreviation of AMP

**a-¹** /ə/ *prefix* **1** in a particular condition or way: *alive* (=living)|*aloud|with nerves all atingle* (=tingling) **2** *old use* in, to, at, or on something: *abed* (=in bed)|*afar* (=far away)

**a-²** /eɪ, æ, ə/ *prefix* showing an opposite or the absence of something; not; without: *amoral* (=not moral)|*atypically* (=not typically)

**A-1** /ˌeɪ ˈwʌn/ *adj old-fashioned* very good or completely healthy: *Everything about the resort was A-1.*

**AA** /eɪ ˈeɪ/ *n* [C] Associate of Arts; a two year college degree in the US

**aard·vark** /ˈɑːdvɑːk‖ˈɑːrdvɑːrk/ *n* [C] a large animal from southern Africa that has a very long nose and eats small insects

**AB** /ˌeɪ ˈbiː/ *n* **1** [U] a common type of blood **2** [C] *AmE* Bachelor of Arts; a university degree in an arts (ART¹ (5)) subject that you get after studying for three or four years

**a·back** /əˈbæk/ *adv* **be taken aback** to be very surprised or shocked by something: *For a moment, I was completely taken aback by her request.*

**ab·a·cus** /ˈæbəkəs/ *n* [C] a wooden frame with small balls used for counting (COUNT¹ (2))

**ab·a·lo·ne** /ˌæbəˈləʊni‖-ˈloʊ-/ *n* [C,U] a kind of SHELLFISH which is used as food and whose shell contains MOTHER-OF-PEARL

**a·ban·don¹** /əˈbændən/ *v* [T] **1** to leave someone, especially someone you are responsible for: *children abandoned by their parents* **2** to go away from a place, vehicle etc, permanently, especially because the situation makes it impossible for you to stay: *We had to abandon the car and walk the rest of the way.|Fearing further attacks, most of the population had abandoned the city.* **3** to stop doing something because there are too many problems and it is impossible to continue: *The game had to be abandoned due to bad weather.* **4** to decide that you no longer believe in a particular idea or principle: *They were accused of abandoning their socialist principles.|***abandon hope (of doing sth)** *Imogen had abandoned all hope of ever seeing her brother again.* **5 abandon yourself to** *literary* to feel an emotion so strongly that you let it control you completely **6 abandon ship** to leave a ship because it is sinking —**abandonment** *n* [U] W3

**abandon²** *n* [U] **with gay/wild abandon** in a careless or uncontrolled way without thinking or caring about what you are doing: *The kids hurled pieces of wood on the fire with gay abandon.*

**a·ban·doned** /əˈbændənd/ *adj* **1** an abandoned building, car, boat etc has been left completely by the people who owned it and is no longer used **2** someone who is abandoned has been left completely alone by the person who was looking after them **3** *literary* behaving in a wild and uncontrolled way

**a·base** /əˈbeɪs/ *v* **abase yourself** to behave in a way that shows you accept that someone has complete power over you —**abasement** *n* [U]

**a·bashed** /əˈbæʃt/ *adj* [not before noun] embarrassed or ashamed because you have done something wrong or stupid: *She looked rather abashed.*

**a·bate** /əˈbeɪt/ *v* [I,T] *formal* to become less strong or decrease, or to make something do this: *We waited for the storm to abate.* —**abatement** *n* [U]

**ab·at·toir** /ˈæbətwɑː‖-ɑːr/ *n* [C] *BrE* a place where animals are killed for their meat; SLAUGHTERHOUSE

**ab·bess** /ˈæbɪ̱s, ˈæbes/ *n* [C] a woman who is in charge of a CONVENT (=religious institution for women)

**ab·bey** /ˈæbi/ *n* [C] a large church, especially one with buildings next to it where MONKS and NUNS live or used to live

**ab·bot** /ˈæbət/ *n* [C] a man who is in charge of a MONASTERY (=place where a group of MONKS live)

**abbr.** also **abbrev.** the written abbreviation of ABBREVIATION

**ab·bre·vi·ate** /əˈbriːvieɪt/ *v* [T] to make a word or expression shorter by missing out letters or using only the first letter of each word: **be abbreviated to** *'Information technology' is usually abbreviated to 'IT'.* —**abbreviated** *adj*

**ab·bre·vi·at·ed** /əˈbriːvieɪtɪ̱d/ *adj* made shorter by missing out letters or missing out parts of a story, statement etc: *Orders were passed to the commander at the front in an abbreviated form.*

**ab·bre·vi·a·tion** /əˌbriːviˈeɪʃən/ *n* **1** [C] a short form

of a word or expression: *'Dr.' is the written abbreviation of 'Doctor'.* **2** [U] the act of abbreviating something

**ABC¹** /ˌeɪ biː ˈsiː/ *n* also **ABCs** *AmE* **1** [singular] the letters of the English alphabet as taught to children **2 the ABC of** the basic facts about a particular subject

**ABC²** *n* [singular, U] American Broadcasting Corporation; one of the national television companies in the US

**ab·di·cate** /ˈæbdɪkeɪt/ *v* [I,T] **1** to give up the position of being king or queen **2 abdicate responsibility** *formal* to refuse to accept responsibility for something any longer —**abdication** /ˌæbdɪˈkeɪʃən/ *n* [C,U]

**ab·do·men** /ˈæbdəmən, æbˈdəʊ-‖-ˈdoʊ-/ *n* [C] **1** the part of your body between your chest and legs which contains your stomach **2** the end part of an insect's body, joined to the THORAX —**abdominal** /æbˈdɒmɪnəl‖-ˈdɑː-/ *adj*: *acute abdominal pains*

**ab·duct** /əbˈdʌkt, æb-/ *v* [T] to take someone away by force; KIDNAP: *Police suspect she was abducted late last night.* —**abductor** *n* [C] —**abduction** /əbˈdʌkʃən/ *n* [C,U]

**a·bed** /əˈbed/ *adj* [not before noun] *old-fashioned* in bed

**a·ber·rant** /ˈæbərənt, əˈberənt/ *adj formal* not usual or normal: *aberrant behaviour*

**ab·er·ra·tion** /ˌæbəˈreɪʃən/ *n* [C,U] an action or event that is different from what usually happens or what someone usually does: *a temporary aberration in US foreign policy | a mental aberration*

**a·bet** /əˈbet/ *v* **abetted, abetting** [T] to help someone do something wrong or illegal —see also **aid and abet** (AID² (2))

**a·bey·ance** /əˈbeɪəns/ *n* **in abeyance** something such as a custom, rule, or system that is in abeyance is not being used at the present time: **fall into abeyance** (=no longer be used)

**ab·hor** /əbˈhɔː‖-əbˈhɔːr, æb-/ *v* **abhorred, abhorring** [T not in progressive] *formal* to hate a kind of behaviour or way of thinking, especially because you think it is morally wrong: *Some genuinely abhorred slavery, others were simply convinced by the economic arguments against it.*

**ab·hor·rence** /əbˈhɒrəns‖-ˈhɔːr-/ *n* [U] *formal* a deep feeling of hatred towards something

**ab·hor·rent** /əbˈhɒrənt‖-ˈhɔːr-/ *adj formal* something that is abhorrent is completely unacceptable because it seems morally wrong; REPUGNANT: **[+ to]** *The practice of killing animals for food is utterly abhorrent to me.*

**a·bide** /əˈbaɪd/ *v* **1 can't abide** to dislike something or someone very much because you think they are very annoying: *I can't abide that man – he's so self-satisfied.* **2** *past tense* also **abode** /əˈbəʊd‖əˈboʊd/ [I always + adv/prep] *old-fashioned* to live somewhere

**abide by** sth *phr v* [T] to accept and obey a decision, rule, agreement etc, even though you may not agree with it: *You have to abide by the referee's decision.*

**a·bid·ing** /əˈbaɪdɪŋ/ *adj* an abiding feeling or belief continues for a long time and is not likely to change

S1 W1 **a·bil·i·ty** /əˈbɪlɪti/ *n plural* **abilities** [C,U] **1** something that you are able to do, especially because you have a particular mental or physical skill: **ability to do sth** *Our ability to think and speak separates us from other mammals.* | **have the ability to do sth** (=be able to do something, especially something that most people, machines etc cannot do) *These creatures have the ability to withstand very low temperatures.* | **of great/exceptional etc ability** (=very good at something) *a player of great ability | No one doubts her abilities as a manager.* **2** someone's, especially a student's, level of intelligence or skill, especially in school or college work: *There are children of all abilities in my class.* | **high/low/average ability** (=having a high, low etc level of intelligence or skill) | **mixed ability class** (=a class of students with different levels of intelligence) **3 to the best of your ability** to do something as well as you can

**-ability** /əˈbɪlɪti/ also **-ibility** *suffix* makes nouns from adjectives ending in -ABLE and -IBLE: *manageability | suitability*

**ab·ject** /ˈæbdʒekt/ *adj* **1 abject poverty/misery/failure etc** the state of being extremely poor, unhappy, unsuccessful etc **2** an abject action or expression shows that you feel very ashamed: *an abject apology* —**abjectly** *adv* —**abjection** /æbˈdʒekʃən,əb-/ *n* [U]

**ab·jure** /əbˈdʒʊə, æb-‖-ˌdʒʊr/ *v* [T] *formal* to state publicly that you will give up a particular belief or way of behaving; RENOUNCE (2) —**abjuration** /ˌæbdʒʊˈreɪʃən/ *n* [U]

**a·blaze** /əˈbleɪz/ *adj* **1 be ablaze** to be burning with a lot of flames, often causing serious damage: *Within minutes the whole house was ablaze.* | **set sth ablaze** (=make something burn a lot) *A tanker was set ablaze in the gunboat attack.* **2** filled with a lot of bright light or colour: *a passing pleasure-boat, with all its lights ablaze* | **[+ with]** *Her yard was ablaze with summer flowers.* **3 ablaze with anger/enthusiasm/excitement etc** very angry, excited etc about something —see also BLAZE

**a·ble** /ˈeɪbəl/ *adj* **1 be able to do sth a)** to have the skill, strength, knowledge etc to do something: *I've always wanted to be able to speak Japanese.* **b)** to be able to do something because the situation makes it possible for you to do it: *Despite his enormous workload the President still seems able to find time to go fishing. | I haven't been able to read that report yet.* —see CAN¹ (USAGE) **2** clever or good at doing something, especially at doing an important job; COMPETENT (1): *one of my more able students* S W

**-able** /əbəl/ also **-ible** *suffix* [in adjectives] **1** that you can do something to: *washable* (=it can be washed) | *unbreakable* (=it cannot be broken) | *loveable* (=easy to love) **2** having a particular quality or condition: *knowledgeable* (=knowing a lot) | *comfortable* —**-ably, -ibly** [in adverbs] *unbelievably*

**able-bod·ied** /ˌ·· ˈ··◂/ *adj* physically strong and healthy, especially when compared with someone who is DISABLED: *Every able-bodied man had to fight for his country.*

**able sea·man** /ˌ·· ˈ··/ *n* [C] a low rank in the navy, or someone who has this rank —see table on page B4

**a·blu·tions** /əˈbluːʃənz/ [plural] *n formal or humorous* the things that you do to make yourself clean, such as washing yourself, cleaning your teeth etc

**a·bly** /ˈeɪbli/ *adv* cleverly, skilfully, or well: *ably assisted by her team of researchers*

**ab·ne·ga·tion** /ˌæbnɪˈgeɪʃən/ *n* [U] *formal* the act of not allowing yourself to have or do something that you want

**ab·norm·al** /æbˈnɔːməl‖-ˈnɔːr-/ *adj* very different from usual in a way that seems strange, worrying, wrong, or dangerous: *abnormal behaviour | an abnormal level of cholesterol* | **abnormal for sb to do sth** *My parents thought it was abnormal for a boy to be interested in ballet.*

**ab·nor·mal·i·ty** /ˌæbnɔːˈmælɪti‖-nər-/ *n* [C,U] an abnormal feature or characteristic, especially something that is wrong with part of someone's body: *tests that can detect genetic abnormalities in the foetus*

**ab·nor·mal·ly** /æbˈnɔːməli‖-ˈnɔːr-/ *adv* **1 abnormally high/low/slow etc** unusually high, low etc, especially in a way that could cause problems: *an abnormally high pulse rate* **2** in an unusual and often worrying or dangerous way

**ab·o** /ˈæbəʊ‖-boʊ/ *n* [C] *taboo* an offensive word for an Australian ABORIGINE

**a·board¹** /əˈbɔːd‖əˈbɔːrd/ *prep* on or onto a ship, plane, or train: **go aboard** *They finally went aboard the plane.*

**aboard²** *adv* **1** on or onto a ship, plane, or train: *The plane crashed killing all 200 people aboard. | The boat swayed as he stepped aboard.* **2 All aboard!** *spoken* used to tell passengers of a ship, bus, or train that they must get on because it will leave soon

**a·bode¹** /əˈbəʊd‖əˈboʊd/ *n* [C] *formal or humorous* someone's home: *Welcome to my humble abode.* | **of no fixed abode** (=having no permanent home)

**abode²** the past tense of ABIDE

**a·bol·ish** /əˈbɒlɪʃ‖əˈbɑː-/ *v* [T] to officially end a law, system etc, especially one that has existed for a long time: *Slavery was abolished in America in the 19th century.* —**abolition** /ˌæbəˈlɪʃən/ *n* [U] *calls for the abolition of the monarchy*

**ab·o·li·tion·ist** /ˌæbəˈlɪʃənɪst/ *n* [C] someone who wants to end a system or law

**A-bomb** /ˈeɪ bɒm‖-bɑːm/ *n* [C] *old-fashioned* an ATOM BOMB

**a·bom·i·na·ble** /əˈbɒmɪnəbəl, -mənə-‖əˈbɑː-/ *adj* extremely unpleasant or of very bad quality —**abominably** *adv*: *Mavis behaved abominably.*

**abominable snow·man** /ˌ···· ˈ··/ *n* [C] a large creature like a human that is supposed to live in the Himalayas; a YETI

**a·bom·i·nate** /əˈbɒmɪneɪt‖əˈbɑː-/ *v* [T not in progressive] *formal* to hate something very much; ABHOR

**a·bom·i·na·tion** /əˌbɒmɪˈneɪʃən‖əˌbɑː-/ *n* **1** [C] someone or something that is extremely offensive or unacceptable: *They considered homosexuality as an abomination.* **2** [U + **of**] *formal* great hatred

**ab·o·rig·i·nal**[1] /ˌæbəˈrɪdʒɪnəl◂/ *adj* **1** *formal* connected with the people or animals that have existed in a place or country from the earliest times; INDIGENOUS **2** connected with the Australian aborigines

**aboriginal**[2] *n* [C] an aborigine

**ab·o·rig·i·ne** /ˌæbəˈrɪdʒɪni/ *n* [C] a member of the group of people who have lived in Australia from the earliest times

**a·bort** /əˈbɔːt‖-ɔːrt/ *v* **1** [T] to stop an activity because it would be difficult or dangerous to continue it: *The shuttle developed a computer problem and the mission had to be aborted.* **2** [T] to deliberately cause a baby to be born too soon so that it cannot live, often because the baby or the mother has medical problems: *Doctors decided to abort the pregnancy.* **3** [I,T] if a woman aborts or aborts her baby, the baby is born too early and is dead when it is born

**a·bor·tion** /əˈbɔːʃən‖əˈbɔːr-/ *n* [C,U] a medical operation in which a baby's development inside a woman is stopped so that it is not born alive: **have an abortion** *an unmarried mother who had an abortion when she was 16* | *anti-abortion campaigners*

**a·bor·tion·ist** /əˈbɔːʃənɪst‖əˈbɔːr-/ *n* [C] someone who does abortions illegally

**a·bor·tive** /əˈbɔːtɪv‖əˈbɔːr-/ *adj* an abortive action is not successful: *an abortive military coup* | **abortive attempt/effort** *an abortive attempt to reform local government*

**a·bound** /əˈbaʊnd/ *v* [I] to exist in very large numbers or quantities: *Rumours abound as to the reasons for his resignation.* | *Examples of this abound in her book.*

**abound with/in** sth *phr v* [T] if a place, situation etc abounds with something it contains a very large number or quantity of that thing

S1 W1 **a·bout**[1] /əˈbaʊt/ *prep* **1** on or dealing with a particular subject: *a book about politics* | *She said something about leaving town.* | **all about** (=all the details of a particular subject) *Naturally, my mother wanted to know all about it.* **2** in many different directions within a particular place, or in different parts of a place: *We spent the whole afternoon walking about town.* | *Books were scattered about the room.* —see also ROUND (USAGE) —see picture on page 1257 **3** in the nature or character of a person or thing: *There's something really odd about Liza.* | *What I like about the movie is the dialogue.* **4 what about/how about** *spoken* **a)** used to ask for news or information about someone or something: *What about Jack? We can't just leave him here.* **b)** used to a make a suggestion: *How about a salad for lunch?* **5** *spoken* used to introduce a subject that you want to talk about: *About that car of yours. How much are you selling it for?* | **it's about** *It's about Tommy, doctor. He's been sick again.* **6 do sth about** to do something to solve a problem or stop a bad situation: *What can be done about the rising levels of pollution?* **7** if an organization, a job, an activity etc is about something, that is its basic purpose: *Basically, the job's all about helping people get the benefits they are entitled to.* **8 be quick about it** *spoken* used to tell someone to do something quickly: *Get me a drink and be quick about it.* **9 while you're about it** *spoken* used to tell someone to do something while they are doing something else because it would be easier to do both at the same time: *Clean up while I'm away and you might as well do the attic while you're about it.* **10 about your person** *formal* if you hide something about your person, you hide it in your clothes: *He had concealed the weapon somewhere about his person.* **11** *literary* surrounding a person or thing: *Jo sensed fear and jealousy all about her.*

**about**[2] *adv* **1** more or less a particular number or amount; approximately (APPROXIMATE[1]): *I live about 10 miles away.* | **round about** (=used when guessing a exact number or amount) *We left the restaurant at round about 10.30.* —see graph at APPROXIMATE[1] **2** in many different directions within a place or in different parts of a place: *Cushions were scattered about on the chairs.* **3** near to you or in the same place as you: *Is Derrick about? There's a phone call for him.* | *Quick! Let's go while there's no-one about.* **4 there's a lot of sth about/there's not much of sth about** *especially spoken* used to say that something is very common, or that not much of it exists or is available: *I hope she hasn't caught that flu bug. There's a lot of it about at the moment.* **5** *informal* almost: *The food's about ready.* —see also **just about** (JUST[1] (8)) **6 that's about it/all** *informal* used to tell someone that you have told them everything you know: *He was a quiet chap, married with kids. That's about it really.* **7** in the opposite direction that you were facing before: *He quickly turned about.* —see also ROUND[3] (USAGE) S1 W1

**about**[3] *adj* **1 be about to do sth** if someone is about to do something or if something is about to happen, they will do it or it will happen very soon: *Sit down everyone. The film's about to start.* **2 not be about to do sth** *informal* used to emphasize that you have no intention of doing something: *I've never smoked in my life and I'm not about to start now.* —see also **out and about** (OUT[1] (33)), **be up and about** (UP[3] (6))

**about-face** /ˌ·ˈ·/ *n* [C usually singular] a complete change in the way someone thinks or behaves: **do an about-face** *The administration seems to have done a complete about-face on gun-control.*

**about-turn** /ˌ·ˈ·/ *n* [C usually singular] *BrE* an about-face

**above**

The picture is above the fireplace / over the fireplace.

The girl jumped over the wall.

The man put his hand over the boy's mouth.

**a·bove**[1] /əˈbʌv/ *prep* **1** in a higher position than something: *Our office is above the hairdresser's.* | *Raise your* S2 

*arms above your head.* —see also OVER[1] —opposite BELOW[1] (1) **2** more than a particular number, amount, or level: *500 feet above sea level | Tonight temperatures should be above freezing.* —opposite BELOW[1] (2) **3** to a greater degree than someone or something else: *The management has always valued hard work above good ideas.* | **above and beyond** (=to a much greater degree) *bravery above and beyond the call of duty* **4** higher in rank, power, or authority: *A captain is above a lieutenant.* —opposite BELOW[1] (3) **5** louder or having a higher PITCH than other sounds: *You can always hear her voice above everybody else's.* **6 be above (doing) sth** to consider yourself so important that you do not have to do all the things that everyone else has to do: *She seems to think she's above doing any housework. | politicians who think they are above the law* **7 above suspicion/reproach/criticism etc** so good that no one can question or criticize you **8 above all (else)** used to emphasize that something is more important than the other things you have already mentioned: *Max is fair, hardworking, and above all honest.* **9 get above yourself** to think you are better or more important than you really are —see also **over and above** (OVER[1] (13))

S2 W1 **above**[2] *adv* **1** in a higher place than something else: *I heard a strange noise coming from the room above.* **2** more than a particular number, amount, or level: *Children aged 10 and above are not allowed in the learner pool.* **3** higher in rank, power, or authority: *officers of the rank of Major and above* **4** *formal* used in a book, article etc to describe someone or something mentioned earlier in the same piece of writing: *See above. | Write to the address given above for further information.* —opposite BELOW[2]

> **USAGE NOTE: ABOVE**
> FORMALITY
> **Above** meaning 'mentioned earlier' is only used in technical or official writing. In everyday writing you are more likely to put: *As I said earlier... (=...stated above) | The facts discussed before... (=...discussed above) | Please contact me at the address I have given you (=...at the above address). | From the last few paragraphs (=from the above paragraphs).*

W3 **above**[3] *adj* **1** [only before noun] used in a book, article etc to describe someone or something mentioned earlier in the same piece of writing: *For the above reasons, the management has no choice but to close the factory.* **2 the above** *formal* [singular or plural] the person or thing mentioned before in the same piece of writing: *The above is the profit before tax. | All the above are asked to attend tomorrow's meeting.*

**above board** /·ˌ· ˈ·◂,·ˈ· ·‖·ˈ· ·/ *adj* [not before noun] honest and legal: **open and above board** *The deal was completely open and above board.*

**above-men·tioned** /·ˌ· ˈ··◂/ *adj* **1** [only before noun] *formal* mentioned on a previous page or higher up on the same page **2 the above-mentioned** people whose names have already been mentioned in a book, document etc —compare UNDERMENTIONED

**ab·ra·ca·dab·ra** /ˌæbrəkəˈdæbrə/ *interjection* a word you say when you do a magic trick, which is supposed to make it successful

**a·brade** /əˈbreɪd/ *v* [I,T] *technical* to rub something so hard that the surface becomes damaged

**a·bra·sion** /əˈbreɪʒən/ *n technical* **1** [C] an area, especially on the surface of your skin, that has been damaged or injured by being rubbed too hard: *minor abrasions* **2** [U] the process of rubbing a surface very hard so that it becomes damaged or disappears

**a·bra·sive**[1] /əˈbreɪsɪv/ *adj* **1** seeming rude or unkind in the way you behave towards people because you say what you think very directly: *a rather abrasive manner* **2** having a rough surface, especially one that can be used to clean other surfaces by rubbing —**abrasively** *adv*

**abrasive**[2] *n* [C usually plural] a substance with a rough surface that you use for cleaning other things by rubbing

**abreast**

They cycled three abreast.

**a·breast** /əˈbrest/ *adv* **1 walk/ride etc abreast** to walk, ride etc next to each other: **two/three/four abreast etc** (=with two or more people next to each other) **2 keep abreast of** to make sure that you know all the most recent facts or information about a particular subject or situation: *Henry tries to keep abreast of the latest developments in computing.*

**a·bridged** /əˈbrɪdʒd/ *adj* an abridged book, play etc has been made shorter but keeps its basic structure and meaning —**abridge** *v* [T] —**abridgement** *n* [C,U]

**a·broad** /əˈbrɔːd‖əˈbrɒːd/ *adv* **1** in or to a foreign country: *I've never lived abroad before.* | **go abroad** *She often goes abroad on business.* **2** *formal* if a feeling, piece of news etc is abroad, a lot of people feel it or know about it: *commercial secrets which we did not want to be spread abroad* **3** *old use* outdoors 

**ab·ro·gate** /ˈæbrəgeɪt/ *v* [T] *formal* to officially end a law, legal agreement, practice etc: *Both governments voted to abrogate the treaty.* —**abrogation** /ˌæbrəˈgeɪʃən/ *n* [C,U]

**a·brupt** /əˈbrʌpt/ *adj* **1** sudden and unexpected: *an abrupt change of plan* | **abrupt halt** *The bus came to an abrupt halt.* **2** seeming rude and unfriendly, especially because you do not waste time in friendly conversation; BRUSQUE: *Sorry, I didn't mean to be so abrupt.* —**abruptly** *adv* —**abruptness** *n* [U]

**ABS** /ˌeɪ biː ˈes/ *n* [U] the abbreviation of ANTI-LOCK BRAKING SYSTEM

**ab·scess** /ˈæbses/ *n* [C] a painful swollen part of your skin or inside your body that has become infected and is full of a yellowish liquid

**ab·scond** /əbˈskɒnd, æb-‖æbˈskɑːnd/ *v* [I] **1** to suddenly leave the place where you work after having stolen money from it: [+ **with**] *The chief accountant had absconded with all the money.* **2** to escape from a place where you are being kept for doing something wrong: *Several boys have absconded from the detention centre.*

**ab·seil** /ˈæbseɪl/ *v* [I + **down**] *BrE* to go down a cliff or a rock by sliding down a rope and touching the cliff or rock with your feet; RAPPEL *AmE*

**ab·sence** /ˈæbsəns/ *n* **1** [C,U] the fact that someone is not in the place where people expect them to be: **in/during sb's absence** (=while they are away) *Ms Leighton will be in charge during my absence.* **2** [U] the lack of something or the fact that it does not exist: [+ **of**] *a complete absence of any kind of planning* | **in the absence of** (=because something is missing or not available) *In the absence of any evidence, the police had to let Myers go.* **3 absence makes the heart grow fonder** S W

used to say that being away from someone makes you like them more —see also **leave of absence** (LEAVE² (3)), **conspicuous by your absence** (CONSPICUOUS (3))

**ab·sent¹** /ˈæbsənt/ *adj* **1** not at work, school, a meeting etc, because you are sick or decide not to go: [+ **from**] *students who are regularly absent from school* **2 absent look/expression etc** a look etc that shows you are not paying attention to or thinking about what is happening —see also ABSENTLY **3** *formal* if something is absent, it is missing or it is not in the place where it is expected to be: [+ **from**] *What was absent from the discussion was any kind of direction or purpose.*

**ab·sent²** /əbˈsent,æb-‖æb-/ *v* [T] **absent yourself (from)** *formal* to not go to a place or take part in an event where people expect you to be

**ab·sen·tee** /ˌæbsənˈtiː◂/ *n* [C] someone who should be in a place or at an event but is not there

**absentee bal·lot** /ˌ··· ˈ··/ *n* [C] *AmE* a process by which people can vote before an election because they will be away during the election

**ab·sen·tee·is·m** /ˌæbsənˈtiːɪzəm/ *n* [U] regular absence from work or school without a good reason

**absentee land·lord** /ˌ··· ˈ··/ *n* [C] someone who lives a long way away from a house or apartment which they rent to other people, and who rarely or never visits it

**absentee vote** /ˌ··· ˈ·/ *n* [C] *AmE* a vote which you send by post in an election because you cannot be in the place where you usually vote; POSTAL VOTE *BrE*

**ab·sen·ti·a** /æbˈsentiə/ *n* **in absentia** *formal* when you are not at a court or an official meeting where a decision is made about you: *They were sentenced in absentia.*

**ab·sent·ly** /ˈæbsəntli/ *adv* in a way that shows that you are not paying attention to or thinking about what is happening: *Laura gazed absently out of the window.*

**absent-mind·ed** /ˌ·· ˈ··◂/ *adj* likely to forget things, especially because you are thinking about something else: *She's getting very absent-minded.* —**absent-mindedly** *adv* —**absent-mindedness** *n* [U]

**ab·sinth, absinthe** /ˈæbsɪnθ/ *n* [U] a bitter green very strong alcoholic drink

S2 W3 **ab·so·lute** /ˈæbsəluːt/ *adj* **1** [only before noun] *especially spoken* used to emphasize your opinion about something or someone, especially when you think they are very bad, stupid, unsuccessful etc: **absolute disgrace/disaster/chaos etc** *The house looked an absolute shambles.* | *I think it's an absolute disgrace the way they treat that child.* | **an absolute genius/fool/idiot etc** *How did you do that? You're an absolute genius.* | **absolute nonsense/rubbish** (=used to say that you think that what someone is saying is completely stupid) **2** absolute silence, freedom, loyalty etc is the state of being completely silent, free etc: *I have absolute confidence in her.* **3** absolute power or authority is complete and unlimited: **absolute ruler/monarch** (=a ruler with unlimited power) **4** definite and not likely to change: *I can't give you any absolute guarantees about your safety.* **5 in absolute terms** measured by itself, not in comparison with other things: *In absolute terms wages have risen, but not in comparison with the cost of living.*

S1 W3 **ab·so·lute·ly** /ˈæbsəluːtli, ˌæbsəˈluːtli/ *adv* **1** *especially spoken* completely and in every way: [+ adj/adv] *He's an absolutely brilliant singer.* | *You can trust her absolutely!* | *You look absolutely fantastic in that dress.* | **absolutely no/nothing** (=none or nothing at all) *He has absolutely no experience of marketing.* | *The burglars took absolutely everything.* **2 absolutely!** *spoken* used to say that you completely agree with someone: *Oh yes, absolutely. I think it's a great idea.* **3 absolutely not!** *spoken* used when saying strongly that someone must not do something or when strongly disagreeing with someone: *"Do you let your kids travel alone at night?" "Absolutely not!"*

Frequencies of the adverb **absolutely** in spoken and written English.

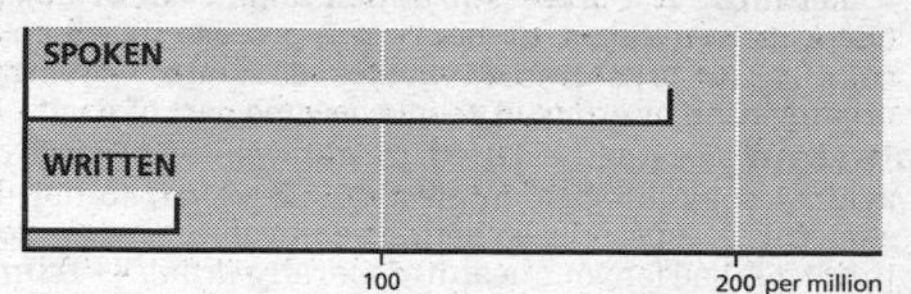


Based on the British National Corpus and the Longman Lancaster Corpus

This graph shows that the adverb **absolutely** is much more common in spoken English than in written English. This is because it is used to emphasize adjectives like **brilliant**, **stupid**, **fantastic** etc in spoken English.

**absolute ze·ro** /ˌ··· ˈ··/ *n* [singular] the lowest temperature that is believed to be possible

**ab·so·lu·tion** /ˌæbsəˈluːʃən/ *n* [U] a process in the Christian religion by which someone is forgiven for the things they have done wrong

**ab·so·lut·is·m** /ˈæbsəluːtɪzəm/ *n* [U] a political system in which one ruler has complete power and authority

**ab·solve** /əbˈzɒlv‖-ɑːlv/ *v* [T] *formal* **1** to say publicly that someone is not guilty or responsible for something: **absolve sb from/of sth** *They were absolved of all responsibility for the accident.* **2** [often passive] to forgive someone for something they have done wrong

**absorb**

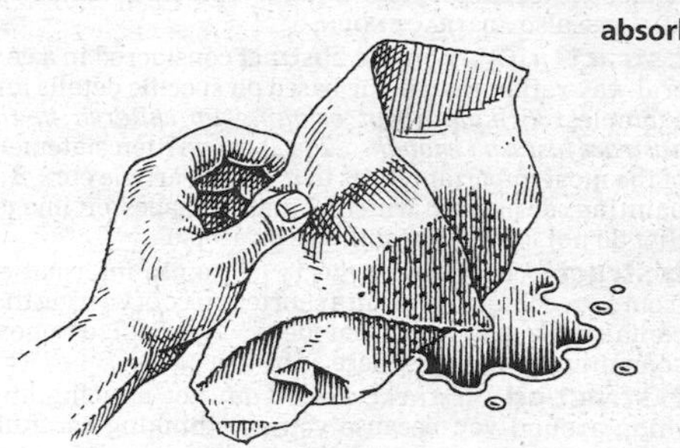

**ab·sorb** /əbˈsɔːb, əbˈzɔːb‖-ɔːrb/ *v* [T] W3

**1** ► **LIQUID** ◄ if something absorbs a liquid, it takes the liquid into itself from the surface or space around it: *Plants absorb nutrients from the soil.*

**2** ► **INFORMATION** ◄ to read or hear a large amount of new information and understand it: *I haven't really had time to absorb everything that he said.*

**3** ► **INTEREST** ◄ to interest someone very much: **be absorbed in** *Judith lay on the settee, absorbed in her book.* | **absorb sb's attention** *The video was totally absorbing the children's attention.*

**4** ► **BECOME PART OF** ◄ to make a smaller country, company, or group of people become part of your country, company, or group: *The US was able to absorb thousands of new immigrants.* | **be absorbed into** *More and more newspapers are being absorbed into the Murdoch empire.*

**5** ► **MONEY/TIME ETC** ◄ if something absorbs money, time etc it uses a lot of it: *Defence spending absorbs almost 20% of the country's wealth.*

**6** ► **FORCE** ◄ to reduce the effect of a sudden violent movement: *The solid walls absorbed much of the impact of the explosion.*

**7** ► **LIGHT/HEAT/ENERGY** ◄ if a substance or object absorbs light, heat, or energy, it keeps it and does not REFLECT it (=send it back) *Black objects absorb heat more.*

**ab·sor·bent** /əbˈsɔːbənt, -ˈzɔː-‖-ɔːr-/ *adj* able to take in liquids easily: *absorbent material*

**ab·sorb·ing** /əbˈsɔːbɪŋ, -ˈzɔː-‖-ɔːr-/ *adj* enjoyable and interesting and holding your attention for a long time: *an absorbing documentary about Communist China*

**ab·sorp·tion** /əbˈsɔːpʃən,-ˈzɔːp-‖-ɔːr-/ *n* [U] **1** [+ **with/in**] the fact of being very interested in something **2** a process in which a material or object takes in liquid, gas, or heat **3** a process in which a country or organization, makes a smaller country, organization or group of people become part of itself

**ab·stain** /əbˈsteɪn/ *v* [I] **1** to not vote either for or against something in an election **2** *formal* to not do something, especially something enjoyable, because you think it is bad for your health or morally wrong: [+ **from**] *Pilots must abstain from alcohol for 24 hours before flying.* —**abstainer** *n* [C]

**ab·ste·mi·ous** /əbˈstiːmiəs/ *adj formal or humorous* careful not to have too much food, drink etc —**abstemiously** *adv* —**abstemiousness** *n* [U]

**ab·sten·tion** /əbˈstenʃən/ *n* [C,U] a vote in an election which is neither for nor against something or someone

**ab·sti·nence** /ˈæbstɪ̣nəns/ *n* [U] the practice of not doing something you enjoy, especially not drinking alcohol —**abstinent** *adj*

**ab·stract¹** /ˈæbstrækt/ *adj* **1** based on general ideas or principles rather than specific examples or real events: **abstract thought/reasoning** (=thought about complicated ideas rather than about things that are around you) *a machine that is capable of abstract thought* **2** existing only as an idea or quality rather than as something real that you can see or touch: *Beauty is an abstract concept.* —compare CONCRETE² (2) **3** abstract paintings, designs etc consist of shapes and patterns that do not look like real people or things —compare FIGURATIVE (2) —see also ABSTRACT NOUN

**abstract²** *n* [C] **1 in the abstract** considered in a general way rather than being based on specific details and examples: *Talking about bringing up children in the abstract just isn't enough.* **2** a short written statement of the most important ideas in a speech, article etc **3** a painting, design etc which contains shapes or images that do not look like real things or people

**ab·stract³** /əbˈstrækt,æb-/ *v* [T] **1** to use information from a speech, article etc in a shorter piece of writing that contains the most important ideas **2** *formal* to remove something from somewhere or from a place

**ab·stract·ed** /əbˈstræktɪ̣d, æb-/ *adj* not noticing anything around you because you are thinking carefully about something else —**abstractedly** *adv*

**ab·strac·tion** /əbˈstrækʃən, æb-/ *n* **1** [C] a general idea about a type of situation, thing, or person, rather than a specific example from real life: *talking in abstractions* **2** [U] a state in which you do not notice what is happening around you because you are thinking carefully about something else

**abstract noun** /ˌ·· ˈ·/ *n* [C] a noun that names a feeling, quality, or state rather than an object, animal, or person: *'Hunger' and 'beauty' are abstract nouns.*

**ab·struse** /əbˈstruːs, æb-/ *adj formal* difficult to understand in a way that seems unnecessarily complicated —**abstrusely** *adv* —**abstruseness** *n* [U]

**ab·surd** /əbˈsɜːd,-ˈzɜːd‖-ɜːrd/ *adj* completely stupid or unreasonable; RIDICULOUS: *Don't be absurd!* | *It seems quite absurd to expect anyone to drive for 3 hours just for a 20 minute meeting.* —**absurdity** *n* [C,U]

**ab·surd·ly** /əbˈsɜːdli,-ˈzɜːd-‖-ɜːr-/ *adv* **absurdly cheap/difficult/easy etc** so cheap, difficult etc that it seems surprising, unusual, or even funny: *Prices on the island seem absurdly low to Western tourists.*

**a·bun·dance** /əˈbʌndəns/ *n* [singular, U] a large quantity of something: **an abundance of** *an abundance of wavy red hair* | **in abundance** *Wild flowers grow in abundance on the hillsides.*

**a·bun·dant** /əˈbʌndənt/ *adj* existing or available in large quantities so that there is more than enough; PLENTIFUL: *abundant supplies*

**a·bun·dant·ly** /əˈbʌndəntli/ *adv* **1** in large quantities: *a force of Marines, abundantly equipped with anti-aircraft guns* | *Melons grow abundantly in this region.* **2 abundantly clear** very easy to understand so that anyone should be able to realize it: *It's abundantly clear what the outcome will be.* | **make sth abundantly clear** (=say something very clearly) *Caroline made it abundantly clear that she didn't want Chuck around.*

**a·buse¹** /əˈbjuːs/ *n* **1** [C,U] the use of something in a way that it should not be used: [+ **of**] *government officials' abuse of power* | **open to abuse** (=able or likely to be used in the wrong way) *The city's metro system is open to abuse by fare dodgers.* | **alcohol/drug/solvent abuse** (=the practice of drinking too much or taking illegal drugs) *The fraud department only deals with the worst abuse.* **2** [U] rude or offensive things that someone says to someone else: *I don't see why I should put up with this kind of abuse from anyone.* | **a stream/torrent of abuse** (=a series of rude or angry words) | **shout/scream/hurl abuse at** *The driver leaned out of his window and started hurling abuse at me.* | **a term of abuse** (=a word or phrase used to insult someone) **3** [U] cruel or violent treatment, often involving forced sexual activity, of someone that you are responsible for or should look after: *child abuse* | *sexual abuse* S W

**a·buse²** /əˈbjuːz/ *v* [T] **1** to deliberately use something such as power or authority, for the wrong purpose: *Williams abused his position as Mayor to give jobs to his friends.* | **abuse sb's trust/confidence etc** (=deceive someone who trusts or depends on you in order to get advantages for yourself) **2** to treat someone in a cruel and violent way, often sexually, especially someone that you should look after: *People who were abused as children often turn into child-abusers themselves.* **3** to say rude or offensive things to someone **4** to treat something so badly that you start to destroy it: *Richards abused his body for years with heroin and cocaine.* **5 abuse yourself** to MASTURBATE

**a·bu·sive** /əˈbjuːsɪv/ *adj* very rude and using offensive language, especially because you are angry: **get/become abusive** *She got quite abusive on the phone.* —**abusively** *adv* —**abusiveness** *n* [U]

**a·but** /əˈbʌt/ also **abut on** *v* [T] *technical* if one piece of land or a building abuts another it is next to it or touches one side of it

**a·bys·mal** /əˈbɪzməl/ *adj* very bad; TERRIBLE (3): *the Labour Party's abysmal performance in the last election* —**abysmally** *adv*: *Educational standards were abysmally low.*

**a·byss** /əˈbɪs/ *n* [C] *literary* **1** a deep empty space, seen from a high point such as a mountain: *The ocean floor drops away into a dark abyss.* **2** a very dangerous or frightening situation: *the abyss of a nuclear war* **3** a great difference which separates two people or groups: *the abyss between rich and poor*

**AC** **1** the written abbreviation of ALTERNATING CURRENT —compare DC (1) **2** the written abbreviation of AIR-CONDITIONING —see also AC/DC

**a/c** *BrE* the written abbreviation of ACCOUNT¹ (2)

**a·ca·cia** /əˈkeɪʃə/ *n* [C] a tree with small yellow or white flowers that grows in warm countries

**ac·a·de·mi·a** /ˌækəˈdiːmiə/ *n* [U] the area of activity and work connected with education in colleges and universities

**ac·a·dem·ic¹** /ˌækəˈdemɪk◂/ *adj* **1** [usually before noun] connected with education, especially at college or university level: *She loved the city, with its academic atmosphere.* | *academic books* | *a program designed to raise academic standards* **2** [usually before noun] concerned with studying from books, as opposed to practical work **3** something that is academic is not important because it cannot happen or have any effect; THEORETICAL: | **purely academic** *The question of where we go on holiday is purely academic since we don't have any money.* **4** good at studying and getting good results at school or university: *He's a popular child, but not very academic.* —**academically** /-kli/ *adv* W

**academic²** *n* [C] a teacher in a college or university

**a·cad·e·mi·cian** /ə,kædə'mɪʃən‖,ækədə-/ *n* [C] a member of an academy

**academic year** /,···· '·/ *n* [C] *especially BrE* the period of the year during which there are school or university classes; school year (SCHOOL[1])

**a·cad·e·my** /ə'kædəmi/ *n* [C] **1** an important official organization consisting of people interested in the development of literature, art, science etc: *the American Academy of Arts and Letters* **2** a college where students are taught a particular subject or skill: *a military academy | the Academy of Music* **3** a school in Scotland for children between 11 and 16

**a cap·pel·la** /,æ kæ'pelə‖,ɑː kə-/ *adj, adv* sung without any musical instruments

**acc.** the written abbreviation of ACCOUNT[1]

**ac·cede** /ək'siːd, æk-/ *v*

**accede to** sth *phr v* [T] *formal* **1** to agree to a demand, proposal etc, especially after first disagreeing with it: *The government would not accede to public pressure.* **2** to achieve a position of power or authority

**ac·cel·e·ran·do** /æk,selə'rændəʊ‖-'rɑːndoʊ/ *adj, adv music* getting gradually faster

**ac·cel·e·rate** /ək'seləreɪt/ *v* **1** [I] if a vehicle or someone who is driving it accelerates, it starts to go faster: *The Ferrari Mondial can accelerate from 0 to 60 mph in 6.3 seconds.* **2** [I,T] if a process accelerates or if something accelerates it, it happens faster than usual or sooner than you expect: *measures to accelerate the rate of economic growth* —opposite DECELERATE

**ac·cel·e·ra·tion** /ək,selə'reɪʃən/ *n* **1** [U] the rate at which a car or other vehicle can go faster: *The latest model has excellent acceleration.* **2** [singular, U] a process in which something happens more and more quickly: *an acceleration in the decline of the coal industry* **3** [U] *technical* the rate at which the speed of an object increases

**ac·cel·e·ra·tor** /ək'seləreɪtə‖-ər/ *n* [C] **1** the part of a vehicle, especially a car, that you press to make it go faster; GAS PEDAL *AmE* —see picture on page 409 **2** *technical* a large machine used to make extremely small pieces of matter move at extremely high speeds

**ac·cent**[1] /'æksənt‖'æksent/ *n* [C] **1** the way someone pronounces the words of a language, showing which country or which part of a country they come from: *Alex spoke Portuguese with a Brazilian accent.* | **strong/broad accent** *a broad Irish accent* —compare DIALECT **2 the accent is on** if the accent is on a particular quality, feeling etc, that quality or feeling is emphasized: *We put the accent on team work at this club rather than individual skills.* **3** the part of a word that you should emphasize when you say it: **[+ on]** *In the word 'corset' the accent is on the first syllable.* —see also STRESS[1] (4) **4** a written mark used above certain letters in some languages to show how to pronounce that letter: *an acute accent*

**ac·cent**[2] /ək'sent‖'æksent/ *v* [T] to emphasize a part of something, especially part of a word in speech

**ac·cen·ted** /ək'sentɪ̣d‖'æksen-/ *adj* **heavily accented** words or speech that are heavily accented are spoken with a very strong accent

**ac·cen·tu·ate** /ək'sentʃueɪt/ *v* [T] to emphasize something, especially the difference between two conditions or situations —**accentuation** /ək,sentʃu'eɪʃən/ *n* [C,U]

1 **ac·cept** /ək'sept/ *v*

1 **1 ► GIFT/OFFER/INVITATION ◄** [I,T] to take something that someone offers you, or to agree to do something that someone asked you to do: *Please accept this small gift. | I've decided to accept the job. | Are you going to accept their invitation? | We've invited her here to give a talk, and she's accepted.* | **accept sth from sb** *He is charged with accepting bribes from local companies.* | **accept a challenge** (=agree to do something difficult) —see REFUSE[1] (USAGE)

**2 ► PLAN/SUGGESTION/ADVICE ◄** [T] to decide to do what someone advises or suggests you should do: *I wish I'd accepted your advice and kept my money in the bank.*

**3 ► IDEA/STATEMENT/EXPLANATION ◄** [T] to agree that what someone says is right or true: *She managed to persuade the jury to accept her version of events.* | **accept that** *I'm willing to accept that some mistakes have been made.*

**4 ► SITUATION/PROBLEM ETC ◄** [T] to decide that there is nothing you can do to change a difficult and unpleasant situation or fact and continue with your normal life: *There's nothing we can do about it so we'll just have to accept it.* | **accept the fact that** *I found it hard to accept the fact that she'd gone.*

**5 ► THINK SB/STH GOOD ENOUGH ◄** [T] to decide that someone has the necessary skill or intelligence for a particular job, course etc or that a piece of work is good enough: **accept sb/sth for** *My story's been accepted for the school magazine.*

**6 ► BECOME PART OF ◄** [T] to allow someone to become part of a group, society, or organization and to treat them in the same way as the other members: *The children gradually began to accept her as one of the family.* | **accept sb into** *It often takes years for immigrants to be accepted into the host community.*

**7 accept blame/responsibility** to admit that you were responsible for something bad that happened: *The ship's owners are refusing to accept any responsibility for the accident.*

**8 accept sb's apology** to say that you are no longer angry with someone after they have said they were sorry about something they have done

**9 ► MONEY ◄** [T] to allow customers to use a particular kind of money to pay for things: *We don't accept travelers' checks.*

**ac·cep·ta·ble** /ək'septəbəl/ *adj* **1** good enough to be S3
used for a particular purpose or to be considered satisfac- W3
tory: *a cheap and acceptable substitute for rubber* | **[+ to]** *The dispute was settled in a way that was acceptable to both sides.* **2** acceptable behaviour is considered to be morally or socially good enough: *Smoking is no longer considered socially acceptable by many people.* | **acceptable for sb to do sth** *I just don't think it's acceptable for children to interrupt all the time.* | **acceptable level/amount** (=neither too high nor too low) *They talk about 'acceptable levels of unemployment'.* —**acceptably** *adv* —**acceptability** /ək,septə'bɪlɪ̣ti/ *n* [U]

**ac·cept·ance** /ək'septəns/ *n* **1** [U] official agreement W3
to take something that you have been offered: **[+ of]** *Russia's acceptance of economic aid from Western countries* | **a letter of acceptance** (=a letter you write in which you agree to accept a job, an opportunity to study somewhere etc) **2** [singular, U] the act of agreeing that an idea, statement, explanation etc is right or true: **gain/find acceptance** (=become accepted) *Feminist ideas have now found widespread acceptance.* **3** [U] the ability to accept an unpleasant situation which cannot be changed, without getting angry or upset about it **4** [singular, U] the process of allowing someone to become part of a group or a society and of treating them in the same way as the other members: *Acceptance by their peer group is important to most youngsters.*

**ac·cess**[1] /'ækses/ *n* [U] **1** the way by which you can S3
enter a building or reach a place: *Access is by means of a* W1
*small door on the right.* | **[+ to]** *Access to the restrooms is through the foyer.* **2** how easy or difficult it is for people to enter a public building or to reach a place: **[+ for]** *We're trying to improve access for disabled visitors.* | **have easy/good access to** (=be able to reach another place easily) *The house is in a central location with good access to the shops.* **3** the right to enter a place: **have access to** *The public don't have access to the site.* **4 have access to** to have the right to see official documents, especially secret documents: *Access to the papers is restricted to Defense Department personnel only.* **5** the legal right to see and spend time with your children, a prisoner, an official etc: *My ex-husband has access to the*

*children once a week.* **6 have access to a phone/a computer etc** to have a telephone, computer etc near you which you can use **7 gain/get access (to)** to succeed in entering a place or in seeing someone or something: *The police managed to gain access through an upstairs window.*

**access²** *v* [T] to find information, especially on a computer

**ac·ces·si·ble** /ək'sesəbəl/ *adj* **1** easy to reach or get into: *The cove is only accessible by boat.* —opposite INACCESSIBLE **2** easy to obtain or use: **easily/readily accessible** *Storing customer details on computer makes them readily accessible.* **3** someone who is accessible is easy to meet and talk to, even if they are very important or powerful: *I think that you'll find she's very accessible.* **4** easy to understand and enjoy: *Buchan succeeds in making a difficult subject accessible to the reader.* —**accessibly** *adv* —**accessibility** /əkˌsesə'bɪləti/ *n* [U]

**ac·ces·sion** /ək'seʃən/ *n formal* **1** [U] a process in which someone becomes king, queen, president etc: **accession to the throne** (=the act of becoming king or queen) —compare SUCCESSION **2** [U + **to**] the act of agreeing to a demand **3** [C,U] an object or work of art that is added to a collection, especially in a MUSEUM

**ac·ces·so·ry** /ək'sesəri/ *n* [C usually plural] **1** something that you add to a machine, tool, car etc so that it can do other things, or in order to make it look attractive: *Accessories include a CD player and alloy wheels.* **2** [C] something such as a bag, belt, jewellery etc that you wear or carry because it is attractive: *fashion accessories* **3** [C] *law* someone who helps a criminal, especially by helping them hide from the police: [+ **to**] *an accessory to murder* | **an accessory before/after the fact** (=someone who helps a criminal before or after the crime)

**access time** /'·· ˌ·/ *n* [C,U] *technical* the time taken by a computer to find and use a piece of information in its memory

S1 W2 **ac·ci·dent** /'æksədənt/ *n* [C] **1 by accident** in a way that is not planned or intended: *I met her quite by accident.* **2** a situation in which someone is injured or something is damaged without anyone intending them to be: **have an accident** *Ken's had an accident at work and he's had to go to hospital.* | **climbing/skiing/riding etc accident** *Five people have been killed in a climbing accident in Nepal.* **3** a crash involving cars, trains, planes etc: **car/automobile/traffic accident** *Her father's been involved in an automobile accident.* | **bad/serious/nasty accident** *A serious accident is blocking the southbound side of the M1.* **4** something that happens without anyone planning or intending it: *I'm really sorry about your camera – it was an accident.* | **a happy accident** (=a lucky or pleasant event or situation which happens without anyone planning it) | **a chapter of accidents** (=a series of unfortunate events that happen without anyone planning them) | **an accident of birth/nature/history etc** (=an event or situation that happens without anyone planning it) **5 accidents will happen** *spoken* used to comfort someone who feels responsible for something bad that has happened **6 have an accident** if a child has an accident, he or she URINATES by mistake

**ac·ci·den·tal** /ˌæksə'dentl◂/ *adj* happening without being planned or intended: *an accidental discharge of toxic waste*

**accidental death** /ˌ···· '·/ *n* [U] *law* an expression used by a British court when it has decided that someone's death was caused by an accident

**ac·ci·den·tal·ly** /ˌæksə'dentl-i/ *adv* **1** without intending to: *I accidentally locked myself out of the house.* **2 accidentally on purpose** *humorous* used to say that someone did something deliberately although they pretend they did not: *I think John lost his homework accidentally on purpose.*

**accident prone** /'··· ·/ *adj* tending to get injured or break things easily

**ac·claim¹** /ə'kleɪm/ *v* [T] **1** to praise someone or something publicly: *His last play was acclaimed by the critics as a masterpiece.* **2 acclaim sb king/queen/leader etc** *formal* to announce publicly that you accept someone as your king, queen etc

**acclaim²** *n* [U] praise for a person or their achievements: **win acclaim** *Gail's artwork has won her international acclaim.*

**ac·claimed** /ə'kleɪmd/ *adj* publicly praised by a lot of people: **highly/widely/universally acclaimed** *Spielberg's highly acclaimed movie, Schindler's List* | **critically acclaimed** (=praised by people who are paid to give their opinion on art, music etc) *a critically acclaimed novel*

**ac·cla·ma·tion** /ˌæklə'meɪʃən/ *n* [C,U] *formal* a loud expression of approval or welcome

**ac·cli·ma·tize** also **-ise** *BrE* /ə'klaɪmətaɪz/ also **acclimate** /ə'klaɪmət‖'ækləmeɪt,ə'klaɪmət/ *AmE v* [I,T] to become used to a new place, situation or type of weather, or to make someone become used to it: **get acclimatized** *It usually takes a while to get acclimatized to living in a new place.* —**acclimatization** /ə'klaɪmətaɪ'zeɪʃən‖-ə-/ *n* [U]

**ac·co·lade** /'ækəleɪd/ *n* [C] praise for someone who is greatly admired or a prize given to them for their work: *She received a 'Grammy Award', the highest accolade in the music business.*

**ac·com·mo·date** /ə'kɒmədeɪt‖ə'kɑː-/ *v* **1** [T] to have or provide enough space for a particular number of people or things: *The hall can only accommodate 200 people.* | *building bigger and bigger highways to accomodate more cars* **2** [T] to give someone a place to stay, live, or work **3** [T] to accept someone's opinions and try to do what they want, especially when their opinions or needs are different from yours: *We've made every effort to accommodate your point of view.* **4** [I + **to**, T] *formal* to get used to a new situation or make yourself do this **5** [T] *formal* to give someone more time to pay you money that they owe you because they have financial problems

**ac·com·mo·dat·ing** /ə'kɒmədeɪtɪŋ‖ə'kɑː-/ *adj* helpful and willing to do what someone else wants

**ac·com·mo·da·tion** /əˌkɒmə'deɪʃən‖əˌkɑː-/ *n* **1** [U] a place for someone to stay, live, or work in: *rented accommodation* **2 accommodations** [plural] *AmE formal* the rooms, food, services etc that are provided in a hotel or on a train, boat etc **3** [singular, U] *formal* a way of ending an argument which aims to satisfy both sides: **reach an accommodation** *We reached an accommodation between both parties.*

**ac·com·pa·ni·ment** /ə'kʌmpənimənt/ *n* **1** [C,U] music played at the same time as a song or a tune played on another instrument: *She starts by singing 'Amazing Grace' with a simple guitar accompaniment.* **2** [C] something that is provided or used with something else: *White wine makes an excellent accompaniment to fish.* **3** [C] *formal* something that happens or exists at the same time as something else: *The job losses are an inevitable accompaniment of this reorganization.* **4 to the accompaniment of** while another musical instrument is being played or another sound can be heard: *Singing to the accompaniment of a piano.* | *She left the stage to the accompaniment of loud cheers.*

**ac·com·pa·nist** /ə'kʌmpənəst/ *n* [C] someone who plays a musical instrument while another person sings or plays the main tune

**ac·com·pa·ny** /ə'kʌmpəni/ *v* [T] **1** to go somewhere with someone, especially in order to look after them: *Children under 14 must be accompanied by an adult.* **2** to play a musical instrument while someone sings a song or plays the main tune **3** [usually passive] to happen or exist at the same time as something else **4** if a book, document etc accompanies something, it

explains what it is about or how it works: *Please see accompanying booklet for instructions.*

**ac·com·plice** /əˈkʌmplɪ̣s‖əˈkɑːm-, əˈkʌm-/ *n* [C] a person who helps someone such as a criminal to do something wrong

**ac·com·plish** /əˈkʌmplɪʃ‖əˈkɑːm-, əˈkʌm-/ *v* [T] to succeed in doing something, especially after trying very hard; achieve: *We have accomplished all we set out to do.*

**ac·com·plished** /əˈkʌmplɪʃt‖əˈkɑːm-, əˈkʌm-/ *adj* an accomplished writer, painter, singer etc is very skilful

**ac·com·plish·ment** /əˈkʌmplɪʃmənt‖əˈkɑːm-, əˈkʌm-/ *n* **1** [C] something successful or impressive that is achieved after a lot of effort and hard work; achievement: *This huge increase in growth would be an impressive accomplishment in any economy.* **2** [C] an ability to do something well; skill: *Playing the piano is one of her many accomplishments.* **3** [U] skill in doing something: *a high level of accomplishment* **4** [U] the act of finishing or achieving something good

**ac·cord¹** /əˈkɔːd‖-ɔːrd/ *n* **1 of your own accord** without being asked or forced to do something: *It's better that she comes of her own accord.* **2** [U] *formal* a situation in which two people, ideas, or statements agree with each other: **be in accord with** *These results are in accord with earlier research.* | **in total/perfect accord** *For once the President and myself were in total accord.* | **speak with one accord** (=if two or more people speak with one accord they show total agreement with each other by what they say) **3** [C] a formal agreement between countries or groups: *the Helsinki accord on human rights* **4 with one accord** *formal* if two or more people do something with one accord they do it together: *With one accord they rushed down to the lake.*

**accord²** *v formal* **1** [T] to give someone or something special attention or treatment: **accord sth to** *The Japanese accord a special reverence to trees and rivers.* **2 accord with** to match or agree with something

**ac·cord·ance** /əˈkɔːdəns‖-əˈkɔːr-/ *n* **in accordance with** *formal* according to a rule, system etc: *accounts prepared in accordance with the Companies Act 1985* | **in accordance with sb's wishes** *He was buried in his home town, in accordance with his wishes.*

**ac·cord·ing as** /əˈkɔːdɪŋ əz, -æz‖əˈkɔːr-/ *conjunction BrE formal* depending on whether

**ac·cord·ing·ly** /əˈkɔːdɪŋli‖-əˈkɔːr-/ *adv* **1** in a way that is suitable for a particular situation or based on what someone has done or said: *I told them what changes I wanted made and they acted accordingly.* **2** [sentence adverb] as a result of something; therefore: *The budget for health care has been cut by 10%. Accordingly, some hospitals may be forced to close.*

2 **according to** /·ˈ·· ·/ **1** as shown by something or said
1 by someone: *According to George, she's a great player.* | *According to our records payment of $56 is now overdue.* **2** in a way that agrees with: *We are paid according to how much work we do.*

**ac·cor·di·on¹** /əˈkɔːdiən‖-əˈkɔːr-/ *n* [C] a musical instrument that you pull in and out to produce sounds while pushing buttons on one side to produce different notes

**accordion²** *adj* [only before noun] having many folds like an accordion: *an accordion file*

**ac·cost** /əˈkɒst‖əˈkɒːst, əˈkɑːst/ *v* [T] to go towards someone you do not know and speak to them in an unpleasant or threatening way: *On the station she was accosted by a man asking for money.*

2 **ac·count¹** /əˈkaʊnt/ *n*
1 **1 ► DESCRIPTION ◄** [C] **a)** a written or spoken description which gives details of an event: *There were several different accounts of the story in the newspapers.* | **give an account** *David gave us a vivid account of his trip to Rio.* | **blow-by-blow account** (=a description of the details of all an event in the order that they happened) | **eyewitness account** (=a description of events by someone who saw them) *an eyewitness account of the robbery* | **firsthand account** (=a description of events by someone who saw or took part in them) *her fascinating firsthand account of the Chinese Cultural Revolution* **b)** a detailed scientific description of a process which explains how it happens and what makes it possible: *Chomsky's account of how children learn their first language*

**2 ► AT A BANK ◄** written abbreviation **a/c** [C] an arrangement that you have with a bank to pay in or take out money: *My salary is paid directly into my bank account.* | **joint account** (=one that is shared by two people) —see also BANK ACCOUNT, CHECKING ACCOUNT, CURRENT ACCOUNT, DEPOSIT ACCOUNT, PROFIT AND LOSS ACCOUNT, SAVINGS ACCOUNT

**3 take account of sth/take sth into account** to consider or include particular facts or details when making a decision or judgment about something: *These figures do not take account of changes in the rate of inflation.*

**4 on account of** because of something else, especially because of a problem or difficulty: *He can't run very fast on account of his asthma.*

**5 accounts a)** [plural] an exact record of the money that a company has received and the money it has spent: *The accounts for last year showed a profit of $2 million.* **b)** [U] a department in a company that is responsible for keeping these records: *Eileen works in accounts.*

**6 on account** if you buy goods on account, you take them away with you and pay for them later

**7 ► WITH A SHOP ◄** [C] an arrangement that you have with a shop which allows you to buy goods and pay for them later; CREDIT ACCOUNT: *Can you charge this to my account please?*

**8 ► BILL ◄** [C] a statement of money that you owe for things you have bought from a shop; bill: **pay/settle your account** (=pay what you owe) *Accounts must be settled within 30 days.*

**9 ► ARRANGEMENT TO SELL GOODS ◄** [C] an arrangement to sell goods and services to another company over a period of time: *Our Sales Manager has secured several big accounts recently.*

**10 by/from all accounts** according to what a lot of people say: *It's a very exciting film by all accounts.*

**11 on my/his etc account** if you do something on someone's account, you do it because you think they want you to: *Please don't leave on my account.*

**12 on your own account** by yourself or for yourself: *Carrie decided to do a little research on her own account.*

**13 on no account/not on any account** used when saying that someone must not, for whatever reason, do something: *On no account must you tell him about our plans.*

**14 by your own account** according to what you have said, especially when you have admitted doing something wrong: *By his own account he was driving too fast.*

**15 on that account/on this account** concerning a particular situation: *There needn't be any more worries on that account.*

**16 give a good/poor account of yourself** to do something or perform very well or very badly: *Kevin gave a good account of himself in today's game.*

**17 bring/call sb to account** *formal* to force someone who is responsible for a mistake or a crime to explain publicly why they did it and punish them for it if necessary: *The people responsible for the accident have never been brought to account.*

**18 put/turn sth to good account** *formal* to use something for a good purpose: *Perhaps she could put some of her talents to good account by helping us*

**19 of no account/of little account** *formal* not important: *Don't worry about what he said, it's of no account.*

**20 of some account** *formal* quite important

**account²** *v* [T] W 2

**account for** sth *phr v* [T] **1** to be the reason why something happens: *Recent pressure at work may account for his behavior.* **2** to give a satisfactory explanation of why something has happened or why you did something: *How do you account for the sudden disappearance of the murder weapon?* **3** to make up a particular amount or part of something: *Imports from Japan accounted for 40%*

*of the total.* **4** to say where all the members of a group of people or things are, especially because you are worried that some of them may be lost: *Is everyone accounted for?* **5 there's no accounting for taste** *informal* used when you find it difficult to understand why someone likes something or wants to do something

**ac·coun·ta·ble** /əˈkaʊntəbəl/ *adj* [not before noun] responsible for the effects of your actions and willing to explain or be criticized for them: [+ **for**] *Managers must be accountable for their decisions.* | **hold sb accountable for sth** (=consider someone responsible) *Should teachers be held accountable for their students' examination results?* | **accountable to** *The bank was effectively accountable to nobody, and could do whatever it liked.* —**accountability** /əˈkaʊntəˈbɪlɪti/ *n* [U] | *demands for greater police accountability*

**ac·coun·tan·cy** /əˈkaʊntənsi/ *n* [U] *especially BrE* the profession or work of keeping or checking financial accounts

S 3 **ac·coun·tant** /əˈkaʊntənt/ *n* [C] someone whose job is to keep and check financial accounts

**ac·coun·ting** /əˈkaʊntɪŋ/ *n* [U] accountancy

**ac·cou·tre·ments** /əˈkuːtrɪmənts/ also **accouterments** /əˈkuːtəmənts‖-tər-/ *AmE n* [plural] *formal or humorous* things that you use or carry when doing a particular activity

**ac·cred·i·ta·tion** /əˈkredɪˈteɪʃən/ *n* [U] official approval for a person or organization

**ac·cred·it·ed** /əˈkredɪtɪd/ *adj* **1** having official approval to do something: *an accredited journalist* **2 be accredited to** if a government official is accredited to another country, they are sent to that country to officially represent their government there **3** officially accepted as being of a satisfactory standard: *an accredited language school*

**ac·cre·tion** /əˈkriːʃən/ *n* **1** [C,U] *technical* a layer of a substance which slowly forms on something **2** [U] *formal* a gradual process by which new things are added and something gradually changes or gets bigger

**ac·crue** /əˈkruː/ *v* [I,T] *formal* **1** if advantages accrue to you, you get those advantages over a period of time: *tax benefits that accrue to investors* **2** if money accrues or is accrued, it gradually increases over a period of time: *The accrued interest will be paid annually.*

**acct** the written abbreviation for ACCOUNT

**ac·cu·mu·late** /əˈkjuːmjʊleɪt/ *v* **1** [T] to gradually get more and more money, possessions, knowledge etc over a period of time: *He accumulated a fortune through property speculation.* **2** [I] to gradually increase in numbers or amount until there is a large quantity in one place: *Leaves had accumulated around the fallen trunks.* —**accumulation** /əˈkjuːmjʊˈleɪʃən/ *n* [C,U] *the accumulation of data*

**ac·cu·mu·la·tive** /əˈkjuːmjʊlətɪv‖-leɪ-, -lə-/ *adj* gradually increasing in amount or degree over a period of time; CUMULATIVE —**accumulatively** *adv*

**ac·cu·mu·la·tor** /əˈkjuːmjʊleɪtə‖-ər/ *n* [C] **1** *technical* a part of a computer that stores numbers **2** *especially BrE* a kind of BATTERY (1) which can take in new supplies of electricity so that it has enough power to keep working **3** a system of betting (BET[1] (1)) on the results of a series of horse races, by which any money you win from a race is bet on the next race

**ac·cu·ra·cy** /ˈækjʊrəsi/ *n* [U] **1** the ability to do something in an exact way without making a mistake **2** the quality of being correct or true: *I wasn't convinced about the accuracy of the report.*

S 2 W 3 **ac·cu·rate** /ˈækjʊrət/ *adj* **1** accurate information, reports, descriptions etc are correct because all the details are true: *She was able to give the police an accurate description of her attacker.* | *a fairly accurate assessment of the situation* **2** an accurate measurement, calculation, record etc has been done in a careful and exact way and is completely correct **3** a machine that is accurate is able to do something in an exact way without making a mistake: *The cutter is accurate to within 1/2 a millimetre.* **4** an accurate shot, throw etc succeeds in hitting or reaching the thing that it is intended to hit: *a devastatingly accurate shot by the Brazilian captain* —**accurately** *adv*: *It's impossible to predict the weather accurately.*

**ac·curs·ed** /əˈkɜːsɪd, əˈkɜːst‖-ɜːr-/ *adj* **1** [only before noun] *formal* very annoying and causing you a lot of trouble **2** *old use* someone who is accursed has had a CURSE[2] (2) put on them

**ac·cu·sa·tion** /ˌækjʊˈzeɪʃən/ *n* [C] a statement saying that someone is guilty of a crime or of doing something wrong: *There isn't a word of truth in your accusations.* | [+ **of**] *accusations of corruption* | **make an accusation against** *Several serious accusations have been made against the former state governor.* | **face an accusation** (=be accused of something) *The school is facing accusations of racism.* | **wild/unfounded accusation** (=one that is completely untrue)

**ac·cu·sa·tive** /əˈkjuːzətɪv/ *n* [C] *technical* a form of a noun in languages such as Latin or German, which shows that the noun is the DIRECT OBJECT of a verb —**accusative** *adj*

**ac·cu·sa·to·ry** /əˈkjuːzətəri‖-tɔːri/ *adj formal* an accusatory remark, look etc from someone shows that they think you have done something wrong

**ac·cuse** /əˈkjuːz/ *v* [T] to say that someone is guilty of a crime or of doing something bad: **accuse sb of (doing) sth** *Are you accusing me of lying?* | *He's accused of murder.* | **stand accused of** (=be officially accused of a serious offence) *Local officials stand accused of gross mismanagement.* —**accuser** *n* [C] W

**ac·cused** /əˈkjuːzd/ *n* **the accused** [singular or plural] the person or group of people who have been officially accused of a crime or offence in a court of law

**ac·cus·ing** /əˈkjuːzɪŋ/ *adj* an accusing look from someone shows that they think that you have done something wrong —**accusingly** *adv*

**ac·cus·tom** /əˈkʌstəm/ *v* [T] to make yourself or another person become used to a situation or place: **accustom yourself to** *It took a while for me to accustom myself to all the new rules and regulations.*

**ac·cus·tomed** /əˈkʌstəmd/ *adj* **1 be accustomed to (doing) sth** to be used to something: *He was accustomed to a life of luxury.* | *I'm not accustomed to getting up so early.* | **get/grow/become accustomed to** *Her eyes quickly became accustomed to the dark* **2** [only before noun] *formal* usual: *her accustomed seat at the head of the table*

**AC/DC** /ˌ· ·ˈ· ·/ *adj slang* sexually attracted to people of both sexes

**ace[1]** /eɪs/ *n* [C] **1** a playing card with a single spot on it, which usually has the highest value in a game: *the ace of hearts* **2 have an ace up your sleeve** to have a secret advantage which could help you to win or be successful **3 hold all the aces** to have all the advantages in a situation so that you are sure to win **4 be/come within an ace of** to very nearly succeed in doing something: *She came within an ace of getting the job as Export Manager.* **5** a first shot in tennis or VOLLEYBALL which is hit so well that your opponent cannot reach the ball and you win the point **6** someone who is extremely skilful at doing something: *a World War II flying ace* | *an ace at chess* **7 ace in the hole** *AmE informal* something that you keep secretly to use when you need it: *That fifty dollars is my ace in the hole.*

**ace[2]** *adj* **1 ace pilot/player/skier etc** someone who is a very skilful pilot, player etc: *ace footballer Diego Maradona* **2** *BrE slang* very good: *The party was ace.*

**ace[3]** *v* [T] **1** *AmE informal* to do very well in an examination, a piece of written work etc: *I think I aced the History test.* **2** to hit your first shot in tennis or VOLLEYBALL so well that your opponent cannot reach the ball

**a·cer·bic** /əˈsɜːbɪk‖-ɜːr-/ *adj* criticizing someone or something in a clever but rather cruel way: *acerbic wit* —**acerbity** *n* [U]

**ac·e·tate** /ˈæsɪ̈teɪt/ *n* [U] **1** a chemical made from acetic acid **2** a smooth artificial cloth used to make clothes

**a·ce·tic ac·id** /əˌsiːtɪk ˈæsɪ̈d/ *n* [U] the acid in VINEGAR

**a·cet·y·lene** /əˈsetɪ̈liːn‖-tlən, -liːn/ *n* [U] a gas which burns with a bright flame and is used in equipment for cutting and joining pieces of metal —see also OXYACETYLENE

**ache[1]** /eɪk/ *v* [I] **1** if part of your body aches, you feel a continuous, but not very sharp pain there: *The noise of the traffic made my head ache.*|*an aching back* **2 ache to do sth/for sth** to want to do or have something very much: *I was aching to tell him the good news.*

**ache[2]** *n* [C] **1** a continuous pain that is not sharp, for example the pain you feel after you have used part of your body too much: *After three days the ache in his legs had almost gone.*|*backache*|**dull ache** (=an annoying ache that is not very painful) *My hand started to hurt with a sort of dull ache.*|**aches and pains** (=many small pains which you feel at the same time) *Apart from the usual aches and pains, she felt all right.* **2** a strong feeling of wanting something **—achy** *adj*: *My arm feels all achy.*

1 **a·chieve** /əˈtʃiːv/ *v* **1** [T] to succeed in doing something
1 good or getting the result you wanted, after trying hard for a long time: *Women have yet to achieve full equality in the workplace.*|*Britain has achieved the highest rate of economic growth in Europe this year.*|*On the test drive Segrave achieved speeds of over 200 mph.* **2** [I] to be successful in a particular kind of job or activity: *We want all our students to achieve within their chosen profession.* **—achievable** *adj* —see OBTAIN (USAGE)

3 **a·chieve·ment** /əˈtʃiːvmənt/ *n* **1** [C] something
2 important that you succeed in doing by your own efforts: *Winning three gold medals is a remarkable achievement.*|**no mean achievement/quite an achievement** (=a very impressive achievement) **2** [U] the act of achieving something: *the achievement of economic stability*|**sense of achievement** (=a feeling of pride when you succeed in doing something difficult) *You get a wonderful sense of achievement when you reach the top.*

**a·chiev·er** /əˈtʃiːvə‖-ər/ *n* [C] someone who is successful because they are determined and work hard

**A·chil·les' heel** /əˌkɪliːz ˈhiːl/ *n* [C] a weak part of something, especially of someone's character, which is easy for other people to attack: *I think Frank's vanity is his Achilles' heel.*

**Achilles ten·don** /əˌkɪliːz ˈtendən/ *n* [C] the part of your body that connects the muscles in the back of your foot with the muscles of your lower leg

**a·choo** /əˈtʃuː/ *n* [C] a word used to represent the sound you make when you SNEEZE

2 **ac·id[1]** /ˈæsɪ̈d/ *n* **1** [C,U] a substance that forms a chemical SALT[1] (4) when combined with an ALKALI. Strong acids can burn holes in material or damage your skin: *sulphuric acid* **2** [U] *slang* the drug LSD

**acid[2]** *adj* **1** having a very sour taste: *The wine had a very acid taste.* **2 acid remark/comment/tone etc** an acid remark etc uses humour in an unkind way to criticize someone **3 the acid test** a way of finding out whether something is as good as people say it is, whether it works, or whether it is true: *The acid test will come when the car goes on sale in the US.* **4** *technical* an acid soil does not contain enough LIME[1] (3) **—acidly** *adv* **—acidity** /əˈsɪdɪ̈ti/ *n* [U]

**acid house** /ˈ·· ·/ *n* [U] a kind of dance music that is played loudly using electronic instruments

**a·cid·ic** /əˈsɪdɪk/ *adj* **1** very sour: *It tastes a bit acidic.* **2** containing acid

**a·cid·i·fy** /əˈsɪdɪ̈faɪ/ *v* [I,T] *technical* to become an acid or make something become an acid

**acid rain** /ˌ·· ˈ·/ *n* [U] rain that contains harmful acid which can damage the environment and is caused by smoke from factories

3 **ac·knowl·edge** /əkˈnɒlɪdʒ‖-ˈnɑː-/ *v* [T]
3 **1 ▶ADMIT◀** to admit or accept that something is true or that a situation exists: *a broadcast message acknowledging their responsibility for the bombing*|**acknowledge that** *By November 1914 the government was forced to acknowledge that its policy had failed.*|*It is now generally acknowledged that he was innocent.*
**2 be acknowledged as** to be thought of as being very important or very good by a large number of people: *Lasalle is widely acknowledged as the world's greatest living authority on Impressionist painting.*
**3 ▶ACCEPT SB'S AUTHORITY◀** to officially accept that a government, court, leader etc has legal or official authority: *Both defendants refused to acknowledge the authority of the court.*|**acknowledge sb as** *The people acknowledged Mandela as their leader.*
**4 ▶LETTER/MESSAGE ETC◀** to tell someone that you have received their message, letter, package etc: **acknowledge receipt of** *Please acknowledge receipt of this document by signing the enclosed form.*
**5 ▶SHOW THANKS FOR◀** to publicly announce that you are grateful for the help that someone has given you: *The author wishes to acknowlege the assistance of the Defense Department.*
**6 ▶SHOW YOU NOTICE SB◀** to show someone that you have seen them or heard what they have said: *Tina was so rude, she didn't even acknowledge my presence.*

**ac·knowl·edge·ment acknowledgment** /əkˈnɒlɪdʒmənt‖-ˈnɑː-/ *n* **1** [C,U] the act of admitting or accepting that something is true: *We have yet to hear any acknowledgement from them that a problem exists.* **2** [C,U] the act of publicly thanking someone for something they have done: **in acknowledgement of** *a special award in acknowledgement of all his hard work* **3** [C,U] a letter written to tell someone that you have received their letter, message etc **4 acknowledgements** [plural] a short piece of writing at the beginning or end of a book in which the writer thanks all the people who have helped him or her

**ac·me** /ˈækmi/ *n* **the acme of** *formal* the best and highest level of something: *the acme of perfection*

**ac·ne** /ˈækni/ *n* [U] a skin problem which causes a lot of small raised spots on the face and neck

**ac·o·lyte** /ˈækəlaɪt/ *n* [C] **1** *formal* someone who serves a leader or believes in their ideas **2** someone who helps a priest at a religious ceremony

**a·corn** /ˈeɪkɔːn‖-ɔːrn, -ərn/ *n* [C] the nut of the OAK tree

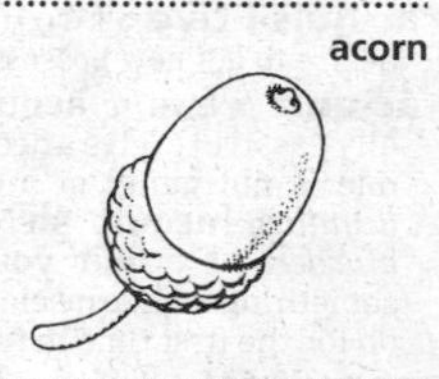
acorn

**a·cous·tic** /əˈkuːstɪk/ *adj* **1** concerned with sound and the way people hear things **2** an acoustic GUITAR or other musical instrument does not have its sound made louder electronically **—acoustically** /-kli/ *adv*

**a·cous·tics** /əˈkuːstɪks/ *n* [plural] **1** the qualities of a room, such as its shape and size, which affect the way sound is heard in it: *The hall has excellent acoustics.* **2** the scientific study of sound

**ac·quaint** /əˈkweɪnt/ *v* [T] **1 be acquainted (with sb)** to know someone, especially because you have met once or twice before: *I am acquainted with him, but only on a professional basis.*|**get/become acquainted** (=start to know someone that you have just met) *I'll leave you two alone for a while so that you can get better acquainted.* **2 be acquainted with sth** *formal* to know about something, because you have seen it, read it, used it etc: *I'm not really acquainted with the southern part of the island.*|**be fully acquainted with sth** *All our employees are fully acquainted with safety precautions.* **3 acquaint yourself with sth** *formal* to deliberately find out about something: *She always took the trouble to acquaint herself with the students' interests.* **4 acquaint sb with sth** *formal* to give someone information about something: *My assistant should be able to acquaint you with all the details.*

**ac·quaint·ance** /əˈkweɪntəns/ *n* **1** [C] someone you know, but who is not a close friend **2 make sb's acquaintance** *formal* to meet someone for the first time:

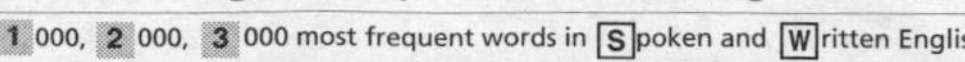

*I'm pleased to make your acquaintance.* **3 of your acquaintance** *formal* a person of your acquaintance is someone that you know: *a certain lawyer of my acquaintance* **4** [U] *formal* knowledge or experience of a particular subject: **have a passing/nodding acquaintance with** (=have only slight knowledge or experience of something) *I must admit I have only a passing acquaintance with his books.* **5 on further/closer acquaintance** *formal* when you start to know someone or something better

**ac·quaint·ance·ship** /əˈkweɪntənsʃɪp/ *n* [U] *formal* **1** your experience or knowledge of a subject **2** the fact of knowing someone socially

**ac·qui·esce** /ˌækwiˈes/ *v* [I] *formal* to unwillingly agree to do what someone wants, or to let them do what they want, without arguing or complaining: [+ **in/to**] *The book accuses him of silently acquiescing in the Nazis' persecution of the Jews.*

**ac·qui·es·cent** /ˌækwiˈesənt◂/ *adj formal* too ready to agree with someone or do what they want, without arguing or complaining —**acquiescence** *n* [U] —**acquiescently** *adv*

W2 **ac·quire** /əˈkwaɪə‖əˈkwaɪr/ *v* [T] **1** *formal* to buy or obtain something, especially something expensive or difficult to get: *The museum has managed to acquire an important work by Dali.* **2** to learn or develop knowledge, skills etc by your own efforts, or to become well known because of your abilities: *I look on it as an opportunity to acquire fresh skills.* | *The team has acquired a fearsome reputation.* **3 acquire a taste for** to begin to like something: *This beer isn't bad. I'm beginning to acquire a taste for it.* **4 be an acquired taste** something that people only begin to like after they have tried it a few times **5** *humorous* to get something by dishonest means

W3 **ac·qui·si·tion** /ˌækwɪ̈ˈzɪʃən/ *n* **1** [U] the act of getting new knowledge, skills etc: *second language acquisition* **2** [U] the act of getting land, power, money etc: *the acquisition of new territory* **3** [C] *formal* something that you have bought or obtained, especially a valuable object: *The National Gallery's latest acquisition is a painting by Goya.*

**ac·quis·i·tive** /əˈkwɪzɪ̈tɪv/ *adj formal* showing too much desire to get new possessions

**ac·quit** /əˈkwɪt/ *v* **acquitted, acquitting 1** [T usually passive] to give a decision in a court of law that someone is not guilty of a crime: *All the defendants were acquitted.* | **acquit sb of sth** *She was acquitted of murder.* **2 acquit yourself well/honourably** to do something well, especially something difficult that you do for the first time in front of other people

**ac·quit·tal** /əˈkwɪtl/ *n* [C,U] an official statement in a court of law that someone is not guilty

**a·cre** /ˈeɪkə‖-ər/ *n* [C] **1** a unit for measuring area, equal to 4047 square metres: *They own 200 acres of farmland.* | *a 200-acre wood* —see table on page B3 **2 acres of space/room** *BrE informal* a large amount of space

**a·cre·age** /ˈeɪkərɪdʒ/ *n* [U] the area of a piece of land measured in acres

**ac·rid** /ˈækrɪ̈d/ *adj* **1** an acrid smell or taste, is strong and unpleasant and stings your nose or throat: *a cloud of acrid smoke* **2** *formal* an acrid comment, discussion etc is very critical or angry

**ac·ri·mo·ni·ous** /ˌækrɪ̈ˈməʊniəs◂‖-ˈmoʊ-/ *adj formal* an acrimonious meeting, argument etc is full of angry comments because people feel very strongly about something: *The meeting ended in an acrimonious dispute.* —**acrimoniously** *adv* —**acrimoniousness** *n* [U]

**ac·ri·mo·ny** /ˈækrɪ̈məni‖-moʊni/ *n* [U] *formal* anger and unpleasantness

**ac·ro·bat** /ˈækrəbæt/ *n* [C] someone who entertains people by doing difficult physical actions such as walking on their hands or balancing on a high rope, especially at a CIRCUS (1)

**ac·ro·bat·ic** /ˌækrəˈbætɪk◂/ *adj* acrobatic movements involve moving your body in a very skilful way, for example by jumping through the air or balancing on a rope: *amazing acrobatic feats* —**acrobatically** /-kli/ *adv*

**ac·ro·bat·ics** /ˌækrəˈbætɪks/ *n* [plural] acrobatic movements

**ac·ro·nym** /ˈækrənɪm/ *n* [C] a word made up from the first letters of the name of something such as an organization. For example NATO is an acronym for the North Atlantic Treaty Organization.

**a·cross¹** /əˈkrɒs‖əˈkrɔːs/ *prep* **1** going, looking etc from one side of a space, area, or line to the other side: *flying across the Atlantic* | *We gazed across the valley.* | *Would you like me to help you across the road?* (=help you to cross it) —see picture on page 1257 **2** reaching or spreading from one side of an area to the other: *a deep crack across the ceiling* | *the only bridge across the river* | *Slowly a smile spread across her face.* | *Do you think this shirt is too tight across the shoulders?* | **right across** *The damn fool has parked right across the entrance to the drive way.* **3** on or towards the opposite side of something: *My best friend lives across the road.* | *Jim yelled across the street to his son.* | **just across** *He knew that just across the border lay freedom.* | **across sth from** *Across the street from where we're standing, you can see the old churchyard.* **4** in every part of a country, organization etc: *a TV series that became popular across five continents* | **right across** *Teachers are expected to teach a range of subjects right across the curriculum.*

**across²** *adv* **1** from one side of something to the other: *There isn't a bridge. We'll have to swim across.* | *We'd got halfway across before Philip realized he'd left his money at home.* **2** if you go, look, shout etc across to someone, you go, look or shout across an area to the place where they are: *There's Brendan. Why don't you go across and say hello?* | *I'm just taking this food across to Sarah. Won't be long.* | **across to/at** *The referee looked across at his linesman before awarding the penalty.* **3 10 feet/10 miles etc across** if something is 10 feet etc across, that is how wide it is: *At its widest point the river is 2 km across.* **4 across from** opposite something or someone: *a woman sitting across from me on the train*

**a·cross-the-board** /·ˌ· · ˈ·◂/ *adj* affecting everyone or everything in a situation or organization: *an across-the-board pay increase* —**across-the-board** *adv*

**a·cros·tic** /əˈkrɒstɪk‖əˈkrɔː-/ *n* [C] a poem or piece of writing in which the first or last letter of each line can be read downwards to spell a word

**a·cryl·ic** /əˈkrɪlɪk/ *adj* acrylic paints or cloth are made from a chemical substance

**a·cryl·ics** /əˈkrɪlɪks/ *n* [plural] acrylic paints

**act¹** *n* [C]

**1 ▶ ACTION ◀** [C] a particular kind of action: *a criminal act* | **act of kindness/revenge/courage etc** *The Bishop condemned the attack as an act of mindless violence.* | *a supreme act of heroism* | **the sexual act** (=the act of having sex)

**2 be in the act of doing sth** to be doing something at a particular moment, especially something that you should not do: **catch sb in the act (of doing sth)** *The photo shows her in the act of raising her gun to fire.* | *The thief was caught in the act.*

**3 ▶ LAW ◀** [C] a law that has been officially accepted by Parliament or Congress: *the 1991 Prevention of Terrorism Act* | *an act of Congress*

**4 ▶ PRETENDING ◀** [singular] insincere behaviour in which you pretend to have a particular kind of feeling: *A lot of people think Betty's very kind and caring, but it's all just a big act.* | **put on an act** (=pretend to have a particular feeling) *He isn't really ill – he's just putting on an act.*

**5 get your act together** *informal* to do something in a more organized way or use your abilities more effectively: *She could be an excellent photographer, if only she got her act together a bit more.*

**6 get in on the act** *informal* to take part in an activity that someone else has started, especially in order to get a share of the advantages for yourself

**7 ▶ PLAY ◀** [C] one of the main parts into which a stage play, OPERA etc is divided: *Hamlet eventually kills the king in Act 5.* | *Everything is resolved in the final act.*
**8 ▶ PERFORMANCE ◀** [C] one of the several short performances in a theatre or CIRCUS (1) show: *They used to do a comedy act together.*
**9 ▶ PERFORMER ◀** [C] a performer, singer, group of musicians etc: *top-selling British act 'The Happy Mondays'*
**10 act of God** an event that is caused by natural forces, such as a storm, flood, or fire, which you cannot prevent or control
**11 act of worship** an occasion when people pray togther and show their respect for God
**12 balancing/juggling act** the action of doing several different kinds of work at the same time —see also **clean up your act** (CLEAN[2])

2 1 **act²** /ækt/ *v*
**1 ▶ DO SOMETHING ◀ a)** [I] to do something to deal with an urgent problem, especially by using your official power or authority: *The UN Security Council must act to end the war in Bosnia.* **b)** [I always + adv/prep] to do something in a particular way or for a particular reason: *The killer claims he was acting in self-defence.* | *I acted more out of compassion than anything else.* | **act in good faith** (=do something honestly without intending to deceive anyone) *The shop manager says they acted in good faith and that they didn't know the camera was damaged.* | **act on (sb's) advice/orders/suggestion etc** (=do what someone has advised, ordered etc) *Acting on a friend's advice, he bought $50,000 of shares in a television company.* | **act on information** (=do something because of information you have received) *The police were acting on information from a member of the public.*
**2 ▶ BEHAVE ◀** [I always + adv/prep] to behave in a particular way: **act strangely/stupidly/correctly etc** *Henry's been acting very strangely recently.* | *The teacher acted perfectly correctly under the circumstances.* | **act like/act as if** *If you act like a child, you're going to be treated like a child.* | *He acted as if he'd never seen me before.* | **act your age** *spoken* (=used to tell someone to be sensible and stop behaving like a child) | **act the fool** (=behave in a stupid and annoying way) *Stop acting the fool, will you!*
**3 ▶ HAVE AN EFFECT ◀ a)** to have a particular effect or use: [+ **as**] *The sugar in the fruit acts as a preservative.* | [+ **on**] *Antibiotics act on the bacteria that cause the disease.* **b)** to start to have an effect: *It takes a couple of minutes for the drug to act.*
**4 ▶ PRETEND ◀** [I,T] to pretend to have particular feelings, qualities etc: **act innocent/stupid/hurt etc** *She suddenly started acting all upset so that the others would feel sorry for her.* | **act the fool/hero etc** *Whenever they're in public he always acts the loving husband.* | **act as if/act like** *They were all trying to act as if nothing had happened.*
**5 ▶ PLAY/FILM ETC ◀** [I,T] to perform in a play or film: *I first started acting when I was 12 years old.* | **act a part/role etc** *Who acted the part of Miss Ceeley?* | **well/badly acted** (=performed well or badly) *I thought the play was extremely well acted.*
**6 ▶ LAWYER ETC ◀ act for sb/act on sb's behalf** to represent someone, especially in a court of law or by doing business for them: *I'm acting on behalf of my client, Mr Harding.*
**7 ▶ DO THE JOB OF ◀ act as** to do a particular job for a short time, for example while the usual person is absent: *Mrs Odell is on holiday, and I'm acting as her replacement till she gets back.* | *My brother speaks French – he will act as interpreter.* —see also ACTING[1]

**act** sth ↔ **out** *phr v* [T] **1** if a group of people act out an event, they show how it happened by pretending to be the people who were involved in it **2** to express your feelings about something through your behaviour or actions, especially when you have been feeling angry or nervous: *Teenagers can act out their anxieties in various aggressive ways.*

**act up** *phr v* [I] *informal* **1** if children act up, they behave badly **2** if a machine or part of your body acts up, it does not work properly: *The photocopier has started acting up again.*

**act·ing¹** /ˈæktɪŋ/ *adj* **acting manager/head teacher/director etc** someone who does an important job while the usual person is not there, or until a new person is chosen for the job

**acting²** *n* [U] the job or skill of performing in plays, films etc

**ac·tion** /ˈækʃən/ *n* S1 W1
**1 ▶ DOING THINGS ◀** [U] the process of doing in order to deal with a problem or difficult situation: *The union is urging strike action.* | *We need more action, and less talk!* | **take action** *The police took firm action to deal with the riots.* | **go/spring into action** (=immediately begin doing something with a lot of energy) *As soon as the SOS call was received, the rescue services sprang into action.* | **course of action** (=a series of actions done in order to deal with something) *One possible course of action would be to raise taxes on alcohol and tobacco.*
**2 ▶ SOMETHING DONE ◀** [C] something that someone does: *The child could not be held responsible for his actions.* | *His prompt action probably saved my life.*
**3 in action** if you see someone or something in action you see them doing the job or activity that they are trained or designed to do: *exciting photos of ski jumpers in action* | *I'd like see the new computer system in action.*
**4 put/call/bring sth into action** to begin to use a plan or idea that you have, and to make it work
**5 be out of action** if something or someone is out of action, they are broken or injured, so that they cannot move or work: *My car's out of action at the moment, so I have to go by bus.* | **put sth/sb out of action** *The torn ligaments in his knee put him out of action for the rest of the season.*
**6 ▶ COURT ◀** [C] the process of taking a case or a claim against someone to a court of law: *They began an action to repossess the house.* | **legal/civil/libel etc action** *The European Commission is threatening legal action against Britain and France to protect the environment.* | **bring an action (against)** *They will bring an action against him if he doesn't repay the loan.*
**7 ▶ FIGHTING ◀** [C,U] fighting or a battle during a war: *When the action ended there were terrible losses on both sides.* | **in/into action** *The navy was sent into action.* | **killed/wounded/missing in action** *Their son was reported missing in action.*
**8 ▶ EXCITING EVENTS ◀** *informal* exciting and important things that are happening: *I was looking for some action in this hick town.* | **where (all) the action is** *This is the design studio – where the action is.*
**9 ▶ STORY ◀ the action** the things that happen in a play or book: *The action of 'Hamlet' takes place in Denmark.*
**10 ▶ BODY MOVEMENT ◀** [C,U] a movement of the body, especially a particular type of movement: *the action of the heart* | *the horse's trotting action*
**11 ▶ MACHINERY ◀** [singular] the movement of the parts of a clock, gun, piano etc: *The action of this piano is rather stiff.*
**12 ▶ EFFECT ◀** [U] the way in which something such as a chemical or process has an effect on something else: *The rock had been worn away by the action of the falling water.*
**13 action group/committee/project etc** a group formed to do something specific, especially to change a social or political situation: *the Child Poverty Action Group*
**14 a piece of the action** *informal* a share of something, such as profits, a business etc
**15 actions speak louder than words** used to say that you are judged by what you do, rather than by what you say you will do
**16 ▶ FILMS ◀ action!** used by film DIRECTORS to tell the actors and other film workers to begin filming

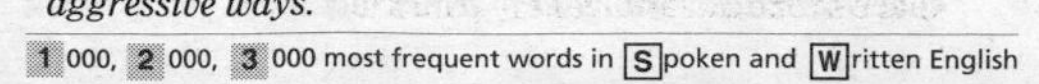

**ac·tio·na·ble** /ˈækʃənəbəl/ *adj* **1** [not before noun] if something you say or do is actionable, it is so serious or damaging that a claim could be made against you in a court of law because of it: *His allegations are actionable in my view.* **2** [usually before noun] an actionable plan, piece of information etc is one that can be done or used

**action-packed** /ˌ·· ˈ·◂/ *adj* an action-packed story or film contains a lot of exciting events

**action re·play** /ˌ·· ˈ··/ *n* [C] *BrE* an important or exciting moment in a sports game on television that is shown again immediately after it happens; INSTANT REPLAY

**action sta·tions** /ˈ·· ˌ··/ *interjection* used to order soldiers etc to go to their positions ready for battle

**ac·tiv·ate** /ˈæktɪ̈veɪt/ *v* [T] **1** to make something, especially an electrical system, start working: *The lock is activated by a magnetic key.* **2** *technical* to make a chemical action or natural process happen: *The manufacture of chlorophyll is activated by sunlight.* **3** *technical* to make something RADIOACTIVE **—activation** /ˌæktɪ̈ˈveɪʃən/ *n* [U]

S2 W2 **ac·tive¹** /ˈæktɪv/ *adj*
**1 ▶DOING THINGS◀** always doing things or ready to do things, especially physical activities: *We had an active holiday, sailing, swimming and water skiing.* | *She may be over 80, but she's still very active!*
**2 ▶IN AN ORGANIZATION◀** involved in an organization, activity etc and always busy doing things to help it: **active member** *an active member of the local Historical Society* | **be active in (doing) sth** *He's very active in local politics.* | *She's been active in raising money for the new church buildings.*
**3 active efforts/discussions etc** efforts, attempts etc to do something, solve a problem etc, that are made with continuous energy and determination: *Active efforts are being made to reach a settlement.*
**4 ▶ELECTRICAL SYSTEM◀** *technical* operating in the way it is supposed to: *The alarm becomes active when the switch is turned on.*
**5 ▶MILITARY◀ a) on active service** a soldier etc who is on active service is fighting in a war **b) on active duty** *AmE* employed by the army etc, as opposed to being in the reserves (RESERVE² (6))
**6 ▶VOLCANO◀** likely to explode and pour out fire
**7 ▶GRAMMAR◀** *technical* if a verb or sentence is active, the person or thing doing the action is the SUBJECT¹(5). In 'The boy kicked the ball', the verb 'kick' is active. —compare PASSIVE¹ (2)
**8 ▶CHEMICAL◀** *technical* producing a reaction in a substance or with another chemical **—actively** *adv*: *The two sides are actively engaged in discussions.*

**active²** *n* **the active/the active voice** *technical* the active form of a verb—compare PASSIVE²

S3 **ac·tiv·ist** /ˈæktɪ̈vɪ̈st/ *n* [C] someone who works hard to achieve social or political change, especially as an active member of a political organization: *Greenpeace activists*

S1 W1 **ac·tiv·i·ty** /ækˈtɪvɪ̈ti/ *n* **1** [U] a situation in which a lot of things are happening or people are doing things, moving around etc: *I missed the noise and activity of the city.* | *a huge amount of media activity during the elections* —opposite INACTIVITY **2** [C] something that you do for interest or pleasure or because you want to achieve something: *leisure activities* | *There'll be plenty of activities laid on for the kids.* | *terrorist activities*

W3 **ac·tor** /ˈæktə‖-ər/ *n* [C] someone who performs in a play, film, or television programme

**ac·tress** /ˈæktrɪ̈s/ *n* [C] a woman who performs in a play, film, or television programme

S1 W2 **ac·tu·al** /ˈæktʃuəl/ *adj* [only before noun] **1** real, especially as compared with what is believed, expected or intended: *a big difference between the opinion polls and the actual election results* | *I'm not joking. Those were his actual words.* | **in actual fact** (=really) *In actual fact, there is not much evidence to support these allegations.* **2 the actual** used to introduce the main part of what you are describing: *The programme starts at 8.00 but the actual film doesn't start until 8.30.*

**ac·tu·al·i·ty** /ˌæktʃuˈælɪ̈ti/ *n* **1** [C usually plural] something that is real; a fact: *the grim actualities of prison life* **2** [U] *formal* the state of being real; EXISTENCE (1) **3 in actuality** *formal* really

**ac·tu·al·ly** /ˈæktʃuəli, -tʃəli/ *adv* **1** [sentence adverb] *spoken* used when you are giving an opinion or adding new information to what you have just said: *I've known Barbara for years. Since we were babies, actually.* | *I do actually think that things have improved.* | *We had quite a good time, actually.* | *Well actually you still owe me $200.* **2** used when you are telling or asking someone what the real and exact truth of a situation is, as opposed to what people may imagine: *He may look young but he's actually 45.* | *Disappointed? No, actually I'm rather glad.* | *Unemployment has actually fallen for the past two months.* | *Did he actually attack you, or just threaten you?*

Frequencies of the adverb **actually** in spoken and written English.

SPOKEN

WRITTEN

500 1000 per million

Based on the British National Corpus and the Longman Lancaster Corpus

This graph shows that the adverb **actually** is much more common in spoken English than in written English.

**USAGE NOTE: ACTUALLY**

WORD CHOICE: **actually, currently, at present**
**Actually** (and **actual**) does not mean 'at the present time' in English. Compare **currently** and **at present**: *"Have you ever met Simon?" "I actually met him two years ago"* (=in fact). *"Is the company doing well?" "Yes." "It's currently doing very well/ It's doing very well at present."*

In conversation, especially in British English, **actually** can be used to make what you are saying softer, especially if you are correcting someone, disagreeing, or complaining: *"Great! I love French coffee!" "Er, it's German actually."* But it can be used with the opposite effect: *I didn't ask your opinion, actually.*

**ac·tu·a·ry** /ˈæktʃuəri‖-tʃueri/ *n* [C] someone who advises insurance companies on how much to charge for insurance, after calculating the various risks

**ac·tu·ate** /ˈæktʃueɪt/ *v* [T] **1 be actuated by** *formal* to behave in a particular way because of a feeling or a quality in your character: *Iago was actuated by malice.* **2** *technical* to make a piece of machinery or electrical equipment start to operate

**a·cu·i·ty** /əˈkjuːɪ̈ti/ *n* [U] *formal* the ability to think, see, or hear quickly and clearly: *mental acuity*

**ac·u·men** /ˈækjʊ̈mən, əˈkjuːmən/ *n* [U] the ability to think quickly and make good judgements: **business/political/financial etc acumen** *The firm's success is due to the director's ingenuity and business acumen.*

**ac·u·pres·sure** /ˈækjʊ̈ˌpreʃə‖-ər/ *n* [U] a method of stopping pain and curing disease by pressing on particular areas of the body

**ac·u·punc·ture** /ˈækjʊ̈ˌpʌŋktʃə‖-ər/ *n* [U] a method of stopping pain and curing disease by putting special needles into particular parts of the body

**a·cute** /əˈkjuːt/ *adj*
**1 ▶SITUATION/FEELING ETC◀** very serious or severe: *an acute shortage of water* | *acute embarrassment*

**2 ▶ PAIN ◀** very severe and sharp
**3 acute hearing/acute sense of smell etc** an ability to hear or smell things that is very sensitive, so that you are able to notice small differences
**4 ▶ INTELLIGENT ◀** quick to notice things and able to think clearly and intelligently: **acute understanding/analysis/observations** *Her book is an acute analysis of Middle Eastern history.*|**acute observer** *De Tocqueville was an acute observer of American ways.*
**5 ▶ MEDICAL ◀** *technical* an acute illness or disease quickly becomes dangerous: *acute tuberculosis* —compare CHRONIC (1)
**6 ▶ MATHEMATICS ◀** *technical* an acute angle is one that is less than 90° —see picture at ANGLE[1]
**7 ▶ PRONUNCIATION MARK ◀** an acute ACCENT (=a mark used to show pronunciation) is the small mark put over a letter, such as é in French —compare GRAVE[3], CIRCUMFLEX —**acuteness** *n* [U]

**a·cute·ly** /əˈkjuːtli/ *adv* very strongly or painfully: *acutely emabarrassed*|**acutely aware/conscious** *The president is acutely conscious of the need for more doctors and nurses.*

**AD** /ˌeɪ ˈdiː◂/ Anno Domini; used to show that a date is a particular number of years after the birth of Christ: *What will world population be by 2000 AD?*|*in the first century AD* —compare BC

S3 W3 **ad** /æd/ *n* [C] *informal* an advertisement —see also CLASSIFIED AD

**ad·age** /ˈædɪdʒ/ *n* [C] a well-known phrase that says something wise about human experience; PROVERB

**a·da·gio** /əˈdɑːdʒəʊ‖-dʒoʊ/ *n* [C] a piece of music to be played or sung slowly —**adagio** *adj, adv*

**Ad·am** /ˈædəm/ *n* **not know someone from Adam** *informal* to not know someone at all

**ad·a·mant** /ˈædəmənt/ *adj formal* determined not to change your opinion, decision, etc: *We tried to negotiate, but they were adamant.*|**adamant that** *Melinda was adamant that she would not travel with us.* —**adamantly** *adv*

**Ad·am's ap·ple** /ˌ·· ˈ··‖ˈ·· ˌ··/ *n* [C] the part at the front of your neck that sticks out slightly and moves when you talk or swallow —see picture at HEAD[1]

W3 **a·dapt** /əˈdæpt/ *v* **1** [I,T] to gradually change your behaviour and attitudes so that you get used to a new situation and can deal with it successfully: **[+ to]** *The children are finding it hard to adapt to their new school.*|*plants that have adapted themselves to desert conditions* **2** [T] to change something so that it can be used in a different way or for a different purpose: *The car's fuel system was adapted to take unleaded gas.*|**[+ for]** *The materials can be adapted for use with older children.* **3 be well adapted to** to be particularly suitable for something: *Alpine flowers which are well adapted to the harsh Swiss winters* **4** [T] to change a book or play so that it can be made into a film, television programme etc —compare ADJUST

**a·dap·ta·ble** /əˈdæptəbəl/ *adj* able to change so as to be suitable or successful in new and different situations: *I'm sure she'll cope with the changes very well – she's very adaptable.*|*The American constitution has proved adaptable in changing political conditions.* —**adaptability** /əˌdæptəˈbɪlɪ̣ti/ *n* [U]

**ad·ap·ta·tion** /ˌædæpˈteɪʃən/ *n* **1** [C] a film or play that was first written in a different form, for example as a book **2** [U] the process by which something changes or is changed so that it can be used in a different way or in different conditions: *adaptation to the environment*

**a·dapt·er, adaptor** /əˈdæptə‖-ər/ *n* [C] **1** something used to connect two pieces of equipment, especially when they are of different sizes **2** *BrE* a special type of PLUG[1] (1) that makes it possible to connect more than one piece of equipment to the electricity supply

**ADC** /ˌeɪ diː ˈsiː/ the abbreviation of AIDE-DE-CAMP

**add** /æd/ *v* S1 W1
**1 ▶ PUT WITH ◀** [T] to put something with something else or with a group of other things: **add sth to sth** *Do you want to add your name to the list?*|*I gave him a rare Swedish stamp to add to his collection.*
**2 ▶ COUNTING ◀** [I,T] to put two or more numbers together in order to calculate the total: *Add 6 and 6 to make 12.*|**add sth to** *Added to what we've already saved, it gives us $550.* —compare SUBTRACT —see picture at MATHEMATICS
**3 ▶ INCREASE ◀** [I,T] to increase the amount or cost of something by putting something more with it: **add sth to** *The sales tax adds 15% to the price of clothes.*|**[+ to]** *Conforming to the new regulations will add to the cost of the project.*
**4 ▶ SAY ◀** [T] to say something more that is related to what has been said already: *That's all I have to say. Is there anything you'd like to add, David?*|*"And I don't care what you think" she added defiantly.*|**add that** *Casey added that everything he had told us was, of course, top-secret.*|**I might add** *spoken* (=used when adding something, especially to complain) *The bus was two hours late, and, I might add, they tried to charge my children the full adult fares.*
**5 ▶ COOKING ◀** [T] to mix one food with another while cooking: *Cream the butter and sugar, then add the eggs.*
**6 ▶ GIVE A QUALITY ◀** [T] to give a particular quality to an event, place, situation etc: *Fine champagne always adds glamour to an occasion.*
**7 added to this/if you add to this** used to introduce another fact, especially one that makes a situation seem even worse: *If you add to this the young age of the victims, it makes the crime unforgiveable.*
**8 add insult to injury** to make a situation even more upsetting for someone, when they have already been badly or unfairly treated
**9 add fuel to the fire/flames** to make a bad situation even worse, especially by making someone more angry

**add** sth ↔ **in** *phr v* [T] to include something with something else: *By the time we added in the cost of the drinks the bill was over £100.*

**add** sth ↔ **on** *phr v* [T] **1** to make a building larger by building another room: *They added on a bedroom at the back.* **2** to increase the amount or cost of something by putting something more with it: *Labor costs could add on a further 25%.*|**[+ to]** *Service is added on to the bill.*

**add to** sth *phr v* [T] to make something such as a feeling or quality stronger and more noticeable: *Our explanation seemed only to add to his bewilderment.*|*a certain diffidence which added to his charm*

**add up** *phr v* **1** [I,T **add** sth ↔ **up**] to calculate the total of several numbers: *Add your scores up and we'll see who won.* **2 not add up** if a set of facts does not add up, it does not provide a reasonable explanation for something: *He had been arrested for murder, but the evidence just didn't add up.* **3** [I not in progressive] *informal* to increase by small amounts until there is a large total: *There are five of us using the phone so it soon adds up.*

**add up to** *phr v* [T not in progressive] to have a particular result: *With a meal included in the cost of the ticket, it all adds up to a really good evening's entertainment.*

**ad·ded** /ˈædɪ̣d/ *adj* in addition to what is usual or expected: *a breakfast cereal with added vitamins*|**added advantage/benefit/precaution etc** (=that makes something better) *She had a deadbolt fitted as an added precaution.*|**added difficulty/problem/complication** (=that makes something worse)

**ad·den·dum** /əˈdendəm/ *n plural* **addenda** /-də/ [C] *technical* something that is added to the end of a speech or book, usually to give more information

**ad·der** /ˈædə‖-ər/ *n* [C] **1** a small poisonous snake living in northern Europe and northern Asia **2** one of several types of snake living in North America

**ad·dict** /ˈædɪkt/ *n* [C] **1** someone who is unable to stop

taking drugs: *treatment centers for addicts* | **drug/heroin/morphine etc addict** *Many heroin addicts have contracted AIDS.* **2** someone who spends too much time doing something they like: *a television addict*

**ad·dic·ted** /əˈdɪktɪ̇d/ *adj* [not before noun] **1** unable to stop taking a harmful substances, especially a drug: [+ **to**] *He is seriously addicted to these tranquillizers.* **2** liking to do or have something so much you do not want to stop: [+ **to**] *kids addicted to computer games*

**ad·dic·tion** /əˈdɪkʃən/ *n* [C,U] the need to have something regularly because you are addicted to it: *drug addiction* | [+ **to**] *a program to deal with addiction to alcohol*

**ad·dic·tive** /əˈdɪktɪv/ *adj* **1** a drug that is addictive makes you unable to stop taking it: **highly addictive** *Crack is a potent, highly addictive form of cocaine.* **2** an activity that is addictive is one that you want to keep doing, especially because you enjoy it so much: *I took up skiing a couple of years ago and I find it quite addictive.*

S3 W1 **ad·di·tion** /əˈdɪʃən/ *n* **1 in addition** used when adding another fact to what has already been mentioned: *The hotel itself can accommodate 80 guests and, in addition, there are several self-catering apartments.* | **in addition to** *He's now running his own research company – that's in addition to his job at the university.* **2** [U] the act of adding something to something else: [+ **of**] *The addition of networking facilities will greatly enhance the system.* **3** [C] something that is added to something else, often in order to improve it: [+ **to**] *A bottle of wine would make a pleasant addition to the meal.* **4** [U] the process of adding numbers or amounts to make a total —compare SUBTRACTION **5** [C] *AmE* a room or a part of a building that is added to the main building: *They built a big addition at the back of their house.*

S2 W2 **ad·di·tion·al** /əˈdɪʃənəl/ *adj* more than what was agreed or expected: *An additional charge is made on baggage over the weight allowance.*

**ad·di·tion·al·ly** /əˈdɪʃənəli/ *adv* in addition; also: [sentence adverb] *A new contract had been agreed. Additionally, staff were offered a bonus scheme.*

**ad·di·tive** /ˈædɪ̇tɪv/ *n* [C] a substance, especially a chemical, that is added to something such as food, to preserve it, give it colour, improve it etc: *Foods sold under this label are guaranteed free from additives.* | *lead additives in petrol*

**ad·dle** /ˈædl/ *v* [T] to make someone confused and unable to think properly: **addle sb's brains** *All that drink has addled his brains!*

**ad·dled** /ˈædld/ *adj* **1** an egg that is addled is no longer good to eat **2** confused and unable to think properly

**add-on** /ˈ· ·/ *n* [C] a piece of equipment that can be connected to a computer, such as a MODEM, to make the computer more useful —compare PERIPHERAL[2]

S2 W2 **ad·dress**[1] /əˈdres‖əˈdres, ˈædres/ *n* **1** [C] the number of the building and the name of the street and town etc where someone lives or works, especially when written on a letter or package: *I wrote the wrong address on the envelope.* | **change of address** *Please notify us of any change of address.* **2** [C] a formal speech made to a group of people who have come especially to listen to it **3** [C] a number that shows where a piece of information is stored in a computer's memory **4 form/style/mode of address** the correct title or name that you use for someone when you are speaking to them

S3 W2 **ad·dress**[2] /əˈdres/ *v* [T] **1** to write on an envelope, package etc the name and address of the person you are sending it to: *If you address the letter, I'll mail it for you.* | **address sth to sb** *The letter is addressed to you, not me.* **2** *formal* to speak directly to someone: *She turned to address the man on her left.* | **address sth to** *You will have to address your complaints to the Head Office.* **3 address a meeting/crowd/conference etc** to make a speech to a large group of people: *The meeting was addressed by Senator Howard.* **4** to use a particular title or name when speaking or writing to someone: **address sb as** *The president should be addressed as 'Mr President'.* **5** *formal* to discuss, think about, or do something about a particular problem or question, especially with the aim of solving a problem: *The article addresses the problems of diseases connected with malnutrition.* | **address yourself to** *Marlowe now addressed himself to the task of searching the room.*

**ad·dress·ee** /ˌædreˈsiː, əˌdresˈiː/ *n* [C] the person a letter, package etc is addressed to

**ad·duce** /əˈdjuːs‖əˈduːs/ *v* [T] *formal* to mention a fact or reason in order to prove, explain, or support what you are claiming is true

**-ade** /eɪd/ *suffix* [in U nouns] a drink made from a particular fruit: *orangeade* (=drink made from orange juice)

**ad·e·noids** /ˈædɪ̇nɔɪdz, ˈædən-/ *n* [plural] the small soft pieces of flesh at the back of your throat that sometimes have to be removed because they become swollen —**adenoidal** /ˌædɪ̇ˈnɔɪdl◂/ *adj*

**ad·ept**[1] /ˈædept, əˈdept‖əˈdept/ *adj* good at doing something that needs care and skill: [**+at/in**] *Melissa soon became adept at predicting his moods.* —**adeptly** *adv*

**ad·ept**[2] /ˈædept/ *n* [C] someone who is good at doing something

S W **ad·e·quate** /ˈædɪ̇kwɪ̇t/ *adj* **1** an adequate amount is enough for a particular purpose: *The research cannot be completed without adequate funding.* | [+ **for**] *Are the parking facilities adequate for fifty cars?* **2** good enough in quality for a particular purpose or activity: *Without the proper resources the department cannot do an adequate job.* | **adequate to do sth** *His explanation did not seem adequate to account for what had happened.* **3** fairly good but not excellent: *Her performance was adequate but lacked originality.* —**adequately** *adv*: *She wasn't adequately insured.* —**adequacy** *n* [U]

**USAGE NOTE: ADEQUATE**

WORD CHOICE: **adequate, sufficient, enough, good enough, satisfactory, (will) do**

**Adequate** and **sufficient** are both more formal than **enough**, but all three can be used to talk about quantity: *Will you have enough/sufficient/adequate money for the trip?* However, **adequate** often sounds a little negative, suggesting that the amount is only just enough: *The water supply here is adequate/sufficient.*

If you want to say that the quality of something is enough, you use **good enough** or **satisfactory**: *"I'm afraid your work isn't good enough/satisfactory."* **Satisfactory** is a more formal word.

**Adequate** can be used to talk about both quality and quantity together, especially with uncountable nouns. For example, if you ask: *Is the food adequate?* you might be asking whether there is enough in amount or whether it is good enough. However, with a plural countable noun the quality meaning is more likely: *adequate resources/training/support etc*

In spoken English people often use **do** (but not in progressive forms) to talk about something being enough in either of these ways: *"Do you have enough money?" "It should do"* (=it should be enough). | *It's not much but it'll have to do.*

**ad·here** /ədˈhɪə‖-ˈhɪr/ *v formal* [I + **to**] to stick firmly to something

**adhere to** sth *phr v* [T] *formal* to continue to behave according to a particular rule, agreement, or belief: *adhere to your principles* | *adhere to the regulations*

**ad·her·ence** /ədˈhɪərəns‖-ˈhɪr-/ *n* [U] the act of behaving according to a particular rule or belief, or supporting a particular idea, even in difficult situations: [+ **to**] *strict adherence to the traditional caste system*

**ad·her·ent** /ədˈhɪərənt‖-ˈhɪr-/ *n* [C] someone who supports a particular idea, plan, political party etc

**ad·he·sion** /ədˈhiːʒən/ *n* **1** [U] the state of one thing sticking to another **2** [C] *technical* a piece of TISSUE (=flesh) that has grown around a small injury or diseased area

**ad·he·sive¹** /əd'hiːsɪv/ *n* [C] a substance such as glue that can be used to make two things stick together

**adhesive²** *adj* adhesive material sticks to surfaces: *adhesive tape*

**ad hoc** /ˌæd 'hɒk‖-'hɑːk, -'hoʊk/ *adj* [usually before noun] *Latin* done or arranged only when the situation makes it necessary, and without any previous planning: *An ad hoc committee has been set up to deal with the problem.* | **on an ad hoc basis** *Decisions were made on an ad hoc basis.* —**ad hoc** *adv*

**a·dieu** /ə'djuː‖ə'duː/ *n plural* **adieux** /ə'djuːz‖ə'duːz/ *or* **adieus** [C] *literary* an act of saying goodbye: **bid sb adieu** *He bid her a fond adieu.* —**adieu** *interjection*

**ad in·fi·ni·tum** /ˌæd ɪnfɪ̈'naɪtəm/ *adv Latin* continuing or repeated without ever ending

**ad·i·os** /ˌædi'os‖-'oʊs/ *interjection Spanish* goodbye

**ad·i·pose** /'ædɪ̈pəʊs‖-poʊs/ *adj technical* consisting of or containing animal fat: *adipose tissue*

**adj** the written abbreviation for ADJECTIVE

**ad·ja·cent** /ə'dʒeɪsənt/ *adj* something that is adjacent to something else, especially a room, building, or area, is next to it: [+ **to**] *The fire started in the building adjacent to the library.*

**ad·jec·ti·val** /ˌædʒɪ̈k'taɪvəl◂/ *adj* **adjectival phrase/clause etc** *technical* a phrase etc that is used as an adjective or that consists of adjectives. For example, 'fully furnished' is an adjectival phrase. —**adjectivally** *adv*

**ad·jec·tive** /'ædʒɪ̈ktɪv/ *n* [C] a word that describes a noun or PRONOUN, such as 'black' in the sentence 'She wore a black hat.', or 'happy' in the sentence 'I'll try to make you happy.' —compare ADVERB

**ad·join** /ə'dʒɔɪn/ *v* [T] if a room, building, or piece of land adjoins another one, it is next to it and joined to it: *The kitchen adjoins the sitting room.* —**adjoining** *adj*: *adjoining rooms*

**ad·journ** /ə'dʒɜːn‖-ɜːrn/ *v* **1** [I,T] if a meeting or law court adjourns, or if the person in charge adjourns it, it finishes or stops for a short time: *The chairman has the power to adjourn the meeting at any time.* | [+ **for/until**] *The trial was adjourned for two weeks.* | *Can I suggest we adjourn for lunch now?* **2 adjourn to** *humorous* to finish an activity and go somewhere: *After the match we adjourned to the pub.* —**adjournment** *n* [C,U]

**ad·judge** /ə'dʒʌdʒ/ *v* [T] *formal* to make a judgement about something or someone: *Any foodstuffs adjudged unacceptable must be disposed of.*

**ad·ju·di·cate** /ə'dʒuːdɪkeɪt/ *v* **1** [I,T] to officially decide who is right in an argument between two groups or organizations: [+ **on/in**] *An independent expert was called in to adjudicate.* | *adjudicate a claim* **2** [I] to be the judge in a competition: *He adjudicated at all the regional music competitions.* —**adjudicator** *n* [C] —**adjudication** /əˌdʒuːdɪ'keɪʃən/ *n* [U]

**ad·junct** /'ædʒʌŋkt/ *n* [C] **1** [+ **to**] something that is added or joined to something but is not part of it **2** *technical* an ADVERBIAL word or phrase that adds meaning to another part of a sentence, such as 'on Sunday' in 'They arrived on Sunday.'

**ad·jure** /ə'dʒʊə‖ə'dʒʊr/ *v* [T] *formal* to try very hard to persuade someone to do something: *Gwendolyn adjured him to be truthful.*

3 **ad·just** /ə'dʒʌst/ *v* **1** [T] to make small changes to something, especially to its position, in order to improve it, make it more effective etc: *Check and adjust the brakes regularly.* **2** [I,T] to gradually get used to a new situation by making small changes to the way you do things: [+ **to**] *Adjusting to the tropical heat was more difficult than they had expected.* | *They'll soon settle in – kids are very good at adjusting.* —see also WELL-ADJUSTED

**ad·just·a·ble** /ə'dʒʌstəbəl/ *adj* something that is adjustable can be changed in shape, size, or position to make it suitable for a particular person or purpose: *an adjustable desk lamp*

**ad·just·ment** /ə'dʒʌstmənt/ *n* [C,U] **1** a small change made to something, such as a machine, a system, or the way something looks: **make adjustments** *We've had to make some adjustments to our original calculations.* | **slight/minor adjustments** (=small changes) **2** a change that someone makes to the way they behave or think: *the adjustments required of someone moving to a foreign country*

**ad·ju·tant** /'ædʒʊ̈tənt/ *n* [C] an army officer responsible for office work

**ad-lib** /ˌæd 'lɪb/ *v* **ad-libbed, ad-libbing** [I,T] to say something in a speech, a performance of a play etc without preparing or planning it: *She forgot her lines and had to ad-lib the rest of the scene.* —**ad-lib** *n* [C] —**ad-lib** /ˌ· '·◂/ *adj, adv*

**ad·man** /'ædmæn/ *n plural* **admen** /-men/ [C] *informal* someone who works in advertsing

**ad·min** /'ædmɪn/ *n* [U] *informal especially BrE* ADMINISTRATION¹ (2): *She works in admin.*

**ad·min·is·ter** /əd'mɪnɪ̈stə‖-ər/ *v* [T] **1** to manage and organize the affairs of a company, government etc: *the bureaucrats who administer welfare programs* | *The Navajo administer their own territory within the United States.* **2** to organize the way a test or punishment is given, or the way laws are used: *the courts administering justice* | *The test was administered fairly and impartially.* **3** *formal* to give someone a medicine or drug to take

**ad·min·is·tra·tion** /ədˌmɪnɪ̈'streɪʃən/ *n* **1** [U] all the activities that are involved in managing and organizing the affairs of a company, institution etc: *We're looking for someone with experience in administration.* | *They spend too much on administration and not enough on doctors and nurses.* **2 the administration** the people who manage a company, insitution etc: *the college administration* **3** [C usually singular] the government of a country at a particular time: *the Kennedy Administration* | *The problem has been ignored by successive administrations.* **4** [U] the act of administering a test, law etc: *the administration of justice*

**ad·min·is·tra·tive** /əd'mɪnɪ̈strətɪv‖-streɪtɪv/ *adj* connected with the work of managing or organizing a company, institution etc: *The job is mainly administrative.* | *administrative duties* —**administratively** *adv*

**ad·min·is·tra·tor** /əd'mɪnɪ̈streɪtə‖-ər/ *n* [C] someone whose job is connected with the management and organization of a company, institution etc

**ad·mi·ra·ble** /'ædmərəbəl/ *adj* something that is admirable has many good qualities that you respect and admire: *an admirable achievement* —**admirably** *adv*

**ad·mi·ral** /'ædmərəl/ *n* [C] a high rank in the British or US navy, or someone who has this rank —see table on page B4

**Ad·mi·ral·ty** /'ædmərəlti/ *n* **the Admiralty** the government department that controls the British navy

**ad·mi·ra·tion** /ˌædmə'reɪʃən/ *n* [U] a feeling of admiring something or someone: *Daniel gazed at her in admiration.* | [+ **for**] *Tippett later developed a deep admiration for Wagner.*

**ad·mire** /əd'maɪə‖-'maɪr/ *v* [T not in progressive] **1** to have a very high opinion of someone because of a quality they have or because of something they have done: *I really admire the way she brings up those kids all on her own.* | **admire sb for sth** *Lewis was admired for his work on medieval literature.* **2** to look at something and think how beautiful or impressive it is: *We stopped half way up the hill to admire the view.* **3 admire sb from afar** to be attracted to someone but without telling them how you feel: *Mary was still a good looking woman and Sid had admired her from afar for a long time.* —**admiring** *adj* —**admiringly** *adv*

**ad·mir·er** /əd'maɪərə‖-'maɪrər/ *n* [C] **1** a man who is attracted to a particular woman: *a beautiful woman with*

*many admirers* | *a secret admirer* **2 be an admirer of** to admire someone, especially a famous person, or their work: *The painter Turner was a great admirer of Byron.*

**ad·mis·si·ble** /əd'mɪsəbəl/ *adj* admissible reasons, facts etc are acceptable or allowed, especially in a court of law: *admissible evidence* —opposite INADMISSIBLE —**admissibility** /əd,mɪsə'bɪləti/ *n* [U]

W3 **ad·mis·sion** /əd'mɪʃən/ *n* **1** [C] a statement in which you admit that something is true or that you have done something wrong: **admission that** *The Senator's admission that he had lied to Congress shocked many Americans.* | **admission of guilt/failure/defeat etc** *The court may interpret your silence as an admission of guilt.* | **by/on your own admission** *By his own admission, he is a complete womanizer.* **2** [U] permission given to someone to enter or become a member of a school, club, building etc: [+ **to**] *seeking admission to a prestigious university* | *This particular college has a very selective admissions policy.* | **gain admission** *Women gained admission to the club only recently.* **3 admissions** [plural] the process of allowing people to enter a university, institution, hospital etc, or the number of people who can enter: *Doctors are reporting a steep rise in admissions.* | **admissions policy/procedures/officer etc** *This particular college has a very selective admissions policy.* **4** [U] the cost of entrance to a concert, sports event etc: *The cost includes free admission to the casinos.* | *Admission: £3.50.* **5** [U] permission to enter a place: *No admission after 10pm.*

> **USAGE NOTE: ADMISSION**
>
> WORD CHOICE: **admission, admittance, admissions**
>
> **Admission** is the usual word. **Admittance** is more formal and only used in the meaning 'permission to go in a building, park etc', usually given by someone in authority. On a notice you might see: *Private Road: No Admittance*
>
> **Admissions** is the word used by official organizations about the number of people entering a university, school, hospital etc: *the admissions officer/policy/procedure* | *We have a lot of emergency admissions.*

S2 W1 **ad·mit** /əd'mɪt/ *v* **admitted, admitting** [T] **1** to accept and agree unwillingly that something is true or that someone else is right: *'I was really scared,' Jenny admitted.* | **admit (that)** *You may not like her, but you have to admit that she's good at her job.* | **I must admit** *spoken* (=when you are admitting something you are embarrassed about) *I must admit I didn't actually do anything to help her.* | **come on, admit it!** *spoken* (=used to try to make someone admit something) *Come on, admit it! You were out with Keith last night?* | **freely/openly admit** (=admit without being ashamed) *Phillips openly admits to being selfish.* **2** also **admit to** to say that you have done something wrong, especially something criminal; CONFESS (1) **admit (to) doing sth** *A quarter of all workers admit to taking time off when they are not ill.* | **admit (to) sth** *After questioning he admitted to the murder.* **3** to allow someone or something to enter a public place to watch a game, performance etc: **admit sb to/into** *Only ticket-holders will be admitted into the stadium.* **4** to allow someone to join an organization, club etc: **admit sb to/into** *The UK was admitted to the EEC in 1973.* **5 be admitted to hospital** *BrE*/**to the hospital** *AmE* to be taken to a hospital because you are ill: *He was admitted to the hospital Tuesday morning with stomach pains.* **6 admit defeat** to stop trying to do something because you realise you cannot succeed: *Sean kept running, refusing to admit defeat.* **7 an admitted alcoholic/atheist etc** someone who has admitted that they are an ALCOHOLIC, etc

**admit of** sth *phr v* [T] *formal* if a situation admits of a particular explanation, that explanation can be accepted as possible: *The facts admit of no other explanation.*

**ad·mit·tance** /əd'mɪtəns/ *n* [U] *formal* permission to enter a place: **gain admittance** (=get admittance) *Gaining admittance to his private club was no easy matter.* —compare ADMISSION (5)

**ad·mit·ted·ly** /əd'mɪtədli/ *adv* [sentence adverb] used when you are admitting that something is true: *The technique is painful, admittedly, but it benefits the patient greatly.* | *This has led to financial losses, though admittedly on a fairly small scale.*

**ad·mix·ture** /əd'mɪkstʃəd-‖-æd'mɪkstʃər/ *n* [C + **of**] *technical* a substance that is added to another substance in a mixture

**ad·mon·ish** /əd'mɒnɪʃ‖-'mɑː-/ *v* [T] *formal* to tell or warn someone severely that they have done something wrong: *The witness was admonished for failing to answer the question.* —**admonishment** *n* [C]

**ad·mo·ni·tion** /,ædmə'nɪʃən/ *n* [C,U] *formal* a warning or expression of disapproval about someone's behaviour —**admonitory** *adj formal*: *an admonitory glance*

**ad nau·se·am** /,æd 'nɔːziəm, -iæm‖-'nɒː-/ *adv* if you say or do something ad nauseam, you say or do it so often that it becomes annoying for other people: *Look, we've been over this ad nauseam – I think we should move on to the next item.*

**a·do** /ə'duː/ *n* [U] **without more/further ado** without delaying or wasting any time: *So without further ado, I'll now ask Mr Davis to open the debate.*

**a·do·be** /ə'dəubi‖ə'dou-/ *n* **1** [U] earth and STRAW (1) that are made into bricks for building houses **2** [C] a house made using adobe

**ad·o·les·cence** /,ædə'lesəns/ *n* [U] the time, usually between the ages of 12 to 18, when a young person is developing into an adult

**ad·o·les·cent** /,ædə'lesənt◂/ *n* [C] a young person who is developing into an adult —see picture at CHILD

**a·dopt** /ə'dɒpt‖ə'dɑːpt/ *v* [T] S W

**1** ▶**CHILD**◀ to legally make another person's child part of your family so that he or she becomes one of your own children: *My mother was adopted when she was four.* —compare FOSTER[1] (1)

**2 adopt an approach/strategy/policy** to start to use a particular method or plan for dealing with something: *The courts have been asked to adopt a more flexible approach to young offenders.*

**3** ▶**STYLE/MANNER**◀ to use a particular style of speaking, writing, or behaving, especially one that you do not usually use: *"I can't say I blame him", Victor replied, adopting a more conciliatory tone.* | *Papers like this tend to adopt a very simple writing style.*

**4** ▶**ACCEPT A SUGGESTION**◀ to formally approve a proposal, especially by voting: *They were trying to persuade the UN to adopt an aggressively anti-American resolution.*

**5 adopt a name/country** to choose it to be your own: *Italy is my adopted country.*

**6** ▶**ELECTION**◀ *BrE* to officially choose someone to represent a political party in an election

**a·dopt·ed** /ə'dɒptəd‖ə'dɑːp-/ *adj* **1** an adopted child has been legally made part of a family that he or she was not born into: *his adopted son* **2** your adopted country is one that you have chosen to live in permanently

**a·dop·tion** /ə'dɒpʃən‖ə'dɑːp-/ *n* **1** [C,U] the act or process of adopting a child **2** [U] the act of deciding to use a particular plan, method, way of speaking etc **3** [U] *BrE* the choice of a particular person to represent a political party in an election

**a·dop·tive** /ə'dɒptɪv‖ə'dɑːp-/ *adj* an adoptive parent is one who has adopted a child

**a·dor·a·ble** /ə'dɔːrəbəl/ *adj* someone or something that is adorable is so attractive that it fills you with feelings of love: *Oh what an adorable little baby!*

**ad·o·ra·tion** /,ædə'reɪʃən/ *n* [U] **1** great love and admiration: *the look of adoration in his eyes* **2** *literary* religious worship

**a·dore** /ə'dɔː‖ə'dɔːr/ *v* [T not in progressive] **1** to love

someone very much and feel very proud of them: *Betty adores her grandchildren.* **2** *informal* to like something very much: *I absolutely adore chocolate.* | *Don't you just adore these cookies?*

**a·dorn** /əˈdɔːn‖-ɔːrn/ *v* [T] *formal* to decorate something: *church walls adorned with religious paintings*

**a·dorn·ment** /əˈdɔːnmənt‖-ɔːr-/ *n* **1** [C] something that you use to decorate something **2** [U] the act of adorning something

**a·dren·a·lin** /əˈdrenəl-ɪn/ *n* [U] **1** a chemical produced by your body when you are afraid, angry, or excited, which makes your heart beat faster so that you can move quickly **2 get the adrenalin going** to make you feel nervously excited and full of energy

**a·drift** /əˈdrɪft/ *adj, adv* **1** a boat that is adrift is not fastened to anything or controlled by anyone **2** someone who is adrift is confused about what to do in their life **3 come adrift** to become separated from something that fastens: *Her hair was forever coming adrift from the pins and combs she used to keep it in place.*

**a·droit** /əˈdrɔɪt/ *adj* clever and skilful, especially in the way you use words and arguments: *an adroit negotiator* —**adroitly** *adv* —**adroitness** *n* [U]

**a·du·ki bean** /əˈduːki biːn/ *n* [C] a brown and red bean that is used in Chinese and Japanese cooking —see picture on page 414

**ad·u·la·tion** /ˌædʒʊˈleɪʃən/ *n* [U] praise and admiration for someone that is more than they really deserve: *basking in the adulation of his fans* —**adulatory** /ˌædʒʊˈleɪˌtəri, ˈædʒʊleitəri‖ˈædʒələtɔːri/ *adj*

2 **ad·ult¹** /ˈædʌlt, əˈdʌlt/ *n* **1** a fully-grown person or animal: *Some children find it difficult to talk to adults.*
2 **2** someone who is old enough to be considered legally responsible, and can for example vote in elections and get married without their parents' permission

3 **adult²** *adj* **1** [only before noun] fully grown or developed: *an adult lion* | **adult life** (=the part of your life when you are an adult) **2** typical of an adult's behaviour or of the things adults do: *dealing with problems in an adult way* **3 adult movie/magazine etc** a film etc that is about sex, shows sexual acts etc

**adult ed·u·ca·tion** /ˌ··· ·ˈ··/ *n* [U] education provided for adults outside the formal educational system, usually by means of classes that are held in the evening

**a·dul·ter·ate** /əˈdʌltəreɪt/ *v* [T] to make food or drink less pure by adding another substance of lower quality to it — see also UNADULTERATED —**adulteration** /əˌdʌltəˈreɪʃən/ *n* [U]

**a·dul·ter·er** /əˈdʌltərə‖-ər/ *n* [C] *old-fashioned* someone who is married and has sex with someone who is not their wife or husband

**a·dul·ter·ess** /əˈdʌltərɪs/ *n* [C] *old-fashioned* a married woman who has sex with a man who is not her husband

**a·dul·ter·y** /əˈdʌltəri/ *n* [U] sex between someone who is married and someone who is not their wife or husband: **commit adultery** *She had committed adultery on several occasions.* —**adulterous** *adj*

**ad·ult·hood** /ˈædʌlthʊd, əˈdʌlt-/ *n* [U] the time when you are an adult

**ad·um·brate** /ˈædʌmbreɪt/ *v* [T] *formal* to suggest or describe something in an incomplete way —**adumbration** /ˌædʌmˈbreɪʃən/ *n* [U]

**adv** the written abbreviation of ADVERB

3 **ad·vance¹** /ədˈvɑːns‖ədˈvæns/ *n*
2 **1 in advance** before something happens or is expected to happen: *I should warn you in advance, we may be delayed.* | **six months/a year in advance** *Rent is payable three months in advance.* | [+ **of**] *Could you distribute copies well in advance of the meeting?*
**2** ► **DEVELOPMENT/IMPROVEMENT** ◄ [C] a change, discovery, or INVENTION that brings progress: *His book argues that there have been major advances for women since 1945.* | [+ **in**] *Recent advances in biotechnology have raised moral questions.*
**3** ► **FORWARD MOVEMENT** ◄ [C] forward movement or progress: *the army's advance*
**4** ► **MONEY** ◄ [C usually singular] money paid to someone before the usual time
**5 advances** [plural] an attempt to start a friendly or sexual relationship with someone: **make advances** *She accused her boss of making advances to her.*
**6** ► **INCREASE** ◄ [C] *technical* an increase in the price or value of something: *a further big advance in the price of gold*

**advance²** *v* W3
**1** ► **MOVE** ◄ [I] to move forward, especially in a slow and determined way: **advance on** (=move forward in order to attack) *Troops advanced on the rebel stronghold.* | [+ **across/through/towards**] *The army slowly advanced across the frozen tundra.*
**2** ► **DEVELOP** ◄ [I] if something such as technical or scientific knowledge advances, it develops and improves: *Our understanding of human genetics has advanced considerably.*
**3 advance a plan/idea/proposal etc** *formal* to suggest a plan etc so that other people can consider it: *A similar plan was advanced by the British delegation.*
**4** ► **MONEY** ◄ [T] to give someone money before they have earned it: **advance sb sth** *Will they advance you some money until your get your first paycheck?*
**5 advance a cause/your interests/your career etc** to do something that will help you achieve advantage of success
**6** ► **PRICE** ◄ [I] *technical* if the price or value of something advances, it increases in amount: *Oil shares advanced today in heavy trading.*
**7** ► **CHANGE TIME** ◄ [T] *formal* to change the time when an event should happen to an earlier time or date: *The time of the meeting has been advanced to ten o'clock.*
**8** ► **FILM/CLOCK** ◄ [T] *formal* if you advance a film, clock etc, you make it go forward —see also ADVANCING

**advance³** *adj* **1 advance planning/warning/booking etc** planning etc that is done before an event: *We received no advance warning of the storm.* **2 advance party/team** a group of people who go first to a place where something will happen to prepare for it

**ad·vanced** /ədˈvɑːnst‖ədˈvænst/ *adj* **1** using the most W3
modern ideas, equipment, and methods: *advanced weapon systems* | *high levels of unemployment in the advanced capitalist economies* —see HIGH¹ (USAGE) **2** studying or dealing with a school subject at a difficult level: *advanced learners of English* | *advanced physics* **3** having reached a late point in time or development: *By this time, the disease was too far advanced to be treated.*

**Advanced lev·el** /·ˈ·· ˌ··/ *n* [C,U] *formal* A LEVEL

**ad·vance·ment** /ədˈvɑːnsmənt‖ədˈvæn-/ *n* [C,U] *formal* progress or development in your job, level of knowledge etc: *career advancement* | *advancements in science*

**advancing** /ədˈvɑːnsɪŋ‖ədˈvæn-/ *adj* **1** moving forward, especially in order to attack: *advancing Serbian forces* **2 advancing years/age** the fact of growing older: *Blake had grown much quieter and more serious – another sign of his advancing years.*

**ad·van·tage** /ədˈvɑːntɪdʒ‖ədˈvæn-/ *n* S1
**1** ► **THAT HELPS YOU** ◄ [C,U] something that helps W1
you to be better or more successful than others: [+ **of**] *the advantages of a university education* | **have an advantage (over)** *For certain types of work wood has advantages over plastic.* | **give sb an advantage** *New tax regulations had given them an advantage over their commerical rivals* | **big/great/definite advantage** *Her previous experience gives her a big advantage over the other applicants.* | **unfair advantage** *Government subsidies give these industries an unfair advantage.* | **be to your advantage** (=give you an advantage) | **be at an advantage** (=have an advantage) *Candidates with computer skills will be at an advantage.* | **gain/seek advantage** (=get or try to get something that will help you against your opponents) *seeking political advantage by exploiting this sensitive issue*
**2 take advantage of sb** to treat someone unfairly to get what you want, especially someone who is generous or

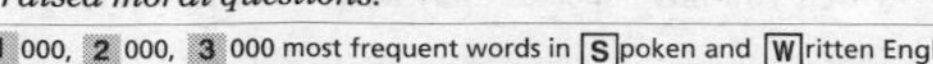

easily persuaded: *Don't lend them the car – they're taking advantage of you!*
**3 take advantage of sth** to use a particular situation to do or get what you want: *I took advantage of the good weather to paint the shed.*
**4 ▶ STH GOOD ◀** [C,U] a good or useful quality or condition that something has: *one of the many advantages of living in the city* | *Is there really any advantage in getting there early?* | **have the advantage of** *For children of this age, cereals have the advantage of being rich in iron.*
**5 to good advantage** in a way that shows the best features of someone or something
**6 ▶ TENNIS ◀ advantage X** used to show that the person named has won the point after DEUCE: *Advantage Agassi.*

**ad·van·ta·geous** /ˌædvənˈteɪdʒəs, ˌædvæn-/ *adj* helpful and likely to make you successful: **[+ to]** *terms advantageous to foreign companies* —**advantageously** *adv*

**Ad·vent** /ˈædvent/ *n* [singular] the period of four weeks before Christmas in the Christian religion

**advent** *n* **the advent of** the time when something first begins to be widely used: *the advent of the motor car*

**ad·ven·ti·tious** /ˌædvənˈtɪʃəs◂, ˌædven-/ *adj formal* happening by chance; unexpected —**adventitiously** *adj*

**ad·ven·ture** /ədˈventʃə‖-ər/ *n* [C,U] an exciting experience in which dangerous or unusual things happen: *a young man looking for adventure* | *Ahab's adventures at sea*

**adventure play·ground** /·ˌ·· ˈ··/ *n* [C] *BrE* an area of ground for children to play on, with exciting equipment and structures for climbing on

**ad·ven·tur·er** /ədˈventʃərə‖-ər/ *n* [C] **1** someone who enjoys adventure: *an adventurer traveling the world* **2** *old-fashioned* someone who tries to become rich or socially important using dishonest or immoral methods

**ad·ven·tur·ous** /ədˈventʃərəs/ *adj* **1** also **adventuresome** *AmE* eager to go to new places and do exciting or dangerous things: *an adventurous expedition up the Amazon* **2** not afraid of taking risks or trying new things: *Andy isn't a very adventurous cook.* —**adventurously** *adv*

**ad·verb** /ˈædvɜːb‖-vɜːrb/ *n* [C] a word or group of words that describes or adds to the meaning of a verb, an adjective, another adverb, or a whole sentence, such as 'slowly' in 'He ran slowly.', 'very' in 'It's very hot.', or 'naturally' in 'Naturally, we want you to come.' —compare ADJECTIVE

**ad·ver·bi·al**[1] /ədˈvɜːbiəl‖-ɜːr-/ *adj* used as an adverb: *an adverbial phrase*

**adverbial**[2] *n* [C] *technical* a word or phrase used as an adverb

**ad·ver·sa·ri·al** /ˌædvɜːˈseəriəl◂‖-vərˈser-/ *adj* an adversarial system, especially in politics and the law, is one in which two sides oppose and attack each other: *the adversarial nature of two-party politics*

**ad·ver·sa·ry** /ˈædvəsəri‖ˈædvərseri/ *n* [C] *formal* a country or person you are fighting or competing against; opponent

**ad·verse** /ˈædvɜːs‖-ɜːrs/ *adj* **1** not favourable: *an adverse report* | *adverse publicity* **2 adverse conditions/effects etc** conditions etc that make it difficult for something to happen or exist: *We had to abandon the climb because of adverse weather conditions.* —**adversely** *adv*

**ad·ver·si·ty** /ədˈvɜːsɪ̇ti‖-ɜːr-/ *n* [U] a situation in which you have a lot of problems that seem to be caused by bad luck: *to keep the family together in times of adversity*

**ad·vert**[1] /ˈædvɜːt‖-ɜːrt/ *n* [C] *BrE* an advertisement

**ad·vert**[2] /ədˈvɜːt‖-ɜːrt/ *v*
**advert to** sth *phr v* [T] *formal* to mention something

**ad·ver·tise** /ˈædvətaɪz‖-ər-/ *v* **1** [I,T] to tell people publicly about a product or service in order to persuade them to buy it: *Have you tried that new shampoo they've been advertising on TV?* **2** [I,T] to make an announcement, for example in a newspaper or on a POSTER, that a job is available, an event is going to happen etc: *a big poster advertising a U2 concert* | **[+ for]** *I see they're advertising for a new Sales Director.* **3** [T] to show or tell something about yourself that it would be better to keep secret: *Don't advertise the fact that you're looking for another job.* —**advertiser** *n* [C]

**ad·ver·tise·ment** /ədˈvɜːtɪ̇smənt‖ˌædvərˈtaɪz-/ *n* [C] **1** a picture, set of words, a film etc that is used to advertise a product or service: *an advertisement for a free day of skiing in Vermont* **2** a statement in a newspaper that a job is available, an event is going to happen etc **3 be an advertisement for** to show the advantages of something: *He's not a very good advertisement for private education.*

**ad·ver·tis·ing** /ˈædvətaɪzɪŋ‖-ər-/ *n* [U] the activity or business of advertising things on television, in newspapers etc: *advertising aimed at 18-25 year olds* | *a career in advertising*

**advertising a·gen·cy** /ˈ···· ˌ···/ *n* [C] a company that designs and makes advertisements for other companies

**ad·vice** /ədˈvaɪs/ *n* [U] an opinion you give someone about what they should do: **[+ on/about]** *There's lots of advice in the book on baby care.* | **give advice** *Can you give me some advice about buying a house?* | **legal/medical/professional advice etc** (=advice from someone with special knowledge) *If I were you, I'd get some legal advice.* | **ask sb's advice** *I want to ask your advice about where to stay in Taipei.* | **follow/take sb's advice** (=do what they advise you) *I followed my father's advice and sold the car.* | *Take my advice and study something practical.* | **a word/piece of advice** (=some advice) *Let me give you a piece of advice. Wear a blue or grey suit to the interview.* | **on sb's advice** (=because they advised you) *On my doctor's advice, I'm taking early retirement.*

This graph shows some of the words most commonly used with the noun **advice**.

advice on
give advice
legal/professional/medical advice
ask advice
take advice
advice about
follow advice
a word/piece of advice

2 4 6 8 10 per million

Based on the British National Corpus and the Longman Lancaster Corpus

**advice col·umn** /ˈ·ˈ· ˌ··/ *n* [C] *especially AmE* part of a newspaper or magazine in which someone gives advice to readers about their personal problems; AGONY COLUMN *BrE* —**advice columnist** *n* [C]

**ad·vi·sab·le** /ədˈvaɪzəbəl/ *adj* [not before noun] something that is advisable should be done in order to avoid problems or risks: *For heavy smokers, regular medical checks are advisable.* | **it is advisable to do sth** *It is advisable to disconnect the computer before you open it up.* —**advisability** /ədˌvaɪzəˈbɪlɪ̇ti/ *n* [U]

**ad·vise** /ədˈvaɪz/ *v* **1** [I,T] to tell someone what you think they should do, especially when you know more than they do about something: **advise sb to do sth** *Passengers are advised not to leave their bags unattended.* | **advise sb against doing sth** *I'd advise you against saying anything to the press.* | **strongly advise** *You are strongly advised to take out medical insurance when visiting China.* | **advise caution/patience/restraint etc** (=advise people to be careful, patient etc) *The makers advise extreme caution when handling this material.* **2** [I,T] to be employed to give advice on a subject about which you have special knowledge or skill: **advise on**

**sth** *She's been asked to advise on training the new team.* | **advise sb on sth** *He advises us on tax matters.* **3** [T] *formal* to inform someone about something: **advise sb of sth** *We'll advise you of any changes in the delivery dates.* | **keep sb advised** (=continue to inform someone) *Keep us advised of the developments.* **4 you would be well/ill advised to do sth** used to tell someone that it is wise or unwise to do something: *You would be well advised to stay in bed and rest.*

**ad·vis·ed·ly** /əd'vaɪzɪ̈dli/ *adv* after careful thought; deliberately: *He behaved like a dictator, and I use the term advisedly.*

3 3 **ad·vis·er** also **advisor** *AmE* /əd'vaɪzə‖-ər/ *n* [C] someone whose job is to give advice because they know a lot about a subject, especially in business, law, or politics: *an independent financial adviser*

**ad·vi·so·ry** /əd'vaɪzəri/ *adj* having the purpose of giving advice: **advisory committee/body** *the Environmental Protection Advisory Committee* | **advisory role/capacity** *employed in a purely advisory role*

**ad·vo·ca·cy** /'ædvəkəsi/ *n* [U] public support for a course of action or way of doing things

**ad·vo·cate**[1] /'ædvəkeɪt/ *v* [T] to publicly support a particular way of doing things: *Extremists were openly advocating violence.*

**ad·vo·cate**[2] /'ædvəkɪ̈t,-keɪt/ *n* [C] **1** someone who publicly supports a particular way of doing things: **be an advocate of** *She's a passionate advocate of natural childbirth.* **2** a lawyer who speaks in a court of law, especially in Scotland —see also **play/be the devil's advocate** (DEVIL (4))

**adze** also **adz** *AmE* /ædz/ *n* [C] a sharp tool with the blade at a right angle to the handle, used to shape pieces of wood

**ae·gis** /'iːdʒɪ̈s/ *n* **under the aegis of** *formal* with the protection or support of a person or organization: *a refugee camp operating under the aegis of the UN*

**ae·on** also **eon** *AmE* /'iːən/ *n* [C] an extremely long period of time

**aer·ate** /'eəreɪt‖'er-/ *v* [T] *technical* to put a gas or air into a liquid under pressure —**aeration** /eə'reɪʃən‖e'reɪ-/ *n* [U]

**aer·i·al**[1] /'eəriəl‖'er-/ *adj* **1** from a plane: *an aerial attack* | *aerial photographs* **2** in or moving through the air

**aerial**[2] *n* [C] a piece of equipment for receiving or sending radio or television signals, usually consisting of a piece of metal or wire; ANTENNA (2) *AmE* —see picture on page 409

**aero-** /eərəʊ, eərə‖eroʊ, -rə/ *prefix* concerning the air or aircraft: *aerodynamics* (=science of movement through air) | *an aeroengine*

**aer·o·bat·ics** /ˌeərə'bætɪks, ˌeərəʊ-‖ˌerə-/ *n* [plural] tricks done in a plane that involve making difficult or dangerous movements in the air

**ae·ro·bic** /eə'rəʊbɪk‖e'roʊ-/ *adj* **1** *technical* using oxygen **2 aerobic exercise** a type of exercise intended to strengthen the heart and lungs: *Examples of aerobic exercise are running, cycling, and swimming.*

**aer·o·bics** /eə'rəʊbɪks‖e'roʊ-/ *n* [U] a very active type of physical exercise done to music, usually in a class

**aer·o·drome** /'eərədrəʊm‖'erədroʊm/ *n* [C] *old-fashioned BrE* a place that small planes fly from

**aer·o·dy·nam·ic** /ˌeərəʊdaɪ'næmɪk◂‖ˌeroʊ-/ *adj* **1** an aerodynamic car, design etc uses the principles of aerodynamics to achieve high speed or low use of petrol **2** *technical* related to or involving aerodynamics: *aerodynamic efficiency* —**aerodynamically** /-kli/ *adv*

**aer·o·dy·nam·ics** /ˌeərəʊdaɪ'næmɪks‖ˌeroʊ-/ *n* [U] **1** the scientific study of how objects move through the air **2** the qualities needed for something to move through the air, especially smoothly and quickly

**aer·o·gramme** /'eərəgræm‖'erə-/ *n* [C] a very light letter you send by AIRMAIL; AIRLETTER *BrE*

**aer·o·nau·tics** /ˌeərə'nɔːtɪks‖ˌerə'nɒː-/ *n* [U] the science of designing and flying planes —**aeronautic** *adj* —**aeronautical** *adj*

**aer·o·plane** /'eərəpleɪn‖'erə-/ *n* [C] *BrE* a flying vehicle with wings and at least one engine; AIRPLANE *AmE* | plane —see picture at AIRCRAFT

**aer·o·sol** /'eərəsɒl‖'erəsɑːl/ *n* [U] a small metal container from which a liquid such as paint can be forced at high pressure —see picture at SPRAY[1]

**aer·o·space**[1] /'eərəʊspeɪs‖'eroʊ-/ *adj* involving the designing and building of aircraft and space vehicles: *the aerospace industry*

**aerospace**[2] *n* [U] the industry that designs and builds aircraft and space vehicles

**aes·thete** *especially BrE* also **esthete** *AmE* /'iːsθiːt‖'es-/ *n* [C] someone who loves and understands beautiful things, such as art and music

**aes·thet·ic** *especially BrE* also **esthetic** *AmE* /iːs'θetɪk, es-‖es-/ *adj* **1** connected with beauty and the study of beauty: *From an esthetic point of view, it's a nice design.* | *a work of great aesthetic appeal* **2** designed in a beautiful way: *The building is aesthetic, but not very practical to heat.* —**aesthetically** /-kli/ *adj*: *aesthetically pleasing*

**aes·thet·ics** *especially BrE* also **esthetics** *AmE* /iːs'θetɪks, es-‖es-/ *n* [U] the study of beauty, especially beauty in art

**ae·ther** /'iːθə‖-ər/ *n* [U] an old spelling of ETHER (=the air or sky)

**ae·ti·ol·o·gy** *BrE* **etiology** *AmE* /ˌiːti'ɒlədʒi‖-'ɑːl-/ *n* [U] the study of what causes disease

**a·far** /ə'fɑː‖ə'fɑːr/ *adv* **from afar** *literary* from a long distance away: *I saw him from afar.*

**af·fa·ble** /'æfəbəl/ *adj* friendly and easy to talk to: *an affable guy* —**affably** *adv* —**affability** /ˌæfə'bɪlɪ̈ti/ *n* [U]

**af·fair** /ə'feə‖ə'fer/ *n* [C] 

**1 affairs** [plural] **a)** public or political events and activities: *world affairs* | *They were accused of interfering in China's internal affairs.* | *the exclusion of women from public affairs* | **foreign affairs** (=political events in other countries) *a foreign affairs correspondent for the CNN* **b)** things connected with your personal life, your financial situation etc: *I am not prepared to discuss my financial affairs with the press.* —see also **state of affairs** (STATE[1] (8))

**2 ▶ EVENT ◀** an event or set of related events, especially one that is impressive or shocking: *the Watergate affair* | *The dinner was an elegant affair.*

**3 ▶ RELATIONSHIP ◀** a secret sexual relationship between two people, when at least one of them is married to someone else: **have an affair (with)** *He had an affair with his boss that lasted six years.* —see also LOVE AFFAIR

**4 ▶ THING ◀** *informal* an object, machine etc of a particular kind: *The computer was one of those little portable affairs.*

**5 be sb's affair** if something is your affair, it only concerns you and you do not want anyone else to get involved in it: *What I do in my time is my affair and nobody else's.*

**af·fect** /ə'fekt/ *v* [T] **1** to do something that produces an effect or change in someone or something: *a disease that affects the central nervous system* | *emergency relief for the areas affected by the hurricane* **2** [usually passive] to make someone feel strong emotions: *How will the tax affect people on low incomes?* | *We were all deeply affected by the news of her death.* **3** *formal* to pretend to have a particular feeling, way of speaking etc: *Simon affected boredom to make me think he didn't care.* | *to affect a foreign accent* S1 W1

**USAGE NOTE: AFFECT**

WORD CHOICE: **affect, effect**

**Affect** is the usual verb and **effect** is the usual noun: *How do you think the changes will affect (v) you?* (NOT affect on/to/in you). *What effect (n) do you think the changes will have on you?*

The verb **effect** is fairly formal and is only used in particular meanings, for example, you might **effect** changes or a plan of action (=make them happen). It does not mean the same as **affect**.

**af·fec·ta·tion** /ˌæfek'teɪʃən/ *n* [C,U] behaviour that is not sincere or natural: *Those beatnik clothes of his are just an affectation.*

**af·fect·ed** /ə'fektɪ̥d/ *adj* not sincere or natural: *that stupid affected laugh of hers*

**af·fect·ing** /ə'fektɪŋ/ *adj formal* producing strong emotions of sadness, pity etc: *a deeply affecting story*

**af·fec·tion** /ə'fekʃən/ *n* [C,U] a gentle feeling of love and caring: [+ **for**] *Bart felt a great affection for the old man.* | **show affection** *Their mother never shows them much affection.*

**af·fec·tion·ate** /ə'fekʃənɪ̥t/ *adj* showing in a gentle way that you love someone: *an affectionate hug* | *a very affectionate child* —**affectionately** *adv*

**af·fi·anced** /ə'faɪənst/ *adj old use* ENGAGED (1)

**af·fi·da·vit** /ˌæfɪ̥'deɪvɪ̥t/ *n* [C] *law* a written statement made under OATH (=after promising to tell the truth), for use as proof in a court of law

**af·fil·i·ate¹** /ə'fɪlieɪt/ *v* **1 be affiliated with/to** if a group or organization is affiliated to a larger one, it is connected with it or controlled by it: *a TV station affiliated to CBS* **2 affiliate yourself to** to join or become connected with a larger group or organization

**af·fil·i·ate²** /ə'fɪliɪ̥t/ *n* [C] a small company, organization etc that is connected with or controlled by a larger one

**af·fil·i·a·tion** /əˌfɪli'eɪʃən/ *n* [C,U] **1** the fact of being involved with or a member of a political or religious organization: *What are her political affiliations?* **2** the act of a smaller group or organization joining a larger one

**af·fin·i·ty** /ə'fɪnɪ̥ti/ *n* **1** [singular] a strong feeling that you like and understand someone because you share the same ideas or interests: [+ **for/between/with**] *I felt an immediate affinity for them.* **2** [C,U] a close connection between two things because of qualities or features that they share: [+ **with/between**] *There is a remarkable affinity between Christian and Chinese concepts of the spirit.*

**af·firm** /ə'fɜːm‖-ɜːrm/ *v* **1** [T] *formal* to state publicly that something is true: *The general affirmed rumors of an attack.* **2** [T] *formal* to strengthen a feeling, belief, or idea: *By submitting to male values, they symbolically affirm male superiority.* **3** [T] *technical* to promise to tell the truth in a court of law, but without mentioning God in the promise —**affirmation** /ˌæfə'meɪʃən‖ˌæfər-/ *n* [C,U]

**af·fir·ma·tive** /ə'fɜːmətɪv‖-ɜːr-/ *adj* **1 answer/reply in the affirmative** to say 'yes' —opposite NEGATIVE¹(3) **2** *formal* a word, sign etc that means 'yes': *an affirmative nod* —**affirmatively** *adv*

**affirmative ac·tion** /ˌ··· '··/ *n* [U] the practice of choosing people for a job or education course who are usually treated unfairly because of their race, sex etc; POSITIVE DISCRIMINATION *BrE*: *an affirmative action employer*

**af·fix¹** /ə'fɪks/ *v* [T + **to**] *formal* to fasten or stick something to something else

**af·fix²** /'æfɪks/ *n* [C] *technical* a group of letters added to the beginning or end of a word to change its meaning or use, such as 'untie', 'misunderstand', 'kindness', or 'quickly' —compare PREFIX¹(1), SUFFIX

**af·flict** /ə'flɪkt/ *v* [T often passive] *formal* to make someone suffer or experience serious problems: **be afflicted with/by** *a country afflicted by famine*

**af·flic·tion** /ə'flɪkʃən/ *n* [C,U] *formal* something, usually a medical condition, that causes pain or unhappiness: *the afflictions of old age*

**af·flu·ent** /'æfluənt/ *adj* having plenty of money, so that you can afford to buy expensive things, live in a nice house etc: *affluent suburbs with large houses and tree-lined streets* —**affluence** *n* [U]

**af·ford** /ə'fɔːd‖-ɔːrd/ *v* [T] **1 can afford a)** to have enough money to buy or pay for something: *Only the bigger clubs can afford the enormous fees that these players demand.* | **afford to do sth** *We can't afford to go on vacation this year.* **b)** to have enough time to do something: *Helena doesn't feel she can afford any more time away from work.* **c)** to be able to do something without causing serious problems for yourself: **afford to do sth** *We simply can't afford to offend such an important customer.* **2** *formal* to provide something or allow something to happen: *The window affords a beautiful view out over the city.* —**affordable** *adj*

**af·for·es·ta·tion** /əˌfɒrɪ̥'steɪʃən‖əˌfɔː-, əˌfɑː-/ *n* [U] *technical* the act of planting trees in order to make a forest —opposite DEFORESTATION —**afforest** /ə'fɒrɪ̥st‖ə'fɔː-, ə'fɑː-/ *v* [T]

**af·fray** /ə'freɪ/ *n* [C] *law* a noisy fight or quarrel in a public place

**af·fri·cate** /'æfrɪkɪ̥t/ *n* [C] *technical* a CONSONANT sound consisting of a PLOSIVE such as /t/ or /d/ that is immediately followed by a FRICATIVE pronounced in the same part of the mouth, such as /ʃ/ or /ʒ/. The word 'church', for example, contains the affricate /tʃ/.

**af·front¹** /ə'frʌnt/ *v* [T usually passive] to offend or insult someone, especially by not showing respect

**affront²** *n* [C usually singular] a remark or action that offends or insults someone: [+ **to**] *an affront to his pride*

**Af·ghan** /'æfgæn/ *n* [C] **1** someone who comes from Afghanistan **2** a warm cover for a bed made of wool knitted (KNIT¹ (1)) in colourful patterns **3** also **Afghan hound** a tall thin dog with a pointed nose and very long silky hair —**Afghan** *adj* —see picture at DOG¹

**a·fi·cio·na·do** /əˌfɪʃə'nɑːdəʊ‖-doʊ/ *n* [C] someone who is very interested in a particular activity or subject and knows a lot about it: *a film aficionado*

**a·field** /ə'fiːld/ *adv* **far afield** far away, especially from home: *Don't go too far afield or you'll get lost.*

**a·fire** /ə'faɪə‖ə'faɪr/ *adj, adv* [not before noun] *literary* **1** burning: *The oil tanker was afire.* **2** filled with strong emotions or excitement: [+ **with**] *afire with patriotism*

**a·flame** /ə'fleɪm/ *adj* [not before noun] *literary* **1** burning **2** very bright with colour or light: [+ **with**] *trees aflame with autumn leaves* **3** filled with strong emotions or excitement —**aflame** *adv*

**AFL-CIO** /ˌeɪ ef ˌel siː aɪ 'əʊ‖-'oʊ/ *n* [singular] the American Federation of Labor and Congress of Industrial Organizations; an association of American TRADE UNIONS, which has a lot of influence in the US

**a·float** /ə'fləʊt‖ə'floʊt/ *adj* [not before noun] **1** floating on water: *Help me get the boat afloat.* **2** having enough money to operate or stay out of debt: *The company was just barely afloat.* **3** *literary* on a ship —**afloat** *adv*

**a·foot** /ə'fʊt/ *adj* [not before noun] **1** being planned or happening: *There were plans afoot for a second attack.* **2** *old use* moving, especially walking —**afoot** *adv*

**a·fore·said** /ə'fɔːsed‖ə'fɔːr-/ also **a·fore·men·tioned** /ə'fɔːmenʃənd‖ə'fɔːr-/ *adj* [only before noun] *law* mentioned before in an earlier part of a document, article, book etc: *The property belongs to the aforesaid Ms Jones.* —**aforesaid** *n* [singular or plural] | *The aforesaid were present at the meeting.*

**a·fore·thought** /ə'fɔːθɔːt‖ə'fɔːrθɒːt/ *adj* —see **with malice aforethought** (MALICE (2))

**a·foul** /ə'faʊl/ *adv* **run/fall afoul of** *formal especially AmE* to cause problems by doing something that is against the rules or that goes against people's beliefs: *run afoul of the school authorities*

**a·fraid** /ə'freɪd/ *adj* [not before noun] **1 I'm afraid** *spoken* used to politely tell someone something that may annoy them, upset them or disappoint them: *That's the most we can offer you, I'm afraid.* | [+ **(that)**] *I'm afraid you've been given the wrong address.* | *Excuse me, but I'm afraid this is a non-smoking area.* | **be afraid** *I could see in his eyes that he was afraid.* | [+ **of**] *Don't be afraid of the dog — he's quite harmless.* | **afraid to do sth** *Don't be afraid to*

*ask for help.* | **be afraid of doing sth** *Luke is afraid of going to bed in the dark.* | **I'm afraid so** (=yes) *"Is she really very ill?" "I'm afraid so."* | **I'm afraid not** (=no) *No, I'm afraid not, but we do have some tickets for tomorrow.* **2** unwilling to do something because you are worried about what will happen if you do it: [+ **of**] *I didn't tell her because I was afraid of upsetting her.* | [+ **(that)**] *I didn't say anything because I was afraid the other kids would laugh at me.* **3** very frightened or worried about something: *The poor little thing looked so afraid.* | **be afraid for** *They've been laying people off, and Charlie is afraid for his job.* **4 afraid of your own shadow** easily frightened or always nervous

This graph shows how common different grammar patterns of the adjective **afraid** are.

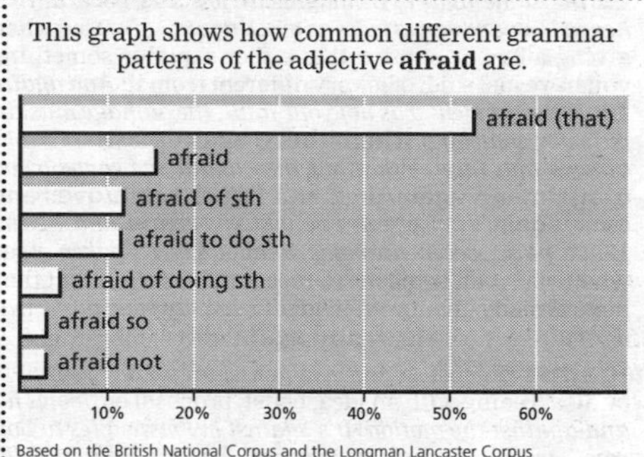


Based on the British National Corpus and the Longman Lancaster Corpus

**a·fresh** /ə'freʃ/ *adv formal* if you do something afresh, you do it again from the beginning: **start afresh** *He moved to America to start his life afresh.*

**Af·ri·can**[1] /'æfrɪkən/ *adj* from or connected with Africa

**African**[2] *n* [C] someone from Africa

**African A·mer·i·can** /ˌ··· ·'···/ *n* [C] *AmE* an American whose family originally came from Africa, especially as slaves —see NEGRO (USAGE)

**Af·ri·kaans** /ˌæfrɪ'kɑːns/ *n* [U] a language of South Africa that is similar to Dutch

**Af·ri·ka·ner** /ˌæfrɪ'kɑːnə‖-ər/ *n* [C] a South African whose family came from the Dutch people who settled there in the 1600s

**Af·ro** /'æfrəʊ‖-roʊ/ *n* [C] a hair style popular with black people in the 1970s in which the hair is cut into a round shape

**Afro-** /æfrəʊ‖-roʊ/ *prefix* **1** of Africa; African: *an Afro-American* (=a black American person) **2** African and: *Afro-Asian* (=of both Africa and Asia)

**aft** /ɑːft‖æft/ *adj, adv technical* in or towards the back part of a boat —opposite FORE[2]

**after-** /ɑːftə‖æftər/ *prefix* coming or happening afterwards: *aftercare* (=care given afterwards) | *after-sales service*

1 1 **af·ter**[1] /'ɑːftə‖'æftər/ *prep* **1** when a particular time or event has happened or is finished: *After the war many soldiers stayed in France.* | *I go swimming every day after work.* | *It's on after the 9 o'clock news.* | *Do you believe in life after death?* | **2 days/3 weeks etc after sth** *A few months after his birth we discovered that our son was deaf.* | **the day/week/year after sth** *We leave the day after tomorrow.* | **soon/not long/shortly after sth** *Not long after the wedding his wife got ill.* | **straight after sth** (=immediately after) *Come home straight after the performance.* | **come after sth** (=happen after something) *The first bomb attack came after midnight* —see SINCE[3] (USAGE). **2** following someone or something else in a list, series, piece or writing, line of people etc: *Whose name is after yours on the roll?* | *The date should be written after the address.* —see picture on page 1257 **3** when a particular amount of time has passed: *After 10 minutes remove the cake from the oven.* | *After a while things started to improve.* | *After months of argument they decided to divorce.* **4** *AmE* used when telling the time to say how many minutes it is after the hour: *The movie starts at a quarter after seven.* **5 day after day/year after year etc** continuously for a very long time: *He's worked in that hell-hole week after week, year after year, since he was 18.* **6** when someone has left a place, has finished doing something etc: *Remember to close the door after you.* | *I spend all day cleaning up after the kids.* **7 go/run/chase etc after sb** to follow someone in order to catch them: *Go after him and apologize.* **8** because of something or as a result of something: *I'm not surprised he walked out, after the way she treated him.* | *After your letter, I didn't think I'd ever see you again.* **9** in spite of something: *After all my hard work she still says it isn't neat enough.* **10 call/shout/gaze etc after sb** to speak to or look towards someone as they move away from you: *"You have a nice day, now!" she called after us.* **11 be after sb/sth a)** to be looking for someone or something: *Police are after a short man with a tattoo on his cheek.* | *"Were you after anything in particular?" "No, we're just looking."* **b)** *informal* to want to have something that belongs to someone else: *I think Chris is after my job.* **12 one after another/one after the other** if a series of events, actions etc happen one after another, each one happens soon after the previous one: *Ever since we moved into this house it's been one problem after another.* **13 after all a)** used to say that something is true or is a fact, in spite of another fact or situation: *He wrote to say they couldn't give me a job after all.* **b)** used to say that something should be remembered or considered, because it helps to explain why something else is true or is a fact: *I don't know why you're so concerned, it isn't your problem after all.* **14** used when listing or naming things, to mean that you have not included a particular thing because that is the first or best one: *After dancing, going to the movies is my favorite weekend activity.* **15** *especially BrE* given the same name as someone else, especially an older member of your family: *His name is Alessandro, after his grandfather.* **16** *formal* in the same style as a particular painter, musician etc: *a painting after Rembrandt* **17 after you** *spoken* **a)** used to say politely that someone else can use or do something before you do: *"Do you need the copier?" "After you."* **b) after you with** used to ask someone if you can have or use something after they have finished: *After you with that knife, please.* —see also **a man/woman after my own heart** (HEART), **take after** (TAKE[1])

**USAGE NOTE: AFTER**

WORD CHOICE: **after (prep), in, after (adv), afterwards, later**

You use **after** (*prep*) to talk about something that happens at the end of a period of time that is different from something that happens within that period: *After a few days I felt much better* (=not until a few days had passed). You use **in** to talk about something that will happen before a period of time has finished: *You'll feel better in a few days* (=by the time a few days has passed).

**After** (*prep*) is more often used to talk about events in the past, and **in** about the future: *She left after an hour* (=after an hour had passed). | *She'll be leaving in an hour* (=after an hour has passed).

**After** (*adv*) with the meaning 'afterwards' usually follows another time adverb: *We arrived just/soon/shortly after*. With words that show a length of time, **afterwards** or **later** is more usual: *She arrived three days afterwards/later* (NOT usually *three days after*, though you could say *after that*).

If you want to use a word with this meaning on its own, you would usually use **afterwards**: *We went swimming and walked home afterwards.* However, in informal British spoken English people sometimes say **after**: *We went swimming and walked home after.* You would not usually begin a sentence with **after**, though: *Afterwards/After that, we left* (NOT *After, we left*).

**after²** *conjunction* when a particular time or event has happened or is finished: *After you'd called the police, what did you do?* | *He changed his name after he left Germany.* | **two days/three weeks etc after** *Ten years after I bought the painting I discovered it was fake.* | **shortly/soon/not long after** *Shortly after the eggs have hatched, the mother goes off in search of food.*

**after³** *adv* after something that has already been mentioned; afterwards: *What are you doing after? Do you want to go for a drink?* | **come after** (=happen after something else has happened) *Having lost the final pages, we can only guess at what might come after.* | **the day/the year etc after** *Once you've purchased the washing machine we guarantee it for up to 5 years after.* | **shortly/soon/not long after** *Not long after, I heard that Mike had been killed in the war.*

**after⁴** *adj* **1 in after years** *literary* in the years after the time that has been mentioned **2** *technical* in the back part of a boat or an aircraft: *the after deck*

**af·ter·birth** /ˈɑːftəbɜːθ‖ˈæftərbɜːrθ/ *n* [U] the substance that comes out of female humans or animals just after they have had a baby

**af·ter·care** /ˈɑːftəkeə‖ˈæftəker/ *n* [U] *BrE* care or treatment given to someone after they have been in hospital

**after ef·fect** /ˈ·· ·,·/ *n* [C usually plural] an unpleasant effect that remains for a long time after the condition or event that caused it: *the after-effects of his illness*

**af·ter·glow** /ˈɑːftəgləʊ‖ˈæftərgloʊ/ *n* [C usually singular] **1** a pleasant feeling that remains after a happy experience: *the afterglow of the party* **2** the light that remains in the western sky after the sun goes down

**af·ter·life** /ˈɑːftəlaɪf‖ˈæftər-/ *n* [singular] the life that some people believe people have after death

**af·ter·math** /ˈɑːftəmæθ‖ˈæftər-/ *n* [singular] the period of time after something such as a war, storm, or accident when people are still dealing with the results: *the danger of disease in the aftermath of the earthquake*

S1 W2 **af·ter·noon** /ˌɑːftəˈnuːn◂‖ˌæftər-/ *n* [C,U] **1** the period of time between midday and sunset or at the end of the day's work: *We went swimming on Tuesday afternoon.* | *Harry went to sleep in the afternoon.* | *Do you want to go shopping tomorrow afternoon?* | *tickets for the afternoon performance* | **this afternoon** (=today in the afternoon) *Could you babysit for a few hours this afternoon?* **2 afternoons** *especially AmE* during the afternoon each day: *She only works afternoons.* —compare EVENING

**af·ters** /ˈɑːftəz‖ˈæftərz/ *n* [plural] *BrE informal* the part of a meal that comes after the main dish; DESSERT

**af·ter·shave** /ˈɑːftəʃeɪv‖ˈæftər-/ *n* [C,U] a liquid with a pleasant smell that a man puts on his face after he shaves (SHAVE¹ (1))

**af·ter·taste** /ˈɑːftəteɪst‖ˈæftər-/ *n* [C usually singular] a taste that stays in your mouth after you have eaten or drunk something: *The wine leaves a strong aftertaste.*

**af·ter·thought** /ˈɑːftəθɔːt‖ˈæftərθɒːt/ *n* [C] **1 as an afterthought** thought of and mentioned after you have finished talking about a particular subject: *He added as an afterthought, 'Bring Melanie too.'* **2** something added later, especially something that was not part of the original plan: *The tiles looked out of place, as if they had been an afterthought.*

S2 W3 **af·ter·wards** /ˈɑːftəwədz‖ˈæftərwərdz/ *adv* also **afterward** *AmE* after an event or time that has already been mentioned: *The ceremony lasts half an hour and afterward there's a meal.* | **2 days/3 weeks etc afterwards** *My parents met during the war but didn't marry till five years afterwards.* —see AFTER¹ (USAGE)

S1 W1 **a·gain** /əˈgen, əˈgeɪn‖əˈgen/ *adv* **1** if something happens again, or someone does something again, it happens or they do it one more time: *Can you say that again? I didn't hear you.* | *I'll never go there again.* | *I'm sorry, Mr Khan's line is busy. Can you try again later?* | **once again** (=again, usually for at least the third time) *Once again the Allies marched in and pushed back the enemy troops.* | **yet again** (=again, after happening many times before) *Can you believe it! He told that story about his teeth yet again.* **2** back to the same state or situation that you were in before: *His parents stayed and nursed him back to health again.* | *It's great to have you home again.* **3 all over again** if you do something all over again, you repeat it from the beginning: *There's no tape in the machine. We'll have to start the interview all over again.* **4 as much/as many/the same again** the same number or amount added to what there already is: *What a fantastic lunch. I could eat the same again.* | *I thought my job was good until I heard Bernard earns twice as much again.* **5** used when giving a fact or opinion that either explains something you have just said, of is very different from it: *And again, while the accident was not your fault, the damage must be paid for somehow.* | **then/there again** *spoken*: *Carol's always had nice clothes but then again she earns a lot.* **6 again and again/time and (time) again/over and over again** very often: *I've told you again and again, Don't play soccer near the windows.* **7** *spoken* used when you want someone to repeat information that they have already given you: *What did you say your name was again?* —see also **now and again** (NOW¹ (6))

**a·gainst** /əˈgenst, əˈgeɪnst‖əˈgenst/ *prep* **1** opposed to  or disagreeing with an idea, belief, proposal etc: *votes for*  *and against the motion* | *It's against my principles to borrow money.* | *Several members spoke against the proposal.* | **be against sth** *I'm against all forms of hunting.* | **against sb's wishes** (=when you know someone does not want something to happen) *They got married against her wishes.* | **against sb's will** (=when someone is forced to do something) *She has been kept in the house against her will.* | **against the law** (=illegal) —see graph at OPPOSED **2** fighting or competing with another person, team, country etc: *He was injured in the game against the Cowboys.* | *We'll be competing against some of the best companies in Europe.* | *the fight against terrorism* **3** in a way that has an unfavourable effect on someone or causes them disadvantage: *discrimination against women* | *Your lack of experience could count against you.* | *The planning regulations tend to work against smaller companies.* **4** touching, hitting, or rubbing another surface: *The rain drummed against the window.* | *I like it when the cat rubs its head against my legs.* | *The car skidded and we could hear the crunch of metal against metal.* —see picture on page 1257 **5** next to and touching an upright surface, especially for support: *There was a ladder propped up against the wall.* | *The younger policeman was leaning against the bureau with his arms folded.* **6** in the opposite direction to: *sailing against the wind* | *swimming against the current* **7** seen or shown with something else behind or as a background: *He caught a glimpse of a man silhouetted against a dimly lit background.* | *knowing what colours look good against your skin* **8** used to describe something in relation to other events that are happening at the same time: *The reforms were introduced against a background of social unrest.* **9** in comparison with: *Only 3% of blacks were registered voters against 97% of the white residents.* | *She checked the contents of the box against the list.* **10** providing protection from harm or damage: *insurance against accident and sickness* | *This spray can be used against weevil and other crop pests.* **11 be/come up against sth** to have to deal with a difficult opponent or problem: *You see, this is what we're up against – the suppliers just aren't reliable.* **12 have sth against sb/sth** to dislike or disapprove of someone or something: *It's not that I have anything against babies. I just don't feel very comfortable with them.*

**a·gape** /əˈgeɪp/ *adj* with your mouth wide open, especially because you are surprised or shocked: *Vince watched, his mouth agape in horror.*

**ag·ate** /ˈægət/ *n* [C] a hard stone with bands of different colours, used in jewellery

**-age** /ɪdʒ/ *suffix* [in nouns] **1** the action or result of doing something: *Buy a larger size to allow for shrinkage.* (=getting smaller) | *several breakages* (=things broken) **2** the cost of doing something: *Postage is extra.* **3** a particular state or rank: *a peerage* (=noble rank)

S1 W1 **age¹** /eɪdʒ/ *n*
**1** ▶ **HOW OLD** ◀ [C,U] the number of years someone has lived or something has existed: *Francis is the same age as me.* | *The boys were six years apart in age.* | *There were dozens of kids there, all different ages.* | **at the age of** (=when someone is a particular age) *Marco won the Grand Prix at the age of 19.* | **4/15 etc years of age** *formal* (=4, 15 etc years old) *The missing girl is 19 years of age.* | **at age 57/4/18 etc** *AmE* (=when someone is 57 etc years old) *Saul entered Yale at age 14.* | **at an early age** (=very young) *girls who become mothers at a very early age* | **act your age** (=behave in a way that is suitable to how old you are) | **sb's age** (=how old someone is) *When you get to my age, it's quite difficult getting up stairs.* | **for his/her age** (=compared with others of the same age) *She's very tall for her age, isn't she.* | **certain age** *Kids get to a certain age and say, right, that's it, and they just go.*
**2** ▶ **LEGAL AGE** ◀ [U] the age when you are legally old enough to do something: *What's the minimum age for getting a driver's license?* | **under age** (=too young) *You're not allowed to be drinking, you're under age.* | **over age** (=too old) *Dan's over age, so the army won't accept him.*
**3** ▶ **PERIOD OF LIFE** ◀ [C,U] one of the particular periods of someone's life: *women of childbearing age* | *Phil's coming up to 13 – rather a difficult age.* —see also OLD AGE, MIDDLE AGE, TEENAGE
**4** ▶ **BEING OLD** ◀ [U] the state or fact of being old: *The newspapers were brown with age.* | *Age had given his face a sort of crumpled look.*
**5** ▶ **PERIOD OF HISTORY** ◀ [C usually singular] a particular period of history: *the last Ice Age* | *We are living in the computer age.* —see also GOLDEN AGE, **in this day and age** (DAY (29))
**6 come of age a)** reach the age when you are legally considered to be a responsible adult **b)** if something comes of age, it reaches a stage of development at which people accept it as being important, valuable etc: *It was during this period that the movies really came of age as a creative art form.*
**7 ages** [plural] also **an age** *informal, especially BrE* a long time: *It'll be ages before we're ready to go.* | **for ages** *Simon! I haven't seen you for ages!* | **it's (been) ages since** *It's ages since we've played that game.* | **take ages** *It takes ages to make that recipe.*

**age²** *v present participle* **ageing** *or* **aging** **1** [I,T] to start looking older or to make someone look older, especially because they have suffered a lot: *Myra's recent illness has aged her considerably.* **2** [I] to become older: *The buildings are ageing, and some are unsafe.* **3** [I] to improve and develop in quality and taste, over a period of time: *a wine that has aged well*

**age brack·et** /ˈ· ˌ··/ *n* [C] the people between two particular ages, considered as a group: *single people in the 40-50 age bracket*

S3 **aged¹** /eɪdʒd/ *adj* **aged 5/30/25 etc** 5, 30 etc years old: *The course is open to children aged 12 and over.* | **[+ between]** *The police are looking for a man aged between 30 and 35.*

**a·ged²** /ˈeɪdʒəd/ *adj* **1** very old: *my aged parents* **2 the aged** old people: *plans to help the aged and infirm*

**age dis·crim·i·na·tion** /ˈ· ···ˌ··/ *n* [U] *AmE* unfair treatment of people because they are old; AGEISM *BrE*

**age group** /ˈ· ·/ *n* [C] all the people between two particular ages, considered as a group: *a book written for children in the 12-14 age group*

**age·ing¹** *BrE* usually **aging** *AmE* /ˈeɪdʒɪŋ/ *adj* [only before noun] becoming old, and usually less useful, attractive, suitable etc: *aging movie stars* | *an ageing population*

**ageing²** *BrE* usually **aging** *AmE n* [U] the process of getting old: *airlines with ageing fleets* | *products that claim to halt the ageing process*

**age·is·m** also **agism** /ˈeɪdʒɪzəm/ *n* [U] *BrE* unfair treatment of people because they are old; AGE DISCRIMINATION *AmE* —**ageist** *adj* —**ageist** *n* [C]

**age·less** /ˈeɪdʒləs/ *adj* **1** never looking old or old-fashioned: *Good clothes should be ageless.* **2** continuing forever: *the ageless fascination of the sea* —**agelessness** *n* [U]

**age lim·it** /ˈ· ˌ··/ *n* [C] the youngest or oldest age at which you are allowed to do something: *The age limit at the new nightclub is 21.*

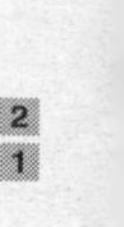

**a·gen·cy** /ˈeɪdʒənsi/ *n* [C] **1** a business that provides information about other businesses and their products, or that provides a particular service: *I got this job through an employment agency.* —see also DATING AGENCY, NEWS AGENCY **2** an organization or department, especially within a government, that does a specific job: *a UN agency responsible for helping refugees* **3 by/through the agency of** being done with or as the result of someone's help S2 W1

**a·gen·da** /əˈdʒendə/ *n* [C] **1** a list of the subjects to be discussed at a meeting: **on the agenda** *the first item on the agenda* **2 be on the agenda** if something is on the agenda, you are planning to do something about it: **be on top of the agenda/be high on the agenda** (=be very important to do) *Health care is on top of President Clinton's agenda.* **3** subjects that everyone has heard of and is talking about: *Environmental issues are racing up the political agenda.* —see also HIDDEN AGENDA S3

**a·gent** /ˈeɪdʒənt/ *n* [C] S3 W2
**1** ▶ **BUSINESS** ◀ a person or company that represents another person or company in business, in their legal problems etc: *Our agent in Rio deals with all our Brazilian business.* | **[+ for]** *We're acting as agents for Mr Watson.* —see also ESTATE AGENT, REAL ESTATE AGENT, LAND AGENT
**2** ▶ **ARTIST/ACTOR** ◀ someone who is paid by actors, musicians etc to find work for them: *My agent has an exciting new script for me to look at.*
**3** ▶ **GOVERNMENT AGENT** ◀ someone who works for a government or police department in order to get secret information about another country or organization; SPY: *a Soviet agent in Czechoslovakia* —see also SECRET AGENT, DOUBLE AGENT
**4** ▶ **CHEMICAL** ◀ *technical* a chemical or substance that makes other substances change: *Soap is a cleansing agent.*
**5** ▶ **FORCE** ◀ someone or something that affects or changes a situation: **agent for/of change** *Technological advances are the chief agents of change.*

**a·gent pro·voc·a·teur** /ˌæʒɒn prɒvɒkəˈtɜː‖ˌɑːʒɑːn proʊvɑːkəˈtɜːr/ *n* [C] *French* someone who is employed to encourage people who are working against a government to do something illegal so that they are caught

**age of con·sent** /ˌ· · ·ˈ·/ *n* [C] the age when someone can legally get married or have a sexual relationship

**age-old** /ˌ· ˈ·◂/ *adj* having existed for a very long time: *age-old customs* | *It's nothing new. It's an age-old problem.*

**ag·glom·er·ate** /əˈglɒmərət‖əˈglɑː-/ *n* [singular, U] *technical* a type of rock formed from pieces of material from a VOLCANO that have melted together

**ag·glom·e·ra·tion** /əˌglɒməˈreɪʃən‖əˌglɑː-/ *n* [C,U] a large collection of things that do not seem to belong together: *an agglomeration of facts* —**agglomerate** *v* /əˈglɒməreɪt‖əˈglɑː-/ —**agglomerate** *adj* /-rət/

**ag·glu·ti·na·tion** /əˌgluːtəˈneɪʃən/ *n* [U] *technical* **1** the state of being stuck together **2** the process of making new words by combining two or more words, such as combining 'ship' and 'yard' to make 'shipyard'

**ag·gran·dize·ment** also **-isement** *BrE* /əˈgrændəzmənt/ *n* [U] a word meaning an increase in power, size, or importance, used especially when you disapprove of this increase: *a war fought for national aggrandizement* | *He did it for his own personal aggrandizement.*

**ag·gra·vate** /ˈægrəveɪt/ *v* [T] **1** to make a bad situation worse: *Their debt problem was aggravated by a rise in interest rates.* **2** *informal* to make someone angry or annoyed: *Stop aggravating the cat!* —**aggravating** *adj* —**aggravatingly** *adv* —**aggravation** /ˌægrəˈveɪʃən/ *n* [C,U]

**ag·gre·gate[1]** /ˈægrɪgɪt/ *n* [C] **1** the total after a lot of different parts or figures have been added together: *Society is not just an aggregate of individuals.* | **on aggregate** *BrE* (=when the points are added together) *Manchester United won 2-1 on aggregate.* | **in (the) aggregate** (=as a group or in total) **2** [singular, U] *technical* sand or small stones that are used in making CONCRETE[1]

**aggregate[2]** *adj* [only before noun] *technical* being the total amount of something, especially money: *aggregate income and investment*

**ag·gre·gate[3]** /ˈægrɪgeɪt/ *v* **1** [linking verb] to be a particular amount when added together: **aggregate £100/20 etc** *Sheila's earnings from all sources aggregated £100,000.* **2** [I,T usually passive] to put things together in a group to form a total; ASSEMBLE: *We made estimates using the aggregated data.*

**ag·gres·sion** /əˈgreʃən/ *n* [U] **1** angry or threatening behaviour or feelings that often result in fighting: *Television violence can encourage aggression in children.* **2** the act of attacking a country, especially when that country has not attacked first: *territorial aggression* | **act of aggression** *an unprovoked act of agression on a peaceful nation*

S 3 **ag·gres·sive** /əˈgresɪv/ *adj* **1** behaving in an angry, threatening way, as if you want to fight or attack someone: *The men were drunk, aggressive and looking for a fight.* **2** someone who is aggressive is very determined to succeed or get what they want: *A successful businessman has to be aggressive.* **3** an aggressive action or plan is intended to achieve the right result: *an aggressive marketing campaign* —**aggressively** *adv* —**aggressiveness** *n* [U]

**ag·gres·sor** /əˈgresə‖-ər/ *n* [C] a person or country that begins a fight or war with another person or country

**ag·grieved** /əˈgriːvd/ *adj* **1** feeling or showing anger and unhappiness because you think you have been unfairly treated: *an aggrieved tone of voice* **2** *law* having suffered as a result of the illegal actions of someone else: **the aggrieved party** (=the person who has suffered)

**ag·gro** /ˈægrəʊ‖-roʊ/ *n* [U] *BrE informal* **1** aggressive behaviour and fighting, especially between young men **2** problems or difficulties that annoy you: *We had so much aggro with our insurance claim.*

**a·ghast** /əˈgɑːst‖əˈgæst/ *adj* [not before noun] feeling or looking shocked by something you have seen or just found out: [+ **at**] *I was aghast at the violence I was witnessing.*

**a·gile** /ˈædʒaɪl‖ˈædʒəl/ *adj* **1** able to move quickly and easily: *Andy climbed the tree, agile as a monkey.* **2 agile mind** the ability to think very quickly and intelligently

**ag·ing** /ˈeɪdʒɪŋ/ an American spelling of AGEING

**ag·is·m** /ˈeɪdʒɪzəm/ an American spelling of AGEISM

**a·gi·tate** /ˈædʒɪteɪt/ *v* **1** [I] to argue strongly in public for something you want, especially a political or social change: [+ **for/against**] *unions agitating for higher pay* **2** [T] to shake or mix a liquid quickly **3** [T] *formal* to make someone feel anxious, upset, and nervous

**a·gi·ta·ted** /ˈædʒɪteɪtɪd/ *adj* so nervous or upset that you are unable to keep still or think calmly: *An agitated waiter rushed up to apologize for the delay.* | *She got rather agitated.*

**a·gi·ta·tion** /ˌædʒɪˈteɪʃən/ *n* **1** [U] feeling of being so anxious, nervous, or upset that you cannot think calmly: *Perry's agitation was so great he could hardly speak.* **2** [C,U] a public argument or action for social or political change: [+ **for/against**] *agitation for civil rights* **3** [U] the act of shaking or mixing a liquid

**a·gi·ta·tor** /ˈædʒɪteɪtə‖-ər/ *n* [C] **1** someone who encourages people to work towards changing something in society: *a political agitator* **2** a machine used to shake or mix liquids

**a·git·prop** /ˌædʒɪtˈprɒp‖-ˈprɑːp/ *n* [U] music, literature, or art that tried to persuade people that SOCIALIST ideas were good: *1970s radical agitprop*

**a·glow** /əˈgləʊ‖əˈgloʊ/ *adj* **1** *literary* bright and shining with warmth, light, or colour: *The morning sun set the sky aglow.* **2** if someone's face or expression is aglow, they seem happy and excited: [+ **with**] *Linda's face was aglow with happiness.*

**AGM** /ˌeɪ dʒiː ˈem/ *n* [C] *BrE* annual general meeting; a meeting held once a year by a club, business, or organization, for the members to discuss the previous year's business, elect officials etc; ANNUAL MEETING *AmE*

**ag·nos·tic** /ægˈnɒstɪk, əg-‖-ˈnɑː-/ *n* [C] someone who believes that people cannot know whether God exists or not —compare **atheist** (ATHEISM) —**agnostic** *adj* —**agnosticism** /-tɪsɪzəm/ *n* [U]

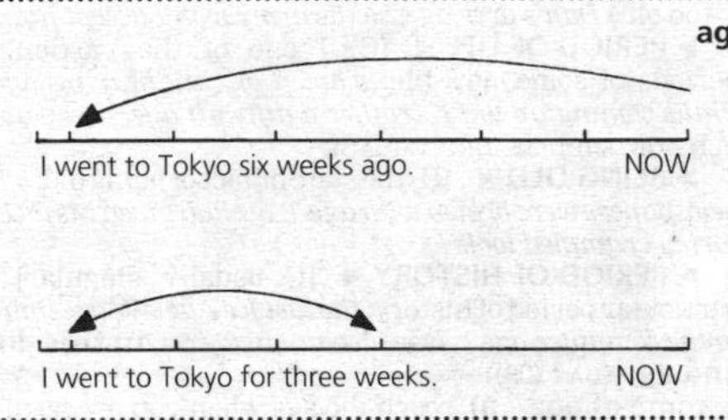
ago
I went to Tokyo six weeks ago.
NOW
I went to Tokyo for three weeks.
NOW

**a·go** /əˈgəʊ‖əˈgoʊ/ *adj* used to show how far back in the past something happened: **5 minutes/an hour/20 years ago** *Michael left the office about half an hour ago.* | **long ago/a long time ago** *I met Aunt Hetty once, a very long time ago.* | **a minute/moment ago** *I had my keys a minute ago, and now I can't find them.* | **a little/short while ago** *Tom got a letter from him just a little while ago.* | **some time ago** (=a fairly long time ago) *They moved to a new house some time ago, a couple of years I think.* —compare FOR[1] (8), SINCE S W

**a·gog** /əˈgɒg‖əˈgɑːg/ *adj* [not before noun] very interested, excited, and surprised, especially at something you are experiencing for the first time: **(be all) agog (at)** *We were all agog at the sights of New York.*

**ag·o·nize** also **-ise** *BrE* /ˈægənaɪz/ *v* [I] to think about a difficult decision very carefully and with a lot of effort: [+ **over/about**] *There's no point in agonizing over which route to take.* —**agonizing** *n* [U] *This time there was none of the agonizing and guilt that had accompanied her earlier decision.*

**ag·o·nized** also **-ised** *BrE* /ˈægənaɪzd/ *adj* expressing very severe pain: *the agonized moans of wounded soldiers*

**ag·o·niz·ing** also **-ising** *BrE* /ˈægənaɪzɪŋ/ *adj* extremely painful or difficult: *agonizing pain* —**agonizingly** *adv*

**ag·o·ny** /ˈægəni/ *n* [C,U] **1** very severe pain: *the agony of arthritis* | **be in agony** *The poor guy was in agony.* | **be agony** *spoken*: *It was agony having my wisdom teeth out.* **2** a very sad, difficult, or unpleasant situation: *It was agony not knowing if she would live.* —see also **pile on the agony** (PILE[2]), **prolong the agony** (PROLONG)(2)

**agony aunt** /ˈ··· ˌ·/ *n* [C] *BrE* someone who writes an agony column

**agony col·umn** /ˈ··· ˌ··/ *n* [C] *BrE* a part of a newspaper or magazine in which someone gives advice to readers about their personal problems; ADVICE COLUMN *AmE*

**ag·o·ra·pho·bi·a** /ˌæɡərəˈfəʊbiə‖-ˈfoʊ-/ *n* [U] *technical* the fear of crowds and open spaces —compare CLAUSTROPHOBIA

**ag·o·ra·pho·bic** /ˌæɡərəˈfəʊbɪk◂‖-ˈfoʊ-/ *n* [C] someone who suffers from agoraphobia —**agoraphobic** *adj*

**a·grar·i·an** /əˈɡreəriən‖əˈɡrer-/ *adj* concerning farming or farmers: *an agrarian revolution in 17th century England|a split between industrial and agrarian interests*

1 **a·gree** /əˈɡriː/ *v*
1 **1 ► SAME OPINION ◄** [I,T not in progressive] to have the same opinion about something as someone else: [+ **with**] *Mr Larsen seems to think it's too risky and I agree with him.*|**agree** *Teenagers and their parents rarely agree.*|[+ **that**] *Most scientists agree that global warming is a serious problem.*|[+ **on/about**] *They belong to the same party, but they don't agree on everything.*|**I quite agree** *BrE spoken* (=I agree completely) *"It's ridiculous." "Yes, I quite agree."*|**I couldn't agree more** *spoken* (=I agree completely) —opposite DISAGREE (1) —see REFUSE[1]
**2 ► DECIDE TOGETHER ◄** [I,T not in progressive] to make a decision with someone after a discussion with them: **agree to do sth** *We agreed to meet up later and talk things over.*|**agree that** *It was agreed that Mr. Rollins would sign the contract May 1st.*|[+ **on**] *They managed to agree on a date for the wedding.*|[+ **to**] *We voted to agree to the latest pay offer.*|**agree a price/plan/strategy etc** *We agreed a price and the car was mine.*|*I think the committee will agree the changes soon.*
**3 ► SAY YES ◄** [I,T not in progessive] to say yes to an idea, plan, suggestion etc: *I suggested we go somewhere for the weekend and she agreed at once.*|**agree to do sth** *Why don't we agree right now to use recycled paper?*
**4 ► BE THE SAME ◄** [I not in progressive] if two pieces of information agree with each other, they are the same: [+ **with**] *Your story doesn't agree with what the police have told us.*
**5 agree to differ** to accept that you do not have the same opinions as someone else and agree not to argue about it

**agree with** *phr v* [T not in passive] **1** to believe that a decision, action, or suggestion is correct or right: *I don't agree with any form of terrorism.* **2 not agree with you** if a type of food does not agree with you, it makes you feel ill **3** if an adjective, verb etc agrees with a word, it matches that word by being plural if the subject is plural etc

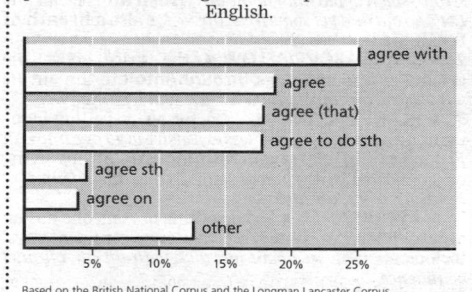

This graph shows how common different grammar patterns of the verb **agree** are in spoken and written English.

agree with
agree
agree (that)
agree to do sth
agree sth
agree on
other

5% 10% 15% 20% 25%

Based on the British National Corpus and the Longman Lancaster Corpus

**USAGE NOTE: AGREE**

GRAMMAR

If you have the same opinion as someone else you **agree with** them. You can also **agree with** (=approve of) their attitude, ideas, plans, rules etc, or an activity or principle that you approve of: *Do you agree with corporal punishment?*

You **agree** with people **about or on** other matters: *I agree (with you) about Mark/on astrology/about this issue* (NOT *I agree this issue*).

If you and others decide on or arrange to do something after discussing it, you **agree on** it: *We finally agreed on a plan/a date/a solution/a deal.* More formally you could also say: *We agreed a plan/a date/a solution/a deal.*

If you accept something, especially something that was not your idea and perhaps you do not like, you **agree to** it. *She agreed to the plan/the date/the solution/the deal.* (NOT *She agreed the plan etc*). You can also **agree to do** something: *They agreed to wait* (NOT *They accepted to wait*).

**a·gree·a·ble** /əˈɡriːəbəl/ *adj* **1** pleasant or acceptable: *an agreeable spot for a picnic* **2** someone who is agreeable is very nice and is liked by other people: *an agreeable young man* **3 be agreeable to sth** *formal* to be willing to do something or willing to allow something to be done: *Are you sure Branson's agreeable to the idea?*

**a·gree·a·bly** /əˈɡriːəbli/ *adv* intended to be pleasant or nice: *He smiled agreeably.*

**a·greed** /əˈɡriːd/ *adj* [only before noun] **1** an agreed plan, price, arrangement etc is one that people have discussed and accepted: *Reform had not yet been achieved, but it remained the party's agreed priority.* **2 be agreed** if people are agreed, they have discussed something and agree about what to do: [+ **on**] *All parties are now agreed on the plan.*

**a·gree·ment** /əˈɡriːmənt/ *n* **1** [C] an arrangement or promise to do something, made by two or more companies, governments, organizations etc: *a trade agreement*|[+ **on**] *an agreement on arms reduction*|**reach an agreement** *What happens if the warring parties fail to reach an agreement?*|**under an agreement** *Under the Sino-British agreement, Hong Kong will come under Chinese rule in 1997.*|**have an agreement that** *We had an agreement that Ms Holst would keep me informed of any changes.* **2** [U] a situation in which people have the same opinion as each other: [+ **that**] *There is agreement among doctors that pregnant women should not smoke.*|[+ **on**] *Is there agreement on how much aid will be sent?*|**be in agreement** *A decision will not be made until everyone is in agreement.* **3** [C] an official document that people sign to show that they have agreed to something: *Please read the agreement and sign it.* S1 W1

**ag·ri·busi·ness** /ˈæɡrɪˌbɪznɪs/ *n* [C,U] the production and sale of farm products, or a company involved in this

**ag·ri·cul·ture** /ˈæɡrɪˌkʌltʃə‖-ər/ *n* [U] the practice or science of farming —compare HORTICULTURE —**agricultural** /ˌæɡrɪˈkʌltʃərəl◂/ *adj* —**agriculturalist** *n* [C] W2

**agro-** /æɡrəʊ‖-roʊ/ *prefix* also **agri-** /æɡrɪ/ concerning farming: *agrobiology|agribusiness*

**a·ground** /əˈɡraʊnd/ *adv* **run/go aground** if a ship runs aground, it becomes stuck in a place where the water is not deep enough

**a·gue** /ˈeɪɡjuː/ *n* [C,U] *old-fashioned* a fever that makes you shake and feel cold

**ah** /ɑː/ *interjection* used to show your surprise, anger, pain, happiness, agreement etc: *Ah! There you are!*

**a·ha** /ɑːˈhɑː/ *interjection* used to show that you understand or realize something: *Aha! So you planned all this, did you?* —see also HA[1]

**a·head** /əˈhed/ *adv*

**1 ► IN FRONT OF ◄** in front of someone or something by a short distance: *He kept his gaze fixed on the car ahead.*|[+ **of**] *Tim pointed to a tree ahead of them.*|**up ahead** *We could see the lights of Las Vegas up ahead.*

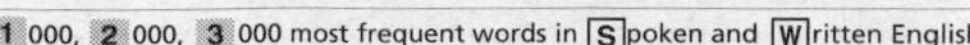
1 000, 2 000, 3 000 most frequent words in S poken and W ritten English

2 ▶ **FORWARD** ◀ if someone or something moves, looks ahead etc, they move or look towards a place in front of them: *Let Tom walk ahead, he knows the way.* | [+ **of**] *One of the group stepped ahead of the others to look at the sign.* | **straight ahead** *He's just staring straight ahead in a complete daze.*
3 ▶ **BEFORE SB ELSE** ◀ arriving, waiting, finishing etc before other people: [+ **of**] *There were four people ahead of me at the doctor's.*
4 ▶ **BEFORE AN EVENT** ◀ *AmE* before an event happens: *You can prepare these salads ahead.* | **ahead of time** *Can you tell me ahead of time if you're coming?*
5 ▶ **FUTURE** ◀ in the future: *Rest now because you have a long journey ahead of you.* | **lie ahead** *We should try to predict the type of problems that may lie ahead.* | **the years/days/months etc ahead** *The decisions you make in the days ahead are going to affect your whole future.* | **plan ahead** (=plan for the future)
6 **ahead of time/schedule etc** earlier than planned or arranged: *We might finish the project ahead of schedule.*
7 ▶ **WINNING** ◀ winning in a competition or election: *Milligan's three-pointer puts them ahead by one.*
8 **go ahead** *spoken* used to tell someone they can do something: *"Can I have the sports section?" "Yeah, go ahead, I've read it."*
9 ▶ **ADVANCED** ◀ ideas, achievements etc that are ahead of others, have made more progress or are more developed: *VEMCO was years ahead of us in their research.* | **be ahead of its time** (=so new that people do not understand or like it) *Her educational theories were way ahead of their time*
10 **get ahead** to make progress and be successful in your job, education etc: *Getting ahead at work is the most important thing to her at the moment.*
11 **go ahead (with sth)** to start doing something: *Frank'll be late but we'll go ahead with the meeting anyway.* —see also GO-AHEAD
12 **get/keep ahead (of the game)** *AmE informal* to get into or be in a position where you are in control of something, so that it is easier to deal with: *I find it hard to keep ahead of the housework.*

**a·hem** /m'hm/ *spelling pronunciation* /ə'hem/ *interjection* a sound you make to attract someone's attention when you want to speak to them, warn them etc

**-aholic** /əhɒlɪk‖əhɒː-, əhɑː-/ *suffix* [in nouns and adjectives] *informal* someone who cannot stop doing something or using something: *a workaholic* (=who loves working and cannot stop) | *a chocaholic* (=who loves chocolate)

**a·hoy** /ə'hɔɪ/ *interjection* used by SAILORS to get someone's attention or greet them: **ship ahoy!** (=used to say that a ship is approaching)

**AI** /ˌeɪ 'aɪ/ *n* [U] the abbreviation of ARTIFICIAL INTELLIGENCE

S2 W2 **aid**[1] /eɪd/ *n* **1** [U] help, such as money or food, given by an organization to a country or to people who are in a difficult situation: *Aid is not getting through to the refugees.* | **in aid of** (=in order to help) *We're collecting money in aid of cancer research.* | **legal aid** (=free legal services) **2** help or advice given to someone who needs it: **come/go to sb's aid** (=help someone) *I didn't speak any French, but a nice man came to my aid and told me where to go.* **3** [C] something such as a machine or tool that helps someone do something: *A video is a useful aid in the classroom.* | **with the aid of** *He was able to prove the existence of the supergun with the aid of a photograph.* **4 what's this in aid of?** *BrE spoken* used to ask what something is used for or why someone is doing something: *What's this meeting tomorrow in aid of, then?* **5** an American spelling of aide —see also FIRST AID

**aid**[2] *v* [T] *formal* **1** to help someone or something by making their situation or what they are doing easier: *an index to aid the reader* | **aid sb in/with sth** *The local community aided us in our investigation.* HELP[1] (USAGE) **2 aid and abet** *law* to help someone do something illegal

**aide** also **aid** *AmE* /eɪd/ *n* [C] someone whose job is to help someone in an important job, especially a politician

**aide-de-camp** /ˌeɪd də 'kɑːmp/ *n plural* **aides-de-camp** (same pronunciation) [C] a military officer who helps an officer of a higher rank to do his duties

**AIDS** /eɪdz/ *n* [U] Acquired Immune Deficiency Syndrome; a very serious disease caused by a VIRUS (1) that stops your body from defending itself against infections

**aid work·er** /'· ˌ··/ *n* [C] someone working for an international organization who brings food and other supplies to people in danger from war, famine etc: *UN aid workers in Yugoslavia*

**ail** /eɪl/ *v* **1** [T] *formal* to cause difficulties for someone or something **2** *old-fashioned* [I,T] to be ill, or to make someone feel ill or unhappy

**ai·ling** /'eɪlɪŋ/ *adj* **1** an ailing company or ECONOMY[1] (1) is having a lot of problems and is not successful: *Vice-Chairman John Smith, who transformed GM's ailing European operations in the 80s* **2** *formal* ill: *aged or ailing parents*

**ail·ment** /'eɪlmənt/ *n* [C] an illness that is not very serious

**aim**[1] /eɪm/ *n* **1** [C] what you are hoping to achieve by a plan, action, or activity: [+ **of**] *The main aim of the course is to improve students' communication skills.* | **with the aim of doing sth** *Research is being done with the specific aim of monitoring customer trends.* **2 take aim** to point a gun or weapon at someone or something you want to shoot: [+ **at**] *Alan took aim at the tiger.* **3 sb's aim** someone's ability to hit what they are aiming at when they throw or shoot something: *Val's aim was very good.* S W

**aim**[2] *v* **1** [I,T] to choose the place, person etc that you want to hit and carefully point your gun, object etc towards them: *Denver aimed his gun but did not shoot.* | [+ **at/for**] *The pitcher aimed at the upper half of the strike zone.* **2** [I] to try or intend to achieve something: [+ **at/for**] *It's important that you should have some sort of a goal to aim for.* | **aim to do sth** *I'm aiming to lose 4kg before the summer holidays.* **3 aim sth at sb** to make something in such a way that a particular person or group of people will like it: *The program is aimed at a teenage audience.* S W

**aim·less** /'eɪmləs/ *adj* without a clear purpose or reason: *drifing through life in a rather aimless fashion* —**aimlessly** *adv* —**aimlessness** *n* [U]

**ain't** /eɪnt/ *spoken* a short form of 'am not', 'is not', 'are not', 'has not', or 'have not', that many people think is incorrect

**air**[1] /eə‖er/ *n* S W
1 ▶ **GAS** ◀ [U] the mixture of gases that we breathe and that surrounds the Earth: *air pollution* | *There was a strong smell of burning in the air.* | **fresh air** (=clean air) *Let's go out and get some fresh air.* —see also **a breath of fresh air** (BREATH (2))
2 ▶ **SPACE ABOVE/BELOW** ◀ the space above the ground or around things **through/into etc the air**: *He fell 2000 metres through the air without a parachute.*
3 ▶ **PLANES/FLYING** ◀ **a) by air** travelling by or using a plane: *It's actually less expensive to go by air to San Francisco.* **b) air travel/crash/industry etc** involving or connected with planes and flying: *the victims of Britain's worst air disaster*
4 ▶ **APPEARANCE** ◀ if something or someone has an air of confidence, mystery etc, they seem confident, mysterious etc: *She set about her task with an air of quiet confidence.*
5 **it's up in the air** *spoken* used to say that something has not been decided yet
6 **be on/off (the) air** to be broadcasting on the radio or television at the present moment, or to stop broadcasting: *We'll be on air in about 3 minutes.*
7 **airs** [plural] a way of behaving in which someone tries to make themselves seem more important than they are: **put on airs/give yourself airs** *Trudy is always putting on airs and pretending she's posh.* | **airs and graces** *Tristan, with his fancy education and his airs and graces.*

aircraft

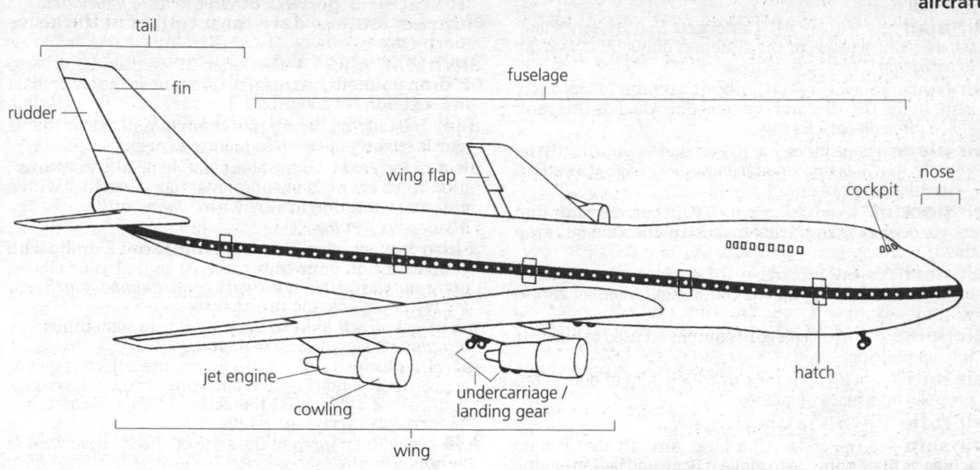


**8 in the air** if a particular emotion is in the air, a lot of people seem to feel it at the same time: *a sense of excitement in the air*
**9 ▶ MUSIC ◀** [C] a name given to a piece of music that means 'tune' —see also **hot air** (HOT¹ (28)), ON-AIR **clear the air** (CLEAR² (13)), **thin air** (THIN¹ (15)), **walk on air** (WALK¹ (14))

**air²** *v*
**1 ▶ CLOTHES ◀** [I,T] also **air** sth↔ **out** *AmE* to put a piece of clothing in a place that is warm or has a lot of air, so that it smells clean: *I've left my sweater on the washing-line to air.*
**2 ▶ ROOM ◀** [I,T] also **air** sth↔ **out** *AmE* to let fresh air into a room, especially one that has been closed for a long time
**3 ▶ TV/RADIO ◀** [T] to broadcast a programme on television or radio
**4 air your views/opinions etc** to say publicly what you think about something important
**5 air your grievances** to tell other people about things that you think are unfair —see also AIRING

**air·bag** /ˈeəbæg‖ˈer-/ *n* [C] a bag in a car that fills with air to protect the driver or passenger in an accident

**air·base** /ˈeəbeɪs‖ˈer-/ *n* [C] a place where military aircraft begin and end their flights

**air·bed** /ˈeəbed‖ˈer-/ *n* [C] a long rubber or plastic bag that you fill with air and lie on —see picture at BED¹

**air·borne** /ˈeəbɔːn‖ˈerbɔːrn/ *adj* **1** a plane that is airborne is in the air **2** airborne soldiers are trained to fight in areas that they get to by jumping out of a plane

**air·bus** /ˈeəbʌs‖ˈer-/ *n* [C] *trademark* a large plane that carries a lot of people for short distances

**air chief mar·shal** /ˌ· · ˈ··◂/ *n* [C] a high rank in the British air force, or someone who has this rank —see table on page B4

**air com·mo·dore** /ˌ· ˈ···◂/ *n* [C] a high rank in the British air force, or someone who has this rank —see table on page B4

**air con·di·tion·ing** /ˈ· ·ˌ···/ *n* [C,U] a system that makes the air in buildings, rooms etc colder, or the machine that does this —**air-conditioned** *adj*: *Our offices are fully air-conditioned.* —**air conditioner** *n* [C]

S2 W2 **air·craft** /ˈeəkrɑːft‖ˈerkræft/ *n plural* **aircraft** [C] a plane or other vehicle that can fly —see also LIGHT AIRCRAFT

**aircraft car·ri·er** /ˈ·· ˌ···/ *n* [C] a type of ship that has a large flat surface that planes fly from

**air·craft·man** /ˈeəkrɑːftmən‖ˈerkræft-/ *n* [C] a low rank in the British air force, or someone who has this rank —see table on page B4

**air·crew** /ˈeəkruː‖ˈer-/ *n* [C] the pilot and the people who are responsible for flying a plane and looking after the passengers

**air·fare** /ˈeəfeə‖ˈerfer/ *n* [C] the price of a journey by plane

**air·field** /ˈeəfiːld‖ˈeər-/ *n* [C] a place where planes can fly from, especially one used by military planes

**air force** /ˈ· ·/ *n* [C] the military organization of a country that uses planes to fight —compare ARMY, NAVY

**air fresh·en·er** /ˈ· ˌ···/ *n* [C,U] a substance used to make the air in a room smell pleasant

**air·gun** /ˈeəgʌn‖ˈer-/ *n* [C] *BrE* a gun that uses air pressure to fire a small round bullet; BB GUN *AmE*

**air·head** /ˈeəhed‖ˈer-/ *n* [C] *slang especially AmE* someone who is stupid

**air host·ess** /ˈ· ··/ *n* [C] *BrE* a woman who serves food and drink to passengers on a plane

**air·i·ly** /ˈeərə̇li‖ˈer-/ *adv* without being serious or concerned: *"I don't really care," he replied airily.*

**air·ing** /ˈeərɪŋ‖ˈer-/ *n* [singular] an occasion when an opinion, idea etc is discussed: **give/get an airing** *The question will get a thorough airing at the next meeting.*

**airing cup·board** /ˈ·· ˌ··/ *n* [C] *BrE* a warm cupboard in a house where sheets and clean clothes are kept

**air·lane** /ˈeəleɪn‖ˈer-/ *n* [C] a path through the air that is regularly used by planes

**air·less** /ˈeələs‖ˈer-/ *adj* not having enough air or having air that does not move, so that it seems difficult to breathe: *The evening was muggy and airless.*

**air·let·ter** /ˈeəˌletə‖ˈerˌletər/ *n* [C] *BrE* a very light letter that you can send by AIRMAIL, AEROGRAMME

**air·lift** /ˈeəˌlɪft‖ˈer-/ *n* [C] an act of taking people or things to an area by plane, when it is difficult or dangerous to use roads: *airlifts of food supplies to famine areas* —**airlift** *v* [T]

**air·line** /ˈeəlaɪn‖ˈer-/ *n* [C] a business that runs a regular service to take passengers and goods to different places by plane S2 W3

**air·lin·er** /ˈeəˌlaɪnə‖ˈerˌlaɪnər/ *n* [C] *old-fashioned* a large passenger plane

**air lock** /ˈ· ·/ *n* [C] **1** a small room used for moving between two places that do not have the same air pressure, such as in a space vehicle or a vehicle under water

2 a BUBBLE [1] (1) in a pipe that stops liquid flowing through it

**air·mail** /ˈeəmeɪl‖ˈer-/ *n* [U] letters etc that are sent somewhere using a plane, or the system of doing this: *Send the letter airmail.*

**air·man** /ˈeəmən‖ˈer-/ *n* [C] *plural* **airmen** /-mən/ a low rank in the US Air Force, or someone who has this rank —see table on page B4

**air·plane** /ˈeəpleɪn‖ˈer-/ *n* [C] *especially AmE* a flying vehicle that has one or more engines; AEROPLANE *BrE* —see picture at AIRCRAFT

**air·pock·et** /ˈeəˌpɒkɪ̣t‖ˈerˌpɑː-/ *n* [C] a current of air that moves downwards and that makes a plane suddenly drop down

S2 W3 **air·port** /ˈeəpɔːt‖ˈerpɔːrt/ *n* [C] a place where planes begin and stop flying, that has buildings for passengers to wait in

**air pump** /ˈ· ·/ *n* [C] a piece of equipment used to blow air into something

**air raid** /ˈ· ·/ *n* [C] an attack in which a lot of bombs are dropped on a place by planes

**air ri·fle** /ˈ· ˌ··/ *n* [C] a type of AIRGUN

**air·ship** /ˈeəˌʃɪp‖ˈer-/ *n* [C] a large aircraft that has no wings, is filled with gas to make it float, and has an engine

**air·sick** /ˈeəˌsɪk‖ˈer-/ *adj* feeling sick because of the movement of a plane —**airsickness** *n* [U]

**air·space** /ˈeəspeɪs‖ˈer-/ *n* [U] the sky above a particular country, that is thought of as being controlled by that country: *The planes had entered Israeli airspace without permission.*

**air·speed** /ˈeəspiːd‖ˈer-/ *n* [singular, U] the speed at which a plane travels

**air strike** /ˈ· ·/ *n* [C] an attack in which a military aircraft drops bombs or shoots guns at a place

**air·strip** /ˈeəˌstrɪp‖ˈer-/ *n* [C] a long narrow piece of land that has been cleared so that planes can fly from it

**air terminal** /ˈ· ˌ···/ *n* [C] **1** a place in a city from where passengers catch buses to the AIRPORT **2** a large building at an AIRPORT where passengers wait to get on planes

**air·tight** /ˈeətaɪt‖ˈer-/ *adj* not allowing air to get in or out: *airtight containers*

**air time** /ˈ· ·/ *n* [U] the amount of time or the number of times that a radio or television station allows a particular song, advertisement etc to be broadcast: *smaller political parties trying to buy more air time*

**air-to-air** /ˌ· · ˈ·◂/ *adj* **air-to-air missile** a weapon that one plane shoots at another plane as they are flying

**air traf·fic con·trol·ler** /ˌ· ˈ·· ·ˌ··/ *n* [C] someone at an airport who gives instructions to pilots by radio —**air traffic control** *n* [U]

**air vice-mar·shal** /ˌ· · ˈ··◂/ *n* [C] a high rank in the British Air Force, or someone who has this rank —see table on page B4

**air·waves** /ˈeəweɪvz‖ˈer-/ *n* [plural] *old-fashioned* **the airwaves** radio broadcasts: **on the airwaves** (=on the radio)

**air·way** /ˈeəweɪ‖ˈer-/ *n* [C] **1** *technical* the passage in your throat that you breathe through **2** an area of the sky that is regularly used by planes: *one of the world's busiest airways*

**air·wor·thy** /ˈeəˌwɜːði‖ˈerˌwɜːrði/ *adj* a plane that is airworthy is safe enough to fly —**airworthiness** *n* [U]

**air·y** /ˈeəri‖ˈeri/ *adj* **1** an airy room or building has plenty of fresh air because it is large or has lots of windows: *an airy first floor restaurant with sea views* **2** cheerful and confident, even when you should be serious or concerned about something: *He dismissed her concerns with an airy wave of the hand.*

**airy fai·ry** /ˌ·· ˈ··◂/ *adj BrE* not very clear or practical; VAGUE: *airy fairy ideas*

**aisle** /aɪl/ *n* [C] **1** a long passage between rows of seats, shelves, etc in a building or a plane —see picture at THEATRE **2** a narrow passage at the side of a church that is separated from the central part by a row of pillars (PILLAR (1)) **3 go/walk down the aisle** *informal* to get married —see also **have them rolling in the aisles** (ROLL[1] (18))

**aitch** /eɪtʃ/ *n* [C] **1** the letter 'h' written as a word **2 drop your aitches** to fail to pronounce the letter 'h' at the beginning of a word.

**a·jar** /əˈdʒɑː‖əˈdʒɑːr/ *adj* [not before noun] a door that is ajar is slightly open —see picture at OPEN[1]

**ak·a** /ˈækə,ˌeɪ keɪ ˈeɪ/ the abbreviation of 'also known as', used when giving someone's real name together with a different name they are known by: *John Phillips, aka The Mississippi Mauler*

**a·kim·bo** /əˈkɪmbəʊ‖-boʊ/ *adj* **(with) arms akimbo** with your hands on your hips (HIP[1] (1)) so that your elbows point outwards: *He stood with arms akimbo, glaring at the intruders.* -see picture at ARM

**a·kin** /əˈkɪn/ *adj* **akin to** very similar to something: *The language is closely akin to Arabic.*

**-al** /əl/ *suffix* also **-ial** **1** [in nouns and adjectives] of or concerning something: *coastal waters* (=near the coast)| *political* **2** [in nouns] the action of doing something: *her arrival* (=arriving)| *a refusal*

**à la** /ˈæ lə,ˈɑː lɑː/ *prep* in the style of: *detective stories à la Agatha Christie*

**al·a·bas·ter** /ˈæləbɑːstə‖-bæstər/ *n* [U] a white stone, used for making STATUES or decorative objects: *an alabaster vase*

**à la carte** /ˌæ lə ˈkɑːt,ˌɑː lɑː-‖-ˈkɑːrt/ *adj, adv* if food in a restaurant is à la carte, each dish has a separate price: *an à la carte menu*

**a·lack** /əˈlæk/ *interjection old use* used to express sorrow

**a·lac·ri·ty** /əˈlækrɪ̣ti/ *n* [U] quickness and eagerness: *They accepted our offer with alacrity.*

**à la mode** /ˌæ lə ˈməʊd,ˌɑː lɑː-‖-ˈmoʊd/ *adj, adv* **1** *old-fashioned* according to the latest fashion **2** *AmE* served with ICE CREAM: *apple pie à la mode*

**alarms**

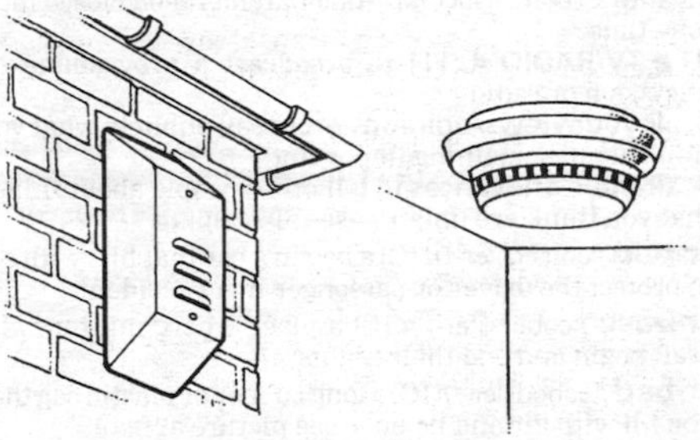

burglar alarm

smoke alarm

**a·larm[1]** /əˈlɑːm‖əˈlɑːrm/ *n* **1** [U] a feeling of fear or anxiety because something dangerous might happen: *I turned in alarm as the wind blew the door open.* **2** [C] something such as a bell or a light that warns people of danger: *a fire alarm*| *Something has set the car alarm off.* **3 sound/raise the alarm** to warn everyone about something bad or dangerous that is already happening: **[+ about]** *The Red Cross has sounded the alarm about the threat of famine.* **4** an alarm clock —see also **false alarm**

**alarm[2]** *v* [T] to make people very worried about a possible danger: *Her high temperature alarmed the doctors.*

**alarm clock** /ˈ· ·/ *n* [C] a clock that will make a noise at a particular time to wake you up: *The alarm clock went off at six.*

**a·larmed** /əˈlɑːmd‖-ɑːr-/ *adj* **1** frightened and worried: *There's no need to look so alarmed!*| **[+by/at/over]**| *Prison authorities have become increasingly alarmed by the number of prisoners trying to escape* **2** protected by an alarm system

**a·larm·ing** /ə'lɑːmɪŋ‖-ɑːr-/ *adj* worrying and frightening: *an alarming increase in violent crime* | **at an alarming rate** (=happening so quickly that it makes people worried) *The rainforest is disappearing at an alarming rate.* —**alarmingly** *adv*

**a·larm·ist** /ə'lɑːmɪ̣st‖-ɑːr-/ *adj* making people unnecessarily worried about dangers that do not exist: *an alarmist report on population growth* —**alarmist** *n* [C]

**a·las¹** /ə'læs/ *adv* [sentence adverb] *formal* unfortunately: *There is, alas, no short way to success.*

**alas²** *interjection old use* used to express sadness, shame, or fear

**al·ba·tross** /'ælbətrɒs‖-trɒːs, -trɑːs/ *n* [C] **1** a very large white sea bird **2 an albatross (around your neck)** something you have done that causes problems for you and prevents you from succeeding: *His friendship with the gangster, Jimmy Hoffa, had become an albatross around his neck.*

**al·be·it** /ɔːl'biːɪ̣t‖ɒːl-/ *conjunction* even though, used to add information or details that are different from what you have already said: *It was a small, albeit very important, mistake.*

**al·bi·no** /æl'biːnəʊ‖æl'baɪnoʊ/ *n* [C] a person or animal with an unusual GENETIC condition, light coloured eyes and very white hair and skin

3 **al·bum** /'ælbəm/ *n* [C] **1** a book in which you put photographs, stamps etc: *a wedding album* **2** a record that has about 20 to 25 minutes music on each side

**al·bu·men** /'ælbjʊmɪ̣n‖æl'bjuː-/ *n* [U] *technical* the white or colourless part of the inside of an egg

**al·che·my** /'ælkəmi/ *n* [U] **1** a science studied in the Middle Ages that involved trying to change ordinary metals into gold **2** *literary* magic: *By what alchemy did he manage to get elected?* —**alchemist** *n* [C]

3 **al·co·hol** /'ælkəhɒl‖-hɒːl/ *n* **1** [U] drinks such as beer or wine that contain a substance that can make you drunk **2** [C,U] a chemical substance, that can be used for medical or industrial purposes to clean things

**al·co·hol·ic¹** /ˌælkə'hɒlɪk◂‖-'hɒː-/ *adj* **1** connected with alcohol or containing alcohol: *alcoholic beverages* **2** caused by drinking alcohol: *an alcoholic stupor* —**alcoholically** /-kli/ *adv*

**alcoholic²** *n* [C] someone who regularly drinks too much alcohol and has difficulty stopping

**al·co·hol·is·m** /'ælkəhɒlɪzəm‖-hɒː-/ *n* [U] the medical condition of being an alcoholic

**al·cove** /'ælkəʊv‖-koʊv/ *n* [C] a place in the wall of a room that is built further back than the rest of the wall: *The bookcase just fits into the alcove in the living room.*

**al den·te** /æl 'denti, -teɪ/ *adj* food, especially PASTA that is al dente is still firm after it has been cooked

**al·der·man** /'ɔːldəmən‖'ɒːldər-/ *n* [C] **1** a member of a town or city council in the US **2** an important member of a town council in Britain in the past

**ale** /eɪl/ *n* [U] **1** a type of beer made from MALT¹ (3) **2** *old-fashioned* beer —see also LIGHT ALE, REAL ALE

**al·eck** /'ælɪ̣k/ *n* —see SMART ALECK

**ale·house** /'eɪlhaʊs/ *n* [C] *old-fashioned* a place where people drank beer

**a·lert¹** /ə'lɜːt‖-ɜːrt/ *adj* **1** always watching and ready to notice anything strange or unusual **2** able to think quickly and clearly: *Despite her years, she still has a lively and alert mind.* | *Please remain alert and report any unattended luggage to the authorities.* **3 be alert to** to realize that you must be careful about something or that something is dangerous: *Tourists need to be alert to the dangers of travelling in the north of the country.*

**alert²** *v* [T] **1** to officially warn someone of something, especially something dangerous, so that they can be ready to deal with it: *Alert air traffic control and tell them one engine isn't working.* | [+ **that**] *Police have been alerted that a second prisoner has escaped.* **2** to make someone notice something important or dangerous: **alert sb to sth** *Montessori alerted teachers to the importance of observing children at play.*

**alert³** *n* **1** a warning to be ready for possible danger: *a full-scale flood alert* —see also RED ALERT **2 be on the alert** to be ready to notice and deal with a situation or problem: *Be on the alert for pickpockets in the crowds.* | **be on full alert** (=completely ready to deal with a dangerous situation) *police on full alert against terrorist attacks*

**A lev·el** /'eɪ ˌlevəl/ *n* [C] an examination in a particular subject taken in schools in England and Wales, usually at the age of 18

**al·fal·fa** /æl'fælfə/ *n* [U] a plant grown especially in the US to feed farm animals

**alfalfa sprout** /·'·· ·/ *n* [C] a young alfalfa plant, eaten raw in SALADS

**al·fres·co** /æl'freskəʊ‖-koʊ/ *adj, adv* in the open air: *an alfresco meal* | *We dined alfresco, on a balcony overlooking the sea*

**al·gae** /'ældʒiː,-giː/ *n* [U] a very simple plant without stems or leaves that grows in or near water

**al·ge·bra** /'ældʒɪ̣brə/ *n* [U] a type of mathematics that uses letters and other signs to represent numbers and values —**algebraic** /ˌældʒɪ̣'breɪ-ɪk◂/ *adj* —**algebraically** /-kli/ *adv*

**al·go·rith·m** /'ælgərɪðəm/ *n* [C] *technical* a set of instructions for solving a mathematical problem, making a computer program etc that are followed in a fixed order

**a·li·as¹** /'eɪliəs/ *prep* used when giving someone's real name together with another name they use: *Velma Johnson, alias Annie Jones*

**alias²** *n* [C] a false name, usually used by a criminal

**al·i·bi** /'ælɪ̣baɪ/ *n* [C] **1** someone or something that proves that someone was not in the area where a crime happened and therefore could not have done it: *I've got an alibi for Tuesday night.* **2** an excuse for something you have failed to do or done wrong

**a·li·en¹** /'eɪliən/ *adj* **1** belonging to another country or race; FOREIGN (1): *an alien culture* **2** very different from what you are used to; strange: [+ **to**] *a way of life that is totally alien to us* **3** [only before noun] connected with creatures from another world: *alien life-forms*

**alien²** *n* [C] **1** *technical* someone who lives or works in your country, but who comes from another country: *illegal aliens entering the country.* **2** a creature from another world: *a film about aliens from Mars*

**a·li·en·ate** /'eɪliəneɪt/ *v* [T] **1** to do something that makes someone unfriendly or unwilling to support you: *The latest tax proposals will alienate many voters.* **2** *law* to give the legal right to a particular piece of land, property etc to someone else

**a·li·en·a·ted** /'eɪliəneɪtɪ̣d/ *adj* feeling separated from society or the group of people around you, and often unhappy: [+ **from**] *the psychological effects of being alienated from normal school life*

**a·li·en·a·tion** /ˌeɪliə'neɪʃən/ *n* [U] **1** the feeling of not being part of society or a group: *the sense of alienation felt by many black people in our culture* **2** separation from a person who you used to be friendly with

**a·light¹** /ə'laɪt/ *adj* [not before noun] **1** burning: **set sth alight** *Several cars were set alight by rioters.* **2** someone whose face or eyes are alight is excited and happy **3** bright with light or colour

**alight²** *v* [I] *formal* **1** if a bird or insect alights on something, it stops flying to stand on something **2** to step out of a vehicle after a journey

**a·lign** /ə'laɪn/ *v* [T] **1 align yourself with** to decide to publicly support a political group or country: *Church leaders have aligned themselves with the opposition.* | **be aligned with** *A country politically aligned with the West.* **2** to arrange things so that they form a line or are parallel to each other

**a·lign·ment** /ə'laɪnmənt/ *n* **1** [U] the state of being arranged in a line with or parallel to something: *the* *correct alignment of spine and pelvis* **2** [C,U] if countries or groups form an alignment, they support each other

**a·like¹** /əˈlaɪk/ *adj* [not before noun] very similar: *My mother and I are alike in many ways.*

**alike²** *adv* **1** in a similar way: *The twins were dressed alike.* **2** equally: *I enjoyed being on this course.|I learned a lot from teachers and students alike.*

**al·i·men·ta·ry ca·nal** /ˌæləmentəri kəˈnæl/ *n* [C] the tube in your body that takes food through your body from your mouth to your ANUS

**al·i·mo·ny** /ˈæləməni‖-mouni/ *n* [U] money that a court orders someone to pay regularly to their former wife or husband after their marriage has ended

**a·lit** /əˈlɪt/ the past tense and past participle of ALIGHT²

S2 W3 **a·live** /əˈlaɪv/ *adj* [not before noun]
**1** ▶**NOT DEAD**◀ still living and not dead: *It was a really bad accident – they're lucky to be alive.|None of my grandparents are alive now.*|**stay alive** (=continue to live) *They managed to stay alive by eating berries and roots.*|**keep sb alive** *He's being kept alive on a life-support machine.*
**2** ▶**CHEERFUL**◀ active and happy; feel alive: *It was the kind of morning when you wake up and feel really alive.*
**3** ▶**STILL EXISTING**◀ continuing to exist: *Ancient traditions are still very much alive in rural areas.*|**keep sth alive** *fighting to keep our academic institutions alive.*
**4 come alive** **a)** if a situation or event comes alive it becomes interesting and seems real: *For me the play only came alive in the final act.* **b)** if someone comes alive they start to be happy and interested in what is happening: *It was as if she came alive when she sat down at the piano.* **c)** if a town or city etc comes alive it becomes busy: *seaside resorts that come alive in the summer.*
**5 bring sth alive** to make something interesting: *Plays need the sound of human voices to bring them alive.*
**6 be alive and well** **a)** to be healthy and enjoy life **b)** *informal humorous* to be popular and successful: *The mini skirt is alive and well in Paris this year.*
**7 be alive and kicking** to be very healthy and active: *"How's your father nowadays?" "Oh, still alive and kicking."*
**8 be alive to** to realize that something is happening and that it is important: *The company is alive to the threat posed by foreign imports.*
**9 be alive with** to be full of people, animals, or things that are moving: *a tree trunk alive with ants* —see also **skin sb alive** (SKIN² (3))

**al·ka·li** /ˈælkəlaɪ/ *n* [C,U] a substance that forms a chemical salt when combined with an acid

**al·ka·line** /ˈælkəlaɪn/ *adj* containing an alkali

**all-** /ɔːl‖ɒːl/ *prefix* **1** consisting or made only of one kind of thing: *an all-male club|an all-wool dress* **2** for the whole of something: *All-India Railways|an all-night party* (=lasting all night)|*an all-night cafe* (=staying open all night)

S1 W1 **all¹** /ɔːl‖ɒːl/ *determiner, predeterminer* **1** the complete amount or quantity of; the whole of: *I've got all day tomorrow to do it.|He had worked all his life in the mine.|Have you done all your homework?|She didn't say a single word all the way back home.*|**all the time** (=very often, especially in a way that is annoying) *It rained all the time we were on holiday!* **2** everyone of: *Someone's taken all my books!|Will all the girls please stand over here.*|**all kinds of** *The course attracts all kinds of people.|All these questions must be answered.*|**you all/they all/it all etc** *They all passed the exam.* **3** the greatest possible amount of: *With all due respect, I really cannot agree with your last statement.* **4 of all people/things/places etc** used to show surprise when mentioning a particular person, thing, or place: *Of course you shouldn't have done it – you of all people should know that!* **5 all innocence/smiles etc** used to emphasize that someone or something has a particular quality of appearance: *Elsie was all smiles when I saw her again the next morning.* **6 for all...** in spite of a particular fact, quality, or situation: *For all her rudeness, she's actually quite a kind-hearted old soul.* **7 go all out/make an all-out effort** to do everything you can to succeed: *We're all out to win the cup this year.*

**all²** *adv* **1** [always + adj/adv/prep] **all alone/new/dark etc**,: *You shouldn't be sitting here by yourself, all alone.|I'm all confused now!|The room suddenly went all dark.*|**all for/all in favour of** (=used to say that you strongly support or agree with something) *One minute he's all for all Labour policy, the next minute he's knocking it.* **2 one, four, ten all** used when giving the score of a game in which both sides have scored the same **3 not all that** *spoken* not very: *It doesn't sound all that good, does it?|I don't think it matters all that much.* **4 all along** *informal* all the time from the beginning while something was happening: *I knew all along that this relationship wouldn't last.|Maybe this is what they were trying to achieve all along.* **5 all at once** **a)** happening all together at the same time: *Obviously they can't do everything all at once.* **b)** suddenly and unexpectedly: *All at once, I knew there was something wrong.* **6 all over** **a)** everywhere on an object or surface: *There were bits of paper all over the floor.|He has cuts all over his legs.* **b)** everywhere in a place: *Antique clocks from all over the world are on display.|People came from all over the country.|They're putting up new offices all over the place.* **c)** finished: *I saw my old girlfriend the other day, but that's all over now.* (=our relationship is finished) **7 that's sb all over** *spoken* that is typical of him or her: *He was late of course, but that's Tim all over!* **8 all the easier/healthier/more effectively etc** used to emphasize how much more easy, etc something is than it would normally have been: *Their success is all the more pleasing when you consider the effort they've made.|The job was made all the easier by having the proper tools.* **9 all the same** *spoken* in spite of something that you have just mentioned: *We realised that the children would have to leave home, but all the same it was difficult when they went.* **10 it's all the same to me** used to say that you do not mind what decision is made, that you would be pleased with any choice or that you do not really care: *You can choose what we do, it's all the same to me.* **11 all but** almost completely: *Their screams of excitement all but drowned out the music.* **12 all too** much more than is desirable: *All too often it's the mother who gets blamed for her children's behaviour.* **13 all told** counting or including everyone; all together: *There were seventeen of us at the meeting, all told.* **14** *informal* **it's all up (with)** used to say that it is impossible for someone to continue doing something, especially when they have been involved in criminal activities **15 (not) all there** *informal* someone who is not all there cannot think in a clear normal way and seems slightly crazy: *I don't think he's quite all there.*

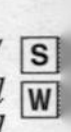

**all³** *pron* **1** every one or every part of something: *I ate the whole packet, all of them!|That's all I know about it.|Not all the children were vaccinated.|I've heard it all before.* **2** used to emphasize the most basic or necessary facts or details about a situation: *All you need is a hammer and some nails.|All I'm asking for is a little respect.* **3 for all sb knows/cares etc** **a)** used to say that something could happen, especially something very unpleasant or serious, and someone would not know or care about it: *The old woman could have been lying dead in the house for all her family cared.* **4 and all** **a)** the whole thing; including everything or everybody mentioned: *They ate the whole fish; bones, tail, head, and all.* **b)** *spoken* an expression meaning as well, used to emphasize what you have just said.: *And you can take that smelly coat out of here and all!|"Look, it's snowing!" "Oh, it is and all!"* **5 it costs all of 50p/took all of 20 minutes etc** *spoken* used to emphasize or express how large or small an amount actually is **6 it was all I could do to...** used to say that you only just succeeded in doing something: *It was all I could do to stop them hitting each other!* **7 (not) at all** used in questions and negative statements to emphasize what you are saying: *They've done nothing at all to try and put the problem right.|They obviously weren't at all happy.|Does he get no pension at all?|Do you know anything about it at all?|He's not looking at all well.* (=he looks ill)|*"Do you mind if I stay for a bit longer?" "Not at all!"* (=certainly not, please do)

**8 all in all** considering every part of a situation: *All in all, it's been a pretty bad year for John Major.* **9 it's all or nothing a)** used to say that unless something is done completely or done in the exact way that you want, something else will happen, especially something unpleasant: *It was all or nothing for Susan; either the company offered her a pay rise or she would leave.* **b)** used to say that someone is using all their effort and energy in order to try and do something —see also **all and sundry** (SUNDRY(1)), EACH, EVERY

**all**[4] *n* **do/give your all** *literary* to do everything possible to try and achieve something: *The coach expects everyone to give their all in every game.*

**Al·lah** /'ælə/ *n* the Muslim name for God

**all-A·mer·i·can** /ˌ· ·'···◂/ *adj* **1** having qualities that are considered to be typically American and that American people admire, such as being healthy and working hard: *an all-American family, cheerful and friendly* **2** belonging to a group of players who have been chosen as the best in their sport at American universities: *an all-American player out of UCLA*

**all-a·round** /ˌ· ·'·/ *adj* [only before noun] *AmE* good at doing many different things, especially at many different sports; ALL-ROUND[1] *BrE*: *an all-around athlete*

**al·lay** /ə'leɪ/ *v* [T] *formal* **allay fear/concern/suspicion etc** to make someone feel less afraid, worried etc: *His reassurances did little to allay their fears for Robert's safety.*

**all clear** /ˌ· '·/ *n* **the all clear a)** official permission to begin doing something: *We've got the all clear from the board for the new project.* **b)** a signal such as a loud whistle that tells you that a dangerous situation has ended: **give/sound the all clear** *The drone of the bombers faded, and the all clear was sounded.*

**all-com·ers** /ˌ· '··/ *n* [plural] anyone who wants to take part in a competition whatever their age or experience: *The marathon is open to all-comers.*

**al·le·ga·tion** /ˌælɪ'geɪʃən/ *n* [C] a statement that has not been proved that someone has done something wrong or illegal: [+ **of**] *allegations of fraud* | **allegation that** *allegations that the election had been fixed.*

**al·lege** /ə'ledʒ/ *v* [T] to say that something is true or that someone has done something wrong even though this has not been proved: **allege (that)** *It was alleged that policemen had accepted bribes.* | **be alleged to be/do sth** *The new missiles are alleged to be capable of travelling enormous distances.*

**al·leged** /ə'ledʒd/ *adj* [only before noun] an alleged fact, quality etc is supposed to be true although there is no proof that it actually is: *reports of alleged police brutality*

**allegedly** /ə'ledʒɪ̈dli/ *adv* [sentence adverb] used when reporting something that other people say is true, although there is no proof: *He was allegedly caught shoplifting in his local supermarket.*

**al·le·giance** /ə'liːdʒəns/ *n* [C,U] loyalty to a leader, country, belief etc: [+ **to**] *allegiance to the king* | **proclaim/pledge allegiance** *I pledge allegiance to the flag of the United States of America.* | **switch allegiance** (=start to support a different person, group etc)

**al·le·go·ry** /'ælɪ̈gəri‖-gɔːri/ *n* [C,U] a story, painting etc in which the events and characters represent ideas or teach a moral lesson —**allegorical** /ˌælɪ̈'gɒrɪkəl‖'gɔːr-/ *adj* —**allegorically** *adv*

**al·leg·ro** /ə'legrəʊ, ə'leɪ-‖-groʊ/ *n* [C] a piece of music played or sung quickly —**allegro** *adj adv*

**al·le·lu·ia** /ˌælɪ̈'luːjə◂/ *interjection* HALLELUJAH

**all-em·brac·ing** /ˌ· '··◂/ *adj* including everyone or everything: *an all-embracing vision of the cosmos*

**Al·len key** /'ælən kiː/ *n* [C] *BrE* a small tool you use to turn an Allen screw (=a type of screw with a hole that has six sides)

**Allen wrench** /'ælən rentʃ/ *n* [C] *AmE* an Allen key

**al·ler·gic** /ə'lɜːdʒɪk‖-ɜːr-/ *adj* **1** having an allergy: **be allergic to sth** *I'm allergic to penicillin.* **2 allergic reaction/rash** an illness or a red painful area on your skin that some people get because of an allergy **3 allergic to sth** *informal* always trying to avoid an activity or thing that you do not like: *I think he's allergic to work!*

**al·ler·gy** /'ælədʒi‖-ər-/ *n* [C,U] a medical condition in which you become ill or in which your skin becomes red and painful because you have eaten certain foods, touched certain things etc: *Do you suffer from any allergies?* | [+ **to**] *an allergy to cat fur*

**al·le·vi·ate** /ə'liːvieɪt/ *v* [T] to make something less painful or difficult: *a medicine to alleviate cold symptoms* | *measures to alleviate poverty* —**alleviation** /əˌliːvi'eɪʃən/ *n* [U]

**al·ley** /'æli/ *n* [C] **1** a narrow street between or behind buildings **2 right up/down sb's alley** *AmE* very suitable for someone: *The job sounds right up your alley.* —see also BLIND ALLEY, BOWLING ALLEY

**alley cat** /'·· ·/ *n* [C] a cat that lives on the streets and does not belong to anyone

**al·ley·way** /'æliweɪ/ *n* [C] an ALLEY (1)

**all-fired** /ˌ· '·◂/ *adv AmE informal* a word meaning completely that you use before describing a quality that you think is extreme: *If he weren't so all-fired sure of himself, I'd like him better.*

**all fours** —see **on all fours** (FOUR (4))

**all go** /ˌ· '·/ *adj* **it's all go** *spoken* used to say that a situation is very busy and full of activity: *It was all go in the office as the deadline approached.*

**al·li·ance** /ə'laɪəns/ *n* [C] **1** an arrangement in which two or more countries, groups etc agree to work together in order to try to change or achieve something: [+ **between**] *The alliance between students and factory workers in the 1960s* | [+ **with**] *Britain's military alliance with her Nato partners.* | **enter into/form an alliance** (=agree to work together) *The two countries entered into a defensive alliance.* **2** a group that is formed when two or more countries, groups etc work together **3 in alliance (with)** if two groups, countries etc are in alliance, they work together to achieve something or protect one another: *Relief workers in alliance with local charities are trying to help the famine victims.* **4** *formal* close relationship, especially a marriage, between people —see also **unholy alliance** (UNHOLY(3)) W3

**al·lied** /'ælaɪd, ə'laɪd/ *adj* **1 Allied** belonging to or connected with the countries that fought together against Germany in the First or Second World War, or against Iraq in the Gulf War: *an Allied bombing raid* | *the Allied forces* **2 allied industries/organizations/trades etc** connected with each other because of being similar or dependent on each other; RELATED: *Agriculture and allied industries provided the state's main source of revenue.* **3 (be) allied to/with** connected with: *Cultural anthropology is closely allied to the field of social psychology.* **4** joined by common political, military, or economic aims: *their allied effort to convince others of the danger of nuclear power*

**Al·lies** /'ælaɪz/ *n* **the Allies** [plural] **a)** the countries, including Britain, the US, and the USSR, that fought together during the Second World War **b)** the countries, including Britain, the US, and France, that fought together during the First World War **c)** the countries that fought together against Iraq in the Gulf War in the early 1990s

**al·li·ga·tor** /'ælɪ̈geɪtə‖-ər/ *n* **1** [C] a large animal with a long mouth and sharp teeth that lives in the hot wet parts of the US and China **2** [U] the skin of this animal used as leather: *alligator shoes*

**all-in** /ˌ· '·◂/ *adj* extremely tired: *You look all-in. Are you o.k.?*

**all in** *adv* **£5000/$100 all in** if you buy or sell something for a particular price all in, that price includes all services, parts etc

**all-in·clu·sive** /ˌ· ·'··◂/ *adj* including everything: *an all-inclusive price*

**al·lit·er·a·tion** /əˌlɪtə'reɪʃən/ *n* [U] the use of words that begin with the same sound in order to make a special effect, especially in poetry

**all-night·er** /ˌ· '··/ *n* [C] *AmE informal* an occasion when you spend the whole night studying or doing written work in university

S2 **al·lo·cate** /ˈæləkeɪt/ *v* [T] to decide officially that a particular amount of money, time etc or something such as a house or job etc should be used for a particular purpose: **allocate sb sth** *The duty officer allocated us a cabin for the night.* | **allocate sth for sth** *one million dollars allocated for disaster relief* | **allocate sth to** *You need to decide how much time to allocate to each exam question.*

**al·lo·ca·tion** /ˌæləˈkeɪʃən/ *n* **1** [C] the amount or share of something that has been allocated to a person or organization **2** [U] the decision to allocate something

**al·lot** /əˈlɒt‖əˈlɑːt/ *v* **allotted, allotting** [T] to decide officially to give something to someone or use something for a particular purpose: **allot sth to** *You may find it useful to allot 20 minutes each day to this task.* | **allot sb sth** *The boys were allotted a room each for studying.*

**al·lot·ment** /əˈlɒtmənt‖əˈlɑːt-/ *n* **1** [C,U] an amount or share of something such as money or time that is given to someone or something, or the process of doing this: *The budget allotment for each district is prepared at the provincial headquarters.* | [+ **of**] *the allotment of funds to schools* **2** [C] a small area of land for growing vegetables that people who live in towns in Britain can rent

**al·lot·ted** /əˈlɒtɪ̣d‖əˈlɑːt-/ *adj* **allotted money/time/resources etc** allotted money etc has been officially given to someone for a particular purpose: *The department has spent its allotted budget.* | **in the allotted time** *I didn't finish the test in the allotted time.*

**all-out** /ˌ· ˈ·◂/ *adj* [only before noun] an all-out effort or attack involves a lot of energy, determination, or anger: *fears of an all-out war* —**all out** *adv*: *Canada will have to go all out on the ice if they want to win.*

S1 W1 **al·low** /əˈlaʊ/ *v* [T] **1** to let someone do or have something, or let something happen: **allow sb to do sth** *The committee allowed the oil company to build a refinery on the island.* | **allow sb sth** *We allow passengers one item of hand luggage each.* | **allow sb in/out/up etc** *I don't allow the cat in the bedroom.* | **be allowed** (=if something is allowed, it is permitted) *"Can I smoke?" "I'm sorry, it's not allowed"* | *Abortions were allowed only for reasons of health.* | **allow swimming/smoking/talking etc** *We do not allow eating in the classrooms.* | **be allowed (to do sth)** (=you are permitted to do something) *I wasn't allowed to stay out after 11 o'clock.* —see graph at PERMIT[1] **2** to be sure that you have enough time, money, food etc available for a particular purpose: *We allowed ourselves plenty of time to get to the airport.* **3** to make it possible for something to happen or for someone to do something, especially something helpful or useful: **allow sb to do sth** *A 24-hour ceasefire allowed the two armies to bury their dead.* | **allow sb sth** *The new seatbelt allows the driver greater freedom of movement.* **4** to accept or agree that something is correct or permitted by the rules or the law: *The judge allowed the evidence.* **5 allow that** *formal* to admit that something is true: *I allow that there may have been a mistake.* **6 allow me!** *spoken* used as a polite way of offering to help someone do something: *"Allow me," the waiter said, helping her with her coat.*

**allow for** sb/sth *phr v* [T] to consider all the possible facts, problems, costs etc involved in a plan or situation and make sure that you can deal successfully with them: *Allowing for inflation, the cost of the project is $2 million.*

**allow of** sth *phr v* [T] *formal* to show that something exists or is possible: *The facts allow of only one interpretation.* —see graphs at FORBID, LET, PERMIT[1]

**al·low·a·ble** /əˈlaʊəbəl/ *adj* **1** acceptable according to the rules: *the maximum allowable dosage* **2** allowable costs are costs that you do not pay tax on: *allowable deductions such as alimony and business expenses*

S2 W3 **al·low·ance** /əˈlaʊəns/ *n* [C] **1** an amount of money that you are given regularly or for a special reason: *His father gave him an allowance of £1000 a year.* | **travel/clothing/housing allowance etc** (=money given officially to spend on travel etc) *Jo's salary includes a monthly clothing allowance.* **2** an amount of something that it is acceptable or safe: *What's your daily calorie allowance?* | *The baggage allowance is 75 pounds per person.* **3** an amount of money that you can earn without paying tax on it: *In 1978 allowances amounted to $7,200 for a family of four.* **4** *especially AmE* a small amount of money that a parent regularly gives to a child; POCKET MONEY (1) *BrE* **5 make allowances** to let someone behave in a way you would not normally approve of, because you know there are special reasons for their behaviour: [+ **for**] *Dad is under a lot of pressure, so we have to make allowances for him.* **6 make (an) allowance for** to consider something when making a decision: **make no allowance for** *My brother made no allowance for my shorter legs, and I had to run to keep up.*

**al·loy**[1] /ˈælɔɪ‖ˈælɔɪ, əˈlɔɪ/ *n* [C,U] a metal that consists of two or more metals mixed together: *Brass is an alloy of copper and zinc.*

**al·loy**[2] /əˈlɔɪ‖əˈlɔɪ, ˈælɔɪ/ *v* [T] **1** [+ **with**] *technical* to mix one metal with another **2** *literary* to lower the value or quality of something by mixing it with something else

**all-pow·er·ful** /ˌ· ˈ···◂/ *adj* having complete power or control: *the all-powerful Senate Foreign Relations Committee*

**all-pur·pose** /ˈ· ˌ··/ *adj* [only before noun] able to be used in any situation: *an all-purpose cleaner*

**all right**[1] *adj, adv* [not before noun] *spoken* S1 W2

**1** ▶ **SATISFACTORY** ◀ satisfactory or acceptable but not excellent: *"What's the food like?" "Well, it's all right I suppose, but the place on Melrose Avenue is better."* | *"How's school going, Steve?" "Oh, all right, I guess."*

**2** ▶ **UNHARMED/WITHOUT PROBLEMS** ◀ not hurt, not upset, or not having any problems: *Katie looked really unhappy – I'd better go and make sure she's all right.* | **be getting on all right** (=not have any problems or difficulties) *The kids seem to be getting on all right at school.*

**3 go all right** to happen without any problems: *Did everything go all right with your test?*

**4 be doing all right** to be successful in your job, life etc: *She's doing all right – she's got a job with Microsoft.*

**5** ▶ **SUITABLE** ◀ used when saying whether something is suitable or at a good time: *I'd really like to see you – would Thursday morning be all right?*

**6 it's all right** used to make someone feel less afraid or worried: *It's all right, Mommy's here.*

**7 it's all right/that's all right a)** used as a reply when someone thanks you: *"Thanks for all your help!" "That's all right – it was nothing really."* **b)** used to tell someone that you are not angry when they say they are sorry for something: *"Sorry I'm late." "That's all right."*

**8 is it all right if/would it be all right if** used when asking if you can do something: *Is it all right if I close the window? It's getting cold in here.*

**9 it's/that's all right by me** used to agree with someone's suggestion: *"Do you think we could finish early today?" "That's all right by me."*

**10 it's all right for you/her etc** used to say that someone else does not have the same problems and difficulties that you have: *It's all right for you – you don't have to work with her every day. She's driving me crazy.*

**11** ▶ **CHECK UNDERSTANDING** ◀ [sentence adverb] used to check that someone has understood what you said, or to show that you have understood: *I'll leave the key with the neighbours, all right?* | *"Connect the positive first and then the negative." "Oh I see, all right."*

**12** ▶ **GREETINGS** ◀ *especially BrE* used when greeting someone and asking about their health, what has happened to them recently etc: *Hi, Stuart – you all right?* | *"How are you John?" "Oh, all right – mustn't grumble!"*

**13 she's/he's all right** *BrE* used when you like someone: *"She's not bad our boss is she?" "No, she's all right."*

**14** ▶ **CERTAINLY** ◀ used to admit that something is true, especially when saying that you also think that something else is not: *Wayne's experienced enough all right, but I don't know if he's right for this particular job.* —see also **a bit of all right** (BIT[1] (20))

**all right**[2] *interjection*

**1** ▶ **YES** ◀ **a)** used when agreeing with someone's suggestion or agreeing to do something: *"Why don't we go*

*to a movie?" "All right. Do you want to stop at Gino's for a pizza first?"* **b)** used when agreeing to do something or to allow something, even though you do not want to: *"Can I play with my new computer game?" "Oh all right then – so long as you don't make too much noise."*
**2** ▶ **ANNOYED** ◀ **a)** used when saying that you have heard and understood what someone has said, especially when you are annoyed: *"The train leaves at 5.30." "All right! I'm just coming!"* **b)** used when asking what has happened or what someone means, especially in an angry or threatening way: *All right, what have you two been doing with that knife?*
**3** ▶ **INTRODUCE/CHANGE SUBJECT** ◀ used to introduce a new subject or activity: *All right, folks, I'd like to introduce our first speaker this evening.*

**all-round**[1] /ˈ· ·/ *adj* [only before noun] *BrE* good at doing many different things, especially at many different sports; ALL-AROUND *AmE*: *an all-round athlete*

**all-round**[2] /ˌ· ˈ·/ *adv BrE informal* used to say that you are thinking about someone or something generally rather than about particular details: *All-round it's not a bad car.*

**all-round·er** /ˌ· ˈ··/ *n* [C] *BrE* someone who is good at many different things

**all-seat·er sta·di·um** /ˌ· ·· ˈ···/ *n* [C] *BrE* a stadium where sports are played and there are seats for everyone who is watching

**all-sing·ing, all-danc·ing** /ˌ· ˈ·· ˌ· ˈ··/ *adj* [only before noun] *BrE humorous* an all-singing, all-dancing machine or system is able to do many different things because it is technically advanced

**all·spice** /ˈɔːlspaɪs‖ˈɒːl-/ *n* [U] a powder used in cooking to give food a special taste, made from the fruit of a tropical American tree

**all-star** /ˈ· ·/ *adj* [only before noun] including many famous actors or sports players: *an all-star cast*

**all-ter·rain bi·cy·cle** /ˌ· ·· ˈ···/ *n* [C] a MOUNTAIN BIKE

**all-ter·rain ve·hi·cle** /ˌ· ·· ˈ···/ *n* [C] a motor vehicle with three or four wheels that you can drive on rough ground

**all-time** /ˈ· ·/ *adj* **1 all-time high/low/best etc** the highest, lowest etc level there has ever been: *The price of wheat reached an all-time low of 42 cents in 1932.* **2 all-time record/classic etc** the best ever known: *He's one of pro football's all-time great receivers.*

**al·lude** /əˈluːd/ *v*
**allude to** sb/sth *phr v* [T] *formal* to mention something or someone indirectly: *The character's evil nature is constantly alluded to throughout the play.*

**al·lure**[1] /əˈljʊə‖əˈlʊr/ *n* [singular, U] a mysterious, exciting, or desirable quality that is very attractive: *Even in her fifties she had lost none of her seductive allure.* | *the allure of foreign travel*

**allure**[2] *v* [T] to attract someone, especially because of an exciting or desirable quality —**allurement** *n* [C]

**al·lur·ing** /əˈljʊərɪŋ‖əˈlʊr-/ *adj* attractive or desirable: *a low, alluring voice*

**al·lu·sion** /əˈluːʒən/ *n* [C,U] something that is said or written that brings attention to a particular subject in a way that is not direct: [+ **to**] *Eliot's poetry is full of allusions to other works of literature.* —**allusive** /-sɪv/ *adj* —**allusively** *adv*

**al·lu·vi·al** /əˈluːviəl/ *adj* made of soil left by rivers, lakes, floods etc: *an alluvial plain*

**al·lu·vi·um** /əˈluːviəm/ *n* [C,U] *technical* soil left by rivers, lakes, floods etc

W3 **al·ly**[1] /ˈælaɪ‖ˈælaɪ, əˈlaɪ/ *n* [C] **1** a country that makes an agreement to help or support another country, especially in a war: *a meeting of the European allies* —see also ALLIES **2** someone who helps and supports you in difficult situations: *Thatcher and Reagan were close allies.*

**al·ly**[2] /əˈlaɪ‖əˈlaɪ, ˈælaɪ/ *v* [I,T] to join with other people or countries to help and support each other: **ally yourself to/with** *They allied themselves to the other western states after the war.*

**al·ma ma·ter** /ˌælmə ˈmeɪtə, -ˈmɑː-‖-ˈmɑːtər/ *n* [singular] **1** the school, college, or university that you used to attend **2** *AmE* the song of a particular school, college, or university

**al·ma·nac** /ˈɔːlmənæk‖ˈɒːl-, ˈæl-/ *n* [C] **1** a book that gives information about the movements of the sun and moon, the times of the TIDES etc for each day of a particular year **2** a book gives information about what happened in a particular subject or activity in a particular year: *a football almanac*

**al·might·y** /ɔːlˈmaɪti‖ɒːl-/ *adj* **1 Almighty God/Father** an expression used to talk about God when you want to emphasize his power **2 the Almighty** God **3 God/Christ Almighty** an expression used when you are angry or upset that some people consider offensive: *God Almighty, what on earth will they do next?* **4 almighty din/crash/row** *informal* a very loud noise, argument etc: *There was an almighty bang in the garden and the shed went up in flames.*

**al·mond** /ˈɑːmənd‖ˈɑː-, ˈæ-, ˈæl-/ *n* [C] a flat pale nut with a slightly sweet taste, or the tree that produces these nuts

**al·mo·ner** /ˈɑːmənə, ˈæl-‖ˈælmənər, ˈɑː-/ *n* [C] an official in a British hospital in former times who helped people who were ill with their financial and social problems

**al·most** /ˈɔːlməʊst‖ˈɒːlmoʊst, ɒːlˈmoʊst/ *adv* very nearly but not completely: *We've almost finished.* | *We stayed there for almost a week.* | **almost every** *They sold almost everything.* | **almost all** *Almost all the children here speak two languages.* | *an almost impossible task* | *wines which are almost as expensive as champagne* | **almost certainly** *The cause is almost certainly a virus.* S1 W1

**USAGE NOTE: ALMOST**

WORD CHOICE: **almost, nearly, hardly, scarcely, very, extremely**

Both **almost** and **nearly** can be used before words like *all, every, and everybody*: *Almost/nearly all (of) my friends came to the party* (NOT *Almost of my friends came...* or *Almost my friends came...*).

Both can also be used before negative verbs: *I almost/nearly didn't get up in time.* However, you do not use **not** with *hardly* or *scarcely*: *There was scarcely enough time to take a shower.*

**Almost** (NOT **nearly**) can be used before *any* and negative words like *no, nobody, never,* and *nothing*: *Almost no one came to the party* (NOT *Nearly no one...*). | *You can find the meaning of almost any word here.* However, it is more usual to use **hardly** or **scarcely** with *any, anybody, ever* etc than **almost** with *no, nobody, never* etc: For example, you are more likely to hear: *Hardly anybody came to the party* than: *Almost no one came to the party.*

You can use *not* before **nearly**, but not usually before **almost**: *She's not nearly as pretty as her sister* (NOT *She's not almost as pretty...*).

Both **nearly** and **almost** can be used with adjectives that have an extreme meaning: *nearly/almost perfect/frozen/dead/impossible*. However, they are not usually used with other, less extreme, adjectives. In these cases you are more likely to use **very** or **extremely**: *The schools are extremely good there* (NOT *nearly good*). | *The coast was very rocky* (NOT *almost rocky*). **Nearly** is more commonly used in British English, while **almost** is more common in American English.

**alms** /ɑːmz‖ɑːmz, ɑːlmz/ *n* [plural] *old-fashioned* money, food, clothes etc that are given to poor people

**alms-house** /ˈ· ·/ *n* [C] a place where poor people could live without paying rent in former times

**a·loe** /ˈæləʊ‖-loʊ/ *n* **1** [U] the wood of an Indian tree that smells sweet **2 aloes** [plural] the juices of the leaves of the aloe plant used for making medicine

**a·loft** /əˈlɒft‖əˈlɒːft/ *adv formal* high up in the air: *a flag flying aloft*

**a·lo·ha** /əˈləʊhə‖əˈloʊhɑː/ *interjection* used as a greeting or to say goodbye in Hawaii

**a·lone¹** /ə'ləʊn‖ə'loʊn/ *adj* **1** [not before noun] without any other people: *She lives alone.* | **alone together** (=if two people are alone together there is no one else in the place where they are) *Suddenly they found themselves alone together in the room.* **2** without any friends or people who you know: **all alone** (=completely alone) *It was scary being all alone in a strange city.* **3** [not before noun] feeling very unhappy and lonely: *He felt terribly alone when June left.* **4 you alone know/have/can do sth** used to say that you are the only person who knows or can do something: *Julie alone knew the terrible truth.* | *Of all the applicants, she alone had the right qualifications.* **5** used to emphasize that one particular thing is very important or has a great effect in a situation: *The price alone was enough to put me off the idea.* **6 be alone in (doing) sth** be the only person to do something: *You're not alone in feeling upset by all this, believe me.*

Frequencies of **alone**, **on your/her own** and **by yourself** in spoken and written English.

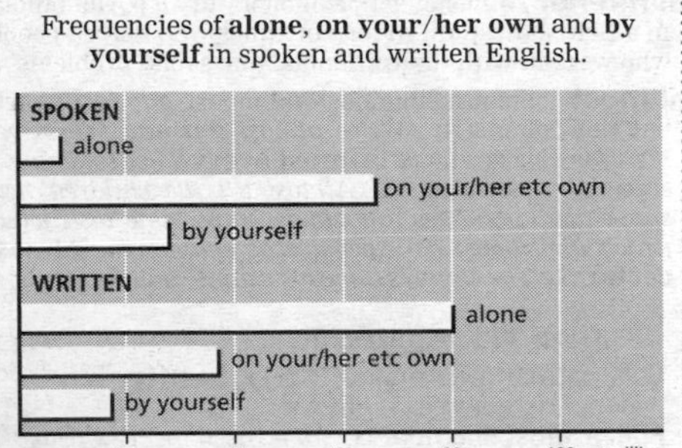


Based on the British National Corpus and the Longman Lancaster Corpus

In spoken English it is more usual to say **on your own** or **by yourself** rather than **alone**. In written or more formal English **alone** is more common.

**USAGE NOTE: ALONE**

WORD CHOICE: **alone, on your own, by yourself, lonely, lonesome, lone, solitary**

If you are **alone**, or less formally, **on your own/by yourself** that just means that no one else is with you, and is neither good nor bad: *I just wanted to stay at home alone/by myself.* With verbs of action, **on your own** and **by yourself** often suggest that no one is helping you: *I want to swim alone* (=with no one else there). | *I want to swim on my own/by myself* (=either with nobody else there or with other people there but not helping).

If you are **lonely** or **lonesome** (*AmE*) you are unhappy because you are alone: *I feel lonely living away from home/a lonely old man.* Places etc can be **lonely** or **lonesome** if they make people feel lonely: *a lonesome little town on the prairie.* Things that you do can also be **lonely**: *a lonely journey/job/life etc.* **Lonely** is never an adverb but **alone** often is: *She travelled alone* (NOT *lonely*).

A **lone** or **solitary** person or thing is simply the only one in a place, and therefore might seem a little lonely: *a lone figure in the middle of the square* (=it is the only one there). In spoken English, you are more likely to talk about: *a figure on its own in the middle of the square.* Sometimes **solitary** can suggest that you choose to be alone: *She is a very solitary person.*

**alone²** *adv* **1** if you do something difficult alone you do it on your own: *Brian was left to put up the tent alone.* **2 go it alone** to start working or living on your own, especially after working or living with other people: *After years of working for a big company I decided to go it alone.* **3 leave/let sb alone** to stop annoying or interrupting someone: *Go away and leave me alone will you.* **4 leave/let sth alone** to stop touching an object or changing something: *Leave that vase alone or you'll break it!* **5 stand alone** if an object or building stands alone it is not near other buildings or objects: *The house stood alone at the end of the road.*

**a·long¹** /ə'lɒŋ‖ə'lɔːŋ/ *adv* **1** if someone or something moves along, they move forward: *I was driving along, thinking about Christmas.* | *He showed me the notes he had made as we went along.* **2 go/come/be along** to go or come to the place where something is happening, someone is waiting etc: *We're having a few drinks in the bar – you're welcome to come along.* | **be along in a minute** (=arrive soon) *There should be another bus along in a minute.* **3 go/come/tag along** to go or come with someone somewhere: *"I'm just out for a walk." "Is it alright if Sharon and I come along too?"* **4 take/bring sb along** to take or bring someone with you somewhere: *Mandy had brought some of her art-school friends along.* **5 come/go/get along** to improve, develop, or make progress in a particular way: **come along fine/nicely/well etc** *"How's she doing after her operation?" "Oh, she's coming along fine."* | *How are things coming along at work?* **6 along with** together with: *Dunne was murdered along with three RUC men near Armagh.* S1 W1

**a·long²** *prep* **1** if someone or something moves or looks along something, they move or look from one end of it to the other: *We're driving along Follyfoot Road.* | *The conductor came hurrying along the corridor.* | *She glanced anxiously along the line of faces.* **2** something that is along something else goes down its whole length: *They've put up a fence along Church Lane.* | *a big crate with some strips of wood along the top* | *We found brambles and wild strawberries growing along the disused railway.* **3** if something is along a passage, wall etc, you can find it at some point there or it has been placed there: **just along** (=a short distance from a particular place) *The bathroom is just along the corridor from my room.* | *a waiting room with a bench along one wall* S1 W1

**a·long·side** /əˌlɒŋ'saɪd‖əˌlɔːŋ-/ *adv prep* **1** next to or along the side of something: *boats moored alongside each other* —see picture on page 1257 **2** if different types of things, ideas etc are used or exist alongside each other, they are used together or exist at the same time: *We like to use these two course books alongside each other.* W3

**a·loof¹** /ə'luːf/ *adj* deliberately staying away from or not talking to other people, especially because you think you are better than they are: **remain/keep/hold yourself aloof** *She preferred to remain distant and aloof.* —**aloofly** *adv* —**aloofness** *n* [U]

**aloof²** *adj* unfriendly, especially because you think you are better than other people: *Alison was polite but aloof when I met her.*

**a·loud** /ə'laʊd/ *adv* **1** if you say something aloud you say it in your normal voice: *Joanne, would you read the poem aloud for us?* **2** in a loud voice: *The pain made him cry aloud.*

**al·pac·a** /æl'pækə/ *n* **1** [C] an animal from Peru that looks like a LLAMA **2** [U] the cloth made from the wool of an alpaca

**al·pha** /'ælfə/ *n* [C usually singular] **1** the first letter of the Greek alphabet **2 the alpha and omega a)** the beginning and the end of something **b)** used to say that something is the best or most important kind of something

**al·pha·bet** /'ælfəbet/ *n* [C] a set of letters, arranged in a particular order, used in writing language: *the Cyrillic alphabet*

**al·pha·bet·i·cal** /ˌælfə'betɪkəl◂/ also **al·pha·bet·ic** /ˌælfə'betɪk◂/ *adj* relating to the alphabet: **in alphabetical order** *The dictionary is arranged in alphabetical order.* —**alphabetically** /-kli/ *adv* —see graph at ORDER¹

**al·pha·nu·mer·ic** /ˌælfənjuːˈmerɪk◂‖-nuː-/ *adj* using letters and numbers: *an alphanumeric code*

**al·pine** /ˈælpaɪn/ *adj* **1** related to the Alps **2** alpine plants grow near the top of a mountain where trees cannot grow

S1 W1 **al·read·y** /ɔːlˈredi‖ɒːl-/ *adv* **1** by or before now, or before a particular time: *The design of the new house is similar to those that have already been built.* | *as I have already mentioned* **2** used to say that something has been done before does not need to be done again: *She asked me to read this chapter, but I've already done it.* | *"Do you want a coffee?" "No, I've already got one thanks."* **3** used to say that something has happened too soon or before the expected time: *Are you leaving already?* | *I've forgotten already!* | *Is it 5 o'clock already?* **4** used to say that a situation, especially a bad one, now exists and it might get worse, greater, etc: *The building's already costing us far too much money as it is.* —see JUST (USAGE), STILL (USAGE)

**al·right** /ˌɔːlˈraɪt‖ˌɒːl-/ *adj, adv* another spelling of ALL RIGHT that many people think is incorrect

**Al·sa·tian** /ælˈseɪʃən/ *n* [C] *especially BrE* a large dog used especially by police or to guard houses; GERMAN SHEPHERD *especially AmE* —see picture at DOG[1]

S1 W1 **al·so** /ˈɔːlsəʊ‖ˈɒːlsoʊ/ *adv* **1** in addition to something else you have mentioned; as well as: *She owns several houses in Leeds and also has business interests in Manchester.* | *I'll take the car because it's a long walk from the station; also the forecast is for rain.* | *We can supply samples and there other laboratories that can be consulted also.* | **not only...but also..** *The report has not only attracted much attention but also some sharp criticism.* **2** used when saying that the same thing is true about another person or thing: *My girlfriend was also called Helen.* —see MOREOVER (USAGE)

**USAGE NOTE: ALSO**

WORD CHOICE: **also, too, as well, either, neither**

When you want to say that something exists or happens in addition to something else, **too** and **as well** are more common than **also** in informal and spoken English. In a scientific report you might see: *The acid also reacts with the coating.* Or it can be used as part of a more formal request: *Could you also type this please?* In spoken English, **as well** is very common: *Can you come too/as well?* | *I was so busy I missed lunch and dinner as well.*

If the verb is negative, you use **either**: *"I don't like grammar." "I don't like it either."* (NOT *I don't like it too* or *I don't also like it*, though *I also don't like it* is possible, but more formal). In informal English people usually say **not...either** rather than **neither**: *She won't come with me or with Grandpa either* (if here you said: *She will neither come with me nor with Grandpa*, it would sound very formal and unnatural).

GRAMMAR

**Also** usually comes after the first auxiliary or modal verb and before the main verb: *The school also has a gymnasium* (NOT usually *The school has also a gymnasium*). | *He can also sing a little* (NOT usually *...also can*). | *Many were bringing up children and also working.*

**Also** usually follows the verb *to be* where it is used alone as a main verb: *Osaka is also worth a visit.* **Also** is not usual at the end of a sentence, where **too** and **as well** are common.

**also-ran** /ˈ· · ·/ *n* [C] someone who has failed to win a competition or election

**al·tar** /ˈɔːltə‖ˈɒːltər/ *n* [C] **1** a table or raised surface that is the centre of many religious ceremonies, especially in Christianity: *the candles on the altar* **2** the part of a church, often at the front, where the priest or minister stands

**altar boy** /ˈ· · ·/ *n* [C] a boy who helps a Catholic priest during the church service

**al·tar·piece** /ˈɔːltəpiːs‖ˈɒːltər-/ *n* [C] a painting or SCULPTURE (2) behind an altar

**al·ter** /ˈɔːltə‖ˈɒːltər/ *v* **1** [I,T] to change or make someone or something change: *Her face hadn't altered much over the years.* | **alter sth** *Nothing can alter the fact that the refugees are our responsbility.* **2** [T] to make a piece of clothing longer, wider etc: *You'll have to have the dress altered for the wedding.* **3** [T] *AmE* to take away the sexual organs of a male cat or dog S3 W3

**al·ter·a·tion** /ˌɔːltəˈreɪʃən‖ˌɒːl-/ *n* [C] a small change that makes someone or something slightly different: *Have you noticed any alteration in the patient's behaviour?* | **to make alterations** *I'm having alterations made to the suit.* | **minor alterations** *Your paper is fine except for some minor alterations I've suggested.*

**al·ter·ca·tion** /ˌɔːltəˈkeɪʃən‖ˌɒːltər-/ *n* [C,U] *formal* a short but usually noisy argument

**al·ter e·go** /ˌæltər ˈiːgəʊ, ˌɔːl-‖ˌæltər ˈiːgoʊ,ˌɒːl-/ *n* [C] **1** another part of your character that is very different from your usual character, or a person in a film, book etc who shows part of the director or writer's character: *Mickey Mouse was Walt Disney's alter ego.* **2** someone who you trust who thinks about things in the same way as you do

**al·ter·nate**[1] /ɔːlˈtɜːnɪt‖ˈɒːltər-, ˈɑːl-/ *adj* [usually before noun] **1** two alternate actions, situations, or states happen one after the other in a repeated pattern: *walls painted with alternate strips of yellow and green* | *alternate rain and sunshine* **2** *especially AmE* used instead of the one that was intended to be used; ALTERNATIVE[1] (1): *We have to have an alternate plan in case it rains.* **3** happening or doing something on one of every two days: *He works alternate days.* | **alternate Mondays/weekends etc** *She visits her parents on alternate weekends.*

**al·ter·nate**[2] /ˈɔːltəneɪt‖ˈɒːltər-/ *v* [I,T] if two things alternate or you alternate them, they happen one after the other in a repeated pattern: [+ **between**] *Her emotions alternated between outrage and sympathy.* | **alternate sth with sth** *We tried to alternate periods of work with sleep.* —**alternation** /ˌɔːltəˈneɪʃən‖ˌɒːltər-/ *n* [C,U]

**al·ter·nat·ing cur·rent** /ˌ· · · · ˈ· ·/ *n* [U] a flow of electricity that regularly changes direction at a very fast rate —compare DIRECT CURRENT

**al·ter·na·tive**[1] /ɔːlˈtɜːnətɪv‖ɒːlˈtɜːr-, æl-/ *adj* **1** [only before noun] an alternative idea, plan etc is one that can be used instead of another one: *There doesn't seem to be an alternative option.* **2** [only before noun] an alternative system or solution is considered less damaging or more effective than the old one: *alternative sources of energy* —see also ALTERNATIVE MEDICINE **3** not based on or believing in the established social or moral standards: *an alternative lifestyle* | *alternative theatre* —**alternatively** *adv*; *We could walk or alternatively we could go in Ted's car.* S2 W2

**alternative**[2] *n* [C] something that you can choose to do or use instead of something else: *Check out the alternatives before deciding whether to go to a nearby college.* | [+ **to**] *a viable alternative to the present system of welfare benefits* | **have no alternative** (=used to say that you feel you must do something) *I had no alternative but to report him to the police.* | **there's no alternative** *I'm sorry, there's no alternative but to sell the car.* S2 W3

**alternative med·icine** /ˌ· · · · ˈ· · ‖ˌ· · · · ˈ· · ·/ *n* [U] one of the ways of treating illnesses that is not based on Western scientific methods: *Homeopathy is a popular form of alternative medicine.*

**al·ter·na·tor** /ˈɔːltəneɪtə‖ˈɒːltərneɪtər, ˈæl-/ *n* [C] an electric GENERATOR for producing ALTERNATING CURRENT —see picture at ENGINE

**al·though** /ɔːlˈðəʊ‖ɒːlˈðoʊ/ *conj* **1** in spite of the fact S1 W1

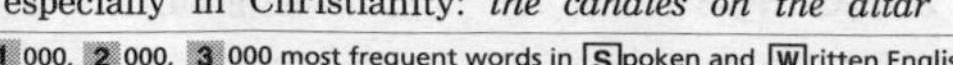

that; THOUGH (1): *Although she joined the company only a year ago, she's already been promoted twice.* | *Although the car is old it still runs well.* **2** but; HOWEVER: *I don't really enjoy sports, although I did watch the game.* | *I can see his point, although, I have to say, I think he's wrong.*

**al·ti·me·ter** /ˈæltɪˌmiːtə‖ælˈtɪmɨtər/ *n* [C] an instrument used in aircraft that tells you how high you are

**al·ti·tude** /ˈæltɨtjuːd‖-tuːd/ *n* **1** [C] the height of an object or place above the sea: *The plane was flying at an altitude of 30,000 feet.* **2 high/low altitudes** a high or low level above the sea: *At high altitudes it is difficult to get enough oxygen.* —compare ELEVATION[1] (1)

**al·to** /ˈæltəʊ‖-toʊ/ *n* [C] **1** a woman with a low singing voice **2** [singular] the part of a piece of music that this person sings

S2 W3 **al·to·geth·er[1]** /ˌɔːltəˈgeðə◂‖ˌɒːltəˈgeðər◂/ *adv* **1** a word meaning completely or thoroughly that is used to emphasize what you are saying: *It seems to have vanished altogether.* | *Eventually they chose an altogether different design.* | *How this is to be achieved is altogether a different matter.* | **not altogether** *I'm not altogether sure if I'd want you as a wife!* | *He did not altogether understand.* **2** used to make a final statement about several things you have just said: *The hotel was nice; the weather was hot; the beaches were beautiful. Altogether I'd say it was a great vacation.* **3** used when you are stating a total amount: *There were five people altogether.* | *How much do I owe you altogether?*

**altogether[2]** *n* **in the altogether** *BrE* without any clothes on; NUDE

**al·tru·is·m** /ˈæltru-ɪzəm/ *n* [U] the practice of thinking of the needs and desires of other people instead of your own —**altruist** *n* [C]

**al·tru·is·tic** /ˌæltruˈɪstɪk◂/ *adj* altruistic behaviour shows that you care about others more than you care for yourself: *Were his motives completely altruistic?* —**altruistically** /-kli/ *adv*

**al·um** /ˈæləm/ *n* [C + **of**] *AmE spoken* a former student of a school, college, university etc

**al·u·min·i·um** /ˌæljʊˈmɪniəm◂, ˌælə-/ *BrE* **a·lu·mi·n·um** *AmE* /əˈluːmɨnəm/ *n* [U] a silver-white metal that is an ELEMENT (=simple substance) and is light and easily made into different shapes

**aluminium foil** /ˌ····ˈ·/ *n* [U] a very thin sheet of shiny metal that you wrap around food to protect it; TINFOIL

**a·lum·na** /əˈlʌmnə/ *n plural* **alumnae** /-niː/ [C] *formal especially AmE* a woman who is a former student of a school, college, or university

**a·lum·ni** /əˈlʌmnaɪ/ *n* [plural] *AmE* the former students of a school, college, or university: *Berkeley alumni* | *the alumni association*

**a·lum·nus** /əˈlʌmnəs/ *n* [C] *formal especially AmE* a former student of a school, college, or university

**al·ve·o·lar** /ˌælviˈəʊlə◂, ælˈviːələ‖ælˈviːələr/ *n* [C] *technical* a CONSONANT sound such as t or d made by putting the end of the tongue at the top of the mouth behind the upper front teeth —**alveolar** *adj*

S1 W1 **al·ways** /ˈɔːlwɨz, -weɪz‖ˈɒːl-/ *adv* **1** all the time, at all times, on every occassion: *Always lock your bicycle to something secure.* | *Tea is always served at 5 o'clock.* | *She had always assumed that Gabriel was a girl's name.* | *Anne had always been pretty.* | *He wasn't always a butler.* (=he had other jobs at other times in his life) —see picture at FREQUENCY **2** for as long as you can remember or for a very long time: *I've always wanted to go to Paris.* **3** if you say that you will always do something, you mean that you will do it forever: *I'll always remember that day.* | *He said he would love me always.* **4** if someone is always doing something, or if something always happens, it happens often, especially in an annoying way: *That wretched car is always breaking down!* | *She's always flirting with him.* **5 you could always.../there is always...** *spoken* used to make a polite suggestion: *You could always try ringing her again.* | *If you can't get it locally, there's always mail order.*

> **USAGE NOTE: ALWAYS**
>
> GRAMMAR
>
> **Always** usually comes after the first auxiliary or modal verb and before the main verb: *He always wanted/had a room of his own* (NOT *He had/wanted always a room of his own*). | *He had always lived there* (*had* is auxiliary here). | *You should always be careful walking alone at night* (NOT usually *should be always careful*).
>
> **Always** usually follows the verb *to be* where it is used alone as a main verb: *I am always hungry* (NOT *I always am hungry*).
>
> SPELLING
>
> Remember it is **always** (NOT *allways* or *all ways*).

**AM** /ˌeɪ ˈem/ *n* [U] amplitude modulation; a system for broadcasting radio programmes that is not as clear as FM

**am[1]** /m, əm/ *v strong* the first person singular of the present tense of the verb to BE

**am[2], AM** /ˌeɪ ˈem/ ante meridiem; used when talking about times that are after MIDNIGHT but before MIDDAY: *I start work at 9 am.* —see also PM

**a·mal·gam** /əˈmælgəm/ *n* **1** [C] *formal* a mixture or combination of different things or substances: [+ **of**] *Her work is a strange amalgam of different musical styles.* **2** [C,U] *technical* a mixture of metals, used to fill holes in teeth

**a·mal·gam·ate** /əˈmælgəmeɪt/ *v* [I + **with** ,T] if two businesses or groups amalgamate, or if one business or group amalgamates with another, they join to form a bigger organization —**amalgamation** /əˌmælgəˈmeɪʃən/ *n* [C,U]

**a·man·u·en·sis** /əˌmænjuˈensɨs/ *n* [C] *formal* someone whose job is to write down what someone else says or copy what they have written

**a·mass** /əˈmæs/ *v* [T] to gradually collect a large amount of money, knowledge, or information: *For twenty-five years Darwin amassed evidence to support his theories.*

**am·a·teur[1]** /ˈæmətə, -tʃʊə, -tʃə, ˌæməˈtɜː‖ˈæmətʃʊr, -tər/ *adj* **1** not doing something as your job, but only for pleasure or interest: *an amateur golfer* | *an amateur orchestra* **2** amateurish

**amateur[2]** *n* [C] someone who does an activity for pleasure or interest, not as a job: *a gifted amateur* —compare PROFESSIONAL[2](1)

**amateur dra·mat·ics** /ˌ··· ·ˈ··/ *n* [U] *BrE* the activity of producing or acting in plays by people who do it for pleasure and not as a job

**am·a·teur·ish** /ˈæmətərɪʃ, ˌæməˈtjʊərɪʃ, -ˈtɜːrɪʃ‖ˌæməˈtʊr-, -ˈtɜːr-/ *adj* not skilfully done or made: *His paintings are amateurish.* —**amateurishly** *adv* —**amateurishness** *n* [U]

**am·a·teur·is·m** /ˈæmətərɨzəm, -tjʊər-‖ˈæmətʃʊr-, -ətər-/ *n* [U] the belief that enjoying a sport or other activity is more important than earning money from it

**am·a·to·ry** /ˈæmətəri‖-tɔːri/ *adj literary* expressing sexual or romantic love

**a·maze** /əˈmeɪz/ *v* [T] to make someone very surprised: *Dave amazed his friends by suddenly getting married.* | *Their loyalty never ceases to amaze me.*

**a·mazed** /əˈmeɪzd/ *adj* **be amazed** extremely surprised: [+ **(that)**] *I'm amazed you've never heard of Jeremy Bentham.* | [+ **at**] *We were amazed at his rapid recovery.* | **amazed to see/hear/find etc** *Visitors are often amazed to discover how little the town has changed.*

**a·maze·ment** /əˈmeɪzmənt/ *n* [U] a feeling of great surprise: **in amazement** *Ralph gasped in amazement.* | **to my amazement** *To my amazement she came up and shook my hand.*

**a·maz·ing** /əˈmeɪzɪŋ/ *adj* **1** extremely good, especially S2

in a surprising and unexpected way: *He's an amazing player to watch.|an amazing bargain.* **2** so surprising that it is hard to believe: *amazing stories of strange happenings during Geller's performances* —**amazingly** *adv*: *an amazingly generous offer*

**am·a·zon** /ˈæməzən‖-zɑːn, -zən/ *n* [C] a tall strong woman —**amazonian** /ˌæməˈzəʊniən◂‖-ˈzoʊ-/ *adj*

**am·bas·sa·dor** /æmˈbæsədə‖-ər/ *n* [C] an important official who represents his or her government in a foreign country —**ambassadorial** /æmˌbæsəˈdɔːriəl/ *adj* —**ambassadorship** /æmˈbæsədəʃɪp‖-dər-/ *n* [C,U]

**am·bas·sa·dress** /æmˈbæsədrɪ̇s/ *n* [C] the wife of an ambassador

**am·ber** /ˈæmbə‖-ər/ *n* [U] **1** a yellowish brown colour **2** a yellowish brown substance used to make jewellery —**amber** *adj*

**ambi-** /æmbɪ/ *prefix* both; double: *ambidextrous* (=using both hands equally well)

**am·bi·ance** /ˈæmbiəns/ *n* [singular, U] another spelling of ambience

**am·bi·dex·trous** /ˌæmbɪˈdekstrəs◂/ *adj* able to use either hand with equal skill

**am·bi·ence** /ˈæmbiəns/ *n* [singular, U] the way a place makes you feel: *a restaurant with a friendly ambience*

**am·bi·ent** /ˈæmbiənt/ *adj technical* **ambient temperature/pressure** the temperature etc of the surrounding area

**ambient music** /ˌ··· ˈ··/ *n* [U] slow electronic music that you listen to when you want to relax

**am·big·u·ous** /æmˈbɪgjuəs/ *adj* **1** having more than one meaning, so that it is not clear which is intended: *an ambiguous sentence* **2** difficult to understand: *His role in the affair is ambiguous.* —**ambiguously** *adv* —**ambiguity** /ˌæmbɪ̇ˈgjuːɪ̇ti/ *n* [C,U] | *Her speech was full of ambiguities and contradictions.*

**am·bit** /ˈæmbɪ̇t/ *n* [singular] *formal* the range or limit of something: *within the ambit of the law*

**am·bi·tion** /æmˈbɪʃən/ *n* **1** [U] determination to be successful, rich, powerful etc: *Your problem is you have no ambition.* **2** [C] a strong desire to achieve something: *My ambition is to become a pilot.*

**am·bi·tious** /æmˈbɪʃəs/ *adj* **1** determined to be successful, rich, powerful etc: *an ambitious and hard-working junior manager* | **be ambitious for sb** (=want them to be very successful) *Mothers are often highly ambitious for their children.* **2** an ambitious plan, idea etc shows a desire to do something good but difficult: *one of the most ambitious engineering projects of modern times* —**ambitiously** *adv* —**ambitiousness** *n* [U]

**am·biv·a·lent** /æmˈbɪvələnt/ *adj* not sure whether you want or like something or not: *Her feelings about getting married are distinctly ambivalent.* —**ambivalence** *n* [U] —**ambivalently** *adv*

**am·ble** /ˈæmbəl/ *v* [I always + adv/prep] to walk in a slow relaxed way: [+ **along/across etc**] *The old man came out and ambled over for a chat.* —**amble** *n* [singular]

**am·bro·si·a** /æmˈbrəʊziə‖-ˈbroʊʒə/ *n* [U] food or drink that tastes or smells extremely good

S3 **am·bu·lance** /ˈæmbjɪ̇ləns/ *n* [C] a special vehicle used for taking people who are ill or injured to hospital

**am·bu·lance·man** /ˈæmjɪ̇lənsmæn/ *n plural* **ambulancemen** /-men/ [C] *BrE* a man whose job is to drive an ambulance or look after the person being taken to hospital

**am·bu·lance·wom·an** /ˈæmjɪ̇ləns,wʊmən/ *n plural* **ambulancewomen** /-ˌwɪmɪn/ [C] *BrE* a woman whose job is to drive an ambulance or look after the person being taken to hospital

**am·bush**[1] /ˈæmbʊʃ/ *n* [C] a sudden attack by people who have been waiting and hiding, or the place where this happens: **wait/lie in ambush** (=wait to ambush someone) *Armed police lay in ambush behind the hedge.*

**ambush**[2] *v* [T] to attack someone from a place where you have been hiding

**a·me·ba** /əˈmiːbə/ *n* [C] an American spelling of AMOEBA

**a·me·bic** /əˈmiːbɪk/ *adj* an American spelling of AMOEBIC

**a·me·li·o·rate** /əˈmiːliəreɪt/ *v* [T] *formal* to make something better: *measures to ameliorate working conditions* —**amelioration** /əˌmiːliəˈreɪʃən/ *n* [U]

**a·men** /ɑːˈmen, eɪ-/ *interjection* **1 Amen** used at the end of a prayer: *Blessed be the Lord, Amen!* **2** used to show that you agree or approve: *"I think we can close the meeting now." "Amen to that."*

**a·men·a·ble** /əˈmiːnəbəl/ *adj* willing to listen or to do something: [+ **to**] *I'm sure they'll be amenable to rational argument.*

**a·mend** /əˈmend/ *v* [T] to make small changes or improvements to a law or document S3

**a·mend·ment** /əˈmendmənt/ *n* **1** [C,U] a written change or improvement to a law or document, or the process of doing this: [+ **to**] *an amendment to the resolution* | **table an amendment** (=say officially that you want to discuss an amendment) **2** [C] one of the rights on the list of rights included in the US Constitution

**a·mends** /əˈmendz/ *n* **make amends** to say you are sorry for the harm you have caused and try to make things better

**a·me·ni·ty** /əˈmiːnɪ̇ti‖əˈme-/ *n* [C usually plural] something such as a piece of equipment, shop, or park that makes it easier to live somewhere: *a town with all the amenities of a larger city* | **basic amenity** *simple huts with only the most basic amenities*

**Am·er·a·sian** /ˌæməˈreɪʒən◂,-ʃən◂/ *n* [C] a word meaning someone who has one American parent and one Asian parent —compare ASIAN-AMERICAN

**A·mer·i·can**[1] /əˈmerɪ̇kən/ *adj* **1** from or connected with the US: *American forces landed on the island at dawn.|The American writer William Boroughs* **2** *especially technical* connected with the CONTINENTS of North and South America: *a species found only in American rivers, especially in Brazil*

**American**[2] *n* [C] someone from the US

**American foot·ball** /ˌ··· ˈ··/ *n* [U] *BrE* a game played by two teams of eleven players, who carry, throw, or kick an OVAL (=egg shaped) ball; FOOTBALL (2) *AmE* —see picture on page 1263

**American In·di·an** /ˌ··· ˈ···/ *n* [C] another name for a NATIVE AMERICAN (someone from one of the first groups of people who lived in America) used especially about people from South America and sometimes considered offensive

**A·mer·i·can·is·m** /əˈmerɪ̇kənɪzəm/ *n* [C] a word, phrase, or sound that is typical of the English language as it is used in the US

**A·mer·i·can·ize** also **-ise** *BrE* /əˈmerɪkənaɪz/ *v* [T] to make something American in character, for example a way of speaking or writing, or the way something is organized —**Americanization** *n* [U] *Opponents of the burger bar said they were resisting the Americanization of our culture.*

**am·e·thyst** /ˈæmɪ̇θɪ̇st/ *n* **1** [C] a valuable purple stone used in jewellery **2** [U] a light purple colour —**amethyst** *adj*

**a·mi·a·ble** /ˈeɪmiəbəl/ *adj* friendly and likeable: *The driver was an amiable young man.* —**amiably** *adv* —**amiability** /ˌeɪmiəˈbɪlɪ̇ti/ *n* [U]

**am·i·ca·ble** /ˈæmɪkəbəl/ *adj* an amicable agreement, relationship etc is one in which people feel friendly towards each other and do not want to quarrel: *an amicable settlement that was acceptable to both sides* —**amicably** *adv* —**amicability** /ˌæmɪkəˈbɪlɪ̇ti/ *n* [U]

**a·mid** /əˈmɪd/ also **amidst** *prep* **1** happening while noisy, busy, or confused events are also happening: *The dollar has fallen in value amid rumors of weakness in the*

US economy. **2** *especially literary* among or surrounded by: *old gabled houses peeped out from amid the trees.*

**a·mid·ships** /əˈmɪdˌʃɪps/ *adv* in the middle part of a ship

**a·midst** /əˈmɪdst/ *prep* amid

**a·mi·no ac·id** /əˌmiːnəʊ ˈæsɪ̈d, əˌmaɪ-‖-noʊ-/ *n* [C] one of the substances that combine to form PROTEINS

**a·miss¹** /əˈmɪs/ *adv* **1 sthg would not come/go amiss** *informal* used to say that something would be suitable or useful in a situation: *A cup of tea wouldn't go amiss.* **2 take sth amiss** to feel upset or offended about something that someone has said or done

**amiss²** *adj* **be amiss** if something is amiss, there is a problem: *Elsa continued as if nothing was amiss.*

**am·i·ty** /ˈæmɪ̈ti/ *n* [U] *formal* friendship, especially between countries: *a spirit of perfect amity*

**am·me·ter** /ˈæmɪtə, ˈæmˌmiːtə‖-ər/ *n* [C] a piece of equipment used to measure the strength of an electric current

**am·mo** /ˈæməʊ‖-moʊ/ *n* [U] *informal* ammunition

**am·mo·ni·a** /əˈməʊniə‖-ˈmoʊ-/ *n* [U] a poisonous gas or clear liquid with a strong smell

**am·mu·ni·tion** /ˌæmjʊ̈ˈnɪʃən/ *n* [U] **1** bullets, shells (SHELL¹ (2)) etc that are fired from guns **2** information that you can use to criticize someone or win an argument against them: *The oil spill was to give environmentalists powerful new ammunition against the oil companies.*

**am·ne·si·a** /æmˈniːziə‖-ʒə/ *n* [U] the medical condition of not being able to remember anything —**amnesiac** /-ziæk‖ʒiæk, -ziæk/ *adj* —**amnesiac** *n* [C]

**am·nes·ty** /ˈæmnəsti/ *n* [C] **1** an official order by a government that allows political prisoners to go free: *an amnesty for all former terrorists* **2** a period of time when you can admit to doing something illegal without being punished: *an amnesty on illegal handguns*

**am·ni·o·cen·te·sis** /ˌæmniəʊsenˈtiːsɪ̈s‖-nioʊ-/ *n* [U] a test to see if an unborn baby has any diseases or other problems, done by taking liquid from the mother's WOMB

**a·moe·ba** also **ameba** *AmE* /əˈmiːbə/ *n plural* **amoebas** or **amoebae** /-biː/ [C] a very small creature that has only one cell

**a·moe·bic** also **amebic** *AmE* /əˈmiːbɪk/ *adj* connected with amoebas

**a·mok** /əˈmɒk‖əˈmɑːk/ also **amuck** *adv* **run amok** to suddenly behave in a very violent and uncontrolled way: *'Gunman runs amok in Shopping Mall'*

S1 W1 **a·mong** /əˈmʌŋ/ also **a·mongst** /əˈmʌŋst/ *prep* **1** in the middle of: *The girl quickly disappeared among the crowd.* | *I could hear voices coming from somewhere among the bushes.* —see picture on page 1257, —see BETWEEN¹ (USAGE) **2 among friends/strangers** with people who are your friends or who you do not know: *Jim relaxed, knowing he was among friends.* **3** through or between: *We walked among the chestnut woods on the mountain slopes.* | *She began rummaging among the books on her desk.* **4** used to say that something such as a feeling or disease affects many people in a particular group, or that many people in a group have the same opinion: *There is widespread concern among scientists about the long-term consequences of storing nuclear waste underground.* | *7,000 job losses among railway workers* **5** used when talking about a particular person or thing in a group of people or things: *She was the eldest among them.* | *Innocent civilians were among the casualties.* | *My grandfather had among his possessions a portrait by Matisse.* **6 among other** used to say that you are only mentioning one or two people or things out of a much larger group: **among other things** *At the meeting they discussed, among other things, recent events in Eastern Europe.* **7** if something is divided or shared among a group of people, each is given a part of it **8 talk/quarrel among yourselves** to talk or quarrel with other people: *Talk among yourselves for a while, I'll be ready soon.*

**a·mor·al** /eɪˈmɒrəl, æ-‖eɪˈmɔː-, -ˈmɑː-/ *adj* having no moral standards at all: *a completely amoral person* —**amorality** /ˌeɪmɒˈrælɪ̈ti, ˌæ-‖ˌeɪmə-/ *n* [U]

**am·o·rous** /ˈæmərəs/ *adj* involving or expressing sexual love: *She resisted his amorous advances.* —**amorously** *adv* —**amorousness** *n* [U]

**a·mor·phous** /əˈmɔːfəs‖-ɔːr-/ *adj formal* having no definite shape or features: *an amorphous mass of twisted metal* —**amorphously** *adv* —**amorphousness** *n* [U]

**a·mor·tize** also **-ise** *BrE* /əˈmɔːtaɪz‖ˈæmər-/ *v* [T] *technical* to pay a debt by making regular payments —**amortizable** *adj* —**amortization** /æˌmɔːtaɪˈzeiʃən‖ˌæmərt-/ *n* [C,U]

**a·mount¹** /əˈmaʊnt/ *n* [C,U] **1** a quantity of something such as time, money, or a substance: [+ **of**] *a considerable amount of money* | **a small/large etc amount** *It's best to cook vegetables in a small amount of water.* **2** the level or degree to which a feeling, quality etc is present: [+ **of**] *Her case has attracted an enormous amount of public sympathy.* | **a certain/fair amount of** (=a fairly high level of something) *Dina encountered a fair amount of envy among her colleagues.* **3 no amount of sth will do sth** used to say that something has no effect: *No amount of persuasion could make her change her mind.* | **any amount of sth** *BrE* (=a lot of) *The school has any amount of resources and equipment.* S1 W1

**USAGE NOTE: AMOUNT**

GRAMMAR

**Amount** is usually used with uncountable nouns, and some people think this is the only correct use: *a large amount of money/food/electricity/hard work.* (Note that you do not usually say a **high** or **big** amount). With plural countable nouns it is best to use **number**: *a large number of mistakes/people*

However, people often use **amount** with plural countable nouns when what they are talking about is thought of as a group: *We didn't expect such a large amount of people.* | *an enormous amount of problems*

**amount²** *v*

**amount to** sth *phr v* [T not in progressive] **1** if figures, sums etc amount to a particular total, they equal that total when they are added together: *Time lost through illness amounted to 1,357 working days.* **2** if an attitude, remark, situation etc amounts to something, it has the same effect: *The court's decision amounts to a not-guilty verdict.* **3 not amount to much/anything/a great deal etc** to not seem important, valuable or successful: *Her academic achievements don't amount to much.*

**a·mour** /əˈmʊə‖əˈmʊr/ *n* [C] *literary* a sexual relationship, especially a secret one

**am·our prop·re** /ˌæmʊə ˈprɒprə‖ˌɑːmʊr ˈproʊprə/ *n* [U] *literary* the quality of feeling respect for yourself

**amp** /æmp/ *n* [C] **1** also **ampere** a unit for measuring electric current: *a 3 amp fuse* **2** *informal* an AMPLIFIER

**am·per·age** /ˈæmpərɪdʒ/ *n* [singular, U] *technical* the strength of an electrical current measured in amps

**am·pere** /ˈæmpeə‖-pɪr/ *n* [C] an amp

**am·per·sand** /ˈæmpəsænd‖-ər-/ *n* [C] the sign '&' that means 'and': *Mills & Boon*

**am·phet·a·mine** /æmˈfetəmiːn, -mɪ̈n/ *n* [C,U] a drug that gives you a feeling of excitement and a lot of energy

**am·phib·i·an** /æmˈfɪbiən/ *n* [C] an animal that can live on both land and water

**am·phib·i·ous** /æmˈfɪbiəs/ *adj* **1** able to live on both land and water **2 amphibious vehicle** a vehicle that is able to move on land and water **3 amphibious operation/force/assault** an amphibious operation etc involves ships and land vehicles

**am·phi·thea·tre** *especially BrE*, **amphitheater** *AmE* /ˈæmfɪ̈ˌθɪətə‖-ər/ *n* [C] a large circular building without a roof and with many rows of seats

**am·pho·ra** /ˈæmfərə/ *n* [C] a tall clay container for oil or wine, used in ancient times

**am·ple** /ˈæmpəl/ *adj* **1** more than enough: *There's ample storage space in the new house.* | **ample time/**

**evidence/opportunity etc** *You will have ample opportunity to state your case later.* **2 ample bosom/figure/torso etc** large a way that is attractive or pleasant —**amply** *adv*: *Recent US history has amply demonstrated the risks of foreign intervention.*

**am·pli·fi·er** /'æmplɪ̈faɪə‖-faɪr/ *n* [C] a piece of electrical equipment that makes sound louder; AMP (2)

**am·pli·fy** /'æmplɪ̈faɪ/ *v* [T] **1** to make a sound louder, especially musical sound: *an amplified guitar* **2** *formal* to explain something that you have said by giving more information about it: *Would you care to amplify that remark?* **3** *formal* to emphasize the importance of something: *Successive reports amplified the case for privatisation.* —**amplification** /ˌæmplɪ̈fɪ̈'keɪʃən/ *n* [U]

**am·pli·tude** /'æmplɪ̈tjuːd‖-tuːd/ *n* [U] *technical* the distance between the middle and the top or bottom of a WAVE² (4) such as a SOUND WAVE

**am·poule** *especially BrE* also **ampule** *AmE* /'æmpuːl/ *n* [C] a small container for medicine that will be put into someone with a special needle

**am·pu·tate** /'æmpjʊ̈teɪt/ *v* [I,T] to cut off someone's arm, leg, finger etc during a medical operation: *Two of her toes were amputated because of frostbite.* —**amputation** /ˌæmpjʊ̈'teɪʃən/ *n* [C,U]

**am·pu·tee** /ˌæmpjʊ̈'tiː/ *n* [C] someone who has had an arm or a leg amputated

**a·muck** /ə'mʌk/ *adv* AMOK

**am·u·let** /'æmjʊ̈lət, -let‖'æmjʊ̈lət/ *n* [C] a small piece of jewellery worn to protect against bad luck, disease etc

**a·muse** /ə'mjuːz/ *v* [T] **1** to make someone laugh or smile: *What amused me most was the thought of Martin in a dress.* **2** to make someone spend time in an enjoyable way without getting bored: *Doing jigsaws would amuse Amy for hours on end.* | **amuse yourself** *The kids amused themselves playing hide-and-seek.*

**a·mused** /ə'mjuːzd/ *adj* **1** someone who is amused by something thinks it is funny so that they smile or laugh: [+ **at/by**] *Clare was highly amused by the little boy's antics.* | *He won't be very amused when he finds out what's happened to his garden.* | *James watched the proceedings with an amused grin.* **2 keep sb amused** to entertain or interest someone for a long time so that they do not get bored: *if you could just keep them amused while I do the shopping*

**a·muse·ment** /ə'mjuːzmənt/ *n* **1** [U] the feeling you have when you think something is funny: *Tom's tricks were a source of endless amusement to the other boys.* | **to sb's amusement** (=in a way that makes someone laugh or smile) *To everyone's amusement he turned up for work in a straw hat and jeans.* **2 amusements** [plural] special things such as machines or games that are intended to entertain people: *The kids can ride on the amusements.* **3** [U] the process of getting or providing pleasure and enjoyment

**amusement ar·cade** /·'·· ·ˌ·/ *n* [C] *BrE* a place where you play games on machines by putting coins into them; VIDEO ARCADE *AmE*

**amusement park** /·'·· ˌ·/ *n* [C] a large park with many special machines that you can ride on, such as ROLLER-COASTERs and MERRY-GO-ROUNDs

**a·mus·ing** /ə'mjuːzɪŋ/ *adj* funny and entertaining: *I don't find his jokes at all amusing.* | **highly/vastly amusing** (=very funny) *a highly amusing film* —**amusingly** *adv*

S1 W1 **an** /ən; *strong*: æn/ *indefinite article, determiner* [used when the following word begins with a vowel sound] a: *an orange* | *an X-ray* | *such an old house* —see also A

**an-** /ən, æn/ *prefix* **1** the form used for A-² before a vowel sound **2** not; without: *anarchy* (=without government) | *anoxia* (=condition caused by lack of oxygen)

**-an** /ən/ *suffix* also **-ean, -ian** **1** [in adjectives and nouns] someone or something of, from, or connected with a particular thing, place, or person: *an American* (=person from America) | *the pre-Tolstoyan novel* **2** [in nouns] someone skilled in or studying a particular subject: *a historian* (=someone who studies history)

**-ana** /ɑːnə‖ænə/ *suffix* [in nouns] another form of the suffix -IANA: *Americana*

**an·a·bol·ic ste·roid** /ˌænəbɒlɪk 'stɪərɔɪd, -'ste-‖-bɑːlɪk 'stɪrɔɪd, -'ster-/ *n* [C] a drug that makes muscles grow quickly, sometimes used illegally by people in sport

**a·nach·ro·nis·m** /ə'nækrənɪzəm/ *n* [C] **1** someone or something that seems to belong to the past, not the present: *The monarchy is something of an anachronism these days.* **2** something in a play, film etc that seems wrong because it is being shown in the wrong period of time —**anachronistic** /əˌnækrə'nɪstɪk◂/ *adj* —**anachronistically** /-kli/ *adv*

**an·a·con·da** /ˌænə'kɒndə‖-'kɑːn-/ *n* [C] a large South American snake

**a·nae·mi·a** *especially BrE*, **anemia** *AmE* /ə'niːmiə/ *n* [U] a medical condition in which there are too few red cells in your blood

**a·nae·mic** *especially BrE*, **anemic** *AmE* /ə'niːmɪk/ *adj* **1** suffering from anaemia **2** seeming weak and uninteresting: *an anaemic performance of King Lear* —**anaemically** /-kli/ *adv*

**an·aer·o·bic** /ˌænə'rəʊbɪk◂‖-'roʊ-/ *adj technical* not needing oxygen in order to live

**an·aes·the·si·a** *especially BrE*, **anesthesia** *AmE* /ˌænɪ̈s'θiːziə‖-ʒə/ *n* [U] **1** the use of anaesthetics in medicine **2** the state of being unable to feel pain

**an·aes·thet·ic** *especially BrE*, **anesthetic** *AmE* /ˌænɪ̈s'θetɪk◂/ *n* [C,U] a drug that stops you feeling pain: **under anaesthetic** (=using an anaesthetic) | **local anaesthetic/general anaesthetic** (=affecting a small part of your body/all of your body) *Wisdom teeth are usually removed under anaesthetic.*

**a·naes·the·tist** *especially BrE*, **anesthetist** *AmE* /ə'niːsθɪ̈tɪst‖ə'nes-/ *n* [C] a doctor or nurse who has been specially trained to give people anaesthetics

**a·naes·the·tize** also **-ise** *BrE*, **anesthetize** *AmE* /ə'niːsθɪ̈taɪz‖ə'nes-/ *v* [T] to give someone an anaesthetic so that they do not feel pain

**an·a·gram** /'ænəgræm/ *n* [C] a word or phrase that is made by changing the order of the letters in another word or phrase: *'Silent' is an anagram of 'listen'.*

**a·nal** /'eɪnl/ *adj* **1** connected with the ANUS **2** showing too much concern with small details, especially in a way that annoys other people: *Don't be so anal.*

**an·al·ge·si·a** /ˌænəl'dʒiːziə‖-ʒə/ *n* [U] *technical* the condition of being unable to feel pain while conscious

**an·al·ge·sic** /ˌænəl'dʒiːzɪk◂/ *n* [C] *technical* a drug that reduces pain: *Aspirin is a mild analgesic.* —**analgesic** *adj*

**a·nal·o·gous** /ə'næləgəs/ *adj formal* similar to another situation or thing so that a comparison can be made: [+ **to/with**] *Scharf's findings are analagous with our own.*

**an·a·logue** /'ænəlɒg‖-lɒːg, -lɑːg/ *n* [C] **1 analogue clock/watch** a clock or watch that uses moving hands, not changing numbers **2** *formal* something that is similar to something else in some way

**analogue com·put·er** /ˌ··· ·'··/ *n* [C] a computer that calculates things by measuring changing quantities such as of VOLTAGE rather than using a BINARY system of counting —compare DIGITAL COMPUTER

**a·nal·o·gy** /ə'nælədʒi/ *n* [C,U] a comparison between two situations, processes etc that seem similar, or the process of making this comparison: **drawing/draw an analogy** (=make a comparison) *analogies between human and animal behaviour* | **by analogy (with)** (=using an analogy) *Dr Wood explained the movement of light by analogy with the movement of water.*

**an·a·lyse** *BrE*, **analyze** *AmE* /'ænəl-aɪz/ *v* [T] **1** to examine or think about something carefully, in order to understand it: *A computer analyzes the photographs sent by the satellite.* | *analyse the text in detail* **2** to examine someone's mental or emotional problems by using analysis (ANALYSIS (3)); PSYCHOANALYSE W3

**a·nal·y·sis** /ə'nælɪ̈sɪ̈s/ *n plural* **analyses** /-siːz/ **1** [C,U] a careful examination of something in order to under- S3 W1

stand it better: *a detailed analysis of the week's news* **2** [C,U] a careful examination of a substance to see what it is made of: *Forensic experts are doing analyses of the samples.* **3** [U] a process in which a doctor makes someone talk about their past experiences, relationships etc in order to help them with mental or emotional problems; PSYCHOANALYSIS **4 in the final/last analysis** used when giving the most basic or important facts about a situation: *In the final analysis, profit is the motive.*

**an·a·lyst** /ˈænəl-ɪ̈st/ *n* [C] **1** someone who makes a careful examination of events or materials in order to make judgments about them: *a food analyst* **2** a doctor who helps people who have mental or emotional problems by making them talk about their experiences and relationships —see also SYSTEMS ANALYST

**an·a·lyt·ic** /ˌænəl-ˈɪtɪk◂/ also **an·a·lyt·i·cal** /-tɪkəl/ *adj* using methods that help you examine things carefully, especially by separating them into their different parts: *an analytic approach*

**an·a·lyze** /ˈænəl-aɪz/ *v* [T] the American spelling of ANALYSE

**an·a·paest** *BrE*, **anapest** *AmE* /ˈænəpest, -piːst/ *n* [C] *technical* part of a line of poetry consisting of two short sounds then one long one —**anapaestic** /ˌænəˈpiːstɪk◂/ *adj*

**an·ar·chic** /æˈnɑːkɪk‖-ɑːr-/ *adj* lacking any rules or order, or not following the moral rules of society: *a lawless, anarchic city | Orton's anarchic sense of humour*

**an·ar·chis·m** /ˈænəkɪzəm‖-ər-/ *n* [U] the political belief that there should be no government and that ordinary people should work together to improve society

**an·ar·chist** /ˈænəkɪ̈st‖-ər-/ *n* [C] someone who believes that governments, laws etc are not necessary —**anarchistic** /ˌænəˈkɪstɪk◂‖-ər-/ *adj* —**anarchistically** /-kli/ *adv*

**an·ar·chy** /ˈænəki‖-ər-/ *n* [U] a situation in which there is no effective government in a country or no order in an organization or situation: *a state of complete anarchy*

**a·nath·e·ma** /əˈnæθɪ̈mə/ *n* [singular, U] something that is completely the opposite of what you believe in: **[+ to]** *The idea of full-blown majority rule was anathema to many Afrikaners.*

**an·a·tom·i·cal** /ˌænəˈtɒmɪkəl◂‖-ˈtɑː-/ *adj* connected with the structure of human or animal bodies: *an anatomical examination* —**anatomically** /-kli/ *adv*

**a·nat·o·my** /əˈnætəmi/ *n* **1** [U] the scientific study of the structure of human or animal bodies **2** [C usually singular] the structure of body, or of a part of a body: *the anatomy of the nervous system* **3** *often humorous* your body: *a part of his anatomy that I'd rather not mention* **4** [C,U] the process of cutting a body into pieces to study its different parts; DISSECTION —**anatomist** *n* [C]

**-ance** /əns/ *suffix*, **-ence** [in nouns] the action, state, or quality of doing something or of being something: *his sudden appearance* (=he appeared suddenly) | *her brilliance* (=she is BRILLIANT)

**an·ces·tor** /ˈænsəstə, -ses-‖-sestər/ *n* [C] **1** a member of your family who lived a long time ago: *My ancestors were French.* **2** the form in which a modern machine, vehicle etc first existed: *Babbage's invention was the ancestor of the modern computer.* —compare DESCENDANT —**ancestral** /ænˈsestrəl/ *adj*: *the family's ancestral home*

**an·ces·try** /ˈænsəstri, -ses-‖-ses-/ *n* [C usually singular, U] the members of your family who lived a long time ago: **of French/Scottish etc ancestry** (=having ancestors who were French, Scottish etc)

**an·chor¹** /ˈæŋkə‖-ər/ *n* [C] **1** a piece of heavy metal that is lowered to the bottom of the sea, lake etc to prevent a ship or boat moving: **weigh anchor** (=lift the anchor so that a ship can start moving) | **drop/cast anchor** *We dropped anchor a few yards offshore.* **2** someone or something that provides a feeling of support and safety **3** *AmE* someone who reads the news on TV and introduces news reports; NEWSREADER *BrE*

**anchor²** *v*
**1** ► **BOAT** ◄ [I,T] to lower the anchor on a ship or boat to hold it in one place: *Three tankers were anchored in the harbor.*
**2** ► **FASTEN** ◄ [T usually passive] to fasten something firmly so that it cannot move: *The panel was firmly anchored by two large bolts.*
**3 be anchored in** to be strongly connected with a particular system, way of life etc: *laws anchored in patriarchal society*
**4** ► **SUPPORT** ◄ [T] to provide a feeling of support or safety for someone: *Her life was anchored by her religion.*
**5** ► **TV NEWS** ◄ [T] *AmE* to be the person who reads the news and introduces reports on TV: *Connie Chung anchors the 6 o'clock news.*

**an·chor·age** /ˈæŋkərɪdʒ/ *n* **1** [C] a place where ships can anchor **2** [C,U] a place where something can be firmly fastened: *Dig deep holes to get good anchorage for your new shrubs.*

**an·cho·rite** /ˈæŋkəraɪt/ *n* [C] *literary* someone who lives alone for religious reasons; HERMIT

**an·chor·man** /ˈæŋkəmæn‖-kər-/ *n plural* **anchormen** /-men/ [C] *AmE* a male anchorperson

**an·chor·per·son** /ˈæŋkəˌpɜːsən‖ˈæŋkərˌpɜːrsən/ *n* [C] *AmE* someone who reads the news on TV and introduces reports

**an·chor·wom·an** /ˈæŋkəˌwʊmən‖-kər-/ *plural* **anchorwomen** /-ˌwɪmɪn/ *n* [C] *AmE* a female anchorperson

**an·cho·vy** /ˈæntʃəvi‖ˈæntʃoʊvi/ *n* [C,U] a very small fish that tastes strongly of salt

**an·cient¹** /ˈeɪnʃənt/ *adj* **1** belonging to a time long ago: *the ancient civilizations of Asia* **2** having existed for a very long time: *an ancient walled city* **3** *usually humorous* very old: *That photo makes me look ancient!* W2

**ancient²** *n* **the ancients** *old use* people who lived long ago, especially the Greeks and Romans: *The ancients believed that the sun and moon were planets.*

**an·cil·la·ry** /ænˈsɪləri‖ˈænsɪ̈leri/ *adj* **1 ancillary workers/staff etc** workers who provide additional help and services for the people who do the main work in hospitals, schools etc **2** connected with or supporting something else, but less important than it: *Agreement was reached on a number of ancillary matters.*

**-ancy** /ənsi/ *suffix*, **-ency** [in nouns] the state or quality of doing something or of being something: *expectancy* (=state of expecting) | *hesitancy* | *complacency* (=being COMPLACENT)

**and** /ənd, ən; *strong* ænd/ *conj* **1** used to join two words, parts of sentences, etc: *Do you want a pen and a bit of paper?* | *The film starred Jack Lemmon and Shirley MacLaine.* | *We've dealt with items one, two, and eleven.* | *We'll have to reduce costs and borrow more money.* | *You need to know what rights you have and how to use them.* **2** then; afterwards: *Have your lunch and get a bath.* | *She picked up the kitten and put it in the box.* | *He knocked on the door and went in.* | **wait and see** *You'll have to wait and see what happens.* **3** used to say that something is caused by something else: *I missed supper and I'm starving!* | *She took some medicine and was sick.* **4** used when adding numbers: *Six and four is ten.* **5 come and .../go and .../try and ... etc** *especially BrE* used instead of 'to': *Shall we go and have a cup of coffee?* | *I'll see if I can try and persuade her to come.* **6** *spoken* used to introduce a statement, comment, question etc: *And now I'd like to introduce our next speaker, Mrs Thompson.* | "We're trying to sort out our next holiday." "And where's the favourite place?" "Oh, America." **7** used between repeated words to emphasize what you are saying: *More and more people are losing their jobs.* | *We waited for hours and hours!* | *That was years and years ago.* | *We ran and ran.* **8 nice and .../good and ...** used to emphasize how nice or good something is: *I like my tea nice and hot.* **9 a hundred and four/three thousand, five hundred and seventy six etc** used after the word 'hundred' and before the numbers 1 to 99 when saying numbers **10 three and three quarters, nineteen and** S1 W1

**a half etc** used after the whole number and before the FRACTION (2) when saying numbers: *in about two and a half month's time|five and a quarter percent* **11** used in descriptions of food and drink to mean served with: *Do you want some fish and chips?|I'll have a gin and tonic.*| **bread and butter** (=bread with butter spread on it) **12 there are experts and experts/computers and computers etc** used to say that some are much better than others **13 and?** *spoken* used when you want someone to add something to what they have just said: *"I'm sorry." "And?" "And I promise it won't happen again."*

**An·dan·te** /æn'dænti,-teɪ‖ɑːn'dɑːn-/ *n* [C] a piece of music played or sung at a speed that is neither very fast or very slow

**andante** *adj* played or sung at a speed that is neither very fast or very slow —**andante** *adv*

**an·di·ron** /'ændaɪən‖-ərn/ *n* [C] one of a pair of iron objects that holds wood in a FIREPLACE

**-andr-** /ændr/ *prefix technical* concerning males or men: *androgynous plants* (=plants which are both male and female)|*polyandry* (=having more than one husband at the same time)

**an·drog·y·nous** /æn'drɒdʒɪnəs‖-'drɑː-/ *adj* **1** having both male and female parts **2** someone who is androgynous looks both female and male: *Bowie had a kind of androgynous sex appeal.*

**an·droid** /'ændrɔɪd/ *n* [C] a ROBOT that looks completely human

**an·ec·dot·al** /ˌænɪk'dəʊtl◂‖-'doʊ-/ *adj* consisting of short stories based on someone's personal experience: *Tom gave an anecdotal account of his recent trip to Morocco.|His findings are based on anecdotal evidence rather than serious research.*

**an·ec·dote** /'ænɪkdəʊt‖-doʊt/ *n* [C] a short story based on your personal experience

**a·ne·mi·a** /ə'niːmiə/ *n* [U] the usual American spelling of ANAEMIA

**a·ne·mic** /ə'niːmɪk/ *adj* the usual American spelling of ANAEMIC

**a·nem·o·ne** /ə'neməni/ *n* [C] a plant with red, white, or blue flowers

**an·es·the·si·a** /ˌænɪs'θiːziə‖-ʒə/ *n* [U] the usual American spelling of ANAESTHESIA

**an·es·the·si·ol·o·gist** /ˌænəsθiːzi'ɒlədʒɪst‖-'ɑːl-/ *n* [C] *AmE* a doctor who gives ANAESTHETICS to a patient

**an·es·thet·ic** /ˌænəs'θetɪk◂/ *n* [C,U] the usual American spelling of ANAESTHETIC

**a·nes·the·tist** /ə'niːsθɪtɪst‖ə'nes-/ *n* [C] the usual American spelling of ANAESTHETIST

**a·nes·the·tize** /ə'niːsθɪtaɪz‖ə'nes-/ *v* [T] the usual American spelling of ANAESTHETISE

**a·new** /ə'njuː‖ə'nuː/ *adv literary* **1 start life anew** to begin a different job, start to live in a different place etc, especially after a difficult period in your life: *She resolved to start life anew in Ireland.* **2** if you do something anew, you start doing it again

**an·gel** /'eɪndʒəl/ *n* [C] **1** a spirit who lives with God in heaven, often shown as a person dressed in white with wings **2** someone who is very kind, very good, or very beautiful: *That little girl of theirs is an angel.*|**be an angel** *spoken* (=used to ask someone to do something for you) *Be an angel and get me my glasses will you?*|**you're an angel** *spoken* (=used to tell someone that you are grateful to them) *Thanks for mailing those letters, you're an angel.*|**sb's no angel** (=used to say that someone behaves very badly) *Sam was no angel at school, believe me.* **3** a way of speaking to a child or woman you love: *How are you angel?* **4** *informal* someone who supports a play, film, music group etc by giving money —see also GUARDIAN ANGEL

**angel dust** /'· ·/ *n* [U] *slang* PCP (=a drug)

**an·gel·ic** /æn'dʒelɪk/ *adj* **1** looking good, kind, and gentle or behaving in this way: *She had an angelic smile, but a dreadful temper.* **2** connected with angels —**angelically** /-kli/ *adv*

**an·gel·i·ca** /æn'dʒelɪkə/ *n* [U] a plant that smells sweet and is used in cooking

**an·ger¹** /'æŋgə‖-ər/ *n* [U] a strong feeling of wanting to harm, hurt or criticize someone because they have done something unfair, cruel, offensive etc: *Paul's face was filled with anger and resentment.*|**do sth in anger** (=do it because you have very strong feelings) *Her mother hardly ever shouted at her in anger.* W3

**anger²** *v* [T often passive] to make someone angry: *What angered me most was his total lack of remorse.*

**an·gi·na** /æn'dʒaɪnə/ *n* [U] a medical condition in which you have bad pains in your chest because your heart is weak

**angle**

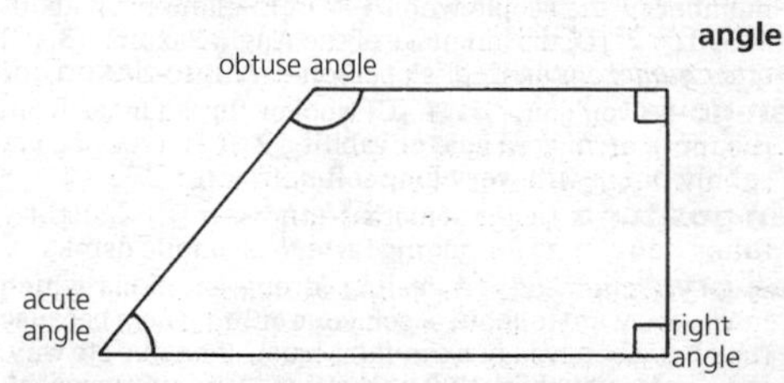


**an·gle¹** /'æŋgəl/ *n* [C] **1** the space between two straight lines or surfaces that touch or cross each other, measured in degrees: *an angle of 45°* —see also RIGHT ANGLE **2** a position from which you look at something or photograph it: *This drawing of the monastery was done from an unusual angle.* **3** a way of considering a problem or situation: *We need to look at the issue from a different angle.* **4 at an angle** leaning to one side and not straight or upright: *The portrait was hanging at an angle.* **5** the shape formed when two lines or surfaces join: *My head struck the angle of the shelf.* S3 W3

**angle²** *v* [I,T] **1** if you angle something in a particular direction or if it angles in that direction, it is not upright or facing straight ahead: *a mirror angled to reflect light from a window* **2** [T] to describe something unfairly by emphasizing some features but not others: *a report was angled in favour of the government*

**angle for** sth *phr v* [T] to try to get something by making suggestions and remarks instead of asking directly: *She was angling for an invitation to that party.*

**an·gle·poise lamp** /ˌæŋgəlpɔɪz 'læmp/ *n* [C] *BrE trademark* a type of lamp that can be moved into different positions —see picture at LIGHT¹

**an·gler** /'æŋglə‖-ər/ *n* [C] someone who catches fish as a sport —compare FISHERMAN

**An·gli·can** /'æŋglɪkən/ *n* [C] a Christian who is a member of the Church of England —**Anglican** *adj* —**Anglicanism** *n* [U]

**an·gli·cis·m** /'æŋglɪsɪzəm/ *n* [C] an English word or expression that is used in another language

**an·gli·cize** also **-ise** *BrE* /'æŋglɪsaɪz/ *v* [T] to make something or someone more English

**an·gling** /'æŋglɪŋ/ *n* [U] **1** the sport of catching fish **2 go angling** to catch fish as a sport

**Anglo-, anglo-** /æŋgləʊ‖-gloʊ/ *prefix* **1** of England or Britain: *an anglophile* (=someone who loves Britain) **2** English or British and: *an Anglo-Scottish family|an improvement in Anglo-American relations*

**Anglo-A·mer·i·can¹** /ˌ·· ·'···◂/ *adj* between or involving both Britain and the US: *Anglo-American relations*

**Anglo-American²** *n* [C] an American whose family come from Britain

**An·glo-Cath·o·lic** /ˌ·· '···◂/ *n* [C] a Christian who is a

member of the part of the Church of England that is similar to the Roman Catholic church —**Anglo-Catholic** *adj* —**Anglo-Catholicism** /ˌ·· ·'····/ *n* [U]

**Anglo-In·di·an** /·· '···◂/ *n* [C] **1** someone whose family is partly British and partly Indian **2** *old use* a British person who was born or lives in India —**Anglo-Indian** *adj*

**an·glo·phile** /'æŋgləʊfaɪl, -glə-‖-gloʊ-,-glə-/ *n* [C] someone who is not British but likes anything British —**anglophilia** /ˌæŋgləʊ'fɪliə, -glə-‖-gloʊ-, -glə-/ *n* [U]

**an·glo·phobe** /'æŋgləʊfəʊb, -glə-‖-gloʊfoʊb,-glə-/ *n* [C] someone who dislikes anything British —**anglophobia** /ˌæŋgləʊ'fəʊbiə, -glə-‖-gloʊ'foʊ-, -glə-/ *n* [U]

**an·glo·phone** /'æŋgləʊfəʊn,-glə‖'-gloʊfoʊn,-glə-/ *adj* anglophone populations or countries have English as one of their languages —**anglophone** *n* [C]

**Anglo-Sax·on** /ˌæŋgləʊ 'sæksən◂‖-gloʊ-/ *n* **1** [C] a member of the people who lived in England from about 600 AD **2** [U] the language of the Anglo-Saxons **3** [C] *often humorous* an English person —**Anglo-Saxon** *adj*

**an·go·ra** /æŋ'gɔːrə/ *n* **1** [U] wool or thread made from the fur of an angora goat or rabbit **2** [C] a type of goat, rabbit, or cat with very long soft hair or fur

**an·gos·tur·a** /ˌæŋgə'stjʊərə◂‖-'stʊrə◂/ *n* [U] a slightly bitter liquid used for adding taste to alcoholic drinks

S3 W3 **an·gry** /'æŋgri/ *adj* **1** feeling strong emotions which make you want to shout at someone or hurt them because they have behaved in an unfair, cruel, offensive etc way, or because you think that a situation is unfair, unacceptable etc: *I was very angry when I heard what happened.* | **angry person/look etc** *an angry letter* | *There were angry scenes when the police broke up the demonstration.* [+ **with/at**] *She was so angry with him that she threatened to throw him out of the house.* | [+ **about/over**] *Parents are justifiably angry about the decision to close the school.* | **make sb angry** *It makes me really angry when I hear people talk about 'humane killing'.* **2 angry with/at yourself** feeling strongly that you wish you had done something or had not done something: *David was angry with himself for letting the others see his true feelings.* **3** *literary* an angry sky or cloud looks dark and stormy **4** *literary* an angry wound etc is painful and red and looks infected —**angrily** *adv*: *"The stupid young fool," he said angrily.*

This graph shows how common different grammar patterns of the adjective **angry** are.

be angry
angry person/look etc
angry with
angry about
angry (that)
angry at
other
10% 20% 30% 40% 50%

Based on the British National Corpus and the Longman Lancaster Corpus

**angst** /æŋst/ *n* [U] strong feelings of anxiety and unhappiness because you are worried about your life, your future, or what you should do in a particular situation: *love letters full of angst*

**an·guish** /'æŋgwɪʃ/ *n* [U] mental or physical suffering caused by extreme pain or worry: *the anguish of not knowing what had happened to her* —**anguished** *adj* | *anguished cries for help*

**an·gu·lar** /'æŋgjʊ̈lə‖-ər/ *adj* **1** thin and not having much flesh on your bones: *a tall, angular young man* **2** having sharp and definite corners: *an angular room* **3** [only before noun] having or forming an angle

S1 W1 **an·i·mal**[1] /'ænɪ̈məl/ *n* [C] **1** a living creature such as a dog or cat, that is not an insect, plant, fish, or person: *farm animals* | **animal welfare/rights etc** *campaigning for animal rights* | **animal products/protein/fats etc** (=things that are made or come from animals) **2** any living creature that is not a plant, including people: *Man is a highly intelligent animal.* **3** *informal* someone who behaves in a cruel, violent, or very rude way: *These football hooligans are just animals.* **4 a very/completely different animal** *informal* something that is very different from the thing you have mentioned: *Communism in North Korea is a very different animal from the Eastern European model.* **5 a political/social animal etc** *informal* someone who is interested in politics, in meeting other people etc

**animal**[2] *adj* [only before noun] **animal urges/instincts etc** human feelings, desires etc that are connected with sex, food, and other basic needs

**animal hus·band·ry** /ˌ··· '···/ *n* [U] farming that involves keeping animals and producing milk, meat etc

**animal rights** /ˌ··· '·/ *n* [U] the idea that people should treat animals well, and especially not use them in tests to develop medicines or other products: **animal rights protestor/campaigner** (=someone who tries to stop cruelty to animals)

**an·i·mate**[1] /'ænɪ̈mɪ̈t/ *adj* living: *animate beings* —opposite INANIMATE

**an·i·mate**[2] /'ænɪ̈meɪt/ *v* [T] to give life or energy to something: *Laughter animated his face for a moment.*

**an·i·ma·ted** /'ænɪ̈meɪtɪ̈d/ *adj* **1** showing a lot of interest and energy: *An animated discussion ensued.* **2 animated cartoon/film/programme** a film made by photographing a series of pictures, clay models etc —**animatedly** *adv*

**an·i·ma·tion** /ˌænɪ̈'meɪʃən/ *n* [U] **1** the process of making animated films **2** liveliness and excitement: *They were talking with animation.*

**an·i·ma·tor** /'ænɪ̈meɪtə‖-ər/ *n* [C] someone who makes animated films

**an·i·mis·m** /'ænɪ̈mɪzəm/ *n* [U] a religion in which animals and plants are believed to have spirits

**an·i·mos·i·ty** /ˌænɪ̈'mɒsɪ̈ti‖-'mɑː-/ *n* [C,U] strong dislike or hatred; HOSTILITY: *There is no personal animosity between the party leaders.*

**an·i·mus** /'ænɪ̈məs/ *n* [singular, U] *formal* a feeling of strong dislike or hatred; HOSTILITY

**an·i·seed** /'ænɪ̈siːd/ *n* [U] the seeds of a plant used in alcoholic drinks and in sweets

**an·kle** /'æŋkəl/ *n* [C] **1** the joint between your foot and your leg —see pictures at FOOT[1] **2 ankle socks/boots** socks or boots that only come up to your ankle

**an·klet** /'æŋklɪ̈t/ *n* [C] a ring or BRACELET worn around your ankle

**an·nals** /'ænlz/ *n* [plural] **1** an official record of events or activities: *the Annals of the Zoological Society* **2 in the annals of history/British politics etc** in the whole history of something: *one of the most disgraceful episodes in the annals of British politics*

**an·neal** /ə'niːl/ *v* [T] to make metal or glass hard by heating it and then slowly letting it get cold

**an·nex** /ə'neks‖ə'neks, 'æneks/ *v* [T] to take control of a country or area next to your own, especially by using force —**annexation** /ˌænek'seɪʃən/ *n* [C,U]

**an·nexe** *BrE*, **annex** *especially AmE* /'æneks/ *n* [C] a separate building that has been added to a larger one

**an·ni·hi·late** /ə'naɪəleɪt/ *v* [T] **1** to destroy something or someone completely: *stock piles of weapons that could annihilate mankind* **2** to defeat someone easily and completely in a game, competition, or election: *Tyson annihilated his opponent in the first round.* —**annihilation** /əˌnaɪə'leɪʃən/ *n* [U]

**an·ni·ver·sa·ry** /ˌænɪ̈'vɜːsəri‖-ɜːr-/ *n* [C] a date on which something special or important happened in a previous year: *our twentieth wedding anniversary*

**An·no Dom·i·ni** /ˌænəʊ 'dɒmɪ̈naɪ‖ˌænoʊ 'dɑː-/ *formal* AD

**an·no·tate** /ˈænəteɪt/ *v* [T] to add short notes to a book or piece of writing to explain parts of it: *an annotated edition of 'Othello'* —**annotation** /ˌænəˈteɪʃən/ *n* [C,U]

2 **an·nounce** /əˈnaʊns/ *v* [T] **1** to officially tell people
1 about a decision or something that will happen: *They announced their engagement in 'The Times'.* | **announce (that)** *A government spokesman announced that the hostages had been released.* **2** to say something in a loud or angry way: **announce (that)** *Winston suddenly announced that he was leaving.* | **announce a visitor/guest** (=say their name loudly, especially at a special event, so other people will know they have arrived) **3** to give information to people using a LOUDSPEAKER or MICROPHONE, especially at an airport or railway station: *announcing the arrival of Flight 207 from Minneapolis* **4** to introduce a programme on television or radio

3 **an·nounce·ment** /əˈnaʊnsmənt/ *n* **1** [C] an import-
3 ant or official statement: [+ **about**] *an important announcement about tax increases* | **announcement that** *We were shocked by the announcement that the mayor was resigning.* | **make an announcement** *Silence please, Mr Dacre has an announcement to make.* **2** [singular] the act of telling people something important is going to happen: *the announcement of the general strike* **3** [C] a small advertisement or statement in a newspaper: **birth/wedding/death announcement** *The wedding announcement appeared on the 16th of June.*

**an·nounc·er** /əˈnaʊnsə‖-ər/ *n* [C] someone who reads news or information on the television or radio

3 **an·noy** /əˈnɔɪ/ *v* [T] to make someone feel slightly angry and unhappy about something: *The way Tina orders us around really annoys me.* | *It annoyed him that the model didn't fit together properly.*

**an·noy·ance** /əˈnɔɪəns/ *n* **1** [U] a feeling of slight anger: *A look of annoyance crossed her face.* | **to your annoyance** *To his annoyance, he discovered they hadn't waited.* **2** [C] something that makes you slightly angry: *Alan found the constant noise of the traffic an annoyance.*

**an·noyed** /əˈnɔɪd/ *adj* slightly angry: *I'll be annoyed if we don't finish by eight.* | [+ **with**] *She was annoyed with Duncan for forgetting to phone.* | [+ **about/by**] *He was annoyed by her apparent indifference.* | **be annoyed that** *Mr Davies was annoyed that the books were missing.*

**an·noy·ing** /əˈnɔɪ-ɪŋ/ *adj* making you feel slightly angry: *an annoying habit of interrupting* | *The annoying thing is he's usually right.* | **it's annoying that** *It's annoying that we didn't know about this before.* —**annoyingly** *adv* | *annoyingly small portions*

2 **an·nu·al¹** /ˈænjuəl/ *adj* **1** happening once a year: *an*
2 *annual conference* **2** based on or calculated over a period of one year: *Steel output reached an annual figure of one million tons.* —**annually** *adv*

**annual²** *n* [C] **1** a plant that lives for one year or season —compare BIENNIAL(2), BIANNUAL **2** a book, especially for children, that is produced once a year with the same title but different stories, pictures etc

**annual meet·ing** /ˌ··· ˈ··/ *n* [C] a meeting held once a year by a club, business, or organization; AGM *BrE*

**an·nu·i·ty** /əˈnjuːəti‖əˈnuː-/ *n* [C] a fixed amount of money that is paid each year to someone, usually until they die

**an·nul** /əˈnʌl/ *v* **annulled, annulling** [T often passive] *technical* to state that a marriage or legal agreement no longer exists —**annulment** *n* [C,U]

**an·ode** /ˈænəʊd‖ˈænoʊd/ *n* [C] *technical* the part of a BATTERY (1) that collects ELECTRONS, often a wire or piece of metal with the sign (+) —compare CATHODE

**an·o·dyne¹** /ˈænədaɪn/ *adj* expressed in a way that is unlikely to offend anyone: *anodyne topics of conversation*

**anodyne²** *n* [C] **1** *technical* a medicine that reduces pain **2** *formal* an activity or thing that comforts people

**a·noint** /əˈnɔɪnt/ *v* [T] to put oil or water on someone's head or body during a religious ceremony —**anointment** *n* [C,U]

**a·nom·a·lous** /əˈnɒmələs‖əˈnɑː-/ *adj* different from what you expected to find: *clearly an anomalous result* —**anomalously** *adv*

**a·nom·a·ly** /əˈnɒməli‖əˈnɑː-/ *n* [C,U] *formal* a strange and unusual feature of a situation or process that often makes it unsatisfactory or unfair, or an example of this: *various anomalies in the tax system* | *a genetic anomaly*

**a·non¹** /əˈnɒn‖əˈnɑːn/ *adv literary* soon: *See you anon.* —see also **ever and anon** (EVER (9))

**anon²** written abbreviation of anonymous

**an·o·nym·i·ty** /ˌænəˈnɪməti/ *n* [U] **1** the state of not letting your name be known: *Every step will be taken to preserve your anonymity.* **2** the state of not having any unusual or interesting features: *the drab anonymity of the city* **3** the state of not showing who is involved in something: *the anonymity of a typed envelope*

**a·non·y·mous** /əˈnɒnəməs‖əˈnɑː-/ *adj* **1** unknown by name: *The benefactor wishes to remain anonymous.* **2** done, sent, or given by someone who does not want their name to be known: *an anonymous donation of £5,000* | **anonymous phone call/letter etc** (=often unpleasant or containing threats) **3** uninteresting features or qualities: *grey, anonymous housing estates* —**anonymity** *n* [U] —**anonymously** *adv*

**a·noph·e·les** /əˈnɒfəliːz‖əˈnɑː-/ *n* [C] a kind of MOSQUITO, especially the kind that spreads MALARIA

**an·o·rak** /ˈænəræk/ *n* [C] *especially BrE* a short coat with a HOOD(1) that keeps out the wind and rain —see picture at COAT¹

**an·o·rex·i·a** /ˌænəˈreksiə◂/ also **anorexia ner·vo·sa** /-nɜːˈvəʊsə‖-nɜːrˈvoʊ-/ *n* [U] a mental illness that makes people, especially young women, stop eating

**an·o·rex·ic** /ˌænəˈreksɪk◂/ *adj* suffering from or connected with anorexia —**anorexic** *n* [C]

**an·oth·er** /əˈnʌðə‖-ər/ *determiner, pron* **1** used to refer to one more person or thing of the same kind: *Can you pass me another mug?* | *I'm going to have another beer.* | *When you've eaten that, you can have another one.* | *"I can't find that pencil you've just given me." "Don't worry, here's another."* | [+ **of**] *Is this another of your schemes to make money?* | **yet another** *He has to go to yet another meeting.* (=he has already been to several) | **from one...to another** *We seem to struggle from one crisis to another.* | **one after another** (=used to talk about a series of similar things of events) *Small businesses have been collapsing one after another.* **2** a different person or thing or some other kind of person or thing: *If that doesn't work, you'll have to find another way of solving the problem.* | *You can press enter to select this value or type another choice (such as N).* | *We'll talk about that another time.* | **another of** *Another of the speakers suggested abandoning the project altogether.* | **... or another** (=used when you cannot be specific about what kind of things or people you mean) *All the kids in this class have learning difficulties of one sort or another.* | **that is another matter/ thing altogether** *You can try it, but whether it will work is another thing altogether.* (=it is likely that it will not work) **3** in addition to a particular amount, distance, period of time etc; FURTHER: *Let the soup simmer for another 10 minutes.* | *I let out another 50 feet of rope.* | *A room with a sea view will cost another £7.* **4 one another** used after a verb to show that two or more people or things do the same thing to each other: *They seem to love one another very much.* **5 another Chernobyl/another Pele etc** used when talking about a situation or person that reminds you of another famous situation or person, especially because they have extremely good or extremely bad qualities

**an·swer¹** /ˈɑːnsə‖ˈænsər/ *n*
**1 ▶ REPLY ◀** [C,U] something you say when you reply to a question that someone has asked you: *I asked Janine what she thought, but I'm still waiting for her answer.* | **give (sb) an answer** *You don't have to give them an answer straight away.* | **the answer is yes/no!** *spoken*: *If it's money you're after again, the answer is no!* | **in answer to** *In answer to your question, I think you can go.*
**2 ▶ TEST/COMPETITION ETC ◀** [C] something that you writes or say in reply to a question in a test, exercise, competition etc: *What was the answer to question 4?*

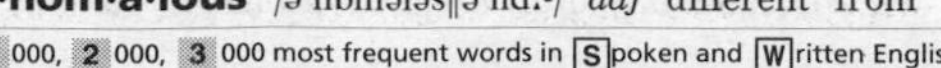

**3 ► INVITATION/LETTER ETC ◄** [C] a written reply to a letter, invitation, advertisement etc: *Did you ever get an answer to your letter?*
**4 ► PROBLEM ◄** [C] a way of dealing with a problem: *There are no easy answers to today's environmental problems.* | **be the answer to sb's problems/worries etc** *If he could get a job it'd be the answer to all his worries.*
**5 not get an answer** to not get a reply when you telephone someone or call at their house: *I tried calling him all day but couldn't get an answer.*
**6 sb's answer to** someone or something that is considered to be just as good as a more famous person or thing: *Britain's answer to the Eiffel Tower*

S1 W2 **answer**[2] *v*
**1 ► REPLY ◄ a)** [I,T] to say something to someone as a reply when they have asked you a question, made a suggestion etc: *I had to answer lots of questions about my childhood.* | **answer that** *When questioned, Hughes answered that he knew nothing about the robbery.* | **answer sb** *How much was it? Come on, answer me.* | *Julie stared at him for a long time before answering.* **b)** [T] to deal with someone's question in a satisfactory way: *You still haven't answered my question.*
**2 answer criticism/charges/accusations etc** to explain why you did something when people are criticizing you: *How do you answer the criticism that your government has done nothing to help the homeless?*
**3 ► TEST ◄** [I,T] to write or say the answer to a question in a test, exercise, competition etc: *Answer as many questions as possible in the time provided.*
**4 answer the phone/door/a call** to pick up the telephone when it rings or go to the door when someone calls
**5 ► LETTER ◄** [T,I] to send a reply to a letter, advertisement etc: *Simon got the job by answering an advertisement in the newspaper.*
**6 ► DO STH AS A REACTION ◄** [I,T] to do something as a reaction to criticism or attack: *The US answered by bombing North Vietnam.*
**7 ► DEAL WITH A PROBLEM ◄** [T] to be a way of dealing with or solving a problem: *"You can borrow my car if you like." "Well, that answers one problem."*
**8 answer a description** if someone answers a description, they match that description: *A man answering the police's description was seen entering the building.*
**9 answer a need** to provide something that is needed

**answer back** *phr v* [I,T] to reply in a rude way to someone that you are supposed to obey: **answer sb back** *Don't answer me back young man!*

**answer for** sth *phr v* [T] **1** to explain to people in authority why you did something wrong or why something happened, and be punished if necessary: *The teachers must answer for their students' disgusting behaviour on the school trip.* **2 have a lot to answer for** *informal* to be responsible for causing a lot of trouble: *That young man's got an awful lot to answer for.* **3 I can answer for him/her etc** *spoken* used to say that someone will definitely do something: *I'm sure John will help us – I can't really answer for the others.*

**answer to** sb/sth *phr v* [T] **1** to give an explanation to someone, especially about something that you have done wrong: *Phipps answers to me and me alone.* **2 answer to the name of a)** if a pet answers to a particular name, it comes when you call that name: *Their dog answers to the name of Fido.* **b)** to be called

**USAGE NOTE: ANSWER**

WORD CHOICE: **answer, reply, respond, give an answer, get back to**

**Answer** is the usual verb you use to talk about answering questions. **Reply** is used especially when you mention the actual words that were said: *I was so nervous I couldn't reply/answer.* | *"Not in the least", he replied.*

**Respond** is more formal and less common and often suggests that a criticism is being replied to: *So far, the travel agent hasn't responded to our complaint.*

If you give someone a piece of information they have asked for, such as a decision you have made, you **give them an answer**: *If we offer you the job, when could you give us an answer?*

If you think you can answer someone later but not at once, you say you will **get back to them**: *Sorry, I'll need to think about that and get back to you.*

GRAMMAR

You **answer** (*v*) a question, advertisement etc., not *to/at* it. Normally you **answer** a person too. If you **answer to** someone, they are the person directly responsible for you in an organization, at work etc, and you have to explain to them if anything goes wrong or if you are not doing something properly.

You give the **answer** (*n*) **to** a question or criticism, not *of* it. You get an **answer** (*n*) **from** someone, not *of* them.

**an·swer·a·ble** /ˈɑːnsərəbəl‖ˈæn-/ *adj* **1 be answerable to** to have to explain your actions to someone in authority: *I am answerable to the government for any decisions I make.* **2** a question that is answerable can be answered

**answering ma·chine** /ˈ··· ·ˌ·/ also **answerphone** *BrE n* [C] a machine that records your telephone calls when you cannot answer them

**ant** /ænt/ *n* [C] **1** a small insect that lives in large groups **2 have ants in your pants** *spoken* to be unable to sit or stand still

**-ant** /ənt/, **-ent** *suffix* [in nouns and adjectives] someone or something that does something: *a servant* (=someone who serves others) | *disinfectant* (=substance for killing germs) | *expectant* (=expecting) | *pleasant* (=pleasing)

**an·tag·o·nis·m** /ænˈtægənɪzəm/ *n* [U] **1** hatred between people or groups of people: *the great antagonism between Futurists and Cubists* **2** opposition to an idea, plan etc: [+ **to/towards**] *his obvious antagonism towards the press*

**an·tag·o·nist** /ænˈtægənɪ̈st/ *n* [C] your opponent in a competition, battle, quarrel etc —compare PROTAGONIST

**an·tag·o·nis·tic** /ənˌtægəˈnɪstɪk◂/ **1** unfriendly; wanting to argue or disagree: *an antagonistic attitude* **2** opposed to an idea or group: [+ **to/towards**] *antagonistic to new ideas* —**antagonistically** /-kli/ *adv*

**an·tag·o·nize** also **-ise** *BrE* /ænˈtægənaɪz/ *v* [T] to annoy someone very much by doing something that they do not like: *Do not do anything to antagonize your customers.*

**An·tarc·tic** /ænˈtɑːktɪk‖-ɑːr-/ *n* [singular] the very cold most southern part of the world

**An·tarc·tic Cir·cle** /·ˌ·· ˈ··/ *n* [singular] an imaginary line drawn around the world at a certain distance from the most southern point (the South Pole) compare ARCTIC CIRCLE —see picture at EARTH[1]

**ante-** /æntɪ/ *prefix* before: *to antedate* (=be earlier than something) | *ante-natal* (=before birth) —compare ANTI-, POST-, PRE-

**an·te**[1] /ˈænti/ *n* **up/raise the ante** to increase your demands or try to get more things from a situation, even though this involves more risks —see also PENNY ANTE

**ante**[2] *v*

**ante up** *phr v past tense* **anted** or **anteed, anteing** [I,T **ante up** sth] *AmE* to pay an amount of money, especially in a game of chance

**ant·eat·er** /ˈæntˌiːtə‖-ər/ *n* [C] an animal that has a very long nose and eats small insects

**an·te·ced·ent** /ˌæntɪ̈ˈsiːdənt/ *n* [C] **1** *formal* an event, organization, or thing that is similar to the one you have mentioned but existed earlier: *historical antecedents* **2 antecedents** [plural] *formal* the people in your family who lived a long time ago; ANCESTORS **3** *technical* a word, phrase, or sentence that is represented by another word, for example a PRONOUN —**antecendent** *adj*

**an·te·cham·ber** /ˈæntɪˌtʃeɪmbə‖-ər/ *n* [C] a small room connected to a larger room

**an·te·date** /ˈæntɪdeɪt, ˌæntɪˈdeɪt/ *v* [T] *formal* to come from an earlier time in history than something else: *It antedates the palace at Nineveh.*

**an·te·di·lu·vi·an** /ˌæntɪdɪˈluːviən◂/ *adj humorous* very old-fashioned; OUTDATED: *antediluvian ideas about women*

**an·te·lope** /ˈæntɪləʊp‖ˈæntəl-oʊp/ *n* [C] an animal with long horns that can run very fast and is very graceful

**an·te·na·tal** /ˌæntɪˈneɪtl◂/ *adj BrE* connected with the medical care given to women who are going to have a baby; PRENATAL *AmE*: *antenatal clinic* —compare POSTNATAL

**an·ten·na** /ænˈtenə/ *n* [C] **1** *plural* **antennae** /-niː/ one of two long thin parts on an insect's head, that it uses to feel things **2** *plural* **antennas** *especially AmE* a wire, ROD (1) etc used for receiving radio and television signals; AERIAL[2] *BrE* —see picture on page 409

**an·ter·i·or** /ænˈtɪəriə‖-ˈtɪriər/ *adj* [no comparative] **1** *technical* at or towards the front: *anterior vertebrae* **2** *formal* happening or existing before something else

**an·te·room** /ˈæntɪrʊm, -ruːm/ *n* [C] a small room that is connected to a larger room, especially where people wait to go into the larger room

**an·them** /ˈænθəm/ *n* [C] **1** a formal or religious song —see also NATIONAL ANTHEM **2** a song that a particular group of people consider to be very important: *The Rolling Stones' 'Satisfaction' became an anthem for a generation.*

**an·ther** /ˈænθə‖-ər/ *n* [C] *technical* the part of a male flower which contains POLLEN

**ant·hill** /ˈæntˌhɪl/ *n* [C] a place where ANTS live

**an·thol·o·gy** /ænˈθɒlədʒi‖ænˈθɑː-/ *n* [C] a set of stories, poems, songs etc by different people collected together in one book: *an anthology of American literature* —**anthologist** *n* [C]

**an·thra·cite** /ˈænθrəsaɪt/ *n* [U] a very hard type of coal that burns slowly and produces a lot of heat

**an·thrax** /ˈænθræks/ *n* [U] a serious disease of cattle and sheep

**anthropo-** /ænθrəpə, -pəʊ‖-pə, -poʊ/ *prefix technical* like or concerning human beings: *anthropomorphic* (=having human form or qualities)

**an·thro·poid** /ˈænθrəpɔɪd/ *adj* an anthropoid animal is very like a human —**anthropoid** *n* [C]

**an·thro·pol·o·gy** /ˌænθrəˈpɒlədʒi‖-ˈpɑː-/ *n* [U] the scientific study of people, their societies, CULTURES etc compare ETHNOLOGY, SOCIOLOGY —**anthropologist** *n* [U] —**anthropological** /ˌænθrəpəˈlɒdʒɪkəl◂‖-ˈlɑː-/ *adj*

**an·thro·po·mor·phis·m** /ˌænθrəpəˈmɔːfɪzəm‖-ɔːr-/ *n* [U] **1** the belief that animals or objects have the same feelings and qualities as humans **2** *technical* the belief that God can appear in a human or animal form —**anthropomorphic** *adj*

**anti-** /æntɪ‖æntɪ, æntaɪ/ *prefix* **1** opposed to; against: *antinuclear* (=opposing the use of atomic weapons and power) | *anti-American* **2** the opposite of something: *anticlimax* (=an unexciting ending instead of the expected CLIMAX[1] (1)) | *antimatter* (=material completely opposite in kind to the ordinary material in the universe) **3** acting to prevent something: *antifreeze* (=a liquid added to prevent freezing) | *antiseptic* (=to stop bacteria) —compare ANTE-, PRO-

**an·ti·air·craft** /ˌæntiˈeəkrɑːft‖-ˈerkræft/ *adj* [only before noun] antiaircraft weapons are used against enemy aircraft: *antiaircraft missiles*

**an·ti·bi·ot·ic** /ˌæntɪbaɪˈɒtɪk◂‖-ˈɑː-/ *n* [C usually plural] a drug that is used to kill BACTERIA and cure infections

**an·ti·bod·y** /ˈæntɪˌbɒdi‖-ˌbɑː-/ *n* [C] a substance produced by your body to fight disease

**an·tic·i·pate** /ænˈtɪsɪpeɪt/ *v* [T] **1** to expect that something will happen and be ready for it: *Organisers are anticipating a large crowd at the carnival.* | **anticipate that** *It is anticipated that next year interest rates will fall.* | **anticipate doing sth** *I didn't anticipate having to do the cooking myself!* **2** to think about something that is going to happen, especially something pleasant: *Daniel was eagerly anticipating her arrival.* **3** to do something before someone else: *Copernicus anticipated in part the discoveries of the 17th and 18th centuries.* **4** *formal* to use or consider something before you should —**anticipatory** /ænˌtɪsɪˈpeɪtəri‖ænˈtɪsəpətɔːri/ *adj* S3

**an·tic·i·pa·tion** /ænˌtɪsɪˈpeɪʃən/ *n* [U] the act of expecting something to happen: *They waited, filled with nervous anticipation.* | **in anticipation of** *The workers have called off their strike in anticipation of a pay offer.*

**an·ti·cler·i·cal** /ˌæntiˈklerɪkəl◂/ *adj* being opposed to priests having any political power or influence —**anticlericalism** *n* [U]

**an·ti·cli·max** /ˌæntɪˈklaɪmæks/ *n* [C,U] a situation or event that does not seem exciting because it happens after something that was much better: *Going back to work after a month travelling in China was bound to be an anticlimax.*

**an·ti·clock·wise** /ˌæntɪˈklɒkwaɪz◂‖-ˈklɑːk-/ *adv, adj BrE* moving in the opposite direction to the hands of a clock; COUNTERCLOCKWISE *AmE*: *Turn the lid anticlockwise* —opposite CLOCKWISE.

**an·tics** /ˈæntɪks/ *n* [plural] behaviour that seems strange, funny, silly, or annoying: *The public quickly grew tired of McEnroe's antics on court.*

**an·ti·cy·clone** /ˌæntɪˈsaɪkləʊn‖-kloʊn/ *n* [C] an area of high air pressure that causes calm weather in the place it is moving over —see also CYCLONE

**an·ti·de·pres·sant** /ˌæntidɪˈpresənt/ *n* [C,U] a drug used to treat DEPRESSION (=a mental illness that makes people very unhappy)

**an·ti·dote** /ˈæntɪdəʊt‖-doʊt/ *n* [C] **1** a substance that stops the effects of a poison: [+ **to**] *There is no known antidote to a bite from this snake.* **2** something that makes an unpleasant situation better: *Laughter, the antidote to stress.*

**an·ti·freeze** /ˈæntɪfriːz/ *n* [U] a substance that is put in the water in car engines to stop it from freezing

**an·ti·gen** /ˈæntɪdʒən/ *n* [C] *technical* a substance that makes the body produce antibodies (ANTIBODY)

**an·ti·her·o** /ˈæntɪˌhɪərəʊ‖-hɪroʊ/ *n* [C] a main character in a book, play, or film who is an ordinary or unpleasant person and lacks the qualities that you expect a hero to have

**an·ti·his·ta·mine** /ˌæntɪˈhɪstəmiːn, -mɪn/ *n* [C,U] a drug that is used to treat an ALLERGY (=an unpleasant reaction to particular foods, substances etc)

**an·ti·knock** /ˌæntɪˈnɒk‖-ˈnɑːk/ *n* [U] a chemical substance that is put in petrol to make car engines operate more smoothly

**anti-lock brak·ing sys·tem** /ˌ.. ˈ.. ˌ../ *n* [U] a piece of equipment that makes a vehicle easier to control when you have to stop very suddenly

**an·ti·ma·cas·sar** /ˌæntɪməˈkæsə‖-ər/ *n* [C] a piece of decorated cloth that is put on the back of a chair to protect it

**an·ti·mat·ter** /ˈæntiˌmætə‖-ər/ *n* [U] a form of MATTER (30) (=substance which the things in the universe are made of) consisting of antiparticles

**an·ti·par·ti·cle** /ˈæntiˌpɑːtɪkəl‖-ˌpɑːr-/ *n* [C] a very small part of an atom that has the opposite electrical charge to the one usually found in atoms

**an·ti·pas·to** /ˈæntipæstəʊ‖ˌæntiˈpɑːstoʊ/ *n* [U] an Italian dish consisting of cold food that you eat before the main part of a meal

**an·ti·pa·thet·ic** /ˌæntɪpəˈθetɪk◂/ *adj* [+ **to**] *formal* having a very strong feeling of disliking or opposing someone or something

**an·tip·a·thy** /ænˈtɪpəθi/ *n* [U + **to/towards**] *formal* strong dislike or opposition towards someone or something: *a strong personal antipathy towards Nixon*

**anti-per·son·nel** /ˌ·· ··ˈ·/ *adj* an anti-personnel weapon is designed to hurt people rather than damage buildings, vehicles etc

**anti-per·spi·rant** /ˌ·· ˈ··/ *n* [U] a substance that prevents you sweating (SWEAT[1] (1))

**An·tip·o·des** /ænˈtɪpədiːz/ *n* **the Antipodes** *often humorous* Australia and New Zealand —**Antipodean** /ænˌtɪpəˈdiːən/ *adj*: *antipodean culture*

**an·ti·quar·i·an** /ˌæntəˈkweəriən◂‖-ˈkwer-/ *adj* [only before noun] an antiquarian bookshop sells old books

**an·ti·quat·ed** /ˈæntəkweɪtəd/ *adj* old-fashioned and not suitable for modern needs or conditions; OUTDATED (1): *antiquated laws*

**an·tique[1]** /ænˈtiːk/ *adj* **1** antique furniture, jewellery etc is old and often valuable: *an antique rosewood desk* **2** *formal* connected with ancient times, especially ancient Rome or Greece

**antique[2]** *n* [C] a piece of furniture, jewellery etc that was made a very long time ago and is therefore valuable: *The palace is full of priceless antiques.* | *an antique dealer*

**an·tiq·ui·ty** /ænˈtɪkwəti/ *n* **1** [U] ancient times: *a tradition that stretches back into antiquity* **2** [U] the state of being very old: *a building of great antiquity* **3** [C usually plural] a building or object made in ancient times: *a collection of Roman antiquities*

**an·tir·rhi·num** /ˌæntəˈraɪnəm/ *n* [C] a garden plant with white, red, or yellow flowers; a SNAPDRAGON

**anti-Se·mite** /ˌænti ˈsiːmaɪt‖-ˈsem-/ *n* [C] someone who hates Jewish people —**anti-Semitic** /ˌænti səˈmɪtɪk◂/ *adj*

**anti-Sem·i·tis·m** /ˌæntɪ ˈseməˌtɪzəm/ *n* [U] hatred of Jewish people

**an·ti·sep·tic[1]** /ˌæntəˈseptɪk◂/ *n* [C] a chemical substance that helps stop a wound becoming infected

**antiseptic[2]** *adj* **1** helping to prevent infection: *antiseptic cream* **2** lacking emotion, interest, or excitement: *dreary antiseptic prose*

**anti-so·cial** /ˌ·· ˈ··◂/ *adj* **1** unwilling to meet people and talk to them, especially in a way that seems unfriendly or rude: *a child who was aggressive and anti-social* **2** an activity that is anti-social does not give you the chance to meet other people: *The job's OK, but I have to work very anti-social hours.* **3** anti-social behaviour shows a lack of concern for other people: *Smoking cigarettes in public is increasingly considered anti-social.*

**anti-tank** /ˌ·· ˈ·◂/ *adj* an anti-tank weapon is designed to destroy enemy tanks (TANK[1] (3))

**an·tith·e·sis** /ænˈtɪθəsəs/ *n* [C usually singular] *formal* the exact opposite of something: *Connie's political views are the complete antithesis of mine.*

**an·ti·thet·i·cal** /ˌæntəˈθetɪkəl/ also **an·ti·thet·ic** /-ˈθetɪk◂/ *adj formal* exactly opposite to something: [+ **to**] *completely antithetical to democratic ideals*

**an·ti·tox·in** /ˌæntiˈtɒksən‖-ˈtɑːk-/ *n* a substance produced by your body or put in a medicine to stop the effects of a poison

**anti trust law** /ˌ·· ˈ· ˌ·/ *n* [C,U] *technical* an American law intended to prevent companies unfairly controlling prices

**ant·ler** /ˈæntlə‖-ər/ *n* [C] one of the two horns of a male DEER

**an·to·nym** /ˈæntənɪm/ *n* [C] a word that means the opposite to another word: *'Good' is the antonym of 'bad'.* —compare SYNONYM —**antonymous** /ænˈtɒnəməs‖-ˈtɑː-/ *adj*

**a·nus** /ˈeɪnəs/ *n* [C usually singular] the hole in your body through which solid waste leaves your BOWELS —see picture at DIGESTIVE SYSTEM

**an·vil** /ˈænvəl/ *n* [C] a heavy iron block on which pieces of metal are shaped using a hammer

S3 W3 **anx·i·e·ty** /æŋˈzaɪəti/ *n* **1** [C,U] the feeling of being very worried about something that may happen or may have happened, so that you think about it all the time: [+ **about/over**] *anxiety among staff about job losses* | *an anxiety attack* **2** [C] something that makes you worry: *the anxieties of parenthood* **3** [U] a feeling of wanting to do something very much but being worried that you will not succeed: **anxiety to do sth** *a natural anxiety to please one's parents*

**anx·ious** /ˈæŋkʃəs/ *adj* **1** very worried about something that may happen or may have happened so that you think about it all the time: [+ **about**] *Helen is anxious about travelling on her own.* | *"Feeling scared, Joe?" "No, just a little anxious."* | **anxious look/expression etc** *an anxious glance at the fuel gauge* | **anxious that** *anxious that it might be cancer* **2** an anxious time or situation is one in which you feel nervous or worried: *an anxious couple of weeks waiting for the test results* **3** feeling strongly that you want to do something or want something to happen: **anxious to do sth** *Peggy is anxious to show that she can cope with extra responsibility.* —**anxiously** *adv*: *waiting anxiously by the phone* —see NERVOUS (USAGE)

S W **an·y[1]** /ˈeni/ *determiner, pron* **1** used to refer to each one or all members of a group, saying it does not matter which: *Any child who attempts to escape is beaten.* | *You can obtain a valuation from any accredited insurance valuer.* | *Any plan chosen should take these factors into account.* | *before you sign any written agreement* | *These tiles are an ideal choice for any bathroom setting.* | **any of** *before touching the computer or any of it's parts* | *Do any of you remember?* | **any other** *Are there any other comments?* **2** used especially in questions or as part of a negative statement to mean some or even the smallest amount: *Few of the students had any knowledge of classical music.* | *I didn't pay any attention to what he said.* | *She promised not to take any chances.* | *He had no friends and didn't deserve any.* | **I haven't any idea** (=I do not know at all) | **any of** *I don't understand what any of this stuff means.* | **any use** *I tried, but it wasn't any use.* (=it was not successful) | **if any** *I don't suppose there will be more than a dozen left, if any.* (=it is likely that there will be none at all) | **in any way** *He was not in any way upset by his wife's decision.* | *If I can help you in any way, let me know.* **3** as much as possible; all: *They're going to need any help they can get* **4** **in any case/at any rate** **a)** no matter what may happen; at least: *There was nothing else to be done. At any rate, I had learnt something.* **b)** besides; also: *In any case, he was a rude old man.* **5** **just any** used to refer to something that is ordinary and not special: *You can't wear just any old clothes to that sort of place, you have to dress up.* **6** **any old how** in any way: *Just pack them in any old how.*

S **any[2]** *adv* **1** used especially in negative statements to mean in the least; at all: *It can't make it any worse, can it?* | *I'm not any better than you.* | *I can't walk any further.* | *The boy could not stand it any longer.* **2** *AmE spoken* used to mean 'at all' at the end of a sentence: *We tried talking to him but that didn't help any.* —compare EITHER, NEITHER.

**an·y·bod·y** /ˈeniˌbɒdi, ˈenibədi‖-ˌbɑːdi/ *pron* any person or all people; anyone

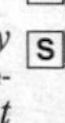

**an·y·how** /ˈenihaʊ/ *adv* **1** [sentence adverb] *especially spoken* used to say that someone does something or something happens in spite of something else: *It was felt that the scandal would damage her reputation but the press reported it anyhow.* **2** in a careless or untidy way: *The cupboard would hardly close, with all the shoes thrown in anyhow.* | **any old how** (=in a very careless way) *The books were arranged any old how on the shelves.* **3** [sentence adverb] *especially spoken* used to add information that limits what has been mentioned before, makes it seem less important etc: *I've never been to a circus, not recently anyhow.* **4** [sentence adverb] *especially spoken* **a)** used when you want to return to the main subject of the conversation: *So anyhow, as I was saying, when I arrived Tom was already there.* **b)** used when you have not included some details in a story and you are saying what the final result was: *Anyhow, when the doctor came he said there was nothing wrong with me.* **5** *AmE spoken* used to mean 'anyway' in spoken American English: *Martin's not feeling too well but he's going to come over anyhow.* | *Anyhow the car finally came out of the garage in a worse state than when it went it.* | *Anyhow, what difference does it make what I think?* | *Why are you calling anyhow?* —see also ANYWAY

**anymore** /ˌeniˈmɔː‖-ˈmɔːr/ *adv* **not ... anymore** not any longer: *Nick doesn't live here anymore.* | *They used to laugh at Sheila. Not anymore.*

**an·y·one** /ˈeniwʌn/ *pron* **1** any person in a group or in the world, when it is not important to say exactly who:

*Anyone can cook risotto – it's easy!* | *He's cleverer than anyone I know.* | **anyone tall/rich etc** *Anyone stupid enough to believe that deserves everything they get!* | **anyone else** (=a different person) *Anyone else would have been too embarrassed, but he walked right up and asked for her autograph.* **2** used in questions and negatives to mean a person: *Is anyone listening to me?* | *If anyone sees Lisa, ask her to call me.* | **anyone interesting/rich etc** *Anyone new coming to tonight's meeting?* | **anyone else** (=a different person) *Do you know anyone else who wants a ticket?* —see also EVERYONE, SOMEONE

**an·y·place** /ˈenipleɪs/ *adv AmE* anywhere: *It's funny, I've never felt anyplace was home before I came to Connecticut.*

S1 W1 **an·y·thing** /ˈeniθɪŋ/ *pron* **1** any thing, event, situation etc, when it does not matter exactly which: *Anything will do to wedge the door open.* | *If you believe that, you'll believe anything!* | *OK, you can borrow the car – anything for a quiet life.* | **anything red/cheap etc** *She'll buy anything reduced in a sale.* | **anything else** (=any different thing) *It's got to be Dior – anything else just isn't good enough.* **2** used in questions, negatives, and statements expressing possibility to mean 'nothing' or 'something': *You can't believe anything she says.* | *Have you heard anything about the new Garrison Keillor book?* | **anything to say/to do etc** *It was a great health farm but there wasn't really anything to do in the evenings.* | **anything new/stupid etc** *We've almost sealed the deal, so don't do anything stupid.* | **anything else** (=any other thing, event etc) *Would you like anything else to eat?* **3 anything but clear/happy etc** used to emphasize that someone or something is not clear, happy etc: *The bridge is anything but safe.* | *We'd been warned he was a frail, withdrawn man but when I met him he was anything but.* —see also SOME

Frequencies of the word **anything** in spoken and written English.

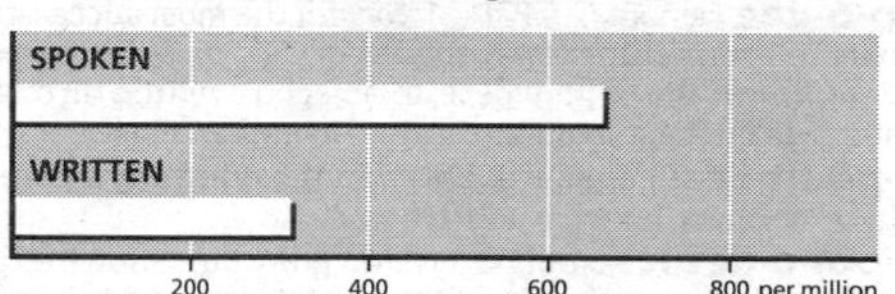


Based on the British National Corpus and the Longman Lancaster Corpus

This graph shows that the word **anything** is more common in spoken English than in written English. This is because it is used a lot in questions, and is used in some common spoken phrases.

**4 anything like** similar in any way to something or someone else: *Does she look anything like her mother?* **5 not anything like/near** *spoken* used to emphasize that someone or something is not in a particular condition or state: *We don't have anything like enough money to buy a new car.* **6 as easy/fast etc as anything** extremely easy, fast etc: *It was a long lecture and as boring as anything.* **7 or anything** or something that is similar: *Would you like a gin and tonic or anything?* **8 for anything** if you will not do something for anything, you will definitely not do it: *After what happened last time, I wouldn't work for them again for anything.* **9 like anything** if you do something like anything, you do it a lot or to a great degree: *Tom only left last week and I already miss him like anything.* **10 anything you say** used to tell someone you agree with what they suggest when actually you do not *"You ought to keep the flat more tidy." "Anything you say."*

S1 W2 **an·y·way** /ˈeniweɪ/ *adv* [sentence adverb] **1** used to say that someone does something or that something happens in spite of a problem: *He said he didn't know much about computers but that he'd try and help us anyway.*

Frequencies of the adverb **anyway** in spoken and written English.

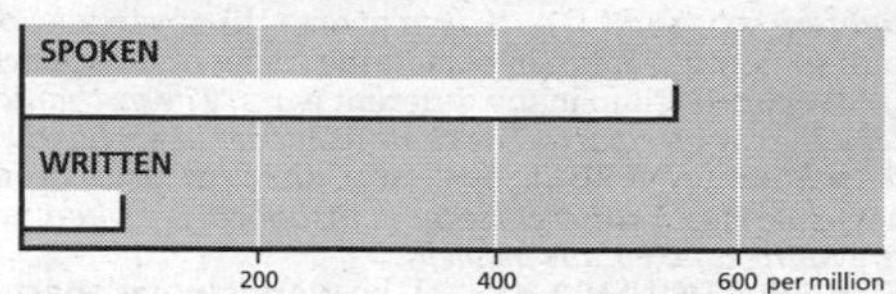


Based on the British National Corpus and the Longman Lancaster Corpus

This graph shows that the adverb **anyway** is much more common in spoken English than in written English. This is because it has some special uses in spoken English.

**2** used when you are changing the subject of a conversation or returning to a previous subject: *Anyway, what was I saying?* **3** used when you want to finish saying something or continue without all the details: *Anyway, I must be going now.* | *Anyway, after three months at the clinic, she'd made a full recovery.* **4** used to add some extra information, an opinion or a question to something that you have just said: *Sam didn't get the job; but he's not worried because it didn't pay well anyway.* | *It was nice of you to offer anyway.* **5** used to find out the real reason for something: *So anyway, what were you doing in the park at two in the morning?* | *Why did he visit Alan anyway?*

**an·y·where** /ˈeniweə||-wer/ also **anyplace** *AmE adv* S1 W3 **1** in or to any place: *Sit anywhere, there are plenty of seats.* | *Tropical fruit used to be hard to find in Britain but now you can buy it anywhere.* | [+ **in**] *Apparently that restaurant does the best curry anywhere in London.* | **anywhere else** (=in or to a different place) *Anywhere else you'd have to pay airport tax but not when you visit this Pacific island.* **2** used in questions, negatives, and statements expressing possibility to mean 'somewhere' or 'nowhere': *I can't find it anywhere. Are you sure you left it here?* | *Do they need anywhere to stay for the night?* | *Would you like a ride anywhere?* | **anywhere interesting/cheap etc** *Did you go anywhere exotic on vacation this year?* | **anywhere else** *The photos are great – have you been anywhere else in Mexico?* **3 not anywhere near a)** used to emphasize that someone or something is not near to another person or thing: *What do you mean it was my fault? My car wasn't anywhere near yours.* **b)** used to emphasize that someone or something is not in a particular condition or state: *The money doesn't come anywhere near compensating for what those people suffered.* **4 anywhere between one and ten/anywhere from one to ten etc** used to mean any age, number, amount etc between one and ten when it is difficult to know exactly which age, number etc: *She was one of those women who could be anywhere between forty five and sixty years of age.* **5 it won't get you anywhere** used to tell someone that they will not be able to change a situation: *You can try writing to complain, but I don't think it will get you anywhere.* **6 not getting/going anywhere** not successful or not having plans for the future: *Terry's a nice enough lad but he's not going anywhere.* —see PLACE[1] (USAGE)

**AOB** /ˌeɪ əʊ ˈbiː||-oʊ-/ *BrE* the abbreviation of 'any other business'; things that have not yet been discussed in the main part of a meeting

**a·or·ta** /eɪˈɔːtə||-ˈɔːr-/ *n* [C] the largest ARTERY (=tube for carrying blood) in the body, taking blood from the heart

**a·pace** /əˈpeɪs/ *adv literary* quickly: *Multimedia developments continue apace.*

**a·part** /əˈpɑːt||-ɑːrt/ *adv, adj* S3 W1
**1 ▶ DISTANCE ◀** if things are apart, they have an amount of space between them: *Joel stood apart from the group, frowning.* | **two miles/six feet etc apart** *The two villages are 6 kilometres apart.*
**2 ▶ TIME ◀ two hours/six weeks etc apart** if things are a particular time apart, they have that much time between them: *Our birthdays are exactly a month apart.*

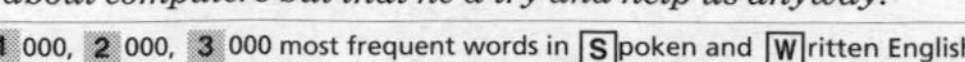

3 **▶ SEPARATE ◀** **a)** if you keep, pull, force etc two things apart, you separate them: *I try to keep my work and private life as far apart as possible.* | *The two boys started fighting so we had to pull them apart.* **b)** if you take or pull something apart, or something comes or falls apart, it is separated into many different parts: *The mechanics took the engine apart.* | *The chair fell apart in my hands.*
4 **▶ SOMEWHERE ELSE ◀** in a different place from someone else: *You never see the twins apart.* | *My wife and I are living apart at the moment.*
5 **▶ RELATIONSHIP ◀** **a) be worlds/poles apart** if people, beliefs, or ideas are worlds or poles apart, they are completely different from each other **b) grow/drift apart** if people or groups grow apart, their relationship slowly ends: *Sadly, the family has grown apart since Auntie Barbara died.*
6 **▶ CONDITION ◀** if something is coming apart or falling apart etc, it is in a very bad condition: *I must get some new trousers; these are all coming apart.* | *Well, the relationship's fallen apart, to be honest.*
7 **joking apart** used to say that you want to consider something seriously: *Joking apart, we must do something about that hole.*
8 **quite apart from** without even considering: *Quite apart from the cost, there's the question of your health to be considered.*
9 **apart from** also **aside from** *especially AmE* **a)** used to introduce one small point which makes a statement not completely true: *This essay's good apart from a couple of spelling mistakes.* **b)** except for: *Apart from the occasional visit, what does Alan do for his kids?*

**a·part·heid** /əˈpɑːtheɪt, -teɪt, -taɪt, -taɪd‖-ɑːr-/ *n* [U] the former South African political and social system in which only white people had full political rights and people of other races, especially black people, were forced to go to separate schools, live in separate areas etc

S2 W3 **a·part·ment** /əˈpɑːtmənt‖-ɑːr-/ *n* [C] **1** *especially AmE* a set of rooms within a larger building, usually on one level, where someone lives; FLAT² (1) *BrE*: *How many bedrooms do you have in your new apartment?* **2** [usually plural] a large room with expensive furniture, decorations etc, used especially by an important person such as a president, prince etc: *the presidential apartments* —see graph at FLAT²

**apartment block** /-ˈ·· ·/ *n* [C] *AmE* a large group of buildings containing many apartments —see picture on page 410

**apartment build·ing** /-ˈ·· ˌ··/ also **apartment house** /-ˈ·· ·/ *n* [C] *AmE* a large building containing many apartments

**ap·a·thet·ic** /ˌæpəˈθetɪk◂/ *adj* not excited about something and not caring whether it happens, or not interested in anything and unwilling to make an effort to change and improve things: *an apathetic electorate* —**apathetically** /-kli/ *adv*

**ap·a·thy** /ˈæpəθi/ *n* [U] the feeling of not being interested or not caring, either about a particular thing or about life: *apathy among the public*

**ape¹** /eɪp/ *n* [C] **1** a large monkey without a tail, or with a very short tail, such as a GORILLA or a CHIMPANZEE **2** an insulting word for a man who behaves in a stupid or annoying way: *Push off you big ape.* **3 go ape** *slang* to suddenly become very angry or excited

**ape²** *v* [T] to copy someone's behaviour, especially in a silly or unkind way

**a·per·i·tif** /əˌperɪ̣ˈtiːf/ *n* [C] an alcoholic drink that is drunk before a meal

**ap·er·ture** /ˈæpətʃə‖ˈæpərtʃʊr/ *n* [C] **1** the hole at the front of a camera or TELESCOPE¹, which can be changed to let more or less light in **2** *technical* a small hole or space in something which is used for a particular purpose: *an inspection aperture*

**ape·shit** /ˈeɪpʃɪt/ *adj* **go apeshit** *slang* to suddenly become very angry or excited

**a·pex** /ˈeɪpeks/ *n* [C] **1** *technical* the top or highest part of something: *the apex of the triangle* **2** *formal* the most successful part: *the apex of his career*

**a·phid** /ˈeɪfɪ̣d, ˈæfɪ̣d/ *n* [C] a type of very small insect that drinks the juices of plants

**aph·o·ris·m** /ˈæfərɪzəm/ *n* [C] a short wise phrase —**aphoristic** /ˌæfəˈrɪstɪk◂/ *adj*

**aph·ro·dis·i·ac** /ˌæfrəˈdɪziæk◂/ *n* [C] a food, drink, or drug that makes you want to have sex —**aphrodisiac** *adj*: *the aphrodisiac properties of the fruit*

**a·pi·a·ry** /ˈeɪpiəri‖ˈeɪpieri/ *n* [C] a place where BEES are kept

**a·piece** /əˈpiːs/ *adv* [only after number or noun] costing or having a particular amount each: **ten pence/fifteen dollars etc apiece** *The tomato plants cost 60p apiece.* | **three pages/a ticket etc apiece** (=having three pages etc each) *We shared the gold out equally – three bags apiece.*

**a·plen·ty** /əˈplenti/ *adj* [only after noun] *old use* in large amounts or numbers, especially more than you need: *There was food aplenty.*

**a·plomb** /əˈplɒm‖əˈplɑːm/ *n* [U] **with aplomb** in a confident and skilful way, especially when you have to deal with difficult problems or a difficult situation: *Ms Sharpe handled their hostile questions with great aplomb.*

**a·poc·a·lypse** /əˈpɒkəlɪps‖əˈpɑː-/ *n* [C] **1 the apocalypse** the destruction and end of the world **2** a dangerous, frightening, and very serious situation causing death, harm, or destruction: *3000 died in the apocalypse of the earthquake.*

**a·poc·a·lyp·tic** /əˌpɒkəˈlɪptɪk◂‖əˌpɑː-/ *adj* **1** warning people about terrible events that will happen in the future: *Orwell's apocalyptic vision of the future* **2** connected with the final destruction and end of the world

**a·poc·ry·phal** /əˈpɒkrɪ̣fəl‖əˈpɑː-/ *adj* an apocryphal story about a famous person or event is well-known but probably not true: *Washington's apocryphal phrase: "Father, I cannot tell a lie."*

**ap·o·gee** /ˈæpədʒiː/ *n* [C] **1** *formal* the most successful part of something: *the apogee of his political career* **2** *technical* the point where an object travelling through space is farthest from the earth —compare PERIGEE

**a·po·lit·i·cal** /ˌeɪpəˈlɪtɪkəl◂/ *adj* not having any interest in or connection with politics

**a·pol·o·get·ic** /əˌpɒləˈdʒetɪk◂‖əˌpɑː-/ *adj* showing or saying that you are sorry that something has happened, especially because you feel guilty or embarrassed about it: *The restaurant manager was very apologetic and said we could have our meal for free.* | *an apologetic letter* —**apologetically** /-kli/ *adv*: *"I know," she said apologetically.*

**ap·o·lo·gi·a** /ˌæpəˈləʊdʒiə, -dʒə‖-ˈloʊ-/ *n* [C + **for**] *formal* a statement in which you defend an idea that you believe in

**a·pol·o·gist** /əˈpɒlədʒɪ̣st‖əˈpɑː-/ *n* [C] someone who tries to defend and explain an idea or system: *one of Stalin's western apologists*

**a·pol·o·gize** also **-ise** *BrE* /əˈpɒlədʒaɪz‖əˈpɑː-/ *v* [I] to tell someone that you are sorry that you have done something wrong: *That was an awful thing to say, I think you should apologize.* | [+ **for**] *I must apologise for the delay in replying to your letter.* | **apologize to** *The US has apologized to Britain for the accident.* | **apologize profusely** (=apologize a lot) *She apologized profusely for being late.* S2

**a·pol·o·gy** /əˈpɒlədʒi‖əˈpɑː-/ *n* [C] **1** something that you say or write to show that you are sorry for doing something wrong: *Your behaviour was outrageous. I demand an apology!* | **accept sb's apology** (=forgive them after they have apologized) *Please accept our sincere apologies.* | **owe sb an apology** (=to have done something bad or unfair to someone) *I owe you an apology for what I said last night – I'm really sorry.* | **make an apology** *The paper was forced to make a grovelling apology.* **2** *literary* a statement in which you defend something you believe in after it has been criticized by other people **3 an apology for** *humorous* a very bad example of something: *an apology for a human being* S3

**ap·o·plec·tic** /ˌæpəˈplektɪk◂/ *adj* **1** *informal* so angry or excited that your face becomes red: *The colonel was apoplectic with rage.* **2** connected with apoplexy

**ap·o·plex·y** /ˈæpəpleksi/ *n* [U] *old-fashioned* an illness caused by a problem in your brain which can damage your ability to move, feel, or think; STROKE[1] (1)

**a·pos·ta·sy** /əˈpɒstəsi‖əˈpɑː-/ *n* [U] *formal* the act of changing your beliefs so that you stop supporting a religion, political party etc

**a·pos·tate** /əˈpɒsteɪt, -stət‖əˈpɑː-/ *n* [C] *formal* someone who has stopped believing in and supporting their old religion or political party

**a pos·ter·i·o·ri** /ˌeɪ pɒsteriˈɔːraɪ, ˌɑː pɒsteriˈɔːri‖ˌɑː poʊstɪriˈɔːri, ˌeɪ pɑː-/ *adj Latin formal* using facts or results to form a judgment about what must have happened before —compare A PRIORI

**a·pos·tle** /əˈpɒsəl‖əˈpɑː-/ *n* [C] **1** one of the 12 people chosen by Christ to teach and spread the Christian religion **2** *formal* someone who believes strongly in a new idea and tries to persuade other people: [+ **of**] *an apostle of revolutionary ideals*

**ap·o·stol·ic** /ˌæpəˈstɒlɪk◂‖-ˈstɑː-/ *adj* **1** connected with the POPE (=leader of the Catholic church) **2** connected with one of Christ's 12 apostles

**a·pos·tro·phe** /əˈpɒstrəfi‖əˈpɑː-/ *n* [C] **a)** the sign (') used in writing to show that numbers or letters have been left out, as in 'don't' (=do not) and '86 (=1986) **b)** the same sign used before 's' to show that something belongs to someone or something, or is connected with them, as in 'John's book', or 'Charles' mother', or 'Nixon's last year as president' **c)** used before 's' to show the plural of letters and numbers as in 'Your r's look like v's.'

**a·poth·e·ca·ry** /əˈpɒθəkəri‖əˈpɑːθəkeri/ *n* [C] someone who mixed and sold medicines in former times

**a·poth·e·o·sis** /əˌpɒθiˈəʊsəs‖əˌpɑːθiˈoʊ-, ˌæpəˈθiːəsəs/ *n plural* **apotheoses** /-siːz/ [C usually singular] *formal* **1** the best and most perfect example of something: [+ **of**] *the apotheosis of French 16th century art* **2** the state of getting to the highest level of something such as honour, importance etc

**ap·pal** *BrE*, **appall** *AmE* /əˈpɔːl‖əˈpɒːl/ *v* [T] to shock someone by being very bad or unpleasant: *The whole idea of killing animals for fur appals me.*

**ap·palled** /əˈpɔːld‖əˈpɒːld/ *adj* very shocked by something very bad or unpleasant: [+ **by/at**] *Rescue workers were appalled at what they saw.*

**ap·pal·ling** /əˈpɔːlɪŋ‖əˈpɒː-/ *adj* **1** so bad or unpleasant that you are shocked: *We heard the appalling news about the earthquake.* **2** very bad: *Morrisson's last album was absolutely appalling.* —**appallingly** *adv*: *You've behaved apallingly.*|*appallingly bad taste*

**ap·pa·loo·sa** /ˌæpəˈluːsə/ *n* [C] *AmE* a kind of horse that is pale coloured with dark spots

**ap·par·at·chik** /ˌɑːpəˈrɑːtʃɪk/ *n* [C] an official working for a government or other organization who obeys orders without thinking

**ap·pa·ra·tus** /ˌæpəˈreɪtəs‖-ˈræ-/ *n plural* **apparatuses** or **apparatus** [C,U] **1** tools and machines used especially for scientific, medical, and technical purposes: *the apparatus shown in the diagram*|*The astronauts have special breathing apparatus.* **2** a system or process for doing something: *the apparatus for settling industrial disputes*

**ap·par·el**[1] /əˈpærəl/ *n* [U] **1** *formal* clothes, especially clothes worn on a special occasion: *the Queen's ceremonial apparel* **2 ladies'/men's/children's apparel** *especially AmE* a word for clothes, often used in shops

**apparel**[2] *v* [T + **in**] *old use* to dress someone, especially in special clothes

W2 **ap·par·ent** /əˈpærənt/ *adj* **1** easily noticed or understood: [+ **to**] *Her anxiety was apparent to everyone.*|**it became apparent that** *It soon became apparent that our opponents were too strong for us.*|**for no apparent reason** (=without a clear reason) *Suddenly, for no apparent reason, he walked away.* **2** seeming to have a particular quality, feeling, or attitude: *I was shocked by Joe's apparent lack of concern for his child.*

**ap·par·ent·ly** /əˈpærəntli/ *adv* **1** [sentence adverb] based on what you have heard is true, although you are not completely sure about it: *Apparently they've run out of tickets for the concert.*|*I wasn't there, but apparently it was a good party.* **2** according to the way someone looks or a situation appears, although you cannot be sure: *She managed to climb out of the car, apparently unhurt.* —compare EVIDENTLY, OBVIOUSLY S1 W2

**ap·pa·ri·tion** /ˌæpəˈrɪʃən/ *n* [C] something that you imagine you can see, especially the spirit of a dead person: *a ghostly apparition*

**ap·peal**[1] /əˈpiːl/ *n* **1** [C] an urgent request for something important such as money or help, especially to help someone in a bad situation: [+ **for**] *The United Nations' appeal for a ceasefire has been largely ignored by both sides.*|**appeal to sb to do sth** *an appeal to parents to supervise their children*|**make/launch an appeal** *In 1988 Bob Geldorf launched an urgent appeal for the famine victims.* **2** [U] a quality that makes you like someone or something, be interested in them, or want them: *Much of Corfu's appeal lies in its lively night life.*|[+ **for**] *The film has great appeal for young audiences.*|**popular/wide appeal** (=liked by many people) *CD-ROMs now have wider popular appeal.*|**sex appeal** (=the quality of being sexually attractive) *Marilyn Monroe had amazing sex appeal.* **3** [C,U] a formal request to a court or to someone in authority asking for a decision to be changed: [+ **to**] *an appeal to the European court of Human Rights* —see also COURT OF APPEAL S2 W1

**appeal**[2] *v* **1** [I] to make a serious public request for help, money, information etc: **appeal (to sb) for sth** *The police are appealing to the public for information about the crime.*|*The Bosnian government appealed for help from Western countries.*|**appeal to sb to do sth** *She appealed to the kidnappers to release her son.* **2 appeal to sb** if someone or something appeals to you, they seem attractive and interesting: *Does the idea of working abroad appeal to you?*|*The magazine is intended to appeal to working women in their 20s and 30s.* **3** [I,T] to make a formal request to a court or someone in authority asking for a decision to be changed: *If you are not satisfied, you can appeal.* **4 appeal to sb's better nature/sense of honour/sense of justice etc** to try to persuade someone to do something by reminding them that it is a good, honourable etc thing to do S3 W3

**Appeal Court** /ˈ·ˈ· ·/ *n* [singular] the COURT OF APPEAL

**ap·peal·ing** /əˈpiːlɪŋ/ *adj* **1** attractive or interesting: **find sb/sth appealing** *I find the idea of $100,000 dollars a year very appealing.*|*She does look rather appealing in that dress.* **2 appealing look/voice etc** a look etc that shows that someone wants help or sympathy: *I said I didn't know anything about computers and gave him an appealing look.* —**appealingly** *adv*

**ap·pear** /əˈpɪə‖əˈpɪr/ *v* S1 W1

**1** ► **SEEM** ◄ [linking verb, not in progressive] a word used especially in formal or written English meaning to seem: **appear upset/calm etc** *Roger appeared very upset.*|*The city appeared calm after the previous night's fighting.*|**appear to be** *There appeared to be no significant difference between the two groups in the test.*|**appear to do sth** *The man appeared to have had a heart attack.*|**it appears that** *It appears that there has been a change in the plans.*|**what appears to be** (=something that looks like) *Police have found what appear to be human remains.*|**make it appear that** *She put the gun next to the body, to make it appear that the victim had shot himself.*|**so it would appear** (=used to say that it seems likely that something is true, although you are not completely sure) *"The boys are completely innocent?" "So it would appear from the press reports."*

**2** ► **START TO BE SEEN** ◄ [I] to start to be seen or to suddenly be seen: *An image appeared on the screen.*|*Two faces appeared at our window.*|[+ **from**] *The manager*

*hardly ever appeared from his office.* | **appear out of nowhere** (=suddenly appear in a way that is very surprising) *I don't know what caused the marks – they just seemed to appear out of nowhere.* | **appear overnight** (=appear very quickly or suddenly) *Software development is a fast-moving business – firms appear and disappear virtually overnight.*
**3 ▶ FILM/TV PROGRAMME ETC ◀** [I] to take part in a film, play, concert, television programme etc: [+ **in/on**] *Roseanne Barr has appeared on the show several times.* | [+ **at**] *Vanessa Redgrave is currently appearing at the Theatre Royal, Drury Lane.*
**4 ▶ BE WRITTEN/SHOWN ◀** [I] to be written or shown on a list, in a book or newspaper, in a document etc: *Her name appears at the front of the book.* | *The story appeared in all the national newspapers.*
**5 ▶ PRODUCT/BOOK ◀** [I] if a product or book appears, it becomes available to be bought for the first time: *When the book finally appeared on the shelves it was a huge success.*
**6 ▶ STH NEW/DIFFERENT ◀** [I] if something new or surprising appears, it happens or exists for the first time: *Several neo-punk bands have recently appeared on the music scene.*
**7 ▶ LAW COURT ◀** [I] to be present in a court of law for a TRIAL[1] (1) that you are involved in: *Smith was ordered to appear in court to face charges on the 15th.* | [+ **on behalf of/for**] *Sir Nicholas Gammon QC appeared on behalf of the defendant.*
**8 ▶ COMMITTEE/INQUIRY ◀ appear before/in front of sth** to answer questions by members of an official group who are trying to find out about something: *The Senator appeared before the Ways and Means Committee.*
**9 ▶ ARRIVE ◀** [I] to arrive, especially when people are not expecting you to: *Karen appeared at about 9 o'clock.*

W2 **ap·pear·ance** /əˈpɪərəns‖əˈpɪr-/ *n*
**1 ▶ WAY SB/STH LOOKS ◀** [C,U] the way someone or something looks to other people: *You mustn't worry about your appearance – you look fine.* | *They've changed the whole appearance of the building.* | **judge by appearances** (=judge someone or something by the way they look) *It's usually best not to judge by appearances.* | **have all the appearances of** (=have all the qualities or features that are typical of something) *The case had all the appearances of a straightforward murder.* | **to/by all appearances** (=based on the way someone or something seems to most people) *He was, to all appearances, a respectable, successful businessman.* | **contrary to/against (all) appearances** (=in spite of the way they appear) *Contrary to appearances, she's actually quite funny when you get to know her.* | **give/create the appearance of** (=seem) *Nigel gives the appearance of being confident, but he isn't really.*
**2 ▶ STH NEW ◀** [singular] the point at which something new begins to exist or starts being used: [+ **of**] *the appearance of the first mammals* | *the appearance of buds on the trees*
**3 ▶ ARRIVAL ◀** [C usually singular] the unexpected or sudden arrival of someone or something: [+ **of**] *The shouting suddenly stopped with the appearance of Peter's father.*
**4 ▶ PLAY/FILM/CONCERT ETC ◀** [C] the act of taking part in a film, play, concert etc: **make an appearance** *He made his first appearance on stage in a Broadway review.* | *the band's only European appearance this year*
**5 keep up appearances** to continue to wear good clothes and behave as though you have plenty of money even though you no longer do
**6 for appearances' sake/for the sake of appearances** if you do something for appearances' sake, you are trying to make people think you are still happy, successful etc
**7 put in an appearance/make an appearance** to go to an event for a short time, because you think you should: *At least Marc managed to put in an appearance at the party.*
**8 ▶ LAW COURT/MEETING ◀** [C] the act of being present at a court of law or official meeting: **make an appearance** *He made a brief appearance in court.*

**ap·pease** /əˈpiːz/ *v* [T] to make someone less angry or stop them from attacking you by giving them what they want

**ap·pease·ment** /əˈpiːzmənt/ *n* [C,U] the act of trying to persuade someone not to attack you or to make them less angry by giving them what they want: *Chamberlain's policy of appeasement towards Hitler in the 30s*

**ap·pell·ate court** /əˌpelət ˈkɔːt‖-ˈkɔːrt/ *n* [C] a court in which people appeal (APPEAL[1] (3)) against decisions made in other courts of law

**ap·pe·lla·tion** /ˌæpəˈleɪʃən/ *n* [C] *literary* a name or title

**ap·pend** /əˈpend/ *v* [T + to] *formal* to add something to a piece of writing

**ap·pend·age** /əˈpendɪdʒ/ *n* [C] **1** something that is connected to a larger or more important thing **2** *formal* an arm, leg or other body part

**ap·pen·dec·to·my** /ˌæpənˈdektəmi/ *n* [C,U] a medical operation in which your APPENDIX (1) is removed

**ap·pen·di·ci·tis** /əˌpendəˈsaɪtəs/ *n* [U] an illness in which your APPENDIX (1) swells and causes pain

**ap·pen·dix** /əˈpendɪks/ *n plural* **appendixes** *or* **appendices** /-dəsiːz/ [C] **1** a small organ near your BOWEL (2) which has little or no use: **have your appendix out** (=have it removed) —see picture at DIGESTIVE SYSTEM **2** a part at the end of a book containing additional information

**ap·per·tain** /ˌæpəˈteɪn‖-ər-/ *v formal*
**appertain to** sth *phr v* [T not in passive] to belong to or concern something

**ap·pe·tite** /ˈæpətaɪt/ *n* **1** [U] a desire for food: *a healthy appetite* | **lose your appetite** *She has completely lost her appetite since the operation.* | **have a huge/big/voracious appetite** (=have the ability to eat a lot of food) | **spoil/ruin your appetite** (=eat before a meal and then not want to eat at the meal) *Don't eat that cake now, you'll spoil your appetite.* | **give sb an appetite** (=make them want to eat) *All that walking has given me a big appetite.* **2** [C] a desire or liking for a particular activity: [+ **for**] *Paul has no appetite for hard work.* | **sexual appetite** *an insatiable sexual appetite* —see also **whet sb's appetite** (WHET (1))

**ap·pe·tiz·er** also **appetiser** *BrE* /ˈæpətaɪzə‖-ər/ *n* [C] a small dish at the beginning of a meal

**ap·pe·tiz·ing** also **appetising** *BrE* /ˈæpətaɪzɪŋ/ *adj* food that is appetizing smells or looks very good: *an appetizing aroma* —**appetizingly** *adv*

**ap·plaud** /əˈplɔːd‖əˈplɒːd/ *v* [I,T] **1** to hit your open hands together to show that you have enjoyed a play, concert, speaker etc; CLAP[1] (1, 2a) **2** to express strong approval of an idea, plan etc: *We applaud the decision to go ahead with the new building.*

**ap·plause** /əˈplɔːz‖əˈplɒːz/ *n* [U] the sound of many people hitting their hands together and shouting, to show that they have enjoyed something: **thunderous applause** (=very loud) | **a round of applause** (=a short period of applause) *Let's have a round of applause for our speakers today.*

**ap·ple** /ˈæpəl/ *n* [C,U] **1** a hard round fruit that has red, light green, or yellow skin and is white inside: *apple pie* —see picture on page 413 **2 be the apple of sb's eye** to be loved very much by someone: *Ben was always the apple of his father's eye.* **3 bob/dunk/dip for apples** to play a game in which you must use your teeth to pick up apples floating in water —see also **upset the apple cart** (UPSET[1] (5)), **a rotten apple** (ROTTEN[1] (5)) S2 W3

**ap·ple·jack** /ˈæpəldʒæk/ *n* [U] *AmE* a very strong alcholic drink made from apples

**apple pie bed** /ˌ·· ·ˈ·/ *n* [C] *BrE* a trick you do to someone's bed in which you fold the sheets in a particular way so that they cannot get into it —see also SHORT-SHEET

**apple-pie or·der** /ˌ·· ·ˈ··/ *n* [U] **be in apple-pie order** to be in perfect order or perfectly arranged: *His tools are always in apple-pie order.*

**apple pol·ish·er** /ˈ.. ˌ../ *n* [C] *AmE spoken* someone who tries to gain something, become popular etc by praising or helping someone else without being sincere

**apple sauce** /ˌ.. ˈ..‖ˈ.. ./ *n* [U] a food made from crushed cooked apples

**ap·pli·ance** /əˈplaɪəns/ *n* [C] a piece of electrical equipment such as a COOKER (1) or WASHING MACHINE, used in people's homes: *labour-saving domestic appliances* —see MACHINE[1] (USAGE)

**ap·plic·a·ble** /əˈplɪkəbəl, ˈæplɪkəbəl/ *adj* affecting or connected with a particular person, group, or situation: [+ **to**] *Please give details about your mortgage, if applicable.* | *Few of these laws are applicable to UK citizens while they are abroad.* —**applicability** /əˌplɪkəˈbɪlɪti/ *n* [U]

**ap·pli·cant** /ˈæplɪkənt/ *n* [C] someone who has formally asked, usually in writing, for a job, university place etc

S1 W1 **ap·pli·ca·tion** /ˌæplɪˈkeɪʃən/ *n*

**1 ▶ WRITTEN REQUEST ◀** [C,U] a formal, usually written, request for something such as a job, place at university, or permission to do something: *Developers have filed a planning application.* | [+ **for**] *There were more than 300 applications for the six jobs.* | **job/membership application** *We received hundreds of job applications.* | **application form** (=the paper on which you write your details) | **on application (to)** (=when you make an application) *Details will be sent on application.*

**2 ▶ PRACTICAL USE ◀** [C,U] practical purpose for which a machine, idea etc can be used, or the act of using it for this: *A micro computer has a wide range of applications for businesses.* | [+ **of/to/in**] *the application of this theory to actual economic practice*

**3 ▶ PAINT/LIQUID ◀** [C,U] the act of putting something such as paint, liquid, medicine etc onto a surface: [+ **of**] *The application of fertilizer increased the size of the plants.*

**4 ▶ EFFORT ◀** [U] attention or effort over a long period of time: *Making your new business successful requires luck, patience, and application.*

**5 ▶ COMPUTERS ◀** a piece of SOFTWARE: *The top software application last year was Microsoft Office.*

**6 ▶ RELATION TO STH ◀** [U] the way in which something can affect or be used on something else: [+ **to**] *That rule has no application to this case.*

**ap·plied** /əˈplaɪd/ *adj* [usually before noun] **applied science/physics/linguistics etc** science etc that has a practical use —compare PURE(10) —opposite THEORETICAL (1)

**ap·pli·qué** /əˈpliːkeɪ‖ˌæplɪˈkeɪ/ *n* [C,U] the process of sewing decorative pieces of material onto a piece of clothing, or the pieces themselves —**appliqué** *v* [T]

S1 W1 **ap·ply** /əˈplaɪ/ *v*

**1 ▶ REQUEST PERMISSION/A JOB ◀** [I] to make a formal, usually written request for something such as a job, place in university, or permission to do something: [+ **to**] *I applied to four universities and was accepted by all of them.* | [+ **for**] *Fletcher applied for the post of Eliot's secretary.*

**2 ▶ USE STH ◀** [T] to use something such as a method, idea, or law in a particular situation, activity, or process: *In some cases tribunals fail to apply the law properly.* | **apply sth to** *New technology is being applied to almost every industrial process.*

**3 ▶ AFFECT STH ◀** [I not in progressive] to have an effect on or to concern a person, group, or situation: [+ **to**] *The questions on this part of the form only apply to married men.* | *Many of the restrictions no longer apply.*

**4 apply yourself** to work hard with a lot of attention for a long time: *Stephen would do very well if only he applied himself.*

**5 ▶ MAKE STH WORK ◀** [T] to do something in order to make something such as a piece of equipment operate: *apply the brakes* | *The crystal vibrates when a small electric current is applied to it.*

**6 ▶ SPREAD PAINT/LIQUID ETC ◀** [T] to put or spread something such as paint, liquid, or medicine onto a surface: *Apply the cream evenly over the skin.*

**7 apply force/pressure** to push on something

**8 ▶ USE A WORD ◀** [T] to use a particular word or name to describe something or someone: *The term 'mat' can be applied to any small rug.*

**ap·point** /əˈpɔɪnt/ *v* [T] **1** to choose someone for a position or a job: *They appointed a new teacher at the school.* | **appoint (sb) as sth** *O'Connell was appointed as Chairman of the Council.* | *The School Board have appointed her Superintendent of the city's schools.* | **appoint sb to sth** *He's been appointed to the State Supreme Court in California.* | **appoint sb to do sth** *She's been appointed to catalog the new books in the library.* **2** *formal* to arrange or decide a time or place for something to happen: *The committee appointed a day in June for celebrations.* | **the appointed time** (=the time that has been arranged) *We met him at the appointed time outside the courtroom.* —**appointee** /əˌpɔɪnˈtiː, ˌæpɔɪn-/ *n* [C] *a presidential appointee* —see also SELF-APPOINTED, WELL-APPOINTED —see HIRE[1] (USAGE) S2 W2

**ap·point·ment** /əˈpɔɪntmənt/ *n* **1** [C] an arrangement for a meeting at an agreed time and place, for some special purpose: *a hospital appointment* | *a five o'clock appointment* | [+ **with**] *an appointment with the doctor at 10.30* | **appointment to do sth** *I have an appointment to see the manager.* | **make an appointment** *Phone his secretary and make an appointment.* | **keep an appointment** (=be present at an appointment as arranged) *If you fail to keep the dentist's appointment you'll have to pay for it.* **2** [C,U] the choosing of someone for a position or job: [+ **as/to/of**] *His appointment as head of department has caused a lot of friction.* | **appointments column** *BrE* (=the part of a newspaper where jobs are advertised) **3 by appointment** if you do something by appointment, you have to arrange it before you do it: *The Director sees students by appointment only.* **4** [C] a job or position, usually involving some responsibility: *He was told he'd got the appointment yesterday morning.* **5 by appointment to the Queen** a phrase that can be used by a business that sells goods or services to the Queen S1 W2

**ap·por·tion** /əˈpɔːʃən‖-ɔːr-/ *v* [T] to decide how something should be shared between various people: [+ **among/between**] *apportioning available funds among the different schools in the district* | **apportion blame/praise etc** (=say who deserves to be blamed or praised) *It's not easy to apportion blame when a marriage breaks up.* —**apportionment** *n* [C,U]

**ap·po·site** /ˈæpəzɪt/ *adj formal* suitable to what is happening or being discussed: *brief but apposite remarks* —**appositely** *adv* —**appositeness** *n* [U]

**ap·po·si·tion** /ˌæpəˈzɪʃən/ *n* [U] an arrangement in grammar in which one simple sentence contains two or more noun phrases that are used in the same way and describe the same thing. For example, in the sentence 'The defendant, a woman of thirty, denies kicking the policeman' the two phrases 'the defendant' and 'a woman of thirty' are in apposition.

**ap·prais·al** /əˈpreɪzəl/ *n* [C,U] a statement or opinion judging the worth, value, or condition of something: [+ **of**] *What's your appraisal of the situation?* | *an annual appraisal of employees' work*

**ap·praise** /əˈpreɪz/ *v* [T] to officially judge how successful, effective, or valuable someone or something is; EVALUATE: *A dealer came to appraise the furniture.*

**ap·pre·cia·ble** /əˈpriːʃəbəl/ *adj* large enough to be noticed or considered important: *There's no appreciable change in the patient's condition.* —**appreciably** *adv*: *The two plans are not appreciably different.*

**ap·pre·ci·ate** /əˈpriːʃieɪt/ *v* **1** [T] to understand how good or useful someone or something is: *Her abilities are not fully appreciated by her employer.* **2** [T] to be grateful for something that someone has done: *I appreciated his help when we moved.* | **I would appreciate it if** (=please do what I ask) *I would appreciate it if you would turn the music down.* **3** [T not in progressive] to understand how serious a situation or problem is or what someone's feelings are: *I don't think you appreciate the* 

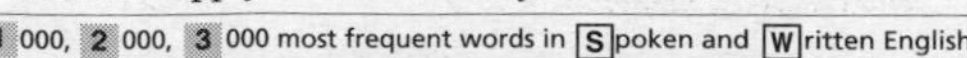
1 000, 2 000, 3 000 most frequent words in S poken and W ritten English

*difficulties his absence will cause.* **4** [I] to gradually become more valuable over a period of time: *Most investments are expected to appreciate at a steady rate.* —opposite DEPRECIATE(1)

**ap·pre·ci·a·tion** /ə,pri:ʃi'eɪʃən/ *n* **1** [U] pleasure you feel when you realize something is good, useful, or well done **2 show sb your appreciation** to show someone that you are grateful for something they have done: *To show our appreciation for all your hard work, we'd like to give you a bonus.* **3** [C,U] an understanding of the importance or meaning of something: [+ **of**] *a realistic appreciation of the situation* **4** [singular, U] a rise in value, especially of land or possessions: *an appreciation of 50% in property values*

**ap·pre·cia·tive** /ə'pri:ʃətɪv/ *adj* feeling or showing admiration or thanks: *an appreciative audience*|[+ **of**] *The visitors were appreciative of all the kindness they'd received.* —opposite UNAPPRECIATIVE —**appreciatively** *adv*

**ap·pre·hend** /,æprɪ'hend/ *v* [T] **1** *formal* if a criminal is apprehended, they are found and taken away by the police; ARREST[1] (1) **2** *old use* to understand something

**ap·pre·hen·sion** /,æprɪ'henʃən/ *n* **1** [C,U] anxiety about the future, especially the worry that you will have to deal with something unpleasant or bad: *a natural apprehension about being in hospital* **2** [U] the act of apprehending someone; ARREST[2] **3** [U] *old use* understanding: *our apprehension of the nature of God*

**ap·pre·hen·sive** /,æprɪ'hensɪv◂/ *adj* worried or nervous about something that you are going to do, or about the future: [+ **about/for**] *feeling a little apprehensive about the treatment* —**apprehensively** *adv*: *I waited apprehensively for his reply.*

**ap·pren·tice¹** /ə'prentɪs/ *n* [C] someone who agrees to work for an employer for a fixed period of time in order to learn a particular skill or job: *She works in the hairdresser's as an apprentice.*|*an apprentice electrician*

**apprentice²** *v* [T usually passive] to make someone an apprentice: **apprentice sb to** *He's apprenticed to a plumber.*

**ap·pren·tice·ship** /ə'prentɪsʃɪp/ *n* [C,U] the job of being an apprentice, or the period of time in which you are an apprentice: *He's serving an apprenticeship as a printer.*|*a five year apprenticeship*

**ap·prise** /ə'praɪz/ *v* [T + **of**] *formal* to inform or tell someone about something: *I write to apprise you of the latest situation.*

S3 W2 **ap·proach¹** /ə'prəʊtʃ‖ə'proʊtʃ/ *v*
**1** ▶ **MOVE TOWARDS** ◀ [I,T] to move towards or nearer to someone or something: *As they approached the wood a rabbit ran out of the trees.*|*The car swerved to avoid an approaching bus.*
**2** ▶ **ASK** ◀ [T] to ask someone for something, or ask them to do something, especially when you are not sure they will be interested: **approach sb for** *Will you be approaching the bank for a loan?*|**approach sb/sth about (doing) sth** *The charity approached several stores about giving food aid.* —see also APPROACHABLE
**3** ▶ **FUTURE EVENT** ◀ [I,T] if an event or a particular time approaches, or you approach it, it is coming nearer and will happen soon: *Our vacation is approaching and we still can't decide where to go.*|*He was in his fifties and approaching retirement.*
**4** ▶ **ALMOST REACH STH** ◀ [T] to almost reach a particular high level or amount, or an extreme condition or state: *temperatures approaching 35° C*|**nothing/not approaching** (=not at all close in amount) *Nothing approaching the $200 million was found by the auditors.*
**5** ▶ **DEAL WITH** ◀ [T] to begin to deal with a difficult situation in a particular way or with a particular attitude: *I don't think refusing to negotiate is the right way to approach this problem.*

S3 W1 **approach²** *n* **1** [C] a method of doing something or dealing with a problem: [+ **to**] *a new approach to teaching languages* **2** [U] movement towards or near to something: *Our approach frightened the birds away.* **3** [C] a road, path etc that leads to a place, and is the main way of reaching it: *The approach to the house was by a minor road.* **4** [C] a request from someone, asking you to do something for them: **make an approach** *They made approaches to the team to buy one of their players.* **5 the approach of** the approach of a particular time or event is the fact that it is getting closer: *The leaves were turning brown with the approach of autumn.*

**ap·proa·cha·ble** /ə'prəʊtʃəbəl‖ə'proʊtʃ-/ *adj* friendly and easy to talk to: *The head teacher is very approachable.* —opposite UNAPPROACHABLE

**ap·pro·ba·tion** /,æprə'beɪʃən/ *n* [U] *formal* official praise or approval

**ap·pro·pri·ate¹** /ə'prəʊpri-ɪt‖ə'proʊ-/ *adj* correct or suitable for a particular time, situation, or purpose: *At an appropriate moment I'll offer the visitors some coffee.*|[+ **for**] *Your clothes are hardly appropriate for a job interview.*|[+ **to**] *objectives and strategies which are appropriate to the markets* —opposite INAPPROPRIATE —**appropriately** *adv*: *Her new job started, appropriately enough, on the first of January.* —**appropriateness** *n* [U] 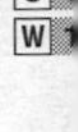

**ap·pro·pri·ate²** /ə'prəʊprieɪt‖ə'proʊ-/ *v* [T] **1** to take something for yourself with no right to do this: *He is suspected of appropriating government funds.* **2** to take something, especially money, to use for a particular purpose: **appropriate sth for** *Congress appropriated $5 million for the International Woman's Year.* —see also MISAPPROPRIATE

**ap·pro·pri·a·tion** /ə,prəʊpri'eɪʃən‖ə,proʊ-/ *n* [C,U] **1** the process of saving money for a special purpose, or the money that is saved, especially by a business or government: [+ **of**] *the appropriation of $2 million for the new hospital* **2** the act of taking control of something without asking permission: *the appropriation by the state of all large, profitable businesses*

**ap·prov·al** /ə'pru:vəl/ *n* [U] **1** the fact of believing that someone or something is good or is doing the right things: **win/earn sb's approval** *By doing well at school he hoped to win his parents' approval.*|**nod/smile/watch etc in approval** *The audience cheered, yelled and whistled in approval.* —opposite DISAPPROVAL **2** the act of officially accepting a plan, decision, or person: *approval of the plans for the new science lab*|**for approval** *He submitted his credentials to the Medical Faculty for approval.*|**meet with sb's approval** (=be accepted by someone) *The budget proposals met with the Senate's approval.*|**seal of approval** (=statement that you accept something) *The IMF has given its seal of approval to the government's economic strategy.* **3** official permission to do something: *We need parental approval before allowing students to go on field trips.* **4 on approval** if you buy something on approval, you have the right to return it to the shop if you decide you do not want it 

**ap·prove** /ə'pru:v/ *v* **1** [T] to officially accept a plan, proposal etc: *The Senate approved a plan for federal funding of local housing programs.* **2** [I] to think that someone or something is good, right, or suitable: [+ **of**] *Catherine's parents now approve of her marriage.* 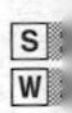

**approved school** /·'· ·/ *n* [C,U] a special school in Britain, where children who have done something illegal are sent if they are under 18

**ap·prov·ing** /ə'pru:vɪŋ/ *adj* showing support or agreement for something: *The professor made no comment about the speech, but gave an approving nod.* —**approvingly** *adv*: *She smiled approvingly at the child.*

**approx** the written abbreviation of approximately

**ap·prox·i·mant** /ə'prɒksɪmənt‖ə'prɑ:k-/ *n* [C] a consonant sound such as /w/ or /L/ made by air passing between the tongue or lip and another part of the mouth without any closing of the air passage

**ap·prox·i·mate¹** /ə'prɒksɪmɪt‖ə'prɑ:k-/ *adj* an approximate number, amount, or time is a little bit more or less than the exact number, amount etc: *What is the approximate cost of the materials?* —**approximately** *adv*: *The plane will be landing in approximately 20 minutes.* 

Frequencies of the adverbs **approximately**, **about**, and **roughly** in spoken and written English.

SPOKEN
approximately
about
roughly
WRITTEN
approximately
about
roughly
200 400 600 800 per million

Based on the British National Corpus and the Longman Lancaster Corpus

All three adverbs are used to mean 'more or less' or 'not exactly'. The graph shows that in this meaning **about** is much more common than **approximately** in both spoken and written English. **Roughly** is also more common than **approximately** in spoken English.

**ap·prox·i·mate²** /ə'prɒksɪ̈meɪt‖ə'prɑːk-/ *v* [I, linking verb] *formal* **1** to be close to a particular number: [+ **to**] *Rainfall during the period we were there approximated to the yearly average.* **2** to be similar to but not exactly the same as something: [+ **to**] *Your story only approximates to the real facts.*

**ap·prox·i·ma·tion** /əˌprɒksɪ̈'meɪʃən‖əˌprɑːk-/ *n* [C,U] **1** a number, amount etc that is not exact, but is almost correct: **rough approximation** (=not exact at all) *Could you give us a rough approximation of the likely cost?* **2** something that is similar to another thing, but not exactly the same: [+ **of/to**] *It was the nearest approximation to a crisis she had ever experienced.*

**ap·pur·te·nance** /ə'pɜːtɪnəns, -tən-‖ə'pɜːrtənəns/ *n* [C usually plural] **1** *formal* things that are an additional and less important part of something larger, for example possessions in a house **2** *technical* an additional right or responsibility connected with owning property

**APR** /ˌeɪ piː 'ɑː‖-'ɑːr/ *n* [C usually singular] Annual Percentage Rate; the rate of INTEREST¹ (4) that you must pay when you borrow money

**ap·rès-ski** /ˌæpreɪ 'skiː◂‖ˌɑː-/ *n* [singular] activities such as eating and drinking that you take part in after skiing (SKI²)

**a·pri·cot** /'eɪprɪ̈kɒt‖'æprɪ̈kɑːt/ *n* **1** [C] a small round fruit that is orange or yellow and has a single large seed —see picture on page 413 **2** [U] the colour of this fruit —see picture on page 411 —**apricot** *adj*

**A·pril** /'eɪprəl/ written abbreviation **Apr** *n* [C,U] the fourth month of the year, between March and May: **on April the sixth/the fifteenth etc** *BrE* | **on April sixth/fifteenth** *AmE*: *I arrived on April seventh.* | **on the sixth/fifteenth etc of April** *My new job starts on the second of April.* | **in April** *This office opened in April 1994.* | **this/last/next April** *I'm going to Africa next April.*

**April fool** /ˌ·· '·/ *n* [C] someone who is tricked on April Fools' Day, or the trick that is played on them

**April Fools' Day** /ˌ·· '· ·/ also **All Fools' Day** *old-fashioned n* [singular] April 1st, a day when people play tricks each other

**a pri·o·ri** /ˌeɪ praɪ'ɔːraɪ, ˌɑː pri'ɔːriː/ *adj, adv Latin* using previous experiences or facts to decide what the probable result or effect of something will be: *an a priori statement such as 'It is raining so the streets must be wet.'*

**a·pron** /'eɪprən/ *n* [C] **1** a piece of clothing that covers the front part of your clothes and ties around your waist, worn to keep your clothes clean, especially while cooking —see picture on page 833 **2 tied to your mother's/wife's apron strings** too easily controlled by your mother or wife **3** also **apron stage** the part of the stage in a theatre that comes forward towards the people watching **4** the hard surface in an airport on which planes are turned around, loaded, unloaded etc

**ap·ro·pos¹** /ˌæprə'pəʊ, 'æprəpəʊ‖-poʊ/ *adv, prep* **apropos of** used to introduce a new subject that is connected with something just mentioned: *He had nothing to say apropos of the latest developments.* | **apropos of nothing** (=not connected with previous conversation) *Apropos of nothing, he suddenly asked me if I liked cats!*

**apropos²** *adj* [not before noun] suitable for a particular situation: *I thought her remarks were very apropos.*

**apse** /æps/ *n* [C] the curved inside end of a building, especially the east end of a church

**apt** /æpt/ *adj* **1 apt to do something** having a natural tendency to do something: *Some of the staff are apt to arrive late on Mondays.* **2** exactly right for a particular situation or purpose: *an apt and telling remark* **3** *formal* quick to learn and understand —**aptness** *n* [U]

**ap·ti·tude** /'æptɪ̈tjuːd‖-tuːd/ *n* [C,U] natural ability or skill, especially in learning: [+ **for**] *She has a real aptitude for drawing and painting.*

**apt·ly** /'æptli/ *adv* **aptly named/described/called etc** named, described etc in a way that seems very suitable: *Lightfoot was aptly named; we never heard him enter.*

**aq·ua·lung** /'ækwəlʌŋ/ *n* [C] a piece of equipment that a swimmer wears on their back under water, that provides air for them to breathe

**aq·ua·ma·rine** /ˌækwəmə'riːn◂‖ˌæ-, ˌɑː-/ *n* **1** [C,U] a greenish blue jewel or the type of stone it comes from **2** [U] a greenish blue colour —**aquamarine** *adj* —see picture on page 411

**aq·ua·plane¹** /'ækwəpleɪn/ *n* [C] a thin board that you stand on while you are pulled over the water by a fast boat

**aquaplane²** *v* [I] **1** to be pulled over the water on an aquaplane **2** *BrE* if a car aquaplanes, it slides over a wet road in an uncontrolled way; HYDROPLANE² (1) *AmE*

**a·quar·i·um** /ə'kweəriəm‖ə'kwer-/ *n plural* **aquariums** *or* **aquaria** /-riə/ [C] **1** a clear glass or plastic container for fish and other water animals **2** a building where people go to look at fish and other water animals

**A·quar·i·us** /ə'kweəriəs‖ə'kwer-/ *n* **1** [singular] the eleventh sign of the ZODIAC, represented by a person pouring water and believed to affect the character and life of people born between January 20 and February 19 **2** [C] someone who was born between January 20 and February 19

**a·quat·ic** /ə'kwætɪk, ə'kwɒ-‖ə'kwæ-, ə'kwɑː-/ *adj* **1** living or growing in water: *an aquatic plant* **2** involving water: *aquatic sports* —**aquatically** /-kli/ *adv*

**aq·ua·tint** /'ækwətɪnt/ *n* [C,U] a method of producing a picture using acid on a sheet of metal, or a picture printed using this method

**aq·ue·duct** /'ækwɪ̈dʌkt/ *n* [C] a structure like a bridge, used to carry a water supply across a valley

**a·que·ous** /'eɪkwiəs, 'ækwiəs/ *adj technical* containing water or similar to water

**aq·ui·line** /'ækwɪ̈laɪn‖-laɪn, -lən/ *adj* **1 aquiline nose** an aquiline nose has a curved shape like the beak of an EAGLE **2** like an EAGLE

**-ar** /ə, ɑː‖ər, ɑːr/ *suffix* **1** [in nouns] the form used for -ER in certain words: *a beggar* (=person who begs) **2** [in adjectives] of or concerning something: *muscular strength* (=strength of muscles) —see also -ULAR

**Ar·ab** /'ærəb/ *n* [C] **1** someone who language is Arabic and whose family have their origin in Arabia or the Middle East **2** also **Arabian** *AmE* a type of fast graceful horse

**ar·a·besque** /ˌærə'besk/ *n* [C] **1** a position in BALLET **2** a decorative pattern of flowing lines

**A·ra·bi·an** /ə'reɪbiən/ *adj* from or connected with Arabia

**Ar·a·bic** /'ærəbɪk/ *n* [U] the language or writing of the Arabs, which is the main language of North Africa, the Middle East, and Arabia —**Arabic** *adj*

**Arabic nu·me·ral** /ˌ··· ˈ···/ *n* [C] a sign, such as 1, 2, or 3, used for numbers in the English alphabet and many others —see also ROMAN NUMERAL

**ar·a·ble** /ˈærəbəl/ *adj* **1 arable land/soil** arable land is suitable for growing crops **2** concerned with growing crops

**ar·bi·ter** /ˈɑːbətə‖ˈɑːrbətər/ *n* [C] **1** someone whose opinions have a lot of influence on what other people do: *an arbiter of taste* **2** someone or something that settles an argument between two opposing sides: **be the final arbiter** (=to make the final decision)

**ar·bi·trage** /ˈɑːbətrɑːʒ‖ˈɑːr-/ *n* [U] *technical* the process of buying something such as a COMMODITY (1) or CURRENCY (1) in one place and selling it in another place at the same time —**arbitrageur** /ˌɑːbətrɑːˈʒɜː‖ˌɑːrbətrɑːˈʒɜːr/ *n* [C]

**ar·bi·tra·ry** /ˈɑːbətrəri, -tri‖ˈɑːrbətreri/ *adj* **1** decided or arranged without any reason or plan, often unfairly: *Management is weak, morale low and punishment is arbitrary.* **2** happening or decided by chance rather than a plan: *The figure of 20% is quite arbitrary.* —**arbitrariness** *n* [U] —**arbitrarily** /ˈɑːbətrərəli‖ˌɑːrbəˈtrerəli/ *adv*: *arbitrarily deprived of his duties*

**ar·bi·trate** /ˈɑːbətreɪt‖ˈɑːr-/ *v* [I,T] to officially judge how an argument between two opposing sides should be settled: *A committee will arbitrate between management and unions.* —**arbitrator** *n* [C]

**ar·bi·tra·tion** /ˌɑːbəˈtreɪʃən‖ˌɑːr-/ *n* [U] the process of judging officially how an argument should be settled: **go to arbitration** (=ask someone to arbitrate)

**ar·bo·re·al** /ɑːˈbɔːriəl‖ɑːr-/ *adj technical* connected with trees or living in trees

**ar·bo·re·tum** /ˌɑːbəˈriːtəm‖ˌɑːr-/ *n* [C] a place where trees are grown for scientific study

**ar·bour** *BrE*, **arbor** *AmE* /ˈɑːbə‖ˈɑːrbər/ *n* [C] a shelter in a garden made by making plants grow together on a frame shaped like an ARCH[1] (4)

**arc** /ɑːk‖ɑːrk/ *n* [C] **1** a curved shape: *the arc of a rainbow* **2** part of a curved line or a circle: *The sun moves across the sky in an arc.* —see picture at CIRCLE[1] **3** a flash of light formed by the flow of electricity between two points —**arc** *v* [T]

**ar·cade** /ɑːˈkeɪd‖ɑːr-/ *n* [C] **1** a covered passage at the side of a row of buildings with PILLARS and arches (ARCH[1] (1)) supporting it on one side **2** a covered passage between two streets with shops on each side of it **3** an AMUSEMENT ARCADE **4** *BrE* also **shopping arcade** a large building or part of a building where there are many shops

**Ar·ca·di·a** /ɑːˈkeɪdiə‖ɑːr-/ *n* [singular] *literary* a place or scene of simple pleasant country life

**ar·cane** /ɑːˈkeɪn‖ɑːr-/ *adj literary* secret and mysterious: *the arcane mysteries and language of the perfume business*

**arch-** /ɑːtʃ, ɑːk‖ɑːrtʃ, ɑːrk/ *prefix* of the highest class or rank; chief; main: *an archbishop* (=a chief BISHOP) | *our archenemy* (=our main worst enemy) | *the company's archrivals* (=main competitors)

S3 **arch¹** /ɑːtʃ‖ɑːrtʃ/ *n* [C] **1** a structure with a curved top and straight sides that supports the weight of a bridge or building **2** a curved structure above a door, window, or gate **3** a curved structure of bones in the middle of your foot —see picture at FOOT[1] **4** something with a curved top and straight sides —see picture on page 835

**arch²** *v* [I,T] to form or make something form a curved shape: *Two rows of trees arched over the driveway.* | *She stretched her arms out and arched her back.*

**arch³** *adj* amused because you think you understand something better than other people: *an arch tone* —**archly** *adv*: *"I think someone here has a little secret," she said archly.*

**ar·chae·ol·o·gy** *especially BrE*, **archeology** *AmE* /ˌɑːkiˈɒlədʒi‖ˌɑːrkiˈɑː-/ *n* [U] the study of ancient societies by examining what remains of their buildings, graves, tools etc —**archaeologist** *n* —**archaeological** /ˌɑːkiəˈlɒdʒəkəl◂‖ˌɑːrkiəˈlɑː-/ *adj*: *an archaeological dig* —**archaeologically** /-kli/ *adv*

**ar·cha·ic** /ɑːˈkeɪ-ɪk‖ɑːr-/ *adj* **1** old and no longer used: *The English used in the letter is an archaic form.* **2** old-fashioned and needing to be replaced: *The central heating in the building is positively archaic.* **3** connected to ancient times

**ar·cha·is·m** /ɑːˈkeɪ-ɪzəm, ˈɑːkeɪ-‖ˈɑːrki-/ *n* [C] an old word or phrase that is no longer used

**arch·an·gel** /ˈɑːkeɪndʒəl‖ˈɑːrk-/ *n* [C] the chief ANGEL (1) in the Jewish, Christian, and Muslim religions

**arch·bish·op** /ˌɑːtʃˈbɪʃəp◂‖ˌɑːrtʃ-/ *n* [C] a priest of the highest rank, who is in charge of all the churches in a particular area

**arch·bish·op·ric** /ˌɑːtʃˈbɪʃəprɪk‖ˌɑːrtʃ-/ *n* [C] **1** the area governed by an archbishop **2** the rank of archbishop

**arch·dea·con** /ˌɑːtʃˈdiːkən◂‖ˌɑːrtʃ-/ *n* [C] a priest of a high rank in the Anglican church who works under a bishop

**arch·di·o·cese** /ˌɑːtʃˈdaɪəsəs, -siːs‖ˌɑːrtʃ-/ *n* [C] the area that is governed by an archbishop

**arch·duke** /ˌɑːtʃˈdjuːk◂‖ˌɑːrtʃˈduːk◂/ *n* [C] a prince who belonged to the royal family of Austria

**archen·e·my** /ˌ· ˈ···/ *n* [C] **1** the main enemy: *Lex Luthor, Superman's archenemy* **2 the archenemy** *literary* the devil

**ar·che·ol·o·gy** /ˌɑːkiˈɒlədʒi‖ˌɑːrkiˈɑː-/ *n* [U] the American spelling of ARCHAEOLOGY

**ar·cher** /ˈɑːtʃə‖ˈɑːrtʃər/ *n* [C] someone who shoots ARROWS (1) from a BOW[3] (1)

**ar·cher·y** /ˈɑːtʃəri‖ˈɑːr-/ *n* [U] the sport of shooting ARROWS (1) from a BOW[3] (1)

**ar·che·type** /ˈɑːkɪtaɪp‖ˈɑːr-/ *n* [C] the most typical example of something, because it has all the most important qualities: *Merlin is the archetype of the wise old man.* —**archetypal** /ˌɑːkɪˈtaɪpəl◂‖ˌɑːr-/ *adj*: *Byron was the archetypal Romantic hero.*

**ar·chi·pel·a·go** /ˌɑːkəˈpeləgəʊ‖ˌɑːrkəˈpeləgoʊ/ *n* [C] a group of small islands and the large area of sea around them

**ar·chi·tect** /ˈɑːkətekt‖ˈɑːr-/ *n* [C] **1** someone whose job is to design buildings **2 the architect of sth** the person who originally thought of an important and successful idea: *Gorbachev was the architect of glasnost.* W

**ar·chi·tec·ture** /ˈɑːkətektʃə‖ˈɑːrkətektʃər/ *n* **1** [U] the style and design of a building or buildings **2** [U] the art and practice of planning and designing buildings: *He studied architecture at university.* **3** [U] the structure and design of something: *the architecture of DNA* **4** [C] *technical* the design of the inside of a computer —**architectural** /ˌɑːkəˈtektʃərəl◂‖ˌɑːr-/ *adj*: *architectural features* **architecturally** *adv*: *Architecturally Chengdu is quite different from most of China.* 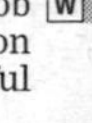

**ar·chive** /ˈɑːkaɪv‖ˈɑːr-/ *n* [C] **1 archives** a large number of records that provide information about the history of a country, organization, family etc: *the State Archives in Paris* **2** a place where a large number of historical records is stored —**archive** *adj*: *interesting archive material* —**archival** /ɑːˈkaɪvəl‖ɑːr-/ *adj*

**ar·chi·vist** /ˈɑːkəvəst‖ˈɑːr-/ *n* [C] someone who works in an archive

**arch·way** /ˈɑːtʃweɪ‖ˈɑːrtʃ-/ *n* [C] **1** a passage under an ARCH[1] (1) or arches **2** an entrance under an arch: *He was standing in the archway outside the club.*

**-archy** /əki, ɑːki‖ərki, ɑːrki/ *suffix* [in nouns] government; rule: *anarchy* (=no government) | *monarchy* (=with one ruler)

**Arc·tic** /ˈɑːktɪk‖ˈɑːrk-/ *n* **the Arctic** the large area of land surrounding the North Pole

**arctic** *adj* **1** connected with or from the most northern part of the world **2** extremely cold: *arctic conditions*

**Arctic Cir·cle** /ˌ·· ˈ··/ *n* [singular] an imaginary line drawn around the world at a certain distance from the most northern point (the North Pole) —compare ANTARCTIC CIRCLE —see picture at EARTH[1]

**arc weld·ing** /ˌ· ˈ··/ *n* [U] a method of joining two pieces of metal together by heating them with a special tool

**-ard** /əd‖ərd/ *suffix* [in nouns] someone who is usually or always in a particular state: *a drunkard*

**ar·dent** /ˈɑːdənt‖ˈɑːr-/ *adj* **1** showing strong positive feelings about an activity and determination to succeed at it: *an ardent supporter of free trade* **2** *literary* showing strong feelings of love: *an ardent suitor* —**ardently** *adv*

**ar·dour** *BrE*, **ardor** *AmE* /ˈɑːdə‖ˈɑːr‖-ər/ *n* [U] **1** very strong positive feelings: *They sang with real ardour.* **2** *literary* strong feelings of love

**ar·du·ous** /ˈɑːdjuəs‖ˈɑːrdʒuəs/ *adj* involving a lot of strength and effort: *an arduous journey through the mountains* —**arduously** *adv* —**arduousness** *n* [U]

**are[1]** /ə; *strong* ɑː‖ər; *strong* ɑːr/ the present tense and plural of 'be'

**are[2]** /ɑː‖ɑːr/ *n* [C] a unit of area —see table on page B2

S1 W1 **ar·e·a** /ˈeəriə‖ˈeriə/ *n* [C] **1** a particular part of a country, town etc: *a working-class area of Birmingham | Many areas of Africa have suffered severe drought this year.* | **the surrounding area** (=the area around a place) *The police have searched the farm and the surrounding area.* **2** a part of a house, office, garden etc that is used for a particular purpose: *a no-smoking area | Come through into the dining area.* **3** a particular subject, range of activities, or group of related subjects: [+ **of**] *reforms in the key areas of health and education* **4** the amount of space that a flat surface or shape covers: *a formula to calculate the area of a circle | an area of 2,000 square miles* —see **grey area** (GREY [1] (6))

> **USAGE NOTE: AREA**
>
> WORD CHOICE: **area, part of the world/the country/town, region, district**
>
> **Area** is the most general word for a part of the Earth's surface. An **area** can be small or large, and is not usually thought of as a fixed land division: *the shopping/downtown area of the city | a rural area of the country | the Houston area.* Informally you might talk instead about a **part of the world/the country/town**: *There's no video shop in our part of town. | New England is a delightful part of the country* (usually =country area).
>
> A **region** is usually large, is usually part of a country, and may or may not be thought of as a fixed land division: *the arctic region of Canada | The south east is the richest region in England.*
>
> A **district** is smaller than a **region,** and is usually an officially fixed area of a country or city: *The financial district of town. | the central district of Hong Kong | the Lake District*

**area code** /ˈ··· ˌ·/ *n* [C] three numbers you use when you want to telephone someone in a different area of the US; DIALLING CODE *BrE*

**a·re·na** /əˈriːnə/ *n* [C] **1** a building with a large flat central area surrounded by seats, where sports or entertainments take place: *The bull was led into the arena.* **2 the political/public/international etc arena** all the activities and people connected with politics, public life etc: *Women are entering the political arena in larger numbers.*

**aren't** /ɑːnt‖ˈɑːrənt/ *v* **a)** the short form of 'are not': *They aren't here.* **b)** the short form of 'am not', used in questions: *I am your friend, aren't I?*

**a·rête** /əˈret,əˈreɪt/ *n* [C] a part of a mountain that consists of a long line of raised rock with steep sides —see picture on page 835

**ar·gent** /ˈɑːdʒənt‖ˈɑːr-/ *n* [U] *poetical* a silver colour —**argent** *adj*

**ar·gon** /ˈɑːgon‖ˈɑːrɑːn/ *n* [U] a chemically inactive gas that is found in the air and is sometimes used in electric lights

**ar·got** /ˈɑːgəʊ‖ˈɑːrgət/ *n* [C,U] informal expressions used by a particular group of people such as criminals

**ar·gu·a·ble** /ˈɑːgjuəbəl‖ˈɑːr-/ *adj* not certainly true or correct and therefore easy to doubt: *Whether or not Webb is the best person for the job is arguable.* | **it is arguable that** (=you can show goods reasons why it might be true) *It's arguable that legislation has little effect on young people's behaviour.* —**arguably** *adv*: *Senna was arguably the greatest racing driver of all time.*

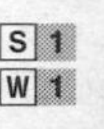

**ar·gue** /ˈɑːgjuː‖ˈɑːr-/ *v* S1 W1

**1** ▶ **DISAGREE** ◀ [I] to disagree with someone in words, often in an angry way: *Did you hear the couple next door arguing last night?* | [+ **with**] *I'm not going to argue with you, but I think you're wrong.* | [+ **about**] *They were arguing about how to spend the money.* | [+ **over**] (=argue about something, especially about who should have something) *The family argued bitterly over who should inherit the house.*

**2** ▶ **STATE** ◀ [I,T] to state, giving clear reasons, that something is true, should be done etc: *a well-argued case* | **argue that** *Croft argued that a date should be set for the withdrawal of troops.* | **argue for/against** (=argue that something should or should not be done) *You can argue against extending the airport on the grounds of cost.* | **argue the point** (=discuss something) *We could argue this point for hours without reaching any sensible conclusions.*

**3 argue sb into/out of sth** *especially BrE* to persuade someone to do or not do something: *Joyce argued me into buying a new jacket.*

**4** ▶ **SHOW CLEARLY** ◀ [T] *formal* to show that something clearly exists or is true: *The commissioner's statement argues a high level of police involvement.*

**5 argue the toss** *BrE informal* to continue to argue about a decision that has been made and cannot be changed: *How stupid of me to argue the toss with the traffic policeman.*

**ar·gu·ment** /ˈɑːgjʊmənt‖ˈɑːr-/ *n* **1** [C] a situation in which two or more people disagree, often angrily: [+ **with**] *an argument with my husband* | [+ **about/over**] *The argument seemed to be about who was going to take the cat to the vet.* | **have an argument** *They were having an argument about the children.* | **get into an argument** *I got into an argument with the other driver.* | **win/lose an argument** *He lost his argument with the doctor.* | **heated argument** (=very angry argument) **2** [C] a set of reasons that show that something is true or untrue, right or wrong etc: *Rose's argument is complex and ingenious.* | [+ **for/against**] *a powerful argument against smoking* | **argument that** *the familiar argument that the costs outweigh the benefits* **3** [U] the act of disagreeing or questioning something: **do sth without (further) argument** *Seamus accepted the suggestion without argument.* | **for the sake of argument** (=in order to discuss all the possibilities) *Let's say for the sake of argument that you don't take the job, then what?* S1 W1

**ar·gu·men·ta·tive** /ˌɑːgjʊˈmentətɪv◂‖ˌɑːr-/ *adj* someone who is argumentative often argues or likes arguing: *When he drinks he becomes argumentative.*

**ar·gy-bar·gy** /ˌɑːdʒi ˈbɑːdʒi‖ˌɑːrdʒi ˈbɑːr-/ *n* [U] *BrE spoken* arguments or quarrelling

**a·ri·a** /ˈɑːriə/ *n* [C] a song that is sung by only one person in an OPERA or ORATORIO

**-arian** /eəriən‖eriən/ *suffix* **1** [in nouns] someone who is connected with or believes in a particular thing: *a vegetarian* (=someone who does not eat meat) | *a librarian* (=someone who works in a library) —see also -GENARIAN **2** [in adjectives] for or connected with people of this type: *a vegetarian restaurant | libertarian principles*

**ar·id** /ˈærɪd/ *adj* **1** arid land is extremely dry and cannot produce many crops: *Much of Namibia is arid country.* **2** an arid discussion, period of time etc does not produce anything new —**aridity** /əˈrɪdɪti/ *adj*

**Ar·ies** /ˈeəriːz,ˈeəri-iːz‖ˈeriːz/ *n* **1** [singular] the first sign of the ZODIAC, represented by a RAM (=male sheep), and believed to affect the character and life of people born between March 21 and April 20 **2** [C] someone who was born between March 21 and April 20

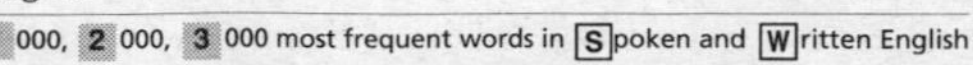

**a·right** /əˈraɪt/ *adv old-fashioned* **1** correctly: *if I remember aright* **2 set things aright** to settle problems or difficulties

S3 W2 **a·rise** /əˈraɪz/ *v past tense* **arose** /əˈrəʊz‖əˈroʊz/ *past participle* **arisen** /əˈrɪzən/ [I] **1** if a problem or difficult situation arises, it begins to happen: *A crisis has arisen in the Foreign Office.* **2** if something arises from or out of a situation, event etc, it is caused or started by that situation etc: [+ **from**] *Can we begin by discussing matters arising from the last meeting?* **3 when the need arises/should the need arise** when or if it is necessary: *Should the need arise for extra staff, we will contact you.* **4** *old-fashioned* to get out of bed, or stand up: *Daniel arose at dawn.* **5** if something arises when you are moving towards it, you are gradually able to see it as you move closer: *As we sped down the highway, the lights of the city arose before us.* **6** *formal* if a group of people arise, they fight for or demand something they want: *Arise and fight for your rights!* —see OCCUR (USAGE)

**ar·is·toc·ra·cy** /ˌærɪ̇ˈstɒkrəsi‖-ˈstɑː-/ *n* **1** [C] the people in the highest social class, who traditionally have a lot of land, money, and power: *dukes, earls, and other members of the aristocracy | the new LA rock 'aristocracy'* —see also UPPER CLASS **2** [U] *technical* the system in which a country is governed by the people of the highest social class —compare DEMOCRACY

**ar·is·to·crat** /ˈærɪ̇stəkræt, əˈrɪ-‖əˈrɪ-/ *n* [C] someone who belongs to the highest social class

**ar·is·to·crat·ic** /ˌærɪ̇stəˈkrætɪk◂, əˌrɪ-‖əˌrɪ-/ *adj* belonging to or typical of the aristocracy: *old, aristocratic families | an aristocratic manner*

**a·rith·me·tic¹** /əˈrɪθmətɪk/ *n* [U] the science of numbers involving adding, multiplying etc —compare MATHEMATICS

**ar·ith·met·ic²** /ˌærɪθˈmetɪk◂/ also **ar·ith·met·i·cal** /-tɪkəl/ *adj* involving or related to arithmetic —**arithmetically** /-kli/ *adv*

**arithmetic pro·gres·sion** /ˌ····ˈ··/ *n* [C] a set of numbers in order of value in which a particular number is added to each to produce the next (as in 2, 4, 6, 8 ...) —compare GEOMETRIC PROGRESSION

**ark** /ɑːk‖ɑːrk/ *n* [C] **1** a large ship **2 the Ark** in the Bible, the large boat built by Noah to save his family and the animals from a flood that covered the earth **3 out of the Ark** *BrE informal* very old or old-fashioned

**Ark of the Cov·e·nant** /ˌ···ˈ···/ *n* [singular] a box containing the laws of the Jewish religion that represented to the Jews the PRESENCE of God

S1 W1 **arm¹** /ɑːm‖ɑːrm/ *n* [C]
**1** ▶ **BODY** ◀ one of the two long parts of your body between your shoulders and your hands: *Mom put her arms around me to comfort me. | Pat appeared carrying a large box under his arm. | a broken arm* | **with arms folded/crossed** (=with your arms bent so that they are resting against your body) | **take sb by the arm** (=lead someone somewhere by holding their arm) *Sid took me by the arm and hurried me out of the room.* | **take sb in your arms** (=gently hold someone with your arms) *Gerry took Fiona in his arms and kissed her.* —see picture at BODY
**2** ▶ **WEAPONS** ◀ **arms** [plural] weapons used for fighting wars: *The government is cutting arms expenditure.* | **take up arms (against sb)** (=get weapons and prepare to fight) *Boys as young as 13 are taking up arms to defend the city.* | **lay down your arms** (=put your weapons down and stop fighting) | **under arms** *BrE* (=with weapons and ready to fight) *All available forces are under arms.* —see also SMALL ARMS, **bear arms** (BEAR)
**3** ▶ **FURNITURE** ◀ the arm of a chair, sofa etc is the part you rest your arms on
**4** ▶ **CLOTHING** ◀ the part of a piece of clothing that covers your arm; SLEEVE
**5 arm in arm** if you walk arm in arm with someone, you are walking next to them with your arm in theirs
**6 be up in arms** *informal* to be very angry and ready to argue or fight: *Residents are up in arms about plans for a new road along the beach.*
**7 welcome sb/sth with open arms** to show that you are happy to see someone or eager to accept an idea, plan etc: *We welcomed Henry's offer with open arms.*
**8 give your right arm** to be willing to do anything to get or do something: *I'd give my right arm to be 21 again.*
**9 at arm's length** if you hold something at arm's length, you hold it away from your body
**10 keep sb at arm's length** to avoid developing a relationship with someone: *Petra keeps all men at arm's length to avoid getting hurt.*
**11 as long as your arm** *informal* a list or written document that is as long as your arm is very long
**12** ▶ **PART OF GROUP** ◀ a part of a large group that is responsible for a particular type of activity: *the political arm of a terrorist organization*
**13** ▶ **OBJECT/MACHINE** ◀ the arm of an object or piece of machinery is the long thin part that looks or moves like an arm: *the arm of a record player* —see picture at GLASS
**14** ▶ **DESIGN** ◀ **arms** [plural] a set of pictures or patterns, usually painted on a SHIELD, that is used as the special sign of a family, town, university etc; COAT OF ARMS
**15 on your arm** *old-fashioned* if a man has a woman on his arm, she is walking beside him holding his arm —see also **arms akimbo** (AKIMBO), babe in arms (BABE (1)), **brothers in arms** (BROTHER¹ (5)), **fold sb/sth in your arms** (FOLD¹ (7)), **twist sb's arm** (TWIST¹ (9))

**arm²** *v* [T] **1** to provide weapons for yourself, an army, a country etc in order to prepare for a fight or a war: **arm sb with sth** *We armed ourselves with whatever we could lay our hands on.* —see also ARMED (1), UNARMED **2** to provide all the information, power etc that are needed to deal with a difficult situation or argument: *I've armed myself with all the facts I need to prove my point.*

**ar·ma·da** /ɑːˈmɑːdə‖ɑːr-/ *n* [C] a large group of something, usually war ships: *a vast armada of foreign visitors*

**ar·ma·dil·lo** /ˌɑːməˈdɪləʊ‖ˌɑːrməˈdɪloʊ/ *n* [C] a small animal that has a shell made of hard bone-like material, and lives in parts of North and South America

**Ar·ma·ged·don** /ˌɑːməˈgedn‖ˌɑːr-/ *n* [singular, U] a terrible battle that will destroy the world: *a nuclear Armageddon*

**ar·ma·ment** /ˈɑːməmənt‖ˈɑːr-/ *n* **1** [C usually plural] the weapons and military equipment used in an army: *nuclear armaments* **2** [U] the process of preparing an army or country for war by giving it weapons —compare DISARMAMENT

**ar·ma·ture** /ˈɑːmətʃə‖ˈɑːrmətʃər/ *n* [C] **1** the part of a GENERATOR, motor etc that turns around to produce electricity, movement etc **2** a frame that you cover with clay or other soft material to make a model

**arm·band** /ˈɑːmbænd‖ˈɑːrm-/ *n* [C] **1** a band of material that you wear around your arm to show that you have an official position, or as a sign of MOURNING **2** [usually plural] *BrE* one of two bands of plastic filled with air that you wear around your arms when you cannot swim

**arm·chair¹** /ˈɑːmtʃeə, ˌɑːmˈtʃeə‖ˈɑːrmtʃer, ˌɑːrmˈtʃer/ *n* [C] a comfortable chair with sides that you can rest your arms on —see picture at CHAIR¹

**arm·chair²** /ˈɑːmtʃeə‖ˈɑːrmtʃer/ *adj* **armchair traveller/critic etc** someone who talks or reads about being a traveller etc, but does not have any real experience of it

S3 W3 **armed** /ɑːmd‖ɑːrmd/ *adj* **1** carrying weapons, especially a gun: *The hostages were kept under armed guard.* | **[+ with]** *The suspect is armed with a shotgun.* | **heavily armed** (=with a lot of weapons) *a heavily armed battleship* | **armed robbery** (=using guns) | **armed combat** (=fighting with weapons) | **armed conflict** (=war) *This political dispute could lead to armed conflict.* | **armed to the teeth** (=carrying a lot of weapons) **2** having something such as knowledge or skills that make it possible for you to do something or deal with something difficult: **[+ with]** *She came to the meeting armed with all the facts and figures to prove us wrong.*

**armed forc·es** /ˌ· ˈ··/ *n* **the armed forces** *plural* a country's military organizations, including the army, navy, and airforce

**arm·ful** /ˈɑːmfʊl‖ˈɑːrm-/ *n* [C] the amount of something that you can hold in one or both arms: **[+ of]** *an armful of books*

**arm·hole** /ˈɑːmhəʊl‖ˈɑːrmhoʊl/ *n* [C] a hole in a shirt, dress, jacket etc that you put your arm through

**ar·mi·stice** /ˈɑːmɪstɪs‖ˈɑːrm-/ *n* [C] an agreement to stop fighting, usually for a short time —compare CEASEFIRE, TRUCE

**ar·mour** *BrE*, **armor** *AmE* /ˈɑːmə‖ˈɑːrmər/ *n* [U] **1** metal or leather clothing that protects your body, worn by soldiers in battles in former times: *a knight in shining armour* | *suit of armor* **2** a strong metal layer that protects military vehicles: *armour-clad warships* **3** a strong layer or shell that protects some plants and animals —see also **a chink in sb's armour** (CHINK¹ (3))

**ar·moured** *BrE*, **armored** *AmE* /ˈɑːməd‖ˈɑːrmərd/ *adj* **1** armoured vehicles have an outside layer made of metal to protect them from attack: *armored personnel carriers* **2** an armoured army used armoured vehicles: *an armoured division*

**armoured car** *BrE*, **armored car** *AmE* /ˌ·· ˈ·/ *n* [C] **1** a car that has special protection from bullets etc, used especially by important people **2** a military vehicle with a strong metal cover and usually a powerful gun

**ar·mour·er** *BrE*, **armorer** *AmE* /ˈɑːmərə‖ˈɑːrmərər/ *n* [C] someone who makes or repairs weapons and ARMOUR

**armour-plat·ed** *BrE*, **armor-plated** *AmE* /ˌ·· ˈ··◂/ *adj* something, especially a vehicle, that is armour-plated has an outer metal layer to protect it —**armour plating** *n* [U] —**armour plate** *n* [U]

**ar·mour·y** *BrE*, **armory** *AmE* /ˈɑːməri‖ˈɑːr-/ *n* [C] a place where weapons are stored

**arm·pit** /ˈɑːmˌpɪt‖ˈɑːrm-/ *n* [C] **1** the hollow place under your arm where it joins your body —see picture at BODY **2** *AmE slang* a very unpleasant or ugly place: *Butte is the armpit of Montana.*

**arms con·trol** /ˈ· ·ˌ·/ *n* [U] the attempts by powerful countries to limit the number and type of war weapons that exist

**arms race** /ˈ· ·/ *n* [C usually singular] the attempt by different countries to produce powerful weapons: *the nuclear arms race*

S1 W1 **ar·my** /ˈɑːmi‖ˈɑːr-/ *n* **1 the army** the part of a country's military force that is trained to fight on land in a war: *He joined the army when he was 17.* | [also + plural verb *BrE*] *The army are helping to clear up after the floods.* | **be in the army** *Both my sons are in the army.* **2** [C] a large organized group of people trained to fight on land in a war: *The rebel armies have taken control of the radio station.* | **raise an army** (=collect and organize an army to fight a battle) **3** [C] a large number of people or animals involved in the same activity: *The village hall is maintained by an army of volunteers.* —compare AIRFORCE, NAVY

**a·ro·ma** /əˈrəʊmə‖əˈroʊ-/ *n* [C] a strong pleasant smell: *the aroma of toast and fresh coffee*

**a·ro·ma·ther·a·py** /əˌrəʊməˈθerəpi‖əˌroʊ-/ *n* [U] a treatment that uses MASSAGE (=rubbing the body) with pleasant smelling natural oils to reduce pain and make you feel well —**aromatherapist** *n* [C]

**ar·o·mat·ic** /ˌærəˈmætɪk◂/ *adj* having a strong, pleasant smell: *aromatic oils* —**aromatically** /-kli/ *adv*

**a·rose** /əˈrəʊz‖əˈroʊz/ the past tense of ARISE

**a·round¹** /əˈraʊnd/ *adv* **1** used to say that something is placed or arranged so that it surrounds something else: *The winner held up his trophy, with many of the spectators crowded around.* | *a bouquet of a dozen red roses, with a silver ribbon wrapped around* | **all around** *The prison was set on an island, with high walls all around.* **2** [only after verb] used to say that someone or something is moving in a circular movement: *She watched the cogs and wheels going around silently.* **3 sit/stand/lie etc around** to sit, stand etc without doing anything in particular, especially so that people think you are wasting time: *There were a few suspicious looking people hanging around outside.* **4 fool/mess etc around** used to mean that someone is wasting time by doing something stupid or dishonest: *Stop messing around! I know you've hidden it.* **5** [only after verb] in many places or in many different parts of a particular area: *Don't leave all your papers lying around —anyone could read them.* | *When I finished college, I travelled around for a while before I got my first job.* | *Since it's your first day here, would you like me to show you around?* **6** if someone is around, they are in the same place as you: *He went down to the sports centre but there was no-one around that he knew.* | *Why is there never a policeman around when you need one?* **7 the best... around/the most exciting... around etc** used to say that someone or something is the best, the most exciting thing of this kind: *East 17 are one of the most popular groups around.* **8 get around to (doing) sth** to finally do something that you have been intending to do for a long time: *I'll get around to the decorating one of these days.* **9** facing in the opposite direction: *Slowly he turned the boat around, hoping the patrol would not hear the engines.* **10 have been around** *informal* to have had experience of many different situations, so that you can deal with new situations confidently **11 2 feet/100 cms etc around** *AmE* having a CIRCUMFERENCE of 2 feet, 100 cms etc —see also ROUND², ROUND³ (USAGE)

S1 W1 (beside a·round¹)

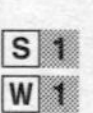

**around²** *prep* **1** used to say that something is placed or arranged so that it surrounds something else: *The whole family were sitting around the dinner table chatting.* | *She had a beautiful woollen shawl wrapped around her shoulders.* **2** used to say that someone or something is moving in a circular movement: *A few wolves were prowling around the deer's carcass.* | *There are reports of a light aircraft flying around and around the Sears Tower.* **3** in many places or parts of a particular area or place: *We took a wander around the garden after breakfast.* | *They have branches dotted around the country.* | **all around** *There were flowers all around the apartment, making it look more homely.* **4** if someone or something is around a particular place, they are in or near that place: *I think he lives somewhere around the centre of town.* | *Is there a bank around here?* **5** if you move or go around something, you move around the side of it instead of going through or over it: *If the gate is locked you'll have to go around the side of the house.* **6** if something is organized around a particular person or thing, it is organized according to their needs, ideas, beliefs etc: *Why does everything have to be organised around what Callum wants to do?* | *Their whole society was built around their belief in their gods.* **7 get around** to avoid or solve

a particular problem or difficult situation: *How do we get around the problem of the new tax laws.* **8 around 200/5000 etc** used when guessing a number, amount etc: *There must have been around 40,000 people in the stadium.* | **around about** *Most guests started to make their way home around about 10 o'clock.* —see also ROUND³

**a·rous·al** /ə'raʊzəl/ *n* [U] excitement, especially sexual excitement

**a·rouse** /ə'raʊz/ *v* [T] **1 arouse interest/expectations etc** to make you become interested, expect something etc: *Matt's behavior was arousing the interest of the neighbors.* **2 arouse anger/fear/dislike etc** to make someone feel very angry, afraid etc **3** to make someone feel sexually excited **4** *formal* to wake someone: [+ **from**] *Anne had to be aroused from a deep sleep.*

**ar·peg·gi·o** /ɑː'pedʒiəʊ‖ɑːr'pedʒioʊ/ *n* [C] the notes of a musical CHORD (1) played separately rather than all at once

**arr** **1** the written abbreviation of arranged by: *music by Mozart, arr Britten* **2** the written abbreviation of arrives or arrival

**ar·raign** /ə'reɪn/ *v* [T] *technical* to make someone come to court to hear what the court says their crime is: *arraigned on a charge of murder* —**arraignment** *n* [C,U]

S2 W2 **ar·range** /ə'reɪndʒ/ *v* **1** [I,T] to organize or make plans for something such as a meeting, party, or trip: *James is arranging a big surprise party for Helen's birthday.* | *I'd like to arrange a business loan.* | **arrange to do sth** *Have you arranged to meet Mark this weekend?* | **arrange for sb to do sth** *I've arranged for the window cleaner to come on Thursday.* | **arrange sth with sb** *Beth arranged a meeting with the marketing director.* | **arrange for sth** *The company will arrange for a taxi to meet you at the airport.* | **arrange when/where/how etc** *We still have to arrange how to get home.* | **as arranged** *Matthew arrived at 2 o'clock as arranged.* **2** [T] to put a group of things or people in a particular order or position: *I've arranged my CDs in alphabetical order.* | **arrange sth in pairs/groups etc** *The children were arranged in lines according to height.* **3** [T] to write or change a piece of music so that it is suitable for particular instruments: [+ **for**] *a symphony arranged for the piano*

**arranged mar·riage** /ˌ.ˌ. '../ *n* [C,U] a marriage in which the parents choose a husband or wife for their child: *Arranged marriages are still common in the Indian community.*

S2 W2 **ar·range·ment** /ə'reɪndʒmənt/ *n* **1** [C usually plural] the things that you must organize so that an event, meeting etc can happen: [+ **for**] *What exactly are the arrangements for the wedding?* | **make arrangements** *The local newspaper made arrangements for an interview with Professor Stein.* | **seating/travel/sleeping etc arrangements** *I'm not very happy about the sleeping arrangements.* **2** [C,U] something that has been organized or agreed on; agreement: *Our loan is by special arrangement with the bank.* | **come to some arrangement** (=make an agreement that is acceptable to everyone) *It would usually cost $500, but I'm sure we can come to some kind of arrangement.* **3** [C,U] a group of things that have been arranged in an attractive or neat way, or the act of arranging a group of things in this way: *a beautiful flower arrangement* **4** [C,U] a piece of music that has been written or changed for a particular instrument: *an arrangement of an old folk song for chorus*

**ar·rant** /'ærənt/ *adj old-fashioned* used to emphasize how bad something is: *arrant nonsense*

**ar·ray¹** /ə'reɪ/ *n* **1** [C usually singular] a group or collection of things, usually arranged so that you can see them all: *The museum has a vast array of uniforms and ceremonial robes.* **2** [C usually singular] a group of people, especially people who are important or special: *a dazzling array of acting talent* **3** [C,U] *literary* fine clothes, especially those worn for a special occasion: *The king came aboard with his guests and family in colourful array.* **4** [C] *technical* a set of numbers or signs, or of computer memory units, arranged in lines across or down

**array²** *v* [T usually passive] **1** *literary* to arrange something in an attractive way **2** *formal* to put soldiers in position ready for battle **3** *literary* to dress in good quality clothes: *She came in arrayed in all her finery.*

**ar·rears** /ə'rɪəz‖ə'rɪərz/ *n* [plural] **1 be in arrears** if someone is in arrears or if their payments are in arrears, they are late in paying something that they should pay regularly, such as rent: *Teachers' pay is in arrears and the school says it can't afford to pay.* | **be four weeks/three months etc in arrears** *The rent money is two months in arrears.* | **fall into arrears** (=become late with payments) **2** money that you owe someone because regular payments such as rent have not been paid at the right time: *We've got 3 months arrears to pay on the video.* **3 be paid in arrears** to be given your wages at the end of the period you have worked: *a salary paid monthly in arrears*

**ar·rest¹** /ə'rest/ *v* [T] **1** if the police arrest you, they take you away because they think you have done something illegal: *Police arrested 26 demonstrators, over half of them women.* | **arrest sb for sth** *Wayne was arrested for dangerous driving.* **2** *formal* to stop something happening or to make it happen more slowly: *drugs used to arrest the spread of the disease* | *arrested development* **3 arrest your attention** *formal* to make you look or listen to something, because it is interesting or exciting: *Her warning tone arrested my attention.* W3

**arrest²** *n* [C,U] the act of taking someone away and guarding them because they may have done something illegal: **make an arrest** *The police made several arrests.* | **be under arrest** (=kept by the police) *He's under arrest and awaiting trial.* | **place/put sb under arrest** (=arrest someone)

**ar·riv·al** /ə'raɪvəl/ *n* **1** [U] the act of arriving somewhere: *the late arrival of the train* | *Joe's sudden arrival spoiled all our plans.* | **arrival at/in** *Shortly after our arrival in Turkey Lisa became very ill.* | **on arrival** (=when you arrive) *He was rushed to the hospital but was dead on arrival.* **2 the arrival of** the time when an important new idea, method, or product is first used or discovered: *The arrival of democracy has thrown the economy into chaos.* **3 new arrival** someone who has just arrived in a particular place to live, work etc: *New arrivals in the camp were greeted with suspicion.* **4** [C] a plane or train that arrives in an airport or station —opposite DEPARTURE W3

**ar·rive** /ə'raɪv/ *v* [I] S2 W1

**1 ▶ GET SOMEWHERE ◀** to get to the place you are going to: *Give me a call to let me know you've arrived safely.* | **arrive in/at/from** *Elaine should be arriving in the States about now.*

**2 ▶ BE DELIVERED ◀** if something arrives, it is brought or delivered to you: *By the time the letter finally arrived, I'd heard the news.*

**3 ▶ EVENT ◀** if an event or particular period of time arrives, it happens: *At last the day of the carnival arrived!*

**4 ▶ STH NEW ◀** if a new idea, method, product etc arrives, it begins to exist or starts being used: *Children don't play outside as much since computer games arrived.*

**5 ▶ BIRTH ◀** to be born: *Sharon's baby arrived just after midnight.*

**6 arrive at a conclusion/agreement/idea etc** to reach an agreement etc after much effort: *After three weeks of confusion we arrived at the conclusion that there was a security leak.*

**7 ▶ SUCCESS ◀** to achieve success: *When he saw his name printed on the door he knew he'd arrived!* —see REACH¹ (USAGE)

**ar·ro·gance** /'ærəgəns/ *n* [U] the quality of thinking that your are very important so that you behave rudely: *The arrogance of that man – pretending he'd never seen us before!*

**ar·ro·gant** /'ærəgənt/ *adj* so proud of your own abilities

or qualities that you behave as if you are much more important than anyone else: *I found him arrogant and overbearing.* —**arrogantly** *adv*: *He strutted about the room arrogantly.*

**ar·ro·gate** /ˈærəgeɪt/ *v* **arrogate sth to yourself** *formal* to claim that you have a particular right, position etc without having the legal right to it: *Having seized power he arrogated to himself the right to change the law.*

**ar·row** /ˈærəʊ‖ˈæroʊ/ *n* [C] **1** a weapon like a thin straight stick with a point at one end that you shoot with a BOW³ (1) **2** a sign in the shape of an arrow, used to show people which direction to go in: *Follow the red arrows to the X-ray department.* —see also STRAIGHT ARROW

**ar·row·head** /ˈærəʊhed‖ˈæroʊ-/ *n* [C] a sharp pointed piece of metal or stone fixed to one end of an arrow

**ar·row·root** /ˈærəʊruːt, ˈærəruːt‖ˈæroʊ-,ˈærə-/ *n* [U] flour made from the root of a tropical American plant

**arse¹** /ɑːs‖ɑːrs/ *n BrE* **1** [C] an impolite word for the part of your body that you sit on **2** [C] *spoken* an impolite word for a stupid and annoying person; arsehole: *Jake's such an arse, I don't know why she's going out with him!* **3 my arse!** *spoken* an impolite way of saying that you do not believe something: *He says he's got a new car? My arse! He hasn't got any money!* **4 shift/move your arse** *spoken* an impolite way of telling someone to hurry up: *Come on! Shift your arse or we'll be late.* **5 be right up sb's arse** *spoken* an impolite way of saying that someone is driving very close to the back of the car in front of them —see also ASS, **pain in the arse/ass etc** (PAIN¹ (3)), SMART ARSE

**arse²** *v* [I] *BrE slang* **can't/couldn't be arsed** to not do something because you are feeling too lazy: *I just can't be arsed making my own lasagne this time – I'll buy one instead.*

**arse about/around** *phr v* [I] to waste time: *He's been arsing about in the garden all day.*

**arse·hole** /ˈɑːshəʊl‖ˈɑːrshoʊl/ *n* [C] *BrE* **1** *spoken* an impolite word for a stupid and annoying person; ASSHOLE *AmE* **2** an impolite word for the ANUS

**ar·se·nal** /ˈɑːsənəl‖ˈɑːr-/ *n* [C] **1** a store of weapons: [+ **of**] *The police found an arsenal of guns in the terrorist's hideout.* **2** a building where weapons are stored

**ar·se·nic** /ˈɑːsənɪk‖ˈɑːr-/ *n* [U] a very poisonous substance sometimes used for killing rats

**ar·son** /ˈɑːsən‖ˈɑːr-/ *n* [U] the crime of deliberately making something burn, especially a building —**arsonist** *n* [C]

1 1 **art¹** /ɑːt‖ɑːrt/ *n* **1** [U] the use of painting, drawing, SCULPTURE etc to represent things or express ideas: *an example of Indian art* | **modern art** *the Museum of Modern Art* **2** [U] objects that are produced by art, such as paintings, drawings etc: *an art exhibition* **3** [U] the skill of drawing or painting: *He excelled at art at school.* **4 the arts** [plural] art, music, theatre, film, literature etc all considered together: *more government funding for the arts* **5 arts** also **the arts** [plural] subjects of study that are not scientific, such as history, languages etc —see also HUMANITIES **6** [C,U] the ability or skill involved in doing or making something: **the art of doing something** *Television is ruining the art of conversation.* | **be quite an art** (=be quite difficult) *Driving a car through central London is quite an art.* | **have/get sth down to a fine art** (=do something very well) *I've got the early morning routine down to a fine art.*

**art²** *v* **thou art** *old use* used to mean 'you are' when talking to one person

**art dec·o** /ˌɑː ˈdekəʊ, ˌɑːt-‖ˌɑːr ˈdeɪkoʊ, ˌɑːrt-/ *n* [U] a style of art and decoration that uses simple shapes and was popular in Europe and America in the 1920s and 1930s

**art di·rec·tor** /ˈ· ·,··/ *n* [C] someone who organizes the clothes, lights, scenery etc for a film

**ar·te·fact, artifact** *n* /ˈɑːtɪfækt‖ˈɑːr-/ [C] an object such as a tool, weapon etc that was made in the past and is historically important: *an exhibition of ancient Egyptian artefacts*

**ar·ter·i·al** /ɑːˈtɪəriəl‖ɑːrˈtɪr-/ *adj* [only before noun] **1** involving the arteries: *arterial blood* **2 arterial road/railway line etc** a main road, railway line etc

**ar·ter·i·o·scle·ro·sis** /ɑːˌtɪəriəʊsklɪˈrəʊsɪs‖ɑːrˌtɪriəʊsklɪˈrəʊ-/ *n* [U] a disease in which your arteries become hard, which stops the blood from flowing through them smoothly

**ar·te·ry** /ˈɑːtəri‖ˈɑːr-/ *n* [C] **1** one of the tubes that carries blood from your heart to the rest of your body —compare VEIN (1) **2** a main road, railway line, river etc

**ar·te·si·an well** /ɑːˌtiːziən ˈwel‖ɑːrˌtiːʒən-/ *n* [C] a WELL⁴ (1) from which the water is forced up out of the ground by natural pressure

**art·ful** /ˈɑːtfəl‖ˈɑːrt-/ *adj* clever at deceiving people: *He's an artful little devil and always gets what he wants.* —**artfully** *adj*: *artfully concealed pockets* —**artfulness** *n* [U]

**art gal·le·ry** /ˈ· ,···/ *n* [C] a building where important paintings are kept and shown to the public

**art house** /ˈ· ·/ *n* [C] a cinema that shows mainly foreign films or films made by small film companies

**ar·thri·tis** /ɑːˈθraɪtɪs‖ɑːr-/ *n* [U] a disease that causes a lot of pain in the joints of your body —**arthritic** /-ˈθrɪtɪk/ *adj*: *arthritic fingers*

**ar·ti·choke** /ˈɑːtɪtʃəʊk‖ˈɑːrtɪtʃoʊk/ *n* [C] **1** also **globe artichoke** a plant with thick pointed leaves that are eaten as a vegetable —see picture on page 414 **2** also **Jerusalem artichoke** a plant that has a root like a potato that you can eat —see picture on page 414

**ar·ti·cle** /ˈɑːtɪkəl‖ˈɑːr-/ *n* [C] **1** a thing, especially one of a group of things: *Most of our wedding presents were household articles that we really needed.* | **article of clothing/furniture/jewellery etc** *She didn't take much with her, just a few articles of clothing.* **2** a piece of writing about a particular subject in a newspaper, magazine etc: *Have you seen that article in the Star about stress management?* **3** a part of a law or legal agreement, especially a numbered part: *Article 1 of the constitution guarantees freedom of religion.* **4** *technical* a word used before a noun to show whether the noun refers to a particular example of something or to a general example of something: **the definite article** (='the' in English) | **the indefinite article** (='a' or 'an' in English) **5 articles** *BrE* an agreement by which someone finishes their education, especially as a lawyer, by working for a company **6 an article of faith** something that you feel very strongly about so that it affects how you think or behave S2 W1

**ar·ti·cled** /ˈɑːtɪkəld‖ˈɑːr-/ *adj* someone who is articled to a company of lawyers, ACCOUNTANTS etc, is employed by that company while they are training to become a lawyer etc: *an articled clerk*

**ar·tic·u·late¹** /ɑːˈtɪkjʊlɪt‖ɑːr-/ *adj* **1** able to talk easily, clearly and effectively about things, especially difficult subjects: *bright, articulate 17-year-olds* —opposite INARTICULATE **2** writing or speech that is articulate is very clear and easy to understand even if the subject is difficult **3** *technical* having joints: *Grasshoppers are articulate insects.* —**articulately** *adv* —**articulateness** *n* [U]

**ar·tic·u·late²** /ɑːˈtɪkjʊleɪt‖ɑːr-/ *v* [I] **1** to express what you are thinking or feeling very clearly: *muddled emotions that I found difficult to articulate* **2** to speak or pronounce your words clearly and carefully

**ar·tic·u·la·ted** /ɑːˈtɪkjʊleɪtɪd‖ɑːr-/ *adj* having two or more parts that are joined together by a moving joint: **articulated bus/vehicle etc** *It's amazing how easily those articulated lorries turn corners.*

**ar·tic·u·la·tion** /ɑːˌtɪkjʊˈleɪʃən‖ɑːr-/ *n* **1** [U] the production of speech sounds: *clear articulation* **2** [U] the expression of thoughts or feelings in words: *the articulation of her suffering* **3** [C] *technical* a joint, especially in a plant

**ar·ti·fact** /ˈɑːtɪ̣fækt‖ˈɑːr-/ *n* [C] another spelling of ARTEFACT

**ar·ti·fice** /ˈɑːtɪ̣fɪ̣s‖ˈɑːr-/ *n formal* **1** [U] the use of clever tricks: *Her charm was all artifice.* **2** [C] a clever trick, especially one used to deceive someone

S3 **ar·ti·fi·cial** /ˌɑːtɪ̣ˈfɪʃəl◂‖ˌɑːr-/ *adj* [usually before noun] **1** not made of natural materials or substances: *artificial sweeteners* **2** not real or natural but deliberately made to look real or natural: *an artificial leg.* **3** artificial behaviour is not natural or sincere because someone is pretending to be something they are not: *an artificial smile* **4** happening because someone has made it happen and not as part of a natural process: *High import taxes give their goods an artificial advantage in the market.* —**artificially** *adv*: *Food prices are being kept artificially low.* —**artificiality** /ˌɑːtɪ̣fɪʃiˈælɪ̣ti‖ˌɑːr-/ *n* [U]

**artificial in·sem·i·na·tion** /ˌ····· ···ˈ··/ *n* [U] the process of making a woman or female animal PREGNANT (1) using a piece of equipment, rather than naturally

**artificial in·tel·li·gence** /ˌ····· ·ˈ···/ also **AI** *n* [U] the study of how to make computers do things that people can do, such as make decisions, see things etc

**artificial res·pi·ra·tion** /ˌ····· ··ˈ··/ *n* [U] a way of making someone breathe again when they have stopped by blowing air into their mouth; MOUTH-TO-MOUTH RESUSCITATION

**ar·til·le·ry** /ɑːˈtɪləri‖ɑːr-/ *n* **1** [U] large guns, especially ones on wheels or fixed in one place, such as on a ship **2 the artillery** the part of the army that uses these weapons

**ar·ti·san** /ˌɑːtɪ̣ˈzæn‖ˈɑːrtɪ̣zən/ *n* [C] someone who does skilled work with their hands; CRAFTSMAN

S3 W2 **art·ist** /ˈɑːtɪ̣st‖ˈɑːr-/ *n* [C] **1** someone who produces art, especially paintings or drawings: *It's not always easy to earn a living as an artist.* **2** a professional performer, especially in music, dance, or the theatre: *Many of the artists in the show donated their fee to charity.* **3** *informal* someone who is extremely good at something: *He's no ordinary baker, the man's an artist.*

**ar·tiste** /ɑːˈtiːst‖ɑːr-/ *n* [C] a professional singer, dancer, actor etc who performs in a show

**ar·tis·tic** /ɑːˈtɪstɪk‖ɑːr-/ *adj* **1** connected with art or culture: *I'm not sure about the artistic merit of much of Dali's work.* **2** showing skill or imagination in any of the arts: *What a beautiful picture, I never realized you were so artistic.* **3** an artistic arrangement, design etc looks attractive and has been done with skill and imagination: *food presented in an artistic way* —**artistically** /-kli/ *adv*

**art·ist·ry** /ˈɑːtɪ̣stri‖ˈɑːr-/ *n* [U] skill in a particular artistic activity: *an example of the photographer's artistry*

**art·less** /ˈɑːtləs‖ˈɑːrt-/ *adj* natural, honest, and sincere: *She chatted away about her life with artless confidence.* —**artlessly** *adj* —**artlessness** *n* [U]

**art nou·veau** /ˌɑː nuːˈvəʊ, ˌɑːt-‖ˌɑːr nuːˈvoʊ,ˌɑːrt-/ *n* [U] a style of art that used pictures of plants and flowers, popular in Europe and America at the end of the 19th century

**arts and crafts** /ˌ· · ˈ·/ *n* [plural] the arts that involve making things with your hands, such as POTTERY etc

**art·work** /ˈɑːtwɜːk‖ˈɑːrtwɜrk/ *n* [U] pictures that are made for a book or magazine, or for another product such as a computer PROGRAM

**art·y** /ˈɑːti‖ˈɑːrti/ *BrE*, **art·sy** /ˈɑːtsi‖ˈɑːrt-/ *AmE adj informal* someone who is arty knows a lot about art or does a lot of art: *arty types gathered in a corner at the party*

**arty-craft·y** /ˌ·· ˈ··◂/ *BrE*, **art·sy craft·sy** /ˌɑːtsi ˈkrɑːftsi◂‖ˌɑːrtsi ˈkræft-/ *AmE adj* someone who is arty-crafty makes things at home and does all kinds of art, especially in a way that is not very professional

**art·y-fart·y** /ˌɑːti ˈfɑːti◂‖ˌɑːrti ˈfɑːr-/ *BrE*, **art·sy-fart·sy** /ˌɑːtsi ˈfɑːtsi◂‖ˌɑːrtsi ˈfɑːr-/ *AmE adj informal* someone who is arty-farty tries too hard to show that they are interested in art

**-ary** /əri‖eri/ *suffix* **1** [in adjectives] of or concerning something; that is something: *planetary bodies* (=that are PLANETS)|*customary* **2** [in nouns] someone connected with something: *the beneficiaries of the will* (=people who get something good from it)|*a functionary* (=someone with duties) **3** [in nouns] a thing or place connected with or containing things of a particular kind: *a library* (=containing books)|*an ovary* (=containing eggs)

**Ar·y·an** /ˈeəriən‖ˈer-/ *n* [C] someone from Northern Europe, especially someone with fair hair and blue eyes —**Aryan** *adj*

**as**[1] /əz; *strong* æz/ *adv, prep* **1 as old/fat/clever etc as sb/sth** equally old, fat etc as someone or something else: *My brother is not as old as me.*|*Her ring is twice as big as mine.*|**as soon as possible** (=as soon as you can)|**just as clever/clean/happy etc** *Tina's clever, but her brother is just as clever.* —see also **as good as** (GOOD[1] (34)) **2 such as** for example: *a heavy land horse such as a Suffolk*|*"There are plenty of opportunities for young people." "Oh yeah, such as?"*|**such ... as** *The disease attacks such birds as parrots and canaries.* —see also **no such ... as** (SUCH[1] (6)) **3 as a teacher/mother/actor etc** used when you are describing someone's job or the main purpose of someone or something: *As parents we are concerned for our children's future.*|*Speaking as your doctor, I would not advise this.*|*It's not bad as a first attempt.*|*The children all dressed up as animals.* **4 as a result of sth** because of something: *Several businesses went under as a result of the recession.* **5 be regarded as sth** to be considered to be something: *'Novecento' is regarded by many as Bertolucci's best film.* —see also **as one** (ONE[2] (15)) S W

**as**[2] *conjunction* **1** used in comparisons: *I can't run as fast as I used to.*|*Jim works in the same office as my sister does.* **2** in the particular way or manner mentioned: *Do as I say!*|*We'd better leave things as they are until the police arrive.*|*As I mentioned in my last letter, I'll be back in Ohio in June.*|*David, as you know, has not been well lately.*|**as usual** *Roberta was late as usual.* **3** while or when: *I saw Peter as I was getting off the bus.*|*As time passed, things seemed to get worse.* **4** used to state why a particular situation exists or why someone does something: *As we're both tired, let's just grab a takeaway.*|**seeing as** (=since) *A cup of tea? I hardly think so, seeing as I'm going out in about two minutes.* **5** though: *Unlikely as it might seem, I'm tired too.*|*Try as she might, Sue couldn't get the door open.*|*As popular as he is, the President hasn't always managed to have his own way.* **6 so cold/heavy/quick etc as to...** or **such an idiot/a disaster etc as to...** used to show the reason that makes something happen or not happen: *The water was so cold as to make swimming quite impossible.*|*How could he have been such an idiot as to trust them in the first place?* **7 so as to do sth** with the purpose of doing something: *The little boy ran off so as not to be caught.* **8 as for sb/sth** *especially spoken* an expression meaning 'concerning'; used when you are starting to talk about someone or something new that is connected with what you were talking about before: *Nick can stay, but as for you, you can get out of my sight.* **9 as yet** [used in negatives] until and including the present time: *We've had no word from Colin as yet.* **10 as if.../as though... a)** in a way that suggests that something is true or not true: *You look as if you've had a good time.*|*It sounds as though she's been really ill.*|*Mandy felt as if they were all ganging up on her.*|**as if to say** *Beckworth shook his head as if to say "don't trust her".* **b)** used to suggest a possible explanation for something although you do not think that this is the actual explanation: *That news reporter always sounds as if he's drunk.*|*You make it sound as if you have to go without food for days on end!* **11 it's not as if...** used to say that something is definitely not true, about a situation or someone's behaviour: *Why do they never go on holiday? I mean it's not as if they're poor is it?*|*I don't know why you're so frightened of her, it's not as if she's got any power over you.* **12 as if you would/as if you care/as if it matters** used to say that someone would S W

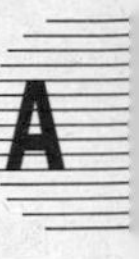

definitely not do something, does not care etc or that something does not matter at all: *Margaret told me she'd never speak to me again! As if I cared.* (=I do not care at all)| *"I reckon Ken's deliberately ignoring us." "As if he would!"* (=he would not ignore us) **13 as it is a)** according to the situation that actually exists, especially when that situation is different from what you expected or need: *They hoped to finish the kitchen by Friday, but as it is they'll probably have to come back next week.* **b)** already: *Just keep quiet, you're in enough trouble as it is.* **14 as from today/15th December/next June etc** also **as of today etc** starting from today, 15th December etc and continuing: *As from today, you are in charge of the office.*| *As of now, there will be no more paid overtime.* **15 as against** in comparison with: *Profits this year are $2.5 million as against $4 million last year.* **16 as to whether/who/which etc** an expression meaning 'concerning' used when speaking about arguments and decisions: *Frank was very uncertain as to whether it was the job for him.*| *advice as to which suppliers to approach* **17 as much as to say** *especially spoken* expressing something in actions rather than words: *He shrugged, as much as to say he wasn't interested.* **18 as it were** used when describing someone or something in a way that is not quite exact: *Jim Radcliffe became our idol as it were, the man we all wanted to be.* **19 as to** according to a particular standard or principle: *The fabrics were arranged as to size and colour.* **20 as is/was/does etc** *formal* in the same way as someone or something else is, does etc: *Eve's very tall, as was her mother.*| *I voted Labour, as did my wife.* —see also **not as such** (SUCH[2] (4)), **as well** (WELL[1] (6)), **as well as** (WELL[1] (5)), **might just as well** (MIGHT[2] (4))

**asap** /ˌeɪ es eɪ ˈpiː, ˈeɪsæp/ the abbreviation of 'as soon as possible'

**as·bes·tos** /æsˈbestəs/ *n* [U] a grey mineral that does not burn easily, used as a building material or in protective clothing

**as·cend** /əˈsend/ *v formal* **1** [I] to move up through the air: *He could feel a current of warm air ascending from the street.* **2** [T] to climb: *We were walking on the forest path, ascending a steep slope.* **3** [I,T] to lead up to a higher position: *The stairs ascended in a graceful curve.* **4 ascend the throne** to become king or queen **5 in ascending order** if a group of things are arranged in ascending order, each thing is higher, or greater in amount, than the one before it —opposite DESCEND

**as·cen·dan·cy**, **ascendency** /əˈsendənsi/ *n* [U] a position of power, influence or control: [+ **over/in**] *He slowly gained ascendancy in the group.*

**as·cen·dant**[1] /əˈsendənt/ also **ascendent** *n* **be in the ascendant** to be or become powerful or popular: *During this period the trade union view was in the ascendant.*

**ascendant**[2] also **ascendent** *adj* **1** becoming more powerful or popular **2** rising

**as·cen·sion** /əˈsenʃən/ *n* [U] the act of moving up

**as·cent** /əˈsent/ *n* **1** [C usually singular] a path or way up to the top of something, for example a mountain: *a rugged and abrupt ascent* **2** [C usually singular] the act of climbing something or moving upwards: *We rested in the valley before beginning the ascent.* **3** [U] the process of becoming more important, powerful, or successful than before: *the ascent of man to modern civilization* —opposite DESCENT (1, 2, 4)

**as·cer·tain** /ˌæsəˈteɪn‖ˌæsər-/ *v* [I,T] *formal* to find out if a fact that you think is true is really true: *The police were never able to ascertain the true facts.*| [+ **how/when/why etc**] *He could not ascertain where the clouds ended and the snow-covered rocks began.* —**ascertainable** *adv*

**as·cet·ic** /əˈsetɪk/ *adj* living without any physical pleasures or comforts, especially for religious reasons: *the ascetic life of Buddhist monks* —**ascetic** *n* [C] —**ascetically** *adv* —**asceticism** *n* [U]

**as·cot** /ˈæskɒt‖-kət/ *n* [C] *AmE* a wide piece of material worn by men loosely folded around their neck inside their collar; CRAVAT

**as·cribe** /əˈskraɪb/ *v*

**ascribe** sth **to** sb/sth *phr v* [T] *formal* **1** to believe that something happens or exists because of someone or something else: *The melody is ascribed to Bach.*| *They ascribe the country's difficulties to the last government's policies.* **2** to believe something or someone has a particular quality: *The Malays ascribe healing properties to this fruit.* —**ascribable** *adj* [+ **to**]

**a·sep·tic** /eɪˈseptɪk, ə-/ *adj* a wound that is aseptic is completely clean without any harmful BACTERIA

**a·sex·u·al** /eɪˈsekʃuəl/ *adj* **1** not having sexual organs or having sex **2 a)** not seeming to have any sexual qualities: *He strikes me as a completely asexual person.* **b)** not interested in sexual relations —**asexually** *adv*: *a plant that reproduces asexually*

**ash** /æʃ/ *n* [C,U] **1** the soft grey powder that remains after something has been burnt: *cigarette ash*| *The house burnt to ashes.* **2** a very hard wood, or the tree, common in Britain and North America, that produces this **3 ashes** [plural] the ash that remains when a dead person's body is burned: *We scattered my father's ashes over the lake.*

**a·shamed** /əˈʃeɪmd/ *adj* [not before noun] **1** feeling shame because of something you have done: **be ashamed of doing sth** *I was ashamed of having lied to my mother.*| **be ashamed that** *Barry was ashamed that he had lost his temper.*| **You ought to be ashamed (of yourself)** *spoken* (=used to tell someone they should feel guilty about something) *You ought to be ashamed of yourself – treating your sister like that!* **2** feeling uncomfortable or upset, especially because someone does something that embarrasses you: [+ **of**] *Sherry is at that age when kids are ashamed of their parents.*| **be ashamed to be/do sth** *That kind of behaviour makes me ashamed to be British.* — see SHAME[1] (USAGE) S3

**ash·can** /ˈæʃkæn/ *n* [C] *AmE old-fashioned* a GARBAGE CAN

**ash·en** /ˈæʃən/ *adj* being a pale grey colour like ash: *her ashen face.*

**a·shore** /əˈʃɔː‖əˈʃɔːr/ *adv* on or towards the shore of a lake, river, sea, or ocean: *Brian pulled the boat ashore.*

**ash·ram** /ˈæʃrəm/ *n* [C] **1** a place where a Hindu holy man lives alone **2** a house where people live together practising the religion of Hinduism

**ash·tray** /ˈæʃtreɪ/ *n* [C] a small dish where you put used cigarettes —see picture at TRAY S3

**Ash Wednes·day** /ˌ· ˈ··/ *n* [C,U] the first day of Lent

**A·sian**[1] /ˈeɪʃən, ˈeɪʒən‖ˈeɪʒən, ˈeɪʃən/ *n* **1** *BrE* someone from Asia, especially India or Pakistan **2** *AmE* someone from Asia, especially Japan, China, Korea etc

**A·sian**[2] *adj* from Asia or related to Asia

**Asian-A·mer·i·can** /ˌ·· ·ˈ···/ *n* [C] an American citizen whose family was originally from Asia

**a·side**[1] /əˈsaɪd/ *adv* **1 move/step aside** to move, step etc to the side: *I stepped aside just in time, and the car whizzed past.* **2 put/set/leave sth aside a)** to save part of an amount of money: *I've been setting aside a little money each week for our holiday.* **b)** to keep something separate or not use it because someone is going to buy or use it later: *One of the rooms was set aside for a yoga class.* **c)** to leave something to be considered at another time: *Let's put this question aside for next week.* **3 brush/sweep sth aside** to treat someone's idea or statement in a way that shows you do not think it is important: *Mr. Coleman brushed my suggestion aside and asked for another question.* **4 aside from** *especially AmE* **a)** except for: *Aside from that one little problem, the day was perfect.* **b)** in addition to: *Aside from physical problems, these patients also show a lot of hostility.* **5** used to show that something you have just said is not as important as what you are going to say next: *These problems aside, we think the plan should go ahead.* S3 W3

**aside**[2] *n* [C] **1** words spoken by an actor to the people watching a play, that the other characters in the play do

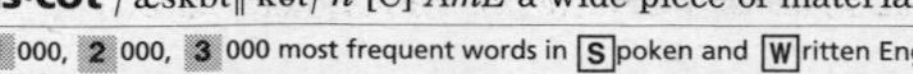

not hear **2** a remark made in a low voice that you only intend certain people to hear **3** a remark or story that is not part of the main subject of a speech

**as·i·nine** /ˈæsɪ̵naɪn/ *adj* extremely stupid or silly; RIDICULOUS: *What an asinine remark!*

S1 W1 **ask** /ɑːsk‖æsk/ *v*
**1** ▶ **QUESTION** ◀ [I,T] to say or write something in order to get an answer, a solution, or information: *"What's your name?" she asked.* | **ask a question** *That kid's always asking awkward questions.* | **ask who/what/where etc** *I was only asking how this could have happened.* | **ask sb sth** *She asked an old man the way to the station.* | **ask sb** *Don't ask him – he won't know anything about it.* | **ask if/whether** *Go and ask Pat whether he's coming tonight.* | **ask (sb) about** *Visitors usually ask about the history of the place.* | **ask around** (=ask in a lot of places or ask a lot of people) *I'm not sure where you can get a good mechanic – you'd better ask around.*
**2** ▶ **FOR HELP ETC** ◀ [I,T] to make a request for help, advice, information etc: *If you need anything, you only have to ask.* | **ask sb to do sth** *Ask John to mail those letters tomorrow.* | **ask to do sth** *Karen asked to see whoever was in charge.* | [+ **for**] *Some people find it difficult to ask for help.* | **ask if you can do sth** *Ask your dad if we can borrow his truck.* —see REQUEST (USAGE)
**3** ▶ **PRICE** ◀ [T] to want a particular amount for money for something you are selling: **ask $50/£1,000 etc for** *I can't believe he's asking £2,000 for that old car.* | **ask the earth/a fortune (for)** (=ask far too much money for something) *They're asking the earth for tickets – we just can't afford it.*
**4** ▶ **INVITE** ◀ [T] to invite someone to your home, to go out with you etc: **ask sb out** (=ask someone, especially someone of the opposite sex, to go to the theatre, a restaurant etc with you) *Jerry's too scared to ask her out.* | **ask sb in** (=invite someone into your house, office etc) *Don't leave them standing on the doorstep – ask them in!* | **ask sb along** (=invite someone to go somewhere with you, especially when you are with a lot of other people) *Get Bill to ask Sheila along.* | **ask sb over** (=invite someone to come to your home)
**5 be asking for it** *spoken* used to say that someone deserves something bad that happens to them: *I don't really care he got beat up on – he was asking for it.*
**6 be asking for trouble** to do something that is very likely to have a bad effect or result: *He thinks anyone who completely trusts anyone else is asking for trouble.*
**7 don't ask me** *spoken* used to say you do not know the answer to something: *"Where's she gone then?" "Don't ask me!"*
**8 asking price** the price that someone wants to sell something for: *At an asking price of just £250, it's got to be a bargain.*
**9 ask yourself** to try to honestly discover the true reason for something: *The government should ask itself where the responsibility for this mess really lies.*
**10 for the asking** if you can have something for the asking, you only have to ask for it and you can have it
**11 I ask you!** *spoken* used to express surprise at and disapproval of something stupid that someone has done: *She sent her kids to camp dressed all in white. I ask you!* —see REQUEST² (USAGE)

**USAGE NOTE: ASK**

WORD CHOICE: **ask, want to know, inquire, question, interrogate**

**Ask** is the usual verb for questions: *"How are you doing?" she asked.* | *That's a stupid question to ask.* Often people use **want to know** when they are talking about what someone else has asked: *He wanted to know where I lived/the train times.*

**Inquire** (or **enquire** *BrE*) has the same meaning but is more formal, and is not followed by a noun or pronoun object. At a meeting: *May I inquire what the committee proposes to do about this?/about the effectiveness of this policy* (NOT *...inquire the effectiveness of this policy*)?

To **question** a person is to ask them a lot of questions, especially officially, and to **interrogate** suggests that someone is being held by force and asked questions that they are unwilling to answer, for example by the police or an enemy.

GRAMMAR

Remember that you do not follow **ask** with a direct question, unless you are repeating the exact words: *Ask what sort of room he would like* (NOT *Ask what sort of room would he like*). | *I asked "What sort of room would you like?"*.

You **ask** people certain things without using *for* or *about*: *I asked him the way/his name/the price/the time/a favour/permission/his advice* (NOT *asked to him the way*). You usually **ask for** or **about** most other things: *Ask one of our guides for directions to Lincoln Center.* | *He asked Sharon for a date* (NOT *He asked a date to Sharon*). | *Can I ask you about the exam results?* (NOT *of the exam results*).

**a·skance** /əˈskæns, əˈskɑːns‖əˈskæns/ *adv* **look askance (at)** to look at or consider something in a way that shows you do not believe it or approve of it

**a·skew** /əˈskjuː/ *adv* not quite straight or in the right position: *Matilda ran towards us with her hat askew.*

**a·slant** /əˈslɑːnt‖əˈslænt/ *adv* [not before noun] *formal* not straight up or down, but across at an angle —**aslant** *adj*

**a·sleep** /əˈsliːp/ *adj* [not before noun] **1** sleeping: *Quiet! The baby is asleep.* | **fast/sound asleep** (=very deeply asleep) *You'll be fast asleep by the time we get home.* **2 fall asleep a)** to begin to sleep: *I always fall asleep watching TV.* **b)** *literary* used to mean that someone dies when you want to avoid saying this directly **3** an arm or leg that is asleep has been in one position for too long, so you cannot feel it —see also **go to sleep** (SLEEP¹ (3)) **4 half asleep** not paying attention to something because you are tired S

**A/S level** /ˌeɪ ˈes ˌlevəl/ *n* **1** [U] an examination in British schools, for pupils who have taken GCSE*s* and want to study a wider range of subjects than is possible at A LEVEL **2** [C] an examination at this standard in a particular subject

**asp** /æsp/ *n* [C] a small poisonous snake from North Africa

**as·par·a·gus** /əˈspærəgəs/ *n* [U] a long thin green vegetable with a point at one end —see picture on page 414

**as·pect** /ˈæspekt/ *n* **1** [C] one part of a situation, idea, plan etc that has many parts: [+ **of**] *Alcoholism affects all aspects of family life.* **2** [C] the direction in which a window, room, front of a building etc faces: *a south-facing aspect* **3** [C,U] *formal* the appearance of someone or something: *Her face wore a melancholy aspect.* **4** [C,U] *technical* the form of a verb in grammar that shows whether an action is continuing, or happens always, repeatedly, or once: *'He sings' differs from 'He is singing' in aspect.* 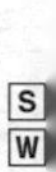

**as·pen** /ˈæspən/ *n* [C] a kind of tree of western North America with leaves that shake in the wind

**as·per·i·ty** /æˈsperɪ̵ti, ə-/ *n* [C,U] *formal* a way of speaking or behaving that is rough or severe: *the asperity of her manner*

**as·per·sion** /əˈspɜːʃən, -ʒən‖-əˈspɜːrʒən, -ʃən/ *n* **cast aspersions on** *formal* to make an unkind remark or an unfair judgment: *Are you casting aspersions on my wife's character?*

**as·phalt** /ˈæsfælt‖ˈæsfɒːlt/ *n* [U] a black sticky substance that becomes hard when it dries, used for making the surface of roads —**asphalt** *v* [T]

**as·phyx·i·a** /æsˈfɪksiə, əs-/ *n* [U] death caused by not being able to breathe

**as·phyx·i·ate** /æsˈfɪksieɪt, əs-/ *v* [I,T] *technical* to be unable to breathe air or make someone unable to do so, especially to die or kill someone in this way; SUFFOCATE (1) —**asphyxiation** /æsˌfɪksiˈeɪʃən, əs-/ *n* [U]

**as·pic** /ˈæspɪk/ *n* [U] a clear brownish JELLY (3) eaten with meat

**as·pi·dis·tra** /ˌæspəˈdɪstrə/ *n* [C] a plant with broad green pointed leaves, often grown in houses

**as·pi·rant** /əˈspaɪərənt, ˈæspərənt‖əˈspaɪr-,ˈæsp-/ *n* [C + **to/for**] *formal* someone who hopes to get a position of importance or honour

**as·pi·rate¹** /ˈæspəreɪt/ *v* [T] *technical* to make the sound of an 'H' when speaking, or to blow out air when pronouncing some consonants

**as·pi·rate²** /ˈæspərət/ *n* [C] *technical* the sound of the letter 'H', or the letter itself

**as·pi·ra·tion** /ˌæspəˈreɪʃən/ *n* **1** [C usually plural, U] a strong desire to have or achieve something: *Hannah has always had political aspirations.* | [+ **of**] *the aspirations of the working classes* **2** [U] the sound of air blowing out that happens when some CONSONANTS are pronounced, such as the /p/ in pin

**as·pire** /əˈspaɪə‖-əˈspaɪr/ *v* [I] to desire and work towards achieving something important: [+ **to/after**] *It was clear that Mrs Thatcher aspired to the leadership of the party.* | **aspire to do sth** *At that time, all serious artists aspired to go to Rome and paint.*

**as·pirin** /ˈæsprən/ *n plural* **aspirins** *or* **aspirin** [C,U] a medicine that reduces pain, INFLAMMATION, and fever

S2 **ass** /æs/ *n* [C]
**1** ▶ **PART OF BODY** ◀ *especially AmE* an impolite word for the part of your body that you sit on: *I tripped and fell flat on my ass.*
**2 get your ass in gear** also **move your ass** *spoken* an impolite way of telling someone to hurry: *Get your ass in gear, or you'll miss your plane!*
**3 get off your ass** *AmE spoken* an impolite way of telling someone to stop being lazy: *If you want to pass this test, you'd better get off your ass and study!*
**4 kick/whip sb's ass** also **kick (some) ass** *AmE slang* to beat someone easily in a fight, game, or sport: *Let's get out there and kick some ass.*
**5 be on sb's ass** *AmE spoken* **a)** an impolite way of saying that someone is annoying you by telling you to do things you do not want to do: *My boss is on my ass all the time.* **b)** an impolite way of saying that someone is driving very close to the back of another car
**6 get your ass over here** *AmE spoken* an impolite way of telling someone to come quickly
**7 my ass!** *AmE spoken* an impolite way of saying that you do not believe something: *"He said he ran twenty miles." "Twenty miles my ass!"*
**8** ▶ **STUPID PERSON** ◀ *informal* a stupid, annoying person: **make an ass of yourself** (=do something stupid or embarrassing)
**9 sb doesn't know their ass from their elbow** *AmE spoken* an impolite way of saying that someone is stupid
**10** ▶ **ANIMAL** ◀ *old use* a DONKEY —see also ARSE, **haul ass** (HAUL¹ (6)), **kiss sb's ass** (KISS), **pain in the arse/ass etc** (PAIN¹ (3)), **piece of ass** (PIECE¹ (21)), **risk your ass** (RISK), SMART ARSE

**as·sail** /əˈseɪl/ *v* [T] **1** [usually passive] if a thought or feeling assails you, it worries or upsets you: *Carla was suddenly assailed by doubts.* **2** to attack someone or something violently: **assail sb with sth** *The angry crowd assailed police with stones and bottles.*

**as·sai·lant** /əˈseɪlənt/ *n* [C] *formal* someone who attacks another person: *Ms Hervey states that she could not see her assailant's face.*

**as·sas·sin** /əˈsæsən/ *n* [C] someone who murders an important person: *Kennedy's supposed assassin, Lee Harvey Oswald*

**as·sas·sin·ate** /əˈsæsəneɪt‖-sə neɪt/ *v* [T] to murder an important person: *a plot to assassinate the President* —see KILL¹ (USAGE)

**as·sas·sin·a·tion** /əˌsæsəˈneɪʃən/ *n* [C,U] the act of assassinating someone: *a terrorist group plotting an assassination* | **assassination attempt** (=a situation in which someone tries but fails to assassinate someone) —see also **character assassination** (CHARACTER (6))

**as·sault¹** /əˈsɔːlt‖əˈsɒːlt/ *n* [C,U] **1** the crime of attacking someone: *increases in violent assaults over the past decade* | **sexual assault** *three years in prison for sexual assault* **2** a military attack to take control of a place controlled by the enemy: *the platoon's unsuccessful assault on the border positions* **3** an attempt to achieve something difficult, especially using physical force: [+ **on**] *an assault on Mt Everest* (=an attempt to climb it) **4 assault on** a strong spoken or written criticism of someone else's ideas, plans etc: *the tobacco industry's recent assault on plans to ban cigarettes* W3

**assault²** *v* [T] **1** to attack someone in a violent way: *Policemen were assaulted by young demonstrators.* **2** to strongly criticize someone's ideas, plans etc: *The MP was assaulted with a barrage of abuse from angry strikers.* **3** if a feeling assaults you, it affects you in a way that makes you uncomfortable or upset: *The noise in the club assaulted our ears.*

**assault and bat·ter·y** /ˌ··· ˈ···/ *n* [U] *law* the official name for a violent attack and the threats that the attacker makes before it

**assault course** /·ˈ· ˌ·/ *n* [C] *BrE* an area of land with special equipment to climb, jump over, run through etc that is used for developing physical strength especially by soldiers; OBSTACLE COURSE *AmE*

**as·say** /əˈseɪ/ *v* [T] **1** to test a metal **2** *literary* to attempt to do something: *to assay the impossible* —**assay** /əˈseɪ,ˈæseɪ‖ˈæseɪ, æˈseɪ/ *n* [C]

**as·se·gai** /ˈæsəgaɪ/ *n* [C] a long thin wooden stick with an iron point, used as a weapon in southern Africa

**as·sem·blage** /əˈsemblɪdʒ/ *n formal* **1** [C] a group of people or things that are together **2** [U] the act of putting parts together in order to make something

**as·sem·ble** /əˈsembəl/ *v* **1** [I] if a group of people assemble in one place, they all go there together: *A large crowd had assembled opposite the American embassy.* **2** [T] to gather a large number of things or people together in one place: *Over the years we've assembled a huge collection of old books.* **3** [T] to put all the parts of something together: *an easy-to-assemble kit*

**as·sem·bly** /əˈsembli/ *n* **1** [C] a group of people who are elected to make laws for a particular country or area: *the New York State Assembly* **2** [C + **of**] a group of people who have gathered together for a particular purpose **3** [C,U] a regular meeting of all the teachers and pupils of a school **4** [U] the process of putting parts together in order to make something: *instructions for assembly* **5 the right of assembly/freedom of assembly** the right of any group to meet together in order to discuss things S3 W2

**assembly line** /·ˈ··· ·/ *n* [C] a system for making things in a factory in which the products move past a line of workers who each make or check one part

**as·sem·bly·man** /əˈsemblimən/ *n* [C] *AmE* a male member of an ASSEMBLY¹ (2)

**as·sem·bly·wom·an** /əˈsembliˌwʊmən/ *n* [C] *AmE* a female member of an ASSEMBLY¹ (2)

**as·sent¹** /əˈsent/ *n* [U] *formal* approval or agreement from someone who has authority: *a nod of assent* | **the Royal assent** (=act of officially signing a new law by the British King or Queen)

**assent²** *v* [I + **to**] *formal* to agree to a suggestion, idea etc after considering it carefully

**as·sert** /əˈsɜːt‖-ɜːrt/ *v* [T] **1 assert your rights/independence etc** to state very strongly your right to do or have something **2 assert yourself** to behave in a determined way so that people do not make you do things you do not want: *You need to assert yourself more.* **3** to state firmly that something is true: **assert that** *The professor asserted that there was nothing wrong with his* *theory.* **4 assert itself** if an idea or belief asserts itself, it begins to influence something: *Milton's influence asserts itself later in his poetry.*

**as·ser·tion** /ə'sɜːʃən‖-ɜːr-/ *n* [C] something that you say or write that you strongly believe: **assertion that** *Wilkinson kept repeating his assertion that he was innocent.*

**as·ser·tive** /ə'sɜːtɪv‖-ɜːr-/ *adj* behaving in a confident way so that people notice you —**assertively** *adv* —**assertiveness** *n* [U] *assertiveness training*

S2 W2 **as·sess** /ə'ses/ *v* [T] **1** to make a judgment about a person or situation after thinking carefully about it: *It's difficult to assess the effects of the new legislation just yet.* | **assess what/how etc** *We've tried to assess what went wrong.* **2** to calculate the value or cost of something: **assess sth at** *They assessed the value of the house at over $250,000.*

S2 W2 **as·sess·ment** /ə'sesmənt/ *n* **1** [C,U] a process in which you make a judgment about a person or situation: *What's your assessment of the situation in Northern Ireland?* **2** [C,U] a calculation about the cost or value of something: *a tax assessment* —see also **continuous assessment** ((CONTINUOUS) (3))

**as·ses·sor** /ə'sesə‖-ər/ *n* [C] **1** someone who decides how well someone has done in an examination **2** someone whose job is to calculate the value of something or the amount of tax someone should pay **3** someone who knows a lot about a subject or activity and who advises a judge or an official committee

S2 W2 **as·set** /'æset/ *n* [C] **1** [usually plural] the things that a company owns, that can be sold to pay debts **2** [usually singular] something or someone that is useful because they help you succeed or deal with problems: *A sense of humor is a real asset in this business.* | **be an asset to** *I think Rachel would be an asset to the department.* —compare LIABILITY —see also LIQUID ASSETS

**asset strip·ping** /'·· ˌ··/ *n* [U] the practice of buying a company cheaply and then selling all the things it owns to make a quick profit

**as·sev·e·rate** /ə'sevəreɪt/ *v* [T + **that**] to state something very firmly and seriously

**ass·hole** /'æshəʊl‖-hoʊl/ *n* [C] **1** an offensive word for someone you think stupid and annoying **2** an offensive word for the ANUS — see also ARSEHOLE

**as·sid·u·ous** /ə'sɪdjuəs‖-dʒuəs/ *adj formal* very careful to make sure that something is done properly or completely: *an assiduous collector of folk songs* —**assiduously** *adv* —**assiduity** /ˌæsɪ̈'djuːɪ̈ti‖-'duː-/ *n* [U]

**as·sign** /ə'saɪn/ *v* [T] **1** to give someone a particular job or make them responsible for a particular person or thing: **assign sb a job/duty/task** *I've been assigned the job of looking after the new students.* | **assign sb to** *Jan's been assigned to the Asian Affairs Bureau.* **2** to decide that something should be done at or during a particular time: *How much time have you assigned for the meeting?* **3** *formal* to give money, equipment etc to someone or decide it should be used for a particular purpose: **assign sth to** *The US has already assigned a large part of its foreign aid budget to Rwanda.*

**as·sig·na·tion** /ˌæsɪg'neɪʃən/ *n* [C] a secret meeting, especially with someone you are having a romantic relationship with: *a secret assignation at midnight*

S2 **as·sign·ment** /ə'saɪnmənt/ *n* **1** [C] a piece of work that is given to someone as part of their job, or that a student is asked to do: *a history assignment* | **on an assignment** *Joanna's going to Italy on a special assignment for her newspaper.* **2** [U] the act of giving people particular jobs to do: *the assignment of chores*

**as·sim·i·late** /ə'sɪmɪ̈leɪt/ *v* **1** [T] to think about new ideas, information etc so that you feel ready to use them: *It will take time to assimilate all these facts.* **2** [I,T] if people assimilate or are assimilated into a country or group, they become part of it and are accepted by other people in it: [+ **into**] *women being assimilated into the workforce* **3** [T] *technical* if you assimilate food, you take it into your mouth and DIGEST[1] (1) it

**as·sim·i·la·tion** /əˌsɪmɪ̈'leɪʃən/ *n* [U] **1** the process of assimilating or being assimilated **2** *technical* the process in which a sound in a word changes because of the effect of another sound next to it, for example the 'p' in 'cupboard'

**as·sist**[1] /ə'sɪst/ *v* **1** [I,T] to help someone to do something, especially by doing all the less important things so that they can spend time doing difficult things: **assist (sb) with/in** *I was employed to assist the manager with his duties.* **2** [T] to make it easier for someone to do something: *They had no maps to assist them.* —see HELP[1] (USAGE) S3 W3

**assist**[2] *n* [C] an action that helps another player on your team to make a point

**as·sist·ance** /ə'sɪstəns/ *n* [U] help or support: *financial assistance* | *Can I be of any assistance?* (=can I help you?) | **with the assistance of** *a report drawn up with the assistance of experts* | **come to sb's assistance** (=help someone) *One of her fellow passengers came to her assistance.* —see HELP[1] (USAGE) S3 W2

**as·sis·tant**[1] /ə'sɪstənt/ *adj* **assistant manager/director/cook etc** someone whose job is just below the level of manager, etc

**assistant**[2] *n* [C] **1** someone who helps someone else in their work, especially by doing the less important jobs: *a clerical assistant* **2** a SHOP ASSISTANT —see also PERSONAL ASSISTANT S3

**assistant pro·fes·sor** /·ˌ·· ·'··/ *n* [C] the lowest rank of PROFESSOR (2) at an American university

**as·siz·es** /ə'saɪzɪ̈z/ *n* [plural] *old use* a meeting of a court in which a judge who travelled to different towns in Britain dealt with cases —**assize** *adj*

**assn** a written abbreviation of ASSOCIATION

**assoc** a written abbreviation of ASSOCIATION

**as·so·ci·ate**[1] /ə'səʊʃieɪt, ə'səʊsi-‖ə'soʊ-/ *v* **1 associate sb/sth with** to make a connection in your mind between one thing or person and another: *I've never associated you with this place.* | *People usually associate Japan with high tech consumer products.* **2 be associated (with)** to be connected with a particular subject, activity, group etc: *problems associated with cancer treatment* | *I wouldn't want to be associated with McKey's project.* **3 associate with sb** to spend time with someone, especially a group who other people disapprove of: *I don't like these layabouts you're associating with.* S3 W2

**as·so·ci·ate**[2] /ə'səʊʃiɪ̈t, ə'səʊsi-‖ə'soʊ-/ *n* [C] **1** someone who you work or do business with: *one of his business associates* **2** someone who has an associate degree

**associate**[3] *adj* **associate member/director/head etc** someone who has some of the same rights or responsibilities as a member etc

**associated com·pa·ny** /·ˌ···· '···/ *n* [C] a company of which 20 to 50 per cent of the shares (SHARE[2] (6)) are owned by another company

**associate de·gree** /·ˌ··· ·'·/ *n* [C] a degree given after two years of study at a JUNIOR COLLEGE in the US

**associate pro·fes·sor** /·ˌ··· ·'··/ *n* [C] a PROFESSOR (2) at an American university whose job is above the level of ASSISTANT PROFESSOR and below the level of FULL PROFESSOR —compare ASSISTANT PROFESSOR, FULL PROFESSOR

**as·so·ci·a·tion** /əˌsəʊsi'eɪʃən, əˌsəʊʃi-‖əˌsoʊ-/ *n* [C] **1** an organization that consists of a group of people who have the same aims, do the same kind of work etc: *the Association of Master Builders* | *an association to help families suffering from alcoholism.* —see also HOUSING ASSOCIATION **2** a connection with a particular person, organization, group etc: *his association with the Green Party* **3** a feeling or memory that is connected with a particular place, event, word etc: *Scotland has all kinds of happy associations for me.* **4 in association with** made or done together with another person, organ- S3 W1 ization etc: *concerts sponsored by the Arts Council in association with several local businesses* —see also FREE ASSOCIATION

**Association foot·ball** /ˌ····ˈ··/ *n* [U] *BrE formal* FOOTBALL (1)

**as·so·nance** /ˈæsənəns/ *n* [U] *technical* similarity in the vowel sounds of words that are close together in a poem, for example between 'born' and 'warm'

**as·sort·ed** /əˈsɔːtɪ̣d‖-ɔːr-/ *adj* of various different kinds: *assorted sizes* | *assorted cookies* —see also ILL-ASSORTED

**as·sort·ment** /əˈsɔːtmənt‖-ɔːr-/ *n* [C] a mixture of different things or of various kinds of the same thing: **[+ of]** *an odd assortment of knives and forks*

**asst** the written abbreviation of ASSISTANT

**as·suage** /əˈsweɪdʒ/ *v* [T] *literary* to make an unpleasant feeling less painful or severe; RELIEVE (1): *Nothing could assuage his guilt.*

S1 W1 **as·sume** /əˈsjuːm‖əˈsuːm/ *v* [T] **1** to think that something is true, although you have no proof of it: **assume (that)** *I didn't see your car, so I assumed you'd gone out.* | *Assuming that the proposal is accepted, when are we going to get the money?* | **we can safely assume** (=used to say that something is certain to happen) *I think we can safely assume that interest rates will go up again soon.* | **assume guilt/innocence** (=assume that someone is guilty or not guilty of a crime) **2 assume control/power/responsibilities etc** to start to do a job, especially an important one: *The President assumes his new responsibilities in January.* **3 assume a manner/air/expression etc** *formal* to behave in a way that does not show how you really feel, especially in order to seem more confident, cheerful etc than you are: *Andy assumed an air of indifference whenever her name was mentioned.* **4** to start to have a particular quality or appearance: *The problem is beginning to assume massive proportions.* **5** to be based on the idea that something else is correct; PRESUPPOSE: **assume (that)** *Your theory assumes that we are willing to pay for services by taxation.*

**as·sumed** /əˈsjuːmd‖əˈsuːmd/ *adj* **under an assumed name** using a false name: *He registered at the hotel under an assumed name.*

S2 W2 **as·sump·tion** /əˈsʌmpʃən/ *n* **1** [C] something that you think is true although you have no proof: **make an assumption** *A lot of people make the assumption that poverty only exists in the Third World.* | **on the assumption that** *I'm working on the assumption that the money will come through.* | **underlying assumption** (=a belief that is used to support a statement or idea, even though this belief may not be correct) *the underlying assumption that scientific progress is always a good thing* **2** [U] *formal* the act of starting to have control or power: **[+ of]** *the assumption of responsibility*

**as·sur·ance** /əˈʃʊərəns‖əˈʃʊr-/ *n* **1** [U] a feeling of calm confidence in your own abilities, especially because you have a lot of experience; SELF-ASSURANCE: *She spoke in a tone of quiet assurance.* **2** [C] a promise that you will definitely do something or that something will definitely happen, especially to make someone less worried: *Despite my repeated assurances Rob still looked very nervous.* | **assurance that** *I give you my personal assurance that the work will be done very soon.* **3** [U] *BrE technical* insurance against events that are certain to happen; INSURANCE(1) *AmE* —see also LIFE ASSURANCE

S2 W3 **as·sure** /əˈʃʊə‖əˈʃʊr/ *v* [T] **1** to tell someone that something will definitely happen or is definitely true so that they are less worried: **assure sb that** *Mom assured us that everything would be all right.* | **I (can) assure you** *spoken*: *The document is genuine, I can assure you.* | **assure sb of sth** *The dealer had assured me of its quality.* —see also **rest assured** (REST² (6)) **2 be assured of** to be able to feel certain that something will happen: *The Liberal Democrats are assured of success in the local elections.* **3** to make something certain to happen or to be achieved; ENSURE: *Excellent reviews have assured the film's success.* —see INSURE (USAGE)

**as·sured** /əˈʃʊəd‖əˈʃʊrd/ *adj* **1** confident about your own abilities; SELF-ASSURED: *an assured manner* **2** certain to happen or to be achieved: *Her political future looks assured.* **3 the assured** *BrE technical* someone whose life has been insured

**as·sur·ed·ly** /əˈʃʊərɪ̣dli‖əˈʃʊr-/ *adv formal* definitely or certainly: *as these three fine examples assuredly demonstrate*

**as·te·risk** /ˈæstərɪsk/ *n* [C] a mark like a star (*), used especially to show something interesting or important —**asterisk** *v* [T]

**a·stern** /əˈstɜːn‖-ɜːrn/ *adv* in or at the back of a ship

**as·te·roid** /ˈæstərɔɪd/ *n* [C] one of the many small PLANETS between Mars and Jupiter

**asth·ma** /ˈæsmə‖ˈæzmə/ *n* [U] an illness that causes difficulties in breathing

**asth·mat·ic** /æsˈmætɪk‖æz-/ *adj* suffering from asthma —**asthmatic** *n* [C] —**asthmatically** /-kli/ *adv*

**as·tig·ma·tis·m** /əˈstɪgmətɪzəm/ *n* [U] difficulty in seeing clearly that is caused by a change in the inner shape of the eye —**astigmatic** /ˌæstɪgˈmætɪk◂/ *adj*

**a·stir** /əˈstɜː‖əˈstɜːr/ *adj* [not before noun] *literary* **1** awake and out of bed **2** excited about something: *The whole village was astir as the visitors arrived.*

**as·ton·ish** /əˈstɒnɪʃ‖əˈstɑː-/ *v* [T] to surprise someone very much: *Diana astonished her family by winning three competitions in a row.* | **what astonishes someone is** *What astonishes me most is his complete lack of fear.*

**as·ton·ished** /əˈstɒnɪʃt‖əˈstɑː-/ *adj* very surprised about something: *We climbed out of the hole, right in front of two astonished policemen.* | **astonished that** *The man seemed astonished that anyone would want to buy the house.* | **astonished to see/hear/find etc** *We were astonished to find the temple still in its original condition.*

**as·ton·ish·ing** /əˈstɒnɪʃɪŋ‖əˈstɑː-/ *adj* so surprising that it is difficult to believe: *an astonishing achievement* —**astonishingly** *adv*: *She looked astonishingly beautiful.*

**as·ton·ish·ment** /əˈstɒnɪʃmənt‖əˈstɑː-/ *n* [U] complete surprise: **in astonishment** *She stared at him in astonishment.* | **to your astonishment** *To my astonishment, the keys were in the door.*

**as·tound** /əˈstaʊnd/ *v* [T] to make someone very surprised or shocked: *The judge's decision astounded everyone.* —**astounded** *adj*: *an astounded look*

**as·tound·ing** /əˈstaʊndɪŋ/ *adj* so surprising that it is almost impossible to believe: *house prices shooting up at an astounding rate* —**astoundingly** *adv*: *astoundingly beautiful scenery.*

**as·tra·khan** /ˌæstrəˈkæn◂‖ˈæstrəkən/ *n* [U] black or grey fur used for making coats and hats

**as·tral** /ˈæstrəl/ *adj formal* connected with stars: *astral bodies*

**a·stray** /əˈstreɪ/ *adv* **1 go astray a)** to become lost: *One of the documents has gone astray.* **b)** *humorous* to start behaving in an immoral way **2 lead sb astray a)** *often humorous* to encourage someone to do bad or immoral things that they would not normally do: *His mother worries that the older boys will lead him astray.* **b)** to make someone believe something that is not true: *It's easy to be led astray by the reports in the papers.*

**a·stride** /əˈstraɪd/ *adv* with one leg on each side of something

**as·trin·gent¹** /əˈstrɪndʒənt/ *adj* **1** *technical* able to make your skin less oily or stop a wound from bleeding: *an astringent lotion* **2** criticizing someone very severely: *astringent remarks* —**astringency** *n* [U]

**astringent²** *n* [C,U] *technical* a substance used to make your skin less oily or to stop a wound from bleeding

**astro-** /æstrəʊ, -trə‖-troʊ, -trə/ *prefix* concerning the stars, the PLANETS, or space: *an astronaut* (=someone who travels in space) | *astrophysics* (=science of the stars)

**as·trol·o·ger** /əˈstrɒlədʒə‖əˈstrɑːlədʒər/ *n* [C] someone

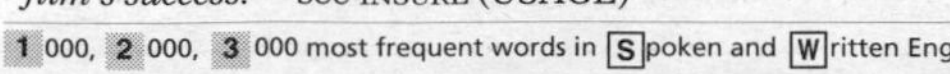

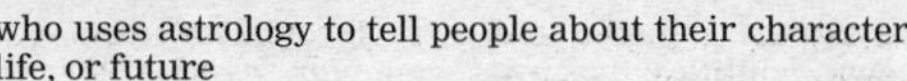

who uses astrology to tell people about their character, life, or future

**as·trol·o·gy** /əˈstrɒlədʒi‖əˈstrɑː-/ *n* [U] the study of the relationship between the movements of the stars and their influence on people and events —see also ZODIAC —**astrological** /ˌæstrəˈlɒdʒɪkəl◂‖-ˈlɑː-/ *adj* —**astrologically** /-kli/ *adv*

**as·tro·naut** /ˈæstrənɔːt‖-nɒːt, -nɑːt/ *n* [C] someone who travels and works in a SPACECRAFT

**as·tro·nom·i·cal** /ˌæstrəˈnɒmɪkəl◂‖-ˈnɑː-/ *adj* **1** astronomical prices, costs etc are extremely high **2** connected with the study of the stars —**astronomically** /-kli/ *adv*: *astronomically high rents*

**as·tron·o·my** /əˈstrɒnəmi‖əˈstrɑː-/ *n* [U] the scientific study of the stars

**as·tro·phys·ics** /ˌæstrəʊˈfɪzɪks‖ ˌæstrə-, -troʊ-/ *n* [U] the scientific study of the chemical structure of the stars and the forces that influence them —**astrophysical** *adj* —**astrophysicist** /-ˈfɪzɪsɪst/ *n* [C]

**as·tro·turf** /ˈæstrəʊtɜːrf/ *n* [U] *trademark* an artificial surface, like grass, that is used in sports such as football

**as·tute** /əˈstjuːt‖əˈstuːt/ *adj* able to understand situations or behaviour very well and very quickly, especially so that you can get an advantage for yourself: *a particularly astute electoral move*|*astute investments* —**astutely** *adv* —**astuteness** *n* [U]

**a·sun·der** /əˈsʌndə‖-ər/ *adv* **be torn asunder** *literary* to be broken violently into many pieces: *The boat was torn asunder on the rocks.*

**a·sy·lum** /əˈsaɪləm/ *n* **1** [U] protection given to someone by a government because they have escaped from fighting or political trouble in their own country —see also POLITICAL ASYLUM **2** [C] *old use* a MENTAL HOSPITAL

**a·sym·met·ri·cal** /ˌeɪsɪˈmetrɪkəl/ also **a·sym·met·ric** /-ˈmetrɪk◂/ *adj* **1** having two sides that are different in shape: *asymmetrical patterns* **2** *formal* not equal —opposite SYMMETRICAL —**asymmetrically** /-kli/ *adv*

**a·symp·to·mat·ic** /æˌsɪmptəmætɪk, eɪ-‖eɪ-/ *adj* if someone or the illness that they have is asymptomatic, there are no signs of the illness

S1 W1 **at** /ət *strong* æt/ *prep* **1** used to show a point in space where someone or something is, or where an event is happening: *We'll meet at my house.*|*a huge queue at the bus stop.*|*They sat down at a corner table.*|**at Jack's/Sue's etc** (=at Jack's house, Sue's house etc) *Pete's round at Mel's.*|**at the doctor's/the bank/the airport etc** (=at a place you go to for a particular purpose) *Guess who I met at the dentist's?* **2 at a party/club/funeral etc** at an event while it is taking place: *I met my wife at a disco.*|*They're all out at the cinema.* **3 at school/work etc** regularly going to school, work etc: *Is Jessica still at school?* (=does she go to school regularly) **4 at lunch/dinner etc** eating your lunch, dinner etc: *I'm sorry, Pam's at lunch just now.* **5** used to show an exact time: *The film starts at 8 o'clock.*|**at the moment** (=now) *We're really busy at the moment.* **6** used to show a particular period of time during which something happens: *My husband often works at night.*|*We like to go to Midnight Mass at Christmas.* **7** used to show the person or thing that an action is directed or aimed at: *Protesters threw rotten eggs at the speakers.*|*Jake shot at the deer but missed.*|*Look at that!*|*Stop shouting at the kids all the time.* **8** used to show the thing that caused an action or feeling: *The children all laughed at his jokes.*|*I'm surprised at you!*|*Dad got really mad at me for scratching the car.* **9** used to show the subject or activity that you are considering when making a judgment about someone's ability: *Barbara's getting on really well at her new job.*|*Rosa's a genius at chemistry.*|**good/bad etc at (doing) sth** *Luis was always good at maths.*|*Matt's bad at handling people.* **10** used to show a continuous state or activity: *two nations at war*|*Many children are still at risk from neglect or abuse.*|*Granny's at peace now.* (=dead)|**at large** (=if someone or something dangerous is at large they are in a particular area and may harm or kill someone) *rumours of a black panther at large* —see picture on page 1257 **11** used to show a price, rate, level, age, speed etc: *old books selling at 10 cents each*|*The house was sold at a price of £250,000.*|*You should have more sense at your age.*|*The car was going at about 50 mph.*|*Amanda rode off at a gallop.* **12 at least/worst/most etc** the least, worst etc thing possible: *John has to practise for at least half an hour every day.*|*At worst, up to 50% of the population could be affected.*|**at the very least/most/worst etc** *That car's worth £250 at the very most.*|**at its/her/their best etc** *The garden is at its best in June.*|*This was Sampras at his most powerful.* **13** used to show that you are trying to do something but are not succeeding or completing it: *George was just picking at his food.*|*Sarah took another sip at her wine.*|*I clutched at the rope but missed.* **14 at sb's invitation/command** because someone asks or orders you to do something: *Rachel attended the dinner at the chairman's command.* **15 at that a)** also or besides: *It's a new idea, and a good one, at that.* **b)** after something happens or as a result of it; then: *Tess called him a liar and at that he stormed out of the room.* —see also **leave it at that** (LEAVE[1] (12)) **16 at a time** at the same time: *Ben was putting chocolates in his mouth two at a time.* **17 where it's at** *informal* used to describe a place or activity that is very popular, exciting, and fashionable: *This Hacienda Club is where it's at.* —see also **(not) at all** (ALL[3]), —see picture on page 1257

**at·a·vis·tic** /ˌætəˈvɪstɪk◂/ *adj formal* atavistic feelings are very basic human feelings, that people have felt since humans have existed

**ate** /et, eɪt‖eɪt/ the past tense of EAT

**-ate** /ɪ̈t, eɪt/ *suffix* **1** [in adjectives] full of or showing a particular quality: *very affectionate* (=showing love) **2** [in verbs] to make something have a particular quality: *to activate* (=make active)|*to regulate* (=make regular; control) **3** [in nouns] a group of people with certain duties: *the electorate* (=voters)|*an inspectorate* **4** [in nouns] the job, rank, or degree of a particular type of person: *She was awarded her doctorate.* (=the degree of doctor) **5** *technical* [in nouns] a chemical salt formed from a particular acid: *phosphate* —**-ately** /ɪ̈tli/ [in adverbs] *fortunately*

**a·the·is·m** /ˈeɪθi-ɪzəm/ *n* [U] the belief that God does not exist —**atheist** *n* [C] —**atheistic** /ˌeɪθiˈɪstɪk◂/ —**atheistical** *adj*

**ath·lete** /ˈæθliːt/ *n* [C] someone who is good at or who often does sports: *a natural athlete*

**athlete's foot** /ˌ·· ˈ·/ *n* [U] a medical condition in which the skin cracks between your toes

**ath·let·ic** /æθˈletɪk, əθ-/ *adj* **1** physically strong and good at sport: *Sven was tall, blonde, and athletic looking.* **2** connected with athletics

**ath·let·ics** /æθˈletɪks, əθ-/ *n* [U] *BrE* sports such as running and jumping; TRACK AND FIELD *AmE*

**-athon** /əθən‖əθɑːn/ *suffix* [in nouns] *informal* an event in which a particular thing is done for a very long time, especially to collect money: *a swimathon*|*a talkathon*

**a·thwart** /əˈθwɔːt‖-ɔːrt/ *prep literary* across

**-ation** /eɪʃən/ *suffix* [in nouns] the act, state, or result of doing something: *an examination of the contents* (=examining them)|*the combination of several factors*

**a·tish·oo** /əˈtɪʃuː/ *spoken* a word used to represent the sound you make when you SNEEZE

**-ative** /ətɪv/ *suffix* [in adjectives] liking something or tending to do something or show a particular quality: *talkative* (=liking to talk a lot)|*argumentative* (=enjoying arguments)|*imaginative* (=showing imagination)

**at·las** /ˈætləs/ *n* [C] a book of maps: *a world atlas*

**ATM** /ˌeɪ tiː ˈem/ *n* [C] *AmE* a machine outside a bank that you use to get money from your account; CASHPOINT *BrE*

**at·mo·sphere** /ˈætməsfɪə‖-fɪr/ *n* [C,U] **1 the atmosphere** the mixture of gases that surrounds the Earth **2** the air inside a room: *a smoky atmosphere* **3** the feeling that an event or place gives you: *The atmosphere at home's been depressing since they had that fight.*| W2

**atmosphere of crisis/optimism etc** *An atmosphere of optimism dominated the party conference.*

**at·mo·spher·ic** /ˌætməsˈferɪk◂/ *adj* **1** [only before noun] related with the Earth's atmosphere: *atmospheric pressure* **2** beautiful and mysterious: *atmospheric music*

**at·mo·spher·ics** /ˌætməsˈferɪks/ *n* [plural] continuous cracking noises that sometimes interrupt radio broadcasts

**at·oll** /ˈætɒl‖ˈætɒːl, ˈætɑːl/ *n* [C] a CORAL[1] island in the shape of a ring: *an atomic bomb detonated on Bikini Atoll in the Pacific*

**at·om** /ˈætəm/ *n* [C] **1** the smallest part of an ELEMENT (1) that can exist alone or combine with other substances to form MOLECULES **2** a very small amount of something: *There isn't an atom of truth in it.*

**atom bomb** /ˈ·· ·/ also **atomic bomb** /·ˌ·· ˈ·/ *n* [C] a NUCLEAR bomb that splits atoms to cause an extremely large explosion

**a·tom·ic** /əˈtɒmɪk‖əˈtɑː-/ *adj* **1** related to the energy produced by splitting atoms or the weapons that use this energy: *atomic warfare | an atomic submarine* **2** connected with the atoms in a substance: *atomic weight*

**atomic en·er·gy** /·ˌ·· ˈ···/ *n* [U] NUCLEAR ENERGY

**at·om·izer** /ˈætəmaɪzə‖-ər/ *n* [C] a thing used to make a liquid such as PERFUME[1] (1) come out of a bottle in very small drops like mist: *a perfume atomizer | a paint atomizer*

**a·ton·al** /eɪˈtəʊnl, æ-‖-ˈtoʊ-/ *adj* a piece of music that is atonal is not based on a particular KEY[1] (4) **—atonally** *adv* **—atonality** /ˌeɪtəʊˈnæləti, ˌæ-‖-toʊ-/ *n* [U]

**a·tone** /əˈtəʊn‖əˈtoʊn/ *v* [I] *formal* to do something to show that you are sorry for having done something wrong: [+ **for**] *Richard was anxious to atone for his thoughtlessness.*

**a·tone·ment** /əˈtəʊnmənt‖əˈtoʊn-/ *n* [U] *formal* something you do to show that you are sorry for having done something wrong

**a·top** /əˈtɒp‖əˈtɑːp/ *prep literary* on top of something

**-ator** /eɪtə‖-ər/ *suffix* [in nouns] someone or something that does something: *a narrator* (=someone who tells a story) | *a generator* (=machine that produces electricity)

**A to Z** /ˌeɪ tə ˈzed‖-ˈziː/ *n* [C] *trademark* a book with maps that show every street in a British city

**at-risk** /ˌ· ˈ·◂/ *adj* **at-risk children/patients etc** people who need special care because they are likely to be in danger from violent parents, to become ill etc: **at-risk register** (=an official list of people in this situation)

**at·ri·um** /ˈeɪtriəm/ *n* [C] **1** one of the two spaces in the top of your heart that push blood into the VENTRICLES **2** a large high open space in a tall building

**a·tro·cious** /əˈtrəʊʃəs‖əˈtroʊ-/ *adj* extremely bad or showing no ability to do something at all: *atrocious weather | Her singing was atrocious. | atrocious housing conditions* **—atrociously** *adv* **—atrociousness** *n* [U]

**a·troc·i·ty** /əˈtrɒsəti‖əˈtrɑː-/ *n* [C usually plural,U] an extremely cruel and violent action, especially during a war: *one of the worst atrocities of the Vietnam War*

**at·ro·phy** /ˈætrəfi/ *v* [I,T] to become weak or make something become weak because of lack of use or lack of blood: *therapy to prevent the leg muscles from atrophying* **—atrophy** *n* [U]

2 **at·tach** /əˈtætʃ/ *v* [T]

2 **1** ▶ **CONNECT** ◀ to connect one thing to another: **attach sth to** *Attach a recent photograph to your application form.* | **be attached to** *a small battery attached to a little loudspeaker | The web was only attached to the leaf by one thread.*

**2** ▶ **LIKE** ◀ **be attached to** to like someone or something very much, because you have known them or had them for a long time: *It's easy to become attached to the children you work with. Too attached, sometimes.*

**3 attach importance/significance etc** to believe that something is important: *People attach too much importance to economic forecasts.*

**4 attach blame** if you attach blame or if blame attaches to someone, they have done something wrong

**5** ▶ **FEELING/QUALITY** ◀ **be attached to** if a quality, feeling, idea etc is attached a person, thing or event, it is connected with them: *It's easy to let the emotions attached to one situation spill over into others.*

**6** ▶ **ORGANIZATION/COMPANY** ◀ **be attached to sth a)** to work for part of a particular organization, especially for a short period of time: *He was attached to the foreign affairs department of a Japanese newspaper.* **b)** to be part of a bigger organization: *the Food Ministry is attached to the Ministry of Agriculture*

**at·taché** /əˈtæʃeɪ‖ˌætəˈʃeɪ/ *n* [C] someone who works in an EMBASSY, and deals with a particular subject: *a cultural attaché*

**attaché case** /·ˈ··· ‖ˌ··ˈ· ·/ *n* [C] a thin case used for carrying business documents

**at·tach·ment** /əˈtætʃmənt/ *n* **1** [C,U] a feeling that you like or love someone or something and that you would be unhappy without them: [+ **to/for**] *I did feel a certain sense of attachment for the strange old guy.* **2** [U] belief in and loyalty towards a particular idea: [+ **to/for**] *old people's attachment to traditional customs and ways* **3** [C] a part that you can put onto a machine to make it do different things: *a versatile food mixer that comes with a range of attachments* **4 on attachment** working for a particular organization, especially for a short period of time: *He was sent on attachment to their offices in Hong Kong.*

**at·tack**[1] /əˈtæk/ *n* S2

**1** ▶ **VIOLENCE AGAINST SB** ◀ [C] an act of deliberately using violence against someone: [+ **on**] *There have been several attacks on foreigners recently.* W1

**2** ▶ **IN A WAR** ◀ [C,U] the act of using weapons against an enemy in a war: *The attack began at dawn.* | [+ **on**] *a carefully planned attack on Iraqi air bases* | **be/come under attack** *Once again we came under attack from enemy fighter planes.* | **launch an attack** (=start an attack)

**3** ▶ **CRITICISM** ◀ [C,U] a statement that criticizes someone strongly: [+ **on**] *recent attacks on the Prime Minister* | **be/come under attack** (=be strongly criticized) *The company came under attack for the firing of 50 employees.* | **go on the attack** (=start to criticize someone severely)

**4** ▶ **ACTIONS TO STOP STH** ◀ [C,U] actions intended to get rid of or stop something such as a system, a set of laws etc: [+ **on**] *Mrs Thatcher's attack on the welfare state*

**5** ▶ **ILLNESS** ◀ [C] a sudden short period of suffering from an illness, especially an illness that you have often: *an attack of asthma*

**6** ▶ **SPORT** ◀ [C,U] **a)** an attempt by a group of players to make a GOAL (2) **b)** the group of players on a team whose job is to make a GOAL (2): *the Arsenal attack*

**7 an attack of fear/panic/anxiety etc** a short period of time when you feel frightened, worried etc: *panic attacks* —see also HEART ATTACK

**attack**[2] *v*

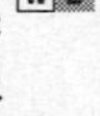

**1** ▶ **ATTACK SOMEONE** ◀ [I,T] to deliberately use physical violence against someone: *Jim was attacked by a man in the park.* | *dogs trained to attack on command* | **attack sb with sth** *She started attacking the burglar with a piece of wood.*

**2** ▶ **IN A WAR** ◀ [I,T] to start using guns, bombs etc against an enemy in a war: *The village had been attacked by the French airforce.*

**3** ▶ **CRITICIZE** ◀ [T] to criticize someone or something very strongly: *The senator made a speech attacking Clinton's healthcare program.* | **attack sb for sth** *The article attacked the government for its policy on education.*

**4** ▶ **SPORT** ◀ [I,T] to move forward and try to make a GOAL (2): *Brazil began to attack more in the second half of the match.*

**5** ▶ **BEGIN DOING** ◀ [T] to begin doing a job or dealing with a problem with determination and eagerness: *She immediately set about attacking the problem.*

6 ▶ **DISEASE** ◀ [T] to damage part of someone's body: *a cruel disease that attacks the central nervous system*

**at·tain** /ə'teɪn/ *v* [T] *formal* **1** to succeed in reaching a particular level or in getting something after trying for a long time: *More women are attaining positions of power in public life.* **2** to reach a high level: *Share prices attained a high of $3.27.* —**attainable** *adj This target should be attainable.*

**at·tain·ment** /ə'teɪnmənt/ *n formal* **1** [U] success in getting something or reaching a particular level: *the attainment of happiness* **2** [C] something that you have succeeded in getting or learning, such as a skill

S2 W1 **attempt¹** *n* [C] **1** an act of trying to do something, especially something difficult: **attempt to do sth** *All attempts to control inflation have failed.* | [+ **at**] *He made one last attempt at the world record.* | **make no attempt** *The protestors made no attempt to resist arrest.* | **in an attempt to do sth** *In an attempt to diffuse the tension I suggested that we break off for lunch.* **2 an attempt on sb's life** an act of trying to kill someone, especially someone famous or important

S2 W2 **at·tempt²** /ə'tempt/ *v* [T] to try to do something that is difficult, dangerous, or has never been done before: **attempt to do sth** *Every time I've attempted to convince her, I've failed completely.* | **attempt sth** *Weather conditions prevented them from attempting the jump.*

S2 W2 **at·tend** /ə'tend/ *v* **1** [I,T] to go to an event such as a meeting or a class: *Only 7 people attended the meeting.* | *Please let us know if you are unable to attend.* —see JOIN¹ (USAGE) **2** [I,T] to go regularly to a school, church etc: *All children between the ages of 5 and 16 must attend school.* **3** [T] *formal* to happen or exist at the same time as something: *the peculiar atmosphere which attends such an event* **4** [T] to look after someone, especially because they are ill

**attend to** sb/sth *phr v* [T] **1** to deal with business or personal matters: *I may be late – I have got one or two things to attend to.* **2** to help a customer in a shop or a restaurant to buy or order something —see JOIN¹ (USAGE)

Frequencies of **attend** and **go to** in spoken and written English.

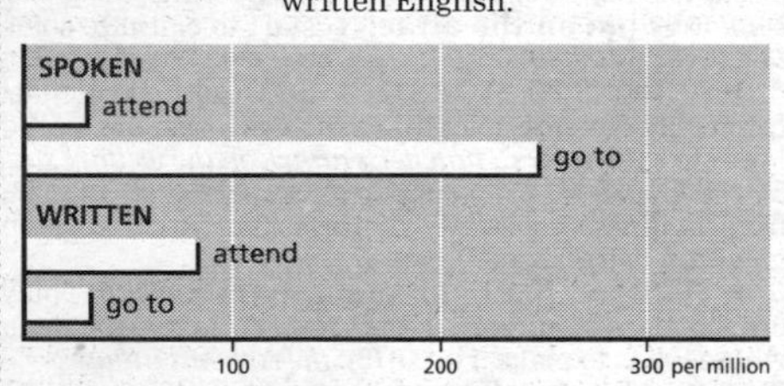


Based on the British National Corpus and the Longman Lancaster Corpus

Both verbs are used to mean 'be at an event'. The graph shows that in this meaning **go to** is much more common than **attend** in spoken English. In written or formal English **attend** is more common.

**at·tend·ance** /ə'tendəns/ *n* **1** [C] the number of people who attend a game, concert, meeting etc: **high/low attendance** *a low attendance at class of 84's reunion* **2** [C,U] the number of times that you go to a meeting, class etc that is held regularly: *Many students have a very poor attendance record.* **3 be in attendance** *formal* to be at a special or important event: *Over 2000 people were in attendance at yesterday's demonstration.* **4 be in attendance on sb** *formal* to look after someone or serve them —see also **dance attendance on** (DANCE¹ (5))

**at·tend·ant¹** /ə'tendənt/ *n* [C] **1** someone whose job is to look after or help customers in a public place: *a car-park attendant* **2** someone who looks after a very important person, such as a king or queen

**attendant²** *adj formal* **1** connected with or caused by something: *nuclear power, with all its attendant risks* **2** going with or being with someone in order to help them

**at·ten·tion** /ə'tenʃən/ *n* S1 W1

**1** ▶ **WATCHING/LISTENING CAREFULLY** ◀ **a) pay attention** to carefully listen to or watch something that is happening, or to be careful about what you are doing: *The teacher got angry with me when I didn't pay attention.* | [+ **to**] *The TV was on but Di wasn't paying much attention to it.* | **pay no attention to** (=used to tell someone to ignore what someone says because it is not true or not important) *Don't pay any attention to him – he's always saying stupid things.* | **pay little attention to/not pay much attention to** (=behave in a way that shows that you do not think something or someone is very important) *We heard noises coming from upstairs, but we didn't pay much attention to them.* **b) give sb/sth your attention** to listen to someone or study something carefully, especially so that you can deal with a problem: **give sb your full/undivided attention** *Now he's gone, I can give you my undivided attention.*

**2** ▶ **INTEREST** ◀ **a)** [U] the interest that people show in someone or something: *She was flattered by all the attention he was giving her.* | **give sth attention** *The press has given the story a lot of attention.* | **the centre of attention** (=a person who everyone looks at and is interested in) *Some people enjoy being the centre of attention.* | **the focus of attention** (=the situation that people are most concerned about or consider to be most important) *The focus of attention has shifted away from domestic issues.* | **hold/keep sb's attention** (=make someone continue to be interested in something) *Follett keeps the reader's attention throughout the book.* | **attention span** (=the period of time during which you continue to be interested in something) *Children generally have a short attention span.*

**3** ▶ **MAKE SB NOTICE** ◀ **a) attract/catch/get sb's attention** to make someone notice you, especially because you want to speak to them or you need their help: *She tried to attract the waiter's attention.* **b) attract attention** if someone or something attracts attention, people notice them, especially because they look very interesting or unusual: *The band members couldn't go out in the street because they attracted too much attention.* **c) get attention** to make someone notice you and be interested in what you are doing: *Children are often bad in order to get attention.* **d) draw attention to** to make people notice and be concerned about something: *The article was intended to draw attention to the situation in Cambodia.* **e) draw attention away from** to make people stop being concerned about something such as a social problem **f) bring sth to sb's attention** to tell someone, especially someone in authority, about something such as a problem: *The matter was first brought to my attention earlier this year.* **g) come to sb's attention** if something such as a problem comes to the attention of someone in authority, they find out about it

**4** ▶ **REPAIR/TREATMENT** ◀ [U] **a)** something you do to repair or clean something, or make it work or be able to be used: *Honda 50cc for sale. Needs some attention.* **b)** treatment given to someone who is ill or injured: *medical attention*

**5** ▶ **CARE** ◀ [C,U] things that you do to help someone which show that you like them: *Pets need a lot of care and attention.*

**6** ▶ **SOLDIERS** ◀ **stand to attention/be at attention** to stand up straight in neat lines: **attention!** (=used when ordering a group of soldiers to stand up straight)

**7** ▶ **SPEECH/ANNOUNCEMENT** ◀ **a) may/could I have your attention?** *spoken* used in a formal situation when you want people to listen to you **b) thank you for your attention** *spoken* used at the end of a speech or statement to thank people for listening

**8** ▶ **LETTER** ◀ **for the attention of** used on the front

of an official letter when you want a particular person to read it or deal with it: *for the attention of the manager*

**at·ten·tive** /əˈtentɪv/ *adj* **1** listening or watching someone carefully because you are interested in them: *The professor was pleased to have such an attentive audience.* **2** to make sure someone has everything they need: *He listened attentively and with growing interest.* | [+ **to**] *The crew were attentive to the passengers' needs.* —opposite INATTENTIVE —**attentively** *adv* —**attentiveness** *n* [U]

**at·ten·u·ate** /əˈtenjueɪt/ *v* [T] *formal* to make something weaker or have less effect: *an attenuated measles vaccine* —**attentuation** *n* [U]

**at·test** /əˈtest/ *v* **1** [I,T] to show or prove that something is is true: [+ **to**] *Luxurious furnishings attested to the wealth of the owner.* **2** [T] to officially state that you believe something is true, especially in a court of law

**at·tes·ta·tion** /ˌæteˈsteɪʃən/ *n* [C,U] *formal* a legal statement made by someone in which they say that something is definitely true

**at·tic** /ˈætɪk/ *n* [C] a space or room under the roof of a house often used for storing things: *She went to college consigning her collection of cuddly toys to the attic.* —see picture on page 410

**at·tire** /əˈtaɪə‖əˈtaɪr/ *n* [U] *formal* clothes: *formal evening attire*

**at·tired** /əˈtaɪrəd‖əˈtaɪrd/ *adj* [not before noun] *formal* dressed in a particular way: *more suitably attired for a rave than for school*

1 **at·ti·tude** /ˈætɪtjuːd‖-tuːd/ *n* **1** [C,U] the opinions and
1 feelings that you usually have about something: [+ **towards**] *Pete's attitude towards women really scares me.* **2** [C,U] the way that you behave towards someone or in a particular situation, especially when this shows how you feel: *an aggressive attitude* | *As soon as they found out I was a doctor their whole attitude changed.* | **attitude problem** (=behaviour that shows that you do not like to help people or do what you should do) | **have a good/bad attitude** *He has a bad attitude towards his schoolwork.* **3** [U] *informal* a style of dressing, decorating etc that shows you have the confidence to do unusual and exciting things without caring what other people think: **with attitude** *a coat with attitude*

2 **at·tor·ney** /əˈtɜːni‖-ɜːr-/ *n* [C] *AmE* a lawyer —see
2 LAWYER (USAGE)

**attorney gen·e·ral** /·ˌ·· ˈ···/ *n* [C] the chief lawyer in a state or of the government in the US

2 **at·tract** /əˈtrækt/ *v* [T] **1** to make someone interested
2 in something, or make them want to take part in something: **attract sb to sth** *What attracted me most to the job was the chance to travel.* | **attract interest/attention etc** *The story has attracted a lot of interest in the media.* **2 be attracted to** to feel that you like someone and want to have a sexual relationship with them: *I'm not usually attracted to blond men.* **3** to make someone like or admire something or feel romantically interested in someone: *I guess it was his eyes that attracted me first.* **4** to make someone or something move towards another thing: *Leftover food attracts flies.* | *low rents designed to attract new businesses to the area*

3 **at·trac·tion** /əˈtrækʃən/ *n* **1** [C,U] a feeling of liking someone, especially in a sexual way: *The attraction between them was almost immediate.* **2** [C] something interesting or enjoyable to see or do: **tourist attraction** (=a place that many tourists visit) | **the main attraction** (=the most popular place, person, or activity) *The beautiful beaches are the island's main attraction.* **3** [C,U] a feature or quality that makes something seem interesting or enjoyable: [+ **of**] *Being your own boss is one of the attractions of owning your own business.* **4** [C,U] *technical* a force which makes things move together or stay together: *gravitational attraction*

2 **at·trac·tive** /əˈtræktɪv/ *adj* **1** someone who is attract-
2 ive is good looking, especially in a way that makes you sexually interested in them: *an attractive young woman* | **find sb attractive** *I must admit I've never found him particularly attractive.* **2** pleasant to look at: *Kitchen utensils should be attractive as well as functional* —see BEAUTIFUL (USAGE). **3** having qualities that make you want to accept something or be involved in it: [+ **to**] *a political movement that is very attractive to the younger generation* | **attractive offer/proposition/package etc** *It's a very attractive offer, and I'll have to give it serious thought.* —**attractively** *adv* —**attractiveness** *n* [U]

**at·trib·u·ta·ble** /əˈtrɪbjʊtəbəl/ *adj* [not before noun] likely to be caused by something: [+ **to**] *Death was attributable to gunshot wounds.*

**at·tri·bute¹** /əˈtrɪbjuːt‖-bjət/ *v*

**attribute** sth **to** sb/sth *phr v* [T] **1** to say that a situation or event is caused by something: *The fall in the number of deaths from heart disease is generally attributed to improvements in diet.* **2** to say that someone was responsible for saying or writing something, painting a famous picture etc: *a saying usually attributed to Confucius* **3** to say that someone or something has a particular quality —**attribution** /ˌætrɪˈbjuːʃən/ *n* [U]

**at·tri·bute²** /ˈætrɪbjuːt/ *n* [C] a quality or feature, especially one that is considered to be good or useful: *What attributes should a good manager possess?*

**at·trib·u·tive** /əˈtrɪbjʊtɪv/ *adj* describing and coming before a noun: *In the phrase 'big city', 'big' is an attributive adjective, and in the phrase 'school bus', 'school' is a noun in an attributive position.* —**attributively** *adv*

**at·tri·tion** /əˈtrɪʃən/ *n* [U] the process of gradually destroying your enemy or making them weak by attacking them continuously: *a war of attrition*

**at·tuned** /əˈtjuːnd‖əˈtuːnd/ *adj* [not before noun] familiar with the way someone thinks or behaves so that you can react to them in a suitable way: [+ **to**] *British companies still aren't really attuned to the needs of the Japanese market.*

**a·typ·i·cal** /eɪˈtɪpɪkəl/ *adj* not typical or usual

**au·ber·gine** /ˈəʊbəʒiːn‖ˈoʊbər-/ *n* [C,U] *BrE* a large dark purple vegetable; EGGPLANT *AmE* —see picture on page 414

**au·burn** /ˈɔːbən‖ˈɒːbərn/ *adj* auburn hair is a reddish brown colour —see picture on page 412

**auc·tion¹** /ˈɔːkʃən‖ˈɒːk-/ *n* [C] a public meeting where land, buildings, paintings etc are sold to the person who offers the most money for them: **put sth up for auction** (=try to sell something at an auction) *The house was put up for auction.* | **auction house** (=a company that arranges auctions)

**auction²** *v* [T + **off**] to sell something at an auction

**auc·tio·neer** /ˌɔːkʃəˈnɪə‖ˌɒːkʃəˈnɪr/ *n* [C] someone who is in charge of an auction and tells people the prices of the goods

**au·da·cious** /ɔːˈdeɪʃəs‖ɒː-/ *adj* brave and shocking: *an audacious robbery* —**audaciously** *adv*

**au·dac·i·ty** /ɔːˈdæsɪti‖ɒː-/ *n* [U] the quality of having enough courage to take risks or say impolite things: **have the audacity to do sth** *I can't believe he had the audacity to ask me for more money!*

**au·di·ble** /ˈɔːdɪbəl‖ˈɒː-/ *adj* a sound that is audible is loud enough for you to hear it: *an audible sigh of relief* | **barely audible** (=difficult to hear) *His voice was barely audible above the roar of the crowd.* —opposite INAUDIBLE —**audibly** *adv* —**audibility** /ˌɔːdɪˈbɪlɪti‖ˌɒː-/ *n* [U]

**au·di·ence** /ˈɔːdiəns‖ˈɒː-, ˈɑː-/ *n* [C] **1** a group of people S 2
who watch and listen to someone speaking or performing W 2
in public: *The audience began clapping and cheering.* **2** the number or kind of people who regularly watch or listen to a particular programme: *The show attracts a regular audience of about 20 million.* | **target audience** (=the kind of people that a programme, advertisement etc is supposed to attract) **3** a formal meeting with a very important person: *The princess was granted an audience with the Pope.*

**au·di·o** /ˈɔːdiəʊ‖ˈɒːdioʊ/ *adj* [only before noun] related to recording and broadcasting sound: *an audio signal*

**au·di·o·tape** /ˈɔːdiəʊteɪp‖ˈɒːdioʊ-/ *n* [C,U] *technical* a

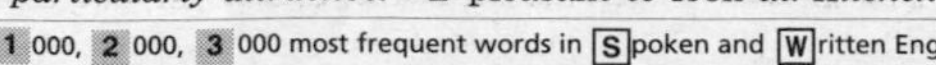

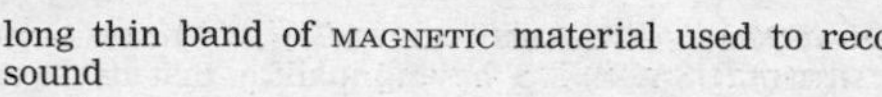

long thin band of MAGNETIC material used to record sound

**au·di·o·ty·pist** /ˈɔːdiəʊˌtaɪpɪ̈st‖ˈɒːdioʊ-/ *n* [C] *BrE* someone whose job is to type letters that have been recorded

**au·di·o·vis·u·al** /ˌɔːdiəʊˈvɪʒuəl◂‖ˌɒːdioʊ-/ *adj* involving the use of recorded pictures and sound: *audiovisual equipment*

**au·dit** /ˈɔːdɪ̈t‖ˈɒː-/ *v* [T] **1** to officially examine a company's financial records in order to check that they are correct **2** *AmE* to attend a university course without having to take any examinations —**audit** *n* [C] *the annual audit*

**au·di·tion¹** /ɔːˈdɪʃən‖ɒː-/ *n* [C] a short performance by an actor, singer etc that someone judges to decide if they are good enough to act in a play, sing in a concert etc: *He failed the audition for the part of the prince.*

**audition²** *v* [I,T] to perform in an audition or judge someone in an audition: [+ **for**] *She's auditioning for Ophelia in 'Hamlet'.* | **audition sb (for)** *They auditioned over 2000 people for 'Grease'.*

**au·di·tor** /ˈɔːdɪ̈tə‖ˈɒːdɪ̈tər/ *n* [C] someone whose job is to officially examine a company's financial records

**au·di·to·ri·um** /ˌɔːdɪ̈ˈtɔːriəm‖ˌɒː-/ *n* [C] **1** the part of a theatre where people sit when watching a play, concert etc **2** a large building used for concerts or public meetings

**au·di·to·ry** /ˈɔːdɪ̈təri‖ˈɒːdɪ̈tɔːri/ *adj* [only before noun] *technical* connected with the ability to hear

**au fait** /əʊ ˈfeɪ‖oʊ-/ *adj* **be au fait with** to be familiar with a system or way of doing something: *I'm not really au fait with the computer system yet.*

**Aug** the written abbreviation of AUGUST

**au·ger** /ˈɔːgə‖ˈɒːgər/ *n* [C] a tool used for making a hole in wood or in the ground

**aught** /ɔːt‖ɒːt, ɑːt/ *pron* **1** *old use* anything **2 for aught I know/care** *old use* used when saying that something may be true but you are not sure or do not care about it

**aug·ment** /ɔːgˈment‖ɒːg-/ *v* [T] *formal* to increase the value, amount, effectiveness etc of something: *new taxes intended to augment government income*

**au·gur** /ˈɔːgə‖ˈɒːgər/ *v* [T] **1 augur well** *formal* to be a sign that something will be successful: *His unfriendly manner did not augur well for our interview.* **2** *literary* to be a sign that a particular thing will happen in the future

**au·gu·ry** /ˈɔːgjɪ̈ri‖ˈɒː/ *n* [C] *literary* a sign of what will happen in the future

**Au·gust** /ˈɔːgəst‖ˈɒː-/ *written abbreviation* **Aug** *n* [C,U] the eighth month of the year, between July and September: **in August** *The new offices open in August 1998.* | **last/next August** *I moved here last August.* | **on August 6th** [also **on 6th August** *BrE*] *The new store opened on August 6th.*

**au·gust** /ɔːˈgʌst‖ɒː-/ *adj literary* old, famous, and respected

**auk** /ɔːk‖ɒːk/ *n* [C] a black and white seabird with short wings

**au lait** /əʊ ˈleɪ‖oʊ-/ *adj French* with milk: *café au lait*

**Auld Lang Syne** /ˌɔːld læŋ ˈzaɪn, ˌəʊld-, -ˈsaɪn‖ˌɒːld-/ a Scottish song that people sing when they celebrate the beginning of the new year at 12 o'clock (MIDNIGHT) on December 31st

**aunt** /ɑːnt‖ænt/ *n* [C] **1** the sister of your father or mother, or the wife of your father's or mother's brother: *Aunt Mary* —see picture at FAMILY **2** a woman who is a friend of a small child's parents —see also AGONY AUNT

**aunty, auntie** /ˈɑːnti‖ˈæn-/ *n* [C] *informal* aunt

**au pair** /ˌəʊ ˈpeə‖oʊ ˈper/ *n* [C] a young woman who stays with a family in a foreign country to learn the language and to look after their children

**au·ra** /ˈɔːrə‖ˈɒːrə/ [C] a quality or feeling that seems to surround or come from a person or a place: [+ **of**] *Hollywood still has an aura of glamour about it.*

**au·ral** /ˈɔːrəl‖ˈɒː-/ *adj* connected with the sense of hearing, or with someone's ability to understand a language —**aurally** *adj*

**au·re·ole** /ˈɔːriəʊl‖-oʊl/ *n* [C] *literary* a bright circle of light; HALO

**au re·voir** /ˌəʊ rəˈvwɑː, ˌɒ-‖ˌoʊ rəˈvwɑːr/ *interjection French* goodbye

**au·ri·cle** /ˈɔːrɪkəl/ *n* [C] one of the two spaces inside the top of your heart

**au·ro·ra bo·re·a·lis** /əˌrɔːrə bɔːriˈeɪlɪ̈s, ɔː-‖-ˈæl-/ *n* [singular] bands of moving light that you can see in the night sky in the far north; the NORTHERN LIGHTS

**aus·pic·es** /ˈɔːspɪ̈sɪ̈z‖ˈɒː-/ *n* [plural] **under the auspices of** *formal* with the help and support of a particular organization: *a relief project set up under the auspices of the United Nations*

**aus·pi·cious** /ɔːˈspɪʃəs‖ɒː-/ *adj formal* likely to be successful: *It was an auspicious moment for a meeting between the heads of state.*

**Aus·sie** /ˈɒzi‖ˈɒːzi/ *n* [C] *informal* someone from Australia —**Aussie** *adj*

**aus·tere** /ɔːˈstɪə, ɒ-‖ɒːˈstɪr/ *adj* **1** plain and simple and without any decoration: *the austere grandeur of the old church* **2** someone who is austere is very strict and looks very serious **3** an austere way of life is very simple and has few things to make it comfortable or enjoyable —**austerely** *adv*

**aus·ter·i·ty** /ɔːˈsterɪ̈ti, ɒ-‖ɒː-/ *n* [U] **1** the quality of being austere **2** bad economic conditions in which people do not have much money to spend: *a time of great austerity after the war*

**Aus·tra·la·sian** /ˌɒstrəˈleɪʒən◂, -ʃən‖ˌɒː-, ˌɑː-/ *adj* connected with Australasia

**Aus·tra·li·an** /ɒˈstreɪliən‖ɒː-, ɑː-/ *n* [C] someone from Australia —**Australian** *adj*: *Australian English*

**Aus·tri·an** /ˈɒstriən‖ˈɒː-,ˈɑː-/ *n* [C] someone who is from Austria —**Austrian** *adj*

**Austro-** /ɒstrəʊ‖ɒːstroʊ, -trə/ *prefix* **1** Australian and: *Austro-Malayan* **2** Austrian and: *Austro-Hungarian*

**au·tar·chy** /ˈɔːtɑːki‖ˈɒːtɑːr-/ *n* [U] *formal* a system of government in which one person or group has unlimited power

**au·tar·ky** /ˈɔːtɑːki‖ˈɒːtɑːr-/ *n technical* **1** [U] an economic system in which a country produces all the things it needs as opposed to buying them from another country **2** [C] a country that has this economic system

**au·then·tic** /ɔːˈθentɪk‖ɒː-/ *adj* **1** done or made in the traditional or original way: *authentic Chinese food* **2** a painting, document, book etc that is authentic has been proved to be by a particular person **3** based on facts: *an authentic account* —**authentically** /-kli/ *adv*

**au·then·tic·ate** /ɔːˈθentɪkeɪt‖ɒː-/ *v* [T] to prove that something is true or real: *authenticated reports of human rights violations* —**authentication** /ɔːˌθentɪ̈ˈkeɪʃən‖ɒː-/ *n* [U]

**au·then·tic·i·ty** /ˌɔːθenˈtɪsɪ̈ti, -θən‖ˌɒː-/ *n* [U] the quality of being real or true: *to establish the painting's authenticity*

**au·thor¹** /ˈɔːθə‖ˈɒːθər/ *n* [C] **1** someone who writes books: *Jeffrey Archer, successful author and politician* | **the author** (=the person who wrote a particular book) *It's clear that the author is a woman.* **2** *formal* the person who starts a plan or idea: *the author of the plan* 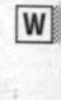

**author²** *v* [T] to be the writer of a book, report etc

**au·thor·ess** /ˈɔːθərɪ̈s‖ˈɒː-/ *n* [C] a woman who writes books

**au·thor·i·tar·i·an** /ɔːˌθɒrɪ̈ˈteəriən◂‖ɒːˌθɑːrɪ̈ˈter-, əˌθɔː-/ *adj* strictly forcing people to obey a set of rules or laws that are often wrong or unfair: *an authoritarian regime | a cruel and authoritarian father* —**authoritarian** *n* [C] —**authoritarianism** *n* [U]

**au·thor·i·ta·tive** /ɔːˈθɒrɪ̣tətɪv, ə-‖əˈθɑːrəteɪtɪv, əˈθɔː-/ *adj* **1** an authoritative book, account etc is respected because the person who wrote it knows a lot about the subject: *Lewis's authorative account of the history of aviation* **2** behaving or speaking in a confident determined way that makes people respect and obey you —**authoritatively** *adv*

1 **au·thor·i·ty** /ɔːˈθɒrɪ̣ti, ə-‖əˈθɑː-, əˈθɔː-/ *n*
**1** ▶ **POWER** ◀ [U] the power you have because of your official position or because people respect your knowledge and experience: *None of us questioned my father's authority.* | **the voice of authority** (=a way of speaking that makes people respect you) *Witten spoke with the voice of authority.*
**2 the authorities** the people or organizations that are in charge of a particular country or area: *British police are cooperating with the Malaysian authorities.*
**3** ▶ **ORGANIZATION** ◀ [C] an official organization or a local goverment department which controls public affairs, provides public services etc: *the Brewer Transit Authority* | **local authority** *BrE*: *You can claim housing benefit from the local authority.*
**4 I have it on good authority** used to say that you are sure that something is true because you trust the person who told you about it
**5** ▶ **EXPERT** ◀ [C] someone who knows a lot about a subject and whose knowledge and opinions are greatly respected: [+ **on**] *Professor Erikson is one of the world's leading authorities on tropical disease.*
**6** ▶ **PERMISSION** ◀ [C,U] official permission to do something: *Whose authority are you acting on?*

**au·thor·i·za·tion** also **-isation** *BrE* /ˌɔːθəraɪˈzeɪʃən‖ˌɒːθərə-/ *n* [C,U] official permission to do something, or the document giving this permission: *You need special authorization to park here.*

**au·thor·ize** also **-ise** *BrE* /ˈɔːθəraɪz‖ˈɒː-/ *v* [T] to give official or legal permission for something: **authorize sb to do sth** *I'm not authorized to answer your questions.*

**authorized cap·i·tal** /ˌ··· ˈ···/ *n* [U] the largest amount of money a company is allowed to get by selling shares (SHARE² (6))

**Authorized Ver·sion** /ˌ··· ˈ··/ *n* [singular] the English translation of the Bible made in England in 1611

**au·thor·ship** /ˈɔːθəʃɪp‖ˈɒːθər-/ *n* [U] **1** the fact that you have written a particular book, document etc: *There's no evidence to dispute his claim to authorship.* **2** *formal* the profession of writing books

**au·tis·m** /ˈɔːtɪzəm‖ˈɒː-/ *n* [U] a severe mental illness that affects children and prevents them from communicating with other people —**autistic** /ɔːˈtɪstɪk‖ɒː-/ *adj*: *an autistic child*

**au·to** /ˈɔːtəʊ‖ˈɒːtoʊ/ *adj AmE old-fashioned* connected with cars: *the auto industry*

**auto-** /ɔːtəʊ, -tə‖ɒːtoʊ, tə/ *prefix* **1** of or by yourself: *an autobiography* (=book about your own life, written by yourself) **2** working by itself without human operation: *an autopump*

**au·to·bi·og·ra·phy** /ˌɔːtəbaɪˈɒgrəfi‖ˌɒːtəbaɪˈɑː-/ *n* **1** [C] the story of your life written by yourself **2** [U] literature that is concerned with people writing about their own lives —**autobiographic** /ˌɔːtəbaɪəˈgræfɪk◂‖ˌɒː-/ *adj* —**autobiographical** *adj* —**autobiographically** /-kli/ *adv* —compare BIOGRAPHY

**au·toc·ra·cy** /ɔːˈtɒkrəsi‖ɒːˈtɑː-/ *n* **1** [U] a system of government in which one person or group has unlimited power **2** [C] a country governed in this way

**au·to·crat** /ˈɔːtəkræt‖ˈɒː-/ *n* [C] **1** someone who makes decisions and gives orders to people without asking them for their opinion **2** someone who has unlimited power to govern a country —**autocratic** /ˌɔːtəˈkrætɪk◂‖ˌɒː-/ *adj*: *his autocratic control of the White House staff* —**autocratically** /-kli/ *adv*

**au·to·cross** /ˈɔːtəʊkrɒs‖ˈɒːtoʊkrɒːs/ *n* [U] *BrE* a sport in which cars race around a grass field

**au·to·cue** /ˈɔːtəʊkjuː‖ˈɒːtoʊ-/ *n* [C] a machine that shows the words that someone must say while they are being filmed for a television programme

**au·to·graph¹** /ˈɔːtəgrɑːf‖ˈɒːtəgræf/ *n* [C] a famous person's signature that they give to someone who admires them: *Can I have your autograph?*

**autograph²** *v* [T] if a famous person autographs a book, photo etc, they sign it

**auto-im·mune dis·ease** *n* [U] a condition in which substances that normally prevent illness in the body, attack and harm parts of it instead

**au·to·mak·er** /ˈɔːtəʊˌmeɪkə‖ˈɒːtoʊˌmeɪkər/ *n* [C] *AmE* a company that makes cars: *US automakers*

**au·to·mat** /ˈɔːtəmæt‖ˈɒː-/ *n* [C] *trademark AmE* a restaurant where you put money in machines to get food

**au·to·mate** /ˈɔːtəmeɪt‖ˈɒː-/ *v* [T] to change to a system where jobs are done or goods are produced by machines instead of people

**au·to·ma·ted** /ˈɔːtəmeɪtɪ̣d‖ˈɒː-/ *adj* using machines to do a job or industrial process: *a highly automated factory*

**au·to·mat·ic¹** /ˌɔːtəˈmætɪk◂‖ˌɒː-/ *adj* **1** an automatic machine, car etc is designed to be operated in a simple way using only a few controls: *an automatic rifle | an automatic time switch* **2** something that is automatic always happens as a result of something you have done, especially because of a rule or law: *Littering results in an automatic fine of $500.* **3** done without thinking, especially because you have done the same thing many times before: *It seems difficult to remember at first, but after a while it becomes automatic.* S3

**automatic²** *n* [C] **1** a weapon that can fire bullets continuously **2** a car with a system of gears (GEAR¹ (1)) that operate themselves without the driver needing to change them

**au·to·mat·i·cally** /ˌɔːtəˈmætɪkli/ *adv* **1** without thinking about what you are doing: *"Of course," I replied automatically.* **2** as the result of a situation: *As a student you are automatically entitled to a grant.* **3** by the action of a machine, without a person making it work: *The doors opened automatically as we approached.* S3 W3

**automatic pi·lot** /ˌ···· ˈ··/ *n* [C] a machine that flies a plane by itself without the need for a pilot

**automatic trans·mis·sion** /ˌ···· ·ˈ··/ *n* [U] a system that operates the gears (GEAR¹ (1)) of a car without the driver needing to change them

**au·to·ma·tion** /ˌɔːtəˈmeɪʃən‖ˌɒː-/ *n* [U] the use of machines instead of people to do a job or industrial process

**au·tom·a·ton** /ɔːˈtɒmətən‖ɒːˈtɑː-/ *n* [C] **1** someone who seems to be unable to feel emotions **2** a machine, especially one in the shape of a human, that moves without anyone controlling it

**au·to·mo·bile** /ˈɔːtəməbiːl‖-ˈɒːtəmoʊ-/ *n* [C] *AmE* a car: *the automobile industry*

**au·ton·o·mous** /ɔːˈtɒnəməs‖ɒːˈtɑː-/ *adj* **1** having the power to govern a region, country etc without being controlled by anyone else: *an autonomous state* **2** *formal* having the ability to work and make decisions by yourself without any help from anyone else —**autonomously** *adv*

**au·ton·o·my** /ɔːˈtɒnəmi‖ɒːˈtɑː-/ *n* [U] **1** freedom to govern a region, country etc without being controlled by anyone else: *a political system that allows a high degree of local autonomy* **2** the ability to make your own decisions without being influenced by anyone else: *the autonomy of the individual*

**au·to·pi·lot** /ˈɔːtəʊˌpaɪlət‖ˈɒːtoʊ-/ *n* [C] AUTOMATIC PILOT

**au·top·sy** /ˈɔːtɒpsi‖ˈɒːtɑːp-/ *n* [C] *especially AmE* an examination of a dead body to discover the cause of death; POSTMORTEM *BrE*

**au·to·sug·ges·tion** /ˌɔːtəʊsəˈdʒestʃən‖ˌɒːtoʊsəgˈdʒe-, -səˈdʒe-/ *n* [U] *technical* the process of making someone believe or feel something, without them realizing that you are doing this

W3 **au·tumn** /ˈɔːtəm‖ˈɒː-/ also **fall** *AmE n* [C,U] the season between summer and winter, when leaves change colour and the weather becomes slightly colder: *autumn mists*

**au·tum·nal** /ɔːˈtʌmnəl‖ɒː-/ *adj* connected with or typical of autumn: *autumnal colours*

**aux** the written abbreviation of AUXILIARY, especially of AUXILIARY VERB

**aux·il·ia·ry¹** /ɔːgˈziljəri, ɔːk-‖ɒːgˈziljəri, -ˈzɪləri/ *adj* **1** auxiliary workers provide additional help for another group of workers, especially nurses or soldiers: *an auxiliary nurse | auxiliary staff* **2** an auxiliary motor, piece of equipment etc is kept ready to be used if the main one stops working properly: *an auxiliary power supply*

**auxiliary²** *n* [C] **1** a worker who provides additional help for another group of workers, especially nurses or soldiers: *a nursing auxiliary* **2** an auxiliary verb: *a modal auxiliary*

**auxiliary verb** /ˌ···· ˈ·/ *n* [C] a verb that is used with another verb to show its tense, person (PERSON (6)), mood (MOOD (6)) etc. In English the auxiliary verbs are 'be', 'do', and 'have' (as in 'I am running', 'I didn't go', 'they have gone') and all the MODALS

**AV** an abbreviation of AUDIO VISUAL

**a·vail¹** /əˈveɪl/ *n* **be to no avail/be of no avail** if something you do is to no avail or of no avail, you do not succeed in getting what you want: *We searched the whole area but all to no avail: Robbie had disappeared.*

**avail²** *v* **avail yourself of** *formal* to accept an offer or use an opportunity to do something: *He availed himself of this privilege.*

S1 W1 **a·vai·la·ble** /əˈveɪləbəl/ *adj* **1** something that is available is able to be used or can easily be bought or found: *Now available in paperback! | We've already used up all the available space.* | **[+ for]** *The university is trying to make more accommodation available for students.* | **[+ to]** *an increase in the number of jobs available to women* | **readily/freely available** (=very easy to obtain by anyone) *Drugs like crack are freely available.* | **every available** (=every one that you can get) *Every available ambulance was rushed to the scene of the accident.* **2** [not before noun] someone who is available is not busy and has enough time to talk to you: *The president was not available for comment.* **3** someone who is available does not have a wife, BOYFRIEND etc, and therefore may want to start a new romantic relationship with someone else —**availability** /əˌveɪləˈbɪlɪti/ *n* [U] *the availability of affordable housing*

**av·a·lanche** /ˈævəlɑːnʃ‖-læntʃ/ *n* [C] **1** a large mass of snow, ice, and rocks that falls down the side of a mountain: *Two skiers were killed in the avalanche.* **2 an avalanche of** a very large number of things such as letters, messages etc that arrive suddenly at the same time

**av·ant-garde** /ˌævɔːŋ ˈgɑːd◂‖ˌævɑːŋ ˈgɑːrd◂/ *adj* **1** avant-garde music, literature etc is extremely modern and often seems strange or slightly shocking: *an avant-garde play* **2 the avant-garde** the group of artists, writers, musicians etc who produce avant-garde books, paintings etc: *a member of the avant-garde*

**av·a·rice** /ˈævərɪs/ *n* [U] *formal* a desire to have a lot of money that is considered to be too strong; GREED —**avaricious** /ˌævəˈrɪʃəs◂/ *adj* —**avariciously** *adv*

**Ave** the written abbreviation of AVENUE (1): *36, Rokesly Ave*

**a·venge** /əˈvendʒ/ *v* [T] *literary* to do something to hurt or punish someone because they have harmed or offended you: *He wanted to avenge his brother's death.* —**avenger** *n* [C]

S3 **av·e·nue** /ˈævɪnjuː‖-nuː/ *n* [C] **1 Fifth Avenue/Shaftesbury Avenue etc** used in the names of streets in a town or city **2** a possible way of achieving something: *We explored every possible avenue, but couldn't find a solution.* **3** *BrE* a road or broad path between two rows of trees, especially one leading to a big house: *an avenue of chestnut trees*

**a·ver** /əˈvɜː‖əˈvɜːr/ *v* [T] *formal* to say something firmly and strongly because you are sure that it is true

**av·e·rage¹** /ˈævərɪdʒ/ *adj* **1** [only before noun] the average amount is the amount you get when you add together several quantities and divide this by the total number of quantities: *Average earnings in the state are about $1500 a month. | What's the average rainfall for July? | an average speed of 200 kph* **2** an average amount or quantity is not unusually big or small: **(of) average height/build/intelligence etc** (=not tall or short, fat or thin etc) *I'd say he was of average height.* **3** having qualities that are typical of most people or things: *The average student spends about two or three hours a night doing homework. | In an average week I drive about 250 miles.* **4** neither very good nor very bad: *There was nothing special about the film – it was just average.*

**average²** *n* **1** [C] the amount calculated by adding together several quantities, and then dividing this amount by the total number of quantities: *The average of 3, 8 and 10 is 7. | House prices have gone up by an average of 2%.* **2 on average** based on a calculation about how many times something usually happens, how much money someone usually gets, how often people usually do something etc: *On average men smoke more cigarettes than women. | Japanese people on average live much longer than Europeans.* **3** [C,U] the usual level or amount for most people or things in a group: **above/below average** (=better or worse than average) *Susie's school work is well above average.* | **the national average** *I suppose the national average is about £20,000 per year.* —see also **law of averages** (LAW (11))

**average³** *v* [linking verb] **1** to usually do something or usually happen a particular number of times, or to usually be a particular size or amount: *I suppose I average about five cups of coffee a day. | The fish averages about two inches in length.* **2** to calculate the average of figures

**average out** *phr v* **1** [**T average** sth ↔ **out**] to calculate the usual number of times that something happens, the usual size of something, or the average amount of a group of figures: *I averaged out the total increase at about 10%.* **2** [linking verb + **to/at**] to usually result in a particular number or amount: *The weekly profits average out at about $1000.*

**a·verse** /əˈvɜːs‖-ɜːrs/ *adj* **1 not be averse to** used to say that someone likes to do something sometimes, especially something that is slightly wrong or bad for them: *I don't smoke cigarettes, but I'm not averse to the occasional cigar.* **2 be averse to** *formal* to be unwilling to do something or to dislike something

**a·ver·sion** /əˈvɜːʃən‖əˈvɜːrʒən/ *n* [singular, U] a strong dislike of something or someone: **[+ to]** *Despite his aversion to publicity, Arnold was persuaded to talk to the press.* | **have an aversion to** *I have an aversion to housework.*

**a·vert** /əˈvɜːt‖-ɜːrt/ *v* [T] **1** to prevent something unpleasant from happening: *The tragedy could have been averted if the crew had followed safety procedures.* **2 avert your eyes/gaze etc** to look away from something that you do not want to see: *Lockwood averted his eyes as she undressed.*

**a·vi·a·ry** /ˈeɪviəri‖ˈeɪvieri/ *n* [C] a large CAGE where birds are kept

**a·vi·a·tion** /ˌeɪviˈeɪʃən‖ˌeɪ-, ˌæ-/ *n* [U] **1** the science or practice of flying in aircraft **2** the industry that makes aircraft

**a·vi·a·tor** /ˈeɪvieɪtə‖ˈeɪvieɪtər, ˈæ-/ *n* [C] *old-fashioned* a pilot

**av·id** /ˈævɪd/ *adj* **avid reader/listener/fan etc** someone who does something, listens to something etc as much as they can: *an avid collector of old jazz records*

**av·o·ca·do** /ˌævəˈkɑːdəʊ◂‖-doʊ/ also **avocado pear** /ˌ···· ˈ·/ *n* [C] a fruit with a thick green or dark purple skin that is green inside and has a large seed in the middle

**a·void** /əˈvɔɪd/ *v* [T] **1** to do something to prevent something bad from happening: *The other car swerved, trying* *to avoid a collision.* | **avoid doing sth** *This leaflet tells you how to avoid getting ill while travelling.* **2** to deliberately stay away from someone or something: *Jon was embarrassed and tried to avoid us the next day.* | *I managed to avoid the worst of the traffic.* | **avoid sb/sth like the plague** (=stay away from someone or something completely, especially because they are very unpleasant) *I used to avoid that class like the plague.* **3** to deliberately not do something, especially because it is dangerous, unpleasant etc: *Loopholes are a way of legally avoiding taxes.* | **avoid doing sth** *Organic gardeners try to avoid using pesticides.*

**a·void·ance** /ə'vɔɪdəns/ *n* [U] the act of avoiding someone or something: [+ **of**] *the avoidance of issues such as domestic violence* | **tax avoidance** (=legal ways of not paying tax) *millions of dollars in lost revenue due to tax avoidance.*

**av·oir·du·pois** /ˌævədə'pɔɪz, ˌævwɑːdjuː'pwɑː‖ˌævərdə'pɔɪz/ *n* [U] the system of weighing things that uses the standard measures of the OUNCE (1), POUND[1] (1), and TON (1) —compare METRIC SYSTEM

**a·vow** /ə'vaʊ/ *v* [T] *formal* to say or admit publicly something you believe or promise: *He avowed his commitment to Marxist ideals.* —**avowal** *n* [C,U] *an avowal of love*

**a·vowed** /ə'vaʊd/ *adj* [only before noun] admitted or said publicly: *an avowed atheist*

**a·vun·cu·lar** /ə'vʌŋkjʊ̈lə‖-ər/ *adj* being like an uncle; kind and concerned about someone who is younger: *an avuncular pat on the shoulder* —**avuncularly** *adv*

**a·wait** /ə'weɪt/ *v* [T] *formal* **1** to wait for something: *Several men are awaiting trial for robbery.* **2** if a situation, event etc awaits you, it is going to happen in the future: *A terrible surprise awaited them at Mr Tumnus' house* —see WAIT[1] (USAGE)

3 **a·wake[1]** /ə'weɪk/ *adj* [not before noun] **1** not sleeping: **be awake** *"Are you awake?" Julie whispered from the door.* | *Les shook her awake.* | **wide awake** (=completely awake) *The baby was wide awake at midnight.* | **keep sb awake** (=prevent someone from sleeping) *The noise of the traffic kept me awake.* | **stay awake** *One of us ought to stay awake and keep watch.* | **lie awake** *I lay awake worrying about my exams.* **2 be awake to** to understand a situation and its possible effects: *The company is awake to the potential of these ideas.*

**awake[2]** *v past tense* **awoke** /ə'wəʊk‖ə'woʊk/ *past participle* **awoken** /ə'wəʊkən‖ə'woʊ-/ [I,T] **1** to wake up, or to make someone wake up: *The child awoke and began to cry.* **2** if something awakes an emotion or if an emotion awakes, you suddenly begin to feel that emotion: *A dull resentment awoke within him.*

**awake** sb ↔ **to** sth *phr v* [T] to make someone understand a situation and its possible effects: *Artists finally awoke to the aesthetic possibilities of photography.*

**a·wak·en** /ə'weɪkən/ *v formal* **1** [T] if something awakens an emotion, it makes you suddenly begin to feel that emotion: *We need to awaken a new faith in the hearts of non-believers.* **2** [I,T] to wake up or to make someone wake up: *The noise outside awakened him.*

**awaken** sb ↔ **to** sth *phr v* [T] to make someone understand a situation and its possible effects: *We must awaken people to the danger to the environment.*

**a·wak·en·ing** /ə'weɪkənɪŋ/ *n* [C] **1** an occasion when you suddenly realize that you understand something or feel something: *the adolescent's sexual awakening* | **rude awakening** (=an occasion when you suddenly realize that something is not true or is unpleasant) *Anyone who thinks marriage will be bliss forever is in for a rude awakening.* **2** the act of waking from sleep

2 **a·ward[1]** /ə'wɔːd‖-ɔːrd/ *n* [C] **1** something such as a
1 prize or money given to someone to reward them for something they have done: *Meryl Streep won the best actress award.* **2** something, especially money, that is officially given to someone as a payment or judgment: *The nurses' pay award was not nearly as much as they had expected.*

**award[2]** *v* [T] **1** to officially give someone something W3
such as a prize or money to reward them for something they have done: **be awarded sth** *Einstein was awarded the Nobel Prize for his work in quantum physics.* | **award sb sth** *The university awarded her a scholarship.* **2** to officially decide that someone should receive a payment or judgment: **be awarded sth** *After seven years of litigation, he was awarded $750,000 compensation.* | **award sb sth** *Management have awarded all factory employees a 5% pay rise.*

**a·ware** /ə'weə‖ə'wer/ *adj* [not before noun] **1** if you are S1
aware that something such as a problem or a dangerous W1
situation exists, you realize that it exists: **aware that** *Were you aware that your son was having difficulties at school?* | [+ **of**] *Most smokers are perfectly aware of the dangers of smoking.* | **make sb aware of sth** *It's time someone made him aware of the effects of his actions.* | **not that I'm aware of** *spoken*: *"Does she have any problems with her marriage?" "Not that I'm aware of."* | **well/acutely aware** (=very aware) *Sara was well aware of Francesca's fear of heights.* **2** if you are aware of something, you notice it, especially because you can see, hear, or smell it: **aware that** *I gradually became aware that there was someone else in the room.* | [+ **of**] *He was aware of a faint smell of gas.* **3** understanding a lot about what is happening around you and paying attention to it, especially because you realize possible dangers and problems: **politically/socially/environmentally etc aware** *Nowadays everyone's much more environmentally aware.* **4 so/as far as I am aware** *spoken* used when you want to emphasize that there may be things that you do not know about a situation: *So far as I'm aware this is the first time a British rider has won the competition.*

**a·ware·ness** /ə'weənə̈s‖ə'wer-/ *n* [U] **1** knowledge or W3
understanding of a particular subject or situation: *political awareness* | **raise awareness** (=improve people's knowledge) *Health officials have tried to raise awareness about AIDS among teenagers.* **2** the ability to notice something using your senses: [+ **of**] *an artist's awareness of light and color*

**a·wash** /ə'wɒʃ‖ə'wɒːʃ, ə'wɑːʃ/ *adj* [not before noun] **1** covered with water or another liquid **2** containing too many things or people of a particular kind: [+ **with**] *TV nowadays is awash with soap operas.*

**a·way[1]** /ə'weɪ/ *adv* **1** to or at a distance from someone S1
or something: *Go away!* | *Dinah was crying as she drove* W1
*slowly away.* | [+ **from**] *The police tried to keep people away from the accident.* | **turn/look away (from sb/sth)** (=turn so that you are not looking at someone or something) **2** if someone is away from school, work or home they are not there: [+ **from**] *You must bring a note from your parents if you've been away from school.* | **away with flu/measles/a cold etc** (=not at school, work etc because you are ill) **3 3 miles/5 kilometres etc away** at a distance of 3 miles, 5 kilometres etc from someone or something: *Geneva is about 20 miles away.* **4 2 days/3 weeks etc away** if an event is 2 days, 3 weeks etc away, it will happen after 2 days etc have passed: *Christmas is only a month away.* | *We live minutes away from the sea.* (=it only takes minutes to get there) **5** into a safe or enclosed place: *Put your money away, I'm paying.* **6** so as to be gone or used up: *The music died away.* | *The farm was swept away in the flood.* | *Ruben gave all his money away to charity.* | *Support for the Democrats has dropped away.* | *The young lovers danced the night away.* (=danced all night) | *Cut away all the dead wood.* **7** used to emphasize a continuous action: *Sue was singing away to herself in the bath.* | *They've been hammering away all day.* **8** if a team is playing away, it is playing a game at its opponent's sports field, STADIUM etc: *Liverpool are playing away at Everton on Saturday.* **9 away with sb/sth!** *literary* used to tell someone to take someone or something away: *Away with the prisoner!* **10 be away** *ScotE* to go or leave a place: *He's just away to the shops.* |

*We're away tomorrow* (=we're leaving tomorrow). —see also **far and away** (FAR[1] (10)), **right away** (RIGHT[2] (2))

**away²** *adj* [only before noun] an away game or match is played at your opponent's field or sports hall —opposite HOME[1] (13)

**awe¹** /ɔː‖ɒː/ *n* [U] **1** a feeling of great respect and admiration for someone or something: **with awe/in awe** *Kate gazed at the mountains with awe.* | **fill sb with awe** *The sight of so many jewels in one place filled them with awe.* **2 be/stand in awe of sb** to have great respect and admiration for and sometimes a slight fear of someone: *Because of his reputation as a dancer we were all rather in awe of him.*

**awe²** *v* [T usually passive] *formal* if you are awed by someone or something, you feel great respect and admiration for them, and are often slightly afraid of them: *The girls were awed by the splendor of the cathedral.* —**awed** *adj*: *an awed silence*

**awe-in·spir·ing** /'· ·,··/ *adj* extremely impressive in a way that makes you feel great respect and admiration: *a truly awe-inspiring achievement*

**awe·some** /'ɔːsəm‖'ɒː-/ *adj* **1** extremely impressive, serious, or difficult so that you feel great admiration, worry, or fear: *an awesome responsibility* | *the awesome sweep of the scenery* **2** *AmE informal* very good: *Their last concert was really awesome.* —**awesomely** *adv*

**awe-strick·en** /'· ··/ *adj* awestruck

**awe·struck** /'ɔːstrʌk‖'ɒː-/ *adj* feeling extremely impressed by the importance, difficulty, or seriousness of someone or something: *She gazed awestruck at the jewels.*

S1 **aw·ful¹** /'ɔːfəl‖'ɒː-/ *adj* **1** very bad or unpleasant: *The weather was awful.* | *a really awful book* | *These canned apricots taste awful!* | *I felt awful about not being able to help.* **2** [only before noun] *spoken* used to emphasize how much or how good, bad etc something is: **an awful lot** (=a very large amount) *I have an awful lot of work to do this week.* | *It made him look an awful fool.* **3 look/feel awful** to look or feel ill: *You look awful – what's wrong with you?* **4** *literary* making you feel great admiration or fear —**awfulness** *n* [U]

**awful²** *adv* [+ adj/adv] *AmE spoken* very: *That kid's awful cute, with her red curls.*

**aw·ful·ly** /'ɔːfəli‖'ɒː-/ *adv spoken* very: *It's awfully cold in here. Is the heater on?*

**a·while** /ə'waɪl/ *adv especially literary* for a short time

S2 **awk·ward** /'ɔːkwəd‖'ɒːkwərd/ *adj* **1** making you feel so embarrassed that you are not sure what to do or say: *The more she tried to get out of the situation, the more awkward it became.* | *an awkward pause* | **make things awkward** (=cause trouble and make a situation very difficult) *She could make things very awkward if she wanted to.* **2** not convenient: *I'm sorry, have I called at an awkward time?* **3** moving or behaving in a way that does not seem relaxed or comfortable, especially because you feel nervous or embarrassed: *I felt a bit awkward on my first day there, but I soon settled in.* | *an awkward wave* | *an awkward teenager* **4** difficult to use or handle: *The camera has a lot of small buttons, which makes it rather awkward to use.* **5** an awkward person is deliberately unhelpful: [+ **about**] *I wish you'd stop being so bloody awkward about everything.* | **an awkward customer** (=someone who is difficult to deal with) —**awkwardly** *adv*: *"Are you the head tutor..." she began awkwardly.* —**awkwardness** *n* [U]

**awl** /ɔːl‖ɒːl/ *n* [C] a pointed tool for making holes in leather

**aw·ning** /'ɔːnɪŋ‖'ɒː-/ *n* [C] a sheet of material outside a shop, tent etc to keep off the sun or the rain

**a·woke** /ə'wəʊk‖ə'woʊk/ the past tense of AWAKE

**a·wok·en** /ə'wəʊkən‖ə'woʊ-/ the past participle of AWAKE

**AWOL** /,eɪ ,dʌbəljuː əʊ 'el, 'eɪwɒl‖-oʊ-,'eɪwɒːl/ *adj* absent without leave; absent from your army group without permission: **go awol** *Two soldiers had gone AWOL the night before.*

**a·wry** /ə'raɪ/ *adj* **1 go awry** if something goes awry, it does not happen in the way that was planned: *My carefully laid plans had already gone awry.* **2** not in the correct position: *He rushed out, hat awry.*

**aw shucks** /,ɔː 'ʃʌks‖,ɒː-/ *interjection AmE* used in a joking way to show that you feel embarrassed or sad

**axe¹** also **ax** *AmE* /æks/ *n* [C] **1** a tool with a heavy metal blade on the end of a long handle, used to cut down trees or split pieces of wood **2 give sb the axe** *informal* to dismiss somone from their job **3 give sth the axe** *informal* to get rid of something such as a plan, a system, or a service **4 have an axe to grind** to do or say something again and again because you want to persuade people to accept your ideas or beliefs: *I have no political axe to grind.*

**axe²** also **ax** *AmE v* [T] *informal* **1** to suddenly dismiss someone from their job: *plans to axe half the workforce* **2** to get rid of a plan, system, or service, or reduce the amount of money that is spent on something: *Student grants have been axed.*

**ax·i·om** /'æksiəm/ *n* [C] *formal* a rule or principle that is generally considered to be true

**ax·i·o·mat·ic** /,æksiə'mætɪk◂/ *adj formal* not needing to be proved because you can easily see that it is true; SELF-EVIDENT —**axiomatically** /-kli/ *adv*

**ax·is** /'æksɪ̈s/ *n plural* **axes** /-siːz/ [C] *technical* **1** the imaginary line around which a large round object, such as the Earth, turns: *The Earth rotates on an axis between the North and South Poles.* —see picture at EARTH[1] **2** a line drawn across the middle of a regular shape that divides it into two equal parts **3** either of the two lines of a GRAPH, by which the positions of points are measured

**ax·le** /'æksəl/ *n* [C] the bar connecting two wheels on a car or other vehicle —see picture at BICYCLE[1]

**ay·ah** /'aɪə/ *n* [C] *IndE, PakE* a nurse who looks after children

**a·ya·tol·lah** /,aɪə'tɒlə‖-'toʊ-/ *n* [C] a religious leader of the Shiite Muslims, especially a very powerful one

**aye¹** /aɪ/ *adv* **1** used to say yes when voting: **the ayes have it** (=used to say that most people in a meeting have voted in favour of something) —opposite NAY **2** *dialect* a word meaning yes, used especially in Scotland

**aye²** *adv ScotE old use or poetic* always

**az·ure** /'æʒə, 'æʒjʊə, 'æzjʊə‖'æʒər/ *adj* having a bright blue colour like the sky —**azure** *n* [U]

# B,b

**B, b** /biː/ *plural* **B's, b's** *n* [C] the second letter of the English alphabet

**B** *n* **1 a)** the seventh note in the musical SCALE[1] (8) of C major **b)** the musical KEY[1] (4) based on this note **2** a mark given to a student's work, to show that it is good but not excellent: *I got a B in History.* —see also B-MOVIE, B-SIDE

**b** the written abbreviation of born: *Andrew Lanham, b 1885*

**B & B** /ˌbiː ənd ˈbiː/ the written abbreviation of BED AND BREAKFAST

**BA** /ˌbiː ˈeɪ/ *n* [C] Bachelor of Arts; the title of a first university degree in a subject such as literature, history etc: *Susan Potter, BA* —compare BSC

**baa** /bɑː/ *v* [I] to make a sound like a sheep —**baa** *n* [C]

**bab·ble**[1] /ˈbæbəl/ *v* **1** [I,T] to speak quickly in a way that is difficult to understand or sounds silly: *I have no idea what he was babbling on about.* **2** [I] to make a sound like water moving over stones —**babbler** *n* [C]

**babble**[2] *n* [singular] **1** the confused sound of many people talking at the same time: *the babble of a crowded party* **2** a sound like water moving over stones

**babe** /beɪb/ *n* **1** *literary* a baby: **babe in arms** (=one that has to be carried) **2** a word for an attractive young woman **3** a way of speaking to a young woman, often considered offensive **4** a way of speaking to someone you love, especially your wife or husband **5 babe in the woods** *AmE* someone who can be easily deceived: *He was like a babe in the woods when he first came to New York.*

**ba·bel** /ˈbeɪbəl‖ˈbeɪ-, ˈbæ-/ *n* [singular, U] the confusing sound of many voices talking together: *a babel of French and Italian*

**ba·boon** /bəˈbuːn‖bæ-/ *n* [C] a large monkey that lives in Africa and South Asia

**ba·bu, baboo** /ˈbɑːbuː/ *n* [C] **1** *IndE old-fashioned* an Indian title of respect **2** *BrE* an Indian CLERK or government official of low rank

**ba·by** /ˈbeɪbi/ *n plural* **babies** [C]
**1 ▶ CHILD ◀** a very young child who has not yet learned to speak or walk: *A baby was crying upstairs.* | *They have a five-year-old boy and a baby girl.* | **have a baby** (=give birth to a baby) *I think she had the baby in June.* | **be expecting a baby** (=have a baby developing inside your body) —see CHILD (USAGE)
**2 ▶ ANIMAL/PLANT ◀** a very young animal or plant: *baby birds* | *baby carrots*
**3 ▶ BROTHER/SISTER ◀** a younger child in a family, often the youngest: *He's the baby of the family.*
**4 ▶ WOMAN ◀** *AmE spoken* **a)** a way of speaking to someone that you love: *Mike baby, could you get me a glass of water?* **b)** a way of speaking to a young woman, often considered offensive
**5 ▶ SILLY ◀** someone who is not behaving in a sensible way: *Don't be such a baby — take your medicine!*
**6 ▶ RESPONSIBILITY ◀** *informal* something special that someone has developed or is responsible for: *Don't ask me about the building contract—that's Robert's baby.*

**baby blues** /ˈ·· ·/ *n* [plural] *informal* a feeling of DEPRESSION (1a) that some women suffer from after they have had a baby: *an attack of the baby blues*

**baby boom·er** /ˈ·· ˌ··/ *n* [C] someone born during a period when a lot of babies were born, especially between 1946 and 1964

**baby car·riage** /ˈ·· ˌ··/ *n* [C] *AmE* a thing like a small bed with four wheels, used for taking a baby from one place to another; PRAM *BrE* —compare PUSHCHAIR —see picture at PRAM

**baby-faced** /ˈ·· ·/ *adj* a baby-faced adult has a face like a child

**Ba·by·gro** /ˈbeɪbigrəʊ‖-groʊ/ *n* [C] *BrE trademark* a piece of clothing for a baby, that covers their whole body

**ba·by·hood** /ˈbeɪbihʊd/ *n* [U] the period of time when you are a baby

**ba·by·ish** /ˈbeɪbi-ɪʃ/ *adj* like a baby or suitable for a baby: *The games were a little babyish for nine-year-olds.*

**baby milk** /ˈ·· ·/ *n* [U] *BrE* dried milk mixed with water and fed to babies instead of breast milk; FORMULA (5) *AmE*

**ba·by·sit** /ˈbeɪbisɪt/ *v past tense and past participle* **babysat** /-sæt/ *present participle* **babysitting** [I,T] to take care of children while their parents are away for a short time —**babysitting** *n* [U] *She earns some extra cash from babysitting.* | *a babysitting service*

**ba·by·sitter** /ˈbeɪbiˌsɪtə‖-ər/ *n* [C] **1** someone who is paid to look after children while their parents are away for a short time. **2** *AmE* someone who is paid to look after children while their parents are at work; CHILDMINDER *BrE*

**baby talk** /ˈ·· ·/ *n* [U] sounds or words that babies use when they are learning to talk

**baby tooth** /ˈ·· ·/ *n plural* **baby teeth** [C] a tooth from the first set of teeth that young children have; MILK TOOTH *BrE*

**baby walk·er** /ˈ·· ˌ··/ *n* [C] a frame on wheels that is used to support a baby while it is learning to walk

**bac·ca·lau·re·ate** /ˌbækəˈlɔːriət/ *n* [C] the last examination you take in French schools and some international schools

**bac·ca·rat** /ˈbækərɑː‖ˌbækəˈrɑː/ *n* [U] a card game usually played for money

**bac·cha·na·li·an** /ˌbækəˈneɪliən◂/ *adj literary* a bacchanalian party, celebration etc involves alcohol, sex, and uncontrolled behaviour: *a bacchanalian orgy*

**bac·cy** /ˈbæki/ *n* [U] *slang* tobacco

**bach** /bætʃ/ *v* **bach it** *AmE old-fashioned* if a man baches it, he lives on his own and looks after himself

**bach·e·lor** /ˈbætʃələ‖-ər/ *n* [C] a man who has never been married: **confirmed bachelor** (=a man who intends never to marry) | **eligible bachelor** (=a rich young man who has not yet married)

**bachelor flat** /ˈ··· ˌ·/ *n* [C] a set of rooms where an unmarried man lives

**bachelor par·ty** /ˈ··· ˌ··/ *n* [C] *AmE* a party for men only, especially the night before a man's wedding; STAG NIGHT *BrE*

**bachelor's de·gree** /ˈ··· ·ˌ·/ *n* [C] the first level of university degree; BA

**ba·cil·lus** /bəˈsɪləs/ *n plural* **bacilli** /-laɪ/ [C] *technical* a rod-shaped BACTERIA, of which some types cause diseases

**back**[1] /bæk/ *adv* S1 W1
**1 ▶ RETURN ◀** in or into the place or position where someone or something was before: *Freddie was supposed to be back at the hotel by six.* | *Put that book back where you found it!* | *"We'd better go back," she said regretfully.* —see graph at RETURN[1]
**2 ▶ AS BEFORE ◀** in or into the condition that someone or something was in before: *I just couldn't get back to sleep.* | *This brings me back to my point about the state of the economy.*
**3 ▶ HOME TOWN ◀** in a place where you or your family lived before: [+ **in/at etc**] *Back in Manitoba we used to skate on the lakes in winter.* | *Back home we never did things this way.*
**4 ▶ NOT FORWARDS ◀** in the direction that you have come from: *George glanced back to see if he was still being followed.* | *He took a few steps back, then took the photo.*
**5 ▶ REPLY ◀** as a reply or reaction to what someone has done: *Can you ask Mr Clark to call me back?* | *I'll pay you back on Friday.* | *I grinned back at him.*

**back**

John's shirt is on back to front *BrE* / on backwards *AmE*.

They stood back to back.

**6 ▶AGAIN◀** once again: *Play the tape back for me, will you?|Let's go back over these figures just to make sure we're right.*
**7 sit/lie/lean back** to sit or lie in a comfortable, relaxed way: *Sit back, relax, and enjoy the show!*
**8 ▶THE PAST◀** in or towards an earlier time: [+ **in/on**] *Back in the fifties, children respected their elders.*| **three years/two months etc back** (=three years ago etc) *If I'd know three years back that stocks were going to crash, I'd have sold everything.*
**9 ▶AWAY FROM SB◀** away from the person who is speaking: *Stay well back! Let the ambulance through.*
**10 ▶AWAY FROM STH◀** away from a surface or area: *Pull back the bandage and see if the wound is healing.|The clouds rolled back and suddenly there was sunlight.*
**11 back and forth** if someone or something goes back and forth, they go in one direction then back to where they started from, and keep repeating this movement: *The shuttle bus runs back and forth between the airport and the downtown area.|pacing back and forth in the waiting room*
**12 ▶BOOK◀** towards the beginning of a book: *There's a picture six pages further back.*
**13 pay/get sb back (for)** to do something unpleasant to someone because they have done something unpleasant to you or someone you care about: *I'll pay him back for hurting my sister – just you wait!*
**14 go back on a promise/agreement etc** to do the opposite of what you promised to do: *You can trust Kate – she'll never go back on her word.*

S1 W1 **back**[2] *n* [C]
**1 ▶BODY◀ a)** the side of a person's or animal's body that is opposite the chest and goes from the neck to the top of the legs: *He lifted the bag of golf clubs onto his back.|The cat arched its back and hissed.*| **on your back** (=with your back on the ground) *They lay on their backs and gazed at the sky.*| **with your back to** *Stand with your back to the wall and don't move.* —see picture at HORSE[1] **b)** the bones that go from your neck to the top of your legs: *He broke his back in a motorbike accident.*
**2 ▶PART◀** the part of something that is furthest from the direction in which it moves or faces: [+ **of**] *He kissed her on the back of her head.|I think there's enough room for your stuff in the back of the truck.*| **at the back** *a small shop with an office at the back* —see FRONT[1] (USAGE)| **in back (of)** *AmE* (=in or at the back of something) *When we go on long journeys by car the kids always ride in back.*| **round the back/out (the) back** *BrE informal* (=behind a house or other building) *We keep the bikes in a shed out the back.* —opposite FRONT[1] (3)
**3 ▶SURFACE◀** the less important side or surface of something such as a paper or card: *Paul scribbled his address on the back of an envelope.|On the back of the canvas we can see the date: 1645.*
**4 ▶CHAIR◀** the part of a seat that you lean against when you are sitting: [+ **of**] *He rested his arm on the back of the sofa.*
**5 ▶BOOK/NEWSPAPER◀** the last pages of a book or newspaper: [+ **of**] *The index is at the back of the book.*
**6 ▶FOOTBALL ETC◀** one of the defending players on a football or hockey team
**7 at your back a)** behind you: *They had the wind at their backs as they set off.* **b)** *literary* supporting you: *Caesar marched into Rome with an army at his back.*
**8 at/in the back of your mind** a thought or feeling that is at the back of your mind is influencing you even though you are not thinking about it: *At the back of Joe's mind was the feeling that he had seen this place before.*
**9 back to back a)** with the backs towards each other: *Stand back to back and we'll see who is taller.* —see also BACK-TO-BACK **b)** *especially AmE* happening one after the other: *a marathon basketball tournament with games played back to back*
**10 back to front** *BrE* in an incorrect position so that what should be the back is at the front; backwards: *You've got your sweater on back to front.*
**11 behind sb's back** if you do something behind someone's back, you do it without them knowing: *She's the kind of person who talks about you behind your back.*
**12 get/put sb's back up** *informal* to annoy someone: *You'll just put people's backs up if you're aggressive all the time.*
**13 get off my back** *spoken* used to tell someone to stop annoying you or asking you to do things you do not want to do: *Do me a favour and get off my back!*
**14 know sth back to front** *BrE* **know sth backwards** *especially AmE* if you know or learn something back to front, you know it very thoroughly: *You can't fool her! She knows the regulations back to front!*
**15 know somewhere like the back of your hand** to know a place extremely well: *I'll drive, if you want – I know New York like the back of my hand.*
**16 the back of beyond** *informal especially BrE* a very distant place that is difficult to get to: *They live on a farm somewhere in the back of beyond.*
**17 be (flat) on your back** to be so ill that you cannot get out of bed: *He's been flat on his back with flu for three weeks.*
**18 be on sb's back** *informal* to be trying to make someone do things they do not want to do: *Dad's on my back about my homework, so I can't go out tonight.*
**19 put your back into it** *informal* to work extremely hard at something: *If we really put our backs into it, we could finish today.*
**20 have your back to the wall** *informal* to be in a very difficult position with no choice about what to do
**21 low-backed/straight-backed/narrow-backed etc** with a low, straight, narrow etc back: *a high-backed chair*
**22 turn your back on** to refuse to be involved with something: *So many of them just turn their backs on their religion when they leave home.*

**back**[3] *adj* [only before noun] **1** at the back: *a back room|the back page|a back seat* —see also BACK DOOR **2** behind something: *in the back yard* **3** from the back: *a back view|Go in the back way so you won't be seen.* **4 back street/lane/road etc** a street etc that is away from the main streets: *a little shop in a back street behind the station* **5 back rent/taxes/pay** money that someone owes from an earlier date **6 back issue/copy/number** an old copy of a magazine or newspaper: *a pile of back copies of 'Punch' magazine* **7** *technical* a back vowel sound is made by raising your tongue at the back of your mouth

**back**[4] *v*
**1 ▶ MOVE SB ◀** [I always + adv/prep, T always + adv/prep] to move backwards, or make someone else move backwards: **back towards/across etc** *Stanley backed slowly across the stage.*
**2 ▶ MOVE VEHICLE ◀** [I, T] to make a car move backwards; REVERSE[1] (2): **back (sth) into/out of etc** *If you back your car out of the driveway I can get mine in* —see picture on page 415.
**3 ▶ SUPPORT ◀** [T] to support someone or something, especially with money, power, or influence: *The bill is backed by environmental lobbyists.|government-backed loans*
**4 ▶ BACK SURFACE ◀** [T usually passive] to put something on the back surface of a flat piece of material: *Back the photo with strong cardboard.|a plastic-backed shower curtain*
**5 ▶ BE BEHIND ◀** [T usually passive] to be at the back of something or behind it: *It was a sunny spot, backed by a wall.*
**6 ▶ MUSIC ◀** [T usually passive] if musicians back a singer or another musician, they play music that makes the main performer sound better
**7 ▶ HORSE/DOG RACE ◀** [T] to risk money on whether a horse, dog, team etc wins something: *We backed Eliamana but it finished fourth.*
**8 back the wrong horse** to support a person, group etc that loses
**9 ▶ WIND ◀** [I] *technical* if the wind backs, it changes direction, moving around the COMPASS (1) in the direction North-West-South-East
**back away** *phr v* [I] **1** to move backwards, away from something, especially because you are afraid, shocked etc: [+ **from**] *The waiter backed away from the table, bowing slightly.* **2** to gradually stop taking part in something or supporting something: *Imperceptibly, the Government has backed away from the plan.*
**back down** *phr v* [I] to accept defeat in an argument, opinion, or claim: *When presented with the evidence, the suspect backed down.*
**back off** *phr v* [I] *especially AmE* **1** to move backwards, away from something: *Back off, you're crowding me.* **2** to stop trying to force someone to do or think something: *I think you should back off for a while and leave Alan to make his own decision.* **3** to gradually stop taking part in something or supporting something: *Jerry backed off when he realized how much work was involved.*
**back onto** sth *phr v* [T] if a building backs onto something such as a river or field, its back faces it
**back out** *phr v* [I] to decide not to do something that you had promised to do: [+ **of**] *They backed out of the contract at the last minute.*
**back up** *phr v* **1** [T **back** sb/sth ↔ **up**] to say that what someone is saying is true: *Peggy would back me up if she were here.|The videotape evidence backed up the manager's story.* **2** [I,T **back** sth ↔ **up**] to make a copy of the information on a computer PROGRAM or DISK **3** [I,T **back** sth ↔ **up**] to make a car go backwards: *Get out of the way – the truck's backing up!* —see picture on page 415 **4** [I] to move backwards: *Back up a bit so that everyone can see.* —see also BACKUP

**back·ache** /ˈbækeɪk/ *n* [C,U] a pain in your back

**back·bench** /ˌbækˈbentʃ◂/ *n* [C] *BrE* the seats in the British parliament where ordinary MPS (MP (1)) sit: *the backbenches* —compare FRONTBENCH

**back·bench·er** /ˌbækˈbentʃə◂‖-ər◂/ *n* [C] *BrE* an ordinary British Member of Parliament rather than one of the party leaders: *Angry backbenchers are threatening to vote against the government.*

**back·bit·ing** /ˈbækbaɪtɪŋ/ *n* [U] unpleasant or cruel talk about someone who is not present: *All this backbiting is destroying company morale.* —**backbiter** *n* [C]

**back·board** /ˈbækbɔːd‖-bɔːrd/ *n* [C] the board behind the basket in the game of BASKETBALL —see picture on page 1263

**back·bone** /ˈbækbəʊn‖-boʊn/ *n* **1** [C] the row of connected bones that go down the middle of your back; SPINE (1) **2 the backbone of** the most important part of an organization, set of ideas etc: *The manufacturing sector forms the backbone of the country's economy.* **3** [U] moral strength: *The army'll give 'em some backbone!*

**back·break·ing** /ˈbækbreɪkɪŋ/ *adj* backbreaking work is physically very difficult and makes you very tired

**back·chat** /ˈbæktʃæt/ *n* [U] *BrE* a reply to someone who is telling you what to do; BACKTALK *AmE*: *None of your backchat, do your homework!*

**back·cloth** /ˈbæk-klɒθ‖-klɒːθ/ *n* [C] **1** a painted cloth hung across the back of a stage **2** the conditions or situation in which something happens: *Against this backcloth of industrial turmoil, violence was always likely.*

**back·comb** /ˈbæk-kəʊm‖-koʊm/ *v* [T] *BrE* to comb your hair against the way it grows in order to style it and make it look thicker; TEASE (4) *AmE*

**back coun·try** /ˈ· ˌ··/ *n* [U] **1** *especially AustrE* a country area where few people live —compare BUSH **2** *AmE* an area, especially in the mountains, away from roads and towns

**back·date** /ˌbækˈdeɪt‖ˈbækdeɪt/ *v* [T] to make something have its effect from an earlier date: **backdate sth from/to** *The pay increase agreed in June will be backdated to January.* —compare ANTEDATE, POSTDATE

**back door** /ˌ· ˈ·/ *n* [C] **1** a door at the back or side of a building **2 get in through the back door** to achieve something by having an unfair secret advantage: *His father works for them so he got in through the back door.*

**back·door** /ˈbækdɔː‖-dɔːr/ *adj* [only before noun] secret, or not publicly stated as your intention: *In what amounts to a backdoor income tax increase, the Chancellor chose to freeze personal tax allowance.*

**back·drop** /ˈbækdrɒp‖-drɑːp/ *n* [C] **1** *literary* the scenery behind something that you are looking at: *the stunning backdrop of the Alps* **2** the conditions or situation in which something happens: *The depression was the backdrop for Steinbeck's greatest works.* **3** a painted cloth hung across the back of a stage

**back·er** /ˈbækə‖-ər/ *n* [C] someone who supports a plan, especially by providing money: *We're still trying to find backers for the housing development scheme.*

**back·fire** /ˌbækˈfaɪə‖ˈbækfaɪr/ *v* [I] **1** if a plan or action backfires, it has the opposite effect to the one you intended **2** if a car backfires, it makes a sudden loud noise because the engine is not working correctly

**back for·ma·tion** /ˈ· ·ˌ··/ *n* [C] *technical* a new word formed from an older word, for example 'televise' formed from 'television'

**back·gam·mon** /ˈbækgæmən/ *n* [U] a game for two players, using flat round pieces and DICE[1] (1) on a special board

**back·ground** /ˈbækgraʊnd/ *n* S2 W2 **1** [C] someone's family history, education, social class etc: *He's always going on about his working class background.|a background in computer engineering* **2** [C,U] the events in the past that explain why something has happened in the way that it has: *Without knowing the background to the case, I couldn't possibly comment.|***background information/details/data etc** *With a bit more background information the report will be fine.* **3** [C] the pattern or colour on top of which something has been drawn, printed etc: *Red lettering on a white background.* **4 in the background a)** behind the main thing that you are looking at: *In the background of this photo you can see a few of my old college friends.* **b)** someone who keeps or stays in the background tries not to be noticed: *A couple of waiters hovered in the background.* **c)** a sound that is in the background is present but is not the main thing that you are listening to: *In the background I could hear the sound of traffic.* **5** [C,U] the sounds that you can hear apart from the main thing that you are listening to:

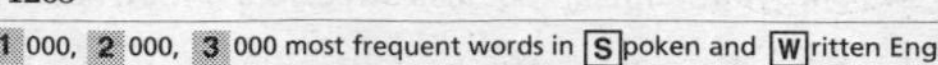

**background noise/music/a lot of background noise** *an irritating background noise of tinny music*

**back·hand** /ˈbækhænd/ *n* [C usually singular] a hit in tennis and some other games in which the back of your hand is turned in the direction of the hit —**backhand** *adj* —see picture on page 1264

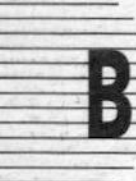

**back·hand·ed** /ˌbækˈhændɪ̣d◂‖ˈbækhændɪ̣d/ *adj* **1** a backhanded remark or COMPLIMENT[1] (1) seems to express praise or admiration but in fact means the opposite: *'Brave' can be a backhanded way of saying 'crazy'.* **2** a backhanded shot etc is made with a backhand

**back·hand·er** /ˈbækhændə‖-ər/ *n* [C] **1** a hit or shot made with the back of your hand **2** *BrE informal* money that you pay illegally and secretly to get something done: *Investigators estimate that £35m had been spent on bribes and backhanders.*

**back·hoe** /ˈbækhəʊ‖-hoʊ/ *n* [C] a large digging machine used for making roads etc

**back·ing** /ˈbækɪŋ/ *n* **1** [U] support or help, especially with money **2** [C] material that is used to make the back of an object **3** [C] the music that is played with a singer's voice to make it sound better —**backing** *adj*

**back·lash** /ˈbæklæʃ/ *n* [C] a strong but usually delayed reaction against recent events, especially against political or social developments: **backlash against** *The 1970s saw the first backlash against the emerging women's movement.* | *The rise in violent crime provoked a backlash against the liberal gun-control laws.*

**back·log** /ˈbæklɒg‖-lɒːg, -lɑːg/ *n* [usually singular] a large amount of work, especially that should already have been completed: *a backlog of letters*

**back·pack**[1] /ˈbækpæk/ *n* [C] *especially AmE* a bag carried on your back, often supported by a light metal frame, used especially by climbers and walkers; RUCKSACK *BrE*

**backpack**[2] *v* [I] *especially AmE* to go walking and camping carrying a BACKPACK[1]: *backpacking along the Appalachian trail* —**backpacker** *n* [C]

**back pas·sage** /ˌ· ˈ··/ *n* [C] a word meaning ANUS (=the hole where food waste comes out of your body) used to avoid offending people

**back·ped·al** /ˌbækˈpedl‖ˈbækˌpedl/ *v* **backpedalled, backpedalling** *BrE* **backpedaled, backpedaling** *AmE* [I] **1** to start to change your opinion about something that you had promised: *They are backpedalling on the commitment to cut taxes.* **2** to PEDAL[2] (2) backwards on a bicycle

**back·room boy** /ˈbækrʊm ˌbɔɪ, -ruːm-/ *n* [usually plural] *informal especially BrE* someone such as an engineer or scientist, whose work is important but who does not get much attention or fame

**back seat** /ˌ· ˈ·◂/ *n* **1** [C] a seat at the back of a car, behind where the driver sits **2 back seat driver a)** a passenger in the back of a car who gives unwanted advice to the driver about how to drive **b)** *especially AmE* someone in business or politics who tries to control things that they are not really responsible for

**back·side** /ˈbæksaɪd/ *n informal* the part of your body that you sit on

**back·slap·ping** /ˈbækslæpɪŋ/ *n* [U] noisy cheerful behaviour when people praise each other's achievements more than they deserve —**backslapper** *n* [C]

**back·slash** /ˈbækslæʃ/ *n* [C] a line (\) used in writing to separate words, numbers, or letters

**back·slide** /ˌbækˈslaɪd‖ˈbækslaɪd/ *v* [I] to start doing the bad things that you used to do, especially after having improved your behaviour: *I haven't had a cigarette for two months, but recently I'm afraid I've begun to backslide.* —**backslider** *n* [C]

**back·space** /ˈbækspeɪs/ *n* [usually singular] the part of a TYPEWRITER that you press to move backwards towards the beginning of the line

**back·spin** /ˈbækspɪn/ *n* [U] a turning movement in a ball that has been hit so that the top of the ball turns backwards as the ball travels forwards

**back·stage** /ˌbækˈsteɪdʒ◂/ *adv* **1** behind the stage in a theatre, especially in the actors' dressing rooms **2** in private, especially within the secret parts of an organization: *That's the official line, but who knows what really goes on backstage?* —**backstage** *adj*

**back·stairs** /ˈbæksteəz‖-sterz/ *adj* [only before noun] secret and probably unfair: *backstairs influence*

**back·street** /ˈ· ·/ *adj* backstreet activities are often illegal and done badly: *a backstreet abortion*

**back·stroke** /ˈbækstrəʊk‖-stroʊk/ *n* [singular] a way of swimming on your back by moving first one arm then the other backwards while kicking your feet

**back·talk** /ˈbæktɔːk‖-tɒːk/ *n* [U] *AmE* a rude reply to someone who is telling you what to do; BACKCHAT *BrE*

**back-to-back** /ˌ· · ˈ·◂/ *n* [C] *BrE* a house in a row or TERRACE (1) built with its back touching the back of the next row of houses

**back·track** /ˈbæktræk/ *v* [I] **1** to change your beliefs, statements etc so that they are not as strong as they were earlier: *Clinton seems to be backtracking on his policy on Bosnia.* **2** to return by the same way that you came

**back·up** /ˈbækʌp/ *n* [C, U] **1** something or someone used to provide support and help when it is needed: *Army units can only operate if they have sufficient backup.* **2 backup plan/system/generator** a plan or system that can be used if the main one does not work

**back·ward** /ˈbækwəd‖-wərd/ *adj* **1** [only before noun] made in a direction towards what is behind you: *She went without a backward glance.* **2** developing slowly and less successfully than most others: *some of the more backward countries* | *a backward child* —compare FORWARD[2] —**backwardly** *adv* —**backwardness** *n* [U]

**back·wards** /ˈbækwədz‖-wərdz/ also **backward** *AmE* *adv* **1** towards the back, the beginning, or the past: *She pushed me and I fell backwards into the chair.* | *Can you say the alphabet backwards?* **2** moving or facing the opposite direction to the usual one: *He walked backwards away from the King.* | *You've got your hat on backwards!* **3** towards a worse state: *The new measures are seen by some as a major step backwards.* **4 backwards and forwards** first in one direction and then in the opposite direction, usually many times **5 bend over/lean over backwards (to do sth)** to try as hard as possible to help or please someone: *We bent over backwards to help them.* **6 know sth backwards** *BrE* **know sth backwards and forwards** *AmE* to know something very well or perfectly: *All the actors know the play backwards and forwards.* —compare FORWARD[1]

**back·wa·ter** /ˈbækwɔːtə‖-wɒː-, -wɑː-/ *n* **1** a very quiet place not influenced by outside events or new ideas: *a rural backwater* **2** a part of a river away from the main stream, where the water does not move

**back·woods** /ˈbækwʊdz/ *n* [plural] a distant and undeveloped area away from any towns

**back·woods·man** /ˈbækwʊdzmən/ *n* [C] **1** someone who lives in the backwoods **2** *BrE* a member of a political party or parliament, especially the House of Lords, who is not very active politically and only sometimes votes, attends meetings etc

**back·yard** /ˌbækˈjɑːd◂‖-ˈjɑːrd◂/ *n* **1** *BrE* a square flat area behind a house, covered with a hard surface **2** *AmE* an area of land behind a house, usually covered with grass: *The old man grew vegetables in his backyard.*

**ba·con** /ˈbeɪkən/ *n* [U] **1** salted or smoked meat from the back or sides of a pig, often served in narrow thin pieces: **bacon and eggs** (=bacon and eggs cooked in hot fat and served together) —see also MEAT **2 bring home the bacon** *informal* to provide enough money to support your family —see also **save sb's bacon** (SAVE)

**bac·te·ri·a** /bæk'tɪəriə‖-'tɪr-/ *n* [plural] *singular* **bacterium** very small living things related to plants, some of which cause disease; MICROBES —compare VIRUS (1, 2) —**bacterial** *adj*: *a bacterial infection*

**bac·te·ri·ol·o·gy** /bæk,tɪəri'ɒlədʒi‖-,tɪri'ɑːl-/ *n* [U] the scientific study of bacteria —**bacteriologist** *n* [C] —**bacteriological** /bæk,tɪəriə'lɒdʒɪkəl‖-,tɪriə'lɑː-/ *adj*

**Bac·tri·an cam·el** /,bæktriən 'kæməl/ *n* [C] a CAMEL from Asia with two HUMPS[1] (2)

1 1 **bad**[1] /bæd/ *adj comparative* **worse** /wɜːs‖wɜːrs/ *superlative* **worst** /wɜːst‖wɜːrst/

**1** ▶ **HARMFUL** ◀ unpleasant, harmful, or likely to cause problems: *I have some bad news for you.* | *I thought things couldn't possibly get any worse.* | *It's bad enough being woken by the baby without you keeping me awake as well.* —opposite GOOD[1] (2)

**2** ▶ **LOW QUALITY** ◀ low in quality or below an acceptable standard: *The failure of the company was due to bad management.* | *Your handwriting is so bad I can hardly read it.* | *bad teachers and a lack of funds* —opposite GOOD[1] (1)

**3** ▶ **WRONG** ◀ morally wrong or evil: *He's a bad man – keep away from him.* —opposite GOOD[1] (23)

**4** ▶ **SERIOUS** ◀ serious or severe: *He is recovering from a bad accident.* | *The pain was really bad.*

**5 bad time/moment etc** a time at which it is very unlucky for something to have happened: *It's a bad time to have to borrow money, with interest rates so high.*

**6 bad for you** harmful to you or to your health: *Too much salt can be bad for you.* | *It is bad for a young girl to be on her own so much.*

**7** ▶ **FOOD** ◀ food that is bad is not safe to eat because it has decayed: *This fish has gone bad.* | *bad apples*

**8 bad at maths/tennis/drawing etc** having no skill or ability in a particular activity: *I'm really bad at chess.* | *Strategic thinking is what so many companies are bad at.*

**9 bad heart/leg/back etc** a heart, leg etc that is injured or does not work correctly: *I haven't been able to do much because of my bad back.* | *Ouch, that was my bad foot!*

**10** ▶ **SWEARING** ◀ bad language contains swearing or rude words: *all these TV programmes with their violence and bad language*

**11 in a bad temper/mood** feeling annoyed or angry: *I didn't mean to take my bad temper out on you.*

**12** ▶ **GUILTY** ◀ **feel bad** to feel ashamed or sorry about something: *I felt bad about not being able to come last night.*

**13 go from bad to worse** to become even more unpleasant or difficult: *The evening went from bad to worse as more and more people left the party.*

**14 be in a bad way** *informal especially BrE* to be very ill, unhappy, injured, or in serious trouble: *She was in a bad way after the funeral.*

**15 get a bad name** to lose people's respect or trust: [+ **for**] *The bar had a bad name and was avoided by all the locals.*

**16 bad egg/lot/sort/type** *BrE old-fashioned* someone who is morally bad or cannot be trusted

**17 bad penny** someone or something that causes trouble and is difficult to avoid: **turn up like a bad penny** (=suddenly appear) *Sure enough, Steve turned up at the party, like a bad penny.*

**18 be taken bad** *informal especially BrE* to become ill: *He was taken bad in the middle of the night.*

**19 in bad faith** if someone does something in bad faith they are behaving dishonestly and have no intention of keeping a promise: *In order to sue, you have to prove that the company was acting in bad faith.*

**20 bad news** *informal* someone or something that always causes trouble: *Look, just avoid him, I warn you. He's bad news!*

**21 bad form** *BrE old-fashioned* socially unacceptable behaviour: *It's bad form to argue with the umpire.*

**22 bad blood** angry or bitter feeling between people; HOSTILITY: *There's too much bad blood between them.*

Frequencies of the adjective **bad** in spoken and written English.

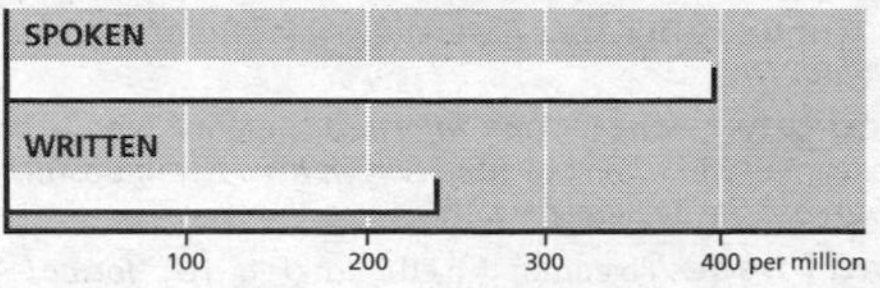


Based on the British National Corpus and the Longman Lancaster Corpus

This graph shows that the adjective **bad** is much more common in spoken English than in written English. This is because it is used in some common spoken phrases.

**bad** (*adj*) **SPOKEN PHRASES**

**23 not bad** *especially BrE* used to say that something is good, or better than you expected: *"How are you?" "Oh, not bad."* | *That's not a bad idea.* | *"Did you enjoy the course?" "Oh it wasn't too bad."*

**24 too bad** **a)** used to say that you do not care that something bad happens to someone: *"I'm going to be late now!" "Too bad, you should have gotten up earlier."* **b)** used to say that you are sorry that something bad has happened to someone: *It's too bad that you couldn't come to the party last night.* **c)** *BrE old-fashioned* used to say that something is very annoying or unreasonable: *They can't increase the price like that, it's just too bad!*

**25 bad girl/boy** used when a child behaves badly: *Bad girl! Put that glass down!*

**26 it's not that bad/it's not as bad as all that** used to say that something is not as bad as someone says it is: *"Yuk! This cheese is revolting!" "Oh, come on, it's not as bad as all that."*

**27 not too bad/not so bad** used to say that something is not as bad as expected: *The exams weren't so bad after all.*

**28 it's bad enough.....** used to say that you already have one problem, so that you cannot worry about or deal with another one: *It's bad enough having to bring up three kids on your own without having to worry about money as well!*

**29 sth can't be bad** used to persuade someone that something is good or worth doing: *You only pay £10 deposit and no interest: that can't be bad, can it?* —see also **make the best of a bad job** (JOB (18)), —**badness** *n* [U]

**bad**[2] *n* **1 take the bad with the good** accept not only the good things in life but also the bad things **2 to the bad** *informal* if you are a particular amount to the bad you are that much poorer or you owe that much: *Thanks to your mistake, I'm £500 to the bad!* **3 go to the bad** *old-fashioned* to begin living in a wrong or immoral way

**bad debt** /,· '·/ *n* [C] a debt that is unlikely to be paid

**bad·die, baddy** /'bædi/ *n* [C] *BrE informal* someone who is bad, especially in a book or film

**bade** /bæd, beɪd/ the past tense and past participle of BID[1]

**badge** /bædʒ/ *n* [C] **1** *BrE* a small piece of metal, cloth, or plastic with a picture or words on it, worn to show rank, membership of a group, support for a political idea or belief, etc: *They were wearing badges that said 'Nuclear Power – No thanks!'.* | *a school blazer with a badge sewn on it* —compare BROOCH —see picture at SIGN[1] **2** a small piece of metal that you wear or carry that shows you have an official position, for example that you are a police officer **3** a small piece of cloth with a picture on it, given to SCOUTS[1] (1), GUIDES[1] (4) etc to show what skills they have learned: *I got my music badge today.* **4 badge of office** an object which shows that you have an official position: *Mayors wear chains around their necks as badges of office.*

**bad·ger**[1] /'bædʒə‖-ər/ *n* [C] an animal which has black and white fur, lives in holes in the ground, and is active at night

**badger²** *v* [T] to try to persuade someone by asking them something several times; PESTER: *The children badgered me into taking them to the cinema.* | **badger someone to do something** *They kept badgering him to get a home computer.*

**bad guy** /ˈ· ·/ *n* [C] *AmE informal* someone who is bad, especially in a book or film: *Screen hero Kevin Costner is playing the bad guy for once.*

**bad·i·nage** /ˈbædɪnɑːʒ‖ˌbædənˈɑːʒ/ *n* [U] *formal or humorous* playful joking talk

**bad·lands** /ˈbædlændz/ *n* [plural] an area of unproductive land in North America with rocks and hills that have been worn into strange shapes by the weather

S2 W3 **bad·ly** /ˈbædli/ *adv comparative* **worse** *superlative* **worst** **1** in an unsatisfactory or unsuccessful way: *The company has been very badly managed.* | *Pearce played pretty badly in yesterday's semi-final.* | *badly made furniture* | **do badly** (=not be successful) *Rob did very badly in the History exam.* **2** to a great or serious degree: *He's been limping badly ever since the ski-ing accident.* | *She badly wanted to be chosen for the school hockey team.* | **badly in need of** (=needing something very much) *He's badly in need of a haircut.* | **go badly wrong** (=if a situation goes badly wrong it becomes very difficult or serious) *Things started to go badly wrong for Eric after he lost his job.* **3 think badly of** to have a bad opinion of someone or something: *I'm sure they won't think badly of you if you tell them you need some time away from work.*

**badly-off** /ˌ·· ˈ·/ *adj comparative* **worse-off, worst-off** [not before noun] **1** not having much money; poor: *We're too badly-off to have a holiday.* **2 badly-off for** not having enough of something that is needed: *The school is rather badly-off for equipment.* —opposite WELL-OFF

**bad·min·ton** /ˈbædmɪntən/ *n* [U] a game like tennis but played with a SHUTTLECOCK (=small feathered object) instead of a ball —see picture on page 1264

**bad-mouth** /ˈ· ·/ *v* [T] *informal especially AmE* to criticize someone or something: *Her former colleagues accused her of bad-mouthing them in public.*

**bad-off** /ˌ· ˈ·◂/ *adj AmE* not having much money; poor

**bad-tem·pered** /ˌ· ˈ··◂/ *adj* easily annoyed or made angry: *He was known as a bad-tempered recluse.*

**baf·fle¹** /ˈbæfəl/ *v* [T] if something baffles someone, they cannot understand or explain it at all: *The question baffled me completely.* —**bafflement** *n* [U] —**baffling** *adj: a baffling mystery*

**baffle²** *n* [C] *technical* a board, sheet of metal etc that controls the flow of air, water, or sound into or out of something

S1 W2 **bag¹** /bæg/ *n* [C]

**1 ▶CONTAINER◀ a)** a container made of paper, cloth etc, which usually opens at the top: *a paper bag* | *a sports bag* **b)** a small bag used by a woman to carry her personal possessions; HANDBAG: *Don't leave your bag in the office when you go for lunch.* **c)** a large bag used to carry your clothes etc when you are travelling: *Just throw your bags in the back of the car.* —see picture at CONTAINER

**2 ▶AMOUNT◀** the amount that a bag will hold: [+ **of**] *two bags of rice per family per month*

**3 ▶WOMAN◀** *spoken* an insulting word for an unpleasant or unattractive woman: *You silly old bag!*

**4 ▶HUNTING◀** [usually singular] the number of birds or animals that someone catches when they go hunting: *We had a good bag that day.*

**5 ▶A LOT OF◀ bags of** *spoken especially BrE* a lot of something; plenty: *She's got bags of money.* | *We're not late, we've got bags of time.*

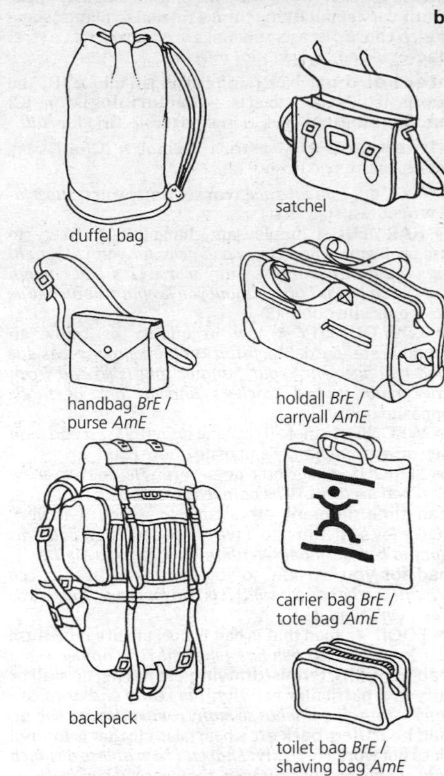


**6 pack your bags** *informal* to leave a place where you have been living, usually after an argument: *We told her to pack her bags at once.*

**7 ▶EYES◀** dark circles or loose skin around your eyes, usually because of old age or being tired

**8 bag of bones** *informal* a very thin person or animal

**9 in the bag** *informal* certain to be won or achieved: *We're sure to win, the match is in the bag.*

**10 ▶TROUSERS◀ bags** [plural] *BrE old-fashioned* loose-fitting trousers: *Oxford bags*

**11 ▶INTERESTED◀ sb's bag** *informal* something that someone is very interested in or very good at: *Sorry, computers aren't really my bag.*

**12 bag and baggage** with all your possessions: *They threw her out of the house bag and baggage.* —see also BAGS, SLEEPING BAG, **let the cat out of the bag** (CAT (2)), **be left holding the bag** (HOLD¹ (20)), **a mixed bag** (MIXED (6))

**bag²** *v* **bagged, bagging** **1** [T] to put materials or objects into bags **2** [T] *informal* to kill or catch animals or birds: *We bagged a rabbit.* **3** [T] *informal* to manage to get something that a lot of people want: *Try to bag a couple of seats at the front.* **4** [I] also **bag out** *informal* to hang loosely, like a bag

**bag** sth ↔ **up** *phr v* [T] to put small objects or loose substances into bags: *We bagged up the money before we closed the shop.*

**bag·a·telle** /ˌbægəˈtel/ *n* **1** [U] a game played on a board with small balls that must be rolled into holes **2** [singular] something that is small and unimportant compared to everything else: *It cost about £25, a mere bagatelle for someone as rich as her.*

**ba·gel** /ˈbeɪɡəl/ *n* [C] a small ring-shaped type of bread

bagel

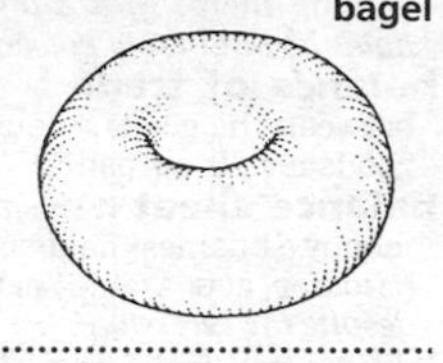

**bag·ful** /ˈbæɡfʊl/ *n plural* **bagfuls,** *or* **bagsful** [C] the amount a bag can hold

**bag·gage** /ˈbæɡɪdʒ/ *n* **1** [U] *especially AmE* the cases, bags, boxes, etc carried by someone who is travelling; LUGGAGE: *Check your baggage in at the desk.* **2** [U] *informal* the beliefs, opinions, and experiences that someone has, which make them think in a particular way: *Throw away all that emotional baggage and start living!* **3** [C] *old-fashioned* a rude, unpleasant, annoying woman

**baggage car** /ˈ·· ˌ·/ *n* [C] *AmE* the part of a train where boxes, bags etc are carried

**baggage room** /ˈ·· ·/ *n* [C] *AmE* a place, usually in a station, where you can leave your bags and collect them later

**bag·gy** /ˈbæɡi/ *adj* baggy clothes hang in loose folds: *She was wearing jeans and a baggy T-shirt.*

**bag la·dy** /ˈ· ˌ··/ *n* [C] a homeless woman who walks around carrying all her possessions with her

**bag·pipes** /ˈbæɡpaɪps/ *n* [plural] a musical instrument played especially in Scotland in which air stored in a bag is forced out through pipes to produce the sound —**bagpipe** *adj*

**bags** /bæɡz/ *spoken BrE* **Bags I!** used by children to claim something that they want: *Bags I the biggest cake!*

**ba·guette** /bæˈɡet/ *n* [C] a long thin LOAF of bread, made especially in France

**bah** /bɑː/ *interjection* used to show disapproval of something: *Bah! That's stupid.*

**bail**[1] /beɪl/ *n* [U] **1** money left with a court of law to prove that a prisoner will return when their TRIAL[1] (1) starts: **release sb on bail/grant sb bail** (=let someone out of prison when bail is paid) *She was released on bail of £5000.* | **be on bail** (=be waiting for your trial after bail has been paid) *While on bail, Marshall committed another assault.* | **stand bail/put up bail** (=pay the bail for someone to be let out) *His father stood bail for him.* **2** one of the two small pieces of wood laid on top of the STUMPS[1] (5) in a game of CRICKET (2)

**bail**[2] *v*

**bail out** *phr v* **1** [T **bail** sb ↔ **out**] to leave a large sum of money with a court so that someone can be let out of prison while waiting for their TRIAL[1] (1): *Clarke's family paid £500 to bail him out.* **2** [I,T **bail** sth ↔ **out**] also **bale out** *BrE* to remove water from the bottom of a boat **3** [T **bail** sb/sth ↔ **out**] to provide money to get someone or something out of financial trouble: *You can't expect the taxpayer to bail out the car industry indefinitely.* **4** [I] *AmE* **a)** to escape from a plane, using a PARACHUTE[1] **b)** *informal* to leave a place or situation as quickly as you can; **bale out** (BALE[2]) *BrE*

**bai·ley** /ˈbeɪli/ *n* [C] an open area inside the outer wall of a castle

**bai·liff** /ˈbeɪlɪf/ *n* [C] **1** *BrE* an official of the legal system who can take people's goods or property when they owe money: *Last year, all his furniture was seized by bailiffs.* **2** *AmE* an official of the legal system who watches prisoners and keeps order in a court of law **3** *BrE* someone who looks after a farm or land that belongs to someone else

**bail-out** /ˈ· ·/ *n* [C] *informal* financial help given to a person or a company that is in difficulty: *The directors were hoping for a government bail-out to save the company.*

**bain ma·rie** /ˌbæn məˈriː/ *n* [C] *French* a pan for cooking things gently usually by cooking them in another pan of water

**bairn** /beən‖bern/ *n* [C] *ScotE, N EngE* **1** a baby **2** a child

**bait**[1] /beɪt/ *n* [singular, U] **1** food used to attract fish, animals, or birds so that you can catch them: *Worms make excellent fish bait.* | **take the bait** (=eat it and be caught) **2** something used to make someone do something, buy something etc: **take the bait** (=accept what someone is offering) *The customer takes the bait and that's it, you've got another sale.* **3 rise to the bait** to become angry when someone is deliberately trying to make you angry: *Senator O'Brien just smiled, refusing to rise to the bait.*

**bait**[2] *v* [T] **1** to put bait on a hook to catch fish or in a trap to catch animals **2** to deliberately try to make someone angry by criticizing them, using rude names etc: *The other children took a vicious pleasure in baiting him.* **3 bear-baiting/badger-baiting etc** the activity of attacking a wild animal with dogs

**baize** /beɪz/ *n* [U] thick cloth, usually green, used especially to cover tables on which games such as BILLIARDS are played

**bake** /beɪk/ *v* **1** [I,T] to cook something using dry heat, in an OVEN: *I'm baking some bread.* | *baked potatoes* —see picture on page 833 **2** [I,T] to make something become hard by heating it: *In former times, bricks were baked in the sun.* **3** [I] *informal* to be too hot: *Open a window it's baking in here!* —see also HALF-BAKED S3

**baked beans** /ˌ· ˈ·/ *n* [U] a dish consisting of beans cooked in a sauce made from tomatoes etc

**Ba·ke·lite** /ˈbeɪkəlaɪt/ *n* [U] *trademark* a hard plastic used especially in the 1930s and 1940s

**bak·er** /ˈbeɪkə‖-ər/ *n* [C] **1** someone who bakes bread and cakes, especially in order to sell them in a shop **2 baker's** *especially BrE* a shop that sells bread, cakes etc; bakery

**baker's doz·en** /ˌ·· ˈ··/ *n* [singular] *old-fashioned* thirteen of something

**bak·er·y** /ˈbeɪkəri/ also **baker's** *BrE* /ˈbeɪkəz‖-ərz/ *n* [C] a place where bread and cakes are baked, or a shop where they are sold

**bak·ing pow·der** /ˈ·· ˌ··/ *n* [U] a powder used in baking cakes to make them light

**baking sheet** /ˈ·· ·/ *n* [C] a baking tray

**baking so·da** /ˈ·· ˌ··/ *n* [U] BICARBONATE OF SODA

**baking tray** /ˈ·· ·/ *n* [C] a flat piece of metal that you bake food on —see picture at TRAY

**bak·sheesh** /ˌbækˈʃiːʃ/ *n* [U] money that people in the Middle East give to poor people, to someone who has helped them, or as a BRIBE

**bal·a·cla·va** /ˌbæləˈklɑːvə◂/ *n* [C] *especially BrE* a warm WOOLLEN hat that covers most of your head and face

**bal·a·lai·ka** /ˌbæləˈlaɪkə/ *n* [C] a musical instrument with strings on a three-sided box, played especially in Russia

balance

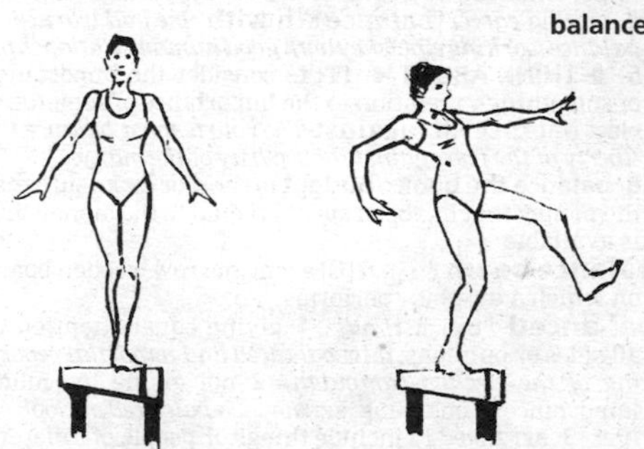

She balanced herself. She lost her balance.

**bal·ance**[1] /ˈbæləns/ *n* S2 W2

**1 ▶ STEADY ◀** [U] a state in which all your weight is evenly spread so that you do not fall: *You need a good sense of balance to ride a bicycle.* | **lose your balance** (=be unable to stay steady and not fall) *I lost my balance and fell on my face.* | **keep your balance** (=manage to stay steady and not fall, especially when this is difficult)

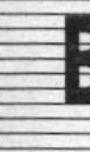

**2 ▶ EQUALITY ◀** [singular] a state in which opposite forces or influences have or are given equal importance: [+ **between**] *the delicate balance between man and nature* | [+ **of**] *a realistic balance of work and relaxation* | **strike a balance** (=manage to balance opposing forces) *We need to strike a balance between the needs of the community and the rights of the individual.* —opposite IMBALANCE
**3 on balance** if you think something on balance, you think it after considering all the facts: *I think on balance I prefer the old system.*
**4 off balance a)** unable to stay steady or upright: *I was still off balance when he hit me again.* **b)** surprised or confused: **throw sb off balance** *The abrupt question threw her off balance and she couldn't reply.*
**5 the balance of evidence/probability etc** the most likely answer or result produced by opposing information, reasons etc: *The balance of evidence suggests that at least some of the politicians received money.*
**6 ▶ FOR WEIGHING ◀** [C] an instrument for weighing things by seeing whether the amounts in two hanging pans are equal
**7 ▶ BANK ◀** [C] the amount of money that you have in your bank account: *Could you tell me what my balance is please?*
**8 ▶ THE REST ◀** [singular] the amount of something that remains after some has been used or spent: [+ **of**] *I'd like to take the balance of my vacation in September.*
**9 ▶ OPPOSITE FORCE ◀** [singular] a force or influence on one side which equals an opposite force or influence: *They work well together – her steadiness acts as a balance to his clever but impractical ideas.*
**10 be/hang in the balance** if the future or success of something hangs in the balance, you cannot yet know whether the result will be bad or good: *Meanwhile the fate of the refugees continues to hang in the balance.*
**11 tip/swing the balance** to influence the result of an event: *Your letter of recommendation swung the balance in his favour.*

S 3 **balance²** *v*
**1 ▶ KEEP STEADY ◀** [I,T] to get into a steady position, without falling to one side or the other, or to put something into this position: **balance sth on** *She balanced the cup on a huge pile of books.* | [+ **on**] *He turned around, balancing awkwardly on one foot.*
**2 ▶ BE EQUAL TO ◀** [I,T] to be equal to something else in weight, amount, or importance: *Exports must go down to balance decreased imports.*
**3 ▶ GO WELL WITH ◀** [T] to have an opposite effect to something else, so that a good result is achieved: *just enough sugar to balance the acidity of the fruit*
**4 ▶ KEEP STH EQUAL ◀** [T] to try to give equal importance to two things: *a working mother, balancing home and career* | **balance sth with** *She had learned to balance working efficiency with good human relationshps.*
**5 ▶ THINK ABOUT ◀** [T] to consider the importance of something in relation to the importance of something else: **balance sth against** *The courts must balance the liberty of the few against the security of the many.*
**6 balance the books/budget** to show or make sure that the money that has been spent is equal to the money that is available

**balance beam** /ˈ·· ˌ·/ *n* [C] a long narrow wooden board on which a GYMNAST performs

**bal·anced** /ˈbælənst/ *adj* **1** giving equal attention to all sides or opinions; fair: *balanced and impartial reporting of the election campaign* **2** not giving too much importance to one thing; SENSIBLE: *a balanced outlook on life* **3** arranged to include things or people of different kinds in the right amount: *a balanced programme of events* | **balanced diet** (=containing the right foods in the right amounts)

**balance of pay·ments** /ˌ··· ˈ··/ *n* [singular] the difference between what a country spends in order to buy goods and services abroad, and the money it earns selling goods and services abroad

**balance of pow·er** /ˌ··· ˈ··/ *n* **the balance of power** a situation in which political or military strength is shared evenly: **hold the balance of power** (=be able to make either side more powerful than the other by supporting them) *In a hung parliament the centre parties hold the balance of power.*

**balance of trade** /ˌ·· · ˈ·/ *n* the difference in value between the goods a country buys from abroad and the goods it sells abroad

**balance sheet** /ˈ·· ·/ *n* [C] a statement of how much money a business has earned and how much money it has paid for goods and services: *a healthy balance sheet despite the recession*

**bal·co·ny** /ˈbælkəni/ *n* [C] **1** a structure you can stand on that sticks out from the upstairs wall of a building **2** the seats upstairs at a theatre —see picture at THEATRE

**bald** /bɔːld‖bɒːld/ *adj* **1** having little or no hair on your head: *His bald head was badly sunburnt.* | **go bald** (=gradually lose your hair) **2** not having enough of what usually covers something: *The car's tires are completely bald.* **3 bald statement/language/truth etc** a statement etc that is correct but gives no additional information to help you understand or accept what is said —**baldness** *n* [U]

**bald ea·gle** /ˌ· ˈ··/ *n* [C] a large North American bird with a white head and neck that is the national bird of the US

**bal·der·dash** /ˈbɔːldədæʃ‖ˈbɒːldər-/ *n* [U] *old-fashioned* talk or writing that is silly nonsense

**bald-faced** /ˌ· ˈ·◂/ *adj AmE* making no attempt to hide that you know what you are doing or saying is wrong; BAREFACED

**bald·ing** /ˈbɔːldɪŋ‖ˈbɒːl-/ *adj* a balding man is losing the hair on his head: *a spare, already balding man in his mid-thirties*

**bald·ly** /ˈbɔːldli‖ˈbɒːld-/ *adj* in a way that is true but makes no attempt to be polite: *To put it baldly, stop smoking or you'll be dead in a year.*

**bale¹** /beɪl/ *n* [C] a large quantity of something such as paper or hay that is tightly tied together especially into a block: *a bale of straw*

**bale²** *v* [T] to tie something such as paper or hay into a large block
**bale out** *phr v* [I] *BrE* **1** to escape from an aircraft by PARACHUTE¹ **2** to leave a place or situation as quickly as you can; **bail out** (BAIL² (4)) *AmE*

**bale·ful** /ˈbeɪlfəl/ *adj literary* expressing anger, hatred, or a wish to harm someone: *a baleful look* —**balefully** *adv*

**balk¹** also **baulk** *BrE* /bɔːk, bɔːlk‖bɒːk, bɒːlk/ *v* **1** [I] to not want to or refuse to do something that is difficult, or frightening: [I + **at**] *Perry seemed interested, but baulked when he heard the price.* **2** [I + **at**] if a horse balks at a fence etc, it stops suddenly and refuses to jump or cross it **3** [T] to stop someone or something from getting what they want: *eager young men balked by rules and regulations* **4** *AmE* to stop, in BASEBALL, in the middle of the action of throwing the ball to the player who is trying to hit it

**balk²** also **baulk** *BrE n* [C] a thick rough wooden beam

**bal·ky** /ˈbɔːki‖ˈbɒː-/ *adj AmE* refusing to do what you are asked or expected to do: *He's a balky man to have to work with.*

**ball¹** /bɔːl‖bɒːl/ *n* [C] S W
**1 ▶ TO PLAY WITH ◀** a round object that is thrown, kicked, or hit in a game or sport: *Bounce the ball to me.* | *a tennis ball*
**2 ▶ ROUND SHAPE ◀** something formed or rolled into a round shape: *a ball of string* | *Shape the dough into balls.*
**3 the ball of the foot/hand/thumb** the rounded part of the foot at the base of the toe, rounded part of the hand at the base of the thumb or fingers —see also EYEBALL¹ (1) —see picture at FOOT¹
**4 a fast/good/curved etc ball** a ball that is thrown, hit, or kicked fast etc in a game or sport: *He hit a long ball to right field.*
**5 no ball** a ball that is thrown too high, low etc towards someone trying to hit it, in the games of CRICKET (2) or ROUNDERS

**6 ▶ BASEBALL ◀** *AmE* a ball thrown in BASEBALL that a player is not expected to hit because it is not within the correct area
**7 ▶ BULLET ◀** a round bullet fired from a type of gun that was used in the past
**8 on the ball** *informal* thinking or acting quickly: *We need an assistant who's really on the ball.*
**9 set/start the ball rolling** to begin an activity or event or make sure it continues: *Let's start the ball rolling with a few suggestions.*
**10 the ball is in your court** it is your turn to take action or to reply: *I've sent him a letter, now the ball's in his court.*
**11 ▶ DANCE ◀** a large formal occasion at which people dance
**12 have a ball** *informal* to have a very good time: *We had a ball at the party last night.*
**13 balls** [plural] **a)** TESTICLES **b)** *taboo spoken* courage or determination: *It's not going to be easy. It'll take fight. Guts. Balls.* **c)** *BrE taboo spoken* something that is stupid or wrong; nonsense: *That's a load of balls!*
**14 a ball of fire** someone who has a lot of energy and is active and successful
**15 the whole ball of wax** *AmE informal* the whole thing; everything
**16 ball-buster/ball-breaker** *AmE slang* **a)** a problem that is very difficult to deal with **b)** an offensive word for a woman who uses her authority over men —see also BALLS, **not play ball** (PLAY[1] (24))

**ball²** *v* [T] **1** also **ball up** to form something into a small round shape so that it takes up less space **2** *AmE spoken taboo* to have sex with a woman
**ball** sth ↔ **up** *phr v AmE spoken* to make a situation confused or difficult to deal with: *No, we're not going now, Lindsay's managed to ball everything up.* —see also BALLS-UP

**bal·lad** /ˈbæləd/ *n* [C] **1** a short story in the form of a poem **2** a simple song, especially a popular love song

**bal·last¹** /ˈbæləst/ *n* [U] **1** heavy material that is carried by a ship to make it more steady in the water **2** material such as sand that is carried in a BALLOON[1] (2) and can be thrown out to make it rise **3** broken stones that are used as a surface under a road, railway lines etc

**ballast²** *v* [T] to fill or supply something with ballast

**ball bear·ing** /ˌ· ˈ··/ *n* [C] **1** an arrangement of small metal balls moving in a ring around a bar so that the bar can turn more easily **2** one of these metal balls

**ball boy** /ˈ· ·/ *n* [C] a boy who picks up tennis balls for people playing in important tennis matches —see picture at TENNIS

**ball·cock** /ˈbɔːlkɒk‖-ˈbɒːlkɑːk/ *n* [C] a hollow floating ball on a stick that opens and closes a hole, to allow water to flow into a container, for example in a TOILET (1)

**bal·le·ri·na** /ˌbæləˈriːnə/ *n* [C] a woman who dances in ballets

**bal·let** /ˈbæleɪ‖bæˈleɪ, ˈbæleɪ/ *n* **1** [C] a performance in which a special style of dancing and music tell a story without any speaking: *Tchaikovsky wrote several famous ballets.* **2** [U] this type of dancing **3** [C] a group of BALLET dancers who work together: *the Bolshoi ballet*

**ballet danc·er** /ˈ·· ˌ··‖·ˈ· ˌ··/ *n* [C] someone who dances in ballets

**ball game** /ˈ· ·/ *n* **1** *AmE* a BASEBALL game **2** *BrE* any game played with a ball **3 a whole new ball game** a situation that is very different from the one you are used to: *I used to be a teacher, so working in an office is a whole new ball game.*

**ball girl** /ˈ· ·/ *n* [C] a girl who picks up tennis balls for people playing in important tennis matches

**bal·lis·tic mis·sile** /bəˌlɪstɪk ˈmɪsaɪl‖-səl/ *n* [C] a MISSILE (1) that is guided up into the air and then falls freely

**bal·lis·tics** /bəˈlɪstɪks/ *n* [U] the scientific study of the movement of objects that are thrown or fired through the air, such as bullets shot from a gun

**bal·loon¹** /bəˈluːn/ *n* [C] **1** a small brightly coloured rubber bag that can be filled with air and used as a toy or decoration for parties **2** a large bag of strong light cloth filled with gas or heated air so that it can float in the air: *hot air balloons drifting toward the horizon* **3** the circle drawn around the words spoken by the characters in a CARTOON **4 balloon payment** *AmE* money borrowed that must be paid back in one large sum after several smaller payments have been made: *a $10,000 balloon payment due in two years* **5 go down like a lead balloon** *informal* if a joke, remark etc goes down like a lead balloon, people do not laugh or react as you expected

**balloon²** *v* [I] **1** to get bigger and and rounder: [+ **out/outwards/up**] *His cheeks ballooned out as he played his trumpet.* **2** to become larger in amount: *Mitch's business debts ballooned to $20,000 in just one year.*

**bal·loon·ing** /bəˈluːnɪŋ/ *n* [U] the sport of flying in a balloon —**balloonist** *n* [C]

**bal·lot¹** /ˈbælət/ *n* **1** [C,U] a system of secret voting or an occasion when you vote in this way: *The Club's officers are always chosen by ballot.* **2** [C] a piece of paper on which you make a secret vote; BALLOT PAPER **3** [C] the number of votes recorded; POLL[1] (5)

**ballot²** *v* [I,T] to vote or to decide something by a vote: *The chairman is elected by balloting all the shareholders.*

**ballot box** /ˈ·· ·/ *n* **1** [C] a box that ballot papers are put in after voting **2 the ballot box** the system or process of voting in an election: *The people have expressed their views through the ballot box.*

**ballot pa·per** /ˈ·· ˌ··/ *n* [C] a piece of paper on which you record your vote

**ball park** /ˈ· ·/ *n* **1** *especially AmE* a field for playing BASEBALL, with seats for watching the game **2 in the right ball park** *informal* close to the amount, price etc that you want or are thinking about: *Their estimate is definitely in the right ball park.* **3 a ball park figure** a number or amount that is almost but not exactly correct: *He said $25,000 but it's just a ball park figure.*

**ball·play·er** /ˈbɔːlˌpleɪə‖ˈbɔːlˌpleɪər/ *n* [C] *AmE* someone who plays BASEBALL

**ball·point** /ˈbɔːlpɔɪnt‖ˈbɔːl-/ also **ballpoint pen** /ˌ·· ˈ·/ *n* [C] a pen with a ball at the end that rolls thick ink onto the paper —see picture at PEN[1]

**ball·room** /ˈbɔːlrʊm, -ruːm‖ˈbɔːl-/ *n* [C] a very large room used for dancing on formal occasions

**ballroom danc·ing** /ˌ·· ˈ··/ *n* [U] a type of dancing that is done with a partner and has different steps for particular types of music, such as the WALTZ[1] (1)

**balls¹** /bɔːlz‖bɒːlz/ *interjection taboo* used to show strong disapproval or disappointment: *Balls to that! I'm not working Saturday morning!*

**balls²** *v*
**balls** sth ↔ **up** *phr v BrE taboo slang* to do something very badly or unsuccessfully: *He totally ballsed up his exams.*

**balls-up** /ˈ· ·/ *n BrE taboo slang* something that has been done very badly or unsuccessfully: *Nigel made a complete balls-up of the arrangements.*

**ball·sy** /ˈbɔːlzi‖ˈbɒːl-/ *adj AmE spoken* brave and determined: *He's a ballsy kind of guy.*

**bal·ly** /ˈbæli/ *adj, adv BrE old-fashioned* an expression meaning BLOODY[1] used to avoid offending other people

**bal·ly·hoo** /ˌbæliˈhuː‖ˈbælihuː/ *n* [U] *informal* a situation in which people publicly express a lot of anger, excitement etc: *After all the promotional ballyhoo, the film flopped.*

**balm** /bɑːm‖bɑːm, bɑːlm/ *n* [C,U] **1** an oily liquid with a strong, pleasant smell that you rub into your skin, often to reduce pain **2** *literary* something that gives you comfort: *Her words were a balm to my shredded nerves.*

**balm·y** /ˈbɑːmi‖ˈbɑːmi, ˈbɑːlmi/ *adj* balmy air, weather etc is warm and pleasant: *a balmy summer night*

**ba·lo·ney** /bəˈləʊni‖-ˈloʊ-/ *n* [U] *informal* **1** something that is silly or not true; nonsense: *"Don't give me that baloney", he said, winking at Christopher.* **2** *AmE* BOLOGNA

**bal·sa** /ˈbɔːlsə‖ˈbɒːl-/ *n* [C,U] a tropical American tree or the wood from this tree, which is very light

**bal·sam** /ˈbɔːlsəm‖ˈbɒːl-/ *n* [C,U] BALM, or the tree that produces it

**bal·us·trade** /ˌbæləˈstreɪd‖ˈbæləstreɪd/ *n* [C] a row of upright pieces of stone or wood with a bar along the top, especially around a BALCONY

**bam·boo** /ˌbæmˈbuː◂/ *n* [C,U] a tall tropical plant with hollow stems that are used for making furniture

**bam·boo·zle** /bæmˈbuːzəl/ *v* [T] *informal* to deceive, trick, or confuse someone

W3 **ban¹** /bæn/ *n* [C] an official order that forbids something from being used or done: *The President supports a global ban on nuclear testing.* —see also TEST BAN

**ban²** *v* **banned, banning** [T] to say that something must not be done, seen, used etc: *Smoking is banned in the building.* | **ban sb from doing sth** *Charlie's been banned from driving for a year.* | **banned book/film/video etc** (=a book etc that is illegal)

**ba·nal** /bəˈnɑːl, bəˈnæl/ *adj* ordinary and not interesting, because of a lack of new or different ideas: *a banal piece of writing* —**banality** /bəˈnæləti/ *n* [C,U]

**ba·na·na** /bəˈnɑːnə‖-ˈnæ-/ *n* [C] a long curved tropical fruit with a yellow skin —see picture on page 413

**banana re·pub·lic** /·ˌ·· ·ˈ··/ *n* [C] *informal* an insulting word for a small poor country with weak government that depends on financial help from abroad

**ba·na·nas** /bəˈnɑːnəz‖-ˈnæ-/ *adj informal* **1** crazy or silly: *People think Mr Allen is bananas because he talks to his plants.* **2 go bananas** become very angry or excited: *Dad will go bananas when he sees this.*

**banana skin** /·ˈ·· ˌ·/ *n* [C] *BrE informal* an embarrassing mistake made by someone in a public position, especially a politician or someone in a government: *This incident could turn into another banana skin for the government.*

**banana split** /·ˌ·· ˈ·/ *n* [C] a sweet dish with bananas and ICE CREAM

S2 W2 **band¹** /bænd/ *n* [C]

**1 ▶ MUSIC ◀** a group of musicians, especially a group that plays popular music: **jazz/rock/big etc band** (=a band that plays JAZZ etc) *He plays saxophone in a little-known jazz band.* | **band leader/singer** (=someone who leads a band, or sings with a band)

**2 ▶ GROUP OF PEOPLE ◀** a group of people formed because of a common belief or purpose: *a small band of enthusiasts*

**3 ▶ PIECE OF MATERIAL ◀** a flat, narrow piece of material with one end joined to the other to form a circle: *papers held together with a rubber band* | *a wide silk band*

**4 ▶ PATTERN ◀** a thick coloured line: *There are orange bands around the snake's back.*

**5 tax/income/age etc band** a particular range of tax, income etc in which a group of people belong: *people within the $20,000 – $30,000 income band*

**6 ▶ RADIO ◀** *technical* a range of radio signals

**band²** *v* [T] to put a band of colour or material on or around something

**band together** *phr v* [I] to unite in order to achieve something: *The two parties banded together to form an alliance.*

**ban·dage¹** /ˈbændɪdʒ/ *n* [C] a narrow piece of cloth that you tie around a wound or around a part of the body that has been injured

bandage

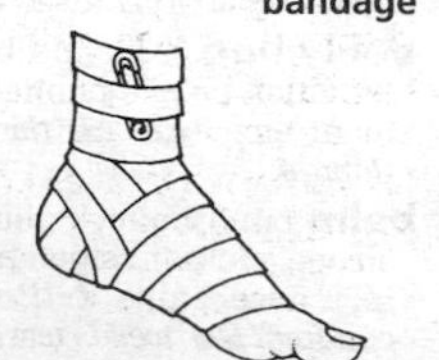

**bandage²** also **bandage up** *v* [T] to tie or cover a part of the body with a bandage: *The nurse bandaged up his sprained ankle.*

**Band-Aid** /ˈ· ·/ *n* [C] *AmE trademark* a piece of thin material that is stuck to the skin to cover cuts and other small wounds; PLASTER¹ (3) *BrE*; ELASTOPLAST *BrE*

**ban·dan·na, bandana** /bænˈdænə/ *n* [C] a large brightly coloured piece of cloth you wear around your head or neck: *hair tied up in a scarlet bandanna*

**B and B** /ˌbiː ənd ˈbiː/ the abbreviation of BED AND BREAKFAST: *a small B and B in the Cotswolds*

**band·box** /ˈbændbɒks‖-bɑːks/ *n* [C] a box for keeping hats in

**ban·deau** /ˈbændəʊ‖bænˈdoʊ/ *n plural* **bandeaux** /-dəʊz‖-ˈdoʊz/ [C] a band of material that you wear around your head to keep your hair in place

**ban·dit** /ˈbændɪt/ *n* [C] someone who robs people, especially one of group of people who attack travellers: *Beware of bandits in the mountains.* —see also ONE-ARMED BANDIT —**banditry** *n* [U]

**band·mas·ter** /ˈbændˌmɑːstə‖-ˌmæstər/ *n* [C] someone who CONDUCTS a military band, BRASS (2) band etc

**ban·do·lier** /ˌbændəˈlɪə‖-ˈlɪr/ *n* [C] a belt that goes over someone's shoulder and is used to carry bullets

**bands·man** /ˈbændzmən/ *n* [C] a musician who plays in a military band, BRASS (2) band etc

**band·stand** /ˈbændstænd/ *n* [C] a structure that has a roof but no walls and is used by a band playing music in a park

**band·wa·gon** /ˈbændˌwægən/ *n* [C] **climb/jump on the bandwagon** to begin to do something that a lot of other people are doing: *Everyone seems to be jumping on the environmental bandwagon.*

**ban·dy¹** /ˈbændi/ *adj* bandy legs curve outwards at the knees —**bandy-legged** *adj*

**bandy²** *v* **bandy words (with)** *old-fashioned* to quarrel with someone

**bandy** sth **about** *phr v* [T] to mention an idea, name, remark etc several times, especially to impress someone: *Several different figures have been bandied about – which is correct?*

**bane** /beɪn/ *n* [singular] something that causes trouble or makes people unhappy: **be the bane of** *Drugs are the bane of the inner cities.* | **the bane of sb's life/existence** (=a cause of continual trouble or unhappiness) *Ask any laser printer user what the bane of their life is and they'll tell you – replacing the toner.*

**bane·ful** /ˈbeɪnfəl/ *adj literary* evil or bad —**banefully** *adv*

**bang¹** /bæŋ/ *n* **1** [C] a sudden loud noise caused by something such as a gun or an object hitting a hard surface: *The front door slammed with a loud bang.* **2** [C] a hard knock or hit against something: *That was a nasty bang on the head.* **3 bangs** [plural] *AmE* hair cut straight across your forehead; FRINGE¹ (1) *BrE* —see picture on page 412 **4** [singular] *AmE informal* a strong feeling of pleasure: *She got a real bang out of seeing the kids in the school play.* **5 go off with a bang** to happen in a very successful way: *The party really went off with a bang!*

**bang²** *v*

**1 ▶ KNOCK/HIT STH ◀** [I,T] to hit something hard against something else, making a loud noise: *She banged the phone down.* | [+ **on**] *They were banging on the door with their fists.*

**2 ▶ CLOSE STH ◀** [I always + adv/prep, T] to close something violently making a loud noise, or to make something close in this way: *She banged the door and stomped up the stairs.* | **bang shut** *The window banged shut.*

**3 ▶ MAKE NOISE ◀** [I] to make a loud noise or noises: [+ **about/around/away**] *I could hear the garage door banging in the wind.*

**4 ▶ HIT STH ◀** [T] to hit a part of your body or something you are carrying against something, especially by accident; BUMP¹ (1): *Bobby fell and banged his knee.* | *I slipped and banged the guitar against the door.*

**5 be banging your head against a brick wall** *informal* to be wasting your efforts by doing something that does not produce any results: *Trying to teach that class is like banging your head against a brick wall.*

6 ▶ **HAVE SEX** ◀ [T] *taboo* to have sex with someone

**bang on** *phr v* [I] *BrE informal* to talk continuously about something in a boring way: [+ **about**] *I'm tired of politicians banging on about family values.*

**bang** sth ↔ **out** *phr v* [T] *informal* **1** to play a tune or song loudly and badly on a piano **2** to write something in a hurry, especially on a TYPEWRITER: *Danielle banged out a few letters, before going home for the day.*

**bang** sb/sth ↔ **up** *phr v* [T] **1** *BrE slang* to put someone in prison **2** *AmE informal* to seriously damage something: *a banged-up old Buick*

**bang**[3] *adv* **1** *informal* directly or exactly: *The train arrived bang on time.* **2 bang on** *spoken* exactly correct: *Yes! Your answer's bang on!* **3 bang goes** *spoken* used to show that you are unhappy because something you had hoped for will not happen: *£750 to repair the car? Bang goes my holiday.* **4** *spoken* in a sudden, violent way: *He slowed down, and bang! The car behind crashed straight into us!*

**bang**[4] *interjection* used to make a sound like a gun or bomb: *"Bang, bang – you're dead," Tommy shouted.*

**bang·er** /ˈbæŋə‖-ər/ *n* [C] *BrE informal* **1** a SAUSAGE **2** an old car in bad condition: *Gary's finally scrapped that old banger of his.* **3** a type of noisy FIREWORK

**ban·gle** /ˈbæŋɡəl/ *n* [C] a solid band of gold, silver etc that you wear loosely around your wrist as jewellery

**bang-up** /ˈ· ·/ *adj AmE informal* very good: *He did a bang-up job fixing the plumbing.*

**ban·ish** /ˈbænɪʃ/ *v* [T] **1** to not allow someone or something to stay in a particular place: **banish sth from/to** *The children were banished to the backyard.* **2** to send someone away permanently from their country or the area where they live, especially as an official punishment: **banish sb from/to** *Many Soviet dissidents were banished to Siberia.* **3 banish sb/sth (from your mind)** to try to stop thinking about something; especially something that worries you —**banishment** *n* [U]

**ban·is·ter** /ˈbænɪstə‖-ər/ *n* [C] a row of upright sticks with a bar along the top, that stops you from falling over the edge of stairs —see picture on page 410

**ban·jo** /ˈbændʒəʊ‖-dʒoʊ/ *n* [C] a musical instrument with four or more strings, a long neck and a round body used especially in COUNTRY AND WESTERN music

1 **bank**[1] /bæŋk/ *n* [C]
1 **1** ▶ **MONEY** ◀ **a)** a business that keeps and lends money and provides other financial services: *The major banks have announced an increase in interest rates.* **b)** a local office of a bank: *I have to go to the bank at lunch time.*
**2** ▶ **RIVER/LAKE** ◀ land along the side of a river or lake: *Roger pushed the boat away from the bank* —see SHORE[1] (USAGE).
**3** ▶ **PILE** ◀ a large pile of earth, sand, snow etc: *There were steep banks of snow at the sides of the road.*
**4 blood/sperm/organ etc bank** a place where human blood etc is stored until someone needs it
**5 cloud/fog bank etc** a large mass of clouds, mist etc
**6 bank of televisions/elevators/computers etc** a large number of machines, television screens etc arranged close together in a row
**7** ▶ **GAME** ◀ the money in a GAMBLING game that people can win —see also **break the bank** (BREAK[1] (32))
**8** ▶ **ROAD** ◀ a slope made at a bend in a road or RACETRACK to make it safer for cars to go around —see also BOTTLE BANK, MEMORY BANK

**bank**[2] *v*
**1** ▶ **MONEY** ◀ [T] to put or keep money in a bank: *Did you bank that check?*
**2** ▶ **PARTICULAR BANK** ◀ [I] to keep your money in a particular bank: [+ **with**] *Who do you bank with?*
**3** ▶ **TURN** ◀ [I] to make a plane, MOTORCYCLE, or car slope to one side when turning: *The plane banked, and circled back toward us.*
**4** ▶ **PILE/ROWS** ◀ also **bank up** *BrE* [T] to arrange something into a pile or into rows: *The walls of the space center are banked high with electronic equipment.*
**5** ▶ **CLOUD/MIST** ◀ also **bank up** [T] to form a mass of cloud, mist etc: *Banked clouds promised rain.*
**6** ▶ **FIRE** ◀ also **bank up** [T] to cover a fire with wood, coal etc to keep it going for a long time: *Josie banked up the fire to last till morning.*

**bank on** sb/sth *phr v* [T] to depend on something happening or someone doing something: **bank on sb doing sth** *We were banking on John being there to show us the way.*

**bank·a·ble** /ˈbæŋkəbəl/ *adj informal* a bankable person or quality is likely to help you get money, success etc: *They need a bankable star for the movie.*

**bank ac·count** /ˈ· ·,·/ *n* [C] an arrangement between a bank and a customer that allows the customer to pay in and take out money

**bank bal·ance** /ˈ· ,··/ *n* [singular] the amount of money someone has in their bank account

**bank book** /ˈ· ·/ *n* [C] a book in which a record is kept of the money you put into and take out of your bank account; PASSBOOK *AmE*

**bank card** /ˈ· ·/ *n* [C] **1** *AmE* a CREDIT CARD provided by your bank **2** *BrE* a CHEQUE CARD

**bank draft** /ˈ· ·/ also **banker's draft** *n* [C] **1** a CHEQUE for one bank to another, especially a foreign bank, to pay a certain amount of money to a person or organization

**bank·er** /ˈbæŋkə‖-ər/ *n* [C] **1** someone who works in a bank in an important position **2** the player who is in charge of the money in some games

**banker's card** /ˈ·· ·/ *n* [C] *BrE* a CHEQUE CARD

**banker's or·der** /,·· ˈ··/ *n* [C] *BrE* a STANDING ORDER

**bank hol·i·day** /,· ˈ···/ *n* [C] **1** *BrE* an official holiday when banks and most businesses are closed: *Next Monday is a bank holiday.* | *stuck in the bank holiday traffic* | **bank holiday weekend** (=a weekend on which there is a bank holiday on Friday or Monday) *Are you going away for the bank holiday weekend?* **2** *AmE* a day during the week when banks are closed by law

**bank·ing** /ˈbæŋkɪŋ/ *n* [U] the business of a bank: *the international banking system*

**bank man·a·ger** /ˈ· ,···/ *n* [C] someone who is in charge of a local bank

**bank note** /ˈ· ·/ *n* [C] *especially BrE* a piece of paper money of a particular value that you use to buy things

**bank rate** /ˈ· ·/ *n* [C] *technical* the rate of INTEREST[1] (4) decided by a country's main bank

**bank·roll**[1] /ˈbæŋkrəʊl‖-roʊl/ *n* [C] a supply of money

**bankroll**[2] *v* [T] *informal* to provide the money that someone needs for a business, a plan etc: *a software company bankrolled by the Samsung Group*

**bank·rupt**[1] /ˈbæŋkrʌpt/ *adj* **1** unable to pay your debts: *Seventeen years of war left the country bankrupt.* **2 go bankrupt** to be unable to pay your debts and to have to sell your property and goods: *The recession has made many small companies go bankrupt.* **3** completely lacking a particular good quality: *The opposition attacked the government as morally bankrupt.*

**bankrupt**[2] *v* [T] to make a person, business or country bankrupt or very poor: *Legal fees almost bankrupted us.*

**bankrupt**[3] *n* [C] someone who has officially said that they cannot pay their debts

**bank·rupt·cy** /ˈbæŋkrʌptsi/ *n* **1** [C,U] the state of being unable to pay your debts: *There has been a sharp increase in bankruptcies in the last two years.* **2** [U] a total lack of a particular good quality: *the moral bankruptcy of this materialistic society*

**bank state·ment** /ˈ· ,··/ *n* [C] a document sent regularly by a bank to a customer that lists the amounts of money taken out of and paid into their BANK ACCOUNT

**banned** /bænd/ *adj* not officially allowed to meet or exist: *Leaders of the banned party were arrested last night.*

**ban·ner¹** /ˈbænə‖-ər/ *n* [C] **1** a long piece of cloth on which something is written, often carried between two poles: *Crowds of people carrying banners joined the demonstration.* —see picture at DEMONSTRATION **2** *literary* a flag **3** a belief or principle: *Many of the poor and unemployed rallied to the Communist banner.* | **under the banner of** (=claiming to support a principle) *The party fought the election under the banner of social justice.*

B

**banner²** *adj AmE* excellent: *a banner year for American soccer*

**banner head·line** /ˌ·· ˈ··/ *n* [C] words printed in very large letters across the top of the first page of a newspaper

**ban·nock** /ˈbænək/ *n* [C] *especially ScotE* a flat cake made of OATMEAL or corn

**banns** /bænz/ *n* [plural] a public statement that two people intend to get married, made in a church in Britain

**ban·quet** /ˈbæŋkwɪ̈t/ *n* [C] a formal dinner for many people on an important occasion

**banqueting hall** /ˈ··· ˌ·/ also **banquet room** /ˈ··· ·/ *AmE* *n* [C] a large room in which banquets take place

**ban·shee** /bænˈʃiː‖ˈbænʃiː/ *n* [C] a spirit whose loud cry is believed to be heard when someone is going to die

**ban·tam** /ˈbæntəm/ *n* [C] a type of small chicken

**ban·tam·weight** /ˈbæntəmweɪt/ *n* [C] a BOXER (1) or WRESTLER who belongs to a group of a particular weight

**ban·ter¹** /ˈbæntə‖-ər/ *n* [U] conversation that has a lot of jokes and teasing (TEASE¹ (1)) remarks in it: *covering his shyness with a good deal of banter*

**banter²** *v* [I] to joke with and TEASE someone —**bantering** *adj* —**banteringly** *adv*

**ban·yan** /ˈbænjən, ˈbænjæn/ *n* [C] an Indian tree with large branches that spread out and form new roots

**bap** /bæp/ *n* [C] *BrE* a round soft bread ROLL² (2)

**bap·tis·m** /ˈbæptɪzəm/ *n* [C,U] **1** a Christian religious ceremony in which someone is touched or covered with water to welcome them into the Christian faith, and sometimes to officially name them **2 baptism of fire** a difficult or painful first experience of something: *We went straight into battle the next day. It was a baptism of fire I'll never forget.* —**baptismal** /bæpˈtɪzməl/ *adj*

**Bap·tist** /ˈbæptɪ̈st/ *n* [C] a member of a Christian group that believes baptism should only be for people old enough to understand its meaning

**bap·tize** also **-ise** *BrE* /bæpˈtaɪz/ *v* [T] **1** to perform the ceremony of baptism on someone **2** to accept someone as a member of a particular Christian church by a ceremony of baptism: *He was baptized a Roman Catholic.* **3** to give a child a name in a baptism ceremony: *She was baptized Sheila Jane.*

S1 W1 **bar¹** /bɑː‖bɑːr/ *n* [C]
**1** ▶ **PLACE TO DRINK IN** ◀ **a)** a place where alcoholic drinks are served —compare PUB **b)** *BrE* one of the rooms inside a pub: *the public bar was crowded*
**2** ▶ **PLACE TO BUY DRINK** ◀ a COUNTER ¹ (1) where alcoholic drinks are served: *There were no free tables so they stood at the bar.*
**3 coffee/snack/salad etc bar** a place where a particular kind of food or drink is served
**4** ▶ **BLOCK OF STH** ◀ a small block of solid material that is longer than it is wide: *a candy bar* | *a bar of soap* —see picture on page 560
**5** ▶ **PIECE OF METAL/WOOD** ◀ a length of metal or wood put across a door, window etc to keep it shut or to prevent people going in or out: *A lot of houses had bars across the windows.*
**6** ▶ **MUSIC** ◀ a group of notes and rests (REST¹ (12)), separated from other groups by vertical lines, into which a line of written music is divided: *She hummed a few bars of the song.*
**7 a bar to (doing) sth** something that prevents you from achieving something that you want: *Bad English is a bar to getting a good job.*
**8** ▶ **GROUP OF LAWYERS** ◀ *law* **a) the bar** *BrE* the group of people who are BARRISTERS (=lawyers who have the right to speak in a court of law) **b)** *AmE* an organization consisting of people who are lawyers
**9 be called to the bar a)** *BrE* to become a BARRISTER **b)** *AmE* to become a lawyer
**10** ▶ **PILE OF SAND/STONES** ◀ a long pile of sand or stones under the water at the entrance to a HARBOUR¹
**11** ▶ **COLOUR/LIGHT** ◀ a narrow band of colour or light
**12** ▶ **UNIFORMS** ◀ a narrow band of metal or cloth worn on a military uniform to show rank
**13** ▶ **HEATER** ◀ the part of an electric heater that provides heat and has a red light
**14 behind bars** *informal* in prison

**bar²** *v* **barred, barring 1** also **bar up** to shut a door or window using a bar or piece of wood so that people cannot get in or out **2** [T] to officially prevent someone from entering a place or from doing something: **bar sb from** *Members voted to bar women from the club.* **3** to prevent people from going somewhere by placing something in their way: *The road ahead was barred by a solid line of policemen.* | **bar sb's way** (=prevent someone passing you by standing in front of them) *A security guard barred her way.*

**bar³** *prep* **1** *formal* except: *No work's been done in the office today, bar a little typing.* **2 bar none** used to emphasize that someone is the best of a particular group: *He's the most talented actor in the country, bar none.* —see also BARRING

**barb** /bɑːb‖bɑːrb/ *n* [C] **1** the sharp curved point of a hook, ARROW (1) etc that prevents it from being easily pulled out **2** a remark that is clever and amusing, but also cruel —see also BARBED (2)

**bar·bar·i·an** /bɑːˈbeəriən‖bɑːrˈber-/ *n* [C] **1** someone from a different tribe or land, who people believe to be wild and not CIVILIZED (1): *The barbarians conquered Rome.* **2** someone who does not behave properly, does not show proper respect for education, art etc: *educational theories apparently written by barbarians*

**bar·bar·ic** /bɑːˈbærɪk‖bɑːr-/ *adj* **1** very cruel and violent; BARBAROUS: *a barbaric act of terrorism* **2** like or belonging to a wild or cruel group or society: *barbaric forest tribes*

**bar·bar·is·m** /ˈbɑːbərɪzəm‖ˈbɑːr-/ *n* **1** [U] a state or condition in which people are not educated, behave violently etc **2** [U] cruel and violent behaviour

**bar·bar·i·ty** /bɑːˈbærɪ̈ti‖bɑːr-/ *n* [C,U] a very cruel act: *The barbarities of the last war must not be repeated.*

**bar·bar·ous** /ˈbɑːbərəs‖ˈbɑːr-/ *adj* **1** shockingly cruel; BARBARIC **2** wild and not CIVILIZED (1): *a savage, barbarous people* —**barbarously** *adv*

**barbecue**

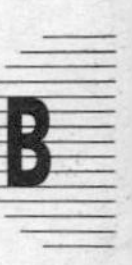

**bar·be·cue**[1] /ˈbɑːbɪkjuː‖ˈbɑːr-/ *n* [C] **1** a metal frame for cooking food on outdoors **2** an outdoor party during which food is cooked and eaten outdoors: *We had a barbecue on the beach.*

**barbecue**[2] *v* [T] to cook food on a metal frame over a fire outdoors: *barbecued chicken*

**barbed** /bɑːbd‖bɑːrbd/ *adj* **1** a hook or ARROW that has one or more sharp, curved points **2** a barbed remark is unkind: *a barbed comment on his appearance*

**barbed wire** also **barbwire** /ˌ· ˈ·◂/ *AmE n* [U] wire with short, sharp points on it: *a high barbed wire fence*

**bar·bell** /ˈbɑːbel‖ˈbɑːr-/ *n* [C] *AmE* a metal bar with weights at each end, which you lift to make you stronger

**bar·ber** /ˈbɑːbə‖ˈbɑːrbər/ *n* [C] **1** a man whose job is to cut men's hair and sometimes to SHAVE[1] (1) them **2 barber's** *BrE* a shop where men's hair is cut

**bar·ber·shop** /ˈbɑːbəʃɒp‖ˈbɑːrbərʃɑːp/ *n* [U] **1** a style of singing popular songs in four parts in close HARMONY: *a barbershop quartet* **2** *AmE* a barber's

**barber's pole** /ˌ·· ˈ·/ *n* [C] a pole with red and white bands used as a sign outside a barber's shop

**bar·bi·can** /ˈbɑːbɪkən‖ˈbɑːr-/ *n* [C] a tower for defence at the gate or bridge of a castle

**bar·bie** /ˈbɑːbi‖ˈbɑːr-/ *n* [C] *BrE & AustrE informal* a BARBECUE

**bar bil·liards** /ˈ· ˌ··/ *n* [U] a game played in PUBs in Britain in which players use long sticks to push balls into holes on a table

**bar·bi·tu·rate** /bɑːˈbɪtʃʊrɪ̣t‖bɑːrˈbɪtʃərɪ̣t, -reɪt/ *n* [C,U] a powerful drug that makes people calm and puts them to sleep

**barb·wire** /ˌbɑːbˈwaɪə◂‖ˈbɑːrbwaɪr/ *n* [U] *AmE* BARBED WIRE

**bar chart** /ˈ· ·/ *n* [C] *BrE* a picture of boxes of different heights, in which each box represents a different amount, for example an amount of profit made in a particular month; BAR GRAPH *AmE* —see picture at CHART[1]

**bar code** /ˈ· ·/ *n* [C] a group of thin and thick lines from which a computer reads information about a product that is sold in a shop

**bar code**

0-582-84223-9

**bard** /bɑːd‖bɑːrd/ *n* [C] *literary* a poet

**bare**[1] /beə‖ber/ *adj*

**1 ▶ WITHOUT CLOTHES ◀** not covered by clothes: *Jonathan's bare feet made no sound in the soft sand.*

**2 ▶ LAND/TREES ◀** not covered by trees or grass, or not having any leaves: *a bare hillside*

**3 ▶ ROOMS ◀** empty, not covered by anything, or not having any decorations: *This room looks very bare—you need some pictures on the walls.*

**4 the bare facts/truth** a statement that tells someone only what they need to know, with no additional details: *a journalist who is not content to simply record the bare facts*

**5 ▶ SMALLEST AMOUNT NECESSARY ◀** [only before noun] the very least amount of something that you need to do something: *He got 40% – a bare pass.* | **the bare essentials/necessities** *The refugees fled, taking only the bare essentials.* | **the bare minimum** (=the smallest amount possible) *carrying the bare minimum of equipment* | **the barest** (=the smallest or simplest possible) *We can provide only the barest outline of the plan.*

**6 the bare bones** the most important parts or facts of something without any detail: *the bare bones of the plan*

**7 lay sth bare a)** to uncover something that was previously hidden: *The excavation laid bare the streets of an ancient city.* **b)** to reveal something that was secret: *The investigation laid bare a million-dollar embezzlement racket.*

**8 with your bare hands** without using a weapon: *He killed her with his bare hands.* —**bareness** *n*

**bare**[2] *v* [T] **1** to let something be seen, by removing something that is covering it: *The dog bared its teeth.* **2 bare your soul** to reveal your most secret feelings

**bare-assed** /ˌbeər æst◂‖ˈberæst/ *adj AmE slang* having no clothes on

**bare·back** /ˈbeəbæk‖ˈber-/ *adj, adv* on the bare back of a horse, without a SADDLE[1] (1): *riding bareback*

**bare·faced** /ˌbeəˈfeɪst◂‖ˈberfeɪst/ *adj* a barefaced lie, remark etc is clear and makes no attempt not to offend someone: *What barefaced cheek – saying that to you!*

**bare·foot** /ˈbeəfʊt‖ˈber-/ also **barefoot·ed** /ˌbeəˈfʊtɪ̣d◂‖ˈberfʊtɪ̣d/ *adj, adv* without shoes on your feet: *kids going barefoot all summer*

**bare·hand·ed** /ˌbeəˈhændɪ̣d◂‖ ˈberhændɪ̣d/ *adj, adv* having no GLOVEs on, or having no tools or weapons: *They fought barehanded.*

**bare·head·ed** /ˌbeəˈhedɪ̣d◂‖ˈberhedɪ̣d/ *adj, adv* without a hat on your head: *You can't go out bareheaded in this weather!*

**bare·leg·ged** /ˌbeəˈlegɪ̣d, -ˈlegd◂‖ˈberlegɪ̣d, -legd/ *adj, adv* with no clothing on your legs

**bare·ly** /ˈbeəli‖ˈberli/ *adv* **1** in a way that almost does not happen, exist etc; just: *Her voice was so low, I could barely hear her.* | *We have barely enough money to live on.* **2** in a way that is simple, with no decorations or details: *The room was furnished barely.* **3** used to emphasize that something happens immediately after a previous action: *She'd barely sat down before he started firing questions at her.*

**barf** /bɑːf‖bɑːrf/ *v* [I] *AmE informal* to VOMIT[1] —**barf** *n* [U] —**barfy** *adj*

**bar·fly** /ˈbɑːflaɪ‖ˈbɑːr-/ *n* [C] *AmE informal* someone who spends a lot of time in bars —**barfly** *adj*

**bar·gain**[1] /ˈbɑːgɪ̣n‖ˈbɑːr-/ *n* [C] **1** something bought cheaply or for less than its usual price: *I might buy a TV, if I can find a bargain in the sales.* | **be a bargain** *These shoes are a bargain at $22.* | **bargain holiday/clothes/prices etc** (=a holiday etc that is very cheap) | **bargain hunting** (=looking for things to buy at a cheap price) *a bargain hunting housewife at the January sales* **2** an agreement, made between two people or groups, to do something in return for something else: **make a bargain** *We've made a bargain that he'll do the shopping and I'll cook.* | **drive a hard bargain** (=succeed in making an agreement that is very much to your advantage) *Fischer was determined to drive a hard bargain.* | **keep your side of the bargain** (=do what you promised as part of an agreement) | **strike a bargain** (=reach an agreement) *Management and unions have struck a bargain over wage increases.* **3 into the bargain** *especially BrE* in addition to everything else: *He was short, fat, and spotty into the bargain.* **4 make the best of a bad bargain** to do the best you can under difficult conditions —**bargainer** *n* [C] *a wage bargainer* —see CHEAP[1] (USAGE)

**bargain**[2] *v* [I] to discuss the conditions of a sale, agreement etc: [+ **for**] *bargaining for better pay*

**bargain for** sth *phr v* also **bargain on** sth [T usually in negatives] to expect that something will happen and make it part of your plans: *We hadn't bargained for such heavy rain, and got really wet.* | **bargain on doing sth** *We can't bargain on finding the right house straight away.* | **more than you bargained for** (=more than you expected) *His wife's angry reaction was more than he bargained for!*

**bargain base·ment** /ˌ·· ˈ··/ *n* [C] a part of a large shop, usually in the floor below ground level, where goods are sold at reduced prices

**bar·gain·ing** /ˈbɑːgənɪŋ‖ˈbɑːr-/ *n* [U] **1** discussion in order to reach agreement about a sale, contract etc: *The 4% pay raise was the result of some hard bargaining.* **2 bargaining position** the power that a person or group has in a discussion or argument

**barge**[1] /bɑːdʒ‖bɑːrdʒ/ *n* **1** [C] a large low boat with a flat bottom used mainly for carrying heavy goods on a CANAL (1) or river **2** a large rowing boat used for an important ceremony

**barge**[2] *v* [I always + adv/prep] to move somewhere in an awkward way, often hitting against things: *She ran* *around the corner and barged into one of the teachers.* | **barge your way** *He barged his way through the room.*

**barge in** *phr v* [I] to enter or rush in rudely: *I wish she wouldn't barge in like that.* | [+ **on**] *Her mother barged in on her and Mike when they were in bed together!*

**barge in on** *phr v* [T] to interrupt someone rudely: *Dan's always barging in on other people's conversations.*

**barg·ee** /bɑːˈdʒiː‖bɑːr-/ *BrE* **barge·man** *AmE n* [C] /ˈbɑːdʒmən‖ˈbɑːr-/ someone who drives or works on a barge

**barge pole** /ˈ· ·/ *n* [C] a long pole used to guide a barge —see also **wouldn't touch sth with a bargepole** (TOUCH[1] (12))

**bar graph** /ˈ· ·/ *n* [C] an American form of BAR CHART

**bar·hop** /ˈbɑːhɒp‖ˈbɑːrhɑːp/ *v* [I] *AmE informal* to visit and drink at several bars, one after another; PUB-CRAWL *BrE*

**bar·i·tone** /ˈbærɪ̈təʊn‖-toʊn/ *n* [C] a male singing voice lower than a TENOR (1a) and higher than a BASS[1] (1), or a male singer whose voice is in this range

**ba·ri·um** /ˈbeəriəm‖ˈber-/ *n* [U] a soft silvery-white metal

**barium meal** /ˌ··· ˈ·/ *n* [U] *technical* a chemical substance that you drink before you have an X-RAY[1] (2)

**bark[1]** /bɑːk‖bɑːrk/ *v* **1** [I] to make the short, loud sound that dogs and some other animals make: [+ **at**] *The dog always barks at strangers.* **2** also **bark out** [T] to say something quickly in a loud voice: *"Listen up!" the teacher barked.* **3 bark up the wrong tree** *informal* to have a wrong idea, especially about how to get a particular result: *You're barking up the wrong tree if you think Sam can help you.* **4 bark at the moon** *AmE informal* to worry and complain about something that you cannot change, and that is not very important **5** [T] to rub the skin off your knee, elbow etc by falling or knocking against something: *I stumbled, barking my shins painfully against the step.*

**bark[2]** *n* [C,U] **1** the sharp, loud sound made by a dog **2** the outer covering of a tree **3** a loud sound or voice: *the bark of the guns* **4 sb's bark is worse than their bite** used to say that although someone talks in an angry way they would not behave violently **5** *literary* BARQUE

**bar·keep·er** /ˈbɑːˌkiːpə‖ˈbɑːrˌkiːpər/ also **bar·keep** /ˈbɑːkiːp‖ˈbɑːr-/ *n* [C] *AmE* someone who serves drinks in a bar; BARTENDER

**bark·er** /ˈbɑːkə‖ˈbɑːrkər/ *n* [C] someone who stands outside a place at a CIRCUS (1), FAIR[2] etc shouting to people to come in

**bar·ley** /ˈbɑːli‖ˈbɑːrli/ *n* [U] a plant that produces a grain used for making food or alcohol

**barley sug·ar** /ˈ·· ˌ··/ *n* [C,U] *BrE* a hard sweet made of boiled sugar

**barley wine** /ˌ·· ˈ·/ *n* [U] *BrE* a kind of very strong beer

**bar·maid** /ˈbɑːmeɪd‖ˈbɑːr-/ *n* [C] *BrE* a woman who serves drinks in a bar

**bar·man** /ˈbɑːmən‖ˈbɑːr-/ *n* [C] *BrE* a man who serves drinks in a bar; BARTENDER *AmE*

**bar mitz·vah** /ˌbɑː ˈmɪtsvə‖ˌbɑːr-/ *n* [C] **1** the religious ceremony held when a Jewish boy reaches the age of 13 and is considered an adult in his religion **2** a boy for whom this ceremony is held

**barm·y** /ˈbɑːmi‖ˈbɑːrmi/ *adj BrE informal* slightly crazy

**barn** /bɑːn‖bɑːrn/ *n* [C] **1** a large farm building for storing crops, or for keeping animals in **2** *informal* a large, plain building: *a great barn of a house*

**bar·na·cle** /ˈbɑːnəkəl‖ˈbɑːr-/ *n* [C] a small sea animal with a hard shell that sticks firmly to rocks and the bottom of boats

**barn dance** /ˈ· ·/ *n* [C] **1** a social event at which COUNTRY DANCING is performed **2** *BrE* a dance performed at this type of event —compare SQUARE DANCE

**bar·ney** /ˈbɑːni‖ˈbɑːrni/ *n* [C usually singular] *BrE informal* a noisy argument

**barn·storm** /ˈbɑːnstɔːm‖ˈbɑːrnstɔːrm/ *v* [I] *AmE* to travel from place to place making short stops to give political speeches, theatre performances, or aircraft flying shows —**barnstormer** *n* [C] —**barnstorming** *adj*

**barn·yard** /ˈbɑːnjɑːd‖ˈbɑːrnjɑːrd/ *n* [C] **1** a space surrounded by farm buildings; FARMYARD **2 barnyard humor** *AmE* humour that is slightly rude

**ba·rom·e·ter** /bəˈrɒmɪ̈tə‖-ˈrɑːmɪ̈tər/ *n* [C] **1** an instrument for measuring changes in the air pressure and weather or calculating height above sea level **2** something that shows or gives an idea of changes that are happening: *Infant mortality is a highly sensitive barometer of social conditions.* —**barometric** /ˌbærəˈmetrɪk◂/ *adj* —**barometrically** /-kli/ *adv*

**bar·on** /ˈbærən/ *n* [C] **1** a man who is a member of the lowest rank of the British NOBILITY (1) or of a rank of European NOBILITY (1) **2** a businessman with a lot of power or influence: *conservative press barons like Beaverbrook* | *Pakistani and Columbian drug barons* —see also ROBBER BARON

**bar·on·ess** /ˈbærənɪ̈s/ *n* **1** [C] a woman who is a member of the lowest rank of the British NOBILITY (1) **2** the wife of a baron

**bar·on·et** /ˈbærənɪ̈t, -net/ *n* [C] a British KNIGHT[1] (2) lower in rank than a baron, whose title passes on to his son when he dies

**bar·on·et·cy** /ˈbærənɪ̈tsi/ *n* [C] the rank of a baronet

**ba·ro·ni·al** /bəˈrəʊniəl‖-ˈroʊ-/ *adj* **1** a baronial room is very large and richly decorated **2** belonging to or involving BARONS (1)

**bar·on·y** /ˈbærəni/ *n* [C] the rank of BARON (1)

**ba·roque** /bəˈrɒk, bəˈrəʊk‖bəˈroʊk, -ˈrɑːk/ *adj* **1** belonging to the very decorated style of art, music, buildings etc, that was common in Europe in the 17th century: *elaborate baroque facades* **2** very detailed and complicated —**baroque** *n* [singular]

**barque** /bɑːk‖bɑːrk/ *n* [C] a sailing ship with three, four, or five MASTS (=poles that the sails are fixed to)

**bar·rack** /ˈbærək/ *v* [I,T] **1** *BrE* to interrupt someone by shouting, sometimes pretending that you agree with them: *The minister was repeatedly barracked during his speech.* **2** *AustrE* to shout to show that you support someone or something

**bar·racks** /ˈbærəks/ *n* [plural] a group of buildings in which soldiers live

**bar·ra·cu·da** /ˌbærəˈkjuːdə‖-ˈkuːdə/ *n* [C] a large tropical fish that eats flesh

**bar·rage[1]** /ˈbærɑːʒ‖bəˈrɑːʒ/ *n* **1** [C usually singular] the continuous firing of guns, especially large heavy guns, to protect soldiers as they move toward an enemy: *a barrage of anti-aircraft fire* **2** [singular] a lot of questions, comments etc, that are said at the same time or very quickly after each other: [+ **of**] *Despite facing a barrage of criticism, Mr Rees pressed ahead with plans for Theatr Clwyd.*

**bar·rage[2]** /ˈbærɑːʒ‖ˈbɑːrɪdʒ/ *n* [C] a wall of earth, stones etc built across a river to provide water for farming or to prevent flooding

**barrage bal·loon** /ˈ·· ·ˌ·‖·ˈ· ·ˌ·/ *n* [C] a large bag that floats in the air to prevent enemy planes from flying near the ground

**barred** /bɑːd‖bɑːrd/ *adj* **1** a barred window, gate etc has bars across it **2** *formal* having bands of different colour: *red barred tail feathers* —see also BAR

**bar·rel[1]** /ˈbærəl/ *n* [C] **1** a large curved container with a flat top and bottom, made of wood or metal: *barrels of beer* —see picture at CONTAINER **2** also **barrelful** the amount of liquid that a barrel contains, used especially as a measure of oil: *Oil was $30 a barrel.* **3** the part of a gun that the bullets are fired through —see picture at GUN[1] **4 have sb over a barrel** to put someone in a situation in which they are forced to accept or do what you want: *The manager had us over a barrel – either we worked on a Saturday or we lost our jobs.* **5 be a barrel of laughs** [often in negatives] to be very enjoyable: *The meeting wasn't exactly a barrel of laughs.* —see also PORK S

BARREL, **scrape (the bottom of) the barrel** (SCRAPE[1] (6)), **lock, stock, and barrel** (LOCK[2] (3))

**barrel**[2] *v* **barreled, barreling** [I] *AmE informal* to move very fast, especially in an uncontrolled way: *He barreled down the road at 90 miles an hour.*

**barrel-chest·ed** /ˌ.. ˈ..◂/ *adj* a man who is barrel-chested has a round chest that sticks out

**barrel or·gan** /ˈ.. ˌ../ *n* [C] a musical instrument that you play by turning a handle, used especially in former times

**bar·ren** /ˈbærən/ *adj* **1** land or soil that is barren has no plants growing on it: *a barren mountainous area* **2** *old use* a woman or a female animal who is barren cannot produce children or baby animals; INFERTILE (2) **3** a tree or plant that is barren does not produce fruit or seeds **4** *literary* without any useful results: *a pointless and barren discussion*

**bar·rette** /bæˈret/ *n* [C] *AmE* a small metal or plastic object used to keep a woman's hair in place; HAIR SLIDE *BrE*

**bar·ri·cade**[1] /ˈbærəkeɪd, ˌbærəˈkeɪd/ *n* [C] a temporary wall or fence across a road, door etc that prevents people from going through: *Soldiers fired over the barricades at the rebels.*

**barricade**[2] *v* [T] to protect or close something by building a barricade: *Terrorists had barricaded themselves inside the embassy.*

3 **bar·ri·er** /ˈbæriə‖-ər/ *n* [C] **1** a type of fence or gate that prevents people from moving in a particular direction: *Crowds burst through the barriers and ran onto the pitch.* **2** a rule, problem etc that prevents people from doing something, or limits what they can do: *an attempt to break down trade barriers* | [**+ to**] *a psychological barrier to success* | **language barrier** (=inability to talk to someone because you speak a different language) **3** a physical object that keeps two areas, people etc apart: [**+ between**] *The mountains form a natural barrier between the two countries.* **4 the 10 second/40% etc barrier** a level or amount of 10 seconds, 40% etc, that is seen as a limit which it is difficult to get beyond: *Sprinters had by then broken the 10 second barrier.* —see also SOUND BARRIER

**barrier reef** /ˌ... ˈ./ *n* [C] a line of CORAL (=pink stone-like substance) separated from the shore by water

**bar·ring** /ˈbɑːrɪŋ/ *prep* **1** unless there are: *Barring any last minute problems, we should finish the job tonight.* **2** except for: *Barring a few suburban services, we may soon lose all passenger trains.*

**bar·ri·o** /ˈbæriəʊ‖ˈbɑːrioʊ/ *n* [C] *AmE* a part of an American town or city where many poor, Spanish-speaking people live

**bar·ris·ter** /ˈbærəstə‖-ər/ *n* [C] a lawyer in Britain who can argue cases in the higher law courts —compare SOLICITOR —see LAWYER (USAGE)

**bar·row** /ˈbærəʊ‖-roʊ/ *n* [C] **1** a small vehicle like a box on wheels, from which fruits, vegetables etc used to be sold **2** a large pile of earth like a small hill that was put over an important grave in ancient times **3** a WHEELBARROW

**barrow boy** /ˈ.. ./ *n* [C] *BrE* a man or boy who sells fruit, vegetables etc from a barrow

**Bart** /bɑːt‖bɑːrt/ the written abbreviation of BARONET

**bar·tend·er** /ˈbɑːˌtendə‖ˈbɑːrˌtendər/ *n* [C] *AmE* someone who makes, pours, and serves drinks in a bar or restaurant; BARMAN *BrE*

**bar·ter**[1] /ˈbɑːtə‖ˈbɑːrtər/ *v* [I,T] to exchange goods, work, or services for other goods or services rather than for money: **barter (with sb) for sth** *I had to barter with the locals for food.* | **barter sth for sth** *They bartered farm products for machinery.*

**barter**[2] *n* [U] **1** a system of exchanging goods and services for other goods and services rather than using money: *an economy based on barter* **2** goods or services that are exchanged in this kind of system: *Beads were used as barter in the early days of settlement.*

**bas·alt** /ˈbæsɔːlt, bəˈsɔːlt‖ˈbæsɒːlt, ˈbeɪ-/ *n* [U] a type of dark green-black rock

**base**[1] /beɪs/ *v* [T] to establish or use somewhere as the main place for your business or work: *a Denver-based law firm* S1 W1

**base** sth **on/upon** sth *phr v* [T often passive] to use particular information or facts as a point from which to develop an idea, plan etc: *The film is based on a novel by Sinclair Lewis.*

**base**[2] *n* S2 W2

**1** ▶ **LOWEST PART** ◀ [C usually singular] the lowest part of something, or the surface at the bottom of something: [**+ of**] *There was a chip in the base of the glass.* | *the base of a triangle* | *Waves crashed and pounded at the base of the cliff.*

**2** ▶ **KNOWLEDGE/IDEAS** ◀ [U] the most important part of something from which new ideas develop: *India has a good scientific research base.* | *This provides a good base for the development of new techniques.*

**3** ▶ **COMPANY/ORGANIZATION** ◀ [C,U] the main place from which a group, company, or organization controls its activities: *Cuba was seen as a base for Communist activity throughout Latin America.* | *Report back to base as soon as you see anything.*

**4** ▶ **MILITARY** ◀ [C] a place where people in a military organization live and work: *a naval base*

**5** ▶ **PEOPLE/GROUPS** ◀ [C usually singular] the people, money, groups etc from which a lot of support or power comes: *an attempt to strengthen the city's economic base* | **tax/customer base** (=all the people who pay tax or buy goods in a particular place) *A reputation for excellent service will expand our customer base.* | **manufacturing base** (=all the factories, companies etc that produce goods in a country) *The country's manufacturing base has shrunk by 20% during the recession.* —see also POWER BASE

**6** ▶ **SUBSTANCE/MIXTURE** ◀ [singular, U] the main part of a substance to which something else is later added: *paint with an oil base*

**7** ▶ **BODY/PLANT** ◀ [C usually singular] the point where part of your body or part of a plant joins with the rest: *She had a dull ache at the base of her neck.*

**8** ▶ **SPORT** ◀ [C] one of the four places that a player must touch in order to get a point in games such as BASEBALL

**9 be off base** *AmE informal* to be completely wrong: *His estimate for painting the kitchen seems way off base.*

**10** ▶ **CHEMISTRY** ◀ [C] *technical* a chemical substance that combines with an acid to form a SALT[1] (3)

**11** ▶ **NUMBERS** ◀ [C usually singular] *technical* the number in relation to which a number system or mathematical table is built up

**12 touch base (with sb)** to telephone someone who you live or work with, or make a short visit, while you are spending time somewhere else —see also **cover (all) the bases** (COVER[1] (13))

**base**[3] *adj literary* not having good moral principles: *base passions* —see also BASE METAL

**base·ball** /ˈbeɪsbɔːl‖-bɒːl/ *n* **1** [U] an outdoor game between two teams of nine players, in which players try to get points by hitting a ball and running around four bases (BASE[1] (8)) —see picture on page 1263 **2** [C] the ball used in this game S3 W2

**baseball cap** /ˈ.. ˌ./ *n* [C] a hat that fits closely around your head with a round part that sticks out at the front —see picture at CAP[1]

**base·board** /ˈbeɪsbɔːd‖-bɔːrd/ *n* [C] *AmE* a narrow board fixed to the bottom of indoor walls where they meet the floor; SKIRTING BOARD *BrE*

**base·less** /ˈbeɪsləs/ *adj formal* not based on facts or good reasons: *baseless accusations*

**base·line** /ˈbeɪslaɪn/ *n* **1** [C usually singular] *technical* a standard measurement or fact to which other measurements or facts are compared, especially in medicine or science **2** the line at the back of the court in games such as tennis or VOLLEYBALL —see picture at TENNIS **3** the area that a player must run in on a BASEBALL field

**base·ment** /ˈbeɪsmənt/ *n* [C] a room or area that is under the level of the ground —see picture on page 410

**base met·al** /ˌ· ˈ··/ *n* [C,U] a metal that is not very valuable, such as iron or lead —compare NOBLE¹ (4)

**base rate** /ˈ· ·/ *n* [C] the standard rate of INTEREST¹ (4) on which a bank bases its charges —compare PRIME RATE

**bas·es** /ˈbeɪsiːz/ the plural of BASIS

**bash¹** /bæʃ/ *v* [I,T] *informal* **1** to hit someone or something hard, in a way that causes pain or damage: **bash sth on/against** *I bashed my toe against the door.* | [+ **into/against**] *Jay bashed into a table in the dark.* | **bash down/in/up etc** (=destroy something by hitting it often) *Police bashed down the door to get in.* **2 union/government etc bashing** *BrE* strong criticism of unions, the government etc **3** to physically attack a type of person that you do not like: *gay bashing* —see also SQUARE-BASHING, **bible basher** (BIBLE (4))

**bash away at** sth *phr v* [T] *BrE informal* to continue working hard at something: *I've been bashing away at this essay for hours.*

**bash on** sth *phr v* [I,T + **with**] *BrE informal* to continue working in order to finish something: *Well, better bash on.*

**bash²** *n* [C] **1** *informal* a hard strong hit: *I gave him a bash on the nose.* **2** *informal* a party or celebration: *a birthday bash* **3 have a bash** *BrE spoken* to try to do something, especially when you are not sure that you will succeed: [+ **at**] *Why not have a bash at windsurfing?*

**bash·ful** /ˈbæʃfəl/ *adj* easily embarrassed in social situations; shy: *a bashful smile* | *Many men are still bashful about discusing their feelings.* —**bashfully** *adv* —**bashfulness** *n* [U]

**Ba·sic** /ˈbeɪsɪk/ *n* [U] a commonly used computer language

S1 W1 **basic** *adj* **1** forming the main or most necessary part of something: *a meeting to discuss the basic structure of the department* | *the basic principles of mathematics* **2** at the simplest or least developed level: *My knowledge of German is pretty basic.* | *The farm lacks even basic equipment.* **3 basic salary/pay etc** the amount of money that you are paid before any special payments are added **4** [only before noun] basic desires, rights etc, are ones that everyone has: *Basic human rights are still denied in many countries.* —see also BASICS

S1 **ba·sic·ally** /ˈbeɪsɪkli/ *adv* **1** [sentence adverb] *spoken* used when giving the most important reason or fact about something, or a simple explanation of something: *Basically, I just don't have enough money.* | *Well, basically, it's a matter of filling in a few forms.* **2** in the main or most important ways, without considering additional details or differences: *The two structures are basically the same.* | *He's basically a nice guy.* **3** in a very simple way, with only the things that are completely necessary: *The office was very basically equipped.*

**ba·sics** /ˈbeɪsɪks/ *n* [plural] the most important and necessary facts about something, from which other possibilities and ideas may develop: *Once you know the basics, you can start experimenting with different methods.* | **the basics of** *I learned the basics of first aid on a weekend course.*

**basic train·ing** /ˌ·· ˈ··/ *n* [U] the period when a new soldier learns military rules and does a lot of exercise

**bas·il** /ˈbæzəl/ *n* [U] a sweet-smelling HERB used in cooking

**ba·sil·i·ca** /bəˈsɪlɪkə, -ˈzɪl-/ *n* [C] a church in the shape of a long room with a round end: *the basilica of St Peter's*

**bas·i·lisk** /ˈbæsɪ̆lɪsk, ˈbæz-/ *n* [C] an imaginary animal like a snake in ancient stories, supposed to be able to kill people by looking at them

**ba·sin** /ˈbeɪsən/ *n* [C] **1** *BrE* a round container fixed to the wall in a bathroom where you wash your hands and face; SINK² (2) **2** *BrE* a bowl for liquids or food: *Pour the sauce into a basin.* **3** also **ba·si·nful** /ˈbeɪsɪ̆nfʊl/ the amount of liquid that a basin can contain: *a basin of hot water* **4** a bowl-shaped area containing water: *Water splashed in the basin of the fountain.* **5** an area of land from which water runs down into a river: *the Amazon basin* —see also PUDDING BASIN (1)

S W **ba·sis** /ˈbeɪsɪ̆s/ *n plural* **bases** /-siːz/ [C] **1** the facts or ideas from which something can be developed: *Their claim had no basis in fact.* | [+ **for**] *The video will provide a basis for class discussion.* | [+ **of**] *a lecture series that later formed the basis of a new book* **2 on the basis of** because of a particular fact or situation: *Employers are not allowed to discriminate on the basis of sex.* **3 on a daily/weekly etc basis** every day, week etc: *All rooms are cleaned on a daily basis.* **4 on a voluntary/part-time etc basis** a system or agreement by which someone or something is VOLUNTARY¹ etc: *The machine has been installed on a trial basis.*

**bask** /bɑːsk‖bæsk/ *v* [I] **1** to enjoy sitting or lying in the heat of the sun or a fire: [+ **in**] *A lizard was basking in the heat of the afternoon sun.* **2** to enjoy the approval or attention that you are getting from other people: [+ **in**] *She basked in the admiration of her family and friends.* —see also **bask/bathe in sb's reflected glory** (GLORY¹ (4))

**baskets**

picnic basket

laundry basket *BrE* / hamper *AmE*

shopping basket

wastepaper basket / wastebasket *AmE*

hanging basket

basket

S **bas·ket** /ˈbɑːskɪ̆t‖ˈbæ-/ *n* [C] **1** a container made of thin pieces of plastic, wire, or wood woven together, used to carry things or put things in: *a shopping basket* | **clothes/laundry basket** (=for putting dirty clothes in) **2** a net with a hole at the bottom hung from a metal ring, through which the ball is thrown in BASKETBALL: **make/shoot a basket** (=get a point in the game) —see also **put all your eggs in one basket** (EGG¹ (5)), WASTEPAPER BASKET —see picture on page 1263

S W **bas·ket·ball** /ˈbɑːskɪ̆tbɔːl‖ˈbæskɪ̆tbɒːl/ *n* [U] a game played indoors between two teams of five players, in which each team tries to win points by throwing a ball through a net, or the ball used in this game —see picture on page 1263

**basket-case** /ˈ·· ·/ *n* [C] *informal* someone who is so nervous or anxious that they cannot deal with simple situations

**bas·ket·ry** /ˈbɑːskɪ̆tri‖ˈbæs-/ also **bas·ket·work** /ˈbɑːskɪ̆twɜːk‖ˈbæskɪ̆twɜːrk/ *n* [U] **1** baskets or other objects made by weaving together thin dried branches **2** the skill of making baskets

**basque** /bæsk/ *n* [C] a piece of underwear for a woman that covers her from under her arms to the top of her legs

**bas-re·lief** /ˌbɑː rɪˈliːf, ˌbæs-/ *n* [C,U] *technical* a style of art in which stone or wood is cut so that shapes are raised above the surrounding surface —compare HIGH RELIEF

**bass¹** /beɪs/ *n* **1** [C] a man whose singing or speaking voice is very low **2** [singular] the part of a piece of music that this person sings **3** [U] the lower half of the whole range of musical notes —compare TREBLE³ (1) **4** [C] a BASS GUITAR: on bass (=playing the bass guitar) *The band features Willie Dixon on bass.* **5** [C] a DOUBLE BASS —**bass** *adj* —**bass** *adv*

**bass²** /bæs/ *n plural* **bass** *or* **basses** [C] a fish that can be eaten and lives both in rivers and the sea

**bass clef** /ˌbeɪs ˈklef/ *n* [C] a sign (𝄢) at the beginning of a line of written music that shows that the top line of the STAVE¹ (1) is the A below MIDDLE C —see picture at MUSIC

**bas·set** /ˈbæsɪ̣t/ also **basset hound** /ˈ··· ·/ *n* [C] a dog with short legs and long ears used for hunting

**bass gui·tar** /ˌbeɪs gɪˈtɑː‖-ˈtɑːr/ also **bass** *n* [C] an electric musical instrument with six strings and a long neck, that plays low notes

**bas·si·net** /ˌbæsɪ̣ˈnet/ *n* [C] *AmE* a small bed that looks like a basket for a young baby

**bas·sist** /ˈbeɪsɪ̣st/ *n* [C] someone who plays a BASS GUITAR or a DOUBLE BASS

**bas·soon** /bəˈsuːn/ *n* [C] a very long wooden musical instrument with a low sound, that is held upright and played by blowing into a thin curved metal pipe

3 **bas·tard** /ˈbɑːstəd, ˈbæ-‖ˈbæstərd/ *n* [C] **1** *slang* an offensive word for someone, especially a man, who you think is unpleasant: *The bastard went and told the police!* **2** *spoken* an insulting or joking word for a man: *The poor bastard's been sacked!|You lucky bastard!* **3** *BrE spoken* something that causes difficulties or problems: *This pan is a bastard to clean.* **4** *old-fashioned* someone whose parents were not married when they were born

**bas·tard·ize** also **-ise** *BrE* /ˈbɑːstədaɪz, ˈbæ-‖ˈbæstər-/ *v* [T] to spoil something by changing its good parts: *a bastardized version of the play*

**bas·tard·y** /ˈbɑːstədi, ˈbæ-‖ˈbæstər-/ *n* [U] *old use* the situation of having parents who were not married to each other when you were born

**baste** /beɪst/ *v* [I,T] **1** to pour liquid or melted fat over meat that is cooking **2** to fasten cloth with long loose stitches, in order to hold it together so that you can SEW it properly later

**bas·ti·on** /ˈbæstiən‖-tʃən/ *n* [C] **1** something that protects a way of life, principle etc that seems likely to change or disappear: **[+ of]** *These clubs are the last bastions of male privilege.* **2** a place where a country or army has strong military defences: *Pearl Harbor was the principal American bastion in the Pacific.* **3** *technical* a part of a castle wall that sticks out from the rest

3 **bat¹** /bæt/ *n* [C]

**1 ▶ ANIMAL ◀** a small animal like a mouse that flies around at night —see also FRUIT BAT

**2 ▶ SPORT ◀ a)** a long wooden stick with a special shape that is used in some sports and games: *a baseball bat* **b)** *BrE* a round flat piece of wood with a handle, used to hit a ball in TABLE TENNIS; PADDLE¹ (3) *AmE*

**3 be at bat** to be the person who is trying to hit the ball in a game of BASEBALL

**4 do sth off your own bat** *BrE informal* to do something without being told to do it: *You did all this work off your own bat?*

**5 do sth right off the bat** *AmE informal* to do something immediately: *I asked him to help, and he said yes right off the bat.*

**6 like a bat out of hell** *informal* very fast: *I drove like a bat out of hell to the hospital.*

**7 old bat** *spoken* an unpleasant old woman

**8 have bats in the belfry** *old-fashioned* to be slightly crazy —see also **as blind as a bat** (BLIND¹ (1c))

**bat²** *v* **batted, batting** **1** [I,T] to hit the ball with a bat in CRICKET (2) or BASEBALL **2 not bat an eye/eyelid** *informal* to not seem to be shocked, surprised, or embarrassed: *He didn't bat an eyelid when I said I was leaving.* **3 bat your eyes/eyelashes** if a woman bats her eyes, she opens and closes them quickly, especially in order to look attractive to men **4 go to bat for** *AmE informal* to help and support someone: *Andy really went to bat for me when I was accused of stealing that money.* **5 bat a thousand** also **bat a 1000** *AmE informal* to be very successful: *She's been batting a thousand ever since she got that new job.*

**bat** sth ↔ **around** *phr v* [T] *informal* to discuss the good and bad parts of a plan, idea etc

**bat·boy** /ˈbætbɔɪ/ *n* [C] a boy whose job is to look after the equipment of a BASEBALL team

**batch** /bætʃ/ *n* [C] **1** a group of people or things that arrive or are dealt with together: *The second batch of student essays was due in.* **2** a quantity of food, medicine etc, that is produced or prepared at the same time

**batch pro·ces·sing** /ˌ· ˈ···/ *n* [U] a type of computer system in which the computer does several jobs one after the other, without needing instructions between each job

**bat·ed** /ˈbeɪtɪ̣d/ *adj* **with bated breath** feeling very anxious or excited: *We waited with bated breath for the results of the test to come through.*

**bath¹** /bɑːθ‖bæθ/ *n plural* **baths** [C] /bɑːðz, bɑːθs‖bæðz, bæθs/ **1** *BrE* a large long container that you fill with water and sit in to wash yourself; BATHTUB *especially AmE*: **run a bath** (=make water flow into a bath) **2** an act of washing your body in a bath: *After a week of camping, I really needed a bath.*|**have a bath** *BrE*/**take a bath** *AmE*: *Do I have time to take a bath before we go out?*|**give sb a bath** (=wash someone in a bath) **3** a container full of liquid in which something is placed for a particular purpose: *Plunge the fabric into a bath of black dye.* **4 baths a)** *BrE old-fashioned* a public building in which there is a swimming pool **b)** a public building where people could go in the past to wash themselves: *the Roman baths at Cirencester* **5 take a bath** *AmE informal* to lose money, especially in a business deal: *We took a bath in the market over that stock.* —see also BIRDBATH, BUBBLE BATH, HIPBATH, **throw the baby out with the bath water** (THROW¹ (34)), TURKISH BATH S2 W3

**bath²** *v BrE* **1** [T] to wash someone in a bath; BATHE¹ (1) *AmE* **2** [I] *old-fashioned* to wash yourself in a bath; BATHE¹ (1)

**USAGE NOTE: BATH**

WORD CHOICE: **bathe, bath, have/take a bath, bathtub, have a swim, take/have a dip, swimming bath(s), sunbathe, bathroom**

You **bathe** (*AmE*) or more formally in British English, **bath** to get clean: *He baths/bathes every morning.* However, you are more likely to say that you **have a bath** (*BrE*) or **take a bath** (*AmE*): *I have/take a bath every day.* The thing that you **have/take a bath** in is a **bath** (*BrE*) or **bathtub** (*AmE*).

You **bathe** something gently to make it clean especially for medical reasons: *to bathe a cut/your eyes.* In British English you say that you **bath** a baby or a sick person, in American English you **bathe** them.

You also **bathe** (*BrE*) when you go swimming, though this meaning is no longer common: *to bathe in the sea* (NOT *take a bath in the sea*). You are more likely to use **have a swim** or **take/have a dip** in the sea or a swimming pool. (A slightly old-fashioned way of saying **swimming pool** in British English is **swimming bath**.) You also **sunbathe** in the sun (NOT *have a sun bath*).

Often you say that you are going to the **bathroom** especially in American English, not because you are going to have a bath, but as a polite way of saying that you are going to the toilet.

SPELLING

Note the spelling of **bathing** and **bathed**. These words can be formed from **bath** with the pronunciation /ˈbɑːθɪŋ/bæθt/. But they can also be formed from **bathe**, with the pronunciation /ˈbeɪðɪŋ/beɪðd/.

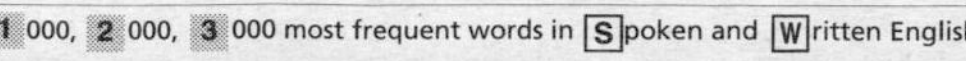

B

**bath chair** /ˈ· ·/ *n* [C] a special chair with wheels and a cover, used in the past for moving someone old or sick around —compare WHEELCHAIR

**bathe¹** /beɪð/ *v* **1** [I,T] *especially AmE* to wash yourself or someone else in a bath; BATH² *BrE*: *I bathed, washed my hair, and got dressed.* **2** [I] *BrE old-fashioned* to swim in the sea, a river, or a lake: *The children ran off to bathe.* **3** [T] to wash or cover part of your body with a liquid, especially as a medical treatment: *Bathe the wound in antiseptic.* **4 be bathed in light/moonlight etc** *literary* an area or building that is bathed in light has light shining onto it in a way that makes it look pleasant or attractive: *The castle was bathed in golden autumn sunlight.* **5 be bathed in tears/sweat etc** *literary* to be covered in tears, sweat etc —see BATH² (USAGE)

**bathe²** *n* [singular] *BrE old-fashioned* an occasion when you swim in the sea, a river, or a lake: *They went for a bathe.*

**bath·er** /ˈbeɪðə‖-ər/ *n* **1** [C] *BrE old fashioned* someone who is swimming in the sea, a river, or a lake **2 bathers** [plural] *AustrE* a piece of clothing that you wear for swimming; SWIMSUIT

**bath·ing** /ˈbeɪðɪŋ/ *n* [U] *BrE old-fashioned* the activity of swimming in the sea, a river, or a lake: *Is the beach safe for bathing?*

**bathing cap** /ˈbeɪθɪŋ kæp/ *n* [C] *old-fashioned* a special hat that you wear for swimming

**bathing cos·tume** /ˈbeɪəɪŋ ˌkɒstjuːm‖-ˌkɑːstuːm/ *n* [C] *BrE old-fashioned* a bathing suit

**bathing ma·chine** /ˈbeɪθɪŋ məˌʃiːn/ *n* [C] a small wooden building on wheels in which people could change their clothes for swimming, in the 18th and 19th centuries

**bathing suit** /ˈbeɪθɪŋ suːt, -sjuːt‖-suːt/ *n* [C] a piece of clothing that you wear for swimming

**bathing trunks** /ˈbeɪθɪŋ trʌŋks/ *n* [C] *BrE old fashioned* a piece of clothing worn by men for swimming

**bath mat** /ˈ· ·/ *n* [C] a piece of thick cloth that you put on the floor next to the bath

**ba·thos** /ˈbeɪθɒs‖-θɑːs/ *n* [U] a sudden change from a beautiful, moral, or serious subject to one that is ordinary, silly, or not important: *a sentimental poem, trembling on the verge of bathos*

**bath·robe** /ˈbɑːθrəʊb‖ˈbæθroʊb/ *n* [C] a long loose piece of clothing shaped like a coat, that you wear especially before or after having a bath —compare DRESSING GOWN

S2 W3 **bath·room** /ˈbɑːθrʊm, -ruːm‖ˈbæθ-/ *n* [C] **1** a room where there is a bath, BASIN (1) etc, and sometimes a toilet **2** *AmE* a room where there is a toilet: *Can you tell me where the bathroom is?* | **go to the bathroom** (=use a toilet) *Mommy, I have to go to the bathroom.*

**bath salts** /ˈ· ·/ *n* [plural] a substance that you put in bath water to make it smell nice

**bath tow·el** /ˈ· ··/ *n* [C] a large TOWEL (=piece of material for drying yourself)

**bath·tub** /ˈbɑːθtʌb‖ˈbæθ-/ *n* [C] *especially AmE* a long large container that you fill with water and sit or lie in to wash yourself; BATH¹ (1) *BrE*

**bath·y·sphere** /ˈbæθɪsfɪə‖-fɪr/ *n* [C] *technical* a strong container used for going deep under the sea, especially to watch plants, animals etc

**ba·tik** /bəˈtiːk, ˈbætɪk/ *n* **1** [U] a way of printing coloured patterns on cloth that involves putting WAX¹ (1) over some parts of the cloth **2** [C,U] cloth that has been coloured in this way —see picture on page 839

**bat·man** /ˈbætmən/ *n plural* **batmen** /-mən/ [C] *technical* an officer's personal servant in the British army

**bat·on** /ˈbætɒn,-tn‖bæˈtɑːn, bə-/ *n* [C] **1** a short thin stick used by a CONDUCTOR (=the leader of a group of musicians) to direct the music **2** a short light stick that is passed from one person to another during a race **3** *especially BrE* a short thick stick used as a weapon by a policeman; TRUNCHEON **4** a short stick that is carried as a sign of a special office or rank **5** a light metal stick that is spun and thrown into the air by a MAJORETTE

**bats·man** /ˈbætsmən/ *n plural* **batsmen** /-mən/ [C] the person who is trying to hit the ball in CRICKET (2)

**bat·tal·ion** /bəˈtæljən/ *n* [C] a large group of soldiers consisting of several companies (COMPANY (9))

**bat·ten¹** /ˈbætn/ *v* **1 batten down the hatches a)** to prepare yourself for a period of difficulty or trouble **b)** to firmly fasten the entrances to the lower part of a ship **2 batten on sb** *especially literary* to live well by using someone else's money, possessions etc

**batten²** *n* [C] a long narrow piece of wood that boards or TILES are fastened to, or that is fixed to other pieces of wood to keep them in place

**bat·ter¹** /ˈbætə‖-ər/ *v* [I always + adv/prep, T] to keep hitting something hard, especially in a way that causes damage: [+ **at/on/against etc**] *The waves battered against the shore.* —**battering** *n* [C,U]

**batter²** *n* **1** [C,U] a liquid mixture of flour, eggs, milk etc, used in cooking: *Fry the fish in batter.* **2** [C,U] *AmE* a thick mixture of flour, eggs, milk etc, used for making cakes **3** [C] the person who is trying to hit the ball in BASEBALL —see picture on page 1263

**bat·tered** /ˈbætəd‖-ərd/ *adj* **1** old and in bad condition: *a battered old suitcase* **2 battered women/children etc** women or children who have been violently treated by their husbands or fathers: *a shelter for battered wives*

**bat·ter·ing ram** /ˈ··· ˌ·/ *n* [C] a long heavy piece of wood used in wars in the past to break through walls or doors

**bat·ter·y** /ˈbætəri/ *n* S

**1 ▸ ELECTRICITY ◂** [C] an object that provides a supply of electricity for something such as a radio or a car: *I need to change the batteries in the flashlight.* | **dead/flat battery** (=a battery that has stopped producing electricity) —see picture at ENGINE

**2 ▸ HENS ◂** [C] a row of small CAGES in which chickens are kept to produce large numbers of eggs: *battery hens* —compare FREE RANGE

**3 ▸ GUNS ◂** [C] several large guns used together: *Enemy anti-aircraft batteries immediately responded to the attack.*

**4 recharge your batteries** *informal* to rest or relax in order to get back your energy: *A week in the mountains should recharge my batteries.*

**5 a battery of** a group of many things of the same kind: *Mayer sat at his desk, surrounded by a battery of telephones.*

**6 ▸ CRIME ◂** [U] *law* the crime of hitting someone —see also ASSAULT AND BATTERY

**bat·tle¹** /ˈbætl/ *n* [C] W

**1 ▸ BETWEEN ARMIES ◂** a fight between opposing armies, groups of ships etc, especially one that is part of a larger war: *the Battle of Trafalgar* | **in/into battle** *Her son was killed in battle.* | *sending troops into battle*

**2 ▸ BETWEEN OPPONENTS ◂** a situation in which opposing groups or people compete or argue with each other when trying to achieve success or control: *a long-running legal battle* | [+ **for**] *The president's advisors were engaged in a battle for power.* | [+ **between**] *a fierce ratings battle between rival TV stations* | [+ **with**] *an ongoing battle with my mother about eating properly*

**3 ▸ ATTEMPT ◂** an attempt to solve a difficult problem or change an unpleasant situation: [+ **against**] *The battle against AIDS will continue for years to come.* | **fight a losing battle** (=try to achieve something that you cannot achieve) *I try to get the kids to pick up their clothes, but I'm fighting a losing battle.*

**4 be half the battle** to be the most difficult or important part of what you have to do: *If you can get an interview, that's half the battle.*

**5 a battle of wits** a disagreement that opposing sides try to win by using their intelligence: *It became a battle of wits between student and teacher.*

**6 do battle (with)** to argue with someone or fight

against someone: *We had to do battle with the authorities over planning permission for the house.*
**7 the battle of the sexes** the relationship between men and women when it is considered as a fight for power

**battle²** *v* **1** [I,T] to be involved in a struggle or argument when you are trying to achieve something difficult or to deal with something unpleasant or dangerous: [+ **against/with**] *She had battled bravely against cancer for many years.*|*I found Maria battling with her maths homework.*|[+ **for**] *a pressure group battling for better schools*|**battle to do sth** *Doctors battled to save his life.*|**battle sth** *AmE*: *I was already battling a cold.* **2 battle it out** to keep fighting or opposing each other until one person or team wins: *I left Adrian and Jo battling it out for the trophy.* **3** [I] *literary* to take part in a fight or war

**bat·tle·axe** *BrE*, **battleax** *AmE* /ˈbætl-æks/ *n* [C] **1** *informal* an unpleasant unfriendly woman who tries to control other people **2** a large AXE (=tool for cutting wood) used as a weapon in the past

**battle cruis·er** /ˈ·· ˌ··/ *n* [C] a large fast ship used in war

**battle cry** /ˈ··· ·/ *n* [C usually singular] **1** a phrase used to encourage people, especially members of a political organization: *'Socialism Now!' was their battle cry.* **2** a loud shout used in war to encourage your side and frighten the enemy

**battle fa·tigue** /ˈ·· ·ˌ·/ *n* [U] a type of mental illness caused by the frightening experiences of war, in which you feel very anxious and upset

**bat·tle·field** /ˈbætlfiːld/ also **bat·tle·ground** /ˈbætlgraʊnd/ *n* [C] **1** a place where a battle is being fought or has been fought **2** a subject that people disagree or argue a lot about: *The housing issue has become a political battleground.*

**bat·tle·ments** /ˈbætlmənts/ *n* [plural] a low wall around the top of a castle, that has spaces to shoot guns or arrows (ARROW (1)) through

**bat·tle·ship** /ˈbætlˌʃɪp/ *n* [C] the largest kind of ship used in war, with very big guns and heavy ARMOUR (2)

**bat·ty** /ˈbæti/ *adj BrE informal* slightly crazy but not in an unpleasant or frightening way; ECCENTRIC¹ (1)

**bau·ble** /ˈbɔːbəl‖ˈbɒː-/ *n* [C] **1** a cheap piece of jewellery **2** *BrE* a brightly coloured decoration that looks like a ball and is used to decorate a CHRISTMAS TREE

**baud** /bɔːd‖bɒːd/ *n* [C] *technical* a unit of measurement of the speed at which information is sent to or from a computer, for example through a telephone line

**baulk** /bɔːk, bɔːlk‖bɒːk, bɒːlk/ a British spelling of BALK

**baux·ite** /ˈbɔːksaɪt‖ˈbɒːk-/ *n* [U] a soft substance that ALUMINIUM (=a type of metal) is obtained from

**bawd·y** /ˈbɔːdi‖ˈbɒːdi/ *adj* bawdy songs, jokes, stories etc are about sex and are funny, enjoyable, and often noisy: *the bawdy 18th century romp, 'Moll Flanders'* —**bawdily** *adv* —**bawdiness** *n* [U]

**bawdy house** /ˈ··· ·/ *n* [C] *old use* a place where women have sex with men for money

**bawl** /bɔːl‖bɒːl/ *v* **1** [I,T] also **bawl out** to shout in a loud unpleasant voice: *The captain stood at the front, bawling orders.* **2** [I] to cry noisily: *a baby bawling*

**bawl** sb ↔ **out** *phr v* [T] *informal especially AmE* to speak angrily to someone because they have done something wrong: *Mom bawled me out for the mess in my room.*

**bay¹** /beɪ/ *n* [C]
**1** ► **SEA** ◄ an area of the sea that curves inwards towards the land: *I had a view across the bay to white sand and pine trees.*|*Montego Bay* —see picture on page 755
**2 keep/hold sth at bay** to prevent something dangerous or unpleasant from happening or from coming too close: *The growling of dogs held the strangers at bay.*|*Economic collapse was held at bay by aid from Russia.*
**3** ► **AREA** ◄ an area within a large room that is separated by shelves, walls etc: *bays in a library*
**4** ► **VEHICLES** ◄ a place where a vehicle can park for a short time: *The bus will depart from bay 3.*|*a loading bay*
**5** ► **TREE** ◄ also **bay tree** a tree that has leaves which smell sweet and are often used in cooking
**6** ► **HORSE** ◄ a horse that is a reddish brown colour

**bay²** *v* [I] **1** if a dog bays, it makes a long high noise, especially when it is chasing something: *the baying of the hounds* **2** to make strong demands to get answers to questions or force someone to give you something: [+ **for**] *a pack of tabloid reporters baying for blood*|*younger men baying at his heels*

**bay³** *adj* a bay horse is a reddish-brown colour

**bay leaf** /ˈ· ·/ *n* [C] a sweet-smelling leaf from the bay tree, often used in cooking

**bay·o·net¹** /ˈbeɪənɪ̆t, -net/ *n* [C] a long blade that is fixed to the end of a RIFLE (=long gun)

**bayonet²** *v* [T] to push the point of a bayonet into someone

**bay·ou** /ˈbaɪuː‖ˈbaɪuː, -oʊ/ *n* [C] a large area of water in the southeast US that moves very slowly and has many water plants

**bay win·dow** /ˌ· ˈ··/ *n* [C] a window that sticks outwards from the wall of a house, usually with glass on three sides

**ba·zaar** /bəˈzɑː‖-ˈzɑːr/ *n* [C] **1** a market or group of shops, especially in India or the Middle East **2** a sale held to collect money for a good purpose: *a charity bazaar*

**ba·zoo·ka** /bəˈzuːkə/ *n* [C] a long light gun that rests on your shoulder and is used especially for firing at tanks (TANK¹ (3))

**BBC** /ˌbiː biː ˈsiː◂/ *n* **1** the British Broadcasting Corporation; the British radio and television company that is paid for by the state **2 BBC English** a standard form of English pronunciation used in Britain; RP

**BB gun** /ˈbiː biː gʌn/ *n* [C] *AmE* a gun that uses air pressure to force out small round metal balls; AIRGUN *BrE*

**BBQ** *n* [C] an abbreviation for BARBECUE

**BC** /ˌbiː ˈsiː/ before Christ; used after a date to show that it was before the birth of Christ: *The Great Pyramid dates from around 2600 BC.* —compare AD

**BCE** /ˌbiː siː ˈiː/ *especially AmE* before common era; used after a date to show that it is before the birth of Christ

**be-** /bɪ/ *prefix* **1** in some verbs, means to treat as a particular thing: *Don't belittle him* (=say he is unimportant).|*He befriended me* (=became my friend). **2** *literary* in some adjectives, means wearing a particular thing: *a bespectacled boy* (=wearing glasses) **3** *old use* completely; thoroughly: *to besmear* (=make very dirty)

**be¹** /bi; *strong* biː/ *auxiliary verb* **1** used with a present participle to form the CONTINUOUS (4) tenses of verbs: **be doing sth** *Don't disturb me while I'm working.*|*Gemma was reading when her son called.*|*They've been asking a lot of questions.*|*He's always causing trouble.* **2** used with past participles to form the PASSIVE²: *Smoking is not permitted.*|*I was told about it yesterday.*|*The house is being painted.*|*She has been invited to the party.*|*The flames could be seen several miles away.*|*The police should have been informed about this.* **3** used to give an order or to tell someone about a rule: *All guests are to vacate their rooms by 10 am on the day of their departure.*|*The children are to be in bed when we get home.* **4** used to show arrangements for the future: *Audrey and Jimmy are to be married in June.*|*We were to have gone away last week but I was ill.*|*I'll be leaving in about half an hour.* **5** used to show what someone should do or what should happen: *What am I to tell her* (=what should I tell her?) *when she finds out?*|*He is more to be* (=should be more) *pitied than blamed.* **6** used to show what cannot or could not happen: *We searched everywhere but the ring was nowhere to be found.* **7** used to show what had to happen or what did happen: *This discovery was to have a major effect on the treatment of heart disease.* **8** used in CONDITIONAL¹ (2) sentences that describe a situation that does not or could not exist: *If I were to do that what would you say?*|*Were we to offer you the job would you take it?* **9** *old use* used instead of 'have' to form the PERFECT³ tenses of some verbs: *Christ is risen* (=has risen) *from the dead.*

 **be²** *v* **1** [linking verb] used to show that someone or something is the same as the subject: *It's me.*|*Lack of money is our biggest problem.*|*If I were you, I shouldn't do it.*|**the problem/difficulty etc is doing sth** *The problem is explaining it to her in a tactful way.*|**the problem/difficulty etc is to do sth** *The difficulty is to know what to do for the best.*|**the fact/idea etc is (that)** *The fact is that you know too much.* **2** [I always + adv/prep] used to show position or time: *Where is Simon?*|*Jane's upstairs.*|*The principal's in his office.*|*How long has she been here?*|*The book is on the table.*|*The concert was last night.*|*The party is on Saturday.* **3** [linking verb] used to show that someone or something belongs to a group or has a particular quality: *Snow is white.*|*Horses are animals.*|*She wants to be a doctor when she leaves school.*|*These shoes are mine.*|*We were hungry.*|*I'm not ready.*|*Be careful!*|*It's hot today.*| *A knife is for cutting with.* **4** used in short phrases and questions: *It's cold isn't it?*|*He isn't leaving, is he?*|*"That's not your coat!" "Yes it is!"* **5** [linking verb] used after 'there' to show that something exists: *There's a hole in your trousers.* **6 be that as it may** *formal* used to say that even though you accept that something is true it does not change a situation: *"James has been under a lot of pressure at work recently." "Be that as it may, he ought to spend time with his family."* **7** [I] to exist: *That's just how it is.* **8** to remain in the same state or stay calm: *If the baby's sleeping let her be.* **9 let/leave sth be** to let a situation remain as it is without trying to change it: *You just have to let some things be.* **10 the be-all and end all** the most important part of a situation or of someone's life: *For Jim making money is the be-all and end all of his job.*

S3 W2 **beach¹** /biːtʃ/ *n plural* **beaches** [C] an area of sand or small stones next to the sea or a lake: *It was a hot day, and the beach was already crowded with people.* —see picture on page 835 —see SHORE¹ (USAGE)

**beach²** *v* [T] **1** to pull a boat onto the shore away from the water **2** if a WHALE (=large sea animal) beaches itself or is beached, it swims onto the shore and cannot get back in the water

**beach ball** /ˈ· ·/ *n* [C] a large coloured plastic ball filled with air and used for playing games on the beach

**beach bug·gy** /ˈ· ˌ··/ *n* [C] a vehicle with very large tyres that can be driven on sand; DUNE BUGGY *AmE*

**beach chair** /ˈ· ·/ *n* [C] *AmE* a folding chair with a seat and back made of cloth or plastic, which is used outdoors, especially at the beach; DECKCHAIR —see picture at CHAIR¹

**beach·comb·er** /ˈbiːtʃˌkəʊmə‖-ˌkoʊmər/ *n* [C] someone who searches beaches for things that might be useful

**beach·head** /ˈbiːtʃhed/ *n* [C] an area of shore that has been taken from an enemy by force and can be used for landing soldiers on: *the Normandy beachheads*

**beach·wear** /ˈbiːtʃweə‖-wer/ *n* [U] clothes that you wear for swimming, lying on the beach etc

**bea·con** /ˈbiːkən/ *n* [C] **1** a special tower with a bright light, or a floating object that sends signals, used to warn boats that they are near the shore **2** a light that is put somewhere to warn or guide people, vehicles, or aircraft **3** a radio or RADAR signal used by aircraft or boats to help them find their position and direction **4** *especially literary* a person, idea etc that guides or encourages you: *a beacon of hope in a dark world* **5** a fire on top of a hill used in former times as a signal —see also BELISHA BEACON

**bead** /biːd/ *n* [C] **1** one of a set of small, usually round pieces of glass, wood, plastic etc, that you can put on a string and wear as jewellery: *a necklace of amber beads* **2** a small drop of liquid such as water or blood: *Beads of sweat stood out on his brow.* **3 draw a bead on** to aim carefully before shooting a weapon —see also WORRY BEADS

**bead·ed** /ˈbiːdʒd/ *adj* **1** decorated with beads **2 beaded with sweat/perspiration** with drops of SWEAT (=liquid produced by your body when you are hot) on your skin

**bead·ing** /ˈbiːdɪŋ/ *n* [U] **1** long thin pieces of wood or stone that are used as a decoration on the edges of walls, furniture etc **2** a lot of beads sewn close together on clothes, leather etc as decoration

**bea·dle** /ˈbiːdl/ *n* [C] **1** an officer in British churches in former times who helped the priest in various ways, especially by keeping order **2** an officer in some British universities who helps at special ceremonies

**bead·y** /ˈbiːdi/ *adj* **1** beady eyes are small, round, and shiny **2 have/keep your beady eye(s) on** *humorous* to watch someone or something very carefully

**bea·gle** /ˈbiːgəl/ *n* [C] a dog with short legs and smooth fur, sometimes used to hunt rabbits

**beak** /biːk/ *n* [C] **1** the hard pointed mouth of a bird **2** *humorous* a large pointed nose **3** *BrE old-fashioned* a judge or a male teacher

**bea·ker** /ˈbiːkə‖-ər/ *n* [C] **1** *BrE* a drinking cup with straight sides and no handle, usually made of plastic **2** a glass cup with straight sides that is used in chemistry for measuring and heating liquids —see picture at LABORATORY

**beam¹** /biːm/ *n* [C]

**1** ▶ **LIGHT** ◀ **a)** a shining line of light from the sun, a lamp etc: *We could see the beams of searchlights scanning the sky.* **b)** a line of light, energy etc that you cannot see: *a laser beam*|*The intruder passed through an infra-red alarm beam.*

**2** ▶ **WOOD/METAL** ◀ a long heavy piece of wood or metal used in building houses, bridges etc

**3** ▶ **SMILE** ◀ a wide happy smile: *"Congratulations!" she said, with a beam of delight.*

**4 off (the) beam** incorrect or mistaken: *We tried to guess the price but we were way off beam.*

**5** ▶ **SPORT** ◀ a long raised wooden bar used in GYMNASTICS , on which you balance and move

**6** ▶ **SHIP** ◀ *technical* the widest part of a ship from side to side —see also **broad in the beam** (BROAD¹ (12))

**beam²** *v* **1** [I] to smile very happily: *The captain beamed with satisfaction.*|*"I got a place!" said Sara, beaming delightedly.* **2** [T always + adv/prep] to send a radio or television signal through the air, especially to somewhere very distant: *the first ever broadcast beamed across the Atlantic* **3** [I,T] to send out a line of light, heat, energy etc: *The sun beamed through the clouds.*|*X-rays are beamed through the patient's body.*

**beam-ends** /ˌ· ˈ·‖ˈ· ·/ *n* **be on your beam-ends** *BrE old-fashioned* to have almost no money

**bean¹** /biːn/ *n* [C] S

**1** ▶ **VEGETABLE** ◀ **a)** a seed from one of many types of climbing plants, that is often used as food **b)** a POD (=seed case) from a bean plant that is used as food when the seeds are young: *green beans* —see picture on page 414

**2** ▶ **PLANT** ◀ a plant that produces beans

**3** ▶ **COFFEE** ◀ one of many types of seed that is used to make coffee, chocolate etc: *coffee beans*|*cocoa beans*

**4 be full of beans** *informal* to be very eager and full of energy: *It's the kids' party today and they're full of beans.*

**5 not have a bean** *informal* to have no money at all: *I can't pay you – I haven't got a bean.*

**6 not know beans (about)** *AmE informal* to know nothing at all about a subject

**7 old bean** *BrE old-fashioned* used by men when talking to a man they know well —see also **spill the beans** (SPILL¹ (3))

**bean²** *v* [T] *informal* to hit someone on the head with an object: *I was beaned on the head by a baseball.* S

**bean·bag** /ˈbiːnbæg/ *n* [C] **1** a very large cloth bag that is filled with pieces of soft plastic and used for sitting on **2** a small cloth bag filled with beans, used for throwing and catching in children's games

**bean curd** /ˈ· ·/ *n* [C] a soft white food made from SOY BEANS; TOFU

**bean·feast** /ˈ· ·/ *n* [C] *BrE informal* a party or celebration

**bea·nie** /ˈbiːni/ *n* [C] *AmE* a small round hat that fits close to your head

**bean·pole** /ˈbiːnpəʊl‖-poʊl/ *n* [C] *humorous* a very tall thin person

**bean·sprout** /ˈbiːnspraʊt/ *n* [C] the small white stem from a bean seed that is eaten as a vegetable —see picture on page 414

W1 **bear¹** /beə‖ber/ *v past tense* **bore** /bɔː‖bɔːr/ *past participle* **borne** /bɔːn‖bɔːrn/ [T]

**1 can't bear** **a)** to dislike something or someone so much that they make you very annoyed or impatient: *Oh, I can't bear that man – he really irritates me!* | *I just can't bear that kind of selfishness.* | **can't bear sb doing sth** *He can't bear people smoking while he's eating.* **b)** to be so upset about something that you feel unable to accept it or let it happen: *Please don't leave me all alone. I couldn't bear it.* | **can't bear the thought of** *We just couldn't bear the thought of selling the farm.* | **can't bear to do sth** *Alison couldn't bear to leave and cried all the way to the airport.*

**2 bear in mind (that)** to remember a fact or piece of information that is important or could be useful in the future: *Bearing in mind that he's only ten, I think he did very well.* | *I think that's excellent advice to bear in mind.*

**3 ▶BE BRAVE◀** to bravely accept or deal with a painful or unpleasant situation: *She bore the pain with tremendous courage.* | *Listening to their screams was more than we could bear.* | **grin and bear it** (=accept something unpleasant without complaining) *It's no good moaning – you'll just have to grin and bear it.*

**4 bear the costs/burden/expense etc** *formal* to pay for something: *As usual, the poorest members of society are bearing the burden of tax increases.*

**5 bear responsibility/the blame etc** *formal* to be responsible, accept the blame etc for something: *In this case, the victim must bear some responsibility for the crime.*

**6 ▶SUPPORT◀** to support the weight of something: *I don't think the table is strong enough to bear your weight.* | *a load-bearing wall*

**7 doesn't bear thinking about** so unpleasant or shocking that you prefer not to think about it: *The long-term consequences of a nuclear leak don't bear thinking about.*

**8 bear a resemblance/relation etc to** to be similar to or connected with someone or something else: *George doesn't bear much resemblance to his father.* | *The things she says bear little relation to what she actually does.*

**9 bear the strain/pressure etc** to be strong enough or firm enough to continue despite problems: *She suddenly became a big star, and their marriage was unable to bear the strain.*

**10 bear the brunt of** to have to accept the most difficult or damaging part of something: *It's the junior staff who will bear the brunt of the redundancies.*

**11 bear (sb) a grudge** to continue to feel annoyed about something that someone did a long time ago: *Despite her treatment of him over the years, he bears her no grudges.*

**12 bear fruit** **a)** if a plan, decision etc bears fruit, it is successful, especially after a long period of time: *Our careful investments were finally bearing fruit.* **b)** if a tree bears fruit, it produces fruit

**13 ▶SHOW SIGNS OF◀** to show physical or emotional signs of a past experience: *Jim proudly bears the scars of his rugby days.*

**14 not bear examination/inspection etc** to not be suitable or good enough to be tested or examined thoroughly: *This line of argument doesn't bear much examination.*

**15 bring influence/pressure etc to bear (on)** to use your influence or power to get what you want: *The tobacco companies are bringing pressure to bear on the government to stop the advertising ban.*

**16 bear witness to** *formal* to show that something is true or exists: *Her latest film bears witness to her versatility as a director.*

**17 bear right/left** to turn towards the right of left: *Bear left at the crossroads.* | *The road bears round to the right.*

**18 ▶BABY◀** *formal* to give birth to a baby: **bear sb a child/son/daughter** (=have their baby) *She bore him three sons.*

**19 bear yourself** *formal* to walk, stand etc in a particular way, especially when this shows your character: *Throughout the trial, she bore herself with great dignity.*

**20 ▶CARRY◀** *literary* to carry someone or something, especially something important: *The emperor was borne along in a sedan chair.* | *A messenger arrived, bearing a message from the prince.*

**21 ▶WIND/WATER◀** *literary* if the wind, sea, or air bears something, it moves it along: *The sound of music was borne along on the wind.*

**22 ▶SIGN/MARK◀** *formal* to have or show a sign or mark: *The letter bore no signature.*

**23 ▶NAME/TITLE◀** *formal* to have a particular name or title: *The chest bears the name of Chippendale.*

**24 bear sb no malice/ill will etc** *formal* not to feel angry towards someone

Frequencies of the verbs **bear**, **stand** and **endure** in spoken and written English.

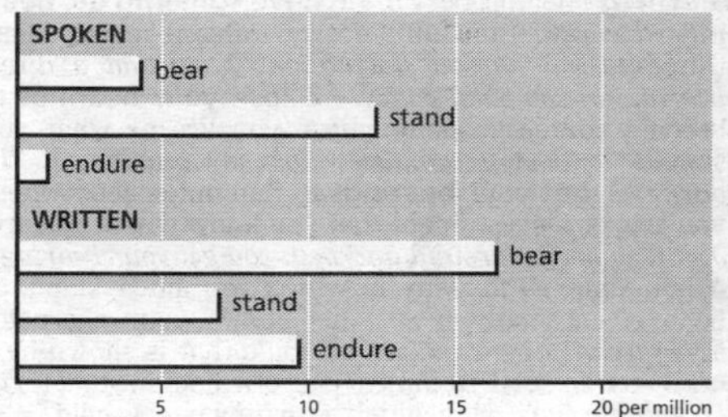


Based on the British National Corpus and the Longman Lancaster Corpus

All three verbs are used to mean 'accept or deal with an unpleasant situation'. The graph shows that in this meaning **stand** and **bear** are much more common than **endure** in spoken English. In written English, **bear** is the most common and **endure**, a formal word, is fairly common.

**bear down** *phr v* **1 bear down on** to move quickly towards someone in a threatening way: *His aunt bore down on him and insisted he joined them for dinner.* | *A powerboat was bearing down on us.* **2** [I] to use all your strength and effort to push or press down on something **3** [T **bear** sb/sth ↔ **down**] *formal* to defeat a person or deal successfully with a difficult situation

**bear on/upon** sth *phr v* [T] *formal* to have a connection with something

**bear** sb/sth **out** *phr v* [T] if facts or information bear out a claim, story, opinion etc, they help to prove that it is true: *Recent evidence bears out the idea that students learn best in small groups.* | *Tell them what really happened. I'll bear you out.*

**bear up** *phr v* [I] to show courage or determination during a difficult or unpleasant time: *How has he been bearing up since the accident?*

**bear with** sb/sth *phr v* [T] **1 bear with me** *spoken* used to ask someone politely to wait while you find out information, finish what you are doing etc: *Bear with me a minute, and I'll check if Mr Garrard's in.* **2** to be patient or continue to do something difficult or unpleasant: *I tried to bear with her tempers.*

**bear²** *n* [C] **1** a large strong animal with thick fur that eats flesh, fruit, and insects —see also TEDDY BEAR, POLAR BEAR **2** *technical* someone who sells shares (SHARE² (6)) or goods when they expect the price to fall: **a bear market** (=when the value of business shares is falling)

3 *informal* a big man who is rough or bad-tempered **4 be like a bear with a sore head** *informal* to be rude to people because you are feeling bad-tempered

**bear·a·ble** /ˈbeərəbəl‖ˈber-/ *adj* something that is bearable is difficult or unpleasant, but you can deal with it: *His friendship was the only thing that made life bearable.* —**bearably** *adv*

**bear claw** /ˈ· ·/ *n* [C] *AmE* fruit covered in PASTRY with long cuts made across the top

S3 **beard¹** /bɪəd‖bɪrd/ *n* [C] **1** hair that grows around a man's chin —compare MOUSTACHE **2** something similar to a beard, such as hair growing on an animal's chin —**bearded** *adj*

**beard²** *v* [T] **beard sb in their den** to go and see someone who has influence or authority, and tell them what you want, why you disagree with them etc

**bear·er** /ˈbeərə‖-ˈberər/ *n* [C] **1** *formal* someone whose job is to carry something such as a flag or a STRETCHER (=light bed for a sick person) **2** someone who brings you information, a letter etc: *I hate to be the bearer of bad news, but...* **3** *law* the bearer of a legal document such as a PASSPORT is the person that it officially belongs to **4** *IndE, PakE* a male servant

**bear hug** /ˈ· ·/ *n* [C] an action in which you put your arms around someone and hold them very tightly because you like them or are pleased to see them

**bear·ing** /ˈbeərɪŋ‖ˈber-/ *n* **1 have some/no etc bearing on** to have some influence, no influence etc on something: *Recent market fluctuations have had a direct bearing on company policy.* **2 lose your bearings** to become confused about where you are or what you should do next: *I completely lost my bearings in the dark.* **3 get your bearings** to find out exactly where you are, or feel confident that you know where you are: *Jim'll show you around and help you get your bearings.* **4** [singular, U] the way in which you move, stand, or behave, especially when this shows your character **5** [C] *technical* a direction or angle that is shown by a COMPASS (1) **6** [C] *technical* part of a machine that turns on another part, or in which a turning part is held

**bear·ish** /ˈbeərɪʃ‖ˈber-/ *adj* **1** rude or bad-tempered **2 a)** a bearish market is one where the prices of shares (SHARE² (6)) are decreasing **b)** someone who is bearish expects the price of business shares to go down —**bearishly** *adv* —**bearishness** *n*

**bear·skin** /ˈbeəˌskɪn‖ˈber-/ *n* **1** [C,U] the skin of a bear **2** [C] a tall hat made of black fur, worn by some British soldiers for special ceremonies

**beast** /biːst/ *n* [C] **1** *literary* an animal, especially a large or dangerous one **2** *old-fashioned especially spoken* someone who is cruel or unpleasant: *You filthy beast!* **3** *spoken* a job, problem etc that is difficult to deal with: *Can you undo this jar? It's a real beast to open.* **4 the beast in sb** the part of someone's character that makes them experience hatred, strong sexual feelings, violence etc: *You bring out the beast in me. Come here!*

**beast·ly** /ˈbiːstli/ *adj old-fashioned especially spoken* very unpleasant; nasty: *What beastly weather!* —**beastly** *adv* —**beastliness** *n* [U]

**beast of bur·den** /ˌ· · ˈ··/ *n* [C] *old use* an animal that does heavy work

S2 W2 **beat¹** /biːt/ *v past tense* **beat** *past participle* **beaten** /ˈbiːtn/

**1 ▶ DEFEAT ◀** [T] **a)** to get the most points, votes etc in a game, race, or competition: *Brazil were beaten in the final 2-1.* | *I could always beat my brother at chess.* | **beat sb hollow** (=defeat them easily) **b)** to successfully deal with or defeat a problem that you have been struggling with: *The Administration claims to have beaten inflation.* —see WIN¹ (USAGE)

**2 ▶ HIT ◀** [T] to hit someone or something many times with your hand or with a stick: *In those days children were often beaten at school.* | *I've been beating the rugs and I'm covered in dust.* | **beat sb to death/beat sb unconscious etc** (=beat them until they die etc) | **beat sb black and blue** (=make marks on their body by beating them hard) | **beat the living daylights out of** *informal* (=beat someone very hard)

**3 beat a record/score etc** to do better than a record etc that already exists: *The record set by Kierson in '84 has yet to be beaten.*

**4 ▶ HIT AGAINST ◀** [I always + adv/prep] to knock or hit against something continuously: **beat on/against etc** *Waves beat against the cliffs.* | *We could hear the rain beating on the roof.*

**5 beat sb to it** *informal* to get or do something before someone else, especially if you are both trying to do it first: *I really wanted that car but someone else had beaten me to it.*

**6 (it) beats me** *spoken* used to say that you cannot understand or explain something: *"How can these kids afford clothes like that?" "Beats me."*

**7 ▶ MIX ◀** [T] to mix things together with a fork or machine when preparing food: *Beat the eggs until they are light and fluffy.*

**8 ▶ DRUMS ◀** [I,T] if you beat the drums or if drums beat, they make a regular continuous sound

**9 ▶ HEART ◀** [I] when your heart beats, it moves in a regular RHYTHM (1) as it pumps your blood: *He's still alive – I can feel his heart beating.*

**10 ▶ WINGS ◀** [I,T] if a bird beats its wings or its wings beat, they move up and down quickly and regularly

**11 you can't beat** *spoken* used to say that someone or something is better than anything else: *You can't beat motor racing for excitement and danger.*

**12 take some beating a)** to be difficult to beat: *Schumacher has 42 points, which will take some beating.* **b)** to be better, more enjoyable etc than almost anything else of the same type: *As a winter sports center, Edmonton takes some beating.*

**13 ▶ BE BETTER ◀** [T not in progressive] *spoken* to be much better and more enjoyable than something else: *This job sure beats tending bar!*

**14 beat the rush** to do something earlier than normal in order to avoid problems when everyone does it: *Shop now and beat the Christmas rush!*

**15 beat about/around the bush** to avoid or delay talking about something embarrassing or unpleasant: *Stop beating about the bush and tell me why you're here.*

**16 beat the system** to find ways of avoiding or breaking the rules of an organization, system etc, in order to achieve what you want

**17 beat it!** *spoken* used to tell someone to leave at once because they are annoying you or should not be there

**18 beat your brains out** *AmE informal* to think about something very hard and for a long time

**19 beat the rap** *AmE informal* to avoid being punished for something you have done

**20 if you can't beat 'em, join 'em** *spoken* used when you decide to take part in something although you disapprove of it, because everyone else is doing it and you cannot stop them

**21 beat time** to make regular movements or sounds to show the speed at which music should be played: *a conductor beating time with his baton*

**22 can you beat that/it?** *spoken* used to show that you are surprised or annoyed by something: *He's taken the money and gone! Can you beat that?*

**23 beat a path (to sb's door)** if people beat a path to your door, they are interested in something you are selling, a service you are providing etc: *They'll be beating a path to your door after this ad.*

**24 to beat the band** *AmE informal* in large amounts or with great force: *It's raining to beat the band.*

**25 beat the heat** *AmE informal* to make yourself cooler: *Let's go swimming to beat the heat.*

**26 ▶ METAL ◀** [T] to hit metal with a hammer in order to shape it or make it thinner

**27 ▶ HUNTING ◀** [I,T] to force wild birds and animals out of bushes, long grass etc so that they can be shot for sport

**28 beat your breast** *literary* to show clearly that you are very upset or sorry about something —see also BEATEN, BEATING

**beat down** *phr v* **1** [I] if the sun beats down, it shines very brightly and the weather is hot **2** [I] if the rain beats down, it is raining very hard **3** [T **beat** sb ↔ **down**] to persuade someone to reduce a price: **beat sb down to sth** *He wanted £4500 for the car but I beat him down to £3850.*

**beat off** *phr v* **1** [T **beat** sb/sth ↔ **off**] to prevent someone who is trying to attack you, harm you, or compete against you: *efforts to beat off our business rivals | We managed to beat off the dogs and run away.* **2** [I,T **beat** sb ↔ **off**] *AmE taboo slang* to MASTURBATE

**beat out** *phr v* **1** [T **beat** sth ↔ **out**] to put out a fire by beating it **2** [T **beat** sth **out of** sb] to force someone to tell you something by beating them: *I had the truth beaten out of me by my father.* **3** [T **beat** sth ↔ **out**] if drums beat out a RHYTHM (1) or you beat out a rhythm on the drums, they make a continuous regular sound **4** [T **beat** sb ↔ **out**] *AmE* to defeat someone in a competition: *Roberts beat out Tony Gwynn for the Most Valuable Player Award.*

**beat up** *phr v* **1** [T **beat** sb ↔ **up**] to hurt someone badly by hitting them: *They claimed they had been beaten up by the police.* **2 beat up on** *AmE* to hit someone and harm them, especially someone younger or weaker than yourself **3 beat up on yourself** *AmE informal* to blame yourself too much for something

3 **beat²** *n* **1** [C] one of a series of movements or hitting actions: *a heartbeat | the slow beat of the drum* **2** [C usually singular] a regular repeated noise: [+ **of**] *the beat of marching feet* **3** [singular] the main RHYTHM (1) that a piece of music or a poem has: *Try to follow the beat.* **4** [C] one of the notes in a piece of music that sounds stronger than the other notes **5** [singular] the area of a town, city etc that a police officer regularly walks around

**beat³** *adj* [not before noun] *informal* very tired: *I'm beat.* | **dead beat** *Come and sit down, you must be dead beat.*

**beat·en** /ˈbiːtn/ *adj* [only before noun] **1** beaten metal has been shaped with a hammer to make it thinner **2** a beaten path, track etc has been made by many people walking the same way: *a well beaten path through the forest* **3 off the beaten track** a place that is off the beaten track is not well known and is far away from the places that people usually visit

**beat·er** /ˈbiːtə‖-ər/ *n* [C] **1** an object that is designed to beat something: *an egg beater | a carpet beater* **2** someone who forces wild birds or animals out of bushes, long grass etc so that they can be shot for sport **3** *AmE informal* an old car in bad condition

**bea·tif·ic** /ˌbiːəˈtɪfɪk◂/ *adj literary* a beatific look, smile etc shows great peace and happiness —**beatifically** /-kli/ *adv*

**be·at·i·fy** /biˈætɪ̣faɪ/ *v* [T] if the Roman Catholic church beatifies someone who has died, it says officially that they are a holy or special person —**beatification** /biˌætɪ̣fɪ̣ˈkeɪʃən/ *n* [U]

**beat·ing** /ˈbiːtɪŋ/ *n* [C] **1** an act of hitting someone many times as a punishment or in a fight: **give sb a beating** (=beat them) **2 take a beating** to lose very badly in a game or competition: *Our team took a real beating on Saturday.* —see also **take some beating** (BEAT¹ (12))

**beat·nik** /ˈbiːtnɪk/ *n* [C] one of a group of young people in the late 1950s and early 1960s, who did not accept the values of society and showed this by their clothes and the way they lived

**beat-up** /ˈ· ·/ *adj informal* a beat-up car, bicycle etc, is old and in bad condition: *a beat-up old Ford Escort*

**beau** /bəʊ‖boʊ/ *n plural* **beaux** /bəʊz‖boʊz/ or **beaus** [C] *old-fashioned* **1** a woman's close friend or lover **2** a fashionable, well-dressed man

**Beau·jo·lais** /ˈbəʊʒəleɪ‖ˌboʊʒəˈleɪ/ *n* [C,U] a type of French red wine

**beau-monde** /ˌbəʊ ˈmɒnd‖ˌboʊ ˈmɔːnd/ *n* [singular] *French* rich and fashionable people

**beaut¹** /bjuːt/ *n* [singular] *AmE & AustrE informal* **a (real) beaut** used to say that something is either very good or very bad: *That last catch was a beaut.*

**beaut²** *adj AustrE informal* very good: *"Had a good day?" "It was beaut."*

**beau·te·ous** /ˈbjuːtiəs/ *adj poetic* beautiful: *the beauteous Helen of Troy* —**beauteously** *adv*

**beau·ti·cian** /bjuːˈtɪʃən/ *n* [C] someone whose job is to give beauty treatments to your skin, hair etc

**beau·ti·ful** /ˈbjuːtɪ̣fəl/ *adj* **1** someone or something that is beautiful is extremely good to look at and gives you a feeling of pleasure: *She was even more beautiful than I had remembered. | a beautiful bunch of flowers* **2** very good: *a beautiful experience | What a beautiful shot! | The weather was beautiful.* —**beautifully** *adv* S1 W2

**USAGE NOTE: BEAUTIFUL**

WORD CHOICE: **beautiful, pretty, handsome, good-looking, attractive, sexy**

**Beautiful** and **pretty** can be used of women, children, and things, but not usually of men, unless you want to suggest that they have female features: *a beautiful girl/house/view | a pretty child/picture/voice.* **Beautiful** is the strongest word to describe a very attractive appearance, it suggests that someone has almost perfect good looks. **Pretty** means good-looking in a more ordinary way, but not really beautiful.

**Handsome** is not common in spoken English. It is usually used to describe men, especially if they have the strong regular features that men in romantic stories are supposed to have. A **handsome** woman is **good-looking** in a strong, healthy way.

**Good-looking** can be used about men and women, but not usually about things: *Gina and Barry are a good-looking couple.* **Attractive** can be used about men, women, and things: *an attractive colour/idea/young man.* An **attractive** person may not be very **good-looking** but makes other people sexually interested in them, though not as much as if they are **sexy**.

**beau·ti·fy** /ˈbjuːtɪ̣faɪ/ *v* [T] to make someone or something beautiful

**beau·ty** /ˈbjuːti/ *n* 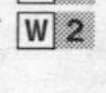

**1 ▶APPEARANCE◀ a)** [U] a quality that a place or person has that makes them very attractive to look at: *Her beauty had faded over the years. | an area of outstanding natural beauty* | **beauty product/tip etc** (=a product etc that is supposed to make you more beautiful) **b)** [C] *old-fashioned* a woman who is very beautiful: *She was considered a great beauty in her youth.*

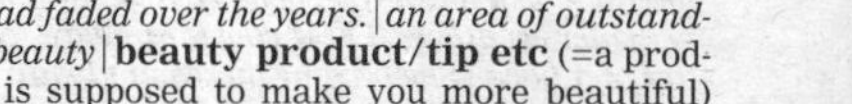

**2 ▶GOOD QUALITY◀** [U] a quality that something such as a poem, song, emotion etc has, which gives you pleasure or joy: *the beauty of Shakespeare's verse*

**3 ▶ADVANTAGE◀ the beauty of** a particularly good quality that makes something especially suitable or useful: *The beauty of golf is that you can play it on your own.*

**4 ▶GOOD EXAMPLE◀** [C] *spoken* a very good example of something or an object that is a particularly good, large, or pleasant one of its type: *We had a turkey at Easter – a real beauty it was. | That black eye's a beauty, Justin!*

**5 ▶APPROVAL◀ (you) beauty!** *AustrE spoken* used to show that you are very pleased by something: *Look at this lunch. Beauty! | You beauty! You've made my day.*

**6 beauty is in the eye of the beholder** used to say that different people have different opinions about what is beautiful

**beauty con·test** /ˈ·· ˌ··/ *n* [C] a competition in which women are judged on how attractive they look

**beauty mark** /ˈ·· ·/ *n* [C] *AmE* a small dark mark on a woman's skin; BEAUTY SPOT (2) *BrE*

**beauty par·lor** /ˈ·· ˌ··/ *n* [C] *AmE* a beauty salon

**beauty queen** /ˈ·· ·/ *n* [C] the winner of a beauty contest

**beauty sal·on** /ˈ·· ˌ··‖ˈ·· ·ˌ·/ *n* [C] a place in which you can receive beauty treatments for your skin, hair etc

**beauty shop** /ˈ·· ·/ *n* [C] *AmE* a beauty salon

**beauty sleep** /ˈ·· ·/ *n* [U] *humorous* enough sleep to keep you healthy and looking good: *I need my beauty sleep.*

**beauty spot** /ˈ·· ·/ *n* [C] **1** a beautiful place in the countryside **2** *BrE* a small dark mark on a woman's skin; BEAUTY MARK *AmE* —see picture on page 412

**bea·ver¹** /ˈbiːvə‖-ər/ *n* [C] a North American animal that has thick fur, a wide flat tail, and cuts down trees with its teeth —see also **eager beaver** (EAGER (3))

**beaver²** *v*

**beaver away** *phr v BrE informal* to work very hard, especially at writing or calculating something: **[+ at]** *He had been beavering away at his homework half the night.*

**be·bop** /ˈbiːbɒp‖-bɑːp/ *n* [U] a type of JAZZ music; BOP² (2)

**be·calmed** /bɪˈkɑːmd‖-ˈkɑːmd, -ˈkɑːlmd/ *adj literary* a ship or boat that is becalmed cannot move because there is no wind

**be·came** /bɪˈkeɪm/ the past tense of BECOME

S1 W1 **be·cause** /bɪˈkɒz, bɪˈkəz‖bɪˈkɒːz, bɪˈkəz/ *conjunction* **1** for the reason that: *I do it because I like it.* | *She got the job because she was the best candidate.* | *"Why can't I go?" "Because you're too young."* **2 because of** as a result of a particular thing or of someone's actions: *He had to retire because of ill health.* | *Sandy's very upset and it's all because of you.* (=your fault) —see OWING (USAGE) **3 just because...** *spoken* used to say that although one thing is true, it does not mean that something else is true: *Just because I'm married doesn't mean that I don't want to see my old friends anymore.* | *David seems to think that just because he's our boss he can talk to us any way he wants.*

**beck** /bek/ *n* **1** *BrE* [C] a small stream **2 be at sb's beck and call** to always be ready to do what someone wants: *I was tired of being at her beck and call all day long.*

**beck·on** /ˈbekən/ *v* [I,T] **1** to make a signal to someone with your hand or arm, to show that you want them to come towards you: **[+ to]** *She beckoned to the child, who came running.* | **beckon sb forward/to/towards etc** *I stood there till she beckoned me across the room.* **2** if something such as money or happiness beckons, it is so attractive that you have to do something in order to get it

S1 W1 **become** /bɪˈkʌm/ *v past tense* **became** /bɪˈkeɪm/ *past participle* **become** **1** [linking verb] to begin to be something, or to develop in a particular way: *He became King at the age of 17.* | *After the death of her father she became the richest woman in the world.* | *The weather became warmer.* | *We soon became acclimatized to the warmer weather.* | *These constant delays are becoming a bit of a bore.* | *She became increasingly anxious about her husband's strange behaviour.* | *He withdrew from the competition when it became clear that he stood no chance of winning.* **2** [T not in progressive] *formal* to suit someone or be suitable for them: *This sort of behaviour hardly becomes a person in your position.* **3 what has become of...?/whatever will become of...?** used to ask what has happened to someone, especially when you have not seen them for a long time, or what will happen to someone that you are worried about: *Whatever will become of Sam when his wife dies?*

**USAGE NOTE: BECOME**

WORD CHOICE: **become**, **get**, **turn**, **go**, **come**

**Become** and **get** can be used with most types of adjective to describe changes in people and things. **Become** is more common in writing, and **get** in spoken English, especially where a quick change is involved: *The sky became/got cloudy.* | *Crime is becoming more widespread.* | *It became clear that he was lying.* | *It gets dark early now.* | *I'm getting wet standing here.* | *Your dinner's getting cold.*

When things change colour, **turn** can be used, or less formally **go** (especially if the change does not last long). Compare: *Jonathan turned/went pale when he heard the news.* | *It's that time of year when the leaves go/turn golden.*

**Go** can also be used where someone's mind or body changes for the worse: *He went crazy/blind/deaf/bald* (but *He fell sick/ill*). **Go** is used in a similar meaning with some things: *The meat's gone bad.* | *Everything went wrong/haywire.* But in other situations **turn** is used: *The milk's turned/gone sour.* | *The situation turned nasty.*

**Come** is used only in very few expressions where something gets better: *It came right in the end.* | *All my dreams have come true* (NOT *become/get* here). Otherwise people use **become** or **get** again: *He eventually got better.*

GRAMMAR

**Become** is never followed by an infinitive though **come** can be: *After a while I came to like Chicago* (NOT *...became to like...*).

**be·com·ing** /bɪˈkʌmɪŋ/ *adj old-fashioned* **1** clothes that are becoming make you look attractive **2** words or actions that are becoming are suitable for you or for the situation you are in —**becomingly** *adv*

**bec·que·rel** /ˌbekəˈrel/ *n* [C] *technical* a unit for measuring RADIOACTIVITY (2)

**beds**

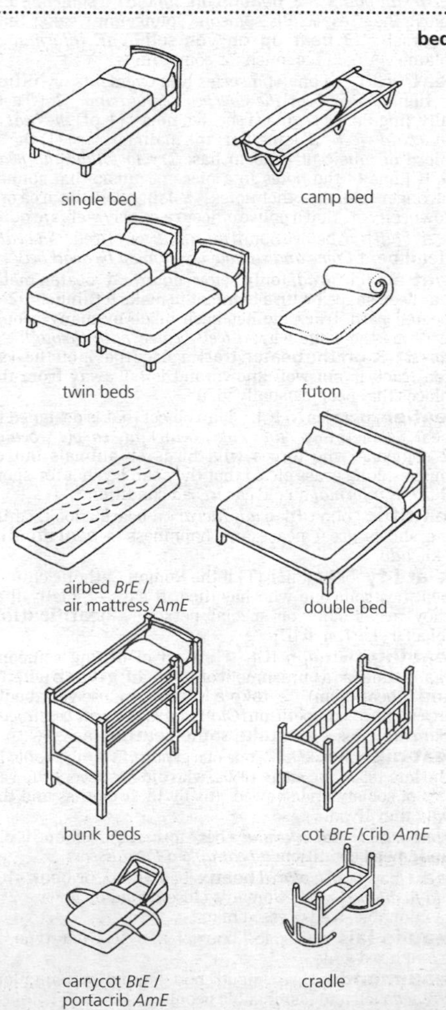

S1 W1 **bed¹** /bed/ *n*
**1 ▶ SLEEP ◀** [C,U] a piece of furniture for sleeping on: *a spare bed | a double bed* | **in bed** *Simon lay in bed reading for hours.* | **go to bed** *In the end, she went to bed without any fuss.* | **make the bed** (=tidy the bed covers) | **put sb to bed** *I'll just put the children to bed.* | **get (sb) out of bed** *Sorry for calling so early – I hope I didn't get you out of bed.* | **time for bed** (=time to go to sleep) | **take to your bed** *old-fashioned* (=stay in bed because you are ill)
**2 go to bed with** *informal* to have sex with someone
**3 get sb into bed** *informal* to persuade someone to have sex with you
**4 ▶ RIVER/LAKE/SEA ◀** [C] the flat ground at the bottom of a river, lake, or sea: *the sea bed*
**5 ▶ GARDEN ◀** [C] an area of a garden, park etc that has been prepared for plants to grow in: *rose beds*
**6 ▶ ROCK ◀** [C] a layer of rock —see also BEDROCK (2)
**7 ▶ BASE ◀** [singular] a layer of something that forms a base that other things are put on top of: [+ **of**] *The hut rests on a bed of concrete.* | *prawns on a bed of lettuce*
**8 oyster/coral etc bed** an area of the bottom of the sea where there are a lot of OYSTERS etc
**9 get out of bed (on) the wrong side** *BrE* **get up on the wrong side of the bed** *AmE* to feel slightly angry or annoyed for no particular reason
**10 not a bed of roses** not a happy, comfortable, or easy situation: *Life isn't always a bed of roses you know.*
**11 you've made your bed and you must lie on it** used to say that you must accept the bad results of your actions
**12 be brought to bed (of)** *old use* to give birth to a baby

**bed²** *v* [T] **1** *old-fashioned* to have sex with someone **2** also **bed out** to put plants into the ground so that they can grow **3** to fix something firmly onto or into a base: *The foundations were bedded in cement.*

**bed down** *phr v* **1** [T **bed** sb/sth ↔ **down**] to make a person or animal comfortable for the night **2** [I] to make yourself comfortable for the night: *Can I bed down on your sofa?*

**bed and board** /ˌ· · ˈ·/ *n* [U] food and a place to sleep

**bed and break·fast** /ˌ· · ˈ··/ *n* [C,U] a private house or small hotel where you can sleep and have breakfast, or this type of place; B AND B

**be·daub** /bɪˈdɔːb‖-ˈdɒːb/ *v* [T usually passive + **with**] *formal* to put paint, mud etc onto something in an untidy way

**be·daz·zle** /bɪˈdæzəl/ *v* [T] to make you think that someone or something is extremely impressive: *He is bedazzled by the status symbols of these crooks.*

**bed bath** /ˈ· ·/ *n* [C] a thorough body wash given to someone who cannot leave their bed

**bed·bug** /ˈbedbʌg/ *n* [C] an insect that sucks blood and lives in houses, especially in beds

**bed·cham·ber** /ˈbedˌtʃeɪmbə‖-ər/ *n* [C] *old-use* a bedroom

**bed·clothes** /ˈbedkləʊðz, -kləʊz‖-kloʊðz, -kloʊz/ *n* [plural] the sheets, covers etc that you put on a bed

**bed·ding** /ˈbedɪŋ/ *n* [U] **1** sheets, covers etc that you put on a bed **2** something soft for animals to sleep on, such as dried grass or STRAW (=dried corn stems)

**be·deck** /bɪˈdek/ *v* [T usually passive] *literary* to decorate something such as a building or street by hanging things all over it: *a balcony bedecked with hanging baskets*

**be·dev·il** /bɪˈdevəl/ *v* **bedevilled** *BrE* **bedeviled** *AmE* [T usually passive] *formal* to cause a lot of problems and difficulties for someone or something: *a society bedevilled by racial tensions* —**bedevilment** *n* [U]

**bed·fel·low** /ˈbedˌfeləʊ‖-loʊ/ *n* [C] **strange/odd/uneasy etc bedfellows** two or more people, ideas etc that are connected or working together in an unexpected way: *Politics and ecology often make uneasy bedfellows.*

**bed·head** /ˈbedhed/ *n* [C] the part of a bed that is behind your head when you are sitting up

**bed·lam** /ˈbedləm/ *n* [U] a wild noisy place or situation: *The courtroom erupted into bedlam as the judge delivered his verdict.*

**bed lin·en** /ˈ· ˌ··/ *n* [U] the sheets and PILLOWCASES for a bed

**Bed·ou·in** /ˈbeduɪn/ *n* [C] a member of an Arab tribe that traditionally lives in tents in the desert

**bed·pan** /ˈbedpæn/ *n* [C] a low wide container used as a toilet by someone who has to stay in bed

**bed·post** /ˈbedpəʊst‖-poʊst/ *n* [C] one of the four main supports at the corners of an old-fashioned bed

**be·drag·gled** /bɪˈdrægəld/ *adj* looking untidy and dirty, especially because you have been out in the rain: *She came in wet and bedraggled.*

**bed·rid·den** /ˈbedˌrɪdn/ *adj* unable to leave your bed, especially because you are old or ill

**bed·rock** /ˈbedrɒk‖-rɑːk/ *n* [U] **1** the basic ideas and principles of a belief etc: *Their determination to remain independent was the bedrock on which the war effort rested.* **2** solid rock in the ground on top of which all the soil rests

**bed·roll** /ˈbedrəʊl‖-roʊl/ *n* [C] *AmE* a number of blankets (BLANKET¹ (1) rolled together and used for sleeping outdoors

**bed·room¹** /ˈbedrʊm, -ruːm/ *n* [C] **1** a room for sleeping in: *a hotel with 50 bedrooms* **2 make/have bedroom eyes** to show that you are sexually attracted to someone S1 W2

**bed·room²** *adj* a bedroom SUBURB is a place from which people travel to a city to work every day; DORMITORY *BrE*

**bed·side** /ˈbedsaɪd/ *n* [C] the area around your bed: *Relatives have been at his bedside all week, hoping he will regain consciousness.* | **bedside lamp/table etc** (=next to your bed)

**bedside man·ner** /ˌ·· ˈ··/ *n* [singular] a doctor's bedside manner is the way that they talk to the people that they are treating

**bed·sit** /ˌbedˈsɪt/ also **bed·sit·ter** /-ˈsɪtə‖-ər/ **bed·sitting room** /ˌbedˈsɪtɪŋ rʊm, -ruːm/ *n* [C] *BrE* a rented room used for both living and sleeping in

**bed·sore** /ˈbedsɔː‖-sɔːr/ *n* [C] a sore place on your skin caused by lying in bed for a long time

**bed·spread** /ˈbedspred/ *n* [C] a decorative cover for a bed that goes on top of all the other covers

**bed·stead** /ˈbedsted/ *n* [C] the wooden or metal frame of a bed

**bed·time** /ˈbedtaɪm/ *n* [C,U] the time when you usually go to bed: *It's way past your bedtime!* | *a bedtime story*

**bed wet·ting** /ˈ· ˌ··/ *n* [U] the problem that some children have of passing URINE (=liquid from the body) while they are asleep —**bed-wetter** *n* [C]

**bee** /biː/ *n* [C] **1** a black and yellow flying insect with a round body that makes HONEY (1) and can sting you: *a swarm of bees* —see also BUMBLEBEE **2 a busy bee** *spoken* someone who enjoys being busy or active **3 have a bee in your bonnet** *informal* to think something is so important, so necessary etc that you keep mentioning it or thinking about it: *Dad's got a bee in his bonnet about saving electricity.* **4 think you're the bee's knees** *BrE spoken* used to describe someone who thinks they are very clever, very good at something etc: *She thinks she's the bee's knees around here.* **5 working/sewing etc bee** *AmE informal* an occasion when people, usually women, meet in order to do a particular type of work —see also SPELLING BEE, **the birds and the bees** (BIRD (3))

**Beeb** /biːb/ *n* **the Beeb** *spoken* the BBC

**beech** /biːtʃ/ *n* [C,U] a large tree with smooth grey BARK² (3) (=outer covering), or the wood from this tree

**beef¹** /biːf/ *n* **1** [U] the meat from a cow: *roast beef* **2** [C] *informal* a complaint: *OK, so what's the beef this time?* **3 where's the beef?** *spoken especially AmE* used when you think someone's words and promises sound good, but you want to know what they actually plan to do —see also BEEF TEA, CORNED BEEF S3

**beef²** *v* [I] *informal* to complain a lot: [+ **about**] *They're always beefing about something or other.*

**beef** sth ↔ **up** *phr v* [T] *informal* to improve

something or make it more interesting, more important etc: *a beefed up news story* | *We need to beef the campaign up a bit.*

**beef·bur·ger** /ˈbiːfbɜːgə‖-bɜːrgər/ *n* [C] *BrE* a flat, circular piece of BEEF[1] (1)

**beef·cake** /ˈbiːfkeɪk/ *n* [C,U] *informal* a strong attractive man with large muscles, or men like this in general —compare CHEESECAKE

**Beef·eat·er** /ˈbiːfˌiːtə‖-ər/ *n* [C] a ceremonial guard at the Tower of London

**beef·steak** /ˈbiːfsteɪk/ *n* [C,U] STEAK (1)

**beef tea** /ˌ· ˈ·/ *n* [U] a hot drink made from BEEF[1] (1) that used to be given to people when they were ill

**beef·y** /ˈbiːfi/ *adj informal* someone who is beefy is big, strong, and often quite fat

**bee·hive** /ˈbiːhaɪv/ *n* [C] **1** a structure where bees (BEE (1)) are kept for producing HONEY (1) **2** a way of arranging a woman's hair in a high pile on the top of her head, which was popular in the 1960s

**bee·line** /ˈbiːlaɪn/ *n* **make a beeline for** *informal* to go quickly and directly towards someone or something: *Rob always makes a beeline for beautiful women at parties.*

**been** /biːn, bɪn‖bɪn/ **1** the past participle of BE **2 have/has been a)** used to say that someone has gone to a place and come back: [+ **to**] *I've never been to Japan.* | **have been to do sth** *Have you been to see the Van Gogh exhibition yet?* **b)** *BrE* used to say that someone has come to a place and left again: *The postman hasn't been yet.* —see GO[1] (USAGE) **3 been there, done that** *spoken* used to say that you are no longer interested in doing something, because you already have a lot of experience of it

**beep**[1] /biːp/ *v* **1** [I] if a machine beeps, it makes a short high sound: *Why does the computer keep beeping?* **2** [I,T] if a car horn beeps or you make it beep, it makes a loud noise

**beep**[2] *n* [C] **1** a short high sound made by an electronic machine: *Leave your message after the beep.* **2** the sound of a car horn: *Look, there's Jan. Give her a beep.*

**beep·er** /ˈbiːpə‖-ər/ *n* [C] a small machine that you carry with you, that makes short high electronic sounds to tell you that you must telephone someone; BLEEPER, PAGER

S2 W3 **beer** /bɪə‖bɪr/ *n* **1** [U] an alcoholic drink made from MALT[1] (3) and hops (HOP[2] (4)): *a pint of beer* | *home-brewed beer* **2** [C] a glass, bottle, or can of beer: *Do you fancy a beer?* **3 not all beer and skittles** *BrE old-fashioned* not just full of pleasure and enjoyment, but involving problems as well —**beery** *adj*

**beer bel·ly** /ˈ· ·ˌ·/ also **beer gut** /ˈ· ·/ *n* [C] an unattractive fat stomach caused by drinking too much beer

**beer mat** /ˈ· ·/ *n* [C] a small circle of card that you put under a glass, especially in a bar

**bees·wax** /ˈbiːzwæks/ *n* [U] **1** a substance produced by bees (BEE (1)), especially for making furniture polish and CANDLES **2 none of your beeswax** *AmE spoken* used to tell someone that what they have asked you is private or personal

**beet** /biːt/ *n* [C,U] **1** also **sugar beet** a vegetable that sugar is made from **2** *AmE* a plant with a round dark red root that you cook and eat as a vegetable; beetroot *BrE* **3 red as a beet** *AmE informal* having a red face, especially because you are embarrassed

**bee·tle**[1] /ˈbiːtl/ *n* [C] one of many types of insect with a round hard, usually black, back

**beetle**[2] *v* [I always + adv/prep] *BrE informal* to go somewhere quickly, especially because you are trying not to be noticed: *He went beetling off down the corridor.*

**beet·root** /ˈbiːtruːt/ *n* [C,U] **1** *BrE* a plant with a round dark red root that you cook and eat as a vegetable; beet *AmE* —see picture on page 414 **2 go beetroot** *BrE informal* to become red in the face, especially because you are embarrassed

**be·fall** /bɪˈfɔːl‖-ˈfɒːl/ *v past tense* **befell** /-ˈfel/ *past participle* **befallen** /-ˈfɔːlən‖-ˈfɒː-/ [T] *formal* if something unpleasant or dangerous befalls you it happens to you: *We prayed that no harm should befall them.*

**be·fit** /bɪˈfɪt/ *v past tense and past participle* **befitted** [T] *formal* to be proper or suitable for someone: *The chairman travelled club class, as befitted his status.* —**befitting** *adj* —**befittingly** *adv*

**before**[1] /bɪˈfɔː‖-ˈfɔːr/ *conjunction* **1** earlier than the time when something happens: *Say goodbye before you go.* | *It will be sometime before we know the full results.* **2** so that something bad does not happen: *Put that money somewhere safe before it gets stolen.* | *That dog ought to be destroyed before it attacks any more children.* **3** used to say that your are willing to suffer or do something unpleasant rather than do something that you do not want to do: *He will die before he tells them what they want to know.* **4 before you know it** *spoken* used to say that something will happen very soon: *We'd better set off or it will be dark before we know it.* **5** used to warn someone not to laugh at, criticize etc someone or something because they have faults and weaknesses themselves: *Before the chairman starts attacking committee members he ought to remember his own mistakes.* **6** used to warn someone that you will do something unpleasant or harmful to them if they do not do something: *Get out before I call the police.* S1 W1

**be·fore**[2] *prep* **1** earlier than something: *I usually take a shower before having my breakfast.* | *The new road should be completed before the end of the year.* | *He arrived home before me.* | *the day before yesterday* (=two days ago) —see FRONT[1] (USAGE) **2** ahead of someone or something else in a list or order: *I think you were before me in the queue.* **3** in the same place, or in front of a person or crowd of people: *Italy will face Brazil this afternoon before a crowd of 100,000 spectators.* **4** if something such as a report or evidence is put before a person or group of people they must consider it and make a decision about it: *The proposal was put before the planning committee.* **5** if one quality or person comes before another, it is more important than it: *I put my wife and kids before anyone else.* | *Quality must come before quantity in my opinion.* **6** *formal* in front of: *The priest stood before the altar.* | *The great plain stretched out before them.* **7** if one place is before another place it is a particular distance in front of that place as you travel towards it: *The pub is 100m before the church on the right.* **8** *formal* if there is a job or situation before you, you have to do the job or face the situation soon: *The task of emptying the house lay before us.* **9** *formal* if a period of time is before you it is about to start and you can do what you want during it: *We had a glorious summer afternoon before us to do as we pleased.* **10** *formal* if you show a particular reaction before someone or something you react in that way: *She trembled before the prospect of meeting him again.*

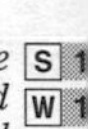

**before**[3] *adv* **1** at an earlier time: *Haven't we met before?* | *I thought she might take notice of what I said but she just carries on as before.* | **the day/week/month before** *Last week she was in Paris, and the week before she was in Rome.* | **before long** *I expect the bus will be here before long.* | *The kids were playing in the mud and before long they were covered in it.* **2** *old use* ahead of someone or something else: *The king's herald walked before.*

**be·fore·hand** /bɪˈfɔːhænd‖-ˈfɔːr-/ *adv* before something else has happened or is done: *The police need to be briefed beforehand on how to deal with this sort of situation.* | *When you give a speech, it's natural to feel nervous beforehand.* S3

**be·friend** /bɪˈfrend/ *v* [T] *formal* to behave in a friendly way towards someone, especially someone who is younger or needs help: *They befriended me when I first arrived in London as a student.*

**be·fud·dled** /bɪˈfʌdəld/ *adj* completely confused: *I felt befuddled by all these changes.*

**beg** /beg/ *v*

**1 I beg your pardon** *spoken* **a)** used to say sorry when you have made a mistake, or said something wrong or embarrassing: *Oh, I beg your pardon. I thought you meant next Tuesday.* **b)** used to show that you strongly disagree with something that someone has said, or think it is unacceptable: *"Chicago's an awful place." "I beg your pardon, that's where I'm from!"* **c)** used to ask someone to repeat what they have just said: *"The meeting's on Wednesday." "I beg your pardon." "I said the meeting's on Wednesday."*

**2 ▶ASK◀** [I,T] to ask for something in an anxious or urgent way, because you want it very much: *She begged and pleaded with them until they finally gave in.* | **beg (sb) to do sth** *The children begged to come with us.* | *I begged Helen to stay but she wouldn't listen.* | **beg (sb) for sth** *I'm begging you for help, Greg.* | **beg forgiveness/a favour/mercy etc** *Can I beg a favour?* | **beg leave to do sth** *formal* (=ask permission to do something)

**3 ▶MONEY/FOOD◀** [I,T] to ask people to give you food, money etc because you are very poor: *a begging letter* | **beg from sb** *a ragged child begging from passing shoppers* | **beg (for) sth** *They were reduced to begging food in the streets.* | **beg sth off sb** *spoken*: *Can I beg a cigarette off you?*

**4 I beg to differ** *spoken formal* to say firmly that you do not agree with something that has been said: *I must beg to differ on this point.*

**5 beg the question** to discuss something in a way that makes it seem that a fact is definitely true when in fact it may not be: *This planning proposal begs the question whether we need more sports facilities at all.*

**6 be going begging** *spoken* if something is going begging, it is available for anyone who wants it: *There's a bottle of wine going begging if anyone's interested.*

**7 ▶DOG◀** [I] if a dog begs, it sits up with its front legs off the ground

**beg off** *phr v* [I] to say that you cannot do something that you had agreed to do: *I'm sorry, but I'm going to have to beg off from the game tonight.*

**be·get** /bɪˈget/ *v past tense and past participle* **begot** /-ˈgɒt‖-ˈgɑːt/ *or past tense* **begat** /-ˈgæt/ *past participle* **begotten** /-ˈgɒtn‖-ˈgɑːtn/ [T] *formal* **1** *old use* to become the father of a child **2** to cause something or make it happen: *Hunger begets crime.*

**beg·gar¹** /ˈbegə‖-ər/ *n* [C] **1** someone who lives by asking people for food and money: *There's been a huge increase in the number of beggars on London's streets.* **2 lucky/lazy/cheeky etc beggar** *BrE spoken* used to describe someone who you think is lucky, lazy etc, in a friendly way: *You lazy little beggar!* | *"How's Dave?" "The lucky beggar's in the south of France!"* **3 beggars can't be choosers** used to say that when you have no money, no power to choose etc, you have to accept whatever is available

**beggar²** *v* [T] **1 beggar description/belief etc** *formal* to be impossible to describe, believe etc: *The scenery was so beautiful that it beggared description.* **2** *formal* to make someone very poor: *Drought combined with falling prices to beggar whole communities of farmers.*

**beg·gar·ly** /ˈbegəli‖-ərli/ *adj literary* a beggarly amount of money is far too small

**beggar-my-neigh·bour** /ˌ‥ · ˈ‥/ *n* [U] a card game in which the aim is to get all your opponent's cards

**beg·gar·y** /ˈbegəri/ *n* [U] *formal* the state of being very poor: *The failure of their farm reduced them to beggary.*

S1 W1 **be·gin** /bɪˈgɪn/ *past tense* **began** /-ˈgæn/ *past participle* **begun** /-ˈgʌn/ *v*

**1 ▶START DOING/FEELING◀** [I,T] to start doing something or start feeling a particular way: **begin to do sth** *We began to wonder if the train would ever arrive.* | **begin** *I'll begin when you're ready.* | **begin sth** *She curled up in bed and began her book.* | **begin doing sth** *I left teaching in 1990 and began working in my present job.* | **begin by doing sth** (=do or say something as the first part of an activity) *Can I begin by thanking you all for being here tonight?*

**2 ▶START HAPPENING◀** [I,T] if something begins, or you begin something, it starts to happen or exist: *Work on the new bridge will begin next year.* | *It was the coldest winter since records began.* | [+ **at**] *The meeting begins at 10.30 am.* | **begin (sth) as** *Roger began his career as a model.*

**3 to begin with a)** *especially spoken* used to introduce the first or most important point that you want to make: *Well, to begin with, he shouldn't even have been driving my car.* **b)** used to say that something was already in a particular condition before something else happened: *I didn't break it! It was like that to begin with.* **c)** during the first part of a process or activity: *The kids helped me to begin with, but they soon got bored.* —see FIRSTLY (USAGE)

**4 ▶SPEECH/BOOK◀** [I] if a speech, book, word etc begins with something, it starts with a particular event, activity, letter etc: [+ **with**] *'Psychosis' begins with a P.*

**5 can't begin to understand/imagine etc** *spoken* used to emphasize how difficult something is to understand etc: *I can't begin to imagine how awful it must be to lose your child.*

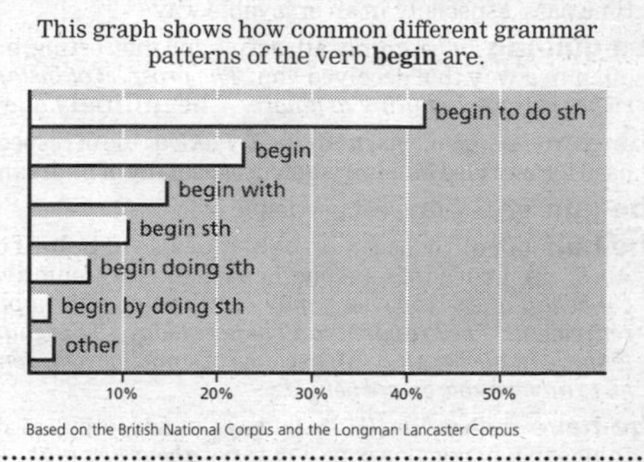


**be·gin·ner** /bɪˈgɪnə‖-ər/ *n* [C] **1** someone who has just started to do or learn something: *an absolute beginner* **2 beginner's luck** unusual success that you have when you start something new

**be·gin·ning** /bɪˈgɪnɪŋ/ *n* [C usually singular] **1** the start or first part of an event, story, period of time etc: [+ **of**] *It will be ready at the beginning of next week.* | *The beginning of the film is very violent.* | **in/at/from the beginning** (=at or from the time when a situation, process etc begins) *We pay our rent at the beginning of every month.* | *I said he would be trouble, right from the beginning.* | **from beginning to end** *The whole trip was a disaster from beginning to end.* —see FIRSTLY (USAGE) **2 beginnings** [plural] the early part or early signs of something that later develops and becomes bigger, more important etc: *the beginnings of the capitalist system* | **from small/humble beginnings** *From humble beginnings in Atlanta, it had developed into a multinational corporation.* **3 the beginning of the end** the time when something good starts to end or become less good S1 W2

**USAGE NOTE: BEGINNING**

WORD CHOICE: **at the beginning of**, **in the beginning**

Something that happens at the very start of an event or period of time happens **at the beginning of** it: *At the beginning of the Civil War Fort Sumter was attacked* (NOT *in the beginning* of it). | *There's a car chase at the beginning* (=at the start of the film).

If something happens **in the beginning** (not usually with *of*) it happens during a period of time near the start of an event or longer period of time: *In the beginning the South had some success* (=during the early part of the Civil War). | *I was too shy to speak to her in the beginning* (=the first few times I saw her).

SPELLING

Remember there are two 'n's in **beginning**.

**be·gone** /bɪˈgɒn‖bɪˈgɒːn/ *interjection old use* used to tell someone to go away

**be·go·ni·a** /bɪˈgəʊniə‖-ˈgoʊ-/ *n* [C] a plant with yellow, pink, red, or white flowers

**be·got** /bɪˈgɒt‖bɪˈgɑːt/ the past tense of BEGET

**be·got·ten** /bɪˈgɒtn‖bɪˈgɑːtn/ the past participle of BEGET

**B**

**be·grudge** /bɪˈgrʌdʒ/ *v* [T] **1** to feel JEALOUS of someone because they have something which you think they do not deserve: **begrudge sb sth** *We shouldn't begrudge her this success.* **2** to feel annoyed or unhappy that you have to pay something, give someone something etc: **begrudge sb sth** *Surely you don't begrudge him the money for his education?* | **begrudge doing sth** *I begrudge spending so much money on train fares.*

**be·guile** /bɪˈgaɪl/ *v* [T] **1** to persuade or trick someone into doing something, especially by saying nice things to them: *Carr beguiled the voters with his good looks and grand talk.* **2** *literary* to do something that makes the time pass, especially in an enjoyable way

**be·guil·ing** /bɪˈgaɪlɪŋ/ *adj* attractive and interesting, but often in a way that deceived you: *The prospect of instant riches was too beguiling to ignore.* —**beguilingly** *adv*

**be·gum** /ˈbeɪgəm, ˈbiː-/ *n* [C] *IndE, PakE* a title of respect, used for married Muslim women, especially of high rank

**be·gun** /bɪˈgʌn/ the past participle of BEGIN

**be·half** /bɪˈhɑːf‖bɪˈhæf/ *n* **on behalf of** also **in behalf of** *AmE* **a)** instead of someone, or as their representative: *On behalf of everyone here, may I wish you a very happy retirement.* | *The President can't be here today, so I'm going to speak in his behalf.* **b)** because of someone: *Oh, don't go to any trouble on my behalf.*

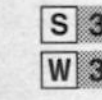
**be·have** /bɪˈheɪv/ *v* [I] **1** [always + adv/prep] to do things in a particular way: *I'm sorry about last night – I behaved like a child.* **2** also **behave yourself** to behave in a way that people think is good or correct, by being polite and obeying people, not causing trouble etc: *Will you children please behave!* | *Did Peter behave himself while I was away?* | **well-behaved/badly-behaved** *a badly-behaved class* —opposite MISBEHAVE **3** [I] to do something according to natural laws: *Quantum mechanics is the study of the way atoms behave.*

**be·hav·iour** *BrE*, **behavior** *AmE* /bɪˈheɪvjə‖-ər/ *n* [U] **1** the way that someone behaves: *Can TV violence cause aggressive behavior?* | **good/bad behaviour** *The headmaster will not tolerate bad behaviour in class.* | [+ **towards**] *Her father's behavior towards him was irrational.* **2 be on your best behaviour** to behave as well and politely as you can, especially in order to please someone: *I want you both to be on your best behaviour at Grandad's.* **3** the way that an object, animal, substance etc normally behaves: *studying the behavior of the AIDS virus* —**behavioural** *adj*: *behavioural science* —**behaviourally** *adv*

**be·hav·iour·is·m** *BrE*, **behaviorism** *AmE* /bɪˈheɪvjərɪzəm/ *n* [U] *technical* the belief that the scientific study of the mind should be based only on people's behaviour, not on what they say about their thoughts and feelings —**behaviourist** *n* [C]

**be·head** /bɪˈhed/ *v* [T] to cut off someone's head as a punishment: *Charles I was beheaded in 1649.*

**be·he·moth** /bɪˈhiːmɒθ‖-mɑːθ/ *n* [C] *literary* something that is very large: *five warships, including two 64,000-ton behemoths*

**be·hest** /bɪˈhest/ *n* [singular] **at the behest of** *formal* because someone has requested or ordered it

S1 W1 **be·hind¹** /bɪˈhaɪnd/ *prep* **1** at or towards the back of something: *The cat ran out from behind a tree.* | *I got stuck behind a truck all the way to the airport.* | *Jane shut the door behind her.* —see FRONT¹ (USAGE) **2** not as successful or advanced as someone or something else: *We're three points behind the other team.* | *Mark's always behind the rest of his class in mathematics.* | **behind schedule** (=not arriving or not ready at the right time) *The new building is already three months behind schedule.* **3 what's behind sth** being the secret or hidden reason for something: *I wonder what's behind this sudden change of plan.* **4** supporting a person, idea etc: *The workers are very much behind these proposals.* | **behind sb/sth all the way** (=supporting someone or something totally) *We're behind you all the way on this one.* **5** responsible for a plan, idea etc or for organizing something: *The police say that organized groups of children are behind the recent spate of thefts.* | *The Rotary Club is behind the fund-raising for the new hospital.* **6** if an unpleasant experience or situation is behind you it no longer upsets you or affects your life: *Now you can put all these worries behind you.* **7** if you have experience behind you, you have learnt valuable skills or got important qualities that can be used: *Marjorie's got ten years of experience as a social worker behind her.* **8** if a quality or attitude is behind an appearance you think that it exists in spite of being hidden: *She suspected that a certain cynicism lay behind his cheerful exterior.* —see also **behind sb's back** (BACK¹ (11)), **behind bars** (BAR² (14))

**behind²** *adv* **1** at or towards the back or something: *an enormous desk with an old man sitting behind* | *The house has a huge garden behind.* | **close behind/not far behind** *The motorcyclists came first, with the President's car following close behind.* **2 be/get behind** to be late or slow in doing something: *This work should have been finished yesterday; I'm getting terribly behind.* | **behind with** *We're already three months behind with the rent.* **3 stay/remain behind** to stay in a place when other people have left it or gone somewhere else: *I decided to stay behind and look after the baby.* **4 leave sth behind** to leave something in a place where you were before **5 fall behind** to be less successful than other people S W

**behind³** *n* [C] *informal* a word meaning BOTTOM¹ (7), sometimes used when you want to avoid saying this directly

**be·hind·hand** /bɪˈhaɪndhænd/ *adv* [+ **with, in**] *formal* late or slow in doing something or paying a debt

**be·hold** /bɪˈhəʊld‖-ˈhoʊld/ *v past tense and past participle* **beheld** /bɪˈheld/ [T] *literary or old use* to see or to look at something —see also LO AND BEHOLD —**beholder** *n* [C]

**be·hold·en** /bɪˈhəʊldn‖-ˈhoʊl-/ *adj* **feel/be beholden to** to feel that you have a duty to someone because they have done something for you: *I hate feeling beholden to anyone.*

**be·hove** /bɪˈhəʊv‖bɪˈhoʊv/ *BrE*, **be·hoove** /bɪˈhuːv/ *AmE v* **it behoves you to do sth** *formal* you should do something because it is right or necessary or it will help you in some way

**beige** /beɪʒ/ *n* [U] a pale dull yellowish brown colour —**beige** *adj* —see picture on page 411

**be·ing¹** /ˈbiːɪŋ/ *v* **1** the present participle of BE **2** used in explanations: *Being a quiet sort of fellow, I didn't want to get involved.* | *You can't expect them just to ignore it, human nature being what it is.* **3 being as** *spoken especially BrE* because; as: *He wasn't that keen to drive, being as he'd had a few drinks.*

**being²** *n* **1 come into being/be brought into being** to begin to exist: *a society that first came into being in 1912* **2** [C] a living thing, especially a person: *a human being* | *strange beings from outer space* **3** [U] *literary* the most important quality or nature of something, especially of a person: **the core/roots/whole of sb's being** *The music seemed to touch the whole of her being.*

**be·jew·elled** *BrE*, **bejeweled** *AmE* /bɪˈdʒuːəld/ *adj* wearing jewels or decorated with jewels: *a bejewelled tiara*

**be·la·bour** *BrE*, **belabor** *AmE* /bɪˈleɪbə‖-ər/ *v* [T] **1 belabour the point** to emphasize an idea or fact too strongly, especially by repeating it many times **2** to attack or criticize someone or something severely **3** *old use* to beat someone or something hard

**be·lat·ed** /bɪˈleɪtɪ̆d/ *adj* happening or arriving late: *belated birthday greetings* —**belatedly** *adv*

**be·lay** /bɪˈleɪ/ *v* [I,T] *technical* to fix a rope on a ship by winding it under and over in the shape of a figure 8 on a special hook

**belch** /beltʃ/ *v* **1** [I] to let air from your stomach come out noisily through your mouth: *He took a mouthful and belched loudly.* —see also BURP[1] **2** [I] to give or send out large amounts of smoke, fire etc: *Blue smoke belched from the car's exhaust pipe* —**belch** *n* [C]

**be·lea·guered** /bɪˈliːgəd‖-ərd/ *adj formal* **1** having many difficulties, especially because everyone is criticizing you or causing trouble for you: *beleaguered parents trying to discipline their children* **2** surrounded by an army and unable to escap;

**bel·fry** /ˈbelfri/ *n* a tower for a bell, especially on a church —see also **have bats in the belfry** (BAT[1] (8))

**Bel·gian[1]** /ˈbeldʒən/ *n* [U] someone from Belgium

**Belgian[2]** *adj* from or connected with Belgium

**be·lie** /bɪˈlaɪ/ *v* [T] *formal* **1** to give someone a false idea about something: *Her pleasant manner belied her true character.* **2** to show that your words, hopes etc are false or mistaken: *Two large tears belied Rosalie's brave words.*

S3 W2 **be·lief** /bɪ̆ˈliːf/ *n* **1** [singular, U] the feeling that something is definitely true or definitely exists: *religious belief* | [+ **in**] *a belief in God* | [+ **that**] *a growing belief that war had become inevitable* | **it is sb's belief that** *It is my belief that racism remains widespread in British society.* | **in the belief that** (=because you think something is true) *She started taking money, in the mistaken belief that she would not be discovered.* | **contrary to popular belief** (=although most people believe the opposite of this) *Contrary to popular belief, eating carrots does not improve your eyesight.* **2** [C] an idea that you believe to be true, especially one that forms part of a system of ideas: *political beliefs* | **hold a belief** (=have a belief) *Some of them hold very right-wing beliefs.* **3** [singular] the feeling that something is good and can be trusted: [+ **in**] *If you're selling, you have to have genuine belief in the product.* | **shake sb's belief in** (=make them doubt what they believe) *The judge's decision shook my belief in the legal system.* **4 be beyond belief** to seem too strange or unreasonable to be true: *These latest proposals are beyond belief!* —see also **to the best of your belief** (BEST[3] (4)) —compare DISBELIEF, UNBELIEF

**be·li·eva·ble** /bɪ̆ˈliːvəbəl/ *adj* something that is believable can be believed because it seems possible, likely, or real: *What I like about the book is that the characters are all very believable.* —**believably** *adv*

S1 W1 **be·lieve** /bɪ̆ˈliːv/ *v* [not in progressive]
**1 ▶ BE SURE STH IS TRUE ◀** [T] to be sure that something is true or that someone is telling the truth: *You shouldn't believe everything you read.* | **believe (that)** *I can hardly believe he's only 25!* | **believe sb** *I don't believe her – it can't be true.* | **believe sth of sb** *Stealing? I would never have believed it of him!* | **not believe a word of it** *spoken* (=not believe something at all)
**2 can't/don't believe** *spoken* used to say that you are very surprised or shocked by something: *It's still raining – I don't believe it!* | *I can't believe he's expecting us to work on Sunday as well!* | *My mum couldn't believe it when I dyed my hair green.*
**3 believe it or not** *spoken* used when you are going to say something that is true but surprising: *Well, believe it or not, they've given me a loan.*
**4 would you believe it!** *spoken* used when you are surprised or angry about something: *And then he just walked out. Would you believe it!*
**5 believe (you) me** *spoken* used to emphasize that something is definitely true: *There'll be trouble when they find out about this, believe you me!*
**6 you'd better believe it!** *spoken* used to emphasize that something is true
**7 don't you believe it!** *spoken* used to emphasize that something is definitely not true
**8 can't believe your eyes/ears** *spoken* to be very surprised by something you see or hear: *I could hardly believe my eyes when he took a gun out of his pocket.*
**9 if you believe that, you'll believe anything** *spoken* used to say that something is definitely not true, and that anyone who believes it must be stupid
**10 ▶ HAVE AN OPINION ◀** [T] to think that something is true, although you are not completely sure: **believe (that)** *I believe you two have met already.* | **believe so/not** (=think that something is true or not) *"Have they arrived yet?" "Yes, I believe so."* | **believe sb to be sth** *The jury believed Beyers to be innocent.* | **be widely believed** (=a lot of people believe this) *They are widely believed to be planning a takeover bid.* | **have reason to believe (that)** (=have information that makes you believe something) *We have reason to believe that she knew the victim quite well.*
**11 seeing is believing** *usually spoken* used to say that you will only believe that something happens or exists when you actually see it
**12 ▶ RELIGION ◀** [I] to have a strong religious faith: *She says that those who believe will go to heaven.* —see also **make believe** (MAKE[1] (19))

**believe in** *phr v* [T] **1** to be sure that someone exists: *Do you believe in God?* | *It's amazing how many people believe in ghosts.* **2** to support or approve of something because you think it is good or right: *I don't believe in all these silly diets.* | **believe in doing sth** *They believe in letting children make their own mistakes.* **3** [T **believe in** sb] to be confident that someone can be trusted: *The people want a President they can believe in.* | *You've got to believe in yourself, or you'll never succeed.*

**be·liev·er** /bɪ̆ˈliːvə‖-ər/ *n* [C] **1** someone who believes in a particular god, religion, or system of beliefs **2 be a (great) believer in** to believe strongly that something is good and brings good results: *I'm a great believer in co-ed schools.*

**Be·li·sha bea·con** /bəˌliːʃə ˈbiːkən/ *n* [C] one of two posts with a round flashing orange light on the top that stand by some road crossings in Britain

**be·lit·tle** /bɪˈlɪtl/ *v* [T] *formal* to make someone or something seem small or unimportant: *He tends to belittle his own efforts.*

**bell** /bel/ *n* [C] **1** a piece of electrical equipment that makes a ringing sound, used as a signal or to get someone's attention: *The door bell rang but no-one answered it.* | *Ring the bell once to make the bus stop.* —see picture at BICYCLE[1] **2** [usually singular] the sound of a bell ringing as a signal or a warning: *I didn't hear the bell, did you?* | **the bell goes** (=makes a noise) *The bell for the end of school went at 3.30.* **3** a hollow metal object shaped rather like a cup, that makes a ringing sound when it is hit by a piece of metal that hangs down inside it: *church bells* **4 give sb a bell** *BrE spoken* to telephone someone: *I must give Vicky a bell later.* **5** something in the shape of a bell, hollow and getting wider at the end: *the bell of a flower* —see also DIVING BELL, **ring a bell** (RING[2] (4)), **as clear as a bell** (CLEAR[1] (10)), **as sound as a bell** (SOUND[3] (5)) S2 W3

**bel·la·don·na** /ˌbeləˈdɒnə‖-ˈdɑːnə/ *n* [U] **1** a poisonous plant; DEADLY NIGHTSHADE **2** a substance from this plant, used as a drug

**bell-bot·toms** /ˈ· ˌ··/ *n* [plural] trousers with legs that become wider at the bottom

**bell·boy** /ˈbelbɔɪ/ *n* [C] *BrE* a young man who carries bags, takes messages etc in a hotel; BELLHOP *AmE*

**belle** /bel/ *n* [C] *old-fashioned* a beautiful girl or woman: **the belle of the ball** (=the most beautiful girl at a dance or party)

**belles-let·tres** /ˌbel ˈletrə/ *n* [U] *French* literature or writings about literary subjects

**bell·hop** /ˈbelhɒp‖-hɑːp/ *n* [C] *AmE* a young man who carries bags, takes messages etc in a hotel; BELLBOY *BrE*

**bel·li·cose** /ˈbelɪkəʊs‖-koʊs/ *adj literary* always wanting to fight or argue; AGGRESSIVE (1) —**bellicosity** *n* [U]

**bel·lig·er·ent** /bə̇ˈlɪdʒərənt/ *adj* **1** very unfriendly and unpleasant: *a belligerent attitude* **2** [only before noun] *formal* a belligerent country is at war with another country —**belligerence, belligerency** *n* [U]

**bel·low¹** /ˈbeləʊ‖-loʊ/ *v* **1** [I,T] to shout loudly, especially in a low voice: *Tony bellowed instructions from an upstairs window.* **2** [I] to make the deep hollow sound that a BULL¹ (1, 2) makes

**bellow²** *n* **1** [C] the deep hollow sound that a BULL¹ (1, 2) makes **2 bellows** [plural] **a)** an object that you use to blow air into a fire **b)** part of a musical instrument, such as an ORGAN (2), that uses air to produce sound

**bell pep·per** /ˈ· ˌ··/ *n* [C] *AmE* a hollow red, green, or yellow vegetable; PEPPER¹ (3) *BrE*, CAPSICUM

**bell-ring·er** /ˈ· ˌ··/ *n* [C] someone who rings church bells, usually as part of a team —**bell-ringing** *n* [U]

S3 **bel·ly¹** /ˈbeli/ *n* [C]
**1** ▶ **PERSON** ◀ **a)** your stomach: *a full belly* **b)** *BrE* the part of your body between your chest and your legs; ABDOMEN (1): *She lay on her belly in the long grass.*
**2** ▶ **ANIMAL** ◀ the underneath of an animal's body —see picture at HORSE¹
**3** ▶ **OBJECT** ◀ a curved or rounded part of an object: *the belly of a plane* —see also POTBELLY

**belly²** *v*
**belly out** *phr v* [I,T **belly** sth ↔ **out**] to swell or become full, or to make something do this: *The sails bellied out in the wind.*

**bel·ly·ache¹** /ˈbeli-eɪk/ *n* [C,U] a pain in your stomach

**bellyache²** *v* [I] *informal* to complain a lot, especially about something unimportant: [+ **about**] *Stop bellyaching about it and get on with the job!*

**belly but·ton** /ˈ·· ˌ··/ *n* [C] *informal* the small round mark in the middle of your stomach; NAVEL

**belly dance** /ˈ··· ·/ *n* [C] a dance from the Middle East performed by a woman using movements of her BELLY¹ (1) and hips (HIP¹ (1)) —**belly dancer** *n* [C]

**belly flop** /ˈ·· ·/ *n* [C] a way of jumping into water, in which the front of your body falls flat against the surface of the water —**bellyflop** *v* [I]

**bel·ly·ful** /ˈbelifʊl/ *n* **have had a bellyful of** *informal* to be annoyed by something because you have heard or experienced too much of it: *I've had a bellyful of your complaints.*

**belly-land·ing** /ˈ·· ˌ··/ *n* [C] the act of landing a plane without using special equipment

**belly laugh** /ˈ·· ·/ *n* [C] *informal* a deep loud laugh

S2 W2 **be·long** /bɪˈlɒŋ‖bɪˈlɔːŋ/ *v* [I] **1** [always + adv/prep] to be in the right place or situation: *Put that chair back where it belongs.* | *Wild animals like this don't belong in a zoo – they should be allowed to go free.* **2** to feel happy and comfortable in a place or situation, because you have the same interests and ideas as other people
**belong to** *phr v* [T] **1** to be the property of: *The house belonged to my grandfather.* | *Who does this scarf belong to?* **2** to be a member of a group or organization: *Do you belong to the tennis club?* | *They were suspected of belonging to a terrorist organization.* **3** to be connected with or form part of: *The film belongs to a rich comic tradition.* | *He belongs to a different generation.*

**be·long·ings** /bɪˈlɒŋɪŋz‖bɪˈlɔːŋ-/ *n* [plural] the things that you own, especially those that you can carry with you: *Please ensure that you have all your belongings when you leave the train.*

**be·lov·ed** /bɪˈlʌvə̇d/ *adj literary or humorous* **1** a beloved place, thing etc is one that you love very much: *She returned at last to her beloved country.* | *He's always talking about his beloved computer!* | [+ **of/by**] *a slogan much beloved of politicians* **2 my/her etc beloved** the person that you love most: *It was a gift from my beloved.* —see also **dearly beloved** (DEARLY (4))

**be·low¹** /bɪˈləʊ‖-ˈloʊ/ *prep* **1** in a lower place or position than, or on a lower level than: *I'd like you to trim my hair just below the ears.* | *Fish were swimming below the surface of the water.* —see picture on page 1257 —see UNDER¹ (USAGE) **2** less than a particular number, amount, level etc: *These families are living below the official poverty line.* | *Bank charges rose at a level slightly below that of inflation.* | **well/way below** (=very much lower than) *Sales figures for January were well below target.* | **below average** (=not as good as the normal standard) *Tom's spelling is well below average.* | **below freezing** (=if the temperature is below freezing it is less than zero degrees) **3** in a lower, less important job than someone else: *A captain is below a general.* S2 W2

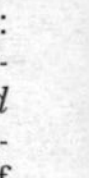

**below²** *adv* **1** in a lower place or position, or on a lower level: *We looked down from the mountain at the valley below.* | *Jim lives on the fourth floor and Jean-Pierre is on the floor below.* **2** on the lower level of a ship or boat: *The Captain told the crew to go below.* **3** less than a particular number, age, price etc: *Children of three and below pay half fare.* **4 10°/15°/20° below etc** if a temperature is 10°, 15°, 20° below etc, it is that number of degrees lower than zero **5** mentioned or shown lower on the same page or on a later page: *See p. 85 below.* | *The information below was compiled by our correspondent.* **6** in a lower, less important rank or job: *officers of the rank of captain and below* **7** *literary* on Earth rather than in Heaven S2 W2

**belt¹** /belt/ *n* [C] S2 W3
**1** ▶ **CLOTHES** ◀ a band of leather, cloth etc that you wear around your waist —see picture on page 840
**2** ▶ **AREA** ◀ a large area of land that has particular characteristics: *America's farming belt* | *the commuter belt* —see also GREEN BELT
**3** ▶ **MACHINE PART** ◀ a circular band of material such as rubber that connects or moves parts of a machine —see also CONVEYOR BELT, FAN BELT
**4 below the belt** *informal* a remark or criticism that is below the belt is unfair or cruel: *That was a bit below the belt, Paul.*
**5 have/get sth under your belt** to have achieved something useful or important: *You need some work experience under your belt.*
**6 (at) full belt** *spoken* moving as quickly as possible: *Willy was off down the road at full belt.*
**7 give sb a belt** *spoken* to hit someone hard —see also CHASTITY BELT, GARTER BELT, SUSPENDER BELT, **tighten your belt** (TIGHTEN (6))

**belt²** *v informal* **1** [T] to hit someone or something hard: *Dan belted the ball at goal.* **2** [I always + adv/prep] *BrE* to travel very fast: [+ **down/along etc**] *We were belting down the motorway at 90 miles per hour.*
**belt** sth ↔ **out** *phr v* [T] *informal* to sing a song or play an instrument loudly: *She was belting out old Broadway favourites.*
**belt up** *phr v* [I] *BrE spoken* used to tell someone rudely to be quiet: *Belt up, for Christ's sake!*

**belt·ed** /ˈbeltə̇d/ *adj* fastened with a belt: *a tightly belted raincoat*

**belt·way** /ˈbeltweɪ/ *n* [C] *AmE* a road that goes around a city to keep traffic away from the centre; RING ROAD *BrE*

**be·moan** /bɪˈməʊn‖-ˈmoʊn/ *v* [T] to complain or say that you are disappointed about something: *As usual, they were all bemoaning the lack of decent training facilities.*

**be·mused** /bɪˈmjuːzd/ *adj* looking as if you are confused: *a bemused expression on his face*

**ben** /ben/ *n* [C] *ScotE* mountain; often used as part of a name: *Ben Nevis*

**bench¹** /bentʃ/ *n* S2 W3
**1** ▶ **SEAT** ◀ [C] a long seat for two or more people, used especially outdoors: *a park bench*
**2** ▶ **COURT** ◀ **the bench** **a)** the seat where a judge

or MAGISTRATE sits in a court of law: *Would the prisoner please approach the bench?* **b)** the position of being a judge or MAGISTRATE in a court of law: *He was appointed to the bench last year.* | **serve/sit on the bench** (=work as a judge or MAGISTRATE)
**3 ▶ POLITICS ◀ benches** [plural] *BrE* the seats in the British parliament where members of a particular party sit: *There were shouts of 'resign!' from the Opposition benches.*
**4 ▶ TABLE ◀** [C] a long heavy table used for working on with tools or equipment: *a carpenter's bench*
**5 ▶ SPORT ◀** [singular] a seat where members of a sports team sit when they are not playing —see also FRONT BENCH, BACKBENCH

**bench²** *v* [T] *AmE* to remove a sports player from a game for a short time: *The number three has been benched for aggressive behavior.*

**bench·mark** /ˈbentʃmɑːk/ *n* [C] **1** something that is used as a standard by which other things can be judged or measured: *a benchmark for future pay negotiations* **2** a mark made on a building, post etc that shows its height above sea level, and is used to measure other heights and distances in a SURVEY² (3)

S3 W3 **bend¹** /bend/ *v past tense and past participle* **bent** /bent/
**1 ▶ MOVE YOUR BODY ◀** [I always + adv/prep] to move the top half of your body forwards or downwards: [**+ towards/across etc**] *He bent towards me and whispered in my ear.* | **bend over** (=bend your body at the waist) *She was bending over the basin, washing her hair.* | **bend down** (=bend your body at the knees or waist) *I bent down to lift the box off the floor.*
**2 ▶ CURVE ◀ a)** [T] to push or press something into a curved shape or fold it at an angle: *Bend your arms and then stretch them upwards.* | **bend sth back/away etc** *I'll bend the branches back so that you can get through.* **b)** [I] to be in the shape of a curve or to change to this shape: *The wire bent easily.*
**3 bend the rules** to do something that is not normally allowed, but will not cause serious problems, usually in order to help someone else: *You should really pay today, but we can bend the rules just this once.*
**4 bend over backwards (to do sth)** to try very hard to be helpful: *I've been bending over backwards to get it done on time for them.*
**5 bend sb's ear** *spoken* to talk to someone, especially about something that is worrying you
**6 on bended knee a)** trying very hard to persuade someone to do something: *If I go on bended knee to the boss, do you think she'd give me my job back?* **b)** in a kneeling position
**7 bend your mind/efforts/thoughts etc to** *formal* to give all your energy or attention to one activity, plan etc

**bend²** *n* [C] **1** a curved part of something, especially a road or river: *The taxi swung around the bend at a terrifying speed.* | [**+ in**] *a sharp bend in the river* **2** an action in which you bend a part of your body: *We started the session with a few knee bends to warm up.* **3 the bends** [plural] a very painful and serious condition that DIVERS get when they come up from under the sea too quickly **4 drive sb round the bend** *spoken especially BrE* to annoy someone **5 be/go round the bend** *spoken especially BrE* to be or become crazy: *You must be round the bend to let her treat you like that.*

**ben·der** /ˈbendə‖-ər/ *n* [C] *BrE informal* **1 go on a bender** to drink a lot of alcohol at one time **2** an insulting word for a man who is attracted to other men; HOMOSEXUAL

**bend·y** /ˈbendi/ *adj informal* **1** easy to bend: *a bendy rubber doll* **2** with many curves or angles: *a bendy road*

W2 **be·neath¹** /bɪˈniːθ/ *prep formal* **1** in or to a lower position than something, or directly under something: *The dolphins disappeared beneath the waves.* | *Jo enjoyed feeling the warm sand beneath her feet.* | **give/buckle/tremble beneath the weight of** (=if something gives, buckles etc beneath the weight of something, it breaks or becomes weaker because it is supporting or carrying a heavy weight): *The shelf was buckling beneath the weight of the books piled on it.* **2** in a lower, less important rank or job than someone else: *She would not speak to people she considered beneath her.* **3** not suitable for someone because of not being good enough: **beneath you** *Vera considered it beneath her even to reply to the insult.*
**4** a feeling or attitude that is beneath another feeling or attitude is covered or hidden by it: *Dave sensed that something more sinister lay beneath the woman's cheerful exterior.* —see picture on page 1257

**beneath²** *adv formal* in or to a lower position: *Madge's skirt was too short and her petticoat was showing beneath.* | *He was standing on the bridge gazing down at the river beneath.*

**Ben·e·dic·tine** /ˌbenɪ̵ˈdɪktɪn◂/ *n* [C] a member of a Christian religious order of MONKS —**Benedictine** *adj*

**ben·e·dic·tine** /ˌbenɪ̵ˈdɪktiːn/ *n* [C,U] a strong alcoholic drink; type of LIQUEUR

**ben·e·dic·tion** /ˌbenɪ̵ˈdɪkʃən/ *n* [C,U] a Christian type of prayer said as a BLESSING (1)

**ben·e·fac·tion** /ˌbenɪ̵ˈfækʃən/ *n formal* **1** [U] the act of doing something good, especially by giving money to someone who needs it **2** [C] money given in this way

**ben·e·fac·tor** /ˈbenɪ̵ˌfæktə‖-ər/ *n* [C] someone who gives money for a good purpose: *An anonymous benefactor donated $2 million.*

**ben·e·fac·tress** /ˈbenɪ̵fæktrɪ̵s/ *n* [C] *old-fashioned* a woman who gives money for a good purpose

**ben·e·fice** /ˈbenɪ̵fɪ̵s/ *n* [C] the pay and position of the priest of a Christian PARISH (1)

**be·nef·i·cent** /bɪˈnefɪ̵sənt/ *adj formal* doing things to help people; generous —**beneficence** *n* [U] —**beneficently** *adv*

**ben·e·fi·cial** /ˌbenɪ̵ˈfɪʃəl◂/ *adj* producing results that bring advantages: *beneficial effects* | [**+ to**] *an agreement that will be beneficial to both parties* —**beneficially** *adv*

**ben·e·fi·cia·ry** /ˌbenɪ̵ˈfɪʃəri‖-ˈfɪʃieri/ *n* [C] **1** someone who gets advantages from an action or change: *The rich were the main beneficiaries of the tax cuts.* **2** someone who receives money or property from someone else who has died: [**+of**] *He was the chief beneficiary of his father's will.*

**ben·e·fit¹** /ˈbenɪ̵fɪt/ *n* **1** [C,U] something that gives you advantages or improves your life in some way: *an aid program that has brought lasting benefits to the region* | **have the benefit of** *She has had the benefit of a first-class education.* | **for sb's benefit** (=in order to help someone or to be useful to them) *All donations are used for the benefit of disabled children.* | **reap the benefit** (=use and enjoy the advantages of something you have worked to achieve) | **be of benefit** *formal* (=be useful or helpful in some way) *The new credit cards will be of great benefit to our customers.* **2** [C,U] *BrE* money provided by the government to people who are sick or unemployed; WELFARE (3) *AmE*: *Are you sure you're getting all the benefits you're entitled to?* | **housing/child/unemployment etc benefit** *How much unemployment benefit do you get?* | **on benefit** (=receiving benefit) *How long have you been on benefit?* **3 benefit concert/performance/match** a concert, performance, etc arranged to make money for CHARITY (2): *a benefit concert for famine relief* **4 give sb the benefit of the doubt** to accept what someone tells you even though you think they may be lying **5** [C usually plural] the money or other advantages that you get from insurance that you have: *The benefits include full medical cover when travelling abroad.* S3 W1

**benefit²** *v* **1** [T] to bring advantages to someone or improve their lives in some way: *a trade agreement that will greatly benefit the developing world* **2** [I] to be helped by something: *I can see the advantages of this for you, but how will I benefit?* | [**+ from/by**] *Many thousands have benefited from the new treatment.* S2 W3 

**Ben·e·lux** /ˈbenɪ̵lʌks/ *n* [singular] the countries of Belgium, the Netherlands, and Luxembourg considered as a group

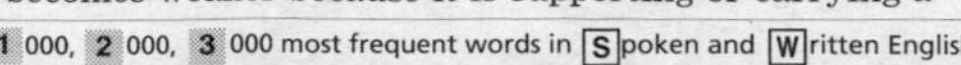

**be·nev·o·lent** /bə̇ˈnevələnt/ *adj* kind and generous: *A benevolent uncle paid for her to have music lessons.* | *a benevolent smile* —**benevolence** *n* [U] —**benevolently** *adv*

**Ben·ga·li**[1] /benˈgɔːli‖-ˈgɒːli/ *n* **1** [U] the language of Bangladesh or West Bengal **2** [C] someone from Bengal

**Bengali**[2] *adj* from or connected with Bengal

**be·night·ed** /bɪˈnaɪtə̇d/ *adj* having no knowledge or understanding —**benightedly** *adv*

**be·nign** /bɪˈnaɪn/ *adj* **1** kind and gentle: *He shook his head in benign amusement.* **2** a benign TUMOUR (=unnatural growth in the body) is not likely to return after treatment —compare MALIGNANT (1) —**benignly** *adv* —**benignity** /bɪˈnɪgnə̇ti/ *n* [U]

**bent**[1] /bent/ the past tense and past participle of BEND[1]

**bent**[2] *adj* **1** something that is bent is no longer flat or straight: *The hinge was bent and the lid wouldn't shut properly.* **2 bent on** completely determined to do something: *He seems bent on success at all costs.* | **bent on doing sth** *She's bent on becoming an actress.* —see also HELL-BENT **3** *informal especially BrE* financially dishonest and willing to use your official position unfairly: *a bent policeman* **4** *BrE slang* an insulting word meaning HOMOSEXUAL **5 bent out of shape** *slang especially AmE* very angry or upset

**bent**[3] *n* [singular] *formal* special natural skill: *He has an artistic bent.*

**ben·zene** /ˈbenziːn, benˈziːn/ *n* [U] a liquid obtained from coal and used for making plastics

**ben·zine** /ˈbenziːn, benˈziːn/ *n* [U] a liquid obtained form PETROLEUM and used to clean clothes

**be·queath** /bɪˈkwiːð, bɪˈkwiːθ/ *v* [T] **1** to officially arrange for someone to have something that you own after your death: **bequeath sth to sb** *She bequeathed her collection of paintings to the National Gallery.* | **bequeath sb sth** *His father bequeathed him a fortune.* **2** to pass knowledge, customs etc to people who come after you or live after you

**be·quest** /bɪˈkwest/ *n* [C] *formal* money or property which you arrange to give to someone after your death: *a bequest of $5000*

**be·rate** /bɪˈreɪt/ *v* [T + **for**] *formal* to speak angrily to someone because they have done something wrong

**be·reaved** /bə̇ˈriːvd/ *adj formal* **1** having lost a close friend or relative because they have recently died: *a bereaved mother* **2 the bereaved** the person or people whose close friend or relative has just died: *Our sympathies go to the bereaved.*

**be·reave·ment** /bə̇ˈriːvmənt/ *n* [C,U] *formal* the fact or state of having lost a close friend or relative because they have died: *depression caused by bereavement or divorce*

**be·reft** /bə̇ˈreft/ *adj formal* **1 bereft of hope/meaning/life etc** completely without any hope etc: *The party's manifesto is bereft of new ideas.* **2** feeling very sad and lonely: *He had left, and she felt completely bereft.*

**be·ret** /ˈbereɪ‖bəˈreɪ/ *n* [C] a round cap with a tight band around the head and a soft loose top part —see picture at CAP[1]

**ber·i·ber·i** /ˌberiˈberi/ *n* [U] a disease of the nerves caused by lack of VITAMIN B

**berk, burk** /bɜːk‖bɜːrk/ *BrE spoken slang n* [C] a stupid person: *I felt a berk in my jeans when everyone else was in suits.*

**ber·ry** /ˈberi/ *n* [C] a small soft fruit with small seeds —see picture on page 413

**ber·serk** /bɜːˈsɜːk, bə-‖bɜːrˈsɜːrk, ˈbɜːrsɜːrk/ *adj* **go berserk** to become very angry and violent

**berth**[1] /bɜːθ‖bɜːrθ/ *n* [C] **1** a place where a ship can stop and be tied up **2** a place for someone to sleep in a ship or on a train; BUNK[1] (1) —see also **give sb/sth a wide berth** (WIDE[1] (7))

**berth**[2] *v* [I,T] to bring a ship into a berth or arrive at a berth

**ber·yl** /ˈberə̇l/ *n* [C] a valuable stone that is usually green or yellow

**be·seech** /bɪˈsiːtʃ/ *v* [T] *literary past tense and past participle* **besought** /bɪˈsɔːt‖-ˈsɒːt/ *or* **beseeched** to eagerly and anxiously ask someone for something

**be·seem** /bɪˈsiːm/ *v* [T] *old use* to be suitable or proper for something

**be·set** /bɪˈset/ *v past tense and past participle* **beset** *present participle* **besetting** [T] *formal* **1** [usually passive] to make someone experience serious problems or dangers: *The business has been beset with financial problems.* **2 besetting sin/weakness** *often humorous* a particular bad feature or habit: *Mark's besetting sin is laziness.*

**be·side** /bɪˈsaɪd/ *prep* **1** next to or very close to someone or something: *Wendy came up and sat beside me.* | *We parked the car beside the sports hall.* —see picture on page 1257 **2** used to compare two people or things: *This year's sales figures don't look very good beside last year's results.* | *Pat looked big and clumsy beside her younger sister.* **3 beside yourself** feeling so angry, excited etc that you find it difficult to control yourself: *He was beside himself with joy when his wife gave birth to their first child.* **4 beside the point** used to say that something that has been mentioned is not directly connected with the main subject or problem that you are talking about: *"How old is she?" "That's beside the point, the question is, can she do the job?"* S W

**be·sides**[1] /bɪˈsaɪdz/ *prep* in addition to a point, statement etc that has just been mentioned: *Will there be anyone else we know at the party besides Will and Janet?* | **besides doing sth** *Besides going to French evening classes twice a week she does yoga on Wednesdays.*

**besides**[2] *adv* used when making another point or statement after one that you have already made: *I don't want to go to the cinema; besides I'm feeling too tired.* | *My wife and I will be there and four of our friends besides.* —see MOREOVER (USAGE)

**be·siege** /bɪˈsiːdʒ/ *v* [T] **1** to surround a city or castle with military force until the people inside let you take control: *In April 655, Osman's palace in Medina was besieged by rebels.* **2** [usually passive] if people, worries, thoughts etc, besiege you, you are surrounded by them: *Miller was besieged by reporters and press photographers.* **3 be besieged with letters/demands/requests etc** to receive a very large number of letters, requests etc

**be·smirch** /bɪˈsmɜːtʃ‖-ɜːrtʃ/ *v* [T] *literary* **besmirch sb's honour/reputation** to spoil the good opinion that people have of someone

**be·som** /ˈbiːzəm/ *n* [C] a large brush made of sticks tied together around a long handle

**be·sot·ted** /bɪˈsɒtə̇d‖bɪˈsɑː-/ *adj* **be besotted (with)** to love or want someone or something so much that you cannot think or behave sensibly: *He's completely besotted with her.*

**be·sought** /bɪˈsɔːt‖-ˈsɒːt/ the past tense and past participle of BESEECH

**be·speak** /bɪˈspiːk/ *v* [T] *literary past tense* **bespoke** /bɪˈspəʊk‖-ˈspoʊk/ *past participle* **bespoken** /bɪˈspəʊkən‖-ˈspoʊ-/ to be a sign of something: *His easy manner bespoke a knowledge of the world.*

**be·spec·ta·cled** /bɪˈspektəkəld/ *adj* wearing glasses

**be·spoke** /bɪˈspəʊk‖-spoʊk/ *adj BrE old-fashioned* a bespoke suit, coat etc has been specially made to fit one person

**best**[1] /best/ *adj* [superlative of *good*] **1** better than anything else or anyone else in quality, skill, effectiveness etc: *He was the best teacher in the school.* | *What's the best way to cook this fish?* | *The best thing to do is to stop worrying.* | **easily the best/by far the best** (=much better than anything else) *I've read all her books but 'Middlemarch' is easily the best.* | **it's best to** *It's best to clean the wall before you paint it* **2 best dress/shoes/clothes etc** clothing that you keep for special occasions: *You ought to wear your best shirt.* **3 best friend** the

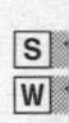

friend that you know and like better than anyone else **4 the next best thing** something that is not exactly what you want but is as similar to it as possible: *The next best thing to being with her was to phone and talk.* **5 best of all** used to introduce the one fact about a situation that is even better than the other good things: *Yeah, my dad's getting a new car – and best of all, he's going to give me the old one!* —see also **be on your best behaviour** (BEHAVIOUR (2)), **your best bet** (BET² (3)), **the best/better part of** (PART¹ (6))

S1 W2 **best²** *adv* [superlative of *well*] **1** in a way that is better than any other; most well: *It works best if you let it warm up first.* | *The glacier can best be viewed from above.* | *the best-dressed man in Paris* **2** to the greatest degree; most: *You know him best – you should ask him.* | *Which did you like best, the music or the dancing?* | *one of our best-loved old cathedrals* **3 for reasons best known to herself/himself** used to say that you cannot understand why someone has done something: *For reasons best known to herself, she arrived dressed in a gorilla suit!* **4 as best you can** *spoken* as well as you can, even if this is not very good: *I'll translate it as best I can, but my German is very rusty.* **5 had best** *spoken* ought to: *You'd best stay at home till you get over that cold.*

**best³** *n* **1 a)** the best, most helpful, most successful etc situation or results that you can achieve: *We all want the best for our children.* | *It's the best we can do in the circumstances.* **b)** the person or thing that is better than any other: *She's the best of the new young writers.* **2 do your best** to try as hard as you can to do something: *As long as you do your best we'll be happy.* | **do your best to do sth** *We'll do our best to finish it on time.* **3 at best** used to emphasize that something is not very good, pleasant, honest, etc even if you consider it in the best possible way: *The city was at best an ordinary sort of place.* | *His answers were at best evasive, at worst very misleading.* **4 to the best of your knowledge/belief/ability** used to say that something is as much as you know, believe, or are able to do: *I'm sure he'll do the work to the best of his ability.* **5 the best of both worlds** a situation in which you have the advantages of two different things without any of the disadvantages: *They live in a village but it's only an hour from London so they have the best of both worlds.* **6 at your best** performing as well or effectively as you are able to: *At her best, she's a really stylish player.* | *He was never at his best early in the morning.* **7 make the best of sth/make the best of a bad job** to accept an unsatisfactory situation, and do whatever you can to make it less bad: *We are stuck here so we might as well make the best of it.* **8 the best of a bad lot** the least bad person or thing in a group of not very good people or things **9 all the best** used to express good wishes to someone for the future: *All the best for the New Year!* **10 Sunday best** *old-fashioned* your best clothes, which you only wear on special occasions **11 be for the best** *especially spoken* used to say that a particular event may not be as bad as it seems: *I still don't want him to go but maybe it's for the best.* **12 at the best of times** if something is not very good, pleasant etc at the best of times, it is usually even worse than this: *It's not a very exciting town at the best of times.*

**best⁴** *v* [T] *old use* to defeat someone

**best-be·fore date** /ˌ· ·ˈ· ˌ·/ *n* [C] a date on containers of food or drink that shows when they will be too old to eat or drink

**bes·ti·al** /ˈbestiəl‖ˈbestʃəl/ *adj* inhuman: *Thousands of them had been murdered in the most bestial manner.* —**bestially** *adv*

**bes·ti·al·i·ty** /ˌbestiˈælʒti‖ˌbestʃi-/ *n* [U] **1** sexual relations between a person and an animal **2** *formal* very cruel behaviour

**bes·ti·ar·y** /ˈbestiəri‖ˈbestʃieri/ *n* [C] an old book about strange animals, written in the Middle Ages

**be·stir** /bɪˈstɜː‖-ˈstɜːr/ *v* [T] **bestir yourself** *formal* to start to do things, after relaxing or being lazy

**best man** /ˌ· ˈ·/ *n* [singular] the man who helps the BRIDEGROOM (=the man getting married) at a wedding ceremony

**be·stow** /bɪˈstəʊ‖-ˈstoʊ/ *v* [T] *formal* to give someone something of great value or importance: **bestow sth on/upon** *honours bestowed on him by the Queen*

**be·stride** /bɪˈstraɪd/ *past tense* **bestrode** /bɪˈstrəʊd‖-ˈstroʊd/ *past participle* **bestridden** /bɪˈstrɪdn/ *v* [T] *literary* to sit or stand on or over something with one leg on each side of it

**best-sel·ler** /ˌ· ˈ··/ *n* [C] a very popular book which many people buy —**best-selling** *adj*: *a best-selling author*

**bet¹** *past tense and past participle* **bet** *or* **betted,** *present participle* **betting** *v* **1** [I,T] to risk money on the result of a race, game, competition, or other future event: **bet (sb) that** *Sean bet that I wouldn't pass my exam.* | **bet (sth) on** *She bet all her money on a horse that came last.* | *No, I don't bet on my own team. It's bad luck.* S1

Frequencies of the verb **bet** in spoken and written English.

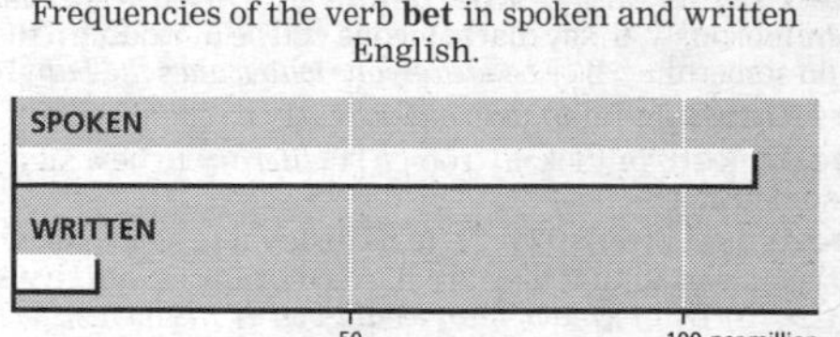


Based on the British National Corpus and the Longman Lancaster Corpus

This graph shows that the verb **bet** is much more common in spoken English than in written English. This is because it is used in some common spoken phrases.

**bet (*v*) SPOKEN PHRASES**

**2 I bet a)** used to say that you are fairly sure that something is true, something is happening etc, although you cannot prove this: *I bet Nigel's sitting at home now laughing his head off.* | *I bet it's quite good actually.* | *I bet you she won't come.* **b)** used to show that you understand or can imagine the situation that someone has just told you about: *"The strawberries dipped in chocolate were gorgeous." "I bet!"* | *"God, I was so angry." "I bet you were."* **c)** used when you are asking someone to guess something: *I bet you'll never guess who I saw this morning.* **d)** used to show that you do not believe what someone has just told you: *"I'm definitely going to give up smoking this time." "Yeah, I bet!"* **3 you bet!** used to emphasize that you agree with someone or are keen to do what they suggest: *"Going to the party on Saturday?" " You bet!"* **4 you can bet your life/your bottom dollar** used when you are sure that you know what someone will do or what will happen: *You can bet your bottom dollar that relationship will end in tears.*

**bet²** /bet/ *n* [C] **1** an agreement to risk money on the result of a race, game, competition etc: **have a bet on** *Mom had a bet on the Yankees and won $20.* | **place a bet** (=choose a horse, team etc and bet on it) **2** money that you risk on a bet: *I've got a £10 bet on the National.* **3 your best bet** *spoken* used when advising someone of what to do: *I think your best bet would be to go back to college and get more qualifications.* **4 my bet is (that)** *spoken* used when saying what you expect to happen in the future: *My bet is that she'll be famous in a few years' time.* **5 a good bet/a safe bet** an action or situation that is likely to be successful or does not involve much risk: *If you're looking for long-term growth, the government's own saving certificates are a pretty good bet.* **6 a safe bet/a sure bet (that)** *spoken* used to say that something seems almost certain: *I think it's a pretty safe bet that he'll get the job.* **7 do sth for a bet** to do something stupid, dangerous etc to win money from someone or to prove that you can do it: *Sandra cut the manager's tie off for a bet!*

**be·ta** /ˈbiːtə‖ˈbeɪtə/ *n* **1** [singular] the second letter of the Greek alphabet, β or B **2** [C] this letter given as a mark for good work by a student

**beta-block·er** /ˈ·· ˌ··/ *n* [C] a drug used to help prevent HEART ATTACKS

**be·take** /bɪˈteɪk/ *v past tense* **betook** /bɪˈtʊk/ *past participle* **betaken** /bɪˈteɪkən/ **betake yourself to** *literary* to go somewhere

**be·tel** /ˈbiːtl/ *n* [U] a plant whose leaves have a fresh taste, and are chewed (CHEW[1] (2)) by people in Asia

**betel nut** /ˈ·· ·/ *n* [C,U] small pieces of red nut with a bitter taste, that are wrapped in a betel leaf and chewed (CHEW[1] (2))

**bête-noire** /ˈbet ˈnwɑː‖-ˈnwɑːr/ *n* [singular] *French* the person or thing that you dislike most

**be·think** /bɪˈθɪŋk/ *past tense and past participle* **bethought** /bɪˈθɔːt‖-ˈθɒːt/ *v* **bethink yourself of** *old use* to remember something or think about something

**be·tide** /bɪˈtaɪd/ *v* **woe betide you** used, especially humorously, to say that someone will be in trouble if they do something: *Woe betide anyone who wakes the baby!*

**be·times** /bɪˈtaɪmz/ *adv old use* early or soon

**be·to·ken** /bɪˈtəʊkən‖-ˈtoʊ-/ *v* [T] *literary* to be a sign of something

**be·tray** /bɪˈtreɪ/ *v* [T] **1** to be disloyal to someone who trusts you so that they are harmed or upset: **betray sb (to sb)** *What kind of man would betray his own sister to the police?* **2** to be disloyal to your country, for example by giving secret information to its enemies: *people who are prepared to betray their country for money* **3 betray your beliefs/principles/ideals etc** to stop supporting your old beliefs and principles, especially in order to get power or avoid trouble **4** [not in progressive or passive] to show feelings that you are trying to hide: *The tremor in his voice betrayed his nervousness.* —**betrayer** *n* [C]

**be·tray·al** /bɪˈtreɪəl/ *n* [C,U] an act of betraying your country, friends, or someone who trusts you: *The tax increases are a ruthless betrayal of election pledges.*

**be·troth·al** /bɪˈtrəʊðəl‖-ˈtroʊ-/ *n* [C] *old use* an agreement that two people will be married; ENGAGEMENT (1)

**be·trothed** /bɪˈtrəʊðd‖-ˈtroʊðd/ *adj old use* **1 be betrothed to** to have promised to marry someone **2 sb's betrothed** the person that someone has agreed to marry —**betroth** *v* [T]

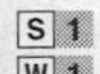
**bet·ter**[1] /ˈbetə‖-ər/ *adj* [comparative of *good*] **1** more useful, interesting, satisfactory, effective, suitable etc: *Your stereo is better than mine.* | *a better job with a better salary* | *It was one of the better Broadway shows I've seen.* | *There must be a better way to do this.* | *a better-quality car* | **much better/far better/a lot better** *It's a much better quality design than the previous model.* **2** [comparative of *well*] **a)** more healthy or less ill or painful than before: *She is a little better today, the doctor says.* | *I'm feeling much better, thank you.* | **feel better for** (=feel better as a result of) *Go for a walk – you'll feel better for getting some fresh air.* —see graph at IMPROVE **b)** completely well again after an illness: *When you're better we can see about planning a trip.* **3 get better a)** to improve: *If the weather gets better we could go out for a walk.* | *Her English isn't really getting any better.* **b)** to recover from an illness or accident: *Are you hungry Sally? I think you must be getting better.* —see graph at RECOVER **4 have seen better days** *informal* to be in a bad condition: *The sofa has seen better days but the chairs are still okay.* **5 be no better than** to be almost as bad as: *He's no better than a thief.* **6 better still** used to say that something is even better than the first thing you mentioned: *Go for a walk around the building, or better still around the block.* **7 against your better judgment** if you do something against your better judgment, you do it even though you think it may not be sensible: *Against our better judgment, we allowed her to stay.* **8 sb's better nature** the part of someone's character that makes them want to be kind and generous, treat people well, etc: *He's become a lot nicer recently. I think she's brought out his better nature.* —see also **your better half/other half** (HALF[1] (9)), **best/better part of** (PART[1] (6)) —opposite WORSE[1]

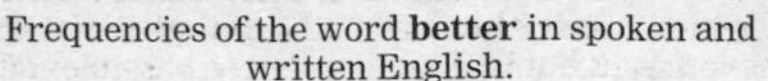
Frequencies of the word **better** in spoken and written English.

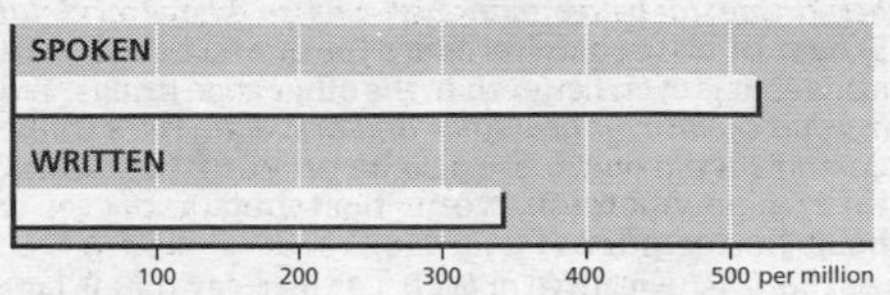


Based on the British National Corpus and the Longman Lancaster Corpus

This graph shows that the word **better** is more common in spoken English than in written English. This is because it is used in a lot of common spoken phrases.

**better (*adj*) SPOKEN PHRASES**

**9 sb had better a)** used to give advice about what someone should do: *She'd better see a doctor if it gets any worse.* **b)** used to threaten someone: *You'd better keep your mouth shut about this.* **10 that's better a)** used to praise or encourage someone: *Try hitting the ball higher. That's better!* **b)** used when trying to comfort someone or make them feel less upset: *Come on, give me a hug. There, that's better, isn't it?.* **11 better** used to say that you or someone else should do something: *Better go and phone her to check she's in.* **12 you'd be better/it would be better to do sth** used to suggest that someone should do one thing rather than another: *It would be better to install a shower rather than a bath.* **13 better luck next time** used to encourage someone who has done badly in an examination, competition etc **14 you'd be better off** used when suggesting that someone should do something differently or change their situation: *Believe me, you'd be better off without him, you really would!* **15 what could be better...?/there's nothing better** used to say that something is perfect: *Three weeks in the sun with nothing to do. What could be better?* | *There's nothing better than a hot shower in the morning.* **16 is that better?** used to ask someone if they are happier with something after you have changed it: *I'll put some more sugar in. There, is that better?* **17 it's better than doing sth** used to say that although your situation is not good, it is better than another situation: *Maybe I'm not well paid, but it's better than being out of a job.* **18 better late than never** used to say that even if something happens late or someone arrives late, this is better than it not happening at all **19 better the devil you know** used to say that something bad that you know about is better than something bad you know nothing about

**better**[2] *adv* [comparative of *well*] **1** in a better way: *He can speak French a lot better than I can.* | *Your bike will run better if you oil it.* | *The private schools tend to be better equipped.* **2** to a higher degree; more: *She knows this town better than you do.* | *I think I like the red one better.* | *Potter is better known for his TV work.* **3 do better** to perform better or reach a higher standard: *You'd do better if you practised more.* | *We did better than all the other schools.* **4 the sooner the better/the later the better etc** used to emphasize that you would prefer something to happen as soon as possible, as late as possible etc: *School finishes at the end of the week, and the sooner the better as far as I'm concerned.* **5 the bigger the better/the faster the better etc** used to emphasize that you want something to be as big as possible, as fast as possible etc: *"Do you want me to bring a bottle of wine?" "Sure – the more the better!"* **6 better off** richer than you were before: *Today's pensioners are better off than they used to be.* | *The average taxpayer will be $80 better off as a result of these changes.* **7 go one better (than)** *informal* to do something more successfully than someone else: *That was a good story but I can go one better.* —compare WORSE[3] 

**better³** *n* **1 the better** used to mean the one that is better when you are comparing two similar people or things: *It's hard to decide which one's the better.* **2 get the better of a)** if your feelings or wishes get the better of you, they make you behave in a way you would not normally behave: *My curiosity finally got the better of me and I opened the letter.*|*I think her nerves got the better of her.* **b)** to defeat someone or deal successfully with a problem **3 for the better** in a way that improves the situation: *a definite change for the better*|**take a turn for the better** (=improve) *The President's fortunes seem, at last, to have taken a turn for the better.* **4 be all the better for** *especially spoken* to be improved by a particular action, change etc: *I think it's all the better for that extra ten minutes' cooking.* **5 so much the better** used to say that something would be even better or bring even more advantages: *They usually cost about $50, but if you can get one for less, then so much the better.* **6 for better or (for) worse** used to say that something must be accepted, whether the results will be good or bad, because it cannot be changed: *This type of farming is, for better or worse, rapidly dying out.* **7 your betters** *old-fashioned* people who are more important than you or deserve more respect —compare worse² —see also **elders and betters** (ELDER² (4))

**better⁴** *v* [T] **1** to be better than something in quality, amount etc: *His total of five gold medals is unlikely to be bettered.* **2 better yourself** to improve your position in society by getting a better education or earning more money **3** *formal* to improve something: *bettering the lot of the working classes*

**bet·ter·ment** /ˈbetəmənt‖-tər-/ *n* [singular] *formal* improvement, especially in someone's social and economic position

S1 W1 **be·tween¹** /bɪˈtwiːn/ *prep* **1** in or into the space or time that separates two things or people: *I sat between Sue and Jane at the Christmas party.*|*There was a low brick wall between our garden and the field beyond.* **2** in the time that separates two events: *Are there any public holidays between Christmas and Easter?*|*You shouldn't eat between meals.* **3** used to show a range of amounts, numbers, distances etc especially when guessing a particular amount, number etc: *The project will cost between eight and ten million dollars.* **4** used to show a connection between two places: *They're building a new road between Manchester and Sheffield.*|*a regular air service between London and Paris* **5** used to show the relationship between two situations, things, people etc: *a long-standing friendship between Bob and Bryan*|*co-operation between the two countries*|*a dispute between management and unions* **6** used to show the fact that something is divided or shared among several people, places, or things: *Tom divided his money between his three children.*|*Between the four of them they managed to lift her into the ambulance.*|*We collected £17 between us.*|**between doing sth** *Between cooking, writing, and running the farm Elsie was kept very busy.* **7 in between** at a point in space or time between two places, events etc: *In between school and university I did a three month crash course in Italian.*|*It's somewhere in between New York and Chicago.* **8 between you and me** *also* **between ourselves** *spoken* used before telling someone something that you do not want them to tell anyone else: *Between you and me, I think Schmidt's about to resign as chairman.* **9 come between you** if something comes between two people, it causes an argument or problems between them **10** *especially spoken* used when it is difficult to give an exact description of, or name to something and you therefore have to compare it to two things that are similar to it: *My job is between a bank-clerk and a messenger boy.*

S3 **between²** *adv* in or into the space that separates two things or people, or in the time that separates two events: *So far I've had temporary jobs with long periods of unemployment between.*|**in between** *She has breakfast and supper but doesn't eat anything in between.*|*a house and stables with a yard in between*

**USAGE NOTE: BETWEEN**

WORD CHOICE: **between, among(st), with, shared by**

**Between** is usually used to talk about two or a few people or things, thought of separately or one after another: *the differences between British and American English*|*the relationship between each member of the family and the other* (NOT *among*)|*the gaps between the fence posts.* In spoken English you will often hear things like *Share this between the twelve of you*, though some people think only **among** is correct where a group of more than two is involved.

**Among(st)** is used to talk about of a group of three or more people or things together, especially using nouns that name groups: *The mountains were hidden among the clouds.*|*Just talk amongst yourselves for a minute.*|*Among the books he found one by Salinger* (*Between the books* would suggest 'between two of them').|

**Amongst** is more formal than **among**.

Where there is little idea of anything different or separate being involved within a group, you can use **with** after adjectives and verbs or **shared by** with nouns: *This offer was very popular with our customers* (NOT *between*, though *among* is possible). *I always eat with them* (NOT usually *among*).|*the knowledge shared by the family*|*an opinion/a view shared by a lot of people* (or *among*)

**be·twixt** /bɪˈtwɪkst/ *prep* **1** *poetic or old use* between **2 betwixt and between** *old-fashioned* not quite belonging to one group or to another

**bev·el** /ˈbevəl/ *n* [C] *technical* **1** a sloping edge or surface, usually along the edge of a piece of wood or glass **2** a tool for making this kind of edge or surface —**bevelled** *adj*: *bevelled glass*

**bev·elled** /ˈbevəld/ *adj* with a sloping edge: *a mirror with bevelled edges*

**bev·er·age** /ˈbevərɪdʒ/ *n* [C] *formal* a hot or cold drink: *alcoholic beverages*

**bev·y** /ˈbevi/ *n* [C] a large group of people of the same kind, especially girls or young women: **[+ of]** *Tom swaggered in surrounded by a bevy of beauties.*

**be·wail** /bɪˈweɪl/ *v* [T] *literary* to express deep sadness or disappointment about something

**be·ware** /bɪˈweə‖-ˈwer/ *v* [I,T only in imperative and infinitive] used to warn someone to be careful because something is dangerous: **[+of]** *Beware of the dog!*|*Beware of doing anything to arouse suspicion.*

**be·wigged** /bɪˈwɪgd/ *adj formal* wearing a WIG

**be·wil·der** /bɪˈwɪldə‖-ər/ *v* [T] to confuse someone

**be·wil·dered** /bɪˈwɪldəd‖-ərd/ *adj* totally confused: *Benny lookd around, a bewildered expression on his face.*

**be·wil·der·ing** /bɪˈwɪldərɪŋ/ *adj* confusing, especially because there are too many choices or things happening at the same time: *There's a bewildering range of skin care products to choose from.* —**bewilderment** *n* [U]

**be·wil·der·ment** /bɪˈwɪldəmənt‖-dər-/ *n* [U] a feeling of being very confused

**be·witch** /bɪˈwɪtʃ/ *v* [T] **1** to make someone feel so interested or attracted by something that they cannot think clearly: *Tim's utterly bewitched by that woman.*|*a bewitching smile* **2** to get control over someone by putting a magic SPELL² (1) on them

**be·yond¹** /bɪˈjɒnd‖bɪˈjɑːnd/ *prep* **1** on or to the further side of something: *Beyond the mountains was the border territory.* —see picture on page 1257 **2** later than a particular time, date etc: *The disco went on until beyond*  

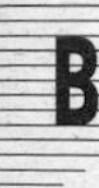

*midnight.* | *The new law extends the ban beyond 1998.* **3** more or greater than a particular amount, level, or limit: *Most people do not choose to work beyond the normal retirement age.* | *Inflation has now risen beyond the level of 5%.* **4** outside the range or limits of someone or something: *Such tasks are beyond the scope of your average schoolkid.* | *The light switch was beyond the child's reach.* **5 beyond belief/doubt/recognition etc** used to say that you cannot believe something, doubt something etc: *The town centre had changed beyond all recognition.* **6 be beyond sb** *especially spoken* to be too difficult for someone: *Algebra was always beyond me.* **7 it is beyond me why/what etc** *spoken* used to say that something seems completely stupid and you cannot understand the reason for it: *Why Joan ever married such an idiot in the first place is beyond me.* **8** used like 'except' in negative sentences: *Fred owns nothing beyond the clothes on his back.* | *I can't tell you anything beyond what you know already.*

**beyond²** *adv* **1** on or to the further side of something: *They crossed the mountains and headed for the valleys beyond.* **2** later than a particular time, date etc: *What changes await us in the year 2000 and beyond?*

**beyond³** *n* **the beyond** *literary* whatever comes after this life

**be·zique** /bɪ̈ˈziːk/ *n* [U] a card game for two or four players, using 64 cards

**bha·ji, bhajee** /ˈbɑːdʒiː/ *n* [C] a hot-tasting Indian vegetable cake cooked in BATTER (=a liquid mixture of flour, egg, and milk or water) *onion bhajis*

**bi-** /baɪ/ *prefix* two; twice; double: *bilingual* (=speaking two languages) | *to bisect* (=cut in two) —compare SEMI- —see also DI-, TRI-

**bi·an·nu·al** /baɪˈænjuəl/ *adj* happening twice each year: *a biannual report* —compare ANNUAL¹, BIENNIAL (2)

**bi·as¹** /ˈbaɪəs/ *n* **1** [U singular] a tendency to consider one person, group, idea etc more favourably than others: *a newspaper with a strong right-wing bias* | [+ **against/towards/in favour of**] *There was a definite bias against commerce and science in the educational curriculum.* **2** [singular] a natural skill or interest in one particular area: *Lydia has a strong artistic bias.* **3 on the bias** in a DIAGONAL direction

**bias²** *v* **biased, biasing** *or* **biassed, biassing** [T] to unfairly influence attitudes, choices, or decisions

**bias bind·ing** /ˌ·· ˈ··/ *n* [U] *BrE* cloth in the form of a narrrow band, used when sewing edges; BIAS TAPE *AmE*

**biased, biassed** /ˈbaɪəst/ *adj* unfairly influenced in favour of or against one particular person, opinion etc: *I admit I'm biased, but I think my son's performance was brilliant!* | [+ **against/towards/in favour of**] *news reporting that was heavily biased towards the government*

**bias tape** /ˌ·· ˈ·/ *n* [U] *AmE* BIAS BINDING

**bib** /bɪb/ *n* [C] **1** a piece of cloth or plastic tied under a baby's chin to protect its clothes when it is eating **2** the upper part of an APRON (1), DUNGAREES, or overalls (OVERALL³ (2)), above the waist **3 your best bib and tucker** *humorous* your best clothes

**bi·ble, Bible** /ˈbaɪbəl/ *n* **1 the Bible** the holy book of the Christian religion, consisting of the OLD TESTAMENT and the NEW TESTAMENT **2** [C] a copy of the Bible **3** [singular] *informal* the most useful and important book on a particular subject: *It's the anatomy student's bible!* **4 bible basher** *BrE,* **bible thumper** *AmE* an insulting expression for someone who tries to spread their own very strong Christian beliefs

**bib·li·cal** /ˈbɪblɪkəl/ *adj* connected with the Bible

**biblio-** /bɪbliəʊ, -liə‖-lioʊ, -liə/ *prefix* concerning books: *a bibliophile* (=someone who likes books)

**bib·li·og·ra·phy** /ˌbɪbliˈɒgrəfi‖-ˈɑːg-/ *n* [C] **1** a list of all the books and articles used in preparing a piece of writing **2** a list of everything that has been written about a particular subject —**bibliographer** *n*

**bib·li·o·phile** /ˈbɪbliəfaɪl/ *n* [C] *formal* someone who likes books

**bib·u·lous** /ˈbɪbjɡ̈ləs/ *adj humorous or formal* liking to drink too much alcohol

**bi·cam·er·al leg·is·la·ture** /baɪˌkæmərəl ˈledʒɡ̈sleɪtʃə, -lətʃə‖-tʃər/ *n* [C] *technical* a law-making body consisting of two parts, like the Senate and the House of Representatives in the US Congress

**bi·car·bon·ate of so·da** /baɪˌkɑːbənɡ̈t əv ˈsəʊdə, -bəneɪt‖-ˌkaːr-,-ˈsoʊdə/ also **bicarbonate**, also **bi·carb** /ˈbaɪkɑːb‖-kɑːrb/ *informal n* [U] a chemical substance used especially in baking, and sometimes taken with water as a medicine

**bi·cen·te·na·ry** /ˌbaɪsenˈtiːnəri‖-ˈtenəri, -ˈsentəneri/ *n* [C] *especially BrE* the day or year exactly 200 years after an important event: *the bicentenary of Mozart's death* —**bicentenary** *adj*

**bi·ce·nten·ni·al** /ˌbaɪsenˈteniəl/ *n* [C] *AmE* the day or year exactly 200 years after an important event: *the bicentennial of the declaration of independence* —**bicentennial** *adj*: *bicentennial celebrations*

**bi·ceps** /ˈbaɪseps/ *n plural* **biceps** [C] the large muscle on the front of your upper arm —see picture at BODY

**bick·er** /ˈbɪkə‖-ər/ *v* [I + **about/over/with**] to argue, especially about something very unimportant: *I wish you two would stop bickering.*

**bi·cy·cle¹** /ˈbaɪsɪkəl/ *n* [C] a two-wheeled vehicle that you ride by pushing its pedals (PEDAL² (1)) with your feet; BIKE: *She goes to work on her bicycle.* | *Can James ride a bicycle yet?* W3

**bicycle²** *v* [I always + adv/prep] *formal* to go somewhere by bicycle —**bicyclist** *n* [C]

**bid¹** /bɪd/ *n* [C] **1** an offer to pay a particular price for something, especially at an AUCTION¹: [+ **for**] *They put in the highest bid for the house.* **2** an offer to do work or provide services for a specific price: [+ **for**] *rival bids for the cleaning contract* **3** an attempt to achieve or obtain something: [+ **for**] *a bid for power* | **bid to do sth** *a desperate bid to free herself from a loveless marriage* **4** a statement of how many points you hope to win in a card game W3

**bid²** *v past tense and past participle* **bid** *present participle* **bidding** **1** [I,T] to offer to pay a particular price for goods, especially in an AUCTION¹: **bid (sb) sth for** *She bid £100 for a Victorian chair.* | *What am I bid for lot 227? Shall we start at $500?* **2** [I] to offer to do work or provide services for a specific price, in competition with other offers: [+ **for**] *Three firms bid for the contract on the new buildings.* **3** [I,T] to say how many points you think you will win in a game of cards —**bidder** *n* [C]

**bid³** *v past tense* **bade** /bæd/ *or* **bid** *past participle* **bidden** /ˈbɪdn/ *or* **bid** *present participle* **bidding** *old use or literary* **1 bid sb good afternoon/good morning etc** to say good morning, good afternoon etc to someone **2** [T] to order or tell someone what to do: **bid sb (to) do sth** *The queen bade us to enter.* **3 bid fair to do sth** to seem likely to do something: *The good weather bids fair to hold.*

**bid·da·ble** /ˈbɪdəbəl/ *adj especially BrE* willing to do what you are told without arguing

**bid·ding** /ˈbɪdɪŋ/ *n* [U] **1** the activity of bidding (BID¹ (1)) for goods, especially in an AUCTION¹: *The bidding was brisk and sales went well.* **2 at sb's bidding** *formal* because someone has told you to **3 do sb's bidding** *formal* to obey someone's requests or orders

**bicycle**

bell
handlebar
crossbar
saddle
rear light
mudguard *BrE* / fender *AmE*
pump
chain
pedal
hub
spokes
valve
gear lever
brake
brake cable
front light
brake
reflector
fork
tyre *BrE* / tire *AmE*
axle

**bide** /baɪd/ *v past tense* **bode** *or* **bided** **1 bide your time** to wait until the right moment to do something: *They are stronger than us and can afford to bide their time.* **2** [I] *old use* to wait or stay somewhere, often for a long time

**bi·det** /ˈbiːdeɪ‖bɪˈdeɪ/ *n* [C] a small, low bath that you sit on to wash the lower part of your body

**bi·en·ni·al** /baɪˈeniəl/ *adj* **1** a biennial event happens once every two years —compare ANNUAL[1] **2** a biennial plant stays alive for two years and produces seeds in the second year —compare ANNUAL[2] (1), BIANNUAL —**biennially** *adv*

**bier** /bɪə‖bɪr/ *n* [C] a frame like a table on which a dead body or COFFIN is placed

**biff** /bɪf/ *v* [T] *informal* to hit someone hard with your FIST —**biff** *n* [C]

**bi·fo·cals** /baɪˈfəʊkəlz‖ˈbaɪfoʊ-/ *n* [plural] special glasses with an upper part made for seeing things that are far away, and a lower part made for reading —**bifocal** *adj*

**bi·fur·cate** /ˈbaɪfəkeɪt‖-ər-/ *v* [I] *formal* if a road, river etc bifurcates, it divides into two separate parts —**bifurcation** /ˌbaɪfəˈkeɪʃən‖-fər-/ *n* [C,U]

S1 W1 **big** /bɪg/ *adj comparative* **bigger,** *superlative* **biggest**
**1 ▶ SIZE ◀** of more than average size, amount, weight etc: *a big house | Your baby's getting big! | a big increase in prices | the biggest hotel in New York | She had a big grin on her face.* | **great big** *spoken* (=extremely big) *There was this great big spider in the sink.* —see WIDE[1] (USAGE)
**2 ▶ IMPORTANT ◀** important and serious: *a big decision | Buying your own house is a big commitment.*
**3 ▶ SUCCESSFUL/POWERFUL ◀** *informal* successful or popular especially in business or entertainment: *Rap music was really big in the 1980s. | It's becoming quite a big area for tourism.* | [+ **in**] *She's very big in the music business.* | **make it big** (=become very successful) *After years as a small-time actor, he suddenly made it big in Hollywood.* | **the big boys** (=the most powerful and influential people or companies) *Small firms like ours can't really compete with the big boys.* —see also BIG CHEESE, **big name** (NAME[1] (4)), BIG NOISE, **big shot** (SHOT[1] (19)), BIG-TIME
**4 ▶ OLDER ◀** *spoken* **a) big sister/brother** your older sister or brother **b)** used especially when speaking to children to mean older or more grown-up: *Come on, don't cry. You're a big girl now.*
**5 ▶ BAD ◀** [only before noun] *spoken* used to emphasize how bad something is: *It's always such a big hassle finding some place to park. | I never said that, you big liar!*
**6 ▶ A LOT ◀** [only before noun] *informal* doing something to a very large degree: **a big eater/drinker/spender etc** *Des is a big gambler you know.* | **be a big fan/admirer of** (=admire someone very much) *I've never been a big fan of REM.*
**7 ▶ BIG DEAL ◀** *spoken* **a) big deal!** used to say that you do not think something is as important or impressive as someone else thinks it is: *So what if he is upset about it? Big deal!* **b) it's no big deal** used to say that something is not really important or not a big problem: *It's no big deal if you can't come – just let us know in time.* **c) make a big deal (out) of** to treat something as if it is more important than it really is: *Why do you have to make such a big deal out of it?*
**8 have big ideas/plans** to have impressive plans for the future: *I've got big plans for this place.*
**9 what's the big idea?** *spoken* used when someone has done something annoying, especially when you want

them to explain why they did it: *Hey, what's the big idea? Who said you could use my computer?*
**10 it is big of sb to do sth** *spoken* **a)** used to say that someone was very kind or generous to do something **b)** used when you really think that someone was not kind or helpful at all: *A whole £5! That was very big of her, I must say!*
**11 big money** also **big bucks** *AmE informal* a lot of money, or the chance to earn a lot of money: *You should go into merchant banking. That's where the big money is.*
**12 big mouth** *spoken* someone who has a big mouth cannot be trusted to keep things secret: *Oh God, me and my big mouth!* —see also BIGMOUTH
**13 be/get too big for your boots** *informal* to be too proud of yourself
**14 use/ward/wield the big stick** *informal* to threaten to use your power to get what you want
**15 big with child** *old use* soon going to have a baby; PREGNANT
**16 big enchilada** *humorous AmE* the most important person; the BOSS —see also **think big** (THINK[1] (17)), —**bigness** *n* [U]

**USAGE NOTE: BIG**

WORD CHOICE: **big**, **large**, **great**

**Big** and **large** are both often used to talk about or to talk about the measurements of things or groups, though **large** is slightly more formal and not so often used of people: *That shirt doesn't fit me – it's too big/large.* | *How big are you round the waist?* | *a big crowd/company/gap* | *a large family/city/university*. See also **fat** WORD CHOICE and **wide** WORD CHOICE.

None of these words are used with uncountable nouns for things you can touch: *There was a lot of traffic/land /space* (NOT *big traffic, large land*).

**Great** means famous or important for something good, or, when it is used about ordinary people, just extremely nice: *Rembrandt was a great painter.* | *Isn't Max a great guy?* See also **famous** WORD CHOICE.

**Great** used about the size of things or events is mainly found in literary writing or names and means 'very large and impressive': *The great city of Samarkand.* | *A great crowd had gathered.* | *a great banquet* | *The Great Wall of China.* Otherwise **great** is used very informally of things just to mean extremely good: *You look great!* | *There's a great view from our hotel room.* | *We had a great time there* (=enjoyable, not necessarily long).

You would usually use **great** rather than **big** to describe the size or extent of things you cannot touch: *She showed great courage/talent/ability.* | *We had great fun.* | *in great detail.* Where both can be used, **great** is stronger and suggests more importance: *It's a big/great pleasure to see you.* | *great/big problem/opportunity/danger.* But note that you usually say *a big difference/mistake/argument* | *It isn't a big deal* (informal=It's not serious or important).

Note that **large** (less often **great** or **big**) is used with these quantity words: *a large amount/scale/number/quantity/extent/proportion/percentage/part/volume/area.* But note only **great** is used in: *a great deal* (= a lot) | *at great length* | *a great height/age*

**big·a·my** /ˈbɪgəmi/ *n* [U] the crime of being married to two people at the same time —compare MONOGAMY, POLYGAMY —**bigamist** *n* [C] —**bigamous** *adj*

**big bang the·o·ry** /ˌ· ˈ· ˌ···/ *n* [singular] *technical* the idea that the universe began with a single large explosion (the 'big bang'), and that the pieces are still flying apart —compare STEADY STATE THEORY

**big brother, Big Brother** *n* [singular] any person, organization, or system that seems to want to control people's lives and restrict their freedom: *Increasingly, the state is taking a big brother role in this area.*

**big busi·ness** /ˌ· ˈ··/ *n* [U] **1** very large companies, considered as a powerful group with a lot of influence **2** a product or type of activity that people spend a lot of money on: *Dieting has become big business.*

**big cat** /ˌ· ˈ·/ *n* [C] *not technical* a large animal of the cat family, such as a lion or tiger

**big cheese** /ˌ· ˈ·/ *n* [C] *informal, often humorous* an important and powerful person in an organization

**big dipper** *n* [C] **1** a small railway in a FUNFAIR, with steep slopes and sharp curves to give an exciting ride **2 the Big Dipper** *AmE* a group of seven bright stars seen only from northern parts of the world; the PLOUGH[1] (3) *BrE*

**big game** /ˌ· ˈ·/ *n* [U] large wild animals hunted for sport, such as lions and ELEPHANTS: *a big game hunter*

**big·gie** /ˈbɪgi/ *n* [C] *informal* something very large, important, or successful: *I think their new CD is going to be a biggie.*

**big gov·ern·ment** /ˈ· ˌ···/ *n* [U] *AmE* too much government involvement in people's lives: *big government welfare policies*

**big gun** /ˌ· ˈ·/ *n* [C] *informal* a person or company that has a lot of power and influence: *He's one of the party big guns.*

**big·head** /ˈbɪghed/ *n* [C] *informal* someone who thinks they are very important, clever etc —**bigheaded** /ˌbɪgˈhedɪd◂/ *adj*

**big-heart·ed** /ˌ· ˈ··◂/ *adj* very kind and generous —**big-heartedly** *adv* **big-heartedness** *n*

**big·horn sheep** /ˌbɪghɔːn ˈʃiːp‖-hɔːrn-/ *n* [C] a wild sheep with long, curved horns that lives in the mountains of western North America

**bight** /baɪt/ *n* [C] **1** a curve in a coast, like a BAY[1] (1) but not as curved **2** a LOOP[1] (1) made in the middle of a rope when tying a knot

**Big Man on Cam·pus** /ˌ· · · ˈ··/ *n* [C] *AmE informal* an important and popular male student at a college or university, especially someone who is good at sports

**big·mouth** /ˈbɪgmaʊθ/ *n* [C] *informal* someone who cannot be trusted to keep secrets

**big name** /ˌ· ˈ·/ *n* [C] a famous person or group, especially a musician, actor etc: *Poor attendance at the concert was put down to the lack of big names.*

**big noise** /ˌ· ˈ·/ *n* [C] *informal* an important and powerful person in an organization

**big·ot** /ˈbɪgət/ *n* [C] someone who is bigoted

**big·ot·ed** /ˈbɪgətɪd/ *adj* having such strong opinions about race, religion, or politics that you are unwilling to listen to anyone else's opinions: *The new sergeant was a bigot, and viewed all black men with suspicion.* | *The decision not to allow disabled athletes to take part was seen as petty and bigoted.*

**big·ot·ry** /ˈbɪgətri/ *n* [U] bigoted behaviour or beliefs: *sensational news stories that just encourage bigotry and intolerance*

**big screen** /ˌ· ˈ·/ *n* **the big screen** the cinema, rather than the television or theatre: *His first big screen part was in a 1957 horror movie, 'The Count'.*

**big shot** /ˈ· ·/ *n* [C] *informal* someone who has a lot of power or influence in a company or an area of business: *Pete Waterman, the record producer and music-biz big shot*

**big tick·et** /ˈ· ··/ *adj AmE informal* expensive: *big ticket items such as cars or refrigerators*

**big time** /ˈ· ·/ *n* **the big time** the position of being very famous or important, for example in the entertainment business or in politics: *He really made it to the big time when his book was turned into a Hollywood movie.* —**big-time** *adj: big-time cocaine dealers*

**big toe** /ˌ· ˈ·/ *n* [C] the largest toe on your foot —see picture at FOOT[1]

**big top** /ˌ· ˈ·/ *n* [C] the very large tent in which a CIRCUS (1) performance takes place

**big wheel** /ˌ· ˈ·/ *n* [C] *BrE* a machine used in AMUSEMENT PARKS, consisting of a very large upright wheel with seats hanging from it, which turns round slowly; FERRIS WHEEL *AmE*

**big·wig** /ˈbɪgwɪg/ *n* [C] *informal* an important person

**bi·jou** /ˈbiːʒuː/ *adj* [only before noun] a bijou house or apartment is small and fashionable: *a bijou residence in Mayfair*

S2 **bike¹** /baɪk/ *n* [C] **1** *informal* a bicycle or MOTORCYCLE **2 on your bike!** *BrE spoken* used to tell someone rudely to go away

**bike²** *v* [I always + adv/prep] *informal* to ride a bicycle: *She bikes to work every day.*

**bik·er** /ˈbaɪkə‖-ər/ *n* [C] someone who rides a MOTORCYCLE, especially as part of a group: *A biker's leather jacket says more about him than a thousand words.*

**bi·ki·ni** /bɪ̆ˈkiːni/ *n* [C] a piece of clothing in two separate parts that women wear for swimming

**bikini line** /-ˈ·· ˈ·/ *n* [C] the place on a woman's legs where the hair around her sexual organs stops growing

**bi·la·bi·al** /baɪˈleɪbiəl/ *n* [C] *technical* a CONSONANT sound such as /p/ or /b/ that is made using both lips —see also LABIAL —**bilabial** *adj*

**bi·lat·er·al** /baɪˈlætərəl/ *adj* **bilateral agreement/arrangement/treaty etc** an agreement etc between two groups or nations —compare MULTILATERAL, UNILATERAL —**bilaterally** *adv*

**bil·ber·ry** /ˈbɪlbəri‖-beri/ *n* [C] a blue-black fruit that grows in Northern Europe or the bush it grows on

**bile** /baɪl/ *n* [U] **1** a bitter green-brown liquid formed in the LIVER (1), which helps you to DIGEST¹ (1) fats **2** *literary* anger and hatred

**bilge** /bɪldʒ/ *n* **1** [C usually plural] the broad bottom part of a ship **2** [U] *old-fashioned informal* nonsense

**bi·lin·gual** /baɪˈlɪŋgwəl/ *adj* **1** written or spoken in two languages: *a bilingual dictionary* **2** able to speak two languages equally well: *Their kids are completely bilingual.* —**bilingual** *n* [C] —compare MONOLINGUAL, MULTILINGUAL

**bil·i·ous** /ˈbɪliəs/ *adj* **1** feeling sick: *Fatty foods make some people bilious.* **2** bad-tempered —**biliousness** *n*

**bilk** /bɪlk/ *v* [T + **out of**] *informal* to cheat someone, especially by taking their money; SWINDLE¹

S1 W1 **bill¹** /bɪl/ *n* [C]

**1 ► PAYMENT ◄ a)** a written list showing how much you have to pay for services you have received, work that has been done etc: [+ **for**] *The bill for the repairs came to $650.* | **pay/settle a bill** *Have you paid the phone bill?* **b)** *BrE* a list showing how much you have to pay for food you have eaten in a restaurant; CHECK² (7) *AmE*: *Could we have the bill, please?* —see picture on page 838

**2 ► LAW ◄** a written proposal for a new law, which is brought to a parliament so that it can be discussed: *a debate in Congress on the President's new transportation bill*

**3 ► MONEY ◄** *AmE* a piece of paper money; NOTE¹ (5) *BrE*: *a five-dollar bill*

**4 fill the bill/fit the bill** to be exactly what you need: *This car fits the bill perfectly. It's cheap and gets good mileage.*

**5 ► CONCERT/SHOW ETC ◄** a programme of entertainment at a theatre, concert, cinema etc, with details of who is performing, what is being shown etc: **top the bill** (=be the most important performer) | **a double bill** (=a show in two parts) *a great double bill with two classic horror movies*

**6 ► ADVERTISEMENT ◄** a printed notice advertising an event

**7 give sb/sth a clean bill of health** to officially state that someone is in good health or that something is working correctly: *Safety inspectors gave all the rides a clean bill of health.*

**8 ► BIRD ◄** a bird's beak

**9 the old bill/the bill** *BrE spoken* the police

**bill²** *v* [T] **1 be billed as** to be advertised or generally described in a particular way: *The election was billed as the make-or-break point for the Liberals.* **2 be billed to play/appear etc** if someone is billed to perform somewhere, it has been advertised that they will perform there: *He was billed to play three successive concerts.* **3** to send someone a bill: *Clients will be billed monthly.* **4 bill and coo** *literary or humorous* if two lovers are billing and cooing, they are kissing and talking softly

**bill·board** /ˈbɪlbɔːd‖-bɔːrd/ *n* [C] a large sign used for advertising; HOARDING (2) *BrE*

**bil·let¹** /ˈbɪlɪ̆t/ *n* [C] a private house where soldiers live temporarily

**billet²** *v* [T + **on/with**] to put soldiers in private house to live there temporarily

**bil·let-doux** /ˌbɪleɪ ˈduː/ *n plural* **billets-doux** /ˌbɪleɪ ˈduːz/ [C] *French humorous or literary* a love letter

**bill·fold** /ˈbɪlfəʊld‖-foʊld/ *n* [C] *AmE* a small flat leather case, used for carrying paper money, CREDIT CARDS etc in your pocket; WALLET (1)

**bill·hook** /ˈbɪlhʊk/ *n* [C] a tool consisting of a blade with a hooked point and a handle, used for cutting off tree branches etc

**bil·liards** /ˈbɪljədz‖-ərdz/ *n* [plural] a game played on a cloth-covered table in which balls are hit with a CUE (=a long stick) against each other and into pockets at the edge of the table —compare POOL¹ (3), SNOOKER¹ —**billiard** *adj* [only before noun] *a billiard table* | *the billiard room*

**bill·ing** /ˈbɪlɪŋ/ *n* **give sb top/star billing** to name a particular performer, actor etc as being the most important person in a show, play etc

**bil·lion** /ˈbɪljən/ *plural* **billion** or **billions** *number* **1** one thousand million —see HUNDRED (USAGE) **2** *BrE old use* a million million —**billionth** *number*

**bill of ex·change** /ˌ· · ·ˈ·/ *n* [C] *technical* a signed document ordering someone to pay someone else a particular amount of money

**bill of fare** /ˌ· · ˈ·/ *n* [C] *old-fashioned* a list of the food that is served in a restaurant; MENU (1)

**bill of lad·ing** /ˌ· · ˈ··/ *n* [C] *technical* a list of the goods being carried, especially on a ship

**bill of rights** /ˌ· · ˈ·/ *n* [C] a written statement of the most important rights of the citizens of a country: *One state has proposed the country adopt a bill of rights and replace the Queen as head of state with a president.*

**bill of sale** /ˌ· · ˈ·/ *n* [C] a written document showing that someone has bought something

**bil·low¹** /ˈbɪləʊ‖-loʊ/ *v* [I] **1** also **billow out** to swell out like a sail: *billowing skirts* **2** *literary* to rise and roll in waves: *smoke billowing upwards*

**billow²** *n* [C usually plural] **1** *literary* a wave, especially a very large one **2** a moving cloud or mass of something such as smoke or cloth

**bil·ly** /ˈbɪli/ also **bil·ly·can** /ˈbɪlikæn/ *n* [C] *BrE, AustrE* a tin pot for cooking or boiling water when you are camping

**billy club** /ˈ·· ·/ *n* [C] *AmE old-fashioned* a short stick carried by a police officer; TRUNCHEON *BrE*

**billy-goat** /ˈ·· ·/ *n* [C] *informal* a word for a male goat used especially by or to children —compare NANNY GOAT

**billy-o** /ˈ·· ·/ *n* **like billy-o** *BrE old-fashioned slang* very fast or with a lot of effort: *We ran like billy-o!*

**bil·tong** /ˈbɪltɒŋ‖-tɔːŋ/ *n* [U] *SAfrE* meat dried in the sun

**bim·bo** /ˈbɪmbəʊ‖-boʊ/ *n* [C] *informal* an insulting word for an attractive but unintelligent young woman: *He picked up some bimbo at the club last night.*

**bi·month·ly** /baɪˈmʌnθli/ *adj* appearing or happening every two months or twice each month: *a bimonthly magazine* —**bimonthly** *adv*

**bin¹** /bɪn/ *n* [C] **1** *BrE* a container for putting waste in: *Throw it in the bin.* —see picture on page 833 **2** a large S2 container for storing things, such as goods in a shop or substances in a factory

**bin²** *v* **binned, binning** [T] *BrE informal* to throw something away: *"What should I do with this letter?" "Just bin it!"*

**bi·na·ry** /ˈbaɪnəri/ *adj technical* **1 the binary system** a system of counting, used in computers, in which only the numbers 0 and 1 are used **2** consisting of two parts; double: *a binary star system*

**bind¹** /baɪnd/ *v past tense and past participle* **bound** /baʊnd/
**1** ▶ **TIE/FASTEN** ◀ [T] *formal or literary* **a)** to tie someone so that they cannot move or escape: *They bound my arms and legs with rope.* | **bound and gagged** (=tied up, and with cloth tied around your mouth so you cannot speak) **b)** also **bind up** to tie things firmly together with cloth or string: *They bound his wounds.*
**2** ▶ **UNITE** ◀ [T] to form a strong emotional or economic connection between two people, countries etc: **bind sth together** *Their shared experiences in war helped to bind the two communities together.*
**3** ▶ **STICK TOGETHER** ◀ [I,T] to stick together in a mass, or to make small pieces of something stick together: *The flour mixture isn't wet enough to bind properly.* | **bind sth** *The rain will help to bind the soil.*
**4** ▶ **RESTRICT** ◀ [T] to reduce someone's freedom of action, for example by giving them a duty or making them promise to do something: *regulations that could bind policy-makers in the future* | *The monks are bound by vows of silence.*
**5** ▶ **STITCH** ◀ [T] to strengthen or decorate something with a border of material: *The edges of the blanket were bound with ribbon.*
**6** ▶ **BOOK** ◀ [T] to fasten the pages of a book together and put them in a cover —see also BOUND

**bind sb over** *phr v* [T] *BrE law* to order someone to cause no more trouble by threatening them with legal punishment: *bound over to keep the peace*

**bind²** *n* **a bind** *informal* an annoying or difficult situation: *It's a real bind having to look after the children.*

**bind·er** /ˈbaɪndə‖-ər/ *n* **1** [C] a removable cover for holding loose sheets of paper, magazines etc —see also RING BINDER **2** [C] a person or machine that fastens the parts of a book together **3** [C,U] a substance that makes things stick together **4** [C] *AmE* an agreement in which you pay something to show that you intend to buy some property

**bind·ing¹** /ˈbaɪndɪŋ/ *adj* **a binding contract/promise/agreement etc** a promise, agreement etc that must be obeyed

**binding²** *n* **1** [C] a book cover **2** [U] material sewn or stuck along the edge of a piece of cloth for strength or decoration

**bind·weed** /ˈbaɪndwiːd/ *n* [U] a wild plant that winds itself around other plants

**binge¹** /bɪndʒ/ *n* [C] *informal* a short period when you do too much of something, especially drinking alcohol: *a week-long binge of shopping and theatre-going* | **on a binge** *Ken's gone on a binge with his mates.*

**binge²** *v* [I] *informal* to eat a lot of food in a short time, especially if you have an EATING DISORDER: [+ **on**] *Whenever she's depressed she binges on chocolates.*

**bin·go¹** /ˈbɪŋgəʊ‖-goʊ/ *n* [U] a game played for money or prizes in which numbers are chosen by chance and called out, and if you have the right numbers on your card you win: *Vera won £20 at bingo.*

**bingo²** *interjection old-fashioned* used when you have just done something successfully and are pleased: *Bingo! That's the one I've been looking for.*

**bin lin·er** /ˈ· ˌ··/ *n* [C] *BrE* a plastic bag used inside a bin (BIN¹ (1)) for holding waste

**bin·man** /ˈbɪnmæn/ *n plural* **binmen** /-men/ [C] *BrE* someone who comes to people's houses to collect their waste; GARBAGE COLLECTOR *AmE*

**bi·noc·u·lars** /bɪˈnɒkjʊləz, baɪ-‖-ˈnɑːkjʊlərz/ *n* [plural] a pair of glasses like short telescopes (TELESCOPE¹), used for looking at distant objects

**binocular vi·sion** /·ˌ··· ˈ··/ *n* [U] *technical* the ability to FOCUS (=see clearly with) both eyes on one object, which humans, monkeys, and some birds have

**bi·no·mi·al** /baɪˈnəʊmiəl‖-ˈnoʊ-/ *n* [C] *technical* a mathematical expression that has two parts connected by the sign + or the sign –, for example 3x + 4y or x – 7 —**binomial** *adj*

**bio-** /baɪəʊ, baɪə‖baɪoʊ, -ˈbaɪə/ *prefix* concerning living things: *biochemistry* (=study of the chemistry of living things)

**bi·o·chem·is·try** /ˌbaɪəʊˈkeməstri‖ˌbaɪoʊ-/ *n* [U] the scientific study of the chemistry of living things —**biochemist** *n* [C] —**biochemical** *adj*

**bi·o·de·gra·da·ble** /ˌbaɪəʊdɪˈgreɪdəbəl◂‖ˌbaɪoʊ-/ *adj technical* materials, chemicals etc that are biodegradable are changed naturally by the action of BACTERIA into substances that are not harmful to the environment

**bi·og·ra·pher** /baɪˈɒgrəfə‖-ˈɑːgrəfər-/ *n* [C] someone who writes about someone else's life

**bi·og·ra·phy** /baɪˈɒgrəfi‖-ˈɑːg-/ *n* **1** [C] an account of a person's life written by someone else: *Boswell's biography of Dr. Johnson* **2** [U] the part of literature that consists of biographies —compare AUTOBIOGRAPHY —**biographical** /ˌbaɪəˈgræfɪkəl◂/ *adj* —**biographically** /-kli/ *adv*

**bi·o·lo·gi·cal** /ˌbaɪəˈlɒdʒɪkəl‖-ˈlɑː-/ *adj* **1** connected with biology: *woman's biological function as a bearer of children* | *the biological sciences* **2 biological father/mother/parent** a child's natural parent, rather than someone who has become its parent through ADOPTION (1)

**biological clock** /ˌ····· ˈ·/ *n* [singular] **1** *technical* the time system in plants and animals that controls behaviour such as sleeping and eating, BODY CLOCK **2** *not technical* the idea that when a woman reaches a certain age, she will soon be too old to have a baby

**biological con·trol** /ˌ····· ·ˈ·/ *n* [U] a method of controlling PESTS (=small insects that harm or destroy crops) by using other insects, birds, or animals to kill them

**biological war·fare** /ˌ····· ˈ··/ *n* [U] methods of fighting a war in which BACTERIA are used to poison people, damage crops etc —compare CHEMICAL WARFARE

**bi·ol·o·gy** /baɪˈɒlədʒi‖-ˈɑːl-/ *n* [U] **1** the scientific study of living things: *She has a degree in biology.* **2** the scientific laws that control the life of a particular type of animal, plant etc: *the biology of bacteria* —**biologist** *n* [C] —**biological** /ˌbaɪəˈlɒdʒɪkəl◂‖-ˈlɑː-/ *adj*: *biological washing powder* (=using special chemicals to wash clothes) —**biologically** /-kli/ *adv*

**bi·o·mass** /ˈbaɪəʊmæs‖ˈbaɪoʊ-/ *n* [U] *technical* plant and animal matter used to provide fuel or energy

**bi·on·ic** /baɪˈɒnɪk‖-ˈɑːn-/ *adj informal* much stronger or faster than a normal person usually because of having electronic arms or legs

**bi·o·phy·sics** /ˌbaɪəʊˈfɪzɪks‖ˌbaɪoʊ-/ *n* [U] the scientific study of matter and natural forces in living things

**bi·o·pic** /ˈbaɪəʊˌpɪk‖ˈbaɪoʊ-/ *n* [C] *informal* a film that tells the story of someone's life: *'Great Balls of Fire', the biopic of Jerry Lee Lewis*

**bi·op·sy** /ˈbaɪɒpsi‖-ɑːp-/ *n* [C] the removal of cells, liquid etc from the body of someone who is ill, in order to find out more about their disease and its effects

**bi·o·rhyth·ms** /ˈbaɪəʊˌrɪðəmz‖ˈbaɪoʊ-/ *n* [plural] regular changes in the speed at which physical processes happen in your body, which some people believe can affect the way you feel and behave

**bi·o·sphere** /ˈbaɪəsfɪə‖-sfɪr/ *n* [singular] *technical* the part of the world in which animals, plants etc can live

**bi·o·tech·nol·o·gy** /ˌbaɪəʊtekˈnɒlədʒi‖ˌbaɪoʊtekˈnɑː-/ *n* [U] *technical* the use in science and industry of living things such as cells and BACTERIA, to make drugs or chemicals, destroy waste matter etc

**bi·par·ti·san** /ˌbaɪpɑːtɪ̮ˈzæn‖baɪˈpɑːrtɪ̮zən/ *adj* consisting of or representing two political parties: *Gore proposed a bipartisan committee drawn especially from both houses.*

**bi·par·tite** /baɪˈpɑːtaɪt‖-ˈpɑːr-/ *adj* **1** *formal* shared by or agreed on by two different groups: *a bipartite treaty* **2** *technical* having two parts: *a bipartite leaf* —compare TRIPARTITE

**bi·ped** /ˈbaɪped/ *n* [C] *technical* an animal with two legs, including humans —compare QUADRUPED —**bipedal** /ˌbaɪˈpedl◂/ *adj*

**bi·plane** /ˈbaɪpleɪn/ *n* [C] an aircraft with two sets of wings, especially of a type built in the early 20th century —compare MONOPLANE

**birch¹** /bɜːtʃ‖bɜːrtʃ/ *n* **1** [C,U] a tree with smooth BARK (=outer covering) and thin branches, or the wood from this tree **2 the birch** the practice of hitting people with a stick as a punishment —see also SILVER BIRCH

**birch²** *v* [T] to hit someone with a stick as a punishment

S2 W2 **bird** /bɜːd‖bɜːrd/ *n* [C]
**1** ▶ **BIRD** ◀ a creature with wings and feathers that lays eggs and can usually fly: *The tree was full of tiny, brightly-coloured birds.*
**2 a little bird told me** *spoken* used to say that you know something, but you will not say how you found out: *A little bird told me that you've got engaged.*
**3 the birds and the bees** *humorous* the facts about sex, especially as told to children
**4 birds of a feather** *informal* people of the same kind
**5 give sb the bird a)** *AmE informal* to make a very rude sign by putting your middle finger up **b)** *BrE* to make rude noises in order to show disapproval of a performer, public speaker etc
**6 a bird in the hand (is worth two in the bush)** used to say that something you already have is worth more than something which is better, but which you cannot be sure of getting
**7 the bird has flown** *informal* used to say that the person you are looking for has already left or escaped
**8 be (strictly) for the birds** *AmE informal* to be silly, useless, or not practical
**9** ▶ **WOMAN** ◀ *BrE old-fashioned* a word meaning a young woman which some women think is offensive —see also DOLLY BIRD
**10** ▶ **PERSON** ◀ *old-fashioned* a person of a particular type, especially one who seems strange or unusual: *He's a strange old bird.*
**11 do bird** *BrE slang* to spend a period of time in prison —see also **eat like a bird** (EAT (1a)), **early bird** (EARLY¹ (10)), **home bird** (HOME³ (5)), **kill two birds with one stone** (KILL¹ (10))

**bird·bath** /ˈbɜːdbɑːθ‖ˈbɜːrdbæθ/ *n* a stone bowl filled with water for birds to wash in, usually in a garden

**bird-brained** /ˈ· ·/ *adj informal* stupid or thoughtless

**bird dog** /ˈ· ·/ *n* [C] *AmE* a dog that is trained to find and bring back birds that have been shot for sport; GUN DOG

**bird·ie¹** /ˈbɜːdi‖ˈbɜːrdi/ *n* [C] **1** *spoken* a word meaning a little bird, used especially by or to children **2** one STROKE¹ (9) less than PAR (=the usual number of strokes) in a game of GOLF **3** *AmE* the small object that you hit across the net in a game of BADMINTON; SHUTTLECOCK *BrE* **4 watch the birdie** *old-fashioned* used to tell people that you are going to take a photograph of them

**birdie²** *v* [T] to hit the ball into the hole in GOLF with one STROKE¹ (9) less than PAR (=the usual number of strokes)

**bird·lime** /ˈbɜːdlaɪm‖ˈbɜːrd-/ *n* [U] a sticky substance spread on branches to catch small birds

**bird of par·a·dise** /ˌ· · ˈ· · ·/ *n* [C] a brightly coloured bird from New Guinea

**bird of pas·sage** /ˌ· · ˈ· ·/ *n* [C] **1** a bird that flies from one area or country to another, according to the seasons **2** *literary* someone who never stays in the same place for long

**bird of prey** /ˌ· · ˈ·/ *n* [C] a bird that kills other birds or small animals for food: *The peregrine falcon, a rare bird of prey, is a protected species.*

**bird·seed** /ˈbɜːdsiːd‖ˈbɜːrd-/ *n* [U] a mixture of seeds for feeding birds

**bird's-eye view** /ˌ· · ˈ·/ *n* [singular] **1** a view of something from high above it: *From the plane we had an amazing bird's-eye view of the town.* **2** a general report or account of something, without many details

**bird·song** /ˈbɜːdsɒŋ‖ˈbɜːrdsɔːŋ/ *n* [U] the musical noises made by birds: *Birdsong and the hum of insects filled the air.*

**bird ta·ble** /ˈ· ˌ· ·/ *n* [C] *BrE* a high wooden structure in a garden that you put seeds, bread etc on for birds to eat

**bird-watch·er** /ˈ· ˌ· ·/ *n* [C] someone who watches wild birds and tries to recognize different types —**bird-watching** *n* [U]

**bi·ret·ta** /bɪ̮ˈretə/ *n* [C] a square cap worn by Roman Catholic priests

**bir·i·a·ni, biryani** /ˌbɪriˈɑːni/ *n* [C,U] an Indian rice dish with meat, fish, or vegetables and spices (SPICE¹ (1))

**bi·ro** /ˈbaɪərəʊ‖ˈbaɪroʊ/ *n* [C] *BrE trademark* a pen with a small ball at the end that rolls ink onto paper; BALLPOINT: *Have you got a red biro?* —see picture at PEN¹

**birth** /bɜːθ‖bɜːrθ/ *n* **1 give birth (to)** if a woman gives birth, she produces a baby from her body: *She gave birth to a fine healthy girl.* **2** [C,U] the time when a baby comes out of its mother's body: *Congratulations on the birth of your daughter!* | *Were you present at the birth?* | **at birth** *He only weighed three pounds at birth.* **3** [U] the character, language, social position etc that you have because of the family or country you come from: *of noble birth* | *She is French by birth.* **4** [singular] the time when something new starts to exist: *the birth of an idea* | *the birth of a nation* **5 the town/country etc of your birth** the town, country etc where you were born S2 W2

**birth cer·tif·i·cate** /ˈ· ·ˌ· · ·/ *n* [C] an official document that shows when and where you were born

**birth con·trol** /ˈ· ·ˌ·/ *n* [U] the practice of controlling, by various methods, the number of children you have; CONTRACEPTION: *a safe method of birth control*

**birth·day** /ˈbɜːθdeɪ‖ˈbɜːr-/ *n* [C] **1** a day that is an exact number of years after the day when you were born: *a birthday present* | *It's my 21st birthday next week.* | **happy birthday!** *spoken* (=what you say on someone's birthday) **2 in your birthday suit** *humorous* not wearing any clothes S2 W3

**birth·mark** /ˈbɜːθmɑːk‖ˈbɜːrθmɑːrk/ *n* [C] a permanent red or brown mark on your skin that you have had since you were born: *Paul had a birthmark on his left cheek.*

**birth·place** /ˈbɜːθpleɪs‖ˈbɜːrθ-/ *n* [C usually singular] **1** the place where someone was born, especially someone famous: *Stratford-upon-Avon was Shakespeare's birthplace.* **2** the place where something first started to happen or exist: *New Orleans is the birthplace of jazz.*

**birth rate** /ˈbɜːθreɪt‖ˈbɜːrθ-/ *n* [C] the number of births for every 100 or every 1000 people in a particular year in a particular place: *a rapidly rising birthrate* —compare DEATH RATE

**birth·right** /ˈbɜːθraɪt‖ˈbɜːrθ-/ *n* [C usually singular] **1** a basic right that you believe you should have because of the family or country you come from: *Freedom of speech is every American's birthright.* **2** property, money etc that you believe you should have because it comes from your family: *Charles felt cheated out of his birthright.*

**bir·y·a·ni** /ˌbɪriˈɑːni/ *n* [C,U] another spelling of BIRIANI

**bis·cuit** /ˈbɪskɪ̮t/ *n* **1** [C] *BrE* a thin, flat, dry, usually sweet cake that is usually sold in packages or tins: *chocolate biscuits* | *cheese and biscuits* —compare COOKIE (1) **2** [C] *AmE* a type of bread baked in small round pieces S3

3 [U] a light yellowish-brown colour **4 take the biscuit** *BrE informal* to be the most surprising, annoying etc thing you have ever heard: *His latest excuse really takes the biscuit!*

**bi·sect** /baɪˈsekt‖ˈbaɪsekt/ *v* [T] *technical* to divide something, especially a line or angle, into two equal parts —**bisection** /baɪˈsekʃən‖ˈbaɪsekʃən/ *n* [U]

**bi·sex·u·al¹** /baɪˈsekʃuəl/ *adj* **1** sexually attracted to both men and women —compare HETEROSEXUAL, HOMOSEXUAL **2** having qualities or features of both sexes: *a bisexual plant* —**bisexually** *adv* —**bisexuality** /ˌbaɪsekʃuˈæləti/ *n* [U]

**bisexual²** *n* [C] someone who is sexually attracted to both men and women: *a club for bisexuals*

W3 **bish·op** /ˈbɪʃəp/ *n* [C] **1** a priest with a high rank in the Christian religion, who is the head of all the churches and priests in a large area: *the Bishop of Durham* **2** a piece in the game of CHESS that can be moved any number of squares from one corner towards the opposite corner

**bish·op·ric** /ˈbɪʃəprɪk/ *n* [C] **1** the area that a bishop is in charge of; DIOCESE **2** the position of being a bishop

**bis·muth** /ˈbɪzməθ/ *n* [U] a grey-white metal that is often used in medicine

**bi·son** /ˈbaɪsən/ *n plural* **bison** or **bisons** [C] an animal like a large cow with long hair, which used to be common in North America; BUFFALO (2): *ancient cave paintings of bison at Lascaux*

**bisque** /bɪsk/ *n* [U] a thick, creamy soup, especially one made from SHELLFISH: *lobster bisque*

**bis·tro** /ˈbiːstrəʊ‖-troʊ/ *n* [C] a small restaurant or bar

S1 W1 **bit¹** /bɪt/ *n* [C]

**1 ▶ SLIGHTLY/FAIRLY ◀ a bit** *informal, especially BrE* **a)** slightly, but not very; a little: *Could you turn the radio down a bit, please?* | *Stay a bit longer – it's still early.* | *I think you're a bit young to be watching this.* | **a bit more/less** *Would you like a bit more cake?* | **a bit like** (=a little similar) *She's a bit like my sister.* **b)** used when you mean 'very' or 'quite a lot', but you do not want to emphasize it too much: *It's all a bit depressing, really.* —see graph at LITTLE

**2 ▶ AMOUNT ◀** *informal, especially BrE* a small amount, especially of something that is not a physical object: **[+ of]** *Let me give you a bit of advice.* | *We may need a bit of help.* | *He still likes to do a bit of gardening.*

**3 ▶ PIECE ◀** a small piece of something: **[+ of]** *The floor was covered with bits of broken glass.* | **break/smash/blow sth to bits** *The bridge was blown to bits by the blast.* | **fall to bits** *That old table's falling to bits.*

**4 ▶ PART ◀** *informal especially BrE* a part or piece of something larger: *You can play on the grass, but keep off the muddy bits.* | **[+ of]** *I liked the last bit of the film best.*

**5 a good bit/quite a bit** *especially BrE* a fairly large amount, or to a fairly large degree: *She knows quite a bit about European history.* | *She's quite a bit older than me.*

**6 not a bit** *especially BrE* not at all: *You're not a bit like your brother, are you?* | *I wasn't a bit worried.*

**7 every bit as** just as much as: *I think she's every bit as pretty as her sister.*

**8 bit by bit** *especially BrE* gradually: *It's a slow process, but we're getting there bit by bit.*

**9 a bit at a time** *especially BrE* in several small parts, not all at the same time: *Just do a bit at a time.*

**10 ▶ TOOL ◀** the sharp part of a tool for cutting or making holes: *a drill bit*

**11 ▶ FOR A HORSE ◀** a metal bar that is put in the mouth of a horse and used for controlling its movements —see picture at HORSE¹

**12 ▶ COMPUTER ◀** the smallest unit of information that can be used by a computer: *a 16-bit processor* —compare BYTE

**13 a bit part** a very small and unimportant acting job in a play or film: *He got a bit part in 'Coronation Street'.*

**14 bits and pieces/bits and bobs** *BrE informal* any small things of various kinds: *Let me get my bits and pieces together.* | *I still had a few bits and bobs of work left to do.*

**15 do your bit** *BrE informal* to do your share of the work that needs to be done: *I don't mind doing my bit, but I'm not organizing the whole thing on my own.*

**16 get the bit between your teeth** *BrE* to start doing something in a very determined way, so that you are not likely to stop until it is done: *Once she'd got the bit between her teeth, there was no stopping her.*

**17 take the bit between your teeth** *AmE* to make a determined effort to deal with something difficult or unpleasant: *I just have to take the bit between my teeth and start writing that essay.*

**18 ▶ US MONEY ◀ a)** *AmE old use* 12½ cents: *I wouldn't give you two bits for that old book.* —see also **two bits** (TWO (7)) **b)** *BrE old use* a small coin: *a threepenny bit*

**19 ▶ YOUNG WOMAN ◀** also **a bit of stuff/fluff/skirt** *spoken* offensive expressions meaning a young woman, especially one who is sexually attractive

**20 a bit of all right** *BrE informal* used to describe someone you think is sexually attractive: *She's a bit of all right.*

**21 a bit on the side** *BrE informal often humorous* the girlfriend or boyfriend of someone who is already married or involved in a sexual relationship with someone else —see also **be champing at the bit** (CHAMP¹ (2)), **a bit of rough** (ROUGH¹ (19))

Frequencies of the noun **bit** in spoken and written English.

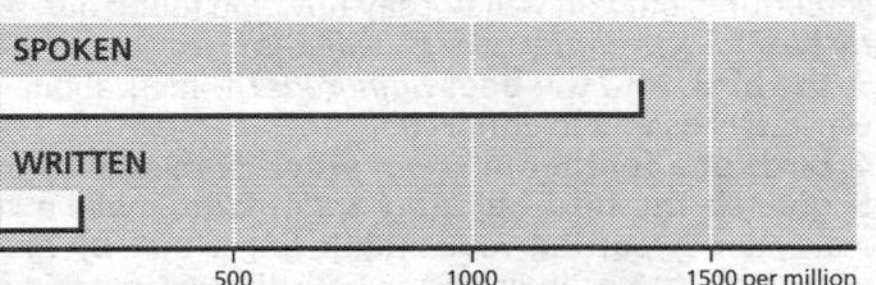


Based on the British National Corpus and the Longman Lancaster Corpus

This graph shows that the noun **bit** is much more common in spoken English than in written English. This is because **a bit** is more common than **a little** in spoken English, and **bit** is used in a lot of common spoken phrases.

**bit (*n*) SPOKEN PHRASES**

**22 a bit of a problem/surprise/fool etc** *BrE* a problem, surprise etc, but not a very big or serious one: *The party was a bit of a disappointment in the end.* | *I had a bit of a shock when I got home.* | *I'm afraid I'm in a bit of a hurry just now – I'll give you a ring later.*

**23 with a bit of luck** *especially BrE* if things go well and there are no problems: *With a bit of luck we should get it finished tomorrow.*

**24 take a bit of doing/fixing etc** *BrE* to be difficult to do, fix etc: *This new system takes a bit of getting used to, doesn't it?*

**25 play the piano a bit/speak French a bit etc** *BrE* to be able to play the piano, speak French etc, but not particularly well or often: *I used to act a bit when I was younger.*

**26 for a bit/in a bit** *BrE* for or after a short period of time: *Could you mind the baby for a bit?* | *I'll see in you in a bit then.*

**27 a bit much** *BrE* used to say that something is not fair or reasonable: *I thought it was a bit much, asking me to drive him all the way home.*

**28 not a bit of it** *especially BrE* used to say that something did not happen, even though you expected that it would: *He should at least have apologized, but not a bit of it!*

**29 the student bit/travelling etc bit** the behaviour or experience that is typical of a student, of travelling etc: *Then she gave us the concerned mother bit.* | *He's really gone in for the whole hippy bit.*

**bit²** the past tense of BITE¹

**bitch¹** /bɪtʃ/ *n* [C] **1** a female dog **2** *informal* an insulting word for a woman that you dislike or think is unpleasant: *She's such a bitch.* | *The silly bitch went and* *told the police.* **3** *AmE spoken* something that causes problems or difficulties: *I love that silk dress, but it's a bitch to wash.* —see also SON OF A BITCH

**bitch²** *v* [I] *informal* **1** to make unpleasant remarks about someone or something: [+ **about**] *We were all bitching about the boss when she walked in.* **2** to complain continuously: *Stop bitching!*|[+ **at**] *AmE*: *He kept bitching at me for waking him up.*

**bitch·in** /ˈbɪtʃən/ *adj AmE slang* very good; excellent: *That's a bitchin car!*|*"We're going to the beach, wanna come?" "Bitchin! Let's go!"*

**bitch·y** /ˈbɪtʃi/ *adj informal* unkind and unpleasant about other people: *a bitchy remark*|*She can be really bitchy sometimes.* —**bitchily** *adv* —**bitchiness** *n* [U]

S 2 **bite¹** /baɪt/ *v past tense* **bit** /bɪt/ *past participle* **bitten** /ˈbɪtn/

bite

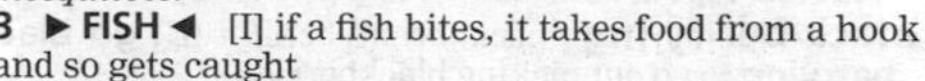

**1 ► WITH YOUR TEETH ◄** [I,T] to cut or crush something with your teeth: *Be careful! My dog bites.*|*Do you bite your fingernails?*|[+ **into/through**] *biting into a juicy apple*|*They had to bite through the rope to escape.*|**bite sth off** *a man whose arm had been bitten off by an alligator*

**2 ► INSECT/SNAKE ◄** [I,T] if an insect or snake bites you, it injures you by making a hole in your skin: *I was bitten all over by mosquitoes.*

**3 ► FISH ◄** [I] if a fish bites, it takes food from a hook and so gets caught

**4 ► NOT SLIP ◄** [I] to hold firmly to a surface, or rest firmly against it; GRIP² (1): [+ **into**] *The ski's edge should bite into the snow.*

**5 ► HAVE AN EFFECT ◄** [I] to have the effect that was intended, especially an unpleasant one: *The new tobacco taxes have begun to bite.*

**6 bite your tongue** to try hard to stop yourself from saying what you really think: *She was really making me angry, but I bit my tongue.*

**7 bite the dust a)** to die, fail, or be defeated: *a welfare programme that bit the dust following budget cuts* **b)** to stop working completely: *My old car's finally bitten the dust.*

**8 bite the bullet** *informal* to bravely accept something unpleasant: *Decisions have to be taken, and as director you have to bite the bullet.*

**9 bite sb's head off** *informal* to answer someone or speak to them very angrily, when there is no good reason for doing this: *I asked if she needed any help, and she bit my head off!*

**10 bite off more than you can chew** to try to do more than you are able to do

**11 he/she won't bite** *spoken* used to say that there is no need to be afraid of someone, especially someone in authority: *Well go and ask him – he won't bite!*

**12 what's biting you/her etc?** *spoken* used to ask why someone is annoyed or upset

**13 once bitten twice shy** used to say that if you have failed or been hurt once, you will be very careful next time

**14 bite the hand that feeds you** to harm someone who has treated you well or supported you

**15 be bitten by the bug/craze etc** to develop a very strong interest in or desire for something: *By then she had been bitten by the travel bug, and could not wait to go again.*

**bite back** *phr v* **1** [T **bite** sth ↔ **back**] to stop yourself from saying something or telling someone what you really feel: *She bit back the insult that rose to her lips.* **2** [I] to react strongly and angrily when someone criticizes you: *Determined to bite back at car thieves, he wired his Sierra Cosworth to an electric fence.*

**bite into** sth *phr v* [T] to cut or press hard against a surface: *The knotted cord bit into my skin.*

**bite²** *n* S 3

**1 ► WITH YOUR TEETH ◄** [C] the act of cutting or crushing something with your teeth: **give sb a bite** *The cat gave Mike a playful bite.*|**have/take a bite of** (=bite a small piece from a larger piece of food) *Can I have a bite of your apple?*

**2 ► WOUND ◄** [C] a wound made when an animal or insect bites you: *My face was covered in mosquito bites!*

**3 a bite (to eat)** *spoken* a small meal: *I haven't had a bite to eat all day.*|*Let's grab a bite at the airport.*

**4 ► COLD ◄** [singular] a feeling of coldness: *There's a real bite in the air tonight.*

**5 ► TASTE ◄** [U] a pleasantly sharp or bitter taste: *I like cheese with a bit of bite.*

**6 ► EFFECTIVENESS ◄** [U] a special quality in a piece of speech or writing that makes its arguments or criticisms effective and likely to persuade people: *a political satire that lacked bite*

**7 ► FISH ◄** [C] an occasion when a fish takes the food from a hook: *Sometimes I sit for hours and never get a bite.*

**8 bite-size/bite-sized** the right size to fit into your mouth easily: *Cut them into bite-size pieces before serving.*

**9 another bite/a second bite at the cherry** *BrE* a second chance to do something

**bit·ing** /ˈbaɪtɪŋ/ *adj* **1** a biting wind is unpleasantly cold: *A biting wind blew down from the hills.* **2** a biting criticism, remark is cruel or unkind: *biting sarcasm* —**bitingly** *adv*

**bit·map** /ˈbɪtmæp/ *n* [C] *technical* a computer image consisting of an arrangement of bits (BIT¹ (12)): *bitmap fonts*

**bit·sy** /ˈbɪtsi/ *adj AmE informal* very small —see also ITSY-BITSY

**bit·ten** /ˈbɪtn/ the past participle of BITE¹

**bit·ter¹** /ˈbɪtə‖-ər/ *adj* S 3 W 3

**1 ► ANGRY/UPSET ◄** full of angry, jealous, and unhappy feelings because you think you have been badly treated or that unfair things have happened to you: *He became bitter and disillusioned as he grew older.*|[+ **about**] *They all lost their jobs when the company was taken over, and obviously they're very bitter about it.*

**2 ► CAUSING UNHAPPINESS ◄** [only before noun] making you feel very unhappy and upset: *Losing the election was a bitter humiliation.*|**a bitter disappointment/blow** *If he failed, it would be a bitter disappointment to his parents.*|**from bitter experience** (=because of your own very unpleasant experiences) *We had learned from bitter experience not to trust their promises.*

**3 ► FULL OF HATRED ◄** a bitter argument, attack, struggle etc is one in which people oppose or criticize each other with strong feelings of hate and anger: *bitter opposition to the President's policies*|*bitter enemies*

**4 ► TASTE ◄** having a strong taste like black coffee without sugar, or very dark chocolate: *The medicine tasted bitter and the child spat it out.* —compare SWEET¹ (1), SOUR¹ (1)

**5 ► COLD ◄** unpleasantly cold: *a bitter east wind*|**bitter cold** *a bitter cold day in February* —see COLD¹ (USAGE)

**6 to the bitter end** continuing until the end, in spite of problems or difficulties: *She stayed with him to the bitter end, although it must have been horrible.*

**7 a bitter pill (to swallow)** something very unpleasant that you have to accept: *His failure was a bitter pill to swallow.* —see also BITTERLY —**bitterness** *n* [U]

**bitter²** *n* **1** [C,U] *BrE* bitter beer of the type drunk in Britain, or a glass of this: *A pint of bitter, please* —compare MILD **2 bitters** [U] a bitter liquid made from a mixture of plant products and used to add taste to alcoholic drinks

**bit·ter·ly** /ˈbɪtəli‖-ər-/ *adv* **1** in a way that makes you very unhappy, or shows that you are very unhappy: *The boys complained bitterly about their chores.*|*I was bitterly disappointed.*|*a decision that she bitterly regretted* **2 bitterly cold** very cold

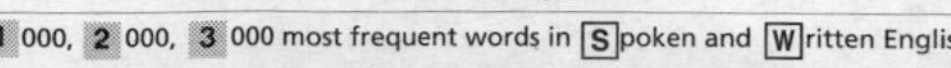

**bit·tern** /ˈbɪtən‖-ərn/ *n* [C] a brown European bird with long legs that lives near water and makes a deep sound

**bit·ter·sweet** /ˌbɪtəˈswiːt◂‖-tər-/ *adj* **1** feelings, memories, or experiences that are bittersweet are happy and sad at the same time: *bittersweet memories of childhood* **2** a taste or smell that is bittersweet is both sweet and bitter at the same time

**bit·ty** /ˈbɪti/ *adj BrE informal* having too many small parts that do not seem to be connected to each other: *I thought the film was rather bitty.* —**bittiness** *n* [U]

**bi·tu·men** /ˈbɪtʃʊmɪ̱n‖bɪ̱ˈtuː-/ *n* [U] a sticky substance made from petrol products that is used for making the surface of roads —**bituminous** /bɪ̱ˈtjuːmɪ̱nəs‖-ˈtuː-/ *adj*

**bi·valve** /ˈbaɪvælv/ *n* [C] *technical* any sea animal that has two shells joined together, such as an OYSTER

**biv·ou·ac¹** /ˈbɪvu-æk/ *n* a temporary camp built outside without any tents

**bivouac²** *v* **bivouacked, bivouacking** [I] to spend the night outside without tents in a temporary camp: *The climbers bivouacked halfway up the mountain.*

**bi·week·ly** /baɪˈwiːkli/ *adj, adv* **1** appearing or happening every two weeks; FORTNIGHTLY: *a biweekly magazine* **2** appearing or happening twice a week; SEMIWEEKLY: *a biweekly television drama*

**biz** /bɪz/ *n* [singular] *informal* a particular type of business, especially one connected with entertainment

**bi·zarre** /bɪ̱ˈzɑː‖-ˈzɑːr/ *adj* very unusual or strange: *a bizarre coincidence | bizarre religious sects* —**bizarrely** *adv*

**blab** /blæb/ *v* [I] *informal* to tell secret information to someone who is not supposed to know it: [+ **to**] *What if they blab to the newspapers?*

**blab·ber** /ˈblæbə‖-ər/ *v* [I] *informal* to talk in a silly or annoying way, especially for a long time: [+ **on**] *I wish she'd stop blabbering on about her boyfriends.*

**blab·ber·mouth** /ˈblæbəmaʊθ‖-ər-/ *n* [C] *informal* someone who tells secrets because they always talk too much

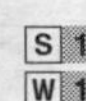
**black¹** /blæk/ *adj*
**1** ▶ **COLOUR** ◀ having the colour of night or coal: *a black evening dress | The mountains looked black against the moon. | She has short black hair.* —see picture on page 411
**2** ▶ **PEOPLE** ◀ **a)** someone who is black is a member of a dark-skinned race, especially the Negro race: *Over half the students here are black.* **b)** [only before noun] connected with or concerning black people: *politics from a black perspective | contemporary black music* —see NEGRO (USAGE)
**3** ▶ **TEA/COFFEE** ◀ black coffee or tea does not have milk in it: *Two black coffees, please.* —opposite WHITE¹ (4)
**4** ▶ **DIRTY** ◀ very dirty: *My hands were black from working on the car.*
**5** ▶ **WITHOUT HOPE** ◀ sad and without much hope for the future; GLOOMY: *Things were beginning to look pretty black for us. | a feeling of black despair |* **a black day** (=when something very sad or upsetting happens) *It's been another black day for the motor industry, with announcements of major job losses.*
**6** ▶ **ANGRY** ◀ full of feelings of anger or hate: *I knew not to irritate him when he was in such a black mood. | Denise gave me a black look.*
**7 not be as black as you are painted** not to be as bad as people say you are
**8** ▶ **EVIL** ◀ *literary* very bad: *black deeds | a black-hearted villain* —see also BLACKLY —**blackness** *n* [C]

**black²** *n* **1** [U] the dark colour of night or coal **2** [U] black clothes: *You look good in black.* **3** [C] someone who belongs to a dark-skinned race, especially the Negro race: *laws that discriminated against blacks* —see NEGRO (USAGE) **4 be in the black** to have money in your bank account —opposite **be in the red** (RED² (5)) **5** [U] black paint, colour etc: *Put some more black around your eyes.*

**black³** *v* [T] **1** *BrE* if a TRADE UNION blacks goods or blacks a company, it refuses to work with them **2** *old-fashioned* to make something black

**black out** *v* **1** [I] to lose consciousness; faint: *I completely blacked out after the accident.* **2** [T **black** sth ↔ **out**] to put a dark mark over something so that it cannot be seen: *The censors had blacked out several words.* **3** [T **black** sth ↔ **out**] to hide or turn off all the lights in a town or city, especially during war —see also BLACKOUT

**black·a·moor** /ˈblækəmʊə‖-mʊr/ *n* [C] *old use* an offensive word for a black person, especially a man

**black and blue** /ˌ· · ˈ·◂/ *adj* skin that is black and blue has BRUISES (=dark marks) on it as a result of being hit: *Ron's been skiing. He's black and blue all over!*

**black and white** /ˌ· · ˈ·◂/ *adj* **1** showing pictures or images only in black, white, and grey: *a black and white photo | an old black and white TV* **2 black and white** considering things in a very simple way, as if there are clear differences between good and bad, right and wrong etc: *a rather black and white presentation of the situation |* **a black and white decision/issue/question** (=where the difference between two choices is completely clear) **3 in black and white** in written form, and therefore definite: *You'd better get a commitment in black and white first. | There it was in black and white – I'd passed the exam!*

**black art** /ˌ· ˈ·/ *n* [U] also **the black arts** [plural] BLACK MAGIC

**black·ball** /ˈblækbɔːl‖-bɒːl/ *v* [T] to vote against someone, especially so that they cannot join a club or social group

**black belt** /ˌ· ˈ·/ *n* [C] **1** a high rank in some types of Eastern self-defence, especially JUDO and KARATE **2** someone who has this rank: *Sandy's a blackbelt in judo.*

**black·ber·ry** /ˈblækbəri‖-beri/ *n* [C] the black or purple fruit of a type of BRAMBLE —see picture on page 413

**black·ber·ry·ing** /ˈblækbəri-ɪŋ‖-beri-/ *n* [U] **go blackberrying** to go out picking blackberries

**black·bird** /ˈblækbɜːd‖-bɜːrd/ *n* [C] a common European and American bird, the male of which is completely black

**black·board** /ˈblækbɔːd‖-bɔːrd/ *n* [C] a board with a dark smooth surface, used in schools for writing on with CHALK¹ (2) —compare WHITEBOARD

**black box** /ˌ· ˈ·/ *n* [C] an electronic unit that controls or records information about a machine, especially on an aircraft; FLIGHT RECORDER

**black com·e·dy** /ˌ· ˈ···/ *n* [C,U] a play, story etc that is funny, but also shows the unpleasant side of human life

**black·cur·rant** /ˌblækˈkʌrənt◂‖-ˈkɜːr-/ *n* [C] **1** a European plant that grows in gardens and has small blue-black berries (BERRY) **2** a berry from this plant: *blackcurrant juice* —compare REDCURRANT

**Black Death** /ˌ· ˈ·/ *n* [singular] the illness that killed large numbers of people in Europe and Asia in the 14th century —see also BUBONIC PLAGUE, PLAGUE¹ (2)

**black e·con·o·my** /ˌ· ·ˈ···/ *n* [singular] business activity that takes place unofficially, especially in order to avoid tax —compare BLACK MARKET

**black·en** /ˈblækən/ *v* **1** [I,T] to become black, or make something black: *Smoke had blackened the ceiling of the room.* **2 blacken sb's name/character/reputation etc** to say unpleasant things about someone in order to make other people have a bad opinion of them

**black En·glish** /ˌ· ˈ··/ *n* [U] the variety of English spoken by some black people in the US

**black eye** /ˌ· ˈ·/ *n* [C] darkness of the skin around your eye, because you have been hit: *Joe came home with a black eye.*

**black-eyed bean** /ˌ· · ˈ·/ *BrE*, **black-eyed pea** *AmE n* [C] a small pale bean with a black spot on it

**black-eyed Su·san** /ˌblæk aɪd ˈsuːzən/ *n* [C] a type of yellow or orange flower that grows in North America

**black gold** /ˌ· ˈ·/ *n* [U] *informal* oil

**black goods** /ˈ· ·/ *n* [plural] *BrE* pieces of equipment used in the house that are usually black, such as televisions or HI-FIS —compare WHITE GOODS

**black·guard** /ˈblægɑːd, -əd‖-ərd, -ɑːrd/ *n* [C] *old use* a man who treats other people very badly; SCOUNDREL

**black·head** /ˈblækhed/ *n* [C] a small spot on the skin, with a black centre

**black hole** /ˌ· ˈ·/ *n* [C] **1** *technical* an area in outer space into which everything near it, including light, is pulled **2** *informal* something that seems to keep using up all your money

**black hu·mour** /ˌ· ˈ··/ *n* [U] jokes, funny stories etc that deal with the unpleasant parts of human life

**black ice** /ˌ· ˈ·/ *n* [U] an area of ice that is very difficult to see: *dangerous driving conditions, with black ice in many areas*

**black·ing** /ˈblækɪŋ/ *n* [U] *old-fashioned* a very thick liquid or polish that is put on objects to make them black

**black·jack** /ˈblækdʒæk/ *n* [U] a card game

**black lead** /ˌblæk ˈled/ *n* [U] a soft black substance; GRAPHITE

**black·leg** /ˈblækleg/ *n* [C] *BrE* someone who continues to work when other workers are on strike (STRIKE[2] (1))

**blacklist[1]** /ˈblækˌlɪst/ *n* [C] a list of people, countries, products etc that are disapproved of, and should therefore be avoided or punished: *Friends of the Earth have produced a blacklist of environmentally damaging products.*

**black·list[2]** *v* [T] to put a person, country, product etc on a blacklist: *I've been blacklisted by the insurance companies just because of one silly accident!*

**black lung** /ˌ· ˈ·/ *n* [U] *AmE informal* a lung disease caused by breathing in coal dust over a long period of time

**black·ly** /ˈblækli/ *adv literary* in an angry, threatening, or unpleasant way: *clouds blackly looming*

**black mag·ic** /ˌ· ˈ··/ *n* [U] magic that is believed to use the power of the Devil for evil purposes —see also WHITE MAGIC

**black·mail[1]** /ˈblækmeɪl/ *v* [T] to demand money or favours from someone by threatening to tell secrets about them: **blackmail sb into doing sth** *Don't think you can blackmail me into helping you!* —**blackmailer** *n* [C]

**blackmail[2]** *n* [U] **1** the practice of getting money from someone or making them do what you want by threatening to tell secrets about them **2** an attempt to make someone do what you want by making threats or by making them feel guilty if they do not: *Staff who refused to work on Sundays faced losing their jobs – it was sheer blackmail.* | **emotional blackmail** (=by making someone feel guilty) *She had already tried emotional blackmail to stop him leaving.*

**black Ma·ri·a** /ˌblæk məˈraɪə/ *n* [C] *BrE old-fashioned* a vehicle used by the police to move prisoners

**black mar·ket** /ˌ· ˈ··◂/ *n* [C] the system by which people illegally buy and sell foreign money, goods that are difficult to obtain etc: [**+ in**] *There's a thriving black market in vehicle parts.* | **on the black market** *The exchange rate for dollars was much higher on the black market.* | *black market cigarettes* —compare BLACK ECONOMY

**black mar·ket·eer** /ˌ· ··ˈ·/ *n* [C] someone who sells things on the black market

**Black Mus·lim** /ˌ· ˈ··/ *n* [C] a member of a group of black people who believe in the religion of Islam and want a separate black society

**black·out** /ˈblækaʊt/ *n* [C] **1** a period of darkness caused by a failure of the electricity supply: *The storm caused a sudden blackout and brought down telephone lines.* **2** a period during a war when all the lights in a town etc must be turned off **3** an occasion when you suddenly lose consciousness: *You'll have to go to the doctor if you keep getting these blackouts.* **4** a situation in which particular pieces of news or information are not allowed to be reported: *A news blackout was imposed during the peace negotiations.*

**black pep·per** /ˌ· ˈ··/ *n* [U] pepper made from crushed seeds from which the dark outer covering has not been removed

**black pud·ding** /ˌ· ˈ··/ *n* [C,U] *BrE* a kind of thick dark SAUSAGE made from animal blood and fat

**black sheep** /ˌ· ˈ·/ *n* [C usually singular] someone who is regarded by other members of their family or group as a failure or embarrassment: *She's the black sheep of the family.*

**Black·shirt** /ˈblækʃɜːt‖-ʃɜːrt/ *n* [C] a member of a FASCIST organization with a black shirt as part of its uniform

**black·smith** /ˈblækˌsmɪθ/ *n* [C] someone who makes and repairs things made of iron, especially HORSESHOES

**black spot** /ˈ· ·/ *n* [C] *especially BrE* **1** part of a road where accidents often happen **2** a place or area where there are more problems than usual: *the worst unemployment black spots* | *an accident blackspot*

**black·strap mo·las·ses** /ˌblækstræp məˈlæsɪz/ *n* [U] *AmE* the darkest, thickest MOLASSES (=thick sweet liquid) produced when sugar is taken from sugar plants

**black·thorn** /ˈblækθɔːn‖-θɔːrn/ *n* [C] a European bush that has small white flowers

**black-tie** /ˌ· ˈ·◂/ *adj* a black-tie party or social occasion is one at which people wear EVENING DRESS (=special formal clothes) *Jan and George are having a party – it's black tie.* —compare WHITE TIE

**black·top** /ˈblæktɒp‖-tɑːp/ *n AmE* **1** [U] a thick black sticky substance that becomes hard as it dries, used to cover roads; BITUMEN **2** [singular] the surface of a road covered by this substance: *We left the blacktop and drove along a forest road.*

**black wa·ter fe·ver** /ˌ· ·· ˈ··/ *n* [U] a very severe form of the disease MALARIA

**black wid·ow** /ˌ· ˈ··/ *n* [C] a very poisonous type of SPIDER that is black with red marks

**blad·der** /ˈblædə‖-ər/ *n* [C] **1** an organ of the body, that is shaped like a bag and contains URINE (=waste liquid from the body) until it is passed out of the body **2** a bag of skin, leather, or rubber, for example inside a football, that can be filled with air or liquid —see also GALL BLADDER

**blade** /bleɪd/ *n* [C] **1** the flat cutting part of a tool or weapon: *Keep the blade of your penknife sharp.* | *a packet of razor blades* —see picture at TOOL[1] and SWORD **2** the flat wide part of an object that pushes against air or water: *the blade of an oar* | *a ceiling fan with polished blades* **3** a long flat leaf of grass or a similar plant: *a blade of grass* **4** the metal part on the bottom of an ICE-SKATE[2] —see also SHOULDER BLADE S3

**blag** /blæg/ *v* [I,T] *BrE slang* to obtain something you want by talking in a clever way: *He blagged his way in by saying he was a friend of the owner.*

**blah[1]** /blɑː/ *n* [U] **1 blah, blah, blah** *spoken* used when you do not need to complete what you are saying because it is boring or because the person you are talking to already knows it: *The answer to question 3, 'which South American country has blah, blah, blah?' is Argentina.* **2** *BrE spoken* remarks or statements that are boring and do not mean much: *the usual blah about everyone working harder* S2

**blah[2]** *adj AmE spoken* **1** not having an interesting taste, appearance, character etc: *The decor of the house was kind of blah.* **2** slightly unwell or unhappy: *I feel really blah today.*

**blame[1]** /bleɪm/ *v* [T] **1** to say or think that someone or something is responsible for something bad: *It's not fair to blame me – it's not my fault we lost.* | **blame sb/sth for** *Mom blamed herself for Danny's problems.* | *The report blames poor safety standards for the accident.* | **blame sth on** *Don't go trying to blame it on me!* | **be to blame** (=be responsible for something bad) *You're not to blame for what happened.* **2 don't blame me** *spoken* used when you are advising someone not to do something: *Buy it then, but don't blame me when it breaks down.* **3 I don't blame you/them etc** *spoken* used to say that you think it S2 W3 was right or reasonable for someone to do what they did: *"She's left her husband." "I don't blame her, after the way he treated her."* **4 only have yourself to blame** *spoken* used to say that someone's problems are their own fault: *If he fails his exams, he'll only have himself to blame.* **5** to criticize someone or something: **blame sb/sth for** *The documentary was blamed for its one-sided presentation of the strike.*

**B**

**blame²** *n* [U] responsibilty for a mistake or for something bad: [+ **for**] *The government cannot escape blame for the state of the economy.* | **get the blame** (=be blamed) *I always get the blame for his mistakes!* | **take the blame** (=say that something is your fault) *You can't expect Terry to take all the blame.* | **put/lay the blame on** (=say that something is someone else's fault) *The other driver kept trying to put the blame on me.*

**blame·less** /ˈbleɪmləs/ *adj formal* not guilty of anything bad; INNOCENT¹ (1): *I don't think he's entirely blameless.* | *a blameless life* —**blamelessly** *adv*

**blame·wor·thy** /ˈbleɪmˌwɜːðiǁ-ɜːr-/ *adj formal* deserving blame or disapproval: *blameworthy conduct*

**blanch** /blɑːntʃǁblæntʃ/ *v* **1** [I] to become pale because you are frightened or shocked: *Robin swallowed and blanched. "Oh, God! Pregnant!"* **2** [T] to put vegetables, fruit, or nuts into boiling water for a short time: *Blanch the peaches and remove the skins.* **3** [T] to make a plant become pale by keeping it away from light

**blanc·mange** /bləˈmɒnʒ, -ˈmɒndʒǁ-ˈmɑː-/ *n* [C,U] *BrE* a cold sweet food made from CORNFLOUR, milk, and sugar

**bland** /blænd/ *adj* **1** without any excitement, strong opinions, or special character: *The principal made a few bland comments about the value of education.* | *Their music is pleasant enough, but a little bland.* **2** food that is bland has very little taste: *a rather bland potato soup* —**blandly** *adv* —**blandness** *n* [U]

**blan·dish·ments** /ˈblændɪʃmənts/ *n* [plural] *formal* praise and nice remarks about someone that are intended to persuade them or influence someone: *She was immune to both their threats and their blandishments.*

S3 **blank¹** /blæŋk/ *adj* **1** showing no expression, understanding, or interest: *Her eyes were blank and stared right through me.* | *a blank look* **2** without any writing, print, or recorded sound: *Leave the last page blank.* | *a blank cassette* **3 go blank a)** to be suddenly unable to remember something: *When I got into the exam room I just panicked and my mind went completely blank.* **b)** to stop showing any images, writing etc: *Suddenly the screen went blank.* —see also BLANK VERSE —**blankly** *adv* —**blankness** *n* [U]

**blank²** *n* [C] **1** an empty space on a piece of paper, where you are supposed to write a word or letter: *Use this information to fill in the blanks on your form.* **2 my mind's a blank** *spoken* used to say that you cannot remember something: *I'm trying to think of his name, but my mind's a complete blank.* **3** a CARTRIDGE (=container for a bullet in a gun) that contains an explosive but no bullet: *Soldiers fired blanks into the crowd.* —see also **draw a blank** (DRAW¹ (36)), —**blankness** *n* [U]

**blank³** *v* **1** [I] *AmE* to be suddenly unable to remember something: *I blanked in the oral exam.* **2** [T] *BrE spoken* to ignore someone who you would usually greet or speak to: *Why did she blank Phil when he came in?*

**blank** sth ↔ **out** *phr v* [T] *informal* **1** to cover something so that it cannot be seen: *The actual names had been blanked out.* **2** to completely forget something, especially deliberately: *I tried to blank out everything he had said from my mind.*

**blank car·tridge** /ˌ· ˈ··/ *n* [C] a CARTRIDGE (1) that contains an explosive but no bullet

**blank cheque** *BrE*, **blank check** *AmE* /ˌ· ˈ·/ *n* [C] **1** a cheque that has been signed, but has not had the amount written on it **2 give sb a blank cheque/check** to give someone permission to do whatever they think is necessary in a particular situation

**blan·ket¹** /ˈblæŋkɪt/ *n* [C] **1** a cover for a bed, usually made of wool **2** a thick covering or area of something: [+ **of**] *The valley was covered with a blanket of mist.* —see also WET BLANKET

**blanket²** *v* [T usually passive] to cover something with a thick layer: [+ **in/with**] *All the rooftops were blanketed in snow.*

**blanket³** *adj* [only before noun] **blanket statement/rule/ban etc** a statement, rule etc that affects everyone or includes all possible cases: *a blanket ban on the use of aerosols* | *We sent out a blanket mailing to every member of Congress.*

**blank·e·ty-blank** /ˌblæŋkɪti ˈblæŋk/ *adj* [only before noun] *AmE spoken* used to show annoyance when you want to avoid swearing: *The blankety-blank key is stuck!*

**blank verse** /ˌ· ˈ·/ *n* [U] poetry that has a fixed RHYTHM (1) but does not RHYME² (1): *Shakespeare's blank verse*—compare FREE VERSE

**blare** /bleəǁbler/ *v* [I,T] to make a very loud unpleasant noise: *Horns blared in the street outside my hotel window.* | *blaring sirens* | **blare out** *a stereo blaring out rock music* —**blare** *n* [singular]

**blar·ney** /ˈblɑːniǁ-ɑːr-/ *n* [U] *informal especially BrE* pleasant but untrue things that you say to someone in order to trick or persuade them

**bla·sé** /ˈblɑːzeɪǁblɑːˈzeɪ/ *adj* not worried or excited about things that most people think are important, impressive etc: *He's very blasé about money now that he's got that job.*

**blas·pheme** /blæsˈfiːm/ *v* [I + **against**] to speak in a way that insults God or people's religious beliefs, or to use the names of God and holy things when swearing —**blasphemer** *n* [C]

**blas·phe·my** /ˈblæsfɪmi/ *n* [C,U] something you say or do that is insulting to God or people's religious beliefs —**blasphemous** *adj*: *The book has been widely condemned as blasphemous.* —**blasphemously** *adv*

**blast¹** /blɑːstǁblæst/ *n*
**1** ▶ **AIR/WIND** ◀ [C] a sudden strong movement of wind or air: [+ **of**] *A blast of cold air swept through the hut.*
**2** ▶ **EXPLOSION** ◀ [C] an explosion, or the very strong movement of air that it causes: *Thirty-six people died in the blast.*
**3** ▶ **NOISE** ◀ [C] a sudden very loud noise: *a blast of rock music* | *The guard gave a blast on his whistle and we were off.*
**4 (at) full blast** as strongly, loudly, or fast as possible: *The radiators were on full blast, but it was still freezing.* | *a radio going at full blast*
**5** ▶ **FUN** ◀ [singular] *AmE informal* an enjoyable and exciting experience: *The concert was a blast.* | *We had a blast at the fair.*

**blast²** *v*
**1** ▶ **EXPLODE** ◀ [I,T] to break a mass of rock into pieces using explosives: [+ **through**] *We had to blast our way through 50 metres of solid rock.* | **blast sth through/in** *Slowly they blasted a path through the mountains.*
**2 blast!** also **blast her/it etc** *spoken* used when you are very annoyed about something: *Oh blast! I've forgotten my key.*
**3** ▶ **MUSIC** ◀ also **blast out** [I,T] to produce a lot of loud noise, especially music: *a radio blasting out pop music* | *Dance music blasted from the stereo.*
**4** ▶ **AIR/WATER** ◀ [T] to direct air or water at something with great force: *Coral can be cleaned by blasting it with a strong jet of water.*
**5** ▶ **ATTACK** ◀ [T] to attack a place or person using bombs or heavy guns: *The town was blasted out of existence.*
**6** ▶ **CRITICIZE** ◀ [T] to criticize something very strongly: *The Senator blasted their plans for educational aid.*
**7 blast sb's hopes** to destroy someone's hope of doing something: *Injury on the team has blasted our hopes of reaching the final.*
**8** ▶ **DESTROY** ◀ [T] *literary* to make something dry

up and die, especially because of heat or cold: *Every green thing was blasted by the icy breath of winter.*

**blast off** *phr v* [I] if a SPACECRAFT blasts off, it leaves the ground —see also BLAST-OFF

**blas·ted** /ˈblɑːstɪ̣d‖ˈblæs-/ *adj* [only before noun] *spoken* used to express annoyance: *I wish that blasted baby would stop crying!*

**blast fur·nace** /ˈ· ˌ··/ *n* [C] a large industrial structure in which iron is separated from the rock that surrounds it

**blast-off** /ˈ· ·/ *n* [U] the moment when a SPACECRAFT leaves the ground: *10 seconds to blast-off* —see also **blast off** (BLAST²)

**bla·tant** /ˈbleɪtənt/ *adj* something bad that is blatant is very clear and easy to see, but the person responsible for it does not seem embarrassed or ashamed: *a blatant abuse of power | blatant discrimination* —**blatantly** *adv* —**blatancy** *n* [C]

**blath·er** /ˈblæðə‖-ər/ *v* [I + **about**] to talk for a long time about things that are not important —**blather** *n* [C,U]

**blaze¹** /bleɪz/ *v* **1** [I] to burn very brightly and strongly: *The room was warm and cosy, with a fire blazing in the hearth.* **2** [I] to shine with a very bright light: *The house still blazed with lights although it was midnight.* **3** also **blaze away** [I] to fire bullets rapidly and continuously: *An enemy plane roared overhead, its guns blazing.* **4 blaze a trail** to develop important new methods or make important new discoveries: *The company has blazed a trail in robotic technology.* **5 be blazed across/all over** if something is blazed across a newspaper etc, it is written in a way that everyone will notice: *News of their divorce was blazed across all the tabloids.* —see also BLAZING

**blaze²** *n*
**1** ▶ **FIRE** ◀ **a)** [singular] the strong bright flames of a fire: *We soon had a cheerful blaze.* **b)** [C] a big dangerous fire: *Wind fanned the blaze, making it impossible for the firefighters to continue.*
**2** ▶ **LIGHT/COLOUR** ◀ [singular] very bright light or colour: [+ **of**] *a blaze of sunshine | The garden is a blaze of colour at this time of year.*
**3** ▶ **GUNS** ◀ [singular] the rapid continuous firing of a gun: [+ **of**] *a blaze of machine gun fire*
**4 a blaze of anger/hatred/passion etc** a sudden show of very strong emotion: *He was surprised by the sudden blaze of anger in her eyes.*
**5 in a blaze of glory/publicity etc** receiving a lot of praise or public attention: *Our team finished the season in a blaze of glory, winning the championship with ease.*
**6 what the blazes/who the blazes etc** *spoken old-fashioned* used to emphasize a question when you are annoyed: *What the blazes is going on here?*
**7 like blazes** *old-fashioned* as fast, as much, or as strongly as possible: *We're going to have to work like blazes to get it done on time!*
**8 go to blazes** *spoken old-fashioned* used to angrily tell someone to go away
**9** ▶ **MARK** ◀ [C usually singular] a white mark, especially one down the front of a horse's face —see also ABLAZE

**blaz·er** /ˈbleɪzə‖-ər/ *n* [C] a JACKET (=piece of clothing like a short coat), sometimes with the special sign of a school, club etc on it: *a school blazer*

**blaz·ing** /ˈbleɪzɪŋ/ *adj* [only before noun] **1** extremely hot: *a blazing August afternoon* **2** full of strong emotions, especially anger: *He jumped to his feet in a blazing fury.* | **blazing row** (=very angry argument)

**bla·zon¹** /ˈbleɪzən/ *n* [C] a COAT OF ARMS

**blazon²** *v* [T] **be blazoned on/across etc** to be written or shown on something in a very noticeable way

**bleach¹** /bliːtʃ/ *n* [U] a chemical used to make things white or to kill GERMS: *I spilled bleach on my blue trousers and ruined them.*

**bleach²** *v* [T] to make something white, especially by using chemicals or sunlight: *bleached blonde hair | Driftwood lined the shore, bleached by the sun.*

**bleach·ers** /ˈbliːtʃəz‖-ərz/ *n* [plural] *AmE* seats arranged in rows with no roof covering them, where you sit to watch sport: *We had a good view from the bleachers.*

**bleak** /bliːk/ *adj* **1** without anything to make you feel cheerful or hopeful: *bleak news* | **a bleak outlook/prospect/future** *With no money and no job, my prospects seemed bleak.* **2** cold and without any pleasant or comfortable features: *a bleak January afternoon | The landscape was bleak and bare.* —**bleakly** *adv* —**bleakness** *n* [U]

**blear·y** /ˈblɪəri‖ˈblɪr-/ also **bleary-eyed** /ˌ·· ˈ·◂/ *adj* unable to see very clearly, because you are tired or have been crying: *Bleary-eyed, she pulled on her robe and went to the kitchen to make coffee.* —**blearily** *adv* —**bleariness** *n* [U]

**bleat** /bliːt/ *v* [I] **1** to make the sound that a sheep or goat makes **2** *informal* to complain in a silly or annoying way: *Oh stop bleating!* —**bleat** *n* [C]

**bleed** /bliːd/ *past tense and past participle* **bled** /bled/ *v*
**1** ▶ **BLOOD** ◀ **a)** [I] to lose blood, especially because of an injury: *Your nose is bleeding.* | **bleed profusely** (=bleed a lot) *Marc lay on the ground, bleeding profusely.* **b)** [T] to take some blood from someone's body in order to treat a disease
**2** ▶ **MONEY** ◀ [T] to make someone pay an unreasonable amount of money: *She bled him for every last cent.* | **bleed sb dry/white** (=take all their money) *developing countries that had been bled dry by massive loan repayments*
**3 my heart bleeds** *spoken* used to say that you feel a lot of sympathy for someone, but often in a joking way when you do not think someone deserves any sympathy: *You can't afford a third car? My heart bleeds!* | [+ **for**] *My heart bleeds for those poor children.*
**4** ▶ **AIR/LIQUID** ◀ [T] to remove air or liquid from a system in order to make it work properly, for example from a heating system: *We need to bleed the radiators.*
**5** ▶ **COLOUR** ◀ [I] to spread from one area of cloth or paper to another: *Wash it in cold water so the colours don't bleed.*

**bleed·er** /ˈbliːdə‖-ər/ *n* [C] *BrE spoken* a rude word for someone, especially a man, that you dislike

**bleed·ing¹** /ˈbliːdɪŋ/ *adj* [only before noun] *BrE spoken* used to emphasize something when you are angry: *Get your bleeding hands off my car!*

**bleeding²** *n* [U] the condition of losing blood from your body: *We tied his arm up tightly to stop the bleeding.*

**bleeding heart** /ˌ·· ˈ·/ also **bleeding heart lib·e·ral** /ˌ·· · ˈ···/ *n* [C] *informal* someone who feels sympathy for poor people or criminals, in a way that you think is not practical or helpful

**bleep¹** /bliːp/ *n* [C] a high electronic sound: *The shrill bleep of the telephone woke him up.*

**bleep²** *v* **1** [I] to make a high electronic sound: *The computer will bleep when it has completed the search.* **2** [T] *BrE informal* to let someone know, through their bleeper, that you want them to telephone you **3** [T] also **bleep out** to prevent an offensive word being heard on television or the radio by making a high electronic sound: *All the swear words had been bleeped out.*

**bleep·er** /ˈbliːpə‖-ər/ *n* [C] *BrE* a small machine that you carry with you, that makes short high electronic sounds to tell you that you must telephone someone; BLEEPER, PAGER

**blem·ish¹** /ˈblemɪʃ/ *n* [C] a small mark, especially a mark on someone's skin or on the surface of an object, that spoils its appearance

**blemish²** *v* [T often passive] to spoil the appearance, beauty, or perfection of something —see also UNBLEMISHED —**blemished** *adj*

**blench** /blentʃ/ *v* [I] to make a sudden movement backwards because you are frightened

**blend¹** /blend/ *v* **1** [T] to thoroughly mix together soft or liquid substances to form a single smooth substance: *Blend the sugar, eggs, and flour.* **2** [I,T] to combine different features or characteristics in a way that produces an effective or pleasant result, or to become combined in this way: *an exciting narrative that blends fact and legend* | [+ **with/together**] *The aroma of woodsmoke blended with the smell of cooking.* **3** [T usually passive] *technical* to produce tea, tobacco, WHISKY etc by mixing several different types together

**blend in** *phr v* [I] if something blends in with the things around it, it matches the background very well or suitably: [+ **with**] *The old house blends in perfectly with the gentle Hampshire countryside.*

B

**blend²** *n* [C] **1** a product such as tea, tobacco, or WHISKY that is a mixture of several different types **2** a mixture of different qualities, characteristics, people etc, that combine together well: *an excellent team, with a nice blend of experience and youthful enthusiasm*

**blend·er** /ˈblendə‖-ər/ *n* [C] an electric machine that you use to mix liquids and soft foods together

S3 **bless** /bles/ *v past tense and past participle* **blessed** *or* **blest** /blest/ [T] **1 bless him/her etc** *spoken* used to show that you are fond of someone, amused by them, or pleased by something they have done: *He loves that toy, bless him!* | *Bless her little heart.* **2 be blessed with** to have a special ability, good quality etc: *Fortunately we're both blessed with good health.* | *Nicole had not been blessed with a sense of humour.* **3** if God blesses someone or something, he helps and protects them: *May God bless you.* **4** to ask God to protect someone or something: *a ceremony to bless their marriage* **5** to make something holy: *Then the priest blesses the bread and wine.* **6 bless you!** *spoken* **a)** what you say when someone SNEEZES **b)** *old-fashioned* used to thank someone for doing something for you **7 bless my soul/I'll be blessed!** *spoken old-fashioned* used to express surprise

**bless·ed** /ˈblesɨd/ *adj* **1** [only before noun] *spoken* used to express annoyance: *Now where have I put that blessed book?* **2** [only before noun] very enjoyable or desirable: *a few moments of blessed silence* **3** holy: *Blessed are the peacemakers.* | *the Blessed Virgin* —**blessedly** *adv* —**blessedness** *n* [U]

**bless·ing** /ˈblesɪŋ/ *n*
**1** ▸ **STH GOOD/HELPFUL** ◂ [C] something that you have or something that happens which is good because it improves your life, helps you in some way, or makes you happy: *This rain will be a blessing for the farmers.* | **be a (great/real) blessing** *The dishwasher has been a real blessing!* | **it is a blessing (that)** *It's a blessing no-one was badly hurt.*
**2 a mixed blessing** a situation that has both good and bad parts: *Getting that job was rather a mixed blessing, as it left me very little time to spend with my family.*
**3 blessing in disguise** something that seems to be bad or unlucky at first, but which you later realize is good or lucky
**4 count your blessings** used to tell someone to remember how lucky they are, especially when they are complaining about something
**5** ▸ **APPROVAL** ◂ [U] someone's approval or encouragement for a plan, activity, idea etc: **with sb's blessing** *They were determined to marry, with or without their parents' blessing.* | **give your blessing to** *The Defense Department has given its blessing to the disarmament proposals.*
**6** ▸ **FROM GOD** ◂ [C,U] protection and help from God, or words spoken to ask for this: *The priest gave the blessing.*

**bleth·er** /ˈbleðə‖-ər/ *v* [I + **on**] *especially ScotE* BLATHER

**blew** /bluː/ *v* the past tense of BLOW¹

**blight¹** /blaɪt/ *n* [singular] **1** an unhealthy condition of plants in which parts of them dry up and die **2** something that makes people unhappy or that spoils their lives or the environment they live in: *Her guilty secret was a blight on her happiness.* | *the blight of poverty*

**blight²** *v* [T] to spoil or damage something, especially by preventing people from doing what they want to do: *a disease which, though not fatal, can blight the lives of its victims* | *a country blighted by poverty* —**blighted** *adj*: *blighted hopes*

**blight·er** /ˈblaɪtə‖-ər/ *n* [C] *BrE old-fashioned* **1** used to talk about someone that you feel sorry for or JEALOUS of: *Poor old blighter.* | *You lucky blighter!* **2** a bad or unpleasant person

**bli·mey** /ˈblaɪmi/ *BrE spoken* used to express surprise: *Blimey, look at that!*

**Blimp** /blɪmp/ *n* [C] someone, especially an old man, with very old-fashioned political ideas —**Blimpish** *adj*

**blimp** *n* [C] **1** a small AIRSHIP (=type of aircraft without wings) **2 Blimp** a COLONEL BLIMP

**blind¹** /blaɪnd/ *adj* S2 W3
**1** ▸ **CAN'T SEE** ◂ **a)** unable to see: *He was nearly blind in one eye.* | **go blind** (=become blind) *In later stages of the disease, sufferers often go blind.* **b) the blind** [plural] people who are unable to see: *talking books for the blind* **c) as blind as a bat** *humorous* not able to see well: *I'm as blind as a bat without my glasses.*
**2** ▸ **IGNORE** ◂ **a) be blind to** to completely fail to notice or realize something: *They seemed to be blind to the consequences of their decision.* **b) turn a blind eye (to)** to deliberately ignore something that you know should not be happening: *The boss sometimes turns a blind eye to smoking in the office.* **c) not take a blind bit of notice** *especially spoken* to completely ignore what someone else is doing, especially in a way that is annoying
**3 not make a blind bit of difference** *BrE informal* used to emphasize that whatever someone says or does will not change the situation at all
**4** ▸ **FEELINGS** ◂ **a) blind faith/loyalty/hate etc** strong feelings that you have without thinking about why you have them: *an unreasoning, blind hatred* **b) blind panic/rage** strong feelings that are out of your control: *In a moment of blind panic she had pulled the trigger and shot the man dead.*
**5 blind corner/bend/curve** a corner on a road that you cannot see beyond when you are driving
**6 the blind leading the blind** *often humorous* used to say that people who do not know much about what they are doing are guiding or advising others who know nothing at all
**7** ▸ **AIRCRAFT** ◂ **blind flying/landing** using only instruments to fly an aircraft because you cannot see through cloud, mist etc
**8 blind drunk** *BrE informal* extremely drunk
**9 swear blind** to say very firmly that something is definitely true: *Phil swears blind it wasn't him.* —see also BLINDLY —**blindness** *n* [U]

**blind²** *v* [T] **1** to permanently destroy someone's ability to see: *He had been blinded in the war.* **2** to make it difficult for someone to see for a short time: *Opening the door, I was immediately blinded by the glare.* **3** to make someone lose their good sense or judgement and be unable to see the truth about something: *blinded by emotion* | **blind sb to** *He had tremendous charm, which blinded us to his dishonesty.* **4 blind sb with science** to confuse or trick someone by using complicated language —see also **effing and blinding** (EFF (1))

**blinds**

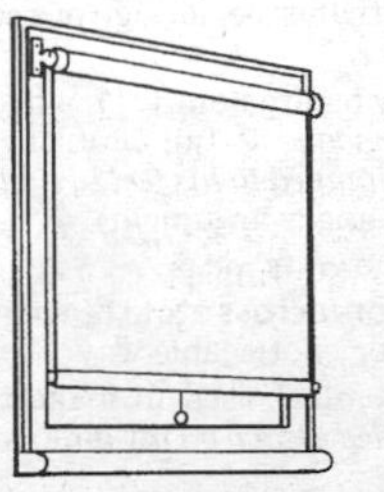
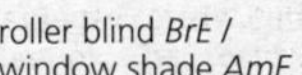
roller blind *BrE* / window shade *AmE*

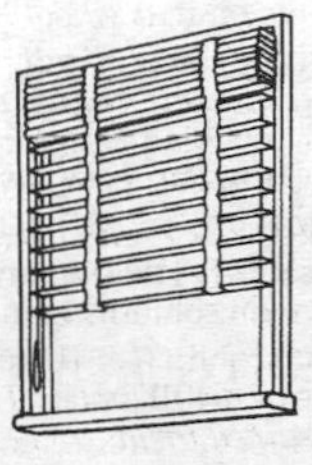
Venetian blind

**blind**[3] *n* [C] **1** a covering that can be pulled down over a window; WINDOW SHADE —see also ROLLER BLIND, WINDOW SHADE *AmE*, VENETIAN BLIND, SHADE[1] (2b) **2** a trick or excuse to stop someone from discovering the truth: *Her accent was a blind – she isn't really an American.* **3** *AmE* a small shelter where you can watch birds or animals without being seen by them; HIDE[2] (1) *BrE*

**blind al·ley** /ˌ· ˈ··/ *n* [C] **1** a small narrow street with no way out at one end **2** an attempt to achieve something, which does not produce useful results

**blind date** /ˌ· ˈ·/ *n* [C] an arranged meeting between a man and woman who have not met each other before

**blind·er** /ˈblaɪndə‖-ər/ *n* **1** [singular] *BrE informal* an excellent performance, especially in sport: *He played an absolute blinder!* **2 blinders** [plural] *AmE* things fixed beside a horse's eyes to prevent it seeing objects on either side; BLINKERS *BrE*

**blind·fold**[1] /ˈblaɪndfəʊld‖-foʊld/ *n* [C] a piece of cloth that covers someone's eyes to prevent them from seeing anything

**blindfold**[2] *v* [T] to cover someone's eyes: *Blindfold the prisoner!*

**blind·fold**[3] *adv* also **blindfolded** /ˈblaɪndfəʊldɪ̣d‖-foʊld-/ **1** with your eyes covered **2 can do sth blindfold** *informal* used to say that it is very easy for you to do something because you have done it so often

**blind·ing** /ˈblaɪndɪŋ/ *adj* **1 blinding light/flash etc** a very bright light that makes you unable to see properly **2 blinding headache/pain etc** a headache, pain etc that is so strong that it makes you unable to think or behave normally **3** *BrE spoken* excellent: *It's a blinding tape, really funny.* —**blindingly** *adv*: *blindingly obvious*

**blind·ly** /ˈblaɪndli/ *adv* **1** not thinking about something or trying to understand it: *Don't just blindly accept what you're told.* **2** not seeing or noticing what is around you: *He felt around blindly for the matches.*

**blind man's buff** /ˌ· · ˈ·/ *n* [U] a children's game in which one player whose eyes are covered tries to catch the others

**blind·side** /ˈblaɪndsaɪd/ *v* [T] *AmE informal* **1** to hit someone unexpectedly from the side: *blindsided by a bus at the intersection* **2** to give someone an unpleasant surprise: *I was blindsided by his suggestion.*

**blind spot** /ˈ· ·/ *n* [C] **1** something that you are unable or unwilling to understand: *I have a blind spot where computers are concerned.* **2** the part of the road that you cannot see when you are driving a car: *The other car was in my blind spot – I just hadn't seen it!* **3** the point in your eye where the nerve enters, which is not sensitive to light

**blink**[1] /blɪŋk/ *v* **1** [I,T] to shut and open your eyes quickly: *I blinked as I came out into the sunlight.* **2** [I] if lights blink, they shine unsteadily or go on and off rapidly: *The light on your answering machine is blinking.* **3 not (even) blink** to not seem at all surprised: *She didn't even blink when I told her how much it would cost.* **4 before you could bl[illegible]** *spoken* extremely quickly

**blink**[2] *n* **1 on the blink** *spoken* not working properly: *The radio's on the blink again.* **2 the blink of an eye** a very short period of time **3** [C] the action of quickly shutting and opening your eyes

**blink·ered** /ˈblɪŋkəd‖-ərd/ *adj* **1** having a limited view of a subject or refusing to accept or consider ideas that are new or different: *blinkered and outdated attitudes* **2** a horse that is blinkered is wearing blinkers

**blink·ers** /ˈblɪŋkəz‖-ərz/ *n* [plural] **1** *BrE* pieces of leather fixed beside a horse's eyes to prevent it seeing objects on either side; BLINDERS *AmE* **2** *AmE informal* the small lights on a car that you flash on and off to show which direction you are turning; WINKERS *BrE*

**blink·ing** /ˈblɪŋkɪŋ/ *adj* [only before noun] *BrE spoken* used to show that you are annoyed: *Whose blinking idea was it to come to this awful place?*

**blip** /blɪp/ *n* [C] **1** a short high electronic sound or a flashing light on the screen of a piece of electronic equipment: *blips on a radar screen* **2** a short pause or change in a process, or activity, especially when the situation gets worse for a while before it improves again: *The drop in sales is only a temporary blip.*

**bliss** /blɪs/ *n* [U] perfect happiness or enjoyment: *wedded bliss* | *I didn't have to get up till 11 – it was sheer bliss.*

**bliss·ful** /ˈblɪsfəl/ *adj* **1** extremely happy or enjoyable: *blissful sunny days* **2 blissful ignorance** a situation in which you do not yet know about something unpleasant —**blissfully** *adv*: *Jean's now married and blissfully happy.*

**blis·ter**[1] /ˈblɪstə‖-ər/ *n* [C] **1** a swelling on your skin containing clear liquid, caused for example by a burn or continuous rubbing: *New shoes always give me blisters.* **2** a swelling on the surface of metal, rubber, painted wood etc

**blister**[2] *v* [I,T] to develop blisters or make blisters form: *The paint will blister in the heat.* —**blistered** *adj*: *Before long, my hands were blistered from all the digging.*

**blis·ter·ing** /ˈblɪstərɪŋ/ *adj* **1** extremely hot: *the blistering heat of the desert* **2 blistering attack/criticism etc** very critical remarks expressing anger and disapproval: *She launched into a blistering attack on her boss.* —**blisteringly** *adv*: *Cover up, as the sun can be blisteringly hot.*

**blithe** /blaɪð‖blaɪð, blaɪθ/ *adj* **1** seeming not to care or worry about the effects of what you do: *a blithe disregard for the facts* **2** *literary or old use* cheerful and having no worries —**blithely** *adv*: *Mollie strolled blithely into the yard.*

**blith·er·ing** /ˈblɪðərɪŋ/ *adj* **blithering idiot** *spoken* someone who has done something very stupid

**blitz** /blɪts/ *n* [usually singular] **1** a sudden military attack, especially from the air **2 have a blitz on** *informal* to work very hard to completely finish something that needs to be done: *We'll have to have a blitz on the house before your parents arrive.* —**blitz** *v* [T]

**blitzed** /blɪtst/ *adj especially AmE informal* very tired or very drunk

**bliz·zard** /ˈblɪzəd‖-ərd/ *n* [C] **1** a severe snow storm: *We got stuck in a blizzard that night.* —see picture on page 836 **2** *AmE informal* a sudden large amount of something that you must deal with: *a blizzard of memos*

**bloat·ed** /ˈbləʊtɪ̣d‖ˈbloʊ-/ *adj* full of liquid, gas, food etc, so that you look or feel much larger than normal: *They've fished a bloated carcass out of the river.* | *I feel really bloated after that meal.*

**bloa·ter** /ˈbləʊtə‖ˈbloʊtər/ *n* [C] a large fat fish eaten smoked

**blob** /blɒb‖blɑːb/ *n* **1** a very small round mass of liquid or sticky substance: [+ **of**] *a blob of honey* —see picture on page 416 **2** something far away that cannot be clearly seen: *The church spire was just a distant blob.*

**bloc** /blɒk‖blɑːk/ *n* [usually singular] a large group of people or countries with the same political aims, working together: *the former Soviet bloc* —see also EN BLOC

**block**[1] /blɒk‖blɑːk/ *n* [C] S2 W2

**1** ► **SOLID MASS** ◄ a solid mass of hard material such as wood or stone with straight sides: [+ **of**] *a block of ice* —see picture on page 416

**2** ► **STREET/STREETS** ◄ **a)** *AmE* the distance along a city street from where one street crosses it to the next: *It's three blocks to the store from here.* | *She lives down the block.* **b)** the four city streets that form a square around an area of buildings: *Let's walk around the block before we go in.*

**3** ► **LARGE BUILDING** ◄ a large building divided into separate parts: *a block of flats* | *a tower block* | *office blocks* —see picture on page 410

**4** ► **QUANTITY OF THINGS** ◄ a quantity of things considered as a single unit: [+ **of**] *a block of shares in a business* | *Highlight this block of text.*

**5 block booking/voting** an arrangement that is made for a whole group, to buy something or to vote together

B

6 ▶ **UNABLE TO THINK** ◀ [usually singular] the temporary loss of your normal ability to think, learn, write etc: **mental/writer's block** *She has a mental block about speaking French.*
7 ▶ **STOPPING MOVEMENT** ◀ [usually singular] something in a pipe, road etc that stops things moving through or along it

8 **the block** a solid block of wood on which someone's head was cut off as a punishment, in former times: *He was prepared to go to the block for his beliefs.*
9 **lay/put your head on the block** to risk destroying other people's opinion of you by doing or saying something
10 ▶ **SPORT** ◀ a movement in sport that stops an opponent going forward
11 ▶ **INFORMATION** ◀ a physical unit of stored information on a MAGNETIC TAPE or DISK
12 ▶ **PRINTING** ◀ a piece of wood or metal with words or line drawings cut into it, for printing
13 ▶ **LAND** ◀ *AustrE, NZE* a large piece of land: *a ten acre block near the city* —see also BLOCK CAPITALS, BUILDING BLOCK, **be a chip off the old block** (CHIP[1] (6)), **I'll knock your block off** (KNOCK[1] (4)), **stumbling block** (STUMBLE (4))

S3 **block[2]** *v* [T] **1** also **block up** to prevent anything moving through a narrow space by placing something across it or in it: *Your truck is blocking the road.* | *My nose is blocked up with this cold.* **2** to stop something happening, developing, or succeeding: *The Senate blocked publication of the report.* **3** also **block off** to be in front of someone so that they cannot see a view, light, the sun etc: *Can you move? You're blocking my light.* **4 block sb's way** to stand in front of someone, so that they cannot go past: *The teacher stood at the entrance, blocking the children's way.* **5** *technical* to limit the use of a particular country's money: *a blocked currency*

**block** sth ↔ **in/out** *phr v* [T] to make a drawing of something that gives a general idea but is not exact: *I'll just block in the main buildings.*

**block** sth ↔ **off** *phr v* [T] to completely close a road or path

**block** sth ↔ **out** **1** to stop light passing: *a heavy curtain blocking out the light* **2** [I,T **block** sth ↔ **out**] to stop yourself thinking about something, or remembering it: *a memory so terrible that she tried to block it out*

**block·ade[1]** /blɒˈkeɪd‖blɑː-/ *n* [usually singular] the surrounding of an area by soldiers or ships to stop people or supplies leaving or entering: *a naval blockade* | **lift/raise the blockade** (=to end a blockade) | **impose a blockade** *They've imposed an economic blockade on the country.*

**blockade[2]** *v* [T] to put a place under a blockade: *The ships blockaded the port.*

**block·age** /ˈblɒkɪdʒ‖ˈblɑː-/ *n* **1** [C] something that is stopping movement in a narrow place: *a blockage in the pipe* **2** [U] the state of being blocked or prevented

**block and tack·le** /ˌ· · ˈ··/ *n* [usually singular] a piece of equipment made with wheels and ropes, used for lifting heavy things

**block·bust·er** /ˈblɒkˌbʌstə‖ˈblɑːkˌbʌstər/ *n* [C] **1** *informal* a book or film that is very good or successful: *the latest blockbuster from Hollywood* **2** a very powerful bomb

**block cap·i·tals** /ˌ· ˈ···/ *n* [plural] letters in their large form, eg A, B, C, rather than a, b, c: *Complete the form in block capitals.*

**block·head** /ˈblɒkhed‖ˈblɑːk-/ *n* [C] *informal* a very stupid person: *You silly blockhead!*

**block·house** /ˈblɒkhaʊs‖ˈblɑːk-/ *n* [C] a small strong building used as a shelter from enemy guns

**block let·ters** /ˌ· ˈ··/ *n* [plural] block capitals

**block par·ty** /ˈ· ˌ··/ *n* [C] *AmE* a party held in the street for all the people living in the area

S3 **bloke** /bləʊk‖bloʊk/ *n* [C] *BrE informal* a man: *The new bloke next door seems a bit weird.*

**blok·ish** /ˈbləʊkɪʃ‖ˈbloʊ-/ *adj BrE humorous* if you do blokish things, you behave in a traditionally male way: *playing football, fixing the car and other blokish activities* —**blokishness** *n* [U] *amiable blokishness*

**blond** /blɒnd‖blɑːnd/ **1** *adj* another spelling of BLONDE **2** a man who is blond has pale or yellow hair

**blonde[1]** /blɒnd‖blɑːnd/ *adj* **1** blonde hair is pale or yellow in colour **2** a woman who is blonde has pale or yellow hair S3

**blonde[2]** *n* [C] *informal* a woman with pale or yellow-coloured hair: *a beautiful blonde* S3

**blood[1]** /blʌd/ *n* S1 W1
1 ▶ **IN YOUR BODY** ◀ [U] the red liquid that your heart pumps round your body: *She lost a lot of blood in the accident.* | **give/donate blood** (=have blood taken from you and stored, to be used to treat someone else) | **draw blood** (=make someone bleed) *The dog bit her but failed to draw blood.*
2 **have sb's blood on your hands** to have caused someone's death
3 **in cold blood** in a cruel and deliberate way: *He murdered the old man in cold blood.*
4 **make your blood boil** to make you extremely angry: *The way they treat those people really makes my blood boil.*
5 **make your blood run cold** to make you feel extremely frightened: *The sudden scream made my blood run cold.*
6 **it's like getting blood out of a stone** used when you find it difficult to persuade someone to give you or tell you something
7 **blood is thicker than water** used to say that family relationships are more important than any other kind
8 **be after sb's blood** to be angry enough to want to hurt or injure someone
9 **sb's blood is up** someone is extremely angry and determined to do something about it: *They tried to stop me, but my blood was up.*
10 ▶ **YOUR FAMILY/GROUP** ◀ [U] the family or group to which you belong from the time that you are born: *There's French blood on his mother's side.*
11 **be/run in sb's blood** if an ability or tendency is in, or runs in, someone's blood, it is natural to them and others in their family
12 **sweat blood** to work extremely hard to achieve something: *Beth sweated blood over that article.*
13 **new/fresh blood** new members in a group or organization who bring new ideas and energy: *It's good to have some new blood in the department.*
14 **young blood** *old-fashioned* a word for a fashionable young man —see also **bad blood** (BAD[1] (22)), BLUE-BLOODED, RED BLOOD CELL, WHITE BLOOD CELL, **your own flesh and blood** (FLESH[1] (5))

**blood[2]** *v* [T] **1** *BrE* to give someone their first experience of an activity, especially a difficult or unpleasant one **2** to give a hunting dog its first taste of blood

**blood-and-guts** /ˌ· · ˈ·◂/ *adj AmE informal* full of action or violence: *a blood-and-guts struggle between the two teams*

**blood-and-thun·der** /ˌ· · ˈ··◂/ *adj* [only before noun] *BrE* a blood-and-thunder film or story is full of exciting and violent action

**blood bank** /ˈ· ·/ *n* [C] a store of human blood to be used in hospital treatment

**blood·bath** /ˈblʌdbɑːθ‖-bæθ/ *n* [singular] the violent killing of many people at one time

**blood broth·er** /ˌ· ˈ··/ *n* [C] a man who promises loyalty to another, often in a ceremony in which the men's blood is mixed together

**blood count** /ˈ· ·/ *n* [C] a medical examination of someone's blood to see if it contains the right substances in the right amounts: *Her blood count is very low.*

**blood·cur·dling** /ˈblʌdˌkɜːdlɪŋ‖-ɜːr-/ *adj* extremely frightening: *a bloodcurdling shriek*

**blood do·nor** /ˈ· ˌ··/ *n* [C] someone who gives their blood to be used in the treatment of other people

**blood feud** /ˈ· ·/ *n* [C] a quarrel that lasts for many years between people or families and in which each side murders or injures members of the other side

**blood group** /ˈ· ·/ *n* [C] *BrE* one of the classes into which human blood can be separated, including A, B, AB and O; BLOOD TYPE *AmE*

**blood heat** /ˈ· ·/ *n* [U] the normal temperature of the human body, about 37° C

**blood·hound** /ˈblʌdhaʊnd/ *n* [C] a large dog with a very good sense of smell, often used for hunting

**blood·less** /ˈblʌdləs/ *adj* **1** without killing or violence: *a bloodless coup* **2** a bloodless part of your body is very pale: *his lips were thin and bloodless* **3** lacking in human feeling —compare BLOODY[2] —**bloodlessly** *adv* —**bloodlessness** *n* [U]

**blood·let·ting** /ˈblʌdˌletɪŋ/ *n* [U] **1** killing people; BLOODSHED: *The violence was a foretaste of the bloodletting to come.* **2** the medical practice in former times of treating people who were ill by removing some of their blood **3** the reduction of the number of people working for an organization

**blood lust** /ˈ· ·/ *n* [U] a strong desire to be violent

**blood mon·ey** /ˈ· ˌ··/ *n* [U] **1** money paid for murdering someone **2** money paid to the family of someone who has been murdered

**blood or·ange** /ˈ· ··/ *n* [C] an orange with red juice

**blood poi·son·ing** /ˈ· ˌ···/ *n* [U] *technical* a serious medical condition in which an infection spreads from a small area of your body through your blood

**blood pres·sure** /ˈ· ˌ··/ *n* [U] the force with which blood travels through your body, that can be measured by a doctor: *high blood pressure*

**blood-red** /ˌ· ˈ·◂/ *adj* dark red, like blood: *blood-red lipstick*

**blood re·la·tion** /ˈ· ·ˌ··/ *n* [C] someone related to you by birth rather than by marriage

**blood·shed** /ˈblʌdʃed/ *n* [U] the killing of people, usually in fighting or war: *taking action to stop the bloodshed*

**blood·shot** /ˈblʌdʃɒt‖-ʃɑːt/ *adj* bloodshot eyes are slightly reddish in colour

**blood sport** /ˈ· ·/ *n* [C] a sport that involves the killing of animals or birds: *a demonstration against blood sports*

**blood·stain** /ˈblʌdsteɪn/ *n* [C] a mark or spot of blood —**bloodstained** *adj*: *a bloodstained handkerchief*

**blood·stock** /ˈblʌdstɒk‖-stɑːk/ *n* [U] horses that have been bred for racing: *a bloodstock auction*

**blood·stream** /ˈblʌdstriːm/ *n* [singular] the blood as it flows around your body: *The drug is injected directly into the bloodstream.*

**blood·suck·er** /ˈblʌdˌsʌkə‖-ər/ *n* [C] **1** [C] a creature that sucks blood from the body of other animals **2** *informal* someone who always uses other people's money or help

**blood·thirst·y** /ˈblʌdˌθɜːsti‖-ɜːr-/ *adj* **1** eager to kill and wound, or enjoying seeing killing and violence: *ruthless and bloodthirsty warriors* **2** describing or showing violence: *The film was too bloodthirsty for me.* —**bloodthirstily** *adv* —**bloodthirstiness** *n* [U]

**blood trans·fu·sion** /ˈ· ·ˌ··/ *n* [C] the process of putting blood into someone's body as a medical treatment

**blood type** /ˈ· ·/ *n* [C] *AmE* one of the classes into which human blood can be separated, including A, B, AB, and O; BLOOD GROUP *BrE*

**blood ves·sel** /ˈ· ˌ··/ *n* [C] **1** any of the tubes through which blood flows in your body —see picture at TEETH **2 burst a blood vessel** to become very angry or upset about something: *My dad nearly burst a blood vessel when I told him I quit college.*

S3 W3 **blood·y[1]** /ˈblʌdi/ *adj, adv spoken especially BrE* used to emphasize what you are saying in a slightly rude way: *It's bloody cold out there!* | *It serves you bloody well right.* | *What a bloody cheek!* | *Bloody hell!* | **not bloody likely** (=definitely not) *"Are you going to go with him?" "Not bloody likely."*

**bloody[2]** *adj* **1** covered in blood or bleeding **2** with a lot of killing and injuries: *a bloody battle* **3 scream/yell bloody murder** *AmE informal* to protest in a loud, very angry way: *She was furious — screaming bloody murder at the manager!* **4 bloody but unbowed** harmed by events but not defeated by them: *He emerged from the discussions bloody but unbowed.* **5** *BrE old-fashioned* unpleasant and nasty or unkind

**bloody[3]** *v* [T] *formal* to injure someone so that blood comes, or to cover something with blood: *The boy punched Jack and bloodied his nose.*

**bloody-mind·ed** /ˌ·· ˈ··◂/ *adj BrE informal* deliberately making things difficult for other people: *Stop being so bloody-minded!* —**bloody-mindedly** *adv* —**bloody-mindedness** *n* [U]

**bloom[1]** /bluːm/ *n* **1** [C,U] a flower or flowers: *beautiful red blooms* | *a mass of bloom on the apple trees* **2 in (full) bloom** with the flowers fully open **3** [U singular] a covering of fine powder that forms on fruit such as GRAPES or PLUMS **4 the bloom of youth/love etc** *literary* the best or happiest time when you are young

**bloom[2]** *v* [I] **1** to produce flowers or to open as flowers **2** to become happy and healthy or successful: *Anne has bloomed since she got her new job.*

**bloom·er** /ˈbluːmə‖-ər/ *n* **1 bloomers** [plural] **a)** *old-fashioned* women's underwear like loose trousers that end at your knees **b)** short loose trousers that end in a tight band at your knees worn by women in Europe and America in the late 19th century **2** [C] *BrE humorous, old-fashioned* an embarrassing mistake in front of other people; BLOOPER (1) *AmE*

**bloom·ing** /ˈbluːmɪŋ, ˈblʊmɪn/ *adj, adv BrE spoken* used for emphasizing a remark or statement: *It's blooming ridiculous!* | *Blooming heck! – look at this!*

**bloop·er** /ˈbluːpə‖-ər/ *n* [C] *AmE informal* **1** an embarrassing mistake made in front of other people; bloomer *BrE*: *I made a real blooper yesterday.* **2** a ball in BASEBALL that is high and slow and easy to catch or hit

**blos·som[1]** /ˈblɒsəm‖ˈblɑː-/ *n* [C,U] **1** a flower or all the flowers on a tree or bush: *orange blossom* **2 in (full) blossom** with the flowers open

**blossom[2]** *v* [I] **1** if trees blossom, they produce flowers: *a blossoming apple tree* **2** also **blossom out** to become happier, more beautiful, more successful etc: *Pete has really blossomed out in his new school.*

**blot[1]** /blɒt‖blɑːt/ **blotted, blotting** *v* [T] **1** to dry a wet surface by pressing soft paper or cloth on it **2 blot your copybook** *informal* to do something that spoils the idea that people have of you

**blot** sth ↔ **out** *phr v* [T] to cover or hide something completely: *Thick, white smoke completely blotted out the sun.* | *She had blotted out all her memories of the accident.*

**blot** sth ↔ **up** *phr v* [T] to remove liquid from a surface by pressing a soft cloth, paper etc onto it

**blot[2]** *n* [C] **1** a mark or spot that spoils something or makes it dirty: *ink blots* **2** a building, structure etc that is ugly and spoils the appearance of a place: **a blot on the landscape** *That new power station is a real blot on the landscape.* **3** something that spoils the good opinion other people have of you: *The Colonel's confession is a blot on the army's honor.*

**blotch** /blɒtʃ‖blɑːtʃ/ *n* [C] a pink or red mark on the skin, or a coloured mark on something —**blotchy** *adj* —**blotched** *adj*

**blot·ter** /ˈblɒtə‖ˈblɑːtər/ *n* [C] **1** a large piece of blotting paper kept on the top of a desk **2** *AmE* a book in which an official daily record is kept: *the police blotter*

**blotting pa·per** /ˈ·· ˌ··/ *n* [U] soft thick paper used for drying wet ink on a page after writing

**blot·to** /ˈblɒtəʊ‖ˈblɑːtoʊ/ *adj BrE old-fashioned* drunk

**blouse** /blaʊz‖blaʊs/ *n* [C] a shirt for women: *a silk blouse*

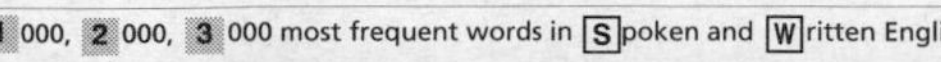

blow up

The car blew up.

Roald's blowing up a balloon.

S2 W3 **blow¹** /bləʊ‖bloʊ/ *past tense* **blew** /bluː/ *past participle* **blown** /bləʊn‖bloʊn/ *v*

**1** [I] ▶ **WIND MOVING** ◀ if the wind or a current of air blows, it moves: *A cold breeze was blowing.*

**2** ▶ **WIND MOVING STH** ◀ [I usually + adv/prep, T] to move something, or to be moved, by the force of the wind or a current of air: *Her hair was blowing in the breeze.* | *A sudden draught blew the door shut.*

**3** ▶ **AIR FROM YOUR MOUTH** ◀ [I,T] to send out a current of air from your mouth: *She blew on her coffee to cool it down.*

**4** ▶ **MAKE A NOISE** ◀ [I,T] to make a sound by passing air through a musical instrument or a horn: *The whistle blew for halftime.*

**5** ▶ **VIOLENCE** ◀ [T] to damage or destroy something violently with an explosion or by shooting: **blow sth away/out/off** *The explosion blew the ship right out of the water.*

**6** ▶ **LOSE MONEY** ◀ [T] *informal* to spend all your money at one time in a careless way: *He's blown all his wages on a new stereo.*

**7** ▶ **LOSE AN OPPORTUNITY** ◀ [T] *informal* to lose a good opportunity by making a mistake or by being careless: *We've blown our chances of getting that new contract.*

**8** ▶ **SURPRISE/ANNOYANCE** ◀ **blow/blow me/blow that etc** *BrE spoken* used to show surprise, annoyance, or determination: *Blow me if she didn't just run off!* | *Blow it! I forgot to phone Jane.*

**9** ▶ **MAKE A SHAPE** ◀ [T] to make or shape something by sending out a current of air from your mouth: **blow a bubble** (=make a ball shape) | **blow glass** (=shape glass by blowing into it when it is very hot)

**10 blow sth (up) out of all proportion** to make something seem much more serious or important than it is

**11** ▶ **LEAVE** ◀ **blow town** *AmE slang* to leave a place quickly

**12** ▶ **ELECTRICITY STOPS** ◀ [I,T] if an electrical FUSE¹ (1) blows, or a piece of electrical equipment blows a FUSE¹ (1), the electricity suddenly stops working because a thin wire has melted

**13** ▶ **TYRE** ◀ [I,T] if a tyre blows or if a car blows a tyre, it bursts

**14** ▶ **MAKE A SECRET KNOWN** ◀ to make known a secret about someone or something: *Your coming here has blown the whole operation.* | **blow sb's cover** (=make known what someone's real job or name is) *It is believed Ames blew the cover of up to twenty agents.* | **blow the gaff** *BrE slang* (=tell something secret, especially without intending to)

**15 blow hot and cold** *informal* to keep changing your attitude towards someone or something: *I can't tell what he wants – he keeps blowing hot and cold.*

**16 blow sb a kiss** to kiss your hand and then pretend to blow the kiss towards someone: *She blew him a kiss from across the street.*

**17 blow your mind** *informal* to make you feel very surprised and excited by something: *Meeting her after so many years really blew my mind.* —see also MIND-BLOWING

**18 blow your nose** to clean your nose by forcing air through it into a cloth or a piece of soft paper

**19 blow sth sky-high a)** to destroy an idea, plan etc by showing that it cannot be true or effective: *This new information blows his theory sky-high.* **b)** to completely destroy a building or structure with an explosion

**20 blow your top/stack** *informal* to become extremely angry quickly or suddenly

**21 blow your own trumpet/horn** *informal* to praise yourself for your own achievements: *You have to blow your own trumpet sometimes – no one else'll do it for you*

**22 blow the whistle on** *informal* to bring something that is wrong to the attention of an authority or the public

**23 blow a gasket/fuse** *informal* to become very angry and upset: *Don't tell her that, she'll blow a fuse!*

**blow away** *phr v informal especially AmE* **1** [T **blow** sb ↔ **away**] to kill someone by shooting them with a gun: *One move and I'll blow you away!* **2** [T **blow** sb ↔ **away**] to defeat someone completely, especially in a game: *Nancy blew away the rest of the skaters.* **3** [T **blow** sb ↔ **away**] to completely surprise someone, especially with something they admire

**blow down** *phr v* [I,T] if the wind blows something down, or if something blows down, the wind makes it fall: **blow sth ↔ down** *trees blown down in the gale*

**blow in** *phr v* [I] *informal especially AmE* to arrive unexpectedly: *Jim blew in about an hour ago – did you see him?*

**blow** sb/sth **off** *phr v* [T] *AmE slang* to treat someone or something as unimportant: *It seems crazy that they blew off Jurassic Park when they were choosing best movies.*

**blow out** *phr v* **1** [I,T] if you blow a flame or a fire out, or if it blows out, it stops burning: **blow sth ↔ out** *Blow out all the candles.* | *The match blew out before I could light the candles.* **2** [I] if a tyre blows out, it bursts **3** [T] **blow itself out** if a storm blows itself out, it ends: *We sheltered in a barn waiting for the storm to blow itself out.* **4** [T **blow** sb ↔ **out**] **a)** *AmE spoken* to easily defeat someone: *We blew them out 28 – zero.* **b)** *BrE spoken* to disappoint someone by not meeting them or not doing what you have agreed to: *He blew me out again last night – I've had enough.* **5** [I] if an oil or gas well blows out, oil or gas suddenly escapes

**blow over** *phr v* **1** [I,T] if the wind blows something over, or it blows over, the wind makes it fall: *Our fence blew over in the storm.* | **blow sth ↔ over** *You could get blown over in a hurricane.* **2** [I] if a storm blows over, it comes to an end **3** [I] if an argument or unpleasant situation blows over, it no longer seems important or is forgotten: *They weren't speaking to each other, but I think it's blown over now.*

**blow up** *phr v* **1** [I,T] to destroy something, or to be destroyed, by an explosion: *The plane blew up in midair.* | **blow sth ↔ up** *Rebels attempted to blow up the bridge.* **2** [T **blow** sth ↔ **up**] to fill something with air or gas: *Stop at the gas station and we'll blow up the tyres.* **3** [T **blow** sth ↔ **up**] if you blow up a photograph, you make it larger: *How much would it cost to have this photo blown up?* **4** [I] if bad weather blows up, it suddenly arrives: *It looks as though there's a storm blowing up.* **5** [I] if a situation, argument etc blows up, it suddenly becomes important or dangerous: *A crisis had blown up over the peace talks.* **6** [I] to become very angry with someone: *Jenny's father blew up when she didn't come home last night.*

W3 **blow²** *n* [C]
**1 ▶ HARD HIT ◀** a hard hit with the hand, a tool, or a weapon: *a blow on the head | three heavy blows from the hammer*
**2 ▶ BAD EFFECT ◀** something that has a bad effect on your confidence or on the possibility of success: [+ **to**] *Her rejection was a serious blow to his pride.* | **deal a blow** *Withdrawal of government funding dealt a serious blow to the project.*
**3 ▶ UNHAPPY EVENT ◀** an event that makes you very unhappy or shocks you: *Her mother's death was a terrible blow.*
**4 ▶ BLOWING ◀** [C] an action of blowing: *It took three blows to put out the candles.*
**5 come to blows** to quarrel seriously and start hitting each other: *They almost came to blows over the money.*
**6 soften/cushion the blow** to help someone accept something unpleasant or bad
**7 ▶ WIND ◀** [singular] a strong wind or storm —see also BODY BLOW, **strike a blow for** (STRIKE¹ (13))

**blow-by-blow** /ˌ· · ˈ·◂/ *adj* [only before noun] a blow-by-blow story, account etc gives all the details of an event as they happened: *Jenny bored us all with a blow-by-blow account of her night out.*

**blow-dry** /ˈ· ·/ *v* [T] to dry hair and give it shape by using an electric dryer —**blow-dry** *n* [C] *a cut and blow-dry*

**blow·er** /ˈbləʊə‖ˈbloʊər/ *n* [C] **1** a machine that blows out air: *a snow blower for clearing the path* **2 on the blower** *BrE old-fashioned* on the telephone in order to talk to someone: *Get on the blower to him at once.* —see also GLASSBLOWER

**blow-fly** /ˈ· ·/ *n* [C] a fly that lays its eggs on meat or wounds

**blow-hard** /ˈ· ·/ *n* [C] *AmE informal* someone who talks about themselves too much

**blow-hole** /ˈ· ·/ *n* [C] **1** a hole in the surface of ice to which water animals such as seals (SEAL¹ (1)) come to breathe **2** a hole in the top of the head of a WHALE, DOLPHIN etc through which they breathe

**blow job** /ˈ· ·/ *n* [C] *taboo slang* the practice of touching a man's sexual organs with your lips and tongue to give him sexual pleasure

**blow-lamp** /ˈ· ·/ *n* [C] *BrE* a piece of equipment that produces a small very hot flame, used especially for removing paint; BLOWTORCH *AmE*

**blown** /bləʊn‖bloʊn/ the past participle of BLOW¹

**blow·out** /ˈbləʊaʊt‖ˈbloʊ-/ *n* [C] **1** a sudden bursting of a TYRE: *A blow-out at this speed could be really dangerous.* **2** [usually singular] *informal* a big expensive meal or large social occasion **3** a sudden uncontrolled escape of oil or gas from a well **4** *AmE informal* an easy victory over someone in a game

**blow·pipe** /ˈbləʊpaɪp‖ˈbloʊ-/ *n* [C] a tube through which you can blow small stones, poisoned arrows (ARROW (1)) etc, used as a weapon

**blow·torch** /ˈbləʊtɔːtʃ‖ˈbloʊtɔːrtʃ/ *n* [C] *AmE* a piece of equipment that produces a small very hot flame, used especially for removing paint; BLOW-LAMP *BrE*

**blow-up** /ˈ· ·/ *n* [C] **1** a photograph, or part of a photograph, that has been made larger **2** [C usually singular] a sudden moment of anger: *I think they've had a blow-up again.* —see also **blow up** (BLOW¹)

**blow·y** /ˈbləʊi‖ˈbloʊi/ *adj BrE informal* windy

**blow·zy, blowsy** /ˈblaʊzi/ *adj* a blowzy woman is fat and looks untidy

**blub·ber¹** /ˈblʌbə‖-ər/ *v* **1** also **blub** [I] to cry noisily, especially in a way that annoys people: *Stop blubbering, for heaven's sake!* **2** also **blubber out** [T] to say something while crying noisily: *"It's not my fault," she blubbered.*

**blubber²** *n* [U] the fat of sea animals, especially WHALES

**bludge** /blʌdʒ/ *v* [I,T] *AustrE, NZE slang* to get something without working or paying for it —**bludger** *n* [C]

**blud·geon¹** /ˈblʌdʒən/ *v* [T] **1** [**into/out of**] to force someone to do something by making threats or arguing with them **2** to hit someone several times with something heavy: *bludgeoned to death*

**bludgeon²** *n* [C] a heavy stick with a thick end, used as a weapon

**blue¹** /bluː/ *adj* S1 W2
**1 ▶ COLOUR ◀** the colour of the clear sky or of the sea on a fine day: *the blue waters of the lake | a dark blue raincoat* —see picture on page 411
**2 ▶ SAD ◀** [not before noun] *informal* sad and without hope; DEPRESSED (1a): *That song always makes me feel blue.*
**3 ▶ CONCERNED WITH SEX ◀** *informal* concerned with sex in a way that might offend some people: *Some of his jokes were a bit blue.* —see also BLUE FILM
**4 once in a blue moon** *informal* hardly ever: *I only ever see him once in a blue moon.*
**5 scream/yell blue murder** *informal* to shout very loudly in protest against something or because you are in pain
**6 do sth till you're blue in the face** *informal* to do something a lot but without achieving what you want: *You can argue till you're blue in the face, she won't change her mind.*
**7 blue with cold** extremely cold
**8 talk a blue streak** *AmE informal* to talk a lot without stopping
**9 go blue** if your skin goes blue, you become blue because you are cold or cannot breathe properly
**10 like blue blazes** *AmE informal* extremely: *It hurts like blue blazes!*

**blue²** *n* **1** [C,U] the colour that is blue: *the rich greens and blues of the tapestry | She nearly always dresses in blue.* **2 blues** [plural] a slow sad style of music that came from the southern US: *a blues singer* —see also RHYTHM AND BLUES **3 the blues** [plural] *informal* feelings of sadness: *Don't be surprised if you get the blues for a while after your baby is born.* **4 out of the blue** *informal* unexpectedly: *a phone call from Jane right out of the blue* —see also **a bolt from/out of the blue** (BOLT¹ (3)) **5 boys in blue** *informal* the police **6** [C] *BrE* **Blue** someone who has represented Oxford or Cambridge University at a sport, or the title given to such a person: *a rugger Blue* **7 the blue** *literary* the sea or the sky

**blue³** *v* [T] *BrE informal* to spend money in a way that is careless or not very responsible: *John blued all his money on drink.*

**blue ba·by** /ˈ· ˌ· ·/ *n* [C] a baby whose skin is slightly blue when it is born because it has a heart problem

**blue·beard** /ˈbluːbɪəd‖-bɪrd/ *n* [C] a man who marries and kills one wife after another

**blue·bell** /ˈbluːbel/ *n* [C] a small plant with blue flowers that grows in woods

**blue·ber·ry** /ˈbluːbəri‖-beri/ *n* [C,U] the small blue fruit of a bushy plant, or the plant itself: *blueberry pie* —see picture on page 413

**blue·bird** /ˈbluːbɜːd‖-bɜːrd/ *n* [C] a small blue bird that lives in North America

**blue-blood·ed** /ˌ· ˈ· ·◂/ *adj* belonging to a royal or NOBLE¹ (3) family: *a blue-blooded French duchess* —**blue-blood** *n* [U]

**blue book** /ˈ· ·/ *n* [C] **1** *BrE* an official report, usually by a committee, printed by the British Government **2** *AmE* a book with a blue cover that is used in American colleges for writing answers to examination questions

**blue·bot·tle** /ˈbluːˌbɒtl‖-ˌbɑːtl/ *n* [C] a large blue fly

**blue cheese** /ˌ· ˈ·/ *n* [C,U] a kind of cheese with blue lines and a strong taste

**blue chip** /ˌ· ˈ·◂/ *adj* a blue-chip company or INVESTMENT (1) is profitable and safe: *blue chip stocks and shares* —**blue chip** *n* [C]

**blue-col·lar** /ˌ· ˈ··◂/ *adj* [only before noun] blue-collar workers do hard or dirty work with their hands —compare PINK-COLLAR, WHITE-COLLAR

**blue-eyed boy** /ˌ· · ˈ·/ *n* [C usually singular] *informal* a man or boy who is liked and approved of by someone in authority: *John was always the blue-eyed boy at school.*

**blue film** /ˌ· ˈ·/ *n* [C] *BrE informal* a film showing sexual activity; BLUE MOVIE

**blue·fish** /ˈbluːˌfɪʃ/ *n plural* **bluefish** [C] a sea fish that is a blueish colour and is caught for sport and to eat off the North American coast

**blue·grass** /ˈbluːgrɑːs‖-græs/ *n* **1** [U] a type of music from the southern and western US, played on instruments such as the GUITAR and VIOLIN **2** a type of grass found in North America, especially in Kentucky

**blue gum** /ˈ· ·/ *n* [C] a tall Australian tree that is a type of EUCALYPTUS

**blue·jay** /ˈbluːˌdʒeɪ/ *n* [C] a common large North American bird with blue feathers

**blue jeans** /ˌ· ˈ·‖ˈ· ·/ *n* [plural] *AmE* dark blue trousers made in a heavy material; JEANS

**blue law** /ˈ· ·/ *n* [C] *AmE* a law to control sexual morals, the drinking of alcohol, working on Sundays etc; LICENSING LAWS *BrE*

**blue mo·vie** /ˌ· ˈ··/ *n* [C] a film showing sexual activity

**blue·print** /ˈbluːˌprɪnt/ *n* [C] **1** a plan for achieving something: *a blueprint for the reform of the tax system* **2** a photographic print of a plan for a building, machine etc

**blue rib·bon** /ˌ· ˈ··/ also **blue riband** *n* [C] a small piece of blue material that you give to the first-prize winner of a competition —**blue ribbon** *adj*: *a blue-ribbon recipe*

**blue-rinse** /ˌ· ˈ·◂/ *adj BrE* **blue-rinse brigade** *humorous* used to describe older women with traditional RIGHT WING values —see also RINSE² (2)

**blue-sky** /ˈ· ·/ *adj* [only before noun] *AmE* blue-sky tests etc are done to test ideas and not for any practical purpose

**blue·stock·ing** /ˈbluːˌstɒkɪŋ‖-ˌstɑː-/ *n* [C] *BrE old-fashioned* a very well-educated woman

**bluff¹** /blʌf/ *v* [I,T] to pretend that you will do something bad or that you are someone else, especially to get something you want when you are in a difficult or dangerous situation: *"I'm an accredited British envoy," he bluffed.* | **bluff your way out of/through/past** (=get out of a difficult situation by deceiving someone) *They bluffed their way past the prison guard.* | **bluff it out** (=escape trouble by continuing to deceive someone) **bluff sb into doing sth** *Rob bluffed the interviewers into believing he'd had lots of experience.*

**bluff²** *n* **1** [C,U] an attempt to deceive someone by making them think you will do something when you have no intention of doing it: *Her threat to fire me was little more than a bluff.* **2 call sb's bluff** to tell someone to do what they threaten because you believe they have no intention of doing it and you want to prove it **3** [C] a very steep cliff or slope

**bluff³** *adj* behaving in a loud, cheerful way, without always considering the way other people feel: *He tried in his bluff, good-natured way to comfort her.* —**bluffly** *adv* —**bluffness** *n* [U]

**blu·ish** /ˈbluːɪʃ/ *adj* slightly blue: *Her skin had a bluish tinge*

**blun·der¹** /ˈblʌndə‖-ər/ *n* [C] a careless or stupid mistake: *A last-minute blunder by the goalkeeper cost them the match.*

**blunder²** *v* **1** [I always + adv/prep] to move in an unsteady way, as if you cannot see properly: **blunder around/about/into** *I could hear someone blundering around downstairs.* **2** [I] to make a big mistake, especially because you have been careless or stupid: *They blundered badly when they appointed him as Chairman.* —**blunderer** *n* [C]

**blun·der·buss** /ˈblʌndəbʌs‖-ər-/ *n* [C] a type of gun used in the past

**blun·der·ing** /ˈblʌndərɪŋ/ *adj* [only before noun] careless or stupid: *You blundering idiot! What did you do that for?*

**blunt¹** /blʌnt/ *adj* **1** not sharp or pointed: *All I could find was a blunt pencil.* —opposite sharp¹ (1,11) —see picture at SHARP¹ **2** speaking in an honest way even if this upsets people: *Jan was straightforward and blunt as always.* —see also BLUNTLY —**bluntness** *n* [U]

**blunt²** *v* [T] **1** to make a feeling less strong: *The bad weather blunted their enthusiasm for camping.* **2** to make the point of a pencil or the edge of a knife less sharp

**blunt·ly** /ˈblʌntli/ *adv* speaking in a direct, honest way that sometimes upsets people: *"You've drunk too much," she said bluntly.* | **to put it bluntly** *spoken*: *To put it bluntly, she's not up to the job.*

**blur¹** /blɜː‖blɜːr/ *n* [singular] **1** [C] a shape that you cannot see clearly: *Everything's a blur without my glasses.* | *the blur of headlights in the distance* **2** an unclear memory of something: *The events of that day gradually became a blur in her mind.*

**blur²** *v* **1** [I,T] to become difficult to see or make something difficult to see, because the edges are not clear: *The ships on the horizon seemed to blur before my eyes.* **2** [I,T] to make the difference between two ideas, subjects etc less clear: *The differences between the two political parties have slowly blurred.* —see also BLURRED —**blurry** *adj*: *a few blurry photos of their holiday together*

**blurb** /blɜːb‖blɜːrb/ *n* [C] a short description giving information about a book, new product etc

**blurred**

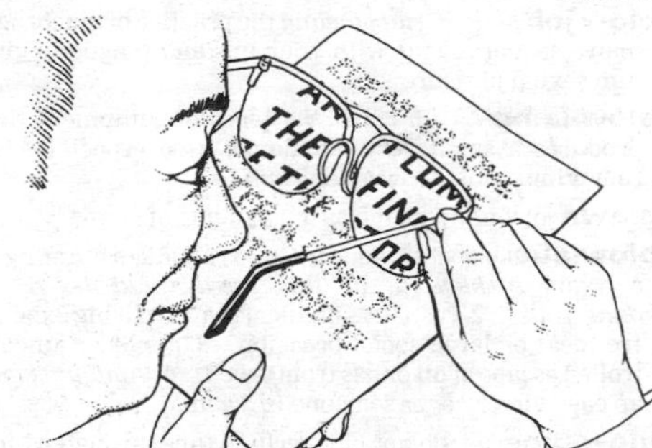

The words were blurred without his glasses.

**blurred** /blɜːd‖blɜːrd/ *adj* **1** unclear in shape, or making it difficult to see shapes: *a blurred photo* **2** difficult to remember or understand clearly: *blurred memories*

**blurt** /blɜːt‖blɜːrt/ *v*

**blurt** sth ↔ **out** *phr v* [T] to say something suddenly and without thinking, usually because you are nervous or excited: *Peter blurted the news out before we could stop him.*

**blush¹** /blʌʃ/ *v* [I] **1** to become red in the face, usually because you are embarrassed: *He blushes every time he speaks to her* **2** to feel ashamed or embarrassed about something: **blush to do sth** *I blush to think of the things I did when I was younger.* **3 the blushing bride** *humorous* a young woman on her wedding day —**blushingly** *adv*

**blush²** *n* **1** [C] the red colour on your face that appears when you are embarrassed: *She felt a blush come to her cheeks when her name was mentioned.* **2 spare my blushes** *old-fashioned* used to say that someone is praising you too much **3 at first blush** *literary* when first thought of or considered: *At first blush this discovery would seem to confirm his theory.* **4** [U] *AmE* blusher

**blush·er** /ˈblʌʃə‖-ər/ *n* [U] cream or powder used for making your cheeks look red or pink; blush *AmE*

**blus·ter** /ˈblʌstə‖-ər/ *v* [I] **1** to speak in a loud, angry way: *He was inclined to bluster when his authority was challenged.* **2** if the wind blusters, it blows violently —**bluster** *n* [U] —**blustering** *adj*: *blustering wintry weather*

**blus·ter·y** /ˈblʌstəri/ *adj* blustery weather is very windy: *a cold and blustery day* —see picture on page 836

**blvd** the written abbreviation of BOULEVARD

**B-mov·ie** /ˈbiː ˌmuːvi/ *n* [C] a cheaply-made film of low quality

**BO** /ˌbiː ˈəʊ‖-ˈoʊ/ *n* [U] body odour; an unpleasant smell from someone's body caused by sweat

**bo·a** /ˈbəʊə‖ˈboʊə/ *n* [C] **1** also **boa con·strict·or** /ˈ·· ·ˌ··/ a large snake that is not poisonous, but kills animals by crushing them **2** a FEATHER BOA

**boar** /bɔː‖bɔːr/ *n* [C] **1** a wild pig **2** a male pig

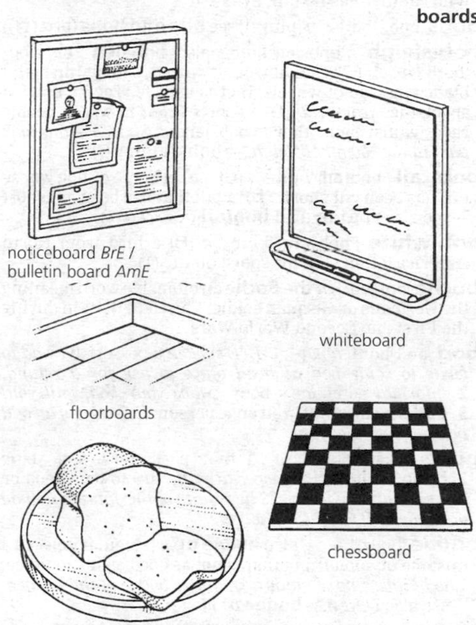


S1 W1 **board¹** /bɔːd‖bɔːrd/ *n*

**1 ▶ INFORMATION ◀** [C] a flat wide piece of wood, plastic etc that shows a particular type of information: *I wrote the examples up on the board.* | *Can I put this notice on the board?* | *I'll check the departure board for train times.* —see also NOTICEBOARD, SCOREBOARD

**2 ▶ FOR PUTTING THINGS ON ◀** [C] a flat piece of wood, plastic, card etc that you use for a particular purpose such as cutting things on, or for playing indoor games: *Cut the bread on the board, not the table!* | *Where's the chess board?* —see also BREADBOARD, CHOPPING BOARD

**3 ▶ GROUP OF PEOPLE ◀** [C also + plural verb *BrE*] a group of people in an organization who make the rules and important decisions: *a board meeting* | **sit on a board** *He sits on the hospital management board.* | **board of directors** *There is still only one woman on the board of directors.*

**4 ▶ FOR BUILDING ◀** [C] a long thin flat piece of wood used for making floors, walls, fences etc: *We'll have to take the boards up to check the wiring.* —see also FLOORBOARD (1)

**5 on board** on a ship or plane: *The ship went down with all its crew on board.* —compare ABOARD

**6 take sth on board** to listen to and accept a suggestion, idea etc: *The school refused to take any of the parents' criticisms on board.*

**7 go by the board** if a plan goes by the board, it is no longer possible: *We just don't have the time – so our idea about meeting to discuss it has had to go by the board.*

**8 across the board** if a plan or situation happens across the board, it affects everyone in a particular group, place etc: *We're aiming to increase productivity across the board.*

**9 ▶ MEALS ◀** [U] the meals that are provided for you when you pay to stay somewhere: *I pay $100 a week for room and board.* | **full/half board** (=all or some meals)

**10 ▶ THEATRE ◀ the boards** [plural] the stage in a theatre —see also **tread the boards** (TREAD¹ (6))

**11 ▶ SPORT ◀ boards** [plural] *AmE* the low wooden wall around the area in which you play ICE HOCKEY

**12 college/medical boards** *AmE* examinations that you take in the US when you apply to a college or medical school —see also ABOVE BOARD, DIVING BOARD, DRAWING BOARD, IRONING BOARD, SURFBOARD, **sweep the board** (SWEEP¹ (9))

**board²** *v* **1** [I,T] *formal* to get on a bus, plane, train etc in order to travel somewhere: *Passengers are asked to board half an hour before departure time.* **2** [I] if a plane or ship is boarding, passengers are getting onto it: *Flight N654 for Kathmandu is now boarding at Gate 16.* **3** [I always + adv/prep] to stay in a room in someone's house that you pay for: *I board with the Nicholsons during the week.* **4** [I] to stay at a school at night as well as during the day: *The students board during the week and go home at weekends.*

**board** sth ↔ **out** *phr v* [T] *BrE* to pay money and arrange for an animal to stay somewhere: *We'll have to board the cat out while we're away.*

**board** sth ↔ **up** *phr v* [T] to cover a window or door with wooden boards: *All the windows were boarded up and the place looked totally deserted.*

**board·er** /ˈbɔːdə‖ˈbɔːrdər/ *n* [C] **1** a student who stays at a school during the night, as well as during the day **2** someone who pays to live in another person's house with some or all of their meals provided; LODGER

**board game** /ˈ· ·/ *n* [C] an indoor game played on a specially designed board made of thick card or wood

**board·ing** /ˈbɔːdɪŋ‖ˈbɔːr-/ *n* [U] **1** the act of getting on a ship, plane etc in order to travel somewhere: *Boarding is now taking place at Gate 38.* **2** narrow pieces of wood that are fixed side by side, usually to cover a broken door or window

**boarding card** /ˈ·· ·/ *n* an official card that you have to show before you get onto a plane

**boarding house** /ˈ·· ·/ *n* [C] a private house where you pay to sleep and eat; GUESTHOUSE —compare PENSION³

**boarding pass** /ˈ·· ·/ *n* [C] a boarding card

**boarding school** /ˈ·· ·/ *n* [C] a school where students live as well as study —compare DAY SCHOOL

**board·room** /ˈbɔːdruːm, -rʊm‖ˈbɔːrd-/ *n* [C] a room where the directors (DIRECTOR (1)) of a company have meetings

**board·walk** /ˈbɔːdwɔːk‖ˈbɔːrdwɔːk/ *n* [C] *AmE* a raised path made of wood, usually built next to the sea —compare PIER (2)

**boast¹** /bəʊst‖boʊst/ *v* **1** [I,T] to talk too proudly about your abilities, achievements, or possessions because you want to make other people admire you: *"I can do better than any of them." she boasted.* | [+ **about**] *I'm fed up hearing Jan boast about her new job.* | [+ **of**] *He enjoyed boasting of his wealth.* | **boast that** *She was boasting that she could speak six languages fluently.* **2** [T] if a place, object, or organization boasts a good feature, it has that good feature: *Few teams can boast such a good record in European football.* | *The hotel boasts the finest view in Wales.* —**boaster** *n* [C]

**boast²** *n* [C] **1** something that you like telling people because you are proud of it: *One of her proudest boasts is that her daughter is a doctor.* **2 no idle boast** used to say that something is not a boast but that it is true

**boast·ful** /ˈbəʊstfəl‖ˈboʊst-/ *adj* talking too proudly about yourself: *We all got drunk and became very loud and boastful.* —**boastfully** *adv* —**boastfulness** *n* [U]

S1 W2 **boat** /bəʊt‖boʊt/ *n* [C] **1** a vehicle that travels across water: *a fishing boat* | *a rowing boat* | **by boat/in a boat** *We went up the river by boat.* **2** *informal* a ship, especially one that carries passengers: *We're getting the night boat to Zeebrugge.* **3 be in the same boat (as)** to be in the same unpleasant situation as someone else: *We're all more or less in the same boat, so there's no use complaining.* **4 push the boat out** *BrE informal* to spend a lot of money on something, especially on celebrating an event: *They really pushed the boat out for their daughter's wedding.* **5 rock the boat** to express a different attitude, opinion, idea etc from what other people are used to, in a way that upsets them: *They rocked the boat by refusing to come to the firm's Christmas lunch.* —see also GRAVY BOAT, SAUCE BOAT **burn your bridges/boats** (BURN¹ (22)), **miss the boat/bus** (MISS¹ (10))

**boat·er** /ˈbəʊtə‖ˈboʊtər/ *n* [C] a hard STRAW (1a) hat with a flat top —see picture at HAT

**boat hook** /ˈ· ·/ *n* [C] a long pole with an iron hook at the end, used to pull or push a small boat

**boat·house** /ˈbəʊthaʊs‖ˈboʊt-/ *n* [C] a building by the side of water that boats are kept in

**boat·ing** /ˈbəʊtɪŋ‖ˈboʊt-/ *n* [U] the activity of travelling in a small boat for pleasure: **go boating** *Let's go boating on the lake.*

**boat·man** /ˈbəʊtmən‖ˈboʊt-/ *n* [C] a man who you pay to take you out in a boat or for the use of a boat

**boat peo·ple** /ˈ· ˌ··/ *n* [plural] people who escape from bad conditions in their country in small boats

**boat·swain** /ˈbəʊsən‖ˈboʊ-/ *n* [C] an officer on a ship whose job is to organize the work and look after the equipment; BOSUN

**boat train** /ˈ· ·/ *n* [C] a train that takes people to or from ships in a port

**Bob** /bɒb‖bɑːb/ *n* **Bob's your uncle!** *BrE spoken* used to say that something will be easy to do: *Just copy the disk, and Bob's your uncle!*

**bob¹** *v*

**1** ▶ **MOVE IN WATER** ◀ [I] to move up and down when floating on the surface of water: **bob up and down** *The boat was bobbing up and down on the waves.*

**2** ▶ **MOVE SOMEWHERE** ◀ [I always + adv/prep] to move quickly in a particular direction: [+ **up/down/out etc**] *She bobbed down behind the wall to avoid being seen.*

**3 bob your head** to move your head down quickly as a way of showing respect, greeting someone or agreeing with them: *Seymour bobbed his head respectfully and said, "Good evening, Sir."*

**4 bob (sb) a curtsy** to make a quick, small CURTSY to someone

**5** ▶ **HAIR** ◀ [T] to cut someone's hair so that it is the same length all the way round their head: *I'm going to get my hair bobbed* —see picture at HAIRSTYLE.

**6 bob for apples** to play a game in which you try to pick up apples floating in water, using only your mouth

**bob²** *n* [C] **1** a way of cutting hair so that it is the same length all the way round your head —see picture at HAIRSTYLE **2** a quick up and down movement of your head, or body, to show respect, agreement, greeting etc: *The maid gave a little bob and left the room.* **3** [plural] *informal* a SHILLING (=coin used in the past in Britain) *In those days the train fare was three bob.* —see also **bits and bobs** (BIT¹ (14))

**bob·bin** /ˈbɒbɪ̣n‖ˈbɑː-/ *n* [C] a small round object that you wind thread onto, especially for a SEWING MACHINE —compare REEL¹ (1a)

**bob·ble¹** /ˈbɒbəl‖ˈbɑː-/ *n* [C] *BrE* a small soft ball, usually made of wool, that is used especially for decorating clothes: *Her pullover had bobbles on the front.* —**bobbly** *adj*: *My sweater's gone all bobbly.*

**bobble²** *v* [T] *AmE* to drop or hold a ball in an uncontrolled way; FUMBLE (3): *The shortstop bobbled the ball and the runner ran home.*

**bobble hat** /ˈ·· ·/ *n* [C] *BrE* a WOOLLEN hat with a bobble on the top

**bob·by** /ˈbɒbi‖ˈbɑːbi/ *n* [C] *BrE informal old-fashioned* a policeman

**bobby pin** /ˈ·· ·/ *n* [C] *AmE* a thin piece of metal bent into a narrow U shape that you use to hold your hair in place; HAIRGRIP *BrE* —see picture at PIN¹

**bobby socks, bobby sox** /ˈ·· ·/ *n* [plural] *AmE* girls' short socks that have the tops turned over

**bob·cat** /ˈbɒbkæt‖ˈbɑːb-/ *n* [C] a large North American wild cat that has no tail; LYNX

**bobs** /bɒbz‖bɑːbz/ *n* [plural] see **bits and bobs** (BIT¹ (14))

**bob·sleigh,** /ˈbɒbsleɪ‖ˈbɑːb-/ also **bobsled** /ˈbɒbsled‖ˈbɑːb-/ *n* **1** [C] a small vehicle with two long thin metal blades instead of wheels, that is used for racing down a special ice track **2** [U] a sports event in which people race against each other in bobsleighs: *Sixteen teams took part in the 400m bobsleigh.* —**bobsleigh** *v* [I]

**bob·tail** /ˈbɒbteɪl‖ˈbɑːb-/ *n* [C] **a)** a horse or dog whose tail has been cut short **b)** a tail that has been cut short —see also **ragtag and bobtail** (RAGTAG (2))

**bob·white** /ˈbɒbwaɪt‖ˈbɑːb-/ *n* [C] a bird from North America, often shot for sport; QUAIL¹ (1)

**boche** /bɒʃ‖bɑːʃ/ *n* **the Boche** an offensive word meaning the Germans or German soldiers, used in Britain during the First and Second World Wars

**bod** /bɒd‖bɑːd/ *n* [C] **1** *BrE spoken* a person: *We had to write to some bod at head office to ask for a refund.* **2** *informal* someone's body: *Move your bod, will you!* **3 odd bod** *informal* a strange person: *He's a bit of an odd bod but very pleasant.*

**bode** /bəʊd‖boʊd/ *v* **1** the past tense of BIDE **2 bode well/ill (for)** *especially literary* to be a good or bad sign for the future: *The results of the opinion poll do not bode well for the Democrats.*

**bodge** /bɒdʒ‖bɑːdʒ/ also **bodge up** *n* [singular] *spoken* a mistake or something that is not as good as it should be: *The builders have made a complete bodge of the kitchen.* —see also BOTCH —**bodge** *v* [T]

**bod·ice** /ˈbɒdɪ̣s‖ˈbɑː-/ *n* [C] **1** the part of a woman's dress above her waist **2** a tight-fitting woman's WAISTCOAT worn over a BLOUSE in former times **3** *old use* a piece of woman's underwear that covered the upper part of her body; CORSET (1)

**bod·i·ly¹** /ˈbɒdɪ̣li‖ˈbɑː-/ *adj* [only before noun] related to the human body: *Many bodily changes occur during adolescence.* | *bodily sensations*

**bodily²** *adv* **1** by moving the whole of your or someone else's body: *He lifted the child bodily aboard.* **2** by moving a large object in one piece: *The column was transferred bodily to a new site by the bank of the river.*

**bod·kin** /ˈbɒdkɪ̣n‖ˈbɑːd-/ *n* [C] a long thick needle without a point

**body**

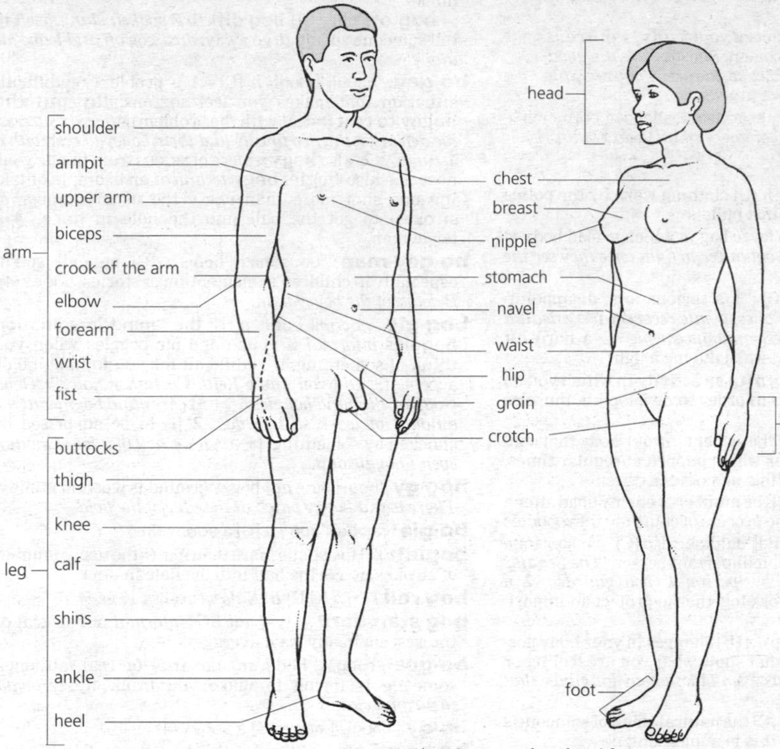

see also pictures at **head** and **foot**

S1 W1 **bod·y** /ˈbɒdi‖ˈbɑːdi/ *n plural* **bodies**

**1 ▶ SB'S BODY ◀** [C] the physical structure of a person or animal: *Many teenagers are self-conscious about their bodies.* | **body heat/temperature/weight etc** *Babies undergo a rapid increase in body weight during the first weeks.* | **body image** (=the mental picture that you have of your own body) *negative feelings associated with a changed body image* | **the body beautiful** (=an idea of the perfect body) *products designed to help you achieve the body beautiful*

**2 ▶ DEAD BODY ◀** [C] the dead body of a person: *Neighbours were called in to identify the body.*

**3 ▶ GROUP OF PEOPLE ◀** [C] a group of people who work together to do a particular job or who are together for a particular purpose: [+ **of**] *Two hundred years ago a body of settlers established themselves on the island.* | **governing body** (=a body that controls the work or activities of an organization or group) | **student body** (=all the students in a particular school or college) *We have a student body from a wide range of background.* | **public body** (=group of people involved in government)

**4 a body of a)** a large amount or collection of something: **body of knowledge/information/literature etc** *Researchers used vast bodies of information to arrive at their findings.* **b)** the main, central, or most important part of something: *The bedrooms were connected to the body of the house by a long corridor.* | *the main body of the report*

**5 in a body** if people do something in a body, they do it together in large numbers: *The demonstrators marched in a body to the main square.*

**6 ▶ CENTRAL PART ◀** [C] the central part of a person or animal's body, not including the head, arms, legs or wings: *Nick has short legs but a long body.*

**7 ▶ SEPARATE OBJECT ◀** [C] *technical* an object that is separate from other objects

**8 ▶ VEHICLE ◀** [C] the main structure of a vehicle not including the engine, wheels etc: *The body's beginning to rust.*

**9 ▶ HAIR ◀** [U] if your hair has body, it is thick and healthy

**10 over my dead body** *spoken* used to show that you are determined to prevent something from happening: *He'll come to the meeting over my dead body.*

**11 long/thick etc bodied etc** having a long, thick etc body: *They were thick-bodied men accustomed to hard labour.* —see also ABLE-BODIED

**12 full/medium/light bodied** used to describe how much FLAVOUR (=taste) a wine or beer has, with full bodied wine or beer having the strongest taste

**13 body and soul** completely: *She threw herself body and soul into her work.*

**14 keep body and soul together** to continue to exist with only just enough food, money etc

**15 ▶ CLOTHES ◀** [C] *BrE* a type of tight fitting shirt worn by women that fastens between their legs; BODY SUIT *AmE* —see picture at UNDERWEAR

**16 body of water** a large area of water such as a lake

**USAGE NOTE: BODY**

WORD CHOICE: **body, figure, build**

A **body** consists of someone's arms, legs, head etc and may be healthy, skinny, dead etc: *I like to look after my body.* If you say someone has a *lovely/*

*good/beautiful body* this may suggest you find them sexually attractive.

Your **figure** is the shape of your **body**. **Figure** is usually used about women: *She has a really good figure.* | *I won't have a cake, thanks. I'm watching my figure* (= trying not to get fat).

**Build** can be used for the size and shape of both men and women: *a man/woman of small/heavy/slim build*

B

**body ar·mour** /ˈ·· ˌ··/ *n* [U] clothing worn by the police that protects them against bullets

**body bag** /ˈ·· ·/ *n* [C] a large bag in which a dead body is removed: *Men will not volunteer to fight once they see the body bags returning.*

**body blow** /ˈ·· ·/ *n* [C] **1** a serious loss, disappointment, or defeat: *Hopes of economic recovery were dealt a body blow by this latest announcement.* **2** a hard hit between your neck and waist during a fight

**body build·ing** /ˈ·· ˌ··/ *n* [U] an activity in which you do hard physical exercise in order to develop big muscles —**body builder** *n* [C]

**body clock** /ˈ·· ·/ *n* [C] the system in your body that controls types of behaviour which happen at regular times, such as sleeping or eating; BIOLOGICAL CLOCK

**body count** /ˈ·· ˌ·/ *n* [C] the number of enemy dead after a period of fighting, or the process of counting their bodies

**bod·y·guard** /ˈbɒdigɑːd‖ˈbɑːdigɑːrd/ *n* [C] **1** someone whose job is to protect an important person: *The Senator arrived, surrounded by personal bodyguards.* **2** a group of people who work together to protect an important person

**body lan·guage** /ˈ·· ˌ··/ *n* [U] changes in your body position and movements that show what you are feeling or thinking: *It was obvious from Luke's body language that he was nervous.*

**body o·dour** /ˈ·· ˌ··/ *n* [C] the natural smell of someone's body, especially when this is unpleasant; BO

**body pol·i·tic** /ˌ·· ˈ···/ *n* [singular] *formal* all the people in a nation forming a state under the control of a single government

**body pop·ping** /ˈ·· ˌ··/ *n* [U] a type of dancing in which the dancer makes short, sudden movements that make them look like a machine or ROBOT (1)

**body search** /ˈ·· ·/ *n* [C] a thorough search for drugs, weapons etc, that might be hidden on someone's body: *They did a body search on all the passengers before they boarded the plane.* —**body-search** *v* [T]

**body snatch·er** /ˈ·· ˌ··/ *n* [C] someone in the past who dug up dead bodies and sold them to doctors for scientific study

**body spray** /ˈ·· ·/ *n* [U] a chemical substance that you put onto your body to make it smell nice

**body stock·ing** /ˈ·· ˌ··/ *n* [C] a close-fitting piece of clothing that covers the whole of your body

**body suit** /ˈ·· ·/ *n* [C] *AmE* a type of tight fitting shirt worn by women that fastens between their legs; BODY (15) *BrE*

**bod·y·work** /ˈbɒdiwɜːk‖ˈbɑːdiwɜːrk/ *n* [U] the metal frame of a vehicle, not including the engine, wheels etc: *The bodywork's beginning to rust.*

**Bo·er**[1] /bɔː, bʊə‖bɔːr bʊr/ *n* [C] someone from South Africa whose family came from Holland

**Boer**[2] *adj* connected with the Boers: *the Boer War*

**bof·fin** /ˈbɒfɪn‖ˈbɑː-/ *n* [C] *BrE* **1** *old-fashioned* a scientist **2** *informal* someone who is very clever but not fashionable: *He was always a bit of a boffin, even at school.*

**bog**[1] /bɒg‖bɑːg, bɔːg/ *n* **1** [C,U] an area of wet muddy ground that you can sink into —compare MARSH, SWAMP[1] **2** [C] *BrE slang* a toilet

**bog**[2] *v*

**bog** sb ↔ **down** *phr v* [T] **1** to become too involved in thinking about or dealing with one particular thing: [+ **in**] *Don't let yourself get bogged down in minor details.* **2** to become stuck in muddy ground and be unable to move

**bog off** phr v [I] **bog off!** *BrE spoken slang* used to tell someone rudely to go away: *Just bog off and leave me alone!*

**bo·gey** /ˈbəʊgi‖ˈboʊgi/ *n* [C] **1** a problem or difficult situation that makes you feel anxious: **lay/put the bogey to rest** (=deal with the problem) *After six successive defeats, Athletico finally laid their bogey to rest with a 3–0 win.* **2** also **bogy** a piece of MUCUS from inside your nose **3** also **bogie**, **bogy** *technical* an example of taking one shot more than PAR (=the usual number of strokes) to get the ball into the hole in GOLF **4** a bogeyman

**bo·gey·man** /ˈbəʊgimæn‖ˈboʊ/ *n* [C] an evil spirit, especially in children's imagination or stories; BOGEY (4): *Beware of the bogey-man.*

**bog·gle** /ˈbɒgəl‖ˈbɑː-/ *v* **1 the mind/imagination boggles** *informal* if your mind etc boggles when you think of something, it is difficult for you to imagine or accept it: *"Did you know Keith's a father now?" "Good God, no, the mind boggles."* | [+ **at**] *My mind boggles at the amount of work still to do.* **2** [I] to be surprised or shocked by something: [+ **at**] *It's a hell of a lot of money, even I boggle at it.*

**bog·gy** /ˈbɒgi‖ˈbɑː-/ *adj* boggy ground is wet and muddy: *There was a boggy patch at the edge of the field.*

**bo·gie**[1] /ˈbəʊgi‖ˈboʊ-/ *n* [C] a BOGEY (3)

**bogie**[2] *v* [T] to use one more than PAR (=the usual number of strokes) to get the ball into the hole in GOLF

**bog roll** /ˈ· ·/ *n* [C,U] *BrE slang* TOILET PAPER

**bog stan·dard** /ˌ· ˈ··◂/ *adj BrE informal* not special or interesting in any way; average

**bo·gus** /ˈbəʊgəs‖ˈboʊ-/ *adj* not true or real, although someone is trying to make you think it is: *bogus insurance claims*

**bo·gy** /ˈbəʊgi‖ˈboʊ-/ *n* [C] a BOGEY (4)

**bo·he·mi·an** /bəʊˈhiːmiən, bə-‖boʊ-, bə-/ *adj* living in a very informal or relaxed way and not accepting society's rules of behaviour: *bohemian cafes frequented by artists, musicians, and actors* —**bohemian** *n* [C]

**boil**[1] /bɔɪl/ *v* **1** [I,T] when a liquid boils it is hot enough to turn into gas: *Put the spaghetti into plenty of boiling, salted water.* | [+ **at**] *Water boils at 100 degrees centigrade.* | *We were advised to boil the water before drinking it.* **2** [I,T] if something containing liquid boils, the liquid inside it is boiling: *The kettle's boiling! Shall I turn it off?* | **put sth on to boil** (=begin to heat something) *I've put the potatoes on to boil.* | **boiled dry** (=heated for too long so there is no liquid left) **3** [I,T] to cook something in boiling water: *a boiled egg* **4** [T] to wash clothes at a very high temperature: *I always boil the cotton sheets.* —see also BOILING POINT, **make your blood boil** (BLOOD[1] (4)) S

**boil away** *phr v* if a liquid boils away it disappears because it has been heated too much: *Oh no! The soup's almost boiled away.*

**boil down** *phr v* **1** [I,T **boil sth ↔ down**] if a food or liquid boils down, it becomes less after cooking: *Spinach tends to boil down a lot.* **2** [T] **boil sth down** to make information shorter by not including anything that is not necessary: *You can boil this down so that there are just two main categories.*

**boil down to** sth *phr v* [T not in progressive] *informal* if a long statement, argument etc boils down to something, that is the main point or cause: *What it boils down to, is that no-one is willing to take on that kind of responsibility.*

**boil over** *phr v* [I] **1** if a liquid boils over, it rises and flows over the side of the container: *Keep an eye on the milk; don't let it boil over.* **2** if a situation or an emotion boils over, the people involved stop being calm: [+ **into**] *The argument boiled over into a fight.*

**boil up** *phr v* **1** [I] if a situation or emotion boils up, it reaches a dangerous level: *She could sense that trouble* *was boiling up at work.* **2** [T **boil sth ↔ up**] to heat food or a liquid until it begins to boil: *Boil the fruit up with sugar.*

**boil²** *n* **1 the boil** the act or state of boiling: **bring sth to the boil** *Bring the sauce to the boil and simmer for 10 minutes.* | **be coming to the boil** (=almost boiling) | **take sth off the boil** (=stop boiling something by taking it off the heat) **2** [C] a painful infected swelling under someone's skin: *The boy's body is covered in boils.* **3 go off the boil** *BrE* to become less good at something that you are usually very good at: *Gower has gone off the boil in terms of batting lately.*

**boiled sweet** /ˌ· ˈ·/ *n* [C] *BrE* a hard SWEET² (1) that often tastes of fruit; HARD CANDY *AmE*

3 **boil·er** /ˈbɔɪlə‖-ər/ *n* [C] a container for boiling water that is part of a steam engine, or is used to provide heating in a house

**boiler suit** /ˈ·· ·/ *n* [C] *BrE* a piece of loose clothing like trousers and a shirt joined together, that you wear over your clothes to protect them

3 **boil·ing** /ˈbɔɪlɪŋ/ *adj* **1** very hot: *Can I open a window? It's boiling in here.* | **boiling hot** *It's been boiling hot all Summer* —see COLD¹ (USAGE). **2** very angry: *I was boiling with pent-up rage.*

**boiling point** /ˈ··· ·/ *n* [C] **1** the temperature at which a liquid boils **2** the point at which emotions get out of control and a situation stops being calm: **reach boiling point** *Relations between the two countries have almost reached boiling point.*

**bois·ter·ous** /ˈbɔɪstərəs/ *adj* someone, especially a child, who is boisterous makes a lot of noise and has a lot of energy: *a class of boisterous five year olds*

**bok choy** /ˌbɒk ˈtʃɔɪ‖ˌbɑːk-/ *n* [U] another spelling of PAK CHOI —see picture on page 414

**bold** /bəʊld‖boʊld/ *adj*
**1 ▶ PERSON/ACTION ◀** not afraid of taking risks and making difficult decisions: *a bold leader* | *It's a bold venture starting a business these days.*
**2 ▶ MANNER/APPEARANCE ◀** so confident or determined that you sometimes offend people: **as bold as brass** (=very confident and not showing enough respect) *He came in here, as bold as brass, and asked if he could have his money back.*
**3 ▶ COLOURS/SHAPES ◀** very strong or bright so that you notice them: *bold geometric shapes*
**4 ▶ LINES/WRITING ◀** written or drawn in a very clear way: **a bold hand** (=bold writing) *Her letter was written in a bold sloping hand.*
**5 in bold (type)** printed in letters that are darker and thicker than ordinary printed letters: *The numbers in this dictionary are in bold type.*
**6 make so bold as to do sth** *formal* to do something that other people feel is rude or not acceptable: *One of the staff made so bold as to ask what the director's salary was.*
**7 if I may be so bold** *spoken formal* used when asking someone a question, to show that you hope it will not offend them: *And what, if I may be so bold, is the meaning of this note?* —**boldly** *adv* —**boldness** *n* [U]

**bold·face** /ˈbəʊldfeɪs‖ˈboʊld-/ *n* [U] *technical* a way of printing letters that makes them thicker and darker than normal —**boldfaced** *adj*

**bole** /bəʊl‖boʊl/ *n* [C] *literary* the main part of a tree; TRUNK (1)

**bo·le·ro¹** /bəˈleərəʊ‖-ˈleroʊ/ *n* [C] a type of Spanish dance, or the music for this dance

**bol·e·ro²** /ˈbɒlərəʊ‖bəˈleroʊ/ *n* [C] a short jacket for a woman

**boll** /bəʊl‖boʊl/ *n* [C] the part of a cotton plant that contains the seeds

**bol·lard** /ˈbɒləd, -lɑːd‖ˈbɑːlərd/ *n* [C] **1** *BrE* a short thick post in the street that is used to stop traffic entering an area or to show a JUNCTION more clearly **2** a thick stone or metal post used for tying ships to when they are in port

**bol·lock** /ˈbɒlək‖ˈbɑː-/ *v* [T] *BrE slang* to tell someone angrily that you do not like what they have done: *I'll bollock him for sticking his rubbish in my cupboard.*

**bol·lock·ing** /ˈbɒləkɪŋ‖ˈbɑː-/ *n* [C] **give sb a bollocking** *BrE* to tell someone that you are very angry about something they have done: *I expect I'll get a bollocking from my boss when she finds out.*

**bol·locks** /ˈbɒləks‖ˈbɑː-/ *n* [plural] *BrE slang* **1** *spoken* used to say rudely that you think something is wrong or stupid: *These statistics are total bollocks.* | **a load of old bollocks** (=complete nonsense) *She's just talking a load of old bollocks.* **2** *spoken* a word used to emphasize that you are annoyed or angry: *Oh bollocks! We've missed it.* **3 bollocks to you/that/it etc** *spoken* used when you refuse to accept or obey something: *Oh yeah? Well, bollocks to you, mate!* **4** the two round male organs that produce SPERM; TESTICLES

**boll wee·vil** /ˌ· ˈ··/ *n* [C] an insect that eats and destroys cotton plants

**bo·lo·gna** /bəˈləʊni, -njə‖-ˈloʊ-/ *n* a type of cooked meat often eaten in sandwiches

**bo·lo·ney** /bəˈləʊni‖-ˈloʊ-/ *n* [U] another spelling of BALONEY

**bo·lo tie** /ˈbəʊləʊ taɪ‖ˈboʊloʊ-/ *n* [C] *AmE* a string worn around your neck that you fasten with a decoration

**Bol·she·vik** /ˈbɒlʃɪ̈vɪk‖ˈboʊl-/ *n* [C] **1** someone who supported the COMMUNIST¹ party at the time of the Russian Revolution in 1917 **2** *old-fashioned* an insulting way of talking about a COMMUNIST² or someone who has strong left-wing views —**bolshevik** *adj*

**bol·shie, bolshy** /ˈbəʊlʃi‖ˈboʊl-/ *adj BrE informal* tending to be angry or annoyed and not to obey people: *Jack was in one of his bolshie moods again!* —**bolshiness** *n* [U]

**bol·ster¹** /ˈbəʊlstə‖ˈboʊlstər/ *n* [C] a long firm PILLOW¹ (1) that you put under other pillows

**bolster²** also **bolster up** *v* [T] **1** to help someone to feel better and more positive: *I did my best to bolster up his confidence.* **2** to improve something by supporting it: *a speech designed to bolster her chances at the election*

**bolt¹** /bəʊlt‖boʊlt/ *n* [C]
**1 ▶ LOCK ◀** a metal bar that you slide across a door or window to fasten it
**2 ▶ SCREW ◀** a screw with a flat head and no point, for fastening two pieces of metal together
**3 a bolt from out of the blue** news that is sudden and unexpected: *It was a bolt out of the blue when Alan resigned – completely unexpected.*
**4 bolt of lightning** lightning that appears as a white line in the sky —see also THUNDERBOLT
**5 make a bolt for (it)** to suddenly try to escape from somewhere
**6 ▶ WEAPON ◀** a short heavy ARROW (1) that is fired from a CROSSBOW
**7 ▶ CLOTH ◀** a large long roll of cloth —see also **shoot your bolt** (SHOOT¹ (21)), **the nuts and bolts of** (NUT¹ (6))

**bolt**
nut washer
bolt
bolt

**bolt²** *v* **1** [I] **a)** to suddenly start to run very fast because you are frightened: *The horse reared up and bolted.* **b)** to escape from somewhere: *Kevin had bolted through the open window.* **2** also **bolt down** [T] to eat very quickly: *Don't bolt your food.* **3** to fasten two things together using a BOLT¹ (2): *We had the safe bolted to the wall.* **4** [I,T] to lock a door or window by sliding a bolt across

**bolt³** *adv* **sit/stand bolt upright** to sit or stand with your back very straight

**bolt·hole** *n* [C] a place where you can escape to and hide: *a bolthole in the country*

**bomb¹** /bɒm‖bɑːm/ *n* [C] 
**1 ▶ WEAPON ◀** a weapon made of material that will

explode: *A bomb was planted at the railway station.* —see also ATOM BOMB, HYDROGEN BOMB, LETTER BOMB, NEUTRON BOMB, STINK BOMB, TIME BOMB
**2 the bomb** used to describe NUCLEAR WEAPONS, and especially the HYDROGEN BOMB: *a 'ban the bomb' campaign*
**3 cost a bomb** *BrE informal* to cost a lot of money
**4 go like a bomb** *BrE informal* **a)** if a car goes like a bomb, it can travel very quickly **b)** if a party goes like a bomb, it is very successful
**5 make a bomb** *BrE informal* to get a lot of money by doing something: **[+out of]** *If you could get some of that cheap pottery back to England, you could make a bomb out of it.*

**B**

**bomb**[2] *v* **1** [T] to attack a place by leaving a bomb there, or by dropping bombs on it from a plane: *The town was heavily bombed in World War II.* **2** [I] *BrE informal* to move or drive very quickly: [+ **down/along/towards]** *Suddenly a police car came bombing down the high street.* **3** [I,T] *AmE informal* to fail a test very badly: *I bombed my mid-term.* **4** [I] *especially AmE* if a play bombs, it is not successful: *His latest play bombed on Broadway.*

**bomb** sth ↔ **out** *phr v* [T] if a building or the people in it are bombed out, the building is completely destroyed: *a bombed out town*

**bom·bard** /bɒm'bɑːd‖bɑːm'bɑːrd/ *v* [T] **1** to attack a place by firing a lot of guns or throwing bombs continuously at it: *British ships began bombarding the port of Alexandria.* **2** to continue asking someone a lot of questions criticizing them, or giving them a lot of information at once: *Both leaders were bombarded with questions from the press.*

**bom·bar·dier** /ˌbɒmbə'dɪə◂‖ˌbɑːmbər'dɪr/ *n* [C] **1** the person on a military aircraft responsible for dropping bombs **2** a low rank in the Royal Artillery (=part of the British Army)

**bom·bard·ment** /bɒm'bɑːdmənt‖bɑːm'bɑːrd-/ *n* [U] a continuous attack on a place by big guns and bombs: *Sarajevo is coming under heavy bombardment from Serb forces.* | **aerial bombardment** (=attack by planes dropping bombs)

**bom·bas·tic** /bɒm'bæstɪk‖bɑːm-/ *adj* bombastic language contains long important sounding words that have no real meaning: *Pennant's pushy and bombastic manner* —**bombast** /'bɒmbæst‖'bɑːm-/ *n* [U]

**bomb dis·po·sal** /'· ·ˌ··/ *n* [U] the job of dealing with bombs that have not exploded, and making them safe: **a bomb disposal expert/squad/unit etc** *Bomb disposal experts were called in to make the device safe.*

**bombed** /bɒmd‖bɑːmd/ *adj* [not before noun] *slang* very drunk or affected by illegal drugs: *I feel like going out and getting completely bombed.*

**bomb·er** /'bɒmə‖'bɑːmər/ *n* [C] **1** a plane that carries and drops bombs **2** someone who puts a bomb somewhere

**bomber jack·et** /'·· ˌ··/ *n* [C] a short jacket which fits tightly around your waist

**bomb·ing** /'bɒmɪŋ‖'bɑːm-/ *n* [C,U] the use of bombs to attack a place: **wave of bombings** (=series of attacks using bombs) *Hundreds have been killed in the current wave of bombings.*

**bomb·proof** /'bɒmpruːf‖'bɑːm-/ *adj* strong enough not to be damaged by a bomb attack: *a bombproof shelter*

**bomb scare** /'· ·/ *n* [C] a situation where someone telephones and says that there is a bomb in a particular place: *a bomb scare in Central London*

**bomb·shell** /'bɒmʃel‖'bɑːm-/ *n* [C] *informal* **1** an unexpected and very shocking piece of news: *His death came as a complete bombshell.* **2 drop a bombshell** to suddenly tell someone a shocking piece of news **3 blonde bombshell** *humorous* an extremely attractive woman with FAIR (=light coloured) hair

**bomb shel·ter** /'· ˌ··/ *n* [C] a room or building that is built to protect people from bomb attacks

**bomb site** /'· ·/ *n* [C] a place where a bomb has destroyed several buildings in a town: *They've pulled down so many buildings around here it looks like a bombsite.*

**bo·na fi·de**, **bonafide** /ˌbəʊnə 'faɪdi‖'bəʊnə faɪd/ *adj* **1** real, true and not intended to deceive someone: *Only bona fide members are allowed to use the club pool.*
**2 bona fides** *BrE* [plural] if you check someone's bona fides, you check that they are who they say they are

**bo·nan·za** /bə'nænzə, bəʊ-‖bə-, boʊ-/ *n* [C] a lucky or successful situation where people can make a lot of money: *Spielberg's movie ET was a box office bonanza.*

**bon·bon** /'bɒnbɒn‖'bɑːnbɑːn/ *n* [C] a type of round SWEET[2] (1)

**bonce** /bɒns‖bɑːns/ *n* [C] *slang* your head

**bond**[1] /bɒnd‖bɑːnd/ *n* [C] 
**1 ▶MONEY◀** an official document promising that a government or company will pay back money that it has borrowed, often with INTEREST[1] (4): *My father put all his money into Canadian Northern Railway bonds.* | *furious trading on the bond market*
**2 ▶UNITE◀** something that unites two or more people or groups, such as love, or a shared interest or idea: [+ **between**] *the natural bond between mother and child* | [+ **of**] *The two countries are linked by bonds of friendship going back many years.* | [+ **with**] | *He felt a strong bond with his audience.*
**3 bonds** [plural] *literary* **a)** something that limits your freedom and prevents you from doing what you want: [+ **of**] *the bonds of slavery* **b)** *literary* chains, ropes etc used for tying up a prisoner: *The prisoners will be freed from their bonds.*
**4 ▶GLUE◀** the way in which two surfaces become fixed to each other using glue
**5 ▶CHEMISTRY◀** *technical* the chemical force that holds atoms together: *In each methane molecule there are four CH bonds.*
**6** a written agreement to do something, that makes you legally responsible for doing it
**7 my word is my bond** *formal* used to say that you will definitely do what you have promised
**8 in/out of bond** *technical* in or out of a BONDED WAREHOUSE

**bond**[2] *v* **1** [I] if two things bond with each other, they become firmly fixed together, especially after they have been joined with glue: *It takes less than 10 minutes for the two surfaces to bond.* **2** [I] to develop a special relationship with someone: *the tendency to bond with others of the same sex* **3** [T] *technical* to keep goods in a bonded warehouse

**bond·age** /'bɒndɪdʒ‖'bɑːn-/ *n* [U] **1** the practice of being tied up for sexual pleasure **2** *literary* the state of being a slave: *Since the age of 13 he had been in bondage.*
**3** the state of having your freedom limited, or being prevented from doing what you want: *He wanted to be free from the bondage of social conventions.*

**bonded ware·house** /ˌ·· '··/ *n* [C] *technical* an official store for goods that have been brought into a country before tax has been paid on them

**bond·hold·er** /'bɒndˌhəʊldə‖'bɑːndˌhoʊldər/ *n* [C] *technical* someone who owns government or industrial bonds (BOND[1] (1))

**bond·ing** /'bɒndɪŋ‖'bɑːn-/ *n* [U] **1** a process in which a special relationship develops between two or more people: *They're in the bar again doing some male bonding!*
**2** *technical* the connection of atoms

**bone**[1] /bəʊn‖boʊn/ *n* 
**1 ▶BODY◀** [C] one of the hard parts that together form the frame of a human or animal body: *The X-ray showed that the bone was broken in two places.* | **thigh/cheek/jaw etc bone** (=the bone in your thigh etc) *very prominent cheek bones* | **big-boned/fine-boned/small-boned etc** (=with big etc bones) *Grace was a tall, big-boned woman* | **good/fine bone structure** (=someone with good bone structure has a well-shaped face)
**2 have a bone to pick with sb** *spoken* used to tell

someone that you are annoyed with them and want to talk about it
**3 the bare bones** the simplest and most important details of something: *This is just the bare bones of the plan – it's still in the early stages.*
**4 make no bones about (doing) sth** to not feel nervous or ashamed about doing or saying something: *We made no bones about our commitment to Marxism.*
**5 be chilled/frozen to the bone** extremely cold
**6 a bone of contention** something that causes arguments between people: *The question of unpaid overtime became the main bone of contention.*
**7 a bag of bones** someone who is much too thin
**8 bones** [plural] *AmE* DICE[1] (1)
**9 close to the bone** a remark, statement etc that is close to the bone, is close to the truth in a way that may offend someone: *Some of his jokes were a bit close to the bone.*
**10 cut sth to the bone** to reduce costs, services etc as much as possible
**11 feel/know it in your bones** to be certain that something is true, even though you have no proof and cannot explain why you are certain: *That boy's trouble, I can feel it in my bones.*
**12 off the bone** meat that is served off the bone has been cut away from the bone
**13 on the bone** meat that is served on the bone is still joined to the bone —see also **dry as a bone** (DRY[1] (1)), **work your fingers to the bone** (WORK[1] (27))

**bone²** *v* [T] to remove the bones from fish, or meat
**bone up** [I] *informal* to study hard for an examination: *I'm having to bone up on criminal law for a test next week.*

**bone chi·na** /ˌ· ˈ··◂/ *n* [U] delicate and expensive cups, plates etc that are made partly with crushed bone

**bone dry** /ˌ· ˈ·◂/ *adj* completely dry: *There had been no rain for months and the land was bone dry.*

**bone·head** /ˈbəʊnhed‖ˈboʊn-/ *n* [C] *informal* a stupid person

**bone i·dle** /ˌ· ˈ··◂/ *adj* extremely lazy: *He's not stupid, just bone idle.*

**bone mar·row** /ˈ· ˌ··/ *n* the soft substance in the hollow centre of bones; MARROW (1): *a bone marrow transplant*

**bone meal** /ˈ· ·/ *n* [U] a substance used to feed plants that is made of crushed bones

**bon·er** /ˈbəʊnə‖ˈboʊnər/ *n* [singular] **1** *AmE taboo* an ERECTION (1) **2** *AmE informal* a stupid or embarrassing mistake

**bone·shak·er** /ˈbəʊnˌʃeɪkə‖ˈboʊnˌʃeɪkər/ *n* [C] *BrE humorous* an old vehicle that is in very bad condition

**bone-tired** /ˌ· ˈ·◂/ *adj* [not before noun] *AmE informal* extremely tired: *Dan sat in the rocker by the fire, bone-tired after his journey.*

**bon·fire** /ˈbɒnfaɪə‖ˈbɑːnfaɪr/ *n* [C] a large outdoor fire, either for burning waste, or for a party: *There was a huge bonfire on Guy Fawkes' night.*

**bonfire night** /ˈ·· ˌ·/ *n* [singular] November 5th, when in Britain people light FIREWORKS and burn a GUY[1] (2) on a large outdoor fire; GUY FAWKES' NIGHT

**bong** /bɒŋ‖bɑːŋ/ *n* **1** [singular] a deep sound made by a large bell **2** [C] *slang* an object used for smoking CANNABIS in which the smoke goes through water to make it cool

**bon·gos**, **bongoes** /ˈbɒŋgəʊz‖ˈbɑːŋgoʊz/ also **bongo drums** /ˈ·· ·/ *n* [plural] a pair of small drums that you play with your hands

**bon·ho·mie** /ˈbɒnəmi‖ˌbɑːnəˈmiː/ *n* [U] *French especially literary* a friendly feeling among a group of people: *The atmosphere of bonhomie was suddenly gone.*

**bonk¹** /bɒŋk‖bɑːŋk/ *v* [I,T] **1** *BrE slang humorous* to have sex with someone **2** *informal* to hit someone lightly on the head or to hit your head on something by mistake: *He fell, bonking his head against a tree.*

**bonk²** *n* **1** [singular] *BrE slang humorous* the action of having sex: *a quick bonk* **2** [C] *informal* the action of hitting someone lightly on the head, or hitting your head against something **3** [C] *informal* a sudden short deep sound, for example, when something hits the ground

**bon·kers** /ˈbɒŋkəz‖ˈbɑːŋkərz/ *adj BrE humorous* **1** slightly crazy: *Fly to Tokyo for one day? You must be bonkers!* **2 drive sb bonkers** to annoy someone: *I wish they'd turn that bloody music down – it's driving me bonkers!*

**bon mot** /ˌbɒn ˈməʊ‖ˌboʊn ˈmoʊ/ *n* [C] *French* a clever remark

**bon·net** /ˈbɒnɪt‖ˈbɑː-/ *n* [C] **1** *BrE* the metal lid over the front of a car: *I'll need to check under the bonnet.* —see picture on page 409 **2 a)** a warm hat that a baby wears which ties under its chin **b)** a type of hat that women wore in the past which tied under their chin and often had a wide BRIM[1] (1) —see also **have a bee in your bonnet** (BEE (3)), —see picture at HAT

**bon·ny** /ˈbɒni‖ˈbɑːni/ *adj especially ScotE* **1** pretty and healthy: *a bonny baby* **2** clever or skilful: *a bonny fighter*

**bon·sai** /ˈbɒnsaɪ, ˈbəʊn-‖boʊnˈsaɪ, ˈbɑːnsaɪ/ *n* [C,U] a tree that is grown so that it always stays very small, or the art of growing trees in this way —**bonsai** *adj*

**bo·nus** /ˈbəʊnəs‖ˈboʊ-/ *n* [C] **1** money added to someone's wages, especially as a reward for good work: *People who stay more than two years in the job receive a special bonus.* **2** something good that you did not expect in a situation: **added bonus** *It's an added bonus being able to work at home.* **3 no-claims bonus** a reduction in the cost of your car insurance when you do not make a claim in a particular year S2

**bon vi·vant** /ˌbɒn viːˈvɒnt‖ˌbɑːn viːˈvɑːnt/ also **bon viveur** /-viːˈvɜː‖-viːˈvɜːr/ *n* [C] *literary French* someone who enjoys good food and wine, and being with people

**bon voy·age** /ˌbɒn vwaɪˈɑːʒ‖ˌbɑːn-/ *French* used to wish someone a good journey

**bon·y** /ˈbəʊni‖ˈboʊ-/ *adj* **1** someone or part of their body that is bony is very thin: *Her hand felt cold and bony.* **2** bony meat or fish contains a lot of small bones **3** a part of an animal that is bony consists mostly of bone

**boo¹** /buː/ *v* [I,T] **1** to shout 'boo' to show that you do not like a person, performance, idea etc: *Some of the audience started booing.* **2 boo sb off (stage)** to shout 'boo' until a performer leaves the stage: *His jokes were so bad he got booed off stage.*

**boo²** *interjection* **1** *plural* **boos** a noise made by people who do not like a person, performance, idea etc **2** a word you shout suddenly to someone as a joke in order to frighten them **3 wouldn't say boo to a goose** an expression used to describe a shy, quiet person: *Christine wouldn't say boo to a goose.*

**boob¹** /buːb/ *n* [C usually plural] **1** *slang* a woman's breast **2** *BrE informal* a silly mistake **3** *AmE old-fashioned* a stupid or silly person

**boob²** *v* [I] to make a stupid mistake: *I think Jean's boobed again.*

**boo-boo** /ˈ· ·/ *n* [C] *informal* a word meaning a mistake: *I made a bit of a boo-boo asking her about David!*

**boob tube** /ˈ· ·/ *n* [C] **1** *BrE* a piece of women's clothing made of stretchy material, that covers only her chest; TUBE TOP *AmE* **2 the boob tube** *AmE informal* the TELEVISION (1): *sitting around watching the boob tube*

**boo·by** /ˈbuːbi/ *n* [C] *informal* a silly or stupid person

**boo·by hatch** /ˈ·· ·/ *n* [singular] *AmE old-fashioned* a mental hospital

**booby prize** /ˈ·· ·/ *n* [C] a prize given as a joke to the person who is last in a competition

**booby trap, booby-trap** /ˈ·· ·/ *n* [C] **1** a hidden bomb that explodes when you touch something else that is connected to it **2** a HARMLESS trap that you arrange for someone as a joke: *The booby trap was a bucket of water resting on top of the door.* —**booby-trapped** *adj*

**boog·er** /ˈbʊgə,ˈbuː-‖-ər/ *n* [C] *AmE slang* **1** used when describing a person or thing: *You wouldn't want to meet him in a dark alley – he's a mean-looking booger.* —compare BUGGER **2** a thick piece of MUCUS from your nose

**boo·gey·man** /ˈbuːgimæn/ *n* a BOGEYMAN

**boo·gie¹** /ˈbuːgi/ *v* [I] *informal* to dance, especially to fast popular music: *Boogie on down!*

**boogie²** *n* **1** also **boogie woo·gie** /ˌbuːgi ˈwuːgi/ [U] *AmE* a type of music played on the piano with a strong fast RHYTHM (1) **2** [C] *informal* a dance, especially to fast popular music: *Do you fancy going for a boogie on Saturday?*

**boo·hoo** /ˌbuː ˈhuː/ *interjection* a word used especially in children's stories to show that someone is crying

S1 W1 **book¹** /bʊk/ *n*

**1** ▶ **PRINTED BOOK** ◀ [C] a set of printed pages that are fastened together in a cover so that you can read them: *I'm reading a book by Graham Greene.* | *Nothing beats curling up with a good book.*

**2** ▶ **BOOK TO WRITE IN** ◀ [C] a set of sheets of paper fastened together in a cover so that you can write on them: *a note book* | **address/exercise etc book** (=a book for a particular purpose)

**3** ▶ **SET OF THINGS** ◀ [C] a set of things such as stamps, matches or tickets, fastened together inside a paper cover

**4 books** [plural] **a)** ▶ **ACCOUNTS** ◀ written records of the accounts of a business: *Their books show a profit.* —see also **cook the books** (COOK¹ (5)) **b)** ▶ **JOBS** ◀ the names of people who use a company's services, or who are sent by a company to work for other people: **on sb's books** (=employed by a company or organization) *informal*: *We have over 100 VDU operators on our books at the moment.*

**5 a closed book** a subject that you do not understand or know anything about: *Chemistry is a closed book to me.*

**6 one for the books** *informal* used to say that something that has happened is unusual or surprising: *Look! Gaynor's buying the drinks. There's one for the books!*

**7 be in sb's good/bad books** *informal* used to say that someone is pleased or annoyed with you

**8 go by the book/do sth by the book** to do something exactly according to rules or instructions: *Tony's the sort of bloke who does everything by the book.*

**9 in my book** *usually spoken* used when giving your opinion: *She's all right in my book.*

**10** ▶ **PART OF A BOOK** ◀ [C] one of the parts that a very large book such as the Bible is divided into: **[+ of]** *the Book of Isaiah*

**11 bring sb to book** *especially BrE* to punish someone for breaking laws or rules, especially when you have been trying to punish them for a long time: *Terry was finally brought to book for fiddling the accounts.* —see also STATUTE BOOK **take a leaf out of sb's book** (LEAF¹ (2)), **read sb like a book** (READ¹ (13)), **suit sb's book** (SUIT² (6)), **a turn-up for the book** (TURN-UP (2)), **throw the book at** (THROW¹ (27))

S2 **book²** *v* **1** [I,T] *BrE* to arrange with a hotel, restaurant, theatre etc to go there at a particular time in the future: *I've booked a table for two at Mario's tonight.* | *We need to book well in advance for Christmas.* | **booked up/fully booked** (=no rooms, tables etc available) *I'm sorry, we're fully booked for the 14th.* | **booked solid** (=all the tickets etc have been sold) *The show's booked solid for months to come.* **2** [T] to arrange for someone such as a singer to perform on a particular date: **booked up/fully booked** (=no time left to do any more performances) *We're booked up right through the summer season.* **3** [T] when a police officer books someone, they write down their name, address etc because they have done something wrong: *Rebecca's been booked for speeding.* **4** [T] *BrE* when a football REFEREE¹ (1) books a player who has broken the rules, they officially write down the player's name in a book

**book in/into** *phr v BrE* **1** [I] to arrive at a hotel and say who you are etc: *I'll call you as soon as I've booked in at my hotel.* **2** [T **book** sb **in/into**] to arrange for someone to stay at a hotel: *Could you book me in at the Hilton for tonight?*

**book** sb **on** sth *phr v* [T] to arrange for someone to travel on a particular plane, train etc: *She asked her secretary to book her on the next flight to London.*

**book·a·ble** /ˈbʊkəbəl/ *adj* **1** *BrE* tickets for a concert, performance etc that are bookable can be ordered before it happens **2 bookable offence** an offence for which a football player can be punished by having their name written in the referee's book (REFEREE¹ (1))

**book·bind·ing** /ˈbʊkˌbaɪndɪŋ/ *n* [U] the art of fastening the pages of books inside a cover —**bookbinder** *n* [C]

**book·case** /ˈbʊk-keɪs/ *n* [C] a set of shelves for keeping books on: *a walnut bookcase*

**book club** /ˈ· ·/ *n* [C] a club that offers books cheaply to its members

**book·end** /ˈbʊkend/ *n* [C usually plural] one of a pair of objects that you put at the end of a row of books to prevent them from falling over

**book·ie** /ˈbʊki/ *n* [C] *BrE informal* a BOOKMAKER

**book·ing** /ˈbʊkɪŋ/ *n* [C] **1** *BrE* an arrangement to travel by train, use a hotel room etc at a particular time in the future: **make a booking** *Can I make a booking for tonight?* | *cancel a booking* **2** an arrangement made by a performer to perform at a particular time in the future **3** the act of writing a football player's name in a book as a punishment for breaking the rules S

**booking of·fice** /ˈ·· ˌ··/ *n* [C] *BrE* a place where you can buy train or bus tickets

**book·ish** /ˈbʊkɪʃ/ *adj* **1** someone who is bookish is more interested in reading and studying than in sports or other activities: *Bill was the studious, bookish type* **2** based on books rather than on practical experience

**book·keep·ing** /ˈbʊkˌkiːpɪŋ/ *n* [U] the job or activity of recording the accounts of an organization

**book·let** /ˈbʊklɪt/ *n* [C] a very short book that usually contains information: *free booklet on drug abuse* S

**book·mak·er** /ˈbʊkˌmeɪkə‖-ər/ *n* [C] someone whose job is to collect money that people want to risk on the result of a race, competition etc, and who pays them if they guess correctly

**book·mark** /ˈbʊkmɑːk‖-mɑːrk/ *n* [C] a piece of paper, leather etc that shows you the last page you have read in a book

**book·mo·bile** /ˈbʊkməbiːl/ *n* [C] *AmE* a vehicle that contains a library and travels to different places so that people can use it

**book·plate** /ˈbʊkpleɪt/ *n* [C] a decorated piece of paper with your name on it, that you stick in the front of your books

**book·rest** /ˈbʊk-rest/ *n* [C] a metal or wood frame that holds a book upright so that you can read it without holding it in your hands

**book·sell·er** /ˈbʊkˌselə‖-ər/ *n* [C] a person or company that sells books

**book·shelf** /ˈbʊkʃelf/ *n plural* **bookshelves** /-ʃelvz/ [C] a shelf that you keep books on

**book·shop** /ˈbʊkʃɒp‖-ʃɑːp/ *n* [C] *especially BrE* a shop that sells books; bookstore *AmE*

**book·stall** /ˈbʊkstɔːl‖-stɒːl/ *n* [C] *BrE* a small shop that has an open front and sells books and magazines, often at a station; NEWSSTAND *AmE*

**book·store** /ˈbʊkstɔː‖-stɔːr/ *n* [C] *AmE* a shop that sells books; bookshop *BrE*

**book to·ken** /ˈ· ˌ··/ *n* [C] *BrE* a card that you can exchange for books: *My aunt always gives me a book token for Christmas.*

**book va·lue** /ˈ· ˌ··/ *n* [C] the standard value that something such as a car of a particular age, style etc is supposed to have

**book·worm** /ˈbʊkwɜːm‖-wɜːrm/ *n* [C] **1** someone who likes reading very much **2** an insect that eats books

3 **boom¹** /buːm/ *n*
**1** [singular] ▶ **INCREASE IN BUSINESS** ◀ a rapid increase of business activity: [+ **in**] *a sudden boom in the housing market* | **consumer/investment/property etc boom** *the post-war property boom* | **boom years/times** *These are boom times for voluntary organizations.* —see also BOOM TOWN
**2** [singular] ▶ **WHEN STH IS POPULAR** ◀ a period when something suddenly becomes very popular or starts happening a lot: **jazz/aerobics etc boom** *the jazz boom of the 1950s*
**3** ▶ **SOUND** ◀ [C] a deep loud sound that you can hear for several seconds after it begins, especially the sound of an explosion or a large gun: *the dull boom of the cannons* —see also SONIC BOOM
**4** ▶ **LONG POLE** ◀ [C] **a)** a long pole on a boat that is attached to a sail at the bottom —see picture at YACHT **b)** a long pole used as part of a piece of equipment that loads and unloads things **c)** a long pole that has a camera or MICROPHONE on the end
**5** ▶ **ON A RIVER** ◀ [C] something that is stretched across a river or a BAY ¹ (1) to prevent things floating down or across it

**boom²** *v* **1** also **boom out a)** [I] to make a loud deep sound: *Guns boomed in the distance.* **b)** [T] to say something in a loud deep voice: *"Come here, boy," boomed the headteacher.* **2** [I usually in progressive] if business, trade, or a particular area is booming, it is very successful: *The steel industry is booming.* —**booming** *adj*

**boom box** /ˈ· ·/ *n* [C] *AmE informal* a GHETTO BLASTER

**boo·me·rang¹** /ˈbuːməræŋ/ *n* [C] a curved stick from Australia that flies in a circle and comes back to you when you throw it

**boomerang²** *v* [I] if a plan boomerangs on someone, it affects them instead of the person who it was intended to affect

**boom town** /ˈ· ·/ *n* [C] a town or city that suddenly becomes very successful because there is a lot of new industry

**boon** /buːn/ *n* [C usually singular] **1** something that is very useful and makes your life a lot easier: *The new bus service will be a real boon to people in the village.* **2** *old use* a FAVOUR¹ (1)

**boon com·pan·ion** /ˌ· ·ˈ··/ *n* [C] *literary* a very close friend

**boon·docks** /ˈbuːndɒks‖-dɑːks/ *n* [plural] *AmE informal* a place that is a long way from the nearest town

**boon·dog·gle** /ˈbuːn ˌdɒgl‖-ˌdɑːgl/ *n* [singular] *AmE informal* an officially organized plan or activity that is very complicated and wastes a lot of time, money, and effort

**boo·nies** /ˈbuːniz/ *n* [plural] *AmE informal* boondocks

**boor** /bʊə‖bʊr/ *n* [C] *old-fashioned* a man who behaves in a very rude way —**boorish** *adj*: *boorish behaviour* —**boorishly** *adv*

**boost¹** /buːst/ *v* [T] **1** to increase something such as production, sales etc because they are not as high as you want them to be: *The advertising campaign is intended to boost sales.* **2 boost sb's confidence/morale/ego** to make someone feel more confident and less worried: *He regularly phones to boost her morale.* **3** to advertise something by discussing or praising it: *a special promotion to boost their new product* **4** also **boost up** to help someone reach a higher place by lifting them: *Can you boost me up onto the horse?*

**boost²** *n* **1** [singular] something that helps someone be more successful and confident, or that helps something increase or improve: [+ **to**] *Last night's victory was a tremendous boost to the team.* | **give (sb/sth) a boost** *Being chosen to attend the conference gave Matthew a real boost.* | **ego/morale boost** (=an increase in confidence) *He wanted a dizzy blonde as a boost to his ego.* **2** [U] an increase in the amount of power available to a ROCKET¹ (1), piece of electrical equipment etc **3 give sb a boost (up)** to lift someone so that they can reach a higher place: *If I give you a boost up, could you reach the window?*

**boost·er** /ˈbuːstə‖-ər/ *n* [C] **1** a small quantity of a drug that increases the effect of one that was given before, so that someone continues to be protected against a disease **2** something that helps someone be more successful or to feel more confident: **morale booster** *The departmental party was a real morale booster.* **3** a ROCKET ¹ (1) that is used to provide additional power for a SPACECRAFT to leave the Earth: *a giant booster rocket* **4** *AmE* someone who gives a lot of support to a person, organization, or an idea

**booster cush·ion** *BrE* /ˈ·· ˌ··/ also **booster seat, booster chair** *AmE* /ˈ·· ·/ *n* [C] a special seat for a small child that lets them sit in a higher position in a car or at a table

**boots**

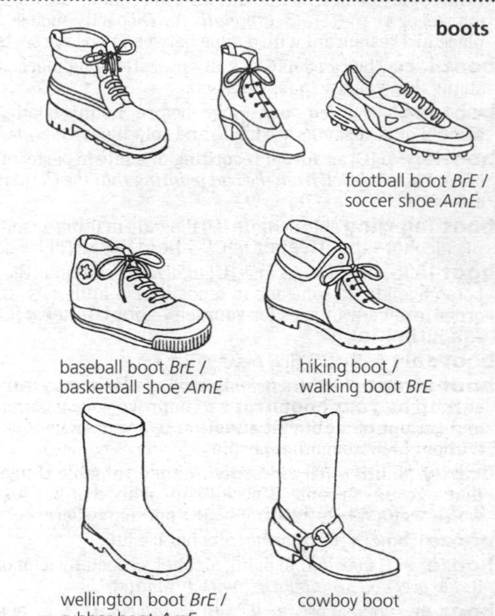


**boot¹** /buːt/ *n* [C] S2 W3
**1** ▶ **SHOE** ◀ a type of shoe that covers your whole foot and the lower part of your leg: *a pair of old army boots*
**2** ▶ **JOB** ◀ *informal* **a) get the boot** to be forced to leave your job **b) give sb the boot** to dismiss someone from their job; SACK² (1): *He was certain they would find out he'd been given the boot.*
**3** ▶ **CAR** ◀ *BrE* an enclosed space at the back of a car, used for carrying bags etc; TRUNK (2) *AmE*: *At least the boot is of reasonable proportions.* —see picture on page 409
**4 put the boot in** *BrE informal* **a)** to say very unkind things to someone who is already upset: *I know you were angry with him but there was no need to put the boot in like that.* **b)** to attack someone by kicking them repeatedly, especially when they are on the ground
**5 give sth a boot** *informal* to give something a quick hard kick: *The door wouldn't open so I gave it a boot.*
**6 the boot is on the other foot** *BrE* used to say that you now have power over someone who used to have power over you
**7 to boot** used at the end of a list of remarks to emphasize them: *He is dishonest, and a coward to boot.* —see also **be/get too big for your boots** (BIG (13)), **lick sb's boots** (LICK¹ (7)), **tough as old boots** (TOUGH¹ (2))

**boot²** *v* **1** [T] *informal* to kick someone or something hard: **boot sth/sb in/round/etc** *The goalkeeper booted the ball upfield.* **2** [I,T] to make a computer

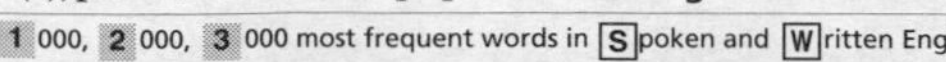

ready to be used by putting in its instructions **3** [T] *AmE* to stop someone from moving their illegally parked vehicle by fixing a piece of equipment to the wheels; CLAMP[1] (3) *BrE*

**boot** sb ↔ **out** *phr v* [T] *informal* to force someone to leave a place, job, or organization, especially because they have done something wrong: *They were booted out of the pub for fighting.*

**boot up** *phr v* [I,T **boot** sth **up**] to make a computer ready to be used by putting in its instructions; BOOT[2] (2)

**boot camp** /ˈ· ·/ *n* [C] a training camp for people who have just joined the US army, Navy, or Marine Corps

**boot·ee**, **bootie** /ˈbuːtiː, buːˈtiː/ *n* [C] a short sock that a baby wears instead of a shoe

**booth** /buːð‖buːθ/ *n* [C] **1** a small partly enclosed place where one person can do something privately, such as use the telephone or vote **2** a tent where you can buy things, play games, or find out information, usually at a market or a FAIR[2] (1) **3** *especially AmE* a partly enclosed place in a restaurant with a table between two long seats

**boot·lace** /ˈbuːtleɪs/ *n* [C usually plural] a long piece of string that you use to fasten a boot

**boot·leg**[1] /ˈbuːtleg/ *adj* [only before noun] bootleg alcohol or recordings are made and sold illegally

**bootleg**[2] *n* [C] an illegal recording of a music performance: *You could tell from the bad printing that the CD was a bootleg.*

**boot·leg·ging** /ˈbuːtlegɪŋ/ *n* [U] illegally making or selling alcohol —**bootlegger** *n* [C] —**bootleg** *v* [I,T]

**boot·lick·ing** /ˈbuːtˌlɪkɪŋ/ *n* [U] *informal* behaviour that is too friendly to someone in a position of authority, in order to get advantages for yourself —**bootlicker** *n* [C] —**bootlicking** *adj*

**boot sale** /ˈ· ·/ *n* [C] *BrE* a CAR BOOT SALE

**boot·straps** /ˈbuːtstræps/ *n* [plural] **pull/haul yourself up by your bootstraps** to improve your position and get out of a difficult situation by your own effort, without help from other people

**boot·y** /ˈbuːti/ *n* [U] *especially literary* valuable things that a group of people, especially an army that has just won a victory, take away or steal from somewhere

**booze**[1] /buːz/ *n* [U] *informal* alcoholic drink

**booze**[2] *v* [I] *informal* to drink alcohol, especially a lot of it: *I expect Jon's out boozing with his mates.*

**booz·er** /ˈbuːzə‖-ər/ *n* [C] *BrE informal* **1** a PUB **2** someone who often drinks a lot of alcohol

**booze-up** /ˈ· ·/ *n* [C] *BrE informal* a party where people drink a lot of alcohol

**booz·y** /ˈbuːzi/ *adj* showing signs of having drunk too much alcohol: *boozy laughter* —**boozily** *adv* —**booziness** *n* [U]

**bop**[1] /bɒp‖bɑːp/ *v* **bopped, bopping** *informal* **1** [T] to hit someone, especially gently: *I bopped him on the head with my book.* **2** [I] *BrE* to dance to popular music

**bop**[2] *n* [singular] **1** *BrE informal* a dance: *It's ages since I had a really good bop.* **2** another word for BEBOP

**bo·rax** /ˈbɔːræks/ *n* [U] a mineral used for cleaning

**Bor·deaux** /bɔːˈdəʊ‖bɔːrˈdoʊ/ *n* [C] a wine that comes from the Bordeaux area in France

**bor·del·lo** /bɔːˈdeləʊ‖bɔːrˈdeloʊ/ *n* [C] *especially literary* a house where men can pay to have sex; BROTHEL

S3 W2 **bor·der**[1] /ˈbɔːdə‖ˈbɔːrdər/ *n* [C] **1** the official line that separates two countries, or the area close to this line: [+ **between**] *The town lies on the border between the US and Mexico.* | [+ **with**] *There has been renewed fighting along the border with Pakistan.* | **on the border** *Jeumont is a small town on the border between France and Belgium.* | **cross the border** *The terrorists were stopped trying to cross the Spanish border.* **2** a band along the edge of something, such as a picture or piece of material: *writing paper with a black border* **3** a band of soil containing plants at the edge of an area of grass: *border plants such as dianthus*

**border**[2] *v* [T] **1** to form a border around the edge of something: *Large trees border the river and the streams.* | [+ **on**] *The valley is bordered on both sides by high limestone cliffs.* **2** if one country borders another country, it is next to it and shares a border with it

**border on** sth *phr v* [T] to be very close to reaching an extreme feeling or quality: *excitement bordering on hysteria*

**bor·der·land** /ˈbɔːdəlænd‖ˈbɔːrdər-/ *n* [C] **1** the land near the border between two countries **2** the borderland between two qualities is an unclear area that contains features of both of them

**bor·der·line**[1] /ˈbɔːdəlaɪn‖ˈbɔːrdər-/ *adj* **borderline case/candidate/decision etc** a situation in which you are not sure whether someone or something is acceptable: *Borderline candidates will take an oral exam to decide their final result.*

**borderline**[2] *n* **1** [singular] the point at which one quality, condition, emotion etc ends and another begins: *slipping gently over the borderline into sleep* **2** [C] a border between two countries

**bore**[1] /bɔː‖bɔːr/ the past tense of BEAR[1]

**bore**[2] *v* **1** [T] to make someone feel bored, especially by talking too much about something they are not interested in: *I'm sorry I spoke for so long – I hope I didn't bore you.* | **bore sb with** *My father's always boring us with his stories about the war.* | **bore sb to death/tears** (=make them very bored) **2** [I,T] to make a deep round hole in a hard surface: [+ **through/into**] *To build the tunnel they had to bore through solid rock.* **3** [I + **into**] if someone's eyes bore into you, they look at you in a way that makes you feel uncomfortable

**bore**[3] *n* **1** [C] someone who is boring, especially because they talk too much about themselves: *He was something of a bore – going on about his charity work all evening.* | **soccer/photography etc bore** (=someone who talks too much about photography etc) **2** [singular] something that you have to do but do not want to do: *Doing housework is a real bore.* **3** **12-bore/small bore etc** the measurement of the size of the inside of a gun BARREL[1] (3) **4** a borehole

S **bored** /bɔːd‖bɔːrd/ *adj* tired and impatient because you do not think something is interesting, or because you have nothing to do: *Children easily get bored.* | [+ **with**] *I'm bored with the same old routine day after day.* | **bored stiff/to tears/to death/out of your mind** (=extremely bored) *You'd be bored stiff in a job like that.*

**USAGE NOTE: BORED**

WORD CHOICE: **bored, boring, interested in, interesting, frightened of, frightening**

With pairs of adjectives like this, the one ending in **-ed** describes the person who has the feeling, the one ending in **-ing** describes whatever gives them that feeling: *I got bored watching TV/talking to Susan.* | *TV/Susan was boring.* | *I'm interested in their summer courses* (NOT *I interested in...* or *I was interesting in/on...* or *I was interested of/on/with/about...*). | *Don't be frightened of it – it isn't really frightening.*

GRAMMAR

You will hear people say they are *bored of* something but many people think only **bored with** is correct: *She's getting really bored with her job.*

**bore·dom** /ˈbɔːdəm‖ˈbɔːr-/ *n* [U] the feeling you have when you are bored: *the sheer boredom of working in a factory*

**bore·hole** /ˈbɔːhəʊl‖ˈbɔːrhoʊl/ *n* [C] a deep hole made using special equipment, especially in order to get water or oil out of the ground

**boring**

The teacher / lecture is boring. / The students are bored.

2 **bor·ing** /'bɔːrɪŋ/ *adj* not interesting in any way: *Her husband is about the most boring person I've ever met.*| **deadly boring** (=very boring) *I always thought maths was deadly boring.*

**born¹** /bɔːn||bɔːrn/ a past participle of BEAR¹

1 **born²** *adj*
2 **1 be born** when a person or animal is born it comes out of its mother's body, or out of an egg: *Forty lambs were born this spring.*|[+ **in**] *Swift was born in 1667.*|*I was born in a small southern town in the USA.*|[+ **at**] *In those days most babies were born at home.*|[+ **on**] *I was born on December 15th 1973.*|**newly-born** recently born: *a newly-born baby*|**be born into/to/of** (=be born in a particular situation, type of family etc) *Frank was born into a wealthy family.*|**be born with** (=have a particular disease, type of character etc since birth) *Jenny was born with a cleft palate.*|**be born blind/deaf/etc** (=be blind, deaf etc when born)|**be born lucky/unlucky etc** (=always be lucky, unlucky etc)|**Australian/French etc born** (=born in or as a citizen of Australia etc) *Australian born rock icon Nick Cave*
**2 be born to do/be sth** to be very suitable for a particular job, activity etc
**3 born leader/teacher/musician etc** someone who has a strong natural ability to lead, teach etc
**4 ▶ START EXISTING ◀** [not before noun] something that is born starts to exist: *And so the concept of the jet engine was born.*
**5 born of/out of** existing as a result of something: *Bill spoke with a cynicism born of bitter experience.*
**6 born and bred** born and having grown up in a particular place and having the typical qualities of someone from that place: *born and bred in Liverpool*
**7 I wasn't born yesterday** *spoken* used to tell someone you think is deceiving you that you are not stupid enough to believe them
**8 in all my born days** *spoken old-fashioned* used to express surprise at something that you have never heard about or experienced before: *Well, I've never heard of such a thing in all my born days!*
**9 there's one born every minute** *spoken* used to say that someone has been very stupid or easily deceived
**10 be born under a lucky/unlucky star** to always have good or bad luck in your life —see also NATURAL-BORN
**11 be born with a silver spoon in your mouth** to be born into a rich family
**12 be born on the wrong side of the blanket** *humorous* to have parents who were not married when you were born

**born-a·gain** /ˌ· ·'·/ *adj* **1 born-again Christian** someone who has become an EVANGELICAL Christian after having a religious experience **2 born-again non-smoker/vegetarian etc** someone who has recently stopped smoking, eating meat etc, and who wants other people to do the same

**borne¹** /bɔːn||bɔːrn/ the past participle of BEAR¹

**borne²** *adj* **1 water-borne/sea-borne/air-borne etc** carried by water, the sea, air etc: *waterborne diseases* **2 be borne in on/upon sb** if a fact is borne in on someone, they realize that it is true: *Slowly it was borne in on the citizens that the enemy had surrounded the entire town.*

**bo·rough** /'bʌrə||-roʊ/ *n* [C] a town, or part of a large city, that is responsible for managing its own schools, hospitals, roads etc: *The New York borough of Queens*|*Lambeth Borough Council* S2

**borough coun·cil** /ˌ·· '··/ *n* [C] *especially BrE* the organization that controls a borough

**bor·row** /'bɒrəʊ||'bɑːroʊ, 'bɔː-/ *v* [I,T] **1** to use something that belongs to someone else and that you must give back to them later: *Can I borrow your pen for a minute?*| **borrow sth from sb** *BrE*: *You are allowed to borrow 6 books from the library at a time.*|**borrow heavily** (=borrow a lot of money) *They borrowed heavily from the bank to start their new business.* —compare LEND (1), LOAN² (1) —see picture at LEND **2** to take or copy someone's ideas, words etc and use them in your own work, language etc: *It is obvious that many ideas in the book have been borrowed.*|[+ **from**] *English borrows words from many languages.* **3 borrow trouble** *AmE informal* to worry about something unnecessarily —see also **be living on borrowed time** (LIVE ¹ (14)) S2 W3

**USAGE NOTE: BORROW**

WORD CHOICE: **borrow, lend, loan, hire, rent, get/have the use of, let somebody use**

You **borrow** something **from** another person who is willing to **lend** it **to** you: *I borrowed some money from my sister* (= my sister lent me some money/I was lent some money by my sister). You will hear some native speakers of English saying things like *My sister borrowed me the money*, but this is not considered to be correct

In American English **loan** is often like **lend**: *The current administration has loaned this country a billion dollars.* In British English **loan** (*v*) is usually used for when someone lends a possession for a long time to a museum etc. so that everybody can see it.

If you **borrow** money you have to pay it back later, and you may have to pay for the use of it as well, if you have borrowed it from a bank rather than a friend. If you **borrow** a car/video etc. you give it back afterwards but you do not usually pay for the use of it, otherwise you would say **hire** or **rent**. See **hire** WORD CHOICE.

People do not usually use **borrow** or **lend/loan** for something that cannot be moved such as a room, house, or piece of land. If you pay for using this sort of thing you **hire** or **rent** it, otherwise you **get the use of** it from someone who is willing to **let** you **use** it: *Could you let us use this hall?/Could we have the use of this hall?*

**bor·row·er** /'bɒrəʊə||'bɑːroʊər , 'bɔː/ *n* [C] someone who is borrowing money: *Most borrowers pay 7% interest.*

**bor·row·ing** /'bɒrəʊɪŋ||'bɑːroʊ-, 'bɔː-/ *n* **1** [C] something such as a word, phrase, or idea that has been copied from another language, book etc: *Names such as Lloyd are Celtic borrowings.*|[+ **from**] *His music is full of borrowings from other composers.* **2** [U] the practice of borrowing money: *The banks announced that borrowing had increased.* **3 borrowings** the total amount of money that a company or organization owes

**borrowing pow·ers** /'··· ˌ··/ *n* [plural] the amount of money that a company is allowed to borrow, according to its own rules

**bor·stal** /'bɔːstl||'bɔːr-/ *n* [C,U] *BrE old-fashioned* a special prison for criminals who are not old enough to be in an ordinary prison: *Shanie was sent to borstal when she was 14.*

**bosh** /bɒʃ‖bɑːʃ/ *interjection* [U] *BrE old-fashioned* a word used when you think that what someone has said is silly or untrue: *"I think Sally has lost weight." "Bosh! She looks fatter than ever."* —**bosh** *n* [U]

B

**bos·om** /ˈbʊzəm/ *n* **1** [singular] the front part of a woman's chest, or the part of her clothes that covers it **2** [C usually plural] a woman's breast **3 the bosom of the family/the Church etc** the situation where you feel safe because you are with people who love and protect you **4** [singular] *literary* a word meaning someone's feelings and emotions, used especially when these are bad or unpleasant: *Drury harboured bitterness and anger in his bosom.* **5 bosom friend/buddy** a very close friend: *We first met in high school and we've been bosom buddies ever since.*

**bos·om·y** /ˈbʊzəmi/ *adj informal* having large breasts

S2 W3 **boss¹** /bɒs‖bɒːs/ *n* [C] **1** the person who employs you or who is in charge of you at work: *I'll have to ask my boss for a day off.* | **be your own boss** (=work for yourself rather than being employed by someone else) **2** *informal* a manager with an important position in a company or other organization: *Prison bosses launched an investigation into major security lapses.* | *Bosses got pay increases of 75%, when the workers' pay was cut to £13,000.* **3** the person who is the strongest in a relationship, who controls a situation etc: *When you first start training a dog it's important to let him see that you're the boss.* | **show sb who's boss** (=make someone realize that you are in control, not them) **4** a round decoration on the surface of something such as the ceiling of an old building

**boss²** *v* [T] to tell people to do things, give them orders etc, especially when you have no authority to do it: **boss sb about** *BrE*/**around** *I'm sick of him bossing us around like that. Who does he think he is?*

**boss³** *adj slang* very attractive or fashionable: *That's boss, that new computer game.*

**bos·sa·no·va** /ˌbɒsəˈnəʊvə‖ˌbɑːsəˈnoʊ-/ *n* [C] a dance that comes from Brazil, or the music for this dance

**boss-eyed** /ˌ· ˈ·◂/ *adj BrE* having both eyes looking in towards your nose; CROSS-EYED

**boss·y** /ˈbɒsi‖ˈbɒːsi/ *adj* **1** always telling other people what to do in a way that is annoying: *I like his approach to things – he can show people what to do without being bossy.* **2 bossy-boots** *BrE informal* someone who you think tells other people what to do too often: *Don't be such a bossy-boots. Let her decide for herself.* —**bossily** *adv* —**bossiness** *n* [U]

**bo·sun** /ˈbəʊsən‖ˈboʊ-/ *n* [C] another spelling of BOATSWAIN

**bo·tan·i·cal** /bəˈtænɪkəl/ *adj* [only before noun] connected with plants or the scientific study of plants —**botanically** /-kli/ *adv*

**botanical gar·den** /ˌ·ˌ·· ˈ··/ *n* [C] a large public garden where many different types of flowers and plants are grown for scientific study

**bot·a·nist** /ˈbɒtənɪst‖ˈbɑː-/ *n* [C] someone whose job is to make scientific studies of wild plants

**bot·a·ny** /ˈbɒtəni‖ˈbɑː-/ *n* [U] the scientific study of plants

**botch¹** /bɒtʃ‖bɑːtʃ/ also **botch up** *v* [T] *informal* to do something badly, because you have been careless or because you do not have the skill to do it properly: *The builders really botched up our patio.* —**botcher** *n* [C]

**botch²** also **botch-up** /ˈ· ·/ *n* [C] *informal especially BrE* a piece of work, job etc that has been badly or carelessly done: **make a botch of** *I've just made an awful botch of my translation.* | **botch job** *That repair was a botch job.*

S1 W1 **both** /bəʊθ‖boʊθ/ *predeterminer, determiner, pron* **1** used to talk about two people, things, situations etc together: *Both Helen's parents are doctors.* | *Both sides are keen to reach an agreement.* | *"I don't know which book to buy." "Why not buy both of them?"* | *They both started speaking together.* —compare EITHER¹ **2 both...and...** used to emphasize that something is true not just of one person, thing, or situation but also of another: *He's lived in both Britain and America.* | *She can both speak and write Japanese.* | *We were treated with both tolerance and compassion.*

**both·er¹** /ˈbɒðə‖ˈbɑːðər/ *v* S W

**1 ▶ MAKE AN EFFORT ◀** [I,T] to make the effort to do something: [**+ about/with**] *BrE*: *I'm too busy to bother about fixing it now.* | **(not) bother to do sth** *Unfortunately he didn't bother to check the exact wording of the contract before he signed it.* | *Nobody listens to me. I don't know why I bother.* | **(not) bother doing something** *I don't know if Sally's coming to the party. I didn't bother asking.* | **don't/didn't/won't etc bother** *"Do you want me to wait for you?" "No, don't bother."*

**2 ▶ WORRY ◀** [I,T] to make someone feel slightly worried or upset: *Being in a crowd really bothers me.* | **it bothers sb that** *It really bothered me that he'd forgotten my birthday.* | **not bother sb** *Mandy hates walking home alone at night but it doesn't bother me.*

**3 ▶ ANNOY ◀** [I,T] to annoy someone by interrupting them when they are trying to do something: *Danny, stop bothering me while I'm trying to work!* | **bother sb about/with sth** *He didn't want to bother her with his financial problems on their honeymoon.*

**4 can't/couldn't be bothered** *BrE* used to say that you do not want to do something because you do not have enough energy or interest: *I knew I ought to clean the car but I just couldn't be bothered.* | **can't/couldn't be bothered to do sth** *My parents could never be bothered to come and see me in the school play.*

**5 not bothered** *especially BrE* if you are not bothered about something, it is not important to you: *"Which chair do you want?" "I'm not bothered."* | [**+ about**] *He's not really bothered about getting the facts right,*

**6 sorry to bother you** *spoken* used as a very polite way of telling someone you want their attention

**7 ▶ FRIGHTEN ◀** [T] to upset or frighten someone by repeatedly trying to hurt them, touch them sexually etc: *Is that man bothering you? Shall I call the police?*

**8 hot and bothered** angry and worried about something, especially unnecessarily: *What are you getting all hot and bothered about? It's not that important.*

**9 not bother yourself/not bother your head** to not take time or energy to do something or to think about something, either because it is not important or because it is too difficult: [**+ with/about**] *Cliff didn't want to bother himself with masses of detail.*

**10 bother it/them etc** *BrE old-fashioned* used to express a sudden feeling of annoyance about something: *Oh bother it! The thread's broken again!*

**bother²** *n* **1** [U] *especially BrE* trouble or difficulty that has been caused by small problems and that usually only continues for a short time: *It's an old car but it's never caused me any bother.* | [**+ with**] *Joe's been having a bit of bother with his back again recently.* | **it's no bother** *spoken* (=used to emphasize that you are happy to help someone and it is not much effort) *"Thanks for your help." "It was no bother at all."* | **go to the bother (of doing sth)** (=make the effort to do something) *I'm not going to go to the bother of writing again. She never writes back.* | **give sb any bother/a lot of bother etc** *Are you sure the station is on your way? I don't want to give you any extra bother.* | **save sb/yourself the bother (of doing sth)** *I should have phoned the shop first and saved myself the bother of going there.* **2** [singular] *BrE* a person or job that is annoying to deal with: *Sorry to be such a bother but could you show me how the photocopier works?*

**bother³** *interjection BrE* used when you are slightly annoyed about something: *Oh bother! I forgot to phone Jean.*

**both·er·a·tion** /ˌbɒðəˈreɪʃən‖ˌbɑː-/ *interjection BrE old-fashioned* used when you are slightly annoyed: *Botheration. I forgot my glasses.*

**both·er·some** /ˈbɒðəsəm‖ˈbɑːðər-/ *adj old-fashioned*

slightly annoying: *She brushed his hand away like a bothersome fly.*

**bottles**

wine bottle | beer bottle | medicine bottle | baby's bottle *BrE*/ baby bottle *AmE* | milk bottle | hot water bottle

1 **bot·tle¹** /'bɒtl||'bɑːtl/ *n*
2 **1** ▶ **CONTAINER** ◀ [C] a container with a narrow top for keeping liquids in, usually made of plastic or glass: *Give the bottle a shake before you open it.* | [+ **of**] *a bottle of champagne*
**2** ▶ **AMOUNT OF LIQUID** ◀ also **bottleful** [C] the amount of liquid that a bottle contains: *Between us, we drank three bottles of wine.*
**3** ▶ **MILK** ◀ [singular] milk given to babies or young animals in a bottle rather than from their mother's breast: *My first baby just wouldn't take a bottle at all.*
**4** ▶ **COURAGE** ◀ [U] *BrE informal* courage to do something that is dangerous or unpleasant: *I never thought she'd have the bottle to do it!*
**5 hit the bottle/take to the bottle** to start drinking a lot of alcohol regularly, in order to forget your problems
**6 be on the bottle** to always be drinking a lot of alcohol
**7 bring a bottle** *BrE* **bring your own bottle** *AmE* used to describe a party to which you must bring your own alcoholic drink

**bottle²** *v* [T] **1** to put a liquid, especially wine or beer, into a bottle after you have made it: *The wine is bottled at the vineyard.* **2** to put vegetables or fruit into special glass containers in order to preserve them

**bottle out** *phr v* [I] *BrE informal* to suddenly decide not to do something because you are frightened: *"Did you tell him?" "No, I bottled out at the last minute."*

**bottle** sth ↔ **up** *phr v* [T] to deliberately not allow yourself to show a strong feeling or emotion: *It is far better to cry than to bottle up your feelings.*

**bottle bank** /'· · ·/ *n* [C] a container in the street that you put empty bottles into, so that the glass can be used again

**bot·tled** /'bɒtld||'bɑː-/ *adj* **bottled water/beer etc** water, beer etc that is sold in a bottle

**bottle-feed** /'·· ·/ *v past tense and past participle* **bottle-fed** /-fed/ [T] to feed a baby or young animal with milk from a bottle rather than from their mother's breast —**bottle-feeding** *n* [U]

**bottle green** /,·· '·◂/ *n* [U] a very dark green colour —**bottle green** *adj* —see picture on page 411

**bot·tle·neck** /'bɒtlnek||'bɑː-/ *n* [C] **1** a place in a road where the traffic cannot pass easily, so that there are a lot of delays **2** a delay in one stage of a process that makes the whole process take longer: *Having only one person to do the clerical work has caused a real bottleneck.*

**bottle o·pen·er** /'·· ,···/ *n* [C] a small tool used for removing the metal lids from bottles

**bot·tom¹** /'bɒtəm||'bɑː-/ *n* S1 W3
**1** ▶ **LOWEST PART** ◀ the lowest part of something: **the bottom** *From the bottom the skyscraper looked as if it touched the clouds.* | [+ **of**] *Hold the bottom of the pole and keep it upright.* | **at the bottom** *Go downstairs and wait for me at the bottom.* | **at the bottom of** *Sign your name at the bottom of the page* —opposite TOP¹ (1)
**2** ▶ **SEA/RIVER** ◀ the ground under a sea, river etc, or the flat land in a valley: **the bottom** *the sea bottom* | [+ **of**] *The bottom of the pool is very slippery.* | **at/on the bottom of sth** *A body was found at the bottom of the canal.*
**3** ▶ **LOWEST SIDE** ◀ the flat surface on the lowest side of an object: **the bottom** *Take the price tag off the bottom.* | [+ **of**] *You have chewing gum stuck to the bottom of your shoe.*
**4** ▶ **CUP/BOX ETC** ◀ the lowest inner surface of something such as a cup or container: **the bottom** *Yuk, this cup's got mould in the bottom.* | [+ **of**] *The flour is at the bottom of the cupboard.*
**5** ▶ **LOWEST POSITION** ◀ the lowest position in an organization or company, or on a list etc: **the bottom** *The team is at the bottom of the league.* | **start at the bottom** *Higgins started at the bottom and worked his way up to managing director.* | **the bottom of the ladder/pile** (=the lowest position in society, an organization etc) —opposite TOP¹ (3)
**6 the bottom of a road/garden etc** *especially BrE* the part of a road, area of land etc that is furthest from where you are: *There's a shop at the bottom of the street.*
**7** ▶ **BODY** ◀ [C] the part of your body that you sit on; BUTTOCKS: *I just sat on my bottom and slid down.*
**8** ▶ **CLOTHES** ◀ [C] also **bottoms** the part of a set of clothes that you wear on the lower part of your body: *bikini bottom* | *pyjama bottoms*
**9 get to the bottom of** to find out the cause of a problem or situation: *I'm going to get to the bottom of this!*
**10 be at the bottom of** to be the basic cause of a problem or situation: *I'm sure Carrie's disturbed childhood is at the bottom of her current problems.*
**11 hit rock bottom/be at rock bottom** to reach a very low level, or be in a very bad situation: *Morale has hit rock bottom.* | *We bought the house when prices were at rock bottom.*
**12 from the bottom of your heart** in a very sincere way: *Thank you from the bottom of my heart.*
**13 big-bottomed/round-bottomed etc** having a bottom or base that is big, round etc
**14 the bottom dropped out of sb's world** used to say that something very bad suddenly happened to someone
**15 the bottom drops out of the market** used to say that people stop buying a particular product
**16 bottoms up!** *spoken* used to tell someone to enjoy or finish their alcoholic drink
**17 bottom gear** the lowest GEAR¹ (1) of a vehicle
**18** ▶ **SHIP** ◀ [C] the part of a ship that is below water
**19 at bottom** the way a person or situation really is, although they may seem different: *She's a good, kind person at bottom.* —compare TOP² —see also **you can bet your bottom dollar** (BET¹ (3)), **knock the bottom out of** (KNOCK¹ (17)), **from top to bottom** (TOP¹ (19))

**bottom²** *adj* [only before noun] **1** in the lowest place or position: *The records are kept on the bottom shelf.* | *the bottom right hand corner of the page* **2** the least important, successful etc: *Tim is in the bottom 10% of his class.* **3** *especially BrE* in the place furthest away from where you are: *Most of the sheep were grazing in the bottom field.* 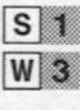

**bottom³** *v*

**bottom out** *phr v* [I] if a situation, price etc bottoms out, it stops getting worse or lower, usually before improving again: *The market price of oil got as low as $10 a barrel before it finally bottomed out.*

**bottom drawer** /,·· '·/ *n* [C] *BrE* all the things, especially things that you use in a house, that a woman collects to use when she is married; HOPE CHEST *AmE*

**bot·tom·less** /'bɒtəmləs||'bɑː-/ *adj* **1** a sea, hole etc that is bottomless is extremely deep **2** seeming to have no end: **a bottomless pit** *a bottomless pit of misery*

**bottom line** /ˌ··ˈ·/ *n* **the bottom line** **a)** the profit or the amount of money that a business makes or loses: *Business today is only interested in the bottom line.* **b)** a situation or fact that exists and that you must accept, even though you may not like it: *The bottom line is that drinking and driving can kill.* **c)** the lowest amount of money that you are willing to pay or take for something: *"What's your bottom line for selling the car?" "I can go down to £450."*

B

**bot·tom·most** /ˈbɒtəmˌməʊst‖ˈbɑːtəmˌmoʊst/ *adj* [only before noun] in the lowest, furthest, or deepest position or place: *the bottommost reaches of the Amazon*

**bottom-up** /ˌ·· ˈ·◂/ *adj BrE* a bottom-up plan is one in which you decide on practical details before thinking about general principles —opposite TOP-DOWN

**bot·u·lis·m** /ˈbɒtʃʊlɪzəm‖ˈbɑː-/ *n* [U] serious food poisoning caused by BACTERIA in preserved meat and vegetables

**bou·doir** /ˈbuːdwɑː‖-wɑːr/ *n* [C] **1** *old use* a woman's bedroom or private sitting room **2** the bedroom seen as the place where sex happens: *secrets of the boudoir*

**bouf·fant** /ˈbuːfɒŋ, -fɒnt‖buːˈfɑːnt/ *adj* a bouffant hair style is one in which your hair is raised away from your head at the top

**bou·gain·vil·le·a** /ˌbuːgənˈvɪliə/ *n* [C,U] a plant that has red or purple flowers and grows up walls

**bough** /baʊ/ *n* [C] a main branch on a tree

**bought** /bɔːt‖bɒːt/ the past tense and past participle of BUY[1]

**bouil·la·baisse** /ˌbuːjəˈbes‖-ˈbeɪs/ *n* [C,U] a strong-tasting soup or STEW[1] (1) made of fish

**bouil·lon** /ˈbuːjɒn‖-jɑːn/ *n* [C,U] a clear soup made by boiling meat and vegetables in water

**bouillon cube** /ˈ·· ·/ *n* [C] *AmE* a solid piece of dried meat or vegetables used in soups; STOCK CUBE *BrE*

**boul·der** /ˈbəʊldə‖ˈboʊldər/ *n* [C] a large stone or piece of rock: *huge boulders choking the stream bed*

**boule·vard** /ˈbuːlvɑːd‖ˈbuːləvɑːrd, ˈbʊ-/ *n* [C] **1 a)** *BrE* a wide road in a town, usually with trees along the sides **b)** *AmE* a wide road in a town or city **2** written abbreviation **Blvd** used as part of the name of a particular road: *Sunset Boulevard*

S 3 **bounce[1]** /baʊns/ *v*

**bounce**

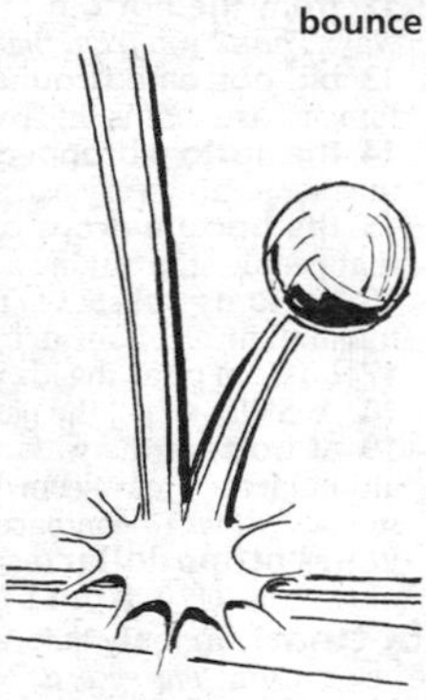

**1 ▶MOVE FROM A SURFACE◀** [I,T] if a ball or other object bounces, it immediately moves away from a surface it has just hit, or you make it move in this way: [+ **off**] *The ball bounced off the crossbar and into the net.* | **bounce sth on/against etc** *The kids were bouncing stones against the walls.*

**2 ▶MOVE UP AND DOWN◀** [I] to move up and down, especially because you are hitting a surface that is made of rubber, has springs etc: [+ **on**] *Lyn was bouncing on the trampoline.* | **bounce up and down** *Stop bouncing up and down on the sofa.*

**3 ▶CHEQUE◀** [I,T] if a cheque bounces or a bank bounces a cheque, the bank will not pay any money because there is not enough money in the account of the person who wrote it: *One bounced cheque could spell ruin for a new business.*

**4 ▶WALK◀** [I always + adv/prep] to walk quickly and with a lot of energy: [+ **across/along/in etc**] *Olivia came bouncing into the room.*

**5 ▶WHEN YOU MOVE◀** [I] if something bounces, it moves quickly up and down as you move: *Her hair bounced when she walked.*

**6 bounce ideas off sb** to ask someone for their opinion about an idea, a plan etc before you make a decision

**7 ▶LIGHT/SOUND◀** [I,T] to REFLECT (1) from a surface: [+ **off**] *radio signals bouncing off the moon*

**8 bounce sb on your knee** to lift a child up and down on your knee

**9 be bounced into (doing) sth** to be forced to decide something quickly or agree with a particular decision, because you have no time to think about it or you will seem to be wrong if you do not agree: *Party members claimed that they had been bounced into choosing him as leader.*

**bounce back** *phr v* [I] to feel better quickly or become successful again after having a lot of problems: *In spite of the difficulties we always managed to bounce back.* | *Becker bounced back in the second set.*

**bounce[2]** *n* **1** [C] the action of moving up and down on a surface: *Try to catch the ball on the second bounce.* **2** [U] the ability to move up and down on a surface, or that surface's ability to make something move up and down: *The ball had completely lost its bounce.* **3** [U] a lot of energy: *The dog has a shiny coat and is full of bounce.* **4** [U] hair that has bounce is in very good condition and goes back to its shape if you press it

**bounc·er** /ˈbaʊnsə‖-ər/ *n* [C] **1** someone whose job is to stand at the door of a club, bar etc and stop unwanted people coming in, or make people leave if they are behaving badly **2** a fast ball in CRICKET (2) that passes or hits the BATSMAN above the chest after it bounces

**bounc·ing** /ˈbaʊnsɪŋ/ *adj* **bouncing baby/child** a very healthy baby or young child

**bounc·y** /ˈbaʊnsi/ *adj* **1** a bouncy ball etc quickly moves away from a surface after it has hit it **2** a bouncy surface is made of a substance that makes people move up and down when they are on it: *The bed is nice and bouncy.* **3** someone who is bouncy is always very happy, confident, and full of energy **4** hair or material that is bouncy goes back to its shape when you press it —**bouncily** *adv* —**bounciness** *n* [U]

**bound[1]** /baʊnd/ the past tense and past participle of BIND[1]

**bound[2]** *adj* [no comparative]

**1 be bound to** to be very likely to do or feel a particular thing: *Don't lie to her. She's bound to find out about it.* | **it is bound to be** (=used to say that something should have been expected) *"It's hot!" "Well, it was bound to be, I just took it out of the oven."* | **bound to happen** *"Why did Max die, Mom?" "He was an old dog, dear. It was bound to happen one day."*

**2 ▶DUTY/PROMISE◀ a) be bound (by)** if someone is bound by a law, promise, agreement etc, they have to do what it says: *We are bound by agreements made at the time of the treaty.* | **bound (by sth) to do sth** *If he's acting as auditor he's bound by law to report.* | **legally bound** *The two parties are not legally bound until the contract has been signed.* **b) be/feel bound to do sth** to feel that you ought to do something: *John felt bound to tell Katherine about the job, even though he didn't want to work with her.* | **I'm bound to say (that)** *I'm bound to say I think you're taking a huge risk.* | **feel duty bound/honour bound to do sth** (=feel very strongly that you have to do or say something, especially because you think it is morally correct)

**3 ▶CONNECTED/INVOLVED◀ a) be bound up with sth** to be closely connected with a particular problem, situation etc: *Henry's problems are all bound up with his mother's death when he was ten.* **b) be bound up in sth** to be so involved in a difficult situation etc that you cannot think about anything else: *Jim's too bound up in his own worries to be able to help us.* **c) be bound (together) by sth** to share a particular feature or quality: *All the stories are bound by a common theme: jealousy.*

**4 ▶PLACE/DIRECTION◀ a) bound for London/college etc** also **London/college etc bound** travelling towards or going to a particular place: *The planes bound for Somalia carry food and medical supplies.* | **homeward bound** (=going home) **b) northbound/southbound/eastbound/westbound** travelling in a

particular direction: *All eastbound trains have been cancelled due to faulty signals.*
**5 snow-bound/strike-bound/tradition-bound etc** controlled or limited by something, so that you cannot do what you want or what other people want you to: *a fog-bound airport*
**6 ▶ BOOK ◀** a bound book is covered on the outside with paper, leather etc: [+ **in**] *a beautiful Bible bound in Moroccan leather* | **leather/velvet etc bound** (=covered in leather, velvet etc)
**7 I'll be bound** *old-fashioned* used when you are very sure that what you have just said is true: *He had good reasons for doing that, I'll be bound.*
**8 bound form** *technical* a part of a word that is always found in combination with another form, such as 'un' and 'er' in the words 'unknown' and 'speaker'

**bound³** *v* **1** [I always + adv/prep] to run with a lot of energy, because you are happy, excited, or frightened: [+ **up/towards/across etc**] *Suddenly a huge dog came bounding towards me.* **2 be bounded by** if a country or area of land is bounded by something such as a wall, river etc it has the wall etc at its edge: *a yard bounded by a rusty fence* | *The US is bounded in the north by Canada and in the south by Mexico.*

**bound⁴** *n*
**1 by leaps and bounds/in leaps and bounds** *BrE* if someone or something increases, develops etc by leaps and bounds, they increase etc very quickly: *Julie's reading is improving in leaps and bounds.*
**2 out of bounds** if a place is out of bounds, you are not allowed to go there: [+ **to/for**] *Parts of the complex are out of bounds to some personnel.*
**3 ▶ LIMITS ◀ bounds** [plural] **a)** limits or rules that are given by law or exist because of social custom: **stay/keep/remain within bounds** *Richards tried to stay within the bounds set by the financial controller.* | **keep sth within bounds** *Talking is permitted in the classroom as long as it is kept within bounds.* **b)** *old-fashioned* the edges of a town, city etc
**4 go beyond the bounds of decency/reason/good taste etc** to not follow the rules that people normally follow when doing something
**5 be within/beyond the bounds of possibility** to be possible or impossible: *Mike's version of events is unlikely, but not beyond the bounds of possibility.*
**6 know no bounds** *formal* if someone's honesty, kindness etc knows no bounds, they are extremely honest etc
**7 in bounds/out of bounds** inside or outside the legal playing area in a sport such as American football or BASKETBALL
**8 ▶ JUMP ◀** [C] a long or high jump made with a lot of energy

2 **bound·a·ry** /ˈbaʊndəri/ *n*
3 **1 ▶ EDGE ◀** [C] the official line that marks the edge of a town, country etc: [+ **between**] *the boundary between the US and Canada* | **draw a boundary** (=decide where one town etc ends and another one starts) | **boundary line** *the county's boundary line*
**2 ▶ WALL/FENCE ◀** [C] something such as a wall or fence that is intended to keep people or things separate: *staying within the boundary of the old city walls*
**3 ▶ LIMIT ◀** [C usually plural] the highest or most extreme limit that something can reach: [+ **of**] *the boundaries of human knowledge*
**4 ▶ BETWEEN FEELINGS/QUALITIES ETC ◀** [C] the point at which one feeling, quality etc stops and another starts: [+ **of/between**] *People disagree about the boundaries of political parties.*
**5 push back the boundaries (of)** to change the way people think about an idea, belief etc, or greatly increase their knowledge of something: *Her new essay really pushes back the boundaries of literary theory.*
**6 ▶ CRICKET ◀** [C] the outer limit of the playing area in CRICKET (2) , or a shot that sends the balls across this limit for points

**bound·en** /ˈbaʊndən/ *adj* **your bounden duty** *old-fashioned* something that you should do because it is morally correct

**bound·er** /ˈbaʊndə‖-ər/ *n* [C] *BrE old-fashioned* a disapproving word for a man who has behaved in a way that you think is morally wrong: *The man's a bounder.*

**bound·less** /ˈbaʊndləs/ *adj* having no limit or end: *enthusiasts with boundless energy for their hobby* —**boundlessly** *adv* —**boundlessness** *n* [U]

**boun·te·ous** /ˈbaʊntiəs/ *adj literary* very generous

**boun·ti·ful** /ˈbaʊntɪfəl/ *adj literary* **1** if something is bountiful, there is more than enough of it: *bountiful harvests* **2** generous: *bountiful God*

**boun·ty** /ˈbaʊnti/ *n* **1** [C] an amount of money that is given to someone by the government as a reward for doing something, such as catching a criminal: *The million-dollar bounty on Noriega's head shows how important it is he is brought to trial.* **2** [U] *literary* the quality of being generous

**bounty hunt·er** /ˈ·· ˌ··/ *n* [C] someone who catches criminals and brings them to the police in return for a reward

**bou·quet** /bəʊˈkeɪ, buː-‖boʊ-, buː-/ *n* **1** [C] an arrangement of flowers, especially one that you give to someone **2** [C,U] the smell of a wine: *a fruity bouquet*

**bour·bon** /ˈbʊəbən‖ˈbɜːr-/ *n* [U] a type of American WHISKEY

**bour·geois¹** /ˈbʊəʒwɑː‖bʊrˈʒwɑː/ *adj* **1** too interested in having a lot of possessions and a high position in society: *the Sixties backlash against bourgeois materialism* **2** belonging to the MIDDLE CLASS **3** belonging to or typical of the part of society that is rich, educated, owns land etc, according to MARXISM —see also PETTY BOURGEOIS —compare PROLETARIAN

**bourgeois²** *n plural* **bourgeois** [C] **1** someone who is too interested in having a lot of possessions and a high position in society **2** a member of the MIDDLE CLASS **3** someone who belongs to the part of society which is rich, educated, owns land etc, according to MARXISM —compare PROLETARIAT

**bour·geoi·sie** /ˌbʊəʒwɑːˈziː‖ˌbʊr-/ *n* **the bourgeoisie** the people in a society who are rich, educated, own land etc, according to MARXISM

**'bout** /baʊt/ *adv, prep spoken* about: *"What are you talking 'bout?"*

**bout** /baʊt/ *n* [C] **1 a bout of flu/nausea/depression etc** a short period of time during which you suffer from an illness **2** a short period of time during which you do something a lot, especially something that is bad for you: *After a near fatal drinking bout, Joe decided to give up alcohol.* **3** a BOXING or WRESTLING match

**bou·tique** /buːˈtiːk/ *n* [C] a small shop that sells very fashionable clothes or other objects

**bou·ton·ni·ere** /buːˌtɒniˈeə‖buːtnˈɪr/ *n* [C] *AmE* a flower that a man wears in the LAPEL of his suit, especially at a wedding; BUTTONHOLE (2) *BrE*

**bo·vine** /ˈbəʊvaɪn‖ˈboʊ-/ *adj* **1** *technical* connected with cows **2** slow and slightly stupid, like a cow: *a bovine expression of contentment*

**bov·ver** /ˈbɒvə‖ˈbɑːvər/ *n* [U] *BrE old-fashioned slang* violent behaviour, especially by a group of young men: **bovver boy** (=someone who behaves in a violent way)

**bow¹** /baʊ/ *v* **1** [I] to bend the top part of your body forward in order to show respect for someone important: [+ **before/to etc**] *He bowed before the king.* **2** [I,T] to bend your body over something, especially in order to see it more closely: [+ **over**] *Professor Teague sat at his desk, bowed over a book.* | **bow your head** (=bend your neck so that you are looking at the ground) | **bow your head in shame** *Phil stood there, his head bowed in shame.* **3 be bowed (under sth)** to be bent because you are carrying something heavy on your back **4 bow and scrape** to show too much respect to someone in authority

**bow down** *phr v* [I] **1** to bend forward from your waist, especially when you are already kneeling, in order to show respect: [+ **before/to etc**] *Maria bowed down before the statue.* **2 bow down to sb** *literary* to let someone give you orders or tell you what to do

**bow out** *phr v* [I] **1** to stop taking part in an activity, job etc, especially one that you have been doing for a long time: **bow out of sth** *Reeves thinks it is time for him to bow out of politics.* **2** to not do something that you have promised or agreed to do

**bow to** sb/sth *phr v* [T] to finally agree to do something that people want you to, even though you do not want to do it: *Congress may bow to public pressure and lift the arms embargo.*

**bow**

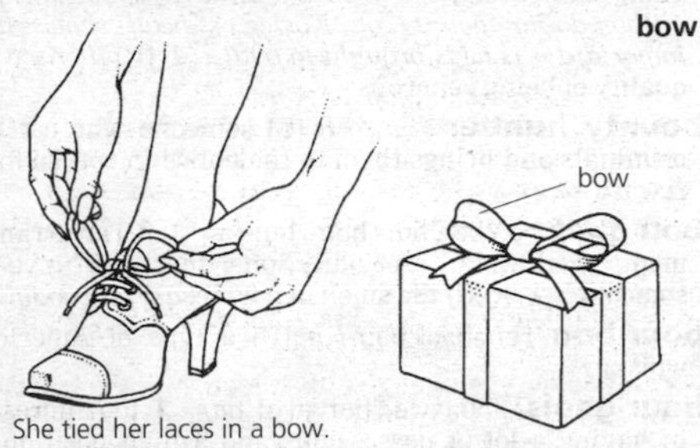


She tied her laces in a bow.

**bow²** /baʊ/ *n* **1** [C] the act of bending the top part of your body forward to show respect for someone **2** also **bows** the front part of a ship —compare STERN² —see picture at YACHT **3 take a bow** if someone takes a bow, they come on the stage at the end of a performance so that people can APPLAUD them

**bow³** /bəʊ‖boʊ/ *n* **1** [C] a weapon used for shooting arrows (ARROW (1)), made of a long thin curved piece of wood **2** [C] a knot of cloth or string with a curved part on either side, used especially for decoration: *Ella wore a big bow in her hair.* **3** [C] a long thin piece of wood with a tight string fastened along it, used to play musical instruments that have strings **4 bow legs** legs that curve outwards at the knees —see also **have more than one string to your bow** (STRING¹ (8))

**bow⁴** /bəʊ‖boʊ/ *v* **1** [I] to bend or curve **2** [I,T] to play a piece of music on a musical instrument with a BOW³ (3)

**bowd·ler·ize** also **-ise** *BrE* /ˈbaʊdləraɪz/ *v* [T] to remove the parts of a book, play etc that you think are offensive, and actually ruin it by doing this —**bowdlerized** *adj*: *a bowdlerized version of 'Antony and Cleopatra'*

**bow·el** /ˈbaʊəl/ *n* **1 bowels** [plural] the system of tubes inside your body where food is made into solid waste material and through which it passes out of your body; INTESTINE: **move/empty your bowels** (=get rid of solid waste from your body) **2** [singular] one part of this system of tubes: *cancer of the bowel* **3 a bowel movement** *formal* an act of getting rid of solid waste from your body **4 the bowels of sth** *literary* the lowest or deepest part of something: **the bowels of the earth** (=deep under the ground)

**bow·er** /ˈbaʊə‖-ər/ *n* [C] *literary* **1** a pleasant place in the shade under a tree, especially in a garden: *a rose-scented bower* **2** *old use* a woman's bedroom

**bow·ing** /ˈbəʊɪŋ‖ˈboʊ-/ *n* [U] the skill of using a BOW³ (3) to play a musical instrument

S2 W3 **bowl¹** /bəʊl‖boʊl/ *n*

**1 ▶ CONTAINER ◀** [C] a wide round container that is open at the top, used to hold liquids, flowers etc: *Mix all the ingredients thoroughly in a bowl.*| [+ **of**] *a bowl of fruit*| **soup/salad/cereal etc bowl** (=a bowl to eat or serve soup, salad etc from)

**2 ▶ AMOUNT ◀** also **bowlful** [C] the amount that a bowl will hold: [+ **of**] *a bowl of rice*

**3 ▶ GAME ◀ a)** *BrE* **bowls** [plural] an outdoor game played on grass in which you try to roll big balls as near as possible to a small ball; LAWN BOWLING *AmE* **b)** [C usually singular] a special game in American football played by the best teams after the normal playing season: *the Rose Bowl*

**4 ▶ BALL ◀** [C] *BrE* a ball that you use in the game of bowls

**5 ▶ SHAPE ◀** [C] the part of an object such as a spoon, pipe, toilet etc that is shaped like a bowl

**6 ▶ SPORT ◀** [C usually singular] *AmE* a large structure shaped like a bowl, where people go to watch special events; STADIUM: *the Hollywood Bowl*

**bowl²** *v* **1** [I,T] to roll a ball along a surface when you are playing the game of bowls **2** [I,T] to throw a ball at the BATSMAN in CRICKET (2) **3** also **bowl out** [T] to make a BATSMAN in CRICKET (2) have to leave the field, by hitting the WICKET (=set of sticks) behind him with a ball

**bowl along** *phr v* [I] to travel or move very quickly and smoothly: *We were really bowling along when suddenly the back wheel fell off.*

**bowl** sb ↔ **out** *phr v* [T] to make a BATSMAN in CRICKET (2) have to leave the field by hitting the WICKET (=set of sticks) behind him with a ball

**bowl** sb/sth ↔ **over** *phr v* [T] **1** to accidentally hit someone so that they fall down, because you are running too quickly: *Some kids running past bowled an old lady over.* **2** to surprise, please, or excite someone very much: *We were absolutely bowled over by the Parthenon.*

**bow-legged** /ˈbəʊˌlegd, -ˌlegɪ̍d‖ˈboʊ-/ *adj* having legs that curve outwards at the knees

**bowl·er** /ˈbəʊlə‖ˈboʊlər/ *n* [C] **1** a player in CRICKET (2) who throws the ball at a BATSMAN **2** also **bowler hat** *especially BrE* a hard round black hat that business men sometimes wear; DERBY (1) *AmE* —see picture at HAT

**bowl·ing** /ˈbəʊlɪŋ‖ˈboʊ-/ *n* [U] **1** an indoor game in which you roll a large heavy ball along a wooden track in order to knock down a group of PINS (=wooden objects shaped like bottles): **go bowling** (=play this game) **2** the act of throwing a ball at the BATSMAN in CRICKET (2)

**bowling al·ley** /ˈ·· ˌ··/ *n* [C] a building where you go bowling

**bowling ball** /ˈ·· ·/ *n* [C] the heavy ball you use in the game of bowling

**bowling green** /ˈ·· ·/ *n* [C] a piece of grass where you play the game of bowls (BOWL¹ (3))

**bow·man** /ˈbəʊmən‖ˈboʊ-/ *n* [C] *old use* a soldier who shoots arrows (ARROW (1)) with a BOW³ (1)

**bow·sprit** /ˈbəʊˌsprɪt‖ˈbaʊ-, ˈboʊ-/ *n* [C] a long pole on the front of a boat that the ropes from the sails are fastened to

**bow tie** /ˌbəʊ ˈtaɪ‖ˌboʊ-/ *n* [C] a short piece of cloth tied in the shape of a bow that men sometimes wear around their neck —see picture on page 840

**bow win·dow** /ˌbəʊ ˈwɪndəʊ‖ˌboʊ ˈwɪndoʊ/ *n* [C] a window that curves outwards

**bow-wow¹** /ˈbaʊ waʊ/ *n* [C] a word meaning a dog, used by and to small children

**bow·wow²** /ˌbaʊˈwaʊ/ *interjection* a word used to make the sound a dog makes, used by and to small children

**box¹** /bɒks‖bɑːks/ *n* S W

**1 ▶ CONTAINER ◀** [C] a container for putting things in, especially one with four stiff straight sides: [+ **of**] *a box of tissues*| *a matchbox*| **cardboard/wooden box** *You need a filing cabinet, not all these cardboard boxes.*| **toolbox/shoebox etc** (=used for keeping tools etc in) —see picture at CONTAINER

**2 ▶ AMOUNT IN A BOX ◀** also **boxful** [C] the amount that a box can hold: [+ **of**] *a box of chocolates*

**3 ▶ SQUARE SHAPE ◀** [C] a small square on a page for people to write information in: *Put an 'X' in the box if you would like to join our mailing list.*

**4 ▶ IN A THEATRE/COURT ◀** [C] a small area of a theatre or court that is separate from where other people are sitting: *the jury box* —see picture at THEATRE

**5 box 25/450 etc** an address at a POST OFFICE that people can use instead of their own address; PO BOX
**6 ► SPORTS FIELD ◄** [C] a special area of a sports field that is marked by lines and used for a particular purpose: *a penalty box*
**7 ► WORN DURING SPORTS ◄** [C] *BrE* a piece of plastic that a man wears over his sex organs to protect them when he is playing a sport, especially CRICKET (2)
**8 ► DEATH ◄◄** [C] *informal* a COFFIN
**9 ► TREE ◄** [C,U] a small tree that keeps its leaves in winter and is often planted around the edge of a garden or field, or the wood from this tree: *a box hedge*
**10 give sb a box on the ears** *old-fashioned* to hit someone on the side of their head
**11 the box** *informal* the television: *What's on the box tonight?*
**12 be out of your box** *BrE slang* to be very drunk —see also BLACK BOX

**box²** *v* **1** [I,T] to fight someone as a sport by hitting them with your closed hands inside big leather gloves (GLOVE (2)) **2** also **box up** [T] to put things in boxes —see also BOXED **3** [T] to draw a box around something on a page **4 box sb's ears** *old-fashioned* to hit someone on the side of their head

**box** sb/sth ↔ **in** *phr v* [T] **1** to park so near to another car that it cannot move **2** to surround someone so that they are unable to move freely: *Steve Cram got boxed in on the final curve.* **3 feel boxed in** **a)** to feel that you cannot do what you want to do because a person or situation is limiting you: *Married for only a year, Connie already felt boxed in.* **b)** to feel that you cannot move freely, because you are in a small space

**box** sth ↔ **off** *phr v* [T] to separate a particular area from a larger one by putting walls around it: *We're going to box off that corner to get extra storage space.*

**box can·yon** /ˈ· ˌ··/ *n* [C] *AmE* a deep narrow valley with very straight sides and no way out

**box·car** /ˈbɒkskɑː‖ˈbɑːkskɑːr/ *n* [C] *AmE* a railway carriage with high sides and a roof, used for carrying goods

**boxed** /bɒkst‖bɑːkst/ *adj* sold in a box or boxes: *a boxed set of CDs*

**box end wrench** /ˌ· · ˈ·/ *n* [C] *AmE* a type of WRENCH² (3) with a hollow end that fits over a NUT¹ (2) that is being screwed or unscrewed; RING SPANNER *BrE* —see picture at TOOL¹

**box·er** /ˈbɒksə‖ˈbɑːksər/ *n* [C] **1** someone who boxes (BOX² (1)), especially as a job **2** a large dog with light brown short hair and a flat nose

**boxer shorts** /ˈ·· ˌ·/ *n* [plural] loose cotton underwear for men —see picture at UNDERWEAR

**box·ing** /ˈbɒksɪŋ‖ˈbɑːk-/ *n* [U] the sport of fighting while wearing big leather GLOVES (2)

**Boxing Day** /ˈ·· ·/ *n* [C,U] *BrE* a national holiday in England and Wales, on the first day after Christmas Day that is not a Sunday

**box junc·tion** /ˈ· ˌ··/ *n* [C] *BrE* a place marked with yellow painted lines where two roads cross each other

**box lunch** /ˈ· ·/ *n* [C] *AmE* a lunch that you take to school or work with you in a LUNCHBOX

**box num·ber** /ˈ· ˌ··/ *n* [C] *BrE* an address at the POST OFFICE that people can use instead of their own address

**box of·fice** /ˈ· ˌ··/ *n* **1** [C] the place in a theatre, cinema etc where tickets are sold **2** [singular] used to describe how successful a film, play, or actor is, by the number of people who pay to see them: **do well/badly at the box office** (=be very successful or unsuccessful) | **a (big) box office draw** (=a successful actor who many people will pay to see)

**box room** /ˈ· ·/ *n* [C] *BrE* a small room in a house where you can store things

1 **boy¹** /bɔɪ/ *n* [C]
1 **1 ► CHILD ◄** a male child or young man: *The boys all wanted to play football.* | **little boy** (=a young male child)
**2 ► SON ◄** a son: *I love my boys, but I'd like to have a girl too.* | **little boy** (=a young son) *How old is your little boy?*
**3 office/paper/delivery etc boy** a young man who does a particular job
**4 the boys** *informal* a group of men who are friends and often go out together: *Friday's his night out with the boys.* | **one of the boys** (=popular with a group of men)
**5 ► ANIMALS ◄** a way of addressing a male horse or dog: *Good boy!*
**6 ► JOB ◄ boys** *informal* **a)** a group of men who do the same job: *Oh no! Wait until the press boys get hold of this story.* **b)** men in the army, navy etc, especially those who are fighting in a war: *our boys on the front lines*
**7 boys will be boys** used to say that you should not be surprised when boys behave badly, are noisy etc
**8 city/local/working-class boy** *informal* a man of any age considered as being affected by the place and social group that he was born in: *the classic story of a local boy who's made good* | *I'm just a country boy.*
**9 old boy/my dear boy** *BrE old-fashioned* a friendly way for one man to speak to another man
**10** *AmE taboo* an offensive way of addressing a black man —see also BLUE-EYED BOY, **jobs for the boys** (JOB (5)), MAMA'S BOY, MUMMY'S BOY, OLD BOY, WIDE BOY

**boy²** *interjection spoken especially AmE* **1** also **oh boy** used when you are excited or pleased about something: *Boy, that was a great meal!* **2 oh boy** used when you are slightly annoyed or disappointed about something: *Oh boy! Bethany's sick again.*

**boy·cott¹** /ˈbɔɪkɒt‖-kɑːt/ *v* [T] to refuse to buy something, use something, or take part in something as a way of protesting: *We boycott all products tested on animals.*

**boycott²** *n* [C] an act of boycotting something, or the period of time when it is boycotted: **[+ of/on/against]** *a boycott on South African fruit in the 70s*

**boy·friend** /ˈbɔɪfrend/ *n* [C] a man that you are having a romantic relationship with: *Have you met Jilly's new boyfriend yet?* —see also GIRLFRIEND

**boy·hood** /ˈbɔɪhʊd/ *n* [U] the time of a man's life when he is a boy: *boyhood memories* —see also GIRLHOOD

**boy·ish** /ˈbɔɪ-ɪʃ/ *adj* **1** a man who is boyish looks or behaves like a boy in a way that is attractive: *boyish good looks* **2** a woman or girl who is boyish looks or behaves a little like a boy: *At 45 May still had a trim, boyish figure.* —**boyishly** *adv* —**boyishness** *n* [U]

**boy scout** /ˌ· ˈ·‖ˈ· ·/ *n* [C] a boy who is a member of an association for boys that teaches them practical skills and develops their characters; SCOUT¹ (1a) —see also GIRL SCOUT, GUIDE

**boy won·der** /ˌ· ˈ··/ *n* [C] a young man who is very successful: *Robson, the boy wonder of the department*

**bo·zo** /ˈbəʊzəʊ‖ˈboʊzoʊ/ *n plural* **bozos** [C] *informal* someone who you think is silly or stupid: *Who's the bozo in the pyjamas?*

**BPhil** /ˌbiː ˈfɪl/ *n* [C usually singular] Bachelor of Philosophy; a first or second degree that you may get after studying at a British university, but that is not as common as a BACHELOR'S DEGREE

**BR** /ˌbiː ˈɑː‖-ˈɑːr/ *n* [singular] British Rail; the organization that controls the British railway system

**Br** **1** the written abbreviation of BROTHER **2** the written abbreviation of BRITISH

**bra** /brɑː/ *n* [C] a piece of underwear that a woman wears to support her breasts —see picture at UNDERWEAR

**brace¹** /breɪs/ *v* **1** [T] to prepare for something unpleasant that is going to happen: **brace yourself for** *Nancy braced herself for the inevitable arguments.* | **brace yourself to do** *Jean, you'd better brace yourself to hear bad news.* | **be braced for** *The entire castle was braced for an attack.* **2** [T] to push part of your body against something solid in order to make yourself more steady: **brace sth against** *Gina braced her foot against the wall and pulled herself up.* | **brace yourself** *Before he could brace himself she'd shoved him out of the door.* **3** [T] to make something stronger by supporting it: *Wait until we've* *braced the ladder.* **4** [I,T] to make your body or part of your body stiff in order to prepare to do something difficult: *Stuart braced his muscles and heaved the fridge aside.*

**brace²** *n*
**1 ▶TEETH◀ a) brace** *BrE* **braces** *especially AmE* a connected set of wires that children sometimes wear on their teeth to make them straight **b)** [C] *BrE* a wire frame that children sometimes have to put over their teeth to make them straight
**2 ▶SUPPORT◀ a)** [C] something that is used to strengthen, stiffen, or support something: *Cath had to wear a neck brace after the accident.* **b)** [C usually plural] *AmE* a metal support that someone with weak legs wears to help them walk; CALLIPERS *BrE*
**3 a brace of sth** two birds or animals that have been killed for food or sport
**4 ▶PRINTED SIGN◀** one of a pair of signs { } used to show that information written between them should be considered together —compare BRACKET¹ (1)
**5 braces** *BrE* two long pieces of material that stretch over someone's shoulders and fasten to their trousers at the front and the back to stop them falling down; SUSPENDERS *AmE*

**brace·let** /ˈbreɪslɪ̈t/ *n* [C] a band or chain that you wear around your wrist or arm as a decoration —compare BANGLE —see picture at JEWELLERY

**brac·ing** /ˈbreɪsɪŋ/ *adj* bracing air or weather is cold and makes you feel very awake and healthy: *a bracing sea breeze*

**brack·en** /ˈbrækən/ *n* [U] a plant that often grows in forests and becomes reddish brown in the autumn

**brack·et¹** /ˈbrækɪ̈t/ *n* [C] **1** [usually plural] **a)** *BrE* also **round bracket**, one of the pair of signs ( ) put around words to show that the rest of the writing can be read and understood without these words; PARENTHESIS *AmE*: **in brackets** *Last year's sales figures are given in brackets.* —see picture at PUNCTUATION MARK **b)** *AmE* **square bracket** *BrE* a sign like this that is square [] **c) angle bracket** a sign like this that is shaped < > —compare BRACE² (4) **2 income/tax/age etc bracket** an income etc that is inside a particular range: *Peter's new job puts him in the highest tax bracket.* **3** a piece of metal, wood, or plastic, often in the shape of the letter L, fixed to a wall to support something such as a shelf

**bracket²** *v* [T] **1** to put brackets around a written word, piece of information etc: *Debit amounts are usually bracketed.* **2** to consider two or more people or things as being the same type: [+ **together/with**] *Women and minors were bracketed together for the legislation.*

**brack·ish** /ˈbrækɪʃ/ *adj* brackish water is not pure because it is slightly salty

**brad** /bræd/ *n* [C] *AmE* a small metal object like a button with two metal sticks that are put through several pieces of paper and folded down to hold the papers together; PAPER FASTENER *BrE*

**brad·awl** /ˈbrædɔːl‖-ɒːl/ *n* [C] *especially BrE* a small tool with a sharp point for making holes; AWL

**brae** /breɪ/ *n* [C] *ScotE* a hill or slope

**brag** /bræg/ *v* **bragged, bragging** [I,T] to talk too proudly about what you have done, what you own etc; BOAST¹ (1): *"I came out top in the test", he bragged* | [+ **about**] *Ben's always bragging about his success with women.* | **brag (that)** *Julia used to brag that her family had a villa in Spain.*

**brag·ga·do·ci·o** /ˌbrægəˈdəʊʃiəʊ‖-ˈdoʊʃioʊ/ *n* [U] *especially literary* proud talk about something that you claim to own, to have done etc

**brag·gart** /ˈbrægət‖-ərt/ *n* [C] someone who is always talking too proudly about what they own or have done

**Brah·man** /ˈbrɑːmən/ also **Brah·min** /ˈbrɑːmɪ̈n/ *n* [C] someone belonging to the highest rank in the HINDU faith

**braid¹** /breɪd/ *n* **1** [U] a narrow band of material formed by twisting threads together, used to decorate the edges of clothes: *a jacket trimmed with red braid* **2** [C] *AmE* a length of hair that has been separated into three parts and then woven together; PLAIT² *BrE* **in braids** *Pippa always wears her hair in braids.* —**braided** *adj* —see picture at HAIRSTYLE

**braid²** *v* [T] *especially AmE* to weave or twist together three pieces of hair or cloth to form one length; PLAIT¹ *BrE*

**braille** /breɪl/ *n* [U] a form of printing with raised parts that blind people can read by touching the paper

**brain¹** /breɪn/ *n* 
**1 ▶ORGAN◀** [C] the organ inside your head that controls how you think, feel, and move: *Messages from the brain are carried by the central nervous system.*
**2 ▶INTELLIGENCE◀** [U] also **brains** *plural* the ability to think clearly and learn quickly: *If you had any brains you'd know what I meant.*
**3 ▶PERSON◀** [C] *informal* someone who is intelligent, with good ideas and useful skills: *Some of our best brains are leaving the country to work in the US.* —see also BRAIN DRAIN
**4 have sth on the brain** *informal* to be always thinking about something: *I've got that song on the brain today.*
**5 be the brains behind sth** to be the person who thought of and developed a particular plan, system, or organization, especially a successful one
**6 brain dead a)** in a state where your brain has stopped working properly even though your heart may still be beating **b)** *informal* stupid and uninteresting, especially because you live a boring life: *If all she does is watch TV all day, no wonder she's brain dead.*
**7 pick sb's brains** to ask someone a lot of questions about something that they know about: *I need to pick your brains about this cashflow forecast.*
**8 brain box** *BrE informal* a very intelligent person —see also BIRD-BRAINED, HARE-BRAINED **beat your brains out** (BEAT¹ (18)), **rack your brain(s)** (RACK² (2))

**brain²** *v* [T] *spoken* to hit someone very hard on the head: *I'll brain you if you do that again!*

**brain·child** /ˈbreɪntʃaɪld/ *n* [singular] an idea, plan, organization etc that someone has thought of without any help from anyone else: [+ **of**] *The festival was the brainchild of Mayor Reeves.*

**brain dam·age** /ˈ· ˌ··/ *n* [U] damage to someone's brain caused by an accident or illness: *Potts suffered severe brain damage in the crash.* —**brain-damaged** *adj*

**brain drain** /ˈ· ·/ *n* **the brain drain** a movement of highly skilled or professional people from their own country to a country where they can earn more money

**brain·less** /ˈbreɪnləs/ *adj* completely stupid: *What a brainless thing to do!* —**brainlessly** *adv*

**brain scan** /ˈ· ·/ *n* [C] a process in which detailed photographs of the inside of your brain are taken and examined by a doctor

**brain·storm** /ˈbreɪnstɔːm‖-stɔːrm/ *n* **1 have a brainstorm** *BrE informal* to suddenly be unable to think clearly or sensibly: *I'm sorry, I must have had a brainstorm that afternoon.* **2** [singular] *AmE* a sudden clever idea; BRAINWAVE *BrE:* **have a brainstorm** *Unless you have a brainstorm, I don't see how we're going to get out of this.*

**brain·stor·ming** /ˈbreɪnstɔːmɪŋ‖-ɔːr-/ *n* [U] the act of meeting with a group of people in order to try to develop ideas and think of ways of solving problems: *a brainstorming session to come up with a slogan for the new shampoo* —**brainstorm** *v* [I]

**brain sur·geon** /ˈ· ˌ··/ *n* [C] a doctor who performs operations on people's brains

**brain teas·er** /ˈ· ··/ *n* [C] a difficult problem that you enjoy trying to solve

**brain·wash** /ˈbreɪnwɒʃ‖-wɒːʃ, -wɑːʃ/ *v* [T] to make someone believe something that is not true, by using force, confusing them, or continuously repeating it over a long period of time: *Young people are being brainwashed by this religious group.* | **brainwash sb into doing sth**

*Commercials can brainwash consumers into buying things they don't need.* —**brainwashing** *n* [U]

**brain·wave** /ˈbreɪnweɪv/ *n* [C] **1** *BrE* a sudden clever idea; BRAINSTORM *AmE*: *I've had a brainwave! Let's go this weekend instead.* **2** an electrical force that is produced by the brain and that can be measured

**brain·y** /ˈbreɪni/ *adj informal* able to learn easily and think quickly; clever: *He always was the brainy one, except at maths.*

**braise** /breɪz/ *v* [T] to cook meat or vegetables slowly in a small amount of liquid in a closed container —**braised** *adj*

**braising steak** /ˈ·· ˌ·/ *n* [U] BEEF[1] (1) that needs long slow cooking

**brake[1]** /breɪk/ *n* [C] **1** a piece of equipment that makes a vehicle go more slowly or stop, usually operated by pressing on a bar with your foot or hand: *Remember to test your brakes regularly:* **put/slam on the brakes** also **apply the brakes** *formal*: *Moira slammed on the brakes and skidded to a halt.* —see also EMERGENCY BRAKE, HANDBRAKE —see picture at BICYCLE[1] **2 act/serve as a brake on sth** to make something slow or difficult: *Rises in interest rates usually act as a brake on expenditure.* **3 put the brakes on sth** to stop something that is happening: *Well, that pretty much puts the brakes on our plans.*

**brake[2]** *v* [I] to make a vehicle or bicycle go more slowly or stop by using its brake: **brake sharply/hard** (=brake quickly) *He braked sharply to avoid the dog.*

**brake flu·id** /ˈ· ˌ··/ *n* [U] liquid used in certain kinds of brakes so that the different parts move smoothly

**brake light** /ˈ· ·/ *n* [C] a light on the back of a vehicle that comes on when you uses the brake —see picture on page 409

**brake shoe** /ˈ· ˌ·/ *n* [C] one of the two curved parts that press against the wheel of a vehicle in order to make it go more slowly or stop

**bram·ble** /ˈbræmbəl/ *n* [C] a wild BLACKBERRY

**bran** /bræn/ *n* [U] the crushed outer skin of wheat or a similar grain that is separated from the rest of the grain when making white flour

1 **branch[1]** /brɑːntʃ‖bræntʃ/ *n* [C]

2 **1 ▶ ON A TREE ◀** a part of a tree that grows outwards from the TRUNK (=stem) and that has leaves, fruit, or smaller branches growing from it: *a fallen tree branch*

**2 ▶ IN A LOCAL AREA ◀** a shop, office etc in a particular area that is part of a large company: *The bank has branches all over the country.* | *a branch office in Boston*

**3 ▶ OF AN ORGANIZATION ◀** a part of a government or other organization that deals with one particular part of its work: *All branches of government are having to cut costs.*

**4 ▶ OF A SUBJECT ◀** one part of a large subject of study or knowledge: [+ **of**] *Newton developed a branch of mathematics called calculus.*

**5 ▶ OF A FAMILY ◀** a group of members of a family who all have the same grandparents or ANCESTORS: *the wealthy South American branch of the family*

**6 ▶ SMALLER PART ◀** a smaller less important part of something that leads away from the larger more important part of it: *a branch of the river Arno*

**branch[2]** *v* [I] to divide into two or more smaller, narrower, or less important parts: **branch into two** *When you reach Germain Street, the road branches into two.*

**branch off** *phr v* [I] **1** if a road, passage, railway etc branches off from another road etc, it separates from it and goes in a different direction: [+ **from**] *a passage branching off from the main tunnel* **2** to leave a main road: [+ **from/into**] *We branched off from the main road and turned down a country lane.* **3** to start talking about something different from what you were talking about before: [+ **into**] *Then the conversation branched off into a discussion about movies.*

**branch out** *phr v* [I] to do something different from what you usually do: *Don't be afraid to branch out and try new ideas.* | **branch out into (doing) sth** *Profits were falling until the bookstore branched out into selling CDs and cassettes.*

**brand[1]** /brænd/ *n* [C] **1** a type of product made by a particular company: [+ **of**] *What brand of detergent do you use?* | **brand leader** (=the brand that sells the most) | **brand loyalty** (=the tendency to always buy a particular brand) | **own brand** *BrE* **store brand** *AmE* (=made and sold by a particular store) **2 brand of humour/politics/religion etc** a particular type of humour, politics etc: *a strange, macabre brand of humour* **3** a mark made or burned on an animal's skin that shows who it belongs to **4** *literary* a piece of burning wood **5** *poetic* a sword

**brand[2]** *v* [T] **1** to describe someone or something as a very bad type of person or thing, often unfairly: **brand sb as** *You can't brand all football supporters as hooligans.* | **brand sb a liar/cheat/whore etc** *In those days, any unmarried mother was branded a whore.* | **brand sb for life** *Stealing that money has branded Jim for life – no-one will trust him again.* **2** [usually passive] to make a mark on something, especially by burning, in order to show who it belongs to: **brand sth with sth** *Each cow was branded with the ranch's logo.*

**brand·ed** /ˈbrændɪd/ *adj* [only before noun] a branded product is made by a well known company and has the company's name on it

**branding i·ron** /ˈ·· ˌ··/ *n* [C] a piece of metal that is heated and used for burning marks on cattle or sheep, to show who they belong to

**bran·dish** /ˈbrændɪʃ/ *v* [T + **at**] to wave something around in a dangerous or threatening way, especially a weapon: *A man leapt out brandishing a kitchen knife.*

**brand name** /ˈ· ˌ·/ *n* [C] the name given to a product by the company that makes it; TRADE NAME

**brand-new** /ˌ· ˈ·◂/ *adj* new and completely unused

**bran·dy** /ˈbrændi/ *n* [C,U] a strong alcoholic drink made from wine, or a glass of this drink

**brandy but·ter** /ˈ·· ˌ··/ *n* [U] a mixture of butter, sugar, and BRANDY, usually eaten with CHRISTMAS PUDDING

**brash** /bræʃ/ *adj* **1** behaving too confidently and speaking too loudly: *Brash, noisy journalists were crowding around the ambassador.* **2** a brash building, place, or object attracts attention by being very colourful, large, exciting etc: *The painting was bold, brash and modern.* —**brashly** *adv* —**brashness** *n* [U]

**brass** /brɑːs‖bræs/ *n*

**1 ▶ METAL ◀** [U] a very hard bright yellow metal that is a mixture of COPPER (1) and ZINC: **brass bed/knob/button etc** *an old brass bedstead*

**2 the brass (section)** the people in an ORCHESTRA or band who play musical instruments made of brass, such as the TRUMPET[1] (1), horn etc

**3 have the brass** *informal* to have the self-confidence and lack of respect to do something that is rude: **have the brass to do sth** *I didn't think she'd have the brass to tell him to his face.*

**4 ▶ DECORATIONS ◀** [C,U] an object made of brass, usually with a design cut into it, or several brass objects

**5 ▶ IN CHURCH ◀** [C] a picture and writing on brass, placed on the wall or floor of a church in memory of someone who died

**6 get down to brass tacks** *informal* to start talking about the real business of a meeting

**7 ▶ PEOPLE IN TOP JOBS ◀ the brass** *AmE informal* people who hold the most important positions; TOP BRASS *BrE*

**8 it's brass monkeys/brass monkey weather** *BrE spoken* used to say that it is very cold: *It's brass monkeys out there today.*

**9 ▶ MONEY ◀** [U] *BrE informal* money

**10 brass hat** *especially BrE slang* a military officer with a high rank —see also **as bold as brass** (BOLD (2))

**brass band** /ˌ· ˈ·/ *n* [C] a band consisting mostly of brass musical instruments such as TRUMPETS, horns etc

**brassed off** /ˌbrɑːst ˈɒf‖ˌbræst ˈɔːf/ *adj BrE informal* tired and annoyed: [+ **with**] *I'm really brassed off with the way he treats me.*

**bras·se·rie** /ˈbræsəri‖ˌbræsəˈriː/ *n* [C] a cheap, informal restaurant usually serving French food

**bras·si·ere** /ˈbræziə‖brəˈzɪr/ *n* [C] *formal* a BRA

**brass knuck·les** /ˌ· ˈ··/ *n* [plural] *AmE* a set of metal rings worn over your KNUCKLES, used as a weapon; KNUCKLE-DUSTER *BrE*

**brass rub·bing** /ˈ· ˌ··/ *n* [C,U] the act of making a copy of a BRASS (5) in a church by putting a piece of paper over it and rubbing it with a soft pencil, or a picture made in this way

**brass·y** /ˈbrɑːsi‖ˈbræsi/ *adj* **1** yellowish in colour like BRASS (1) **2** sounding hard and loud like the sound made by a BRASS (2) musical instrument **3** a woman who is brassy is too loud, confident, or brightly dressed: *Who's that brassy woman with Les?*

**brat** /bræt/ *n* [C] *informal* a child, especially a badly behaved one: **spoilt/spoiled brat** *That kid of theirs is a real spoilt brat.*

**bra·va·do** /brəˈvɑːdəʊ‖-doʊ/ *n* [U] behaviour that is deliberately intended to show how brave and confident you are: *youthful bravado*

S3 **brave**[1] /breɪv/ *adj* **1** facing danger, pain, or difficult situations with courage and confidence: *a brave cancer victim* | *It was very brave of you to tell her the truth.* **2** very good: *his original brave intentions* | **a brave attempt** *Fran didn't win, but it was a brave attempt.* **3 put on a brave face/front** to pretend that you are happy when you are really very upset —**bravely** *adv*

**brave**[2] *v* [T] to deal with a difficult, dangerous, or unpleasant situation: *Braving their parents' displeasure, they announced their engagement.* | **brave the elements** (=go out in bad weather)

**brave** sth ↔ **out** *phr v* [T] to deal bravely with something that is frightening or difficult

**brave**[3] *n* **1** [plural] brave people: *Today we remember the brave who died in the last war.* **2** [C] a young fighting man from a Native American tribe

**brav·e·ry** /ˈbreɪvəri/ *n* [U] actions, behaviour, or an attitude that shows courage and confidence: *an act of great bravery*

**bra·vo** /ˈbrɑːvəʊ, brɑːˈvəʊ‖-voʊ/ *interjection* used to show your approval when someone, especially a performer, has done something very well: *Bravo! Encore!*

**bra·vu·ra** /brəˈvjʊərə‖-ˈvjʊrə/ *n* [U] **1** the act of showing a lot of skill in the way you perform, write, paint etc, especially when you do something very difficult **2** the act of showing great courage

**braw** /brɔː‖brɒː/ *adj ScotE* **1** a braw woman is beautiful, especially because she is big and strong **2** braw weather is good

**brawl**[1] /brɔːl‖brɒːl/ *n* [C] a noisy quarrel or fight among a group of people, especially in a public place: *a drunken brawl in the street* —**brawler** *n* [C]

**brawl**[2] *v* [I] to quarrel or fight in a noisy way, especially in a public place

**brawn** /brɔːn‖brɒːn/ *n* [U] **1** physical strength, especially when compared with intelligence: *Mina has the brains, I have the brawn.* **2** *BrE* meat from a pig's head that has been boiled and pressed in a container and is often served in thin flat pieces; HEADCHEESE *AmE*

**brawn·y** /ˈbrɔːni‖ˈbrɒː-/ *adj* very large and strong: *His brawny arms glistened with sweat.*

**bray** /breɪ/ *v* [I] **1** if a DONKEY brays, it makes a loud sound **2** if someone brays, they laugh or talk in a loud, slightly unpleasant way —**bray** *n* [C] —**braying** *adj*

**bra·zen** /ˈbreɪzən/ *adj* **1** behaving in an immoral way without being embarrassed or ashamed: **a brazen hussy** (=a woman who behaves this way, especially sexually) **2 brazen lie/attitude** a lie or bad attitude that is shocking because the person responsible is not ashamed of it **3** *literary* having a shiny yellow colour

**brazen** sth ↔ **out** *phr v* [T] to deal with a situation that is difficult or embarrassing for you by appearing to be confident rather than ashamed

**bra·zen·ly** /ˈbreɪzənli/ *adv* without showing or feeling any shame: *She brazenly admitted she had spent the night with Greg.*

**bra·zi·er** /ˈbreɪziə‖-ʒər/ *n* [C] a metal container that holds a fire and is used to keep people warm in the outside

**breach**[1] /briːtʃ/ *n* **1 breach of the law/rules/agreement etc** an action that breaks a law, rule, or agreement between people, groups, or countries: *a clear breach of the 1994 Trade Agreement* | **be in breach of sth** *We will expel any member found to be in breach of the rules.* | **breach of contract** *If they fail to deliver the goods, we will sue them for breach of contract.* **2 breach of confidence/trust/etiquette etc** an action that breaks the rules of what people consider good or moral behaviour: *Bond shook the Queen's hand in a deliberate breach of etiquette.* | *The company regards revealing confidential information as a serious breach of trust.* **3** [C] a serious disagreement between people, groups, or countries with the result that they do not have a good relationship any more: *Britain could not risk a breach with the US over sanctions.* | **heal the breach** (=make people etc stop disagreeing and be friends again) **4 breach of the peace** *BrE law* an action such as fighting that annoys people in a public place **5 step into the breach** to help by doing someone else's job or work when they are suddenly unable to do it **6** [C] a hole or broken place in a wall or similar structure, especially one made during a military attack: *a breach in the castle wall* **7 a breach of security/duty etc** the result of someone breaking a system, not doing their duty etc: *There had been a major breach of security at the air base.* W

**breach**[2] *v* [T] **1** to break a hole in a wall or similar structure so that something can pass through: *The storm had breached the sea wall in two places.* **2** to break a law, rule, agreement etc: *The committee ruled that Payne was guilty of breaching the rules on sponsorship.*

**bread** /bred/ *n* [U] **1** a common important food made from flour, water, and YEAST: *Would you like some bread with your soup?* | **a loaf of bread** (=a large piece of bread that you buy and cut into pieces) | **a slice of bread** (=a thin piece of bread that you cut from a loaf) | **white/brown bread** (=bread baked with white or brown flour) **2** *old-fashioned* money **3 your/sb's bread and butter** *informal* the work that provides you with most of the money that you need in order to live: *I don't write just for fun – it's my bread and butter.* **4 earn your (daily) bread** to earn the money that you need in order to live **5 know which side your bread is buttered on** to know who to be nice to in order to get advantages for yourself —see also FRENCH BREAD, SLICED BREAD

**bread-and-but·ter** /ˌ· · ˈ··◂/ *adj* [only before noun] **bread-and-butter question/issue** *BrE* a question that is concerned with the most important and basic things: *bread-and-butter political issues such as jobs and housing*

**bread·bas·ket** /ˈbredˌbɑːskɪ̣t‖-ˌbæ-/ *n* **1** [C] a basket for holding or serving bread **2** [singular] the part of a country or other large area that provides most of its food: *Zambia could be the breadbasket of Africa.*

**bread bin** /ˈ· ·/ *n* [C] *BrE* a container for keeping bread in so that it stays fresh —see picture on page 833

**bread·board** /ˈbredbɔːd‖-bɔːrd/ *n* [C] a wooden board on which you cut bread —see picture at BOARD[1]

**bread·box** /ˈ· ·/ *AmE n* [C] a BREADBIN

**bread·crumbs** /ˈbredkrʌmz/ *n* [plural] very small pieces of bread left after cutting bread, or deliberately prepared for cooking: *Coat the fish with breadcrumbs and fry in a little oil.*

**bread·ed** /ˈbredɪ̣d/ *adj* covered in breadcrumbs: *breaded plaice*

**bread·fruit** /ˈbredfruːt/ *n* [C,U] a large tropical fruit that looks like bread

**bread·line** /'bredlaɪn/ *n* **1 be/live on the breadline** to be extremely poor **2 be near/below the breadline** to be quite poor or extremely poor, according to official standards

**breadth** /bredθ, bretθ/ *n* **1** [C,U] the distance from one side of something to the other; width: *What is the breadth of this room?* | **5 metres/3 feet etc in breadth** *The boat measured eight feet in breadth* —compare LENGTH (1), WIDTH (1) **2 breadth of vision/mind/outlook etc** an ability to consider and understand a range of ideas, attitudes, and customs that are very different from your own: *a statesman with the breadth of vision of Abraham Lincoln* **3** [U] the fact or quality of including a great variety of people, subjects etc: *a novel of the breadth and magnitude of Tolstoy's 'War and Peace'* **4** [C,U] the quality of being very large from one side to the other: *the breadth of the ocean* —see also BROAD, HAIR'S BREADTH, **the length and breadth of** (LENGTH (6))

**breadth·ways** /'bredθweɪz, 'bretθ-/ also **breadth·wise** /-waɪz/ *adj, adv* with the broad side nearest to the person who is looking at it: *The box should fit in the case breadthways.*

**bread·win·ner** /'bredˌwɪnə||-ər/ *n* [C] the member of a family who earns the money to support the others

S1 **break¹** /breɪk/ *v past tense* **broke** /brəʊk||broʊk/ *past*
W1 *participle* **broken** /'brəʊkən||'broʊkən/

**1 ► IN PIECES ◄ a)** [T] to make something separate into two or more pieces, for example by hitting it, dropping it, or bending it: *The thieves got in by breaking a window.* | **break sth in two/in half/into pieces etc** *He broke the roll in two and handed a piece to me.* **b)** [I] to separate into two or more pieces: *The frames are made of plastic and they tend to break easily.*

**2 ► PART OF YOUR BODY ◄** [T] to damage part of your body, especially a bone, and make it split into two or more pieces: *She fell downstairs and broke her hip.*

**3 ► NOT WORKING ◄ a)** [T] to damage something such as a machine so that it cannot work or be used: *Someone's broken my camera – I can't get it to focus properly.* | *There's no point in buying him expensive toys, he'll only break them.* **b)** [I] if something such as a part of a machine breaks, it stops working: *I think the spring's broken.*

**4 ► SURFACE/SKIN ◄** [I,T] if the surface of something breaks or if you break it, it splits or gets a hole in it: *The seal on the jar did not seem to have been broken.*

**5 ► RULE/LAW ETC ◄** [T] to disobey a rule, law etc: *Anyone who rides a motorbike without a helmet is breaking the law.*

**6 ► PROMISE/AGREEMENT ◄ break a promise/break an agreement/break your word** to not do what you have promised to do or signed an agreement to do: *I felt I had to take her to the film – I didn't want to break my promise.*

**7 break free/break loose** to escape from someone or somewhere by using force: *I managed to break free by elbowing him in the stomach.*

**8 break loose** if violent feelings or a violent situation breaks loose, they suddenly start to happen: **all hell broke loose** (=people started behaving in a wild, uncontrolled way) *The moment the shot rang out all hell broke loose.*

**9 break even** to neither make a profit nor lose money: *Things have been so bad we'll be lucky if we break even.*

**10 break a habit** to stop wanting to keep doing something, especially something that you should not do: *Smoking is a difficult habit to break.*

**11 why break the habit of a lifetime?** *humorous spoken* used when telling someone that you expect that they will behave in the same way that they have always done, and make the same mistakes: *"I'd better hurry up or I'll be late." "Why break the habit of a lifetime?"*

**12 break sb's heart** to make someone very unhappy by ending a relationship with them or by doing something that they do not want you to do: *He's really good looking – I expect he broke all the girls' hearts when he was at school.* | *It'll break your father's heart if you tell him you're giving up college.*

**13 you're breaking my heart/it's breaking my heart** *humorous spoken* used when saying jokingly that you are very sad about something, even though you are not

**14 break your neck** *spoken* to hurt yourself very badly, especially by falling onto the ground: *The path was really icy and I was lucky I didn't break my neck.*

**15 I'll break his/her neck** *spoken* used when threatening to hurt someone because you are very angry about what they have done: *If I get hold of the guy who hit my car I'll break his neck.*

**16 break the back of** to finish the main or worst part of something: *The engineers are confident they have broken the back of the problem.*

**17 break your back** *spoken* to work very hard to try and do something: *We've been breaking our backs trying to get the work done on time.*

**18 break sb's fall** to stop someone from falling straight onto the ground, so that they are not badly hurt: *Luckily some trees at the bottom of the cliff broke his fall.*

**19 break a record** to do something even faster or even better than the previous best time, amount etc: *Christie has broken his own European record in the 100 meters.* | **break all records** (=to be much better or much more successful than anything before) *This year's sales performance is expected to break all records.*

**20 break for lunch/coffee/dinner etc** to stop for a short time in order to have lunch, a drink etc: *At 12.30 we'll break for lunch, and start again at 2 o'clock.*

**21 break sb's concentration/flow/train of thought** to interrupt someone and stop them from being able to continue thinking or talking about something: *I never listen to music when I'm working – it breaks my concentration.*

**22 ► END A SITUATION ◄** [T] to stop an unpleasant situation from continuing: **break the monotony** *We took turns driving, in order to try and break the monotony.* | **break the deadlock/stalemate** (=end a situation in which an agreement or a solution cannot be found) *a way of ending the deadlock in Bosnia*

**23 break a strike** to force workers to end a STRIKE² (1): *threats to use the army to break the 10 month old strike*

**24 break the silence/calm** to end a period of silence or calm by talking or making a noise: *The silence was broken by a burst of machine-gun fire.*

**25 break your silence** to start talking about something in public after refusing to do so for a long time: *She has finally broken her silence about the divorce.*

**26 break your links/ties/connection etc** to end your connection or relationship with a person, group, organization etc: *The US broke all diplomatic links with North Korea for a 3 month period..*

**27 break sb** to completely destroy someone's chances of success or make them feel that they cannot continue: *the scandal that finally broke him*

**28 break sb's spirit/resolve** to make someone stop trying to achieve something, or start doing what you want: *They could not break her spirit.*

**29 break ranks** to behave differently from the other members of a group, who are expecting you to support them: *No one in the party was prepared to break ranks and vote against their leader.*

**30 break the ice a)** to make people who have just met each other less nervous and more willing to talk, for example at a party or meeting: *Sharon tried to break the ice by suggesting that we all play a game.* **b)** to do something that shows you want to end an argument, quarrel etc: *Yeltsin offered a ceasefire to the rebels in an attempt to break the ice.*

**31 it won't break the bank** used to say that you can afford to buy something: *It's time we had a holiday, and it won't break the bank.*

**32 break the bank** to win more money in a game of cards than a CASINO or a DEALER (3) is able to pay you

**33 break fresh/new ground** to do something completely new that no one has ever done before, or find out

new information about a subject: *Researchers claim they are breaking new ground and are getting closer to discovering the causes of the disease.*
**34 break cover** to move out of a place where you have been hiding so that you can be seen: *One of the rhinos broke cover and charged straight at them.*
**35 break camp** to pack tents and other equipment and leave the place where you have been camping
**36 ► DAY/DAWN ◄** [I] if the day or the dawn breaks, light starts to shine in the sky: *We arrived at Narita just as the dawn was breaking.*
**37 ► STORM ◄** [I] if a storm or the MONSOON breaks, it suddenly begins: *Bonington's team were nearing the summit when the monsoon broke.*
**38 ► WEATHER ◄** [I] if the weather breaks, it suddenly changes
**39 ► WAVE ◄** [I] if a wave breaks, the top part starts to fall down, usually because it is hitting or getting near the shore: *waves breaking against the foot of the cliffs*
**40 ► VOICE ◄** [I] if a boy's voice breaks, it becomes lower and starts to sound like a man's voice: *I was in the school choir until my voice broke.*
**41 ► NEWS ◄** [I] if news about an important event breaks, it finally becomes known: *The Watergate scandal was about to break.*
**42 ► CODE ◄** [T] to succeed in understanding what the letters or numbers in a secret CODE[1] (4) mean: *Polish scientists broke the Enigma code shortly before World War II.*
**43 break wind** to allow gas to escape from your BOWELS, making a noise and an unpleasant smell; FART[1] (1)
**44 break (sb's) serve** to win a game in tennis when your opponent is serving (SERVE[1] (10): *Courier broke Sampras' serve in the first game of the third set.*
**45 break!** used when telling BOXERS or WRESTLERS to stop fighting
**46 break a leg!** *humorous spoken* used to wish someone good luck

**break away** *phr v* [I] **1** to leave a group or political party to form another group, usually because of a disagreement: [+ **from**] *The Nottingham miners broke away from the NUM to form their own union.* **2** to move away from someone or something: [+ **from**] *They kissed, then she broke away from him and ran to the window.*

**break down** *phr v*
**1 ► MACHINE ◄** [I] if a large machine, especially a car, breaks down, it stops working: *The elevators in this building are always breaking down.*
**2 ► FAIL ◄** [I] if a discussion, system etc breaks down, it fails because there are problems: *Peace talks have broken down over the question of reparations.*
**3 ► DOOR ◄** [T **break** sth ↔ **down**] if you break down a door, you hit it so hard that it breaks and falls to the ground
**4 ► CHANGE FIXED IDEAS ◄** [T **break** sth ↔ **down**] to change the fixed ideas or feelings that someone or a group of people have so that they agree with yours: *It'll be difficult to break down their prejudices about lesbians.*
**5 ► CHANGE CHEMICALLY ◄** [I,T] if a substance breaks down or something breaks it down, it changes as a result of a chemical process: **break sth ↔ down** *Bacteria break down the animal waste to form methane gas.*
**6 ► CRY ◄** [I] to be unable to stop yourself crying, especially in public: *If I go to the funeral, I'll break down.*
**7 ► BECOME ILL ◄** [I] to become mentally or physically ill: *If Tim carries on working like this, he'll break down sooner or later.*
**8 ► MAKE STH SIMPLE ◄** [T **break** sth ↔ **down**] to separate something such as a job or report into parts, especially so that it is easier to do or understand: *a recipe that breaks down the making of creme brulee into simple steps* —see also BREAKDOWN (4)

**break for** sth *phr v* [T] *AmE* to suddenly run or drive somewhere, especially in order to escape from someone: *Sharkey broke for the exit, but got nabbed.*

**break in** *phr v* **1** [I] to enter a building by using force, in order to steal something: *Someone broke in and took several computers.* —see also BREAK-IN **2** [T **break** sb/sth ↔ **in**] to make a person or animal get used to a certain way of behaving or working: *Don't worry about doing the accounts, we'll break you in gently.* **3** [I] to join a conversation by interrupting someone or saying something suddenly: [+ **with**] *Dad would occasionally break in with a suggestion.* | [+ **on**] *Sorry to break in on you, but your wife is on the line.* **4** [T **break** sth ↔ **in**] to make new shoes or boots less stiff and more comfortable, by wearing them

**break into** sth *phr v* [T]
**1 ► STEAL ◄** to enter a building by using force, in order to steal something: *Thieves broke into the bank vault by digging a tunnel.*
**2 break into a run/gallop/trot etc** to suddenly start running etc: *Suzie heard footsteps behind her and broke into a run.*
**3 break into a sweat** to start sweating (SWEAT[2] (1)): *The game was over before I'd even broken into a sweat!*
**4 ► NEW BUSINESS ACTIVITY ◄** to become involved in a new activity, especially a business activity: *British Airways is trying to break into the American market.*
**5 ► MONEY ◄** to start to spend money that you did not want to spend: *We'll have to break into the £500 your dad gave us.*
**6 ► INTERRUPT ◄** to interrupt an activity by saying or doing something: *Sorry to break into your lunch hour, but I must speak to you urgently.*
**7 break into tears/laughter/cheers etc** to suddenly start crying, laughing etc

**break** sb **of** sth *phr v* [T] to make someone stop having a bad habit: *What can we do to break him of sucking his thumb?*

**break off** *phr v* **1** [I,T] to suddenly stop doing something, especially talking to someone: *Fay told her story, breaking off now and then to wipe the tears from her eyes.* | **break sth ↔ off** *I broke off the conversation and answered the phone.* **2** [T **break** sth ↔ **off**] to stop a relationship: **break off relations/an engagement** *Britain was about to break off diplomatic relations with Libya.* **3** [T] to break a piece from the main part of something: **break sth ↔ off** *I broke off a piece of bread.* | **break sth off sth** *Why don't you break a branch off the tree and make a walking stick?*

**break out** *phr v* [I]
**1 ► ESCAPE ◄** to escape from a prison or similar place: [+ **of**] *a plan to break out of jail* —see also BREAKOUT
**2 ► WAR/FIRE ETC ◄** if something unpleasant such as a fire, war, or disease breaks out, it starts to happen: *Several scuffles broke out in the crowd.*
**3 ► CHANGE YOUR LIFE ◄** to change the way you live or behave, especially because you feel bored: **break out of a routine/rut etc** *I've got to break out of the same old dull routine or I'll go crazy.*
**4 break out in spots/a rash etc** if you break out in spots etc, a lot of red spots appear on your skin: *Talcum powder makes me break out in a rash.*
**5 break out in a sweat** to start sweating (SWEAT[2] (1))

**break through** *phr v* **1** [I,T] to force a way through something: **break through sth** *At dawn 300 tanks prepared to break through the enemy lines.* **2** [I,T] if the sun or light breaks through, you can see it through something such as clouds or mist **3** [T **break through** sth] to deal successfully with something, especially unreasonable behaviour or bad feelings: *How could I break through his reserve?* —see also BREAKTHROUGH

**break up** *phr v*
**1 ► BREAK INTO PIECES ◄** [I,T] to break or make something break into many small pieces: *The stricken tanker began to break up on the rocks.* | **break** sth ↔ up *Jim started to break the ice up on the frozen lake.*
**2 ► SEPARATE ◄** [T **break** sth ↔ **up**] to separate something into several smaller parts: *I want to plant more bushes to break up the garden a bit.*
**3 ► FIGHT ◄** [I,T] if a fight etc breaks up or someone breaks it up, the people stop fighting each other: **break**

sth ↔ **up** *Three policemen were needed to break up the fight.* | **break up a demonstration/meeting etc** *The army is on hand to break up any demonstrations against the regime.*

**4 ▶ MARRIAGE/ORGANIZATION ◀** [I] if a marriage, group of people, or organization breaks up, the people in it separate and do not live or work together any more: *If a parent dies, the family may break up.* —see also BREAKUP (1)

**5 ▶ CROWD ◀** [I] if a crowd or meeting breaks up, people start to leave

**6 ▶ SCHOOL ◀** [I] *BrE* if a school or the students of a school break up, they begin a holiday: [+ **for**] *When do you break up for Easter?*

**7 ▶ MAKE SB LAUGH ◀** [T] *AmE* to say or do something that is so funny that people cannot stop laughing: **break sb up** *Hal really broke me up with that story about the alligator.*

**break with** sb/sth *phr v* [T] **1** to leave a group of people or an organization, especially because you have had a disagreement with them: **break with sb/sth over sth** *Powell broke with the Conservative Party over Europe.* **2 break with tradition/the past** to stop following old customs and do something in a completely different way

S2 W2 **break²** *n*

**1 ▶ A REST ◀** **a)** [C] a period of time when you stop what you are doing in order to rest, eat etc: **without a break** *Larry had worked all day without a break.* | **tea/coffee/lunch break** *It's time for a coffee break.* | **have/take a break** *Let's take a ten minute break.* **b)** [C] a short holiday: **weekend break** *a travel agent specializing in weekend breaks* | **the Easter/Christmas etc break** (=the public or school holiday at Easter etc) **c)** [U] also **break time** *BrE* the time during the school day when classes stop and teachers and students can rest, eat, play etc; RECESS¹ (2) *AmE*: *I'll speak to you at break.*

**2 ▶ A PAUSE IN STH ◀** **a)** [C] a period of several weeks or years during which something stops, before continuing again: [+ **in**] *a welcome break in my normal routine* | **career break** *Demi Moore planned to take a career break to have children.* **b)** [C] a pause in a conversation or in what someone is saying: [+ **in**] *She waited for a break in the conversation.* **c)** also **commercial break** a pause for advertisements during a television or radio programme: *Join us again after the break.*

**3 ▶ END/CHANGE ◀** [singular] an occasion when you end a relationship with a person, organization etc, or change the way that things have always been done in the past: [+ **from**] *Medieval thought represents a sharp break from that of the Greeks.* | [+ **with**] *In a break with tradition, they held their wedding at home.* | **a clean break** (=a very clear and definite end to a relationship) *I don't want a messy divorce, just a quick, clean break.* | **make the break** *She's wanted to leave Dave for years, and last week she finally made the break.*

**4 ▶ A SPACE ◀** [C] a space between two things or between two parts of something: *The sun shone through a break in the clouds.* | **a break in the weather** (=a short period of good weather)

**5 ▶ A CHANCE ◀** [C] *informal* a sudden or unexpected chance to do something, especially be successful in your job: **big/lucky break** *My big break came when I was spotted singing in a club by a talent scout.*

**6 make a break for sth** to suddenly start running towards something in order to escape from a place: *As soon as the guard's back was turned they made a break for the door.* | **make a break for it** (=try to escape)

**7 ▶ BROKEN PLACE ◀** [C] the place where a bone in your body has broken: *It's a nasty break, the bone has splintered.*

**8 give sb/sth a break!** *spoken* used when you want someone to stop talking about something or doing something because it is annoying you: *I'm sick of hearing about your problems. Just give it a break.*

**9 give me a break!** *AmE spoken* used when you do not believe something someone has said

**10 ▶ TENNIS ◀** also **break of serve** [C] a situation in a game of tennis in which you win a game when your opponent is serving (SERVE¹ (10)): **break point** (=the moment when if you win the point, you win a game)

**11 ▶ POINTS ◀** [C] the number of points won by a player when it is their turn to hit the ball in a game such as BILLIARDS or SNOOKER¹

**12 the break of day** *literary* the time early in the morning when it starts getting light

**break·a·ble** /ˈbreɪkəbəl/ *adj* made of a material such as glass or clay that breaks easily

**break·age** /ˈbreɪkɪdʒ/ *n* **1 breakages** [plural] things that have been broken, especially things that belong to someone else that you must pay for: *a £5 deposit on hiring glasses, in case of breakages* **2** [U] *formal* the act of breaking

**break·a·way** /ˈbreɪkəweɪ/ *adj* **breakaway group/party/movement** a breakaway group etc has been formed by people who left another group because of a disagreement: *the breakaway state of Slovenia* —**breakaway** *n* [C]

**break·dance** /breɪkdɑːns‖-dæns/ *v* [I] to do a type of dance involving ACROBATIC movements —**breakdancing** *n* [U] —**breakdancer** *n* [C]

**break·down** /ˈbreɪkdaʊn/ *n* **1** [C,U] the failure of a system or relationship: *Family breakdown can lead to behavioral problems in children.* | [+ **in**] *a serious breakdown in relations between the two countries* | [+ **of**] *the gradual breakdown of authority* **2** also **nervous breakdown** [C] a serious medical condition in which someone becomes mentally ill and is unable to deal with even the simplest situations: **have/suffer a breakdown** *After the trial Paul had a breakdown.* **3** [C] an occasion when a car or a piece of machinery breaks and stops working **4** [C] a written statement explaining the details of something such as a bill or the cost of a plan: [+ **of**] *Can you prepare a full breakdown of labour costs?*

**breakdown truck** /ˈ·· ˌ·/ also **breakdown lor·ry** /ˈ·· ˌ··/ *n* [C] *BrE* a vehicle with special equipment used to pull a car that does not work to a place where it can be repaired; TOWTRUCK *AmE*

**break·er** /ˈbreɪkə‖-ər/ *n* [C] a large wave with a white top that rolls onto the shore

**break·e·ven** /ˌbreɪkˈiːvən◂/ *n* [U] the level of business activity at which a company is making neither a profit nor a loss: **breakeven point** *The firm should reach breakeven point after one year.* —see also **break even** (BREAK¹ (9))

**break·fast** /ˈbrekfəst/ *n* [C,U] the meal you have in the morning: **have sth for breakfast** *We had coffee and toast for breakfast.* | **working breakfast** (=a breakfast at which you talk about business) —see also BED AND BREAKFAST, CONTINENTAL BREAKFAST, **make a dog's breakfast/dinner of sth** (DOG¹ (8)), —**breakfast** *v* [I + **on**] S2 W2

**breakfast tel·e·vi·sion** /ˌ·· ˈ····ˌ|ˌ·· ˈ··ˈ·/ *n* [U] *BrE* television programmes that are broadcast in the early part of the morning

**break-in** /ˈ· ·/ *n* [C] an act of entering a building illegally and by force, especially in order to steal things: *Since the break-in we've had all our locks changed.* —see also **break in** (BREAK¹)

**breaking and en·ter·ing** /ˌ·· · ˈ···/ *n* [U] *law* the crime of entering a building illegally and by force

**break·neck** /ˈbreɪknek/ *adj* **at breakneck speed** extremely and often dangerously fast

**break·out** /ˈbreɪkaʊt/ *n* [C] an escape from a prison, especially one involving a lot of prisoners

**break·through** /ˈbreɪkθruː/ *n* [C] an important new discovery in something you are studying, especially one made after trying for a long time: **make a breakthrough** *Scientists have made a major breakthrough in the treatment of cancer.*

**break·up** /ˈbreɪkʌp/ *n* [C,U] **1** the act of ending a marriage or relationship: *the consequences of marital breakup on children* **2** the separation of a group, organization, or country into smaller parts, especially because it has become weaker or there are serious disagreements: [+ **of**] *the breakup of the Soviet Union*

**break·wa·ter** /ˈbreɪkˌwɔːtə‖-ˌwɔːtər, -ˌwɑː-/ *n* [C] a large strong wall built out into the sea to protect the shore from the force of the waves: *forming a natural breakwater against the sea*

**breast¹** /brest/ *n*
**1** ▶ **PART OF A WOMAN'S BODY** ◀ [C] one of the two round raised parts of a woman's body that produce milk when she has a baby: *a woman with a baby at the breast* | *breast cancer* —see picture at BODY
**2** ▶ **CHEST** ◀ [C] the part of your body between your neck and your stomach, especially the upper part of this area: *Dick cradled her photograph against his breast.*
**3** ▶ **PART OF A BIRD** ◀ [C] the front part of a bird's body: *a robin with a red breast*
**4** ▶ **MEAT** ◀ [U] meat that comes from the front part of the body of a bird such as a chicken: *turkey breast*
**5 make a clean breast of it/things** to admit that you have done something wrong: *Why not make a clean breast of it and tell them you took the money?*
**6 single-breasted/double-breasted** a coat, dress etc that is single-breasted etc has one or two rows of buttons down the front
**7 bare-breasted/small-breasted/red-breasted etc** having bare etc breasts
**8** ▶ **EMOTIONS** ◀ [C] *literary* where your feelings of sadness, love, anger, fear etc come from: *a troubled breast* —see also **beat your breast** (BEAT¹ (28))

**breast²** *v* [T] **1** to reach the top of a hill or slope **2** to push against something with your chest

**breast·bone** /ˈbrestbəʊn‖-boʊn/ *n* [C] a long flat bone in the front of your chest to which the top seven pairs of RIBS¹ (1) are connected —see picture at SKELETON

**breast-feed** /ˈbrestfiːd/ *v past tense and past participle* **breastfed** /-fed/ [I,T] to feed a baby with milk from your breast rather than from a bottle —compare SUCKLE, NURSE¹ (16)

**breast·plate** /ˈbrestpleɪt/ *n* [C] a leather or metal protective covering worn over the chest by soldiers during battles in former times

**breast-pock·et** /ˌ· ˈ··/ *n* [C] a pocket on the outside of a shirt or JACKET (1), above the breast

**breast·stroke** /ˈbrest-strəʊk‖-stroʊk/ *n* [U] a way of swimming in which you push your arms out and then bring them back in a circle towards you while bending your knees towards your body and then kicking out

S3 W2 **breath** /breθ/ *n*
**1** ▶ **AIR YOU BREATHE** ◀ **a)** [U] the air that you take in and out of your lungs when you breathe: *Paul smelt the cigarette smoke on her breath.* | **bad breath** (=breath that smells unpleasant) **b)** the process of breathing in and out: *Her breath was coming more easily now.* **c)** [U, singular] the air in your lungs or the act of breathing it in: *Let your breath out slowly.* | **take a (big/deep) breath** (=breathe in once) *Shaun took a deep breath and dived in.* | **be out of breath** (=have difficulty breathing because you have just been running, climbing stairs etc) | **get your breath back** (=breathe normally again after running or making a lot of effort) *At the top of the stairs she stopped to get her breath back.* | **short of breath** (=unable to breath easily, especially because you are unhealthy)
**2 a breath of fresh air a)** something that is new and different in a way you find exciting and enjoyable: *Osborne's play brought a breath of fresh air to the British theatre.* **b) take a breath of fresh air** to go outside because it is unpleasantly hot where you are
**3 hold your breath a)** to breathe in and close your mouth to keep the air in your lungs: *I just held my breath and prayed I wouldn't sneeze.* **b)** to wait anxiously to see what is going to happen: *We held our breath while Mr Evans read the exam results.*
**4 take your breath away** to be so beautiful or exciting that you feel as if you nearly stop breathing: *a view that takes your breath away*
**5 under your breath** in a quiet voice so that no-one can hear you: *"Son of a bitch," he muttered under his breath.*
**6 in the same breath a)** used to say that someone has said two things at once that are so different from each other they cannot both be true: *They said that women should have equal pay, and added in the same breath that men need more money.* **b)** if you mention two people or things in the same breath, you show that you think they are alike: *a player who has been mentioned in the same breath as Pete Sampras*
**7 with your last/dying breath** at the moment when you are dying: *With his last breath he cursed his captors.*
**8 a breath of air/wind** *literary* a slight movement of air: *Scarcely a breath of air disturbed the stillness of the day.*
**9 be the breath of life to sb** to be the most important thing in someone's life —see also **with bated breath** (BATED), **catch your breath** (CATCH¹ (23)), **draw a breath** (DRAW¹ (23)), **gasp for breath** (GASP¹ (2)), **save your breath** (SAVE¹ (15)), **waste your breath** (WASTE² (2))

**breath·a·lyse** *BrE*, **breathalize** *AmE* /ˈbreθəl-aɪz/ *v* [T] to make someone breathe into a special piece of equipment in order to see if they have drunk too much alcohol

**breath·a·lys·er** *BrE*, **breathalyzer** *AmE* /ˈbreθəl-aɪzə‖-ər/ *n* [C] *trademark* a piece of equipment used by the police to see if drivers have drunk too much alcohol

**breathe** /briːð/ *v* S W
**1** ▶ **AIR** ◀ [I,T] to take air into your lungs and send it out again: *When you get an asthma attack you can't breathe.* | *People are concerned about the quality of the air they breathe.* | **breathe deeply** (=take in a lot of air)
**2** ▶ **BLOW** ◀ [I,T] to blow air or smoke out of your mouth: [+ **on**] *Roy breathed on his hands and rubbed them together vigorously.* | **breathe sth over sb** *The fat man opposite was breathing garlic all over me.*
**3 breathe again/more easily** to relax because something dangerous or frightening has finished: *The all-clear was given and we could breathe again.*
**4 breathe a sigh of relief** to no longer be worried about something that had been worrying or frightening you
**5 be breathing down sb's neck** to pay very close attention to what someone is doing in a way that makes them feel nervous or annoyed: *How can I concentrate with you breathing down my neck all the time?*
**6 not breathe a word** to not tell anyone anything at all about something, because it is a secret: *Don't breathe a word, it's supposed to be a surprise.*
**7** ▶ **WINE** ◀ [I] if you let wine breathe, you open the bottle to let the air get to it before you drink it
**8** ▶ **SAY STH QUIETLY** ◀ [T] to say something very quietly, almost in a whisper: *"Wait," he breathed."*
**9 breathe your last** *literary* to die
**10 breathe life/excitement/enthusiasm into sth** to change a situation so that people feel more excited or interested: *Let's hope Doug can breathe a bit of life into these rather dull people.*
**11 breathe fire** to behave and talk very angrily

**breathe in** *phr v* **1** [I] to take air into your lungs: *The doctor made me breathe in while he listened to my chest.* **2** [T **breathe** sth ↔ **in**] to breathe air, smoke, a particular kind of smell etc into your lungs: *They may be in danger of breathing in asbestos dust.*

**breathe out** *phr v* **1** [I] to send air out from your lungs: *Jim breathed out deeply.* **2** [T **breathe** sth ↔ **out**] to send out air, oxygen, a particular kind of smell etc: *Green plants breathe out oxygen in sunlight.*

**breath·er** /ˈbriːðə‖-ər/ *n* **have/take a breather** *informal* to stop what you are doing for a short time in order to rest —see also HEAVY BREATHER

**breath·ing** /ˈbriːðɪŋ/ *n* [U] the process of breathing air in and out: **heavy breathing** (=loud breathing) *When I picked up the phone all I heard was heavy breathing.*

**breathing space** /ˈ·· ·/ *n* [C,U] a short time when you stop doing something difficult, tiring etc, so that you have time to think more clearly about a situation

**breath·less** /ˈbreθləs/ *adj* **1** having difficulty breathing, especially because you are very tired, excited, or frightened: *The long climb left Jan feeling breathless.* **2** unpleasantly hot with no fresh air or wind: *the* *breathless heat of a midsummer night in Rome* —**breathlessly** *adv* —**breathlessness** *n* [U]

**breath·tak·ing** /ˈbreθˌteɪkɪŋ/ *adj* very impressive, exciting, or surprising: *the breathtaking natural beauty of the rain forests | a man of quite breathtaking stupidity* —**breathtakingly** *adv*

**breath test** /ˈ· ˌ·/ *n* [C] a test in which the police make a car driver breathe into a special bag to see if he has drunk too much alcohol

**breath·y** /ˈbreθi/ *adj* if someone's voice is breathy, you can hear their breath when they speak

**breech birth** /ˈbriːtʃ bɜːθ‖-bɜːrθ/ also **breech de·liv·e·ry** /ˈ· ·ˌ···/ *n* [C] a birth in which the lower part of a baby's body comes out of its mother first

**breech·es** /ˈbrɪtʃɪ̇z/ *n* [plural] short trousers that fasten just below the knees: *riding breeches*

3 **breed**[1] /briːd/ *v past tense and past participle* **bred** /bred/ **1** [I] if animals breed they have babies: *Eagles breed during the cooler months of the year.* **2** [T] to keep animals or plants in order to produce babies or new plants, or in order to develop new or better animals or plants: *commercially bred animals* **3** [T] to cause a particular feeling or condition: *living conditions that breed violence and despair* **4 breed like rabbits** to produce a lot of babies quickly, especially more than you think is desirable —see also WELL-BRED

**breed**[2] *n* [C] **1** a type of animal or plant, especially one that people have kept to breed, such as cats, dogs, and farm animals: *Spaniels are my favourite breed of dog.* **2** a particular kind of person or type of thing: **a rare/dying breed** *Honest salesmen are a rare breed nowadays.* | **a new breed of** *the first of a new breed of satellites*

**breed·er** /ˈbriːdə‖-ər/ *n* [C] someone who breeds animals or plants as a job: *a dog breeder*

**breed·ing** /ˈbriːdɪŋ/ *n* [U] **1** the act or process of animals producing babies: **breeding season** (=the time of the year when an animal has babies) **2** the activity of keeping animals or plants in order to produce new or better types: *the breeding of pedigree dogs* | **breeding stock** (=animals you keep to breed from) **3** polite social behaviour that someone learns from their family: *The young lieutenant had an air of wealth and good breeding.*

**breeding ground** /ˈ·· ·/ *n* [C] **1** a place or situation where something bad or harmful grows and develops: [+ **for**] *overcrowded slums that are breeding grounds for crime* **2** a place where animals go in order to breed: *In spring, the birds migrate north to their breeding grounds.*

**breeze**[1] /briːz/ *n* [C] **1** a gentle wind: *flowers waving in the breeze* —see picture on page 836 **2 be a breeze** *informal* to be something that is very easy to do —see also **shoot the breeze** (SHOOT[1] (11))

**breeze**[2] *v* [I always + adv/prep] to walk somewhere in a calm confident way: [+ **in/into/out etc**] *She just breezed into my office and said she wanted a job.*

**breeze through** sth *phr v* [T] to finish a piece of work or pass an exam very easily: *She breezed through the exam.*

**breeze-block** /ˈ· ·/ *n* [C] *BrE* a light brick used in building, made of CEMENT and CINDERS; CINDER BLOCK *AmE*

**breez·y** /ˈbriːzi/ *adj* **1** a breezy person is cheerful, confident, and relaxed: *a breezy and relaxed air of confidence* **2** breezy weather is when the wind blows quite strongly —**breezily** *adv* —**breeziness** *n* [U]

**breth·ren** /ˈbreðrən/ *n* [plural] *old-fashioned* a way of addressing or talking about the members of an organization or association, especially a religious group

**breve** /briːv/ *n* [C] *BrE* a musical note which continues for twice as long as a SEMIBREVE; DOUBLE WHOLE NOTE *AmE*

**bre·vi·a·ry** /ˈbriːviəri, ˈbre-‖-ieri/ *n* [C] a prayer book used in the Roman Catholic church

**brev·i·ty** /ˈbrevɪ̇ti/ *n* [U] **1** the quality of expressing something in very few words **2** shortness of time: *In the interests of brevity I will summarize my views.*

**brew**[1] /bruː/ *v* **1** [T] to make beer **2** [I,T] if tea or coffee brews or you brew it, you pour boiling water over it to make it ready to drink **3** [I] if something unpleasant is brewing, it will happen soon: *There's trouble brewing at work.*

**brew up** *phr v* [I] *BrE informal* to make a drink of tea

**brew**[2] *n* [C] a drink such as tea or beer —see also HOME BREW

**brew·er** /ˈbruːə‖-ər/ *n* [C] a person or company that makes beer

**brew·er·y** /ˈbruːəri/ *n* [C] a place where beer is made, or a company that makes beer

**bri·ar**, **brier** /ˈbraɪə‖-ər/ *n* **1** [C,U] a wild bush with prickly branches **2** [C] a tobacco pipe made from a briar

**bribe**[1] /braɪb/ *v* [T] to pay money to someone to persuade them to help you, especially by doing something dishonest: **bribe sb to do sth** *We bribed the doorman to let us in.* | **bribe sb for sth** *prisoners bribing guards with cigarettes*

**bribe**[2] *n* [C] an amount of money or something valuable that you give someone to persuade them to help you or to do something dishonest: *a New York judge charged with accepting bribes* —compare PAYOLA[1]

**brib·er·y** /ˈbraɪbəri/ *n* [U] dishonestly giving money to someone in order to persuade them to do something that will help you: *We tried persuasion, bribery and threats, but the guard still wouldn't let us pass.* | *He was arrested on suspicion of accepting bribery.* | **bribery and corruption** (=bribery and dishonest behaviour)

**bric-a-brac** /ˈbrɪk ə ˌbræk/ *n* [U] small objects that are not worth very much money but are interesting or attractive

**brick**[1] /brɪk/ *n* **1** [C,U] a hard block of baked clay used for building walls, houses etc: *a brick wall* **2** [C] *BrE* a small square block of wood, plastic etc used as a toy **3** [C] *old-fashioned* a good person who you can depend on when you are in trouble: *Janet's a real brick.* **4 you can't make bricks without straw** used to say you cannot do a job if you do not have the necessary materials —see also **bang your head against a brick wall** (BANG[1] (5)), **drop a brick** (DROP[1] (34)), **come down on sb like a ton of bricks** (TON (5)) S2 W3

**brick**[2] *v*

**brick** sth ↔ **off** *phr v* [T] to separate an area from a larger area by building a wall of bricks: *Some of the rooms had been bricked off.*

**brick** sth ↔ **up/in** *phr v* [T] to fill or close a space by building a wall of bricks in it: *bricked up windows*

**brick·lay·er** /ˈbrɪkˌleɪə‖-ər/ *n* [C] someone whose job is to build walls, buildings etc with bricks —**bricklaying** *n* [U]

**brick·work** /ˈbrɪkwɜːk‖-wɜːrk/ *n* [U] bricks, or the way they have been used to build a wall, house etc: *The brickwork was cracked and in need of repair.*

**brick·yard** /ˈbrɪkjɑːd‖-jɑːrd/ *n* [C] a place where bricks are made

**brid·al** /ˈbraɪdl/ *adj* **1** concerning a bride or a wedding: *a bridal car* **2 the bridal party** the group of people who arrive at the church with the bride **3 bridal suite** a special set of rooms in a hotel for a newly married couple **4 bridal shower** *AmE* a party for a woman who is going to be married, given by her friends and family

**bride** /braɪd/ *n* [C] a woman at the time she gets married or just after she is married: *You may kiss the bride.*

**bride·groom** /ˈbraɪdgruːm, -grʊm/ also **groom** *n* [C] a man at the time he gets married, or just after he is married

**brides·maid** /ˈbraɪdzmeɪd/ *n* [C] a girl or woman, usually unmarried, who helps the bride on her wedding day and is with her at the wedding

**bride-to-be** /ˌ· · ˈ·/ *n* [C] a woman who is going to be married soon: *That's Jonathan's bride-to-be.*

S2 W2 **bridge¹** /brɪdʒ/ *n* [C]
**1 ▶ OVER A RIVER/ROAD ETC◀** a structure built over a river, road etc, that allows people or vehicles to cross from one side to the other
**2 ▶ CONNECTION◀** something that provides a connection between two things; LINK² (1): *The training programme is seen as a bridge between school and work.*

**3 ▶ SHIP◀** the raised part of a ship from which the officers control it
**4 ▶ CARD GAME◀** [U] a card game for four players who play in pairs
**5 the bridge of your nose** the bony upper part of your nose between your eyes
**6 ▶ PAIR OF GLASSES◀** the part of a pair of glasses that rests on the bridge of your nose —see picture at GLASS¹
**7 ▶ MUSICAL INSTRUMENT◀** a small piece of wood under the strings of a VIOLIN or GUITAR, used to keep them in position
**8 ▶ FOR TEETH◀** a small piece of metal for keeping false teeth in place —see also **build bridges** (BUILD¹ (7)), **burn your bridges** (BURN¹ (22)), **cross that bridge when you come to it** (CROSS¹ (7)), **be (all) water under the bridge** (WATER¹ (7))

**bridge²** *v* [T] **1** to build or form a bridge over something: *a fallen tree bridging the stream* **2 bridge the gap (between)** to reduce or get rid of the difference between two things: *an attempt at bridging the economic gap between North and South*

**bridge·head** /ˈbrɪdʒhed/ *n* [C] a strong position far forward in enemy land from which an army can go forward or attack

**bridging loan** /ˈ·· ˌ·/ *n* [C] *BrE* an amount of money lent by a bank to cover the period between buying a new house and selling the old one

**bri·dle¹** /ˈbraɪdl/ *v* **1** [T] to put a bridle on a horse **2** [I,T] to show you are angry about something, especially by making a sudden upward movement of your chin: *She bridled at his autocratic tone.*

**bridle²** *n* [C] a set of leather bands put around a horse's head and used to control its movements —see picture at HORSE¹

**bridle path** /ˈ·· ·/ also **bri·dle·way** /ˈbraɪdlweɪ/ *n* [C] a path intended for horse-riding, and not suitable for cars

**Brie** /briː/ *n* [U] a soft French cheese

S2 W2 **brief¹** /briːf/ *adj*
**1 ▶ TIME◀** continuing for a short time: *a brief visit*
**2 have a brief word** to have a short conversation: *Could I have a brief word with you, Mr Thomas?*
**3 be brief** to say or write something using only a few words, especially because there is little time
**4 ▶ SPEECH/LETTER◀** using very few words or including few details: *a brief note of thanks*
**5 in brief a)** in as few words as possible: *We should, in brief, invest heavily in digital systems.* **b)** without any details: *a report in brief*
**6** someone who is brief does not say very much to someone, often in a rude way: *She was very brief with me when I asked about the contracts.*
**7 ▶ CLOTHES◀** clothes which are brief are short and cover only a small area of your body: *a very brief bikini*

**brief²** *n* [C] **1** official instructions that explain what someone's job is, what their duties are, how they should behave etc: *The architects's brief is to design an extension that is modern but blends with the rest of the building.* **2** a short spoken or written statement giving facts about a law case **3 briefs** [plural] men's or women's underwear worn on the lower part of the body

**brief³** *v* [T] to give someone all the necessary information about a situation, so that they are prepared for it: **brief sb on sth** *The president has been fully briefed on the current situation in Haiti* —compare DEBRIEF.

**brief·case** /ˈbriːfkeɪs/ *n* [C] a case used for carrying papers or documents —see picture at SUITCASE

**brief·ing** /ˈbriːfɪŋ/ *n* [C,U] information or instructions that you get before you have to do something

**brief·ly** /ˈbriːfli/ *adv* **1** for a short time: *We stopped off briefly in London on our way to Geneva.* **2** in as few words as possible: *Sonia explained briefly what we were to do.* [sentence adverb] *Briefly, I think we should accept their offer.* S W

**bri·er** /ˈbraɪə‖-ər/ *n* [C] a BRIAR

**brig** /brɪg/ *n* [C] a ship with two MASTS (=poles) and large square sails

**bri·gade** /brɪˈgeɪd/ *n* [C] **1** a large group of soldiers forming part of an army **2** an insulting word for a group of people who have the same beliefs: *the anti-nuclear brigade* —see also FIRE BRIGADE S

**brig·a·dier** /ˌbrɪgəˈdɪə◂‖-ˈdɪr◂/ *n* [C] a high military rank in the British Army or the person who has this rank —see table on page B4

**brigadier-gen·e·ral** /ˌ··· ˈ···/ *n* [C] a high army rank or someone holding this rank —see table on page B4

**brig·and** /ˈbrɪgənd/ *n* [C] *literary* a thief, especially one of a group that attacks people in mountains or forests

**brig·an·tine** /ˈbrɪgəntiːn/ *n* [C] a ship like a BRIG but with fewer sails

**bright** /braɪt/ *adj* S W
**1 ▶ LIGHT◀** shining strongly or with plenty of light: *bright sunlight | bright lights | a new, bright, fully air-conditioned office*
**2 ▶ INTELLIGENT◀** intelligent and likely to be successful: *Rosa's a bright child – she should do well at school.* | **(have) a bright idea** *We've no money and the last bus has gone. Any bright ideas?*
**3 ▶ COLOURS◀** bright colours are strong and easy to see: *bright red | Wash bright colours separately.*
**4 ▶ CHEERFUL◀** cheerful or full of life: *a bright smile* | [+ **with**] *Her eyes were bright with excitement*
**5 as bright as a button** clever and full of life
**6 not too/very bright a)** if your future is not too bright, there is no reason to hope that good things will happen: *The future doesn't look too bright for these youngsters on the dole.* **b)** *informal* not sensible: *That wasn't very bright, was it?*
**7 look on the bright side** to see the good points in something that is bad in other ways: *Look on the bright side – not having a holiday will mean you save money!*
**8 bright and early** very early in the morning: *Max was up bright and early, keen to get started.*
**9 bright spark** *informal* an intelligent person, often used jokingly about someone who has done something stupid: *What bright spark forgot to turn the oven off?*
**10 bright and breezy** cheerful and confident
**11 have a bright future/have bright prospects** to be likely to be successful in whatever you do as a job
**12 bright-eyed and bushy-tailed** *humorous* keen to start doing something, especially because it is new or interesting
**13 the bright lights** the interesting exciting life that people are supposed to have in big cities: *June went off in search of the bright lights in London.*
**14 bright spot** an event or a period of time that is more pleasant when everything else is unpleasant: *The only bright spot of the weekend was our trip to the theatre.* —**brightly** *adv*: *The sun shone brightly.* —**brightness** *n* [U]

**bright·en** /ˈbraɪtn/ *v* **1** [T] to make something brighter in colour **2** [I] to become brighter in colour, or to shine with more light: *The sky had already begun to brighten.* **3** [I,T] to become happier or more excited, or make someone else feel like this: *His expression brightened when I mentioned the money.*

**brighten** sth ↔ **up** *phr v* **1** [T] to make something more attractive or interesting: *New curtains would brighten up this room.* **2** [I] to start to become happy again: *She brightened up as soon as she saw us.* **3** [I] to become brighter: *The weather soon brightened up.*

**brights** /braɪts/ *n* [plural] *AmE* car HEADLIGHTS when they are on as brightly as possible —see also HIGH-BEAM

**brill¹** /brɪl/ *adj BrE spoken* very good; BRILLIANT¹ (3)

**brill²** *n* [C] a European fish with a thin flat body

**bril·liance** /ˈbrɪljəns/ *n* [U] **1** a very high level of intelligence or skill: *Hendrix's brilliance as a rock guitarist has never been matched.* **2** brightness of colour

3 **bril·liant¹** /ˈbrɪljənt/ *adj* **1** brilliant light or colour is
3 very bright and strong: *The stage was flooded with brilliant light.* | *brilliant reds and blues* **2** extremely good, clever, or skilful: *Cox's performance was brilliant.* | **a brilliant idea** *Hugh came up with a brilliant idea for a book.* **3** *BrE* excellent: *"How was your holiday?" "It was brilliant!"* **4** very successful: *a long and brilliant career* —**brilliantly** *adv*

**brilliant²** *n* [C] *technical* a precious stone cut with a lot of surfaces that shine

**bril·lian·tine** /ˈbrɪljəntiːn/ *n* [U] an oily substance used on men's hair

**Bril·lo pad** /ˈbrɪləʊ pæd‖-loʊ-/ *n* [C] *trademark* a ball of wire filled with soap, used for cleaning pans

**brim¹** /brɪm/ *n* [C] **1** the bottom part of a hat that sticks out to protect you from sun and rain —see picture at HAT **2 be full to the brim (with)** if a container such as a glass is full to the brim, it is as full as possible: *Dave poured whisky till the glass was full to the brim.*

**brim²** *v* **brimmed, brimming** [I] to be very full of something: [+ **with**] *Andy's eyes brimmed with tears.* | *Eve was brimming with confidence.*

**brim over** *phr v* [I] **1** if a container is brimming over, it is so full of something that this is coming out over its top edge: [+ **with**] *The barrel was brimming over with water.* **2 brim over with confidence/excitement etc** to be very confident, excited etc

**brim·ful**, **brimfull** /ˈbrɪmˌfʊl/ *adj* [not before noun] very full: [+ **of/with**] *John is brimful of ambition, and ready to fight his way to the top.*

**brim·stone** /ˈbrɪmstəʊn, -stən‖-stoʊn, -stən/ *n* [U] *old use* SULPHUR —see also **fire and brimstone** (FIRE¹ (13))

**brin·dled** /ˈbrɪndld/ *adj* a brindled cow, cat etc is brown with marks or bands of another colour

**brine** /braɪn/ *n* [U] **1** water which contains a lot of salt, used for preserving food: *sardines in brine* **2** sea water

1 **bring** /brɪŋ/ *v past tense and past participle* **brought**
1 /brɔːt‖brɒːt/ [T] **1** to take someone or something to the place you are now, to the place you are going to, or to the place that you have been talking about: *Did you bring anything to drink?* | *Sheila was at the party and she brought that awful Ronnie with her!* | **bring sb sth** *Could you bring me that chair?* **2** to cause something such as a problem or reaction: *The minister's speech brought an angry reaction from the Teachers' Association.* | *This whole venture has brought nothing but trouble!* **3 bring with it** if a change, action etc brings with it something such as a problem or advantage, the two things are connected and come together: *Every scientific advance brings with it its own risks.* **4** if something such as an event or fact brings people to a place, it makes them go there: *The discovery of gold brought thousands of prospectors flocking to the Transvaal.* **5 bring charges** if the police bring charges against someone, they decide to charge them with a crime: *There was a six-month investigation, but eventually no charges were brought.* **6 not bring yourself to do sth** if you cannot bring yourself to do something, you cannot make yourself do it: *She couldn't bring herself to touch it.* **7 bring sth into being** *formal* to make something start to exist: *The bureau was brought into being during the Second World War.* **8 bring sth to the boil** to heat liquid until it starts to boil **9 bring tears to your eyes/bring a lump to your throat** to make you start to feel strong emotions such as pity, sadness, or happiness: *To see them meet after all this time, it really brings a lump to your throat!* **10 bring sth to an end/a close/a conclusion etc** to make something finish or stop: *It's time we brought this whole sordid affair to a close.* **11 bring sth to bear** *formal* to use pressure, influence etc to change a situation: *Unfair pressure has been brought to bear upon the strikers to make them return.* **12 bring sth to sb's attention/notice** *formal* to tell someone about something: *Thank you for bringing this mistake to our attention.* **13 what brings you here?** *spoken* used to show that you are surprised to see someone **14 bring home the bacon** *informal* to earn the money that your family needs to live —see also **bring sth to a head** (HEAD¹ (45)), **bring sb to heel** (HEEL¹ (9)), **bring sb to their senses** (SENSE¹ (6)), **bring sth home to sb** (HOME² (4)), **bring sb/sth to their knees** (KNEE¹ (6))

**bring** sth ↔ **about** *phr v* [T] to make something happen: *Computers have brought about many changes in the workplace.*

**bring** sb/sth **around/round** *phr v* [T] **1 bring the conversation around/round to** to deliberately and gradually introduce a new subject into a conversation: *I'll try to bring the conversation around to the subject of money.* **2** to make someone become conscious again: *We managed to bring her round with some smelling salts.* **3** to manage to persuade someone to do something or to agree with you: *Give me a day or two and I'll see if I can bring her around.* **4** to bring someone or something to someone's house: *If I bring it round tomorrow you can check it out.*

**bring back** *phr v* [T] **1** [**bring** sth ↔ **back**] to start to use something such as a law, method, or process that was used in the past: *They should bring back the death penalty, that's what I think!* | *bringing back the old electric trams* **2 bring back** sth to make you remember something: *The smell of new paper always brings back memories of school.* **3 bring** sth ↔ **back** to take something or someone with you when you come back from somewhere: **bring sb back sth** *Hey, Freddie! Bring me back a few beers would ya!* | **bring sth back (for sb)** *I brought these back from Kenya for the children.* **4 it brings us/me back to** used when you want to talk about a particular problem again: *This brings us back to the important question of money.*

**bring** sb/sth ↔ **down** *phr v* [T] **1** to fly an aircraft down to the ground and stop: *He brought the Cessna down in a hay-meadow by the river.* **2** to move your arm or a weapon, tool etc quickly downwards: *He brought down the axe with a thud.* **3** to shoot at a plane, bird, or animal so that it falls to the ground: *A bomber had been brought down by anti-aircraft fire.* **4 bring down the government/president etc** to force the government etc to stop ruling **5** to knock someone over in a game of football, RUGBY etc: *Klinsmann was brought down on the edge of the area.*

**bring** sth ↔ **down on/upon** *phr v* [T] *formal* to make something bad happen to someone, especially yourself: *His recklessness brought down disaster on the whole family.*

**bring** sth ↔ **forth** *phr v* [T] *formal* to produce something or make it appear: *a tragic love affair that brought forth only pain*

**bring** sth ↔ **forward** *phr v* [T] **1** to change an arrangement in the future so that something happens sooner: *The meeting's been brought forward to Thursday.* **2 bring forward legislation/plans/policies etc** to officially introduce plans etc for people to discuss: *The government has brought forward a plan to tackle urban crime.* **3** *technical* to move the total from one set of calculations onto the next page, so that more calculations can be done: *The balance brought forward is £21,765.*

**bring in** *phr v* [T] **1** [**bring in** sth] to earn a particular amount or produce a particular amount of profit: *The sale of the house only brought in about £45,000.* **2** [**bring** sb ↔ **in**] to allow or invite someone to become involved in a discussion, INVESTIGATION etc: *It all became very serious and the police were brought in.* | *Could I just bring in some members of the audience to get their views.*

**3 bring in a verdict** when a court or JURY brings in a verdict, it says whether someone is guilty or not

**bring** sb/sth ↔ **off** *phr v* [T] **1** to succeed in doing something very difficult: *Together they brought off a daring diamond robbery.* **2** *technical* to help people to leave a ship that is sinking

**bring** sth ↔ **on** *phr v* [T] **1** to make something bad or unpleasant happen: *a bad cold brought on by going out in the rain*| *Whatever has brought this on? Have I upset you somehow?* **2** to make plants or crops grow faster: *The hot weather has really brought on the roses.*

**bring** sth **on/upon** sb *phr v* [T] to make something bad happen to someone: *You have brought disaster on the whole village!*

**bring out** *phr v* [T] **1** [**bring** sth/sb ↔ **out**] to make something easier to see, taste, notice etc: *The oregano really brings out the flavour of the meat.*| *Fatherhood seems to have brought out his sense of responsibility.* **2 bring out the best/worst in sb** to make someone behave in the best or worst way that they can: *Alcohol just brings out the worst in her.* **3** [**bring** sth ↔ **out**] to produce a book, record etc to be sold to the public: *The Food Association has brought out a handy guide.* **4** [**bring** sb **out**] to make someone feel more confident, happy, and friendly: *When he went to college it really brought him out.* **5** [**bring** sb ↔ **out**] *BrE* to make workers stop working and go on strike (STRIKE[2] (1)): *They are threatening to bring out the power workers next.*

**bring** sb **out in** *phr v* [T] *BrE* if something brings you out in spots, a RASH[2] (1) etc, it makes spots etc appear on your skin: *Chocolate always brings me out in spots.*

**bring** sb **round** —see **bring sb around/round**

**bring** sb **through** (sth) *phr v* [T] to help someone to successfully deal with a very difficult event or period of time: *It was Churchill, above all, who brought us through the war.*

**bring** sb **together** *phr v* [T] to introduce two people to each other or to be the thing that does this: *What brought them together was their mutual love of opera.*

**bring** sb/sth ↔ **up** *phr v* [T] **1** to mention a subject or start to talk about it: *Why did you have to bring up the subject of money?*| *I shall bring up this question at the next meeting.* —see RAISE[1] (USAGE) **2** [usually passive] to educate and care for a child until it is grown up: *He left her to bring up three young children on her own.*| **be brought up (as) a Catholic/Muslim etc** *I was brought up a Lutheran.*| **be brought up to do sth** *In my day, children were brought up to respect the law.* **3** *BrE* to VOMIT[1] something up from your stomach: *He can't eat anything without bringing it up.* **4 bring sb up short/with a start** to make someone suddenly stop talking or doing something: *Her question brought me up short.* **5 bring sb up on a charge of theft/treason etc** to charge someone with a particular crime

**USAGE NOTE: BRING**

WORD CHOICE: **bring, take, fetch, carry**

**Bring** means to take someone or something with you to the place where you are now, to your home, or to the place you have been talking about: *They came to my party and brought me a present.* | *When I'm next in San Francisco, bring your new boyfriend to see me.* | *Have you brought your camera?* **Bring** is also used in the same way for taking something towards the person being spoken to or talked about: *Hold on, I'll bring you a towel.* | *They brought her everything she needed.*

**Take** involves moving in the opposite direction to **bring**: *We went to her party and took her a present.* | *When I'm in San Francisco I'll take you to Alcatraz.* | *Take your camera when you go out* (=NOT usually *carry* here). | *Can you take me home now?*

**Fetch** in British English means to go and get something or someone and bring them back: *Can you fetch Janice from the station?* **Carry** does not give any idea as to the direction of movement, but suggests that you are holding something in your arms or with your hands: *Will you carry the baby/the groceries for me?*

**bringing-up** /ˌ·· ˈ·/ *n* [singular] *AmE* the care and training that parents give their children when they are growing up; UPBRINGING

**brink** /brɪŋk/ *n* **1 be on the brink of** to be almost in a new and very different situation: *Karl is on the brink of a brilliant acting career.* **2 the brink of** *literary* the edge of a very high place such as a cliff

**brink·man·ship** /ˈbrɪŋkmənʃɪp/ *BrE*, **brinks·man·ship** /ˈbrɪŋksmən-/ *AmE* —*n* [U] a method of gaining political advantage by pretending that you are willing to do something very dangerous

**brin·y** /ˈbraɪni/ *adj* water that is briny contains a lot of salt

**bri·oche** /ˈbriːɒʃ, briːˈəʊʃ‖briːˈoʊʃ, -ˈɒːʃ/ *n* [C] a type of sweet bread made with flour, eggs, and butter

**bri·quette** /brɪˈket/ *n* [C] a block of pressed coal dust, to burn in a fire or BARBEQUE

**brisk** /brɪsk/ *adj* **1** quick and full of energy: *a brisk walk* **2** quick, practical and showing that you want to get things done quickly: *She spoke in a brisk tone.* **3** trade or business that is brisk is very busy, with a lot of products being sold **4** weather that is brisk is cold and clear —**briskly** *adv* —**briskness** *n* [U]

**bris·ket** /ˈbrɪskɪ̥t/ *n* [U] meat from an animal's chest, especially a cow

**bris·tle[1]** /ˈbrɪsəl/ *n* [C,U] **1** short stiff hair that feels rough: *His chin was covered with bristles.* **2** a short stiff hair, wire etc that forms part of a brush —see picture at BRUSH[1]

**bristle[2]** *v* [I] **1** to behave in a way that shows you are very angry or annoyed: [+ **with**] *bristling with rage*| [+ **at**] *He bristled at the mere suggestion.* **2** if an animal's hair bristles, it stands up stiffly because the animal is afraid or angry

**bristle with** sth *phr v* [T] to have a lot of something or be full of something: *a battleship bristling with guns*

**bris·tly** /ˈbrɪsli/ *adj* **1** bristly hair is short and stiff **2** a bristly part of your body has short stiff hairs on it: *a bristly chin*

**Brit** /brɪt/ *n* [C] *informal* someone from Britain

**britch·es** /ˈbrɪtʃɪ̥z/ *n* [plural] *AmE* trousers

**Brit·ish** /ˈbrɪtɪʃ/ *adj* **1** from or connected with Great Britain: *the British government* **2 the British** people from Britain

**British Broad·cast·ing Cor·po·ra·tion** /ˌ·· ˈ··· ··ˌ··/ *n* the BBC

**Brit·ish·er** /ˈbrɪtɪʃə‖-ər/ *n* [C] *AmE* someone from Britain

**British Isles** /ˌ·· ˈ·/ *n* the group of islands that includes Great Britain, Ireland, and the smaller islands around them

**British Sum·mer Time** /ˌ·· ˈ·· ·/ *n* [U] the time one hour ahead of Greenwich Mean Time, that is used in Britain from late March to late October —compare DAYLIGHT SAVING TIME

**Brit·on** /ˈbrɪtn/ *n* [C] *formal* someone from Britain: *the ancient Britons*

**brit·tle** /ˈbrɪtl/ *adj* **1** hard but easily broken: *The branches were dry and brittle.* **2** a system, relationship etc that is brittle is easily damaged or destroyed: *a very brittle friendship* **3** showing no warm feelings: *a brittle laugh*

**bro** /brəʊ‖broʊ/ *n* [C] *spoken* **1** your brother **2** *AmE* a way of greeting a friend

**broach** /brəʊtʃ‖broʊtʃ/ *v* [T] **1 broach the subject/question/matter etc** to mention a subject that may be embarrassing, unpleasant or cause an argument: *It's often difficult to broach the subject of sex.* **2** to open a bottle or BARREL (1) containing wine, beer etc

S2 W2 **broad**[1] /brɔːd‖brɒːd/ *adj*
**1** ▶ **WIDE** ◀ a road, river, or part of someone's body etc that is broad is wide: *We went along a broad carpeted passage.*|*He was six feet tall, with broad shoulders and slender hips.*|**6 feet/3 metres etc broad** *The track was three metres broad* —compare NARROW.
**2** ▶ **INCLUDING A LOT** ◀ including many different kinds of things: **broad range/spectrum of** *She has a very broad range of interests.*|**broad category/field/area etc** *In general, the paintings fall into two broad categories.*
**3** ▶ **GENERAL** ◀ concerning the main ideas or parts of something rather than all the details: **broad sense/term/definition etc** *This is education in the broadest sense of the word.*|**broad consensus/agreement etc** *All the members were in broad agreement.*
**4** ▶ **LARGE AREA** ◀ covering a large area of land or water: *They came to a broad expanse of water.*
**5 broad grin/smile** a big smile which clearly shows that you are happy: *"A great win," he said with a broad grin.*
**6 in broad daylight** if something such as a crime happens in broad daylight, it happens in the daytime when you would expect someone to prevent it: *The attack happened in broad daylight, in one of the busiest parts of town.*
**7** ▶ **WAY OF SPEAKING** ◀ a broad ACCENT[1](1) clearly shows where you come from: *a broad Scottish accent*
**8 broad hint/sarcasm** a HINT (=suggestion) etc that is very clear and easy to understand: *dropping broad hints about what she wanted for Christmas*
**9 broad humour/wit etc** humour etc that is slightly rude
**10 it's as broad as it's long** *spoken* used to say that it does not matter which of two things you choose, because neither is clearly better
**11 have a broad back** to be easily able to deal with hard-work, problems etc
**12 broad in the beam** *informal* having large or fat HIPS
**13 a broad church** an organisation that contains a wide range of opinions: *The Labour Party has to be a broad church.* —see also BREADTH

**broad**[2] *n* **1 the Broads** used in the names of some wide parts of rivers in Eastern England: *the Norfolk Broads* **2** [C] *AmE spoken* an offensive way of referring to a woman

**broad·band** /'· ,·/ *n* [U] *technical* a system of sending radio signals which allows several messages to be sent at the same time

**broad bean** /,· '·‖'· ·/ *n* [C] *BrE* a round pale green bean; FAVA BEAN *AmE* —see picture on page 414

**broad·brush, broad-brush** /'brɔːdbrʌʃ‖'brɒːd-/ *adj* dealing only with the main parts of something, and not with the details: *a broadbrush strategy for increasing sales*

**broad·cast**[1] /'brɔːdkɑːst‖'brɒːdkæst/ *n* [C] a programme on the radio or on television: *a radio news broadcast*|**live broadcast** (=a programme that you see or hear at the same time as the events are happening)

**broadcast**[2] *v past tense and past participle* **broadcast** **1** [I,T] to send out radio or television programmes: *The interview was broadcast live across Europe.* **2** [T] to tell something to a lot of people: *There was no need to broadcast the fact that he lost his job.*

**broad·cast·er** /'brɔːdkɑːstə‖'brɒːdkæstər/ *n* [C] someone who speaks on radio or television programmes: *a well-known journalist and broadcaster*

**broad·cast·ing** /'brɔːdkɑːstɪŋ‖'brɒːdkæstɪŋ/ *n* [U] the business of making television and radio programmes: *a career in broadcasting*

**broad·en** /'brɔːdn‖'brɒːdn/ *v* **1** [T] to increase something such as knowledge, experience, or your range of activities: *Broaden your knowledge of English with this book.*|**broaden your horizons** (=increase your activities and opportunities) **2** [I,T] to make something broader or to become broader: *The road broadened into an imposing avenue.* **3 broaden your mind** if an experience broadens your mind, it makes it easier for you to accept other people's beliefs, ways of doing things etc: *Travel broadens the mind.*
**broaden out** *phr v* [I] to gradually become wider: *The river broadens out at this point.*

**broad gauge** /'· ·/ *n* [C] a size of railway track that is wider than the normal size

**broad jump** /'· ·/ *n* [U] *AmE* a sport in which you try to jump as far as possible; LONG JUMP

**broad·loom** /'brɔːdluːm‖'brɒːd-/ *n* [U] *technical* CARPET[1](1) that is woven in a single wide piece

**broad·ly** /'brɔːdli‖'brɒːd-/ *adv* **1** in a general way, covering the main facts rather than details: *She knows broadly what to expect.*|**broadly speaking** *There are, broadly speaking, four types of champagne.*|**broadly similar** *We reached broadly similar conclusions.* **2 smile/grin broadly** to have a big smile on your face which clearly shows that you are happy or amused **3 broadly based** including a range of different things or subjects: *a broadly based approach to education*

**broad·mind·ed, broad-minded** /,brɔːd'maɪndɪd◂‖,brɒːd-/ *adj* willing to respect opinions or behaviour that are very different from your own: *Her parents were broadminded, tolerant and liberal.* —opposite NARROW-MINDED —compare SMALL-MINDED —**broad-mindedly** *adv* —**broad-mindedness** *n* [U]

**broad·sheet** /'brɔːdʃiːt‖'brɒːd-/ *n* [C] a newspaper printed on large sheets of paper, especially a serious newspaper that people respect —compare TABLOID

**broad·side**[1] /'brɔːdsaɪd‖'brɒːd-/ *n* [C] **1** a strong criticism of someone or something especially a written one: *Can the government survive this latest broadside from its own supporters?* **2** an attack in which all the guns on one side of a ship are fired at the same time

**broadside**[2] *AmE* **broadside on** *BrE adv* with the longest side facing something: [+ **to**] *I brought the boat in broadside to the beach.*

**broadside**[3] *v* [T] *especially AmE* to crash into the side of another vehicle

**broad·sword** /'brɔːdsɔːd‖'brɒːdsɔːrd/ *n* [C] a heavy sword with a broad flat blade

**bro·cade** /brə'keɪd‖broʊ-/ *n* [U] thick heavy decorative cloth which has a pattern of gold and silver threads: *brocade curtains* —**brocaded** *adj*

**broc·co·li** /'brɒkəli‖'brɑː-/ *n* [U] a green vegetable that has short branch-like stems —see picture on page 414

**bro·chure** /'brəʊʃə, -ʃʊə‖broʊ'ʃʊr/ *n* [C] a thin book giving information or advertising something: *a glossy holiday brochure*

**brogue** /brəʊg‖broʊg/ *n* [C] **1** a thick strong leather shoe with a pattern in the leather —see picture at SHOE[1] **2** [usually singular] an ACCENT (=way of pronouncing words), especially the one used by the Irish or Scottish people

**broil** /brɔɪl/ *v* [T] *AmE* to cook something under direct heat, or over a flame on a BARBECUE[1] (1) ; GRILL[1] (1) *BrE*: *broiled chicken*

**broil·er** /'brɔɪlə‖-ər/ *n* [C] **1** *AmE* a special area of a STOVE[1] (1) used for cooking food under direct heat; GRILL[2] (1) *BrE* **2** *AmE* a very hot day **3** a broiler chicken

**broiler chick·en** /'·· ,··/ *n* [C] a chicken that is suitable to be cooked by broiling

**broil·ing** /'brɔɪlɪŋ/ *adj AmE* broiling weather, sun etc makes you feel extremely hot: *a day in the broiling sun*

**broke**[1] /brəʊk‖broʊk/ the past tense of BREAK[1]

**broke**[2] *adj* [not before noun] **1** having no money: *I'm fed up with being broke all the time.*|**flat broke** *AmE* **stony broke** *BrE* (=completely broke) **2 go broke** if a company or business goes broke, it can no longer operate because it has no money: *A lot of small businesses went broke in the recession.* **3 go for broke** *informal* to take big risks trying to achieve something: *Why not go for broke and set up your own business?*

**bro·ken**[1] /'brəʊkən‖'broʊ-/ the past participle of BREAK[1]

S3 W3 **broken²** *adj*
**1 ▶ PIECE OF EQUIPMENT ◀** not working properly: *The vacuum cleaner's broken again.* | **get broken** (=become broken) *Somehow the heaters got broken.*
**2 ▶ OBJECT ◀** in small pieces because it has been hit, dropped etc: *Mind the broken glass.* | **get broken** (=become broken) *It got broken in the mail.* —see picture on page 1258
**3 ▶ BONE ◀** cracked because you have had an accident: *a broken leg*
**4 ▶ INTERRUPTED ◀** interrupted and not continuous: *a broken white line* | **broken sleep** (=with interruptions) *sixteen nights of broken sleep because of the baby*
**5 ▶ PERSON ◀** extremely mentally or physically weak because you have suffered a lot: *He returned a broken man.*
**6 broken agreement/promise etc** a promise etc in which someone did not do what they promised
**7 broken English/French etc** English, French etc that is spoken very slowly by someone who only knows a little of the language
**8 broken home** a family that no longer lives together because the parents have divorced (DIVORCE² (1))
**9 broken marriage** a marriage that has ended because the husband and wife do not live together any more
**10 a broken heart** a feeling of extreme sadness, especially because someone you love has died or left you

**broken-heart·ed** /ˌ·· ˈ··◂/ *adj* extremely sad, especially because someone you love has died or left you: *He dumped her for no apparent reason, and left her broken-hearted.* —**broken-heartedly** *adv*

**bro·ker¹** /ˈbrəʊkə‖ˈbroʊkər/ *n* [C] someone who buys and sells shares (SHARE² (6)) in a company, INSURANCE (1), foreign money etc for other people: *an insurance broker*

**broker²** *v* [T] **broker a deal/settlement/treaty etc** to arrange the details of a deal etc so that everyone can agree to it

**bro·ker·age** /ˈbrəʊkərɪdʒ‖ˈbroʊ-/ *n* [U] **1** the business of being a broker **2** the amount of money a broker charges **3 brokerage house/firm** a company of brokers, or the place where they work

**brol·ly** /ˈbrɒli‖ˈbrɑːli/ *n* [C] *BrE informal* an UMBRELLA (1)

**bro·mide** /ˈbrəʊmaɪd‖ˈbroʊ-/ *n* **1** [C,U] a chemical compound, sometimes used in medicine to make people feel calm **2** [C] *formal* a statement which is intended to make someone less angry but which is not effective

**bronc** /brɒŋk‖brɑːŋk/ *n* [C] *informal* a BRONCO

**bron·chi·al** /ˈbrɒŋkiəl‖ˈbrɑːŋ-/ *adj* affecting the bronchial tubes: *a bronchial infection*

**bronchial tube** /ˈ··· ˌ·/ *n* [C usually singular] one of the small tubes that take air into your lungs —see picture at RESPIRATORY

**bron·chi·tis** /brɒŋˈkaɪtɪ̣s‖brɑːŋ-/ *n* [C] an illness which affects your bronchial tubes and makes you cough —**bronchitic** /-ˈkɪtɪk/ *adj*

**bron·co** /ˈbrɒŋkəʊ‖ˈbrɑːŋkoʊ/ *n* [C] a wild horse from the western US: *a bucking bronco*

**bron·to·sau·rus** /ˌbrɒntəˈsɔːrəs‖ˌbrɑːn-/ *n* [C] a large DINOSAUR with a small head and a long neck

**Bronx cheer** /ˌbrɒŋks ˈtʃɪə‖ˌbrɑːŋks ˈtʃɪr/ *n* [C] *AmE* a rude sound you make by putting your tongue between your lips and blowing; RASPBERRY (2) *BrE*

**bronze¹** /brɒnz‖brɑːnz/ *n* **1** [U] a hard metal that is made of a mixture of COPPER (1) and TIN¹ (1) **2** [U] the dark red-brown colour of bronze **3** [C] a work of art such as a STATUE (=model of a person), made of bronze **4** [C] a BRONZE MEDAL

**bronze²** *adj* **1** made of bronze: *a bronze statuette by Degas* **2** having the red-brown colour of bronze

**Bronze Age** /ˈ· ·/ *n* [singular] the time, between about 6000 and 4000 years ago, when bronze was used for making tools, weapons etc —compare IRON AGE, STONE AGE

**bronzed** /brɒnzd‖brɑːnzd/ *adj* having skin that is attractively brown because you have been in the sun

**bronze med·al** /ˌ· ˈ··/ *n* [C] a MEDAL made of bronze given to the person who comes third in a race or competition —**bronze medallist** *n* [C] —see also GOLD MEDAL, SILVER MEDAL

**brooch** /brəʊtʃ‖broʊtʃ/ *n* [C] a piece of jewellery that you fasten to your clothes; PIN¹ (2) *AmE* —see picture at PIN¹

**brood¹** /bruːd/ *v* [I] **1** to keep thinking for a long time about something that you are worried, angry, or upset about: *After the argument Simon sat in his room, brooding.* | **[+ over/about/on]** *There's no point brooding over it – she's gone.* **2** if a bird broods, it sits on its eggs to make the young birds break out

**brood²** *n* [C] **1** a family of young birds all born at the same time **2** *humorous* a family with a lot of children: *Mary has a whole brood of grandchildren.*

**brood·er** /ˈbruːdə‖-ər/ *n* [C] **1** a heated structure for young birds to live in **2** someone who broods a lot

**brood·ing** /ˈbruːdɪŋ/ *adj* mysterious and threatening: *a brooding menacing atmosphere* —**broodingly** *adv*

**brood·y** /ˈbruːdi/ *adj* **1** silent because you are thinking or worrying about something: *Damian's been really broody lately.* **2** *informal* wishing that you had a baby: *I get broody when I see baby clothes in shop windows.* **3** if a female bird is broody, it wants to lay eggs or to sit on them to make the young birds break out —**broodily** *adv* —**broodiness** *n* [U]

**brook¹** /brʊk/ *n* [C] a small stream: *a babbling brook*

**brook²** *v* **not brook sth/brook no sth** *formal* to not allow or accept something: *He would brook no interruptions from subordinates.*

**broom** /bruːm, brʊm/ *n* **1** [C] a large brush with a long handle, used for sweeping floors —see picture at BRUSH¹ **2** [U] a large bush with small yellow flowers that grows on unused land

**broom·stick** /ˈbruːmˌstɪk, ˈbrʊm-/ *n* [C] a broom with a long handle and small sticks tied at one end that a WITCH (1) is supposed to fly on in children's stories

**Bros** the written abbreviation of Brothers, used in the names of companies: *Jones Bros., tailors*

**broth** /brɒθ‖brɒːθ/ *n* [U] thick soup with meat, rice, or vegetables: *chicken broth* —see also SCOTCH BROTH

**broth·el** /ˈbrɒθəl‖ˈbrɑː-, ˈbrɒː-/ *n* [C] a house where men pay to have sex with PROSTITUTES

**broth·er¹** /ˈbrʌðə‖-ər/ *n* [C] **1** a male who has the same parents as you: *This is a picture of my brother Andrew.* | **elder/older/younger/little etc brother** *My younger brother is a doctor.* —see picture at FAMILY **2** a male member of a group with the same interests, religion, profession etc as you: *Brothers, we must stand together to fight the inequalities of the system!* **3** *plural* **brothers** or **brethren** a male member of a religious group, especially a MONK: *Brother Justin* **4** *AmE* a member of a FRATERNITY (=a club of male university students) **5 brothers in arms** soldiers who have fought together in a war —see also BIG BROTHER, BLOOD BROTHER S W

**brother²** *interjection AmE* used to express annoyance or surprise: *Oh brother! Did he really say that?*

**broth·er·hood** /ˈbrʌðəhʊd‖-ər-/ *n* **1** [U] a feeling of friendship between people: *peace and brotherhood among men* **2** [C] an organization or society formed for a particular purpose, especially a religious one: *the Franciscan brotherhood* **3** [C] *old-fashioned* a union of workers in a particular trade **4** [U] the relationship between brothers

**brother-in-law** /ˈ··· ·ˌ·/ *n plural* **brothers-in-law** *or* **brother-in-laws** [C] **1** the brother of your husband or wife **2** the husband of your sister **3** the husband of your husband or wife's sister —see picture at FAMILY

**broth·er·ly** /ˈbrʌðəli‖-ər-/ *adj* showing the helpfulness, love, loyalty etc that you would expect a brother to show: *brotherly love* | *He offered me some brotherly advice.* —**brotherliness** *n* [U]

**brough·am** /ˈbruːəm/ *n* [C] a light carriage used in the past which had four wheels and a roof and was pulled by a horse

**brought** /brɔːt‖brɒːt/ the past tense and past participle of BRING

**brou·ha·ha** /ˈbruːhɑːhɑː‖bruːˈhɑːhɑː/ *n* [U] *old-fashioned* unnecessary noise and activity; COMMOTION

**brow** /braʊ/ *n* **1** [C] the part of your face above your eyes and below your hair; FOREHEAD: **mop/wipe your brow** (=dry your brow with your hand or a piece of cloth when you are hot or nervous) | **crease/wrinkle/knit etc your brow** (=tighten the skin on your brow, making lines appear when you are angry or thinking very hard) *"I don't understand," he said, wrinkling his brow.* **2** an EYEBROW **3 the brow of the hill** *especially BrE* the top part of a slope or hill

**brow·beat** /ˈbraʊbiːt/ *v past tense* **browbeat** *past participle* **browbeaten** /-biːtn/ [T + **into**] to make someone do something by continuously asking them to, especially in an unpleasant threatening way: *The witness was being browbeaten under cross-examination.*

S2 W2 **brown¹** /braʊn/ *adj* **1** having the colour of earth, wood, or coffee: *I'd like a pair of dark brown shoes please.* | *brown bread* **2** having skin that has been turned brown by the sun: *You're very brown – have you been on vacation?* | **brown as a berry** (=very brown) *She came back as brown as a berry.*

**brown²** *n* [C,U] the colour of earth, wood, or coffee: *the different browns and greens of the landscape* —see picture on page 411

**brown³** *v* [I,T] **1** to heat food so that it turns brown or to become brown in this way by being heated: *First brown the meat in a frying pan.* **2** to become brown because of the sun's heat or to make something brown in this way: *The children's faces were browned by the sun.* **3 browned off** *BrE informal* annoyed and bored

**brown-bag** /ˈ· ·/ *v* [I] *AmE* **1** to bring your LUNCH to work, usually in a small brown paper bag: *I'm brown-bagging it this week.* **2** to bring your own alcohol to a restaurant which does not serve alcohol —**brown-bagging** *n* [U]

**brown goods** /ˈ· ·/ *n* [plural] *BrE* electrical goods bought to provide entertainment at home, such as televisions and computers —compare WHITE GOODS

**Brown·ie** /ˈbraʊni/ also **Brownie Guide** /ˈ·· ·/ *n* **1 the Brownies** the part of the Girl Guides Association that is for younger girls **2** [C] a member of this organization

**brownie** *n* [C] **1** a thick flat American chocolate cake: *fudge brownies* **2 get/earn brownie points** *informal* if you do something to get brownie points you want people to praise you

**brown-nose** /ˈ· ·/ *v* [I,T] *informal* to try to make your manager, teacher etc like you by being very nice to them: *You're not going to get that promotion just by brown-nosing!* —**brown-nose** *n* [C]

**brown out** /ˈ· ·/ *n* [C] *AmE* a power failure affecting some but not all the electrical lights in an area

**brown rice** /ˌ· ˈ·/ *n* [U] rice which still has its outer layer

**brown·stone** /ˈbraʊnstəʊn‖-stoʊn/ *n* **1** [U] a type of reddish-brown stone, often used for building **2** [C] a house in the US with a front made of this stone, common in New York City: *office buildings side by side with the more elegant brownstones*

**browse** /braʊz/ *v* [I] **1** to look through the pages of a book, magazine etc without a particular purpose, just reading the most interesting parts: [+ **through**] *I was browsing through a newspaper when I spotted your name.* **2** to look at the goods in a shop without wanting to buy any particular thing: *Can I help you, madam, or are you just browsing?* **3** [+ **on**] if a goat, DEER etc browses, it eats plants **4** to search computer material: *a fast effective browsing tool*

**bruise¹** /bruːz/ *n* [C] **1** a purple or brown mark on your skin that you get because you have fallen, been hit etc **2** a mark on a piece of fruit that spoils its appearance

**bruise²** *v* [I,T] **1** if part of you body bruises or if you bruise it, it gets hit or hurt and a bruise appears: *She fell off her bike and bruised her knee.* **2** if a piece of fruit bruises or is bruised, it gets a bruise by being hit, dropped etc —**bruising** *n* [U] *severe bruising to the face and head*

**bruised** /bruːzd/ *adj* **1 bruised ribs/knee/elbow etc** a part of your body with a bruise on it **2** upset or emotionally harmed by an experience

**bruis·er** /ˈbruːzə‖-ər/ *n* [C] *informal* a big strong rough man: *Two ugly bruisers barred the door.*

**bruit** /bruːt/ *v*

**bruit** sth ↔ **abroad** *phr v* [T] *formal* to tell a lot of people about something

**brunch** /brʌntʃ/ *n* [C,U] a meal eaten in the late morning, as a combination of breakfast and LUNCH

**bru·nette** /bruːˈnet/ *n* [C] a woman with dark brown hair: *a slim brunette*

**brunt** /brʌnt/ *n* **bear/take the brunt of sth** to receive the worst part of an attack, criticism etc: *The southern part of the town bore the brunt of the attack.*

**brushes**

**brush¹** /brʌʃ/ *n* S3

**1** ▶ **FOR CLEANING** ◀ [C] an object that you use for cleaning, painting etc, made with a lot of hairs, bristles (BRISTLE¹ (2)), or thin pieces of plastic fixed to a handle: *a hairbrush* | *Get a brush and sweep up all that rubbish.*

**2** [singular] a movement which brushes something, to remove dirt, make something smooth, tidy etc: *I'll just give my hair a quick brush.*

**3** ▶ **TOUCH** ◀ [singular] a quick light touch, made by chance when two things or people pass each other: *the brush of her silk dress as she walked past*

**4** ▶ **BUSHES/TREES** ◀ [U] **a)** *AmE* small bushes and trees covering an open area of land **b)** branches which have broken off bushes and trees

**5 a brush with death/a brush with the law etc** an occasion when something bad almost happens to you, but you just manage to avoid it

**6** ▶ **TAIL** ◀ [C] the tail of a FOX¹ (1) —see also **daft as a brush** (DAFT (1))

**brush²** *v* **1** [T] to clean something or make something smooth and tidy using a brush: *Don't forget to brush your teeth.* **2** [T always + adv/prep] to remove something with a brush or with your hand: **brush sth off/away etc** *Brush the crumbs off your jacket, you messy thing.|He brushed his hair out of his eyes.* **3** [I always + adv/prep, T] to touch someone or something lightly by chance when passing them: [+ **against**] *I felt her hair brush against my arm.|* **brush sth** *The car brushed the hedges of the narrow lane.* **4 brush yourself down** *BrE* **brush yourself off** *AmE* to tidy yourself, especially after a fall, by using your hands to brush your clothes etc: *I got up, brushed myself down, and carried on walking.*

**brush** sb/sth ↔ **aside** *phr v* [T] to refuse to listen to or consider something: *He simply brushed all my objections aside.*

**brush** sth ↔ **down** *phr v* [T] to clean your clothes or an animal thoroughly using a brush

**brush** sth ↔ **off** *phr v* [T] refuse to listen to someone or their ideas, especially by ignoring them or saying something rude: *The President brushed off their pleas for an investigation.*

**brush up (on)** sth *phr v* [I] to quickly practise and improve your skills or knowledge: *I must brush up on my French before I go to Paris.*

**brushed** /brʌʃt/ *adj* [only before noun] a brushed cloth has been specially treated to make it feel much softer: *brushed cotton*

**brush-off** /ˈ· ·/ *n* [singular] a clear sign that you do not want someone's friendship, invitations etc: **give sb the brush-off** *I thought Andy liked me, but he gave me the brush-off.*

**brush·wood** /ˈbrʌʃwʊd/ *n* [U] small dead branches broken from trees or bushes

**brush·work** /ˈbrʌʃwɜːk‖-wɜːrk/ *n* [U] the particular way in which someone puts paint on a picture using a brush

**brusque** /bruːsk, brʊsk‖brʌsk/ *adj* using very few words in a way that seems rude but is not intended to be: *He was rather brusque on the phone.* —**brusquely** *adv*: *"You'd better leave," she said brusquely.* —**brusqueness** *n* [U]

**brus·sels sprout** /ˌbrʌsəlz ˈspraʊt/ *n* [C] a small round green vegetable with many tightly folded leaves; SPROUT[2] (1) —see picture on page 414

**bru·tal** /ˈbruːtl/ *adj* **1** very cruel and violent: *a brutal and savage crime* **2** unkind and not sensitive to people's feelings: **brutal honesty/frankness etc** *They told us all the details with brutal honesty.* —**brutally** *adv*: *brutally honest* —**brutality** /bruːˈtælɪti/ *n* [C,U]|*the brutalities of war*

**bru·tal·ize** also **-ise** *BrE* /ˈbruːtəl-aɪz/ *v* [T usually passive] **1** to affect someone so badly that they lose their normal human feelings: *brutalized by their experiences in jail* **2** to treat someone in a cruel or violent way: *systematically abused and brutalized* —**brutalization** /ˌbruːtəl-aɪˈzeɪʃən‖-lə-/ *n* [U]

**brute**[1] /bruːt/ *n* [C] **1** *often humorous* a man who is rough, cruel and not sensitive: *Don't hit him, you brute!* **2** *literary* an animal, especially a large or strong one

**brute**[2] *adj* **brute force/strength etc** physical strength rather than thought or intelligence: *He won, not so much by skill as by brute force.*

**brut·ish** /ˈbruːtɪʃ/ *adj* showing no human intelligence or feeling —**brutishly** *adv* —**brutishness** *n* [U]

**Bryl·creem** /ˈbrɪlkriːm/ *n* [U] *trademark* a type of oil used on men's hair to make it shiny and smooth

**BS** /ˌbiː ˈes/ *n* [U] *AmE informal* an abbreviation of BULLSHIT

**BSc** /ˌbiː es ˈsiː/ Bachelor of Science; a first university degree in a science subject: *Barbara Stone, BSc* —compare BA

**BSE** /ˌbiː es ˈiː/ *n* [U] bovine spongiform encephalitis; a deadly brain disease in cows

**B-side** /ˈbiː saɪd/ *n* [C] the less important side of a record

**BST** /ˌbiː es ˈtiː/ *n* [U] the abbreviation of British Summer Time

**bub** /bʌb/ *n* [C] *AmE slang* used to speak to a man, especially when you are angry: *Hey, what do you think you're doing, bub?*

**bub·ble**[1] /ˈbʌbəl/ *n* [C] **1** a ball of air in liquid: *When water boils, bubbles rise to the surface.|soap bubbles|* **blow bubbles** *She was blowing bubbles in her milk with a straw.* **2** a small amount of air trapped in a solid substance: *Examine the glass carefully for bubbles.* **3** also **speech bubble** *BrE* a circle around the words said by someone in a CARTOON (1) **4 prick/burst the bubble** to make someone suddenly realize the unpleasant truth about something that seemed wonderful or perfect: *The relationship was great at first but that bubble soon burst.* **5 burst sb's bubble** to destroy someone's beliefs or hopes about something: *Coming second in the contest really burst his bubble.* **6** a large clear plastic tent used to protect a seriously ill person from infection

**bubble**[2] *v* **1** [I] to produce bubbles: *Heat the cheese until it bubbles.|*[+ **up**] *The cola bubbled up when I unscrewed the lid.* **2** [I] to make the sound that water makes when it boils: [+ **away**] *The water was bubbling away on the stove.* **3** [I] also **bubble over** to be excited: [+ **with**] *bubbling over with enthusiasm*

**bubble and squeak** /ˌ·· ·ˈ·/ *n* [U] a British dish of potatoes and CABBAGE (1) mixed together and cooked in fat

**bubble bath** /ˈ·· ·/ *n* **1** [U] a liquid soap that smells pleasant and makes bubbles in your bath water **2** [C] a bath with this in the water

**bubble gum**[1] /ˈ·· ·/ *n* [U] a type of CHEWING GUM that you can blow into a BUBBLE[1] (2)

**bubble gum**[2] *adj AmE* connected with children between about seven and thirteen years old: *a magazine aimed at the bubble gum set*

**bubble jet print·er** /ˈ·· · ˌ··/ *n* [C] a type of machine for printing from a computer that SPRAYs ink onto the paper

**bub·bly**[1] /ˈbʌbli/ *adj* **1** full of BUBBLES **2** someone who is bubbly always seems cheerful, friendly, and eager to do things: *Angie's irresistably bubbly personality*

**bubbly**[2] *n* [U] *informal* CHAMPAGNE

**bu·bon·ic plague** /bjuːˌbɒnɪk ˈpleɪg‖buːˌbɑː-/ *n* [U] a very serious disease spread by rats, that killed large numbers of people in the Middle Ages —see also BLACK DEATH, PLAGUE[1] (2)

**buc·ca·neer** /ˌbʌkəˈnɪə‖-ˈnɪr/ *n* [C] **1** someone who attacks ships at sea and steals from them; PIRATE[1] (3) **2** someone who succeeds, especially in business, by using any method, including cheating

**buck**[1] /bʌk/ *n* [C]

**1** ▶ **MONEY** ◀ *AmE, AustrE informal* a dollar: *He owes me ten bucks.|* **big bucks** (=a lot of money)| **make a fast buck** (=make some money quickly, often dishonestly)

**2 pass the buck** to try to blame someone else or make them responsible for something that you should deal with: *You were the one who took on this job. Don't try to pass the buck.*

**3 the buck stops here** used to say that you are the person who is responsible when no-one else will accept the responsibility

**4** ▶ **MALE ANIMAL** ◀ *plural* **buck** or **bucks** a male DEER, rabbit etc —compare DOE

**5 feel/look like a million bucks** *AmE informal* to feel or look very healthy, happy, and beautiful

**6 buck naked** *AmE informal* wearing no clothes at all

**7** ▶ **WELL-DRESSED MAN** ◀ a well-dressed young man in early 19th-century England: *a Regency buck*

**buck**[2] *v*

**1** ▶ **HORSE** ◀ [I] if a horse bucks, it kicks its back feet into the air, or jumps with all four feet off the ground

**2** ▶ **THROW SB** ◀ [T] to throw a rider off by jumping in this way

**3** ▶ **CAR** ◀ [I] *AmE* if a car bucks, it moves forward in a way which is not smooth, but stops and starts suddenly

**4** ▶ **OPPOSE** ◀ *informal* to oppose something in a direct way; RESIST [+ **against/at**] *Initially he bucked against her restraints, but later came to accept them.|* **buck the system** (=avoid the usual rules) *natural rebels, with the guts it takes to buck the system|* **buck a**

**trend** *The growth of the company has bucked the current recessionary trend in the industry.*

**buck for** sth *phr v* [T] to try very hard to get something, especially a good position at work: *He's bucking for promotion.*

**buck up** *phr v* **1** [I,T **buck** sb **up**] to become more cheerful or make someone more cheerful: *Come on, buck up, things aren't that bad!* **2 buck up!** *BrE spoken* used to tell someone to hurry up: *Buck up, John! We'll be late.* **3 buck your ideas up** *BrE informal* used to tell someone to try harder to improve their behaviour or attitude

**buck·a·roo** /ˌbʌkəˈruː/ *n* [C] *AmE informal* a word meaning COWBOY (1), used especially when speaking to children

**buck·board** /ˈbʌkbɔːd‖-bɔːrd/ *n* [C] a light vehicle which has four wheels and is pulled by a horse, used in the US in the 19th century

**bucked** /bʌkt/ *adj* [not before noun] *BrE old-fashioned* very pleased: [+ **at/by**] *We were bucked at the news.*

S 2 **buck·et¹** /ˈbʌkɪ̈t/ *n* [C]

**1 ▶ CONTAINER ◀** an open container with a handle, used for carrying and holding things, especially earth or water: *a bucket of water*

**2** also **bucketful** the quantity of liquid that a bucket can hold: [+ **of**] *It took four buckets of water to wash the car.*

**3 ▶ PART OF MACHINE ◀** a part of a machine shaped like a large bucket and used for moving earth, water etc

**4 by the bucket/bucketful** *informal* in large quantities: *drinking beer by the bucket*

**5 sweat/weep buckets** *informal* to SWEAT¹ (1) or cry a lot

**6 in buckets** *informal* if rain comes down in buckets, it is raining very heavily —see also **kick the bucket** (KICK¹ (12)), **a drop in the bucket** (DROP² (8))

**bucket²** *v*

**bucket down** *phr v* [I] *BrE informal* to rain very hard: *It's been bucketing down all day.*

**bucket shop** /ˈ·· ·/ *n* [C] *BrE informal* a business that sells cheap tickets for air travel

**buck·le¹** /ˈbʌkəl/ *v* **1** [I,T] to fasten a buckle or be joined together with a buckle: *The strap buckles at the side.* | **buckle sth** *buckle a satchel* | **buckle sth on/up/together** *Lou was buckling on his revolver.* **2** [I,T] to become bent or curved because of heat or pressure, or to make something bend or curve in this way: *The rails buckled under the intense heat of the fire.* **3** [I] if your knees or legs buckle, they become weak and bend: *I felt a blow and my knees started to buckle.*

**buckle down** *phr v* [I] to start working seriously: [+ **to**] *You'd better buckle down to some revision now.*

**buckle up** *phr v* [I] *especially AmE* to fasten your SEAT BELT in a car, aircraft etc

**buckle²** *n* [C] a metal fastener used for joining the two ends of a belt or STRAP¹, for fastening a shoe, bag etc, or for decoration —see picture at FASTENER

**buck·ler** /ˈbʌklə‖-ər/ *n* [C] *especially literary* a small circular SHIELD¹ (1a) with a raised centre

**buck·ram** /ˈbʌkrəm/ *n* [U] stiff cloth, used in the past for covering books, making the stiff parts of clothes etc

**Buck's Fizz** /ˌbʌks ˈfɪz/ *n* [C, U] a mixture of CHAMPAGNE and orange juice, or a glass of this

**buck·shee** /ˌbʌkˈʃiː◂/ *adv BrE old-fashioned* without payment; free —**buckshee** *adj*

**buck·shot** /ˈbʌkʃɒt‖-ʃɑːt/ *n* [U] a lot of small metal balls that you fire together from a gun

**buck·skin** /ˈbʌkˌskɪn/ *n* [U] strong soft leather made from the skin of a DEER or goat

**buck teeth** /ˌ· ˈ·/ *n* [plural] teeth that stick forward out of your mouth —**buck-toothed** /ˌ· ˈ·◂/ *adj*

**buck·wheat** /ˈbʌkwiːt/ *n* [U] a type of small grain used as food for chickens, and for making FLOUR

**bu·col·ic** /bjuːˈkɒlɪk‖-ˈkɑː-/ *adj literary* connected with the countryside: *a church, lovely in its bucolic setting* —**bucolically** /-kli/ *adv*

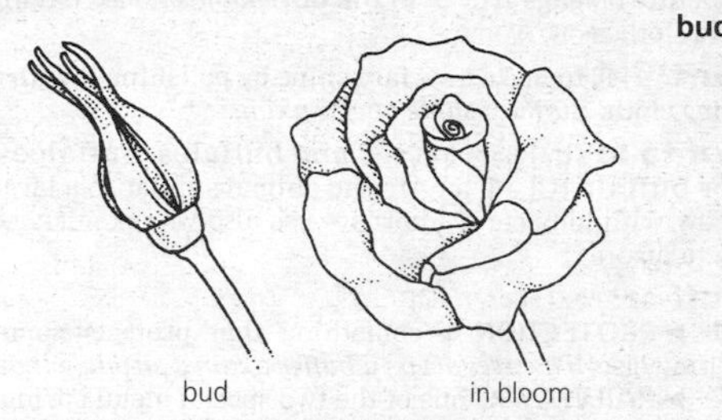


**bud¹** /bʌd/ *n* [C] **1** a young tightly rolled up flower or leaf before it opens: *rose buds* | **in bud** (=having buds but no flowers yet) | **come into bud** (=start to produce buds) **2** *AmE informal* BUDDY —see also COTTON BUD, TASTE BUD **nip sth in the bud** (NIP¹ (3))

**bud²** *v* **budded, budding** [I] to produce buds

**Bud·dhis·m** /ˈbʊdɪzəm‖ˈbuː-, ˈbʊ-/ *n* [U] a religion of east and central Asia, based on the teaching of Gautama Buddha —**Buddhist** *n* [C] —**Buddhist** *adj*

**bud·ding** /ˈbʌdɪŋ/ *adj* **1 budding singer/actor/writer etc** someone who is just starting to sing, act etc and will probably be successful at it **2** [only before noun] beginning to develop: *a budding relationship*

**bud·dy** /ˈbʌdi/ *n* [C] **1** *informal* a friend: *We're good buddies.* **2** *AmE spoken* used to speak to a man you do not know; BUD¹(2): *Hey, buddy! This your car?* **3** someone who offers to look after and become a friend to a person who has AIDS

**buddy-bud·dy** /ˈ·· ˌ··/ *adj AmE informal* very friendly with someone

**buddy sys·tem** /ˈ·· ˌ··/ *n* [C] *AmE* a system in which two people help each other or keep each other safe

**budge** /bʌdʒ/ *v* [I,T usually in negatives] *informal* **1** to move, or move someone or something from one place to another: *Come on – budge. I can't get past.* | **budge sth** *The car was stuck in the snow and we couldn't budge it.* | [+ **from**] *Will hasn't budged from his room all day.* **2** to make someone change their opinion: *It's no good, Dad won't budge.* | **not budge an inch** (=not change at all)

**bud·ge·ri·gar** /ˈbʌdʒərɪgɑː‖-gɑːr/ *n* [C] a small brightly-coloured bird that people keep at home as a pet; BUDGIE

**bud·get¹** /ˈbʌdʒɪ̈t/ *n* [C] **1** a plan of how a person or organization will spend the money that is available in a particular period of time, or the money itself: *planning the annual budget* | [+ **of**] *a welfare program with a budget of $2 billion* | **defence/advertising etc budget** (=money available for defence etc) | **over/under budget** (=having spent more or less than the amount allowed in a budget) | **budget deficit** (=a situation in which more money has been spent than is available) | **balance the budget** (=make sure that only money available is spent) | **be on a tight budget** (=not have much money to spend) **2** an official statement that a government makes about how much it intends to spend and what taxes will be necessary  S 1 W 2

**budget²** *v* **1** [I] to carefully plan and control how much you spend: *We'll just have to budget more sensibly in the future.* | **budget for** (=plan how much you need for something) *We've budgeted for a new car next year.* **2** [I,T] to plan carefully how much of something will be needed: *She's learned how to budget her time carefully.*

**budget³** *adj* [only before noun] very low in price; cheap: *a budget flight*

**bud·get·a·ry** /ˈbʌdʒɪ̈təri‖-teri/ *adj* connected with the way money is spent in a budget: *budgetary restrictions*

**bud·gie** /ˈbʌdʒi/ *n* [C] *BrE* a small brightly coloured bird that people keep at home as a pet; BUDGERIGAR

**buff¹** /bʌf/ *n* **1** [C] **film/computer/jazz etc buff** someone who is interested in films, computers etc and knows a lot about them **2** [U] a pale yellow-brown colour —see picture on page 411 **3 in the buff** *old-fashioned* having no clothes on; NAKED

**buff²** *v* [T] to make a surface shine by polishing it with a dry cloth: *Buff to a shine after waxing.*

B

**buf·fa·lo** /ˈbʌfələʊ‖-loʊ/ *n plural* **buffalos, buffaloes,** or **buffalo** [C] **1** an African animal similar to a large cow with long curved horns —see also WATER BUFFALO **2** a BISON

**buff·er¹** /ˈbʌfə‖-ər/ *n* [C]
**1** ▶ **PROTECTION** ◀ something that protects something else: *The trees act as a buffer against strong winds.*
**2** ▶ **RAILWAY** ◀ one of the two special metal springs on the front or back of a train or at the end of a railway track to take the shock if the train hits something
**3 buffer zone** an area between two armies, which is intended to separate them so that they do not fight
**4 buffer state** a smaller peaceful country between two larger countries, which makes war between them less likely: *Part of the settlement was to create a Serbian buffer state.*
**5** ▶ **COMPUTER** ◀ a place in a computer's memory for storing information temporarily
**6** ▶ **PERSON** ◀ *BrE old-fashioned* an old man who seems silly: *You stupid old buffer!*
**7** ▶ **FOR POLISHING** ◀ something used to polish a surface: *Where's my nail buffer?*
**8 hit the buffers** *informal* an official discussion that hits the buffers does not have a successful result

**buffer²** *v* [T] to reduce the bad effects of something: *buffering the effects of the recession*

**buf·fet¹** /ˈbʊfeɪ‖bəˈfeɪ/ *n* [C] **1** a place in a railway station, bus station etc where you can buy and eat food or drink **2** a meal of cold food at a party or other occasion, in which people serve themselves at a table and then move away to eat: **buffet lunch/supper** *We had a buffet lunch for Hayley's christening*|**finger buffet** (=with food that you eat with your hands) **3** *BrE* the part of the train where you can buy food and drink; DINING CAR **4** a piece of furniture in which you keep the things you use to serve and eat a meal

**buffet²** /ˈbʌfɪ̟t/ *v* [T usually passive] **1** if wind, rain, or the sea buffets something, it hits it with a lot of force: *London was buffeted by storms last night.* **2** *literary* to treat someone unkindly: *weary of being buffeted by life* —**buffeting** *n* [C]

**buffet** sb/sth **about** *phr v* [I] to knock or hit something and make it move

**buf·foon** /bəˈfuːn/ *n* [C] *old-fashioned* someone who does silly things that make you laugh —**buffoonery** *n* [U]

**bug¹** /bʌg/ *n* [C] **1** *especially AmE* a small insect, especially one that people think is unpleasant **2** *informal* an illness that people catch very easily from each other but is not very serious: **pick up a bug** (=get a bug)|**tummy/stomach bug** (=illness affecting your stomach) **3 the travel/ski/parachuting etc bug** *informal* a sudden strong interest in doing something that usually lasts only a short time: *bitten by the fitness bug.* **4** a small fault in the system of instructions that operates a computer —see also DEBUG **5** a small piece of electronic equipment for listening secretly to other people's conversations.

**bug²** *v* **bugged, bugging** [T] **1** *informal* to annoy: *It really bugs me when the car behind me drives too close.* **2** to put a BUG¹ (5) somewhere secretly in order to listen to conversations: *Do you think the room is bugged?*

**bug·a·boo** /ˈbʌgəbuː/ *n* [C] *old-fashioned* an imaginary thing or person that children are scared of

**bug·bear** /ˈbʌgbeə‖-ber/ *n* [C] something that makes people feel worried or scared: *the old bugbear – communism*

**bug-eyed** /ˌbʌgˈaɪd◂/ *adj* having eyes that stick out

**bug·ger¹** /ˈbʌgə‖-ər/ *n* [C] *spoken especially BrE* S2
**1** *taboo* someone who is very annoying or unpleasant: *Bill's an obnoxious little bugger.* **2** a rude word meaning someone that you pretend to be annoyed with, although you actually like them: *What are you doing, you daft bugger?* **3** a rude word meaning a job or activity that is very difficult: *Having to commute so far is a real bugger.* **4 bugger all** rude expression meaning nothing, used especially when you are angry: *There's bugger all we can do about the car now.*|**bugger all help/thanks/work etc** (=none at all) *I got bugger all thanks for driving my boss to the airport.* **5 play silly buggers** a rude expression meaning to behave in a stupid way that annoys other people: *Stop playing silly buggers and get on with your homework!* **6** *taboo* a man who regularly has ANAL SEX, especially with other men or boys

**bugger²** *v* [T] *BrE* **1 bugger (it)!** *spoken* a rude expression used when you are angry because something bad has happened: *Bugger it! The car battery is dead.* **2 I'll be buggered/bugger me!** *spoken* a rude expression used when you are surprised about something **3 bugger the ...** *slang* used to say that you do not care about the person or thing you are talking about: *Bugger the expense, I'm going to buy it!* **4 I'll be buggered if..** *slang* used to say angrily that you will not do something: *I'll be buggered if I help them any more.* **5** *taboo or law* to have ANAL sex with someone

**bugger about** also **bugger around** *phr v BrE* **1** [I] to behave in a stupid way or waste time: *Stop buggering about and get on with your work* **2** [T **bugger** sb **about**] to cause unnecessary problems for someone: *Don't let Peter bugger you about, tell him to leave.*

**bugger off** *phr v* [I often imperative] *BrE* an impolite expression meaning to go away, or leave a place, which is very rude when used directly: *Bugger off and leave me alone!*|*Simon's always buggering off home early.*

**bugger** sth ↔ **up** *phr v* [T] *BrE* to do something stupid that ruins something or causes trouble: *You really buggered up our plans by arriving late.*

**bug·gered** /ˈbʌgəd‖-ərd/ *adj* [not before noun] **1** *BrE slang* a rude word meaning extremely tired: *That's the last time I work so late. I'm buggered!* **2** *BrE slang* a rude word meaning completely ruined or broken: *The washing machine's buggered.* **3 I'm buggered** *BrE spoken* used to say that you are very surprised by something or cannot understand it: *I'm buggered if I know why they didn't come!*

**bug·ger·y** /ˈbʌgəri/ *n* [U] *BrE law* ANAL sex

**bug·gy** /ˈbʌgi/ *n* [C] **1** *BrE* a light folding chair on wheels that you push small children in; STROLLER (1) *AmE* **2** a light carriage pulled by a horse **3** *AmE* a thing like a small bed on wheels, that a baby lies in; PRAM *BrE*

**bu·gle** /ˈbjuːgəl/ *n* [C] a musical instrument like a TRUMPET¹ (1) which is used in the army to call soldiers —**bugler** *n* [C]

**build¹** /bɪld/ *v past tense and past participle* **built** /bɪlt/ 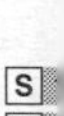
**1** ▶ **MAKE STH** ◀ [I,T] to make something, especially a building or something large: *Are they going to build on this land?*|**build sb sth** *Nick said he'd build us a fitted wardrobe.*
**2** ▶ **MAKE STH DEVELOP** ◀ [T] to make something develop or form: *Kate's working hard to build a career.*|**build (up) a picture of sb/sth** (=form a clear idea about someone or something) *The police are trying to build up a picture of Haig's daily routine.*
**3** ▶ **FEELING** ◀ [I,T] if a feeling builds or you build it, it increases gradually over a period of time: *Tension is building between the two countries.*

**4 well-built/brick-built etc** used for describing how large someone is, what something is made of, or how it was built: *a heavily-built man|a brick-built house*
**5 be built of** to be made using particular materials: *a cottage built of Cumbrian slate*
**6 be built on/around** to happen as a result of something: *The company's success is built on its very popular home computers.*
**7 build bridges** to try to establish a better relationship between people who do not like each other

**build** sth ↔ **in** *phr v* [T usually passive] to make something so that it is a permanent part of a wall, room etc

**build** sth ↔ **into** *phr v* [T] **1** to make something so that it is a permanent part of a wall, room etc **2** to make something a permanent part of a system, agreement etc: *A completion date was built into the contract.* —see also BUILT-IN

**build on** sth *phr v* **1** [T **build** sth ↔ **on**] to add another room etc to a building in order to have more space **2** [**build on** sth] to use your achievements as a base for further development: *Now we must build on our success in Italy.* —see also **be built on** (BUILD[1] (5))

**build up** *phr v*
**1** ▶ **PRAISE** ◀ [T **build** sb/sth ↔ **up**] to praise someone or something so that other people think they are really good: *You have to build kids up – make them feel important.*
**2** ▶ **MAKE STRONGER** ◀ [T **build** sb ↔ **up**] to make someone well and strong again, especially after an illness: *Build your mother up with nourishing food.*
**3** ▶ **FEELING** ◀ [I,T **build** sth ↔ **up**] if a feeling builds up or you build it up, it increases gradually over a period of time: *Try and build up his confidence a bit.*
**4** ▶ **INCREASE GRADUALLY** ◀ [I,T **build** sth ↔ **up**] if a substance, force, or activity builds up somewhere or you build it up, it gradually becomes bigger and stronger: *Both sides have built up huge stockpiles of arms.* —see also BUILD-UP (1)
**5 build up sb's hopes** to unfairly encourage someone to think that they will get what they hope for

**build up to** sth *phr v* [T] to prepare for a particular moment or event: *I could tell she was building up to some kind of announcement.* —see also BUILD-UP (3)

**build²** *n* [singular,U] the shape and size of someone's body: *a powerful build* —see BODY (USAGE)

3 **build·er** /ˈbɪldə‖-ər/ *n* [C] *especially BrE* a person or a company that builds or repairs buildings

**builders' mer·chant** /ˈ·· ˌ··/ *n* [C] *BrE* a company that stores and sells building materials such as bricks, cement, and sand

1 **build·ing** /ˈbɪldɪŋ/ *n* [C] **1** a structure such as a house,
1 church, or factory, that has a roof and walls: *one of the tallest buildings in the world* **2** [U] the process or business of building things: *The next major step is the building of a gym.*|**building costs/programmes/regulations etc** *Building costs will have to be reduced.*

**building block** /ˈ··· ·/ *n* [C] **1** a block of wood or plastic for young children to build things with **2 building blocks** [plural] the pieces or parts which together make it possible for something big or important to exist: *Amino acids are the fundamental building blocks of protein.*

**building con·trac·tor** /ˈ·· ·ˌ··‖ˈ··ˌ··/ *n* [C] someone whose job is to organize the building of a house, office, factory etc

**building site** /ˈ·· ·/ *n* [C] a place where a house, factory etc is being built

**building so·ci·e·ty** /ˈ·· ·ˌ···/ *n* [C] *BrE* a type of bank that you pay money into in order to save it and earn interest and that will lend you money to buy a house or apartment; SAVINGS AND LOAN ASSOCIATION *AmE*

**build-up** /ˈ· ·/ *n* **1** [U singular] an increase over a period of time: *a heavy build-up of traffic on the motorway* **2** [C] a description of someone or something in which you say they are very special or important: **give sb a big build-up** *The presenter gave her a big build-up.* **3** [C] the length of time spent preparing an event: [+ **to**] *the long build-up to the opening of the Channel Tunnel* —see also **build up** (BUILD[1])

**built** /bɪlt/ the past tense and past participle of BUILD

**built-in** /ˌ· ˈ·◂/ *adj* forming a part of something that cannot be separated from it: *a built-in microphone* —see also **build in** (BUILD[1])

**built-up** /ˌ· ˈ·◂/ *adj* a built-up area has a lot of buildings and not many open spaces: *speeding in a built-up area*

**bulb** /bʌlb/ *n* [C] **1** the glass part of an electric light, that the light shines from; LIGHT BULB: *a 100 watt bulb* —see picture at LIGHT[1] **2** a root shaped like a ball that grows into a flower or plant: *tulip bulbs*

**bul·bous** /ˈbʌlbəs/ *adj* fat and round and unattractive: *a bulbous nose*

**bulge¹** /bʌldʒ/ *n* [C] **1** a curved mass on the surface of something, usually caused by something under or inside it: *The wallet made a fat bulge in his pocket.* **2** a sudden temporary increase in the amount or level of something: *a bulge in the birthrate* —**bulgy** *adj*: *bulgy-eyed*

**bulge²** *v* [I] **1** also **bulge out** to stick out in a rounded shape, especially because something is very full or too tight: [+ **with**] *His pockets were bulging with candy.* **2** [+ **with**] *informal* to be very full of people or things

**bul·gur** /ˈbʌlgə‖-ər/ *n* [U] a type of wheat which has been dried and broken into pieces

**bu·lim·i·a** /bjuːˈlɪmiə,bʊ-/ *n* [U] an illness in which a person cannot stop themselves from eating too much, and then vomits (VOMIT[1]) in order to control their weight —**bulimic** *adj*

**bulk¹** /bʌlk/ *n* **1 the bulk (of sth)** the main or largest part of something: *the bulk of the workforce* **2** [C usually singular] a big mass of something **3** [U] the size of something or someone: *The dough will rise until it is double in bulk.* **4 in bulk** if you buy goods in bulk, you buy large amounts each time you buy them

**bulk²** *adj* **1 bulk buying/orders etc** the buying etc of goods in large quantities at one time **2** [only before noun] bulk goods are sold or moved in large quantities: *bulk flour for commercial bakeries* **3 bulk mail** the posting of large amounts of mail for a smaller cost than usual

**bulk³ bulk large** *v literary* to be the main or most important part of something

**bulk** sth ↔ **out** *phr v* [T] to make something look bigger or thicker, by adding something else: *We can bulk out the report with lots of diagrams.*

**bulk·head** /ˈbʌlkhed/ *n* [C] a wall which divides the structure of a ship or aircraft into separate parts

**bulk·y** /ˈbʌlki/ *adj* **1** something that is bulky is bigger than other things of its type and is difficult to carry or store: *a bulky parcel|a new elastic that is less bulky* **2** someone who is bulky is big and heavy —**bulkiness** *n* [U]

**bull¹** /bʊl/ *n* [C]
**1** ▶ **MALE COW** ◀ an adult male animal of the cattle family: *A mean-looking bull was standing in the path.*
**2** ▶ **MALE ANIMAL** ◀ the male of some other large animals such as the ELEPHANT or WHALE
**3 take the bull by the horns** to bravely or confidently deal with a difficult, dangerous, or unpleasant problem: *She decided to take the bull by the horns and ask him outright.*
**4** ▶ **NONSENSE** ◀ [U] *AmE informal* nonsense or something that is completely untrue: *You never went to Hawaii – that's pure bull.*
**5 be like a bull in a china shop** to keep knocking things over, dropping things, breaking things etc
**6 like a bull at a gate** if you move somewhere like a bull at a gate, you move there very fast, ignoring everything in your way

**7 ▶ RELIGION ◀** an official statement from the POPE
**8 ▶ CENTRE ◀** the centre of a TARGET[1] (3) that you are shooting at
**9 ▶ BUSINESS ◀** someone who buys shares (SHARE[2] (6)) because they expect prices to rise —compare BEAR[2] (2) —see also **like a red rag to a bull** (RED[1] (6)), **shoot the bull** (SHOOT[1] (9))

**bull²** *interjection slang* used to say that you do not believe or agree with what someone has said: *Bull! Where did you get that idea?*

**bull·dog** /ˈbʊldɒg‖-dɔːg/ *n* [C] a powerful dog with a large head, a short neck, and short thick legs

**bulldog clip** /ˈ·· ·/ *n BrE* [C] a small metal object that shuts tightly to hold papers together

**bull·doze** /ˈbʊldəʊz‖-doʊz/ *v* [T] **1** to destroy buildings etc with a bulldozer **2** to push objects such as earth and rocks out of the way with a bulldozer **3 bulldoze sb into (doing) sth** to force someone to do something that they do not really want to do

**bull·doz·er** /ˈbʊldəʊzə‖-doʊzər/ *n* [C] a powerful vehicle with a broad metal blade, used for moving earth and rocks, destroying buildings etc

**bul·let** /ˈbʊlɪ̣t/ *n* [C] a small piece of metal that you fire from a gun: *a bullet through the heart* | **bullet holes/wounds etc** *The door was riddled with bullet holes.* —compare SHELL[1] (2) SHOT[1] (4) —see also PLASTIC BULLET **bite the bullet** (BITE[1] (8)), —see picture at GUN[1]

**bul·le·tin** /ˈbʊlətɪ̣n/ *n* [C] **1** a news report on radio or television **2** an official statement that is made to inform people about something important **3** a letter or printed statement that a group or organization produces to tell people its news

**bulletin board** /ˈ··· ˌ·/ *n* [C] **1** *AmE* a board on the wall that you put information or pictures on; NOTICE-BOARD *BrE*: *a windows bulletin-board due out next year* —see picture on page 837 **2 electronic bulletin board** a place in a computer information system where you can read or leave messages

**bullet proof** /ˈ·· ·/ *adj* something that is bullet proof is designed to stop bullets from going through it

**bull·fight** /ˈbʊlfaɪt/ *n* [C] a type of entertainment popular in Spain, in which a man fights and kills a BULL[1] (1) —**bullfighter** *n* [C] —**bullfighting** *n* [U]

**bull·finch** /ˈbʊlˌfɪntʃ/ *n* [C] a small grey and red European bird

**bull·frog** /ˈbʊlfrɒg‖-frɑːg, -frɔːg/ *n* [C] a kind of large FROG that makes a loud noise

**bull-head·ed** /ˌ· ˈ··◂/ *adj* determined to get what you want without really thinking enough about it —**bull-headedly** *adv* —**bullheadedness** *n* [U]

**bull·horn** /ˈbʊlhɔːn‖-hɔːrn/ *n* [C] *AmE old-fashioned* a piece of equipment that you hold up to your mouth to make your voice louder; MEGAPHONE *BrE*

**bul·lion** /ˈbʊljən/ *n* [U] bars of gold or silver: *gold bullion*

**bul·lish** /ˈbʊlɪʃ/ *adj* **1** [not before noun] feeling confident about the future: *very bullish about the company's prospects* **2** *technical* in a business market that is bullish the prices of shares (SHARE[2] (6)) tend or seem likely to rise —**bullishly** *adv* —**bullishness** *n* [U]

**bull·necked** /ˌbʊlˈnekt◂/ *adj* having a short and very thick neck

**bul·lock** /ˈbʊlək/ *n* [C] a young male cow that cannot breed

**bull pen** /ˈ· ·/ *n* [C] *AmE* **1** the area in a BASEBALL field in which PITCHERS practise throwing **2** the PITCHERS of a BASEBALL team

**bull·ring** /ˈbʊlˌrɪŋ/ *n* [C] the place where a BULLFIGHT is held

**bull ses·sion** /ˈ· ˌ··/ *n* [C] *AmE informal* an occasion when a group of people meet to talk in a relaxed and friendly way: *an all-night bull session*

**bull's-eye**

The arrow hit the bull's-eye.

**bull's-eye** /ˈ· ·/ *n* [C] **1** the centre of a TARGET[1] (3) that you try to hit when shooting or in games like darts (DART[2] (2)) **2** *BrE* a large hard round sweet

**bull·shit¹** /ˈbʊlˌʃɪt/ *n* [U] *informal* a rude word meaning something that is stupid and completely untrue: *Forget all that bullshit and listen to me!* | **a load of bullshit** *Your so-called plan is a load of bullshit.*

**bullshit²** *v* [I,T] *informal* a rude word meaning that something said is stupid or completely untrue, especially in order to deceive or impress someone: *Don't believe him, he's probably bullshitting.* —**bullshitter** *n* [C]

**bull ter·ri·er** /ˌ· ˈ···/ *n* [C] a strong short-haired dog —see also PIT BULL TERRIER

**bul·ly¹** /ˈbʊli/ *n* [C] someone who uses their strength or power to frighten or hurt someone who is weaker: *Bullies are often cowards.*

**bully**

**bully²** *v* [T] to threaten to hurt someone or frighten them, especially someone smaller or weaker —**bullying** *n* [U] *an attempt to tackle the problem of bullying in schools*

**bully off** *phr v* [I] to start a game of HOCKEY (1) —**bully-off** *n* [C]

**bully³** *adj* **bully for you/him etc** *spoken* used when you do not think that someone has done anything special but they want you to praise them: *Yes. I know you've done all the dishes. Bully for you!*

**bully beef** /ˈ·· ·/ *n* [U] *BrE* CORNED BEEF

**bully boy** /ˈ·· ·/ *n* [C] *BrE informal* someone who behaves in a violent and threatening way

**bul·rush** /ˈbʊlrʌʃ/ *n* [C] a tall plant that looks like grass and grows by water

**bul·wark** /ˈbʊlwək‖-wərk/ *n* [C] **1** something that protects you from an unpleasant situation: [+ **against**] *The Soviet Union was our only bulwark against fascism.* **2 bulwarks** [plural] the sides of a boat or ship above the DECK[1] (1) **3** a strong structure like a wall, built for defence

**bum¹** /bʌm/ *n* [C] *informal* **1** *AmE* someone, especially a man, who has no home or job, and who asks people for money **2** *BrE* the part of your body that you sit on; BOTTOM[1] (3) **3 beach/ski etc bum** someone who spends all their time on the beach, skiing (SKI[2]) etc without having a job **4** someone who is very lazy S

**bum**[2] **bummed, bumming** *v* [T] *slang* to ask someone for something such as money, food, or cigarettes

**bum around** *phr v slang* **1** also **bum about** [I] to spend time lazily doing nothing **2** [T **bum around** sth] to travel around in an unplanned way living very cheaply: *a year bumming around Australia*

**bum**[3] *adj* [only before noun] *slang* bad and useless: *It must be a bum copy. It sounds terrible!*

**bum bag** /ˈ· ·/ *n* [C] a small bag that you wear around your waist to hold money, keys etc

**bum·ble** /ˈbʌmbəl/ *v* [I] **1** also **bumble on** to speak in a confused way so that no-one can understand you: *I really don't know what Karl was bumbling on about.* **2** also **bumble around** to move in an unsteady way

**bum·ble·bee** /ˈbʌmbəlbiː/ *n* [C] a large hairy BEE

**bum·bling** /ˈbʌmblɪŋ/ *adj* [only before noun] behaving in a careless way and making a lot of mistakes: *bumbling incompetence*

**bumf, bumph** /bʌmf/ *n* [U] *BrE informal* boring written information that you have to read: *I got a load of bumf from the gas board.*

**bum·mer** /ˈbʌmə‖-ər/ *n* **a bummer** *slang* a situation that is disappointing or annoying: *It was a real bummer being ill on holiday.*

S3 **bump**[1] /bʌmp/ *v* **1** [I always + adv/prep, T] to hit or knock against something: [+ **against/into etc**] *It was so dark I bumped into a tree* | **bump sth on/against etc** *I bumped my head on the ledge.* **2** [I always + adv/prep] to move up and down as you move forward, especially in a vehicle: [+ **along/across etc**] *The bus bumped along the rutted road.*

**bump into** sb *phr v* [T] to meet someone that you know when you were not expecting to: *I bumped into Jean in town this morning.*

**bump** sb ↔ **off** *phr v* [T] *informal* to kill someone

**bump** sth ↔ **up** *phr v* [T] *informal* to suddenly increase something by a large amount: *In the summer they bump up the prices by ten percent.*

**bump**[2] *n* [C] **1** an area of skin that is raised up because you have hit it on something: *How did you get that bump over your eye?* **2** a small raised area on a surface: *bumps on the road* **3** *informal* a slight accident in which your car hits something but you are not hurt: *Jim had a bump in the car.* **4** the sound of something hitting a hard surface: *We heard a bump in the next room.* | **fall/sit down etc with a bump** *Don sat down with a bump.*

**bump·er**[1] /ˈbʌmpə‖-ər/ *n* [C] **1** *BrE* a bar fixed on the front and back of a car to protect it if it hits anything; FENDER (1) *AmE* —see picture on page 409 **2 bumper-to-bumper** bumper-to-bumper traffic is very close together and moving slowly

**bumper**[2] *adj* [only before noun] unusually large: *a bumper crop* | *a bumper edition of a magazine*

**bumper car** /ˈ·· ·/ *n* [C] a small electric car that you drive in a special area at a FUNFAIR and deliberately try to hit other cars

**bumper stick·er** /ˈ·· ˌ··/ *n* [C] a small sign on the BUMPER[1] (1) of a car, with a humorous, political, or religious message

**bumph** /bʌmf/ *n* [U] another spelling of BUMF

**bump·kin** /ˈbʌmpkɨn/ *n* [C] *informal* someone from the countryside who is considered to be stupid

**bump·tious** /ˈbʌmpʃəs/ *adj* too proud of your abilities in a way that annoys other people —**bumptiously** *adv* —**bumptiousness** *n* [U]

**bump·y** /ˈbʌmpi/ *adj* **1** a bumpy surface is flat but has a lot of raised parts so it is difficult to walk or drive on it: *a bumpy lane* **2** a bumpy journey by car or plane is uncomfortable because of bad road or weather conditions **3 have a bumpy ride/time** to have a lot of problems for a long time: *Professional soccer has had a bumpy ride in the US.* —opposite SMOOTH[1]

**bun** /bʌn/ *n* [C] **1** *BrE* a small round sweet cake: *a sticky bun* **2** *especially AmE* a small round type of bread: *a hamburger bun* **3** a hairstyle in which a woman with long hair fastens it in a small round shape at the back of her head —see picture at HAIRSTYLE **4 have a bun in the oven** *BrE humorous* to be PREGNANT (=going to have a baby)

**bunch**[1] /bʌntʃ/ *n* **1 bunch of flowers/keys/grapes etc** a group of flowers, keys etc that are fastened or held together **2** [singular] *informal* a group of people: *Our new neighbours are a weird bunch.* **3 the pick of the bunch** the best among a group of people or things **4** [singular] *especially AmE* a large number of people or things, or a large amount of something: [+ **of**] *The doctor asked me a bunch of questions.* **5 in bunches** *BrE* if a girl wears her hair in bunches, she ties it together at each side of her head —see picture at HAIRSTYLE **6 thanks a bunch** an expression meaning thank you very much, used jokingly when you are not grateful at all S2

**bunch**[2] *v* also **bunch together, bunch up** **1** [I] to stay close together in a group: *The children bunched together in little groups in the playground.* **2** [T] to tighten part of your body: *Sean bunched his fists and strode towards them.* **3** [T] to hold or tie things together in a bunch **4** [I,T] to pull material together tightly in folds

**bun·dle**[1] /ˈbʌndl/ *n* [C] **1** a group of things such as papers, clothes, or sticks that are fastened or tied together **2** [singular] *informal* a lot of money: **cost a bundle** *The trip will cost a bundle and we can't pay for it ourselves.* | **make a bundle** (=earn or win a lot of money) **3 be a bundle of nerves** *informal* to be very nervous **4 be a bundle of fun/laughs** *informal* an expression meaning a person or situation that is fun or makes you laugh, often used jokingly when they are not fun at all: *You were a bundle of fun last night. What's wrong?* **5 not go a bundle on sth** *BrE informal* to not like something very much: *Jim never drank, and certainly didn't go a bundle on gambling.*

**bundle**[2] *v* **1** [T always + adv/prep] to quickly push someone or something somewhere because you are in a hurry or you want to hide them: **bundle sb into/through etc** *They bundled Perez into the car, and drove off.* **2** [I always + adv/prep] to move somewhere quickly in a group: [+ **into/through etc**] *Six of us bundled into a taxi.*

**bundle** sb **off** *phr v* [T] to send someone somewhere in a hurry

**bundle up** *phr v* **1** [T **bundle** sth ↔ **up**] to make a bundle by tying things together: *Bundle up the newspapers and take them to the skip.* **2** [I,T **bundle** sb **up**] to dress warmly because it is cold

**bung**[1] /bʌŋ/ *n* [C] **1** a round piece of rubber, wood etc used to close the top of a container —see picture at LABORATORY **2** *BrE slang* money given to someone secretly, and usually illegally, to make them do something

**bung**[2] *v* [T always + adv/prep] *BrE informal* to put something somewhere quickly and without thinking carefully: **bung sth in/on etc** *Can you bung these clothes in the washing machine?*

**bung** sth ↔ **up** *phr v* [T] **1** to block a hole by putting something in it **2 be bunged up** *informal* to find it difficult to breathe because you have a COLD

**bun·ga·low** /ˈbʌŋgələʊ‖-loʊ/ *n* [C] **1** *BrE* a house which is all on ground level **2** *AmE* a small house which is often on one level —see picture on page 410 S2

**bung·hole** /ˈbʌŋhəʊl‖-hoʊl/ *n* [C] a hole for emptying or filling a BARREL[1] (1)

**bun·gle** /ˈbʌŋgəl/ *v* [T] to do something unsuccessfully, because you have made stupid or careless mistakes: *The whole police operation was bungled.* —**bungle** *n* [C] —**bungler** *n* [C] —**bungling** *n* [U] —**bungled** *adj*: *a bungled rescue attempt*

**bun·ion** /ˈbʌnjən/ *n* [C] a painful red sore area on the first joint of your big toe

**bunk¹** /bʌŋk/ *n* **1** [C] a narrow bed that is fixed to the wall, for example on a train or ship **2 bunk beds** [plural] two beds that are fixed together, one on top of the other —see picture at BED¹ **3 do a bunk** *BrE informal* to suddenly leave a place without telling anyone **4** [U] *informal* nonsense; BUNKUM: *What a load of bunk!*

**bunk²** *v* [I] *informal* also **bunk down** to lie down to sleep in a particular place: *You can bunk down on the sofa for tonight.*

**bunk off** *phr v BrE informal* [I,T **bunk off** sth] to stay away from somewhere such as school or to leave somewhere early without permission: *I think I'll bunk off classes this afternoon.*

**bun·ker** /ˈbʌŋkə‖-ər/ *n* [C] **1** a place where you store coal, especially on a ship or outside a house **2** a strongly built shelter for soldiers, usually underground **3** *BrE* a large hole on a GOLF course, filled with sand; SANDTRAP *AmE* —see picture on page 1264

**bunk·house** /ˈbʌŋkhaʊs/ *n* [C] a building where workers sleep

**bun·kum** /ˈbʌŋkəm/ *n* [U] *informal* nonsense

**bunk-up** /ˌ· ˈ·/ *n BrE* [singular] *informal* an act of pushing someone up from below to help them get higher

S3 **bun·ny** /ˈbʌni/ also **bunny rab·bit** /ˈ·· ˌ··/ *n* [C] a word for a rabbit, used especially by or to children

**bun·sen bur·ner** /ˌbʌnsən ˈbɜːnə‖ˈbɜːrnər/ *n* [C] a piece of equipment that produces a hot gas flame, for scientific EXPERIMENTS —see picture at LABORATORY

**bunt** /bʌnt/ *v* [I] *AmE* to deliberately hit the ball a short distance in a game of BASEBALL —**bunt** *n* [C]

**bun·ting** /ˈbʌntɪŋ/ *n* [U] small paper or cloth flags on strings, used to decorate buildings and streets on special occasions

**buoy¹** /bɔɪ‖ˈbuːi, bɔɪ/ *n* [C] an object that floats on the sea to mark a safe or dangerous area

**buoy²** also **buoy up** *v* [T] **1** to make someone feel happier or more confident: *buoyed by a two goal lead* **2** to keep profits, prices etc at a high level: *The company's profits were buoyed by a successful publishing venture.* **3** to keep something floating

**buoy·an·cy** /ˈbɔɪənsi‖ˈbɔɪənsi, ˈbuːjənsi/ *n* [U] **1** the ability of an object to float: *the buoyancy of light wood* **2** the power of a liquid to make an object float: *Salt water has more buoyancy than fresh water.* **3** a feeling of cheerfulness and belief that you can deal with problems easily **4** the ability of prices, a business etc to quickly get back to a high level after a difficult period

**buoy·ant** /ˈbɔɪənt‖ˈbɔɪənt, ˈbuːjənt/ *adj* **1** cheerful and confident: *Phil was in buoyant mood.* **2** buoyant prices etc tend to rise: *a buoyant economy* **3** able to float or keep things floating: *Cork is a very buoyant material.* —**buoyantly** *adv*

**bur** /bɜː‖bɜːr/ *n* [C] another spelling of BURR

**Bur·ber·ry** /ˈbɜːbəri‖ˈbɜːrbəri, -beri/ *n* [C] *trademark* a kind of RAIN COAT

**bur·ble** /ˈbɜːbəl‖ˈbɜːr-/ *v* **1** [I,T] to talk about something in a confused way that is difficult to understand: *Maggie kept burbling away about how difficult things were.* **2** [I] to make a sound like a stream flowing over stones —**burble** *n* [C]

**burbs** /bɜːbz‖bɜːrbz/ *n* **the burbs** *AmE informal* the SUBURBS (=areas around a city)

S3 W3 **bur·den¹** /ˈbɜːdn‖ˈbɜːrdn/ *n* **1** [C] something difficult or worrying that you are responsible for: **heavy burden** *We're in no position to take on another heavy financial burden.* **2** [singular] *formal* the main meaning of what someone is saying **3 the burden of proof** *law* the duty to prove that something is true **4** something that is carried; load —see also BEAST OF BURDEN

**burden²** *v* **1 be burdened by** to have a lot of problems because of a particular thing: *a big company burdened by debt* —see also UNBURDEN **2 be burdened with** to be carrying something heavy: *burdened with grocery bags.*

**bur·den·some** /ˈbɜːdnsəm‖ˈbɜːr-/ *adj* causing problems or additional work: *burdensome responsibilities*

**bu·reau** /ˈbjʊərəʊ‖ˈbjʊroʊ/ *n plural* **bureaux** /-rəʊz‖-roʊz/ *BrE*, **bureaus** *AmE* [C] **1** an office or organization that collects or provides information: *an employment bureau* **2** *especially AmE* a government department or a part of a government department: *the Federal Bureau of Investigation* **3** *BrE* a large desk or writing table **4** *AmE* a piece of furniture with several drawers, used to keep clothes in; CHEST OF DRAWERS

**bu·reauc·ra·cy** /bjʊəˈrɒkrəsi‖bjʊˈrɑː-/ *n* **1** [U] a complicated official system which is annoying or confusing because it has a lot of rules, processes etc: *plans to eliminate unnecessary bureaucracy* **2** [C,U] the officials who are employed rather than elected to do the work of a government, business etc

**bu·reau·crat** /ˈbjʊərəkræt‖ˈbjʊr-/ *n* [C] someone who works in a bureaucracy and uses official rules very strictly

**bu·reau·crat·ic** /ˌbjʊərəˈkrætɪk◂‖ˌbjʊr-/ *adj* involving a lot of complicated official rules and processes —**bureaucratically** /-kli/ *adv*

**bureau de change** /ˌbjʊərəʊ də ˈʃɒndʒ‖ˌbjʊroʊ də ˈʃɑːndʒ/ *n* [C] *French* an office or shop where you can change foreign money

**bur·geon** /ˈbɜːdʒən‖ˈbɜːr-/ *v* [I] *formal* to grow or develop quickly

**burgeoning** /ˈbɜːdʒənɪŋ‖ˈbɜr-/ *adj* increasing or developing very quickly: *a project to improve water supplies to Denver's burgeoning population*

**burg·er** /ˈbɜːgə‖ˈbɜːrgər/ *n* [C] **1** a flat round piece of finely cut BEEF¹ (1), which is cooked and usually eaten in a bread ROLL² (2); a HAMBURGER: **cheeseburger** (=a burger with cheese on top of the meat) **2 vegeburger/nutburger** something like a HAMBURGER but made of vegetables, nuts etc

**burgh** /ˈbʌrə‖bɜːrg, ˈbʌroʊ/ *n* [C] *ScotE* a BOROUGH

**bur·gher** /ˈbɜːgə‖ˈbɜːrgər/ *n* [C] *old use* someone who lives in a particular town

**bur·glar** /ˈbɜːglə‖ˈbɜːrglər/ *n* [C] someone who gets into houses, shops etc to steal things —compare ROBBER, THIEF —see also CAT BURGLAR

**burglar a·larm** /ˈ·· ·ˌ·/ *n* [C] a piece of equipment that makes a loud noise when a burglar gets into a building —see picture at ALARM¹

**bur·gla·rize** /ˈbɜːgləraɪz‖ˈbɜːr-/ *v* [T] *AmE* to get into a building and steal things from it or from the people inside; burgle *BrE*

**bur·glar·y** /ˈbɜːgləri‖ˈbɜːr-/ *n* [C,U] the crime of getting into a building to steal things: *Burglaries in the area have risen by 5%.*

**bur·gle** /ˈbɜːgəl‖ˈbɜːr-/ *v* [T] *BrE* to get into a building and steal things from it or from the people inside; burglarize *AmE*: *We've been burgled three times!* —see STEAL¹ (USAGE)

**bur·gun·dy** /ˈbɜːgəndi‖ˈbɜːr-/ *n* **1** [C,U] red or white wine from the Burgundy area of France **2** [U] a dark red colour —see picture on page 411

**bur·i·al** /ˈberiəl/ *n* [C,U] the act or ceremony of putting a dead body into a grave

**burk** /bɜːk‖bɜːrk/ *n* [C] another spelling of BERK

**bur·lap** /ˈbɜːlæp‖ˈbɜːr-/ *n* [U] *AmE* a type of thick rough cloth; HESSIAN *BrE*

**bur·lesque¹** /bɜːˈlesk‖bɜːr-/ *n* **1** [C,U] speech, acting, or writing in which a serious subject is made to seem silly or an unimportant subject is treated in a serious way **2** *AmE* a performance involving a mixture of comedy and STRIPTEASE, popular in America in the past: *a burlesque house*

**burlesque²** *v* [T] to make a serious subject seem silly to amuse people

**bur·ly** /ˈbɜːli‖ˈbɜːrli/ *adj* a burly man is big and strong: *burly rugby players* —**burliness** *n* [U]

S2 W3

B

# burn¹ /bɜːn‖bɜːrn/ *v past and past participle* **burnt** /bɜːnt‖bɜːrnt/ *or* **burned**

① FIRE
② CHEMICALS
③ KILL
④ PRODUCE POWER/LIGHT
⑤ FEELING/EMOTION
⑥ MONEY
⑦ CARS
⑧ OTHER MEANINGS

## ① FIRE

**1 ► PRODUCE HEAT ◄** [I] to produce heat and flames: *Is the fire still burning?*

**2 ► DESTROY WITH FIRE ◄** [I,T] to be destroyed by fire or destroy something with fire: **burn sth** *I burnt all his old letters.*

**3 burn to the ground/burn to ashes** if a building burns to the ground, it is completely destroyed by fire

**4 burn sth to a crisp/cinder** to burn something until it is black, especially by cooking it for too long —see picture on page 833

**5 ► DAMAGE BY FIRE ◄** [I,T] to damage something or hurt someone with fire or heat, or be hurt or damaged in this way: *I've burnt my hand.* | *Quick, the toast's burning!* | **burn a hole in** *Be careful you don't burn a hole in the chair with your cigarette.*

## ② CHEMICALS

**6** [T] to damage or destroy something by a chemical action; CORRODE

## ③ KILL

**7 be burned to death/burned alive** to be killed in a fire

**8 burn sb at the stake** to kill someone by tying them to a post on top of a fire

## ④ PRODUCE POWER/LIGHT

**9** [I,T] if you burn a FUEL , or if it burns, it is used to produce power, heat, light etc: *The central heating boiler burns oil.*

**10 ► SHINE ◄** [I] if a light or lamp burns, it shines or produces light: *A light was burning in her window.*

## ⑤ FEELING/EMOTION

**11** [I,T] to feel unpleasantly hot or make part of your body feel like this: *I'm afraid the ointment might burn a bit.*

**12 ► BE EMBARRASSED ◄** [I] if your face or cheeks are burning, they feel hot because you are embarrassed or upset

**13 be burning with rage/desire etc** to feel an emotion very strongly

**14 be burning to do sth** to want to do something very much: *Hannah's burning to tell you her news.*

**15 it burns me/her/John etc that** *AmE* used to say that something makes someone feel angry or jealous: *It really burns me the way they treat us.*

**16 be/get burned** to be emotionally hurt by someone or something

## ⑥ MONEY

**17 burn a hole in your pocket** if money is burning a hole in your pocket, you want to spend it as soon as you can

**18 burn your fingers/get your fingers burned** *informal* to suffer the unpleasant results of something that you have done: *George got his fingers badly burned when the travel company collapsed.*

**19 be/get burned** to lose a lot of money, especially in a business deal: *A lot of people got burned buying junk bonds.*

## ⑦ CARS

**20 ► GO FAST ◄** [I always + adv/prep] to travel very fast: [+ **along/through/up etc**] *a sports car burning up the motorway*

**21 burn rubber** *AmE informal* to start a car moving so quickly that the tyres become very hot and make a loud high noise

## ⑧ OTHER MEANINGS

**22 burn your bridges/boats** *informal* to do something that you cannot change, that often makes a situation difficult for you

**23 burn the candle at both ends** *informal* to work too hard for too long

**24 burn the midnight oil** *informal* to work or study until late at night

**burn away** *phr v* [I,T] if something burns away or is burned away, it is destroyed or reduced to something much smaller by fire

**burn down** *phr v* **1** [I,T **burn** sth ↔ **down**] if a building burns down or is burned down, it is destroyed by fire **2** [I] if a fire burns down, the flames become weaker and it produces less heat —compare **burn out** (BURN¹), **burn up** (BURN¹)

**burn** sth ↔ **off** *phr v* [T] **1** to remove something by burning it: *farmers burning off the stubble from the fields* **2 burn off energy/fat/calories etc** to use energy etc by doing physical exercise: *I think I'll go for a walk and burn off a few calories!*

**burn out** *phr v*

**1 ► FIRE ◄** [I,T **burn** sth **out**] if a fire burns out or burns itself out, it stops burning because there is no coal, wood etc left

**2 be burnt out** if something is burnt out, the inside of it is destroyed by fire: *The hotel was completely burnt out; only the walls remained.*

**3 burn yourself out** to ruin your health and feel very tired through working too hard, drinking too much alcohol etc

**4 ► ENGINE ◄** [I,T **burn** sth ↔ **out**] if an engine or electric wire burns out or is burned out, it stops working because it has been damaged by getting too hot

**5 ► AIRCRAFT ◄** [I] if a ROCKET¹ or JET¹ (1) burns out, it stops operating because all its FUEL has been used —see also BURNOUT (1)

**burn up** *phr v*

**1 ► DESTROY ◄** [I,T **burn** sth ↔ **up**] if something burns up or is burnt up, it is completely destroyed by fire or great heat

**2 ► BURN BRIGHTER ◄** [I] if a fire burns up, it gets stronger and brighter

**3 ► BE HOT ◄** [I] *spoken* if someone is burning up, they are very hot

**4 ► MAKE SB ANGRY ◄** [T **burn** sb **up**] *informal especially AmE* to make someone angry: *The way he treats her really burns me up.*

**5 be burned up with anger/jealousy etc** to have your mind full of a strong emotion

**6 burn up energy/fat/calories etc** to use energy etc by doing physical exercise

**USAGE NOTE: BURN**
SPELLING
In American English the past tense and past participle of the verb is **burned**: *She burned a hole in my new shirt.* In British English **burnt** is used, though **burned** is also used, especially when the action goes on for some time: *The fire burned brightly.* | *I've burnt my hand.* | *The house burnt down.*

In both American and British English, **burnt** is used when the word is used as an adjective: *burnt toast* | *a burnt tree* (=made black by burning)

This is also true of **spoiled/spoilt, learned/learnt, spilled/spilt, spelled/spelt, smelled/smelt**, and, with a pronunciation difference as well, **leaned/leant, leaped/leapt, dreamed/dreamt, kneeled/knelt**. e.g. *I learned English for ten years.* | *a spoilt child*

S3 **burn²** *n* [C] **1** an injury or mark caused by fire, heat, or acid: **severe/minor burns** (=burns that are serious or not serious) **2 the burn** *informal* a painful hot feeling in your muscles when you exercise a lot: *Go for the burn.* **3** *especially ScotE* a small stream

**burn·er** /ˈbɜːnə‖ˈbɜːrnər/ *n* [C] **1** *AmE* the part of an OVEN or heater that produces heat or a flame: *a gas burner* —see picture at FONDUE; GAS RING *BrE* **2 put sth on the back burner** *informal* to delay dealing with something until a later time: *We've had to put the vacation plans on the back burner because of Bob's ill health.*

**burn·ing¹** /ˈbɜːnɪŋ‖ˈbɜːr-/ *adj* [only before noun] **1** on fire: *You could see the burning house for miles around.* **2** feeling very hot: *burning cheeks* **3 burning ambition/need etc** a very strong need etc: **burning ambition** *My burning ambition is to travel around the world.* **4 burning question/issue** a very important and urgent question: *The burning question is will Rob agree to come?*

**burning²** *adv* **burning hot** very hot

**bur·nish** /ˈbɜːnɪʃ‖ˈbɜːr-/ *v* [T] to polish metal until it shines —**burnished** *adj*: *burnished copper*

**bur·nous** also **burnoose** *AmE* /bɜːˈnuːs‖bɜːr-/ *n* [C] a long loose dress or coat worn by Arab men and women

**burn·out** /ˈbɜːnaʊt‖ˈbɜːrn-/ *n* [C,U] **1** the time when a ROCKET (1) or JET¹ (1) has finished all of its FUEL and stops operating **2** a state in which you have ruined your health by working too hard: *teachers suffering from burnout*

S3 **burnt¹** /bɜːnt‖bɜːrnt/ the past tense and past participle of BURN¹

**burnt²** *adj* **1** damaged or hurt by burning: *The cake's a little bit burnt, I'm afraid.* **2 burnt offering a)** something that is offered as a gift to a god by being burnt on an ALTAR (1) **b)** *humorous* food that you accidentally burnt while you were cooking it

**burp** /bɜːp‖bɜːrp/ *v informal* **1** [I] to pass gas noisily from your stomach out through your mouth; BELCH (1) **2** [T] to help a baby to do this, especially by rubbing or gently hitting its back; WIND¹ (9) —**burp** *n* [C]

**burr** /bɜː‖bɜːr/ *n* [C] **1** a fairly quiet regular sound like something turning quickly; WHIRR: *the burr of a sewing machine* **2** a way of pronouncing English with a strong 'r' sound **3** also **bur** the seed container of some plants, covered with PRICKLES¹ (1) that make it stick to things

**bur·ri·to** /bəˈriːtəʊ‖-toʊ/ *n plural* **burritos** [C] Mexican dish made with a TORTILLA (=flat thin bread) folded around meat or beans with cheese

**bur·ro** /ˈbʊrəʊ‖ˈbɜːroʊ/ *n plural* **burros** [C] *especially AmE* a DONKEY (1), usually a small one

**bur·row¹** /ˈbʌrəʊ‖ˈbɜːroʊ/ *v* **1** [I always + adv/prep, T] to make a hole or passage in the ground: *burrowing a hole* | [+ **into/under etc**] *The dog managed to burrow under the fence.* **2** [T always + adv/prep] to press your body close to someone or under something because you want to get warm, feel safe etc: **burrow sth into/under etc** *The baby burrowed her head into my shoulder.* **3** [I always + adv/prep] to search for something that is hidden in a container or under other things: [+ **into/through etc**] *Helen burrowed into her pocket for a handkerchief.*

**burrow²** *n* [C] a passage in the ground made by a rabbit or FOX¹ (1) as a place to live

**bur·sar** /ˈbɜːsə‖ˈbɜːrsər/ *n* [C] *especially BrE* someone at a school or college who deals with the accounts and office work

**bur·sa·ry** /ˈbɜːsəri‖ˈbɜːr-/ *n* [C] an amount of money given to someone so that they can study at a university or college; SCHOLARSHIP

**burst**

The balloon burst.

**burst¹** /bɜːst‖bɜːrst/ *v past tense and past participle* **burst**
**1 ▶ BREAK OPEN ◀** [I,T] if something bursts or if you burst it, it breaks open or apart suddenly and violently so that its contents come out: *You're going to burst the balloon, if you're not careful.*
**2 bursting with** so full of something that there is no room for any more: *The barracks were bursting with refugees.*
**3 ▶ MOVE SUDDENLY ◀** [I always + adv/prep] to move somewhere suddenly or quickly, especially into or out of a place: [+ **through/into/in etc**] *Don't burst into my bedroom without knocking!*
**4 burst open** to suddenly be open: *The door burst open to reveal Francis holding a tray.*
**5 be bursting to do sth** *informal* to want to do something very much: *Mona's bursting to tell you the news.*
**6 be bursting with pride/confidence/energy etc** to be very proud, confident etc
**7 be bursting** *informal* to need to go to the toilet very soon
**8 full to bursting** so full that there is no room for any more: *I can't eat any more, I'm full to bursting!*
**9 bursting at the seams** so full that nothing else can fit inside —see also **burst sb's bubble** (BUBBLE¹ (5)), **burst the bubble** (BUBBLE¹ (4))

**burst in on/upon** sb/sth *phr v* [T] to interrupt something at an embarrassing moment: *I burst in on the meeting thinking that the room was empty.*

**burst into** sth *phr v* [T] **1** to suddenly begin to make a sound, especially to start singing, crying, or laughing: *The audience burst into applause.* | **burst into song** *Everyone on the bus burst into song as we got closer to home.* | **burst into tears** *Benny suddenly burst into tears.* **2 burst into flames** to suddenly start to burn very strongly: *The plane crashed into the hillside and burst into flames.*

**burst out** *phr v* **1 burst out laughing/crying etc** to suddenly start to laugh, cry etc: *They all burst out laughing at the expression on her face.* **2** [T] to suddenly say something forcefully: *"I don't believe it!" she burst out angrily.* —see also OUTBURST (1)

**burst²** *n* [C] **1** the act of something bursting or the place where it has burst: *a burst in the water pipe* **2 a burst of sth a)** a short sudden effort or increase in activity: *a burst of speed on the last lap* **b)** a short sudden and usually loud sound: *sharp bursts of machine gun fire* **c)** a sudden strong feeling or emotion: *bursts of violent temper*

**bur·then** /ˈbɜːðən‖ˈbɜːr-/ *n* [C] *literary* a BURDEN

**bur·ton** /ˈbɜːtn‖ˈbɜːrtn/ *n* **gone for a burton** *BrE spoken* lost, broken, or dead: *This radio's gone for a burton.*

W3 **bur·y** /ˈberi/ *v* [T]
**1 ▶ PUT SB IN GRAVE ◀** to put someone who has died in a grave: **bury sb in/at etc** *Gretta wanted to be buried at St Peter's.*
**2 have buried sb** to have had someone you love die: *Jessie has already buried two husbands.*
**3 ▶ PUT STH UNDER EARTH ◀** to put something under the earth, often in order to hide it
**4 ▶ COVER WITH STH ◀** [usually passive] to cover something with other things so that it can not be found: **bury sth under/beneath etc** *The climbers were buried under a pile of rocks.*
**5 ▶ FEELING/MEMORY ◀** to ignore a feeling or memory and pretend that it does not exist: *a deeply buried memory*
**6 bury your face/head etc (in sth)** to press your face etc into something soft, usually to get comfort, to avoid someone, or to be able to smell something: *Noel turned away, burying his face in the pillow.* | **bury your face/head in your hands** (=cover your face etc with your hands because you are very upset)
**7 dead and buried** completely finished and no longer important: *All the prewar ideas about defence are now dead and buried.*
**8 bury the hatchet/bury your differences** to agree to stop arguing about something and become friends again
**9 ▶ PUSH STH INTO A SURFACE ◀** to push something, especially something sharp, into something else with a lot of force: *The dog buried its teeth in my leg.* | **bury itself** (=be pushed, thrown, or shot somewhere and stick there) *The knife buried itself in the wall a few inches from my head.*
**10 bury yourself in your work/studies etc** to give all your attention to something: *After the divorce, she buried herself in her work.*
**11 bury your head in the sand** to ignore an unpleasant situation and hope it will stop if you do not think about it

S1 W2 **bus¹** /bʌs/ *n plural* **buses** also **busses** *AmE* [C] a large vehicle that people pay to travel on: *Hurry up or we'll miss the bus!* | **by bus** *I go to work by bus.* | **bus driver/fare etc** *The bus fare is 60p.*

**bus²** *v* **bussed, bussing** also **bused, busing** *AmE* [T]
**1** to take a group of people somewhere in a bus that you HIRE (=pay to use) for the journey: **bus sb to/into etc** *Children had to be bussed to neighbouring schools.*
**2** *AmE* to take away dirty dishes from the tables in a restaurant: **bus tables** *Shelley had a job bussing tables.*

**bus·boy** /ˈbʌsbɔɪ/ *n* [C] *AmE* a young man whose job is to help in a restaurant by taking away dirty dishes

**bus·by** /ˈbʌzbi/ *n* [C] a tall fur hat worn by some British soldiers

**bush** /bʊʃ/ *n* [C] **1** a low thick plant smaller than a tree and with a lot of thin branches: *a rose bush* **2 the bush** wild country that has not been cleared, especially in Australia or Africa —see also **beat about the bush** (BEAT¹ (15))

**bush ba·by** /ˈ· ··/ *n* [C] a small African animal that lives in trees and has large eyes and ears, and a long tail

**bushed** /bʊʃt/ *adj* [not before noun] *informal* very tired

**bush·el** /ˈbʊʃəl/ *n* [C] a unit for measuring grain or vegetables equal to 8 gallons or 36.4 litres —see also **hide your light under a bushel** (HIDE¹ (7)) —see table on page B2

**bush league** /ˈ· ·/ *adj AmE informal* badly done or of such bad quality that it is not acceptable: *His work is still strictly bush league.*

**bush·man** /ˈbʊʃmən/ *n* [C] **1 Bushman** a member of a southern African tribe who live in the bush **2** someone who lives in the Australian BUSH (2)

**bush tel·e·graph** /ˌ· ˈ···/ *n* [U] *BrE humorous* the way in which people pass important news to each other very quickly: *I'd better warn you, the bush telegraph here works faster than the speed of light.*

**bush·whack** /ˈbʊʃwæk/ *v AmE* **1** [T] to attack someone suddenly from a hidden place; AMBUSH² **2** [I,T] to push or cut your way through thick trees or bushes —**bushwhacker** *n* [C]

**bush·y** /ˈbʊʃi/ *adj* bushy hair or fur grows thickly: *a bushy tail* —**bushiness** *n* [U] —see picture on page 412

S1 W1 **busi·ness** /ˈbɪznɨs/ *n*

① WORK DONE BY COMPANIES
② COMPANY
③ SUBJECT
④ STH THAT CONCERNS YOU
⑤ WORK TO BE DONE
⑥ OTHER MEANINGS

① **WORK DONE BY COMPANIES**
**1** [U] the activity of buying or selling goods or services that is done by companies: *Students on the course learn about all aspects of business.* | **in business** *Most of my family are in business.* | **do business with** *We do a lot of business with Italian companies.* | **the business community** (=important people who work in business) *The policy is backed by the international business community.*
**2 be in business/go into business** to be operating as a company or to begin operating as a company: *Pam's going into business with her sister.*
**3 go out of business** to stop operating as a company: *Higher interest rates will drive smaller firms out of business.*
**4 ▶ AMOUNT OF COMPANY WORK ◀** [U] the amount of work a company is doing or its value: *We're now doing twice as much business as we did last year.* | **business is good/bad/slow etc** *Business is slow during the summer.* | **drum up business** (=increase it) *Sidney's doing the rounds of the customers, trying to drum up business.*
**5 ▶ NOT PLEASURE ◀** [U] work that you do as part of your job: **on business** *Chris is in London this week, on business.* | **business trip/lunch/meeting etc** *I try to avoid too many business lunches.*
**6 business is business** used to say that profit is the most important thing to consider: *Harry may be a friend but business is business, and he's not the best man for the job.*

② **COMPANY**
**7** [C] an organization such as a shop or factory which produces or sells goods or services: *Paul's decided to start his own business.* | **run a business** *Mrs Taylor runs an office equipment business.*
**8 the advertising/printing/shipping etc business** work or a job involved with advertising, printing etc: *Steve works in the movie business.*

③ **SUBJECT**
**9 ▶ SUBJECT/EVENT ◀** [singular] a subject, event, or activity that you have a particular opinion of: *Politics is a serious business.* | *Tanya found the whole business ridiculous.* [continued on next page]

[continued from previous page]

**10 ▶ STH UNCLEAR ◀** [U] used when you talk about something in general and do not give any details: *He handles the mail and all that business.*

④ **STH THAT CONCERNS YOU**

**11 none of your business** *spoken* not something that you have a right to know about: *I know it's none of my business, but what did you decide?* | *It's none of your business how much I weigh.*

**12 mind your own business a)** *spoken* used to tell someone that something is private and you do not want them to ask about it or know about it: *"Where did you go last night?" "Mind your own business!"* **b)** to do your normal activities, without showing any interest in what other people are doing: *I was driving along, minding my own business, when the police pulled me over.*

**13 not your business** not something that you are responsible for or that affects you

**14 your/sb's business** something that affects you but not other people, so other people have no right to know about it: *"Are you going out with Kate tonight?" "That's my business".*

**15 make it your business to do sth** to make a special effort to do something: *Ruth made it her business to get to know the customers.*

⑤ **WORK TO BE DONE**

**16** [U] work that must be done in a particular job or period of time: *We discussed this week's business.* | [+ **of**] *the routine business of government*

**17 get down to business** to start dealing with an important subject: *We'd better stop chatting and get down to business.*

**18 business as usual** used to tell you that a shop or business is working normally when you might think it was closed

**19 any other business** subjects to be discussed in a meeting after the main subjects have been dealt with

⑥ **OTHER MEANINGS**

**20 be in business** *informal* to have all that you need to start doing something: *Gillian brought the food, Jack the wine and I had some rugs to sit on, so we were in business.*

**21 mean business** *informal* to be determined to do something even if it involves harming someone or making them upset: *I could tell from the look on his face that he meant business.*

**22 go about your business** to do the things that you normally do: *ordinary people going about their business*

**23 have no business doing sth/have no business to do sth** to behave wrongly in doing something: *He was very drunk and had no business driving.*

**24 like nobody's business** *spoken* very well, very much, or very fast: *Wanda can play the piano like nobody's business.*

**25 not in the business of doing sth** not planning to do something, because it is thought to be wrong: *This government is not in the business of increasing public spending.*

**26 (it's) the business** *BrE slang* used to say that something is very good or works well: *Have you seen David's new car? It's the business.* —see also BIG BUSINESS **funny business** (FUNNY (3)), **monkey business** (MONKEY¹ (3)), SHOW BUSINESS

**business card** /ˈ·· ˌ·/ *n* [C] a card that shows the business person's name, position, company, and address —see picture on page 837

**business class** /ˈ·· ·/ *n* [U] travelling conditions on an aircraft that are more expensive than TOURIST CLASS but not as expensive as FIRST CLASS (1) —compare ECONOMY CLASS

**business end** /ˈ·· ·/ *n* **the business end (of sth)** *informal* the end of a tool or weapon that does the work or causes the damage: *the business end of a gun*

**business hours** /ˈ·· ·/ *n* [plural] the normal hours that shops and offices are open

**busi·ness·like** /ˈbɪznə̇s-laɪk/ *adj* effective and practical in the way that you do things: *a businesslike manner*

**busi·ness·man** /ˈbɪznə̇smən/ *n plural* **businessmen** /-mən/ [C] **1** a man who works at a fairly high level in a company **2 be a good businessman** to know how to deal with money and be successful in business

**business park** /ˈ·· ˌ·/ *n* [C] an area where many companies and businesses have buildings and offices

**business plan** /ˈ·· ˌ·/ *n* [C] a document which explains what a company wants to do in the future

**business stud·ies** /ˈ·· ˌ··/ *n* [plural] a course of study on economic and financial subjects

**business suit** /ˈ·· ˌ·/ *n* [C] *AmE* a suit that a man wears during the day, especially in the office; LOUNGE SUIT *BrE*

**busi·ness·wom·an** /ˈbɪznə̇sˌwʊmən/ *n plural* **businesswomen** /-ˌwɪmɪn/ [C] **1** a woman who works at a fairly high level in a company **2 be a good businesswoman** to know how to deal with money and be successful in business

**busk** /bʌsk/ *v* [I] *BrE* to play music in a public place in order to earn money —**busker** *n* [C]

**bus lane** /ˈ· ·/ *n* [C] a part of a wide road that only buses are allowed to use

**busman's hol·i·day** /ˌbʌsmənz ˈhɒlə̇di‖-ˈhɑːlə̇deɪ/ *n* [singular] a holiday spent doing the same work as you do in your job

**bus pass** /ˈ· ·/ *n* [C] a special ticket giving cheap or free bus travel

**buss** /bʌs/ *v* [T] *AmE* to kiss someone in a friendly rather than sexual way: *politicians bussing babies*

**bus·ser** /ˈbʌsə‖-ər/ *n* [C] *AmE* someone who works in a restaurant taking away dirty dishes

**bus shel·ter** /ˈ· ˌ··/ *n* [C] *especially BrE* a small structure with a roof that keeps people dry while they are waiting for a bus

**bus sta·tion** /ˈ· ˌ··/ *n* [C] a place where buses start and finish their journeys

**bus stop** /ˈ· ·/ *n* [C] a place at the side of a road, marked with a sign, where buses stop for passengers

**bust¹** /bʌst/ *v past tense and past participle* **bust** *BrE* **busted** *especially AmE* [T] *informal*

**1 ▶ BREAK ◀** to break something: *I bust my watch this morning.* | *Tony busted the door down.*

**2 ▶ POLICE ◀** *informal* **a) bust sb (for sth)** if the police bust someone, they charge them with a crime **b)** if the police bust a place, they go into it to look for something illegal: *The party was busted by the vice squad.*

**3 bust a gut** *informal* to try extremely hard to do something: *I bust a gut trying to finish that work on time.*

**4 ... or bust!** *informal* used to say that you will try very hard to go somewhere or do something: *San Francisco or bust!*

**5 ▶ MILITARY ◀** *especially AmE* to give someone a lower military rank as a punishment; DEMOTE

**6 ▶ BURST ◀** *AmE* to burst

**bust out** *phr v* [I] *informal* to escape from a place, especially prison

**bust up** *phr v informal* **1** [I] to argue angrily and stop being lovers, partners, or friends: *They bust up after six years of marriage.* **2** [T **bust** sth ↔ **up**] to prevent something from continuing: *Angry protesters bust up the meeting.* **3** [T **bust** sth ↔ **up**] *AmE* to damage or break something: *Hey! Don't bust up my bar!* —see also BUST-UP

**bust²** *n* [C] **1** a model of someone's head, shoulders and upper chest, made of stone or metal: [+ **of**] *a bust of Beethoven* **2** a woman's breasts, or the part of her clothes that covers her breasts **3** a measurement around a woman's breast and back: *Do you have this bra in a bigger bust size?* **4** *informal* a situation in which the police go into a place looking for something illegal: *major drugs bust*

**bust³** *adj* [not before noun] *informal* **1 go bust** a business that goes bust cannot continue operating: *Dad lost his job when the firm went bust.* **2** broken: *The television's bust again.*

**bus·ter** /ˈbʌstə‖-ər/ *n AmE spoken* used to speak to a man who is annoying you or who you do not respect: *You're under arrest, buster!*

**bus·tle¹** /ˈbʌsəl/ *v* [I always + adv/prep] to move around quickly, looking very busy: [+ **about/round etc**] *Madge bustled round the room putting things away.*.

**bustle²** *n* **1** [singular] busy and usually noisy activity: [+ **of**] *a continual bustle of people coming and going* —see also **hustle and bustle** (HUSTLE² (1)) **2** [C] a frame worn by women in the past to hold out the back of their skirts

**bus·tling** /ˈbʌsəlɪŋ/ *adj* a bustling place is very busy

**bust-up** /ˈ· ·/ *n* [C] *informal* **1** a very bad quarrel or fight: *Cathy and I had a real bust-up yesterday.* **2** [C] the end of a relationship: *the bust-up of their marriage* —see also **bust up** (BUST¹)

**bust·y** /ˈbʌsti/ *adj informal* a woman who is busty has large breasts

S1 W2 **bus·y¹** /ˈbɪzi/ *adj*

**1 ▶ WORKING NOW ◀** someone who is busy at a particular time is working and is not available: *She's busy now, can you phone later?*|[+ **with**] *Mr Haynes is busy with a customer at the moment.*

**2 busy doing sth** giving something a lot of your time and attention: *Rachel's busy studying for her exams.*

**3 ▶ TIME ◀** a busy period is full of work or other activities: *December is the busiest time of year for shops.*

**4 ▶ PLACE ◀** a busy place is very full of people or vehicles and movement: *We live on a very busy road.*|*a busy office*

**5 ▶ WORKS HARD ◀** having very little free time because you always have so much to do: *a busy mother of four with a full time job*

**6 keep sb/yourself busy** to find plenty of things to do: *I kept myself busy to take my mind off smoking.*

**7 ▶ TELEPHONE ◀** *especially AmE* a telephone that is busy, is being used; ENGAGED (2) *BrE*: *I'm sorry, the line's busy at the moment, can you try later?*

**8 ▶ PATTERN ◀** a pattern or design that is busy is too full of small details

**9 as busy as a bee** very active: *The children have been as busy as bees making a collage this afternoon.* —**busily** *adv*

**busy²** *v* [T] **busy yourself with** to use your time dealing with something: *He busied himself with answering letters.*

**bus·y·bod·y** /ˈbɪziˌbɒdi‖-ˌbɑːdi/ *n* [C] someone who is too interested in other people's private activities: *You interfering old busybody!*

**busy Liz·zie** /ˌbɪzi ˈlɪzi/ *n* [C] a small plant with bright flowers

**bus·y·work** /ˈbɪziwɜːk‖-wɜːrk/ *n* [U] *AmE* work that seems to be producing a result but is really only keeping someone busy

S1 W1 **but¹** /bət/; *strong* /bʌt/ *conjunction* **1** in spite of something, or not as you would expect: *The situation looked desperate but they didn't give up hope.*|*The car was very cheap but it's been extremely reliable.* **2** used to add another statement to one that you have already made, to say that both things are true: *These changes will cost quite a lot, but they will save us money in the long run.*|*an expensive but immensely useful book* **3** used like however, to explain why something did not happen, why you did not do something etc: *He would have won easily, but he fell and broke his leg.*|*I'd like to go but I'm too busy.* **4** used after a negative to emphasize that it is the second part of the sentence that it is true: *They own not one but three houses.*|*The purpose of the scheme is not to help the employers but to provide work for young people.*|**no choice/alternative etc but to...** *We had no alternative but to fire him.*|**no question/doubt but that...** (=used to say that you are sure that something is true) *There's no doubt but that Evans is guilty.* **5 but for** without: *But for these interruptions the meeting would have finished half an hour ago.* **6 but then (again)** *spoken* **a)** used before a statement that makes what you have just said seem less true, useful, or valuable: *We could ask John to help again, but then I don't want to bother him.* **b)** used before a statement that may seem surprising, to say that it is not really surprising: *Apparently Dinah hasn't been to work all week, but then she always was unreliable wasn't she?* **7** used to express strong feelings such as anger, surprise etc: *But that's marvellous news!* **8 you cannot but.../you could not but...** *formal* used to say that you have to do something or cannot stop yourself from doing it: *I could not but admire her.* **9** used to emphasize a word or statement: *It'll be a great party – everyone, but everyone, is coming.* **10** used to change the subject of a conversation: *But now to the main question.* **11** [usually in negatives] *literary* used to emphasize that a statement includes every single person or thing: *Not a day goes by but that I think of Geoff.* (=I think of Geoff every day)

**USAGE NOTE: BUT**

WORD CHOICE: **but, however**

**But** is very frequent in spoken English, where it is often used at the beginning of a sentence: *"I read it in a newspaper." "But newspapers aren't always right!"*

**But** is also used in writing, though not usually at the beginning of a sentence. **However** is used especially in more formal writing, often with commas before and after it in the middle of a sentence: *This had been reported in a newspaper. One must remember, however, that newspapers are not always accurate.*

GRAMMAR

**But** or **however** is never used in a main clause beside another clause with **although**: *Although they're very busy, I think they enjoy it* (NOT ... *but/however I think they enjoy it*). You can begin a clause with *but although*, or *however although*: *I tried doing the accounts, but although I know some maths I found it very difficult* (=and I know some maths but I still found it difficult).

**but²** *prep* **1** apart from; except: *What can we do but sit and wait?*|*I could come any day but Thursday.*|**nothing but** (=used when talking about a bad quality or situation to emphasize how bad it is) *This car's been nothing but trouble.*|**anything but** (=used to say that a person or situation does not have a good quality) *Those receptionists are anything but helpful.* **2 the last but one/the next but two etc** *especially BrE* the last or next thing or person except for one, two etc: *Pauline and Derek live in the next house but one.* (=they live two houses away from us) S2 W3

**but³** *adv* **1** *especially literary* only: *You can but try.* **2** *AmE spoken* used to emphasize what you are saying: *Go there but fast!*|*They're rich, but I mean rich!* S2 W3

**but⁴** /bʌt/ *n* **no buts (about it)** *spoken* used to say that there is no doubt about something: *No buts, you are going to school today!*

**bu·tane** /ˈbjuːteɪn/ *n* [U] a gas stored in liquid form, used for cooking and heating

**butch** /bʊtʃ/ *adj informal* **1** a woman who is butch looks, behaves, or dresses like a man **2** a man who is butch seems big and strong, and typically male

**butch·er¹** /ˈbʊtʃə‖-ər/ *n* [C] **1** someone who owns or works in a shop that sells meat **2 the butcher's** a shop where you can buy meat **3** someone who has killed a lot of people cruelly and unnecessarily **4 have/take a butcher's** *BrE slang* to have a look at something S3

**butcher²** *v* [T] **1** to kill animals and prepare them to be used as meat **2** to kill people cruelly or unnecessarily,

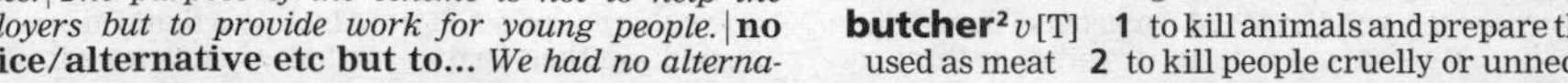

especially in large numbers **3** *informal* to spoil something by working carelessly: *That hairdresser really butchered my hair!*

**butch·er·y** /ˈbʊtʃəri/ *n* [U] **1** cruel and unnecessary killing: *the butchery of battle* **2** the preparation of meat for sale

**but·ler** /ˈbʌtlə‖-ər/ *n* [C] the main male servant of a house

**butt¹** /bʌt/ *n* [C]
**1 be the butt of** to be the person or thing that other people often make jokes about: *Paul quickly became the butt of everyone's jokes.*
**2 ► CIGARETTE ◄** the end of a cigarette after most of it has been smoked
**3 ► GUN ◄** the thick end of the handle of a gun: *a rifle butt*
**4 ► CONTAINER ◄** a large round container for collecting or storing liquids: *a rainwater butt*
**5 ► ACT OF STRIKING STH ◄** the act of striking someone with your head
**6 ► PART OF YOUR BODY ◄** *AmE informal* the part of your body that you sit on; BUTTOCK —see also **a pain in the ass/butt** (PAIN¹ (3))
**7 get your butt in/out/over** *AmE spoken* used to rudely tell someone to go somewhere or do something: *Get your butt out of that bathroom now.*

**butt²** *v* [I,T] **1** to hit or push against something or someone with your head **2** if an animal butts someone, it hits them with its horns

**butt in** *phr v* [I] **1** to interrupt a conversation rudely: *Stop butting in!* **2** *AmE* to become involved in a private situation that does not concern you: *Things were going real well until you had to butt in!*

**butt out** *phr v* [I] *AmE spoken* used to tell someone to stop being involved in something: *This has got nothing to do with you, so just butt out!*

**butte** /bjuːt/ *n* [C] *AmE* a hill with steep sides and a flat top

S2 **but·ter¹** /ˈbʌtə‖-ər/ *n* [U] **1** a solid yellow food made from milk or cream that you spread on bread or use in cooking: *Beat the butter and sugar together.* **2 butter wouldn't melt in sb's mouth** used to say that someone seems to be very kind and sincere but is not really —**buttery** *adj*

**butter²** *v* [T] to spread butter on something: *buttered toast*

**butter** sb ↔ **up** *phr v* [T] *informal* to say nice things to someone so that they will do what you want: *Don't think you can butter me up that easily.*

**but·ter·ball** /ˈbʌtətbɔːl‖-tərbɒːl/ *n* [C] *AmE informal* someone who is fat, especially a child

**butter bean** /ˈ·· ·/ *n* a large pale yellow bean —see picture on page 414

**but·ter·cream** /ˈbʌtəkriːm‖-ər-/ *n* [U] a soft mixture of butter and sugar used inside or on top of cakes

**but·ter·cup** /ˈbʌtəkʌp‖-ər-/ *n* [C] a small shiny yellow wild flower

**but·ter·fat** /ˈbʌtəfæt‖-ər-/ *n* [U] the natural fat in milk

**but·ter·fin·gers** /ˈbʌtəˌfɪŋgəz‖ˈbʌtərˌfɪŋgərz/ *n* [singular] *informal* someone who often drops things they are carrying or trying to catch

**but·ter·fly** /ˈbʌtəflaɪ‖-ər-/ *n* [C] **1** a type of insect that has large wings, often with beautiful colours **2 have butterflies (in your stomach)** *informal* to feel very nervous before doing something: *I always get butterflies before an exam.* **3 butterfly stroke** a way of swimming by lying on your front and moving your arms together over your head **4** someone who usually moves on quickly from one activity or person to the next

butterfly

**butterfly nut** /ˈ··· ˌ·/ *n* [C] a WING NUT

**but·ter·milk** /ˈbʌtəˌmɪlk‖-ər-/ *n* [U] the liquid that remains after butter has been made

**but·ter·scotch** /ˈbʌtəskɒtʃ‖-ərskɑːtʃ/ *n* [U] a type of sweet made from butter and sugar boiled together

**butt·hole** /ˈbʌthəʊl‖-hoʊl/ *n* [C] *AmE taboo slang* **1** someone's ANUS **2** used to insult someone: *You butthole!*

**but·tock** /ˈbʌtək/ *n* [C usually plural] one of the fleshy parts of your body that you sit on —see picture at BODY

**but·ton¹** /ˈbʌtn/ *n* **1** [C] a small round flat object on your shirt, coat etc which you pass through a hole to fasten it: **do up/undo a button** (=fasten or unfasten a button) —see picture at FASTENER **2** [C] a small round object on a machine that you press to make it work: *Press the pause button.* —see also PUSH-BUTTON **3** *AmE* a small metal or plastic BADGE (1,2), often with a message on it **4 button nose/eyes** a nose or eyes that are small and round **5 on the button** *informal especially AmE* exactly right, or at exactly the right time —see also **as bright as a button** (BRIGHT (5)) S2

**button²** *v* [I,T] also **button up** **1** to fasten clothes with buttons or to be fastened with buttons: *I don't like pants that button at the side.* | *Sam, make sure Nina buttons up her jacket.* **2 button it!** *spoken* used to tell someone impolitely to stop talking

**button-down** /ˈ·· ·/ *adj* a button-down shirt or collar has the ends of the collar fastened to the shirt with buttons —see picture on page 840

**but·ton·hole** /ˈbʌtnhəʊl‖-hoʊl/ *n* [C] **1** a hole for a button to be put through to fasten a shirt, coat etc —see picture on page 840 **2** *BrE* a flower you fasten to your clothes; BOUTONNIERE *AmE*

**button-through** /ˈ·· ·/ *adj BrE* a button-through dress or skirt fastens from the top to the bottom with buttons

**but·tress¹** /ˈbʌtrəs/ *n* [C] a brick or stone structure built to support a wall

**buttress²** *v* [T] to support a system, idea, argument etc, especially by providing money: *The evidence seemed to buttress their argument.*

**but·ty** /ˈbʌti/ *n* [C] *BrE informal* a SANDWICH

**bux·om** /ˈbʌksəm/ *adj* a woman who is buxom is attractively large and healthy and has big breasts

**buy¹** /baɪ/ *v past tense and past participle* **bought** /bɔːt‖bɒːt/ **1 a)** [I,T] to get something by paying money for it: *Where did you buy that dress?* | **buy sb sth** *Let me buy you a drink.* | **buy sth for** *Sally's buying new curtains for the bedroom.* | **buy sth from sb** *I bought this from an old guy in the market.* | **buy sth for $10/£200 etc** *I bought it for two bucks at a garage sale.* | **buy sth for a song** (=buy something very cheaply) —opposite SELL¹ (1) **b)** [T] if a sum of money buys something, that is what you can get with it: *A dollar doesn't buy much these days.* **2 buy time** to get more time to do something, especially by making excuses: *Tell them we've got problems with the software, it might buy us more time.* **3** [T] *informal* to believe an explanation or reason, especially one that is not very likely to be true: *We could say it was an accident, but he'd never buy that.* **4** [T] *AmE informal* to pay money to someone, especially someone in an official position, in order to persuade them to do something dishonest; BRIBE: *They say the judge was bought.* **5 (have) bought it** *informal* to be killed, especially in an accident or war: *Vic bought it somewhere in the desert.* S1 W1

**buy in** sth *phr v* [T] *BrE* to buy something in large quantities: *We'd better buy in more beer for the party.*

**buy into** sth *phr v* [T] **1** to buy part of a business or organization, especially because you want to control it: *Clegg used the money to buy into a printing business.* **2** *informal* to believe an idea

**buy** sb ↔ **off** *phr v* [T] to pay someone money to stop them causing trouble or threatening you; BRIBE¹

**buy out** *phr v* **1** [T **buy** sb/sth ↔ **out**] to buy someone's shares (SHARE² (6)) of a business that you previously owned together, so that you have complete control —see also BUYOUT **2** [T **buy** sb **out of** sth] to pay money so that someone can leave an organization such as the army before their contract has finished

**buy up** sth ↔ *phr v* [T] to quickly buy as much as you can of something such as land, tickets, food etc: *Much of the land has been bought up by property developers.*

Frequencies of the verbs **buy**, **get** and **purchase** in spoken and written English.

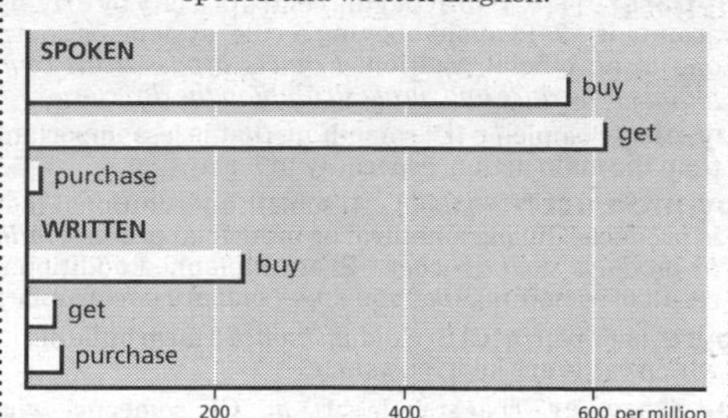


Based on the British National Corpus and the Longman Lancaster Corpus

All three verbs are used to mean 'get something by paying for it'. The graph shows that in this meaning **get** is extremely common in spoken English. However, **get** is informal and is not at all common in written English. **Purchase** is used in formal or business contexts. It is not very common and is used more in written English than in spoken English.

**buy**[2] *n* **be a good/bad buy** to be worth or to be not worth the price you paid: *The wine is a good buy at £3.49* see CHEAP[2] (USAGE).

S3 W3 **buy·er** /ˈbaɪə‖-ər/ *n* [C] **1** someone who buys something expensive such as a house or car: *We hope lower house prices will attract more buyers* —opposite SELLER (1). **2** someone whose job is to choose and buy the goods for a shop or company

**buyer's mar·ket** /ˌ.. ˈ.., ˈ.. ˌ../ *n* [singular] a situation in which there is plenty of something available so that buyers have a lot of choice and prices tend to be low —opposite SELLER'S MARKET

**buy·out** /ˈbaɪaʊt/ *n* [C] a situation in which someone gains control of a company by buying all or most of its shares (SHARE[2] (6)): *a management buyout*

**buzz**[1] /bʌz/ *v*

**1** ▶ **MAKE A SOUND** ◀ [I] to make a continuous sound, like the sound of a BEE: *The machine made a loud buzzing noise.*

**2** ▶ **MOVE AROUND** ◀ **a)** [I always + adv/prep] to move around in the air making a continuous sound like a BEE **buzz round/around/about** *A fly buzzed round the room.* **b)** to move quickly and busily around a place: **buzz around/round/about** *I spent the day buzzing around town in Dad's car.*

**3** ▶ **EXCITEMENT** ◀ [I] if a group of people or a place is buzzing, people are making a lot of noise because they are excited: [+ **with**] *Lineker had the crowd buzzing with excitement.*

**4 sb's head/mind is buzzing (with sth)** if your head or mind is buzzing with thoughts, ideas etc, your cannot stop thinking about them

**5** ▶ **EARS** ◀ [I] if your ears or head are buzzing you can hear a continuous low unpleasant sound

**6** ▶ **CALL** ◀ [I + **for,** T] to call someone by pressing a BUZZER: *I'll just buzz my secretary and ask for the file.*

**7** ▶ **AIRCRAFT** ◀ [T] *informal* to fly an aircraft low and fast over buildings, people etc

**buzz off** *phr v* [I] *spoken* **1 buzz off!** used to tell someone impolitely to go away **2** to go away: *I've finished everything, so I'll buzz off now.*

**buzz**[2] *n* **1** [C] a continuous noise like the sound of a BEE —see picture on page 1261 **2** [singular] the sound of people talking a lot in an excited way: [+ **of**] *a buzz of anticipation* **3** [singular] *informal* a strong feeling of excitement, pleasure, or success: **give sb a buzz** *You know Steve, driving fast gives him a real buzz.* **4 give sb a buzz** *informal* to telephone someone **5 the buzz** *informal* unofficial news or information that is spread by people telling each other: *The buzz is that Jack is leaving.*

**buz·zard** /ˈbʌzəd‖-ərd/ *n* [C] **1** *BrE* a type of large HAWK[1] (1) (=hunting bird) **2** *AmE* a type of large bird that eats dead animals

**buzz·cut** /ˈbʌzkʌt/ *n* [C] *AmE* a very short style of cutting hair —see picture at HAIRSTYLE

**buzz·er** /ˈbʌzə‖-ər/ *n* [C] a small electric machine that buzzes (BUZZ[1] (1)) when you press it: *Press the buzzer if you know the answer.*

**buzz saw** /ˈ. ./ *n* [C] *AmE* a SAW[2] (1) with a round blade that is spun around by a motor; CIRCULAR SAW

**buzz·word** /ˈbʌzwɜːd‖-wɜːrd/ *n* [C] a word or phrase from one special area of knowledge that people suddenly think is very important: *The 'information superhighway' became a buzzword in the 90s.*

**by-, bye-** /baɪ/ *prefix* less important: *a by-product* (=something made in addition to the main product) | *a by-election* (=one held between regular elections)

**by**[1] /baɪ/ *prep* **1** used especially with a PASSIVE[1] (2) verb to show the person or thing that does something or makes something happen: *I was attacked by a dog.* | *The building was designed by a famous architect.* | *We are all alarmed by the rise in violent crime.* **2** using or doing a particular thing: *You can reserve the tickets by phone.* | *Send it by airmail.* | *I know her by sight.* (=recognize her face) **by doing sth** | *She earns her living by selling insurance.* | **by train/plane/car** *We're travelling to London by train.* **3** passing through or along a particular place: *They came in by the back door.* | *It's quicker to go by the country route.* **4** beside or near something: *She stood by the window looking out over the fields.* | *Jane went and sat by Patrick.* **5** if you move or travel by someone or something, you go past them without stopping: *He walked by without noticing me.* | *I go by the Vicarage every day on my way to work.* **6** used to show the name of someone who wrote a book, produced a film, wrote a piece of music etc: *the 'New World Symphony' by Dvorak* **7** not later than a particular time date etc: *The documents need to be ready by next Friday.* | *I reckon the film should be over by 9.30.* **8** according to a particular rule, method, or way of doing things: *You've got to play by the rules.* | *Profits were £6 million, but by their standards this is low.* **9** used to show the amount or degree of something: *The price of oil fell by a further $2 a barrel.* | *I was overcharged by £3.* | **by far** (=by a large amount or degree) *Godard's first film was better by far.* **10** used to show the part of a piece of equipment or of someone's body that someone takes or holds: *He took her by the arm and led her across the road.* | *She grabbed the hammer by the handle.* **11** used when expressing strong feelings or making serious promises: *By God, I'll kill that boy when I see him!* **12** used between two numbers that you are multiplying or dividing: *What's 48 divided by 4?* **13** used when giving the measurements of a room, container etc: *a room 15 metres by 23 metres* **14** used to show a rate or quantity: *We're paid by the hour.* **15 day by day/bit by bit etc** used to show the way in which something happens: *Day by day he grew weaker.* **16** used to show the situation or period of time during which you do something or something happens: *You could ruin your eyes reading by torchlight.* | **by day/night** *a tour of Paris by night* **17** used to show the connection between one fact or thing and another: *Colette's French by birth.* | *It's fine by me if you want to go.* **18** as a result of an action or situation: **by accident** *I saw Maureen quite by accident in the supermarket the other day.* | **by mistake** *I managed to delete an afternoon's work on the computer by mistake.* **19** if a woman has children by a particular man, that man is the children's father: *Ann's got two children by her previous husband.* **20 (all) by yourself** completely alone: *Dave spent Christmas all by himself.* S1 W1

**by**[2] *adv* **1** if someone or something moves or goes by, they go past: *As I was standing on the platform the Liverpool train went whizzing by.* | *Ten years had gone by since I*

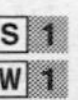

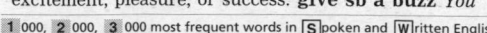

*had last seen Marilyn.|James walked by without even looking in my direction.* **2** beside or near someone or something: *A crowd of people were standing by waiting for an announcement.* **3 put/keep/lay sth by etc** to put something somewhere in order to use it in the future: *Her mother gave her a dinner service to put by for when she got married.* **4 call/stop/go by** to go to someone's house in order to visit them for a short time: *Why don't you stop by for a drink after work?* **5 by and large** *especially spoken* used when talking generally about someone or something: *Charities are, by and large, exempt from income tax.* **6 by the by** *spoken* used when mentioning something that may be interesting but is not particularly important: *By the by, Ian said he might call round tonight.* **7 by and by** *especially literary* soon

**bye-** /baɪ/ *prefix* another spelling of BY-

S1 **bye¹** /baɪ/ also **bye-bye** /ˌ· ˈ·‖ˈ· ·/ *interjection informal* goodbye: **bye for now** (=used to say that you will see or speak to someone again soon)

S3 **bye²** *n* [C] a situation in a sports competition in which a player or a team does not have an opponent to play against and continues to the next part of the competition

**bye-byes** /ˈ· ·/ *n* **go (to) bye-byes** *BrE* an expression meaning go to sleep, used by or to children

**by-e·lec·tion**, **bye-election** /ˈ· ·ˌ··/ *n* [C] *especially BrE* a special election to replace a politician who has left parliament or died

**by·gone** /ˈbaɪgɒn‖-gɒːn/ *adj* **bygone age/era/days etc** an expression meaning a period of time in the past: *The buildings reflect the elegance of a bygone era.*

**by·gones** /ˈbaɪgɒnz‖-gɒːnz/ *n* **let bygones be bygones** to forget something bad that someone has done to you and forgive them

**by·law** /ˈbaɪlɔː‖-lɒː/ *n* **1** [C] a law made by a local government that people in that area must obey **2** *AmE* a rule made by an organization to control the people who belong to it

**by-line** /ˈ· ·/ *n* [C] a line at the beginning of some writing in a newspaper or magazine giving the writer's name

**by·pass¹** /ˈbaɪpɑːs‖-pæs/ *n* [C] **1** a road that goes around a town or other busy area rather than through it **2** *technical* a tube that allows gas or liquid to flow around something rather than through it **3 heart bypass/bypass surgery** an operation to direct blood through new VEINS (=blood tubes) outside the heart

**bypass²** *v* [T] **1** to avoid the centre of a city by driving around it **2** to avoid obeying a rule, system, or someone in an official position: *Francis bypassed the complaints procedure and wrote straight to the director.*

**by·play** /ˈbaɪpleɪ/ *n* [U] something that is less important than the main action, especially in a play

**by-prod·uct** /ˈ· ˌ··/ *n* [C] **1** something additional that is produced during a natural or industrial process: *milk by-products such as whey* **2** an unplanned additional result of something that you do —compare END PRODUCT

**byre** /baɪə‖baɪr/ *n* [C] *BrE old-fashioned* a farm building in which cattle are kept; COWSHED

**by·stand·er** /ˈbaɪˌstændə‖-ər/ *n* [C] someone who watches what is happening without taking part; ONLOOKER: **innocent bystander** *Several innocent bystanders were killed by the blast.*

**byte** /baɪt/ *n* [C] *technical* a unit of computer information equal to eight bits (BIT¹ (12))

**by·way** /ˈbaɪweɪ/ *n* [C] a small road or path which is not used very much

**by·word** /ˈbaɪwɜːd‖-wɜːrd/ *n* [C] **1 be a byword for** to be so well known for a particular quality that your name is used to represent that quality: *The political system had become a byword for fraud.* **2** [singular] a phrase or saying that is very well known

**by·zan·tine** /baɪˈzæntaɪn, -tiːn, bɪ-‖ˈbɪzəntiːn, -taɪn/ *adj formal* complicated and difficult to understand: *the byzantine complexity of our tax laws*

**C, c** /siː/ *plural* **C's, c's** *n* [C] **1** the third letter of the English alphabet **2** the number 100 in the system of ROMAN NUMERALS

**c** **1** the written abbreviation of CENTIMETRE(s) **2** a written abbreviation of CIRCA (=about): *born c 1830* **3** the written abbreviation of CUBIC **4** the written abbreviation of COPYRIGHT when printed inside a small circle

**C[1]** /siː/*n* **1 a)** the first note in the musical SCALE[1] (8) of C MAJOR[1] (4) **b)** the musical KEY[1] (4) on this note **2** a mark given to a student's work to show that it is of average quality

**C[2]** the written abbreviation of CELSIUS: *Water boils at 100°C.*

**C&W** /ˌsiː ən ˈdʌbəljuː/ *n* [U] COUNTRY AND WESTERN (=type of music)

**ca** a written abbreviation of CIRCA (=about) *dating from ca 1900*

**cab** /kæb/ *n* [C] **1** a taxi: **call (sb) a cab** (=telephone for a taxi) **2** the part of a bus, train or TRUCK[1] (1) in which the driver sits **3** a carriage pulled by horses that was used like a taxi in former times

**ca·bal** /kəˈbæl/ *n* [C] a small group of people who make secret plans, especially in order to have political power

**cab·a·ret** /ˈkæbəreɪ‖ˌkæbəˈreɪ/ *n* **1** [C,U] entertainment, usually with music, songs, and dancing, performed in a restaurant or club while the customers eat and drink **2** [C] a restaurant or club where this is performed: *the most famous Parisian cabaret, the Moulin Rouge*

**cab·bage** /ˈkæbɪdʒ/ *n* **1** [C,U] a large round vegetable with thick green or purple leaves —see picture on page 414 **2** [C] *BrE informal* **a)** someone who is lazy and shows no interest in anything **b)** someone who cannot think, move, speak etc as a result of brain injury; VEGETABLE (2)

**cab·bie, cabby** /ˈkæbi/ *n* [C] *informal* a taxi driver

**ca·ber** /ˈkeɪbə‖-ər/ *n* [C] a long heavy wooden pole that is thrown into the air as a test of strength in sports competitions in Scotland: *tossing the caber*

**cab·in** /ˈkæbɪ̈n/ *n* [C] **1** a small house, especially one built of wood in an area of forest or mountains **2** a small room on a ship in which you live or sleep **3** an area inside a plane where the passengers sit or where the pilot works: *the First Class cabin*

**cabin boy** /ˈ·· ·/ *n* [C] a young man who works as a servant on a ship

**cabin class** /ˈ·· ·/ *n* [U] travelling conditions on a ship that are better than TOURIST CLASS but not as good as FIRST CLASS (1)

**cabin cruis·er** /ˈ·· ˌ··/ *n* [C] a large motor boat with one or more cabins for people to sleep in

S2 W2 **cab·i·net** *n* [C] **1** [also + plural verb BrE] the politicians with important positions in a government who meet to make decisions or advise the leader of the government: *a cabinet meeting* **2** a piece of furniture with doors and shelves or drawers, used for storing or showing things: *a drinks cabinet* – see also FILING CABINET

**cabinet-mak·er** /ˈ··· ˌ··/ *n* [C] someone whose job is to make good quality wooden furniture

**cabin fe·ver** /ˈ·· ˌ··/ *n* [U] *AmE* a state in which you feel bad-tempered, because you have not been outside for a long time

W3 **ca·ble[1]** /ˈkeɪbəl/ *n* **1** [C] a plastic or rubber tube containing wires that carry telephone messages, electronic signals etc **2** [C,U] a thick strong metal rope used on ships, to support bridges etc **3** [U] CABLE TELEVISION: *a cable channel* **4** [C] a TELEGRAM

**cable[2]** *v* [I,T] to send someone a CABLE[1] (4) **cable sb sth** *I cabled Mary the good news.*

**cable car** /ˈ·· ·/ *n* [C] **1** a vehicle pulled by a moving CABLE[1] (2), used to take people to the top of mountains **2** a vehicle used in cities, that is pulled along by a moving CABLE[1] (2)

cable car

**ca·ble·gram** /ˈkeɪbəlgræm/ *n* [C] a TELEGRAM

**cable rail·way** /ˈ·· ˌ··/ *n* [C] a railway on which vehicles are pulled up steep slopes by a moving CABLE[1] (2)

**cable stitch** /ˈ·· ·/ *n* [C,U] a knotted pattern of stitches used in KNITTING

**cable tel·e·vi·sion** /ˌ·· ˈ···· ˌ·· ··ˈ··/ also **cable TV** /ˌ·· ··ˈ·/ *n* [U] a system of broadcasting television programmes by CABLE[1] (1) —compare SATELLITE TELEVISION

**ca·boo·dle** /kəˈbuːdl/ *n* **the whole (kit and) caboodle** *informal* everything: *slash costs by abolishing the whole caboodle: ballot papers, polling booths, even town halls.*

**ca·boose** /kəˈbuːs/ *n* [C] *AmE* the part of a train where the official in charge of it travels, usually at the back; GUARD'S VAN *BrE*

**cab rank** /ˈ· ·/ *n* [C] *BrE* a place where taxis wait; CABSTAND *AmE*

**cab·ri·o·let** /ˈkæbriəleɪ‖ˌkæbriəˈleɪ/ *n* [C] a car with a roof that can be folded back; CONVERTIBLE[2]

**cab·stand** /ˈkæbstænd/ *n* [C] *AmE* a place where taxis wait for customers; TAXI RANK *BrE*

**ca·cao** /kəˈkaʊ/ *n* [C] the seed from which chocolate and COCOA are made

**cache[1]** /kæʃ/ *n* [C] a number of things that have been hidden, or the place where they have been hidden: *Police found a cache of explosives in a garage in South London.*

**cache[2]** *v* [T] to hide something in a secret place

**cach·et** /ˈkæʃeɪ‖kæˈʃeɪ/ *n* [U] *formal* if something has cachet, people think it is especially good and desirable: *a good college but without the cachet of Harvard or Yale.*

**cack-hand·ed** /ˌkæk ˈhændɪ̈d◂/ *adj BrE informal* careless or tending to drop things; CLUMSY (1)

**cack·le[1]** /ˈkækəl/ *v* [I] **1** to laugh in a loud unpleasant way, making short high sounds: *Rumplestiltskin rubbed his hands and cackled with delight.* **2** when a chicken cackles, it makes a loud unpleasant sound

**cackle[2]** *n* **1** [C,U] a short high unpleasant laugh: *loud cackles of amusement* **2 cut the cackle** *BrE old-fashioned* used to tell someone to stop talking about unimportant things

**ca·coph·o·ny** /kəˈkɒfəni‖kəˈkɑː-/ *n* [singular] a loud unpleasant mixture of sounds: *a cacophony of car horns and shouting* —**cacophonous** *adj*

**cac·tus** /ˈkæktəs/ *n plural* **cacti** /-taɪ/ or **cactuses** [C] a prickly plant that grows in hot dry places

**CAD** /ˌsiː eɪ ˈdiː, kæd/ *n* [U] computer-aided design; the use of COMPUTER GRAPHICS to plan cars, aircraft, buildings etc

**cad** /kæd/ *n* [C] *old-fashioned* a man who cannot be trusted —**caddish** *adj*

**ca·dav·er** /kəˈdævə, kəˈdeɪ-‖kəˈdævər-/ *n* [C] *technical* a dead human body: *He looked like a walking cadaver.*

**ca·dav·er·ous** /kəˈdævərəs/ *adj formal* looking extremely pale, thin, and unhealthy: *cadaverous cheeks*

**CAD/CAM** /ˈkædkæm/ *n* [U] computer-aided design and manufacture; the use of computers to plan and make industrial products

**cad·dy[1]** /ˈkædi/ *n* [C] **1** also **caddie** someone who carries the GOLF CLUBS for someone who is playing GOLF **2** a small box for storing tea

**caddy[2], caddie** *v* [I + **for**] to carry GOLF CLUBS

for someone who is playing GOLF —see picture on page 1264

**ca·dence** /ˈkeɪdəns/ *n* [C] **1** the way someone's voice rises and falls, especially when reading out loud **2** *technical* a set of CHORDS at the end of a line or piece of music

**ca·den·za** /kəˈdenzə/ *n* [C] *technical* a difficult part of a CONCERTO in which the performer plays without the ORCHESTRA to show their skill

**ca·det** /kəˈdet/ *n* [C] **1** someone who is training to be an officer in the army, navy, air force, or police force **2** someone who is in a CADET CORPS

**cadet corps** /·ˈ· ·/ *n* [C] an organization that gives simple military training to pupils in some British schools

**cadge** /kædʒ/ *v* [I,T] *BrE informal* to ask someone for food or cigarettes because you do not have any or do not want to pay; MOOCH *AmE*: **cadge sth from/off** *I managed to cadge a lift from Joanna.* —**cadger** *n* [C]

**Cad·il·lac** /ˈkædɪlæk,-dəl-/ *n* [C] *trademark* **1** a very expensive and comfortable car made by an American company **2** *AmE informal* something that is regarded as the highest quality example of a particular type of product; ROLLS ROYCE *BrE*: *the Cadillac of stereo systems*

**cad·mi·um** /ˈkædmiəm/ *n* [U] a type of metal used in batteries (BATTERY (1))

**ca·dre** /ˈkɑːdə, -drə, ˈkeɪdə‖ˈkædri, ˈkɑːdrə/ *n formal* [C also + plural verb *BrE*] a small group of specially trained people in a profession, political party, or military force: *a cadre of highly trained scientists*

**cae·sar·e·an** /sɪ̇ˈzeriən‖-ˈzer-/ also **caesarean section** /·,··· ˈ··/ *n* [C] an operation in which a woman's body is cut open to take a baby out; C-SECTION *AmE*

**cae·su·ra** /sɪˈzjʊərə‖sɪˈʒʊrə, sɪˈzʊrə/ *n* [C] *technical* a pause in the middle of a line of poetry

**café** /ˈkæfeɪ‖kæˈfeɪ, kə-/ *n* [C] **1** a small restaurant where you can buy drinks and simple meals **2** a place on a computer NETWORK[1] (4), where people with similar interests discuss things electronically: *You can set up a special interest café on e-mail or Internet.*

**caf·e·te·ri·a** /ˌkæfɪ̇ˈtɪəriə‖-ˈtɪr-/ *n* *n* [C] a restaurant where you choose your own food and carry it to the table, often in a factory, college etc: *the school cafeteria*

**caf·e·tiere** /ˌkæfəˈtjeə‖-ˈtjer/ *n* [C] a special pot for making coffee, with a metal FILTER[1] (1) that you push down

**caff** /kæf/ *n* [C] *informal BrE* a café

**caf·feine** /ˈkæfiːn‖kæˈfiːn/ *n* [U] a substance in tea and coffee that makes you feel more active

**caf·tan** /ˈkæftæn‖kæfˈtæn/ *n* [C] a long loose piece of clothing like a coat, usually made of silk or cotton and worn in the Middle East

**cage**[1] /keɪdʒ/ *n* [C] a structure made of wires or bars in which birds or animals can be kept

cage

**cage**[2] *v* **1** [T] to put or keep something in a cage: *caged birds* **2 feel caged in** to feel uncomfortable and annoyed because you cannot go outside

**cag·ey** /ˈkeɪdʒi/ *adj informal* unwilling to tell people definitely what your plans, intentions, or opinions are: [**+ about**] *Senator King is being very cagey about whether he'll run for president* —**cagily** *adv* —**caginess** *n*

**ca·goule** /kəˈguːl/ *n* [C] *BrE* a thin coat with a HOOD (=cover for your head) that stops you from getting wet

**ca·hoots** /kəˈhuːts/ *n* **be in cahoots (with)** to be working secretly with another person or group, especially in order to do something dishonest: *Perhaps O'Brien was in cahoots with the thieves.*

**cairn** /keən‖kern/ *n* [C] a pile of stones, especially at the top of a mountain, to mark a place

**cais·son** /ˈkeɪsən, kəˈsuːn‖ˈkeɪsɑːn, -sən/ *n* [C] **1** a large box filled with air, that allows people to work under water **2** a large box for carrying AMMUNITION (1)

**ca·jole** /kəˈdʒəʊl‖-ˈdʒoʊl/ *v* [I,T] to gradually persuade someone to do something by being nice, etc: **cajole sb into doing sth** *Can't you cajole her into coming?*

**cake**[1] /keɪk/ *n* **1** [C, U] a soft sweet food made by baking a mixture of flour, fat, sugar and eggs: *a birthday cake* | *Would you like a slice of chocolate cake?* —compare BISCUIT **2 fish cake/rice cake etc** fish, rice etc that has been formed into a flat round shape and then cooked **3** [C] a small block of something: [**+ of**] *a cake of soap* **4 be a piece of cake** *spoken* to be very easy: *"How do you do that?" "It's a piece of cake! Watch!"* **5 take the cake** *AmE informal* to be worse than anything else you can imagine; **take the biscuit** (BISCUIT (4)) *BrE*: *I've heard some pretty dumb ideas, but that takes the cake!* **6 you can't have your cake and eat it** *spoken* used to tell someone that they cannot have the advantage of something without its disadvantages **7 a slice of the cake** a part of the money, help etc that is available for everyone to share —see also **sell like hot cakes** (HOT CAKE)

**cake**[2] *v* **1 be caked with/in** to be covered with a layer of something thick and hard: *Look at your boots! They're caked with mud.* **2** [I] if a substance cakes, it forms a thick hard layer when it dries

**cake·hole** /ˈkeɪk-həʊl‖-hoʊl/ *n* [C] *BrE spoken* someone's mouth: *Shut your cakehole!*

**cake pan** /ˈ· ·/ *n* [C] *AmE* a CAKE TIN (1)

**cake tin** /ˈ· ·/ *n* [C] *BrE* **1** a metal container in which you bake a cake —see picture at PAN[1] **2** a metal container with a lid, that you keep a cake in

**cake·walk** /ˈkeɪkwɔːk‖-wɒːk/ *n* [singular] *AmE informal* a very easy victory

**cal·a·bash** /ˈkæləbæʃ/ *n* [C] a large tropical fruit with a shell that can be dried and used as a bowl

**cal·a·brese** /ˈkæləbriːs/ *n* [U] a type of BROCCOLI

**cal·a·mine lo·tion** /ˈkæləmaɪn ˌləʊʃən‖-ˌloʊ-/ *n* [U] a pink liquid for sore, itchy or sunburnt (SUNBURN) skin

**ca·lam·i·ty** /kəˈlæmɪ̇ti/ *n* [C] a terrible and unexpected event that causes a lot of damage or suffering: *It would be a calamity for the farmers if the crops failed again.* —**calamitous** *adj* —**calamitously** *adv*

**cal·ci·fy** /ˈkælsɪ̇faɪ/ *v* [I,T] *technical* to become hard, or make something hard, by adding LIME[1] (3)

**cal·ci·um** /ˈkælsiəm/ *n* [U] a simple chemical substance in bones, teeth, and CHALK[1] (1)

**cal·cu·la·ble** /ˈkˈlkjɡ̇ləbəl/ *adj* something that is calculable can be measured by using numbers: *clear and calculable beneficial effects*

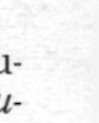

**cal·cu·late** /ˈkælkjɡ̇leɪt/ *v* [T] **1** to find out how much something will cost, how long something will take etc, by using numbers: *Oil prices are calculated in dollars.* | **calculate how much/how many etc** *I'm trying to calculate how much paint we need.* | **calculate (that)** *Sally calculated that she'd have about £100 left.* **2** to guess something using as many facts as you can find: *It's difficult to calculate what effect all these changes will have on the company.* **3 be calculated to do sth** to be intended to have a particular effect: *a comment calculated to annoy traditionalists in the party*

**calculate on** sth *phr v* [T] if you calculate on something you are depending on it for your plans to succeed: *We're calculating on an early start.* | **calculate on sb/sth doing sth** *Ken hadn't calculated on Polson refusing his offer.*

**cal·cu·lat·ed** /ˈkælkjɡ̇leɪtɪ̇d/ *adj* **1** a calculated crime or dishonest action is deliberately and carefully planned: *a calculated attempt to deceive the American public* **2 take a calculated risk** to do something that involves a risk after thinking carefully about what might happen —see also CALCULATE —**calculatedly** *adv*

**cal·cu·lat·ing** /ˈkælkjɡ̊leɪtɪŋ/ *adj* making careful and clever plans to get what you want, without caring about anyone else: *a criminal with a cold, calculating mind*

S2 **cal·cu·la·tion** /ˌkælkjɡ̊ˈleɪʃən/ *n* **1** [C,U] a way of using numbers in order to find out an amount, price, or value: *Dee looked at the bill and made some rapid calculations.*
**2** [U] careful planning in order to get what you want

S3 **cal·cu·la·tor** /ˈkælkjɡ̊leɪtə‖-ər/ *n* [C] a small electronic machine that can do calculations such as adding and multiplying: *a solar calculator* (=working using the power of the sun)

**cal·cu·lus** /ˈkælkjɡ̊ləs/ *n* [U] the part of mathematics that deals with changing quantities, such as the speed of a falling stone or the slope of a curved line

**cal·dron** /ˈkɔːldrən‖ˈkɒːl-/ *n* [C] the American spelling of CAULDRON

**cal·en·dar** /ˈkælɡ̊ndə‖-ər/ *n* [C] **1** pages printed to show the days, weeks, and months of a particular year, that you hang on the wall **2** *AmE* **a)** a book with separate spaces or pages for each day of the year, on which you write down the things you have to do; DIARY (2) *BrE* **b)** all the things you plan to do in the next days, months etc: *The President's calendar is already very full.* **3** a system for dividing time, that fixes the event from which all years are measured and arranges days into months and years: *the Gregorian calendar* **4** all the events in a year that are important for a particular organization or activity: *The Derby is a major event in the racing calendar.*

**calendar month** /ˌ··· ˈ·/ *n* [C] **1** one of the twelve months of the year: *Salaries will be paid at the end of the calendar month.* **2** a period of time from a specific date in one month to the same date in the next month

**calendar year** /ˌ··· ˈ·/ *n* [C] a period of time from January 1st to December 31st

**calf** /kɑːf‖kæf/ *n plural* **calves** /kɑːvz‖kævz/ [C] **1** the part of the back of your leg between your knee and your ANKLE —see picture at BODY **2** the baby of a cow, or of some other large animals such as the ELEPHANT **3 be in calf** if a cow is in calf, it is going to have a baby —see also **kill the fatted calf** (KILL[1] (14))

**calf love** /ˈ· ·/ *n* [U] PUPPY LOVE

**cal·i·ber** /ˈkælɡ̊bə‖-ər/ *n* the American spelling of CALIBRE

**cal·i·brate** /ˈkælɡ̊breɪt/ *v* [T] *technical* to mark an instrument or tool so that you can use it for measuring

**cal·i·bra·tion** /ˌkælɡ̊ˈbreɪʃən/ *n* [U] *technical* a set of marks on an instrument or tool used for measuring

**cal·i·bre** *BrE*, **caliber** *AmE* /ˈkælɡ̊bə‖-ər/ *n* **1** [U] the level of quality or ability that someone or something has achieved: *We've been lucky in the high calibre of directors we've been able to recruit.* **2** [C] *technical* **a)** the width of the inside of a gun or tube **b)** the width of a bullet

**cal·i·co** /ˈkælɪkəʊ‖-koʊ/ *n* [U] **1** *BrE* heavy cotton cloth that is usually white **2** *AmE* light cotton cloth with a small printed pattern **3 calico cat** *AmE* a cat that has black, white and brown fur

**cal·i·pers** /ˈkælɡ̊pəz‖-ərz/ *n* [plural] the American spelling of CALLIPERS

**ca·liph** /ˈkeɪlɡ̊f/ *n* [C] a MUSLIM ruler

**ca·li·phate** /ˈkeɪlɡ̊feɪt/ *n* [C] the country a caliph rules, or the period of time when they rule it

**cal·is·then·ics** /ˌkælɡ̊sˈθenɪks/ *n* [plural] the American spelling of CALLISTHENICS

**calk** /kɔːk‖kɒːk/ *v* [T] an American spelling of CAULK

## call[1] /kɔːl‖kɒːl/ *v* S1 W1

① HAVE/USE A NAME
② DESCRIBE SB/STH
③ TELEPHONE
④ SAY STH LOUDLY
⑤ TELL/ORDER
⑥ VISIT
⑦ AGREE
⑧ ARRANGE STH
⑨ OTHER MEANINGS

### ① HAVE/USE A NAME

**1** [T] **be called sth** to have a particular name or title: *They have a three-year-old son called Matthew.* | *What was that book called?*

**2** [T] to use a particular name or title when you speak to someone: *My name's Alan, but you can call me Al.* | *Do you want to be called Miss or Ms?* | **call sb by** *I prefer to be called by my middle name.*

**3** [T] to give someone or something the name they will be known by in the future: **call sb/sth sth** *They've decided to call the baby Louise.*

### ② DESCRIBE SB/STH

**4** [T] to use a particular word or phrase to describe someone or something that clearly shows what you think of them: **call sb/sth sth** *Are you calling me a liar?* | *You may call it harmless fun, but I call it pornography.*

**5 call yourself sth** to claim that you are a particular type of person, although you do nothing to show this is true: *He calls himself a Christian, but I've never seen him go to church.*

**6 call sb names** to insult someone by using unpleasant words to describe them: *The other kids used to call me names.* —see also **call a spade a spade** (SPADE (3))

### ③ TELEPHONE

**7** [I,T] to telephone someone: *I tried calling last night but you weren't home.* | *He said he'd call me later to make arrangements.* —see TELEPHONE[1] (USAGE)

**8** [T] to ask someone to come to you by telephoning them: *I think we should call the doctor.* | *I swear, I'm gonna call the cops!* —see graph at TELEPHONE[2] —see also **call in**

**9 call collect** *AmE* to make a telephone call that is paid for by the person who receives it; **reverse the charges** (REVERSE[1] (5)) *BrE*

### ④ SAY STH LOUDLY

**10** [I,T] to say or shout something loudly so that someone can hear you: *I thought I heard Dad calling me.* | [+ **through/down/up**] *"I'm coming!" she called down the stairs.*

**11** [T] also **call out** to read names or numbers in a loud voice in order to get someone's attention: *OK, when I call your name, go and stand in line.*

### ⑤ TELL/ORDER

**12** [T] to ask or order someone to come to you, either by speaking loudly or sending them a message: **call sb into/over** *Later, the boss called Dan into her office.* | **call sb up/down** *AmE*: *Marcie got called up to the Principal's office for smoking.*

**13** [T usually passive] to tell someone that they must come to a law court or official committee: **call sb to do sth** *They were called to give evidence at the trial.*

**14 be/feel called to do sth** if you are called to do

[continued on next page]

[continued from previous page]
something, you feel that God is telling you to do it: *Simon felt called to do missionary work.*
**15 call sb/sth to order** *formal* to tell people to obey the rules of a formal meeting: *I now call this meeting to order.*

## ⑥ VISIT

**16** [I] *BrE* also **call round** to stop at a house or other place for a short time to see someone or do something: *The milkman called while you were out.* | **call on sb** *We thought we'd call on James on the way home.* | **call at sth** *I called at the drycleaner's to collect your suit.*

## ⑦ AGREE

**17 call it £10/2 hours etc** *spoken* used to ask someone to agree with a particular suggestion you are making, especially in order to make things simpler: *"I owe you £10.20." "Oh, call it £10!"*
**18 call it a draw** if two opponents in a game call it a draw, they agree that neither of them has won —see also **call it quits** (QUITS (2))

## ⑧ ARRANGE STH

**19 call a meeting/election/rehearsal etc** to arrange for something to happen at a definite time: *We've called an emergency meeting of the governors.*
**20 call a huddle** *AmE informal* to arrange for people to come together to have a meeting

## ⑨ OTHER MEANINGS

**21 call into question** to make people uncertain about whether something is right or true: *I feel that my competence is being called into question here.*
**22 call it a day** *informal* to decide to stop working, especially because you have done enough or you are tired: *Come on, let's call it a day and go home.*
**23 call attention to** to ask people to pay attention to a particular subject or problem: *May I call your attention to item seven on the agenda.*
**24 ▶TRAINS◀** [I + at] if a train calls at a place, it stops there for a short time: *This train will call at all stations to Broxbourne.*
**25 call the tune/shots** *informal* to be in a position of authority so that you can give orders and make decisions
**26 call sth to mind a)** to remind you of something: *Don't those two call to mind the days when we were courting?* **b)** to remember something: *Can you call to mind when you last saw her?*
**27 ▶GAMES/SPORTS◀** [I,T] to guess which side of a coin will land upwards when it is thrown in the air, in order to decide who will play first in a game: *It's your turn to call.* —see also SO-CALLED **call sb's bluff** (BLUFF[2] (2))

**call back** *phr v* **1** [I,T] to telephone someone again, especially because one of you was not in or was busy: *No problem, I'll call back later.* | **call sb back** *Can you ask John to call me back when he gets in?* **2** [I] *BrE* to return to a place you have been to earlier, especially a house or a shop: *I'll call back with my car and pick up the painting.*

**call by** *phr v* [I] *BrE informal* to stop and visit someone when you are near the place where they live or work: *I thought I'd call by and see how you were.*

**call** sb/sth ↔ **down** *phr v* [T] *literary* to pray loudly that something unpleasant will happen to someone or something: *calling down the wrath of God*

**call for** sb/sth *phr v* [T] **1** to need a particular action, behaviour, quality etc: *Really, Susan, that kind of attitude just isn't called for.* —see also UNCALLED-FOR **2** to ask strongly and publicly for money, justice etc in order to change a situation: *farmers calling for larger government subsidies* **3** *BrE* to meet someone at their home in order to take them somewhere: *I'll call for you at 8 o'clock.* **4** *AmE* to say that something is likely to happen, especially when talking about the weather: *The forecast calls for more rain.*

**call** sth ↔ **forth** *phr v* [T] *formal* to make something such as a quality appear so that you can use it; SUMMON

**call in** *phr v* [I] **1** to telephone somewhere, especially the place where you work, to tell them where you are, what you are doing etc: **call in sick** (=telephone to say you are too ill to come to work) **2** [T **call** sb ↔ **in**] to ask someone to come and see you to help you with a difficult situation: *Police have been called in to help find missing Sandra Day, aged 7.* **3** [**call in a loan/favour**] to ask someone to pay back money or to help you with something because you helped them earlier **4** [I + **at/on**] *BrE* to visit a person or place while you are on your way somewhere else: *Could you call in on Mum on your way home?*

**call** sb/sth ↔ **off** *phr v* [T] **1** to order a dog or person to stop attacking someone: *Call off the alsation – it's frightening my son.* **2** to decide that a planned event will not take place; CANCEL: *There's no rush now – the game's been called off.* **3** [**call off a strike/search etc**] to decide officially that something should be stopped after it has already started: *Rescuers had to call off the search due to worsening weather.*

**call on/upon** sb/sth *phr v* [T] **1** to visit someone for a short time: *Why don't you call on my sister when you're in Brighton?* **2** to formally ask someone to do something: **call on sb to do sth** *The UN has called on both sides to observe the ceasefire.*

**call out** *phr v* **1** [I,T **call** sth ↔ **out**] to say something loudly: *Call out the numbers so that we can hear them at the back.* **2** [T **call** sb/sth ↔ **out**] **a)** to order an organization to help, especially in a dangerous situation: *The National guard has been called out to help fight fires.* **b)** *BrE* to order workers to go on strike (STRIKE[2] (1))

**call up** *phr v* **1** [I, T **call** sb ↔ **up**] *informal especially Am E*] to telephone someone **2** [T **call** sb ↔ **up** *BrE*] to officially order someone to join the army, navy, or air force; DRAFT[2] (2) *AmE I was called up three months after war broke out.* **3** [T **call** sb ↔ **up**] to choose someone for a national sports team, especially football: *Hurst was called up for the game against Mexico.* **4** [T **call** sth ↔ **up**] if you call up information on a computer, you make the computer show it to you **5** [T **call** sb/sth **up**] to make something appear again after it has gone or been forgotten: *calling up the spirits of the dead*

S1 W1 **call**[2] *n*
**1 ▶TELEPHONE◀** [C] **a)** an attempt to speak to someone by telephone: *Were there any phone calls for me while I was out?* | **get/receive a call** *I got a call from Jane in Australia last week.* | **give sb a call** *I'll give you a call at the weekend.* | **make a call** *It's cheaper to make calls after 6pm.* | **take a call** (=answer a call) *I'll take the call in my office.* | **return a call** (=telephone someone who tried to telephone you earlier) **b)** a telephone call asking a doctor, the police etc to go somewhere where they are needed: *We're getting calls about a disturbance at a pub in Camden.*
**2 be on call** if someone such as a doctor or engineer is on call, they are ready to go and help whenever they are needed as part of their job: *Don't worry, there's a doctor on call 24 hours a day.*
**3 ▶SHOUT/CRY◀** [C] **a)** the sound or cry that a bird or animal makes **b)** a shout or cry that you make to get someone's attention
**4 ▶VISIT◀** [C] a visit, especially for a particular reason: *Sorry, Doctor Pugh is out on a call at the moment.* | **pay/make a call (on)** (=visit someone) *Why not pay a call on your aunt while you're in Leeds?*
**5 there isn't much call for** used to say that something is not popular or is not needed: *There isn't much call for black and white televisions these days.*

**6 there is no call for** *spoken* used to tell someone that their behaviour is wrong and unnecessary: *There's no call for swearing – I'm doing my best!*
**7 ▶REQUEST/ORDER◀** [C] a request or order for someone to do something or go somewhere: *a strike call*| **call for sb to do sth** *There have been calls for the secretary to resign.*
**8 ▶PLANE◀** [C] an official message at an airport that a plane for a particular place will soon leave: *This is the last call for flight BA872 to Moscow.*
**9 ▶DECISION◀** [singular] **a)** the decision made by a REFEREE (=judge) in a sports game **b)** *AmE informal* a decision: **make a call** (=decide)| **easy/hard call** (=a difficult or easy decision)| **it's your call** *spoken*
**10 have first call on a)** to have the right to be the first person to use something **b)** to be the first person that someone will help because you are important to them
**11 the call of** *literary* the power that a place or way of life has to attract someone: *the call of the sea*
**12 the call of nature** a need to URINATE (=pass liquid from your body) —see also **be at sb's beck and call** (BECK (2)), PORT OF CALL, ROLL-CALL

**call box** /ˈ· ·/ *n* [C] **1** *AmE* a public telephone beside a road used to telephone for help **2** *BrE* a small structure that is partly or completely enclosed, containing a public telephone; PHONE BOOTH *AmE*

**call·er** /ˈkɔːlə‖ˈkɒːlər/ *n* [C] **1** someone making a telephone call: *An anonymous caller warned the police about the bomb.* **2** someone who visits your house: *If you're not sure who the caller is, ask to see some identification.*

**call girl** /ˈ· ·/ *n* [C] a PROSTITUTE who makes arrangements to meet men by telephone

**cal·lig·ra·phy** /kəˈlɪgrəfi/ *n* [U] the art of producing beautiful writing using special pens or brushes, or the writing produced this way —**calligrapher** *n* [C]

**call-in** /ˈ· ·/ *n* [C] *AmE* a radio or television programme in which people telephone to give their opinions; PHONE-IN *BrE*

**call·ing** /ˈkɔːlɪŋ‖ˈkɒː-/ *n* [C] **1** a strong desire or feeling of duty to do a particular kind of work, especially religious work; VOCATION (3) **2** *formal* someone's profession or trade

**calling card** /ˈ·· ·/ *n* [C] *AmE* a small card with a name and often address printed on it, that people used to give to people they visited; VISITING CARD

**cal·li·pers** *BrE*, **calipers** *AmE* /ˈkæləpəz‖-ərz/ *n plural* **1** a tool used for measuring thickness, the distance between two surfaces, or the DIAMETER (=inside width) of something **2** *BrE* metal bars that someone wears on their legs to help them walk; BRACE[2] (2b) *AmE*

**cal·lis·then·ics** *BrE*, **calisthenics** *AmE* /ˌkæləsˈθenɪks/ *n* [U] a set of physical exercises that are intended to make you thin and healthy

**call let·ters** /ˈ· ˌ··/ *n* [plural] *AmE* a name made up of letters and numbers used by people operating communication radios to prove who they are; CALL SIGN *BrE*

**call op·tion** /ˈ· ˌ··/ *n* [C] *technical* the right to buy a particular number of shares (SHARE[2] (6)) at a different price within a fixed period of time

**cal·lous** /ˈkæləs/ *adj* not caring that other people are suffering: *We were shocked at the callous disregard for human life.*| *the callous slaughter of thousands of seals* —**callously** *adv* —**callousness** *n* [U]

**cal·loused** /ˈkæləst/ *adj* calloused skin is rough and covered in CALLUSES

**cal·low** /ˈkæləʊ‖-loʊ/ *adj literary* young and without experience; IMMATURE: *a callow youth*

**call sign** /ˈ· ·/ *n* [C] *BrE* a name made up of letters and numbers used by people operating communication radios to prove who they are; CALL LETTERS *AmE*

**call-up** /ˈ· ·/ *n* [C] *BrE* an order to join the army, navy etc; DRAFT[1] (2) *AmE*: *He got his call-up papers in July.* —see also **call up** (CALL[1])

**cal·lus** /ˈkæləs/ also **callosity** /kəˈlɒsəti‖-ˈlɑː-/ *n* [C] an area of thick hard skin: *The rowers had calluses on their hands.*

**calm**[1] /kɑːm‖kɑːm, kɑːlm/ *adj* **1** quiet and without excitement, nervous activity, or strong feeling: *Richard spoke with calm authority.*| *Keep calm, and try not to panic!* **2** weather that is calm is not windy **3** a sea, lake etc that is calm is smooth or has only gentle waves —**calmly** *adv* —**calmness** *n* [U] S3

**calm**[2] *n* [U] **1** a situation that is quiet and peaceful: *They remained on the terrace after dinner, enjoying the calm of the evening.* **2 the calm before the storm** a calm peaceful situation before a big argument, problem etc

**calm**[3] *v* [T] to make someone or something quiet after strong emotion or nervous activity: *Charlie tried to calm the frightened children.*
**calm** (sb/sth ↔) **down** *phr v* [I,T] to become quiet after strong emotion or nervous activity, or make someone or something become quiet: *Calm down and tell me what happened.*

**Cal·or gas** /ˈkælə gæs‖-lər-/ *n* [U] *BrE trademark* a type of gas that is sold in metal containers and used where there is no gas supply

**cal·o·rie** /ˈkæləri/ *n* [C] **1** a unit for measuring the amount of ENERGY that food will produce: *An average potato has about 90 calories.*| *a calorie-controlled diet.*| *Burn off the calories with this new exercise bike.* **2** *technical* the amount of heat that is needed to raise the temperature of one gram of water by one degree centigrade **3 count your calories** to control your weight, especially by calculating the number of calories you eat

**cal·o·rif·ic** /ˌkæləˈrɪfɪk◂/ *adj* **1** food that is calorific tends to make you fat **2** *technical* producing heat

**ca·lum·ni·ate** /kəˈlʌmni-eɪt/ *v* [T] *formal* to say untrue and unfair things about someone; SLANDER[2]

**cal·um·ny** /ˈkæləmni/ *n* **1** [C] an untrue and unfair statement about someone intended to give people a bad opinion of them **2** [U] the act of saying things like this —see also SLANDER[1]

**cal·va·ry** /ˈkælvəri/ *n* [C] a model that represents the death of Jesus Christ

**calve** /kɑːv‖kæv/ *v* [I] to give birth to a CALF (=young cow)

**calves** /kɑːvz‖kævz/ *n* the plural of CALF

**Cal·vin·is·m** /ˈkælvənɪzəm/ *n* [U] the Christian religious teachings of John Calvin, based on the idea that events on Earth are controlled by God and cannot be changed by humans

**Cal·vin·ist** /ˈkælvənəst/ *adj* **1** following the teachings of CALVINISM **2** also **Calvinistic** /ˌkælvəˈnɪstɪk◂/ having severe moral standards and tending to disapprove of pleasure; PURITANICAL —**Calvinist** *n* [C]

**ca·lyp·so** /kəˈlɪpsəʊ‖-soʊ/ *n* [C] a West Indian song based on subjects of interest in the news

**ca·lyx** /ˈkælɪks, ˈkeɪ-‖ˈkeɪ-/ *n plural* **calyxes** or **calyces** [C] the green outer part of a flower that protects it before it opens

**cam** /kæm/ *n* [C] a wheel or part of a wheel that is shaped to change circular movement into backwards and forwards movement

**ca·ma·ra·de·rie** /ˌkæməˈrɑːdəri‖-ˈræ-, -ˈrɑː-/ *n* [U] friendliness between people who like each other or work together as part of a group: *camaraderie of soldiers in the trenches*

**cam·ber** /ˈkæmbə‖-ər/ *n* [C,U] *technical* a slight curve from the centre to the side of a road or other surface that makes water run off to the side

**cam·bric** /ˈkeɪmbrɪk/ *n* [U] thin white cloth made of LINEN (2) or cotton

**cam·cor·der** /ˈkæmˌkɔːdə‖-ˌkɔːrdər/ *n* [C] a VIDEO camera and recorder in one machine, that you can carry around

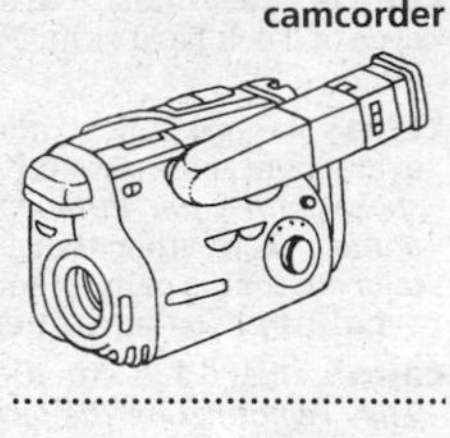

camcorder

**came** /keɪm/ the past tense of COME

**cam·el** /ˈkæməl/ *n* [C] a large desert animal with a long neck and either one or two HUMPS (=large raised parts) on its back

**cam·el·hair** /ˈkæməlheə/ *n* [U] a thick yellowish brown cloth usually used for making coats

**ca·mel·li·a** /kəˈmiːliə/ *n* [C] a red, pink, or white flower like a rose

**cam·em·bert** /ˈkæməmbeə‖-ber/ *n* [C,U] a small round French cheese, that is white outside and yellow inside

**cam·e·o** /ˈkæmi-əʊ‖-oʊ/ *n plural* **cameos** [C] **1** a short appearance in a film or play by a well-known actor: *Denholm Eliot in a cameo role as a butler* **2** a small piece of jewellery with a raised figure or shape fixed to a flat surface of a different colour **3** a short piece of writing that gives a clear idea of a person, place, or event

camera

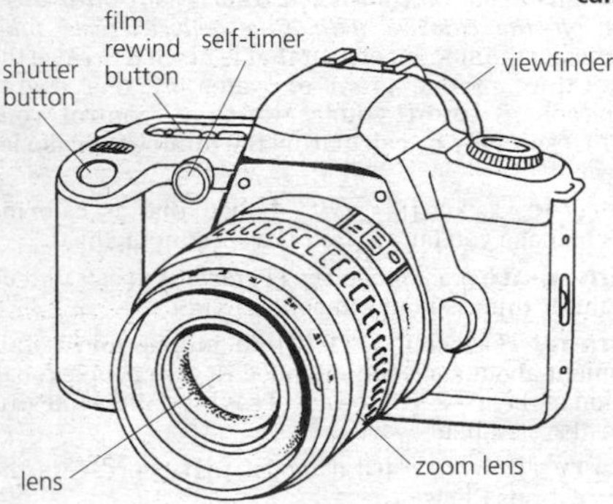


S2 W3 **cam·e·ra** /ˈkæmərə/ *n* [C] **1** a piece of equipment used to take photographs or moving pictures **2** the part of the equipment used for making television pictures that changes images into electrical signals **3 in camera** a law case that is held in camera takes place secretly or privately

**cam·e·ra·man** /ˈkæmərəmən/ *n* [C] someone who operates a camera for films or television

**camera-shy** /ˈ··· ·/ *adj* not liking to have your photograph taken

**cam·i·knick·ers** /ˈkæmiˌnɪkəz‖-ərz/ *n* [plural] *BrE* a piece of women's underwear that combines CAMISOLE and KNICKERS

**cam·i·sole** /ˈkæmɪsəʊl‖-soʊl/ *n* [C] a short piece of women's underwear worn on the top half of the body —see picture at UNDERWEAR

**cam·o·mile, chamomile** /ˈkæməmaɪl/ *n* [C,U] a plant with small white and yellow flowers that are sometimes used to make tea: *camomile tea*

**cam·ou·flage¹** /ˈkæməflɑːʒ/ *n* **1** the way in which the colour or shape of something makes it difficult to see in the place where it lives: *The insect's colour provides camouflage from its enemies.* **2** a way of hiding something, especially a military object, using branches, paint etc: *anti-aircraft camouflage netting* **3** behaviour that is designed to hide something: *Aggression is often a camouflage for insecurity.*

**camouflage²** *v* [T] to hide something by making it look the same as the things around it, or by making it seem like something else: *The trucks were well camouflaged with branches.* | *symptoms of illness camouflaged by other factors*

**camp¹** /kæmp/ *n* **1** [C,U] a place where people stay in temporary shelters, such as tents, usually for a short time: *Let's go back to the camp – it's getting dark.* | **break camp** (=take down a tent or shelter you have been using) **2 prison/labour etc camp** a place where people are kept for a particular reason, when they do not want to be there: *a refugee camp* —see also CONCENTRATION CAMP **3** [C,U] a place where young people go to relax and take part in activities, often as members of an organization: *scout camp* | *summer camp* —see also DAY CAMP, HOLIDAY CAMP **4** [C] a group of people or organizations who have the same ideas or principles, especially in politics: *the extreme right-wing camp of the party* S3 W3

**camp²** *v* [I] **1** to set up a tent or shelter and stay there for a short time: *We'll camp by the river for the night, and move on tomorrow.* | *camping equipment* **2 go camping** to visit an area and stay in a tent: *We went camping in the mountains last weekend.*

**camp out** *phr v* [I] **1** to sleep outdoors, usually in a tent **2** to stay somewhere where you do not have all the usual things that a house has: *We'll just have to camp out until our furniture arrives.*

**camp** sth ↔ **up** *phr v* [T] *informal* to deliberately behave in a funny, unnatural way, with too much movement or expression

**camp³** *adj informal* **1** a man who is camp moves or speaks in the way that people used to think was typical of HOMOSEXUALS **2** clothes, decorations etc that are camp are very strange, bright, or unusual: *Only you could get away with wearing that outfit – it's so camp!*

**cam·paign¹** /kæmˈpeɪn/ *n* [C] **1** a series of actions intended to achieve a particular result, especially in politics or business: [+ **for**] *a campaign for equal rights* | [+ **against**] *educational campaigns against smoking* | *an advertising campaign* **2** a series of battles, attacks etc intended to achieve a particular result in a war S3 W1

**campaign²** *v* [I] to lead or take part in a series of actions intended to achieve a particular result: [+ **for/against**] *a group campaigning against the destruction of the rainforests* —**campaigner** *n* [C]

**cam·pa·ni·le** /ˌkæmpəˈniːli/ *n* [C] a high bell tower that is usually separate from any other building

**cam·pa·nol·o·gy** /ˌkæmpəˈnɒlədʒi‖-ˈnɑː-/ *n* [U] the skill of ringing bells —**campanologist** *n* [C]

**camp bed** /ˌ· ˈ·‖ˈ· ·/ *n* [C] *especially BrE* a light, narrow bed that folds flat and is easy to carry; COT (2) *AmE* —see picture at BED¹

**camp·er** /ˈkæmpə‖-ər/ *n* [C] **1** someone who is staying in a tent or shelter **2** *AmE* a sort of room fitted onto or pulled behind a large vehicle that has cooking equipment and beds in it **3 happy camper** *spoken* someone who seems to be happy with their situation

**camp·fire** /ˈkæmpfaɪə‖-faɪr/ *n* [C] a fire made outdoors by people who are camping

**camp fol·low·er** /ˈ· ˌ···/ *n* [C] **1** someone who supports an organization or a political party, but who is not actually a member of the main group **2** someone who was not a soldier but who followed an army from place to place to provide services, especially in the past

**camp·ground** /ˈkæmpgraʊnd/ *n* [C] *AmE* an area where people can camp, that often has a water supply and toilets; CAMPSITE *BrE*

**cam·phor** /ˈkæmfə‖-ər/ *n* [U] a white substance with a strong smell, that is used especially to keep insects away

**camp rob·ber** /ˈ· ˌ··/ *n* [C] a grey North American bird that does not seem afraid of people and often flies away with food

**camp·site** /ˈkæmpsaɪt/ *n* [C] **1** *BrE* an area where people can camp, that often has a water supply and toilets; CAMPGROUND *AmE* **2** *AmE* a place, usually within a CAMPGROUND, where one person or group can camp

**camp·stool** /ˈkæmpstuːl/ *n* [C] a small folding seat with no back

**cam·pus** /ˈkæmpəs/ *n* **1** the land and buildings of a university or college **2 big man on campus** *AmE* someone who is well-known for being involved in a lot of student activities, and thinks they are important because of this

**cam·shaft** /ˈkæmʃɑːft‖-ʃæft/ *n* [C] a metal bar that a CAM is fastened to in an engine

S1 W1 **can¹** /kənˑ *strong* kæn/ *v* [modal verb] **1** to be able to: *He's so tall he can touch the ceiling.* | *This machine can perform two million calculations per second.* | *I can't remember where I put it.* | *They have everything that money can buy.* | *The police still haven't found her but they're doing all they can.* **2** *spoken* used when asking someone to do something or give you something: *Can I have a cigarette please?* | *Can you help me lift this box?* **3** *especially spoken* to have permission to do something or to be allowed to do something: *You can't play football here.* | *"Can we go home now please?" "No you can't."* | *The goalkeeper can't handle the ball outside the penalty area.* (=it is against the rules) **4** to have a particular skill or know how to do a particular activity: *Gabriella can speak French, Russian, and Italian.* | *Can you drive?* **5** used to show what is possible or likely: *I am confident that a solution can be found.* | *There can be no doubt that he is guilty.* | *The word "bank" can have several different meanings.* | *Can he still be alive after all this time?* **6** used with verbs connected with the five senses and with verbs connected with thinking: *I can hear you easily from here.* | *You can really taste the garlic in that soup.* | *I can't understand why you're so upset.* | *You can imagine how annoyed she was!* **7** [usually in questions and negatives] used especially when you think there is only one possible answer to a question or one possible thing to do in a particular situation: *Jill's left her husband but can you blame her after the way he treated her?* | *It's a very kind offer, but I really can't accept it.* **8** to have to do something; must: *If you won't keep quiet you can get out.* **9** used especially in expressions of surprise: *What can it possibly be?* | *You can't be serious!* | *They can't have arrived already surely!* **10** used to show what sometimes happens or how someone sometimes behaves: *It can be quite cold here at night.* | *Gerard can be annoying, I know.*

Frequencies of the verb **can** in spoken and written English.

SPOKEN

WRITTEN

1000 2000 3000 per million

Based on the British National Corpus and the Longman Lancaster Corpus

This graph shows that the verb **can** is much more common in spoken English than in written English. This is because it is used a lot in questions and has some special uses in spoken English.

**USAGE NOTE: CAN**

WORD CHOICE: **can, may, could, might, be allowed to, let, do/would you mind if..., be able to**

In everyday conversation, **can** is used much more commonly than **may** to talk about permission: *You can go now* (=you are allowed to go). Some people say that **may** is more correct, however its use tends to be limited to formal contexts. When talking about permission in the past, people often use **was/were allowed to** or change the sentence and use **let**: *He was allowed to leave at ten.* | *I let him leave at ten* (=I allowed him to go and he did).

When you are asking permission, **could** (also **might**, especially in American English) is often used instead of **can** because it seems less direct and more polite: *Could I borrow your car?* **May** is more formal, and is used especially by officials. For example at an airport: *May I see your passport, madam?* In everyday English people often say: **Do/would you mind if...** or **Is it alright if...** when asking permission: *Do you mind if I smoke?*

**Can** is also used to say that you have the ability to do something: *I can swim now* (=I am able to swim). To talk about something you will have the ability to do in the future, you use **will be able to**: *I'll be able to speak better if I practise more.* For past ability either **could** or **was/were able to** is used, but sometimes with slightly different meaning. **Could** often suggests more someone's ability that they had for some time (but perhaps did not use): *I could swim when I was eight* (=I knew how to). | *She couldn't buy a ticket* (=She didn't have enough money). **Was/were able to** may suggest more that the situation allowed someone to do something (perhaps with effort): *By arriving at two I was able to swim for an hour* (=The pool was open long enough to allow this). | *I wasn't able to buy a ticket* (=There were none left/I didn't manage to get one). **Used to be able to** is used to talk about something that you could do before, but can no longer do now: *He used to be able to run a 100 metres in under 10 seconds, but he's getting a bit old these days.*

When you are talking about something that is not certain, you often use **may**, or, with more doubt, **might** or **could**: *The road may/might/could be blocked* (=Perhaps/It is possible the road is blocked). | *The road could be blocked* (=It is possible to block the road). For past time **may have/might have/could have** are used: *There may have been an accident* (=Perhaps there was an accident). *Might* or *could have* would be more often used here when we now know that there was no accident.

**Can** is usually used to ask whether something is possible: *Can this really be true?* (=Is it possible this is true?) and to say that something is not possible: *That can't be true.* Again **could** shows more doubt (and is commoner in American English): *Could that really be true?*

**Can** is often used with verbs related to the senses and the mind, such as *see, hear, feel, believe*: *Look at this photo – can you see somebody famous in it?*

GRAMMAR

Remember **can, could, may** and **might** are NEVER used with the *to* infinitive of a verb: *I can help you* (NOT *I can to help you*).

**can²** /kæn/ *n* [C] **1** a metal container in which food or drink is preserved without air: *a Coke can* | [+ **of**] *All we've got is a couple of cans of soup.* —see picture at CONTAINER **2** a special metal container that keeps the liquid inside it under pressure, releasing it as a SPRAY² (1) when you press the button on the lid: *a can of hairspray* **3** *especially AmE* a metal container with a lid that can be removed, used for holding liquid: *Two large cans of paint ought to be enough.* **4 can of worms** a very complicated situation that causes a lot of problems when you start to deal with it: *I just don't know what to do – every solution I can think of would just open up a whole new can of worms.* **5 in the can** *informal* a film that is in the can is complete and ready to be shown **6 the can** *slang* **a)** a prison **b)** *AmE* a toilet —see also **carry the can** (CARRY¹ (31)) S2

**can³** *v* **canned, canning** [T] *especially AmE* **1** to preserve food by putting it into a metal container from which all the air is removed; TIN³ *BrE* —see also CANNED (1) **2** *AmE informal* to dismiss someone from a job; SACK² (1) **3 can it!** *AmE spoken* used to tell someone to stop talking or making noise

**Ca·na·di·an ba·con** /kəˌneɪdiən 'beɪkən/ *n* [U] *AmE* meat from the back or sides of a pig, served in thick, round pieces; BACON *BrE*

**ca·nal** /kə'næl/ *n* [C] **1** a passage dug out of the ground, either to connect two areas of water so boats can travel between them, or to bring or remove water from somewhere: *the Panama Canal* **2** a passage in the body of a person or animal —see also ALIMENTARY CANAL

**canal boat** /·'· ·/ *n* [C] a long narrow boat that is used on a canal

**can·a·lize** also **-ise** *BrE* /'kænəl-aɪz/ *v* [T] **1** *formal* to direct the actions, energy, etc of a person or group to one particular purpose; CHANNEL[2] (1) **2** to make a river deeper, straighter etc, especially in order to prevent flooding —**canalization** /ˌkænəlaɪ'zeɪʃən‖-nəl-ə/ *n* [U]

**can·ap·é** /'kænəpeɪ‖-pi, -peɪ/ *n* [C] a small piece of bread with cheese, meat, fish, etc on it, served with drinks at a party

**ca·nard** /kæ'nɑːd‖kə'nɑːrd/ *n* [C] *French* a deliberately false report or piece of news

**ca·nar·y** /kə'neəri‖-'neri/ *n* [C] a small yellow bird that sings and is often kept as a pet

**ca·nas·ta** /kə'næstə/ *n* [U] a card game in which two sets of cards are used

**can·can** /'kænkæn/ *n* [C] a fast dance from France danced by women in a show in which they kick their legs high into the air

S 2 **can·cel** /'kænsəl/ *v* **cancelled, cancelling** *BrE*, **canceled, canceling** *AmE* [T] **1** to arrange that a planned activity or event will not now happen: *The football game had been cancelled due to rain.* **2** to end an agreement or arrangement that exists in law: *I've cancelled my subscription to the magazine.*

**cancel** sth ↔ **out** *phr v* [T] to have an equal but opposite effect on something, so that a situation does not change: *The losses in our overseas division have cancelled out this year's profits.*

**can·cel·la·tion** /ˌkænsə'leɪʃən/ *n* [C,U] a decision or statement that a planned or regular activity will not happen: *The restaurant is fully booked for tonight, but sometimes there are cancellations.*

**Can·cer** /'kænsə‖-ər/ *n* **1** [singular] the fourth sign of the ZODIAC represented by a CRAB[1] (1), and believed to affect the character and life of people born between June 22 and July 22 **2** [C] someone who was born between June 22 and July 22

S 2 W 2 **cancer** *n* **1** [C,U] a very serious disease in which cells in one part of the body start to grow in a way that is not normal, often causing death: *smoking causes lung cancer.*|*cancer of the jaw* **2** [C] an activity that is increasing, and causes a lot of harm: *Corruption is the cancer of society.* —**cancerous** *adj*: *a cancerous growth*

**can·de·la·brum** /ˌkændʒ'lɑːbrəm/ *n* plural **candelabra** [C *usually plural*] a decorative holder for several candles or lamps

**can·did** /'kændʒd/ *adj* directly truthful, even when the truth may be unpleasant or embarassing: *The Governor's brutally candid assessment struck a new blow to Mr Major's reputation.* —see also CANDOUR —**candidly** *adv*

**can·di·da** /'kændʒdə/ *n* [U] *technical* a FUNGUS that causes an infection in the mouth and throat of children or in a woman's VAGINA; THRUSH[1] (2)

**can·di·da·cy** /'kændʒdəsi/ also **candidature** /'kændʒdətʃə‖-ər/ *especially BrE n* [C,U] the position of being one of the people who are competing to be elected

W 2 **can·di·date** /'kændʒdʒt‖-deɪt, -dʒt/ *n* [C] **1** someone who is being considered for a job or is competing to be elected: [+ **for**] *They're interviewing three candidates for the post of sales manager.* **2** *especially BrE* someone who is taking an examination **3** a person, group, or idea that is suitable for something or likely to get something: [+ **for**] *You smoke, drink, and never get any exercise: you're a prime candidate for a heart attack!*

**can·died** /'kændid/ *adj* [only before noun] boiled or baked in sugar as a means of preservation: *candied cherries*

**can·dle** /'kændl/ *n* [C] **1** a round stick of WAX[1] (1) around a WICK (=piece of string) that is burnt to provide light **2 can't hold a candle to** *informal* to be not as good as someone or something else: *When it came to giving a good party, no one could hold a candle to the Andersons.* —see also **burn the candle at both ends** (BURN[1] (23)) S 3

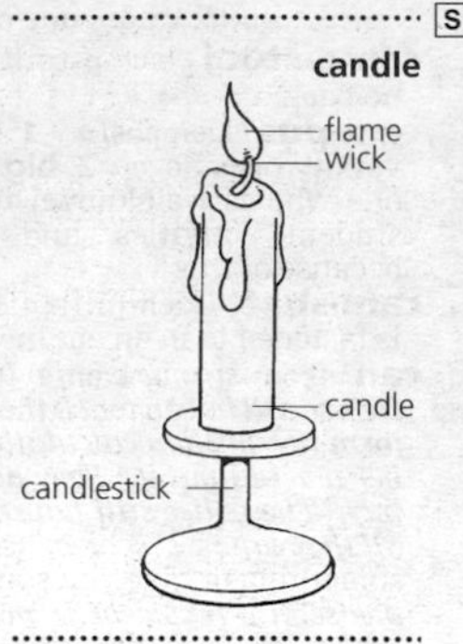


**can·dle·light** /'kændl-laɪt/ *n* [U] the light produced when a candle burns

**candle-lit** /'·· ·/ *adj* lit by candles: *a candle-lit dinner for two*

**can·dle·stick** /'kændlˌstɪk/ *n* [C] a specially shaped metal or wooden stick that you put a candle into —see picture at CANDLE

**can·dle·wick** /'kændlˌwɪk/ *n* [U] **1** also **candlewicking** thick, soft cotton thread **2** cloth decorated with patterns of raised rows of this thread

**can-do** /ˌ·'·/ *adj* [only before noun] *informal* willing to try anything and expect that it will work: *a can-do attitude towards work*

**can·dour** *BrE*, **candor** *AmE* /'kændə‖-ər/ *n* [U] sincere HONESTY and truthfulness: *I appreciate your candour in this matter* —see also CANDID.

**can·dy** /'kændi/ *n* [C,U] *AmE* sweet food made of sugar or chocolate, or a piece of this; SWEET[2] (1) *BrE* —see graph at SWEET[2] S 3

**candy ap·ple** /'·· ˌ··/ *n* [C] *AmE* TOFFEE APPLE

**candy cane** /'·· ·/ *n* [C] *AmE* a stick of hard red and white sugar with a curved end

**can·dy·floss** /'kændiflɒs‖-flɑːs, -flɒːs/ *n* [U] *BrE* sticky threads of pink sugar wound around a stick and eaten as a sweet; COTTON CANDY *AmE*

**can·dy-striped** /'·· ˌ·/ *adj* candy-striped cloth has narrow coloured lines on a white background

**candy strip·er** /'kændi ˌstraɪpə‖-ər/ *n* [C] *AmE* a young person, usually a girl, who does unpaid work as a nurse's helper in a hospital in order to learn about hospital work

**cane[1]** /keɪn/ *n* **1** [C] a long thin stick with a curved handle used to help someone walk —see also STICK **2** [U] thin pieces of the stems of plants used for making furniture, baskets etc: *a cane chair* **3** [C] a long, hard, yellow stem of a BAMBOO, used for supporting other plants in the garden **4** [singular] a long thin stick used especially in former times by teachers to hit children with as a punishment

**cane[2]** *v* [T] to punish someone, especially a child, by hitting them with a long thin stick

**ca·nine** /'keɪnaɪn, 'kæ-‖'keɪ-/ *adj* being or related to dogs: *a canine welfare organization* | *his canine companion, Rex*

**canine tooth** /'·· ·/ *n* [C] one of four sharp pointed teeth in the front of the human mouth; EYE TOOTH —see picture at TEETH

**can·is·ter** /'kænʒstə‖-ər/ *n* [C] **1** a round metal case that bursts when thrown or fired from a gun, scattering what is inside: *Police fired canisters of tear gas into the crowd.* **2** a small round container, usually made of metal, for keeping food, liquid etc in: *discovered an early copy of 'Napoleon' in an old film canister* **3** a round metal container of gas

**can·ker** /'kæŋkə‖-ər/ *n* [C,U] **1** an evil influence that spreads quickly and is difficult to destroy: *the canker of violence in modern society* **2** a disease that affects trees or plants —**cankerous** *adj* —**cankered** *adj*

**can·na·bis** /ˈkænəbɪ̣s/ *n* [U] an illegal drug obtained from HEMP plants and smoked in cigarettes

**canned** /kænd/ *adj* **1** canned food is preserved in a round metal container; TINNED *BrE*: *canned tomatoes* **2 canned music/laughter etc** music, laughter etc that has been recorded and is used on television or in radio programmes **3** [never before noun] *slang* drunk

**can·nel·lo·ni** /ˌkænɪ̣ˈləʊni‖-ˈloʊ-/ *n* [U] small tubes of PASTA filled with meat and sometimes cheese, and covered in SAUCE[1]

**can·ne·ry** /ˈkænəri/ *n* [C] a factory where food is put into cans

**can·ni·bal** /ˈkænɪ̣bəl/ *n* [C] **1** someone who eats human flesh: *the cannibal killer, Jeffrey Dahmer* **2** an animal that eats the flesh of other animals of the same kind —**cannibalism** *n* [U] —**cannibalistic** /ˌkænɪ̣bəˈlɪstɪk◂/ *adj*

**can·ni·bal·ize** also **-ise** *BrE* /ˈkænɪ̣bəlaɪz/ *v* [T] to take something apart, especially a machine, so that you can use its parts to build something else

**can·non**[1] /ˈkænən/ *n* [C] a large, heavy, powerful gun, usually fixed to two wheels, used in the past

**cannon**[2] *v* [I always + adv/prep] to hit or knock into someone or something, especially while running: *She came hurtling round the corner and cannoned straight into me.*

**can·non·ade** /ˌkænəˈneɪd/ *n* [C] a continuous heavy attack by large guns

**can·non·ball** /ˈkænənbɔːl‖-bɒːl/ *n* [C] a heavy iron ball fired from an old type of large gun

**cannon fod·der** /ˈ·· ˌ··/ *n* [U] *informal* ordinary members of the army, navy etc whose lives are not considered to be very important

**can·not** /ˈkænət, -nɒt‖-nɑːt/ *modal verb* **1** a negative form of 'can': *Mrs. Armstrong regrets that she cannot accept your kind invitation.* **2 cannot but** *formal* used to say that you feel you have to do something: *One cannot but admire her determination.*

**can·ny** /ˈkæni/ *adj* **1** clever, careful, and not easily deceived, especially in business or politics: *a canny political advisor* **2** *ScotE* nice, good: *a canny lass* —**cannily** *adv*

**canoe**

**ca·noe**[1] /kəˈnuː/ *n* [C] a long light boat that is pointed at both ends and which you move along using a PADDLE[1] (1) —see also **paddle your own canoe** (PADDLE[2] (5))

**canoe**[2] *v* [I] to travel by canoe —**canoeist** *n* [C]

**can·on** /ˈkænən/ *n* [C] **1** a Christian priest who has special duties in a CATHEDRAL **2** a piece of music in which a tune is started by one singer or instrument and is copied by each of the others **3** *formal* a generally accepted rule or standard on which an idea, subject, or way of behaving is based: *Her behaviour offends all the canons of good taste.* **4** *formal* a list of books or pieces of music that are officially recognized as being the work of a certain writer: *the Shakespearian canon* **5** an established law of the Christian church

**ca·non·i·cal** /kəˈnɒnɪkəl‖kəˈnɑː-/ *adj* **1** according to CANON LAW **2** *technical* in the simplest mathematical form

**can·on·ize** also **ise** *BrE* /ˈkænənaɪz/ *v* [T] to officially state that a dead person is a SAINT (1) —**canonization** /ˌkænənaɪˈzeɪʃən‖-nənə-/ *n* [C,U]

**canon law** /ˌ·· ˈ·/ *n* [U] the laws of Christian Church

**ca·noo·dle** /kəˈnuːdl/ *v* [I] *BrE old-fashioned* if two people canoodle, they kiss and hold each other in a sexual way

**can o·pen·er** /ˈ· ˌ···/ *n* [C] *especially AmE* a tool for opening a can of food; TIN OPENER *BrE* —see picture on page 833

**can·o·py** /ˈkænəpi/ *n* [C] **1** a cover fixed above a bed, seat etc as a decoration or as a shelter **2** *literary* something that spreads above you like a roof: *a canopy of branches* —**canopied** *adj*

**canst** /kənst, kænst/ *strong v* **thou canst** *old use* used to mean 'you can' when talking to one person

**can't** /kɑːnt‖kænt/ **1** the short form of cannot: *I can't understand what this means.* | *You can swim, can't you?* **2** used as the opposite of 'must', to say that something is impossible or unlikely: *They can't have gone out because the light's on.*

**cant**[1] /kænt/ *n* **1** [U] insincere talk about moral or religious principles by someone who is pretending to be better than they really are: *a politician's cant about family values* **2** [U] special words used by a particular group of people, especially in order to keep things secret: *thieves' cant* **3** [C] a sloping surface or angle

**cant**[2] *v* [I,T] to lean, or make something lean

**cantab** /ˈkæntæb/ used after the title of a degree from Cambridge University: *Jane Smith MA (Cantab)*

**can·ta·loup, cantaloupe** /ˈkæntəluːp‖-loʊp/ *n* [C,U] a type of MELON with a hard green skin and sweet orange flesh —see picture on page 413

**can·tan·ker·ous** /kænˈtæŋkərəs/ *adj* bad-tempered and complaining a lot: *a cantankerous old man* —**cantankerously** *adv* —**cantankerousness** *n* [U]

**can·ta·ta** /kænˈtɑːtə, kən-‖kən-/ *n* [C] a piece of religious music sung by a CHOIR and single performers

**can·teen** /kænˈtiːn/ *n* [C] **1** a place in a factory, school etc where meals are provided, usually quite cheaply: *lunch in the works' canteen* **2** a small container in which water or other drink is carried by soldiers, travellers etc **3** *BrE* a set of knives, forks and spoons in a box

**canter**[1] /ˈkæntə‖-ər/ *v* [I,T] to ride or make a horse run quite fast, but not as fast as possible

**can·ter**[2] *n* **1** [singular] the movement of a horse when it is running fairly fast, but not as fast as possible **2** [C] a ride on a horse at this speed **3** a short or quick journey: *Paris is now only a canter away due to the Channel Tunnel.*

**can·ti·cle** /ˈkæntɪkəl/ *n* [C] a short religious song usually using words from the Bible

**can·ti·le·ver** /ˈkæntɪ̣liːvə‖-tl-iːvər/ *n* [C] a beam that sticks out from an upright post or wall and supports a shelf, the end of a bridge etc

**can·to** /ˈkæntəʊ‖-toʊ/ *n plural* **cantos** [C] one of the parts into which a very long poem is divided

**can·ton** /ˈkæntɒn, kænˈtɒn‖ˈkæntən, -tɑːn/ *n* [C] one of the areas with limited political powers that make up a country such as Switzerland

**Can·to·nese** /ˌkæntəˈniːz◂/ *n* [U] a Chinese language spoken in Southern China and Hong Kong

**can·ton·ment** /kænˈtuːnmənt‖-ˈtɑːn-/ *n* [C] *technical* a camp for soldiers

**can·tor** /ˈkæntə, -tɔː‖-ər, -ɔːr/ *n* [C] **1** a man who leads the prayers and songs in a Jewish religious service **2** the leader of a CHOIR in a church

**can·vas** /ˈkænvəs/ *n* **1** [U] strong cloth used to make bags, tents, shoes etc **2** [C] a painting done with oil paints, or the piece of cloth it is painted on **3 under canvas** *BrE* in a tent: *We spent the night under canvas.*

**can·vass** /ˈkænvəs/ *v* **1** [I,T] to try to get information, support for a political party etc, by going from place to place within an area and talking to people: *The company canvassed 600 people who use their product.* | *We'll have to canvass the entire area before the referendum.* **2** [T] to talk about a problem, suggestion etc in detail: *The suggestion is being widely canvassed as a possible solution to the dispute.* —**canvass** *n* [C] —**canvasser** *n* [C]

**can·yon** /ˈkænjən/ *n* [C] a deep valley with very steep sides of rock that usually has a river running through it

**cap.** also **caps.** the written abbreviation of capital letter (CAPITAL[1] (3))

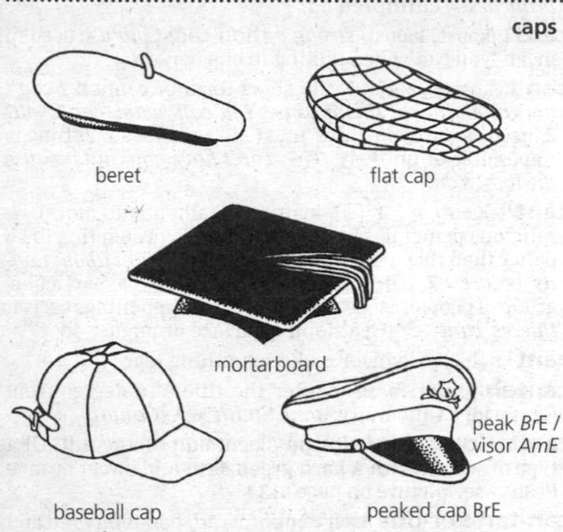


see also picture at **hat**

S3 **cap¹** /kæp/ *n* [C]
**1 ▶ HAT ◀** **a)** a type of soft flat hat that has a curved part sticking out at the front **b)** a covering that fits very closely to your head and is worn for a particular purpose: *a swimming cap* | *a shower cap* **c)** a special type of hat that is worn by a particular profession or group of people: *a nurse's cap*
**2 ▶ TOP/COVERING ◀** a protective covering that you put on the end or top of an object: *Make sure that you put the cap back on that pen.* —see also ICE CAP, TOECAP —see picture at TOP[1]
**3 go cap in hand (to)** to ask someone for something, especially money, in a very polite way that makes you seem unimportant: *going cap in hand to the bank for a loan*
**4 if the cap fits** *spoken* used to say that someone should regard a remark as criticism of them if they think that the criticism is suitable: *I never said you were a liar, but if the cap fits...*
**5 ▶ EXPLOSIVE ◀** a small paper container with explosive inside it, used especially in toy guns
**6 ▶ LIMIT ◀** an upper limit that is put on the amount of money that can be spent or borrowed in a particular situation: *a cap on local council spending*
**7 ▶ SEX ◀** a CONTRACEPTIVE made of a round piece of rubber that a woman puts inside her VAGINA
**8 set your cap at** *old-fashioned* if a woman sets her cap at a man, she tries to attract him, especially in order to marry him —see also **a feather in your cap** (FEATHER[1] (2)), **put your thinking cap on** (THINKING[1])

**cap²** *v* **capped, capping** [T] **1** to say or do something that is better, worse, funnier etc than what someone else has just said or done: *She capped my story with an hilarious account of the party.* **2 to cap it all** *spoken* used before describing the worst, funniest etc part at the end of a story or description: *And to cap it all, I found I'd left my purse at home!* **3 be capped with** to have a particular substance on top: *snow-capped mountains* | *a graceful tower capped with a gilded dome* **4** *BrE* to choose someone for a national sports team: *He's been capped three times for England.* **5** to cover a tooth with a special white substance **6** *BrE* to put a limit on the amount of money that can be charged or spent, especially by local government

**ca·pa·bil·i·ty** /ˌkeɪpəˈbɪlʒti/ *n* [C] **1** the natural ability, skill, or power that makes you able to do something: *a child's language capability* | **capability to do sth** *A willingness and a capability to change are necessary to meet the market's needs.* | **beyond sb's capabilities** (=too difficult for someone) *I have a good knowledge of French, but simultaneous translation is beyond my capabilities.* **2** the ability that a country has to take a particular kind of military action: *a nuclear weapons capability* S3

**ca·pa·ble** /ˈkeɪpəbəl/ *adj* **1 capable of (doing) sth** having the skills, power, intelligence etc needed to do something: *I don't think Banks is capable of murder.* | *The company isn't capable of handling an order that large.* **2** skilled or very good at doing something: *a very capable doctor* —**capably** *adv* S2 W2

**ca·pa·cious** /kəˈpeɪʃəs/ *adj formal* able to contain a lot: *a capacious suitcase* —**capaciousness** *n* [U]

**ca·pa·ci·tor** /kəˈpæsʒtə‖-ər/ *n* [C] a piece of equipment that collects and stores electricity

**ca·pac·i·ty** /kəˈpæsʒti/ *n* **1** [singular] the amount of space a container, room etc has to hold things or people: [+ **of**] *The fuel tank has a capacity of 12 gallons.* | *seating capacity of 500* | **capacity crowd** (=one that fills all the seats in a room, hall etc) *The orchestra played to a capacity crowd in the Queen Elizabeth Hall.* | **filled to capacity** (=completely full) **2** [C,U] someone's ability to do something: [+ **for**] *a child's capacity for learning* | *an infinite capacity for love* | **capacity to do sth** *a capacity to think in an original way* **3** [singular] *formal* someone's job, position, or duty; ROLE (1): *Rollins will be working in an advisory capacity on this project.* | **do sth in your capacity as** *I attended in my capacity as chairman of the safety committee.* **4** [singular, U] the amount of something that a factory, company, machine etc can produce or deal with: *Our factories have been working at full capacity all year.* S3 W2

**ca·par·i·soned** /kəˈpærʒsənd/ *adj* in medieval times a caparisoned horse was one covered in a decorated cloth

**cape** /keɪp/ *n* [C] **1** a long loose piece of clothing without SLEEVES that fastens around your neck and hangs from your shoulders **2** a large piece of land surrounded on three sides by water: *the Cape of Good Hope*

**ca·per¹** /ˈkeɪpə‖-ər/ *v* [I always + adv/prep] to jump about and play in a happy, excited way: *lambs capering in the fields*

**caper²** *n* [C] **1** a small dark green part of a flower used in cooking to give a sour taste to food **2** *informal* a planned activity, especially an illegal or dangerous one: *If he thinks I'm going along with him on this caper, he's wrong.* **3** a short jumping or dancing movement: **cut a caper** (=dance with little steps or jumps)

**ca·pil·la·ry** /kəˈpɪləri‖ˈkæpəleri/ *n* [C] **1** a very small tube as thin as a hair **2** the smallest type of BLOOD VESSEL (=tube carrying blood) in the body

**capillary at·trac·tion** /ˌ·,···ˈ··‖ˈ····ˌ··/ also **capillary ac·tion** /ˌ·,··· ˈ··‖ˈ···· ˌ··/ *n* [U] *technical* the force that makes a liquid rise up a narrow tube

**cap·i·tal¹** /ˈkæpʒtl/ *n* S3 W1
**1 ▶ CITY ◀** [C] an important town or city where the central government of a country, state etc is: *Albany is the capital of New York State.*
**2 ▶ FINANCIAL ◀** [singular, U] money or property, especially when it is used to start a business or to produce more wealth: *You'll need more capital if you want to open your own business.* —see also WORKING CAPITAL, VENTURE CAPITAL

3 ► **LETTER** ◄ [C] a letter of the alphabet written in its large form as it is, for example at the beginning of someone's name —compare LOWER CASE
4 ► **CENTRE OF ACTIVITY** ◄ [C] a place that is a centre for an industry, business, or other activity: *Hollywood is the capital of the movie industry.*
5 **make capital out of** to use a situation or event to help you get an advantage: *The Republicans are sure to make capital out of the closure of the plant.*
6 ► **BUILDING** ◄ the top part of a COLUMN (=a long stone post used in some buildings)

S3 W3 **capital²** *adj* **1 capital letter** a letter that is written or printed in its large form —compare LOWER CASE **2 capital offence/crime** an offence etc that is punished by death **3** *old-fashioned* excellent: *That's a capital suggestion!*

**capital as·sets** /ˌ··· ˈ··/ *n* [plural] *technical* machines, buildings, and other property belonging to a company

**capital gains** /ˌ··· ˈ·/ *n* [plural] profits you make by selling your possessions

**capital gains tax** /ˌ··· ˈ· ·/ *n* [C] a tax that you pay on profits that you make when you sell your possessions

**capital goods** /ˈ··· ˌ·/ *n* [plural] goods such as machines or buildings that are made for the purpose of producing other goods —compre CONSUMER GOODS

**capital in·ten·sive** /ˌ··· ·ˈ··◂/ *adj* a capital intensive business, industry etc needs a lot of money for it to operate properly —compare LABOUR-INTENSIVE

**cap·i·tal·is·m** /ˈkæpɪ̈tl-ɪzəm/ *n* [U] a system of production and trade based on property and wealth being owned privately, with only a small amount of industrial activity by the government —compare COMMUNISM

**cap·i·tal·ist¹** /ˈkæpɪ̈tl-ɪ̈st/ *n* [C] **1** someone who supports capitalism: *the class struggle between workers and capitalists* **2** someone who owns or controls a lot of money and lends it to businesses, banks etc to produce more wealth

**capitalist²** also **cap·i·ta·lis·tic** /ˌkæpɪ̈tlˈɪstɪk◂/ *adj* using or supporting capitalism: *Marx argued against the capitalist system.* | *capitalist societies of the rich West*

**cap·i·tal·ize** also **-ise** *BrE* /ˈkæpɪ̈tl-aɪz/ *v* [T] **1** to write a letter of the alphabet using a CAPITAL¹ (3) letter **2** to supply a business with money so that it can operate **3** *technical* to calculate the value of a business based on the value of its shares (SHARE² (6)) or on the amount of money it makes —**capitalization** /ˌkæpɪ̈tl-aɪˈzeɪʃən‖-əˈzeɪ-/ *n* [U]

**capitalize on** sth *phr v* [T] to get as much advantage out of a situation, event etc as you can: *We are well-placed to capitalize on the growth of cable TV.*

**capital lev·y** /ˌ··· ˈ··/ *n* [C] *technical* a tax on private or industrial wealth that is paid to the government

**capital pun·ish·ment** /ˌ··· ˈ···/ *n* [U] punishment by legal killing

**capital trans·fer tax** /ˌ··· ˈ·· ˌ·/ *n* [C,U] *BrE* a tax paid when you receive money, either as a gift or when someone dies —see also INHERITANCE TAX

**cap·i·ta·tion** /ˌkæpɪ̈ˈteɪʃən/ *n* [C] a tax or payment of the same amount from each person

**Cap·i·tol** /ˈkæpɪ̈tl/ *n* **1 the Capitol** the building in Washington D.C. where the US Congress meets **2** [C] the building or group of buildings of the central government of one of the 50 states of the US

**Capitol Hill** /ˌ··· ˈ·/ *n* [singular] **1** the US Congress **2** the hill where the Capitol building stands

**ca·pit·u·late** /kəˈpɪtʃɪ̈leɪt/ *v* [I] **1** to accept or agree to something that you have been opposing until now: *Helen finally capitulated and let her son have a car.* **2** *formal* to accept defeat by your enemies in a war; SURRENDER¹ (1) —**capitulation** /kəˌpɪtʃɪ̈ˈleɪʃən/ *n* [C,U]

**ca·pon** /ˈkeɪpən‖-pɑːn, -pən/ *n* [C] a male chicken that has had its sex organs removed to make it grow big and fat

**cap·puc·ci·no** /ˌkæpɪ̈ˈtʃiːnəʊ‖-noʊ/ *n* [C,U] Italian coffee made with hot milk and with chocolate powder on top

**ca·price** /kəˈpriːs/ *n* **1** [C,U] a sudden and unreasonable change of mind or behaviour: *the caprices of a spoilt child* **2** [U] the tendency to change your mind suddenly or behave in an unexpected way

**ca·pri·cious** /kəˈprɪʃəs/ *adj* **1** likely to change your mind suddenly or behave in an unexpected way: *as capricious and manipulative as her mother had been* **2** changing quickly and suddenly: *a capricious wind* —**capriciously** *adv*

**Cap·ri·corn** /ˈkæprɪkɔːn‖-kɔːrn/ *n* **1** [singular] the tenth sign of the ZODIAC represented by a goat and believed to affect the character and life of people born between December 22 and January 19 **2** [C] someone who was born between December 22 and January 19

**cap·si·cum** /ˈkæpsɪkəm/ *n* [C,U] *technical* a kind of PEPPER (=a green, red, or yellow vegetable)

**cap·size** /kæpˈsaɪz‖ˈkæpsaɪz/ *v* [I,T] if a boat capsizes or if you capsize it, it turns over in the water

**cap·stan** /ˈkæpstən/ *n* [C] **1** a round machine shaped like a drum, used to wind up a rope that pulls or lifts heavy objects **2** the round bar that goes round to move the TAPE¹ (12) in a TAPE RECORDER

**cap·sule** /ˈkæpsjuːl‖-səl/ *n* [C] **1** a plastic container shaped like a very small tube with medicine inside that you swallow whole **2** the part of a SPACECRAFT in which people live and work

**cap·tain¹** /ˈkæptɪ̈n/ *n* [C] **1** someone who commands a ship or aircraft: *The Captain and crew welcome you aboard.* **2** a rank in the navy, army or US Air Force or Marines —see also GROUP CAPTAIN —see table on page B4 **3** someone who leads a team or other group of people: *Julie's the school tennis captain.* **4 captain of industry** someone who owns an important company W3

**captain²** *v* [T] to lead a group or team of people and be their captain

**cap·tain·cy** /ˈkæptɪ̈nsi/ *n* [C,U] the position of being captain of a team, or the period during which someone is captain

**cap·tion** /ˈkæpʃən/ *n* [C] words printed above or below a picture in a book or newspaper or on a television screen to explain what the picture is showing

**cap·tious** /ˈkæpʃəs/ *adj literary* always criticizing unimportant things

**cap·ti·vate** /ˈkæptɪ̈veɪt/ *v* [T often passive] to attract someone very much: *I was captivated by his charm and good looks.*

**cap·ti·va·ting** /ˈkæptɪ̈veɪtɪŋ/ *adj* very attractive: *a captivating smile and beautiful eyes*

**cap·tive¹** /ˈkæptɪv/ *adj* **1** [only before noun] unable to move about freely because of being kept in prison or in a small space: *Captive soldiers passed by in chains.* | *captive animals* **2 take/hold sb captive** to keep someone as a prisoner: *The American officers were held captive for three months.* **3 captive audience** people who listen or watch someone or something because they have to, not because they are interested

**captive²** *n* [C] someone who is kept as a prisoner, especially in a war

**cap·tiv·i·ty** /kæpˈtɪvɪ̈ti/ *n* [U] the state of being kept in a prison, CAGE etc and not allowed to go where you want: *The hostages were released from captivity.* | **in captivity** *Many animals do not breed well when kept in captivity.*

**cap·tor** /ˈkæptə‖-ər/ *n* [C] someone who is keeping another person prisoner: *He managed to escape from his captors.*

**cap·ture¹** /ˈkæptʃə‖-ər/ *v* [T] W3
1 ► **PERSON** ◄ to catch someone in order to make them a prisoner: *Government troops have succeeded in capturing the rebel leader.*
2 ► **PLACE** ◄ to get control of a place that previously

belonged to an enemy by fighting for it: *The town of Moulineuf was captured after a siege lasting ten days.*
3 ▶ **ANIMAL** ◀ to catch an animal after chasing or following it
4 ▶ **BOOK/PAINTING/FILM** ◀ to succeed in showing or describing a situation or feeling using words or pictures: *These photographs capture the essence of working-class life at the turn of the century.*
5 **capture sb's imagination/attention etc** to make someone feel very interested and attracted: *His stories of foreign adventure captured my imagination.*
6 **capture sb's heart** to seem attractive to someone so that they become very fond of you or love you

7 ▶ **BUSINESS/POLITICS** ◀ to get something that previously belonged to one of your competitors: *Japanese firms have captured over 60% of the electronics market.*
8 ▶ **COMPUTERS** ◀ *technical* to put something in a form that a computer can use: *The data is captured by an optical scanner.*
9 ▶ **CHESS** ◀ to remove one of your opponent's PIECES from the board in CHESS

**capture**[2] *n* 1 [U] the act of catching someone in order to make them a prisoner: *The two soldiers somehow managed to avoid capture.* 2 **the capture of Rome/Jerusalem etc** the act of getting control of a place that previously belonged to an enemy

S1 W1 **car** /kɑː‖kɑːr/ *n* [C] 1 a small vehicle with four wheels and an engine, that you use to travel from one place to another: *I go to work by car.* | *Cars were parked on both sides of the road.* —see picture on page 409 2 **sleeping/dining/buffet car** a train carriage used for sleeping etc 3 *AmE* a train carriage 4 the part of a lift, BALLOON[1] (2), or AIRSHIP in which people or goods are carried

**ca·rafe** /kəˈræf, kəˈrɑːf/ *n* [C] a glass container with a wide neck, used for serving wine or water at meals

**car a·larm** /ˈ· ·ˌ·/ *n* [C] a special system for protecting cars against thieves that makes a loud noise if anyone touches the car

**car·a·mel** /ˈkærəməl, -mel/ *n* 1 [C] a brown sweet made of sticky boiled sugar 2 [U] burnt sugar used for giving food a special taste and colour —see also CRÈME CARAMEL —**caramelize** *v* [I,T]

**car·a·pace** /ˈkærəpeɪs/ *n* [C] *technical* a hard shell on the outside of some animals such as CRABS or TORTOISES, that protects them

**car·at** /ˈkærət/ *n* [C] 1 also **karat** *AmE* a measurement that shows how pure gold is: *a 22-carat gold chain* 2 a measurement equal to 200 MILLIGRAMS on the scale of measurement for the weight of jewels

**car·a·van** /ˈkærəvæn/ *n* [C] 1 *BrE* a vehicle that a car can pull and in which people can live and sleep when they are on holiday; TRAILER (1) *AmE* 2 *BrE* a covered vehicle pulled by a horse in which people such as gipsies (GIPSY) live; WAGON (1) *AmE* 3 a group of people with animals or vehicles who travel together for protection through dangerous areas such as deserts

**car·a·van·ning** /ˈkærəvænɪŋ/ *n* [U] *BrE* the practice of having holidays in a caravan: *a caravanning holiday in Cornwall*

**car·a·van·se·rai** /ˌkærəˈvænsəraɪ/ *n* [C] a hotel with a large open central area, used in the past in Eastern countries by groups of people and animals travelling together

**car·a·way** /ˈkærəweɪ/ *n* [C,U] a plant whose strong-tasting seeds are used to give a special taste to food

**car·bine** /ˈkɑːbaɪn‖ˈkɑːr-/ *n* [C] a short light RIFLE (=type of gun)

**car·bo·hy·drate** /ˌkɑːbəʊˈhaɪdreɪt, -drət‖ˌkɑːrboʊ-/ *n* 1 *technical* [C,U] one of several food substances such as sugar which consist of oxygen, HYDROGEN and CARBON (1), and which provide your body with heat and energy 2 [C usually plural] foods such as rice, bread, and potatoes that contain carbohydrates

**car·bol·ic a·cid** /kɑːˌbɒlɪk ˈæsəd‖kɑːrˌbɑː-/ *n* [U] a liquid that kills BACTERIA, used for preventing the spread of disease or infection

**carbolic soap** /·ˌ·· ˈ·/ *n* [U] a strong soap made from coal TAR[1] (1)

**car bomb** /ˈ· ·/ *n* [C] a bomb hidden inside a car

**car·bon** /ˈkɑːbən‖ˈkɑːr-/ *n* 1 [U] a simple substance that exists in a pure form as diamonds, GRAPHITE etc or in an impure form as coal, petrol etc 2 [C,U] CARBON PAPER 3 [C] a CARBON COPY (1)

**car·bon·at·ed** /ˈkɑːbəneɪtəd‖ˈkɑːr-/ *adj* carbonated drinks contain small BUBBLES: *carbonated spring water*

**carbon black** /ˈ·· ·/ *n* [U] a black powder made by partly burning oil, wood etc, used for making rubber

**carbon cop·y** /ˌ·· ˈ··/ *n* [C] 1 a copy, especially of something that has been typed (TYPE[2] (1)), made using CARBON PAPER 2 someone or something that is very similar to another person or thing: [+ **of**] *The robbery is a carbon copy of one that took place last year.*

**carbon dat·ing** /ˌ·· ˈ··/ *n* [U] a method used to find out the age of very old objects

**carbon di·ox·ide** /ˌ·· ·ˈ··/ *n* [U] the gas produced when animals breathe out, when carbon is burned in air, or when animal or vegetable substances decay

**car·bon·if·er·ous** /ˌkɑːbəˈnɪfərəs◂‖ˌkɑːr-/ *adj* producing or containing carbon or coal: *carboniferous rocks*

**car·bon·ize** also **-ise** *BrE* /ˈkɑːbənaɪz‖ˈkɑːr-/ *v* [I,T] to change or make something change into CARBON (1) by burning without air —**carbonized** *adj*

**carbon mo·nox·ide** /ˌ·· ·ˈ··/ *n* [U] a poisonous gas produced when CARBON (1), especially petrol, burns in a small amount of air

**carbon pa·per** /ˈ·· ˌ··/ *n* [C,U] thin paper with a blue or black substance on one side, that you put between sheets of paper when typing (TYPE[2] (2)) in order to make copies

**carbon tet·ra·chlo·ride** /ˌkɑːbən tetrəˈklɔːraɪd‖ˌkɑːr-/ *n* [U] a colourless liquid used for cleaning dirty marks off clothes

**car boot sale** /ˌ· ˈ· ˌ·/ *n* [C] *BrE* a sale in a CAR PARK or other open space, where people sell things from the back of their cars

**car·bo·run·dum** /ˌkɑːbəˈrʌndəm‖ˌkɑːr-/ *n* [U] an extremely hard substance made from CARBON (1) and SILICON used for polishing things

**car·boy** /ˈkɑːbɔɪ‖ˈkɑːr-/ *n* [C] a large round bottle used for holding dangerous chemical liquids

**car·bun·cle** /ˈkɑːbʌŋkəl‖ˈkɑːr-/ *n* [C] 1 a large painful lump under someone's skin 2 a red jewel, especially a GARNET (1)

**car·bu·ret·tor** *BrE*, **carburetor** *AmE* /ˌkɑːbjəˈretə, -bə-‖ˈkɑːrbəreɪtər/ *n* [C] a part of a car engine that mixes the air and petrol which burns in the engine to provide power —see picture at ENGINE

**car·cass** /ˈkɑːkəs‖ˈkɑːr-/ *n* [C] 1 the body of a dead animal, especially one that is ready to be cut up as meat 2 **shift/move your carcass!** *spoken* used to tell someone to move from the place where they are sitting or standing 3 the decaying outer structure of a building, vehicle, or other object

**car·cin·o·gen** /kɑːˈsɪnədʒən‖kɑːr- / *n* [C] a substance that can cause CANCER

**car·cin·o·genic** /ˌkɑːsɪnəˈdʒenɪk◂‖ˌkɑːr-/ *adj* likely to cause CANCER: *the carcinogenic effects of high-fat diets*

**car·ci·no·ma** /ˌkɑːsəˈnəʊmə‖ˌkɑːrsəˈnoʊ-/ *n* [C] *technical* a CANCER

**card**[1] /kɑːd‖kɑːrd/ *n* S1 W2
1 **library/membership/identity etc card** a small piece of plastic or paper that shows that someone belongs to a particular organization, club etc: *Employees must show their ID cards at the gate.*
2 ▶ **BIRTHDAY/CHRISTMAS ETC** ◀ [C] a piece of thick stiff paper with a picture on the front, that you send to people on special occasions: *Did you remember to send Val a birthday card?*
3 ▶ **HOLIDAY** ◀ [C] a card with a photograph or picture on one side, that you send to someone when you are

on holiday; POSTCARD: *Don't forget to send us a card from Greece!*
**4 ► INFORMATION ◄** [C] a small piece of stiff paper or plastic that shows information about someone or something, especially one that is part of a set used for storing information: *a card index system|an expansion card for 386 machines*
**5 ► STIFF PAPER ◄** [U] *BrE* thick stiff paper
**6 ► BANK ◄** [C] a small piece of plastic that you use to pay for goods or to get money from a special machine at a bank: *Lost or stolen cards must be reported immediately.* — see also CHARGE CARD, CHEQUE CARD, CREDIT CARD
**7 ► GAMES ◄** [C] a small piece of thick stiff paper with numbers and signs or pictures on, that is one of a set of fifty two used to play games such as POKER (1) or BRIDGE[1] (4): **play cards** (=play a game with cards) | **pack of cards** (=a complete set of cards)
**8 cigarette/football/baseball etc card** a small piece of thick stiff paper with a picture on one side that is part of a set which people collect
**9 ► BUSINESS ◄** [C] a small piece of thick stiff paper that shows your name, job, and the company you work for; BUSINESS CARD; VISITING CARD: *I'll leave my card and you can contact me when it suits you.*
**10 be on the cards** *BrE*, **be in the cards** *AmE* to seem likely to happen: *Another resignation could be on the cards.*
**11 play your cards right** to deal with a situation in the right way so that you are successful in getting what you want: *If he plays his cards right Tony might get a promotion.*
**12 put/lay your cards on the table** to tell people what your plans and intentions are in a clear, honest way: *I think it's time I put my cards on the table. You see, I'm not really a student.*
**13 play/keep your cards close to your chest** to keep your plans, thoughts, or feelings secret
**14 hold all the cards** *informal* to have all the advantages in a particular situation so that you can control what happens
**15 get/be given your cards** *BrE informal* to have your job taken away from you
**16 have another card up your sleeve** to have another advantage that you can use to be successful in a particular situation
**17 best/strongest/winning/trump card** something that gives you a big advantage in a particular situation: *The promise of tax cuts proved, as always, to be the Republican Party's trump card.*
**18 sb's card is marked** if someone's card is marked, they have done something that makes people in authority disapprove of them
**19 ► AMUSING / UNUSUAL PERSON ◄** [singular] *old-fashioned* an amusing or unusual person: *Old Fred's a real card, isn't he!*
**20** [C] the thing inside a computer that the chips (CHIP[1] (4a)) are fixed to, that allows the computer to do specific things
**21 ► TOOL ◄** [C] *technical* a tool that is similar to a comb and is used for combing, cleaning and preparing wool or cotton for spinning (SPIN[1] (2))
**22 ► FOOTBALL ◄** [C] a small piece of stiff red or yellow paper, shown to a player who has done something wrong in a game of football

**card²** *v* [T] **1** to comb, clean, and prepare wool or cotton, before making cloth **2** *AmE* to ask someone to show a card proving that they are old enough to be in a particular place, especially a bar

**car·da·mom** /ˈkɑːdəməm‖ˈkɑːr-/ *n* [C,U] the seeds of an Asian fruit, used to give a special taste to Indian and Middle Eastern food

**card·board¹** /ˈkɑːdbɔːd‖ˈkɑːrdbɔːrd/ *n* [U] a stiff brown material like very thick paper, used especially for making boxes: *We covered the hole with a sheet of cardboard.*

**cardboard²** *adj* **1** made from cardboard: *a cardboard box* **2** [only before noun] seeming silly and not real: *a romantic novel full of cardboard characters*

**cardboard cit·y** /ˌ·· ˈ··/ *n* [C] an area usually in a large town or city where people who have no home sleep outside using cardboard boxes to try to keep warm

**cardboard cut-out** /ˌ·· ˈ· ·/ *n* [C] **1** a picture drawn on cardboard so that it can stand up on a surface **2** a person or character in a book, film etc who seems silly or unreal

**card-car·ry·ing** /ˈ· ˌ···/ *adj* **card-carrying member** someone who has paid money to an organization and is a keen member of it: *a card-carrying member of the Labour Party*

**card cat·a·log** /ˈ· ˌ···/ *n* [C] *AmE* a box of cards that contain information about something and are arranged in order, for example in a library; CARD INDEX *BrE*

**card·hold·er** /ˈkɑːdˌhəʊldə‖ˈkɑːrdˌhoʊldər/ *n* [C] someone who has a CREDIT CARD

**car·di-** /kɑːdi‖kɑːrdi/ *prefix* another form of the prefix CARDIO-

**car·di·ac** /ˈkɑːdi-æk‖ˈkɑːr-/ *adj* [only before noun] *technical* connected with the heart: **cardiac arrest/failure** (=when the heart stops working)

**car·di·gan** /ˈkɑːdɪgən‖ˈkɑːr-/ also **car·die** /ˈkɑːdi‖ˈkɑːr-/ *BrE informal n* [C] a knitted JACKET[1] (1) or SWEATER, fastened at the front with buttons

**car·di·nal¹** /ˈkɑːdənəl‖ˈkɑːr-/ *n* [C] **1** a priest of high rank in the Roman Catholic Church **2** a North American bird of which the male is a bright red colour **3** a CARDINAL NUMBER

**cardinal²** *adj* [only before noun] very important or basic: *Having clean hands is one of the cardinal rules when preparing food.* | **cardinal error** (=very serious and basic mistake)

**cardinal num·ber** /ˌ··· ˈ··/ *n* [C] a number such as 1, 2 or 3, that shows how many of something there are —compare ORDINAL NUMBER

**cardinal point** /ˌ··· ˈ·/ *n* [C] *technical* one of the four main points (north, south, east, or west) on a COMPASS (1)

**cardinal sin** /ˌ··· ˈ·/ *n* [C] **1** *informal* something bad or stupid that you must avoid doing: *the cardinal sin of ignoring public opinion* **2** a serious SIN[1] (1) in the Christian religion

**cardinal vir·tue** /ˌ··· ˈ··/ *n* [C] *formal* a moral quality that someone has which people greatly respect or value

**card in·dex** /ˈ· ˌ··/ *n* [C] *BrE* a box of cards that contain information about something and are arranged in order, for example in a library; CARD CATALOG *AmE*

**cardio-** /kɑːdiəʊ, -diə‖kɑːrdioʊ, -diə/ *prefix* also **cardi-** /kɑːdi‖kɑːr-/ *technical* concerning the heart: *a cardiograph* (=instrument that measures movements of the heart)

**car·di·ol·o·gy** /ˌkɑːdiˈɒlədʒi‖ˌkɑːrdiˈɑː-/ *n* [U] the study or science of the heart

**card phone** /ˈ· ·/ *n* [C] a public telephone in which you must use a special plastic card rather than coins

**card·sharp** /ˈkɑːdʃɑːp‖ˈkɑːrdʃɑːrp/ also **card·sharp·er** /-ˌʃɑːpə‖-ˌʃɑːrpər/ *n* [C] someone who cheats when playing cards in order to make money

**card ta·ble** /ˈ· ˌ··/ *n* [C] a small light table that you can fold, used for playing cards

**card vote** /ˈ· ·/ *n* [C] *BrE* a way of voting at a TRADE UNION meeting in which your vote represents the votes of all the members of your organization

**care¹** /keə‖ker/ *v* [I,T] S1 W3
**1 ► OBJECTS/EVENTS ◄** to feel that something is important, so that you are interested in it, worried about it etc: **[+ about]** *The only thing he seems to care about is money.* | **care who/what/how etc** *Don't you care what happens to them?* | *I don't care whether we win or lose.*
**2 ► PEOPLE ◄** to mind about what happens to someone, because you like or love them: *I care about him, and hate to see him hurt like this.* | *She felt that nobody cared.*

**3 who cares?** *spoken* used to say that something does not worry or upset you because it is not important: *It's rather old and scruffy, but who cares?*
**4 couldn't care less** *spoken* used to say rudely that you do not care at all about something: *I really couldn't care less what you think!*
**5 what do I/you/they care?** *spoken* used to say that someone does not care at all about something: *What do I care? It's your responsibility now!*
**6 as if I cared!** *spoken* used to say that something is not important to you at all: *As if I cared whether he comes with us or not!*
**7 for all sb cares** *spoken* used to say that something does not matter at all to someone: *We could be starving for all they care!*

**8 not care to** *old-fashioned* not to like to do something: *She doesn't care to spend much time with her relatives.*
**9 I wouldn't care to** *spoken* used to say that you think that something would be an unpleasant experience: *I wouldn't care to meet him in a dark alley!*
**10 would you care to?** *spoken formal* used to ask someone politely whether they want to do something: *Would you care to join us for a drink?* —see also CARING

**care for** sb/sth *phr v* [T] **1** to look after someone who is not able to look after themselves: *She cared for her father all through his long illness.* | *The children are being well cared for.* **2** [usually in negative and questions] *formal* to like or want something or someone: *Would you care for a drink?* | *I don't much care for his parents.*

S2 W2 **care²** *n*
**1 ▶ LOOKING AFTER SB/STH ◀** [U] the process of looking after someone or something, especially because they are weak, ill, old etc: *high standards of medical care* | *They shared the care of the children.* | *advice on skin care* —see also DAY CARE, INTENSIVE CARE
**2 ▶ CAREFULNESS ◀** [U] carefulness to avoid damage, mistakes etc: *Fragile – handle with care.* —see also **tender loving care** (TENDER¹ (4))
**3 take care** to be careful: *It's very icy, so take care on the roads.* | **take care (that)** *Take care that you don't drop it!* | **take care to do sth** *Take care to keep the power cable away from the blade.* | **take care with/over sth** *Paul always takes great care over his appearance.*
**4 take care of a)** to look after someone or something: *Who's taking care of the dog while you're away?* **b)** to deal with all the work, arrangements etc that are necessary for something to happen: *Her secretary always took care of the details.* | *Don't worry about your accommodation – it's all taken care of.* **c)** an expression meaning to pay for something; used when you want to avoid saying this directly: *We'll take care of the fees.*
**5 take care!** *spoken* used when saying goodbye to family or friends: *Bye! Take care! See you on Sunday.*
**6 in care** *BrE* a child who is in care is being looked after in a local council home, not by their parents: **take sb into care** *When he was sent to prison, the children were taken into care.*
**7 ▶ PROBLEM/WORRY ◀** [C,U] *literary* something that causes problems and makes you anxious or sad: *At last I felt free from my cares.* | **not have a care in the world** (=not have any problems or worries) | **take the cares of the world on your shoulders** (=worry about other people's problems as well as your own)
**8 care of** used when sending letters to someone at someone else's address; c/o
**9 driving without due care and attention** *BrE law* the crime of driving a car without being careful enough
**10 have a care!** *spoken old-fashioned* used to tell someone to be more careful

**ca·reen** /kəˈriːn/ *v* [I always + adv/prep] *AmE* to move quickly forwards making sudden sideways movements; LURCH: [+ **down/over/along**] *The car careened around the corner and skidded to a halt.*

S2 W2 **ca·reer¹** /kəˈrɪə‖-ˈrɪr/ *n* [C] **1** a job or profession that you have been trained for and intend to do for several years: *a career in banking* | *He realized that his acting career was over.* | **career change** (=when you start a completely different job or profession) | **career structure** (=the opportunities that you have to move upwards in your job or profession) —see JOB (USAGE) **2 career soldier/teacher etc** someone who intends to be a soldier, teacher etc for most of their life, not just for a particular period of time **3** the period of time in your life that you spend doing a particular activity: *She had not had a very impressive school career up till then.* | *My career as an English teacher didn't last long.*

**career²** *v* [I always + adv/prep] to move forwards very fast and often without control: [+ **down/along/towards**] *The truck careered down the hill and into a tree.*

**career break** /·ˈ· ˌ·/ *n* [C] a short period of time when you do not work in your usual job or profession, for example because you want to look after your children

**career coun·sel·or** /·ˈ· ˌ···/ *n* [C] *AmE* a CAREERS OFFICER

**ca·reer·ist** /kəˈrɪərɪst‖-ˈrɪr-/ *n* [C] *especially AmE* someone whose career is more important to them than anything else so that they will do whatever is necessary to be successful —**careerist** *adj* —**careerism** *n* [U]

**careers of·fic·er** /·ˈ· ˌ···/ also **careers ad·vis·er** /·ˈ· ·ˌ··/ *n* [C] *BrE* someone whose job is to give people advice about what jobs and professional training might be suitable for them; CAREER COUNSELOR *AmE*

**career wom·an** /·ˈ· ˌ··/ *n* [C] a woman whose career is very important to her, so that she may not want to get married or have children: *a fiercely independent career woman*

**care·free** /ˈkeəfriː‖ˈker-/ *adj* having no worries or problems: *With the exams over, we felt happy and carefree at last.* | *Travel in carefree comfort to your hotel near Paris.*

**care·ful** /ˈkeəfəl‖ˈker-/ *adj* **1 (be) careful!** *spoken* used to tell someone to think about what they are doing so that they do not have an accident **2** trying to avoid damaging, harming, or losing something: *a careful driver* | **careful to do sth** *I was careful not to say anything about it to the boss.* | [+ **with**] *Be careful with that vase – it's very fragile.* | **careful who/what/how etc** *Be careful how you handle those glasses.* | *I had taught them to be careful crossing the road.* | [+ **about**] *Mara was extremely careful about what she ate.* | **careful (that)** *We were very careful that he didn't find out.* **3** paying a lot of attention to detail, so that something is done correctly and thoroughly: *After careful consideration, we've decided to accept their offer.* | *a careful study of all aspects of the problem* **4 careful with money** not spending more money than you need to **5 you can't be too careful** *spoken* used to say that you should do everything possible to avoid problems or danger —**carefulness** *n* [U] S1 W2

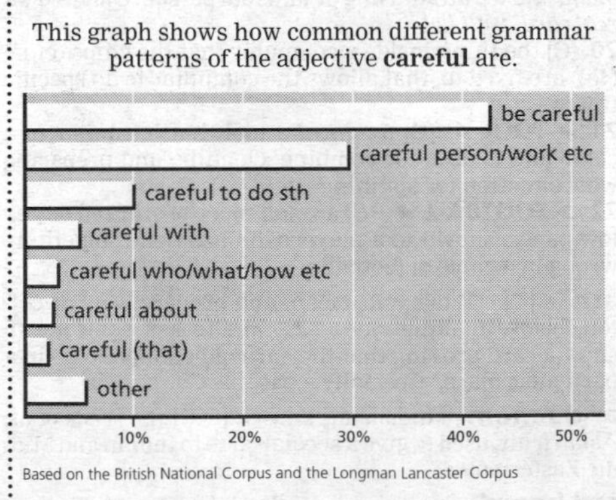


**care·ful·ly** /ˈkeəfəli‖ˈkeərfəli/ *adv* in a careful way: *I carried the bowl carefully in both hands.* | **carefully planned/chosen etc** *a carefully planned operation* S2 W2

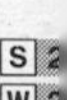

**care·giv·er** /ˈkeəˌgɪvə‖ˈkerˌgɪvər/ *n* [C] *AmE* someone who takes care of a child or sick person

**care la·bel** /ˈ· ˌ··/ *n* [C] a small piece of cloth in a piece of clothing that tells you how to wash it

**care·less** /ˈkeələs‖ˈker-/ *adj* **1** not paying enough attention to what you are doing, so that you make mistakes, damage things etc: *I had been careless and left the window unlocked.* | *a careless student* **2** done without much effort or attention to detail: *This is a very careless piece of work – do it again!* | *a careless mistake* **3** natural and not done with any deliberate effort or attention: *He ran a hand through his hair with a careless gesture.* | *careless charm* **4 careless of** *formal* deliberately ignoring something: *She turned and, careless of the pain, headed blindly for the door.* **5** *rare* without problems or worries; CAREFREE —**carelessly** *adv* —**carelessness** *n* [U]

**care pack·age** /ˈ· ˌ··/ *n* [C] *AmE* a package of food, sweets etc that is sent to someone living away from home, especially a student at college

**car·er** /ˈkeərə‖ˈkerər/ *n* [C] *BrE* someone who stays at home to look after a relative who is old, ill etc

**ca·ress**[1] /kəˈres/ *v* [T] **1** to gently touch someone in a way that shows you love them: *She lovingly caressed the baby's cheek.* **2** *poetic* to touch something gently, in a way that seems pleasant or romantic: *Waves caressed the shore.*

**caress**[2] *n* [C] a gentle loving touch or kiss

**car·et** /ˈkærɪ̇t/ *n* [C] *technical* the mark (‸) or (ʌ) used in writing and printing to show where something is to be added

**care·tak·er** /ˈkeəˌteɪkə‖ˈkerˌteɪkər/ *n* [C] **1** *BrE* someone whose job is to look after a building, especially a school; JANITOR *AmE* **2** someone who looks after a house or land while the person who owns it is not there **3** *AmE* someone who looks after other people, especially a teacher, parent, nurse etc

**caretaker gov·ern·ment** /ˈ··· ˌ···/ *n* [C] a government that has power only for a short period of time between the end of one government and the start of another

**care·worn** /ˈkeəwɔːn‖ˈkerwɔːrn/ *adj* looking sad, worried, or anxious: *the careworn face of a mother with hungry children to feed*

**car·fare** /ˈkɑːfeə‖ˈkɑːrfer/ *n* [U] *AmE old-fashioned* the amount of money that it costs to travel on a TROLLEY (3) in some cities in the US

**car·go** /ˈkɑːgəʊ‖ˈkɑːrgoʊ/ *n plural* **cargoes** *or* **cargos** [C,U] the goods being carried in a ship, plane, TRUCK[1] (1) etc: *We sailed from Jamaica with a cargo of rum.* | *a cargo vessel*

**car·hop** /ˈkɑːhɒp‖ˈkɑːrhɑːp/ *n* [C] *AmE old-fashioned* **1** someone who takes care of your car if you are staying a large hotel **2** someone who carries food to people's cars at a DRIVE-IN restaurant

**Car·ib·be·an** /ˌkærɪ̇ˈbiːən◂/ *adj* from or connected with the islands in the Caribbean sea —**Caribbean** *adj*: *Caribbean literature*

**car·i·bou** /ˈkærɪ̇buː/ *n* [C] a North American REINDEER

**car·i·ca·ture**[1] /ˈkærɪkətʃʊə‖-tʃʊr/ *n* **1** [C] a funny drawing of someone that makes some of their features look bigger or more amusing than they really are: *Newspapers often have caricatures of politicians.* **2** [C] a description of someone that shows only some parts of their character, especially parts that are silly or amusing: *a caricature of a semi-educated village teacher* **3** [U] the skill of making pictures, or writing about people in this way

**caricature**[2] *v* [T] to draw or describe someone in a way that makes them seem silly or stupid: *They are always being caricatured as hardworking bores.*

**car·i·ca·tur·ist** /ˈkærɪkətʃʊərɪ̇st‖-tʃʊr-/ *n* [C] someone who draws or writes caricatures

**car·ies** /ˈkeəriz‖ˈker-/ *n* [U] *technical* decay in someone's teeth: *dental caries*

**car·ill·on** /ˈkærɪ̇ljən, kəˈrɪ-‖ˈkærəljɑːn, -lən/ *n* [C] a set of bells in a tower that are controlled from a piano KEYBOARD[1] (1), or a tune played on these bells

**car·ing** /ˈkeərɪŋ‖ˈker-/ *adj* **1** someone who is caring thinks about what other people need or would like, and tries to help them: *a warm and caring man* | *a very caring attitude* **2 be past caring** *informal* to not worry about something because you are very tired, upset, or worried about something else **3 caring profession** a job that involves looking after other people: *Like most of the caring professions, nursing is very badly paid.*

**car·jack·ing** /ˈkɑːˌdʒækɪŋ‖ˈkɑːr-/ *n* [C,U] the crime of forcing the driver of a car to drive you somewhere or give you their car, by using threats and violence —compare HIJACKING —**carjacker** *n* [C] —**carjack** *v* [T]

**car·mine** /ˈkɑːmɪ̇n, -maɪn‖ˈkɑːr-/ *n* [U] a deep purplish red colour —**carmine** *adj*

**car·nage** /ˈkɑːnɪdʒ‖ˈkɑːr-/ *n* [U] the killing and wounding of lots of people, especially in a war: *The battlefield was a scene of terrible carnage.*

**car·nal** /ˈkɑːnl‖ˈkɑːrnl/ *adj* a word meaning connected with the body or sex, used especially in religious language: *carnal desires* —**carnally** *adv*

**car·na·tion** /kɑːˈneɪʃən‖kɑːr-/ *n* [C] a white, pink, or red flower that smells sweet and is often worn as a decoration at formal ceremonies

**car·ne** /ˈkɑːni‖ˈkɑːr-/ *n* [U] —see CHILLI (1)

**car·ne·li·an** /kɑːˈniːliən‖kɑːr-/ *n* [C] another spelling of CORNELIAN

**car·ney** /ˈkɑːni‖ˈkɑːr-/ *n* [C] *AmE* another spelling of CARNY

**car·ni·val** /ˈkɑːnɪ̇vəl‖ˈkɑːr-/ *n* **1** [C,U] a celebration with dancing, drinking, and a PROCESSION (1) through the streets: *Carnival in Rio* | *the Notting Hill carnival* | *the carnival atmosphere after they won the game* **2** [C] *AmE* a noisy outdoor event at which you can ride on special machines and play games for prizes; FUNFAIR *BrE* **3** [C] *AmE* an event held at a school in which students play games for prizes

**car·ni·vore** /ˈkɑːnɪ̇vɔː‖ˈkɑːrnɪ̇vɔːr/ *n* [C] **1** an animal that eats flesh —compare HERBIVORE, OMNIVORE **2** *humorous* someone who eats meat —compare VEGETARIAN —**carnivorous** *adj*

**car·ny, carney** /ˈkɑːni‖ˈkɑːr-/ *n* [C] *AmE informal* someone who works in a CARNIVAL (2)

**car·ob** /ˈkærəb/ *n* [U] the fruit of a Mediterranean tree, that tastes similar to chocolate and is sometimes eaten instead of chocolate

**car·ol**[1] /ˈkærəl/ also **Christmas carol** *n* [C] a traditional Christmas song

**carol**[2] *v* **carolled, carolling** *BrE*, **caroled, caroling** *AmE* [I] to sing carols or other songs in a lively way

**ca·rot·id ar·te·ry** /kəˈrɒtɪ̇d ˌɑːtəri‖-ˈrɑːtɪ̇d ˌɑːr-/ *n* [C] *technical* one of the two arteries (ARTERY (1)) in your neck, that supply blood to your head

**ca·rouse** /kəˈraʊz/ *v* [I] *literary* to drink a lot, be noisy, and laugh loudly —**carousal** *n* [C,U]

**car·ou·sel, carrousel** /ˌkærəˈsel/ *n* [C] **1** *AmE* a machine with wooden horses on it that turns round and round, which people can ride on for fun; MERRY-GO-ROUND (1) **2** the circular moving belt that you collect your bags and cases from at an airport **3** a circular piece of equipment that you put slides (SLIDE[2] (4)) into for showing on a SLIDE PROJECTOR

**carp**[1] /kɑːp‖kɑːrp/ *v* [I usually in progressive] to complain about something or criticize someone continually: *Stop carping!*

**carp**[2] *n plural* **carp** [C] a large fish that lives in lakes, pools, and rivers, which you can eat

**car·pal tun·nel syn·drome** /ˌkɑːpəl ˈtʌnl ˌsɪndrəʊm‖ˌkɑːr-, -droʊm/ *n* [U] *technical* a medical condition in which someone gets a lot of pain and weakness in their wrist

**car park** /ˈ· ·/ *n* [C] *BrE* **1** an open area where cars can park; PARKING LOT *AmE* **2** an enclosed building for cars to park in; PARKING GARAGE *AmE*

**car·pen·ter** /ˈkɑːpɪ̣ntə‖ˈkɑːrpɪ̣ntər/ *n* [C] someone whose job is making and repairing wooden objects

**car·pen·try** /ˈkɑːpɪ̣ntri‖ˈkɑːr-/ *n* [U] the skill or work of a carpenter

**car·pet¹** /ˈkɑːpɪ̣t‖ˈkɑːr-/ *n* **1** [C,U] heavy woven material for covering floors or stairs, or a piece of this material: *a beautiful persian carpet* | **fitted carpet** (=one that is cut to fit the shape of a room) —compare RUG (1) **2 carpet of leaves/flowers etc** *literary* a thick layer of leaves etc —see also MAGIC CARPET, **sweep sth under the carpet** (SWEEP¹ (13))

C

**carpet²** *v* [T] **1** [usually in passive] to cover a floor with carpet: *a carpeted corridor* **2** *informal especially BrE* to blame someone for something they have done; REPRIMAND **3 carpeted with grass/flowers etc** *literary* covered with a thick layer of grass etc

**car·pet·bag** /ˈkɑːpɪtbæg‖ˈkɑːr-/ *n* [C] a bag used for travelling, usually made of carpet

**car·pet·bag·ger** /ˈkɑːpɪ̣tˌbægə‖ˈkɑːrpɪtˌbægər/ *n* [C] someone who tries to become active in the political life of another area for their own advantage, especially someone from the North of the US active in the South in the 1860s and 1870s

**carpet bomb** /ˈ·· ˌ·/ *v* [T] to drop a lot of bombs over a small area to destroy everything in it.

**car·pet·ing** /ˈkɑːpɪ̣tɪŋ‖ˈkɑːr-/ *n* [U] heavy woven material for making CARPETS

**carpet slip·per** /ˈ·· ˌ··/ *n* [C] a type of soft shoe that you wear indoors

**carpet sweep·er** /ˈ·· ˌ··/ *n* [C] a simple machine for sweeping CARPETS

**car pool¹** /ˈ· ·/ *n* [C] **1** a group of car owners who agree to drive everyone in the group to work, school etc on different days so that only one car is used at a time **2** a group of cars owned by a company or other organization that its members can use; MOTOR POOL

**car pool²** *v* [I] *AmE* if a group of people car pool, they agree to drive everyone in the group to work, school etc on different days so that only one car is used at a time

**car·port** /ˈkɑːpɔːt‖ˈkɑːrpɔːrt/ *n* [C] a shelter for a car that has a roof and one or two walls, often built against the side of a house —compare GARAGE¹ (1)

**car·rel** /ˈkærəl/ *n* [C] a small enclosed space with a desk and a light for one person to use in a library

**car·riage** /ˈkærɪdʒ/ *n* **1** [C] a vehicle with wheels that is pulled by a horse, used in former times **2** [C] *BrE* one of the connected parts of a train that passengers sit in; CAR (3) *AmE* **3** [U] *formal* the way someone walks and moves their head and body **4** something with wheels that is used to move a heavy object, especially a gun **5** [U] *formal especially BrE* the act of moving goods from one place to another or the cost of moving them **6** [C] the movable part of a machine that supports another part: *the carriage of a typewriter* —see also BABY CARRIAGE

**carriage clock** /ˈ·· ·/ *n* [C] a small clock inside a glass case with a handle on top

**car·riage·way** /ˈkærɪdʒweɪ/ *n* [C] *BrE* the part of a road that a single line of traffic moves along —see also DUAL CARRIAGEWAY

**car·ri·er** /ˈkæriə‖-ər/ *n* [C] **1** a company that moves goods or passengers from one place to another **2** a military vehicle or ship used to move soldiers, weapons etc —see also AIRCRAFT CARRIER **3** *technical* someone who passes a disease to other people without having it themselves **4** a metal frame that is fixed to a bicycle or other vehicle and holds bags etc **5** a carrier bag

**carrier bag** /ˈ··· ˌ·/ *n* [C] *BrE* a bag that you are given in a shop, to carry the things you have bought —see picture at BAG¹

**carrier pi·geon** /ˈ··· ˌ··/ *n* [C] a PIGEON (=type of bird) that has been trained to carry messages

**car·ri·on** /ˈkæriən/ *n* [U] dead flesh that is decaying: *Some birds feed on carrion.*

**car·rot** /ˈkærət/ *n* **1** [C,U] a plant with a long thick orange pointed root that you eat as a vegetable —see picture on page 414 **2** [C] *informal* something that is promised to someone in order to try and persuade them to work harder: **carrot and stick approach/method etc** (=a way of persuading someone to do something using a mixture of promises and threats)

**car·rot·y** /ˈkærəti/ *adj* hair that is carroty is orange

**car·rou·sel** /ˌkærəˈsel/ *n* [C] another spelling of CAROUSEL

**car·ry¹** /ˈkæri/ *v* **carried, carrying** S1 W1

**1 ▶ LIFT AND TAKE ◀** [T] to take something somewhere in your hands or arms, on your back etc: *A porter helped me carry my luggage.* | *Let me carry that for you.* | **carry sth around/out/to etc** *I'm not carrying it around all day!* —see BRING (USAGE)

**2 ▶ VEHICLE/SHIP/PLANE ◀** [T] to take people or things from one place to another: **carry sth to/down/away etc** *The ship was carrying oil from Kuwait to Japan.* | **carry sb/sth** *a coach carrying 44 American tourists*

**3 ▶ HOW STH IS MOVED ◀** [T] if a pipe, river, wire etc carries something such as liquid or electricity, the liquid etc flows along it: **carry sth along/through/across etc** *Pipes carry the water across the desert.* | *Soil from the river banks is carried down towards the sea.* | **carry sth** *Two lines are dedicated to carrying teletext data.* | **be carried out to sea/downstream etc** (=be taken somewhere by a current of water)

**4 ▶ DISEASE ◀** [T] if a person, animal, or insect carries a disease the disease is spread by them: *Brown rats carried the plague.* | *Many serious diseases are carried by insects.*

**5 carry sth in your head/mind** to remember information that you need, without writing it down: *He was required to carry a detailed map of the aiport in his head.*

**6 ▶ HAVE WITH YOU ◀** [T] to take money, a weapon, or something that you need, with you in your pocket, on your belt, in your bag etc: *I don't usually carry that much cash on me.* | **carry a gun/knife etc** *The police here don't carry guns.* | **carry arms** (=carry weapons) *a society where men carried arms as a matter of course*

**7 ▶ SHOP ◀** [T] if a shop carries goods, it has a supply of them for sale: **carry a range/selection** *Selfridges carries a good range of sports equipment.* | *I'm afraid we don't carry that line any more.*

**8 be carrying too much weight/extra pounds etc** to weigh too much: *He's carrying at least ten kilos too many around.*

**9 ▶ BUILDING ◀** [T] if a pillar, wall etc carries something, it supports the weight of that thing: *These two columns carry the whole roof.*

**10 be/get carried away** to be so excited, angry, interested etc that you are no longer really in control of what you do or say, or you forget everything else: *Sorry I shouted – I get a little carried away at times!* | *We got carried away by the beauty of the music.*

**11 carry yourself well/stiffly etc** to stand and move in a particular way: *He carried himself upright, like the old soldier he was.*

**12 ▶ CHILD ◀** [T] *old-fashioned* if a woman is carrying a child, she is PREGNANT (=going to have a baby)

**13 ▶ NEWSPAPER/BROADCAST ◀** [T] if a newspaper or a television or radio broadcast carries a piece of news, an advertisement etc, it prints it or broadcasts it: *The trade press carried details of the new laws.*

**14 ▶ LABEL/WRITING ◀** [T] if an object, container etc carries a warning, information etc it is written on it: *These new perfumes carry an 'exclusive' tag.* | *a card carrying details of your blood group*

**15 carry insurance/a guarantee etc** to have insurance etc: *All our products carry a 12 month guarantee.*

**16 ▶ HAVE A QUALITY ◀** [T] to have a particular quality such as authority or confidence that makes you believe or not believe someone: *Her manner carried an unmistakable air of authority.* | **carry conviction** (=to seem very sure about something) *Matthew's voice did not carry much conviction.* | **carry weight** (=to have some influence over someone) *Her views carry a lot of weight with the committee.*
**17 ▶ CRIME ◀** [T] if a crime carries a particular punishment, that is the usual punishment for the crime: *Rape carries the death penalty here.* | *a serious crime which carries a long jail sentence*
**18 carry a (heavy) load/burden** to have a lot of work to do or a lot of responsibility for something: *Each team member is expected to carry a fair share of the workload*
**19 ▶ USELESS PERSON ◀** [T] if you carry someone who is not doing as much as they should, you manage without the work they should be doing, or the money they should be earning: *The team simply can't afford to carry anyone.*
**20 carry sth too far/to extremes/to excess** to do or say too much about something: *Don't you think you're carrying discipline a bit too far? They're only children!*
**21 carry sb to victory/to the top etc** to be the reason that a person or group is successful: *It's that extra enthusiasm that will carry you to the top.*
**22 ▶ PERSUADE ◀** [T] if someone carries a group of people, they persuade those people to support them: *Her tearful pleas carried the meeting.*
**23 carry the day** to persuade a group of people to support you: *His appeal to common sense was what finally carried the day.*
**24 as fast as his/her legs could carry him/her** as fast as possible: *She ran to her mother as fast as her legs could carry her.*
**25 carry all/everything before you** *literary* to be completely successful in a struggle against other people
**26 ▶ VOTE ◀ be carried** if a suggestion, proposal etc is carried, most of the people at an official meeting vote for it and it is accepted: *The amendment to the bill was carried unanimously.* (=everyone agreed to it) | **be carried by 20 votes/50 votes etc** (=20, 50 etc more people voted for something than voted against it) *the motion to ban the sale of guns was carried by 76 votes.* | **declare sth carried** (=to state officially that something has been accepted) *I declare the resolution carried.*
**27** [I] **▶ SOUND/SMELL ◀** if a sound or smell carries to a particular place, it goes as far as that place: *The sounds of laughter carried as far as the lake.*
**28 carry one/two/three etc** to put a number into the next row to the left when you are adding numbers together: *Nine and three make twelve, put down two and carry one.*
**29 ▶ BALL ◀** [I] if the ball carries a particular distance in GOLF, CRICKET (2) etc, that is how far it travels when it is hit
**30 carry a torch for sb** to be in love with someone who does not love you
**31 carry the can (for sb/sth)** *BrE informal* to be blamed or punished for something that is someone else's fault as well as your own: *Why am I always left to carry the can?*
**32 carry a tune** to sing correctly —see also CARD-CARRYING, CARRIER, CASH AND CARRY, **fetch and carry** (FETCH (4))

**carry** sth ↔ **forward** *phr v* [T] **1** to move a total to the next page for adding to other numbers **2** to make an amount of something such as money or holiday time available for use at a later time

**carry** sb/sth ↔ **off** *phr v* [T] **1** to do something difficult successfully: *It's a demanding role, but I'm sure she'll be able to carry it off.* **2** to win a prize: *Jackie carried off most of the awards that evening.*

**carry on** *phr v* **1** [I,T **carry on** sth] *especially BrE* to continue doing something: *Don't stop – carry on, everyone!* | **carry on doing sth** *We all carried on singing as if nothing odd was happening.* | **carry on with sth** *Please carry on with your work.* | **carry on as normal/as usual/as you are/regardless** *I think we should just carry on as we are for now.* **2** [I] to continue moving: *We carried on down the freeway for a while.* | *Carry straight on until you get to the traffic lights.* **3** [T **carry on** sth] to continue something that has been started by someone else: *He is relying on his son to carry on the family business.* | *When she left I carried on her research.* **4** [T **carry on** *sth*] to do something for a period of time: *Negotiations were being carried on, in spite of the fighting.* | **carry on a conversation** *They carried on a curious conversation, never looking at each other.* **5** [I] *spoken* to behave in a silly, excited, or anxious way: *Stop carrying on, you two!* | *Anyone would think they owned the business, the way they carry on!* **6** [I] *old-fashioned* to have a sexual relationship with someone, when you should not: *she's been carrying on with the milkman, I'm certain of it.*

**carry** sth ↔ **out** *phr v* [T] **1** to do something that needs to be organized and planned: *They are carrying out urgent repairs.* | *A survey is now being carried out nationwide.* | *It won't be an easy plan to carry out.* **2 carry out a promise/a threat/an intention/an order etc** to do something that you have said you will do or that someone has asked you to do: *We carried out her instructions to the letter.*

**carry** sth ↔ **over** *phr v* [T] **1** if something is carried over into a new set of conditions, it continues to exist when conditions change: *aspects of the dream which are carried over into wakefulness* **2** to carry something forward: *Holiday time can be carried over into next year.*

**carry through** *phr v* [T] **1** [**carry** sth **through**] to complete or finish something successfully, in spite of difficulties: *I'm determined to carry this through.* **2 carry sb through (sth)** to help someone to manage during an illness or a difficult period: *Her confidence carried her through.*

**carry**[2] *n* [C,U] *technical* the distance a ball or bullet travels after it has been thrown, hit or fired

**car·ry·all** /ˈkæri-ɔːl‖-ɒːl/ *n* [C] *AmE* a large soft bag or case; HOLDALL *BrE* —see picture at BAG[1]

**car·ry·cot** /ˈkærikɒt‖-kɑːt/ *n* [C] *BrE* a small bed used for carrying a baby; PORTACRIB *AmE* —see picture at BED[1]

**carrying charge** /ˈ··· ˌ·/ *n* [C] *AmE* a charge added to the price of something you have bought by INSTALLMENT PLAN (=paying over several months)

**carry-on**[1] /ˈ·· ·/ *n* [singular] *BrE spoken* behaviour or a situation that is silly or annoying: *What a carry-on!* —see also **carry on** (CARRY[1])

**carry-on**[2] *adj* [only before noun] carry-on cases or bags are ones that passengers take onto a plane with them

**carry-out** /ˈ·· ·/ *n* [C] *AmE, ScotE* food that you can take away from a restaurant to eat somewhere else, or a restaurant that sells food like this; TAKEAWAY *BrE*

**carry-o·ver** /ˈ·· ˌ··/ *n* [singular] **1** something that affects an existing situation but is the result of a past one: [+ **from**] *Grandma is still frugal, a carry-over from the war years.* **2** an amount of money that has not been used and is available to use later: [+ **of**] *a carry-over of funds to next year's budget* —see also **carry over** (CARRY[1])

**car·sick** /ˈkɑːˌsɪk‖ˈkɑːr-/ *adj* feeling sick because you are travelling in a car —**carsickness** *n* [U]

**cart**[1] /kɑːt‖kɑːrt/ *n* [C] **1** a vehicle with two or four wheels that is pulled by a horse and used for carrying heavy things —see also HANDCART **2** *AmE* a large wire basket on wheels that you use in a SUPERMARKET; TROLLEY (1) *BrE* **3** *AmE* a small table with wheels, used to move and serve food and drinks; TROLLEY (2) *BrE* **4 put the cart before the horse** to do things in the wrong order —see also **upset the apple cart** (UPSET[1] (5))

**cart**[2] *v* [T always + adv/prep] **1** *informal* to carry something that is awkward or heavy: *I was really tired after carting all that furniture upstairs.* **2** to carry something in a cart: [+ **away**] *The corn sacks were carted away.*

**cart** sb **off** *phr v* [T] *informal* to take someone away, especially to prison: *The police carted him off this morning.*

**car tax** /ˈ· ·/ *n* [C,U] ROAD TAX

**carte blanche** /ˌkɑːt ˈblɑːnʃ‖ˌkɑːrt-/ *n* [U] complete freedom to do whatever you like in a particular situation, especially to spend money: **give sb carte blanche** *We were given carte blanche to redecorate the hotel.*

**car·tel** /kɑːˈtel‖kɑːr-/ *n* [C] a group of companies who agree to fix prices to limit competition so that they can increase their profits: *an illegal international oil cartel*

**cart·er** /ˈkɑːtə‖ˈkɑːrtər/ *n* [C] *old use* someone whose job is to drive a CART[1] (1)

**cart·horse** /ˈkɑːthɔːs‖ˈkɑːrthɔːrs/ *n* [C] a large strong horse, often used for pulling heavy loads

**car·ti·lage** /ˈkɑːtɪlɪdʒ‖ˈkɑːrtəlɪdʒ/ *n* [C,U] a strong stretchy substance, or piece of this, that is around the joints in a person or animal's body

**cart·load** /ˈkɑːtləʊd‖ˈkɑːrtloʊd/ *n* [C] the amount that a CART can hold: [+ **of**] *cartloads of hay*

**car·tog·ra·phy** /kɑːˈtɒgrəfi‖kɑːrˈtɑː-/ *n* [U] the skill or practice of making maps —**cartographer** *n* [C]

**car·ton** /ˈkɑːtn‖ˈkɑːrtn/ *n* [C] **1** a box made of CARDBOARD (=stiff paper) or plastic that contains food or drink: *a carton of fruit juice*|*a milk carton* —see picture at CONTAINER **2** *AmE* a large container with smaller containers of goods inside it: *a carton of cigarettes*

S3 **car·toon** /kɑːˈtuːn‖kɑːr-/ *n* [C] **1** a funny drawing in a newspaper, often including humorous remarks about news events —compare COMIC STRIP **2** a short film that is made by photographing a series of drawings **3** a drawing that is used as a model for a painting or other work of art

**car trans·port·er** /ˈ· ·ˌ··/ *n* [C] a large vehicle on the road or railway, that carries several new cars to a place where they will be sold

**car·tridge** /ˈkɑːtrɪdʒ‖ˈkɑːr-/ *n* [C] **1** a metal, CARDBOARD, or plastic tube containing explosive and a bullet that you use in a gun **2** the small part of a RECORD PLAYER containing the STYLUS (=needle) that takes sound signals from the record **3** a container with ink, film, or MAGNETIC TAPE in it, that you put into a pen, camera, or TAPE RECORDER

**cartridge pa·per** /ˈ·· ˌ··/ *n* [U] *BrE* thick strong paper used for drawing on

**cart-track** /ˈ· ·/ *n* [C] a narrow road with a rough surface, usually on a farm

**cart·wheel** /ˈkɑːt-wiːl‖ˈkɑːrt-/ *n* [C] a movement in which you turn right over by throwing your body sideways onto your hands while bringing your legs over your head —**cartwheel** *v* [I]

**carve** /kɑːv‖kɑːrv/ *v* **1** [I,T] to cut a large piece of cooked meat into smaller pieces using a big knife: *Carve the lamb into slices and arrange in a hot serving dish.* —see picture on page 834 **2** [T] to cut shapes out of solid wood or stone: *Michelangelo carved this figure from a single block of marble.* **3** [T] to cut a pattern or letter on the surface of something: **carve sth on/in etc** *Someone had carved their initials on the tree.*

**carve** sth ↔ **out** *phr v* [T] **carve out a career/niche/reputation etc** to become successful and be respected: *She's carved out a very successful career as a photographer.*

**carve** sb/sth ↔ **up** *phr v* [T] **1** if two or more people, governments etc carve something up, they divide it into separate parts and share it between them eventhough this is wrong: *Hitler and Stalin ruthlessly carved up Poland between them.* —see also CARVE-UP **2** *BrE informal* to drive past another car going in the same direction and then turn in front of it too quickly

**carv·er** /ˈkɑːvə‖ˈkɑːrvər/ *n* [C] **1** someone who carves **2** a big knife used for cutting meat; CARVING KNIFE

**car·ver·y** /ˈkɑːvəri‖ˈkɑːr- / *n* [C] *BrE* a restaurant that serves ROAST[3] meat

**carve-up** /ˈ· ·/ *n* [singular] an arrangement between two or more people, governments etc by which they divide something among themselves even though this is wrong

**carv·ing** /ˈkɑːvɪŋ‖ˈkɑːr-/ *n* **1** [C] an object or pattern made by cutting a shape in wood or stone for decoration **2** [U] the activity or skill of carving

**carving fork** /ˈ·· ·/ *n* [C] a large fork used to hold cooked meat firmly while you are cutting it

**carving knife** /ˈ·· ·/ *n* [C] a large knife used for cutting cooked meat —see picture at KNIFE[1]

**car wash** /ˈ· ·/ *n* [C] a place where there is special equipment for washing cars

**car·y·at·id** /ˌkæriˈætɪd/ *n* [C] *technical* a PILLAR (1) in the shape of a female figure

**Cas·a·no·va** /kæsəˈnəʊvə‖-ˈnoʊ-/ *n* [C] a man who has had, or says he has had, a lot of lovers: *a man with a reputation as a womaniser, a Casanova*

**cas·bah** /ˈkæzbɑː/ *n* [C] an ancient Arab city or the market in it

**cas·cade[1]** /kæˈskeɪd/ *n* [C] **1** a small steep WATERFALL that is one of several together **2** something that hangs down in large quantities: [+ **of**] *Her hair fell over her shoulders in a cascade of curls.*

**cascade[2]** *v* [I always + adv/prep] to flow, fall or hang down in large quantities: *Geraniums cascaded over the balcony.*|*a cascading stream*

**case[1]** /keɪs/ *n* S1 W1

**1 ▶ EXAMPLE ◀** [C] an example of a particular situation, problem etc: *In some cases, it is necessary to operate.*|[+ **of**] *an extreme case of anorexia*|**case in point** (=a clear example of a situation, problem etc that you are discussing or explaining) *This latest policy is a case in point.*|**classic case of** (=a typical example of a situation, problem etc) *a classic case of food poisoning*

**2 ▶ SITUATION ◀** [C usually singular] a situation that exists, especially as it affects a particular person or group: **be the case** *This was found to be the case in many third-world countries.*|**it is the case (that)** *It is simply not the case that standards have fallen.*|**in sb's case** *In Sandra's case, the reasons are less easy to pinpoint.*|*I'm not supposed to let anyone in without a card, but I'll make an exception in your case.*|**understate/overstate the case** (=make a situation seem less or more serious than it really is)

**3 in that case** *spoken* used to describe what you will do, or what will happen, as a result of a particular situation or event: *"I'm afraid I can't come after all." "Well, in that case I'm not going either."*

**4 in any case** *spoken* used to say that a fact or part of a situation stays the same even if other things change: *We have to go past your house in any case, so we'll take you home.*

**5 (just) in case** *especially spoken* **a)** as a way of being safe from something that might happen or might be true: *Take an umbrella, in case it rains.*|*I'm sure Harry will remember, but why not give him a ring just in case?* **b)** *AmE* if: *In case I'm late, start without me.*

**6 it's a case of** *spoken* used before describing a situation, especially the one you are now in: *We don't want to sell the car, but it's a case of having to.*|*It's a case of too many people and not enough jobs.*

**7 in case of** used to describe what you should do in a particular situation, especially on official notices: *In case of fire, break the glass.*

**8 ▶ BOX/CONTAINER ◀** [C] **a)** a large box or container in which things can be stored or moved: *a packing case*|*a case of wine* **b)** a special box used as a container for holding or protecting something: *a jewellery case*|*The exhibits were all in glass cases.* **c)** *BrE* a SUITCASE: *Shall I take your cases down to the car?* —see also BOOKCASE, BRIEFCASE, PILLOWCASE

**9 ▶ LAW/CRIME ◀** [C] **a)** a question or problem that will be dealt with by a law court: *a libel case*|**win/lose a case** *They lost their case in the High Court, and had*

*to pay damages.* **b)** all the reasons that one side in a legal argument can give against the other side: *the case for the prosecution*|**have a case** (=have enough good arguments to go to a law court) *The police have a clear case against him.* **c)** an event or set of events that need to be dealt with by the police: *investigating a murder case*|**be on the case** (=be in charge of dealing with a particular crime) *Inspector Hacker is on the case.*
**10 ▶REASON/ARGUMENT◀** [C,U] the facts, arguments, or reasons for doing something, supporting something etc: [+ **for/against**] *the case against hanging*|*There may be a case for abandoning the scheme altogether.*|**make out a case for** (=provide good reasons for something) *I'm sure we can make out a good case for a pay rise.*
**11 get off my case** *spoken* used to tell someone to stop criticizing you or complaining about you: *OK, OK, just get off my case already!*
**12 be on sb's case** *informal* to be criticizing someone continuously: *Dad's always on my case about something or another.*
**13 ▶PERSON◀** [C] someone who is being dealt with by a doctor, a SOCIAL WORKER, the police etc —see also **sad case** (SAD (4)), NUTCASE, BASKET-CASE
**14 ▶GRAMMAR◀** [C,U] *technical* the way in which the form of a word changes, showing its relationship to other words in a sentence: *case endings* —see also LOWER CASE, UPPER CASE

**case²** *v* [T] **1 be cased in** to be completely surrounded by a material or substance: *The reactor will be cased in metal.* **2 case the joint** *slang* to look around a place that you intend to steal from in order to find out information —see also CASING

**case·book** /ˈkeɪsbʊk/ *n* [C] a detailed written record kept by a doctor, SOCIAL WORKER, or police officer of the cases (CASE¹ (9)) they have dealt with

**case his·tory** /ˈ· ˌ···/ *n* [C] a detailed record of someone's past illnesses, problems etc that a doctor or SOCIAL WORKER studies

**case law** /ˈ· ·/ *n* [U] *law* a type of law that is based on decisions judges have made in the past

**case·load** /ˈkeɪsləʊd‖-loʊd/ *n* [C] the number of people a doctor, SOCIAL WORKER etc has to deal with

**case·ment** /ˈkeɪsmənt/ *n* [C] a window that opens like a door with HINGES¹ at one side

**case stud·y** /ˈ· ˌ··/ *n* [C] a detailed account of the development of a particular person, group, or situation that has been studied over a period of time

**case work** /ˈ· ·/ *n* [U] work that a SOCIAL WORKER does which is concerned with the problems of a particular person or family that needs help —**caseworker** *n* [C]

S2 W2 **cash¹** /kæʃ/ *n* [U] **1** money in the form of coins or notes rather than cheques, CREDIT CARDS etc: **in cash** *I'm bringing $400 in travellers' checks and $100 in cash.* —see MONEY (USAGE)|**pay in cash** (=not by cheque etc)|*Is there any discount if I pay in cash?*|**hard cash** (=notes and coins only) *In terms of hard cash, we've raised over £200 and in pledges about £8500.* **2** *informal* money: *The company's a bit short of cash right now.*|**be strapped for cash** (=not have enough money) **3 pay cash** to pay immediately using a cheque or cash, but not by adding a debt to your account: *Are you paying cash or do you have a trade account?*|**cash bonus/sale/deposit** (=one in which a direct payment is made) **4 cash down** if you pay for something cash down, you pay for it before you receive it **5 cash on delivery** COD; used to mean that the customer pays the person delivering the goods to them —see also PETTY CASH

S3 **cash²** *v* [T] **cash a cheque/postal order/draft etc** to exchange a cheque etc for the amount of money it is worth: *Can you cash my traveller's cheques here?*|*Where can I get this cashed?* —**cashable** *adj*: *cashable at any bank*
**cash in** *phr v* **1** [I] to make a profit from a situation in a way that other people think is wrong or unfair: [+ **on**] *He's just cashing in on the fact that his father is a big movie director.* **2** [T **cash** sth ↔ **in**] to exchange something such as an insurance POLICY (2) for its value in money **3 cash in your chips** *humorous* to die
**cash up**, also **cash out** *AmE phr v* [T] to add up the amount of money received in a shop in a day so that it can be checked

**cash and car·ry** /ˌ· · ˈ··/ *n* [C] a very large shop where customers representing a business or organization can buy large amounts of goods at cheap prices

**cash·book** /ˈkæʃbʊk/ *n* [C] a book in which you keep a record of money received and paid out

**cash box** /ˈ· ·/ *n* [C] a small metal box with a lock that you keep money in

**cash card** /ˈ· ·/ *n* [C] a special plastic card used for getting money from a machine outside a bank —compare CHEQUE CARD, CREDIT CARD, DEBIT CARD

**cash cow** /ˈ· ·/ *n* [C] the part of a business you can always depend on to make enough profits: *seeing the product as a high-yielding cash cow, requiring little investment in the mature stage of its life-cycle*

**cash crop** /ˈ· ·/ *n* [C] a crop grown in order to be sold rather than to be used by the people growing it —compare SUBSISTENCE CROP

**cash desk** /ˈ· ·/ *n* [C] the desk in a shop where you pay

**cash dis·count** /ˌ· ˈ··/ *n* [C] an amount by which a seller reduces a price if the buyer pays immediately or before a particular date

**cash dis·pens·er** /ˈ· ·ˌ··/ *n* [C] *especially BrE* a CASH MACHINE

**ca·shew** /ˈkæʃuː, kəˈʃuː/ *n* [C] **1** a small curved nut **2** the tropical American tree that produces this

**cash flow** /ˈ· ·/ *n* [singular, U] **1** the movement of money coming into a business as income and going out as wages, materials etc: *maintaining a healthy cash flow* **2 have cash flow problems** to not have enough money

**cash·ier¹** /kæˈʃɪə‖-ˈʃɪr/ *n* [C] someone whose job is to receive or pay out money in a shop, bank, hotel etc

**cashier²** *v* [T] to force an officer to leave the army, navy etc because they have done something wrong

**cash-in-hand** /ˌ· · ˈ·◂/ *adj* a cash-in-hand payment is made in the form of notes and coins so that there is no record of the payment

**cash·less** /ˈkæʃləs/ *adj* done or working without using actual money: *a cashless transaction between two banks*|*the cashless society*

**cash ma·chine** /ˈ· ·ˌ·/ *n* [C] a machine in or outside a bank from which you can obtain money with a special plastic card; CASH DISPENSER *especially BrE*, ATM *AmE*

**cash·mere** /ˈkæʃmɪə‖ˈkæʒmɪr, ˈkæʃ-/ *n* [U] a type of fine soft wool: *I wish I could afford a cashmere sweater.*

**cash·point** /ˈkæʃpɔɪnt/ *n* [C] *BrE* a cash machine

**cash reg·is·ter** /ˈ· ˌ···/ *n* [C] a machine used in shops to keep the money in and record the amount of money received from each sale: TILL²

**cash-strapped** /ˈ· ·/ *adj* not having enough money: *higher school meal prices imposed by a cash-strapped county council*

**cas·ing** /ˈkeɪsɪŋ/ *n* [C] an outer layer of metal, rubber etc that covers and protects something such as a wire or tyre

**ca·si·no** /kəˈsiːnəʊ‖-noʊ/ *n plural* **casinos** [C] a place where people try to win money by playing card games or ROULETTE: *Doesn't that club have a casino upstairs?*

**cask** /kɑːsk‖kæsk/ *n* [C] a round wooden container used for storing wine or other liquids, or the amount of liquid contained in this: *a cask of rum*

**cas·ket** /ˈkɑːskɪt‖ˈkæs-/ *n* [C] **1** a small decorated box in which you keep jewellery and other valuable objects **2** *especially AmE* a COFFIN

**cas·sa·va** /kəˈsɑːvə/ *n* [C,U] a tropical plant with thick roots that you can eat, or the flour made from these roots

**cas·se·role¹** /ˈkæsərəʊl‖-roʊl/ *n* [C] **1** food that is cooked slowly in liquid in a covered dish in the OVEN: *chicken casserole* **2** a deep covered dish used for cooking food in the oven

**casserole²** *v* [T] to cook food in a casserole

**cas·sette** /kə'set/ *n* [C] **1** a small flat plastic case containing MAGNETIC TAPE, that can be used for playing or recording sound: *Now available on cassette or CD!* **2** a closed container with photographic film in it, that can be fitted into a camera

**cassette play·er** /·'· ˌ··/ *n* [C] a piece of electrical equipment used for playing cassettes

**cassette re·cord·er** /·'· ·ˌ··/ *n* [C] a piece of electrical equipment used for recording sound or for playing cassettes on; TAPE RECORDER

**cas·sock** /'kæsək/ *n* [C] a long, usually black, piece of clothing worn by priests

W3 **cast¹** /kɑːst‖kæst/ *v past tense and past participle* **cast**
**1 cast (a) light on/onto a)** to provide new information which makes something easier to understand: *research findings that cast new light on the origin of our universe* **b)** *literary* to send light onto a surface: *The candle cast a flickering light on the wall.*
**2 cast a shadow** *literary* **a)** if something casts a shadow over an event, period of time etc, it makes people feel less happy or hopeful because they are worried about it: [+ **over**] *My father's illness cast a shadow over the wedding celebrations.* **b)** to make a shadow appear on a surface or area: [+ **on/over/across etc**] *The oak tree casts a long shadow across the lawn in the afternoon.*
**3 ▶ LOOK ◀ a) cast a look/glance** *literary* to look at someone or something: [+ **at/towards/around etc**] *Sandra waited, casting nervous glances over her shoulder.* **b) cast an eye over** to check or look at something quickly: *Could you just cast an eye over these figures before I show them to the bank?*
**4 cast doubt on** to make people feel less certain about something: *Preliminary results from an Anglo-French trial cast doubts on the usefulness of the drug.*
**5 cast a vote** also **cast a ballot** *AmE* to vote in an election: *Barely one in three voters will bother to cast a ballot on February 26th.*
**6 cast a spell on/over a)** to use magic words or ceremonies to change someone or something: *She's a witch! She'll cast a spell on you if she sees you in the wood!* **b)** to make someone feel very strongly attracted and keep their attention completely: *Within minutes Sinatra's voice had cast its spell on the audience.*
**7 cast your mind back** to try to remember something that happened a long time ago: [+ **to**] *Cast your mind back to your first day at school.*
**8 cast sth from your mind** if you cast worries, fears, doubts etc from your mind, you stop feeling worried, afraid etc
**9 cast aspersions on** *formal* to make unfavourable remarks about someone or something: *Under the censorship rules, they could not cast aspersions on a foreign power.*
**10 ▶ METAL ◀** [T] to pour liquid metal, plastic etc into a MOULD (=specially shaped container) , or to make an object in this way: *a statue of a horse cast in bronze*
**11 ▶ ACTOR ◀** [T] to choose which people will act particular parts in a play, film etc
**12 cast sb as/cast sb in the role of** to regard or describe someone as a particular type of person: *Clarke's trying to cast me in the role of the villain in all of this.*
**13 ▶ FISHING ◀** [I,T] to throw a fishing line or net into the water: *There's a trick to casting properly.*
**14 ▶ THROW ◀** [T always + adv/prep] *literary* to throw something somewhere: *Sparks leapt as more wood was cast onto the bonfire.*
**15 cast sb into prison/into a dungeon/into Hell etc** *literary* to force someone to go somewhere unpleasant: *Memet should, in her opinion, be cast into prison.*
**16 be cast away** to be left alone on a lonely shore or island, as a result of your ship sinking: *If you were cast away on a desert island, what would you miss most?*
**17 be cast down** *literary* to feel sad and discouraged: *Malcolm too seemed quite cast down.*
**18 cast your net wide** to consider or try as many things as possible in order to find what you want: *We'll be casting our net wide to get the right person for the job.*
**19 ▶ CAST ITS SKIN ◀** if a snake casts its skin, it gets rid of the top layer
**20 cast a shoe** if a horse casts a shoe, it loses one of them
**21 cast a horoscope** to calculate the details of someone's HOROSCOPE
**22 cast pearls before swine** to offer something that is very valuable or beautiful to someone who does not understand how valuable it is —see also **the die is cast** (DIE² (3)), **throw in/cast your lot with** (LOT (16))

**cast about/around for** sth *phr v* [T] to try to think of something to do or say: *Having retired early, I am casting about for a way to supplement my income.*

**cast** sb/sth ↔ **aside** *phr v* [T] to get rid of someone or something because you no longer like them or they are no longer useful: *When Henry became King, he cast aside all his former friends.* | **cast aside your inhibitions/doubts etc** (=get rid of your feelings of shyness, doubt etc)

**cast off** *phr v* **1** [T **cast** sb/th ↔ **off**] *literary* to get rid of something or someone: *a haven of tranquility where you can cast off the strains and stresses of life* **2** [I,T **cast** sth ↔ **off**] to untie the rope that fastens your boat to the shore so that you can sail away **3** [I,T **cast** sth ↔ **off**] to finish a piece of KNITTING by taking the last stitches off the needle in a way that stops them from coming undone

**cast on** *phr v* [I,T **cast** sth ↔ **on**] to start a piece of KNITTING by making the first stitches on the needle

**cast** sb/sth ↔ **out** *phr v* [T] *literary* to force someone or something to go away: *an exorcist who casts out demons*

**cast** sth ↔ **up** *phr v* [T] if the sea casts up something, it brings it onto the shore: *A body had been cast up on the rocks.*

**cast²** *n* [C]
**1 ▶ ACTORS ◀** all the people who act in a play or film: *Films like 'Ben Hur' have a cast of thousands.*
**2 ▶ ON YOUR BODY ◀** a hard protective case used around a part of your body to support a broken bone: *a plaster cast* | *Murray has his leg in a cast.*
**3 ▶ FOR SHAPING METAL ◀ a)** a MOULD (=specially shaped container) into which you pour liquid metal, plastic etc in order to make an object of a particular shape **b)** an object made in this way
**4 cast of (sb's) mind/features** *formal* the way someone thinks, behaves, or looks: *a philosophical cast of mind*
**5 ▶ IN FISHING ◀** the act of throwing a fishing line
**6 have a cast in your eye** *old-fashioned* to have a problem with your eye which forces it to look to the side
**7 ▶ COLOUR ◀** a small amount of a particular colour: *Sage leaves have a silvery cast.*
**8 ▶ EARTH ◀** a small pile of earth thrown out of the ground by WORMS when they make a hole

**cas·ta·nets** /ˌkæstə'nets/ *n* [plural] a musical instrument made of two small round pieces of wood or plastic that you knock together in your hand

**cast·a·way** /'kɑːstəweɪ‖'kæst-/ *n* [C] someone who is left on a lonely shore or island after their ship has sunk

**caste** /kɑːst‖kæst/ *n* [C,U] **1** one of the fixed and unchangeable social classes into which people are born in India, or the system of having these classes **2** a group of people who have the same position in society: **lose caste** *BrE* (=lose your social position)

**cas·tel·lat·ed** /'kæstəleɪtəd/ *adj technical* built to look like a castle: *a castellated bell tower*

**cast·er, castor** /'kɑːstə‖'kæstər/ *n* [C] **1** a small wheel fixed to the bottom of a piece of furniture so that it can move in any direction **2** *BrE* a small container with holes in the top, used to spread sugar, salt etc on food SHAKER (1) *AmE*

**caster sug·ar, castor sugar** /'·· ˌ··/ *n* [U] *BrE* sugar with very small grains used for cooking

**cast·i·gate** /'kæstəgeɪt/ *v* [T] *formal* to criticize or punish someone severely —**castigation** /ˌkæstə'geɪʃən/ *n* [U]

**cast·ing** /'kɑːstɪŋ‖'kæstɪŋ/ *n* **1** [U] the process of choosing the actors for a film or play: *a casting director* **2** [C] an object made by pouring liquid metal, plastic etc into a MOULD (=specially shaped container) **3 the casting couch** *humorous* a situation in which an actress is persuaded to have sex in return for a part in a film, play etc

**casting vote** /ˈ·· ˌ·/ *n* [C usually singular] the vote of the person in charge of a meeting, which can be used to make a decision when there is an equal number of votes supporting and opposing a proposal

**cast i·ron** /ˌ· ˈ··/ *n* [U] a type of iron that is hard, breaks easily, and is shaped in a MOULD[1] (2)

**cast-i·ron** /ˌ· ˈ··◂/ *adj* **1 a cast-iron excuse/alibi/guarantee etc** an excuse etc that is very certain and cannot fail **2** made of cast iron: *a cast-iron frying pan* **3** extremely strong or determined: *You need a cast-iron stomach to eat Imran's curry!*

3 **cas·tle** /ˈkɑːsəl‖ˈkæ-/ *n* [C] **1** a very large strong building, built in the past as a safe place that could be easily defended against attack: *Warwick Castle* **2** one of the pieces used in a game of CHESS; ROOK[1] (2) **3 castles in the air** plans or hopes that you have that are unlikely ever to become real; DAYDREAMS

**cast-off** /ˈ· ·/ *adj* [only before noun] cast off clothes or other goods that are not wanted or have been thrown away

**cast-offs** /ˈ· ·/ *n* [C] clothes that you do not wear any more and give to someone else: *As the youngest of five kids I was always dressed in other people's cast-offs.*

**cast·or** /ˈkɑːstə‖ˈkæstər/ *n* [C] another spelling of CASTER

**castor oil** /ˌ·· ˈ·◂/ *n* [U] a thick oil made from the seeds of a plant and used in the past as a medicine to make the BOWELS empty

**castor sug·ar** /ˈ·· ˌ··/ *n* [U] another spelling of CASTER SUGAR

**cas·trate** /kæˈstreɪt‖ˈkæstreɪt/ *v* [T] to remove the sexual organs of a male animal or a man —**castration** /kæˈstreɪʃən/ *n* [U]

**cas·u·al** /ˈkæʒuəl/ *adj*

**1 ▶ NOT CARING ◀** not caring or seeming not to care about something: *His casual manner annoyed me.* | *Karla tried to sound casual, but her excitement was obvious.*

**2 ▶ CLOTHES ◀** casual clothes are comfortable clothes that you wear in informal situations: *casual shoes*

**3 casual worker/employment/labour etc** a worker, employment etc that a company uses or offers only for a short period of time: *They're making do with casual staff.*

**4 ▶ WITHOUT ATTENTION ◀** without any clear aim or serious interest: *a casual glance at the Times* | **casual observer** (=someone not looking very carefully) *Even to the most casual observer it was obvious she was sick.*

**5 ▶ NOT PLANNED ◀** happening by chance without being planned: *a casual meeting* | **casual remark** (=something you say for no particular reason)

**6 casual sex** sex that you have without intending to have a serious relationship with the other person

**7 casual visitor/user etc** someone who does not often visit a place, use something etc: *a casual user of the library service* —**casually** *adv*: *a casually dressed young man* —**casualness** *n* [U]

**cas·u·al·ty** /ˈkæʒuəlti/ *n* **1** [C] someone who is hurt or killed in an accident or battle: *First reports of the air crash tell of more than 50 casualties.* | **heavy casualties** (=a lot of people hurt or killed) **2 be a casualty of** someone or something that suffers as a result of a particular event or situation: *The Safer City Project became a major casualty of financial cutbacks.* **3 Casualty** [U] *BrE* the part of a hospital that people are taken to when they are hurt in an accident or suddenly become ill; EMERGENCY ROOM *AmE*: *Steph works nights in casualty.*

**cas·u·ist** /ˈkæʒuɪ̵st/ *n* [C] *formal* someone who is skilled in casuistry

**cas·u·is·try** /ˈkæʒuɪ̵stri/ *n* [U] *formal* the use of clever but often false arguments to answer moral or legal questions

**ca·sus bel·li** /ˌkɑːsəs ˈbeli, ˌkeɪsəs ˈbelaɪ/ *n* [C] *Latin* an event or political action which directly causes a war

**cat** /kæt/ *n* [C] S1 W3

**1 ▶ ANIMAL ◀ a)** a small animal with four legs that is often kept as a pet or used for catching mice (MOUSE (1)) **b)** a large animal that is related to this, such as a lion or tiger

**2 let the cat out of the bag** to tell a secret, especially without intending to

**3 put/set the cat among the pigeons** to cause trouble by doing or saying something that upsets people, causes arguments etc

**4 play cat and mouse with** to let someone think they are getting or doing what they want, then prevent them from getting or doing it

**5 like a cat on hot bricks** *BrE*, **like a cat on a hot tin roof** *AmE* so nervous or anxious that you cannot keep still or keep your attention on one thing

**6 ▶ WOMAN ◀** *old-fashioned* an insulting word for a woman who you think is unkind or unpleasant —see also CATTY, **raining cats and dogs** (RAIN[2] (4)), **no room to swing a cat** (ROOM[1] (2))

**cat·a·clys·m** /ˈkætəklɪzəm/ *n* [C] *literary* a violent and sudden event or change, such as a serious flood or EARTHQUAKE —**cataclysmic** /ˌkætəˈklɪzmɪk/ *adj*

**cat·a·combs** /ˈkætəkuːm‖-koʊm/ *n* [C usually plural] an area of passages and rooms below the ground where dead people are buried

**cat·a·falque** /ˈkætəfælk/ *n* [C] a decorated raised structure on which the dead body of an important person is placed before their funeral

**Cat·a·lan** /ˈkætəlæn‖-tl-ən/ *n* [U] a language spoken in part of Spain around Barcelona

**cat·a·lep·sy** /ˈkætəlepsi/ *n* [U] a medical condition in which you cannot control your movements so that your body becomes stiff like a dead body or remains in whatever position it is placed —**cataleptic** /ˌkætəˈleptɪk◂/ *adj*

**cat·a·logue**[1] also **catalog** *AmE* /ˈkætəlɒg‖-lɒːg, -lɑːg/ *n* [C] **1** a book containing pictures and information about goods that you can buy: *the Sears catalog* **2 catalogue of failures/disasters/errors etc** a series of failures, disasters etc that happen one after the other and never seem to stop: *the latest addition to the catalogue of terrorist crimes* **3** a list of all the objects, paintings etc at an EXHIBITION (1) or sale, of all the books in a library etc W3

**catalogue**[2] also **catalog** *AmE v* [T] **1** to put a list of things into a particular order and write it in a catalogue **2** to give a list of all the events or qualities connected with someone or something

**ca·tal·y·sis** /kəˈtælɪ̵sɪ̵s/ *n* [U] the process of making a chemical reaction quicker by adding a catalyst

**cat·a·lyst** /ˈkætl-ɪ̵st/ *n* [C] **1** a substance that makes a chemical reaction happen more quickly without being changed itself **2** something or someone that causes an important change or event to happen: [+ **for**] *The police beatings served as a catalyst for the escalation of violence.* —**catalytic** /ˌkætəˈlɪtɪk◂/ *adj*

**catalytic con·vert·er** /ˌ···· ·ˈ··/ *n* [C] a piece of equipment fitted to the EXHAUST[1] (1) of a car that reduces the amount of poisonous gases sent out into the air when the engine is operating

**cat·a·ma·ran** /ˌkætəməˈræn/ *n* [C] a sailing boat with two separate HULLS (=the part that goes in the water)

**cat-and-dog** /ˌ· · ˈ·/ *adj* [only before noun] *BrE informal* a cat-and-dog life is full of quarrels and arguments

**cat·a·pult**[1] /ˈkætəpʌlt/ *n* [C] **1** a large weapon used in former times to throw heavy stones, iron balls etc **2** *BrE* a small stick in the shape of a Y with a thin band of rubber fastened over its ends, used by children to throw stones; SLINGSHOT *AmE* **3** a piece of equipment used to send an aircraft into the air from a ship

**catapult**[2] *v* **1** [T always + adv/prep] to push or throw something very hard so that it moves through the air very quickly: **catapult sb into/over/out etc** *Sam was catapulted into the air by the force of the blast.* **2 catapult sb to fame/stardom etc** to suddenly make someone very famous: *The movie 'Rebel Without a Cause' catapulted James Dean to stardom.*

**cat·a·ract** /ˈkætərækt/ *n* [C] **1** a medical condition of the eye in which the LENS (3) of your eye becomes white instead of clear, so that you cannot see **2** *literary* a large WATERFALL

**ca·tarrh** /kəˈtɑː‖-ˈtɑːr/ *n* [U] an uncomfortable condition in which your nose and throat are almost blocked with thick liquid, for example when you have a cold

**ca·tas·tro·phe** /kəˈtæstrəfi/ *n* [C,U] **1** a terrible event in which there is a lot of destruction or many people are injured or die: *the catastrophe of a worldwide conflict* | *The oil spill threatens an unparalleled ecological catastrophe.* **2** an event or situation which is extremely bad for the people involved: *If the contract is cancelled, it'll be a catastrophe for everyone concerned.* | *It's a minor catastrophe, isn't it? Plymouth losing?* —**catastrophic** /ˌkætəˈstrɒfɪk◂‖-ˈstrɑː-/ *adj*: *a catastrophic fall in the price of rice* —**catastrophically** /-kli/ *adv*

**cat·a·ton·ic** /ˌkætəˈtɒnɪk◂‖-ˈtɑː-/ *adj technical* caused or affected by a condition in which you cannot think, speak, or move any part of your body: *a catatonic trance*

**cat·bird seat** /ˈkætbɜːd ˌsiːt‖-bɜːrd-/ *n AmE informal* **be (sitting) in the catbird seat** to be in a position where you have an advantage

**cat bur·glar** /ˈ· ˌ··/ *n* [C] a thief who gets into a building by climbing up walls, pipes etc

**cat·call** /ˈkætkɔːl‖-kɒːl/ *n* [C] a loud whistle or shout expressing dislike or disapproval of a speech or performance: *jeers and catcalls from the audience* —**catcall** *v* [I]

S1 W1 **catch¹** /kætʃ/ *v past tense and past participle* **caught**

**1** ▶ **STOP/TRAP SB** ◀ [T] **a)** to stop someone after you have been chasing them and prevent them from escaping: *"You can't catch me!" she yelled, running away across the field.* | *If the guerillas catch you, they will kill you.* **b)** if the police catch a criminal, they find the criminal and stop him or her from escaping: *State police have launched a massive operation to catch the murderer.* | *The jewel thieves were never caught.*

**2** ▶ **FIND SB DOING STH** ◀ [T] to find or see someone while they are actually doing something wrong or illegal: **catch sb doing sth** *I caught Howard reading my private letters.* | **catch sb in the act (of)/catch sb red-handed** (=catch someone in the middle of doing something bad) *a shoplifter caught in the act* | *They say Buster was caught red-handed.* | **catch sb at it** *BrE spoken*: *We know he's been cheating, but we've never caught him at it.*

**3** ▶ **FIND SB UNPREPARED** ◀ **catch sb unawares/catch sb off guard/catch sb on the hop** *BrE* to do something or happen when someone is not expecting it and not ready to deal with events: *a night attack that caught the enemy unawares* | *Her question caught him off guard.* | *The dramatic fall in share prices caught even the experts on the hop.* | **be caught napping** *informal* (=not be ready to deal with something unexpected that happens) | **catch sb with their pants/trousers down** *informal* (=make someone feel embarrassed by arriving or doing something when they are not ready)

**4** ▶ **ANIMAL/FISH** ◀ [T] to trap an animal or fish by using a trap, net, or hook, or by hunting it: *It's a useless cat, no good at catching mice.* | *Last time we went fishing I caught a huge trout.* | *catching butterflies*

**5** ▶ **HOLD** ◀ **a)** [I,T] to get hold of and stop an object such as a ball that is moving through the air: *Watch – if you throw the ball, Bouncer can catch it in his mouth.* | *"Chuck me over those cigarettes, would you." "Here you are. Catch!"* —see picture on page 1263 **b)** [T] to suddenly take hold of someone: *She stumbled forward but Calum caught her in his arms.* | **catch hold of** *Miss Perry caught hold of my sleeve and pulled me back.*

**6** ▶ **ILLNESS** ◀ [T] to get a disease or illness: *My sister has mumps. I hope I haven't caught it.* | **catch sth from/off** *I think I'm getting the flu – I must have caught it off Gerry.* | **catch your death (of cold)** (=get a very bad cold) *Don't stand out there in the rain. You'll catch your death.*

**7 catch a train/plane/bus** to get on a train etc in order to travel, or to be in time to get it: *Every morning I catch the 7.15 train to London.* | *There's a train in now. If you run, you'll just catch it.* | **have a train etc to catch** *I have to hurry – I have a bus to catch* —see REACH¹ (USAGE).

**8** ▶ **BE IN TIME** ◀ [T] to not be too late to see something, talk to someone etc: *I managed to catch her just as she was leaving.* | **catch the post** *BrE* (=post letters in time for them to be collected that day) —opposite MISS¹ (5)

**9** ▶ **GET STUCK** ◀ [I,T] if your hand, finger, clothing etc catches or is caught in something, it becomes stuck or fastened there: *"What happened to your finger?" "It got caught in the car door."* | *Bobby caught his shirt on a wire fence.*

**10 catch sb's attention/interest/imagination etc** if something catches your attention etc, you notice it or feel interested in it: *The unusual panelling on the wall caught our attention.* | *a story that will catch the imagination of every child* | **catch sb's eye** (=get sb's attention) *We need big, bold headlines – something to catch the reader's eye.*

**11** ▶ **HEAR/UNDERSTAND** ◀ **not catch sth** to not hear or not understand what someone says: *Could you say that again? I didn't catch the last bit.* | *I'm afraid I didn't catch your name.* | *Did you catch the announcement?*

**12** ▶ **NOTICE** ◀ [T not in progressive] to see or notice something for a moment: **catch sight of/catch a glimpse of** *I suddenly caught sight of her in the crowd.* | *Fans waited at the airport hoping to catch a glimpse of Gloria Estefan.* | **catch a whiff of** (=notice a smell for a moment) *Brad caught a whiff of smoke in the air.*

**13** ▶ **DESCRIBE WELL** ◀ [T] to show or describe very successfully the character or quality of something, in a picture, a piece of writing etc: *a novel that catches the mood of pre-war Britain*

**14** ▶ **BURN** ◀ **a) catch fire** if something catches fire, it starts to burn accidentally: *Two farm workers died when a barn caught fire.* —see FIRE¹ (USAGE) **b)** [I] if a fire catches it starts to burn: *For some reason the charcoal isn't catching.*

**15 you won't catch me doing sth** *spoken* used to say that you would never do something: *You won't catch me ironing all his cotton shirts!*

**16 be caught up in** to be involved in something unwillingly: *Children who were caught up in the crime are getting a lot of media attention.*

**17 catch yourself doing sth** to suddenly realize that you are doing something: *Monica sometimes caught herself envying her students.*

**18** ▶ **PROBLEM** ◀ [T] to discover a problem and stop it from developing any more: *This kind of cancer can be cured, provided it is caught early enough.*

**19** ▶ **HIT** ◀ [T] to hit someone: **catch sb on the chin/face etc** *I caught him on the chin with a heavy punch.*

**20** ▶ **SPORT** ◀ **a)** also **catch out** [T] to end a player's INNINGS in CRICKET (2) by taking and holding a ball hit off their BAT¹ (2a) before it touches the ground **b)** [I] to be the CATCHER in a game of BASEBALL

**21** ▶ **BE PUNISHED** ◀ **you'll catch it** *BrE spoken* used to tell someone that they are going to be in trouble because they have done something wrong: *You'll catch it if your mother finds out where you've been.*

**22** ▶ **IN A BAD SITUATION** ◀ **be caught in/without etc** to be in a situation that is difficult, because you cannot easily get out of it or because you do not have what you need: *We got caught in a rainstorm on the way here.* | *an actor caught without a script*

**23 catch your breath a)** to stop breathing for a moment because something has surprised, frightened or shocked you **b)** to pause for a moment after a lot of physical effort in order to breathe normally again: *Hang on a minute, let me catch my breath!*

**24** ▶ **SHINE ON** ◀ [T] if the light catches something or if something catches the light, the light shines on it making it look bright: *The sunlight caught her hair and turned it to gold.*

**25** ▶ **CONTAINER** ◀ [T] if a container catches liquid, it is in a position where the liquid falls into it: *Steve! Bring me something to catch the drips under this pipe.*

**26 catch the sun** *informal* to become sunburned (SUNBURN) so that your skin is red: *You've caught the sun on the back of your neck.*

**catch at** sth *phr v* [T] to try to take hold of something: *"You mean there's a real fire?" Heather caught at his arm.*

**catch on** *phr v* [I] **1** to become popular and fashionable: *It was a popular style in Britain but it never really caught on in America.* **2** to begin to understand or realize something: [+ **to**] *It was a long time before the police caught on to what he was really doing.*

**catch** sb ↔ **out** *phr v* [T] *BrE* **1** to make someone make a mistake, especially in order to prove that they are lying: *It's a useful technique for handling people who are trying to catch you out.* **2** if an unexpected event catches you out, it puts you in a difficult situation, because you were not ready to deal with it: *Didn't they ever tell you they in fact got caught out by the weather?*

**catch up** *phr v* **1** [I,T] to improve so much that you reach the same standard as other people in your class, group etc: *If you miss a lot of lessons, it's very difficult to catch up.* | [+ **with**] *At the moment our technology is more advanced, but other countries are catching up with us.* **2** [I,T] to come from behind and reach someone in front by going faster: [+ **with**] *Drive faster, they're catching up with us.* | **catch sb up** *You go on ahead. I'll catch you up later.* **3** [I] to do what needs to be done because you have not been able to do it until now: [+ **on**] *I have some work to catch up on.* | *a chance to catch up on some sleep* (=after a period without enough sleep) | *You have a lot of catching up to do.*

**catch up with** sb *phr v* [T] **1** to finally find someone who has been doing something illegal and punish them: *It took six years for the law to catch up with them.* **2** if troubles, duties etc catch up with you, you cannot avoid them any longer

**catch²** *n* **1** [C] *informal* a hidden problem or difficulty; SNAG¹(1): *The rent is only £40 a week – there must be a catch somewhere.* | **the catch is (that)** *The catch is that you can't enter the competition unless you've spent $100 in the store.* **2** [C] a hook or something similar for fastening a door or lid and keeping it shut **3** [C] an act of catching a ball that has been thrown or hit: *Hey! Nice catch!* **4** [C] an amount of fish that has been caught: *Local fishermen are reporting record catches.* **5** [U] a simple game in which two or more people throw a ball to each other: *Let's go outside and play catch.* **6 be a good catch** *old-fashioned* if a man is a good catch, he is regarded as a very desirable husband, because he is rich and good-looking

**catch-22** /ˌkætʃ twentiˈtuː/ *n* [U] a situation in which you cannot do one thing until you do another thing, but you cannot do that until you have done the first thing, with the result that you can do neither: **catch-22 situation** *It's a catch-22 situation – without experience you can't get a job and without a job you can't get experience.*

**catch·all¹** /ˈ· ·/ *adj* intended to include all situations or possibilities: **catch-all clause/list etc** *a vague catch-all clause in an employment contract*

**catch·all²** *n* [C] *AmE* a drawer, cupboard etc where you put any small objects

**catch crop** /ˈ· ·/ *n* [C] a vegetable crop that grows quickly, planted between two rows of another crop

**catch·er** /ˈkætʃə‖-ər/ *n* [C] the player who sits on his heels behind the BATTER²(3) in a game of baseball —see picture on page 1263

**catch·ing** /ˈkætʃɪŋ/ *adj* [not before noun] *informal* **1** a disease or illness that is catching is infectious: *Well, I hope it's not catching.* **2** an emotion or feeling that is catching spreads quickly among people

**catch·ment ar·e·a** /ˈkætʃmənt ˌeəriə‖-ˌeriə/ *n* [C] **1** the area that a school takes its students from, that a hospital takes its patients from etc **2** the area that a river or lake gets water from

**catchpen·ny** /ˈ· ·ˌ·/ *adj old-fashioned* cheap and of bad quality but made to look attractive

**catch·phrase** /ˈkætʃfreɪz/ *n* [C] a short well-known phrase used regularly by an entertainer or politician, so that people think of that person when they hear it

**catch·word** /ˈkætʃwɜːd‖-wɜːrd/ *n* [C] a word or phrase that is easy to remember and is repeated regularly by a political party, newspaper etc; SLOGAN

**catch·y** /ˈkætʃi/ *adj* **catchy song/tune** a song or tune that is pleasant and easy to remember: *a catchy advertising slogan like 'Go to Work on an Egg'* —**catchily** *adv*

**cat·e·chis·m** /ˈkætɪ̣ˌkɪzəm/ *n* [singular] a set of questions and answers about the Christian religion that people learn in order to become full members of a church

**cat·e·chize** also **-ise** *BrE* /ˈkætɪ̣kaɪz/ *v* [T] to teach someone about a religion by using a series of questions and answers

**cat·e·gor·i·cal** /ˌkætɪ̣ˈgɒrɪkəl◂‖-ˈgɔː-, -ˈgɑː-/ *adj* a categorical statement is a clear statement that something is definitely true: **categorical denial/statement/assurance etc** *Can you give us a categorical assurance that no jobs will be lost?*

**cat·e·gor·i·cally** /ˌkætɪ̣ˈgɒrɪkli‖-ˈgɔː-, -ˈgɑː-/ *adv* in such a sure and certain way that there is no doubt: **categorically deny/refuse etc** *Forbes has categorically denied his guilt all along.*

**cat·e·go·rize** also **– ise** *BrE* /ˈkætɪ̣gəraɪz/ *v* [T] to put people or things into groups according to what type they are, or to say which group they are in; CLASSIFY: *The population is categorized according to age, sex, and socio-economic group.* | **categorize sth/sb as** *Keene doesn't like to be categorized as a socialist.* —**categorization** /ˌkætɪ̣gəraɪˈzeɪʃən‖-rə-/ *n* [C,U]

**cat·e·go·ry** /ˈkætɪ̣gəri‖-gɔːri/ *n* [C] a group of people or things that all have the same particular qualities: **fall into a category** (=belong to a category) *Voters fall into three main categories.* S2 W2

**ca·ter** /ˈkeɪtə‖-ər/ *v* [I,T] to provide and serve food and drinks at a party, meeting etc, usually as a business: [+ **for/at**] *Who's catering at your daughter's wedding?* | **cater sth** *AmE*: *Shouldn't we get bids for catering the 20th class reunion?*

**cater for** sb/sth *phr v* [T] to provide a particular group of people with everything that they need or want: *a holiday company that caters more for the elderly*

**cater to** sb/sth *phr v* [T] to provide something that a particular type of person wants but that you think is bad, stupid etc: *It's the kind of movie that caters to the worst side of human nature.*

**ca·ter·er** /ˈkeɪtərə‖-rər/ *n* [C] a person or company that is paid to provide and serve food and drinks at a party, meeting etc: *What time will the caterers get here?*

**ca·ter·ing** /ˈkeɪtərɪŋ/ *n* [U] the activity of providing and serving food and drinks at parties for money: *Who did the catering?* —see also SELF-CATERING

**cat·er·pil·lar** /ˈkætəˌpɪlə‖-tərˌpɪlər/ *n* [C] **1** a small creature like a WORM with a lot of legs that feeds on leaves and is the LARVA of a BUTTERFLY or other insect **2** also **caterpillar track** a belt made of metal plates that is fastened over the wheels of a heavy vehicle to help it to move over soft ground **3** also **caterpillar tractor** a heavy vehicle that is fitted with these belts

**cat·er·waul** /ˈkætəwɔːl‖-tərwɒːl/ *v* [I] to make a loud high unpleasant noise like the sound a cat makes —**caterwaul** *n* [singular]

**cat flap** /ˈ· ·/ *n* [C] an entrance to the house for your pet cat, consisting of a piece of wood or plastic which hangs down over a hole at the bottom of the door, and which can swing open

**cat·gut** /ˈkætgʌt/ *n* [U] strong thread made from the INTESTINES of animals and used for the strings of musical instruments

**ca·thar·sis** /kəˈθɑːsɪ̣s, kæ-‖kəˈθɑːr-/ *n* [C,U] *formal* a way of dealing with bad or strong feelings and emotions, by expressing or experiencing them through writing, talking, DRAMA etc —**cathartic** /-tɪk/ *adj*: *It was actually a cathartic exprience to write my autobiography.*

**ca·the·dral** /kəˈθiːdrəl/ *n* [C] a very large church, which is the main church of a particular area under the control of a BISHOP (1): *Durham cathedral* | **cathedral city** (=one with a cathedral)

**cath·er·ine wheel** /ˈkæθərɨ̆n wiːl/ *n* [C] a round FIREWORK that spins around

**cath·e·ter** /ˈkæθɨ̆tə‖-ər/ *n* [C] a thin tube that is put into your body to take away liquids —**catheterize** also **-ise** *BrE v* [T]

**cath·ode** /ˈkæθəʊd‖-θoʊd/ *n* [C] *technical* the negative ELECTRODE from which electric current leaves a piece of equipment like a BATTERY (1) —compare ANODE

C

**cathode ray tube** /ˌ·· ˈ· ·/ *n* [C] a piece of equipment used in televisions and computers, in which negative ELECTRONS from the cathode produce an image on a screen

**Cath·o·lic** /ˈkæθəlɪk/ *adj* connected with the Roman Catholic Church: *a Catholic school* —**Catholic** *n* [C] —**Catholicism** /kəˈθɒlɨ̆sɪzəm‖kəˈθɑː-/ *n* [U]

**catholic** *adj formal* **have catholic tastes** to like a wide variety of things —**catholicity** /ˌkæθəˈlɪsɨ̆ti/ *adj*

**cat·kin** /ˈkætkɪn/ *n* [C] *especially BrE* a soft flower that grows in long thin groups and hangs from the branches of trees such as the WILLOW OR BIRCH[1]

**cat lit·ter** /ˈ· ˌ··/ *n* [U] a substance that people put down in boxes for cats that live indoors, so that they can pass waste from their BOWELS into it

**cat·nap** /ˈ· ·/ *n* [C] *informal* a very short sleep: *"Where's Grandma?" "She's having a catnap."* —**cat nap** *v* [I]

**cat-o'-nine-tails** /ˌkæt ə ˈnaɪn teɪlz/ *n* [C] a whip made of nine strings with knots on the end, used in the past for punishing people

**CAT scan** /ˈkæt skæn/ *n* [C] the image produced by a CAT scanner

**CAT scan·ner** /ˈkæt ˌskænəˈ‖-ər/ *n* [C] an electronic machine used in a hospital to look inside someone's body

**cat's cra·dle** /ˌ· ˈ··/ *n* [U] a game children play with string which they wind around the fingers of both hands to make different patterns

**cat's eye** /ˈ· ·/ *n* [C] one of the line of small flat objects fixed in the middle of the road, that shine when lit by car lights, to guide traffic in the dark

**cat's paw** /ˈ· ·/ *n* [C] *old-fashioned* someone who does unpleasant or dangerous jobs because someone else has ordered them to

**cat suit** /ˈ· ·/ *n* [C] a tight piece of women's clothing that covers all of the body and legs in one piece

**cat·sup** /ˈkætsəp/ *n* [U] *AmE* an American spelling of KETCHUP

**cat·te·ry** /ˈkætəri/ *n* [C] *BrE* a place where you can leave cats to be looked after while you are away from home

**cat·tle** /ˈkætl/ *n* [plural] cows and BULLS kept on a farm for their meat or milk: *herds of cattle* | **20/100 etc head of cattle** (=20, 100 etc cattle)

**cattle grid** /ˈ·· ·/ *BrE*, **cattle guard** *AmE n* [C] a set of bars placed over a hole in the road, so that animals cannot go across but cars can

**cat·tle·man** /ˈkætlmən/ *n* [C] someone who looks after or owns cattle

**cattle mar·ket** /ˈ·· ˌ··/ *n* [C] *BrE* **1** a place where cattle are bought and sold **2** *informal* a disapproving word for a beauty competition or a social event where women are judged only by their sexual attractiveness

**cattle truck** /ˈ·· ·/ *n* [C] *BrE* a vehicle or part of a train that is made to carry cattle

**cat·ty** /ˈkæti/ *adj* someone who is catty is unpleasant and often says nasty things about people: *She's a liar. Does that sound catty, too?* —**cattily** *adv* —**cattiness** *n* [U]

**catty-cor·ner** /ˈ·· ˌ··/ *adv AmE* KITTY CORNER

**cat·walk** /ˈkætwɔːk‖-wɒːk/ *n* [C] **1** a long raised path that MODELS walk on in a fashion show **2** a temporary structure for walking on, built around the outside of buildings or between them when they are being built or repaired

**Cau·ca·sian** /kɔːˈkeɪziən‖kɒːˈkeɪʒən/ *adj* someone who is Caucasian belongs to the race that has white or pale skin —**Caucasian** *n* [C]

**cau·cus** /ˈkɔːkəs‖ˈkɒː-/ *n* [C] a group of people in a political party, who meet to discuss and decide on political plans

**cau·dal** /ˈkɔːdl‖ˈkɒːdl/ *adj technical* at or related to an animal's tail —**caudally** *adv*

**caught** /kɔːt‖kɒːt/ the past tense and past participle of CATCH[1]

**caul·dron, caldron** /ˈkɔːldrən‖ˈkɒːl-/ *n* [C] a large round metal pot for boiling liquids over a fire: *a witch's cauldron* —see picture at WITCH

**cau·li·flow·er** /ˈkɒlɪˌflaʊə‖ˈkɒːliˌflaʊər, ˈkɑː-/ *n* [C,U] a garden vegetable with green leaves around a large firm white centre —see picture on page 414

**cauliflower cheese** /ˌ···· ˈ·/ *n* [U] *BrE* the white part of a cauliflower cooked and eaten with cheese SAUCE

**cauliflower ear** /ˌ···· ˈ·/ *n* [C] an ear permanently swollen into a strange shape, especially as a result of an injury

**caulk, calk** /kɔːk‖kɒːk/ *v* [T] to fill the holes or cracks in something, especially a ship, with an oily or sticky substance that keeps water out

**caus·al** /ˈkɔːzəl‖ˈkɒː-/ *adj* **1 causal relationship/link/connection etc** a relationship etc that exists between two or more events or situations, where one causes the other to happen: *a causal relationship between unemployment and crime* **2** *technical* a causal CONJUNCTION (3), for example 'because', introduces a statement about the cause of something —**causally** *adv*

**cau·sal·i·ty** /kɔːˈzælɨ̆ti‖kɒː-/ *n* [U] *formal* the relationship between a cause and the effect that it has

**cau·sa·tion** /kɔːˈzeɪʃən‖kɒː-/ *n* [U] *formal* **1** the action of causing something to happen or exist **2** causality

**caus·a·tive** /ˈkɔːzətɪv‖ˈkɒː-/ *adj formal* **1** acting as the cause of something: *causative factors* **2** *technical* a causative verb expresses an action that causes something to happen or be —**causatively** *adv*

**cause¹** /kɔːz‖kɒːz/ *n* 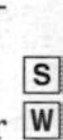

**1 ▶ WHAT CAUSES STH ◀** [C] a person, event, or thing that makes something happen: [**+ of**] *What was the cause of the accident?* | *The doctor had recorded the cause of death as heart failure.* | **root/underlying etc cause** (=the basic cause) *The root cause of the crime problem is poverty.* | **cause and effect** (=the idea or fact of one thing directly causing another) —see REASON[1] (USAGE)

**2 ▶ GOOD REASON ◀** [U] something that makes it right or fair for you to feel or behave in a particular way: [**+ for**] *There is no cause for alarm.* | **cause for complaint** (=a reason to complain) *I've got no cause for complaint – I'm doing all right.* | **cause for concern** (=a reason to be worried) *The patient's condition is giving cause for concern.* | **have good cause to** *God knows he's got good cause to be relieved.* | **with/without good cause** *Many people are worried about the economy, and with good cause.*

**3 ▶ STH YOU SUPPORT ◀ a)** [C] an organization, principle, or aim that a group of people support or fight for: *How many of them are sympathetic to our cause?* | [**+ of**] *her lifelong devotion to the cause of women's rights* **b) be in/for a good cause** if something you do is for a good cause, it is worth doing because it is intended to help other people, especially through a CHARITY (2): *Well, I don't mind giving if it's for a good cause.*

**4 make common cause (with)** *formal* to join with other people or groups for a particular purpose: *Faced by an enemy on their territory, the French parties tried to make common cause.*

**5 ▶ LAW ◀** [C] a case that is brought to a court of law —see also **lost cause** (LOST[1] (13))

**cause²** *v* [T] to make something happen: *Heavy traffic is causing long delays on the freeway.* | **cause sb/sth to do** 

sth *A dog ran into the road, causing the cyclist to swerve.* | **cause concern/uncertainty/embarrassment etc** (=make people feel worried, unsure, embarrassed etc) *The constant changes of policy have caused a great deal of uncertainty in the workforce.* | **cause sb trouble/problems/inconvenience etc** *Jimmy's behaviour is causing me a lot of problems.* | **cause offence** (=offend someone) *I'm sorry; I didn't mean to cause offence.*

**USAGE NOTE: CAUSE**

GRAMMAR

Something can **cause** death/crime/trouble etc, or **cause** somebody inconvenience/a problem etc: *His behaviour caused everyone a lot of worry* (NOT *caused to everyone...*).

Something can **cause** someone or something **to** do something: *The disease caused his face to swell* (NOT *caused that his face swelled*, or *caused his face swell*, though you could say less formally *...made his face swell*).

SPELLING

Remember the difference between **cause**, and *because* and *of course*.

**cause cé·lè·bre** /ˌkəʊz seˈlebrə, ˌkɔːz-‖ˌkɒːz-, ˌkoʊz-/ *n* [C] *French* an event or legal case that a lot of people become interested in, because it is an exciting subject to discuss or argue about

**cause·way** /ˈkɔːzweɪ‖ˈkɒːz-/ *n* [C] a raised road or path across wet ground or through water

**caus·tic** /ˈkɔːstɪk‖ˈkɒːs-/ *adj* **1** a caustic substance can burn through things by chemical action **2** a caustic remark criticizes someone in a way that is unkind but often cleverly humorous —**caustically** /-kli/ *adv*

**caustic so·da** /ˌ·· ˈ··/ *n* [U] a very strong chemical substance that you can use for some difficult cleaning jobs

**cau·ter·ize** also **-ise** *BrE* /ˈkɔːtəraɪz‖ˈkɒː-/ *v* [T] *technical* to burn a wound with hot metal or a chemical to stop the blood or stop it becoming infected

**cau·tion¹** /ˈkɔːʃən‖ˈkɒː-/ *n* **1** [U] the quality of being very careful, not taking any risks, and trying to avoid danger: **with caution** *We must proceed with caution.* | **great/extreme caution** *the need for extreme caution when handling these animals* | **treat sth with caution** (=think carefully about something because it might not be true) *Evidence given by convicted criminals should always be treated with caution.* **2 word/note of caution** a warning to be careful: *One note of caution, don't let your children try this trick.* **3 throw/fling/cast caution to the winds** to start to take more risks in what you do or say: *Throwing all caution to the winds, she swung around to face him.* **4** [C] *BrE* a spoken official warning given by someone in authority when you have done something wrong that is not a serious crime: *The judge let him off with a caution.* **5** [singular] *old-fashioned* an amusing person

**caution²** *v* [T] **1** to warn someone that something might be dangerous, difficult etc: **caution sb about/against** *Geraldine cautioned the boys about talking to strange men.* | **caution (sb) that** *Foreign Office officials were quick to caution that these remarks did not mean there would be a new peace initiative.* **2** *BrE* to warn someone officially that the next time they do something illegal they will be punished: **caution sb for/about** *She got cautioned for speeding.*

**cau·tion·ar·y** /ˈkɔːʃənəri‖ˈkɒʃəneri/ *adj* giving a warning or advice: *a cautionary note on the abuse of power* | **cautionary tale** (=the story of an event that can be used to warn people) *It's a cautionary tale about how not to buy a computer.*

**cau·tious** /ˈkɔːʃəs‖ˈkɒː-/ *adj* careful to avoid danger or risks: *a cautious driver* | **cautious about doing sth** *I've always been very cautious about giving my address to strangers.* | **cautious optimism** (=hopes for a good result while being careful not to expect too much) —**cautiously** *adv*: *Sara opened the door cautiously and peeped in.* —**cautiousness** *n* [U]

**cav·al·cade** /ˌkævəlˈkeɪd, ˈkævəlkeɪd/ *n* [C] a line of people on horses or in cars or carriages moving along as part of a ceremony

**Cav·a·lier** /ˌkævəˈlɪə◂‖-ˈlɪr◂/ *n* [C] a supporter of the King against parliament in the English Civil War of the 17th century —compare ROUNDHEAD

**cavalier** *adj* not caring or thinking about other people's feelings: *The complaints show these companies have been treating the issue in a cavalier way*

**cav·al·ry** /ˈkævəlri/ *n* [U] **1** the part of an army that fights on horses, especially in the past **2** the part of a modern army that uses tanks (TANK¹ (3))

**cav·al·ry·man** /ˈkævəlrimən/ *n* [C] a soldier who fights on a horse

**cave¹** /keɪv/ *n* [C] a large natural hole in the side of a cliff or hill, or under the ground —see picture on page 835

**cave²** *v*

**cave in** *phr v* [I] **1** if the top or sides of something cave in, they fall down or inwards: [+ **on**] *The roof of the tunnel just caved in on us.* **2** [I] to finally stop opposing something, especially because someone has persuaded or threatened you: *You don't know, they might cave in straight away and give us what we want.* —**cave-in** *n* [C]

**ca·ve·at** /ˈkeɪviæt, ˈkæv-/ *n* [C] *formal* a warning that you must pay attention to something before you make a decision or take a particular action

**caveat emp·tor** /ˌkeɪviæt ˈemptɔː, ˌkæv-‖-tɔːr/ *n* [U] *Latin* the principle that when goods are sold, the buyer is responsible for checking the quality of the goods

**cave·man** /ˈkeɪvmæn/ *n* [C] **1** someone who lived in a CAVE¹ many thousands of years ago **2** *informal* a man who behaves rudely or violently: *He used caveman tactics of rough behaviour towards women.*

**cav·ern** /ˈkævən‖-ərn/ *n* [C] a large CAVE¹

**cav·ern·ous** /ˈkævənəs‖-ərnəs/ *adj* a cavernous room, space, or hole is very large and deep: *a cavernous dining hall* —**cavernously** *adv*

**cav·i·ar, caviare** /ˈkæviɑː‖-ɑːr/ *n* [U] **1** the preserved eggs of various large fish, eaten as a special very expensive food **2 caviar to the general** *BrE literary* something that only a sensitive and educated person can enjoy or understand

**cav·il** /ˈkævəl/ *v* **cavilled, cavilling** *BrE* **caviled, caviling** *AmE* [I + **at**] *formal* to make unnecessary complaints about someone or something

**cav·ing** /ˈkeɪvɪŋ/ *n* [U] the sport of going deep under the ground in CAVES; SPELUNKING *AmE*

**cav·i·ty** /ˈkævəti/ *n* [C] **1** *formal* a hole or space inside something **2** *technical* a hole in a tooth made by decay

**cavity wall** /ˈ··· ˌ·/ *n* [C] a wall consisting of two walls with a space between them to keep out cold and noise

**cavity wall in·su·la·tion** /ˌ··· ··ˈ··/ *n* [U] a substance put inside a cavity wall to keep heat inside a building

**ca·vort** /kəˈvɔːt‖-ɔːrt/ *v* [I] to jump or dance around noisily in a playful or sexual way: *Pictures appeared in newspapers of the two of them cavorting on a beach.*

**caw** /kɔː‖kɒː/ *n* [C] the loud unpleasant sound made by some types of bird, especially the CROW¹ (1) —**caw** *v* [I]

**cay** /kiː, keɪ/ *n* [C] *AmE* a very small low island formed of CORAL¹ or sand

**cay·enne pep·per** /ˌkeɪen ˈpepə‖-ər/ *n* [U] the red powder made from a PEPPER¹ (3) that has a very hot taste

**cay·man** /ˈkeɪmən/ *n* [C] a South American animal like an ALLIGATOR

**CB** /ˌsiː ˈbiː◂/ *n* [U] Citizen's Band; a radio on which people can speak to each other over short distances, especially when they are driving —**CB-er** *n* [C]

**CBE** /ˌsiː biː ˈiː/ *n* [C] Commander of the British Empire; an honour given to some British people for things they have done for their country

**cc** **1** carbon copy to; used at the end of a business letter to show that you are sending a copy to someone else: *To Neil Fry, cc. Anthea Baker, Matt Fox* **2** the abbreviation of CUBIC CENTIMETRE: *a 200 cc engine*

**CCTV** the written abbreviation of CLOSED CIRCUIT TELEVISION

**CD** /ˌsiː ˈdiː◂/ *n* [C] compact disc; a small circular piece of hard plastic on which high quality recorded sound or large quantities of information can be stored

C D player

**CD player** /ˈ· ·ˌ··/ *n* [C] a piece of equipment used to play COMPACT DISCS

**CD-ROM** /ˌsiː diː ˈrɒm‖-ˈrɑːm/ *n* [C,U] compact disc read-only memory; a CD on which large quantities of information can be stored to be used by a computer —see picture on page 837

**CDT** /ˌsiː diː ˈtiː/ *n* [U] Craft, Design, and Technology; a practical subject studied in British schools

W3 **cease¹** /siːs/ *v* [I,T] *formal* to stop doing something or stop happening: **cease (doing) sth** *The company ceased trading at 6 pm today.* | *It rained all day without ceasing.* | **cease sth** *The committee decided to cease financial support.* | **cease to do sth** *Most people had already ceased to obey the curfew.* | **cease to exist** *The town which Joyce wrote about has long since ceased to exist.* | **cease fire!** (=used to order soldiers to stop shooting) —see also CEASEFIRE, **wonders will never cease** (WONDER² (6))

**cease²** *n* **without cease** *formal* without stopping

**cease·fire** /ˈsiːsfaɪə‖-faɪr/ *n* [C] an agreement to stop fighting for a period of time, especially so that a more permanent agreement can be made: *negotiating a ceasefire* —compare ARMISTICE, TRUCE

**cease·less** /ˈsiːsləs/ *adj formal* happening or existing for a long time without changing or stopping: *the ceaseless fight against crime* —**ceaselessly** *adv*

**ce·dar** /ˈsiːdə‖-ər/ *n* **1** [C] a large EVERGREEN² tree with leaves shaped like needles **2** also **cedarwood** [U] the hard reddish wood of this tree that smells pleasant

**cede** /siːd/ *v* [T] *formal* to give something such as an area of land or a right to a country or person, especially when you are forced to: *Hong Kong was ceded to Britain in 1842.* —see also CESSION

**ce·dil·la** /sɪˈdɪlə/ *n* [C] a mark put under the letter 'c' in French and some other languages, to show that it is an 's' sound instead of a 'k' sound. It is written 'ç'.

**Cee·fax** /ˈsiːfæks/ *n* [U] *trademark* an information service that has no sound and is provided on television by the BBC in Britain

**cei·lidh** /ˈkeɪli/ *n* [C] an evening entertainment with Scottish or Irish singing and dancing

S3 W3 **cei·ling** /ˈsiːlɪŋ/ *n* [C] **1** the inner surface of the top part of a room —compare ROOF¹ (2) **2** the largest number or amount of something that is officially allowed: *a budget ceiling of $5000* | *The government imposed a ceiling on imports of foreign cars.* **3** *technical* the greatest height an aircraft can fly at or the level of the clouds —see also **glass ceiling** (GLASS¹ (7))

**ce·leb** /səˈleb/ *n* [C] *informal* a CELEBRITY

**cel·e·brant** /ˈseləbrənt/ *n* [C] someone who performs or takes part in a religious ceremony

**cel·e·brate** /ˈseləbreɪt/ *v* **1** [I,T] to show that an event or occasion is important by doing something special or enjoyable: *It's Dad's birthday and we're going out for a meal to celebrate.* | *We've bought champagne to celebrate Jan's promotion.* | **celebrate sth** *My folks are celebrating their 50th anniversary.* | **celebrate Christmas/Thanksgiving etc** *The Chinese celebrate their New Year in January or February.* **2** [T] *formal* to praise someone or something in speech or writing: *poems that celebrate the joys of love* **3** [T] to perform a religious ceremony, especially the Christian Mass W

**cel·e·brat·ed** /ˈseləbreɪtəd/ *adj* famous; talked about a lot: *a celebrated professor* | *a celebrated legal case*

**cel·e·bra·tion** /ˌseləˈbreɪʃən/ *n* **1** [C] an occasion or party when you celebrate something: *I don't feel like getting involved in any New Year's celebrations.* **2** [U] the act of celebrating: **in celebration of** (=in order to celebrate something) *There'll be a reception in celebration of the Fund's 70th Anniversary.* S

**cel·e·bra·to·ry** /ˌseləˈbreɪtəri◂‖ˈseləbrətɔːri/ *adj* [only before noun] done in order to celebrate a particular event or occasion: *Join us for a celebratory drink in the bar.*

**ce·leb·ri·ty** /səˈlebrəti/ *n* **1** [C] a famous person, especially someone in the entertainment business **2** [U] *formal* the state of being famous; fame

**ce·ler·i·ty** /səˈlerəti/ *n* [U] *formal* great speed

**cel·e·ry** /ˈseləri/ *n* [U] a vegetable with long pale green stems that you can eat cooked or uncooked: *a stick of celery* —see picture on page 414

**ce·les·ti·al** /səˈlestiəl‖-tʃəl/ *adj formal* **1** related to the sky or heaven: **celestial bodies** (=the sun, moon, stars etc) **2** *literary* very beautiful

**cel·i·bate** /ˈseləbət/ *adj* not married and not having sex, especially because of your religious beliefs: *Catholic priests are required to be celibate.* —**celibate** *n* [C] —**celibacy** /-bəsi/ *n* [U] *a vow of celibacy*

**cell** /sel/ *n* [C] **1** the smallest part of a living thing that can exist independently: *cancer cells* | *red blood cells* **2** a small room in a prison, MONASTERY, or CONVENT where someone sleeps **3** a piece of equipment for producing electricity from chemicals, heat, or light: *alkaline battery cells* **4** a small group of people who are working secretly as part of a larger political organization: *a terrorist cell* **5** a small space that an insect or other small creature has made to live in or use: *the cells of a honeycomb* W

**cel·lar** /ˈselə‖-ər/ *n* [C] **1** a room under a house or other building, often used for storing things **2** a store of wine belonging to a person, restaurant etc

**cel·lar·age** /ˈselərɪdʒ/ *n* [U] **1** the charge for storing something in a cellar **2** the size of a cellar

**cell di·vi·sion** /ˈ· ·ˌ··/ *n* [C,U] the process by which plant and animal cells increase their numbers

**cel·list** /ˈtʃeləst/ *n* [C] someone who plays the cello

**cel·lo** /ˈtʃeləʊ‖-loʊ/ *n* [C] a large musical instrument shaped like a VIOLIN that you hold between your knees and play by pulling a special stick across wire strings

**Cel·lo·phane** /ˈseləfeɪn/ *n* [U] *trademark* thin transparent material used for wrapping things

**cell·phone** /ˈselfəʊn‖-foʊn/ *n* [C] a cellular phone

**cel·lu·lar** /ˈseljələ‖-ər/ *adj* **1** consisted of or related to the cells of plants or animals **2 cellular blanket/clothes etc** loosely woven covers, clothes etc that keep you warm **3** having a lot of holes; POROUS: *cellular rock*

**cellular phone** /ˌ··· ˈ·/ *n* [C] a telephone that you can carry around with you, that works from a system that uses a network of radio stations to pass on signals

**cel·lu·lite** /ˈseljəlaɪt/ *n* [U] fat that is just below someone's skin and makes it look uneven and unattractive

**cel·lu·loid** /ˈseljəlɔɪd/ *n trademark* **1 on celluloid** on cinema film: *Chaplin's comic genius is preserved on celluloid.* **2** [U] a plastic substance made mainly from

CELLULOSE (2) that used to be made into photographic film

**cel·lu·lose** /ˈseljᵊləʊs‖-loʊs/ *n* [U] **1** the material that the cell walls of plants are made of and that is used to make plastics, paper etc **2** also **cellulose acetate** *technical* a plastic that is used for many industrial purposes, especially making photographic film and explosives

**Cel·si·us** /ˈselsiəs/ abbreviation **C** *n* [U] a temperature scale in which water freezes at 0° and boils at 100°; CENTIGRADE —**Celsius** *adj*: *a Celsius thermometer | 12° Celsius*

**Cel·tic** /ˈkeltɪk, ˈseltɪk/ *adj* related to the Celts, an ancient European people, or to their languages

**ce·ment¹** /sɪˈment/ *n* [U] **1** a grey powder made from LIME¹ (3) and clay, that becomes hard when it is mixed with water and allowed to dry, and that is used in building: *I think he's outside mixing cement and laying bricks.* **2** a thick sticky substance that becomes very hard when it dries and is used for filling holes or sticking things together

**cement²** *v* [T] **1** also **cement over** to cover something with cement **2** to make a relationship between people or countries firm and strong: *His marriage to Lucy Brett cemented important business ties with her family.*

**cement mix·er** /·ˈ· ˌ··/ *n* [C] a machine with a round drum that turns around, into which you put cement, sand, and water to make CONCRETE; CONCRETE MIXER

**cem·e·tery** /ˈsemᵻtri‖-teri/ *n* [C] a piece of land, usually not belonging to a church, in which dead people are buried —compare CHURCHYARD, GRAVEYARD

**cen·o·taph** /ˈsenətɑːf‖-tæf/ *n* [C] a MONUMENT built to remind you of soldiers, sailors etc who were killed in a war and are buried somewhere else

**cen·sor¹** /ˈsensə‖-ər/ *n* [C] someone whose job is to examine books, films, letters etc and remove anything considered to be offensive, morally harmful, or politically dangerous

**censor²** *v* [T] to examine books, films, letters etc to remove anything that is considered offensive, morally harmful, or politically dangerous etc

**cen·so·ri·ous** /senˈsɔːriəs/ *adj formal* always looking for mistakes and faults in other people and wanting to criticize them: *She didn't used to be so censorious of others' behaviour.* —**censoriously** *adv* —**censoriousness** *n* [U]

**cen·sor·ship** /ˈsensəʃɪp‖-sər-/ *n* [U] the practice or system of censoring something: *the censorship of television programmes*

**cen·sure¹** /ˈsenʃə‖-ər/ *n* [U] *formal* the act of expressing strong disapproval and criticism: *a vote of censure*

**censure²** *v* [T] *formal* to officially criticize someone for something they have done wrong: *The inspector was officially censured for his handling of the demonstration.*

**cen·sus** /ˈsensəs/ *n plural* **censuses** [C] **1** an official process of counting a country's population and finding out about the people **2** an official process of counting something for government planning: *a traffic census*

S1 W1 **cent** /sent/ *n* [C] **1** 0.01 of the main unit of currency in some countries, or a coin worth this amount. For example, there are 100 cents in one US dollar. **2 put in your two cents' worth** *AmE* to give your opinion about something, when other people do not want to hear it —see also **red cent** (RED¹ (18))

**cen·taur** /ˈsentɔː‖-tɔːr/ *n* [C] a creature in ancient Greek stories with the head, chest, and arms of a man and the body and legs of a horse

**cen·te·nar·i·an** /ˌsentᵻˈneəriən‖-ˈner-/ *n* [C] someone who is 100 years old or older

**cen·te·na·ry** /senˈtiːnəri‖-ˈte-, ˈsentəneri/ also **cen·ten·ni·al** /senˈteniəl/ *AmE n* [C] the day or year exactly 100 years after a particular event: *a concert to mark the centenary of the composer's birth*

**cen·ter** /ˈsentə‖-ər/ *n v* the American spelling of CENTRE

**centi-** /sentᵻ/ *prefix* also **cent-** /sent/ **1** 100: *a centipede* (=creature with 100 legs) **2** 100th part of a unit: *a centimetre* (=0.01 metres) —see table on page B2

**Cen·ti·grade** /ˈsentᵻgreɪd/ *n* [U] CELSIUS —**Centigrade** *adj*

**cen·ti·gram**, **centigramme** /ˈsentᵻgræm/ *n* [C] a unit for measuring weight. There are 100 centigrams in one gram. —see table on page B2

**cen·time** /ˈsɒntiːm‖ˈsɑːn-/ *n* [C] 0.01 of a FRANC or some other units of money, or a coin worth this amount

**cen·ti·me·tre** *BrE*, **centimeter** *AmE* /ˈsentᵻˌmiːtə‖-ər/ written abbreviations **c** and **cm** *n* [C] a unit for measuring length. There are 100 centimetres in one metre. —see table on page B2 S3

**cen·ti·pede** /ˈsentᵻpiːd/ *n* [C] a small creature like a WORM with a lot of very small legs

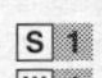

**cen·tral** /ˈsentrəl/ *adj* **1** [only before noun, no comparative] a central organization, system etc makes decisions or controls the operation of a whole country or large organization: *central planning | the central committee of the Communist Party | I'm not advocating central government. | All the money is allocated from a central fund.* **2** [only before noun, no comparative] in the middle of an object or an area: *Central Asia | The houses face onto a central courtyard.* **3** more important and having more influence than anything else: *Owen played a central role in the negotiations.* | [+ **to**] *The inevitability of mass poverty is central to Malthus's argument.* | **of central importance** *Environmental issues are rapidly taking a position of central importance in the political debate.* | **central idea/theme/concern etc** *A responsible press was a central theme running through the speech.* **4** a place that is central is easy to reach because it is near the middle of a town or area: *The house is near Leicester Square, it's very central.* —**centrally** *adv*: *Our office is very centrally situated.* —**centrality** /senˈtrælᵻti/ *n* [C]

**central bank** /ˌ·· ˈ·/ *n* [C] a national bank that does business with the government, and controls the amount of money available and the general system of banks

**central gov·ern·ment** /ˌ·· ˈ···/ *n* [C,U] the government of a whole country, as opposed to LOCAL GOVERNMENT

**central heat·ing** /ˌ·· ˈ··/ *n* [U] a system of heating buildings in which water or air is heated in one place and then sent around the rest of the building through pipes and RADIATORS or VENTS

**cen·tral·is·m** /ˈsentrəlɪzəm/ *n* [U] a way of governing a country or controlling an organization in which one central group has power and tells people in other places what to do

**cen·tral·ize** also **-ise** *BrE* /ˈsentrəlaɪz/ *v* [T] to organize the control of a country or organization so that one central group has power and tells people in other places what to do: *an attempt to centralize the economy* —compare DECENTRALIZE —**centralized** *adj*: *centralized planning* —**centralization** /ˌsentrəlaɪˈzeɪʃən‖-lə-/ *n* [U]

**central lock·ing** /ˌ·· ˈ··/ *n* [U] a system for locking the doors on a car in which all the locks are operated when you turn the key in one lock

**central nerv·ous sys·tem** /ˌ·· ˈ·· ˌ··/ *n* [C] the main part of your NERVOUS SYSTEM consisting of your brain and your SPINAL CORD

**central pro·ces·sing u·nit** /ˌ·· ˈ··· ˌ··/ *n* [C] a CPU

**central res·er·va·tion** /ˌ·· ··ˈ··/ *n* [C] *BrE* a narrow piece of ground that separates the two parts of a MOTORWAY; MEDIAN¹ (1) *AmE* —see picture on page 415

**cen·tre¹** *BrE*, **center** *AmE* /ˈsentə‖-ər/ *n*

**1 ▸ MIDDLE ◂** [C] the middle of a space, area, or object, especially the exact middle: *Draw a line through the centre of the circle. | Tony only likes chocolates with soft centres.* | [+ **of**] *There was an enormous oak table in the center of the room.*

**2 ▸ PLACE/BUILDING ◂** [C] a place or building which

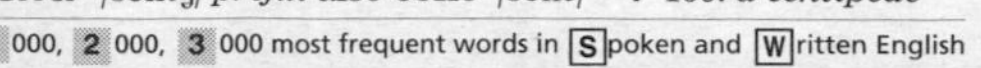

is used for a particular purpose or activity: *the Fred Hutchinson Cancer Research Center | a huge new suburban shopping center | I'll just get a cab to the conference centre.* —see also GARDEN CENTRE, JOB CENTRE
**3 ▶ CENTRE OF ACTIVITY ◀** [C] a place where most of the important things happen that are connected with a particular business or activity: *a major banking centre | It's not exactly a cultural center like Paris.* | [+ **of**] *The main Control Room is the centre of the communications system.* | *a center of academic excellence*
**4 ▶ OF A TOWN ◀** [C] *BrE* the part of a town or city where most of the shops, restaurants, cinemas, theatres etc are; DOWNTOWN *AmE*: city/town centre *parking facilities in the town centre*

**5 centre of population/urban centre** an area where a large number of people live: *Nuclear installations are built well away from the main centres of population.*
**6 ▶ OF ATTENTION/INTEREST ◀** someone or something to which people give a lot of attention: **be the centre of attention** *Betty just loves being the center of attention.* | **be at the centre of a row/dispute/controversy etc** (=be the person or thing most involved in a quarrel etc and therefore getting the most attention)
**7 ▶ IN POLITICS ◀ the centre** a MODERATE (=middle) position in politics which does not support extreme ideas: *The party's new policies show a swing towards the centre.* | **left/right of centre** *As far as I can tell, her political views are slightly left of centre.*
**8 ▶ IN SPORT ◀** [C] a player in games such as football or BASKETBALL who plays in or near the middle of the field or playing area: *the Sonics' six-foot-four-inch center*

**centre²** *BrE*, **center** *AmE v* [T] to move something to a position at the centre of something else: *The title isn't quite centred on the page, is it?*
**centre on/upon** *phr v* [T] if your attention centres on something or someone, or is centred on them, you pay more attention to them than anything else: *The debate centred on the morality of fox hunting.* | **be centred on** *Anyone could see that his interest was centered on Bess.*
**centre around** also **centre round** *BrE phr v* [I,T] if your thoughts, activities etc centre around something or are centred around it, it is the main thing that you are concerned with or interested in: *In the 16th century, village life centred around religion.*

**cen·tre·fold** *BrE*, **centerfold** *AmE* /ˈsentəfəʊld‖-tərfoʊld/ *n* [C] **1** the two pages that face each other in the middle of a magazine or newspaper **2** a picture covering these two pages, especially one of a young woman with no clothes on

**centre for·ward** /ˌ·· ˈ··/ *n* [C] an attacking player who plays in the centre of the field in football

**centre of grav·i·ty** /ˌ·· · ˈ···/ *n* [singular] the point in any object on which it can balance

**cen·tre·piece** *BrE*, **centerpiece** *AmE* /ˈsentəpiːs‖-ər-/ *n* [C] **1** a decoration, especially an arrangement of flowers in the middle of a table **2** [singular] the most important, noticeable or attractive part of something: [+ **of**] *The centrepiece of Bevan's policy was the National Health Service.*

**cen·tri·fu·gal force** /ˌsentrɪˈfjuːgəl◂ ˈfɔːs, senˌtrɪfjʊ̈gəl-‖senˌtrɪfjʊ̈gəl ˈfɔrs/ *n* [U] *technical* a force which makes things move away from the centre of something when they are moving around the centre

**cen·tri·fuge** /ˈsentrɪ̈fjuːdʒ/ *n* [C] a machine that spins a container around very quickly so that the heavier liquids and any solids are forced to the outer edge or bottom

**cen·trip·e·tal force** /senˌtrɪpɪ̈tl ˈfɔːs‖-ˈfɔːrs/ *n* [U] *technical* a force which makes things move towards the centre of something

**cen·trist** /ˈsentrɪ̈st/ *adj* having political beliefs that are not extreme; MODERATE¹ (2) —**centrist** *n* [C]

**cen·tu·ri·on** /ˌsenˈtʃʊəriən‖-ˈtʊr-/ *adj* an army officer of ancient Rome, who was in charge of about 100 soldiers

S1 W1 **cen·tu·ry** /ˈsentʃəri/ *n* [C] **1** one of the 100-year periods counted forwards or backwards from the year of Christ's birth: *twentieth-century art forms such as Cubism | the worst air disaster this century* | **at the turn of the century** (=in or around the year 1900) **2** a period of 100 years **3** 100 runs (RUN² (17)) made by one player in the game of CRICKET (2) in one INNINGS

**CEO** /ˌsiː iː ˈəʊ‖-ˈoʊ/ *n* [C] Chief Executive Officer; the person with the most authority in a large company

**ce·phal·ic** /sɪ̈ˈfælɪk/ *adj technical* connected with or affecting your head

**ce·ram·ics** /sɪ̈ˈræmɪks/ *n* **1** [U] the art of making pots, bowls, TILES etc, by shaping pieces of clay and baking them until they are hard **2** [plural] things that are made this way: *an exhibition of ceramics at the crafts museum* —**ceramic** *adj*: *ceramic tiles*

**ce·re·al** /ˈsɪəriəl‖ˈsɪr-/ *n* **1** [C,U] a breakfast food made from grain and usually eaten with milk **2** [C] a plant grown to produce grain for foods, such as wheat, rice etc: *cereal crops* S3

**cer·e·bel·lum** /ˌserɪ̈ˈbeləm/ *n* [C] *technical* the bottom part of your brain that controls your muscles

**cer·e·bral** /ˈserɪ̈brəl‖səˈriː-, ˈserɪ̈-/ *adj* **1** *technical* connected with or affecting your brain: *cerebral hemorrhage* **2** thinking or explaining things in a very complicated way that takes a lot of effort to understand: *If I'd wanted something cerebral on a Friday night, I'd have stayed at home and read Proust!* | *a cerebral film*

**cerebral pal·sy** /ˌ··· ˈ··‖·ˌ·· ˈ··, ˌ··· ˈ··/ *n* [U] a disease caused by damage to the brain before or during birth which results in difficulties of movement and speech

**cer·e·bra·tion** /ˌserɪ̈ˈbreɪʃən/ *n* [U] *formal* the process of thinking

**cer·e·mo·ni·al¹** /ˌserɪ̈ˈməʊniəl◂‖-ˈmoʊ-/ *adj* used in a ceremony or done as part of a ceremony: *the Mayor's ceremonial duties | Native American ceremonial robes*

**ceremonial²** *n* [C,U] a special ceremony or the practice of having ceremonies: *an occasion for public ceremonial*

**cer·e·mo·ni·ous** /ˌserɪ̈ˈməʊniəs◂‖-ˈmoʊ-/ *adj* paying great attention to formal, correct behaviour; as if you were in a ceremony —**ceremoniously** *adv*: *He ceremoniously burnt the offending documents in the bin.* —**ceremoniousness** *n* [U]

**cer·e·mo·ny** /ˈserɪ̈məni‖-moʊni/ *n* **1** [C] a formal or traditional set of actions used at an important social or religious event: *the wedding ceremony | a graduation ceremony* **2** [U] the special actions and formal words traditionally used on particular occasions: *The queen was crowned with due ceremony.* **3 without ceremony** in a very informal way, without politeness: *Without further ceremony, Ed pushed back his chair and went out.* —see also **not stand on ceremony** (STAND¹ (46))

**ce·rise** /səˈriːz‖səˈriːs, -riːz/ *n* [U] bright pinkish red —**cerise** *adj*

**cert** /sɜːt‖sɜːrt/ *n* **be a (dead) cert** *BrE informal* to be certain to happen or to succeed: *So you reckon that this horse is a dead cert to win?*

**cert.** the written abbreviation of CERTIFICATE

**cer·tain¹** /ˈsɜːtn‖ˈsɜːrtn/ *determiner, pronoun* **1** a certain thing, person, place etc is a particular thing, person etc that you are not naming or describing exactly: *You can get cheaper fares on certain days of the year.* | *There are certain things I just can't discuss with my mother.* | **certain of** *formal* (=several particular people or things in a group) *Certain of the older members objected strongly to the proposal.* **2** some, but not a lot: **a certain amount of** *a certain amount of flexibility* | **to a certain extent/degree** (=in a limited way, but not completely) *I agree with you to a certain extent but there are other factors to consider.* **3 a certain a)** enough of a particular quality to be noticed: *There's a certain prestige about going to a private school.* **b)** *formal* used to talk about someone you do not know but whose name you have been told: *There's a certain Mrs. Myles on the phone for you.*

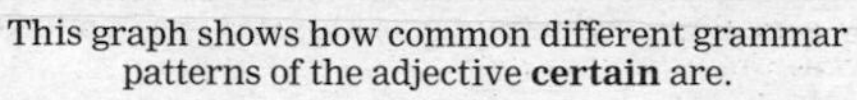

This graph shows how common different grammar patterns of the adjective **certain** are.

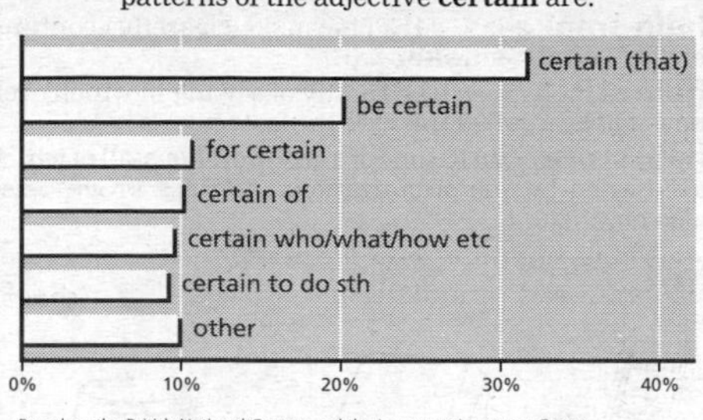


Based on the British National Corpus and the Longman Lancaster Corpus

1 1 **certain²** *adj* **1** [not before noun] confident and sure, without any doubts: *Just so we're absolutely certain, can I check these figures?* | **certain (that)** *We're certain that by tomorrow, Mr Knowles, you'll have an answer.* | **certain who/what/how etc** *I'm not certain whether there's a bus service on Sundays.* | [+ **about/of**] *Now are you certain about that?* | *I'm not quite certain of how much is left in that account.* **2 know/say for certain** to know something without any doubt: *"How much will the repairs cost." "I couldn't say for certain."* **3 make certain a)** to do something in order to be sure that something will happen: **make certain (that)** *Can you draw Harry a map just to make certain he'll find the hotel?* **b)** to check that something is correct or true: [+ **of**] *I suggest you make certain of your facts before you accuse anybody.* **4** if something is certain, it will definitely happen or is definitely true: *a business facing certain bankruptcy* | **it is certain (that)** *It now seems certain that Pam will lose her license.* | **certain to do sth** *There's one boy who's certain to succeed!* | **it is not certain who/what/how etc** *It's not certain where he lived.* (=no one knows definitely)

1 1 **cer·tain·ly** /ˈsɜːtnli‖ˈsɜːr-/ *adv* [sentence adverb] **1** without any doubt; of course: *Certainly we'll consider your suggestion, Alan.* | *That certainly does change the situation.* | *"Not smoking has made a real difference." "It certainly has."* —see OF COURSE (USAGE), SURELY (USAGE)

Frequencies of the adverb **certainly** in spoken and written English.

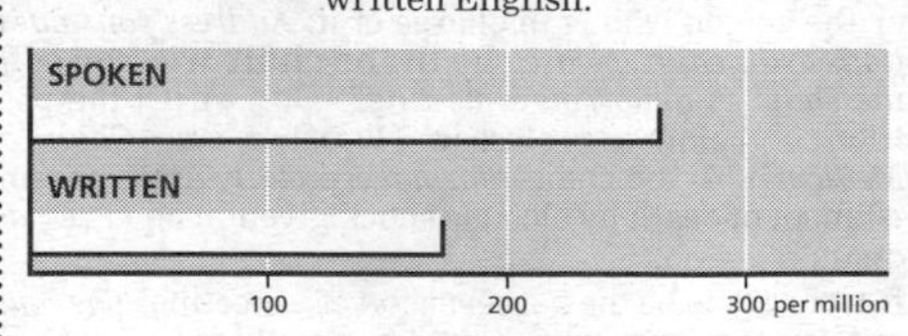


Based on the British National Corpus and the Longman Lancaster Corpus

This graph shows that the adverb **certainly** is more common in spoken English than in written English. This is because it has some special uses in spoken English.

**certainly** (*adv*) **SPOKEN PHRASES**

**2** used to agree or give your permission: *"I'd like a beer, please" "Certainly, sir."* | *"Can I come along?" "Certainly."* **3 certainly not!** used to disagree completely, or to refuse to give permission: *"Did you break my camera?" "Certainly not!"*

**cer·tain·ty** /ˈsɜːtnti‖ˈsɜːr-/ *n* **1** [C] something that is definitely true or that will definitely happen: *It's a certainty that prices will go up soon.* | *Dying's the only certainty in this life.* **2** [U] the state of being completely certain: *Nowadays there's less certainty about church teachings.* | **with certainty** *You can't say with any certainty where you might be in the future.*

**cer·ti·fi·ab·le** /ˈsɜːtʒfaɪəbəl‖ˈsɜːr-/ *adj* **1** *informal* crazy, especially in a way that is dangerous: *If you ask me, that man is certifiable.* **2** *especially AmE* good enough or correct enough to be officially approved: *a certifiable statement* | *grade A certifiable beef*

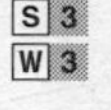

**cer·tif·i·cate** /səˈtɪfɪkət‖sər-/ *n* [C] **1** an official document that states that a fact or facts are true: **birth/death/marriage certificate** (=giving details of someone's birth, death, or marriage) **2** an official paper stating that you have completed a course of study S3 W3

**cer·tif·i·cat·ed** /səˈtɪfɪkeɪtʒd‖sər-/ *adj especially BrE* having successfully completed a training for a profession: *a certificated nurse* —**certification** /sə͵tɪfʒˈkeɪʃən‖sər-/ *n* [U]

**certified mail** /͵··· ˈ·/ *n* [U] *AmE* a method of sending mail in which the fact that you have sent it is recorded and the person it is sent to must sign their name to prove they have received it; RECORDED DELIVERY *BrE*

**certified pub·lic ac·coun·tant** /͵··· ͵··ˈ··/ *n* [C] a CPA

**cer·ti·fy** /ˈsɜːtʒfaɪ‖ˈsɜːr-/ *v* [T] **1** to state that something is correct or true, especially after some kind of test: *You have to get these accounts certified by an auditor.* | **certify sb/sth** *Remember that gas boiler we had that was certified dangerous?* | **certify (that)** *Sign here to certify that this statement is correct.* **2** to give an official paper to someone which states that they have completed a course of training for a profession: *She was certified as a teacher in 1990.* **3** to officially state someone to be mentally ill

**cer·ti·tude** /ˈsɜːtʒtjuːd‖ˈsɜːrtʒtuːd/ *n* [U] *formal* the state of being or feeling certain about something

**ce·ru·le·an** /sʒˈruːliən/ *adj technical or literary* deep blue like a clear sky

**cer·vi·cal** /ˈsɜːvɪkəl, səˈvaɪkəl‖ˈsɜːrvɪkəl/ *adj technical* **1** related to the neck: *cervical vertebrae* (=the bones in the back of your neck) **2** related to the cervix: *cervical cancer*

**cervical smear** /͵··· ˈ·, ·͵·· ˈ·‖͵··· ˈ·/ *n* [C] *technical* a test for CANCER of a woman's CERVIX; PAP SMEAR *AmE*

**cer·vix** /ˈsɜːvɪks‖ˈsɜːr-/ *n* [C] the narrow passage into a woman's UTERUS

**ce·sar·e·an** /sʒˈzeəriən‖-ˈzer-/ *n* [C] another spelling of CAESAREAN

**ces·sa·tion** /seˈseɪʃən/ *n* [C,U + **of**] *formal* a pause or stop: *a cessation of hostilities* (=when the fighting stops in a war)

**ces·sion** /ˈseʃən/ *n* [C,U] *formal* the act of giving up land, property, or rights, especially to another country after a war, or something that is given up in this way: *John's cession of his kingdom in 1213.* —see also CEDE

**cess·pit** /ˈses͵pɪt/ *n* [C] **1** also **cesspool** /ˈsesːpul/ a large hole or container under the ground in which waste from a building, especially from the toilets, is collected **2** a place or situation in which people behave immorally: *For weeks the affair threatened to be a cesspit of scandal.*

**ce·tac·ean** /sɪˈteɪʃən/ *n* [C] *technical* a MAMMAL (=an animal which feeds its babies on milk) that lives in the sea, such as a WHALE —**cetacean** *adj*

**cf** used in writing to introduce something else that should be compared or considered

**CFC** /͵siː ef ˈsiː/ *n* also **chlorofluorocarbon** a gas used in FRIDGES and AEROSOL cans, now believed to be responsible for damaging the OZONE LAYER

**cha-cha** /ˈtʃɑː tʃɑː/ also **cha-cha-cha** /͵· · ˈ·/ *n* [C] a dance from South America with small, fast steps

**chafe** /tʃeɪf/ *v* **1** [I,T] if a part of your body chafes or if something chafes it, it becomes sore because of something rubbing against it: *Put a soft pad under the saddle to avoid chafing the horse's back.* **2** [T] to rub part of your body to make it warm **3** [I] to be or become impatient or annoyed: [+ **at/under**] *Some hunters are chafing under the new restrictions.*

**chaff¹** /tʃɑːf‖tʃæf/ *n* [U] **1** the HUSKS (=outer seed covers) separated from grain before it is used as food; **2** dried grasses and plant stems used for food for farm animals —see also **separate the wheat from the chaff** (WHEAT (3))

**chaff[2]** *v* [T] *old fashioned* to make jokes about the person you are talking to, in a friendly way

**chaf·finch** /ˈtʃæfɪntʃ/ *n* [C] a common small European bird

**chafing dish** /ˈ· · ·/ *n* [C] a container with a HEATER under it, used for cooking food in or for keeping food warm at the table

**chag·rin[1]** /ˈʃægrɪn‖ʃəˈgrɪn/ *n* [U] *formal* annoyance and disappointment because something has not happened the way you hoped: **to sb's chagrin** *To the chagrin of the Pentagon, the USSR exploded a nuclear bomb in 1949.*

**chagrin[2]** *v* **be chagrined** *formal* to feel annoyed and disappointed: *Dale was chagrined that she wasn't impressed.*

S3 W2 **chain[1]** /tʃeɪn/ *n*

**1 ► JOINED RINGS ◄** [C,U] a series of rings, usually made of metal, which are joined together in a line and used for fastening things, supporting weights, decoration etc: *Look at the gold chain Tim bought me!* | *a length of chain* | *a bridge supported on heavy chains* | *We had to stop and put chains on the tires.* | **a bicycle chain** (=that makes the wheels turn) | **chain of office** *BrE* (=a decoration worn by some officials at ceremonies) —see picture at BICYCLE[1]

**2 chain of events/circumstances etc** [C] a connected series of events etc: *the chain of events that led to World War I* —see also CHAIN OF COMMAND, FOOD CHAIN

**3 ► SHOPS/HOTELS ◄** [C] a number of shops, hotels, cinemas etc owned or managed by the same company or person: [+ **of**] *a chain of restaurants* | **hotel/restaurant/retail etc chain** *a major American hotel chain*

**4 ► CONNECTED LINE ◄** [C] people, mountains, islands etc forming a line: *the largest mountain chain in North America* | *Everybody link arms to make a chain.*

**5 ► PRISONER ◄ chains** [plural] chains fastened to a prisoner's legs and arms, to prevent them from escaping: **in chains** *There were a number of men in chains, all sentenced to death.*

**6 ► BUYING A HOUSE ◄** [C usually singular] *BrE* a number of people buying houses in a situation where each person must complete the sale of their own house before they can buy the next person's house

**7 ► MEASURE ◄** [C] a measurement of length, used in the past —see table on page B2

**chain[2]** *v* **1** to fasten someone or something to something else, especially in order to prevent them from escaping or being stolen: **chain sb/sth up** *She wouldn't chain her dog up, and it got killed on the main road.* | **chain sb/sth together** *convicts working all chained together* | **chain sb/sth to sth** *There's a bicycle chained to the railings out front.* **2 be chained to something** to have your freedom restricted because of a responsibility you cannot excape: *With a sick husband she's chained to the house all day.*

**chain gang** /ˈ· ·/ *n* [C] a group of prisoners chained together to work outside their prison

**chain let·ter** /ˈ· ˌ· ·/ *n* [C] a letter sent to several people asking them to send a copy of the letter to several more people

**chain mail** /ˈ· ·/ *n* [U] a piece of protective clothing made by joining small metal rings together, worn by soldiers in the past

**chain of com·mand** /ˌ· · ·ˈ·/ *n* [C] a system in an organization by which decisions are made and passed from people at the top of the organization to people lower down: *Symonds is third in the chain of command.*

**chain re·ac·tion** /ˌ· ·ˈ· ·/ *n* [C] a series of related events or chemical reactions, each of which causes the next: *A student playing with chemicals set off a chain reaction in a public toilet and blew it to bits.*

**chain saw** /ˈ· ·/ *n* [C] a tool used for cutting wood, consisting of a circular chain fitted with teeth and driven by a motor —compare CIRCULAR SAW —see picture at TOOL[1]

**chain-smoke** /ˈ· ·/ *v* [I,T] to smoke cigarettes continuously —**chain-smoker** *n* [C]

**chain stitch** /ˈ· ·/ *n* [C,U] a way of sewing in which each new stitch is pulled through the last one

**chain store** /ˈ· ·/ *n* [C] one of a group of shops, all of which are owned by one organization; MULTIPLE STORE —see also CHAIN[1] (3)

**chairs**

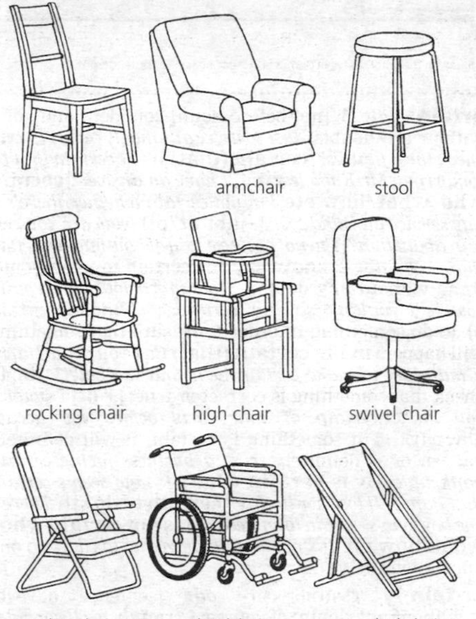

**chair[1]** /tʃeə‖tʃer/ *n* **1** [C] a piece of furniture for one person to sit on, which has a back, a seat, and four legs: *Grandpa's in his favorite chair by the fireplace.* **2** [singular] the position of being in charge of a meeting, or the person who is in charge of it: *Address your questions to the chair, please.* | **be in the chair** *Who will be in the chair at tomorrow's meeting?* **3 a)** [C] the position of being a professor: [+ **of**] *a new Chair of Medicine* **4 the chair** *informal especially AmE* the punishment of death by electric shock given in an ELECTRIC CHAIR

**chair[2]** *v* [T] to be the CHAIRPERSON of a meeting: *The commission of inquiry was chaired by a well-known judge.*

**chair·lift** /ˈtʃeəlɪft‖ˈtʃer-/ *n* [C] a line of chairs hanging from a moving wire, used for carrying people up and down mountains, especially when they are skiing (SKI[2])

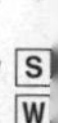
**chair·man** /ˈtʃeəmən‖ˈtʃer-/ *n plural* **chairmen** /-mən/ [C] **1** someone, especially a man, who is in charge of a meeting or directs the work of a committee or organization: *Potts was elected chairman of the education committee.* **2** *BrE* someone who is in charge of a large company or organization: *I think he was the chairman of a big building society before he came here.*

**chair·man·ship** /ˈtʃeəmənʃɪp‖ˈtʃer-/ *n* **the chairmanship** the position of being a chairman, or the time when someone has this position: *A committee was set up under the chairmanship of Edmund Compton.*

**chair·per·son** /ˈtʃeəˌpɜːsən‖ˈtʃerˌpɜːrsən/ *n plural* **chairpersons** [C] someone who is in charge of a meeting or directs the work of a committee or organization

**chair·wom·an** /ˈtʃeəˌwʊmən‖ˈtʃer-/ *n plural* **chair·women** /-ˌwɪmɪn/ [C] a woman who is a chairperson

**chaise** /ʃeɪz/ *n* [C] a light carriage pulled by one horse, used in former times

**chaise longue** /ˌʃeɪz ˈlɒŋ‖-ˈlɔːŋ/ *n* [C] *French* **1** a long chair[1] (1) with an arm only at one end, on which you can sit and stretch your legs out. **2** *AmE* a long chair with a back that can be upright for sitting, or can lie flat for lying down

**chal·et** /ˈʃæleɪ‖ʃæˈleɪ/ *n* [C] **1** a house with a steeply sloping roof, common in places with high mountains and snow such as Switzerland **2** *especially BrE* a small house, especially in a HOLIDAY CAMP

**chal·ice** /ˈtʃælɪ̣s/ *n* [C] a gold or silver decorated cup used for example to hold wine in Christian religious services —see also **poisoned chalice** (POISON[2] (7))

**chalk[1]** /tʃɔːk‖tʃɒːk/ *n* [U] **1** soft white or grey rock formed a long time ago from the shells of small sea animals; LIMESTONE: *chalk hills* **2** also **chalks** [plural] small sticks of this substance, white or coloured, used for writing or drawing: *a box of coloured chalks|writing in chalk on the blackboard* **3 as different as chalk and cheese** *BrE* completely different from each other —see also **not by a long chalk** (LONG[1] (16))

**chalk[2]** *v* [T **+up/on**] to write, mark, or draw something with chalk

**chalk** sth ↔ **up** *phr v* [T] *informal* **1** to succeed in getting something, especially points in a game: *Seattle chalked up another win last night over Denver.* **2** to record what someone has done, what someone should pay etc: *You can chalk the drinks up to my account.* **3 chalk it up to experience** to accept a failure or disappointment calmly and regard it as an experience that you can learn something from

**chalk·board** /ˈtʃɔːkbɔːd‖ˈtʃɒːkbɔːrd/ *n* [C] *AmE* a BLACKBOARD: *Thanks, but the janitor cleans the chalkboard.*

**chalk·y** /ˈtʃɔːki‖ˈtʃɒː-/ *adj* similar to chalk or containing chalk: *white chalky soil|I can't stand those chalky tasting antacid tablets.* —**chalkiness** *n* [U]

2 **challenge[1]** /ˈtʃælɪ̣ndʒ/ *n*

2 **1 ▶STH DIFFICULT◀** [C,U] something that tests strength, skill, or ability especially in a way that is interesting: *I liked the speed and challenge of racing.*|**face a challenge** (=be ready to deal with one) *The White House has to face yet another foreign policy challenge.*|**meet a challenge/rise to a challenge** (=successfully deal with one) *a new and vibrant initiative to meet the challenge of the 21st century*

**2 ▶QUESTIONING OF RIGHTNESS◀** [C] a refusal to accept that something is right and legal: [+ **to**] *a direct challenge to the Governor's authority|feminist challenges to the traditional social order*

**3 ▶INVITATION TO COMPETE◀** a suggestion to someone that they should try to defeat you in a fight, game etc: *The champions are ready to accept a challenge from any team that is a serious contender.*

**4 ▶A DEMAND TO STOP◀** [C] a demand from someone such as a guard to stop and give proof of who you are, and an explanation of what you are doing

**5 ▶IN LAW◀** [C] *law* a statement made before the beginning of a court case that a JUROR is not acceptable: *Each lawyer may issue up to six challenges.*

3 **chal·lenge[2]** *v* [T] **1** to refuse to accept that something
3 is right or legal: *What happens if the Finance Committee challenges us on these figures?|political offenders who challenge the authority of our law courts|* **challenge sb to do sth** *I challenge Dr. Carver to deny his involvement!* **2** to invite someone to compete or fight against you: **challenge sb to sth** *After lunch Carey challenged me to a game of tennis.* —compare DARE[1] (5) **3** to test the skills or abilities of someone or something; STIMULATE: *I'm really at my best when I'm challenged.|* **challenge sb to do sth** *Every teacher ought to be challenging kids to think about current issues.* **4** to stop someone and demand proof of who they are, and an explanation of what they are doing: *We were challenged by the sentry guarding the gate.* **5** *law* to state that a JUROR is not acceptable before a TRIAL[1] (1) begins —**challenger** *n* [C]

**chal·lenged** /ˈtʃælɪ̣ndʒd/ *adj* **visually/physically/mentally challenged** *AmE* an expression for describing someone who has difficulty doing things because of blindness etc, used when you want to avoid saying this directly

**chal·leng·ing** /ˈtʃælɪ̣ndʒɪŋ/ *adj* difficult in an interesting or enjoyable way: *Teaching young children is a challenging and rewarding job.|a challenging problem* —**challengingly** *adv*

**cham·ber** /ˈtʃeɪmbə‖-ər/ *n* **1** [C] an enclosed space, W3
especially in your body or inside a machine: *a combustion chamber|The heart has four chambers.* **2** [C] a room used for a special purpose, especially an unpleasant one: **gas/torture chamber** (=used for killing people by gas or for hurting them) **3** [C] a large room in a public building used for important meetings **4** [C] one of the two parts of a parliament or of the US Congress. For example, in Britain the upper chamber is the House of Lords and the Lower Chamber is the House of Commons: *the council chambers* **5** [C] *old use* a bedroom or private room: *the Queen's private chambers* **6 chambers** [plural] *especially BrE* an office or offices used by BARRISTERS or judges **7** [C] the place inside a gun where you put the bullet —see picture at GUN[1]

**cham·ber·lain** /ˈtʃeɪmbəlɪ̣n‖-bər-/ *n* [C] an important official who manages things like cooking, cleaning, buying food etc in a king's or NOBLEMAN's court

**cham·ber·maid** /ˈtʃeɪmbəmeɪd‖-ər-/ *n* [C] a female servant or worker whose job is to clean and tidy bedrooms, especially in a hotel

**chamber mu·sic** /ˈ·· ˌ··/ *n* [U] CLASSICAL music written for a small group of instruments

**chamber of com·merce** /ˌ·· · ˈ··/ *n* [C] a group of business people in a particular town or area, working together to improve trade

**chamber or·ches·tra** /ˈ·· ˌ···/ *n* [C] a small group of musicians who play CLASSICAL music together

**chamber pot** /ˈ·· ·/ *n* [C] a round container for URINE used in a bedroom and kept under the bed in the past

**cha·me·le·on** /kəˈmiːliən/ *n* [C] **1** a LIZARD that can change its colour to match the colours around it **2** someone who changes their ideas, behaviour etc to fit different situations: *He was a chameleon, able to blend with the customs and people he was living among.*

**cham·ois** /ˈʃæmwɑː/ *n* **1** [C] a wild animal like a small goat that lives in the mountains of Europe and SW Asia **2** also **chamois leather** /ˈ·· ˌ··/ [C,U] soft leather prepared from the skin of chamois, sheep, or goats and used for cleaning or polishing, or a piece of this leather

**cham·o·mile** /ˈkæməmaɪl/ *n* [C,U] another spelling of CAMOMILE

**champ[1]** /tʃæmp/ *v* [I,T] **1** to bite food noisily; CHOMP **2 be champing at the bit** to be unable to wait for something patiently

**champ[2]** *n* [C] a CHAMPION[1] (1): *The Cowboys are the next World Champs!*

**cham·pagne** /ʃæmˈpeɪn/ *n* [U] a French white wine with a lot of BUBBLES, drunk on special occasions

**cham·pers** /ˈʃæmpəz‖-pərz/ *n* [U] *BrE informal* champagne

**cham·pi·on[1]** /ˈtʃæmpiən/ *n* [C] **1** someone or some- W2
thing that has won a competition, especially in sport: *the world heavyweight boxing champion|* **reigning champion** (=the champion at the present time) **2 champion of** someone who publicly fights for and defends an aim or principle, such as the rights of a group of people: *a champion of women's rights*

**champion²** *v* [T] to publicly fight for and defend an aim or principle, such as the rights of a group of people: *championing the cause of religious freedom*

W2 **cham·pi·on·ship** /ˈtʃæmpiənʃɪp/ *n* **1** [C] also **championships** [plural] a competition to find which player, team, etc is the best in a particular sport: *the women's figure skating championships* **2** [C] the position or period of being a champion; TITLE¹ (5): *fighting for the world championship* **3** [U + **of**] the act of championing something or someone

S1 W1 **chance¹** /tʃɑːns‖tʃæns/ *n*

**1** ► **POSSIBILITY** ◄ [C,U] how possible or likely it is that something will happen, especially something that you want: **chance/chances of** *What are her chances of survival?* | **there's a chance (that)** *There's always the chance that something will go wrong.* | **a good/fair/slight chance (of)** *The day will be cloudy with a slight chance of some rain later tonight.* | **some/no/little chance** *There seems to be little chance of a ceasefire.* | **chances are** *spoken* (=used to say that something is likely) *Chances are they'll be out when we call.* | **a fifty-fifty chance** (=when the chances of something happening or not happening are equal) | **a chance in a million** (=a chance that you are very unlikely to have again) *I couldn't pass up going to Japan; it was a chance in a million.* | **a million to one chance** (=when something is extremely unlikely to happen)

**2** ► **HOW LIKELY TO SUCCEED** ◄ **a) sb's chances** how likely it is that someone will succeed: *Ryan will be a candidate in next month's elections, but his chances are not good.* | **not fancy/not rate sb's chances** *BrE* (=think someone is unlikely to succeed) **b) stand/have a chance (of)** if someone or something stands a chance of doing something, it is possible that they will succeed: **stand a good chance** (=be likely to succeed) *If we did move to London, I'd stand a much better chance of getting a job.* | **have an outside chance** (=has a slight chance of success) | **have a sporting chance** (=have a fairly good chance of success) | **have a fighting chance** (=have a small but real chance of success if a great effort can be made) **c) be in with a chance** if a competitor is in with a chance, it is possible that they will win: *There's three of us going for promotion, but I figure I'm in with a chance.*

**3 by any chance** *spoken* used to ask politely whether something is true: *Are you Mrs Grant, by any chance?*

**4 any chance of ...** *spoken* used to ask whether you can have something or whether something is possible: *Any chance of a cup of coffee?* | *Any chance of you coming to the party on Saturday?*

**5 no chance!/fat chance!** *spoken* used to emphasize that you are sure something could never happen: *"Maybe your brother would lend you the money?" "Huh, fat chance!"*

**6 on the off chance** if you do something on the off chance, you do it hoping for a particular result, although you know it is not likely: *I didn't really expect her to be at home. I just called on the off chance.*

**7** ► **OPPORTUNITY** ◄ [C] a time or situation which you can use to do something that you want to do: **chance to do sth** *Ralph was waiting for a chance to introduce himself.* | [+ **of**] *our only chance of escape* | **have/get a chance** *I never get a chance to relax these days.* | **give sb a chance** *I can explain everything if you'll just give me a chance.* | **take the chance** (=use the opportunity) *You should take the chance to travel while you're still young.* | **grab the chance/jump at the chance** (=eagerly and quickly use an opportunty) *You're so lucky. If someone invited me over to Florida, I'd jump at the chance.* | **miss a chance** (=fail to use the opportunity) *Denise never misses the chance of a free meal.* | **a second chance/another chance** (=another chance after you have failed the first time) *Students will be given further training and a second chance to pass the exam.* | **last chance** *Friday is your last chance to see the show before it closes.* | *You really ought to be punished, but I'll give you one last chance.* (=opportunity to behave well) | **the chance of a lifetime** (=an opportunity you are not likely to get more than once) | **now's your chance** *spoken* (=used to tell someone to do something immediately because there is a good opportunity) *Quick! Now's your chance to ask her, before she leaves.* | **given half a chance** *spoken* (=if someone were given even a small opportunity) *Rick could do really well, given half a chance.*

**8** ► **RISK** ◄ **take a chance** to do something that involves risks: *The rope might break but that's a chance we'll have to take.* | **take chances** *After losing $20,000 on my last business venture, I'm not taking any chances this time.* | **take a chance on** (=take a chance hoping things will happen in the way you want) *I haven't reserved a table. I'm taking a chance on the restaurant not being full.*

**9** ► **LUCK** ◄ [U] the way some things happen without being planned or caused by people: *Success is rarely a matter of chance. You have to work at it.* | **by chance** (=without being planned or intended) *I bumped into her quite by chance in Oxford Street.* | **pure/sheer/blind chance** (=nothing except chance) *It was pure chance that they ended up working in the same office in the same town.* | **as chance would have it** (=happening in a way that was not expected or intended) *As chance would have it, the one time I wanted to see her, she wasn't in.*

**10 chance would be a fine thing!** *spoken* used to mean that the thing you want to happen is very unlikely: *"If he asked me to marry him, I might say yes." "Chance would be a fine thing!"* (=he's unlikely to ask) —see also **game of chance** (GAME¹ (11))

> **USAGE NOTE: CHANCE**
>
> WORD CHOICE: **chance, opportunity, occasion**
>
> Both **chance** and **opportunity** can be used for a situation that is suitable for doing something that you want to do: *I'll have a chance/an opportunity to visit Niagara Falls when I'm in the States.* You can *get/take/grab/jump at/miss the opportunity/chance* to do something and *give someone the opportunity/chance* to do something.
>
> **Chance** is also used to say it is possible that something might happen. *There is a chance that I'll see him* (=perhaps I'll see him).
>
> An **occasion** is a moment when something happens, especially when the same thing happens several times: *I met her on several occasions* (=several times). | *On this occasion I was late* (NOT *In this occasion...* or just *This occasion...*). An **occasion** can also be an event: *Christmas is a special occasion.*
>
> In formal English **occasion** (usually [U]) can also mean 'reason': *The poor service gave them occasion to complain* (=caused them to complain).
>
> SPELLING
>
> Remember the two 'p's in **opportunity**.

**chance²** *v* **1** *informal* to do something that you know involves a risk: **chance it** *If we creep in quietly, maybe no one will notice. Anyway, let's chance it.* | **chance your luck** *You may lose all you money, but you'll just have to chance your luck like everyone else.* **2** *literary* to happen in an unexpected and unplanned way: **chance to do sth** *She chanced to be passing when I came out of the house.* | **it chanced that** *It chanced that we were both working in Paris that year.*

**chance on/upon** sb/sth *phr v* [T] to find something or meet someone when you are not expecting to: *Henry chanced upon some valuable coins in the attic.*

**chance³** *adj* [only before noun] not planned; ACCIDENTAL: *Their chance meeting brought them back together after seven years apart.*

**chan·cel** /ˈtʃɑːnsəl‖ˈtʃæn-/ *n* [C] the part of a church where the priests and the CHOIR (=singers) sit

**chan·cel·ler·y** /ˈtʃɑːnsələri‖ˈtʃæn-/ *n* [C] **1** the building in which a CHANCELLOR has his office **2** the officials who work in a CHANCELLOR's office **3** the offices of an official representative of a foreign country; CHANCERY

3 **chan·cel·lor** /ˈtʃɑːnsələ‖ˈtʃænsələr/ *n* [C] **1** the Chancellor of the Exchequer **2 a)** the person who officially represents a British university on special occasions **b)** the person in charge of an American university **3** the chief minister of some countries: *Willy Brandt the former West German Chancellor*

**Chancellor of the Ex·cheq·uer** /ˌ·······ˈ··/ *n* [C] the British government minister in charge of taxes and government spending

**chan·ce·ry** /ˈtʃɑːnsəri‖ˈtʃæn-/ *n* [singular] **1** *especially BrE* a government office that collects and stores official papers **2** the part of the British system of law courts which deals with EQUITY (4) **3** the offices of an official representative of a foreign country; CHANCELLERY

**chanc·y** /ˈtʃɑːnsi‖ˈtʃænsi/ *adj informal* uncertain or involving a lot of risk: *Acting professionally is a chancy business.* —**chanciness** *n* [U]

**chan·de·lier** /ˌʃændəˈlɪə‖-ˈlɪr/ *n* [C] a large round structure for holding CANDLES or lights that hang from the ceiling and is decorated with many small pieces of glass

**chand·ler** /ˈtʃɑːndlə‖ˈtʃændlər/ *n* [C] *old use* someone who makes or sells candles CANDLE —see also SHIP'S CHANDLER

1 **change[1]** /tʃeɪndʒ/ *v*

1 **1 ▶ BECOME DIFFERENT ◀** [I,T] to become different: *Susan has changed a lot since I last saw her.* | **changing circumstances/attitudes etc** *Animals must be able to adapt to changing conditions in order to survive.* | **change out of all recognition** (=change completely) *The town I grew up in has changed out of all recognition.* | **change colour** *The leaves are slowly changing colour.* | **not change your spots** (=never change your character or habits)

**2 ▶ MAKE STH/SB DIFFERENT ◀** [T] to make something or someone different: *plans to change the voting system* | *Having a baby changes your life completely.*

**3 ▶ FROM ONE THING TO ANOTHER ◀** [I,T] to stop having or doing one thing and start having or doing something else instead: **change (from sth) to sth** *We've changed from traditional methods of production to an automated system.* | **change your name/address/job etc** *Emma refused to change her name when she married.* | **change jobs/cars etc** (=change from one to another) | **change course/direction** (=start to move in a different direction) *Our ship changed course and headed south.* | **change the subject** (=talk about something else) *I'm sick of politics. Let's change the subject.* | **change tack** (=try a different method of dealing with a situation) *Perhaps my cold reaction persuaded him to change tack in his dealings with the committee.* | **change sides** (=leave one side and join the other one) *Paul decided to change sides halfway through the debate.* | **change ends** (=to move to opposite ends of a TENNIS COURT or football field during a game) *The two teams change ends at half-time.*

**4 change your mind** to change your decision, plan, or opinion about something: **[+ about]** *If you change your mind about the job, just give me a call.*

**5 ▶ CLOTHES ◀ a)** [I,T] to take off your clothes and put on different ones: *I'm just going upstairs to change.* | **[+ into/out of]** *Why don't you change into something more comfortable?* | *It's time you changed your socks.* | **get changed** (=put on different clothes) **b)** [T] to put fresh clothes on a baby or fresh covers on a bed: *I'm just going to change the baby.*

**6 ▶ REPLACE STH ◀** [T] to put something new in place of something old, damaged, or broken: *Can you change the light bulb for me?* | *changing a tyre*

**7 ▶ EXCHANGE GOODS ◀** [T] to exchange something that you have bought, or that a customer has bought from you, especially because there is something wrong with it: *I bought these gloves for my daughter, but they're too large. Can I change them for a smaller size?*

**8 ▶ EXCHANGE MONEY ◀** [T] **a)** to exchange a larger unit of money for smaller units that add up to the same value: *Can you change a £20 note?* **b)** to exchange money from one country for money from another: **change sth into/for** *I want to change my sterling into dollars.*

**9 ▶ TRAINS/BUSES ◀** [I,T] to get out of one train or bus and into another in order to continue your journey: **[+ at]** *Passengers for Liverpool should change at Crewe.* | **change trains/buses** *You can travel all the way to Paris without having to change trains.* | **all change!** *BrE* (=used to tell passengers to get off a train because it does not go any further)

**10 change hands** if property changes hands, it passes from one owner to another: *The house has changed hands three times in the last two years.*

**11 change places (with) a)** to give someone your place and take their place: *Would you mind changing places with me so I can sit next to my friend?* **b)** to take someone else's social position or situation in life instead of yours: *She may be very rich, but I wouldn't want to change places with her.*

**12 change gear** to put the engine of a vehicle into a higher or lower GEAR[1] (1) in order to go faster or slower: **change into/out of** *Change into second gear as you approach the corner.* | **change up/down** *BrE*: *Change down before you get to the hill.*

**13 change your tune** to start expressing a different attitude and reacting in a different way, after something has happened: *When I offered him a share of the profits, he soon changed his tune.*

**14 ▶ WIND ◀** [I] if the wind changes, it starts to blow in a different direction —see also **chop and change** (CHOP[1] (5))

**change** sth ↔ **around** *phr v* [T] to move things into different positions: *When we'd changed the furniture around, the room looked quite different.*

**change into** *phr v* [T] **1** [**change into** sth] to become something different: *When the princess kissed the frog, it changed into a handsome prince.* **2** [**change** sth/sb **into** sth] to make something or someone become something different: *You can't change iron into gold.*

**change[2]** *n* 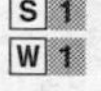

**1 ▶ THINGS BECOMING DIFFERENT ◀** [C,U] the process or result of something or someone becoming different: **[+ in]** *a change in the weather* | *I've noticed a big change in Louise since she got married.* | *changes in the immigration laws* | *Many old people find it hard to cope with change.* | **[+ of]** *a change of temperature* | **change for the better/worse** (=a change that makes a situation better or worse) *When Bill Clinton was elected, we all believed the new administration would be a change for the better.* | **change of heart** (=change in someone's attitude) *He didn't want kids at first but recently he's had a real change of heart.*

**2 ▶ FROM ONE THING TO ANOTHER ◀** [C] the fact of one thing or person being replaced by another: **[+ of]** *a change of government* | *a change of address* | **change from sth to** *the change from city life to living right out in the countryside* | *The car needs an oil change.*

**3 ▶ PLEASANT NEW SITUATION ◀** [singular] a situation or experience that is different from what happened before, and is usually interesting or enjoyable: **[+ from]** *Roast lamb is a welcome change from the usual junk food.* | **for a change** *Let's go out to a restaurant for a change.* | **it makes a change** *spoken* (=used to say that something is different from usual and better) *"The train was on time today." "Well, that makes a change."* | **change of scene/air etc** (=a stay in a different place that is pleasant) *How about a week by the sea? The change of air would do you good.*

**4 ▶ MONEY ◀** [U] **a)** the money that you get back when you have paid for something with more money than it costs: *I waited for the shopkeeper to hand me my change.* **b)** money in the form of coins: **in change** *I have about a dollar in change.* | **change for £1/$10** (=coins that you give someone in exchange for the same money in a larger unit) *Excuse me, have you got change for a pound?* | **loose change** *Matt emptied the loose change from his pockets.* | **small change** (=coins of low value) *When travelling by bus in a strange place, have small change ready.* —see MONEY (USAGE)

**5 change of clothes/underwear etc** an additional set of clothes that you have with you, for example when you are travelling

**6 ▶ TRAIN/BUS ◀** [C] a situation in which you get off one train or bus and get on another in order to continue your journey

**7 get no change out of** *spoken* to get no useful information or help from someone: *I wouldn't bother asking Richard, you'll get no change out of him.* —see also **ring the changes** (RING² (6))

**change·a·ble** /ˈtʃeɪndʒəbəl/ *adj* likely to change or changing often: *The weather was very changeable.* —**changeably** *adv* —**changeableness** *n* [U] —**changeability** /ˌtʃeɪndʒəˈbɪlɪ̈ti/ *n* [U]

**changed** /tʃeɪndʒd/ *adj* **1 a changed man/woman** someone who has become very different from what they were before as a result of a powerful experience: *Since she stopped drinking, she's a changed woman.* **2 changed circumstances** a change in someone's financial situation: *When planning ahead, be aware of the possibility of changed circumstances.*

**change·less** /ˈtʃeɪndʒləs/ *adj literary* never seeming to change: *a changeless desert landscape* —**changelessly** *adv*

**change·ling** /ˈtʃeɪndʒlɪŋ/ *n* [C] *literary* a baby that is said to have been secretly exchanged for another baby by fairies (FAIRY (1))

**change of life** /ˌ· · ˈ·/ *n* [singular] the MENOPAUSE

**change·o·ver** /ˈtʃeɪndʒˌəʊvə‖-ˌoʊvər/ *n* [C] a change from one activity, system, or way of working to another: *working to ensure that the changeover to the new method is as smooth as possible*

**change purse** /ˈ· ·/ *n* [C] *AmE* a small bag in which coins are kept; PURSE¹ (1) *BrE* —see picture at PURSE¹

**change ring·ing** /ˈ· ˌ··/ *n* [U] the art of ringing a set of bells in an order that keeps changing

**changing room** /ˈ·· ·/ *n* [C] a room where people change their clothes when they play sports; LOCKER ROOM *AmE*

S3 W2 **chan·nel¹** /ˈtʃænl/ *n* [C]

**1 ▶ TELEVISION ◀** a television station and all the programmes broadcast by it: *We watched the news on Channel 4.* | *This is boring – I'm going to switch to another channel.*

**2 ▶ RADIO ◀** a particular range of SOUND WAVES which can be used to send and receive radio messages

**3 ▶ SYSTEM OF INFORMATION ◀** also **channels** [plural] a system or method that you use to send or obtain information about a particular subject: *If you go through official channels, your application will take months.*

**4 ▶ FOR WATER ◀** a passage that water or other liquids flow along: *an irrigation channel*

**5 ▶ SEA/RIVER ◀ a)** a passage of water connecting two seas: **the Channel** (=the English Channel) **b)** the deepest part of a river, HARBOUR¹, or sea passage, especially one that is deep enough to allow ships to sail in

**6 ▶ IN A SURFACE ◀** a long deep line cut into a surface or a long deep space between two edges; GROOVE¹ (1): *Slide the plastic door strip into the channel provided.*

**7 ▶ WAY TO EXPRESS YOURSELF ◀** a way of expressing your thoughts, feelings, or physical energy: *The kids need a channel for all that energy.*

**channel²** *v* **channelled, channelling** *BrE*, **channeled, channeling** *AmE* [T] **1** to control and direct something such as money or energy towards a particular purpose: **channel sth into** *Nancy channels her creativity into her home life.* | **channel sth through** *The famine relief money was channelled through the UN.* **2** to cut a long deep line in something: *Water had channelled grooves in the rock.* **3** to send water through a passage: *An efficient irrigation system channels water to the crops.*

**channel hop** /ˈ·· ·/ *BrE*, **channel surf** *AmE v* [I] to repeatedly change from one television channel to another, only watching a few minutes of any programme

**chan·nel·ling** *BrE*, **channeling** *AmE* /ˈtʃænl-ɪŋ/ *n* [U] a practice based on the belief that messages can be received from other PLANETS or from dead people —**channeller** *n* [C]

**chant¹** /tʃɑːnt‖tʃænt/ *v* [I,T] **1** to repeat a word or phrase again and again: *an angry crowd chanting slogans and waving banners* **2** to sing or say a religious song or prayer in a way that involves singing phrases on one note: *a priest chanting the liturgy*

**chant²** *n* [C] **1** words or phrases that are repeated again and again by a group of people: **take up a chant** *Dave took up the crowd's chant of "More Jobs! More Money!"* **2** a regularly repeated tune, often with many words sung on one note, especially used for religious prayers —see also GREGORIAN CHANT —**chanter** *n* [C]

**chan·try** /ˈtʃɑːntri‖ˈtʃæ-/ also **chantry cha·pel** /ˌ·· ˈ··/ *n* [C] a small church or part of a church paid for by someone so that priests can pray for them there after they die

**chan·ty** also **chantey** *AmE* /ˈʃænti/ *n* [C] a song sung by sailors as they did their work in former times; SHANTY

**Cha·nu·kah** /ˈhɑːnʊ̈kə‖ˈkɑːnəkə, ˈhɑː-/ *n* HANUKKAH

**cha·os** /ˈkeɪ-ɒs‖-ɑːs/ *n* [U] **1** a situation in which everything is happening in a confused way and nothing is organized or arranged in order: **complete/utter/absolute chaos** *There was absolute chaos when the air controllers came out on strike.* | **in chaos** (=in a state of chaos) *I arrived home to find the house in chaos.* **2** the state of the universe before there was any order

**cha·ot·ic** /keɪˈɒtɪk‖-ˈɑːtɪk/ *adj* a chaotic situation is one in which everything is happening in a confused way: *Traffic conditions tonight are chaotic.*

**chap** /tʃæp/ *n BrE informal* **1** [C] a man, especially a man you know and like: *a decent sort of chap* **2 chaps** [plural] protective leather covers worn over your trousers when riding a horse S

**chap·ar·ral** /ˌʃæpəˈræl, ˌtʃæp-/ *n* [U] *AmE* land on which small OAK trees grow close together

**chap·book** /ˈtʃæpbʊk/ *n* [C] *AmE* a small printed book, usually consisting of writings about literature or poetry

**chap·el¹** /ˈtʃæpəl/ *n* **1** [C] a small church or a room in a hospital, prison etc in which Christians pray and have religious services **2** [C] a small church or a room or area in a church with its own ALTAR used especially for private prayer and religious services: *a wedding chapel in Las Vegas* **3** [C] **a)** a building in England or Wales where Christians who are Nonconformists have religious services **b)** a Roman Catholic church in Scotland **4** [U] the religious services held in a chapel: **go to chapel** *Bethann goes to chapel every Sunday.* **5** [C] *BrE* the members of a UNION (=workers' organization) in the newspaper or printing industry

**chapel²** *adj BrE informal* Nonconformist: *He's chapel but his wife is Roman Catholic.*

**chap·e·rone¹, chaperon** /ˈʃæpərəʊn‖-roʊn/ *n* [C] **1** an older woman in former times who went out with a young unmarried woman on social occasions and was responsible for her behaviour: *I will only allow it if you have Maria as a chaperone.* **2** *AmE* someone, usually a parent or teacher, who attends school dances or visits to help watch the children

**chaperone², chaperon** *v* [T] to go out somewhere with a woman as her chaperone

**chap·lain** /ˈtʃæplɪ̈n/ *n* [C] a priest or other religious minister responsible for the religious needs of a club, the army, a hospital, etc: *the prison/school chaplain* —see PRIEST (USAGE)

**chap·lain·cy** /ˈtʃæplɪ̈nsi/ *n* [C] the position of a chaplain or the place where a chaplain works

**chap·let** /ˈtʃæplɪ̈t/ *n* [C] *literary* a band of flowers worn on the head

**chapped** /tʃæpt/ *adj* chapped lips or hands are sore, dry, and cracked, especially as a result of cold weather or wind —**chap** *v* [T]

S3 W1 **chap·ter** /ˈtʃæptə‖-ər/ *n* [C]
**1** ▶ **IN A BOOK** ◀ one of the parts into which a book is divided: *I've only read as far as Chapter 5.*
**2** ▶ **PERIOD** ◀ a particular period or event in someone's life or in history: [+ **of**] *That summer an important chapter of my life came to an end.*
**3** ▶ **PRIESTS** ◀ all the priests connected with a CATHEDRAL, or a meeting of these priests
**4** ▶ **CLUB** ◀ *especially AmE* the local members of a large organization such as a club: *the San Fernando Valley chapter of the Sierra Club*
**5 give/quote sb chapter and verse** to give someone exact details about where to find some information
**6 a chapter of accidents** *BrE* a series of unfortunate events coming one after another

**chap·ter·house** /ˈtʃæptəhaʊs‖-ər-/ *n* [C] a building where the priests connected with a CATHEDRAL meet

**char¹** /tʃɑː‖tʃɑːr/ *v past tense and past participle* **charred, charring** **1** [I,T] to burn something so that its outside becomes black: *Roast the peppers until the skin begins to char and blister.* —see also CHARRED **2** [I] *BrE old fashioned* to work as a cleaner in a house, office, public building etc

**char²** *n* **1** [C] *BrE old fashioned* a CHARWOMAN **2** [U] *BrE old-fashioned* tea: *a cup of char*

**char·a·banc** /ˈʃærəbæŋ/ *n* [C] *BrE old-fashioned* a large comfortable bus used for pleasure trips

S1 W1 **char·ac·ter** /ˈkærɪ̯ktə‖-ər/ *n*
**1** ▶ **ALL SB'S QUALITIES** ◀ [C usually singular] the particular combination of qualities that makes someone a particular kind of person: *There is a serious side to her character.* | **be in/out of character** (=be typical or untypical of someone's character) *I can't believe she lied to me – it seems so out of character.* | **the English/French etc character** *Openness is at the heart of the American character.* —see CHARACTERISTIC¹
**2** ▶ **QUALITIES OF STH** ◀ [singular, U] the particular combination of features and qualities that makes a thing or place different from all others: *the unspoilt character of the coast* | [+ **of**] *In only ten years the whole character of the school has changed.* | **in character** *Liquids are different in character from both solids and gases.*
**3** ▶ **INTERESTING QUALITY** ◀ [U] a quality that makes someone or something special and interesting: *These new houses have very little character.*
**4** ▶ **MORAL STRENGTH** ◀ [U] a combination of qualities such as courage and loyalty that are admired and regarded as valuable: *a woman of great character* | **character building** (=activity aimed at developing these qualities) *outdoor programs that are meant to be character building*
**5** ▶ **PERSON** ◀ [C] **a)** a person in a book, play, film etc: *Hardy's main character is a young milkmaid whose life ends in tragedy.* **b)** a person of a particular kind, especially a strange or dishonest one: *a couple of suspicious-looking characters standing outside the house* **c) be a character** to be an interesting, and unusual person: *Kurt's quite a character – he has so many tales to tell.*
**6** ▶ **REPUTATION** ◀ [U] *formal* reputation: *a man of previous good character* | **a slur on your character** (=something that harms your character in other people's opinion) | **character assassination** (=a cruel and unfair attack on someone's character)
**7** ▶ **LETTER/SIGN** ◀ [C] a letter, mark, or sign used in writing, printing, or computing: *Chinese characters*

**char·ac·ter·ise** /ˈkærɪ̯ktəraɪz/ *v* a British spelling of CHARACTERIZE

S3 W2 **char·ac·ter·is·tic¹** /ˌkærɪ̯ktəˈrɪstɪk◂/ *n* [C usually plural] a quality or feature of something or someone that is typical of them and easy to recognize: *A characteristic of this species is the blue stripe on its back.* | *Obstinacy remains one of Gail's less endearing characteristics.*

**characteristic²** *adj* very typical of a particular thing or of someone's character: *Larry, with characteristic generosity, invited us all back to his house.* | [+ **of**] *The flint walls are characteristic of the local architecture.* —**characteristically** /-kli/ *adv*

**char·ac·ter·i·za·tion** /ˌkærɪ̯ktəraɪˈzeɪʃən‖-tərə-/ *n* **1** [C,U] the way in which a writer makes a person in a book, film, or play seem like a real person: *He writes exciting stories but his characterization is weak.* **2** [U] the way in which the character of a real person or thing is described: **characterization of sb/sth as** *the characterization of the enemy as 'cruel fanatics'*

**char·ac·ter·ize** also **-ise** *BrE* /ˈkærɪ̯ktəraɪz/ *v* [T] **1** to be typical of a person, place, or thing: *Bright, vibrant colours characterize his paintings.* **2** to describe the character of someone or something in a particular way; PORTRAY: **characterize sb as sth** *I would characterize Captain Hill as a born leader of men.* W3

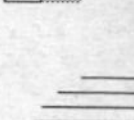

**char·ac·ter·less** /ˈkærɪ̯ktələs‖-tər-/ *adj* not having any special or interesting qualities: *snack-bars selling mass-produced, characterless food*

**character ref·e·rence** /ˈ··· ˌ···/ *n* [C] REFERENCE (4)

**cha·rade** /ʃəˈrɑːd‖ʃəˈreɪd/ *n* **1 charades** [U] a game in which one person acts the meaning of a word or phrase and the others have to guess what it is **2** [C] a situation in which people pretend that something is true and behave as if it were true, when everyone knows it is not really true: *Their marriage is an empty charade, continued only for the sake of the children.*

**char·broil** /ˈtʃɑːbrɔɪl‖ˈtʃɑːr-/ *v* [T] *AmE* to cook food over a very hot charcoal fire —**charbroiled** *adj*

**char·coal** /ˈtʃɑːkəʊl‖ˈtʃɑːrkoʊl-/ *n* [U] a black substance obtained by burning wood, that can be used as FUEL, or sticks of this substance used for drawing: *a sketch drawn in charcoal* | *a charcoal grill*

**chard** /tʃɑːd‖tʃɑːrd/ *n* [U] a vegetable with large leaves

**charge¹** /tʃɑːdʒ‖tʃɑːrdʒ/ *n* S1
**1** ▶ **PRICE** ◀ [C,U] the amount of money you have to pay for goods or services: *Gas charges will rise in July.* | [+ **for**] *When you buy a suit, there is no charge for any alterations.* | **free of charge** (=at no cost) *Your order will be delivered free of charge within a ten-mile limit.* | **at no extra charge** (=without having to pay more money) —see COST¹ (USAGE) W1
**2** ▶ **CONTROL** ◀ **a) be in charge (of)** to be the person who controls or is responsible for a group of people or an activity: *Who's in charge around here?* | *the officer in charge of the investigation* —see CONTROL¹ (USAGE) **b) put sb in charge (of)** to give someone complete responsibility over an activity, group of people, organization etc: *I've been put in charge of the team.* **c) take charge (of)** to take control of a situation, organization, or group of people: *Harry will take charge of the department while I'm away.*
**3** ▶ **RESPONSIBILITY/CARE FOR** ◀ **a) be in/under sb's charge** if someone or something is in your charge, you are responsible for looking after them: *The child was in my charge when he ran away.* | *The files were left in your charge.* **b)** [C] *formal* someone that you are responsible for looking after: *Sarah bought some chocolate for her three young charges.*
**4** ▶ **THAT SB IS GUILTY** ◀ [C] an official statement made by the police saying that someone is guilty of a crime: [+ **against**] *The charge against her was arson.* | **on a charge** *Young appeared in court on a murder charge.* | **charge of burglary/theft/fraud etc** *Owen is facing a charge of armed robbery.* | **bring/press/prefer charges** (=state officially that someone is guilty of a crime) *As it was his first offence, the store agreed not to press charges.* | **drop the charges** (=decide to stop making charges)
**5** ▶ **BLAME** ◀ [C] a written or spoken statement blaming someone for doing something bad or illegal; ALLEGATION: *the charge of being an uncaring mother* | *a group which earlier rejected the charge that it had put undue pressure on the Prime Minister* | **counter a charge** (=say that a charge is untrue) | **lay/leave yourself open to a charge of** (=be likely to be blamed for something) *The*

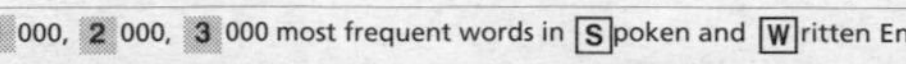

*procedures the doctor followed laid him open to charges of negligence.*
**6 ► ATTACK ◄** [C] an attack in which soldiers, wild animals etc rush with great force against someone
**7 ► ELECTRICAL FORCE ◄** [U] an electrical force that is put into a piece of electrical equipment such as a BATTERY (1): **on charge** (=taking in a charge of electricity) *Leave the battery on charge all night.*
**8 ► EXPLOSIVE ◄** [C] an amount of explosive, especially the amount needed to work successfully
**9 ► STRENGTH OF FEELINGS ◄** [U] the power of strong feelings: *a novel with a strong emotional charge*
**10 get a charge out of sth** *AmE* to be excited by something and enjoy it very much: *I got a real charge out of seeing my niece take her first steps.*

**11 ► AN ORDER TO DO STH ◄** [C] *formal* an order to do something: **a charge to do sth** *The old servant fulfilled his master's charge to care for the children.* —see also **reverse the charges** (REVERSE[1] (5))

S1 W2 **charge²** *v*
**1 ► MONEY ◄ a)** [I,T] to ask someone a certain amount of money for something you are selling: **charge sb £10/$50 etc (for sth)** *The restaurant charged us £40 for the wine.* | [+ **for**] *We won't charge for delivery if you pay now.* **b) charge sth to sb's account** to record the cost of something on someone's account, so that they can pay for it later: *Charge the room to the company's account.* **c)** [T] *AmE* to pay for something with a CREDIT CARD: *I charged the shoes on Visa.* | **charge it** *"Do you have enough cash for that?" "No, but I can charge it."*
**2 ► RUSH/ATTACK ◄ a)** [I,T] to deliberately rush quickly towards someone or something in order to attack them: [+ **at/towards/into**] *a three-ton rhino charging towards us* | **charge sb** *We drew our swords and charged the enemy.* **b)** [I always+ adv/prep] to deliberately run or walk somewhere quickly: [+ **around/through/out etc**] *At playtime, the children charged wildly out of the building.*
**3 ► WITH A CRIME ◄** [T] to state officially that someone is guilty of a crime: **be charged with** *The man they arrested last night has been charged with murder.*
**4 ► BLAME SB ◄** [T] *formal* to say publicly that you think someone has done something wrong: **charge that** *Labour's Bryan Gould charged that Mr. Mellor acted 'improperly'.*
**5 ► ELECTRICITY ◄** [I,T] if a battery charges or if you charge it, it takes in and stores electricity: *If the light comes on, the battery isn't charging.*
**6 ► ORDER SB ◄** [T] *formal* to order someone to do something or make them responsible for it: **be charged with doing sth** *The commission is charged with investigating all the alleged breaches of the rules.*
**7 ► GUN ◄** [T] *old use* to load a gun
**8 ► GLASS ◄** [T] *formal* to fill a glass: *Charge your glasses and drink a toast to the happy couple.*

**charge·a·ble** /ˈtʃɑːdʒəbəl‖ˈtʃɑːr-/ *adj* **1** chargeable costs must be paid: *Living expenses are chargeable to my account.* **2** chargeable asets or gains have to have tax paid on them **3** a chargeable offence is serious enough for the police to officially state that you are guilty of it

**charge ac·count** /ˈ· ·ˌ·/ *n* [C] *AmE* an account you have at a shop that allows you to take goods away with you now and pay later; CREDIT ACCOUNT

**charge card** /ˈ· ·/ *n* [C] a plastic card that you can use to buy goods in a particular shop and pay for them later

**charged** /tʃɑːdʒd‖tʃɑːrdʒd/ *adj* a charged situation or subject makes people feel very angry, anxious, or excited, and is likely to cause arguments or violence: **highly charged** *a highly charged press conference*

**char·gé d'af·faires** /ˌʃɑːʒeɪ dæˈfeə‖ˌʃɑːrʒeɪ dæˈfer/ *n* [C] *French* an official who represents their government during the absence of an AMBASSADOR or in a country where there is no ambassador

**charge hand** /ˈ· ·/ *n* [C] *BrE* a worker in charge of other workers whose position is below that of a FOREMAN (1)

**charge nurse** /ˈ· ·/ *n* [C] a nurse in charge of one part of a hospital

**charg·er** /ˈtʃɑːdʒə‖ˈtʃɑːrdʒər/ *n* [C] **1** a piece of equipment used to put electricity into a BATTERY (1) **2** *literary* a horse that a soldier or KNIGHT rides in battle

**charge sheet** /ˈ· ·/ *n* [C] a record kept in a police station of the names of people the police have stated are guilty of a particular crime

**char·i·ot** /ˈtʃæriət/ *n* [C] a vehicle with two wheels pulled by a horse, used in ancient times in battles and races

**char·i·o·teer** /ˌtʃæriəˈtɪə‖-ˈtɪr/ *n* [C] the driver of a chariot

**cha·ris·ma** /kəˈrɪzmə/ *n* [U] a powerful attractive personal quality that has a strong influence over other people and makes them admire you: *Few Presidents have had the charisma of Kennedy.*

**charismatic** /ˌkærɪ̣zˈmætɪk◂/ *adj* **1** able to attract and influence other people because of a powerful personal quality you have: *Martin Luther King was a very charismatic speaker.* **2 charismatic church/movement** groups of Christians who believe that God can give them special powers, for example the power to cure illness

**char·i·ta·ble** /ˈtʃærɪ̣təbəl/ *adj* **1** kind and sympathetic in the way you judge people: *Let's be charitable and say he didn't know the car was stolen.* —opposite UNCHARITABLE **2** concerned with giving help to the poor: *a charitable institution* —**charitably** *adv*

**char·i·ty** /ˈtʃærɪ̣ti/ *n* **1** [U] money or gifts given to help people who are poor, sick etc: *All the money raised by the concert will go to charity.* | *refugees living on charity* **2** [C] an organization that collects money or goods in order to help people who are poor, sick etc: *Several charities sent aid to the flood victims.* | **charity event/walk/concert etc** (=an event organized to collect money for a charity) **3** [U] a kind sympathetic attitude you have when judging or criticizing someone: **show charity** *The newspaper stories reporting his suicide showed little charity.* **4 charity begins at home** you should help your own family, country etc before you help other people S2 W3

**charity shop** /ˈ··· ˌ·/ *n* [C] *BrE* a shop that sells things given by people in order to collect money for a charity

**char·la·dy** /ˈtʃɑːˌleɪdi‖ˈtʃɑːr-/ *n* [C] *BrE old-fashioned* a CHARWOMAN

**char·la·tan** /ˈʃɑːlətən‖ˈʃɑːr-/ *n* [C] someone who pretends to have special skills or knowledge: *The man's a complete charlatan, only in it for the money.*

**Charles·ton** /ˈtʃɑːlstən‖ˈtʃɑːrl-/ *n* **the Charleston** a quick dance popular in the 1920s

**char·ley horse** /ˌtʃɑːli ˈhɔːs‖ˌtʃɑːrli ˈhɔːrs/ *n* [C singular] *AmE informal* a pain in a large muscle, for example in your leg, caused by the muscle becoming tight; CRAMP[1] (1)

**char·lie** /ˈtʃɑːli‖ˈtʃɑːr-/ *n* [C] *BrE spoken* a stupid person: **feel a right/proper charlie** (=feel very stupid)

**charm¹** /tʃɑːm‖tʃɑːrm/ *n* **1** [C,U] a pleasant quality someone or something has that makes people like them, feel attracted to them, or be easily influenced by them: *Dick still has a certain boyish charm.* | *the charms of rural life* | **turn on the charm** (=use your charm) *Wait till Grace turns on the charm, you won't be able to resist.* **2** a piece of magic which involves saying special words; SPELL[2] (1) **3** a very small object worn on a chain or BRACELET that people think will bring them good luck: *a small gold horseshoe worn as a lucky charm.* **4 work like a charm** to work perfectly or immediately: *I don't know what you sprayed on the roses, but it worked like a charm.*

**charm²** *v* [T] **1** to attract someone and make them like you, especially so that you can easily influence them: *Collette was charmed by the stranger's elegant manners and rugged good looks.* **2** to gain power over someone or something by using magic **3 have/lead a charmed life** to be lucky all the time, so that although you are often in dangerous situations nothing ever harms you —**charmed** *adj*

**charm·er** /ˈtʃɑːmə‖ˈtʃɑːrmər/ *n* [C] someone who uses their charm to please or influence people: *Even at ten years old, he was a real charmer.* —see also SNAKE CHARMER

**charm·ing** /ˈtʃɑːmɪŋ‖ˈtʃɑːr-/ *adj* very pleasing or attractive; nice: *What a charming house!|Harry can be charming when he wants.* —**charmingly** *adv*

**charm school** /ˈ· ·/ *n* [C] *especially AmE* a school where young women were sometimes sent in the past to learn how to behave politely and gracefully

**char·nel house** /ˈtʃɑːnl haʊs‖ˈtʃɑːr-/ *n* [C] *literary* a place where the bodies and bones of dead people are stored

**charred** /tʃɑːd‖tʃɑːrd/ *adj* burnt black: *the charred remains of a corpse*

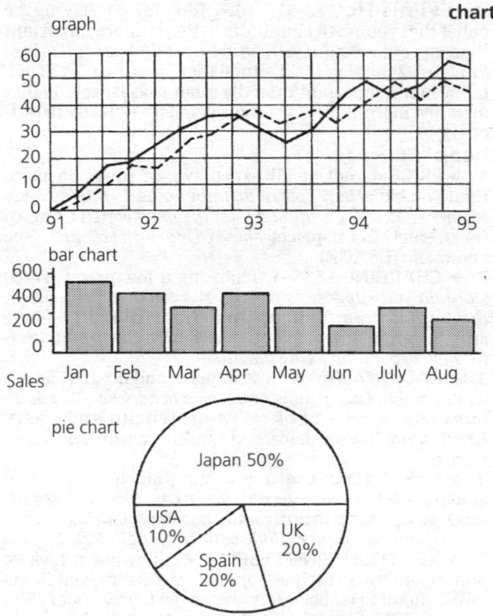


3 3 **chart¹** /tʃɑːt‖tʃɑːrt/ *n* [C] **1** information that is clearly arranged in the form of a simple picture, sets of figures, GRAPH etc, or a piece of paper with this information on it: *a flow chart|a weather chart* **2** a detailed map, especially of an area of the sea **3 the charts** a list, which comes out weekly, of the most popular records: **top the charts** *Madonna's song topped the charts for over ten weeks.* —see also BAR CHART, PIE CHART, FLOW CHART

**chart²** *v* [T] **1** to record information about a situation or set of events over a period of time in order to see how it changes or develops: *a study charting the steady progress of women in the 19th century* **2** to make a map of an area of land or sea, or draw lines on a map to show where you have travelled —see also UNCHARTED

3 **char·ter¹** /ˈtʃɑːtə‖ˈtʃɑːrtər/ *n* **1** [C] a statement of the principles, duties, and purposes of an organization: *freedoms embodied in the UN charter* **2** [singular] *BrE informal* a law or official decision that seems to give someone the right to do something most people consider morally wrong: *Proposals to cut customs staff amount to little more than a drug-smuggler's charter.* **3** [C] a signed statement from a government or ruler which allows a town, organization, or university to officially exist and have special rights **4** [U] the practice of paying money to a company to use their boats, aircraft, etc: *boats available for charter*

**charter²** *v* [T] **1** to pay for the use of a plane, boat, train etc: *a chartered plane* **2** to say officially that a town, organization, or university officially exists and has special rights —see HIRE¹ (1)

**chartered ac·coun·tant** /ˌ·· ·ˈ··/ *n* [C] *BrE* an ACCOUNTANT who has successfully completed special examinations; CPA *AmE*

**charter flight** /ˈ·· ·/ *n* [C] a low cost journey in a plane on which all the places have been paid for in advance by travel companies for their customers —compare **scheduled flight** (SCHEDULE²)

**charter mem·ber** /ˌ·· ˈ··/ *n* [C] *AmE* an original member of a club or organization; FOUNDER MEMBER *BrE*

**char·treuse** /ʃɑːˈtrɜːz‖ʃɑːrˈtruːz/ *n* [U] **1** a strong green or yellow alcoholic drink **2** a bright green colour

**chart-top·ping** /ˈ· ˌ··/ *adj* **chart-topping record/group/hit etc** a record, group etc that has sold the most records in a particular week

**char·wom·an** /ˈtʃɑːˌwʊmən‖ˈtʃɑːr-/ *n* [C] *BrE old-fashioned* a woman who works as a cleaner, especially in someone's house

**char·y** /ˈtʃeəri‖ˈtʃeri/ *adj* **be chary of doing sth** to be unwilling to risk doing something: *Many census authorities have been chary of asking for information on sensitive subjects such as ethnic background.*

**chase¹** /tʃeɪs/ *v* S 3

**1 ▶FOLLOW◀** [I,T] to quickly follow someone or something in order to catch them: *Outside in the yard, kids were yelling and chasing each other.*|**chase sb along/down/up etc** *The dog spotted a cat and chased it up a nearby tree.*|**chase sb away/off** (=chase someone in order to make them leave) *Harry chased the boys off with a stick.*|**[+ after]** *A favorite game was to chase after a passing farm cart and try to grab its tailboard.*

**2 ▶HURRY◀** [I always + adv/prep] *especially BrE* to rush or hurry somewhere: **around/up/down etc** *Mum's been chasing round the shops all day.*

**3 ▶TRY TO GET STH◀** [I + **after**, T] to use a lot of time and effort trying to get something such as work or money: *The solicitor's doing everything she can to chase the contract.*

**4 ▶MAN/WOMAN◀** [T] to try hard to make someone notice you and pay attention to you, because you want to have a sexual relationship with them: *It was embarrassing – Louise spent the entire party chasing me.*

**5 ▶METAL◀** [T] *technical* to decorate metal with a special tool: *chased silver*

**6 chase the dragon** *slang* to smoke the drug HEROIN

**chase** sb/sth ↔ **up** *phr v* [T] **1** to remind someone to do something they promised to do for you: *I had to chase Dick up to get those reports I asked for last week.* **2** to try to make something happen or arrive more quickly, because it has been taking too long: *Can you chase up those photos for me by tomorrow?*

**chase²** *n* **1** [C] the act of following someone or something quickly in order to catch them: *The movie began with a dramatic car chase.* **2 give chase** *literary* to chase someone or something: *The hounds gave chase across the fields.* —see also PAPER CHASE, WILD-GOOSE CHASE

**chas·er** /ˈtʃeɪsə‖-ər/ *n* [C] a weaker alcoholic drink which is drunk after a strong one, or a stronger alcoholic drink which is drunk after a weak one: *a pint of bitter and a whisky chaser*

**chas·m** /ˈkæzəm/ *n* **1** [C] a very deep space between two high areas of rock, especially one that is dangerous: *a rope bridge across the chasm* **2** [singular] a big difference between the opinions, experience, ways of life, etc of different groups of people, especially when this means they cannot understand each other: *the chasm between rich and poor*

**chas·sis** /ˈʃæsi/ *n plural* **chassis** /ˈʃæsiːz/ [C] **1** the frame on which the body, engine, wheels etc of a vehicle are built **2** the landing equipment of a plane

**chaste** /tʃeɪst/ *adj* **1** *old-fashioned* having very high personal moral standards in your sexual behaviour: *Wives are expected to remain chaste, whatever their* *husbands' behaviour.* —compare CELIBATE —see also CHASTITY **2** simple and plain in style —**chastely** *adv*

**chas·ten** /ˈtʃeɪsən/ *v* [T usually passive] to make someone realize that their behaviour is wrong or mistaken: *Party workers have returned to their home towns, chastened by their overwhelming defeat.*

**chas·tise** /tʃæˈstaɪz/ *v* [T] **1** *formal* to criticize someone severely: *He should be chastised for his insolence.* **2** *old-fashioned* to physically punish someone —**chastisement** *n* [C,U]

**chas·ti·ty** /ˈtʃæstɪ̩ti/ *n* [U] the principle or way of behaving in which you do not behave in a way that is sexually immoral, especially for religious reasons

**chastity belt** /ˈ··· ˌ·/ *n* [C] a special belt with a lock, used in former times to prevent women from having sex

S2 **chat**[1] /tʃæt/ *n* [C,U] *especially BrE* an informal friendly conversation: *Drop in for a chat if you have an hour to spare this evening.* | **have a chat** *We had a chat about the old days.* —see also BACKCHAT

**chat**[2] **chatted, chatting** *v* [I] *especially BrE* also **chat away** to talk in a friendly informal way, especially about things that are not important: *Danny and Paul chatted away like old friends.* | [+ **about**] *We sat in the café for hours chatting about our experiences.* | [+ **with/to**] *Helen chatted with most of the guests at the party.*

**chat** sb↔ **up** *phr v* [T] *BrE* to talk to someone in a way that shows you are sexually attracted to them: *We found Doug in the bar trying to chat up a waitress.*

**chat·eau** /ˈʃætəʊ‖ʃæˈtoʊ/ *n plural* **chateaux** /-təʊz‖-ˈtoʊz/ or **chateaus** [C] a castle or large country house in France

**chat·e·laine** /ˈʃætl-eɪn/ *n* [C] **1** *formal* the female owner, or wife of the owner, of a large country house or castle in France **2** a short thin chain fastened to a woman's belt, used in the past for carrying keys

**chat line** /ˈ· ·/ *n* [C] *BrE* a telephone service that people call to talk to other people who have called the same service

**chat show** /ˈ· ·/ *n* [C] *BrE* a television or radio show on which people are asked questions and talk about themselves; TALK SHOW *AmE*

**chat show host** /ˈ· · ˌ·/ *n BrE* the person who introduces people and asks questions on a chat show

**chat·tel** /ˈtʃætl/ *n* [C] *law old-fashioned* something that belongs to you: *In those days women and children were considered chattels.* —see also GOODS AND CHATTELS

**chat·ter**[1] /ˈtʃætə‖-ər/ *v* [I] **1** to talk quickly in a friendly way without stopping, especially about things that are not serious or important: [+ **to**] *You've been chattering to Tom on the phone for ages.* **2** if birds or monkeys chatter, they make short high sounds **3** if your teeth are chattering, you are so cold or frightened your teeth are knocking together and you cannot stop them **4 the chattering classes** *BrE* those people in society who are keen to discuss and have opinions about important or fashionable ideas, subjects, and events

**chatter**[2] *n* [U] **1** a friendly informal conversation about something unimportant **2** a series of short high sounds made by some birds or monkeys **3** a hard quick repeated sound made by your teeth knocking together or by machines: *the chatter of the printer*

**chat·ter·box** /ˈtʃætəbɒks‖-tərbɑːks/ *n* [C] *informal* someone, especially a child, who talks too much

**chat·ty** /ˈtʃæti/ *adj especially BrE* **1** liking to talk a lot in a friendly way: *Lorna's normally very quiet, but she was quite chatty yesterday.* **2** a piece of writing that is chatty has a friendly informal style: *a chatty letter*

**chat-up line** /ˈ· · ˌ·/ [C] *n BrE* something that someone says in order to start a conversation with someone they find sexually attractive; LINE[1] (23) *AmE*

**chauf·feur**[1] /ˈʃəʊfə, ʃəʊˈfɜː‖ˈʃoʊfər, ʃoʊˈfɜːr/ *n* [C] someone whose job is to drive a car for someone else

**chauffeur**[2] *v* [T] **1** to drive a car for someone as your job **2** also **chauffeur around** to drive someone in your car, especially when you do not want to: *I seem to spend most of Saturday chauffeuring the kids around.*

**chauf·feuse** /ʃəʊˈfɜːz‖ʃoʊ-/ *n* [C] a woman whose job is to drive a car for someone else

**chau·vin·is·m** /ˈʃəʊvɪ̩nɪzəm‖ˈʃoʊ-/ *n* [U] **1** a strong belief that your country is better or more important than any other: *cultural chauvinism* **2** the attitude that your own sex is better, more intelligent, or more important than the other sex, especially the male sex: **male chauvinism** *The club is a bastion of male chauvinism.*

**chau·vin·ist** /ˈʃəʊvɪ̩nɪ̩st‖ˈʃoʊ-/ *n* [C] **1** someone, especially a man, who believes that their own sex is better and more important than the other sex: **male chauvinist (pig)** *My boss is a male chauvinist who thinks no woman could do his job.* **2** someone who believes that their own country is better or more important than any other country —**chauvinist** *adj*

**chau·vi·nis·tic** /ˌʃəʊvɪ̩ˈnɪstɪk◂‖ˌʃoʊ-/ *adj* **1** having the belief that your own country is better or more important than any other country: *a chauvinistic dislike of all things foreign* **2** having the attitude that your own sex is better or more important than the other sex, especially that men are more important than women —**chauvinistically** /-kli/ *adv*

**cheap**[1] /tʃiːp/ *adj* S W

**1** ▶ **PRICE** ◀ not at all expensive, or lower in price than you expected: *You're just not going to find a cheap leather coat.* | *the cheapest TV on the market* | **dirt cheap** (=extremely low in price) *These CDs are dirt cheap.* —see ECONOMIC (USAGE)

**2** ▶ **CHARGING LESS** ◀ charging a low price: *Which store do you suppose is cheaper?* | *As taxi companies go, they're quite cheap.* | **cheap and cheerful** *BrE* (=simple and charging a low price, but pleasant) *a cheap and cheerful bistro, popular with students*

**3** ▶ **BAD QUALITY** ◀ low in price and quality, or not worth much: *Cheap wine gives me a headache.* | *You don't think these earrings look too cheap?* | **cheap and nasty** *BrE* (=very low in price and quality) *cheap and nasty t-shirts*

**4** ▶ **CHEAP TO USE** ◀ not costing much to use or to employ: *I'll have to have a cheaper car, this one uses too much gas.* | **cheap labour** *multinational clothing companies exploiting cheap child labour in Bangladesh*

**5** ▶ **NOT DESERVING RESPECT** ◀ showing a lack of honesty, moral principles, or sincere feelings, and therefore difficult to respect: *It makes me feel cheap, but I can't face seeing Mother.* | **(just) some cheap sth** *He acts like I'm just some cheap little bimbo.* | *This is not some cheap pastime! This is art!* | **cheap thrill** (=excitement that you do not have to work hard for or pay for) *Glue-sniffing is a cheap thrill, and a trend among some schoolchildren.* | **cheap remark/joke etc** (=one that attacks people who cannot defend themselves)

**6** ▶ **NOT GENEROUS** ◀ *AmE* not liking to spend money; MEAN[2] (2) *BrE*: *Frank's so cheap that he re-uses Christmas wrapping paper.*

**7 on the cheap** spending less money than is needed to do something properly: *I'm not surprised the roof is leaking – the landlord does everything on the cheap.*

**8 cheap at the price/at any price** of such high value, or so good or useful, that the cost is not important

**9 life is cheap** used to say that it is not important if people die: *Everyone carried a gun or knife during the war, and life was cheap.* —**cheaply** *adv*: *a cheaply furnished room* —**cheapness** *n* [U]

**USAGE NOTE: CHEAP**

WORD CHOICE: **cheap, low-priced, inexpensive, not cost a lot, reasonable, good value, a good buy, a bargain, a steal, a snip, low**

Saying that something is **cheap** often suggests it is also bad in quality: *Buying cheap shoes is not a good idea in the long run.* | *That necklace looks really cheap and nasty.* **Low-priced** and **inexpensive** do not suggest this, but are not so common in

> informal spoken English: *The university needs more low-priced accommodation.* In everyday English people often just say that something **doesn't cost a lot/much**.
>
> If you want to say that something is good and does not cost as much as it might, you say it is **reasonable**, **good value**, or **a good buy**: *$200 for a leather jacket seems pretty reasonable to me.*
>
> If something is **a bargain** it cost very much less than you expected to pay. In informal conversation people often say instead that something is **a steal** (American English) or **a snip** (British English).
>
> The cost of something, a bill, someone's salary etc can be **low** or **reasonable** but not **cheap**.

**cheap**[2] *adv* at a low price: *Sharon has some really nice furniture she picked up cheap in a sale.* | *They're selling linen off cheap in Lewis's.* | **sth does not come cheap** (=something is expensive) *Houses like that don't come cheap.* | **(be) going cheap** (=selling for a lower price than usual) *Ask if they've got any flights going cheap.*

**cheap·en** /ˈtʃiːpən/ *v* **1** [T] to make something or someone seem to have lower moral standards than they had before: **cheapen yourself by doing sth** *Don't cheapen yourself by accepting their bribe.* **2** [I,T] to become or make something become lower in price or value: *The dollar's increase in value has cheapened imports.*

**cheap·skate** /ˈtʃiːpskeɪt/ *n* [C] *informal* someone who does not like spending money and does not care if they behave in an unreasonable way to avoid spending it: *The cheapskate didn't even offer to pay for the cab.*

**cheat**[1] /tʃiːt/ *v* **1** [I] to behave in a dishonest way in order to win or to get an advantage, especially in a competition, game, or examination: *You're doing it again, you're trying to cheat!* | [+ **at**] *Jack always cheats at cards.* | **that's cheating** *Hey, don't look at the next page – that's cheating!* **2** [T] to trick or deceive someone who trusts you: *Don't just jump to conclusions that you've been deliberately cheated.* | **cheat sb (out) of sth** *Guy figures he was cheated out of that job by office politics.* **3 feel cheated** to feel that you have been treated wrongly or unfairly and have not got what you deserve: *I feel cheated really. I was meant to go to France and now it's only Leeds.* **4 cheat death/fate etc** to manage to avoid death etc even though it seemed that you would not be able to

**cheat on** sb *phr v* [T] to be unfaithful to your husband, wife, or sexual partner by secretly having sex with someone else: *I think Winnie's been cheating on me, but I can't prove it.*

**cheat**[2] *n* [C] **1** someone who is dishonest and cheats: *I saw you look at that card, you cheat!* **2 a cheat** something that is dishonest or unfair: *That's a cheat! The box is half empty!*

1 **check**[1] /tʃek/ *v*
2 **1 ▶ FIND OUT ◀** [I,T] to do something in order to find out whether something that you think is correct, true, or safe really is correct, true, or safe: *"Are all the windows shut?" "I'll just go and check."* | **check sth** *I'll check my calendar and get back to you.* | [+ **that**] *They're entitled to check that the will is valid, of course.* | [+ **whether/how/who etc**] *Let me just check whether the potatoes are cooked.* | [+ **for**] *Have these cables been checked for faults?* | **check sth against/with sth** (=compare something with something else to see whether they are the same) *Upon delivery, the items are checked against the original order.* | **double check** (=look at something twice to be sure about something) *Double check all the spellings, especially of people's names.*
**2 ▶ ASK SB ◀** [I] to ask someone for permission to do something or ask whether something is correct: *I'm not authorized to give you a refund – I'll have to check first.* | [+ **that**] *We'd better check that these are the right pills.* | [+ **whether/how/who etc**] *Let's stop and check whether this is the right road.* | **check with sb** *It's wise to check with your doctor before going on a diet.*
**3 ▶ NOT DO STH ◀** [T] to suddenly stop yourself from saying or doing something because you realize it would be better not to: *Susan quickly turned aside, checking an urge to laugh out loud.* | **check yourself** *"You shouldn't have..." he checked himself, trying to stay calm.*
**4 ▶ STOP STH ◀** [T] to stop something bad from getting worse or continuing to happen etc: *Speed bumps will be installed to check the neighborhood traffic.*
**5 ▶ MAKE A MARK ◀** [T] *AmE* to make a mark (✓) next to an answer, something on a list etc to show that it is correct or that you have dealt with it; TICK[2] (2) *BrE*
**6 ▶ BAGS/CASES ETC ◀** [T] *AmE* to leave your bags etc at an official place so they can be put on a plane or a train, or to take someone's bags in order to do this: *Any luggage over 5 kilos must be checked.*

**check in** *phr v* **1** [I, T **check** sb **in**] to go to the desk at a hotel or airport and report that you have arrived: *You need to check in one hour before the flight.* | **check in at** *Let's check in at the hotel before we get something to eat.* —see also CHECK-IN **2** [T **check** sth ↔ **in**] *AmE* to take a book you have borrowed back to a library

**check** sth ↔ **off** *phr v* [T] to write a mark next to something on a list when you have dealt with it or made sure that it is correct: *Check off the names as people arrive.*

**check out** *phr v*
**1 ▶ MAKE SURE ◀ a)** [T **check** sth ↔ **out**] to make sure that something is actually true, correct, or acceptable; INVESTIGATE: *Why don't I check out the bar and see if it's OK?* | **check it out (with)** *Check it out with Mark if you don't believe me.* **b)** [I] if information checks out, it is proven to be true, correct, or acceptable: *If your credit record checks out, they give you a $1000 limit right away.*
**2 ▶ LOOK AT SB/STH ◀** [T **check** sb/sth ↔ **out**] to look at someone or something because they are interesting or attractive: *Hey, check this out!*
**3 ▶ GET INFORMATION ◀** [T **check** sb ↔ **out**] *informal* to get information about someone, especially to find out if they are suitable for something: *It's routine, they check members out before letting them join.*
**4 ▶ TEST STH ◀** [T **check** sth ↔ **out**] to test something to find out if it works, how it works, whether it is suitable for what you want etc: *In here, they stripped down the aircraft and checked them out for airworthiness.*
**5 ▶ HOTEL ◀** [I] to leave a hotel after paying the bill: *We checked out at noon.*
**6 ▶ BOOKS ◀** [T **check** sth ↔ **out**] *AmE* to borrow books from a library: *The library allows you to check out six books at a time.* —see also CHECKOUT

**check** sth ↔ **over** *phr v* [T] **1** to look closely at something to make sure it is correct or acceptable: *Will you check over my essay before I hand it in?* **2** to examine someone to make sure they are healthy: *They've checked her over and given her all these tests and she's fine.*

**check up on** sb *phr v* [T] to try and make sure that someone is doing what they said they would do or what you want them to do, especially secretly: *Are you trying to check up on me, or what?*

**check on** sb *phr v* [T] to make sure that someone is safe, has everything they need, etc: *Honey, can you go upstairs and check on the kids?*

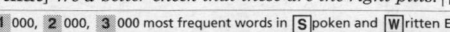

**check**[2] *n* S1
**1 ▶ ON SAFETY/CORRECTNESS/TRUTH ETC ◀** [C] W3
an act of finding out if something is safe, correct, true, or in the condition it should be: *the airport's routine security checks* | [+ **on**] *the need for tighter checks on arms sales* | **have a check** *Have a check in your bag first and see if it's there.* | **eye/blood pressure/dental etc check** (=done to make sure you are healthy) | **carry out a check (on)** *We will carry out a check on options available to you.* | **spot check** (=a quick check of one thing among a group of things, that you do without warning) *Customs officers will do spot checks for drugs and other illegal goods.*
**2 keep a check (on sb/sth)** to watch or listen to something or someone regularly or continuously, in order to

control something or gather information: *Keep a check on your speed.* | *Their phones had even been tapped to keep a check on their activities.*
**3 run/do a check** to organize an examination of something or someone in order to find out information: **run a check on sb** *Troy's staying late to run some background checks on suspects.* | **do a check for sth** *I'd better do a check for gas leaks.*
**4 ▶ A CONTROL ON STH ◀** something that controls something else and stops it from getting worse, continuing to happen etc: *Higher interest rates will act as a check on public spending.* | **keep/hold sb/sth in check** (=keep someone or something under control) *It was obvious she was barely holding her temper in check.*

**5 ▶ PATTERN ◀** [C,U] a pattern of squares, especially on cloth: *I don't like checks or stripes, just plain colors.* | **a check shirt/jacket etc** (=made with this cloth) —see also CHECKED —see picture on page 839
**6 ▶ FROM YOUR BANK ◀** [C] *AmE* one of a set of printed pieces of paper that you can sign and use instead of money to pay for things; CHEQUE *BrE* [+ **for**] *a check for $30* | **by check** *Is it okay to pay by check?*
**7 ▶ IN A RESTAURANT ◀** [C] *AmE, ScotE* a list that you are given in a restaurant showing what you have eaten and how much you must pay; BILL[1] (1b) —see picture on page 838
**8 ▶ FOR YOUR COAT/BAG ◀** *AmE* **a) coat check/hat check** a place in a restaurant, theatre etc where you can leave your coat, bag etc to be guarded until you go home **b)** [C] a ticket that you are given so you can claim your things from this place
**9 ▶ MARK ◀** [C] *AmE* a mark (✓) that you put next to an answer to show that it is correct or next to something on a list to show that you have dealt with it; TICK[1] (1) *BrE*
**10 ▶ CHESS ◀** [U] the position of the KING (=most important piece) in CHESS when it can be directly attacked by the opponent's pieces

**check·book** /ˈtʃekbʊk/ *n* [C] *AmE* a small book of checks that your bank gives you; CHEQUEBOOK *BrE*

**checked** /tʃekt/ *adj* checked cloth has a regular pattern of differently coloured squares: *a checked blouse*

**check·er** /ˈtʃekə‖-ər/ *n* **1** [C] *AmE* someone who works at the CHECKOUT in a SUPERMARKET **2 checkers** [U] a game that two people play with 12 round pieces each, in which the purpose is to take the other player's pieces by jumping over them with your pieces; draughts (DRAUGHT[1] (2)) *BrE* —see also CHINESE CHEQUERS

**check·er·board** /ˈtʃekəbɔːd‖-kərbɔːrd/ *n* [C] *AmE* a board used to play checkers, with 32 white squares and 32 black squares; DRAUGHTBOARD *BrE*

**check·ered** also **chequered** *BrE* /ˈtʃekəd‖-ərd/ *adj* **1** having a pattern made up of squares of two different colours: *a checkered tablecloth* | *checkered tiles in the bathroom* **2 have a checkered history/past/career etc** to have had periods of failure as well as successful times in your past: *The company has a pretty checkered history. I'd think carefully before investing.*

**checkered flag** also **chequered flag** *BrE* /ˌ·· ˈ·/ *n* [C] a flag covered with black and white squares that is waved at the beginning and end of a motor race

**check-in** /ˈ· ·/ *n* **1** [singular] a place where you report your arrival, especially at an airport: *Make sure you're at the check-in by 5.30.* | **check-in desk** *BrE*, **check-in counter** *AmE*: *Go to the check-in desk in zone C.* **2** [U] the process of reporting your arrival, especially at an airport: *The whole check-in process seems to take forever.* —see also **check in** (CHECK[1])

**checking ac·count** /ˈ·· ·ˌ·/ *n* [C] *AmE* a bank account that you can take money out of at any time; CURRENT ACCOUNT *BrE* —compare DEPOSIT ACCOUNT

**check·list** /ˈtʃekˌlɪst/ *n* [C] a list that helps you by reminding you of the things you need to do for a particular job or activity: *The guide contains a handy checklist of points to look for when buying a car.*

**check·mate** /ˈtʃekmeɪt/ *n* [C,U] the position of the KING (=most important piece) in CHESS at the end of the game, when it is being directly attacked and cannot escape

**check·out** /ˈtʃek-aʊt/ *n* **1** [C] the place in a SUPERMARKET where you pay for the goods you have collected: *Why can't they have more checkouts open?* **2** [C,U] the time by which you must leave a hotel room: *Checkout is at noon.* —see also **check out** (CHECK[1])

**check·point** /ˈtʃekpɔɪnt/ *n* [C] a place, especially on a border, where an official person examines vehicles or people: *Vehicles were stopped at the checkpoint.*

**check·room** /ˈtʃek-rʊm, -ruːm/ *n* [C] *AmE* a place in a restaurant, theatre etc where you can leave your coat, bags etc to be guarded; CLOAKROOM (1) *BrE*

**check stub** /ˈ· ·/ *n* [C] the American spelling of CHEQUE STUB

**check·up, check-up** /ˈtʃek-ʌp/ *n* [C] a general medical examination that a doctor or DENTIST gives you to make sure you are healthy

**ched·dar** /ˈtʃedə‖-ər/ *n* [U] a hard, smooth, usually yellow or orange cheese

**cheek[1]** /tʃiːk/ *n* **1** [C] the soft round area of flesh on each side of your face below your eye: *Would you let him kiss you on the cheek?* | *the smooth pink cheeks of a baby* —see picture at HEAD[1] **2** [singular, U] *BrE* disrespectful or rude behaviour, especially towards someone in a position of authority: *I've had enough of that boy's cheek.* | **have the cheek to do sth** *Billy had the cheek to say it was boring round here, right in front of Nan.* | **have a cheek** *They've got a cheek, charging her for a call when it's her own phone!* **3 what a cheek!** *BrE spoken* used to show surprise that someone has behaved rudely or without enough respect **4 cheek by jowl** if people live or work cheek by jowl they live or work very close together: *Families were living cheek by jowl in impossible conditions.* **5 cheek to cheek** if two people dance cheek to cheek, they dance very close to each other in a romantic way **6 turn the other cheek** to deliberately avoid reacting in an angry or violent way when someone has hurt or upset you **7** [C] *informal* one of the two soft fleshy parts of your bottom; BUTTOCK **8 red-cheeked/hollow-cheeked/rosy-cheeked etc** having red, hollow etc cheeks: *He was a merry-faced, ruddy-cheeked little man.* —see also **tongue in cheek** (TONGUE (3)) W

**cheek[2]** *v* [T] *BrE* to speak rudely or disrespectfully to someone, especially to someone older such as your teacher or parents; SASS *AmE*: *Don't you cheek your mother like that! Go and apologise!*

**cheek·bone** /ˈtʃiːkbəʊn‖-boʊn/ *n* [C usually plural] one of the two bones above your cheeks, just below your eyes

**cheek·y** /ˈtʃiːki/ *adj BrE* **1** rude or disrespectful, especially towards someone older such as a teacher or parent: *Don't be so cheeky!* | *The cheeky devil!* | **cheeky monkey** *Cheeky monkey! Get your hand out of the biscuit tin.* **2** *approving* disrespectful or not proper, but in a way that is amusing rather than rude: *a scruffy little boy with a cheeky grin* | *a rather cheeky mini skirt* —**cheekily** *adv* —**cheekiness** *n* [U] —see also SASSY

**cheep** /tʃiːp/ *v* [I] if a young bird cheeps, it makes a weak, high noise: *baby birds cheeping for food* —**cheep** *n*

**cheer[1]** /tʃɪə‖tʃɪr/ *n* [C] **1** a shout of happiness, praise, approval, or encouragement: **a cheer rises/goes up** *A deafening cheer rose from the crowd as the band walked onto the stage.* | **give a cheer** *Everyone gave a cheer when Gilmore crawled out of the wreck, unhurt.* **2 three cheers for sb!** used to tell a group of people to shout three times as a way of showing support, happiness, thanks etc: *Three cheers for the birthday girl!* **3** [U] *formal or literary* a feeling of happiness and confidence: *Christmas cheer* —see also CHEERS **4** [C] a special CHANT (=kind of poem) that the crowds at a US sports game shout in order to encourage their team to win

**cheer[2]** *v* **1** [I,T] to shout as a way of showing happiness, praise, approval, or support of someone or something: *Everybody cheered when the firemen arrived.* | **cheer sb** *It says here that thousands packed the city centre* *to cheer her.* **2** [T usually passive] to make someone feel more hopeful when they are worried: *cheering news | Kerrie was visibly cheered when we finally saw a light in the distance.*

**cheer up** *phr v* **1** [I,T] to become less sad, or to make someone feel less sad: *He'll cheer up if you get him a beer.* | **cheer sb ↔ up** *I'm taking Angie out to cheer her up.* **2 cheer up!** *spoken* used to tell someone not to be so sad: *"Cheer up, Mandy!" "Oh, I'm all right, really."* **3 cheering up** the act of trying to make someone feel less sad: **need/want cheering up** *Craig needs cheering up. What should we do? | All I want is a little cheering up.*

**cheer** sb/sth ↔ **on** *phr v* [T] to shout encouragement at a person or team to help them do well in a race or competition: *They were behind by two touchdowns and she was still cheering them on!*

**cheer·er** /ˈtʃɪərə‖ˈtʃɪrər/ *n* [C] *AmE* someone who shouts encouragement at a person or team to help them do well in a race or competition: *the loudest cheerer in the grandstand*

**cheer·ful** /ˈtʃɪəfəl‖ˈtʃɪr-/ *adj* **1** behaving in a way that shows you are happy, for example by smiling or being very friendly: *Despite feeling ill, she managed to keep cheerful.* | **a cheerful grin/smile/face** (=showing that you are happy) *Nancy gave me a cheerful grin and waved me over.* **2** something that is cheerful makes you feel happy because it is so bright or pleasant: *I must say I like a cheerful kitchen. | a cheerful letter full of good news* **3** tending to be happy most of the time: *Basically I'm a cheerful person.* **4** [only before noun] a cheerful attitude shows that you are willing to do whatever is necessary in a happy way: *cheerful enthusiasm for the job* —see also **cheap and cheerful** (CHEAP[1] (2)), **—cheerfully** *adv*: *"Morning!" she called cheerfully.* **—cheerfulness** *n* [U]

S3 **cheer·i·o** /ˌtʃɪəriˈəʊ‖ˌtʃɪriˈoʊ/ *interjection BrE informal* goodbye

**cheer·lead·er** /ˈtʃɪəˌliːdə‖ˈtʃɪrˌliːdər/ *n* [C] a member of a team of young women who encourage a crowd to cheer at a US sports game by shouting special words and dancing: *cheerleaders practicing their routines*

**cheer·lead·ing** /ˈtʃɪəˌliːdɪŋ‖ˈtʃɪr-/ *n* [U] **1** the activity of being a cheerleader: *a cheerleading uniform* **2** *AmE* the act of loudly supporting an organization, idea etc and not being willing to listen to criticism of it

**cheer·less** /ˈtʃɪələs‖ˈtʃɪr-/ *adj* cheerless weather, places, or times make you feel sad, bored, or uncomfortable: *the dark, cheerless rooms upstairs | a grey and cheerless day* **—cheerlessly** *adv* **—cheerlessness** *n* [U]

**cheers** /tʃɪəz‖tʃɪrz/ *interjection* **1** used when you lift a glass of alcohol before you drink it, in order to say that you hope the people you are drinking with will be happy and have good health **2** *BrE informal* thank you **3** *BrE informal* goodbye

**cheer·y** /ˈtʃɪəri‖ˈtʃɪri/ *adj* cheerful, or making you feel happy: *a cheery greeting | Oh she's fine, as cheery as ever.* **—cheerily** *adv*

**cheese** /tʃiːz/ *n* [C,U] **1** a solid food made from milk, which is usually yellow or white in colour, and can be soft or hard: *half a pound of cheese | a cheese sandwich | a selection of English cheeses* | **cow's/goat's/sheep's cheese** (=from the milk of a cow etc) **2 say cheese** used to tell people to smile when you are going to take their photograph: *Come on everybody, say cheese!* —see also BIG CHEESE, **as different as chalk and cheese** (CHALK[1] (3))

**cheese·board** /ˈtʃiːzbɔːd‖-bɔːrd/ *n* [C] **1** a board used to cut cheese on **2** a board used for serving a variety of cheeses —see picture on page 838.

**cheese·bur·ger** /ˈtʃiːzbɜːgə‖-bɜːrgər/ *n* [C] a HAMBURGER cooked with a piece of cheese on top of the meat

**cheese·cake** /ˈtʃiːzkeɪk/ *n* **1** [C,U] a cake made from a mixture containing soft cheese **2** [U] *old-fashioned* photographs of pretty women with few clothes on —compare BEEFCAKE

**cheese·cloth** /ˈtʃiːzklɒθ‖-klɒːθ/ *n* [U] thin cotton cloth used for putting around some kinds of cheeses, and sometimes for making clothes

**cheesed off** /ˌtʃiːzd ˈɒf‖-ˈɒːf/ *adj BrE informal* bored and annoyed with something: *You sound cheesed off. What's the matter?*

**cheese-par·ing** /ˈ· ··/ *n* [U] *BrE* behaviour that shows you are unwilling to give or spend money **—cheeseparing** *adj*

**chee·tah** /ˈtʃiːtə/ *n* [C] a member of the cat family that has long legs and black spots on its fur, and can run extremely fast

**chef** /ʃef/ *n* [C] a skilled cook, especially the chief cook in a hotel or restaurant: *a pastry chef* —see picture on page 838

**chef d'oeu·vre** /ˌʃeɪ ˈdɜːvrə‖-ˈdɜːvrə, -ˈdɜːrv/ *n* [C] *French formal* the best piece of work by a painter, writer, etc; MASTERPIECE

**Chel·sea bun** /ˌtʃelsi ˈbʌn/ *n* [C] *BrE* a small, round, sweet cake with dried fruit in it

S3 W3 **chem·i·cal[1]** /ˈkemɪkəl/ *n* [C] a substance used in chemistry or produced by chemistry: *mixing chemicals in a test tube*

W3 **chemical[2]** *adj* connected with or used in chemistry, or made by a chemical process: *the chemical composition of bleach | the chemical industry | chemical engineering* **—chemically** /-kli/ *adv*: *Chemically, the two substances are very similar.*

**chemical re·ac·tion** /ˌ··· ·ˈ··/ *n* [C, U] a natural process in which the atoms of chemicals mix and arrange themselves differently to form new substances

**chemical war·fare** /ˌ··· ˈ··/ *n* [U] methods of fighting a war using chemical weapons —compare BIOLOGICAL WARFARE

**chemical weap·on** /ˌ··· ˈ··/ *n* [C] a poisonous substance, especially a gas, used as a weapon in war

**che·mise** /ʃəˈmiːz/ *n* [C] **1** a piece of women's underwear worn on the top half of her body **2** a simple dress that hangs straight from a woman's shoulders

S3 **chem·ist** /ˈkemɪst/ *n* [C] **1** a scientist who has a special knowledge in chemistry **2** *BrE* someone who is trained to prepare drugs and medicines, who works in a shop; DRUGGIST *AmE* —compare PHARMACIST

S2 **chem·is·try** /ˈkemɪstri/ *n* [U] the science that is concerned with studying the structure of substances and the way that they change —compare PHYSICS

**chemistry set** /ˈ··· ˌ·/ *n* [C] a box containing equipment for children to do simple chemistry at home

**chem·ist's** /ˈkemɪsts/ *n* [C] *BrE* a shop where medicines and TOILETRIES are sold; DRUGSTORE *AmE* —see also PHARMACY

**chem·o·ther·a·py** /ˌkiːməʊˈθerəpi, ˌke-‖-moʊ-/ *n* [U] the use of drugs to control and try to cure CANCER

**che·nille** /ʃəˈniːl/ *n* [U] twisted thread with a surface like a soft brush, or cloth made from this and used for decorations, curtains etc

S2 **cheque** /tʃek/ *n* [C] *BrE* one of a set of printed pieces of paper that you can sign and use instead of money to pay for things: [+ **for**] *a cheque for £200*| **write a cheque** *How much should I write the cheque for?*| **by cheque** (=with a cheque) *Can I pay by cheque?*| **cash a cheque** (=get cash by writing a cheque); CHECK *AmE* —see also DRAFT[1] (3), BLANK CHEQUE, TRAVELLERS CHEQUE

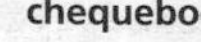


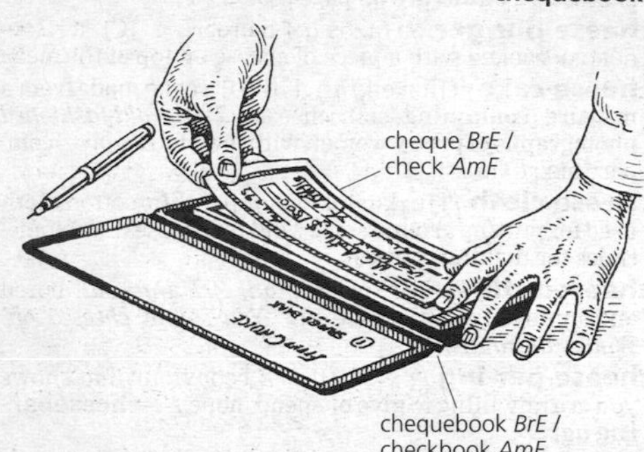


**cheque·book** /ˈtʃekbʊk/ *n* [C] *BrE* a small book of cheques that your bank gives you; CHECKBOOK *AmE*

**chequebook jour·nal·is·m** /ˌ·· ˈ····/ *n* [U] *BrE* low quality writing in newspapers that pay large amounts of money for details of famous people's private lives

**cheque card** /ˈ· ·/ also **cheque guarantee card** /ˌ·····ˈ· ·/ *n* [C] *BrE* a card given to you by your bank that you must show when you write a cheque, which promises that the bank will pay out the money written on the cheque —compare CASH CARD, CREDIT CARD, DEBIT CARD

**chequ·ered** /ˈtʃekəd‖-ərd/ *adj* a British spelling of CHECKERED

**chequered flag** /ˌ··ˈ·/ *n* [C] a British spelling of CHECKERED FLAG

**cheq·uers** /ˈtʃekəz‖-ərz/ *n* —see CHINESE CHEQUERS

**cheque stub** *BrE*, **check stub** *AmE* /ˈ· ·/ *n* [C] the part of a cheque that is left when you tear it out of a cheque book, used for recording the amount you have spent

**cher·ish** /ˈtʃerɪʃ/ *v* [T usually passive] **1** to love someone or something very much and take care of them well: *his most cherished possession* **2** to be very important to someone: **cherished hopes/dreams/ideas etc** *one of our cherished hopes, a community centre for the village*| *cherished memories*

**che·root** /ʃəˈruːt/ *n* [C] a CIGAR with both ends cut straight

S3 **cher·ry** /ˈtʃeri/ *n* **1** [C] a small red or black round fruit with a long thin stem: *a bunch of cherries*| *cherry tart* —see picture on page 413 **2 a)** [C] also **cherry tree** the tree on which this fruit grows **b)** [U] the wood of this tree, used for making furniture **3** a bright red colour **4 the cherry on the cake/on the top** something additional that you did not expect, that is pleasant to have —see also **another bite/a second bite at the cherry** (BITE[2] (9))

**cherry bomb** /ˈ·· ·/ *n* [C] *AmE* a large round red FIRECRACKER (=small loud explosive)

**cherry bran·dy** /ˌ·· ˈ··/ *n* [U] a sweet alcoholic drink that tastes of cherries

**cherry·pick** /ˈtʃeri pɪk/ *v* [I, T] to choose exactly the things or people you want, from a group

**cherry to·ma·to** /ˈ·· ·ˌ··/ *n plural* **cherry tomatoes** [C] a very small TOMATO

**cher·ub** /ˈtʃerəb/ *n* [C] **1** a picture or figure of a fat, pretty, usually male child with small wings, used as a decoration **2** *informal* a young pretty child who behaves very well **3** *spoken* used to address a young child in a friendly way: *Come to Mummy, my cherub!* **4** *plural* **cherubim** /ˈtʃerəbɪm/ *biblical* one of the ANGELS that guard the seat where God sits —**cherubic** /tʃəˈruːbɪk/ *adj*: *a smile of cherubic innocence*

**cher·vil** /ˈtʃɜːvɪl‖ˈtʃɜːr-/ *n* [U] a strong-smelling garden plant used as a HERB

**chess** /tʃes/ *n* [U] a game for two players, who move their playing pieces according to fixed rules across a board in an attempt to CHECKMATE (=trap) their opponent's KING (=most important piece)

**chess·board** /ˈtʃesbɔːd‖-bɔːrd/ *n* [C] a square board with 64 black and white squares, each square being next to a square of a different colour, on which chess is played —see picture at BOARD[1]

**chess·man** /ˈtʃesmæn/ also **chesspiece** /ˈtʃespiːs/ *n plural* **chessmen** /-men/ [C] any of the 16 black or 16 white playing pieces used in the game of chess

**chest** /tʃest/ *n* [C] **1** the front part of your body between your neck and your stomach: *a hairy chest*| *The doctor is going to listen your chest, Cindy.* —see also FLAT-CHESTED —see picture at BODY **2** a large, strong box that you use to store things in or to move your personal possessions from one place to another: *We keep the summer clothes in a chest in the attic.*| *a blanket chest* —see also CHEST OF DRAWERS, HOPE CHEST, MEDICINE CHEST, TEA CHEST, WAR CHEST **3 get something off your chest** to tell someone about something that has been worrying or annoying you for a long time, so that you feel better afterwards S W

**ches·ter·field** /ˈtʃestəfiːld‖-ər-/ *n* [C] a soft comfortable SOFA, usually covered with leather

**chest·nut**[1] /ˈtʃesnʌt/ *n* **1** [C] a smooth red-brown nut that you can eat: *roast chestnuts*| *chestnut stuffing* **2** also **chestnut tree** [C] the tree on which this nut grows **3** [U] a reddish brown colour **4** [C] a horse that is this colour **5 an old chestnut** a joke or story that has been repeated many times **6** [C] a HORSE CHESTNUT —see also WATER CHESTNUT

**chestnut**[2] *adj* red-brown in colour: *her chestnut hair*

**chest of drawers** /ˌ· · ˈ·/ *n* a piece of furniture with drawers, used for storing clothes; BUREAU (4) *AmE*

**chest·y** /ˈtʃesti/ *adj* **1** *informal especially BrE* having a lot of CATARRH (=thick liquid) in your lungs: *a chesty cough*| *He was a bit chesty, so I didn't send him to school.* **2** *informal* an impolite word used to describe a woman with large breasts

**chev·a·lier** /ˌʃevəˈlɪə‖-ˈlɪr/ *n* [C] *French* **1** a title for someone who has a high rank in a special association in France: *a Chevalier of the Legion of Honour* **2** a member of the lowest rank of the French NOBILITY in the past

**che·val mir·ror** /ʃəˈvæl mɪrə‖-rər/ *n* [C] a long mirror in a frame which stands upright without being fixed to a wall

**chev·ron** /ˈʃevrən/ *n* [C] **1** a pattern in a V shape **2** a piece of cloth in the shape of a V which a soldier has on their SLEEVE (1) to show their rank

**chew**[1] /tʃuː/ *v* **1** [I,T] to bite food several times before swallowing it: *This meat's so tough I can hardly chew it!*| [+ **at/on**] *a dog chewing on a bone* **2** [I + T] to bite something repeatedly in order to taste it or because you are nervous: *We gave the dog an old shoe to chew on.*| *Stop chewing your nails – it's disgusting.* **3 chew the cud a)** if a cow or sheep chews the cud, it repeatedly bites food it has brought up from its stomach. **b)** *informal* to think very carefully before making a decision **4 chew the fat** *informal* to have a long, friendly conversation —see also **bite off more than you can chew** (BITE[1] (10))

**chew on** sth *phr v* [T] **chew on it** *informal* to think about something carefully for a period of time

**chew** sb **out** *phr v* [T] *AmE, informal* to talk angrily to someone in order to show them that you disapprove of what they have done: *I know I'm late, you don't have to chew me out!*

**chew** sth ↔ **over** *phr v* [T] to think carefully about a question, problem, idea etc. over a period of time: *Let me chew it over for a few days, and then I'll let you have my answer.*

**chew** sth ↔ **up** *phr v* [T] to bite something repeatedly with your teeth so that you can make it smaller or softer and swallow it: *That dog's chewed the carpet up again!*

**chew²** *n* [C] **1** the act of biting something repeatedly with the teeth **2** something such as a sweet you chew or special tobacco which you chew but do not swallow: *a chew of tobacco*

**chewing gum** /ˈ·· ·/ *n* [U] a type of sweet, that you chew for a long time but do not swallow

**chew·y** /ˈtʃuːi/ *adj* food that is chewy has to be chewed a lot before it is soft enough to swallow: *chewy toffees | wonderfully chewy chocolate brownies*

**Chey·enne** /ʃaɪˈæn/ *n* **1 the Cheyenne** a Native American people that live in the West of the US **2** [C] a member of the Cheyenne people

**chic** /ʃiːk/ *adj* very fashionable and expensive and showing good judgment of what is attractive and good style: *a chic black dress | Provençal cuisine has become very chic. | a chic restaurant* —**chic** *n* [U]

**chi·cane** /ʃɪˈkeɪn/ *n* [C] an S shaped bend in a straight road, especially on a track for racing cars

**chi·ca·ne·ry** /ʃɪˈkeɪnəri/ *n* [U] *formal* the use of clever plans or actions to deceive people: *The legal system got to the truth and settled cases fairly and without chicanery.*

**Chi·ca·no** /tʃɪˈkɑːnəʊ‖-noʊ/ *n* [C] *plural* **Chicanos** *AmE* a US citizen who was born in Mexico or whose family came from Mexico —**Chicano** *adj*

**chi-chi** /ˈʃiː ʃiː/ *adj informal* stylish or attractive, especially in a way that you think uses too much decoration: *a chi-chi nightclub*

**chick** /tʃɪk/ *n* [C] **1** a baby bird: *a robin chick* **2** a word meaning a young woman, that some people think is offensive

**chick-a-dee** /ˈtʃɪk ə diː/ *n* [C] a North American bird with a black head

2 **chick·en¹** /ˈtʃɪkɪn/ *n*
**1 ▶ BIRD ◀** [C] a common farm bird that is kept for its meat and eggs: *He keeps chickens on his farm.* —see also HEN, COCK¹ (1), ROOSTER
**2 ▶ MEAT ◀** [U] the meat from this bird eaten as food: *roast chicken | fried chicken | chicken soup*
**3 ▶ SB WHO IS NOT BRAVE ◀** [C] *informal* someone who is not at all brave; COWARD: *Don't be such a chicken!*
**4 ▶ GAME ◀** [U] a game in which children must do something dangerous to show that they are brave
**5 which came first, the chicken or the egg?** used to say that it is difficult or impossible to decide which of two things came first or which action is the cause and which is the effect
**6 a chicken and egg situation/problem/thing etc** a situation in which it is impossible to decide which part caused another and which is the effect of another
**7 your chickens have come home to roost** your bad or dishonest actions in the past have caused the problems that you have now —see also **don't count your chickens before they've hatched** (COUNT¹ (8)), SPRING CHICKEN

**chicken out** *phr v* [I] *informal* to decide at the last moment not to do something you said you would do because you are afraid: **chicken out of doing sth** *I knew you'd chicken out of telling Dad you want to leave school.*

**chicken²** *adj* [not before noun] *informal* not brave enough to do something: *Your brother is chicken.*

**chick·en·feed** /ˈtʃɪkɪnfiːd/ *n* [U] *informal* an amount of money that is so small that it is almost not worth having: *The bank offered to lend us £1000, but that's chickenfeed compared to what we need.*

**chicken-fried steak** /ˌ··· ˈ·/ *n* [C,U] *AmE* a thin piece of BEEF¹ (1) covered in BREADCRUMBS and cooked in hot fat

**chicken-heart·ed** /ˌ·· ˈ··◂/ also **chicken-livered** *adj* not brave; COWARDLY

**chick·en·pox** /ˈtʃɪkɪnpɒks ‖ -pɑːks/ *n* [U] an infectious illness which causes a slight fever and spots on your skin

**chicken run** /ˈ·· ·/ *n* [C] an area surrounded by a fence where you keep chickens

**chick·en·shit** /ˈtʃɪkɪnʃɪt/ *n* [C] *AmE informal* a rude word meaning someone who is not at all brave; COWARD

**chicken wire** /ˈ·· ·/ *n* [U] a type of thin wire net used to make fences for chickens

**chick·pea** /ˈ· ·/ *n* [C] a large brown PEA which is cooked and eaten; GARBANZO

**chick·weed** /ˈtʃɪkwiːd/ *n* [U] a garden WEED¹ (1) with small white flowers

**chic·le** /ˈtʃɪkəl/ *n* [U] the GUM (=thick juice) of a tropical American tree used in making CHEWING GUM

**chic·o·ry** /ˈtʃɪkəri/ *n* [U] a European plant with blue flowers whose leaves are eaten and whose roots are sometimes used as coffee; ENDIVE (2) *AmE*

**chide** /tʃaɪd/ *v past* **chided** *or* **chid** /tʃɪd/ *past participle* **chided, chid** *or* **chidden** /ˈtʃɪdn/ [I,T] *literary* to speak angrily to someone because you do not approve of something they have done; REBUKE: *"You naughty children!" she chided.* | **chide sb for sth** *Louise often chided her son for his idleness.* | **chide sb for doing sth** *Mr Jones chided the children for not wearing their coats.*

**chief¹** /tʃiːf/ *adj* **1** most important; main: *One of the chief causes of crime today is drugs. | the prosecution's chief witness* —see also CHIEFLY **2** highest in rank: *the chief accountant | the chief political correspondent of the Washington Post* **3 chief cook and bottle washer** *humorous* someone in charge of an event, especially someone who must do a lot of small unimportant jobs to make sure it is a success: *"Is there any more wine?" "Ask my husband, he's chief cook and bottle washer today!"* S2 W2

**chief²** *n* [C] W3
**1 ▶ RULER OF TRIBE ◀** a ruler of a tribe: *an American Indian tribal chief*
**2 ▶ SB IN CHARGE OF AN ORGANIZATION ◀** the most important person in a company or organization: *the chief of Austria's army intelligence | Industry chiefs yesterday demanded tough measures against inflation.*
**3 the chief** *informal* the person in charge of the company or organization you work for: *The chief wants to see you right away.*
**4 big/great white chief** *humorous* the person in charge of a group of people, company, organization etc
**5 too many chiefs and not enough Indians** used to say there are too many people saying how something should be done and not enough people doing it
**6 ▶ MAN ◀** *BrE old-fashioned* used to speak in a friendly way to a man you think is more important that you

**chief con·stab·le** /ˌ· ˈ··/ *n* [C] a police officer in charge of the police in a large area of Britain

**Chief Ex·ec·u·tive** /ˌ· ·ˈ···/ *n AmE* **the Chief Executive** the President of the US

**chief executive of·fi·cer** /ˌ· ·ˈ··· ˌ···/ *n* [C] the person with the most authority in a large company

**chief in·spect·or** /ˌ· ·ˈ··◂/ *n* [C] a British police officer of middle rank

**chief jus·tice** /ˌ· ˈ··◂/ *n* [C] the most important judge in a court of law, especially of the US Supreme Court

**chief·ly** /ˈtʃiːfli/ *adv* mostly but not completely; mainly: *The work consists chiefly of interviewing members of the public. | I lived abroad for years, chiefly in Italy.*

**chief of staff** /ˌ· · ˈ·/ *n plural* **chiefs of staff** [C] **1** an officer of high rank in the army, navy etc who advises the officer in charge of a particular military group or operation **2** an official of high rank who advises the man in charge of an organization or government: *the White House chief of staff*

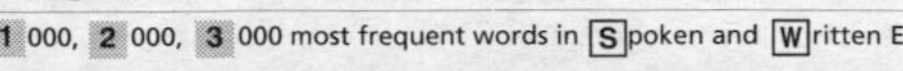

**Chief Rab·bi** /ˌ· ˈ··/ *n* **the Chief Rabbi** the main leader of the JEWISH religion in a country

**chief su·per·in·ten·dent** /ˌ· ····ˈ··◂/ *n* [C] a British police officer of high rank

**chief·tain** /ˈtʃiːftən/ *n* [C] the leader of a tribe or a Scottish CLAN —**chieftainship** *n* [C,U]

**Chief Whip** /ˌ· ˈ·/ *n* **the Chief Whip** an important member of a British political party whose job is to make sure that members of his party elected to parliament obey party orders

**chif·fon** /ˈʃɪfɒn‖ʃɪˈfɑːn/ *n* [U] a soft thin silk or NYLON material that you can see through: *a pink chiffon ballgown*

**chi·gnon** /ˈʃiːnjɒn‖-jɑːn/ *n* [C] *French* a smooth knot of hair that a woman wears at the back of her head

**chi·hua·hua** /tʃɪˈwɑːwə/ *n* [C] a very small dog from Mexico with smooth hair

**chil·blain** /ˈtʃɪlbleɪn/ *n* [C] a painful red place on your fingers or toes that is caused by cold and a weak supply of blood

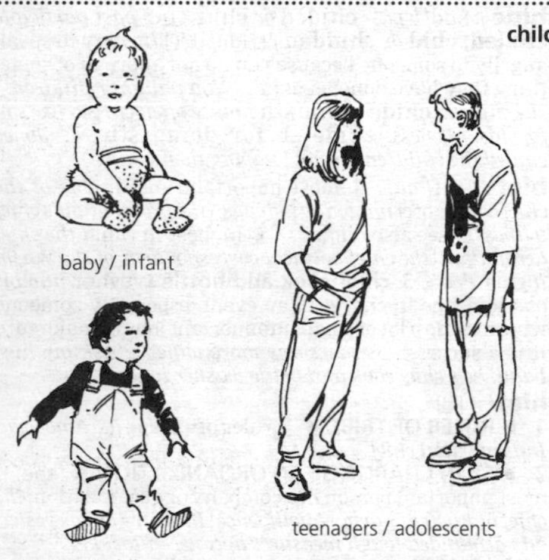


S1 W1 **child** /tʃaɪld/ *n* [C] *plural* **children** /ˈtʃɪldrən/

**1 ► YOUNG PERSON ◄** a young person from the time they are born until they are aged 14 or 15: *We've always competed, ever since we were children.*|*Can you sell me a bike suitable for a seven-year-old child?*|**as a child** (=when you were a child) *As a child I remember Grandma singing me to sleep.*|**a child killer/victim/prostitute etc** (=a child who is a killer etc)

**2 ► SON/DAUGHTER ◄** a son or daughter of any age: *How many children did Victoria have?*|*We'll come if we can find a babysitter for the children.*|*Is this her first child?* (=is this her first PREGNANCY?)|**have a child** (=give birth)|**an only child** (=someone with no brothers or sisters)

**3 ► SB INFLUENCED BY AN IDEA ◄** someone who is very strongly influenced by the ideas and attitudes of a particular person or period of history: *Thatcher's children are finding that the world has moved on.*|**[+ of]** *a real child of the sixties*

**4 ► SB WHO IS LIKE A CHILD ◄** someone who is not very experienced in doing something, or who behaves like a child: *Richard's such a child – he can't even do his own washing and cooking.*

**5 children should be seen and not heard** an expression meaning that children should be quiet and not talk, used when you disapprove of the way the children are behaving

**6 be with child** *old use* to be PREGNANT

**7 be heavy/great with child** *old use* to be nearly ready to give birth —see also CHILD'S PLAY

**USAGE NOTE: CHILD**

WORD CHOICE: **child, baby, infant, toddler, teenager, adolescent, youth, young people, kid**

A very young **child** is a **baby** or more formally an **infant**: *Many infants have died in the refugee camps.* A child who has just learned to walk is a **toddler**.

Young people aged 13 to 19 are **teenagers** and a younger teenager may also be called an **adolescent**, but this word is rather formal, and may show a negative attitude: *a group of giggly adolescent girls*

The word **youth** is often used for an older male teenager (15+) in official reports about crimes or bad behaviour: *The police are seeking two youths who raped a teenage girl.* In official names **youth** includes both sexes: *a youth club/group/scheme/worker/centre/hostel.* Often the phrase **young people** is used for this age group in everyday English: *a disco full of young people dancing*

**Kid** is informal and used both for **child** (up to around 14): *The kids are playing in the yard,* and for **young people**: *We met a group of college kids.*

GRAMMAR

Remember the plural of **child** is **children**, never *childs* or *childrens.* But in the possessive form you say: *this child's education*|*these children's education*

**child·bear·ing** /ˈtʃaɪldˌbeərɪŋ‖-ˌber-/ *n* [U] **1** the process of giving birth to a baby **2 childbearing age** the time in a woman's life when she can have babies

**child ben·e·fit** /ˌ· ˈ···/ *n* [U] an amount of money that the British government gives to families with children

**child·birth** /ˈtʃaɪldbɜːθ‖-bɜːrθ/ *n* [U] the act of having a baby: *His mother died in childbirth.*

**child·care** /ˈtʃaɪldkeə‖-ker/ *n* [U] an arrangement in which someone who is trained to look after children cares for them while the parents are at work: *The company pays £20 a week towards childcare.*

**child·hood** /ˈtʃaɪldhʊd/ *n* [C,U] the period of time when you are a child: *I had a happy childhood.* —see also SECOND CHILDHOOD W

**child·ish** /ˈtʃaɪldɪʃ/ *adj* **1** related to or typical of a child: *a high childish laugh* **2** behaving in a silly way that makes you seem much younger than you really are: *Stop messing around, it's so childish.* —compare CHILDLIKE —**childishly** *adv* —**childishness** *n* [U]

**child·less** /ˈtʃaɪldləs/ *adj* having no children: *a childless couple* —**childlessness** *n* [U]

**child·like** /ˈtʃaɪldlaɪk/ *adj* having qualities that are typical of a child, especially qualities such as INNOCENCE and trust: *an expression of childlike innocence* —compare CHILDISH

**child·min·der** /ˈtʃaɪldˌmaɪndə‖-ər/ *n* [C] *BrE* someone who is paid to look after young children while their parents are at work; BABYSITTER *AmE* —**childminding** *n* [U]

**child prod·i·gy** /ˌ· ˈ···/ *n* [C] a child who is unusually skilful at doing something such as playing a musical instrument

**child·proof** /ˈtʃaɪldpruːf/ *adj* something that is childproof is designed to prevent a child from opening, damaging, or breaking it: *a childproof lock*

**chil·dren** /ˈtʃɪldrən/ *n* the plural of CHILD

**children's home** /ˈ·· ·/ *n* [C] a place in Britain where children live if their own parents cannot look after them

**child's play** /ˈ· ·/ *n* [U] something that it is very easy to do: *Cracking such a simple code was child's play to him.*

**child sup·port** /ˈ· ˌ··/ *n* [U] *AmE* money that someone pays regularly to their former wife or husband in order to support their children; MAINTENANCE (2) *BrE*

**chil·i** /ˈtʃɪli/ *n* [C,U] the American spelling of CHILLI

**chill**[1] /tʃɪl/ *v* **1** [I,T] if you chill something such as food or drink or if it chills, it becomes very cold but does not freeze: *Chill the champagne in a bucket of ice.* | *Serve the melon chilled.* **2** [T usually passive] to make someone very cold: **chilled to the bone/marrow** *Come and sit by the fire, you look chilled to the bone.* **3** [T] *literary* to frighten someone, especially by seeming very cruel or violent: *The look in her eye chilled me.* **4** [T] *literary* if you chill someone's hopes or keenness for doing something, you discourage them

**chill out** *phr v* [I] *especially AmE* to relax completely instead of feeling angry, tired, or nervous: *Chill out, man, I didn't mean to insult you.*

**chill**[2] *n* **1** [singular] a feeling of coldness: *There's a real chill in the air.* | **take the chill off** (=heat something slightly) *Heat the baby's milk just enough to take the chill off.* **2** [C] a feeling of fear caused by something that is very unpleasant or cruel: *Her description of the massacre sent a chill through the audience.* | **send a chill down sb's spine** (=make them feel very frightened) **3** [C] a mild illness with a fever: **catch a chill** *It began to snow on the way home and I caught a nasty chill.* **4** [singular] a way of behaving or speaking that is very unfriendly: *There was a marked chill in his voice when he answered.*

**chill**[3] *adj* unpleasantly cold: *a chill wind*

**chil·ler** /ˈtʃɪlə‖-ər/ *n* [C] *informal* a film or book that is intended to frighten you: *the black magic chiller, 'Rosemary's Baby'*

**chil·li** *BrE*, **chili** *AmE* /ˈtʃɪli/ *n plural* **chillies, chilies** **1** [U] a dish made with beans and usually meat cooked with chillies: **chilli con carne** (=this dish made with meat) **2** [C] a small, thin type of PEPPER[1] (3) with a very strong, hot taste **3** [U] a hot-tasting red powder made from this PEPPER[1] (3) and used in cooking

**chil·ling** /ˈtʃɪlɪŋ/ *adj* something that is chilling makes you feel frightened, especially because it is cruel, violent, or dangerous: *the chilling sound of wolves howling*

**chilli pow·der** /ˈ·· ˌ··/ *n* [U] CHILLI (3)

**chil·lum** /ˈtʃɪləm/ *n* [C] *slang* a type of pipe used for smoking CANNABIS

**chill·y** /ˈtʃɪli/ *adj* **1** cold enough to make you feel uncomfortable: *The wind's a bit chilly.* **2** unfriendly: *The speech met with a chilly reception.* —see COLD[1] (USAGE) —**chilliness** *n* [singular, U]

**chilly bin** /ˈ·· ·/ *n* [C] *NZE* a large container used for keeping food or drink cold

**chi·mae·ra** /kəɪˈmɪərə, kɪ‖-ˈɪrə/ *n* [C] another spelling of CHIMERA

**chime**[1] /tʃaɪm/ *v* **1** [I,T] if a bell or clock chimes, it makes a ringing sound, especially to tell you what time it is: *The grandfather clock chimed six.* **2** [I + **with**] to be the same as something else or to have the same effect: *Her views on art chime completely with mine.*

**chime in** *phr v* [I] to say something in a conversation, especially to agree with what someone has just said: *"We'll miss you too," the children chimed in.*

**chime**[2] *n* [C] **1** a ringing sound made by a bell or clock: *the chime of the doorbell* **2 chimes** [plural] a set of bells or other objects that produce musical sounds

**chi·me·ra, chimaera** /kaɪˈmɪərə, kɪ‖-ˈmɪrə/ *n* [C] **1** an imaginary creature that breathes fire and has a lion's head, a goat's body, and a snake's tail **2** something, especially an idea or hope, that is not really possible and can never exist: *trying to present that impossible chimera, 'a balanced view'*

**chi·me·ri·cal** /kaɪˈmerɪkəl, kɪ-/ *adj literary* imaginary or not really possible

**chim·ney** /ˈtʃɪmni/ *n* [C] **1** a pipe inside a building that goes from a fire to the roof in order to let smoke out: *a factory chimney belching smoke* —see picture on page 410 **2** a narrow opening in tall rocks or cliffs that you can climb up **3** the glass cover that is put over the flame in an oil lamp

**chimney breast** /ˈ·· ·/ *n* [C] *BrE* the part of a wall in a room that encloses a chimney

**chimney-piece** /ˈ·· ·/ *n* [C] *BrE* a decoration, usually made of brick or stone, built above a FIREPLACE

**chimney pot** /ˈ·· ·/ *n* [C] a short wide pipe made of baked clay or metal, that is fixed to the top of a CHIMNEY —see picture on page 410

**chimney stack** /ˈ·· ·/ *n* [C] *BrE* **1** the tall CHIMNEY of a building such as a factory; SMOKESTACK *AmE* **2** a group of small chimneys on a roof

**chimney sweep** /ˈ·· ·/ *n* [C] someone whose job is to clean CHIMNEYS using special long brushes

**chim·pan·zee** /ˌtʃɪmpænˈziː, -pən-/ also **chimp** /tʃɪmp/ *informal n* [C] an intelligent African animal that is like a monkey without a tail

**chin** /tʃɪn/ *n* [C] **1** the front part of your face below your mouth: *She sat with her chin in her hands.* —see picture at HEAD[1] **2 (keep your) chin up!** *spoken* used to tell someone to make an effort to stay cheerful when they are in a difficult situation: *Chin up! It'll be over soon.* S3

**chi·na** /ˈtʃaɪnə/ *n* [U] **1** a hard white substance produced by baking a type of clay at a high temperature: *china teacups* **2** also **chinaware** plates, cups etc made of china: *We were given a lot of china as wedding presents.*

**Chi·na·town** /ˈtʃaɪnətaʊn/ *n* [C,U] an area in a city where there are Chinese restaurants, shops, and clubs, and where a lot of Chinese people live

**chin·chil·la** /ˌtʃɪnˈtʃɪlə/ *n* **1** [C] a small South American animal bred for its fur **2** [U] the pale grey fur of the chinchilla

**Chi·nese**[1] /ˌtʃaɪˈniːz◂/ *n* **1** [U] the language of China **2 the Chinese** people from China **3** [C] *BrE informal* a meal of Chinese food, or a restaurant that sells Chinese food

**Chinese**[2] *adj* from or connected with China

**Chinese che·quers** *BrE*, **Chinese checkers** *AmE n* [U] /ˌ·· ˈ··/ a game in which you move small balls from hole to hole on a board in the shape of a star

**Chinese fire drill** /ˌ·· ˈ· ·/ *n* [singular] *AmE informal* a very confusing situation

**Chinese lan·tern** /ˌ·· ˈ··/ *n* [C] a small box made of thin paper that you put a light inside as a decoration

**Chinese leaves** /ˌ·· ˈ·/ *n* [U] a type of CABBAGE eaten especially in East Asia —see picture on page 414

**Chinese medi·cine** /ˌ·· ˈ··‖ˌ·· ˈ···/ *n* [U] a kind of medicine that uses HERBS (=dried plants) and ACUPUNCTURE

**Chinese whis·pers** /ˌ·· ˈ··/ *n* [U] *BrE* the passing of information from one person to another, and then others, when the information gets slightly changed each time: *Chinese whispers started about child abuse in Cleveland and developed into a national scandal.*

**Chink** /tʃɪŋk/ *n* [C] a very offensive word for a Chinese person

**chink**[1] *n* **1** [C] a small hole in a wall, or between two things that join together, that lets light or air through: *The sun came through a chink in the curtains.* **2** [C] a high ringing sound made by metal or glass objects hitting each other: *the chink of coins* **3 a chink in sb's armour** a weakness in someone's character, argument etc that you can use to attack them

**chink**[2] *v* [I,T] if glass or metal objects chink or you chink them, they make a high ringing sound when they knock together: *They chinked their glasses and drank a toast to the couple.*

**chin·less** /ˈtʃɪnləs/ *adj* **1** having a chin that is small or slopes inwards **2** *BrE* lacking courage or determination **3 chinless wonder** a young man from an upper class family who is weak and stupid

**chi·no** /ˈtʃiːnəʊ‖-noʊ/ *n* **1** [U] a strong material made of woven cotton **2 chinos** [plural] trousers made from this material

**chin·strap** /ˈtʃɪnstræp/ *n* [C] a band of cloth under your chin to keep a hat or HELMET in place

**chintz** /tʃɪnts/ *n* [U] smooth cotton cloth that is printed with flowery patterns and used for making curtains, furniture covers etc: *pink chintz curtains*

**chintz·y** /ˈtʃɪntsi/ *adj* **1** covered with chintz: *a chintzy sofa* **2** *AmE informal* cheap and badly made: *a chintzy chest of drawers* **3** *AmE informal* unwilling to give people things or spend money; STINGY: *We don't need to be chintzy over the Christmas presents this year.*

**chin up** /ˈ· ·/ *n* [C] *AmE* an exercise in which you hang on a bar and pull yourself up until your chin is above the bar; PULL-UP

**chin·wag** /ˈtʃɪnwæɡ/ *n* [singular] *informal especially BrE* an informal conversation; CHAT² —**chinwag** *v* [I]

S2 W3 **chip¹** /tʃɪp/ *n* [C]
**1 ▶ MARK ◀** a small hole or mark on a plate, cup etc where a piece has broken off: [+ **in**] *There's a chip in this plate.*
**2 ▶ PIECE ◀** a small piece of wood, stone, metal etc that has broken off something: *Wood chips covered the floor of the workshop.* —see picture on page 416
**3 a) ▶ FOOD ◀** *BrE* a long thin piece of potato cooked in oil; FRENCH FRY *AmE*: *fish and chips* **b)** *AmE* a thin, flat round piece of potato cooked in very hot oil and eaten cold; CRISP¹ *BrE*
**4 ▶ COMPUTER ◀ a)** a small piece of SILICON that has a set of complicated electrical connections on it and is used to store and PROCESS² (4) information in computers **b)** the main MICROPROCESSOR of a computer
**5 have a chip on your shoulder** to easily become offended or angry because you think you have been treated unfairly in the past: *He's always had a chip on his shoulder about not going to university.*
**6 be a chip off the old block** *informal* to be very similar to your mother or father in appearance or character
**7 ▶ GAME ◀** a small flat coloured piece of plastic used in GAMBLING to represent a particular amount of money
**8 ▶ SPORT ◀** a kick in football, RUGBY etc that makes the ball go high into the air for a short distance
**9 when the chips are down** *spoken* a serious or difficult situation, especially one in which you realize what is really true or important: *When the chips are down, you've only got yourself to depend on.*
**10 have had your chips** *BrE informal* to be in a situation in which you no longer have any hope of improvement —see also BLUE CHIP, **cash in your chips** (CASH²), COW CHIP

**chip²** *v* **chipped, chipping** **1** [I,T] if something such as a plate chips or if you chip it, a small piece of it breaks off accidentally: *Gary fell and chipped one of his front teeth.* | *These cheap plates chip really easily.* **2** [T] to cut potatoes into thin pieces ready to be cooked in hot oil **3** [T] to hit or kick a ball in football, RUGBY etc so that it goes high into the air for a short distance

**chip** sth ↔ **away** *phr v* [T] to remove something, especially something hard that is covering a surface, by hitting it with a tool so that small pieces break off: *Sandy chipped away the plaster covering the tiles.* | [+ **at**] *Archaeologists were carefully chipping away at the rock.*

**chip away at** sth *phr v* [T] to gradually make something less effective or destroy it: *The emphasis on testing has chipped away at teachers' autonomy.*

**chip in** *phr v* **1** [I] to interrupt a conversation by saying something that adds more detail: *They kept chipping in with facts and figures.* **2** [I,T] if each person in a group chips in, they each give a small amount of money so that they can buy something together: *I'd like to chip in if you're getting Mike a birthday present.*

**chip** sth ↔ **off** *phr v* [T] to remove something by breaking it off in small pieces: *Bert chipped the paint off the front door and varnished it.*

**chip·board** /ˈtʃɪpbɔːd‖-bɔːrd/ *n* [U] a type of board made from small pieces of wood pressed together with glue

**chip·munk** /ˈtʃɪpmʌŋk/ *n* [C] a small American animal similar to a SQUIRREL¹ with black lines on its fur

**chip·o·la·ta** /ˌtʃɪpəˈlɑːtə◂/ *n* [C] *BrE* a small thin SAUSAGE

**chip pan** /ˈ· ·/ *n* [C] *BrE* a deep pan with a wire basket inside used for cooking food in hot oil, especially chips (CHIP¹ (3))

**chipped** /tʃɪpt/ *adj* a cup, plate etc that is chipped has a small piece broken off the edge of it —see picture on page 1258

**chip·per** /ˈtʃɪpə‖-ər/ *adj AmE* cheerful and active: *Grandma's over her illness and feeling pretty chipper again.*

**chip·pings** /ˈtʃɪpɪŋz/ *n* [plural] *BrE* small pieces of stone used when putting new surfaces on roads or railway tracks

**chip shop** /ˈ· ·/ also **chip·py** /ˈtʃɪpi/ *informal n* [C] *BrE* a shop that cooks and sells FISH AND CHIPS and other food

**chi·rop·o·dist** /kɪ̵ˈrɒpədɪst, ʃɪ̵-‖-ˈrɑː-/ *n* [C] *BrE* someone who is trained to examine and treat foot injuries and diseases; PODIATRIST *AmE* —**chiropody** *n* [U]

**chi·ro·prac·tic** /ˈkaɪrəpræktɪk/ *n* [U] a way of treating illness by pressing on and moving the bones in someone's SPINE (1) —**chiropractor** *n* [C]

**chirp** /tʃɜːp‖tʃɜːrp/ also **chirrup** *v* [I] **1** if a bird or insect chirps, it makes short high sounds **2** to speak in a cheerful, high voice: *"Yes, all finished," he chirped.* —**chirp** *n* [C]

**chirp·y** /ˈtʃɜːpi‖ˈtʃɜːrpi/ *adj BrE informal* cheerful and active: *You're very chirpy this morning – have you had some good news?* —**chirpily** *adv* —**chirpiness** *n* [U]

**chir·rup** /ˈtʃɪrəp‖ˈtʃɪ-, ˈtʃɜː-/ *v* [I] CHIRP

**chis·el¹** /ˈtʃɪzəl/ *n* [C] a metal tool with a sharp edge, used to cut wood or stone —see picture at TOOL¹

**chisel²** *v* **chiselled, chiselling** *BrE* **chiseled, chiseling** *AmE* [T] **1** to use a chisel to cut wood or stone into a particular shape: **chisel sth into/from/in etc** *Martin chiselled a hole in the door for the new lock.* **2** *old-fashioned* to cheat or deceive someone, by getting more than you deserve —**chiseller** *BrE*, **chiseler** *AmE n* [C]

**chit** /tʃɪt/ *n* [C] **1** an official note that shows that you are allowed to have something: *Take the chit to the counter and collect your books.* **2** *old-fashioned* a young woman who behaves badly and does not respect older people

**chit-chat** /ˈ· ·/ *n* [U] *informal* conversation about things that are not very important: *boring social chit-chat*

**chit·ter·lings** /ˈtʃɪtəlɪŋz‖-ər-/ also **chit·lings** /ˈtʃɪtlɪŋz/ **chitlins** /-lɪ̵nz/ *n* [plural] the INTESTINE of a pig eaten as food, especially in the southern US

**chit·ty** /ˈtʃɪti/ *n* [C] *BrE informal* a CHIT (1)

**chiv·al·rous** /ˈʃɪvəlrəs/ *adj* a man who is chivalrous behaves in a polite, kind, generous, and honourable way, especially towards women: *a chivalrous attitude towards the loser* —**chivalrously** *adv*

**chiv·al·ry** /ˈʃɪvəlri/ *n* [U] **1** behaviour that is honourable, kind, generous, and brave, especially men's behaviour towards women **2** a system of religious beliefs and honourable behaviour that KNIGHTS in the Middle Ages were expected to follow

**chive** /tʃaɪv/ *n* [C usually plural] a long thin green plant that looks and tastes like an onion, and is used in cooking

**chiv·vy, chivy** /ˈtʃɪvi/ *v* **chivvied, chivvying** [T] *BrE* to try to make someone do something more quickly, especially in an annoying way: **chivvy sb along/up** *Go and see if you can chivvy the kids up a bit.*

**chlo·ro·fluo·ro·car·bon** /fluərəʊˈkɑːbən‖-roʊˈkɑːr-/ /ˌklɔːrəʊ/ *n* [C] *technical* a CFC

**chlo·ride** /ˈklɔːraɪd/ *n* [C,U] *technical* a chemical compound that is a mixture of chlorine and another substance: *sodium chloride*

**chlo·ri·nate** /ˈklɔːrɪ̵neɪt/ *v* [T] to add chlorine to water to kill BACTERIA

**chlo·rine** /ˈklɔːriːn/ *n* [U] a greenish-yellow gas that is a chemical ELEMENT (=simple substance) and is often used to keep the water in swimming pools clean

**chlor·o·form** /ˈklɒrəfɔːm, ˈklɔː-‖ˈklɔːrəfɔːrm/ *n* [U] a liquid that makes you become unconscious if you breathe it —**chloroform** *v* [T]

**chlo·ro·phyll** /ˈklɒrəfɪl, ˈklɔː-‖ˈklɔː-/ *n* [U] the green-coloured substance in plants

**choc** /tʃɒk‖tʃɑːk, tʃɒːk/ *n* [C] *BrE informal* a CHOCOLATE (2)

**choc·a·hol·ic** /ˌtʃɒkəˈhɒlɪk‖ˌtʃɑːkəˈhɒː-, ˌtʃɒːk-/ *n* [C] another spelling of CHOCOHOLIC

**choc·cy** /ˈtʃɒki‖ˈtʃɑːki, ˈtʃɒːki/ *n* [C] *BrE spoken* a CHOCOLATE (2)

**choc-ice** /ˈ· ·/ *n* [C] *BrE* a small block of ICE CREAM covered with chocolate

**chock** /tʃɒk‖tʃɑːk/ *n* [C] a block of wood or metal put in front of a wheel, door etc to prevent it from moving —**chock** *v* [T]

**chock-a-block** /ˌtʃɒk ə ˈblɒk◂‖ˈtʃɑːk ə ˌblɑːk/ *adj* [not before noun] **a)** full of people or things that are very close to each other: **[+ with]** *Disneyland was chock-a-block with people that day.*

**chock-full** /ˌ· ˈ·◂/ *adj* [not before noun] *informal* completely full: **[+ of]** *The bus was chock-full of people.*

**choc·o·hol·ic**, also **chocaholic** /ˌtʃɒkəˈhɒlɪk‖ˌtʃɑːkəˈhɒː-, -ˈhoː-, ˌtʃo-, ˌtʃɒːk-/ *n* [C] someone who likes chocolate very much and eats it all the time

S2 **choco·late** /ˈtʃɒklɪ̥t‖ˈtʃɑːkəlɪ̥t, ˈtʃɒːk-/ *n* **1** [U] a sweet brown food eaten for pleasure or used to give foods such as cakes a special sweet taste: *a chocolate bar* | **chocolate cake/cookie/ice cream etc** (=cake etc that tastes of chocolate) | **milk chocolate** (=chocolate made with a lot of milk in it) | **dark** *AmE*/**plain** *BrE* **chocolate** (=chocolate that does not have much milk in it) | **plain** *AmE* **cooking** *BrE* **chocolate** (=chocolate with no milk in it, used for cooking) | **white chocolate** (=chocolate that is white) **2** [C] a small sweet that consists of something such as a nut or CARAMEL covered with chocolate: *a box of chocolates* **3** [C,U] a hot sweet drink made with milk and chocolate, or a cup of this drink

**chocolate box** /ˈ··· ·‖ˈ··· ·/ *adj* [only before noun] *BrE informal* very pretty, but in a way that seems false or artificial: *a chocolate box village*

**chocolate chip cook·ie** /ˌ··· ˈ··‖ˌ··· ˈ··/ *n* [C] a kind of flat COOKIE containing small pieces of chocolate

**choco·lat·ey** /ˈtʃɒklɪ̥ti‖ˈtʃɑːkələti, ˈtʃɒːk-/ *adj* tasting or smelling of chocolate

S1 W1 **choice¹** /tʃɔɪs/ *n*

**1 ▶ABILITY TO CHOOSE◀** [singular, U] the right to choose or the chance to choose between several things: *Nowadays both men and women are able to exercise choice as to whom they marry.* | **[+ between]** *a genuinely free choice between candidates* | **[+ of]** *a choice of accommodation* | **have a choice** (=be able to choose) | **give sb a choice** *I'll give you a choice – we can go to the movies or out for a meal.* | **have no choice** (=be forced to do something because it is the only thing you can do) *I had to go back. I was short of money and had no choice.* | **leave sb with no choice** (=be forced to do something because it is the only thing you can do) *He was left with no choice but to resign.*

**2 ▶ACT OF CHOOSING◀** [C] the act of choosing something: *The board denied that financial considerations had influenced their choice.* | **[+ of]** *Alf left the choice of where they would go to Jenny.* | **make a choice** (=choose) *You should find out more before making your final choice.*

**3 ▶RANGE TO CHOOSE FROM◀** [singular] the range of people or things that you can choose from: *There's a small general store in town, but I don't think there will be much choice.* | **[+ of]** *There is a choice of dozens of magazines aimed at women readers.* | **have a choice** *In your exam you will have a choice of five questions.*

**4 ▶THING CHOSEN◀** [C usually singular] the person or thing that someone has chosen: *The choices you make now will affect you for many years.* | **[+ of]** *The choice of Cannes as the venue for the conference was inspired.* | **first/second etc choice** *Italy was our second choice – all the flights to Greece were booked up.*

**5 ▶THING YOU MAY CHOOSE◀** [C] one of several things that you can choose: *The computer will show you several search choices.*

**6 of your choice** chosen by you without anything limiting what you can choose from: *Chill and serve with the garnishes of your choice.*

**7 by choice** if you do something by choice, you do it because you want to do it and not because you are forced to do it: *The government has claimed that many people are homeless by choice.*

**8 the drug/treatment/newspaper etc of choice** the thing that a certain group of people prefer to use: *It is the drug of choice for this type of illness.* —see also CHOOSE, HOBSON'S CHOICE

**choice²** *adj* **1** *formal* of a very high quality or standard, used especially of food: *choice apples* | *a choice collection of antique books* **2** choice meat, especially BEEF¹ (1), is of a standard that is good but not the best: *choice steak* **3 a few choice words/phrases** if you use a few choice words, you say exactly what you mean in an angry way: *He dismissed the objection in a few choice words.*

**choir** /ˈkwaɪə‖kwaɪr/ *n* [C] **1** a group of people who sing together, especially in a church or school **2** [usually singular] the part of a church in which the choir sits

**choir·boy** /ˈkwaɪəbɔɪ‖ˈkwaɪr-/ *n* [C] a young boy who sings in a church choir

**choir loft** /ˈ· ·/ *n* [C] *AmE* the part of a church, usually at the front, in which the choir sits

**choir·mas·ter** /ˈkwaɪəˌmɑːstə‖ˈkwaɪrˌmæstər/ *n* [C] *BrE* someone who trains a choir; DIRECTOR (3) *AmE*

**choke¹** /tʃəʊk‖tʃoʊk/ *v*

**1 ▶STOP BREATHING◀** [I,T] to prevent someone from breathing, or to be prevented from breathing, because your throat is blocked or because there is not enough air: *The fumes were choking me.* | **[+ on]** *He choked to death on a fish bone.*

**2 ▶INJURE◀** [T] to prevent someone from breathing and hurt them by putting your hands around their throat and pressing on it: *Stop it – you're choking me!*

**3 ▶BLOCK◀** [I,T] to fill an area or passage so that it is difficult to move through it: *Weeds choked the canal.* | *The roads were choked with traffic.*

**4 ▶VOICE◀** [I,T] if your voice is choked or you choke with laughter or anger, your emotions make your voice sound strange and not very loud: **[+ with]** *"She's been raped," he said in a voice choked with emotion.*

**5 ▶SAY STH◀** [T] also **choke** sth↔ **out** to say something one word or phrase at a time in a strange voice, because you are very upset or angry or because you have been laughing: *"George," he choked out, "is that you, George?"*

**6 ▶SPORTS◀** [I] *AmE informal* to fail at doing something, especially a sport, because there is a lot of pressure on you: *They choked in the playoffs and lost the series 4 games to 2.*

**7 ▶PLANTS◀** [T] to kill a plant by surrounding it with other plants that take away its light and room to grow: *The thistles choked the corn.*

**8 choke a horse** *AmE spoken* if something is big enough to choke a horse, it is very big or larger than usual: *a wad of bills big enough to choke a horse*

**choke** sth↔ **back** *phr v* [T] to control your anger, sadness etc so that you do not show it: *I stood there trembling and trying to choke back the tears.*

**choke** sth↔ **down** *phr v* [T] **1** to eat something with difficulty, especially because you are ill or upset: *He managed to choke down a sandwich.* **2** to choke something back

**choke off** *phr v* [T] to prevent someone from doing

something or stop something happening: *A higher interest rate will choke off the demand for money.*

**choke up** *phr v* [I] **be choked up** to be very upset about something: *She and Mark broke up last week, and she's pretty choked up about it.*

**choke²** *n* **1** [C] a piece of equipment in a vehicle that controls the amount of air going into the engine, and that is used to help the engine start **2** [U] the controlling of the amount of air going into an engine by using this piece of equipment: *Give it a bit more choke.* **3** [C] the act or sound of choking

**choke chain** /ˈ· ·/ *n* [C] a chain that is fastened around the neck of a dog to control it

**choke·cher·ry** /ˈtʃəʊktʃeri‖ˈtʃoʊk-/ *n* [C] a North American tree that produces small sour fruit

**choked** /tʃəʊkt‖tʃoʊkt/ *adj* [not before noun] *BrE* upset or angry: *I was really choked to hear he'd died.*

**chok·er** /ˈtʃəʊkə‖ˈtʃoʊkər/ *n* [C] a piece of jewellery or narrow cloth that fits closely around your neck

**chok·y, chokey** /ˈtʃəʊki‖ˈtʃoʊki/ *n* [U] **in choky** *BrE old-fashioned* in prison

**chol·er** /ˈkɒlə‖ˈkɑːlər/ *n* [U] *literary* bad temper

**chol·e·ra** /ˈkɒlərə‖ˈkɑː-/ *n* [U] a serious disease of the stomach and BOWELS that is caused by bad water or infected food

**chol·e·ric** /ˈkɒlərɪk‖ˈkɑː-/ *adj literary* bad tempered or angry: *an unbalanced choleric individual*

**cho·les·te·rol** /kəˈlestərɒl‖-roʊl/ *n* [U] a chemical substance found in fat, blood, and other cells in your body, which doctors think may cause heart disease

**chomp** /tʃɒmp‖tʃɑːmp, tʃɒːmp/ *v* [I + **away/on**] to bite food noisily: *chomping away on an apple*

**choo-choo** /ˈtʃuː tʃuː/ *n* [C] *spoken* a word meaning a train, used by or to children

S1 W1 **choose** /tʃuːz/ *v past tense* **chose** /tʃəʊz‖tʃoʊz/ *past participle* **chosen** /ˈtʃəʊzən‖ˈtʃoʊ-/ [I,T] **1** to decide which one of a number of things, possibilities, people etc that you want because it is the best or most suitable: **choose sth** *The party has finally chosen a woman as leader.* | **choose to do sth** *He chose to learn German rather than French in school.* | *Eleanor was chosen to play the role of Juliet.* | **choose** *I don't know which one to get. You choose* | [+ **between**] *Maria was forced to choose between happiness and duty.* | **choose whether/which/when etc** *You should choose where we eat – I don't mind.* | **choose from** *a story chosen from a collection of fairy tales* **2** to decide or prefer to do something or behave in a particular way: *We can, if we choose, take the case to appeal.* | **choose to do sth** *We chose to ignore her rudeness.* **3 there is little/nothing to choose between** used when you think that two or more things are equally good and you cannot decide which is better: *There was little to choose between the two candidates.* —see also CHOICE¹

This graph shows how common different grammar patterns of the verb **choose** are.

choose sth
choose to do sth
choose
choose between
choose whether/which/when etc
choose from
other

10% 20% 30% 40% 50% 60%

Based on the British National Corpus and the Longman Lancaster Corpus

**choos·y, choosey** /ˈtʃuːzi/ *adj especially BrE* someone who is choosy will only accept food, clothes, jobs etc that they consider to be very good; PICKY: *She didn't much like the job, but she knew she couldn't afford to be choosy.*

**chop¹** /tʃɒp‖tʃɑːp/ *v* **chopped, chopping**

**1 ▶ CUT STH ◀** [T] also **chop up** to cut something such as food or wood into smaller pieces: *Can you chop some firewood?* | **chop sth into pieces/chunks/segments** *Chop an onion into pieces.* —see picture on page 834

**2 ▶ REDUCE STH ◀** [T] to reduce by a large amount the money that can be spent: *Next year's budget has been chopped by fifty percent.*

**3 ▶ SWING A TOOL ◀** [I] to swing a heavy tool such as an AXE¹ (1) in order to cut something: [+ **away/at**] *Ben's been chopping away at that tree for two hours now.*

**4 ▶ MAKE A PATH ◀** [T] to make a path by cutting down plants: *The leader chopped a rough trail through the jungle.* | **chop your way through** *We chopped our way through the underbrush.*

**5 chop and change** *BrE informal* to keep changing your mind

**6 ▶ HIT STH ◀** [T] to hit something by moving your hand downward quickly and suddenly: *I chopped his wrist and he dropped the knife.*

**chop** sth ↔ **down** *phr v* [T] to make a tree or strong plant fall down by cutting it with a sharp tool such as an AXE¹ (1)

**chop** sth ↔ **off** *phr v* [T] to remove something by cutting it with a sharp tool such as an AXE¹ (1) so that it is no longer connected to something else: *Charles I had his head chopped off.*

**chop²** *n* [C]

**1 ▶ MEAT ◀** a small flat piece of meat on a bone, usually cut from a sheep or pig: *a grilled pork chop*

**2 get the chop** *BrE informal* **a)** to lose your job: *Six more salesmen got the chop yesterday.* **b)** to officially stop something or reduce the amount you are paying for it: *The project got the chop in the last board meeting.*

**3 be for the chop** *BrE informal* to be very likely to be closed or stopped: *One of the three factories is for the chop.*

**4 ▶ WITH YOUR HAND ◀** a sudden downward movement with your hand: *a karate chop*

**5 ▶ WITH A TOOL ◀** the act of hitting something once with a sharp tool such as an AXE¹ (1)

**6 the chops** *informal* the part of your face that includes your mouth and jaw: *I hit him in the chops.*

**chop-chop** /ˌ· ˈ·/ *interjection especially BrE* an expression used when you want someone to hurry: *Come on! Chop-chop!*

**chop·per** /ˈtʃɒpə‖ˈtʃɑːpər/ *n* [C] **1** *BrE* a large square knife used for cutting large pieces of meat **2** *informal* a HELICOPTER **3** a type of MOTORCYCLE on which the front wheel is in front of the bars you use to control the vehicle instead of underneath them **4 choppers** [plural] *slang* teeth

**chopping board** /ˈ·· ·/ also **chopping block** *n* [C] *especially BrE* a large piece of wood or plastic that you cut meat or vegetables on; CUTTING BOARD *AmE*

**chop·py** /ˈtʃɒpi‖ˈtʃɑːpi/ *adj* choppy water has many small waves and is very rough to sail on —**choppiness** *n* [U]

**chop·stick** /ˈtʃɒp-stɪk‖ˈtʃɑːp-/ *n* [C usually plural] one of the two thin sticks that you use to eat food in many countries in Asia —see picture at STICK²

**chop su·ey** /ˌtʃɒp ˈsuːi‖ˌtʃɑːp-/ *n* [U] a Chinese dish made of pieces of vegetables and meat served with rice

**cho·ral** /ˈkɔːrəl/ *adj* [only before noun] involving singing by a CHOIR (=group of people), or intended to be sung by a choir: *choral music* | *a choral concert*

**cho·rale** /kɒˈrɑːl‖kəˈræl, -ˈrɑːl/ *n* [C] a piece of music praising God usually sung in a church by a CHOIR (=group of people): *a Bach chorale*

**choral so·ci·e·ty** /ˈ·· ˌ···/ *n* [C] *BrE* a group of people who sing together

**chord** /kɔːd‖kɔːrd/ *n* [C] **1** a combination of two or more musical notes played at the same time **2 strike/touch a chord** to do or say something that people feel is familiar or true: *His writings struck a chord in the hearts of the rebellious students.* **3** *technical* a straight line joining two points on a curve —see picture at CIRCLE[1]

**chore** /tʃɔː‖tʃɔːr/ *n* [C] **1** a job that you have to do regularly, especially work that you do to keep a house clean: *household chores* **2** something you have to do that is very boring and unpleasant: *I find motorway driving a chore.*

**chor·e·og·raph** /ˈkɒriəgrɑːf, ˈkɔː-‖ˈkɔːriəgræf/ *v* [T] to arrange how dancers should move during a performance

**chor·e·og·ra·phy** /ˌkɒriˈɒgrəfi, ˌkɔː-‖ˌkɔːriˈɑːg-/ *n* [U] the art of arranging how dancers should move during a performance —**choreographer** *n* [C]

**chor·is·ter** /ˈkɒrɪstə‖ˈkɔːrɪstər-, ˈkɑː/ *n* [C] a singer in a CHOIR, especially a boy in a school choir that sings in a church

**chor·tle** /ˈtʃɔːtl‖ˈtʃɔːrtl/ *v* [I] to laugh because you are amused or pleased about something: *Harry chortled with delight.* —**chortle** *n* [C]

**cho·rus[1]** /ˈkɔːrəs/ *n* [C]
**1 ▶ SONG ◀** the part of a song that is repeated after each VERSE (=main part in a song) *Everyone joined in the chorus.*
**2 ▶ SINGERS ◀** a large group of people who sing together —compare CHOIR (1): *the university chorus*
**3 ▶ MUSIC ◀** a piece of music written to be sung by a large group of people: *the Hallelujah Chorus*
**4 ▶ GROUP IN MUSICAL PLAY ◀** a group of singers, dancers, or actors who act together in a show but do not have the main parts: *a member of the chorus in the musical '42nd Street'*
**5 a chorus of thanks/disapproval/protest etc** something expressed by many people at the same time: [+ **of**] *Peggy's announcement brought a chorus of congratulation.*
**6 in chorus** if people say something in chorus, they say the same thing at the same time: *"Mom!", the kids cried in chorus*
**7 a) ▶ PLAY ◀** in ancient Greek plays, the chorus is the group of actors who give explanations or opinions about the play **b)** in English drama of the early 1600s, the chorus is usually one person who gives explanations or opinions about the play, especially at the beginning or the end

**chorus[2]** *v* [T] if two or more people chorus something, they say it at the same time: *"Good morning," we chorused.*

**chorus girl** /ˈ·· ·/ *n* [C] a woman who sings and dances in a group in a play or film

**chorus line** /ˈ·· ·/ *n* [C] a group of people who sing and dance together, especially while standing in a straight line, in a play or film

**chose** /tʃəuz‖tʃouz/ the past tense of CHOOSE

**cho·sen** /ˈtʃəuzən‖ˈtʃou-/ the past participle of CHOOSE —see also WELL-CHOSEN

**chow[1]** /tʃau/ *n* **1** [U] *slang* food: *It's chow time!* **2** also **chow chow** /ˈ· ·/ [C] a dog with long thick fur and a dark-coloured tongue that first came from China

**chow[2]** *v*
**chow down** *phr v* [I] *AmE informal* to eat: *We were chowing down on powdered donuts.*

**chow·der** /ˈtʃaudə‖-ər/ *n* [U] a thick soup usually made with CLAMS or fish, vegetables, and milk

**chow·der·head** /ˈtʃaudəhed‖-ər-/ *n* [singular] *AmE slang* a stupid person

**chow mein** /ˌtʃau ˈmeɪn/ *n* [U] a Chinese dish made with meat, vegetables and NOODLES

**Christ[1]** /kraɪst/ *n* **1** also **Jesus Christ, Jesus** the man on whose life, death and teaching Christianity is based, believed to be the son of God —see JESUS[1] (USAGE) **2 the Christ** the religious leader who Christians believe saves the world

**Christ[2]** *interjection* used to express annoyance, surprise etc: *Christ! I've left my keys at home.*

**chris·ten** /ˈkrɪsən/ *v* [T] **1** to be officially given your name at a Christian religious ceremony soon after you are born: **be christened** *She was christened Sarah.* **2** to invent a name for someone because it describes them well: *Tony's colleagues christened him Romeo.* **3** *BrE informal* to use something for the first time: *We haven't christened the new dinner service yet.*

**Chris·ten·dom** /ˈkrɪsəndəm/ *n* [U] *old-fashioned* all the Christian people or countries in the world

**chris·ten·ing** /ˈkrɪsənɪŋ/ *n* [C,U] a Christian religious ceremony at which someone is officially given their name and becomes a member of a Christian church

**Chris·tian[1]** /ˈkrɪstʃən, -tiən/ *n* [C] **1** a person who believes in the ideas taught by Jesus Christ or belongs to a Christian church **2** *informal* a good person

**Christian[2]** *adj* **1** believing the ideas taught by Jesus Christ, or belonging to a Christian church: *Christian ministers* **2** based on the ideas taught by Jesus Christ: *Christian doctrine* **3** also **christian** behaving in a good, kind way: *Laughing at his misfortune wasn't a very christian act.*

**Christian e·ra** /ˌ·· ˈ··/ *n* [singular] the period from the birth of Christ to the present

**Chris·ti·an·i·ty** /ˌkrɪstiˈænəti/ *n* [U] the religion based on the life and teachings of Jesus Christ

**Christian name** /ˈ·· ·/ *n* [C] the name someone is given when they are christened (CHRISTEN (1)), or someone's first name; GIVEN NAME *especially AmE*: *His Christian name is Michael.*

**Christian Sci·ence** /ˌ·· ˈ··/ *n* [U] a religion started in America in 1866, which includes the belief that illnesses can be cured by faith —**Christian Scientist** *n* [C]

**Christ·mas** /ˈkrɪsməs/ *n* [C,U] **1** also **Christmas Day** December 25th, the day when Christians celebrate the birth of Christ: *Are you going home for Christmas?* **2** the period before and after this day: *It snowed all over Christmas.*

**Christmas cake** /ˈ·· ·/ *n* [C,U] a special cake eaten in Britain at Christmas

**Christmas card** /ˈ·· ·/ *n* [C] a card that you send to friends and relatives at Christmas with your good wishes

**Christmas car·ol** /ˌ·· ˈ··/ *n* [C] a Christian song sung at Christmas; CAROL[1]

**Christmas cook·ie** /ˌ·· ˈ··/ *n* [C] a COOKIE eaten in the US at Christmas

**Christmas crack·er** /ˌ·· ˈ··/ *n* [C] a brightly coloured tube of paper containing a small toy that two people pull at Christmas parties

**Christmas Day** /ˌ·· ˈ·/ *n* [C,U] December 25th, the day when Christians celebrate the birth of Christ

**Christmas din·ner** /ˌ·· ˈ··/ *n* [C] a special meal eaten on Christmas Day, consisting mainly of TURKEY (2) and vegetables, followed by Christmas pudding

**Christmas Eve** /ˌ·· ˈ·/ *n* [C,U] the day before Christmas Day

**Christmas pud·ding** /ˌ·· ˈ··/ *n* [C] a PUDDING containing a lot of dried fruit eaten at Christmas

**Christmas stock·ing** /ˌ·· ˈ··/ *n* [C] a long sock which children leave out on Christmas Eve to be filled with presents

**Christ·mas·sy** /ˈkrɪsməsi/ *adj informal* typical of or connected with Christmas: *a nice Christmassy feeling*

**Christ·mas·time** /ˈkrɪsməstaɪm/ *n* [U] the period during Christmas when people celebrate

**Christmas tree** /ˈ·· ·/ *n* [C] a FIR tree either real or artificial that you decorate specially for Christmas

**chro·mat·ic** /krəuˈmætɪk, krə-‖krou-, krə-/ *adj* **1** connected with or containing bright colours **2** related to the musical scale which consists of SEMITONES: *the chromatic scale*

**chrome** /krəum‖kroum/ *n* [U] a hard ALLOY (=a combination of metals) of chromium and other metals used for covering objects with a shiny protective surface

**chrome yel·low** /ˌ· ˈ··◂/ *n* [U] a very bright yellow colour

**chro·mi·um** /ˈkrəʊmiəm‖ˈkroʊ-/ *n* [U] a blue or white metal that is an ELEMENT (=simple substance) and is used for covering objects with a shiny protective surface: *chromium plated*

**chro·mo·some** /ˈkrəʊməsəʊm‖ˈkroʊməsoʊm/ *n* [C] *technical* a part of every living cell that is shaped like a thread which controls the character, shape etc that a plant or animal has: *x and y chromosomes*

**chron-** /krɒn‖krɑːn/ *prefix* another form of the prefix CHRONO-

**chron·ic** /ˈkrɒnɪk‖ˈkrɑː-/ *adj* [usually before noun] **1** a chronic disease or illness is one that cannot be cured: *He's been suffering from chronic arthritis for years now.* **2** a problem or difficulty that you cannot get rid of or that keeps coming back: *a chronic shortage of language teachers|chronic unemployment* **3 chronic alcoholic/gambler etc** someone who suffers from a particular problem or type of behaviour for a long time and cannot stop: *Jake was a chronic alcoholic who could not hold down a job.* **4** *BrE informal* extremely bad: *Don't go to that new restaurant, I've heard the food's chronic.* —**chronically** /-kli/ *adj*: *chronically ill*

**chron·i·cle¹** /ˈkrɒnɪkəl‖ˈkrɑː-/ *n* [C] a written record of a series of events, especially historical events, written in the order in which they happened: [+ **of**] *The book provides a detailed chronicle of the events leading up to his death.*

**chronicle²** *v* [T] to give an account of a series of events in the order in which they happened: *The effect of her parents' separation on her childhood is carefully chronicled in the book.* —**chronicler** *n* [C]

**chrono-** /krɒnəʊ, -nə‖krɑːnoʊ, -nə/ also **chron-** *prefix* concerning time: *a chronometer* (=instrument for measuring time very exactly)

**chron·o·graph** /ˈkrɒnəgrɑːf‖ˈkrɑːnəgræf/ *n* [C] a scientific instrument for measuring and recording periods of time

**chron·o·log·i·cal** /ˌkrɒnəˈlɒdʒɪkəl◂‖ˌkrɑːnəˈlɑː-/ *adj* arranged according to when something happened: **chronological order** *Put the following battles in chronological order.* —**chronologically** /-kli/ *adv*

**chro·nol·o·gy** /krəˈnɒlədʒi‖-ˈnɑː-/ *n* [U] the science of giving times and dates to events

**chro·nom·e·ter** /krəˈnɒmɪ̣tə‖-ˈnɑːmɪ̣tər/ *n* [C] a very exact clock for measuring time, used for scientific purposes

**chrys·a·lis** /ˈkrɪsəlɪ̣s/ *n* [C] a MOTH or BUTTERFLY at the stage of development when it has a hard outer shell, before being a LARVA and an adult

**chry·san·the·mum** /krɪˈsænθɪ̣məm/ *n* [C] a garden plant with large brightly coloured flowers

**chub·by** /ˈtʃʌbi/ *adj* fat in a pleasant healthy-looking way: *I was chubby even as a baby.|chubby cheeks* —**chubbiness** *n* [U] —see FAT¹ (USAGE)

S2 **chuck¹** /tʃʌk/ *v* [T] *informal* **1** to throw something in a careless or relaxed way: **chuck sth on /out of/into etc** *Tania chucked her bag down on the sofa.*|**chuck sb sth** *Chuck me that magazine, would you?* **2 chuck sb** *BrE* to end a romantic relationship with someone: *Why did Judy chuck him?* **3 chuck sb under the chin** to gently touch someone under their chin, especially a child

**chuck** sth ↔ **away/out** *phr v* [T] to throw something away: *We had to chuck a lot of stuff out when we moved.*

**chuck** sb ↔ **out** *phr v* [T] to make someone leave a place, especially because they are behaving badly: *We got chucked out of the pub last night.*

**chuck** sth ↔ **in** *phr v* [T] *BrE* to stop doing something, especially something that is boring or annoying: *What on earth made him chuck his job in so suddenly?*

**chuck up** *phr v* [I,T] *especially BrE slang* to VOMIT¹: *I was chucking up all night.*

**chuck²** *n* **1** [C] part of a machine that holds something so that it does not move **2** *spoken* a word used to address someone in some parts of Northern England

**chuck·le** /ˈtʃʌkəl/ *v* [I] to laugh quietly: *What are you chuckling about?* —**chuckle** *n* [C]

**chuck·le·head** /ˈtʃʌkəlhed/ *n* [C] *AmE informal* a stupid person

**chuck steak** /ˌ· ˈ·/ *n* [U] meat that comes from just above the shoulder of an animal

**chuck wag·on** /ˈ· ˌ··/ *n* [C] *AmE old-fashioned* a vehicle that carries food for a group of people

**chuffed** /tʃʌft/ *adj BrE informal* very pleased or happy: *He's really chuffed about passing the exam.*

**chug** /tʃʌg/ *v* **chugged, chugging** [I always + adv/prep] if a car, train etc chugs, it moves slowly making a repeated low sound: [+ **along/up/around etc**] *The boat chugged out of the harbour.* —**chug** *n* [C usually sing]

**chug-a-lug** /ˈ· · ˌ·/ *v* [I] *AmE informal* to drink all of something in a glass or bottle without stopping: *He chug-a-lugged the entire thing.*

**chum¹** /tʃʌm/ *n* [C] *old-fashioned* a good friend: *Freddie's an old school chum of mine.*

**chum²**

**chum up** *phr v* [I] *old-fashioned* to become someone's friend: [+ **with**] *She soon chummed up with the girl in the next room.*

**chum·my** /ˈtʃʌmi/ *adj old-fashioned* friendly —**chummily** *adv* —**chumminess** *n* [U]

**chump** /tʃʌmp/ *n* [C] *BrE* **1** *old-fashioned* someone who is silly or not very clever **2 chump chop/steak** *BrE* a thick piece of meat with a bone in it **3 be off your chump** *BrE old-fashioned* to be doing or intend to do something extremely silly

**chun·der** /ˈtʃʌndə‖-ər/ *v* [I] *informal* to VOMIT¹

**chunk** /tʃʌŋk/ *n* [C] **1** a large piece of something that does not have an even shape: [+ **of**] *a chunk of cheese* —see picture on page 416 **2** a large part or amount of something: *The rent takes a large chunk out of my monthly salary.|It's sad to see another chunk of the old Liverpool gone.*

**chunk·y** /ˈtʃʌŋki/ *adj* **1** thick, solid and heavy: *She wore a lot of chunky silver jewellery.* **2** someone who is chunky has a broad, heavy body

**church** /tʃɜːtʃ‖tʃɜːrtʃ/ *n* **1** [C] a building where Chris- S1
tians go to worship **2** [U] the religious ceremonies in a W1
church: *Mrs Dobson invited us to dinner after church.* **3 the church** the profession of the CLERGY (=priests and other people employed by the church) **4** [singular, U] the institution of the Christian religion: *separation of church and state*

**church·go·er** /ˈtʃɜːtʃˌgəʊə‖ˈtʃɜːrtʃˌgoʊər/ *n* [C] someone who goes to church regularly

**church·key** /ˈtʃɜːtʃkiː‖ˈtʃɜːrtʃ-/ *n* [C] *AmE informal* a BOTTLE OPENER

**church·man** /ˈtʃɜːtʃmən‖ˈtʃɜːrtʃ-/ *n* [C] *plural* **churchmen** /-mən/ a priest; CLERGYMAN

**Church of Eng·land** /ˌ· · ˈ··◂/ *n* **the Church of England** the state church in England, the official leader of which is the Queen or King —**Church of England** also **C of E** *adj*

**Church of Scot·land** /ˌ· · ˈ··◂/ *n* [singular] the state church in Scotland

**church school** /ˈ· ˌ·/ *n* [C] a school in Britain that is partly controlled by the church

**church·war·den** /ˌtʃɜːtʃˈwɔːdn‖ˈtʃɜːrtʃwɔːrdn/ *n* [C] someone who looks after church property and money

**church·yard** /ˈtʃɜːtʃjɑːd‖ˈtʃɜːrtʃjɑːrd/ *n* [C] a piece of land around a church where people are buried

**churl·ish** /ˈtʃɜːlɪʃ‖ˈtʃɜːr-/ *adj* bad-tempered or impolite: *It seemed churlish to refuse his invitation.* —**churl** *n* [C] —**churlishly** *adv* —**churlishness** *n* [U]

**churn¹** /tʃɜːn‖tʃɜːrn/ *n* [C] **1** a container used for shaking milk in order to make it into butter **2** *BrE* a large metal container used to carry milk in —see picture at CONTAINER

**churn²** *v* **1** [I] if your stomach churns you feel sick because you are nervous or frightened: *My stomach was churning on the day of the exam.* **2** [T] to make milk by using a churn **3** also **churn up** [I,T] if water churns or if it is churned, it moves about violently

**churn** sth ↔ **out** *phr v* [T] to produce large quantities of something, especially without caring about quality: *The factory churns out thousands of these awful plastic toys every week.*

**churn up** *phr v* **1** [T **churn** sth ↔ **up**] to damage the surface of something, especially by walking on it or driving a vehicle over it: *The lawn had been churned up by the tractor.* **2** [T **churn** sb **up**] to make someone upset or angry: *The argument had left her feeling all churned up.* **3** [I,T] to CHURN² (3)

**chute** /ʃuːt/ *n* [C] **1** a long narrow structure that slopes down, used for sliding things from one place to another or for people to slide down: *The pool had the added attraction of a water chute.* **2** *informal* a PARACHUTE¹

**chut·ney** /ˈtʃʌtni/ *n* [U] a mixture of fruits, hot-tasting seeds and sugar, that is eaten with meat or cheese: *mango chutney*

**chutz·pah** /ˈhʊtspə/ *n* [U] *slang* too much confidence, which is often considered to be rude; NERVE¹ (3): *He wouldn't have the chutzpah to deliver that message.*

**CIA** /ˌsiː aɪ ˈeɪ/ *n* **the CIA** the Central Intelligence Agency; the department of the US government that collects information about other countries, especially secretly —compare FBI

**ciao** /tʃaʊ/ *interjection informal* used to say goodbye

**ci·ca·da** /sɪ̇ˈkɑːdə‖sɪ̇ˈkeɪdə, -ˈkɑː-/ *n* [C] an insect that lives in hot countries, has large transparent wings, and makes a high singing noise

**cic·a·trice** /ˈsɪkətrɪs/ also **cic·a·trix** /-trɪks/ *n* [C] *technical* a mark remaining from a wound; SCAR¹ (1)

**ci·ce·ro·ne** /ˌsɪsəˈrəʊni, ˌtʃɪtʃə-‖-ˈroʊ-/ *n* [C] *literary* someone who shows tourists interesting places; GUIDE¹ (1a)

**CID** /ˌsiː aɪ ˈdiː/ *n* **the CID** the Criminal Investigation Department; the department of the British police that deals with very serious crimes

**-cide** /saɪd/ *suffix* [in nouns] another form of the suffix -ICIDE: *genocide* (=killing a whole race of people) —**-cidal** *in adjectives* —**-cidally** *in adverbs*

**ci·der** /ˈsaɪdə‖-ər/ *n* [C,U] **1** *BrE* an alcoholic drink made from apples or a glass of this drink **2** *AmE* also **sweet cider** a non-alcoholic drink made from apples or a glass of this drink —see also HARD CIDER *AmE*

**ci·gar** /sɪˈɡɑː‖-ˈɡɑːr/ *n* [C] a thing that people smoke made from tobacco leaves that have been rolled into a thick tube shape

S2 W3 **cig·a·rette** /ˌsɪɡəˈret‖ˌsɪɡəˈret, ˈsɪɡəˌret/ *n* [C] a thin tube of paper filled with finely cut tobacco that people smoke: *a packet of cigarettes*

**cigarette butt** /..ˈ. ˌ., ˈ... ˌ./ also **cigarette end** *especially BrE n* [C] the part of a cigarette that remains when someone has finished smoking it

**cigarette hol·der** /..ˈ. ˌ.., ˈ... ˌ../ *n* [C] a narrow tube for holding a cigarette

**cigarette light·er** /..ˈ. ˌ.., ˈ... ˌ../ also **lighter** *n* [C] a small object that produces a flame for lighting cigarettes, CIGARS etc

**cigarette pa·per** /..ˈ. ˌ.., ˈ... ˌ../ *n* [C,U] thin paper used to make your own cigarettes

**cig·gy** /ˈsɪɡi/ *n* [C] *BrE spoken* a cigarette

**ci·lan·tro** /sɪ̇ˈlæntrəʊ‖ sɪ̇ˈlɑːntroʊ, -ˈlæn-/ *n* [U] *AmE* the strong-tasting leaves of a small plant, used for giving a special taste to food, especially in Asian and Mexican cooking; CORIANDER *especially BrE*

**C-in-C** /ˌsiː ɪn ˈsiː/ *n* an abbreviation of COMMANDER IN CHIEF

**cinch¹** /sɪntʃ/ *n* [singular] *informal* **1** something that is very easy: *"How was the exam?" "Oh, it was a cinch!"* **2** something that will definitely happen: *It's an absolute cinch that this horse is going to win!*

**cinch²** *v* [T] *AmE* **1** to pull a belt, STRAP¹ (1) etc tightly around something **2** to do something so that you can be sure something will happen: *They cinched a place in the play-off.*

**cinch³** *adj AmE* **cinch belt/strap etc** a thin belt etc, made of ELASTIC¹, that you pull so that it is very tight

**cinc·ture** /ˈsɪŋktʃə‖-ər/ *n* [C] *literary* a belt

**cin·der** /ˈsɪndə‖-ər/ *n* [C usually plural] a very small piece of burnt wood, coal etc: *a cold hearth full of cinders* | **burnt to a cinder** (=completely burnt) *The cake was burnt to a cinder.*

**cinder block** /ˈ.. ˌ./ *n* [C] *AmE* a large brick for building made from CEMENT and cinders; BREEZE-BLOCK *BrE*

**cinder track** /ˈ.. ˌ./ *n* [C] a race track covered with cinders

**cine-** /sɪni/ *prefix BrE* concerning films or the film industry: *a cine-camera*

**cine-cam·e·ra** /ˈsɪni ˌkæmərə/ *n* [C] *BrE* a camera for making moving films, rather than photographs

**cine-film** /ˈsɪni fɪlm/ *n* [U] *BrE* film used in a cine-camera

**cin·e·ma** /ˈsɪnɪ̇mə/ *n especially BrE* **1** [C] a building in which films are shown; MOVIE THEATER *AmE*: *What's on at the cinema?* **2** [singular, U] the skill or industry of making films: *a leading figure in Italian cinema* S3

**cin·e·mat·ic** /ˌsɪnɪ̇ˈmætɪk◂/ *adj* connected with films for the cinema: *a lack of cinematic output*

**cin·e·ma·to·gra·phy** /ˌsɪnɪ̇məˈtɒɡrəfi‖-ˈtɑː-/ *n* [U] *technical* the skill or study of making films: *with impressive cinematography by Robert Surtees* —**cinematographer** *n* [C]

**cin·na·mon¹** /ˈsɪnəmən/ *n* [U] a sweet-smelling substance used for giving a special taste to cakes etc

**cinnamon²** *adj* having a light yellowish-brown colour

**ci·pher¹**, **cypher** /ˈsaɪfə‖-ər/ *n* [C] **1** a system of secret writing; CODE¹ (4) **2** someone who is not important and has no power or influence: *a mere cypher* **3** *literary* the number 0; zero

**cipher²** *v* [T] to put a message into CODE (=a system of secret writing) —compare DECIPHER

**cir·ca** /ˈsɜːkə‖ˈsɜːr-/ *prep formal* used before a date to show that something happened on nearly, but not exactly that date: *manuscripts dating from circa 1100*

**cir·ca·di·an** /sɜːˈkeɪdiən‖sɜːr-/ *adj* [only before noun] *technical* connected with a period of 24 hours, used especially when talking about changes in people's bodies

**cir·cle¹** /ˈsɜːkəl‖ˈsɜːr-/ *n* [C] S2 W2
**1** ▶ **SHAPE** ◀ a completely round shape, like the letter O: *Draw a circle 10cm in diameter.* | *Cut the pastry into circles.* | **perfect circle** (=exactly round) —see picture at SHAPE¹

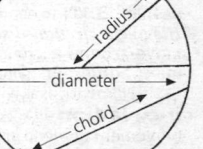

circle

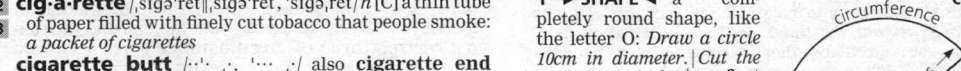

**2** ▶ **GROUP OF PEOPLE/THINGS** ◀ a group of people or things forming a round shape: *The children stood round in a circle.* | *a circle of chairs*
**3** ▶ **SOCIAL GROUP** ◀ also **circles** a group of people who know each other: *a large circle of friends* | *well-known in fashionable circles* | **move in different circles** (=have different friends, jobs, interests etc)
**4** **political/literary/scientific etc circles** the people who are involved in politics, literature, science etc: *These ideas have caused an uproar in literary and academic circles.*

5 ▶ THEATRE ◀ *BrE* the upper floor of a theatre, that has seats arranged in curved rows; BALCONY (2) *especially AmE* —see picture at THEATRE
6 **go round in circles** to think or argue about something without deciding anything or making progress: *Let's have a break – we're just going round in circles.*
7 **come/turn full circle** if a process, argument etc comes full circle, it ends in the same situation in which it began: *By August her feelings had turned full circle.* —see also **square the circle** (SQUARE³ (6)), VICIOUS CIRCLE

**circle²** *v* 1 [T] to draw a circle around something: *Circle the correct answer.* 2 [I,T] to move around in a circle in the air: *The plane circled the airport before landing.*

**cir·clet** /ˈsɜːklɪ̈t‖ˈsɜːr-/ *n* [C] a narrow band of gold, silver, or jewels worn around someone's head or arms

W3 **cir·cuit** /ˈsɜːkɪ̈t‖ˈsɜːr-/ *n* [C] 1 a path that forms a circle around an area, or a journey along this path: *We did a circuit of the old city walls.* 2 a track that cars, MOTORBIKES etc race around 3 **the tennis/lecture/cabaret etc circuit** all the places that are usually visited by someone who plays tennis etc: *a well-known entertainer on the club circuit* 4 the complete circle that an electric current travels 5 **do circuits** *BrE informal* to do CIRCUIT TRAINING —see also PRINTED CIRCUIT, SHORT CIRCUIT

**circuit board** /ˈ·· ·/ *n* [C] a set of connections between points on a piece of electrical equipment which uses a thin line of metal to CONDUCT (=carry) the electricity; PRINTED CIRCUIT

**circuit break·er** /ˈ·· ˌ··/ *n* [C] a piece of equipment that stops an electric current if it becomes dangerous

**circuit court** /ˈ·· ˌ·/ *n* [C] a court of law that happens in a small town when a judge visits from a larger town

**cir·cu·i·tous** /sɜːˈkjuːɪ̈təs‖sɜːr-/ *adj* **circuitous route/course etc** a way of getting from one place to another that is longer than the most direct way —**circuitously** *adv*

**cir·cuit·ry** /ˈsɜːkɪ̈tri‖ˈsɜːr-/ *n* [U] a system of electric circuits

**circuit train·ing** /ˈ·· ˌ··/ *n* [U] *BrE* several different exercises done quickly after each other, in order to make you able to do sport better

**cir·cu·lar¹** /ˈsɜːkjɪ̈lə‖ˈsɜːrkjɪ̈lər/ *adj* 1 shaped like a circle: *a circular table* 2 moving around in a circle: *a circular bus route* 3 **circular argument/discussion etc** an argument in which you always return to the same statements or ideas that were expressed at the beginning —**circularity** /ˌsɜːkjɪ̈ˈlærɪ̈ti‖ˌsɜːr-/ *n* [U]

**circular²** *n* [C] a printed advertisement, notice etc that is sent to lots of people at the same time

**cir·cu·lar·ize** also **-ise** *BrE* /ˈsɜːkjɪ̈ləraɪz‖ˈsɜːr-/ *v* [T] to send printed notices or advertisements to a lot of people

**circular saw** /ˌ··· ˈ·/ *n* [C] a round metal blade with small sharp parts around the edge, used for cutting wood —compare CHAIN SAW

**cir·cu·late** /ˈsɜːkjɪ̈leɪt‖ˈsɜːr-/ *v* 1 [I,T] to move around within a system, or to make something do this: *Blood circulates around the body.* 2 [I] if information, facts, ideas etc circulate, they become known by many people 3 [T] to send goods, information etc to people: *His agent circulated several copies of the book.* 4 [I] to move around a group, especially at a party, talking to many different people; MINGLE (2) —**circulatory** /ˌsɜːkjɪ̈ˈleɪtəri, ˈsɜkjɪ̈lətəri‖ˈsɜːrkjɪ̈lətɔːri/ *adj*

**cir·cu·la·tion** /ˌsɜːkjɪ̈ˈleɪʃən‖ˌsɜːr-/ *n* 1 [C,U] the movement of blood around your body: *Exercise improves the circulation.* 2 [U] the exchange of information, money etc from one person to another in a group or society: **in circulation** *Several thousand of the fake notes are in circulation.* 3 [singular] the average number of copies of a newspaper or magazine that are usually sold each day, week, month etc: *Circulation fell when the price was increased to 45p.* 4 **out of circulation** *informal* not taking part in social activities for a period of time: *Sandy's out of circulation until after her exams.* 5 [C,U] the movement of liquid, air etc in a system

**circum** /sɜːkəm‖sɜːr-/ *prefix* all the way round something: *to circumnavigate the world* (=sail round it) | *to circumvent* (=avoid something by finding a way round)

**cir·cum·cise** /ˈsɜːkəmsaɪz‖ˈsɜːr-/ *v* [T] 1 to cut off the skin at the end of the PENIS (=male sex organ) 2 to cut off the CLITORIS of a female

**cir·cum·ci·sion** /ˌsɜːkəmˈsɪʒən‖ˌsɜːr-/ *n* [C,U] the act of circumcising someone, or an occasion when a baby is circumcised as part of a religious ceremony

**cir·cum·fer·ence** /səˈkʌmfərəns‖sər-/ *n* 1 [C,U] the distance measured around the outside of a circle: *the circumference of the Earth* | *3 metres in circumference* —see picture at CIRCLE¹ 2 [singular] the measurement around the outside of any shape; PERIPHERY —**circumferential** /səˌkʌmfəˈrenʃəl‖sər-/ *adj* —see table on page B3

**cir·cum·flex** /ˈsɜːkəmfleks‖ˈsɜːr-/ *n* [C] a mark placed above a letter in a French word to show its pronunciation, for example, ô —compare GRAVE³, ACUTE (7)

**cir·cum·lo·cu·tion** /ˌsɜːkəmləˈkjuːʃən‖ˌsɜːr-/ *n* [C,U] *formal* the practice of using too many words to express an idea, instead of saying it directly —**circumlocutory** /ˌsɜːkəmˈlɒkjɪ̈təri, -ləˈkjuːtəri‖-ˈlɑːkjɪ̈tɔːri/ *adj*

**cir·cum·nav·i·gate** /ˌsɜːkəmˈnævɪ̈geɪt‖ˌsɜːr-/ *v* [T] to sail completely around the Earth, an island etc —**circumnavigation** /ˌsɜːkəmnævɪ̈ˈgeɪʃən‖ˌsɜːr-/ *n* [C,U]

**cir·cum·scribe** /ˈsɜːkəmskraɪb‖ˈsɜːr-/ *v* [T] 1 [often passive] *formal* to limit power, rights, or abilities; RESTRICT: *All our minds are heavily circumscribed by habit.* 2 *technical* to draw a line around something: *a circle circumscribed by a square* —**circumscription** /ˌsɜːkəmˈskrɪpʃən‖ˌsɜːr-/ *n* [U]

**cir·cum·spect** /ˈsɜːkəmspekt‖ˈsɜːr-/ *adj* 1 thinking carefully about things before doing them; CAUTIOUS: *The journalist was circumspect, only tentatively linking the escape with the murder.* 2 a circumspect action or answer is done or given only after careful thought —**circumspectly** *adv* —**circumspection** /ˌsɜːkəmˈspekʃən‖ˌsɜːr-/ *n* [U]

**cir·cum·stance** /ˈsɜːkəmstæns, -stəns‖ˈsɜːr-/ *n* S1 W1
1 **circumstances** [plural] the conditions that affect a situation, action, event etc: *The rules can only be waived in exceptional circumstances.* | **in suspicious circumstances** (=in a way that makes you think something illegal or dishonest has happened) *He was found dead in suspicious circumstances.* | **extenuating circumstances** (=things that have happened which excuse or explain someone's bad behaviour or actions) 2 **under/in no circumstances** used to emphasize that something must definitely not happen: *Under no circumstances are you to leave the house.* 3 **under/in the circumstances** used to say that a particular situation makes an action, decision etc necessary or acceptable when it would not normally be: *The result was the best that could be expected under the circumstances.* 4 [U] the combination of facts, events etc that influence your life, and that you cannot control: **force of circumstance** *Force of circumstance compelled us to leave.* | **victim of circumstance** (=someone who is harmed because of the situation they are in, not because they have done anything wrong) 5 **live in reduced circumstances** *old-fashioned* to have much less money than you used to have 6 **pomp and circumstance** *literary* grand ceremonial activity, especially on a formal or important occasion

**cir·cum·stan·tial** /ˌsɜːkəmˈstænʃəl◂‖ˌsɜːr-/ *adj* 1 **circumstantial evidence** *law* facts that make you believe something probably happened, but do not definitely prove that it did 2 **circumstantial account/description etc** *formal* a description etc that includes all the details —**circumstantially** *adv*

**cir·cum·vent** /ˌsɜːkəmˈvent‖ˌsɜːr-/ *v* [T] 1 to avoid a problem or rule that restricts you, especially in a clever or dishonest way: *The company opened an account abroad, in order to circumvent the tax laws.* 2 *formal* to change the direction in which you are travelling in order to avoid something: *We went north in order to circumvent the mountains.* —**circumvention** /-ˈvenʃən/ *n* [U]

**cir·cus** /ˈsɜːkəs‖ˈsɜːr-/ *n* **1** [C] a group of people and animals who travel around performing skilful tricks as entertainment: **circus act** (=a trick performed in a circus)|**circus ring** (=the round area where tricks are performed) **2** [singular] *informal* a meeting, group of people etc that is very noisy and uncontrolled: *The first day of school is always such a circus.* **3** [C] in ancient Rome, a place where fights, races etc took place, with seats built in a circle **4** [singular] *BrE* used sometimes as the name of a round open area where several streets join together: *Piccadilly Circus*

**cirque** /sɜːk‖sɜːrk/ *n* [C] *technical* a CORRIE —see picture on page 855

**cir·rho·sis** /sɪ̈ˈrəʊsɪ̈s‖-ˈroʊ-/ *n* [U] a serious disease of the LIVER (1), often caused by drinking too much alcohol

**cir·rus** /ˈsɪrəs/ *n* [U] a form of cloud that is light and shaped like feathers, high in the sky —compare CUMULUS, NIMBUS (1)

**CIS** /ˌsiː aɪ ˈes/ *n* the Commonwealth of Independent States; the name given to a group of states of which the largest is Russia

**cis·sy** /ˈsɪsi/ *n* [C] *BrE informal* SISSY —**cissy** *adj*

**cis·tern** /ˈsɪstən‖-ərn/ *n* [C] a container in which water is stored inside a building

**cit·a·del** /ˈsɪtədəl, -del/ *n* [C] **1** a strong FORT (=small castle), intended to be somewhere people can go for safety if their city is attacked **2 the citadel of sth** *literary* a place or situation in which an idea, principle, system etc that you think is important is kept safe; STRONGHOLD: *the last citadel of freedom*

**ci·ta·tion** /saɪˈteɪʃən/ *n* [C] **1** [C] an official statement about someone's character or actions, especially one saying that they have been brave in battle: *a citation for bravery* **2** [C] a line taken from a book, speech etc; QUOTATION (1) **3** [U] an occasion when someone cites or is cited

**cite** /saɪt/ *v* [T] **1** to mention something as an example, especially one that supports, proves, or explains an idea or situation: **cite sth as sth** *Several factors have been cited as the cause of the student unrest.* **2** to give the exact words of something that has been written in order to support an opinion or prove an idea; QUOTE[1] (1): *the passage cited above* **3** to call someone to appear before a court of law: *Two managers had been cited for similar infractions.* **4** to mention someone by name in a court case: *Penny was cited in the divorce proceedings.* **5** *formal* to mention someone because they deserve praise: **cite sb for sth** *Joe was cited for bravery.*

**cit·i·fied** /ˈsɪtɪfaɪd/ *adj* connected with the city or the way people in cities live, especially when this is considered bad: *a rural area that has become industrialized and citified*

**cit·i·zen** /ˈsɪtɪ̈zən/ *n* [C] **1** someone who lives in a particular town, country, or state and has rights and responsibilities there: *teaching our children to be good citizens* **2** someone who belongs to a particular country, whether they are living there or not: *tax advantages for British citizens living and working abroad* —compare NATIONAL[2] **3 second-class citizen** someone who feels unimportant because of the way other people treat them: *I was made to feel like a second-class citizen as soon as I walked through the door.* —see also SENIOR CITIZEN

**cit·i·zen·ry** /ˈsɪtɪ̈zənri/ *n* [U] all the citizens in a particular place

**citizen's ar·rest** /ˌ···· ˈ·/ *n* [C] the act of taking someone to a police station because you think they have done something wrong: **make a citizen's arrest** *The stallholder made a citizen's arrest.*

**Cit·i·zens' Band** /ˌ··· ˈ·◂/ *n* [U] —see CB

**cit·i·zen·ship** /ˈsɪtɪ̈zənʃɪp/ *n* [U] the legal right of belonging to a particular country: **French/US/Brazilian citizenship** *an application for French citizenship*|**dual citizenship** (=belonging to two different countries) *dual citizenship of Canada and the US*

**cit·ric ac·id** /ˌsɪtrɪk ˈæsɪ̈d/ *n* [U] a weak acid found in some fruits, such as lemons

**cit·ron** /ˈsɪtrən/ *n* [C] a fruit like a LEMON (1) but bigger

**cit·ron·el·la** /ˌsɪtrəˈnelə/ *n* [U] an oil used for keeping insects away

**cit·rus** /ˈsɪtrəs/ also **citrus tree** /ˈ·· ·/ *n* [C] a type of tree that produces citrus fruits —**citrus, citrous** /ˈsɪtrəs/ *adj*

**citrus fruit** /ˈ·· ·/ *n* [C,U] a fruit with a thick skin such as an orange or LEMON (1) —see picture on page 413

**cit·y** /ˈsɪti/ *n* **1** [C] a large important town, especially one with a CATHEDRAL: *New York City*|*a capital city*|**city dweller** (=someone who lives in a city) **2** the people who live in a city: *The city has been living in fear since last week's earthquake.* **3 the City** *BrE* the area of London which is Britain's financial centre, and the important institutions there: **City banker/stockbroker etc** (=a banker etc who works in the city) —see also INNER CITY S1 W1

**city cen·tre** /ˌ·· ˈ··/ *n* [C] *BrE* the main shopping or business area in a city; DOWNTOWN *AmE*

**city desk** /ˈ·· ·/ *n* [C] *AmE* a department of a newspaper that deals with local news

**city ed·it·or** /ˈ·· ˌ···/ *n* [C] **1** also **financial editor** *BrE* a JOURNALIST responsible for the financial part of a newspaper **2** *AmE* a JOURNALIST responsible for local news

**city fa·ther** /ˌ·· ˈ··/ *n* [C usually plural] *old use* a member of the group of people who govern a city

**city hall** /ˌ·· ˈ·/ *n* [C,U] *AmE* the local government of a city and the building it uses as its offices

**city plan·ning** /ˌ·· ˈ··/ *n* [U] *AmE* the study of the way cities work, so that roads, houses, services etc can be provided effectively; TOWN PLANNING *BrE*

**city slick·er** /ˌ·· ˈ··/ *n* [C] someone who lives and works in a city and has no experience of anything outside it

**city-state** /ˌ·· ˈ·‖ˈ·· ·, ˌ·· ˈ·/ *n* [C] a city, especially in former times, that forms an independent state with the surrounding country area: *the city-state of Athens*

**cit·y·wide** /ˈsɪtiwaɪd/ *adj especially AmE* involving all the areas of a city: *a citywide campaign to fight racism*

**civ·et** /ˈsɪvɪ̈t/ *n* **1** [C] also **civet cat** a small animal like a cat, that lives in Asia and Africa **2** [U] a strong-smelling liquid from a civet cat, used to make PERFUME

**civ·ic** /ˈsɪvɪk/ *adj* [only before noun] **1** connected with a town or city: *the civic authorities*|**civic centre** (=an area in a city where all the public buildings are) **2** connected with the people who live in a town or city: *It is your civic duty to vote in the local elections.*|**civic pride** (=people's pride in their own city)

**civ·ics** /ˈsɪvɪks/ *n* [U] *especially AmE* a school subject dealing with the rights and duties of citizens and the way government works

**civ·ies** /ˈsɪviz/ *n* [plural] CIVVIES

**civ·il** /ˈsɪvəl/ *adj* **1** [only before noun] connected with the people who live in a country: *civil order*|**civil conflict/disturbance/unrest etc** (=fighting etc between different groups of people living in the same country) *the continuing civil conflict in Rwanda*|**civil liberty/liberties** (=the freedom that the people in a country have to behave and think as they wish within the law) **2** [only before noun] connected with the ordinary people or things in a country rather than the military ones: *The military and civil authorities are working together to quell the unrest.* **3** [only before noun] involving or dealing with private legal matters, not with criminal ones: *Many civil cases can be settled out of court.* —see also CIVIL LAW —compare CRIMINAL[1] (2) **4** polite in a formal and not a friendly way: *Try at least to be civil.*

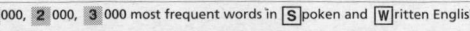

**civil de·fence** /ˌ·· ˈ··/ *n* [U] **1** the organization of ordinary rather than military people to help defend their country from military attack **2 civil defences** *plural* the things a country does to prepare for a military attack by an enemy: *We need to strengthen our civil defences.*

**civil dis·o·be·di·ence** /ˌ·· ··ˈ···/ *n* [U] action that breaks the law usually taken by a large number of people to protest against something done by the government

**civil en·gi·neer·ing** /ˌ·· ··ˈ··/ *n* [U] the planning, building, and repair of roads, bridges, large buildings, etc —**civil engineer** *n* [C]

**ci·vil·ian** /sɪ̆ˈvɪljən/ *n* [C] anyone who is not a member of the army, navy, airforce, or police: *the killing of innocent civilians during the bombing campaign* —**civilian** *adj: a return to civilian government after years of military rule*

**ci·vil·i·ty** /sɪ̆ˈvɪlɪ̆ti/ *n* **1** [U] polite behaviour which most people consider normal: *Please have the civility to knock before you enter next time.* **2 civilities** [plural] *formal* something that you say or do in order to be polite: *We exchanged civilities when we were neighbours but nothing more.*

**civ·i·li·za·tion** also **-isation** *BrE* /ˌsɪvəl-aɪˈzeɪʃən‖ -vələˈzeɪ-/ *n* **1** [C,U] a society that is well organized and developed: *contemporary American civilization*|[+ **of**] *the ancient civilizations of Greece and Rome* **2** [U] all the societies in the world considered as a whole: *The book explores the relationship between religion and civilization.* **3** [U] the process in which societies become developed and organized **4** [U] *humorous* a place where you feel comfortable or where there is plenty to do: *After a week in the mountains all I wanted to do was get back to civilization!*

**civ·i·lize** also **-ise** *BrE* /ˈsɪvəl-aɪz/ *v* [T] *BrE often humorous* to make someone behave in a more sensible or gentle way: *men who need to be domesticated and civilized*

**civ·i·lized** also **-ised** *BrE* /ˈsɪvəl-aɪzd/ *adj* **1** being well organized and developed socially: *Such things should not be allowed to happen in a civilized society.* **2** pleasant and comfortable: *"This is very civilized." she said, lying back in the sun with a gin and tonic.* **3** behaving in a polite sensible way instead of getting angry: *Let's try and be civilized about this shall we?*

**civil law** /ˌ·· ˈ·/ *n* [U] the area of law deals with the affairs of private citizens rather than with crime

**civil lib·er·ty** /ˌ·· ˈ···/ also **civil liberties** *n* [U] [plural] the right of all citizens to be free to do whatever they want while respecting the rights of other people

**civil list** /ˈ·· ·/ *n* [singular] the sum of money given every year by Parliament to the King or Queen of Britain and to some other people

**civil rights** /ˌ·· ˈ·/ *n* [plural] the rights that every person should have, such as the right to vote or to be treated fairly by the law, whatever their sex, race, or religion: **civil rights campaigner/movement etc** *50,000 people attended the civil rights demonstration.* —see also BILL OF RIGHTS

**civil ser·vant** /ˌ·· ˈ··/ *n* [C] someone employed in the civil service

**civil ser·vice** /ˌ·· ˈ··/ *n* [singular] the government departments that manage the affairs of the country

**civil war** /ˌ·· ˈ·/ *n* [C,U] a war in which opposing groups of people from the same country fight each other in order to gain political control

**civ·vies, civies** /ˈsɪviz/ *n* [plural] *slang* ordinary clothes, as opposed to military uniform, used mainly by people in the army, navy, or airforce: *sailors on leave wearing their civvies*

**civ·vy** /ˈsɪvi/ *n* [C] *BrE* **1** *slang* a word meaning someone who is not in the army, navy, or airforce, used mainly by people who are **2 civvy street** *old-fashioned* ordinary life as it is lived outside the army, navy, or airforce

**cl** the written abbreviation of CENTILITRE

**clack** /klæk/ *v* **1** [I,T] if you clack something or if it clacks, it makes a continuous short hard sound **2** [I] *informal* if tongues are clacking, people are talking a lot about something shocking or surprising: *News of her pregnancy had already set tongues clacking in the neighbourhood.* —**clack** *n* [singular]

**clad** /klæd/ *adj* **1** *literary* wearing a particular kind of clothing: *a model clad in silk and lace*|**warmly/poorly/scantily clad** (=dressed in a particular way) **2 snow-clad/ivy-clad etc** covered in a particular thing: *an armor-clad ship*

**clad·ding** /ˈklædɪŋ/ *n* [U] a cover of hard material that protects the outside of a building, tank, or engine

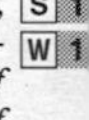

**claim¹** /kleɪm/ *v* **1** [I,T] to state that something is true, even though it has not been proved: **claim (that)** *Gascoigne claimed he'd been dining with friends at the time of the murder.*|**claim to be** *She claims to be a descendant of Charles Dickens.*|**claim to have done** *Doctors claimed to have discovered a cure for the disease.*|**claim responsibility/innocence/credit** (=say officially that you are responsible, innocent etc) **2** [I,T] to officially demand or receive money from an organization: [+ **on**] *You can claim on the insurance if you have an accident while on vacation.*|*The government intends to make legal aid harder to claim.*|**claim benefit/an allowance/damages** (=officially receive money because you do not have a job, are injured etc) **3** [T] to state that you have a right to something or to take something that belongs to you: *Viscount Lander will claim the title on his father's death.*|*Lost property can be claimed between 10 a.m. and 4 p.m.* **4** [T] if a war, accident etc claims lives, people die because of it: *The Kobe earthquake has so far claimed over 3000 lives.* **5** [T] if something claims someone's attention or time, they have to consider it carefully: *The issue of a united Ireland continues to claim our undivided attention.*

**claim²** *n* [C] S2 W1

**1 ▶ MONEY ◀ a)** a request for money, especially money that you have a right to: [+ **for**] *claims for compensation*|**make a claim/put in a claim** *They put in a claim on the insurance for the stolen luggage.*|**pay claim** (=a request made by workers for more money)|**claim form** (=an official form that you must fill in in order to get money from an organization) **b)** the sum of money you request when making such a claim: *The insurance company cannot meet such enormous claims.*

**2 ▶ STATEMENT ◀** a statement that something is true, even though it has not been proved: **claim that** *Dino denies claims that he is involved in a drugs ring.*|**claim to do/be sth** *the Democratic claim to be the party of women's rights*|**make a claim** *Photographs make a claim to protray reality in a way that paintings never can.*|**make no claim to do something** (=used to say that you do not pretend to be able to do something) *I make no claim to understand the complexities of the situation.*|**dispute a claim** (=say publicly that a statement is not true)

**3 ▶ FOR PRAISE/RESPECT ETC ◀** something that you say or do, that shows that you deserve to be successful: [+ **to**] *Judging by last night's performance Ryan must have a claim to a place on the Olympic team.*

**4 ▶ TO OWN OR TAKE SOMETHING ◀** a right to have or get something such as land, a title etc that belongs to you: [+ **to**] *No one can dispute Oliver's claim to the inheritance.*|**have a claim on/to sth** *Surely they have a rightful claim to their father's land?*

**5 lay claim to sth** to say that you have a right to own something: *Ellen resented the stranger who laid claim to her brother's fortune.*

**6 stake your claim** to say that you have a right to own something, especially when other people also say they have a right to own it: *If you want some of the furniture now's the time to stake your claim.*

**7 claim to fame** an expression meaning a reason why someone or something is famous, often used jokingly when mentioning something that is not very important: *My main claim to fame is that I once shook Elvis' hand.*

**8 have a claim on sb** to have a right to demand some-

one's time, attention etc: *She seems to think she's got an exclusive claim on my time.*
9 ► **LAND** ◄ something such as a piece of land that contains valuable minerals —see also **jump a claim** (JUMP[1] (19))

**clai·mant** /ˈkleɪmənt/ *n* [C] **1** someone who claims something, especially money, from the government, a court etc because they think they have a right to it: *The company was ordered to recompense the claimant for damages.* **2** someone who makes a claim, for example under a WILL[2] (2)

**clair·voy·ant** /kleəˈvɔɪənt‖kler-/ *n* [C] someone who says they can see what will happen in the future —**clairvoyance** *n* [U] —**clairvoyant** *adj*

**clam[1]** /klæm/ *n* [C] **1** a SHELLFISH that you can eat, which has a shell in two parts that open and close **2** *AmE informal* someone who does not say what they are thinking or feeling **3** **as happy as a clam** *AmE informal* very happy

**clam[2]** *v*
**clam up** *phr v* [I] *informal* to suddenly stop talking, especially when you are nervous or shy: *I just clammed up when her father came in.*

**clam·bake** /ˈklæmbeɪk/ *n* [C] *AmE* an informal party by the sea where clams are cooked and eaten

**clam·ber** /ˈklæmbə‖-ər/ *v* [I always + adv/prep] to climb slowly, using your hands and feet: [+ **up/over/to etc**] *They clambered over the slippery rocks.*

**clam·my** /ˈklæmi/ *adj* feeling wet, cold, and sticky in a way that is unpleasant: *clammy with sweat* —**clammily** *adv* —**clamminess** *n* [U]

**clam·our[1]** *BrE*, **clamor** *AmE* /ˈklæmə‖-ər/ *n* [singular,U] **1** a very loud noise, often made by a large group of people or animals: *the clamor of factory machinery* **2** strong feeling expressed loudly by a large group of people: [+ **for**] *the clamour for an all-out strike* —**clamorous** *adj*

**clamour[2]** *BrE*, **clamor** *AmE* *v* [I] **1** [always + adv/prep] to demand something loudly: [+ **for**] *The audience were on their feet clamouring for more.* **2** to talk or shout loudly: *Children clamored in the playground.*

**clamp[1]** /klæmp/ *v* [T] **1** [always + adv/prep] to fasten or hold two things together using a clamp: **clamp sth together/onto etc** *Clamp the two parts together until the glue dries.* **2** [always + adv/prep] to put or hold something in a position where it does not move: **clamp sth over/between/around etc** *He clamped a hand over my mouth* **3** *BrE* to put a clamp on a car that is illegally parked; BOOT[2] (3) *AmE*
**clamp down** *phr v* [I] to take firm action to stop a crime or other illegal activity happening: [+ **on**] *The police are really clamping down on drunk drivers.*

**clamp[2]** *n* [C] **1** a piece of equipment for fastening or holding things together **2** a piece of equipment fastened to the wheel of a car that is parked illegally; DENVER BOOT *AmE*

**clamp·down** /ˈklæmpdaʊn/ *n* [C usually singular] sudden firm action that is taken to try and reduce crime

**clan** /klæn/ *n* [C] **1** a large group of families that often share the same name: *the Campbell clan* **2** *humorous* a word meaning a large family, used especially when they are all together on a special occasion: *The whole clan will be here over Christmas.*

**clan·des·tine** /klænˈdestɪ̯n/ *adj* clandestine activities or organizations are secret: *a clandestine affair*

**clang** /klæŋ/ *v* [I,T] if a metal object clangs or if you clang it, it makes a loud ringing sound —**clang** *n* [singular]

**clang·er** /ˈklæŋə‖-ər/ *n* **drop a clanger** *BrE informal* to make a careless remark that upsets or embarrasses someone very much

**clang·our** *BrE*, **clangor** *AmE* /ˈklæŋə‖-ər/ *n* [U] the hard ringing sound that is made when metal is hit

**clank** /klæŋk/ *v* [I,T] if a metal object clanks or if you clank it, it makes a loud heavy sound —**clank** *n* [C] *the clank of machinery*

**clans·man** /ˈklænzmən/ *n* [C] a male member of a CLAN

**clans·wom·an** /ˈklænzˌwʊmən/ *n* [C] a female member of a CLAN

**clap[1]** /klæp/ *v* **clapped, clapping** **1** [I] to hit your hands together loudly and continuously to show that you enjoyed a performance or that you approve of something: *The crowd roared with approval and clapped.* —see picture on page 1259 **2** **clap your hands** **a)** to hit your hands together loudly and continuously to show that you approve, agree, or have enjoyed something **b)** to hit your hands together to attract someone's attention or to stop them doing something: *She clapped her hands and shouted, "Rosie, stop that now!"* **3** **clap sb on the back/shoulder etc** to hit someone lightly with your open hand in a friendly way or to show that you are amused **4** **clap eyes on** *BrE informal* to suddenly see someone or something: *Until this morning I'd never clapped eyes on him.* **5** **clap your hand on/over etc** to put your hand somewhere quickly and suddenly: *Babs clapped her hand over her mouth saying, "My God, I think I left the oven on."* **6** **clap hold of** to take hold of someone or something suddenly: *I clapped hold of him by the shoulder and pushed him out of the front door.* **7** **clap sb in prison/jail/irons** to suddenly put someone in prison or chains —**clapping** *n* [U]

**clap[2]** *n* **1** [singular] a sudden loud sound that you make when you hit your hands together, especially to show that you enjoyed something or that you agree: **give sb a clap** *BrE*: *Come on everyone let's give Tommy a clap.* **2** **a clap on the back/shoulder** an act of hitting someone on the back or shoulder to show that you are friendly or amused **3** **a clap of thunder** a loud sound made by thunder **4** **the clap** *slang* GONORRHOEA

**clap·board** /ˈklæpbɔːd‖ˈklæbərd, ˈklæpbɔːrd/ *n* [C,U] *AmE* a set of boards that cover the outside walls of a building, or one of these boards; WEATHERBOARD (1) *BrE*: *a clapboard house*

**clapped-out** /ˌ· ˈ·◄/ *adj BrE informal* a clapped-out car, machine etc is in very bad condition because it is old and has been used a lot

**clap·per** /ˈklæpə‖-ər/ *n* [C] **1** the metal thing inside a bell that hits it to make it ring **2** *BrE* a piece of equipment used by farmers that makes a noise to frighten birds away **3** **run like the clappers** *BrE informal* to run extremely fast: *You'll have to run like the clappers if you want to catch that bus.*

**clap·trap** /ˈklæptræp/ *n* [U] *informal* stupid talk

**clar·et** /ˈklærət/ *n* [C,U] **1** red wine from the Bordeaux area of France **2** [U] a dark red colour —**claret** *adj*

**clar·i·fied but·ter** /ˌ··· ˈ··/ *n* [U] butter that has been made clean and pure by heating it

**clar·i·fy** /ˈklærɪ̯faɪ/ *v* [T] to make something clearer and easier to understand: *Can you clarify that statement?* | **clarify how/what etc** *The report aims to clarify how these conclusions were reached.* | **clarify your position** (=tell people what you think about a particular subject and what you intend to do about it) *Reporters asked the Congressman to clarify his position on welfare reform.* —**clarification** /ˌklærɪ̯fɪ̯ˈkeɪʃən/ *n* [U]

**clar·i·net** /ˌklærɪ̯ˈnet/ *n* [C] a musical instrument shaped like a long black tube, which you play by blowing into it and pressing keys (KEY[1] (3)) to change the notes —**clarinettist** *n* [C]

**clar·i·on call** /ˈklæriən ˌkɔːl‖-ˌkɒːl/ *n* [C] a strong and direct request for people to do something

**clar·i·ty** /ˈklærɪ̯ti/ *n* [U] the quality of expressing ideas or thoughts in a clear way: *the clarity and precision of his prose* | **clarity of vision/purpose** *Churchill's clarity of vision impressed all who knew him.*

**clash[1]** /klæʃ/ *v* **1** [I] if two armies, or groups of people clash, they suddenly start fighting each other: *Troops clashed near the border.* | [+ **with**] *Police have clashed with demonstrators again today.* **2** [I] if two people or groups of people clash, they argue because their opinions and beliefs are very different: [+ **with**] *Democrats clashed with Republicans in a heated debate.* **3** [I] if two colours or patterns clash, they look very bad together: [+ **with**] *That purple tie clashes with your red shirt.* **4** [I] if two events clash, they happen at the same time in a way that is inconvenient: [+ **with**] *Unfortunately the concert clashed with Ann and Jim's dinner party.* **5** [I,T] if two pieces of metal clash or if you clash them, they make a loud ringing sound: *The cymbals clashed.*

**clash²** *n* [C] **1** a short fight between two armies or groups of people: *border clashes* **2** an argument between two people or groups of people: *a clash of temperament* | [+ **between**] *angry clashes between Tory and Labour ministers* | **personality clash** (=a situation in which two people do not like each other) **3** a loud sound made by two metal objects being hit together: *the clash of swords* **4** a combination of two colours, designs etc that look bad together **5** a situation in which two events happen at the same time in a way that is inconvenient: *a scheduling clash on TV*

**clasp¹** /klɑːsp‖klæsp/ *n* **1** [C] a small metal object for fastening a bag, belt, piece of jewellery etc **2** [singular] a tight hold; GRIP¹ (1): *the firm, reassuring clasp of her hand*

**clasp²** *v* [T] **1** to hold someone or something tightly, closing your fingers or arms around them: *A baby monkey clasps its mother's fur tightly.* | **clasp sb/sth in your hands/arms** *She clasped the photograph in her hands.* | **clasp sb to your chest/bosom** (=hold someone tightly because you love them or are upset, frightened etc) **2** to fasten something with a clasp

**clasp knife** /ˈ· ·/ *n* [C] a large knife with blades that fold into the handle; JACKKNIFE¹ (1)

S1 W1 **class¹** /klɑːs‖klæs/ *n*

**1 ▶ IN A SOCIETY ◀ a)** [C] one of the groups in a society that people can be divided into according to their jobs, income, the kind of family they have etc: *the professional classes* | **class differences/distinctions/privileges etc** *Class divisions are as evident in Britain today as ever.* —see also LOWER CLASS, MIDDLE CLASS, UPPER CLASS, WORKING CLASS **b)** [U] the system in which people are divided into such groups: **class system** *The old class system is slowly disappearing.*

**2 ▶ GROUP OF STUDENTS ◀** [C] a group of pupils or students who are taught together: *We're in the same class in math.* [also + plural verb *BrE*]: *My class are going on an outing to the Lake District.*

**3 ▶ TEACHING PERIOD ◀** [C,U] a period of time during which someone teaches a group of people, especially in a school; LESSON (2) *BrE*: **in class** (=during the class) *No talking in class!* | **take a class** *BrE* (=teach a class) | **geography/French/cooking class** (=a period of time during which a particular subject is taught)

**4 ▶ LESSONS ◀** [C] *AmE* a set of classes you attend in order to study a particular subject; COURSE¹ (3) *BrE*: *a class in photography at night school*

**5 ▶ COLLEGE ◀** [C] *especially AmE* a group of students who finished studying together in the same year: *I missed a semester and couldn't graduate with my class.* | **the class of 1965/1973 etc** *The class of '69 spent almost as much time protesting as learning.*

**6 ▶ OF ANIMALS/PLANTS ETC ◀** [C] a group of people, animals, or other things that can be considered or studied together because they are similar in some way

**7 ▶ QUALITY ◀** [C] a group into which people or things are divided according to their quality: *You get a nicer class of people living in this area.* | **in a class of its own** (=used to say someone or something is excellent) *Your mother's cooking is in a class of its own.* | **not in the same class** (=not as good as someone or something) *He's not in the same class as her at tennis.* —see also BUSINESS CLASS, CABIN CLASS, CLUB CLASS, ECONOMY CLASS, FIRST CLASS, HIGH-CLASS, LOW-CLASS, SECOND CLASS, THIRD CLASS, TOURIST CLASS

**8 ▶ STYLE ◀** [U] *informal* style or skill that you show in the way you do something, that makes people notice and admire you: **have/show class** *The team showed real class in this afternoon's match.* | **class player/actress etc** (=very good player, actress, etc) | **class act** (=used to describe someone who is very skilful, attractive etc) *The company's very well managed, the class act of the industry.*

**9 ▶ DEGREE ◀** [C] *BrE* one of the three levels into which a university degree is divided according to the quality of the work: *a second class degree*

**class²** *v* [T often passive] to consider people, things etc as belonging to a particular group, especially according to an official system: **class sb/sth as** *Heroin and cocaine are classed as hard drugs.*

**class ac·tion** /ˌ· ˈ··◂/ *n* [C,U] *AmE* a LAWSUIT arranged by a group of people for themselves and also for others with the same problem

**class-con·scious** /ˈ· ˌ··/ *adj* always judging other people according to the social class they belong to —**class-consciousness** *n* [U]

**clas·sic¹** /ˈklæsɪk/ *adj* **1** a classic book, play, film etc is important or special and remains popular for a long time: *The Coca-Cola bottle is one of the classic designs of our century.* **2** of excellent quality: *Roy scored a classic goal in the 90th minute.* **3** a classic style of art or clothing is attractive in a simple traditional way: *a classic raincoat* **4 a classic example/case etc** a very typical example of something, sometimes in an impressive or humorous way: *Tom made the classic mistake of trying to drive away without releasing the hand brake.* W3

**classic²** *n* [C] **1** a book, play, or film that is important and has been popular for a long time: *'La Grande Illusion' is one of the classics of French cinema.* **2** something that is very good and one of the best examples of its kind: *The 1976 semi-final between Borg and Gerulaitis was a classic.* **3 classics** [plural] the language, literature, and history of Ancient Rome and Greece: *Judith studied classics at Oxford.* **4 that's (a) classic!** *spoken* used when you think something is extremely funny

**clas·si·cal** /ˈklæsɪkəl/ *adj* **1** based on or belonging to a traditional style or set of ideas, especially in art or science: *classical physics, as opposed to quantum physics* **2** connected with the language, literature etc of Ancient Greece and Rome: **classical education** (=an education that includes studying Latin and Greek) 

**classical mu·sic** /ˌ··· ˈ··/ *n* [U] music that people consider to be serious and that has been popular for a long time

**clas·si·cis·m** /ˈklæsɪ̇sɪzəm/ *n* [U] a style of art that is simple, regular, and does not show too much emotion, based on the models of Ancient Greece or Rome —compare REALISM, ROMANTICISM

**clas·si·cist** /ˈklæsɪ̇sɪ̇st/ *n* [C] someone who studies classics (CLASSIC² (3))

**clas·si·fi·ca·tion** /ˌklæsɪ̇fɪ̇ˈkeɪʃən/ *n* **1** [U] a process in which you put something into the group or class it belongs to: *the classification of wines according to qualilty* **2** [C] a group or class into which something is put: *job classifications*

**clas·si·fied** /ˈklæsɪ̇faɪd/ *adj* classified information or documents are ones which the government has ordered to be kept secret

**classified ad** /ˌ··· ˈ·/ also **classified** *BrE n* [C] a small advertisement you put in a newspaper if you want to buy or sell something; SMALL AD, WANT AD *AmE*

**classified di·rec·to·ry** /ˌ··· ·ˈ···/ *n* [C] *BrE* a book that gives a list of the addresses and telephone numbers of companies under the title of their job or business

**clas·si·fy** /ˈklæsɪ̇faɪ/ *v* [T] **1** to decide what group a plant, animal, book etc belong to according to a system: **classify sth as** *Is this plant classified as a moss or a lichen?* **2** to regard people or things as belonging to a particular type because they have the same physical features, qualities etc —**classifiable** *adj*

**class·is·m** /ˈklɑːsɪzəm‖ˈklæ-/ *n* [U] the belief that one social class, especially the one you belong to, is better than another —**classist** *adj*

**class·less** /ˈklɑːsləs‖ˈklæs-/ *adj* **1** a classless society is one in which people are not divided into different social classes **2** a classless person does not clearly belong to one particular social class —**classlessness** *n* [U]

**class·mate** /ˈklɑːsmeɪt‖ˈklæs-/ *n* [C] a member of the same class in a school, college or, in the US, a university

S3 W3 **class·room** /ˈklɑːs-rʊm, -ruːm‖ˈklæs-/ *n* [C] a room that you have lessons in at a school or college

**class strug·gle** /ˌ· ˈ··/ *n* [singular,U] the Marxist theory that social reality is a continuing struggle for political and economic power between CAPITALISTS (=the owners of property, factories etc) and the PROLETARIAT (=the workers)

**class·work** /ˈklɑːswɜːk‖ˈklæswɜːrk/ *n* [U] school work done by students in a class rather than at home —compare HOMEWORK (1)

**class·y** /ˈklɑːsi‖ˈklæsi/ *adj informal* fashionable and expensive: *classy restaurants*

**clat·ter** /ˈklætə‖-ər/ *v* **1** [I,T] if heavy hard objects clatter, or if you clatter them, they make a loud unpleasant noise: *The tray fell clattering to the ground.* **2** [I always + adv/prep] to move quickly and noisily: **clatter over/down/along etc** *The horse went clattering over the cobbles.* —**clatter** *n* [singular,U] *the clatter of dishes*

S3 W2 **clause** /klɔːz‖klɒːz/ *n* [C] **1** a part of a written law or legal document covering a particular subject of the whole law or document: *A confidentiality clause was added to the contract.* **2** *technical* a group of words that contains a subject and a verb, but which is usually only part of a sentence —compare PHRASE[1] (2)

**claus·tro·pho·bi·a** /ˌklɔːstrəˈfəʊbiə‖ˌklɒːstrəˈfoʊ-/ *n* [U] a strong fear of being in a small enclosed space or among a crowd of people —compare AGORAPHOBIA

**claus·tro·pho·bic** /ˌklɔːstrəˈfəʊbɪk◂‖ˌklɒːstrəˈfoʊ-/ *adj* **1** feeling extremely anxious when you are in a small enclosed space: *I get claustrophobic in elevators.* **2** making you feel anxious and uncomfortable as if you are enclosed in a small space: *a claustrophobic atmosphere*

**clav·i·chord** /ˈklævɪ̮kɔːd‖-kɔːrd/ *n* [C] a musical instrument like a piano that was played especially in the past

**clav·i·cle** /ˈklævɪkəl/ *n* [C] *technical* a COLLARBONE —see picture at SKELETON

**claw**[1] /klɔː‖klɒː/ *n* [C] **1** a sharp curved nail on the toe of an animal or bird: *The cat dug his claws into my leg.* **2 get your claws into sb a)** if a woman gets her claws into a man, she shows that she is determined to marry him **b)** to say unpleasant things about someone in order to upset them: *Wait till the papers get their claws into him.* **3** [usually plural] the part of the body of some insects and sea animals that is used for attacking and holding things —see picture at CRAB[1] **4** the curved end of a tool or machine used for pulling nails out of wood and lifting things: *a claw hammer*

**claw**[2] *v* [I,T] **1** to tear or pull at something using claws: [+ **at**] *The cat keeps clawing at the rug.* **2** to try very hard to get hold of something: *Mary clawed at her husband's sleeve, trying to stop him.* | **claw your way up/along/across etc** (=move somewhere slowly by holding tightly onto things as you move)

**claw** sth ↔ **back** *phr v* [T] **1** to get back something that you had lost, by working very hard: *Through aggressive advertising, the company managed to claw back its share of the market.* **2** *BrE* if a government claws back money that ordinary people have been allowed to keep or get, it gets it back by increasing taxes

**clay** /kleɪ/ *n* [U] heavy sticky soil that can be used for making pots, bricks etc —see also **feet of clay** (FOOT[1] (22)), —**clayey** *adj*

**clay pi·geon shoot·ing** /ˌ· ˈ·· ˌ··/ *n* [U] *BrE* a sport in which you shoot at pieces of hard clay that are thrown up into the air; SKEET SHOOTING *AmE*

S2 W2 **clean**[1] /kliːn/ *adj*

**1** ▶ **WITHOUT DIRT** ◀ without any dirt or marks: *Are your hands clean?* | *a clean towel* | **sweep/scrub etc sth clean** *Wipe that sink clean when you're done.* | **clean and tidy/neat** *Try to keep your room clean and tidy.* | **spotlessly clean** (=very clean) *a spotlessly clean kitchen*

**2** ▶ **HABITS/APPEARANCE** ◀ behaving in a way that keeps things clean or having a clean appearance: *Cats are wonderfully clean creatures.*

**3** ▶ **AIR/WATER** ◀ containing nothing that is dirty or harmful, such as poisons: *Smell that clean air!*

**4** ▶ **FAIR/LEGAL** ◀ **a)** done in a fair or legal way: *a clean fight* **b)** showing that you have followed the rules or the law: *a clean driving licence* | *Well, she has a clean record.* (=she is not a criminal)

**5** ▶ **JOKES/HUMOUR** ◀ not offensive or not dealing with sex: **good, clean fun** *Oh, don't get mad – it was just good, clean fun!* | **keep it clean** (=used to tell someone not to do or say anything morally offensive) | **clean living** (=a way of life in which you do not drink, take drugs, or behave in an immoral way)

**6 make a clean breast of it** to admit that you have done something wrong so that you no longer feel guilty

**7 a clean break a)** a quick sudden separation from a person, organization, place etc: *Den left the next day, needing to make a clean break.* **b)** a break in a bone or other object that is complete and has not left any small pieces

**8** ▶ **SMOOTH** ◀ having a smooth or regular edge or surface: *a clean cut*

**9 come clean** *informal* to finally tell the truth or admit that you have done something wrong: [+ **about**] *It's time you came clean about your affair.*

**10 a clean sheet/slate** a situation that shows that someone has behaved well or not made any mistakes: *Jed looked forward to starting life again with a clean sheet.*

**11 a clean bill of health** a report that says you are healthy or that a machine or building is safe: *Inspectors gave the factory a clean bill of health.*

**12 a clean sweep a)** a complete change in a company or organization, made by getting rid of people **b)** a victory in all parts of a game or competition, especially by winning the first three places: *The 200m race was a clean sweep for France.*

**13** ▶ **PAPER** ◀ a piece of paper that is clean has not yet been used

**14 a clean copy** a piece of writing that contains no mistakes

**15** ▶ **WITHOUT WEAPONS/DRUGS** ◀ [not before noun] *slang* not having any hidden weapons or illegal drugs: *They searched him at the airport, but he was clean.*

**16** ▶ **NOT HAVING DRUGS** ◀ [not before noun] no longer taking illegal drugs: *Dave's been clean for two years now.*

**17** ▶ **POWER/ENERGY** ◀ producing energy or power without causing POLLUTION: **clean energy** (=energy that is produced safely)

**18** ▶ **MOVEMENT** ◀ a clean movement in sport is skilful and exact

**19 as clean as a new pin** *BrE* **as clean as a whistle** very clean —see also CLEANLY, CLEAN-CUT, **keep your nose clean** (NOSE[1] (13)) —**cleanness** *n* [U]

S1 W3 **clean**[2] *v* **1** [I,T] to remove dirt from something by rubbing or washing: *Your shoes need cleaning.* —see also DRY-CLEAN, SPRING-CLEAN **2** [I] to clean a building or other people's houses as your job: *Anne comes in to clean twice a week.* **3** [T] to cut out the inside parts of an animal or bird that you are going to cook **4 clean your plate** to eat all your food

**clean** sb/sth **out** *phr v* [T] **1** [**clean** sth ↔ **out**] to make the inside of a room, house etc clean or tidy: *We'd better clean out the attic this week* **2** [**clean** sb/sth ↔ **out**] *informal* to steal everything from a place or all someone's possessions: *Burglars completely cleaned the place out.* **3** [**clean** sb **out**] *informal* if something expensive cleans someone out, they spend all their money on it so that they have none left: *The Paris trip cleaned us out.*

clean

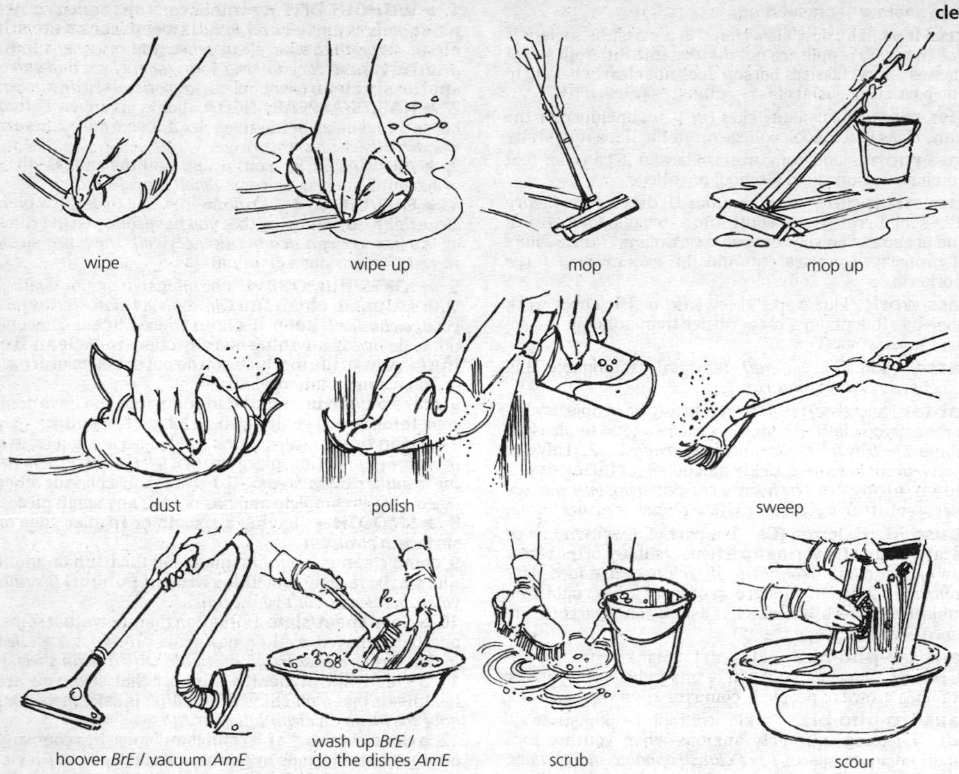


**clean up** *phr v* **1** [I,T] to make something completely clean and tidy: *We spent all Saturday morning cleaning up.*|*a plan to clean up the bay* **2** [I,T] to wash yourself after you have got very dirty: **clean sb/yourself up** *Let me just go clean myself up.*|**get cleaned up** *Dad's upstairs getting cleaned up.* **3 clean up your act** *informal* to start behaving in a responsible way: *If you don't clean up your act I'll kick you out.* **4** [I] *informal* to win a lot of money or make a lot of money in a business deal: *We really cleaned up at the races today!* **5** [T **clean** sth ↔ **up**] to improve moral standards in a place or organization: *It's high time British soccer cleaned up its image.* —see also CLEAN-UP

**clean³** *adv informal* used to emphasize the fact that an action or movement takes place completely and thoroughly: **clean away/through/past** *The robbers got clean away.*|*The knife went clean through his finger.*|**clean forget** (=forget completely) *Sorry, I clean forgot your birthday.*

**clean⁴** *n* [singular] a process in which you clean something: *The car needs a good clean.*

**clean-cut** /ˌ· ˈ·◂/ *adj* someone who is clean-cut looks neat and clean: *clean-cut college boys*

S3 **clean·er** /ˈkliːnə‖-ər/ *n* [C] **1** someone whose job is to clean other people's houses, offices etc **2** a machine or substance used for cleaning: *a vacuum cleaner* **3 the cleaner's** a DRY CLEANER'S **4 take sb to the cleaner's** *informal* **a)** to cheat someone out of all their money or possessions **b)** to defeat someone completely: *The Lakers took the Bulls to the cleaner's, winning 96 – 72.*

**clean·ing** /ˈkliːnɪŋ/ *n* [U] a process in which you clean other people's houses, offices etc: **the cleaning** *Liz comes on Thursday to do the cleaning.*

**cleaning lady** /ˈ·· ˌ··/ also **cleaning woman** *n* [C] a woman who cleans offices, houses etc as her job

**clean-limbed** /ˌ· ˈ·◂/ *adj* tall and active-looking: *a clean-limbed athlete*

**clean·li·ness** /ˈklenlinɪ̮s/ *n* [U] the practice of keeping yourself or the things around you clean

**clean·ly** /ˈkliːnli/ *adv* quickly and smoothly with just one movement: *The branch snapped cleanly in two.*

**cleanse** /klenz/ *v* [T] **1** to get rid of any dirt from a wound or from your skin: *Use a piece of gauze to cleanse the cut.* **2** [+ **of/from**] *biblical* to make someone no longer guilty for things they have done wrong

**cleans·er** /ˈklenzə‖-ər/ *n* [C,U] **1** a liquid used for removing dirt or MAKE-UP (1) from your face **2** a chemical liquid or powder used for cleaning surfaces inside a house, office etc: *cream cleanser for the bathroom*

**clean-shav·en** /ˌ· ˈ··◂/ *adj* a man who is clean-shaven does not have hair on his face —see picture on page 412

**clean-up** /ˈ· ·/ *n* [C, usually singular] a process by which you get rid of dirt or waste from a place: *a clean up program designed to tackle car pollution*|**clean-up campaign/programme/measures** *The mayor launched the clean-up campaign.*

**clear¹** /klɪə‖klɪr/ *adj* S1 W1

**1 ► EASY TO UNDERSTAND ◄** expressed in a simple and direct way so that people understand: *clear instructions*|*You must never do that again. Is that clear?*|**be clear on** *The rules are quite clear on the point.*|**clear to sb** *Is all this clear to you?*|**make sth clear** (=express something strongly) *Taylor's book makes the subject exquisitely clear.*|**make it clear (that)** *Mr Tate made it*

*clear there was to be no compromise.* | **make yourself clear** (=express something well) *To make yourself clear without using facial expressions can be very difficult.* | **get sth clear** *Let's get one thing clear; you have my whole-hearted support.* | **Do I make myself clear?** (=used when you are angry and are telling someone to do or not to do something) *If I catch you smoking again you're grounded. Do I make myself clear?* | **a clear picture/idea** (=a good understanding) | **crystal clear** (=very easy to understand)
**2 ▶ IMPOSSIBLE TO DOUBT ◀** impossible to doubt, question, or be mistaken about: *clear evidence of guilt* | *They won by a clear majority.* | **clear whether/why/how etc** *It is not yet clear whether we will benefit or not.* | **it is clear that** *It is clear that this situation cannot last much longer.* | **become clear** *It has become increasingly clear that privileges have been abused.* | **a clear case/example of sth** *a clear case of theft*
**3 ▶ CERTAIN ◀ be clear** to feel certain that you know or understand something: [+ **about/on**] *Are you all clear now about what you have to do?* | **clear whether/what/how etc** *I'm still not really clear how this machine works.*
**4 ▶ SUBSTANCE/LIQUID ◀** transparent: *a clear gel*
**5 ▶ WATER/AIR ◀** clean and fresh: *a crystal clear mountain lake*
**6 clear sky/day etc** without clouds, mist, smoke etc
**7 ▶ EYES ◀** very pure in colour and without any redness
**8 ▶ SKIN ◀** smooth and without any red spots
**9 ▶ EASY TO SEE ◀** easy to see: *The photo was fuzzy, not clear at all*
**10 ▶ EASY TO HEAR ◀** easy to hear, and therefore easy to understand: *a clear speaking voice* | *The radio reception isn't very clear.* | **clear as a bell** (=very easy to hear and understand)
**11 ▶ AFTER TAX ◀** a clear amount of profit, wages etc is what is left after taxes have been paid on it; NET³ (1): *I get £200 a week clear.* | **a clear $10,000/£400 etc** *It pays a clear $30,000 per year.*
**12 a clear month/two clear weeks/five clear days etc** used to say that you have a whole month, two weeks etc to do something without having to do anything else
**13 see your way clear (to doing sth)** *informal* to have the necessary time or willingness to be able to do something: *I was hoping you could see your way clear to lending me $150.*
**14 a clear conscience** the knowledge that you have done the right thing: *Now I've explained what happened, I can go with a clear conscience.*
**15 ▶ NOT BLOCKED ◀** not covered or blocked by anything that stops you from doing or seeing what you want: *Finally! A clear desk.* | **clear view/look** *From the top floor you get a clear view of the bay.*
**16 ▶ NOT BUSY ◀** without any planned activities or events: *Next Monday is clear; shall we meet then?*
**17 a clear head** the ability to think clearly and quickly: *I won't drink now – I'll need a clear head to face Susan.*
**18 be clear of** to not touch something or to be ahead of someone or something: *He parked the car clear of the entrance.* | *United are clear of their nearest rivals.*
**19 as clear as mud** *spoken humorous* used to say that something is very difficult to understand —see also ALL CLEAR, CLARITY, CLEARLY, **the coast is clear** (COAST (2)), —**clearness** *n* [U]

S1 W2 **clear²** *v*
**1 ▶ SURFACE/PLACE ◀** [T] to make a surface or place emptier or tidier by removing things that cover it: **clear sth of** *The room had been cleared of all his possessions.* | **clear sth off sth** *Can you clear your things off my desk please?* | **clear a space for** (=move things so that there is room for something else) *Sally cleared a space on her desk for the computer.* | **clear the table** (=take plates, forks, knives etc off the table after you have eaten)
**2 ▶ UNBLOCK ◀** [T] to remove something that is blocking something else or causing a problem: *Snowploughs have been out clearing the roads.* | **clear sb/sth from sth** *Police cleared crowds from the area.*
**3 ▶ OF A CRIME/BLAME ETC ◀** [T usually passive] to prove that someone is not guilty of something: *Rawlings was cleared after new evidence was produced.* | **clear sb of (doing) sth** *Maya was cleared of manslaughter.* | **clear sb's name** *He fought for years to clear his name.*
**4 ▶ GIVE/GET PERMISSION ◀** [T] **a)** to give or get official permission for something to be done: *The plans have not yet been cleared by the council.* | **clear sth with sb** *I'll have to clear that with my boss first.* **b)** to give official permission for a person, ship, or aircraft to enter or leave a country: *The plane took off as soon as it was cleared.*
**5 clear sth through customs/clear customs** to be allowed to take things through customs (CUSTOM (4))
**6 ▶ WEATHER ◀** [I] if the weather, sky, mist etc clears, conditions become brighter or easier to see through: *We'll wait till the fog clears.*
**7 ▶ LIQUID ◀** [I] if a liquid clears, it becomes more transparent
**8 ▶ CHEQUE ◀** [I,T] if a cheque clears or if a bank clears it, the money is moved from one bank to another
**9 clear a debt/loan** to get rid of a debt by paying what you owe
**10 ▶ EARN ◀** [T] *informal* to earn a particular amount of money after taxes have been paid on it: *Diane clears £20,000 a year.*
**11 clear a fence/hurdle/wall etc** to jump over a fence etc without touching it
**12 clear your head/mind** to stop worrying or thinking about something or get rid of the effects of drinking too much alcohol: *A good walk might clear my head a bit.*
**13 clear the air** to talk calmly and seriously with someone in order to try to end an argument and feel better
**14 clear the decks** to do a lot of work that needs to be done before you can do other things: *I'm trying to clear the decks before Christmas.*
**15 clear your throat** to cough in order to be able to speak properly
**16 ▶ FACE/EXPRESSION ◀** [I] if your face or expression clears, you stop looking worried or angry: *Her brow cleared and she smiled.*
**17 ▶ JOB/DUTY ◀** [T] to deal with work that needs to be done: *Look! I've got all this to clear before the week-end.*
**18 ▶ SKIN ◀** [I] to no longer have spots
**19 clear the way for** to make preparations so that a process can happen: *This agreement will clear the way for further talks.*
**20 ▶ MESSAGE ◀** [T] *technical* to discover the meaning of a message in a secret language; DECODE (1)

**clear away** *phr v* [I,T] to make a place look tidier by putting things back where they belong: *Come on children, time to start clearing away.* | **clear sth ↔ away** *Let's clear these files away.*

**clear off** *phr v* [I] *BrE informal* to leave a place quickly: *They cleared off when they saw the police coming.* | **clear off!** *spoken* (=used to tell someone angrily to go away)

**clear out** *phr v* **1** [T] to make a place tidy by removing unwanted things: **clear sth ↔ out** *It's time I cleared those drawers out.* **2** [I] to leave a place or building quickly: *I'll give you ten minutes to clear out of here.* | **clear out!** *spoken* (=used to tell someone angrily to go away) —see also CLEAR-OUT

**clear up** *phr v* **1** [I,T] to make a place look tidier by putting things back where they belong: *We'd better start clearing up.* | **clear** sth **↔ up** *Come on, Jamie, clear those toys up.* **2** [T **clear** sth **↔ up**] to find the whole explanation for something that is strange and hard to understand, such as a crime: *The Dreyfus case was never completely cleared up.* **3** [T **clear** sth **↔ up**] to make sure that everyone involved in something understands all the facts and agrees, so that there will be no problems: *There are a couple of points we need to clear up before the meeting begins.* **4** [I] if the weather clears up, it gets better **5** [I] if an illness or infection clears up, it disappears

**clear up after** sb *phr v* [T] to make somewhere clean

and tidy after someone else has made it dirty and untidy: *I'm sick of clearing up after you!*

**clear**[3] *adv* **1** away from or out of the way: *They managed to pull her clear of the wreckage.* **2 keep/stay/steer clear (of)** to avoid someone or something because of possible danger or trouble: *Steer clear of Marilyn, she's a troublemaker.* **3 see clear** *especially AmE* to see something that is a long way away clearly: *You can see clear to the mountains today.* —see also **loud and clear**

**clear**[4] *n* **in the clear a)** not guilty of something: *If Middlemass had spoken to Potter at 8:45, Potter was in the clear.* **b)** no longer having a particular illness or infection

**clear·ance** /ˈklɪərəns‖ˈklɪr-/ *n* **1** [C,U] the amount of space around one object that is needed to avoid it touching another object: *The clearance between the bridge and the top of the bus was only ten centimetres.* **2** [U] a process in which official permission is given for a person, ship, or aircraft to leave or enter a country: *The pilot requested clearance for an emergency landing.* **3** [C,U] a process by which a cheque goes from one bank to another **4** [C,U] the removal of unwanted things from a place: **slum/land/snow clearance** *a slum clearance project* **5** [U] SECURITY CLEARANCE

**clearance sale** /ˈ·· ·/ *n* [C] an occasion when goods in a shop are sold cheaply in order to get rid of them

**clear-cut**[1] /ˌ· ˈ·◂/ *adj* **1** definite or easy to understand: *There's no clear-cut distinction between severe depression and mental illness.* **2** having a definite outer shape: *the clear-cut outline of the mountains*

**clear-cut**[2] *n* [C] *AmE* an area of forest that has been completely cut down

**clear-head·ed** /ˌ· ˈ··◂/ *adj* thinking clearly —**clearheadedly** *adv* —**clear-headedness** *n* [U]

**clear·ing** /ˈklɪərɪŋ‖ˈklɪr-/ *n* [C] a small area where there are no trees in the middle of a wood

**clearing bank** /ˈ·· ˌ·/ *n* [C] one of the banks in Britain that uses a clearing house when dealing with other banks

**clearing house** /ˈ·· ·/ *n* [C] a central office that deals with financial affairs of clearing banks

S1 W1 **clear·ly** /ˈklɪəli‖ˈklɪrli/ *adv* **1** [sentence adverb] used to show that what you are saying is true and cannot be doubted; OBVIOUSLY: *Clearly, the situation is more complicated than we first thought.* **2** in a way that is easy to see, hear, or understand: *Please speak clearly.* **3** in a way that is sensible: *What's wrong with you today? You're not thinking clearly.*

**clear-out** /ˈ· ·/ *n* [C usually singular] *Br E* a process in which you get rid of unwanted objects or possessions: **have a clear-out** *I must have a clear-out one of these days.*

**clear-sight·ed** /ˌ· ˈ··◂/ *adj* able to understand a problem or situation well: *a clear-sighted analysis* —**clearsightedly** *adv* —**clear-sightedness** *n* [U]

**clear·way** /ˈklɪəweɪ‖ˈklɪr-/ *n* [C] a road in Britain on which vehicles must not stop

**cleat** /kliːt/ *n* [C] **1** a small bar with two short arms around which ropes can be tied, especially on a ship **2** [usually plural] one of a set of pieces of rubber, iron etc fastened to the bottom of a shoe to stop it slipping —see picture at STUD[1] **3 cleats** [plural] *AmE* a pair of shoes with these pieces —compare **spikes** (SPIKE[1] (2))

**cleav·age** /ˈkliːvɪdʒ/ *n* [C,U] **1** the space between a woman's breasts **2** *formal* a difference between two people or things that often causes problems or arguments

**cleave** /kliːv/ *v* [T] *formal past tense* **cleaved, clove** /kləʊv‖kloʊv/ **cleft** /kleft/ *past participle* **cleaved, cloven** /ˈkləʊvən‖ˈkloʊ-/ **cleft 1** [I always + adv/prep,] [T always + adv/prep] to cut something into separate parts using a heavy tool or to be able to be cut in this way: *The wooden door had been cleft in two.* **2** [T] to divide something into two completely separate parts: *Class divisions have cleft the society.* **3 cleave the air/darkness etc** to move quickly through the air etc: *His fist cleft the air.*

**cleave to** sb/sth *phr v* [T] **1** *formal* to continue to think that a method, belief etc is true or valuable, even when this seems unlikely: *John still cleaves to his romantic ideals.* **2** to stick to someone or something or seem to surround them

**cleav·er** /ˈkliːvə‖-ər/ *n* [C] a heavy knife for cutting up large pieces of meat

**clef** /klef/ *n* [C] a sign at the beginning of a line of written music to show the PITCH[1] (6) of the notes: *the treble clef etc*

**cleft**[1] /kleft/ *n* [C] a natural crack in the surface of rocks or the Earth etc: *a deep cleft in his chin*

**cleft**[2] *adj* **be in a cleft stick** *BrE* to be in a very awkward situation

**cleft**[3] a past tense and past participle of CLEAVE

**cleft pal·ate** /ˌ· ˈ··/ *n* [C] a split in the top of someone's mouth that makes it difficult for them to speak clearly

**clem·a·tis** /ˈklemətɪ̈s, klɪ̈ˈmeɪtɪ̈s/ *n* [C,U] a plant with spreading branches and white, yellow, or pale flowers

**clem·ent** /ˈklemənt/ *adj formal* **1** willing not to punish someone too severely **2** clement weather is neither too hot nor too cold; MILD[1] (3) —opposite INCLEMENT —**clemency** *n* [U] —**clemently** *adv*

**clem·en·tine** /ˈkleməntiːn, -taɪn/ *n* [C] a kind of small, sweet orange —see picture on page 413

**clench** /klentʃ/ *v* [T] **clench your fists/teeth/jaw etc** to hold your hands, teeth etc together tightly, usually because you feel angry or determined: *She muttered "Go away" through clenched teeth.*

**clere·sto·ry** /ˈklɪəstəri‖ˈklɪrˌstɔːri/ *n* [C] *technical* the upper part of the wall of a large church, that has windows in it and rises above the lower roofs

**cler·gy** /ˈklɜːdʒi‖ˈklɜːr/ *n* **the clergy** [plural] the priests in the Christian church: *the power of the clergy in the Middle Ages.*

**cler·gy·man** /ˈklɜːdʒimən‖ˈklɜːr-/ *n* [C] *plural* **clergymen** /-mən/ a male priest in the Christian church —see PRIEST (USAGE)

**cler·gy·wom·en** /ˈklɜːdʒiˌwʊmən‖ˈklɜːr-/ *n* [C] *plural* **clergywomen** /-ˌwɪmɪn/ a female priest in the Christian church

**cler·ic** /ˈklerɪk/ *n* [C] *old-fashioned* a member of the clergy

**cler·i·cal** /ˈklerɪkəl/ *adj* **1** connected with office work: *a clerical error* **2** connected with priests: *a clerical collar*

**clerk**[1] /klɑːk‖klɜːrk/ *n* [C] **1** someone who keeps records or accounts in an office: *a clerk in a commercial firm* **2** an official in charge of the records of a court, town council etc **3** *AmE* someone who deals with people arriving in a hotel: *Leave the keys with the desk clerk.* **4** *AmE old-fashioned* someone who serves people in a shop **5** *old use* a priest in the Church of England

**clerk**[2] *v* [I] *informal especially AmE* to work as a clerk

**clerk of works** /ˌ· · ˈ·/ *n* [C] *BrE* someone who is in charge of repairs to the buildings in a particular place

**clev·er** /ˈklevə‖-ər/ *adj* **1** *especially BrE* able to learn and understand things quickly; INTELLIGENT: *a clever student* | *You tied your shoes up yourself? What a clever girl!* **2** able to use your intelligence to get what you want, especially in a slightly dishonest way: *a clever lawyer's tricks* **3** *especially BrE* skilful at doing a particular thing: *Bill's very clever with his hands.* | **clever at doing sth** *Deborah's clever at getting people to cooperate.* **4** designed in an unusual way that is very effective: *What a clever little gadget!* | *Now that's a clever idea.* **5** *BrE spoken* used jokingly when someone has done something silly or stupid: *"When I got to the library I found I'd left the books at home." "That was clever!"* **6 clever clogs/dick** *BrE spoken* used to describe someone who is annoying because they are always right or always think they are right: *All right, clever clogs, we'll do it your way!* **7 be too clever by half** *BrE spoken* to be annoying because you are confident about your own intelligence or abilities —**cleverly** *adv* —**cleverness** *n* [U] S2

**cli·ché** /ˈkliːʃeɪ‖kliːˈʃeɪ/ *n* [C] an expression that is used too often and has lost most of its meaning: *the old cliché that a chain is only as strong as its weakest link* —**clichéd** *adj*

S3 **click** /klɪk/ *v* **1** [I,T] to make a short hard sound or make something produce this sound: *The man opposite kept clicking his ballpoint pen.* | **click your fingers/tongue** (=make a short hard sound with your fingers or tongue, especially in order to get someone's attention or to express annoyance) | **click your heels** (=knock the heels of your shoes or boots together in a way that soldiers do) | **click shut/click into place** *The bolt clicked into place.* **2** [I] *informal* to suddenly understand or realize something: **it clicked (with sb)** *It suddenly clicked. The man at the station must have been her brother.* | *For ages I couldn't do algebra then one day it clicked.* **3** [I] *informal* to like someone and share their ideas, opinions etc: *Petra and I clicked straight away.*

**click on** sth *phr v* [T] to press a button on a computer MOUSE (2) in order to do a computer operation —**click** *n* [singular]

S3 W1 **cli·ent** /ˈklaɪənt/ *n* [C] someone who pays for services or advice from a person or organization: *meeting with an important client*

**cli·en·tele** /ˌkliːənˈtel‖ˌklaɪənˈtel, ˌkliː-/ *n* [singular] all the people who regularly use a shop, restaurant etc: *a very select clientele*

**client state** /ˌ·· ˈ·◂/ *n* [C] a country that is dependent on the support and protection of a more powerful country

**cliff** /klɪf/ *n* [C] a high rock with a very steep side, near the sea —see picture on page 835

**cliff·hang·er** /ˈklɪfˌhæŋə‖-ər/ *n* [C] a situation or competition that makes you feel very excited or nervous because you have to wait a long time to see how it will end: *The election in Russia was a real cliffhanger.* —**cliff-hanging** *adj*

**cli·mac·tic** /klaɪˈmæktɪk/ *adj* a climactic period of time or situation is one in which very important or exciting events happen: *the hero, dodging bullets in the movie's climactic scene*

W3 **cli·mate** /ˈklaɪmɪ̣t/ *n* [C] **1** a situation that exists at a particular time, especially one which involves people's opinions and attitudes: **social/political/economic climate** *Small businesses are finding it hard to survive in the present economic climate.* | **climate of suspicion/hostility/distrust** *a climate of growing racial intolerance* **2** the typical weather conditions in a particular area: *Los Angeles' warm, dry climate* **3** an area with particular weather conditions: *I could not bear living in a tropical climate.*

**cli·mat·ic** /klaɪˈmætɪk/ *adj* [only before noun] connected with the weather in a particular area: *climatic conditions*

**cli·max¹** /ˈklaɪmæks/ *n* [C usually singular] **1** the most exciting or important part of a story or experience that normally comes near the end: [+ **of**] *the climax of an exciting expedition* | **reach a climax** *The opera reaches its climax in the third act.* **2** an ORGASM

**climax²** *v* **1** [I,T] if a situation, process, or story climaxes it reaches its most important or exciting part: [+ **in**] *Her determination and hard work climaxed in her appointment as chairwoman.* **2** [I] to have an ORGASM

W2 **climb¹** /klaɪm/ *v*

**1** ▶ **MOVE UP/DOWN** ◀ [I always + adv/prep, T] to move up, down, or across something, especially something tall or steep, using your feet and hands: [+ **up/down/along etc**] *Some spectators climbed onto the roof to get a better view.* | **climb a wall/tree/mountain etc** *The kids are always climbing trees.*

**2** ▶ **WITH DIFFICULTY** ◀ [I always + adv/prep] to move into, out of, or through something slowly and awkwardly: [+ **through/over/into etc**] *Ian managed to climb through a hole in the hedge.* | **climb into/out of clothes** (=put on or remove clothing slowly)

**3** ▶ **SPORT** ◀ [I,T] to climb mountains as a sport: *Sir Edmund Hillary was the first man to climb Mount Everest.* —see also CLIMBING

**4** ▶ **PATH/SUN/PLANE** ◀ [I] to move gradually to a higher position: [+ **into/up etc**] *The path climbs high into the hills.* | *The plane slowly began to climb.*

**5** ▶ **PLANT** ◀ [I] to grow up a wall or other structure: *Ivy climbed up the front of the building.*

**6** ▶ **TEMPERATURE/PRICES ETC** ◀ [I] to increase in number, amount, or level: *The temperature was climbing steadily.* | [+ **to**] *The original estimate of $500 million has now climbed to a staggering $1300 million.*

**7** ▶ **IN A LIST** ◀ [I,T] to move higher in a list of teams, records etc as you become more popular or successful: [+ **to**] *Madonna's new record has climbed to number 2 in the US charts.*

**8** ▶ **IN YOUR LIFE/PROFESSION** ◀ [I,T] to move to a better position in your social or professional life: *Steve climbed rapidly in the firm.* | **climb the ladder** (=become more successful)

**9 be climbing the walls** *spoken* to become extremely anxious, annoyed, or impatient: *When Colin hadn't arrived home by midnight I was climbing the walls.*

**climb down** *phr v* [I] *informal* to admit that you were wrong, especially after being certain that you were right —**climb-down** *n* [singular] *a humiliating climb-down*

**climb²** *n* [C usually singular] **1** a process in which you go up towards a place and that usually involves a lot of effort: *It's quite a climb to the fifth floor!* | *a tough climb to the top of the hill* **2** an increase in value or amount: *After a fairly steady climb, prices stabilized at around $1.65 a litre.* **3** an improvement in your professional or social position **4** a process in which someone or something gets a higher position in a list because of being popular or successful: **a climb up the charts/table/league etc** *a sensational climb up the charts for Elton's new album* **5** a steep rock or cliff you climb up: *You'll need a rope for that climb.*

**climb·er** /ˈklaɪmə‖-ər/ *n* [C] **1** someone who climbs as a sport **2** a person or animal that can climb easily: *Monkeys are good climbers.* **3** a plant that grows up a wall or other structure —see also **social climber**

**climb·ing** /ˈklaɪmɪŋ/ *n* [U] the sport of climbing mountains or rocks: **climbing boots/equipment etc** *Remember to bring climbing boots.* | **rock/mountain climbing** *Rock climbing can be very dangerous.* | **go climbing** (=climb mountains or rocks as a sport)

**climb·ing frame** /ˈ·· ˌ·/ *n* [C] *BrE* a structure for children to climb on, made from metal bars, wood, or rope; JUNGLE GYM *AmE*

**climb·ing i·ron** /ˈ·· ˌ··/ *n* [C usually plural] a small piece of metal with sharp points that is fastened under boots to make climbing less difficult or dangerous; CRAMPON

**clime** /klaɪm/ *n* [C] *poetic* CLIMATE: *They retired to sunnier climes.*

**clinch¹** /klɪntʃ/ *v* **1** [T] to succeed in getting or winning something after trying very hard: **clinch the deal/contract** *It was the BM40's superior design that clinched the deal.* | **clinch the contest/championship/title etc** *Germany scored twice in the last ten minutes to clinch the championship.* **2 clinch it** *informal* if an event, situation, process etc clinches it, it makes someone finally decide to do something that they were already thinking of doing: *The offer of a company car clinched it and I accepted the job.* **3** [I] if two people clinch, they hold each other's arms tightly, especially when they are fighting **4** [T] to fix a nail firmly by bending the point over

**clinch²** *n* [C] **1** a situation in which two people hold each other's arms tightly, especially when they are fighting **2** a situation in which two people who love each other hold each other tightly; EMBRACE²

**clinch·er** /ˈklɪntʃə‖-ər/ *n* [C] *informal* a fact or remark that ends an argument or discussion: *The clincher came when police found his fingerprints on the stolen car.*

**cline** /klaɪn/ *n* [C] *technical* a series of very small differences in a group of things of the same kind; CONTINUUM

**cling** /klɪŋ/ *v past tense and past participle* **clung** /klʌŋ/

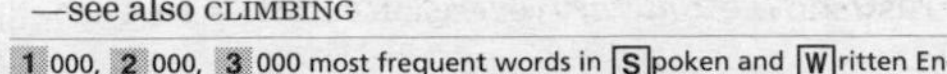

[I] **1** [always + adv/prep] to hold someone or something tightly, especially because you do not feel safe: [+ **to/on/at etc**] *I clung onto Duncan for comfort.* **2** [always + adv/prep] to stick to someone or something or seem to surround them: [+ **to/around etc**] *His wet shirt clung to his body.* **3** to stay close to someone all the time because you are too dependent on them or do not feel safe: *Some children tend to cling their first day at school.*

**cling to** sth *phr v* [T] if you cling to a belief, idea, or feeling, you continue to think that it is true even when this seems extremely unlikely: **cling to the hope that** *We clung to the hope that we might see her again one day.*

**cling·film** /ˈklɪŋfɪlm/ *n* [U] *BrE trademark* very thin transparent plastic used to cover food and keep it fresh; PLASTIC WRAP *AmE*

**cling·y** /ˈklɪŋi/ also **clinging** /ˈklɪŋɪŋ/ *adj* **1** someone who is clingy is too dependent on another person: *a timid, clingy child* **2** clingy clothing or material sticks tightly to your body and shows its shape

**clin·ic** /ˈklɪnɪk/ *n* [C] **1** a building, often part of a hospital, where people come for special medical treatment or advice: **dental/family planning/ante-natal clinic** *I'll meet you at the family planning clinic.* **2** *especially BrE* a period of time during which doctors give treatment or advice to people with particular health problems: **hold a clinic** *The baby clinic is held on Monday afternoons.* **3** a meeting during which a professional person gives advice or help to people: *an M.P.'s clinic* —compare SURGERY (3) **4** *AmE* a place where medical treatment is given at a low cost **5** *especially AmE* a small hospital in an area far away from large cities which provides medical treatment: *a rural health clinic with ten to fifteen beds* **6** *AmE* a group of doctors who work together and share the same offices; PRACTICE[1] (4) *BrE* **7** an occasion when medical students are taught how to decide what illness a patient has and how to treat it

 W3 **clin·i·cal** /ˈklɪnɪkəl/ *adj* **1** [only before noun] clinical work, training etc is practical medical work that is done in a hospital or clinic: *The drug has undergone a number of clinical trials.* | *clinical medicine* **2** connected with a hospital or clinic **3** considering only the facts and not seeming influenced by personal feelings: *He regarded her suffering with clinical detachment.* **4** a clinical building or room is very plain and clean but not attractive or comfortable: *The walls were painted a clinical white.* —**clinically** /-kli/ *adv*: *clinically tested*

**clinical ther·mom·e·ter** /ˌ··· ·ˈ···/ *n* [C] a THERMOMETER for measuring the temperature of your body

**clink**[1] /klɪŋk/ *v* [I,T] if two glass or metal objects clink or if you clink them, they make a short ringing sound: **clink glasses** *I clinked glasses with the other guests.*

**clink**[2] *n* **1** [singular] the short ringing sound made by metal or glass objects hitting each other: *the clink of glasses.* —see picture on page 1261 **2** *slang* prison: *They threw him in the clink for two years.*

**clink·er** /ˈklɪŋkə‖-ər/ *n* **1** [C,U] the hard material like rocks which is left after coal has been burnt **2** [singular] *AmE* a bad note in a musical performance: *The singer hit a real clinker.* **3** [singular] *AmE old-fashioned* something or someone that is a total failure: *That movie was a total clinker.*

**clip**[1] /klɪp/ *n*

**1** ▶ **FOR FASTENING** ◀ [C] a small metal or plastic object for holding or fastening things together: *Fasten the microphone clip to your shirt front.* | **hair clip** (=a piece of metal or plastic for keeping hair in the right place) —see also BULLDOG CLIP, PAPERCLIP

**2** ▶ **CUT** ◀ [singular] a process in which you make something shorter or tidier by cutting it: *I'll have to give that hedge a clip.*

**3** ▶ **FILM** ◀ [C] a short part of a film that is shown by itself: *Clips from Mel Gibson's new movie*

**4 a clip round the ear/earhole** *BrE informal* a short blow on the side of someone's head

**5** ▶ **GUN** ◀ [C] a container for bullets which passes them rapidly into the gun so that they can be fired

**6** ▶ **NEWSPAPER** ◀ [C] an article that is cut from a newspaper or magazine for a particular reason

**7 $100/50 cents etc a clip** *AmE informal* if things cost $100, 50 cents etc a clip, they cost that amount of money each

**8 at a good/fair etc clip** quickly: *Traffic was going by at a fair clip.*

**9** ▶ **WOOL** ◀ [C] *AustrE, NZE* the total amount of wool that is taken from a group of sheep at one time

**clip**[2] *v* **clipped, clipping**

**1** ▶ **FASTEN** ◀ [I always + adv/prep, T] to fasten something together or to be fastened together using a CLIP[1] (1): **clip sth into/onto/together etc** *The invoices had been carefully clipped together.* | [+ **on/to etc**] *The keys will clip onto your belt.*

**2** ▶ **CUT** ◀ [T] to cut small amounts of something in order to make it tidier: *clipping the hedge*

**3** ▶ **CUT FROM NEWSPAPER** ◀ [T always + adv/prep] to cut an article or picture from newspaper, magazine etc: **clip sth out of/from** *Elsa clipped the article out of the evening paper.*

**4** ▶ **HIT** ◀ [T] to hit the surface of something quickly but hard: *The bullet clipped the car's side mirror.*

**5** ▶ **REDUCE** ◀ [T] to slightly reduce an amount, quantity etc: *Gunnell clipped a second off the world record.*

**6 clip sb's wings** to restrict someone's freedom, activities, or power: *Getting married has really clipped his wings.*

**7 clip sb round the ear/earhole** *BrE informal* to hit someone quickly on the side of the head

**8** ▶ **TICKET** ◀ [T] to make a hole in a bus or train ticket to show that it has been used

**9 clip your words** to say words in a quick, short, and not very friendly way

**clip·board** /ˈklɪpbɔːd‖-bɔːrd/ *n* [C] a small flat board with a clip[1] (1) on top used for holding pieces of paper so that you can write on them

**clip-clop** /ˌ· ˈ·/ *n* [singular] the sound made by a horse as it walks on a hard surface —**clip-clop** *v* [I]

**clip joint** /ˈ· ·/ *n* [C] *slang* a restaurant or NIGHTCLUB that charges too much for food, drinks etc

**clip-on** /ˈ· ·/ *adj* [only before noun] —**clip-on** *n* [C] fastened to something with a CLIP[1] (1): *clip-on earings* —see picture at JEWELLERY

**clipped** /klɪpt/ *adj* **1** cut so that it is short and neat: *a neatly clipped hedge* **2** a clipped voice is quick and clear but not very friendly

**clip·per** /ˈklɪpə‖-ər/ *n* [C] **1 clippers** [plural] a special tool with two blades for cutting small pieces from something: *nail clippers* **2** a fast sailing ship used in the past

**clip·ping** /ˈklɪpɪŋ/ *n* [C] **1** an article or picture that has been cut out of a newspaper or magazine; CUTTING[1] (2) **2** [usually plural] a small piece cut from something bigger: *He swept the hedge clippings into a heap.*

**clique** /kliːk/ *n* [C] a small group of people who think they are special and do not let other people join them: *A small clique of right-wingers controls local affairs.*

**cliqu·ey** /ˈkliːki/ also **cliquish** /ˈkliːkɪʃ/ *adj* a cliquey organization, club etc has a lot of cliques or is controlled by them: *That tennis club is too cliquey for my liking.*

**clit·o·ris** /ˈklɪtərɪ̆s/ *n* [C] a part of a woman's outer sexual organs where she can feel sexual pleasure

**Cllr** *BrE* the written abbreviation of COUNCILLOR

**cloak**[1] /kləʊk‖kloʊk/ *n* **1** [C] a warm piece of clothing like a coat without SLEEVES that hangs loosely from your shoulders **2** [singular] an organization, activity, or way of behaving that deliberately protects someone or keeps something secret: [+ **for**] *The political party is used as a cloak for terrorist activities.* | **under the cloak of** *prejudice and hypocrisy hiding under the cloak of religion*

**cloak**[2] *v* [T usually passive] **1** to deliberately hide facts, feelings etc so that people do not see or understand them: **cloaked in secrecy** *The early stages of the talks have been cloaked in secrecy.* **2 cloaked in darkness/rust/snow etc** *literary* covered in darkness, rust etc

**cloak-and-dag·ger** /ˌ· · ˈ· ·◂/ *adj* [usually before noun] a cloak-and-dagger situation, activity etc, is very secret and mysterious, often in a way that seems unnecessary: *Cloak-and-dagger tactics were used to get the bill through Parliament.* | **cloak-and-dagger stuff** (=mysterious activities or ways of behaving) *I'm sick of all this cloak-and-dagger stuff.*

**cloak·room** /ˈkləʊkrʊm, -ruːm‖ˈkloʊk-/ *n* [C] **1** a small room where you can leave your coat; COATROOM *AmE* **2** *BrE* a word meaning a room in a public building where there are toilets, used because you want to avoid saying this directly; REST ROOM *AmE*: *Excuse me, where's the ladies' cloakroom?*

**clob·ber¹** /ˈklɒbə‖ˈklɑːbər/ *v* [T] *informal* **1** to hit someone very hard: *I'll clobber you if you say that again.* **2** to defeat someone very easily in a way that is embarrassing for the team that loses: *The Dallas Cowboys clobbered the Buffalo Bills last night.* **3** to affect someone or something badly, especially by making them lose money: *companies clobbered by foreign competitors* **4** to punish someone severely when they break a law: *Motorists caught driving without insurance will be clobbered.*

**clobber²** *n* [U] *informal especially BrE* someone's possessions, especially their clothes: *Don't forget all your clobber if you're staying the night.* | **fishing/swimming/football clobber etc** (=clothes and equipment needed for a particular activity)

**cloche** /klɒʃ‖kloʊʃ/ *n* [C] **1** a hat shaped like a bell, worn by women in the 1920s **2** a glass or transparent plastic cover put over young plants to protect them during cold weather

**clock¹** /klɒk‖klɑːk/ *n* [C] **1** an instrument in a room or on a public building that shows what time it is: *The clock was ticking on the mantelpiece.* | **the clock strikes three/half past four etc** *The church clock struck midnight.* | **the clock says...** (=the clock shows a particular time) | **by the hall/kitchen/church etc clock** (=according to a particular clock) *It's 4.30 by the kitchen clock.* | **wind (up) the clock** (=turn a key in a clock so that it keeps working) | **set the clock by sth** (=change the time on a clock according to the time on the television, radio etc) | **set the clock for sth** (=turn a screw at the back of a clock so that it will ring at a certain time) *Mary set her clock for 6.30 a.m* | **the clock is slow/fast** (=used to show that the clock is showing an earlier or later time than the actual time) *Your clock's ten minutes slow.* | **clock face** (=the front part of a clock with the numbers on) —see also ALARM CLOCK, CARRIAGE CLOCK, CUCKOO CLOCK, GRANDFATHER CLOCK —compare WATCH² (1) **2 put the clock(s) back** *especially BrE*, **set the clock(s) back** *AmE* to change the time shown on the clock to an earlier time, when the time changes officially **3 put the clock(s) forward** *BrE*, **set the clock(s) ahead** *AmE* to change the time shown on the clock to a later time, when the time changes officially **4 put/turn the clock back** to go back to the ideas or methods tried before instead of doing things in a new or modern way: *The new employment bill will put the clock back fifty years.* **5 put the clock back/forward** to remember a particular time in the past or imagine a time in the future: *It put the clock back forty years seeing that old Bette Davis movie.* **6 around the clock/round the clock** *BrE* all day and all night without stopping: *Charles has been working round the clock preparing the case.* **7 against the clock a)** if you work against the clock, you work as quickly as you can because you do not have much time: *We're working against the clock to get this proposal finished.* **b)** if you run, swim etc against the clock, you run or swim a particular distance as fast as possible **8 watch the clock** to keep looking at the clock to see what time it is because you are bored **9 live by the clock** to organize your life so that you always do the same things at the same time and are never late **10 the twenty-four hour clock** a system for measuring time in which the hours of the day and night have numbers from 0 to 23 **11 start/stop the clock** to start or stop measuring how much time is left in a game or sport that has a time limit: *They stopped the clock when Baggio was injured.* **12 the clock a)** an instrument in a vehicle that measures how many miles or kilometres it has travelled: *The car had 43,000 miles on the clock.* **b)** an instrument in a vehicle that measures the speed at which it is travelling **13 run out the clock/kill the clock** *AmE* if a team runs out the clock at the end of a game, it does not allow the opponents to get the ball so that they cannot earn points —see also BIOLOGICAL CLOCK, BODY CLOCK, DANDELION CLOCK, TIME CLOCK

**clock²** *v* [T] **1** to travel at a particular speed, or to measure the speed at which someone or something is travelling: *The police clocked him at 95 miles an hour on the freeway.* **2** to record the time taken to travel a certain distance: **clock sb at** *She was clocked at 59 seconds for the first lap.* **3 clock this/that!** *BrE spoken* used to tell someone to notice or pay attention to something **4 clock sb one** *BrE informal* to hit someone: *I clocked him one in the eye.* **5 clock a car** *BrE slang* to change the number of miles shown on the CLOCK¹ (12) of a car, in order to sell it for more money

**clock in/on** *phr v* [I] to record on a special card the time you arrive at or begin work; punch in (PUNCH¹): *I clock on at 8:30.*

**clock off/out** *phr v* [I] to record on a special card the time you stop or leave work; punch out (PUNCH¹): *I'm clocking off early today.*

**clock up** sth *phr v* [T] to reach a particular number or amount: *The Dodgers have clocked up six wins in a row so far this season.* | *I clocked up 90,000 miles in my Ford.*

**clock-ra·di·o** /ˌ· ˈ· · ·/ *n* [C] a clock that can be set to turn on a radio in order to wake someone up

**clock·watch·ing** /ˈklɒkˌwɒtʃɪŋ‖ˈklɑːkˌwɑːtʃɪŋ-, -ˌwɔːtʃ-/ *n* [U] the practice of looking often at a clock to see what time it is because you are bored or want to stop working —**clockwatcher** *n* [C]

**clock·wise** /ˈklɒk-waɪz‖ˈklɑːk-/ *adv* in the same direction in which the hands HAND¹ (40) of a clock move: *Screw the lid on clockwise.* —**clockwise** *adj* —opposite ANTICLOCKWISE *BrE*, COUNTERCLOCKWISE *AmE*

**clock·work** /ˈklɒk-wɜːk‖ˈklɑːk-wɜːrk/ *n* [U] **1** clockwork toys, trains, soldiers etc have machinery inside them to make them move when you turn a key **2 go like clockwork** if something you have arranged goes like clockwork, it happens in exactly the way you planned: *The concert went like clockwork.* **3 (as) regular as clockwork** very regular: *Walter came round every Friday, regular as clockwork.* **4 with clockwork precision/accuracy** in an extremely exact way

**clod** /klɒd‖klɑːd/ *n* [C] **1** a lump of mud or earth —see picture on page 416 **2** *informal* a stupid person who behaves insensitively —**cloddish** *adj*

**clod·hop·per** /ˈklɒdˌhɒpə‖ˈklɑːdˌhɑːpər/ *n* [C] **1** *informal* someone who is awkward and rough **2 clodhoppers** [plural] *humorous* a pair of heavy strong shoes

**clog¹** /klɒg‖klɑːg/ *v* also **clog up** [I,T] if something clogs a road, pipe etc, or a road or a pipe clogs, it gradually becomes blocked and no longer works properly: *Don't put potato peelings down the drain, they'll clog up the pipe.* | **clog sth with** *The roads were clogged with traffic.* —**clogged** *adj*: *clogged pores*

**clog²** *n* [C usually plural] a shoe made of wood with a leather top that covers the front of your foot but not your heel —see also **clever clogs** (CLEVER (6)) **pop your clogs** (POP¹ (9)), —see picture at SHOE¹

**clois·ter¹** /ˈklɔɪstə‖-ər/ *n* [C] **1** [usually plural] a covered passage that surrounds one side of a square garden in a church, MONASTERY etc **2** a building where MONKS or NUNS live

**cloister²** *v* **cloister yourself (away)** to spend a lot of time alone in a room or building, especially because you need to study or work

**clois·tered** /ˈklɔɪstəd‖-ərd/ *adj* **1** protected from the difficulties and demands of ordinary life: *a cloistered existence* **2** a cloistered building contains cloisters

**clone**[1] /kləʊn||kloʊn/ *n* [C] **1** *technical* an animal or plant produced in an ASEXUAL way from a particular cell and looking exactly like this cell **2** *technical* a computer that can use SOFTWARE that was written for a different computer: *an IBM clone* **3** *informal* someone or something that seems to be an exact copy of someone or something else: *She's a bit of a Madonna clone.*

**clone**[2] *v* [T] to make an exact copy of a plant or animal by taking a cell from it and developing it artificially

**clonk** /klɒŋk||klɑːŋk/ *n* [singular] the sound made when a heavy object falls to the ground or hits another heavy object —**clonk** *v* [I,T]

**clop** /klɒp||klɑːp/ *v* **clopped, clopping** [I] if a horse clops, its hooves (HOOF[1] (1)) make a loud sound as they touch the ground —**clop** *n* [singular] —**clopping** *n* [singular]

S1 W1 **close**[1] /kləʊz||kloʊz/ *v*

**1** ► **SHUT** ◄ [I, T] to shut something so that there is no longer a space or hole, or to become shut in this way: *Ann closed her book and stood up.* | **close a door/window/gate** *Would you mind if I closed the window?* | **close the curtains/blinds/shutters** *Close the curtains – it's getting dark.* | **close your eyes** *Beth closed her eyes and tried to sleep.* —see OPEN[2] (USAGE)

**2** ► **NO LONGER EXIST** ◄ also **close down** [I,T] if a company, shop etc closes or you close it, it stops operating permanently: *We have reluctantly decided to close the factory.*

**3** ► **FOR A PERIOD OF TIME** ◄ also **close up** [I, T] if a shop or building closes or you close it, it stops being open to the public for a period of time; SHUT[1] (15): *The shops close at six.*

**4** ► **BOOK/SPEECH ETC** ◄ [I always + adv/prep, T always + adv/prep] if a book, play, speech etc closes or someone closes it, it ends in a particular way: **close sth/with/by etc** *The Prime Minister closed his speech by making an appeal for peace.* | [+ **with/by/when**] *The novel closes when the family are re-united in Prague.* | **closing remarks** (=something that you say at the end of an official talk or speech)

**5 close an account** to stop having an account with a bank

**6** ► **FINANCIAL/ECONOMIC** ◄ [I always + adv/prep] if business shares (SHARE[2] (6)) or CURRENCY (1) closes at a particular price, they are worth that amount at the end of a day's trade on the STOCK MARKET: [+ **at/down etc**] *Portland shares closed only 4p down at 112p.*

**7 close a deal/sale/contract etc** to successfully arrange a business deal, sale etc

**8** ► **OFFER** ◄ [I] to finish on a particular date: *Special offer closes June 3.*

**9** ► **DISTANCE/DIFFERENCE** ◄ [I,T] to make the distance or difference between two things smaller: *Society needs to close the gap between rich and poor.* | [+ **on**] *The other car was closing on us fast.*

**10** ► **REDUCE ACTIVITIES ETC** ◄ [T] to make an activity or opportunity no longer available: *The legislation closes a lot of loopholes in the tax law.*

**11 be closed** if a particular subject is closed, you are no longer willing to discuss it: *It was a regrettable incident but I now consider the matter closed.*

**12** ► **HOLD STH** ◄ [I always + adv/prep, T always + adv/prep] if someone's hands, arms etc close around something or they close them around something, they hold it firmly: [+ **around/round/over etc**]: *The baby's tiny hand closed over Ken's finger.*

**13** ► **WOUND** ◄ also **close up** [I,T] if a wound closes or you close it, it grows back together and becomes healthy, or you sew it together for it to become healthy: *The surgeon closed the incision neatly.*

**14 close ranks a)** if people close ranks, they join together to protect each other, especially because their group, organization etc is being criticized **b)** if soldiers close ranks, they stand closer together

**15 close the book(s) on sth** to stop working on something, especially a police inquiry, because it is impossible to continue —see also CLOSED, CLOSING DATE, CLOSING TIME, **close/shut the door on** (DOOR (16)), **close your eyes to sth** (EYE[1] (39))

**close down** *phr v* **1** [I, T **close** sth ↔ **down**] if a company, shop etc closes down or is closed down, it stops operating permanently **2** [I] *BrE* to stop broadcasting radio or television programmes at the end of the day: *BBC 2 closes down at 12:45 tonight.*

**close in** *phr v* [I] **1** to move closer to someone or something, especially in order to attack them: *The snake closed in for the kill.* | [+ **on/around/upon etc**] *The gang closed in on Larry brandishing sticks.* **2** if the night, bad weather etc closes in, it becomes darker or gets worse **3** if the days close in, they become shorter because it is autumn

**close** sth ↔ **off** *phr v* [T] to separate a road, room etc from the area around it so that people cannot go there or use it: *One of the lanes is closed off for repairs.*

**close out** *phr v* [T] *AmE* if a store closes out a type of goods, they sell all of them cheaply: **close sth ↔ out** *We're closing out this line of swimwear.*

**close up** *phr v* **1** [I, T **close** sth ↔ **up**] if a shop or building closes up or is closed up, it stops being open to the public for a period of time **2** [I,T] if a group of people close up, they move nearer together: **close up the ranks!** (=used to order soldiers to stand closer together) **3** [I,T] if a wound closes up or if something closes it up, it grows together or is sewn together and becomes healthy again **4** [I] to deliberately not show your true emotions or thoughts: *Every time I ask Jenny about it she just closes up.*

**close with** sb/sth *phr v* [T] *BrE* **1** to agree to do a business deal with someone: *It was such a good offer that I closed with him on the spot.* **2** *literary* to begin a fight or battle: *The two armies closed with each other around about midday.*

S1 W1 **close**[2] /kləʊs||kloʊs/ *adj*

① NEAR
② LIKELY
③ CAREFUL
④ SIMILAR
⑤ ALMOST LOST/DANGEROUS ETC
⑥ FRIENDLY
⑦ ALMOST CORRECT
⑧ SPOKEN PHRASES
⑨ OTHER MEANINGS

**① NEAR**

**1** ► **NEAR IN SPACE** ◄ not far: *The shops on Roland Way are the closest.* | [+ **to**] *They chose a spot close to the river for their picnic.* | **in close proximity** *The new housing estate is in close proximity to a nuclear power station.*

**2 at close range/quarters** very near: *The victim had been shot at close range.*

**3** ► **NEAR IN TIME** ◄ near to something in time: [+ **to**] *Your birthday's close to mine.*

**② LIKELY**

**4** ► **LIKELY TO HAPPEN** ◄ seeming likely to happen or to do something soon: [+ **to**] *close to death* | **close to doing sth** *The two countries are close to signing a peace agreement.*

③ **CAREFUL**

**5** a close examination, inspection, observation is one in which you look at something very carefully and thoroughly: **take a close look at sth** *Take a closer look at the photo; doesn't it remind you of someone?* | **keep a close watch/eye on** (=watch someone or something very carefully) *I'll keep a close eye on the kids; don't worry.*
**6 close confinement/arrest** if a prisoner is kept in close confinement or under close arrest, someone guards them carefully to make sure they do not escape

④ **SIMILAR**

**7** if two things are close, they are very similar: [+ **to**] *There was a look of resentment in her eyes which was close to hatred.*
**8 close to sth** if a number or amount is close to another number or amount, it is similar to it: *During the recession, the country's growth rate was close to zero.*

⑤ **ALMOST LOST/DANGEROUS ETC**

**9 ▶ COMPETITION/ELECTIONS ETC ◀** won or lost by a very small amount: **close game/contest etc** *a close match that could have gone either way* | **a close second/third etc** (=almost finish a competition in the position ahead of the one you actually get)
**10 ▶ BE TOO CLOSE TO CALL ◀** if a competition, election, or result is too close to call the two sides have almost exactly the same number of votes, points etc
**11 ▶ ALMOST DANGEROUS / EMBARRASSING ◀** *spoken* used when you have only just managed to avoid a dangerous or embarrassing situation: **that was close** *"Phew, that was close," Frank said as he swerved to avoid the cyclist.* | **a close call/shave/thing** (=a situation in which something dangerous, embarrassing etc almost happens)

⑥ **FRIENDLY**

**12** if two people are close, they like or love each other very much: *Mom and I are much closer now than we were when I was a teenager.* | [+ **to**] *I felt closer to Rob that evening than ever before.* | **close friends** *Fiona and I have always been close friends.*
**13 close relation/relative** a member of your family such as your brothers, sisters, parents etc
**14 keep in close contact/touch** if two people keep in close contact, they see, talk to, or write to each other regularly
**15 close association/connection/link etc** if a relationship, association etc is close, the people in it work or talk together a lot: *The school encourages close links between teachers and parents.* | **close cooperation** *What we need now is closer cooperation between the club and supporters.* | **close partners/colleagues** *Dr Henke and I were close colleagues on the research project.*

⑦ **ALMOST CORRECT**

**16 you're close/that's close** *spoken* used to tell someone that they have almost guessed or answered something correctly: *"Where did you go on holiday this year – Turkey?" "You're close, we went on a 10 day tour to Syria."*
**17 close, but no cigar** *AmE spoken* used when something someone does or says is almost correct or successful: *It was close, but no cigar for the Dodgers as they lost to the Reds 4-3.*

⑧ **SPOKEN PHRASES**

**18 the closest thing to/the closest you'll get to** something that is very similar to, but not exactly the same as the thing mentioned: *The island was the closest thing to an earthly paradise I can imagine.*
**19 too close for comfort** if something that happens is too close for comfort, it frightens you or makes you nervous: *That car came around the corner just a little too close for comfort.*
**20 close to home a)** if something unpleasant happens close to home, you are directly affected by it because you see it in your daily life: *It's one thing seeing violence on the television but when it happens so close to home it's a different matter.* **b)** if a remark or criticism is close to home, it makes someone feel embarrassed or uncomfortable: *Allegations of elitism were too close to home as far as the committee was concerned.*

⑨ **OTHER MEANINGS**

**21 ▶ WEATHER ◀** very warm in a way that is uncomfortable because there seems to be no air: *It's very close today.*
**22 ▶ SECRET ◀** [not before noun] unwilling to tell people your thoughts or feelings; SECRETIVE: [+ **about**] *Wanda's always been very close about her past.*
**23 ▶ NOT GENEROUS ◀** [not before noun] not generous; MEAN[2] (2): [+ **with**] *You won't get a penny out of him, he's very close with his money.*
**24 close shave/haircut** a process in which someone's hair is cut very close to the skin on the face or head
**25 close print/stitches etc** print etc with little space between the letters, lines etc: *I find it difficult to read such close print.*
**26 close work** a process or activity which involves looking at or handling things in a very skilful and careful way: *Embroidery is very close work.*
**27 close vowel** *technical* a close vowel is pronounced with only a small space between the tongue and the top of the mouth —**closeness** *n* [U] —see also **close to the bone** (BONE[1] (9)), **play your cards close to your chest** (CARD[1] (13))

S3 W2 **close**[3] /kləʊs‖kloʊs/ *adv* **1** not far away; near: [+ **to**] *Ships can anchor close to the shore there.* | **close by** *The Abbots live quite close by.* | **close at hand/close together** (=very near) *Three men were standing very close together on the corner.* | **close behind** *James heard footsteps close behind him.* | **get close** *I couldn't get close enough to see what was happening.* | **stay/keep close** *We must all stay close together.* | **hold/draw sb close** (=hold someone against your body because you love them or want to protect them) *He drew her close to him.* **2 close up/close to/up close** from only a short distance away: *When I saw her close up I realised she wasn't Jane.* **3 close on/close to** used when you are guessing a number, age, amount etc or cannot give the exact number etc: *The walk took three whole days and covered close on forty miles.* **4 close to sth** to be very similar to something: *When I saw Henry with another woman I felt something close to jealousy.* **5 come close to (doing) sth** to almost do something: *I tell you I was so angry I came close to hitting her.* | *She came close to tears when she heard the news.* **6** near to the surface of something: *An electric razor doesn't really shave as close as a blade.* **7 run sb close** to be almost as successful, skilful etc as someone else: *Maxwell runs him close as one of this country's most exciting musicians.* —see also **sail close to the wind** (SAIL[2] (6))

**close**[4] /kləʊz‖kloʊz/ *n* **1** [singular] *formal* the end of an activity or of a period of time: **the close of** *They returned home tired but happy at the close the day.* **2 bring sth to a close** end a meeting, lesson etc: *The chairman brought the meeting to a close by thanking everyone for their hard work.* **3 come/draw to a close** if a period of time or an activity draws to a close, it ends: *And so, as 1994 draws to a close let's look at some of the major events of the year.*

**close**[5] /kləʊs‖kloʊs/ *n* **1** [C] *BrE* a word used in street names for a road that has only one way in or out: *They live at 26 Hillside Close.* **2** the area and buildings surrounding a CATHEDRAL

**close-cropped** /ˌkləʊs ˈkrɒpt◂‖ˌkloʊs ˈkrɑːpt◂/ *adj* close-cropped grass or hair is cut very short

S3 **closed** /kləʊzd‖kloʊzd/ *adj* **1** shut, especially overnight or for a certain period of time: *The shops are closed on Sundays.* | **closed to the public/visitors etc** *The gardens are closed to visitors in winter.* **2** restricted to a particular group of people: **closed membership** *The golf club has closed membership.* **3** not willing to accept ideas or influences from outside: **closed society/world/way of life** *Army officers and their families live in a very closed world.* | **closed mind** (=someone who has a closed mind does not accept new ways of thinking or doing things) **4 behind closed doors** if official meetings or decisions take place behind closed doors, they take place secretly **5 a closed book** a subject or problem that someone knows or understands nothing about: *Most of mathematics is just a closed book to me.*

**closed cir·cuit tel·e·vi·sion** /ˌ· ·· ˈ····, ˌ· ·· ··ˈ··/ *n* [C,U] a system in which cameras send pictures to television sets that is used in many public buildings to protect them from crime

**closed-door** /ˌ· ˈ·/ *adj* [only before noun] closed-door meetings or talks take place secretly

**close·down** /ˈkləʊzdaʊn‖ˈkloʊz-/ *n* **1** [C] a situation in which work in a company, factory etc is stopped, especially permanently **2** [C, U] *BrE* the end of radio or television broadcasts each day

**closed sea·son** /ˌ· ˈ··/ *n* [C] the American form of CLOSE SEASON

**closed shop** /ˌ· ˈ·◂/ *n* [C] a company, factory etc where all the workers must belong to a particular TRADE UNION

**close-fist·ed** /ˌkləʊs ˈfɪstɪ̣d◂‖ˌkloʊs-/ *adj* unwilling to spend money; TIGHT-FISTED

**close-fit·ting** /ˌkləʊs ˈfɪtɪŋ◂‖ˌkloʊs-/ *adj* close-fitting clothes are tight and show the shape of your body

**close-grained** /ˌkləʊs ˈgreɪnd◂‖ˌkloʊs-/ *adj* close-grained wood has a fine natural pattern

**close-knit** /ˌkləʊs ˈnɪt◂‖ˌkloʊs-/ also **closely-knit** /ˌ·· ˈ·◂/ *adj* a close-knit group of people have strong friendly relationships with each other: *a close-knit community*

S2 W2 **closely** /kləʊsli/ *adv* **1** if you look at or study something closely, you look at it etc hard, trying to notice everything about it: **watch sb closely** *The detective was watching him closely, waiting for a reply.* **2** if two things are closely connected or related, there is a strong connection between them or they are very much like each other: *These two subjects were closely linked, and it makes sense to consider them together.* | **closely resembles** *Their dialect closely resembles that of the northern provinces.* **3** in a way that makes things close together: *a flash of lightning, closely followed by thunder* | *We were so closely packed in the elevator, I could hardly move.*

**close-mouthed** /ˌkləʊs ˈmaʊðd◂,-ˈmaʊθt◂‖ˌkloʊs-/ *adj* not willing to say much because you are trying to keep a secret

**close·out** /ˈkləʊzaʊt‖ˈkloʊz-/ *adj* **closeout sale/price** *AmE* a sale or price that is to get rid of goods cheaply: *There's a closeout sale on swimwear at Penney's this week.* —**closeout** *n* [C]

**close sea·son** /ˈkləʊs ˌsiːzən‖ˈkloʊs-/ *n* [C] *BrE* **1** the period each year when particular animals, birds, or fish cannot legally be killed for sport; CLOSED SEASON *AmE* —opposite OPEN SEASON **2** the period during the summer when football teams do not play important games

**close-set** /ˌkləʊs ˈset◂‖ˌkloʊs-/ *adj* close-set eyes are near to each other: *Lessing's angry, close-set eyes followed him.*

S3 **clos·et¹** /ˈklɒzɪ̣t‖ˈklɑː-, ˈklɒː-/ *n* [C] **1 come out of the closet a)** to tell people that you are HOMOSEXUAL after hiding the fact **b)** to admit you believe something or to discuss something that was previously kept secret **2** *especially AmE* a cupboard built into the wall of a room from the floor to the ceiling: *Jean had a closet full of clothes that most teenages would kill for.* —compare WARDROBE **3** *old use* a small room where people went to study, pray etc alone —see also WATER CLOSET, **a skeleton in the closet** (SKELETON (4))

**closet²** *adj* **closet homosexual/alcoholic etc** someone who is a HOMOSEXUAL, ALCOHOLIC etc but who does not want to admit it: *Not all teachers are closet radicals.*

**closet³** *v* [T, usually passive] to shut someone in a room away from other people in order to be alone or to discuss something private: **closet yourself away** *Bill closeted himself away in his study for hours on end.*

**close-up** /ˈkləʊs ʌp‖ˈkloʊs-/ *n* [C] a photograph taken from very near: *a close-up of the kitten's face* | **in close up** (=from very near) *Much of the movie is shot in close-up.*

**clos·ing¹** /ˈkləʊzɪŋ‖ˈkloʊ-/ *adj* [only before noun] happening or done at the end of a period of time or event **closing remarks/words/speech/ceremony**: *Yeltsin's closing speech was a call for a referendum on land ownership.* **closing stages/seconds/minutes etc** | *The UN was set up during the closing stages of the Second World War.*

**closing²** *n* [U] another word for CLOSURE

**closing date** /ˈ·· ˌ·/ *n* [C] the last date on which it is possible to make a request to do something: *Closing date for applications is 6th August.*

**closing time** /ˈ·· ·/ *n* [C,U] the time when a PUB in Britain must stop serving drinks and close: *Finish your drinks please – it's well past closing time!*

**clo·sure** /ˈkləʊʒə‖ˈkloʊʒər/ *n* [C, U] **1** a process in which a factory, school, hospital etc permanently stops operating or providing services: *Today the government announced the closure of Bart's Hospital in London.* **2 closure of a road/bridge etc** a process in which a road, bridge etc is blocked for a short time so that people cannot use it

**clot¹** /klɒt‖klɑːt/ **clotted, clotting** *v* [I, T] if blood or milk clots or if something clots it, it becomes thicker and more solid as it dries — see also CLOTTED CREAM

**clot²** *n* [C] **1** a thick almost solid mass formed when blood or milk dries **2** *BrE informal* a stupid person: *What did you put the matches in the fridge for, you clot?*

**cloth** /klɒθ‖klɒːθ/ *n* **1** [U] material used especially for making clothes: *cotton cloth* **2** [C] a piece of cloth used to cover a table; TABLECLOTH **3** [C] a piece of cloth used for a particular purpose: *She rubbed at the stain with a damp cloth.* | **dishcloth/floorcloth etc** *Tim grabbed a dishcloth and mopped up.* —see picture on page 833 **4 the cloth** *literary* used to mean priests in the Christian church considered as a group **5 make sth up out of whole cloth** *AmE informal* if a story, explanation, etc is made up out of whole cloth, it is not true: *I could tell his excuse was made up out of whole cloth.*

**cloth cap** /ˌ· ˈ·/ *n* [C] *BrE* a soft flat cap with a stiff pointed piece at the front

**clothe** /kləʊð‖kloʊð/ *v* [T usually passive] *literary* **1** to put clothes on your body: *Helen was clothed in a simple dress of brown wool.* | **fully/partly/brightly clothed etc** (=dressed in a particular way) *The children lay on the bed, fully clothed and fast asleep.* **2** to provide clothes for yourself or other people: *Volunteers ensure that the children are adequately clothed.* **3 be clothed in** *literary* to be completely covered by something: *an angel clothed in flames*

**clothes** /kləʊðz, kləʊz‖kloʊðz, kloʊz/ *n* [plural] the things that people wear to cover their body or keep warm: *I need some new clothes.* | **work/school clothes** (=clothes suitable for work or school) S2 W2

**USAGE NOTE: CLOTHES**

WORD CHOICE: **clothes, clothing, piece/item of clothing, garment, something to wear, cloth, material, fabric, dress**

**Clothes** is the usual word for things we wear: *She's got some beautiful clothes* (NOT *cloths*). **Clothing** [U] is a more formal word for **clothes** in general: *The workers here all have to wear protective clothing* (NOT *clothings*). | *a clothes/clothing shop.* When you are talking about clothes for a particular event, you often say **something to wear**: *It's Gloria's wedding tomorrow and I haven't got anything to wear* (=I have no suitable clothes).

**Clothes** is not used with numbers, and in conversation if you want to talk about one **piece/item of clothing** you would usually call it by its name: *I want to buy a new coat* (NOT *a new cloth/clothing*). **Garment** [C] is a rather formal word for a single **piece of clothing**. On a shop notice: *Only three garments may be taken into the fitting room* (NOT *three clothes*).

**Clothes** are made from various kinds of **material, fabric** or **cloth** [U], such as woven wool, silk, cotton or acrylic: *I brought back a lovely piece of cloth from Thailand to make a dress out of.* A **cloth** ([C] with plural **cloths**) is a piece of cloth, used for cleaning surfaces, dishes etc: *Oh dear, I've spilt my beer – have you got a cloth?*

A **dress** [C] is a kind of clothing worn by women: *What a pretty dress she's wearing!* In certain expressions **dress** [U] is used to mean a particular type of **clothes**. *The men were expected to wear casual dress/formal evening dress/national dress/fancy dress for the dinner.*

**clothes**

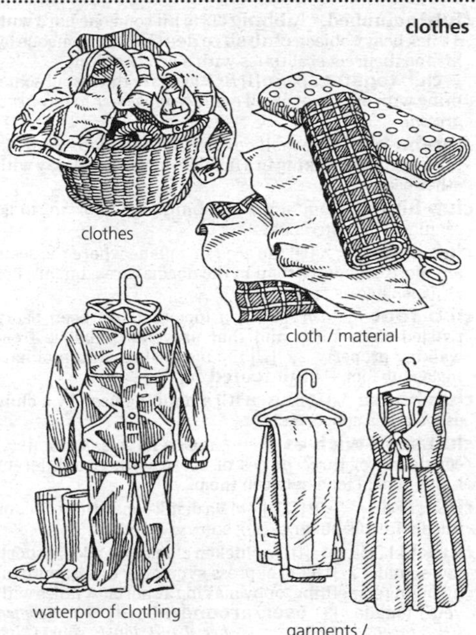


**clothes bas·ket** /ˈ· ˌ··/ *especially BrE n* [C] a large basket for clothes that need to be washed, dried, or ironed (IRON²)

**clothes brush** /ˈ· ·/ *n* [C] a brush used to remove dirt, dust etc from clothes

**clothes hang·er** /ˈ· ˌ··/ *n* [C] a HANGER

**clothes·horse** /ˈkləʊðzhɔːs, ˈkləʊz-‖ˈkloʊðzhɔːrs, ˈkloʊz-/ *n* [C] **1 a)** *BrE* a frame on which you hang clothes to dry indoors **2** *AmE informal* someone who thinks too much about clothes and who likes to have many different clothes

**clothes·line** /ˈkləʊðzlaɪn, ˈkləʊz-‖ˈkloʊðz-, ˈkloʊz-/ *n* [C] a rope on which you hang clothes to dry outdoors; WASHING LINE *BrE*

**clothes peg** /ˈ· ˌ·/ *BrE* **clothespin** /ˈkləʊðzˌpɪn, ˈkləʊz-‖ˈkloʊðz-, ˈkloʊz-/ *AmE n* [C] a wooden or plastic object that you use to fasten wet clothes to a clothesline —see picture at PIN¹

**cloth·i·er** /ˈkləʊðiə‖ˈkloʊðiər/ *n* [C] *old-fashioned* someone who makes or sells men's clothes or material for clothes

**cloth·ing** /ˈkləʊðɪŋ‖ˈkloʊ-/ *n* [U] clothes considered as a group, especially the clothes someone is wearing, or a particular type of clothes: *Remember to bring a change of clothing.* | **clothing manufacturer/industry** *Clothing manufacturers have reported a drop in profits.* | **item/article of clothing** *Bring several warm items of clothing.* | **waterproof/protective clothing** *Lab workers should wear protective clothing.*

**clotted cream** /ˌ·· ˈ·/ *n* [U] thick cream made by slowly heating milk and taking the cream from the top

**clo·ture** /ˈkləʊtʃə‖ˈkloʊtʃər/ *n* [C] *AmE technical* a way of ending an argument over a BILL¹ (2) in the US government and forcing a vote on it

**cloud¹** /klaʊd/ *n* **1** [C, U] a white or grey mass in the sky that consists of very small drops of water: *Dark clouds gathered overhead.* **2 a cloud of dust/smoke/gas etc** a mass of dust etc in the air **3** [C] something that makes you feel afraid or worried: [+ **of**] *The clouds of war began to threaten our peaceful life.* | **a cloud on the horizon** (=something that threatens to spoil a happy situation) *The only cloud on the horizon was her mother's illness.* | **cast a cloud** (=spoil a happy situation) *The news that several competitors had been taking drugs cast a cloud over the event.* **4 on cloud nine** *informal* very happy about something: *Adam was on cloud nine after the birth of his son.* **5 under a cloud** *informal* if someone is under a cloud, people have a bad opinion of them because they have done something wrong: *He left the company under a cloud.* **6 be/live in cloud-cuckoo-land** to think that a situation is much better than it actually is in a way that makes you seem stupid: *If Ben thinks he's getting a pay rise, he's living in cloud-cuckoo-land.* **7 every cloud has a silver lining** used to say that there is something good even in a situation that seems very sad or difficult —see also **have your head in the clouds** (HEAD¹ (11)) S W 3

**cloud²** *v*

**1** ▶ **GLASS** ◀ also **cloud over/up** [I,T] if a transparent material such as glass clouds or something clouds it, you cannot see through it properly any more: *Steam had clouded the windows up.*

**2** ▶ **LIQUID** ◀ also **cloud up** [I,T] if a liquid clouds or if something clouds it, it becomes less clear: *Don't shake the barrel, you'll cloud the beer.*

**3** ▶ **THOUGHTS/MEMORIES** ◀ [T] to make someone less able to think clearly or remember things: **cloud sb's judgement/memory** *Don't let your personal feelings towards this woman cloud your judgement.*

**4 cloud the issue** to make a subject or problem difficult to understand by introducing ideas or information that are not connected with it: *Bringing in unnecessary details at this stage will only cloud the issue.*

**5** ▶ **FACE** ◀ also **cloud over** [I,T] if someone's expression clouds or if something clouds it, they start to look angry or sad: *His face clouded when he saw her.*

**6** ▶ **SPOIL STH** ◀ [T] to make something less pleasant than it should have been: *Half a billion people vote in a general election clouded by violence and charges of poll-rigging.*

**7** ▶ **COVER WITH CLOUD** ◀ [T] to cover something with clouds: *Thick mist clouded the mountaintops.*

**cloud over** *phr v* [I] **1** if the sky clouds over, it becomes dark because it is full of black clouds. *The sky's really clouding over; I think we're in for a storm.* **2** [I] if someone's expression clouds over, they start to look angry or sad: *Anne's face clouded over as she remembered.*

**cloud·bank** /ˈklaʊdbæŋk/ *n* [C] a thick mass of low cloud

**cloud·burst** /ˈklaʊdbɜːst‖-bɜːrst/ *n* [C] a sudden storm

**cloud·ed** /ˈklaʊdɪ̵d/ *adj* **1** not clear or transparent: *clouded glass* **2** a clouded face or expression shows that someone is unhappy or angry

**cloud·less** /ˈklaʊdləs/ *adj* a cloudless sky is clear and bright: *sip exotic cocktails under a cloudless sky*

**cloud·y** /ˈklaʊdi/ *adj* **1** cloudy weather is dark because the sky is full of clouds: *cloudy with outbreaks of rain* **2** cloudy liquids are not clear or transparent **3** cloudy thoughts, memories etc are not very clear or exact

**clout¹** /klaʊt/ *n* **1** [U] *informal* the power or authority to influence other people's decisions: *His job carries a lot of clout.* **2** [C] *informal* a hard blow given with the hand: *I'll give you a clout round the ear!*

**clout²** *v* [T] *informal* to hit someone hard: *Dad clouted me before I had a chance to explain.*

**clove¹** /kləʊv‖kloʊv/ *n* [C] **1** a SPICE (=something used to give a special taste to food) that has a strong smell, is black, and looks like a pin **2 a clove of garlic** one of the parts of a GARLIC root (=a plant similar to an onion)

**clove²** a past tense of CLEAVE

**clo·ven** /ˈkləʊvən‖ˈkloʊ-/ a past participle of CLEAVE

**cloven hoof** /ˌ·· ˈ·/ *n* [C] a HOOF that is divided into two parts: *Sheep and goats have cloven hooves.*

**clo·ver** /ˈkləʊvə‖ˈkloʊvər/ *n* [U] **1** a small plant with three leaves on each stem **2 in clover** *informal* living comfortably because you have plenty of money

**clo·ver·leaf** /ˈkləʊvəliːf‖ˈkloʊvər-/ *n* [C] **1** the leaf of a clover plant **2** a network of curved roads which connect two main roads where they cross

**clown¹** /klaʊn/ *n* [C] **1** someone who entertains people in a CIRCUS (1) by dressing in funny clothes, and doing things to make people laugh **2** someone who often makes jokes or behaves in a funny way: *Frankie was a bit of a clown – always up to mischief and practical jokes.* | **class clown** (=someone in a school class who behaves in a funny or silly way) **3** a stupid or annoying person: *I can't understand what she sees in that clown.* **4 make a clown of yourself** *informal* to do something stupid or embarrassing

clown

**clown²** *v* also **clown around/about** [I] to behave in a silly or funny way: *Stop clowning around, you lot, and get back to your seats!*

**clown·ish** /ˈklaʊnɪʃ/ *adj* silly or stupid —**clownishly** *adv* —**clownishness** *n* [U]

**cloy** /klɔɪ/ *v* [I] if something sweet or pleasant cloys, it begins to annoy you because there is too much of it: *Her sweet submissive smile began to cloy after a while.*

**cloy·ing** /ˈklɔɪ-ɪŋ/ *adj* **1** a cloying attitude or quality annoys you because it is too pleasant: *cloying sentimentality* **2** cloying food or smells are sweet and make you feel sick: *The cloying stench of cheap perfume.*

**cloze test** /ˈkləʊz test‖ˈkloʊz-/ *n* [C] a test in which students have to write the correct words into the spaces that have been left empty in a short piece of writing

S1 W1 **club¹** /klʌb/ *n* [C]
**1** ▶ **FOR AN ACTIVITY/SPORT** ◀ [also + plural verb *BrE*] an organization for people who share a particular interest or enjoy similar activities, such as sports or politics: *the Ramblers Club* | **rugby/golf/squash club etc** (=a club for people who play a particular sport) | **join a club** *It costs £15 to join the club.* | **belong to a club** *She belongs to the local tennis club.*
**2** ▶ **PROFESSIONAL SPORT** ◀ a professional organization including the players, managers, and owners of a sports team: *Tottenham Hotspur Football Club* | [also + plural verb *BrE*] *The club have added a new fast bowler to their line-up.* | **ball club** *AmE* (=a BASEBALL team)
**3** ▶ **FOR MEN** ◀ an organization, usually for men only, where they can relax and enjoy social activities
**4** ▶ **BUILDING** ◀ the building or place where people who belong to an organization meet in order to do activities or play sports: *There's a party at the golf club.*
**5 book/record club etc** an organization which people join in order to buy books, records etc cheaply
**6** ▶ **FOR DANCING/MUSIC** ◀ a place where usually young people go to dance, listen to music, and meet socially: *a jazz club* | *Shall we go to a club?*
**7** ▶ **FOR HITTING BALL** ◀ a special stick used in GOLF to hit the ball; GOLF CLUB (2)
**8** ▶ **WEAPON** ◀ a thick heavy stick used to hit people or things
**9** ▶ **IN CARD GAMES** ◀ **a)** a black shape with three leaves printed on cards for games **b)** the SUIT (=group of cards) that has this shape printed on them: *the ace of clubs*
**10 in the club** *BrE humorous* if a woman is in the club, she is going to have a baby; PREGNANT
**11 join the club** *BrE* **welcome to the club** *AmE* used after someone has described a bad situation that they are in, to tell them that you are in the same situation —see also COUNTRY CLUB, **fan club** (FAN¹ (1)), YOUTH CLUB

**club²** *v* **clubbed, clubbing** [T] to hit someone hard with a thick heavy object: **club sb to death** (=kill someone by hitting them several times with a heavy object)
**club together** *phr v* [I] *BrE* to share the cost of something with other people: *We clubbed together to buy her a present.*

**club·ba·ble** /ˈklʌbəbəl/ *adj BrE old-fashioned* interesting and good at talking in a friendly and relaxed way with other people

**club·bing** /ˈklʌbɪŋ/ *n* **go clubbing** *BrE informal* to go regularly to NIGHTCLUBS

**club class** /ˈ· ·/ *n* [U] the area in a plane where the seats are more expensive than in the normal area, but are not as expensive as FIRST CLASS

**club foot** /ˌ· ˈ·/ *n* **1** [C] a foot that has been badly twisted since birth and that prevents someone from walking properly **2** [U] the medical condition of having a club foot —**club-footed** *adj*

**club·house** /ˈklʌbhaʊs/ *n* [C] a building used by a club, especially a sports club

**club sand·wich·es** /ˌ· ˈ···/ *n* [C] a large SANDWICH¹ (1) consisting of three pieces of bread with two different kinds of cold food between them

**club so·da** /ˌ· ˈ··/ *n* [C,U] *AmE* a drink consisting of water filled with gas BUBBLES (1)); SODA WATER *BrE*

**cluck¹** /klʌk/ *v* **1** [I] if a chicken clucks, it makes a short, low sound **2** [I,T] to express sympathy or disapproval by saying something, or by making a short low noise with your tongue: [+ **over/around/about**] *The women stood together clucking over her scandalously short skirt.* —**clucking** *adj*

**cluck²** *n* [C usually singular] **1** a low short noise made by hens **2** a sound made with your tongue, used to show disapproval or sympathy: *a disapproving cluck* **3** *especially AmE* a stupid person: *You dumb cluck, why'd you tell him?*

**clue¹** /kluː/ *n* [C] **1** an object or piece of information that helps someone solve a crime or mystery: *He didn't know who had sent the letter, and the envelope provided no clue.* | [+ **to/about**] *We now have a clue to the time at which the murder took place.* | **search for clues** *Our search for clues proved fruitless.* **2** a question that you must solve in order to find the answer to a CROSSWORD or PUZZLE² (2) | **give sb a clue** *I'll give you a clue, Kevin, it's a kind of bird.* **3 not have a clue:** *informal* **a)** to know nothing at all about the answer to a question or about how to do something: *"Do you know how to switch this thing off?"* S2

"I'm afraid I haven't got a clue." | **not have a clue where/why etc** *We haven't got a clue where they could have disappeared to.* **b)** to be very stupid, or very bad at a particular activity: *Myra just hits her kids when they start crying; she hasn't got a clue.* | [+ **about**] *No point asking Jill, she hasn't got a clue about maths.* | **not have a clue how/why etc** *Evans hasn't got a clue how to get on with people.* **4** a reason why something happens that you find by studying events, someone's behaviour etc: *Childhood experiences may provide a clue as to why some adults develop phobias.*

**clue²** *v*

**clue** sb ↔ **in** *phr v* [T] *informal* to give someone information about something: *Mark clued me in on how the computer system works.*

**clued-up** /ˌ· ˈ·/ *BrE* **clued-in** *AmE adj informal* knowing a lot about something: *Ask Margaret. She's pretty clued-up about that sort of thing.*

**clue·less** /ˈkluːləs/ *adj informal* having no understanding or knowledge of something: *He was completely clueless about the rules of the game.*

**clump¹** /klʌmp/ *n* **1** [C] a group of trees, bushes, or other plants growing very close together: [+ **of**] *a clump of grass* **2** [C] a piece of earth or mud **3** [singular] the sound of someone walking with heavy steps: *I heard the clump of Ralph's boots going up the stairs.*

**clump²** *v* **1** [I always + adv/prep] to walk with slow noisy steps: [+ **up/down/along etc**] *Grandpa clumped along in his workboots.* **2** [I always + adv/prep, T always + adv/prep] to put something heavy down with a loud noise: *She clumped the books down on the desk.*

**clump together** *phr v* [I,T] if separate objects clump together, or are clumped together they form a group or solid mass: *Rinse the rice to prevent the grains clumping together.*

**clum·sy** /ˈklʌmzi/ *adj* **1** moving in an awkward way and tending to break things: *At 17, she was clumsy, shy and awkward.* | *a clumsy attempt to catch the ball* | *"Look, you've just knocked that cup over." "Sorry, how clumsy of me."* **2** a clumsy object is not easy to use and is often large and heavy **3** said or done carelessly or in a way that is not delicate and sensitive: *David made a clumsy but well-meaning attempt to comfort us.* | **clumsy excuse/apology** *Becky stammered a clumsy apology.* —**clumsily** *adv* —**clumsiness** *n* [U]

**clung** /klʌŋ/ the past tense and past participle of CLING

**clunk** /klʌŋk/ *n* [singular] a loud sound made when two solid objects hit each other —**clunk** *v* [I, T]

**clunk·er** /ˈklʌŋkə‖ər/ *n* [C] *AmE informal* an old car or other machine that does not work well

**clunk·y** /ˈklʌŋki/ *adj* clunky shoes are heavy with thick SOLES (=bottoms)

**clus·ter¹** /ˈklʌstə‖-ər/ *n* [C] **1** a group of things of the same kind that are very close together: [+ **of**] *a cluster of low farm buildings* **2** a group of people all in the same place **3** *AmE* a small piece of metal pinned to a soldier's uniform to show a high class of honour

**cluster²** *v* [I always + adv/prep, T always + adv/prep] if a group of people or things cluster somewhere or are clustered somewhere, they form a small group in that place: [+ **around/together etc**] *A group of children had clustered around the toy shop window.*

**cluster bomb** /ˈ·· ˌ·/ *n* [C] a bomb that sends out smaller bombs when it explodes —**cluster-bomb** *v* [T]

**clutch¹** /klʌtʃ/ *v* [I] to hold something or someone tightly, especially because you are frightened, in pain, or do not want to lose something: *Tom fell to the ground clutching his stomach.* | *A woman clutching a baby stole an elderly woman's purse.*

**clutch at** *phr v* **1** [T] to try hard to hold something, especially when you are in a dangerous situation: *Suzie clutched desperately at the muddy river bank.* **2 clutch at straws** to try hard to find a sign of hope or a solution, even when these are not likely to exist, in a difficult or dangerous situation: *The doctors are really clutching at straws with this new treatment, but they've tried everything else.*

**clutch²** *n* **1** [C] the PEDAL¹ (2) that you press with your foot when driving a vehicle in order to change GEAR¹ (1): let in the clutch/let out the clutch (=put your foot on or take your foot off the clutch) **2 clutches** *plural* the power, influence, or control that someone has: **in sb's clutches** (=controlled or influenced by someone) *Many state organizations fell into the clutches of the Mafia.* **3** [singular] a tight hold that someone has on something: *I shook myself free of her clutch.* **4 a clutch of** a small group of similar things: **a clutch of eggs/chickens** (=a group of eggs which a hen produces at one time, or the chickens born from these eggs) **5 when it comes to the clutch** *AmE informal* when a difficult situation happens: *When it comes to the clutch, you can always count on Tom.*

**clutch bag** /ˈ· ·/ *n* [C] a small bag that women carry in their hand, used especially on formal social occasions

**clut·ter¹** /ˈklʌtə‖-ər/ also **clutter up** *v* [T] **1** to cover or fill a space or room with too many things, so that it looks very untidy: *Piles of books and papers cluttered his desk.* | **be cluttered (up) with** *The front room was cluttered up with ornaments and antique furniture.* **2** to fill your mind with unnecessary information: *Don't clutter up your mind with useless detail.* —**cluttered** *adj*

**clutter²** *n* [singular, U] a large number of things that are scattered somewhere in an untidy way: *Could you get rid of some of that clutter in your bedroom?*

**cm** the written abbreviation of CENTIMETRE

**CNN** /ˌsiː en ˈen/ *n* [U] Cable News Network; an American organization that broadcasts television news programmes to countries all over the world

**C-note** /ˈsiː nəʊt‖-noʊt/ *n* [C] *AmE slang* a 100 dollar note

**C.O.** /ˌsiː ˈəʊ◂‖-ˈoʊ◂/ *n* [C] Commanding Officer; an officer who commands a military unit

**Co.** /kəʊ‖koʊ/ **1** the abbreviation of COMPANY: *James Smith & Co.* **2 and co** *spoken* used after mentioning a person or thing to mean the other people or things that you consider to belong to their group: *I can't say I'm looking forward to seeing Angela and co again.* **3** the written abbreviation of COUNTY: *Co. Durham*

**c/o** the written abbreviation of care of; used especially in addresses when you are sending a letter or parcel to someone who is living in someone else's house etc: *John Hammond, c/o Dowling Music College, Bethesda, Maryland*

**co** /kəʊ‖koʊ/ *prefix* **1** together with: *to coexist* (=exist together or at the same time) | *coeducation* (=of boys and girls together) **2** doing something with someone else as an equal or with less responsibility: *my co-author* (=someone who wrote the book with me) | *the co-pilot* (=someone who helps a pilot)

**coach¹** /kəʊtʃ‖koʊtʃ/ *n* [C] S3 W3

**1 ▶ IN A SPORT ◀** [C] someone who trains a person or team in a sport: *a tennis coach* —see TEACH (USAGE)

**2 ▶ IN A SCHOOL SUBJECT ◀** [C] *especially BrE* someone who gives special instruction to a student in a particular subject, especially so that they can pass an examination

**3 ▶ BUS ◀** [C] *BrE* a bus with comfortable seats used for long journeys; BUS¹ *AmE*: *We went to Paris by coach.*

**4 ▶ IN A TRAIN ◀** [C] *BrE* one of the parts of the train in which the passengers sit; CAR (3) *AmE*

**5 ▶ PULLED BY HORSES ◀** [C] a large carriage pulled by horses

**6 ▶ A CLASS OF TRAVEL ◀** [U] *AmE* the cheapest type of seats on a plane or train: *We flew coach out to Atlanta.*

**coach²** *v* [I,T] **1** to teach a person or team the skills they need for a sport: *Nigel coaches a cricket team in his spare time.* **2** *especially BrE* to give someone special instruction in a particular subject, especially so that they can pass an examination: **coach sb in/for** *Chorley had to be coached in most subjects for the first two terms.* **3** to give someone instruction in what they should say or do in a particular situation: **coach sb in sth** *The Callaghan girl must be carefully coached in the story she will tell in court.*

**coach·buil·der** /ˈkəʊtʃˌbɪldə‖ˈkoʊtʃˌbɪldər/ *n* [C] *BrE* a worker who builds the main outer structure of a car

**coach·ing** /ˈkəʊtʃɪŋ‖ˈkoʊ-/ *n* [U] **1** a process in which you teach a person or team the skills they need for a sport: **tennis/football/rugby coaching etc** *tennis coaching sessions* **2** a process in which you give a student special instruction in a particular subject

**coach·load** /ˈkəʊtʃləʊd‖ˈkoʊtʃloʊd/ *n* [C] all the people travelling in a COACH[1] (3), especially when it is full: *coach loads of football supporters*

**coach·man** /ˈkəʊtʃmən‖ˈkoʊtʃ-/ *n* [C] someone who drove a COACH[1] (5) pulled by horses in the past

**coach sta·tion** /ˈ· ˌ··/ *n* [C] *BrE* the place where people begin or end their journeys on buses that travel a long distance

**coach·work** /ˈkəʊtʃwɜːk‖ˈkoʊtʃwɜːrk/ *n* [U] *BrE* the main outer structure of a car

**co·ag·u·late** /kəʊˈægjʊleɪt‖koʊ-/ *v* [I,T] if a liquid coagulates or something coagulates it, it becomes thick and almost solid: *The heat will coagulate the egg mixture.* —**coagulation** /kəʊˌægjʊˈleɪʃən‖koʊ-/ *n* [U]

S3 W2 **coal** /kəʊl‖koʊl/ *n* **1** [U] a black mineral which is dug from the earth and burnt to produce heat: *Bring in some coal for the fire.* | *the coal industry* **2** [C usually plural] a piece of coal, especially one that is burning **3 carry/take coals to Newcastle** *BrE informal* to take something to a place where there is already plenty of it available **4 haul/rake/drag sb over the coals** to speak angrily to someone because they have done something wrong

**coal bunk·er** /ˈ· ˌ··/ *n* [C] a small building or large container where coal is stored

**co·a·lesce** /ˌkəʊəˈles‖ˌkoʊ-/ *v* [I] *formal* if objects or ideas coalesce, they combine to form one single group: *These three themes coalesce at the end of the book.* —**coalescence** *n* [U]

**coal·face** /ˈkəʊlfeɪs/ *n* **1** [C] the part of a coal mine where the coal is cut from the earth **2 at the coalface** *BrE* actually doing a particular kind of work rather than planning or managing it: *These new methods will help teachers working at the coalface.*

**coal·field** /ˈkəʊlfiːld‖ˈkoʊl-/ *n* [C] an area where there is coal under the ground

**coal gas** /ˈ· ·/ *n* [U] gas produced by burning coal, used especially for electricity and heating —compare NATURAL GAS

**coal·hole** /ˈkəʊlhəʊl‖ˈkoʊlhoʊl/ *n* [C] *BrE* a small underground room where coal is stored

**coal·house** /ˈkəʊlhaʊs‖ˈkoʊl-/ *n* [C] a small building where coal is stored

**Coal·ite** /ˈkəʊlaɪt‖ˈkoʊl-/ *n* [U] *trademark* a substance similar to coal that does not produce smoke when it is burned

W3 **co·a·li·tion** /ˌkəʊəˈlɪʃən‖ˌkoʊə-/ *n* **1** [C] a union of two or more political parties that allows them to form a government or fight an election together: *a three-party coalition* | **coalition government** (=a government consisting of different political parties) **2** [C] a group of people who join together to achieve a particular purpose, usually a political one: *policies designed by a coalition of public officials and local businessmen* **3** [U] a process in which two or more political parties or groups join together

**coal·man** /ˈkəʊlmən‖ˈkoʊl-/ *n* [C] a man who delivers coal to people's houses

**coal mine** /ˈ· ·/ also **coal pit** *n* [C] a mine from which coal is dug

**coal scut·tle** /ˈ· ˌ··/ *n* [C] a specially shaped container with a handle for carrying coal

**coal tar** /ˈ· ·/ *n* [U] a thick black sticky liquid made by heating coal without air, from which many drugs and chemical products are made: *coal tar soap*

**coarse** /kɔːs‖kɔːrs/ *adj* **1** having a rough surface that feels slightly hard: *Hannah's skin was coarse from years of working outdoors.* **2** consisting of threads or parts that are thicker or larger than usual: *The coarse sand was hot and rough under her feet.* **3** talking in a rude and offensive way, especially about sex: *coarse jokes* —**coarsely** *adv* —**coarseness** *n* [U]

**coarse fish·ing** /ˌ· ˈ··/ *n* [U] *BrE* the sport of catching fish other than TROUT or SALMON in rivers and lakes

**coars·en** /ˈkɔːsən‖ˈkɔːr-/ *v* [I,T] **1** to become thicker or rougher, or to make something thicker or rougher: *Hard work had coarsened his hands.* | *His face swollen and puffy, the features coarsened by over-indulgence.* **2** to become or to make someone become less polite in the way they talk or behave, especially about sex: *Drinking had coarsened his sexual appetites.*

**coast**[1] /kəʊst‖koʊst/ *n* [C] **1** the area where the land meets the sea: *We drove along the Pacific coast to Seattle.* | **on the coast** (=on the land near the sea) *I used to live in a small village on the coast of Brittany.* | **off the coast** (=in the sea near the land) *a small island off the coast of Scotland* | **coast to coast** (=from one coast of a country to the other coast of the same country) *They walked coast to coast across England.* —see SHORE (USAGE) **2 the coast is clear** *informal* if the coast is clear, it is safe for you to do something without having to risk being seen or caught: *We raced towards them as soon as the coast was clear.*

**coast**[2] *v* [I] **1** [always + adv/prep] to move in or on a vehicle, especially down a hill, without using any effort or any power from the engine: [+ **down/around/along etc**] *Bev coasted downhill on her bicycle.* **2** to achieve something without having to try very hard: *Janey's teacher says she's just coasting and could do even better if pushed.* | [+ **to/through**] *Polls predict that the party will coast to victory in the next election.* **3** *AmE* to slide down a hill covered in snow on a SLEDGE[1]: *The kids went coasting all afternoon.* **4** to sail along the coast while staying close to land

**coast·al** /ˈkəʊstl‖ˈkoʊstl/ *adj* [only before noun] in the sea or on the land near the coast: *the coastal waters of Britain*

**coast·er** /ˈkəʊstə‖ˈkoʊstər/ *n* [C] **1** a small thin object on which you put a glass, or cup, to protect a table from heat or liquids **2** a ship that sails from port to port along a coast, but does not go further out to sea —see also ROLLER COASTER

**coaster brake** /ˈ··· ·/ *n* [C] *AmE* a BRAKE[1] on some types of bicycle that works by moving the pedals (PEDAL[1] (1)) backwards

**coast·guard** /ˈkəʊstgɑːd‖ˈkoʊstgɑːrd/ *n* **1 the Coastguard** [also + plural verb *BrE*] the organization that helps swimmers and ships that are in danger and helps prevent illegal activities such as SMUGGLING: *The operation required the cooperation of the Coastguard.* **2** [C] a member of this organization

**coast·line** /ˈkəʊstlaɪn‖ˈkoʊst-/ *n* [C] the land on the edge of the coast, especially the shape of this land as seen from the air: *rocky coastline*

**coat**[1] /kəʊt‖koʊt/ *n* [C] **1** a piece of clothing that is worn over your clothes to protect them or to keep you warm: *The lab assistants wear long white coats.* | **put on/take off your coat** *Billy! Put your coat on, it's cold outside!* **2** *BrE old-fashioned or AmE* a piece of clothing that covers the top part of your body and is worn as part of a suit; JACKET (1): *A business suit usually consists of matching pants, coat, and vest.* **3** the fur, wool, or hair that covers an animal's body: *a dog with a glossy coat* **4** a thin layer of a liquid or other substance that you spread thinly over a surface: [+ **of**] *He applied a light coat of varnish.* **5 white-coated/fur-coated/winter-coated etc** wearing a white, fur etc coat —see also **cut your coat according to your cloth** (CUT (33)), MORNING COAT

**coat**[2] *v* [T] **1** to cover something, especially food, with a thin layer of liquid or another substance: *Dust coated the furniture and everything smelled damp.* | **coat sth with/in** *Herring is good coated in oatmeal and fried.* **2 metal-coated/plastic-coated etc** covered with a thin layer of metal etc **3 sugar-coated a)** covered with sugar **b)** making something seem more attractive, desirable etc than it really is: *The program depicts a sugar-coated version of family life.*

**coat check** /ˈ· ·/ *n* [C] *AmE* a room in a public building where you can leave your coat while you are in the building; CLOAKROOM

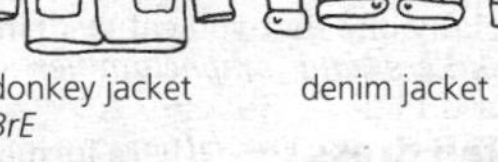

**coat hang·er** /ˈ· ˌ··/ *n* [C] an object that you use to hang up clothes on; HANGER

**coat·ing** /ˈkəʊtɪŋ‖ˈkoʊ-/ *n* [C] a thin layer of something that covers a surface: *The tank's metal coating is made from a mixture of copper and zinc.*

**coat of arms** /ˌ· · ˈ·/ *n* [C] *plural* **coats of arms** a set of pictures or patterns painted on a SHIELD[1] (3) and used as the special sign of a family, town, university etc

**coat of mail** /ˌ· · ˈ·/ *n* [C] a coat made of metal rings that was worn to protect the top part of a soldier's body in the Middle Ages

**coat rack** /ˈ· ·/ *n* [C] a board or pole with hooks on it that you hang coats on —see picture on page 838

**coat·room** /ˈkəʊtrʊm, -ruːm‖ˈkoʊt-/ *n* [C] *AmE* a room in a public building where you may leave your coat, hat etc while you are there; CLOAKROOM (1)

**coat·stand** /ˈkəʊtstænd‖ˈkoʊt-/ *n* [C] a tall pole with hooks at the top that you hang coats on

**coat·tails** /ˈkəʊt-teɪlz‖ˈkoʊt-/ *n* [plural] **1 (ride/hang) on sb's coattails** if you achieve something on someone's coattails, you achieve it with the help or influence of someone powerful: *A number of Republican congressmen were elected on Reagan's coattails.* **2** the cloth at the back of a TAILCOAT that is divided into two pieces

**coax** /kəʊks‖koʊks/ *v* **1** [I,T] to persuade someone to do something that they do not want to do by talking to them in a kind, gentle, and patient way: *"Please, Vic, come with us," Nancy coaxed.* | **coax sb into/out of doing (sth)** *We had to coax Alan into going to school.* | **coax sb to do sth** *The bear coaxed its cubs to enter the water.* | **coax sb down/out/back etc** *I managed to coax her round to my point of view.* **2** [T] to make something such as a machine do something by dealing with it in a slow, patient, and careful way: **coax sth out of/from sth** *He coaxed a fire out of some dry grass and twigs.* | **coax sth down/round/back etc** *We coaxed the pennies out of the piggybank with the blade of a knife.* —**coaxing** *n* [U] —**coaxingly** *adv*

**cob** /kɒb‖kɑːb/ *n* [C] **1** a CORNCOB **2** *BrE* a round LOAF of bread **3** a type of large nut from the HAZEL[1] tree; COBNUT **4** a type of horse that is strong and has short legs **5** a male SWAN[1]

**co·balt** /ˈkəʊbɔːlt‖ˈkoʊbɒːlt/ *n* [U] **1** a shiny silver-white metal that is a chemical ELEMENT (=simple substance), and that is used to make some metals and to give a blue colour to some substances **2** a bright blue-green colour: *the parrot's cobalt feathers* —**cobalt** *adj*

**cob·ber** /ˈkɒbə‖ˈkɑːbər/ *n* [C] *AustrE, NZE informal* a word meaning a friend, used especially by men talking to other men

**cob·ble**[1] /ˈkɒbəl‖ˈkɑː-/ *v* [T] **1** *old-fashioned* to repair or make shoes **2** to put COBBLESTONES on a street

**cobble** sth ↔ **together** *phr v* [T] *informal* to quickly make something that is useful but not perfect: *The diplomats cobbled together an agreement.* | *She cobbled together a tent from a few pieces of string and a sheet.*

**cobble**[2] *n* [C] a cobblestone

**cob·bled** /ˈkɒbəld‖ˈkɑː-/ *adj* a cobbled street is covered with cobblestones

**cob·bler** /ˈkɒblə‖ˈkɑːblər/ *n* [C] **1** *AmE* cooked fruit covered with a sweet, bread-like mixture: *peach cobbler* **2** someone who makes and repairs shoes **3 cobblers** *BrE spoken informal* something that someone says which you think is stupid or untrue: **a load of (old) cobblers** *I've never heard such a load of old cobblers in my life!*

**cob·ble·stone** /ˈkɒbəlstəʊn‖ˈkɑːbəlstoʊn/ *n* [C] a small round stone set in the ground, especially in the past, to make a hard surface for a road

**cob·nut** /ˈkɒbnʌt‖ˈkɑːb-/ *n* [C] a nut from the HAZEL[1] tree; COB (3)

**co·bra** /ˈkəʊbrə‖ˈkoʊ-/ *n* [C] a poisonous African or Asian snake that can spread the skin of its neck to make itself look bigger

**cob·web** /ˈkɒbweb‖ˈkɑːb-/ *n* [C] **1** a net of sticky threads made by a SPIDER to catch insects; SPIDERWEB *AmE* **2 blow/brush/clear the cobwebs away** to do something, especially go outside, in order to help yourself to think more clearly and have more energy —**cobwebbed** *adj* —**cobwebby** *adj*

**co·ca** /ˈkəʊkə‖ˈkoʊ-/ *n* [U] a South American bush whose leaves are used to make the drug COCAINE

**Coca-Co·la** /ˌ·· ˈ··/ *n* [C,U] *trademark* a sweet brown non-alcoholic drink

**co·caine** /kəʊˈkeɪn, kə-‖koʊ-/ *n* [U] a drug, usually in the form of a white powder, that is taken illegally for pleasure or used in some medical situations to prevent pain: *Jimmy was high on cocaine.* —see also CRACK[2] (10)

**coc·cyx** /ˈkɒksɪks‖ˈkɑːk-/ *n plural* **coccyxes** *or* **coccyges** /kɒkˈsaɪdʒiːz‖ˈkɑːksɨ-/ [C] *technical* the small bone at the bottom of your SPINE (1); TAILBONE —see picture at SKELETON

**coch·i·neal** /ˌkɒtʃɨˈniːl◂‖ˌkɑː-/ *n* [U] a red substance used to give food a red colour

**coch·le·a** /ˈkɒkliə‖ˈkɑː-/ *n plural* **cochleas** *or* **cochleae** /-li-aɪ/ [C] *technical* a part of the inner ear

**cock**[1] /kɒk‖kɑːk/ *n*
**1** ► **CHICKEN** ◄ [C] *especially BrE* an adult male chicken; ROOSTER *AmE* —see also COCK-A-DOODLE-DOO
**2** ► **SEX ORGAN** ◄ [C] *taboo* a PENIS
**3 cock and bull story** a story or excuse that is silly and unlikely but is told as if it were true: *She gave me some cock and bull story about the dog eating her homework.*
**4** ► **CONTROL FLOW** ◄ [C] something that controls the flow of liquid out of a pipe or container; TAP[1] (1) —see also BALLCOCK, STOPCOCK
**5** ► **MALE BIRD** ◄ [C] an adult male bird of any kind: *a cock robin*
**6** ► **MAN** ◄ [C] *BrE old-fashioned* a word used by a man when talking to another man he knows well

**7 cock of the walk** *old-fashioned* if you describe someone as behaving like the cock of the walk, they are behaving as if they were better or more important than other people —see also **half cocked** (HALF[2] (11))

**cock**[2] *v* [T] **1** to lift a part of your body so that it is upright, or hold a part of your body at an angle: *Paul cocked his head to one side as he considered my idea.* | *The little dog cocked a leg against the lamppost and urinated.* **2** to pull back the HAMMER[1] (5) of a gun so that it is ready to be fired **3** to put your hat on at an angle; TILT[1] (1) **4 keep an ear cocked** *informal* to pay close attention because you want to be sure you hear something you expect or think may happen: *She kept an ear cocked for the sound of Joe's key in the front door.* **5 cock a snook** *BrE informal* to show clearly that you do not respect someone or something: [+ **at**] *The artist cocked a snook at the critics by exhibiting an empty frame.*

**cock** sth ↔ **up** *phr v* [T] *BrE informal* to spoil something such as an arrangement or plans, especially by making a stupid mistake: *His secretary really cocked up his travelling schedule and he's furious about it.* —see also COCK-UP

**cock·ade** /kɒˈkeɪd‖kɑː-/ *n* [C] a small piece of cloth used as a decoration on a hat to show rank, membership of a club etc

**cock-a-doo·dle-doo** /ˌkɒk ə ˌduːdl ˈduː‖ˌkɑːk-/ *n* [C] the loud sound made by an adult male chicken

**cock-a-hoop** /ˌkɒk ə ˈhuːp‖ˌkɑːk-/ *adj* [not before noun] pleased and excited about something, especially something you have done: [+ **at/about**] *Robert's cock-a-hoop about his new job.*

**cock-a-leek·ie** /ˌkɒk ə ˈliːki‖ˌkɑːk-/ *n* [U] a type of Scottish soup made with chicken, vegetables, and LEEKS

**cock·a·ma·mie** /ˌkɒkəˈmeɪmi◂‖ˌkɑːk-/ *adj AmE informal* a cockamamie story or excuse is not believable or does not make sense: *What cockamamie idea will he think up next?*

**cock·a·too** /ˌkɒkəˈtuː‖ˈkɑːkətuː/ *n* [C] an Australian PARROT[1] (1) with a lot of feathers on the top of its head

**cock·chaf·er** /ˈkɒktʃeɪfə‖ˈkɑːktʃeɪfər/ *n* [C] a European BEETLE (=a kind of insect) that damages trees and plants

**cock·crow** /ˈkɒk-krəʊ‖ˈkɑːkkroʊ/ *n* [U] *literary* the time in the early morning when the sun rises; DAWN[1] (1)

**cocked hat** /ˌ· ˈ·/ *n* [C] **1 knock/beat sb/sth into a cocked hat** to be a lot better than someone or something else: *My mother is such a good cook she knocks everybody else into a cocked hat.* **2** a hat with the edges turned up on three sides, worn in the past

**cock·e·rel** /ˈkɒkərəl‖ˈkɑː-/ *n* [C] a young male chicken

**cocker span·iel** /ˌkɒkə ˈspænjəl‖ˌkɑːkər-/ *n* [C] a dog with long ears and long silky fur

**cock-eyed** /ˌ· ˈ·◂/ *adj informal* **1** an idea, situation, plan etc that is cock-eyed is strange and not practical: *The whole idea is completely cock-eyed.* **2** not straight but set at an angle: *I think you put that shelf up cock-eyed.*

**cock fight** /ˈ· ·/ *n* [C] a sport, illegal in many countries, in which two male chickens are made to fight —**cockfighting** *n* [U]

**cock·horse** /ˌkɒkˈhɔːs‖ˈkɑːkhɔːrs/ *n* [C] *old use* a HOBBYHORSE

**cock·le** /ˈkɒkəl‖ˈkɑː-/ *n* [C] **1** a common European SHELLFISH that is often used for food **2 warm the cockles of sb's heart** to make someone feel happy and full of good feelings towards other people: *Seeing her delight in her new baby just warms the cockles of your heart.*

**cock·le·shell** /ˈkɒkəlʃel‖ˈkɑː-/ *n* [C] **1** the heart-shaped shell of the cockle **2** *literary* a small light boat

**cock·ney** /ˈkɒkni‖ˈkɑːk-/ *n* **1** [C] someone, especially a WORKING CLASS person, who comes from the eastern area of London **2** [U] a way of speaking English that is typical of someone from this area —**cockney** *adj*

**cock·pit** /ˈkɒkˌpɪt‖ˈkɑːk-/ *n* [C] **1** the area in a plane, small boat, or racing car where the pilot or driver sits —see pictures at AIRCRAFT and YACHT **2** a small, usually enclosed area where COCK FIGHTS took place in former times

**cock·roach** /ˈkɒk-rəʊtʃ‖ˈkɑːk-roʊtʃ-/ *n* [C] a large black insect often found in old or dirty houses; ROACH (1) *AmE*

**cocks·comb** /ˈkɒks-kəʊm‖ˈkɑːks-koʊm/ *n* [C] **1** the red flesh that grows from the top of a male chicken's head **2** also **coxcomb** the cap worn by a JESTER (=someone employed to amuse a king in the past)

**cock·suck·er** /ˈkɒkˌsʌkə‖ˈkɑːkˌsʌkər/ *n* [C] *AmE taboo* an insulting way of talking to a man

**cock·sure** /ˌkɒkˈʃʊə‖ˌkɑːkˈʃʊr/ *adj informal* too confident of your abilities or knowledge, in a way that is annoying to other people: *He seemed to be rather cocksure, this young man.*

**cock·tail** /ˈkɒkteɪl‖ˈkɑːk-/ *n* [C] **1** an alcoholic drink made from a mixture of different drinks **2 seafood/prawn/lobster cocktail** a mixture of small pieces of fish, PRAWNS, or LOBSTER, served cold and eaten at the beginning of a meal **3 fruit cocktail** a mixture of small pieces of fruit **4** a mixture of dangerous substances, especially one that you eat or drink: *a lethal cocktail of pain-killers and amphetamines* —see also MOLOTOV COCKTAIL

**cocktail dress** /ˈ·· ˌ·/ *n* [C] a formal dress for wearing to parties or other evening social events

**cocktail lounge** /ˈ·· ·/ *n* [C] a public room in a hotel, restaurant etc, where alcoholic drinks may be bought

**cocktail par·ty** /ˈ·· ˌ··/ *n* [C] a party at which alcoholic drinks are served and for which people usually dress formally

**cocktail shak·er** /ˈ·· ˌ··/ *n* [C] a container in which cocktails are mixed

**cocktail stick** /ˈ·· ·/ *n* [C] a short pointed stick on which small pieces of food are served —see picture at STICK[2]

**cocktail wait·ress** /ˈ·· ˌ··/ *n* [C] *AmE* a woman who serves drinks to people sitting at tables in a BAR[2] (1)

**cock-up** /ˈ· ·/ *n* [C] *BrE spoken* something that has been done very badly, so that it spoils someone's plans or arrangements: *God, what a cock-up!*

**cock·y** /ˈkɒki‖ˈkɑːki/ *adj informal* too confident about yourself and your abilities, especially in a way that annoys other people: *He's very clever, but far too cocky.* —**cockily** *adv* —**cockiness** *n* [U]

**co·coa** /ˈkəʊkəʊ‖ˈkoʊkoʊ/ *n* [U] **1** also **cocoa powder** a brown powder made from the crushed cooked seeds of a tropical tree, used to make chocolate and to give a chocolate taste to foods **2** a sweet hot drink made with this powder, sugar, and milk or water: *a cup of cocoa*

**cocoa bean** /ˈ·· ·/ *n* [C] the small seed of a tropical tree, that is used to make cocoa

**cocoa but·ter** /ˈ·· ˌ··/ *n* [U] a fat obtained from the seeds of a tropical tree, used in making some COSMETICS

**co·co·mat** /ˈkəʊkəmæt‖ˈkoʊ-/ *n* [U] *AmE* COCONUT MATTING

**co·co·nut** /ˈkəʊkənʌt‖ˈkoʊ-/ *n* **1** [C] the large brown seed of a tropical tree, which has a hard shell containing white flesh that you can eat and a milky liquid —see picture on page 413 **2** [U] the white flesh of this seed, often used in cooking: *shredded coconut*

**coconut mat·ting** /ˌ··· ˈ··/ *n* [U] *BrE* a rough material used to cover floors that is made from the outer part of a coconut shell; cocomat *AmE*

**coconut milk** /ˈ··· ˌ·/ *n* [U] the liquid inside a coconut

**coconut shy** /ˈ··· ˌ·/ *n plural* **coconut shies** [C] *BrE* a game in which you try to knock coconuts off posts by throwing balls at them

**co·coon**[1] /kəˈkuːn/ *n* [C] **1** a silk cover that young MOTHS and other insects make to protect themselves while they are growing **2** something that wraps around you completely, especially to protect you: [+ **of**] *The baby peered out of its cocoon of blankets.*

**cocoon**[2] *v* [T] to protect or surround someone or something completely, especially so that they feel safe: [+ **in**] *cocooned in a reassuring network of friends and relatives* —**cocooned** *adj*: *a rich, cocooned existence on the East Side*

**COD** /ˌsiː əʊ ˈdiː‖-oʊ-/ the abbreviation of cash on delivery; a situation in which you pay for goods when they are delivered to you

**cod** /kɒd‖kɑːd/ *n* **1** [C] a large sea fish that lives in the North Atlantic **2** [U] the white flesh of this fish, eaten as food: *Cod and chips twice, please.*

**co·da** /ˈkəʊdə‖ˈkoʊ-/ *n* [C] **1** an additional part at the end of a piece of music that is separate from the main part **2** a separate piece of writing at the end of a work of literature or a speech

**cod·dle** /ˈkɒdl‖ˈkɑːdl/ *v* [T] to treat someone in a way that is too kind and gentle and that protects them from pain or difficulty: *Don't coddle the child – he's fine!*

S2 W2 **code¹** /kəʊd‖koʊd/ *n* [C]
**1** ▶ **BEHAVIOUR** ◀ a set of rules that tell people how to behave in their life or in certain situations: **code of conduct/behaviour** *Fry rejected the accepted code of behaviour and married one of his servants.*
**2** ▶ **RULES/LAWS** ◀ a set of written rules or laws: *Each state in the US has a different criminal and civil code.* | **dress code** (=rule about what clothes you must wear in a school, business etc)
**3** **code of practice** a set of rules that people in a particular business or profession agree to obey: *The film industry wants to produce a code of practice for employers.*
**4** ▶ **SECRET MESSAGE** ◀ a system of words, letters, or signs that you use instead of ordinary words when you are writing something that you want to keep secret: **in code** *Send your reports in code.* | **break/crack a code** (=manage to understand a secret code)
**5** ▶ **SIGNS GIVING INFORMATION** ◀ a set of numbers, letters, or signs that show what something is or give information about it: *Most countries have some form of postal code that speeds mail delivery.* —see also BAR CODE, POSTCODE, ZIP CODE
**6** ▶ **TELEPHONES** ◀ also **dialling code, STD code** *BrE* the group of numbers that come before a telephone number when you are calling from a different area; AREA CODE *AmE*: *What's the code for Aberdeen?*
**7** ▶ **COMPUTERS** ◀ a set of instructions that tell a computer what to do —see also MACHINE CODE, SOURCE CODE
**8** ▶ **SOUNDS/SIGNALS** ◀ a system of sounds or signals that represent words or letters when they are sent by machine: *a telegraphic code* —see also MORSE CODE

**code²** *v* [T] **1** to put a set of numbers, letters, or signs on something to show what it is or give information about it: *Product orders should be coded according to where they will be shipped.* **2** to put a message in code so that it is secret **3** **colour code** to mark a group of things with different colours so that you can tell the difference between them —**coded** *adj*: *a coded message*

**co·deine** /ˈkəʊdiːn‖ˈkoʊ-/ *n* [U] a drug used to stop pain

**code name** /ˈ· ·/ *n* [C] a name that keeps secret someone's real name or a real plan —**code name** *v* [T]

**co·dex** /ˈkəʊdeks‖ˈkoʊ-/ *n* [C] *plural* **codices** /-dʒsiːz/ *technical* an ancient book written by hand: *a sixth-century codex*

**cod·fish** /ˈkɒdˌfɪʃ‖ˈkɑːd-/ *n* [C] a COD

**cod·ger** /ˈkɒdʒə‖ˈkɑːdʒər/ *n* [C] *informal* **old codger** an old man: *He's a charming old codger.*

**co·di·fy** /ˈkəʊdɪ̈faɪ‖ˈkɑː-/ *v* [T] to arrange laws, principles, facts etc in a system —**codification** /ˌkəʊdɪ̈fɪ̈ˈkeɪʃən‖ˌkɑː-/ *n* [C,U]

**cod-liver oil** /ˌ· ·· ˈ·◂/ *n* [U] a yellow oil from a fish that contains a lot of substances that are important for good health

**cod·piece** /ˈkɒdpiːs‖ˈkɑːd-/ *n* [C] a piece of coloured cloth worn by men in the 15th and 16th centuries to cover the opening in the front of their trousers

**cods·wal·lop** /ˈkɒdzˌwɒləp‖ˈkɑːdzˌwɑː-/ *n* [U] *BrE* *spoken* **a load of codswallop** something that someone says which you think is stupid or untrue

**co·ed¹** /ˌkəʊˈed◂‖ˈkoʊed/ *adj* using a system in which students of both sexes are educated together: *The university became coed in 1967.*

**coed²** *n* [C] *AmE old-fashioned* a woman student at a university

**co·ed·u·ca·tion** /ˌkəʊedjʊ̈ˈkeɪʃən‖ˌkoʊedʒə-/ *n* [U] a system in which students of both sexes are educated together —**coeducational** *adj formal*

**co·ef·fi·cient** /ˌkəʊɪ̈ˈfɪʃənt‖ˌkoʊ-/ *n* [C] *technical* the number by which something that varies is multiplied: *In 8pq the coefficient of pq is 8.*

**co·e·qual** /ˌkəʊˈiːkwəl◂‖ˌkoʊ-/ *adj formal* if people are coequal, they have the same rank, ability, importance etc: *three managers of coequal status* —**coequally** *adv*

**co·erce** /kəʊˈɜːs‖koʊˈɜːrs/ *v* [T] to force someone to do something they do not want to do by threatening them: **coerce sb into doing sth** *The rebels coerced the villagers into hiding them from the army.*

**co·er·cion** /kəʊˈɜːʃən‖koʊˈɜːrʒən/ *n* [U] the use of threats or orders to make someone do something they do not want to do: *Soames said he had been under coercion when he confessed.*

**co·er·cive** /kəʊˈɜːsɪv‖koʊˈɜːr-/ *adj* using threats or orders to make someone do something they do not want to do: *coercive measures to reduce absenteeism* —**coercively** *adv*

**co·e·val** /kəʊˈiːvəl‖koʊ-/ *adj formal* happening or existing during the same period of time: [+ **with**] *The development of stone tools was coeval with the appearance of farming settlements.*

**co·ex·ist** /ˌkəʊɪgˈzɪst‖ˌkoʊ-/ *v* [I] *formal* to exist at the same time or in the same place, especially peacefully: [+ **with**] *great wealth coexisting with extreme poverty*

**co·ex·ist·ence** /ˌkəʊɪgˈzɪstəns‖ˌkoʊ-/ *n* [U] *formal* **1** the state of existing together at the same time or in the same place: *the coexistence of the traditional novel with experimental writing* **2** **peaceful coexistence** if two or more countries or people have a peaceful coexistence, they are not fighting one another —**coexistent** *adj*

**C of E** /ˌsiː əv ˈiː/ *n BrE* an abbreviation for Church of England

**cof·fee** /ˈkɒfi‖ˈkɒːfi, ˈkɑːfi/ *n* [U] **1** a hot, dark brown drink that has a slightly bitter taste: *Do you want a cup of coffee?* | **black coffee** (=coffee with no milk added) | **white coffee** *BrE* (=coffee with milk added) **2** [C] *especially BrE* a cup of this drink: *Who wants a coffee?* **3** a brown powder that you use to make coffee: *a pound of coffee* | **instant coffee** (=a powder that you use to make coffee quickly) **4** [U] a light brown colour —see picture on page 411 —see also **wake up and smell the coffee** (WAKE¹) S1 W2

**coffee bar** /ˈ·· ·/ *n* [C] *BrE* a small restaurant that serves coffee and other non-alcoholic drinks, sandwiches (SANDWICH¹ (1)) and cakes etc —compare COFFEE SHOP

**coffee bean** /ˈ·· ·/ *n* [C] the seed of a tropical tree that is used to make coffee

**coffee break** /ˈ·· ·/ *n* [C] a short time when you stop working to have a cup of coffee; TEA BREAK

**cof·fee·cake** /ˈkɒfikeɪk‖ˈkɒː-, ˈkɑː-/ *n* [C,U] **1** *AmE* a sweet heavy cake usually eaten with a cup of coffee **2** *BrE* a cake tasting of coffee

**coffee grind·er** /ˈ·· ˌ··/ *n* [C] a small machine that crushes coffee beans

**coffee house** /ˈ·· ·/ *n* [C] a restaurant that serves coffee, cakes etc

**coffee ma·chine** /ˈ·· ·ˌ·/ *n* [C] a machine that gives you a cup of coffee, tea etc, when you put money in it

**cof·fee·mak·er** /ˈkɒfiˌmeɪkə‖ˈkɒːfiˌmeɪkər, ˈkɑː-/ *n* [C] an electric machine that makes a pot of coffee

**coffee mill** /ˈ·· ·/ *n* [C] a COFFEE GRINDER

**coffee morn·ing** /ˈ·· ˌ··/ *n* [C] *BrE* a social occasion when a group of people meet to talk and drink coffee, and usually give money to help a church or another organization

**coffee pot** /ˈ·· ·/ *n* [C] a container from which coffee is served

**coffee shop** /ˈ·· ·/ *n* [C] **1** *AmE* a restaurant that serves cheap meals **2** *BrE* a place in a large shop or a hotel that serves meals and non-alcoholic drinks

**coffee ta·ble** /ˈ·· ˌ··/ *n* [C] **1** a low table on which you put cups, newspapers etc **2 coffee table book** a large expensive book that usually has a lot of pictures in it and is meant to be looked at rather than read

**cof·fer** /ˈkɒfə‖ˈkɒːfər, ˈkɑː-/ *n* [C] **1 coffers** the money that an organization, government, etc, has available to spend: *What happened to the money put into the union coffers three years ago?* **2** a large strong box often decorated with jewels, silver, gold etc, and used to hold valuable or religious objects **3** a cofferdam

**cof·fer·dam** /ˈkɒfədæm‖ˈkɒːfər-, ˈkɑː-/ *n* [C] a large box filled with air that allows people to work under water

**cof·fin** /ˈkɒfɪn‖ˈkɒː-, ˈkɑː-/ *n* [C] a long box in which a dead person is buried or burnt; CASKET *AmE* —see also **a nail in sb's/sth's coffin** (NAIL¹ (3))

**cog** /kɒg‖kɑːg/ *n* [C] **1** a wheel with small bits sticking out around the edge, that fit together with the bits of another wheel as they turn around in a machine **2** one of the small bits that stick out on a cog **3 a cog in the machine/wheel** someone who is not important or powerful, who only has a small job or part in a large business or organization

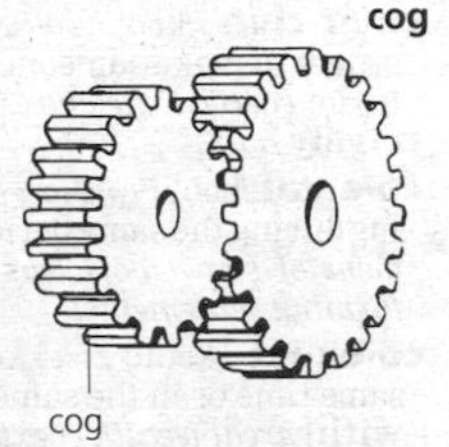


**co·gent** /ˈkəʊdʒənt‖ˈkoʊ-/ *adj formal* something such as an argument that is cogent is reasonable, so that people are persuaded that it is correct: **cogent argument/reasons/answers etc** *Professor Calder presented a cogent examination of the facts.* —**cogently** *adv* —**cogency** *n*

**cog·i·tate** /ˈkɒdʒɪteɪt‖ˈkɑː-/ *v* [I + **about/on**] *formal* to think carefully and seriously about something —**cogitation** /ˌkɒdʒɪˈteɪʃən‖ˌkɑː-/ *n* [U]

**co·gnac** /ˈkɒnjæk‖ˈkoʊ-, ˈkɑː-/ *n* [C,U] a kind of BRANDY (=strong alcoholic drink) made in France, or a glass of this drink

**cog·nate¹** /ˈkɒgneɪt‖ˈkɑːg-/ *adj* cognate words or languages have the same origin

**cognate²** *n* [C] a word in one language that has the same origin as a word in another language: *The German 'hund' is a cognate of the English 'hound'.*

**cog·ni·tion** /kɒgˈnɪʃən‖kɑːg-/ *n* [U] **1** *formal* understanding **2** *technical* the process by which you see or hear something, recognize it, and understand it: *the regions of the brain that are responsible for memory and cognition*

**cog·ni·tive** /ˈkɒgnɪtɪv‖ˈkɑːg-/ *adj formal or technical* related to the process of knowing, understanding, and learning something: *cognitive psychology* —**cognitively** *adv*

**cog·ni·zance** also **cognisance** *BrE* /ˈkɒgnɪzəns‖ˈkɑːg-/ *n* [U] *formal* **1** knowledge or understanding of something **2 take cognizance of** to understand something and consider it when you take action or make a decision

**cog·ni·zant** also **cognisant** *BrE* /ˈkɒgnɪzənt‖ˈkɑːg-/ *adj* [not before noun] having knowledge or information about something; AWARE: *Colby was cognizant of these goals, but was unmoved by them.*

**cog·no·men** /kɒgˈnəʊmən‖kɑːgˈnoʊ-, ˈkɑːgnə-/ *n* [C] **1** *formal* a name used instead of someone's real name, or a description added to someone's name, for example 'the Great' in 'Alexander the Great' **2** *technical* a SURNAME (=last name or family name), especially in ancient Rome

**co·gno·scen·ti** /ˌkɒnjəʊˈʃenti‖ˌkɑːnjə-/ *n* **the cognoscenti** people who have special knowledge about a particular subject, especially art, literature, or food

**cog·wheel** /ˈkɒg-wiːl‖ˈkɑːg-/ *n* [C] a COG (1)

**co·hab·it** /ˌkəʊˈhæbɪt‖ˌkoʊ-/ *v* [I] *formal* to live with another person as though you were married —**cohabitation** /kəʊˌhæbɪˈteɪʃən‖koʊ-/ *n* [U]

**co·here** /kəʊˈhɪə‖koʊˈhɪr/ *v* [I] *formal* **1** if the ideas or arguments in a piece of writing cohere, they are connected in a clear and reasonable way **2** if two objects cohere, they stick together

**co·her·ence** /kəʊˈhɪərəns‖koʊˈhɪr-/ also **co·her·en·cy** /-rənsi/ *n* [U] **1** a reasonable connection or relation between ideas, arguments, statements etc: *An overall theme will help to give your essay coherence.* **2** if a group has coherence, its members are connected or united because they share common aims, qualities, or beliefs: *A common religion ensures the coherence of the tribe.*

**co·her·ent** /kəʊˈhɪərənt‖koʊˈhɪr-/ *adj* **1** if a piece of writing, set of ideas etc is coherent, it is easy to understand because the information is presented in an orderly and reasonable way: *Finally! A textbook that provides a coherent approach to the subject.* **2** if someone is coherent, they are talking in a way that is clear and easy to understand: *My head hurt so much I couldn't give a coherent answer.* —**coherently** *adv*

**co·he·sion** /kəʊˈhiːʒən‖koʊ-/ *n* [U] **1** if there is cohesion among a group of people, a set of ideas etc, all the parts or members of it are connected or related in a reasonable way to form a whole: *Religious beliefs can provide cohesion in diverse societies.* **2** a close relationship, based on grammar or meaning, between two parts of a sentence or a larger piece of writing —**cohesive** /-ˈhiːsɪv/ *adj* —**cohesively** *adv* —**cohesiveness** *n* [U]

**co·hort** /ˈkəʊhɔːt‖-ˈkoʊhɔːrt/ *n* [C] a word meaning a person or group of people who support a particular leader, used especially when you disapprove of them: *Get the Mayor and his crooked cohorts out of City Hall!*

**coif·fure** /kwɒˈfjʊə‖kwɑːˈfjʊr/ *n* [C] *formal* the way someone's hair is arranged; HAIRDO —**coiffured** *adj*

**coil¹** /kɔɪl/ *v* [I,T] to wind or twist into a series of rings, or to make something do this; SPIRAL³ (1): *snakes coiled in the grass* | **coil sth** *Please coil the cords neatly before you put them away.* —**coiled** *adj*

**coil²** *n* [C] **1** a continuous series of circular rings into which something such as wire or rope has been wound or twisted: [+ **of**] *Coils of barbed wire were stretched around the compound.* **2** a wire or a metal tube in a continuous circular shape that produces light or heat when electricity is passed through it: *the coil in a light bulb* **3** the part of a car engine that sends electricity to the SPARK PLUGS —see picture at ENGINE **4** a CONTRACEPTIVE that is a flat curved piece of metal or plastic that is fitted inside a woman's UTERUS ; IUD

**coin¹** /kɔɪn/ *n* **1** [C] a piece of metal, usually flat and round, that is used as money —compare BILL¹ (3), NOTE¹ (5) **2 toss/flip a coin** to choose or decide something by throwing a coin into the air and guessing which side of it will show when it falls: *Let's toss a coin to see who goes first.* **3 the other side of the coin** a different or opposite way of thinking about something: *Children should learn to respect the police, but the other side of the coin is that the police should earn that respect.* **4 two sides of the same coin** two problems or situations that are so closely connected that they are really just two parts of the same thing: *You can't cure poverty without also doing something about improving education; they're two sides of the same coin.* **5** [U] money in the form of metal coins **6 pay sb back in their own coin** *BrE old-fashioned* to treat someone in the same unpleasant way as they have treated you

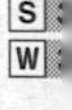

**coin²** *v* [T] **1** to invent a new word or expression,

especially one that many people start to use: *The term 'Information Highway' was coined a few years ago.* **2 to coin a phrase** *spoken* used as a joke when you have just said something so familiar and ordinary that it is funny: *"Alone at last," he said, "to coin a phrase!"* **3 coin money/coin it** *BrE spoken* to earn a lot of money very quickly: *That new restaurant on the corner must be coining it.* **4** to make pieces of money from metal

**coin·age** /ˈkɔɪnɪdʒ/ *n* **1** [U] the system of money used in a country: *Britain did not use decimal coinage until 1971.* **2** [C] a word or phrase that has been recently invented: *The phrase 'glass ceiling' is a fairly recent coinage.* **3** [U] the use of new words or phrases **4** [U] the making of coins

**co·in·cide** /ˌkəʊɪnˈsaɪd‖ˌkoʊ-/ *v* [I] **1** to happen at the same time as something else, especially by chance; CONCUR (2): *Suspects are interviewed in separate rooms to see if their stories coincide.* | [+ **with**] *The Suez crisis happened to coincide with the uprising in Hungary.* | **be planned/timed/arranged to coincide** *The Queen's visit has been planned to coincide with the school's 200th anniversary.* **2** [not in progressive + **with**] if two people's ideas, opinions etc coincide, they are the same

**co·in·ci·dence** /kəʊˈɪnsɪdəns‖koʊ-/ *n* **1** [C,U] a surprising and unexpected situation in which two things that are connected happen at the same time, in the same place, or to the same people: *What a coincidence! I didn't know you were going to be in Geneva too!* | **by coincidence** *My mother is called Anna, and by a funny coincidence my wife's mother is also called Anna.* | **be sheer/pure coincidence** (=happen completely by chance) | **not a coincidence/more than coincidence** (=used when you think something did not happen by chance) *It can't be a coincidence that four jewelry stores were robbed in one night.* **2** [singular] *formal* if there is a coincidence between two ideas, opinions etc, the ideas etc are the same: [+ **of**] *a coincidence of opinion among the board members*

**co·in·ci·dent** /kəʊˈɪnsɪdənt‖koʊ-/ *adj formal* existing or happening at the same place or time

**co·in·ci·den·tal** /kəʊˌɪnsɪˈdentl‖koʊ-/ *adj* happening completely by chance without being planned: **purely/completely coincidental** *Any similarity between this film and real events is purely coincidental.* —**coincidentally** *adv* [sentence adverb] *Coincidentally, two of the men came up with similar improvements concerning pumps.*

**co·in·sur·ance** /ˌkəʊɪnˈʃʊərəns‖ˌkoʊɪnˈʃʊr-/ *n* [U] *AmE* **1** a type of insurance in which the payment is split between two people, especially between an employer and a worker: *health coinsurance* **2** insurance that will only pay for part of the value of something

**co·in·sure** /ˌkəʊɪnˈʃʊə‖ˌkoʊɪnˈʃʊr/ *v* [T] *AmE* to buy or provide insurance in which the payment is split between two people, or insurance that will only pay for part of the value of something

**coir** /kɔɪə‖kɔɪr/ *n* [U] the rough material that covers the shell of a COCONUT, used for making MATS, ropes etc

**co·i·tus** /ˈkəʊɪtəs, ˈkɔɪtəs‖ˈkoʊ-, ˈkɔɪ-/ *n* [U] *technical* the act of having sex; SEXUAL INTERCOURSE —**coital** *adj*

**coke** /kəʊk‖koʊk/ *n* **1 Coke** [C,U] *trademark* the drink COCA-COLA: *Regular fries and a large Coke, please.* **2** [U] *informal* COCAINE **3** [U] a solid black substance produced from coal and burned to provide heat

**Col.** *n* the written abbreviation for COLONEL

**col**[1] /kɒl‖kɑːl/ *n* [C] a low point between two high places in a mountain range; PASS[2] (5)

**col**[2] the written abbreviation for COLUMN

**col-** /kəl, kɒl‖kəl, kɑːl/ *prefix* the form used for CON- before l: *to collaborate* (=work together)

**co·la** /ˈkəʊlə‖ˈkoʊ-/ *n* [C,U] a brown, sweet, CARBONATED drink: *a can of cola*

**col·an·der** /ˈkʌləndə, ˈkɒ-ˈkʌləndər, ˈkɑː-/ *n* [C] a metal or plastic bowl with a lot of small holes in the bottom and sides, used to separate liquid from food

**cold**[1] /kəʊld‖koʊld/ *adj* S1 W1

**1 ▶ OBJECTS/SURFACES/LIQUIDS/ROOMS ETC ◀** having a low temperature: *a blast of cold air* | *We slept on the cold ground.* | **feel cold** *The office always feels so cold first thing on Monday morning.* | **ice/stone/freezing cold** (=very cold) *The radiator is stone cold; isn't the heating working?* | **as cold as ice** (=very cold) | **go cold** *BrE*/**get cold** (=become cold) *My tea's gone cold.* | *Come and eat or your dinner will get cold!* —see picture at HOT[1]

**2 ▶ WEATHER ◀** when there is cold weather, the temperature of the air is very low: *It was so cold this morning I had to scrape the ice off my windshield.* | **cold winter/evening/January etc** *the coldest winter on record* | **be cold out/outside** *Put on a coat; it's cold out.* | **get cold** (=become cold) *The weather gets colder around the middle of October.* | **turn cold** (=become cold or colder, especially suddenly)

**3 ▶ PEOPLE ◀ be/feel/look/get cold** if you are cold, your body is at a low temperature: *Could you turn up the heater, I'm cold.* | **be blue with cold** (=be so cold that your skin looks slightly blue) | **as cold as ice** (=very cold) *My feet are as cold as ice.*

**4 ▶ LACKING FEELING ◀** lacking normal human feelings such as sympathy, pity, humour etc: *a cold, calculated murder* | *He's a very cold man, very aloof and arrogant.*

**5 ▶ UNFRIENDLY ◀** unfriendly and behaving as though you do not care much about other people: *Martin was really cold towards me at the party.*

**6 ▶ FOOD EATEN COLD ◀** cold food is cooked but not eaten hot: *We brought cold chicken and a bottle of wine to the picnic.* | *a cold buffet which the guests helped themselves to*

**7 get/have cold feet** *informal* to suddenly feel that you are not brave enough to do something you planned to do: *You're not getting cold feet about marrying him, are you?*

**8 give sb the cold shoulder** *informal* to deliberately ignore someone or be unfriendly to them, especially because they have upset or offended you

**9 cold (hard) cash** *AmE informal* money in the form of paper money and coins rather than cheques or CREDIT CARDS

**10 leave sb cold** to not interest someone or affect their feelings in any way: *Opera just leaves me cold – I can't understand why people like it.*

**11 cold shower** a SHOWER[1] (2) without any hot water: **take a cold shower** (=used to tell someone to stop feeling sexually excited)

**12 ▶ TRAIL/SCENT ◀** if someone's trail or scent is cold, you cannot find out which way they have gone because it has been a long time since they passed a particular place: *We had the dogs after him, but the trail had gone cold.*

**13 ▶ GAME ◀** [never before noun] used in a children's game, to say that someone is far away from the hidden object they are trying to find: *You're getting colder!*

**14 ▶ LIGHT/COLOUR ◀** a cold colour or light reminds you of things that are cold: *The moon shone with a cold, clear light.* | **in the cold light of day** (=in the morning, when you see things clearly) *In the cold light of day, we wondered whether we'd made the right decision.*

**15 cold steel** *literary* a weapon such as a knife or sword —see also **in cold blood** (BLOOD[1] (3)), **cold fish** (FISH[1] (8)), **blow hot and cold** (BLOW[1] (15)), **cold comfort** (COMFORT[1] (7)), **pour cold water over/on** (POUR[1] (7)), **a cold sweat** (SWEAT[2] (3)), —**coldly** *adv* —**coldness** *n* [U]

**USAGE NOTE: COLD**

WORD CHOICE: **cold, cool, hot, warm, chilly, freezing, boiling, baking, heated**

**Cold** means at a lower temperature than **cool**, often one that is not comfortable. **Cool** often suggests a pleasantly low temperature: *I hate cold weather.* | *It's lovely and cool in here.*

In the same way, **hot** suggests a higher temperature than **warm**, or a temperature which would not be comfortable for a long period. **Warm** often

C

suggests a pleasantly high temperature: *The handle is too hot to touch.*|*I could lie in a warm bath for hours.*

When talking of **cold** air or weather people often say it is **chilly** or, if it is very cold, **freezing** or **bitterly cold**. Very **hot** weather is **boiling** or **baking**. Cold weather may be called **the cold**: *My feet were purple with the cold* (=because of the cold, NOT *purple because of cold*).|*I don't like the cold* (NOT *I don't like cold*).

**A cold** is an illness: *My nose runs when I have a cold* (NOT *have cold*).|*I've caught a cold from my husband* (NOT *caught cold*). Compare: *I got cold waiting for the bus without a coat* (=felt cold, not the same as ...*got a cold* = caught the illness).

When talking about people's character or behaviour, **cold** usually means lacking any emotion or friendly feelings: *a cold start*|*His manner towards her was very cold.* **Cool** can mean less friendly, enthusiastic etc than usual: *When Bill arrived, more than an hour later, he got a rather cool reception.* **Cool** can also mean calm and not getting excited or showing your emotions: *a cool head in a crisis.* **Warm** often means friendly and welcoming: *a warm smile.*

**Heated** arguments, discussions etc are ones in which people disagree and get angry.

**cold**[2] *n* **1** [U] **the cold** a very low temperature outside: *Don't go out in the cold without your coat!* **2** [C] a slight illness that makes it difficult to breathe through your nose and makes your throat hurt: *I've got a bad cold.*| **catch a cold** (=become ill) *Keep your feet dry so you don't catch a cold.*| **catch your death of cold** (=used to warn someone that they may become very ill if they do not keep themselves warm in cold weather) —see also COMMON COLD **3 come in from the cold** to become accepted or recognized, especially by a powerful group of people **4 leave sb out in the cold** *informal* to not include someone in an activity: *If you don't start working harder, you'll be left out in the cold when it comes time for promotion.*

**cold**[3] *adv* **1** *AmE* suddenly and completely: *Then Paul stopped cold. "What was that noise?"* **2 out cold** unconscious, especially because you have been hit on the head: **knock sb (out) cold** (=hit someone so that they become unconscious) **3** without preparation: *I can't just get up there and make a speech cold!*

**cold-blood·ed** /ˌ· ˈ··◂/ *adj* **1** a cold-blooded animal, such as a snake, has a body temperature that changes with the temperature of the air or ground around it —compare WARM-BLOODED **2 cold-blooded killer/murder/violence etc** a person or their actions that show they feel no pity and do not care if other people suffer —**cold-bloodedly** *adv* —**cold-bloodedness** *n* [U]

**cold call** /ˌ· ˈ·/ *n* [C] if someone who is selling something makes a cold call, they telephone someone they have never met and try to sell something

**cold cream** /ˈ· ·/ *n* [U] a thick, white, sweet-smelling, oily cream used for cleaning your face and making it softer

**cold cuts** /ˈ· ·/ *n* [plural] *especially AmE* thinly cut pieces of various types of cold cooked meat

**cold-heart·ed** /ˌ· ˈ··◂/ *adj* behaving in a way that shows no pity or sympathy —**cold-heartedly** *adj* —**cold heartedness** *n* [U]

**cold snap** /ˈ· ·/ *n* [C] a sudden short period of extremely cold weather

**cold sore** /ˈ· ·/ *n* [C] a painful spot on your lips or inside your mouth that you may get when you are ill with a cold

**cold spell** /ˈ· ·/ *n* [C] a period of several days or weeks when the weather is much colder than usual

**cold stor·age** /ˌ· ˈ··/ *n* [U] **1** if you keep something such as food in cold storage, you keep it in a cold place so that it will stay fresh and in good condition **2 put/go/be in cold storage** to not take action on a plan or idea until later in the future: *We'll have to put the project into cold storage until we can get the funding.*

**cold store** /ˈ· ·/ *n* [C] a very cold room that is kept cold by a machine and used to store food, fur coats etc to keep them fresh or in good condition

**cold sweat** /ˌ· ˈ·/ *n* [singular] a reaction by your body when you are nervous or afraid, in which you SWEAT[1] (1) but still feel cold: *The thought of the trial made him break out in a cold sweat.*

**cold tur·key** /ˌ· ˈ··/ *n* [U] **go cold turkey** to suddenly stop taking a drug you are addicted to and to experience a sort of illness because of it: *Marcia went cold turkey off heroin.*

**cold war** /ˌ· ˈ·◂/ *n* [singular U] an unfriendly political relationship between two countries who do not actually fight each other, usually used of the unfriendly relationship between the US and the USSR after the Second World War

**cole·slaw** /ˈkəʊlslɔː‖ˈkoʊlslɒː/ *n* [U] a SALAD made with thinly cut raw CABBAGE (1)

**co·ley** /ˈkəʊli‖ˈkoʊ-/ *n* [C,U] a large North Atlantic sea fish or the flesh of this fish eaten as food

**col·ic** /ˈkɒlɪk‖ˈkɑː-/ *n* [U] if a baby suffers from colic, it has severe pain in its stomach and BOWELS (1) —**colicky** *adj*

**co·li·tis** /kəˈlaɪtɪ̆s/ *n* [U] *technical* an illness in which part of your COLON (2) swells, causing pain

**col·lab·o·rate** /kəˈlæbəreɪt/ *v* [I] **1** to work together with someone in order to achieve something, especially in science or art: [+ **on/with**] *He was one of the scientists who collaborated with Oppenheimer on the atomic bomb.*| **collaborate to do sth** *The gallery and the university collaborated to mount an exhibition of rare drawings.*| **collaborate in doing sth** *Watson and Crick collaborated in discovering the structure of DNA.* **2** [+ **with**] to be disloyal to your country by helping an enemy army or government that has taken control of your country

**col·lab·o·ra·tion** /kəˌlæbəˈreɪʃən/ *n* [U] **1** [+ **between/with**] the act of working together with another person or group to achieve something, especially in science or art: **in collaboration with** *The company is building the centre in collaboration with the Institute of Offshore Engineering.* **2** [+ **with**] help given to an enemy army or government that has taken control of your country

**col·lab·o·ra·tive** /kəˈlæbərətɪv‖-reɪ-/ *adj* [only before noun] **collaborative effort/work/project etc** involving two or more people working together to achieve something

**col·lab·o·rat·or** /kəˈlæbəreɪtə‖-ər/ *n* [C] **1** someone who helps their country's enemies, for example by giving them information, when the enemy has taken control of their country: *Their job was to identify enemy collaborators.* **2** someone who works with other people in order to achieve something, especially in science or art: *collaborators on a biography of Dickens*

**col·lage** /ˈkɒlɑːʒ‖kəˈlɑːʒ/ *n* **1** [C] a picture made by sticking other pictures, photographs, cloth etc onto a surface **2** [U] the art of making such pictures

**col·la·gen** /ˈkɒlədʒən‖ˈkɑː-/ *n* [U] a PROTEIN substance, sometimes put into women's face creams

**col·lapse**[1] /kəˈlæps/ *v* S

**1 ▶STRUCTURE◀** [I] if a building, wall, piece of furniture etc collapses, it suddenly falls down because its structure is weak or because it has been hit with a sudden violent force: *The roof is in danger of collapsing.*|*Uncle Ted's chair collapsed under his weight.*

**2 ▶FAIL◀** [I] if a system, idea, or organization collapses, it suddenly fails or becomes too weak to continue: *The business finally collapsed because of rising debts.*

**3 ▶ILLNESS◀** [I] to suddenly fall down or become unconscious because you are ill: *He collapsed with a heart attack while he was dancing.*

**4 ▶SIT◀** to suddenly sit down, especially because you are very tired: *I was so exhausted when I got home, I just collapsed on the sofa.*

5 ▶ **MAKE STH SMALLER** ◀ [I,T] if a piece of furniture or equipment collapses or you collapse it, you can fold it so that it becomes smaller: *The legs on our card table collapse so we can store it in the closet.*
6 ▶ **MEDICAL** ◀ [I] if a lung or a BLOOD VESSEL collapses, it suddenly becomes flat, so that it no longer has any air or blood in it

**collapse²** *n*
1 ▶ **BUSINESS/SYSTEM/IDEA ETC** ◀ [singular, U] a sudden failure in the way something works, so that it cannot continue: *The country's economic collapse led to political chaos.*
2 ▶ **BUILDING / STRUCTURE / FURNITURE ETC** ◀ [U] the act of suddenly falling down because of a weakness in something's structure or because something has hit it violently: *the collapse of an apartment building during the earthquake*
3 ▶ **ILLNESS** ◀ [singular] a sudden illness that makes you fall down or become unconscious
4 ▶ **MONEY/PRICES ETC** ◀ [singular] a sudden decrease in the value of something: *the collapse of the stock market in 1987*

**col·lap·si·ble** /kəˈlæpsɪ̈bəl/ *adj* something collapsible can be folded so that it takes less space: *a collapsible bicycle*

**col·lar¹** /ˈkɒlə‖ˈkɑːlər/ *n* [C]
1 ▶ **CLOTHING** ◀ a stiff band of material on a shirt, dress, or coat that fits around someone's neck —see picture on page 840
2 ▶ **CAT/DOG** ◀ a narrow band of leather or plastic that is fastened around an animal's neck
3 **hot under the collar** *spoken* angry or excited: *Calm down! There's no need to get all hot under the collar.*
4 ▶ **COLOURED FUR/FEATHERS** ◀ a band of fur, feathers, or skin around an animal's neck that is a different colour from the rest of the fur etc
5 ▶ **WORK ANIMAL** ◀ a thick leather ring put over the shoulders of a work animal to help it pull machinery or a vehicle
6 ▶ **MACHINE** ◀ a part of a machine that is shaped like a ring
7 ▶ **POLICE** ◀ *slang* if the police make a collar, they catch a criminal —see also BLUE-COLLAR, WHITE-COLLAR, DOG COLLAR

**collar²** *v* [T] *informal* **1** to catch someone and hold them so that they cannot escape: *The police collared him before he could get out of the country.* **2** to find someone so that you can talk to them: *See if you can collar Tim. I need to know when he'll be ready.*

**col·lar·bone** /ˈkɒləbəʊn‖ˈkɑːlərboʊn/ *n* [C] one of the pair of bones that go from the bottom part of your neck to your shoulders —see picture at SKELETON

**col·lard greens** /ˌkɒləd‖ˈkɑːlərd ˈgriːnz/ *n* a green leafy vegetable cooked and eaten as food

**collar stud** /ˈ·· ·/ *n* [C] an object like a button, used to fasten old-fashioned collars to shirts

**col·late** /kəˈleɪt/ *v* [T] **1** to arrange sheets of paper in the correct order before they are in a book etc: *a photocopier that collates and staples* **2** *formal* to gather information together, examine it carefully, and compare it with other information to find any differences

**col·lat·e·ral¹** /kəˈlætərəl/ *n* [U] *technical* property or other goods that you promise to give someone if you cannot pay back the money they lent you; SECURITY (4) | **put sth up as collateral** (=promise it in this way)

**collateral²** *adj formal* **1** connected with something or happening as a result of it, but not as important: *A collateral aim of better education is reducing unemployment.* **2** collateral relatives are members of your family who are not closely related to you

**col·la·tion** /kəˈleɪʃən/ *n formal* **1** [U] the examination and comparing of information **2** [U] the arranging of sheets of paper in the correct order **3** [C] *formal* a small, usually cold meal

S3 W2 **col·league** /ˈkɒliːg‖ˈkɑː-/ *n* [C] someone you work with, used especially by professional people or managers: *a colleague of mine at the bank*

**col·lect¹** /kəˈlekt/ *v* S1 W2
1 ▶ **BRING TOGETHER** ◀ [T] to get things of the same type from different places and bring them together: *Researchers spent 6 months collecting facts and figures.* | *Could you collect some branches for a fire?*
2 ▶ **KEEP OBJECTS** ◀ [T] to get and keep objects because you think they are attractive or interesting: *The family's been collecting modern art for thirty years.*
3 ▶ **MONEY** ◀ **a)** [T] to ask for or obtain money you are owed or something you have won: *He's collected his second gold medal of these Olympics.* **b) collect (money) for sth** to ask people to give you money for a particular purpose: *We're collecting for Save the Children.*

4 ▶ **INCREASE IN AMOUNT** ◀ [I,T] if something collects in a place or you collect it there, it gradually increases in amount: *Rain collected in pools on the uneven road.* | *solar panels for collecting the sun's heat*
5 ▶ **CROWD** ◀ [I] to come together gradually to form a group of people: *A crowd was beginning to collect around the scene of the accident.*
6 ▶ **DUST/DIRT** ◀ [T] to become covered in dust etc: *All the furniture had collected a fine layer of dust.*
7 ▶ **TAKE SB/STH FROM A PLACE** ◀ [T] *especially BrE* to come to a particular place in order to take someone or something away: *Martin's gone to collect the children from school.*
8 **collect yourself/collect your thoughts etc** to make an effort to remain calm and think clearly and carefully about something: *He paused for a moment to collect himself, then pushed open the door.*

**collect²** /kəˈlekt/ *adv AmE* **1 call/phone sb collect** when you telephone someone collect, the person who received the call pays for it **2 collect call** a telephone call paid for by the person who receives it

**col·lect³** /ˈkɒlɪkt, -lekt‖ˈkɑː-/ *n* [C] a short prayer in some Christian services

**col·lect·a·ble** /kəˈlektəbəl/ also **col·lect·i·ble** /-ɪ̈bəl/ *adj* something that is collectable is likely to be bought and kept as part of a group of similar things, especially because it might increase in value: *Art Deco glassware is very collectable right now.*

**col·lect·ed** /kəˈlektɪ̈d/ *adj* **1** in control of yourself and your thoughts, feelings, etc. **2 collected works** all of someone's books, poems etc printed in one book or set of books

**col·lect·i·ble** /kəˈlektkbəl/ also **collectable** *n* [C] an object that you keep as part of a group of similar things: *Miss Kelly's house was full of collectibles, displayed on every possible surface.*

**col·lec·tion** /kəˈlekʃən/ *n* S2 W1
1 ▶ **SET/GROUP** ◀ **a)** [C] a set of similar things that are kept or brought together because they are attractive or interesting: *a stamp collection* | **[+ of]** *a magnificent collection of prehistoric tools* **b)** [C] a group of things that are put together: *A collection of empty wine bottles stood on the back porch.*
2 ▶ **MONEY** ◀ **a)** [C] the act of asking for money from people for a particular purpose: **have a collection** *Every Christmas we have a collection and give the money to a charity.* | **take (up) a collection** *We'll be taking up a collection at the end of tonight's service.* **b)** [U] the act of obtaining money that is owed to you: *Resistance to the new tax is making collection difficult.*
3 ▶ **TAKING STH AWAY** ◀ [C,U] the act of taking something from a place, especially when this is done regularly: *Garbage collections are made every Tuesday morning.*
4 ▶ **BRINGING TOGETHER** ◀ [U] the act of bringing together things of the same type from different places to form a group: *the collection of reliable data*
5 ▶ **CLOTHES** ◀ [C] a number of different pieces of clothing designed by someone for a particular time of year: *the Paris spring collections*
6 ▶ **PEOPLE** ◀ [C usually singular] a group of people,

especially people you think are strange or unusual in some way: *There was an interesting collection of people at the wedding.*
7 ▶ **BOOKS/MUSIC** ◀ [C] several stories, poems, pieces of music etc that are in one book or on one record: *A new collection of Frost's poetry*

**collection box** /ˈ·ˈ·· ˌ·/ *n* [C] a container with a small opening in the top into which people put money for CHARITY (2)

**collection plate** /ˈ·ˈ·· ˌ·/ *n* [C] a large, almost flat dish in which you put money during some religious services

W3 **col·lec·tive**[1] /kəˈlektɪv/ *adj* [only before noun] involving a group, or shared or made by every member of a group: **collective decision/responsibility etc** *a collective decision on the part of the management*

**collective**[2] *n* [C] **1** a group of people who work together to run something such as a business or farm **2** the business or farm that is run by this group

**collective bar·gain·ing** /·ˌ·· ˈ···/ *n* [U] the discussions held between employers and a union in order to reach agreement on wages, working conditions etc

**collective farm** /·ˌ·· ˈ·/ *n* [C] a large farm that is owned by the government and controlled by the farm workers

**col·lec·tive·ly** /kəˈlektɪvli/ *adv* as a group: *The islands, which are northwest of Australia, are collectively known as Indonesia.*

**collective noun** /·ˌ·· ˈ·/ *n* [C] *technical* a noun, such as 'committee' or 'family', that is the name of people or things considered as a unit

**col·lec·tiv·is·m** /kəˈlektɪvɪzəm/ *n* [U] a political system in which all businesses, farms etc are owned by the government —**collectivize** *v* [T] —**collectivist** *adj*

**col·lec·tor** /kəˈlektə‖-ər/ *n* [C] **1** someone whose job is to collect taxes, tickets, debts etc **2** someone who collects things that are interesting or attractive: *a coin collector* **3 collector's item** something that a collector would like to have: *Original teddy bears have become real collectors' items.*

S1 W2 **col·lege** /ˈkɒlɪdʒ‖ˈkɑː-/ *n*
1 ▶ **ADVANCED EDUCATION** ◀ [C,U] **a)** *especially BrE* a school for advanced education, especially in a particular subject or skill: *a teacher training college* —see also SIXTH FORM COLLEGE **b)** *AmE* a school for advanced education where you can get a BACHELOR'S DEGREE: *Which colleges have you applied to?* | **college campus/class/graduate etc** *Many firms will only hire college graduates.* | **go to college** (=attend a college or university) —see also JUNIOR COLLEGE —compare UNIVERSITY
2 ▶ **PART OF UNIVERSITY** ◀ [C] one of the groups of teachers and students that form a separate part of some universities, especially in Britain: *Trinity College, Cambridge*
3 ▶ **BUILDINGS** ◀ [C] the buildings used by any of these organizations
4 ▶ **STUDENTS AND TEACHERS** ◀ [C also + plural verb *BrE*] the students and teachers of one of these organizations: *The whole college turned up to the memorial service.*
5 ▶ **ORGANIZATION** ◀ [C] a group of people who have special rights and duties within a profession or organization: *the Royal College of Nursing* —see also ELECTORAL COLLEGE
6 ▶ **SCHOOL** ◀ [C] *BrE* a word used in the name of some large schools, especially PUBLIC SCHOOLS

**college boards** /ˌ·· ˈ·/ *n* [plural] a set of examinations that students in the US must take in order to enter a college or university

**col·le·gi·ate** /kəˈliːdʒiət/ *adj* **1** involving or related to a college: *inter-collegiate competition* **2** organized into colleges: *a collegiate university*

**col·lide** /kəˈlaɪd/ *v* [I] **1** to hit something or someone that is moving in a different direction from you: *Two supertankers collided in the rough seas.* | [+ **with**] *Donna swerved to avoid colliding with a taxi.* **2** to have an argument with a person or group, especially on a particular subject: [+ **with**] *The President has again collided with Congress over his budget plans.*

**col·lie** /ˈkɒli‖ˈkɑːli/ *n* [C] a middle sized dog with long hair, kept as a pet or trained to look after sheep —see picture at DOG[1]

**col·li·er** /ˈkɒliə‖ˈkɑːliər/ *n* [C] *BrE* **1** *formal* someone whose job is to cut coal in a mine; MINER **2** a ship that carries coal

**col·lie·ry** /ˈkɒljəri‖ˈkɑːl-/ *n* [C] *BrE* a COAL MINE and the buildings and machinery connected with it

**col·li·sion** /kəˈlɪʒən/ *n* [C,U] **1** an accident in which two or more people or vehicles hit each other while moving in different directions: [+**with**] *The school bus was involved in a collision with a truck.* | **head-on collision** (=between two vehicles moving directly towards each other) **2** [+ **between**] a strong disagreement between two people or groups **3 be on a collision course a)** to behave in a way that will cause a serious disagreement or even a war: *Environmentalists and loggers are on a collision course, with no compromise in sight.* **b)** to be moving in a direction in which you will hit another person or vehicle

**col·lo·cate** /ˈkɒləkeɪt‖ˈkɑː-/ *v* [I + **with**] *technical* when words collocate, they are often used together and sound natural together —**collocate** /ˈkɒləkɪ̵t‖ˈkɑː-/ *n* [C]

**col·lo·ca·tion** /ˌkɒləˈkeɪʃən‖ˌkɑː-/ *n* [U] *technical* [C,U] the way in which some words are often used together, or a particular combination of words used in this way: *"Commit a crime" is a typical collocation in English.*

**col·loid** /ˈkɒlɔɪd‖ˈkɑː-/ *n* [C] *technical* a mixture of substances in which one substance is completely mixed with another but not DISSOLVE*d* —compare SUSPENSION (4)

**col·lo·qui·al** /kəˈləʊkwiəl‖-ˈloʊ-/ *adj* language or words that are colloquial are used mainly in conversation rather than in writing or formal speech —**colloquially** *adv*

**col·lo·qui·al·is·m** /kəˈləʊkwiəlɪzəm‖-ˈloʊ-/ *n* [C] an expression or word used mainly in conversation

**col·lo·quy** /ˈkɒləkwi‖ˈkɑː-/ *n* [C] *formal* a conversation —compare SOLILOQUY

**col·lude** /kəˈluːd/ *v* [I] *formal* to work with someone secretly, especially in order to cheat or deceive other people: [+ **with**] *He was accused of colluding with the occupying forces.*

**col·lu·sion** /kəˈluːʒən/ *n* [U] *formal or law* a secret agreement that two or more people make in order to do something dishonest

**col·ly·wob·bles** /ˈkɒliˌwɒbəlz‖ˈkɑːliˌwɑː-/ *n* **the collywobbles** *BrE informal* an uncomfortable feeling that you get when you are very nervous

**co·logne** /kəˈləʊn‖-ˈloʊn/ *n* [U] a liquid that smells slightly of flowers or plants that you put on your neck or wrists —compare PERFUME[1] (1)

**co·lon** /ˈkəʊlən‖ˈkoʊ-/ *n* [C] **1** the sign (:) that is used in writing and printing to introduce an explanation, example, QUOTATION (1) etc —compare SEMICOLON —see picture at PUNCTUATION MARK **2** *technical* the lower part of the BOWELS, in which food is changed into waste matter —see picture at DIGESTIVE SYSTEM

**colo·nel** /ˈkɜːnl‖ˈkɜːr-/ *n* [C] a high rank in the Army, Marines, or the US Air Force, or someone who has this rank —see table on page B4

**Colonel Blimp** /ˌ·· ˈ·/ *n* [C] *BrE* an old man with very old-fashioned ideas, who thinks he is important

**co·lo·ni·al**[1] /kəˈləʊniəl‖-ˈloʊ-/ *adj* **1** connected with or related to a country that controls and rules other countries: *a major colonial power* **2** made in a style that was common in the US in the 18th century: *a large colonial house* **3** connected with the US when it was under British rule: *an old colonial port on the coast* **4** *BrE* behaving in a way that shows you believe you are better than the people in the foreign country where you live: *He still has a colonial mentality.* —see also COLONY

**colonial**[2] *n* [C] someone who lives in a COLONY but who is a citizen of the country that rules the colony

**co·lo·ni·al·is·m** /kəˈləʊniəlɪzəm‖-ˈloʊ-/ *n* [U] the principle or practice in which a powerful country rules a weaker one and establishes its own trade and culture there —compare IMPERIALISM

**co·lo·ni·al·ist** /kəˈləʊniəl̩ɪst‖-ˈloʊ-/ *n* [C] a supporter of colonialism —**colonialist** *adj*: *a savage colonialist war*

**col·o·nist** /ˈkɒlən̩ɪst‖ˈkɑː-/ *n* [C] someone who settles in a new colony: *Dutch colonists in South America*

**col·o·nize** /ˈkɒlənaɪz‖ˈkɑː-/ *v* [T] to establish political control over an area or over another country, and send your citizens there to settle —**colonization** /ˌkɒlənaɪˈzeɪʃən‖ˌkɑːlənə-/ *n* [U] —**colonizer** *n* [C]

**col·on·nade** /ˌkɒləˈneɪd‖ˌkɑː-/ *n* [C] a row of upright stone posts that usually support a roof or row of arches —**colonnaded** *adj*

**col·o·ny** /ˈkɒləni‖ˈkɑː-/ *n* [C] **1** a country or area that is under the political control of a more powerful country, usually one that is far away: *Algeria was formerly a French colony.* —see also CROWN COLONY, DOMINION (3), PROTECTORATE **2** a group of people who live in a colony **3** one of the 13 areas of land on the east coast of North America that later became the United States: *Connecticut was one of the original colonies.* **4** a particular group of people or the place where they live: *an artists' colony* | *a leper colony* **5** a group of animals or plants of the same type that are living or growing together: *Breeding colonies of rare birds were threatened by the oil spill.*

**col·or** /ˈkʌlə‖-ər/ the American spelling of COLOUR

**col·o·ra·tion** /ˌkʌləˈreɪʃən/ *n* [U] the way something is coloured or the pattern these colours make; COLOURING

**col·o·ra·tu·ra** /ˌkɒlərəˈtʊərə, -ˈtjʊə-‖ˌkʌlərəˈtʊrə/ *n* **1** [U] a difficult piece of music that is meant to be sung fast **2** [C] a woman, especially a SOPRANO, who sings this type of music

**col·or·ize** *AmE*, **col·our·ize** also **-ise** *BrE* /ˈkʌləraɪz/ *v* [T] to add colour to an old film that was made in black and white —**colourization** *n* [U]

**color line** /ˈ·· ·/ *n* [singular] *AmE* the set of laws or social customs in some places that prevents people of different races from going to the same places or taking part in the same activities; COLOUR BAR *BrE*: *Friendship across the color line was rare then.*

**co·los·sal** /kəˈlɒsəl‖kəˈlɑː-/ *adj* extremely large: *a colossal statue* | *Their secret to success was manufacturing cheap goods on a colossal scale.* —**colossally** *adv*

**co·los·sus** /kəˈlɒsəs‖kəˈlɑː-/ *n* [C] someone or something that is very big or very important: *An intellectual colossus like Leonardo comes along only once in a generation.*

S1 W1 **colour**[1] *BrE*, **color** *AmE* /ˈkʌlə‖-ər/ *n*

**1 ▶ A COLOUR ◀** [C] red, blue, yellow, green, brown, purple etc: *"What colour are your eyes?" "They're brown."* | *My favourite colour is purple.* | **light/bright/pastel etc colour** *Children like bright colors.* | **be an orange/greenish etc colour** *It was kind of an orangey-red colour.* —see picture on page 411

**2 ▶ COLOUR IN GENERAL ◀** [C,U] the appearance of something, especially something with a lot of different colours: *Chameleons can change colour to match their surroundings.* | *I had always wanted to go to New England to see the fall colors.* (=the colours of the trees)

**3 in (full) colour** a television programme or film that is in colour contains colours such as red, green, and blue rather than just black and white

**4 ▶ SB'S RACE ◀** [C,U] how dark or light someone's skin is, which shows which race they belong to: *people of all colours* | *discrimination on the basis of color* —see also COLOURED

**5 ▶ SB'S FACE ◀** [C,U] the general appearance and colour of a person's skin, especially when this shows the state of their health or emotions: *Well, you look better than you did. You've got some colour in your face now.* | **a high colour** (=a red colour in someone's face that shows they are ill)

**6 ▶ SUBSTANCE ◀** [U] a substance that makes something red, blue, yellow etc: *After a few washes, dark clothes begin to lose their color.*

**7 ▶ STH INTERESTING ◀** [U] interesting and exciting details or qualities that a place or person has: *The old market is lively, full of colour and activity.* | **add/give colour to** (=make something more interesting) *A few illustrations or anecdotes will add colour to your report.*

**8 lend/give colour to sth** to make something, especially something unusual, appear likely or true: *We now have independent evidence that lends colour to the accusation of fraud.*

**9 off colour a)** not in good health: *You look a little off colour today.* **b)** jokes, stories etc that are off-colour are rude and often about sex

**10 colours** [plural] **a)** the colours that are used as a sign to represent a team, school, club etc: *The national colours of Italy are green, white, and red.* **b)** *especially BrE* a flag, RIBBON, BADGE etc that you wear or carry to show that you belong to or support a team, school etc

**11 show yourself in your true colours** to behave in a way that shows what your real character is, especially if you are unpleasant or dishonest

**12 see the colour of sb's money** *spoken* to have definite proof that someone has enough money to pay for something: *"A whiskey, please." "Let's see the color of your money first."*

**13 nail your colours to the mast** to say clearly what your opinion is on a particular subject

colour in *BrE* /color in *AmE*

**colour**[2] *BrE*, **color** *AmE* *v* **1** [T] to make something coloured rather than just black, white, or plain: *Do you colour your hair or is it naturally red?* | **colour sth red/blue etc** *Sunset came and coloured the sky a brilliant red.* **2** also **colour in** [I,T] use coloured pencils to put colours inside the lines of a picture: *As a kid, I used to love colouring in shapes.* **3** [I] when someone colours, their face becomes redder because they are embarrassed **4** [T] **colour sb's judgment/opinions/attitudes etc** to influence the way someone thinks about something, especially so that they become less fair or reasonable: *Don't you think your opinions are colored by prejudice?* —see also **colour code** (CODE (3))

**colour**[3] *BrE*, **color** *AmE* *adj* **colour television/photograph/monitor etc** a television etc that produces or shows pictures in colour rather than in black, white and grey —opposite MONOCHROME

**colour bar** *BrE*, **color bar** *AmE* /ˈ·· ·/ *n* [C usually singular] a set of laws or social customs that prevent people of different races from going to the same places or taking part in the same activities; COLOR LINE *AmE*

**colour-blind** *BrE*, **color-blind** *AmE* /ˈ·· ·/ *adj* **1** unable to see the difference between all or some colours **2** treating people from different races equally and fairly: *The law should be colour-blind.* —**colour-blindness** *n* [U]

**colour-co·or·di·nat·ed** *BrE*, **color-coordinated** *AmE* /ˈ···,····/ *adj* clothes, decorations etc that are colour-coordinated have colours which look good together —**colour-coordination** /,·· ···ˈ··/ *n* [U]

**col·oured**[1] *BrE*, **colored** *AmE* /ˈkʌləd‖-ərd/ *adj* **1** having a colour such as red, blue, yellow etc, rather than being black, white, or plain: *coloured glass* | *brightly colored tropical birds* **2** an offensive word for someone who belongs to a race of people with dark or black skin —see NEGRO (USAGE) **3** *SAfrE* someone whose parents or grandparents were both white and black

**coloured**[2] *BrE*, **colored** *AmE n* [C] an offensive word for someone belonging to a race of people with dark skin —see NEGRO (USAGE)

**col·our·fast** *BrE*, **colorfast** *AmE* /ˈkʌləfɑːst‖ˈkʌlərfæst/ *adj* cloth that is colourfast will not lose its colour when it is washed —**colourfastness** *n* [U]

**col·our·ful** *BrE*, **colorful** *AmE* /ˈkʌləfəl‖-lər-/ *adj* **1** having bright colours or a lot of different colours: *a colourful display of flowers* **2** interesting, exciting, and full of variety: **colourful career/life/period etc** *Charlie Chaplin had a long and colorful career.* | **colourful character/figure** (=someone who is interesting and unusual) *The old galley cook was the most colourful character on the ship.* **3** colourful language, speech etc uses a lot of swearing —**colourfully** *adv*

**col·our·ing** *BrE*, **coloring** *AmE* /ˈkʌlərɪŋ/ *n* **1** **food colouring** a substance used to give a particular colour to food **2** [U] the colour of someone's skin, hair, and eyes: *Mandy has her mother's fair coloring.* **3** [U] the colours of an animal, bird, or plant: *The black and yellow colouring of some insects acts as a warning to predators.*

**col·our·less** *BrE*, **colorless** *AmE* /ˈkʌlələs‖ˈkʌlər-/ *adj* **1** having no colour: *Water is a colorless liquid.* **2** not interesting or exciting; DULL[1] (1): *Everything about this town seems drab and colourless to me.* —**colourlessly** *adv* —**colourlessness** *n* [U]

**colour scheme** *BrE*, **color scheme** *AmE* /ˈ·· ·/ *n* [C] the combination of colours that someone chooses for a room, painting etc: *a sophisticated colour scheme*

**colour sup·ple·ment** /ˈ·· ,···/ *n* [C] *BrE* a magazine printed in colour and given free with a newspaper, especially a Sunday newspaper

**Colt** /kəʊlt‖koʊlt/ *n* [C] *trademark* a kind of PISTOL: *a Colt 45*

**colt** *n* [C] a young male horse —compare FILLY

**colt·ish** /ˈkəʊltɪʃ‖ˈkoʊlt-/ *adj* a young person or animal that is coltish has a lot of energy but moves in an awkward way: *her long coltish limbs*

**col·um·bine** /ˈkɒləmbaɪn‖ˈkɑː-/ *n* [C] a garden plant with delicate leaves and bright flowers that hang down

S2 W2 **col·umn** /ˈkɒləm‖ˈkɑː-/ *n* [C] **1** a tall, solid, upright, stone post used to support a building or as a decoration: *a graceful Ionic column* **2** a long moving line of people or things: *A long, winding column of soldiers marched through the streets.* **3** one of two or more lines of print that go down the page of a newspaper or book and that are separated from each other by a narrow space: *Turn to Page 5, column 2.* **4** a line of numbers or words written under each other that goes down a page: *Add up the numbers in each column separately.* **5** an article on a particular subject or by a particular writer that appears regularly in a newspaper or magazine: *a weekly column* | *She writes the gardening column in the Express.* **6** something that has a long, thin shape, like a column: [+ **of**] *a column of smoke* —see also FIFTH COLUMN, PERSONAL COLUMN, SPINAL COLUMN

**col·umn·ist** /ˈkɒləmɪ̈st, -ləmnɪ̈st‖ˈkɑː-/ *n* [C] someone who writes articles, especially about a particular subject, that appear regularly in a newspaper or magazine

**com-** /kəm, kɒm‖kəm, kɑːm/ *prefix* the form used for CON- before b, m, or p: *compassion* (=sympathy)

**co·ma** /ˈkəʊmə‖ˈkoʊ-/ *n* [C] a state in which someone remains unconscious for a long time, usually caused by a serious illness or injury: **be/lie in a coma** *Marina Stefani, 25, has been in a coma for the past four months.*

**co·ma·tose** /ˈkəʊmətəʊs‖ˈkoʊmətoʊs/ *adj* **1** *technical* in a coma **2** *informal* so tired that you cannot think properly: *Working till you're comatose doesn't help anybody.*

**comb**[1] /kəʊm‖koʊm/ *n* **1** [C] a flat piece of plastic, metal etc with a row of thin teeth on one side, used for making your hair tidy **2** [C] a small flat piece of plastic, metal etc with a row of thin teeth on one side, used for keeping your hair back or for decoration **3** [singular] a process in which you make your hair tidy or straight using a comb: *Your hair needs a good comb.* **4** [C] the red piece of flesh that grows on top of a male chicken's head **5** [C] a HONEYCOMB —see also FINE-TOOTH COMB

**comb**[2] *v* [T] **1** to make hair or fur tidy or straight using a comb: *Your hair's a mess! Go comb it.* **2** to search a place thoroughly: **comb sth for** *The police combed the woods for the missing boy.*

**comb** sb/sth ↔ **out** *phr v* [T] **1** to make hair or fur straight and smooth using a comb: *It took over an hour to comb out all the tangles in Buster's fur.* **2** *informal* to get rid of unnecessary people from within a group **3** [+ **from**] to find and collect specific pieces of information from a larger amount of information —**comb out** *n* [singular]

**comb through** *phr v* [T] to search through a lot of objects or information in order to find a specific thing or piece of information: *Marta combed through a box of old photographs, looking for the baby portrait.*

**com·bat**[1] /ˈkɒmbæt‖ˈkɑːm-/ *n* **1** [U] organized fighting, especially in a war: **active/armed combat** *These troops have very little experience of active combat.* | **in combat (with)** *Corporal Gierson was killed in combat.* | **combat mission/activity/unit etc** *The women were excluded from the combat units.* | **combat plane/jacket/boots** *A combat plane flew overhead.* | **locked in mortal combat** (=fighting until one of the opponents dies) **2** [C] a fight or battle: [+ **between/against**] *a combat between good and evil* | **single combat** (=a formal fight between only two people)

**com·bat**[2] /ˈkɒmbæt, kəmˈbæt‖kəmˈbæt, ˈkɑːmbæt/ *v* **combatted, combatting** *BrE* [T] *formal* **1** to take action in an organized way in order to oppose something bad or harmful: *a neighborhood watch system to help combat crime* | *new strategies to combat inflation* **2** to fight against an enemy or opponent in order to try and defeat them

**com·ba·tant** /ˈkɒmbətənt‖kəmˈbætnt/ *n* [C] someone who fights in a war

**combat fa·tigue** /ˈ·· ·,·/ *n* [U] *technical* BATTLE FATIGUE

**com·ba·tive** /ˈkɒmbətɪv‖kəmˈbætɪv/ *adj* ready and willing to fight or argue: *a combative committee member* —**combatively** *adv* —**combativeness** *n* [U]

**com·bi·na·tion** /,kɒmbɪ̈ˈneɪʃən‖,kɑːm-/ *n* **1** [C,U] two or more different things, qualities, substances etc that are used or put together: *a perfect wine and food combination* | [+ **of**] *A combination of factors may be responsible for the increase in cancer.* | *a screen heroine who is a combination of the modern and the traditional* | *A combination of tact and authority was needed to deal with the situation.* | **in combination (with)** *Certain drugs which are safe when taken separately are lethal in combination.* **2** [C] a number of things chosen from a group and put in a particular order: *Certain combinations of sounds are not possible in English.* | *an unusual combination of colours* **3** [C] the series of numbers or letters you need to open a combination lock: *I've forgotten the combination for my bicycle lock!* **4** **a winning combination** a mixture of different people or things that work successfully together **5** [U] *especially AmE* used before a noun in some phrases to mean that something does more than one job or uses more than one method: *a combination of washer and dryer* | *combination* S W *chemotherapy* **6 combinations** [plural] *BrE old-fashioned* a piece of underwear covering the upper part of your body and legs, worn especially in the past; UNION SUIT

**combination lock** /.. '.. ./ *n* [C] a lock which can only be opened by using a series of numbers or letters in a particular order

S3 W2 **com·bine¹** /kəm'baɪn/ *v* **1** [I,T] if you combine two or more different things, ideas, or qualities or if they combine, they begin to exist or work together: *I'm looking for a job in which I can combine the different aspects of my experience so far.* | **combine to do sth** *Several factors had combined to harm our friendship.* | **combine sth with** *The new software package combines power with maximum flexibility.* | **combined with** *Heat treatment is most effective if combined with regular physiotherapy.* | **combined effect/effects** (=the result of two or more different things used or mixed together) *The combined effects of the heat and too much alcohol made Sheila feel nauseous.* **2** [I,T] if two or more different substances, liquids etc combine or if you combine them, they mix or join together to produce a new single substance, liquid etc: **combine to do sth** *Different amino acids combine to form proteins.* | **combine sth** *Combine all the ingredients in a salad bowl.* | **combine sth with** *Steel is produced by combining iron with carbon.* **3** [T] to do two very different activities at the same time: **combine sth with** *You can't combine studying for your exams with a wild social life!* | **combine sth and sth** *It's no easy task combining family responsibilities and a full-time job!* | **combine business with pleasure** (=work and enjoy yourself at the same time) **4** [I,T] if two or more groups, organizations etc combine or if you combine them, they join or work together in order to do something: **combine to do sth** *Two of the smaller groups had combined to form one large team.* | **combine sth** *a report on the advantages of combining small village schools*

**com·bine²** /'kɒmbaɪn‖'kɑːm-/ *n* [C] **1** also **combine harvester** a machine used by farmers to cut grain, separate the seeds from it, and clean it **2** a group of people or organizations who work together for a particular purpose: *The factory was sold to a British combine after the war.*

**com·bined** /kəm'baɪnd/ *adj* **1** [only before noun] done, made, or achieved by several people or groups working together: **combined effort/action/operation** *"Who cooked the dinner?" "Well, it was a combined effort really."* | **combined salaries** (=the total amount of money that two or more people earn) **2** having two very different feelings at the same time: *Ann felt a combined relief and sadness.*

**combining form** /.'.. ./ *n* [C] *technical* a form of a word that has a meaning but cannot be used alone, and is used with other words to make new ones such as 'Anglo', meaning 'English', in the word 'Anglo-American'

**com·bo** /'kɒmbəʊ‖'kɑːmboʊ/ *n* [C] *informal* **1** a small band that plays JAZZ¹ (1) or dance music **2** *AmE* any combination of different things, especially a meal at a FAST FOOD restaurant: *I'll have the fish combo to go.*

**com·bus·ti·ble** /kəm'bʌstəbəl/ *adj* able to burn easily: *Alcohol is highly combustible.*

**com·bus·tion** /kəm'bʌstʃən/ *n* [U] **1** the process of burning **2** *technical* chemical activity which uses oxygen to produce light and heat **3 combustion chamber** the enclosed space in which combustion happens —see also INTERNAL COMBUSTION ENGINE

## come¹ /kʌm/ *v past tense* came /keɪm/ *past participle* come

S1 W1

① MOVE
② TRAVEL
③ ARRIVE
④ REACH A CONDITION/STATE
⑤ HAPPEN/EXIST
⑥ REACH AS FAR AS
⑦ SPOKEN PHRASES
⑧ IN AN ORDER/POSITION
⑨ OTHER MEANINGS
⑩ PHRASAL VERBS

### ① MOVE

**1** [I] a word meaning to move towards someone, or to visit or arrive at a place, used when the person speaking or the person listening is in that place: *Come a little closer.* | *Sarah's coming later on.* | *I've come about the job you advertised.* | [+ **to/towards/here etc**] *Come here and look at this.* | *When are you coming back?* | **come and do sth** *Can I come and see you tomorrow?* | **come to do sth** *A man comes to clean the windows on Fridays.* | **come for sb** (=in order to take them somewhere) *When is Anton coming for you?* | **come running/flying/speeding etc** *Jess came flying round the corner and banged straight into me.* | **come to dinner/lunch** *What day are your folks coming to dinner?*

**2 ▶ MOVE WITH SB ◀** [I] to move to a particular place with the person who is speaking: *Can Billy come too?* | [+ **with**] *Would you like to come to the concert with me?* | [+ **along**] *There's room for one more, if you want to come along.*

### ② TRAVEL

**3** [I] to travel a particular distance or in a particular way to reach the place you are in or talking about: *We rode back the way we had come.* | **come by/on/with etc** *Did you come on a coach or by train?* | **come far/miles/a long way etc** *Some of the birds have come thousands of miles to winter here.* | *It would be a shame to have come all this way and not see them.*

### ③ ARRIVE

**4** [I] to arrive or be sent somewhere: *The phone bill has come at a bad time.*

**5 ▶ TIME/EVENT ◀** [I] if a time or event comes, it arrives or happens: *The moment had come for me to break the news to her.* | *Christmas seems to come earlier every year.* | **coming soon** (=used especially in advertisements) *Coming soon, to a theater near you!* | **the time is coming/will come** *The time will come when you'll thank me for this.*

### ④ REACH A CONDITION/STATE

**6 come to sth** an expression used in some phrases, meaning to reach a particular state or position: **come to a decision/the conclusion** *I've come to the conclusion that we've made a mistake.* | **come to power/trial etc** *When does Alan's case come to court?* | **come to an end/halt/stop etc** *Yes, I saw the van come to a screeching halt right there.*

**7 come open/undone etc** to become open etc: *Your shoelace is coming untied.* | *The bottle came open in my bag!* —see also **a dream come true** (DREAM¹ (5))

**8 come to do sth** to begin to do something, especially to have a particular feeling or opinion about someone or something as a result of time or experience: *In time you may come to like it here.* | *That's the kind of behavior*

[continued on next page]

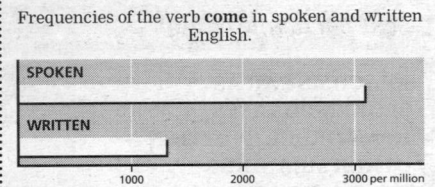

[continued from previous page]
*we've come to expect from him.* | *You've come to mean a lot to me.*
**9 come into sth** to begin to be in a particular state or position: *As we turned the corner, the town came into view.* | *The new law comes into effect next month.*

### ⑤ HAPPEN/EXIST

**10** [I] to happen or appear: *Your chance will come one day.* | *No good will come from all this.* | **sth comes and goes** *"How's the pain?" "Well, it comes and goes."* | **come in twos/threes etc** (=happen two, three etc times, closely together) *Trouble always comes in threes.*
**11** [I] to exist: **come in different shapes and sizes** *Cats come in many shapes and sizes.*
**12 as nice/as stupid etc as they come** extremely nice, stupid etc: *Don't get Bill angry—he's as mean as they come.*
**13 take it as it comes** to accept something exactly as it happens or is given to you, without trying to change it or plan ahead: *For the moment I'm just taking each day as it comes.*
**14 the best/worst is yet to come** used to say that better or worse things can be expected to happen in the future
**15 come what may** whatever happens: *Come what may, I'll never leave you.*
**16 come to pass** *literary* to happen after a period of time: *It came to pass that they had a son.*

### ⑥ REACH AS FAR AS

**17** [I always + adv/prep] to reach a particular place: **come up to/down to etc** *The water is pretty deep – it comes right up to my neck.* | *Carrie's hair comes down to her waist.*

Frequencies of the verb **come** in spoken and written English.

Based on the British National Corpus and the Longman Lancaster Corpus

This graph shows that the verb **come** is much more common in spoken English than in written English. This is because it is used in a lot of common spoken phrases.

### ⑦ SPOKEN PHRASES

**18 here comes John/Shelia etc** used when someone is coming towards you and you want the person you are with to notice them: *Look out, here comes the boss!*
**19 how come?** used to ask someone why something has happened: *How come Tyler's still here?*
**20 come to think of it/come to that** used when you want to add something you have just realized or been reminded of: *It was really fun – come to think of it, I should write Jim a thank-you note.* | *I haven't seen her for weeks – or her parents, come to that.*
**21 come again?** used to ask someone to repeat what they have just said
**22 come July/next year/the wedding etc** at a particular time in the future: *Come Monday, we'll be in our new house.*
**23 come (now)** *old-fashioned* used to comfort or gently encourage someone: *Come, Sarah, don't cry.*
**24 come, come!/come now** *old-fashioned* used to tell someone that you do not accept what they are saying or doing: *Come now, try to be more polite.*
**25 don't come the innocent/victim etc with me** *BrE* used to tell someone not to pretend to you that they are innocent, a victim etc: *Don't come the poor struggling artist with me. You're just lazy!*

### ⑧ IN AN ORDER/POSITION

**26** [I always + adv/prep] to be in a particular position or rank in order, importance, or quality: **come before/after** *The singing comes before the Mayor's speech.* | **come first/second etc** *"How was the tournament?" "We came last."* (=we did not win any games) | *My family always comes first.* (=is the most important thing in my life)

### ⑨ OTHER MEANINGS

**27 ► BE SOLD/AVAILABLE ◄** [I] to be sold, produced, or available: *Yogurt comes in many flavors.* | *The camera comes complete with batteries.* | **come cheap** *Houses like that don't come cheap.*
**28 have come a long way** to have made a lot of progress: *Computer technology has come a long way since the 1970's.*
**29 come as a surprise/relief/blow etc (to sb)** to make someone feel surprised, RELIEVED etc: *The news came as a complete shock to him.* | **it comes as no surprise that** (=used to say that you were expecting something) *It comes as no surprise that their marriage is over.*
**30 come of age a)** to reach an age, usually 18 or 21, when you are considered by law to be an adult **b)** if an artist, style, or organization comes of age, they reach their best, most successful period of time: *Mozart's music came of age when the baroque style was at its height.*
**31 come easily/naturally (to sb)** to be easy for someone to do, say etc: *Acting has always come naturally to her.*
**32 years/weeks/days etc to come** used to emphasize that something is still in the future or will continue into the future: *Nuclear waste will remain hazardous for generations to come.* —see also COMING[1]
**33 ► SEX ◄** [I] *slang* to have an ORGASM
**34 come to hand** things that come to hand are easy to reach or use, or are easily available: *Just use whatever comes to hand.*
**35 come to mind** if someone or something comes to mind, you think of them when you are trying to find a solution to something: *We need a new secretary. Does anyone good come to mind?*
**36 come to life a)** to become exciting or seem almost real: *When he reads out loud, Papa makes stories come to life.* **b)** to wake up or begin to grow again: *spring buds coming to life*
**37 come clean** *informal* to admit that you have done something wrong: [+ **about**] *I think you should come clean about where you were last night.*
**38 come right out and say sth** to speak in a direct, often surprising way: *Susie came right out and asked Bert what he thought of her.*
**39 not know whether you are coming or going** *informal* to feel confused because you are doing too many things, so that nothing is organized
**40 come good/right** *BrE informal* to end or finish well or correctly: *Don't worry, it'll all come right in the end.*

### ⑩ PHRASAL VERBS

**come about** *phr v* [I] **1** to happen, especially in a way that seems impossible to control: **how did it come about that** *How did it come about that humans speak so many different languages?* **2** when a ship comes about, it changes direction

**come across** *phr v* **1** [T not in passive] to meet, find, or discover someone or something by accident or by chance: *He had never come across a person quite like Sheila.* | *I came across some old photos in the attic.* **2** [I] **a)** if an idea comes across to someone, they understand it clearly: *Your point really came across at the meeting.* **b)** if someone comes across in a particular way, they give other people that feeling or opinion about them: *He came across as being rather arrogant.* | **come across well/badly** *I don't think I came across very well in the interview.* | **come across as (being) sth** *Sometimes you come across as being nervous.*

**come across with** sth *phr v* [T] *BrE spoken* **come**

**across with the goods** to provide money or information when it is needed

**come after** sb *phr v* [T not in passive] to look for someone until you find them so you can hurt them, punish them, or get something from them: *I heard the tax people are coming after him for unpaid VAT.*

**come along** *phr v* [I] **1 be coming along** *informal* to be developing, or improving, especially in education or health: [+ **with**] *How's Martin coming along with his English?*|*Mother's coming along nicely, thank you.* **2** to appear or arrive at a time you do not expect or cannot know about: *Take any job opportunity that comes along.*|*A bus should come along any minute now.* **3 a)** to follow someone somewhere: *You go on ahead – I'll come along later.* **b)** to go somewhere with someone: *Do you mind if I come along with you?* **4 come along!** *especially BrE spoken* **a)** used to tell someone to hurry up: *Come along now, children.* **b)** used to encourage someone to try harder: *Come along, surely someone knows the answer.*

**come apart** *phr v* [I] **1** to split or fall into pieces without anyone using force: *The book just came apart in my hands.* **2 come apart at the seams** to become unable to deal with a situation, or impossible to be dealt with: *It felt as if his whole life was coming apart at the seams.*

**come around** *phr v* [I] **1** *AmE* to visit someone at home or at the place where they are: *Mind if I come around after work?* **2** *AmE* to change your opinion so that you now agree with someone: *It took some persuading, but he finally came around.* **3** if a regular event comes round, it arrives or happens as usual: *Thanksgiving comes around so quickly, doesn't it?* **4** *AmE* to become conscious again: *It was three weeks before she came around.*

**come at** sb/sth *phr v* [T not in passive] **1** to move towards someone in a threatening way: *Meg came at me with a knife.* **2** if pieces of information, images etc come at you, you feel confused because there are a lot of them all at the same time **3** *informal* to consider or deal with a problem: *We need to come at the problem from a different angle.*

**come away** *phr v* [I] **1** if part of something comes away from something else, it becomes separated when you are using it normally: *I didn't break it! The handle came away in my hand.* **2** to leave a place: *Come away, Ben. There's going to be trouble.*

**come back** *phr v* [I] **1 it's all coming back to me** *spoken* to say that you are finally beginning to remember something **2** to become fashionable or popular again: [+ **in**] *Miniskirts have come back in this season.* **3** to reply in a forceful, quick, and often unkind way; RETORT[1] [+ **at**] *I don't want anyone coming back at me over this.*|[+ **with**] *coming back with a nasty retort* —see also COMEBACK

**come before** sb *phr v* [T] *formal* to be sent to a person or group in authority in order to be considered or judged: *When you come before the judge, tell the whole truth.*

**come between** sb *phr v* [T not in passive] **1** to cause trouble between two or more people: *Why should a little argument come between friends?* **2** to prevent someone from giving enough attention to something: *I don't let anything come between me and my work.*

**come by** sth *phr v* [T not in passive] **1** to obtain something that is rare or difficult to find: *How on earth did you come by these tickets?*|**be hard to come by** (=to be difficult to obtain or find) *Jobs are hard to come by these days.* **2** *AmE* to make a short visit to a place on your way to somewhere else: *I'll come by the house and get my stuff later, OK?*

**come down** *phr v* [I]
**1 ▶ BECOME LOWER ◀ a)** if a price, level etc comes down, it becomes lower: *Wait to buy a house until interest rates come down.* **b)** [+ **to**] to offer or accept a lower price: *Do you think the dealer would come down at all?*
**2 ▶ TRAVEL SOUTH ◀** to travel south or away from an important place such as a big city, to the place where the speaker is: *Come down for the weekend sometime.*|[+ **to**] *Are you coming down to Knoxville for Christmas?*
**3 ▶ BUILDING ◀** if a building comes down, it is destroyed by being pulled down
**4 come down on the side of** also **come down in favour of** to decide to support someone or something after thinking about a problem for a long time
**5 come down in sb's opinion/estimation** to do something that makes someone respect you less: *John really came down in my opinion after that.*
**6 come down in the world** to become poorer or less successful than you used to be.
**7 come (back) down to earth** to suddenly have to start dealing with ordinary practical problems after ignoring them for a time: *"Charles!" He stopped daydreaming and came back down to earth, startled.*
**8 ▶ DRUGS ◀** [+ **off/from**] *informal* to stop being affected by a powerful drug such as HEROIN or LSD that you have taken
**9 ▶ LEAVE UNIVERSITY ◀** [+ **from**] *BrE* to leave a university, especially Oxford or Cambridge, after completing a period of study

**come down on** sb/sth *phr v* [T not in passive] to punish someone or criticize them severely: **come down on sb for doing sth** *My parents really came down on me for being out so late.*|**come down hard on** (=punish someone very severely) *We're going to come down hard on car theft.*|**come down like a ton of bricks** (=punish someone extremely severely)

**come down to** sb/sth *phr v* [T not in passive] **1** if a complicated situation or problem comes down to something, it is the single most important point or choice: **it comes down to** *It all came down to a choice between cutting wages or cutting staff.* **2** if a document, object, idea etc comes down to someone, it has survived from a long time ago until the present: *The text which has come down to us is only a fragment of the original.*

**come down with** sth *phr v* [T not in passive] *informal* to become ill with something infectious, especially something that is not very serious: *I think I'm coming down with a cold.*

**come for** sth/sb *phr v* [T] **1** to arrive to collect someone or something: *I've come for the carpet I ordered.*|*Shall I come for you at about six then?* **2** to try to harm someone or take them away where they do not want to go: *When the secret police come for you, you'll talk, believe me!*

**come forward** *phr v* [I] **1** to offer yourself for a job, election etc: [+ **as**] *More women are coming forward as candidates than ever before.*|**come forward to do sth** *We need more volunteers to come forward to help.* **2** to offer help to someone in authority who needs it or has asked for it: [+ **with**] *A young girl has come forward with a description of the attacker.*

**come from** sb/sth *phr v* [T not in progressive] **1** to have started, been produced or first existed in a particular place, thing or time: *Where do you come from originally?*|*Milk comes from cows.*|*The passage she quoted came from Dickens.* **2 coming from him/her/you etc** *spoken* used to criticize what someone has said because they say one thing and behave in the opposite way: *Pretentions? Me? That's rich, coming from you!* **3 come from doing sth** also **come of doing sth** to be the result of doing something: *"I feel sick." "That's what comes from drinking too much."*

**come in** *phr v* [I]
**1 ▶ ARRIVE ◀** to arrive or be received: *As long as money's coming in, I'm happy.*|*Reports are coming in of a bad earthquake in Mexico.*|*Jenny's train comes in at eight.*
**2 ▶ ENTER ◀** to enter a room or house: *Come in! Take a seat.*
**3 ▶ BE INVOLVED ◀ a)** to be involved in a plan, deal etc: *We need financial advice – that's where Kate*

[continued on next page]

[continued from previous page]
*comes in.* | [+ **on**] *It'll cost you $1000 to come in on the scheme.* **b)** to interrupt or enter a conversation or discussion: *Excuse me, can I come in here?*
**4 ► BECOME FASHIONABLE ◄** to become fashionable or popular to use: *When platform shoes came in I thought they looked ridiculous.* —opposite **go out** (GO[1])
**5 come in first/second etc** to finish first, second etc in a race or competition: *I came in a long way behind everyone else.*
**6 come in useful/handy** to be useful: *Bring some rope along; it might come in handy.*
**7 ► SEA ◄** when the TIDE (=level of the sea) comes in, it rises —opposite **go out** (GO[1]), —see also **come in from the cold** (COLD[2] (3))

**come in for** sth *phr v* [T] **come in for criticism/blame/scrutiny** to be criticized, blamed etc for something: *The police came in for a lot of criticism for excess brutality.*

**come into** sth *phr v* [T, not in passive] **1 come into money/a fortune** to receive money, land etc after someone has died; INHERIT (1) **2** to be involved in something: *Mary, a minor character, doesn't come into the story much.* **3 luck/love/pride etc doesn't come into it!** *spoken* used to say that what someone has just mentioned is completely unimportant: *"Your brother was very lucky to win." "It was skill – luck didn't come into it."* **4 come into fashion** to become a popular thing to wear or do: *A-line skirts are coming into fashion again.* **5 come into your own** to become very good, useful, or important in a particular situation: *On icy roads like these, a four-wheel drive really comes into its own.*

**come of** sth *phr v* [T] to result from something: *Nothing came of my attempts to find her.* | *"I'm fat." "That's what comes of not exercising."*

**come off** *phr v* **1** [I,T not in passive] to stop being connected to something or stop sticking to something: *How did your button come off?* | [+ **onto**] *Some wet paint came off onto her hands.* | **come off sth** *The hook came off the wall when I hung my coat on it.* **2 come off well/badly etc a)** to happen well, badly etc: *Despite the problems, the wedding came off very well.* **b)** to do something successfully, badly etc: *The vice-president came off badly in the TV debate.* **3 come off it!** *spoken* **a)** used to tell someone that you think they are lying, or saying something stupid: *"I can't stand Claire." "Come off it, Joe, you asked her out last week!"* **b)** used to tell someone to stop doing or saying something annoying: *Come off it, Dave, that's enough now!* **4** [I] to have the intended effect; succeed: *Irene tried, but her joke didn't quite come off.*
**5 come off heroin/tranquillizers etc** to stop taking a drug that is ADDICTIVE (=makes you want to keep taking it)

**come on** *phr v*
**1 ► START ◄** [I] **a)** if a light or machine comes on, it starts working: *A dog started barking and lights came on in the house.* **b)** if a slight illness comes on, you start to have it: *I can feel a headache coming on.* **c)** if a television or radio programme comes on, it starts: *What time does the movie come on?* **d) it comes on to do sth** *BrE spoken* it starts to do something: *It came on to rain.*
**2 come on!** *spoken* **a)** used to tell someone to hurry up: *Come on, we'll be late!* **b)** also **come along!** *BrE* used to encourage someone to try harder: *Come on, guys, you can do it!* **c)** used to encourage someone to be more cheerful: *Come on, let's see a smile.* **d)** used to show someone that you know that what they have just said was not true or right: *Oh come on, don't lie to me!*
**e)** used to make someone angry enough to want to fight you, or to do something they would not normally do: *Come on, then, hit me! I dare you!*
**3 be coming on** to be improving or making progress, especially in education or health: [+ **with**] *How are you coming on with your training?*
**4 ► DISCOVER ◄** [T **come on** sb/sth] to find or discover someone or something by chance: *Turning the corner, I came on a group of picnickers.*
**5 come on strong** *informal* to make it very clear to someone that you think they are sexually attractive

**come on to** sb/sth *phr v* [T] **1** *spoken* to move forward in a speech or discussion to a new subject: *I'll come on to this question in a few moments.* **2** *informal* if someone comes on to another person, they make it very clear that they are sexually interested in them

**come out** *phr v* [I]
**1 ► BECOME KNOWN ◄** to become publicly known, especially after being hidden: *It was several weeks before the truth of the matter came out.*
**2 ► BECOME CLEAR ◄** if a fact comes out when you consider something, it becomes much easier to see than it was before: *The family resemblances come out strongly in the wedding photos.*
**3 ► BECOME AVAILABLE ◄** if a book, record etc comes out, it becomes publicly available: *A second edition will come out next year.*
**4 ► BE SAID ◄** if something you say comes out in a particular way, that is how it sounds or how it is understood: *The words came out in little more than a whisper.* | **come out all wrong** (=not sound the way you had intended)
**5 ► FINISH IN A PARTICULAR WAY ◄ come out well/badly/ahead etc** to finish an action, process etc in a particular way or with a particular result: *If you spend a little more time on your work now, you'll come out ahead in the end.* | *I can never get cakes to come out right.*
**6 ► SAY PUBLICLY ◄** [always + adv/prep] to say publicly that you strongly support or oppose a particular plan, belief etc: [+ **for/against etc**] *The board of directors has come out strongly in favour of a merger.* | **come out and say/state etc sth** *No one will come out and say it, but basically they can't stand her.*
**7 ► DISAPPEAR ◄** if colour or a mark comes out, it disappears, especially because it has been washed: *Ink stains will usually come out if you use a little methanol.*
**8 ► SUN ◄** if the sun, moon, or stars come out, they appear in the sky
**9 ► FLOWER ◄** if a flower comes out, it opens: *I love it when the snowdrops start to come out.*
**10 ► PHOTOGRAPH ◄** if a photograph or a subject of a photograph comes out, it looks the way the photographer wanted it to: *Some of the wedding photos didn't come out.* | *That sunset really came out well, didn't it?*
**11 ► HOMOSEXUAL ◄** [+ **to**] if someone comes out, they say openly that they are HOMOSEXUAL
**12 ► WORKER ◄** *BrE* to refuse to work; STRIKE[2] (1): *The teachers are coming out in support of their pay claim.*
**13 ► GIRL ◄** *old-fashioned* if a young woman comes out, she is formally introduced into UPPER-CLASS society, usually at a dance

**come out in** sth *phr v* [T not in passive] *BrE* **come out in spots/a rash etc** to become partly covered by marks because you are ill or sensitive to particular foods or drugs: *If I eat eggs, I come out in a rash.*

**come out with** sth *phr v* [T not in passive] *informal* to say something, especially suddenly or in a way that is not expected: *Tanya came out with a really stupid remark.*

**come over** *phr v* **1** [I] **a)** to visit someone's house or the place where they are: *Can I come over and see you on Friday night?* **b)** to make a journey, from another country and travelling east or west, to a place where you are now: [+ **to/from**] *When did your family first come over to America?* **2** [T **come over sb** not in passive] **come over** if a strong feeling comes over someone, they suddenly experience it: *A wave of sleepiness came over me.* | **not know what has come over sb** (=be unable to explain someone's strange behaviour) *I'm sorry I was so rude – I don't know what came* *over me!* **3** [I] **a)** if an idea comes over to someone, they understand it clearly **b)** if someone comes over in a particular way, they give other people that feeling or opinion about them: [+ **as**] *I don't think I came over as a confident manager at the interview.* **4 come over (all) shy/nervous etc** *informal especially BrE* to become shy, nervous etc

**come round** *BrE phr v* [I] **1** to visit someone at home or at the place where they are: *Why don't you come round for lunch?* **2** to change your opinion so that you now agree with someone: [+ **to**] *I'm sure Bradley will come round to our way of thinking.* **3** if a regular event comes round, it arrives or happens as usual: *Your birthday's coming round again, isn't it?* **4** to become conscious again: *Kim was muttering, and seemed to be coming round.*

**come through** *phr v* **1 a)** [I] if a piece of news, a result etc comes through, it becomes known or heard: *Listen! There's something coming through on the radio now.* | *We're still waiting for our exam results to come through.* **b)** if an official document comes through, it arrives: *Has your giro come through yet?* **2** [T **come through** sth] to continue to live, exist, be strong, or succeed after a difficult or dangerous time: *We're so relieved that Bill came through the operation all right.* | *Amazingly, our house came through the storm without much damage.*

**come through with** sth *phr v* [T] to give people something important, especially when they have been worried that you would not produce it in time: *Our representative in Hong Kong finally came through with the figures.*

**come to** *phr v*

**1 ▶ REACH A STATE ◀** [T **come to** sth] **a) it has come to this** *spoken* used to express shock that a situation has become so bad: *"I want back all the jewellery I gave you." "So, it's come to this, has it, our wonderful marriage?"* **b)** to reach a particular state or position, especially a bad one: *All those years, and in the end it came to nothing.* | *If it comes to a fight, you can depend on me!* **c) what's it all coming to?/what's the world coming to?** *spoken* used to show how shocked or disappointed something has made you feel

**2 come to £20/$30 etc** to be a total amount of £20, $30 etc: *That comes to £23.50, madam.*

**3** [T not in passive] if a thought or idea comes to you, you realize or remember it, especially suddenly: *The solution came to him in a flash.* | *I've forgotten her name, but maybe it'll come to me later.*

**4** [I] to become conscious again: *When Jack came to, he was lying in an alley and his wallet was gone.*

**5 when it comes to** *informal* **a)** on the subject of: *I can use a computer, but when it comes to repairing them, I know nothing.* **b)** when you are dealing with something: *When it comes to relationships, everyone makes mistakes.*

**6 have sth coming (to you)** *informal* to deserve to be punished or to have something bad happen to you: *"Ron's been expelled from school." "Well, he had it coming."* | *I hope you get what's coming to you, you sod!*

**7 come to yourself** *old-fashioned informal* to gain control of your emotions again

**come under** sth *phr v* [T not in passive] **1** to be governed, controlled, or influenced by something: *Your case comes under the jurisdiction of the county courts.* | *All doctors come under the same rules of professional conduct.* **2 come under attack/fire/scrutiny** to be attacked, shot at etc: *Some members in the party have come under attack from radicals in recent weeks.* **3** if a piece of information comes under a particular title, subject etc, it can be found there in a book, library etc: *'Phobias' – that will come under Psychology in section twelve.* —see also **come under the hammer** (HAMMER[1] (2))

**come up** *phr v* [I]

**1 ▶ APPEAR OR HAPPEN ◀ a)** to be mentioned or suggested as something to be considered or given attention: *A lot of new questions came up at the meeting.* | *Your name came up in our conversation once or twice.* **b) be coming up** if an important event is coming up, it is being arranged and will happen soon: *Don't you have a birthday coming up soon?* **c)** if a legal case comes up, it is dealt with in a court of law: *Your case comes up next week.* **d)** if a job or position comes up, it becomes available: *A vacancy has come up in the accounts department.*

**2 ▶ TRAVEL NORTH ◀** to travel north or towards an important place such as a big city: [+ **to**] *Why don't you come up to New York for the weekend?*

**3 ▶ MOVE NEAR ◀** to move near someone or something, especially by walking: [+ **to/behind etc**] *Come up to the front of the room so everyone can see you.* | *Aagh! Don't come up behind me like that!*

**4 ▶ SUN/MOON ◀ a)** when the sun or moon comes up, it rises: *The sun was coming up by the time I finished the essay.* **b)** when a plant comes up, it begins to be seen above the ground: *Look, the daffodils are coming up.* **c)** when food comes up, it rises back from your stomach after being swallowed: *I suddenly felt nauseous and then the whole lot came up.*

**5 ▶ PROBLEM ◀** if a problem or difficulty comes up, it suddenly appears or starts to affect you: **sth comes up** *Sorry I can't go with you—something has suddenly come up.*

**6 coming (right) up!** *spoken* used to say that something, especially food or drink, will be ready very soon: *"Two martinis, please." "Coming up!"*

**7 come up in the world** to become richer or more successful in society: *She had come up in the world since her days on the flower stall.*

**8 ▶ BEGIN AT UNIVERSITY ◀** *BrE* to begin studying at a university, especially Oxford or Cambridge

**come up against** sth/sb *phr v* [T not in passive] to have to deal with opposition, problems, unfairness etc; ENCOUNTER[1] (1): *You've got no idea of what you're going to come up against.*

**come up for** sth *phr v* **1** [T] **come up for review/re-examination etc** to have a fixed time in the future when something will be examined, changed etc: *The new regulations come up for review in April.* **2 come up for re-election/selection** to reach the time when people have to vote about whether you should continue in your political position

**come upon** sth/sb *phr v* [T not in passive] *literary* to find or discover something or someone by chance: *Suddenly I came upon a clearing in the wood.*

**come up to** sth *phr v* [T] to be as good as something else or as an expected standard: *This doesn't come up to the standard of your usual work.* —see also **not come/be up to scratch** (SCRATCH[2] (3))

**come up with** sth *phr v* [T] **1** to think of an idea, plan, reply etc: *Is that the best excuse you can come up with?* | *Someone had better come up with a solution fast.* **2** to produce a sum of money that is needed: *How am I supposed to come up with $10,000?*

**come²** *n* [U] *slang* a man's SEMEN (=the liquid he produces during sex)

**come·back** /ˈkʌmbæk/ *n* [C usually singular] **1 make/stage a comeback** if a person, activity, style etc makes a comeback, they become popular again after being unpopular for a long time: *The miniskirt made a comeback in the late 1980s.* **2** a quick reply that is often clever, funny, and insulting; RETORT[2] (1): *I couldn't think of a good comeback.* —see also **come back** (COME[1]) **3** a way of getting payment or a reward for something wrong or unfair that has been done to you: *Check your contract carefully, or you may have no comeback if something goes wrong.*

**co·me·di·an** /kəˈmiːdiən/ *n* [C] **1** someone whose job is to tell jokes and make people laugh **2** *old use* someone who plays funny characters in plays or films

**co·me·di·enne** /kəˌmiːdiˈen/ *n* [C] *old-fashioned* a female comedian

**come·down** /ˈkʌmdaʊn/ *n* [C usually singular] *informal* a situation that is not as good, important, interesting etc as the situation you had previously: *The 'King of Wall Street' is bankrupt! What a comedown!* —see also **come down** (COME¹)

**com·e·dy** /ˈkɒmɪ̆di‖ˈkɑː-/ *n* **1** [C,U] a play, film etc that is intended to entertain people and make them laugh: *a comedy starring Eddie Murphy | Come to Comedy Night at the Albion!* **2** [U] the quality in something such as a book or play that makes people laugh; HUMOUR¹ (1): *Can't you see the comedy of the situation?* —see also BLACK COMEDY, SITUATION COMEDY

**comedy of man·ners** /ˌ··· · ˈ··/ *n* [C] a comedy that makes the behaviour of a particular group, especially the UPPER CLASS, seem silly

**come-hith·er** /ˌ· ˈ··/ *adj old-fashioned* **come-hither look/eyes** a way of looking at someone that shows you think they are sexually attractive

**come·ly** /ˈkʌmli/ *adj literary* a comely woman has an attractive appearance —**comeliness** *n* [U]

**come-on** /ˈ· ·/ *n* [C] **1** *informal* something that a business offers cheaply or free in order to persuade you to buy something: *The competition for a free trip is just a come-on.* **2 give sb the come-on** *BrE spoken* to behave in a way that shows someone very clearly that you are sexually interested in them —see also **come on** (COME¹)

**com·er** /ˈkʌmə‖-ər/ *n* **all comers** *informal* anyone who is interested, especially anyone who wants to take part in a competition: *The contest is open to all comers.* —see also LATECOMER, NEWCOMER

**co·mes·ti·bles** /kəˈmestɪ̆bəlz/ *n* [plural] *formal* food

**com·et** /ˈkɒmɪ̆t‖ˈkɑː-/ *n* [C] an object in space like a bright ball with a long tail that moves around the sun: *Halley's comet*

**come·up·pance** /kʌmˈʌpəns/ *n* [singular] *informal* a punishment or something bad that happens to you which you really deserve: **get your comeuppance** *You'll get your comeuppance one day, you'll see!*

W3 **com·fort¹** /ˈkʌmfət‖-ərt/ *n*

**1 ▶ EMOTIONAL ◀** [U] a feeling of being more calm, cheerful, or hopeful after you have been worried or unhappy: *I looked to my family for comfort when things got difficult at work.* | **bring/give comfort** *The service is there to give the advice and comfort people need.* | **take/draw/derive comfort from** *Mrs. Oliphant drew great comfort from the familiar hymns.* | **it's no/some/any comfort** *If it's any comfort, we didn't win anything either.*

**2 ▶ PHYSICAL ◀** [U] a feeling of being physically relaxed and satisfied, so that nothing is hurting you, making you feel too hot or cold etc: **for comfort** *I usually dress for comfort rather than style.* | **too cold/hot/high etc for comfort** (=physically unpleasant for a particular reason) | **in comfort/in the comfort of** *Now you can watch your favorite movies in the comfort of your own home.* | **built/made/designed for comfort** *a new climbing boot designed for comfort and safety*

**3 ▶ MONEY/POSSESSIONS ◀** [U] a way of living in which you have all the possessions, money etc that you need or want: *I intend to retire in comfort!*

**4 comforts** [plural] the things that make your life more pleasant and comfortable, especially things that are not necessary: **all the comforts of home** *The beach cabin has all the comforts of home.* | **material comforts** (=money and possessions) | **creature comforts** (=things such as comfortable chairs and warm rooms) *Alicia was too fond of her creature comforts to go camping.*

**5 ▶ SB/STH THAT HELPS ◀** [C] someone or something that helps you feel happier or calmer when you have been worried or unhappy: **be a comfort to** *Jerry's been a real comfort to me since Max died.* | **comfort eating/shopping etc** (=eating etc that makes you feel better) | **it's a comfort** *It's a comfort to know there's someone to keep an eye on the kids.*

**6 too close/near etc for comfort** something that is too close for comfort makes you feel worried, unhappy, or uncomfortable, because it is dangerous in some way: *The cars were whizzing past us much too close for comfort.*

**7 cold/small comfort** a small piece of good news that does not make you feel better about a bad situation: *The promise that I might one day be rehoused was cold comfort.* —**comfortless** *adj*

**comfort²** *v* [T] to make someone feel calmer and more hopeful by being kind and sympathetic to them when they are worried or unhappy: *Nothing I could do or say could comfort Diane when her son died.* —**comforting** *adj* —**comfortingly** *adv*

**com·for·ta·ble** /ˈkʌmftəbəl, ˈkʌmfət-‖ˈkʌmfərt-, ˈkʌmft-/ *adj* S W

**1 ▶ FEELING PHYSICALLY COMFORTABLE ◀** feeling physically relaxed and satisfied, without feeling any pain or being too hot, cold etc: *I was so comfortable and warm in bed I didn't want to get up.* | **make yourself comfortable** *Sit down and make yourself comfortable while I put the kettle on.*

**2 ▶ CLOTHES / FURNITURE / PLACES ETC ◀** making you feel physically relaxed and satisfied: *Joyce has a comfortable apartment in Portland.* | *comfortable shoes* | **comfortable to sit/lie/stand on etc** *Is your chair comfortable to sit on?*

**3 ▶ NOT WORRIED ◀** if you are comfortable with an idea, person, or activity, you do not feel worried about it: *I'm not comfortable with the idea of you having a motorcycle.* | **feel comfortable** *an office environment you can feel comfortable in*

**4 ▶ MONEY ◀** having enough money to live on without worrying about paying for things: *The Austins aren't rich, but they're comfortable.*

**5 ▶ ILL/INJURED ◀** if someone who is ill or injured is comfortable, they are not in too much pain

**6 ▶ RACE/COMPETITION ◀** a number of points or a distance that will allow you to win easily: *Cantona scored to give United a comfortable 3-0 lead at half-time.*

**7 ▶ BELIEF/IDEA/OPINION ◀** a belief etc that you do not think very seriously about and that ignores problems or difficulties: *the comfortable middle class belief that everyone who works hard will succeed* —**comfortably** *adv* —see also UNCOMFORTABLE

**com·fort·er** /ˈkʌmfətə‖-fərtər/ *n* [C] **1** someone who comforts you **2** *AmE* a cover for a bed that is filled with a soft warm material such as feathers; DUVET *BrE* **3** *old use* a warm SCARF

**com·fy** /ˈkʌmfi/ *adj spoken* comfortable: *a comfy chair*

**com·ic¹** /ˈkɒmɪk‖ˈkɑː-/ *adj* amusing you and making you want to laugh: *a comic performance* | **comic writer/actress/performer etc** (=someone who writes or performs things that make you laugh) | **comic relief** (=a situation in a serious story that makes you relax a little because it is funny) | **comic verse/song etc** (=a song etc that entertains you and makes you laugh) —opposite TRAGIC (2)

**comic²** also **comic book** /ˈ··· ·/ *AmE n* [C] **1** a magazine for children that tells a story using comic strips **2** someone whose job is to tell jokes and make people laugh; COMEDIAN: *a stand-up comic*

**com·i·cal** /ˈkɒmɪkəl‖ˈkɑː-/ *adj* behaviour or situations that are comical are funny in a strange or unexpected way: *The cat looked so comical with the bow on its head!* —**comically** /-kli/ *adv*

**comic op·e·ra** /ˌ·· ˈ···/ *n* [C,U] an OPERA with an amusing story in which the singers speak as well as sing

**comic strip** /ˈ·· ·/ *n* [C] a series of drawn pictures inside boxes that tell a story —compare CARTOON (1)

**com·ing¹** /ˈkʌmɪŋ/ *n* **1 the coming of sth/sb** the time when something new begins, especially something that will cause a lot of changes: *With the coming of railways, new markets opened up.* **2 comings and goings**

*informal* the movements of people as they arrive at and leave places: *Mrs Williams next door knows all the comings and goings of everyone in the neighbourhood.*

**coming²** *adj* [not before noun] *formal* happening soon: *the clouds of the coming storm* —see also UP-AND-COMING

**coming of age** /ˌ·· · ˈ·/ *n* [singular] the point in a young person's life, usually the age of 18 or 21, at which their society considers them to be an adult

**com·ma** /ˈkɒmə‖ˈkɑːmə/ *n* [C] the mark (,) used in writing and printing to show a short pause —see also INVERTED COMMA —see picture at PUNCTUATION MARK

**W2** **command¹** /kəˈmɑːnd‖kəˈmænd/ *n*
**1 ▶ ORDER ◀** [C] an order that should be obeyed: *Fire when I give the command.*
**2 ▶ CONTROL ◀** [U] the control of a group of people or a situation: **be in command** *Judge Hathaway was in complete command of the courtroom.* | **have sth under your command** *We suspect that Don Sacco has several gangs under his command.* | **take command** (=begin controlling and making decisions) *Janet took command of the situation and got everyone out of the building safely.* | **at sb's command** (=available to be used by someone whenever they want) *Each congressman has a large staff at his command.* | **have command** *Flynn had command of a squadron on the Western Front.*
**3 ▶ MILITARY ◀** [C also + plural verb *BrE*] **a)** a part of an army, navy etc that is controlled separately and has a particular job: *pilots of the Southern Air Command* **b)** a group of officers or officials who give orders: *Are you criticizing the High Command?* **c)** the group of soldiers that an officer is in control of
**4 have (a) command of** to have a good knowledge of something, especially a subject such as a language: *Jill has an impressive command of French.*
**5 ▶ COMPUTER ◀** [C] an instruction to a computer to do something
**6 at your command** if you have a particular skill at your command, you are able to use that skill well and easily: *a carpenter with years of experience at his command*
**7 be in command of yourself/your faculties** to be able to control your emotions and thoughts: *Kathleen walked in, tall, slim, confident and in total command of herself.*

**com·mand²** *v*
**1 ▶ ORDER ◀** [I,T] to tell someone officially to do something, especially if you are a military leader, a king etc: **command sb to do sth** *Captain Picard commanded the crew to report to the main deck.* | **command that** *The General commanded that the regiment attack at once.*
**2 ▶ LEAD THE MILITARY ◀** [I,T] to be responsible for giving orders to a group of people in the army, navy etc: *He commands the 4th Battalion of the Scots Guard.*
**3 ▶ DESERVE AND GET ◀** to get something such as attention or respect because you are important or popular: *Dr. Young commands a great deal of respect as a surgeon.* | *"Supermodels" can command extremely high fees.*
**4** [T] **▶ CONTROL ◀** to control something: *The party which commands a majority of seats in Parliament forms the government.*
**5 ▶ VIEW ◀** if a place commands a view, you can see something clearly from it: *The Ramses Hilton commands a magnificent view of Cairo.*

**com·man·dant** /ˌkɒmənˈdænt‖ˈkɑːməndænt/ *n* [C] the chief officer in charge of a military organization: *the commandant of a prison camp*

**com·man·deer** /ˌkɒmənˈdɪə‖ˌkɑːmənˈdɪr/ *v* [T] to take someone else's property for your own use, especially during the war: *The local hotel was commandeered for the wounded.*

**com·mand·er** /kəˈmɑːndə‖kəˈmændər/ *n* [C] **1** an officer of any rank who is in charge of a group of soldiers or a particular military activity: *the American Commander, General Otis* | *our platoon commander* **2** a high rank in the navy, or someone who holds this rank —see table on page B4 **3** a British police officer of high rank —see also WING COMMANDER

**commander in chief** /ˌ·,·· · ˈ·/ *n* [C usually singular] someone of high rank who is in control of all the military organizations in a country or of a specific military activity: *The Queen is Commander in Chief of the British armed forces.*

**com·mand·ing** /kəˈmɑːndɪŋ‖kəˈmæn-/ *adj* **1** having the authority or position that allows you to give orders: *a commanding officer* | *Japan's commanding economic position* **2** making people respect and obey you: *Papa's commanding presence* **3** a commanding view or position is one from which you can clearly see a long way **4** being in a position from which you are likely to win a race or competition easily: *a commanding lead*

**com·mand·ment** /kəˈmɑːndmənt‖kəˈmænd-/ *n* [C] **1** one of the ten rules given by God in the Bible that tell people how they must behave **2** *literary* a command

**command mod·ule** /·ˈ· ˌ··/ *n* [C] *technical* the part of a space vehicle from which its activities are controlled

**com·man·do** /kəˈmɑːndəʊ‖kəˈmændoʊ/ *n plural* **commandos** or **commandoes** [C] **1** a soldier or a small group of soldiers who are specially trained to make quick attacks into enemy areas: *a commando raid* **2 the commandoes** a UNIT (1) of the British Royal Marines

**command per·form·ance** /·ˌ· ·ˈ··/ *n* [C usually singular] a special performance at a theatre that is given at the request of a king, president etc

**command post** /·ˈ· ·/ *n* [C] the place from which military leaders and their officers control activities

**com·mem·o·rate** /kəˈmeməreɪt/ *v* [T] to do something to show that you remember and respect someone important or an important event in the past: *a parade to commemorate the town's bicentenary* —**commemorative** /kəˈmemərətɪv/ *adj* | *a commemorative plaque*

**com·mem·o·ra·tion** /kəˌmeməˈreɪʃən/ *n* [U] something that makes you remember and respect someone important or an important event in the past: **in commemoration of** *a service in commemoration of those who died in the war*

**com·mence** /kəˈmens/ *v* [I,T] *formal* to begin or to start something: **[+ with]** *A trial commences with opening statements.* | **commence sth** *Your first evaluation will be six months after you commence employment.* | **commence doing sth** *You may commence reading, Jeremy.*

Frequencies of **commence**, **start** and **begin** in spoken and written English.

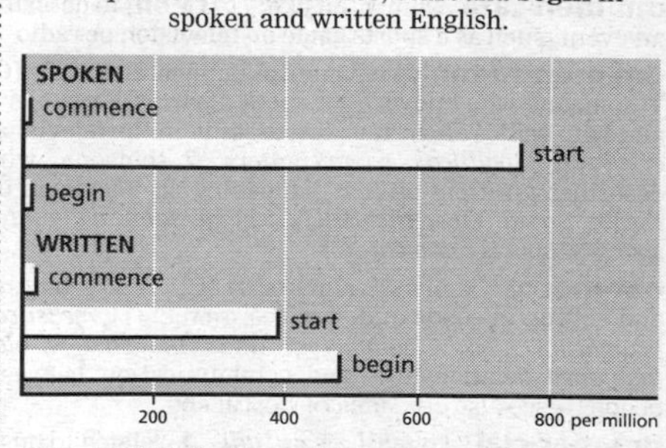


Based on the British National Corpus and the Longman Lancaster Corpus

This graph shows that in spoken English **start** is the most common of the three verbs. In written English **begin** is the most common. **Commence**, a formal word, is the least common of the three verbs in spoken and written English.

**com·mence·ment** /kəˈmensmənt/ *n formal* **1** [C,U] beginning: **[+ of]** *the commencement of the proceedings* **2** [C] *AmE* a ceremony at which university, college, or high school students receive their DIPLOMAS; GRADUATION

**com·mend** /kəˈmend/ *v* [T] *formal* **1** to praise or approve of someone or something, especially publicly:

**commend sb for sth** *A Chester man was commended for his public-spirited action.* | **highly commended** *Bartholomew's work has been highly commended.* **2** to tell someone that something is good or deserves attention; RECOMMEND: *I commend this bill to the House.* | **not have much to commend it** (=not be satisfactory) *The hotel doesn't have much to commend it.* **3** *old use* to give someone to someone else to take care of

**com·men·da·ble** /kəˈmendəbəl/ *adj formal* deserving praise: *a highly commendable effort* | *Baldwin answered with commendable frankness.* —**commendably** *adv*

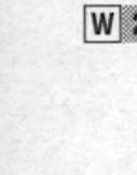

**com·men·da·tion** /ˌkɒmənˈdeɪʃən‖ˌkɑː-/ *n formal* [C,U] an official statement praising someone, especially someone who has been brave or very successful

**com·men·su·rate** /kəˈmenʃərɪ̈t/ *adj formal* matching something in size, quality, or length of time: [+ **with**] *a salary commensurate with your experience*

S1 W2 **com·ment¹** /ˈkɒment‖ˈkɑː-/ *n* **1** [C,U] an opinion that you express about someone or something: *Does anyone have any questions or comments?* | **make a comment (on/about)** *The police chief made no comment about the bomb attack.* | **be fair comment** *BrE spoken* (=be criticism that is reasonable or deserved) **2** [U] criticism or discussion of something someone has said or done: *The Prime Minister's speech received much comment in the press.* | **no comment** *spoken* (=used by people in public life when they do not want to answer questions about a subject) **3 be a comment on** to be a sign of the bad quality of something: *The number of adults who cannot read is a comment on the quality of our schools.*

S2 W3 **comment²** *v* [I,T] to express an opinion about someone or something: [+ **on**] *People were always commenting on my sister's looks.* | **comment that** *Some critics have commented that the film is unnecessarily violent.*

**com·men·ta·ry** /ˈkɒməntəri‖ˈkɑːmənteri/ *n* **1** [C] a spoken description of an event, given while the event is happening, especially on the television or radio: *Stop shouting! I can't hear the baseball commentary.* | [+ **on**] *Do they have a commentary on the parade?* | **running commentary** (=a continuous description of something) **2** [C,U] something such as a book or article that explains or discusses a book, poem, idea etc: *political commentary* **3 be a sad commentary on** to be a sign of how bad a particular situation is: *The whole incident was a sad commentary on the state of British football.*

**com·men·tate** /ˈkɒmənteɪt‖ˈkɑː-/ *v* [I + **on**] to describe an event, such as a sports game on television or radio

**com·men·ta·tor** /ˈkɒmənteɪtə‖ˈkɑːmənteɪtər-/ *n* [C] **1** someone who knows a lot about a particular subject, and who writes about it or discusses it on the television or radio: *political commentators* **2** someone who describes an event as it is happening on television or radio: *David Vine, the BBC's commentator on winter sports* | *a sports commentator*

**com·merce** /ˈkɒmɜːs‖ˈkɑːmɜːrs/ *n* [U] **1** the buying and selling of goods and services; TRADE¹ (1): *measures promoting local commerce and industry* **2** *old-fashioned* relationships and communication between people —see also CHAMBER OF COMMERCE

S2 W2 **com·mer·cial¹** /kəˈmɜːʃəl‖-ɜːr-/ *adj* **1** related to business and the buying and selling of goods and services: *Our top priorities must be profit and commercial growth.* **2** related to the ability of a product or business to make a profit: *Gibbons failed to see the commercial value of his discovery* | **a commercial success/failure** | *The film was a huge commercial success.* **3** [only before noun] a commercial product is one that is produced in large quantities and sold to the public rather than only to other businesses: *All commercial milk is pasteurized.* **4** commercial business or activity produces goods and services in large quantities: *a large commercial fish farm* **5** more concerned with money than with quality: *I used to like their music but they've become very commercial.* **6 commercial radio/TV/channel etc** radio or television broadcasts that are produced by companies that earn money through advertising

**commercial²** *n* **1** [C] an advertisement on television or radio: *a soap powder commercial* **2 commercial break** the time when advertisements are shown during a television or radio programme S

**commercial bank** /·ˌ·· ˈ·/ *n* [C] *technical* the kind of bank that provides services for customers and businesses and that is used by most ordinary people

**com·mer·cial·is·m** /kəˈmɜːʃəlɪzəm‖-ɜːr-/ *n* [U] the principle or practice of being more concerned with making money from buying and selling goods than you are about their quality: *the commercialism of modern culture*

**com·mer·cial·ize** /kəˈmɜːʃəlaɪz‖-ɜːr-/ also **-ise** *BrE v* [T] **1** [usually passive] to be more concerned with making money from something than about its quality: *Christmas has become so commercialized nowadays.* **2** to sell something to the public in order to make a profit, especially something that would not usually be sold: *commercializing space launches to help pay for more space research* —**commercialization** /kəˌmɜːʃəlaɪˈzeɪʃən‖-ˌmɜːrʃələ-/ *n* [U]

**com·mer·cial·ly** /kəˈmɜːʃəli‖-ɜːr-/ *adv* **1** considering whether a business or product is making a profit [sentence adverb] *Commercially, the movie was a flop.* | **commercially viable** *The project is no longer commercially viable.* **2** produced or used in large quantities as a business: *commercially farmed land* **3** if a new product is commercially available, you can buy it in shops

**commercial trav·el·ler** /·ˌ·· ˈ···/ *n* [C] *BrE old-fashioned* someone who travels from place to place selling goods for a company

**com·mie** /ˈkɒmi‖ˈkɑː-/ *n* [C] *especially AmE* an insulting word for a COMMUNIST

**com·mis·e·rate** /kəˈmɪzəreɪt/ *v* [I + **with**] *formal* to express your sympathy for someone who is unhappy about something

**com·mis·e·ra·tion** /kəˌmɪzəˈreɪʃən/ *n formal* **1** [U] a feeling of sympathy for someone when something unpleasant has happened to them **2 commiserations** [plural] used to express sympathy to someone, especially someone who has lost a competition: *Our commiserations to the losing team.*

**com·mis·sar·i·at** /ˌkɒmɪ̈ˈseəriət‖ˌkɑːmɪ̈ˈser-/ *n* [C] a military department that is responsible for supplying food

**com·mis·sa·ry** /ˈkɒmɪ̈səri‖ˈkɑːmɪ̈seri/ *n* [C] **1** *BrE* an officer in the army who is in charge of food supplies **2** *AmE* a shop that supplies food and other goods in a military camp **3** *AmE* a place where you can eat in a large organization such as a film STUDIO (2), factory etc

**com·mis·sion¹** /kəˈmɪʃən/ *n*
**1 ▶ PEOPLE ◀** [C] a group of people who have been given the official job of finding out about something or controlling something: *The Government has set up a commission to suggest improvements to the education system.*
**2 ▶ MONEY ◀** [C,U] an amount of money that is paid to someone according to the value of the goods they have sold: *The dealer takes a 20% commission on the sales he makes.* | **be on commission** (=be paid according to what you sell)
**3 ▶ JOB ◀** [C] **a)** a request for an artist or musician to make a piece of art or music, for which they are paid: *a commission from the Academy for a new sculpture* **b)** *formal* a duty or job that you ask someone to do
**4 out of commission a)** not working or not able to be used at the present time: *One of the ship's anchors was out of commission.* **b)** *informal* ill or injured
**5 ▶ ARMY/NAVY ETC ◀** [C] an officer's position in the army, navy etc and the authority that is given to them
**6 ▶ CRIME ◀** [U] *formal* the commission of a crime is the act of doing it
**7 in commission** if a military ship is in commission, it is still being used by the navy

**commission²** *v* [T] **1** to formally ask someone to

write an official report, produce a work of art for you etc: *We'll be commissioning a report on teenage alcoholism.* | **commission sb to do sth** *I've been commissioned to write a new play!* **2 be commissioned** be given an officer's rank in the army, navy etc

**com·mis·sion·aire** /kəˌmɪʃəˈneə‖-ˈner/ *n* [C] *BrE* someone whose job is to stand at the entrance to a hotel, theatre, or cinema and help people; DOORMAN *AmE*

**commissioned of·fic·er** /ˌ·ˌ·· ˈ···/ *n* [C] a military officer who has a commission

**com·mis·sion·er** /kəˈmɪʃənə‖-ər/ *n* [C] **1** someone who is officially in charge of a government department in some countries: *Commissioner Addo is responsible for Education.* **2** the head of the police department in some parts of the US **3** a member of a COMMISSION[1] (1) **4 commissioner for oaths** *BrE* a lawyer who may legally be a WITNESS to particular legal documents

2 **com·mit** /kəˈmɪt/ *v* **committed, committing** [T]
2 **1 ▶ CRIME ◀** to do something wrong or illegal: **commit a crime** *Women commit fewer crimes than men.* | **commit murder/rape/adultery etc** *Brady committed a series of brutal murders.* | **commit suicide** (=kill yourself deliberately)

**2 ▶ SAY THAT SB WILL DO STH ◀** to say that someone will definitely do something or must do something: **commit sb to sth** *My agent has already committed me to an appearance.* | **commit sb to doing sth** *The contract commits him to playing for the team for the next three years.*

**3 commit yourself** to say that you will definitely do something: *You don't have to commit yourself at this stage.* | *We can't commit ourselves to any concrete proposals.* | **commit yourself to doing sth** *Sorry, I've already committed myself to working for Clive.* | **not commit yourself** (=refuse to say whether you will do something) *Roxburgh decided that it would be wiser not to commit himself.*

**4 ▶ MONEY/TIME ◀** to decide to use money, time, people etc for a particular purpose: **commit sth to sth** *A large amount of money has been committed to this project.*

**5 ▶ PRISON/HOSPITAL ◀** to order someone to be put in a hospital or prison: *You're crazy! You ought to be committed!*

**6 commit sth to memory** to learn something so that you remember it

**7 commit sth to paper** to write something down

2 **com·mit·ment** /kəˈmɪtmənt/ *n* **1** [C] a promise to do
2 something or to behave in a particular way: *Jim's afraid of emotional commitments.* | [+ **to**] *a commitment to equal pay and opportunities* **2** [U] the hard work and loyalty that someone gives to an organization, activity etc: *I was impressed by the energy and commitment shown by the players.* | [+ **to**] *Her commitment to work is beyond question.* **3** [C] something that you have previously arranged to do at a certain time and that prevents you from doing anything else at that time: *She's got several teaching commitments over the summer.* **4** [C] an amount of money that you have to pay regularly and that prevents you from spending your money on other things: *a heavy mortgage commitment* **5** [U] *especially AmE* the use of money, time, people etc for a particular purpose: *The plan involves commitment of money and staff time.*

**com·mit·tal** /kəˈmɪtl/ *n* [C,U] **1** the process in which a court sends someone to a mental hospital or prison **2** *formal* the burying or cremating (CREMATE) of a dead person

**com·mit·ted** /kəˈmɪtɨd/ *adj* willing to work very hard at something: *a committed group of environmentalists*

3 **com·mit·tee** /kəˈmɪti/ *n* **1** [C] a group of people cho-
1 sen to represent a larger group in order to do a particular job, make decisions etc: *He's on the finance committee.* | [also + plural verb *BrE*] *The committee have decided to raise membership fees for next year.* **2 welcoming committee** a group of people often sent by a large organization to welcome an important visitor

**com·mode** /kəˈməʊd‖-ˈmoʊd/ *n* [C] **1** *BrE* a piece of furniture shaped like a chair that can be used as a TOILET **2** *AmE dialect* a TOILET **3** *old use* a piece of furniture with drawers or shelves

**com·mo·di·ous** /kəˈməʊdiəs‖-ˈmoʊ-/ *adj formal* a house or room that is commodious is very big —**commodiously** *adv*

**com·mod·i·ty** /kəˈmɒdɨti‖kəˈmɑː-/ *n* [C] **1** a product that can be sold to make a profit: *agricultural commodities* **2** *formal* a useful quality: *Time is a precious commodity.*

**com·mo·dore** /ˈkɒmədɔː‖ˈkɑːmədɔːr/ *n* [C] **1** a high rank in the navy, or someone who has this rank —see table on page B4 **2** the CAPTAIN in charge of a group of ships that are carrying goods

**com·mon**[1] /ˈkɒmən‖ˈkɑː-/ *adj* S 1
**1 ▶ A LOT/LARGE AMOUNT ◀** existing in large W 1
numbers or happening often and in many places: *Heart disease is one of the commonest causes of death.* | [+ **among**] *Bad dreams are fairly common among children.* | **it is common for sth to happen** *It's very common for new fathers to feel jealous of the baby.* | **common belief/assumption/practice etc** *It's a common but false assumption that all mentally ill people are violent.*

**2 ▶ SAME/SIMILAR ◀** [usually before noun, no comparative] common aims, beliefs, ideas etc are shared by several people or groups: *They had a satisfying sense of working towards a common goal.* | [+ **to**] *a theme that is common to all her novels* | **common ground** (=shared opinions, beliefs etc among people who are usually separate) *The two parties met to establish some common ground.*

**3 ▶ SHARED BY EVERYONE ◀** [usually before noun, no comparative] belonging to or shared by everyone in a society: [+ **to**] *These problems are common to all societies.* | **the common good** (=the advantage of everyone) *Do they seriously think they're acting for the common good?* | **common knowledge** (=something everyone knows) *In a small town everyone's actions are common knowledge.* | **common land** (=owned by the public) | **by common consent** (=agreed by everyone) *Joe was chosen as captain by common consent.*

**4 common courtesy/decency** a polite way of behaving that you expect from people: *It's only common courtesy to write and thank them for the present.*

**5 ▶ ORDINARY ◀** [only before noun, no comparative] ordinary and not special in any way: *The common people will not benefit from these reforms.* | *common salt* | **the common man** (=ordinary people) | **common-or-garden** *BrE slang* (=very common and ordinary)

**6 ▶ PERSON ◀** *especially BrE old-fashioned* an offensive word for someone from a low social class: *Stop that! People will think we're common.* | **as common as muck** *BrE* (=extremely common)

**7 common practice** a usual or accepted way of doing things: *Sending kids away to school was common practice among the upper classes.*

**8 the common touch** the ability of someone in a position of power or authority to talk to and understand ordinary people: *He's made it to the top without losing the common touch.*

**common**[2] *n* **1 have sth in common (with sb)** to have the same interests, attitudes etc as someone else: *To my surprise, I found I had a lot in common with this stranger.* **2 have sth in common (with sth)** if objects or ideas have something in common, they share the same features: *Their methods have a lot in common.* **3 in common with sb/sth** in the same way as someone or something else: *In common with a lot of other countries, we're in an economic recession.* **4** [C] a large area of grass in a village that people walk or play sport on **5** *technical* having the same relationship to two or more quantities: *5 is a common factor of 10 and 20*

**common cold** /ˌ·· ˈ·/ *n* [C] a slight illness in which your throat hurts and it is difficult to breathe normally

**common de·nom·i·na·tor** /ˌ·· ·ˈ····/ *n* [C] **1** an attitude or quality that all the different members of a group have: *The common denominator in these very different* *schemes is that they aim to reduce pollution.* **2** *technical* a number that can be divided exactly by all the DENOMINATORS (=bottom number) in a set of fractions (FRACTION (2)) **3 the lowest common denominator** the least attractive, least intelligent people or features in a situation: *trashy TV programs that appeal to the lowest common denominator*

**com·mon·er** /ˈkɒmənə‖ˈkɑːmənər/ *n* [C] someone who is not a member of a NOBLE[1] (3) family: *Sarah Ferguson was a commoner before she married the Duke Of York.*

**common frac·tion** /ˌ·· ˈ··/ *n* [C] *AmE* a FRACTION[1] (2) that is shown by a number above and a number below a line, such as ½, rather than as a DECIMAL[2]; VULGAR FRACTION *BrE*

**common law[1]** /ˈ·· ·/ *adj* [only before noun] **1 common-law marriage/husband/wife** a relationship that is considered to be a marriage because the man and woman have lived together for a long time **2** according to or related to COMMON LAW[2]: *common law rules*

**common law[2]** /ˌ·· ˈ·/ *n* [U] the law of England that has developed from common customs and the decisions of judges rather than from laws made by Parliament

W3 **com·mon·ly** /ˈkɒmənli‖ˈkɑː-/ *adv* usually or by most people: *commonly agreed principles* | *Sodium chloride is more commonly known as salt.*

**Common Mar·ket** /ˌ·· ˈ··◂/ *n* **the Common Market** *old-fashioned* the EUROPEAN UNION

**common noun** /ˌ·· ˈ·/ *n* [C] *technical* in grammar, a common noun is any noun that is not the name of a particular person, place, or thing: *'Book' and 'sugar' are common nouns.* —compare PROPER NOUN —see also NOUN

**com·mon·place[1]** /ˈkɒmənpleɪs‖ˈkɑː-/ *adj* happening or existing in many places, and therefore not special or unusual: *Car thefts are commonplace in this part of town.*

**commonplace[2]** *n* **1** [C usually singular] something that happens or exists in many places, so that it is not unusual: *One-parent families are now a commonplace in our society.* **2 the commonplace** ordinary or boring: *In my view, his paintings verge on the commonplace.*

**common room** /ˈ·· ·/ *n* [C] *BrE* a room in a school or college that a group of teachers or students use when they are not teaching or studying

**Com·mons** /ˈkɒmənz‖ˈkɑː-/ *n* **the Commons** the larger and more powerful of the two parts of the British parliament, whose members are elected by citizens: *enough votes to force a bill through the Commons* | **in the Commons** (=among the Members of Parliament) —compare **the Lords** (LORD (2))

**common sense** /ˌ·· ˈ·◂/ *n* [U] the ability to behave in a sensible way and make practical decisions: *Use your common sense for once!* —**common-sense** *adj*: *a common-sense approach to the economy*

**com·mon·wealth** /ˈkɒmənwelθ‖ˈkɑː-/ *n* **1 the Commonwealth** an organization of about 50 countries that were once part of the British EMPIRE (1) and which are now connected politically and economically: *the Commonwealth Games* **2** [C] *formal* an association of countries with political or economic links: *In 1991 the USSR became the Commonwealth of Independent States.*

**com·mo·tion** /kəˈməʊʃən‖-ˈmoʊ-/ *n* [singular, U] sudden noisy activity: *They heard a commotion downstairs.* | **cause a commotion** *The bar was packed, and the winning touchdown caused an immense commotion.*

**com·mu·nal** /ˈkɒmjʊ̈nəl, kəˈmjuːnl/ *adj* **1** shared by a group, especially a group of people who live together: *a communal bathroom* **2** involving people from many different races, religions, or language groups: *rising communal tension in India*

**com·mune[1]** /ˈkɒmjuːn‖ˈkɑː-, kəˈmjuːn/ *n* [C] **1** a group of people who live together and who share the work and their possessions **2** a group of people who work as a team, especially on a farm, and give what they produce to the state **3** the smallest division of local government in countries such as France and Belgium

**com·mune[2]** /kəˈmjuːn/ *v* [I] *formal* to share your thoughts and feelings with someone or with nature without using words: *communing with nature*

**com·mu·ni·ca·ble** /kəˈmjuːnɪkəbəl/ *adj* **1** a communicable illness is infectious **2** able to be communicated: *Her ideas were not easily communicable to others.* —**communicably** *adv*

**com·mu·ni·cant** /kəˈmjuːnʒ̈kənt/ *n* [C] someone who receives COMMUNION (2) regularly in the Christian church

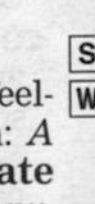

**com·mu·ni·cate** /kəˈmjuːnʒ̈keɪt/ *v* [C]
**1 ▶ EXPRESS ◀** [T] to express your thoughts and feelings clearly, so that other people understand them: *A baby communicates its needs by crying.* | **communicate sth to sb** *Without meaning to, she communicated her anxiety to her child.* | **communicate itself** *Dissatisfaction with working conditions communicated itself throughout the workforce.*
**2 ▶ EXCHANGE INFORMATION ◀** to exchange information or conversation with other people, using words, signs etc: *He learnt how to use sign language to communicate with deaf customers.*
**3 ▶ CONTACT ◀** [I] *formal* to contact someone, especially by telephone or by writing a letter
**4 ▶ UNDERSTAND ◀** [I] if two people communicate, they can easily understand each other's thoughts and feelings: [+ **with**] *Parents sometimes find it difficult to communicate with their teenage children.*
**5 ▶ ROOMS ◀** [I] if rooms or parts of a building communicate, you can get directly to one from the other
**6 ▶ DISEASE ◀** [T usually passive] to pass a disease from one person or animal to another: *research into how the AIDS virus is communicated*

**com·mu·ni·ca·tion** /kəˌmjuːnʒ̈ˈkeɪʃən/ *n* **1** [U] the process by which people exchange information or express their thoughts and feelings: *Good communication is vital in a large organization.* | **means of communication** *Radio was the pilot's only means of communication.* **2 communications** [plural] **a)** ways of sending information, especially using radio, telephone or computers: *Modern communications enable more and more people to work from home.* **b)** ways of travelling and sending goods, such as roads, railways etc: [+ **with**] *Paris has good communications with many European cities.* **3** [C] *formal* a letter, message or telephone call: *a communication from the Ministry of Defence* **4 communication skills** ways of expressing yourself well so that other people will understand: *a week's course in improving communication skills* **5 be in communication with** *formal* to talk or write to someone regularly or occasionally

**communication cord** /·ˌ··ˈ·· ·/ *n* [C] *BrE* a chain that a passenger pulls to stop a train in an EMERGENCY (=a sudden dangerous situation)

**communications sat·el·lite** /·ˌ··ˈ·· ˌ···/ *n* [C] a piece of equipment in space that travels around the Earth and is used for radio, television, and telephone signals around the world

**com·mu·ni·ca·tive** /kəˈmjuːnʒ̈kətɪv‖-keɪtɪv/ *adj* **1** able to talk easily to other people: *It's hard to know what she's thinking; she's not very communicative.* **2** relating to the ability to communicate, especially in a foreign language: *students' communicative skills*

**com·mu·nion** /kəˈmjuːnjən/ *n* **1** [U] *formal* a special relationship with someone or something in which you feel that you understand them very well: [+ **between/with**] *He sought meaningful communion with another human being.* **2** [U] also **Holy Communion** the Christian ceremony in which people eat bread and drink wine as signs of Christ's body and blood **3** [C] *formal* a group of people or organizations that share the same religious beliefs: *He belongs to the Anglican communion.*

**com·mu·ni·qué** /kəˈmjuːnʒ̈keɪ‖kəˌmjuːnʒ̈ˈkeɪ/ *n* [C] an official report or announcement: *The palace has issued a communiqué denying the paper's allegations.*

**Com·mu·nis·m** /ˈkɒmjɡ̈nɪzəm‖ˈkɑː-/ *n* [U] **1** a political system in some countries in which the government controls the production of all food and goods, and which has no different social classes **2** the belief in this political system

**Com·mu·nist**[1] /ˈkɒmjɡ̈nɟst‖ˈkɑː-/ *adj* connected with Communism: *Communist countries | a communist regime*

**Communist**[2] *n* [C] **1** someone who is a member of a political party that supports Communism **2** someone who believes in Communism

**communist bloc** /ˌ··· ˈ·/ *n* [singular] the group of countries, mostly in Eastern Europe, that had Communist governments and supported the former Soviet Union

S1 W1 **com·mu·ni·ty** /kəˈmjuːnɟti/ *n*
**1 ▶ PEOPLE ◀** [C, also + plural verb *BrE*] *BrE* all the people who live in the same area, town etc: *an arts centre built to serve the whole community* | **community affairs/needs/relations etc** *We meet once a month to discuss community problems.* | **community spirit** (=the desire to be friendly with and help other people who live in the same community)
**2 ▶ PARTICULAR GROUP ◀ sense of community** the feeling that you belong to a group of people because you live in the same area
**3** [C] a group of people who share the same nationality or religion or who are similar in another way: *There are many different ethnic communities living in New York.* | *the gay community*
**4 the community** society and the people in it: *The trend is towards reintegrating mentally ill people into the community.* | **the international community** (=all the countries of the world) —see also EC
**5 ▶ PLANTS/ANIMALS ◀** [C] a group of plants or animals that live in the same environment: *Communities of otters are slowly returning to several British rivers.*

**community cen·tre** *BrE* **community center** *AmE* /·ˈ··· ˌ··/ *n* [C] a place where people from the same area can go for social events, classes etc

**community chest** /·ˈ··· ˌ·/ *n* [C] *AmE* money that is collected by the people and businesses in an area to help poor people

**community col·lege** /·ˈ··· ˌ··/ *n* [C,U] a college in the US that students can go to for two years in order to learn a skill or to prepare for university; JUNIOR COLLEGE

**community prop·er·ty** /·ˈ··· ˌ···/ *n* [U] *law* property such as houses or land, that is considered to be owned by both a husband and wife in US law

**community ser·vice** /·ˌ··· ˈ··/ *n* [U] **1** work that someone does without being paid to help other people **2** a punishment given for some crimes, in which the criminal has to do useful work to help people

**com·mu·ta·ble** /kəˈmjuːtəbəl/ *adj* **1** *law* a punishment that is commutable can be made less severe **2** payments that are commutable can be exchanged for another type of payment

**com·mu·ta·tion** /ˌkɒmjɡ̈ˈteɪʃən‖ˌkɑː-/ *n* **1** [C,U] a reduction in how severe a punishment is: *commutation of a death sentence to life* **2** [U] *formal* the act of replacing one method of payment with a different method **3** [C] *technical* a payment of one type made instead of an equal payment of another type

**com·mu·ta·tive** /kəˈmjuːtətɪv‖ˈkɑːmjəteɪtɪv/ *adj technical* a mathematical operation that is commutative can be done in any order

**com·mute**[1] /kəˈmjuːt/ *v* **1** [I] to regularly travel a long distance to get to work: [+ **to/from/between**] *Jim commutes from Weehawken to Manhattan every day.* **2** [T] to change the punishment given to a criminal to one that is less severe: **commute a sentence (to)** *The sentence was later commuted to life imprisonment.* **3 commute sth for/into sth** to exchange one thing, especially one kind of payment, for another: *He commuted his pension for a lump sum.*

**commute**[2] *n* [C usually singular] *especially AmE* the journey to work every day: *My morning commute takes 45 minutes.*

commuters

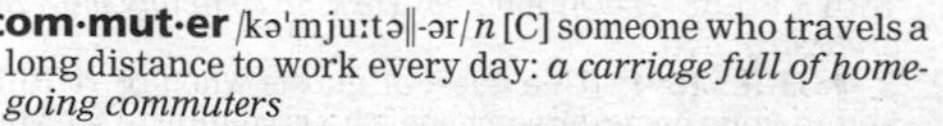

**com·mut·er** /kəˈmjuːtə‖-ər/ *n* [C] someone who travels a long distance to work every day: *a carriage full of home-going commuters*

**commuter belt** /·ˈ·· ˌ·/ *n* [C] an area around a large city from which many people travel to work every day

**comp** /kɒmp‖kɑːmp/ *n* [C] **1** *AmE informal* a ticket for a play, sports game etc that is given away free **2** *BrE spoken* a COMPREHENSIVE SCHOOL

**com·pact**[1] /kəmˈpækt, ˈkɒmpækt‖kəmˈpækt/ *adj* **1** small and easy to carry: *a compact camera* **2** small but arranged so that everything fits neatly into the space available: *The dormitory rooms were compact, with a desk, bed and closet built in.* **3** firmly and closely packed together; DENSE (1): *The bushes grew in a compact mass.* **4** small but solid and strong: *a small compact-looking man* **5** expressing things clearly in only a few words —**compactly** *adv* —**compactness** *n* [U]

**com·pact**[2] /ˈkɒmpækt‖ˈkɑːm-/ *n* [C] **1** a small flat container with a mirror, containing powder for a woman's face **2** *AmE* a small car **3** *formal* an agreement between two or more people, countries etc

**com·pact**[3] /kəmˈpækt/ [T] *v* to press something soft or something made of small pieces together, so that it becomes smaller or more solid —**compacted** *adj*

**compact disc** /ˌ·· ˈ·/ *n* [C] a small circular piece of hard plastic on which music, or large quantities of information can be stored; CD: *The new album is available on vinyl, cassette, or compact disc.*

**compact disc play·er** /ˌ·· ˈ· ˌ··/ *n* [C] CD PLAYER

**com·pan·ion** /kəmˈpænjən/ *n* [C] **1** someone you spend a lot of time with especially someone you are travelling with or a friend: *His dog became his closest companion during the last years of his life.* | **constant companion** (=someone you are always with) **2** one of a pair of things that go together or can be used together: [+ **to**] *This book is a companion to the author's first work.* | **companion volume/album/statement etc** *Paul Simon has just released a companion album to his Greatest Hits.* **3** someone, especially a woman, who is paid to live or travel with an older person **4** used as part of the title of a book on a particular subject, especially a book that explains something W3

**com·pan·io·na·ble** /kəmˈpænjənəbəl/ *adj* pleasantly friendly: *They sat together in companionable silence.* —**companionably** *adv*

**com·pan·ion·ship** /kəmˈpænjənʃɪp/ *n* [U] a friendly and comfortable relationship with someone: *When Stan died, it was the companionship I missed.*

**com·pan·ion·way** /kəmˈpænjənweɪ/ *n* [U] the steps going from one DECK (=level) of a ship to another deck

**com·pa·ny** /ˈkʌmpəni/ *n* S1
**1 ▶ BUSINESS ◀** [C] an organization that makes or sells goods or services in order to get money: *Craig got a job working for an insurance company.* | [also + plural W1

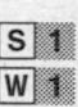

verb *BrE*]: *The company are hoping to expand their operations abroad.* | **manage/run a company** *In ten years Geoff went from working in the mail room to running the company.* | **set up/start a company** *The company was set up just after the war.* | **a company goes bankrupt/bust/out of business** (=stops doing business because it owes so much money) *Quite a few companies went bankrupt in the late 1980s.* | **company directors/employees/policy etc** *It's not company policy to exchange goods without a receipt.* —see also PUBLIC COMPANY
**2** ▶ **OTHER PEOPLE** ◀ [U] another person, or other people, that you can talk to or who stop you feeling lonely: *They obviously enjoy each other's company.* | **keep sb company** *Rita's husband is away for the week, so I thought I'd go over and keep her company.* | **be good company** (=if someone is good company, you enjoy being with them) | **as company** *Bessie was glad to have the dog as company.* | **in sb's company/in the company of sb** (=with someone) *I couldn't help feeling uneasy in the company of such an important man.* | **in company with sb** (=together with another person or with a group) *He left for New York, in company with the orchestra.*
**3** ▶ **GUESTS** ◀ [U] a guest or guests who are visiting you in your home, or someone who is coming to see you: **have company** *It looks like the Hammills have company—there are three cars in the driveway.* | **expect company** (=be waiting for guests to arrive) *We're expecting company this evening.*
**4** ▶ **FRIENDS** ◀ [singular, U] the group of people that you are friends with or that you spend time with: **in pleasant/elevated etc company** *She was too shy to mix in such elevated company.* | **the company sb keeps** (=the people you spend time with) *People do tend to judge you by the company you keep.* | **bad company** (=people who do things you disapprove of) *parents worry that their children are being led into bad company* | **not like the company sb is keeping** (=disapprove of the people someone is friends with) | **keep company with sb** *old-fashioned* (=spend time with someone)
**5** ▶ **PERFORMERS** ◀ [C] a group of actors, dancers, or singers who work together: *Our local theatre gets a lot of touring companies.*
**6 be in good company** used to tell someone that important or respected people have done something similar to what they have done, so they should not be ashamed
**7** ▶ **GROUP** ◀ [U] a group of people who are together in the same place, often for a particular purpose or for social reasons: *These remarks made the assembled company burst into sudden applause.* | **in company** (=surrounded by other people, especially at a formal or social occasion) *Parents need to teach their children how to behave in company.*
**8 and company** *especially spoken* used after a person's name to mean that person and their friends: *"Who's going to the party?" "Jim and company, I guess."*
**9** ▶ **ARMY** ◀ [C] a group of about 120 soldiers who are usually part of a larger group
**10 two's company, three's a crowd** used to suggest that two people would rather be alone together than have other people with them
**11 in company with sth** if something happens in company with something else, both things happen at the same time: *Democracy progressed in company with the emancipation of women.* —see also **part company** (PART[2] (3)), **present company excepted** (PRESENT[3] (5))

**company car** /ˌ··· ˈ·/ *n* [C] a car that your employer gives you while you work for them

**company law** /ˌ··· ˈ·/ *n* [U] the area of law that concerns how businesses operate and what their duties are to each other, to customers, and to governments

**company sec·re·ta·ry** /ˌ··· ˈ····/ *n* [C] *BrE* a member of a company who deals with money, legal matters etc.

**com·pa·ra·ble** /ˈkɒmpərəbəl‖ˈkɑːm-/ *adj* **1** similar to something else in size, number, quality etc, so that you can make a comparison: *A comparable car would cost far more abroad.* | [+ **with/to**] *Is the pay rate comparable to that of other companies?* | **comparable in size/importance etc** *The planet Pluto is comparable in size to the moon.* **2** being equally important, good, bad etc: *In my view these two artists just aren't comparable.* | [+ **with/to**] *His poetry is hardly comparable with Shakespeare's.* —**comparability** /ˌkɒmpərəˈbɪlʒti‖ˌkɑːm-/ *n* [U]

**com·pa·ra·bly** /ˈkɒmpərəbli‖ˈkɑːm-/ *adv* in a similar way or to a similar degree: *Earnings have risen comparably in the industrial sector.*

**com·par·a·tive**[1] /kəmˈpærətɪv/ *adj* **1 comparative comfort/freedom/wealth etc** comfort, freedom etc that is fairly satisfactory when compared to another state of comfort etc: *After a lifetime of poverty, his last few years were spent in comparative comfort.* **2 comparative beginner/newcomer/genius etc** someone who is not really a beginner etc, but who seems to be one when compared to other people: *After living here five years, we're still considered comparative newcomers.* **3 comparative study/analysis/literature etc** a study etc that involves comparing something to something else: *a comparative study of different sociological groups* **4** the comparative form of an adjective or adverb shows an increase in size, degree etc when it is considered in relation to something else. For example, 'bigger' is the comparative form of 'big,' and 'more comfortable' is the comparative form of 'comfortable.'

**comparative**[2] *n* **the comparative** the form of an adjective or adverb that shows an increase in size, degree etc when something is considered in relation to something else. For example, 'bigger' is the comparative of 'big,' and 'more comfortable' is the comparative of 'comfortable.'

**com·par·a·tive·ly** /kəmˈpærətʒvli/ *adv* as compared to something else or to a previous state: *The children were comparatively well-behaved today.* | **comparatively speaking** *This part of the coast is still unspoiled, comparatively speaking.*

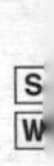

**compare**[1] /kəmˈpeə‖-ˈper/ *v*
**1** ▶ **SIMILAR/DIFFERENT** ◀ [T] to consider two or more things, people, ideas etc, in order to show how they are similar to or different from each other: *The report compares the different types of home computer currently available.* | **compare sth to/with** *There is nothing to compare with a nice cold drink when you get home after work.* | **compare and contrast** (=an expression used when telling students to write about the similarities and differences in works of literature, or art)
**2 compared to/with** used when considering the size, quality, or amount of something in relation to something similar: *Compared to our small apartment, our uncle's house seemed like a palace.* | *Statistics show a 20% reduction in burglary compared with last year.*
**3** ▶ **LIKE/EQUALLY GOOD** ◀ [T] to say that something or someone is like someone or something else, or that it is equally good, large etc: **compare sth/sb to** *You can't compare the war in Somalia to the Vietnam War.*
**4 does not compare** if something or someone does not compare with something else, it is not as good, large etc: *My old car was a real beauty. This one just doesn't compare.*
**5** ▶ **BETTER/WORSE** ◀ to be better or worse in some way than someone or something else: [+ **with**] *How does life in Britain compare with life in the States?* | **compare favourably/unfavourably** *The imported fabrics are 30% cheaper and compare very favorably in quality.*
**6 compare notes** if two people compare notes, they talk about something they have both done, in order to see if they have the same opinions, ideas etc about it: *The pair got together in Paris to compare notes on current research.*

**compare**[2] *n* **beyond/without compare** *literary* a quality that is beyond compare is the best of its kind: *a beauty and an elegance beyond compare*

**com·pa·ri·son** /kəmˈpærʒsən/ *n*
**1** ▶ **COMPARING** ◀ [U] the process of comparing two people or things: [+ **with**] *Comparison with the director's earlier movies seems inevitable.* | **by comparison**

(=compared to someone or something else) *After months of being in a tropical climate, Spain seemed cool by comparison.* | **for comparison** (=for the purpose of comparing) *He showed us the original text for comparison.* | **in comparison with/to** (=compared to someone or something else) *In comparison with the States, the UK is tiny.* | **invite comparison** (=if an object, idea etc invites comparison with something else, it reminds you of it so that you compare them) *Her paintings invite comparison with those of the early Impressionists.* | **on comparison** (=after you have compared two things to see if they are similar or different) *On comparison, the Escort was the more reliable car.* | **stand/bear comparison** (=compare favourably with someone or something) *Irving's work bears comparison with the best of the modern novelists.*
**2** ▶ **JUDGEMENT** ◀ [C] a statement or examination that considers how similar or different two people, places, things etc are: [+ **of**] *a comparison of smog levels in Chicago and Detroit* | [+ **between**] *a comparison between the two novels*
**3** ▶ **BE LIKE STH** ◀ [C] a statement that someone or something is like someone or something else: [+**to**] *The comparison of the mall to a zoo seemed entirely appropriate.* | **make a comparison** (=consider the similarities between two things) *You can't make a comparison between American and Japanese schools – they're too different.* | **draw a comparison** (=show a similarity between two ideas or things) *It's tempting to draw a comparison between this and the Watergate scandal.*
**4 there's no comparison** *spoken* used when you think that someone or something is much better than someone or something else: *There's just no comparison between the junk he sings now and his earlier songs.*
**5** ▶ **GRAMMAR** ◀ [U] a word used in grammar meaning the way an adverb or adjective changes its form to show whether it is COMPARATIVE[1] (4) or SUPERLATIVE[1] (2)

**com·part·ment** /kəm'pɑːtmənt‖-ɑːr-/ *n* [C] **1** one of the separate areas into which a plane, ship, or train is divided: *a non-smoking compartment* **2** one of the separate parts of something such as a desk or box, where you can keep things: *Put the ice cream back in the freezer compartment..* —see also GLOVE COMPARTMENT

**com·part·men·tal·ize** also **-ise** *BrE* /ˌkɒmpɑːt'mentl-aɪz‖kəmˌpɑːrt-/ *v* [T] to divide things into separate groups, especially according to what type of things they are —**compartmentalized** *adj* —**compartmentalization** /ˌkɒmpɑːtˌmentl-aɪ'zeɪʃən‖kəmˌpɑːrtmentl-ə-'zeɪʃən/ *n* [U]

**com·pass** /'kʌmpəs/ *n* **1** [C] an instrument that shows directions: *a map and compass* | **compass point** (=one of the 32 marks on a compass that shows you the exact direction) **2** [C] an instrument that you use to draw circles or measure distances on maps **3** [U] *formal* the area or range of subjects that someone is responsible for or that is discussed in a book: [+ **of**] *Within the brief compass of a single page the author covers most of the major points.*

**com·pas·sion** /kəm'pæʃən/ *n* [U] a strong feeling of sympathy for someone who is suffering, and a desire to help them: [+ **for**] *compassion for the poor and sick* | **feel/show compassion** *"Come have a drink," offered Cook, feeling compassion.* | **be filled with compassion** (=feel a lot of compassion)

**com·pas·sion·ate** /kəm'pæʃənət/ *adj* feeling sympathy for people who are suffering: *a caring, compassionate man* | *a compassionate smile* —**compassionately** *adv*

**compassionate leave** /ˌ.... '.ˌ/ *n* [U] special permission to have time away from work because one of your relatives has died or is very ill

**com·pat·i·bil·ity** /kəmˌpætəˈbɪləti/ *n* [U] **1** the ability to exist or be used together without causing problems **2** *technical* the ability of one piece of computer equipment to be used with another one, especially when they are made by different companies

**com·pat·i·ble¹** /kəm'pætəbəl/ *adj* **1** *technical* compatible machines, methods, ideas etc can exist together or be used together without causing problems: *The new software is IBM compatible.* (=can be used with IBM computers) | [+ **with**] *The project is not compatible with the company's long-term aims.* **2** two people that are compatible are able to have a good relationship

**compatible²** *n* [C] a piece of computer equipment that can be used with another piece, especially one made by a different company: *IBM compatibles*

**com·pat·ri·ot** /kəm'pætriət‖-'peɪt-/ *n* [C] someone who was born in or is a citizen of the same country as someone else; COUNTRYMAN: *Stich defeated his compatriot Becker in the quarter final.*

**com·pel** /kəm'pel/ *v* **compelled, compelling** [T] **1** to force someone to do something: **compel sb to do sth** *reports that children were compelled to participate in bizarre rituals* | **feel compelled to do sth** (=feel very strongly that you must do something) *Harrison felt compelled to resign because of the allegations in the press.* **2** *formal* to make people have a particular feeling or attitude: *His appearance on stage compelled the audience's attention.* —compare IMPEL

**com·pel·ling** /kəm'pelɪŋ/ *adj* **1** extremely interesting or exciting: *a compelling personality* **2 compelling argument/reason/cases etc** an argument etc that makes you feel it is true or that you must do something about it: *He felt a compelling need to tell someone about his idea.* —**compellingly** *adv*

**com·pen·di·ous** /kəm'pendiəs/ *adj formal* a book that is compendious gives information in a short but complete form —**compendiously** *adv*

**com·pen·di·um** /kəm'pendiəm/ *n plural* **compendiums** *or* **compendia** /-diə/ [C] *formal* **1** a book that contains a complete collection of facts, drawings etc on a particular subject: *a cricketing compendium* **2** *BrE* a set of different BOARD GAMES in one box

**com·pen·sate** /'kɒmpənseɪt‖'kɑːm-/ *v* **1** [I] to replace or balance something good that has been lost or is lacking, by providing or doing something equally good: *Because my left eye is so weak, my right eye has to work harder to compensate.* | [+ **for**] *Her intelligence more than compensates for her lack of experience.* **2** [I,T] to pay someone money because they have suffered injury, loss or damage: **compensate sb for sth** *The firm agreed to compensate its workers for their loss of earnings.*

**com·pen·sa·tion** /ˌkɒmpən'seɪʃən‖ˌkɑːm-/ *n* **1** [U] W3 money that someone pays you because they have harmed or hurt you in some way: [+ **for**] *compensation for injuries at work* | **in compensation** *The plane was cancelled, and all we got in compensation was a free meal.* | **as compensation** *The workers were given 30 days' pay as compensation.* | **pay sb compensation** *The idea is that criminals should pay compensation to their victims.* | **seek/claim compensation** (=ask officially for compensation) | **award/grant compensation** (=pay compensation) *The court awarded Jamieson £15,000 compensation.* **2** [C,U] something that makes a sad or an unpleasant situation better or happier: *One of the few compensations of being unemployed was seeing more of the family.* | **by way of compensation** (=in order to make a situation better) *By way of compensation he offered to take her out for a meal.* **3** [C,U] actions, behaviour etc that replace or balance something that is lacking: [+ **for**] *Linda's aggressiveness is really just a compensation for her feelings of insecurity.* | **as compensation** *Lip reading can act as compensation for loss of hearing.*

**com·pen·sa·to·ry** /ˌkɒmpən'seɪtəri‖kəm'pensəˌtɔːri/ *adj* [usually before noun] **1** intended to reduce the harmful effects of something or to make them easier to bear **2** compensatory payments are paid to someone who has been harmed or hurt in some way: *She was awarded a large sum in compensatory damages.*

**com·pere** /'kɒmpeə‖'kɑːmper/ *n* [C] *BrE* someone who introduces the people who are performing in a television programme, theatre show etc; EMCEE *AmE*: *He plays a* *sleazy, no-talent TV compere.* —**compere** *v* [I,T] *BrE*| *UTV's Pamela Ballentine will compere the show.*

S3 W3 **com·pete** /kəm'piːt/ *v* [I]
**1** ▶ **PERSON/BUSINESS** ◀ to try to be more successful than another person or organization, especially in business: [+ **with**] *They found themselves competing with foreign companies for a share of the market.*|[+ **for**] *She and her sister are always competing for attention.*|[+ **against**] *businesses competing against each other*| **compete to do sth** *Several advertising agencies are competing to get the contract.*|**can't compete** (=be unable to compete, especially with something bigger or better) *Small, independent bookstores simply can't compete with the big national chains.*

**2** ▶ **IN A COMPETITION** ◀ to take part in a competition or sporting event: *How many runners will be competing in the marathon?*
**3 can't compete with sb/sth** to not be as interesting, attractive etc as someone or something else: *Melinda was plain and knew she couldn't compete with her sister where boys were concerned.*
**4** ▶ **SOUND/SMELL** ◀ [I + **with**] if a sound or smell competes with another sound or smell, you can hear both equally well: *The songs of the birds competed with the sound of the church bells.*
**5** ▶ **IDEAS/ARGUMENTS** ◀ if two ideas, arguments, claims etc compete with each other, they cannot both be right or cannot both be successful

**com·pe·tence** /'kɒmpɪ̈təns‖'kaːm-/ *n* **1** [U] the ability and skill to do what is needed: *No one questioned his competence as a doctor.*|*a high level of managerial competence* **2** [U] *law* the legal power of a court of law to hear and judge something in court **3** [U] a special area of knowledge: *It is not within my competence to make such judgements.* **4** [C] a skill needed to do a particular job: *Typing is considered by most employers to be a basic competence.*

**com·pe·tent** /'kɒmpɪ̈tənt‖'kaːm-/ *adj* **1** having enough skill or knowledge to do something to a satisfactory standard: *She's a highly competent linguist.*| **competent to do sth** *I don't feel competent to give an opinion at the moment.* **2** a piece of work, performance etc that is competent is satisfactory but not especially good: *The workmen did a competent job.* **3** [not before noun] having the legal power to deal with something in a court of law: **be competent to do sth** *This court is not competent to hear your case.* —**competently** *adv*

**com·pet·ing** /kəm'piːtɪŋ/ *adj* **competing claims/interests/theories etc** competing claims etc are two claims that cannot both be accepted: *We've got several competing priorities to decide between.*

S1 W1 **com·pe·ti·tion** /ˌkɒmpɪ̈'tɪʃən‖ˌkaːm-/ *n* **1** [U] a situation in which people or organizations compete with each other: [+ **between**] *Sometimes there's a lot of competition between children for their mother's attention.*|[+ **for**] *Competition for the job was intense.*|[+ **among**] *This price reduction is due to competition among suppliers.*|**be in competition with** (=be competing with)|**fierce/stiff/intense etc competition** *There is fierce competition between the three leading soap manufacturers.*|**in the face of competition** (=in a situation where you are competing) *In the face of such strong competition, small grocery stores are going out of business.* **2** [singular, U] the people or groups that are competing against you, especially in business or in a sport: **the competition** *Going to trade fairs is an ideal opportunity to size up the competition.*|**no/not much/little etc competition** (=no one who is likely to be better than you) *Lewis is bound to win the race; there's just no competition.*|**a lot of/considerable/fierce etc competition** (=people who are very strong or skilful) *The team overcame fierce competition for their place in the finals.*|**foreign competition** (=companies from other countries that you are competing with) **3** [C] an organized event in which people or teams compete against each other, especially using their skill: *United were knocked out of the competition in the first round.*|*a crossword competition*| **competition to do sth** *a competition to find a designer for the new airport building*|**win/lose a competition** *Who won the volleyball competition?*|**enter a competition** *Teams from high schools all over the state have entered the competition.*

**com·pet·i·tive** /kəm'petɪ̈tɪv/ *adj* **1** a competitive situation is one in which people or organizations try very hard to be more successful than others: *an extremely competitive market*|**highly/fiercely/intensely competitive** *Advertising is an intensely competitive business.* **2** products or prices that are competitive are cheaper than others but still of good quality: *The hotel offers a high standard of service at competitive rates.* **3** someone who is competitive is determined to be more successful than other people: *I hate playing tennis with Steve. He's too competitive.* **4 competitive edge** a strong desire to win or do well that gives someone an advantage: *The team seems to have lost their competitive edge in recent months.* —**competitively** *adv* S W

**com·pet·i·tive·ness** /kəm'petɪ̈tɪvnɪ̈s/ *n* [U] **1** the ability of a company or a product to compete with others: *New machinery has enhanced the company's productivity and competitiveness.* **2** the desire to be more successful than other people: *Her enthusiasm and competitiveness rubbed off on everyone.*

**com·pet·i·tor** /kəm'petɪ̈tə‖-ər/ *n* [C] **1** a person, team, company etc that is competing with another: *The firm's major competitors are all in France.* **2** someone who takes part in a competition: *Two of the competitors failed to turn up for the race.*

**com·pi·la·tion** /ˌkɒmpɪ̈'leɪʃən‖ˌkaːm-/ *n* **1** [C] a book or list, record etc which is made up of different pieces of information, songs etc: **compilation album/cassette** *a compilation album of Christmas music* **2** [U] the process of making a book, list, record etc from different pieces of information, songs etc: *the compilation of a dictionary*

**com·pile** /kəm'paɪl/ *v* [T] **1** to make a list, record etc using different pieces of information, songs etc: *The document was compiled by the Department of Health.*| **compile sth from/for sth** *These notes were compiled from lectures and seminars.* **2** to put a set of instructions into a computer in a form that you can understand and use

**com·pil·er** /kəm'paɪlə‖-ər/ *n* [C] **1** someone who collects different pieces of information or facts to be used in a book, report, or list **2** a set of instructions in a computer that changes a computer language known to the computer user into the form needed by the computer

**com·pla·cen·cy** /kəm'pleɪsənsi/ *n* [U] a feeling of satisfaction with what you have achieved which makes you stop trying to improve or change things: *There are no grounds for complacency in today's competitive environment.*

**com·pla·cent** /kəm'pleɪsənt/ *adj* pleased with what you have achieved so that you stop trying to improve or change things: *There's a danger of becoming complacent if you win a few games.*|[+ **about**] *We simply cannot afford to be complacent about the future of our car industry.* —**complacently** *adv*

**com·plain** /kəm'pleɪn/ *v* **1** [I, T not in passive] to say that you are annoyed, dissatisfied, or unhappy about something or someone: *They've already been given a 10% raise so why are they complaining?*|*"You never ask my opinion about anything," Rod complained.*|[+ **about**] *She often complains about not feeling appreciated at work.*|**complain (that)** *People complain that they don't get enough information.*|**complain to sb** *Neighbours complained to the police about the dogs barking.*| **complain bitterly** *Employees complained bitterly about working conditions.* **2 can't complain** *spoken* used to say that a situation is satisfactory generally in spite of the fact there may be a few problems: *Old age is creeping up, but I can't complain.* S W

**complain of** sth *phr v* [T] to say that you feel ill or

have a pain in a part of your body: *Dan's been complaining of severe headaches recently.*

**com·plain·ant** /kəmˈpleɪnənt/ *n* [C] *law* someone who makes a formal complaint in a court of law; PLAINTIFF

2 3 **com·plaint** /kəmˈpleɪnt/ *n* **1** [C,U] a written or spoken statement in which someone complains about something: *The sales assistants were trained to deal with customer complaints in a friendly manner.* | **[+ about]** *We have received a number of complaints about your conduct.* | **[+ against]** *All complaints against police officers are carefully investigated.* | **complaint that** *We are concerned by complaints that children are being bullied.* | **make a complaint** (=complain formally to someone) *If you wish to make a complaint you should see the manager.* | **have/receive a complaint** *The BBC received a stream of complaints about the programme.* | **file/lodge/submit a complaint** *formal* (=complain officially to someone) *"I wish to lodge an official complaint," the woman said.* | **letter of complaint** *The Council received over 10,000 letters of complaint.* | **reason/cause/grounds for complaint** *Anyone dismissed because of their race has legitimate grounds for complaint.* | **complaints procedure** (=a system for dealing with official complaints) **2** [C] something that you complain about: *Our main complaint is the poor standard of service.* **3** [C] an illness that affects a particular part of your body: *Mr Riley is suffering from a chest complaint.* | *minor skin complaints*

**com·plai·sance** /kəmˈpleɪzəns/ *n* [U] *formal* willingness to do what pleases other people —**complaisant** *adj* —**complaisantly** *adv*

**com·plect·ed** /kəmˈplektɪ̆d/ *adj* **fair/dark complected** *AmE* having fair or dark skin

**com·ple·ment¹** /ˈkɒmplɪ̆mənt‖ˈkɑːm-/ *n* [C] **1** someone or something that emphasizes the good qualities of another person or thing: **[+ to]** *A fine wine is a complement to a good meal.* **2** the number or quantity needed to make a group complete: **a full complement (of)** (=all the people or things that form a complete group) *Each new cell will carry its full complement of chromosomes.* **3** *technical* a word or phrase in grammar that follows a verb and describes the subject of the verb: *In 'John is cold' and 'John became chairman', 'cold' and 'chairman' are complements.* **4** *technical* an angle that together with another angle already mentioned makes 90 degrees —compare COMPLIMENT¹

**com·ple·ment²** /ˈkɒmplɪ̆ment‖ˈkɑːm-/ *v* [T] to show up the good qualities in someone or something, or make them seem more attractive: *The white silk of her blouse complements her olive skin perfectly.* | *Sally's tact and reserve complemented John's go-getting attitude.* —compare COMPLIMENT²

**com·ple·men·ta·ry** /ˌkɒmplɪ̆ˈmentəri◂‖ˌkɑːm-/ *adj* **1** making someone or something better or more attractive by emphasizing its good qualities or having qualities that the other person or thing lacks: *The computer and the human mind have different but complementary abilities.* **2** *technical* two angles that are complementary add up to 90 degrees

**com·plete¹** /kəmˈpliːt/ *adj* **1** a word used to emphasize that a quality you are describing is as great or extreme as possible: *Their engagement came as a complete surprise to me.* | *The police were in complete control of the situation.* | **a complete idiot/failure/wimp etc** *I felt a complete fool.* **2** having all parts, details, facts etc included and with nothing missing: *The captain ordered a complete baggage check.* | *Buy one of those plates every month until your collection is complete.* | *The party didn't seem complete without Clare.* | **the complete works of** (=a book or books containing every play, story or poem by a particular person) *the complete works of Shakespeare* **3** [not before noun] finished: *The work on the new building is nearly complete.* **4 complete with** having equipment or features: *The house comes complete with swimming pool and sauna.* **5 the complete footballer/host etc** someone who is good at all parts of an activity: *Best's vision and ball control made him the complete footballer.* —**completeness** *n* [U]

**complete²** *v* [T] **1** to finish doing something especially when it has taken a long time: *The students have just completed their course.* | *The building took two years to complete.* **2** to make something whole or perfect by adding what is missing: *This exercise involves completing sentences.* | *He only needs one more stamp to complete his collection.* | **complete a form/questionnaire** (=give information that is needed) S2 W1

**com·plet·ed** /kəmˈpliːtɪ̆d/ *adj* containing all the necessary parts or answers needed to finish something: *Send your completed form to the following address.*

**com·plete·ly** /kəmˈpliːtli/ *adv* in every way; totally: *I completely forgot that it was his birthday yesterday.* | [+ adj/adv] *She was bored with work and wanted to do something completely different.* | *I felt completely relaxed.* 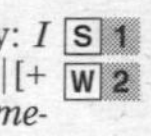

**com·ple·tion** /kəmˈpliːʃən/ *n* [U] **1** the state of being finished: **near completion** (=almost finished) *The new houses are nearing completion.* | **completion date** (=the time by which something must or will be finished) *The builders have given us December 22nd as a completion date.* **2** the act of completing or finishing something: **[+ of]** *The job is subject to your satisfactory completion of the training course.* | **on completion** *We paid them on completion of the work.* **3** the final point in the sale of a property, such as a house, when the documents have all been signed and all the money paid

**com·plex¹** /ˈkɒmpleks‖ˌkɑːmˈpleks◂/ *adj* **1** consisting of many different parts or processes that are closely connected: *There is a complex network of roads round the city.* | *Photosynthesis is a highly complex process.* **2** difficult to understand or deal with: *Mental illness is by its nature very complex.* | *a complex problem* **3** *technical* a complex word or sentence contains a main part and one or more other parts S3 W2

**com·plex²** /ˈkɒmpleks‖ˈkɑːm-/ *n* [C] **1** a group of buildings that are close together, or a large building containing smaller buildings that are used for the same purpose: *They are building a vast new shopping complex in the town.* | **leisure/sports/cinema complex** *a 12-screen cinema complex* **2** an emotional problem in which someone is unnecessarily anxious about something or thinks too much about something: **have a complex about sth** *She's has some kind of a complex about her nose.* | **give sb a complex** *You'll give Graham a complex if you keep going on about how fat he is.* **3 a complex of roads/regulations etc** a large number of things which are closely connected and difficult to understand —see also INFERIORITY COMPLEX, OEDIPUS COMPLEX, SUPERIORITY COMPLEX, PERSECUTION COMPLEX

**com·plex·ion** /kəmˈplekʃən/ *n* **1** [C] the natural colour or appearance of the skin on your face: *Drinking lots of water is good for the complexion.* | **a pale/ruddy complexion etc** (=a pale, red face etc) **2** [singular] the general character or nature of something: **put a (whole) new complexion on** (=change a situation) *These latest findings have put a whole new complexion on the affair.*

**com·plex·i·ty** /kəmˈpleksɪ̆ti/ *n* [U] **1** the state of being complicated: *Many claimants are put off by the sheer complexity of insurance company rules.* **2 the complexities of** the problems and difficulties involved in a situation or process: *the complexities of the tax laws*

**com·pli·ance** /kəmˈplaɪəns/ *n* [U] *formal* **1** OBEDIENCE to a rule, agreement, or demand: *Compliance with the law is expected of all citizens.* | **in compliance with** *In compliance with her wishes, she was buried next to her husband.* **2** the tendency to agree too willingly to someone else's wishes or demands: *Her compliance with everything we suggested made it difficult to know what she really felt.*

**com·pli·ant** /kəmˈplaɪənt/ *adj* willing to obey, or agree to other people's wishes and demands: *He soon settled down and became a compliant patient.* —**compliantly** *adv* —see also COMPLY

**com·pli·cate** /ˈkɒmplɪkeɪt‖ˈkɑːm-/ *v* [T] **1** to make a problem or situation more difficult: *The situation is complicated by the fact that I've got to work late on Friday.* | **to complicate matters/things** *Just to complicate things, the car has broken down!* **2** [usually passive] to make an illness worse: *a heart condition complicated by pneumonia*

S2 **com·pli·cat·ed** /ˈkɒmplɪkeɪtɪd‖ˈkɑːm-/ *adj* **1** difficult to understand or deal with: *They had to begin the complicated task of sorting out his legal affairs.* | *a complicated set of instructions* | **extremely/highly complicated** *a highly complicated situation* **2** consisting of many closely related or connected parts: *The human brain is an incredibly complicated organ.*

**com·pli·ca·tion** /ˌkɒmplɪˈkeɪʃən‖ˌkɑːm-/ *n* **1** [C,U] a problem or situation that makes something more difficult to understand or deal with: *The fact that the plane was late added a further complication to our journey.* **2** [C, usually plural] a medical problem or illness that happens while someone is already ill and makes medical treatment more difficult: *Pneumonia is one of the common complications faced by bed-ridden patients.*

**complicit** /kəmˈplɪsɪt/ *adj* involved in or knowing about a situation, especially one that is morally wrong or dishonest: *They exchanged complicit smiles.* | **complicit in sth** *The careers of the officers complicit in the cover-up were ruined.*

**com·plic·i·ty** /kəmˈplɪsɪti/ *n* [U] *formal* a process in which someone is involved in a crime or illegal activity together with other people: [+ **in**] *Jennings denied complicity in the murder.*

**com·pli·ment¹** /ˈkɒmplɪmənt‖ˈkɑːm-/ *n* [C] **1** a remark that expresses admiration of someone or something: *"You have lovely hair", Bob told Emma, who blushed at the compliment.* | *Maria's used to receiving compliments on her appearance.* | **pay sb a compliment** (=tell someone that they look nice, have done something well, etc) | **take sth as a compliment** (=be pleased about what someone has said about you) *"James described you as a bold, brave feminist." "Oh well, I'll take that as a compliment."* | **shower sb with compliments** (=praise someone very much) | **return a compliment** (=say something nice to someone after they have said something nice to you) | **fish for compliments** (=try to make someone say something nice about you, usually by asking them a question) **2 pay sb the compliment of doing sth** to do something that shows you trust someone else and have a good opinion of them: *They paid me the ultimate compliment of electing me as their representative.* **3 compliments** *plural* used to express praise, admiration or good wishes: **my compliments to the chef** (=used to tell someone that they cook very well) *This Stilton and celery soup is delicious; my compliments to the chef!* | **compliments of the season** (=used as a spoken or written greeting at Christmas and New Year) **4 a) with the compliments of.../with our compliments** an expression printed on a small piece of paper used by a company or organization when they send goods or information: *With the compliments of J. Nocuold & Son* **b)** used when a person or company gives you something such as a free ticket, meal etc: *Please accept these tickets with our compliments.* **5 a) return the compliment** to do something to help someone after they have helped you: *Thanks for helping me move the furniture; I'll try to return the compliment one day.* **b)** to say or do something unpleasant to someone after they have behaved badly towards you: *"Gemma called you a fat liar." "Gee thanks. Remind me to return the compliment."* **6 back-handed compliment** *BrE* **left-handed compliment** *AmE* something that someone says to you which is unpleasant and pleasant at the same time: *"A lot of people seem to resent you, but I like you", she said. Talk about a back-handed compliment.* —compare COMPLEMENT¹

**com·pli·ment²** /ˈkɒmplɪment‖ˈkɑːm-/ *v* [T] to say something nice to someone in order to praise them: **compliment sb on sth** *Bob complimented me on my new hairstyle.* —compare COMPLEMENT²

**com·pli·men·ta·ry** /ˌkɒmplɪˈmentəri◂‖ˌkɑːm-/ *adj* **1** expressing admiration, praise or respect: *Your teacher made some very complimentary remarks about your work.* | [+ **about**] *Donleavy was highly complimentary about Coleman's work.* **2** given free to people: *There was a complimentary bottle of champagne in the hotel room.* | **complimentary ticket/seat etc** *We've got two complimentary tickets for the Barcelona game.*

**compliment slip** /ˈ... ˌ·/ *n* [C] a small piece of paper with a company's name and address on it, that it sends with goods instead of a proper letter

**com·pline** /ˈkɒmplɪn‖ˈkɑːm-/ *n* [U] a Christian church service held late in the evening, especially in the Roman Catholic church —compare EVENSONG, VESPERS

**com·ply** /kəmˈplaɪ/ *v* [I] *formal* to do what you have to do or are asked to do: [+ **with**] *Failure to comply with the regulations will result in prosecution.* —see also COMPLIANCE

**com·po·nent** /kəmˈpəʊnənt‖-ˈpoʊ-/ *n* [C] one of several parts that together make up a whole machine or system: *The repair shop sells electrical components.* | *Counselling is an important component of our rehabilitation programme.* —compare CONSTITUENT¹ (2)

**com·port** /kəmˈpɔːt‖-ɔːrt/ *v* **comport yourself** *formal* to behave yourself in a particular way: *He always comported himself in an exemplary manner.* —**comportment** *n* [U]

**com·pose** /kəmˈpəʊz‖-ˈpoʊz/ *v* **1 be composed of** to be formed from a group of substances or parts: *Water is composed of hydrogen and oxygen.* **2** [T not in progressive] if different things or people compose something else, they combine together to form it: *the individual letters that compose a word* **3** [I,T] to write a piece of music: *Could you compose a piece for the concert?* **4 compose a letter/poem/speech etc** to write a letter, poem etc, thinking very carefully about it as you write it: *compose a letter of complaint* **5 compose your thoughts/features** to make yourself feel or look calm: *He felt he needed a quiet place where he could compose his thoughts.* | **compose yourself** (=try hard to become calm after feeling very angry, upset, or excited) **6** [T] to arrange the parts of a painting, photograph or scene etc in a way that achieves a particular result: *The photographer will need plenty of time to compose the shot.*

**com·posed** /kəmˈpəʊzd‖-ˈpoʊzd/ *adj* seeming calm and not upset or angry: *He appeared very composed despite the stress he was under.*

**com·pos·er** /kəmˈpəʊzə‖-ˈpoʊzər/ *n* [C] someone who writes music

**composite¹** /ˈkɒmpəzɪt‖kɑːmˈpɑː-/ *adj* [only before noun] made up of different parts or materials: *a composite problem* | *composite molecules*

**com·po·site²** *n* [C] **1** something made up of different parts or materials: *Behaviour is a composite of individual and group influences.* | *If she wants to be a model, she'll need a composite of good photographs.* **2** a method used by the police for producing a picture of a possible criminal from descriptions given by a WITNESS or WITNESSES; IDENTIKIT *BrE*

**com·po·si·tion** /ˌkɒmpəˈzɪʃən‖ˌkɑːm-/ *n*

**1 ▶ MAKING A WHOLE ◀** [U] the way in which something is made up of different parts, things, members etc: *There were dramatic changes in the composition of the committee after the election.* | [+ **of**] *He's doing research into the chemical composition of plants.* | **in composition** *The suburbs are mainly working class in composition.*

**2 ▶ MUSIC/ART ETC ◀ a)** [C] a piece of music or art, or a poem: *She's very fond of Bach's later compositions.* **b)** [U] the art or process of writing pieces of music, poems etc

**3 ▶ PHOTOGRAPH/PICTURE ◀** [U] the way in which the different parts that make up a photograph or painting

are arranged: *The composition of these photographs is superb.*
**4 ▶ SCHOOL SUBJECT ◀** [C,U] *old-fashioned* a short piece of writing about a particular subject that is done especially at school: *a 400-word composition about Autumn*
**5 ▶ PRINTING ◀** [U] *technical* the process of arranging words, pictures etc on a page before they are printed

**com·pos·i·tor** /kəm'pɒzʒtə‖-'pɑːzʒtər/ *n* [C] someone who arranges letters, pictures etc on a page before they are printed

**com·pos men·tis** /ˌkɒmpəs 'mentʒs‖ˌkɑːm-/ *adj* [not before noun] *often humorous* able to think clearly and be responsible for your actions: *It's too early in the morning – I'm not compos mentis!*

**com·post¹** /'kɒmpɒst‖'kɑːmpoʊst/ *n* [U] a mixture of decayed plants, leaves etc used to improve the quality of soil: **compost heap** (=a place in a garden where you pile decayed leaves, plants etc in order to make compost)

**compost²** *v* [T] **1** to make plants, leaves etc into compost **2** to put compost onto soil

**com·po·sure** /kəm'pəʊʒə‖-'poʊʒər/ *n* [singular, U] a calm feeling which you have when you feel confident about dealing with a situation: **keep/maintain your composure** (=stay calm) *They maintained an admirable composure throughout the ordeal.* | **lose your composure** (=get angry or upset) | **recover/regain your composure** (=become calm after feeling angry or upset)

**com·pote** /'kɒmpɒt, -pəʊt‖'kɑːmpoʊt/ *n* [C,U] fruit cooked in sugar and water and eaten cold

**com·pound¹** /'kɒmpaʊnd‖'kɑːm-/ *n* [C] **1** *technical* a substance containing atoms from two or more elements (ELEMENT (1)): *Sulphur dioxide is a compound of sulphur and oxygen.* **2** a combination of two or more things or qualities that make up a situation: *social unrest caused by a compound of unemployment and poverty* **3** an area that contains a group of buildings and is surrounded by a fence or wall: *a prison compound* **4** *technical* a noun or adjective made up of two or more words: *The noun 'flower shop' and the adjective 'self-made' are compounds.*

**compound²** *adj* **1 compound eye/leaf etc** *technical* a single eye, leaf etc that is made up of two or more parts or substances **2 compound noun/adjective** *technical* a noun or adjective that is made up of two or more words

**com·pound³** /kəm'paʊnd/ *v* [T] **1** to make a difficult situation even worse by adding more problems: **be compounded by** *Our difficulties were compounded by the language barrier.* **2** to make something by mixing different parts or substances together: *Scientists are able to compound an increasing number of substances to produce new drugs.* **3** *AmE* to pay INTEREST¹ (4) that is calculated on both the sum of money and the INTEREST¹ (4): *My bank compounds interest quarterly.*

**compound frac·ture** /ˌ·· '··/ *n* [C] *technical* a broken bone that cuts through someone's skin

**compound in·terest** /ˌ·· '···/ *n* [U] INTEREST¹ (4) that is calculated on both the sum of money lent or borrowed and on the unpaid INTEREST already earned or charged —compare SIMPLE INTEREST

**com·pre·hend** /ˌkɒmprɪ'hend‖ˌkɑːm-/ *v* [I,T not in progressive] *formal* to understand something that is complicated or difficult: *Even scientists do not comprehend these phenomena.* | **comprehend how/why/what etc** *I fail to comprehend how this was allowed to happen.* | **fully comprehend** (=understand completely)

**com·pre·hen·si·ble** /ˌkɒmprɪ'hensʒbəl‖ˌkɑːm-/ *adj* easy to understand: *The book offers an easily comprehensible explanation of the subject.* | **[+ to]** *Such detailed analyses are not comprehensible to the average person.* —opposite INCOMPREHENSIBLE —**comprehensibly** *adv* —**comprehensibility** /ˌkɒmprɪhensʒ'bɪlʒti‖ˌkɑːm-/ *n* [U]

**com·pre·hen·sion** /ˌkɒmprɪ'henʃən‖ˌkɑːm-/ *n* **1** [U] the ability to understand something: *a reasonable comprehension of the subject* | **beyond (sb's) comprehension** (=impossible to understand) *How she managed to pass her exam after doing so little work is beyond my comprehension.* **2** [U] knowledge of what a situation is really like: *Most politicians have no real comprehension of what it is like to be poor.* **3** [C,U] an exercise given to students to test how well they understand written or spoken language: **reading/listening comprehension** (=a piece of written or spoken language which tests how well students understand)

**com·pre·hen·sive** /ˌkɒmprɪ'hensɪv◂‖ˌkɑːm-/ *adj* **1** including all the necessary facts, details, or problems that need to be dealt with; thorough: *There was a comprehensive inspection of the nuclear plant.* | **comprehensive study/list/coverage etc** *a comprehensive account of the events leading up to the Second World War* | **comprehensive insurance/cover/policy** (=a type of insurance that pays for damage whether it is caused by you or someone else) **2 comprehensive education/system** a system of education in which pupils of different abilities go to the same school or are taught in the same class —**comprehensively** *adv* —**comprehensiveness** *n* [U] W3

**comprehensive school** /··'·· ˌ·/ also **comprehensive** *n* [C] a state school in Britain for pupils of different abilities over the age of 11: *Kylie goes to the local comprehensive.*

**com·press¹** /kəm'pres/ *v* **1** [I,T] if you compress something it is pressed so that it takes up less space: **compress sth into** *The machine compresses old cars into blocks of scrap metal.* | **compressed air/gas etc** *Compressed gas was escaping through a hole in the cylinder.* **2** [T] to write or express something using fewer words: *Try to compress and simplify your notes so that they are easier to learn.* **3** [T usually passive] to reduce the amount of time that it takes for something to happen or be done: **compress sth into** *What would normally have been a three-year training course had to be compressed into eighteen months* —**compressible** *adj* —**compression** /-'preʃən/ *n* [U]

**com·press²** /'kɒmpres‖'kɑːm-/ *n* [C] a small thick piece of material that you put on part of someone's body to stop blood flowing out or to make it less painful: **cold/hot compress** *Apply a cold compress to the injured part of the limb.*

**com·pres·sor** /kəm'presə‖-ər/ *n* [C] a machine or part of a machine that compresses air or gas

**com·prise** /kəm'praɪz/ *v* [not in progressive] *formal* **1** [linking verb] to consist of particular parts, groups etc: *The house comprises 2 bedrooms, a kitchen, and a living room.* | **be comprised of** *The city's population is largely comprised of Asians and Europeans.* **2** [T] if different people or things comprise something they combine together to form it: *Women comprise a high proportion of part-time workers.* —see also CONSTITUTE W3

**USAGE NOTE: COMPRISE**

WORD CHOICE: **make up, consist of, compose, comprise, include, constitute**

Things **consist of** or **are made up of** a series of parts, or more formally **are composed of/comprise** all their parts: *New York City comprises Manhattan, Queens, Brooklyn, The Bronx and Staten Island.* | *a street composed mainly of detached houses* (NOT *composed by/from*) | *a family made up of six people* | *Dinner consisted of a starter, a main course and a dessert* (NOT *consisted in/on* or *was consisted of*).

You will sometimes hear native speakers using **comprise** with *of*, but some people think this is incorrect: *The company comprises of/is comprised of five divisions.*

If you only mention some of the parts, you use **include**: *New York City includes Brooklyn and Queens.*

All the parts of something together **make up** or more formally **constitute** or (less frequently) **comprise** the whole: *Manhattan, Queens, Brooklyn, The Bronx and Staten Island constitute/comprise New York City.*|*How many people make up a basket ball team?*

GRAMMAR

These words are not used in progressive tenses in these meanings.

**com·pro·mise¹** /ˈkɒmprəmaɪz‖ˈkɑːm-/ *n* **1** [C,U] an agreement between two people that is achieved by both people accepting less than they wanted at first: *Compromise is an inevitable part of marriage.*| **reach a compromise** *Talks continue in the hope that the two factions will reach a compromise.*| **make a compromise** *Everybody has to be prepared to make compromises.* **2** [C] an idea or thing that is the result of an agreement between two people or groups who want different things: [+ **between**] *The treaty represents a political compromise between the two nations.*

**compromise²** *v* **1** [I] to reach an agreement with someone by both of you accepting less than you wanted at first: *She was forced to compromise in order to avoid a major argument.*| [+**on**] *We managed to compromise on a price for the car.*| [+ **with**] *Can't you boys compromise with each other? Play football this morning and tennis this afternoon.* **2 compromise your principles/beliefs/ideas etc** to do something that is against your principles etc and which therefore seems dishonest or shameful: *He tried to make money without compromising his moral values.*| **compromise yourself** (=do something dishonest or embarrassing that puts you in a difficult position) **3 compromise your chances** to spoil the chances of something good happening: *That kind of behaviour will compromise your chances of promotion.*

**com·pro·mis·ing** /ˈkɒmprəmaɪzɪŋ‖ˈkɑːm-/ *adj* making it seem or proving that you have done something morally wrong or embarrassing: **compromising situation/position etc** *The magazine had shown him in a compromising position with his political researcher.*| **compromising letter/photograph/picture etc** *A large number of compromising letters fell into the hands of Tsarist investigators.*

**comp·trol·ler** /kənˈtrəʊlə, kəmp-‖-ˈtroʊlər/ *n* [C] *formal* an official title for a CONTROLLER (2)

**com·pul·sion** /kəmˈpʌlʃən/ *n* **1** [C] a strong and unreasonable desire that is difficult to control: *Constantly washing her hands became a compulsion that needed treatment.*| **compulsion to do sth** *I had a sudden compulsion to hit her.* **2** [singular, U] a force or influence that makes someone do something: **compulsion to do sth** *Please note that you are under no compulsion to sign the agreement.* —see also COMPEL

**com·pul·sive** /kəmˈpʌlsɪv/ *adj* **1** compulsive behaviour is very difficult to stop or control, and is often a result of or a sign of a mental problem: *Compulsive spending is often a symptom of deep unhappiness.* **2 a compulsive liar/gambler/drinker etc** someone who has such a strong desire to lie etc that they are unable to control it **3** a book, programme etc that is compulsive is so interesting that you cannot stop reading or watching it: **compulsive reading/viewing** (=very interesting to read or watch) *'Gardening World' – compulsive viewing for gardeners.* —**compulsively** *adv* —**compulsiveness** *n* [U]

**com·pul·so·ry** /kəmˈpʌlsəri/ *adj* something that is compulsory must be done because it is the law or because someone in authority orders you to; OBLIGATORY: *In Britain, education is compulsory between the ages of 5 and 16.*|*compulsory lay-offs* —**compulsorily** *adv* —compare VOLUNTARY¹ (4)

**com·punc·tion** /kəmˈpʌŋkʃən/ *n* [U] *formal* a deep feeling of shame or guilt

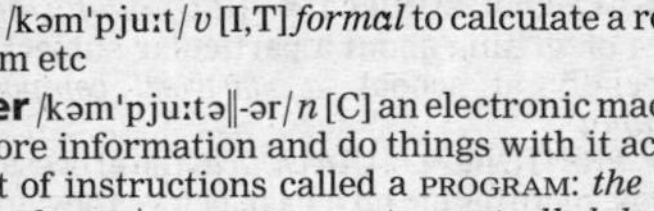

**com·pu·ta·tion** /ˌkɒmpjʊˈteɪʃən‖ˌkɑːm-/ *n* [C,U] *formal* the process of calculating or the result of calculating

**com·pute** /kəmˈpjuːt/ *v* [I,T] *formal* to calculate a result, answer, sum etc

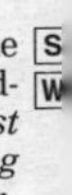

**com·put·er** /kəmˈpjuːtə‖-ər/ *n* [C] an electronic machine that can store information and do things with it according to a set of instructions called a PROGRAM: *the latest computer software*|*a new computer-controlled heating system*|*The doctor has all the patient's details on computer.*| **computer system/analysis/applications/networks etc** *We've just had a new computer system installed at work.*| **computer literacy** (=basic knowledge of and ability to use computers)| **computer literate** (=able to use a computer) —see also MICROCOMPUTER, MINICOMPUTER, PERSONAL COMPUTER, LAPTOP

**Computer-aid·ed de·sign** /ˌ·· ·· ·ˈ·/ *n* [U] CAD

**computer dat·ing a·gency** /·ˌ·· ˈ·· ˌ···/ *n* [C] a company that uses computers to try to find suitable partners for people by matching their interests etc

**computer game** /·ˈ·· ·/ *n* [C] a game that you play on a computer

**computer graph·ics** /·ˌ·· ˈ··/ *n* [plural] the pictures and images that you see on a computer screen

**com·put·er·ize** also **-ise** *BrE* /kəmˈpjuːtəraɪz/ *v* [T] to use a computer to control an operation, system etc: *They have decided to computerize the accounts department.*| *Our local supermarket now has a fully computerized checkout system.* —**computerization** /kəmˌpjuːtəraɪˈzeɪʃən‖-rə-/ *n* [U]

**computer mod·el·ling** /·ˌ·· ˈ···/ *n* [U] the representation of a problem, situation, or real object in a form in which you can see it from all angles on a computer: *computer modelling of the city's traffic flow*

**computer pro·gram** /·ˌ·· ˈ··/ *n* [C] a list of instructions that you need to give to a computer in order to make it do a particular thing —**computer programmer** *n* [C]

**computer sci·ence** /·ˌ·· ˈ··/ *n* [U] the study of computers and what they can do: *a BSc in Computer Science*

**computer vi·rus** /·ˌ·· ˈ··/ *n* [C] a VIRUS (3)

**com·put·ing** /kəmˈpjuːtɪŋ/ *n* [U] the use of computers as a job or in business etc: *Have you ever done any computing?*

**com·rade** /ˈkɒmrɪd, -reɪd‖ˈkɑːmræd/ *n* [C] **1** *formal* a friend, especially someone who shares difficult work or danger: *He misses his comrades from his days in the Army.* **2** someone who is a fellow member of a union, political party etc at the same time as you are, used especially of people in Communist groups: *Comrades, please support this motion.* —**comradely** *adj*

**comrade in arms** /ˌ·· · ˈ·/ *n* [C] someone who has worked, fought with you or worked with you to achieve particular aims

**com·rade·ship** /ˈkɒmrɪdʃɪp, -reɪd-‖ˈkɑːmræd-/ *n* [U] *formal* friendship and loyalty among people who work together, fight together etc: *It was the spirit of comradeship that made victory possible.*

**Con** the written abbreviation of CONSERVATIVE or conservative party

**con-** /kən, kɒn‖kən, kɑːn/ *prefix* together; with: *a confederation*|*to conspire* (=plan together)

**con¹** /kɒn‖kɑːn/ *v* **conned, conning** [T] *informal* **1** to get money from someone by deceiving them: **con sb out of** *He conned me out of £5!* **2** to persuade someone to do something by deceiving them: **con sb into doing sth** *We were conned into signing the contract.*

**con²** *n* [C] **1** a method or process of getting money from someone, especially by pretending to be someone else: *There are hardly any chocolates in this box at all – what a con!* —see also MOD CONS, **the pros and cons** (PRO¹ (3)) **2** *slang* a prisoner

**con-artist** /ˈ· ˌ··/ *n* [C] *informal* someone who tricks or deceives people in order to get money from them

**con·cat·e·nation** /kɒnˌkætɪ̯ˈneɪʃən‖kɑːn-/ *n* [C,U] *formal* a series of events or things joined together one after another: *a strange concatenation of events*

**con·cave** /ˌkɒnˈkeɪv◂, kən-‖ˌkɑːnˈkeɪv◂, kən-/ *adj* a concave surface is curved inwards in the middle —opposite CONVEX

**con·cav·i·ty** /kənˈkævɪ̯ti/ *n formal* **1** [U] the state of being concave **2** [C] a place or shape that is curved inwards

**con·ceal** /kənˈsiːl/ *v* [T] *formal* **1** to hide something carefully: *Customs officers found the cannabis concealed inside the case.*|*The path was concealed by long grass.* **2** to hide your real feelings or the truth: **conceal sth from sb** *Don't try to conceal anyting from me.* —**concealment** *n* [U]

**con·cede** /kənˈsiːd/ *v*

**1** ▶ **ADMIT STH IS TRUE** ◀ [T] to admit that something is true or correct although you wish it was not true: *"You could be right I suppose", Sheila conceded.*| **concede (that)** *I concede that he's a good runner, but I still think I can beat him.*

**2** ▶ **ADMIT DEFEAT** ◀ [I,T] to admit that you are not going to win a battle, argument, or game because you are not strong enough or good enough to win: *The army conceded and the enemy claimed victory.*| **concede defeat** *Matthew kept on arguing, unwilling to concede defeat.*

**3 concede a goal/point etc** to not be able to stop your opponent from getting a goal, point etc during a game: *Manchester United were unlucky to concede a goal before half-time.*

**4** ▶ **GIVE STH AS A RIGHT** ◀ [T] to give something to someone as a right or PRIVILEGE (1): **concede sth to** *The richer nations will never concede equal status to the poorer countries.*

**5** ▶ **GIVE STH UNWILLINGLY** ◀ [T] to give something to someone unwillingly after trying to keep it: **concede sth to** *After the First World War Germany conceded a lot of land to her neighbours.* —see also CONCESSION

**con·ceit** /kənˈsiːt/ *n* **1** [U] an attitude that shows you have too high an opinion of your own abilities or importance; CONCEITEDNESS: *The conceit of the woman – it's unbelievable!* **2** [C] *technical* an unusual, cleverly expressed comparison of two very different things, especially in poetry

**con·ceit·ed** /kənˈsiːtɪ̯d/ *adj* behaving in a way that shows you think you are very clever, skilful, beautiful etc: *He's a conceited little so-and-so.* —**conceitedly** *adv*: *I knew that, he said conceitedly.*

**con·cei·te·dness** /kənˈsiːtɪ̯dnɪ̯s/ *n* [U] CONCEIT

**con·cei·va·ble** /kənˈsiːvəbəl/ *adj* able to be believed or imagined: *He could talk intelligently on almost any conceivable subject.*|*What conceivable reason could they have for doing such crazy things?*| **conceiveable (that)** *It is conceivable that the peace mission will succeed.* —opposite INCONCEIVABLE —**conceivably** *adv*

**con·ceive** /kənˈsiːv/ *v* **1** [T] to think of a new idea, plan etc and develop it in your mind: *Scientists first conceived the idea of the atomic bomb in the 1930's.* **2** [T] *formal* to imagine a particular situation: **conceive what/why/how etc** *I find it difficult to conceive why the government introduced the policy in the first place.*| **conceive of sth** *I can't conceive of any reason why we can't come.*| **conceive of doing sth** *I would never conceive of treating someone the way Helen treats John.* **3** [I,T] to become PREGNANT: *fertility treatment for women who have difficulty conceiving*

2 2 **con·cen·trate¹** /ˈkɒnsəntreɪt‖ˈkɑːn-/ *v* **1** [I] to think very carefully about something that you are doing: *Keep the noise down will you – I'm trying to concentrate.*| [+ **on**] *She was too distracted to concentrate properly on her book.* **2 be concentrated on/in/around etc** to be present in particularly large numbers or amounts in a particular place: *Italian industry is concentrated mainly in the north of the country.*|*The mass of the sphere is concentrated at its center.* **3** if something concentrates the mind it makes you think very clearly: *Relaxing in a jacuzzi concentrates the mind wonderfully.* **4** [T] to make a liquid stronger by removing some of the water from it

**concentrate** sth ↔ **on** *phr v* [T] to pay particular attention to something, work particularly hard at it etc, and make that the most important thing you are doing: *Doctors are aiming to concentrate more on prevention than cure.*| **concentrate your attention/efforts/thoughts etc on** *Virgos should concentrate their efforts on work this month.*

**concentrate²** *n* [C,U] a substance or liquid which has been made stronger by removing the water from it: *orange concentrate*

**con·cen·trat·ed** /ˈkɒnsəntreɪtɪ̯d‖ˈkɑːn-/ *adj* **1** a concentrated liquid or substance is made stronger by removing water from it: *concentrated hydrochloric acid*|*concentrated orange juice* **2** [only before noun] showing determination to do something: *He made a concentrated effort to improve his work.*

**con·cen·tra·tion** /ˌkɒnsənˈtreɪʃən‖ˌkɑːn-/ *n* **1** [U] the ability to think about something carefully or for a long time: *Her work as a simultaneous translator requires strong powers of concentration.* **2** [U] a process in which you put a lot of attention, energy etc into a particular activity: [+ **on**] *Concentration on strengthening the team's defence is essential.* **3** [C,U] a large amount of something in one place or area: [+ **of**] *There is an increasing concentration of power in central government.* **4** [C] *technical* the amount of a substance contained in a liquid: *a high concentration of sulphuric acid* S3 W2

**concentration camp** /ˌ..ˈ.. ˌ./ *n* [C] a prison where large numbers of ordinary people are kept, especially during a war, and are treated extremely cruelly

**con·cen·tric** /kənˈsentrɪk/ *adj technical* having the same centre: *concentric circles* —compare ECCENTRIC¹ (2)

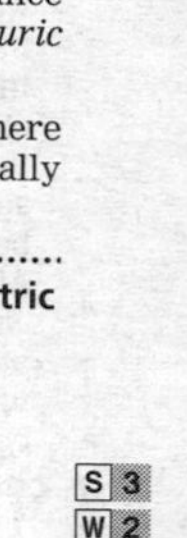


**con·cept** /ˈkɒnsept‖ˈkɑːn-/ *n* [C] someone's idea of how something is, or should be done: *a revolutionary concept in industry*| [+ **of**] *It's difficult to grasp the concept of infinite space.* S3 W2

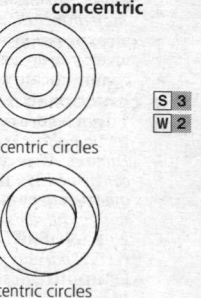

**con·cep·tion** /kənˈsepʃən/ *n* **1** [C,U] a general idea about what something is like, or a general understanding of something: [+ **of**] *He's got a really strange conception of friendship.*| **have no conception of** *You've no conception of what conditions are like.* **2** [U] a process in which someone forms a plan or idea: *The conception of the book took five minutes, but writing it took a year.* **3** [C,U] the process by which male and female sex cells join together in a woman's body and the woman becomes PREGNANT

**con·cep·tu·al** /kənˈseptʃuəl/ *adj formal* based on ideas: *the conceptual framework of the play* —**conceptually** *adv*

**conceptual art** /.ˌ... ˈ./ *n* [U] *technical* art in which the main aim of the artist is to show an idea

**con·cep·tu·al·ize** also **-ise** *BrE* /kənˈseptʃuəlaɪz/ *v* [I,T] to form an idea: *two schools of thought that conceptualize things differently*

**con·cern¹** /kənˈsɜːn‖-ɜːrn/ *n*

**1** ▶ **WORRY** ◀ **a)** [C] something that worries you: *The main concern is that the health of the employees will be at risk.* **b)** [U] a feeling of worry, especially about something such as a social problem, someone's health etc: *The recent rise in crime is a matter of considerable public concern.*| [+ **about/over**] *There is growing concern*

*about the effects of pollution on health.* | **concern for sb** *A government spokesman expressed concern for the lives of the hostages.* | **cause concern/be a cause for concern** *The depletion of the ozone layer is causing widespread concern among scientists.*

**2 be of concern (to sb)** if something is of concern to you, it is important to you and you feel worried about it: *The rise in unemployment is of great concern to the government.*

**3** [C,U] something that is important to you or that involves you: *His main concern is to be able to provide for his family.*

**4 ▶ FEELING FOR SB ◀** [singular, U] a feeling of wanting someone to be happy and healthy: [**+ for**] *parent's loving concern for their children*

**5 sb's concern** if something is your concern, you are responsible for it: *The money side of the business is your concern.*

**6 not sb's concern/none of sb's concern** if something is not your concern, you are not interested in it and you do not need to worry about it or become involved in it: *How much money I earn is none of your concern.*

**7 ▶ BUSINESS ◀** [C] a business or company: *The restaurant is a family concern.* | **a going concern** (=a business that is financially successful)

W3 **concern²** *v* [T] **1** if an activity, situation, rule etc concerns you, it affects you or involves you: *The tax changes will concern large corporations rather than small businesses.* **2** [not in passive] to make someone feel worried or upset: *The fact that she spends so much time on her own really concerns me.* **3** [not in passive] if a story, book, report etc concerns someone or something, it is about them: *This article concerns a man who was wrongly imprisoned.* **4 concern yourself with/about sth** to become involved in something because you are interested in it or because it worries you: *More and more people are concerning themselves with environmental problems.* **5 to whom it may concern** an expression written at the beginning of a formal letter when you do not know the name of the person you want to communicate with —see also CONCERNED

S1 W1 **con·cerned** /kənˈsɜːnd‖-ɜːr-/ *adj*

**1** [not before noun] involved in something or affected by it: *The affair is greatly regretted by everyone concerned.* | *Divorce is very painful, especially when children are concerned.* | [**+ in**] *Everyone concerned in the incident was questioned by the police.* | [**+ with**] *all the people concerned with children's education*

**2 ▶ WORRIED ◀** worried about something: *Concerned parents approached the school about the problem.* | [**+ about**] *Ross has never been particularly concerned about what other people think of him.* | [**+ for**] *Rescuers are concerned for the safety of two men trapped in the mine.* | **concerned that** *He's concerned that he won't get his money back.* —see NERVOUS (USAGE)

**3 as far as I'm concerned** *spoken* used when giving your opinion about something or saying how it affects you, especially when you do not care what other people think: *As far as I'm concerned the whole idea is crazy.*

**4 ▶ BE IMPORTANT TO ◀** [never before noun] believing that something is important: [**+ with**] *Congressmen seem to be far more concerned with getting elected than with passing legislation.* | **be concerned to do sth** *We are concerned to sort this out as quickly as possible.*

**5 where/as far as sth is concerned** *spoken* used when saying what particular thing you are talking about: *Where money is concerned, I always try to be very careful.*

**6 ▶ LOVE/CARE ◀** caring about someone and whether they are happy and healthy: [**+ for/about**] *How can you expect me not to be concerned about my own son?*

**7 be concerned with** if a book, story etc is concerned with a person, subject etc it is about that subject: *This story is concerned with a Russian family in the 19th century.* —**concernedly** /kənˈsɜːnɪ̆dli‖-ɜːr-/ *adv*

W3 **con·cern·ing** /kənˈsɜːnɪŋ‖-ɜːr-/ *prep formal* a word meaning 'about', used to show you are talking or writing about a particular thing or person: *Police are anxious to hear any information concerning his whereabouts.*

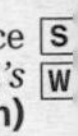

**con·cert** /ˈkɒnsət‖ˈkɑːnsərt/ *n* [C] **1** a performance given by musicians: *We went to a concert of Vivaldi's 'Four Seasons'.* | *a pop concert* **2 in concert (with)** *formal* **a)** people who do something in concert do it together after having agreed on it: *The various governments decided to act in concert over this matter.* **b)** playing or singing at a concert: *Michael Jackson in concert at the Palladium*

**con·cert·ed** /kənˈsɜːtɪ̆d‖-ɜːr-/ *adj* **concerted effort/attempt/action etc** a concerted effort etc is done by people working together in a carefully planned and very determined way: *a concerted campaign to raise public awareness of environmental issues* —**concertedly** *adv*

**con·cert·go·er** /ˈkɒnsətˌgəʊə‖ˈkɑːnsərtˌgoʊər/ *n* [C] someone who often goes to concerts

**concert hall** /ˈ·· ·/ *n* [C] a large public building where concerts are performed

**con·cer·ti·na¹** /ˌkɒnsəˈtiːnə‖ˌkɑːnsər-/ *n* [C] a small musical instrument like an ACCORDION that you hold in your hands and play by pressing in from each side

**concertina²** *v past and past participle* **concertinaed** [I] *BrE* if something concertinas, it folds together upon itself: *The bonnet of the car had concertinaed as a result of the crash.*

**con·cert·mas·ter** /ˈkɒnsətˌmɑːstə‖ˈkɑːnsərtˌmæstər/ *n* [C] *AmE* the most important VIOLIN player in an ORCHESTRA

**con·cer·to** /kənˈtʃɜːtəʊ‖-ˈtʃertoʊ/ *n plural* **concertos** [C] a piece of music for one or more SOLO¹ (2) instruments and an ORCHESTRA

**con·ces·sion** /kənˈseʃən/ *n*

**1 ▶ STH YOU ALLOW SB ◀** [C] something that you allow someone to have in order to end an argument or a disagreement: **make a concession** *We will never make any concessions to terrorists.* —see also CONCEDE

**2 ▶ A RIGHT ◀** [C] a special right that a particular person or group of people is allowed to have, for example by the government or an employer: *tax concessions* | *Greyhound Inc won the concession of running hotels in Glacier Park.*

**3 ▶ PRICE REDUCTION ◀** [C] *BrE* a reduction in the price of tickets, FARES etc for certain groups of people, for example old people or children

**4 concessions** [plural] *AmE* the things sold at a concession stand

**5 ▶ ACT OF ALLOWING ◀** [U] *formal* the act of giving or allowing something as a right

**6 ▶ RIGHT TO SELL STH ◀** [C] *AmE* the right to sell something within the building of a larger business, or the area you are allowed to sell something in: *a hamburger concession in the mall*

**con·ces·sion·aire** /kənˌseʃəˈneə‖-ˈner/ *n* [C] *informal* someone who has been given a CONCESSION (2), especially to run a business

**con·ces·sion·ar·y** /kənˈseʃənəri‖-neri/ *adj* **1** given as a concession **2** *BrE* specially reduced in price, for example for old people or children: *Local authorities have the power to set up concessionary fare schemes.*

**concession stand** /·ˈ·· ·/ *n* [C] *AmE* a small business that sells food, drinks or SOUVENIRS at sporting events, places that tourists visit and some theatres

**con·ces·sive clause** /kənˌsesɪv ˈklɔːz‖-ˈklɒːz/ *n* [C] *technical* a CLAUSE (2), often introduced by 'although,' that introduces a fact or idea that seems to be the opposite of the main fact or idea. For example, the sentence 'Although it's old, it works well,' begins with a concessive clause.

**conch** /kɒntʃ, kɒŋk‖kɑːntʃ, kɑːŋk/ *n* [C] the large twisted shell of a tropical sea animal that looks like a SNAIL

**con·chie** /ˈkɒntʃi‖ˈkɑːn-/ *n* [C] *BrE old-fashioned informal* an insulting word for a CONSCIENTIOUS OBJECTOR

**con·ci·erge** /ˌkɒnsiˈeəʒ‖ˌkɑːnsiˈerʒ/ *n* [C] *French* **1** someone who looks after a building, usually by watching the entrance to see who comes in and goes out, especially in France **2** *especially AmE* someone whose job in a hotel is helping guests, for example by giving them advice about local restaurants etc

**con·cil·i·ate** /kənˈsɪlieɪt/ *v* [T] *formal* to do something to make people more likely to stop arguing, especially by giving them something they want: *Negotiators were called in to conciliate between the warring factions.* —**conciliator** *n* [C]

**con·cil·i·a·tion** /kənˌsɪliˈeɪʃən/ *n* [U] the process of trying to get people to agree: *peaceful negotiation attempts at conciliation through compromise*

**con·cil·i·a·tory** /kənˈsɪliətərili‖-tɔːri/ *adj* doing something that is intended to make someone stop arguing with you: **conciliatory gesture/message/tone etc** *We'd like to offer you free theater tickets as a conciliatory gesture.*

**con·cise** /kənˈsaɪs/ *adj* short and clear, with no unnecessary words: *a concise explanation* —**concisely** *adv* —**conciseness** also **concision** /kənˈsɪʒən/ *formal n* [U]

**con·clave** /ˈkɒŋkleɪv‖ˈkɑːŋ-/ *n* [C] a private and secret meeting: *A conclave of cardinals was held to elect a new pope.*

3 **con·clude** /kənˈkluːd/ *v* [T] **1** to decide that something
2 is true after considering all the information you have: **conclude that** *The enquiry concluded that the accident had been caused by human error.* | **conclude from sth that** *Davis concludes from an analysis of traffic accidents that the speed limit should be lowered.* **2** [T] to complete something you have been doing, especially for a long time: **conclude your work/investigation/research etc** *I will be publishing my results only when I have concluded my research.* **3** [I always + adv/prep, T] to end something such as a meeting or speech by doing or saying one final thing: [+ **with/on/as/by etc**] *The session usually concludes with an informal discussion.* | **conclude sth** *We were finally able to conclude the meeting and go home.* | **conclude sth with/by etc** *The service was concluded with a hymn.* **4 conclude an agreement/treaty/contract etc** to finish arranging an agreement etc successfully: *After months of negotiations they concluded the sale.*

**con·clu·ding** /kənˈkluːdɪŋ/ *adj* **concluding sentence/remark/stages etc** the last sentence, stage etc in an event or piece of writing: *He makes his position perfectly clear in the concluding paragraph.*

2 **con·clu·sion** /kənˈkluːʒən/ *n* **1** [C] something you
2 decide after considering all the information you have: *These are the report's main conclusions.* | [+ **that**] *Becky came to the conclusion that he must have forgotten.* | **lead to/point to/support the conclusion (that)** *All the evidence pointed to the conclusion that he was guilty.* | **draw a conclusion** *From these facts we can draw some conclusions about how the pyramids were built.* | **jump to conclusions** (=decide that something is true too quickly, without knowing all the facts) *Don't jump to conclusions – just because they're late doesn't mean they've had an accident!* **2** [C] the end or final part of something: *I found the conclusion of his book very interesting.* **3 in conclusion** used in a piece of writing or a speech to show that you are about to finish what you are saying: *In conclusion, I would like to say how much I have enjoyed myself today.* **4** [U] the final arrangement of something such as a business deal: [+ **of**] *The conclusion of a peace treaty.* **5 be a foregone conclusion** to be certain to happen even though it has not yet officially happened: *The outcome of the battle was a foregone conclusion.*

**con·clu·sive** /kənˈkluːsɪv/ *adj* something that is conclusive is certainly true, so there is no doubt or uncertainty: **conclusive proof/evidence/findings etc** *The investigation failed to provide any conclusive evidence.* —opposite INCONCLUSIVE —**conclusively** *adv*

**con·coct** /kənˈkɒkt‖-ˈkɑːkt/ *v* [T] **1** to invent a clever story, excuse, or plan, especially in order to deceive someone: *John concocted an elaborate excuse for being late.* **2** to make something, especially food or drink, by mixing different things, especially things that are not usually combined: *Jean concocted a great meal from the leftovers.*

**con·coc·tion** /kənˈkɒkʃən‖-ˈkɑːk-/ *n* [C] something, especially a drink, made by mixing different things, especially things that are not usually combined: *She offered him a green concoction with fruit floating in it.*

**con·com·i·tant**[1] /kənˈkɒmɪtənt‖-ˈkɑː-/ *adj formal* existing or happening together, especially as a result of something: *war with all its concomitant sufferings.* —**concomitantly** *adv*

**concomitant**[2] *n* [C] *formal* something that often or naturally happens with something else [+ *of*]: *Deafness is a frequent concomitant of old age.*

**con·cord** /ˈkɒŋkɔːd‖ˈkɑːŋkɔːrd/ *n* [U] **1** *formal* the state of having a friendly relationship, so that you agree on things and live in peace **2** *technical* in grammar, concord between words happens when they match correctly, for example when a plural noun has a plural verb following it

**con·cor·dance** /kənˈkɔːdəns‖-ɔːr-/ *n* **1** [U] the state of being similar to something else or in agreement with it: *the concordance between the proposals* **2** [C] *technical* an alphabetical list of all the words used in a book or set of books by one writer, with information about where they can be found and usually about how they are used: *a Shakespeare concordance* | *computerized concordances*

**con·cor·dant** /kənˈkɔːdənt‖-ɔːr-/ *adj formal* being in agreement or having the same regular pattern

**con·course** /ˈkɒŋkɔːs‖ˈkɑːŋkɔːrs/ *n* [C] **1** a large hall in a building such as an airport or train station where crowds of people can gather **2** a large crowd that has gathered together: *a large concourse of people.*

**con·crete**[1] /ˈkɒŋkriːt‖kɑːnˈkriːt/ *adj* **1** made of con- S3
crete: *a concrete floor* **2** clearly based on fact, rather than on beliefs or guesses: *concrete information about the identity of the murderer* —compare ABSTRACT[1] (2) **3** definite and specific rather than general: *Have you got any concrete proposals as to what we should do?* —**concretely** *adv*

**con·crete**[2] /ˈkɒŋkriːt‖ˈkɑːŋ-/ *n* [U] a substance used for building that is made by mixing sand, very small stones, cement, and water

**con·crete**[3] /ˈkɒŋkriːt‖ˈkɑːŋ-/ *v* [T] to cover something such as a path, wall etc with concrete

**concrete jun·gle** /ˌ·· ˈ··/ *n* [C usually singular] an unpleasant area in a city that is full of big ugly buildings and has no open spaces

**concrete mix·er** /ˈ·· ˌ··/ *n* [C] a CEMENT MIXER

**con·cu·bi·nage** /kɒnˈkjuːbɪnɪdʒ‖kɑːn-/ *n* [U] *formal* the system or practice of living together as man and wife without being married

**con·cu·bine** /ˈkɒŋkjʊbaɪn‖ˈkɑːŋ-/ *n* [C] a woman who lives with and has sex with a man who already has a wife or wives, but who is socially less important

**con·cur** /kənˈkɜː‖-ˈkɜːr/ *v* **concurred, concurring** [I] *formal* **1** to agree with someone or have the same opinion as them: [+ **with**] *The judge stated that he concurred with the ruling.* **2** to happen at the same time; COINCIDE (1) **concur to do sth** *Everything concurred to produce the desired effect.*

**con·cur·rence** /kənˈkʌrəns‖-ˈkɜːr-/ *n formal* **1** [U] agreement: [+ **with**] *Jules expressed his concurrence with the suggestion.* **2** [C] an example of events, actions etc happening at the same time: [+ **of**] *a strange concurrence of events*

**con·cur·rent** /kənˈkʌrənt‖-ˈkɜːr-/ *adj* **1** existing or happening at the same time: *He is serving two concurrent prison sentences.* **2** *formal* in agreement: [+ **with**] *My opinions are concurrent with yours.* —**concurrently** *adv*: *two prison sentences to run concurrently*

**con·cuss** /kənˈkʌs/ *v* [T often passive] if something hits your head and concusses you, it makes you lose consciousness or feel sick for a short time because you brain is temporarily damaged: *The driver of the car was badly concussed.*

**con·cus·sion** /kən'kʌʃən/ *n* [U] a small amount of damage to the brain that makes you lose consciousness or feel sick for a short time, usually caused by something hitting your head

**con·demn** /kən'dem/ *v* [T]
**1 ▶ DISAPPROVE ◀** to say very strongly that you do not approve of something or someone, especially because you think it is morally wrong: *Politicians were quick to condemn the bombing.* | **condemn sth/sb as** *The law has been condemned as an attack on personal liberty.* | **condemn sb/sth for doing sth** *She knew that society would condemn her for leaving her children.*
**2 ▶ PUNISH ◀** to give someone a severe punishment after deciding they are guilty of a crime: **condemn sb to death** *The prisoner was condemned to death.*
**3 ▶ FORCE TO DO STH ◀** if a particular situation condemns someone to something, it forces them to live in an unpleasant way or to do something unpleasant: **condemn sb to sth** *people condemned to a life of poverty* | **condemn sb to do sth** *A significant proportion of such children are condemned to fail.*
**4 ▶ BUILDING ◀** to state officially that a building is not safe enough to be used: *an old house that had been condemned*
**5 ▶ SHOW GUILT ◀** if the way you look or behave condemns you, it shows that you are guilty of something: *His nervousness condemned him.*

**con·dem·na·tion** /ˌkɒndəm'neɪʃən, -dem-‖ˌkɑːn-/ *n* [C,U] an expression of very strong disapproval of someone or something: **[+ of]** *Condemnation of the latest violence came from all political parties.*

**con·dem·na·to·ry** /kən'demnətəri, ˌkɒndem'neɪtəri‖kən'demnətɔːri/ *adj* expressing strong disapproval

**con·demned** /kən'demd/ *adj* someone who is condemned is going to be punished by being killed

**condemned cell** /·ˌ· '·, ·'· ·/ *n* [C] *BrE* a room for a prisoner who was going to be punished by death

**con·den·sa·tion** /ˌkɒnden'seɪʃən, -dən-‖ˌkɑːn-/ *n*
**1** [U] small drops of water that are formed when gas changes to liquid: *There was a lot of condensation on the windows.* **2** [U] *technical* the process of change from gas to liquid: *the condensation of steam into water* **3** [C,U] *formal* the act of making something shorter: *the condensation of his report*

**con·dense** /kən'dens/ *v* **1** [I,T] if gas condenses or is condensed, it becomes a liquid as it becomes cooler: *Steam condensed on the bathroom mirror.* | **[+ into]** *The gaseous metal is cooled and condenses into liquid zinc.* **2** [T] to make a liquid thicker by removing some of the water: *condensed soup* **3** [T] to make something that is spoken or written shorter, by not giving as much detail or using fewer words to give the same information: **condense sth into sth** *This whole chapter could be condensed into a few paragraphs.*

**condensed milk** /·ˌ· '·/ *n* [U] a type of thick sweet milk sold in cans —compare EVAPORATED MILK

**con·dens·er** /kən'densə‖-ər/ *n* [C] **1** a piece of equipment that makes a gas change into liquid **2** a machine for storing electricity, especially in a car engine

**con·de·scend** /ˌkɒndɪ'send‖ˌkɑːn-/ *v* [I] **1** to behave as if you think you are better or more important than other people: *She'd be a better teacher if she didn't condescend to her students.* **2** to do something in a way that shows you think it is below your social or professional position: **condescend to do sth** *The managing director condescended to have lunch with us in the canteen.* —**condescension** /-'senʃən/ *n* [U]

**con·de·scend·ing** /ˌkɒndɪ'sendɪŋ◂‖ˌkɑːn-/ *adj* behaving as though you think you are better or more important than other people: *Professor Hutter's manner is extremely condescending.* —**condescendingly** *adv*

**con·di·ment** /'kɒndɪmənt‖'kɑːn-/ *n* [C] *formal* a powder or liquid, such as salt or KETCHUP that you use to give special taste to food

**con·di·tion¹** /kən'dɪʃən/ *n* S W
**1 ▶ STATE ◀** [singular] the state that something is in: **[+ in]** *What sort of condition is your new house in?* | **[+ of]** *The garden was in a condition of total neglect.* | **be in good/bad/perfect/awful etc condition** *The car has been well maintained and is in excellent condition.* | **in that condition** *spoken* (=in a bad state) *You can't wear a jacket in that condition!*
**2 a) conditions** [plural] the situation in which people live or work, especially the physical things such as pay or food that affect the quality of their lives: **working/driving/living etc conditions** *Poor working conditions lead to demoralized and unproductive employees.* | **under excellent/terrible etc conditions** *The people are living in makeshift tents under the most appalling conditions.* **b)** the weather at a particular time, especially when you are considering how this will affect you: *Police are advising people to stay at home until weather conditions improve.* | **freezing/stormy/icy conditions** *Blizzard conditions are making the roads extremely hazardous.* **c)** all the things that affect the way something happens: *The experiment must be done under laboratory conditions.*
**3 ▶ AGREEMENT/CONTRACT ◀** [C] something that is stated in a contract or agreement that must be done: *Have you read the conditions of employment carefully?* | **[+ for]** *There were strict conditions for letting us use their information.* | **lay down/impose conditions** (=state what must be done) *The allies laid down several conditions for their continued support.* | **meet/satisfy a condition** (=obey what is demanded by a condition) *The bank agreeed to extend the loan if certain conditions were met.* | **under the conditions of sth** *Under the conditions of the agreement the work must be completed by the end of the month.* | **on condition that/on one condition** (=only if a particular thing happens) *Ron lent me the money on condition that I pay it back next month.*
**4 ▶ STH THAT MUST BE DONE ◀** [C] something that must happen first before something else can happen: **[+ for/of]** *Finance ministers claimed that all the conditions for an economic revival were in place.*
**5 ▶ AN ILLNESS ◀** [C] an illness or health problem that affects you permanently or for a very long time: *People suffering from this condition should not smoke.* | **a heart/lung etc condition** *She has a serious heart condition.*
**6 ▶ STATE OF HEALTH ◀** [U, singular] a person or animal's state of health: *The hospital described his condition as 'satisfactory'.* | **out of condition** (=unhealthy or unfit) *The horse is still out of condition after a serious illness.* | **in no condition to do sth** (=too ill, drunk, or upset to be able to do something) *After a whole bottle of wine he was in no condition to drive.*
**7 on no condition** never, in no possible situation: *This equipment should on no condition be used by untrained staff.*
**8 ▶ SITUATION OF GROUP ◀** [singular] the situation or state of a particular group of people: *Few people can really appreciate the condition of the poor in our cities.*

**condition²** *v* [T] **1** to make a person or an animal think or behave in a certain way by influencing or training them over a period of time: *People are conditioned by the society and age they live in.* | **condition sb to do sth** *The animals were conditioned to expect food at the sound of the bell.* —see also CONDITIONING **2** *formal* to control or decide the way in which something can happen or exist: *What I buy is conditioned by the amount I earn.* **3** to keep hair or skin healthy by putting a special liquid on it: *This shampoo conditions your hair as well as washing it.* —see also CONDITIONER

**con·di·tion·al¹** /kən'dɪʃənəl/ *adj* **1** if an offer, agreement etc is conditional, it will only be done if something else happens: **be conditional on/upon** *a conditional acceptance* | *His agreement to buy our house was con-*

*ditional on our leaving all the furniture in it.* —opposite UNCONDITIONAL **2** in grammar, a conditional sentence is one that begins with 'if' or 'unless' and expresses something that must be true or happens before something else can be true or happen —**conditionally** *adv*

**conditional**[2] *n* [C] a sentence or CLAUSE (2) that is expressed in a conditional form

**conditional dis·charge** /·,··· '··/ *n* [C usually singular] a judgment made by a court that allows someone who has done something illegal not to be punished as long as they obey rules set by the court

**con·di·tion·er** /kən'dɪʃənə‖-ər/ *n* [C,U] **1** a liquid that you put onto your hair after washing it to make it softer **2** a liquid that you wash clothes in to make them softer

**con·di·tion·ing** /kən'dɪʃənɪŋ/ *n* [U] the process by which people or animals are trained to behave in a particular way when particular things happen: *Most adults are unaware of the social conditioning they have been subject to since childhood.* —see also AIR CONDITIONING

**con·do** /'kɒndəʊ‖'kɑːndoʊ/ *n* [C] *AmE informal* a CONDOMINIUM

**con·dole** /kən'dəʊl‖-'doʊl/ *v*

**condole with** sb *phr v* [T] *formal* to express sympathy for someone's problems

**con·do·lence** /kən'dəʊləns‖-'doʊ-/ *n* [C usually plural, U] sympathy for someone who has had something bad happen to them, especially when someone has died: *a letter of condolence* | **send/offer your condolences** (=formally express your sympathy when someone has died) *I'd like to offer my condolences to the victim's parents.* —compare COMMISERATION

**con·dom** /'kɒndəm‖'kɑːn-, 'kʌn-/ *n* [C] a thin rubber bag that a man wears over his PENIS (=sex organ) during sex, to prevent a woman having a baby, or to protect against disease

**con·do·min·i·um** /,kɒndə'mɪniəm‖,kɑːn-/ *n* [C] **1** *especially AmE* one apartment in a building with several apartments, each of which is owned by the people living in it **2** a building containing several of these apartments

**con·done** /kən'dəʊn‖-'doʊn/ *v* [T] to accept or forgive behaviour that most people think is morally wrong: *I cannot condone the use of violence under any circumstances.*

**con·dor** /'kɒndɔː‖'kɑːndər, -dɔːr/ *n* [C] a very large South American VULTURE (=a bird that eats dead animals)

**con·duce** /kən'djuːs‖-'duːs/ *v*

**conduce to/towards** sth *phr v* [T] *formal* to help to produce a particular quality or state

**con·du·cive** /kən'djuːsɪv‖-'duː-/ *adj* **be conducive to** *formal* if a situation is conducive to something such as work, rest etc, it provides conditions that make it easy for you to work etc: *With so much noise outside, the room is hardly conducive to work.*

3 **con·duct**[1] /kən'dʌkt/ *v*

2 **1 conduct a survey/experiment/inquiry etc** to carry out a particular process, especially in order to get information or prove facts: *The company conducted a survey to find out local reaction to the leisure centre.*

**2 ▶MUSIC◀** [I,T] to stand in front of a group of musicians and direct their playing: *The orchestra is conducted by John Williams.*

**3 ▶ELECTRICITY/HEAT◀** [T] if something conducts electricity or heat, it allows the electricity or heat to travel along or through it: *Plastic and rubber won't conduct electricity, but copper will.*

**4 ▶SHOW SB STH◀** [T always + adv prep] to show someone a building or place by leading them around it: *The guide conducted us round the castle.*

**5 conduct yourself** *formal* to behave in a particular way, especially in a situation where people judge you by the way you behave: *Public figures have a duty to conduct themselves responsibly.*

3 **con·duct**[2] /'kɒndʌkt‖'kɑːn-/ *n* [U] *formal* **1** the way someone behaves, especially in public, in their job etc: *The reporter was accused of unprofessional conduct.* **2** the way a business, activity etc is organized: *There was great dissatisfaction with the conduct of the negotiations.*

**con·duc·tion** /kən'dʌkʃən/ *n* [U] the passage of electricity through wires, heat through metal, water through pipes etc

**con·duc·tive** /kən'dʌktɪv/ *adj technical* able to conduct electricity, heat etc: *Copper is a very conductive metal.* —**conductivity** /,kɒndʌk'tɪvɪ̈ti‖,kɑːn-/ *n* [U]

**con·duc·tor** /kən'dʌktə‖-ər/ *n* [C] **1** someone who stands in front of a group of musicians or singers and directs their playing or singing **2** someone whose job is to collect payments from passengers on a bus or train **3** something that allows electricity or heat to travel along it or through it: *Wood is a poor conductor of heat.* **4** *AmE* someone who is in charge of a train or the workers on a train

**con·duc·tress** /kən'dʌktrɪ̈s/ *n* [C] *old-fashioned* a female conductor

**con·duit** /'kɒndɪt, 'kɒndjuɪ̈t‖'kɑːnduɪ̈t/ *n* [C] **1** a pipe or passage through which water, gas, a set of electric wires etc pass **2** a connection between two things that allows people to pass ideas, news, money, weapons, drugs etc from one place to another: *The countries have been a conduit for the arms supplied to the terrorists.*

**cone**[1] /kəʊn‖koʊn/ *n* [C] **1** a solid or hollow shape with a round base, sloping sides, and a point at the top, or something with this shape **2** an object shaped like a large cone that is put on a road to prevent cars from going somewhere or to warn drivers about something **3** the fruit of a PINE[1] (1) or FIR tree —see also CONIFER **4** a piece of thin, cooked cake, shaped like a cone, that you put ICE CREAM (2) in; CORNET (2) *BrE*

**cone**[2] *v*

**cone** sth ↔ **off** *phr v* [T] to close a road or part of a road by putting a row of cones across it or along it

**co·ney** /'kəʊni‖'koʊ-/ *n* [C] another spelling of CONY

**con·fab** /'kɒnfæb‖'kɑːn-/ *n* [C] *informal* a conversation that is private and friendly: *We'll have a quick confab to talk about what he wants.*

**con·fab·u·late** /kən'fæbjɪ̈leɪt/ *v* [I] *formal* to talk together

**con·fab·u·la·tion** /kən,fæbjɪ̈'leɪʃən/ *n* [C] *formal* a private conversation

**con·fec·tion** /kən'fekʃən/ *n* [C] *formal* a beautifully prepared sweet food

**con·fec·tion·er** /kən'fekʃənə‖-ər/ *n* [C] someone who makes or sells sweets, cakes etc

**confectioner's sug·ar** /·'··· ,··/ *n* [U] *AmE* a kind of sugar that is very powdery; ICING SUGAR *BrE*

**con·fec·tion·e·ry** /kən'fekʃənəri/ *n* **1** [U] sweets, cakes etc **2** [C] a shop that sells sweets, cakes etc

**con·fed·e·ra·cy** /kən'fedərəsi/ *n* [C] a union of people, parties, or states, especially for political purposes or trade

**con·fed·e·rate**[1] /kən'fedərɪ̈t/ *n* [C] **1** someone who helps someone else do something, especially something secret or illegal: *It was important that they didn't think he was John's confederate in the robbery.* **2** a member of a confederacy

**confederate**[2], **Confederate** *adj* belonging to a confederacy or the Confederacy: *The Confederate Army.*

**con·fed·e·rate**[3] /kən'fedəreɪt/ *v* [I,T] to combine or to combine something in a confederacy: [+ **with**] *In 1949 Newfoundland was confederated with Canada through a referendum.*

**con·fed·e·ra·tion** /kən,fedə'reɪʃən/ *n* [C] a confederacy

**con·fer** /kən'fɜː‖-'fɜːr/ *v* **conferred, conferring** *formal* **1** [I] to discuss something with other people, so that everyone can express their opinions and decide on something: [+ **with**] *The congresswoman is conferring with her advisors on the matter.* **2 confer a title/degree/honour etc** [T] to officially give someone a title etc, especially as a reward for something they have achieved: [+ **on/upon**] *An honorary degree was conferred on him by the University.* —**conferment** *n* [C,U]

S3 W1 **con·fe·rence** /ˈkɒnfərəns‖ˈkɑːn-/ *n* [C] **1** a large formal meeting where a lot of people discuss important matters such as business or politics, especially for several days: [+ **on**] *a scientific conference on the ozone layer* | **hold a conference** (=have a conference) | **attend a conference** (=go to a conference) *Representatives from over 100 countries attended the International Peace Conference in Geneva.* | **conference centre/table/room** (=a building, table etc used for conferences) *The university has a conference center in the mountains.* —see also PRESS CONFERENCE **2** a private meeting for a few people to have formal discussions: [+ **with**] *After a brief conference with his aides, he left for the airport.* | **have/hold a conference** *Everyone go and rest, and we'll have a conference about our next move later.* | **in conference** *The manager cannot see you now; she's in conference.* **3** *AmE* a group of teams that play against each other; LEAGUE[1] (1): *College football has two main conferences, the Pac Ten and the Big Ten.*

C

**conference call** /ˈ··· ˌ·/ *n* [C] a telephone call in which several people in different places can all talk to each other

**con·fess** /kənˈfes/ *v* [I,T] **1** to admit that you have done something wrong or illegal, especially to the police: *After three hours of questioning the suspect broke down and confessed.* | **confess to doing sth** *Edwards confessed to being a spy for the KGB.* | **confess that** *She confessed that she killed her husband.* | **confess to murder/a crime/robbery etc** *Occasionally people confess to crimes they haven't committed just to get attention.* **2** to admit something that you feel embarrassed about: **confess that** *Marsha confessed that she didn't really know how to work the computer.* | **confess to doing sth** *He confessed to having a secret admiration for his opponent.* | **confess yourself puzzled/baffled etc** *The police have confessed themselves baffled by this strange and savage crime.* | **I (must) confess** *spoken* (=used when admitting something you feel slightly embarrassed about) *I must confess I don't visit my parents as often as I should.* **3** to tell a priest or God about the wrong things you have done so that you can be forgiven

**con·fessed** /kənˈfest/ *adj* [only before noun] having admitted publicly that you have done something: *a confessed criminal* —see also SELF-CONFESSED —**confessedly** /-ˈfesɪ̈dli/ *adv*

**con·fes·sion** /kənˈfeʃən/ *n* **1** [C] a formal statement that you have done something wrong or illegal: *The police officer wrote down every word of Smith's confession.* | [+ **of**] *a confession of failure* | **make a confession** *At 3 a.m. Higgins broke down and made a full confession.* **2** [C,U] a private statement to a priest about the bad things that you have done **3** [C] *formal* a statement of what your religious beliefs are: *a confession of faith*

**con·fes·sion·al**[1] /kənˈfeʃənəl/ *n* [C] a place in a church, usually an enclosed room, where a priest hears people make their confessions

**confessional**[2] *adj* confessional speech or writing contains private thoughts or facts that you normally want to keep secret, especially private information about things you have done that were wrong

**con·fes·sor** /kənˈfesə‖-ər/ *n* [C] the priest who someone regularly makes their confession to

**con·fet·ti** /kənˈfeti/ *n* [U] small pieces of coloured paper that you throw over a man and woman who have just been married, especially when they come out of church

**con·fi·dant** /ˈkɒnfɪ̈dænt, ˌkɒnfɪ̈ˈdænt, -ˈdɑːnt‖ˈkɑːnfɪ̈dænt/ *n* [C] someone you tell your secrets to or who you talk to about personal things

**con·fi·dante** /ˈkɒnfɪ̈dænt, ˌkɒnfɪ̈ˈdænt, -ˈdɑːnt‖ˈkɑːnfɪ̈dænt/ *n* [C] a female confidant

**con·fide** /kənˈfaɪd/ *v* [T] **1** to tell someone you trust about personal things that you do not want other people to know: **confide to sb that** *He confided to his friends that he didn't have much hope for his marriage.* **2** *formal* to give something you value to someone you trust so they look after it for you: **confide sth to sb** *He confided his money to his brother's safe-keeping.*

**confide in** sb *phr v* [T] to tell someone about something very private or secret, especially a personal problem, because you feel you can trust them: *It's important to have someone that you can confide in.*

**con·fi·dence** /ˈkɒnfɪ̈dəns‖ˈkɑːn-/ *n* S W 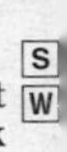
**1** ▶ **FEELING SB/STH IS GOOD** ◀ [U] the feeling that you can trust someone or something to be good, work well, or produce good results: [+ **in**] *Our first priority is to maintain the customer's confidence in our product.* | **have confidence in** *We have every confidence in your abilities.* | **win/gain/lose sb's confidence (in)** *Opinion polls show that voters have lost confidence in the administration.* | **inspire/restore/undermine confidence (in)** (=make people feel more or less confident about something or someone) *These miscarriages of justice have undermined confidence in our legal system.* | **show confidence (in)** *Middle-aged people generally do not show as much confidence in what the future holds as do the young.*
**2** ▶ **BELIEF IN YOURSELF** ◀ [U] the belief that you have the ability to do things well or deal with situations successfully: *Joyce always had an abundance of confidence. She seemed to fear no one.* | **lack confidence/be lacking in confidence** *She's a good student but she lacks confidence in herself.* | **lack of confidence** *A lack of confidence seems to be her main problem.* | **give sb confidence** *Living on her own in a foreign country for a year gave her a lot of confidence.* | **give sb the confidence to do sth** *Good training will give a beginner the confidence to enjoy skiing.* | **restore/lose confidence** *Going back to work restored my confidence and made me feel more capable.* | **boost/shake sb's confidence** (=make someone feel more or less confident) *Julie's confidence was badly shaken by her car accident.*
**3** ▶ **FEELING STH IS TRUE** ◀ [U] the feeling that something is definite or true: *How can anyone say with confidence that the recession is over?* | **have confidence that** *At that time he had little confidence that God existed.*
**4** ▶ **FEELING OF TRUST** ◀ [U] a feeling of trust in someone, so that you can tell them something and be sure they will not tell other people: **have/gain/get sb's confidence** (=make someone feel they can trust you) *It took me a long time to gain his confidence, but he trusts me now.* | **in (strict) confidence** (=if you tell someone something in confidence, you tell them in secret and they must not tell anyone else) *I'm giving you this information in the strictest confidence.* | **take sb into your confidence** (=tell someone something secret) *Tanya took Liane into her confidence about her marital problems.*
**5** ▶ **A SECRET** ◀ [C] a secret or a piece of information that is private or personal: *They spent their evenings drinking wine by the fire and sharing confidences.* —see also VOTE OF CONFIDENCE, VOTE OF NO CONFIDENCE

**confidence-build·ing** /ˈ··· ˌ··/ *adj* an event, action etc that is confidence-building increases your confidence: *The outdoor training is meant to be a confidence-building exercise for youngsters.*

**confidence trick** /ˈ··· ˌ·/ *n* [C] *formal* a dishonest trick played on someone in order to get their money; CON[2] (1) —**confidence trickster** *n* [C]

**con·fi·dent** /ˈkɒnfɪ̈dənt‖ˈkɑːn-/ *adj* **1** sure that you can do something or deal with a situation successfully: *He gave her a confident smile.* | **be confident about** *Joyce is very confident about using computers.* **2** [not before noun] very sure that something is going to happen or that you will be able to do something: **be confident (that)** *We are confident that next year's profits will be higher.* —see also SELF-CONFIDENT —**confidently** *adv* S W

**con·fi·den·tial** /ˌkɒnfɪ̈ˈdenʃəl◂‖ˌkɑːn-/ *adj* **1** spoken or written in secret and intended to be kept secret: *a confidential naval report on the failure of equipment* | **keep sth confidential** *Doctors are required to keep patients'* *records completely confidential.* | **strictly confidential** (=completely confidential) *What I'm telling you is strictly confidential.* **2** a confidential way of speaking or behaving shows that you do not want other people to know what you are saying: *His voice sank into a confidential whisper as he mentioned who was involved.* **3** a confidential secretary or CLERK[1] (1) is one who is trusted with secret information —**confidentially** *adv*

**con·fi·den·ti·al·i·ty** /ˌkɒnfɪ̈denʃiˈælɪ̈ti‖ˌkɑːn-/ *n* [U] a situation in which you trust someone not to tell secret or private information to anyone else: *The relationship between attorneys and their clients is based on confidentiality.* | **breach of confidentiality** (=an occasion when someone tells a secret) *It is a breach of confidentiality for a priest to reveal what someone has said in the confessional.*

**con·fid·ing** /kənˈfaɪdɪŋ/ *adj* behaving in a way that shows you want to tell someone about something that is private or secret: *She allowed a confiding note to enter her voice.* —**confidingly** *adv*: *She spoke gaily, innocently, and confidingly.*

**con·fig·u·ra·tion** /kənˌfɪgjʊ̈ˈreɪʃən/ *n* [C,U] **1** *formal or technical* the shape or arrangement of the parts of something; LAYOUT: [+ **of**] *the configuration of pistons in an engine* **2** *technical* the combination of equipment needed to run a computer system

**con·fig·ure** /kənˈfɪgə‖-gjər/ *v* [T] *technical* to arrange something, especially computer equipment, so that it works with other equipment

3 **con·fine** /kənˈfaɪn/ *v* [T]

**1** ▶ **LIMIT** ◀ to keep someone or something within the limits of a particular activity or subject; RESTRICT: **be confined to** *The police cadet's duties were confined to taking statements from the crowd.* | *a former editor now confined to organizing the letter page* | **confine yourself to sth** *We must confine ourselves to the subject at hand.*

**2 be confined to a)** to affect or happen to only one group of people, or in only one place or time: *This disease is not just confined to children.* **b)** to have to stay in a place, especially because you are ill: *an elderly woman confined to a small apartment* | **confined to bed** *I was confined to bed for 10 days with a nasty bout of flu.* | **confined to a wheelchair** (=unable to walk) *Although confined to a wheelchair, she is very active in church life.*

**3** ▶ **KEEP SB IN A PLACE** ◀ to keep someone in a place that they cannot leave, such as a prison: **confine sb to** *Any soldier who leaves his post will be confined to the barracks.* | **be confined in** *He was allegedly confined in a narrow, dark room for two months.*

**4** ▶ **STOP SPREADING** ◀ to stop something bad from spreading to another place: **confine sth to sth** *Firefighters quickly confined the blaze to the factory floor.*

**5** ▶ **STAY IN BED** ◀ [usually passive] to make someone stay in bed because they are ill: *I had flu and was confined to bed.*

**con·fined** /kənˈfaɪnd/ *adj* a confined space or area is one that is very small: *It wasn't easy to sleep in such a confined space.*

**con·fine·ment** /kənˈfaɪnmənt/ *n* **1** [U] the act of putting someone in a room, prison etc, or the state of being there: *her years of confinement* | *They were held in confinement for three weeks.* —see also SOLITARY CONFINEMENT **2** [C,U] an act of giving birth to a child; LYING-IN

**con·fines** /ˈkɒnfaɪnz‖ˈkɑːn-/ *n* [plural] limits or borders: **within/beyond the confines of** *within the confines of the prison*

2 **con·firm** /kənˈfɜːm‖-ɜːrm/ *v* [T] **1** to show that some-
2 thing is definitely true, especially by providing more proof: *The new evidence has confirmed the first witness's story.* | **confirm that** *Research has confirmed that the risk is higher for women.* | **confirm what** *The new results confirm what most of us knew already.* **2** to make an idea or feeling stronger or more definite: *This just confirms my fears.* | **confirm you in your belief/opinion/view etc (that)** (=make you believe something more strongly) *The expression on his face confirmed me in my suspicions.* **3** to say that something is definitely true: *The President refused to confirm the rumor.* | **confirm that** *Walsh confirmed that the money had been paid.* | **confirm what** *My brother will confirm what I have told you.* **4** to tell someone that a possible arrangement, date, or time is now definite: *Could you confirm the dates we discussed.* | **be confirmed in office** (=be formally accepted in a new position of responsibility, especially as leader of a country) **5 be confirmed** to be made a full member of the Christian church in a special ceremony

**con·fir·ma·tion** /ˌkɒnfəˈmeɪʃən‖ˌkɑːnfər-/ *n* [C,U] **1** a statement etc that says that something is definitely true, or the act of stating this: [+ **of**] *There's still no official confirmation of the report.* | **confirmation that** *verbal confirmation that payment has been made* **2** a letter etc that tells you that a possible arrangement, date, time etc is now definite: *I'm still waiting for confirmation from them about my visit.* **3** a religious ceremony in which someone is made a full member of the Christian church

**con·firmed** /kənˈfɜːmd‖-ɜːr-/ *adj* **a confirmed bachelor/alcoholic/vegetarian etc** someone who seems completely happy with the way of life they have chosen

**con·fis·cate** /ˈkɒnfɪ̈skeɪt‖ˈkɑːn-/ *v* [T] to officially take private property away from someone, usually as a punishment: *Miss Williams confiscated all our sweets.* —**confiscation** /ˌkɒnfɪ̈ˈskeɪʃən/ *n* [C,U]: *the confiscation of pornographic material* —**confiscatory** /ˈkɒnfɪ̈skeɪtəri, kənˈfɪskətəri‖kənˈfɪskətɔːri/ *adj*

**con·fla·gra·tion** /ˌkɒnfləˈgreɪʃən‖ˌkɑːn-/ *n* [C] *formal* **1** a very large fire that destroys a lot of buildings, forests etc **2** a violent situation or war: *a nuclear conflagration*

**con·flate** /kənˈfleɪt/ *v* [T] *formal* to combine two or more things to form a single new thing: *This idea conflates two issues.* —**conflation** /-ˈfleɪʃən/ *n* [C,U]

**con·flict**[1] /ˈkɒnflɪkt‖ˈkɑːn-/ *n* [C,U] **1** a state of dis- S2
agreement or argument between people, groups, coun- W2
tries etc: *serious political conflict* | [+ **over**] *conflicts over wage settlements* | [+ **between**] *the conflict between tradition and innovation* | **in conflict** *permanently in conflict with her superiors* | **come into conflict** (=start arguing with) *She had often come into conflict with her mother-in-law.* **2** a situation in which you have to choose between two or more opposite needs or influences: [+ **between**] *a conflict between the demands of one's work and one's family* | **in conflict with** *The principles of democracy are sometimes in conflict with political reality.* **3** fighting or a war: *a violent conflict* | **armed conflict** *the frightening prospect of armed conflict* **4** a situation in which you have two opposite feelings about something: *an agonizing state of inner conflict* **5 conflict of interest/interests a)** a situation in which you cannot do your job fairly because you will be affected by the decision you make: *There is a growing conflict of interest between her position as a politician and her business activities.* **b)** a situation in which different people want different things

**con·flict**[2] /kənˈflɪkt/ *v* [I] if two ideas, beliefs, opinions etc conflict, they cannot exist together or both be true: [+ **with**] *This conflicts with the police evidence.* | **conflicting opinions/demands/interests etc** *I had rung a few friends, and been given a great deal of conflicting advice.*

**con·flu·ence** /ˈkɒnfluəns‖ˈkɑːn-/ *n* [singular + **of**] **1** *technical* the place where two or more rivers flow together **2** the point at which two or more ideas, principles etc are very similar —**confluent** *adj*

**con·form** /kənˈfɔːm‖-ɔːrm/ *v* [I] **1** to behave in the way that most other people in your group or society behave: *the pressure on schoolchildren to conform* **2 conform to a law/rule etc** to obey a law, rule etc: *You must conform to the rules or leave the school.* | *conform to the official safety standards* **3 conform to the pattern/model/ideal etc** *formal* to happen or develop in the way that is normal or that you expect —see also CONFORMIST —**conformer** *n* [C] —**conformance** *n* [U]

**con·for·ma·tion** /ˌkɒnfɔːˈmeɪʃən‖ˌkɑːnfɔːr-/ *n* [C,U] *technical* the shape of something or the way in which it is formed: *the conformation of the earth*

**con·form·ist** /kənˈfɔːmɪ̈st‖-ɔːr-/ *adj* thinking and behaving like everyone else, because you do not want to be different: *conformist thinking* —**conformist** *n* [C] *his refusal to be a conformist*

**con·for·mi·ty** /kənˈfɔːmɪ̈ti‖-ɔːr-/ *n* [U] *formal* **1** behaviour that obeys the accepted rules of society or a group, and is the same as that of most other people: *an emphasis on conformity and control* | [+ **to**] *conformity to an agreed standard of taste* **2 in conformity with** *formal* in a way that obeys rules, customs etc: *We must act in conformity with the local regulations.*

**con·found** /kənˈfaʊnd/ *v* [T] **1** to confuse and surprise people by being unexpected: *His amazing recovery confounded the medical specialists.* **2** *formal* to defeat an enemy, plan etc **3** *formal* if a problem etc confounds you, you cannot understand it or solve it: *Her question completely confounded me.* **4 confound it/him/them** *old-fashioned* used to show that you are annoyed

**con·found·ed** /kənˈfaʊndɪ̈d/ *adj* [only before noun] *old-fashioned* used to show that you are annoyed: *That confounded dog has run away again!*

**con·fra·ter·ni·ty** /ˌkɒnfrəˈtɜːnɪ̈ti‖ˌkɑːnfrəˈtɜːr-/ *n* [C] a group of people, especially religious people who are not priests, who work together for some good purpose

**con·frère** /ˈkɒnfreə‖ˈkɑːnfrer/ *n* [C] *French, formal* a friend or someone you work with

**con·front** /kənˈfrʌnt/ *v* [T] **1** to behave in a threatening way towards someone, as though you are going to attack them: *Opening the door, he found himself confronted by a dozen policemen with guns.* **2** to deal with something very difficult or unpleasant in a brave and determined way: *We try to help people confront their problems.* **3** [usually passive] to suddenly appear and need to be dealt with: *On my first day at work I was confronted with the task of chairing a meeting.* **4** to accuse someone of doing something by showing them the proof: **confront sb with the evidence/proof** *When the police confronted her with the evidence, she admitted everything.*

**con·fron·ta·tion** /ˌkɒnfrənˈteɪʃən‖ˌkɑːn-/ *n* [C,U + **with/between**] **1** a situation in which there is a lot of angry disagreement between two people or groups with very different opinions: *She had stayed in her room to avoid another confrontation.* **2** a fight or battle

**con·fron·ta·tion·al** /ˌkɒnfrənˈteɪʃənəl◂‖ˌkɑːn-/ *adj* intended to cause arguments or make people angry: *a confrontational style of government*

**con·fuse** /kənˈfjuːz/ *v* [T] **1** to make someone feel that they cannot think clearly or do not understand: *Don't give me so much information – you're confusing me!* **2** to think wrongly that one person, thing, or idea etc is someone or something else: **confuse sb/sth with** *I always confuse you with your sister – you look so alike.* | *Donald Reagan, not to be confused with former President Ronald Reagan* **3 confuse the issue/matter/argument etc** to make it even more difficult to think clearly about a situation or problem or to deal with it: *He kept asking unnecessary questions which only confused the issue.*

S3 **con·fused** /kənˈfjuːzd/ *adj* **1** unable to understand clearly what someone is saying or what is happening: *I am totally confused. Could you explain that again?* | [+ **about**] *If you're confused about anything, phone my office.* **2** not clear or not easy to understand: *There was an argument and a confused fight followed.* | *a lot of confused ideas* —**confusedly** /-ˈfjuːzɪ̈dli/ *adv*

S3 **con·fus·ing** /kənˈfjuːzɪŋ/ *adj* difficult to understand because there is no clear order or pattern: *The instructions were so confusing I've done it all wrong.* | *It was a very confusing situation.* —**confusingly** *adv*

S3 W3 **con·fu·sion** /kənˈfjuːʒən/ *n* [U] **1** a state of not understanding what is happening or what something means because it is not clear: [+ **about/over/as to**] *There was some confusion as to whether we had won or lost.* | **create/lead to confusion** *This complicated situation has led to considerable confusion.* **2** a situation in which someone wrongly thinks that one person, thing, or idea is someone or something else: *To avoid confusion, the teams wore different colours.* | [+ **between**] *confusion between 'tax avoidance' and 'tax evasion'* **3** a feeling of not being able to think clearly what you should say or do, especially in an embarrassing situation: *His confusion at meeting her there was quite apparent.* | **in confusion** *She stopped in confusion as everyone turned to look at her.* **4** a very confusing situation, usually with a lot of noise and action, so that it is difficult to understand or control: *a scene of indescribable confusion*

**con·fute** /kənˈfjuːt/ *v* [T] *formal* to prove that a person or belief is completely wrong —**confutation** /ˌkɒnfjuːˈteɪʃən‖ˌkɑːn-/ *n* [C,U]

**con·ga** /ˈkɒŋɡə‖ˈkɑːŋɡə/ *n* [C,U] a Latin American dance in which people hold onto each other and dance in a line, or the music for this

**con·geal** /kənˈdʒiːl/ *v* [I] if a liquid such as blood congeals, it becomes thick or solid

**con·ge·ni·al** /kənˈdʒiːniəl/ *adj* pleasant in a way that makes you feel comfortable and relaxed: [+ **to**] *The club provides a social atmosphere which is congenial to the average business man.* —**congenially** *adv*

**con·gen·i·tal** /kənˈdʒenɪ̈tl/ *adj* **1** a congenital medical condition or disease has affected someone since they were born: *congenital abnormalities* | *congenital defect* **2** existing as a part of your character and unlikely to change: *his congenital inability to make decisions* | *a congenital liar* —**congenitally** *adv*

**con·ger eel** /ˌkɒŋɡər ˈiːl‖ˌkɑːŋ-/ *n* [C] a large fish that looks like a snake

**con·ges·ted** /kənˈdʒestɪ̈d/ *adj* **1** a congested street, city etc is very full of traffic: *congested air space* **2** a part of your body that is congested is very full of liquid, usually blood or MUCUS —**congestion** /-ˈdʒestʃən/ *n* [U] *traffic congestion*

**con·glom·e·rate** /kənˈɡlɒmərɪ̈t‖-ˈɡlɑː-/ *n* **1** [C] a large business organization consisting of several different companies that have joined together: *a large multinational conglomerate* **2** [C,U] *technical* a rock consisting of different sizes of stones held together by clay **3** [C] a group of things gathered together

**con·glom·e·ra·tion** /kənˌɡlɒməˈreɪʃən‖-ˌɡlɑː-/ *n* [C + **of**] a group of many different things gathered together

**con·grats** /kənˈɡræts/ *n* [plural] *informal* CONGRATULATIONS

**con·grat·u·late** /kənˈɡrætʃʊ̈leɪt/ *v* [T] **1** to tell someone that you are happy because they have achieved something or because something nice has happened to them: *He never even stopped to congratulate me.* | **congratulate sb on** *She congratulated me warmly on my exam results.* **2 congratulate yourself (on)** to feel pleased and proud of yourself because you have achieved something or something good has happened to you: *I congratulated myself on my good fortune.* —**congratulation** /kənˌɡrætʃʊ̈ˈleɪʃən/ *n* [U] —**congratulatory** /kənˌɡrætʃʊ̈ˈleɪtəri‖-ˈɡrætʃʊ̈lətɔːri/ *adj*

**con·grat·u·la·tions** /kənˌɡrætʃʊ̈ˈleɪʃənz/ *n* [plural] S **1** words saying you are happy that someone has achieved something: *Give Marie my congratulations and tell her I'll come soon.* **2** an expression used when you want to congratulate someone: *"I've just passed my driving test!" "Congratulations!"* | [+ **on**] *Congratulations on a superb performance!*

**con·gre·gate** /ˈkɒŋɡrɪ̈ɡeɪt‖ˈkɑːŋ-/ *v* [I] to come together in a group: *Crowds began to congregate to hear the President's speech.*

**con·gre·ga·tion** /ˌkɒŋɡrɪ̈ˈɡeɪʃən‖ˌkɑːŋ-/ *n* [C also + plural verb *BrE*] **1** a group of people gathered together in a church: *The congregation knelt to pray.* **2** the people who usually go to a particular church: *Several members of the congregation were sick.* —**congregational** *adj*

**Con·gre·ga·tion·al·is·m** /ˌkɒŋɡrɪ̈ˈɡeɪʃənəlɪzəm‖ˌkɑːŋ-/ *n* [U] one type of Christianity, in which each congregation is responsible for making its own decisions —**Congregational** *adj* —**Congregationalist** *n* [C]

**con·gress** /ˈkɒŋɡres‖ˈkɑːŋɡrɪ̈s/ *n* **1** [C,U] a formal meeting of representatives of different groups, countries etc, to discuss ideas, give information etc: *the annual congress of the miners' union* **2** [C] the group of people chosen or elected to make the laws in countries **3 Congress** the group of people elected to make laws in the US, consisting of the Senate and the House of Representatives: *The President has lost the support of Congress.* —**congressional** /kənˈɡreʃənəl/ *adj* [only before noun] *a congressional committee*

**con·gress·man** /ˈkɒŋɡrɪ̈smən‖ˈkɑːŋ-/ *n* [C] a man who is a member of a congress, especially the US House of Representatives: *Congressman Stephen Richards Rojack*

**con·gress·wom·an** /ˈkɒŋɡrɪ̈sˌwʊmən‖ˈkɑːŋ-/ *n* [C] a woman who is a member of a congress, especially the US House of Representatives: *an interview with Congresswoman Anne Harding*

**con·gru·ent** /ˈkɒŋɡruənt‖ˈkɑːŋ-/ *adj* **1** [+ **with**] *formal* fitting together well; suitable **2** *technical* congruent triangles (TRIANGLE (1)) are the same size and shape —**congruence** *n* [U] —**congruently** *adv* —opposite INCONGRUENT

**con·gru·ous** /ˈkɒŋɡruəs‖ˈkɑːŋ-/ *adj* [+ **with**] fitting together well; suitable —**congruity** /kənˈɡruːɪ̈ti/ *n* [C,U] —opposite INCONGRUOUS

**con·ic** /ˈkɒnɪk‖ˈkɑː-/ *adj* connected with or shaped like a CONE[1] (1)

**con·i·cal** /ˈkɒnɪkəl‖ˈkɑː-/ *adj* shaped like a CONE[1] (1): *There were several huts with conical roofs.*

**conic sec·tion** /ˌ·· ˈ··/ *n* [C] *technical* a shape made in GEOMETRY when an imaginary flat surface is passed through a CONE[1] (1)

**co·ni·fer** /ˈkəʊnɪ̈fə, ˈkɒ-‖ˈkɑːnɪ̈fər/ *n* [C] a tree that has leaves like needles that stay on it during the winter and brown cones (CONE[1] (3)) that contain its seeds —**coniferous** /kəˈnɪfərəs‖koʊ-, kə-/ *adj*

**conj** the written abbreviation of CONJUNCTION

**con·jec·ture**[1] /kənˈdʒektʃə‖-ər/ *n formal* **1** [U] the act of thinking of reasons, explanations etc without having very much information to base them on: *She didn't know the facts, so what she said was pure conjecture.* | *conjecture about their role in the affair* **2** [C] an idea or opinion formed by guessing: *My results show that this conjecture was, in fact, correct.* —**conjectural** *adj*

**conjecture**[2] *v* [I,T] *formal* to form an idea or opinion without having much information to base it on; guess: [+ **that**]: *It seems reasonable to conjecture that these conditions breed violence.*

**con·join** /kənˈdʒɔɪn/ *v* [I,T] *formal* to join together or make things or people do this

**con·joint** /kənˈdʒɔɪnt/ *adj* joined together, united —**conjointly** *adv*: *conjointly working for peace*

**con·ju·gal** /ˈkɒndʒʊ̈ɡəl‖ˈkɑːn-/ *adj* [only before noun] *formal* connected with marriage: *They lived together in conjugal bliss.*

**con·ju·gate** /ˈkɒndʒʊ̈ɡeɪt‖ˈkɑːn-/ *v technical* **1** [I] if a verb conjugates, it has different grammatical forms to show different tenses etc: *The verb 'to go' conjugates irregularly.* **2** [T] if you conjugate a verb, you state the different grammatical forms that it can have

**con·ju·ga·tion** /ˌkɒndʒʊ̈ˈɡeɪʃən‖ˌkɑːn-/ *n* [C] *technical* **1** a set of verbs in languages such as Latin that conjugate in the same way **2** the way that a particular verb conjugates

**con·junc·tion** /kənˈdʒʌŋkʃən/ *n* **1 in conjunction with** working, happening, or being used with someone or something else: *The worksheets are designed to be used in conjunction with the new course books.* **2** [C] a combination of different things that have come together by chance: *a happy conjunction of events* **3** [C] *technical* a word such as 'but', 'and', or 'while' that connects parts of sentences, phrases, or clauses (CLAUSE (2))

**con·junc·tive** /kənˈdʒʌŋktɪv/ also **con·junct** /ˈkɒndʒʌŋkt, kənˈdʒʌŋkt‖ˈkɑːn-/ *n* [C] *technical* a word that joins phrases together —**conjunctive** also **conjunct** /ˈkɒndʒʌŋkt, kənˈdʒʌŋkt‖ˈkɑːn-/ *adj*: *a conjunctive adverb*

**con·junc·ti·vi·tis** /kənˌdʒʌŋktɪˈvaɪtɪ̈s/ *n* [U] a painful and infectious disease of the eye that makes it red

**con·junc·ture** /kənˈdʒʌŋktʃə‖-ər/ *n* [C] *formal* a combination of events or situations, especially one that causes problems: *the historic conjuncture from which Marxism arose*

**con·jure** /ˈkʌndʒə‖ˈkɑːndʒər, ˈkʌn-/ *v* **1** [I,T] to perform clever tricks in which you seem to make things appear, disappear, or change as if by magic: *The magician conjured a rabbit out of his hat.* **2** [T] to make something appear or happen unexpectedly **3 a name to conjure with a)** the name of a very important person **b)** a very long name that is difficult to say

**conjure** sth ↔ **up** *phr v* [T] **1** to bring a thought, picture, idea, or memory to someone's mind: *The word 'China' conjured up a whole new set of images in his mind.* **2** to make something appear when it is not expected, as if by magic: *Somehow we have to conjure up another $10,000.* **3** to make the spirit of a dead person appear by saying special magic words

**con·jur·er, conjuror** /ˈkʌndʒərə‖ˈkɑːndʒərər-, ˈkʌn/ *especially BrE n* [C] someone who entertains people by performing clever tricks in which things appear, disappear, or change as if by magic

**con·jur·ing** /ˈkʌndʒərɪŋ‖ˈkɑːn-, ˈkʌn-/ *n* [U] the skill of performing clever tricks in which you seem to make things appear, disappear, or change as if by magic

**conk**[1] /kɒŋk‖kɑːŋk, kɒːŋk/ *n* [C] *BrE slang* a nose

**conk**[2] *v* [T] *slang* to hit someone hard, especially on the head

**conk out** *phr v* [I] *informal* **1** if a machine or car conks out, it suddenly stops working: *Our car conked out on the way home.* **2** *especially AmE* if someone conks out, they fall asleep because they are very tired: *I got home from work and I just conked out on the sofa.*

**con·ker** /ˈkɒŋkə‖ˈkɑːŋkər/ *n* [C] *BrE* **1** the large shiny brown seed of the HORSE CHESTNUT tree **2 conkers** *BrE* a children's game in which you try to break your opponent's conker by hitting it with your own

**con·man** /ˈkɒnmæn‖ˈkɑːn-/ *n* [C] someone who tries to get money from people by tricking them

**con·nect** /kəˈnekt/ *v* S2 W2

**1** ▶ **JOIN** ◀ [T] to join two or more things together: *This railway line connects London and Edinburgh.* | **connect sth to/with** *Connect the speakers to the record player and plug it in.* | **connecting passage/door etc** (=one that joins two rooms, buildings etc) *We'd like two rooms with connecting doors.*

**2** ▶ **REALIZE** ◀ [T] to realize that two facts, events, or people are related to each other: *She did not connect the two events in her mind.* | **connect sb/sth with** *They did not at first connect her with the crime.*

**3** ▶ **ELECTRICITY/GAS ETC** ◀ [T] to join something to the main supply of electricity, gas, or water, or to the telephone network: *Has the phone been connected yet?* —opposite DISCONNECT

**4** ▶ **TELEPHONES** ◀ [T] to join two telephone lines so that two people can speak: *Please hold the line. I'm trying to connect you.*

**5** ▶ **TRAINS/BUSES** ◀ [I] if one train, bus, etc connects with another, it arrives just before the other one leaves so that you can continue your journey: *I missed the connecting flight.* | [+ **with**] *This train connects with the one to Glasgow.*

**6** ▶ **HIT STH** ◀ [I] *AmE* to succeed in hitting someone or something: *He swung at the ball, but didn't connect.*

**7 ► UNDERSTAND PEOPLE ◄** [I + **with**] *especially AmE* if people connect, they feel that they like each other and understand each other: *They valued her ability to empathize and connect with others.*

**connect** sth ↔ **up** *phr v* [I,T] to join something to the main supply of electricity, gas, or water, or to the telephone network: *Is the washing machine connected up yet?*

**con·nect·ed** /kəˈnektɪ̣d/ *adj* **1** if two things are connected, they are joined together: *The two continents were once connected.* | [+ **to**] *The wire is connected to an electrode.* **2** if two facts, events, etc are connected, they affect each other or are related to each other: [+ **with**] *problems connected with drug abuse* | **closely connected** *The two ideas are closely connected, and should be dealt with together.* **3 connected with sb** having a social or professional relationship with someone: *Aren't they connected with his father's business in some way?* **4 well connected** having important or powerful friends or relatives

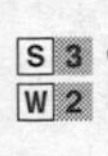

S3 W2 **con·nec·tion** also **connexion** *BrE* /kəˈnekʃən/ *n*

**1 ► STH THAT CONNECTS THINGS ◄** [C] the way in which two facts, ideas, events etc are related to each other, and one is affected or caused by the other: [+ **between**] *the connection between smoking and cancer* | [+ **with**] *His statement had no connection with anything that had gone before.* | **find/establish a connection** (=prove or discover that something is connected with something else) *Police have so far failed to establish a connection between the two murders.* | **make a connection** (=realize that there is a connection) *The evidence was there in the file but no one made the connection.* —see RELATIONSHIP (USAGE)

**2 ► JOINING THINGS TOGETHER ◄** [U] the joining together of two or more things: *Connection to the water mains takes only a few minutes.*

**3 in connection with** concerning something: *The police are interviewing two men in connection with the robbery.*

**4 ► ELECTRICAL WIRE ◄** [C] a wire or piece of metal joining two parts of a machine or electrical system: **loose connection** (=one that is not joined properly) *My radio isn't working properly – I think it's got a loose connection.*

**5 ► TRAIN/BUS ETC ◄** [C] a train, bus, or plane which is arranged to leave at a time which allows passengers from an earlier train, bus, or plane to use it to continue their journey: *If this train gets delayed we'll miss our connection to Paris.*

**6 ► ROAD/RAILWAY ETC ◄** [C] a road, railway etc that joins two places and allows people to travel between them: *Cheshunt has good rail connections to London, with trains every half hour.*

**7 ► PEOPLE ◄ connections** [plural] **a)** people who you know who can help you by giving you money, finding you a job etc: *He used his Mafia connections to find Pablo another job.* **b)** people who are related to you, but not very closely: *He is English, but has Irish connections.* —see RELATIONSHIP (USAGE)

**8 ► TELEPHONE ◄** if you have a bad connection on the telephone, you are unable to hear properly because there is a lot of noise in the telephone: *We had such a bad connection we gave up.*

**con·nec·tive**[1] /kəˈnektɪv/ *adj* joining two or more things together: *a lack of connective knowledge*

**connective**[2] *n* [C] *technical* a word that joins phrases, parts of sentences etc

**connective tis·sue** /ˌ·ˌ·· ˈ··/ *n* [U] parts of the body such as muscle or fat, that support or join organs and other body parts together

**con·ne·xion** /kəˈnekʃən/ *n* a British spelling of CONNECTION

**conning tow·er** /ˈ·· ˌ··/ *n* [C] *technical* the structure on top of a SUBMARINE (=underwater ship)

**con·nip·tion fit** /kəˈnɪpʃən ˌfɪt/ *n* [C] *AmE, humorous* a way of behaving which shows that you are very angry: **have/throw a conniption fit** *My mother threw a conniption fit when I didn't come home till two in the morning.*

**con·nive** /kəˈnaɪv/ *v* [I] **1** to not try to stop something wrong from happening: [+ **at**] *He would not be the first politician to connive at a shady business deal.* **2 connive to do sth** to work together secretly to achieve something, especially something wrong; CONSPIRE: *They connived with their mother to deceive me.* —**connivance** *n* [C]: *We could not have escaped without the connivance of the guards.*

**con·niv·ing** /kəˈnaɪvɪŋ/ *adj* behaving in a way that does not prevent something wrong from happening, or actively helps it to happen: *He knew all along, the conniving bastard!*

**con·nois·seur** /ˌkɒnəˈsɜː‖ˌkɑːnəˈsɜːr/ *n* [C] someone who knows a lot about something such as art, food, music etc: *a wine connoisseur*

**con·no·ta·tion** /ˌkɒnəˈteɪʃən‖ˌkɑː-/ *n* [C] a feeling or an idea that a word makes you think of that is not its actual meaning: *'Bermuda', with its connotations of sun, sea and sand* | *a negative connotation* —compare DENOTATION —**connotative** /ˈkɒnəteɪtɪv‖ˈkɑːn-, kəˈnoʊtətɪv/ *adj*

**con·note** /kəˈnəʊt‖-ˈnoʊt/ *v* [T] *formal* if a word connotes something, it makes you think of feelings and ideas that are not its actual meaning: *The word 'plump' connotes cheerfulness.* —compare DENOTE

**con·nu·bi·al** /kəˈnjuːbiəl‖-ˈnuː-/ *adj* **connubial bliss** *formal* the state of being happily married: *living in connubial bliss*

**con·quer** /ˈkɒŋkə‖ˈkɑːŋkər/ *v* **1** [I,T] to take land by attacking people or win it by fighting a war: *The Normans conquered England in 1066.* **2** [I,T] to defeat an enemy: *The Zulus conquered all the neighbouring tribes.* **3** [T] to gain control over something that is difficult, using a lot of effort: *Gemma felt ashamed that she hadn't been able to conquer her fear.* | *efforts to conquer inflation* **4** [T] to succeed in climbing to the top of a mountain when no one has ever climbed it before **5** [T] to become very successful in a place: *English comedians find it difficult to conquer America.* | **conquer sb's hearts** (=make someone love you) *She had conquered the hearts of the local people.* —**conqueror** *n* [C] —**conquering** *adj*: *conquering heroes*

**con·quest** /ˈkɒŋkwest‖ˈkɑːŋ-/ *n* **1** [singular, U] the act of defeating an army or taking land by fighting: *the Norman Conquest* **2** [C] land that is won in a war: *French conquests in Asia* **3** [C] *often humorous* someone that you have persuaded to love you or to have sex with you: *He boasts about his many conquests.* **4** [singular] the act of gaining control of or dealing successfully with something that is difficult or dangerous: [+ **of**] *the conquest of space*

**con·quis·ta·dor** /kɒnˈkwɪstədɔː‖kɑːnˈkiːstədɔːr/ *n* [C] [plural] one of the Spanish conquerors of Mexico and Peru in the 18th century

**con·san·guin·i·ty** /ˌkɒnsæŋˈgwɪnɪ̣ti‖ˌkɑːn-/ *n* [U] *formal* the state of being members of the same family

**con·science** /ˈkɒnʃəns‖ˈkɑːn-/ *n* [C,U]

**1 ► MIND ◄** the part of your mind that tells you whether what you are doing is morally right or wrong: *Be guided by your conscience.* | **a social conscience** (=a moral sense of how society should be) | **a guilty/bad conscience** (=feel guilty because you have done something wrong) *It was his guilty conscience that made him offer to help.* | **a clear conscience** (=a feeling that you have done nothing wrong) *Well at least I can face them all with a clear conscience.* | **a twinge/pang of conscience** (=guilty feeling) *Ian felt a pang of conscience at having misjudged her.* | **have no conscience (about sth)** (=not feel guilty about something) *They've no conscience at all about cheating.* | **a prisoner of conscience** (=someone who is in prison because of their political or religious beliefs) | **a matter of conscience** (=something that you must make a moral judgment about) *I can't tell you what to do – it's a matter of conscience.*

**2 on your conscience** if you have something on your

conscience it makes you feel guilty: *If anything happens to her I'll always have it on my conscience.*
**3 prick your conscience** if an action or event pricks your conscience, it makes you feel guilty: *The dog's sad look pricked her conscience and she took him home.*
**4 clear your conscience** to make yourself stop feeling guilty by telling someone about what you did wrong: *Terry decided to clear his conscience and confess.*
**5 in all conscience** *formal* if you cannot in all conscience do something, you cannot do it because you think it is wrong: *I couldn't in all conscience tell him that his job was safe.*
**6 in good conscience** if you do something in good conscience, you do it because you think it is the right thing to do: *statements made in good conscience*

**conscience clause** /ˈ·· ˌ·/ *n* [C] a part of a law that says that the law does not have to be obeyed by people who feel that it would be morally wrong to obey it

**conscience-strick·en** /ˈ·· ˌ··/ also **conscience-smitten** *adj* very sorry that you have done something wrong: *Kate hurried home, conscience-stricken at leaving her mother alone.*

**con·sci·en·tious** /ˌkɒnʃiˈenʃəs◂‖ˌkɑːn-/ *adj* showing a lot of care and attention: *a conscientious and methodical worker* —**conscientiously** *adv* —**conscientiousness** *n* [U] *praised for her conscientiousness*

**conscientious ob·jec·tor** /ˌ···· ˈ··/ *n* [C] someone who refuses to become a soldier because of their moral or religious beliefs —see also DRAFT DODGER

2 3 **con·scious** /ˈkɒnʃəs‖ˈkɑːn-/ *adj* **1** [not before noun] noticing or realizing something; AWARE: **conscious of (doing) sth** *I was very conscious of the fact that I had to make a good impression.* | **conscious that** *I was conscious that she was ill at ease.* **2** awake and able to understand what is happening around you: *The driver was still conscious when the ambulance reached the scene of the accident.* **3 a conscious effort/decision/attempt etc** an effort etc that is deliberate and intended: *Vivien had made a conscious effort to be friendly.* **4 safety-conscious/fashion-conscious etc** thinking a lot about safety, fashion etc: *recipes for calorie-conscious slimmers* —see also SELF-CONSCIOUS —opposite UNCONSCIOUS[1] —**consciously** *adv*

3 **con·scious·ness** /ˈkɒnʃəsnɪ̈s‖ˈkɑːn-/ *n* **1** [U] the condition of being awake and able to understand what is happening around you: **lose consciousness** (=go into a deep sleep) *David lost consciousness at eight o'clock and died a few hours later.* | **regain consciousness** (=wake up) *She could faintly hear voices as she began to regain consciousness.* **2** [U] your mind and your thoughts: *Even the most important issues eventually fade from your consciousness.* **3** [U] someone's ideas, feelings, or opinions about politics, life etc: *The experience helped to change her political consciousness.* **4** [singular] the state of knowing that something exists or is true; AWARENESS: *a consciousness of danger* —see also STREAM OF CONSCIOUSNESS

**consciousness rais·ing** /ˈ··· ˌ··/ *n* [U] the process of making people understand and care more about a moral, social, or political problem

**cons·cript**[1] /kənˈskrɪpt/ *v* [T + **into**] **1** to make someone join the army, navy etc: *young Frenchmen who were conscripted into the army and forced to fight in Algeria.* **2** to make someone become a member of a group or take part in a particular activity —compare RECRUIT[1]

**con·script**[2] /ˈkɒnskrɪpt‖ˈkɑːn-/ *n* [C] someone who has been made to join the army, navy etc —compare RECRUIT[2]

**con·scrip·tion** /kənˈskrɪpʃən/ *n* [U] the practice of making people join the army, navy etc; DRAFT[1] (2a) —see also NATIONAL SERVICE

**con·se·crate** /ˈkɒnsɪ̈kreɪt‖ˈkɑːn-/ *v* [T] **1** to officially state in a special religious ceremony that a place or building is holy and can be used for religious purposes. **2** to officially state in a special religious ceremony that someone is now a priest, BISHOP (1) etc —**consecrated** *adj*: *consecrated ground* —**consecration** /ˌkɒnsɪ̈ˈkreɪʃən‖ˌkɑːn-/ *n* [U]

**con·sec·u·tive** /kənˈsekjʊ̈tɪv/ *adj* consecutive numbers or periods of time follow one after the other without any interruptions: *It had rained for four consecutive days.* —**consecutively** *adv*: *Number the pages consecutively.*

**con·sen·sus** /kənˈsensəs/ *n* [singular, U] an opinion that everyone in a group will agree with or accept: **reach a consensus on** *The EC Council of Finance Ministers failed to reach a consensus on the pace of integration.* | **consensus politics** (=political ideas and actions that everyone accepts in a general way)

**con·sent**[1] /kənˈsent/ *n* [U] **1** permission to do something especially by someone in authority or by someone who is responsible for something: **Without sb's consent** *He took the car without the owner's consent.* | **give your consent** (=allow something to happen) —see also AGE OF CONSENT **2** agreement about something: **by common consent** (=with most people agreeing) *The chairman was elected by common consent.* | **by mutual consent** (=by agreement between both the people or groups of people involved) *divorce by mutual consent* **3 with one consent** *old use* if people do something with one consent, they all agree to do it —see also ASSENT, DISSENT 

**consent**[2] *v* [I] to give your permission for something or agree to do something: [+ **to**] *Her father reluctantly consented to the marriage.*

**consenting ad·ult** /ˌ·ˌ·· ˈ··, ˌ·ˌ·· ˈ·ˈ·/ *n* [C] *law* someone who is considered to be old enough to decide whether they want to have sex —see also AGE OF CONSENT

**con·se·quence** /ˈkɒnsɪ̈kwəns‖ˈkɑːnsɪ̈kwens/ *n* **1** [C] something that happens as a result of a particular action or set of conditions: *the harmful social consequences of high levels of unemployment.* | *The safety procedures had been ignored, with potentially tragic consequences.* | **take/suffer/face the consequences (of sth)** (=to accept the bad results of something you have done) *He broke the law, and now he must face the consequences of his actions.* **2 as a consequence (of sth)/in consequence (of sth)** *formal* as a result of something: *the rise in sea levels predicted as a consequence of global warming.* **3 of little/no/any consequence** *formal* of little importance or value: *Your opinion is of little consequence to me.* 

**con·se·quent** /ˈkɒnsɪ̈kwənt‖ˈkɑːn-/ *adj formal* happening as a result of a particular event or situation: *the rise in inflation and consequent fall in demand* —compare SUBSEQUENT

**con·se·quen·tial** /ˌkɒnsɪ̈ˈkwenʃəl◂‖ˌkɑːn-/ *adj formal* **1** happening as a direct result of a particular event or situation: *redundancy and the consequential loss of earnings* **2** important; SIGNIFICANT: *a consequential decision* —opposite INCONSEQUENTIAL —**consequentially** *adv*

**con·se·quent·ly** /ˈkɒnsɪ̈kwəntli‖ˈkɑːnsɪ̈kwentli/ *adv* [sentence adverb] as a result: *We talked until the early hours, and consequently I overslept.* | *The bank refused to give the company more time. Consequently, it went bankrupt.* —see THUS (USAGE) W3

**con·ser·van·cy** /kənˈsɜːvənsi‖-ɜːr-/ *n* [U] *BrE* **1** a group of officials who control and protect an area of land, a river etc: *the Thames Conservancy* **2** the protection of natural things such as animals, plants, forests etc; CONSERVATION (1)

**con·ser·va·tion** /ˌkɒnsəˈveɪʃən‖ˌkɑːnsər-/ *n* [U] **1** the protection of natural things such as animals, plants, forests etc, to prevent them being spoiled, or destroyed: *wildlife conservation* **2** the act of preventing something from being lost or wasted: [+ **of**] *conservation of energy* 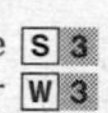

**conservation a·re·a** /ˌ··ˈ·· ˌ···/ *n* [C] **1** an area where animals and plants are protected **2** an area where interesting old buildings are protected and new buildings are carefully controlled

**con·ser·va·tion·ist** /ˌkɒnsəˈveɪʃənɪst‖ˌkɑːnsər-/ *n* [C] someone who works to protect animals, plants etc or to protect old buildings —**conservationism** *n* [U]

**con·ser·va·tis·m** /kənˈsɜːvətɪzəm‖-ɜːr-/ *n* [U] **1** dislike of change and new ideas: *people's innate conservatism in matters of language* **2** also **Conservatism** the political belief that society should change as little as possible **3 Conservatism** the political beliefs of the Conservative Party

**con·ser·va·tive¹** /kənˈsɜːvətɪv‖-ɜːr-/ *adj* **1 Conservative** belonging to or concerned with the Conservative Party in Britain: *Conservative policies|a Conservative MP* **2** not liking changes or new ideas: *a very conservative attitude to education* **3** not very modern in style, taste etc; traditional: *a very conservative suit* **4 a conservative estimate/guess** a guess which is deliberately lower than the real amount: *At a conservative estimate, the holiday will cost about £1500.* —**conservatively** *adv*

**conservative²** *n* [C] **1 Conservative** someone who supports or is a member of the Conservative Party in Britain **2** someone who does not like changes in ideas or fashion: *Aunt May is a real conservative. She's totally opposed to mothers going out to work.*

**Conservative Par·ty** /·ˈ··· ˌ··/ *n* **the Conservative Party** a British political party on the RIGHT

**con·ser·va·toire** /kənˈsɜːvətwɑː‖-ˈsɜːrvətwɑːr/ *n* [C] *BrE* a school where people are trained in music or acting; CONSERVATORY *AmE*

**con·ser·va·to·ry** /kənˈsɜːvətəri‖-ˈsɜːrvətɔːri/ *n* [C] **1** a room with glass walls and a glass roof, where plants are grown, that is usually added on to the side of a house **2** *AmE* a school where people are trained in music or acting; CONSERVATOIRE *BrE*

**con·serve¹** /kənˈsɜːv‖-ɜːrv/ *v* [T] **1** to protect something and try to prevent it from changing or being damaged: *We must conserve our woodlands for future generations.* **2** to use as little water, energy etc as possible so that it is not wasted: *conserving electricity*

**con·serve²** /ˈkɒnsɜːv‖ˈkɑːnsɜːrv/ *n* [C,U] *formal* fruit that is preserved by being cooked with sugar; JAM¹ (1)

S1 **con·sid·er** /kənˈsɪdə‖-ər/ *v*
W1 **1 ▶THINK ABOUT◀** [I,T] to think about something, especially about whether to accept something or do something: *He paused to consider his options.|Any reasonable offer will be considered.*|**consider doing sth** *I'm considering applying for that job.*|**consider where/how/why etc** *We're still considering where to move to.*
**2 ▶HAVE AN OPINION◀** [T] to think of someone or something in a particular way: **consider sb/sth (to be) wise/important etc** *A further increase in interest rates is now considered unlikely.*|**consider sth an honour/a duty etc** *I consider it a great honour to be invited.*|**consider sb (to be) a fool/hero etc** *Liz Quinn was considered an excellent teacher.*
**3 consider yourself lucky** to think you are fortunate: *Consider yourself lucky you weren't in the car at the time.*
**4 ▶REMEMBER TO THINK OF◀** [T] to remember to think carefully about something before making a judgment or a decision: *Before you resign you should consider the effect it will have on your family.*|**consider that** *If you consider that she's only been studying English for six months, she speaks it very well.*|**consider what/how/who etc** *Have you considered how difficult it is for these refugees?*
**5 ▶PEOPLE'S FEELINGS◀** [T] to think about someone or their feelings etc and try to avoid upsetting or hurting them: *God, you're so selfish! You've got to learn to consider other people!*
**6 all things considered** used when saying what you think about something after considering all the facts: *All things considered, I'm sure we made the right decision.*
**7 ▶DISCUSS FORMALLY◀** [T] to discuss something such as a report or problem, so that you can make a decision about it: *The committee has been considering the report.*
**8 ▶LOOK AT◀** [T] *formal* to look at someone or something carefully: *Henry considered the sculpture with an expert eye.*
**9 be considering your position** *formal* to be deciding whether or not to leave your job

**con·sid·e·ra·ble** /kənˈsɪdərəbəl/ *adj* fairly large, S
especially large enough to have an effect or be important: W
*She has considerable influence with the President.|A statue was erected at considerable public expense.* —compare INCONSIDERABLE

**con·sid·e·ra·bly** /kənˈsɪdərəbli/ *adv* **considerably** S
**more/colder/higher etc** much more, much colder etc: W
*It's considerably colder today.*

**con·sid·er·ate** /kənˈsɪdərɪt/ *adj* always thinking of what other people need or want and taking care not to upset them: *Diana is a considerate boss who is always willing to listen.*|**considerate of sb (to do sth)** *It was very considerate of you to let us know you were going to be late.* —opposite INCONSIDERATE —**considerately** *adv* —**considerateness** *n* [U]

**con·sid·e·ra·tion** /kənˌsɪdəˈreɪʃən/ *n* S
**1 ▶THOUGHT◀** [U] *formal* careful thought and W
attention: **under consideration** (=being discussed and thought about so that an official decision can be made) *There are several amendments under consideration.*|**due/long consideration** *After due consideration, I have decided to tender my resignation.*|**give sth your fullest consideration** (=think about it very carefully before making an official decision)
**2 take sth into consideration** to remember to think about something important when you are making a decision or judgement: *Your teachers will take your recent illness into consideration when marking your exams.*
**3 ▶STH THAT AFFECTS A DECISION◀** [C] something that you must think about when you are planning to do something, which affects what you decide to do: *Political rather than economic considerations influenced the location of the new factory.*
**4 ▶KINDNESS◀** [U] the quality of thinking about other people's feelings and taking care not to upset them: **out of consideration for** *The murdered woman's name has not been released, out of consideration for her parents.*|**show consideration for** *Jeff never shows any consideration for his mother's feelings.*
**5 of no consideration/of little consideration** *formal* if something is of no consideration it is not at all important
**6 in consideration of** *formal* as payment for something: *a small payment in consideration of your services*
**7 ▶MONEY◀** [singular] *formal* a payment for a service: **for a small consideration** *I might be able to help you, for a small consideration.*

**con·sid·ered** /kənˈsɪdəd‖-ərd/ *adj* **1 considered opinion/judgement etc** an opinion based on careful thought **2 well/poorly/highly considered** thought to be good, bad etc: *Her paintings are very well considered abroad.* **3 all things considered** *usually spoken* used to say what you believe after thinking about all the facts: *All things considered, I'm sure we made the right decision.*

**con·sid·er·ing¹** /kənˈsɪdərɪŋ/ *prep conjunction* used when describing a situation, before stating a fact that you know has had an effect on that situation: *Considering the strength of the opposition, we did very well to score two goals.*|**considering that/who/how etc** *John did quite well in his exams considering how little he studied.*

**considering²** *adv spoken* used at the end of a phrase when you are expressing an opinion about something in spite of another fact: *Mum didn't look too bad, considering.*

**con·sign** /kənˈsaɪn/ *v* [T] *formal* **1** to put someone or something somewhere, especially in order to get rid of them: **consign sb/sth to** *I consigned his letter to the dustbin.*|*She preferred to take care of her mother at home, rather than consigning her to institutional care.*|**consign sb/sth to the flames** *literary* (=burn someone or something) *The body was consigned to the flames.* **2** to send or deliver something to someone who has bought it **3** to make someone or something be in a particular situation, especially an unpleasant one: **consign sb/sth to** *consigning Cambodia to a decade of civil war*

**con·sign·ee** /ˌkɒnsaɪˈniː, -sə̇-‖ˌkɑːn-/ *n* [C] *technical* the person that something is delivered to

**con·sign·ment** /kənˈsaɪnmənt/ *n* **1** [C] a quantity of goods delivered at the same time: [+ **of**] *a new consignment of computer games* **2** [U] the act of delivering things

**con·sign·or, consigner** /kənˈsaɪnə‖-ər/ *n* [C] *technical* the person who sends goods to someone else

3 **con·sist** /kənˈsɪst/ *v*

**consist in** sth *phr v* [T not in progressive] *formal* to be based on or depend upon something: *The beauty of Venice consists largely in the style of its ancient buildings.*

**consist of** sth *phr v* [T not in progressive] used to say what something is made of when it contains a number of parts or things: *Bolognaise sauce consists of minced beef, onion, tomatoes, garlic and seasoning.*

**con·sis·ten·cy** /kənˈsɪstənsi/ *n* **1** [U] the quality of always being the same or always being good: *Replies to these questions showed no real consistency.* —opposite INCONSISTENCY **2** [C,U] how firm or thick a mixture is: *Beat the butter and sugar until the mixture has the consistency of thick cream.*

3 **con·sis·tent** /kənˈsɪstənt/ *adj* **1** always having the
3 same beliefs, behaviour, attitudes, quality etc: *one of the most consistent players on the tennis circuit|a consistent supporter of constitutional rights* **2** continuing to develop in the same way: *a consistent improvement in the country's economy* **3** a consistent argument or idea is organized so that each part agrees with the others **4 be consistent with** if something that is said, written, or done is consistent with a particular idea or piece of information, it says the same thing or follows the same principles: *This evidence is not consistent with what you said earlier.* —opposite INCONSISTENT —**consistently** *adv*: *I'm fed up with your consistently negative attitude.*

**con·so·la·tion** /ˌkɒnsəˈleɪʃən‖ˌkɑːn-/ *n* [C,U] someone or something that makes you feel better when you are sad or disappointed: *It was some consolation for me to know that I had only failed by 2%.*

**consolation prize** /ˌ··ˈ·· ·/ *n* [C] a prize that is given to someone who has not won a competition: *Ten runners-up each received a T-shirt as a consolation prize.*

**con·sol·a·to·ry** /kənˈsɒlətəri, -ˈsəʊlə-‖-ˈsoʊlətɔːri, -ˈsɑː-/ *adj formal* intended to make someone feel better

**con·sole**[1] /kənˈsəʊl‖-ˈsoʊl/ *v* [T] to make someone feel better when they are feeling sad or disappointed: *No one could console her when Peter died.*|**console sb with** *Console yourself with the thought that no one was injured!*

**con·sole**[2] /ˈkɒnsəʊl‖ˈkɑːnsoʊl/ *n* [C] **1** a flat board that contains the controls for a machine, piece of electrical equipment, computer etc: *a games console* **2** a special cupboard in which a television, computer etc is fitted

**con·sol·i·date** /kənˈsɒlə̇deɪt‖-ˈsɑː-/ *v* [I,T] **1** to make your position of power stronger and more likely to continue, or maintain the same level of achievement, profit, success etc so that it seems likely to continue: *His successful negotiations with the Americans helped him to consolidate his position.*|*Canon has consolidated its hold on the European market.* **2** to join together a group of companies, organizations etc, or to become joined together **3** to combine several jobs, duties etc together —**consolidated** *adj* —**consolidation** /kənˌsɒlə̇ˈdeɪʃən‖-ˌsɑː-/ *n* [C,U]

**con·som·mé** /kənˈsɒmeɪ, ˈkɒnsəmeɪ‖ˌkɑːnsəˈmeɪ/ *n* [U] clear soup made from meat or vegetables

**con·so·nance** /ˈkɒnsənəns‖ˈkɑːn-/ *n* **1 in consonance with** *formal* agreeing with something or existing together without any problems **2** [C,U] *technical* a combination of musical notes that sound pleasant: HARMONY (1)

**con·so·nant**[1] /ˈkɒnsənənt‖ˈkɑːn-/ *n* [C] **1** a speech sound made by partly or completely stopping the flow of air through the mouth **2** a letter that represents one of these sounds. The letters 'a', 'e', 'i', 'o', and 'u' represent vowels, and all the other letters are consonants

**consonant**[2] *adj* **1 consonant with** *formal* not seeming to show that a statement or belief is wrong: *This policy is scarcely consonant with the government's declared aims.* **2** *technical* being a combination of musical notes that sounds pleasant

**con·sort**[1] /ˈkɒnsɔːt‖ˈkɑːnsɔːrt/ *n* [C] **1 in consort (with sb)** *formal* doing something together with someone: *The prince ruled in consort with his father.* **2** the wife or husband of a ruler —see also PRINCE CONSORT **3** a group of people who play music from former times or the group of old-fashioned instruments they use

**con·sort**[2] /kənˈsɔːt‖-ɔːrt/ *v formal* [I + **with/together**] to spend time with someone who other people disapprove of: **consorting with the enemy** (=spending time with and helping the enemies of your country)

**con·sor·ti·um** /kənˈsɔːtiəm‖-ɔːr-/ *n plural* **consortiums** *or* **consortia** [C] a combination of several companies, banks etc working together to buy something, build something etc

**con·spec·tus** /kənˈspektəs/ *n* [C] *formal* a short report giving the most important ideas of a subject

**con·spic·u·ous** /kənˈspɪkjuəs/ *adj* **1** someone or something that is conspicuous is very easy to notice, especially because they are different from everything or everyone else around them: *I felt very conspicuous in my suit – everyone else was in jeans.* **2** unusually good, bad, skilful etc; REMARKABLE: *The campaign had been a conspicuous success.* **3 conspicuous by your absence** used to say that people noticed that you were not in the place you should have been —opposite INCONSPICUOUS —**conspicuously** *adv* —**conspicuousness** *n* [U]

**con·spi·ra·cy** /kənˈspɪrəsi/ *n* [C,U] a secret plan made by two or more people to do something that is harmful or illegal: **conspiracy to (do) sth** *a conspiracy to smuggle drugs into the country*|**conspiracy against** *A conspiracy against the elected government.*|**conspiracy of silence** (=an agreement to keep quiet about something that should not be a secret)|**conspiracy theory** (=the idea that an event was caused by a conspiracy) *conspiracy theories about President Kennedy's assassination*

**con·spi·ra·tor** /kənˈspɪrətə‖-ər/ *n* [C] someone who is involved in a secret plan to do something harmful or illegal

**con·spi·ra·to·ri·al** /kənˌspɪrəˈtɔːriəl/ *adj* **1** connected with a secret plan to do something harmful or illegal: *conspiratorial discussions* **2 conspiratorial grin/giggle/wink etc** one between two people who know a secret —**conspiratorially** *adv*

**con·spire** /kənˈspaɪə‖-ər/ *v* [I] **1** to plan something harmful or illegal together secretly: **conspire (with sb) to do sth** *He had conspired with an accomplice to rob the bank.*|**conspire against sb** *Mentally ill people sometimes believe that relatives are conspiring against them.* **2** if events conspire to make something happen, they happen at the same time and make something bad happen: **conspire to do sth** *Technological failure and atmospheric conditions conspired to make take-off impossible.*

**con·sta·ble** /ˈkʌnstəbəl‖ˈkɑːn-/ *n* [C] a British police officer of the lowest rank —see also PATROLMAN (1)

**con·stab·u·la·ry** /kənˈstæbjə̇ləri‖-leri/ *n* [C] *BrE* the police force of a particular area or country —see also PATROL[2] (2)

**con·stan·cy** /ˈkɒnstənsi‖ˈkɑːn-/ *n* [U] *formal* **1** the quality of staying the same even though other things change: *constancy of purpose* **2** loyalty and faithfulness to a particular person: *constancy between husband and wife*

**con·stant**[1] /ˈkɒnstənt‖ˈkɑːn-/ *adj* **1** staying the same S2
for a period of time: *A thermostat kept the temperature* W2
*constant.* **2** happening all the time or regularly: *Sam*

*was in constant pain.* **3** *literary* loyal and faithful: *a constant friend*

**constant²** *n* [C] *technical* **1** a number or quantity that never varies **2** *formal* something that stays the same even though other things change —compare VARIABLE²

S3 W3 **con·stant·ly** /ˈkɒnstəntli‖ˈkɑːnstəntli/ *adv* all the time, or very often: *As I walked through the town, I was constantly reminded of my childhood.* | **constantly changing** *the constantly changing membership of our group*

**con·stel·la·tion** /ˌkɒnstʒˈleɪʃən‖ˌkɑːn-/ *n* [C] **1** a group of stars that forms a particular pattern and has a name **2 a constellation of** *literary* a group of people or things that are similar: *a constellation of famous television performers*

**con·ster·na·tion** /ˌkɒnstəˈneɪʃən‖ˌkɑːnstər-/ *n* [U] a feeling of shock or worry, especially one that makes it difficult to think about what to do; DISMAY¹: *The thought of living alone filled her with consternation.*

**con·sti·pa·tion** /ˌkɒnstʒˈpeɪʃən‖ˌkɑːn-/ *n* [U] the condition of finding it difficult to empty your bowels (BOWEL (1)) —**constipated** *adj*

W3 **con·sti·tu·en·cy** /kənˈstɪtʃuənsi/ *n* [C] **1** an area of the country that elects a representative to a parliament: *John Major, speaking from his Huntingdon constituency* **2** [also + plural verb *BrE*] the people who live and vote in a particular area —compare WARD¹ (2) **3** any group that supports or is likely to support a politician or a political party: *The Unions were no longer the constituency of the Labour Party alone.*

**con·sti·tu·ent¹** /kənˈstɪtʃuənt/ *n* [C] **1** someone who votes and lives in a particular area represented by one politician **2** one of the parts that combine to form something: *the constituents of gunpowder* —compare COMPONENT

**constituent²** *adj* [only before noun] being one of the parts that makes a whole: *the EC and its constituent members*

W3 **con·sti·tute** /ˈkɒnstʒtjuːt‖ˈkɑːnstʒtuːt/ *v* **1** [linking verb, not in progressive] if several parts constitute something, they form it together; make up (MAKE¹): *the 50 states that constitute the USA* —see also COMPRISE **2** [linking verb not in progressive] to be considered to be something: *Boarding a train without a ticket constitutes a breach of the regulations.* **3** [T] *formal* to make something from a number of different parts

W2 **con·sti·tu·tion** /ˌkɒnstʒˈtjuːʃən‖ˌkɑːnstʒˈtuː-/ *n* **1** [C] the system of basic laws and principles that a DEMOCRATIC country is governed by, which cannot easily be changed by the political party in power: *The First Amendment of the Constitution guarantees freedom of speech.* **2** [singular] the ability of your body to fight disease and illness: **have a strong/good/weak etc constitution** *She's got a strong constitution – she'll recover in no time.* **3** [C] *formal* the way something is formed and how it is organized: [+ **of**] *objections to the constitution of the committee* **4** the system of rules and principles that an organization is governed by

W3 **con·sti·tu·tion·al¹** /ˌkɒnstʒˈtjuːʃənəl◂‖ˌkɑːnstʒˈtuː-/ *adj* **1** officially allowed or limited by the system of rules of a country or organization: *The government can't refuse to hold an election; it's not constitutional.* | **a constitutional monarchy** (=a country ruled by a king or queen whose power is restricted by a constitution) —opposite UNCONSTITUTIONAL **2** connected with the constitution of a country or organization: *a constitutional crisis* | **a constitutional amendment** (=a change to the original constitution) **3** connected with someone's health and their ability to fight illness —see also CONSTITUTIONALLY

**constitutional²** *n* [C] *old-fashioned* a walk you take because it is good for your health

**con·sti·tu·tion·al·is·m** /ˌkɒnstʒˈtjuːʃənəlɪzəm‖ˌkɑːnstʒˈtuː-/ *n* [U] the belief that a government should be based on a constitution —**constitutionalist** *n* [C]

**con·sti·tu·tion·al·i·ty** /ˌkɒnstʒtjuːʃəˈnælʒti‖ˌkɑːnstʒtuː-/ *n* [U] the quality of being acceptable according to the constitution: *The senator questioned the constitutionality of the proposed law.*

**con·sti·tu·tion·al·ly** /ˌkɒnstʒˈtjuːʃənəli‖ˌkɑːnstʒˈtuː-/ *adv* **1** in a way that obeys the rules of a country: *The government must always act constitutionally.* **2** in a way that is related to someone's character or health and physical ability

**con·strain** /kənˈstreɪn/ *v* [T] **1** to stop someone from doing what they want to do: **constrain by** *Many women feel constrained by their roles as wife and mother.* **2** to prevent something from developing and improving: *Our research has been constrained by lack of funding.*

**con·strained** /kənˈstreɪnd/ *adj* **1 constrained to do sth** feeling that you are forced to do something: *In the recession companies felt constrained to make job cuts where possible.* **2** a constrained smile, manner etc seems too controlled and is not natural —**constrainedly** /kənˈstreɪnʒdli/ *adv*

**con·straint** /kənˈstreɪnt/ *n* **1** [C] something that limits your freedom to do what you want; RESTRICTION: [+ **on**] *These new policies place additional constraints on housing projects.* | **financial/legal/cultural etc constraints** *Financial constraints limited her choice of accommodation.* **2** [U] control over the way people are allowed to behave, so that they cannot do what they want: *freedom from constraint* **3 under constraint** if you do something under constraint, you do it because you have been forced to W

**con·strict** /kənˈstrɪkt/ *v* [T] **1** to make something smaller, narrower, or tighter **2** to limit someone's freedom to do what they want: *Poverty constricts people's choices.* —**constricted** *adj* —**constriction** *n* [C,U] —**constrictive** *adj*

**con·struct¹** /kənˈstrʌkt/ *v* [T] **1** to build a large building, bridge, road etc: *The Golden Gate Bridge was constructed in 1933-1937.* | **be constructed of/from etc** *huge skyscrapers constructed entirely of concrete and glass* **2** to form something such as a sentence, argument, or system by joining words, ideas etc together: *attempts to construct a programme that will meet the educational needs of every child* **3** *technical* to draw a mathematical shape: *Construct a square on this line.* W

**con·struct²** /ˈkɒnstrʌkt‖ˈkɑːn-/ *n* [C] **1** an idea formed by combining pieces of knowledge: *the central constructs of role theory* **2** *formal* something that is built or made

**con·struc·tion** /kənˈstrʌkʃən/ *n* S W

**1** ▶ **BUILDINGS/ROADS ETC** ◀ [U] the process or method of building large buildings, bridges, roads etc: *Local labor is used in the construction of the dam.* | *the construction industry* | **construction site** (=the place where something is being constructed) | **under construction** (=being built) *When we got to the hotel, it was still under construction.*

**2** ▶ **MAKING STH USING MANY PARTS** ◀ [U] the process or method of building or making something using many parts: *Titanium is used in the construction of aircraft fuselages.*

**3** ▶ **PHRASE** ◀ [C] the order in which certain words are put together in a sentence, phrase etc: *difficult grammatical constructions*

**4** ▶ **STH BUILT** ◀ [C] *formal* something that has been built: *a strange construction made of wood and glass*

**5** ▶ **IDEAS/KNOWLEDGE** ◀ [U] the method or process of forming something from knowledge or ideas: *the construction of sociological theory*

**6 of simple/strong etc construction** *formal* built in a simple way, built to be strong etc: *Your home is not secure if the doors are not of strong construction.*

**7 put a construction on** *formal* to think that a statement has a particular meaning or that something was done for a particular reason: *The judge put an entirely different construction to his remarks.* —**constructional** *adj*

**con·struc·tive** /kənˈstrʌktɪv/ *adj* **1** intended to be helpful and to suggest improvements, rather than to upset or offend people: **constructive advice/criticism** *I don't mind constructive criticism but if you're just going to insult me I'm not staying.* **2** having a good effect or likely to produce good results: *Young people in inner cities need constructive outlets for their energy.* —**constructively** *adv* —**constructiveness** *n* [U]

**con·struc·tor** /kən'strʌktə‖-ər/ *n* [C] a company or person that builds things

**con·strue** /kən'struː/ *v* **1 construe sth as** to understand a remark or action in a particular way: *Party leaders felt that such an action would be construed as political persecution.* **2** [I,T] to translate each word in a piece of writing, especially one in Greek or Latin

**con·sub·stan·ti·a·tion** /ˌkɒnsəbstænʃi'eɪʃən‖ˌkɑːn-/ *n* [U] *technical* the belief that the real body and blood of Christ are present in the bread and wine offered by the priest at a Christian religious service

**con·sul** /'kɒnsəl‖'kɑːn-/ *n* [C] **1** a representative of the government who lives in a foreign country in order to help and protect citizens of their own country who live there: *the French Consul in Addis Ababa* **2** one of the two chief public officials of the ancient Roman republic, each elected for one year —**consular** *adj*: *a consular official* —**consulship** *n* [C,U]

**con·su·late, Consulate** /'kɒnsjʊlɪt‖'kɑːnsəlɪt/ *n* [C] the official building in which a consul lives and works

S3 W3 **con·sult** /kən'sʌlt/ *v* [I,T] **1** to ask for information or advice from someone because it is their job to know about it: *If symptoms persist, consult a doctor without delay.* | **consult sb about sth** *An increasing number of clients are consulting them about Social Security changes.* **2** to ask for someone's permission or to discuss something with someone so that you can make a decision together: *I can't believe you sold the car without consulting me!* | [+ **with**] *The President consulted with European leaders before taking action.* **3** to look for information in a book, map, list etc: *Have you consulted a dictionary?*

**con·sul·tan·cy** /kən'sʌltənsi/ *n* [C] a company that gives advice and training in a particular area to people in other companies

S3 W3 **con·sul·tant** /kən'sʌltənt/ *n* [C] **1** someone who has a lot of experience and whose job it is to give advice and training in a particular area: *a management consultant* **2** *BrE* a senior hospital doctor who has a lot of knowledge about a particular kind of medical treatment; SPECIALIST (2) *AmE*

S3 W3 **con·sul·ta·tion** /ˌkɒnsəl'teɪʃən‖ˌkɑːn-/ *n* **1** [U] a discussion in which people who are affected by a decision can say what they think should be done: *Parents are demanding a greater consultation over their children's future.* | **in consultation with** (=with the agreement and help of someone) *The decision was made in consultation with union members.* **2** [U] advice given by a professional person: *The school counselor was always available for consultation.* **3** [C] a meeting with a professional person, especially a doctor, for advice or treatment: *A follow-up consultation was arranged for two weeks' time.* **4** [U] the act of looking for information or help in a book: *Leaflets were regularly displayed for consultation by students.*

**con·sul·ta·tive** /kən'sʌltətɪv/ *adj* providing advice and suggesting solutions to problems: *a consultative document*

**con·sult·ing¹** /kən'sʌltɪŋ/ *n* [U] the service of providing financial advice to companies

**consulting²** *adj* providing financial or other types of advice to companies: *a major international consulting firm*

**consulting room** *n* [C] *BrE* a room where a doctor sees patients

**con·sume** /kən'sjuːm‖-'suːm/ *v* [T] **1** to use time, energy, goods etc: *As a country, we consume a lot more than we produce.* **2 time-consuming** something that is time-consuming takes a long time: *a very time-consuming process* **3** *formal* to eat or drink something: *He's able to consume vast quantities of food.* **4 consumed with** if you are consumed with a feeling, you feel it very strongly and cannot forget it: *He was consumed with guilt after the accident.* **5** *formal* if fire consumes something, it destroys it completely —see also CONSUMING

**con·sum·er** /kən'sjuːmə‖-'suːmər/ *n* [C] someone who buys and uses products and services: *a wider choice of goods for the consumer* —compare PRODUCER (1) S2 W2

**consumer con·fi·dence** /ˌ·,·· '···/ *n* [U] a measure of how satisfied people are with the present economic situation, as shown by how much money they spend: *Consumer confidence was reported to hit an all-time low in September.*

**consumer du·ra·bles** /ˌ·,·· '···/ *BrE n* [plural] large things such as cars, televisions, or furniture that you do not buy often or regularly; DURABLE GOODS *AmE*

**consumer goods** /·'·· ·/ *n* [plural] goods such as food, clothes, and equipment that people buy, especially to use in the home —compare CAPITAL GOODS

**con·sum·er·ism** /kən'sjuːmərɪzəm‖-'suː-/ *n* [U] **1** the idea or belief that the buying and selling of products is the most important or useful activity for an individual and a society **2** actions to protect people from unfair prices, advertising that is not true etc

**consumer price in·dex** /·,·· '·,··/ *n* [C] *AmE* a list of the prices of products that is prepared to show how much prices have increased during a particular period of time: RETAIL PRICE INDEX *BrE*

**consumer so·ci·e·ty** /·'·· ·,···/ *n* [C] a society in which the buying of products and services is considered extremely important

**con·sum·ing** /kən'sjuːmɪŋ‖-'suː-/ *adj* [only before noun] a consuming feeling is so strong that it controls you and often has a bad effect on your life: *It was her consuming ambition to become party leader.* | **consuming passion** (=something you are extremely interested in) *Sandy's consuming passion is still the martial arts.*

**con·sum·mate¹** /kən'sʌmɪt/ *adj formal* **1** very skilful: *a great performance from a consummate actress* **2** complete and perfect in every way: *a consummate example of Picasso's artistry* **3** used to emphasize how bad someone or something is: *a man with a consummate lack of tact* —**consummately** *adv*

**con·sum·mate²** /'kɒnsəmeɪt‖'kɑːn-/ *v* [T] *formal* **1** to make a marriage or a relationship complete by having sex **2** to make something complete or perfect

**con·sum·ma·tion** /ˌkɒnsə'meɪʃən‖ˌkɑːn-/ *n* [U] *formal* **1** the act of making a marriage or relationship complete by having sex **2** *formal* the point at which something is complete or perfect: *the consummation of his ambitions*

**con·sump·tion** /kən'sʌmpʃən/ *n* [U] W3

**1 ▶ AMOUNT OF STH USED ◀** the amount of oil, electricity etc that is used: *Fuel consumption has risen dramatically in the last few years.*

**2 ▶ EATING/DRINKING ◀** *formal* the act of eating or drinking: *The consumption of alcohol was forbidden according to their religion.* | **fit/unfit for human consumption** (=safe or not safe for people to eat) *The meat was declared unfit for human consumption.*

**3 ▶ BUYING ◀** the act of buying and using products: *The consumption of luxury goods is governed by psychological values like social prestige.* | **conspicuous consumption** (=buying expensive goods in order to show other people how rich you are)

**4 ▶ AMOUNT OF FOOD/DRINK ◀** the amount of food or drink that is eaten or drunk: *Patients are advised to cut down on their consumption of alcohol.*

**5 ▶ ILLNESS ◀** a word used in the past for the lung disease TUBERCULOSIS

**6 for sb's consumption** if a piece of information or remark is for a particular person or group's consumption, it is intended to be heard or read by them: *secret policy documents that are not for public consumption*

**con·sump·tive** /kən'sʌmptɪv/ *adj* a word used in the past to describe someone who had the lung disease TUBERCULOSIS —**consumptive** *n* [C]

containers

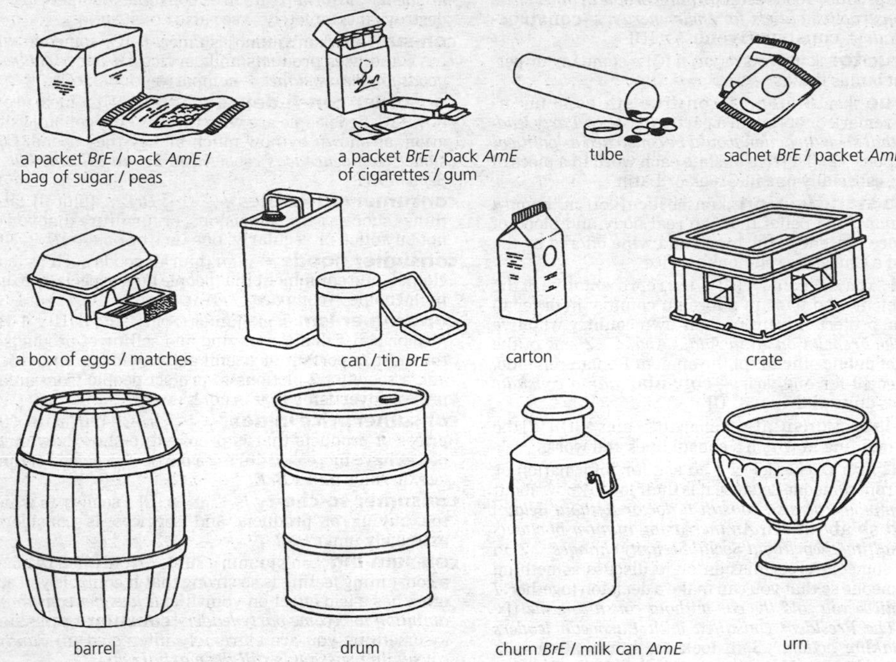

**cont.** the written abbreviation for CONTAINING, CONTENTS, CONTINUED, CONTINENT

S3 W2 **con·tact¹** /ˈkɒntækt‖ˈkɑːn-/ *n*

**1 ▶ COMMUNICATION ◀** [U] communication with a person, organization, country etc: [+ **with**] *He's not had any contact with his son for months.* | [+ **between**] *There is very little contact between the two tribes.* | **be/get/stay in contact (with)** *We stay in contact with each other by telephone.* | **make/lose contact with** (=succeed in communicating or stop communicating with someone) *I've lost contact with most of my school friends.* | **put sb in contact (with)** (=make it possible for someone to communicate with another person by giving them that person's address or telephone number) *Sarah put me in contact with an expert in the field.*

**2 ▶ TOUCH ◀** [U] a state in which two people or things touch each other: [+ **with**] *Children need close physical contact and interaction with a caring adult.* | [+ **between**] *This disease is spread by contact between the animals.* | **in contact (with)** *For a second, his hand was in contact with mine.* | **come into contact (with)** *She screamed as her body came into contact with the water.* | **on contact (with)** (=at the moment of touching something) *The bomb exploded on contact with the ground.* | **contact points/area/surfaces etc** *The contact points of the two surfaces must be clean and dry.*

**3 come into contact with sb** to meet someone: *Diana dazzled everyone who came into contact with her.*

**4 ▶ PERSON WHO CAN HELP ◀** [C] a person you know who may be able to help you or give you advice about something: *He has a lot of contacts in the media.*

**5 ▶ SITUATION/PROBLEM ◀** [U] experience of dealing with a particular kind of situation or problem: **bring sb into contact with sth** *Pat's job brought her into contact with the problems people face when they retire.*

**6 point of contact a)** a place that you go to or a person that you meet when dealing with an organization: *Primary health care teams are the first point of contact for users of the health service.* **b)** a way in which two very different things are connected: *It's difficult to find a point of contact between theory and practice.*

**7 ▶ ELECTRICAL PART ◀** [C] an electrical part that completes a CIRCUIT (4) when it touches another part

**8 ▶ EYES ◀** [C] a contact lens —see also **eye contact** (EYE¹ (9))

**contact²** *v* [T] to write to or telephone someone: *Give the names of two people who can be contacted in case of emergency.* 

**contact³** *adj* [only before noun] **1** a contact number or address is a telephone number or address where someone can be found if necessary: *The school requires a contact number for each child.* **2** contact explosives or chemicals become active when they touch something: *Contact poisons are widely used in pest control.*

**contact lens** /ˈ·· ·/ *n* [C] a small round piece of plastic you put on your eye to help you see clearly

**con·ta·gion** /kənˈteɪdʒən/ *n* [C,U] **1** *technical* a situation in which a disease is spread by people touching each other: *The danger of contagion was now very small.* **2** *technical* a disease that can be passed from person to person by touch **3** *formal* a feeling or attitude that spreads quickly from person to person

**con·ta·gious** /kənˈteɪdʒəs/ *adj* **1** a disease that is contagious can be passed from person to person by touch **2** a person who is contagious has a disease that can be passed to another person by touch: *The patient is still* *highly contagious.* **3** if a feeling, attitude, or action is contagious, other people quickly begin to feel it, believe it, do it etc: *Her enthusiasm was contagious* —**contagiousness** *n* [U] —**contagiously** *adv*

S2 W1 **con·tain** /kən'teɪn/ *v* [T] **1** to have something inside, or have something as a part: *He opened the bag, which contained a razor, soap and a towel.* | *The letter contained important information about Boulestin's legal affairs.* **2** to keep a strong feeling or emotion under control: *Jane couldn't contain her amusement a moment longer.* | **contain yourself** (=keep your emotions under control) *He was so excited he could hardly contain himself.* **3** to stop something from spreading or escaping: *Doctors are struggling to contain the epidemic.* —see also SELF-CONTAINED **4** *formal* to surround an area or an angle: *How big is the angle contained by these two sides?*

**con·tain·er** /kən'teɪnə‖-ər/ *n* [C] **1** something such as a box or bowl that can be used for keeping things in: *Ice cream comes in plastic containers.* **2** a very large metal box in which goods are packed to make it easy to lift or move them onto a ship or vehicle: *The deck was full of big cargo containers.*

**con·tain·ment** /kən'teɪnmənt/ *n* [U] **1** the act of keeping something under control: *containment of public expenditure* **2** the use of political actions to prevent an unfriendly country from becoming more powerful: *a policy of containment*

**con·tam·i·nant** /kən'tæmɪ̈nənt/ *n* [C] *technical* a poisonous substance that makes something impure

**con·tam·i·nate** /kən'tæmɪ̈neɪt/ *v* [T] **1** to make a place or substance dirty and dangerous by adding something to it, for example chemicals or poison: *fears that dumped waste might contaminate water supplies* **2** to influence something in a way that has a bad effect —**contamination** /kən,tæmɪ̈'neɪʃən/ *n* [U]

**con·tam·i·nat·ed** /kən'tæmɪ̈neɪtɪ̈d/ *adj* **1** water, food etc that is contaminated has dangerous or harmful things in it, such as chemicals or poison: *Several outbreaks of infection have been traced to contaminated food.* **2** influenced in a way that produces a bad effect

**contd.** the written abbreviation for CONTINUED

**con·tem·plate** /'kɒntəmpleɪt‖'kɑːn-/ *v* **1** [T] to think about something that you intend to do in the future: *Aren't you a little young to be contemplating marriage?* | **contemplate doing sth** *I've never even contemplated leaving my job.* **2** [T] to accept the possibility that something is true: **too dreadful/horrifying etc to contemplate** *The thought of the letter never having reached him was too terrible to contemplate.* **3** [I,T] to think seriously about something for a long time, especially in order to understand it better: *contemplating the meaning of life*

**con·tem·pla·tion** /,kɒntəm'pleɪʃən‖,kɑːn-/ *n* [U] quiet, serious thinking about something, especially in order to understand it better: *The monks spend an hour in contemplation each morning.*

**con·tem·pla·tive¹** /kən'templətɪv, 'kɒntəmpleɪtɪv‖kən-, 'kɑːntem-/ *adj* spending a lot of time thinking seriously and quietly: *a contemplative mood* —**contemplatively** *adv*

**contemplative²** *n* [C] *formal* someone who spends their life thinking deeply about religious matters

**con·tem·po·ra·ne·ous** /kən,tempə'reɪniəs/ *adj formal* happening in the same period of time; CONTEMPORARY (2): [+ **with**] *Built in the 13th and 14th centuries, they are contemporaneous with many of the great Gothic cathedrals.* —**contemporaneously** *adv* —**contemporaneity** /kən,tempərə'niːɪ̈ti/ *n* [U]

W2 **con·tem·po·ra·ry¹** /kən'tempərəri, -pəri‖-pəreri/ *adj* **1** belonging to the present time; MODERN: **contemporary music/art/dance etc** *an exhibition of contemporary Japanese prints* **2** happening or existing in the same period of time

**contemporary²** *n* [C] someone who was in a particular place or who lived at the same time as someone else: *Oswald was much admired by his contemporaries at the Royal Academy.*

**con·tempt** /kən'tempt/ *n* [U] **1** a feeling that someone or something is not important and deserves no respect: [+ **for**] *His contempt for his fellow students was quite obvious.* | **with contempt** *He had been treated with nothing but contempt ever since he arrived.* | **hold sb in contempt** (=feel contempt for someone) *They'd always held that family in contempt.* | **beneath contempt** (=so unacceptable that you have no respect for the person involved) *That sort of behavior is simply beneath contempt.* **2** disobedience or disrespect towards a court of law: **in contempt of** *He was found in contempt of the order.* | **contempt of court** (=not doing what a judge or court of law has told you to do) **3** complete lack of fear towards something difficult or dangerous: *contempt for danger*

**con·temp·ti·ble** /kən'temptɪ̈bəl/ *adj* so unacceptable that you have no respect for the person involved: *They were portrayed as contemptible cowards.* —**contemptibly** *adv*

**con·temp·tu·ous** /kən'temptʃuəs/ *adj* **1** showing that you feel that someone or something is not important and deserves no respect: *Cordelia threw him a contemptuous look.* | **be contemptuous of** *He was openly contemptuous of his elder brother.* **2** not feeling any fear in a dangerous situation: *Contemptuous of the risks, she ran into the burning building.* —**contemptuously** *adv*

**con·tend** /kən'tend/ *v* **1** [I] to compete against someone in order to gain something: *contending for the World Heavyweight Title* **2** [T + **that**] to argue or state that something is true: *Some astronomers contend that the universe may be younger than previously believed.*

**contend with** sth *phr v* [T] **have to contend with sth/have sth to contend with** to have to deal with something difficult or unpleasant: *He had to contend with a lot of shouting and jeering from the audience.*

**con·tend·er** /kən'tendə‖-ər/ *n* [C] someone who takes part in a competition or a situation in which they have to compete with other people: *a serious contender for the Democratic nomination*

**con·tent¹** /'kɒntent‖'kɑːn-/ *n* **1 contents** [plural] **a)** the things that are inside a box, bag, room etc: *The box had fallen over, and some of the contents had spilled out.* | *The customs official rummaged through the contents of the briefcase.* **b)** the things that are written in a letter, book etc: *If the contents of this letter become known to the Foreign Secretary, there would be grave consequences.* | **table of contents** (=a list at the beginning of a book, which shows the different parts into which the book is divided) | **contents page** (=the page in a book on which the table of contents appears) **2** [singular] the amount of a substance that is contained in something: *the fat content of cheese* **3** [singular] the ideas, facts, or opinions that are contained in a speech or a piece of writing: *They said they liked the content of your article, but the style wasn't quite right for the magazine.* 

**con·tent²** /kən'tent/ *adj* [not before noun] **1** happy and satisfied: *Tarka lay drowsy and content in the sun.* | **content to do sth** *John is quite content to watch television for hours at a stretch.* | [+ **with**] *She is content with her job at the moment.* **2 not content with** if someone is not content with doing something, they do not think that it is good enough, and so want to do more: *Not content with sentencing him to ten years in prison, the judge ordered that he leave the country on his release.* 

**content³** *n* [U] **1** *literary* a feeling of quiet happiness and satisfaction **2 do sth to your heart's content** to do something as much as you want: *We sang away to our hearts' content.*

**content⁴** *v* [T] **1 content yourself with sth** to do or have something that is not what you really wanted, but is still satisfactory: *This is all I have, so you'll have to content yourself with £5 for the moment.* **2** to make someone feel happy and satisfied: *I was no longer satisfied with the life that had hitherto contented me.*

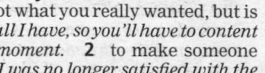

**con·tent·ed** /kənˈtentɨd/ *adj* happy and satisfied because your life is good: *a fat and contented black cat* —**contentedly** *adv*: *The baby gurgled contentedly in its crib.*

**con·ten·tion** /kənˈtenʃən/ *n* **1** [C] *formal* an opinion that someone expresses: *Her main contention is that doctors should do more to encourage people to lead healthy lives.* **2** [U] *formal* argument and disagreement between people: *The issue of subsidies is a great source of contention in Europe.* **3 a bone of contention** a subject that causes disagreement or argument: *Their aunt's will has always been a bone of contention between them.* **4 in contention** *formal* being the subject of argument and disagreement: *The issue is no longer in contention.*

**con·ten·tious** /kənˈtenʃəs/ *adj* **1** causing a lot of argument and disagreement between people: *Animal welfare did not become a contentious issue until the late 1970s.* **2** someone who is contentious often argues with people —**contentiously** *adv* —**contentiousness** *n* [U]

**con·tent·ment** /kənˈtentmənt/ *n* [U] the state of being happy and satisfied: *He gave a sigh of contentment, turned over and went to sleep.* —opposite DISCONTENT

**con·test¹** /ˈkɒntest‖ˈkɑːn-/ *n* [C] **1** a competition: *a beauty contest* **2** a struggle to win control or power: *the contest for leadership of the party* **3 no contest** used to mean that you will easily be the best or win the contest

**con·test²** /kənˈtest/ *v* [T] **1** to say formally that you do not accept something or do not agree with it: *His brothers are contesting the will.* **2** to compete for something or try to win it: *contesting a seat on the council*

**con·tes·tant** /kənˈtestənt/ *n* [C] someone who competes in a contest: *The next contestant is Vera Walker of Lincoln.*

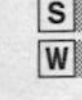

S3 W1 **con·text** /ˈkɒntekst‖ˈkɑːn-/ *n* [C] **1** the situation, events, or information that are related to something, and that help you to understand it better: *These changes must be seen in their historical and social context.* | **in context** (=considered together with the related situation, events etc rather than considered alone) *I think we need to look at these events in context.* **2** the words and sentences that come before and after a particular word, and that help you to understand the meaning of the word: *'Mad' can mean 'foolish', 'insane', or 'angry', depending on the context.* **3 take/quote sth out of context** to repeat a sentence or statement, without describing the situation in which it was said, with the result that it seems to mean something different: *Jones was furious that the papers had quoted his remarks completely out of context.*

**con·tex·tu·al** /kənˈtekstʃuəl/ *adj* relating to a particular context: *contextual information* —**contextually** *adv*

**con·tex·tu·al·ize** also **-ise** *BrE* /kənˈtekstʃuəlaɪz/ *v* [T] to consider something together with the situation, events, or information that relate to it, rather than alone —**contextualization** /kənˌtekstʃuəlaɪˈzeɪʃən‖-lə-/ *n* [U]

**con·tig·u·ous** /kənˈtɪgjuəs/ *adj* [+ **with**] *formal* next to something, or near something in time or order: [+ **with**] *Canada is contiguous with the US along much of its border.* —**contiguously** *adv* —**contiguity** /ˌkɒntɨˈgjuːɨti‖ˌkɑːn-/ *n* [U]

**con·ti·nence** /ˈkɒntɨnəns‖ˈkɑːn-/ *n* [U] *formal* the practice of controlling your desire for sex

**con·ti·nent¹** /ˈkɒntɨnənt‖ˈkɑːn-/ *n* [C] **1** a large mass of land surrounded by sea: *the continents of Asia and Africa* **2 the Continent** *especially BrE* Western Europe not including Britain: *a holiday on the Continent*

**continent²** *adj* **1** able to control your BLADDER (1) and bowels (BOWEL (1)) **2** *old use* controlling your desire to have sex —opposite INCONTINENT

**con·ti·nen·tal¹** /ˌkɒntɨˈnentl◂‖ˌkɑːn-/ *adj* **1** [only before noun] belonging to the North American continent: *The continental United States does not include Hawaii.* **2** relating to a large mass of land: *birds and reptiles from continental South America* **3** *especially BrE* belonging to or in the European continent: *We visited all the major continental cities.* **4** characteristic of the warmer countries in Western Europe: *That café looks very continental with its tables set out on the pavement like that.*

**continental²** *n* [C] *BrE old-fashioned* someone who comes from Europe but not from Britain

**continental break·fast** /ˌ····ˈ··/ *n* [C] a breakfast consisting of coffee and bread with butter and JAM¹ (1) —compare ENGLISH BREAKFAST

**continental drift** /ˌ····ˈ·/ *n* [U] *technical* the very slow movement of the continents (CONTINENT¹ (1)) across the surface of the Earth

**continental shelf** /ˌ····ˈ·/ *n plural* **continental shelves** [C] *technical* the part of a CONTINENT¹ (1) that slopes down under the ocean and ends in a steep slope down to the bottom of the ocean

**con·tin·gen·cy** /kənˈtɪndʒənsi/ *n* **1** an event or situation that might happen in the future, especially one that might cause problems: **contingency plan** (=a plan that you make in order to deal with a problem that might happen) *contingency plans to cope with a major computer failure* **2 contingency fee** *AmE* an amount of money that a lawyer in the US will be paid only if the person they are advising wins in court

**con·tin·gent¹** /kənˈtɪndʒənt/ *adj formal* dependent on something that is uncertain or that will happen in the future: [+ **on/upon**] *Further investment would be contingent upon the company's profit performance.* —**contingently** *adv*

**contingent²** *n* [C also + plural verb *BrE*] **1** a group of people who all have the same aim or are from the same area, and who are part of a larger group: *Has the Scottish contingent arrived yet?* **2** a group of soldiers sent to help a larger group: *A large contingent of field artillery was dispatched.*

**con·tin·u·al** /kənˈtɪnjuəl/ *adj* **1** continuing for a long time without stopping: *five weeks of continual rain* | *The hostages lived in continual fear of violent death.* **2** repeated often and over a long period of time; frequent: *The continual trips to my mother's house took up a lot of my time.* **3** used to describe actions that are repeated many times over a period of time and are annoying: *I wish you'd stop that continual chattering!* —**continually** *adv*: *continually reassessing the situation*

**USAGE NOTE: CONTINUAL**

WORD CHOICE: **continual(ly), continuous(ly)**

**Continual** describes separate actions (often annoying actions you do not like) which are repeated over a period of time: *These continual interruptions are driving me mad.* | *She's continually flying off to different places.*

**Continuous** especially describes things and events that go on without a break: *The police formed a continuous line round the building.* | *This product is the result of years of continuous development.* | *We landed after flying continuously for 16 hours.*

The uses just described are regarded by many as the correct ones, but native speakers often use **continuous(ly)** also, like **continual(ly)**, to describe repeated separate actions: *There were continuous interruptions.* As a result, **continuous(ly)** is much more frequent in spoken English. Where both might be used, **continuous(ly)** may carry less of the idea that the repeated action is annoying: *It rained continuously all summer, which was good for the rice crop.* Compare: *It rained continually all summer, which completely spoiled our vacation.*

**con·tin·u·ance** /kənˈtɪnjuəns/ *n* **1** [singular, U] the state of continuing for a long period of time: *the continuance in power of the Nationalist party* **2** [C usually singular] *law* the act of allowing the events in a court of law to stop for a period of time, usually so a lawyer can find more facts about the case

**con·tin·u·a·tion** /kənˌtɪnjuˈeɪʃən/ *n* **1** [U] The act or state of continuing for a long period without stopping: *A royal child will ensure the continuation of the family line.* **2** [C] something that follows after something else without stopping or changing: [+ **of**] *The present economic policy is a continuation of the earlier one.* **3** [C] something that is joined to something else as if it were part of it: [+ **of**] *The Baltic Sea is a continuation of the North Sea.*

S1 W1 **con·tin·ue** /kən'tɪnjuː/ *v* **1** [I,T] to keep happening, existing, or doing something for a longer period of time without stopping: *He will be continuing his education in the US.* | *The fighting continued for a week.* [+ **with**] *Continuing with this argument is very pointless.* | **continue to do sth** *Silvina continued to work after she had had her baby.* | **continue doing sth** *They continued talking after the meal.* **2** [I,T] to start again after an interruption: *After a brief ceasefire the fighting continued.* | **continue doing sth** *Are you going to continue seeing her when she comes back?* **3** [I] to walk, travel, or go further on or along: [+**down/in/after etc**] *We continued along the road for some time.* **4** [I,T] to say something else after you have been interrupted: *"And so," he continued, "we will try harder next time."* —see also CONTINUAL, DISCONTINUE

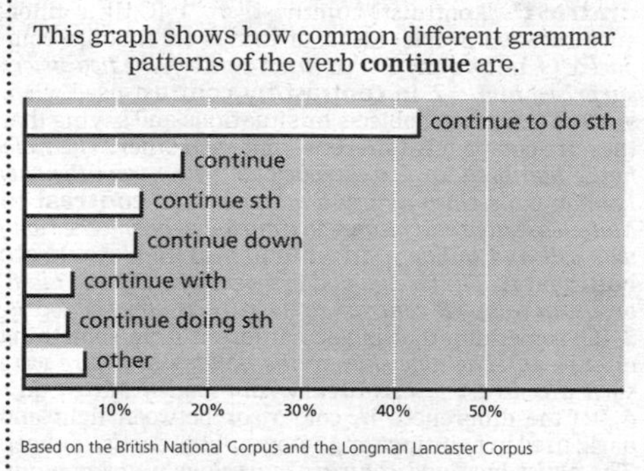


**con·tin·ued** /kən'tɪnjuːd/ *adj* [only before noun] continuing to happen for a long time, or happening many times: *The continued failure of the police caused a public outcry.* | *continued press speculation*

**continuing ed·u·ca·tion** /ˌ·‚·· ··'··/ *n* [U] education provided for adults outside the formal educational system, usually by means of classes that are held in the evening

**con·ti·nu·i·ty** /ˌkɒntɪ̵'njuːɪ̵ti‖ˌkɑːntɪ̵'nuː-/ *n* [U] **1** the continuing of an event, system etc over a long period of time, without problems happening when there is a change: *We should ensure continuity of care between hospital and home.* **2** *technical* the organization of a film or television programme to give the appearance that the action happens without pauses or interruptions

**con·tin·u·o** /kən'tɪnju-əʊ‖-oʊ/ *n* [C] *technical* a musical part consisting of a line of low notes with figures showing the higher notes that are to be played with them

S2 W3 **con·tin·u·ous** /kən'tɪnjuəs/ *adj* **1** continuing to happen or exist without stopping or without any interruptions: *The brain needs a continuous supply of blood.* | *The Blood Transfusion Service has a long and continuous tradition of public service.* **2** something such as a line that is continuous does not have any spaces or holes in it **3 continuous assessment** *BrE* a way of judging how well a student is doing by looking at the work they do during the year rather than by testing them in an examination **4** *technical* the continuous form of a verb is used to show that an action or activity is continuing to happen, and is shown in English by the verb 'be', followed by a PRESENT PARTICIPLE, as in 'I was waiting for the bus' —**continuously** *adv*

**con·tin·u·um** /kən'tɪnjuəm/ *n* [C] *plural* **continuums** *or* **continua** /-juə/ something that changes or develops very gradually, so that each part is very similar to previous and following parts; CLINE: *a learning continuum along which all learners fit*

**con·tort** /kən'tɔːt‖-ɔːrt/ *v* [I,T] to twist something so that it does not have its normal shape, and looks strange or unattractive, or to twist in this way: [+ **with**] *His face was contorted with rage.*

**con·tor·tion** /kən'tɔːʃən‖-ɔːr-/ *n* [U] **1** the act of twisting something so that it does not have its normal shape, and looks strange or unattractive, or the fact of being twisted in this way: *the involuntary contortion of muscles brought on by the illness* **2** [C] a twisted position or movement that looks strange: *They turned as they danced with the most amazing contortions.* **3** [C] complicated activity in order to do something: *He went through a series of amazing contortions to get Karen a work permit.*

**con·tor·tion·ist** /kən'tɔːʃənɪ̵st‖-ɔːr-/ *n* [C] someone who entertains people by twisting their body into strange and unnatural shapes and positions

**con·tour** /'kɒntʊə‖'kɑːntʊr/ *n* [C] **1** the shape of the outer edges of something such as an area of land or someone's body: *the contours of the hills and ridges* | *the contour of her face* **2** also **contour line** a line on a map that connects points of equal height above sea level, which together with others show hills, valleys etc

**con·toured** /'kɒntʊəd‖'kɑːntʊrd/ *adj* **1** shaped to fit closely next to something else, or in a shape like this: *The cushion was still warm, contoured to the shape of his body.* **2** having an attractive, curved shape: *the smoothly contoured lines and attractive styling of this sofa*

**contra-** /kɒntrə‖kɑːn-/ *prefix* **1** acting to prevent something: *contraceptive devices* (=against CONCEPTION) **2** opposite: *plants in contradistinction to animals*

**con·tra·band** /'kɒntrəbænd‖'kɑːn-/ *n* [U] goods that are brought into a country illegally, especially without tax being paid on them: *contraband steel imported illegally into Turkey* —**contraband** *adj*

**con·tra·bass** /ˌkɒntrə'beɪs‖ˌkɑːn-/ *n* [C] a DOUBLE BASS

**con·tra·cep·tion** /ˌkɒntrə'sepʃən‖ˌkɑːn-/ *n* [U] the practice of making it possible for a woman to have sex without having a baby, or the methods for doing this; BIRTH CONTROL: *The pill is a popular method of contraception.*

**con·tra·cep·tive** /ˌkɒntrə'septɪv◂‖ˌkɑːn-/ *n* [C] a drug, object, or method used to make it possible for a woman to have sex without having a baby: *You can get free contraceptives from the family planning clinic.* —**contraceptive** *adj* [only before noun]: *a contraceptive device*

**con·tract¹** /'kɒntrækt‖'kɑːn-/ *n* [C] **1** a formal written agreement between two or more people, which says what each person must do for the other: *His contract of employment specifies that he must get at least one month's training.* | [+ **with**] *Tyler has just agreed a seven year contract with a Hollywood studio.* | **sign a contract** *Read the contract carefully before you sign it.* | **enter into a contract** *They have just entered into a lucrative contract with a clothing store.* | **be on a contract/be under contract** (=be working for someone with whom you have a contract) | **be in breach of contract** (=have done something that is not allowed by the contract) *If they don't get the test version of the software to us by tomorrow they'll be in breach of contract.* **2 subject to contract** if an agreement is subject to contract, it has not yet been agreed formally by a contract: *We've agreed to their offer on our house, subject to contract.* **3** *informal* an agreement to kill a person for money: *There is a contract out on him and he's in hiding.*

**con·tract²** /kən'trækt/ *v* **1** [I] to become smaller or narrower: *Metal contracts as it becomes cool.* | *The economy continues to contract, raising fears of further political problems.* —opposite EXPAND (1) **2** [T] *formal* to begin to have an illness: *He contracted pneumonia.* **3 contract to do sth** to sign a contract in which you agree formally that you will do something: *They contracted to work fixed hours each week.* **4 contract a marriage/alliance etc** to agree formally that you will marry someone or have a particular kind of relationship with them: *Most of the marriages were contracted when the brides were very young.*

**contract in** *phr v* [I] *formal especially BrE* to agree or promise, especially officially, to take part in something: *They contracted in to the share deal.*

**contract out** *phr v* **1** [T **contract** sth ↔ **out**] to arrange to have a job done by a person or company outside your own organization: *The company has contracted the catering out to an outside firm.* **2** [I] [+ **of**] *formal especially BrE* to agree or promise, especially officially, not to take part in something such as a PENSION SCHEME

**contract bridge** /ˌ·· ˈ·/ *n* [U] a form of the card game BRIDGE[1] (4), in which one of the two pairs say how many tricks (TRICK (11)) they will try to win

**con·trac·tion** /kənˈtrækʃən/ *n* **1** [C] *technical* a very strong and painful movement of a muscle, especially of the muscles around the WOMB during the process of birth **2** [U] the process of becoming smaller or narrower: *the contraction of metal as it cools* **3** [C] a shortened form of a word or words: *'Haven't' is a contraction of 'have not'.*

**con·trac·tor** /kənˈtræktə‖ˈkɑːntræktər/ *n* [C] a person or company that makes an agreement to do work or provide goods in large amounts for another company: *a roofing contractor*

**con·trac·tu·al** /kənˈtræktʃuəl/ *adj* agreed in a contract: *College teachers have a contractual obligation to research and publish.* —**contractually** *adv*

**con·tra·dict** /ˌkɒntrəˈdɪkt‖ˌkɑːn-/ *v* **1** [T] to disagree with something by saying that it is wrong or not true, especially by saying that the opposite is true: **contradict sb** *Don't contradict your father!* | **flatly contradict** *The article flatly contradicts what the lobbyists have claimed.* **2** [T] if one statement, story etc contradicts another statement etc, the facts in it are different so that both statements cannot be true: *The witnesses' statements contradicted each other and the facts remained unclear.* **3 contradict yourself** to say something that is the opposite of what you said before: *The stupid fool can't speak two sentences without contradicting himself.*

**con·tra·dic·tion** /ˌkɒntrəˈdɪkʃən‖ˌkɑːn-/ *n* **1** [C] a difference between two statements, beliefs, or ideas about something that means they cannot both be true: *The prosecution pointed out the contradictions in the defendant's testimony.* | [+ **between**] *There is a contradiction between the government's radical ideas and its actual urban policy.* **2** [U] the act of saying that someone else's opinion, statement etc is wrong or not true: *You can say what you like without fear of contradiction.* **3 a contradiction in terms** a combination of words that seem to mean opposite things, so that the phrase has no clear meaning: *'Permanent revolution' is a contradiction in terms.* **4 in (direct) contradiction to** in a way that is opposite to a belief or statement: *Your behavior is in direct contradiction to the principles you claim to have.*

**con·tra·dic·to·ry** /ˌkɒntrəˈdɪktəri◂‖ˌkɑːn-/ *adj* two statements, beliefs etc that are contradictory, are different and therefore cannot both be true: *The witnesses gave two completely contradictory accounts.* —see also SELF-CONTRADICTORY

**con·tra·dis·tinc·tion** /ˌkɒntrədɪˈstɪŋkʃən‖ˌkɑːn-/ *n* [C] **in contradistinction to** *formal* as opposed to: *plants in contradistinction to animals*

**con·tra·flow** /ˈkɒntrəfləʊ‖ˈkɑːntrəfloʊ/ *n* [C,U] *BrE* a temporary arrangement on a large road by which traffic in both directions uses only one side of the road because the other side is being repaired

**con·trail** /ˈkɒntreɪl‖ˈkɑːn-/ *n* [C] *AmE* a line of white steam made in the sky by a plane

**con·tral·to** /kənˈtræltəʊ‖-toʊ/ *n* [C] the lowest female singing voice, or a woman who has this voice

**con·trap·tion** /kənˈtræpʃən/ *n* [C] *informal* a strange looking piece of equipment or machinery, especially one that you think is unlikely to work well: *a funny old contraption for pumping up water*

**con·tra·ri·wise** /ˈkɒntrəriwaɪz, kənˈtreri-‖ˈkɑːntreri-/ *adv old-fashioned* in the opposite way or direction; CONVERSE[3]

**con·tra·ry**[1] /ˈkɒntrəri‖ˈkɑːntreri/ *n formal* **1 on the contrary** used for showing that you disagree completely with what has just been said: *It wasn't a good thing; on the contrary it was a huge mistake.* **2 to the contrary** showing that the opposite is true: *Unless there is evidence to the contrary, we ought to believe them.* **3 the contrary** the opposite of what has been said or suggested: *They say he is guilty, but I believe the contrary.*

**contrary**[2] *adj* **1** contrary ideas or opinions are completely different from each other and opposed to each other: *Two contrary views emerged in the discussion.* **2** someone who is contrary deliberately does things differently from the way that other people do them, or from the way that people expect: *Evans was his usual contrary self.* **3 contrary to** if something is contrary to someone's belief or opinion, it is true even though that person believes or thinks the opposite: *Contrary to popular belief the desert can be a beautiful place.* **4** *formal* contrary weather conditions are ones that cause difficulties: *Contrary winds delayed the boats' return.* —**contrariness** *n* [U]

**con·trast**[1] /ˈkɒntrɑːst‖ˈkɑːntræst/ *n* **1** [C,U] a difference between people, ideas, or things etc that are compared: [+ **between**] *The contrast between the two sisters surprised him.* **2 in contrast/by contrast** used when you are comparing objects or situations and saying that they are completely different from each other: *Their old house had been large and spacious; by contrast the new London flat seemed cramped and dark.* | **in contrast to** *Mary was short and plump, in contrast to her mother who was tall and willowy.* | **in sharp/marked/stark etc contrast to** *The foreign visitors were wealthy and glamorous, in complete contrast to the poverty-stricken locals.* **3** [C] something that is very different from something else: [+ **to**] *The blue skies of the holiday brochure were such a contrast to this dreary rain-sodden March day.* **4** [U] the differences in colour, or between light and dark, used in paintings or photographs for artistic effect: *The artist has used contrast marvelously in his paintings.* **5** [U] the degree of difference between the light and dark parts of a television picture: *Can you adjust the contrast please?* W2

**con·trast**[2] /kənˈtrɑːst‖-ˈtræst/ *v* **1** [T] to compare two things, ideas, people etc to show how different they are from each other: **contrast sth with sth** *In the film, the peaceful life of a farmer is contrasted with the violent existence of a gangster.* **2** [I] if two things contrast, the difference between them is very easy to see and is sometimes surprising: [+ **with**] *The snow was icy and white, contrasting with the brilliant blue sky.* | **contrast sharply/strikingly with** (=be extremely different from) *These results contrast sharply with other medical tests carried out in Australia.*

**con·tras·ting** /kənˈtrɑːstɪŋ‖-ˈtræs-/ *adj* two or more things that are contrasting are different from each other, especially in a way that is interesting or attractive: *a blue shirt with a contrasting collar*

**con·tra·vene** /ˌkɒntrəˈviːn‖ˌkɑːn-/ *v* [T] *formal* to do something that is not allowed according to a law or rule: *Milk from an unhealthy cow may contravene public health regulations.*

**con·tra·ven·tion** /ˌkɒntrəˈvenʃən‖ˌkɑːn-/ *n* **1** [C,U] the act of doing something that is not allowed by a law or rule: *Sending the troops was a contravention of the treaty.* **2 in contravention of** in a way that is not allowed by a law or rule: *They employed minors in contravention of the law.*

**con·tre·temps** /ˈkɒntrətɒŋ‖ˈkɑːntrətɑːn/ *n plural* **contretemps** [C] *French often humorous* **1** an argument: *I had a little contretemps with Mr Willard on the phone.* **2** an unlucky and unexpected event, especially an embarrassing one

S2 W2 **con·trib·ute** /kənˈtrɪbjuːt/ *v* **1** [I,T] to give money, help, ideas etc to something that a lot of other people are also involved in: **contribute to/towards sth** *Most people contributed something towards the new church buildings.* | **contribute sth to/towards sth** *The volunteers contribute huge amounts of their own time to the project.* **2 contribute to sth** to help to cause something: *Various factors contributed to his downfall.* **3** [I,T] to write articles, stories, poems etc for a newspaper or magazine: *one of several authors contributing to the book*

S2 W2 **con·tri·bu·tion** /ˌkɒntrɪˈbjuːʃən‖ˌkɑːn-/ *n* **1** [C] something that you give or do in order to help something be successful: [+ **to/towards**] *Einstein was awarded the Nobel Prize for his contribution to Quantum Theory.* | **make a contribution** *Day centres for the elderly make a valuable contribution to the overall service.* **2** [C] an amount of money that you give in order to help pay for something: [+ **to/towards**] *We are asking for contributions to disaster relief.* | **make a contribution** *Would you like to make a contribution to the hospital rebuilding fund?* **3** [C] a regular payment that you make to your employer or to the government to pay for benefits that you will receive when you are no longer working, for example a PENSION[1] **4** [C] a story, poem, or piece of writing that you write and that is printed in a magazine or newspaper: *This week's issue has contributions from several well-respected journalists.* **5** [U] the act of giving money, time, help etc: *All the money has been raised by voluntary contribution.*

**con·trib·u·tor** /kənˈtrɪbjətə‖-ər/ *n* [C] **1** someone who writes a story, article etc that is printed in a magazine or newspaper: [+ **to**] *I became a regular contributor to the paper, writing film reviews.* **2** someone who gives money, help, ideas etc to something that a lot of other people are also involved in: [+ **to**] *Dr Win was a major contributor to the research.* **3** *formal* someone or something that helps to cause something to happen: [+ **to**] *Order and quiet are important contributors to a good learning environment.*

**con·trib·u·to·ry** /kənˈtrɪbjətəri‖-tɔːri/ *adj* **1** [only before noun] being one of the causes of a particular result: *Smoking is a contributory cause of lung cancer.* **2** a contributory PENSION[1] or insurance plan is one that is paid for by the workers as well as by the company —opposite NONCONTRIBUTORY

**contributory neg·li·gence** /ˌ····ˈ····/ *n* [U] *law* failure to take enough care to avoid or prevent an accident, so that you are partly responsible for any loss or damage caused

**con trick** /ˈ· ·/ *n* [C] a CONFIDENCE TRICK

**con·trite** /ˈkɒntraɪt‖ˈkɑːn-/ *adj* feeling guilty and sorry for something bad that you have done: *her contrite expression* —**contritely** *adv* —**contrition** /kənˈtrɪʃən/ *n* [U]

**con·triv·ance** /kənˈtraɪvəns/ *n* **1** [C,U] a clever plan to get something for yourself by deceiving someone, or the practice of doing this: *Their story was a clumsy contrivance to persuade me to help them.* **2** [C] a machine or piece of equipment that has been made or invented for a special purpose: *a steam-driven contrivance used in 19th century clothing factories*

**con·trive** /kənˈtraɪv/ *v* [T] **1** to arrange an event or situation in a clever way, especially secretly or by deceiving people: *He managed to contrive a meeting between Janet and her ex-boyfriend.* **2** *formal* to succeed in doing something in spite of difficulties: **contrive to do sth** *She didn't speak any English, but we contrived to communicate using sign language.* **3** to make or invent something in a clever way, especially because you need it suddenly: *Peter had contrived a tolerable substitute for our sled.*

**con·trived** /kənˈtraɪvd/ *adj* a story, situation etc that is contrived has been written or arranged in a way that seems false and not natural: *The film had a ridiculously contrived story line.*

**control**[1] /kənˈtrəʊl‖-ˈtroʊl/ *n* S1 W1

**1 ► MAKE SB/STH DO WHAT YOU WANT ◄** [U] the ability or power to make someone or something do what you want: *Generally your driving's OK, but your clutch control isn't very good.* | [+ **of/over**] *Babies are born with very little control over their movements.* | **have control of/over** *I prefer living alone because I feel I have more control over my life.* | **under control** (=being controlled or dealt with successfully) *Don't worry, everything's under control.* | **out of control** (=no longer possible to be controlled) *The car spun out of control and hit a tree.* | **get out of control** (=become impossible to control) *The street party went on, getting louder and louder and more out of control.* | **lose control (of)** (=not be able to control something any longer) *He took a corner too fast, and lost control of the car.* | **beyond/outside sb's control** (=impossible for you to control) *Ten people had been killed, and it was obvious that the situation had gotten beyond the control of the authorities.* | **take/gain control (of)** (=gain the ability to control something) *Students are encouraged to take control of their own learning, rather than just depending on the teacher.* | **circumstances beyond sb's control** (=a situation that you cannot control) *Tonight's performance has been cancelled due to circumstances beyond our control.*

**2 ► POLITICAL/MILITARY POWER ◄** [U] the power to rule or govern a place, or the fact that you have more power than other political parties: **have control of/over** *By the end of the year, the rebels had control of the northern territories.* | **gain/take control (of)** (=get control of a place that someone else was controlling) *When the communists gained control they abolished the monarchy.* | **lose control** (=not be able to control a place any longer) *The Democrats have just lost control of Congress.* | **be/come under sb's control** *The whole of this area came under Soviet control.* | **under the control of** (=being controlled by a political party etc) *The government has been overthrown and the country is now under the control of the military.* | **under British/Communist/enemy control** *The city is now under Serbian control.* | **regain control** (=gain control after you had lost it) *The Conservatives are hoping to regain control of the seats taken from them in the last election.* | **have overall control** *BrE* (=have more members of your political party in a council than other parties have, so that you control the council) | **assume control** (=get control of a country by defeating the government using military power) *Lij Yasu seized the palace and assumed control of the country.*

**3 ► WAY OF LIMITING STH ◄** [C,U] a method or law for limiting the amount or growth of something: [+ **of**] *the control of inflation* | *control of pests and diseases* | [+ **on**] *The authorities imposed strict controls on the movement of cattle.* | **arms control** (=control of the amount of weapons a country has) *An arms control agreement between the superpowers has just been announced.* | **crowd control** *Crowd control is a problem for the police at these demonstrations.* | **tight/rigid controls** (=strict controls) *The government favours the introduction of tighter controls on immigration.* | **rent/price/wage etc controls** *Rent controls ensured that no one paid too much for housing.*

**4 ► DISEASE/FIRE ETC ◄** [U] the ability to stop something dangerous from getting worse or affecting more people: **have sth under control** *Firefighters now have the blaze under control.* | **bring sth under control** *The plant was given six months to bring the pollution under control.* | **keep sth under control** *Johnson's been struggling for years to keep his drinking under control.*

**5 ► ABILITY TO CONTROL EMOTIONS ◄** [U] the ability to remain calm even when you feel very angry, upset, or excited: *It took a lot of control, but she managed not to cry.* | **lose control** (=become extremely angry or upset and not be able to control your behaviour) *Jim made me so mad, I just lost control and hit him.* | **self-control** (=the ability to behave calmly even when you feel very upset, angry etc) | **regain control** (=succeed in

behaving calmly again after you have been upset or angry) *She felt tears welling up inside her again, but she managed to regain control.*
**6 be in control a)** to be able to control a situation, organization, or area because you have more power than anyone else: [+ **of**] *The anti-government forces are still in control of the area.* **b)** to be able to control your emotions, deal with problems, and organize your life well: *Weber's one of those guys who always seems to be in control.* **c)** to manage to control a difficult situation: [+ **of**] *The police chief assured reporters that he was in control of events.*

**7 ▶ COMPANY/ORGANIZATION ◀** [U] the power to make all the important decisions in an organization or part of an organization: **take control (of)** *Anne Williams will take control of the research division on August 5th.* | **have control of** (=own a larger part of a company than other people so that you control that company) *The Johnson family has effective control of the company, owning almost 60% of the shares.* | **lose control (of)** (=not be able to control a company etc any longer) *McAllister lost control of the company in 1988.* | **under the control of** (=being controlled by someone) *The college was under the control of a group of trustees.*
**8 ▶ MACHINE/VEHICLE ◀** [C] the thing that you press or turn to make a machine, vehicle, television etc work: *Who's got the control for the video?* | *the volume control of a television set* | **be at the controls** (=be controlling a vehicle or aircraft) *The co-pilot is at the controls.* —see also REMOTE CONTROL
**9 ▶ SKILL ◀** [U] the ability to make very skilful movements with a ball, pencil, tool etc: *Johnson passes with good control, over to Abdul-Jabber.*
**10 ▶ AIRCRAFT ETC ◀** [U] the people who direct an activity, especially by giving instructions to an aircraft or SPACECRAFT : *air-traffic control*
**11 ▶ SCIENTIFIC TEST ◀** *technical* [C] **a)** a person, group etc against which you compare another person or group that is very similar, in order to see if a particular quality is caused by something or happens by chance: **control group/population** *a control group of non-smoking women were compared to four groups of women smokers.* **b)** a thing that you already know the result for that is used in a scientific test, in order to show that your method is working correctly —see also CONTROLLED EXPERIMENT
**12 ▶ COMPUTER ◀** also **control key** [singular] a particular button on a computer that allows you to do certain operations: *Press control and F2 to exit.*
**13 ▶ YOUR BODY ◀** the ability to control the movements of your body by using your muscles when dancing or doing physical excercise
**14 ▶ CHECKING SOMETHING ◀** [U] the process of checking that something is correct, or the place where this is done: *passport control* | *stock control* —see BIOLOGICAL CONTROL, BIRTH CONTROL, QUALITY CONTROL, REMOTE CONTROL

S2 W1 **con·trol²** *v* **controlled, controlling** [T]
**1 ▶ MAKE SB STH DO WHAT YOU WANT ◀** to make someone or something do what you want or behave in the way you want them to behave: *The teacher can't control the class.* | *a huge company controlling half the world's coffee trade*
**2 ▶ MACHINE/PROCESS/SYSTEM ◀** to make a machine, process, or system work in a particular way: *This button controls the temperature in the building.* | **control how/what/which etc** *The valves in the heart control how quickly the blood is pumped around the body.*
**3 ▶ LIMIT ◀** if a government etc controls something, it uses laws or other methods to limit the amount or growth of something: *Development in areas of outstanding natural beauty is strictly controlled.*
**4 ▶ POLITICAL/MILITARY POWER ◀** to rule or govern a place, or to have more power than other political parties: *The Democrats continued to control the House until 1994.* | **Labour/Republican/Democrat controlled** *a Conservative-controlled council*
**5 ▶ DISEASE/FIRE ETC ◀** to stop something dangerous from getting worse or affecting more people: *The Ministry of Health has set up a programme to control the spread of AIDS.*
**6 ▶ EMOTION ◀** if you control your emotions, you succeed in behaving calmly and sensibly, even though you feel angry, upset, or excited: *Sarah just can't control her temper.* | **control yourself** (=succeed in behaving calmly and sensibly, even though you feel angry etc) *She annoyed me intensely, but I managed to control myself and remain polite.*
**7 ▶ VOICE/EXPRESSION ◀** if you control your voice or the expression on your face, you make it seem normal, so that people cannot see that you are upset, angry, or excited: *He controlled his voice, betraying nothing but a casual interest.*
**8 ▶ ANIMALS ◀** to kill animals when there are so many of them that they cause problems: *measures to control rats in the city's sewers*
**9 ▶ BUSINESSES/ORGANIZATIONS ◀** to make sure that something is done correctly: *The company strictly controls the quality of its products.*

### USAGE NOTE: CONTROL

WORD CHOICE: **control, manage, run, be in charge of, check on, inspect, monitor**

Most meanings of **control** (*n,v*) involve the idea of a person or other force having the power to change or stop something, without the people or things affected being able to do anything about it. People, organizations, machines etc **control** other people, organizations, their own or others actions, events, etc, sometimes from far away.

Where you want to give the idea of people directing businesses etc, where the other people involved are nearby and perhaps allowed some say in the activity, you may use **manage**, **run**, or **be in charge of**: *He's managing/running an electrical shop/project group/rock band.* | *Margaret is in charge of the school while Mrs Williams is away.*

When you want to talk about people, things, or activities, in order to see if they are correct, but without directly affecting them, you may use **check on** or **inspect**: *We need to check on our sales.* | *The department is going to be inspected next week.* | *a security check.* **Control** means the same as **check on** only in a few contexts, and usually only as the noun: *quality control, stock control*

**Monitor** is a word meaning to watch and check on someone or something over a period of time. This can be done by a person or by a machine, often in a technical or official context.

**control key** /·'· ·/ *n* [C] a particular button on a computer that allows you to do certain operations
**con·trol·la·ble** /kən'trəʊləbəl‖-'troʊl-/ *adj* possible to be controlled: *Central heating makes the temperature of your home easily controllable.*
**con·trolled** /kən'trəʊld‖-'troʊld/ *adj* **1** calm and not showing emotion, even if you feel angry, afraid etc: *Her voice was resonant and controlled as she delivered her resignation speech.* **2** a movement, action, situation etc that is controlled is one that is carefully and deliberately done in a particular way, or made to have particular qualities: *The chicks are hatched in a controlled environment.* **3** limited by a law or rule: *controlled parking zones*
**controlled drug** /·,· '·/ *n* [C] *law* a drug that is illegal to possess or use
**controlled ex·per·i·ment** /·,· ·'···/ *n* [C] *technical* a scientific test done in a place where you can control all the things that might affect the test: *a controlled experiment to determine the effects of light and nutrients on plant growth*

**controlled sub·stance** /ˌ· ˈ··/ *n* [C] *law* a drug that it is illegal to possess or use: *Heroin is a controlled substance.*

**con·trol·ler** /kənˈtrəʊlə‖-ˈtroʊlər/ *n* [C] **1** someone who is in charge of a particular organization or part of an organization: *the Controller of Channel 4* **2** also **comptroller** *formal* someone who is in charge of the money received or paid out by a company or government department

**controlling in·terest** /ˌ·.. ˈ··/ *n* [C usually singular] *technical* if you have a controlling interest in a company, you own enough shares (SHARE² (6)) to be able to make decisions about what happens to the company

**control room** /·ˈ· ·/ *n* [C] the room that a process, service, large machine, factory etc is controlled from

**control tow·er** /·ˈ· ˌ··/ *n* [C] a tall building in an airport from which people direct the movement of aircraft on the ground and in the air

**con·tro·ver·sial** /ˌkɒntrəˈvɜːʃəl◂‖ˌkɑːntrəˈvɜːrʃəl◂/ *adj* causing a lot of disagreement, because many people have strong opinions about the subject being discussed: *Contraception is still a controversial issue in this part of the world.* | **a controversial plan/decision etc** *a highly controversial plan to flood the valley in order to build a hydro-electric dam* | **a controversial figure** (=someone who does things that are controversial) *Maxwell soon became a controversial figure in the world of big business.* —**controversially** *adv*

**con·tro·ver·sy** /ˈkɒntrəvɜːsi, kənˈtrɒvəsi‖ˈkɑːntrəvɜːrsi/ *n* [C,U] a serious argument or disagreement, especially about something such as a plan or decision, that continues for a long time: *The proposals to reduce the strength of the army have been the subject of much controversy.* | *a political controversy* | [+ **over/about/surrounding**] *the controversy surrounding the nuclear energy program*

**con·tu·ma·cious** /ˌkɒntjʊˈmeɪʃəs◂‖ˌkɑːntə-/ *adj formal* unreasonably disobedient —**contumaciously** *adv*

**con·tume·ly** /ˈkɒntjuːmli, -tjʊmɪli‖kənˈtuːməli/ *n* [C,U] disrespectful and offensive behaviour or language

**con·tuse** /kənˈtjuːz‖-ˈtuːz/ *v* [T] *technical* to BRUISE²

**con·tu·sion** /kənˈtjuːʒən‖-ˈtuː-/ *n* [C,U] *technical* a BRUISE² or BRUISING

**co·nun·drum** /kəˈnʌndrəm/ *n* [C] **1** a confusing and difficult problem: *I don't know the answer – it's a conundrum.* **2** a trick question asked for fun; RIDDLE¹ (1)

**con·ur·ba·tion** /ˌkɒnɜːˈbeɪʃən‖ˌkɑːnɜːr-/ *n* [C] a group of towns that have spread and joined together to form an area with a high population, often with a large city as its centre: *urban conurbations on the west coast*

**con·va·lesce** /ˌkɒnvəˈles‖ˌkɑːn-/ *v* [I] to spend time getting well after an illness: *After her operation my wife was sent abroad to convalesce.*

**con·va·les·cence** /ˌkɒnvəˈlesəns‖ˌkɑːn-/ *n* [singular] the length of time a person spends getting well after an illness: *a long and painful convalescence*

**con·va·les·cent** /ˌkɒnvəˈlesənt◂‖ˌkɑːn-/ *n* [C] a person spending time getting well after an illness —**convalescent** *adj*: *a convalescent nursing home*

**con·vect** /kənˈvekt/ *v* [I] *technical* to move heat by convection

**con·vec·tion** /kənˈvekʃən/ *n* [U] the movement in a gas or liquid caused by warm gas or liquid rising, and cold gas or liquid sinking: *Warm air rises by convection.*

**convection ov·en** /·ˈ·· ˌ··/ *n* [C] a special OVEN that makes hot air move around inside it so that all the parts of the food get the same amount of heat

**con·vec·tor** /kənˈvektə‖-ər/ also **convector hea·ter** /·ˈ·· ˌ··/ *n* [C] an electrical heater that uses hot air

**con·vene** /kənˈviːn/ *v* [I,T] *formal* if a group of people convene, or someone convenes them, they come together, especially for a formal meeting: *The President's foreign policy advisers convened for an emergency session.* | *Shouldn't we convene a meeting about this?*

**con·ve·ni·ence** /kənˈviːniəns/ *n* **1** [U] the quality of being suitable for a particular purpose, especially because it is easy to use or saves you time: *Many women prefer the convenience of working at home while their children are small.* | **for convenience** *We bought this house for convenience; it's near the shops and the railway station.* **2** [U] what is easiest and best for a particular person: **for sb's convenience** *I'm not going to organize my day entirely for your convenience!* | **suit sb's convenience** *We can call at your home at any time to suit your convenience.* | **at sb's convenience** (=at a time that is best and easiest for someone) *Meetings are always arranged at the management's convenience and staff are expected to fit in.* **3 at your earliest convenience** *formal* as soon as possible; usually in letters: *We should be grateful if you would reply at your earliest convenience.* **4** [C] something that is useful because it saves you time or means that you have less work to do: *The supermarket offers a bag-packing service, as a convenience to customers.* **5** also **public convenience** [C usually plural] *formal* a public toilet —see also FLAG OF CONVENIENCE **6 a marriage of convenience** a marriage that has been agreed for a particular purpose, not because the two people love each other: *In the past most royal marriages were marriages of convenience, arranged for political reasons.*

**convenience food** /·ˈ··· ˌ·/ also **convenience foods** *n* [C,U] food that is frozen, or in tins, packages etc, and can be prepared quickly and easily: *People with busy lifestyles tend to rely more and more on convenience foods.*

**convenience store** /·ˈ··· ˌ·/ *n* [C] *AmE* a shop where you can buy food, alcohol, magazines etc, that is often open 24 hours each day —see also CORNER SHOP

**con·ve·ni·ent** /kənˈviːniənt/ *adj* **1** helpful for you because it saves you time or does not spoil your plans or cause you problems: *I find going to the supermarket once a month the most convenient way to shop.* | **convenient for sb** *Is three o'clock convenient for you?* | **convenient time/moment** *I'm afraid this isn't a very convenient time — Could you call back later?* **2** near and easy to reach: *The bus stop around the corner is probably the most convenient.* | **convenient for sth** *Our house is very convenient for schools and stores.* —opposite INCONVENIENT S3

**con·ve·ni·ent·ly** /kənˈviːniəntli/ *adv* **1** in a way that is helpful for you because it saves you time or does not spoil your plans or cause you problems: *The results can be summarized conveniently in the following table.* **2** in a place that is near or easily reached: *The hotel is conveniently situated near the airport.* **3** if someone has conveniently forgotten, ignored, lost etc something, they are pretending to have forgotten etc because this helps them to avoid doing something: *Mary conveniently forgot that she had promised to help clean the kitchen.*

**con·vent** /ˈkɒnvənt‖ˈkɑːnvent/ *n* [C] a building or set of buildings where NUNS live —see also CONVENT SCHOOL

**con·ven·tion** /kənˈvenʃən/ *n* **1** [C,U] behaviour and attitudes that most people in a society consider to be normal and right: *The handshake is a social convention.* | *She went against all convention and married outside her religion.* | **by convention** *By convention, the bride's father gives her away at her wedding.* —see HABIT (USAGE) **2** [C] a formal agreement, especially between countries, about particular rules or behaviour: *the European convention on human rights* —compare PACT, TREATY **3** [C] a large formal meeting for people who belong to the same profession or organization: *a teacher's convention* **4** [C] a method or style often used in literature, art, the theatre etc to achieve a particular effect: *The omniscient narrator is a convention of the nineteenth century novel.* W2

**con·ven·tion·al** /kənˈvenʃənəl/ *adj* **1** [only before noun] a conventional object or way of doing something is of a type that has been used or available for a long time and is considered the usual type: *The water purifying system fits neatly under a conventional sink unit.* **2** always following the opinions and behaviour that most people in a society consider to be normal, right, and socially acceptable but sometimes slightly boring: *Her opinions*

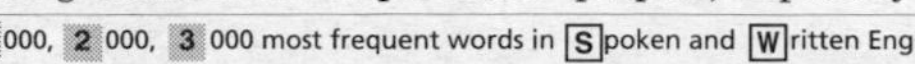

*are rather narrow and conventional.* | [+ **in**] *John is fairly conventional in his tastes.* —opposite UNCONVENTIONAL —see HABIT (USAGE) **3 the conventional wisdom** the opinion that most people consider to be normal and right: *This idea has become part of the conventional wisdom of a whole generation of educationalists.* **4** [only before noun] conventional weapons and wars are not NUCLEAR ones **5 conventional medicine** the usual form of medicine practised in most European and North American countries; WESTERN MEDICINE —**conventionally** *adv* —**conventionality** /kən,venʃə'nælɪ̈ti/ *n* [U]

**conventional ov·en** /.'... ,../ *n* [C] an ordinary OVEN, not a MICROWAVE[1] (1): *This will take 3 minutes in a microwave, or 25 minutes in a conventional oven.*

**convent school** /'.. ,./ *n* [C] a school for girls that is run by Roman Catholic NUNS

**con·verge** /kən'vɜːdʒ‖-'vɜːrdʒ/ *v* [I] **1** to come from different directions and meet at the same point: *The two streams converge here to form a river.* **2** if groups of people converge in a particular place, they come there from many different places and meet together to form a large crowd: [+ **on**] *The two armies converged on the enemy capital.* **3** if different ideas or aims converge, they become the same: *Here the two distinct theories converge.* —opposite DIVERGE

**con·ver·sant** /kən'vɜːsənt‖-ɜːr-/ *adj* [not before noun] **1** *formal* having knowledge or experience of something: [+ **with**] *Are you fully conversant with the facts of the case?* **2** *AmE* able to hold a conversation in a foreign language, but not to be able to speak it perfectly: [+ **in**] *He's conversant in French but not really fluent.*

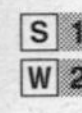

**con·ver·sa·tion** /,kɒnvə'seɪʃən‖,kɑːnvər-/ *n* **1** [C] an informal talk in which people exchange news, feelings, and thoughts: *a telephone conversation* | *He stood silent in the doorway, unwilling to interrupt their conversation.* | **have/hold a conversation** *I had a long conversation with my brother on his birthday.* | **carry on a conversation** (=have a conversation) *It's impossible to carry on a conversation with all this noise in the background.* | **turn a conversation to sth** (=begin talking about something) *The conversation turned to the subject of Sarah's new boyfriend.* **2** [U] informal talk in which people exchange news, feelings, and thoughts: *the buzz of conversation* | **make conversation** (=talk to someone in an informal way that actually needs some effort to think of what to say) *I'm not very good at making polite conversation.* | **be in conversation with** (=be talking to someone) *In today's programme, three well-known artists are in conversation with Jenny Murray.* **3 get into conversation** *especially BrE* also **get into a conversation** *especially AmE* to begin to talk to someone, especially someone you do not know: *I got into conversation with the bus driver today, and he told me that fares are going up again soon.*

**con·ver·sa·tion·al** /,kɒnvə'seɪʃənəl◂‖,kɑːnvər-/ *adj* **1** a conversational style, phrase etc is informal and commonly used in conversation: *Business letters are not usually written in conversational style.* **2** concerning or relating to conversation: *I go to evening classes to do conversational German.* —**conversationally** *adv*

**con·ver·sa·tion·al·ist** /,kɒnvə'seɪʃənəlɪ̈st‖,kɑːnvər-/ *n* [C] someone whose conversation is intelligent, amusing, and interesting: *a good conversationalist*

**conversation piece** /..'.. ,./ *n* [C] something that provides a subject for conversation, often said in a joking way about objects that seem very strange or ugly

**con·verse**[1] /kən'vɜːs‖-'vɜːrs/ *v* [I] *formal* to talk informally, or to have a conversation: [+ **with**] *It's difficult to converse rationally with people who hold extremist views.*

**con·verse**[2] /'kɒnvɜːs‖'kɑːnvɜːrs/ *n formal* **the converse** the converse of a fact, word, statement etc is the opposite of it: *I think the converse of what you just said is true.*

**con·verse**[3] /'kɒnvɜːs‖kən'vɜːrs/ *adj formal* a converse opinion, belief, statement etc is the opposite opinion etc: *I hold the converse opinion.*

**con·verse·ly** /kən'vɜːsli, 'kɒnvɜːsli‖kən'vɜːrsli, 'kɑːnvɜːrsli/ *adv formal* used when one situation is the opposite of another: *$1 will buy 100 yen. Conversely, 100 yen will buy $1.*

**con·ver·sion** /kən'vɜːʃən‖-'vɜːrʒən/ *n* [C,U] **1** the act or process of changing something from one form, purpose, or system to a different one: [+ **into**] *The company buys raw material such as wool for conversion into cloth.* | [+ **of**] *The conversion of the old classrooms into a new library has greatly improved the school.* | [+ **to**] *The British conversion to the metric system took place in the 1970s.* | **house conversion** (=the act or process of changing a large house into several apartments) *a company that does house conversions* **2** an act of changing from one religion or belief to a different one: [+ **to**] *His sudden conversion to the anti-nuclear movement may make voters suspicious.* | [+ **from**] *Her conversion from the Protestant to the Catholic faith surprised many people.* **3** a score that you can make in RUGBY football by kicking the ball over the top part of the GOAL (3)

**con·vert**[1] /kən'vɜːt‖-'vɜːrt/ *v* **1** [I,T] to change or make something change from one form, system, or purpose to a different one: **convert sth to/into sth** *This is part of the process of converting iron into steel.* | [+ **to**] *The whole office converted to a new computer system last year.* | *Our house is a converted barn.* **2** [I] to be able to be changed from one object into another: [+ **to/into**] *This sofa converts to a bed.* | *I can't see how this plastic sheet converts into a tent.* **3** [I,T] to change or make someone change their opinion or habit: [+ **to**] *I've converted to decaffeinated coffee.* | **convert sb to sth** *My daughter has finally converted me to Guns 'n' Roses.* **4** [I,T] to change or make someone change from one religion or belief to another: [+ **to**] *Anne has converted to Islam recently.* W3

**con·vert**[2] /'kɒnvɜːt‖'kɑːnvɜːrt/ *n* [C] someone who has been persuaded to change their opinion and accept a particular religion or belief: *a convert to Christianity*

**con·vert·er, convertor** /kən'vɜːtə‖-'vɜːrtər/ *n* [C] a machine that changes the form of things, especially one that makes steel from melted iron

**con·ver·ti·ble**[1] /kən'vɜːtɪ̈bəl‖-ɜːr-/ *adj* **1** an object that is convertible can be folded or arranged in a different way so that it can be used as something else: *They bought a convertible sofa-bed.* **2** money that is convertible can be exchanged for the money of another country **3** a car that is convertible has a roof that you can fold back or remove: *a convertible sports car* **4** *technical* a financial document such as an insurance arrangement or BOND[1] (1) that is convertible can be changed, or exchanged for something else: *convertible life insurance policy* —**convertibility** /kən,vɜːtɪ̈'bɪlɪ̈ti‖-,vɜːr-/ *n* [U]

**convertible**[2] *n* [C] a car with a soft roof that you can fold back or remove —compare HARDTOP —see also CABRIOLET

**con·vex** /,kɒn'veks◂, kən-,'kɒnveks‖,kɑːn'veks◂, kən-, 'kɑːnveks/ *adj* curved outwards like the surface of the eye: *a convex lens* | *a convex mirror* —**convexly** *adv* —**convexity** /kən'veksɪ̈ti/ *n* [C,U] —opposite CONCAVE

**con·vey** /kən'veɪ/ *v* [T] **1** to express what you are thinking or feeling without stating it directly: *His tone conveyed an unmistakable warning.* | *Jan's office conveyed an impression of efficiency and seriousness.* **2** to communicate information or a message: *All this information can be conveyed in a simple diagram.* | *Please convey my best wishes to her.* **3** *formal* to take or carry something from one place to another: *Your luggage will be conveyed to the hotel by taxi.* **4** *law* to legally change the possession of property from one person to another

**con·vey·ance** /kən'veɪəns/ *n* **1** [C] *formal* a vehicle: *There was no conveyance available, so we were obliged to walk.* **2** [U] *formal* the act of taking something from one place to another **3** [C] *law* a legal document that gives land, property etc from one person to another

**con·vey·anc·ing** /kən'veɪənsɪŋ/ *n* [U] *law* the work done, usually by a lawyer, to change the possession of property, especially a house, from one person to another

**con·vey·or, conveyer** /kən'veɪə‖-ər/ *n* [C] **1** a person or thing that carries or communicates something: *the conveyer of good news* **2** a conveyor belt

**conveyor belt** /·'·· ·/ *n* [C] a long continuous moving band of rubber, cloth, or metal, used for moving goods or partly finished products from one place to another in a factory, or bags from one place to another in an airport

**con·vict¹** /kən'vɪkt/ *v* [T] to prove or officially announce that someone is guilty of a crime after a TRIAL¹ (1) in a law court: **be convicted of sth** *Buxton was convicted of rape.*|*a convicted murderer* —opposite ACQUIT

**con·vict²** /'kɒnvɪkt‖'kɑːn-/ *n* [C] someone who has been proved to be guilty of a crime and sent to prison: *There was a report on the news about an escaped convict.*

W3 **con·vic·tion** /kən'vɪkʃən/ *n* **1** [C] a very strong belief or opinion: *a woman of strong political convictions* **2** [U] the feeling of being sure about something and having no doubts: *The speech lacked style and conviction.*|*"Maybe it was all a mistake," said Tom, without conviction.*|**carry conviction** (=show that someone feels sure about something and has no doubts) *Their shouts and threats carried little conviction.* **3** [C] a decision in a court of law that someone is guilty of a crime: *They had no previous convictions.*|[+ **for**] *This was her third conviction for theft.* **4** [U] the process of proving that someone is guilty in a court of law: *The trial and conviction of Jimmy Malone took over three months.* —opposite ACQUITTAL —see also **have the courage of your convictions** (COURAGE (2))

S3 W3 **con·vince** /kən'vɪns/ *v* [T] **1** to make someone feel certain that something is true: *Her arguments didn't convince me.*|**convince sb (that)** *I managed to convince them that the story was true.*|**convince sb of sth** *We finally convinced them of our innocence.* **2** to persuade someone to do something: **convince sb to do sth** *I've been trying to convince Jean to come with me.*

**con·vinced** /kən'vɪnst/ *adj* **1 be convinced** to feel certain that something is true: *Molly agreed, but she did not sound very convinced.*|*I was convinced that we were doing the right thing.*|**convinced of sth** *We are all convinced of his innocence.*|**convinced (that)** *I felt convinced that they were right.* **2 convinced Muslim/Christian etc** someone who believes very strongly in a particular religion

**con·vinc·ing** /kən'vɪnsɪŋ/ *adj* **1** making you believe that something is true or right: *You're not a very convincing liar!*|*There is now convincing evidence that smoking causes lung cancer.* **2 a convincing victory/win** an occasion when a person or team wins a game by a lot of points —**convincingly** *adv*

**con·viv·i·al** /kən'vɪviəl/ *adj* friendly and pleasantly cheerful: *a convivial atmosphere*|*She seemed to be in a convivial mood.* —**convivially** *adv* —**conviviality** /kənˌvɪvi'æləti/ *n* [U]

**con·vo·ca·tion** /ˌkɒnvə'keɪʃən‖ˌkɑːn-/ *n formal* **1 a)** [C] an organization of church officials or members of some universities that holds formal meetings **b)** [C] formal meetings held in this way: *He first gave the speech at a German university convocation in March.* **2** [U] the process of arranging for a large meeting to be held **3** [C] *AmE* the ceremony held when students have passed their examinations and are leaving university

**con·voke** /kən'vəʊk‖-'voʊk/ *v* [T] *formal* to tell people that they must come together for a formal meeting

**con·vo·lut·ed** /'kɒnvəluːtəd‖'kɑːn-/ *adj* **1** complicated and difficult to understand: *The whole thing was written in the most convoluted and obscure language possible.*|*a convoluted argument* **2** *formal* having many twists and bends: *They used some convoluted glass apparatus for measuring the expansion of the gas.* —**convolutedly** *adv*

**con·vo·lu·tion** /ˌkɒnvə'luːʃən‖ˌkɑːn-/ *n* [C usually plural] **1** the complicated details of a story, explanation etc, which make it difficult to understand: *It was an effort to follow the endless convolutions of the plot.* **2** a fold or twist in something which has many of them: *the many convolutions of the small intestine*

**con·voy¹** /'kɒnvɔɪ‖'kɑːn-/ *n* [C] **1** a group of vehicles or ships travelling together: *A convoy of lorries arrived bringing supplies of food and medicine.*|**in convoy** *We decided to travel in convoy so that no-one could lose their way.* **2** a group of armed vehicles or ships whose purpose is to travel with others in order to protect them: *They were escorted through the danger area by a naval convoy.*|**under convoy** (=protected by a convoy) *The weapons were sent under convoy.*

**convoy²** *v* [T] to travel with something in order to protect it: *Battleships helped to convoy much-needed supplies to Britain in 1917.*

**con·vulse** /kən'vʌls/ *v* **1** [I] if a part of your body convulses, it moves violently and you are not able to control it: *He sat down, his shoulders convulsing with sobs.* **2** [I] if you convulse, your body shakes violently and you are not able to control it, especially because of illness or injury **3 be convulsed with laughter/anger** to be laughing so much or feel so angry that you shake and are not able to stop yourself

**con·vul·sion** /kən'vʌlʃən/ *n* **1** [C usually plural] an act of shaking violently and uncontrollably because you are ill: *His temperature was very high and he started having convulsions.* **2 be in convulsions** *informal* to be laughing a lot: *The story was so funny, we were in convulsions.*

**con·vul·sive** /kən'vʌlsɪv/ *adj* sudden, violent and impossible to control: *The drunken man made convulsive efforts to stand up.* —**convulsively** *adv*

**co·ny, coney** /'kəʊni‖'koʊni/ *n* **1** [C] *old use* a rabbit **2** [U] rabbit fur used for making coats

**coo¹** /kuː/ *v* [I] **1** to make the low soft cry of a DOVE¹ (1) or PIGEON **2** to make soft quiet sounds: *He was cooing in her ear.* —see also **bill and coo** (BILL² (4)) —**coo** *n* [C]

**coo²** *interjection* used to express surprise: *Coo! That must have cost a lot!*

**cook¹** /kʊk/ *v* **1** [I,T] to prepare food for eating by using heat: *Mmm! That's delicious! Where did you learn to cook like that?*|**cook dinner/supper/a meal etc** *I'm tired. Will you cook dinner today?*|**cook sth for sb** *Sarah cooked lasagne for her parents when they visited.*|**cook sb sth** *He decided to cook his parents a special meal for their wedding anniversary.* **2** [I] to be prepared for eating by using heat: *The potatoes are cooking and will be ready in ten minutes.* **3** [T] *informal* to change facts, numbers etc dishonestly, for your own advantage; FALSIFY: *I'm sure the police have been cooking the evidence to get more convictions.* **4 be cooking** *informal* being planned in a secret way: *Everyone in the office has been whispering this morning – I'm sure there's something cooking.* **5 cook the books** to dishonestly change official records and figures in order to steal money: *The company accountant was charged with cooking the books.* **6 cook sb's goose** to get someone into serious trouble: *It would really cook his goose if I told his wife where he was last night.* **7 be cooking with gas** *AmE spoken* used to say that someone is doing something very well S2

**cook** sth↔ **up** *phr v* [T] **1** to make a meal quickly, often using food that has been left from a previous meal: *I volunteered to cook up a risotto using the rice from last night.* **2** *informal* to invent a story or excuse in order to prevent someone blaming you for something: *Rachel cooked up some story about her car breaking down, to explain why she was so late.*

**cook²** *n* [C] **1** someone who prepares and cooks food as their job: *Jane works as a cook in a local restaurant.* —compare CHEF **2 be a good/excellent etc cook** to be good at preparing and cooking food: *My dad's a really good cook.* **3 too many cooks (spoil the broth)**

used when you think there are too many people trying to do the same job at the same time, so that the job is not done well —see also **chief cook and bottle-washer** (CHIEF (3))

**cook·book** /ˈkʊkbʊk/ *n* [C] *AmE* a book that tells you how to prepare and cook food; COOKERY BOOK *BrE*

**cook-chill** /ˌ· ˈ·◂/ *adj BrE* cook-chill foods have already been cooked when you buy them, and are stored at a low temperature, but not frozen

**cooked** /kʊkt/ *adj* cooked food is not raw and is ready for eating: *cooked meats*

**cook·er** /ˈkʊkə‖-ər/ *n* [C] *BrE* **1** a large piece of equipment for cooking food on or in; STOVE[1] (1) *AmE* —see picture on page 833 **2** a fruit, especially an apple, that is suitable for cooking but not for eating raw

**cook·e·ry** /ˈkʊkəri/ *n* [U] *BrE* the art or skill of cooking; COOKING[1] (1) *AmE*: *Jane's favourite subject at school is cookery.* | *French provincial cookery*

**cookery book** /ˈ··· ˌ·/ *n* [C] *BrE* a book that tells you how to prepare and cook food; COOKBOOK *AmE*

**cook·house** /ˈkʊkhaʊs/ *n* [C] *old-fashioned* an outdoor kitchen where you cook food, especially in a military camp

**cook·ie** /ˈkʊki/ *n* [C] **1** *especially AmE* a flat, dry, sweet cake usually sold in packets; BISCUIT (1) *BrE*: *Karen had a glass of milk and a cookie.* **2 tough/smart cookie** *informal* someone who is clever, successful, and strongly defends what they believe in **3 that's the way the cookie crumbles** *informal* used when something unpleasant has happened to say that you must accept things the way they are, even though you do not like it **4** *AmE old-fashioned* an attractive young woman **5** *ScotE* a BUN (1)

**cookie cut·ter** /ˈ·· ˌ··/ *n* [C] *AmE* **1** an instrument that cuts cookies into special shapes before you bake them **2** something that is almost exactly the same as other things of the same type, and is not interesting in any way: *The new business park was totally different from the cookie cutter approach of the other buildings in the area.*

**cookie sheet** /ˈ·· ·/ *n* [C] *AmE* a flat piece of metal that you bake food on; BAKING TRAY

S3 **cook·ing[1]** /ˈkʊkɪŋ/ *n* [U] **1** the act of making food and cooking it: *I hate cooking.* **2** food made in a particular way or by a particular person: *Gail's cooking is always good.* | *Indian cooking* | **home cooking** (=good food like you get in your own house)

**cooking[2]** *adj* [only before noun] **1** suitable for or used in cooking: *Fry the vegetables in cooking oil.* **2** *AmE* doing something very well: *The band is really cooking tonight.*

**cooking ap·ple** /ˈ·· ˌ··/ *n* [C] a kind of apple used in cooking —compare EATING APPLE

**cooking oil** /ˈ·· ·/ *n* [U] oil from plants, such as sunflowers or olives (SUNFLOWER or OLIVE (2))

**cook·out** /ˈkʊk-aʊt/ *n* [C] *AmE informal* a party or occasion when a meal is cooked and eaten outdoors

**cook·ware** /ˈkʊkweə‖-wer/ *n* [U] containers and equipment used for cooking

W3 **cool[1]** /kuːl/ *adj*

**1 ▶ TEMPERATURE ◀** low in temperature, but not cold, often in a way that feels pleasant: *There was a cool breeze blowing off the sea.* | *sipping a cool drink* —see COLD (USAGE)

**2 ▶ CALM ◀** calm and not nervous, upset, embarrassed etc: *Now just stay cool. Everything's OK.* | **(as) cool as a cucumber** (=very calm) *Robert walked into the exam looking cool as a cucumber.* | **cool customer** (=someone who behaves calmly in a difficult situation) | **cool head** (=ability to remain calm in a difficult situation) *The job is quite demanding, so we need someone with a cool head.* | **cool, calm, and collected** (=calm) *Although she was nervous before the interview she managed to appear cool, calm and collected.*

**3 ▶ NOT FRIENDLY ◀** behaving in a way that is not as friendly as you expect: *Her gaze was decidedly cool.* | [+ **towards**] *The boss didn't actually say anything critical, but he was very cool towards me.*

**4 ▶ FASHIONABLE ◀** *informal* very attractive, fashionable, relaxed etc, in a way that people admire: *You look really cool in those sunglasses.*

**5 it's cool** *spoken* used to say that something is not a problem: *Don't worry about the work – it's cool!*

**6 ▶ COLOUR ◀** a cool colour is one, such as blue or green, that makes you think of cool things

**7 a cool million/hundred thousand etc** *informal* a surprisingly large amount of money that someone seems to earn very easily: *He earns a cool half million every year.* —**coolness** *n* [U] —**coolly** *adv* —**coolish** *adj*

**cool[2]** *v* **1** [I,T] also **cool down** to become cool or cooler, or make something do this: *You'll need to let your tea cool before you drink it.* | *They opened the windows to cool the room down.* **2** [I] if a feeling, emotion, or relationship cools, it becomes less strong: *Our initial enthusiasm cooled when we saw how much work was involved.* **3 cool it** *spoken* **a)** used to tell someone to stop being angry, violent etc: *That's enough arguing, you two – cool it!* **b)** to stop putting as much effort into something, or pressure on someone as you have been: *The more you chase after him, the less likely he is to go out with you. You'd better cool it a bit.* **4 cool your heels** to be forced to wait: *The receptionist kept me cooling my heels for at least an hour.* S3

**cool down** *phr v* **1** [I,T] to become cool or cooler, or make something do this: *Let the engine cool down, and then try starting it.* | **cool sth ↔ down** *Blow on your cocoa to cool it down.* **2** [I] to become calm after being angry: *His father took a long time to cool down after their last argument.*

**cool off** *phr v* [I] **1** to return to a normal temperature after being hot: *We'd been in the sun all day, so went for a swim to cool off.* **2** to become calm after being angry: *Maybe you should go away and cool off before we talk any more.*

**cool[3]** *n* **1 the cool** a temperature that is pleasantly cold: [+ **of**] *They went for a stroll in the cool of the evening.* **2 keep your cool** to remain calm in a frightening or difficult situation **3 lose your cool** to stop being calm in an annoying or frightening situation: *I couldn't help it, I just lost my cool and started shouting at him.*

**cool[4]** *adv* **play it cool** to behave in a calm way because you do not want someone to know that you are really nervous, angry etc: *Don't worry, just listen to what they say and play it cool.*

**coo·lant** /ˈkuːlənt/ *n* [C,U] *technical* a liquid or gas used to cool something, especially an engine —see picture at ENGINE

**cool·box** /ˈkuːlbɒks‖-bɑːks/ also **cool·bag** /ˈkuːlbæg/ *n* [C] *BrE* a container that keeps food and drink cool and fresh, which you use on a PICNIC[1] (1); COOLER (2) *AmE*

**cool·er** /ˈkuːlə‖-ər/ *n* [C] **1** a container in which something, especially drinks, is cooled or kept cold: *Mike went to fetch a bottle of wine from the cooler.* **2** *AmE* a coolbox **3** *AmE* a machine that provides AIR-CONDITIONING **4 the cooler** *slang* prison

**cool-head·ed** /ˌ· ˈ··◂/ *adj* not easily excited or upset: *We need a quick-thinking, cool-headed person for the job.*

**coo·lie** /ˈkuːli/ *n* [C] *old-fashioned* an unskilled worker who is paid very low wages, especially in parts of Asia

**cooling-off pe·ri·od** /ˌ·· ˈ· ˌ···/ *n* [C] **1** a period of time when two people or groups who are arguing about something can go away and think about how to improve the situation **2** a period of time after you have signed some types of sales agreement, when you can change your mind about buying something: *a 14-day cooling-off period on a pension plan*

**cooling sys·tem** /ˈ·· ˌ··/ *n* [C] a system for keeping the temperature in a machine, engine etc low: *a fault in the power station's cooling system*

**cooling tow·er** /ˈ·· ˌ··/ *n* [C] a large, round, tall building, used in industry for making water cool

**coon** /kuːn/ *n* [C] **1** *AmE informal* a RACCOON **2** *taboo* a very offensive word for a black person **3 in a coon's age** *AmE informal* in a long time: *This is the best meal I've had in a coon's age!*

**coon·skin** /ˈkuːnskɪn/ *adj* made from the skin of a RACCOON: *Pictures of traders in coonskin caps*

S3 **co-op** /ˈkəʊɒp‖ˈkoʊɑːp/ *n* [C] a COOPERATIVE²

**coop¹** /kuːp/ *n* [C] a building for small animals, especially chickens

**coop²** *v*

**coop** sb/sth↔ **up** *phr v* [T usually passive] to restrict the freedom of someone or something by keeping them in a place that is too small: [+ **in**] *The fresh air felt good after being cooped up in the house for so long.*

**coo·per** /ˈkuːpə‖-ər/ *n* [C] someone who makes barrels (BARREL¹ (1))

**co·op·e·rate** also **co-operate** *BrE* /kəʊˈɒpəreɪt‖ˈɑːp-/ *v* [I] **1** if two people or groups cooperate, they work together in order to achieve a result that is good for both of them: *a classroom ethos which enables children to cooperate* | [+ **with**] *Leopards cooperate with each other when hunting game.* | [+ **in**] *Russia and the US are cooperating in joint space ventures.* | **cooperate to do sth** *Aid agencies and the UN are cooperating to deliver supplies to the area.* | **cooperate closely** (=work a lot together to achieve something) **2** to help someone willingly when they ask for your help: [+ **with**] *I will advise my client to cooperate fully with the police.*

S3 W2 **co·op·e·ra·tion** also **co-operation** *BrE* /kəʊˌɒpəˈreɪʃən‖koʊˌɑːp-/ *n* [U] **1** things that you do with someone else to achieve a common purpose: [+ **between**] *a lack of cooperation between police and fire services* | **in cooperation with** *The film was produced in cooperation with KBC of Australia.* **2** help that is willingly given: *Have your passports ready, and thank you for your cooperation.* | **full/complete cooperation** *If we're going to succeed, I'll need your full cooperation.*

**co·op·e·ra·tive¹** also **co-operative** *BrE* /kəʊˈɒpərətɪv‖koʊˈɑːp-/ *adj* **1** willing to cooperate; helpful: *a cooperative witness* | *The woman in the bank wasn't very cooperative.* **2** done or operated by people working together: *The Food Stamp Program is a cooperative activity of local, state and Federal governments.* **3 cooperative factory/firm/association etc** a cooperative firm etc is operated by people working together as a cooperative

**cooperative²** also **co-operative** *BrE*—*n* [C] an organization such as a company or factory in which all the people working there own an equal share of it; CO-OP: **housing/farm cooperative** *The produce is supplied by a farm cooperative.*

**co·opt** also **co-opt** /kəʊˈɒpt‖koʊˈɑːpt/ *v* [T] *formal* **1** to add someone to an organization such as a committee, sometimes against their will, by the agreement of all the other members: *The Student's Union can have a maximum of 5 coopted members.* | **coopt sb onto/into sth** *Mr King has been coopted onto the board.* **2** to include someone in something, especially against their will: *a vision of the world which co-opts and misrepresents us*

**co·or·di·nate¹** also **co-ordinate** *BrE* /kəʊˈɔːdɪ̥neɪt‖koʊˈɔːr-/ *v* [T] **1** to organize an activity so that the people involved in it work well together and achieve a good result: *Harris is coordinating a campaign to make people aware of the importance of exercise.* **2** to make the movements of the parts of your body work well together when performing a particular action: *a young child unable to coordinate her movements*

**co·or·din·ate²** also **co-ordinate** *BrE* /kəʊˈɔːdɪ̥nɪ̥t‖koʊˈɔːr-/ *n* [C] **1** *technical* one of a set of numbers which give the exact position of a point on a map, computer screen etc **2 coordinates** *plural* women's clothes that can be worn together because their colours match

**coordinate³** also **co-ordinate** *BrE adj technical* **1** equal in importance or rank: *coordinate clauses in a sentence joined by 'and'* —compare SUBORDINATE¹ **2** involving the use of coordinates

**coordinating con·junc·tion** /·ˈ···· ·ˌ··/ *n* [C] a word such as 'and' or 'but', which joins two clauses of the same type

**co·or·di·na·tion** /kəʊˌɔːdɪ̥ˈneɪʃən‖koʊˌɔːr-/ *n* [U] **1** the way in which your muscles move together when you perform a movement: *Too much alcohol affects your coordination.* **2** the act of coordinating: *the careful coordination of research*

**co·or·di·na·tor** /kəʊˈɔːdɪ̥neɪtə‖koʊˈɔːrdɪ̥neɪtər/ *n* [C] someone who organizes the way people work in an activity

**coot** /kuːt/ *n* [C] **1** a small black and white water bird with a short beak **2 old coot** *AmE informal* an old man who you think is strange or unpleasant: *crazy old coot*

**coo·ties** /ˈkuːtiz/ *n* [plural] *AmE informal* **1** *old use* lice (LOUSE¹ (1)) that you have in your hair **2 have cooties** *spoken* used by children to insult another child: *Jenny has cooties!*

**cop¹** /kɒp‖kɑːp/ *n* [C] **1** *informal* a police officer: *a motorcycle cop* **2 not be much cop** *BrE slang* to not be very good: *The film wasn't much cop, was it?* **3 it's a fair cop** *BrE spoken humorous* used when someone has discovered that you have done something wrong and you want to admit it S3

**cop²** *v* **copped, copping** [T] *slang* **1 cop it** *BrE spoken* to be punished: *You'll cop it from your Mum when she finds out!* **2 cop (a load of) this** *BrE spoken* used to say look at or listen to this **3 cop hold of** [only in imperative] *BrE spoken* used to tell someone to take or hold something: *Cop hold of my bag while I go and get the tickets.* **4 cop a plea** *AmE* to agree to say you are guilty of a crime in order to receive a less severe punishment **5 cop a feel** *AmE* to touch someone in a sexual way when they do not want you to

**cop off** *phr v* [I,T] *BrE slang* to meet someone and start a sexual relationship with them: *So, what's the gossip? Did you cop off?* | [+ **with**] *Who was it he copped off with at the Christmas party?*

**cop out** *phr v* [I,T] *slang* to not do something that you are supposed to do: *It's your turn to sing – you can't cop out now.* —see also COP OUT

**cope¹** /kəʊp‖koʊp/ *v* [I] **1** to succeed in dealing with a difficult problem or situation: *I've never driven a big van before, but I'm sure I can cope.* | [+ **with**] *A family and a full time job is a lot to cope with.* **2** if a machine or system can cope with a particular amount of work, it can do it: *The system can cope with up to 40 terminals.* S2 W2

**cope²** *n* [C] a long loose piece of clothing worn by priests on special occasions

**cop·i·er** /ˈkɒpiə‖ˈkɑːpiər/ *n* [C] a machine that quickly makes photographic copies of documents; PHOTOCOPIER

**co·pi·lot** /ˈkəʊˌpaɪlət‖ˈkoʊ-/ *n* [C] a pilot who shares the control of an aircraft with the main pilot

**cop·ing** /ˈkəʊpɪŋ‖ˈkoʊ-/ *n* [C,U] a layer of rounded stones or bricks at the top of a wall or roof

**co·pi·ous** /ˈkəʊpiəs‖ˈkoʊ-/ *adj* existing or being produced in large quantities: *Jill sat through the meeting and made copious notes.* —**copiously** *adv*: *Then she wept copiously.*

**cop out** /ˈ· ·/ *n* [C] *slang* an occasion when you do or say something in order to avoid doing what you should do, or the actual words you use to make this excuse

**cop·per** /ˈkɒpə‖ˈkɑːpər/ *n* **1** [U] a reddish-brown metal used for making wire **2 coppers** [plural] *BrE* money of low value made of this metal or of BRONZE¹ (1): *He pulled a pawn ticket and a few coppers out of his pocket.* **3** [U] a reddish-brown colour: *flowing copper hair* **4** [C] *BrE informal* a police officer

**copper beech** /ˌ·· ˈ·/ *n* [C] a large tree with purple-brown leaves

**cop·per·head** /ˈkɒpəhed‖ˈkɑːpər-/ *n* [C] a poisonous yellow and brown North American snake

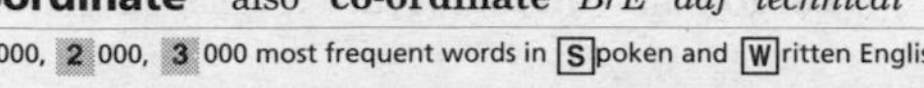

**cop·per·plate** /ˈkɒpəpleɪt‖ˈkɑːpər-/ *n* [U] neat, regular, curving handwriting with the letters all joined together in a very specific style, used especially in the past

**copse** /kɒps‖kɑːps/ also **cop·pice** /ˈkɒpɪs‖ˈkɑː-/ *n* [C] a group of trees or bushes growing close together; a small wood

**cop shop** /ˈ· ·/ *n* [C] *informal* the office from which the police work; POLICE STATION

**cop·u·la** /ˈkɒpjʊlə‖ˈkɑːp-/ *n* [C] *technical* a type of verb that connects the subject of a sentence to its COMPLEMENT[1] (3): *In the sentence 'The house seems big', 'seems' is the copula.*

**cop·u·late** /ˈkɒpjʊleɪt‖ˈkɑːp-/ *v* [I] *technical* to have sex —**copulation** /ˌkɒpjʊˈleɪʃən/ *n* [U]

**cop·u·la·tive** /ˈkɒpjʊlətɪv‖ˈkɑːpjʊleɪ-/ *n* [C] *technical* a word or word group that connects other word groups —**copulative** *adj*

S1 W2 **cop·y**[1] /ˈkɒpi‖ˈkɑːpi/ *n* **1** [C] something that is made to be exactly like another thing: *I haven't got the original letter, but I have got a copy.*| [+ **of**] *Please send a copy of your marriage certificate.*| **make a copy** *I made a copy of the ad and sent it to my brother.* **2** [C] one of many books, magazines etc that are all exactly the same: [+ **of**] *He was reading a copy of the daily newspaper.* **3** [U] *technical* written material that is to be printed in a newspaper, magazine etc: *All copy must be on my desk by Monday morning.* **4 make good copy** *informal* to be interesting news —see also FAIR COPY, HARD COPY, SOFT COPY

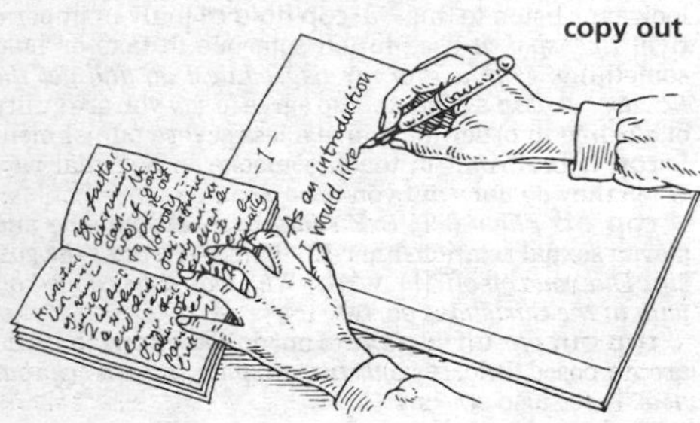


S2 **copy**[2] *v* **1** [T] to make something exactly like another thing: *Could you copy this letter and send it out, please?* **2** [T] to deliberately do things that someone else has done, or do things in the same way that someone else does them: *Street fashion tends to copy the ideas of the top fashion designers.* **3** [I,T] to cheat in an examination, school work etc by looking at someone else's work and writing the same thing that they have: [+ **off**] *If I catch anyone copying off their neighbor, they'll be sent to the principal's office!*| [+ **from**] *Jeremy had copied from the girl next to him.*

**copy** sth ↔ **out** *phr v* [T] *BrE* to write something again exactly as it is written somewhere else: *The monks copied their manuscripts out by hand.*| *Just copy out of the book.*

**cop·y·book**[1] /ˈkɒpibʊk‖ˈkɑː-/ *n* [C] a book used in the past containing examples of good handwriting to copy —see also **blot your copybook** (BLOT[1] (2))

**copybook**[2] *adj* [only before noun] *BrE* completely suitable or correct: *a copybook answer*

**cop·y·cat** /ˈkɒpikæt‖ˈkɑː-/ *n* [C] **1** *informal* a word used by children to criticize someone who copies other people's clothes, behaviour, work etc **2 copycat crime/killing etc** a crime, murder etc which is similar to a famous crime that another person has done

**copy ed·i·tor** /ˈ·· ˌ···/ *n* [C] someone whose job is to be sure that the words in a book, newspaper etc are ready to be printed

**cop·y·ist** /ˈkɒpi-ɪst‖ˈkɑː-/ *n* [C] someone who made written copies of documents, books etc in the past

**cop·y·right** /ˈkɒpiraɪt‖ˈkɑː-/ *n* [C,U] the legal right to be the only producer or seller of a book, play, film, or record for a specific length of time: *Who owns the copyright of this book?*| *an infringement of copyright* —**copyright** *adj* —**copyright** *v* [T]

**cop·y·writ·er** /ˈkɒpiˌraɪtə‖ˈkɑːpiˌraɪtər/ *n* [C] someone who writes the words for advertisements

**coq au vin** /ˌkɒk əʊ ˈvæn‖ˌkoʊk oʊ-/ *n* [U] *French* a dish of chicken cooked in red wine

**coq·ue·try** /ˈkɒkɪtri‖ˈkoʊ-/ *n* [C,U] *literary* behaviour that is typical of a coquette

**co·quette** /kəʊˈket, kɒ-‖koʊ-/ *n* [C] *literary* a woman who frequently tries to attract the attention of men without having sincere feelings for them; FLIRT[2] —**coquettish** *adj* —**coquettishly** *adv*

**cor** /kɔː‖kɔːr/ *interjection BrE spoken* used when you are very surprised or impressed by something

**cor-** /kə, kɒ‖kə, kɔːr, kɑːr/ *prefix* the form used for CON- before r: *to correlate* (=connect together)

**cor·a·cle** /ˈkɒrəkəl‖ˈkɔː-,ˈkɑː-/ *n* [C] a small round boat that you move with a PADDLE[1] (1)

**cor·al**[1] /ˈkɒrəl‖ˈkɔː-, ˈkɑː-/ *n* [U] a hard red, white, or pink substance formed from the bones of very small sea creatures, that is often used to make jewellery: *a coral necklace*

**coral**[2] *adj* pink or reddish orange in colour

**coral reef** /ˌ·· ˈ·/ *n* [C] a line of hard rocks formed by coral, found in warm sea water that is not very deep

**cor an·glais** /ˌkɔːr ˈɒŋgleɪ‖-ɔːŋˈgleɪ/ *n* [C] *especially BrE* a long wooden musical instrument which is like an OBOE but with a lower sound; ENGLISH HORN *especially AmE*

**cor bli·mey** /ˌkɔː ˈblaɪmi‖ˌkɔːr-/ also **blimey** *interjection BrE old-fashioned* used to express surprise

**cord**[1] /kɔːd‖kɔːrd/ *n* **1** [C,U] a piece of thick string or thin rope: *We need some cord to hang the picture.*| *He pulled explosives and some tangled cord from his bag.* **2 cords** [plural] trousers made from a thick strong cotton cloth with thin raised lines on it **3** [C,U] *especially AmE* an electrical wire or wires with a protective covering, usually for connecting electrical equipment to the supply of electricity: *the phone cord*| *How much cord do you need to connect the washing machine?* **4** [C] *AmE* a specific quantity of wood cut for burning in a fire: [+ **of**] *We use three cords of wood in a winter.* —see also **cut the cord** (CUT[1] (29)), COMMUNICATION CORD, CORDLESS, SPINAL CORD, UMBILICAL CORD, VOCAL CORDS

**cord**[2] *v* [T] to tie or connect something with rope, string, etc: *Bundles of hay were corded and tossed onto the wagon.*

**cord·age** /ˈkɔːdɪdʒ‖ˈkɔːr-/ *n* [U] rope or cord in general, especially on a ship

**cor·di·al**[1] /ˈkɔːdiəl‖ˈkɔːrdʒəl/ *n* [C,U] **1** *BrE* sweet fruit juice that you add water to before you drink it: *a lime cordial* **2** *AmE old-fashioned* a strong sweet alcoholic drink; LIQUEUR: *We were offered an after-dinner cordial.*

**cordial**[2] *adj* friendly but quite formal and polite: *a cordial note from Mrs Thomas* —**cordiality** /ˌkɔːdiˈælɪti‖ˌkɔːrdʒiˈæ-, kɔːrˈdʒæ-/ *n* [U]

**cor·di·al·ly** /ˈkɔːdiəli‖ˈkɔːrdʒəli/ *adv* **1** in a friendly but polite and formal way: *You are cordially invited to our wedding on May 9.* **2 cordially disliked/hated** to dislike someone very strongly: *He was cordially disliked by the whole street.*

**cor·dite** /ˈkɔːdaɪt‖ˈkɔːr-/ *n* [U] a smokeless explosive used in bullets and bombs

**cord·less** /ˈkɔːdləs‖ˈkɔːrd-/ *adj* a piece of equipment that is cordless is not connected to its power supply by wires: *a cordless phone*

**cor·don**[1] /ˈkɔːdn‖ˈkɔːrdn/ *n* [C] a line of police officers, soldiers, or vehicles put around an area to stop people going there: *The police immediately put up a cordon around the scene of the accident.*

**cordon**[2] *v*

**cordon** sth ↔ **off** *phr v* [T] to surround and protect an area with police officers, soldiers, or vehicles: *Police have cordoned off the street where the murder took place.*

**cor·don bleu** /ˌkɔːdɒn ˈblɜː‖ˌkɔːrdɒːn-/ *adj* [only before noun] concerning food cooked to the highest standard: **cordon bleu chef** (=someone who is trained to prepare food to this standard)

**cor·du·roy** /ˈkɔːdʒ̆ərɔɪ, -djə̆-‖ˈkɔːrdə-/ *n* [U] a thick strong cotton cloth with thin raised lines on it, used for making clothes: *a corduroy jacket* —see picture on page 839

W3 **core[1]** /kɔː‖kɔːr/ *n* [C]
**1** ▶ **FRUIT** ◀ the hard central part of fruit such as an apple: *Remove the cores, fill with raisins and cinnamon, and bake the apples for 40 minutes.*
**2** ▶ **CENTRAL PART** ◀ the most important or central part of something: [+ **of**] *Houston is the central core of a metropolitan area of about 2.6 million residents.*
**3 core values/beliefs/concerns** the values etc that are most important to someone
**4** ▶ **PEOPLE** ◀ a number of people who form a strong group which is very important to an organization: *The club was beginning to develop a core of young people who were very active in the community.*
**5 to the core** in a way that affects all of your feelings or your character: *That woman is rotten to the core!* | *When I saw the accident, I was shaken to the core.*
**6** ▶ **PLANETS** ◀ the central part of the Earth or any other PLANET
**7** ▶ **NUCLEAR REACTOR** ◀ the central part of a NUCLEAR REACTOR

**core[2]** *v* [T] to take the centre from a piece of fruit

**core cur·ric·u·lum** /ˌ· ·ˈ···/ *n* [U] the basic subjects that someone must study in school

**co·re·li·gion·ist** /ˌkəʊrɪ̆ˈlɪdʒənɪ̆st‖ˌkoʊ-/ *n* [C] *formal* someone who is a member of the same religion as you

**cor·er** /ˈkɔːrə‖-ər/ *n* [C] a specially shaped knife for taking the hard centres out of fruit

**co-res·pon·dent** /ˌkəʊrɪ̆ˈspɒndənt‖ˌkoʊrɪ̆ˈspɑːn-/ *n* [C] *law* someone whose name is given in a DIVORCE[1] (1) because they have had sex with the wife or husband of the person who wants the divorce —compare RESPONDENT

**core time** /ˈ· ·/ *n* [U] the period during the middle part of the day when an office or other place of work that has FLEXITIME expects all its people to be working

**cor·gi** /ˈkɔːgi‖ˈkɔːrgi/ *n plural* **corgis** [C] a small dog with short legs and a pointed nose: *the Queen's famous corgis*

**co·ri·an·der** /ˌkɒriˈændə‖ˌkɔːriˈændər/ *n* [U] *BrE* a plant used to give a special taste to food, especially in Indian cooking; CILANTRO *AmE*

**Co·rin·thi·an** /kəˈrɪnθiən/ *adj* of a style of Greek architecture that uses decorations of leaves cut into stone: *a Corinthian column*

**cork[1]** /kɔːk‖kɔːrk/ *n* **1** [U] the BARK (=outer part) of a tree from southern Europe and North Africa, used to make things: *cork mats* **2** [C] a long round piece of cork which is put into the top of a bottle, especially a wine bottle, to keep liquid inside

**cork[2]** *v* [T] to close a bottle by blocking the hole at the top tightly with a long, round piece of cork —opposite UNCORK

**cork·age** /ˈkɔːkɪdʒ‖ˈkɔːr-/ *n* [U] the charge made by a hotel or restaurant for allowing people to drink alcoholic drinks which they bought somewhere else

**corked** /kɔːkt‖kɔːrkt/ *adj* corked wine tastes bad because a decaying cork has allowed air into the bottle

**cork·er** /ˈkɔːkə‖ˈkɔːrkər/ *n* [C] *BrE old-fashioned* someone or something you think is very good —**corking** *adj*

**cork·screw[1]** /ˈkɔːkskruː‖ˈkɔːrk-/ *n* [C] a tool made of twisted metal which you use to pull a CORK[1] (2) out of a bottle —see picture on page 833

**corkscrew[2]** *adj* [only before noun] twisted or curly; SPIRAL[1]: *corkscrew curls*

**cor·mo·rant** /ˈkɔːmərənt‖ˈkɔːr-/ *n* [C] a large black sea bird which has a long neck and eats fish

S3 **corn** /kɔːn‖kɔːrn/ *n* **1** [U] *BrE* grains of plants such as wheat, BARLEY, and OATS or their seeds **2** [U] *AmE, AustrE* **a)** a tall plant with large yellow grains at the top, which is cooked whole and eaten as a food; MAIZE **b)** the grains of this plant —see also SWEETCORN **3** [C] a painful area of thick hard skin on your foot

**corn·ball** /ˈkɔːnbɔːl‖ˈkɔːrnbɒːl/ *adj* [only before noun] *AmE informal* cornball humour is too simple, old-fashioned, unoriginal, and silly: *At lunchtime he bored us with these awful cornball jokes.*

**corn bread** /ˈ· ·/ *n* [U] bread made from CORNMEAL

**corn chip** /ˈ· ·/ *n* [C] crushed MAIZE formed into a small flat piece and cooked in oil, eaten especially in the US

**corn cir·cle** /ˈ· ˌ··/ also **crop circle** *n* [C] patterns that appeared in British farm fields which some people believe were made by creatures from another world

**corn·cob** /ˈkɔːnkɒb‖ˈkɔːrnkɑːb/ also **cob** *n* [C] the top part of a MAIZE plant after its yellow grains have been removed

**corn·crake** /ˈkɔːnkreɪk‖ˈkɔːrn-/ *n* [C] a European bird with a loud sharp cry

**corn dol·ly** /ˈ· ˌ··/ *n* [C] a figure made from the heads and stems of wheat plants, made especially in former times to celebrate the HARVEST[1] (1)

**cor·ne·a** /ˈkɔːniə‖ˈkɔːr-/ *n* [C] the transparent protective covering on the outer surface of your eye —**corneal** *adj*: *an operation for a corneal graft* —see picture at EYE[1]

**corned beef** /ˌkɔːnd ˈbiːf◂‖ˌkɔːrnd-/ *n* [U] *BrE* **1** a kind of pressed cooked BEEF[1] (1) sold in a tin; **2** *AmE* beef that has been covered in salt water and SPICES to preserve it

**cor·ne·li·an** /kɔːˈniːliən‖kɔːr-/ *n* [U] a red or white stone used in jewellery

S1 W2 **cor·ner[1]** /ˈkɔːnə‖ˈkɔːrnər/ *n*
**1** ▶ **WHERE TWO LINES/EDGES MEET** ◀ [C] the point at which two lines or edges meet: *He pulled a dirty handkerchief out by its corner and waved it at me.* | **in/on the corner** *Write your name in the top left-hand corner of the page.* | **three-cornered/four-cornered etc** *a three-cornered hat*
**2** ▶ **ROADS** ◀ [C often singular] **a)** the point where two roads meet: **on/at the corner** *He stopped at the corner of 5th and Main to buy a newspaper.* **b)** a point in a road where it turns sharply: *I think the gas station should be just around the next corner.*
**3** ▶ **CORNER OF A ROOM/BOX** ◀ [C often singular] the place inside a room or box where two walls or sides meet: **in/at the corner** *Jim and his cousin sat in the corner talking about people back home.*
**4** ▶ **MOUTH** ◀ [C] the corners of your mouth are the sides of your mouth: *A small smile appeared at the corners of his mouth.*
**5** ▶ **DIFFICULT SITUATION** ◀ [singular] a difficult situation that is difficult to escape from: **force sb into a corner** *The president is likely to be forced into a corner over his latest plans for welfare spending.* | **tight corner** (=very difficult situation)
**6** ▶ **SPORT** ◀ [C] **a)** a kick in SOCCER that one team is allowed to take from one of the corners of their opponent's end of the field —see picture on page 1264 **b)** any of the four corners of the area in which the competitors fight in BOXING or WRESTLING
**7** ▶ **DISTANT PLACE** ◀ [C] a distant place in another part of the world: [+**of**] *She's gone off to do voluntary work in some remote corner of the world.* | **the four corners of the Earth/world** (=all the distant places in the world) *People came from the four corners of the world to see this spectacle.*
**8 see sth out of the corner of your eye** to notice something accidentally, without turning your head towards it or looking for it: *Out of the corner of her eye she saw the dog running towards her.*
**9 just around the corner** likely to happen soon: *Economic recovery is just around the corner.*
**10 turn a corner** to start to improve: *She's been ill for a long time, but the doctors think she's turned a corner now.*

**11 cut corners** to do things too quickly, and not as carefully as you should, especially to save money or time: *Don't try to cut corners when you're decorating.*
**12 cut a corner** to go across the corner of something, especially a road, instead of keeping to the edges
**13 have a corner on the market** to have a position in which you control all of the supply of a particular type of goods: *The company had a corner on the silver market.* —see also KITTY-CORNER

**corner²** *v* **1** [T] to force a person or animal into a position from which they cannot easily escape: *As the dog was cornered, it began to growl threateningly.|Janet cornered Marty in the hall.* **2 corner sb** also **back sb into a corner** to put someone into a position in which they cannot choose to do what they want to do: *They have backed us into a corner – if we don't accept their terms, we'll lose our jobs.* **3 corner the market** to gain control of the whole supply of a particular kind of goods: *They're trying to corner the market by buying up all the wheat in sight.* **4** [I] if a car corners, it goes around a corner or curve in the road

**corner shop** /ˈ· · ·/ *n* [C] *BrE* a small shop, usually but not always on a corner, that sells food, cigarettes, and other things needed every day —see also CONVENIENCE STORE

**cor·ner·stone** /ˈkɔːnəstəʊn‖ˈkɔːrnərstoʊn/ *n* [C] **1** a stone set at one of the bottom corners of a building, often put in place at a special ceremony: *The mayor laid the cornerstone for the new city hall yesterday.* **2** something that is extremely important because everything else depends on it: **[+ of/for]** *Trust and commitment are the cornerstones of any marriage.* —compare FOUNDATION STONE

**cor·net** /ˈkɔːnɪ̣t‖kɔːrˈnet/ *n* [C] **1** a musical instrument like a TRUMPET¹ (1) often used in military bands **2** *BrE* a thin container shaped like a cone that you eat ICE-CREAM from —see also CONE

**corn ex·change** /ˈ· ·ˌ·/ *n* [C] a place where corn used to be bought and sold

**corn·flakes** /ˈkɔːnfleɪks‖ˈkɔːrn-/ *n* [plural] small flat pieces of crushed corn, usually eaten at breakfast with milk and sugar

**corn·flour** /ˈkɔːnflaʊə‖ˈkɔːrnflaʊr/ *n* [U] *BrE* fine white flour made from corn, used in cooking to make liquids thick; CORNSTARCH *AmE*

**corn·flow·er** /ˈkɔːnflaʊəʳ‖ˈkɔːrnflaʊər/ *n* [C] a wild plant with blue flowers

**cor·nice** /ˈkɔːnɪ̣s‖ˈkɔːr-/ *n* [C] a decorative area at the top edge of a wall or PILLAR (1)

**cor·niche** /kɔːˈniːʃ‖kɔːr-/ *n* [C] a road built along a coast

**Cor·nish** /ˈkɔːnɪʃ‖ˈkɔːr-/ *adj* from or related to Cornwall

**Cornish pas·ty** /ˌ·· ˈ··/ *n* [C] *BrE* a folded piece of PASTRY (1), baked with meat and potatoes in it, usually for one person to eat

**corn liq·uor** /ˈ· ˈ··/ also **corn whiskey** *n* [U] a strong American alcoholic drink made from corn

**corn·meal** /ˈkɔːnmiːl‖ˈkɔːrn-/ *n* [U] flour made from MAIZE

**corn on the cob** /ˌ· · · ˈ·/ *n* [U] the top part of a MAIZE plant, cooked and eaten whole

**corn pone** /ˈkɔːn pəʊn‖ˈkɔːrn poʊn/ *n* [U] a kind of American bread made from corn meal

**corn·row** /ˈkɔːnrəʊ‖ˈkɔːrnroʊ/ *n* [C] a way of arranging hair, especially by women of West Indian and West African origin, in which hair is put into small tight plaits (PLAIT²) in lines along your head

**corn·starch** /ˈkɔːnstɑːtʃ‖ˈkɔːrnstɑːrtʃ/ *n* [U] *AmE* cornflour

**corn syr·up** /ˌ· ˈ··/ *n* [U] a very sweet thick liquid made from MAIZE, used in cooking

**cor·nu·co·pi·a** /ˌkɔːnjʊ̣ˈkəʊpiə‖ˌkɔːrnəˈkoʊ-/ *n* [singular] **1** a decorative container in the shape of an animal's horn, full of fruit and flowers, used to represent plenty **2** a lot of good things: *the cornucopia of delights on display*

**corn whis·key** /ˈ· ˌ··/ *n* [U] CORN LIQUOR

**corn·y** /ˈkɔːni‖ˈkɔːrni/ *adj informal* not new, different, interesting, or surprising: *My dad loves telling corny jokes.|I know it sounds corny, but I dream about her every night.* —**cornily** *adv* —**corniness** *n* [U]

**co·rol·la·ry** /kəˈrɒləri‖ˈkɔːrəleri, ˈkɑː-/ *n* [C] *formal* something that is the direct result of something else: *This is the inevitable corollary of his determination to succeed.*

**co·ro·na** /kəˈrəʊnə‖-ˈroʊ-/ *n* [C] the shining circle of light seen around the sun when the moon passes in front of it in an ECLIPSE¹ (1)

**cor·o·na·ry** /ˈkɒrənəri‖ˈkɔːrəneri, ˈkɑː-/ *adj* concerning or about the heart: *coronary disease*

**cor·o·na·tion** /ˌkɒrəˈneɪʃən◂‖ˌkɔː-, ˌkɑː-/ *n* [C] the ceremony at which someone is officially made king or queen

**cor·o·ner** /ˈkɒrənə‖ˈkɔː-, ˈkɑːrənər/ *n* [C] someone whose job is to discover the cause of someone's death, especially if they died in a sudden or unusual way: *The coroner recorded a verdict of death by natural causes.*

**cor·o·net** /ˈkɒrənɪ̣t‖ˌkɔːrəˈnet, ˌkɑː-/ *n* [C] **1** a small CROWN¹ (1a) worn by princes or other members of a royal family, especially on formal occasions **2** anything that you wear on your head that looks like a CROWN¹ (1b): *a coronet of flowers*

**corp** /kɔːp‖kɔːrp/ **1** the abbreviation of CORPORAL¹ **2** the abbreviation of CORPORATION

**cor·po·ra** /ˈkɔːpərə‖ˈkɔːr-/ *n* [plural] plural of CORPUS

**cor·po·ral¹** /ˈkɔːpərəl‖ˈkɔːr-/ *n* [C] a low rank in the army, air force etc —see table on page B4

**corporal²** *adj formal literary* of or about the body

**corporal pun·ish·ment** /ˌ··· ˈ···/ *n* [U] a way of officially punishing someone by hitting them, especially in schools and prisons: *Corporal punishment was abolished in Britain in 1986.*

**cor·po·rate** /ˈkɔːpərɪ̣t‖ˈkɔːr-/ *adj* [only before noun] W2 **1** belonging to or connected with a business: *This policy is a key feature of our long-term corporate planning.* **2** shared by or involving all the members of a group: *corporate responsibility|corporate identity* **3** forming a single group: *The university is a corporate body made up of several different colleges.* **4 corporate hospitality** ways in which companies entertain their customers in order to gain business —**corporately** *adv*

**cor·po·ra·tion** /ˌkɔːpəˈreɪʃən‖ˌkɔːr-/ *n* [C] **1** a big company, or a group of companies acting together as a single organization: *He works for a large American corporation.|a multinational corporation* **2** *BrE old use* a group of people elected to govern a town or city **3 corporation tax** a tax paid by companies on their profits S3 W2

**cor·po·re·al** /kɔːˈpɔːriəl‖kɔːr-/ *adj formal* **1** related to the body as opposed to the mind, feelings, or spirit: *He paid little attention to corporeal needs like food.* **2** able to be touched; MATERIAL² (2)

**corps** /kɔː‖kɔːr/ *n technical* **1** a group in an army with special duties and responsibilities: *the medical corps* **2** *technical* a trained army unit made of two or more DIVISIONS (=group of soldiers) **3** a group of people who work together to do a particular job: *the president's press corps*

**corpse** /kɔːps‖kɔːrps/ *n* [C] the dead body of a person: *Her corpse was found floating in the river.*

**cor·pu·lent** /ˈkɔːpjʊ̣lənt‖ˈkɔːr-/ *adj formal* very fat: *He was a corpulent, pompous, and short-tempered little man.* —**corpulence** *n* [U]

**cor·pus** /ˈkɔːpəs‖ˈkɔːr-/ *n plural* **corpora** /-pərə/ *or* **corpuses** [C] **1** *formal* a collection of all the writing of a particular kind or by a particular person: *They aim to study the entire corpus of Shakespeare's works.* **2** *technical* a collection of information or material to be studied: *a corpus of spoken English* —see also HABEAS CORPUS

**cor·pus·cle** /ˈkɔːpəsəl, kɔːˈpʌ-‖ˈkɔːrpə-/ *n* [C] one of the red or white cells in the blood

**cor·ral¹** /kəˈrɑːl‖kəˈræl/ *n* [C] an enclosed area where cattle, horses etc can be temporarily kept, especially in North America

**corral²** *v* -ll- [T] **1** to make animals move into a corral: *They corralled the cattle before loading them onto the truck.* **2** to keep people in a particular area in order to control them: *They corralled the protesters, keeping them away from the president's car.*

S1 W2 **cor·rect¹** /kəˈrekt/ *adj* **1** without any mistakes: *I'm not sure of the correct spelling.* | *Make sure you replace the parts in the correct order.* **2** suitable and right for a particular situation: *What's the correct procedure in cases like this?* | *When lifting heavy weights it is very important that your back is in the correct position.* **3** correct behaviour is formal and polite: *Simpson always knew what was correct and proper.* —**correctly** *adv* —**correctness** *n* [U] —opposite INCORRECT

S3 **correct²** *v* [T]
**1** ▶ **SHOW STH IS WRONG** ◀ to show someone that something is wrong, and make it right: *Correct my pronunciation if it's wrong.* | *I'd like to correct the impression that library work is boring.* | **correct sb** (=tell someone that what they have said is wrong)
**2** ▶ **IMPROVE BY CHANGING** ◀ to make something work the way it should: *Some eyesight problems are relatively easy to correct.*
**3** ▶ **EXAMS/ESSAYS ETC** ◀ to make marks on a piece of written work to show the mistakes in it: *She spent the whole evening correcting exam papers.*
**4 correct me if I'm wrong** *spoken* used when you are not sure that what you are going to say is true or not: *Correct me if I'm wrong, but didn't you say you were going to London today?*
**5 I stand corrected** *formal spoken* used to admit that something you have said is wrong after someone has told you it is wrong

**cor·rec·tion** /kəˈrekʃən/ *n* **1** [C] a change made in something in order to correct it: *The page was covered in crossings-out and corrections.* | **make a correction** *She makes all her corrections with a green pen.* **2** [U] the act of changing something in order to make it right or better **3** *spoken* used to say that what you have just said is wrong and you want to change it: *That figure was 30,000... correction, make that 31,000.*

**correctional fa·ci·li·ty** /·ˈ··· ·ˌ···/ *n* [C] *AmE technical or humorous* a prison

**correction flu·id** /·ˈ·· ˌ··/ *n* [U] *formal* a special white liquid used for covering written mistakes

**cor·rec·ti·tude** /kəˈrektɪ̣tjuːd‖-tuːd/ *n* [U] *formal* correctness of behaviour

**cor·rec·tive¹** /kəˈrektɪv/ *adj formal* intended to make a fault or mistake right again: *corrective treatment* | *This condition may require corrective surgery.* —**correctively** *adv*

**corrective²** *n* [C] *formal* something that is intended to correct a fault or mistake: [+ **to**] *The idea is that this will function as a corrective to complacency.*

**cor·rel·ate¹** /ˈkɒrɪ̣leɪt‖ˈkɔː-, ˈkɑː-/ *v* [I,T] if two or more facts, ideas etc correlate, or you correlate them, they are closely connected or one causes another: *They found that the two sets of results seemed to be correlated.* | [+ **with**] *Scientists have been unable to correlate their findings with recent increases in radioactivity levels.*

**cor·re·late²** /ˈkɒrɪ̣lɪ̣t‖ˈkɔː-, ˈkɑː-/ *n* [C] either of two things that correlate with each other

**cor·re·la·tion** /ˌkɒrɪ̣ˈleɪʃən‖ˌkɔː-, ˌkɑː-/ *n* **1** [C,U] a connection between two ideas, facts etc, especially when one may be the cause of the other: [+ **between**] *They found a strong correlation between urban deprivation and poor health.* | [+ **with**] *There was also some correlation with social class.* **2** [U] the process of correlating two or more things

**cor·rel·a·tive¹** /kəˈrelətɪv/ *adj* **1** two or more facts, ideas etc that are correlative are closely related or dependent on each other: *correlative theories and beliefs* | *Profits were directly correlative to the popularity of the product.* **2** *technical* two words that are correlative are frequently together but not usually used next to each other: *'Either' and 'or' are correlative conjunctions.*

**correlative²** *n* [C] *formal* one of two or more facts, ideas etc that are closely related or that depend on each other

**cor·re·spond** /ˌkɒrɪ̣ˈspɒnd‖ˌkɔːrɪ̣ˈspɑːnd, ˌkɑː-/ *v* [I] **1** if two things or ideas correspond, the parts or information in one relate to the parts or information in the other: *The two halves of the document did not correspond.* | [+ **with/to**] *The numbers correspond to distinct points on the map.* **2** to be very similar or the same as something else: [+ **to**] *The French 'baccalauréat' roughly corresponds to British 'A-levels'.* **3** to write letters to someone and receive letters from them: *For the next three years they corresponded regularly.* | [+ **with**] *She stopped corresponding with him after the death of her mother.*

**cor·re·spon·dence** /ˌkɒrɪ̣ˈspɒndəns‖ˌkɔːrɪ̣ˈspɑːn-, ˌkɑː-/ *n* [U] **1** letters exchanged between people, especially official or business letters: *A secretary came in twice a week to deal with his correspondence.* **2** the process of sending and receiving letters: *All correspondence between us must cease.* **3** a relationship or connection between two or more ideas or facts: [+ **between**] *There was no correspondence between the historical facts and Johnson's account of them.*

**correspondence course** /··ˈ·· ˌ·/ *n* [C] a course of lessons in which the student works at home and sends completed work to their teacher by mail: *I'm taking a correspondence course in business studies.*

**cor·re·spon·dent¹** /ˌkɒrɪ̣ˈspɒndənt‖ˌkɔːrɪ̣ˈspɑːn-, ˌkɑː-/ *n* [C] **1** someone who is employed by a newspaper or a television station etc to report news from a particular area or on a particular subject: *Our correspondent in South Africa sent this report.* | *the political correspondent for The Times* **2** someone who writes letters: **good/bad correspondent** (=someone who is good or bad at writing letters regularly) *I'm not a very good correspondent, I'm afraid.*

**correspondent²** *adj formal* being right for a particular situation: [+ **with**] *The result was correspondent with the government's wishes in this matter.*

**cor·re·spon·ding** /ˌkɒrɪ̣ˈspɒndɪŋ◂‖ˌkɔːrɪ̣ˈspɑːn-, ˌkɑː-/ *adj* [only before noun] **1** caused by or dependent on something you have already mentioned: *The war, and the corresponding fall in trade, have had a devastating effect on the country.* **2** having similar qualities or a similar position to something you have already mentioned; matching; EQUIVALENT¹: *The corresponding chromosome in the other parent was found to be defective.* —**correspondingly** *adv*

**cor·ri·dor** /ˈkɒrɪ̣dɔː‖ˈkɔːrɪ̣dər, ˈkɑː-/ *n* [C] **1** a long, narrow passage between two rows of rooms in a building or a train, with doors leading off it: *Room 101 is at the end of the corridor.* | *She hurried down the corridor.* **2** a narrow area of land, within a bigger area, that has different qualities or features from the land that surrounds it: *the industrial corridor that connects Queretaro with Mexico City* | *the Polish corridor* **3 corridors of power** the places where important government decisions are made: *Who can tell what really goes on in the corridors of power?* S2 W3

**corrie** /ˈkɒri‖ˈkɔː- ˈkɑː-/ *n* [C] a deep bowl-shaped area on a mountain —see picture on page 835

**cor·rob·o·rate** /kəˈrɒbəreɪt‖kəˈrɑː-/ *v* [T] *formal* to provide information that supports or helps to prove someone else's statement, idea etc: *We now have new evidence to corroborate the defendant's story.* —**corroboration** /kəˌrɒbəˈreɪʃən‖-rɑː-/ *n* [U] —**corroborative** /kəˈrɒbərətɪv‖-ˈrɑːbəreɪ-/ *adj*

**cor·rode** /kəˈrəʊd‖-ˈroʊd/ *v* [I,T] if metal corrodes or something corrodes it, it is slowly destroyed by the effect of water, chemicals etc: *All the electrical components have corroded.*

**cor·ro·sion** /kəˈrəʊʒən‖-ˈroʊ-/ *n* [U] **1** the gradual destruction of substances such as metal by the effect of water, chemicals etc **2** a substance such as RUST (=red weakened metal) that is produced by the process of corrosion

**cor·ro·sive** /kəˈrəʊsɪv‖-ˈroʊ-/ *adj* **1** a corrosive liquid such as an acid can destroy metal, plastic etc: *Danger! Corrosive material.* **2** gradually making something weaker, and possibly destroying it: *Fear of unemployment is having a corrosive effect on the country's economy.*

**cor·ru·gated** /ˈkɒrəgeɪtɪ̇d‖ˈkɔː-, ˈkɑː-/ *adj* in the shape of waves or folds, or made like this in order to give something strength: *corrugated cardboard|corrugated iron* —**corrugation** /ˌkɒrəˈgeɪʃən‖ˌkɔː-, ˌkɑː-/ *n* [C]

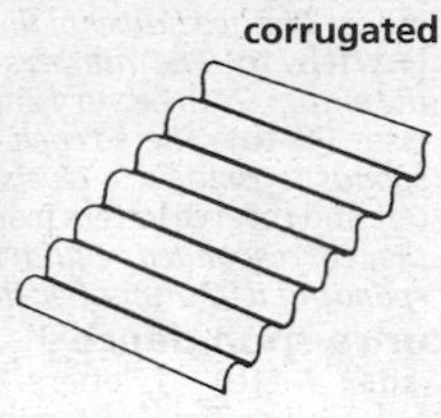

corrugated iron

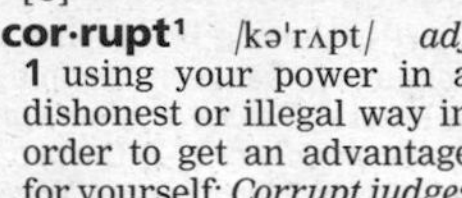

**cor·rupt¹** /kəˈrʌpt/ *adj* **1** using your power in a dishonest or illegal way in order to get an advantage for yourself: *Corrupt judges have taken millions of dollars in bribes.* **2** very bad morally: *a corrupt society* **3** something that is corrupt is not pure or is not the way it was made or intended —see also INCORRUPTIBLE —**corruptly** *adv* —**corruptness** *n* [U]

**corrupt²** *v* [T] **1** to encourage someone to start behaving in an immoral or dishonest way; PERVERT¹ (2): *Young prisoners are being corrupted by the older, long term offenders.|They say power corrupts.* **2** to change the traditional form of something, such as a language, so that it becomes worse than it was **3** to change the information in a computer, so that the computer does not work properly any more —**corruptible** *adj* —**corruptibility** /kəˌrʌptɪ̇ˈbɪlɪ̇ti/ *n* [U]

**cor·rup·tion** /kəˈrʌpʃən/ *n* **1** [U] dishonest, illegal, or immoral behaviour, especially from someone with power: *The Chief Executive is being investigated for alleged corruption.* **2** [C usually singular] a changed form of something, for example a word: *The word Thursday is a corruption of Thor's Day.*

**cor·sage** /kɔːˈsɑːʒ‖kɔːr-/ *n* [C] a group of small flowers that a woman fastens to her clothes on a special occasion such as a wedding

**cor·sair** /ˈkɔːseə‖ˈkɔːrser/ *n* [C] *old use* the name of a North African PIRATE¹ (3), or their ship

**corse** /kɔːs‖kɔːrs/ *n* [C] *old use or poetical* a CORPSE

**cor·set** /ˈkɔːsɪ̇t‖ˈkɔːr-/ *n* [C] **1** a tightly fitting piece of underwear that women wore in the past to make them look thinner **2** a strong, tightly fitting piece of clothing that supports your back when it is injured

**cor·tege** /kɔːˈteɪʒ‖kɔːrˈteʒ/ *n* [C] a line of people, cars etc that move along slowly in a funeral

**cor·tex** /ˈkɔːteks‖ˈkɔːr-/ *n plural* **cortices** /-tɪ̇siːz/ [C] *technical* the outer layer of an organ such as your brain —**cortical** /ˈkɔːtɪkəl‖ˈkɔːr-/ *adj*

**cor·ti·sone** /ˈkɔːtɪ̇zəʊn‖ˈkɔːrtɪ̇soʊn/ *n* [U] a HORMONE that is used especially in the treatment of diseases such as ARTHRITIS

**cor·us·ca·ting** /ˈkɒrəskeɪtɪŋ‖ˈkɔː-, ˈkɑː-/ *adj formal* flashing with light: *coruscating jewels*

S1 **cos¹** /kəz/ *conjunction nonstandard* an abbreviation of because

**cos²** /kɒs‖kɑːs/ *n* the abbreviation of COSINE

**cosh¹** /kɒʃ‖kɑːʃ/ *n* [C] *BrE informal* a heavy weapon in the shape of a short thick pipe

**cosh²** *v* [T] *informal especially BrE* to hit someone with a cosh

**co·sig·na·to·ry** /ˌkəʊˈsɪgnətəri‖ˌkoʊˈsɪgnətɔːri/ *n* [C] *formal* one of a group of people who sign a legal document for their department, organization, country etc: *We will need both cosignatories to sign the cheque.*

**co·sine** /ˈkəʊsaɪn‖ˈkoʊ-/ *n* [C] *technical* the measurement of an ACUTE (6) angle in a TRIANGLE (1) with a RIGHT ANGLE that is calculated by dividing the length of the side next to it by the length of the HYPOTENUSE —compare SINE

**cos·met·ic** /kɒzˈmetɪk‖kɑːz-/ *adj* [only before noun] **1** dealing with the outside appearance rather than the important part of something; SUPERFICIAL (1): *We're making a few cosmetic changes to the house before we sell it.*| **cosmetic exercise** (=something you do that looks good but does not achieve anything) **2** intended to make your hair or skin look more attractive: *the cosmetic industry|Are you on the diet for health or cosmetic reasons?*

**cos·me·ti·cian** /ˌkɒzməˈtɪʃən‖ˌkɑːz-/ *n* [C] someone who is professionally trained to put cosmetics on other people

**cos·met·ics** /kɒzˈmetɪks‖kɑːz-/ *n* [plural] creams, powders etc that you use on your face and body in order to look more attractive

**cosmetic sur·ge·ry** /ˌ·· ˈ···/ *n* [U] medical operations that improve your appearance after you have been injured, or because you want to feel more attractive

**cos·mic** /ˈkɒzmɪk‖ˈkɑːz-/ *adj* **1** connected with space or the universe **2** extremely large: *a scandal of cosmic proportions* —**cosmically** /-kli/ *adv*

**cosmic ray** /ˌ·· ˈ·/ *n* [C usually plural] a stream of RADIATION (2) reaching the Earth from space

**cos·mog·o·ny** /kɒzˈmɒgəni‖kɑːzˈmɑː-/ *n* [C,U] the origin of the universe, or a set of ideas about this

**cos·mol·o·gy** /kɒzˈmɒlədʒi‖kɑːzˈmɑː-/ *n* [U] the science of the origin and structure of the universe, especially as studied in ASTRONOMY

**cos·mo·naut** /ˈkɒzmənɔːt‖ˈkɑːzmənɒːt/ *n* [C] an ASTRONAUT from the former Soviet Union

**cos·mo·pol·i·tan¹** /ˌkɒzməˈpɒlɪ̇tən◂‖ˌkɑːzməˈpɑː-/ *adj* **1** a cosmopolitan place consists of people from many different parts of the world: *the cosmopolitan bustle of San Francisco* **2** a cosmopolitan person, belief, opinion etc shows a wide experience of different people and places: *Brigitta has such a cosmopolitan outlook on life.*

**cosmopolitan²** *n* [C] someone who has travelled a lot and feels at home in any part of the world

**cos·mos** /ˈkɒzmɒs‖ˈkɑːzməs/ *n* **the cosmos** the whole universe, especially when you think of it as a system

**cos·set** /ˈkɒsɪ̇t‖ˈkɑː-/ *v* [T] to give someone as much care and attention as you can, especially when it is too much: *No-one in the family gets as much cossetting as that cat!*

**cost¹** /kɒst‖kɔːst/ *n*  S1 W1

**1** ▶ **MONEY PAID** ◀ [C] the amount of money that you have to pay in order to buy, do, or produce something: *I'll give you $15 to cover the cost of the gas.*| **at a cost of** *The new building's going up at a cost of $82 million.*| **high/low cost** *a low cost source of electric power*| **full cost** *If no scholarships or other aid are available, students will have to pay the full cost of their education.*| **cost of living** (=the cost of buying all the food, clothes etc that you need to live) *The cost of living rose two percent in the last year.*| **at no extra cost** *A cassette/radio is included at no extra cost.*

**2** ▶ **LOSS/DAMAGE** ◀ [C,U] something that you lose, give away, damage etc in order to achieve something: **at (a) cost to** *Duncan always puts Hannah's needs before his own, at considerable cost to himself.*| **whatever the cost** (=no matter how much work, money, risk etc is needed) *He's determined to win, whatever the cost.*| **at all costs** (=whatever happens) *We must avoid a scandal at all costs.*

**3 costs** [plural] **a)** the money that you must regularly spend in order to continue having a home, car, business etc: **increase costs** *Businesses protested that the new taxes would increase production costs unreasonably.*| **reduce/cut costs** *We've got to cut costs and we're starting with the phone bill.*| **cover costs** (=make enough money to pay for the things you have bought) *At this rate we'll barely cover our costs.*| **running costs** (=the cost of owning and using a car or machine) *Because of the engine's efficiency the car has very low running costs.*

**b) costs** also **court costs** *AmE* the money that you must pay to lawyers etc if you are involved in a legal case in court, especially if you are guilty: *Bellisario won the case and was awarded costs.*
**4** ▶ **PRICE PAID** ◀ [singular] *especially AmE* the price that someone pays for something that they are going to sell; COST PRICE: **at cost** *His uncle's a car dealer and let him buy the car at cost.*
**5 find/know/learn etc sth to your cost** to realize something is true because you have had a very unpleasant experience: *Driving fast in wet conditions is dangerous, as my brother discovered to his cost!* —see also **count the cost** (COUNT[1] (9))

This graph shows some of the words most commonly used with the noun **cost**.

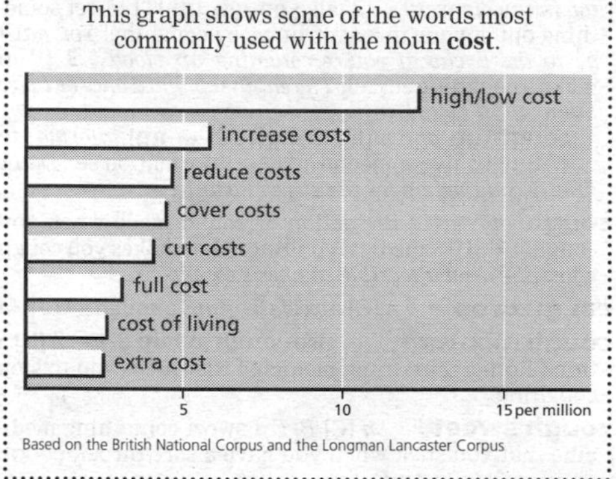


**USAGE NOTE: COST**
WORD CHOICE: **price, cost, charge, fare, fees, rent, rental**
When you are talking about the money you need to buy a particular thing, the usual word is **price**: *The price of a CD/piece of land/packet of cigarettes/cauliflower.*
**Cost** (*n*) is like **price,** but is used less for objects, and more for services or activities: *the cost of having the house painted/going on holiday*. It is also used for general things: *the cost of living* (NOT *of life*)| *the cost of food* | *the cost of production/postage* (NOT ... *for postage*). The **cost** of something may be *high* or *low* but not *free* or *expensive*.
The amount of money you pay for something is what it **costs** (*v*) you: *How much did this CD cost you?*| *It cost £1000 to have the house painted.* Things may **cost** *a lot* but not *cost high/expensive*.
The person who is selling goods or services to you **charges** you for them: *How much did he charge you for mending the car/for that CD?* A **charge** (*n*) is a sum of money asked, especially for allowing someone to do something or for a service: *There will be a small charge for admission to the museum/for reconnecting your gas supply.*
A charge for travelling on a plane, train, bus etc. is the **fare**. The charge for professional services, for a course etc is the **fees** (plural). The charge for living in someone else's room or house for some time is the **rent**. In a hotel, however, you pay the **price** of the room. The charge when you rent/hire a car etc is the **rental**.
GRAMMAR
Remember that the past tense and past participle of **cost** is **cost**, not *costed*: *This trip has cost her a fortune.*

S1 W2 **cost²** *v*
**1** ▶ **PRICE** ◀ *past tense and past participle* **cost** [linking verb] to have a particular price: *Buy one of your own – they don't cost much.*|**cost (sb) sth** *How much did the work cost you?*|**cost a (small) fortune/the earth** (=cost a lot of money) *The meal cost a small fortune, but it was well worth it.*|**cost a bomb** *BrE* (=cost a lot of money) *What a fantastic dress. It must have cost a bomb!*
**2 cost sb their job/life/marriage etc** to do something that makes you lose your job etc: *Joe's brave action cost him his life.*
**3 it will cost you** *spoken* used to say that something will be expensive: *Tickets are still available, but they'll cost you!*
**4** ▶ **CALCULATE COST** ◀ *past tense and past participle* **costed** [T usually passive] to calculate the cost of something or decide how much something should cost: *We'll get the plan costed before presenting it to the board.*
**5 cost an arm and a leg/cost a pretty penny** to have a price that is too high: *We'd like to send the children to private school but it would cost us an arm and a leg.*
**6 cost sb dear/dearly** to make someone suffer a lot: *The delay in sending our report cost us dearly because it meant we lost the contract.*
**7 sth costs money** *spoken* used to remind or warn someone that they should be careful because something is expensive: *Don't leave your sneakers in the rain! Shoes cost money, you know.*

**co-star¹** /ˈkəʊ stɑː‖ˈkoʊ stɑːr/ *n* [C] one of two or more famous actors that work together in a film or play

**co-star²** *v* [I + **with**] to be working in a film or play with other famous actors

**cost-ben·e·fit a·nal·y·sis** /ˌ· ˈ··· ·ˌ···/ *n* [C] *technical* a way of calculating the methods or plans that will bring you the most benefits for the smallest cost

**cost ef·fec·tive** /ˌ· ·ˈ··◂/ *adj* bringing the best possible profits or advantages for the lowest possible costs: *Recruitment and training have to be planned in the most cost effective way.* —**cost effectively** *adv* —**cost effectiveness** *n* [U]

**cos·ter·mon·ger** /ˈkɒstəˌmʌŋgə‖ˈkɑːstərˌmɑːŋgər, -ˌmʌŋ-/ *n* [C] *BrE old use* someone who sells fruit and vegetables in the street

**cost·ing** /ˈkɒstɪŋ‖ˈkɒːst-/ *n* [C,U] the process of calculating the cost of a future business activity, product etc, or the calculation itself: *Have we got the costings through yet?*

**cost·ly** /ˈkɒstli‖ˈkɒːstli/ *adj* **1** too expensive and wasting a lot of money: *Replacing all the windows would be too costly.* **2** something that is costly causes a lot of problems or trouble: *Hawksworth letting that goal in proved a costly mistake.* —**costliness** *n* [U]

**cost-plus** /ˌ· ˈ·◂/ *adj technical* a cost-plus contract gives the person selling all of their costs (COST[1] (3)) and part of the profit as well

**cost price** /ˌ· ˈ·◂/ *n* [U] the price that someone pays for something that they are going to sell; COST[1] (4) *especially AmE*

**cos·tume** /ˈkɒstjʊm‖ˈkɑːstuːm/ *n* **1** [C,U] a set of clothes that are typical of a particular place or historical period of time: *The dancers were all in national costume.* **2** [C] a set of clothes worn to make you look like something such as an animal, GHOST[1] (1) etc or to hide who you are: *Hallowe'en costumes* **3** [C] *BrE* a SWIMMING COSTUME

**costume dra·ma** /ˈ·· ˌ··/ *n* [C] a play that is about a particular time in history, in which people wear costumes from that time

**costume jew·elle·ry** /ˈ·· ˌ···/ *n* [U] cheap jewellery that is often designed to look expensive

**co·sy¹** *especially BrE*, **cozy** *AmE* /ˈkəʊzi‖ˈkoʊzi/ *adj* **1** a place that is cosy is small, comfortable, and warm: *a cosy room* **2** a situation that is cosy is comfortable and friendly: *a cosy chat* **3** having a close connection or relationship, especially one you do not approve of: *cosy deals with local councils* —**cosily** *adv* —**cosiness** *n* [U]

**cosy²** *n* [C] a covering for a teapot etc that keeps the tea inside from getting cold too quickly: *a tea cosy*

**cot** /kɒt‖kɑːt/ *n* [C] **1** *BrE* a small bed with high sides for a young child; CRIB[1] (1) *AmE* —see picture at BED[1] **2** *AmE* a CAMP BED

**co·tan·gent** /kəʊˈtændʒənt‖koʊ-/ *n* [C] *technical* the measurement of an angle in a TRIANGLE (1) with a RIGHT ANGLE that is calculated by dividing the length of the side opposite it by the length of the side next to it —compare TANGENT (3)

**cot death** /ˈ· ˌ·/ *n* [C] *BrE* the sudden and unexpected death of a healthy baby while it is sleeping; CRIB DEATH *AmE*

**co·te·rie** /ˈkəʊtəri‖ˈkoʊ-/ *n* [C] a small group of people who enjoy doing the same things together, and do not like including others

**co·ter·mi·nous** /kəʊˈtɜːmɪ̣nəs‖koʊˈtɜːr-/ *adj formal* coterminous countries share the same border

**co·til·lion** /kəˈtɪljən/ *n* [C] a formal occasion when people dance; BALL[1] (11)

S2 W3 **cot·tage** /ˈkɒtɪdʒ‖ˈkɑː-/ *n* [C] *especially BrE* a small house in the country: *We're staying in a holiday cottage in Dorset.*

**cottage cheese** /ˌ·· ˈ·‖ˈ·· ·/ *n* [U] soft white cheese made from sour milk

**cottage hos·pi·tal** /ˌ·· ˈ···/ *n BrE* a small hospital, usually in a country area

**cottage in·dus·try** /ˌ·· ˈ···/ *n* [C] an industry that consists of people working at home: *a programme to promote cottage industry in rural areas*

**cot·tag·er** /ˈkɒtɪdʒə‖ˈkɑːtɪdʒər/ *n* [C] *BrE slang* a man who looks for HOMOSEXUAL partners in a public place such as a toilet

**cot·tag·ing** /ˈkɒtɪdʒɪŋ/ *n* [U] *BrE slang* the practice of looking for male HOMOSEXUAL partners in a public place such as a toilet

**cot·ton[1]** /ˈkɒtn‖ˈkɑːtn/ *n* [U] **1** cloth or thread made from the white hair of the cotton plant: *a crisp cotton shirt* **2** a plant with white hairs on its seeds that are used for making cotton cloth and thread **3** *BrE* thread used for sewing **4** *AmE* COTTON WOOL

**cotton[2]** *v*

**cotton on** *phr v* [I] *informal* to begin to understand something: *I dropped about six hints before he cottoned on.*

**cotton to** *phr v* [T] *AmE informal* to begin to like a person, idea etc: *I didn't cotton to her at first, but she's really nice.*

**cotton bud** /ˌ·· ˈ·/ *n* [C] *BrE* a small thin stick with COTTON WOOL at each end, used for cleaning places that are hard to reach, such as inside your ears; Q-TIP *AmE*

**cotton can·dy** /ˌ·· ˈ··/ *n* [U] *AmE* CANDYFLOSS

**cotton gin** /ˈ·· ·/ *n* [C] a machine that separates the seeds of a cotton plant from the cotton

**cotton pick·ing** /ˈ·· ˌ··/ *adj* [only before noun] *AmE spoken* used to emphasize that you are annoyed or surprised: *Mind your own cotton picking business!*

**cotton reel** /ˈ·· ·/ *n* [C] *BrE* the small object that cotton thread is wound around; SPOOL (2) *AmE*

**cot·ton·tail** /ˈkɒtnteɪl‖ˈkɑːtn-/ *n* [C] *AmE* a small rabbit with a white tail

**cot·ton·wood** /ˈkɒtnwʊd‖ˈkɑː-/ *n* [C,U] a North American tree with seeds that look like white cotton

**cotton wool** /ˌ·· ˈ·◂/ *n* [U] *BrE* **1** a soft mass of cotton that you use especially for cleaning and protecting wounds: *Cotton wool pads are good for removing make-up.* **2 wrap sb in cotton wool** to protect someone completely from the dangers, difficulties etc of life: *You can't wrap those kids in cotton wool all their lives.*

**cot·y·le·don** /ˌkɒtɪˈliːdn‖ˌkɑːtlˈiːdn/ *n* [C] *technical* the first leaf that grows from a seed

**couch[1]** /kaʊtʃ/ *n* [C] **1** a comfortable piece of furniture for two or three people to sit on, or for one person to lie down on; SOFA **2** *literary* a bed

**couch[2]** *v* **be couched in** *formal* to be expressed in a particular way: *The offer was couched in obscure legal jargon.*

**cou·chette** /kuːˈʃet/ *n* [C] **1** a narrow bed that folds down from the wall in a train **2** a comfortable seat on a night boat or train —compare SLEEPING CAR

**couch po·ta·to** /ˈ· ·ˌ··/ *n* [C] *informal* someone who spends a lot of time sitting and watching television

**cou·gar** /ˈkuːgə, -gɑː‖-gər, -gɑːr/ *n* [C] a large brown wild cat from the mountains of Western North America and South America; MOUNTAIN LION

**cough[1]** /kɒf‖kɒːf/ *v* **1** [I] to suddenly push air out of your throat with a short sound: *coughing from smoking too many cigarettes* **2** also **cough up** [T] to get something out of your throat or lungs by coughing: *You must go to the doctor if you're coughing up blood.* **3** [I] to make a coughing sound: *The engine coughed once or twice but wouldn't start.*

**cough up** *phr v* [I,T **cough** sth ↔ **up**] *informal* to unwillingly give someone money, information etc: *Dad's finally coughed up for the stereo I wanted.*

**cough[2]** *n* **1** [C] the action or sound made when you cough **2** [U] a medical condition that makes you cough a lot: *She's got a terrible smoker's cough.*

**cough drop** /ˈ· ·/ *n* [C] *especially AmE* a cough sweet

**cough mix·ture** /ˈ· ˌ··/ also **cough syrup** *BrE*— *n* [U] a thick liquid containing medicine that helps you to stop coughing

**cough sweet** /ˈ· ·/ *n* [C] *BrE* a sweet containing medicine that you suck when you have a sore throat; COUGH DROP *especially AmE*

**could** /kəd ; *strong* kʊd/ *modal verb 3rd person singular* **could** *negative short form* **couldn't** **1** the past tense of 'can': *Could you hear that all right?* | *I couldn't get tickets after all, they were sold out.* | *Marcia said we could smoke, it was okay with her.* —see CAN[1] (USAGE) **2** used to ask if someone is able or allowed to do something: *Could I ask you a couple of questions?* | *What about Sam? Could he come along too?* **3** used to express something that might be possible or might happen, when it is not certain that it will happen or be possible: *Most accidents in the home could be easily prevented.* | *It could be weeks before the construction is actually finished.* | *If you're not careful, you could find yourself without enough stock to fill the order.* **4** used to be polite when you are asking someone to do something: *Could you pay this check into the bank for me tomorrow?* | *Yeah, there are a couple of things you could do for me if you're going into town.* **5** used to suggest what you think someone should do or might be able to do: *We could get the bus instead.* | *You could always try phoning her at the office.* | *If you could let us know your decision as soon as possible, it would be a great help.* **6** used to show that you are annoyed about something: *You could have told me you were going to be late!* | *I'm sure John could be more careful when he's washing up.* | *How could you say such an insulting thing to her! She's my best friend!* **7 I couldn't care less** used when you are not at all interested in or concerned about something: *I said I couldn't care less if I got paid triple time, I'm not coming in on a Sunday.* | *A lot of the students just couldn't care less about learning anything.* **8 I couldn't agree more** used when you completely agree with someone: *I couldn't agree more. There's just far too much sex and violence on TV.* **9 I could have strangled/hit/killed etc sb** used to emphasize that you were very angry with someone: *I could have murdered Ryan for telling Jason that!* **10 couldn't be more wonderful/exciting/boring etc** also **couldn't be better/prettier/worse etc** used to emphasize how good, exciting etc something is: *It couldn't have been a more restful vacation.* | *Things couldn't be worse, everything seems to be going wrong at once.* **11 I couldn't** used to politely say that you do not want any more food or drink: *"Would you like another piece of pie?" "Oh, no thanks, I couldn't."* S1 W1

**couldst** /kʊdst/ *v* **thou couldst** *old use* you could

**cou·lee** /ˈkuːli, -leɪ/ *n* [C] *AmE* a small valley with steep sides

S2 W1 **coun·cil** /ˈkaʊnsəl/ *n* [C] **1** a group of people that are chosen to make rules, laws or decisions, or to give advice: *the council for civil liberties* **2** the organization that is responsible for local government in a particular region in Britain: *Bob Jones has been on the Borough Council for years.* | **council offices/housing/worker etc** *BrE* (=owned, employed etc by local government) *Dave's got his name down for a council flat.* **3** a group of people elected to the government of a city in the US: *the Los Angeles city council* **4 council of war** *humorous* a meeting to decide how to deal with a particular problem

**council es·tate** /ˈ·· ·ˌ·/ *n* [C] *BrE* an area consisting of streets of council houses

**council house** /ˈ·· ·/ *n* [C] a house or flat in Britain that is provided by the local council for a very low rent

S3 W3 **coun·cil·lor** *BrE*, **councilor** *AmE* /ˈkaʊnsələ‖-ər/ *n* [C] a member of a council: *Write to your local councilor to complain.*

**coun·cil·man** /ˈkaʊnsəlmən/ *n* [C] a man who is a member of the government of a city in the US

**coun·cil·wom·an** /ˈkaʊnsəlˌwʊmən/ *n* [C] a woman who is a member of the government of a city in the US

**coun·sel**[1] /ˈkaʊnsəl/ *n technical* **1** [singular] a type of lawyer who represents you in court: *The judge asked counsel for the defence to explain.* **2 keep your own counsel** to keep your plans, opinions etc secret **3** [U] *literary* advice

**counsel**[2] *v* [T] **1** *formal* to advise someone: **counsel sb to do sth** *She counselled them not to accept this settlement.* **2** to listen and give support to someone with problems: *a new unit to counsel alcoholics*

**coun·sel·ling** *BrE*, **counseling** *AmE* /ˈkaʊnsəlɪŋ/ *n* [U] the act of listening to people and giving them support with their problems, especially as your job: *She's been undergoing counseling for depression.*

**coun·sel·lor** *BrE*, **counselor** *AmE* /ˈkaʊnsələ‖-ər/ *n* [C] someone whose job is to help and support people with problems: *Have you thought of seeing a counsellor?* —see LAWYER (USAGE)

S1 W3 **count**[1] /kaʊnt/ *v*

**1 ▶ SAY NUMBERS ◀** also **count up** [I] to say numbers in their correct order: [+ **to**] *Sarah can count up to five now.* | *Try to count to ten before you lose your temper.*

**2 ▶ FIND THE TOTAL ◀** also **count up** [T] to count the people, objects, numbers etc in a group in order to find a total: *The teacher was counting the children as they got on the bus.* | **count sheep** (=count imaginary sheep as a way of getting to sleep)

**3 ▶ INCLUDE ◀** [T] to include someone or something in a total: *There are five people in the family counting my parents.* | **count sb/sth among** *I count Jules and Ady among my closest friends.*

**4 ▶ BE ALLOWED ◀** [I,T] to be officially allowed or accepted; VALID: *Illegible entries do not count.*

**5 count yourself lucky/fortunate etc** to feel that you are lucky etc: *After the avalanche we counted ourselves lucky to be alive.*

**6 ▶ IMPORTANT ◀** [I not in progressive] to be a very important or valuable thing: *First impressions really do count.* | **count for something/anything/more etc** *His promises don't count for much.*

**7 be able to count sb/sth on (the fingers of) one hand** *spoken* used to emphasize how small the number of something is: *You could have counted the number of people in the theater on one hand.*

**8 don't count your chickens (before they're hatched)** *especially spoken* used to say that you should not make plans because you hope something good will happen: *It should be worth a few million, but I don't like to count my chickens.*

**9 count the cost** to start having problems as a result of your earlier decisions or mistakes: *We're now counting the cost of not taking out medical insurance.*

**10 who's counting?** used to say that you are not worried about the number of times something happens: *"But I always smoke your cigarettes." "No problem, who's counting?"* —see also **stand up and be counted** (STAND[1]), **it's the thought that counts** (THOUGHT[2] (12))

**count** sb/sth **as** *phr v* [I] to consider or regard someone or something in a particular way: *For tax purposes this counts as unearned income.*

**count down** *phr v* [I] to record the time passing until an important event happens: *We're counting down to our holiday.* —see also COUNTDOWN

**count** sb **in** *phr v* [T] *informal* to include someone in a planned activity: *Mark, can we count you in for the cricket team?*

**count on/upon** sb/sth *phr v* [T] **1** to depend on or be certain of someone or something: *You can count on my vote.* | *If I got into trouble I could always count on Rusty.* | **count on doing sth** *We're all counting on winning this contract.* | **count on sb/sth doing sth** *Just don't count on Bev being too thrilled about the news.* | **count on sb/sth to do sth** *You can count on Dean to ruin any party.* **2** to plan or expect to do something: **count on (sb/sth) doing sth** *We didn't count on so many people being on vacation.*

**count** sb/sth **out** *phr v* [T] **1** to lay things down one by one as you count them: *The teller counted out ten $50 bills.* **2** *informal* to not include someone or something: *If you're looking for trouble you can count me out.*

**count**[2] *n* [C]

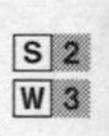

**1 ▶ TOTAL ◀** the total that you get by counting a particular set of things, or the process of doing this: *The vote was so close that we had to have several counts.*

**2 ▶ MEASUREMENT ◀** a measurement that shows how much of a substance is present in the area or thing being examined: *The pollen count is high today.* | *a low sperm count*

**3 at the last count** used to give the latest information about a particular situation: *At the last count, 46 students were interested in the trip.*

**4 on all/several etc counts** in every way, in several ways etc: *Their education policy has failed on several counts.*

**5 keep count** to keep a record of the changing total of something over a period of time: *I never manage to keep count of what I spend on the credit card.*

**6 lose count** to forget a number you were calculating or a total you were trying to count: *Shut up – you've made me lose count now!*

**7 be out for the count a)** to be in a deep sleep: *There's no point in asking George – he's out for the count.* **b)** if a BOXER (1) is out for the count, he has been knocked down for ten seconds or more

**8 ▶ LAW ◀** *technical* one of the crimes that someone is charged with: *Davis was found not guilty on all counts.*

**9 ▶ RANK/TITLE ◀** a European NOBLEMAN whose rank is similar to a British EARL: *the Count of Monte Cristo*

**count·a·ble** /ˈkaʊntəbəl/ *adj* a countable noun has both a singular and a plural form: *Countable nouns like 'table' or 'tables' are marked [C] in this book.* —see also COUNT NOUN —compare UNCOUNTABLE

**coun·te·nance**[1] /ˈkaʊntɪnəns/ *n formal* **1** [C] your face or your expression: *the gloomy countenance of a disappointed child* **2** [U] support or approval

**countenance**[2] *v* [T] to accept, support, or approve of something: **countenance doing sth** *Her father won't countenance her getting married so young.*

**counter-** /kaʊntə‖-tər/ *prefix* **1** the opposite of something: *a counterproductive thing to do* (=producing results opposite to what you wanted) **2** matching something: *my counterpart in the American system* (=someone who has the same job as mine) **3** done or given as a reaction to something, especially to oppose it: *proposals and counter-proposals* **4** acting to prevent

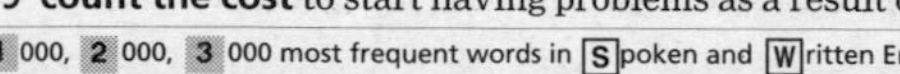

something: *a counterinsurgency strategy* (=to prevent INSURGENTS)

S3 **coun·ter¹** /ˈkaʊntə‖-ər/ *n* [C]
**1 ▶ SHOP ◀** the place where you pay or are served in a shop, bank, restaurant etc
**2 over the counter** drugs, medicines etc that are bought over the counter are ones that you can buy in a shop without a PRESCRIPTION (1) from a doctor
**3 under the counter** if you buy something under the counter, you buy it secretly and usually illegally: *It's risky, but you can get alcohol under the counter.*
**4 ▶ KITCHEN ◀** *AmE* a flat surface on top of a piece of furniture, especially in a kitchen, used for working on, preparing food etc; WORK-SURFACE *BrE*: *Just leave my keys on the kitchen counter.* —see picture on page 833

**5 ▶ GAME ◀** a small round object that you use in some games that are played on a board
**6 ▶ EQUIPMENT ◀** a piece of electrical equipment that counts something: *Set the video counter to zero before you press play.* —see also GEIGER COUNTER
**7 ▶ ACTION AGAINST STH ◀** an action that is used to try to prevent something bad from happening, or an argument used to prove that something is wrong: [+ **to**] *Britain began its pro-Japanese policy as a counter to Russian advances in Asia.*

**counter²** *v* **1** [I,T] to say something in order to try to prove that what someone said was not true: [+ **that**] *"That's not what James told me," he countered.* | **counter an argument/allegation etc** *He was determined to counter the bribery allegations.* **2** [T] to do something in order to reduce the bad effects of something, or to defend yourself against them: *One way of countering these problems would be to redistribute wealth among the poor.*

**counter³** *adv* [not before noun] in a way that is opposite to something: **run counter to** *The child is asked to behave in ways which run counter to his natural desires.* —**counter** *adj*: *To publicize this revolting film is counter to the standards of your newspaper.*

**coun·ter·act** /ˌkaʊntərˈækt/ *v* [T] to reduce or prevent the bad effect of something, by doing something that has the opposite effect: *a drug that counteracts the poison* —**counteraction** /-ˈækʃən/ *n* [C,U]

**coun·ter·at·tack** /ˈkaʊntərətæk/ *n* [C] an attack that you make against someone who has attacked you, in a war, sport, or an argument: *I decided on a swift counterattack.* —**counterattack** *v* [I,T] —**counterattacker** *n* [C]

**coun·ter·bal·ance** /ˌkaʊntəˈbæləns‖-tər-/ *v* [T] to have an equal and opposite effect to something such as a change, feeling etc: *His fear of his father is counterbalanced by a genuine respect.* —**counterbalance** /ˈkaʊntəˌbæləns‖-tər-/ *n* [C]

**coun·ter·clock·wise** /ˌkaʊntəˈklɒkwaɪz◂‖-tərˈklɑːk-/ *adv AmE* moving in the opposite direction to the hands of a clock; ANTICLOCKWISE *BrE*: *To remove the lid, turn it counterclockwise.* —opposite CLOCKWISE

**coun·ter·feit¹** /ˈkaʊntəfɪt‖-tər-/ *adj* made to look exactly like something else: *The task force were looking for counterfeit money.*

**counterfeit²** *v* [T] to copy something exactly in order to deceive people

**coun·ter·foil** /ˈkaʊntəfɔɪl‖-tər-/ *n* [C] the part of something such as a cheque that you keep so that you can remember how much money you have spent

**coun·ter·in·sur·gen·cy** /ˌkaʊntərɪnˈsɜːdʒənsi‖-ɜːr-/ *n* [U] military action against people who are fighting against their own country's government

**coun·ter·in·tel·li·gence** /ˌkaʊntərɪnˈtelɪdʒəns/ *n* [U] action that a country takes in order to stop other countries discovering their secrets

**coun·ter·mand** /ˌkaʊntəˈmɑːnd, ˈkaʊntəmɑːnd‖ˌkaʊntər‖ˈkaʊntərˈmænd/ *v* [T] to officially tell people to ignore an order, especially by giving them a different one: *Senior officers persuaded the general to countermand the order.*

**coun·ter·mea·sure** /ˈkaʊntəmeʒə‖-tərmeʒər/ *n* [C usually plural] an action taken to prevent another action from having a harmful effect: *new countermeasures against terrorism*

**coun·ter·pane** /ˈkaʊntəpeɪn‖-ər-/ *n* [C] *old-fashioned* a thick cover that you put over all the other covers on a bed; BEDSPREAD

**coun·ter·part** /ˈkaʊntəpɑːt‖-tərpɑːrt/ *n* [C] someone or something that has the same job or purpose as someone or something else in a different place: *Belgian officials are discussing this with their French counterparts.*

**coun·ter·point** /ˈkaʊntəpɔɪnt‖-ər-/ *n* **1** [U] a combination of two or more tunes that are played together to sound like one tune **2** [C] a tune that is one part of counterpoint

**coun·ter·pro·duc·tive** /ˌkaʊntəprəˈdʌktɪv◂‖-tər-/ *adj* achieving the opposite result to the one that you want: *Sending young offenders to prison can be counterproductive.*

**counter-rev·o·lu·tion** /ˌ·· ··ˈ··/ *n* [C,U] political or military actions taken to get rid of a government that is in power because of a previous REVOLUTION (2) —**counter-revolutionary** *adj*

**counter-rev·o·lu·tion·a·ry** /ˌ·· ··ˈ····/ *n* [C] someone who is involved in a counter-revolution

**coun·ter·sign** /ˈkaʊntəsaɪn‖-ər-/ *v* [T] to sign a paper that has already been signed by someone else: *The note must be countersigned by a doctor.*

**coun·ter·ten·or** /ˌkaʊntəˈtenə‖ˈkaʊntərˌtenər/ *n* [C] a man who is trained to sing with a very high voice

**counter-ter·ror·ist** /ˈ·· ˌ···/ *adj* **counter-terrorist operation/team/unit etc** a plan or group that tries to prevent the violent activities of political groups who use force —**counter-terrorist** *n* [C]

**coun·ter·vail·ing** /ˌkaʊntəˈveɪlɪŋ◂‖-ər-/ *adj formal* with an equally strong but opposite effect: *the need for countervailing forces to that of the state*

**coun·tess** /ˈkaʊntɪs/ *n* [C] a woman with the same rank as an EARL or a COUNT² (9)

**counting house** /ˈ·· ·/ *n* [C] an office where accounts and money were kept in former times

**count·less** /ˈkaʊntləs/ *adj* too many to be counted: *It has saved my life, and the lives of countless others.* | *I spent countless hours on trains and buses.*

**count noun** /ˈ· ·/ *n* [C] *technical* a noun that has both singular and plural forms, can be used with numbers and with words such as many, few etc, or can be used with a or an —see also NOUN

**coun·tri·fied** /ˈkʌntrifaɪd/ *adj* typical of the countryside, or made to seem typical of the countryside: *the countrified existence of the newly rich*

**coun·try¹** /ˈkʌntri/ *n* **1** [C] an area of land that is controlled by its own government, president, king etc: *Pakistan became a fully independent country shortly after the Second World War.* —compare NATION (1) —see also MOTHER COUNTRY —see LAND¹ (USAGE) **2 the country a)** land that is outside towns and cities, including land used for farming; the countryside: *I've always wanted to live in the country.* **b)** all the people who live in a particular country: *The President has the support of over 50 per cent of the country.* **3 farming country/walking country etc** land that is suitable for a particular activity: *The Peak District is good walking country.* S1 W1
**4 go to the country** *BrE* if a Prime Minister goes to the country, they ask for a GENERAL ELECTION to be held

**country²** *adj* [only before noun] belonging to or connected with the countryside: *They much preferred country life to life in the city.*

**country and west·ern** /ˌ·· · ˈ··/ *n* [U] popular music in the style of music from the southern and western US

**country bump·kin** /ˌ·· ˈ··/ *n* [C] someone from the countryside who seems stupid

**country club** /ˈ·· ˌ·/ *n* [C] a sports and social club in the countryside, especially one for rich people

**country danc·ing** /ˌ·· ˈ··/ *n* [U] a traditional form of dance in which pairs of dancers move in rows and circles

**country house** /ˌ·· ˈ·/ *n* [C] *BrE* a large house in the countryside, especially one that is of historical interest

**coun·try·man** /ˈkʌntrimən/ *n plural* **countrymen** /-mən/ [C] **1** someone from your own country; COMPATRIOT: *During the war, the loyalty of fellow countrymen was all-important.* **2** a man who lives in the country rather than a town or city

**country mu·sic** /ˈ·· ˌ··/ *n* [U] COUNTRY AND WESTERN

**country seat** /ˌ·· ˈ·/ *n* [C] *BrE* the countryside house of someone who is rich and owns land

S2 W3 **coun·try·side** /ˈkʌntrisaɪd/ *n* [U] land that is outside cities and towns: *Our new house is surrounded by the most beautiful countryside.*

**coun·try·wom·an** /ˈkʌntriˌwʊmən/ *n plural* **countrywomen** /-ˌwɪmɪn/ [C] a woman who lives in the country rather than a town or city

S1 W2 **coun·ty¹** /ˈkaʊnti/ *n* [C] an area of Great Britain, the US and some other countries that contains several towns that are governed together

**county²** *adj BrE informal* belonging to or typical of people from the upper classes in Britain

**county coun·cil** /ˌ·· ˈ··/ *n* [C] an organization consisting of a group of people who are elected to organize schools, HOUSING etc, in a county in Britain

**county court** /ˌ·· ˈ·/ *n* [C] *BrE* a local court of law that deals with private quarrels between people rather than with serious crimes

**county fair** /ˌ·· ˈ·/ *n* [C] *AmE* an event that happens each year in a particular county, with games and competitions for the best farm animals, cooking etc

**county town** /ˌ·· ˈ·/ *BrE*, **county seat** *AmE*— *n* [C] the town in a COUNTY¹ where its government is

**coup** /kuː/ *n* [C] **1** a sudden and sometimes violent attempt by citizens or the army to take control of the government; coup d'état: *There were rumours of a coup in Moscow before Gorbachev was actually overthrown.* **2** an achievement that is extremely impressive because it was very difficult: *Getting a former International as coach was a real coup for the club.*

**coup de grâce** /ˌkuː də ˈgrɑːs/ *n* [singular] *French* **1** an action or event that ends or destroys something that has gradually been getting weaker: *The nuclear atoms delivered the coup de grâce to classical physics.* **2** a hit or shot that kills someone or something

**coup d'état** /ˌkuː deɪˈtɑː‖-deˈtɑː/ *n plural* **coups d'état** (*same pronunciation*) *French* [C] a COUP (1)

**cou·pé** /ˈkuːpeɪ‖kuːˈpeɪ/ *n* [C] *especially BrE* a car with two doors and a sloping back

S1 W1 **cou·ple¹** /ˈkʌpəl/ *n* **1 a couple a)** two things or people of the same kind: *We just need a couple more chairs so everyone can sit down.*|[+ **of**] *There's a couple of girls waiting for you outside.* **b)** a small number of things: [+ **of**] *I don't know why I feel so bad, I only had a couple of drinks.* —see PAIR¹ (USAGE) **2** [C] two people who are married or having a sexual or romantic relationship: *This hotel is a favourite with young honeymoon couples.*|*the couple next door*

**couple²** *v* **1** [T] to join or fasten two things together, especially two vehicles **2** [I] *formal* to have sex

**couple with** *phr v* [T usually passive] if one thing is coupled with another, they happen or exist together and produce a particular result: *Lack of rain coupled with high temperatures caused the crops to fail.*

**coup·let** /ˈkʌplɪ̣t/ *n* [C] two lines of poetry, one following the other, that are the same length: *rhyming couplets*

**coup·ling** /ˈkʌplɪŋ/ *n* [C] **1** something that connects two things together, especially two vehicles **2** *formal* an act of coming together to have sex

**cou·pon** /ˈkuːpɒn‖-pɑːn/ *n* [C] **1** a small piece of printed paper that gives you the right to pay less for something or get something free: *The coupon entitles you to 10 cents off your next purchase.* **2** a printed form, that you write your name and address on, in order to send for information or enter a competition

S3 **cour·age** /ˈkʌrɪdʒ‖ˈkɜːr-/ *n* [U] **1** the ability to be brave when you are in danger, in pain, in a difficult situation etc: *Sue showed great courage throughout her illness.*|**summon up the courage/pluck up the courage** (=try to make yourself be brave enough) *Liz was trying to summon up the courage to tell Paul it was all over between them.*|**take courage** (=need courage) *Driving again after his accident must have taken a lot of courage.* **2 have the courage of your (own) convictions** to be brave enough to say or do what you think is right even though other people may not agree or approve —see also DUTCH COURAGE

**cou·ra·geous** /kəˈreɪdʒəs/ *adj* brave: *a courageous and independent woman*|*a courageous decision* —**courageously** *adv* —**courageousness** *n* [U]

**cour·gette** /kʊəˈʒet‖kʊr-/ *n* [C] *BrE* a long vegetable with a dark green skin; ZUCCHINI *AmE* —see picture on page 414

**cou·ri·er¹** /ˈkʊriə‖-ər/ *n* [C] **1** someone who is employed to take a package, documents etc somewhere **2** *BrE* someone who is employed by a travel company to help people on holiday, by giving them information, helping them with problems etc

**courier²** *v* [T] to send something somewhere by using a courier

S1 W1 **course¹** /kɔːs‖kɔːrs/ *n*

**1 of course a)** used when you are mentioning something that you think other people already know, or should know: *Your car insurance must, of course, be renewed every year.* **b)** used to say that what you or someone else has just said is not surprising: *Hannah applied for the job and got it, of course.* **c)** *spoken* also **course** *informal* used to agree with someone, or to give permission to someone: *"Can I borrow the car tonight?"– "Yeah, course you can."* **d)** also **course** *spoken* used to emphasize that what you are saying is true or correct: *"You promise you won't forget?" "Of course I won't!"* —see OF COURSE (USAGE)

**2 of course not/course not** *spoken* used to emphasize that you are saying no to something, or that something is not true or correct: *"Do you think they'll mind if I arrive late?" "No, of course not."*

**3 ▶ LESSONS ◀** [C] *especially BrE* a series of lessons, or studies in a particular subject: *Andy's doing a one-year journalism course.*|[+ **on**] *a course on the French Revolution*|[+ **in**] *She's taking a course in flower arranging.* —see also CORRESPONDENCE COURSE, CRASH COURSE, REFRESHER COURSE, SANDWICH COURSE

**4 in the course of/during the course of** *formal* during a process or period of time: *During the course of our conversation it emerged that Bob had been in prison.*

**5 ▶ ACTIONS ◀** [C] an action or series of actions that you could take in order to deal with a particular situation: *In this case, the best course would be to avoid talking about it altogether.*|**course of action** *One possible course of action would be to increase tax on alcohol.*

**6 ▶ USUAL/NATURAL ◀** [C] the usual or natural way that something happens, develops, or is done: *Once the story is begun, it must follow its course.*|**course of history/nature etc** *When he met Sally it changed the whole course of his life.*|**in the normal course of events** *In the normal course of events a son would take over the farm from his father.*

**7 let sth take its course** to wait for something to develop in the usual way: *Just relax and let nature take its course.*

**8 run its course** to develop in the usual way and come to a natural end: *The illness has run its course.*

**9 ▶ PLANE/BOAT ◀** [C] the planned direction that a boat or plane takes to go somewhere: **on/off course** (=going in the right or wrong direction) *The ship had been blown off course in the storm.*

**10 ▶ PART OF A MEAL ◀** [C] one of the separate parts of a meal: **3-course meal/5-course meal etc** *That restaurant has excellent 3-course meals for very reasonable*

*prices.* | **first/second/main course etc** *We're having fish for the main course.*

**11 be on course** to be likely to achieve something because you have already had some success: [+ **for**] *The company is on course for record profits this year.* | **be on course to do sth** *Brazil are on course to win the World Cup.*

**12 ▶ RACE ◀** [C] an area of land or water where races happen: *The course is a particularly difficult one.* —see also ASSAULT COURSE, OBSTACLE COURSE

**13 golf course** [C] an area of land that is designed for you to play golf on

**14 ▶ MEDICAL TREATMENT ◀** [C] *especially BrE* an amount of medicine or medical treatment given or taken regularly for a fixed period of time: *If your doctor prescribes antibiotics, you should finish the course.* | **course of injections/drugs/treatment etc** *a course of injections for weight loss*

**15 in (the) course of time** after some or enough time has passed: *She'll get used to school in the course of time.*

**16 ▶ RIVER ◀** [C] the direction a river moves in: *The course of the water was shown by a line of willow trees.*

**17 ▶ BRICKS/STONE ◀** [C] a layer of bricks, stone etc —see also **as a matter of course** (MATTER[1] (18)), **par for the course** (PAR (3)), **stay the course** (STAY[1] (7)), **in due course** (DUE[1] (6))

**course[2]** *v* **1** [I always + adv/prep] *literary* if a liquid courses somewhere, it flows rapidly: [+ **down/along/through etc**] *He could not stop the tears coursing down his cheeks.* **2** [I always + adv/prep] *literary* if a feeling or thought courses through your body or mind, you feel it very strongly, or think it quickly: [+ **down/through**] *The shock was so great, it coursed down every nerve in Sam's body.* **3** [I,T] to chase a rabbit with dogs as a sport

**coursebook** /ˈ· ·/ *n* [C] *BrE* a book that you use regularly during a set of lessons on a particular subject; TEXTBOOK[1]

S1 W1 **court[1]** /kɔːt‖kɔːrt/ *n*

**1 ▶ LAW ◀** [C,U] a building or room where all the information concerning a crime is given so that it can be judged: *There was a large crowd of reporters gathered outside the court.* | **in court** *He was summoned to appear in court as a witness.* | **go to court** (=start the legal process to have a case dealt with in a court) *She was prepared to go to court to get compensation if necessary.* | **take sb to court** (=make someone be judged in a court) *Davis was taken to court for assaulting a policeman.* | **settle out of court** (=agree without being judged in a court) *We decided to settle the matter out of court.* | **court case/appearance/judge etc** *The court case lasted six weeks.*

**2 the court** [U] the people in a court, especially the judge and the JURY (1): *The defendant told the court that he was in Newcastle at the time of the alleged rape.*

**3 ▶ SPORT ◀** an area that has been specially made for playing games such as tennis on: *There are three squash courts available this evening.* | **on/off court** (=playing or not playing) *Becker and Edberg are due on court in an hour.* —see picture at TENNIS

**4 ▶ KING/QUEEN ETC ◀** [C] **a)** the official place where a king or queen lives and works: *This was one of the most splendid of the royal courts of Europe.* | **court painter/jester/adviser etc** (=someone who is employed by the court to paint etc) **b)** the royal people and the people who work for them or advise them: *Several members of the court were under suspicion.*

**5 hold court** to speak in an interesting and amusing way so that people gather to listen to you: *Gary was holding court in the pub last night.*

**6 pay court to** *old-fashioned* to give a lot of your attention to someone in order to impress them: *Stefan was dancing with everyone and paying court to all the girls.*

**7 ▶ CASTLE/LARGE HOUSE ◀** [C] an open space that is completely or partly surrounded by buildings, especially one that is part of a castle or large house; COURTYARD

**8 Court** *especially BrE* used as part of the name of a short street or of an apartment building —see also **the ball is in your court** (BALL[1] (10)), **be laughed out of court** (LAUGH[1] (7))

**court[2]** *v* **1** [T] *old-fashioned* if a man courts a woman, he visits her, takes her to restaurants etc because he hopes to marry her: *Richard courted Lindsay for years before she agreed to marry him.* **2** [I,T] *old-fashioned* if a man and a woman are courting, they are having a romantic relationship and may get married: *We were courting for two years before we even got engaged.* **3 court danger/death/punishment etc** to behave in a way that makes danger etc more likely: *You realize you're simply courting danger by driving that old car?* **4** [T] to try to get something you want, especially support from other people, by doing something to please them: *The directors are courting the support of the shareholders.*

**court card** /ˈ· ·/ *n* [C] *BrE* the king, queen or JACK[1] (2) in a set of playing cards; FACE CARD *AmE*

**cour·te·ous** /ˈkɜːtiəs‖ˈkɜːr-/ *adj* having good manners and respect for other people: *The staff are always courteous and helpful.* | *I received a courteous reply from the manager.* —opposite DISCOURTEOUS —**courteously** *adv* —**courteousness** *n* [U]

**cour·te·san** /ˌkɔːtʃˈzæn‖ˈkɔːrtʃzən/ *n* [C] a woman in former times who had sex with rich or important men for money

**cour·te·sy** /ˈkɜːtʃsi‖ˈkɜːr-/ *n* **1** [U] polite behaviour that shows that you have respect for other people: *Lack of courtesy is sometimes seen as a disease of modern day society.* —opposite DISCOURTESY **2** [C] something you do or say in order to be polite: *The managers exchanged courtesies before getting down to business.* **3 by courtesy of/courtesy of** by the permission or kindness of someone rather than by paying them: *Paul had his own flat and sports car courtesy of his celebrity father.*

**courtesy bus** /ˈ··· ˌ·/ *n* [C] a bus provided by a hotel near an airport that their guests can use to travel to and from the airport

**courtesy call** /ˈ··· ˌ·/ *n* [C] a visit to someone that you make to be polite or to show your respect for them

**courtesy car** /ˈ··· ˌ·/ *n* [C] a car that a garage, hotel etc lends to its customers while they are having their own car fixed, are staying at the hotel etc

**court·house** /ˈkɔːthaʊs‖ˈkɔːrt-/ *n* [C] *especially AmE* a building containing courts of law

**court·ier** /ˈkɔːtɪə‖ˈkɔːrtɪr/ *n* [C] someone in former times who had an important position in the COURT[1] (4b)

**court·ly** /ˈkɔːtli‖ˈkɔːrtli/ *adj* graceful and polite: *He answered with a courtly bow.* —**courtliness** *n* [U]

**court-mar·tial[1]** /ˌ· ˈ··‖ˈ· ˌ··/ *n* [C] **1** a military court that deals with people who break military law: *Soldiers were often court-martialled for cowardice.* **2** an occasion on which someone is judged by one of these courts

**court-martial[2]** *v past tense and past participle* **court-martialled** *BrE* , **court-martialed** *AmE* [T] to hear and judge someone's case in a military court: *Soldiers were often court-martialled for cowardice.*

**Court of Ap·peal** /ˌ· · ·ˈ·/ *n* [singular] the highest court of law in Britain apart from the HOUSE OF LORDS

**Court of Ap·peals** /ˌ· · ·ˈ·/ *n* [singular] one of 12 law courts in the US that deals with cases when people are not satisfied with the judgment given by a lower court —see also APPELLATE COURT

**court of en·quir·y, court of inquiry** /ˌ· · ·ˈ···‖ˌ· · ˈ···/ *n* [C] *BrE* a group of people chosen to discover the facts about something or the causes of something, for example a serious accident —compare GRAND JURY

**court of law** /ˌ· · ˈ·/ *n* [C] a place where law cases are judged; COURT[1] (1)

**court or·der** /ˌ· ˈ··/ *n* [C] an order given by a court of law that someone must do or must not do something

**court re·port·er** /ˌ· ·ˈ··/ *n* [C] someone who works in a court and records everything that is said during a case, on a special machine similar to a TYPEWRITER

**court·room** /ˈkɔːtruːm, -rʊm‖ˈkɔːrt-/ *n* [C] a room in a law court where cases are judged

**court·ship** /ˈkɔːt-ʃɪp‖ˈkɔːrt-/ *n* **1** [C,U] the period of time during which a man and woman have a romantic relationship before getting married **2** [U] special behaviour used by animals to attract each other for sex

**court shoe** /ˈ· ·/ *n* [C] *BrE* a type of woman's formal shoe that is very plain and has no fastening; PUMP[1] (3) *AmE* —see picture at SHOE[1]

**court·yard** /ˈkɔːtjɑːd‖ˈkɔːrtjɑːrd/ *n* [C] an open space that is completely or partly surrounded by buildings, especially one that is part of a castle or large house

**cous·cous** /ˈkuːskuːs/ *n* [U] a North African dish made of crushed wheat, served with meat and vegetables

S3 **cous·in** /ˈkʌzən/ *n* [C] **1** the child of your UNCLE or AUNT —see also FIRST COUSIN, SECOND COUSIN, KISSING COUSIN —see picture at FAMILY **2** *rare* someone who is similar to you, or something that is similar to something else

**cou·ture** /kuːˈtjʊə‖-ˈtʊr/ *n* [U] *French* expensive and fashionable clothes

**cove** /kəʊv‖koʊv/ *n* [C] **1** part of the coast where the land bends around, partly enclosing the sea so the shore is protected from the wind, rain etc **2** *BrE old-fashioned* a man: *He's an odd cove.*

**cov·en** /ˈkʌvən/ *n* [C] a meeting of witches (WITCH (1))

**cov·e·nant** /ˈkʌvənənt/ *n* a formal agreement between two or more people —**covenant** *v* [T]

**Cov·en·try** /ˈkʌvəntri, ˈkɒv-‖ˈkʌv-, ˈkɑːv-/ *n* **send sb to Coventry** *BrE informal* to refuse to speak to someone in order to punish them or show disapproval

S1 W1 **cov·er**[1] /ˈkʌvə‖-ər/ *v* [T]

**1** ▶ **PUT STH OVER STH** ◀ also **cover up** to put something over the top of something in order to hide or protect it: *Cover the pan when the sauce boils and let it simmer.* | **cover sth with sth** *They covered the tables with clean white cloths.*

**2** ▶ **BE OVER STH** ◀ to be on top of something or spread over something: *Colourful pictures covered the walls.* | **be covered with sth** *If it carries on snowing the ground will be covered by morning.* | **be covered in sth** *The children were covered in paint.*

**3** ▶ **AN AREA** ◀ to spread over an area: *The city covers 25 square miles.*

**4** ▶ **DISTANCE** ◀ to travel a particular distance: *They were hoping to cover 40 miles yesterday.* | **cover a lot of ground** (=travel a long way) *We covered a lot of ground during those two weeks in Spain.*

**5** ▶ **DEAL WITH/INCLUDE** ◀ to include or deal with something: *The course covers all aspects of business and law.* | *Most of the key points are covered in this book.* | *This scheme would cover only a few of the three million people without jobs.* | *development officers whose work would cover a local area*

**6** ▶ **RULES** ◀ to deal with a particular situation: *The rules, while they cover a wide range of issues, do not cover every possible situation.*

**7** ▶ **NEWS** ◀ to report the details of an event for a newspaper, television, or radio: *Simonson was sent to Switzerland to cover the Winter Olympics.*

**8** ▶ **PAY FOR STH** ◀ money that covers a cost is enough to pay for it: *He should get enough money from the council to cover his rent.* | **cover the cost of sth** *You will have to pay an extra amount to cover the cost of insurance.*

**9** ▶ **INSURANCE** ◀ if an insurance agreement covers someone or something, it states that money will be given to the person if they are injured, if something is damaged etc: *The policy will cover any medical expenses that you incur while you are abroad.* | **cover sb against sth** *We're not covered against theft.*

**10** ▶ **GUNS** ◀ **a)** to protect someone by being ready to shoot anyone who attacks them: *We'll cover you while you run for it.* **b)** to aim a gun at a person, or the door of a building with people in it, so that they cannot escape: *Don't move – we've got you covered.* | *The police had the back entrance covered.*

**11** ▶ **SPORT** ◀ to stay close to a member of the opposing team or a part of the field in a game, in order to prevent your opponents from gaining points: *Who's covering second base?*

**12 cover for sb a)** to do the work that someone else usually does because they are ill or not present: *Who's going to cover for you when you're on holiday?* **b)** to prevent someone from getting into trouble by lying, especially about where they are or what they are doing: *Cover for me, will you? Just say I'm at the dentist's.*

**13 cover (all) the bases** *AmE* to be prepared to deal with any situation, and be sure that nothing bad will happen and no one can criticize you: *Just be sure to cover all your bases if you join in their business venture.*

**14 cover your back** *BrE spoken* to be careful to do nothing that would make people criticize you

**cover up** *phr v* **1** [T **cover** sth ↔ **up**] to put something over the top of something in order to hide it or protect it: *She put a cloth over the floor to cover up the mess.* **2** [T **cover** sth ↔ **up**] to prevent mistakes or unpleasant facts from being known about: *The whole thing was very well covered up and never reached the newspapers.* —see also COVER-UP **3 cover up for sb** to protect someone by hiding unpleasant facts about them: *They covered up for Kirk by refusing to answer any of the questions.* **4** [I] to put clothes on in order to keep warm or to prevent people from seeing your body: *Cover up well against the cold.* **5 cover yourself up** to put clothes, sheets etc over yourself so that your body is covered: *Some religions require that women cover themselves up completely.*

S1 W2 **cover**[2] *n*

**1** ▶ **STH THAT PROTECTS STH** ◀ [C] something that is put over or onto something to protect it or keep dirt etc out: *a cushion cover* | *Put a cover over the bowl.*

**2** ▶ **BOOKS** ◀ [C] the outer front or back page of a magazine, book etc: *a picture of President Clinton on the cover of Newsweek* | **read sth from cover to cover** (=read everything in a book, magazine etc)

**3** ▶ **SHELTER/PROTECTION** ◀ [U] shelter or protection from bad weather or attack: *The soldiers ran for cover when the shooting began.* | **take cover** (=find shelter or protection) *Come on, we can take cover in that barn over there!* | **break cover** (=come out from the place where you have been sheltered or protected)

**4 covers** [plural] the sheets, blankets etc on a bed: *The covers had slipped off the bed during the night.*

**5** ▶ **INSURANCE** ◀ [U] insurance against injury, damage etc: *The policy gives you temporary medical cover for your holiday.* | [+ **against**] *cover against fire and theft*

**6 a cover for** a business that seems normal and honest, but is really used to hide illegal activities: *He used the shop as a cover for various illegal activities.*

**7 under cover** pretending to be someone else in order to do something without being noticed: *She was working under cover to get information on the drug dealers.*

**8 under cover of darkness** hidden by darkness: *They escaped under cover of darkness.*

**9 under plain cover/under separate cover** if a letter etc is sent under plain cover or under separate cover, it is sent in a plain envelope or a separate envelope: *The bill will be sent to you later under separate cover.*

**cov·er·age** /ˈkʌvərɪdʒ/ *n* [U] **1** the way in which a subject or event is reported on television or radio, or in newspapers: *ABC gave the story extensive coverage in the evening news.* **2** the amount of protection given to you by an insurance agreement: *Make sure your policy will give you adequate coverage in case of a break-in.* **3** the range of subjects and facts included in a course, class etc: *The syllabus includes coverage of all the outdoor skills.*

**cov·er·alls** /ˈkʌvərɔːlz‖-ɒːlz/ *n* [plural] *AmE* a piece of clothing that you wear over all your clothes to protect them; overalls (OVERALL[3] (3)) *BrE*

**cover charge** /ˈ·· ·/ *n* [C] money that you have to pay in a restaurant in addition to the cost of the food and drinks

**covered wag·on** /ˌ·· ˈ··/ *n* [C] a large vehicle with a

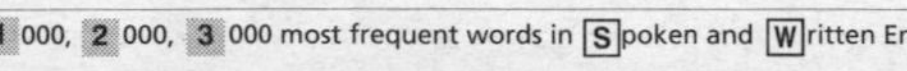

curved cloth top that is pulled by horses, used in former times in North America

**cover girl** /ˈ·· ·/ *n* [C] a young attractive woman whose photograph is on the front cover of a magazine

**cov·er·ing** /ˈkʌvərɪŋ/ *n* [singular] something that covers or hides something: *a light covering of snow*

**covering let·ter** /ˌ··· ˈ··/ *n* [C] *BrE* a letter that you send with documents or a package explaining what it is or giving additional information; COVER LETTER *AmE*

**cov·er·let** /ˈkʌvəlɪ̠t‖-vər-/ *n* [C] a cloth cover for a bed; BEDSPREAD

**cover let·ter** /ˈ·· ˌ··/ *n* [C] *AmE* a covering letter

**cover note** /ˈ··· ·/ *n* [C] *BrE* a document that proves that you have car insurance

**cover sto·ry** /ˈ·· ˌ··/ *n* [C] the story that goes with a picture on the cover of a magazine

**cov·ert¹** /ˈkʌvət,-ˈkəʊvɜːt‖ˈkoʊvərt/ *adj* secret or hidden: *illegal, covert actions of enemy agents* —opposite OVERT —**covertly** *adv*

**covert²** *n* [C] a group of small bushes growing close together in which animals can hide

**cover-up** /ˈ·· ·/ *n* [C] an attempt to prevent the public from discovering the truth about something —see also **cover up** (COVER¹)

**cov·et** /ˈkʌvɪ̠t/ *v* [T] *formal* to have a very strong desire to have something that someone else has: *He possessed rare and much coveted works of art.*

**cov·et·ous** /ˈkʌvɪ̠təs/ *adj* having a very strong desire to have something that someone else has, especially wealth: *They began to cast covetous eyes on their neighbours' fields.* —**covetously** *adv* —**covetousness** *n* [U]

S 2 **cow¹** /kaʊ/ *n* [C] **1** a large female animal that is kept on farms and produces milk —compare BULL¹ (1) **2** a male or female animal of this type **3** the female of some large land and sea animals, such as the ELEPHANT or the WHALE **4** *BrE spoken* an impolite way of saying that a woman is stupid or very unpleasant: *Linda's a silly cow – just ignore her!* **5 have a cow** *AmE informal* to be very angry or surprised about something **6 till the cows come home** *informal* for a very long time, or for ever

**cow²** *v* [T] to make someone behave in the way you want them to by using violence or threats: *I was determined not to be cowed by their threats.*

**cow·ard** /ˈkaʊəd‖-ərd/ *n* [C] someone who is not at all brave: *He called me a coward because I would not fight.*

**cow·ard·ice** /ˈkaʊədɪ̠s‖-ər-/ also **cow·ard·li·ness** /ˈkaʊədlinɪ̠s‖-ərd-/ *n* [U] lack of courage: *cowardice in the face of danger*

**cow·ard·ly** /ˈkaʊədli‖-ər-/ *adj* behaving in a way that shows that you are not brave: *That was a very cowardly thing to do.* | *a cowardly attack on a defenceless man*

**cow·bell** /ˈkaʊbel/ *n* [C] a bell that is put around a cow's neck so that it can be found easily

**cow·boy** /ˈkaʊbɔɪ/ *n* [C] **1** a man who rides a horse and is employed to look after cattle in North America **2** *BrE informal* someone who is dishonest in business, or who produces very bad quality work: *a firm of cowboy builders* **3 cowboys and Indians** a game played by children who pretend to be cowboys and Native Americans, fighting each other (NATIVE AMERICAN)

**cowboy hat** /ˈ·· ˌ·/ *n* [C] a hat with a wide circular edge and a soft round top; STETSON

**cow·catch·er** /ˈkaʊˌkætʃə‖-ər/ *n* [C] a piece of metal on the front of a train used to push things off the track

**cow chip** /ˈ· ·/ *n* [C] *AmE* a round flat mass of dry solid waste from a cow

**cow·er** /ˈkaʊə‖-ər/ *v* [I] to bend low and move back, especially because you are frightened: *They were cowering in the cellars, trapped by the shelling.* | *He cowered against the wall.*

**cow·girl** /ˈkaʊgɜːl‖-gɜːrl/ *n* [C] a woman who rides a horse and is employed to look after cattle in North America

**cow·hand** /ˈkaʊhænd/ *n* [C] someone who is employed to look after cattle

**cow·hide** /ˈkaʊhaɪd/ *n* [C,U] the skin of a cow or the leather that is made from this

**cowl** /kaʊl/ *n* [C] **1** a very large hood that covers your head and shoulders, especially worn by MONKS **2** a cover for a chimney that protects it from wind and rain; HOOD (4)

**cow·lick** /ˈkaʊˌlɪk/ *n* [C] hair that sticks up on top of your head

**cow·ling** /ˈkaʊlɪŋ/ *n* [C] a metal cover for an aircraft engine —see picture at AIRCRAFT

**cowl neck** /ˌ· ˈ·/ *n* [C] the neck on a piece of clothing that falls in folds at the front

**co-work·er** /ˌkəʊ ˈwɜːkə‖ˈkoʊ ˌwɜːrkər/ *n* [C] someone who works with you and has a similar position

**cow·pat** /ˈkaʊpæt/ *n* [C] *BrE* a round flat mass of solid waste from a cow

**cow pie** /ˌ· ˈ·/ *n* [C] *AmE* a COW CHIP

**cow·poke** /ˈkaʊpəʊk‖-poʊk/ *n* [C] *AmE old-fashioned* a COWBOY (1)

**cow·pox** /ˈkaʊpɒks‖-pɑːks/ *n* [U] a disease that cows suffer from and that can be given to humans to protect them from SMALLPOX

**cow·rie** /ˈkaʊri/ *n* [C] a shiny brightly-coloured tropical shell, used in former times as money in parts of Africa and Asia

**cow·shed** /ˈkaʊʃed/ *n* [C] a building where cows live in the winter, or where their milk is taken from them

**cow·slip** /ˈkaʊˌslɪp/ *n* [U] a small European wild plant with sweet smelling yellow flowers

**cox** /kɒks‖kɑːks/ *n* [C] someone who controls the direction of a rowing boat, especially in races —**cox** *v* [T]

**cox·comb** /ˈkɒkskəʊm‖ˈkɑːkskoʊm/ *n* [C] *old use* a stupid man who spends too much time and money on his clothes and appearance

**cox·swain** /ˈkɒksən, -sweɪn‖ˈkɑːk-/ *n* [C] a cox

**coy** /kɔɪ/ *adj* **1** pretending to be shy in order to attract interest, or to avoid dealing with something difficult: *She gave him a coy smile.* **2** unwilling to give information about something: [+ **about**] *Tania was always coy about her age.* —**coyly** *adv* —**coyness** *n* [U]

**coy·ote** /ˈkɔɪ-əʊt, kɔɪˈəʊti‖ˈkaɪ-oʊt, kaɪˈoʊti/ *n* [C] a small wild dog that lives in North West America and Mexico

**coy·pu** /ˈkɔɪpuː/ *n* [C] an animal like a BEAVER, kept on farms for its fur; NUTRIA

**coz** /kʌz/ *n old use* a way of addressing a cousin

**coz·en** /ˈkʌzən/ *v* [T] *old use* to trick or deceive someone

**co·zy** /ˈkəʊzi‖ˈkoʊzi/ *adj* the American spelling of COSY —**cozily** *adv* —**coziness** *n* [U]

**CPA** /ˌsiː piː ˈeɪ/ *n AmE* [C] Certified Public Accountant; an ACCOUNTANT who has passed all their examinations; CHARTERED ACCOUNTANT *BrE*

**CPU** /ˌsiː piː ˈjuː/ *n* the part of a computer that controls and organizes all its activities; CENTRAL PROCESSING UNIT

**crab¹** /kræb/ *n* **1** [C] a sea animal whose body is covered with a shell and that has five legs on each side and two large CLAWS on the front legs **2** [U] the flesh of this animal that you can cook and eat as food **3 crabs** [plural] a medical condition in which a kind of LOUSE is in the hair around the sexual organs **4** [singular] *AmE informal* someone who easily becomes annoyed about unimportant things: *He's a real crab – always finding fault with everything.*

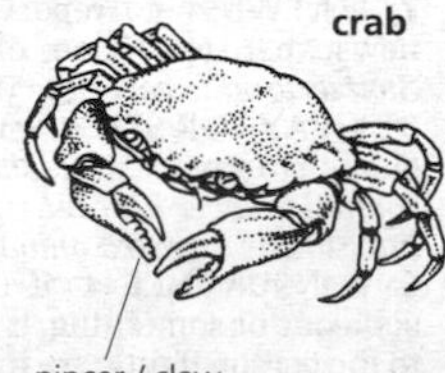


**crab²** *v* **crabbed, crabbing** [I] *informal* to complain about something in an annoyed way; GRUMBLE¹ (1)

**crab ap·ple** /ˈ· ˌ··/ *n* [C] a small apple that tastes sour, or the tree that it grows on

**crab·bed** /ˈkræbɪ̆d/ *adj* **1** writing which is crabbed is difficult to read because the letters are small and untidy **2** *old-fashioned* someone who is crabbed always behaves as if they are annoyed; BAD-TEMPERED

**crab·by** /ˈkræbi/ *adj informal* someone who is crabby easily becomes annoyed about unimportant things; BAD-TEMPERED: *a rather crabby old man | I was feeling crabby.*

**crab·grass** /ˈkræbgrɑːs‖-græs/ *n* [U] a kind of rough grass

**crab·wise** /ˈkræbwaɪz/ also **crabways** /-weɪz/ *adv* sideways, especially in a way that seems difficult: *I moved crabwise along the edge of the cliff.*

S3 **crack**¹ /kræk/ *v*

**1 ▶ BREAK ◀** [I,T] to break or make something break so that it gets one or more lines on its surface: *Don't put that delicate china in the dishwasher – it may crack. | She fell off her bike and cracked a bone in her leg.*

**2 ▶ LOUD SOUND ◀** [I,T] to make a sudden quick sound like the sound of something breaking, or to make something do this: *The branch cracked loudly and broke off. | He had a habit of cracking his knuckles.*

**3 ▶ HIT STH ◀** [I always + adv/prep, T always + adv/prep] to hit something hard but not deliberately, especially part of your body: [+ **against/on**] *The rock cracked against my shoulder.* | **crack sth against/on** *He fell, cracking his head on the wall.*

**4 ▶ HIT SB ◀** [T] to hit someone hard and deliberately on part of their body: **crack sb over/in/on** *He cracked the burglar over the head with a vase.*

**5 ▶ LOSE CONTROL ◀** also **crack up** [I] to be unable to continue doing something or working well because of great pressure: *We're hoping the prisoner will crack under interrogation. | The whole political system is beginning to crack up.*

**6 ▶ MENTALLY ILL ◀** also **crack up** [I] to become mentally ill because of too much pressure: *Many of the soldiers cracked up on returning from the war.*

**7 ▶ VOICE ◀** [I] if your voice cracks, it changes from one level to another suddenly because of strong emotions: *Her voice cracked as she tried to explain what had happened.*

**8 ▶ NERVE ◀** [I] if your nerve cracks, you no longer feel confident that you can do something difficult: *At the last moment his nerve cracked.*

**9 ▶ EGG/NUT ◀** [T] to break the outside part of something, such as an egg or a nut, in order to get what is inside it: *The foxes crack the eggs, and suck out the yolk.*

**10 ▶ STEAL ◀** [T] to open a SAFE² illegally, in order to steal what is inside

**11 ▶ SOLVE ◀** [T] to find the answer to a problem or find how to use a CODE¹ (4): *His skill at cracking codes proved invaluable during the war. | This is a national problem, we're not going to crack it here this afternoon.*

**12 ▶ STOP CRIME/ENEMY ◀** [T] to find a way of destroying an enemy or stopping something they are doing: *Police are hoping to crack the drug-smuggling ring.*

**13 crack it** *BrE* to succeed in some way

**14 crack a deal** *AmE informal* to succeed in making a business deal, especially when this has been difficult: *We finally managed to crack that deal with the Japanese.*

**15 crack a joke** *informal* to tell a joke: *He kept cracking jokes about my appearance.*

**16 crack a smile** *AmeE informal* to smile when you have been serious, sad, or angry: *She finally cracked a smile, although she had tears in her eyes.*

**17 crack open a bottle** *informal* to open a bottle of alcohol for drinking: *Let's crack open a bottle to celebrate!*

**18 not all/everything it's cracked up to be** *informal* not as good as people say it is: *The film wasn't all it's cracked up to be – I was quite bored in parts.*

**19 get cracking** *informal* to start doing something or going somewhere as quickly as possible: *The train goes at ten so let's get cracking.*

**20 crack the whip** *informal* to make people you have control over work very hard

**crack down** *phr v* [I] to become more strict in dealing with a problem and punishing the people involved: [+ **on**] *The police are cracking down on illegal parking.* —see also CRACKDOWN

**crack on** *phr v* [I] *BrE informal* to continue working hard at something in order to try to finish it: [+ **with**] *I'm hoping to crack on with that translation this weekend.*

**crack up** *phr v informal* **1** [I,T] to laugh a lot at something, or to make someone laugh a lot: *Everyone in the class just cracked up.* | **crack sb up** *She's so funny. She cracks me up.* **2** [I] to become unable to think or behave sensibly because you have too many problems, too much work etc: *I must be cracking up – I've lost those papers again!* —see also CRACK-UP

**crack**² *n* [C]

**1 ▶ THIN SPACE ◀** a very narrow space between two things or two parts of something: [+ **in**] *A thin ray of light shone through a crack in the curtains.* | [+ **between**] *The children carefully avoided the cracks between the paving stones.* | **open sth a crack** (=open something very slightly) *She opened the door a crack and peeped out.*

**2 ▶ BREAK ◀** a thin line on the surface of something when it is broken but has not actually come apart: [+ **in**] *There were several cracks in the glass.*

**3 ▶ PROBLEM ◀** a fault in an idea, system, or organization: [+ **in**] *Cracks were appearing in the government's economic policy.*

**4 ▶ SOUND ◀** a sudden loud very sharp sound like the sound of a stick being broken: *There was a loud crack as the wood finally broke in two.* —see picture on page 1261

**5 ▶ JOKE/REMARK ◀** a clever joke or rude remark: [+ **about**] *I've had enough of your cracks about my weight.* | **make a crack** *I wish I hadn't made that crack about lawyers.*

**6 ▶ CHANCE TO DO STH ◀** *informal* an opportunity or attempt to achieve something, especially for the first time: [+ **at**] *I'd like a crack at climbing that mountain.* | **have/take a crack at sth** *Why don't you have a crack at that competition – you might win!* | **a (fair) crack of the whip** *BrE* (=a chance to do something or be in control) *They'll do well if we give them a fair crack of the whip.*

**7 a crack on the head** what you feel when you are hit on the head, usually not deliberately: *I got a nasty crack on the head as I went through the low doorway.*

**8 a crack in sb's voice** a sudden change in the level of someone's voice, especially because they are very upset: *He noticed the crack in her voice as she tried to continue.*

**9 crack of dawn** very early in the morning: *We'll have to get up at the crack of dawn tomorrow.*

**10 ▶ DRUG ◀** [U] a very pure form of the drug COCAINE that some people take illegally for pleasure

**11 good crack** *IrE, BrE spoken* friendly, enjoyable talk in a group: *We go there for the crack.*

**12 what's the crack?** *BrE spoken* used to ask someone what is happening, or what has been happening recently —see also **paper over the cracks** (PAPER³ (2))

**crack**³ *adj* [only before noun] **1** having a very high level of quality or skill, or being very highly trained: *A crack regiment was sent in to deal with the situation.* **2 crack shot** someone who always hits what they shoot at

**crack·down** /ˈkrækdaʊn/ *n* [C usually singular] severe action that is taken in order to deal with a problem: [+ **on**] *They're having a crackdown on drunk driving.* —see also **crack down** (CRACK¹)

**cracked** /krækt/ *adj* **1** something that is cracked has been damaged and has one or more lines on its surface: *cracked cups and saucers | Her skin was cracked and dry.* —see picture on page 1258 **2** [not before noun] *informal* someone who is cracked is slightly crazy **3** someone's voice that is cracked sounds rough and uncontrolled because they are upset

**crack·er** /ˈkrækə‖-ər/ *n* [C] **1** a small thin BISCUIT often eaten with cheese **2** also **Christmas cracker** a brightly coloured paper tube that makes a small exploding sound when you pull it apart, and that usually contains a small gift and a joke, used at Christmas in

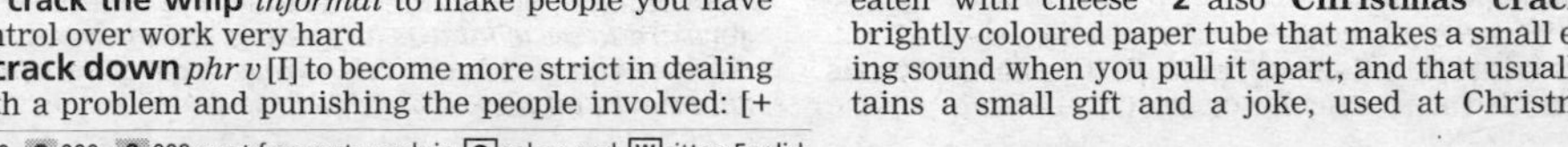

Britain **3** a FIRECRACKER **4** *BrE spoken* something that is very good or very funny: *Did you hear his joke? It was a real cracker!* **5** *BrE old-fashioned* a very attractive woman

**crack·ers** /ˈkrækəz‖-ərz/ *adj* [not before noun] *BrE informal* crazy: *You lent him all that money? You must be crackers!*

**crack·ing** /ˈkrækɪŋ/ *adj* [only before noun] **1** very fast: *We set off at a cracking pace.* **2** *BrE spoken* very good: *It's going to be a cracking good race.*

**crack·le** /ˈkrækəl/ *v* [I] to make a repeated short sharp sound like something burning in a fire: *The dry sticks crackled as they caught fire.* | *The radio crackled so much we could hardly hear what was said.* —**crackle** *n* [C] —**crackly** *adj* —see picture on page 1261

**crack·ling** /ˈkræklɪŋ/ *n* **1** [singular] the sound made by something when it crackles: *There was a silence after that, except for the crackling of the fire.* **2** *BrE* **cracklings** *AmE* [U] the hard skin of a pig when it has been cooked and is easily broken

**crack·pot** /ˈkrækpɒt‖-pɑːt/ *n* [C] *humorous* someone who is slightly crazy —**crackpot** *adj*

**crack-up** /ˈ· ·/ *n* [C] *AmE informal* **1** a NERVOUS BREAKDOWN **2** a car accident —see also **crack up** (CRACK¹)

**-cracy** /krəsi/ *suffix* [in nouns] another form of the suffix -OCRACY: *bureaucracy* (=government by officials who are not elected)

**cra·dle¹** /ˈkreɪdl/ *n* [C]

**1** ▶ **BED** ◀ a small bed for a baby, especially one that you can move gently from side to side: *She rocked the cradle to quieten the child.* —see picture at BED¹

**2 the cradle of** the place where something important began: *Athens is often regarded as the cradle of democracy.*

**3 from/in the cradle** from or in the earliest years of your life: *Sara had learned that language from the cradle.*

**4 from the cradle to the grave** all through your life: *a promise of security from the cradle to the grave*

**5** *BrE* a structure that people working on the sides of high buildings stand in which can be moved up and down: *a window-cleaner's cradle*

**6** the part of a telephone where the part that you hold in your hand is put when it is not being used —see also CAT'S CRADLE, **rob the cradle** (ROB (5))

**cradle²** *v* [T] to hold something gently in your hands or arms, as if to protect it: *John cradled the baby in his arms.* | *The wine-glass looked tiny cradled in his big hands.*

**cradle-snatch·er** BrE **cradle-robber** *AmE* /ˈ·· ,··/ *n* [C] someone who has a romantic relationship with someone much younger than they are —**cradle-snatch** *v* [I]

S3 **-craft** /krɑːft‖kræft/ *suffix* [in nouns] **1** a vehicle of a particular kind: *a spacecraft* | *a hovercraft* | *several aircraft* **2** skill of a particular kind: *statecraft* (=skill in government) | *stagecraft* (=skill in acting or directing plays)

**craft¹** /krɑːft‖kræft/ *n* **1** *plural* **craft** [C] **a)** a small boat: *I steered the craft carefully round the rocks.* **b)** an aircraft or SPACECRAFT **2** *plural* **crafts** [C] an activity, especially a traditional one that needs a lot of skill, in which you make something with your hands: *a craft such as needlework* **3** [C] a profession, especially one needing a special skill: *the anthropologist takes years to learn his craft* **4** [U] skill in deceiving people: *Craft and cunning were necessary for the scheme to work.* —see also LANDING CRAFT

**craft²** *v* [T usually passive] to make something using a special skill, especially with your hands: *Each doll will be crafted individually by specialists.* | **hand-crafted** (=made by hand, not by machine) *a hand-crafted silver cigarette case*

**craft knife** /ˈ· ·/ *n BrE* [C] a very sharp knife used for cutting paper, thin wood etc, when the cutting needs to be exact

**crafts·man** /ˈkrɑːftsmən‖ˈkræfts-/ *n* [C] someone who is very skilled at a particular CRAFT¹ (2)

**crafts·man·ship** /ˈkrɑːftsmənʃɪp‖ˈkræfts-/ *n* [U] **1** the special skill that someone uses to make something beautiful with their hands: *These works of art combine precious materials with exquisite craftsmanship.* **2** very detailed work that has been done using a lot of skill, so that the result is beautiful: *the fine craftsmanship of the carved Georgian table*

**crafts·wom·an** /ˈkrɑːftsˌwʊmən‖ˈkræfts-/ *n* [C] a woman who is very skilled at a particular CRAFT¹ (2)

**craft·y** /ˈkrɑːfti‖ˈkræf-/ *adj* good at getting what you want by clever planning and secretly deceiving people; CUNNING¹ (1, 2): *You crafty devil, you!* —**craftily** *adv* —**craftiness** *n* [U] S3

**crag** /kræg/ *n* [C] a high and very steep rough rock or mass of rocks

**crag·gy** /ˈkrægi/ *adj* **1** a mountain that is craggy is very steep and covered in rough rocks **2** having a face with many deep lines on it: *craggy good looks*

**cram** /kræm/ *v* **crammed, cramming** **1** [T always + adv/prep] to force something into a small space: **cram sth into/onto/down etc** *Jessica crammed her clothes into the bag.* **2 cram into sth** if people cram into a place, they fill it: *Thousands of people crammed into the stadium to see the final game.* **3 a)** [I] to prepare yourself for an examination by learning a lot of information very quickly; SWOT² *BrE*: *I've been cramming hard all week.* | [+ **for**] *He'd crammed for the test until four in the morning.* **b)** [T] *BrE* to help someone prepare for an examination by cramming: *The college is cramming the students hard for the summer exams.*

**crammed** /kræmd/ *adj* **crammed with/crammed full of** completely full of things or people: *monthly reports crammed full of information*

**cram·mer** /ˈkræmə‖-ər/ *n* [C] *BrE* a special school that prepares people quickly for examinations

**cramp¹** /kræmp/ *n* **1** [C,U] a severe pain that you get in part of your body when a muscle becomes too tight, making it difficult for you to move that part of your body: *I woke up in the middle of the night with cramp in my leg.* | **have/get cramp** *BrE* **have/get a cramp** *AmE* —*The swimmer got a cramp and had to quit the race.* —see also WRITER'S CRAMP **2 cramps** [plural] *especially AmE* severe pains in the stomach, especially the ones that women get during MENSTRUATION

**cramp²** *v* [T] **1** to prevent the development of someone's ability to do something: *Her education was cramped by lack of money.* **2 cramp sb's style** to prevent someone from doing something they want to do, especially by going with them when they do not want you: *He left Helen in the ski lodge. He didn't want anyone cramping his style on the slopes.*

**cramped** /kræmpt/ *adj* **1** a cramped room, building etc does not have enough space for the people in it: *I couldn't sleep on the plane, it was too cramped.* | *cramped living conditions* | *cramped offices* **2** also **cramped up** unable to move properly and uncomfortable because there is not enough space: *We all felt stiff from having been cramped up in the back of the car for so long.* **3** writing that is cramped is very small and difficult to read

**cram·pon** /ˈkræmpɒn‖-pɑːn/ *n* [C usually plural] a piece of metal with sharp points on the bottom that you fasten onto your boots to help in mountain climbing in the snow

**cran·ber·ry** /ˈkrænbəri‖-beri/ *n* [C] a small red sour fruit: *cranberry sauce* —see picture on page 413

**crane¹** /kreɪn/ *n* [C] **1** a large tall machine used by builders for lifting heavy things **2** a tall water bird with very long legs

**crane²** *v* [I always + adv/prep, T] to look around or over something by stretching or leaning: *The children craned forward to see what was happening.* | **crane your neck** *Everyone on the bus craned their necks out of the windows and stared at them.*

**crane fly** /ˈ· ·/ *n* [C] a flying insect with long legs; DADDY LONGLEGS (1) *BrE*

**cra·ni·um** /ˈkreɪniəm/ *n* [C] *technical* the part of your head that is made of bone and covers your brain

**crank**[1] /kræŋk/ *n* [C] **1** *informal* someone who has unusual ideas and behaves strangely: *I was treated like a troublemaker and a crank.* | **crank caller/letters** *We get quite a few crank phone calls.* **2** *AmE informal* someone who easily gets angry or annoyed with people **3** a piece of equipment with a handle that you can turn in order to move something

**crank**[2] also **crank up** *v* [T] **1** to make something move by turning a crank: *crank an engine* **2** *informal* to make music louder: *Crank up the volume!*

**crank** sth ↔ **out** *phr v* [T] *informal especially AmE* to produce a lot of something very quickly: *He cranks out detective novels at the rate of three a year.*

**crank·shaft** /ˈkræŋkʃɑːft‖-ʃæft/ *n* [C] a long piece of metal in a vehicle that is connected to the engine and helps to turn the wheels

**crank·y** /ˈkræŋki/ *adj* **1** bad-tempered: *The baby's a little cranky this morning.* **2** *BrE* having very strange ideas, or behaving strangely; ECCENTRIC[1] (1): *She's just a cranky old woman.* —**crankiness** *n* [U]

**cran·ny** /ˈkræni/ *n* [C] a small narrow hole in a wall or rock: *The toad hid itself in a cranny in the wall.* —see also **nook and cranny** (NOOK (3)) —**crannied** *adj*

**crap**[1] /kræp/ *n slang* **1** [U] something someone says that you think is completely wrong or untrue: *Jane doesn't really think we believe all that crap, does she?* | **be full of crap** (=often say things that are untrue or completely wrong) *We all knew Mark was full of crap, but we still had to listen to him.* | **cut the crap** (=used to tell someone to stop saying things that are completely wrong or untrue) **2 be a load of crap** *also* **be a bunch of crap** *AmE* to be very bad, or completely untrue: *That new comedy last night was a load of crap, I thought.* **3** [U] things that are useless or unimportant: *What is all this crap doing on my desk?* **4** [singular] solid waste that is passed from your bowels: **have/take a crap** (=to pass solid waste from the BOWELS) **5 not take crap from someone** to refuse to allow someone to treat you badly or to say something unfair to you: *I don't have to take that crap from her – I'm leaving!* **6 I don't need this (kind of) crap** used when you are angry at the way someone is talking or behaving to you **7 craps** [plural] *AmE* a game played for money in the US, using two DICE[1] (1): **shoot craps** (=play this game)

**crap**[2] *adj slang* of very bad quality: *Everyone knows those cars are crap!*

**crap**[3] *v* **crapped, crapping** [I] *spoken taboo* to pass waste matter from the bowels

**crape** /kreɪp/ *n* [U] **1** CREPE (1) **2** black material that people wore in former times as a sign of their sadness when someone died

**crap·per** /ˈkræpə‖-ər/ *n* **the crapper** *BrE slang* a rude word meaning the toilet

**crap·py** /ˈkræpi/ *adj spoken slang* not very good: *We arrived late and ended up staying in a crappy hotel.*

**crash**[1] /kræʃ/ *v*
**1 ▶ CAR/PLANE ETC ◀** [I,T] to have an accident in a car, plane etc by violently hitting another vehicle or something such as a wall or tree: *The DC10 crashed shortly after take-off.* | **[+ into/onto etc]** *The car crashed straight into a tree.* | **crash a car/bus/plane etc** *Rick crashed his bike before he'd finished paying for it.*
**2 ▶ HIT STH/SB HARD ◀** [I always + adv/prep, T always +adv/prep] to hit something or someone extremely hard while you are moving, causing a lot of damage, or making a lot of noise: **[+ into/through etc]** *The ladder came crashing through the window.* | **crash sth down** *Rod's face went bright red and he crashed his fist down on the table.* | **go crashing into** *He lost his balance on the ice and went crashing into the crowd.* | **come crashing down** *A branch came crashing down onto the greenhouse.*
**3 ▶ MAKE A LOUD NOISE ◀** [I] to make a sudden, loud noise: *The cymbals crashed, and the symphony came to an end.* —see picture on page 1261
**4 ▶ SLEEP ◀** also **crash out** [I] *spoken* **a)** to go to bed, or go to sleep very quickly, especially because you are very tired: *I was so tired last night, I got home and just crashed out on the sofa.* **b)** to stay at someone's house for the night, especially when you have not planned to: *Can I crash at your place on Saturday night?*
**5 ▶ COMPUTER ◀** [I,T] if a computer crashes or you crash the computer, it suddenly stops working: *The system crashed at nine this morning, so we haven't been able to do anything.*

**6 ▶ FINANCIAL ◀** [I] if a STOCK MARKET crashes, the stocks (STOCK[1] (3a)) suddenly lose a lot of value
**7 ▶ PARTY ◀** *informal* [T] to go to a party that you have not been invited to: *She crashes parties all the time even though she always gets thrown out.*
**8 crashing bore** *BrE old-fashioned* someone who is very boring

**crash**[2] *n* [C] **1** a violent accident involving one or more vehicles: **plane/car etc crash** *41 people were killed in a plane crash in the Himalayas last week.* **2** a sudden loud noise made by something falling, breaking etc: **[+ of]** *Jessica heard the crash of breaking glass behind her.* | **with a crash** *There was a loud crack and the branch came down with a crash.* **3** a sudden, unexpected failing of a computer or computer system **4** an occasion on which the stocks (STOCK[1] (3a)) in a STOCK MARKET suddenly lose a lot of value: *Nobody was prepared for the crash on Black Monday in 1987.* S3

**crash bar·ri·er** /ˈ· ˌ···/ *n* [C] *BrE* a strong fence or wall built to keep cars apart or to keep them away from people, in order to prevent an accident

**crash course** /ˈ· ·/ *n* [C] a course in which you learn the most important things about a particular subject in a very short period of time: **[+ in]** *a crash course in Spanish*

**crash di·et** /ˈ· ˌ··/ *n* [C] an attempt that someone makes to lose a lot of weight in a very short period of time

**crash-dive** /ˈ· ·/ *v* [I] if a SUBMARINE[1] crash-dives, it sinks quickly to a great depth

**crash hel·met** /ˈ· ˌ··/ *n* [C] a very strong hat that covers your whole head, worn by racing car drivers, motorcyclists etc —see picture at HELMET

**crash-land** /ˈ· ·/ *v* [I,T] to crash a plane in a controlled way because it is damaged and cannot be flown any more

**crass** /kræs/ *adj* behaving in a way that shows you do not understand other people's feelings, or care about them: *crass stupidity* | *a crass commercial adventure* —**crassly** *adv*

**-crat** /kræt/ *suffix* [in nouns] another form of the suffix -OCRAT

**crate**[1] /kreɪt/ also **crate up** *v* [T] to pack things into a crate

**crate**[2] *n* [C] **1** a box made of wood or plastic that is used for carrying fruit, bottles etc: *They lifted the crates onto the wagon.* —see picture at CONTAINER **2** *old-fashioned* a very old car or plane that does not work very well

**cra·ter** /ˈkreɪtə‖-ər/ *n* [C] **1** the round open part of a VOLCANO **2** a round hole in the ground, especially made by an explosion or by something that has fallen from the sky: *the craters on the moon*

**cra·vat** /krəˈvæt/ *n* [C] a wide piece of loosely folded material that men wear around their necks —compare TIE[1] (1)

**crave** /kreɪv/ *v* [T] **1** to have an extremely strong desire for something, especially a drug: *She's an insecure child who craves attention.* **2** *formal* to ask seriously for something: *May I crave your pardon?*

**cra·ven** /ˈkreɪvən/ *adj formal* completely lacking courage; COWARDLY: *You craven coward.* —**cravenly** *adv* —**cravenness** *n* [U]

**crav·ing** /ˈkreɪvɪŋ/ *n* [C] an extremely strong desire for something: [+ **for**] *a craving for some chocolate*

**craw** /krɔː‖krɒː/ *n* [C] *AmE* —see **stick in your craw** (STICK[1] (11))

**craw·dad** /ˈkrɔːdæd‖ˈkrɒː-/ *n* [C] *AmE informal* a small animal like a LOBSTER that lives in rivers and streams; CRAYFISH

**crawl[1]** /krɔːl‖krɒːl/ *v* [I]

**1 ▶ MOVE ON HANDS AND KNEES ◀** to move along on your hands and knees with your body close to the ground: [+ **along/across etc**] *She suddenly got down and crawled along behind the wall so that Carl wouldn't see her.* | *Is your baby crawling yet?* —see picture at KNEEL

**2 ▶ INSECT ◀** if an insect crawls, it moves using its legs: [+ **over/up etc**] *Watch out! There's a wasp crawling up your leg.*

**3 ▶ CARS ETC ◀** if a vehicle crawls, it moves forward very slowly: [+ **by/along etc**] *The traffic was crawling by at 5 miles an hour.*

**4 ▶ TOO HELPFUL ◀** to be too pleasant or helpful to someone in authority, especially because you want them to help you: **crawl to sb** *Just look at Janice – crawling to the director of studies again!*

**5 be crawling with** to be completely covered with insects, people etc: *Eugh! This floor is crawling with ants.*

**6 make your skin crawl** if something or someone makes your skin crawl, you think they are extremely unpleasant: *The way Jonathan looks at her really makes my skin crawl.*

**crawl[2]** *n* [singular] **1** a very slow speed: *The traffic had slowed down to a crawl.* **2** a fast way of swimming in which you lie on your stomach and move one arm and then the other over your head

**crawler lane** /ˈ·· ˌ·/ *n* [C] *BrE* a special part of a road that can be used by slow vehicles so that other vehicles can go past

**cray·fish** /ˈkreɪˌfɪʃ/ *n* [C,U] a small animal like a LOBSTER that lives in rivers and streams, or the flesh of this animal eaten as food

**cray·on[1]** /ˈkreɪən, -ɒn‖-ɑːn, -ən/ *n* [C] a stick of coloured WAX[1](1) or CHALK[2](2) used for writing or drawing, especially on paper: *children's crayons*

**crayon[2]** *v* [I,T] to draw with a crayon

**craze** /kreɪz/ *n* [C] a fashion, game, type of music etc that suddenly becomes very popular but usually only remains popular for a very short time: *This computer game is the latest craze.*

**crazed** /kreɪzd/ *adj* behaving in a wild and uncontrolled way as if you are crazy: *a crazed expression* | [+ **with**] *He was crazed with grief.*

S3 W3 **cra·zy[1]** /ˈkreɪzi/ *adj informal*

**1 ▶ STRANGE ◀** behaving in a way that is very strange: *Don't mind her, she's crazy.* | *The neighbors must think we're crazy.* | *You have some crazy friends.*

**2 ▶ NOT SENSIBLE ◀** an action or behaviour that is crazy is not sensible and likely to cause problems: **it's crazy** *spoken*: *I get more money if I don't work – it's crazy.* | *That's the craziest idea I've ever heard.* | **be crazy to do sth** *It'd be crazy to try and drive home in this weather.*

**3 ▶ ANGRY ◀** angry or annoyed: **drive sb crazy** (=make sb angry or annoyed) *Turn that music down, it's driving me crazy!*

**4 be crazy about sb/sth** to like someone very much, or be very interested in something: *Frank is just crazy about you!*

**5 like crazy** very quickly or very hard: *We're going to have to work like crazy to get this finished on time.*

**6 ▶ ILL ◀** mentally ill: *He lived alone and they were sure he was crazy.* | **go crazy** *Kurtz had gone crazy, alone in the jungle.*

**7 crazy as a loon** *AmE informal* very strange and possibly mentally ill —**crazily** *adv* —**craziness** *n* [U]

**crazy[2]** *n* [C] *AmE informal* someone who is crazy

**crazy golf** /ˌ·· ˈ·/ *n* [U] *BrE* a game like GOLF in which the players hit the ball through various amusing OBSTACLES; MINIATURE GOLF *AmE*

**crazy pav·ing** /ˌ·· ˈ··/ *n* [U] *especially BrE* pieces of stone of different shapes fitted together to make a path or flat place

**crazy quilt** /ˌ·· ˈ·/ *n* [C] *AmE* a cover for a bed made from small pieces of cloth of different shapes that have been sewn together

**creak[1]** /kriːk/ *v* [I] if something such as a door, bed, stair etc creaks, it makes a long high noise when someone opens it, sits on it, walks on it etc: *The window shutters creaked in the wind.*

**creak[2]** *n* [C] the sound made by something when it creaks: [+ **of**] *the creak of a door*

**creak·y** /ˈkriːki/ *adj* something such as a chair, bed etc that is creaky creaks when you sit on it, stand on it etc —**creakily** *adv* —**creakiness** *n* [U]

**cream[1]** /kriːm/ *n* [U] **1** a thick yellowish-white liquid that rises to the top of milk: *Have some cream in your coffee.* | *strawberries and cream* **2** [C,U] a food containing this: *cream of chicken soup* | *cream cakes* **3** [C,U] a thick soft substance that you put on your skin in order to make it soft, treat a medical condition etc: *Put some sun cream on before you go out.* **4 the cream of** the cream of a group of people are the best people in that group: *a team representing the cream of Britain's young athletes*

**cream[2]** *adj* yellowish-white in colour: *a cream coloured carpet* —**cream** *n* [U] —see picture on page 411

**cream[3]** *v* [T] **1** to make something into a thick soft mixture: *Cream the butter and sugar together.* | *creamed potatoes* **2** to take cream from the surface of milk **3** *AmE informal* to defeat someone completely

**cream** sb/sth **off** *phr v* [T] to choose the best people or things from a group, especially so that you can use them for your own advantage: *We cream off the best athletes and put them into a special squad.*

**cream cheese** /ˌ· ˈ·‖ˈ· ·/ *n* [U] a type of soft white smooth cheese

**cream crack·er** /ˌ· ˈ··/ *n* [C] *BrE* a light BISCUIT (1) often eaten with cheese

**cream·er** /ˈkriːmə‖-ər/ *n* **1** [U] a liquid that you can use instead of cream in drinks **2** [C] a small container for holding cream

**cream·e·ry** /ˈkriːməri/ *n* [C] *old-fashioned* a place where milk, butter, cream, and cheese are produced or sold

**cream·y** /ˈkriːmi/ *adj* **1** containing cream: *creamy milk* **2** thick smooth and soft like cream: *This make-up has a lovely creamy consistency.* **3** yellowish-white in colour

**crease[1]** /kriːs/ *n* **1** [C] a line on cloth, paper etc, made by folding, crushing or pressing it: *You've got a crease in your dress where you've been sitting.* | *I can never get the creases straight in these trousers.* **2 [singular]** the line where the player has to stand to hit the ball in CRICKET(2)

**crease[2]** *v* [I,T] to become marked with a line or lines, or to make a line appear on cloth, paper etc by folding or crushing it: *Don't sit on my paper, you'll crease it!* | *This material creases really easily.*

**crease (sb) up** *phr v* [I,T] *BrE spoken* to laugh or make someone laugh a lot: *That guy really creases me up!*

**creased** /kriːst/ *adj* cloth or paper that is creased has a line or lines on it because it has been folded or crushed: *She wanted to wear her black dress but it was too creased.*

**cre·ate** /kriˈeɪt/ *v* **1** [T] to make something exist that did not exist before: *Her behaviour is creating a lot of problems.* | *Government promises to create more public sector jobs.* **2** [T] to invent something: *The writer creates his own special language.* | [+ **by**] *This dish was created by our chef Jean Richard.* **3 create sb/sth** *BrE* to officially give someone special rank or title: *James I created him Duke of Buckingham.* **4** [I] *BrE old-fashioned* to be noisily angry: *Don't tell Grandad – he'll only start creating.* S W

S3 W2 **cre·a·tion** /kri'eɪʃən/ *n* **1** [U] the act of creating something: [+ **of**] *The report proposed the creation of an independent Scottish parliament.* | *a job-creation scheme* **2** [C] something that has been created: *The story was a fanciful creation.* | *this year's new fashion creations from Paris* **3** [U] the whole universe, and all living things: *Are we the only thinking species in creation?* **4 the Creation** the act by God, according to the Bible, of making the universe, including the world and everything in it

**cre·a·tion·ist** /kri'eɪʃənɪst/ *n* [C] someone who believes that God created the universe in the way described in the Bible —**creationism** *n* [U]

S3 W3 **cre·a·tive** /kri'eɪtɪv/ *adj* **1** producing or using new and effective ideas, results etc: *He came up with a really creative solution to the problem.* | *I enjoy my job, but I'd like to do something more creative.* **2** someone who is creative is very imaginative and good at making things, painting etc: *You're so creative! – I could never make my own clothes.* —**creatively** *adv* —**creativeness** *n* [U] —**creativity** /ˌkriːeɪ'tɪvɪti/ *n* [U]

**creative ac·count·ing** /·ˌ·· ·'··/ *n* [U] the act of changing business accounts to achieve the result you want in a way that hides the truth but is not illegal

**cre·a·tor** /kri'eɪtə‖-ər/ *n* [C] **1** someone who made or invented a particular thing: *Walt Disney, the creator of Mickey Mouse* **2 the Creator** God

W3 **crea·ture** /'kriːtʃə‖-ər/ *n* [C]
**1** ▶ **LIVING THING** ◀ anything that is living, but not a plant: *The crocodile is a strange-looking creature.* | **living creature** *He has great respect for all living creatures.*
**2** ▶ **STRANGE** ◀ a strange and sometimes frightening living thing: *creatures from outer space*
**3 stupid/adorable/horrid etc creature** someone who has a particular character or quality: *"Lady Jones is a charming creature", he sighed.*
**4** ▶ **SB CONTROLLED BY STH** ◀ someone who is controlled by, or completely in the power of a particular person or organization: [+ **of**] *He was a creature of the military government.*
**5 a creature of habit** someone who always does things in the same way or at the same times
**6** ▶ **STH MADE OR INVENTED** ◀ something, especially something bad, that has been made or invented by a particular person or organization

**creature com·forts** /ˌ·· '··/ *n* [plural] all the things that make life more comfortable and enjoyable such as good food, a warm house etc

**crè·che** /kreʃ‖kreʃ, kreɪʃ/ *n* [C] **1** *BrE* a place where babies are looked after while their parents are at work —compare DAY CARE (1) *AmE* **2** *AmE* a model of the scene of Jesus' birth, often placed in churches and homes at Christmas; CRIB[1](3) *BrE*

**cre·dence** /'kriːdəns/ *n* [U] *formal* the acceptance of something as true: *The amount of credence accorded to written records will undoubtedly vary.* | **gain credence** (=to become more widely accepted or believed) *This doctrine gained credence in academic circles over the next few decades.* | **give credence to sth** (=to believe or accept something as true) *I don't give any credence to these rumors.* | **lend credence to sth** (=to make something more believable)

**cre·den·tials** /krɪ'denʃəlz/ *n* [plural] **1** the things that show people that you have the ability to do something, are suitable for something etc, such as your education, experience, and achievements: *He spent the first hour trying to establish his credentials as a financial expert.* **2** a letter or other document which proves your good character or your right to have a particular position: *The commissioner presented his credentials to the State Department.*

**cred·i·bil·i·ty** /ˌkredɪ'bɪlɪti/ *n* [U] **1** the quality of deserving to be believed and trusted: *This latest scandal has damaged his credibility as a leader.* | [+ **of**] *There are serious questions about the credibility of these reports.* | **gain/lose credibility** *Predictions of economic recovery have now lost all credibility.* **2 credibility gap** the difference between what someone, especially a politician, says and what people can believe

**cred·i·ble** /'kredɪbəl/ *adj* deserving or able to be believed or trusted: *a credible witness* —**credibly** *adv*

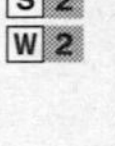
**cred·it**[1] /'kredɪt/ *n* S2 W2
**1** ▶ **DELAYED PAYMENT** ◀ [U] an arrangement with a shop, bank etc that makes it possible for you to buy something and pay for it later: **on credit** (=bought using this arrangement) *stores that sell goods on credit* | **interest-free credit** (=credit with no additional charge) —compare DEBIT[1] (2)
**2** ▶ **PRAISE** ◀ [U] approval or praise that you give to someone for something they have done: **give (sb) credit (for sth)** *You could at least give him some credit for all the effort he's put in.* | **take/claim/deserve etc (the) credit** *Sam never once accepted all the credit for himself.* | **to sb's credit** (=making someone deserve praise or admiration) *It is much to her credit that Joy persevered in spite of all the difficulties.*
**3 be a credit to sb/sth** also **do sb/sth credit** to behave so well or be so successful that everyone who is connected with you can be proud of you: *She's a credit to the team.* | *Your children really do you credit.*
**4 have sth to your credit** to have achieved something: *She already has two successful novels to her credit.*
**5 be in credit** to have money in your bank account: *There are no bank charges if you stay in credit.*
**6** ▶ **FILM** ◀ **the credits** [plural] the list of names of actors and other people involved shown at the beginning or end of a film or television programme
**7 on the credit side** used to say that the things you are going to mention are the good or positive things about someone or something: *On the credit side, the school has considerable success in sport and music.*
**8** ▶ **UNIVERSITY** ◀ [C] a successfully completed part of a course at a university or college: *The drama course should give me enough credits to finish my degree.*
**9** ▶ **TRUE/CORRECT** ◀ [U] the belief that something is true or correct

**credit**[2] *v* [T not in progressive] **1** to believe that something is true: *He told me he'd just won first prize – would you credit it?* | *I find that statement rather hard to credit.* **2** to add money to a bank account: [+ **to**] *The cheque has been credited to your account.* —compare DEBIT[2] (1) **3 credit sb with sth** to believe that someone has a quality, or has done something good: *Do credit me with a little intelligence!* | *This symbol was credited with magical powers.* **4 be credited to** if something is credited to someone or something, they have achieved it or are the reason for it: *Much of their success can be credited to Wilson – an expert.*

**cred·i·ta·ble** /'kredɪtəbəl/ *adj* deserving praise or approval: *a creditable piece of factual research* | **a creditable performance** *Sue gave a very creditable performance as Lady Macbeth.* —**creditably** *adv*

**credit ac·count** /'·· ·ˌ·/ *n* [C] *BrE* an account with a shop which allows you to take goods and pay for them later; CHARGE ACCOUNT *AmE*

**credit card** /'·· ·/ *n* [C] a small plastic card that you use to buy goods or services: *We accept all major credit cards.* —compare CASH CARD, CHEQUE CARD, DEBIT CARD

**credit freeze** /'·· ˌ·/ *n* [C] a period during which the government makes it more difficult for people to borrow money, to reduce the amount of money people spend

**credit note** /'·· ·/ *n* [C] a document which a shop gives you when you return goods allowing you to exchange them for goods of the same value

**cred·i·tor** /'kredɪtə‖-ər/ *n* [C] someone who money is owed to —compare DEBTOR

**credit rat·ing** /'·· ˌ··/ *n* [C] a judgement made by a financial institution about how likely a person or business is to pay their debts

**credit voucher** /'·· ··/ *n* [C] *AmE* a credit note

**cred·it·wor·thy** /'kredɪtˌwɜːθi‖-ˌwɜːr-/ *adj* considered to be able to repay debts —**creditworthiness** *n* [U]

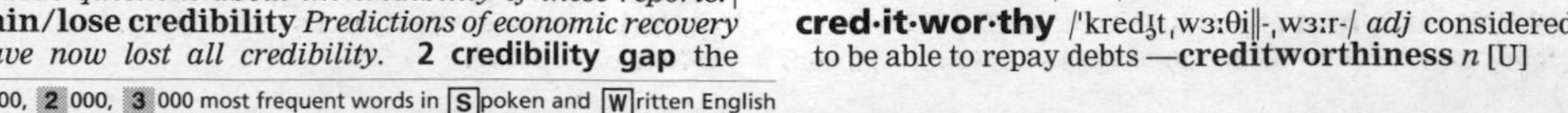

**cre·do** /ˈkriːdəʊ, ˈkreɪ-‖-doʊ/ *n* [C] a formal statement of the beliefs of a religion etc

**cre·du·li·ty** /krɪˈdjuːlɪ̣ti‖-ˈduː-/ *n* [U] willingness or ability to believe that something is true: *childish credulity* | **strain/stretch credulity** *This explanation strained my credulity too far.*

**cred·u·lous** /ˈkredjʊ̣ləs‖-dʒə-/ *adj* always believing what you are told, and therefore easily deceived: *This man has coaxed millions of pounds from a credulous public.* —**credulously** *adv* —**credulousness** *n* [U]

**creed** /kriːd/ *n* [C] **1** a set of beliefs or principles: *the Marxist-Leninist creed* | *people of every creed* (=all different religious beliefs) **2 the Creed** a formal statement of belief spoken in certain Christian churches

**creek** /kriːk/ *n* [C] **1** *BrE* a long narrow area of water that flows from the sea, a river, or a lake into the land **2** *AmE, AusE* a small narrow stream or river **3 be up the creek** *spoken* to be in a difficult situation: *If I don't get my passport by Friday, I'll be completely up the creek.* **4 be up shit creek (without a paddle)** *slang* an impolite way of saying that you are in serious trouble

**creel** /kriːl/ *n* [C] a fisherman's basket for carrying fish

**creep¹** /kriːp/ *v past tense and past participle* **crept** /krept/ [I always + adv/prep] **1** to move in a quiet, careful way, especially to avoid attracting attention: [+ **into/over/around etc**] *Johann would creep into the gallery to listen to the singers.* | *He crept back up the stairs, trying to avoid the ones that creaked.* —see picture on page 1262 **2** if something such as an insect, small animal, or car creeps, it moves slowly and quietly: [+ **down/along/away etc**] *a caterpillar creeping down my arm* **3** to gradually enter something and change it: [+ **in/into/over etc**] *Funny how religion is creeping into the environmental debate.* **4** if a plant creeps it grows or climbs up or along a particular place: [+ **up/over/around etc**] *ivy creeping up the walls of the building* **5** if mist, clouds etc creep, they gradually fill or cover a place: [+ **into/over etc**] *Fog was creeping into the valley.* **6** *BrE informal* to be insincerely nice to someone, especially someone in authority, in order to gain an advantage for yourself: **creep (up) to sb** *I'm not the kind of person to creep to anybody.* **7 sb/sth makes my flesh creep** used to say that someone or something makes you feel strong dislike or fear: *His glassy stare made my flesh creep.*

**creep up on** sb/sth *phr v* [T] **1** to surprise someone by walking up behind them silently: *Don't yell – let's creep up on them and scare them.* **2** if a feeling or idea creeps up on you, it gradually increases: *The feeling she had for Malcolm, had crept up on her and taken her by surprise.* **3** to seem to come sooner than you expect: *Somehow, the end of term had crept up on us.*

**creep²** *n* **1** *informal especially AmE* someone who you dislike extremely: *Get lost, you little creep!* **2** [C] *BrE informal* someone who tries to make you like them or do things for them by being insincerely nice to you: *Don't try and flatter her – she doesn't approve of creeps.* **3 give sb the creeps** if a person or place gives you the creeps, they make you feel nervous and a little frightened, especially because they are strange: *That house gives me the creeps.*

**creep·er** /ˈkriːpə‖-ər/ *n* [U] a plant that grows up trees or walls or along the ground

**creep·y** /ˈkriːpi/ *adj* making you feel nervous and slightly frightened: *There's something creepy about the way he looks at me.* | *a creepy old house*

**creepy-crawl·y** /ˌ·· ˈ··/ *n* [C] *spoken especially BrE* an insect, especially one that you are frightened of

**cre·mate** /krɪ̣ˈmeɪt‖ˈkriːmeɪt/ *v* [T] to burn the body of a dead person at a funeral ceremony —**cremation** /krɪˈmeɪʃən/ *n* [C,U]

**crem·a·to·ri·um** /ˌkreməˈtɔːriəm‖ˌkriː-/ **crem·a·to·ry** /ˈkremətəri‖ˈkriːmətɔːri/ *especially AmE n* [C] a building in which the bodies of dead people are burned at a funeral ceremony

**crème car·a·mel** /ˌkrem ˈkærəməl, -mel/ *n* [C] a sweet food made from milk, eggs, and sugar

**crème de la crème** /ˌkrem də lɑː ˈkrem/ *n* [singular] *French* the very best of a kind of thing or group of people: *The chefs there are the crème de la crème of the culinary world.*

**crème de menthe** /ˌkrem də ˈmɒnθ‖-ˈmɑːnt/ *n* [U] a strong, sweet, green alcoholic drink

**cren·el·lat·ed** *BrE*, **crenelated** *AmE* /ˈkrenəleɪtɪ̣d/ *adj technical* a wall or tower that is crenellated has BATTLEMENTS

**cre·ole** /ˈkriːəʊl‖-oʊl/ *n* **1** [C,U] a language that is a combination of a European language with one or more other languages —compare PIDGIN **2** [C] someone descended from both Europeans and Africans **3** [C] a white person born in the West Indies or parts of Spanish America, or descended from the original French settlers in the southern US **4** [U] food prepared in the hot strong-tasting style of the southern US: *shrimp creole* —**creole** *adj*

**cre·o·sote** /ˈkriːəsəʊt‖-soʊt/ *n* [U] a thick, brown, oily liquid used for preserving wood —**creosote** *v* [T]

**crepe, crêpe** /kreɪp/ *n* **1** also **crape** [U] light, soft, thin cloth, with very small folded lines on the surface, made from cotton, silk, wool, etc. **2** [U] tightly pressed rubber used especially for making the bottoms of shoes: *crepe-soled shoes* **3** [C] a very thin PANCAKE (1)

**crepe pa·per** /ˌ· ˈ··‖ˈ· ˌ··/ *n* [U] thin, brightly coloured paper with very small folded lines on the surface, especially used as decorations

**crept** /krept/ the past tense and past participle of CREEP¹

**cre·scen·do** /krɪ̣ˈʃendəʊ‖-doʊ/ *n* [C] **1** a sound or a piece of music that becomes gradually louder: **rise to/reach a crescendo** (=to gradually become louder) *The violins had reached a crescendo.* | *Her voice rose to a crescendo.* —opposite DIMINUENDO **2** a time when people are becoming more and more excited, anxious, or angry: *A crescendo of resentment built up between the two women.* | **rise to/reach a crescendo** *the clamour of telephones as the working day reached its crescendo of activity* —**crescendo** *adj*

**cres·cent** /ˈkresənt/ *n* [C] **1** a curved shape, wider in the middle and pointed at the ends: **crescent moon/knife/biscuit etc** *A new crescent moon rose above the town.* —see picture at SHAPE¹ **2** the curved shape as a sign of the Muslim religion **3** a word meaning a street with a curved shape, often used in the street's name: *Turn left into Badgerly Crescent.*

**cress** /kres/ *n* [U] a small plant with round green leaves that can be eaten and has a slightly hot taste: *egg and cress sandwiches*

**crest¹** /krest/ *n* **1** [C usually singular] the top or highest point of something such as a hill or a wave: [+ **of**] *He climbed over the crest of the hill.* —see picture on page 835 **2** [C] a special picture used as a sign of a family, town, school etc: *the school colours and crest* | *the family crest on his notepaper* **3** [C] a pointed group of feathers on top of a bird's head, or a raised area on the body of an animal: *the dramatic feathery crest of the cockatoo* **4** [C] a decoration of bright feathers, worn, especially in former times, on top of soldiers' helmets (HELMET) **5 be riding the crest of a wave** to be very successful, happy etc: *The President is currently riding the crest of a wave of popularity.*

**crest²** *v* **1** [T] to reach the top of a hill, mountain etc: *They'd crested another ridge by the afternoon.* **2** [I] if a wave crests it reaches its highest point before it falls

**crest·ed** /ˈkrestɪ̣d/ *adj* **1** having a crest: *crested birds* **2** marked by a crest: *the Duke's crested notepaper*

**crest·fal·len** /ˈkrestˌfɔːlən‖-ˌfɒːl-/ *adj* disappointed especially because you have failed to do something: *The kids came back from the game looking crestfallen.*

**cre·ta·ceous** /krɪ̣ˈteɪʃəs/ *adj technical* **1** similar to CHALK¹ (1) or containing chalk **2 the Cretaceous period** the time when rocks containing chalk were formed

**cret·in** /ˈkretɪ̣n||ˈkriːtn/ *n* [C] *especially spoken* someone who is extremely stupid: *Don't be such a cretin! Don't you know anything?* —**cretinous** *adj*

**cre·vasse** /krɪˈvæs/ *n* [C] a deep open crack in thick ice, especially in a GLACIER —see picture on page 835

**crev·ice** /ˈkrevɪ̣s/ *n* [C] a narrow crack, especially in rock: *He climbed the cliff, finding footholds in the crevices.*

S3 W3 **crew¹** /kruː/ *n* **1** [C] all the people working on a ship, plane etc: *These planes carry over 300 passengers and crew.* **2** [C] all the people working on a ship, plane etc except the most important officers: *How many crew does he need to sail his yacht?* **3** [C] a group of people working together with special skills for a particular purpose: *a TV camera crew* —see also GROUND CREW **4** [singular] a group of people: *We found a happy crew of foreign students in the hostel.* | **motley crew** (=a group of people who are a strange mixture of types) *My son came home from college with this motley crew.* **5** [C] a team of people who compete in rowing (ROW³) races: *Who will be on the college crew?*

**crew²** *v* [I,T] to be part of the crew on a boat: *He asked me to crew for him in the sailing races.*

**crew³** *old use* the past tense of CROW²

**crew cut** /ˈ· ·/ *n* [C] a very short hair style for men —see picture at HAIRSTYLE

**crew·man** /ˈkruːmən/ *n plural* **crewmen** /-mən/ [C] a member, especially a male member, of a CREW¹ (2)

**crew mem·ber** /ˈ· ,··/ *n* [C] a member of a CREW¹ (2)

**crew neck** /ˈ· ·/ *n* [C] a plain, round neck on a SWEATER —see picture on page 840 —compare V-NECK

**crib¹** /krɪb/ *n especially AmE* **1** [C] a bed for a baby or young child, especially one with bars to keep the baby from falling out; COT (1) *BrE* —see picture at BED¹ **2** [C] an open box or wooden frame holding food for animals; MANGER **3** [C] *BrE* a model of the scene of Jesus' birth, often placed in churches and homes at Christmas; CRÈCHE *AmE* **4** [C] *informal* **a)** something copied dishonestly from someone else's work, especially at school **b)** a book giving a translation or answers to questions, often used dishonestly by students **5** [U] the card game of cribbage

**crib²** *v* **cribbed, cribbing** [I,T] to copy school or college work dishonestly from someone else: **crib sth off/from sb** *He cribbed the answers off his friend.*

**crib·bage** /ˈkrɪbɪdʒ/ also **crib** *informal n* [U] a card game in which points are shown by putting small pieces of wood in holes in a small board

**crib death** /ˈ· ·/ *n* [C] *AmE* COT DEATH *BrE*

**crick¹** /krɪk/ *n* [C] a sudden, painful stiffening of the muscles, especially in the back or the neck: [+ **in**] *Reading over your shoulder gives me a crick in my neck.*

**crick²** *v* [T] to do something that produces a crick in your back or neck: *He bent to lift the case and cricked his back.*

S3 W3 **crick·et** /ˈkrɪkɪ̣t/ *n* **1** [C] a small brown jumping insect, which makes a noise by rubbing its wings together **2** [U] an outdoor game between two teams of 11 players in which players try to get points by hitting a ball and running between two sets of STUMPS (=special sticks)

**crick·et·er** /ˈkrɪkɪ̣tə||-ər/ *n* [C] someone who plays CRICKET (2)

**cri·er** /ˈkraɪə||-ər/ *n* [C] a TOWN CRIER

**cri·key** /ˈkraɪki/ *interjection BrE informal* used to show that you are surprised or annoyed: *Oh crikey, I'm going to miss the bus!*

S2 W2 **crime** /kraɪm/ *n*

**1 ▶ CRIME IN GENERAL ◀** [U] illegal activities in general: *We moved here ten years ago because there was very little crime.* | **crime prevention** (=work done to stop crime from happening) *Neighborhood watch groups have been a very effective means of crime prevention.* | **serious crime** *Police need more personnel to tackle serious crime in the inner cities.* | **crime rate** (=the amount of crime in society) *Voters are becoming frustrated with the growing crime rate.* | **violent crime** *a worrying increase in violent crime* | **petty crime** (=crime that is not very serious) *Kids living on the streets are likely to be involved in petty crime.* | **crime wave** (=a sudden increase in the amount of crime) | **turn to crime** (=start doing illegal things) *Rich kids don't generally need to turn to crime.* | **a life of crime** (=a way of living and getting money by doing illegal activities) | **white-collar crime** (=crimes done by professional people that involve clever and complicated ways of illegally getting money)

**2 ▶ A PARTICULAR CRIME ◀** [C] a dishonest, violent, or immoral action that can be punished by law: *A thirty-four year old man was charged with the crime after the murder weapon was found in his home.* | [+ **against**] *Crimes against the elderly are becoming more common.* | **commit a crime** (=do something illegal) *Most crimes are committed by males under the age of 30.* | **scene of the crime** (=place where a particular crime happened) *They say a murderer always returns to the scene of the crime.*

**3 it's a crime** *spoken* used to say that you think something is completely immoral: *It's a crime to waste all that good food.*

**4 crime against humanity** a cruel crime against a lot of ordinary people, that is considered unacceptable in any situation, even a war: *The commandant of the prison camp was found guilty of crimes against humanity.*

**5 crime of passion** a crime, usually murder, that happens as a result of someone's sexual jealousy

**6 crime doesn't pay** used to say that it is wrong to think that being involved in crime will bring you any advantage, because you will probably be caught and punished for it —see also ORGANIZED CRIME, **partners in crime** (PARTNER¹ (5)), WAR CRIME, **white collar crime**, (WHITE-COLLAR (2))

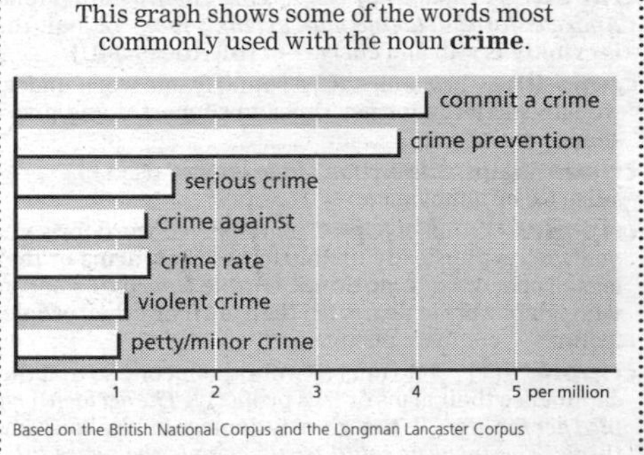


**crim·i·nal¹** /ˈkrɪmɪ̣nəl/ *adj* **1** related to or connected with crime: *criminal behaviour* | *The boy had shown criminal tendencies since early adolescence.* | **a criminal offence** (=a crime that can be punished by law) | **criminal element** (=people within a particular group who are known to be involved in crime) *Ray got mixed up with the local criminal element.* | **criminal negligence** (=the illegal act of not doing something you should do, with the result that someone is hurt) | **criminal damage** (=the illegal act of damaging someone else's property) **2** [no comparative] related to the part of the legal system that is concerned with crime: *criminal court* | *criminal case* | *criminal attorney* | **criminal charges** (=official statements saying that someone has done something illegal) *Wharton faces criminal charges and will be tried in May.* —compare CIVIL (3) **3** wrong, dishonest, and unacceptable: *There was a criminal lack of foresight in the planning of this venture.* —**criminally** *adv* S3 W2

**criminal²** *n* [C] someone who is involved in illegal activities or has been proved guilty of a crime: *The man is a criminal. How could the people elect him to office?* | **hardened criminal** (=someone who has been involved in crime for a long time) *Teenagers should not be sent to prison with hardened criminals.*

**crim·i·nal·ize** also **-ise** *BrE* /ˈkrɪmɪ̣nəl-aɪz/ *v* [T] to make

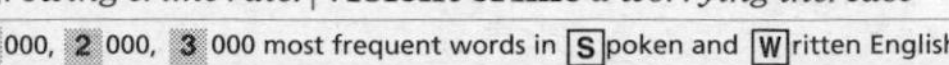

something illegal: *The police have tried in the past to criminalize hitchhiking.*

**criminal law** /ˌ··· ˈ·/ *n* [U] laws or the study of laws concerning crimes and their punishments —see also CANON LAW, CIVIL LAW, COMMON LAW[2]

**criminal rec·ord** /ˌ··· ˈ··/ also **record** *n* [C] an official record kept by the police of any crimes a person has committed: *The defendant has no previous criminal record.*

**crim·i·nol·o·gy** /ˌkrɪmɪˈnɒlədʒi‖-ˈnɑː-/ *n* [U] the scientific study of crime and criminals —**criminologist** *n* [C]

**crimp** /krɪmp/ *v* [T] **1** to press something, especially cloth, paper etc into small regular folds **2** to make your hair slightly curly by using a special heated tool

**crim·son¹** /ˈkrɪmzən/ *adj* having a deep purplish red colour: *a crimson sky | She turned crimson when he made the remark.* —**crimson** *n* [C] —see picture on page 411

**crimson²** *v* [I] if your face crimsons, it becomes red because you are embarrassed

**cringe** /krɪndʒ/ *v* [I] **1** to move back or away from someone or something, especially because you are afraid or in pain: *The dog cringed and whimpered when the tall man appeared.* **2** to feel embarrassed by something that seems stupid: *I cringe when I think what I used to wear in the Sixties. | They sing this song that makes me cringe.* —**cringe** *n* [C]

**crin·kle¹** /ˈkrɪŋkəl/ *v* [I,T] also **crinkle up** to become covered with small folds, or make something do this: *The heat was beginning to make the cellophane crinkle.* —compare WRINKLE[2] —**crinkled** *adj*

**crinkle²** *n* [C usually singular] a thin fold, especially in your skin or on cloth, paper etc —compare WRINKLE¹ (1, 2)

**crin·kly** /ˈkrɪŋkli/ *adj* **1** having many thin folds: *Andrew stared at the old man's crinkly face.* **2** hair that is crinkly is stiff and curly —**crinkliness** *n* [U]

**crin·o·line** /ˈkrɪnəlɪn/ *n* [C] a round frame worn under a woman's skirt in former times to support it and give it shape

**cripes** /kraɪps/ *interjection old-fashioned* used to express surprise or annoyance

**crip·ple¹** /ˈkrɪpəl/ *n* [C] **1** an offensive word for someone who is physically unable to use their arms or their legs properly **2 emotional cripple** *informal* someone who is not able to deal with their own or other people's feelings —compare DISABLED

**cripple²** *v* [T] **1** to hurt or wound someone so that they cannot use their arms or legs properly: *The accident crippled her for life.* **2** to seriously damage or weaken something: *The incident could easily cripple the peace talks.* —**crippled** *adj* —**crippling** *adj*

S2 W2 **cri·sis** /ˈkraɪsɪs/ *n plural* **crises** /-siːz/ [C,U] **1** a period or moment of great danger, difficulty, or uncertainty, especially in politics or economics: *the energy crisis of 1972 | the Cuban missile crisis* **2** a time when a personal emotional problem or situation has reached its worst point: *In times of crisis you find out who your real friends are.* | **be at a crisis point** (=be in a condition that cannot get any worse) *I think Paul and Lucinda are at a crisis point in their marriage.* **3** the time during a serious illness when it could get either better or worse: *The crisis came that night.* **4 crisis management** the skill or process of dealing with unusually dangerous or difficult situations **5 crisis of confidence** a situation in which people no longer believe a government, economy, system etc is working properly, and will no longer support it, work with it etc: [+ **in**] *a crisis of confidence in the foreign exchange when interest rates were cut* —see also MIDLIFE CRISIS

**crisp¹** /krɪsp/ *n* [C] *BrE* a very thin, flat round piece of potato cooked in oil and eaten cold; CHIP¹ (3b) *AmE* —see also **burn sth to a crisp** (BURN¹ (4))

**crisp²** *adj* **1** pleasantly dry, hard, and easily broken: *crisp bacon | His feet broke through the crisp outer layer of snow.* **2** a fruit, vegetable, or plant that is crisp is firm and fresh: *a crisp apple | a crisp salad* **3** paper or cloth that is crisp is fresh, clean, and new: *a crisp, new five dollar bill* **4** weather that is crisp is cold and dry: *a crisp winter day* **5** someone's behaviour or manner that is crisp is quick, confident, and shows no doubts or slowness; BRISK (1, 2): *The general's voice was crisp and clear as he addressed the meeting.* —**crisply** *adv* —**crispness** *n* [U]

**crisp³** *v* [T] to make something become crisp, especially by cooking or heating it

**crisp·bread** /ˈkrɪspbred/ *n* [C,U] a thin dry biscuit that is not sweet

**crisp·y** /ˈkrɪspi/ *adj* a word meaning CRISP² (1) used especially to talk about food: *crispy bacon*

**criss·cross¹, criss-cross** /ˈkrɪskrɒs‖-krɔːs/ *n* [C] a pattern made up of straight lines, usually a lot of them, that cross each other: *the crisscross of scars on his back* —**crisscross** *adj: trees planted in a crisscross pattern*

**crisscross², criss-cross** *v* [I,T] to make a regularly repeated pattern of straight lines that cross each other, or to make this pattern on something: *The flyovers crisscross the city above the congested streets.*

**cri·te·ri·on** /kraɪˈtɪəriən‖-ˈtɪr-/ *n plural* **criteria** /-riə/ [C often plural] a standard which is established so that a judgment or decision, especially a scientific one, can be made: *More detailed criteria are necessary before a logical decision can be reached.* | [+ **for**] *What are your criteria for judging a bottle of wine?* W2

**crit·ic** /ˈkrɪtɪk/ *n* [C] **1** someone whose job is to make judgments about the good and bad qualities of something, especially art, music, films etc: *The jazz critic for The Times panned the show, calling it 'a joke'.* **2** someone who expresses strong disapproval or dislike of a person, idea, organization etc: [+ **of**] *He became an outspoken critic of the country's educational policies.* **3 armchair critic** someone who does nothing themselves but criticizes others for what they do W3

**crit·i·cal** /ˈkrɪtɪkəl/ *adj* S2

**1 ▶ MAKING SEVERE JUDGMENTS ◀** someone who is critical makes severe and often unfair judgments of people or things: *I don't mean to be over critical, but isn't all of this completely unnecessary?* | [+ **of**] *Pat is always very critical of her son's appearance.* W2

**2 ▶ IMPORTANT ◀** very important because what happens in the future depends on it: *We need an immediate decision on this critical issue.* | **be critical to** *Parental attention is critical to the child's socialization.* | **of critical importance** (=very important) *Finding the source of the gas leak was of critical importance.*

**3 ▶ DANGEROUS/UNCERTAIN ◀** a critical time or moment is one that is dangerous or uncertain because a sudden change to a better or a worse condition is possible: *David is at a critical stage in the illness.*

**4 ▶ MAKING FAIR JUDGMENTS ◀** providing careful and fair judgments of the good and bad characteristics of something: *a critical analysis of Stevens' poem*

**5 ▶ ART/FILM/BOOKS ETC ◀** produced by or resulting from the work of CRITICS: *'The Piano' got a lot of critical acclaim, but I didn't like the music in it.* | *a critical success* (=the critics liked it)

**6 in a critical condition** *BrE*, **in critical condition** *AmE* so ill that you could die: *The patient is in critical condition at Bellvue Hospital tonight.*

**7 the critical list** a list of people in hospital who are so ill that they could die: *He was taken off the critical list last night, so we're very relieved.*

**8 with a critical eye** if you look at or examine something with a critical eye, you examine it carefully in order to judge its good and bad qualities

**critically** /ˈkrɪtɪkli/ **critically ill/injured/important, etc** very seriously ill, very important etc: *10 people died and 30 were critically injured in a rail crash yesterday.* **2** in a way that shows you have thought about the good and bad qualities of something: *You need to critically assess your lifestyle.*

**critical mass** /ˌ··· ˈ·/ *n* [C,U] *technical* the amount of a substance necessary for an ATOMIC, CHAIN REACTION to start

**critical path a·nal·y·sis** /ˌ··· ˌ· ·'···/ *n plural* **critical path analyses** [C] *technical* a method of planning a large piece of work so that there will be few delays and the cost will be as low as possible

S2 W2 **crit·i·cis·m** /'krɪtʒsɪzəm/ *n* **1** [C,U] the act of giving your opinion or judgment about the good and bad qualities of someone or something: *Kate doesn't take any kind of criticism very well.* | **constructive criticism** (=intended to help someone or something improve) **2** [C,U] written or spoken remarks that express your disapproval or bad opinion of someone or something: *We all felt that Wanda's criticism was unjustified.* | [+ **of**] *My only criticism of the book is that it's a little too academic.* **3 a)** [U] the activity of forming and expressing judgments about the good or bad qualities of books, films, music etc: *literary criticism* **b)** [C,U] the written work that results from this activity

S3 W3 **crit·i·cize** also **-ise** *BrE* /'krɪtʒsaɪz/ *v* **1** [I,T] to express your disapproval of someone or something, or to talk about their faults: *Ron does nothing but criticize and complain all the time.* | **criticize sb for (doing) sth** *The report strongly criticizes the police for failing to deal with the problem quickly.* **2** [T] to express judgments about the good and bad qualities of something: *Criticizing your own work is very difficult.*

**cri·tique**[1] /krɪ'ti:k/ *n* [C,U] an article, book etc expressing judgments about the good and bad qualities of something such as the work of a writer or artist: [+ **of**] *The final article is a critique of John Updike's latest novel.*

**critique**[2] *v* [I,T] *AmE* to make remarks about the good and bad qualities of something, especially artistic or literary work: *I asked my professor to critique the paper before I turned it in to the examining board.*

**crit·ter** /'krɪtə‖-ər/ *n* [C] *AmE spoken* a creature, especially an animal: *Be careful, that horse is a mean critter!*

**croak**[1] /krəʊk‖kroʊk/ *v* **1** [I] to make a deep low sound like the sound a FROG makes **2** [I,T] to speak in a low, rough voice as if you have a sore throat: *He was shivering and croaking in a voice they barely recognized as his.* **3** [I] *slang* to die

**croak**[2] *n* [C] a low sound made in an animal's or person's throat, like one that a FROG makes

**cro·chet** /'krəʊʃeɪ‖kroʊ'ʃeɪ/ *v* [I,T] to make clothes, blankets etc from wool using a special needle with a hook at one end —compare KNIT (1) —**crochet** *n* [U] —**crotcheting** *n* [U]

**crock** /krɒk‖krɑ:k/ *n* [C] **1** *old use* a clay pot **2 crocks** [plural] **a)** *BrE old-fashioned* plates, cups etc, especially made of baked clay **b)** pieces of broken EARTHENWARE (=baked clay) **3** *spoken* **a crock of shit** *AmE taboo* something that is unbelievable, unfair, untrue etc: *You can't expect me to believe that! What a crock of shit!* **4 old crock** *BrE slang* **a)** an old car **b)** an old person: *We old crocks can't run like you.*

**crocked** /krɒkt‖krɑ:kt/ *adj* [never before noun] **1** *BrE old-fashioned* injured or broken **2** *AmE spoken* drunk: *Don't mind Roger. He's always crocked by noon.*

**crock·e·ry** /'krɒkəri‖'krɑ:-/ *n* [U] *especially BrE* cups, plates etc, especially made of CHINA

crocodile

**croc·o·dile** /'krɒkədaɪl‖'krɑ:-/ *n* **1** [C] a large REPTILE (1) with a long mouth and many sharp teeth that lives in lakes and rivers in hot wet parts of the world **2** [U] the skin of this animal, used for making things such as shoes **3** [singular] *BrE* a long line of people, especially school children, walking in pairs **4 shed crocodile tears** to pretend you feel sad, sorry, or upset when you do not really feel that way

**cro·cus** /'krəʊkəs‖'kroʊ-/ *n* [C] a small purple, yellow, or white flower that comes up in early spring

**croft** /krɒft‖krɒ:ft/ *n* [C] a very small farm in Scotland

**croft·er** /'krɒftə‖'krɒ:ftər/ *n* [C] someone who lives and works on a croft

**croft·ing** /'krɒftɪŋ‖'krɒ:f-/ *n* [U] the system of farming on crofts in Scotland

croissant

**crois·sant** /'kwɑ:sɒŋ‖krɒ:'sɑ:nt/ *n* [C] *French* a piece of bread, shaped in a curve and usually eaten for breakfast

**crone** /krəʊn‖kroʊn/ *n* [C] an ugly or unpleasant old woman

**cro·ny** /'krəʊni‖'kroʊni/ *n* [C usually plural] one of a group of people, who spend a lot of time with each other and will usually help each other, even if this involves dishonesty: *Nixon gave positions of power to many of his political cronies.*

**crook**[1] /krʊk/ *n* [C] **1** *informal* someone who is dishonest: *I wouldn't buy a car from them – they're a bunch of crooks.* **2** a long stick with a curved end, used by people who look after sheep —see picture at STICK[2] **3 the crook of your arm** the part of your arm where it bends, used for holding things: *She cradled the little dog in the crook of her arm.* —see picture at BODY[1]

**crook**[2] *v* [T] if you crook your finger or your arm, you bend it: *She beckoned me, crooking her finger.*

**crook**[3] *adj* [never before noun] *informal AustrE* ill

**crook·ed** /'krʊkʒd/ *adj* **1** dishonest: *a crooked cop* **2** bent, twisted, or not in a straight line: *Her teeth were all crooked.* —**crookedly** *adv* —**crookedness** *n* [U]

**croon** /kru:n/ *v* [I,T] to sing or speak in a soft gentle voice, especially about love: *Sinatra crooning mellow tunes*

**crop**[1] /krɒp‖krɑ:p/ *n* [C] **1** a plant such as wheat, rice, or fruit that is grown by farmers, especially in order to be eaten: *The main crop in China is rice.* | *Most of the land is used for growing crops.* | *crops being harvested in September* **2** the amount of wheat, rice, fruit etc that is produced in a season: *Wheat farmers have had a record crop this year.* | **bumper crop** (=a very large amount of wheat, rice etc produced in a season) **3 a crop of** a group of people that arrive or things that happen at the same time: *There was the usual crop of problems to deal with when I got back to the office.* | *this season's crop of young players* **4** a short whip used in horse riding —see picture at WHIP[1] **5** the part under a bird's throat where food is stored **6** a very short hairstyle **7 a crop of dark hair/blonde curls etc** hair that is short, thick, and attractive W3

**crop**[2] *v* [I] **1** to cut someone's hair short **2** to cut a part off a photograph or picture so that it is a particular size or shape **3** if an animal crops grass or other plants, it makes them short by eating them **4** if a plant crops, it produces fruit, grain etc: *The apple trees cropped well that year.*

**crop up** *phr v* [I] **1** if something, especially a problem, crops up, it happens or appears suddenly and unexpectedly: *Please let me know if anything crops up while I'm away.* —see OCCUR (USAGE) **2** if something such as a name or a subject crops up, it appears in something you read or hear: *Your name kept cropping up in conversation.*

**crop cir·cle** /'· ˌ··/ *n* [C] a CORN CIRCLE

**crop-dust·ing** /'· ˌ··/ *n* [U] *AmE* CROP-SPRAYING

**crop·per** /'krɒpə‖'krɑ:pər/ **come a cropper** *BrE informal* **a)** to fail in something, especially unexpectedly: *I came a cropper on the last question in the test.* **b)** to accidentally fall onto the ground from a horse or bicycle: *Jimmy came a cropper as he turned the corner.*

**crop ro·ta·tion** /'· ·ˌ··/ *n* [U] the practice of changing the crops that you grow in a field each year to preserve the good qualities in the soil

**crop·spray·ing** /ˈ· ˌ··/ *n* [U] the practice of spreading crops with chemicals that kill insects; CROP-DUSTING *AmE*

**cro·quet** /ˈkrəʊkeɪ, -ki‖kroʊˈkeɪ/ *n* [U] a game played on grass in which players hit balls with wooden MALLETS (=long-handled hammers) so that they roll under curved wires

**cro·quette** /krəʊˈket‖kroʊ-/ *n* [C] a piece of crushed meat, fish, potato etc that is made into a small round piece, covered in BREADCRUMBS, fried (FRY[1] (1)) and eaten

**cro·sier, crozier** /ˈkrəʊʒə, -ziə‖-ər/ *n* [C] a CROZIER

**cross-** /krɒs‖krɔːs/ *prefix* **1** going from one side to the other; across: *a cross-Channel ferry* (=sailing from Britain to France) **2** going between two things and joining them: *cross-cultural influences*

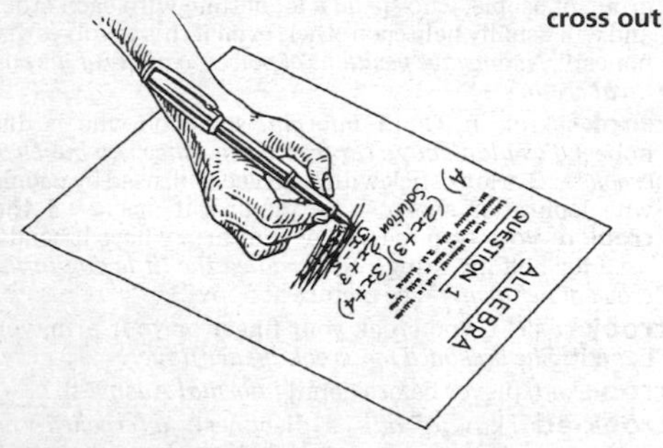


**cross out**

S2 W2 **cross[1]** /krɒs‖krɔːs/ *v*

**1 ▶ GO FROM ONE SIDE TO ANOTHER ◀** [I,T] to go or stretch from one side of something such as a road, river, room etc to the other: *It took them four weeks to cross the desert.* | *Look both ways before you cross the road.* | *The railway line from Leeds to Manchester crosses the Pennines.*

**2 ▶ CROSS A LINE ETC ◀** [T] if you cross a line, track etc you go over and beyond it: *Two cyclists crossed the finish line together in first place.*

**3 ▶ TWO ROADS/LINES ETC ◀** [T] if two or more roads, lines, etc cross, they go across each other: *There's a shopping mall near where Ventura Boulevard crosses Sepulveda.* | **cross sth** *Station Avenue crosses East Street about a mile down the road.*

**4 ▶ LEGS/ARMS ◀** [T] if you cross your legs or arms, you put one on top of the other: *She was sitting on the floor with her legs crossed.*

**5 cross your fingers** used to say that you hope something will happen in the way you want: *Cross your fingers that I get the job.*

**6 cross sb's mind** if an idea, thought etc crosses someone's mind, it comes into their mind for a short time: *It never crossed my mind to check whether the deal was genuine.* | **the thought has crossed my mind** (=used to tell someone you have thought of the thing they are suggesting)

**7 cross sb's face** if an expression crosses someone's face, it appears on their face: *A look of horror crossed Ken's face when he realized what he had done.*

**8 cross that bridge when you come to it** used to say that you will not think or worry about something until it actually happens: *Don't worry about running out of money. We'll cross that bridge when we come to it.*

**9 ▶ BREED OF PLANT/ANIMAL ◀** [T] to mix two or more different breeds of animal or plant to form a new breed: *This flower has been produced by crossing several different varieties.* | [+ **with**] *If you cross a horse with a donkey, you get a mule.* —see also CROSS[2] (3), CROSSBREED[1]

**10 cross my heart (and hope to die)** *spoken informal* used to say that you promise that you will do something or that what you are saying is true: *I didn't take it, cross my heart!*

**11 sb's paths cross** if two people's paths cross they meet, usually unexpectedly: *I know Irving quite well – our paths first crossed when we were at Yale.*

**12 ▶ MAKE SB ANGRY ◀** [T] to make someone angry by opposing their plans or orders: *Anyone who dares to cross me will find themselves in serious trouble.*

**13 ▶ SPORT ◀** [I,T] to kick, throw, or hit the ball across the playing area in a sport such as football, HOCKEY etc

**14 ▶ CHEQUE ◀** [T] *BrE* to draw two lines across a cheque to show that it must be paid into a bank account

**15 cross swords (with)** to argue with someone: *He has crossed swords with the District Attorney several times.*

**16 cross yourself** to move your hand across your upper body in the shape of a cross, especially as a sign of the Roman Catholic faith

**17 cross sb's palm with silver** *especially BrE* to give money to someone —see also **dot the i's and cross the t's** (DOT[2] (4)), **keep your fingers crossed** (FINGER[1] (3)), **cross the Rubicon** (RUBICON)

**cross sth off** *phr v* [I,T] to draw a line through one or more things on a list because you have dealt with them or they are not needed any more: *As you do each job, cross it off the list.*

**cross sth ↔ out** *phr v* [T] to draw a line or lines through something you have written or drawn, usually because it is wrong

**cross over** *phr v* [I] **1** if an entertainer crosses over from one area of entertainment to another, they become successful in the second one as well as the first **2** *BrE old use* to die

**cross[2]** *n* [C] S3 W3

**1 ▶ CHRISTIAN SIGN ◀** **a)** an upright post of wood with another crossing it, that people were nailed to and left to die on as a punishment in the past: *Christians believe that Jesus Christ died on a cross.* **b)** an object or picture in the shape of a cross used as a sign of the Christian faith or for decoration: *Pauline wore a tiny gold cross around her neck.* | **the Cross** (=cross that Christ died on, used as a sign of Christian faith)

**2 ▶ A MARK ON PAPER ◀** *especially BrE* **a)** a mark (x or +) used on paper, to represent where something is, or where something should be: *I've put a cross on the map to mark where our house is.* | *Please sign your name by the cross, to give your consent.* **b)** a mark (x) used on paper to show that something that has been written or printed is not correct: *There were more crosses than ticks on Mark's French homework.* **c)** a mark (x or +) used by someone who cannot write to write their name

**3** a mixture of two things, breeds, or qualities: *Their dog is a Jack Russell cross.* | [+ **between**] *He seems to think his girlfriend is a cross between Naomi Campbell and Tina Turner.*

**4 ▶ MILITARY AWARD ◀** a decoration in the shape of a cross worn as an honour, especially for military bravery: *He was awarded the George Cross.*

**5 ▶ SPORT ◀** **a)** a kick or hit of the ball in a sport such as football, HOCKEY etc that goes across the field **b)** a way of hitting someone in the sport of BOXING in which your arm goes over theirs as they try to hit you

**6 a (heavy) cross to bear** a problem that makes you very unhappy or worried, often one that continues for a long time: *His mother's illness has been a very heavy cross to bear.* —see also **the sign of the cross** (SIGN[1] (10))

**cross[3]** *adj especially BrE* angry or annoyed. **get cross** S3 *Charlotte, Mummy will get very cross if you do it again.* | **get/be cross with sb** *Alright you two, don't get cross with each other!* —see also CROSSWIND

**cross·bar** /ˈkrɒsbɑː‖ˈkrɔːsbɑːr/ *n* [C] **1** a bar that joins two upright posts especially two GOALPOSTS **2** the metal bar between the seat and the HANDLEBARS on a man's bicycle —see picture at BICYCLE[1]

**cross·bones** /ˈkrɒsbəʊnz‖ˈkrɔːsboʊnz/ *n* —see SKULL AND CROSSBONES

**cross·bow** /ˈkrɒsbəʊ‖ˈkrɒːsboʊ/ *n* [C] a weapon like a small BOW³ (1) fixed onto a longer piece of wood, used for shooting bolts (=short, heavy sticks)

**cross·breed¹** /ˈkrɒsbriːd‖ˈkrɒːs-/ *v* [I,T] **a)** to make one kind of a plant or animal breed with a different breed **b)** if a plant or animal crossbreeds it breeds with one of a different breed —**crossbred** /ˈkrɒsbred‖ˈkrɒːs-/ *adj*

**crossbreed²** *n* [C] an animal or plant that is a mixture of breeds —compare INTERBREED

**cross-Chan·nel** /ˌ· ˈ··◂/ *adj* travelling across the English Channel: *There are several cross-Channel ferries from Dover every day.*

**cross·check** /ˌkrɒsˈtʃek‖ˌkrɒːs-/ *v* [T] to make certain that results or calculations are correct by using a different method of calculation from the one you first used —**crosscheck** *n* [C]

**cross-coun·try¹** /ˌ· ˈ··◂/ *adj* across fields or open country: *Duncan prefers cross-country skiing to downhill.* —**cross-country** *adv*: *travelling cross-country*

**cross-country²** *n* [C,U] *BrE* a race that is run across countryside and fields, not on a track

**cross-cul·tu·ral** /ˌ· ˈ···◂/ *adj* belonging to or involving two or more different societies, countries or cultures (CULTURE (1))

**cross·cur·rent** /ˈkrɒsˌkʌrənt‖ˈkrɒːsˌkɜːr-/ *n* [C] a current in the sea, a river etc that moves across the general direction of the main current

**cross-dress·ing** /ˌ· ˈ··/ *n* [U] *AmE* the practice of wearing the clothes of the opposite sex, especially for sexual pleasure —**cross-dresser** *n* [C]

**crossed** /krɒst‖krɒːst/ *adj* if a telephone line is crossed, it is connected by mistake to two or more telephones, so that you can hear other people's conversations

**crossed cheque** /ˌ· ˈ·/ *n* [C] a cheque in Britain that has two lines across it showing that it must be paid into a bank account

**cross-ex·am·ine** /ˌ· ·ˈ··/ *v* [T] to question someone very thoroughly, especially a WITNESS in a law court —**cross-examination** /ˌ· ···ˈ··/ *n* [C;U] —**cross-examiner** /ˌ· ·ˈ···/ *n* [C]

**cross-eyed** /ˌ· ˈ·◂‖ˈ· ·/ *adj* having eyes that look in towards the nose; BOSS-EYED *BrE*

**cross-fer·ti·lize** also **-ise** *BrE* /ˌ· ˈ···/ *v* [T] **1** to combine the male sex cells from one type of plant with female sex cells from another **2** [often passive] to influence someone or something with ideas from other areas: *Europe has been cross-fertilized by contact with many other societies.* —**cross-fertilization** /ˌ· ···ˈ··/ *n* [U]

**cross·fire** /ˈkrɒsfaɪə‖ˈkrɒːsfaɪr/ *n* [U] **1 be caught in the crossfire** to be involved in a situation in which other people are arguing, when you do not want to be: *I left the room to avoid being caught in the crossfire between Dad and William.* **2** two or more lines of bullets being fired across a particular point

**cross-grained** /ˌ· ˈ·◂/ *adj* wood that is cross-grained has lines that go across it instead of along it

**cross-hatch·ing** /ˈ· ˌ··/ *n* [U] lines drawn across part of a picture, DIAGRAM etc to show that something is made of different material, or to produce the effect of shade

**cross·ing** /ˈkrɒsɪŋ‖ˈkrɒː-/ *n* [C] **1** a marked place where you can safely cross a road, railway, river etc —see also LEVEL CROSSING, PEDESTRIAN CROSSING, PELICAN CROSSING, ZEBRA CROSSING **2** a place where two lines, roads, tracks etc cross **3** a journey across the sea: *The crossing was rough and lots of people were seasick.*

**cross-legged** /ˌkrɒs ˈlegd◂‖ˌkrɒːs ˈlegɪd◂/ *adv* in a sitting position with your knees wide apart and ankles crossed: *children sitting cross-legged on the floor* —**cross-legged** *adj*

**cross·o·ver** /ˈkrɒsəʊvə‖ˈkrɒːsoʊvər/ *n* [C] the change a popular performer makes from working in one area of entertainment to another: [+ **from**] *Madonna has made a crossover from rock music to the movies.* —see also **cross over** (CROSS¹)

cross-legged

She sat with her legs crossed. Paul is sitting cross-legged.

**crossover pri·ma·ry** /ˈ··· ˌ···/ *n* [C] *AmE* an OPEN PRIMARY

**cross·patch** /ˈkrɒspætʃ‖ˈkrɒːs-/ *n* [C] *old-fashioned* someone who is bad-tempered

**cross·piece** /ˈkrɒspiːs‖ˈkrɒːs-/ *n* [C] something that lies across another thing, especially in a building, railway track etc

**cross·ply** /ˈkrɒsplaɪ‖ˈkrɒːs-/ *adj* RADIAL

**cross-pur·pos·es** /ˌ· ˈ···/ *n* **at cross-purposes** two people who are at cross-purposes do not understand each other, because they are talking about different things but do not realize it

**cross-ques·tion** /ˌ· ˈ··/ *v* [T] to CROSS-EXAMINE someone —**cross-questioner** *n*

**cross-re·fer** /ˌ· ·ˈ·/ *v* [I,T] to tell a reader to look in another place in the book they are reading so that they can get further information: [+ **to/from**] *The author cross-refers you to Chapter 10 for more details.*

**cross-ref·er·ence** /ˌ· ˈ···‖ˈ· ˌ···/ *n* [C] a note that tells the reader of a book to go to another place in the book, to get further information

**cross·roads** /ˈkrɒsrəʊdz‖ˈkrɒːsroʊdz/ *n plural* **crossroads** **1** a place where two roads meet and cross each other **2** a time in your life when you have to make a very important decision that will affect your future: *When my marriage ended, I felt as if I had reached a crossroads in my life.*

**cross-sec·tion** /ˈ· ˌ··/ *n* [C] **1** something that has been cut in half so that you can look at the inside, or a drawing of this: *cross-section of a plant stem* **2** a group of people or things that is typical of a much larger group: *a cross-section of the American public*

**cross-stitch** /ˈ· ·/ *n* [C,U] a stitch in a cross shape used in decorative sewing

**cross street** /ˈ· ·/ *n* [C] *AmE* a smaller street that crosses the street you are on

**cross·town** /ˈkrɒstaʊn‖ˈkrɒːs-/ *adj* [only before noun] *AmE* moving in a direction across a town or city: *the crosstown bus*

**cross trees** /ˈ· ·/ *n* [plural] *technical* two beams fastened across the top of a ship's MAST (1)

**cross·walk** /ˈkrɒswɔːk‖ˈkrɒːswɒːk/ *n* [C] *AmE* a special place for people to cross the road; PEDESTRIAN CROSSING *BrE*

**cross·wind** /ˈkrɒsˌwɪnd‖ˈkrɒːs-/ *n* [C] a wind that blows across the direction that you are moving in

**cross·wise** /ˈkrɒsˌwaɪz‖ˈkrɒːs-/ *adv* **1 lay/cut sth crosswise** to lay etc something from one corner of something to the opposite corner **2** two things that are placed crosswise are arranged to form the shape of an 'x'

**cross·word** /ˈkrɒsˌwɜːd‖ˈkrɒːsˌwɜːrd/ also **crossword puz·zle** /ˈ·· ˌ··/ *n* [C] a word game in which you write the answers to questions in a pattern of numbered boxes

**crotch** /krɒtʃ‖krɑːtʃ/ also **crutch** *BrE n* [C] the part of your body between the tops of your legs, or the part of a piece of clothing that covers this —see picture at BODY[1]

**crotch·et** /ˈkrɒtʃɪ̈t‖ˈkrɑː-/ *n* [C] *BrE* a musical note which continues for a quarter of the length of a SEMIBREVE; QUARTER NOTE *AmE* —see picture at MUSIC

**crotch·et·y** /ˈkrɒtʃɪ̈ti‖ˈkrɑː-/ *adj* often slightly angry or annoyed: *a crotchety old man*

**crouch**

squat crouch / squat crouch

**crouch** /kraʊtʃ/ *v* [I] **1** also **crouch down** to lower your body close to the ground by bending your knees completely: *My legs began to ache from crouching for so long.* | *The boy crouched down to fix his sandal.* **2** if an animal crouches it sits as low as possible, often because it is frightened or is going to attack something: *The cat crouched, its eyes following the mouse as it scurried away.*

**croup** /kruːp/ *n* [U] an illness in children which makes them cough and have difficulty breathing

**crou·pi·er** /ˈkruːpiə‖-ər/ *n* [C] someone whose job is to collect and pay out money where people play cards, ROULETTE etc for money

**crou·ton** /ˈkruːtɒn‖-tɑːn/ *n* [C usually plural] a small square piece of bread cooked in fat and served with soup or on salad

**crow[1]** /krəʊ‖kroʊ/ *n* **1** [C] a large shiny black bird with a loud cry **2** [singular] the loud sound a COCK[1] (1) makes **3 as the crow flies** in a straight line: *ten miles from here as the crow flies* —see also **eat crow** (EAT (5))

**crow[2]** *v* [I] **1** if a COCK[1] (1) crows, it makes a loud high sound **2** if a baby crows, it makes a noise that shows it is happy: *The baby crowed with delight at the toy.* **3** [+ **over/about**] to talk about what you have done in a very proud way

**crow·bar** /ˈkrəʊbɑː‖ˈkroʊbɑːr/ *n* [C] a heavy iron bar used to lift or open things

**crowd[1]** /kraʊd/ *n* **1** [C] a large group of people in a public place: *A vast crowd had assembled in the main square.* **2** [C] a large number of a particular kind of people or things: [+ **of**] *a crowd of supporters* | *Kemp stepped out to face a crowd of cameras.* | **crowds of** *streets filled with crowds of people* **3** [singular] *informal* a group of people who know each other, work together etc: *"Who'll be at the party?" "Oh, the usual crowd – Maura, Tom, Joe, Jen, Turi...."* **4 follow the crowd/go with the crowd** to always do what other people do, without thinking for yourself

S2 W2 **crowd[2]** *v* **1** [I,T] to gather together in large numbers, filling a particular place, or moving in a particular direction: *Supporters crowded the stadium.* | [+ **around/into etc**] *We all crowded around the speaker.* **2** [T] if thoughts or ideas crowd your brain, mind, head etc, they fill it: *A jumble of confused thoughts crowded my brain.* **3** [T] **a)** to make someone angry by moving too close to them: *The guy standing behind me was crowding me, so I poked him in the ribs.* **b)** *especially AmE* to make someone angry or upset by making too many unfair demands on them: *Stop crowding me! I need time to make this decision.*

**crowd** sb/sth ↔ **out** *phr v* [T] to force someone or something out of a place or situation: *The bigger software firms are crowding small businesses out.*

**crowd·ed** /ˈkraʊdɪ̈d/ *adj* too full of people or things: *Sometimes the classes were very crowded.* | *a crowded street* | [+ **with**] *It was two weeks before Christmas and the mall was crowded with shoppers.*

**crown[1]** /kraʊn/ *n* **1** [C] **a)** a circle made of gold and decorated with jewels, worn by kings and queens on their heads **b)** a similar circle, sometimes made of other things such as leaves or flowers, worn by someone who has won a special honour **2 the crown a)** the position of being king or queen: *when the crown passed to George the Third...* **b)** the government of a country such as Britain that is officially led by a king or queen: *The islands are possessions of the Crown.* **3** [usually singular] the top part of a hat, head, or hill: *a hat with a high crown* —see picture at HAT **4 a)** a unit of money in several European countries: *Swedish crowns* **b)** an old British coin, four of which made a pound **5** [C] an artificial top for a damaged tooth **6** a mark, sign, BADGE etc in the shape of a crown, used especially to show rank or quality **7** *informal* the fact of winning an important sports competition: *Can she retain her Wimbledon crown?* S W

**crown[2]** *v* [T] **1** to place a crown on someone's head as a sign of royal power: *The Empress was crowned ten years ago.* | **crown sb king/queen** *Henry was crowned king.* **2** to make something complete or perfect by adding success, beauty, happiness etc to it: **crown sth with** *All their efforts have been crowned with success.* **3 crowned with** *literary* having something on top: *mountain peaks crowned with snow* **4** to put a protective top on a damaged tooth **5** *slang* to hit someone on the head **6 to crown it all** *informal* used to say that the next thing that happened was the worst in a series of bad things: *And then, to crown it all, I lost my purse.*

**crown col·o·ny** /ˌ· ˈ···/ *n* [C] a COLONY[1] controlled by the British government

**crown court** /ˈ· ·/ *n* [C,U] a court of law in Britain that deals with serious criminal cases and is higher than a Magistrates' Court

**crowned head** /ˌ· ˈ·/ *n* [C usually plural] a king or queen: *All the crowned heads of Europe were present at the funeral.*

**crown·ing glory** /ˈkraʊnɪŋ/ *n* [singular] **1** something that is more valuable, beautiful, or important than anything else you have or do: *The hotel's crowning glory was a stunning roof garden with a panoramic view.* **2** *humorous* your hair

**crown jew·els** /ˌ· ˈ··/ *n* [plural] the crown, sword, jewels etc worn by a king or queen for ceremonies

**crown prince** /ˌ· ˈ·◂/ *n* [C] the boy or man who is expected to become the next king: *Crown Prince Frederick*

**crown prin·cess** /ˌ· ˈ··◂‖ˌ· ˈ··◂/ *n* [C] the girl or woman who is expected to become queen: *the Crown Princess of Prussia*

**crow's feet** /ˈ· ·/ *n* [plural] very small lines in the skin near your eyes

**crow's nest** /ˈ· ·/ *n* [C] a small box at the top of a ship's MAST[1] from which someone can watch for danger, land etc

**cro·zier, crosier** /ˈkrəʊʒə, -ziə‖-ər/ *n* [C] a long stick with a decorative curved end carried by a BISHOP (1)

**CRT** /ˌsiː ɑː ˈtiː‖-ɑːr-/ *n* [C] the abbreviation of CATHODE RAY TUBE

**cru·cial** /ˈkruːʃəl/ *adj* **1** something that is crucial is extremely important because everything else depends on it: *crucial decisions involving millions of dollars* **2** *slang* excellent —**crucially** *adv* S W

**cru·ci·ble** /ˈkruːsɪ̈bəl/ *n* [C] a container in which substances are heated to very high temperatures

**cru·ci·fix** /ˈkruːsɪ̈fɪks/ *n* [C] a cross with a figure of Christ on it

**cru·ci·fix·ion** /ˌkruːsɪ̈ˈfɪkʃən/ *n* **1** [C,U] the act of killing someone by fastening them to a cross and leaving them to die **2 the Crucifixion** the death of Christ in this way **3** [C] also **Crucifixion** a picture or other object representing Christ on the cross

**cru·ci·form** /ˈkruːsɪ̟fɔːm‖-fɔːrm/ *adj* shaped like a cross

**cru·ci·fy** /ˈkruːsɪ̟faɪ/ *v* [T] **1** to kill someone by fastening them to a cross **2** to criticize someone severely and cruelly for something they have done, especially in public: *If the newspapers find out you'll be crucified.*

**crud** /krʌd/ *n* [U] *informal* something unpleasant to look at, smell, taste etc: *I can't eat this crud!* —**cruddy** *adj*

**crude**[1] /kruːd/ *adj* **1** offensive or rude, especially in a sexual way; VULGAR (1): *a crude gesture|crude jokes* **2** not developed to a high standard or made with great skill: *crude tools made of stone* **3** crude oil, rubber etc is in its natural or raw condition before it is treated with chemicals **4** done without attention to detail: *a crude comparison of different engines* **5 in crude terms** expressed in a simple way: *In crude terms, the gulf between wealth and poverty is growing wider each year.* —**crudely** *adv*: *crudely built shacks* —**crudity** also **crudeness** *n* [C,U]

**crude**[2] also **crude oil** /ˌ· ˈ·/ *n* [U] the oil that comes out of OIL WELLS, before it is separated into different products: *1000 barrels of crude*

**cru·dit·és** /ˈkruːdɪ̟teɪ‖ˌkruːdɪ̟ˈteɪ/ *n* [plural] *French* pieces of raw vegetable served before a meal —see picture on page 838

W3 **cru·el** /ˈkruːəl/ *adj* **1** causing unfair or unnecessary pain or suffering: *a cruel twist of fate*|**a cruel blow** (=a sudden event that is painful and unfair) *My brother's death was a cruel blow.* **2** deliberately making people or animals suffer: *The older kids played cruel jokes on her little brother.*|**cruel look/smile/laugh etc** *Cilla gave a cruel laugh and left him standing there alone.* **3 be cruel to be kind** to do something to someone that will make them upset or unhappy in order to help them in another way —**cruelly** *adv*: *cruelly neglected by his parents*

**cru·el·ty** /ˈkruːəlti/ *n* **1** [U] a willingness or desire to make people or animals suffer: *There was a hint of cruelty in Brian's smile.* **2** [U] behaviour that deliberately causes pain to people or animals: *The children had suffered cruelty and neglect.*|[+ **to**] *cruelty to animals* **3** [C] a cruel action: *horrifying cruelties that occur in wartime* **4** [U] the unfairness of something that happens: *Ruth's eyes filled with tears at life's cruelty.*

**cru·et** /ˈkruːɪ̟t/ *n* [C] a thing that holds the containers for salt, pepper etc on a table

**cruise**[1] /kruːz/ *v* **1** [I] to sail along slowly, especially for pleasure: *cruising in the Mediterranean* **2** [I] to move at a steady speed in a car, aircraft etc: *cruising at 50 miles per hour* **3** [I,T] to drive a car slowly through a place with no particular purpose: *We were out cruising Friday night, and I saw Jerry with Kimberly.* **4** [I,T] *slang* to look in a public place for a sexual partner: *cruising the singles bars*

**cruise**[2] *n* [C] **1** a holiday on a large ship: *a Caribbean cruise* **2** a journey by boat for pleasure

**cruise con·trol** /ˈ· ·ˌ·/ *n* [C] a piece of equipment in a car that makes it go at a steady speed

**cruise li·ner** /ˈ· ˌ··/ *n* [C] a large ship for cruising

**cruise mis·sile** /ˌ· ˈ··/ *n* [C] a large explosive weapon that flies close to the ground and can be aimed at an exact point hundreds of kilometres away

**cruis·er** /ˈkruːzə‖-ər/ *n* [C] **1** a large fast warship: *a battle cruiser* **2** a boat used for pleasure **3** *AmE* a police car

**cruise ship** /ˈ· ·/ *n* [C] a large ship with restaurants, bars etc that people have holidays on

**crul·ler** /ˈkrʌlə‖-ər/ *n* [C] *AmE* a small piece of sweet bread with a twisted shape

**crumb** /krʌm/ *n* [C] **1** a very small piece of dry food, especially bread or cake: *Brush the crumbs off the table.* —see picture on page 416 **2 crumb of comfort/hope etc** a very small amount of comfort, hope etc: *Marie's offer of help was our only crumb of comfort.* **3** *AmE old-fashioned* someone who has done something unpleasant

**crum·ble**[1] /ˈkrʌmbəl/ *v* **1** [I,T] also **crumble away** to break apart into little pieces, or make something do this: *Billy crumbled the bread in his fingers.* **2** [I] if a building crumbles, it is old and starting to fall down: *Britain's crumbling schools* **3** [I] also **crumble away** if your determination, courage etc crumbles, it becomes weak or fails: *Brigg's resolve crumbled and he reached for the whisky bottle.* **4** [I] if a military operation, government etc crumbles, it loses its power and its effectiveness: *a crumbling empire*

**crumble**[2] *n* [U] a cooked dish of fruit covered with a dry mixture of flour, butter, and sugar: *apple crumble*

**crum·bly** /ˈkrʌmbli/ *adj* something such as food or soil that is crumbly breaks easily into small pieces: *a nice, crumbly cheese*

**crumbs** /krʌmz/ *interjection BrE informal* used to express surprise

**crum·my** /ˈkrʌmi/ *adj informal* **1** of bad quality: *a crummy book|What a crummy idea!* **2** ill or upset: *I felt pretty crummy the next morning.*

**crum·pet** /ˈkrʌmpɪ̟t/ *n* **1** [C] a small round bread with holes in one side, eaten hot with butter **2** [U] *BrE slang* an offensive word for a sexually attractive woman

**crum·ple** /ˈkrʌmpəl/ *v* **1** [I,T] also **crumple up** to crush something so that it becomes smaller and bent, or to be crushed in this way: *I had crumpled up about ten sheets, trying to write the letter.* **2** [I] if your face crumples you suddenly look sad or disappointed, as if you might cry **3** [I] if your body crumples, you fall in an uncontrolled way because you are unconscious, drunk etc: *Watkins crumpled in a heap and the referee stopped the fight.*

**crum·pled** /ˈkrʌmpəld/ *adj* **1** also **crumpled up** crushed into a smaller bent shape: *a crumpled banknote* —see picture on page 1258 **2** cloth or clothes that are crumpled have a lot of lines or folds in them: *Don't sit around in your suit. It'll get crumpled.* **3** someone who is crumpled somewhere, is lying still in a strange position after they have fallen

**crumple zone** /ˈ·· ·/ *n* [C] part of a car that crumples easily in an accident to protect the people inside

**crunch**[1] /krʌntʃ/ *n* [singular] **1** a noise like the sound of something being crushed: *the crunch of footsteps on gravel|a horrible crunch* —see picture on page 1261 **2** *AmE* a difficult situation caused by a lack of money: *The company's in a crunch right now.*|**feel the crunch** (=not have enough money) **3 when/if it comes to the crunch** used to say what you will do when something important happens or when a difficult decision has to be made: *If it comes to the crunch, whose side will you take?*

**crunch**[2] *v* **1** [I] to make a sound like something being crushed: *Our feet crunched on the frozen snow.* **2** [I always + adv/prep, T] to eat hard food in a way that makes a noise: [+ **on**] *The dog was crunching on a bone.*|**crunch sth** *crunching a biscuit*

**crunch·y** /ˈkrʌntʃi/ *adj* food that is crunchy is firm and fresh, and makes a noise when you bite it: *a crunchy apple* —**crunchiness** *n* [U]

**cru·sade**[1] /kruːˈseɪd/ *n* [C] **1** one of a series of wars fought in the 11th, 12th, and 13th centuries by Christian armies trying to take Palestine from the Muslims **2** a determined attempt to change something because you think you are morally right: [+ **against/for**] *He seems to be running a one-man crusade against cigarette smoking.*

**crusade**[2] *v* [I] to take part in a CRUSADE[1]: [+ **against/for**] *crusading against nuclear weapons* —**crusader** *n* [C]

**cruse** /kruːz/ *n* [C] *old use* a small pot for oil, wine etc

**crush**[1] /krʌʃ/ *v* [T] **1** to press something so hard that it breaks or is damaged: *His leg was crushed in the accident.*|**be crushed to death** (=die by being crushed) *Two people were crushed to death in the rush to escape.*

2 to press something in order to break it into very small pieces, or into a powder: *Crush two cloves of garlic.* —see picture on page 834 **3 crush a rebellion/uprising/revolt etc** to use severe methods to stop people from fighting you or opposing you: *The revolution was crushed within days.* **4 crush sb's hopes/enthusiasm/confidence etc** to make someone lose all hope, confidence etc **5** to make someone feel extremely upset or shocked: *Sara was crushed by their insults.*

**crush up** *phr v* [I] *BrE informal* if people crush up, they fit into a small space by moving closer to each other: *"Is there room for one more in your car?" "Yes, but you'll have to crush up."*

**crush**[2] *n* **1** [singular] a crowd of people pressed so close together that it is difficult for them to move: *There's always such a crush on the train in the mornings.* **2** [C] an uncontrollable feeling of love for someone, especially that a young person has for someone older: **have a crush on** *Did you have a crush on one of your teachers when you were at school?* **3 orange/lemon etc crush** a drink made by crushing the juice out of a fruit

**crush bar·ri·er** /ˈ· ˌ···/ *n* [C] a fence used to control crowds at football matches, public events etc

**crush·ing** /ˈkrʌʃɪŋ/ *adj* **1** very hard to deal with, and making you lose hope and confidence: *the crushing burden of debt*| **crushing blow** (=something that makes you lose hope and confidence) *Failing his final exams was a crushing blow.*| **crushing defeat** *his party's crushing defeat in the local elections* **2** a crushing remark, reply etc contains a very strong criticism —**crushingly** *adv*: *"That's fairly obvious," she replied crushingly.*

**crust** /krʌst/ *n* [C,U] **1** the hard brown outer surface of bread: *cucumber sandwiches with the crusts cut off* **2** the baked pastry on a PIE (1,2) **3** a thin hard dry layer on the surface of something: *the Earth's crust*

**crus·ta·cean** /krʌˈsteɪʃən/ *n* [C] *technical* an animal such as a LOBSTER or a CRAB that has a hard outer shell and several pairs of legs, and usually lives in water —**crustacean** *adj*

**crust·ed** /ˈkrʌstɪ̯d/ *adj* [+ **with**] having a thin hard dry layer on the surface: *old boots crusted with mud*

**crust·y** /ˈkrʌsti/ *adj* **1** bread that is crusty is pleasant to eat because it has a hard crust **2** *informal* someone who is crusty is bad-tempered: *crusty old ladies in big hats* **3** having a thin dry hard layer of something on the surface: *walls crusty with dirt* —**crustiness** *n* [U]

**crutch** /krʌtʃ/ *n* [C] **1** [usually plural] one of a pair of long sticks that you put under your arms to help you walk when you have hurt your leg: *walking on crutches* **2** something that gives you support or help: *Joan's religion was a crutch to her when her husband died.* **3** *BrE* the part of your body between the tops of your legs

**crux** /krʌks/ *n* **the crux** the most important part of a problem, question, argument etc: *The crux of the play is his inability to accept his wife as an equal.*| *The crux of the matter is whether or not he'd intended to commit a crime.*

S2 W2 **cry**[1] /kraɪ/ *v past tense and past participle* **cried** /kraɪd/ *present participle* **crying**

**1 ▶PRODUCE TEARS◀** [I] to produce tears from your eyes, usually because you are unhappy or hurt: *Don't cry, Laura. It's OK.*| *I always cry at weddings.*| [+ **over/about**] *I know it's stupid to cry over something so unimportant.*| [+ **with/in**] *Zack began to cry with frustration.*| [+ **for**] *The baby was crying for attention.*| **cry your eyes out/cry your heart out** *informal* (=be extremely sad and cry a lot)| **cry yourself to sleep** (=cry until you fall asleep)

**2 ▶SAY LOUDLY◀** [T] to shout something loudly: *"Stop!" she cried.*

**3 ▶ANIMALS/BIRDS◀** [I] if animals and birds cry they make a loud sound: *seagulls on the cliffs crying loudly*

**4 cry on sb's shoulder** *informal* to tell someone why you are unhappy or worried: *I've had Glen crying on my shoulder all afternoon about his love life.*

**5 cry over spilt milk** to waste time feeling sorry about an earlier mistake or problem that cannot be changed: *It's no use crying over spilt milk.*

**6 cry into your beer** *informal* to feel too much pity for yourself, especially because you think you have been treated unfairly

**7 cry wolf** to ask for help when you do not need it, so that people do not believe you when you really need help

**8 for crying out loud** *spoken* used when you feel annoyed or impatient with someone: *For crying out loud, stop nagging me about it!*

**9** [T] *literary* to make something known to the public by shouting: **cry your wares** *market traders crying their wares* —see also **cry for the moon** (MOON[1] (4))

**cry off** *phr v* [I] *BrE* to say that you will not do something that you have already promised to do: *Paul tried to cry off at the last moment saying he had to work late.*

**cry out** *phr v* **1** [I] to make a loud sound of fear, shock, pain etc: *He was in a lot of pain, but he didn't cry out.*| [+ **in/with**] *Even the smallest movement made him cry out in pain.* **2** [I,T] to shout something loudly: *Maria cried out sharply, "Don't touch it!"*| [+ **for**] *I was so scared, I couldn't even cry out for help.* **3 be crying out for** *informal* to need something urgently: *The kitchen is crying out for a coat of paint.* **4 cry out against** to complain strongly or protest strongly about something

**cry**[2] *n plural* **cries** W

**1 ▶SOUND EXPRESSING FEELING◀** [C] a loud sound showing fear, pain, shock etc: *a baby's cry*| **a cry of alarm/anger/despair etc** *A cry of protest rose from the crowd.*| *a cry of delight*| **give a cry/let out a cry** *Hugh let out a startled cry as he fell into the water.*

**2 ▶SHOUT◀** [C] a loud shout: [+ **of**] *As they left the stage there were cries of "More! More!"*

**3 ▶ANIMAL/BIRD◀** [C] a sound made by a particular animal: *the cries of seagulls wheeling over the docks*

**4 ▶TIME WHEN SB CRIES◀** [singular] *especially BrE* a period of time during which you cry: **have a cry** *You'll feel better after you've had a good cry.*

**5 be a far cry from** *informal* to be very different from something else: *It was a far cry from the leafy suburbs she was used to.*

**6 cry for help** something someone says or does that shows that they are very unhappy and need help: *Janie's suicide attempt was obviously a cry for help.*

**7 ▶PHRASE◀** [C] a phrase that is used to unite people in support of a particular action or idea; SLOGAN| **war/battle cry** (=a phrase shouted at the enemy in a fight)

**8 in full cry a)** if someone is in full cry they are strongly or loudly criticizing someone or something: *The Democrats were in full cry over Reagan's defence spending plans.* **b)** if a group of dogs is in full cry, they are making loud noises as they hunt an animal —see also HUE AND CRY

**cry·ing** /ˈkraɪ-ɪŋ/ *adj* **1 a crying need for sth** a serious need for something: *There is a crying need for improvements to our public transport system.* **2 it's a crying shame** *spoken* used to say you are angry and upset about something: *It's a crying shame the way she works so hard to have Ken waste it all gambling.*

**crypt** /krɪpt/ *n* [C] a room under a church, used in former times for burying people

**cryp·tic** /ˈkrɪptɪk/ *adj* deliberately mysterious, or having a secret meaning: **cryptic remark/comment/statement etc** *What are we supposed to understand from a cryptic remark like that?* —**cryptically** /-kli/ *adv*

**crypto-** /krɪptəʊ, -tə‖-toʊ, -tə/ *prefix formal* secret or hidden: *a crypto-Communist*

**cryp·to·gram** /ˈkrɪptəgræm/ *n* [C] a message written in code (CODE[1] (4))

**cryp·to·gra·phy** /krɪpˈtɒgrəfi‖-ˈtɑː-/ *n* [U] the study of secret writing and codes (CODE[1] (4)) —**cryptographer** *n* [C]

**crys·tal** /ˈkrɪstl/ *n* **1** [C,U] rock that is transparent like ice, or a piece of this **2** [U] very high quality transparent glass: *On the sideboard was his mother's collection* *of crystal and cut-glass.* **3** [C] a small regular shaped piece of a substance, formed naturally when this substance becomes solid: *crystals of ice|copper sulphate crystals* **4** [C] *AmE* the transparent cover on a clock or watch

**crystal ball** /ˌ·· ˈ·/ *n* [C] a glass ball that you can look into to magically see what is going to happen in the future

**crystal clear** /ˌ··ˈ·◂/ *adj* very clearly stated, easy to understand: *I want to make one thing crystal clear – I do not agree with these proposals.*

**crys·tal·line** /ˈkrɪstəlaɪn, -liːn‖-lən/ *adj* **1** very clear or transparent, like crystal **2** made of crystals

**crys·tal·lize** also **-ise** *BrE* /ˈkrɪstəlaɪz/ *v* **1** [I,T] if a liquid crystallizes, it forms crystals (CRYSTAL (3)): *The liquid will crystallize at 50 degrees centigrade.* **2** [I,T] if an idea, plan etc crystallizes or if you crystallize it, it becomes very clear in your mind: *a number of related ideas that gradually crystallized into a practical plan* —**crystallization** /ˌkrɪstəlaɪˈzeɪʃən‖-lə-/ *n* [U]

**crys·tal·lized** /ˈkrɪstəlaɪzd/ *adj* crystallized fruit is made by a special process which covers it with sugar: *crystallized ginger*

**crystal set** /ˈ··· ·/ *n* [C] a very simple old-fashioned radio

**CSE** /ˌsiː es ˈiː/ *n* [C] Certificate of Secondary Education; an examination taken at the age of 16 in schools in Britain before 1988

**C-section** /ˈsiː ˌsekʃən/ *n* [C] *AmE informal* a CAESAREAN

**CS gas** /ˌsiː es ˈgæs/ *n* [U] *BrE* TEAR GAS

**ct** **1** the written abbreviation of CARAT: *a 24ct gold necklace* **2** a written abbreviation for CENT: *These cost 75 cts.*

**cu** the written abbreviation of CUBIC: *40 cu m of rock*

**cub** /kʌb/ *n* [C] **1** a young lion, bear, etc: *a lion cub|A fox and her cubs were crossing the field.* **2 the Cubs** *BrE* the CUB SCOUT organization **3** a member of the CUB SCOUT organization

**cub·by·hole** /ˈkʌbihəʊl‖-hoʊl/ *n* [C] a very small space in a house, used for storing things or hiding in

**cube¹** /kjuːb/ *n* [C] **1** a solid object with six equal square sides: *a sugar cube|an ice cube|Cut the meat into small cubes.* —see picture at SHAPE¹ **2 the cube of sth** the number you get when you multiply a number by itself twice, so for example 4 x 4 x 4 = 64 so the cube of 4 is 64

**cube²** *v* [T] **1** to multiply a number by itself twice: *4 cubed is 64* **2** to cut food into cubes; DICE² (1)

**cube root** /ˌ· ˈ·‖ˈ· ·/ *n* [C] *technical* the cube root of a particular number is the number that when multiplied by itself twice will give that number: *4 is the cube root of 64*

**cu·bic** /ˈkjuːbɪk/ *adj* **cubic centimetre/metre/inch etc** a measurement of space which is calculated by multiplying the length of something by its width and height: *What's the cubic capacity of this engine?*

**cu·bi·cle** /ˈkjuːbɪkəl/ *n* [C] a small part of a room that is separated from the rest of the room so that you cannot be seen by other people, cannot hear any noise etc

**cub·is·m** /ˈkjuːbɪzəm/ *n* [U] a 20th century style of art, in which objects and people are represented by GEOMETRIC shapes —**cubist** *adj*: *cubist paintings* —**cubist** *n* [C]

**cu·bit** /ˈkjuːbɪt/ *n* [C] *biblical* an ancient measure of length equal to the length of your arm between your wrist and your elbow

**Cub Scout** /ˈ· ˌ·/ *n* [C] *BrE* **1 the Cub Scouts** the part of the SCOUT¹ (1a) organization for younger boys **2** a young boy who is a member of this organization

**cuck·old¹** /ˈkʌkəld, ˈkʌkəʊld‖-kəld/ *n old-fashioned* an insulting name for a man whose wife has deceived him by having sex with another man

**cuckold² 2** *v* [T] *old-fashioned* if a wife or her LOVER cuckold her husband, they deceive him by having sex with each other

**cuck·oo¹** /ˈkʊkuː‖ˈkuːkuː, ˈkʊ-/ *n* [C] a grey European bird that puts its eggs in other birds' NESTS and that makes a sound that sounds like its name

**cuckoo²** *adj* [not before noun] *informal* crazy or silly: *You're completely cuckoo!*

**cuckoo clock** /ˈ·· ·/ *n* [C] a clock with a wooden bird inside that comes out every hour and makes the sound of a cuckoo to show what time it is

**cu·cum·ber** /ˈkjuːkʌmbə‖-ər/ *n* [C,U] a long thin round vegetable with a dark green skin and a light green inside usually eaten raw: *tomato and cucumber salad* —see picture on page 414

**cud** /kʌd/ *n* [U] **1** food that a cow has eaten, swallowed, and brought back into its mouth to eat a second time **2 chew the cud a)** *informal* to think very hard about something before making a decision **b)** if a cow chews the cud, it eats cud

**cud·dle¹** /ˈkʌdl/ *v* [I,T] to hold someone or something very close to you with your arms around them, especially to show that you love them: *Dawn and her boyfriend were cuddling on the sofa.* —see picture on page 1260

**cuddle up** *phr v* [I] to lie or sit very close to someone or something: [+ **to/together**] *The children cuddled up to each other for warmth.*

**cuddle²** *n* [singular] an act of cuddling someone: **give sb a cuddle** *Come over here and let me give you a cuddle.*

**cud·dly** /ˈkʌdli/ *adj* someone or something that is cuddly makes you want to cuddle them: *a cuddly little baby*

**cud·gel¹** /ˈkʌdʒəl/ *n* **1** [C] a short thick stick used as a weapon **2 take up the cudgels** to start to fight for an idea that you believe in

**cudgel²** *v* [T] **1** to hit someone with a cudgel **2 cudgel your brains** to think very hard about something

**cue¹** /kjuː/ *n* [C] **1** an action or event that provides a signal: *The fall in interest rates may be a cue for an upturn in consumer spending.* **2** a word, phrase, or action in a play that is a signal for the next person to speak or act: *She stood nervously in the wings waiting for her cue.*| **miss your cue** (=not speak or act when you are supposed to) **3 (right) on cue** happening or done at exactly the right moment: *I had just suggested Philip's name when he walked in, right on cue.* **4 take your cue from** to copy what someone else does, especially in order to behave in the right way: *With interest rates, the smaller banks will take their cue from the Federal Bank.* **5** a long straight wooden stick used for hitting the ball in games such as BILLIARDS and SNOOKER¹

**cue²** *v* [T] to give someone a sign that it is the right moment for them to speak or do something especially during a performance: *The studio manager will cue you when it's your turn to come on.*

**cue ball** /ˈ· ·/ *n* [C] the ball which a player hits with the CUE in a game such as BILLIARDS

**cuff¹** /kʌf/ *n* [C] **1** the end of a SLEEVE (=the arm of a shirt, dress etc) —see picture on page 840 **2** *AmE* a narrow piece of cloth turned upwards at the bottom of a trouser leg; TURN-UP *BrE* **3** an action in which you hit someone lightly on the head with your hand open **4 cuffs** [plural] HANDCUFFS —see also OFF-THE-CUFF

**cuff²** *v* [T] **1** to hit someone lightly, especially in a friendly way: *She cuffed him playfully on the side of the head.* **2** to put HANDCUFFS on someone

**cuff link** /ˈ· ·/ *n* [C] one of a pair of small round objects used for fastening shirt cuffs —see picture on page 840

**cui·rass** /kwɪˈræs/ *n* [C] a piece of metal or leather that covers a soldier's chest and back, worn for protection in battle in former times

**cui·sine** /kwɪˈziːn/ *n* [U] *French* **1** a particular style of cooking: *French cuisine|vegetarian cuisine* **2** the food cooked in a particular restaurant or hotel, especially when it is very good: *Enjoy the delicious cuisine created by our award-winning chef.*

**cul-de-sac** /ˈkʌl də ˌsæk, ˈkʊl-‖ˌkʌl də ˈsæk, ˌkʊl-/ *n* [C] **1** a road which is closed at one end so that there is only one way in and out **2** an unhelpful situation in which you cannot make any more progress: *These ideas lead us into a philosophical cul-de-sac.*

**cul·i·na·ry** /ˈkʌlɪnəri‖ˈkʌlɪneri, ˈkjuːl-/ *adj* [only before noun] *formal* connected with cooking: *culinary herbs* | *culinary skills* | **culinary delights** (=food that tastes very good) *the region's culinary delights*

**cull**[1] /kʌl/ *v* **1** [T] *formal* to find or choose information from many different places: **cull sth from** *photographs culled from various sources* **2** [I,T] to kill the weakest animals in a group so that the size of the group does not increase too much **3** *literary* [T] to gather flowers or fruit

**cull**[2] *n* [C] the act of killing the weakest animals in a group so that the size of the group does not increase too much

C

**cul·len·der** /ˈkʌlɪndə‖-ər/ another spelling of COLANDER

**cul·mi·nate** /ˈkʌlmɪneɪt/

**culminate in sth** *phr v* [T] if a process culminates in something, it finally reaches the highest point of development or the most important result: *a series of minor clashes culminating in a full scale war*

**cul·mi·na·tion** /ˌkʌlmɪˈneɪʃən/ *n* [U] **the culmination of** the final or highest point that is reached after a long period of effort or development: *This little book represented the culmination of 15 years' work.*

**cu·lottes** /kjuːˈlɒts‖kjʊˈlɑːts/ *n* [plural] women's trousers which stop at the knee and are shaped to look like a skirt

**cul·pa·ble** /ˈkʌlpəbəl/ *adj* **1** *formal* deserving blame: *Both parties were held to be to some extent culpable.* **2** *technical* an action that is criminal: **culpable homicide/negligence etc** *He pleaded guilty to culpable homicide.* —**culpably** *adv* —**culpability** /ˌkʌlpəˈbɪlɪti/ *n* [U]

**cul·prit** /ˈkʌlprɪt/ *n* [C] **1** the person who is guilty of a crime, or responsible for damage, a problem etc: *Police finally managed to catch the culprit.* **2** *informal* the reason for a particular problem or difficulty: **the main culprit** *High production costs are the main culprit.*

**cult** /kʌlt/ *n* **1** [C] an extreme religious group that is not part of an established religion: *Anyone who betrayed the cult could be punished by death.* **2 cult film/figure/TV show etc** a film, music group etc that has become very popular but only among a particular group of people: *a cult band* | *James Dean acquired the status of a cult hero.* **3** [C] a fashionable belief, idea, or attitude that influences people's lives: *Diet, therapy, exercise... It's all part of this cult of self-improvement.* **4** [C,U] *formal* a system of religious beliefs and practices

**cul·ti·va·ble** /ˈkʌltɪvəbəl/ *adj* land which is cultivable can be used to grow crops

**cul·ti·vate** /ˈkʌltɪveɪt/ *v* **1** [T] to prepare and use land for growing crops and plants: *Some of the land would be impossible to cultivate.* **2** to develop a particular skill or quality in yourself: *The company have been successful in cultivating a very professional image.* **3** to make an effort to develop a friendly relationship with someone because you want something from them: *Professor Gladwyn would be an acquaintance worth cultivating.*

**cul·ti·vat·ed** /ˈkʌltɪveɪtɪd/ *adj* **1** someone who is cultivated is intelligent and knows a lot about music, art, literature etc: *It was a pleasure to talk to such a cultivated audience.* **2** land that is cultivated is used for growing crops or plants: *cultivated fields* **3** crops or plants that are cultivated are grown in order to be sold

**cul·ti·va·tion** /ˌkʌltɪˈveɪʃən/ *n* [U] **1** the preparation and use of land for growing crops: *different methods of soil cultivation* | **under cultivation** (=used for growing crops and plants) *These fields have been under cultivation for years.* **2** the planting and growing of plants and crops: *Terraces for rice cultivation covered the hillsides.* | [+ **of**] *the successful cultivation of tobacco* **3** the deliberate development of a particular quality or skill

**cul·ti·va·tor** /ˈkʌltɪveɪtə‖-ər/ *n* [C] **1** *formal* someone who grows crops or plants, especially a farmer **2** a tool or machine that is used to prepare land for growing crops

**cul·tu·ral** /ˈkʌltʃərəl/ *adj* **1** belonging to or connected with a particular society and its way of life: *a wide range of cultural influences* | **cultural heritage/traditions etc** (=ideas, customs etc that have existed in a particular society for a long time) **2** related to art, literature, music etc: **cultural activity** *They enjoy cultural activities like going to the theatre and the opera.* | **cultural centre** (=a place, usually a big city, where a lot of artistic and musical events happen) *Vienna is a real cultural centre for music lovers.* | **cultural desert** *informal* (=a place such as a small town where there are no cultural activities) W

**cul·tu·ral·ly** /ˈkʌltʃərəli/ *adv* **1** in a way that is related to the ideas, beliefs, or customs of a society: *culturally approved patterns of behaviour* **2** in a way that is related to art, music, literature etc: *The French are a culturally sophisticated people.* | [sentence adverb] *Culturally, the city has a lot to offer.*

**cul·ture** /ˈkʌltʃə‖-ər/ *n* S W

**1** ▶ **IN A SOCIETY** ◀ [C,U] the ideas, beliefs, and customs that are shared and accepted by people in a society: *Our culture teaches us to hide a lot of our true feelings.* | *black culture* | **Western/British/Japanese etc culture** *Western culture places a high value on material acquisition.*

**2 culture shock** the feelings of shock and anxiety that someone has when they visit a foreign country or a new place for the first time: *John found life in London a bit of a culture shock at first.*

**3** ▶ **IN A GROUP** ◀ [C,U] the attitudes and beliefs about something that are shared by a particular group of people or in a particular organization: *Working late hours for very little money seems part of the company culture.* | **drug/computer etc culture** *90's rave culture* | *youth culture* —see also SUBCULTURE

**4** ▶ **ART/MUSIC/LITERATURE ETC** ◀ [U] activities that are related to art, music, literature etc: *If it's culture you're looking for, the city has plenty of museums and art galleries.* | **popular culture** (=the music, books, films etc that are liked by most people in a society)

**5** ▶ **SOCIETY** ◀ [C] a society that existed at a particular time in history: *primitive cultures* | *the Ancient Greek and Roman cultures* —see also CIVILIZATION

**6** ▶ **CROPS** ◀ [U] *technical* the practice of growing crops: *strawberry culture*

**7** ▶ **SCIENCE** ◀ [C,U] the process of growing BACTERIA for scientific use, or the bacteria produced by this

**cul·tured** /ˈkʌltʃəd‖-ərd/ *adj* having had a good education so that you are interested in art, literature, music etc: *a well-read and cultured woman*

**cultured pearl** /ˌ.. ˈ./ *n* [C] a PEARL (1) that has been grown artificially

**cul·vert** /ˈkʌlvət‖-ərt/ *n* [C] a pipe that takes a stream under a road, railway line, etc

**cum** /kʊm, kʌm/ *prep* used between two nouns to show that something or someone has two purposes: *a kitchen-cum-dining room* | *a lunch-cum-business meeting*

**cum·ber·some** /ˈkʌmbəsəm‖-bər-/ *adj* **1** a process or system that is cumbersome is slow and difficult: *The technique was cumbersome and created problems with sound reproduction.* **2** heavy and difficult to move: *cumbersome equipment that slowed us down considerably* **3** words or phrases that are cumbersome are long or complicated

**cum·in** /ˈkʌmɪn/ *n* [U] the seeds of a plant that have a sweet smell and are used in cooking, or the plant that they grow on

**cum lau·de** /kʌm ˈlɔːdi, kʊm-, -ˈlaʊdeɪ‖kʊm ˈlaʊdi/ *adv* *AmE* if you GRADUATE[3] (1) cum laude, you finish a university degree in the US and are given official praise for special achievement

**cum·mer·bund** /ˈkʌməbʌnd‖-ər-/ *n* [C] a wide piece of cloth that a man wears around his waist as part of a suit worn to very formal occasions

**cum·quat, kumquat** /ˈkʌmkwɒt‖-kwɑːt/ *n* [C] a fruit that looks like a very small orange

**cu·mu·la·tive** /ˈkjuːmjələtɪv‖-leɪtɪv/ *adj* increasing gradually as more of something is added or happens: *Learning is a cumulative process.* | **cumulative effect (of)** *Depression is often caused by the cumulative effects of stress and over-work.*

**cu·mu·lus** /ˈkjuːmjələs/ *n* [C,U] a thick white cloud with a flat bottom edge

**cu·nei·form** /ˈkjuːnifɔːm, ˈkjuːni-əfɔːm‖kjuːˈniːəfɔːrm/ *adj* connected with the writing used by the people of ancient Mesopotamia —**cuneiform** *n* [U]

**cun·ni·lin·gus** /ˌkʌnɪˈlɪŋgəs/ *n* [U] the act of touching the female sex organs with the lips and tongue in order to give sexual pleasure —compare FELLATIO

**cun·ning¹** /ˈkʌnɪŋ/ *adj* **1** someone who is cunning is good at deceiving people in order to get what they want: *She can be very cunning when she wants to be.* **2** behaviour or actions that are cunning are dishonest and unfair, and are used to get what you want: *That was a cunning trick!* **3** a cunning object or piece of equipment is clever and unusual: *a cunning little device for keeping out draughts* **4** *AmE old-fashioned* attractive: *That's a cunning little dress you're wearing.* —**cunningly** *adv*: *There was a microphone cunningly placed behind the picture.*

**cunning²** *n* [U] the ability to achieve what you want by deceiving people in a clever way: *the tiger's ferocity and cunning* | **low cunning** (=unpleasant dishonest methods) *She would use low cunning in order to win people's sympathy.*

**cunt** /kʌnt/ *n* [C] *spoken taboo* **1** a stupid or unpleasant person: *Shut up, you stupid cunt!* **2** a woman's VAGINA (=sex organ)

**cups**

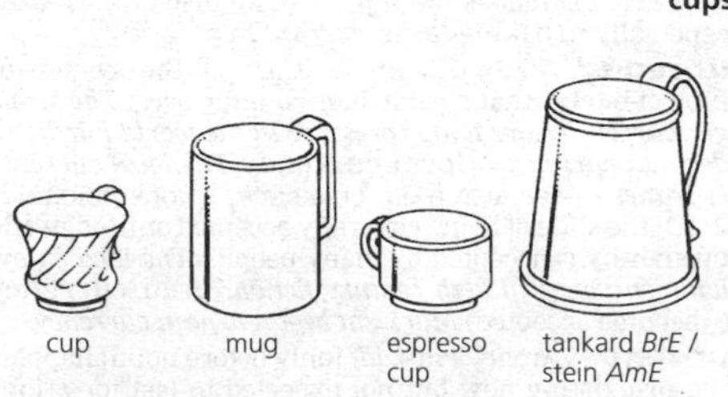


S1 W1 **cup¹** /kʌp/ *n*

**1** ▶ **FOR DRINKING FROM** ◀ [C] a small round container with a handle, that you use to drink tea, coffee etc: *a cup and saucer* | **tea cup/coffee cup** *a beautiful set of tea cups* —compare MUG¹ (1)

**2** ▶ **DRINK** ◀ [C] the liquid contained inside a cup: *Would you like another cup?* | [+ **of**] *a nice hot cup of coffee*

**3** ▶ **AMOUNT OF LIQUID** ◀ [C] **a)** also **cupful** the amount of liquid a cup can hold: *She came round to borrow a cupful of sugar.* **b)** *AmE* an exact measure of quantity used in cooking in the US, Canada, and New Zealand: *Stir half a cup of sugar and one cup of flour into the batter.*

**4** ▶ **ROUND THING** ◀ [C] something round and hollow that is shaped like a cup: *acorn cups* | [+ **of**] *the cup of a flower* | *She held it in the cup of her hand.*

**5** ▶ **SPORT** ◀ **a)** [C] a specially shaped silver container that is given as a prize in a competition, especially a sports competition: *The president of the club came to present the cup to the winners.* **b)** [singular] *especially BrE* a sports competition: *She's been picked to play in the Wightman Cup.* **c)** *AmE* a hole in the ground that you have to try to get the ball into in the game of GOLF —see picture on page 1264

**6** ▶ **CLOTHING** ◀ [C] the part of a BRA that covers a woman's breast

**7** ▶ **MIXED DRINK** ◀ *BrE* [C,U] a mixed alcoholic drink: *cider cup* | *a glass of champagne-cup*

**8 not be your cup of tea** *spoken* to not be the sort of thing that you like: *Jazz just isn't my cup of tea – I prefer classical music.*

**9 in your cups** *BrE old-fashioned* drunk, or when drunk: *He sometimes attempted to speak French, in his cups.* —see also EGGCUP, LOVING CUP

**cup²** *v* **cupped, cupping** [T] **1** to hold something in your hands, so that your hands form part of a circle around it: *Phil cupped her face in his hands and kissed her.* **2 cup your hand(s)** to make a shape like a cup with your hand or hands: *He cupped his hands and I poured some water into them.*

C

**cup·bear·er** /ˈ· ˌ··/ *n* [C] someone in a royal court who serves wine on official occasions

**cup·board** /ˈkʌbəd‖-ərd/ *n* [C] a piece of furniture with doors, and sometimes shelves, used for storing clothes, plates, food etc: *It's in the kitchen cupboard.* | *The cupboard doors were open.* —see also AIRING CUPBOARD, **skeleton in the cupboard** (SKELETON (4)) —see picture on page 833 S2

**cup·cake** /ˈkʌpkeɪk/ *n* [C] a small round cake

**cup fi·nal** /ˈ· ˌ··/ *n* [C] *BrE* the last and most important game in a competition, especially a football competition

**cup·ful** /ˈkʌpfʊl/ *n* [C] the amount that a cup can hold —see CUP¹ (3)

**cu·pid** /ˈkjuːpɪd/ *n* **1** the Roman god of sexual love, represented as a beautiful boy with wings who is carrying a BOW³ (1) and ARROW (1): *a sentimental picture with cupids around the edge* **2 play cupid** to try to arrange for two people to fall in love with each other: *She vowed never to play cupid again.*

**cu·pid·i·ty** /kjʊˈpɪdɪti/ *n* [U] *formal* very strong desire for something, especially money or property; GREED (2): *We were astounded by the young man's cupidity.*

**cu·po·la** /ˈkjuːpələ/ *n* [C] a small round part on top of a building: *a golden edifice with an onion-shaped cupola*

**cup·pa** /ˈkʌpə/ *n* [C] *BrE spoken* a cup of tea: *I'm dying for a cuppa!*

**cu·pric** /ˈkjuːprɪk/ *adj technical* containing COPPER (1)

**cup tie** /ˈ· ·/ *n* [C] *BrE* a game between two teams in a competition in which only the winning team will play any more games: *Saturday's FA Cup tie against Spurs*

**cur** /kɜː‖kɜːr/ *n* [C] **1** *old-fashioned* an unfriendly dog, especially a MONGREL **2** *old use* an unpleasant person

**cu·ra·ble** /ˈkjʊərəbəl‖ˈkjʊr-/ *adj* an illness that is curable can be cured —opposite INCURABLE (1)

**cu·ra·çao** /ˈkjʊərəsəʊ, ˌkjʊərəˈsəʊ‖ˈkjʊrəsoʊ, ˌkjʊrəˈsoʊ/ *n* [U] a strong thick alcoholic drink that tastes of oranges

**cu·ra·cy** /ˈkjʊərəsi‖ˈkjʊr-/ *n* [C] the job or position of curate or the period of time that someone has this position: *My first curacy was in St Luke's.*

**cu·rate** /ˈkjʊərɪt‖ˈkjʊr-/ *n* [C] **1** a priest of the lowest rank, whose job is to help the priest who is in charge of an area **2 curate's egg** something that has good and bad parts: *The book is something of a curate's egg.*

**cu·ra·tive** /ˈkjʊərətɪv‖ˈkjʊr-/ *adj* able to, or intended to cure illness: *the curative effects of lemon juice on scurvy victims* —**curative** *n* [C] | *This herb was once thought to be a curative.*

**cu·ra·tor** /kjʊˈreɪtə‖-ər/ *n* [C] someone who is in charge of a MUSEUM: *He's Curator of Prints at the Metropolitan.*

**curb¹** /kɜːb‖kɜːrb/ *v* [T] to control or limit something in order to prevent it from having a harmful effect: *measures to curb the spread of the virus*

**curb²** *n* [C] **1** an influence which helps to control or limit something: [+ **on**] *We are trying to keep a curb on their activities.* **2** *AmE* the edge of the part of a road where people can walk; KERB *BrE*

**curb crawler** /ˈ· ˌ··/ *n* [C] the American spelling of KERB CRAWLER

**curd** /kɜːd‖kɜːrd/ *n* [U] also **curds** *plural* the thick substance that forms in milk when it becomes sour

**cur·dle** /ˈkɜːdl‖ˈkɜːrdl/ *v* [I,T] **1** to become thicker or form curd, or to make a liquid do this: *Milk may curdle in warm weather.* **2 make your blood curdle** to make you very frightened —see also BLOODCURDLING

**cu·r·é** /ˈkjʊəreɪ‖kjʊˈreɪ/ *n* [C] a PARISH (1) priest in France

**cure¹** /kjʊə‖kjʊr/ *v* [T] **1** to make someone who is ill well again: *The doctors did everything they could to cure her, but she died three months later.* | *When I left hospital I was completely cured.* **2** to make an illness disappear completely, usually by medical treatment: *an operation to cure a hernia problem* **3** to remove a problem, or improve a bad situation: *Attempts to cure unemployment have so far failed.* | **cure sb of** *Even whisky could not cure him of his anxieties.* **4** to preserve food, tobacco etc by drying it, hanging it in smoke, or covering it with salt: *cured ham* —see also REST CURE

**cure²** *n* [C] **1** a medicine or medical treatment that can cure an illness: [+ **for**] *a cure for cancer* **2** something that removes a problem, or improves a bad situation: *a cure for inflation* **3** the act of making someone well again after an illness: *The new treatment effected a miraculous cure.* **4 take the cure** the practice in former times of going to a SPA (1) in order to improve your health

**cure-all** /ˈ· ·/ *n* [C] something that people think will cure any problem: *Privatisation is seen as a cure-all.*

**cu·ret·tage** /kjʊəˈretɪdʒ‖ˌkjʊrəˈtɑːʒ/ *n* [U] *technical* medical treatment to remove unhealthy flesh or skin

**cur·few** /ˈkɜːfjuː‖ˈkɜːr-/ *n* **1** [C] a law forcing everyone to stay indoors from a particular time in the evening until a particular time in the morning: *The military regime decided to impose a curfew.* **2** [singular, not with *the*] the time after which everyone must stay indoors, according to this law: *Anyone found in the streets after curfew will be shot.*

**cu·ri·o** /ˈkjʊəriəʊ‖ˈkjʊrioʊ/ *n plural* **curios** [C] a small object that is valuable because it is old, beautiful, or rare: *Sue came across a shop selling curios and antiques.*

**cu·ri·os·i·ty** /ˌkjʊəriˈɒsɪ̣ti‖ˌkjʊriˈɑːs-/ *n* **1** [singular, U] the desire to know about something, or to know about a lot of different things: [+ **about**] *Children have a natural curiosity about the world around them.* | **out of curiosity** *Just out of curiosity, how old are you?* | **burning/bursting with curiosity** (=having an extremely strong desire to know something) | **idle curiosity** (=the desire to know something that you do not need to know) *It's not just idle curiosity.* | **satisfy your curiosity** (=find out what you want to know) *I just had to satisfy my curiosity, so I opened the parcel.* **2** [C] something that is interesting because it is unusual or strange: *His house was full of old maps and other curiosities.* **3 curiosity killed the cat** an expression used to tell someone not to ask questions about something that does not concern them

S3 **cu·ri·ous** /ˈkjʊəriəs‖ˈkjʊr-/ *adj* **1** wanting to know about something: *When I mentioned her name everyone was very curious.* | [+ **about**] *I'm curious about this book she's supposed to be writing.* | **curious to see/hear/know etc** *Mandy was curious to hear what Peter had to say for himself.* —opposite INCURIOUS **2** strange or unusual: *a curious noise coming from the cellar* | **curious that** *It's very curious that she left without saying goodbye.* —**curiously** *adv* | *She watched curiously as I opened the box.*

**curl¹** /kɜːl‖kɜːrl/ *n* **1** [C] a small mass of hair that hangs in a curving shape: *a little boy with beautiful blonde curls* **2** [C] something that forms a curved shape: *A curl of smoke rose from her cigarette.* **3 a curl of your lip/mouth** a sideways and upwards movement of your lip or mouth, showing that you disapprove of someone or something

**curl²** *v* [I,T] **1** to form a twisted or curved shape or to make something do this: *Ivy curled round the trunk of the tree.* | **curl sth** *Maria used to curl her hair each week.* **2** [I always + adv/prep T, always + adv/prep] to move, forming a twisted or curved shape, or to make something do this: [+ **across/along etc**] *Morning mists curled across the surface of the river.* | **curl sth around/round/over etc** *The baby curled his fingers around my thumb.* **3** if you curl your lip, or if your lip curls, you move it upwards and sideways, to show that you disapprove of someone or something: *Her lip curled in contempt.* **4 make your hair curl** *spoken* if a story, experience etc would make your hair curl it is very surprising, frightening, or shocking: *The stories they tell about him would make your hair curl.* —see also **make sb's toes curl** (TOE¹ (5))

**curl up** *phr v* [I] **1** to lie or sit with your arms and legs bent close to your body: *I just wanted to curl up and go to sleep.* **2** if something flat curls up, its edges start to become curved and point upwards: *The letter was now yellow and beginning to curl up.* **3** to move upwards in the form of a curl or curls: *Wisps of smoke were already curling up from the fireplace.*

**curl·er** /ˈkɜːlə‖ˈkɜːrlər/ *n* [C] *usually plural* a small plastic or metal tube used for making hair curl: *Edith came to the door with her hair in curlers.*

**cur·lew** /ˈkɜːljuː‖ˈkɜːrluː/ *n* [C] a brown and grey bird with long legs and a curved beak, that lives near water or damp areas of land

**cur·li·cue, curlycue** /ˈkɜːlɪkjuː‖ˈkɜːr-/ *n* [C] a decorative twisted pattern

**curl·ing** /ˈkɜːlɪŋ‖ˈkɜːr-/ *n* [U] a winter sport played on ice by sliding flat heavy stones towards a marked point

**curling tongs** /ˈ·· ·/ *BrE* also **curling i·rons** /ˈ·· ˌ··/ *especially AmE n* [plural] a piece of electrical equipment that you heat and use to put curls in your hair

**curl·y** /ˈkɜːli‖ˈkɜːrli/ *adj* having a lot of curls: *long dark curly hair* —**curliness** *n* [U] S

**cur·mud·geon** /kɜːˈmʌdʒən‖kɜːr-/ *n* [C] *old-fashioned* an old person who is often angry or annoyed —**curmudgeonly** *adj*

**cur·rant** /ˈkʌrənt‖ˈkɜːr-/ *n* [C] a small dried GRAPE used especially in baking cakes: *currant bun*

**cur·ren·cy** /ˈkʌrənsi‖ˈkɜːr-/ *n* [C,U] **1** the system or type of money that a particular country uses: *The stronger currencies are under pressure in the world markets.* | *decimal currencies* | **local currency** *The local currency is francs.* —see also HARD CURRENCY, SINGLE CURRENCY **2** [U] the state of being generally accepted or used: **wide currency** (=accepted by many people) *The idea enjoys wide currency in 20th century fiction.* | **gain currency** (=become accepted) *Marxism began to gain currency.* W

**cur·rent¹** /ˈkʌrənt‖ˈkɜːr-/ *adj* [only before noun] happening or existing now but not expected to last for a long time: *her current boyfriend* —**currently** *adv*: *Sir Ranulph is currently occupied writing a book about his Antarctic expedition.* S W

**current²** *n* [C] **1** a continuous movement of water in a particular direction in the sea or in a river: *The current was very strong.* **2** a flow of electricity through a wire

**current ac·count** /ˈ·· ·ˌ·/ *n* [C] *BrE* a bank account that you can take money out of at any time; CHECKING ACCOUNT *AmE* —compare DEPOSIT ACCOUNT

**current af·fairs** /ˌ·· ·ˈ·/ *n* [U] important political events or other events in society that are happening now

**currently** /ˈkʌrəntli‖ˈkɜːrəntli/ *adv* at the present time: *Two major changes are currently being considered.* | *They need more help than is currently available.* —see PRESENTLY (USAGE), ACTUALLY (USAGE) S W

**cur·ric·u·lum** /kəˈrɪkjʊ̣ləm/ *n plural* **curricula** /-lə/ or **curriculums** [C] the subjects that are taught by a school, college etc, or the things that are studied in a particular subject: *Has computer studies been introduced into the school curriculum?* —compare SYLLABUS W

**curriculum vi·tae** /kəˌrɪkjʊ̣ləm ˈviːtaɪ/ *n* [C] **1** *BrE* a CV; RESUMÉ² (2) *AmE* **2** *AmE* a document on which a university teacher writes a list of their teaching experience and articles, books etc they have written when they are applying for a job

**cur·ry¹** /ˈkʌri‖ˈkɜːri/ *n* [C,U] a type of food from India consisting of meat or vegetables covered in a thick liquid with a hot taste

**curry²** *v* [T] **1** to make meat or vegetables into curry **2 curry favour with** to try to make someone like you or notice you in order to get something that you want: *currying favour with the teachers*

**curry pow·der** /ˈ·· ˌ··/ *n* [U] a mixture of SPICES (=dried vegetable parts with a hot taste) crushed into a fine powder, used in cooking

**curse¹** /kɜːs‖kɜːrs/ *v* **1** [I] to swear: *You should have heard him cursing when he tripped over the cat.* **2** [T] to say or think bad things about someone or something because they have made you angry: **curse sb/sth for (doing) sth** *I cursed myself for not buying a phrase book.* **3** [T] to ask God or a magical power to harm someone: *The man had been cursed by a witch doctor and was in despair.*

**curse²** *n* [C] **1** a word or words that you use when you swear or when you express anger etc: *The convict screamed out curses at them.* **2** a word or sentence used to ask God or a magical power to make something happen to someone or something: **put a curse on** *The witch doctor put a curse on him.* **3** something that causes trouble, harm etc: [+ **to**] *Foxes can be a curse to farmers.* **4 the curse** *old-fashioned* an expression meaning MENSTRUATION

**curs·ed** /ˈkɜːsɪ̆d‖ˈkɜːr-/ *adj* **1 be cursed with** to suffer because of a problem that you have: *She had always been cursed with ill-health.* **2** [only before noun] *old-fashioned* unpleasant or annoying: *I'm sick to death of being stuck in this cursed place.* **3** *literary* suffering as a result of a punishment by God or a god —**cursedly** *adv*

**cur·sive** /ˈkɜːsɪv‖ˈkɜːr-/ *adj* written in a flowing rounded style of writing with the letters joined together: *cursive script* —**cursively** *adv*

**cur·sor** /ˈkɜːsə‖ˈkɜːrsər/ *n* [C] a mark or a small light which can be moved around a computer screen to show where you are working

**cur·so·ry** /ˈkɜːsəri‖ˈkɜːr-/ *adj* quick and done without enough attention to details: *After only a cursory glance he tore up the note.* —**cursorily** *adv*

**curt** /kɜːt‖kɜːrt/ *adj* replying with very few words in a way that does not seem polite: *With a curt nod, he turned away and sat down.* —**curtly** *adv* —**curtness** *n* [U]

**cur·tail** /kɜːˈteɪl‖kɜːr-/ *v* [T] *formal* to reduce something such as the amount of money you spend: *The Government wants private firms to curtail wage rises.* | *Our evening's enjoyment was curtailed when Alfred became ill.* —**curtailment** *n* [C,U]

S2 W3 **cur·tain** /ˈkɜːtn‖ˈkɜːrtn/ *n* [C] **1** a piece of hanging cloth that can be pulled across to cover a window, door etc to divide a room etc: **draw the curtains** (=close the curtains) **2** a sheet of heavy material that can be made to come down across the front of the stage in a theatre —see picture at THEATRE **3** a thick layer of something that stops anything behind it from being seen: *a thick curtain of smoke* | *a curtain of trailing branches* **4 the curtain falls on** *literary* if the curtain falls on an event or period of history, it ends **5 it'll be curtains for sb/sth** *informal* used to say that someone will die, or that something will end: *It'll be curtains for you if they find you here!*

**curtain call** /ˈ·· ·/ *n* [C] the time at the end of a performance when the actors come out to receive APPLAUSE

**curtain hook** /ˈ·· ·/ *n* [C] a small hook which is joined to the top of a curtain so that you can hang it up

**curtain rail** /ˈ·· ·/ *n* [C] a long piece of plastic or metal that you hang a curtain on

**curtain rais·er** /ˈ·· ˌ··/ *n* [C] **1** a short play, film etc that is performed or shown before the main one **2** a small thing that happens or is done just before something more important: *a curtain raiser for the main programme of research*

**curt·sy, curtsey** /ˈkɜːtsi‖ˈkɜːr-/ *n* [C] a sign of respect that a woman makes to a more important person by bending her knees with one foot behind the other —**curtsy** *v* [I] —compare BOW² (1)

**cur·va·ceous, curvacious** /kɜːˈveɪʃəs‖kɜːr-/ *adj* having an attractively curved body shape: *curvacious female models* —**curvaceousness** *n* [U]

**cur·va·ture** /ˈkɜːvətʃə‖ˈkɜːrvətʃər/ *n* [C,U] *technical* **1** the state of being curved, or the degree to which something is curved: *the curvature of the Earth's surface* **2** a medical condition in which part of someone's body curves in a way that is not natural: *curvature of the spine*

**curve¹** /kɜːv‖kɜːrv/ *n* [C] **1** a line which gradually bends like part of a circle: *a curve on a graph* | *the curve of her hips* **2** a rounded bend in a road, river etc: *The car took the curve much too quickly.* **3 curve ball** a throw in BASEBALL in which the ball spins so that it curves suddenly and is difficult to hit **4** *AmE* **throw sb a curve** to surprise someone with a question or problem that is difficult to deal with: *They threw us a curve and asked us about Longfellow when we were ready for a question on Thoreau.* S3 W3

**curve²** *v* [I,T] to bend or move in the shape of a curve, or to make something do this: *The track curved into the woods.*

**curved** /kɜːvd‖kɜːrvd/ *adj* having a shape that is rounded and not straight: *a sword with a curved blade*

**curv·y** /ˈkɜːvi‖ˈkɜːrvi/ *adj* having a shape with several curves: *her curvy red lips* | *Eileen has a curvy figure.*

**cush·ion¹** /ˈkʊʃən/ *n* [C] **1** a cloth bag filled with soft material that you put on a chair to make it more comfortable —compare PILLOW¹ (1) **2** something that stops one thing from hitting another thing: *The hovercraft rides on a cushion of air.* **3** something, especially money, that prevents you from being affected by a situation immediately: *I have some savings – hopefully they'll act as a cushion while I'm looking for a job.* **4** the soft rubber edge of the table that is used for playing BILLIARDS or SNOOKER¹ S3

**cushion²** *v* [T] **1** to make a fall or knock less painful, for example by having something soft in the way: *They had put mattresses on the ground to cushion his fall.* **2** to reduce the effects of something unpleasant: **cushion the blow** *generous leaving allowances to help cushion the blow of redundancy* | **be cushioned against** (=be protected from something unpleasant) *The rich are cushioned against the effects of the recession.*

**cush·y** /ˈkʊʃi/ *adj* **cushier, cushiest** *informal* very easy: *I wish I had a nice cushy job like her.* | **a cushy number** *BrE* (=an easy job)

**cusp** /kʌsp/ *n* [C] **1** *technical* the point formed by two curves meeting **2 on the cusp** someone who was born on the cusp was born near the time when one STAR SIGN ends and another one begins

**cus·pi·dor** /ˈkʌspɪ̆dɔː‖-ɔːr/ *n* [C] *AmE* a container for people to SPIT¹ (1,2) in; SPITTOON

**cuss¹** /kʌs/ *v* [I,T] *AmE informal, BrE old-fashioned* to use rude words because you are annoyed by something: *It does a fella good to cuss if he wants to.*

**cuss** sb **out** *phr v* [T] *AmE spoken* to swear and shout at someone because you are angry: *My Mom cussed me out for breaking the lamp.*

**cuss²** *n* [C] *AmE old-fashioned* **stubborn/stupid/ornery etc cuss** a very annoying person

**cuss·ed** /ˈkʌsɪ̆d/ *adj* behaving in a deliberately unhelpful way —**cussedness** *n* [U]

**cuss word** /ˈ· ·/ *n* [C] *AmE* a SWEAR WORD

**cus·tard** /ˈkʌstəd‖-ərd/ *n* **1** [U] *especially BrE* a yellow liquid that is eaten with sweet dishes, made with milk, sugar, eggs, and flour **2** [C,U] a soft baked mixture of milk, sugar, and eggs

**custard pie** /ˌ·· ˈ·/ *n* [C] a PIE filled with custard, which people throw at each other as a joke in films etc

**cus·to·di·al** /kʌˈstəʊdiəl‖-ˈstoʊ-/ *adj formal* connected with the custody of someone: *custodial care*

**custodial sen·tence** /ˌ···· ˈ··/ *n* [C] *law* a period of time that someone has to spend in prison as a punishment

**cus·to·di·an** /kʌˈstəʊdiən‖-ˈstoʊ-/ *n* [C] **1** someone who is responsible for looking after a public building or a collection of valuable objects **2 custodian of tradition/moral values etc** someone who tries to protect a traditional set of beliefs, attitudes etc

**cus·to·dy** /ˈkʌstədi/ *n* [U] **1** the right to take care of a child, especially when the child's parents are legally separating from each other: [+ **of**] *In most divorce cases the mother is awarded custody of the children.* | **have custody** *a dispute over who should have custody* **2 in custody** being kept in prison by the police until you go to court, because the police think you are guilty: **hold/keep sb in custody** *A man is being held in police custody in connection with the murder.* | **take sb into custody** (=catch someone and keep them in custody) **3 in sb's custody** *formal* being kept and looked after by someone: *The silver seal was placed in the custody of the mayor.*

W3 **cus·tom** /ˈkʌstəm/ *n* **1** [C,U] something that is done by people in a particular society because it is traditional: **local/tribal/ancient/Swedish etc custom** *"Why the pile of salt?" "It's an old Japanese custom."* | **it is the custom (for sb) to do sth** *It's the custom for the bride's father to pay for the wedding.* | **the custom of doing sth** *the old French custom of serving the vegetables separate from the meat* | **by custom/according to the custom** *By custom we had to stop and speak to every person we met.* **2** [singular] *especially literary* something that you usually do every day, or in a particular situation: *He awoke early, as was his custom.* —see HABIT (USAGE) **3** [U] *formal* the practice of regularly using a particular shop or business **4 customs** [plural] the place where your bag is checked for illegal drugs, guns etc when you go into a country: *She was stopped at customs and questioned.* | **clear customs** (=be allowed through customs after being checked)

**cus·tom·a·ry** /ˈkʌstəməri‖-meri/ *adj* **1** something that is customary is normal because it is the way something is usually done: **it is customary (for sb) to do sth** *It is customary for the most important person to sit at the end of the table.* **2** someone's customary behaviour is the way they usually do things: *Barbara answered with her customary frankness.* —**customarily** /ˈkʌstəmərəli‖ˌkʌstəˈmerəli/ *adv*

**custom-built** /ˌ.. ˈ.◂/ *adj* a custom-built car, house etc has been specially designed and made for a particular person

S1 W1 **cus·tom·er** /ˈkʌstəmə‖-ər/ *n* [C] **1** someone who buys goods or services from a shop, company etc: *Next customer please!* | *the customer complaints department* | **regular customer** *keeping the shop's regular customers happy* | **sb's biggest/best customer** (=someone who buys the most goods or services) *We don't want to lose them – they're one of our biggest customers.* —compare PATRON (2) —see picture on page 838 **2 a cool customer** *informal* someone who is always calm and very confident but in an unpleasant way **3 awkward/tricky etc customer** someone who is difficult to deal with because they behave in a deliberately unhelpful way

**cus·tom·ize** also **-ise** *BrE* /ˈkʌstəmaɪz/ *v* [T] to change something to make it more suitable for you, or to make it look special or unusual: *The program allows computer users to customize the menu.* | *a customized car*

**custom-made** /ˌ.. ˈ.◂/ *adj* a custom-made pair of shoes, shirt etc is specially made for a particular person

**Customs and Ex·cise** /ˌ.. . ˈ../ *n* [singular] the department of the British government that is responsible for collecting the tax on goods that are being bought or sold or have been brought into the country

S1 W1 **cut¹** /kʌt/ *v past tense and past participle* **cut** *present participle* **cutting**

**1** ▶ **DIVIDE WITH KNIFE ETC** ◀ [T] to divide something into two or more pieces using a sharp tool such as a knife: *Do you want me to cut the cake?* | *The thieves had cut the phone wires.* | **cut sth in half/in two** *cut the orange in half* | **cut sth into quarters/pieces/four** *Cut each one into about 6 pieces.*

**2** ▶ **REMOVE A PIECE OF** ◀ [T] to use a knife to remove a piece from the main part of something: **cut sth** *I cut another slice of bread.* | **cut sb sth** *Cut me a big slice of that lemon cake, will you?*

**3** ▶ **MAKE A SHAPE** ◀ [T] to make something into a particular shape by using a sharp tool such as a knife: **cut sth into chunks/rings etc** *Cut the carrots into small cubes.*

**4** ▶ **MAKE A HOLE** ◀ [I,T] to make a hole in the surface of something, or to open it by using a sharp tool such as a knife: [+ **into/through etc**] *a knife that will cut through glass* | **cut a hole in sth** *Firefighters had to cut a hole in the car roof.* | **cut sth open** *Ben cut the sack open in a great hurry to see what was inside.*

**5** ▶ **GRASS/HAIR ETC** ◀ [T] to make something shorter with a knife, scissors etc in order to improve its appearance: **cut the lawn/the grass/the hedge** *I think I'll cut the grass this afternoon if it doesn't rain.* | **have/get your hair cut** (=pay someone to cut your hair) *Where do you have your hair cut?*

**6 cut sb free/loose** to allow someone to escape by using a knife to cut the rope that they are tied by

**7** ▶ **CROPS** ◀ [T] to take the top part off crops such as wheat before gathering them: *cutting corn*

**8** ▶ **WOUND** ◀ [T] to injure yourself when a sharp object or surface breaks open your skin so that you start bleeding: **cut your finger/knee/hand etc** *Be careful not to cut your fingers with that knife – it's very sharp.* | **cut yourself (on sth)** *I cut myself quite badly on a piece of glass.* | **cut sth open** (=injure part of your body by cutting it on something) *He fell and cut his head open.*

**9** ▶ **REDUCE PRICES/TIME/MONEY ETC** ◀ [T] to reduce something a lot, especially prices, time, or money: *A secure home will cut the risk of burglary.* | **cut sth by a quarter/25% etc** *Marston's is to cut its workforce by 20%.* | **cut sth off/from/to etc** *The new direct service will cut 2 hours off the flying time between London and Seoul.*

**10** ▶ **FILM/SPEECH** ◀ [T] **a)** to reduce the length of a film, speech etc: *The original version was cut by more than 30 minutes.* **b)** to remove part of a film, speech, or piece of writing, for example because it might offend people **c)** to put the parts of a film together so that they make a continuous story and get rid of the parts you do not want **d) Cut!** *spoken* said by the director of a film to tell everyone to stop acting, stop filming etc

**11** ▶ **DIVIDE AN AREA** ◀ [T] to divide an area into two or more parts: **cut sth in/into** *The river cuts the valley in two.*

**12** ▶ **PLAYING CARDS** ◀ [I,T] to divide a pack of cards into two

**13** ▶ **MUSIC/RECORD** ◀ [T] if a musician cuts a record, they make a record of their music

**14** ▶ **LINE** ◀ [T] if a line cuts another line, they cross each other at a particular point

**15** ▶ **TOOTH** ◀ if a baby cuts a tooth, the tooth starts to grow

**16 cut your teeth on sth** to get your first experience of doing something by practising on something simple

**17 cut in line** *AmE* to unfairly go in front of other people who are waiting to buy or do something; **jump the queue** *BrE* JUMP¹ (17)

**18 cut class** *AmE informal* to deliberately not go to a class that you should go to: *I cut class to go hang out in the bar.*

**19 cut corners** to do something in a way that is not perfect, in order to save time, effort, or money

**20 cut sth short** to stop doing something earlier than was planned: *She had to cut short her vacation when she heard that her mother was ill.*

**21 cut sb short** to stop someone from finishing what they wanted to say: *I tried to explain, but he cut me short.*

**22 cut the crap** *spoken* an impolite way of telling someone to deal only with the most important things without wasting time on unimportant details: *I wish they'd cut the crap and get on with this meeting!*

**23 cut sb dead** to deliberately ignore someone when you meet them: *I saw Ian in town but he just cut me dead!*
**24 cut sb to the quick** to upset someone very much by saying something cruel
**25 cut the ground from under sb's feet** to make someone or their ideas seem less impressive by having better ideas yourself, doing something before they do etc
**26 cut your own throat** to behave in a way that will harm you, especially because you are proud or angry: *He'd just be cutting his own throat if he left now.*
**27 cut a fine figure/cut an odd figure etc** *literary* to have an impressive, strange, etc appearance: *Steve cut an odd figure in his cloak and Spanish riding hat.*
**28 it cuts both ways** *informal* used to say that something has advantages but also disadvantages
**29 cut the cord** to stop depending on someone, especially your parents
**30 cut and run** *informal* to leave a situation suddenly when it becomes too difficult, especially when you should have stayed: *Don't worry. He won't cut and run.*
**31 cut your losses** to stop trying to do something that is already failing in order to prevent the situation becoming even worse
**32 not cut the mustard** *AmE informal* to not be good enough: *Lawrence tries really hard but his work just doesn't cut the mustard.*
**33 ▶ ILLEGAL DRUG ◀** [T usually passive] to mix an illegal drug such as HEROIN with some other substance
**34 cut your coat according to your cloth** to spend only as much money as you can afford
**35 cut no ice/not cut much ice** if something cuts no ice with someone, it will not persuade them to change their mind: *I don't expect anything I say will cut much ice with him.* —see also **cut a long story short** (STORY (12)), **cut a swathe through** (SWATHE[1] (4)), **cut it fine** (FINE[3] (5))

**cut across** *phr v* [T] **1** to go across an area of land instead of going around it, in order to save time: *Come on, if we cut across the field we'll get there before Frank.* **2** if a problem or feeling cuts across different groups of people, they are all affected by it: *The drug problem cuts across all social classes.*

**cut** sth ↔ **away** *phr v* [T] to remove the unwanted or unnecessary parts from something: *Cut away all the dead wood.*

**cut back** *phr v* **1** [I, T **cut back** sth] to reduce the numbers of something, or the time or money that is spent on something, especially because you do not have enough money: *Defence spending is to be cut back.* | [+ **on**] *Many schools are cutting back on staff at the moment.* **2** [T **cut** sth ↔ **back**] to remove the top part of a plant in order to help it to grow: *I must cut that holly bush back a bit.* —see also CUTBACK

**cut down** *phr v*
**1 ▶ REDUCE ◀** [I,T] to reduce the amount of something that you eat, buy, use etc: *You smoke too much – you should try to cut down.* | **cut sth ↔ down** *The coal industry was cut down to half its former size.* | [+ **on**] *My doctor's told me to cut down on carbohydrates.*
**2 ▶ TREE ◀** [T **cut** sth ↔ **down**] to cut through the TRUNK of a tree so that it falls on the ground
**3 ▶ KILL/INJURE ◀** *literary* [T **cut** sb ↔ **down**] to kill or injure someone with a sword or gun: *Our men were cut down by a hail of machine-gun fire.*
**4 ▶ MAKE SHORTER ◀** [T **cut** sth ↔ **down**] to reduce the length of something such as a piece of writing: *The essay's too long – it needs cutting down a little.*
**5 cut sb down to size** to make someone realize that they are not as important, successful etc as they think they are

**cut in** *phr v* **1** [I] to interrupt someone who is speaking by saying something: [+ **on**] *I wish Marie would stop cutting in on our conversation all the time.* **2** [I] to suddenly drive into the space between two moving cars in a dangerous way: *This idiot cut in right in front of me.* **3** [I] if a part of a machine cuts in, it starts to operate when it is needed: *The safety device cuts in automatically when needed.* **4 cut sb in on** *informal* to allow someone to take part in a secret plan to make money: *Come on, Joey, you said you were going to cut me in on this one!*

**cut off** *phr v*
**1 ▶ PIECE OF STH ◀** [T **cut** sth ↔ **off**] to separate something by cutting it from the main part: *She cut off a big piece of meat.* | *One of his fingers was cut off in the accident.*
**2 ▶ STOP THE SUPPLY ◀** [T **cut** sth ↔ **off**] to stop the supply of something such as electricity, gas, water etc: *The electricity company are threatening to cut us off.* | *The US has cut off aid to Cambodia.*
**3 get cut off** to suddenly not be able to hear someone that you were speaking to on the telephone: *I don't know what happened – we just got cut off.*

**4 ▶ PLACE/PEOPLE ◀** [T **cut** sb/sth ↔ **off**] to surround a place so that the people there are completely separated from other places or people: *In winter the town is often cut off by snow.* | *They were cut off by the Russian army and forced to surrender.*
**5 ▶ STOP BEING FRIENDLY ◀** [T **cut** sb **off**] to stop having a friendly relationship with someone: *Julia had been completely cut off by all her family and friends.* | **cut yourself off (from)** (=avoid people) *After his wife died he cut himself off completely from the rest of the world.*
**6 ▶ MONEY/PROPERTY ◀** [T **cut** sb ↔ **off**] to take away someone's right to receive your money or property, especially when you die: **cut sb off without a penny** *My parents have threatened to cut me off without a penny if I marry him.*
**7 ▶ STOP SB TALKING ◀** [T **cut** sb **off**] to prevent someone from finishing what they are saying: *She cut me off in mid sentence.*
**8 be cut off a)** if a place is cut off, it is difficult to get to and is a long way from any other place: *The village is so cut off from civilization that it receives almost no visitors.* **b)** if someone is cut off they are lonely because they are not able to meet people: [+ **from**] *Mothers with very young children often feel cut off from the rest of the community.*
**9 cut off your nose to spite your face** to do something because you are angry even though it will harm you

cut out

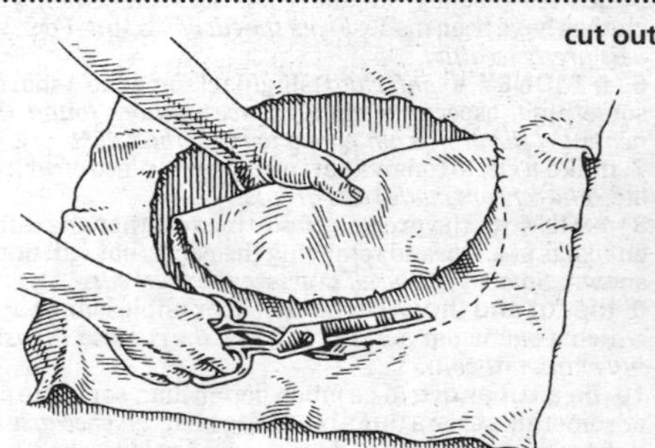

**cut out** *phr v*
**1 ▶ REMOVE STH ◀** [T **cut** sth ↔ **out**] to remove something by cutting: *I cut the advertisement out of the newspaper.* | *The surgeon cut out the tumour.*
**2 ▶ MAKE STH INTO A SHAPE ◀** [T **cut** sth ↔ **out**] to cut a piece of paper, cloth etc so that it becomes a particular shape: *The children were cutting out squares from the scraps of material.*
**3 ▶ PIECE OF WRITING/NEWS REPORT ETC ◀** [T **cut** sth ↔ **out**] to take out part of a piece of writing, a news report etc, especially because it might offend people
**4 ▶ STOP DOING STH ◀** [T **cut** sth ↔ **out**] to stop doing or eating something, especially because it is harmful to you: *If you cut out the drink you'd feel much healthier.*
**5 cut it/that out** *spoken* used to tell someone to stop doing something because it is annoying you: *Hey, you guys, cut it out – Mom's trying to get some sleep.*
**6 ▶ STOP SB FROM DOING STH ◀** [T **cut** sb **out**] to stop someone from doing something or taking part in something: *Todd's injuries cut him out of being selected for the team.*

7 ▶ **MOTOR** ◀ [I] if a motor cuts out, it suddenly stops working: *The engine cut out halfway across the lake.*
8 ▶ **STOP STH BEING SEEN** ◀ [T] to prevent light from reaching somewhere, or prevent a particular view from being seen: *The tinted windows help cut out the glare from the sun.*
9 **cut sb out of your will** to remove someone's name from the list of people who will receive your money or property when you die
10 **be cut out for/cut out to be** [usually in questions and negatives] to have the qualities that you need for a particular job or activity: *In the end I decided I wasn't cut out for the army.* | *Are you sure you're really cut out to be a teacher?* —see also **have your work cut out** (WORK² (14))

**cut up** *phr v* **1** [T **cut** sth ↔ **up**] to cut something into small pieces: *His mother has to cut up all his food for him.* **2** [I] *AmE informal* if a class cuts up, the students in it behave badly **3 be badly cut up** to have a lot of injuries because you have been in an accident or fight **4 cut up (about sth)** *informal* very upset because something bad has happened to you: *She still seems very cut up about it.* **5 cut up rough** *BrE informal* to react in an angry or violent way

S2 W2 **cut²** *n* [C]
1 ▶ **WOUND** ◀ a wound that is caused when something sharp cuts your skin: *The driver escaped with a few cuts and bruises.*
2 ▶ **HOLE/MARK** ◀ a hole in something, or a mark in the surface of something, made by something sharp: *The kitchen counter is covered with cuts.*
3 ▶ **REDUCTION** ◀ [often plural] a planned reduction in the size or amount of something: **job cuts/wage cuts/tax cuts etc** *A shorter working week will mean pay cuts for millions of workers.* | [+ **in**] *a massive cut in public spending*
4 ▶ **HAIR** ◀ [usually singular] **a)** the act of cutting someone's hair: *How much do they charge for a cut and blow-dry?* **b)** the style in which your hair has been cut
5 **clothes** [usually singular] the style in which your clothes have been made: *From the cut of his suit, I'd say he was pretty wealthy.*
6 ▶ **MONEY** ◀ *informal* [singular] someone's share of something, especially money: *Investigators found that her cut of the profits amounted to more than 25%.*
7 **make a cut** to remove part of a speech, piece of writing etc: *The censors made several cuts.*
8 ▶ **FILM** ◀ the process of putting together the different parts of a film and removing the parts that will not be shown: *Spielberg himself oversaw the final cut.*
9 **the cut and thrust of** the violent or unpleasant way in which a particular activity is done: *the cut and thrust of international politics*
10 **be a cut above** to be much better than someone else or something else: **a cut above the rest** *Just because she went to a private school, Jayne seems to think she's a cut above the rest of us.*
11 ▶ **MEAT** ◀ a piece of meat that has been cut so that you can cook it: *cuts of fresh lamb*
12 ▶ **ROAD** ◀ *AmE* a road that has been made through a hill —see also POWER CUT

**cut and dried** /ˌ· · ˈ·◂/ *adj* a decision or result that is cut and dried cannot now be changed: *I think we can say that the result of the election is now cut and dried.*

**cut·a·way** /ˈkʌtəweɪ/ *adj* a cutaway model, drawing etc is open on one side so that you can see the details inside it

**cut·back** /ˈkʌtbæk/ *n* [C usually plural] a reduction in something, such as the number of workers in an organization, the amount of money spent by the government etc: [+ **in**] *recommended cutbacks in social programmes* —see also **cut back** (CUT¹)

S3 **cute** /kjuːt/ *adj informal* **1** very pretty or attractive: *Jenny's such a cute little girl.* **2** attractive in a sexual way: *an all-American type – cute, blonde and vivacious* **3** *especially AmE* clever and practical when dealing with people, sometimes in an unpleasant way: *He's one cute lawyer!* | **get cute with** (=try to deceive someone) *Don't get cute with me – I know what those tires cost.* —**cutely** *adv* —**cuteness** *n* [U]

**cute·sy** /ˈkjuːtsi/ *adj AmE* **1** something that is cutesy is too pretty or clever in a way you think is annoying: *That greeting card is too cutesy.*

**cute·y** /ˈkjuːti/ *n* [C] *spoken* someone who is attractive, kind, and helpful: *He's such a cutey!*

**cut glass** /ˌ· ˈ·◂/ *n* [U] glass that has patterns cut into its surface

**cut-glass** *adj* **1** made of cut glass: *a cut-glass decanter* **2 cut-glass accent/vowel** an accent or vowel that is typical of someone from a high social class

**cu·ti·cle** /ˈkjuːtɪkəl/ *n* [C] an outer layer of hard skin, especially around the base of your nails

**cut·lass** /ˈkʌtləs/ *n* [C] a short sword with a curved blade, used by sailors or PIRATES in former times —see picture at SWORD

**cut·ler** /ˈkʌtlə‖-ər/ *n* [C] someone who makes or sells cutlery

**cut·le·ry** /ˈkʌtləri/ *n* [U] knives, forks, spoons, and other things used for eating with; SILVERWARE *AmE*: *Can you put the cutlery on the table.* —see pictures on pages 833 and 838

**cut·let** /ˈkʌtlɪt/ *n* [C] **1** a small flat piece of meat on a bone, usually LAMB¹ (2) or VEAL: *a grilled lamb cutlet* **2 vegetable/nut/prawn cutlet** a flat mass of vegetables, nuts etc covered with egg and BREADCRUMBS and cooked in hot fat

**cut·off** also **cut-off** *BrE* /ˈkʌtɒf‖-ɔːf/ *n* **1** [C] a fixed limit or level at which you decide to or have to stop doing something: **cutoff date/score/point** (=the date etc when you stop doing something) *The cutoff point for this sample was a score of 50% or more.* **2 cutoffs** [plural] short trousers that you make by cutting off the bottom part of a pair of trousers **3** [C] a part of a pipe that you open and shut to control the flow of gas or liquid

**cut·out** /ˈkʌtaʊt/ *n* [C] **1** the shape of a person, object etc that has been cut out of wood or paper: *a life-size cardboard cutout of Margaret Thatcher* **2** a piece of equipment that stops a machine when something is not working properly

**cut-price** /ˌ· ˈ·◂/ *adj* **1** sold at less than the usual price: *cut-price petrol* **2** a cut-price shop, supermarket etc sells goods at reduced prices: *a cut-price garage*

**cut·purse** /ˈkʌtpɜːs‖-pɜːrs/ *n* [C] *old use* a PICKPOCKET

**cut-rate** /ˈ· ·/ *adj* sold at less than the usual price

**cut·ter** /ˈkʌtə‖-ər/ *n* [C] **1** a small ship **2** [often plural] a tool that is used for cutting: *wire cutters*

**cut·throat¹** /ˈkʌtθrəʊt‖-θroʊt/ *adj* [only before noun] a cutthroat activity involves people who are all trying to get the same thing, often behaving badly or unfairly to each other: *Cutthroat competition led to a lot of bankruptcies and mergers.*

**cut·throat²** *n* [C] *old use* a murderer

**cut-throat ra·zor** /ˌ·· ˈ··/ *n* [C] a RAZOR with a very long sharp blade —see picture at RAZOR

**cut·ting¹** /ˈkʌtɪŋ/ *n* [C] **1** a stem or leaf that is cut from a plant and put in soil or water to grow into a new plant **2** *BrE* a piece of writing that is cut from a newspaper, magazine etc; CLIPPING (1) *AmE*: **press/newspaper cuttings** *Margot had sent him a bunch of press cuttings about the wedding* **3** *BrE* something that is produced by cutting, especially a passage cut through a hill for a road or railway; CUT² (12) *AmE*

**cutting²** *adj* **1** very unkind and intended to upset someone: *Danny can be so cutting at times.* | *Sue made a cutting remark about my clothes.* **2** a cutting wind is very cold and you can feel it through your clothes **3 be (at) the cutting edge of sth** to be the most advanced form of an activity, in which the newest methods, systems, equipment etc are developed and used: *The information highway is the cutting edge of the electronic revolution.*

**cutting board** /ˈ·· ·/ *n* [C] *AmE* a large piece of wood or plastic used for cutting meat or vegetables on; CHOPPING BOARD *BrE*

**cutting room** /'· · ·/ *n* [C] a room where the final form of a film is prepared by cutting and putting the different parts into the correct order

**CV** /ˌsiː 'viː/ also **curriculum vitae** *n* [C] *BrE* a short written document giving your education and past employment, used when you are looking for a job; RESUMÉ[2] (2) *AmE*: *Please send a CV and brief letter to the address below.*

**cwt** the written abbreviation of HUNDREDWEIGHT

**-cy** /si/ *suffix* [in nouns] **1** the state or quality of being something: *privacy* (=state of being private)| *accuracy*| *bankruptcy* **2** a particular rank or position: *a baronetcy* (=the rank of a BARONET)

**cy·an** /'saɪən‖'saɪ-æn, -ən/ *adj* dark greenish blue —**cyan** *n* [U]

**cy·a·nide** /'saɪənaɪd/ *n* [U] a very strong poison

**cyber-** /saɪbə‖-ər/ *prefix* connected with computers, especially with the sending of messages on the INTERNET

**cy·ber·net·ics** /ˌsaɪbə'netɪks‖-bər-/ *n* [U] the scientific study of the way in which information is moved about and controlled in machines, the brain and the NERVOUS SYSTEM —**cybernetic** *adj*

**cy·ber·punk** /'saɪbəpʌŋk‖-ər-/ *n* [U] stories about imaginary events connected with computer science: *cyberpunk fiction*

**cy·ber·space** /'saɪbəspeɪs‖-ər/ *n* [U] a word from SCIENCE FICTION, used to mean the place where electronic messages, information, pictures etc exist when they are sent from one computer to another: *We didn't meet in San Francisco – we met in cyberspace!*

**cy·borg** /'saɪbɔːg‖-bɔːrg/ *n* [C] a creature that is partly human and partly machine

**cyc·la·men** /'sɪkləmən/ *n* [C] a plant with pink, red, or white flowers

S3 W3 **cy·cle¹** /'saɪkəl/ *n* [C] **1** a number of events happening in a regularly repeated order: [+ **of**] *the cycle of the seasons*| *the endless cycle of violence in this part of the world* —see also LIFE CYCLE **2** a bicycle or MOTORCYCLE **3** the period of time needed for a machine to finish a process: *This washing machine has a 50 minute cycle.* **4** a group of songs, poems etc that are all about a particular important event

**cycle²** *v* [I] *especially BrE* to travel by bicycle: *Do you cycle to work?*

**cy·clic** /'saɪklɪk/ also **cyc·li·cal** /'sɪklɪkəl, 'saɪ-/ *adj* happening in cycles (CYCLE¹ (1)): *the cyclical nature of history* —**cyclically** /-kli/ *adv*

**cy·clist** /'saɪklɪst/ *n* [C] someone who rides a bicycle: *Andrew and Merv are very keen cyclists.*

**cy·clone** /'saɪkləʊn‖-kloʊn/ *n* [C] a very violent storm that moves very rapidly in a circle: *Darwin was flattened by Cyclone Tracy in 1974.* —compare HURRICANE, TYPHOON

**cy·clops** /'saɪklɒps‖-klɑːps/ *n* [singular] a very big man in ancient Greek stories who only had one eye in the middle of his forehead

**cy·der** /'saɪdə‖-ər/ *n* [U] *BrE* another spelling of CIDER

**cyg·net** /'sɪgnɪt/ *n* [C] a young SWAN¹

**cyl·in·der** /'sɪlɪndə‖-ər/ *n* [C] **1** a shape, object, or container with circular ends and long straight sides: *The gases are stored under pressure in separate cylinders.* —see picture at SHAPE² **2** the tube within which a PISTON moves forwards and backwards in an engine: *a four cylinder engine*

**cy·lin·dri·cal** /sɪ'lɪndrɪkəl/ *adj* in the shape of a cylinder: *A huge cylindrical oil tank stood beside the engine.*

**cym·bal** /'sɪmbəl/ *n* [C] a musical instrument made of a thin round metal plate that you play by hitting it with a stick, or by hitting two of them together: *The sudden clash of cymbals.*

**cyn·ic** /'sɪnɪk/ *n* [C] someone who is not willing to believe that people have good, honest, or sincere reasons for doing something: *Even the most hardened cynic must agree that charity does some good.* —**cynicism** *n* [U]

**cyn·i·cal** /'sɪnɪkəl/ *adj* unwilling to believe that people have good, honest, or sincere reasons for doing something: *You're just so cynical, Dave! Don't you believe in anything?*| [+ **about**] *Since her divorce she's become very cynical about men.* —**cynically** /-kli/ *adv*

**cy·no·sure** /'sɪnəzjʊə‖'saɪnəʃʊr/ *n* [usually singular] *formal* someone or something that everyone is interested in or attracted to

**cy·pher** /'saɪfə‖-ər/ *n* [C] another spelling of CIPHER

**cy·press** /'saɪprɪs/ *n* [C] a tree with dark green leaves and hard wood, that does not lose its leaves in winter

**Cy·ril·lic** /sɪ'rɪlɪk/ *adj* Cyrillic writing is written in the alphabet used for Russian, Bulgarian, and other Slavonic languages: *a Cyrillic typewriter*

**cyst** /sɪst/ *n* [C] a mass containing liquid that grows in your body or under your skin: *an ovarian cyst*

**cystic fi·bro·sis** /ˌsɪstɪk faɪ'brəʊsɪs‖-'broʊ-/ *n* [U] a serious medical condition, especially in children, in which breathing and digesting (DIGEST¹ (1)) food is very difficult

**cyst·i·tis** /sɪ'staɪtɪs/ *n* [U] an infection of the BLADDER¹ (1), especially in women

**cy·tol·o·gy** /saɪ'tɒlədʒi‖-'tɑː-/ *n* [U] the scientific study of cells from living things —**cytologist** *n* [C]

**czar** /zɑː‖zɑːr/ *n* [C] **1** another spelling of TSAR **2 banking/drug/health etc czar** *AmE* someone who is very powerful in a particular job or activity

**cza·ri·na** /zɑː'riːnə/ *n* [C] another spelling of TSARINA

# D,d

**D** /diː/ **d** *plural* **D's, d's** *n* [C] **1** the fourth letter of the English alphabet **2** the number 500 in the system of ROMAN NUMERALS

**D** **1** the second note in the SCALE[1] (8) , or the musical KEY[1] (4) based on this note **2** a mark that a teacher gives to a student's work, showing that it is not very good —see also D AND C, D-DAY

**d** **1** the written abbreviation of died: *John Keats d 1821* **2** the abbreviation of PENNY (4) in the system of money used in Britain before 1971

D

**d'** *spoken* the short form of do: *D'you know how many people are going to be there?*

**-'d** **1** the short form of would: *I asked if she'd be willing to help.* **2** the short form of had: *Nobody knew where he'd gone.*

**-d** /d, t/ *suffix* the form used for -ED after 'e': *baked*

**DA** /ˌdiː ˈeɪ/ *n* [C] the abbreviation of DISTRICT ATTORNEY

**dab¹** /dæb/ *n* [C] **1** a small amount of something that you put onto a surface with your hand, a cloth etc: [+ **of**] *Add a dab of butter and some parsley.* **2** a light touch with your hand, a cloth etc: *She wiped her tears away with a dab of her handkerchief.* **3** a small flat fish **4 dabs** [plural] *BrE old-fashioned* your FINGERPRINTS[1]

**dab²** *v* **dabbed, dabbing** **1** [I,T] to touch something lightly, usually several times: [+ **at**] *He dabbed at his bleeding lip.* **2** [T] to put a substance onto something with quick, light movements of your hand: **dab sth on/onto etc** *She hastily dabbed some cream on her face.*

**dab·ble** /ˈdæbəl/ *v* **1** [I] to do something or be involved in something in a way that is not very serious: [+ **at/in**] *James dabbles in politics.* **2** [T + **in**] to move your hands, feet etc about in water: *dabbling in the sea*

**dab hand** /ˌ· ˈ·/ *n* **be a dab hand at** *BrE informal* to be very good at a particular activity

**dach·shund** /ˈdækshʊnd,-sənd/ *n* [C] a type of small dog with short legs and a long body —see picture at DOG[1]

**Dac·ron** /ˈdækrɒn‖ˈdeɪkrɑːn/ *n* [U] *trademark AmE* a kind of cloth that is not made from natural materials

**dac·tyl** /ˈdæktɪl‖-tl/ *n* [C] *technical* a repeated sound pattern in poetry, consisting of one long sound followed by two short sounds as in the word 'carefully' —**dactylic** /dækˈtɪlɪk/ *adj*

S1 W2 **dad** /dæd/ *n* [C] *informal* father: *She lives with her Mom and Dad.*

S1 **dad·dy** /ˈdædi/ *n* [C] a word meaning father, used especially by or to young children: *Look, Daddy's home!* —see also SUGAR DADDY

**daddy long·legs** /ˌdædi ˈlɒŋlegz‖-ˈlɔːŋ-/ *n* [C] **1** *BrE* a flying insect with long legs; CRANE FLY **2** *AmE* an insect with long legs that is similar to a SPIDER

**da·do** /ˈdeɪdəʊ‖-doʊ/ *n plural* **dadoes** [C] the lower part of a wall in a room, especially when it is decorated differently to the upper part of the wall

**dae·mon** /ˈdiːmən/ *n* [C] a spirit in ancient Greek stories that is half a god and half a man —compare DEMON

**daf·fo·dil** /ˈdæfədɪl/ *n* [C] a tall yellow spring flower with a central tube-shaped part

**daft** /dɑːft‖dæft/ *adj BrE informal* **1** silly or not very sensible: *What a daft thing to say!* | **don't be daft** *spoken* (=used to tell someone not to be silly) | **as daft as a brush** (=extremely silly) *Jay's a nice bloke but he's as daft as a brush.* **2 be daft about** to be extremely interested in: *Tony's still daft about cars!* —**daftness** *n* [U]

**dag** /dæg/ *n* [C] *AustrE spoken* a strange or stupid person

**dag·ger** /ˈdægə‖-ər/ *n* [C] **1** a short pointed knife used as a weapon —see picture at KNIFE[1] **2 look daggers at** *BrE* to look at someone angrily —see also CLOAK-AND-DAGGER **3 be at daggers drawn** if two people are at daggers drawn, they are extremely angry with each other

**da·go** /ˈdeɪgəʊ‖-goʊ/ *n* [C] an extremely offensive word for someone from Spain, Italy, Portugal etc

**da·guer·ro·type** /dəˈgerəʊtaɪp‖-rə-/ *n* [C,U] an old type of photograph

**dahl** /dɑːl/ *n* [C,U] an Indian dish with a hot taste, made with beans, PEAS, or LENTILS

**dah·li·a** /ˈdeɪliə‖ˈdæliə/ *n* [C] a large garden flower with a bright colour

**dai·ly¹** /ˈdeɪli/ *adj* [only before noun] **1** happening or done every day: *daily flights to Miami* **2 daily life** the ordinary things that you usually do or experience **3** connected with a single day: *a daily rate of pay* S3 W2

**daily²** *adv* done or happening every day: *The zoo is open daily, from 9am to 5 pm.*

**daily³** *n* **1** [C usually plural] a DAILY PAPER **2** [C] *BrE old-fashioned* a DAILY HELP **3 dailies** [plural] *AmE* the first prints of a film before it has been edited (EDIT (1)); rushes (RUSH[2] (7)) *BrE*

**daily help** /ˌ·· ˈ·/ *n* [C] *BrE old-fashioned* someone, especially a woman, who is employed to clean someone's house

**daily pa·per** /ˌ·· ˈ··/ *n* [C] a newspaper that is printed and sold every day except Sunday

**dain·ty¹** /ˈdeɪnti/ *adj* **daintier, daintiest** **1** small, pretty, and delicate: *a dainty white handkerchief* **2** dainty movements are small and careful —**daintily** *adv* —**daintiness** *n* [U]

**dainty²** *n* [C] something small that is good to eat such as a sweet cake

**dai·qui·ri** /ˈdaɪkɪ̈ri, ˈdæk-/ *n* [C,U] a sweet alcoholic drink made with RUM[1] and fruit juice

**dai·ry** /ˈdeəri‖ˈderi/ *n* [C] **1** a place on a farm where milk is kept and butter and cheese are made **2** a company which sells milk and makes other dairy products

**dairy cat·tle** /ˈ·· ˌ··/ *n* [plural] cattle that are kept to produce milk rather than for their meat

**dairy farm** /ˈ·· ˌ·/ *n* [C] a farm that has cows and produces milk

**dai·ry·maid** /ˈdeərimeɪd‖ˈder-/ *n* [C] a woman who worked in a dairy in the past

**dai·ry·man** /ˈdeərimən‖ˈderɪ-mən, -mæn/ *n* [C] a man who works in a dairy

**da·is** /ˈdeɪɪ̈s, deɪs/ *n* [singular] a low stage that you stand on when you are making a speech or performing, so that people can see and hear you

**dai·sy** /ˈdeɪzi/ *n* [C] **1** a white flower with a yellow centre **2 pushing up the daisies** *humorous* someone who is pushing up the daisies is dead —see also **fresh as a daisy** (FRESH (12))

**daisy chain** /ˈ·· ·/ *n* [C] daisies tied together into a string to wear around your neck or wrist

**dai·sy·wheel print·er** /ˈdeɪziwiːl ˌprɪntə‖-ər/ *n* [C] a type of PRINTER (1) that produces good quality writing

**Dal·ai La·ma** /ˌdælaɪ ˈlɑːmə‖ˌdɑː-/ *n* [C] **the Dalai Lama** the leader of the Tibetan Buddhist religion

**dale** /deɪl/ *n* [C] a word meaning valley, used in former times or in the names of places, especially in the North of England

**dal·li·ance** /ˈdæliəns/ *n* [U] *old-fashioned* the behaviour of two people who are dallying with each other

**dal·ly** /ˈdæli/ *v* [I] *old-fashioned* to waste time, or do something very slowly: *Don't dally along the way!*

**dally with** sb/sth *phr v* [T] **1** to think about something but not in a very serious way: *They'd dallied with the idea of going on a world tour many times.* **2** *old-fashioned* to start a romantic relationship with someone but not in a serious way

**dal·ma·tian** /dælˈmeɪʃən/ *n* [C] a large dog with short white hair and black or brown spots —see picture at DOG[1]

**dam**

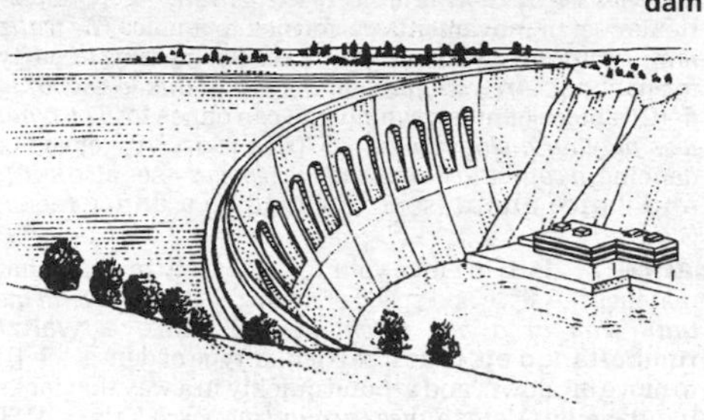

**dam¹** /dæm/ *n* [C] **1** a special wall built across a river, stream etc to stop the water from flowing, especially to make a lake or produce electricity: *the Aswan dam in Egypt* **2** *technical* the mother of a four-legged animal, especially a horse —compare SIRE¹ (2)

**dam²** *v* **dammed, damming** [T] to stop the water in a river, stream etc from flowing by building a special wall across it

**dam** sth ↔ **up** *phr v* [T] to dam a river, stream etc: *The stream had been dammed up.*

S2 W2 **dam·age¹** /ˈdæmɪdʒ/ *n* [U]
**1** ▶ **PHYSICAL HARM** ◀ physical harm caused to something or someone: [+ **to**] *damage to property* | **serious/severe/extensive damage** (=very bad damage) *The earthquake caused extensive structural damage.* | **minor/superficial damage** (=damage that is not very serious) | **do/cause damage** *Don't you realize the damage these chemicals are doing to our environment?* | **brain/liver/lung etc damage** (=damage caused to someone's brain etc) *permanent brain damage from the accident* | **irreparable/irreversible damage** (=damage that cannot be repaired) | **water/storm/flood etc damage** (=damage caused by water, a storm etc)
**2** ▶ **EMOTIONAL HARM** ◀ harm caused to someone's emotions or mind: *Such a traumatic childhood experience can cause terrible emotional damage.*
**3** ▶ **BAD EFFECT** ◀ a bad effect on something: [+ **to**] *The damage to his reputation was considerable.*
**4** ▶ **MONEY** ◀ **damages** [plural] *law* money that a court orders someone to pay to someone else for harming them or their property: *The court awarded him £15000 in damages.*
**5 the damage is done** used to say that something bad has happened which makes it impossible to go back to the way things were before it happened: *She immediately regretted her outburst, but the damage was done.*
**6 what's the damage?** *spoken* used humorously to ask how much you have to pay
**7 damage limitation** an attempt to limit the damage to something: *a damage limitation exercise to save the Prime Minister*

This graph shows some of the words most commonly used with the noun **damage**.

| Phrase | Frequency (per million) |
|---|---|
| damage to | ~7 |
| do damage | ~5.5 |
| cause damage | ~2.7 |
| brain damage | ~2.2 |
| severe/extensive damage | ~1.6 |
| serious damage | ~1.1 |
| irreparable/irreversible damage | ~0.8 |

Axis: 2, 4, 6, 8, 10 per million

Based on the British National Corpus and the Longman Lancaster Corpus

**damage²** *v* [T] **1** to cause physical harm to something or to part of someone's body: *Take care not to damage the timer mechanism.* | *I've damaged a knee ligament.* **2** to have a bad effect on something or someone in a way that makes them weaker or less successful: *Taylor felt her reputation had been damaged by the newspaper article.* —**damaging** *adj* | *Unemployment has had a damaging effect on morale.* S3 W3

**dam·ask¹** /ˈdæməsk/ *n* [U] a type of cloth with a pattern in it, often used to cover furniture

**damask²** *adj* **1** made of damask: *a damask tablecloth* **2** *literary* pink: *her damask cheek*

**damask rose** /ˈ·· ˌ·/ *n* [C] a pink rose with a beautiful smell

**Dame** /deɪm/ *n* a British title of honour given to a woman as a reward for the good things she has done

**dame** *n* [C] **1** *AmE old-fashioned* a woman **2** a character in a PANTOMIME (=a special play at Christmas) dressed as an ugly old woman but acted by a man **3** a woman who has been given the British title Dame: *Dame Edith Evans*

**dam·mit** /ˈdæmɪ̥t/ *interjection* used to show that you are annoyed: *Hurry up, dammit!*

**damn¹** /dæm/ *adj* [only before noun] *spoken* used to show that you are angry or annoyed with someone or something: *I can't get this damn button undone!* S2

**damn²** *adv* [+ adj/adv] *spoken* **1** used to emphasize how good something is, how bad something is etc; very: *We've been so damn busy all day, I'm shattered!* | *It's damn cold in here.* | **damn good/fine etc** *He was damn lucky he didn't have an accident.* **2 damn well** used to emphasize how determined or sure you are about something: *I damn well will go, and I'd like to see anyone try and stop me!* **3 know damn well** used to say that someone definitely knows something, especially when you are angry: *Chris knew damn well we wanted to leave at 8. Where the hell is he?* **4 damn all** *especially BrE* nothing at all: *Make him wash the dishes, there's damn all else he's good for.*

**damn³** *interjection* used to show that you are very annoyed or disappointed: *Damn! I've forgotten the keys.*

**damn⁴** *n spoken* **1 not give a damn** used to show that you do not care about something: *I don't give a damn about her.* **2 not worth a damn** used to say that you think something has no value at all: *Her promise isn't worth a damn.*

**damn⁵** *v* [T] **1 damn you/them/it etc** *spoken* used to show that you are extremely angry with someone or something: *Damn you! If you think you can do this to me, you're wrong!* **2** to state that something is very bad: *The critics damned the play on the first night.* | **damn with faint praise** (=show that you think someone or something is very bad by only praising them a little) —see also **(as) near as damn it** (NEAR² (5))

**dam·na·ble** /ˈdæmnəbəl/ *adj old-fashioned* very bad or annoying: *This damnable heat!* —**damnably** *adv*

**dam·na·tion¹** /dæmˈneɪʃən/ *n* [U] the act of deciding to punish someone by sending them to HELL¹ (3) for ever, or the state of being in hell for ever

**damnation²** *interjection old-fashioned* used to show that you are very angry or annoyed

**damned¹** /dæmd/ *adj* **1** [only before noun] *spoken* used to show that you are angry or annoyed with something: *a damned nuisance* **2 be damned** be sent by God to punishment without end after death **3 I'll be damned** *spoken* used as a strong expression of surprise **4 I'm damned if/I'll be damned if** *spoken* used to emphasize that you do not want something to happen, or that you do not know something: *I'll be damned if I let her come into my house.* | *I'm damned if I know.* **5 damned if you do, damned if you don't** used to mean that whatever you say or do will be considered to be wrong

**damned²** *adv* [+ adj/adv] *spoken* used to say how good something is, how bad something is etc: *War is a damned expensive business.* —see also DAMN¹ (1)

**damned**³ *n* **the damned** the people who God will send to HELL¹ (3) when they die because they have been so bad

**damned·est** /ˈdæmdɨst/ *adj informal especially AmE* **1 the damnedest thing/luck etc** the most unusual or surprising thing etc: *That machine was the damnedest thing you ever saw!* **2 do your damnedest** to try very hard to make something work or succeed: *I'll do my damnedest to fix it, but I can't promise anything.*

**damn-fool** /ˈ· ·/ *adj* [only before noun] *spoken* very stupid: *That was the biggest damn-fool mistake I ever made.*

**damn·ing** /ˈdæmɪŋ/ *adj* **damning indictment/comment/account** something that shows someone or something is very bad: *a damning indictment of the government's economic record.*

**Dam·o·cles** /ˈdæməkliːz/ —see **sword of Damocles** (SWORD (3))

**damp¹** /dæmp/ *adj* **1** slightly wet, often in an unpleasant way: *Wipe the leather with a damp cloth.* **2 damp squib** *BrE informal* something that is intended to be exciting, effective etc, but which is disappointing —**damply** *adv*

**USAGE NOTE: DAMP**

WORD CHOICE: **damp, moist, humid**

**Damp** is often used about something you would prefer to be dry: *damp clothes/weather | a damp bed/wall/room | In the rainy season everything gets damp I'm afraid.*

**Moist** is used especially when something is not too wet and not too dry: *a moist ginger cake|Keep houseplant soil moist – don't let it dry out.*

**Humid** is a more technical word used mainly to describe the climate or weather, or air that feels wet: *It gets very humid here in the summer* (=the air is hot and damp).

You do not usually use these words to talk about people who get wet.

**damp²** *n* [U] *BrE* a part or area that is slightly wet: *There's a patch of damp on my bedroom wall.*

**damp³** *v* [T] to make a sound less loud: *Damp the sound with the pedal after each beat.*

**damp** sth ↔ **down** *phr v* [T] **1** to make a fire burn more slowly, often by covering it with ash **2** to control, reduce or limit something, especially a feeling: *damping down a child's high spirits*

**damp course** /ˈ· ·/ *n* [C] *BrE* a layer of material which is put into the bottom of a wall to prevent water rising through it

**damp·en** /ˈdæmpən/ *v* [T] **1** to make something slightly wet **2 dampen sb's enthusiasm/spirits** to make people feel less confident, happy, or ENTHUSIASTIC: *The accident had done nothing to dampen his competitive spirit.*

**dampen** sth ↔ **down** *phr v* [T] to damp something down

**damp·er** /ˈdæmpə‖-ər/ *n* [C] **1** a piece of equipment that stops a piano string from making a sound **2** a piece of metal that is opened or closed to control how strongly a fire burns **3 put a damper on** to affect something in a way that makes people sad, disappointed, or less hopeful: *This unwelcome news put a damper on the celebrations.*

**damp·ness** /ˈdæmpnɨs/ *n* [U] the state or condition of being slightly wet

**dam·sel** /ˈdæmzəl/ *n* [C] **1** *old use* a young woman who is not married **2 damsel in distress** *humorous* a young woman who needs help or protection

**dam·son** /ˈdæmzən/ *n* [C] a small bitter dark purple PLUM¹ (1)

**dan** /dæn/ *n* [C, singular] a level of skill in a fighting sport such as JUDO, including a BLACK BELT

S2 W3 **dance¹** /dɑːns‖dæns/ *n* **1** [C] an act of dancing: **have a dance** *Let's have one more dance before we go home.* | **do a dance** (=move as if you are dancing) *When Claire heard the news she did a little dance of excitement.* **2** [C] a particular set of movements performed to music: *The waltz is an easy dance to learn.* **3** [C] a social meeting or party for dancing: *Are you going to the dance this weekend?* **4** [C] a piece of music which you can dance to: *The band was playing a slow dance.* **5** [U] the activity or art of dancing: *a course in dance and movement* —see also **song and dance about** (SONG (5)), **lead sb a dance** (LEAD¹ (17))

**dance²** *v* **1** [I] to move your feet and body in a way that matches the style and speed of music: *She danced with me until 3am at a bar downtown.* **2 dance a waltz/rumba/tango etc** to do a particular type of dance **3** [I] to move up, down, and around quickly in a way that looks like dancing: *Moths danced around the porch light.* **4** [T always + adv/prep] to make someone or something move as if they were dancing: *She danced the baby up and down on her knee.* **5 dance attendance on** to do everything possible in order to please someone: *a movie star with several young men dancing attendance on her* **6 dance to sb's tune** to do what someone wants you to do in a way that shows complete obedience: *They control all the funding so we have to dance to their tune.* —**dancing** *n* [U] *her love of dancing* S3

**dance-band** /ˈ· ·/ *n* [C] a group of musicians who play music that you dance to

**dance floor** /ˈ· ·/ *n* [C] a special floor in a restaurant, hotel etc for people to dance on

**dance hall** /ˈ· ·/ *n* [C] a large public room where people used to pay to go and dance

**danc·er** /ˈdɑːnsə‖ˈdænsər/ *n* [C] **1** someone who dances as a profession: **ballet/ballroom etc dancer** *I want to be a ballet dancer when I grow up.* **2 good/bad etc dancer** someone who dances well, badly etc

**D and C** /ˌdiː ənd ˈsiː/ *n* [C] a medical operation to clean out the inside of a woman's WOMB

**dan·de·li·on** /ˈdændɨlaɪən/ *n* [C] a wild plant with yellow flowers, and white balls of seeds that travel a long way in the air

**dandelion clock** /ˈ···· ˌ·/ *n* [C] the soft ball of white seeds that grows on the dandelion plant

**dan·der** /ˈdændə‖-ər/ **get sb's dander up** *n old-fashioned* to make someone angry

**dan·di·fied** /ˈdændɪfaɪd/ *adj old-fashioned* a man who is dandified wears very fashionable clothes in a way that shows he cares too much about his appearance

**dan·dle** /ˈdændl/ *v* [T] *old-fashioned* to play with a baby or small child by moving them up and down in your arms or on your knee

**dan·druff** /ˈdændrəf, -drʌf/ *n* [U] pieces of dead skin from your head that can be seen as a white dust in your hair and on your shoulders

**dan·dy¹** /ˈdændi/ *n* [C] *old-fashioned* a man who spends a lot of time and money on his clothes and appearance

**dandy²** *adj old-fashioned especially AmE* very good: *"Let's go the movies" "That'll be dandy."*

**Dane** /deɪn/ *n* [C] someone from Denmark

**dang** /dæŋ/ *interjection AmE spoken* a less offensive word for DAMN

**dan·ger** /ˈdeɪndʒə‖-ər/ *n* **1** [U] the possibility that someone or something will be harmed or killed: *Danger! High Voltage.* | [+ **of**] *Is there any danger of infection, doctor?* | [+ **from**] *danger from radioactive sources* | **in danger** (=in a situation in which you may be harmed or killed) *I had a sudden feeling that Petra was in danger.* | **out of danger** (=not in danger any more) *The patient is now out of danger.* **2** [C often plural] something or someone that may harm or kill you: *I think he enjoys the dangers of rock climbing.* | **face dangers** (=do something that involves dangers) *All boxers are well aware of the dangers they face in the ring.* | **be a danger to** *The wreck is a danger to other ships.* **3** [C,U] the possibility that something unpleasant will happen: **danger that** *There* S2 W2 *is always the danger that Elizabeth will go back on her promise.* | [+ **of**] *Is there much danger of losing money?* | **be in danger of** (=be in a situation in which something unpleasant may happen) *Carlos is in danger of losing his job.* **4 be on the danger list** to be so ill that you may die **5 there's no danger of that** used to mean that something bad will not happen

**danger mon·ey** /'·· ,··/ *n* [U] *especially BrE* additional money that you are paid for doing dangerous work; DANGER PAY *AmE*

S2 W2 **dan·ger·ous** /'deɪndʒərəs/ *adj* **1** able or likely to harm or kill you: *dangerous animals* | *Neil thought the man looked dangerous.* | **it is dangerous (for sb) to do sth** *It's dangerous for women to walk alone at night.* | **highly/very dangerous** *It would be highly dangerous to attempt to cross the river just here.* **2** a belief, situation, or action that is dangerous involves a lot of risk, or is likely to cause problems: *The business is in a dangerous financial position.* **3 dangerous ground/territory** a situation or subject that could make someone very angry or upset: *You're on dangerous ground when you talk politics with Ed.* —**dangerously** *adv*: *driving dangerously* | *dangerously high temperatures*

**danger pay** /'·· ,·/ *n* [U] *AmE* DANGER MONEY *BrE*

**dan·gle** /'dæŋgəl/ *v* **1** [I,T] to hang or swing loosely, or make something do this: *a leather purse dangled from his belt* | **dangle sth** *I dangled my feet in the clear blue water.* **2 dangle sth in front of sb** to offer something good to someone in order to persuade them to do something: *The promise of an ice-cream cone was dangled in front of us, as a reward for washing the car.*

**Da·nish¹** /'deɪnɪʃ/ *n* [U] **1** the language of Denmark **2** [C] *AmE* a Danish pastry

**Danish²** *adj* connected with the people or language of Denmark

**Danish pas·try** /,·· '··/ *n* [C] a very sweet cake made of light PASTRY (1)

**dank** /dæŋk/ *adj* unpleasantly wet and cold: *a dank prison cell* —**dankness** *n* [U]

**dap·per** /'dæpə‖-ər/ *adj* **1** a man who is dapper is small and has a neat appearance: *He was small, dapper, and wore a green bow tie.* **2** nicely dressed: *You're looking very dapper in your new suit!*

**dap·ple** /'dæpəl/ *v* [T] *literary* to mark something with spots of colour, light, or shade

**dap·pled** /'dæpəld/ *adj* marked with spots of colour, light, or shade: *a sky dappled with clouds*

**dapple-grey** /,·· '·◂/ *n* [C] a horse that is grey with spots of darker grey

**Dar·by and Joan** /,dɑːbi ən 'dʒəʊn‖,dɑːrbi ən 'dʒoʊn/ *n* **be like Darby and Joan** *BrE humorous* used when talking about an old husband and wife who live very happily together

W3 **dare¹** /deə‖der/ *v*

**1 ▶ DO STH DANGEROUS ◀** [I not in progressive] to be brave enough to do something dangerous or that you are afraid to do: *The others used to steal things from stores, but I would never dare.* | **dare (to) do sth** *Would you dare to do a parachute jump?*

**2 ▶ DO STH RUDE/SHOCKING ETC ◀** [I] to be confident enough, rude enough, or dishonest enough to do something that is very rude, shocking, or wrong: *Tell her what I really think? I wouldn't dare!*

**3 how dare you** *spoken* used to show that you are very angry and shocked about what someone has done or said: *How dare you accuse me of lying!*

**4 don't you dare!** *spoken* used to warn someone not to do something because it makes you angry: *Don't you dare talk to me like that!*

**5 ▶ PERSUADE SB TO DO STH ◀** [T] to try to persuade someone to do something dangerous or embarrassing as a way of proving that they are brave: **dare sb to do sth** *They dared Lenny to climb to the very top branch.* | **I dare you!** *spoken*: *Go on! Ask her for her telephone number. I dare you!*

**6 dare I say/suggest** *formal spoken* used when adding information that you think people may not accept or believe: *I found him intelligent, observant, and, dare I say it, a sparkling wit!*

**7 I dare say** *spoken especially BrE* used when saying or agreeing that something may perhaps be true: *I dare say things will improve.*

**dare²** *n* [C] something dangerous that you have dared someone to do: *a dare to run through the field with the bull in it* | **for a dare** (=because someone has dared you to) *I only did it for a dare.*

**dare·dev·il** /'deədevəl‖'der-/ *n* [C] someone who likes doing dangerous things: *a daredevil motorcyclist* —**daredevil** *adj*

**daren't** /deənt‖dernt/ *spoken* the short form of 'dare not' (DARE¹ (1))

**dare·say** /,deə'seɪ◂‖,der-/ *v* **I daresay** *especially BrE* used when saying or agreeing that something may perhaps be true: *I daresay you're right.*

**dar·ing¹** /'deərɪŋ‖'der-/ *adj* **1** willing to do something that is dangerous or that involves a lot or risk: *the daring lifeboatmen* | *a daring rescue attempt* **2** new or unusual in a way that is sometimes shocking: *a daring film* | *Sometimes her outfits were more daring than usual.* —**daringly** *adv*:*daringly close to the edge*

**daring²** *n* [U] courage that makes you willing to take risks: *a plan of great daring*

S2 W1 **dark¹** /dɑːk‖dɑːrk/ *adj*

**1 ▶ PLACE ◀** a dark place is one where there is little or no light: *The church was dark and quiet.* | *I waited for them in a dark alley.* | **go dark** (=become dark) *Suddenly, the room went dark and somebody screamed.* —opposite LIGHT³ (3)

**2 ▶ COLOUR ◀** not light or pale in colour: **dark blue/green/pink etc** *a dark blue dress* —opposite LIGHT³ (1)

**3 it gets dark** when it gets dark in the evening the light disappears and night begins: *Come on, let's go in, it's getting dark.*

**4 ▶ HAIR/EYES ◀** someone who is dark has hair and eyes that are black or brown: *a tall, dark man* —opposite FAIR¹ (5)

**5 ▶ THREATENING/MYSTERIOUS ETC ◀** threatening, mysterious, or evil: *the dark forces of the night* | *There was a darker side to his character.*

**6 ▶ FEELINGS/THOUGHTS ◀** dark thoughts are sad and show that you think something very bad may happen: *I sat there gloomily, thinking dark thoughts.*

**7 keep sth dark** *informal* to keep something secret: *You're getting married! You kept that dark!*

**8 ▶ UNHAPPY TIME ◀** a dark time is unhappy or without hope: *in the dark days of the war* | *Even in the darkest moments, I still had you, my love.*

**9 dark horse a)** someone who people do not know much about who surprises everyone by winning a competition **b)** *BrE* someone who does not tell people much and who has surprising qualities or abilities: *She's a dark horse. I didn't know she'd written a novel.*

**10 darkest Africa/South America etc** *old-fashioned* the parts of Africa etc about which we know very little —see also PITCH-BLACK

**dark²** *n* [U] **1 the dark** a situation in which there is no light: *Children are sometimes afraid of the dark.* | **in the dark** *Be careful if you're walking home in the dark.* **2 after dark** at night: *Some of my friends won't go out after dark.* **3 before dark** before the time when it gets dark at night: *You can go out, but make sure you come home before dark.* **4 be in the dark** *informal* to know nothing about something important because you have not been told about it: *Well, I'm afraid we're in the dark as much as you are.* | **keep sb in the dark** *The public was kept in the dark about the assassination attempt.* —see also **a shot in the dark** (SHOT¹ (14))

**Dark Ag·es** /'· ,··/ *n* **the Dark Ages** the period in European history from 476 AD to about 1000 AD

**dark·en** /'dɑːkən‖'dɑːr-/ *v* [I,T] **1** to become dark, or

D

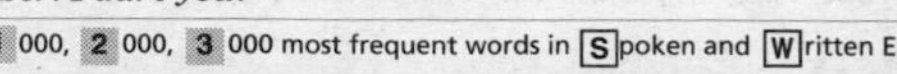

make something dark: *the skies darkened | The sun had darkened his skin.* **2** to become less happy or positive or make someone feel this way: *The news darkened their view of the situation.* **3 never darken my door again** *old-fashioned humorous* used to tell someone that you do not want them in your house again

**dark glass·es** /ˌ· ˈ··/ *n* [plural] glasses with dark glass in them, that you wear to protect your eyes from the sun or to hide your eyes

**dark·ie** /ˈdɑːki‖ˈdɑːr-/ *n* [C] *old-fashioned* an offensive word for a black person

**dark·ly** /ˈdɑːkli‖ˈdɑːrk-/ *adv* **1** in an unpleasant or threatening way: *'Don't you be too sure,' said Marcus darkly.* **2** with a dark colour: *Philip flushed darkly.*

W3 **dark·ness** /ˈdɑːknəs‖ˈdɑːrk-/ *n* [U] **1** a place or time when there is no light: *Beyond the glittering street was darkness.* | **total darkness** (=complete darkness) *The clouds moved across the moon, leaving us in total darkness.* | **darkness falls** (=it becomes night) **2 forces/powers of darkness** evil or the devil **3** the dark quality of a colour

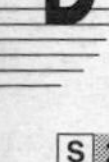

**dark·room** /ˈdɑːkruːm, -rʊm‖ˈdɑːrk-/ *n* [C] a dark room where film is taken out of a camera and made into a photograph

S2 **dar·ling¹** /ˈdɑːlɪŋ‖ˈdɑːr-/ *n* [C] **1** a way of speaking to someone that you love: *Hurry up, darling.* **2** someone who seems very nice, generous, friendly etc: *He's such a darling.* **3 the darling of** the most popular person in a particular group or area of activity: *She's the darling of the fashion world.*

**darling²** *adj* [only before noun] *spoken* used when you love someone or something very much, or when you think something is very attractive: *My two darling daughters. | What a darling little house!*

**darn¹** /dɑːn‖dɑːrn/ *v* [T] **1** to repair a hole in a piece of clothing by stitching wool over it: *darning socks* **2 darn it!** *spoken* used when you are annoyed about something: *Darn it! I'll have to do it all myself!* **3 I'll be darned!** *spoken* used when you are surprised about something: *Did they really? Well, I'll be darned!*

**darn²** *n* [C] a place where a hole in a piece of clothing has been repaired neatly with wool

**darn³** also **darned** /dɑːnd‖dɑːrnd/ *adj spoken* used to emphasize how bad, stupid, unfair etc someone or something is: *The darn fool got lost on the way.* —**darn** also **darned** *adv*: *It was a darned good movie.*

**darn·ing** /ˈdɑːnɪŋ‖ˈdɑːr-/ *n* [U] the practice of repairing holes in clothing by using wool

**dart¹** /dɑːt‖dɑːrt/ *v* **1** [I always + adv/prep] to move suddenly and quickly in a particular direction: [+ **forward/across/off etc**] *Jill darted forward and pulled him away from the fire.* **2 dart a glance/look** to look at someone or something very quickly and suddenly: *Tom darted a terrified glance over his shoulder.*

**dart²** *n* **1** [C] a small pointed object that is thrown or shot as a weapon or thrown in the game of darts: *a poisoned dart* **2 darts** a game in which darts are thrown at a round board with numbers on it **3** [singular] a sudden, quick movement in a particular direction: **make a dart at/for** *The prisoner made a dart for the door.* **4** [C] a small fold put into a piece of clothing to make it fit better

**dart·board** /ˈdɑːtbɔːd‖ˈdɑːrtbɔːrd/ *n* [C] a round board used in the game of darts

**dash¹** /dæʃ/ *v* **1** to go or run somewhere very quickly: [+ **into/across/behind etc**] *Olive dashed into the room, grabbed her bag and ran out again.* **2** [T always + adv/prep] to make something move violently against a surface, usually so that it breaks: **dash sth against/onto/to etc** *The ship was dashed against the rocks.* **3 dash sb's hopes** to disappoint someone by telling them that what they want is not possible: *Budget cuts dashed hopes for several plans proposed by NASA.* **4 (I) must dash/(I) have to dash** *BrE spoken* used to tell someone that you must leave quickly: *I must dash – I said I'd meet Daniel at eight o'clock.* **5 dash it (all)!** *BrE spoken* used to show that you are slightly annoyed or angry about something: *Dash it! I can't find my scissors!* **6** [I always + adv/prep] if a wave or rain dashes against something it hits it hard: *Stormy waves dashed against the shore.*

**dash off** *phr v* **1** [I] to leave somewhere very quickly: *Harry dashed off before she had a chance to thank him.* **2** [T **dash** sth ↔ **off**] to write or draw something very quickly: *She dashed off a quick letter excusing him from school that day.*

**dash²** *n*
**1** ▶ **LINE** ◀ [C] a line [–] used in writing and printing, for example in the sentence 'Go home – they're waiting for you.' —compare HYPHEN
**2 make a dash for** to run very quickly in order to get away from something or in order to reach something: **make a dash for cover/freedom etc** *The prisoners made a dash for freedom.* | **make a dash for it** *It's pouring with rain – we'll have to make a dash for it.*
**3** ▶ **SMALL AMOUNT** ◀ [singular] a very small amount of a liquid or other substance: [+ **of**] *Add salt, pepper and a dash of vinegar.* —see picture on page 416
**4 a mad dash** *informal* an attempt to get somewhere or do something extremely quickly: *When the alarm went there was a mad dash for the exit.*
**5** ▶ **SOUND** ◀ [C] a long sound or flash of light used for sending messages in MORSE CODE —compare DOT¹ (4)
**6** ▶ **CAR** ◀ [C] *AmE informal* DASHBOARD
**7** ▶ **STYLE** ◀ [U] *old-fashioned* style, energy, and courage in someone such as a soldier
**8 cut a dash** to look very impressive and attractive in particular clothes: *Edmond really cut a dash in that white linen suit.*

**dash·board** /ˈdæʃbɔːd‖-bɔːrd/ *n* [C] the board at the front of a car that has the controls on it —see picture on page 409

**dashed** /dæʃt/ *adj* [only before noun] *BrE old-fashioned* used to emphasize what you are saying: *Harry talked dashed nonsense all evening.*

**dash·ing** /ˈdæʃɪŋ/ *adj* a man who is dashing is very attractive, fashionable, and confident —**dashingly** *adv*

**dast·ard·ly** /ˈdæstədli‖-ərd-/ *adj old-fashioned* very cruel or evil: *a dastardly plot*

**DAT** /ˌdiː eɪ ˈtiː/ *n* [U] digital audio tape; a system used to record music, sound, or information in DIGITAL form

**da·ta** /ˈdeɪtə, ˈdɑːtə/ *n* [U, plural] **1** information or facts: *We cannot tell you the results until we have looked at all the data.* **2** information in a form that can be stored and used: *data retrieval system*

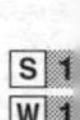

**data bank** /ˈ·· ˌ·/ *n* [C] a place, especially a computer, where information on a particular subject is stored: *a missing persons data bank*

**da·ta·base** /ˈdeɪtəˌbeɪs/ *n* [C] a large amount of data stored in a computer system so that you can find and use it easily: *Put the new customers on the database.* S2 W2

**data bus** /ˈ·· ·/ *n* [C] *technical* an electronic path along which DATA travels from one part of a computer to another

**data pro·cess·ing** /ˌ·· ˈ···/ *n* [U] the use of computers to store and organize data, especially in business

**date¹** /deɪt/ *n* [C] **1** the numbers or words you use to talk about a particular day, month, and year: *The date on the letter was the 30th August 1962.* | **date of birth** (=the day you were born) *Please write your name, address, and date of birth on the form.* **2** a particular day: *a date for the next meeting* | **set a date** (=choose a particular date) *Have you set a date for the wedding?* **3 at a later date** *formal* at some time in the future: *We'll deal with this problem at a later date.* **4 to date** up to now: *To date there has been no improvement in his condition.* **5 a)** an occasion when you arrange to meet someone that you like in a romantic way: *Do you have a date tonight?* | **go (out) on a date** *"So, what did he say?" "Well, we're going on a date Friday night."* —see also BLIND DATE S1 W1

**b)** *AmE* someone that you have a date with: *Can I bring my date to the party?* **6 make a date** to agree on a time to meet someone socially: *Let's make a date to go and see 'Arcadia' one day next week.* **7** a sweet sticky brown fruit with a long hard seed inside —see also CLOSING DATE, **expiry date** (EXPIRY (2)), SELL-BY DATE, OUT-OF-DATE, UP-TO-DATE

S 3 W 3 **date²** *v* **1** [T] to write or print the date on something: *a newspaper dated November 23, 1963* **2** [T] to find out when something old such as a book, painting, building etc was made: *The rocks are dated by examing the fossils found in the same layer.* **3** [I] if clothing, art etc dates, it looks old-fashioned: *His designs are so successful, they've hardly dated at all.* **4** [T] *AmE* to have a romantic relationship with someone: **be dating sb** *Is he still dating Sarah?* **5** [T] if something that you say, do, or wear dates you, it shows that you are fairly old: *Yes, I remember the moon landings – that dates me doesn't it?*

**date from** also **date back to** *phr v* [I] to have existed since a particular time in the past: *This church dates from the 13th century.*

**dat·ed** /ˈdeɪtɪ̣d/ *adj* old-fashioned: *That dress looks dated now.* —compare OUT-OF-DATE

**date·line** /ˈdeɪtlaɪn/ *n* [singular] the INTERNATIONAL DATE LINE

**date rape** /ˈ· ·/ *n* [C,U] a RAPE that is done by someone the woman has met in a social situation

**date stamp** /ˈ· ·/ *n* [C] **a)** a piece of equipment used for printing the date on letters, documents etc **b)** the mark that it makes

**dating a·gen·cy** /ˈ·· ˌ···/ *n* [C] a business that helps people to meet other people, to have a romantic relationship

**da·tive** /ˈdeɪtɪv/ *n* [C] *technical* a particular form of a noun in some languages such as Latin and German, which shows that the noun is the INDIRECT OBJECT of a verb —**dative** *adj*

**daub¹** /dɔːb‖dɒːb/ *v* [T] to paint or cover something with a soft substance, without being very careful: *faces daubed with black mud*

**daub²** *n* **1** [U] *technical* mud or clay used for making walls —see also **wattle and daub** (WATTLE (2)) **2** a small amount of a soft or sticky substance: [+ **of**] *a daub of paint*

S 1 W 1 **daugh·ter** /ˈdɔːtə‖ˈdɒːtər/ *n* [C] **1** someone's female child: *My daughter's at university now.* —see picture at FAMILY **2** *technical* something new that forms or develops when something else divides or ends: *a daughter language*

**daughter-in-law** /ˈ·· ˌ· ·/ *n plural* **daughters-in-law** [C] your son's wife — compare SON-IN-LAW —see picture at FAMILY

**daugh·ter·ly** /ˈdɔːtəli‖ˈdɒtər-/ *adj old-fashioned* behaving in a way that a daughter is supposed to behave

**daunt** /dɔːnt‖dɒːnt/ *v* [T usually passive] **1** to make someone feel afraid or less confident: *He felt utterly daunted by the prospect of moving to another country.* **2 nothing daunted** *formal* not at all discouraged: *It was steep but, nothing daunted, he started climbing.*

**daunt·ing** /ˈdɔːntɪŋ‖ˈdɒːn-/ *adj* frightening in a way that makes you feel less confident: *It's a daunting task, but we're optimistic.* | **daunting prospect** (=something daunting that you are going to do) *the daunting prospect of asking for a loan*

**daunt·less** /ˈdɔːntləs‖ˈdɔːnt-/ *adj literary* confident and not easily frightened: *dauntless optimism* —**dauntlessly** *adv*

**dau·phin** /ˈdɔːfɪn‖ˈdɒːfən/ *n* [C] the oldest son of a King of France

**dau·phine** /ˈdɔːfiːn‖dɒːˈfiːn/ *n* [C] the wife of the oldest son of a King of France

**dav·en·port** /ˈdævənpɔːt‖-pɔːrt/ *n* [C] *AmE* a large SOFA, especially one that can be made into a bed

**dav·it** /ˈdævɪ̣t, ˈdeɪvɪ̣t/ *n* [C] one of a pair of long curved poles that sailors swing out over the side of a ship in order to lower a boat into the water

**daw·dle** /ˈdɔːdl‖ˈdɒː-/ *v* [I] to take a long time to do something or go somewhere: *Don't dawdle – we're late already!* | [+ **over**] *I dawdled over a second cup of coffee.* —**dawdler** *n* [C]

**dawn¹** /dɔːn‖dɒːn/ *n* [C,U] **1** the time at the beginning of the day when light first appears: *We talked almost until dawn.* | **at dawn** *The first boats set off at dawn.* | **dawn breaks** (=the first light of the day appears) *When dawn broke we were still 50 miles from Calcutta.* | **at the crack of dawn** (=very early in the morning) *I was up at the crack of dawn to get the plane.* —compare DUSK **2 the dawn of civilization/time etc** the time when something began or first appeared: *People have been falling in love since the dawn of time.* **3 a false dawn** something that seems positive or hopeful but really is not: *another false dawn on the road to recovery*

**dawn²** *v* [I] **1** if day or morning dawns, it begins: *The morning dawned fresh and clear after the storm.* **2** *literary* if a period of time or situation dawns, it begins: *The age of Darwin had dawned.* **3** *formal* if a feeling or idea dawns, you think of it for the first time

**dawn on** sb *phr v* [T not in passive] if a fact dawns on you, you realise it for the first time: *Then the ghastly truth dawned on me.* | **it dawns on sb that** *It dawned on me that Joanna had been right all along.*

**dawn cho·rus** /ˌ· ˈ··/ *n* [singular] *especially BrE* the sound of many birds singing at dawn

**dawn raid** /ˌ· ˈ·/ *n* [C] an attack or operation that happens very early in the morning, especially involving the police

## day /deɪ/ *n*

S 1 W 1

| | |
|---|---|
| ① PERIOD OF TIME | ⑧ NOW |
| ② THE TIME YOU ARE AWAKE | ⑨ BAD THINGS HAPPEN |
| ③ FUTURE | ⑩ GOOD THINGS HAPPEN |
| ④ PAST | ⑪ PLEASURE |
| ⑤ SB'S LIFE/STH'S EXISTENCE | ⑫ SUCCESS/FAME |
| ⑥ WORK | ⑬ SPOKEN PHRASES |
| ⑦ EACH DAY/EVERY DAY | ⑭ OTHER MEANINGS |

### ① PERIOD OF TIME

**1** [C] a period of 24 hours: *We spent three days in Paris then went south.* | *What day is it today – Tuesday?* | **the day before yesterday** *I just saw Pat the day before yesterday.* | **the day after tomorrow** *We're leaving for LA the day after tomorrow.*

**2** [C,U] the period of time between when it becomes light in the morning and the time it becomes dark: *I'm usually out during the day.* | *It rained all day.* | **by day** (=during the day) *Owls usually sleep by day and hunt by night.*

[continued on next page]

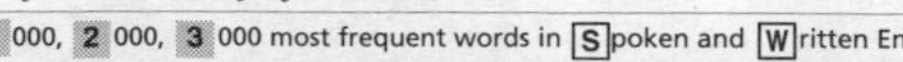
1 000, 2 000, 3 000 most frequent words in S poken and W ritten English

[continued from previous page]

**day**

| Monday | the day before yesterday |
|---|---|
| Tuesday | yesterday |
| Wednesday | TODAY |
| Thursday | tomorrow |
| Friday | the day after tomorrow |
| Saturday | |
| Sunday | |

② THE TIME YOU ARE AWAKE
**3** [C usually singular] the time during the day when you are awake: *His day begins at six.* | **long day** (=a day when you had to get up early and were busy all day) *It's been a very long day.* | **all day (long)** (=during the whole time you are awake) *I've been studying all day. I'm beat!*

③ FUTURE
**4 one day** also **some day** at an unknown time in the future: *One day I'll buy a boat and sail around the world.*
**5 one of these days** *informal* at some time in the future: *I might find the time to paint the bedroom one of these days.*
**6 any day (now)** *spoken* very soon: *She's expecting the baby any day now.*
**7 the day will come (when)** used to emphasize that something will definitely happen at some time in the future: *The day will come when he loses his eyesight completely.*

④ PAST
**8 one day** on a particular day in the past: *One day, she just didn't turn up for work, and we never saw her again.*
**9 childhood/student/army days** the time when you were a child, student, soldier etc
**10 the good old days** time in the past that you think was better than the present time: *In the good old days people never had to lock their doors.*
**11 those were the days** *spoken* used to say that a time in the past was better than the present time
**12 the other day** a few days ago; recently: *We had a letter from Kim the other day.*
**13 in those days** during a period of time in the past: *Women wore long skirts in those days.*
**14 in my day** used to describe what things were like when you were young: *In my day we used to have to get up at six o'clock.*
**15 in his or her day** during the most successful part of someone's life: *Your grandfather was a famous radio personality in his day.*
**16 the standards/fashion/wages etc of the day** the standards etc that existed in a particular period of time in the past
**17 five/three/nine years to the day** exactly five years, three years, etc ago: *It's two years to the day since we moved here.*

⑤ SB'S LIFE/STH'S EXISTENCE
**18 sb's days** someone's life: *She ended her days in poverty.*
**19 sb's/sth's days are numbered** someone or something will not continue to exist or be effective: *The days of the vinyl record are numbered.*

⑥ WORK
**20** [C] the time spent working during a 24-hour period: *I work an eight-hour day.* | *Did you have a good day at the office?* —see also WORKING DAY
**21 day off** a day when you do not have to work: *I'm taking a day off next week.*
**22 be on days** *spoken* to be working during the day doing a job that you often have to do at night, for example, if you work in a hospital: *I'm on days this week.*

⑦ EACH DAY/EVERY DAY
**23 day after day** happening continuously for a long time so that you become annoyed or bored: *I couldn't stand sitting at a desk day after day.*
**24 from day to day** if something changes from day to day it change often —compare DAY-TO-DAY
**25 day by day** slowly and gradually: *Her health was improving day by day.*
**26 day in, day out** every day for a long time: *She cooked and cleaned day in, day out for forty years.*
**27 night and day** also **day and night** all the time; continuously: *He was attended by nurses night and day.*

⑧ NOW
**28 these days** used to talk about your situation, behaviour, feelings etc now, especially if they used to be different: *I don't go out much these days – once or twice a month at the most.*
**29 in this day and age** used when you are surprised or annoyed that something still happens: *I find it incredible that such punishments still exist in this day and age.*
**30 to this day** even now, after so much time has passed: *To this day I don't know who told Katy about Duncan.*
**31 up to/until/to the present day** from a time in the past until now: *This tradition has continued right up until the present day.*

⑨ BAD THINGS HAPPEN
**32 it's not my/your/his day** *spoken* used when several unpleasant things have happened to someone in one day: *It's really not Chris's day – he overslept, his car broke down, and he spilt coffee on his new pants.*
**33 have an off day** to be less successful or happy than usual, for no particular reason: *His work isn't usually this bad – he must have had an off day.*
**34 it's (just) one of those days** *spoken* used when everything seems to be going wrong: *It's just been one of those days.*

⑩ GOOD THINGS HAPPEN
**35 make sb's day** to make someone very happy: *Hearing her voice on the phone really made my day.*
**36 it's your/his/my lucky day!** used when something very good happens to someone: *Ruth just found a ten pound note in the street. It must be her lucky day!*

⑪ PLEASURE
**37 make a day of it** *spoken* to choose to spend all day doing something, usually for pleasure, when you could have spent only part of the day doing it: *We were going into New York for the concert anyway, so we decided to make a day of it.*
**38 day out** *especially BrE* a day spent at the beach, in the countryside, at the zoo etc

⑫ SUCCESS/FAME
**39 sb's day will come** used to say that someone will have a chance to succeed in the future, even if they are not successful now
**40 have had your day** to be no longer successful, powerful, or famous: *It seems as if Communism has had its day.*

⑬ SPOKEN PHRASES
**41 that'll be the day** *spoken* used to say that you think something is very unlikely to happen: *"Bill says he'll wash the dishes tonight." "That'll be the day!"*

⑭ OTHER MEANINGS
**42 not have all day** *spoken* to not have much time available: *Hurry up, we don't have all day!*
**43 it's not every day (that)** *spoken* used to say that something does not happen often and is therefore very special: *Let's go out and celebrate. After all, it's not every day you get a new job.*
**44 (live to) see the day** *spoken* to experience something that you thought would never happen: *I never*

*thought I'd live to see the day when women became priests.*
**45 40/50/60 etc if she's a day** *spoken* used to emphasize that someone is at least as old as you are saying: *She's ninety if she's a day.*
**46 from one day to the next** if something changes from one day to the next, it does not stay the same for very long: *I never know where he'll be from one day to the next.*
**47 soup/dish/fish of the day** the special soup etc that a restaurant serves on a particular day
**48 day of action** *BrE* a day when the workers in a particular place stop working for one day, to protest about something; a STRIKE[2] (1)
**49 the day of reckoning** the time when you are punished or made to suffer for the things you have done wrong —see also **call it a day** (CALL[1] (27)), **carry the day** (CARRY[1] (23)), **every dog (has) its day** (DOG[1] (11)), **have a field day** (FIELD DAY (1)), HALF-DAY, **it's early days** (EARLY[1] (5)), **it's (a little) late in the day** (LATE[1] (9)), OPEN DAY, **save the day** (SAVE[1] (11)), SPEECH DAY, SPORTS DAY

**USAGE NOTE: DAY**

WORD CHOICE: **from day to day, day by day, day after day**

Something that changes or goes on **day by day** or **from day to day** is a continuous action: *The problem is getting worse day by day.* | *We just muddle along from day to day.*

Separate events that are repeated happen **day after day**: *Day after day he tramps the streets looking for work* (=he does the same thing every day).

GRAMMAR

Remember that *on* is used with days and the word **day** itself: *on Thursday/on that day/on the same day/on the second day* (NOT **in** or **at**)

**On** is never used with the phrase **the other day**, when you do not say the exact day when something happened: *I saw Joey in Dick's Bar the other day* (=a few days ago). Compare: *We spent two days in the mountains —on one day we went hiking and on the other we went fishing.*

Note that you say **in those days** but **these days** (NOT **in these days**): *In those days not many people had TVs, but these days a lot of households have more than one.*

Remember that the phrase is **during the day**: *I couldn't get much work done during the day* (NOT *during day* or *in the day*, though you can say *in the daytime*).

You do not use **the** with **all day**.

SPELLING

Remember that **today** is one word.

**day boy** /ˈ· ·/ *n* [C] *BrE* a boy DAY PUPIL
**day·break** /ˈdeɪbreɪk/ *n* [U] the time of day when light first appears: *We arrived in Cairo at daybreak.*
**day camp** /ˈ· ·/ *n* [C] *AmE* a place where children can go in the day during the school holidays to do sports, art etc
**day care centre** *BrE*, **day care center** *AmE n* /ˈ·· ˌ··/ [C] **1** *AmE* a place where babies are looked after while their parents are at work; CRÈCHE *BrE* **2** a place in Britain where people who are old or ill can be looked after during the day
**day·dream¹** /ˈdeɪdriːm/ *v* [I] to think about something pleasant, especially when this makes you forget what you should be doing: *Stop daydreaming! You were meant to finish that hours ago.* —**daydreamer** *n* [C]
**daydream²** *n* [C] pleasant thoughts you have while you are awake, that make you forget what you are doing
**day girl** /ˈ· ·/ *n* [C] *BrE* a girl DAY PUPIL
**Day·Glo** /ˈdeɪgləʊ‖-gloʊ/ *adj trademark* having a very bright orange, green, yellow, or pink colour: *Dayglo socks*
**day·light** /ˈdeɪlaɪt/ *n* [U] **1** the light produced by the sun during the day: *We'll keep working while there's still enough daylight.* **2 daylight robbery** *BrE informal* a situation in which something costs you a lot more than it should: *£2.50 for a cup of coffee? It's daylight robbery!* **3 see daylight** *informal* to begin to understand something that you have found difficult to understand before: *Joan explained it again, and at last I began to see daylight.* **4 scare/frighten the (living) daylights out of** *informal* to frighten someone a lot: *It scared the living daylights out of me when the flames shot out.* **5 beat/knock the (living) daylights out of** *informal* to hit someone a lot and seriously hurt them —see also **in broad daylight** (BROAD[1] (6))

**daylight sav·ing time** /ˌ·· ˈ·· ˌ ·/ also **daylight savings** /ˌ·· ˈ··/ *n* [U] *AmE* the time during the summer when clocks are one hour ahead of standard time —compare BRITISH SUMMER TIME
**day nur·se·ry** /ˈ· ˌ···/ *n* [C] *BrE* a place where small children can be left while their parents are at work
**day of judge·ment** /ˌ· · ˈ··/ *n* [singular] JUDGMENT DAY
**day pu·pil** /ˈ· ˌ··/ *n* [C] *BrE* a pupil who goes to a BOARDING SCHOOL but who lives at home
**day re·lease** /ˌ· ·ˈ·/ *n* [U] *BrE* a system that allows workers to spend one day a week studying a subject at a college
**day re·turn** /ˌ· ·ˈ·/ *n* [C] *BrE* a train or bus ticket that lets you go somewhere at a cheaper price than usual, if you go there and back on the same day
**day room** /ˈ· ·/ *n* [C] a room in a hospital where patients can go to read, watch television etc
**day school** /ˈ· ·/ *n* [C,U] a school where the students go home in the evening rather than one where they live —compare BOARDING SCHOOL
**day·time** /ˈdeɪtaɪm/ *n* [U] the time during the day between the time when it gets light and the time when it gets dark; DAY (2): *I can't sleep in the daytime.*
**day-to-day** /ˌ· · ˈ·◂/ *adj* **day-to-day management/running/administration etc** work that is done as a normal part of your life, your job etc: *The manager is responsible for the day-to-day running of the hotel.*
**day trip** /ˈ· ·/ *n* [C] a visit to the beach, the zoo etc when you go there and come back the same day
**day-trip·per** /ˈ· ˌ··/ *n* [C] *BrE* someone who visits a place for pleasure but spends only one day there: *Yarmouth is crowded with day-trippers at this time of year.*
**dazed** /deɪzd/ *adj* **1** unable to think clearly, especially because of a shock, accident etc: *Dazed survivors staggered from the wreckage.* **2 in a daze** unable to think clearly: *I've been wandering around in a daze all day.*
**daz·zle** /ˈdæzəl/ *v* [T often passive] **1** if a very bright light dazzles you it stops you from seeing properly for a short time: *a deer dazzled by the headlights* **2** to make someone feel strong admiration: *As children, we were dazzled by my uncle's good looks and charm.* —**dazzle** *n* [U] *BrE*
**daz·zling** /ˈdæzəlɪŋ/ *adj* **1** a light that is dazzling makes you unable to see properly for a short time **2** very impressive and attractive: *a dazzling display of football skills*
**dbl** the written abbreviation of double
**DC** /ˌdiː ˈsiː/ **1** direct current; electric current that always flows in one direction —compare AC **2** the abbreviation of District of Columbia, in the US: *Washington, DC*

**D-Day** /ˈdiː deɪ/ *n* [singular] **1** 6th June 1944; the day the British, Americans, and other armies landed in France during the Second World War **2** *informal* a day on which an important action is planned to happen or begin: *So Friday is D-Day, then?*

**DDT** /ˌdiː diː ˈtiː/ *n* [U] a chemical used to kill insects that harm crops

**de-** /diː, dɪ/ *prefix* **1** in some verbs and nouns, shows an opposite: *a depopulated area* (=which all or most of the population has left) | *deindustrialization* (=becoming less industrial) **2** in some verbs, means to remove something or remove things from something: *to debone the fish* (=remove its bones) | *The king was dethroned.* (=removed from power) **3** in some verbs, means to make something less; reduce: *to devalue the currency*

**dea·con** /ˈdiːkən/ *n* [C] a religious official, in some Christian churches, who is just below the rank of a priest

**dead¹** /ded/ *adj* [no comparative]

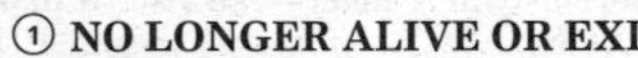

① NO LONGER ALIVE OR EXISTING
② HAVING NO POWER/NOT WORKING
③ HAVING NO FEELING OR ENERGY
④ NOT INTERESTING, USEFUL, OR IMPORTANT
⑤ SPOKEN PHRASES
⑥ OTHER MEANINGS

### ① NO LONGER ALIVE OR EXISTING

**1** no longer alive: *Her mother had been dead for ten years.* | *dead leaves* | **dead body** (=the body of a person who has died) | **dead as a doornail/stone dead** *informal* (=completely dead with no signs of life at all) | **drop dead** (=die suddenly when no-one expects it) *37 years old, no health problems, and he just dropped dead at work!* —compare LIVE² (1)

**2 the dead** people who have died, especially people who have been killed: *There wasn't even time to bury the dead.*

**3 rise from the dead/come back from the dead** according to Christian beliefs, to become alive again after dying

### ② HAVING NO POWER/NOT WORKING

**4 dead battery/engine etc** an engine etc that no longer works because it has no electricity

**5 ▶TELEPHONES ETC◀** a telephone line, radio etc that is dead is not working and makes no sound when you try to use it: *All the lines out of town are dead.* | **go dead** *Suddenly the radio went dead.*

### ③ HAVING NO FEELING OR ENERGY

**6 arm/leg etc** a part of your body that is dead has no feeling in it: **go dead** *When I got up my leg had gone totally dead.*

**7 ▶NO EMOTION◀** showing no emotion or sympathy: *Jennie's eyes were cold and dead.* | **[+to]** *dead to all feelings of compassion*

**8 ▶TIRED◀** *spoken* very tired: *I can't go out tonight. I'm absolutely dead!*

**9 dead to the world** very deeply asleep or unconscious: *Better leave Craig – he's dead to the world.*

### ④ NOT INTERESTING, USEFUL, OR IMPORTANT

**10 ▶BORING◀** a town that is dead is boring because nothing interesting or exciting happens there, and there is nothing interesting to do: *This place is dead after nine o'clock.*

**11 ▶IDEA/SUBJECT◀ dead and buried** an argument, problem, plan etc that is dead and buried is not worth considering again: *You're talking as if the issue of low pay is dead and buried.*

**12 a dead duck** *informal* a plan, idea etc that is not worth considering because it is very likely to fail

**13 be a dead loss** *informal* to be completely useless: *That building firm's a dead loss.*

**14 dead as a dodo** no longer important or useful, and no longer having any influence: *The extreme Right of this country is as dead as a dodo.*

### ⑤ SPOKEN PHRASES

**15 drop dead** *spoken* used to rudely and angrily tell someone to go away and leave you alone

**16 over my dead body** *spoken* used to say that you are determined not to allow something to happen: *You'll marry him over my dead body!*

**17 I wouldn't be seen/caught dead** *spoken* used to say that you would never wear particular clothes, go to particular places, or do particular things, because you would feel embarrassed: **[+ in/on/with etc]** *I wouldn't be seen dead in a dress like that!*

**18 be in dead trouble** *BrE spoken* to be in serious trouble: *You'll be in dead trouble if your Dad finds out.*

**19 dead from the neck up** *BrE spoken* very stupid

### ⑥ OTHER MEANINGS

**20 ▶LANGUAGE◀** a dead language is no longer used by ordinary people: *What's the point of learning a dead language like Latin?* —opposite LIVING² (6)

**21 the dead centre** the exact centre

**22 ▶GLASS/BOTTLE◀** *BrE informal* a glass etc that is dead is no longer being used

**23 dead silence** complete silence: *Everyone stood and waited in dead silence.*

**24 ▶PLANET◀** a dead PLANET (1) has no life on it

**25 ▶IN SPORT◀** when the ball is dead in some games it is no longer on the playing area

**26 a dead cert** *BrE spoken* something that is definitely going to happen or is definitely going to win a race

**27 in a dead faint** completely unconscious

**28 dead ringer** someone who looks exactly like someone else: *Dave's a dead ringer for Paul McCartney.*

**29 dead weight** something that is very heavy and difficult to carry: *The boy was unconscious, a dead weight.*

**30 dead wood** the people or things within an organization that are useless or no longer needed

**31 more dead than alive** in a very weak physical condition: *They were more dead than alive when they were airlifted off the ice.* —**deadness** *n* [U]

S3 **dead²** *adv* **1** *BrE informal* completely: *Ben's dead against coming with us.* **2** *BrE spoken* very: *He was dead good-looking.* **3** [+ adj/adv] *informal* directly or exactly: **dead ahead/in front/at etc** *I stared dead ahead at the doorway.* | **dead on time** *informal* (=exactly at a particular time or the arranged time) *The bus arrived dead on time.* **4 dead beat** *informal* very tired: *I can't go any further – I'm dead beat.*

**dead³** *n* **the dead of night/winter** the middle of the night or the middle of the winter

**dead beat** /ˈ· ˌ·◀/ *n* [C] *AmE informal* **1** someone who is lazy and who has no plans in life **2** someone who avoids paying their debts

**dead bolt** /ˈ· ·/ *n* [C] *AmE* a strong lock often used on doors; MORTICE LOCK *BrE*

**dead·en** /ˈdedn/ *v* [T] to make a feeling or sound less strong: *medicine to deaden the pain*

**dead end** /ˌ· ˈ·◂/ *n* [C] **1** a street with no way out at one end **2** a situation from which no more progress is possible: **come to/reach a dead end** *The negotiations have reached a dead end.* **3 dead-end job** a job with low wages and no chance of progress

**dead·head**[1] /ˈdedhed/ *v* **1** [T] *BrE* to remove the dead flowers from a plant **2** [I] *AmE* to drive a train, bus, or TRUCK[1] (1) with no passengers or goods

**deadhead**[2] *n* [C] *AmE* a vehicle that has no passengers or goods

**dead heat** /ˌ· ˈ·/ *n* [C] the result of a race in which two or more competitors finish at exactly the same time

**dead let·ter** /ˌ· ˈ··/ *n* [C] **1** a law, idea that still exists but that people no longer obey, or are not interested in: *An arts education is a dead letter as far as many students are concerned.* **2** a letter that cannot be delivered or returned

**dead·line** /ˈdedlaɪn/ *n* [C] a date or time by which you have to do or complete something: *The deadline is May 27th.* | **work to a deadline** (=plan your work so that it can be finished by the deadline) | **meet a deadline** (=finish by the deadline) *The deadlines are very short and difficult to meet.* | **tight deadline** (=a deadline that is difficult)

**dead·lock** /ˈdedlɒk‖-lɑːk/ *n* [singular, U] a situation in which a disagreement cannot be settled; STALEMATE (1): *The talks have reached a complete deadlock.* | **break the deadlock** (=end the deadlock) —**deadlock** *v* [I,T] —**deadlocked** *adj*

**dead·ly**[1] /ˈdedli/ *adj*
**1** ▶ **VERY DANGEROUS** ◀ likely to cause death: *a deadly poison*
**2 deadly enemy** someone who will always be your enemy and will try to harm you as much as possible: *The inhabitants soon came to regard the white settlers as their deadly enemy.*
**3** ▶ **COMPLETE** ◀ complete or total: *We sat in deadly silence.*
**4** ▶ **VERY EFFECTIVE** ◀ causing harm in a very effective way: *She hit the target with deadly accuracy.*
**5** ▶ **LIKE DEATH** ◀ [only before noun] like death in appearance: *His face had a deadly paleness.*
**6** ▶ **BORING** ◀ *spoken* not at all interesting or exciting: *"How was the party?" "Pretty deadly."*

**deadly**[2] *adv* **deadly serious/dull/boring etc** very serious, dull etc: *I'm deadly serious, this isn't a game!*

**deadly night·shade** /ˌ·· ˈ··/ *n* [C,U] a poisonous European plant; BELLADONNA

**dead-man's float** /ˌ· · ˈ·/ *n* [singular] *AmE* a way of floating in water with your body and face turned downwards

**dead·pan** /ˈdedpæn/ *adj* sounding and looking completely serious when you are not really: *telling a joke in a deadpan voice* —**deadpan** *adv*

**dead reck·on·ing** /ˌ· ˈ···/ *n* [U] the practice of calculating the position of a ship or aircraft without using the sun, moon, or stars

3 **deaf** /def/ *adj* **1** physically unable to hear anything or unable to hear well: *He's quite deaf and needs a hearing aid.* | **stone deaf/deaf as a post** *informal* (=completely deaf) —see also TONE-DEAF **2 the deaf** people who are deaf: *a school for the deaf* **3 deaf to** *literary* unwilling to hear or listen to something: *She was deaf to his pleas.* **4 turn a deaf ear** be unwilling to listen to what someone is saying or asking: *The factory owners turned a deaf ear to the demands of the workers.* **5 fall on deaf ears** if advice or a warning falls on deaf ears, everyone ignores it —**deafness** *n* [U]

**deaf-aid** /ˈ· ·/ *n* [C] *BrE informal* a small electric machine, worn near your ear, that helps you to hear better; HEARING AID

**deaf-and-dumb** /ˌ· · ˈ·◂/ *adj* unable to hear or speak —**the deaf and dumb** *n* [plural]

**deaf·en** /ˈdefən/ *v* [T usually passive] **1** if a noise deafens you, it is so loud that you cannot hear anything else: *deafened by the roar of the engine* **2** to make someone unable to hear

**deaf·en·ing** /ˈdefənɪŋ/ *adj* noise or music that is deafening is very loud

**deaf-mute** /ˌ· ˈ·‖ˈ· ·/ *n* [C] someone who is unable to hear or speak

**deal**[1] /diːl/ *v past tense and past participle* **dealt** /delt/ S1 W1
**1** also **deal out** [I,T] to give playing cards to each of the players in a game: **deal sth (out) to sb** *Deal out three cards to each player.* **2** [I] *informal* to buy and sell illegal drugs: *Many users end up dealing to support their habit.* **3 deal a blow** *literary* **a)** to cause harm to someone or something: **deal a crippling/decisive etc blow** (=cause very serious harm) *The recession dealt many small businesses a fatal blow.* **b)** to hit someone

**deal in** sth *phr v* [T] **1** to buy and sell a particular type of product: *dealing in 19th century watercolours* —see also DEALER (1) **2** to have a particular attitude to your work: *As a scientist, I do not deal in speculation.*

**deal out** sth *phr v* [T] **1** to give playing cards to each of the players in a game **2** to decide what kind of punishment someone will get

**deal with** sb/sth *phr v* [T] **1** to take the correct action for a piece of work, type of work etc: *Who's dealing with the Glaxo account?* **2** to succeed in solving a problem: *Don't worry, Mr Symes, it's already been dealt with.* **3** to succeed in controlling an emotional problem so that it does not affect your life: *It's OK, I'm dealing with it so far.* **4** to do business with someone or have a business connection with someone: *I've dealt with them for a long time.* **5** if a book, speech, work of art etc deals with a particular subject, it is about that subject: *These ideas are dealt with more fully in Chapter Four.*

**deal**[2] *n* S1 W1
**1 a great deal** also **a good deal** a large quantity of something: [+ **of**] *A great deal of their work is unpaid.* | **a great deal more/a great deal longer etc** (=a lot more, longer etc) *He knew a good deal more than I did.*
**2** ▶ **AGREEMENT** ◀ [C] an agreement or arrangement, especially in business or politics, that helps both sides involved: *The band has negotiated a new deal with their record company.* | **get a good deal** (=buy something at a good price) *You can get some really good deals from travel agents right now.* | **strike/make/cut/do a deal** (=produce or make an agreement) *The two teams did a deal and Robson was traded.*
**3 it's a deal** *spoken* used to say that you agree to do something: *"OK, $500, but that's my last offer." "OK, it's a deal."*
**4** ▶ **TREATMENT** ◀ [C usually singular] treatment of a particular type that is given or received: **a better/fairer deal** *a better deal for nurses* | **a new deal** (=a new and fairer system of social or political treatment) *The prime minister promised a new deal for farmers.* | **a rough/raw deal** (=unfair treatment) *Women tend to get a raw deal from employers.*
**5** ▶ **GAME** ◀ [singular] the process of giving out cards to players in a card game: *It's your deal, Alison.* —see also DEALER (3)
**6** ▶ **WOOD** ◀ [U] *BrE* FIR or PINE[1] (2) wood used for making things: *a deal table*
**7 a deal of** *old-fashioned* a large quantity of something —see also **big deal** (BIG[1] (7))

**USAGE NOTE: DEAL**
GRAMMAR
**A great/good deal of...** is usually only used with uncountable nouns: *a great deal of time/money/difficulty/pressure/interest.* Compare: *There's been a good deal of change* with: *There have been a good many changes.*

W3 **deal·er** /ˈdiːlə‖-ər/ *n* [C] **1** someone who buys and sells a particular product, especially an expensive one: *a car dealer* **2** someone who sells illegal drugs **3** someone who gives out playing cards in a game —see also DOUBLE-DEALER

**deal·er·ship** /ˈdiːləʃɪp‖-ər-/ *n* [C] a business that sells a particular company's product, especially cars: *Nissan dealerships*

**deal·ing** /ˈdiːlɪŋ/ *n* **1 dealings** [plural] the business activities or relationships that you have been involved in: *The secret dealings of his department were made public.* | **have dealings with** (=have a business relationship with someone) *We've had dealings with ITBF for the past few years.* **2 plain dealing/honest dealing etc** a particular way of doing business with people

**dealt** /delt/ *v* the past tense and past participle of DEAL[1]

**dean** /diːn/ *n* [C] **1** a priest of high rank, especially in the Anglican church, who is in charge of several priests or churches **2** someone in a university who is in charge of an area of study, or in charge of students and their behaviour

**dean·e·ry** /ˈdiːnəri/ *n* [C,U] the area controlled by a dean or the place where a dean lives

**dean's list** /ˈ· ·/ *n* [C] *AmE* a list of the best students at a university

S1 **dear**[1] /dɪə‖dɪr/ *interjection* The phrases 'oh dear', 'dear oh dear', 'dear dear', and 'dear me' are all used to show that you are surprised, upset, or annoyed because you have done something wrong, because something bad has happened etc. 'Oh dear' is much more common than the others. 'Dear oh dear' and 'dear dear' are used to emphasize how surprised, upset, or annoyed you are. 'Dear me' is a little old-fashioned: *Oh dear I've broken the lamp.* | *"He's been taken into hospital." "Oh dear!"* | *Dear oh dear, that's terrible news.* | *Dear, dear, I am sorry. Hope I didn't hurt you.* | *Dear me! I forgot to call Kathy and now it's too late.*

S2 **dear**[2] *n* [C] **1** used when speaking to someone you love: *How did the interview go, dear?* **2** *spoken* a friendly way of speaking to someone you do not know, for example, to a customer in a shop: *Can I help you, dear?* **3** *spoken especially BrE* someone who is very kind and helpful: *Be a dear and make me some coffee.* **4 old dear** *BrE* a fairly rude expression meaning an old woman

Frequencies of the word **dear** in spoken and written English.

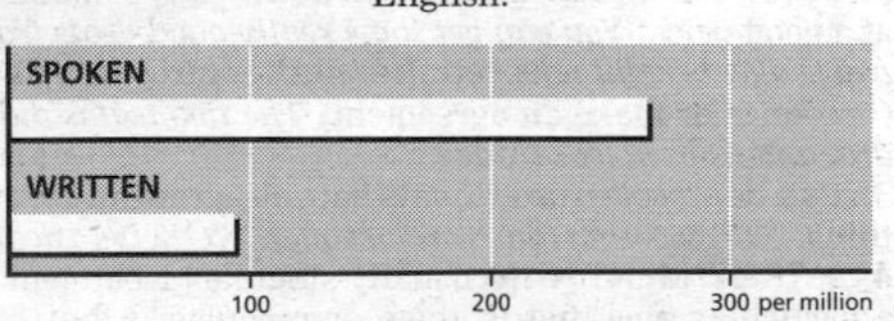


Based on the British National Corpus and the Longman Lancaster Corpus

This graph shows that the word **dear** is much more common in spoken English than in written English. This is because it has some special uses in spoken English and is used in some common spoken phrases.

S2 W2 **dear**[3] *adj* **1 Dear** used before someone's name or title when you begin a letter: *Dear Madam* | *Dear Meg* **2** *BrE* expensive: *I didn't buy it because it was too dear.* **3** *formal* a dear friend or relative is very important to you and you love them a lot: *Mark had become a dear friend.* | **be dear to sb** *His sister was very dear to him.* **4 for dear life** if you run, fight, climb etc for dear life, you do it as fast or as well as you can because you are afraid

**dear**[4] *adv* **cost sb dear** to cause a lot of trouble and suffering for someone: *Carolyn's marriage to Pete cost her dear.*

**dear·est** /ˈdɪərɪ̣st‖ˈdɪr-/ *n* [C] used when speaking to someone you love: *Well, dearest, I was a little worried.*

**dear·ie** /ˈdɪəri‖ˈdɪr-/ *n* [C] another spelling of DEARY

**dear John let·ter** /ˌ· ˈ· ˌ··/ *n* [C] a letter to a man from his wife or GIRLFRIEND, saying that she no longer loves him

**dear·ly** /ˈdɪəli‖ˈdɪrli/ *adv* **1** if you love someone dearly, want something dearly etc, you do so with strong emotions: *James loved his sister dearly.* **2 cost sb dearly** to cause a lot of trouble or suffering: *Vandalism costs schools dearly.* **3 pay dearly** to suffer a lot for something that you have done: *They've paid dearly for not explaining beforehand.* **4 dearly beloved** used by a priest or minister at the beginning of a Christian marriage or funeral

**dearth** /dɜːθ‖dɜːrθ/ *n* [singular] *formal* a lack of something: [+ **of**] *problems owing to the dearth of experienced personnel*

**dear·y, dearie** /ˈdɪəri‖ˈdɪri/ *n* [C] *old-fashioned* **1** used as a way of speaking to someone you love **2 dearie me** *old-fashioned* used when you are surprised or sad about something

S W **death** /deθ/ *n*

**1** ▶ **THE END OF SB'S LIFE** ◀ [U] the end of the life of a person or animal: [+ **of**] *The death of his mother was a great shock.* | *shortly after Lenin's death in 1924* | *the risk of death or serious injury at work* | **bleed/burn/starve etc to death** (=die in a particular way) *He choked to death on a fishbone.* | **put sb to death** (=kill someone, especially after an official decision) *Caesar ordered the prisoners to be put to death.* | **meet your death** *literary* (=die) —see also ACCIDENTAL DEATH

**2** ▶ **EXAMPLE OF SB DYING** ◀ [C] an example of someone dying: *a campaign to reduce the number of deaths on Britain's roads* | [+ **from**] *deaths from lung cancer*

**3 die a horrible/terrible etc death** to die in a terrible etc way: *The animals in the traps can die a slow and agonizing death.*

**4** ▶ **IN ART** ◀ **Death** [singular] a creature that looks like a SKELETON (1a) , used in paintings, stories etc as a sign of death and destruction

**5 scared/bored to death** *informal* extremely frightened or bored

**6 sick to death of** very unhappy with something because it has been annoying you for a long time: *I am sick to death of your complaining!*

**7 you'll catch your death (of cold)** *spoken* used as a warning to someone when you think they are likely to become ill because it is wet or cold: *Don't go out without a coat! You'll catch your death of cold!*

**8 at death's door** be very ill and likely to die

**9 like death warmed up/warmed over** *informal* if someone looks or feels like death warmed up, they look or feel very ill or tired

**10** ▶ **THE END** ◀ [singular] the permanent end of an idea, custom etc: *an article lamenting the death of classical music*

**11 you'll/he'll be the death of me!** *spoken* used, especially humorously, when someone makes you very worried and anxious: *That boy is going to be the death of me!*

**12 fight to the death** **a)** to fight until one person is killed **b)** to fight very hard to achieve something even if it means that you suffer

**13 death blow** an action or event that makes something fail or end: *The new evidence dealt a death blow to the prosecution case.* —see also BLACK DEATH, **kiss of death** (KISS[2] (2)), **a matter of life and death** (LIFE (11))

**death·bed** /ˈdeθbed/ *n* **1 on your deathbed** just before you die **2 deathbed confession/conversion/reconciliation** something that you admit or do just before you die: *a deathbed conversion to Catholicism*

**3 be on your deathbed a)** to be close to death **b)** *humorous* to be feeling very ill

**death camp** /ˈ· ·/ *n* [C] a place where large numbers of prisoners are killed or die, usually in a war

**death cer·tif·i·cate** /ˈ· ·ˌ···/ *n* [C] a legal document, signed by a doctor, that states the time and cause of someone's death

**death du·ty** /ˈ· ˌ··/ *n* [U] *BrE law* tax on the money or property that you give to someone else after you die: INHERITANCE TAX

**death knell** /ˈ· ·/ *n* [singular] **sound the death knell** to be a sign that something will soon stop existing or stop being used: *Plans to build a bridge across the river sounded the death knell for the ferry.*

**death·less** /ˈdeθləs/ *adj* **deathless prose/verse/lines etc** *humorous* writing that is very bad or boring

**death·ly** /ˈdeθli/ *adj* reminding you of death or of a dead body: *Rachel felt deathly cold.* | **a deathly hush** (=complete silence) *A deathly hush fell over the room when the manager walked in.* —**deathly** *adv*

**death mask** /ˈ· ·/ *n* [C] a model of a dead person's face, made by pressing a soft substance over their face and letting it become hard

**death pen·al·ty** /ˈ· ˌ···/ *n* [singular] punishment by killing, used in some countries for serious crimes

**death rate** /ˈ· ·/ *n* [C] the number of deaths for every 100 or every 1000 people in a particular year and in a particular place —compare BIRTHRATE

**death rat·tle** /ˈ· ˌ··/ *n* [C] a strange noise sometimes heard from the throat or chest of someone who is dying

**death row** /ˌdeθ ˈrəʊ‖-ˈroʊ/ *n* [U] the part of a prison where prisoners are kept while waiting to be punished by being killed: **on death row** *a murderer on death row*

**death sen·tence** /ˈ· ˌ··/ *n* [C] the punishment of death given by a judge: *Gilmore received a death sentence.*

**death's head** /ˈ· ·/ *n* [C] a human SKULL used as a sign of death

**death squad** /ˈ· ·/ *n* [C] a group of people who kill their political opponents, often because they have been ordered to by a political party

**death throes** /ˈ· ·/ *n* [plural] **1** the final stages before something fails or ends: *The coalition seems to be in its death throes.* **2** sudden violent movements sometimes made by someone who is dying

**death toll** /ˈ· ·/ *n* [C] the total number of people who die in a particular accident, war etc: *As the civil unrest continued, the death toll rose.*

**death trap** /ˈ· ·/ *n* [C] *informal* a vehicle or building that is in dangerously bad condition: *Some of those second-hand cars are real death traps.*

**death war·rant** /ˈ· ˌ··/ *n* [C] **1** an official document stating that someone is to be killed as a punishment for their crimes **2 sign your own death warrant** to do something that seems likely to cause you very serious trouble

**death wish** /ˈ· ·/ *n* [singular] a desire to die: *He's going out with Debbie; What does he have, a death wish?*

**deb** /deb/ *n* [C] *informal* a DEBUTANTE

**de·ba·cle, débâcle** /deɪˈbɑːkəl, dɪ-‖-ˈbæ/ *n* [C] an event or situation that is a complete failure because plans have failed

**de·bar** /dɪˈbɑː/ *v* **debarred, debarring** [T] to officially prevent someone from doing something: [+ **from**] *He was debarred from the golf club for stealing club funds.* —compare DISBAR

**de·base** /dɪˈbeɪs/ *v* [T] **1** *informal* to reduce the quality or value of something: *a once rational society debased by war and corruption* **2 debase yourself** to do something that makes other people have less respect for you: *women forced to debase themselves by selling their bodies* —**debasement** *n* [C,U]

**de·ba·ta·ble** /dɪˈbeɪtəbəl/ *adj* a question or opinion that is debatable is not clear because different people express different views about it: *That is a highly debatable point.* | **it is debtatable whether/how long etc** *It is debatable whether nuclear weapons actually prevent war.*

**de·bate¹** /dɪˈbeɪt/ *n* **1** [C,U] discussion or argument on a subject that people have different opinions about: [+ **on/over/about**] *As yet there has been little public debate on these issues.* | **fierce/heated/intense debate** (=discussion involving very strong opinions) | **the welfare/abortion etc debate** *the gun control debate in the US* **2** [C] a formal discussion on a subject: [+ **about/on**] *a lively debate on the relevance of Marx today* **3 be open to debate** also **be a matter for debate** if an idea is open to debate no-one has proved yet whether it is true or false: *Whether that would have made any difference is open to debate.* **4 under debate** being discussed: *The whole question of compensation is still under debate.* 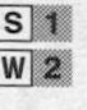 S1 W2

**debate²** *v* [I,T] **1** to discuss a subject formally when you are trying to make a decision or find a solution: *We debated for several hours before taking a vote.* | **debate whether/what/how etc** *debating whether to raise the price of school meals* | **hotly debated** (=argued about strongly) *His conclusions are hotly debated among academics.* **2** to consider something in your own mind before reaching a decision: **debate with yourself** *He debated with himself for a moment then replied.* | **debate who/what/how etc** *I wasn't feeling well and was debating whether to go to work.* —**debater** *n* [C]

**de·bauch** /dɪˈbɔːtʃ‖dɪˈbɒːtʃ, dɪˈbɑːtʃ/ *v* [T] *formal* to make someone behave in an immoral way, especially with alcohol, drugs, or sex

**de·bauched** /dɪˈbɔːtʃt‖-ˈbɒːtʃt,-ˈbɑːtʃt/ *adj* someone who is debauched is immoral because they drink a lot of alcohol, take drugs, or have an immoral attitude to sex

**de·bauch·e·ry** /dɪˈbɔːtʃəri‖dɪˈbɒː-, dɪˈbɑː-/ *n* **1** [U] immoral behaviour involving drugs, alcohol, sex etc: *a life of total debauchery* **2** [C] an occasion when someone behaves in this way

**de·ben·ture** /dɪˈbentʃə‖-ər/ *n* [C] *technical* an official document given by a company, showing that it has borrowed money and that it will pay a fixed rate of INTEREST¹ (4) , whether or not it makes a profit

**de·bil·i·tate** /dɪˈbɪlʒteɪt/ *v* [T] **1** if illness, heat, hunger etc debilitates someone, it makes their body or mind weak: *debilitated by fever* **2** if an action debilitates an organization or structure, it weakens its authority or effectiveness

**de·bil·it·at·ing** /dɪˈbɪlʒteɪtɪŋ/ *adj* **1** a debilitating disease or condition makes your body or mind weak: *debilitating heat* **2** a debilitating action, result etc weakens an organization, structure etc: *the debilitating effect of economic decline*

**de·bil·i·ty** /dɪˈbɪlʒti/ *n* [C,U] *formal* weakness, especially as the result of illness

**deb·it¹** /ˈdebʒt/ *n* [C] *technical* **1** something in a book of accounts that shows money spent or owed **2** a sum of money taken out of a bank account —compare CREDIT¹ (1) —see also DIRECT DEBIT

**debit²** *v* [T] *technical* **1** to take money out of a bank account: *the sum of £25 debited from your account* **2** [+ **against**] to record the amount of money taken from a bank account —compare CREDIT² (2)

**debit card** /ˈ·· ·/ *n* [C] a special plastic card that you can use to pay for things directly from your bank account —compare CASH CARD, CHEQUE CARD, CREDIT CARD

**debit note** /ˈ·· ·/ *n* [C] a document sent by a company to a customer telling them how much money they owe

**deb·o·nair** /ˌdebəˈneə◂‖-ˈner◂/ *adj* a man who is debonair is fashionable and well dressed and behaves in an attractively confident way: *a stylish, debonair young man*

**de·bouch** /dɪˈbaʊtʃ, -ˈbuːʃ/ *v* [I always + adv/prep] **1** *technical* if a river, road etc debouches somewhere, it comes out from a narrow place into a wider place **2** *formal* if people debouch from one place to another, they move out of one place into somewhere larger

**de·brief** /ˌdiːˈbriːf/ *v* [T] to talk to someone to get information from them after they have done a job that you told them to do: *The returning bomber crews were debriefed.* —compare BRIEF³ —**debriefing** *n* [U]

**de·bris** /ˈdebriː, ˈdeɪ-‖dəˈbriː, deɪ-/ *n* [U] all the pieces that are left after something has been destroyed in an accident, explosion etc: *The beach was littered with debris.*

S2 W2 **debt** /det/ *n* **1** [C] a sum of money that you owe: **pay off/repay/clear your debts** *He now had enough money to pay off his father's outstanding debts.* | **[+ of]** *The company has debts of around $1,000,000.* | **run up a debt** (=borrow money without paying it back on time.) *students running up massive credit card debts* **2** [U] the state of owing money: *He was imprisoned for debt.* | **be in debt** (=owe money) | **£200/$1000 etc in debt** *She was still $600 in debt.* | **go/get/run/slip etc into debt** (=spend so much money that you need to borrow money) *Malone was sinking hopelessly into debt.* | **be heavily/deeply/up to your ears in debt** (=owe a lot of money) **3 your debt to sb** the degree to which you have learned from or been influenced by someone else: *Marx's debt to earlier thinkers such as Hegel* **4 be in debt** also **owe a debt of gratitude to sb** to be very grateful to someone for what they have done for you —see also BAD DEBT, NATIONAL DEBT

**debt coll·ect·or** /ˈ· ·,··/ *n* [C] someone who is employed to get back the money that people owe

**debt·or** /ˈdetə‖-ər/ *n* [C] a person, group, or organization that owes money —compare CREDITOR

**de·bug** /ˌdiːˈbʌg/ *v* **debugged, debugging** [T] **1** to take the mistakes out of a computer's PROGRAM (=set of instructions) **2** to find and remove secret listening equipment in a room or building

**de·bunk** /ˌdiːˈbʌŋk/ *v* [T] to show that an idea or belief is false: *debunking the myth that British cuisine is bad* —**debunker** *n* [C]

**de·but** /ˈdeɪbjuː, ˈdebjuː‖deɪˈbjuː, dɪ-/ *n* [C] the first public appearance of someone such as an entertainer or a sports player or of something new and important: *Their debut album was recorded in 1991.* | **make your debut** *a young actress making her debut on Broadway*

**deb·u·tante** /ˈdebjʊtɑːnt/ *n* [C] a young UPPER CLASS woman who goes to special parties as a way of being formally introduced to upper-class society

**Dec** the written abbreviation of DECEMBER

**deca-** /dekə/ *prefix* ten: *decalitre* (=ten litres) | *the decathlon* (=a sports competition with 10 different events) —see table on page B2

S3 W2 **dec·ade** /ˈdekeɪd, deˈkeɪd/ *n* [C] a period of ten years

**dec·a·dence** /ˈdekədəns/ *n* [U] the state of having low moral standards and being more concerned with pleasure than with serious matters: *the corruption and decadence of the nobility*

**dec·a·dent** /ˈdekədənt/ *adj* having low moral standards and being more concerned with your own pleasure than serious matters: *Pop music was condemned as decadent and crude.* —**decadently** *adv*

**de·caf** /ˈdiːkæf/ *n* [U] *spoken* decaffeinated coffee or tea

**de·caf·fein·a·ted** /diːˈkæfɪ̣neɪtɪ̣d/ *adj* coffee or tea that is decaffeinated has had CAFFEINE (=a drug that keeps you awake) removed

**de·cal** /ˈdiːkæl, ˈde-‖diːˈkæl, ˈdekəl/ *n* [C] *AmE* a piece of paper with a pattern or picture on it that you stick onto another surface; TRANSFER[2] (3) *BrE*

**Dec·a·logue** /ˈdekəlɒg‖-lɔːg, -lɑːg/ *n* [singular] the Ten Commandments

**de·camp** /dɪˈkæmp/ *v* [I] to leave a place quickly and usually secretly: *The secretary decamped with the members' money.*

**de·cant** /dɪˈkænt/ *v* [T] to pour liquid, especially wine, from one container into another

**de·cant·er** /dɪˈkæntə‖-ər/ *n* [C] a glass container for holding alcoholic drinks

**de·cap·i·tate** /dɪˈkæpɪ̣teɪt/ *v* [T] to cut off someone's head —**decapitation** /dɪˌkæpɪ̣ˈteɪʃən/ *n* [C,U]

**de·cath·lon** /dɪˈkæθlɒn‖-lɑːn, -lən/ *n* [singular] a competition including ten different sports —compare PENTATHLON

**de·cay[1]** /dɪˈkeɪ/ *v* **1** [I,T] to be slowly destroyed by a natural chemical process, or to make something do this: *The carcass was already starting to decay.* **2** [I often in progressive] if buildings, structures, or areas decay, their condition gradually becomes worse: *The Metropole Hotel was now decaying after years of neglect.* **3** [I often in progressive] if traditional beliefs, morals, standards etc decay, people do not believe in them or support them any more: *Educational standards have decayed.*

**decay[2]** *n* **1** [U] the natural chemical change that causes the slow destruction of something: *The house had stood empty for years and smelled of decay.* | **tooth decay** *Use a fluoride toothpaste to fight tooth decay.* **2** [singular] the part of something that has been destroyed in this way: *The dentist used a drill to remove the decay.* **3** [U] the gradual destruction of ideas, beliefs, social or political organizations etc: *moral and spritual decay* **4** [U] the change from economic success to a state of being poor: *urban decay* **5** [U] the gradual destruction of buildings and structures caused by a lack of care: **fall into decay/fall into a state of decay** *the old fortress falling into a state of decay*

**de·cease** /dɪˈsiːs/ *n* [U] *formal* death: *Upon your decease the house will pass to your wife.*

**de·ceased** /dɪˈsiːst/ *n* **the deceased** *formal* someone who has died, especially recently: *The deceased left a large sum of money to his children.* —**deceased** *adj*

**de·ceit** /dɪˈsiːt/ *n* [C,U] behaviour that is intended to make someone believe something that is not true, or an example of this behaviour: *hypocrisy and deceit*

**de·ceit·ful** /dɪˈsiːtfəl/ *adj* someone who is deceitful tells lies in order to get what they want —**deceitfully** *adv* —**deceitfulness** *n* [U]

**de·ceive** /dɪˈsiːv/ *v* [T] **1** to make someone believe something that is not true in order to get what you want: *You deceived me, and I can't forgive you.* | **deceive sb into doing sth** *They deceived the old man into signing the papers.* **2 deceive yourself** to pretend to yourself that something is not true, because the truth is unpleasant: *I thought she loved me, but really I was deceiving myself.* **3 are my eyes deceiving me?** *spoken* used when you see someone or something that you are very surprised to see: *Are my eyes deceiving me, or is that a genuine Persian carpet.* —**deceiver** *n* [C]

**de·cel·e·rate** /ˌdiːˈseləreɪt/ *v* [I] *technical* to go slower, especially in a vehicle: *Decelerate when approaching a corner.* —opposite ACCELERATE —**deceleration** /ˌdiːseləˈreɪʃən/ *n* [U]

**De·cem·ber** /dɪˈsembə‖-ər/ written abbreviation **Dec** *n* [C,U] the 12th and last month of the year, between November and January: **in December** *The course starts in December.* | **last/next December** *I arrived here last December.* | **on December 6th** (also **on 6th December** *BrE*) *The meeting will be on December 6th* (spoken as *on the sixth of December* or *on December the sixth* or *AmE on December 6th*)

**de·cen·cy** /ˈdiːsənsi/ *n* [U] **1** a quality in someone's character that makes them honest and polite and makes them have respect for other people: *a judgement that reflects the decency and good sense of the American people* **2** acceptable behaviour, especially moral and sexual behaviour: **sense of decency** *They have no sense of honour or decency.* | **common decency** (=basic standards of behaviour that everyone should follow) *It's common decency to let someone know if you are going to arrive late.* | **have the decency to do sth** (=behave in a way that follows the basic standards of acceptable behaviour) *You could have had the decency to ask me before you invited all your friends to stay!* **3 decencies** *old-fashioned* standards of behaviour that people think are acceptable

**de·cent** /ˈdiːsənt/ *adj* **1** acceptable and good enough: *Haven't you got a decent pair of shoes?* | *a house with a decent sized yard* **2** treating people in a fair and kind way: *I decided her father was a decent guy, after all.* | **be decent of sb to do sth** *It was decent of him to offer to help us paint the house.* | **be decent about something** S *especially BrE* (=treat someone fairly and sympathetically when they have done something wrong) *The lecturers were really decent about my absences.* **3** following the standards of moral behaviour accepted by most people: *Decent citizens have nothing to fear from this legislation.* | **do the decent thing** (=do something because you feel you ought to) *When Tom found out that his girlfriend was pregnant, he did the decent thing and married her.* **4** *usually humorous* wearing enough clothes to not show too much of your body: *Don't come in – I'm not decent!* —opposite INDECENT (1) **5 a decent burial/funeral** if someone is given a decent burial, they are buried in an acceptable way —**decently** *adv*

**de·cen·tral·ize** also **-ise** *BrE* /ˌdiːˈsentrəlaɪz/ *v* [T] to move parts of a government, organization etc from one central place to several different smaller ones: *Many firms are decentralizing parts of their operations.* —**decentralized** *adj*: *a decentralized economy* —**decentralization** /ˌdiːsenrəlaɪˈzeɪʃən‖-lə-/ *n* [U]

**de·cep·tion** /dɪˈsepʃən/ *n* [C,U] the act of deliberately making someone believe something that is not true: *outrage at the government's deception*

**de·cep·tive** /dɪˈseptɪv/ *adj* **1** something that is deceptive seems to be one thing but is in fact very different: *A boa constrictor can move with deceptive speed.* **2** deliberately intended to make someone believe something that is not true: *deceptive behavior* —**deceptively** *adj* —**deceptiveness** *n* [U]

**deci-** /desɪ/ *prefix* a 10th part of a unit: *a decilitre* (=0.1 litres) —see table on page B2

**dec·i·bel** /ˈdesɪ̈bel,-bəl/ *n* [C] *technical* a unit of measurement for the loudness of sound: *The noise level in factories must not exceed 85 decibels.*

This graph shows how common the different grammar patterns of the verb **decide** are.

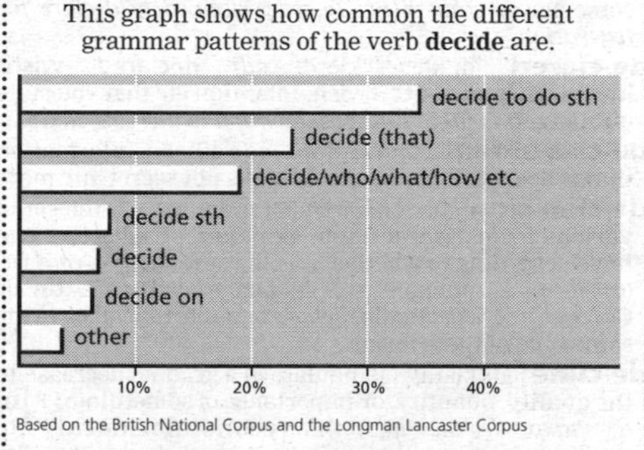


S1 W1 **de·cide** /dɪˈsaɪd/ *v* **1** [I,T] to make a choice or judgment about something, especially after a period of not knowing what to do or in a way that ends disagreement: **decide to do sth** *Tina's decided to go to Prague for her holidays.* | **decide that** *It was eventually decided that four London hospitals should be closed.* | **decide who/what/how etc** *I can't decide what to do.* | **decide whether/if** *Women now have greater freedom to decide whether or not to get married.* | [+ **between**] *I'm trying to decide between the green and the blue for the bathroom.* | **decide sth** *I'm eighteen now —I have a right to decide my own future.* | **decide for yourself** (=make your own choice or judgment, without asking anyone else to do it for you) *You must decide for yourself whether to leave college.* —see also DECISION (1) **2** [T] to be the reason for someone making a particular judgment or choice: **decide sb to do sth** *What was it that finally decided you to give up your job?* | **deciding factor** (=a very strong reason that forces you to make a particular decision) *Money should not be the deciding factor over who runs a TV station.* **3** [T] if an event, action etc decides something, it influences events so that one particular result will happen: *A goal in the last minute decided the match.* | **the deciding vote** (=the person who has the deciding vote makes the final decision, because all the other votes are equally divided) **4 decide in favour of/decide against a)** to choose or not choose someone or something: *After long discussion they decided in favour of the younger candidate.* **b)** if a judge or JURY (1) decides in favour of someone or against someone, they say in court that someone is guilty or not guilty: *The jury decided in favour of the plaintiff.*

**decide on** sth *phr v* [T] to choose one thing from many possible choices: *Have you decided on a date for your wedding?*

**de·cid·ed** /dɪˈsaɪdɪ̈d/ *adj* definite and easily noticed: *a decided change for the better*

**de·cid·ed·ly** /dɪˈsaɪdɪ̈dli/ *adv* **1** [+ adj/adv] *especially BrE* definitely or in a way that is easily noticed: *The man was decidedly drunk.* **2** in a way that shows that you are very sure and determined about what you want to do: *"I'm not going to do it," said Margaret decidedly.*

**de·cid·er** /dɪˈsaɪdə‖-ər/ *n* [C] *informal* the last part of a game or competition, which will show who the winner is: *This next round will be the decider.*

**de·cid·u·ous** /dɪˈsɪdʒuəs/ *adj* deciduous trees lose their leaves in winter —compare EVERGREEN[2]

**dec·i·mal**[1] /ˈdesɪ̈məl/ *adj* a decimal system is based on the number 10: *decimal currency*

**decimal**[2] *n* [C] *technical* a FRACTION (=a number less than one) that is shown as a FULL STOP followed by the number of TENTHS, then the number of HUNDREDTHS etc, as in the numbers 0.5, 0.175, 0.661 etc

**dec·i·mal·ize** also **-ise** *BrE* /ˈdesɪ̈məlaɪz‖ˈdesəmə-/ *v* [I,T] to change to a decimal system of money or measurements —**decimalization** /ˌdesɪ̈məlaɪˈzeɪʃən‖ˌdesəmələ-/ *n* [U]

**decimal place** /ˌ··· ˈ·/ *n* [C] *technical* one of the positions after a FULL STOP in a decimal: *measurements accurate to three decimal places*

**decimal point** /ˌ··· ˈ·/ *n* [C] *technical* the FULL STOP in a decimal, used to separate whole numbers from TENTHS, HUNDREDTHS, etc

**decimal sys·tem** /ˈ··· ˌ··/ *n* [singular] a system of counting that is based on the number 10

**dec·i·mate** /ˈdesɪ̈meɪt/ *v* [T usually passive] to destroy a large part of something: *The population has been decimated by disease.* —**decimation** /ˌdesɪ̈ˈmeɪʃən/ *n* [U]

**de·ci·pher** /dɪˈsaɪfə‖-ər/ *v* [T] to find the meaning of something that is difficult to read or understand: *I can't decipher his handwriting.* —see also INDECIPHERABLE

This graph shows some of the words most commonly used with the noun **decision**.

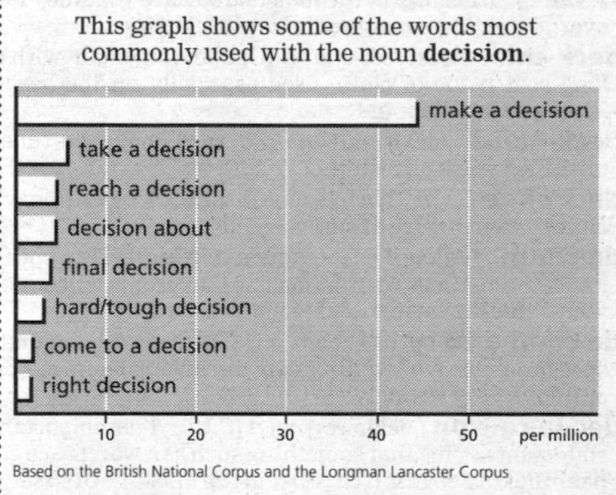


**de·ci·sion** /dɪˈsɪʒən/ *n* **1** [C] a choice or judgment that you make after a period of discussion or thought: *The judges' decision is final.* | **decision to do sth** *his wife's decision to leave him* | **make/take a decision** (=decide) *The committee is due to make its decision this week.* | **come to/reach a decision** (=finally decide) *We finally came to a firm decision.* | [+ **about**] *a decision about whether to expand the business* | **final decision** (=a decision that will not be changed) *I'm afraid I don't have the final decision in these matters.* | **big decision** (=an important S1 W1 decision) | **difficult/hard/tough decision** *It was a tough decision, but I decided to leave my job.* **2** [U] the quality someone has that makes them able to make choices or judgments quickly and confidently: *This job requires the ability to act with speed and decision.* —opposite INDECISION **3** [U] the act of deciding something: *The burden of decision rests with the Supreme Court.*

**decision-mak·ing** /'·· ˌ··/ *n* [U] the process of thinking about a problem, idea etc, and then making a choice or judgment: *an attempt to make workers more involved in decision-making*

**de·ci·sive** /dɪ'saɪsɪv/ *adj* **1 a decisive step/role/battle etc** an action, event etc that has a powerful effect on the final result of something: *Waterloo was the decisive battle of the entire war.* **2** good at making decisions quickly and with confidence: *a decisive leader* | **decisive action** (=action taken quickly and confidently in order to solve a problem) *She demonstrated a talent for quick, decisive action.* **3** leading to a clear result and ending doubt: *a decisive election victory* **4 play a decisive role (in sth)** to be one of the most important causes of something: *a decisive role in the recent peace process* **5 a decisive step** something that results in important change: *The covenant at Sinai was the decisive step in the creation of Israel.* **6** definite and not able to be doubted: *The answer was a decisive no.* —**decisively** *adv*

**de·ci·sive·ness** /dɪ'saɪsɪvnɪ̈s/ *n* [U] the ability to make decisions quickly with confidence and determination: *David acted with speed and decisiveness.*

**deck¹** /dek/ *n* [C] **1** the outside top level of a ship that you can walk on: **on deck** *Let's go up on deck and sit in the sun.* | **above/below deck(s)** *Peter stayed below decks.* —see picture at YACHT **2** one of the levels on a ship or bus: **lower/upper deck** (=on a ship) *Our cabin is on the lower deck.* | **top/bottom deck** (=on a bus) *The kids love riding on the top deck.* **3** *AmE* a wooden floor built out from the back of a house, used for relaxing on **4** *especially AmE* a set of playing cards; PACK² (8) *BrE* **5 all hands on deck** *informal* used when everyone must work together to do something as quickly as possible —see also **clear the decks** (CLEAR² (14)), **hit the deck** (HIT¹ (21)), FLIGHT DECK, TAPE DECK

**deck²** *v* [T] **1** also **deck sth out** to decorate something with flowers, flags etc, especially for a special occasion: [+ **with**] *The street was decked with flags for the royal wedding.* **2** *slang* to hit someone so hard that they fall over: *Gerry just swung round and decked him.*

**deck·chair** /'dektʃeə‖-tʃer/ *n* [C] a folding chair with a long seat made of cloth, used especially on the beach —see picture at CHAIR¹

**deck·hand** /'dekhænd/ *n* [C] someone who does unskilled work on a ship

**deck shoe** /'· ·/ *n* [C] a flat shoe made of CANVAS (=heavy cloth) —see picture at SHOE¹

**de·claim** /dɪ'kleɪm/ *v* [I + **against/about** T] to speak loudly, sometimes with actions, so that people will notice you —**declamation** /ˌdeklə'meɪʃən/ *n* [C,U]

**de·clam·a·to·ry** /dɪ'klæmətəri‖-tɔːri/ *adj* a declamatory speech or piece of writing expresses your feelings and opinions very strongly

W3 **dec·la·ra·tion** /ˌdeklə'reɪʃən/ *n* [C,U] **1** an important statement saying that something such as a war, peace etc has officially begun: *a ceasefire declaration* | [+ **of**] *issue a declaration of war* **2** an official or serious statement of what someone believes: [+ **of**] *the United Nations Declaration of Human Rights* **3** a statement in which you officially give information, especially about yourself: *a declaration of taxable earnings*

**de·clar·a·tive** /dɪ'klærətɪv/ *adj technical* a declarative sentence has the form of a statement

W2 **de·clare** /dɪ'kleə‖-kler/ *v*

**1 ▶ STATE OFFICIALLY ◀** [T] to state officially and publicly that a particular situation exists or that something is true: **declare that** *The doctor finally declared that the man was dead.* | **declare sth (to be) sth** *The government of New South Wales declared 8000 hectares of forest a national park.* | **declare sth open** *I declare this exhibition open.* | **declare sth unsafe/a failure/a success etc** *The use of certain chemicals has now been declared illegal.* | **declare sb insane/unfit/a traitor etc** (=state officially that someone is crazy etc) | **declare sb the winner/the champion etc** *Ali was declared the winner of the fight.*

**2 declare war (on sb) a)** to decide and state officially that you will begin fighting another country **b)** *informal* to say that something is wrong and that you will do everything you can to stop it: *Police have now declared war on drug dealers in the area.*

**3 ▶ SAY WHAT YOU THINK/FEEL ◀** [T] to say very clearly and publicly what you think or feel: *"On that point, I cannot agree with you," he declared.* | **declare that** *Jane declared that she would rather resign than change her decision.* | **declare sth** *The opposition declared their support for the bill.* | **declare yourself (to be) sth** *She had publicly declared herself a lesbian.*

**4 ▶ MONEY/PROPERTY ETC ◀** [T] to make an official statement saying how much money you have earned, what property you own etc: *All investment income must also be declared.*

**5 declare an interest** to tell people that you are connected with something that is being discussed: *I should declare an interest here; Mr Hackett used to work for me.*

**6 declare bankruptcy** to state officially that you are unable to pay your debts

**7 ▶ SURPRISE ◀ (Well) I declare!** *spoken old-fashioned* used as an expression of surprise: *Well I declare! What a pretty little village.* —**declarable** *adj*

**declare against** sb/sth *phr v* [T] to state that you oppose someone or something

**declare for** sb/sth *phr v* [T] to state that you support someone or something: *Paredes decided to declare for federation.*

**de·clared** /dɪ'kleəd‖-'klerd/ *adj* **declared wish/intention/policy etc** a wish, intention etc that you state publicly: *It is their declared intention to increase taxes.*

**de·clas·si·fied** /ˌdiː'klæsɪ̈faɪd/ *adj* official information that is declassified was secret but is not secret any more

**de·clen·sion** /dɪ'klenʃən/ *n* [C] *technical* **1** the set of various forms that a noun, PRONOUN, or adjective can have according to whether it is the SUBJECT¹ (5), OBJECT¹ (6) etc of a sentence in a language such as Latin or German **2** a particular set of nouns etc that all have the same type of these forms

**de·cline¹** /dɪ'klaɪn/ *n* [singular, U] a gradual decrease in the quality, quantity, or importance of something: [+ **in**] *a sharp decline in profits* | **economic/moral etc decline** *Economic decline is often tangled up with political turmoil.* | **fall/go into decline** (=start to decrease) *The activities of Welsh mines went into decline after about 1980.* W

**decline²** *v* W

**1 ▶ BECOME LESS ◀** [I] to decrease in quantity or importance: *In regions such as New England textile industries had declined and unemployment was high.* | *declining prices*

**2 ▶ BECOME WORSE ◀** [I] to become gradually worse in quality: *Do you think standards of education have declined in recent years?* | *declining health*

**3 ▶ SAY NO ◀** [I,T] to say no when someone invites you somewhere or offers you something: *Talbot had been invited but declined on the grounds that he was too busy.* | **decline an offer/proposal etc** *We declined their offer of financial help.*

**4 ▶ REFUSE ◀** to refuse to do something: **decline to do sth** *Allen angrily declined to discuss the matter.* —see REFUSE¹ (USAGE)

**5 sb's declining years** *formal* the last years of someone's life

**6 ▶ GRAMMAR ◀** *technical* **a)** [I] if a noun, PRONOUN, or adjective declines, its form changes according to whether it is the SUBJECT¹ (5), OBJECT¹ (6) etc of a sentence **b)** [T] if you decline a noun etc, you show these various forms that it can take

**de·code** /ˌdiːˈkəʊd‖-ˈkoʊd/ *v* [T] **1** to discover the meaning of a secret or complicated message: *a computer that can decode and implement complex instructions.* **2** *technical* to understand the meaning of a word rather than use a word to express meaning —opposite ENCODE

**dé·colle·tage** /ˌdeɪkɒlˈtɑːʒ‖deɪˌkɑːləˈtɑːʒ/ *n* [U] *French* the top edge of a woman's dress that is cut very low to show part of her shoulders and breasts —**décolleté** /deɪˈkɒlteɪ‖ˌdeɪkɑːləˈteɪ/ *adj*: *a satin dress, high-waisted and decolleté*

**de·col·o·nize** also **-ise** *BrE* /ˌdiːˈkɒlənaɪz‖-ˈkɑː-/ *v* [T] to make a former COLONY politically independent —**decolonization** /diːˌkɒlənaɪˈzeɪʃəl‖-ˌkɑːlənə-/ *n* [U]

**de·com·mis·ion** /ˌdiːkəˈmɪʃən/ *v* [T] to stop using a NUCLEAR weapon or REACTOR and prepare to take it to pieces

**de·com·pose** /ˌdiːkəmˈpəʊz‖-ˈpoʊz/ *v* **1** [I,T] to decay or make something decay: *a partially-decomposed body* **2** [I,T] *technical* to divide into smaller parts or to make something do this —**decomposition** /ˌdiːkɒmpəˈzɪʃən‖-ˌkɑːm-/ *n* [U]

**de·com·press** /ˌdiːkəmˈpres/ *v* [T] to reduce the pressure of air on something

**de·com·pres·sion cham·ber** /ˌdiːkəmˈpreʃən ˌtʃeɪmbə‖-bər/ *n* [C] a special room where people go after they have been deep under the sea, in order to slowly return to normal air pressure

**decompression sick·ness** /ˌdiːkəmˈpreʃən ˌsɪknɪ̈s/ *n* [U] a dangerous medical condition that people get when they come up from deep under the sea too quickly; **bends** (BEND² (3))

**de·con·gest·ant** /ˌdiːkənˈdʒestənt◂/ *n* [C,U] medicine that you can take if you have a cold to help you breathe more easily

**de·con·struc·tion** /ˌdiːkənˈstrʌkʃən/ *n* [U] *technical* a method used in the criticism of literature which claims that there is no single explanation of the meaning of a piece of writing

**de·con·tam·i·nate** /ˌdiːkənˈtæmɪ̈neɪt/ *v* [T] to remove a dangerous substance from somewhere: *It may cost over $5 million to decontaminate the whole site.* —**decontamination** /ˌdiːkəntæmɪ̈ˈneɪʃən/ *n* [U]

**de·cor** /ˈdeɪkɔː‖-kɔːr/ *n* [C,U] the way that the inside of a building is decorated: *tacky furniture and tasteless decor*

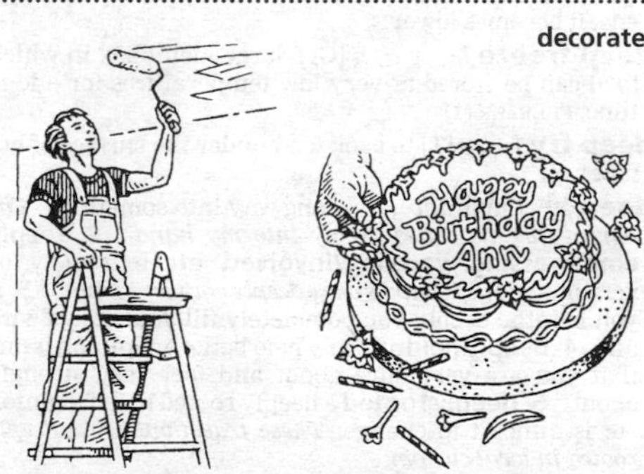


S3 **dec·o·rate** /ˈdekəreɪt/ *v especially BrE* **1** [I,T] to make the inside of a building look more attractive by painting it, putting paper on the walls etc: *I'm going to decorate the bathroom next.* **2** [T] to make something look more attractive by putting something pretty on it: **decorate sth with** *We decorated the Christmas tree with tinsel and lights.* **3** [T + **for**] to give someone a MEDAL as an official sign of honour —**decorating** *n* [U]

S3 **dec·o·ra·tion** /ˌdekəˈreɪʃən/ *n* **1** [C often plural] something pretty that you put onto something else in order to make it more attractive: *Christmas decorations* **2** [U] the way in which something is decorated: *The Rococo decoration inside the palace is delightful.* **3** [C,U] *especially BrE* the act or process of decorating: *The decoration of the house had taken months to complete.* **4** [C] something such as a MEDAL that is given to someone as an official sign of honour

**dec·o·ra·tive** /ˈdekərətɪv‖ˈdekərə-, ˈdekəreɪ-/ *adj* pretty or attractive, but not always necessary or useful: *a decorative panel above the door* —**decoratively** *adv*

**dec·o·ra·tor** /ˈdekəreɪtə‖-ər/ *n* [C] someone who paints houses and puts paper on the walls as their job

**dec·o·rous** /ˈdekərəs/ *adj formal* having the correct appearance or behaviour for a particular occasion —**decorously** *adv*: *A servant was hovering decorously behind them.*

**de·co·rum** /dɪˈkɔːrəm/ *n* [U] *formal* correct behaviour that shows respect: *I hope you will behave with suitable decorum at the prize-giving tomorrow.*

**de·coy** /ˈdiːkɔɪ/ *n* [C] **1** someone or something used to trick someone into going where you want them to go so that you can catch them, attack them etc: *Police have been using mocked-up patrol cars as decoys to make drivers slow down.* **2** a model of a bird used to attract wild birds so that you can watch them or shoot them —**decoy** /dɪˈkɔɪ/ *v* [T]

**de·crease¹** /dɪˈkriːs/ *v* [I,T] to go down to a lower level, or to make something do this: *In the last ten years cars have generally decreased in size.*|*making further efforts to decrease military spending* —opposite INCREASE¹ —**decreasing** *adj*

**de·crease²** /ˈdiːkriːs/ *n* [C,U] the process of reducing something, or the amount by which it reduces: [+ **in**] *There has been a decrease in the annual birth rate for the last twenty years.*|[+ **of**] *He refused to accept a decrease of 20% to his salary.*

**de·cree¹** /dɪˈkriː/ *n* [C] **1** an official command or decision, especially one made by the ruler of a country: *On 13 November the Emperor issued the decree.* **2** a judgment in a court of law

**decree²** *v* [T] to make an official judgment or give an official command: **decree that** *The King decreed that there should be an end to the fighting.*

**decree ab·sol·ute** /·ˌ· ˈ···/ *n* [C] *BrE law* an order by a court of law which officially ends a marriage

**decree ni·si** /dɪˌkriː ˈnaɪsaɪ/ *n* [C] *BrE law* an order by a court of law that a marriage will end at a particular time in the future unless there is a good reason not to end it

**de·crep·it** /dɪˈkrepɪ̈t/ *adj* old and in bad condition: *The buildings were in a decrepit state.* —**decrepitude** *n* [U]

**de·crim·in·a·lize** also **-ise** *BrE* /diːˈkrɪmɪ̈nəlaɪz/ *v* [T] to state officially that something is not illegal any more: *the campaign to decriminalize cannabis* —**decriminalization** *n* [U]

**de·cry** /dɪˈkraɪ/ *v* **decried, decrying** [T] *formal* to state publicly that you do not approve of something

**ded·i·cate** /ˈdedɪ̈keɪt/ *v* [T] **1 a)** to say that something such as a book or film has been written, made, or sung to express love, respect etc for someone: **dedicate sth to sb** *I'd like to dedicate this song to my wife.* **b)** to state in an official ceremony that a building will be given someone's name in order to show respect for them: **dedicate sth to sb** *a chapel dedicated to St Francis* **2 dedicate yourself/your life to sth** to decide to spend all your time on and put all your efforts into one particular thing: *Sheila dedicated herself to a life of religion.*

**ded·i·cat·ed** /ˈdedɪ̈keɪtɪ̈d/ *adj* **1** someone who is dedicated works very hard at what they do because they care a lot about it: *He's certainly dedicated but really not very talented.*|[+ **to**] *dedicated to one's art*|**dedicated sportsman/musician/Marxist etc** *Simon has been a dedicated Marxist all his life.* **2** made for or used for only one particular purpose: *the transmission of software code through dedicated satellite channels* **3** *technical* a dedicated computer, computer system etc is only used for one particular job, such as controlling a machine —**dedicatedly** *adv*

**ded·i·ca·tion** /ˌdedʒ'keɪʃən/ *n* **1** [U] hard work or effort that someone puts into a particular activity because they care about it a lot: *The success of the festival is a tribute to the dedication of one man.* | [+ **to**] *single-minded dedication to her art* **2** [C] an act of dedicating something to someone **3** [C] a ceremony in which a building is given someone's name in order to show respect for them

**de·duce** /dɪ'djuːs‖dɪ'duːs/ *v* [T] *formal* to make a judgment about something, based on the information that you have: **deduce that** *I deduced that she was married by the ring on her finger.* | [+ **from**] *What did Darwin deduce from the presence of these species?* —**deducible** *adj*

**de·duct** /dɪ'dʌkt/ *v* [T] to take away an amount or part from a total; subtract: **deduct sth from** *The dues will be deducted from his weekly pay-cheques.* —**deductible** *adj*

**de·duc·tion** /dɪ'dʌkʃən/ *n* [C,U] **1** the process of making a judgment about something, based on the information that you have: *His powers of deduction were impressive.* **2** the process of taking away an amount from a total, or the amount that is taken away: *After deductions for tax etc your salary is about £700 a month.*

**de·duc·tive** /dɪ'dʌktɪv/ *adj* using the knowledge that you have to make a judgment about a fact or situation: *deductive reasoning*

**deed** /diːd/ *n* [C] **1** *literary* something someone does that is very good or very bad: *heroic deeds in battle* **2** *law* an official paper that is a record of an agreement, especially an agreement concerning who owns property **3 your good deed for the day** *humorous* something kind or helpful that you do

**deed poll** /'· ·/ *n* [C] a legal document signed by only one person, for example in order to officially change your name

**deem** /diːm/ *v* [T not in progressive] *formal* to think of something in a particular way; consider: **deem that** *They deemed that he was no longer capable of managing the business.* | **deem sth necessary/appropriate etc** *They were told to take whatever action they deemed necessary.*

S2 W1 **deep¹** /diːp/ *adj*
**1 ▶ GOING FAR DOWN ◀** going far down from the top or from the surface: *a deep hole in the ground* | *Come on, get in! The water's not very deep here.* | **2 metres/6 feet etc deep** *At this point the lake is ninety metres deep.*
**2 knee-deep/ankle-deep etc** deep enough to come up to your knees etc: *Soon they were in waist-deep mud.*
**3 ▶ GOING FAR IN ◀** going far in from the outside or from the front edge of something: *He had a deep wound on his forehead.* | **deep in the forest/mountains etc** (=far from the edge of the forest etc) *The path led them deep into the forest.*
**4 ▶ FEELING/BELIEF ◀** a deep feeling or belief is very strong and sincere: *Even Rob's parents regarded him with deep suspicion.*
**5 run/go deep** if a feeling such as hatred or anger runs deep in someone, they feel it very strongly, especially because of things that have happened in the past: *Resentment against the police runs deep in the community.* —see also **still waters run deep** (STILL² (5))
**6 ▶ SOUND ◀** a deep sound is very low: *his deep voice* | *There was a flash and a deep roar.*
**7 ▶ COLOUR ◀** a deep colour is dark and strong: *the deep blue sky* —compare LIGHT³ (1), PALE¹ (2)
**8 ▶ BREATH ETC ◀** a deep SIGH², GULP² etc involves taking a lot of air into your lungs before letting it out again with a loud sound: *He took a deep breath and began to sing.*
**9 ▶ SERIOUS ◀ a)** someone who is deep or has deep thoughts thinks very hard about things, often in a way that other people find difficult to understand: *Hal seems to me to be a very deep, sensitive type of person.* **b)** a deep book, conversation, thought etc involves serious, complicated, or mysterious subjects that are often difficult to understand: *a deep conversation about the meaning of life*
**10 deep in debt** owing a lot of money
**11 deep sleep** if someone is in a deep sleep it is difficult to wake them
**12 be in deep trouble** also **be in deep shit** *slang* to be in a bad situation because you have done something wrong or stupid: *Don't say another word. You're in deep shit already.*
**13 in deep water** in trouble or in a difficult or serious situation: *He had an uneasy feeling he was getting into deep water.*
**14 to be in deep** *informal* to be very involved in a situation, especially one that causes you problems
**15 deep in thought/conversation etc** thinking so hard, or paying attention to something so much that you do not notice anything else that is happening around you
**16 jump/be thrown in at the deep end** to choose to do or be made to do a very difficult job without having prepared for it: *Our policy is to throw trainee representatives right in at the deep end.*
**17 go off at the deep end** *informal* to become angry suddenly and violently, usually without good reason —**deepness** *n* [U]

**deep²** *adv* **1** [always + adv/prep] a long way into or below the surface of something; deeply: [+ **down/below etc**] *He pushed his stick deep down into the mud.* | *Carl was looking deep into her eyes.* **2 deep down a)** if you know or feel something deep down, you are sure about it even though you do not admit it: *I knew deep down that I would probably never see Marie again.* **b)** if someone is good, evil etc deep down, that is what they are really like even though they usually hide it: *She may seem unfriendly, but deep down she's very nice.* **3 deep into the night** until very late: *They talked deep into the night.* **4 two/three etc deep** if things or people are two deep, there are two rows or layers of things or people: *People were standing three deep at the bar.* W

**deep³** *n* **the deep** *poetical* the sea

**deep·en** /'diːpən/ *v* **1** [I,T] if a feeling such as love or sadness deepens, it gradually becomes stronger: *Enid's sorrow deepened as she thought of the long years ahead without him.* **2** [I] if a serious situation deepens, it gets worse: *a deepening recession* **3** [I,T] if you deepen your knowledge or understanding of something, you learn more about it and understand it better: *an opportunity for young people to deepen their understanding of the world* **4** [I] if water deepens, it becomes deeper **5** [I] if a colour deepens, it becomes darker **6** [I] if a sound deepens, it becomes lower

**deep freeze** /ˌ· '·‖'· ·/ *n* [C] a large metal box in which food can be stored at very low temperatures for a long time; FREEZER (1)

**deep fry** /'· ·/ *v* [T] to cook food under the surface of hot fat or oil

**deep·ly** /'diːpli/ *adv* **1** a long way into something: *The parrot dug its claws deeply into my hand.* **2 deeply embarrassing/worrying/involved etc** extremely or very much: *His remarks were deeply embarrassing.* **3** if you breathe deeply you completely fill your lungs with air **4 deeply held** a deeply held belief or opinion is one that you are very sure about and feel very strongly about **5 deeply rooted** a deeply rooted belief, opinion etc is difficult to change: *These traditions were deeply rooted in local custom.* W

**deep-root·ed** /ˌ· '··◂/ also **deeply rooted** /ˌ·· '··◂/ *adj* a deep-rooted habit, idea, belief etc is so fixed in a person or society that it is very difficult to change or destroy it: *a deep-rooted suspicion of lawyers*

**deep-seat·ed** /ˌ· '··◂/ *adj* a deep-seated attitude, feeling, or idea is strong and is very difficult to change: *a deep-seated fear of failure*

**deep-set** /ˌ· '·◂/ *adj* deep-set eyes seem to be further back into the face than most people's

**deep six** /ˌ· '·/ *v* [T] *AmE informal* to decide not to use something such as a plan: *We decided to deep six the whole project.*

**Deep South** /ˌ· ˈ·/ *n* [singular] the most southern states of the US

**deer** /dɪə‖dɪr/ *n plural* **deer** or **deers** [C] a large grass-eating wild animal that can run very fast and has wide branching horns

**deer·stalk·er** /ˈdɪəˌstɔːkə‖ˈdɪrˌstɒːkər/ *n* [C] a type of soft hat with pieces of cloth that cover your ears

**de·face** /dɪˈfeɪs/ *v* [T] to spoil the surface or appearance of something, especially by writing or making marks on it: *Most of the monuments had been broken or defaced.* —**defacement** *n* [U]

**de fac·to** /ˌdeɪ ˈfæktəʊ‖ ˌdɪˈfæktoʊ, ˌdeɪ/ *adj Latin* really existing although not legally stated to exist: *a de facto state of war* —**de facto** *adv*

**def·a·ma·tion** /ˌdefəˈmeɪʃən/ *n* [U] *formal* the act of defaming someone: **defamation of character** *Chambers sued the newspaper for defamation of character.*

**de·fame** /dɪˈfeɪm/ *v* [T] *formal* to write or say something that makes people have an unfairly bad opinion of someone or something —**defamatory** /dɪˈfæmətəri‖-tɔːri/ *adj*

**de·fault¹** /dɪˈfɒlt‖-ˈfɒːlt/ *n* **1 by default** if you win a game, competition etc by default, you win it because your opponent did not play or because there were no other competitors **2** [U] *formal* failure to do something that you are supposed to do according to the law or because it is your duty: *the risk of default by borrowers* **3 in default of** *formal* because of the lack or absence of something **4** [C usually singular] *technical* the way in which things will be arranged on a computer screen unless you decide to change them

**default²** *v* [I] to not do something that you are legally supposed to, especially not to pay money you are supposed to pay: **[+ on]** *He defaulted on his child support payments.* —**defaulter** *n* [C]

3 **de·feat¹** /dɪˈfiːt/ *n* **1** [C,U] failure to win or succeed: *an election defeat* | **serious defeat** *The government has suffered a serious defeat.* | **admit defeat** (=stop trying to succeed) *She's told him she won't marry him, but he'll never admit defeat.* **2** [U] victory over someone or something: **[+ of]** *We made the defeat of fascism our major priority.*

**defeat²** *v* [T] **1** to win a victory over someone in a war, competition, game etc; BEAT¹ (1): *After a long campaign Wellington's army finally defeated Napoleon.* | **defeat sb by 10 points/ by 3 goals to 2 etc** *We defeated the other team by six runs.* —see WIN (USAGE) **2** if something defeats you, you cannot understand it and therefore cannot answer or deal with it: *It was the last question on the paper that defeated me.* **3** to make something fail: *It was a lack of money, not effort, that defeated their plan.*

**de·feat·ist** /dɪˈfiːtɪst/ *n* [C] someone who believes that they will not succeed —**defeatist** *adj*: *a defeatist attitude* —**defeatism** *n* [U]

**def·e·cate** /ˈdefɪkeɪt/ *v* [I] *formal* to get rid of waste matter from your BOWELS —**defecation** /ˌdefɪˈkeɪʃən/ *n* [U]

**de·fect¹** /dɪˈfekt, ˈdiːfekt/ *n* [C] a fault or a lack of something that means that something is not perfect: *All the cars are tested for defects before they leave the factory.*

**de·fect²** /dɪˈfekt/ *v* [I] to leave your own country or a group in order to go to or join an opposing one: *a talented Russian actor who defected to the West* —**defector** *n* [C] —**defection** /dɪˈfekʃən/ *n* [C,U]

**de·fec·tive** /dɪˈfektɪv/ *adj* **1** not made properly, or not working properly: *defective components* **2** *technical* **defective verb** a verb such as 'must' or 'can' that cannot be used in all the forms that a verb can usually be used in —**defectively** *adv* —**defectiveness** *n* [U]

2 **de·fence** *BrE*, **defense** *AmE* /dɪˈfens/ *n*

1 **1 ▶ PROTECTING ◀** [U] the act of protecting something or someone from attack: **come to sb's defence** (=help someone by protecting them from attack) *Several people witnessed the attack, but no one came to her defence.* | **in defence of** *Hundreds gave their lives in defence of freedom.* —see also SELF-DEFENCE

**2 ▶ PROTECT A COUNTRY ◀** [U] all the systems, people, materials etc that a country uses to protect itself from attack: *He's one of the President's top advisors on defense.* | **defence cuts/spending/budget etc** *There are plans to increase defence spending by 6%.*

**3 defences** *BrE* **defenses** *AmE* all the armies and weapons that are available to defend a place: *The city's defenses were not strong enough to withstand the attack.*

**4 ▶ AGAINST CRITICISM ◀** [C,U] something that you say or do in order to protect someone or something from criticism: **in sb's/sth's defence** *Speaking in defence of the proposal, he pointed out how much cheaper it would be.*

**5 ▶ IN A LAW COURT ◀ a)** [C] the things that are said in a court of law to prove that someone is not guilty of a crime: *Our defense looked pretty solid.* **b) the defence** all the people who are concerned with showing in a court of law that someone is not guilty of a crime: *The defense's case is strong.* —compare PROSECUTION (2)

**6 ▶ AGAINST ILLNESS ◀** [C] something that your body produces naturally as a way of preventing illness: *The body's immune system is its defence against infection.*

**7 ▶ EMOTIONS ◀** [C] something you do or a way of behaving that prevents you from being upset or seeming weak: **[+ against]** *Dean's aggressive behaviour is his defence against depression.*

**8 ▶ SPORT ◀** [C] *BrE* the players in a game of football etc whose main job is to try to prevent the other team from getting points: *Barnaby cut through the heart of Arsenal's defence.*

**de·fence·less** *BrE*, **defenseless** *AmE* /dɪˈfensləs/ *adj* weak and unable to protect yourself from attack or harm: *a defenceless old lady*

**defence mech·a·nis·m** *BrE*, **defense mechanism** *AmE* /ˈ·· ˌ···/ *n* [C] **1** a process in your brain that makes you forget things that are painful for you to think about **2** a reaction in your body that protects you from an illness or danger

**de·fend** /dɪˈfend/ *v* **1** [T] to do something in order to protect someone or something from being attacked: **defend sth against/from** *They needed more troops to defend the border against possible attack.* | **defend yourself** *I picked a stick up to defend myself.* **2** to do something in order to stop something being taken away or in order to make it possible for something to continue: *The union said they would take action to defend their members' jobs.* **3** [T] to use arguments to protect something or someone from criticism, or to prove that something is right: *How can you defend the torture of animals for scientific research?* | **defend sb against/from** *He had to defend himself against their charges.* | **defend yourself** *As a politician, you have to be able to defend yourself when things get tough.* **4** [I,T] to protect your own team's end of the field in a game such as football, to prevent your opponents from getting points **5 defend a title/championship** to take part in a regular competition that you won the last time it was held **6** [T] to be a lawyer for someone who has been charged with a crime: *Who is defending the case?* —compare PROSECUTE (2) S3 W3

**de·fen·dant** /dɪˈfendənt/ *n* [C] *law* the person in a court of law who has been accused (ACCUSE) of doing something illegal: *We find the defendant not guilty.* —compare PLAINTIFF W2

**de·fend·er** /dɪˈfendə‖ər/ *n* [C] **1** one of the players in a game such as football who have to defend their team's GOAL (3) from the opposing team **2 a defender of the poor/liberty/privilege etc** someone who defends a particular idea, belief, person etc

**de·fense¹** /dɪˈfens/ *n* the American spelling of DEFENCE

**de·fense²** /dɪˈfens‖ˈdiːfens/ *n* [C,U] *AmE* the players in a game of football etc whose main job is to try to prevent the other team from getting points: *He plays defense for the New York Giants.* —opposite OFFENSE²

**de·fen·si·ble** /dɪˈfensɪbəl/ *adj* **1** a defensible opinion or idea seems reasonable and you can easily support it: *Richmond's theories are not morally defensible.* **2** a defensible building or area is easy to protect against attack —**defensibly** *adv*

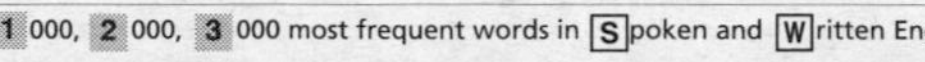

**de·fen·sive¹** /dɪˈfensɪv/ *adj* **1** used or intended to protect people against attack: *The rockets are a purely defensive measure against nuclear attack.* —opposite OFFENSIVE¹ (3) **2** behaving in a way that shows you think someone is criticizing you even if they are not: *There's no need to be so defensive, I just asked how old you are!* **3** *AmE* concerned with stopping the other team from getting points in a game: *defensive play | the defensive coach* —**defensively** *adv* —**defensiveness** *n* [U]

**defensive²** *n* **on the defensive** behaving in a way that shows that you think that someone is criticizing you even if they are not

**de·fer** /dɪˈfɜː‖-ˈfɜːr/ *v* **deferred, deferring** [T] to delay something until a later date: *Let's defer the decision for a few weeks.*

**defer to** sb/sth *phr v* [T] *formal* to agree to accept someone's opinion or decision because you have respect for that person

**def·er·ence** /ˈdefərəns/ *n* [U] *formal* behaviour that shows that you respect someone and are therefore willing to accept their opinions or judgment: *He had the arrogance of someone who had always been accustomed to deference.* | **in/out of deference to** (=done because you respect someone's beliefs, opinions etc) *They were married in church out of deference to their parents' wishes.* —**deferential** /ˌdefəˈrenʃəl◂/ *adj* —**deferentially** *adv*

**de·fi·ance** /dɪˈfaɪəns/ *n* [U] behaviour that shows you clearly refuse to do what someone tells you to do: *The boy gave me a look of hatred and defiance as he slammed the door.* | **in defiance of** *The company had been dumping their waste into the sea, in defiance of government regulations.*

**de·fi·ant** /dɪˈfaɪənt/ *adj* refusing clearly to do what someone tells you to do: *He gave a short, defiant laugh.* —**defiantly** *adv*

**de·fi·cien·cy** /dɪˈfɪʃənsi/ *n* [C,U] **1** a lack of something that is necessary: *The disease is caused by a vitamin deficiency.* **2** a weakness or fault in something

**deficiency dis·ease** /-ˈ··· ·ˌ·/ *n* [C,U] a disease caused by a lack of a food substance that is necessary for good health: *deficiency diseases such as rickets*

**de·fi·cient** /dɪˈfɪʃənt/ *adj* **1** not containing or having enough of something: *zinc deficient plants* | [+ **in**] *a diet deficient in calcium* **2** not good enough: *Some of the methods used were deficient.*

**def·i·cit** /ˈdefɪ̈sɪ̈t/ *n* [C] the difference between the amount of something that you have and the higher amount that you need: [+ **of**] *The directors have reported a deficit of £2.5 million.* | [+ **in**] *a deficit in magnesium*

**de·file¹** /dɪˈfaɪl/ *v* [T] *formal* to make something less pure or good: *These disgusting videos defile and corrupt the minds of the young.*

**de·file²** /dɪˈfaɪl, ˈdiːfaɪl/ *n* [C] *formal* a narrow passage, especially through mountains

S3 W2 **de·fine** /dɪˈfaɪn/ *v* [T] **1** to describe something correctly and thoroughly: *the ability to define clients' needs* | **define sth clearly/precisely** *The powers of the President are clearly defined in the Constitution.* **2** to explain exactly the meaning of a particular word or idea: *Each of us might define the concept of freedom in a very different way.* | **define sth as** *The dictionary defines it as 'a narrow passage'.* | **define sth loosely/broadly** (=define something in a way that is less exact) **3** to show the edge or shape of something clearly: **sharply/clearly defined** *sharply defined footprints in the fresh snow* **4** to have particular features or qualities that make you different or separate from other people or things: **define sth as** *Which qualities define us as human?* —**definable** *adj*

S3 **def·i·nite** /ˈdefɪnɪ̈t, ˈdefənɪ̈t/ *adj* **1** clearly known, seen, or stated: *Amanda saw a definite change in her son that year.* **2** a definite arrangement, promise etc will happen in the way that someone has said: *We have to set a definite date for the concert.* **3 be definite (about)** to say something very firmly so that people understand exactly what you mean: *She was very definite about how she felt.*

**definite ar·ti·cle** /ˌ··· ˈ···/ *n* [C usually singular] **1** the word 'the' in English **2** a word in another language that is like 'the' —compare INDEFINITE ARTICLE —see also ARTICLE¹ (4)

**def·i·nite·ly** /ˈdefɪnɪ̈tli, ˈdefənɪ̈tli/ *adv* with no chance of being wrong; certainly: *Max knew that he had definitely been wrong about Diana.* | *"It's not worth that much, is it?" "No, definitely not!"* —see OF COURSE (USAGE), SURELY (USAGE) S

**def·i·ni·tion** /ˌdefɪ̈ˈnɪʃən/ *n* **1** [C] a phrase or sentence that says exactly what a word, phrase, or idea means: *a definition in a dictionary* | [+ **of**] *No one has yet come up with a satisfactory definition of terrorism.* **2 by definition** if something has a particular quality by definition, it must have that quality because all things of that type have it: *A message that cannot be seen or heard is, by definition, not effective.* **3** [U] the degree to which something such as a picture, sound etc is clear: **lack definition** *The photograph lacks definition.* S W

**de·fin·i·tive** /dɪˈfɪnɪ̈tɪv/ *adj* **1** [usually before noun] a definitive book, study of something etc is considered to be the best ever produced and cannot be improved: *She has written the definitive book on the poet Wordsworth.* **2** a definitive statement, VERDICT etc will not be changed —**definitively** *adv*

**de·flate** /ˌdiːˈfleɪt, dɪ-/ *v* **1** [I,T] if a tyre, BALLOON¹ (1,2) etc deflates, or if you deflate it, it gets smaller because the gas inside it comes out **2** [T] to make someone feel less important or less confident: *I'd love to deflate that ego of his!* **3** [T] to show that a statement, argument etc is wrong **4** [T] *technical* to change economic rules or conditions in a country so that prices fall or stop rising —**deflation** /ˌdiːˈfleɪʃən, dɪ-/ *n* [U]

**de·flat·ed** /ˌdiːˈfleɪtɪ̈d, dɪ-/ *adj* feeling less cheerful or confident than before: *I felt utterly deflated and let down.*

**de·fla·tion·a·ry** /ˌdiːˈfleɪʃənəri, dɪ-‖-neri/ *adj technical* causing a situation in which prices fall or stop rising: *deflationary policies*

**de·flect** /dɪˈflekt/ *v* **1** [I,T] to turn in a different direction, especially after hitting something else, or to make something do this: *The waves are deflected by the lifeboat's high narrow bows.* **2 deflect attention/criticism/anger etc** to stop people criticizing something, getting angry about it etc: *a transparent attempt to deflect public criticism* **3** [T] if something deflects you from what you are doing, it takes your attention away from it: *Nothing could deflect him from his goal.*

**de·flec·tion** /dɪˈflekʃən/ *n* [C,U] **1** the action of making something change its direction: *the deflection of the bullet* **2** *technical* the degree to which the moving part on a measuring instrument moves away from zero

**de·flow·er** /ˌdiːˈflaʊə, dɪ-‖-ər/ *v* [T] *literary* to have sex with a woman who has never had sex before

**de·fog** /diːˈfɒg‖-ˈfɔːg, ˈfɑːg/ *v* **defogged, defogging** [T] *AmE* to remove the CONDENSATION from the window inside a car, by using heat or warm air; DEMIST *BrE*

**de·fo·li·ant** /diːˈfəʊliənt‖-ˈfoʊ-/ *n* [C,U] a chemical substance used on plants to make their leaves drop off

**de·fo·li·ate** /diːˈfəʊlieɪt‖-ˈfoʊ-/ *v* [T] to use defoliant on a plant or tree

**de·for·es·ta·tion** /diːˌfɒrɪ̈ˈsteɪʃən‖-ˌfɔː-,-ˌfɑː-/ *n* [U] the cutting or burning down of all the trees in an area —**deforest** /diːˈfɒrɪ̈st‖-fɔː-, -ˈfɑː/ *v* [T usually passive]

**de·form** /dɪˈfɔːm‖-ɔːrm/ *v* [T] to change the usual shape of something so that its usefulness or appearance is spoiled: *The heat had deformed the plastic.*

**de·for·ma·tion** /ˌdiːfɔːˈmeɪʃən‖-ɔːr-/ *n* **1** [C,U] a change in the usual shape of something, especially one that makes it worse: *deformation of the telescope's mirror* **2** [U] the process of changing the shape of something in a way that spoils its usefulness or appearance

**de·formed** /dɪˈfɔːmd‖-ɔːrmd/ *adj* something that is deformed has the wrong shape, especially because it has grown or developed wrongly: *a deformed foot*

**de·for·mi·ty** /dɪˈfɔːmɪ̈ti‖-ɔːr-/ *n* [C,U] a condition in which part of someone's body is not the normal shape

**de·fraud** /dɪˈfrɔːd‖-ˈfrɒːd/ *v* [T] to trick a person or organization in order to get money from them: **defraud sb of** *She defrauded her employers of thousands of pounds.*

**de·fray** /dɪˈfreɪ/ *v* [T] **defray costs/expenses** *formal* to pay someone's costs etc: *The company will defray any expenses you have on the journey.*

**de·frock** /ˌdiːˈfrɒk‖-ˈfrɑːk/ *v* [T] to officially remove a priest from his job because he has done something wrong —**defrocked** *adj*

**de·frost** /ˌdiːˈfrɒst‖-ˈfrɒːst/ *v* **1** if frozen food defrosts, or if you defrost it, it gets warmer until it is not frozen **2** [I,T] if a FREEZER or REFRIGERATOR defrosts, or if you defrost it, it is turned off so that the ice inside it melts **3** [T] *AmE* to remove ice from inside the windows of a car by using heat or warm air; DEMIST *BrE* —compare DEFOG

**deft** /deft/ *adj* **1** a deft movement is skilful, and often quick: *With one deft movement, she flipped the pancake over.* **2** skilful at doing something: *a deft political operator* —**deftly** *adv* —**deftness** *n* [U]

**de·funct** /dɪˈfʌŋkt/ *adj formal* not existing any more, or not useful any more

**de·fuse** /ˌdiːˈfjuːz/ *v* [T] **1** to improve a difficult or dangerous situation, for example by making people less angry or by dealing with the causes of a problem: *We believe that greater economic stability might defuse the current crisis.* | **defuse tension/anger/fears etc** *In an attempt to defuse the tension, Rob put some music on.* **2** to remove the FUSE[1] (2) from a bomb in order to stop it exploding

**de·fy** /dɪˈfaɪ/ *v* **defied, defying** [T] **1** to refuse to obey a law or rule, or refuse to do what someone in authority tells you to do: *He defied his father's wishes and married Agnes.* **2 defy description/analysis/imagination etc** to be so extreme or unusual that it is almost impossible to describe or understand: *The beauty of the scene defies description.* **3 I defy you (to)** *spoken formal* used when asking someone to do something that you think is impossible, in order to prove that you are right: *I defy you to think of one way in which this government has helped the poor.*

**de·gen·e·rate[1]** /dɪˈdʒenəreɪt/ *v* [I] to become worse: [+ **into**] *The debate soon degenerated into petty squabbling.* —**degeneration** /dɪˌdʒenəˈreɪʃən/ *n* [U]

**de·gen·e·rate[2]** /dɪˈdʒenərɪ̈t/ *adj* **1** *formal* having become worse in character or quality than before: *the last degenerate member of a noble family* **2** having very low standards or moral behaviour: *The Emperor was denounced as a degenerate debauchee.*

**degenerate[3]** *n* [C] someone whose behaviour is considered to be morally unacceptable

**de·gen·era·tive** /dɪˈdʒenərətɪv/ *adj* a degenerative illness gradually gets worse and cannot be stopped

**de·grad·a·tion** /ˌdegrəˈdeɪʃən/ *n* **1** [singular, U] an experience that makes you feel ashamed and angry: *a life of poverty and degradation* **2** [U] the process by which something changes to a worse condition

**de·grade** /dɪˈgreɪd/ *v* **1** [T] to treat someone without respect or make people lose their respect for someone; DEBASE: *a movie that degrades women* | **degrade yourself** *How can you degrade yourself by writing such trash?* **2** [T] to make a situation or the condition of something worse **3** [I,T] *technical* to change a substance, chemical etc to a simpler form

**de·grad·ing** /dɪˈgreɪdɪŋ/ *adj* a degrading experience, event etc makes you lose respect for yourself: *We oppose flogging and other cruel, inhuman, or degrading punishments.*

S3 W1 **de·gree** /dɪˈgriː/ *n*
**1** ▶ **ANGLES/TEMPERATURE** ◀ [C] a unit of measurement, especially for temperature or angles —see table on page B3
**2** ▶ **AMOUNT** ◀ [C,U] the amount of a quality that exists or how much something happens: [+ **of**] *People will choose the party that offers some degree of social change.* | *There are different views about the degree to which unemployment is society's fault.*
**3 to a degree** also **to some degree/to a certain degree** partly: *I think that's true to a degree, but the situation isn't quite as simple as that.*
**4** ▶ **UNIVERSITY** ◀ [C] **a)** a course of study at a university or college: *a law degree* | *a degree course* | [+ **in**] *a degree in Economics* | **take/do a degree** *Isabelle's doing her degree at the Sorbonne.* **b)** a QUALIFICATION (1) given to someone who has successfully completed this course of study: **have/hold a degree** *Lori has a degree in Chemistry from Harvard.*
**5 by degrees** very slowly; gradually: *By degrees, the music drove all thoughts from his head.*
**6** ▶ **POSITION IN SOCIETY** ◀ [U] *old use* your position in society

**de·hu·man·ize** also **-ise** *BrE* /ˌdiːˈhjuːmənaɪz/ *v* [T often passive] to treat people so badly that they lose their good human qualities such as kindness etc: *War dehumanizes people.* —**dehumanizing** *adj* —**dehumanization** /diːˌhjumənaɪˈzeɪʃən‖-nə-/ *n* [U]

**de·hy·drate** /ˌdiːhaɪˈdreɪt‖diːˈhaɪdreɪt/ *v* **1** [T] to remove the liquid from a substance such as food or chemicals: *The substance is dehydrated and stored as powder.* **2** [I] to lose too much water from your body —**dehydrated** *adj* —**dehydration** /ˌdiːhaɪˈdreɪʃən/ *n* [U]

**de-ice** /ˌdiːˈaɪs/ *v* [T] to remove the ice from something

**de·i·fy** /ˈdiːɪ̈faɪ, ˈdeɪ-/ *v* **deified, deifying** [T] *formal* to treat someone or something with far too much respect and admiration —**deification** /ˌdiːɪ̈fɪ̈ˈkeɪʃən, ˌdeɪ/ *n* [U]

**deign** /deɪn/ *v* **deign to do something** an expression meaning to agree to do something, often used jokingly when you think someone should do that thing all the time: *Ah, so you've deigned to grace us with your presence I see!*

**de·is·m** /ˈdiːɪzəm, ˈdeɪ-/ *n* [U] the belief in a God who made the world but has no influence on human lives —compare THEISM

**De·i·ty** /ˈdiːɪ̈ti,ˈdeɪ-/ *n formal* **the Deity** God

**deity** *n* [C] a god or GODDESS: *the deities of ancient Greece*

**dé·jà vu** /ˌdeɪʒɑː ˈvjuː/ *n* [U] *French* the feeling that you have previously experienced exactly the same thing as you are experiencing now: *Madeleine felt a strange sense of déjà vu as she walked into the room.*

**de·jec·ted** /dɪˈdʒektɪ̈d/ *adj* unhappy, disappointed, or sad —**dejectedly** /dɪˈdʒektɪ̈dli/ *adv* —**dejection** /dɪˈdʒekʃən/ *n* [U]

**de ju·re** /ˌdiː ˈdʒʊəri,ˌdeɪ ˈdʒʊəreɪ‖-ˈdʒʊr-/ *adj law* true or right because of a law

**de·lay[1]** /dɪˈleɪ/ *n* **1** [C usually singular] the length of time between the moment when something should start and the moment it actually does start: *Sorry for the delay, Mr Weaver.* | [+ **of**] *a delay of twenty minutes* | **short/long etc delay** *There was a slight delay before the show.* | **without delay** (=immediately) **2** [C] a situation in which someone or something is made to wait: **severe delays** *There are severe delays on Route 95 this morning because of an accident.* | [+ **in**] *delays in transporting the goods to London* **3** [U] the situation in which something does not happen or start when it should do: **be subject to delay** (=likely to be delayed) S2 W3

**delay[2]** *v* **1** [I,T] to wait until a later time to do something: *She delayed for months before deciding.* | **delay sth until** *Ralph decided to delay his trip until April or May.* | **delay doing sth** *Don't delay claiming or you may lose benefit.* **2** [T often passive] to make someone or something late: *The plane was badly delayed by fog.* —**delayed** *adj* S3

**delayed-ac·tion** /ˌ· ˈ··◂/ *adj* designed to work or start only after a fixed period of time has passed: *a delayed-action bomb*

**delaying tac·tic** /ˈ···ˌ··/ *n* [C usually plural] something you do deliberately in order to delay something so that you gain an advantage for yourself

**de·lec·ta·ble** /dɪˈlektəbəl/ *adj literary* extremely pleasant to taste, smell etc: *a delectable mixture of flavours* —**delectably** *adv*

**de·lec·ta·tion** /ˌdiːlekˈteɪʃən/ *n* [U] *formal* enjoyment, pleasure, or amusement

**del·e·gate¹** /ˈdelɪ̈gɪ̈t/ *n* [C] someone who has been elected or chosen to speak, vote, or take decisions for a group: *We sent five delegates to the conference.*

**del·e·gate²** /ˈdelɪ̈geɪt/ *v* **1** [I,T] to give part of your power or work to someone in a lower position than you: *A good manager knows when to delegate.* | **delegate sth to sb** *Minor tasks should be delegated to your assistant.* **2** [T] to choose someone to do a particular job, or to be a representative of a group, organization etc: **delegate sb to do sth** *I've been delegated to organize the weekly meetings.*

**del·e·ga·tion** /ˌdelɪ̈ˈgeɪʃən/ *n* **1** [C] a group of people who represent a company, organization etc: *A small delegation had been sent to address the UN.* **2** [U] the process of giving power or work to someone else so that they are responsible for part of what you normally do

**de·lete** /dɪˈliːt/ *v* [T] to remove a letter, word etc from a piece of writing: *His name was deleted from the list.*

**del·e·ter·i·ous** /ˌdelɪ̈ˈtɪəriəs◂‖-ˈtɪr-/ *adj formal* damaging or harmful: *the deleterious effects of smoking*

**de·le·tion** /dɪˈliːʃən/ *n* **1** [U] the act or process of removing something from a piece of writing **2** [C] a letter or word that has been removed from a piece of writing

**del·i** /ˈdeli/ *n* [C] *informal* a DELICATESSEN

**de·lib·e·rate¹** /dɪˈlɪbərɪ̈t/ *adj* **1** intended or planned, and not happening accidentally: *a deliberate act of disobedience* **2** deliberate speech, thought, or movement is slow and careful: *He began working in his usual deliberate and meticulous manner.* —**deliberateness** *n*[U]

**de·lib·e·rate²** /dɪˈlɪbəreɪt/ *v* [I] to think about something very carefully: *We really can't afford to deliberate any longer.* | [+ **on/about**] *They met to deliberate on possible solutions to the problem.*

S3 W3 **de·lib·er·ate·ly** /dɪˈlɪbərɪ̈tli/ *adv* **1** done in a way that is intended or planned: *I don't think he deliberately tried to shove you.* | *They're deliberately choosing a cautious policy.* **2** done or said in a slow, careful way

**de·lib·e·ra·tion** /dɪˌlɪbəˈreɪʃən/ *n* **1** [C often plural, U] careful consideration or discussion of something: *Their deliberations went on for hours.* **2** [U] if you speak or move with deliberation, you speak or move slowly and carefully

**de·lib·e·ra·tive** /dɪˈlɪbərətɪv‖-bəreɪtɪv/ *adj* existing for the purpose of discussing or planning something

**del·i·ca·cy** /ˈdelɪkəsi/ *n* **1** [C] something good to eat that is expensive or rare: *Snails are considered a delicacy in France.* **2** [U] a careful and sensitive way of speaking or behaving so that you do not upset anyone; TACT **3** [U] the quality of being easy to harm, damage, or break

**del·i·cate** /ˈdelɪkɪ̈t/ *adj*
**1** ▶ **EASILY DAMAGED** ◀ easily damaged or broken; FRAGILE (1): *a delicate bubble of Venetian glass*
**2** ▶ **NEEDING SENSITIVITY** ◀ needing to be dealt with carefully or sensitively in order to avoid problems or failure: *The negotiations are at a delicate stage.*
**3** ▶ **PERSON** ◀ someone who is delicate is hurt easily or easily becomes ill: *a delicate child*
**4** ▶ **PART OF THE BODY** ◀ a part of the body that is delicate is attractive and graceful: *He looked down at his long white delicate fingers.*
**5** ▶ **SKILFULLY MADE** ◀ made skilfully and with attention to the smallest details: *a delicate pattern of butterflies and leaves*
**6** ▶ **TASTE/SMELL/COLOUR** ◀ a taste, smell, or colour that is delicate is pleasant and not strong: *a delicate shade of blue* —compare INDELICATE —**delicately** *adv*

**del·i·cates** /ˈdelɪkɪ̈ts/ *n* [plural] clothes that are made from material that needs careful treatment

**del·i·ca·tes·sen** /ˌdelɪkəˈtesən/ *n* [C] a shop that sells high quality cheeses, SALADS, cooked meats etc

**de·li·cious** /dɪˈlɪʃəs/ *adj* **1** very pleasant to taste or smell: *This cake is absolutely delicious!* **2** *literary* extremely pleasant or enjoyable: *It was a delicious but unlikely fantasy.*

**de·light¹** /dɪˈlaɪt/ *n* **1** [U] feelings of great pleasure and satisfaction: **with/in delight** *The kids rushed down to the beach, shrieking with delight.* | **to sb's delight** *To my secret delight, Sarah announced that she was leaving.* | **scream/gasp etc of delight** *With a cry of delight he ran towards Jen.* **2** [C] something that makes you feel very happy or satisfied: **the delights of** *the delights of owning your own home* **3 take delight in (doing) sth** to enjoy something very much, especially something you should not do: *Chris takes great delight in teasing his sister.*

**delight²** *v* [T] to give someone great satisfaction and enjoyment: *a book that is certain to delight any reader* | **delight sb with sth** *He delighted them with his charm and sparkling wit.*

**delight in** sth *phr v* [T not in passive] to enjoy something very much, especially something unpleasant

**de·light·ed** /dɪˈlaɪtɪ̈d/ *adj* very pleased and happy: *The puppies ran around the delighted children.* | **be delighted to do sth** *Thanks for the invitation. I'd be delighted to come!* | **delighted (that)** *We're delighted that you'll be there.* | [+ **at/by**] *Tom was delighted at the sensation he was creating.* —**delightedly** *adv* S

**de·light·ful** /dɪˈlaɪtfəl/ *adj* very pleasant: *a delightful young man* —**delightfully** *adv*

**de·lim·it** /dɪˈlɪmɪ̈t/ *v* [T] *formal* to fix or say exactly what the limits of something are —**delimitation** /dɪˌlɪmɪ̈ˈteɪʃən/ *n* [C]

**de·lin·e·ate** /dɪˈlɪnieɪt/ *v* [T] *formal* to describe or draw something carefully so that people can understand it: *Make sure your ideas are clearly delineated in your speech.* —**delineation** /dɪˌlɪniˈeɪʃən/ *n* [U]

**de·lin·quen·cy** /dɪˈlɪŋkwənsi/ *n* **1** [U] illegal or immoral behaviour, especially by young people **2** [C] *formal* an action that is illegal or immoral

**de·lin·quent¹** /dɪˈlɪŋkwənt/ *adj* **1** behaving in a way that is illegal or that society does not approve of: *delinquent behaviour* **2** *technical* a delinquent debt, account etc has not been paid on time

**delinquent²** *n* [C] someone, especially a young person, who breaks the law or behaves in ways their society does not approve of: *juvenile delinquents vandalizing telephones*

**del·i·ques·cent** /ˌdelɪ̈ˈkwesənt◂/ *adj technical* a deliquescent substance becomes a liquid because of water in the air

**de·lir·i·ous** /dɪˈlɪriəs‖-ˈlɪr-/ *adj* **1** talking continuously in an excited or anxious way, especially because you are ill: *One patient had been babbling all night, delirious with a high fever.* **2** extremely excited or happy —**deliriously** *adv*

**de·lir·i·um** /dɪˈlɪriəm/ *n* **1** [C,U] a state in which someone is delirious, especially because they are very ill: *High doses of certain drugs produce delirium.* **2** [singular] extreme excitement

**delirium tre·mens** /dɪˌlɪriəm ˈtremənz‖-ˈtriː-/ *n* [U] *technical* a medical condition, caused especially by drinking too much alcohol, in which someone's body shakes and they see things that are not there

**de·liv·er** /dɪˈlɪvə‖-ər/ *v*

**1** ▶ **TAKE STH SOMEWHERE** ◀ [I] to take goods, letters etc to the place where they have been sent: *Do you deliver on Saturdays?* | **deliver sth to** *Could you deliver this letter to the accounts department?* | **have sth delivered** *I'm having some flowers delivered for her birthday.*
**2 deliver a speech/lecture/talk etc** to make a speech etc to a lot of people: *The President, as was customary, delivered the opening address.*

**3 ▶ DO STH YOU SHOULD DO ◀** [I,T] to do or provide the things you are expected to, because you are responsible for them or they are part of your job: *Local councils are responsible for delivering most basic services.* | **deliver the goods** (=do or provide what you are expected to) *They made all kinds of promises before the election, but have since failed to deliver the goods.* | **deliver on a promise** *AmE* (=do what you promised to do)
**4 ▶ BABY ◀** [T] to help a woman give birth to a baby: *Traditionally, local midwives would deliver all the babies in the area.* | **deliver sb of** *formal*: *On May 14th, she was safely delivered of a daughter.*
**5 deliver a blow/shock etc to** to hit someone, give them a shock etc: *He delivered a wild, desperate blow to Derek's jaw.*
**6 deliver a verdict/judgment/ruling etc** to officially state a formal decision or judgment
**7 ▶ PERSON ◀** [T always + adv/prep] to put someone into someone else's control: **deliver sb to** *Sharett had betrayed him and delivered him to the enemy.*
**8 ▶ VOTES ◀** [T] *especially AmE* to get the votes or support of a particular group of people in an election: *We're counting on you to deliver the blue collar vote.*
**9 ▶ MAKE SB FREE OF ◀** [T] *literary or Biblical* to help someone escape from something bad or evil: **deliver sb from** *Deliver us from temptation.* —**deliverer** *n* [C]

**deliver** sth **up** *phr v* [T often passive] *formal* to give something to someone else: **[+ to]** *All documents must be delivered up to the trustee.*

**de·liv·er·a·ble** /dɪˈlɪvərəbəl/ *n* [C usually plural] something that a company has promised to have ready for a customer, especially parts of computer systems: *a list of software deliverables*

**de·liv·er·ance** /dɪˈlɪvərəns/ *n* [U + **from**] *formal* the state of being saved from harm or danger

S2 W3 **de·liv·er·y** /dɪˈlɪvəri/ *n* **1** [C,U] the act or process of bringing goods, letters etc to the person or place they have been sent to: *postal deliveries* | *a delivery charge* | **take delivery of** (=officially accept something that has been brought or sent to you) **2** [C] something that is delivered: *Deliveries to the restaurant should be made at the back entrance.* **3** [C] the process of giving birth to a child: *Mrs Howell had an easy delivery.* | **delivery room/ward etc** (=a room in a hospital for births) **4** [singular] the way in which someone speaks or performs in public: *You'll have to work on your delivery.*

**de·liv·er·y·man** /dɪˈlɪvərimən/ *n* [C] someone who delivers goods to people

**dell** /del/ *n* [C] *literary* a small valley with grass and trees

**de·louse** /ˌdiːˈlaʊs/ *v* [T] to remove lice (LOUSE¹ (1)) or similar animals from someone's hair, clothes etc

**del·phin·i·um** /delˈfɪniəm/ *n* [C] a tall garden plant with many blue flowers along its stem

**del·ta** /ˈdeltə/ *n* [C] **1** the fourth letter of the Greek alphabet **2** an area of low land where a river spreads into many smaller rivers near the sea: *the Nile delta* —see picture on page 835

**de·lude** /dɪˈluːd/ *v* [T] to make someone believe something that is not true; deceive: **delude sb/yourself** *You're deluding yourself if you think you'll change Rob's mind.* | **delude sb into doing sth** *That new job title is just a way of deluding her into thinking she's been promoted.*

**del·uge¹** /ˈdeljuːdʒ/ *n* **1** [C usually singular] a large flood, or period when there is a lot of rain **2 deluge of letters/questions etc** a lot of letters, questions etc that all come at the same time: *a deluge of complaints about the show*

**deluge²** *v* [T] **1** [usually passive] to send a very large number of letters, questions etc to someone all at the same time: **be deluged with/by** *The response has been great – we've been deluged with new orders.* **2** *formal* to cover something with a lot of water —see also INUNDATE

**de·lu·sion** /dɪˈluːʒən/ *n* **1** [C,U] a false belief about yourself or the situation you are in: **be under the delusion that** (=wrongly believe that) *I was still under the naive delusion that everyone was good at heart.* **2 delusions of grandeur** the belief that you are much more important or powerful than you really are —**delusive** /-sɪv/ *adj* —**delusively** *adv*

**de·luxe** /dɪ̆ˈlʌks‖-ˈlʊks/ *adj* [usually before noun] something that is of better quality than other things of the same type: *The deluxe model costs a lot more.*

**delve** /delv/ *v* [I] **1** [always + adv/prep] to search for something by putting your hand deeply into a bag, container etc: **delve in/among/between etc** *Hank delved in his pockets for some change.* **2** *poetic* to dig

**delve into** *phr v* [T] to try to find more information about someone or something: *I wouldn't delve too deeply into his past if I were you.*

**Dem** /dem/ the written abbreviation of Democrat or Democratic

**de·mag·ne·tize** also **-ise** *BrE* /ˌdiːˈmægnətaɪz/ *v* [T] **1** to take away the MAGNETIC qualities of something **2** *technical* to remove sounds from a MAGNETIC TAPE —**demagnetization** /ˌdiːmægnətaɪˈzeɪʃən‖-nətə-/ *n* [U]

**dem·a·gogue** also **demagog** *AmE* /ˈdeməgɒg‖-gɑːg/ *n* [C] someone who gives political speeches that try to persuade people by using emotional language rather than reason —**demagogy, demagogery** *n* [U] —**demagogic** /ˌdeməˈgɒgɪk◂‖-ˈgɑː-/ *adj* —**demagogically** /-kli/ *adv*

**de·mand¹** /dɪˈmɑːnd‖dɪˈmænd/ *n* S1 W1
**1 ▶ FIRM REQUEST ◀** [C] a very firm request for something that you think someone should give you, or think you have a right to: *The government refused to give in to the demands of the terrorists.* | **[+ for]** *a demand for a 10% pay increase* —see REQUEST² (USAGE)
**2 demands** [plural] the difficult, annoying, or tiring things that someone or something makes you do: **the demands of** *the pace and demands of modern life* | **make demands (on)** *The job makes great demands on my time.*
**3 ▶ GOODS/SERVICES ◀** [singular, U] people's need or desire to buy or use particular goods and services: **[+ for]** *There's not much demand for oil heaters any more.* | **meet demand** (=supply or sell enough goods etc for people to buy) *Ford have increased production in order to meet demand.* | **be in demand** (=be wanted by a lot of people) *Her books are in great demand at the moment.* —see also **supply and demand** (SUPPLY² (4))
**4 by popular demand** because a lot of people have asked for something to be done, performed etc: *Here they are, back by popular demand, The Wild Ones!*
**5 on demand** *formal* done or given whenever someone asks: *This note entitles the bearer to $20 on demand.*

**demand²** *v* **1** [T] to ask for something very firmly, especially something that someone does not want to give you: *The Governor has demanded your resignation.* | **demand to know/see etc** *I demand to know what's going on!* | **demand that** *Protesters went on hunger strike to demand that all political prisoners be freed.* **2** [I,T] to ask a question or order something to be done very firmly: *"Did you do this?" Kathryn demanded angrily.* | **demand sth of sb** (=ask someone for something) **3** [T] to need someone's time, energy, skill etc: *There are just too many things all demanding my attention at once.* W2

**de·mand·ing** /dɪˈmɑːndɪŋ‖dɪˈmæn-/ *adj* **1** needing a lot of ability, effort, or skill: *a demanding job* **2** expecting a lot of attention, especially in a way that is not fair: *Her mother could be very demanding at times.* S3

**de·mar·cate** /ˈdiːmɑːkeɪt‖dɪˈmɑːr-/ *v* [T] *formal* to state or fix the limits of an area, system etc: *The development of clearly demarcated territories is fairly recent in history.*

**de·mar·ca·tion** /ˌdiːmɑːˈkeɪʃən‖-ɑːr-/ *n* [U] **1** the point at which one person's area of work, responsibility etc ends and someone else's begins: *There is no clear demarcation between the responsibilities of our two departments.* **2** a way of separating one area of land from another

**de·mean** /dɪˈmiːn/ *v* [T] *formal* to do something that you think you are too good for: *Don't demean yourself by taking that job.* —**demeaning** *adj*: *Cleaning the toilets was the most demeaning task at the camp.*

**de·mea·nour** *BrE*, **demeanor** *AmE* /dɪˈmiːnə‖-ər/ *n* [singular, U] the way someone behaves or looks that gives you a general idea of their character: *There was certainly a large element of irony in his demeanour.*

**de·men·ted** /dɪˈmentɨd/ *adj* **1** behaving as if you are crazy, especially because of an upsetting experience: *The woman was almost demented with grief.* **2** *old-fashioned* suffering from a mental illness

**de·men·tia** /dɪˈmenʃə, -ʃiə‖-tʃə/ *n* [U] *technical* an illness that affects the brain and memory, and makes you gradually lose the ability to think and behave normally

**dem·e·ra·ra sug·ar** /ˌdemərеərə ˈʃʊgə‖-rerə ˈʃʊgər/ *n* [U] a type of rough brown sugar

**de·mer·it** /diːˈmerɨt/ *n* [C] **1 the merits and demerits of** *formal* the good and bad qualities or features of something **2** *AmE* a mark showing that a student has done something wrong at school

**de·mesne** /dɪˈmeɪn/ *n* [C] *old use or law* a very big house and all the land that belongs to it, especially in former times

**demi-** /demi/ *prefix* **1** half: *a demisemiquaver* (=very short musical note) **2** partly something: *a demigod* (=partly human and partly a god)

**dem·i·god** /ˈdemigɒd‖-gɑːd/ *n* [C] **1** someone who is so important and powerful that they are treated like a god: *a dictator with demigod status* **2** a man in ancient stories, who is half god and half human

**dem·i·john** /ˈdemidʒɒn‖-dʒɑːn/ *n* [C] a large bottle with a short narrow neck, often used for making wine

**de·mil·i·ta·rize** also **-ise** *BrE* /ˌdiːˈmɪlɨtəraɪz/ *v* [T usually passive] to remove the weapons, soldiers etc from a country or area so that there can be no fighting there —**demilitarization** /diːˌmɪlɨtəraɪˈzeɪʃən‖-rə-/ *n* [U]

**de·mise** /dɪˈmaɪz/ *n* [U] **1** *formal* the end of something that used to exist: [+ **of**] *the sad demise of the local newspaper* **2** *formal or law* death —**demise** *v* [I] *especially AmE*: *The sport has continued to demise over the years.*

**de·mist** /ˌdiːˈmɪst/ *v* [T] *BrE* to remove mist from a car window using heat; DEFROST (3) *AmE* —**demister** *n* [C]

**dem·o** /ˈdeməʊ‖-moʊ/ *n* [C] *informal* **1** an event at which a large group of people publicly protest about something **2 give sb a demo** to show someone how something works or is done **3** a piece of recorded music that is sent to a record company so that they can decide whether to sell it or not: *a demo tape* —compare DEMONSTRATION (2)

**de·mob** /diːˈmɒb‖-ˈmɑːb/ *v* **demobbed, demobbing** [T] *BrE informal* to demobilize

**de·mo·bi·lize** also **-ise** *BrE* /diːˈməʊbɨlaɪz‖-moʊ-/ *v* [T usually passive] to send home the members of an army, navy etc, especially at the end of a war: *Unemployed demobilized soldiers drifted toward the cities.* —**demobilization** /diːˌməʊbɨlaɪˈzeɪʃən‖-ˌmoʊbələ-/ *n* [U]

W2 **de·moc·ra·cy** /dɪˈmɒkrəsi‖dɪˈmɑː-/ *n* **1** [U] a system of government in which everyone in the country can vote to elect its members **2** [C] a country that has a government which has been elected by the people of the country **3** [U] a situation or system in which everyone is equal and has the right to vote, make decisions etc

**dem·o·crat** /ˈdeməkræt/ *n* [C] **1** someone who believes in, or works to achieve democracy **2 Democrat** a member or supporter of the Democratic party of the US

W2 **dem·o·crat·ic** /ˌdeməˈkrætɪk◂/ *adj* **1** controlled by representatives who are elected by the people of a country: *a democratic government* **2** organized according to the principle that everyone has a right to be involved in making decisions: *a democratic management style* —**democratically** /-kli/ *adv*: *democratically-elected councils*

**de·moc·ra·tize** also **-ise** *BrE* /dɪˈmɒkrətaɪz‖dɪˈmɑː-/ *v* [T] to change the way in which a government, company etc is organized, so that the people in it have more power —**democratization** /dɪˌmɒkrətaɪˈzeɪʃən‖-ˌmɑːkrətə-/ *n* [U]

**dé·mo·dé** /ˌdeɪˈməʊdeɪ‖ˌdeɪmoʊˈdeɪ/ *adj formal* not fashionable any more

**de·mog·ra·phy** /dɪˈmɒgrəfi‖-ˈmɑː-/ *n* [U] the study of human populations and the ways in which they change —**demographer** *n* [C] —**demographic** /ˌdeməˈgræfɪk◂/ *adj*

**de·mol·ish** /dɪˈmɒlɪʃ‖dɪˈmɑː-/ *v* [T] **1** to completely destroy a building, especially so that the land it is on can be used for something else: *Several houses were demolished to make way for the new road.* **2** to prove that an idea or opinion is completely wrong: *He demolished my argument in minutes.* **3** *informal especially BrE* to eat all of something very quickly

**dem·o·li·tion** /ˌdeməˈlɪʃən/ *n* [C,U] the act, or process of demolishing a building

**de·mon** /ˈdiːmən/ *n* [C] **1** an evil spirit **2** *humorous* someone who is very good at a game, especially cards: *Pete is a demon poker player.* **3 the demon drink** *humorous* alcoholic drink —compare DAEMON

**de·mo·ni·a·cal** /ˌdiːməˈnaɪəkəl◂/ also **de·mo·ni·ac** /dɪˈməʊniæk‖-ˈmoʊ-/ *adj formal* wild, uncontrolled, and evil: *demoniacal cruelty* —**demoniacally** /-kli/ *adv*

**de·mon·ic** /dɪˈmɒnɪk‖dɪˈmɑː-/ *adj* **1** wild and cruel: *demonic laughter* **2** like a demon: *demonic possession* —**demonically** /-kli/ *adv*

**de·mon·stra·ble** /dɪˈmɒnstrəbəl, ˈdemən-‖dɪˈmɑːn-/ *adj formal* able to be shown or proved —**demonstrably** *adv*: *These conclusions are demonstrably wrong.* —**demonstrability** /dɪˌmɒnstrəˈbɪlɨti‖dɪˌmɑːn-/ *n* [U]

**dem·on·strate** /ˈdemənstreɪt/ *v* **1** [T] to show or prove something clearly: *These findings clearly demonstrate the fact that unemployment leads to poor health.* | **demonstrate that** *Edwin Hubble demonstrated that ours was not the only galaxy.* **2** [T] to show or describe how something works or is done **3** [I] to march through the streets with a large group of people in order to publicly protest about something: *Supporters demonstrated outside the courtoom during the trial.* | **demonstrate against** *What are they demonstrating against?* **4** [T] to show that you have a particular skill, quality, or ability: *At last she had the chance to demonstrate her musical talents.* W2

**demonstration**

**dem·on·stra·tion** /ˌdemənˈstreɪʃən/ *n* **1** [C] an event at which a large group of people march through the streets, in order to publicly protest about something: *The new tax proposals sparked mass demonstrations.* S3 W

|[+ **against**] *a demonstration against the war*|**stage/hold a demonstration** *Students staged a demonstration to protest about the rises in tuition fees.*|**break up a demonstration** *Police used tear gas to break up the demonstration.* **2** [C,U] an act of explaining and showing how something works or is done: **give a demonstration** *He gave a demonstration of how the program works.* **3** *formal* [C] the expression of a feeling: *a demonstration of her love*

**de·mon·stra·tive** /dɪˈmɒnstrətɪv‖dɪˈmɑːn-/ *adj* willing to show loving feelings towards people: *Dave's not very demonstrative, but I know he loves me.* —**demonstratively** *adv*

**demonstrative pro·noun** /-ˌ··· ˈ··/ *n* [C] *technical* a PRONOUN such as 'that' or 'this' that shows which person or thing is meant, and separates it from others

**dem·on·stra·tor** /ˈdemənstreɪtə‖-ər/ *n* [C] **1** someone who takes part in a DEMONSTRATION: *Thousands of demonstrators gathered outside the Capitol building.* **2** someone who shows people how something works or is done

**de·mor·al·ize** also **-ise** *BrE* /dɪˈmɒrəlaɪz‖dɪˈmɔː-, dɪˈmɑː-/ *v* [T] to reduce or destroy someone's courage or confidence: *Such a move would undermine standards in schools and demoralize teachers.* —**demoralized** *adj*: *Defeated and demoralized, the protesters made their way home.* —**demoralizing** *adj*: *a series of demoralizing failures* —**demoralization** /dɪˌmɒrəlaɪˈzeɪʃən‖-ˌmɔːrələ-, -ˌmɑː-/ *n* [U] *widespread demoralization in the police force*

**de·mote** /dɪˈməʊt‖-ˈmoʊt/ *v* [T often passive] to make someone's rank or position lower or less important —opposite PROMOTE (2) —**demotion** /-ˈməʊʃən‖-ˈmoʊ-/ *n* [C,U]

**de·mot·ic** /dɪˈmɒtɪk‖dɪˈmɑː-/ *adj formal* used by or popular with most ordinary people

**de·mo·ti·vate** /ˌdiːˈməʊtɪ̈veɪt‖-ˈmoʊ-/ *v* [T] to make someone less eager or willing to do their job —**demotivating** *adj*: *Lack of sufficient challenge at work can be very demotivating.* —**demotivation** /ˌdiːməʊtɪ̈ˈveɪʃən‖diːˌmoʊ-/ *n* [U]

**de·mur**[1] /dɪˈmɜː‖-ˈmɜːr/ *v* **demurred, demurring** [I] *formal* to express doubt about or opposition to a plan or suggestion: *They demurred at the idea of working on a Sunday.*

**demur**[2] *n* [U] *formal* disagreement or disapproval: **without demur** *I agreed to this without demur.*

**de·mure** /dɪˈmjʊə‖-ˈmjʊr/ *adj* a word meaning quiet, serious, and always behaving well, used especially about women in former times —**demurely** *adv*: *She lowered her eyes demurely.* —**demureness** *n* [U]

**de·mys·ti·fy** /ˌdiːˈmɪstɪ̈faɪ/ *v* [T] to make a subject that seems difficult or complicated easier to understand, especially by explaining it in simpler language: *This book attempts to demystify the whole subject of computers.* —**demystification** /diːˌmɪstɪ̈fɪ̈ˈkeɪʃən/ *n* [U]

**den** /den/ *n* [C] **1** the home of some types of animal, for example lions or foxes (FOX[1] (1)) **2** a place where secret or illegal activities take place: *a gambler's den*|*a den of thieves* **3** an enclosed and secret place where children play **4** *especially AmE* a room in someone's house where they can relax, watch television etc **5** *AmE* a group of CUB SCOUTS **6** *BrE old-fashioned* a small room in someone's house where they can work, read, etc without being disturbed: *Father retreated to his den.* **7 den of iniquity** *often humorous* a place where activities that you think are immoral or evil happen: *Her mother saw the city as a den of iniquity.*

**de·na·tion·al·ize** also **-ise** *BrE* /diːˈnæʃənəlaɪz/ *v* [T] to sell a business or industry that is owned by the state, so that it is then owned privately; PRIVATIZE —**denationalization** /diːˌnæʃənəlaɪˈzeɪʃən‖-lə-/ *n* [U]

**de·ni·a·ble** /dɪˈnaɪəbəl/ *adj* something that is deniable can be proved not to be true —opposite UNDENIABLE

**de·ni·al** /dɪˈnaɪəl/ *n* **1** [C,U] a statement saying that something is not true: [+ **of**] *The government issued a firm denial of the rumour.* **2 denial of justice/humanity/rights etc** a situation in which someone is not allowed to have justice, their rights etc: *protests against the denial of human rights* **3** [U] *technical* a condition in which someone cannot or will not admit what they are really feeling

**den·i·er** /ˈdeniə‖-ər/ *n* [U] *BrE* a measure of how thin NYLON or silk threads are: *a pair of 15-denier tights*

**den·i·grate** /ˈdenɪ̈greɪt/ *v* [T] to say that something or someone is not good or important: *men who denigrate the status of women* —**denigration** /ˌdenɪ̈ˈgreɪʃən/ *n* [U]

**den·im** /ˈdenɪ̈m/ *n* **1** [U] a type of strong cotton cloth, used especially to make JEANS —see picture on page 839 **2 denims** [plural] *old-fashioned* a pair of trousers made of this material; JEANS

**den·i·zen** /ˈdenɪ̈zən/ *n* [C + **of**] *literary* an animal, plant, or person that lives or is found in a particular place

**den moth·er** /ˈ· ˌ··/ *n* [C] *AmE* a woman who leads a group of CUB SCOUTS

**de·nom·i·nate** /dɪˈnɒmɪ̈neɪt‖dɪˈnɑː-/ *v* [T] *formal* to give a name to something; DESIGNATE[1] (2)

**de·nom·i·na·tion** /dɪˌnɒmɪ̈ˈneɪʃən‖dɪˌnɑː-/ *n* [C] **1** a religious group that is part of a larger religious organization: *Christians of all denominations* **2** *technical* the value of a coin or NOTE[1] (5) **3** *formal* a name for a group or type

**de·nom·i·na·tion·al** /dɪˌnɒmɪ̈ˈneɪʃənəl‖dɪˌnɑː-/ *adj* connected with or belonging to a particular religious denomination

**de·nom·i·na·tor** /dɪˈnɒmɪ̈neɪtə‖dɪˈnɑːmɪ̈neɪtər/ *n* [C] *technical* the number below the line in a FRACTION (2) —compare NUMERATOR —see also LOWEST COMMON DENOMINATOR

**de·no·ta·tion** /ˌdiːnəʊˈteɪʃən‖-noʊ-/ *n* [C] *technical* the thing that is actually described by a word rather than the feelings or ideas it suggests —compare CONNOTATION

**de·note** /dɪˈnəʊt‖-ˈnoʊt/ *v* [T] *formal* **1** to mean: *The word 'family' is used here to denote the members of a household, whether or not they are related.* **2** to be a sign of something; INDICATE (4): *Crosses on the map denote villages and hamlets.* —**denotative** *adj*

**de·noue·ment** /deɪˈnuːmɒŋ‖ˌdeɪnuːˈmɑːŋ/ *n* [C] the explanation at the end of a story or play

**de·nounce** /dɪˈnaʊns/ *v* [T] **1** to express strong disapproval of someone or something, especially in public: *The President's statement was denounced by all parties.*|**denounce sb/sth as** *He denounced the waste of public money as 'criminally negligent'.* **2** to give information to the police or other authority about someone's illegal political activities: **denounce sb to sb** *She eventually denounced him to the secret police.* —see also DENUNCIATION

**dense** /dens/ *adj*
**1** ▶ **CLOSE TOGETHER** ◀ made of several things that are closely packed together: *He forced his way through the dense crowd.*|*Dense jungle covered the whole area.*
**2** ▶ **SMOKE/MIST** ◀ difficult to see through or breathe in: *dense fog*|*a dense black cloud*
**3** ▶ **STUPID** ◀ *informal* not able to understand things easily; stupid: *Oh, don't be so dense!*
**4** ▶ **WRITING** ◀ a dense piece of writing is difficult to understand because it contains a lot of information or uses complicated language
**5** ▶ **SUBSTANCE** ◀ *technical* a substance that is dense has a lot of MASS[1] (6) in relation to its size: *Water is eight hundred times denser than air.* —**densely** *adv*: *a densely populated area* —**denseness** *n* [U]

**den·si·ty** /ˈdensɪ̈ti/ *n* [U] **1** the degree to which an area is filled with things or people: *population density* **2** *technical* the relationship between something's MASS[1] (6) and its size

**dent¹** /dent/ *n* [C] **1** a hollow area in the surface of something, usually made by something hitting it: [+ **in**] *There was a dent in the door where he'd kicked it.* **2** a reduction in the amount of something, especially money or supplies: *The trip made a big dent in our savings.*

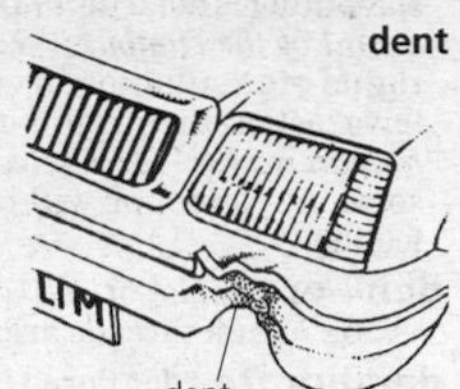

**dent**

**dent²** *v* [T] **1** to make a hollow area in the surface of something, usually by hitting it: *I'm afraid I've dented the car.* **2** to damage or harm something: *Diesel sales have been badly dented by environmental concerns.*

**den·tal** /ˈdentl/ *adj* connected with your teeth: *dental treatment*

**dental floss** /ˌ·· ˈ·/ *n* [U] a kind of thin string that you use for cleaning between your teeth

**dental hy·gien·ist** /ˌ·· ˈ··ˌ·· ·ˈ··/ *n* [C] someone who works with a dentist and cleans people's teeth, or gives them advice about how to look after their teeth

**dental nurse** /ˈ·· ·/ *n* [C] someone whose job is to help a dentist

**dental sur·geon** /ˌ·· ˈ··/ *n* [C] *formal* a dentist

**den·tine** /ˈdentiːn/ also **den·tin** /ˈdentɪn/ *AmE* —*n* [U] the type of bone that your teeth are made of —see picture at TEETH

**den·tist** /ˈdentɪ̵st/ *n* [C] someone whose job is to treat people's teeth: *I'm going to the dentist's this afternoon.*

**den·tis·try** /ˈdentɪ̵stri/ *n* [U] the medical study of the mouth and teeth, or the work of a dentist

**den·tures** /ˈdentʃəz‖-ərz/ *n* [plural] a set of artificial teeth worn by someone who does not have their own teeth any more; FALSE TEETH

**de·nude** /dɪˈnjuːd‖dɪˈnuːd/ *v* [T] *formal* to remove a natural layer or part of something: **denude sth of** *The trees were now denuded of their leaves.* —**denudation** /ˌdiːnjuːˈdeɪʃən‖-nuː-/ *n* [U]

**de·nun·ci·a·tion** /dɪˌnʌnsiˈeɪʃən/ *n* [C] a public statement that someone or something is wrong or bad

**Den·ver boot** /ˌdenvə ˈbuːt‖-vər-/ *n* [C] *AmE informal* a metal object that the police fasten to an illegally parked car so that it cannot be moved; WHEEL CLAMP

S2 W2 **de·ny** /dɪˈnaɪ/ *v* [T]
**1** ▶ **SAY STH IS UNTRUE** ◀ to say that something someone has said about you is not true: *I saw you, so don't try to deny it!* | **deny (that)** *Do you deny that this is your writing?* | *I can't deny her remarks hurt me.* | **deny doing sth** *He denied ever having been there.* | **flatly/categorically deny** (=deny very strongly) *Jackson categorically denied any involvement in the affair.*
**2** ▶ **NOT ALLOW** ◀ [often passive] to refuse to allow someone to have or do something: *Permission was denied.* | **deny sb sth** *She could deny her son nothing.* | **deny sth to sb** *The campaign aims to deny contraceptive advice to girls under sixteen.* —see REFUSE¹ (USAGE)
**3 there's no denying** *spoken* used to say that it is very clear that something is true: *There's no denying that this is a serious blow.*
**4** ▶ **PRINCIPLES/BELIEFS** ◀ *formal* to do something that is the opposite of something you strongly believe in
**5** ▶ **FEELINGS** ◀ to refuse to admit that you are feeling something: *I realized I'd been denying a lot of angry feelings towards my mother.*
**6 deny yourself** to decide not to have something that you would like, especially for moral or religious reasons

**de·o·do·rant** /diːˈəʊdərənt‖-ˈoʊ-/ *n* [C,U] a chemical substance that you put on your skin to hide or destroy unpleasant smells

**de·o·do·rize** *also* **-ise** *BrE* /diːˈəʊdəraɪz‖-ˈoʊ-/ *v* [T] to remove or hide the unpleasant smell of something

**dep** the written abbreviation of DEPART or DEPARTURE

**de·part** /dɪˈpɑːt‖-ɑːrt/ *v* **1** [I] to leave, especially when you are starting a journey: *The train for Edinburgh will depart from platform 5.* **2 depart this life** *formal* to die —see also DEPARTURE

**depart from** sth *phr v* [T] to start to do something differently from the usual, traditional, or expected way: *Her approach departs radically from normal educational practices.*

**de·part·ed** /dɪˈpɑːtɪ̵d‖-ɑːr-/ *adj* [only before noun] **1** a word meaning dead, used to avoid saying this directly: *our dear departed father* **2** *literary* a period of time that is departed has gone for ever: *departed youth*

**de·part·ment** /dɪˈpɑːtmənt‖-ɑːr-/ *n* [C] **1** one of the groups of people working together to form part of a large organization such as a hospital, university, or company: **the English/sales etc department** *She's in charge of the personnel department.* | [+ **of**] *the Department of Genetic Research* **2** one of the parts that the government is divided into which is responsible for a particular problem or part of people's lives: *the State Department* | *the Department of Transport* **3** [C] one of the areas that sells a particular type of product in a large shop: *the toy department* **4** one of the separate areas that some countries are divided into, for example in France **5 be sb's department** *spoken* to be something that a particular person is responsible for: *Don't ask me – cooking's John's department.* —see also FIRE DEPARTMENT, POLICE DEPARTMENT —**departmental** /ˌdiːpɑːtˈmentl◂‖-ɑːr-/ *adj*: *a departmental meeting* S3 W1

**de·part·men·ta·lize** -ise *BrE* /ˌdiːpɑːtˈmentl-aɪz‖-ɑːr-/ *v* [T] to divide something into different departments: *Most large organizations are departmentalized.*

**department store** /-ˈ··· ·/ *n* [C] a large shop that is divided into separate departments, each selling a different type of goods

**de·par·ture** /dɪˈpɑːtʃə‖-ˈpɑːrtʃər/ *n* **1** [C,U] an act of leaving a place, especially at the start of a journey: [+ **for**] *I saw Simon shortly before his departure for Russia.* **2** [C,U] an act of leaving an organization or position: *His sudden departure from the political scene took everyone by surprise.* **3** [C] a flight, train etc that leaves at a particular time: *There are several departures for New York every day.* **4** [C] a way of doing something that is different from the usual, traditional, expected way: **new/fresh/radical etc departure** (=a completely new and usually better way of doing something) *This approach represents a radical departure from previous policy.* —opposite ARRIVAL 

**departure lounge** /-ˈ··· ˌ·/ *n* [C] the place at an airport where people wait until their plane is ready to leave

**departures board** /-ˈ··· ·/ *n* [C] a board in an airport or station that shows the times at which planes or trains leave

**de·pend** /dɪˈpend/ *v* **it/that depends** *spoken* used to say that you cannot give a definite answer to something, because the answer could change according to what happens: *"Are you going to visit him?" "Well, it depends."* S1 W2

**depend on/upon** *phr v* [T] **1** to need the support, help, or existence of someone or something else: *The country depends heavily on its tourist trade.* | *We depend entirely on donations from the public.* | **depend on sb/sth for** *Children depend on their parents for all of their material needs.* | **depend on sb/sth to do sth** *I'm depending on you to get this done.* | **depend on sb/sth doing sth** *We're depending on him finishing the job by Friday.* **2** to trust or have confidence in someone or something: *You can depend on Jane – she always keeps her promises.* | **depend upon it** *spoken* (=you can be sure) *Depend upon it, he'll turn up.* **3** [not in progressive] to change according to what else happens or whether something else changes: *The length of the treatment depends on the severity of the illness.* | **depending on** *The plant may grow to a height of several meters, depending on soil conditions.* | **depend on who/what/how etc** *The amount you pay depends on where you live.*

**de·pen·da·ble** /dɪˈpendəbəl/ *adj* someone or something

that is dependable can be trusted to do what you need or expect: *Ed Duncan was a dependable, hardworking detective.*|*a dependable source of income* —**dependably** *adv* —**dependability** /dɪˌpendəˈbɪlɪ̈ti/ *n* [U]

**de·pen·dant** /dɪˈpendənt/ *n* [C] someone, especially a child, who depends on you for food, clothes, money etc

**de·pen·dence** /dɪˈpendəns/ *n* [U] **1** a situation in which you depend on the help and support of someone or something else in order to exist or be successful: [+ **on/upon**] *We need to reduce our dependence on oil as a source of energy.* —opposite INDEPENDENCE **2 drug/alcohol dependence** the state of being ADDICTED (1) to drugs or alcohol **3** *formal* trust; RELIANCE: *I always place a lot of dependence on what she says.*

**de·pen·den·cy** /dɪˈpendənsi/ *n* **1** [U] a state of dependence **2** [C] a country that is controlled by another country

S3 W3 **de·pen·dent** /dɪˈpendənt/ *adj* **1** needing someone or something else in order to exist, be successful, be healthy etc: *Do you have any dependent children?*| **be dependent on/upon sth (for)** *The young are totally dependent on their parents for food and shelter.* **2 drug/alcohol etc dependent** ADDICTED (1) to drugs, alcohol etc **3 be dependent on/upon** *formal* to change according to what else happens or whether something else changes: *How much you get paid is dependent on how much you produce.*

**dependent clause** /·ˌ·· ˈ·/ *n* [C] a CLAUSE (2) in a sentence that gives information related to the main clause, but cannot exist alone

**de·pict** /dɪˈpɪkt/ *v* [T] to describe something, especially in writing or pictures, in a way that gives a clear idea of a real situation: *a book that depicts life in pre-revolutionary Russia* —**depiction** /dɪˈpɪkʃən/ *n* [C,U]

**de·pil·a·to·ry** /dɪˈpɪlətəri‖-tɔːri/ *n* [C] a substance that gets rid of unwanted hair from your body —**depilatory** *adj* [only before noun] *Try one of our depilatory creams.*

**de·plete** /dɪˈpliːt/ *v* [T usually passive] to reduce the amount of something that is available: *Our food reserves had been severely depleted over the winter.* —**depletion** /dɪˈpliːʃən/ *n* [U] *the depletion of the ozone layer*

**de·plor·a·ble** /dɪˈplɔːrəbəl/ *adj formal* very bad, unpleasant, and shocking: *Conditions in the prison were deplorable.*|*a deplorable waste of tax-payers' money* —**deplorably** *adv*

**de·plore** /dɪˈplɔː‖-ˈplɔːr/ *v* [T] to disapprove very strongly of something and criticize it severely, especially publicly: *The UN deplored the invasion as a 'violation of international law'.*

**de·ploy** /dɪˈplɔɪ/ *v* [T] to organize people or things, especially soldiers, military equipment etc, so that they are in the right place and ready to be used: *They decided it was time to deploy more troops.* —**deployment** *n* [C,U]

**de·pop·u·late** /ˌdiːˈpɒpjɪ̈leɪt‖-ˈpɑːp-/ *v* [T usually passive] to greatly reduce the number of people living in a particular area: *Many rural areas were completely depopulated by the end of the century.* —**depopulation** /diːˌpɒpjɪ̈ˈleɪʃən‖-ˌpɑːp-/ *n* [U]

**de·port** /dɪˈpɔːt‖-ɔːrt/ *v* [T] **1** to make someone who is not a citizen of a particular country leave that country, especially because they do not have a legal right to stay **2 deport yourself** *formal* to behave in a particular way, especially in the proper or corrrect way

**de·por·ta·tion** /ˌdiːpɔːˈteɪʃən‖-ɔːr-/ *n* [C,U] the act of deporting someone: *a deportation order*

**de·por·tee** /ˌdiːpɔːˈtiː‖-ɔːr-/ *n* [C] someone who has been deported or is going to be deported

**de·port·ment** /dɪˈpɔːtmənt‖-ɔːr-/ *n* [U] **1** *especially BrE* the way that someone stands and walks: *As a girl, she had lessons in elocution and deportment.* **2** *old-fashioned especially AmE* the way that a person, especially a young woman, behaves in public

**de·pose** /dɪˈpəʊz‖-ˈpoʊz/ *v* [T] **1** to remove a king, queen, or ruler from a position of power: *The army was threatening to depose him.* **2** *law* to officially give information about something, after you have promised to tell the truth

**de·pos·it¹** /dɪˈpɒzɪ̈t‖dɪˈpɑː-/ *n* [C] W3

**1 ▶ SUM OF MONEY ◀** the first part of the money for a house, car, holiday etc, that you pay so that it will be kept for you: **put down a deposit (on)** (=pay a deposit) *We put down a deposit on a house last week.*

**2 ▶ RENT ◀** money that you pay when you rent or HIRE something, which will be given back if you do not damage the thing you are renting or hiring: *You will have to pay one month's rent in advance, plus a deposit of $500.*

**3 ▶ BANK ◀** an amount of money that is paid into a bank account: **make a deposit** *I'd like to make a deposit, please.*

**4 ▶ SOIL/MINERALS ◀** a layer of a mineral, metal etc that is left in soil or rocks through a natural process: *rich deposits of gold in the hills*

**5 ▶ LAYER ◀** an amount or layer of a substance that gradually develops in a particular place: *fatty deposits on the heart*

**6 ▶ ELECTION ◀** money paid by someone who is a CANDIDATE (1) in a political election in Britain, that will be returned to them if they get enough votes: **lose your deposit** (=not get enough votes)

**deposit²** *v* **1** [T always + adv/prep] *formal* to put something down in a particular place: [+ **on/in/by etc**] *The female deposits her eggs directly into the water.* **2** [T] to leave a layer of a substance on the surface of something: *As the river slows down, it deposits a layer of soil.* **3** [T] to put money or something valuable in a bank or other place where it will be safe: *You are advised to deposit your valuables in the hotel safe.*

**deposit ac·count** /·ˈ·· ·ˌ·/ *n* [C] *especially BrE* a bank account that pays INTEREST¹ (4) on condition that you keep money there for a particular length of time —compare CHECKING ACCOUNT, CURRENT ACCOUNT

**dep·o·si·tion** /ˌdepəˈzɪʃən, ˌdiː-/ *n* **1** [C] *law* a statement written for a court of law, by someone who has promised to tell the truth **2** [U] *technical* the natural process of depositing a substance in rocks or soil **3** [C,U] the act of removing someone from a position of power

**de·pos·i·tor** /dɪˈpɒzɪ̈tə‖dɪˈpɑːzɪ̈tər/ *n* [C] someone who puts money in a bank or other financial organization

**de·pos·i·to·ry** /dɪˈpɒzɪ̈təri‖dɪˈpɑːzɪ̈tɔːri/ *n* [C] a place where something can be safely kept —**depository** *adj*

**deposit slip** /·ˈ·· ·/ *n* [C] *AmE* a form that you use to pay money into your bank account; PAYING-IN SLIP *BrE*

**dep·ot** /ˈdepəʊ‖ˈdiːpoʊ/ *n* [C] **1** a place where goods are stored until they are needed **2** a place where buses are kept and repaired **3** *AmE* a railway station or bus station, especially a small one

**de·prave** /dɪˈpreɪv/ *v* [T] *formal* to be an evil influence on someone, especially someone who is young or not very experienced —**depravity** /dɪˈprævɪ̈ti/ *n* [U] *scenes of depravity* —**depravation** /ˌdeprəˈveɪʃən/ *n* [U]

**de·praved** /dɪˈpreɪvd/ *adj* completely evil or morally unacceptable: *a vicious and depraved man*

**dep·re·cate** /ˈdeprɪ̈keɪt/ *v* [T] *formal* to strongly disapprove of or criticize something —**deprecation** /ˌdeprɪ̈ˈkeɪʃən/ *n* [U]

**dep·re·cat·ing** /ˈdeprɪ̈keɪtɪŋ/ *also* **dep·re·ca·to·ry** /ˈdeprɪ̈keɪtəri‖-kətɔːri/ *adj* **1** expressing criticism or disapproval: *She made several deprecating remarks about my dress sense.* **2** words or actions that are deprecating are intended to make someone feel less annoyed or disapproving: *"He's not here at the moment," she said with a deprecating smile.* —see also SELF-DEPRECATING —**deprecatingly** *adv*

**de·pre·ci·ate** /dɪˈpriːʃieɪt/ *v* **1** [I] to decrease in value or price: *A new car will depreciate quite fast.* —opposite APPRECIATE (4) **2** [T] *formal* to make something seem unimportant

**de·pre·ci·a·tion** /dɪˌpriːʃiˈeɪʃən/ *n* [U] a reduction in the value or price of something: *the depreciation of the dollar* —**depreciatory** /dɪˈpriːʃiətəri‖-ʃətɔːri/ *adj*

**dep·re·da·tion** /ˌdeprəˈdeɪʃən/ *n* [C often plural] *formal* an act of cruelty, violence, or destruction

**de·press** /dɪˈpres/ *v* [T] **1** to make someone feel very unhappy: *The thought of having to take the exam again depressed him.* **2** to prevent something from working properly or being as active as it usually is: *Several factors combined to depress the American economy.* **3** *formal* to press something down, especially a part of a machine: *Depress the clutch fully.* **4** *formal* to reduce the value of prices or wages: *Competition between workers will depress wage levels.*

**de·press·ant** /dɪˈpresənt/ *n* [C] a substance or drug that makes your body's processes slower and makes you feel very relaxed or sleepy —compare STIMULANT —**depressant** *adj*

**de·pressed** /dɪˈprest/ *adj* **1 a)** feeling very unhappy: *She felt lonely and depressed.* | [+ **about/at**] *Carter seemed depressed about the situation.* **b)** suffering from a medical condition in which you are so unhappy that you cannot live a normal life **2** an area, industry etc that is depressed does not have enough economic or business activity **3** a depressed level or amount is lower than normal: *During the illness certain hormone levels are depressed.*

D

**de·press·ing** /dɪˈpresɪŋ/ *adj* making you feel very sad: *I found the whole experience very depressing.* | *It's a depressing thought.* —**depressingly** *adv*: *a depressingly familiar story*

**de·pres·sion** /dɪˈpreʃən/ *n* **1** [C,U] **a)** a feeling of sadness that makes you think there is no hope for the future: *She was overcome by depression.* | **deep/severe depression** *Peter fell into a deep depression on hearing the news.* **b)** a medical condition that makes you so unhappy and anxious you cannot live a normal life **2 a)** [C,U] a long period during which there is very little business activity and lots of people do not have jobs: *the long years of economic depression* —compare RECESSION **3 the Depression** the period when there was not much business activity and not many jobs in the 1930s **4** [C] a part of a surface that is lower than the other parts: *The rain had collected in several depressions on the ground.* **5** [C] *technical* a mass of air that has a low pressure and usually causes rain

**de·press·ive¹** /dɪˈpresɪv/ *adj* often feeling DEPRESSED

**depressive²** *n* [C] someone who suffers from DEPRESSION

**dep·ri·va·tion** /ˌdeprəˈveɪʃən/ *n* **1** [C usually plural] something you need or usually have that you are prevented from having: *People suffered terrible deprivations during the war.* **2** [U] a lack of something that you need or want: *Sleep deprivation can result in mental disorders.*

**de·prive** /dɪˈpraɪv/ *v*

**deprive** sb **of** sth *phr v* [T often passive] to take something from someone, especially something that they need or want: *A lot of these children have been deprived of a normal home life.*

**de·prived** /dɪˈpraɪvd/ *adj* not having the things that are considered to be necessary for a comfortable or happy life: *a deprived childhood*

**de·pro·gram** /ˌdiːˈprəʊgræm‖-ˈproʊ-/ *v* [T] to help someone who has been involved in a religious CULT to stop obeying its orders and to start thinking for themselves again

**dept** the written abbreviation of DEPARTMENT

S3 W3 **depth** /depθ/ *n*

**1** ▶ **DISTANCE** ◀ [C usually singular, U] **a)** the distance down from the top surface to the bottom of something: *What depth is the lake?* | **to/at a depth of** *Plant the seeds at a depth of ten centimetres.* | **a metre/foot etc in depth** *The pond is no more than a metre in depth.* **b)** the distance from the front to the back of an object: *The depth of the shelves is about 35cm.*

**2** ▶ **EMOTION/SITUATION** ◀ [U] how strong an emotion is or how serious a situation is: *Lawmakers underestimated the depth of public feeling on this issue.*

**3** ▶ **KNOWLEDGE** ◀ [U] *approving* the quality of knowing or giving a lot of details about a subject: *I was impressed by the depth and complexity of the book.* | *The network's news coverage lacks depth.* | **in depth** (=considering all the details) *We'll need to study the report in some depth.* —see also IN-DEPTH

**4 be out of your depth a)** to be involved in a situation or activity that is too difficult for you to understand: *I felt completely out of my depth when they started discussing philosophy.* **b)** to be in water that is too deep for you to stand in and be able to breathe

**5 be in the depths of despair/depression etc** to feel very unhappy

**6 the depths of the countryside/forest etc** the middle of a place where there are not many people

**7 the depths of winter** the middle of winter, especially when it is very cold

**8 hidden depths** a part of someone's character that you do not notice when you first meet them: *I didn't know she wrote poety – she obviously has hidden depths.*

**9** ▶ **SEA** ◀ **the depths** *literary* the deepest parts of the sea

**depth charge** /ˈ· ·/ *n* [C] a bomb that explodes at a particular depth under water

**dep·u·ta·tion** /ˌdepjəˈteɪʃən/ *n* [C] a group of people who are sent to talk to someone in authority, as representatives of a larger group

**de·pute** /dɪˈpjuːt/ *v* [T] **depute sb to do sth** *formal* to tell or allow someone to do something instead of you

**dep·u·tize** also **-ise** *BrE* /ˈdepjətaɪz/ *v* [I] to do the work of someone of a higher rank than you for a short time because they are unable to do it: [+ **for**] *Who's going to deputize for Liam while he's away?*

**dep·u·ty** /ˈdepjəti/ *n* [C] **1** someone who is directly below a manager in rank, and who is officially in charge when the manager is not there **2** a member of the LOWER HOUSE of parliament in some countries, for example France **3** someone whose job is to help a SHERIFF (1) in the US: *On the third day, a deputy unlocked my cell.* W2

**de·rail** /ˌdiːˈreɪl, dɪ-/ *v* **1** [usually passive] to make a train go off the railway line **2** [T] to spoil or interrupt a plan, agreement etc: *The dispute has temporarily derailed the arms control agreement.* —**derailment** *n* [C,U]

**de·ranged** /dɪˈreɪndʒd/ *adj* behaving in a crazy or dangerous way —**derangement** *n* [C,U]

**der·by** /ˈdɑːbi‖ˈdɜːrbi/ *n* [C] **1** *AmE* a man's round hard hat that is usually black; **bowler hat** (BOWLER (2)) *BrE* —see picture at HAT **2** *BrE* a sports match between two teams from the same area or city **3** a race that anyone can enter: *a donkey derby* **4** *AmE* a type of horse race

**de·reg·u·late** /ˌdiːˈregjəleɪt/ *v* [T] to remove government rules and controls from some types of business activity: *Data communications have largely been deregulated in Europe.* —**deregulation** /diːˌregjəˈleɪʃən/ *n* [U]

**der·e·lict¹** /ˈderəlɪkt/ *adj* a building or piece of land that is derelict is in very bad condition because it has not been used for a long time

**derelict²** *n* [C] someone who has no money or home and who has to live on the streets

**der·e·lic·tion** /ˌderəˈlɪkʃən/ *n* **1 dereliction of duty** *formal* failure to do what you should do as part of your job **2** [U] the state of being derelict

**de·ride** /dɪˈraɪd/ *v* [T] *formal* to make remarks or jokes that show you think someone or something is silly or useless: *You shouldn't deride their efforts.* | **deride sb as sth** *Wayne was derided as a mere playboy.*

**de ri·gueur** /də riːˈgɜː‖-ˈgɜːr/ *adj* [not before noun] *French* considered to be necessary if you want to be fashionable: *Hats are de rigeur at society weddings.*

**de·ri·sion** /dɪˈrɪʒən/ *n* [U] remarks that show you think someone or something is stupid or silly: *There was a note of derision in his voice.*

**de·ri·sive** /dɪˈraɪsɪv/ *adj* showing that you think someone or something is stupid or silly: *derisive laughter* —**derisively** *adv*

**de·ri·so·ry** /dɪˈraɪsəri/ *adj* **1** an amount of money that is derisory is so small that it is not worth considering seriously: *Unions described the pay offer as derisory.* **2** derisive: *derisory comments* —**derisorily** *adv*

**de·riv·able** /dɪˈraɪvəbəl/ *adj formal* something that is derivable can be calculated from something else

**der·i·va·tion** /ˌderɪ̣ˈveɪʃən/ *n* **1** [C,U] the origin of something, especially a word: *the derivation of place names* **2** [C] a word that comes from another word or language

**de·riv·a·tive**[1] /dɪˈrɪvətɪv/ *n* [C] something that has developed or been produced from something else: **[+ of]** *Heroin is a derivative of morphine.*

**derivative**[2] *adj* not new or invented, but copied or taken from something else: *a largely derivative text*

**de·rive** /dɪˈraɪv/ *v* **1** [T] to get something, usually a pleasant feeling, from something or someone: **derive sth from** *He derived some comfort from the fact that he wasn't the only one to fail the exam.* **2** [I] to develop or come from something else: **[+ from]** *This word is derived from Latin.* **3** [T] *technical* to get a chemical substance from another substance

**der·ma·ti·tis** /ˌdɜːməˈtaɪtɪ̣s‖ˌdɜːr-/ *n* [U] a disease of the skin that causes redness, swelling, and pain

**der·ma·tol·o·gy** /ˌdɜːməˈtɒlədʒi‖ˌdɜːrməˈtɑː-/ *n* [U] the part of medical science that deals with the skin, its diseases, and their treatment —**dermatologist** *n* [C]

**de·rog·ate** /ˈderəgeɪt/ *v*

**derogate from** sth *phr v* [T] *formal* to make something seem less important or less good

**de·rog·a·to·ry** /dɪˈrɒgətəri‖dɪˈrɑːgətɔːri/ *adj* insulting and disapproving: **derogatory remark/comment/term etc** *Many gay men still regard 'queer' as a very derogatory term.* —**derogatorily** *adv*

**der·rick** /ˈderɪk/ *n* [C] **1** a tall machine used for lifting heavy weights, used especially on ships **2** a tall tower built over an oil well to raise and lower the DRILL[1] (1)

**der·riè·re** /ˈderieə‖ˌderiˈer/ *n* [C] *humorous* your bottom: *sitting around on your derriere*

**der·ring-do** /ˌderɪŋ ˈduː/ *n* [U] **deeds/acts etc of derring-do** *humorous* very brave actions like the ones that happen in adventure stories

**derv** /dɜːv‖dɜːrv/ *n* [U] *trademark BrE* an oil product like petrol that is used in DIESEL ENGINES

**der·vish** /ˈdɜːvɪʃ‖ˈdɜːr-/ *n* [C] a member of a Muslim religious group, some of whom dance fast and spin around as part of a religious ceremony

**de·sal·i·nate** /diːˈsælɪ̣neɪt/ *v* [T] to remove the salt from sea water so that it can be used in homes and factories —**desalination** /diːˌsælɪ̣ˈneɪʃən/ *n* [U]

**de·scale** /ˌdiːˈskeɪl/ *v* [T] to remove the white substance that forms on the inside of pipes, KETTLES etc

**des·cant** /ˈdeskænt/ *n* [C,U] a tune that is played or sung above the main tune in a piece of music

**de·scend** /dɪˈsend/ *v* **1** [I,T] *formal* to move from a higher level to a lower one: *The plane started to descend.* | **[+ from]** *He descended slowly from the railway carriage.* | **descend sth** *Mrs Danvers descended the stairs.* —opposite ASCEND **2** [I] *literary* if darkness, night etc descends, it begins to get dark **3 in descending order** numbers, choices etc that are in descending order are arranged from the highest or most important to the lowest or least important

**descend from** sth *phr v* [T] **1** to have developed from something that existed in the past: *These ideas descend from those of the ancient philosophers.* **2 be descended from sb** to be related to someone who lived a long time ago: *My mother claims she is descended from Abraham Lincoln.*

**descend on/upon** sb/sth *phr v* [T] **1** if a feeling descends on someone, they begin to feel it: *Gloom descended on the office when we heard the news.* **2** *informal* if a large number of people descend on you, they come to your home: *My in-laws are descending on us this weekend.*

**descend to** sth *phr v* [T] to behave or speak in an unpleasant way that is not what people expect from you: **descend to (doing) sth** *I refused to descend to petty personal attacks.* | **descend to sb's level** (=behave or speak in the same unpleasant way as someone else)

**de·scen·dant** /dɪˈsendənt/ *n* [C] someone who is related to a person who lived a long time ago: **direct descendant** (=from one father or mother to the next) *He reckons he's a direct descendant of Napoleon Bonaparte.* —compare ANCESTOR (1)

**de·scent** /dɪˈsent/ *n* **1** [C,U] *formal* the process of going down: *Passengers must fasten their seat belts prior to descent.* **2** [C] a path or road that goes steeply downwards: *a slippery descent* **3** [U] your family origins, especially in connection with the country that you come from: **by descent** *They're Irish by descent.* | **be of Russian/Chinese etc descent** *She's of German descent.* **4** [singular] a gradual change towards behaviour that is wrong or not acceptable: **[+ into]** *her descent into a life of crime* **5** [singular] a sudden unwanted visit or attack: *the descent on the town by a motorcycle gang*

**de·scribe** /dɪˈskraɪb/ *v* [T] **S1** **W1** **1** to say what something or someone is like by giving details about them: *The police asked her to describe the two men.* | *An alternative approach to the problem is described in Chapter 3.* | **describe how/why/what etc** *It's difficult to describe how I feel.* | **describe sb/sth as** *Sarah described him as shy.* | **describe sb/sth to sb** *So describe this new boyfriend to me!* | **describe doing sth** *He described going downstairs and finding his mother lying on the floor.* —see SPEAK (USAGE) **2** *formal* to make a shape in the air by moving your hands in a particular way: *Her hand described a circle in the air.*

**de·scrip·tion** /dɪˈskrɪpʃən/ *n* **S2** **W2** **1** [C,U] a piece of writing or speech that says what someone or something is like: *Berlin sounds fascinating from your description.* | **detailed/accurate description** *The police have issued a detailed description of the missing woman.* | **give a description** *I gave them a description of my car.* | **brief/general description** *a brief description of what the job involves* | **full/complete description** *I'll need a full description of the stolen property.* | **answer/fit a description** (=be like the person or thing described) *A man fitting that description was seen outside the bank.* **2 be beyond/past description** to be too good, bad, big etc to be described easily: *I found the play boring beyond description.* **3** [C] a type of thing, person etc: **of every/some/that etc description** *flowers and plants of every description* | **of all descriptions** *People of all descriptions came to see the show.*

This graph shows some of the words most commonly used with the noun **description**.

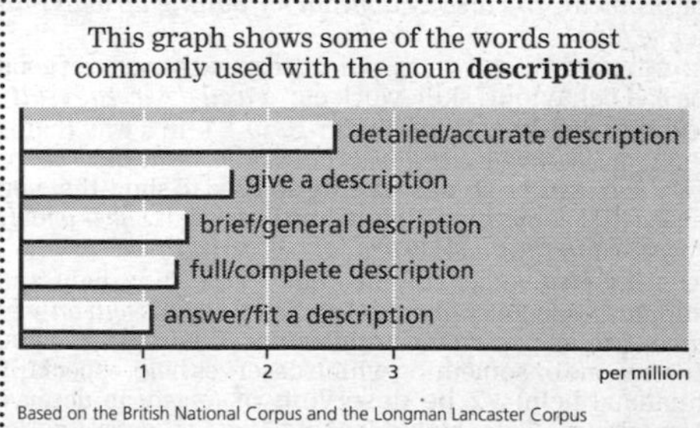


Based on the British National Corpus and the Longman Lancaster Corpus

**de·scrip·tive** /dɪˈskrɪptɪv/ *adj* **1** giving a description of something in words or pictures: *The book is full of descriptive passages.* **2** *technical* describing how the words of a language are actually used, rather than saying how they ought to be used —**descriptively** *adv* —**descriptiveness** *n* [U]

**de·scry** /dɪˈskraɪ/ *v* [T] *literary* to notice or see something, especially when it is a long way away

**des·e·crate** /ˈdesɪkreɪt/ *v* [T] to spoil or damage something holy —**desecration** /ˌdesɪˈkreɪʃən/ *n* [U]

**de·seg·re·gate** /diːˈsegrɪgeɪt/ *v* [T] to end a system by which people of different races are kept separate —**desegregation** /ˌdiːsegrɪ̇ˈgeɪʃən‖diːˌseg-/ *n* [U]

**de·sel·ect** /ˌdiːsəˈlekt/ *v* [T] **1** to remove something from a list of choices on a computer **2** *BrE* to refuse to choose an existing Member of Parliament as a CANDIDATE (1) at the next election —**deselection** /-ˈlekʃən/ *n* [U]

**de·sen·si·tize** also **-ise** *BrE* /diːˈsensɪ̇taɪz/ *v* [T] **1** to make someone react less strongly to something by making them become used to it: [+ **to**] *Many children have become desensitized to violence* **2** *technical* to make photographic material less sensitive to light —**desensitization** /diːˌsensɪ̇taɪˈzeɪʃən‖-tə-/ *n* [U]

**des·ert¹** /ˈdezət‖-ərt/ *n* **1** [C,U] a large area of sand where it is always very hot and dry: *the Sahara Desert* **2** [C] a place where there is no activity or where nothing interesting happens: *a cultural desert*

**de·sert²** /dɪˈzɜːt‖-ˈzɜːrt/ *v* **1** [T] to leave someone alone and refuse to help or support them any more: *Mike just deserted her when she got pregnant.* **2** [T] to leave a place so that it is completely empty: *They deserted their homes and fled to the hills.* **3** [T] if a feeling or quality deserts you, you no longer have it, especially at a time when you need it: *Mike's confidence seemed to have deserted him.* **4** [I + **from**] to leave the army without permission

**de·sert·er** /dɪˈzɜːtə‖-ˈzɜːrtər/ *n* [C] a soldier who leaves the army without permission

**de·ser·tion** /dɪˈzɜːʃən‖-ɜːr-/ *n* **1** [C,U] the act of leaving the army without permission **2** [U] *law* the act of leaving your wife or husband because you do not want to live with them any longer

**desert is·land** /ˌ·· ˈ··/ *n* [C] a small tropical island far from other places with no people living on it

**deserts get your just deserts** to be punished in a way that you deserve

S2 W3 **de·serve** /dɪˈzɜːv‖-ɜːrv/ *v* [T] **1** to have earned something by good or bad actions or behaviour: *You've been working all morning – I think you deserve a rest.* | **deserve to do sth** *The team deserves to win.* | **deserve it** *Yeah, I hit him but he deserved it.* | **get what you deserve** (=be punished or have something unpleasant happen in a way that you deserve) | **deserve all you get** (=deserve any unpleasant things that may happen to you) | **deserve better** (=deserve more pleasant treatment or situations than you are getting) **2 deserve consideration/attention etc** if a suggestion, idea, or plan deserves consideration etc, it is good or sensible enough to be considered: *These proposals deserve serious consideration.* **3 deserve a medal** *spoken* used to say that you admire the way someone dealt with a situation or problem: *You deserve a medal for putting up with Phil for so long!*

**de·served** /dɪˈzɜːvd‖-ˈzɜːrvd/ *adj* earned because of good or bad behaviour, skill, work etc: *a well-deserved result*

**de·serv·ed·ly** /dɪˈzɜːvɪ̇dli‖-ɜːr-/ *adv* **1** in a way that is right or deserved: *Her novels have been, quite deservedly, very successful.* **2 deservedly so** used to show that you agree that something is right and deserved: *She is widely respected in the music world, and deservedly so.*

**de·serv·ing** /dɪˈzɜːvɪŋ‖-ɜːr-/ *adj* **1** needing help and support, especially financial support: *Grants will only be awarded to deserving applicants.* | **deserving case** (=someone or something which deserves help, especially financial help) **2 be deserving of** *formal* to deserve something: *This stupid-looking hat is deserving of ridicule!*

**de·sex·u·al·ize** also **-ise** *BrE* /diːˈsekʃuəlaɪz/ *v* [T] to remove the sexual quality from something —**desexualization** /diːˌsekʃuəlaɪˈzeɪʃən‖-lə-/ *n* [C,U] *desexualization of the body*

**dés·ha·bil·lé** /ˌdeɪzæˈbiːeɪ/ also **dishabille** *AmE* —*n* [U] *literary or humorous* the state of being only partly dressed, used especially of a woman

**des·ic·cant** /ˈdesɪ̇kənt/ *n* [C,U] *technical* a substance that takes water from the air so that it keeps other things dry

**des·ic·cate** /ˈdesɪ̇keɪt/ *v* [T] *formal* to remove all the water from something —**desiccation** /ˌdesɪ̇ˈkeɪʃən/ *n* [U]

**des·ic·cat·ed** /ˈdesɪ̇keɪtɪ̇d/ *adj* **1** dessicated food has been dried in order to preserve it: *desiccated coconut* **2** *formal* completely dry

**de·sid·e·ra·tum** /dɪˌzɪdəˈreɪtəm, -ˈrɑː-, dɪˌsɪ-/ *n plural* **desiderata** /-tə/ [C] *Latin formal* something that is wanted or needed

**de·sign¹** /dɪˈzaɪn/ *n* S3 W1

**1** ▶ **ARRANGEMENT OF PARTS** ◀ [U] the way that something has been planned and made, including its appearance, how it works etc: *One or two changes have been made to the computer's basic design.* | *the importance of good design*

**2** ▶ **PATTERN** ◀ [C] a decorative pattern on something: *wallpaper with a floral design*

**3** ▶ **DRAWING PLANS** ◀ [U] the art or process of making a drawing of something to show how you will make it or what it will look like: *graphic design*

**4** ▶ **DRAWN PLAN** ◀ [C] a drawing showing how something will be made or what it will look like: [+ **for**] *The Council has just approved the design for the new sports centre.*

**5** ▶ **INTENTION** ◀ [C] a plan that someone has in their mind: *Did he have some sinister design in doing this?* | **by design** (=intentionally) *Whether this happened by design or not we shall never know.*

**6 have designs on sb** to want a sexual relationship with someone: *It soon became obvious that he had designs on her.*

**7 have designs on sth** to be interested in something because you want it for yourself, especially if it will bring you money: *I reckon they have designs on their uncle's business.*

**design²** *v* **1** [I,T] to make a drawing or plan of something that will be made or built: *A local architect designed the theatre.* | **well/badly etc designed** *a well designed office* **2** [T usually passive] to plan or develop something for a specific purpose: **design sth to do sth** *These exercises are designed to develop and strengthen muscles.* | **be designed for** *coursebooks designed for intermediate students* | **be designed as** *a short film designed as an introduction to road safety* —see also DESIGNER¹ 

**des·ig·nate¹** /ˈdezɪgneɪt/ *v* [T] **1** to choose someone or something for a particular job or purpose: **designate sth as/for** *We're going to designate this room as a no-smoking area.* | **designate sb to do sth** *She has been designated to take over the position of treasurer.* **2** to show or mean something, especially by using a special name or sign: *Buildings are designated by red squares on the map.*

**des·ig·nate²** /ˈdezɪgnɪ̇t, -neɪt/ *adj* [only after noun] *formal* a word used after the name of an official job showing that someone has been chosen for that job but has not yet officially started work: *the ambassador designate*

**designated dri·ver** /ˌ···· ˈ··/ *n* [C] *AmE informal* someone who agrees to drive their friends and not drink alcohol when they go out together to a party, bar etc

**designated hi·tter** /ˌ···· ˈ··/ *n* [C] *AmE* **1** someone in the game of BASEBALL whose job is usually to hit the ball, but who replaces the PITCHER (=person who throws the ball) when it is their turn to hit **2** *informal* someone who does a job for someone else, especially in politics or business

**des·ig·na·tion** /ˌdezɪgˈneɪʃən/ *n* **1** [U] the act of choosing someone or something for a particular purpose, or of giving them a particular description: *the designation of a student library assistant* **2** [C] *formal* a name or title: *Her official designation is Systems Manager.*

**de·sign·ed·ly** /dɪˈzaɪnɪ̇dli/ *adv formal* on purpose; intentionally

**de·sign·er¹** /dɪˈzaɪnə‖-ər/ *n* [C] someone whose job is to make plans or patterns for clothes, furniture, equipment etc: *a dress designer* 

**designer²** *adj* [only before noun] **1** made by a well-known and fashionable designer: *designer jeans* **2** *not technical* changed by GENETIC ENGINEERING: *a designer virus*

**designer drug** /ˌ·ˌ·· ˈ·/ *n* [C] a drug similar to COCAINE or HEROIN that is produced artificially but is not illegal itself

**de·sign·ing¹** /dɪˈzaɪnɪŋ/ *adj* someone who is designing tries to deceive people in order to get what they want

**designing²** *n* [U] DESIGN ¹ (1)

**de·sir·a·ble** /dɪˈzaɪərəbəl‖-zaɪ-/ *adj formal* **1** something that is desirable is worth having or doing because it is useful or popular: **highly desirable** (=very desirable)| **it is desirable that** *It is desirable that you should have some familiarity with computers.* —compare UNDESIRABLE **2** someone who is desirable is very sexually attractive —**desirably** *adv* —**desirablility** /dɪˌzaɪərəˈbɪlᵻti-ˌzaɪr-/ *n* [U]

W 2 **de·sire¹** /dɪˈzaɪə‖-ˈzaɪr/ *v* [T not in progressive] **1** *formal* to want or hope for something very much: *the qualities we desire in our employees*| **desire to do sth** *Anyone desiring to vote must come to the meeting.*| **desire sb to do sth** *The prince desired her to be his queen.* **2 leave a lot to be desired** *especially spoken* used to say that something is not as good as you think it should be: *The standard of cooking here leaves a lot to be desired.* **3** *old-fashioned* to want to have sex with someone —**desired** *adj*: *My remarks had the desired effect.*

**desire²** *n* **1** [C,U] a strong hope or wish: [+ **for**] *a desire for knowledge*| **desire to do sth** *Anna has a great desire to travel.*| **desire that** *a desire that his books should reach as many people as possible*| **show/express a desire** *They did not show the slightest desire to accompany us.*| **overwhelming/burning desire** (=very strong desire) *He fought a burning desire to break into the conversation.*| **have no desire to do sth** (=used to emphasize that you do not want to do something) *I have no desire to see him hurt, I assure you.* **2 sb's heart's desire** a very strong wish that someone has **3** [U + **for**] *formal* a strong wish to have sex with someone

**de·sir·ous** /dɪˈzaɪərəs‖-ˈzaɪr-/ *adj formal* wanting something very much: [+ **of**] *No one had ever been so openly desirous of my attention.*

**de·sist** /dɪˈzɪst, dɪˈsɪst/ *v* [I] *formal* to stop doing something: [+ **from**] *You are ordered to desist from such behaviour.*

S 2 **desk** /desk/ *n* [C] **1** a piece of furniture like a table, usu-
W 2 ally with drawers in it, that you sit at to write and work **2** a place where you can get information in a hotel, airport etc: *the check-in desk* **3** an office that deals with a particular subject, especially in newspapers or television: *Lloyd is running the sports desk.*

**desk clerk** /ˈ· ·/ *n* [C] *AmE* someone who works at the main desk in a hotel

**de·skill** /ˌdiːˈskɪl/ *v* [T] to remove or reduce the need for skill in a job, usually by changing to machinery

**desk job** /ˈ· ·/ *n* [C] a job that involves working mostly at a desk in an office

**desk ti·dy** /ˈ· ˌ··/ *n* [C] *BrE* a container for putting pens, pencils etc in, that you keep on your desk

**desk·top, desktop** /ˈdesktɒp‖-tɑːp/ *adj* **1 desktop computer** a computer that is small enough to be used on a desk —see picture on page 837 **2 desktop publishing** the work of getting a magazine, small book etc ready to be produced, using a small computer

**des·o·late¹** /ˈdesələt/ *adj* **1** a place that is desolate is empty and looks sad because there are no people there and not much activity: *desolate moorland* **2** someone who is desolate feels very sad and lonely —**desolately** *adv* —**desolation** /ˌdesəˈleɪʃən/ *n* [U]

**des·o·late²** /ˈdesəleɪt/ *v* [T usually passive] *literary* **1** to make someone feel very sad and lonely: *Martin was desolated by his wife's death.* **2** to make a place seem empty and sad: *He returned to the desolated camp.*

**despair¹** *n* [U] **1** a feeling that you have no hope at all for the future: **in despair** *I spent ages trying to fix it, but gave up in despair.*| **the depths of despair** (=very strong feelings of despair)| **drive sb to despair** *Norman's constant drinking drives his family to despair.* **2 the despair of sb** someone or something that makes someone feel very worried, upset, or unhappy: *That Jones girl is the despair of her teachers.*

**de·spair²** /dɪˈspeə‖-ˈsper/ *v* [I] to feel that there is no hope that a situation will improve: *Dirk came close to despairing in those months of unemployment.*| **despair of (doing) sth** *They despaired of finding the children alive.*

**de·spair·ing** /dɪˈspeərɪŋ‖-ˈsper-/ *adj* showing a feeling of despair: *He raised his eyes in a despairing gesture.* —**despairingly** *adv*: *Don was shaking his head despairingly.*

**de·spatch** /dɪˈspætʃ/ another spelling of DISPATCH

**des·pe·ra·do** /ˌdespəˈrɑːdəʊ‖-doʊ/ *n* [C] *old-fashioned* a violent criminal who is not afraid of danger

**des·per·ate** /ˈdespərᵻt/ *adj* **1** willing to do anything W 3
and not caring about danger, because you are in a very bad situation: *We had no food left at all and were getting desperate.*| *an appeal from the teenager's desperate parents* **2** [not before noun] needing or wanting something very much: [+ **for**] *By then I was desperate for a holiday.*| **desperate to do sth** *Ben was desperate to get a job.*| **in desperate need** *We're in desperate need of help.* **3** a desperate situation is very bad or serious: *There was a desperate shortage of doctors.* **4** a desperate action is something that you only do because you are in a very bad situation: **desperate attempt/effort/measures** *The victim had made a desperate attempt to escape.*

**des·pe·rate·ly** /ˈdespərᵻtli/ *adv* **1** in a desperate way: *He looked round desperately for someone to help him.*| **try desperately** *The doctors were trying desperately to save her life.* **2** very much: *Joe's work is desperately important to him.*| **desperately need** *He desperately needs reassurance.*

**des·per·a·tion** /ˌdespəˈreɪʃən/ *n* [U] the state of being desperate: *a look of desperation in his eyes*| **in desperation** *Finally, in desperation, we went to a pawnbroker.*

**des·pic·a·ble** /dɪˈspɪkəbəl, ˈdespɪ-/ *adj* extremely unpleasant;: *a despicable liar*| *It's despicable the way he treats those kids.* —**despicably** *adv*: *grinning despicably*

**de·spise** /dɪˈspaɪz/ *v* [T not in progressive] to dislike someone or something very much: *Mrs Morel had come to despise her husband.*

**de·spite** /dɪˈspaɪt/ *prep* **1** in spite of something: S 2
*Despite all our efforts to save the school, the County decided* W 1
*to close it.*| **despite the fact that** *She went to Spain despite the fact the doctor had told her to rest.* **2 despite yourself** if you do something despite yourself, you do it although you did not intend to: *Despite herself, she found his attention rather enjoyable.*

**de·spoil** /dɪˈspɔɪl/ *v* [T] *literary* **1** to make a place much less attractive by removing or damaging things **2** to steal from a place using force, especially in a war

**de·spon·dent** /dɪˈspɒndənt‖dɪˈspɑːn-/ *adj* unhappy and not hopeful: *Gill had been out of work for a year and was getting very despondent.* —**despondency** *n* [U] —**despondently** *adv*: *He was staring despondently into the distance.*

**des·pot** /ˈdespɒt, -ət‖ˈdespət, -ɑːt/ *n* [C] someone such as a ruler who used power in a cruel and unfair way —**despotic** /deˈspɒtɪk‖-ˈspɑː-/ *adj* —**despotically** /-kli/ *adv*

**des·pot·is·m** /ˈdespətɪzəm/ *n* [U] rule by a despot

**des res** /ˌdez ˈrez/ *n* [C] *BrE informal* a house that a lot of people admire and would like to live in

**des·sert** /dɪˈzɜːt‖-ɜːrt/ *n* [C,U] sweet food served after the main part of a meal: *There's ice-cream for dessert.*

**des·sert·spoon** /dɪˈzɜːtspuːn‖-ˈzɜːrt-/ *n* [C] **1** *especially BrE* a spoon that is between the sizes of a TEASPOON and a TABLESPOON —see picture at SPOON¹ **2** also **dessertspoonful** /-fʊl/ the amount held by a dessertspoon

**dessert wine** /ˌ·ˈ· ·/ *n* [C,U] a sweet wine served with dessert

**de·sta·bil·ize** also **-ise** *BrE* /diːˈsteɪbɪ̈laɪz/ *v* [T] to make something less likely to remain politically successful: *an attempt to destabilize the government* —**destabilization** /ˌdiːsteɪbɪ̈laɪˈzeɪʃən‖diːˌsteɪbɪ̈lə-/ *n* [C]

**des·ti·na·tion** /ˌdestɪ̈ˈneɪʃən/ *n* [C] the place that someone or something is going to: *holiday destinations*

**des·tined** /ˈdestɪ̈nd/ *adj* **1** [not before noun] certain to have something or do something at some time in the future: [+ **for**] *She seemed destined for a long and successful career.* | **destined to do sth** *We were destined never to meet again.* **2 be destined for** to be travelling towards a particular place: *a flight destined for Cairo* **3 destined lover/profession etc** *literary* the person, thing etc that you will have in the future

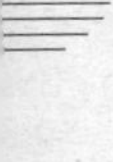

**des·ti·ny** /ˈdestɪ̈ni/ *n* **1** [C usually singular] the things that will happen to someone in the future, especially those that cannot be changed or controlled; FATE (1) | **your/my/his etc destiny** *Juan accepted his destiny without complaint.* **2** [U] the power that some people believe decides what will happen to them in the future: *I'm a great believer in destiny.*

**des·ti·tute** /ˈdestɪ̈tjuːt‖-tuːt/ *adj* **1** having no money, no food, and nowhere to live: *Many people were so destitute they lived out of garbage cans.* **2 be destitute of** *formal* to be completely without something: *a man destitute of all compassion* —**destitution** *n* [U]

**de·stroy** /dɪˈstrɔɪ/ *v* [T] **1** to damage something so badly that it cannot be repaired or so that it no longer exists: *The school was completely destroyed by fire.* | *an accident that destroyed her ballet career* **2** to kill an animal, especially because it is sick, or dangerous **3 destroy sb** to ruin someone's life completely so that they have no hope for the future —see also DESTRUCTION

**USAGE NOTE: DESTROY**

WORD CHOICE: **destroy, ruin, spoil**

**Destroy** means to damage something so badly that it no longer exists or cannot be repaired: *Whole areas of the city were destroyed.* | *a drug to destroy cancer cells* | *Their traditional way of life has been destroyed.*

You **ruin** or (less strong) **spoil** something good or useful. It then usually still exists, but no longer has its good qualities or features: *Too much sugar can ruin your teeth.* | *You've completely spoiled my day.*

**de·stroy·er** /dɪˈstrɔɪə‖-ər/ *n* [C] **1** a small fast military ship with guns **2** someone or something that destroys things or people: *They feared photography would be the destroyer of art.*

W3 **de·struc·tion** /dɪˈstrʌkʃən/ *n* [U] **1** the act or process of destroying something: *the threat of nuclear destruction* **2 be sb's destruction** *formal* to be the thing that completely ruins someone's life: *Gambling was his destruction.* —see also DESTROY

**de·struc·tive** /dɪˈstrʌktɪv/ *adj* causing damage to people or things: *Jealousy is a very destructive emotion.* —**destructively** *adv* —**destructiveness** *n* [U]

**des·ul·to·ry** /ˈdesəltəri, ˈdez-‖-tɔːri/ *adj formal* done without any particular plan or purpose: *They talked in a desultory manner for a few minutes.* —**desultorily** /ˈdesəltərɪ̈li, ˈdez-ˌdesəlˈtɔːrɪ̈li, ˌdez-/ *adv*

**Det** the written abbreviation of DETECTIVE

**de·tach** /dɪˈtætʃ/ *v* [T] **1** to remove a piece or part of something that is designed to be removed: *If you are interested in the course, detach and fill out the application form.* | **detach sth from** *You can detach the hood from the jacket.* **2 detach yourself** to try to be less involved in, or less concerned about a situation: *I try to detach myself from my patients.*

**de·tach·a·ble** /dɪˈtætʃəbəl/ *adj* able to be removed and put back: *a detachable handle*

**de·tached** /dɪˈtætʃt/ *adj* **1** not reacting in an emotional way, so that you can do your job properly or make the right decisions: *Try to take a more detached view.* **2** *BrE* a detached house or garage is not joined to another building on any side: *a large detached house on the outskirts of the town* —compare SEMIDETACHED, TERRACED HOUSE —see picture on page 410

**de·tach·ment** /dɪˈtætʃmənt/ *n* **1** [U] the state of not reacting in an emotional way, so that you can do your job properly or make the right decisions: *Doctors need to have some degree of emotional detachment.* **2** [C] a group of soldiers who are sent away from the main group to do a special job

**de·tail**[1] /ˈdiːteɪl‖dɪˈteɪl/ *n* **1** [C,U] a single feature, fact, or piece of information, or many small features considered together: *Todd had planned the journey down to the smallest detail.* | *We need to discuss a few details before you start.* | **attention to detail** *Editing requires great attention to detail.* | **go into detail/details** (=include a lot of details when describing or explaining something) | **read/describe etc sth in detail** (=pay attention to all the details) *Study the contract in detail before signing.* | **have an eye for detail** (=be skilled at noticing details) **2 details** [plural] all the additional information you need about something you already know a little about: [+ **of**] *Send for details of the course.* | **full/further details** *For further details, contact the personnel department.* **3** [singular, U] *technical* a specific duty in the army, or the person or group who have that duty: *the security detail* S2 W1

**detail**[2] *v* [T] **1** to give all the facts or information about something: *The paper then goes on to detail a number of joint initiatives.* **2 detail sb to do sth** to officially order someone, especially soldiers, to do a particular job: *Vance, you're detailed to the night watch.*

**de·tailed** /ˈdiːteɪld‖dɪˈteɪld/ *adj* including a lot of information and detail: *a detailed account of the development of the atom bomb* W2

**de·tail·ing** /ˈdiːteɪlɪŋ‖dɪˈteɪlɪŋ/ *n* [U] decorations that are added to something such as a car or piece of clothing

**de·tain** /dɪˈteɪn/ *v* [T] **1** to officially prevent someone from leaving a place: *Police detained the terrorists.* **2** to delay someone who wants to leave, by talking to them, asking them to do something etc: *I want a quick word, but I won't detain you long.*

**de·tain·ee** /ˌdiːteɪˈniː/ *n* [C] someone who is officially kept in a prison, usually because of their political views

**de·tan·gle** /ˌdiːˈtæŋgəl/ *v* [I,T] *especially AmE* to remove the knots in hair

**de·tect** /dɪˈtekt/ *v* [T] to notice or discover something, especially something that is not easy to see, hear etc: *Many forms of cancer can be cured if detected early.* | *Do I detect a note of sarcasm in your voice?* —**detectable** *adj* W3

**de·tec·tion** /dɪˈtekʃən/ *n* [U] the process of detecting, or the fact of being detected: *the early detection of cancer*

**de·tec·tive** /dɪˈtektɪv/ *n* [C] **1** a police officer whose job is to discover information that will result in criminals being caught —see also STORE DETECTIVE **2** someone who is paid to discover information about someone or something: *She hired a detective to find out where her husband was going after work.* **3 detective story/novel etc** a story about a crime, often a murder, and a detective who tries to find out who did it W3

**de·tec·tor** /dɪˈtektə‖-ər/ *n* [C] a piece of equipment that makes a signal if it discovers something: *smoke detectors* | *a metal detector* —see also LIE DETECTOR

**dé·tente** /ˈdeɪtɒnt,deɪˈtɑːnt‖deɪˈtɑːnt/ *n* [C,U] a state of more friendly political relations between countries that have previously been unfriendly

**de·ten·tion** /dɪˈtenʃən/ *n* **1** [U] the state of being kept somewhere by the police, because they think you have done something illegal: *Willis spent over 100 days in detention.* **2** [C,U] a punishment in which children who have behaved badly are forced to stay at school for a short time after the others have gone home

**detention cen·tre** *BrE*, **detention center** *AmE* /·'·· ,··/ *n* [C] a place where young people who have done something illegal are kept, because they are too young to go to prison

**de·ter** /dɪ'tɜː‖-'tɜːr/ *v* **deterred, deterring** [T] to persuade someone not to do something, by making them realize it will be difficult or will have unpleasant results: *security measures aimed at deterring shoplifters* | **deter sb from doing sth** *a new program designed to deter kids from experimenting with drugs* —see also DETERRENT

**de·ter·gent** /dɪ'tɜːdʒənt‖-ɜːr-/ *n* [C,U] a liquid or powder that contains soap used for washing clothes, dishes etc

**de·te·ri·o·rate** /dɪ'tɪəriəreɪt‖-'tɪr-/ *v* [I] **1** to become worse: *deteriorating health* | *Relations between the two countries have since deteriorated.* **2** [+ **into**] to develop into a bad or unpleasant situation *The meeting soon deteriorated into a fight.* —**deterioration** /dɪ,tɪəriə'reɪʃən‖-,tɪr-/ *n* [U] *environmental deterioration*

**de·ter·mi·nant** /dɪ'tɜːmɪnənt‖-ɜːr-/ *n* [C] *formal* something that strongly influences what you do or how you behave: [+ **of**] *Social class is a major determinant of consumer spending patterns.*

**de·ter·mi·nate** /dɪ'tɜːmənət‖-ɜːr-/ *adj formal* strictly controlled or limited: *A firm will act in a determinate way to maximize its profits.*

W3 **de·ter·mi·na·tion** /dɪ,tɜːmə'neɪʃən‖-ɜːr-/ *n* **1** [U] the ability to continue trying to achieve what you have decided to do even when this is difficult: **determination to do sth** *Her determination to do well made her keep on studying.* | **dogged determination** (=very strong determination) *They were admired for their dogged determination to learn the language.* **2** [U] *formal* the act of deciding something officially: *the determination of government policy* **3** [C] *technical* the act of finding the exact level, amount, or causes of something: *determination of the cause of death* —see also SELF-DETERMINATION

W1 **de·ter·mine** /dɪ'tɜːmən‖-ɜːr-/ *v* [T] **1** to find out the exact details or facts about something: *Your parents' income is used to determine your level of financial aid.* | [+ **how/what/who etc**] *The purpose of the exercise is to determine where we want to go from here.* **2** to have a strong influence or effect on something: *Usually the size of the practice will determine the number of doctors.* **3** to officially decide something: *The date of the court case was yet to be determined.* **4** *formal* to form a firm intention to do something: **determine to do sth** *We determined to leave at once.*

W3 **de·ter·mined** /dɪ'tɜːmənd‖-ɜːr-/ *adj* **1** having a strong desire to do something, so that you will not let anyone stop you: *a determined young woman* | **determined to do sth** *I am determined to find out who is responsible for this.* | **determined that** *Determined that his son would do well, Eliot sent him to a private school.* **2** showing determination, especially in a difficult situation: **determined attempts/opposition etc** *The library was closed down despite determined opposition.*

**de·ter·min·er** /dɪ'tɜːmənə‖-'tɜːrmənər/ *n* [C] *technical* a word that comes before an adjective that describes a noun, for example 'his' in 'his new car' or 'that' in 'that big tree'

**de·ter·min·is·m** /dɪ'tɜːmənɪzəm‖-ɜːr-/ *n* [U] the belief that what you do and what happens to you are caused by things that you cannot control —**deterministic** /dɪ,tɜːmə'nɪstɪk◂‖-ɜːr-/ *adj*

**de·ter·rent** /dɪ'terənt‖-'tɜːr-/ *n* [C] **1** something that makes someone less likely to do something: **be a deterrent to sb** *Window locks are an effective deterrent to potential burglars.* **2 nuclear deterrent** NUCLEAR weapons that a country has, that are supposed to prevent other countries from attacking —**deterrence** *n* [U]

**de·test** /dɪ'test/ *v* [T not in progressive] to hate something or someone very much: *I detest computers.* —**detestation** /,diːte'steɪʃən/ *n* [U]

**de·test·able** /dɪ'testəbəl/ *adj* very bad, and deserving to be criticized or hated: *a detestable little man* —**detestably** *adv*

**de·throne** /dɪ'θrəʊn‖-'θroʊn/ *v* [T] **1** to remove a king or queen from power **2** to remove someone from a position of authority or importance —**dethronement** *n* [U]

**det·o·nate** /'detəneɪt/ *v* [I,T] to explode or make something explode, using special equipment

**det·o·na·tion** /,detə'neɪʃən/ *n* [C,U] an explosion, or the action of making a bomb etc explode

**det·o·na·tor** /'detəneɪtə‖-ər/ *n* [C] a piece of equipment that is used to start an explosion

**de·tour¹** /'diːtʊə‖-tʊr/ *n* [C] a way of going from one place to another that is longer than the usual way, for example because you want to avoid traffic problems or to visit something: **make/take a detour** *BrE*: *We took a detour to avoid the town centre.*

**detour²** *v* [I,T] *especially AmE* to make a detour

**de·tox** /'diːtɒks‖-tɑːks/ *n* [U] special treatment at a hospital to help people stop drinking alcohol or taking drugs

**de·tox·i·fi·ca·tion** /,diːtɒksəfə'keɪʃən‖diː,tɑːk-/ *n* [U] **1** the process of removing harmful chemicals or poison from something **2** detox: *detoxification unit* —**detoxify** /diː'tɒksəfaɪ‖-'tɑːk-/ *v* [T]

**de·tract** /dɪ'trækt/ *v*

**detract from** sth *phr v* [T not in progressive] to make something seem less good than it really is: *One mistake is not going to detract from your achievement.* —**detraction** /dɪ'trækʃən/ *n* [C,U]

**de·trac·tor** /dɪ'træktə‖-ər/ *n* [C] someone who says bad things about someone or something, in order to make them seem less good than they really are: *The President's detractors expressed their usual low expectations of his policies.*

**det·ri·ment** /'detrəmənt/ *n* [U] *formal* the state of being harmed or damaged by something: **to the detriment of** (=resulting in harm or damage to something) *He worked longer and longer hours, to the detriment of his marriage.*

**de·tri·men·tal** /,detrə'mentl◂/ *adj formal* causing harm or damage: [+ **to**] *Smoking is detrimental to health.* —**detrimentally** *adv*

**de·tri·tus** /dɪ'traɪtəs/ *n* [U] *technical* pieces of waste that remain after something has been broken up or used

**de trop** /də 'trəʊ‖-'troʊ/ *adj* [not before noun] *French* a word meaning too much or not necessary, used when you are trying too hard to sound important or educated

**deuce** /djuːs‖duːs/ *n* **1** the situation in tennis when both players have 40 points, after which the next player must win two points to win the game **2 what/where/who etc the deuce?** *spoken old-fashioned* used to add force to a question: *What the deuce is going on?* **3 a deuce of** *old-fashioned* a very severe example or case of something: *She had a deuce of a row with her father.*

**deuc·ed** /'djuːsəd, djuːst‖'duː-/ *adj, adv old-fashioned* very or very great: *I'm deuced glad you turned up when you did.*

**Deutsch·mark** /'dɔɪtʃmɑːk‖-mɑːrk/ *n* [C] the standard unit of money in Germany; MARK² (8)

**de·val·ue** /diː'væljuː/ *v* **1** [I,T] to reduce the value that the money of one country has when it is exchanged for the money of another country **2** [T] to make someone or something seem less important or valuable than they really are: *The skills of women were not recognized and often devalued.* —**devaluation** /diː,vælju'eɪʃən/ *n* [C,U]

**dev·a·state** /'devəsteɪt/ *v* [T usually passive] **1** to cause so much damage to a place or area that most of it is destroyed: *The bomb devastated the city centre.* **2** to make someone feel extremely shocked and sad: *Rob was devastated by the news of her death.* | *a country devastated by war* —**devastation** /,devə'steɪʃən/ *n* [U] *A cyclone came over the island, causing complete devastation.*

**dev·a·stat·ing** /'devəsteɪtɪŋ/ *adj* **1** destroying or badly damaging something: *Acid rain has a devastating* *effect on the environment.* **2** shocking and upsetting: *the devastating news of a plane crash* **3** almost impossible to argue against or deal with: *a devastating argument in favour of legalization* **4** *old-fashioned* extremely attractive —**devastatingly** *adv*: *Mathew looked devastatingly handsome in his white linen suit.*

S3 W1 **de·vel·op** /dɪˈveləp/ *v*
**1 ▶ GROW ◀** [I,T] to grow or gradually change into a larger, stronger, or more advanced state, or to make someone or something do this: *Children develop very rapidly.* | [+ **into**] *James has developed into a charming young man.* | [+ **from**] *In less than ten years it develops from a seed into a full-grown tree.* | **develop sth** *exercises designed to develop your muscles*
**2 ▶ PLAN/PRODUCT ◀** [T] to make a new idea, plan, or product become successful over a period of time: *Scientists are developing new drugs to treat arthritis.*
**3 ▶ START TO HAVE ◀** [I] to gradually begin to have a quality, illness, problem etc: *Some alcoholics develop liver disease.*

**4 ▶ BECOME MORE ACTIVE ◀** [I] to become more active or more of a problem, and therefore become more noticeable: *Trouble is developing in the cities.*
**5 ▶ IDEA/ARGUMENT ◀** [T] to make an argument or idea clearer, by studying it more or by speaking or writing about it in more detail: *We will develop a few of these points in the seminar.*
**6 ▶ LAND ◀** [T] to use land for the things that people need, for example by taking minerals out of it or by building on it: *We're waiting to hear if permission to develop the land will be granted.*
**7 ▶ PHOTOGRAPHY ◀** [I,T] to make a photograph out of a photographic film, using chemicals

**de·vel·oped** /dɪˈveləpt/ *adj* **1 developed country/nation/society** a rich industrial country, nation etc with a lot of business activity: *a study of farming methods used in developed countries* —compare DEVELOPING, UNDERDEVELOPED **2** in a larger or more advanced state

**de·vel·op·er** /dɪˈveləpə‖-ər/ *n* **1** [C] a person or company that buys land or buildings and hopes to make a profit by building new houses, roads etc: *an industrial developer* **2** [C,U] *technical* a chemical substance used for developing photographs **3 late developer** a child whose mental or physical growth happens more slowly than other children of the same age

**de·vel·op·ing** /dɪˈveləpɪŋ/ *adj* **developing country/nation** a poor country that is trying to increase its industry and improve trade: *One of the basic needs in many developing countries is water.* —compare DEVELOPED, UNDERDEVELOPED

W1 **de·vel·op·ment** /dɪˈveləpmənt/ *n* **1** [U] the gradual growth of something, so that it becomes bigger or more advanced: *an expert in child development* | [+ **of**] *a course on the development of Greek thought* **2** [C] a new event or piece of news that is likely to have an effect on the present situation: *recent political developments in the former Soviet Union* **3** [C] the act or result of making a product or design better and more advanced: *There have been significant computer developments during the last decade.* **4** [U] the process of planning and building new houses, offices etc on a piece of land: *The land was sold for development.* **5** [C] a group of new buildings that have all been planned and built together on the same piece of land: *a new housing development* —**developmental** /dɪˌveləpˈmentl◂/ *adj* —**developmentally** *adv*

**de·vi·ance** /ˈdiːviəns/ also **de·vi·an·cy** /ˈdiːviənsi/ *n* [U] deviant behaviour: *sexual deviance*

**de·vi·ant** /ˈdiːviənt/ *adj* deviant behaviour, especially sexual behaviour, is considered to be strange and morally unacceptable: *Many formerly deviant activities have graually become accepted forms of behaviour.* —**deviant** *n* [C] —**deviance, deviancy** *n* [U]

**de·vi·ate**[1] /ˈdiːvieɪt/ *v* [I] *formal* to change what you are doing so that you are not following an expected plan, idea, or type of behaviour: [+ **from**] *The plane had to deviate from its normal flight path.*

**de·vi·ate**[2] /ˈdiːviǝt/ *adj AmE formal* deviant

**de·vi·a·tion** /ˌdiːviˈeɪʃən/ *n* **1** [C,U] a noticeable difference from what is expected or acceptable: [+ **from**] *deviation from the norm* **2** [C] *technical* a difference between a number or measurement in a set and the average of all the numbers or measurements in that set —see also STANDARD DEVIATION

**de·vi·a·tion·ist** /ˌdiːviˈeɪʃənǝst/ *n* [C] a word for someone who disagrees with some parts of a system of political beliefs, used to show disapproval —**deviationism** *n* [U]

**de·vice** /dɪˈvaɪs/ *n* [C] W2
**1 ▶ PIECE OF EQUIPMENT ◀** a piece of equipment intended for a particular purpose, for example for recording or measuring something: [+ **for**] *a useful device for detecting electrical activity* | *modern labour-saving devices* —see MACHINE[1] (USAGE)
**2 leave sb to their own devices** to leave someone alone to do whatever they want: *I just gave her a brush and paints, and left her to her own devices.*
**3 ▶ PLAN/TRICK ◀** a plan or trick, especially for a dishonest purpose: *Their proposal was only a device to confuse the opposition.*
**4 ▶ SPECIAL METHOD ◀** a special way of doing something that makes it easier to do: *Testing yourself with information on cards is a useful device for studying.*
**5 ▶ BOMB ◀** a bomb or other explosive weapon: *an explosive device*
**6 ▶ LITERATURE/THEATRE ◀** the special use of words in literature, or of words, lights etc in a play, to achieve an effect: *Metaphor is a common literary device.*
**7 ▶ PICTURE ◀** *technical* a picture or design used by a NOBLE[1] (3) family as their sign: *the device on his shield*

**dev·il** /ˈdevəl/ *n*
**1 ▶ EVIL ◀ a) the Devil** the most powerful evil spirit in Christianity; SATAN **b)** [C] any evil spirit: *The villagers believed a devil had taken control of his body.*
**2 ▶ PERSON ◀** [C] *informal* someone who behaves very badly, especially a child: *Tommy's a little devil!*
**3 speak/talk of the devil** *spoken* used when someone you have just been talking about walks into the room where you are
**4 play/be devil's advocate** to pretend that you disagree with something so that there will be a discussion about it
**5 be a devil** *BrE spoken* used to persuade someone to do something they are not sure they should do: *Go on, be a devil, have another gin and tonic.*
**6 lucky/poor/silly etc devil** *spoken* someone who is lucky, unlucky, silly etc
**7 what/who/why etc the devil?** *spoken old-fashioned* used to show that you are surprised or annoyed: *What the devil d'you think you're doing?*
**8 a devil of a job/mess etc** *old-fashioned* a very unpleasant job, mess etc: *We had a devil of a job trying to get the carpet clean again.*
**9 go to the devil!** *spoken* used to tell someone rudely to go away or stop annoying you
**10 have the luck of the devil** to be very lucky
**11 better the devil you know (than the devil you don't)** used to say that it is better to deal with someone or something you know, even if you do not like them, than to deal with someone or something new that might be worse
**12 be between the devil and the deep blue sea** to be in a difficult situation in which you have to choose between two unpleasant things
**13 do sth like the devil** *old-fashioned* to do something very fast or using a lot of force: *They rang the bell and ran like the devil.*
**14 devil take the hindmost** used to describe a situation in which people think about their own success and do not care what happens to anyone else

**dev·il·ish** /ˈdevəlɪʃ/ *adj* very bad, difficult, or unpleasant: *devilish schemes*

**dev·il·ish·ly** /ˈdevəlɪʃli/ *adv old-fashioned* [+ adj/adv] a word meaning very, used to show annoyance: *The collector was a devilishly hard fellow to talk to.*

**dev·illed** *BrE*, **deviled** *AmE* /ˈdevəld/ *adj* devilled food is cooked in or mixed with very hot pepper

**devil-may-care** /ˌ··· ˈ·◂/ *adj* cheerful, careless, and willing to take risks: *a devil-may-care attitude to life*

**dev·il·ment** /ˈdevəlmənt/ *n* [U] *literary* wild or bad behaviour that causes trouble: *eyes blazing with devilment*

**dev·il·ry** /ˈdevəlri/ *n* [U] devilment

**devil's food cake** /ˈ·· ·ˌ·/ *n* [C,U] an American chocolate cake

**de·vi·ous** /ˈdiːviəs/ *adj* **1** using dishonest tricks and deceiving people in order to get what you want: *I wouldn't trust him – he's devious.* **2** *formal* not going in the most direct way to get to a place: *a devious route* —**deviously** *adv* —**deviousness** *n* [U]

**de·vise** /dɪˈvaɪz/ *v* [T] to plan or invent a way of doing something, especially something complicated and clever: *She devised a method for quicker communications between offices.*

**de·vi·tal·ize** also **-ise** *BrE* /ˌdiːˈvaɪtl-aɪz/ *v* [T] to take the power or strength away from something —**devitalization** /diːˌvaɪtl-aɪˈzeɪʃən‖-tl-ə-/ *n* [U]

**de·void** /dɪˈvɔɪd/ *adj* **be devoid of** to be completely lacking in something: *That man is totally devoid of all humour.*

**de·vo·lu·tion** /ˌdiːvəˈluːʃən/ *n* [U] the act of giving power from a national government to a group or organization at a lower or more local level —**devolutionist** *adj* —**devolutionist** *n* [C]

**de·volve** /dɪˈvɒlv‖dɪˈvɑːlv/ *v*

**devolve on/upon** sb *phr v* [T not in passive] *formal* to give work, responsibility etc to someone at a lower level: **devolve sth on/upon sb** *The Governor devolved the choice upon the committee.* | **it devolves on/upon sb** *It devolved upon the deputy to make a speech.*

**devolve to** sb *phr v* [T not in passive] *formal* **1** to give work, responsibility etc to someone at a lower level **2** if land, goods etc devolve to someone they become the property of that person when their owner dies

**de·vote** /dɪˈvəʊt‖-ˈvoʊt/ *v* **1 devote time/effort/money etc to** to use your time, effort etc in order to do something or help something be successful: *I'm devoting all my time and energy to being a mom right now.* **2 devote yourself to** to do everything you can to achieve something or help someone: *Mother Teresa has devoted herself to caring for the poor.*

**de·vot·ed** /dɪˈvəʊtɪ̣d‖-ˈvoʊ-/ *adj* showing great love and loyalty for someone or something: *a devoted father* | **[+ to]** *Kiko is devoted to her music.* —**devotedly** *adv*

**dev·o·tee** /ˌdevəˈtiː/ *n* [C] **1** someone who admires someone or something very much: **[+ of]** *a devotee of 1930s films* **2** a very religious person: *a Sikh devotee*

**de·vo·tion** /dɪˈvəʊʃən‖-ˈvoʊ-/ *n* **1** [U] great love or loyalty: **[+ to]** *Alanna has always shown intense devotion to her children.* **2** [U] the act of spending a lot of time and energy on something: **[+ to]** *her total devotion to her job* **3** [U] great loyalty to a religion **4 devotions** [plural] prayers and other religious acts

**de·vo·tion·al** /dɪˈvəʊʃənəl‖-ˈvoʊ-/ *adj* related to or used in religious services: *devotional music*

**de·vour** /dɪˈvaʊə‖-ˈvaʊr/ *v* [T] **1** to eat something quickly because you are very hungry: *The boys devoured their pancakes with great joy.* **2** to read something quickly and eagerly: *Joseph devoured the contents of the book avidly.* **3 be devoured by** to be filled with a strong feeling that seems to control you: *Cindy felt devoured by jealousy.* **4** to destroy someone or something: *beams devoured by rot* **5 devour sb/sth with your eyes** to look eagerly at someone or something and notice everything about them

**de·vout** /dɪˈvaʊt/ *adj* **1** someone who is devout has a very strong belief in a religion: *a devout Catholic* **2** *formal* a devout hope or wish is one that you feel very strongly: *It is my devout hope that we can work together in peace.* —**devoutly** *adv* —**devoutness** *n* [U]

**dew** /djuː‖duː/ *n* [U] the small drops of water that form on outdoor surfaces during the night

**dew·drop** /ˈdjuːdrɒp‖ˈduːdrɑːp/ *n* [C] a small drop of dew: *dewdrops sparkling in the morning sunlight*

**dew·fall** /ˈdjuːfɔːl‖ˈduːfɒːl/ *n* [U] *literary* the forming of dew or the time when dew begins to appear

**dew·lap** /ˈdjuːlæp‖ˈduː-/ *n* [C] a hanging fold of loose skin under the throat of a cow, dog etc

**dew·y** /ˈdjuːi‖ˈduːi/ *adj* wet with drops of DEW: *The dewy woodland was solitary and still.*

**dewy-eyed** /ˌ·· ˈ·◂/ *adj* having eyes that are slightly wet with tears

**dex·ter·i·ty** /dekˈsterɪ̣ti/ *n* [U] the ability to be very quick and skilful with your hands: *He used his knife with speed and dexterity.*

**dex·ter·ous** /ˈdekstərəs/ also **dextrous** /ˈdekstrəs/ *adj* able to use your hands in a skilful way: *dextrous use of the needle* —**dexterously, destrously** *adv*

**dex·trose** /ˈdekstrəʊz, -strəʊs‖-stroʊz, -stroʊs/ *n* [U] a type of sugar that is in many sweet fruits

**dex·trous** /ˈdekstrəs/ *adj* another spelling of DEXTEROUS

**dho·ti** /ˈdəʊti‖ˈdoʊti/ *n* [C] a piece of clothing worn by some Hindu men, consisting of a piece of cloth that is wrapped around the waist and between the legs

**dhow** /daʊ/ *n* [C] an Arab ship with one large sail

**DI** /ˌdiː ˈaɪ/ *n* [C] Detective Inspector; a middle rank in the British police

**di-** /daɪ, dɪ/ *prefix* two; twice; double: *A dipthong is a vowel made up of two sounds.* —compare SEMI —see also BI-, TRI-

**di·a·be·tes** /ˌdaɪəˈbiːtiːz, -tɪ̣s/ *n* [U] a serious disease in which there is too much sugar in your blood

**di·a·bet·ic¹** /ˌdaɪəˈbetɪk◂/ *adj* **1** having diabetes: *Sarah is diabetic.* **2** caused by diabetes: *a diabetic coma* **3** produced for people who have diabetes: *diabetic chocolate*

**diabetic²** *n* [C] someone who has diabetes

**di·a·bol·i·cal** /ˌdaɪəˈbɒlɪkəl◂‖-ˈbɑː-/ *adj* **1** also **diabolic** /ˌdaɪəˈbɒlɪk◂‖-ˈbɑː-/ evil or cruel: *diabolical abuse* | *a diabolical plan to destroy him* **2** *informal especially BrE* extremely unpleasant or bad: *The toilets were in a diabolical state.* —**diabolically** /-kli/ *adv*

**di·achron·ic** /ˌdaɪəˈkrɒnɪk◂‖-ˈkrɑː-/ *adj technical* dealing with something such as a language as it changes over time: *a diachronic study* —**diachronically** /-kli/ *adv*

**di·a·crit·ic** /ˌdaɪəˈkrɪtɪk/ *n* [C] a mark placed over, under, or through a letter in some languages, to show that the letter should be pronounced differently from the letter without a mark —**diacritical** *adj*

**di·a·dem** /ˈdaɪədem/ *n* [C] *literary* a circle of jewels, flowers etc that you wear on your head

**di·ae·re·sis, dieresis** /daɪˈɪərɪ̣sɪ̣s, -ˈe-‖-ˈe-/ *n plural* **diaereses** /-siːz/ [C] *technical* a sign (¨) put over the second of two VOWELS to show that it is pronounced separately from the first

**di·ag·nose** /ˈdaɪəgnəʊz‖-noʊs/ *v* [T] to find out what is wrong with someone or something, especially what illness someone has, by examining them carefully: *diagnosing computer faults* | **diagnose sth as** *The illness was diagnosed as mumps.*

**di·ag·no·sis** /ˌdaɪəgˈnəʊsɪ̣s‖-ˈnoʊ-/ *n plural* **diagnoses** /-siːz/ [C,U] the discovery of exactly what is wrong with someone or something, by examining them closely: **[+ of]** *diagnosis of kidney disease* | **make/give a diagnosis** *An exact diagnosis can only be made by obtaining a blood sample.* —compare PROGNOSIS

**di·ag·nos·tic** /ˌdaɪəgˈnɒstɪk◂‖-ˈnɑː-/ *adj* related to or used for diagnosis: *diagnostic tests*

**di·ag·o·nal** /daɪˈægənəl/ *adj* **1** a diagonal line is straight and joins two opposite corners of a flat shape, usually a square —compare HORIZONTAL¹ —see picture at VERTICAL **2** a diagonal pattern follows a sloping direction —**diagonal** *n* [C] —**diagonally** *adv*: *The path goes diagonally across the field.*

**di·a·gram** /ˈdaɪəgræm/ *n* [C] a drawing or plan that shows exactly where something is, what something looks like, or how something works: *a diagram of the human body* —**diagrammatic** /ˌdaɪəgrəˈmætɪk◂/ *adj* —**diagrammatically** /-kli/ *adv*

**dial**[1] /daɪəl/ *n* [C] **1** the part of a machine or piece of equipment such as a watch, that is usually covered in glass and shows the time or a measurement: *She looked at the dial to check her speed.* **2** the wheel on a telephone with numbered holes for your fingers, that you move around in order to make a call **3** part of a piece of equipment such as a radio, that you turn around to listen to different radio stations

**dial**[2] *v* **dialled, dialling** *BrE,* **dialed, dialing** *AmE* [I,T] to move the numbered wheel or press the buttons on a telephone in order to make a telephone call

**di·a·lect** /ˈdaɪəlekt/ *n* [C,U] a variety of a language spoken only in one area, in which words or grammar are slightly different from other forms of the same language —compare ACCENT[1] (1), IDIOLECT

**di·a·lec·tic** /ˌdaɪəˈlektɪk/ also **dialectics** *n* [U] a method of examining and discussing ideas in order to find the truth, that follows rules developed by Socrates, Plato and Hegel —**dialectical** /ˌdaɪəˈlektɪkəl◂/ *adj*

**dialling code** /ˈ··· ·/ *n* [C] *BrE* the numbers at the beginning of a telephone number that represent a specific area of a city or country; AREA CODE *AmE*

**dialling tone** /ˈ··· ·/ *n* [C] *BrE* the sound you hear when you pick up the telephone that lets you know that you can make a call; DIAL TONE *AmE*

**di·a·logue** *BrE,* **dialog** *AmE* /ˈdaɪəlɒg‖-lɔːg, -lɑːg/ *n* [C,U] **1** a conversation in a book, play, or film: *a boring movie full of bad dialog* **2** *formal* a discussion between two groups, countries etc: *There is a need for constructive dialogue between leaders.* —compare MONOLOGUE

**dial tone** /ˈ· ·/ *n* [C] *AmE* the sound you hear when you pick up the telephone that lets you know that you can make a call; DIALLING TONE *BrE*

**di·al·y·sis** /daɪˈælǝsǝs/ *n* [U] the process of taking harmful substances out of someone's blood using a special machine, because their KIDNEYS do not work properly

**di·a·mant·é** /ˌdiːəˈmɒnteɪ◂‖ˌdiːəmɑːnˈteɪ◂/ *adj* decorated with artificial diamonds: *a diamanté necklace*

**di·am·e·ter** /daɪˈæmǝtǝ‖-ǝr/ *n* [C] a straight line going from one side of a circle to the other side, passing through the centre of the circle | **3 inches/1 metre etc in diameter** *Draw a circle six centimetres in diameter.* —see picture at CIRCLE

**di·a·met·ri·cally** /ˌdaɪəˈmetrɪkli/ *adv* **diametrically opposed/opposite** completely different and opposite: *The two ideas are diametrically opposed.*

**di·a·mond** /ˈdaɪəmənd/ *n*
**1 ▶ STONE ◀** [C,U] a very hard valuable stone, that usually has no colour and is used in jewellery: *Did you see the size of that diamond engagement ring?*
**2 ▶ SHAPE ◀** [C] a shape with four straight sides of equal length that stands on one of its points —see picture at SHAPE[1]
**3 ▶ ON A PLAYING CARD ◀** [C] **a)** a diamond shape printed in red on a playing card **b)** [C] one of the cards in the set that are printed in this way: *the queen of diamonds*
**4 ▶ SPORTS FIELD ◀** [C] **a)** the area in a BASEBALL field within the diamond shape formed by the four bases (BASE[1] (8)) **b)** the whole playing field used in BASEBALL —see picture on page 1263

**diamond an·ni·ver·sa·ry** /ˌ··· ··ˈ···/ *n* [C] *especially AmE* the date that is exactly 60 years after the date when two people were married; DIAMOND WEDDING *BrE*

**diamond in the rough** /ˌ··· · ˈ·/ *n* [C] *AmE informal* someone who behaves in a slightly rude way, but is really kind and generous; ROUGH DIAMOND *BrE*

**diamond ju·bi·lee** /ˌ··· ˈ···/ *n* [C] the date that is exactly 60 years after the date of an important event, especially of someone becoming a king or queen —compare GOLDEN JUBILEE, SILVER JUBILEE

**diamond wed·ding** /ˌ··· ˈ··/ *n BrE* the date that is exactly 60 years after the date when two people were married; DIAMOND ANNIVERSARY *AmE* —compare GOLDEN WEDDING, SILVER WEDDING ANNIVERSARY

**di·a·per** /ˈdaɪəpə‖ˈdaɪpər/ *n* [C] *AmE* a piece of soft cloth that is put between a baby's legs and fastened around its waist to hold liquid and solid waste; NAPPY *BrE* S3

**diaper rash** /ˈ··· ˌ·‖ˈ·· ˌ·/ *n* [U] *AmE* sore skin between a baby's legs and on its BUTTOCKS, caused by a wet diaper; NAPPY RASH *BrE*

**di·aph·a·nous** /daɪˈæfənəs/ *adj* diaphanous cloth is so fine and thin that you can almost see through it

**di·a·phragm** /ˈdaɪəfræm/ *n* [C] **1** the muscle that separates your lungs from your stomach **2** a round rubber object that some women wear inside their VAGINA so that they can have sex without having children; DUTCH CAP **3** *technical* any thin piece of stretched material that is moved by sound

**di·a·rist** /ˈdaɪərǝst‖ˈdaɪr-/ *n* [C] someone who keeps a diary and later sells this as a book

**di·ar·rhoea, diarrhea** /ˌdaɪəˈrɪə/ *n* [U] a medical condition that makes you empty your BOWELS very often and in a very liquid form

**di·a·ry** /ˈdaɪəri‖ˈdaɪri/ *n* [C] **1** a book in which you write down the things that happen to you each day; JOURNAL (2): **keep a diary** (=write things in a diary regularly) **2** *BrE* a book with marked separate spaces for each day of the year, in which you write down the meetings, events etc that are planned for each day; CALENDAR (2a) *AmE*: *Did you put the meeting date in your diary?*

**di·as·po·ra** /daɪˈæspərə/ *n* [C] *formal* **1 the Diaspora** the movement of the Jewish people away from ancient Palestine, to settle in other countries **2** the spreading of people from a national group or culture to other areas

**di·a·ton·ic scale** /ˌdaɪətɒnɪk ˈskeɪl‖-tɑː-/ *n* **the diatonic scale** a set of eight musical notes that uses a fixed pattern of spaces between the notes

**di·a·tribe** /ˈdaɪətraɪb/ *n* [C] a long speech or piece of writing that criticizes someone or something very severely: [**+ against**] *a diatribe against contemporary American civilization*

**dibs** /dɪbz/ *n* **dibs on sth** *AmE spoken* an expression used especially by children in order to claim a right to something: *Dibs on the seat near the window!*

**dice**[1] /daɪs/ *n plural* **dice** **1** [C usually plural] a small block of wood, plastic etc that has six sides with a different number of spots on each side, used in games of chance: **throw/roll the dice** *She threw the dice and moved her counter across the board.* **2** [U] any game of chance that is played with dice **3 no dice** *especially AmE spoken* used to refuse to do something or to say that something is not possible: *"Can I borrow some cash?" "Sorry, no dice."*

dice

**dice**[2] *v* **1** also **dice up** [T] to cut food into small square pieces: *diced carrots* —see picture page 834 **2 dice with death** to put yourself in a very dangerous situation **3** [I + **for**] *literary* to play dice with someone, for money, possessions etc

**dic·ey** /ˈdaɪsi/ *adj informal* slightly dangerous and uncertain: *The future looks pretty dicey for small businesses.*

**di·chot·o·my** /daɪˈkɒtəmi‖-ˈkɑː-/ *n* [C] *formal* a separation between two things or ideas that are completely opposite: [**+ between**] *a dichotomy between his public and private lives*

**dick** /dɪk/ *n* [C] **1** *slang* a PENIS **2** *slang* a stupid annoying person, especially a man: *He's acting like a complete dick.* **3** *AmE old-fashioned* a PRIVATE DETECTIVE —see also **clever dick** (CLEVER (6)), SPOTTED DICK

**dick·ens** /ˈdɪkɪ̥nz/ *n* **1 what/who/where the dickens** *spoken* used when asking a question to show that you are very surprised or angry: *What the dickens is the matter with her?* **2 as pretty/smart etc as the dickens** *AmE informal* very pretty, clever etc: *Isn't she as cute as the dickens!*

**Dic·ken·si·an** /dɪˈkenziən/ *adj* Dickensian buildings, living conditions etc are poor, dirty,and unpleasant: *a single mother living in a Dickensian block of flats*

**dick·ey** /ˈdɪki/ *n* another spelling of DICKY[2]

**dick·head** /ˈdɪkhed/ *n* [C] *slang* a stupid annoying person, especially a man: *Don't be such a dickhead!*

**dick·y[1]** /ˈdɪki/ *adj BrE informal* weak, and likely to break or not work properly: **dicky heart/ticker** (=a heart that is weak and not very healthy)

**dicky[2]**, **dickey** *n* [C] a false shirt front sometimes worn by a man under a jacket

**dick·y·bird** /ˈdɪkibɜːd‖-bɜːrd/ *n* [C] *BrE* **1** a word meaning any small bird, used by or to children **2 not hear a dickybird** *informal* to not hear any news about someone or something: *"Have you heard from them since they moved?" "No, not a dickybird."*

**dicky bow** /ˈdɪki bəʊ‖-boʊ/ *n* [C] *informal* a BOW TIE

**dic·ta** /ˈdɪktə/ the plural of DICTUM

**Dic·ta·phone** /ˈdɪktəfəʊn‖-foʊn/ *n* [C] *trademark* an office machine on which you can record speech so that someone can listen to it and TYPE [2] (1) it later

**dic·tate[1]** /dɪkˈteɪt‖ˈdɪkteɪt/ *v* **1** [I,T] to say words for someone else to write down: **dictate sth to sb** *She's dictating a letter to her secretary right now.* **2** [I,T] to tell someone exactly what they must do or how they must behave: [+ **to**] *I refuse to be dictated to by some mindless bureaucrat!* | **dictate who/what/how etc** *Can they dictate how the money will be spent?* | **as dictated by** (=according to what someone said) *Federal funds have to be used as dictated by Washington.* | **dictate that** *The custom dictates that men should be clean-shaven.* **3** [T] to control or influence something; DETERMINE (2): *Funds dictate what we can do.*

**dic·tate[2]** /ˈdɪkteɪt/ *n* [C] *formal* an order, rule, or principle that you have to obey

**dic·ta·tion** /dɪkˈteɪʃən/ *n* **1** [U] the act of saying words for someone to write down: **take dictation** (=write down words that someone else is saying) **2** [C] a piece of writing that a teacher reads out to test your ability to hear and write the words correctly: *I hate doing French dictations.*

**dic·ta·tor** /dɪkˈteɪtə‖ˈdɪkteɪtər/ *n* [C] **1** a ruler who has complete power over a country, especially when their power has been gained by force: *the downfall of the hated dictator* **2** someone who tells other people what they should do, in a way that seems unreasonable: *a real little dictator*

**dic·ta·to·ri·al** /ˌdɪktəˈtɔːriəl◂/ *adj* **1** a dictatorial government or ruler has complete power over a country **2** a dictatorial person tells other people what to do in an unreasonable way: *Professor Clement's dictatorial attitude* —**dictatorially** *adv*

**dic·ta·tor·ship** /dɪkˈteɪtəʃɪp‖-ˈteɪtər-/ *n* **1** [C,U] government by a ruler who has complete power **2** [C] a country that is ruled by one person who has complete power

**dic·tion** /ˈdɪkʃən/ *n* [U] **1** the way in which someone pronounces words: *Actors have training in diction.* **2** the choice and use of words and phrases to express meaning, especially in literature or poetry

**dic·tion·a·ry** /ˈdɪkʃənəri‖-neri/ *n* [C] **1** a book that gives a list of words in alphabetical order and explains their meanings in the same or another language: *a German – English dictionary* **2** a book like this that deals with the words and phrases used in a particular subject: *a science dictionary*

**dic·tum** /ˈdɪktəm/ *n plural* **dicta** /-tə/ or **dictums** [C] **1** a formal statement of opinion by someone who is respected or has authority **2** a short phrase that expresses a general rule or truth: *He followed the age-old dictum of 'age before beauty'.*

**did** /dɪd/ the past tense of DO[1]

**di·dac·tic** /daɪˈdæktɪk, dɪ̥-/ *adj formal* **1** speech or writing that is didactic is intended to teach people a moral lesson: *His novel has a didactic tone.* **2** someone who is didactic is too eager to teach people things or give instructions —**didactically** /-kli/ *adv*

**did·dle** /ˈdɪdl/ *v* [T] **diddle sb (out of sth)** *informal* to get money from someone by deceiving them: *They'll diddle you out of your last penny if you give them the chance.*

**did·dly** /ˈdɪdli/ also **diddly-squat** /ˈ·· ·/ *n* **not know/mean diddly** *AmE informal* to know or mean nothing at all: *Brad? He doesn't know diddly about baseball.*

**did·dums** /ˈdɪdəmz/ *interjection BrE* a word used to someone who is upset or annoyed in a way you think seems childish

**did·ge·ri·doo** /ˌdɪdʒəriˈduː/ *n* [C] a long wooden musical instrument, played especially in Australia

**did·n't** /ˈdɪdnt/ the short form of 'did not': *You saw him, didn't you?*

**didst** /dɪdst/ **thou didst** *old use* you did

**die[1]** /daɪ/ *v past tense and past participle* **died** *present participle* **dying** [I] S1 W1

**1 ▶ BECOME DEAD ◀** to stop living and become dead: *He was very sick and we knew he might die.* | **of/from** *The animals died of starvation in the snow.* | *My grandfather died from a heart attack.* | [+ **for**] *Do you believe in anything enough to die for it?* | **die happy/poor/young etc** *He died young, at the age of 27.* | **die a hero/martyr/rich man etc** *Van Gogh died a broken man.* | **die a natural/horrible etc death** (=die in a particular way) | **to your dying day** (=until you die) | **die by your own hand** *literary* (=kill yourself) | **die in your sleep** *She died peacefully in her sleep at the age of 98.*

**2 ▶ DISAPPEAR ◀** to disappear or stop existing: *Our love will never die.* | **die with sb** (=disappear or be finished when someone dies) *The family name will die with him.*

**3 ▶ MACHINES ◀** *informal* to stop working: *The car's engine spluttered and died.* | **die on sb** (=stop working while they are using it) *The mower just died on me.*

**4 be dying for** *spoken* to want something very much: *I'm dying for a cup of coffee.*

**5 be dying to do sth** *spoken* to want to do something very much, so that it is difficult to wait: *We're dying to get started.*

**6 be dying of hunger/thirst** *spoken* to be very hungry or thirsty

**7 I nearly died/I could have died** *spoken* used to say that you felt very surprised or embarrassed: *I nearly died when my ex-husband walked into the room!*

**8 I'd rather die** *spoken* used to say very strongly that you do not want to do something: *I'd rather die than work for him!*

**9 old habits die hard** used to say that it takes a long time to change to a new way of doing something

**10 never say die** *spoken* used to encourage someone to continue doing something that is difficult

**11 die laughing** *spoken* to laugh a lot: *I nearly died laughing when I saw him with that ridiculous haircut.*

**12 die the death** *informal* to gradually fail or be destroyed: *Eventually the photography club died the death.*

**13 dying breath/wish** someone's very last breath or wish before they die: *No matter what you think, say nothing about it to your dying breath.*

**14 die on the vine** *literary* to fail, especially at an early stage, because of a lack of support

**15 sth to die for** something that is so nice or attractive that you would do anything to have it: *cream cakes to die for*

**die away** *phr v* [I] if sound, wind, or light dies away, it becomes gradually weaker and finally stops: *The strange noise died away and an absolute silence closed in upon us.*

**die back** *phr v* [I] if a plant dies back, it dies above the ground but remains alive at its roots

**die down** *phr v* [I] if something dies down, it becomes less strong, active, or violent: *Don't worry, the gossip will soon die down.*

**die off** *phr v* [I] if a group of people, animals etc die off, they die one by one until there are no more of them

**die out** *phr v* [I] to disappear or stop existing completely: *Smallpox has completely died out in this country.*

**die²** *n* [C] **1** a metal block used to press or cut something into a particular shape **2** a DICE¹ (1) **3 the die is cast** used to say that a decision has been taken and cannot now be changed

**die cast·ing** /ˈ· ˌ··/ *n* [U] the process of making metal objects by forcing liquid metal into a hollow container with a particular shape, and then allowing it to become hard

**die·hard** /ˈdaɪhɑːd‖-hɑːrd/ *n* [C] someone who opposes change and refuses to accept new ideas —see also **old habits die hard** (DIE¹ (9)), **—diehard** *adj*: *a diehard bigot*

**di·e·re·sis** /daɪˈɪərɪ̇sɪ̇s,-ˈe‖-ˈe-/ *n plural* **diereses** /-siːz/ [C] another spelling of DIAERESIS

**die·sel** /ˈdiːzəl/ *n* **1** [U] a type of heavy oil used instead of petrol in diesel engines **2** [C] *informal especially AmE* a vehicle that uses diesel

**diesel en·gine** /ˈ·· ˌ··/ *n* [C] an engine that burns diesel instead of petrol used especially for buses, trains, and goods vehicles

**diesel fu·el** /ˈ·· ˌ··/ also **diesel oil** /ˈ·· ·/ *n* [U] DIESEL (1)

S3 W2 **di·et¹** /ˈdaɪət/ *n*
**1 ▶KIND OF FOOD◀** [C,U] the kind of food that someone eats each day: *It is important to have a balanced, healthy diet.* | *a vegetarian diet* | [+ **of**] *They exist on a diet of fish.*
**2 ▶TO GET THIN◀** [C] a limited range and amount of food that you eat when you want to get thinner: **go/be on a diet** *Lyn always seems to be on a diet.*
**3 ▶FOR HEALTH◀** [C] a limited type of food and drink that someone is allowed because they have a health problem: *a salt-free diet*
**4 a diet of** too much of an activity that you think is boring or has bad effects: *Kids today are raised on a constant diet of pop music and television.*
**5 ▶MEETING◀** [C] *old use* an official meeting to discuss political or church matters

**diet²** *v* [I] to limit the amount and type of food that you eat in order to become thinner

**di·e·ta·ry** /ˈdaɪətəri‖-teri/ *adj* related to someone's diet: *special dietary requirements*

**di·e·tet·ics** /ˌdaɪəˈtetɪks/ *n* [U] the science that is concerned with what people eat and drink and how this affects their health

**di·e·ti·cian, dietitian** /ˌdaɪəˈtɪʃən/ *n* [C] someone who is specially trained in dietetics

W3 **dif·fer** /ˈdɪfə‖-ər/ *v* **1** [I] to be different from something in quality, features etc: [+ **from**] *Humans differ from other mammals in their ability to speak.* | **differ widely/greatly** *Opinions on the subject differ widely.* **2** [I] if two people or groups differ about something, they have opposite opinions: [+ **about/on/over**] *The two lawyers differed about how to present the case.* **3 agree to differ** to stop arguing with someone and accept that you will never agree **4 I beg to differ** *spoken formal* used to say that you disagree with someone

S1 W1 **dif·fe·rence** /ˈdɪfərəns/ *n* **1** [C] something that makes one thing or person different from another thing or person: [+ **between**] *It's hard to see many differences between the centrist political parties.* **2** [singular, U] the fact of being different, or an amount by which one thing is different from another: **difference in age/size etc** *There's not much difference in price.* | **tell the difference** (=recognize that two similar things are different) *The twins are so alike, it's difficult to tell the difference.* | **a world of difference** (=a big difference) *There's a world of difference between going abroad on holiday and going there to live.* **3 your/their etc differences** the disagreements that people have: **have your differences** *We've had our differences in the past, but we get on OK now.* | **settle your differences** (=agree not to argue any more) **4 difference of opinion** a slight disagreement: *The two sides have a difference of opinion over aims and methods.* **5 make a (big) difference/make all the difference** to have an important effect on a thing or a situation: *Having a good teacher has made all the difference for Alex.* **6 make no difference a)** to have no effect at all on something: *Even if you'd tried to help, it wouldn't have made the slightest difference.* **b)** to be unimportant to someone: *It doesn't make any difference to me whether you go or stay.* **7 with a difference** used to express approval about something that is different and better: *That was a meal with a difference!* —see also **split the difference** (SPLIT¹ (8))

**dif·fe·rent** /ˈdɪfərənt/ *adj* **1** not like something or someone else, or not like before: *You look different. Have you had your hair cut?* | [+ **from**] *Our two sons are very different from each other.* | [+ **to**] *Her jacket's a bit different to mine.* | [+ **than**] *(AmE)*: *The estimate is different than we expected.* **2** [only before noun] separate; DISTINCT: *He took the photo from three different angles.* | *There are many different types of fabric.* **3** [only before noun] another: *I think she's moved to a different job now.* | [+ **from**] *This is a different girl from the one he used to go out with.* **4** various; several: *There are several different books on the subject.* **5** *spoken* unusual, often in a way that you do not like: *His new jacket is certainly different, but I can't imagine wearing it myself!* **—differently** *adv*: *The two words sound the same but they're spelled differently.* S1 W1

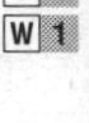

**USAGE NOTE: DIFFERENT**
GRAMMAR
Teachers often prefer **different(ly) from**, but **different(ly) to** is equally common in spoken British English (though not usual in American English). **Different(ly) than** is also used, especially in American English. Note that you never say **different of**.
SPELLING
The noun is **difference**: *The difference between your country and mine* (NOT *the different.*).

**dif·fe·ren·tial¹** /ˌdɪfəˈrenʃəl◂/ *n* [C] **1** an amount or degree of difference between things, especially difference in the wages of people doing different types of jobs in the same industry or profession: *pay differentials* **2** a differential gear

**differential²** *adj* based on or depending on a difference: *differential rates of pay for skilled and unskilled workers*

**differential cal·cu·lus** /ˌ···· ˈ···/ *n* [U] *technical* a way of measuring the speed at which an object is moving at a particular moment

**differential gear** /ˌ···· ˈ·/ *n* [C] an arrangement of gears (GEAR¹ (1)) that allows one back wheel of a car to turn faster than the other when the car goes around a corner

**dif·fe·ren·ti·ate** /ˌdɪfəˈrenʃieɪt/ *v* **1** [I,T] to recognize or express the difference between things or people: [+ **between**] *The reviews don't even differentiate between good books and bad books.* | **differentiate sb/sth from** *It's sometimes hard to differentiate one sample from another.* **2** [T] to be the quality, condition etc that shows the difference between things or people: **differentiate sth/sb from** *Its unusual nesting habits differentiate this bird from others.* | **differentiate sth** *What differentiates these two periods of history?* **3** [I] to behave differently towards someone or something, especially in an unfair way; DISCRIMINATE (2) [+ **between**] *He shouldn't differentiate between the quiet and the talkative children.* **—differentiation** /ˌdɪfərenʃiːˈeɪʃən/ *n* [U] *socio-economic differentiation*

S1 W1 **dif·fi·cult** /ˈdɪfɪkəlt/ *adj* **1** very hard to do, understand, or deal with; not easy: *Was the exam very difficult?* | *a difficult job* | **difficult to do** *She finds it difficult to climb stairs.* **2** someone who is difficult never seems pleased or satisfied: *Don't be so difficult!* **3** involving a lot of problems and causing a lot of trouble or worry: *Things are a bit difficult at home at the moment.* | **make life difficult for sb** (=cause problems for someone) *They've done everything in their power to make life difficult for me.*

S1 W1 **dif·fi·cul·ty** /ˈdɪfɪkəlti/ *n* **1** [U] the state of being hard to do, understand or deal with: **have difficulty doing sth** *We have enough difficulty paying the rent as it is!* | **with difficulty** *With difficulty, we hauled it up the stairs.* | **be in difficulty** (=be having problems) *The business is in financial difficulty.* | **get/run into difficulty** (=get into a difficult situation) *I had to sell my sewing machine when we got into difficulty with an electric bill.* **2** [C] a problem or something that causes trouble: *If you have any difficulties, give me a shout.* **3** [U] how difficult something is: *The tests vary in difficulty.*

**dif·fi·dent** /ˈdɪfɪ̈dənt/ *adj* shy and unwilling to make people notice you or talk about you: *He suddenly felt diffident in the presence of these people* | [+ **about**] *She was diffident about her prize.* —**diffidently** *adv* —**diffidence** *n* [U]

**dif·fract** /dɪˈfrækt/ *v* [T] *technical* to divide light into coloured bands or into light and dark bands —**diffraction** /dɪˈfrækʃən/ *n* [U]

**diffuse**

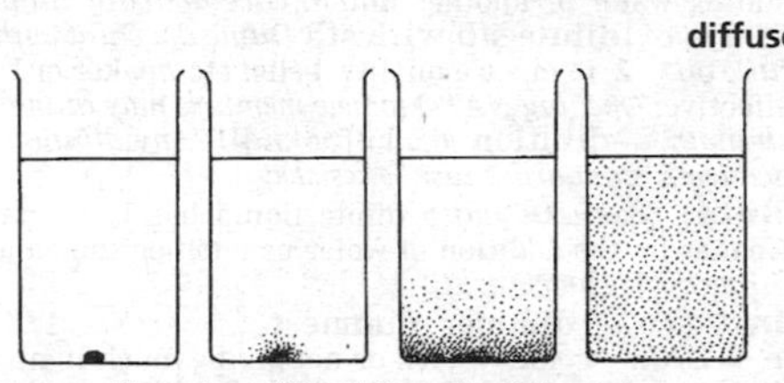

The colour diffused throughout the water.

**dif·fuse¹** /dɪˈfjuːz/ *v* [I,T] *formal* **1** to make heat, a gas etc spread so that it mixes with the surrounding air or water: *The kitchen stove diffused its warmth all over the house.* **2** to spread ideas, information etc among a lot of people: *Their ideas diffused quickly across Europe.* —**diffusion** /dɪˈfjuːʒən/ *n* [U]

**dif·fuse²** /dɪˈfjuːs/ *adj* **1** scattered over a large area: *The organization is large and diffuse.* **2** using a lot of words and not explaining things clearly and directly: *His writing is diffuse and difficult to understand.* —**diffusely** *adv* —**diffuseness** *n* [U]

S3 **dig¹** /dɪg/ *v past tense and past participle* **dug** /dʌg/ *present participle* **digging** **1** [I,T] to move earth or make a hole in it using a SPADE or your hands: *They escaped by digging an underground tunnel.* | **dig for sth** (=dig in order to find something) *They're digging for treasure.* **2** [T] to remove vegetables from under the earth using a SPADE: *She's digging potatoes at the moment.* **3** [T] *old-fashioned* to like something: *I really dig that dress!* **4 dig your own grave** to do something that will cause serious problems for you in the future **5 dig sb in the ribs** to touch someone with your elbow, especially because you want them to notice something amusing

**dig in** *phr v* **1** [T **dig** sth ↔ **in**] to mix something into soil by digging: *I need to dig some manure in before I plant the potatoes.* **2 dig your heels in** to refuse to do something in spite of other people's efforts to persuade you **3** [I] *informal* to start eating food that is in front of you: *Dig in! There's plenty for everyone!* **4** [I,T] if soldiers dig in or dig themselves in, they make a protected place for themselves by digging

**dig into** *phr v* **1** [T **dig** sth **into** sth] to mix something into soil by digging: *Dig some fertilizer into the soil first.* **2** [I,T **dig** sth **into** sth] to push hard into something, or to make something do this: *Her nails were digging into his arm.* **3** [T **dig into** sth] to start using a supply of something, especially money: *I'm going to have to dig into my savings again.*

**dig** sth ↔ **out** *phr v* [T] **1** to get something out of a place, using a SPADE or your hands: *We had to dig the car out of a snow drift.* **2** to find something you have not seen for a long time, or that is not easy to find: *I must remember to dig out that book for you.*

**dig** sth ↔ **up** *phr v* [T] **1** to remove something from under the earth using a SPADE: *I'll dig up that plant and move it.* **2** to find hidden or forgotten information by careful searching: *They tried to dig up something from his past to spoil his chances of being elected.*

**dig²** *n* **1 give sb a dig** to push someone quickly and lightly with your finger or elbow: *John's falling asleep – give him a dig will you?* **2** [C] a joke or remark that you make to annoy or criticize someone: [+ **at**] *I thought that last comment was a dig at the boss.* **3** [C] the process of digging in an ancient place in order to find objects for study: *an archaeological dig* **4 digs** [plural] *BrE old-fashioned* a room that you pay rent to live in

**di·gest¹** /daɪˈdʒest, dɪ̈-/ *v* [T] **1** to change food that you have just eaten into substances that your body can use: *Most babies can digest a wide range of food easily.* —compare INGEST **2** to understand new information, especially when there is a lot of it or it is difficult to understand: *I struggled to digest the news.*

**di·gest²** /ˈdaɪdʒest/ *n* [C] a short piece of writing that gives the most important facts from a book, report etc

**di·gest·i·ble** /daɪˈdʒestɪ̈bəl, dɪ̈-/ *adj* food that is digestible can be easily digested —opposite INDIGESTIBLE

**di·ges·tion** /daɪˈdʒestʃən, dɪ̈-/ *n* **1** [U] the process of digesting food **2** [C] your ability to digest food easily: **a good/poor etc digestion** *I've always had a poor digestion.*

**di·ges·tive** /daɪˈdʒestɪv, dɪ̈-/ *adj* [only before noun] connected with the process of digestion: *the digestive system*

**digestive bis·cuit** /·ˌ·· ˈ··/ *n* [C] a type of plain, slightly sweet BISCUIT (1) that is popular in Britain

**digestive system**

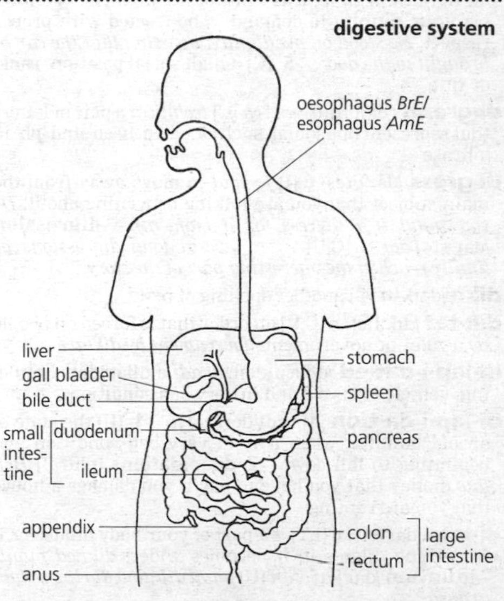


the human digestive system

**digestive sys·tem** /·ˈ·· ˌ··/ *n* [C] the system of organs in which your body digests (DIGEST¹ (1)) food

D

**dig·ger** /ˈdɪgə‖-ər/ *n* [C] a large machine that digs and moves earth —see also **gold digger**

**dig·gings** /ˈdɪgɪŋz/ *n* [plural] a place where people are digging for metal, especially gold

**di·git** /ˈdɪdʒɪ̟t/ *n* [C] **1** one of the written signs that represent the numbers 0 to 9: **three-digit/four-digit etc number** *4305 is a four-digit number.* **2** *technical* a finger or toe

**di·gi·tal** /ˈdɪdʒɪ̟tl/ *adj* **1** using a system in which information is represented in the form of changing electrical signals: **digital cassette/compact disc/audio-tape etc** *recorded on digital audiotape* **2** giving information in the form of numbers: *a digital watch* **3** *formal* of the fingers and toes

**digital com·put·er** /ˌ··· ·ˈ··/ *n* [C] a type of computer that uses a BINARY (1) system

**digital re·cord·ing** /ˌ··· ·ˈ··/ *n* [C,U] a high quality recording of sound made by changing information about the sound into the binary system (BINARY (1))

**di·gi·tize** also **-ise** *BrE* /ˈdɪdʒɪ̟taɪz/ *v* [T] to put information into a digital form

**dig·ni·fied** /ˈdɪgnɪ̟faɪd/ *adj* behaving in a calm and serious way, even in a difficult situation, which makes people respect you: *a dignified old lady* | *She made a dignified departure.*

**dig·ni·fy** /ˈdɪgnɪ̟faɪ/ *v* [T] to make something or someone seem better or more important than they really are by using a particular word to describe them: **dignify sb/sth with** *I cannot dignify him with the name 'physician'.*

**dig·ni·ta·ry** /ˈdɪgnɪ̟təri‖-teri/ *n* [C] someone who has an important official position: *Flowers were presented to visiting dignitaries.*

**dig·ni·ty** /ˈdɪgnɪ̟ti/ *n* **1** [U] the ability to behave in a way that shows you respect yourself and stay calm, even in a very difficult situation: *The family faced their ordeal with dignity and courage.* | **human dignity** | *Even in the prison camp we tried to retain some human dignity.* **2** [U] a calm and serious manner or quality: *The dignity of the occasion was spoilt when she fell down the steps.* **3 be beneath your dignity** if something is beneath your dignity, you think you are too good or important to do it: *Such arguing was beneath her dignity.* **4 stand on your dignity** to demand to be treated with proper respect: *He stood on his dignity, insisting that the car be brought to the door.* **5** [C] a high social position, rank, or title

**di·graph** /ˈdaɪgrɑːf‖-græf/ *n* [C] *technical* a pair of letters that represent one sound, such as 'ea' in 'head' and 'ph' in 'phrase'

**di·gress** /daɪˈgres/ *v* [I] *formal* to move away from the main subject that you are talking or writing about: *Do you mind if I digress for a moment?* —**digression** /daɪˈgreʃən/ *n* [C,U] *After several long digressions he finally reached the interesting part of the story.*

**dike** /daɪk/ *n* [C] another spelling of DYKE

**dik·tat** /dɪkˈtæt/ *n* [C,U] an order that is forced on people by a ruler or government: *government by diktat*

**di·lap·i·dat·ed** /dɪ̟ˈlæpɪ̟deɪtɪ̟d/ *adj* a dilapidated building, vehicle etc is old and in very bad condition

**di·lap·i·da·tion** /dɪ̟ˌlæpɪ̟ˈdeɪʃən/ *n* **1** [U] the state of an old building when it is in very bad condition and beginning to fall down **2 dilapidations** [plural] *BrE law* money that you have to pay if you damage a house that you are renting

**di·late** /daɪˈleɪt/ *v* [I,T] if a part of your body dilates or if something dilates it, it becomes wider: *dilated pupils* —**dilation** /daɪˈleɪʃən/ *n* [U] *pupil dilation during sexual arousal*

**dilate on/upon sth** *phr v* [T] *formal* to speak or write a lot about something: *He dilated upon their piety and heroism.*

**dil·a·to·ry** /ˈdɪlətəri‖-tɔːri/ *adj formal* slow and tending to delay decisions or actions: *dilatory attempts to reach an agreement*

**dil·do** /ˈdɪldəʊ‖-doʊ/ *n* [C] an object shaped like a male sex organ that some women put inside their VAGINA for sexual pleasure

**di·lem·ma** /dɪ̟ˈlemə, daɪ-/ *n* [C] a situation in which it is very difficult to decide what to do, because all the choices seem equally good or equally bad: *a moral dilemma* | **be in a dilemma** *I'm in a dilemma about this job offer.* | **be on the horns of a dilemma** (=be unable to decide between two unpleasant choices)

**dil·et·tan·te** /ˌdɪlɪ̟ˈtænti‖-ˈtɑːnti/ *n* [C] someone who seems or pretends to be interested in a subject but is not seriously interested and does not know very much about it —**dilettante** *adj*

**dil·i·gent** /ˈdɪlɪ̟dʒənt/ *adj* someone who is diligent works hard and is careful and thorough: *Philip is a diligent worker and should do well in the examinations.* —**diligently** *adv*: *They worked diligently all morning.* —**diligence** *n* [U]

**dill** /dɪl/ *n* [U] a garden plant used to give a special taste to food

**dill pick·le** /ˌ· ˈ··/ *n* [C] a whole CUCUMBER which has been preserved in vinegar

**dil·ly** /ˈdɪli/ *n* [C] *AmE old-fashioned* something or someone exciting or special: *That's a dilly of a rollercoaster!*

**dilly-dal·ly** /ˈ·· ˌ··/ *v* [I] *informal* to waste time, because you cannot decide about something: *Don't dilly-dally, just get on with it!*

**di·lute**[1] /daɪˈluːt/ *v* [T] **1** to make a liquid weaker by adding water or another liquid: *Give the baby diluted fruit juice.* | **dilute sth with sth** *Dilute the paint with a little oil.* **2** to make a quality, belief etc weaker or less effective: *Opening NATO to new members may dilute its strength.* —**dilution** /daɪˈluːʃən/ *n* [U] *Any dilution of academic standards must be resisted.*

**dilute**[2] /ˌdaɪˈluːt◂/ *adj* a dilute liquid has been made weaker by the addition of water or another substance: *dilute hydrochloric acid*

**dim**[1] /dɪm/ *adj* **dimmer, dimmest**

**1 ▶ DARK ◀** fairly dark or not giving much light, so that you cannot see well: *in the dim light of the early dawn*

**2 ▶ SHAPE ◀** a dim shape is one which is not easy to see because it is too far away, or there is not enough light: *The dim outline of a large building loomed up out of the mist.*

**3 ▶ EYES ◀** *literary* dim eyes are weak and cannot see well: *The dim eyes of the old woman were surprisingly attractive.*

**4 dim recollection/awareness etc** a memory or understanding of something that is not clear in your mind; VAGUE (2): *Laura had a dim recollection of someone telling her this before.*

**5 FUTURE CHANCES** if your chances of success in the future are dim, they are not good: *Prospects for an early settlement of the dispute are dim.*

**6 in the dim and distant past** *humorous* a very long time ago

**7 take a dim view of** to disapprove of something: *We took a dim view of his disobedience.*

**8 ▶ UNINTELLIGENT ◀** *informal especially BrE* not intelligent: *You can be really dim sometimes!* —**dimly** *adv*: *a dimly lit room* | *She was only dimly aware of the risk.* —**dimness** *n* [U]

**dim**[2] *v* **dimmed, dimming** **1** [I,T] if a light dims, or if you dim it, it becomes less bright: *The lights in the theatre began to dim.* **2** [I,T] if a feeling or quality dims or is dimmed, it grows weaker: *Her beauty had not dimmed over the years.* | *His words dimmed our hopes of a peaceful settlement.* **3 dim your headlights/lights** *AmE* to lower the angle of the front lights of your car, especially when someone is driving towards you; DIP[1] (3) *BrE*

**dime** /daɪm/ *n* [C] **1** a coin of the US and Canada, worth one tenth of a dollar —compare CENT **2 a dime a dozen** *AmE informal* very common and not valuable: *PhDs are a dime a dozen nowadays.*

**dime nov·el** /ˈ· ˌ··/ *n* [C] *AmE* a cheap book with a story that contains a lot of exciting events

W3 **di·men·sion** /daɪˈmenʃən, dʒ-/ *n* **1** [C] a part of a situation that makes you regard the situation in a particular way; ASPECT (1): **new/different dimension** *The baby has added a new dimension to their lives.*| **political/social/spiritual dimension** *We should not forget that education has an important spiritual dimension.* **2** [C] a measurement in space, for example length, height etc: *A diagram represents things in only two dimensions.* —see also FOURTH DIMENSION **3 dimensions** [plural] **a)** the size of something, especially when this is given as its length, height, and width: *What are the room's dimensions?* **b)** how great or serious a problem is: *We're heading for a catastrophe of enormous dimensions.*

**dime store** /ˈ· ·/ *n* [C] *AmE* a shop that sells many different kinds of cheap goods, especially for the house

**di·min·ish** /dʒˈmɪnɪʃ/ *v* **1** [I,T] to become or make something become smaller or less important: *The party's share of the electorate has diminished steadily.*| **diminish sth** *These drugs diminish blood flow to the brain.* **2** [T] to deliberately make someone or something appear less important or valuable than they really are: *Don't let him diminish your achievements.* **3 diminishing returns** the idea that a point can be reached at which the profits or advantages you are getting stop increasing in relation to the effort you are making

**diminished re·spon·si·bil·i·ty** /ˌ·, ·· ···ˈ···/ *n* [U] *law* a state in which someone is not considered to be responsible for their actions because they are mentally ill

**di·min·u·en·do** /dʒˌmɪnjuˈendəʊ||-doʊ/ *n* [C] *technical* a part in a piece of music where it becomes gradually quieter —opposite CRESCENDO —**diminuendo** *adj adv*

**dim·i·nu·tion** /ˌdɪmʒˈnjuːʃən||-ˈnuː-/ *n* [C,U] a reduction in the size, number, or amount of something: **[+ of/in]** *a diminution in value*

**di·min·u·tive¹** /dʒˈmɪnjʒtɪv/ *adj formal* small or short: *a shy diminutive man*

**diminutive²** *n* [C] a word formed by adding a diminutive suffix

**diminutive suf·fix** /ˌ··· ˈ··/ *n* [C] *technical* an ending that is added to a word to express smallness, for example 'ling' added to 'duck' to make 'duckling'

**dim·i·ty** /ˈdɪmʒti/ *n* [U] a strong cotton cloth with a slightly raised pattern on it

**dim·mer** /ˈdɪmə||-ər/ also **dimmer switch** *n* [C] **1** an electric light SWITCH² (1) that can change the brightness of the light **2** a SWITCH for lowering the beam of a car's front lights —DIPSWITCH *BrE*

**dim·ple** /ˈdɪmpəl/ *n* [C] a small hollow place on your cheek or chin, especially one that forms when you smile —see picture on page 412

**dim·pled** /ˈdɪmpəld/ *adj* having dimples: *her dimpled cheeks*

**dim·wit** /ˈdɪmwɪt/ *n* [C] *spoken* a stupid person: *dimwits not worthy of our attention* —**dim-witted** /ˌ· ˈ··◂/ *adj*

**din¹** /dɪn/ *n* [singular] a loud unpleasant noise that continues for a long time: *The kids were making a horrendous din.*

**din²** *v* **dinned, dinning**

**din** sth **into** sb *phr v* [T] to make someone learn and remember something by repeating it to them again and again: *Respect for our elders was dinned into us at school.*

**di·nar** /ˈdiːnɑː||dɪˈnɑː, ˈdiːnɑːr/ *n* [C] the standard unit of money used in the former Yugoslavia and in several muslim countries

**dine** /daɪn/ *v* [I] *formal* to eat dinner: *We dined at the Ritz.* —see also **wine and dine** (WINE²)

**dine on/off sth** *phr v* [T] *formal* to eat a particular kind of food for dinner, especially expensive food: *We dined on lobster and strawberries.*

**dine out** *phr v* [I] **1** *formal* to eat dinner in a restaurant or in someone else's house: *They would dine out together once a month.* —see also **eat out** (EAT (1b)) **2 dine out on** *BrE humorous* to keep using a story about something that has happened to you in order to entertain people at meals

**din·er** /ˈdaɪnə||-ər/ *n* [C] **1** someone who is eating dinner in a restaurant **2** *AmE* a small restaurant that serves cheap meals: *She's a waitress in an all-night diner in North Vegas.* **3** *AmE* a DINING CAR

**di·nette** /daɪˈnet/ *n* [C] *AmE* a small area, usually in or near the kitchen, where people eat meals

**dinette set** /·ˈ· ˌ·/ *n* [C] *AmE* a table and matching chairs

**ding-a-ling** /ˈdɪŋ ə lɪŋ/ also **ding·bat** /ˈdɪŋbæt/ *n* [C] *AmE spoken* a stupid person: *Who's that fat dingbat over there?*

**ding-dong** /ˈdɪŋ dɒŋ||-dɔːŋ/ *n* [U] **1** [U] the noise made by a bell **2** [singular] *BrE informal* a noisy argument: *They were having a real ding-dong in the kitchen.*

**din·ghy** /ˈdɪŋgi, ˈdɪŋi/ *n* [C] **1** a small open sailing boat used especially for racing **2** a small open boat used for pleasure or for taking people between a ship and the shore —see also RUBBER DINGHY

**din·gle** /ˈdɪŋgəl/ *n* [C] *literary* a small valley with trees in it: *He went alone to the dingle to clear his thoughts.*

**din·go** /ˈdɪŋgəʊ||-goʊ/ *n plural* **dingoes** [C] an Australian wild dog

**din·gy** /ˈdɪndʒi/ *adj* a dingy room, street, or place is dark, dirty, and in bad condition: *a dingy back street* —**dingily** *adv*: *dingily furnished* —**dinginess** *n* [U]

**din·ing car** /ˈ··· ·/ *n* [C] a carriage on a train where meals are served; RESTAURANT CAR

**dining room** /ˈ··· ·/ *n* [C] a room where you eat meals in a house, hotel etc

**dining ta·ble** /ˈ·· ˌ··/ *n* [C] a table for having meals on —compare DINNER TABLE

**dink** /dɪŋk/ *n* [C] *informal* Double Income No Kids; one of two young people who are married to each other and who both earn a lot of money, but who have no children; DINKY² *BrE*

**din·kum** /ˈdɪŋkəm/ *adj* —see FAIR DINKUM

**din·ky¹** /ˈdɪŋki/ *adj* **1** *BrE informal* small and attractive: *What a dinky little cottage!* **2** *AmE* small and not very nice: *It was a really dinky hotel room.*

**dinky²** *n* [C] *BrE* a dink

**din·ner** /ˈdɪnə||-ər/ *n* **1** [C,U] the main meal of the day, eaten in the middle of the day or the evening: *Would you like to come over for dinner on Friday?*| *We're having fish for dinner tonight.*| **Sunday/Christmas/Thanksgiving dinner etc** (=a special meal eaten on Sunday, at Christmas, at Thanksgiving, etc)| **school dinner** (=a meal provided at school in the middle of the day) **2** [C] a formal occasion when an evening meal is eaten, often to celebrate something: *They're giving a dinner in honour of her retirement.* **3 had more ... than you've had hot dinners** *BrE spoken humorous* used to say that someone has had a lot of experience of something and has done it many times: *She's nursed more babies than you've had hot dinners.* —see also TV DINNER, **be dressed up like the dog's dinner** (DOG¹ (9)) S1 W2

**dinner dance** /ˈ·· ˌ·/ *n* [C] a social event in the evening, that includes a formal meal and music for dancing: *the annual dinner dance*

**dinner jack·et** /ˈ·· ˌ··/ *n* [C] *BrE* a black or white JACKET (1) worn by men on very formal occasions, usually with a BOW TIE; TUXEDO *AmE*

**dinner la·dy** /ˈ·· ˌ··/ *n* [C] *BrE* a woman who serves meals to children at school

**dinner par·ty** /ˈ·· ˌ··/ *n* [C] a social event when people are invited to someone's house for an evening meal

**dinner ser·vice** /ˈ·· ˌ··/ also **dinner set** /ˈ·· ·/ *n* [C] a complete set of plates, dishes etc, used for serving a meal

**dinner ta·ble** /ˈ·· ˌ··/ *n* **the dinner table a)** an occasion when people are eating dinner together: *That's not a very pleasant topic for the dinner table.* **b)** the table at which people eat dinner —compare DINING TABLE

**dinner thea·ter** /ˈ·· ˌ··/ *n* [C] *AmE* a restaurant in which you see a play after your meal

**din·ner·time** /ˈdɪnətaɪm‖-ər-/ *n* [singular] the time when you usually have dinner, especially in the middle of the day: *He always seems to call me at dinnertime.*

**di·no·saur** /ˈdaɪnəsɔː‖-sɔːr/ *n* [C] **1** one of a group of REPTILES that lived about 200 million years ago **2** *informal* something very large and old-fashioned that no longer works well or effectively: *one of the dinosaurs of the computer industry*

**dint** /dɪnt/ *n* **1 by dint of** by using a particular method: *By dint of persistent questioning, I finally got to the truth.* **2** a small hollow in the surface of something made by hitting it: *a dint in the car door*

**di·o·cese** /ˈdaɪəsɪ̵s/ *n* [C] the area under the control of a BISHOP (1), in the Christian church **—diocesan** /daɪˈɒsɪ̵sən‖-ˈɑː-/ *adj*

**di·ox·ide** /daɪˈɒksaɪd‖-ˈɑːk-/ *n* [C, U] *technical* a chemical compound containing two atoms of oxygen to every atom of another ELEMENT (=simple substance) —see also CARBON DIOXIDE

**di·ox·in** /daɪˈɒksɪ̵n‖-ˈɑːk-/ *n* [C, U] a very poisonous chemical used for killing plants

**Dip** the written abbreviation of DIPLOMA

**dip**[1] /dɪp/ *v* **dipped, dipping** **1** [T] to put something into a liquid and quickly lift it out again: *Dip your finger in the batter and taste it.* —see picture on page 834 **2** [I] to go downwards: *We watched the sun dip below the horizon.* **3 dip your headlights/lights** *BrE* to lower the angle of the front lights of your car, especially when someone is driving towards you; DIM[2] (3) *AmE* **4** [T] to make animals go through a bath containing a chemical that kills insects on their skin —see also SKINNY-DIPPING

**dip into** sth *phr v* [T] **1** to read short parts of a book, magazine etc, but not the whole thing: *It's the kind of book you can dip into now and again.* **2** to use some of an amount of money that you have: **dip into your savings** *Medical bills forced her to dip into her savings.* | **dip into your pocket** (=pay for something with your own money) | *Parents are being asked to dip into their pockets for new school books.* **3** to put your hand into a bag or box in order to take out one of the things inside: *On her lap was a bag of candy which she kept dipping into.*

**dip**[2] *n*
**1** ▸ **SWIM** ◂ [C] *informal* a quick swim: *Are you coming in for a dip?* | **have/take a dip** *They've decided to take a dip in the lake before lunch.*
**2** ▸ **DECREASE** ◂ [C] a slight decrease in the amount of something: *an unexpected dip in profits*
**3** ▸ **IN A SURFACE** ◂ [C] a place where the surface of something goes down suddenly, then goes up again: *a dip in the road*
**4** ▸ **FOOD** ◂ [C,U] a thick mixture that you can dip food into before you eat it: *sour cream and onion dip* —see picture on page 838
**5** ▸ **FOR ANIMALS** ◂ [C,U] a liquid that contains a chemical which kills insects on sheep and other animals
**6** ▸ **PERSON** ◂ [C] *AmE spoken* a stupid person —see also LUCKY DIP

**diph·ther·i·a** /dɪfˈθɪəriə, dɪp-‖-ˈθɪr-/ *n* [U] a serious infectious throat disease that makes breathing difficult

**diph·thong** /ˈdɪfθɒŋ, ˈdɪp-‖-θɒːŋ/ *n* [C] *technical* **1** a compound vowel sound made by pronouncing two vowels quickly one after the other. For example, the vowel sound in 'my' is a dipthong. —see also GLIDE[2] (3) **2** a DIGRAPH

**di·plo·ma** /dɪ̵ˈpləʊmə‖-ˈploʊ-/ *n* [C] **1** *BrE* a document showing that someone has successfully completed a course of study or passed an examination: *I'm hoping to get my teaching diploma this year.* | [+ **in**] *a diploma in catering* **2** *AmE* a document showing that a student has successfully completed their HIGH SCHOOL, college, or university education: *a master's diploma*

**di·plo·ma·cy** /dɪ̵ˈpləʊməsi‖-ˈploʊ-/ *n* [U] **1** the work of managing the relationships between countries: *a major player in post-war diplomacy* **2** skill in dealing with people and persuading them to agree to something without upsetting them: *The job requires tact and diplomacy.* —see also **gunboat diplomacy** (GUNBOAT (2))

**dip·lo·mat** /ˈdɪpləmæt/ *n* [C] **1** someone who officially represents their government in a foreign country **2** someone who is good at dealing with people without upsetting them: *As a natural diplomat, Baxter found it easy to placate the two sides.*

**dip·lo·mat·ic** /ˌdɪpləˈmætɪk◂/ *adj* **1** concerning or involving the work of diplomats: *She was hoping for a diplomatic post in the Middle East.* **2** dealing with people politely and skilfully without upsetting them: *They were always very diplomatic with awkward clients.* | *a diplomatic answer* **—diplomatically** /-kli/ *adv*: *Maria handled the situation very diplomatically.*

**diplomatic corps** /ˈ·ˈ·· ˌ·/ *n* [U] all the diplomats working in a particular country

**diplomatic im·mu·ni·ty** /ˌ···· ·ˈ···/ *n* [U] *law* a diplomat's special rights in the country where they are working, which protect them from local taxes and PROSECUTION (1)

**diplomatic re·la·tions** /ˌ···· ·ˈ··/ *n* [plural] the arrangement between two countries that each should keep representatives at an EMBASSY in the other country: **break off diplomatic relations** *Britain broke off diplomatic relations after the crisis of 1982.*

**Diplomatic Ser·vice** /·ˈ·· ˌ··/ *n* [singular] all the people who work for their government abroad in an EMBASSY or a CONSULATE

**di·plo·ma·tist** /dɪ̵ˈpləʊmətɪ̵st‖ˈploʊ-/ *n* [C] a DIPLOMAT

**dip·per** /ˈdɪpə‖-ər/ *n* [C] **1** a large spoon with a long handle used for taking liquid out of a container **2** a small bird that feeds in mountain streams —see also BIG DIPPER

**dip·py** /ˈdɪpi/ *adj informal* silly or crazy

**dip·shit** /ˈdɪpʃɪt/ *n* [C] *AmE spoken* an impolite word meaning a stupid person

**dip·so** /ˈdɪpsəʊ‖-soʊ/ *n* [C] *slang* a dipsomaniac

**dip·so·ma·ni·ac** /ˌdɪpsəˈmeɪniæk/ *n* [C] someone who has a very strong desire for alcoholic drinks, which they cannot control **—dipsomania** /-niə/ *n* [U]

**dip·stick** /ˈdɪpˌstɪk/ *n* [C] **1** a stick for measuring the amount of liquid in a container, especially the amount of oil in a car's engine —see picture at ENGINE **2** *spoken* a stupid person

**dip switch** /ˈ· ·/ *n* [C] *BrE* a SWITCH[2] (1) for lowering the beam of a car's front lights; DIMMER (2) *AmE*

**dip·tych** /ˈdɪptɪk/ *n* [C] a picture made in two parts which can be closed like a book —compare TRIPTYCH

**dire** /daɪə‖daɪr/ *adj* **1** extremely serious, bad or terrible: *He was in dire trouble and he knew it.* | *That makes the situation sound dire.* | **in dire need/poverty** *The country was in dire need of financial aid.* | **dire consequences** *Increasing fuel prices will have dire consequences for the poor.* | **be in dire straits** (=be in an extremely difficult or serious situation) **2 dire warning/threat** a dire warning or threat warns people about something terrible that will happen in the future

**di·rect**[1] /dɪ̵ˈrekt, ˌdaɪˈrekt◂/ *adj* S2 W1
**1** ▸ **WITHOUT ANYTHING BETWEEN** ◂ done without any other people, actions, processes etc coming between: *Can we have direct access to the information on file?* | *She has direct control over the business.* | *I'm not in direct contact with them.*
**2** ▸ **FROM ONE PLACE TO ANOTHER** ◂ going straight from one place to another without stopping or changing direction: *Which is the most direct route to London?* | *We can get a direct flight to New York.*
**3** ▸ **EFFECT** ◂ likely to change something immediately: *The change in the law will have a direct bearing on the way benefits are calculated.*
**4** ▸ **EXACT** ◂ [only before noun] exact or total: *Weight increases in direct proportion to mass.* | *These ideas are in direct contrast with the themes of her earlier essays.* |

**direct quote** (=what someone said in their exact words)
**5 ▶ BEHAVIOUR/ATTITUDE ◀** saying exactly what you mean in an honest clear way: *If only she'd been less direct in her approach, he might have helped.*
**6 direct descendant** someone who is related to someone else through their parents and grandparents, not through their AUNTS, UNCLES, brothers, sisters etc: *She claimed to be a direct descendant of Wordsworth.*
**7 direct result/consequence** something that happens only because of one particular thing: *They were suffering from stress, and their physical symptoms were a direct result.*
**8 direct question/answer** a question that asks for information exactly and specifically, with no possibility of misunderstanding, or an answer that gives information in this way: *Now, let me ask you a direct question, and I expect a direct answer.*
**9 direct heat/sunlight** strong heat or sunlight that someone or something is not protected from: *Never change the film in direct sunlight.* —opposite INDIRECT

S2 W2 **direct²** *v* [T]
**1 ▶ AIM ◀** [always + adv/prep] to aim something in a particular direction or at a particular person, group etc: **[+ at/towards/away from etc]** *The machine directs an X-ray beam at the patient's body.* | *For once her sarcasm was not directed at us.* | *Environmental policy was traditionally directed at pollution control.* | **direct your efforts towards sth** (=try hard to do one particular thing) *I want to direct my efforts more towards my own projects.* | **direct your attention towards sth** *None of them had ever directed serious attention to the problem.*
**2 ▶ BE IN CHARGE ◀** to be in charge of something or control it: *Stella had been asked to direct a research project.*
**3** to tell someone how to get to a place: *A policeman stood in the middle of the road, directing the traffic.* | **[+ to]** *Could you direct me to Trafalgar Square, please?* —see LEAD¹ (USAGE)
**4** *formal* to tell someone what they should do: *We were directed to hand over our passports.* | **direct that** *Judge Rice directed that a verdict of 'not guilty' be entered.*
**5 ▶ ACTING ◀** to give the actors in a play, film, or television programme instructions about what they should do: *Who directed that movie we saw last week?*

**direct³** *adv* **1** without stopping or changing direction: *Can we fly direct to Chicago, or do we stop in Salt Lake City first?* **2** without dealing with anyone else first: *Esther decided to contact the manager direct.* | *It is usually cheaper to buy the goods direct from the wholesaler.*

**direct cur·rent** /ˌ· ˈ··/ *n* [U] a flow of electricity that moves in one direction only —compare ALTERNATING CURRENT

**direct deb·it** /ˌ· ˈ··, ˌ·· ˈ··/ *n* [C,U] *especially BrE* an instruction you give your bank to pay money directly out of your account regularly to a particular person or organization —compare STANDING ORDER

**direct de·pos·it** /ˌ· ·ˈ··/ *n* [U] *AmE* a method of paying someone's wages directly into their bank account

**direct dis·course** /ˌ· ˈ··/ *n* [U] an American form of the expression DIRECT SPEECH

**direct hit** /ˌ· ˈ·/ *n* [C] an occasion when something thrown or dropped, for example a bomb, exactly hits the object it was aimed at: *The railway station suffered two direct hits that night.*

S1 W1 **di·rec·tion** /dʒ̍ˈrekʃən, daɪ-/ *n*
**1** [C] the way something or someone moves, faces, or is aimed: **in the direction of** (=towards) *The suspects were last seen heading in the direction of Miami.* | **in sb's direction** (=towards someone) *Tristram glanced in her direction and their eyes met.* | **in the opposite direction** *The girls giggled and pointed in the opposite direction.* | **change direction** *On seeing me, Maurice changed direction and went along the wharf instead.* | **in a southerly/easterly etc direction** *Continue in a southerly direction until you reach the road.* | **in all directions** *As shots rang out, the crowd ran screaming in all directions.*
**2 directions** [plural] instructions about how to get from one place to another, or about what to do: *A very helpful woman gave me directions to the police station.*
**3 ▶ WAY STH DEVELOPS ◀** [C] the general way in which someone or something changes or develops: **take a direction** *Drayson was surprised at the direction his career had taken.* | *The company is hoping to extend its operations in this direction.*
**4 ▶ WHERE FROM OR WHERE TO ◀** [C] where something comes from or where something leads: *The evidence all points in this direction.* | *Help came from a wholly unexpected direction.*
**5 ▶ CONTROL ◀** [U] control, management, or advice: **under sb's direction** *The project progressed well, under the capable direction of Magnus Armstrong.*
**6 ▶ FILM ◀** [U] the instructions and advice given by a film DIRECTOR (2)
**7 ▶ PURPOSE ◀** [U] a general purpose or aim: *Her mother felt that Rachel's life lacked direction.*
**8 sense of direction a)** the ability to know which way you should be going in a place you do not know well: *"Are we going north?" "Don't ask me! I've got no sense of direction at all."* **b)** an idea about what your aims in life are: *Doing the course gave her more sense of direction.*

**di·rec·tion·al** /dʒ̍ˈrekʃənəl, daɪ-/ *adj technical* **1** pointing in a particular direction **2** a directional piece of equipment receives or gives out radio signals from some directions more strongly than others

**di·rec·tive¹** /dʒ̍ˈrektɪv, daɪ-/ *n* [C] an official order or instruction: *the EU directive on paternity leave*

**directive²** *adj* giving instructions: *It is important in these cases that doctors take a less directive approach.*

**di·rect·ly¹** /dʒ̍ˈrektli, daɪ-/ *adv* **1** with no other person, action, process etc between: *The new law won't directly affect us.* | *I know where you can get that directly from the manufacturers.* **2** exactly: *Have you noticed how he never looks directly at you?* | *Her practical ideas seemed directly opposed to the department's academic style.* **3 speak/ask/answer etc directly** to say exactly what you mean without trying to hide anything: *Cindy has a job in mind, but refuses to say directly what it is.* **4** *BrE old-fashioned* very soon: *He should be here directly, if you don't mind waiting.* **5** *BrE old-fashioned* immediately S2 W2

**directly²** *conjunction BrE* as soon as: *I came directly I got your message.*

**direct mail** /ˌ· ˈ·/ *n* [U] advertisements that are sent by post to many people

**direct meth·od** /ˌ· ˈ··/ *n* [singular, U] a method of teaching a foreign language without using the student's own language

**direct ob·ject** /ˌ· ˈ··, ˌ·· ˈ··/ *n* [C] *technical* the noun, noun phrase, or PRONOUN that you need to complete the meaning of a statement using a TRANSITIVE verb, for example 'Mary' in the statement 'I saw Mary' —compare INDIRECT OBJECT

**di·rec·tor** /dʒ̍ˈrektə, daɪ-‖-ər/ *n* [C] **1** one of the committee of top managers who control a company: *a former director of Gartmore Pensions Ltd* | **board of directors** (=the committee of directors) **2** the person who gives instructions to the actors, CAMERAMAN etc in a film or play —compare PRODUCER (2) **3** someone who is in charge of a particular activity or organization: *the director of transport operations* | *Greta has been appointed project director.* | **financial/sales/personnel director** (=a director in charge of the financial department etc) —see also MANAGING DIRECTOR, NON-EXECUTIVE DIRECTOR W1

**di·rec·tor·ate** /dʒ̍ˈrektərʒ̍t, daɪ-/ *n* [C] **1** the BOARD (=committee) of directors of a company **2** a directorship

**Director of Stud·ies** /ˌ··· ˈ··/ *n* [singular] a teacher in a British university or language school who is in charge of organizing the students' programmes of study

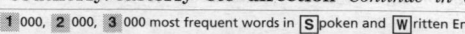

**di·rec·tor·ship** /dʒ̍ˈrektəʃɪp, daɪ-‖-ər-/ *n* [C] the position of being a director of a company

**di·rec·to·ry** /daɪˈrektəri, dʒ̇-/ *n* [C] a book or list of names, facts etc, usually arranged in alphabetical order: *I couldn't find your number in the telephone directory.|a new business directory*

**directory en·qui·ries** /ˌ···· ·ˈ··/ *BrE*, **directory assistance** /ˌ···· ·ˈ··/ *AmE n* [U] a service on the British telephone network that you can use to find out someone's telephone number

**direct speech** /·ˌ· ˈ·ˌ,·· ˈ·/ *n* [U] *technical* the style used to report what someone says by giving their actual words, for example 'I don't want to go,' said Julie; DIRECT DISCOURSE *AmE* —compare INDIRECT SPEECH, REPORTED SPEECH

**direct tax** /·ˌ· ˈ·/ *n* [C, U] *technical* a tax, such as income tax, which is actually collected from the person who pays it, as opposed to a tax on goods or services —opposite INDIRECT TAXATION —**direct taxation** /·ˌ· ·ˈ··/ *n* [U]

**dirge** /dɜːdʒ‖dɜːrdʒ/ *n* [C] **1** a slow sad song sung at a funeral: *When I die, I don't want any of those awful dirges.* **2** a song or piece of music that is too slow and boring

**dir·i·gi·ble** /ˈdɪrɪ̣dʒɪ̣bəl, dɪ̣ˈrɪ-/ *n* [C] an AIRSHIP

**dirk** /dɜːk‖dɜːrk/ *n* [C] a heavy pointed knife used as a weapon in Scotland in the past

S3 **dirt** /dɜːt‖dɜːrt/ *n* [U] **1** any substance that makes things dirty, such as mud or dust: *You should have seen the dirt on that car!*|**dog dirt** (=waste from a dog's BOWELS (1)) **2** loose earth or soil: *Michael threw his handful of dirt onto the coffin.* **3** *informal* information about someone's private life or activities which could give people a bad opinion of them if it became known: *Apparently, confidential files were combed for dirt on the candidates.* **4** talk, writing, films etc that are considered unpleasant or immoral because they are about sex —see also **dish the dirt** (DISH[2] (1)), **hit the dirt** (HIT[1] (21)), **treat sb like dirt** (TREAT[1] (1))

**dirt bike** /ˈ· ˌ·/ *n* [C] a small MOTORCYCLE for young people, usually ridden on rough paths or fields

**dirt cheap** /ˌ· ˈ·◂/ *adj, adv informal* extremely cheap: *We got the cow dirt cheap because the Parsons sold off their farm.*

**dirt farm·er** /ˈ· ˌ··/ *n* [C] *AmE* a poor farmer who works to feed himself and his family, without paying anyone else to help

**dirt poor** /ˌ· ˈ·◂/ *adj AmE informal* extremely poor

**dirt road** /ˈ· ·/ *n* [C] a road made of hard earth

**dirt track** /ˈ· ·/ *n* [C] a track used for MOTORCYCLE races

S2 W3 **dirt·y[1]** /ˈdɜːti‖ˈdɜːr-/ *adj* **dirtier, dirtiest**

**1** ▶ **NOT CLEAN** ◀ covered in dirt or marked with dirt: *Just stack the dirty dishes in the sink.|Look how dirty your hands are! Go wash them right now!*

**2** ▶ **IMMORAL** ◀ connected with sex in a way that is considered immoral or unpleasant: *Mick's always telling dirty jokes.|There were a bunch of dirty magazines under his bed.*|**a dirty mind** (=a mind that often thinks about sex)|**dirty weekend** *humorous* (=a weekend when a man and woman who are not married to each other go away to have sex)

**3** ▶ **UNPLEASANT** ◀ *spoken* used to emphasize that you think someone or something is very bad: *You're a dirty liar!|Yeah, they gave us all the dirty jobs.*

**4** ▶ **DISHONEST** ◀ unfair or dishonest: *a dirty fighter|There's been some dirty business over these contracts.*|**dirty trick** (=an unkind dishonest way of treating someone) *I'm so sorry anyone should play such a dirty trick!*|**do the dirty on sb** *BrE* (=treat someone in a way that is unfair or dishonest)|**dirty pool** *AmE* (=unfair or dishonest behaviour)

**5 be a dirty word** if something is a dirty word, people believe it is a bad thing even if they do not know or think much about it: *Nowadays power tends to be a slightly dirty word as far as organizations are concerned.*

**6 give sb a dirty look** to look at someone in a very disapproving way: *When I went in there she gave me a dirty look and told me to take a seat.*

**7 do sb's dirty work** to do an unpleasant or dishonest job for someone so that they do not have to do it themselves: *I told them to do their own dirty work.*

**8** ▶ **DRUGS** ◀ *AmE slang* containing or possessing illegal drugs —see also **wash your dirty linen in public** (WASH[1] (6)) —**dirtily** *adv*

**dirty[2]** *adv* [I,T] **1 dirty rotten** *spoken* extremely nasty: *the dirty rotten bastard!|What a dirty rotten trick!* **2 play dirty a)** to behave in a very unfair and dishonest way **b)** to cheat in a game **3 talk dirty** to talk rudely about sex **4 dirty great/dirty big** *BrE spoken* extremely big: *We suddenly saw this dirty great truck coming towards us.*

**dirty[3]** *v* **dirtied, dirtying** [I,T] **1** to put or leave marks on something and make it no longer clean: *Max wiped his dirtied hands on his thighs.* **2 dirty your hands on sth** to become involved in something bad that will affect people's opinion of you

**dirty old man** /ˌ··· ˈ·/ *n* [C] *informal* an older man who is too sexually interested in younger women

**dirty tricks** /ˌ·· ˈ·/ *n* [plural] secret, dishonest, and often criminal activities by a government, political group, or company, for example spreading false information about their competitors or opponents: **dirty tricks campaign** (=a planned series of dirty tricks) *The airline was accused of a dirty tricks campaign against their rivals.*

**dis-** /dɪs/ *prefix* **1** shows an opposite or negative: *I disapprove* (=do not approve)|*his dishonesty* (=lack of honesty)|*a discontented look* **2** shows the stopping or removing of a condition: *Disconnect the machine from the electricity supply.* (=so that it is no longer connected)|*Disinfect the wound first.* **3** [in verbs] to remove something: *a dismasted ship*

**dis·a·bil·i·ty** /ˌdɪsəˈbɪlɪ̣ti/ *n* **1** [C] a physical problem that makes someone unable to use a part of their body properly: *She manages to lead a normal life in spite of her disabilities.* **2** [U] the state of not being able to use parts of your body properly: *learning to cope with disability*

**dis·a·ble** /dɪsˈeɪbəl/ *v* [T] **1** [often passive] to make someone unable to use a part of their body properly: *Carter was permanently disabled in the war.* **2** to deliberately make a machine or piece of equipment impossible to use: *This system is designed to destroy or disable enemy ballistic missiles.* —**disablement** *n* [C,U]

**dis·a·bled** /dɪsˈeɪbəld/ *adj* **1** someone who is disabled cannot use a part of their body properly: **severely disabled** (=unable to use most of your body)|**disabled parking/toilet/entrance** (=for disabled people) W3
**2 the disabled** people who are disabled: *The theatre has good access for the disabled.* —compare CRIPPLE[1] (1), HANDICAPPED

**dis·a·buse** /ˌdɪsəˈbjuːz/ *v* [T] *formal* to persuade someone that what they believe is untrue: [+ **of**] *I never did anything to disabuse him of that idea.*

**dis·ad·van·tage** /ˌdɪsədˈvɑːntɪdʒ‖-ˈvæn-/ *n* [C, U] an unfavourable condition or quality that makes someone or something less likely to be successful or effective: [+ **of**] *The main disadvantage of the project is the cost.*|[+ **to**] *There are some disadvantages to his proposal.*|**be at a disadvantage** (=have a disadvantage) *I was at a disadvantage because I didn't speak French.*|**put sb at a disadvantage/be to sb's disadvantage** (=give someone a disadvantage) *Her height will be very much to her disadvantage if she wants to be a dancer.*

**dis·ad·van·taged** /ˌdɪsədˈvɑːntɪdʒd◂‖-ˈvæn-/ *adj* having social disadvantages, such as a lack of money or education, which make it difficult for you to succeed: *disadvantaged kids from the ghetto*

**dis·ad·van·ta·geous** /ˌdɪsædvənˈteɪdʒəs, -væn-/ *adj* [+ **to/for**] unfavourable and likely to cause problems for you —**disadvantageously** *adv*

**dis·af·fec·ted** /ˌdɪsəˈfektɪ̣d◂/ *adj* no longer loyal because you are not at all satisfied with your leader, ruler etc: *Some of the government's most loyal supporters are now becoming disaffected.* —**disaffection** /-ˈfekʃən/ *n* [U]

**dis·af·fil·i·ate** /ˌdɪsəˈfɪlieɪt/ *v* [I, T + **from**] if an organization disaffiliates from another organization or is disaffiliated from it, it breaks the official connection it has with it —compare AFFILIATE[1]

S2 **dis·a·gree** /ˌdɪsəˈgriː/ *v* [I] **1** to have or express a different opinion from someone else: [+ **with**] *Peter may disagree with this, but I don't really care.* | [+ **about/on**] *We often disagree about politics.* | **I disagree** *spoken*: *I disagree; I think it's a bad idea.* **2** if statements or reports about the same event or situation disagree, they are different from each other

**disagree with** sb *phr v* [T] if something such as food or weather disagrees with you, it has a bad effect on you or makes you ill: *Seafood always disagrees with me.*

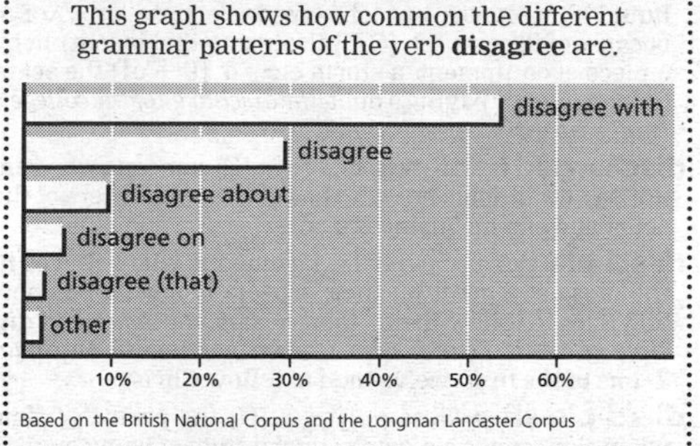


**dis·a·gree·a·ble** /ˌdɪsəˈgriːəbəl◂/ *adj* **1** not at all enjoyable or pleasant: *a disagreeable experience* **2** unfriendly and bad-tempered: *a rude, disagreeable woman* —**disagreeably** *adv*

**dis·a·gree·ment** /ˌdɪsəˈgriːmənt/ *n* **1** [C,U] a situation in which people express different opinions about something and sometimes quarrel: *Just because we've had a few disagreements, it doesn't mean we aren't still friends.* | [+ **about/over/as to**] *There is some disagreement as to whether the disease is curable.* | [+ **among/between**] *There is a lot of disagreement among doctors about this.* | **be in disagreement** (=disagree) **2** [U] differences between two statements, reports etc that ought to be similar: [+ **between**] *There is considerable disagreement between these two estimates.*

**dis·al·low** /ˌdɪsəˈlaʊ/ *v* [T] to officially refuse to allow something such as a claim, because a rule has been broken: *Leeds had a goal disallowed for being offside.*

S2 W2 **dis·ap·pear** /ˌdɪsəˈpɪə‖-ˈpɪr/ *v* [I] **1** to become impossible to see or find: *Where are my keys? They seem to have disappeared.* | **disappear behind/under/into etc** *Grab the cat quick! Before he disappears out the door!* | **disappear from view/sight** *David watched her car until it disappeared from view.* **2** to stop existing: *So what happens when the rain forest disappears for ever?* —**disappearance** *n* [C,U]: *Her sudden disappearance was very worrying.*

**dis·ap·point** /ˌdɪsəˈpɔɪnt/ *v* [T] **1** to make someone feel sad because something they hoped for or expected did not happen: *I'm sorry to disappoint you, but I can't come after all.* | *You disappoint me, Eric. I expected better.* **2 disappoint sb's hopes/expectations** to prevent something from happening that someone hoped for or expected

**dis·ap·point·ed** /ˌdɪsəˈpɔɪntɪ̆d◂/ *adj* **1** sad because something you hoped for did not happen, or because someone or something was not as good as you expected: *Dad seemed more disappointed than angry.* | [+ **about**] *Nathan's really disappointed about not being able to go.* | **disappointed in sb** *I'm disappointed in you! How could you have lied like that?* | **disappointed (that)** *Of course I'm disappointed I didn't get an invitation.* | [+ **with**] *I have to say we're disappointed with your work.* | [+ **at**] *Are you disappointed at not being chosen?* | **disappointed to hear/see/find** *We were disappointed to find the museum closed.* | **bitterly/terribly disappointed** *Gordon was bitterly disappointed when he failed that course.* **2 disappointed hope/plan/expectation** something you hope for, plan, or expect that does not happen or is not as good as you expected

**dis·ap·point·ing** /ˌdɪsəˈpɔɪntɪŋ◂/ *adj* not as good as you hoped or expected: *disappointing profit figures* | *Well, Bill was really negative about it, which was pretty disappointing.* —**disappointingly** *adv*

**dis·ap·point·ment** /ˌdɪsəˈpɔɪntmənt/ *n* **1** [U] sadness that something is not as good as you expected it to be, or has not happened in the way you hoped it would: **to sb's (great) disappointment** *To her great disappointment none of her tomatoes grew well.* **2** [C] someone or something that is not as good as you hoped or expected: *The movie was kind of a disappointment.* | **be a disappointment to sb** *Frankly, I've been a disappointment to my father; he wanted me to be a lawyer.*

**dis·ap·pro·ba·tion** /ˌdɪsæprəˈbeɪʃən/ *n* [U] *formal* disapproval of someone or something because you think they are morally wrong

**dis·ap·prov·al** /ˌdɪsəˈpruːvəl/ *n* [U] an attitude that shows you think that someone or their behaviour, ideas etc are bad or unsuitable: [+ **of**] *We intend to express our disapproval of the marriage.* | **with disapproval** *Baxter eyed our dirty clothes with obvious disapproval.* | **in disapproval** *Aunt Clarissa snorted in disapproval.*

**dis·ap·prove** /ˌdɪsəˈpruːv/ *v* [I] to think that someone or their behaviour, ideas etc are bad or unsuitable: [+ **of**] *Mother disapproves of every boyfriend I bring home.* | **strongly disapprove** *I strongly disapprove of couples living together before marriage.*

**dis·ap·prov·ing** /ˌdɪsəˈpruːvɪŋ◂/ *adj* showing that you think someone or something is bad or unsuitable: *a disapproving frown* —**disapprovingly** *adv*: *Tyler shook his head disapprovingly.*

**dis·arm** /dɪsˈɑːm‖-ˈɑːrm/ *v* **1** [I] to reduce the size of your armed forces and the number of weapons: *Getting the rebels to disarm will not be easy.* **2** [T] to take away someone's weapons: *Captured soldiers were disarmed and put into camps.* **3** [T] if your manner or behaviour disarms someone, it is so pleasant that it makes them stop feeling angry or disapproving towards you: *That charm of hers can disarm even her sternest critics.* —see also DISARMING **4** [T] to take the explosives out of a bomb, MISSILE (1) etc

**dis·ar·ma·ment** /dɪsˈɑːməmənt‖-ˈɑːr-/ *n* [U] the reduction of the size of a country's military forces and the number of weapons that it has: **nuclear disarmament** (=reduction in the number of atomic weapons)

**dis·arm·ing** /dɪsˈɑːmɪŋ‖-ˈɑːr-/ *adj* making you trust someone or feel less angry with them than before: *Kenneth has such a disarming smile!* —**disarmingly** *adv*

**dis·ar·range** /ˌdɪsəˈreɪndʒ/ *v* [T] *formal* to make something untidy —**disarrangement** *n* [U]

**dis·ar·ray** /ˌdɪsəˈreɪ/ *n* [U] *formal* the state of being completely confused or untidy: **in disarray** *Troops retreated in disarray under heavy gunfire.* | *Manuscripts lay in wild disarray on the side table.* | **throw sth into disarray/fall into disarray** *Gray's plans have been thrown into disarray because of injuries.*

**dis·as·so·ci·ate** /ˌdɪsəˈsəʊʃieɪt, -sieɪt‖-ˈsoʊ-/ *v* [T] another form of DISSOCIATE

**di·sas·ter** /dɪˈzɑːstə‖dɪˈzæstər/ *n* [C,U] **1** a sudden event such as a flood, storm, or accident which causes great damage or suffering: *108 people died in the mining disaster.* | **natural disaster** (=caused by nature, not by an accident) *The 1987 hurricane was the worst natural disaster to hit England for decades.* | **disaster area** (=a place where a disaster has happened) | **disaster strikes** *Disaster struck on the first day, when all our equipment was* 

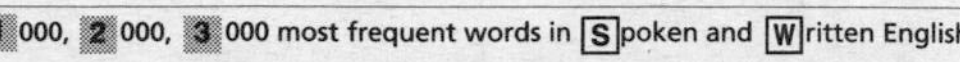

*stolen.* **2** a complete failure: *The party was a total disaster – half the guests didn't even turn up!*

**di·sas·trous** /dɪˈzɑːstrəs‖dɪˈzæ-/ *adj* very bad, or ending in failure: *Warrington's disastrous early marriage* | *Chemical leaks have had a disastrous effect on wildlife.* —**disastrously** *adv*

**dis·a·vow** /ˌdɪsəˈvaʊ/ *v* [T] *formal* to state that you are not responsible for something, or that you have no knowledge of it: *He later disavowed any connection with the Fascist collaborators.* —**disavowal** *n* [C,U]

**dis·band** /dɪsˈbænd/ *v* [I,T] if a club or organization disbands or is disbanded, its activities are officially stopped, and it no longer exists

**dis·bar** /dɪsˈbɑː‖-ˈbɑːr/ *v* **disbarred, disbarring** [T] to make a lawyer leave the bar (BAR² (8)) or the legal profession —compare DEBAR —**disbarment** *n* [U]

**dis·be·lief** /ˌdɪsbɪ̵ˈliːf/ *n* [U] a feeling that something is not true or does not exist: *My initial response was one of utter disbelief.* | **stare/gasp/blink etc in disbelief** *Marta shook her head in disbelief, shocked by the damage.* —compare UNBELIEF, BELIEF

**dis·be·lieve** /ˌdɪsbɪ̵ˈliːv/ *v* [I + **in** , T] *formal* to not believe something or someone: *I see no reason to disbelieve him.* —**disbelieving** *adj*: *disbelieving laughter*

**dis·burse** /dɪsˈbɜːs‖-ɜːrs/ *v* [T] *formal* to pay out money, especially from a large sum that is available for a special purpose: *Over $25 million has been disbursed from the fund.* —**disbursement** *n* [C,U]

S3 **disc** also **disk** *AmE* /dɪsk/ *n* [C] **1** a round, flat shape or object: *a revolving metal disc* **2** a COMPACT DISC **3** a record that you play on a RECORD PLAYER **4** *BrE* a computer DISK **5** a flat piece of CARTILAGE between the bones of your back: **slipped disc** (=one that has slipped out of its correct place)

**dis·card¹** /dɪsˈkɑːd‖-ɑːrd/ *v* **1** [T] to get rid of something because it is useless: *What was more worrying was a box of used syringes that hadn't been properly discarded.* **2** [I,T] to put down unwanted cards in a card game —**discarded** *adj*: *old discarded clothes*

**discard²** /ˈdɪskɑːd‖-ɑːrd/ *n* [C] an unwanted card that is put down in a card game

**disc brakes** /ˈ· ·/ *n* [plural] BRAKES¹ that work by means of a pair of hard surfaces pressing against a DISC (1) in the centre of a car wheel

**di·scern** /dɪˈsɜːn‖-ɜːrn/ *v* [T not in progressive] *formal* to see, notice, or understand something only after looking at it or thinking about it carefully; PERCEIVE (2): *In the distance I could just discern the hills near Tendaho.* | **discern who/what/how etc** *It was difficult to discern which of them was telling the truth.* —**discernible** *adj*: *There is still no discernible improvement in the economic situation.* —**discernibly** *adv*

**di·scern·ing** /dɪˈsɜːnɪŋ‖-ɜːr-/ *adj* showing the ability to make good judgments, epecially about art, music, style etc: *Amanda liked to think she was discerning in her tastes.* | *With prices down by a third, there are many bargains around for the discerning buyer.*

**di·scern·ment** /dɪˈsɜːnmənt‖-ɜːr-/ *n* [U] *formal* the ability to make good judgments about people or about art, music, style etc: *I hope Pam shows more taste and discernment in choosing a husband.*

**dis·charge¹** /dɪsˈtʃɑːdʒ‖-ɑːr-/ *v*

**1** ▶ **SEND SB AWAY** ◀ [T] to officially allow a person to go or send them away, especially after being ill in hospital or working in the army, navy etc: [+ **from**] *I think Oliver gets discharged from the RAF in August.* | **discharge yourself** (=leave hospital before your treatment is complete)

**2** ▶ **LET STH OUT** ◀ [I always + adv/prep, T] to send out gas, liquid, smoke etc, or allow it to escape: [+ **into**] *pollutants being discharged into the atmosphere*

**3** ▶ **SHOOT** ◀ [T] to fire a gun or shoot an ARROW (1) etc

**4 discharge a duty/promise/responsibility etc** *formal* to do properly everything that is part of a particular duty etc: *the failure of the council to discharge its duty*

**5 discharge a debt** *formal* to pay a debt

**6** ▶ **GOODS/PASSENGERS** ◀ [T] to unload goods or passengers from a ship, plane etc

**7** ▶ **ELECTRICITY** ◀ [I,T] if a piece of electrical equipment discharges or is discharged, it sends out electricity

**8** ▶ **A WOUND** ◀ [I,T] to send out PUS (=infected liquid)

**discharge²** /ˈdɪstʃɑːdʒ‖-tʃɑːrdʒ/ *n* **1** [U] the action of allowing someone to go away, especially someone who has been ill in hospital or working in the army, navy etc: [+ **from**] *Patents' needs after discharge from hospital will be monitored.* —see also DISHONOURABLE DISCHARGE **2** [C,U] the act of sending out gas, liquid, smoke etc, or the substance that is sent out: [+ **of**] *the discharge of toxic waste into the sea* | **nasal/vaginal discharge** (=a thick liquid that comes out of someone's nose or VAGINA because of illness) **3** [C,U] electricity that is sent out by a piece of equipment, a storm etc **4** [U + **of**] the act of doing a duty or paying a debt: *the discharge of the college's legal responsibilities*

**discharged bank·rupt** /·ˌ· ˈ··/ *n* [C] someone who cannot pay their debts but who has obeyed the orders of the court and can do business again

**di·sci·ple** /dɪˈsaɪpəl/ *n* [C] **1** someone who believes in the ideas of a great teacher, especially a religious one, and tries to follow them: *Dian Fossey, the American disciple of Louis Leakey who studied gorillas in Rwanda.* **2** one of the first twelve men to follow Christ

**di·sci·ple·ship** /dɪˈsaɪpəlʃɪp/ *n* [U] the period of time when someone is a disciple, or the state of being one

**dis·ci·pli·nar·i·an** /ˌdɪsɪ̵plɪ̵ˈneəriən‖-ˈner-/ *n* [C] someone who believes people should obey orders and rules, and who makes them do this: *a strict disciplinarian*

**dis·ci·pli·na·ry** /ˈdɪsɪ̵plɪnəri, ˌdɪsɪ̵ˈplɪ-‖ˈdɪsɪ̵plɪ̵neri/ *adj* connected with the punishment of someone who has not obeyed rules, or with trying to make people obey rules: **disciplinary action/measures** (=things you do to punish someone) *The investigation led to disciplinary action against several officers.* | **disciplinary hearing/committee** (=to decide if someone should be punished)

**dis·ci·pline¹** /ˈdɪsɪ̵plɪ̵n/ *n* **1** [U] the practice of making people obey rules and orders, or the controlled situation that results from this practice: *We have high standards of discipline at this school that must be maintained.* | *strict military discipline* | **keep discipline** *teachers who can't keep discipline in the classroom* **2** [C,U] a method of training your mind or learning to control your behaviour: *Learning poetry is a good discipline for the memory.* **3** [U] the ability to control your own behaviour and way of working: *He'll never finish that course – he's got no discipline!* —see also SELF-DISCIPLINE **4** [U] punishment for not obeying rules: *That child needs discipline.* **5** [C] an area of knowledge such as history, chemistry, mathematics etc that is studied at a university S W

**discipline²** *v* [T] **1** to teach someone to obey rules and control their own behaviour: *At least I'm not afraid of disciplining my kids!* **2 discipline yourself (to do sth)** to control the way you work, how regularly you do something etc, because you know it is good for you: *It's a question of disciplining yourself to write every day.* **3** to punish someone in order to keep order and control: *One director left today and two others have been disciplined.*

**dis·ci·plined** /ˈdɪsɪ̵plɪ̵nd/ *adj* behaving in a controlled way according to strict rules: *the most disciplined, effective army in the world* | *a disciplined approach*

**disc jock·ey** /ˈ· ˌ··/ *n* [C] someone who introduces and plays records of popular music on a radio show or at a dance club

**dis·claim** /dɪsˈkleɪm/ *v* [T] **disclaim responsibility/knowledge etc** *formal* to state that you are not responsible for something, that you do not know anything about it, etc: *I can't believe the insurance company disclaimed liability for the accident.*

**dis·claim·er** /dɪsˈkleɪmə‖-ər/ *n* [C] a statement that you are not responsible for something, that you are not connected with it etc

**dis·close** /dɪsˈkləʊz‖-ˈkloʊz/ *v* [T] **1** to make something publicly known, especially after it has been kept secret from the public: *The Security Service is unlikely to disclose any information.* | **disclose that** *It has recently been disclosed that 30% of donations are spent on publicity.* **2** to show something by removing the thing that covers it: *The curtains rose, disclosing a stage bathed in red light.*

**dis·clo·sure** /dɪsˈkləʊʒə‖-ˈkloʊʒər/ *n* **1** [U] the act of telling or showing something that has been kept secret: *MPs called for public disclosure of the committee's findings.* **2** [C] a fact which is made known after being kept secret: *Following sensational disclosures concerning his personal life, he has offered to resign.*

**dis·co** /ˈdɪskəʊ‖-koʊ/ *n* [C] a club or social event at which people dance to recorded popular music

**dis·cog·ra·phy** /dɪˈskɒgrəfi‖-ˈskɑːg-/ *n* [C] a list of the music and songs recorded by a musician or musical group

**dis·col·or** /dɪsˈkʌlə‖-ər/ *v* [T] the American spelling of discolour

**dis·col·o·ra·tion** /dɪsˌkʌləˈreɪʃən/ *n* **1** [U] the process of becoming discoloured **2** [C] a place on the surface of something where it has become discoloured

**dis·col·our** *BrE*, **discolor** *AmE* /dɪsˈkʌlə/ *v* [I,T] if something is discoloured or if it discolours, its colour changes, making it look dirty or unattractive: *Sprinkle the apple slices with lemon juice to prevent them from discolouring.*

**dis·com·bob·u·late** /ˌdɪskəmˈbɒbjʊ̈leɪt‖-ˈbɑːb-/ *v* [T] *humorous* to make someone feel completely confused or upset

**dis·com·fit** /dɪsˈkʌmfɪ̈t/ *v* [T] *formal* to make someone feel slightly uncomfortable, annoyed, or embarrassed: *Expecting a handshake, Jenny was discomfited by his kiss.* —**discomfiture** *n* [U]

**dis·com·fort** /dɪsˈkʌmfət‖-ərt/ *n* **1** [U] a feeling of slight pain or of being physically uncomfortable: *You may experience some discomfort for a few days after the operation.* **2** [U] a feeling of embarrassment, shame, or slight worry: [+ **at**] *Paul's discomfort at facing criticism tends to make him too defensive.* **3** [C] something that makes you uncomfortable: *the discomforts of travel*

**dis·com·mode** /ˌdɪskəˈməʊd‖-ˈmoʊd/ *v* [T] *formal* to cause trouble or difficulties for someone; INCOMMODE

**dis·com·pose** /ˌdɪskəmˈpəʊz‖-ˈpoʊz/ *v* [T] *formal* to make someone feel worried and no longer calm —**discomposure** /-ˈpəʊʒə‖-ˈpoʊʒər/ *n* [U]

**dis·con·cert** /ˌdɪskənˈsɜːt‖-ɜːrt/ *v* [T often passive] to make someone feel slightly confused or worried: *It was that cold, steady gaze of his that disconcerted her most.*

**dis·con·cert·ing** /ˌdɪskənˈsɜːtɪŋ◂‖-ɜːr-/ *adj* making you feel slightly confused or worried —**disconcertingly** *adv*: *It all seemed disconcertingly familiar.*

**dis·con·nect** /ˌdɪskəˈnekt/ *v* [T] **1** to take out the wire, pipe etc that connects a machine or piece of equipment to something: *Disconnect the cables before you try to move the computer.* **2** to remove the supply of power from a machine or building: *You realize if we don't pay that bill soon they'll disconnect our gas?* **3** to break the telephone connection between two people: *Operator? We've been disconnected.* —**disconnection** /-ˈnekʃən/ *n* [C, U]

**dis·con·nect·ed** /ˌdɪskəˈnektɪ̈d◂/ *adj* disconnected thoughts or ideas do not seem to be related to each other

**dis·con·so·late** /dɪsˈkɒnsəlɪ̈t‖-ˈkɑːn-/ *adj* feeling extremely sad and hopeless: *A few disconsolate men sat in the foyer with their hats in their hands.* —**disconsolately** *adv*: *O'Grady trudged disconsolately back home.*

**dis·con·tent¹** /ˌdɪskənˈtent/ *n* [U] a feeling of being unhappy and not satisfied with the situation you are in: [+ **with**] *There is no evidence whatsoever of customer discontent with our credit terms.* —opposite CONTENTMENT

**discontent²** *v* [T] to make someone feel discontented

**dis·con·tent·ed** /ˌdɪskənˈtentɪ̈d◂/ *adj* unhappy or not satisfied with the situation you are in: [+ **with**] *Eva was ambitious and was discontented with her job at the post office.* —**discontentedly** *adv*

**dis·con·tin·ue** /ˌdɪskənˈtɪnjuː/ *v* [T] to stop doing or providing something that you have regularly done or provided until now: *Bus Route 51 is being discontinued as of March 1st.* | *a discontinued china pattern* | **discontinued line** (=a type of product that is no longer being produced) —**discontinuation** /ˌdɪskəntɪnjuˈeɪʃən/ *n* [U] —**discontinuance** /ˌdɪskənˈtɪnjuəns/ *n* [U]

**dis·con·ti·nu·i·ty** /ˌdɪskɒntɪ̈ˈnjuːɪ̈ti‖-kɑːntɪ̈ˈnuː-/ *n* **1** [U] the fact of a process not being continuous **2** [C] a sudden change or pause in a process

**dis·con·tin·u·ous** /ˌdɪskənˈtɪnjuəs◂/ *adj* not continuous: *Women are particularly affected because of their discontinuous employment patterns.* —**discontinuously** *adv*

**dis·cord** /ˈdɪskɔːd‖-ɔːrd/ *n* **1** [U] *formal* disagreement or quarrelling between people: *marital discord* | *discord within NATO* **2** [C,U] an unpleasant sound made by a group of musical notes that do not go together well —compare HARMONY (4)

**dis·cord·ant** /dɪsˈkɔːdənt‖-ɔːr-/ *adj* **1 strike/sound a discordant note** *literary* to seem strange and unsuitable in relation to everything around: *The modern decor strikes a discordant note in this 17th century building.* **2** a discordant sound is unpleasant because it is made up of musical notes that do not go together well **3** not in agreement: *discordant results from the experiment*

**dis·co·theque** /ˈdɪskətek, ˌdɪskəˈtek/ *n* [C] a DISCO

**dis·count¹** /ˈdɪskaʊnt/ *n* [C] **1** a reduction in the cost of goods that you are buying: *Do I get a discount if I buy a whole case of wine?* | **discount price/fare** (=cheaper than the usual price) | **discount store/shop/warehouse** (=where you can buy goods cheaply) **2 at a discount a)** bought or sold for less than the usual price **b)** *informal* not wanted or not regarded as valuable: *a ridiculous place where intelligence is at a discount* S3

**discount²** /dɪsˈkaʊnt‖ˈdɪskaʊnt/ *v* [T] to regard an idea, opinion, or piece of news as unimportant or unlikely to be true: *Larry tends to discount any suggestion I make in meetings.* | **discount the possibility of** (=think that something is very unlikely to happen) *General Hausken had not discounted the possibility of aerial attack.*

**dis·coun·te·nance** /dɪsˈkaʊntɪ̈nəns/ *v* [T] *formal* to stop someone from doing something by showing that you disapprove of their behaviour

**dis·cour·age** /dɪsˈkʌrɪdʒ‖-ˈkɜːr-/ *v* [T] **1** to prevent or try to prevent someone from doing something by making the action difficult or unpleasant, or by showing them that it would not be a good thing to do: *You should install locks on all your windows to discourage burglars.* | **discourage sb from doing sth** *We ought to be focusing on discouraging kids from smoking.* **2** to make someone think that they will not be able to succeed in doing something so that they no longer want to continue doing it: *Students soon get discouraged if you criticize them too often.* —opposite ENCOURAGE

**dis·cour·age·ment** /dɪsˈkʌrɪdʒmənt‖-ˈkɜːr-/ *n* **1** [U] a feeling that you have lost confidence or determination and no longer want to continue doing something **2** [U] the act of trying to discourage someone from doing something **3** [C] something that discourages you

**dis·cour·a·ging** /dɪsˈkʌrɪdʒɪŋ‖-ˈkɜːr-/ *adj* making you lose the confidence or determination you need to continue doing something: *The test results so far encountered have been very discouraging.* —**discouragingly** *adv*

**dis·course¹** /ˈdɪskɔːs‖-ɔːrs/ *n* **1** [C] a serious speech or piece of writing on a particular subject: [+ **on/upon**] *Professor Grant delivered a long discourse on aspects of moral theology.* **2** [U] serious conversation between people: *You can't expect meaningful discourse when you two disagree so violently.* **3** [U] the language used in particular kinds of speech or writing: *scientific discourse* W3

**discourse²** /dɪs'kɔːs‖-ɔːrs/ *v*

**discourse on/upon** sth *phr v* [T] to make a long formal speech about something: *Mrs. Hitchins discoursed at length on the ignorance of the frontier people.*

**dis·cour·te·ous** /dɪs'kɜːtiəs‖-ɜːr-/ *adj formal* not polite, and not showing respect for other people: *Cameron was not really interested, but it would be discourteous to say so.* —**discourteously** *adv* —**discourteousness** *n* [U]

**dis·cour·te·sy** /dɪs'kɜːtəsi‖-ɜːr-/ *n* [C, U] *formal* an action or behaviour that is not polite

S2 W1 **dis·cov·er** /dɪs'kʌvə‖-ər/ *v* [T] **1** to find something that was hidden or that people did not know about before: *I've just discovered a secret drawer in my old desk.* | *The Curies are best known for discovering radium.* —see INVENT (USAGE) **2** to find out something yourself, without being told about it: **discover that** *Police discovered that Kim's son was dealing in drugs.* | [+ **who/what/how etc**] *Emily's not even two, but she's discovered how to open doors.* **3** to notice someone who is very good at something and help them to become successful and well-known —**discoverer** *n* [C]

W3 **dis·cov·e·ry** /dɪs'kʌvəri/ *n* **1** [C] a fact or thing that someone discovers that was hidden or not known about before: *recent archaeological discoveries* | **make a discovery** *Astronomers have made significant discoveries about our galaxy.* **2** [C] something that you learn or find out yourself, without being told about it: [+ **that**] *The discovery that her assistant had lied made Patty decide to fire him.* **3** [U] the act of discovering something: [+ **of**] *The discovery of oil in Alaska was a boon to the economy.*

**dis·cred·it¹** /dɪs'kredɪ̈t/ *v* [T] **1** to make people stop respecting or trusting someone or something: *Black's remarks were taken out of context in an effort to discredit him.* **2** to make people stop believing in a particular idea: *Some of Freud's theories have now been discredited.*

**discredit²** *n* loss of other people's respect or trust: **to sb's discredit** *I know enough to her discredit* (=enough bad things about her) *not to vote for her.* | **bring discredit on/to** (=make people stop respecting someone or something) *Their outrageous behaviour has brought discredit on English football.*

**dis·cred·i·ta·ble** /dɪs'kredɪ̈təbəl/ *adj* bad or wrong, and making people lose respect for you or trust in you: *a discreditable secret* —**discreditably** *adv*

**di·screet** /dɪ'skriːt/ *adj* **1** done or said in a careful way so that you do not offend, upset, or embarrass people: *It wasn't very discreet of you to ring me up at the office.* | *That morning I began making discreet inquiries.* **2** careful not to talk about things that other people want to keep secret: *Don't worry about my secretary hearing us; he's very discreet.* —opposite INDISCREET —compare DISCRETE —**discreetly** *adv*

**di·screp·an·cy** /dɪ'skrepənsi/ *n* [C,U] a difference between two amounts, details, reports etc that ought to be the same: [+ **in**] *How do you explain these discrepancies in the accounts?* | [+ **between**] *There are big discrepancies between what Margaret says and what you say.*

**di·screte** /dɪ'skriːt/ *adj formal* separate: *There are two discrete breeding groups on the island.* —compare DISCREET —**discretely** *adv* —**discreteness** *n* [U]

**di·scre·tion** /dɪ'skreʃən/ *n* [U] **1** the ability and right to decide exactly what should be done in a particular situation: *Promotions are left to the discretion of the supervisor.* | **at sb's discretion** (=according to someone's decision or wishes) *The size of your payment may be changed at your discretion.* **2** the ability to deal with situations in a way that does not offend or embarrass people, especially by keeping other people's secrets: *It's a delicate matter, Mr Nagel, that must be handled with the utmost discretion.* | **be the soul of discretion** (=be extremely discreet) **3 discretion is the better part of valour** used to say that it is better to be careful than to take unnecessary risks

**di·scre·tion·a·ry** /dɪ'skreʃənəri‖-neri/ *adj* not controlled by strict rules, but left for someone to make a decision about in each particular situation: *the court's discretionary powers*

**di·scrim·i·nate** /dɪ'skrɪmɪ̈neɪt/ *v* **1** [I,T] to recognize a difference between things: [+ **between**] *It's sometimes difficult to discriminate between edible and poisonous mushrooms.* | **discriminate sth from** *You must learn to discriminate fact from opinion.* **2** [I] to treat people differently from each other in an unfair way: [+ **against**] *Are you saying the law discriminates against the disabled?* | **discriminate in favour of** *As an employer, she always discriminates in favour of women.*

**di·scrim·i·nat·ing** /dɪ'skrɪmɪ̈neɪtɪŋ/ *adj* able to judge what is of good quality and what is not: *We have a large wine list for those of discriminating taste.*

**di·scrim·i·na·tion** /dɪˌskrɪmɪ̈'neɪʃən/ *n* [U] **1** the practice of treating one particular group in society in an unfair way: [+ **against**] *Laws have got to be tougher to stop discrimination against the disabled.* | [+ **in favour of**] *discrimination in favour of university graduates* | **racial discrimination** (=discrimination against someone who is of another race or colour) | **sex discrimination** (=discrimination against women) —see also POSITIVE DISCRIMINATION, REVERSE DISCRIMINATION **2** the ability to judge what is of good quality and what is not

**di·scur·sive** /dɪ'skɜːsɪv‖-ɜːr-/ *adj* changing from one subject to another without any clear plan: *a discursive style of writing* —**discursively** *adv* —**discursiveness** *n* [U]

**dis·cus** /'dɪskəs/ *n* [C] a heavy plate-shaped object which is thrown as far as possible as a sport

**di·scuss** /dɪ'skʌs/ *v* [T] **1** to talk about something with another person or a group in order to exchange ideas or decide something: *Sandy won't ever discuss money.* | **discuss sth with sb** *I'd like to discuss my contract with you.* | **discuss what/who/where etc** *We're here to discuss what we can do to prevent crime.* —see SPEAK (USAGE) **2** to talk or write about something in detail and consider different ideas or opinions about it: *Chapter One discusses the rise of the city-state on the European continent.*

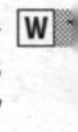

**di·scus·sion** /dɪ'skʌʃən/ *n* [C,U] **1** the act of discussing something, or a conversation in which people discuss something: **have a discussion (about)** *Yes, on Friday we had a long discussion about the wording of the proposal.* | **under discussion** (=being discussed) *The section now under discussion focuses on tenants' rights.* | **be up for discussion** (=be something that can be discussed and possibly changed) *Joe, I'm sorry, but item three is not up for discussion.* **2** something that is written about a subject that considers different ideas or opinions about it: *the report's discussion of the legislation*

**dis·dain¹** /dɪs'deɪn/ *n* [U] a complete lack of respect that you show for someone or something because you think they are not at all worth paying attention to: [+ **for**] *He maintained an obvious disdain for the customs of the local people.* | **treat sb/sth with disdain** *Mrs Strachan's evidence was treated with disdain by the prosecution.*

**disdain²** *v* **1** [T] to have no respect for someone or something, and believe they are unimportant **2 disdain to do sth** to refuse to do something because you are too proud to do it: *Tom Butler disdained to reply to such a trivial question.*

**dis·dain·ful** /dɪs'deɪnfəl/ *adj* showing that you do not respect someone or something and think that they are unimportant: *a long disdainful look* | [+ **of**] *There are some in the sport who are disdainful of amateurs.* —**disdainfully** *adv*

**dis·ease** /dɪ'ziːz/ *n* **1** [C,U] an illness or unhealthy condition in your body, especially one caused by infection: **eye/liver/kidney etc disease** *Heart disease runs in our family.* | **cause disease** *filthy insanitary conditions that cause disease* | **infections/contagious disease** (=easily passed from one person to another) *vaccination against infectious diseases such as typhoid* | **suffer from a disease** (=have a disease) *She suffers from a rare disease of the central nervous system.* | **catch/contract a**

**disease** (=get a disease by being infected) **2** [C] something that is seriously wrong with society or with someone's mind, behaviour etc: *Loneliness is a disease of our urban communities.* —see also HEART DISEASE, SOCIAL DISEASE —**diseased** *adj*: *diseased muscles | a diseased plant*

**USAGE NOTE: DISEASE**

WORD CHOICE: **disease, illness**

Though **illness** and **disease** are often used in the same way and are equally common in spoken English, **illness** is really the state, or length of time, of being unwell (usually caused by some **disease). ***She died after a long illness. | How many working days have you missed through illness?*

It is **diseases** that have medical names, are related to parts of the body, and can be caught, carried and passed on if they are infectious: *a kidney/sexually-transmitted disease/infectious disease/Alzheimer's disease.* However, you would usually talk about *mental illness* or a *terminal/critical illness.*

This graph shows some of the words most commonly used with the noun **disease**.

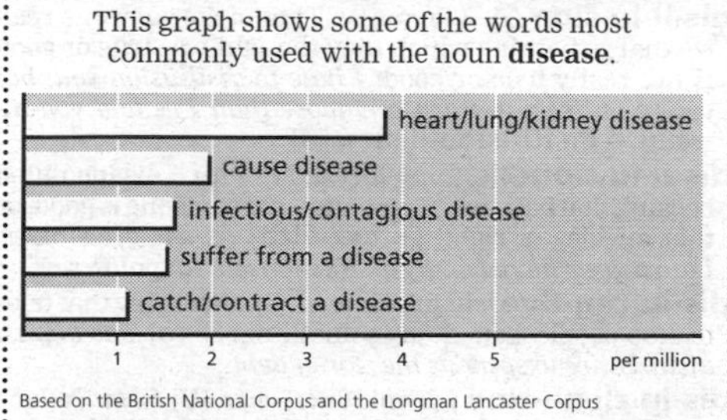


Based on the British National Corpus and the Longman Lancaster Corpus

**dis·em·bark** /ˌdɪsɪ̵mˈbɑːk‖-ɑːrk/ *v* **1** [I] to get off a ship or aircraft —opposite EMBARK **2** [T] to put people or goods onto the shore from a ship —**disembarkation** /ˌdɪsembɑːˈkeɪʃən‖-bɑːr-/ *n* [U]

**dis·em·bod·ied** /ˌdɪsɪ̵mˈbɒdid◂‖-ˈbɑː-/ *adj* **1** existing without a body or separated from a body: *disembodied spirits* **2** a disembodied sound or voice comes from someone who cannot be seen

**dis·em·bow·el** /ˌdɪsɪ̵mˈbaʊəl/ *v* **disembowelled, disembowelling** *BrE*, **disemboweled, disemboweling** *AmE* [T] to remove someone's bowels (BOWEL (1)) —**disembowelment** *n* [U]

**dis·en·chant·ed** /ˌdɪsɪ̵nˈtʃɑːntɪ̵d‖-ˈtʃænt-/ *adj* disappointed with someone or something, and no longer believing that they are good, exciting, or right: [+ **with**] *By that time I was becoming disenchanted with the whole idea.* —**disenchantment** *n* [U]

**dis·en·fran·chise** /ˌdɪsɪnˈfræntʃaɪz/ *v* [T] to take away from someone their right to vote —**disenfranchisement** /-tʃɪzmənt‖-tʃaɪz-/ *n* [U]

**dis·en·gage** /ˌdɪsɪ̵nˈgeɪdʒ/ *v* **1** [T] to separate something from something else that is fastened to it or holding it: **disengage yourself** *Sally found it difficult to disengage herself from his embrace.* **2** [I,T] if you disengage part of a machine or if it disengages, you make it move away from another part that it was connected to: *Disengage the gears when you park the car.* **3** [I] if two armies disengage, they stop fighting —**disengagement** *n* [U]

**dis·en·tan·gle** /ˌdɪsɪ̵nˈtæŋgəl/ *v* [T] **1 disentangle yourself (from)** to escape from a difficult situation that you are involved in **2** to remove knots from ropes, strings etc that have become twisted or tied together **3** to separate different ideas or pieces of information that have become confused together: *It's very difficult to disentangle fact from fiction in what she's saying.* —**disentanglement** *n* [U]

**dis·e·qui·lib·ri·um** /ˌdɪsekwɪ̵ˈlɪbriəm, ˌdɪsiː-/ *n* [U] *formal* a lack of balance in something

**dis·es·tab·lish** /ˌdɪsɪ̵ˈstæblɪʃ/ *v* [T] *formal* to officially decide that a particular church is no longer the official church of your country

**dis·fa·vour** *BrE*, **disfavor** *AmE* /dɪsˈfeɪvə‖-ər/ *n* [U] *formal* a feeling of dislike and disapproval: **look with disfavour on/upon** *The job creation program is looked upon with disfavor by the local community.*

**dis·fig·ure** /dɪsˈfɪgə‖-ˈfɪgjər/ *v* [T] to spoil the beauty that something naturally has: *good looks marred by a disfiguring scar* —**disfigured** *adj* —**disfigurement** *n* [C,U]

**dis·fran·chise** /dɪsˈfræntʃaɪz/ *v* [T] *especially AmE* to DISENFRANCHISE someone

**dis·gorge** /dɪsˈgɔːdʒ‖-ɔːrdʒ/ *v* **1** [T] *literary* if a vehicle or building disgorges people, they come out of it in a large group **2** [T] if something disgorges what was inside it, it lets it pour out: *Chimneys in the valley were disgorging smoke into the air.* **3** [I,T] if a river disgorges, it flows into the sea: *The Mississippi disgorges its waters into the Gulf of Mexico.* **4** [T] to give back something that you have taken illegally **5** [T] to bring food back up from your stomach through your mouth

**dis·grace¹** /dɪsˈgreɪs/ *n* **1** [U] the complete loss of other people's respect because you have done something they strongly disapprove of: *Smith faced total public disgrace after the incident.* | **in disgrace** *Toranaga's father sent my mother away in disgrace.* **2 sth is a disgrace** used to say that something should not be allowed to happen because it is very wrong or unfair: **it's an absolute/utter disgrace** *It's an absolute disgrace, the way he treats his wife.* **3 be a disgrace to** to have a very bad effect on people's opinion of the family or other group that you belong to: *Your conduct is a disgrace to the medical profession, and I'll see your licence is revoked.*

**disgrace²** *v* [T] to do something so bad that people lose respect for your family or for the group you belong to: *How could you disgrace us all like that?* | **disgrace yourself** *Well, I'm not the one who disgraced herself at a friend's wedding!* | **be (publicly) disgraced** (=be made to feel ashamed, especially in public)

**dis·grace·ful** /dɪsˈgreɪsfəl/ *adj* extremely bad or unacceptable: *It's a disgraceful state of affairs when decent folk are afraid to leave their homes.* —**disgracefully** *adv*

**dis·grun·tled** /dɪsˈgrʌntld/ *adj* annoyed, unhappy, and disappointed, especially because things have not happened in the way that you wanted: *a disgruntled client*

**dis·guise¹** /dɪsˈgaɪz/ *v* [T] **1** to change someone's appearance so that they look like someone else and people cannot recognize them: **disguise yourself as** *Maybe you could disguise yourself as a waiter and sneak in there.* | **be disguised as** *He escaped across the border disguised as a priest.* **2** to change the appearance, sound, taste etc of something so that people do not recognize it: *There's no way you can disguise that southern accent.* **3** to hide something so that people will not notice it: *Try as he might, Dan couldn't disguise his feelings for Katie.* | **disguise the fact (that)** *There's no disguising the fact that business is bad.* | **thinly disguised** (=only slightly disguised) *The speech was seen by many as a thinly disguised attack on the president.*

**disguise²** *n* **1** [C, U] something that you wear to change your appearance and hide who you are, or the act of wearing this: *The beard, the glasses, and the German accent were all part of his disguise.* **2 in disguise a)** wearing a disguise: *I kept forgetting I was in disguise, and got a lot of funny looks.* **b)** made to seem like something else that is better: *'Tax reform' is just a tax increase in disguise.* —see also **blessing in disguise** (BLESSING (3))

**dis·gust¹** /dɪsˈgʌst, dɪz-/ *n* [U] **1** a very strong feeling of dislike that almost makes you sick, caused by something unpleasant: **with disgust** *Everybody except Joe looked at me with disgust.* **2** a feeling of annoyance and disappointment because of someone's unacceptable behaviour, the bad quality of something etc: **in disgust** *Sam threw his books down in disgust and stormed out of the room.* | **much to sb's disgust** *Much to my disgust I found that there were no toilets for the disabled.*

**disgust²** *v* [T] **1** to make someone feel very annoyed and disappointed about something unacceptable: *Enid said she was disgusted by the sex in the film.* | **be disgusted to find/hear/see etc** *Dear Sir: I was disgusted to see the picture on page one of Sunday's feature section.* **2** to make someone feel almost sick because of something unpleasant: *The thought of dissecting a frog disgusts me.*

S2 **dis·gust·ing** /dɪsˈɡʌstɪŋ, dɪz-/ *adj* **1** extremely unpleasant and making you feel sick: *"Here, hold this a minute." "Yuck! It's disgusting!"* **2** shocking and unacceptable: *Sixty pounds for a thirty-minute consultation. I think that's disgusting!* | *Man, do you have a disgusting imagination.* —compare NAUSEATING —**disgustingly** *adv: They're disgustingly rich.*

S3 **dish¹** /dɪʃ/ *n* [C] **1** a flat round container with not very high sides, from which food is served on the table: *a serving dish* | *a vegetable dish* —compare BOWL¹ (1) **2 the dishes** all the plates, cups, bowls etc that have been used to eat a meal and need to be washed: **do/wash the dishes** *I'll just do the dishes before we go.* —see picture at CLEAN² **3** food cooked or prepared in a particular way as a meal: *a wonderful pasta dish* **4 be a dish** *informal* to be sexually attractive —see also SIDE DISH, SATELLITE DISH

**dish²** *v* [T] *old-fashioned* **1 dish the dirt** *informal* to spend time talking about other people's private lives and saying unkind or shocking things about them **2 dish sb's hopes/chances** *especially BrE* to prevent someone from doing something that they hoped to do

**dish** sth ↔ **out** *phr v* [T] *informal* **1** to give something to various people in a careless way: *We'll probably dish out some leaflets there too.* | *Portnoy still tends to dish out unwanted advice.* **2** to serve food to people: *Sam's dishing out sandwiches if you want one.* **3 sb can dish it out but they can't take it** used to say that someone is quick to criticize others but does not accept criticism well

**dish up** *phr v* [I,T] to put food for a meal into dishes, ready to be eaten: **dish sth ↔ up** *Could you dish up the vegetables? They're there, on the sideboard.*

**dis·ha·bille** /ˌdɪsəˈbiːl/ *n* [U] *AmE* the usual American form of DÉSHABILLÉ

**dis·har·mo·ny** /dɪsˈhɑːməni‖-ɑːr-/ *n* [U] *formal* disagreement about important things that makes people be unfriendly to each other —**disharmonious** /ˌdɪshɑːˈməʊniəs‖-hɑːrˈmoʊ-/ *adj*

**dish·cloth** /ˈdɪʃklɒθ‖-klɔːθ/ *n* [C] a cloth used for washing dishes —see picture on page 833

**dis·heart·ened** /dɪsˈhɑːtnd‖-ɑːrtn/ *adj* disappointed so that you lose hope and the determination to continue doing something: *If young children don't see quick results they grow disheartened.* —**dishearten** *v* [T]

**dis·heart·en·ing** /dɪsˈhɑːtn-ɪŋ‖-ɑːr-/ *adj* making you lose hope and determination: **be disheartening to hear/see etc sth** *It's disheartening to see what little progress has been made.* —**dishearteningly** *adv*

**di·shev·elled** *BrE*, **disheveled** *AmE* /dɪˈʃevəld/ *adj* dishevelled clothes, hair etc are very untidy: *Pam arrived late, dishevelled and out of breath.*

**dis·hon·est** /dɪsˈɒnɪst‖-ˈɑː-/ *adj* not honest: *Unfortunately there are dishonest traders about.* —**dishonestly** *adv*

**dis·hon·est·y** /dɪsˈɒnɪsti‖-ˈɑː-/ *n* [U] dishonest behaviour

**dis·hon·our¹** *BrE*, **dishonor** *AmE* /dɪsˈɒnə‖-ˈɑːnər/ *n* [U] *formal* loss of respect from other people because you have behaved in a morally unacceptable way: **bring dishonour on** *You've brought enough dishonour on your family already without causing any more trouble.*

**dishonour²** *BrE*, **dishonor** *AmE* *v* [T] **1** *formal* to make your family, country, profession etc lose the respect of other people **2** if a bank dishonours a cheque, it refuses to pay out money for it

**dis·hon·ou·ra·ble** *BrE*, **dishonorable** *AmE* /dɪsˈɒnərəbəl‖-ˈɑː-/ *adj* not morally correct or acceptable: *There's nothing dishonourable in charging for advice.*

**dishonourable dis·charge** /·ˌ···· ˈ··/ *n* [C,U] an order to someone to leave the army because they have behaved in a morally unacceptable way

**dish·pan** /ˈdɪʃpæn/ *n* [C] *AmE* a large bowl which you use for washing dishes in

**dish tow·el** /ˈ· ˌ··/ *n* [C] *AmE* a cloth used for drying dishes; TEA TOWEL *BrE*

**dish·wash·er** /ˈdɪʃˌwɒʃə‖,-ˌwɒːʃər, -ˌwɑː-/ *n* [C] a machine that washes dishes —see picture on page 833

**dish·wash·ing liq·uid** /ˈdɪʃwɒʃɪŋ ˌlɪkwɪd‖-wɒː-, -wɑː-/ *n* [U] *AmE* liquid soap used to wash dishes; WASHING-UP LIQUID *BrE* —see picture on page 833

**dish·wa·ter** /ˈdɪʃˌwɔːtə‖-ˌwɒːtər, -ˌwɑː-/ *n* [U] **1** dirty water that dishes have been washed in **2 like dishwater** *informal* tea or coffee that tastes like dishwater tastes unpleasantly weak

**dishwater blond** /ˌ··· ˈ·/ *adj AmE old-fashioned* dishwater blond hair is a dull brown colour

**dish·y** /ˈdɪʃi/ *adj old-fashioned* sexually attractive

**dis·il·lu·sion** /ˌdɪsɪ̈ˈluːʒən/ *v* [T] to make someone realize that something which they thought was true or good is not really true or good: *I hate to disillusion you, but you're unlikely to learn any more than I've told you already.* —**disillusionment** *n* [U]

**dis·il·lu·sioned** /ˌdɪsɪ̈ˈluːʒənd◂/ *adj* disappointed because you have lost your belief that someone is good, or that an idea is right: [+ **by/with**] *As she grew older, Laura grew increasingly disillusioned with politics.*

**dis·in·cen·tive** /ˌdɪsɪ̈nˈsentɪv/ *n* [C] something that tries to stop people from doing something: [+ **to**] *The biggest disincentive to spend is the fear of debt.*

**dis·in·cli·na·tion** /ˌdɪsɪŋklɪ̈ˈneɪʃən/ *n* [U] *formal* a lack of willingness to do something: *Very naturally there has been a disinclination to face up to these issues.*

**dis·in·clined** /ˌdɪsɪnˈklaɪnd/ *adj* **be/feel disinclined to do sth** *formal* to be unwilling to do something: *In the present case I feel disinclined to interfere in the matter.*

**dis·in·fect** /ˌdɪsɪ̈nˈfekt/ *v* [T] to clean something with a chemical that destroys BACTERIA: *First use some iodine to disinfect the wound.* | *Disinfect the area thoroughly.*

**dis·in·fec·tant** /ˌdɪsɪ̈nˈfektənt/ *n* [C,U] a chemical that destroys BACTERIA, or a cleaning product that does this

**dis·in·for·ma·tion** /ˌdɪsɪnfəˈmeɪʃən ‖ -fər-/ *n* [U] false information which is given intentionally in order to hide the truth or confuse people, especially in political situations: *government disinformation about the effects of nuclear testing* —compare MISINFORMATION

**dis·in·gen·u·ous** /ˌdɪsɪ̈nˈdʒenjuəs◂/ *adj* not sincere and slightly dishonest: *McEwan's claims about the incident strike me as disingenuous.* —**disingenuously** *adv*

**dis·in·her·it** /ˌdɪsɪ̈nˈherɪ̈t/ *v* [T] to take away from someone, especially your son or daughter, their legal right to receive your money or property after your death —**disinheritance** *n* [U]

**dis·in·te·grate** /dɪsˈɪntɪ̈ɡreɪt/ *v* [I,T] **1** to break up or make something break up into very small pieces: *The whole plane just disintegrated in mid-air.* **2** to become weaker or less united and be gradually destroyed: *a society disintegrating under economic pressures* —**disintegration** /dɪsˌɪntɪ̈ˈɡreɪʃən/

**dis·in·ter** /ˌdɪsɪnˈtɜː‖-ˈtɜːr/ *v* **disinterred, disinterring** [T] *formal* to dig a dead body from a grave —opposite INTER —**disinterment** *n* [U]

**dis·in·terest** /dɪsˈɪntrɪ̈st/ *n* [U] a lack of interest: [+ **in**] *The exception to Balfour's disinterest in social issues was education.*

**dis·in·terest·ed** /dɪsˈɪntrɪ̈stɪ̈d/ *adj* **1** able to judge a situation fairly because you are not concerned with gaining any personal advantage from it; OBJECTIVE² (1): *disinterested advice* **2** sometimes used to mean 'uninterested', although many people think this is wrong —**disinterestedly** *adv* —**disinterestedness** *n* [U]

**USAGE NOTE: DISINTERESTED**

WORD CHOICE: **uninterested (in), disinterested (in)**

**Uninterested (in** something) means not interested in it: *I'm completely uninterested in football.*|*an uninterested student* (=bored)

If someone is **disinterested** they are able to be fair because they are not involved in a situation where other people are fighting, disagreeing etc, and not expecting to gain anything themselves from it: *We need the advice of a disinterested party* (=someone who is not directly involved).

Native speakers of English also sometimes say that people are **disinterested in** things, meaning the same as **uninterested in**, though is usually considered to be incorrect: *I'm completely disinterested in football.*

**dis·in·vest·ment** /ˌdɪsɪnˈvestmənt/ *n* [U] *BrE technical* the act of taking your money out of a company, by selling your shares (SHARE[2] (6)) in it; DIVESTMENT *AmE*

**dis·joint·ed** /dɪsˈdʒɔɪntɪd/ *adj* a disjointed speech or piece of writing is one in which the words or ideas are not well connected together or arranged in a reasonable order —**disjointedly** *adv* —**disjointedness** *n* [U]

**dis·junc·tive** /dɪsˈdʒʌŋktɪv/ *adj technical* a disjunctive CONJUNCTION (3) expresses a choice or opposition between two ideas. For example, 'or' is a disjunctive conjunction

**dis·junc·ture** /dɪsˈdʒʌŋktʃə‖-ər/ *n* [C,U] a difference between two things that you would expect to be in agreement: *a disjuncture between his private and public life*

S 2 W 3 **disk** /dɪsk/ *n* [C] **1** a flat circular piece of plastic or metal used for storing computer information —see picture on page 837 **2** the usual American spelling of DISC —see also COMPACT DISC, FLOPPY DISK, HARD DISK, LASER DISK

**disk drive** /ˈ· ·/ *n* [C] a piece of equipment in a computer system that is used to pass information to or from a disk

**dis·kette** /dɪsˈket‖ˈdɪsket/ *n* [C] *AmE* a FLOPPY DISK

**dis·like**[1] /dɪsˈlaɪk/ *v* [T, not in progressive] to think someone or something is unpleasant and not like them: *Why do you dislike her so much?*|**dislike doing sth** *Tom dislikes going to the dentist, that's why he's crabby.*

**dislike**[2] /dɪsˈlaɪk, ˈdɪslaɪk/ *n* **1** [C,U] a feeling of not liking someone or something: **[+ of/for]** *She shared her mother's dislike of housework.*|**intense dislike** (=very strong dislike) *His colleagues regarded him with intense dislike.*|**take a dislike to** (=decide that you dislike someone) *When the two men met, they took an instant dislike to each other.* **2 dislikes** [plural] the things that you do not like: **likes and dislikes** *A good hotel manager should know his regular guests' likes and dislikes.*

**dis·lo·cate** /ˈdɪsləkeɪt‖-loʊ-/ *v* [T] **1** to injure a joint so that the two bones at the joint are moved out of their normal position: *I dislocated my shoulder playing football.* **2** to spoil the way in which a plan, system, or service is aranged, so that it cannot work normally; DISRUPT —**dislocated** *adj*: *a dislocated shoulder* —**dislocation** /ˌdɪsləˈkeɪʃən‖-loʊ-/ *n* [C,U]|*The storm caused considerable dislocation of air traffic.*

**dis·lodge** /dɪsˈlɒdʒ‖-ˈlɑːdʒ/ *v* [T] **1** to force or knock something out of its position: *Ian dislodged a few stones as he climbed up the rock.* **2** to make someone leave a place or lose a position of power: *the revolution that failed to dislodge the British in 1919* —compare LODGE[1] (3) —**dislodgement** *n* [U]

**dis·loy·al** /dɪsˈlɔɪəl/ *adj* unfaithful to your friends, your country, or the group you belong to: **[+ to]** *He felt he had been disloyal to his friends.* —**disloyally** *adv* —**disloyalty** *n* [C,U]

**dis·mal** /ˈdɪzməl/ *adj* **1** a dismal place, situation, thought etc has nothing pleasant in it and makes it difficult for you to feel happy and hopeful: *The future looks pretty dismal right now.*|*a dismal, grey November afternoon* **2** bad and unsuccessful: *Your record so far is pretty dismal.*|**be a dismal failure** *His scheme was a dismal failure.* —**dismally** *adv*

**dis·man·tle** /dɪsˈmæntl/ *v* **1** [T] to take a machine or piece of equipment apart so that it is in separate pieces: *Chris dismantled the bike in five minutes.* **2** [T] to gradually get rid of a system or organization: *an election promise to dismantle the existing tax legislation*

**dis·may**[1] /dɪsˈmeɪ/ *n* [U] the worry, disappointment, and unhappiness you feel when something unpleasant happens: **with/in dismay** *Amanda read her exam results with dismay.*|*They stared at each other in dismay.*|**to sb's dismay** *I found to my dismay that I had left my notes behind.*|**fill sb with dismay** *The thought of making the journey filled him with dismay.*

**dismay**[2] *v* [T] to make someone feel worried, disappointed, and upset: **be dismayed to see/hear etc** *Brenda was dismayed to find that work on the roof had not even begun.*|**be dismayed at** *We were dismayed at the cost of the repairs.*

**dis·mem·ber** /dɪsˈmembə‖-ər/ *v* [T] **1** to cut a body into pieces or tear it apart **2** to divide a country, area, or organization into smaller parts —**dismemberment** *n* [U]

**dis·miss** /dɪsˈmɪs/ *v* [T] W 3

**1** ▶ **IDEA** ◀ to refuse to consider someone's idea, opinion etc, without thinking carefully about it: **dismiss sth as** *He just laughed and dismissed my suggestion as unrealistic.*|**dismiss sth out of hand** (=dismiss something completely)

**2** ▶ **JOB** ◀ to remove someone from their job: **dismiss sb for** *Will they dismiss Woods for stealing the money?*|**dismiss sb from** *Bryant was dismissed from his post.*

**3** ▶ **SEND AWAY** ◀ to send someone away or allow them to go: *The teacher might dismiss the class early today because of the snow.*

**4** ▶ **IN A COURT** ◀ if a judge dismisses a court CASE[1] (9a), they stop it before a result is reached: *The case was dismissed owing to lack of evidence.*

**5** ▶ **SPORT** ◀ to end the INNINGS of a player or a team in the game of CRICKET (2)

**dis·miss·al** /dɪsˈmɪsəl/ *n* **1** [C,U] an act of removing someone from their job: **unfair dismissal** *Wilson was claiming compensation for unfair dismissal.* **2** [U] a refusal to consider something seriously

**dis·miss·ive** /dɪsˈmɪsɪv/ *adj* refusing to consider someone or something seriously: **[+ of]** *Why, I wonder, is Mr Sykes so dismissive of the protesters?* —**dismissively** *adv*

**dis·mount** /dɪsˈmaʊnt/ *v* **1** [I + **from**] to get off a horse, bicycle, or MOTORCYCLE **2** [T] to take something, especially a gun, down from its base or support

**dis·o·be·di·ent** /ˌdɪsəˈbiːdiənt, ˌdɪsəʊ-‖ˌdɪsə-, ˌdɪsoʊ-/ *adj* deliberately not doing what you are told to do by your parents, teacher, employer etc —**disobediently** *adv* —**disobedience** *n* [U] —see also CIVIL DISOBEDIENCE

**dis·o·bey** /ˌdɪsəˈbeɪ, ˌdɪsəʊ-‖ˌdɪsə-, ˌdɪsoʊ-/ *v* [I,T] to refuse to do what someone with authority tells you to do, or refuse to obey a rule or law: *Remember you're in the army; if you disobey orders you'll get a court martial.*

**dis·o·bli·ging** /ˌdɪsəˈblaɪdʒɪŋ/ *adj formal* unwilling to help someone or do what they want —**disoblige** *v* [T]

**dis·or·der** /dɪsˈɔːdə‖-ˈɔːrdər/ *n* **1** [U] a situation in which things or people are very untidy or disorganized: **in disorder** *Everything was in disorder, but nothing seemed to be stolen.* **2** [C,U] a situation in which many people disobey the law, especially in a violent way, and are impossible to control: **civil/public disorder** *a campaign of civil disorder* **3** [C] an illness which prevents part of your body from working properly: **skin/stomach/liver etc disorder** *a rare genetic disorder* 

**dis·or·dered** /dɪsˈɔːdəd‖-ˈɔːrdərd/ *adj* **1** untidy or not arranged, planned, or done in a clear order **2** if someone is mentally disordered, their mind is not working in a normal and healthy way

**dis·or·der·ly** /dɪsˈɔːdəli‖-ˈɔːrdər-/ *adj* **1** untidy or lacking order: *Joe left his clothes in a disorderly heap.* **2** behaving in a noisy violent way and causing trouble in a public place: **drunk and disorderly** (=behaving very badly in a public place because you have drunk too much alcohol) —**disorderliness** *n* [U]

**disorderly house** /·ˌ··· ˈ·/ *n* [C] *BrE law* a place where men pay to have sex; BROTHEL

**dis·or·gan·ized** also **-ised** *BrE* /dɪsˈɔːgənaɪzd‖-ˈɔːr-/ *adj* not arranged or planned in a clear order, or lacking any kind of plan or system: *The conference arrangements were completely disorganized.* | *The whole thing's being run by a bunch of disorganized amateurs.* —compare UNORGANIZED

**dis·or·i·en·tate** /dɪsˈɔːriənteɪt/ also **dis·or·i·ent** /dɪsˈɔːriənt/ *AmE v* [T] **1** to make someone not know which direction they have come from or are going in **2** to make someone uncertain about what is happening around them and unable to think clearly —**disorientating, disorienting** *adj* **disorientation** /dɪsˌɔːriənˈteɪʃən/ *n* [U]

**dis·or·ien·tat·ed** /dɪsˈɔːriənteɪtɪ̣d/ also **dis·or·i·ent·ed** /dɪsˈɔːrienteɪtɪ̣d/ *adj, adv* **1** confused and not understanding what is happening around you: *His wife said he was disoriented and begged to be allowed to sleep.* **2** confused about which direction you are facing or which direction you should go

**dis·own** /dɪsˈəʊn‖-ˈoʊn/ *v* [T not in progressive] to say that you no longer have any connection with someone or something; REPUDIATE (3) *Frankly, I'm not surprised her family disowned her.*

**di·spar·age** /dɪˈspærɪdʒ/ *v* [T] *formal* to criticize someone or something in a way that shows you do not think they are very good or important: *Matcham's threatres were widely disparaged by architects.* —**disparagement** *n* [C, U]

**di·spar·a·ging** /dɪˈspærədʒɪŋ/ *adj* disparaging remarks criticize someone or something and show that you do not think they are very good —**disparagingly** *adv*

**dis·pa·rate** /ˈdɪspərɪ̣t/ *adj formal* very different and not connected with each other: *The challenge is to make disparate computer systems work together.* —**disparately** *adv*

**di·spar·i·ty** /dɪˈspærɪ̣ti/ *n* [C, U] *formal* a difference between two or more things, especially an unfair one: [+ **in/between**] *We are still seeing a disparity between the rates of pay for men and women.* —see also PARITY

**dis·pas·sion·ate** /dɪsˈpæʃənɪ̣t/ *adj* not influenced by emotion and therefore able to make fair decisions: *a dispassionate view* —**dispassionately** *adv*

**di·spatch¹** also **despatch** *BrE* /dɪˈspætʃ/ *v* [T] **1** *formal* to send someone or something somewhere for a particular purpose: **dispatch sb/sth to** *A reporter was dispatched to Naples to cover the riot.* **2** *old-fashioned* to deliberately kill a person or animal **3** *old-fashioned* to finish all of something

**dispatch²** also **despatch** *BrE n* **1** [C] a message sent between military or government officials: *a dispatch from headquarters* **2** [C] a report sent to a newspaper from one of its writers who is in another town or country **3 with dispatch** *formal* if you do something with dispatch, you do it well and quickly **4** [singular] the act of sending people or things to a particular place —see also **mentioned in dispatches** (MENTION¹ (7))

**dispatch box** /ˈ·· ·/ *n* **1** [C] a box for holding official papers **2 the dispatch box** a box on a central table in the British Parliament next to which important members of parliament stand to make speeches

**dispatch rid·er** /ˈ·· ˌ··/ *n* [C] someone whose job is to take messages or packages by MOTORCYCLE or bicycle

**di·spel** /dɪˈspel/ *v* **dispelled, dispelling** [T] to stop someone believing or feeling something, especially because it is wrong or harmful: *The film aims to dispel the notion that AIDS only affects gay men.*

**di·spen·sa·ble** /dɪˈspensəbəl/ *adj* easy to get rid of because not really needed: *Part-time workers are considered dispensable in times of recession.* —opposite INDISPENSABLE

**di·spen·sa·ry** /dɪˈspensəri/ *n* [C] a place where medicines are prepared and given out, especially in a hospital —compare PHARMACY

**dis·pen·sa·tion** /ˌdɪspənˈseɪʃən, -pen-/ *n* **1** [C, U] special permission from someone in authority or a religious leader to do something that is not usually allowed: **special dispensation** *Caroline's marriage was annulled by special dispensation from the Church.* **2** [C] *formal* a religious or political system that has control over people's lives at a particular time **3** [U] *formal* the act of providing people with something as part of an official process: *the dispensation of justice*

**di·spense** /dɪˈspens/ *v* [T] **1** *formal* to give something to people, especially in fixed amounts: *Villagers dispensed tea to people involved in the accident.* **2** to prepare and give medicines to people **3** to officially provide something for people in a society: **dispense justice/punishments** (=decide whether or not someone is guilty of a crime and what punishment they should receive)

**dispense with** sb/sth *phr v* [T] *formal* to not use or do something that you usually use or do, because it is no longer necessary: **can dispense with** *I think we can dispense with a translator.* | **dispense with the formalities** (=not use very polite behaviour, such as introducing people to each other)

**di·spens·er** /dɪˈspensə‖-ər/ *n* [C] a machine in a public place which gives you things such as drinks or money when you press a button —see also CASH DISPENSER

**dispensing chem·ist** /·ˈ·· ˌ··/ *n* [C] *BrE* someone who is trained to sell medicines and advise people about them; PHARMACIST

**di·sper·sal** /dɪˈspɜːsəl‖-ɜːr-/ *n* [U] the act of spreading things over a wide area: *the dispersal of information*

**di·sperse** /dɪˈspɜːs‖-ɜːrs/ *v* [I,T] **1** if a group of people disperses or is dispersed, they separate and go away in different directions: *The police used tear gas to disperse the crowd.* **2** if something disperses or is dispersed, it spreads over a wide area: *The clouds dispersed as quickly as they had gathered.* —**dispersal** *n* [U]

**Dis·per·sion** /dɪˈspɜːʃən‖dɪˈspɜːrʒən/ *n* **the Dispersion** the DIASPORA

**dispersion** *n* [U] *technical* dispersal

**di·spir·ited** /dɪˈspɪrɪ̣tɪ̣d/ *adj* discouraged or without hope: *After six hours, dispirited and weary, they gave up the search.* —**dispiritedly** *adv*

**dis·place** /dɪsˈpleɪs/ *v* [T] **1** to take the place of someone or something: *Coal is being displaced by natural gas as a major source of energy.* **2** to make a group of people or animals have to leave the place where they normally live —**displaced** *adj*

**displaced per·son** /ˌ·· ˈ··/ *n plural* **displaced persons** [C] *technical* someone who has been forced to leave their country because of war or cruel treatment; REFUGEE

**dis·place·ment** /dɪsˈpleɪsmənt/ *n* **1** [U] the act of forcing a group of people or animals to leave the place where they usually live **2** [singular] *technical* the weight or VOLUME (1) of liquid that something such as a ship floating on it takes the place of

**displacement ac·tiv·i·ty** /·ˈ·· ·ˌ···/ *n* [C,U] *technical* something that is done in order to avoid doing something else that you do not want to think about

**di·splay¹** /dɪˈspleɪ/ *n* W3

**1** ▶ **ATTRACTIVE ARRANGEMENT** ◀ [C,U] an attractive arrangement of objects for people to look at or buy: [+ **of**] *a display of African tribal masks*

**2** ▶ **PERFORMANCE** ◀ [C] a public performance of something that is intended to entertain people: *a fireworks display* | [+ **of**] *a display of juggling*

**3 be on display** something that is on display is in a

public place where people can look at it: **put sth on display** *Mapplethorpe's photographs were first put on display in New York.*
**4 display of affection/temper/loyalty etc** an occasion when someone clearly shows a particular feeling, attitude, or quality
**5 ▶EQUIPMENT◀** [C] a piece of equipment that can show changing information, for example the screen of a computer

W2 **display**[2] *v* [T] **1** to show goods for sale in a shop, or paintings, historical objects etc in a public place: *shop windows displaying the latest fashions* **2** to clearly show a feeling, attitude, or quality by what you do or say: *All the musicians displayed considerable skill.* **3** if a computer or notice displays information, it shows information in a way that can be clearly seen: *Local train and bus times are displayed on the noticeboard.*

**dis·pleased** /dɪsˈpliːzd/ *adj formal* not satisfied and annoyed: *"We are most displeased," said the Queen.* —**displease** *v* [T]

**dis·plea·sure** /dɪsˈpleʒə‖-ər/ *n* [U] *formal* the feeling of being annoyed with someone because you do not approve of their behaviour: **incur sb's displeasure** (=make someone displeased)

**dis·port** /dɪˈspɔːt‖-ɔːrt/ *v* [T] **disport yourself** *old-fashioned* to amuse yourself by doing active enjoyable things: *a charming painting of lords and ladies disporting themselves by a lake*

**dis·po·sa·ble** /dɪˈspəʊzəbəl‖-ˈspoʊ-/ *adj* **1** intended to be used once or for a short time and then thrown away: *disposable nappies* **2** available to be used: *disposable resources*

**disposable in·come** /·,··· ˈ··/ *n* [U] the amount of money you have left to spend after you have paid your taxes, bills etc

**dis·pos·al** /dɪˈspəʊzəl‖-ˈspoʊ-/ *n* **1** [U] the act of getting rid of something: [+ **of**] *the safe disposal of radioactive waste* **2 at sb's disposal** available for someone to use: *Tanner had a considerable amount of cash at his disposal.* | **sb is at your (complete) disposal** (=someone is ready to help you in any way) **3** [C] *AmE informal* a small machine under the kitchen SINK[2] which breaks vegetable waste into small pieces; WASTE DISPOSAL *BrE* **4** [U] *formal* the act of putting people or things in a particular place or in a particular order

**dis·pose** /dɪˈspəʊz‖-ˈspoʊz/ *v* [T] *formal* to arrange things or put them in their places

**dispose of** sth *phr v* [T] **1** to get rid of something, especially something that is difficult to get rid of: *How did Dahmers dispose of his victims' bodies?* **2** to deal with something such as a problem or question successfully **3** to defeat an opponent

**dispose** sb **to** sth *phr v* [T usually in passive] to make someone more likely to feel or think a particular way about something

**dis·posed** /dɪˈspəʊzd‖-ˈspoʊzd/ *adj* [not before noun] **1 well/favourably/kindly disposed (to)** liking or approving of someone or something such as an idea or plan: *Management is favourably disposed to the idea of job-sharing.* **2 be disposed to do sth** *formal* feel willing to do something or behave in a particular way: *Johnson disagreed, but did not feel disposed to argue.* **3 be disposed to sth** *formal* to have a tendency towards something: *a man disposed to depression*

**dis·po·si·tion** /ˌdɪspəˈzɪʃən/ *n formal* **1** [C] a particular type of character which makes someone more likely to behave or react in a certain way; TEMPERAMENT: **have a cheerful/sunny disposition** (=have a happy character and behave in a happy way) | **people of a nervous disposition** *The film is not suitable for people of a nervous disposition.* **2** [U] a tendency to behave in a particular way: **have/show a disposition to do sth** *Neither side shows the slightest disposition to compromise.* **3** [C] the position or arrangement of something in a particular place: [+ **of**] *a map showing the disposition of the American forces* **4** [C,U] *law* the act of formally giving property to someone

**dis·pos·sess** /ˌdɪspəˈzes/ *v* [T, usually passive] *formal* to take property or land away from someone: **be dispossessed of sth** *black South Africans who had been dispossessed of their homes* —**dispossession** /-ˈzeʃən/ *n* [U]

**dis·pos·sessed** /ˌdɪspəˈzest◂/ *adj* **1** having had property or land taken away **2 the dispossessed** [plural] people who are dispossessed

**dis·proof** /dɪsˈpruːf/ *n* [C,U] *formal* a fact, argument etc that proves that something is wrong or false, or the act of proving that something is wrong or false

**dis·pro·por·tion** /ˌdɪsprəˈpɔːʃən‖-ɔːr-/ *n* [C,U] *formal* the lack of a suitable or equal relation between two or more things

**dis·pro·por·tion·ate** /ˌdɪsprəˈpɔːʃənɪ̣t◂‖-ɔːr-/ *adj* too much or too little in relation to something else: *the disproportionate amount of money being spent on defence projects* —**disproportionately** *adv*

**dis·prove** /dɪsˈpruːv/ *v* [T] to prove something false or wrong: *She was able to quote figures that disproved Smith's argument.*

**di·spu·ta·ble** /dɪˈspjuːtəbəl, ˈdɪspjʊ̣-/ *adj* something that is disputable is not definitely true or right and therefore is something that you can argue about; DEBATABLE —opposite INDISPUTABLE —**disputably** *adv*

**dis·pu·ta·tion** /ˌdɪspjʊ̣ˈteɪʃən/ *n* [C,U] *formal* a formal discussion about a subject which people cannot agree on

**dis·pu·ta·tious** /ˌdɪspjʊ̣ˈteɪʃəs/ *adj formal* tending to argue; ARGUMENTATIVE —**disputatiously** *adv*

**di·spute**[1] /dɪˈspjuːt, ˈdɪspjuːt/ *n* [C,U] W2
**1 ▶SERIOUS DISAGREEMENT◀** a situation in which two countries or groups of people quarrel or disagree with each other: *a border dispute* | *A prolonged labor dispute disrupted rail services.*
**2 be beyond dispute** if something is beyond dispute, everyone agrees that it is true or that it really happened: *It is beyond dispute that advances in medicine have enabled people to live longer.*
**3 be in/under dispute** if facts are in or under dispute, people do not agree about them
**4 be in dispute (with sb)** to disagree publicly with another person or group: *The miners were in dispute with their employers over pay.*
**5 be open to dispute** if something is open to dispute, it is not completely certain and not everyone agrees about it: *His interpretation of the poem is open to dispute.*

**dis·pute**[2] /dɪˈspjuːt/ *v* **1** [T] to say that you think something such as a fact or idea is not correct or true: *Few would dispute that travel broadens the mind.* **2** [I,T] to argue or disagree with someone: **hotly disputed** (=argued about with strong feelings or with anger) **3** [T] to argue with another country, group etc about who owns a piece of land: *The defending army disputed every inch of ground.*

**disputed ter·ri·to·ry** /·,·· ˈ····/ *n* [C,U] an area of land that is claimed by two or more countries

**dis·qual·i·fi·ca·tion** /dɪsˌkwɒlɪ̣fɪ̣ˈkeɪʃən‖-ˌkwɑː-/ *n* [C,U] a situation in which someone is stopped from doing an activity or taking part in a competition because they have broken a rule: *Drug-taking is punished by instant disqualification from the game.*

**dis·qual·i·fy** /dɪsˈkwɒlɪ̣faɪ‖-ˈkwɑː-/ *v* [T] **1** to stop someone taking part in a competition because they have broken a rule: [+ **from**] *Schumacher was disqualified from the race for ignoring a black flag.* **2** to prevent someone from doing a job or taking part in an activity, often unfairly: [+ **from**] *women in their 50's who are disqualified from working simply because of their age*

**dis·qui·et** /dɪsˈkwaɪət/ *n* [U] *formal* feelings of being anxious or not satisfied about something: [+ **over**] *Growing disquiet was voiced over police handling of terrorist investigations.*

**dis·qui·si·tion** /ˌdɪskwɪ̣ˈzɪʃən/ *n* [C] *formal* a long speech or written report

**dis·re·gard¹** /ˌdɪsrɪˈgɑːd‖-ɑːrd/ *v* [T] to ignore something or treat it as unimportant: *The judge ordered the jury to disregard the witness's last statement.*

**disregard²** *n* [U] the act of ignoring something that other people think is important: **complete/total/blatant disregard for** *Rudi drove with blatant disregard for his passengers' safety.*

**dis·re·pair** /ˌdɪsrɪˈpeə‖-ˈper/ *n* [U] buildings, roads etc that are in disrepair are in bad condition because they have not been repaired or looked after: **be in disrepair/fall into disrepair** *a fine Georgian mansion that had been allowed to fall into disrepair*

**dis·rep·u·ta·ble** /dɪsˈrepjətəbəl/ *adj* a disreputable person or organization is not respected because they are thought to be involved in dishonest or illegal activities —**disreputably** *adv* —**disreputableness** *n* [U]

**dis·re·pute** /ˌdɪsrɪˈpjuːt/ *n* [U] **bring sb/sth into disrepute** to make people stop trusting or having a good opinion of an activity, idea, organization etc: *When one policeman is convicted of corruption, it brings the whole system into disrepute.*

**dis·re·spect** /ˌdɪsrɪˈspekt/ *n* [U] **1** lack of respect for someone or for something such as the law **2 no disrespect (to)** *spoken* used when you are criticizing someone or something to say that you do not want to seem rude: *No disrespect to Adrian, but he's not very experienced.* —**disrespectful** *adj* —**disrespectfully** *adv*

**dis·robe** /dɪsˈrəʊb‖-ˈroʊb/ *v* [I] *formal or humorous* to take off your clothes

**dis·rupt** /dɪsˈrʌpt/ *v* [T] to prevent a situation, event, system etc from continuing in its usual way by causing problems: *We hope the move to Kansas won't disrupt the kids' schooling too much.*

**dis·rup·tion** /dɪsˈrʌpʃən/ *n* [C,U] a situation in which something is prevented from continuing in its normal way because of problems and difficulties: *The strike caused widespread disruption to train services.*

**dis·rup·tive** /dɪsˈrʌptɪv/ *adj* disruptive behaviour prevents something from continuing in its usual way and causes trouble: *a child who was disruptive in class* —**disruptively** *adv*

**diss** /dɪs/ *v* [T] *AmE slang* to make unfair and unkind remarks about someone

**dis·sat·is·fac·tion** /dɪˌsætəsˈfækʃən, dɪsˌsæ-/ *n* [U] a feeling of not being satisfied

**dis·sat·is·fied** /dɪˈsætəsfaɪd, dɪsˈsæ-/ *adj* not satisfied because something is not as good as you had expected: [+ **with**] *If for any reason you are dissatisfied with this product, please return it to the address below.*

**dis·sat·is·fy** /dɪˈsætəsfaɪ, dɪsˈsæ-/ *v* [T] to fail to satisfy someone or something

**dis·sect** /dɪˈsekt, daɪ-/ *v* [T] **1** to cut up the body of a dead person or animal in order to study it **2** to examine something in great detail so that you discover its faults or understand it better

**dis·sec·tion** /dɪˈsekʃən, daɪ-/ *n* [C,U] the act of cutting up the body of a dead person or animal to study it

**dis·sem·ble** /dɪˈsembəl/ *v* [I,T] *formal* to hide your true feelings, ideas, desires etc

**dis·sem·i·nate** /dɪˈseməneɪt/ *v* [T] *formal* to spread information, ideas etc to as many people as possible, especially in order to influence them —**dissemination** /dɪˌseməˈneɪʃən/ *n* [U] *the dissemination of information about new tax rules*

**dis·sen·sion** /dɪˈsenʃən/ *n* [C,U] disagreement and argument among a group of people: *On the issue of the single market, there was little dissension.*

**dis·sent¹** /dɪˈsent/ *n* **1** [U] refusal to accept an official opinion or an opinion that most people accept: *political dissent* **2** [C] *AmE* a judge's written statement giving their reasons for disagreeing with the other judges in a law case **3** [U] *old use* a disagreement with accepted religious beliefs, especially one that makes someone leave an established church —see also CONSENT¹, ASSENT¹

**dissent²** *v* [I] to say that you strongly disagree with an official opinion or decision, or one that is accepted by most people —**dissenter** *n* [C]

**dis·ser·ta·tion** /ˌdɪsəˈteɪʃən‖ˌdɪsər-/ *n* [C] a long piece of writing about a subject, especially one that you write as part of a university degree

**dis·ser·vice** /dɪˈsɜːvəs, dɪsˈsɜː‖-ɜːr-/ *n* **do a disservice to** to do something that harms someone or something, especially by giving other people a bad opinion about them: *The fans' behaviour has done the game a great disservice.*

**dis·si·dent** /ˈdɪsədənt/ *n* [C] someone who publicly criticizes a government or political party, especially in a country where this is not allowed —**dissident** *adj*: *a group of dissident writers* —**dissidence** *n* [U]

**dis·sim·i·lar** /dɪˈsɪmələ, dɪsˈsɪ-‖-ər/ *adj* not the same —**dissimilarity** /dɪˌsɪməˈlærəti, dɪsˌsɪ-/ *n* [C,U]

**dis·sim·u·late** /dɪˈsɪmjəleɪt/ *v* [I,T] *formal* to hide your true feelings or intentions, especially by lying to people

**dis·si·pate** /ˈdɪsəpeɪt/ *v formal* **1** [I,T] to scatter or disappear, or make something do this: *England's arrogance was dissipated by a 1-0 defeat by the United States.* **2** [T] to gradually waste something such as money or energy by trying to do a lot of different or unnecessary things

**dis·si·pat·ed** /ˈdɪsəpeɪtəd/ *adj* spending too much time on physical pleasures such as drinking alcohol, in a way that is harmful to your health

**dis·si·pa·tion** /ˌdɪsəˈpeɪʃən/ *n* [U] *formal* **1** the process of making something disappear or scatter: [+ **of**] *the dissipation of heat* **2** the enjoyment of physical pleasures such as drinking too much alcohol, that are harmful to your health: *a life of luxury and dissipation* **3** the act of wasting money, time, energy etc

**dis·so·ci·ate** /dɪˈsəʊʃieɪt, -sieɪt‖-ˈsoʊ-/ *v* [T] **1 dissociate yourself from** to do or say something to show that you do not agree with a person or organization, especially so that you avoid being criticized for their behaviour or views: *I wish to dissociate myself from the views expressed by Mr Irving.* **2 dissociate sb/sth from** to regard two things or people as separate and not connected to each other —**dissociation** /dɪˌsəʊʃiˈeɪʃən -siˈeɪ-‖-ˌsoʊ-/ *n* [U]

**dis·so·lute** /ˈdɪsəluːt/ *adj* having an immoral way of life, for example drinking too much alcohol, having sex with many people etc: *Dylan Thomas, then an intensely romantic, though dissolute figure* —**dissolutely** *adv* —**dissoluteness** *n* [U]

**dis·so·lu·tion** /ˌdɪsəˈluːʃən/ *n* [U] **1** the act of formally ending a parliament **2** the act of formally ending a marriage or business arrangement **3** the process by which something gradually becomes weaker and disappears: *the dissolution of the Roman Empire*

**dissolve**

**dis·solve** /dɪˈzɒlv‖dɪˈzɑːlv/ *v*

**1** ▶ **STH SOLID** ◀ **a)** [I] if a solid dissolves, it mixes with a liquid and becomes part of it: [+ **in**] *Sugar dissolves in water.* **b)** [T] to make something solid become part of a liquid by putting it in a liquid and mixing it: **dissolve sth in** *Dissolve the tablets in water.*

**2 dissolve into laughter/tears** start to laugh or cry
**3 ▶ BECOME WEAKER ◀** [I] to become weaker and disappear: *Her objections to the plan began to dissolve.*
**4 ▶ PARLIAMENT ◀** [T] to formally end a parliament before an election
**5 ▶ MARRIAGE/BUSINESS/ORGANIZATION ◀** [T usually passive] to formally end a marriage, business arrangement, or organization

**dis·so·nance** /ˈdɪsənəns/ *n* **1** [C,U] a combination of musical notes that have a strange sound because they are not in HARMONY (1) **2** [U] *formal* a lack of agreement between different ideas or opinions —**dissonant** *adj*

**dis·suade** /dɪˈsweɪd/ *v* [T] to persuade somebody not to do something: **dissuade sb from doing sth** *a campaign to dissuade young people from smoking* | —compare PERSUADE —**dissuasion** /dɪˈsweɪʒən/ *n* [U]

S2 W2 **dis·tance¹** /ˈdɪstəns/ *n* [C,U]
**1 ▶ HOW FAR ◀** the amount of space between two places or things: **short/long distance** *Sylvia could only run a short distance without getting out of breath.* | [+ **from**] *What's the distance from Chicago to Detroit?* | **at a distance of 5 metres/2 miles etc** (=5 metres etc away) *Place the rod at a distance of 40mm from the light source.* | **some distance from/a good distance away from** (=a fairly long distance from) *Gareth's cottage is some distance from the road.*
**2 in the distance** in a place that is far away, but close enough to be seen or heard: *That's Long Island in the distance over there.*
**3 at/from a distance a)** from a place that is not very close: **follow sb from a distance** (=follow them by walking a long way behing them) *The detective followed him at a distance.* **b)** a long time after something happened: *It's difficult to remember exactly what they looked like at this distance in time.*
**4 within walking/driving distance** near enough to walk or drive to: [+ **of**] *There are two good Chinese restaurants within walking distance of my house.*
**5 within spitting distance of** *informal* very near
**6 keep your distance a)** to avoid becoming too friendly with someone or too closely involved in something **b)** to not go too close to someone or to another car
**7 keep sb at a distance** to not become too friendly with someone: *Ann likes to keep people at a distance.*
**8 ▶ UNFRIENDLY FEELING ◀** a situation in which two people do not tell each other what they really think or feel, in a way that seems unfriendly: [+ **between**] *There was still a certain distance between me and my father.*
**9 go the distance** *informal* if you go the distance in a sport or competition, you continue playing or competing until the end —see also LONG-DISTANCE, MIDDLE DISTANCE

**distance²** *v* **distance yourself** to say that you are not involved with someone or something, or try to become less involved, especially to avoid being connected with them: *The Soviet Union distanced itself from the US position.*

**distance learn·ing** /ˈ·· ˌ··/ *n* [U] *BrE* a method of study that involves watching television programmes and sending work to teachers instead of going to a school

W3 **dis·tant** /ˈdɪstənt/ *adj*
**1 ▶ FAR AWAY ◀** far from where you are now: *the distant sound of traffic* | *Nora gazed at the distant hills.*
**2 ▶ UNFRIENDLY ◀** unfriendly and showing no emotion: *After the quarrel Susan remained cold and distant.*
**3 ▶ RELATIVE ◀** [only before noun] not very closely related to you: *a distant cousin*
**4 in the (dim and) distant past** a long time ago
**5 in the not too distant future** used when talking about what will happen in a few months or years from now: *The President hopes to visit Ireland in the not too distant future.* —**distantly** *adv*

**dis·taste** /dɪsˈteɪst/ *n* [U] a feeling of dislike for someone or something that you think is unpleasant or morally offensive: [+ **for**] *her distaste for any form of compromise*

**dis·taste·ful** /dɪsˈteɪstfəl/ *adj* very unpleasant or morally offensive: *What follows is John's story. Parts of it may seem distasteful, even shocking.* —**distastefully** *adv* —**distastefulness** *n* [U]

**dis·tem·per** /dɪˈstempə‖-ər/ *n* [U] **1** an infectious disease that affects dogs and cats **2** *BrE* a type of paint that you mix with water used for painting walls

**dis·tend** /dɪˈstend/ *v* [I,T] to swell or make something swell because of pressure from inside —**distended** *adj*: *a distended stomach* —**distension** /-ˈtenʃən/ *n* [U] *technical*

**dis·til** also **distill** *AmE* /dɪˈstɪl/ *v* **distilled, distilling** [T] **1** to make a liquid such as water or alcohol more pure by heating it so that it becomes a gas and then letting it cool **2** to make a strong alcoholic drink such as WHISKY by this method **3** to get ideas, information etc from a large amount of knowledge or experience —**distillation** /ˌdɪstəˈleɪʃən/ *n* [C,U]

**dis·til·ler** /dɪˈstɪlə‖-ər/ *n* [C] a person or company that makes strong alcoholic drinks such as WHISKY

**dis·til·le·ry** /dɪˈstɪləri/ *n* [C] a factory where strong alcoholic drink is produced by distilling

**dis·tinct** /dɪˈstɪŋkt/ *adj* **1** clearly different or belonging to a different type: **quite/entirely distinct** (=completely distinct) *two entirely distinct languages* | [+ **from**] *The behavior of men as individuals is distinct from their behavior in a group.* **2 as distinct from** used when emphasizing that you are talking about a particular kind of thing and not something else: *childhood as distinct from adolescence* **3** something that is distinct can clearly be seen, heard, smelled etc: *The outline of the ship became more distinct.* **4** [only before noun] a distinct possibility, feeling, quality etc definitely exists or is definitely important and cannot be ignored: *a distinct lack of interest among the general public* | **have a distinct advantage** *Oxbridge graduates have a distinct advantage when applying for jobs in the civil service.* W3

**dis·tinc·tion** /dɪˈstɪŋkʃən/ *n* **1** [C] a clear difference between two similar things: [+ **between**] *the distinction between formal and informal language* **2 make/draw a distinction** to say that two things or groups are different or treat them in a different way: *The school makes no distinction between male and female students.* **3** [U] the quality of being excellent and important: *No one today doubts Eliot's distinction as a poet.* | **of (great) distinction** (=very good and very important) *Collingwood was a scholar of great distinction.* **4** [C] a special honour given to someone to show them respect or to reward their achievements: **have the distinction of doing sth** *Dinah had the great distinction of being invited to meet the Prime Minister.* **5** [C] a special mark given to a student who has done very well: *Bianca got a distinction in her chemistry exam.* S3 W2

**dis·tinc·tive** /dɪˈstɪŋktɪv/ *adj* having a special quality, character, or appearance that is different and easy to recognize: *a rock band with a distinctive sound* —**distinctively** *adv* —**distinctiveness** *n* [U]

**dis·tinct·ly** /dɪˈstɪŋktli/ *adv* **1** clearly: *I distinctly heard him say my name.* **2** used when saying that someone or something has a particular quality, character etc that is easy to recognize: *The rest of the passengers had distinctly Indian names.* **3** used when emphasizing an adjective that you are using to describe something or someone: *Paul was feeling distinctly foolish.* **4 distinctly remember doing sth** used to say that you definitely remember details about something very clearly

**dis·tin·guish** /dɪˈstɪŋgwɪʃ/ *v* **1** [I,T] to be able to recognize and understand the difference between two similar things or people: *Dogs can distinguish a greater range of sounds than humans.* | [+ **between**] *It's important to distinguish between tax avoidance and tax evasion.* | **distinguish sb/sth from** *The twins are so alike it's difficult to distinguish one from the other.* **2** [T not in S3 W3

progressive] to be able to see the shape of something or hear a particular sound: *The light was too dim for me to distinguish anything clearly.* **3** [T not in progressive] *formal* to be the thing that makes someone or something different from other people or things: **distinguish sb/sth from** *There's not much to distinguish her from the other candidates.* | **distinguishing feature/mark** (=a feature or mark that makes someone or something look different) **4 distinguish yourself** to do something so well that people notice you and remember you: *McEnroe first distinguished himself by winning a junior tournament at Wimbledon.*

**dis·tin·guish·a·ble** /dɪˈstɪŋgwɪʃəbəl/ *adj* easily recognized as being different from other things or people: [+ **from**] *The copy was barely distinguishable from the original painting.*

**dis·tin·guished** /dɪˈstɪŋgwɪʃt/ *adj* **1** very successful and therefore respected and admired: *a school with a distinguished academic record* —see FAMOUS (USAGE) **2** someone who has a distinguished appearance looks important in a way that makes you respect and admire them: *a tall, distinguished-looking man*

**dis·tort** /dɪˈstɔːt‖-ɔːrt/ *v* [T] **1** to explain a fact, statement, idea etc in a way that changes its real meaning: *The journalist was accused of distorting the facts.* **2** to change the appearance, sound, or shape of something so that it is strange or unclear: *Tall buildings can distort radio signals.* —**distorted** *adj* —**distortion** /dɪˈstɔːʃən‖-ɔːr-/ *n* [U]

**dis·tract** /dɪˈstrækt/ *v* [T] to make someone who is working, studying etc unable to continue what they are doing by making them look at or listen to something else: *Try not to distract the other students.* | **distract sb from** *Meg was distracted from her work by the noise outside.* | **distract sb's attention** (=deliberately stop someone paying attention to what they are doing) —**distracting** *adj*

**dis·tract·ed** /dɪˈstræktɪ̈d/ *adj* anxious and unable to think clearly: *After the argument, Kathryn felt too distracted to work.* —**distractedly** *adv*

**dis·trac·tion** /dɪˈstrækʃən/ *n* **1** [C,U] something that makes you stop paying attention to what you are doing: *I have to study in the library – there are too many distractions at home.* **2** [C] a pleasant and not very serious activity that you do for amusement **3 drive sb to distraction** to annoy someone so much, that they become angry, upset, and no longer able to think clearly: *The baby's constant crying was driving me to distraction.*

**dis·trait** /dɪˈstreɪ/ *adj French* distracted

**dis·traught** /dɪˈstrɔːt‖-ˈstrɒːt/ *adj* so upset and worried that you cannot think clearly: *The distraught woman was yesterday giving police a description of her attacker.*

**dis·tress**[1] /dɪˈstres/ *n* [U]
**1 ▶ EXTREME WORRY ◀** a feeling of extreme worry and unhappiness: *Luke's destructive behaviour caused his parents great distress.* | **in distress** *The girl was crying and clearly in distress.*
**2 ▶ PAIN ◀** *formal* great physical pain
**3 ▶ LACK OF MONEY/FOOD ◀** a situation in which you suffer or have great problems because you have no money, food etc: **in distress** *charities that aid families in distress* | *acute financial distress*
**4 distress signal** a message sent from a ship, aircraft etc asking for help
**5 be in distress** if a ship, aircraft etc is in distress, it is in danger of sinking or crashing

**distress**[2] *v* [T] to make someone feel extremely upset and worried

**dis·tressed** /dɪˈstrest/ *adj* **1** extremely upset and shocked: **deeply distressed** *Hannah was deeply distressed by the news about her father.* **2** experiencing a lot of pain: *The animal was clearly distressed.* **3** *formal* having very little money: *a family living in distressed circumstances*

**dis·tress·ing** /dɪˈstresɪŋ/ also **distressful** *adj* making you feel extremely upset and anxious: *a distressing experience* —**distressingly** *adv*

**dis·trib·ute** /dɪˈstrɪbjuːt/ *v* [T] **1** to give something such as food, medicine, books etc to a large group of people, especially in a planned way: **distribute sth among/to** *Clothes and blankets have been distributed among the refugees.* | *a man distributing leaflets to passers-by* **2** to supply goods to shops and companies in a particular area: *Milk is distributed to the local shops by Herald's Dairies.* **3** to share something such as wealth or power among different people or organizations **4** to spread something over a large area: *The flowers rely on the wind to distribute their pollen.*

**dis·tri·bu·tion** /ˌdɪstrɪ̈ˈbjuːʃən/ *n* **1** [U] the act of giving things to a large group of people or delivering goods to companies, shops etc: [+ **of**] *the distribution of aid supplies* **2** [C,U] the way in which people, buildings etc are arranged over a large area: *population distribution* **3** [U] *technical* the way in which wealth, property etc is shared among the members of a society

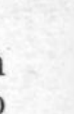

**dis·trib·u·tive** /dɪˈstrɪbjʊ̈tɪv/ *adj* **1** connected with distribution: *distributive costs* **2** *technical* referring to each single member of a group; distributing words in English include 'each', 'every' and 'either'

**dis·trib·u·tor** /dɪˈstrɪbjʊ̈tə‖-ər/ *n* [C] **1** a company or person that supplies shops and companies with goods **2** the part of a car's engine that sends an electric current to the SPARK PLUGS —see picture at ENGINE

**dis·trict** /ˈdɪstrɪkt/ *n* [C] **1** a particular area of a town or the countryside: *a semi-detached house in a pleasant suburban district* —see AREA (USAGE) **2** an area of a country, city etc that has official borders: *a postal district*

**district at·tor·ney** /ˌ·· ·ˈ··/ *n* [C] a lawyer in the US who is responsible for bringing legal charges against criminals in a particular area

**district coun·cil** /ˌ·· ˈ··/ *n* [C] a group of people elected in Britain to organize local services such as education, cleaning the streets etc in a particular area

**district court** /ˌ·· ˈ·/ *n* [C] a local court in the US where people are judged in cases involving national rather than state law

**district nurse** /ˌ·· ˈ·/ *n* [C] a nurse who visits and treats people in their own homes in Britain

**dis·trust**[1] /dɪsˈtrʌst/ *n* [U] a feeling that you cannot trust someone: *The local people regard the police with suspicion and distrust.* | [+ **of**] *Dylan's distrust of journalists makes him difficult to interview.* —**distrustful** *adj* —**distrustfully** *adv* —compare MISTRUST[1]

**distrust**[2] *v* [T] to not trust someone or something

**dis·turb** /dɪˈstɜːb‖-ɜːrb/ *v* [T]
**1 ▶ INTERRUPT ◀** to interrupt someone so that they cannot continue what they are doing by asking a question, making a noise etc: *Sorry to disturb you, but I have an urgent message from your husband.*
**2 ▶ WORRY ◀** to make someone feel worried or slightly shocked: *What disturbs me most is his total lack of remorse.*
**3 ▶ MOVE ◀** to move something or change its position: *If you find a bird's nest, never disturb the eggs.*
**4 do not disturb** a sign that you put on a door when you do not want anyone to interrupt you
**5 disturb the peace** *law* to behave in a noisy and unpleasant way in public

**dis·turb·ance** /dɪˈstɜːbəns‖-ɜːr-/ *n* **1** [C,U] something that stops you from being able to continue doing something, or the act of stopping someone from being able to continue doing something: *The noise of the traffic is a continual disturbance.* | *I need a place where I can work without disturbance.* **2** [C] a situation in which people fight or behave violently in public: *There were disturbances in the crowd as fans left the stadium.* **3** [U] a state in which someone is emotionally upset and does not behave normally: *a long history of mental disturbance*

**dis·turbed** /dɪˈstɜːbd‖-ɜːr-bd/ *adj* someone who is disturbed does not behave in a normal way, because they have had very shocking or upsetting experiences

**dis·turb·ing** /dɪˈstɜːbɪŋ‖-ɜːr-/ *adj* making you feel worried or shocked: *a disturbing increase in the crime rate*

**dis·u·nite** /ˌdɪsjuːˈnaɪt/ *v* [T] *formal* to prevent people from agreeing with each other and working together —**disunited** *adj*

**dis·u·ni·ty** /dɪsˈjuːnɪ̈ti/ *n* [U] a situation in which a group of people cannot agree with each other or work together

**dis·use** /dɪsˈjuːs/ *n* [U] a situation in which something is no longer used: **fall into disuse** (=stop being used) *The building eventually fell into disuse.*

**dis·used** /ˌdɪsˈjuːzd◂/ *adj* no longer used: *a disused mine*

**di·syl·lab·ic** /ˌdaɪsɪ̈ˈlæbɪk◂, ˌdɪ-/ *adj technical* having two SYLLABLES

**ditch¹** /dɪtʃ/ *n* [C] a long narrow hole cut into the ground at the side of a field, road etc, especially for water to flow through —see also LAST-DITCH

**ditch²** *v* **1** [T] to get rid of something because you no longer need it **2** [T] *informal* to end a romantic relationship with someone: *Julie's ditched her boyfriend.* **3** [I,T] to deliberately crash an aircraft into the sea

**ditch·wa·ter** /ˈdɪtwɔːtə‖-wɒːtər,-wɑː-/ *n* **as dull as ditchwater** *BrE* very boring

**dith·er¹** /ˈdɪðə‖-ər/ *v* [I] to not do something because you are unable to decide what to do: *Stop dithering, Linda, and get on with it!* —**ditherer** *n* [C]

**dither²** *n* **be (all) in a dither** *BrE informal* to be nervous and confused because you cannot decide what to do

**di·tran·si·tive** /ˌdaɪˈtrænsɪ̈tɪv, -zɪ̈-/ *adj technical* a ditransitive verb has an INDIRECT OBJECT and a DIRECT OBJECT. 'Give' in the sentence 'Give me the book.' is ditransitive —compare INTRANSITIVE, TRANSITIVE —**ditransitive** *n* [C]

**dit·to¹** /ˈdɪtəʊ‖-toʊ/ *adv spoken* used to say that something is the same as something else, or that you think the same as someone else: *"I'm absolutely fed up with this job." "Ditto."*

**ditto²** *n* plural **dittos** [C] a mark (") you use instead of repeating what you have already written, usually immediately above in a list

**dit·ty** /ˈdɪti/ *n* [C] *humorous* a short simple poem or song

**di·u·ret·ic** /ˌdaɪjʊˈretɪk◂/ *n* [C] a substance that increases the flow of URINE —**diuretic** *adj*

**di·ur·nal** /daɪˈɜːnəl‖-ˈɜːr-/ *adj technical* **1** happening in the daytime **2** happening every day

**Div** *n* the written abbreviation of DIVISION

**di·van** /dɪˈvæn‖ˈdaɪvæn/ *n* [C] **1** a bed with a thick base **2** a long low soft seat that has no back or arms

**dive¹** /daɪv/ *v past tense* **dived** also **dove** /dəʊv‖doʊv/ *AmE* [I]

**1** ▶ **JUMP INTO WATER** ◀ to jump into water with your head and arms first: [+ **into/off etc**] *Sally dived expertly into the pool.*|*Diving off the cliffs is very dangerous.*

**2** ▶ **GO DEEPER** ◀ to go deeper under water: *The submarine began to dive.*

**3** ▶ **SWIM UNDER WATER** ◀ to swim under water using special breathing equipment: *frogmen diving for sunken treasure*

**4** ▶ **BIRD/AIRCRAFT** ◀ if a bird or an aircraft dives, it goes down through the air very quickly and steeply, head first

**5** ▶ **JUMP FORWARDS** ◀ [always + adv/prep] to jump forwards or to one side in order to catch something or to avoid something: [+ **after/towards/aside etc**] *Jackson dived after the ball.*

**6** ▶ **INTO BUILDING/CROWD** ◀ to quickly go into a building or a crowd of people: [+ **into**] *We dived into a coffee shop to avoid the rain.*

**7 dive into your bag/pockets etc** to put your hand into your bag, pockets etc so that you can get something out

**dive in** *phr v* [I] **1** to start doing something eagerly and energetically: *Harvey dived in with several questions.* **2 dive in!** *spoken* used to invite people to start eating a meal

**dive²** *n* [C] **1** a jump into the water with your head and arms first **2 make a dive for** to move quickly and suddenly towards something **3** *informal* a place such as a bar or club that is cheap and dirty: *I've heard the new club's a bit of a dive.*

**dive-bomb** /ˈ· ·/ *v* [I,T] to attack someone or something by flying down towards them from the air

**dive bomb·er** /ˈ· ˌ··/ *n* [C] a type of military plane that flies low over a place and drops bombs on it

**div·er** /ˈdaɪvə‖-ər/ *n* [C] **1** someone who swims or works underwater using special breathing equipment: *a deep sea diver* **2** someone who jumps into water with their head and arms first

**di·verge** /daɪˈvɜːdʒ, dɪ̈-‖-ɜːrdʒ-/ *v* [I] **1** if two lines or paths diverge, they go in different directions **2** if two things diverge, they become different although they used to be the same: *Our business interests diverged and we had to sell the company.* —opposite CONVERGE

**di·ver·gence** /daɪˈvɜːdʒəns, dɪ̈-‖-ɜːr-/ *n* [C,U + **between/of**] a difference between two or more things such as opinions or interests

**di·ver·gent** /daɪˈvɜːdʒənt, dɪ-‖-ɜːr-/ *adj* divergent opinions, interests etc are very different from each other

**di·vers** /ˈdaɪvəz‖-ərz/ *adj* [only before noun] *old-fashioned* of many different kinds

**di·verse** /daɪˈvɜːs‖dɪ̈ˈvɜːrs, daɪ-/ *adj* very different from each other: *subjects as diverse as pop music and archeology* —**diversely** *adv*

**di·ver·si·fy** /daɪˈvɜːsɪ̈faɪ‖dɪ̈ˈvɜːr-, daɪ-/ *v* **1** [I] if a business or a country's ECONOMY¹ (1) diversifies, it starts to produce a range of different products and services, instead of just one or two: *a publishing company that is diversifying into the software market* **2** [T] to make a business or ECONOMY ¹ (1) start to produce a range of different products or services **3** [I,T] to change something so that there is more variety —**diversification** /daɪˌvɜːsɪ̈fɪ̈ˈkeɪʃən‖dɪ̈ˈvɒːr-, daɪ-/ *n* [U]

**di·ver·sion** /daɪˈvɜːʃən, dɪ̈-‖-ɜːrʒən/ *n* **1** [C] something that stops you from paying attention to what you are doing or what is happening: **create a diversion** (=deliberately take someone's attention away from something else) *Some of the prisoners created a diversion while Riggs climbed the wall.* **2** [C,U] a change in the direction or purpose of something: [+ **of**] *the massive diversion of resources into the military budget* **3** [C] *formal* an activity that you do for pleasure: *The cinema is always a pleasant diversion.* **4** [C] *especially BrE* a different road for traffic to travel on when the usual road cannot be used

**di·ver·sion·a·ry** /daɪˈvɜːʃənəri, dɪ̈-‖-ˈvɜːrʒəneri/ *adj* intended to take someone's attention away from something

**di·ver·si·ty** /daɪˈvɜːsɪ̈ti, dɪ̈-‖-ɜːr-/ *n* [singular] **1** a range of different people or things; variety: *the cultural diversity of the United States*|*a diversity of opinion* **2** [U] the quality of having variety and including a wide range of different people or things

**di·vert** /daɪˈvɜːt, dɪ̈-‖-ɜːrt/ *v* [T] **1** to change the direction or purpose of something: *diverted traffic*|**divert sth into** *The company should divert more resources into research.* **2 divert attention/criticism etc** to stop people from paying attention to something or criticizing it: *The tax cuts diverted attention from the real economic problems.* **3** *formal* to entertain someone

**di·vert·ing** /daɪˈvɜːtɪŋ, daɪ-‖-ɜːr-/ *adj formal* entertaining and amusing: *a mildly diverting film comedy*

**di·vest** /daɪˈvest, dɪ̈-/ *v*

**divest** sb **of** sth *phr v* [T] *formal* **1 divest yourself of** to take off something you are wearing or carrying: *Pedro divested himself of his overcoat and boots.* **2** to get rid of something that you own: **divest yourself of** *A new minister must divest himself of his business interests.* **3** to take away someone's power, rights, etc: *The king was divested of all his wealth and power.*

**di·vest·ment** /daɪˈvestmənt/ *n* [U] *AmE technical* the act of taking your money out of a company or place where you had put it in order to make a profit; DISINVESTMENT *BrE*

S1 W2 **di·vide¹** /dɪ̇ˈvaɪd/ *v*
**1** ▶ **SEPARATE** ◀ **a)** [T] to separate something such as an area, group, or object into two or more parts: **divide sth into** *Take the orange and divide it into quarters.* | *The USA is divided into 50 states.* | **divide sth between** *Hitler and Stalin divided Poland between them.* **b)** [I] to become separated into two or more different parts: [+ **in/into**] *The cell quickly divides in two.*
**2** ▶ **KEEP SEPARATE** ◀ also **divide off** [T] to keep two areas separate from each other: *The Berlin Wall used to divide East and West Berlin.* | **divide sth from** *The chapel is divided from the rest of the church by a screen.*
**3** ▶ **SHARE** ◀ also **divide up** [T] to separate something into two or more parts and share them between two or more people: **divide sth between/among** *The money is to be divided up equally among the six grandchildren.*

**4** ▶ **MATHEMATICS** ◀ **a)** [T] to find out how many times one number is contained in another larger number: **divide sth by sth** *Divide 21 by 3.* | **divided by sth** *6 divided by 3 is 2.* **b)** [I] to be contained in another, usually larger, number one or more times: [+ **into**] *8 divides into 64.* —compare MULTIPLY (2)
**5** ▶ **DISAGREE** ◀ [T] to make people disagree with each other and form groups with opposing views: **be divided over/about** (=disagree about something) *Voters are bitterly divided over the issue of gun control.*
**6 dividing line** the difference between two types or groups of similar things: [+ **between**] *There's a thin dividing line between genius and madness.*
**7 divide and rule** to control people by making them argue or fight with each other instead of opposing you —**divided** *adj*

**divide²** *n* [C usually singular] **1** a difference between two groups of people, especially in their beliefs or way of life, that makes them seem separate from each other: *two politicians on either side of a political divide* **2** *AmE* a line of high ground between two river systems; WATERSHED (3)

**divided high·way** /ˌ·‚·· ˈ··/ *n* [C] *AmE* a main road on which the traffic travelling in opposite directions is kept apart by a piece of land or a low fence; DUAL CARRIAGEWAY *BrE*

W3 **div·i·dend** /ˈdɪvɪ̇dənd, -dend/ *n* [C] **1** a part of a company's profit that is divided among the people who have shares (SHARE² (6)) in the company **2 pay dividends** if something you do pays dividends, you get an advantage from it later: *All Ken's hard work eventually paid dividends.* **3** *BrE* the money you can win in a national competition that involves guessing the results of football games **4** *technical* a number that is to be divided by another number

**di·vid·er** /dɪ̇ˈvaɪdə‖-ər/ *n* [C] **1** something that divides something else into parts **2** a piece of card that separates pages in a FILE¹ (2) **3 dividers** [plural] an instrument used for measuring or marking lines or angles, that consists of two pointed pieces of metal joined together at the top

**div·i·na·tion** /ˌdɪvɪ̇ˈneɪʃən/ *n* [U] the act of finding out what will happen in the future by means of special powers, or the ability to do this

**di·vine¹** /dɪ̇ˈvaɪn/ *adj* **1** having the qualities of a god or connected with, or coming from God: *the authority of divine law* | **divine service** (=a formal ceremony involving prayers etc to God) **2 divine help/intervention/inspiration/retribution** help etc from God **3** *old fashioned* very pleasant or good; WONDERFUL: *You look simply divine!*

**divine²** *v* **1** [T] *literary* to discover or guess something: *He must have divined from my expression that I was angry.* **2** [I] to search for underground water or minerals using a special Y-shaped stick

**divine³** *n* [C] *old use* a priest

**di·vin·er** /dɪ̇ˈvaɪnə‖-ər/ *n* [C] someone who searches for underground water or minerals using a special Y-shaped stick

**divine right** /ˌ·‚· ˈ·/ *n* **1** [singular] the right given to a king or queen by God to rule a country, that in former times could not be questioned or opposed **2 have a divine right to do sth** *informal* to be able to do what you want without having to ask permission: *You don't have a divine right to open all my mail, you know.*

**div·ing** /ˈdaɪvɪŋ/ *n* [U] **1** the activity of swimming under water using special breathing equipment **2** the activity of jumping into water with your head and arms first: *a diving competition*

**diving bell** /ˈ·· ·/ *n* [C] a metal container shaped like a bell, in which people can work under water

**diving board** /ˈ·· ·/ *n* [C] a board fixed above a SWIMMING POOL and used for diving

**diving suit** /ˈ·· ·/ *n* [C] a special protective suit worn when swimming deep under water

**di·vin·ing rod** /·ˈ·· ‚·/ *n* [C] a special Y-shaped stick used to search for underground water or minerals

**di·vin·i·ty** /dɪ̇ˈvɪnɪ̇ti/ *n* **1** [U] the study of God and religious beliefs; THEOLOGY **2** [U] the quality or state of being like God or a god **3** [C] God or a god

**divinity school** /·ˈ··· ‚·/ *n* [C] *AmE* a college where students study to become priests

**di·vis·i·ble** /dɪ̇ˈvɪzɪ̇bəl/ *adj* able to be divided, especially by another number: *6 is divisible by 3.*

**di·vi·sion** /dɪ̇ˈvɪʒən/ *n* S3 W1
**1** ▶ **SEPARATING** ◀ [C,U] the act of dividing something into different parts or the way it is divided: [+ **between**] *the division between public and private life* | [+ **of sth into**] *the division of people into winners and losers*
**2** ▶ **SHARING** ◀ [C,U] the act of dividing something so that it can be shared or the way it is divided: [+ **of sth between**] *the division of power between church and state*
**3** ▶ **DISAGREEMENT** ◀ [C,U] a disagreement among the members of a group, especially one that makes them form smaller groups: *There are deep divisions in the party over Europe.*
**4** ▶ **MATHEMATICS** ◀ [U] the process of finding out how many times one number is contained in another —compare MULTIPLICATION (1) —see also LONG DIVISION
**5** ▶ **PART OF AN ORGANIZATION** ◀ [C] a large part of an organization, company etc, consisting of several smaller parts: *I work in the Computer Services Division.*
**6** ▶ **SPORT** ◀ [C] *BrE* one of the groups of teams that a sports competition, especially football, is divided into: **the First/Second Division** *Brighton play in the Second Division.*
**7** ▶ **ARMY** ◀ [C] a part of an army larger than a BRIGADE (1): *the Guards Division*
**8** ▶ **IN PARLIAMENT** ◀ [C] *technical* a process in which members of the British parliament vote for something by dividing into groups: *MP's forced a division on the bill.*

**di·vi·sion·al** /dɪ̇ˈvɪʒənəl/ *adj* connected with a DIVISION (=one of the parts into which a large organization or army is divided): *divisional headquarters*

**division bell** /·ˈ·· ·/ *n* [C] a bell that is rung to tell members of the British parliament to vote

**division lob·by** /·ˈ·· ‚··/ *n* [C] one of the two places to which a British Member of Parliament must go to vote

**division of la·bour** /ˌ·‚·· · ˈ··/ *n* [C,U] a way of organizing work in which each member of a group has a particular job to do

**di·vi·sive** /dɪ̇ˈvaɪsɪv/ *adj* having the effect of dividing people into groups with opposing opinions: *Religious schools were seen as socially divisive.*

**di·vi·sor** /dɪ̇ˈvaɪzə‖-ər/ *n* [C] *technical* the number by which another number is to be divided

**di·vorce¹** /dɪ̇ˈvɔːs‖-ɔːrs/ *n* **1** [C,U] the legal ending of a S3 marriage: *In Britain, one in three marriages ends in divorce.* | **get a divorce** *Why doesn't she get a divorce?* | **divorce case** (=the legal process of divorce) | **divorce proceedings** (=the official actions to legally end your marriage) | **divorce rate** (=the number of divorces each year) | **divorce settlement** (=the legal decision about how much money, property etc you get after a divorce) —compare SEPARATION (2) **2** [C] a separation of ideas, subjects, values etc: [+ **between**] *the divorce between power and ideology*

**divorce²** *v* **1** [I,T] if someone divorces their husband or wife, or if two people divorce, they legally end their marriage: *David's parents divorced when he was six.* **2** [T] to separate two ideas, subjects, values etc completely: **divorce sth from** *It is difficult to divorce sport from politics.* | **be divorced from reality** (=not based on real things or sensible thinking) *Some of his ideas are completely divorced from reality.*

**di·vorced** /dɪ̆ˈvɔːst‖-ɔːrst/ *adj* no longer married to your former wife or husband: *75% of divorced women remarry.* | **get divorced** (=legally end your marriage) *My parents are getting divorced.*

**di·vor·cee** /dɪ̆ˌvɔːˈsiː‖dəˌvɔːrˈseɪ/ *n* someone who is no longer legally married to their former wife or husband

**div·ot** /ˈdɪvət/ *n* [C] a small piece of earth and grass that you dig out accidentally while playing sport

**di·vulge** /daɪˈvʌldʒ, dɪ̆-/ *v* [T] to give someone information, especially about something secret: *Staff may not divulge confidential information.* | **divulge sth to sb** *Do not divulge the conclusions of the report to anyone.* | **divulge what/where etc** *Adams refused to divulge what he had done with the money.* | **divulge your sources** (=say who told you)

**div·vy** /ˈdɪvi/ *n* [C] *BrE slang* a stupid person

**Di·wa·li** /dɪˈwɑːli/ *n* an important Hindu FESTIVAL (2) that is celebrated in the autumn

**Dix·ie** /ˈdɪksi/ *n* [singular] *AmE informal* the southern states of the US

**dix·ie·land** /ˈdɪksilænd/ *n* [U] a type of JAZZ¹ (1) with a strong rhythm

**DIY** /ˌdiː aɪ ˈwaɪ/ *n* [U] *especially BrE* do-it-yourself; the activity of making or repairing things yourself instead of buying them or paying someone else to do it

**diz·zy** /ˈdɪzi/ *adj* **1** feeling unable to balance, especially after spinning around or because you feel ill: *Greg felt sick and dizzy in the hot sun.* | **dizzy spell** (=a short period when you feel dizzy) **2 the dizzy heights** *humorous* an important position: *Naomi had reached the dizzy heights of manageress.* **3** *informal* careless and forgetful: *A dizzy blonde works at the front desk.* **4 dizzy height/peak** *literary* a dizzy height or peak is very high —**dizzily** *adv* —**dizziness** *n* [U]

**dizzy**

**DJ** /ˌdiː ˈdʒeɪ◂/ *n* [C] a disc jockey; someone who plays records on a radio show or in a club

**djinn** /dʒɪn/ *n* [C] a magical spirit in Arab fairy stories; GENIE

**DNA** /ˌdiː en ˈeɪ/ *n* [U] an acid that carries GENETIC information in a cell

S 1 W 1 **do¹** /duː/ *auxiliary verb past tense* **did** /dɪd/ *past participle* **done** /dʌn/ *3rd person singular present tense* **does** /dəz; *strong* dʌz/

**1 ▶ IN QUESTIONS/NEGATIVES ◀ a)** used with another verb to form questions or negatives: *Do you like bananas?* | *I don't feel like going out tonight.* | *Ian didn't answer.* | *Where do you live?* | *Doesn't Rosie look wonderful?* | *Don't just stand there – do something!* | *Why don't you come for the weekend?* (=please come) | *Don't let's invite her.* (=let's not invite her) **b)** *especially spoken* used to form QUESTION TAGS: *You know Tony, don't you?* | *She didn't pay cash, did she?*

**2 ▶ FOR EMPHASIS ◀** used to give emphasis to the main verb: *Do take care!* | *"Why didn't you tell me?" "I did tell you."* | *He owns, or did own, a yacht.*

**3 ▶ IN POLITE REQUESTS ◀** used as a polite way of offering someone something: *Do have a cup of tea.*

**4 ▶ INSTEAD OF VERB ◀** used to avoid repeating another verb: *Omar speaks English better than he did.* (=better than he used to speak it) | *"You broke my pencil!" "No I didn't!"* | *"You left the door open." "So I did."* (=you are right) | *"Will Kay come?" "She may do."* | *"You ought to phone your mother." "I have done."* | *So he plays the piano, does he?* | **so do I** *Emma loves chocolate, and so do I.* | **neither do I** *"I don't want any more." "Neither do I."*

**5 what is sb/sth doing?** used to ask why someone or something is in a particular place, when you think they should not be there: *What's this cake doing on the floor?* | *What was that man doing in our garden anyway?*

**6 ▶ WITH ADVERB ◀** used to reverse the order of the subject and the verb when an adverb or adverbial phrase starts a sentence: *Not only did I see him, I spoke to him, too.*

D

Frequencies of the verb **do** in spoken and written English.

SPOKEN
WRITTEN
2000 4000 6000 8000 10,000 per million

Based on the British National Corpus and the Longman Lancaster Corpus

This graph shows that the verb **do** is much more common in spoken English than in written English. This is because it is used to form questions and negatives and is used in some common spoken phrases.

**do up**

She's doing up her blouse.

She's undoing her blouse.

**do²** *v* 

**1 ▶ ACTIVITY/JOB ◀** [T] to PERFORM (2) and finish a particular activity or job: *Have you done your homework*

*yet?* | *Jo does aerobics three times a week.* | *It's a pleasure doing business with you.* | **do the dishes/washing up/laundry etc** *It's your turn to do the washing.* —see JOB (USAGE), MAKE[1] (USAGE)
**2 do your hair/teeth/nails** to spend time making your hair look nice, brushing your teeth etc: *Jan spends ages doing her hair in the mornings.*
**3 what do you do (for a living)?** *spoken* used to ask someone what their job is
**4 ▶ SUCCEED/FAIL ◀** [I] used to ask or say whether someone is being successful: *How are you doing?* | [+ **with/in etc**] *How are you doing in your new job?* | **do well/badly** *The children are doing very well at school.*
**5 do nothing for/do a lot for etc** [T] to have a particular effect on something or someone: **do nothing for sb** (=not improve someone's appearance) *That colour does nothing for her.* | **do a lot for** (=have a good effect on) *Getting the job has done a lot for her self-esteem.* | **do wonders for** (=have a very good effect on) *Moving to the city has done wonders for my social life.*

**6 ▶ SPEND TIME ◀** [T] *informal* to spend a period of time doing something difficult or something that you have to do: *I did two years of teaching before that.*
**7 ▶ FOOD ◀** [T] *informal* to make a particular kind of food: *I was thinking of doing a casserole tonight.*
**8 ▶ A SERVICE ◀** [T] to provide a particular service: *Do you do theatre bookings here?* | *We don't do food after 2 o'clock.*
**9 ▶ COPY ◀** [T] *informal* to copy someone's behaviour, in order to entertain people: *He does Clinton very well.*
**10 ▶ STUDY ◀** [T not in passive] *BrE* to study a particular subject in a school or university: *I did French for 5 years.*
**11 do sb good** to make someone feel better, more cheerful etc: *A break will do you good.*
**12 do 10 miles/do 20 kms etc** to achieve a particular speed, distance etc: *We did 300 miles on the first day.* | *The car can do 120 mph.*
**13 ▶ VISIT ◀** [T] to visit a particular place, especially when you are going to see a lot of other places: *Let's do the Eiffel Tower today and the Pompidou Centre tomorrow.*
**14 ▶ ENOUGH/SUITABLE ◀** *especially spoken* [I,T not in progressive] used to say that something will be enough or be suitable: [+ **for**] *Ten bottles of wine should do for the party.* | *That vase would do for your Mum's birthday present.* | *"I've got a saucepan." "That'll do."* | **should/will do sb** *Here's £20 – that should do you.* | **should/will do sb for** *A few sandwiches will do us for lunch.*
**15 that will do!** *spoken* used to tell a child that you want them to stop behaving in the way they are behaving
**16 do as you're told** *spoken* used to tell a child to behave in the way you tell them to
**17 would do well to do sth** used to advise someone that they should do something: *You'd do well to avoid that restaurant.*
**18 ▶ CHEAT ◀** [T] *BrE spoken* to cheat someone: *That painting's a fake. You've been done.*
**19 ▶ PUNISH ◀** [T] *BrE spoken* to punish someone: *Your Dad'll do you when he finds out.* | **get done** *I got done for speeding yesterday.*
**20 do it** *informal* to have sex
**21 ▶ HAPPEN ◀** [I] *spoken* to happen: *What's doing at your place tonight?*
**22 do sth to death** to talk about or do something so often that it becomes boring: *That joke has been done to death.*
**23 do well by sb** to treat someone well: *He's left home, but he still does well by his kids.* —see also **do your bit** (BIT[1] (15)), **how do you do** (HOW[1] (10)), **nothing doing** (NOTHING[1] (13)), **do sb proud** (PROUD (4))

**do away with** sb/sth *phr v* [T] **1** to get rid of something so that it does not exist any longer: *The government has done away with free eye tests for everyone.* **2** *informal* to kill someone

**do** sb **down** *phr v* [T] *BrE informal* to criticize someone, especially when they are not there

**do for** sb/sth *phr v* [T] **1 what will you do for sth?** *spoken* used to ask someone what arrangements they have made for a particular thing: *What will you do for transport tonight?* **2** *BrE slang* to kill someone **3** *old-fashioned* to make someone feel so tired that they cannot do anything: *All that travelling around really did for me.* | **be done for** *I'm going to bed, I'm done for.* **4** *BrE old-fashioned* to have a job cleaning someone else's house, cooking for them etc

**do in** *phr v* [T] **1** [**do** sb ↔ **in**] *informal* to kill someone: *They say Bates did his wife in.* **2** [**do** sb **in**] to make someone feel extremely tired: *That walk really did me in.*

**do** sth ↔ **out** *phr v* [T] **1** to make a room look nice by decorating it: *The room was beautifully done out in pastel colours.* **2** *informal especially BrE* to clean a room or cupboard thoroughly: *I'll do out the kitchen cupboards tonight.*

**do** sb **out of** sth *phr v* [T often passive] *informal* to cheat someone by not giving them something that they deserve, or something that they are owed: *I was done out of £10 in the shop this morning.*

**do over** *phr v* [T] **1** [**do** sth ↔ **over**] to decorate a room, wall etc **2** [**do** sth **over**] *AmE* to do something again because you did it wrong the first time: *Your homework's full of mistakes, you'd better do it over.* **3** [**do** sth ↔ **over**] *slang* to steal things from a place: *The factory was done over last night.* **4** [**do** sb ↔ **over**] *BrE slang* to attack and injure someone

**do up** *phr v* **1** [I,T] to fasten or tie: *This skirt does up at the back.* | **do** sth ↔ **up** *I can't do my shoelaces up.* | *Do up your coat or you'll be cold.* —see OPEN[2] (USAGE) **2** [T **do** sth ↔ **up**] to repair or redecorate a building or old car, so that it looks much better: *They did up the house and sold it for a vast profit.* **3 do yourself up** to make yourself look neat and attractive: *Sue spent ages doing herself up for her date.*

**do with** sth *phr v* [T] **1 could do with** *spoken* to need or want something: *I could do with a drink.* | *I could have done with some help this morning.* **2 what you do with yourself** what you spend your time doing: *What do you do with yourself when you're not working?* | **not know what to do with yourself** *June didn't know what to do with herself after she retired.* **3 what shall we do with?/ what have you done with?** *spoken* used to ask someone about arrangements that have been made or something that has been done: *What shall we do with the kids while you're working?* | *I can't find my pen, what have you done with it?* **4 have/be to do with** to have a connection with something: *The programme is to do with mental illness.* | **be nothing to do with you** (=used to say that someone should not ask about something) *What I do when you're out is nothing to do with you.* | **not have anything to do with** (=not have any connection with) *Do you think his bad mood has anything to do with what I said?* | **be something to do with** (=having some connection, but you are not sure what) *Judy's job is something to do with marketing.* **5 what is someone doing with?** used to ask why someone has something: *What are you doing with my diary?*

**do without** *phr v* **1** [I,T] to manage to live without something or someone: *I can't afford a car, so I guess I'll just have to do without.* | **do without sth** *You'll have to do without your dinner if you don't get back in time.* **2 can do without** used to say that you prefer not to have something: *"Oh shut up, I can do without all this hassle."*

**do**[3] *n* [C] *informal* **1** a party or other social event: *Are you going to this do at John's tonight?* **2 dos and don'ts** things that you must and must not do in a particular situation

**do**[4], **doh** /dəʊ‖doʊ/ *n* [singular, U] the first note in a musical SCALE[1] (8) according to the SOL-FA system

**D.O.A.** /ˌdiː əʊ ˈeɪ‖-oʊ-/ *adj AmE* dead on arrival; someone who is dead on arrival is declared to be dead as soon as they are brought to a hospital

**d.o.b.** the written abbreviation of date of birth

**doc** /dɒk‖dɑːk/ *n* [C] *spoken* a doctor

**do·cent** /dəʊˈsent‖doʊ-/ *n* [C] *AmE* **1** a university teacher **2** someone who guides visitors through a MUSEUM, etc

**do·cile** /ˈdəʊsaɪl‖ˈdɑːsəl/ *adj* quiet and easily controlled: *a docile child* —**docilely** *adv* —**docility** /dəʊˈsɪlɪ̇ti‖dɑː-/ *n* [U]

**dock¹** /dɒk‖dɑːk/ *n* **1** [C] a place in a port where ships are loaded and unloaded: *A crowd was waiting at the dock to greet them.* | **in dock** *The ship is now in dock for repairs.* —see also DRY DOCK **2** [C] the part of a law court where the person being tried (TRY¹ (7)) stands **3** [C,U] a plant with thick green leaves that grows wild in Britain

**dock²** *v* **1** [I,T] if a ship docks or you dock a ship, it sails into a dock: *We'll be docking in about half an hour.* **2 dock sb's wages/pay** to reduce the amount of money you pay someone: *Your wages will be docked if you're away for too long.* **3** [I] if two spaceships dock, they join together in space **4** [T] to cut an animal's tail short

**dock·er** /ˈdɒkə‖ˈdɑːkər/ *n* [C] *BrE* someone whose job is loading and unloading ships; LONGSHORE-MAN, STEVEDORE

**dock·et** /ˈdɒkɪ̇t‖ˈdɑː-/ *n* [C] **1** [C] *technical* a short document used in business that shows what is in a package or describes goods that are being delivered **2** *AmE law* a list of legal cases (CASE¹ (9a)) that will take place in a particular court

**dock·land** /ˈdɒklənd, -lænd‖ˈdɑːk-/[U] also **docklands** *plural n* [U] *BrE* the area surrounding the place where ships are loaded and unloaded in a large port

**dock·side** /ˈdɒksaɪd‖ˈdɑːk-/ *n* [singular] the area around the place in a port where ships are loaded and unloaded

**dock·yard** /ˈdɒkjɑːd‖ˈdɑːkjɑːrd/ *n* [C] a place where ships are repaired or built

S2 W1 **doc·tor¹** /ˈdɒktə‖ˈdɑːktər/ *n* [C] **1** someone who is trained to treat people who are ill: **go to a doctor/see a doctor** *I think you'd better go to the doctor about your chest.* | **Doctor Smith/Brown etc** *I'd like to make an appointment to see Doctor Pugh.* **2** someone who holds the highest level of degree given by a university: *a Doctor of Law* **3** *AmE* a way of addressing or referring to a DENTIST

**doctor²** *v* [T] **1** to dishonestly change something in order to make it seem better: *The figure had been doctored to read $5000 instead of $500.* **2** to add a substance, especially a drug or poison, to food or drink: *Paul suspected that his drink had been doctored.* **3** to remove the sex organs of an animal, especially a cat or dog, so that it cannot produce babies

**doc·tor·al** /ˈdɒktərəl‖ˈdɑːk-/ *adj* [only before noun] done as part of work for the university degree of DOCTOR¹ (2): *a doctoral thesis on Kant*

**doc·tor·ate** /ˈdɒktərɪ̇t‖ˈdɑːk-/ *n* [C] a university degree of the highest level

**Doctor of Phi·los·o·phy** /ˌ· · · ·ˈ···/ *n* [C] a PHD

**doc·tri·naire** /ˌdɒktrɪ̇ˈneə‖ˌdɑːk-trɪ̇ˈner◂/ *adj formal* certain that your beliefs or opinions are completely correct and unable to consider the practical problems involved in making them work: *a facile doctrinaire argument*

**doc·trine** /ˈdɒktrɪ̇n‖ˈdɑːk-/ *n* [C] a belief or set of beliefs that form the main part of a religion or system of ideas: *the doctrine of predestination* —**doctrinal** /dɒkˈtraɪnl‖ˈdɑːktrɪ̇nəl/ *adj*

**doc·u·dra·ma** /ˈdɒkjʊˌdrɑːmə‖ˈdɑːkjʊˌdrɑːmə,-dræmə/ *n* [C] *AmE* a film, usually for television, that presents a true story as a play

W2 **doc·u·ment¹** /ˈdɒkjɪ̇mənt‖ˈdɑːk-/ *n* [C] a piece of paper that gives official written information about something: *legal documents*

**doc·u·ment²** /ˈdɒkjɪ̇ment‖ˈdɑːk-/ *v* [T] to write about something, film it, or take photographs of it, in order to record information about it: *photographs documenting the early history of the motor car*

**doc·u·men·ta·ry¹** /ˌdɒkjɪ̇ˈmentəri◂‖ˌdɑːk-/ *n* [C] a film or television programme that gives facts and information about something: [+ **on/about**] *a documentary about volcanoes*

**documentary²** *adj* **1 documentary film/programme** a film or television programme that gives facts and information about something **2** [only before noun] documentary proof or evidence is proof in the form of documents

**doc·u·men·ta·tion** /ˌdɒkjɪ̇mənˈteɪʃən, -men-‖ˌdɑːk-/ *n* [U] official documents that are used to prove that something is true or correct

**DOD** the written abbreviation of the US Department of Defence

**dod·der** /ˈdɒdə‖ˈdɑːdər/ *v* [I] to walk in an unsteady way shaking slightly, especially because you are very old

**dod·der·ing** /ˈdɒdərɪŋ‖ˈdɑː-/ *adj informal* shaking slightly and unable to walk properly because you are old or ill

**dod·dery** /ˈdɒdəri‖ˈdɑː-/ *adj informal* weak and unable to walk properly or do things quickly because you are old or ill: *Some of the patients are a bit doddery.*

**dod·dle** /ˈdɒdl‖ˈdɑːdl/ *n* **be a doddle** *BrE informal* to be extremely easy: *The exam was a doddle!*

**dodge¹** /dɒdʒ‖dɑːdʒ/ *v* **1** [T] to move quickly in order to avoid being hit by someone or something: *I managed to dodge the shot that came flying through the air.* —see picture on page 1263 **2** [I always + adv/prep] to move quickly in a particular direction to avoid someone or something: [+ **into/out/behind**] *He dodged in and out of the traffic.* **3** [T] to avoid a law or unpleasant duty in a dishonest way: *Senator O'Brian skillfully dodged the crucial question.* **4 dodge the issue** to avoid considering or discussing something that needs to be dealt with

**dodge²** *n* [C] **1** *informal* something dishonest you do in order to avoid a responsibility or law: *Jake was full of clever dodges to avoid paying his debts.* | **tax dodge** *He'll claim the car was a present as a tax dodge.* **2 make a dodge** to make a sudden forward or sideways movement to avoid something

**dodge ball** /ˈ· ·/ *n* [U] a game played by children in which you try to avoid being hit by a large rubber ball thrown by the other players

**dodg·em car** /ˈdɒdʒəm kɑː‖ˈdɑːdʒəm kɑːr/ *n* [C] *BrE* a small electric car that people drive around an enclosed area at a FUNFAIR; BUMPER CAR *AmE*

**dodg·ems** /ˈdɒdʒəmz‖ˈdɑː-/ *n* **the dodgems** a form of entertainment at a FUNFAIR in which people drive small electric cars around an enclosed space, chasing and hitting other cars: *Let's go on the dodgems.*

**dodg·er** /ˈdɒdʒə‖ˈdɑːdʒər/ *n* [C] **tax/draft dodger** someone who uses dishonest methods to avoid paying taxes or serving in the army

**dodg·y** /ˈdɒdʒi‖ˈdɑː-/ *adj BrE informal* **1** containing false information, often for a dishonest purpose: *dodgy accounts* **2** uncertain or difficult: *It's a dodgy situation.* **3** not working properly: *The gears in the car are a bit dodgy.* **4** dishonest or not to be trusted: *a dodgy character* —**dodginess** *n* [U]

**do·do** /ˈdəʊdəʊ‖ˈdoʊdoʊ/ *n* [C] **1** a large bird that no longer exists and was unable to fly **2** *AmE* a stupid person —see also **dead as a dodo** (DEAD¹ (14))

**doe** /dəʊ‖doʊ/ *n* [C] a female rabbit, DEER, etc —compare BUCK¹ (4)

**do·er** /ˈduːə‖-ər/ *n* [C] **1** someone who does things instead of just thinking or talking about them: *She's a doer, not a thinker* **2 evildoer/wrongdoer** someone who does evil or wrong

**does** /dəz; *strong* dʌz/ the 3rd person singular of the present tense of DO¹

**does·n't** /ˈdʌzənt/ the short form of 'does not'

**doff** /dɒf‖dɑːf, dɒːf/ *v* [T] *old-fashioned* to take off a piece of clothing, especially your hat: *Everyone called him 'Sir' and doffed their hats.* —opposite DON²

**dog¹** /dɒg‖dɒːg/ *n* [C]  S1 W1

**1 ▶ ANIMAL ◀** a very common animal that people keep as a pet or to guard a building: *I could hear a dog barking.*

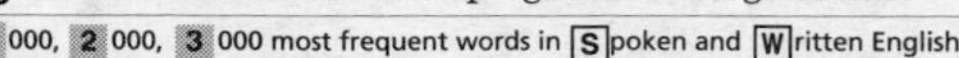

**2** ► **MALE ANIMAL** ◄ a male dog, FOX[1] (1) etc —compare BITCH[1] (1)
**3 be going to the dogs** *informal* if an organization is going to the dogs, it is getting much worse and will be difficult to improve: *This country's really going to the dogs!*
**4** ► **WOMAN** ◄ *slang* an offensive word used by men meaning an unattractive woman
**5 it's dog eat dog** an expression used to describe a situation in which people compete strongly and will do anything to get what they want: *Show business isn't all glamour, it's dog eat dog out there.* | *Advertising is a dog-eat-dog business.*
**6 it's a dog's life** *spoken* used to say that life is difficult and full of hard work and worry, with very little pleasure
**7 not have a dog's chance** *informal* to have no chance of being successful
**8 make a dog's breakfast of sth** *BrE informal* to do something very badly: *You've made a real dog's breakfast of putting those shelves up.*
**9 be dressed up like a dog's dinner** *BrE informal* to be wearing expensive clothes that you think are suitable for a social event, but that other people think are silly
**10 dog in the manger** someone who will not let other people use or have something, even though they do not need it themselves
**11 every dog has its day** an expression used to mean that even the most unimportant person has a time in their life when they are successful and noticed
**12 sth is a dog** *AmE informal* used to say that something is very poor quality: *This radio is a dog.*
**13 the dogs** *BrE informal* a sports event which consists of a series of races for dogs
**14 put on the dog** *AmE old-fashioned* to pretend to be richer than you really are or to know more than you really do —see also DOGHOUSE, **the hair of the dog** (HAIR[1] (10)), SHAGGY DOG STORY, **as sick as a dog** (SICK[1] (1)), **let sleeping dogs lie** (SLEEP[2] (6)), **the tail wagging the dog** (TAIL[1] (11)), **top dog** (TOP[2] (7)), **treat someone like a dog** (TREAT[1] (1))

**dog**[2] *v* **dogged, dogging** [T] **1** if a problem or bad luck dogs you, it causes trouble for a long time: *Maradona had been dogged by injury all season.* **2** to follow close behind someone: *A mob of youths had been dogging us for some time.*

**dog bis·cuit** /ˈ· ˌ··/ *n* [C] a small dry hard BISCUIT for dogs

**dog·cart** /ˈdɒgkɑːt‖ˈdɒːgkɑːrt/ *n* [C] **1** a vehicle pulled by a horse, that has two wheels and two seats **2** a small vehicle pulled by a large dog

**dog·catch·er** /ˈdɒgˌkætʃə‖ˈdɒːgˌkætʃər/ *n* [C] *AmE* someone whose job is to collect dogs without owners; DOG WARDEN *BrE*

**dog col·lar** /ˈ· ˌ··/ *n* [C] **1** a collar worn by dogs, onto which a LEAD (=length of leather, rope, chain etc) can be fastened **2** a stiff round white collar worn by priests

**dog days** /ˈ· ·/ *n* [plural] *literary* the hottest days of the year: *the dog days of summer*

**doge** /dəʊdʒ‖doʊdʒ/ *n* [C] the highest government official in Venice and in Genoa in the past

**dog-eared** /ˈ· ·/ *adj* dog-eared books or papers have been used so much that the corners are turned over or torn: *a dog-eared novel* —see picture on page 1258

**dog-end** /ˈ· ·/ *n* [C] **1** *BrE informal* the small part of a cigarette that is left after it has been smoked **2** something left over and not considered to be worth very much

**dog·fight** /ˈdɒgfaɪt‖ˈdɒːg-/ *n* [C] **1** an organized fight between dogs **2** a fight between armed aircraft

**dog·fish** /ˈdɒgˌfɪʃ‖ˈdɒːg-/ *n* [C] *plural* **dogfish** a kind of small SHARK (1)

**dog·ged** /ˈdɒgɪ̈d‖ˈdɒː-/ *adj* dogged actions or behaviour show that you are very determined to continue doing something: *her dogged determination to succeed* —**doggedly** *adv* —**doggedness** *n* [U]

**dog·ge·rel** /ˈdɒgərəl‖ˈdɒː-, ˈdɑː-/ *n* [U] poetry that is silly or funny and not intended to be serious

**dog·gie** /ˈdɒgi‖ˈdɒː-/ *n* [C] another spelling of DOGGY

**dog·go** /ˈdɒgəʊ‖ˈdɒːgoʊ/ *adv* **lie doggo** *old-fashioned* to stay quiet and still so that people will not notice you or find you

**dog·gone** /ˈdɒgɒn‖ˈdɒːgɒːn/ *v* [T] **doggone it** *AmE old-fashioned spoken* used when you are slightly annoyed that something has happened: *The door blew open and, doggone it, if the chickens didn't get loose!* —**doggone**, **doggoned** *adj*: *That doggone cat!*

**dog·gy, doggie** /ˈdɒgi‖ˈdɒːgi/ *n* [C] **1** a word meaning dog, used especially by or to young children **2 doggy style/fashion** a position in which two people have sex that is similar to the position that dogs or other animals use

**doggy bag** /ˈ·· ˌ·/ *n* [C] a small bag for taking home food that is left over from a meal, especially from a restaurant

**doggy pad·dle** /ˈ·· ˌ··/ *n* DOG PADDLE

**dog han·dler** /ˈ· ˌ··/ *n* [C] a police officer who works with a trained dog

**dog·house** /ˈdɒghaʊs‖ˈdɒːg-/ *n* **be in the doghouse** *informal* to be in a situation in which someone is annoyed with you because you have done something wrong: *I'm in the doghouse because I forgot Sam's birthday.*

**do·gie** /ˈdəʊgi‖ˈdoʊ-/ *n* [C] *AmE* a baby cow without a mother

**dog·leg** /ˈdɒgleg‖ˈdɒːg-/ *n* [C] a place in a road, path etc where it changes direction suddenly

**dog-like** /ˈ· ·/ *adj* faithful and loving without asking for anything for yourself: *dog-like fidelity*

**dog·ma** /ˈdɒgmə‖ˈdɔːgmə, ˈdɑːgmə/ *n* [C,U] a fixed belief, or set of beliefs that people are expected to accept without question: *party dogma*

**dog·mat·ic** /dɒgˈmætɪk‖dɔːg-, dɑːg-/ *adj* having ideas or beliefs that you are completely certain about and expect other people to accept without question: *Her staff find her bossy and dogmatic.* —**dogmatically** /-kli/ *adv*

**dog·ma·tise** /ˈdɒgmətaɪz‖ˈdɔːg-,ˈdɑːg-/ *v* a British spelling of DOGMATIZE

**dog·ma·tis·m** /ˈdɒgmətɪzəm‖ˈdɔːg-, ˈdɑːg-/ [U] attitudes or behaviour that are dogmatic —**dogmatist** *n* [C]

**dog·ma·tize** /ˈdɒgmətaɪz‖ˈdɔːg-,ˈdɑːg-/ *v* also **-ise** *BrE* [I + **about**] to speak, write, or act in a dogmatic way

**do-good·er** /ˌ· ˈ··‖ˈ· ˌ··/ *n* [C] someone who thinks they are being helpful but who annoys other people because they get involved in situations where they are not wanted

**dog pad·dle** /ˈ· ˌ··/ also **doggy paddle** *informal n* [singular] a simple way of swimming by moving your legs and arms like a swimming dog

**dogs·bod·y** /ˈdɒgzˌbɒdi‖ˈdɔːgzˌbɑːdi/ *n* [C] *BrE* someone who has to do all the jobs that nobody else wants to do: *I'm just the general dogsbody around here.*

**dog·sled** /ˈdɒgsled‖ˈdɔːg-/ *n* [C] a SLEDGE (=low flat vehicle on metal blades) pulled by dogs over snow

**dog tag** /ˈ· ˌ·/ *n* [C] *AmE* a small piece of metal that soldiers wear around their necks with their name, blood type, and number written on it

**dog-tired** /ˌ· ˈ·◂/ *adj informal* extremely tired

**dog war·den** /ˈ· ˌ··/ *n* [C] *BrE* someone whose job is to collect dogs without owners; DOGCATCHER *AmE*

**dog·wood** /ˈdɒgwʊd‖ˈdɔːg-/ *n* [C,U] a tree or bush with red or pink berries (BERRY) and red stems

**DoH** /ˌdiː əʊ ˈeɪtʃ‖-oʊ-/ *n* the abbreviation of the Department of Health

**doh, do** /dəʊ‖doʊ/ *n* [singular, U] the first or eighth note in the SOL-FA musical SCALE[1] (8)

**doi·ly** /ˈdɔɪli/ *n* [C] a circle of paper or cloth with a pattern cut into it that you put on a plate before putting cakes etc on it

**do·ing** /ˈduːɪŋ/ *n* **1 be sb's doing** if something bad is someone's doing, they did it: *This mess is all your doing.* **2 take some doing** to be hard work: *Sorting this lot out is going to take some doing.* **3 doings** *BrE* **a)** [plural] things that someone does **b)** [C] *informal* a small thing whose name you have forgotten or do not know: *Pass me that doings.*

**do-it-your·self** /ˌ· · ˈ·◂/ *n* [U] DIY

**Dol·by** /ˈdɒlbi‖ˈdɔːl-, ˈdoʊl-/ *n* [U] *trademark* a system for reducing unwanted noise when you record music or sounds

**dol·drums** /ˈdɒldrəmz‖ˈdoʊl-, ˈdɑːl-, ˈdɔːl-/ *n* **1 be in the doldrums** *informal* **a)** to be feeling sad: *Fay's really in the doldrums today.* **b)** to not be growing or improving: *The car industry has been in the doldrums for several years.* **2 the doldrums** an area in the ocean just north of the EQUATOR where the weather can be so calm that sailing ships cannot move

**dole**[1] /dəʊl‖doʊl/ *n* [U] *BrE* **1** money given by the government in Britain to people who are unemployed: **be/go on the dole** (=be or become unemployed and receive money from the government) *Kevin was on the dole for a year before he got a job.* **2 the dole queue a)** the line of people waiting to claim this money each week **b)** the number of people who are unemployed and claiming money from the state: *As two factories closed today, 500 people joined the dole queue.*

**dole**[2] *v*

**dole** sth ↔ **out** *phr v* [T] *informal* to give money or food to more than one person: [+ **to**] *Vera was doling out candy to all the kids.*

**dole·ful** /ˈdəʊlfəl‖ˈdoʊl-/ *adj* very sad: *a doleful song about lost love* —**dolefully** *adv* —**dolefulness** *n* [U]

S3 **doll**[1] /dɒl‖dɑːl, dɔːl/ *n* **1** [C] a child's toy that looks like a small person **2** [C] *slang* a word meaning an attractive young woman, that is now usually considered offensive **3** [singular] *AmE informal* a very nice person: *Jim's a real doll – he let me borrow his car.*

**doll**[2] *v*

**doll** sb **up** *phr v* [T] *informal* if a woman dolls herself up, she gets ready for a social occasion by putting on attractive clothes and MAKE-UP (1): **doll yourself up** *I can't be bothered to doll myself up tonight.* | **be/get dolled up** *The girls were all dolled up for a party.*

**dol·lar** /ˈdɒlə‖ˈdɑːlər/ *n* [C] **1** the standard unit of money in the US, Australia, Canada, Hong Kong and other countries, for which the sign is $: *This book costs ten dollars.* **2** a piece of paper or coin worth this amount of money **3 the dollar** the value of US money in relation to the money of other countries: *The pound has risen against the dollar.* —see also **you can bet your bottom dollar** (BET[1] (3)), **feel/look like a million dollars** (MILLION (4)) S1 W3

**dollars-and-cents** /ˌ·· · ˈ·/ *adj AmE* considered in a financial way: *It's an interesting idea, but from a dollars-and-cents point of view it just won't work.*

**doll house** /ˈ· ·/ *n* [C] *AmE* a DOLL'S HOUSE *BrE*

**dol·lop**[1] /ˈdɒləp‖ˈdɑː-/ *n* [C] a mass of soft food, usually dropped from a spoon: [+ **of**] *a large dollop of cream* —see picture on page 416

**dollop**[2] *v* [T always + adv/prep] *informal* to drop a mass of soft food onto a surface: **dollop sth onto/into** *May dolloped the mixture into the frying pan.*

**doll's house** /ˈ· ˌ·/ *n* [C] *BrE* a child's toy house with small furniture in it; DOLL HOUSE *AmE*

**dol·ly** /ˈdɒli‖ˈdɑːli, ˈdɔːli/ *n* [C] **1** another word for a DOLL[1], used by and to children **2** *technical* a flat frame on wheels used for moving heavy objects

**dolly bird** /ˈ·· ·/ *n* [C] *BrE old-fashioned* a pretty young woman, especially one who wears fashionable clothes

**dol·men** /ˈdɒlmen, -mən‖ˈdoʊlmən, ˈdɔːl-, ˈdɑːl-/ *n* [C] *technical* two or more large upright stones supporting a large flat piece of stone, built in ancient times

**dol·our** *BrE*, **dolor** *AmE* /ˈdɒl‖ˈdoʊ-lər/ *n* [U] *literary* great sadness —**dolorous** *adj*

**dol·phin** /ˈdɒlfɪn‖ˈdɑːl-, ˈdɔːl-/ *n* [C] a very intelligent sea animal like a fish with a long grey pointed nose

**dolphin**

**dol·phi·na·ri·um** /ˌdɒlfɪˈneəriəm‖ˌdɑːlfɪˈner-, ˌdɔːl-/ *n* [C] a pool where dolphins are kept and people can go to see them

**dolt** /dəʊlt‖doʊlt/ *n* [C] *old-fashioned* a silly or stupid person —**doltish** *adj* —**doltishly** *adv*

**-dom** /dəm/ *suffix* [in U nouns] **1** the state of being something: *freedom* **2 a)** [in C nouns] a particular rank: *He was rewarded with a dukedom.* (=was made a DUKE) **b)** an area ruled by a particular type of person: *kingdom* **3** [in U nouns] *informal* all the people who share the same set of interests, have the same job, etc: *officialdom* (=all officials) | *yuppiedom*

**do·main** /dəˈmeɪn, dəʊ-‖də-, doʊ-/ *n* [C] *formal*

**1** ► **ACTIVITY/KNOWLEDGE** ◄ an area of activity, interest, or knowledge: *This problem lies outside the domain of medical science.*

**2 sb/sth's domain** an area of activity controlled by someone: *Mortgages were until recently the domain of building societies.*

**3** ► **LAND** ◄ an area of land owned and controlled by one person or government: *feudal domains*

**4 in the public domain** if information is in the public domain, it is not kept secret: *Details of the arms deals must be brought into the public domain.*

5 ▶ **QUANTITIES** ◀ *technical* the set of possible quantities by which something can vary

**dome** /dəʊm‖doʊm/ *n* [C] **1** a round roof on a base like a circle **2** a shape like a ball cut in half: *the dome of his bald head*

**domed** /dəʊmd‖doʊmd/ *adj* covered with a dome or shaped like a dome: *a high domed ceiling*

W2 **do·mes·tic¹** /də'mestɪk/ *adj*
1 ▶ **WITHIN ONE COUNTRY** ◀ happening within a country and not involving any other countries: *the domestic market* | *Domestic flights go from Terminal 1.*
2 ▶ **USED AT HOME** ◀ used in the house or home: **domestic appliance/equipment etc** *Electricity charges can be at business or domestic rate.*
3 ▶ **ABOUT FAMILY AND HOME** ◀ [only before noun] concerning family relationships and life at home: **domestic life** *I suspect Tony's domestic life isn't very happy.* | **domestic violence/problem/trouble etc** (=violence etc between members of the same family)
4 ▶ **PERSON** ◀ someone who is domestic enjoys spending time at home and is good at cooking, cleaning etc
5 ▶ **ANIMAL** ◀ a domestic animal lives on a farm or in someone's home —**domestically** /-kli/ *adv*

**domestic²** *n* [C] a servant who works in a large house

**do·mes·ti·cate** /də'mestɨkeɪt/ *v* [T] to make an animal able to live with people as a pet or work for them on a farm —compare TAME² (2) —**domestication** /dəˌmestɨ'keɪʃən/ *n* [U]

**do·mes·ti·cat·ed** /də'mestɨ'keɪtɨd/ *adj* someone who is domesticated enjoys spending time at home and doing work in the home: *Ray's very domesticated – he loves cooking.*

**do·mes·tic·i·ty** /ˌdəʊmes'tɪsɨti‖ˌdoʊ-/ *n* [U] life at home with your family: *a scene of happy domesticity*

**domestic sci·ence** /·ˌ·· '··/ *n* [U] *BrE old-fashioned* the study in schools of cooking, SEWING etc

**domestic ser·vice** /·ˌ·· '··/ *n* [U] the work of a servant in a large house

**dom·i·cile** /'dɒmɨsaɪl‖'dɑː-, 'doʊ-/ *n* [C] *law* a place where someone lives: *His last known domicile was 11 Park Road, London, N8.*

**dom·i·ciled** /'dɒmɨsaɪld‖'dɑː-,'doʊ-/ *adj law* **be domiciled in** to live in a particular place

**dom·i·cil·i·a·ry** /ˌdɒmɨ'sɪliəri‖ˌdɑːmɨ'sɪlieri, ˌdoʊ-/ *adj law* **domiciliary services/care/visits etc** care or services at someone's home

**dom·i·nance** /'dɒmɨnəns‖'dɑː-/ *n* [U] the fact of being more powerful, more important, or more noticeable than other people or things: *military dominance* | **[+of]** *Japan's dominance of the market*

W3 **dom·i·nant¹** /'dɒmɨnənt‖'dɑː-/ *adj* **1** stronger, more powerful, or more noticeable than other people or things: *The dominant male gorilla is the largest in the group.* | *a dominant personality* **2** *technical* a dominant physical feature can appear in a child even if it has been passed on from only one parent: *Brown eyes are dominant.* —compare RECESSIVE **3** high and easily seen: *The castle was built in a dominant position on a hill.*

**dominant²** *n* [singular] the fifth note of a musical SCALE¹ (8) of eight notes

W3 **dom·i·nate** /'dɒmɨneɪt‖'dɑː-/ *v* **1** [I,T] to have power and control over someone or something: *a society in which males dominate* | **dominate sth** *Sue's very nice, but she does tend to dominate the conversation.* **2** [I,T] to be the most important feature of something: *Education issues dominated the election campaign.* **3** [T] to be the largest and most impressive thing in a place: *The cathedral dominates the city.* —**domination** /ˌdɒmɪ'neɪʃən‖ˌdɑː-/ *n* [U] *a fight to free the country from foreign domination*

**dom·i·na·trix** /ˌdɒmɨ'neɪtrɪks‖ˌdɑː-/ *n* [C] a woman who is the stronger partner in a sado-masochistic (SADOMASOCHISM) sexual relationship

**dom·i·neer·ing** /dɒmɨ'nɪərɪŋ◂‖ˌdɑːmɨ'nɪr-/ *adj* someone who is domineering tries to control other people without considering how they feel or what they want: *a domineering mother* —**domineer** *v* [I]

**Do·min·i·can** /də'mɪnɪkən/ [C] a member of a Christian religious group who leads a holy life —**Dominican** *adj*

**do·min·ion** /də'mɪnjən/ *n* **1** [U] *literary* the power or right to rule people: **have/hold dominion over** *Alexander the Great held dominion over a vast area.* **2** [C] *formal* the land owned or controlled by one person or a government: *the king's dominion* **3** [C] one of the countries that was a member of the British COMMONWEALTH in the past —see also COLONY (1), PROTECTORATE

**dom·i·no** /'dɒmɨnəʊ‖'dɑːmɨnoʊ/ *n plural* **dominoes**
**1** [C] one of a set of small flat pieces of wood, plastic etc, with different numbers of spots on, used for playing a game **2 dominoes** [U] the game played using dominoes **3 the domino effect** a situation in which one event or action causes several other things to happen one after the other

**don¹** /dɒn‖dɑːn/ *n* [C] *BrE* a university teacher, especially one who teaches at the universities of Oxford or Cambridge

**don²** *v* **donned, donning** [T] *formal* to put on a hat, coat etc —opposite DOFF

**do·nate** /dəʊ'neɪt‖'doʊneɪt/ *v* [I,T] **1** to give something, especially money, to a person or an organization in order to help them: **donate sth to sb/sth** *Last year he donated $1,000 to cancer research.* **2 donate blood** to allow some blood to be removed from your body so that it can be used in a hospital to help someone who is ill or injured

**do·na·tion** /dəʊ'neɪʃən‖doʊ-/ *n* **1** [C] something, especially money, that you give to a person or an organization in order to help them: *All donations will be gratefully received.* | **make a donation** (=give money) **2** [U] the act of giving something, especially money, to help a person or an organization

**done¹** /dʌn/ the past participle of DO¹

**done²** *adj* [not before noun, no comparative]
1 ▶ **FINISHED** ◀ finished or completed: *The job's nearly done.* | *As soon as I'm done I'll give you a call.* | **over and done with** (=completely finished) *I'll be glad when this wedding is over and done with!*
2 ▶ **COOKED** ◀ cooked enough to eat: *Is the pasta done yet?* —compare OVERDONE, UNDERDONE
3 **be done for** *informal* to be in serious trouble or likely to fail: *If we're caught we're done for.*
4 **done in** *informal* extremely tired: *I've got to sit down – I'm done in.*
5 **be done/be the done thing** to be socially acceptable: *It just isn't the done thing to call teachers by their first names.*
6 **be/have done with it** to finish dealing with something or someone, and never deal with them again: *I know it's unfair but let's just pay the fine and have done with it.*
7 **be done** *BrE informal* to be deceived or cheated: *You paid £50 for that! You were done mate!*
8 **be/get done** *BrE informal* to be caught by the police for doing something illegal, but usually not too serious: **[+ for]** *I got done for speeding on the M1 last night.* —see also **be hard done by** (HARD² (5))

**done³** *interjection* used to agree to and accept the conditions of a deal: *"I'll give you $90 a day for the job." "Done!"*

**dong** /dɒŋ‖dɑːŋ, dɒːŋ/ *n* [C] *taboo slang* the male sex organ

**don·jon** /'dɒndʒən‖'dɑːn-/ *n* [C] the strong main tower of a MEDIEVAL castle

**Don Ju·an** /ˌdɒn 'hwɑːn, -'wɑːn, -'dʒuːən‖ˌdɑːn-/ *n* [C] a man who is good at persuading women to have sex with him

**don·key** /'dɒŋki‖'dɑːŋki/ *n* [C] **1** a grey or brown animal like a horse, but smaller and with long ears **2** a stupid person **3 donkey's years** *BrE informal* a very long time: *It's donkey's years since I went to the pictures.*

**donkey der·by** /ˈ·· ˌ··/ *n* [C] *BrE* a race on donkeys done for amusement or to raise money

**donkey en·gine** /ˈ·· ˌ··/ *n* [C] a small additional engine used for special jobs, especially on a ship

**donkey jack·et** /ˈ·· ˌ··/ *n* [C] *BrE* a short thick coat, usually very dark blue, that has a piece of leather or plastic across the shoulders —see picture at COAT[1]

**don·key·work** /ˈdɒŋkiwɜːk‖ˈdɑːŋkiwɜːrk/ *n* [U] *informal* hard boring work; GRUNT WORK *AmE*: *Why do I always have to do the donkeywork?*

**don·nish** /ˈdɒnɪʃ‖ˈdɑːnɪʃ/ *adj especially BrE* clever, serious, and more interested in ideas than real life —**donnishly** *adv*

**do·nor** /ˈdəʊnə‖ˈdoʊnər/ *n* [C] **1** a person, group etc that gives something, especially money, to an organization in order to help people: *Funding for the clinic has come mostly from private donors.* **2** someone who gives a part of their body so that it can be used in the medical treatment of someone else: *The search is under way for a suitable donor.* **3 donor card** a card that you carry to show that when you die, a doctor can take parts of your body to use in the medical treatment of someone else

**do-noth·ing** /ˈ· ˌ··/ *n* [C] *informal* a lazy person

**Don Quix·ote** /ˌdɒn ˈkwɪksət, -kɪˈhəʊti‖ˌdɑːn-, -ˈhoʊti/ *n* [singular] someone who is determined to change what is wrong, but who does it in a way that is silly or not practical —see also QUIXOTIC

**don't** /dəʊnt‖doʊnt/ **1** the short form of 'do not': *Don't worry!*|*You know him, don't you?* —see also **dos and don'ts** (DO[3] (2)) **2** *spoken* an incorrect short form of 'does not': *She don't like it.*

**do·nut** /ˈdəʊnʌt‖ˈdoʊ-/ *n* [C] an American spelling of DOUGHNUT

**doo·dah** /ˈduːdɑː/ *BrE*, **doo·dad** /ˈduːdæd/ *AmE n* [C] *informal* a small object whose name you have forgotten or do not know: *Where's the control doodah for the TV?*

**doo·dle** /ˈduːdl/ *v* [I] to draw shapes, lines, or patterns without really thinking about what you are doing: *I always doodle when I'm on the phone.* —**doodle** *n* [C]

**doo·dle·bug** /ˈduːdlbʌg/ *n* [C] a flying bomb used by the Germans in World War II

**doo-doo** /ˈduːduː/ *n* [U] *informal* a word for solid waste from your body, used by or to children —**doo-doo** *v* [I]

**doo·fer** /ˈduːfə‖-ər/ also **doo·fah** /ˈduːfə/ *n* [C] *informal* a small object whose name you have forgotten or do not know

**doo·fus** /ˈduːfəs/ *n* [C] *AmE informal* a silly or stupid person

**doo·hick·ey** /ˈduːˌhɪki/ *n* [C] *AmE informal* a small object whose name you have forgotten or do not know, especially a part of a machine

**doo·lal·ly** /duːˈlæli/ *adj informal* crazy

**doom**[1] /duːm/ *v* [T usually passive] to make someone or something certain to fail, die, be destroyed etc: **doom sth to sth** *The species is doomed to extinction.*|**doom sb/sth to do sth** *Marx's theory was that capitalist economies are eventually doomed to collapse.*|**doomed to failure** *The marriage seems doomed to failure.* —**doomed** *adj*

**doom**[2] *n* [U] the end of something especially by destruction or death, that will soon come and that you cannot avoid: *a terrible sense of impending doom*|**meet your doom** *Thousands of soldiers met their doom on this very field.*|**spell doom for** (=mean that something will end) *The budget cuts spelled doom for the mining community.*|**doom and gloom** (=a feeling that the future will be terrible)

**Dooms·day** /ˈduːmzdeɪ/ *n* [singular] **1 till/until Doomsday** *informal* forever: *You could wait till Doomsday and he'd never show up.* **2** the last day of the Earth's existence

**doom·ster** /ˈduːmstə‖-ər/ *n* [C] *informal* someone who always thinks something bad is going to happen

**door** /dɔː‖dɔːr/ *n* [C] S1 W1 **1** the large flat object that you open and close at the entrance to a building, room, vehicle etc: **open/close/shut/slam the door** *Could you open the door for me?*|*Close the door behind you.*|**knock on/at the door** *Knock on the door and see if they're home.*|**kitchen/bathroom/bedroom etc door** *Don't forget to lock the office door.*|**front/back/side door** *Is the front door open?*|**revolving/sliding/swing doors** *Nathan got stuck in the revolving doors!* —compare GATE[1] (1) —see picture on page 410 **2** the space made by an open door; DOORWAY: *Rick turned around and ran out of the door.*|*I glanced through the open door.* **3 at the door** if someone is at the door they are waiting for you to open it so they can come inside: *There's somebody at the door.* **4 answer the door** to open the door to see who is there **5 show/see sb to the door** to take someone to the main way out of a building: *Goodbye, Mr Carter. My secretary will show you to the door.* **6 two/three doors down etc** a place that is a particular number of houses or buildings away from where you are: *The Rigbys live two doors down from us.* **7 (from) door to door a)** between one place and another: *My commute takes forty minutes, door to door.* **b)** going to each house in a street or area to sell something, collect money or ask for votes: *Joe sold vacuum cleaners door to door for years.* —see also DOOR-TO-DOOR **8 out of doors** outside; OUTDOORS **9 behind closed doors** where other people cannot see you; secretly: *The meeting took place behind closed doors.* **10 show sb the door** to make it clear to someone that you want them to leave: *I'm warning you, if he gets drunk I'll show him the door.* **11 lay sth at sb's door** to say that something is someone's fault **12 be on the door** to work at the entrance to a theatre, club, etc collecting tickets **13 an open door policy** willingness to allow people to come in: *an open door policy for immigration* **14 open doors for sb** to give someone an opportunity they would not have had otherwise: *I think your new job will really open doors for you.* **15 open the door to** to make something possible: *You're opening the door to trouble by hitchhiking.* **16 shut/close the door on** to make something impossible: *Sasha's accident shut the door on her ballet career.* —see also BACK DOOR, FRONT DOOR, NEXT DOOR, **at death's door** (DEATH (8))

**door·bell** /ˈdɔːbel‖ˈdɔːr-/ *n* [C] a button outside a house that you push to make a sound so that people inside know you are there: **ring the doorbell** (=push the button)

**do-or-die** /ˌ· · ˈ·/ *adj* very determined: *a do-or-die attitude*

**door·jamb** /ˈdɔːdʒæm‖ˈdɔːr-/ *n* [C] one of two upright posts on either side of a doorway; DOORPOST

**door·keep·er** /ˈdɔːˌkiːpə‖ˈdɔːrˌkiːpər/ *n* [C] someone who guards the main door of a large building and lets people in and out

**door·knob** /ˈdɔːnɒb‖ˈdɔːrnɑːb/ *n* [C] a round handle that you turn to open a door

**door·knock·er** /ˈdɔːˌnɒkə‖ˈdɔːrˌnɑːkər/ *n* [C] a heavy metal ring or bar on a door that visitors use to knock with

**door·man** /ˈdɔːmæn, -mən‖ˈdɔːr-/ *n plural* **doormen** /-men, -mən/ [C] a man in a hotel or theatre who watches the door, helps people find taxis, and usually wears a uniform —compare PORTER (2)

**door·mat** /ˈdɔːmæt‖ˈdɔːr-/ *n* [C] **1** a piece of material just inside a door for you to clean your shoes on **2** *informal* someone who lets other people treat them badly and never complains: *Ted lets Tracy treat him like a doormat.*

**door·nail** /ˈdɔːneɪl‖ˈdɔːr-/ *n* [singular] —see **dead as a doornail** (DEAD[1] (1))

**door·plate** /ˈdɔːpleɪt‖ˈdɔːr-/ *n* [C] a flat piece of metal fixed to the door of a house or building showing the name of the person or company that works inside

**door·post** /ˈdɔːpəʊst‖ˈdɔːrpoʊst/ *n* [C] one of two upright posts on either side of a doorway; DOORJAMB

**door prize** /ˈ· ·/ *n* [C] *AmE* a prize given to someone who has the winning number on their ticket for a show, dance, or party

**door·sill** /ˈdɔːˌsɪl‖ˈdɔːr-/ *n* [C] the part of a door frame that you step across when you go through a doorway

D

**door·step¹** /ˈdɔːstep‖ˈdɔːr-/ *n* [C] **1** a step just outside a door to a house or building **2 on your doorstep** very near to where you live or are staying: *Wow! You've got the beach right on your doorstep!* **3** *BrE informal* a very thick piece of bread cut from a loaf

**doorstep²** *v* [I] if politicians wanting votes or JOURNALISTS looking for a news story go doorstepping, they visit people who do not want to see them

**door·stop** /ˈdɔːstɒp‖ˈdɔːrstɑːp/ also **door·stop·per** /-ˌstɒpə‖-ˌstɑːpər/ *n* [C] **1** something you put under or against a door to keep it open **2** a rubber object fixed to a wall to stop a door hitting it when it is opened

**door-to-door** /ˌ· · ˈ·◂/ *adj* visiting each house in a street or area, usually to sell something, collect money, or ask for votes

**door·way** /ˈdɔːweɪ‖ˈdɔːr-/ *n* [C] the space where the door opens into a room or building: *I looked up and there was Paolo, standing in the doorway.*

**door·yard** /ˈdɔːjɑːd‖ˈdɔːrjɑːrd/ *n* [C] *AmE* an area in front of the door of a house

**doo·zy, doozie** /ˈduːzi/ *n* [C] *AmE informal* something that is so good, bad, strange etc that you can hardly believe it: *I've heard lies before, but that one was a real doozy!*

**dope¹** /dəʊp‖doʊp/ *n informal* **1** [U] a drug that is not legal, especially MARIJUANA: *a dope dealer* **2** [C] someone who is stupid: *Pam, you dope!* **3 the dope on** new information about someone or something, especially information that not many people know: *Give me all the dope on the new teacher.* **4** [U] medicine, especially medicine that makes you sleep easily

**dope²** *v* [T] *informal* **1** also **dope up** to give someone a drug, often in their food or drink, to make them sleep or feel better: *They dope the elephants in order to tag them.* | *If we dope you up enough you'll still be able to sing with a cold.* **2** to give an animal a drug that makes it perform better in a race or competition

**dope·head** /ˈdəʊphed‖ˈdoʊp-/ *n* [C] *slang* someone who takes a lot of drugs

**dop·ey, dopy** /ˈdəʊpi/ *adj informal* **1** slow to react mentally or physically, as if you have taken a drug: *I'm still a little dopey from the anesthetic.* **2** slightly stupid: *Dan gave me a dopey grin.*

**dop·pel·gang·er** /ˈdɒpəlgæŋə, -geŋ-‖ˈdɑːpəlgæŋər/ *n* [C] *German* **1** a spirit that looks exactly like a living person **2** someone who looks exactly like someone else

**do·py** /ˈdəʊpi‖ˈdoʊpi/ *adj* another spelling of DOPEY

**Dor·ic** /ˈdɒrɪk‖ˈdɔː-, ˈdɑː-/ *adj* in the oldest and most simple of the Greek building styles: *a Doric column* —compare CORINTHIAN, IONIC

**dork** /dɔːk‖dɔːrk/ *n* [C] *AmE informal* someone who you think is stupid, because they behave strangely or wear strange clothes: *You look a real dork in that outfit.* —**dorky** *adj*

**dorm** /dɔːm‖dɔːrm/ *n* [C] *informal* a dormitory

**dor·mant** /ˈdɔːmənt‖ˈdɔːr-/ *adj* not active or not growing at the present time but able to be active later: *The seeds remain dormant in the soil all winter.* | **lie dormant** *Stress may activate the virus which has lain dormant in the blood.* —**dormancy** *n* [U]

**dor·mer** /ˈdɔːmə‖ˈdɔːrmər/ also **dormer win·dow** /ˈ·· ˌ··/ *n* [C] a window built upright in the slope of a roof

**dor·mi·to·ry¹** /ˈdɔːmɪtəri‖ˈdɔːrmɪtɔːri/ *n* [C] **1** a large room in a BOARDING SCHOOL or HOSTEL for several people to sleep in **2** *AmE* a large building in a college or university where students live; HALL OF RESIDENCE *BrE*

**dormitory²** *adj* [only before noun] *especially BrE* a dormitory town is a place from which people travel into a city to work every day

**dor·mo·bile** /ˈdɔːməbiːl‖ˈdɔːr-/ *n* [C] *trademark BrE* a vehicle big enough to live in when you travel, with cooking equipment and beds in it

**dor·mouse** /ˈdɔːmaʊs‖ˈdɔːr-/ *n* [C] a small European forest animal with a long furry tail

**dor·sal** /ˈdɔːsəl‖ˈdɔːr-/ *adj* [only before noun] *technical* on or related to the back of an animal or fish: *a shark's dorsal fin* —see picture at FISH¹

**do·ry** /ˈdɔːri/ *n* **1** [C] a rowing boat that has a flat bottom and is used for fishing **2** [C,U] a flat sea fish that can be eaten, or the flesh of this fish

**DOS** /dɒs‖dɑːs/ *n* [U] *trademark* Disk Operating System; SOFTWARE that is loaded onto a computer system to make all the different parts work together

**dos·age** /ˈdəʊsɪdʒ‖ˈdoʊ-/ *n* [C usually singular] the amount of medicine that you should take at one time: *Do not exceed the recommended dosage.*

**dose¹** /dəʊs‖doʊs/ *n* [C] **1** a measured amount of a medicine: **[+ of]** *a dose of antibiotics* **2** an amount of something unpleasant that you experience at one time: **[+ of]** *Workers were exposed to a large dose of radiation.* | *a bad dose of flu* | **in small doses** (=for a short time) *I can only tolerate Joseph in small doses.* **3 like a dose of salts** *BrE informal* very quickly and easily: *The new owners went through the company like a dose of salts, stripping it of its assets.* **4 have a dose** *slang* to be infected with VENEREAL DISEASE

**dose²** also **dose up** *v* [T] to give someone medicine: **dose sb with** *Sumi dosed herself with aspirin and went to bed.*

**dosh** /dɒʃ‖dɑːʃ/ *n* [U] *BrE spoken* money

**do-si-do** /ˌdəʊ si ˈdəʊ‖ˌdoʊ si ˈdoʊ/ *n* [singular] an action in COUNTRY DANCING in which partners pass each other sideways —**do-si-do** *v* [I]

**doss¹** /dɒs‖dɑːs/ *v*

**doss around/about** *phr v* [I] *BrE informal* to do very little: *We just dossed around all day Saturday.*

**doss down** *phr v* [I] *BrE informal* to sleep somewhere that is not your usual place or not a real bed: *Hundreds dossed down in the theatre because of the blizzards.*

**doss²** *n* **a doss** *BrE informal* work that does not need much effort: *This job's a real doss.*

**doss·er** /ˈdɒsə‖ˈdɑːsər/ *n* [C] *BrE informal* someone who has nowhere to live and sleeps in the street or in cheap HOSTELS

**doss-house** /ˈ· ·/ *n* [C] *BrE slang* a place where people who have nowhere to live can stay cheaply; FLOPHOUSE *AmE*

**dos·si·er** /ˈdɒsieɪ‖ˈdɒːsjeɪ, ˈdɑː-/ *n* [C] a set of papers containing detailed information on a person or subject; FILE¹ (1): **keep a dossier on** *The secret police kept dossiers on all opponents of the regime.*

**dost** /dʌst/ *v* **thou dost** *old use or biblical* you do

**dot¹** /dɒt‖dɑːt/ *n* [C] **1** a small round mark or spot S2
**2 on the dot** *informal* exactly at a particular time: **on the dot of five (o'clock)/at five (o'clock) on the dot** *Mr Green arrived at six on the dot.* **3** something that looks like a small spot because it is so far away: *The plane was just a dot in the sky.* **4** a short sound or flash of light used when sending messages by MORSE CODE —compare DASH² —see also **the year dot** (YEAR (11))

**dot²** *v* **dotted, dotting** [T] **1** to mark something by putting a dot on it or above it: *She never dots her i's.* —see picture on page 839 **2** [often passive] to spread things over a wide area and quite far apart: **be dotted with** *The lake was dotted with sailboats.* | **be dotted about/around etc** *The company now has over 20 stores dotted around the country.* **3** to put a very small amount of something on a surface or in several places on a surface: *Dot some rouge on your cheeks, then blend carefully.* **4 dot the i's and cross the t's** *informal* to pay attention to all the details when you are finishing something: *Well, we haven't dotted the i's and crossed the t's, but the contract's nearly ready.* —see also DOTTED LINE

**do·tage** /ˈdəʊtɪdʒ‖ˈdoʊ-/ *n* **in your dotage** in your old age

**dote** /dəʊt‖doʊt/ *v*

**dote on/upon** sb *phr v* [T] to love someone and to show this by your actions: *I can't help doting on my* *granddaughter.* —**doting** *adj* [only before noun] *a doting parent* —**dotingly** *adv*

**doth** /dʌθ/ *old use or biblical* does

**dot-ma·trix print·er** /ˈ· ·· ˌ··/ *n* [C] a machine connected to a computer that prints letters, numbers etc using many small dots

**dot·ted line** /ˌ·· ˈ·/ *n* [C] **1** a series of printed or drawn DOTS that form a line: *Cut along the dotted lines.* **2 sign on the dotted line** *informal* to officially agree to something, especially by signing a contract

**dot·ty** /ˈdɒti‖ˈdɑːti/ *adj informal especially BrE* **1** slightly crazy or likely to behave strangely **2 dotty about sb/sth** very fond of or interested in someone or something: *Gemma's dotty about horses.*

S1 W2 **doub·le**[1] /ˈdʌbəl/ *adj*
**1** ▶ **OF TWO PARTS** ◀ consisting of two parts that are similar or exactly the same: *You can't park on double yellow lines.*
**2 double l/s/9 etc** *BrE spoken* used when you are spelling a word or telling someone a number, to show that a letter or number is repeated: *My number is 869 34 double 2.*|*That's Robbins with a double 'b'.*
**3** ▶ **TWICE AS BIG** ◀ twice as big, twice as much, or twice as many as usual, or twice as big, much, or many as something else: *Leave the dough in a warm place to rise until it is double in bulk.*|*I'll have a double whisky please.*
**4** ▶ **FOR TWO PEOPLE** ◀ made to be used by two people: *a double room* —compare SINGLE[1] (4)
**5** ▶ **WITH TWO DIFFERENT USES** ◀ combining two different uses or qualities; DUAL: *a double-action corkscrew*|*the double advantage of money and a good education*
**6** ▶ **DECEIVING** ◀ seeming to be one thing while actually being another; deceiving: *There was a double meaning in Sybil's words.*|**lead a double life** (=pretend to be one type of person but really be another)
**7** ▶ **FLOWER** ◀ a double flower has more than the usual number of PETALS —see also DOUBLY, **double figures** (FIGURE[1] (1b))

**double**[2] *n*
**1** ▶ **TWICE THE SIZE** ◀ [C, U] something that is twice the size, quantity, value, or strength of something else: *Scotch and water, please – make it a double.*|*"What did they offer you?" "Ten thousand." "I'll give you double."*
**2** ▶ **SIMILAR PERSON** ◀ [C] someone who looks very much like someone else: *Caroline's her mother's double.*
**3** ▶ **IN FILMS** ◀ [C] an actor who takes the place of another actor in a film because the acting involves something very dangerous: *a stunt double*
**4 at the double** *BrE* **on the double** *AmE* very quickly and without any delay: *The firemen came around on the double.*
**5** ▶ **TENNIS** ◀ **doubles** [U] a game played between two pairs of players: *the men's doubles* —compare **singles** (SINGLE[2] (3))—see also MIXED DOUBLES
**6 double or nothing** *AmE* **double or quits** *BrE* a decision in a game when you must decide to do something that will either win you twice as much money or make you lose it all
**7** ▶ **IN RACING** ◀ [C] a BET[2] (1) on the results of two races in which any money won on the first race is risked on the second
**8** ▶ **A THROW** ◀ [C] a throw in the game of darts (DART[2] (2)) that hits a point between the two outer circles on the board, and has twice the usual value
**9** ▶ **A HIT** ◀ [C] a hit which allows the BATTER[2] (3) in BASEBALL to reach second BASE[1] (8)

**double**[3] *v* **1** [I,T] to become twice as much or as many, or to make something twice as big: *Unemployment more than doubled in 1921.*|*The Federal government has doubled its tax on liquor.* **2** also **double sth over** [T] to fold something in half: *Take a sheet of paper and double it.* **3** [I] if a BATTER[2] (3) in a game of BASEBALL doubles, he hits the ball far enough to get to second BASE[1] (8) **4 double your fists** *AmE* to curl your fingers tightly to make FISTS ready to fight

**double as** sb/sth *phr v* [T] to have a second use, job, or purpose as something else: *Our local police chief doubles as the fire chief.*

**double back** *phr v* [I] to turn around and go back the way you have come: *I doubled back along the main highway to LA.*

**double up** *phr v* **1** also **double over** [I,T **double** sb **up**] to suddenly bend at the waist because you are laughing too much or are in pain and cannot stand up: *Emilio doubled over, grabbing his leg.*|**be doubled up/over with** *We leant against the table, doubled over with laughter.* **2** [I] to share something, especially a bedroom: *There aren't enough textbooks. Can you double up?*|[+ **with sb**] *You'll have to double up with Susie while Aunt Clara is visiting.*

**double**[4] *adv* **1 see double** to have something wrong with your eyes so that you see two things instead of one: *I was feeling dizzy and seeing double.* **2 be bent double** to be bent over a long way: *The trees were almost bent double in the wind.* **3 fold sth double** to fold something in half to make it twice as thick

**double**[5] *predeterminer* twice as much or twice as many: *It's worth double the amount I paid for it.*

**double-act** /ˈ·· ·/ *n* [C] two actors, especially COMEDIANS, who perform together

**double a·gent** /ˌ·· ˈ··/ *n* [C] someone who finds out an enemy country's secrets for their own country but who also gives secrets to the enemy —compare SPY[1]

**double-bar·relled** *BrE* **double-barreled** *AmE* /ˌ·· ˈ··◂/ *adj* **1** a double-barrelled gun has two places where the BULLETS come out **2** *BrE* a double-barrelled family name has two parts **3** *AmE* with two purposes: *a double-barreled plan* **4** *AmE* very strong or using a lot of force: *a double-barreled attack*

**double bass** /ˌdʌbəl ˈbeɪs/ also **bass** *n* [C] a very large musical instrument shaped like a VIOLIN that the musician plays standing up

**double bed** /ˌ·· ˈ·/ *n* [C] a bed made for two people to sleep in —see picture at BED[1]

**double bill** /ˌ·· ˈ·/ *n* [C] a cinema or theatre performance in which two films or plays are shown one after the other; DOUBLE FEATURE *AmE*

**double bind** /ˌ·· ˈ·/ *n* [C usually singular] a situation in which any choice you make will have unpleasant results

**double-blind** /ˌ·· ˈ·◂/ *adj technical* a double-blind EXPERIMENT[1] (1) or study compares two or more groups in which neither the scientists nor the people being studied know which group is being tested and which group is not

**double bluff** /ˌ·· ˈ·/ *n* [C] an attempt to deceive someone by telling them the truth, hoping that they will think you are lying

**double boil·er** /ˌ·· ˈ··/ *n* [C] a pot for cooking food, consisting of one pan resting on top of another pan with hot water in it

**double-book** /ˌ·· ˈ·/ *v* [I,T] to promise the same seat in a theatre, on a plane, etc to more than one person —**double-booking** *n* [U]

**double-breast·ed** /ˌ·· ˈ··◂/ *adj* a double-breasted jacket, coat etc has two sets of buttons —compare SINGLE-BREASTED —see picture on page 840

**double-check** /ˌ·· ˈ·/ *v* [I,T] to check something again so that you are completely sure

**double chin** /ˌ·· ˈ·/ *n* [C] a fold of loose skin under someone's chin that looks like a second chin —see picture on page 412

**double cream** /ˌ·· ˈ·/ *n* [U] *BrE* very thick cream —compare SINGLE CREAM

**double-cross** /ˌ·· ˈ·/ *v* [T] to cheat someone, especially after you have already agreed to do something dishonest with them: *Shorty's murder was blamed on a gang he'd double-crossed in the past.* —**double cross** *n* [C] —**double-crosser** *n* [C]

**double date** /ˌ·· ˈ·/ *n* [C] *especially AmE* an arranged social meeting for two couples (COUPLE[1] (2)) —**double-date** *v* [I, T]

**double-deal·er** /ˌ·· '··/ *n* [C] *informal* someone who deceives other people —**double-dealing** *n* [U]

**double-deck·er** /ˌ·· '··◂/ *n* [C] **1** a bus with two levels **2** a SANDWICH[1] (1) made with three pieces of bread leaving two spaces to be filled with food

**double-di·git** /ˌ·· '··/ *adj AmE* related to the numbers 10 to 99, especially as a PERCENTAGE: *double-digit inflation* —see also DOUBLE FIGURES

**double-dip[1]** /ˌ·· '·/ *n* [C] *AmE* an ice-cream CONE[1] (4) with two balls of ice-cream

**double-dip[2]** *v* [I] *AmE* to collect pay or money from two places at once, usually in a way that is not legal or not approved of; MOONLIGHT[2] (2)

**double-dutch** /ˌ·· '·/ *n* [U] **1** *informal* speech or writing that you cannot understand; nonsense **2** *AmE* a skipping (SKIP[1] (1)) game using two long ropes

**double du·ty** /ˌ·· '··/ *n* [U] *AmE* **do double duty** to do more than one job or be used for more than one thing at the same time: *The lids on the camping pans do double duty as plates.*

**double-edged** /ˌ·· '·◂/ *adj* **1** with two very different meanings: *a double-edged remark* **2** with two cutting edges: *a double-edged sword*

**double en·ten·dre** /ˌduːblɒn'tɒndrə‖-blɑːn'tɑːn-/ *n* [C] *French* a word or phrase that may be understood in two different ways, one of which is often sexual

**double fault** /ˌ·· '·/ *n* [C] two mistakes, one after another, when you are serving (SERVE[1] (10)) in tennis, that make you lose a point

**double fea·ture** /ˌ·· '··/ *n* [C] *AmE* a cinema performance in which two films are shown one after the other; DOUBLE BILL

**double fig·ures** /ˌ·· '··/ *n* [plural] *BrE* the numbers from 10 to 99: *The death toll is thought to have reached double figures.* —see also DOUBLE-DIGIT

**double first** /ˌ·· '·/ *n* [C] a British university degree in which a student reaches the highest standard in two subjects

**double-glaz·ing** /ˌ·· '··/ *n* [U] *especially BrE* glass on a window or door in two separate sheets with a space between them, in order to keep noise out and heat in —**double-glaze** *v* [T]

**double-head·er** /ˌ·· '··/ *n* [C] *AmE* two BASEBALL games played one after the other

**double he·lix** /ˌ·· '··/ *n* [C] *technical* a shape consisting of two parallel spirals (SPIRAL[2] (1)) that twist around the same centre, found especially in the structure of DNA

**double in·dem·ni·ty** /ˌ·· ·'···/ *n* [U] *AmE law* a feature of a life insurance POLICY that allows double the value of the contract to be paid in the case of death by accident

**double jeop·ar·dy** /ˌ·· '···/ *n* [C] *AmE law* the act of taking someone to court a second time for the same offence, in some rare situations

**double-joint·ed** /ˌ·· '··◂/ *adj* able to move the joints in your fingers, arms etc backwards as well as forwards

**double neg·a·tive** /ˌ·· '···/ *n* [C] a sentence in which two negatives (NEGATIVE[2] (1)) are used when only one is needed in correct English grammar, for example in the sentence 'I don't want nobody to help me!'

**double-park** /ˌ·· '·/ *v* [I,T] to leave a vehicle on a road beside another vehicle that is already parked there

**double play** /ˌ·· '·/ *n* [C] *AmE* the action of making two runners in a game of BASEBALL have to leave the field by throwing the ball quickly from one BASE[1] (8) to another before the runners reach either one

**double-quick** /ˌ·· '·◂/ *adv BrE informal* as quickly as possible: *Call an ambulance double-quick!*

**double stand·ard** /ˌ·· '··/ *n* [C] a rule, principle etc that is unfair because it treats one group or type of people more severely than another in the same situation

**doub·let** /'dʌblɪ̇t/ *n* [C] a man's shirt, worn in Europe from about 1400 to the middle 1600s

**double take** /ˌ·· '·/ *n* [C] **do a double take** to react to something after a short delay because you are surprised

**double-talk** /'·· ·/ *n* [U] *informal* speech that seems to be serious and sincere, but has another meaning or is a mixture of sense and nonsense: *legal double-talk* —**double-talk** *v* [I,T] —**double-talker** *n* [C]

**double·think** /'dʌbəlˌθɪŋk/ *n* [U] a dishonest belief in two opposing ideas at the same time

**double time** /ˌ·· '·/ *n* [U] **1** double wages paid to someone when they work on a day or at a time when people do not normally work —compare **time and a half** (TIME[1] (84)) **2** *AmE* a fast military march

**double-time** *adv AmE informal* as quickly as possible: *C'mon get upstairs and clean your room – double-time!*

**double vi·sion** /ˌ·· '··/ *n* [U] a medical condition in which you see two of everything, for example after hitting your head or drinking too much alcohol

**double wham·my** /ˌ·· '··/ *n* [C] *informal* two bad things that happen together, or one after the other: *the double whammy of higher prices and more taxes*

**double whole note** /ˌ·· '· ·/ *n* [C] *AmE* a musical note that continues for twice the length of a WHOLE NOTE; BREVE *BrE*

**dou·bloon** /dʌ'bluːn/ *n* [C] a gold coin used in the past in Spain and Spanish America

**doub·ly** /'dʌbli/ *adv* **1** by twice the amount, or to twice the degree: *Be doubly careful when driving in fog.* **2** in two ways or for two reasons: *You are doubly mistaken.*

**doubt[1]** /daʊt/ *n* **S1**

**1** ► **UNCERTAIN FEELING** ◄ [C,U] a feeling or feelings of being uncertain about something: **[+ about/as to]** *Maisie expressed private doubts about Lawrence's sanity.* | **[+ whether/who/what etc]** *There's no doubt who was responsible for this outrage.* | **[+ (that)]** *I have little doubt that the coup will succeed.* | **cast doubt(s) on sth/raise doubts about sth** (=say that something may not be true or real) *The new evidence cast some doubt on his reliability as a witness.* | **an element of doubt** (=a slight doubt) | **without a shadow of a doubt** (=there is no doubt at all) **W1**

**2 no doubt** used when you are saying that you think something is probably true: *No doubt she was disturbed by the noise.* | **no doubt about it** (=it is certainly true) *Someone had been eavesdropping, no doubt about it.*

**3 have your doubts (about)** used to say that you have reasons for not feeling certain about something or someone: *"Don't you think she'd be a good candidate?" "Well, I have my doubts."*

**4 if/when in doubt** used when advising someone what to do: *If in doubt, don't eat it.*

**5 be in doubt** if someone's or something's future or success is in doubt, they may not be able to continue or succeed: *The future of the public library is in doubt.*

**6 be in doubt about** to not be certain about something: *He's still in some doubt about what to do.*

**7 be beyond doubt** if something is beyond doubt, it is completely certain: *Patel's integrity is beyond doubt.* | **beyond reasonable doubt** *law*: *Her guilt was established beyond reasonable doubt.*

**8 without/beyond doubt** *formal* used to emphasize an opinion: *Sally was without doubt one of the finest swimmers in the school.*

**9 open to doubt** something that is open to doubt has not been proved to be definitely true or real: *The authenticity of the relics is open to doubt.* —see also SELF-DOUBT, **give sb/sth the benefit of the doubt** (BENEFIT[1] (4))

**doubt[2]** *v* [T not in progressive] **1** to think that something may not be true: *Kim never doubted his story.* | **doubt (that)** *I don't doubt that he's a brilliant scientist, but can he teach?* **2** *especially spoken* to think that something is unlikely: **doubt if/whether** *You can complain, but I doubt if it'll make any difference.* | **doubt sth** *"Do you think there'll be any tickets left?" "I very much doubt it."* | **doubt (that)** *I doubt that we'll ever see George again.* **3** to not trust or have confidence in someone: *If* **S2**

*anyone doubts my ability to handle this, they should say so.* | **doubt sb's word** (=think that someone may not be telling the truth) —**doubter** *n* [C]

**doubt·ful** /'daʊtfəl/ *adj* **1** having doubts about something: *The journalist looked doubtful when he heard her story.* | [+ **if/whether**] *I'm still doubtful whether I should accept this job.* | **doubtful about (doing) sth** *At first we were doubtful about employing Charlie.* **2** something that is doubtful may not be true or may not happen in the way you want: *The company's prospects are starting to look more doubtful.* | [+ **if/whether**] *It was doubtful whether the patient would survive the operation.* **3** unlikely: [+ **that**] *It now seems doubtful that the missing airmen will ever be found.* **4** probably false or of no value; DUBIOUS: *Pringle was given the doubtful privilege of leading the troops.* —**doubtfully** *adv*

**doubt·ing Thom·as** /ˌdaʊtɪŋ 'tɒməs‖-'tɑːm-/ *n* [singular] *humorous* someone who tends to doubt things if they have not seen proof of them

**doubt·less** /'daʊtləs/ *adv formal* used when saying something that you believe to be true although you have no proof: *Renee was doubtless reassured by the news.*

**douche** /duːʃ/ *n* [C usually singular] **1** a mixture of water and something such as VINEGAR, that a woman puts into her VAGINA to wash it **2** water that is poured over part of someone's body —**douche** *v* [I,T]

**dough** /dəʊ‖doʊ/ *n* **1** [singular, U] a mixture of flour and water ready to be baked into bread, PASTRY etc **2** [U] *informal* money

**dough·nut** /'dəʊnʌt‖'doʊ-/ *n* [C] **1** a small round cake, often in the form of a ring **2 do doughnuts** *AmE informal* to make a car spin around in circles

**dough·ty** /'daʊti/ *adj* [only before noun] *literary* brave and determined: *a doughty fighter*

**dough·y** /'dəʊi‖'doʊi/ *adj* **1** looking and feeling like DOUGH (1) **2** doughy skin is unhealthily pale and soft

**dour** /dʊə,'daʊə‖'daʊər, dʊ'r/ *adj* **1** severe and never smiling **2** making you feel anxious or afraid; GRIM (1): *a dour reminder* —**dourly** *adv*

**douse, dowse** /daʊs/ *v* [T] **1** to put out a fire by pouring water on it **2** [+ **with/in**] to cover something in water or other liquid

**dove¹** /dʌv/ *n* [C] **1** a kind of small PIGEON (=bird) often used as a sign of peace **2** someone in politics who prefers peace and discussion to war —opposite HAWK¹ (2)

**dove²** /dəʊv‖doʊv/ *especially AmE* a past tense of DIVE¹

**dove·cot** /'dʌvkɒt‖-kɑːt/ *also,* **dove·cote** /'dʌvkəʊt,kɒt‖-koʊt, -kɑːt/ *n* [C] a small house built for doves to live in

**dove·tail¹** /'dʌvteɪl/ *v* **1** [I,T] to fit perfectly together or to make two plans, ideas etc fit together perfectly: [+ **with**] *My vacation plans dovetail nicely with Joyce's.* **2** [T + **together**] to join two pieces of wood by means of dovetail joints

**dovetail²** also **dovetail joint** /ˌ·· '·/ *n* [C] a type of JOINT¹ (3) fastening two pieces of wood together

**dov·ish** /'dʌvɪʃ/ *adj* preferring peace and discussion to war

**dow·a·ger** /'daʊədʒə‖-ər/ *n* [C] **1** a woman from a high social class who has land or a title from her dead husband: *the dowager Duchess of Devonshire* **2** *informal* a respected and impressive old lady

**dow·dy** /'daʊdi/ *adj* **1** unattractive or unfashionable: *a dowdy frock* **2** a dowdy woman wears dull or unfashionable clothes —**dowdily** *adv* —**dowdiness** *n* [U]

**dow·el** /'daʊəl/ *n* [C] a wooden pin for holding two pieces of wood, metal, or stone together

**Dow Jones Av·e·rage** /ˌdaʊ dʒəʊnz 'ævərɪdʒ‖-dʒoʊnz-/ *n* [singular] a daily list of prices of shares (SHARE² (6)) on the American STOCK EXCHANGE, based on the daily average prices of 30 industrial shares

**down-** /daʊn/ *prefix* **1** to a lower position: *to downgrade a job* (=make it lower in importance) | *a downpour* (=heavy rain) **2** in some adverbs and adjectives, means at or towards the bottom or end of something: *downstairs* | *downriver* (=nearer to its mouth) **3** in some adverbs and adjectives, means at or towards the lower or worst part of something: *down-market* (=meeting the demand of the lower social groups) —compare UP-

**down¹** /daʊn/ *adv* **S1** **W1** **1** from above towards a lower place or position: *David bent down to tie his shoelace.* | *The sun beat down on their heads all day long.* **2** at a lower place or position than usual: *You can't cross here, the bridge is down.* **3** at or towards a lower position or floor: *We heard the sound of laughter down below.* | *Let's go down to the kitchen.* **4** into a sitting or lying position: *Please sit down.* | *I think I'll go and lie down for a while.* **5** firmly and tightly into place or position: *Have you stuck down the envelope?* **6** towards the south: *They drove all the way down from Boston to Miami.* —opposite UP¹ (4) **7** *BrE* away from a university at the end of a period of study: *Sarah went down from Oxford in 1966.* **8** at or towards a lower level in price or amount: *Keep your speed down.* | *House prices have come down in recent months.* **9** into a weaker, smaller, or quieter state: *Would you mind turning the radio down?* | *The heels of his shoes had worn down.* | [+ **to**] *Sharif cut his report down to only three pages.* **10 be down to your last pound/dollar/litre** to be left with only a small amount of something: *We're down to our last five dollars.* **11 write/note/jot/take down** to write something on paper: *I'll write down the address for you.* **12 pass/hand down** to give or tell something to people in the next GENERATION (1): *The jewels were passed down through the family.* **13** paid to someone immediately in CASH¹ (1): *A top quality freezer for only £20 down and £5 a week for a year.* **14** from top to bottom: *I want you to wash my car down.* **15** in or into the body as a result of swallowing: *Meg's been very ill and can't keep her food down.* **16 be down to sb** if something is down to someone they are responsible for it or must make a decision about it: *It's down to Tom to decide whether to pay it or not.* —see also **be up to sb** (UP¹ (16)) **17 be/come down to sth** to be mainly the result of one particular thing: *Most of the problems came down to bad management.* **18 Down!** *spoken* used to tell a jumping dog to get down **19 down to** including something or someone at a low level or rank: *Everyone uses the cafeteria, from the managing director down to the office boy.* **20 down under** *informal* in or to Australia or New Zealand **21 Down with...** *spoken* used to express opposition and a wish for someone or something to go: *Down with the government!* **22 be/go down with sth** to have a particular illness: *Jane's down with flu.*

**down²** *prep* **S1** **1** towards the ground or a lower point, or in a lower position: *The bathroom is down those stairs.* **2** along: *The wind raced down the alley.* **3 down the river** in the direction of the river's current: *We sailed down the river.* **4 down the shops/park/market etc** *BrE informal* an expression meaning to or at the shops etc, that some people think is not correct: *Bob's just gone down the pub.* **5 down the road/pike/line etc** *AmE* at some time in the future: *You'll understand better a few years down the line when you've had some experience.*

**down³** *adj*
**1** ►**SAD**◄ [not before noun] sad and discouraged: *Andy's been feeling down lately.*
**2** ►**IN A GAME**◄ [not before noun] behind an opponent by a certain number of points: *Agassi was down by two sets to one.*
**3** ►**COMPLETED**◄ [not before noun] *informal* done or finished: *Three exercises down and two to go.*
**4 be down on sb/sth** *informal* to have a low opinion of someone or something: *Why is Mark so down on her at the moment?*
**5** ►**COMPUTER**◄ [not before noun] if a computer is down, it is not working —opposite UP³ (3)
**6 have/put sb down for sth** to have or put someone's name on a list of people who want to do something: *Put me down to bring the desserts.*

**7 down escalator/staircase** an ESCALATOR (=moving stairs) or stairs which take you down to a lower level —see also **be down on your luck** (LUCK[1] (14))

**down[4]** *v* [T] **1** to drink or eat something quickly: *Jack downed three beers with his steak and fries.* **2** to knock or force someone to the ground: *O'Malley downed his opponent in the first round.* **3 down tools** *BrE* to stop working at the end of a day or to STRIKE (=protest about conditions by stopping work)

**down[5]** *n* **1** [U] soft hair like a baby's **2** [U] the soft fine feathers of a bird **3** [C] one of the four chances that an American football team has to move forward when it is their turn to have the ball **4 the downs** low round hills covered with grass, as in the south of England **5 have a down on sb** *BrE informal* to dislike or have a bad opinion of someone: *Mark had a down on Utopians.* —see also **ups and downs** (UP[4] (2))

**down-and-out** /ˌ· · ˈ·◂/ *n* [C] *informal* someone who has no job, no money, and nowhere to live —**down-and-out** *adj*

**down-at-heel** /ˌ· · ˈ·◂/ *adj especially BrE* dressed in old clothes and looking as if you do not have much money

**down·beat[1]** /ˈdaʊnbiːt/ *n* [C] **1** the first note in a BAR (1) of music **2** the movement a CONDUCTOR makes to show when this note is to be played or sung

**downbeat[2]** *adj informal* not showing any strong feelings, especially not happy ones: *Al was surprisingly downbeat about the party.* —compare UPBEAT

**down·cast** /ˈdaʊnkɑːst‖-kæst/ *adj* **1** sad or upset because of something bad that has happened: *Keith is very downcast at the moment – he misses his wife terribly.* **2** downcast eyes are looking down

**down·er** /ˈdaʊnə‖-ər/ *n informal* **1** [C] a drug that makes you feel very relaxed or sleepy —compare UPPER[2] (2) **2** [singular] a person or situation that stops you feeling cheerful or happy: *"Nick can't come." "What a downer."* **3 be on a downer** *BrE* to be sad or experiencing a series of sad events: *What's up with Ruth? She's been on a downer all week.*

**down·fall** /ˈdaʊnfɔːl‖-fɒːl/ *n* [singular] complete loss of your money, moral standards, social position etc, or the sudden failure of an organization: *The scandal led to the family's downfall.* | **be sb's downfall** *That one error of judgment was his downfall.*

**down·grade** /ˈdaʊngreɪd/ *v* [T] **1** to make a job less important or move someone to a less important job: **downgrade sb/sth to sth** *Harris was downgraded to Assistant Manager.* —opposite UPGRADE **2** to make something seem less important or valuable than it is

**down·heart·ed** /ˌdaʊnˈhɑːtɪd◂‖-ɑːr-/ *adj* discouraged or made sad by something: *When no replies came, I began to feel downhearted.*

**down·hill[1]** /ˌdaʊnˈhɪl◂/ *adv* [only after verb] **1** towards the bottom of a hill or lower land: *I had to run downhill as fast as I could.* **2 go downhill** to become worse: *They won the first game but after that things went downhill.*

**downhill[2]** *adj* **1** on a slope that goes down to a lower point: *downhill skiing* | *The path was all downhill.* **2** [not before noun] easy to do, especially after you have been doing something difficult: **all downhill/downhill all the way** *The worst is over – it's all downhill from here.*

**down·home** /ˈdaʊnhəʊm‖-hoʊm/ *adj AmE* related to the values and customs of people who live in the countryside

**Dow·ning Street** /ˈdaʊnɪŋ striːt/ *n* [not with *the*] the government or PRIME MINISTER of Great Britain: *Downing Street declined to comment on the allegations.*

**down·load** /ˌdaʊnˈləʊd‖-ˈloʊd/ *v* [T] to move information or PROGRAMS from one part of a computer system to another

**down·mar·ket** /ˌdaʊnˈmɑːkɪt◂‖-ɑːr-/ *adj BrE* downmarket goods or services are cheap and not of very good quality: *a downmarket magazine aimed at working mums* —compare UPMARKET —**downmarket** *adv*

**down pay·ment** /ˌ· ˈ· ·/ *n* [C] a payment you make when you buy something that is only part of the full price, with the rest to be paid later: **make a down payment** *We've made a down payment on a washing machine.* —compare DEPOSIT[2]

**down·play** /ˌdaʊnˈpleɪ/ *v* [T] to make something seem less important than it really is; play down (PLAY[1]): *Officials are downplaying last month's drop in exports.*

**down·pour** /ˈdaʊnpɔː‖-pɔːr/ *n* [C often singular] a lot of rain that falls in a short time —see picture on page 836

**down·right[1]** /ˈdaʊnraɪt/ *adj* [only before noun] used to emphasize that someone or something is completely bad, false, or unpleasant: *That's a downright lie!*

**downright[2]** *adv* [+ adj/adv] used to emphasize that someone or something is completely bad, untrue, unpleasant etc: *Jed's just downright lazy.*

**down·riv·er** /daʊnˈrɪvə‖-ər/ *adv* in the direction that the water in a river is flowing: *The bridge was another mile downriver.* —compare DOWNSTREAM

**down·side** /ˈdaʊnsaɪd/ *n* **the downside** the negative side of something: *The downside of the plan is that we lose a lot of time.*

**down·size** /ˈdaʊnsaɪz/ *v* [I,T] if a company or organization downsizes, or downsizes its operations, it reduces the number of people it employs in order to reduce costs —**downsizing** *n* [U]

**down·spout** /ˈdaʊnspaʊt/ *n* [C] *AmE* a pipe that carries water away from the roof of a building; DRAINPIPE *BrE*

**Down's syn·drome** /ˈ· ˌ··/ *n* [U] a condition that someone is born with, that stops them from developing in a normal way, both mentally and physically

**down·stage** /ˌdaʊnˈsteɪdʒ◂/ *adv* towards or near the front of the stage in a theatre —**downstage** *adj* —opposite UPSTAGE[2]

**down·stairs** /ˌdaʊnˈsteəz◂‖ˈsterz/ *adv* **1** towards or on a lower floor of a building, especially a house: *Rosie ran downstairs.* **2 the downstairs** the rooms on the ground floor in a house: *We have still got to paint the downstairs.* —compare UPSTAIRS —**downstairs** *adj*: *a downstairs room* S2

**down·stream** /ˌdaʊnˈstriːm◂/ *adv* in the direction the water in a river or stream is flowing: *a boat drifting downstream* —compare DOWNRIVER, UPSTREAM

**down·time** /ˈdaʊntaɪm/ *n* [U] the time when a computer is not working

**down-to-earth** /ˌ· · ˈ·◂/ *adj* practical and direct in a sensible honest way: *a down-to-earth approach to health care*

**down·town** /ˌdaʊnˈtaʊn◂/ *adv especially AmE* towards or in the centre or main business area of a town or city; CITY CENTRE *BrE*: **go downtown** *I have to go downtown later.* —**downtown** *adj* [only before noun] *downtown restaurants* —compare UPTOWN S3 W3

**down·trod·den** /ˈdaʊnˌtrɒdn‖-ˌtrɑː-/ *adj* downtrodden people, workers etc are treated badly and without respect by people who have power over them

**down·turn** /ˈdaʊntɜːn‖-tɜːrn/ *n* [C usually singular] a period or process in which business activity, production etc is reduced and conditions become worse: *a sharp economic downturn* | [+ **in**] *a downturn in shipbuilding orders* —opposite UPTURN

**down·ward** /ˈdaʊnwəd‖-wərd/ *adj* [only before noun] going down to a lower level or place: *a gentle downward slope* | *Share prices continued their downward trend.* —opposite UPWARD

**down·ward·ly mo·bile** /ˌ··· ˈ··/ *adj* someone who is downwardly mobile is becoming poorer

**down·wards** /ˈdaʊnwədz‖-wərdz/ also **downward** *adv* **1** towards a lower level or position: *Nina glanced downwards.* | **face downwards** (=with the front towards the ground) *The body lay face downwards on the rug.* —opposite UPWARDS (1) **2** down to and including the lowest position in a set: *Everyone from the chairman downwards is taking a pay cut.* —opposite UPWARDS (1)

**down·wind** /ˌdaʊnˈwɪnd/ *adv* in the direction that the wind is moving

**down·y** /ˈdaʊni/ *adj* covered in or filled with soft fine hair or feathers: *the baby's downy head*

**dow·ry** /ˈdaʊəri‖ˈdaʊri/ *n* [C] property and money that a woman gives to her husband when they marry in some societies

**dowse¹** /daʊz/ *v* [I + **for**] to look for water or minerals under the ground using a special stick that points to where they are; DIVINE² (2)

**dowse²** /daʊs/ *v* [T] another spelling of DOUSE

**dow·ser** /ˈdaʊzə‖-ər/ *n* [C] someone who dowses for water or minerals

**dows·ing rod** /ˈ·· ·/ *n* [C] a special stick in the shape of a Y used by a dowser

**doy·en** /ˈdɔɪən/ *n* [C] the oldest, most respected, or most experienced member of a group: **the doyen of** *the doyen of sports commentators*

**doy·enne** /dɔɪˈen/ *n* [C] the oldest, most respected, or most experienced woman in a group: **the doyenne of** *the doyenne of gossip columists*

**doz** *n* the written abbreviation of DOZEN

**doze** /dəʊz‖doʊz/ *v* [I] to sleep lightly for a short time: *Pam often dozes in her chair after lunch.* —**doze** *n* [singular] *especially BrE*: *having a doze in front of the telly*

**doze off** *phr v* [I] to go to sleep, especially when you did not intend to; **drop off** (DROP¹), **nod off** (NOD¹): *I was just dozing off when the phone rang.*

S2 W3 **doz·en** /ˈdʌzən/ written abbreviation **doz** *determiner plural* **dozen** *or* **dozens** **1 a dozen/two dozen/three dozen** a group of twelve: *a dozen eggs|half a dozen* **2 dozens (of)** *informal* a lot of: *I've been there dozens of times.*|**dozens and dozens** *They collected dozens and dozens of shells on the beach.* —see also BAKER'S DOZEN, **a dime a dozen** (DIME (2)), **nineteen to the dozen** (NINETEEN (2)), **six of one and half a dozen of another** (SIX (2))

**doz·y** /ˈdəʊzi‖ˈdoʊ-/ *adj* **1** not feeling very awake: *I was feeling dozy after lunch.* **2** *BrE informal* slow to understand things; stupid: *Those kids are really dozy!* —**dozily** *adv* —**doziness** *n* [U]

**DP** /ˌdiː ˈpiː/ the abbreviation of DATA PROCESSING

**D Phil** /ˌdiː ˈfɪl/ the abbreviation of Doctor of Philosophy

**Dr** **1** the written abbreviation of DOCTOR **2** the written abbreviation of DRIVE² (7): *88 Park Dr*

**drab¹** /dræb/ *adj* not bright in colour or not interesting: *The city looked drab and colorless to me.*

**drab²** *n* [C] *old use* a dirty, untidy, and perhaps immoral woman —see also DRIBS AND DRABS

**drach·ma** /ˈdrækmə/ *n* [C] *plural* **drachmas** *or* **drachmae** /-miː/ **1** the unit of money in modern Greece **2** an ancient Greek silver coin and weight

**dra·co·ni·an** /drəˈkəʊniən‖-ˈkoʊ-/ *adj* very strict and cruel: **draconian laws/measures/methods etc** *draconian measures to control population growth*

S2 W3 **draft¹** /drɑːft‖dræft/ *n*

**1 ▶ UNFINISHED FORM ◀** [C] a piece of writing, a drawing, or a plan that is not yet in its finished form: **make a draft** *Let's make a rough draft of the letter.*|**first/final draft** *the first draft of a poem*|**draft proposal/copy/version etc** *a draft copy of a newspaper article*

**2 ▶ ARMY ◀ the draft** *AmE* **a)** *informal* a system in which people are ordered to fight for their country when it is involved in a war; CONSCRIPTION **b)** the group of people who are ordered to do this

**3 ▶ MONEY ◀** [C] *especially BrE* a written order for money to be paid by a bank, especially from one bank to another: **by draft** *Payment must be made by bank draft.*

**4 ▶ SPORTS ◀** [C] a system in some American sports in which PROFESSIONAL¹ (3) teams pick players from colleges for their teams

**5 ▶ COLD AIR/DRINKS ◀** [C] the American spelling of DRAUGHT

**draft²** *v* [T] **1** to write a plan, letter, report etc that will need to be changed before it is in its finished form: *Eva's busy drafting her speech for the conference.* **2** *AmE* to order someone to serve in their country's military during a war; CALL-UP *BrE*; CONSCRIPT¹ (1): **be drafted into sth** *Joe's been drafted into the army.*

**draft board** /ˈ· ·/ *n* [C] *AmE* the committee that decides who will be drafted into the military

**draft card** /ˈ· ·/ *n* [C] *AmE* a card sent to someone telling them they have been drafted

**draft dod·ger** /ˈ· ˌ··/ *n* [C] *AmE* someone who illegally avoids joining the military even though they have been drafted

**draft·ee** /drɑːfˈtiː‖dræf-/ *n* [C] *AmE* someone who has been drafted

**drafts·man** /ˈdrɑːftsmən‖ˈdræfts-/ *n plural* **draftsmen** /-mən/ [C] **1** someone who puts a suggested law or a new law into the proper words **2** the American spelling of DRAUGHTSMAN

**draft·y** /ˈdrɑːfti‖ˈdræfti/ *adj* the American spelling of DRAUGHTY

S3 W3 **drag¹** /dræg/ *v* **dragged, dragging**

**1 ▶ PULL ALONG THE GROUND ◀** [T] to pull someone or something along the ground, often because they are too heavy to carry: **drag sth away/along/through etc** *Inge managed to drag the table into the kitchen.*|*Angry protesters were dragged away by police.*|**drag a leg/foot etc** (=let it touch the ground as you move) *a bird dragging its broken wing* —see picture on page 1260

**2 ▶ NOT GENTLY ◀** [T always + adv/prep] to pull someone or something somewhere in a way that hurts or damages them: **drag sth up/over etc** *The plants had been dragged out by the roots.*|*Harvey dragged her over to the window.*|**drag sb to the ground** (=pull someone down to the ground)

**3 drag yourself up/down/into etc** *informal* to move somewhere with difficulty: *Jacob could hardly drag himself up the stairs.*

**4 ▶ PERSUADE SB TO COME ◀** [T always + adv/prep] *informal* if you drag someone somewhere, you persuade or force them to come when they do not want to: **drag sb along/away etc** *Try and drag her along to the meeting tonight.*|*Carla can't drag him away from the football on TV.*

**5 drag yourself away (from)** to leave someone or something, or stop doing something, although you do not want to: *It's well worth a visit if you can drag yourself away from the pool.*

**6 ▶ TIME ◀** [I] if time or an event drags, it seems to go very slowly because nothing interesting is happening: *Friday afternoons always drag.*

**7 ▶ TOUCH THE GROUND ◀** [I] if something is dragging along the ground, in the mud etc, part of it is touching the ground, the mud etc as you move: [+ **along/in**] *Your coat's dragging in the mud.*

**8 drag your feet/heels** *informal* to take too much time to do something because you do not want to do it: *The authorities are dragging their feet over banning cigarette advertising.*

**9 drag sb's name through the mud/mire** to tell people about the bad things that someone has done, so that they will have a bad opinion of them

**10 drag (along) behind sb** to go more slowly than someone so that you are always behind them

**11 ▶ COMPUTER ◀** [T always + adv/prep] to move something on a computer screen by pulling it along with the MOUSE (2)

**12 drag a pond/river etc** to look for something in a lake, river etc by pulling a heavy net along the bottom: *They dragged the lake for the missing girl's body.*

**13 ▶ BOAT ◀** [T] if a boat drags its ANCHOR¹ (1), it pulls the anchor away from its place on the sea bottom

**drag** sb ↔ **down** *phr v* [T] **1** to make someone feel unhappy or discouraged: *All these criticisms were dragging her down.* **2 drag sb down to your level** *informal often humorous* to make someone behave like you, in a worse way than they would usually behave: *"Look at this mess – it's not like you!" "I know – Ken's dragged me down to his level."*

**drag** sb/sth ↔ **in** *phr v* [T] to start to talk about someone or something that is not connected with what you are talking or arguing about: *Why drag Jules in? He has nothing to do with it.*

**drag** sb/sth **into** sth *phr v* [T] to make someone get involved in a particular situation, discussion etc even though they do not want to: *I'm sorry to drag you into this mess.*

**drag on** *phr v* [I] if an event drags on, it seems to continue for longer than is necessary, often because you are bored: [+ **for**] *The meeting dragged on for hours.*

**drag** sth ↔ **out** *phr v* [T] to make a meeting, an argument etc last longer than is necessary: *"How long can she drag this argument out?" Calvin wondered.*

**drag** sth **out of** sb *phr v* [T] to make someone tell you something when they had not intended to or were not supposed to do so: *He'll tell me, even if I have to drag it out of him!*

**drag** sb/sth ↔ **up** *phr v* [T] **1** to mention an unpleasant subject or event, even though it is not necessary and it upsets the people who were involved in it: *The newspapers are dragging up her alleged affair again.* **2** *BrE informal often humorous* to RAISE[1] (4) a child so badly that when they are adult they behave badly, have bad manners etc: *That child must have been dragged up.*

**drag**[2] *n*

**1** ▶ **SB/STH BORING** ◀ **a drag** *informal* something or someone that is unexciting or boring: *The party was a real drag.* | *Don't be such a drag! Come out with us.*

**2 be a drag on** a person or thing that is a drag on someone makes it hard for them to make progress towards what they want: *Marriage would be a drag on my career.*

**3** ▶ **ON CIGARETTE** ◀ [C] the act of breathing in smoke from your cigarette: **take a drag on** *Pran took a deep drag on his cigarette.*

**4** ▶ **CLOTHES** ◀ [U] women's clothes worn by a man, or men's clothes worn by a woman: **in drag** *The whole performance is done in drag.*

**5** ▶ **FORCE** ◀ [singular, U] the force of air that pushes against an aircraft or a vehicle that is moving forward: *Increasing the car's height increases aerodynamic drag.*

**6** ▶ **BORING JOURNEY** ◀ [U] *BrE informal* a long and boring journey: *It's a terrible drag all the way from Tijuana.*

**7 the main drag** *AmE informal* the biggest or longest street that goes through a town: *We passed the last buildings on the main drag of Encino.*

**8** ▶ **STH THAT IS PULLED** ◀ [C] something that is made to be pulled along: *a drag harrow*

**drag·gled** /ˈdræɡəld/ *adj literary* BEDRAGGLED

**drag·gy** /ˈdræɡi/ *adj informal* boring or unpleasant

**drag·net** /ˈdræɡnet/ *n* [C] **1** a net that is pulled along the bottom of a river or lake, to bring up things that may be there **2** a system in which the police look for criminals, using very thorough methods: *a police dragnet*

**drag·on** /ˈdræɡən/ *n* [C] **1** a large imaginary animal that has wings and a long tail and can breathe out fire **2** *informal* a woman who behaves in an angry, unfriendly way: *Casey's new teacher's a real dragon.* —see also **chase the dragon** (CHASE[1] (6))

dragon

**drag·on·fly** /ˈdræɡənflaɪ/ *n* [C] a brightly coloured insect with a long thin, often coloured body and transparent wings

**dra·goon**[1] /drəˈɡuːn/ *n* [C] a soldier in past times who rode a horse and carried a gun and sword

**dragoon**[2] *v*

**dragoon** sb **into** sth *phr v* [T] to force someone to do something they do not want to do: **dragoon sb into doing sth** *Monica was dragooned into being on the management committee.*

**drag queen** /ˈ· ·/ *n* [C] *slang* a HOMOSEXUAL man who dresses as a woman

**drag race** /ˈ· ·/ *n* [C] *AmE* a car race that is won by the car that can increase its speed fastest over a very short distance —**drag racing** *n* [U]

**drag·ster** /ˈdræɡstə‖-ər/ *n* [C] a car used in drag races that is long, narrow, and low

**drain**[1] /dreɪn/ *v*

**1** ▶ **LIQUID** ◀ **a)** [T] to make the water or liquid flow away from something: *Can you drain the spaghetti, please?* | *Deep ditches were dug to drain the fields.* | **drain sth from sth** *Brad drained all the oil from the engine.* | **well/poorly etc drained** *Carrots grow best in a well drained soil.* —see picture on page 834 **b)** [I] if liquid drains, it flows away: [+ **away**] *I watched the bath water drain away.* **c)** [I] if something drains, the liquid that is in it or on it flows away and it becomes dry: *Open ditches drain very efficiently.*

**2 drain a glass/cup etc** to drink all the liquid in a glass, cup etc: *Hannah drained her mug in one gulp.*

**3** ▶ **USE TOO MUCH** ◀ [T] to use too much of something so that there is not enough left: *Huge imports were draining the country's currency reserves.* | **drain sb/sth of sth** *Our country is being drained of many of its best scientists.*

**4** ▶ **MAKE TIRED** ◀ [T] to make someone feel very tired and without any energy: *Working with sick children every day really drains you.*

**5** ▶ **COLOUR** ◀ [I always + adv/prep] if the colour drains from your face, your skin becomes very pale usually because you are frightened or shocked: [+ **from/away etc**] *All the colour had drained from Zelda's cheeks.*

**6** ▶ **BE REDUCED** ◀ [I always + adv/prep] to gradually be reduced: [+ **away/out of etc**] *The family's wealth has slowly drained away.*

**drain** sth ↔ **off** *phr v* [T] to make water or a liquid flow off something, leaving it dry: *Leave to simmer for 40 minutes then drain off the stock.*

**drain**[2] *n* [C] **1** *especially BrE* a pipe that carries water or waste liquids away: **blocked drains** *The drains were blocked and the streets were full of water.* **2** the frame of metal bars over a drain where water etc can flow into it: *Clear the leaves out of the drain.* **3 a drain on sth** something that continuously uses time, money, strength etc: *Not having anybody to rent my room is a serious drain on my financial resources.* **4 down the drain** *informal* wasted or having no result: *The fire meant two years' hard work down the drain.* —see also BRAIN DRAIN

**drain·age** /ˈdreɪnɪdʒ/ *n* [U] **1** a system of pipes or passages in the ground for carrying away water or waste liquids: *drainage channels* **2** the process by which water or waste liquid flows away though this system

**drained** /dreɪnd/ *adj* very tired and without any energy: *Steve felt so drained he could hardly make it to the car.*

**drain·ing board** /ˈ·· ·/ *n* [C] a slightly sloping area next to the kitchen SINK[2] where you put wet dishes to dry —see picture on page 833

**drain·pipe** /ˈdreɪnpaɪp/ *n* [C] **1** *BrE* a pipe that carries rain water away from the roof of a building **2** *BrE* a pipe that carries waste water away from buildings; DOWNSPOUT *AmE* —see picture on page 410

**drainpipe trou·sers** /ˌ·· ˈ··/ *n* [plural] *BrE* trousers with narrow legs

**drake** /dreɪk/ *n* [C] a male duck —see also DUCKS AND DRAKES

**dram** /dræm/ *n* [C] **1** also **drachm** a small unit of weight or of liquid —see table on page B2 **2** a small alcoholic drink, especially WHISKY: *Would you like a wee dram before you go?*

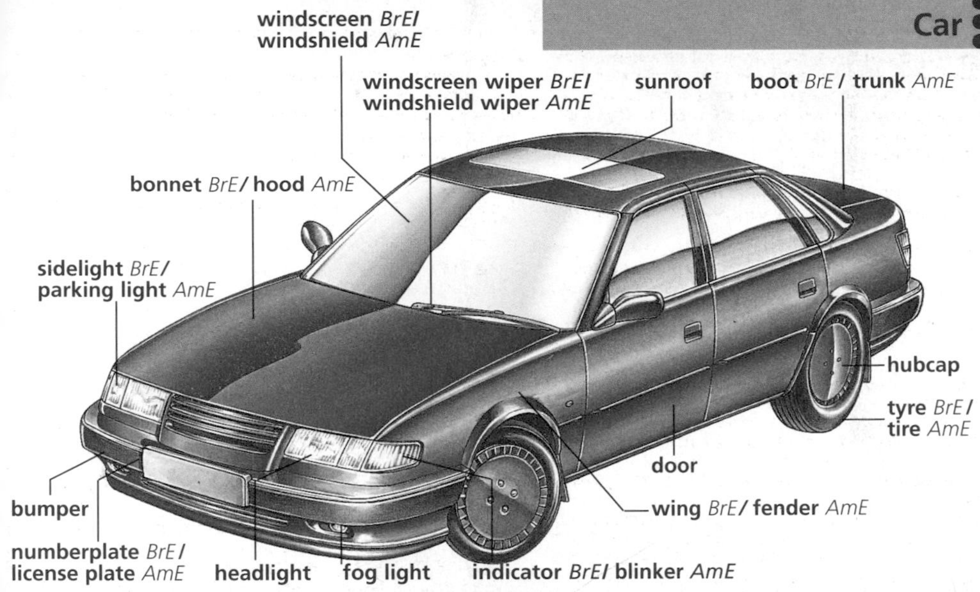

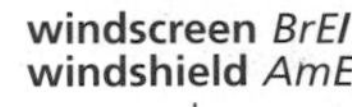

windscreen BrE/
windshield AmE
windscreen wiper BrE/
windshield wiper AmE
sunroof
boot BrE/ trunk AmE
bonnet BrE/ hood AmE
sidelight BrE/
parking light AmE
hubcap
tyre BrE/
tire AmE
door
bumper
wing BrE/ fender AmE
numberplate BrE/
license plate AmE
headlight
fog light
indicator BrE/ blinker AmE

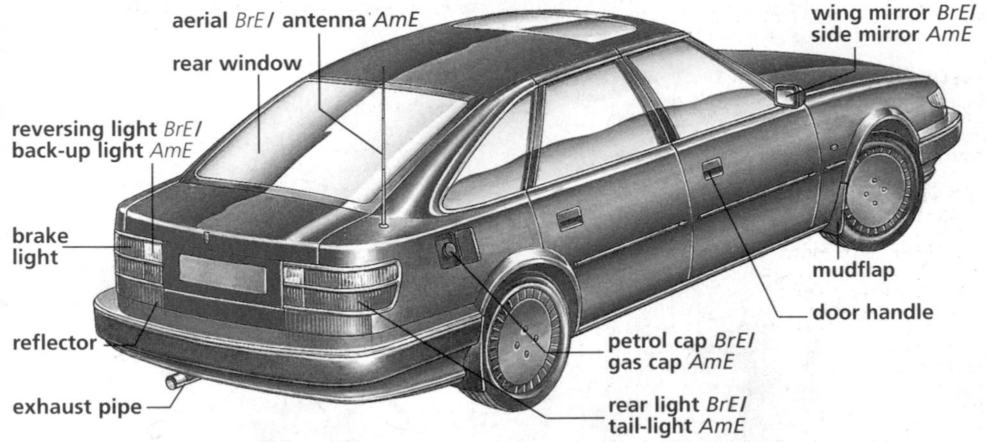

aerial BrE/ antenna AmE
wing mirror BrE/
side mirror AmE
rear window
reversing light BrE/
back-up light AmE
brake
light
mudflap
door handle
reflector
petrol cap BrE/
gas cap AmE
exhaust pipe
rear light BrE/
tail-light AmE

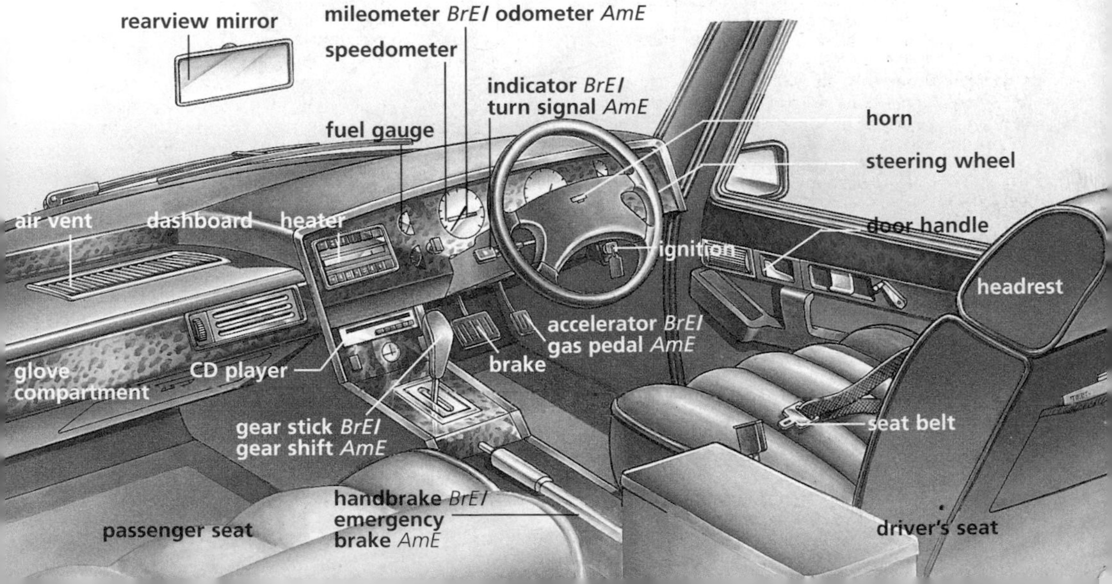

rearview mirror
mileometer BrE/ odometer AmE
speedometer
indicator BrE/
turn signal AmE
horn
fuel gauge
steering wheel
air vent
dashboard
heater
door handle
ignition
headrest
accelerator BrE/
gas pedal AmE
brake
glove
compartment
CD player
seat belt
gear stick BrE/
gear shift AmE
handbrake BrE/
emergency
brake AmE
passenger seat
driver's seat

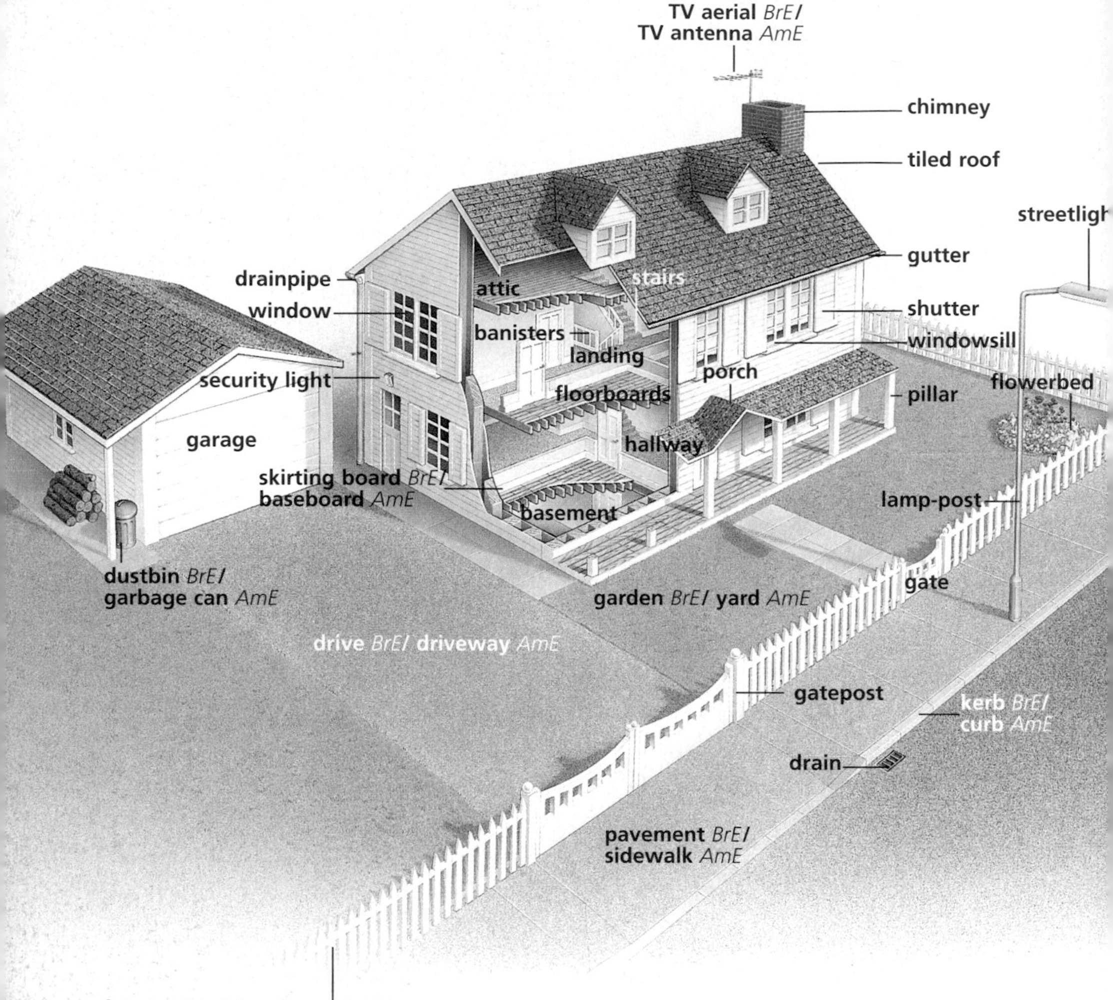

TV aerial *BrE*/ TV antenna *AmE*
chimney
tiled roof
streetlight
gutter
drainpipe
stairs
attic
window
shutter
banisters
windowsill
landing
porch
security light
pillar
flowerbed
floorboards
garage
hallway
skirting board *BrE*/ baseboard *AmE*
lamp-post
basement
dustbin *BrE*/ garbage can *AmE*
garden *BrE*/ yard *AmE*
gate
drive *BrE*/ driveway *AmE*
gatepost
kerb *BrE*/ curb *AmE*
drain
pavement *BrE*/ sidewalk *AmE*
fence *BrE*/ picket fence *AmE*

bungalow

semi-detached *BrE*/ duplex *AmE*

terraced houses *BrE*/ row houses *AmE*

ranch house

block of flats *BrE*/ apartment building *AmE*

sky-blue
lime
jade
olive
beige
violet
scarlet
poppy
golden
navy blue
ottle green
tan
khaki
cream
russet
mustard
royal blue
turquoise
peach
maroon
emerald
lemon
burgundy
magenta
rose
tangerine
mauve
apricot
green
coffee
lilac
pink
buff
purple
red
blue
crimson
black
white
orange
grey
yellow
brown
uamarine

Emma has long wavy gingery-brown hair, with a centre parting *BrE*/ center part *AmE*. She has freckles, hazel eyes and wears her hair pushed back behind her ears.

Roald has short spiky fair hair. He's got thick bushy eyebrows, a five o'clock shadow and sideburns.

Kaori has straight shoulder-length hair, a side parting *BrE*/ side part *AmE* and a short fringe *BrE*/ short bangs *AmE*. She has dark brown eyes and high cheekbones.

Eduardo is clean-shaven with greying hair and a receding hairline. He has a small scar on his jaw and a dimple in his chin.
His wife, Nadia, has long straggly dark hair.

Sue has blonde hair with a wispy fringe. She has a beauty spot on her cheek and a pointed chin.

John is slightly tanned with wavy ginger hair and a roman nose. He has stubble, a double chin and wears half moon spectacles *BrE*/ reading glasses *AmE*.
Nick has lank auburn hair, a pale complexion, and is growing a goatee beard.

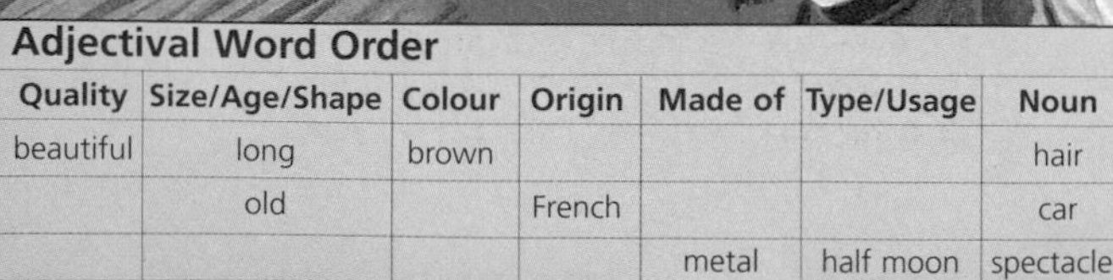

**Adjectival Word Order**

| Quality | Size/Age/Shape | Colour | Origin | Made of | Type/Usage | Noun |
|---|---|---|---|---|---|---|
| beautiful | long | brown | | | | hair |
| | old | | French | | | car |
| | | | | metal | half moon | spectacles |

1 strawberries
2 cranberries
3 blackberries
4 raspberries
5 gooseberries
6 grapes
7 blueberries
8 loganberries
9 oranges
10 grapefruit
11 limes
12 lemon
13 clementines
14 cantaloup *BrE*/ cantaloupe *AmE*
15 watermelon
16 honeydew melon
17 pineapple
18 mango
19 coconuts
20 plantains
21 bananas
22 papaya
23 lychee
24 passion fruit
25 starfruit
26 persimmons
27 quinces
28 figs
29 peaches
30 nectarines
31 pears
32 plums
33 kiwi fruit
34 cherries
35 apricots
36 apples

1 garlic
2 leeks
3 spring onions *BrE*/ green onions *AmE*
4 onions
5 yam
6 sweet potato
7 potatoes
8 Jerusalem artichoke
9 cucumbers
10 marrow *BrE*/ squash *AmE*
11 courgettes *BrE*/ zucchini *AmE*
12 pumpkin
13 butter beans
14 green beans
15 broad beans
16 aduki beans
17 peas
18 kidney beans
19 runner beans
20 beansprouts
21 swede *BrE*/ rutabaga *AmE*
22 beetroot *BrE*/ beet *AmE*
23 white radish
24 ginger
25 radishes
26 carrots
27 parsnips
28 turnips
29 cabbage
30 corn cobs
31 chinese leaves *BrE*/ bok choy *AmE*
32 celery
33 artichoke
34 okra
35 asparagus
36 cauliflower
37 lettuce
38 spinach
39 red pepper
40 green pepper
41 broccoli
42 aubergine *BrE*/ egg plant *AmE*
43 mushrooms
44 tomatoes
45 brussels sprouts

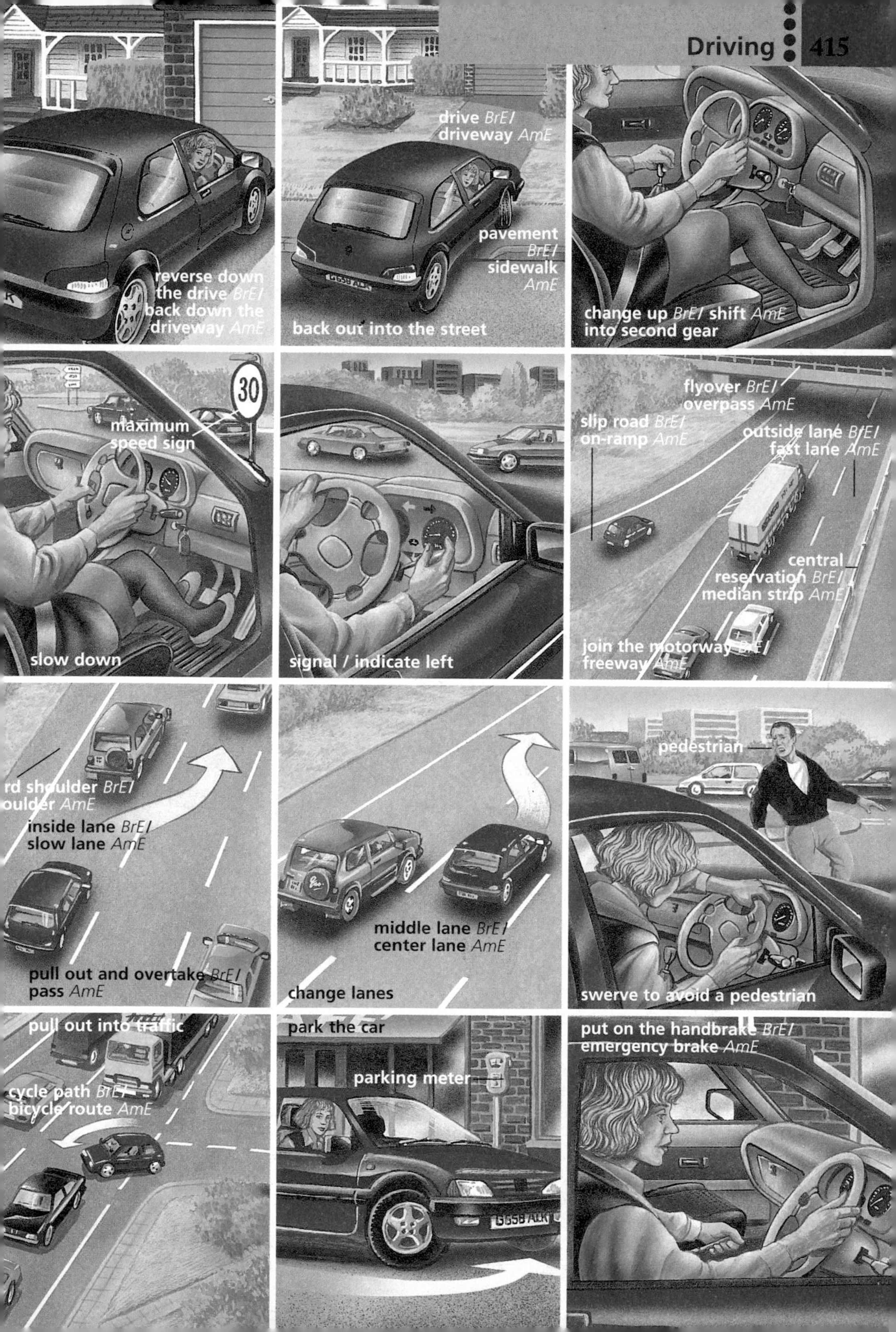

reverse down the drive *BrE*/
back down the driveway *AmE*

drive *BrE*/
driveway *AmE*

pavement *BrE*/
sidewalk *AmE*

back out into the street

change up *BrE*/ shift *AmE*
into second gear

maximum speed sign

slow down

signal / indicate left

flyover *BrE*/
overpass *AmE*

slip road *BrE*/
on-ramp *AmE*

outside lane *BrE*/
fast lane *AmE*

central reservation *BrE*/
median strip *AmE*

join the motorway *BrE*/
freeway *AmE*

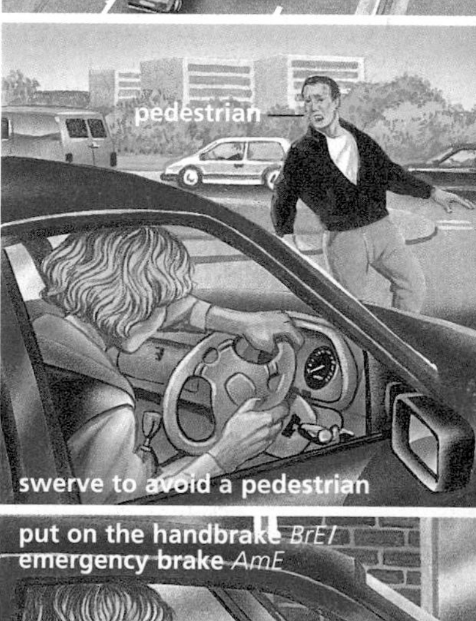

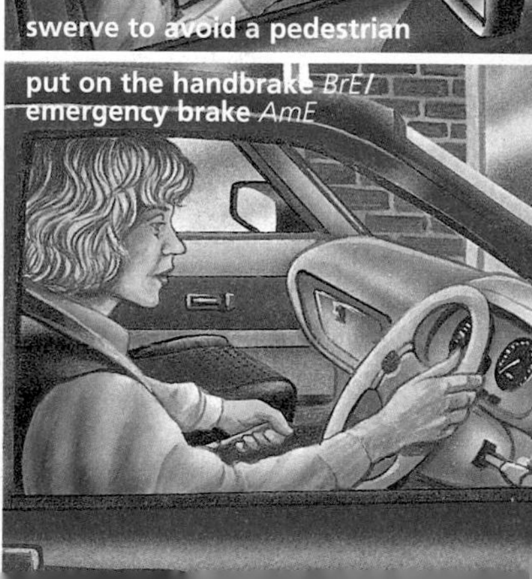

**chunk** of rock

**hunk** of cheese

**bar** of chocolate

**bar** of soap

**cube** of sugar

**block** of ice

**rasher** of bacon *BrE*

**slab** of concrete

**clod** of earth

**wad** of banknotes *BrE*/ bills *AmE*

**slice** of bread

**slice** of cake

**dollop** of jam

**lump** of butter

**sheet** of newspaper

**pane** of glass

**blob** of paint

**trickle** of rain

**square** of chocolate

**segment** of orange

**pinch** of salt

**squeeze** of lemon

**squirt** of liquid

**drop** of sauce

**dash** of sauce

**wisp** of smoke

**puff** of perfume

**crumb** of cake

**speck** of dirt

**grain** of sand

**flake** of paint

**shred** of cloth

**chip** of china

**splinter** of wood

**sliver** of glass

**scrap** of paper

3 **dra·ma** /ˈdrɑːmə‖ˈdrɑːmə, ˈdræmə/ *n* **1** [C] a play for the theatre, television, radio etc **2** [U] plays considered as a form of literature: *drama classes*|**drama school** (=place for students to study drama) **3** [C,U] an exciting and unusual situation or set of events: *Maggie's life is always full of drama.*|**the drama of** *We all shared in the drama of the rescue.* **4 make a drama out of sth** to make things seem worse than they really are: *We won't make a drama out of a crisis.*

**dra·mat·ic** /drəˈmætɪk/ *adj* **1** impressive, sudden, and often surprising: *the dramatic changes taking place in Eastern Europe* **2** exciting: *a dramatic point in the story* **3** connected with drama or the theatre: *a dramatic production* **4** in a way that you intend to be impressive and exciting: *Tristan immediately threw up his hands in a dramatic gesture.* —**dramatically** /-kli/ *adv*: *Output has increased dramatically.*

**dramatic i·ron·y** /ˌ·ˌ·· ˈ···/ *n* [U] a special effect in a play in which the people watching know something that the characters in the play do not, and can understand the real importance or meaning of what is happening

**dra·mat·ics** /drəˈmætɪks/ *n* **1** [U] the study or practice of skills used in drama, such as acting: *amateur dramatics* **2** [plural] behaviour that shows too much feeling, and that is often insincere; HISTRIONICS

**dram·a·tis per·so·nae** /ˌdræmətɪ̣s pɜːˈsəʊnaɪ, pəˈsəʊniː‖-pərˈsoʊniː/ *n* [plural] *Latin* the characters in a play

**dram·a·tist** /ˈdræmətɪ̣st/ *n* [C] someone who writes plays, especially serious ones; PLAYWRIGHT

**dram·a·tize** also **-ise** *BrE* /ˈdræmətaɪz/ *v* **1** [T] to change a story so that it can be performed as a play: *a novel dramatized for television* **2** [I,T] to make a situation seem more exciting, terrible etc than it really is: *Why do you have to dramatize everything?*—**dramatization** /ˌdræmətaɪˈzeɪʃən‖-tə-/ *n* [C,U]

**drank** /dræŋk/ the past tense of DRINK[1]

**drape¹** /dreɪp/ *v* [T] **1** to cover or decorate something with folds of cloth: **drape sth over/around etc sth** *Jack emerged with a towel draped around him.*|**drape sth with/in etc sth** *a coffin draped in the national flag* **2** to let something hang or lie somewhere loosely: **drape sth over/around sth** *Mina lay back, her arms draped lazily over the cushions.*

**drape²** *n* **drapes** [plural] *especially AmE* curtains, especially long thick curtains

**drap·er** /ˈdreɪpə‖-ər/ *n* [C] *BrE old-fashioned* someone who sells cloth, curtains, etc

**drap·er·y** /ˈdreɪpəri/ *n* **1** [C,U] cloth arranged in folds: *a casket covered with embroidered silk drapery* **2** [U] *BrE* cloth and other goods sold by a draper; DRY GOODS (2) *AmE* **3** [U] *BrE* the trade of selling cloth, curtains, etc

**dras·tic** /ˈdræstɪk/ *adj* strong, sudden, and often severe: *NATO threatened more drastic action if its terms were not met.* —**drastically** /-kli/ *adv*: *The size of the army was drastically cut.*

**drat** /dræt/ *interjection old-fashioned* used to show you are annoyed: *Drat! The car won't start!* —**dratted** *adj*: *Where are my dratted keys?*

**draught¹** *BrE*, **draft** *AmE* /drɑːft‖dræft/ *n* [C]
**1 ▶ COLD AIR ◀** a current of cold air flowing through a room: *Shut the window – there's a draught in here!*
**2 ▶ GAME ◀ draughts** [plural] *BrE* **a)** a game played by two people, each with 12 round pieces, on a board of 64 squares; CHECKERS (2) *AmE* **b)** the pieces used in a game of draughts
**3 ▶ SWALLOW ◀** the act of swallowing liquid, or the amount of liquid swallowed at one time: *Mick took a long draught of lager.*
**4 on draught** *especially BrE* a beer that is on draught is served from a large container rather than a bottle; on tap (TAP[1] (4b))
**5 ▶ MEDICINE ◀** *literary* a medicine that you drink: *a sleeping draught*
**6 ▶ FIRE ◀** the flow of air to a fire
**7 ▶ SHIP ◀** the depth of water needed by a ship so that it will not touch the bottom of the sea, a river etc

**draught²** *BrE*, **draft** *AmE adj* [only before noun] **1** a draught animal is used for pulling heavy loads **2** a draught beer is served from a large container, not a bottle

**draught·board** /ˈdrɑːftbɔːd‖ˈdræftbɔːrd/ *n* [C] *BrE* a board with 64 squares on which the game of draughts (DRAUGHT[1] (2)) is played; CHECKERBOARD *AmE*

**draughts·man** *BrE*, **draftsman** *AmE* /ˈdrɑːftsmən‖ˈdræfts-/ *n* [C] **1** someone who draws all the parts of a new building or machine that is being planned **2** someone who draws well

**draugh·ty** *BrE*, **drafty** *AmE* /ˈdrɑːfti‖ˈdræfti/ *adj* with currents of air blowing through it: *a draughty old house*

S1 W1

**draw¹** /drɔː‖drɒː/ *v past tense* **drew** /druː/ *past participle* **drawn** /drɔːn‖drɒːn/

① PICTURE/DESCRIPTION
② MOVE
③ GET/CAUSE STH
④ MAKE COMPARISON/JUDGMENT
⑤ MAKE SB NOTICE
⑥ MONEY
⑦ AIR/WATER
⑧ BY CHANCE
⑨ STOP/END
⑩ SPORT
⑪ OTHER MEANINGS

**① PICTURE/DESCRIPTION**
**1 ▶ WITH PENCIL ◀** [I,T] to make a picture of something with a pencil or pen: *Can I draw your portrait?*|*I've never been able to draw well.*|**draw sb sth/draw sth for sb** *Hans drew her a map showing her how to get there.*
**2 ▶ DESCRIBE ◀** [T] to describe something in speech or writing: *the vividly drawn character of Heathcliff*

**② MOVE**
**3 ▶ MOVE IN ONE DIRECTION ◀** [I always + adv/prep] to move steadily in a particular direction: **draw towards/past etc** *We watched from the deck as their boat drew alongside.*
**4 draw near/close** to move closer in time or space: *Maria grew anxious as the men drew closer.*|*Christmas is drawing near.*
**5 draw level** to move into a position where you are equal to someone else in a race, game, or competition: *Black drew level with the other runners.*
**6 ▶ PULL ◀** [T always + adv/prep] to make someone or something move by pulling them gently: **draw aside/up/across etc** *Drawing the covers around her, Zoe curled up in bed.*|*Hussain drew me aside to whisper in my ear.*

[continued on next page]

[continued from previous page]
**7 draw the curtains** to open or close the curtains
**8 ▶ PULL A VEHICLE ◀** [T] if an animal draws a vehicle, it pulls it along: *a carriage drawn by six horses*
**9 ▶ TAKE OUT ◀** [T always + adv/prep] to take something out of a container, cover etc: **draw sth out/from etc** *Smedley drew some papers from his pocket.*
**10 draw a gun/pistol/sword etc** to take a weapon from its container or from your pocket: *Jack drew his knife with a flourish.*
**11 draw a tooth/cork/nail** to pull a tooth etc out

**③ GET/CAUSE STH**
**12 ▶ GET STH IMPORTANT ◀** [T] to get something that you need or that is important from someone or something: *I drew a lot of comfort from her kind words.* | *Plants draw nourishment from the soil.*
**13 ▶ GET A REACTION ◀** to get a particular kind of reaction from someone because of something you have said or done: **draw praise/criticism etc (from)** *Reagan's remarks drew an angry response from the Democrats.* | **draw fire (from)** (=be criticized) *The new proposals drew fire from all sides for being elitist.*

**④ MAKE COMPARISON/JUDGMENT**
**14 draw a comparison/analogy etc** to compare two things, people, ideas etc: *Do you think we can draw a parallel between the two novels?*
**15 draw a distinction/line etc** to say that you think two things are different and show why you think so: *We have to draw a line between fantasy and reality.*
**16 draw a conclusion/moral etc (from sth)** to decide that a particular fact or principle is true after thinking carefully about it: *Now that you've heard the evidence, you can draw your own conclusions.*

**⑤ MAKE SB NOTICE**
**17 draw sb's attention (to sth)** to deliberately make someone notice something: *I'd like to draw your attention to the no smoking rule.*
**18 draw sb's eye** if something draws your eye, it is so interesting that you notice it: *The intentness of his gaze drew all eyes towards him.*

**⑥ MONEY**
**19 ▶ FROM YOUR BANK ACCOUNT ◀** also **draw out** [T] to take money from your bank account: *Hughes had drawn $8000 in cash from a bank in Toronto.*
**20 ▶ BE PAID ◀** [T] to receive an amount of money regularly from your employer or from the government: *How long have you been drawing unemployment benefit?*
**21 draw a cheque (on sth)** *BrE* **draw a check (on sth)** *AmE* to write a cheque for taking money out of a bank: *a check drawn on a Swiss bank*

**⑦ AIR/WATER**
**22 ▶ LIQUID ◀** [T] to take water, beer etc from a well or container
**23 ▶ INTO YOUR LUNGS ◀** [T] to take air or smoke into your lungs: **draw breath** *I was having trouble just drawing breath, but Meg ran on up the hill.*
**24 ▶ FIRE/CHIMNEY ◀** [I] if a fire or CHIMNEY draws, it lets the air flow through to make the fire burn well

**⑧ BY CHANCE**
**25 ▶ PLAYING CARD/TICKET ◀** [I,T] to choose a card, ticket etc by chance: *I drew the ace of spades.*
**26 draw the short straw** used to say that someone has been unlucky because they were chosen by chance to do an unpleasant job: *I'm only here because I drew the short straw.*
**27 draw lots** to decide who will do something by taking pieces of paper etc out of a container: *We drew lots to see who would go first.*
**28 be drawn against sb** *BrE* to be chosen by chance to play or compete against someone

**⑨ STOP/END**
**29 draw to a halt/stop** if a vehicle draws to a halt, it slows down and stops
**30 draw to a close/end** if an event or a period of time draws to a close etc, it ends or finishes
**31 draw a line under sth** to say that something is completely finished: *The agreement draws a line under the recent rail dispute.*

**⑩ SPORT**
**32 ▶ GAME ◀** [I,T] *especially BrE* to end a game or match without either side winning: *They drew 3 – 3.* | *Inter drew with Juventus last night.*
**33 draw a bow** to bend a BOW[3] (1) by pulling back the string in order to shoot an ARROW (1)

**⑪ OTHER MEANINGS**
**34** [T] to attract someone: *Beth felt drawn to this gentle stranger.* | **draw a crowd** *The festival is likely to draw huge crowds.*
**35 draw the line (at sth)** to refuse to do something because you disapprove of it: *I'd really like to help you, but I draw the line at lying.*
**36 draw a blank** *informal* to be unsuccessful, especially when you have been trying to find information or the answer to a problem: *Detectives hunting the missing girl have drawn a blank.*
**37 ▶ PERSUADE SB ◀** [T usually passive] to persuade someone to talk about something: *She refused to be drawn on the subject of her divorce.*
**38 draw blood** to make someone BLEED
**39 draw breath** to find time to have a rest when you are busy: *I didn't have time to draw breath this morning.*
**40 draw a veil over sth** to deliberately keep something unpleasant or embarrassing from being known: *It might be best to draw a veil over Peter's past for now.*
**41 ▶ SHIP ◀** *technical* if a ship draws a certain depth, it needs that depth of water to float in —see also **be at daggers drawn** (DAGGER (3))

**draw back** *phr v* [I] **1** to move yourself away from something: *He drew back in horror when he saw the cuts on her face.* **2** to be afraid or unwilling to do something: [+ **from**] *The company drew back from making a firm commitment.*

**draw in** *phr v* **1** [I] if the days or nights draw in, it gets dark earlier in the evening and so there are fewer hours of daylight: *In October the nights start drawing in.* **2** [T usually passive] to involve someone in something, often when they do not really want to take part: **draw sb in** *We invited Al along to our meetings but he was wary of getting drawn in.* **3 draw your horns in** *BrE* to spend less money because you have financial problems

**draw** sb **into** sth *phr v* [T] to involve someone in something, often when they do not really want to take part: *Homeless children often get drawn into crime.*

**draw** sth ↔ **off** *phr v* [T] to remove some liquid from a larger supply: *We had to draw off some water from the radiator.*

**draw on** *phr v* **1 draw on a cigarette/cigar etc** to breathe in smoke from a cigarette etc **2** [T] to use money, experiences etc for a particular purpose: **draw on/upon sth** *It was a challenge but luckily we had the expertise to draw on.* | **draw on your savings** *I had to draw on my savings to pay for the repairs.* **3** [I] if a period of time draws on, it comes nearer: *Winter is drawing on.*

**draw out** *phr v* **1** [T] to make someone feel less nervous and more willing to talk: **draw sb out** *Try to draw the new boy out a bit if you can.* **2** [T] to make an event last longer than usual: **draw sth ↔ out** *The final questions drew the meeting out for another hour.* **3** [I] if the days draw out, it stays light until later in the evening and so there are more hours of daylight: *It's nice when the days start drawing out again.*

**draw up** *phr v*
**1 ▶ LIST/CONTRACT ETC ◀** [T] to prepare a written document: **draw sth ↔ up** *They drew up a list of candidates.*
**2 ▶ VEHICLE ◀** [I] to arrive somewhere and stop: *The taxi drew up at the gate.*
**3 draw up a chair** [T] to bring a chair closer to someone or something: *Ben drew his chair up to the fireplace.*
**4 draw yourself up (to your full height)** to stand up very straight because you are angry or determined about something: *Drawing himself up to his full height, he ordered me out of the room.*
**5 draw up your knees** to bring your legs closer to your body: *I found him rolling on the floor in pain, with his knees drawn up to his chest.*
**6 ▶ SOLDIERS ◀** [T usually passive] to arrange people in a special order: **draw sth up** *troops drawn up in ranks*

**draw²** *n* [C] **1** *especially BrE* a game that ends with both teams having the same number of points **2** the act of choosing a winning number, ticket etc in a LOTTERY (1): *Bill picked the winning number on the first draw.* **3** a performer, show, sports team etc that a lot of people are willing to pay to see: *Whitney Houston is always a big draw.* **4 quick/fast on the draw a)** able to pull a gun out quickly in order to shoot **b)** good at reacting quickly and intelligently to difficult questions or in difficult situations: *Amit was very quick on the draw in his interview.* —see also **the luck of the draw** (LUCK[1] (15))

**draw·back** /ˈdrɔːbæk‖ˈdrɒː-/ *n* [C] a disadvantage of a situation, product etc: **[+ of/to (doing sth)]** *One drawback of New York in the summer is the heat.*

**draw·bridge** /ˈdrɔːbrɪdʒ‖ˈdrɒː-/ *n* [C] a bridge that can be pulled up to let ships pass, or to stop people from entering or attacking a castle

3 **drawer** /drɔː‖drɒːr/ *n* **1** [C] part of a piece of furniture, such as a desk, that you pull out and push in and use to keep things in: *The scissors are in the kitchen drawer.* —see also BOTTOM DRAWER, TOP-DRAWER —see picture on page 833 **2 drawers** [plural] *old-fashioned* underwear that women and girls wear between their waist and the tops of their legs; KNICKERS

2 **draw·ing** /ˈdrɔːɪŋ‖drɒː-/ *n* **1** [C] a picture that you
2 draw with a pencil, pen etc: *She's done some beautiful charcoal drawings.* **2** [U] the art of making pictures, plans etc with a pen or pencil: *Drawing has never been my strong point.*

**drawing board** /ˈ·· ·/ *n* **1** [C] a large flat board that artists and DESIGNERS work on **2 (go) back to the drawing board** to start working on a plan or idea again after something that you have tried has failed: *We didn't raise enough money so it's back to the drawing board.*

**drawing pin** /ˈ·· ·/ *n* [C] *BrE* a short pin with a round flat head, used especially for putting notices on boards or walls; THUMBTACK *AmE* —see picture at PIN[1]

**drawing room** /ˈ·· ·/ *n* [C] *old-fashioned* a room, especially in a large house, where you can entertain guests or relax

**drawl** /drɔːl‖drɒːl/ *v* [I,T] to speak in a slow unclear way with vowel sounds that are longer than normal —**drawl** *n* [singular] *a Southern drawl*

**drawn¹** /drɔːn‖drɒːn/ the past participle of DRAW[1]

**drawn²** *adj* someone who looks drawn has a thin pale face, usually because they are ill or worried

**drawn-out** /ˌ· ˈ·◂/ *adj* taking more time than usual or more time than you would like: **long drawn-out** *a long drawn-out dispute*

**draw·string** /ˈdrɔːstrɪŋ‖ˈdrɒː-/ *n* [C] a string through the top of a bag, piece of clothing etc that you can pull tight or make loose —see picture on page 840

**dray** /dreɪ/ *n* [C] a flat CART[1] (1) with four wheels that was used in the past for carrying heavy loads, especially BARRELS of beer

**dread¹** /dred/ *v* **1** [T] to feel anxious or worried about something that is going to happen or you think will happen in the future: *I've got an interview tomorrow and I'm dreading it.* | **dread doing sth** *I'm dreading going back to work.* | **dread sb doing sth** *Tim dreaded his parents finding out.* | **dread (that)** *I'm dreading that I'll be asked to help on Sunday.* **2 I dread to think** *spoken* used to show that you think a situation is very worrying: *I dread to think what the children will get up to when I'm away.*

**dread²** *n* **1** [U] a fear of something in the future: *The prospect of meeting Mark's relatives filled her with dread.* | **a dread of** *a dread of the unknown* **2 be/live in dread of** to continuously be very anxious or afraid of what may happen: *The people of the war-torn city live in dread of further shelling.*

**dread·ed** /ˈdredɪ̆d/ also **dread** *literary adj* [only before noun] *sometimes humorous* making you feel afraid or anxious: *I hear the dreaded Miss Jones is going to be at the meeting.*

**dread·ful** /ˈdredfəl/ *adj especially BrE* **1** extremely unpleasant: *We've had some dreadful weather lately.* **2** [only before noun] used to emphasize how bad something or someone is: *It's a dreadful waste of money.*

**dread·ful·ly** /ˈdredfəli/ *adj especially BrE* **1** [+ adj/adv] extremely: *They're dreadfully busy at the moment.* **2** very badly: *The team played dreadfully.* **3** very much: *Would you mind dreadfully if I didn't come?*

**dread·locks** /ˈdredlɒks‖-ɑːks/ *n* [plural] a way of arranging your hair, popular with RASTAFARIANS, in which it hangs in thick lengths like pieces of rope —see picture at HAIRSTYLE

**dread·nought** /ˈdrednɔːt‖-nɒːt/ *n* [C] a type of WARSHIP used at the beginning of the 20th century

**dream¹** /driːm/ *n* S2 W2
**1 ▶ ASLEEP ◀** [C] a series of thoughts, images, and feelings that you experience when you are asleep: *In my dream, I was playing football with the children.* | **have a dream** *I had a really weird dream last night.* | **bad dream** (=frightening or unpleasant) *He claims that eating cheese late at night gives him bad dreams.* | **recurring dream** (=a dream you have again and again)
**2 ▶ WISH ◀** [C] something you hope for and want to happen very much: *Mike's big dream was to be a professional racing driver.* | **[+ of]** *a dream of becoming rich* | **dream house/car etc** (=the house, car etc you really want) *Three weeks in Barbados is my idea of a dream holiday.* | **the house/job of your dreams** *I have just met the man of my dreams!* | **beyond your wildest dreams** (=better than anything you ever imagined or hoped for)
**3 ▶ UNREAL SITUATION ◀** [singular] a situation that does not seem real or part of normal life: **be/seem like a dream** *After a few weeks back at work our vacation seems like a dream.*
**4 ▶ PLEASANT THOUGHTS ◀** [C usually singular] a set of pleasant thoughts that make you forget about what is really happening; DAYDREAM[2]: *Peter's lost in a dream again.*
**5 a dream come true** something that you wanted to happen for a long time: *Finding my real mother after all these years was a dream come true.*
**6 like a dream** *usually spoken* extremely well or effectively: *The plan worked like a dream.* | **go like a dream** (=work perfectly) *The new motorbike goes like a dream.*
**7 a dream** *usually spoken* a very attractive person or thing: *Her latest boyfriend is an absolute dream.*
**8 be/live in a dream world** to have ideas or hopes that are not practical or likely to happen: *If you think he'll change, you're living in a dream world.*
**9 in your dreams** *spoken* used to say that something is not likely to happen: *"I'm going to ask her to go out with me." "In your dreams!"*

**dream²** *v past tense and past participle* **dreamed** or **dreamt** /dremt/ S3

**1 ▶ THINK ABOUT ◀** [I,T] to think about something that you would like to happen: **[+ of]** *We dream of buying our own house.* | **dream (that)** *She dreamed that one day she would be famous.* | **[+ about]** *We used to dream about living abroad.*
**2 ▶ WHILE SLEEPING ◀** [I,T] to have a dream while you are asleep: **[+ about]** *I dreamt about you last night.* | **dream (that)** *It's quite common to dream that you're falling.*
**3 ▶ IMAGINE ◀** [I,T] to imagine that you have done, seen, or heard something that you have not: *I was sure I posted the letter but I must have dreamt it.*
**4 wouldn't dream of (doing) sth** *spoken* used to say that you would never do something because you do not approve of it or think it is unpleasant: *We wouldn't dream of letting our daughter go out on her own at night.*
**5 who would have dreamt it?** *spoken* used to express surprise about something that has happened: *"Did you hear that Bruno's been made Managing Director?" "Yes, who would have dreamt it?"*

**dream** sth ↔ **away** *phr v* [T] to waste time by thinking about what may happen: *She would just sit in her room dreaming away the hours.*

**dream on** *phr v* [I] *spoken* **dream on!** used to tell someone that they are hoping for something that will not happen: *You think I'm going to help you move house? Dream on!*

**dream** sth ↔ **up** [T] to think of a plan or idea, especially an unusual one: *Who on earth dreams up the plots for these soap operas?*

**dream·boat** /ˈdriːmbəʊt‖-boʊt/ *n* [C] *old-fashioned* someone who is very good-looking and attractive

**dream·er** /ˈdriːmə‖-ər/ *n* [C] **1** someone who has ideas or plans that are not practical **2** someone who dreams while they are asleep

**dream·i·ly** /ˈdriːmɪ̆li/ *adv* thinking about pleasant things and not about what is actually happening: *"I'm coming" he replied dreamily, without moving.*

**dream·land** /ˈdriːmlænd/ *n* [U] a happy place or situation that exists only in your imagination

**dream·less** /ˈdriːmləs/ *adj* dreamless sleep is very deep and peaceful

**dream·like** /ˈdriːmlaɪk/ *adj* as if happening in a dream; unreal: *There was a dreamlike quality about the film.*

**dreamt** /dremt/ a past tense and past participle of DREAM[2]

**dream tick·et** /ˌ· ˈ··/ *n* [C] a combination of people who you think will be sure to win an election for a political party: *Clinton and Gore were the Democrats' dream ticket.*

**dream·y** /ˈdriːmi/ *adj* **1** someone who is dreamy has a good imagination but is not very practical: *a bright, but dreamy child* **2** looking as though you are thinking about something pleasant rather than things happening around you: *a dreamy look* **3** a dreamy sight, sound etc is peaceful and relaxing: *She loved the dreamy music of those old songs.* **4** *informal* very attractive and desirable: *a dreamy new sports car* —**dreaminess** *n* [U]

**drear·y** /ˈdrɪəri‖ˈdrɪri/ also **drear** /drɪə‖drɪr/ *poetical adj* not interesting or cheerful: *the same old dreary routine* | *a dreary winter's day*

**dredge** /dredʒ/ *v* **1** [T] to remove mud or sand from the bottom of a river, HARBOUR[1] etc **2** [I,T] to search for something on the bottom of a river, lake, etc with a dredge **3** [T] to cover food lightly with flour, sugar etc

**dredge** sth ↔ **up** *phr v* [T] **1** *informal* to start talking again about something that happened a long time ago: *Come on now, let's not dredge up old quarrels.* **2** to pull something up from the bottom of a river

**dredg·er** /ˈdredʒə‖-ər/ also **dredge** *n* [C] a machine or ship used for digging or removing mud and sand from the bottom of a river, HARBOUR[1] etc

**dregs** /dregz/ *n* **1** [plural] small pieces that sink to the bottom of wine, coffee etc —compare LEE (3) **2 the dregs of society/humanity** an offensive expression used to describe the people that you consider are the least important or useful

**drench** /drentʃ/ *v* [T] to make something or someone extremely wet —**drenching** *adj*

**drenched** /drentʃt/ *adj* **1** extremely wet: *Come on in – you're drenched!* | **[+ with/in]** *I came back from aerobics drenched in sweat.* | **drenched to the skin** (=wearing completely wet clothes) **2** covered in something: **[+ in]** *women drenched in cheap perfume* | **rain-drenched/sun-drenched etc** (=covered in rain, or in the effects of something such as the sun) *sun-drenched deserts*

**dress**[1] /dres/ *n* **1** [C] a piece of clothing worn by a woman or girl that covers her body from her shoulder to somewhere on her leg: *Sheila wore a long red dress.* —compare SKIRT[1] (1) **2** [U] the way someone dresses: *His dress is always very formal.* **3 dress code** a standard of what you should wear for a particular situation: *This restaurant has a strict dress code – no tie, no service.* **4 evening/national/battle etc dress** a special set of clothes that you wear for a particular occasion —see also DRESS SENSE, CLOTHES (USAGE)

**dress**

He got dressed.

He put on a jacket.

He wore a dark suit.

**dress**[2] *v*
**1 ▶ PUT ON CLOTHES ◀ a)** [I] to put on clothes, etc, especially before a special occasion: *I've got to go home to dress.* | **dress for** (=put on clothes you wear for a particular activity) *How do you normally dress for work?* | **dress for dinner** (=put on formal clothes for your evening meal) **b)** [T] to put clothes on yourself or someone else: *I dress the kids before I go to work.* —see also DRESSED
**2 ▶ WEAR CLOTHES ◀** [I] to wear a particular kind of clothes: *Dress warmly if you're going out for a walk.*
**3 dress a wound/cut etc** to clean and cover a wound etc
**4 dress a salad** to put a mixture of oil, VINEGAR, salt etc onto a SALAD (=cold vegetables) *Don't dress the salad until just before you're ready to eat.*
**5 dress poultry/crab etc** to clean and prepare meat or fish so that it is ready to cook or eat

**6 ▶ MAKE CLOTHES ◀** [T] to make or choose clothes for someone: *The Princess is dressed by one of Britain's most famous designers.*
**7 ▶ HAIR ◀** [T] *formal* to arrange someone's hair into a special style
**8 ▶ HORSE ◀** [T] to brush a horse in order to make it clean
**9 dress wood/metal/leather etc** *technical* to polish or put a special surface onto wood etc
**10 dress stone** *technical* to cut and shape stone so that it can be used in building
**11 ▶ SOLDIERS ◀** [I,T] *technical* a word used in the army to tell soldiers to form a straight line

**dress down** *phr v* **1** [I] to wear clothes that are more informal than you would usually wear **2** [T **dress sb ↔ down**] to speak angrily or severely to someone about something they have done wrong —see also DRESSING-DOWN

**dress up**

The kids are dressing up in their room.

Jill's getting dressed up for the dinner party.

**dress up** *phr v* **1** [I,T] to wear special clothes, MAKE-UP (1), etc for fun: [+ **as**] *He went to the party dressed up as a Chicago gangster.* | [+ **in**] *I keep a box of old clothes for the children to dress up in.* [**dress sb ↔ up**] | *We dressed him up as a gorilla.* **2** [I] to wear clothes that are more formal than you would usually wear: *It's a small informal party – you don't have to dress up.* **3** [T **dress** sth **↔ up**] to make something sound more interesting or attractive than it really is: *It was the old offer dressed up as something new.*

**USAGE NOTE: DRESS**

WORD CHOICE: **dress, get dressed, put on, dress up, dress yourself, have on, wear, dress in, be in**

If you **dress** (slightly formal) or **get dressed** you **put on** all your clothes. But you usually use **put on** if you are talking about just one piece of clothing or things like glasses and jewellery: *It's ten o'clock – isn't time you got dressed?*|*We had to wash and dress in a freezing bathroom.*|*OK, you can put your shirt back on.*|*Wait a moment while I put my shoes on.*

You **dress up** only in special clothes or for a special occasion. These may be particularly good or formal ones: *What kind of party is it? Will we have to dress up?* Or they may be unusual clothes that make you look like someone else, for example if you are acting in a play: *He had to dress up as a clown.*

You only talk about someone **dressing themselves** if a special effort is involved: *Can Tara dress herself yet?* (=Tara is a small child)|*Since the accident he can't feed or dress himself.*

After you have **put on** your clothes etc, you **have** them **on**: *They all had dark glasses on.*

**Wear** means to **have** clothes, jewellery etc **on** and is often used to describe someone's usual style of dressing: *She always wears earrings/casual clothes/black.*|*I'll be wearing a red coat.*|*All visitors to the site must wear a protective helmet.* You can also use **dress (in)** and **be (dressed) in** to talk about what clothes someone is wearing, or their style of clothes: *She always dresses casually/in black.*|*The band were all (dressed) in green and red jackets.*

GRAMMAR

You **dress in** clothes, or **dress** someone **in** them. You cannot *dress clothes* or *dress with clothes*.

**dres·sage** /ˈdresɑːʒ‖drɪˈsɑːʒ/ *n* [U] a competition in which a horse performs a complicated series of actions in answer to signals from its rider

**dress cir·cle** /ˌ· ˈ··/ *n* [C] the lowest of the curved rows of seats upstairs in a theatre

**dressed** /drest/ *adj* **1 get dressed** to put your clothes on: *Go and get dressed!* **2** having your clothes on: *Aren't you dressed yet?*| **fully dressed** (=with all your clothes on) **3** wearing a particular type of clothes: [+ **in/as**] *The older woman was dressed in a suit.* | **well/neatly/badly etc dressed** *a very well-dressed young man* **4 dressed to kill** *informal* wearing very attractive clothes so that everyone notices you **5 dressed (up) to the nines** *informal* wearing your best or most formal clothes: *Where on earth's he going dressed up to the nines like that?*

**dress·er** /ˈdresə‖-ər/ *n* [C] **1** *BrE* a large piece of furniture with open shelves for storing plates, dishes etc; WELSH DRESSER **2** *AmE* a piece of furniture with drawers for storing clothes, sometimes with a mirror on top; CHEST OF DRAWERS **3 a fashionable/stylish/sloppy etc dresser** someone who dresses in a fashionable etc way: *Stanley was an impeccable dresser, with plenty of money.* **4** someone who looks after an actor's clothes in the theatre and helps them to dress for a play

**dress·ing** /ˈdresɪŋ/ *n* **1** [C,U] a mixture of liquids, usually made from oil and VINEGAR, that you put on raw vegetables: *a vinaigrette dressing* —see also FRENCH DRESSING, SALAD DRESSING **2** [C,U] *AmE* a mixture of food that you put inside a piece of meat, for example a chicken, before you cook it; STUFFING (1) **3** [C] a special piece of material used to cover and protect a wound: *Put the soiled dressings in this bin.* —see also CROSS-DRESSING, POWER DRESSING, WINDOW DRESSING

**dressing-down** /ˌ·· ˈ·/ *n* **give sb a dressing-down** to talk to someone angrily because they have done something wrong: *He gave the children a good dressing-down.*

**dressing gown** /ˈ·· ·/ *n* [C] *especially BrE* a piece of clothing like a long loose coat that you wear inside the house; BATHROBE

**dressing room** /ˈ·· ·/ *n* [C] **1** a room where an actor or performer can get ready, before going on stage, appearing on television etc **2** a small room next to a BEDROOM

**dressing ta·ble** /ˈ·· ˌ··/ *n* [C] *BrE* a piece of furniture like a table with a mirror on top, sometimes with drawers, that you use when you are doing your hair, putting on MAKE-UP (1) etc; VANITY TABLE *AmE*

**dressing-up** /ˌ·· ˈ·/ *n* [U] a children's game in which they put on special clothes and MAKE-UP (1) and pretend that they are someone else: *a box of dressing-up clothes*

**dress·mak·er** /ˈdresˌmeɪkə‖-ər/ *n* [C] someone who makes their own clothes, or makes clothes for other people as a job —**dressmaking** *n* [U]

**dress re·hears·al** /ˈ· ·ˌ··/ *n* [C] the final practice of a play, OPERA etc, using all the clothes that will be worn for the actual performance

**dress sense** /ˈ· ·/ *n* [U] the ability to choose clothes that make you look attractive

**dress shirt** /ˈ· ·/ *n* [C] a formal shirt, sometimes with a special decoration at the front, that you wear under a DINNER JACKET

**dress u·ni·form** /ˈ· ˌ···/ *n* [C,U] a uniform that officers in the army, navy etc wear for formal occasions or ceremonies

**dress·y** /ˈdresi/ *adj* **1** dressy clothes are suitable for formal occasions: *Her outfit was just right for a summer evening – smart, but not too dressy.* **2** someone who is dressy likes to wear very fashionable or formal clothes: *Mr Menendez is a very dressy sort of person.*

**drew** /druː/ the past tense of DRAW[1]

**drib·ble[1]** /ˈdrɪbəl/ *v* **1** [I] *BrE* to let SALIVA (=natural liquid in your mouth) flow out of your mouth onto your chin; DROOL (1) *AmE*: *Watch out, the baby is dribbling on your shirt!* **2** [I always + adv/prep] if a liquid dribbles, it flows very slowly in small irregular drops: [+ **down/from/out etc**] *There was a tiny hole in the pipe and water was dribbling out.* **3** [T] to pour something out slowly in an irregular way: *This artist works by dribbling paint straight from the tube.* **4** [I,T] to move the ball along with you, by short kicks, BOUNCES, or hits, in a game of football, BASKETBALL etc: *We've been learning how to dribble the ball.* —see picture on page 1264

**dribble[2]** *n* **1** [U] *BrE* a flow of SALIVA (=natural liquid in your mouth) from your mouth; SALIVA *AmE* **2 a dribble of sth** a small amount of liquid: *He wiped a dribble of ice-cream from his chin.* **3** [C] the way in which you move the ball along with you in football, BASKETBALL etc

**drib·let** /ˈdrɪblɪ̈t/ *n* [C] a very small amount of something

**dribs and drabs** /ˌdrɪbz ən ˈdræbz/ *n* [plural] **in dribs and drabs** in small irregular amounts or numbers over a period of time: *The guests arrived in dribs and drabs.*

**dried** /draɪd/ *adj* dried substances, such as food or flowers, have had the water removed

**dried fruit** /ˌ· ˈ·/ *n* [C,U] fruit that has been dried and is used in cooking or eaten on its own

**dried milk** /ˌ· ˈ·/ *n* [U] milk that is made into a powder and can be used by adding water

**dri·er** /ˈdraɪə‖-ər/ *n* [C] another spelling of DRYER

**drift[1]** /drɪft/ *v* [I] **1** to move slowly on water or in the air: [+ **out/towards etc**] *The rubber raft drifted out to sea.* **2** [always + adv/prep] to move or go somewhere without any plan or purpose: [+ **around/along etc**] *Jenni spent the year drifting around Europe.* | **drift from sth to sth** *The conversation drifted from one topic to another.* **3 drift into sth** to go from one situation or condition to another without realizing it: *She was just drifting into sleep when the alarm went off.* **4** if snow, sand etc drifts, the wind blows it into large piles: *The snow was drifting in great piles against the house.* **5 let sth drift** to allow something to continue in the same way: *He couldn't let the matter drift for much longer.*

**drift apart** *phr v* [I] if people drift apart, their relationship gradually ends: *Over the years my college friends and I have drifted apart.*

**drift off** *phr v* [I] to gradually fall asleep: *I was just drifting off when the phone rang.*

**drift[2]** *n*
**1** ▶ **SNOW** ◀ [C] a large pile of snow, sand etc that has been blown by the wind: [+ **of**] *The road is blocked with massive drifts of snow.*
**2** ▶ **SHIP** ◀ [U] the degree to which a ship or plane changes its direction because of the movement of the wind or water
**3** ▶ **GENERAL MEANING** ◀ **the drift** the general meaning of what someone is saying: [+ **of**] *So what's the drift of the argument?* | **follow/get/catch sb's drift** (=understand the general meaning) *I didn't hear every word of her speech, but I got the drift.*
**4** ▶ **CHANGE** ◀ [singular] a slow change or development from one situation, opinion etc to another: *the drift of public opinion towards the political left* | **the broad/whole/general drift** (=the general change in direction) *A general drift towards anarchy must be prevented at all costs.*
**5** ▶ **MOVEMENT OF PEOPLE** ◀ a slow and unplanned movement of large numbers of people: [+ **from/to/into**] *the drift from the countryside to the cities*

**drift·er** /ˈdrɪftə‖-ər/ *n* [C] **1** someone who is always moving from one job or place to another **2** a fishing boat that uses a floating net

**drift-ice** /ˈ· ·/ *n* [U] pieces of broken ice floating in a sea, river etc

**drift·net** /ˈdrɪftnet/ *n* [C] a large net behind a boat, used to catch fish

**drift·wood** /ˈdrɪftwʊd/ *n* [U] wood floating in the sea or left on the shore

**drills**

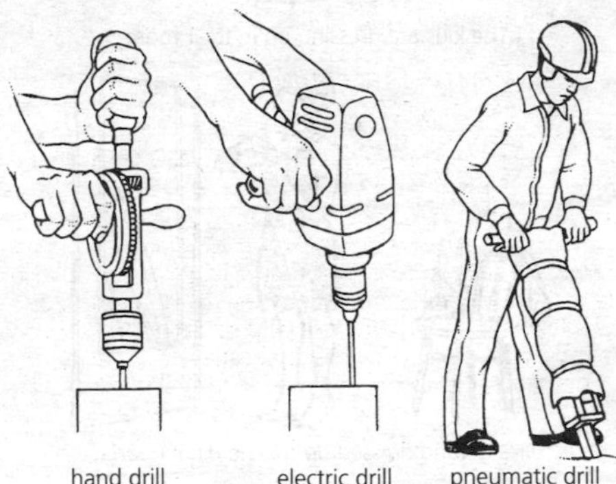


**drill[1]** /drɪl/ *n*
**1** ▶ **TOOL** ◀ [C] a tool or machine used for making holes in something: *an electric drill*
**2** ▶ **WAY OF LEARNING** ◀ [U] a way of learning something by repeating it many times: *a pronunciation drill*
**3 fire/emergency drill** a practice of the things you should do in a dangerous situation such as a fire
**4** ▶ **MILITARY TRAINING** ◀ [U] military training in which soldiers practice marching and other actions: *rifle drill*
**5** ▶ **CLOTH** ◀ [U] a type of strong cotton cloth
**6 the drill** *BrE old-fashioned* the correct way of doing something: *What's the drill for getting money after four o'clock?*
**7** ▶ **SEEDS** ◀ **a)** [C] a machine for planting seeds in rows **b)** a row of seeds planted by machine

**drill[2]** *v* **1** [I,T] to make a hole in something using a drill: *You need to drill holes for the fittings.* | **drill for oil/water/gas etc** *The Saudi government has announced plans to drill for water in the desert.* **2** [T] to teach someone by making them repeat something many times: *She was drilling the class in the forms of the past tense.* | **well-drilled** *The well-drilled cabin crew evacuated the passengers in minutes.* **3** [I,T] to practice marching and other military actions, or to train soldiers to do this **4** [T] to plant seeds in rows

**drill** sth **into sb** *phr v* [T] to keep telling someone something until they know it very well: *Mother had drilled it into me not to talk to strangers.*

**drilling plat·form** /ˈ·· ˌ··/ *n* [C] a large structure in the sea used for drilling for oil, gas etc

**dri·ly** /ˈdraɪli/ *adv* another spelling of DRYLY

S1 W2 **drink¹** /drɪŋk/ *n* **1** [C] an amount of liquid that you drink: *Can I have a drink of water, please?* | **soft drink** (=a non-alcoholic drink) *They sell ice-cream and soft drinks.* **2** [C,U] alcohol, or a glass or bottle of alcohol: *Have another drink.* | *There was lots of food and drink left over from the party.* | **a stiff drink** (=very strong alcohol) *After that news I need a stiff drink!* | **go out for a drink** *BrE* (=go to a PUB) | **take to drink** (=start drinking a lot of alcohol regularly) | **stand sb a drink** (=buy someone a drink, especially because they do not have enough money) | **a drink problem** (=difficulty in limiting the amount of alcohol you drink so that it affects your life) **3 drinks** [plural] *BrE* a social occasion when you have alcoholic drinks and sometimes food: *Don't forget we're invited to the Jones' for drinks on Sunday.* **4 the drink** *informal* the sea, a lake, or other large area of water —see also **drive sb to drink** (DRIVE¹ (4))

S2 W2 **drink²** *v past tense* **drank** /dræŋk/ *past participle* **drunk** /drʌŋk/ **1** [I,T] to take liquid into your mouth and swallow it: *I don't need a glass, I'll drink from the bottle.* | *If you have a fever, drink plenty of water.* | *What would you like to drink?* **2** [I] to drink alcohol, especially regularly or too much: *He's been drinking heavily since his wife died.* | **don't/doesn't drink** (=never drink alcohol) *Whisky? No thanks, I don't drink.* | **drink and drive** (=driving after you have drunk too much alcohol) *a new campaign to stop drinking and driving at Christmas* | **drink like a fish** (=regularly drink a lot of alcohol) | **drink yourself unconscious/silly etc** (=drink so much alcohol that you become unconscious etc) *If he goes on this way he'll drink himself to death.* | **drink someone under the table** (=drink more alcohol than someone else but not be as ill as them) **3 what are you drinking?** *spoken* used to offer to buy someone a drink, especially in a PUB

**drink** sth ↔ **in** *phr v* [T] to look at or listen to something carefully and enjoy it: *We spent the day drinking in the sights and sounds of Paris.*

**drink to sth** *phr v* [T] **1** to wish someone success, good luck, good health etc before having an alcoholic drink: *Let's drink to your success in your new job.* **2 I'll drink to that!** *spoken* used to agree with what someone has said

**drink** sth ↔ **up** *phr v* [T] to drink all of something: *Come on, drink up your milk.*

**drin·ka·ble** /ˈdrɪŋkəbəl/ *adj* **1** water that is drinkable is safe to drink **2** wine, beer etc that is drinkable is of good quality and tastes pleasant

**drink-dri·ving** /ˌ· ˈ··/ *n* [U] *BrE* driving a car after having drunk too much alcohol; DRUNK-DRIVING *AmE*

**drink·er** /ˈdrɪŋkə‖-ər/ *n* [C] **1** someone who regularly drinks alcohol: *Dave has always been a bit of a drinker.* | **hard/heavy drinker** (=someone who drinks a lot) **2 coffee/wine/champagne etc drinker** someone who regularly drinks coffee etc: *There's no wine – we're all beer drinkers, I'm afraid.*

**drink·ing foun·tain** /ˈ·· ˌ··/ *n* [C] a piece of equipment in a public place that produces a stream of water for you to drink from; WATER FOUNTAIN *AmE*

**drinking-up time** /ˌ·· ˈ· ·/ *n* [U] *BrE* the time, after a PUB has closed, when people are allowed to finish their drinks

**drinking wa·ter** /ˈ·· ˌ··/ *n* [U] water that is pure enough for you to drink

**drinks ma·chine** /ˈ· ·ˌ·/ *n* [C] a machine that serves hot and cold drinks when you put money into it

**drinks par·ty** /ˈ· ˌ··/ *n* [C] *BrE* a party where you mainly talk to people and have alcoholic drinks; COCKTAIL PARTY

**drip¹** /drɪp/ *v* **dripped, dripping** **1** [I] to produce small drops of liquid: *The tap's dripping.* | *Be careful – your paintbrush is dripping.* **2** [I,T] to fall or let something fall in very small drops: [**+ down/from etc**] *Sweat dripped from his body.* | *Water was dripping through the ceiling.* | **drip water/blood etc** *John came in, his arm dripping blood.* | **be dripping with sth** *It's so hot, I'm dripping with sweat.* **3 be dripping with jewels/diamonds etc** to be wearing too much jewellery etc

**drip²** *n* **1** [singular, U] the sound or action of a liquid falling in very small drops: *There was no noise except for the drip drip drip of water.* **2** [C] one of the very small drops of liquid that falls from something: *I put some plastic on the floor to catch the drips.* **3** [C] a piece of equipment used in hospitals for putting liquids directly into your blood; IV *AmE*: *They put her on a drip to speed up the contractions* **4** [C] *informal* someone who is boring and has a weak character

**drip-dry** /ˌ· ˈ·◂/ *adj* drip-dry clothing does not need ironing (IRON²) —**drip-dry** *v* [I,T]

**drip·ping¹** /ˈdrɪpɪŋ/ *n* [U] *BrE* the oily substance that comes out of meat when you cook it

**dripping²** *adj* extremely wet: **dripping wet** *Take off that jacket, you're dripping wet.*

**drip·py** /ˈdrɪpi/ *adj* very emotional and weak: *Don't be so drippy, just call Kate and ask her out!*

**drive¹** /draɪv/ *v past tense* **drove** /drəʊv‖droʊv/ *past participle* **driven** /ˈdrɪvən/ S1 W1

**1 ► OPERATE A VEHICLE ◄** [I,T] to sit in a car, bus etc and make it travel from one place to another: *Do you drive?* | *She drove the pick-up and got our supplies.* —see picture on page 415

**2 ► TRAVEL SOMEWHERE ◄** [I,T] to travel in a car: *Shall we drive or take the bus?*

**3 ► TAKE SB SOMEWHERE ◄** [T] to take someone somewhere in a car: *Just tell us when you have to go, and Jim will drive you.* | **drive sb back/down/over etc** *Can I drive you home?*

**4 ► FEELING ◄** [T] to make someone feel or do something bad or unpleasant: **drive sb to sth** *The children are driving me to despair.* | **drive sb to do sth** *It was hunger that drove them to steal the bread.* | **be driven by sth** (=be encouraged to do something by an unpleasant feeling or quality) *Phil, driven by jealousy, started spying on his wife.* | **drive sb to drink** (=upset someone very much) *This job's enough to drive anyone to drink!* | **drive sb mad/crazy etc** *The noise from the neighbours is driving me mad.*

**5 ► FORCE SB/STH ◄** [T] to force someone or something to go somewhere: *Tourists were driven indoors by the rain.* | *Cowhands drove the cattle into the corral.*

**6 ► PROVIDE POWER ◄** [T] to provide the power for something: *a steam-driven generator*

**7 ► HIT STH INTO STH ◄** [T] to hit something, such as a nail, into something else: *We watched Dad drive the posts into the ground.*

**8 ► SPORT ◄** [I,T] to move a ball in a game of football, GOLF etc by kicking, hitting, or bouncing (BOUNCE¹ (1)) it hard and fast: *Bonds drove the ball to center field.* —see picture on page 1264

**9 drive a hard bargain** to make an agreement difficult by demanding a lot or refusing to give too much

**10 drive sb out of their mind** to do something that makes someone feel as if they are crazy

**11 drive a coach and horses through sth** to destroy an argument, plan etc completely: *The new bill will drive a coach and horses through recent trade agreements.*

**12 ► MAKE A HOLE ◄** [T] to make a large hole in something using heavy equipment or machinery: *They're planning to drive a tunnel through the mountains.*

**13 drive home a point** to make something completely clear to someone: *I tried to drive home the point that we need extra people, but the boss wasn't interested.*

**14 drive a wedge between** to do something that makes people disagree or start to dislike each other: *Lisa's lies drove a wedge between the couple.*
**15 drive yourself too hard** to force yourself to work too hard, because you want to be successful

**drive at** sth *phr v* [T] **what sb is driving at** the thing someone is really trying to say: *He didn't mention the word 'redundancy' but I knew what he was driving at.*

**drive** sb ↔ **away** *phr v* [T] to behave in a way that forces someone to leave: *Your possessiveness will drive Liz away if you're not careful.*

**drive off** *phr v* **1** [I] if a car, driver etc drives off, they leave: *After the accident the other car just drove off.* **2** [T **drive** sb/sth ↔ **off**] to force someone or something that is attacking or threatening you to go away: *We keep dogs in the yard to drive off intruders.* **3** [I] to hit the first ball in a game of GOLF

**drive** sb/sth ↔ **out** *phr v* [T] to force someone or something to leave: *Downtown stores are being driven out by crime.*

**drive** sth ↔ **up** *phr v* [T] to force prices, costs etc to rise quickly: *The oil shortage drove gas prices up by 20 cents a gallon.*

S2 W2 **drive²** *n*
**1** ► **IN A CAR** ◄ [C] a trip in a car: *It's a four day drive to Prague.* | **go for a drive** *Let's go for a drive along the coast.*
**2** ► **OUTSIDE YOUR HOUSE** ◄ [C] the area or road between your house and the street; DRIVEWAY: *He parked his car in the drive.* —see picture on page 415
**3** ► **SPORT** ◄ [C] an act of hitting a ball hard, especially in tennis or GOLF: *He hit a long, high drive to right field.*
**4** ► **A FIGHT FOR STH** ◄ [C] a planned effort by an organization or government to achieve a change that will improve people's lives: *a big anti-smoking drive* | **economy drive** (=effort to reduce spending)
**5** ► **NATURAL NEED** ◄ [C] a strong natural need which must be satisfied: *Hunger is a human drive.* | *sex drive*
**6** ► **SB'S ENERGY** ◄ [U] determination and energy that make you successfully achieve something: *Brian has got tremendous drive.*
**7 Drive** used in the names of roads: *They live at 141 Park Drive.*
**8** ► **POWER** ◄ [singular] the power from an engine that makes the wheels of a vehicle go round: *four wheel drive*
**9** ► **MILITARY ATTACK** ◄ [C] several military attacks: *a drive deep into enemy territory* —see also DISK DRIVE, WHIST DRIVE

**drive-by** /ˈ· ·/ *adj* **drive-by shooting/killing** the act of shooting someone from a moving car

**drive-in** /ˈ· ·/ *adj* [only before noun] a drive-in restaurant, cinema etc allows you to buy food or watch a film without leaving your car —**drive-in** *n* [C]

**driv·el¹** /ˈdrɪvəl/ *n* [U] something that is said or written that is silly or does not mean anything: *Don't talk such drivel!*

**drivel²** *v* **drivelled, drivelling** [I] *BrE* **drivel on/away** to speak continuously without saying anything important —**drivelling** *adj*: *a drivelling idiot*

**driv·en¹** /ˈdrɪvən/ the past participle of DRIVE¹

**driven²** *adj* trying extremely hard to achieve what you want —see also **as pure as the driven snow** (PURE (8))

S1 W2 **driv·er** /ˈdraɪvə‖-ər/ *n* [C] **1** someone who drives a car, bus etc **2** a GOLF CLUB (2) with a wooden head —see also **back seat driver** (BACK SEAT (2)), **Sunday driver** (SUNDAY (3))

**driv·er's ed·u·ca·tion** /ˌ·· ··ˈ··/ *n* [U] *AmE* a course that you usually take at school, that teaches you how to drive a car

**driver's lic·ense** /ˈ·· ˌ··/ *n* [C] *AmE* an official document that allows you to drive on public roads; DRIVING LICENCE *BrE*

**drive shaft** /ˈ· ·/ *n* [C] *technical* a part of a vehicle that takes power from the GEARBOX to the wheels

**drive-through** /ˈ· ·/ *n* [singular] *especially AmE* a restaurant, bank etc where you can buy food or do business without getting out of your car

**drive·way** /ˈdraɪvweɪ/ *n* [C] the area or road between your house and the street; DRIVE² (2) —see picture on page 415

**driv·ing** /ˈdraɪvɪŋ/ *adj* **1 driving rain/snow** rain or snow that falls very hard and fast **2 driving force/ambition/politician** someone or something that produces a strong effect on people or situations: *Hawksworth was the driving force behind the project.*

**driving li·cence** /ˈ·· ˌ··/ *n* [C] *BrE* an official document that allows you to drive on public roads; DRIVER'S LICENSE *AmE*

**driving range** /ˈ·· ·/ *n* [C] an open outdoor area where people practice hitting GOLF balls

**driving school** /ˈ·· ·/ *n* [C] an organization that teaches you to how to drive a car

**driving seat** /ˈ·· ·/ *n* **be in the driving seat** *BrE* **be in the driver's seat** *AmE* to be the person who is in control of a situation: *Fiona led the meeting but Marie was the one in the driving seat.*

**driving test** /ˈ·· ·/ *n* [C] the official test that you must pass in order to drive a car on public roads

**driving un·der the in·flu·ence** /ˌ·· ·· ·ˈ···/ *n* [U] *AmE* DUI

**driz·zle¹** /ˈdrɪzəl/ *v* [I] to rain slightly: *The rain isn't too bad – it's only drizzling.*

**drizzle²** *n* [singular, U] weather that is between mist and rain: *A light drizzle had started by the time we left.* —**drizzly** *adj*

**droll** /drəʊl‖droʊl/ *adj old-fashioned or humorous* amusing: *Oh! Very droll!*

**droll·e·ry** /ˈdrəʊləri‖ˈdroʊl-/ *n* [C,U] *old-fashioned* humour

**-drome** /drəʊm‖droʊm/ *suffix* [in nouns] *old-fashioned* a large place for a particular purpose: *an aerodrome* (=an airport)

**drom·e·da·ry** /ˈdrɒmədəri‖ˈdrɑːməderi/ *n plural* **dromedaries** [C] a CAMEL with one raised part on its back

**drone¹** /drəʊn‖droʊn/ *v* [I] to make a continuous low dull sound: *An airplane droned overhead.*

**drone on** *phr v* [I] to speak in a boring way, usually for a long time: [+ **about**] *Tom was droning on about work.*

**drone²** *n* [C] **1 the drone (of)** a continuous low dull sound: *the steady drone of traffic* **2** a male BEE that does no work **3** someone who does a lot of dull work without many rewards **4** someone who has a good life but does not work to earn it: *idle drones living at the expense of society*

**dron·go** /ˈdrɒŋgəʊ‖ˈdrɑːŋgoʊ/ *n* [C] *informal, especially AustrE* a boring and stupid person

**drool** /druːl/ *v* [I] **1** to let SALIVA (=the liquid in your mouth) flow from your mouth; DRIBBLE¹ (1) *BrE* **2** to show great pleasure in looking at someone or something: [+ **over**] *Janet was drooling over the two little kittens.* —compare SLOBBER

**droop¹** /druːp/ *v* [I] **1** to hang or bend downwards: *The plant needs some water – it's starting to droop.* **2** to become sad or weak: *Our spirits drooped as we faced the long trip home.*

**droop²** *n* [singular] **1** an act of drooping **2 brewer's/drinker's droop** *humorous* a condition in which a man cannot get an ERECTION (1) because he has drunk too much alcohol

# drop¹ /drɒp‖drɑːp/ *v*

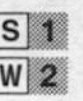

① FALL/ALLOW TO FALL
② DECREASE
③ STOP (DOING STH)
④ NOT USE
⑤ GO SOMEWHERE
⑥ OTHER MEANINGS

## ① FALL/ALLOW TO FALL

**1** [T] to stop holding or carrying something so that it falls: *I must have dropped my scarf on the bus.* | *The dog dropped a stick at George's feet.*
**2 ▶FALL◀** [I] to fall suddenly, especially from a high place: *A bottle rolled across the table, dropped onto the floor and smashed.* | *Your button has dropped off.*
**3 ▶LOWER YOUR BODY◀** [I always + adv/prep, T] to lower yourself or part of your body suddenly: [+ **to/into/down etc**] *He dropped into a chair with a sigh.*
**4 ▶GROUND◀** [I always + adv/prep] if a path, land etc drops it goes down suddenly, forming a steep slope: *At that point the path dropped sharply to the right.* | [+ **away**] *The cliff dropped away to the sea.*
**5 drop anchor** to lower a boat's ANCHOR¹ (1) to the bottom of the sea, lake etc so that the boat stays in the same place
**6 ▶HIT◀** [T] to hit someone so hard that they fall down: *Ali dropped him with one punch.*

## ② DECREASE

**7 ▶LEVEL/AMOUNT◀** [I] to fall to a lower level or amount: *The town's population is expected to drop in the next decade.* | [+ **to/from**] *The number of people out of work has dropped to 2 million.* | **drop sharply** *House prices have dropped sharply in the recession.*
**8 ▶TEMPERATURE◀** [I] to become colder quite quickly: *The temperature dropped below zero.*
**9 ▶LOWER A LEVEL/AMOUNT◀** [T] to lower the level or amount of something: *Drop your speed as you approach the bend.*
**10 drop your voice/let your voice drop** to speak more quietly: *Barbara saw the manager coming and dropped her voice to a whisper.*

## ③ STOP (DOING STH)

**11 ▶STOP DOING STH◀** [T] to stop doing something or planning to do something: *Plans for a new swimming pool were dropped due to lack of funding.*
**12 ▶TO STOP TALKING◀** to stop talking about something because it upsets people: **drop it/drop the subject** *spoken*: *Just drop it can't you? I'm tired of arguing.* | **let the matter drop** *I wish you'd let the matter drop.*
**13 drop everything** to stop what you are doing in order to do something else: *I can't just drop everything and go, I've got far too much work.*
**14 ▶RELATIONSHIP◀** [T] to end a relationship with someone, usually without thinking about how the other person will feel: *Sally drops her boyfriends as soon as she gets bored.*
**15 drop history/physics/German etc** to decide to stop studying history etc at school or university: *I wish I hadn't dropped French, it would've been useful for this job.*

## ④ NOT USE

**16 ▶NOT USE◀** [T] to decide not to use something that you had planned to use: *This article won't be of interest to our readers. Let's drop it.*
**17 ▶NOT INCLUDE◀** [T] to no longer include someone in a team or group: [+ **from**] *Jeff's been dropped from the team for Saturday's game.*
**18 ▶WORD OR LETTER◀** [T] to not use a particular word or letter: *He often drops his 'h's' when he talks.* | *Oh, drop the 'senator', just call me Gordon.*

## ⑤ GO SOMEWHERE

**19 ▶VISIT◀** [I always + adv/prep] to visit someone informally without arranging a particular time: [+ **in/over/round/by**] *Drop by whenever you're in the area.* | **drop in on sb** *I think I'll drop in on Jill on my way home.*
**20 ▶TAKE SB SOMEWHERE◀** [T always + adv/prep] to take someone by car to a particular place that you are driving past: **drop sb off/at etc** *She usually drops the kids off at school on her way to work.*
**21 ▶TAKE STH SOMEWHERE◀** [T always + adv/prep] to take something to a particular place and leave it there: **drop sth off/at/in etc** *I'll drop the books off at your place after my class.*
**22 drop behind/back** to move slowly so that you get separated from the group you are with: *Don't drop behind the others on the trail in case you get lost.*

## ⑥ OTHER MEANINGS

**23 drop sb a line/note** to write a short letter to someone: *Drop me a line when you get to Hawaii.*
**24 work until you drop** to work until you are extremely tired: *They worked until they dropped.*
**25 (let) drop a hint/suggestion/remark etc** to say something informally and without emphasizing it: *He let drop a remark about his childhood which quite surprised me.*
**26 drop your eyes/gaze** to stop looking at someone and look down, usually because you feel embarrassed or uncomfortable: *She blushed and dropped her gaze.*
**27 drop dead a)** to die suddenly and unexpectedly without having previously been ill: *One day he just dropped dead in the street.* **b)** *spoken* used angrily to tell someone to be quiet, stop annoying you etc
**28 ▶MONEY◀** [T] *informal* to lose money in business, a game etc: *Phil dropped $200 playing poker yesterday.*
**29 ▶NOT CATCH◀** [T] to fail to catch a ball hit by a BATSMAN in the game of CRICKET (2)
**30 ▶LOSE◀** [T] to lose a point, game etc in a sports competition: *Davison has dropped three points in the fourth round.*
**31 ▶DRUGS◀** [T] *informal* to swallow an illegal drug: *She dropped acid in the 60s.*
**32 drop names** to use the names of famous or important people in conversations to make yourself seem important
**33 drop a stitch** to let the wool fall off the needle when you are knitting (KNIT¹ (1))
**34 drop a clanger/brick** *BrE* to say something socially embarrassing
**35 drop a bombshell** *informal* to suddenly tell someone a shocking piece of news: *Then she dropped a bombshell and told me she wanted a divorce.*

**drop away** *phr v* [I] to become lower in level or amount: *Sales have dropped away in recent months.*

**drop off** *phr v* [I] **1** to begin to sleep: *Just as I was dropping off, I heard a noise in the house.* **2** to become lower in level or amount: *Interest in the game has dropped off recently.*

**drop out** *phr v* [I] **1** to leave an activity, course etc before it has finished: [+ **of**] *He dropped out of college.* | *Dwyer had to drop out of the race because of injury.* **2** to move away from or refuse to take part in society because you do not agree with its principles —see also DROPOUT (2) **3** if a word or expression drops out of a language, it is no longer used

S2 W3 **drop²** *n*
**1 ▶ LIQUID ◀** [C] a very small amount of liquid that falls in a round shape: [+ **of**] *Big drops of rain rolled down the window.*|*a tear drop* —see picture on page 416
**2 ▶ A SMALL AMOUNT ◀ a drop** *informal* **a)** a small amount of liquid that you drink: *I like my whisky with just a drop of soda.* **b)** a small amount of something: *He hasn't a drop of sense in his head.*
**3 ▶ DISTANCE ◀** [singular] a distance from something down to the ground: *a path that ended in a vertical drop of fifty feet*
**4 ▶ LESS IN AMOUNT ◀** [singular] if there is a drop in the amount, level, or number of something, it goes down or becomes less: *a drop in interest rates*|*a sudden drop in air pressure*
**5 at the drop of a hat** used to say that you would do something immediately if you had the opportunity: *I'd go to the Far East at the drop of a hat.*
**6 ▶ DELIVER ◀** [C] an act of dropping or leaving something, such as food or medical supplies, especially from an aircraft: *an air drop to the war-torn region* —see also MAIL DROP

**7 lemon/fruit/chocolate etc drop** a sweet that tastes of LEMON etc —see also COUGH DROP
**8 a drop in the ocean** *BrE*, **a drop in the bucket** *AmE* a very small amount of something compared to what is actually needed or wanted: *The fund raising is going well, but it's really only a drop in the ocean.*
**9 eye/ear etc drops** a type of medicine that you put in your eye etc, one drop at a time
**10 not touched a drop** used to say that you have not drunk any alcohol at all

**drop cloth** /ˈ· ·/ *n* [C] *AmE* a large cloth for covering furniture, floors, etc in order to protect them from dust or paint; DUSTSHEET *BrE*

**drop-dead gor·geous** /ˌ· · ˈ··/ *adj BrE spoken* very attractive

**drop goal** /ˈ· ·/ *n* [C] a GOAL in RUGBY football made with a dropkick

**drop-in cent·re** /ˈ· · ˌ··/ *n* [C] *BrE* a place where people who have no job, nowhere to live etc can get information, relax, and talk

**drop·kick** /ˈdrɒpkɪk‖ˈdrɑːp-/ *n* [C] a kick in a game such as RUGBY football, made by dropping the ball and kicking it immediately —see picture on page 1263

**drop·let** /ˈdrɒplɪ̣t‖ˈdrɑːp-/ *n* [C] a very small drop of liquid

**drop·out** /ˈdrɒpaʊt‖ˈdrɑːp-/ *n* **1** [C] someone who leaves school or college before they have finished: *a high-school dropout* **2** [C] someone who refuses to join ordinary society because they do not agree with its social practices, moral standards etc **3** [C,U] *technical* a short loss of signal when an electronic machine is working

**drop·per** /ˈdrɒpə‖ˈdrɑːpər/ *n* [C] a short glass tube with a hollow rubber part at one end, that you use to measure out liquid one drop at a time

**drop·pings** /ˈdrɒpɪŋz‖ˈdrɑː-/ *n* [plural] solid waste from animals or birds

**drop scone** /ˈ· ·/ *n* [C] a small flat plain cake

**drop shot** /ˈ· ·/ *n* [C] a shot in a game such as tennis in which the ball falls quickly at the front of the court

**drop·sy** /ˈdrɒpsi‖ˈdrɑːpsi/ *n* [U] a medical condition in which liquid forms in parts of your body

**dross** /drɒs‖drɑːs, drɒːs/ *n* [U] **1** *BrE* something that is of very low quality: *That film was utter dross!* **2** waste or useless substances: *gold with impurities or dross*

**drought** /draʊt/ *n* [C,U] a long period of dry weather when there is not enough water for plants and animals to live

**drove¹** /drəʊv‖droʊv/ the past tense of DRIVE¹

**drove²** *n* [C] **1** a group of animals that are being moved together: *a drove of cattle* **2 droves** [plural] a crowd of people: **in droves** *Tourists come in droves to see the White House.*

**drov·er** /ˈdrəʊvə‖ˈdroʊvər/ *n* [C] someone who moves cattle or sheep from one place to another in groups

**drown** /draʊn/ *v* **1** [I,T] to die from being under water for too long or to kill someone in this way: *The woman drowned while swimming in the sea.* **2** also **drown out** [T] to prevent a sound from being heard by making a loud noise: *His voice was drowned out by the traffic.* **3** [T] to cover something completely with liquid: **drown sth with/in** *Grant drowned his pancakes in syrup.* **4 drown your sorrows** to drink a lot of alcohol in order to forget your problems

**drowse** /draʊz/ *v* [I] to be in a light sleep or feel pleasantly as though you are almost asleep: *I was drowsing in front of the television when you called.*

**drow·sy** /ˈdraʊzi/ *adj* **1** tired and almost asleep, usually because of food, drugs, or because you are in a warm place: *The cat lay drowsy and content in the sunshine.* **2** so peaceful that you feel relaxed and tired: *a drowsy summer afternoon* —**drowsily** *adv* —**drowsiness** *n* [U] *The tablets may cause drowsiness.*

**drub·bing** /ˈdrʌbɪŋ/ *n* [C] *informal* an occasion when one team easily beats another team in sport: **give sb a drubbing** *We gave the other team a good drubbing.*

**drudge** /drʌdʒ/ *n* [C] someone who does hard boring work —**drudge** *v* [I]

**drudg·e·ry** /ˈdrʌdʒəri/ *n* [U] hard boring work

**drug¹** /drʌg/ *n* [C] **1** an illegal substance that people smoke, INJECT (1) etc to make them feel happy or excited: *He was arrested for selling drugs.*|**take/use drugs** *My cousin has been taking drugs for years.*|**do drugs** *slang* (=take drugs habitually) *Has she been doing drugs, or does she always act like this?*|**be on drugs** (=use drugs regularly) *My grandfather thinks all kids these days are on drugs.*|**illegal drugs** *They test their employees for traces of illegal drugs.*|**drug abuse** (=the use of illegal drugs) *the problem of drug abuse in the inner city*|**hard drug** (=a dangerous drug such as HEROIN, COCAINE etc)|**soft drug** (=one that is not considered very harmful such as MARIJUANA)|**dangerous drugs** *a well-known expert on the abuse of dangerous drugs* **2** a medicine or a substance for making medicines: *a drug used in the treatment of cancer*|**prescribe a drug** *Doctors should only prescribe drugs when it's really necessary.* **3 a drug on the market** something that cannot be sold because there is too much of it available —see also **miracle drug** (MIRACLE (3)), DESIGNER DRUG S2 W1

This graph shows some of the words most commonly used with the noun **drug**.

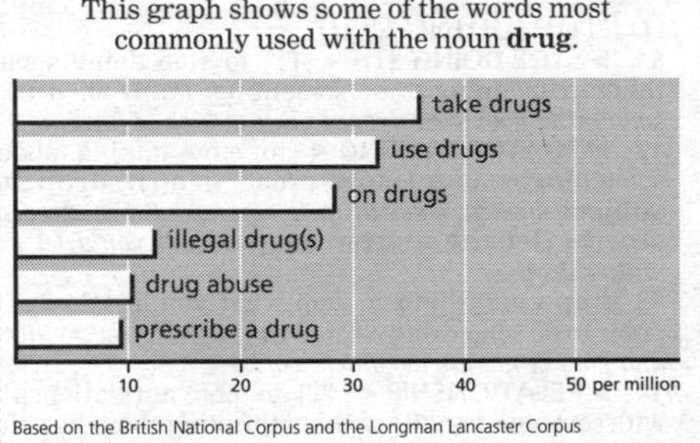


Based on the British National Corpus and the Longman Lancaster Corpus

**drug²** *v* **drugged, drugging** [T] **1** to give someone a drug, especially in order to make feel them tired or go to sleep: *They had to drug the lion before they transported it.* **2** to add drugs to someone's food or drink to make them feel tired or go to sleep **3 be drugged up (to the eyeballs)** *especially BrE* to have been given a lot of drugs by a doctor: *I tried to speak to her after the operation, but she was drugged up to the eyeballs.* **4 drugged out** *AmE* always taking and influenced by drugs: *Greg's a real smart guy, it's too bad he's drugged out all the time.* —**drugged** *adj*

**drug ad·dict** /ˈ· ˌ··/ *n* [C] someone who cannot stop taking drugs, such as HEROIN or COCAINE —**drug addiction** /ˈ· ˌ··/ *n* [U]

**drug bar·on** /ˈ· ˌ··/ *n* [C] someone who leads an organization that deals in large quantities of illegal drugs

**drug czar** /ˈ· ·/ *n* [C] an official employed by the US government to try to stop the trade of illegal drugs

**drug deal·er** /ˈ· ˌ··/ *n* [C] someone who sells illegal drugs

**drug·get** /ˈdrʌgɪ̆t/ *n* [C,U] rough heavy cloth used especially as a floor covering, or a piece of this material

**drug·gie** /ˈdrʌgi/ *n* [C] *informal* someone who often takes illegal drugs

**drug·gist** /ˈdrʌgɪ̆st/ *n* [C] *AmE old-fashioned* someone who is trained to prepare drugs and medicines, and works in a shop; CHEMIST (2) *BrE* —compare PHARMACIST

**drug mis·use** /ˈ· ·ˌ·/ *n* [U] *BrE* the practice of using drugs for pleasure rather than for medical reasons

**drug re·hab·il·i·ta·tion** /ˌ· ····ˈ··/ also **drug rehab** /ˌdrʌg ˈriːhæb/ *AmE n* [U] the process of helping someone to live without drugs after they have been ADDICTED to them

**drug run·ner** /ˈ· ˌ··/ *n* [C] someone who brings illegal drugs from one country to another

**drug·store** /ˈdrʌgstɔː‖-stɔːr/ *n* [C] *AmE* a shop where you can buy medicines, beauty products etc; PHARMACY, CHEMIST's *BrE*

**dru·id** /ˈdruːɪ̆d/ *n* [C] a member of an ancient Celtic group of priests, in Britain, Ireland, and France, before the Christian religion

**drum¹** /drʌm/ *n* [C] **1** a musical instrument made of skin stretched over a circular frame that you hit with your hand or a stick: *the steady rhythmic beating of the drums* **2** something that looks like a drum, especially part of a machine: *The brake drums are gone on my car.* **3** a large round container for storing liquids such as oil, chemicals etc: *dirty, green oil drums at the back of the yard* —see picture at CONTAINER **4 the drum of** a sound like the sound a drum makes: *the steady drum of the rain on the window* **5 bang/beat the drum for sb/sth** to speak eagerly in support of someone or something: *He's always banging the drum for better schools.*

**drum²** *v* **drummed, drumming 1** [I] to play a drum **2** [I,T] to make a sound similar to a drum by hitting a surface again and again: *Rain drummed on the windows.* | **drum your fingers** *Drumming your fingers can be a sign of anxiety.*

**drum** sth **into** sb *phr v* [T] to keep telling someone something until they cannot forget it: *It was drummed into me to never borrow money.*

**drum** sb **out of sth** *phr v* [T] to force someone to leave an organization: *He was drummed out of the army.*

**drum** sth ↔ **up** *phr v* [T] to obtain something by asking a lot of people for help, information etc: *We managed to drum up support for the idea.*

**drum·beat** /ˈdrʌmbiːt/ *n* [C] a sound of someone hitting a drum

**drum kit** /ˈ· ·/ *n* [C] a set of drums used especially by professional musicians

**drum ma·jor** /ˌ· ˈ··‖ˈ· ˌ··/ *n* [C] the male leader of a BAND (=a group of marching musicians), especially in the army

**drum ma·jor·ette** /ˌ· ··ˈ·‖ˈ· ··ˌ·/ *n* [C] a MAJORETTE

**drum·mer** /ˈdrʌmə‖-ər/ *n* [C] someone who plays drums

**drum·ming** /ˈdrʌmɪŋ/ *n* [U] the act of playing a drum or the sound a drum makes

**drum-roll** /ˈ· ·/ *n* [C] a quick continuous beating of a drum, usually used to introduce an important event

**drum·stick** /ˈdrʌmˌstɪk/ *n* [C] **1** the lower part of the leg of a chicken or other bird, cooked as food **2** a stick that you use to hit a drum —see picture at STICK²

**drunk¹** /drʌŋk/ the past participle of DRINK¹

**drunk²** *adj* **1** [not before noun] unable to control your behaviour, speech etc because you have drunk too much alcohol: *Graham was too drunk to remember what happened last night.* | **get drunk (on)** *As students we used to go out and get drunk most nights.* | *I got hideously drunk on tequila last night.* | **blind drunk** (=very drunk) *I'm fed up of you coming home blind drunk.* | **drunk as a skunk/lord** (=very drunk) **2 drunk and disorderly** *law* the crime of behaving in a violent noisy way in a public place when you are drunk **3 drunk with power/happiness etc** so excited by a feeling of power etc that you behave in a strange way —see also **roaring drunk** (ROARING (4)), PUNCH-DRUNK —compare SOBER¹ (1)

**drunk³** *also* **drunkard** /ˈdrʌŋkəd‖-ərd/ *n* [C] someone who is drunk or often gets drunk —compare ALCOHOLIC

**drunk-driv·ing** /ˌ· ˈ··/ *n* [U] driving a car after having drunk too much alcohol; DRINK-DRIVING *BrE*

**drunk·en** /ˈdrʌŋkən/ *adj* [only before noun] **1** drunk or showing that you are drunk: *drunken shouting* | **be in a drunken stupor** (=almost asleep because you are so drunk) **2 drunken party/orgy etc** a party etc where people are drunk —**drunkenly** *adv* —**drunkenness** *n* [U]

**drunk tank** /ˈ· ·/ *n* [C] *AmE informal* a cell in a prison for people who have drunk too much alcohol

**dry¹** /draɪ/ *adj comparative* **drier** *superlative* **driest** S2
**1 ▶NOT WET◀** without water or liquid inside or on W2 the surface: *The floor was made of hard dry earth.* | *The paint isn't dry yet – be careful!* | *Can you check if the washing's dry?* | **shake/rub/wipe sth dry** *Give it to me and I'll wipe it dry.* | **as dry as a bone** (=very dry)
**2 ▶WEATHER◀** having very little rain or MOISTURE: *The air was dry, and the sun beat down fiercely.* | *the dry season*
**3 run/go dry** if a lake, river etc runs dry, all the water gradually disappears, especially because there has been no rain
**4 ▶HUMOUR◀** someone with a dry sense of humour pretends to be serious when they are really joking
**5 ▶THIRSTY◀** *informal* thirsty: *I'm really dry – do you have any orange juice?*
**6 dry mouth/skin/lips etc** without enough of the liquid that is normally in your mouth etc: *I felt nervous and dizzy and my mouth was dry.*
**7 dry cough** a cough which does not produce any PHLEGM (1)
**8 ▶SPEECH/WRITING◀** boring: *I found the lecture dry and uninspired.* | **as dry as dust** (=very boring)
**9 dry wine/sherry etc** wine etc that is not sweet: *dry white wine*
**10 dry bread** bread eaten on its own without butter, JAM¹ (1) etc
**11 ▶TOWN/COUNTRY◀** not allowing any alcohol to be sold there: *There are still some dry states in the US.*
**12 ▶VOICE◀** showing no emotion
**13 not a dry eye in the house** *often humorous* used to say that everyone was crying because something was very sad —see also DRIP-DRY —**dryly, drily** *adv* —**dryness** *n* [U]

**dry²** *v* [I,T] to make something dry or become dry: *My* S2 *boots haven't dried yet.* | **dry sth** *Sit up and dry your eyes.* W3 —see also CUT AND DRIED, DRIED

**dry off** *phr v* [I,T] to become dry or make something dry, especially on the surface: *It was lovely being able to swim and then dry off in the sun.* | **dry sth ↔ off** *Put the washing near the fire to dry it off.*

**dry out** *phr v* [I,T] **1** to become or make something completely dry after it has been very wet: **dry sth ↔ out** *Dry your anorak out on the radiator.* **2** to stop drinking alcohol after you have become an ALCOHOLIC

**dry up** *phr v*
**1 ▶RIVER/LAKE ETC◀** [I,T] if something such as a river dries up, the water in it disappears: *During the drought all the reservoirs dried up.* | **dry sth ↔ up** *The sun has completely dried up the soil and the crops are dying.*
**2 ▶SUPPLY OF STH◀** [I] to come to an end and have no more available: *The research is finishing because the money's dried up.*
**3 ▶PLATES/DISHES ETC◀** [I,T] to rub dry with a cloth: **dry sth ↔ up** *Would you mind drying up the supper things?*
**4 dry up!** *spoken* used to angrily tell someone to be quiet, especially when they are complaining about something: *Just dry up! I'm enjoying the film even if you're not!*

**5 ► STOP TALKING ◄** [I] to stop talking because you have forgotten what you were going to say or what you should say when speaking or acting

**dry·ad** /ˈdraɪæd/ *n* [C] a female spirit in ancient Greek stories who lived in a tree

**dry bat·te·ry** /ˈ· ˌ···/ also **dry cell** /ˈ· ·/ *n* [C] an electric BATTERY (1) containing chemicals that are not in a liquid form

**dry-clean** /ˌ· ˈ·/ *v* [T] to clean clothes etc with chemicals instead of water

**dry clean·er's** /ˌ· ˈ··/ *n plural* **dry cleaner's** [C] a shop where you can take clothes etc to be dry-cleaned

**dry dock** /ˈ· ·/ *n* [C] a place where a ship can be taken out of the water for repairs

**dry·er** /ˈdraɪə‖-ər/ *n* [C] **hairdryer/spin-dryer** a machine that dries things

**dry-eyed** /ˌ· ˈ·◄/ *adj* not crying

**dry ginger** *n* [U] a drink that tastes of GINGER and can be mixed with WHISKY or other alcoholic drinks

**dry goods** /ˈ· ·/ *n* [plural] **1** goods such as tobacco, tea, coffee **2** *AmE* things that are made from cloth such as clothes, sheets, and curtains: *a dry goods store*

**dry ice** /ˌ· ˈ·/ *n* [U] mist produced by a machine that is used as a special effect in the theatre, DISCOs etc

**dry land** /ˌ· ˈ·/ *n* [U] land rather than water: *After three weeks at sea we were glad to be back on dry land again.*

**dry·ly** /ˈdraɪli/ *adv* if you say something dryly, you do not put any emotion in your voice, especially in order to sound funny: *"If you're lucky," said Harrison dryly, "they'll only hang you."*

**dry rot** /ˌ· ˈ·/ *n* [U] a disease in wood, that turns it into powder

**dry run** /ˌ· ˈ·/ *n* [C] an event that you use as a way of practising for a more important event: *Both the parties are treating the local elections as a dry run.*

**dry-shod** /ˌ· ˈ·/ *adv literary* without getting your feet wet

**dry-stone wall** /ˌ· · ˈ·/ *n* [C] a wall built with pieces of stone that fit closely together and no cement

**dry wall** /ˌ· ˈ·/ *n* [U] *AmE* a hard substance used as the inside wall of a house —**dry-wall** *v* [I,T]

**DTI** /ˌdiː tiː ˈaɪ/ *n* **the DTI** the abbreviation of the Department of Trade and Industry

**DTP** /ˌdiː tiː ˈpiː/ *n* [U] DESKTOP PUBLISHING; the production of books, newspapers etc using computers

**DT's** /ˌdiː ˈtiːz/ *n* **the DT'S** *humorous* a condition caused by drinking too much alcohol in which your body shakes, and you see imaginary things

**du·al** /ˈdjuːəl‖ˈduːəl/ *adj* [only before noun] **dual nationality/controls/purpose etc** having two nationalities, sets of controls etc —**duality** /djuˈæləti‖du-/ *n* [U]

**dual car·riage·way** /ˌ·· ˈ···/ *n* [C] *BrE* a main road that has two lines of traffic travelling in each direction and has a strip of land in the centre; DIVIDED HIGHWAY *AmE*

**dual cit·i·zen·ship** /ˌ·· ˈ····/ *n* [U] the state of being a citizen of two countries

**dub¹** /dʌb/ *v* **dubbed, dubbing** [T] **1** [usually passive] to give something or someone a humorous name that describes their character: *Mrs Thatcher was dubbed 'The Iron Lady'.* **2** to change the original spoken language of a film or television programme into another language: **dub sth into sth** *It's a Swedish film dubbed into English.* **3** *especially BrE* to make a record out of two or more different pieces of music or sound mixed together **4** *literary* if a king or queen dubs someone, they give the title of KNIGHT¹ (2) to that person in a special ceremony

**dub²** *n* [U] a style of poetry or music from the West Indies with a strong regular beat

**dub·bin** /ˈdʌbən/ *n* [U] a thick oily substance used to make leather softer and to stop water going through it

**du·bi·e·ty** /djuːˈbaɪəti‖duː-/ *n* [U] *formal* doubt

**du·bi·ous** /ˈdjuːbiəs‖ˈduː-/ *adj* **1 be dubious** to not be sure whether something is good or true: [+ **about**] *I'm a bit dubious about the idea of lending Jim my car.* **2** making you doubt whether someone or something is honest, safe etc: *He looks like a dubious character.* | **highly dubious** *This deal sounds highly dubious to me.* —**dubiously** *adv* —**dubiousness** *n* [U]

**du·cal** /ˈdjuːkəl‖ˈduː-/ *adj* like a DUKE (1) or belonging to a duke

**duc·at** /ˈdʌkət/ *n* [C] a gold coin that was used in several European countries in the past

**duch·ess** /ˈdʌtʃəs/ *n* [C] a woman with the highest social rank below a princess, or the wife of a DUKE (1): *the Duchess of York*

**duch·y** /ˈdʌtʃi/ *n* [C] the land and property of a DUKE (1) or DUCHESS (1); DUKEDOM (2)

**duck¹** /dʌk/ *n*

**1 ► BIRD ◄** [C] a very common water bird with short legs and a wide beak that is used for its meat, eggs, and soft feathers

**2 ► FEMALE BIRD ◄** [C] a female duck

**3 ► MEAT ◄** [U] the meat of this bird used as food: *roast duck with orange sauce*

**4 take to something like a duck to water** to learn how to do something very easily: *Don't worry, you'll take to it like a duck to water.*

**5 ► PERSON ◄** also **ducks** *BrE spoken* a friendly way of speaking to someone, especially a woman or child: *What can I get you, ducks?*

**6 ► PERSON ◄** [C] a SCORE¹ (1) of zero by a BATSMAN in a game of CRICKET (2)

**7 duck shoot** *AmE slang* a very easy job or piece of work —see also **a dead duck** (DEAD¹ (12)), **lame duck** (LAME¹ (3)), **like water off a duck's back** (WATER¹ (5)), DUCKS AND DRAKES

**duck²** *v* **1** [I,T] to lower your head or body very quickly, especially to avoid being seen or hit: *He saw a policeman coming, and ducked behind a car.* | **duck sth** *We had to duck our heads to get through the doorway.* **2** [T] to push someone under water for a short time as a joke: *The children were busy ducking each other in the swimming pool.* **3** [T] *informal* to try to avoid something, especially a difficult or unpleasant duty; DODGE¹ (1,2): *His speech ducked all the major issues.*

**duck**

**duck out of** sth *phr v* [T] *informal* to avoid doing something that you have to do or have promised to do: **duck out of doing sth** *Don't try and duck out of cleaning the kitchen!*

**duck·billed plat·y·pus** /ˌdʌkbɪld ˈplætəpəs/ *n* [C] a PLATYPUS

**duck·boards** /ˈdʌkbɔːdz‖-bɔːrdz/ *n* [plural] long narrow boards that you use to make a path over muddy ground

**duck·ing stool** /ˈ·· ·/ *n* [C] a seat on the end of a long pole, used to DUCK² (2) a woman in water as a punishment in the past

**duck·ling** /ˈdʌklɪŋ/ *n* [C] a small young duck

**ducks and drakes** /ˌ· · ˈ·/ *n* [U] a children's game in which you make flat stones jump across the surface of water

**duck·weed** /ˈdʌkwiːd/ *n* [U] a plant that grows on the surface of fresh water

**duck·y¹** /ˈdʌki/ *n BrE spoken* a friendly way of speaking to someone, especially a woman or child

**ducky²** *adj AmE old-fashioned* **1** perfect or satisfactory: *That's just ducky!* **2** attractive in an amusing or interesting way; CUTE (1): *That's a ducky dress you're wearing!*

**duct** /dʌkt/ *n* [C] **1** a pipe or tube for carrying liquids, air, cables (CABLE[1] (1)) etc: *the air duct* **2** a thin narrow tube that carries air, liquid etc inside your body, in a plant etc: *a tear duct*

**duc·tile** /ˈdʌktaɪl‖-tl/ *adj* **1** ductile metals can be pressed or pulled into shape without needing to be heated **2** *formal* someone who is ductile can be easily influenced or controlled —**ductility** /dʌkˈtɪlɪti/ *n* [U]

**duct·less gland** /ˌdʌktləs ˈglænd/ *n* [C] an ENDOCRINE GLAND

**dud** /dʌd/ *n* [C] *informal* **1** something that is useless, especially because it does not work correctly: *Several of the fireworks were duds.* **2 duds** [plural] *slang* clothes —**dud** *adj*: *a dud light bulb*

**dud cheque** /ˌ· ˈ·/ *n* [C] a cheque that is useless because the person who writes it has no money in their bank account

**dude** /djuːd‖duːd/ *n* [C] **1** *slang especially AmE* a man: *a real cool dude* **2** *AmE old-fashioned* an American man from a city, who is living in or visiting the countryside

**dude ranch** /ˈ· ·/ *n* [C] a holiday place in the US where you can ride horses and live like a COWBOY (1)

**dud·geon** /ˈdʌdʒən/ *n* **in high dudgeon** *formal* angry because someone has treated you badly: *She slammed the door and flounced out in high dudgeon.*

S1 W1 **due[1]** /djuː‖duː/ *adj*
**1 be due** to be expected to happen or arrive at a particular time: *When is your baby due?*| **be due at five o'clock/thirteen hundred hours etc** *The flight from Boston is due at 9:30.*| **be due in an hour/two days etc** *The bus is due any minute now.*| **be due to do sth** *The meeting isn't due to start until three.*| **be due for sth** (=expect to get something) *I'm due for a pay rise soon.*| **due back/out/in etc** *You were due back an hour ago.*
**2 due to** because of: *The company's problems are due to a mixture of bad luck and poor management.*| *The 15.30 train to Sheffield has been cancelled due to circumstances beyond our control.* —see OWING (USAGE)
**3 ▶ OWED ◀** owed to someone either as a debt or because they have a right to it: *You're due three weeks holiday this year.*| **be due to** *Treat him with the respect that is due to a world champion.*
**4 ▶ MONEY ◀** [not before noun] an amount of money that is due is the amount that should be paid now: *The first interest payments will be due in August.*
**5 with (all) due respect** *spoken* used when you disagree with someone or criticize them in a polite way: *With all due respect, you don't have as much experience as she does.*
**6 in due course** at some time in the future when it is the right time, but not before: *The committee will consider your application in due course.*
**7 ▶ PROPER ◀** [only before noun] *formal* proper or suitable: *She was convicted of driving without due care and attention.* —see also DULY

**due[2]** *n* **1 give sb his/her due** used when criticizing someone to admit that not all the things they did were bad, wrong, unpleasant etc: *John was a lousy teacher, but to give him his due he tried hard.* **2 dues** [plural] regular payments you make to an organization of which you are a member: **pay your dues** *All the union members have already paid their dues.* **3 your/his etc due** the amount of money someone is owed, or something they have a right to: *Gwen never takes more than her due.*

**due[3]** *adv* **due north/south/east/west** directly or exactly north etc

**due date** /ˌ· ˈ·/ *n* [usually singular] the date on which something is supposed to happen, especially when money must be paid

**du·el[1]** /ˈdjuːəl‖ˈduːəl/ *n* [C] **1** a fight with weapons between two people, used in the past to settle a quarrel: *The officer challenged him to a duel.* **2** a situation in which two people or groups are involved in an angry disagreement

**duel[2]** *v* **duelling, duelled** *BrE*, **dueling, dueled** *AmE* [I + **with**] to fight a duel

**du·en·na** /djuˈenə‖du-/ *n* [C] an older woman whose job was to look after the daughters in a Spanish or Portuguese family in former times; CHAPERON

**due pro·cess** /ˌ· ˈ··/ *n* [U] *AmE law* the correct process that should be followed in law and is designed to protect someone's legal rights

**du·et** /djuˈet‖duˈet/ *n* [C] a piece of music for two performers —compare QUARTET (2), SOLO[2] (1), TRIO (3)

**duff[1]** /dʌf/ *n* **1 up the duff** *slang* PREGNANT (=with a baby growing inside you) **2** [U] a type of cake: *plum duff*

**duff[2]** *adj BrE informal* useless and broken

**duff[3]** *v*
**duff** sb ↔ **up** also **duff** sb ↔ **in** *phr v* [T] *BrE slang* to fight someone and injure them: *Let's go and duff him up!*

**duf·fel bag** /ˈdʌfəl bæg/ *n* [C] a bag made of strong cloth, with a round bottom and a string around the top —see picture at BAG[1]

**duffel coat, duffle coat** /ˈdʌfəl kəʊt‖-koʊt/ *n* [C] *especially BrE* a coat made of rough heavy cloth, usually with a HOOD (1) and TOGGLES (=buttons shaped like tubes) —see picture at COAT

**duf·fer** /ˈdʌfə‖-ər/ *n* [C] *old-fashioned* someone who is stupid or not very good at something

**dug** /dʌg/ the past tense and past participle of dig

**dug·out** /ˈdʌgaʊt/ *n* [C] **1** a small boat made by cutting out a hollow space in a tree trunk: *a dugout canoe* **2** a shelter dug into the ground for soldiers to use —compare TRENCH (2) **3** a low shelter at the side of a sports field, where players and team officials sit

**DUI** /ˌdiː juː ˈaɪ/ *n* [U] *AmE* driving under the influence; the crime of driving when you have had too much alcohol to drink: *a large number of DUI arrests on New Year's Eve*

**duke** /djuːk‖duːk/ *n* [C] **1** a man with the highest social rank below a prince: *the Duke of Norfolk* —see also DUCHESS **2 dukes** [plural] *old-fashioned* FISTS: *Put up your dukes and fight!*

**duke·dom** /ˈdjuːkdəm‖ˈduːk-/ *n* [C] **1** the rank of a duke **2** the land and property belonging to a duke; DUCHY

**dul·cet** /ˈdʌlsɪt/ *adj* **1 sb's dulcet tones** *humorous* someone's voice: *Is the boss in yet? I thought I heard his dulcet tones.* **2** *literary* dulcet sounds are soft and pleasant to hear

**dul·ci·mer** /ˈdʌlsɪmə‖-ər/ *n* [C] **1** a musical instrument with up to 100 strings, played with light hammers **2** a small instrument with strings that is popular in American FOLK MUSIC, and is played across your knees

**dull[1]** /dʌl/ *adj* S3
**1 ▶ BORING ◀** not interesting or exciting: *Bill's friends are a pretty dull bunch.*| *the dull routine of the office*| **as dull as ditchwater** *BrE informal* (=very boring)
**2 never a dull moment** *often humorous* used to say that a lot of interesting things are happening or that you are very busy
**3 ▶ COLOUR/LIGHT ◀** not bright or shiny: *Nina's hair was a dull, darkish brown.*
**4 ▶ SOUND ◀** not clear or loud: *The sack hit the floor with a dull thud.*
**5 ▶ PAIN ◀** a dull pain is not severe but does not stop: *a dull throbbing at the base of the spine* —see graph at PAIN[1]
**6 ▶ WEATHER ◀** not bright and with lots of clouds: *It'll be dry but dull today, with outbreaks of rain this evening.*
**7 ▶ NOT INTELLIGENT ◀** not able to think quickly or understand things easily
**8 ▶ KNIFE/BLADE ◀** not sharp; BLUNT[1] (1)
**9 ▶ TRADE ◀** if business on the Stock Exchange is dull, few people are buying and selling —**dully** *adv* —**dullness** *n* [U]

**dull[2]** *v* [T] to make something such as pain or a feeling become less sharp, less clear etc —see graph at PAIN[1]: *tranquillizers to dull the pain*

**dull·ard** /ˈdʌləd‖-ərd/ *n* [C] *old-fashioned* someone who is stupid and has no imagination

**du·ly** /ˈdjuːli‖ˈduːli/ *adv* **1** in the proper or expected way: *Here are your travel documents, all duly signed.* **2** at the proper time or as expected: *The Queen duly appeared on the balcony to wave to the crowds.*

S 3 **dumb** /dʌm/ *adj* **1** *not technical* a word used to describe someone who is permanently unable to speak, which some people find offensive: **deaf and dumb** (=unable to hear or speak) *She's been deaf and dumb since birth.* **2** *informal especially AmE* stupid: *What a dumb question.* | *That was a dumb thing to do!* | **play dumb** (=pretend to be stupid) | **dumb blonde** (=a woman who is sexually attractive, but seems stupid) **3** unable to speak, because you are angry, surprised, shocked etc: *He stared in dumb misery at the wreckage of the car.* | **be struck dumb** (=be so shocked that you cannot speak) **4 dumb animals/beasts** used to emphasize that animals cannot speak and that people often treat them badly: *It's cruel to bait dumb animals.* —**dumbly** *adv*: *They all stood dumbly staring at the coffin.* —**dumbness** *n* [U]

D

**dumb·bell** /ˈdʌmbel/ *n* [C] **1** two weights connected by a short bar, that you can lift in each hand to strengthen your arms and shoulders **2** *informal especially AmE* someone who is stupid

**dumb·found** /dʌmˈfaʊnd/ *v* [T] to shock or surprise someone so much that they are very confused: *Pollini's piano playing continues to dumbfound the critics.*

**dumb·found·ed** /dʌmˈfaʊndɪ̇d/ *adj* so surprised that you are confused and cannot speak: *Victor stared dumbfounded as the woman continued to scream abuse at him.*

**dum·bo** /ˈdʌmbəʊ‖-boʊ/ *n* [C] *informal* someone who is stupid

**dumb show** /ˈ· ·/ *n* [C,U] a performance or action in which you do not say anything, but instead use movements to express your meaning

**dumb·struck** /ˈdʌmstrʌk/ *adj* so shocked or surprised that you cannot speak

**dumb wait·er** /ˌ· ˈ··/ *n* [C] **1** a small LIFT[2] (1) used to move food, plates etc from one level in a restaurant, hotel etc to another **2** a small table that turns around on a base, used for serving food

**dum-dum** *n* [C] a soft bullet that causes serious wounds because it breaks into pieces when it hits you

**dum·my¹** /ˈdʌmi/ *n* [C]
**1 ▸ COPY ◂** an object that is made to look like a tool, weapon, vehicle etc but which you cannot use: *Don't worry about the gun, it's a dummy.*
**2 ▸ FOR CLOTHES ◂** a large model in the shape of a person, especially used when you are making clothes or to show them in a shop: *a dressmaker's dummy*
**3 ▸ FOR BABIES ◂** *BrE* a specially shaped rubber object that you put in a baby's mouth for it to suck; PACIFIER (1) *AmE*
**4 ▸ STUPID PERSON ◂** *informal especially AmE* someone who is stupid
**5 ▸ IN CARD GAME ◂** cards that are placed on the table by one player for all the other players to see in a game of BRIDGE[1] (4)

**dummy²** *adj* [only before noun] a dummy tool, weapon, vehicle etc is made to look like a real one but you cannot use it: *a dummy rifle*

**dummy³** *v*
**dummy up** *phr v* [I] *AmE slang* to stay silent and not speak: *When I asked her name she just dummied up.*

**dummy run** /ˌ·· ˈ·/ *n* [C] an occasion when you practise doing something in complete detail to see if it works

**dump¹** /dʌmp/ *v*
**1 ▸ PUT STH SOMEWHERE ◂** [T always + adv/prep] to put something such as a load, bag etc somewhere in a careless, untidy way: **dump sth in/on/there etc** *Who dumped all these books on my desk?*
**2 ▸ GET RID OF ◂** [T] to get rid of someone or something that you do not want: *I hear Lucy has dumped her boyfriend.* | *Let's dump the car and walk the rest of the way.*
**3 ▸ SELL GOODS ◂** [T] to get rid of goods by selling them in a foreign country at a much lower price
**4 ▸ COPY INFORMATION ◂** [T] *technical* to copy information stored in a computer's memory on to something else such as a DISK or MAGNETIC TAPE
**5 dumping ground** a place where you send people or things that you want to get rid of: *The estate is a dumping ground for problem tenants.*
**dump on** sb *phr v* [T] *AmE informal* **1** to criticize someone very strongly and often unfairly: *Don't dump on the teachers we've got, they're doing a good job.* **2** to tell someone all your problems: *Sorry to dump on you like that, I was feeling kind of low.*

**dump²** *n* [C]
**1 ▸ WASTE ◂** a place where unwanted waste is taken and left: *the town rubbish dump*
**2 ▸ WEAPONS ◂** a place where military supplies are stored, or the supplies themselves: *an ammunition dump*
**3 ▸ UNPLEASANT PLACE ◂** *informal* a place that is unpleasant to live in because it is dirty, ugly, untidy etc: *Do something about your room, it's a dump.*
**4 down in the dumps** *informal* very sad and without much interest in life: *I've been feeling a bit down in the dumps lately.*
**5 ▸ COMPUTER ◂** *technical* the act of copying the information stored in a computer's memory onto something else, such as a DISK

**dump·er truck** /ˈ·· ·/ *n* [C] *BrE* a vehicle with a large open container at the back that can move up to pour sand, soil etc onto the ground; DUMP TRUCK *AmE*

**dump·ling** /ˈdʌmplɪŋ/ *n* [C] **1** a round lump of flour and fat mixed with water, cooked in boiling liquid and served with meat: *mince and dumplings* **2** a sweet dish made of PASTRY filled with fruit: *apple dumplings*

**Dump·ster** /ˈdʌmpstə‖-ər/ *n* [C] *trademark AmE* a large metal container used for waste in the US; SKIP[2] (2) *BrE*

**dump truck** /ˈ· ·/ *n* [C] *AmE* a DUMPER TRUCK *BrE*

**dump·y** /ˈdʌmpi/ *adj informal* someone who is dumpy is fat, short, and unattractive: *a dumpy little man*

**dun** /dʌn/ *n* [C,U] a dull brownish-grey colour —**dun** *adj*

**dunce** /dʌns/ *n* [C] *old-fashioned* someone who is slow at learning things: *the dunce of the class*

**dunce's cap** /ˈ·· ·/ *n* [C] a tall pointed hat that a stupid student had to wear in school in the past

**Dun·dee cake** /dʌnˈdiː ˌkeɪk/ *n* [C,U] a British cake made with fruit and nuts

**dun·der·head** /ˈdʌndəhed‖-ər-/ *n* [C] *old-fashioned* someone who is stupid

**dune** /djuːn‖duːn/ *also n* [C] a hill made of sand near the sea or in the desert; SAND DUNE

**dune bug·gy** /ˈ· ˌ··/ *n* [C] *AmE* a car with big wheels and no roof that you can drive across sand; BEACH BUGGY

**dung** /dʌŋ/ *n* [U] solid waste from animals, especially cows

**dun·ga·rees** /ˌdʌŋgəˈriːz/ *n* [plural] **1** *BrE* loose trousers that have a square piece of cloth that covers your chest, and long thin pieces that fasten over your shoulders; OVERALL[3] (2) *AmE* **2** *AmE* heavy cotton trousers used for working in

**dun·geon** /ˈdʌndʒən/ *n* [C] a dark underground prison used in the past, especially under a castle

**dunk** /dʌŋk/ *v* [T] **1** to dip something that you are eating into coffee, tea etc: *Don't dunk your biscuit in your tea!* **2** *AmE* to push someone under water for a short time as a joke; DUCK[2] (2) **3** to throw the ball downwards into the basket in BASKETBALL —see also **dunk for apples** (APPLE (3)), SLAM DUNK —**dunk** *n* [C] —see picture on page 1263

**dun·no** /ˈdʌnəʊ/ *spoken* a way of saying 'I don't know', that some people think is incorrect: *"Do you want to come?" "I dunno, I might."*

**du·o** /ˈdjuːəʊ‖ˈduːoʊ/ *n* [C] **1** a piece of music for two performers **2** two people who perform together or are often seen together: *comedy duo Reeves and Mortimer*

**du·o·dec·i·mal** /ˌdjuːəˈdesɪ̣məl◂‖ˌduː-/ *adj technical* a duodecimal system of numbers is based on the number 12, instead of the usual system based on ten

**du·o·de·num** /ˌdjuːəˈdiːnəm‖ˌduː-/ *n* [C] *technical* the top part of your BOWEL, below your stomach —**duodenal** /ˌdjuːəˈdiːnl◂‖ˌduː-/ *adj*: *a duodenal ulcer* —see picture at DIGESTIVE SYSTEM

**du·o·logue** /ˈdjuːəlɒg‖ˈduːəlɒːg, -lɑːg/ *n* [C] *formal* a conversation or discussion between two people, especially in a play

**dupe¹** /djuːp‖duːp/ *n* [C] someone who is tricked, especially into becoming involved in something illegal

**dupe²** *v* [T usually passive] to trick or deceive someone: **dupe sb into doing sth** *Consumers are being duped into buying faulty electronic goods.*

**du·plex** /ˈdjuːpleks‖ˈduː-/ *n* [C] *AmE* **1** a type of house divided into two parts, with two separate homes in it —see picture on page 410 **2** an apartment with rooms on two levels

**du·pli·cate¹** /ˈdjuːplɪ̣kɪ̣t‖ˈduː-/ *n* [C] **1** an exact copy of something that you can use in the same way: *If you've lost your key I can give you a duplicate.* **2 in duplicate** if something is written in duplicate, there are two copies of it —**duplicate** *adj*: *a duplicate copy*

**duplicate²** /ˈdjuːplɪ̣keɪt‖ˈduː-/ *v* [T] **1** to copy something exactly: *It can duplicate the movements of the human hand.* | *piles of duplicated notes* **2** *formal* to succeed in repeating something: *Scientists were not able to duplicate the effect under laboratory conditions.* —**duplication** /ˌdjuːplɪ̣ˈkeɪʃən‖ˌduː-/ *n* [U]

**du·pli·ca·tor** /ˈdjuːplɪ̣keɪtə‖ˈduː-plɪ̣keɪtər/ *n* [C] *BrE old-fashioned* a machine used to make copies of written pages

**du·plic·i·ty** /djuːˈplɪsɪ̣ti‖duː-/ *n* [U] *formal* dishonest behaviour that is intended to deceive someone —**duplicitous** *adj*

**dur·a·ble** /ˈdjʊərəbəl‖ˈdʊr-/ *adj* **1** staying in good condition for a long time even if used a lot: *Plastic window frames are more durable than wood.* **2** continuing for a long time: *a durable peace between France and Germany* —see also CONSUMER DURABLES —**durably** *adv* —**durability** /ˌdjʊərəˈbɪlɪ̣ti‖ˌdʊr-/ *n* [U]

**durable goods** /ˈ··· ˌ·/ *n* [plural] *AmE* large things such as cars, televisions, and furniture, that you do not buy often; CONSUMER DURABLES *BrE*

**du·ra·tion** /djʊˈreɪʃən‖dʊ-/ *n* [U] *formal* the length of time that something continues: *an illness of relatively short duration* | **for the duration (of)** *He was interned and had to stay in the US for the duration of the war.*

**du·ress** /djʊˈres‖dʊ-/ *n* [U] *formal* illegal or unfair threats: **under duress** (=using unfair threats) *The confession was obtained under duress.*

**dur·ex** /ˈdjʊəreks‖ˈdʊr-/ *n trademark* **1** [C] *BrE* a rubber CONTRACEPTIVE that a man wears over his PENIS during sex **2** [U] *AustrE* clear narrow plastic that is sticky on one side and is used for fastening paper

S1 W1 **dur·ing** /ˈdjʊərɪŋ‖ˈdʊr-/ *prep* **1** all through a length of time: *We didn't see a soul during the holidays.* | *Children were evacuated to the country during the war.* **2** at some point in a period of time: *Henry died during the night.* | *There will be one ten-minute interval during the performance.*

**USAGE NOTE: DURING**

WORD CHOICE: **during, for**

If someone asks you a question beginning with *When...?*, you can answer with **during** but not **for**: *"When did he get those scars?" "During the last war."* If someone asks you a question beginning with *How long...?* you can answer with **for** but not with **during**: *"How long did you stay in Mexico City?" "For about three months."*

When you want to talk about the time within which something happens, you use **during**: *Call me sometime during the vacation.* | *Thieves broke in during the night.*

When you are talking about how long something lasts, you use **for**: *I was only out of the room for a few minutes.* | *They were married for 20 years.*

**During** is common with words for something that continues for a length of time: *during the program/the semester/the war/a conversation.* You also use it to talk about specific periods of time: *during office hours/the day/last week/ that year/the 80s.* **For** is more usual with phrases used to measure length of time: *for two hours/a week/many years/a long period.*

GRAMMAR

**During** is never used with a clause like a **while** clause: *While I was at home, I met a nice boy* (NOT *During I was...*, but you can say *During my time at home,..*). Also, you would say: *I did the dishes while you were asleep* (NOT *during you were asleep*).

**durst** /dɜːst‖dɜːrst/ *old use* the past tense of DARE

**dusk** /dʌsk/ *n* [U] the time before it gets dark when the sky is becoming less bright: **at dusk** *The street lights go on at dusk.* —compare DAWN¹

**dusk·y** /ˈdʌski/ *adj* dark or not very bright in colour: *The room was filled with dusky shadows.* | **dusky pink/orange/blue etc** *a dusky pink room*

**dust¹** /dʌst/ *n* **1** [U] dry powder consisting of extremely small bits of earth or sand: *The truck drove off in a cloud of dust.* | *the heat and dust of an Indian town* **2** [U] dry powder consisting of extremely small bits of dirt which you find in buildings on furniture, floors etc: *The table was covered with a layer of dust.* **3 coal dust/gold dust/wood dust etc** [U] powder consisting of extremely small bits of coal or gold etc **4 a dust** the act of dusting something: *Can you give the room a quick dust?* **5 let the dust settle/wait for the dust to settle** to allow or wait for a confused situation to become clear **6 not see sb for dust** *BrE informal* if you do not see someone for dust, they leave a place very quickly in order to avoid something: *Tell him it's his turn to pay for the drinks and you won't see him for dust.* —see also **bite the dust** (BITE¹ (7)), DUSTY

**dust²** *v* **1** [I,T] to clean the dust from a surface by moving something such as a soft cloth across it: *Could you dust the dining room?* —see picture at CLEAN **2** also **dust off** [T] to remove something such as dust or dirt from your clothes by brushing them with your hands: *Jim got to his feet and dusted the knees of his trousers.* **3** [T] to shake a fine powder over something: *Dust icing sugar over the pastry.*

**dust** sth ↔ **down** *phr v* [T] to remove something such as dirt or dust from your clothes by brushing them with your hands: *Burt stood there dusting down his overalls.* | **dust yourself down** *The horse threw him, but Joe just laughed, picked himself up and dusted himself down.*

**dust** sth ↔ **off** *phr v* [T] **1** to clean something by brushing it or wiping it with a cloth: *She dusted the snow off Billy's coat.* **2** to get something ready in order to use it again after not using it for a long time: *Investors are at last dusting off their cheque books as the economy recovers.*

**dust·bin** /ˈdʌstbɪn/ *n* [C] *BrE* a large container outside your house, used for holding food waste, empty containers etc; GARBAGE CAN *AmE* —see picture on page 170

**dustbin man** /ˈ·· ˌ·/ *n* [C] *BrE informal* a DUSTMAN

**dust bowl** /ˈ· ·/ *n* [C] an area of land that has DUST STORMS and very long periods without rain

**dust cart** /ˈ· ·/ *n* [C] *BrE* a large vehicle that goes from house to house to collect waste from dustbins; GARBAGE TRUCK *AmE*

**dust cov·er** /ˈ· ˌ··/ *n* [C] *AmE* a dust jacket

**dust·er** /ˈdʌstə‖-ər/ *n* [C] **1** a cloth for removing dust from furniture **2** *AmE* a light coat that you wear to protect your clothes while you are cleaning the house **3** *AmE informal* a DUST STORM

**dust jack·et** /ˈ· ˌ··/ *n* [C] a paper cover of a book, which you can remove; DUST COVER *AmE*

**dust·man** /ˈdʌstmən/ *n* [C] *BrE* someone whose job is to remove waste from DUSTBINS; GARBAGE COLLECTOR *AmE*

**dust·pan** /ˈdʌstpæn/ *n* [C] a flat container with a handle that you use with a brush to remove dust and waste from the floor —see picture at BRUSH[1]

**dust·sheet** /ˈdʌst-ʃiːt/ *n* [C] *BrE* a large sheet of cloth used to protect furniture from dust or paint; DROP CLOTH *AmE*

**dust storm** /ˈ· ·/ *n* [C] a storm with strong winds that carries large amounts of dust

**dust·up** /ˈdʌst-ʌp/ *n* [C] *BrE slang* a fight

**dust·y** /ˈdʌsti/ *adj* **1** covered with dust: *a dusty road* | *The shelves are really dusty.* —see picture on page 1258 **2 dusty blue/pink etc** blue etc that is not bright but is slightly grey: *The curtains had faded to a dusty pink.* **3** *literary* subjects, facts etc that are dusty are not interesting

**Dutch**[1] /dʌtʃ/ *n* **1** [U] the language of the Netherlands **2 the Dutch** [plural] people from the Netherlands —see also DOUBLE-DUTCH

**Dutch**[2] *adj* **1** from or connected with the Netherlands **2 go Dutch (with sb)** to share the cost of a meal in a restaurant **3 talk (to sb) like a Dutch uncle** to tell someone severely that you disapprove of what they have done **4 Dutch treat** *AmE* an occasion when you share the cost of something such as a meal in a restaurant

**Dutch auc·tion** /ˌ· ˈ··/ *n* [C,U] a public sale at which the price is gradually reduced until someone will pay it

**Dutch barn** /ˌ· ˈ·/ *n* [C] a farm building with a curved roof on a frame that has no walls, used for storing HAY

**Dutch cap** /ˌ· ˈ·/ *n* [C] *informal* a round rubber CONTRACEPTIVE, that a woman wears inside her VAGINA during sex; DIAPHRAGM (2)

**Dutch cour·age** /ˌ· ˈ··/ *n* [U] courage or confidence that you get when you drink alcohol

**Dutch elm dis·ease** /ˌ· ˈ· ·ˌ·/ *n* [U] a disease that affects and kills ELM trees

**Dutch·man** /ˈdʌtʃmən/ *n* [C] **1** someone from the Netherlands **2 and I'm a Dutchman** *BrE spoken* used when someone has just said something you do not believe is true: *"I've got a date with Cindy." "Oh yeah, and I'm a Dutchman!"*

**Dutch ov·en** /ˌ· ˈ··/ *n* [C] *old-fashioned* a kind of container used for cooking

**du·ti·a·ble** /ˈdjuːtiəbəl‖ˈduː-/ *adj* dutiable goods are those that you must pay DUTY (4) on

**du·ti·ful** /ˈdjuːtɪfəl‖ˈduː-/ *adj* always doing what you are expected to do and always behaving in a loyal and obedient way: *I'm not going to play the dutiful little housewife any more!*

**dut·i·ful·ly** /ˈdjuːtɪfəli‖ˈduː-/ *adv* if you do something dutifully you do it because you think it is the correct way to behave: *I dutifully wrote down every word.*

S1 W1 **du·ty** /ˈdjuːti‖ˈduː-/ *n*

**1 ▶ STH YOU HAVE TO DO ◀** [C,U] something that you have to do because it is morally or legally right: [+ **to/towards**] *Ian felt a sense of duty towards his parents.* | **have a duty to do sth/be your duty to do sth** *The company has a duty to its shareholders to accept the highest bid.* | *As Christians it's our duty to help the less fortunate.* | **do your duty** *You must do your duty and report him to the police.* | **be (in) duty bound to do sth** (=have a duty to do something)

**2 ▶ PART OF YOUR JOB ◀** [C usually plural, U] something you have to do as part of your job or because of your social position: *Your duties will also include coordinating secretarial support to the Head of Planning.* | **medical/official etc duties** *Illness prevented her from carrying out her official duties.* | **report for duty** (=go somewhere and officially say you are ready to work) *Private Jones reporting for duty, Sir.*

**3 be on/off duty** to be working or not working at a particular time, especially doing a job which people take turns to do so that someone is always doing it: *It was the same nurse who was on duty when you had your accident.* | **be on night duty** *Helen is on night duty all next week.*

**4 ▶ TAX ◀** [C,U] a tax you pay on something you buy: *The duty on wine has gone up.* | **customs duty** (=tax paid on goods coming into the country) —see also DEATH DUTY, STAMP DUTY, TAX (USAGE)

**5 do duty as/for sth** to be used as something

**duty-free**[1] /ˌ·· ˈ·◂/ *adj* duty-free goods can be brought into a country without paying tax on them: *duty-free cigarettes* | *the duty-free shop* —**duty-free** *adv*

**duty-free**[2] *n* [C,U] *informal* alcohol, cigarettes etc that you can bring into a country without paying tax on them

**du·vet** /ˈduːveɪ, ˈdjuː-‖duːˈveɪ/ *n* [C] *especially BrE* a large cloth bag filled with feathers or similar material that you use to cover yourself in bed; COMFORTER (2) *AmE*

**dwarf**[1] /dwɔːf‖dwɔːrf/ *n plural* **dwarves** /dwɔːvz‖dwɔːrvz/ or **dwarfs** [C] **1** an imaginary creature that looks like a small man: *Snow White and the Seven Dwarfs.* **2** a word that some people find offensive, for someone who does not continue growing to the normal height but stays very short

**dwarf**[2] *adj* [only before noun] a dwarf plant or animal is much smaller than the usual size: *a dwarf conifer*

**dwarf**[3] *v* [T usually passive] to be so big that other things are made to seem very small: *The cathedral is dwarfed by its surrounding skyscrapers.*

**dwell** /dwel/ *v past tense and past participle* **dwelt** /dwelt/ or **dwelled** [I] *literary* to live in a particular place: *A woodsman and his family dwelt in the middle of the forest.*

**dwell on/upon** sth *phr v* [T] to think or talk for too long about something, especially something unpleasant: *Don't dwell on the past – try and be more positive.*

**dwel·ler** /ˈdwelə‖-ər/ *n* [C] **city/town/cave/forest dweller** a person or animal that lives in a particular place: *City-dwellers suffer higher pollution levels.*

**dwell·ing** /ˈdwelɪŋ/ *n* [C] *formal* a house, apartment etc where people live S2

**dwelling house** /ˈ·· ·/ *n* [C] *law* a house that people live in, not one that is being used as a shop, office etc

**dwelt** /dwelt/ a past tense and past participle of DWELL

**dwin·dle** /ˈdwɪndl/ *v* [I] also **dwindle away** to gradually become less and less or smaller and smaller: *The workforce has dwindled since its pre-war heyday.* | **dwindle (away) to nothing/one/two etc** *Their supply of food had dwindled to almost nothing.* —**dwindling** *adj*: *a dwindling population*

**dye**[1] /daɪ/ *n* [C,U] **1** a substance you use to change the colour of your clothes, hair etc: *hair dye* **2 dye job** *informal* someone who has had a dye job has used a substance to change the colour of their hair

**dye**[2] *v* **dyes, dyed, dyeing** [T] to give something a different colour using a dye: **dye sth black/blue/blonde etc** *Priscilla's hair was dyed jet black.* —**dyed** *adj*

**dyed-in-the-wool** /ˌ· · · ˈ·◂/ *adj* having strong beliefs or opinions that will never change: *Even dyed-in-the-wool republicans admitted he had talent.*

**dy·ing** /ˈdaɪ-ɪŋ/ the present participle of die

**dyke, dike** /daɪk/ *n* [C] **1** a wall or bank built to keep back water and prevent flooding **2** an offensive word for a LESBIAN (=woman who is sexually attracted to women) **3** *especially BrE* a narrow passage to carry water away

**dy·nam·ic**[1] /daɪˈnæmɪk/ *adj* **1** full of energy and new ideas, and determined to succeed: *a dynamic young businesswoman* **2** *technical* continuously moving or changing: *Markets are dynamic and a company must learn to adapt.* **3** *technical* connected with a force or power that causes movement **4** *technical* a dynamic verb describes an action or event, not a state —**dynamically** /-kli/ *adv*

**dynamic**[2] *n* [singular] **1 dynamics a)** [plural] the way in which things or people behave, react, and affect each other: *the dynamics of capitalist economies* | **group**

**dynamics** (=the way in which the members of a group behave towards each other) **b)** [U] the science concerned with the movement of objects and with the forces related to movement **c)** [plural] changes of loudness in music **2** *formal* something that causes action or change: *Feminism is seen as a dynamic of social change.*

**dy·na·mis·m** /ˈdaɪnəmɪzəm/ *n* [U] energy and determination to succeed: *entrepreneurial dynamism*

**dy·na·mite¹** /ˈdaɪnəmaɪt/ *n* [U] **1** a powerful explosive used especially for breaking rock **2** something or someone that is very exciting or is likely to cause a lot of trouble: *They've only been playing together for six months but they're dynamite.*

**dynamite²** *v* [T] to damage or destroy something with dynamite

**dy·na·mo** /ˈdaɪnəməʊ‖-moʊ/ *n plural* **dynamos** [C] **1** a machine that changes some other form of power directly into electricity: *bicycle lights powered by a dynamo* **2** someone who is very keen and energetic: *Gordon Strachan, Leeds midfield dynamo*

**dyn·a·sty** /ˈdɪnəsti‖ˈdaɪ-/ *n* [C] **1** a family of kings or other rulers whose parents, grandparents etc have ruled the country for many years: *The Habsburg dynasty ruled in Austria from 1278 to 1918.* **2** a period of time when a particular family ruled a country or area: *Shang dynasty*

**d'you** /djʊ, dʒə/ *spoken* the short form of 'do you': *D'you know what I mean?*

**dys·en·te·ry** /ˈdɪsəntəri‖-teri/ *n* [U] a serious disease of your BOWELS (1) that makes them bleed and pass much more waste than usual

**dys·func·tion·al** /dɪsˈfʌŋkʃənəl/ *adj technical* **1** not following the normal patterns of social behaviour, especially with the result that someone cannot behave in a normal way or have a satisfactory life: *dysfunctional family relationships* **2** not working properly or normally

**dys·lex·i·a** /dɪsˈleksiə/ *n* [U] *technical* a difficulty with reading and writing because you are unable to see the difference between the shapes of letters; WORD BLINDNESS —**dyslexic** *adj*: *Two of the children in the class are dyslexic.*

**dys·pep·si·a** /dɪsˈpepsiə, -ˈpepʃə/ *n* [U] *technical* a problem that your body has in dealing with the food you eat; INDIGESTION

**dys·pep·tic** /dɪsˈpeptɪk/ *adj* **1** suffering from dyspepsia **2** *old-fashioned* bad-tempered

# E,e



**E, e** /iː/ *plural* **E's, e's** *n* [C] the fifth letter of the English alphabet

**E¹** *n* **a)** the third note in the musical SCALE¹ (8) of C major **b)** the musical KEY¹ (4) based on this note

**E²** **1** the written abbreviation of east or eastern **2** *BrE technical* the written abbreviation of earth, a connection between a piece of electrical equipment and the ground **3** *slang* the abbreviation of ECSTASY (2), an illegal drug **4** short for E NUMBER **5** a very low mark for an exam or piece of school work

S1 W1 **each¹** /iːtʃ/ *determiner, pronoun* **1** every single one of two or more things or people considered separately: *Jane had a blister on each foot.* | *There are four bedrooms, each with its own shower.* | *The price is $60 for a week, then $10 for each extra day.* | *My sister's got two boys and I've got one of each.* (=one son and one daughter) [+ **of**] *I gave a piece of cake to each of the children.* | **we/you/they each** *My wife and I each have our own bank accounts.* | **one/half/a piece etc each** *Biscuits! Can we have two each, Mum?* **2 each and every one** an expression used to emphasize that you are talking about every single person or thing in a group: *These are issues that affect each and every one of us.* **3 each to his own** *old-fashioned* used to mean that we all have different ideas about how to do things, what we like etc —see also ALL, EVERY

**USAGE NOTE: EACH**

WORD CHOICE: **each, every, both, everybody/everyone, nobody/no one, neither**

**Each** is used for any number of people or things considered separately, **every** for any number considered together: *Each item is carefully checked* (=probably one by one).|*Every item has been carefully checked* (=all of them).|*Each child was given a small gift* (=a gift of their own).|*Every child was given a small gift* (=they were all given one).

**Both** is used for two things taken together: *Both my children* (=I have two children) *go to the same school.*|*Each of my children* (=I have two or more children) *goes to a different school.*

You usually use **everyone** or **everybody** rather than *every person*, though in a formal report you might read: *The document was signed by every person present* (NEVER *every persons/people).*

You do not usually use **everyone** or **everybody** followed by **not**. Instead you say **not everybody/everyone...** or **no one/nobody...**, depending on which you mean: *Not everybody here is a vegetarian* (=some people are but not all).| *No one here is a vegetarian* (=none of the people here is a vegetarian). You would almost NEVER say: *Everyone here isn't a vegetarian.*

Similarly instead of using **both...** followed by **not...** you would say **only one...** or **neither...**: *Only one of them knows the answer.*|*Neither of them knows the answer.* You would not usually say: *Both of them don't know the answer.*

GRAMMAR

**Both** is always plural: *Both these books are mine.*

A noun immediately after **each** or **every** is always singular: *Each/every area of the country* (NOT *areas*).

**Every, everyone, everything** etc always take a singular verb: *Every state elects its own governor.*

**Each** takes a singular verb except when it comes after a plural word: *Each of them won $50.*| *They each won/have each won $50.* However in informal spoken English people sometimes use a plural verb, especially when there are a lot of words between **each of** and the verb: *Each of the kids arriving for the first time are shown around the school.* However, some people think only the singular verb is correct.

**Each** and **every** may be followed by a plural pronoun, especially when you are talking about both males and females: *Each girl must make up her own mind.*|*Each person must make up their own mind.* It sounds a little formal to say: *Each person must make up his or her own mind* and it is considered sexist to use *he* unless you are only talking about men or boys.

In a similar way plural pronouns (but not plural verbs) can go with **everyone, everybody, anyone, no one, someone** etc: *Has everyone finished their drinks?*|*Somebody's left their umbrella behind.*|*No one here seems to know what they are doing.*

**each²** *adv* for or to every one: *The tickets are $5 each.*

**each oth·er** /ˌ· ˈ··/ *pron* [not used as the subject of a sentence] used to show that each of two or more people does something to the other or others: *Susan and Robert kissed each other passionately.* | *They were holding each other's hands.* | *We had a lot to tell each other about our trip.* | *Stop arguing with each other.* —see also **be at each other's throats** (THROAT (5)) —compare ONE ANOTHER 

**each way** /ˌ· ˈ·/ *adv* if you BET (=try to win money by guessing the winner of a race) money each way, you will win if the horse or dog you choose comes first, second, or third —**each way** *adj*: *a £10 each way bet*

**ea·ger** /ˈiːɡə‖-ər/ *adj* **1** very keen and excited about something that is going to happen or about something you want to do: *There was a queue of eager schoolchildren outside the theatre.* | **eager to do sth** *Clara was eager to tell her side of the story.* | **eager for** (=eager to get or have) *fans eager for a glimpse of the singer* **2 eager to please** willing to do anything to be helpful to people: *She's a very hard worker and very eager to please.* **3 eager beaver** *informal* someone who is too keen and works harder than they should —**eagerly** *adv*: *the eagerly awaited sequel to 'Star Wars'* —**eagerness** *n* [U] *In his eagerness to secure peace Roosevelt was duped, it was said, by Stalin.*

**ea·gle** /ˈiːɡəl/ *n* [C] a very large strong bird with a beak like a hook that eats small animals, birds etc

**eagle-eyed** /ˌ·· ˈ·◂/ *adj* very good at seeing or noticing things: *One eagle-eyed passer-by noticed that the window was slightly open.*

**ea·glet** /ˈiːɡlɪ̈t/ *n* [C] a young EAGLE

**-ean** /iən/ *suffix* [in adjectives and nouns] another form of the suffix -AN: *Mozartean* (=of or like Mozart)

**ear** /ɪə‖ɪr/ *n* 

**1 ▶ PART OF YOUR BODY ◀** [C] one of the organs on either side of your head that you hear with: *Lou turned to Mark and whispered something in his ear.* —see picture at HEAD¹

**2 ▶ HEARING ◀** [U] the ability to hear sounds: *too high-pitched to be heard by the human ear* | **have good ears** (=be able to hear quiet noises)

**3 ▶ GRAIN ◀** [C] the top part of plants, such as wheat, that produces grain: *an ear of corn*

**4 long-eared/short-eared etc** having long etc ears: *a long-eared rabbit*

**5 be all ears** *informal* to be very keen to hear what someone is going to tell you: *As soon as I mentioned money, Karen was all ears.*

**6 be out on your ear** *informal* to be forced to leave a job, organization etc, especially because you have done

something wrong: *You'd better start working harder, or you'll be out on your ear.*
**7 be up to your ears in work/debt/problems etc** to have a lot of work etc: *I'm up to my ears in work at the moment. Can we discuss this later?*
**8 close/shut your ears to** to refuse to listen to bad or unpleasant news
**9 smile/grin etc from ear to ear** to show that you are very happy or pleased by smiling so much: *She came out of his office, grinning from ear to ear. 'I've been promoted.'*
**10 give sb a thick ear** *BrE informal* to hit someone: *Behave yourself or I'll give you a thick ear!*
**11 go in (at) one ear and out (at) the other** *informal* if information goes in one ear and out the other, you forget it as soon as you have heard it: *I don't know why I tell her anything. It just goes in one ear and out the other.*
**12 have an ear for music/languages etc** to be very good at learning music, copying sounds etc: *She has no ear for languages at all.* | *a good ear for dialogue*
**13 have sb's ear** to be trusted by someone so that they will listen to your advice, opinions etc: *While Ross Perot had the ear of the nation, he did spout a number of home truths.*
**14 keep your/an ear to the ground** to make sure that you always know what is happening in a situation: *I haven't heard any more news but I'll keep my ear to the ground.*
**15 lend an ear** to listen to what someone is saying sympathetically: *I'm always ready to lend an ear, if you need to talk.*
**16 play sth by ear** to play music without having to read written music —see also **play it by ear** (PLAY[1] (11))
**17 sb's ears are burning** used to say that someone thinks that people are talking about them
**18 sb's ears are flapping** *BrE* used to say that someone is trying to listen to your private conversation —see also **bend sb's ear** (BEND[1] (5)), **send sb off with a flea in their ear** (FLEA (2)), **make a pig's ear of** (PIG[1] (5)), **prick (up) your ears** (PRICK[1] (5)), **turn a deaf ear** (DEAF[1] (4)), **wet behind the ears** (WET[1] (6))

**ear·ache** /ˈɪəreɪk‖ˈɪr-/ *n* [singular, U] a pain inside your ear

**ear drops** /ˈ· ·/ *n* [plural] medicine to put in your ear

**ear·drum** /ˈ· ·/ *n* [C] a tight thin skin over the inside of your ear which allows you to hear sound

**ear·ful** /ˈɪəfʊl‖ˈɪr-/ *n* **give sb an earful** *informal* to tell someone how angry you are about something they have done: *He gave me a real earful about being late so often.*

**earhole** /ˈɪəhəʊl‖ˈɪrhoʊl/ *n* [C] *BrE informal* your ear: *If you don't shut up I'll give you a clip round the earhole!* (=hit you)

**earl** /ɜːl‖ɜːrl/ *n* [C] a man with a high social rank: *the Earl of Warwick*

**earl·dom** /ˈɜːldəm‖ˈɜːrl-/ *n* [C] **1** the rank of an earl **2** the land or property belonging to an earl

**ear·li·est** /ˈɜːliəst‖ˈɜːr-/ *n* **at the earliest** no earlier than the time or date mentioned: *Work will begin in October at the very earliest.*

**ear lobe** /ˈ· ·/ *n* [C] the soft piece of flesh at the bottom of your ear —see picture at HEAD[1]

S1 W1 **ear·ly[1]** /ˈɜːli‖ˈɜːrli/ *adj*
**1 ► NEAR THE BEGINNING ◄** near to the beginning of a day, year, someone's life etc: *We've booked two weeks' holiday in early May.* | *Her early life was miserably unhappy.* | **in the early days** (=at the beginning of a process, project etc) *In the early days we used to work Saturdays as well.*
**2 ► BEFORE THE USUAL TIME ◄** arriving or happening before the usual or expected time: *Hey, you're early! It's only five o'clock!* | *The rains are early this year.* | **five minutes early/three hours early etc** *The bus was ten minutes early.* | **an early grave** (=dying too soon)
**3 ► NOT TOO LATE ◄** near enough to the beginning of a process to prevent something bad from happening: *There is far less risk with cancer if it is detected early.*
**4 ► FIRST ◄** [only before noun] being one of the first people, events, machines etc: *Early motor cars had very poor brakes.* | *early man*
**5 it's early days** *spoken* used to say that it is too soon to be sure about what the result of something will be: *She's having a few problems with the coursework at school but it's early days yet.*
**6 at/from an early age** at or since a time when you were very young: *At an early age she decided she wanted to be a surgeon.*
**7 make an early start** to start an activity, journey etc very early in the day because you have a lot to do, far to go etc
**8 the early hours** the time between MIDNIGHT and morning: *Order was restored in the prison in the early hours of Saturday morning.*
**9 early night** if you have an early night you go to bed earlier than usual: *I could really do with an early night!*
**10 early bird** someone who always gets up very early in the morning: *Seven? No problem! I'm a real early bird!*
**11 the early bird catches the worm** used to say that someone is successful because they were the first to do something
**12 early riser** someone who always gets up early in the morning
**13 early potatoes/lettuces/avocados etc** potatoes etc that are ready to be picked before any others

**early[2]** *adv* **1** before the usual, arranged, or expected time: *I arrived early, to make sure of a seat.* | *The play ended early so we still had time for a drink.* **2** near the beginning of a day, week, or other period of time: *Early the following day he phoned to apologize.* **3** near the beginning of an event, story, process etc: *Early in the film we see Paul's violent temper.* **4 early on** at an early stage in a relationship, process etc: *I realized early on I'd never pass the exam.* S1 W1

**early warn·ing sys·tem** /ˌ·· ˈ·· ˌ··/ *n* [C] a series of RADAR stations that give a warning when enemy aircraft are going to attack

**ear·mark** /ˈɪəmɑːk‖ˈɪrmɑːrk/ *v* [T usually passive] to decide that someone or something will be used for a particular purpose in the future: **earmark sb/sth for** *80% of the funds have been earmarked for education.* | *schools earmarked for closure* | **earmark sb/sth as** *The building has been earmarked as a new treatment center.*

**ear·muffs** /ˈɪəmʌfs‖ˈɪr-/ *n* [plural] two pieces of material joined by a band over the top of your head, that you wear to keep your ears warm

**earn** /ɜːn‖ɜːrn/ *v* S2 W2
**1 ► GET MONEY ◄** [I,T] to receive a particular amount of money for the work that you do: *He earns nearly £20,000 a year.* | *If you aren't earning you simply can't afford a holiday.* | **earn a fortune** (=earn a lot of money) —see GAIN[1] (USAGE)
**2 ► MAKE A PROFIT ◄** [T] to make a profit from business or from putting money in a bank, lending it to a company etc: *'Dracula' earned £7 million on its first day.*
**3 ► GET STH YOU DESERVE ◄** [T] to get something that you deserve, because of your qualities or actions: *I think you should have a rest. You've certainly earned it.*
**4 earn sb praise/a reputation etc** if something earns you praise, a name etc it makes other people think of you in a particular way: *Her perfectionism earned her a reputation as a 'difficult' star.*
**5 earn a living** to make money in order to pay for the things you need: *I earned my living mainly from teaching.*
**6 earn your keep** to do jobs etc as a way of paying the owner of the place where you live: *Harry is unemployed at the moment but he does lots of jobs around the house to earn his keep.*

**earn·er** /ˈɜːnə‖ˈɜːrnər/ *n* **1** [C] someone who earns money for the job that they do: **high earner/low earner etc** *Private childcare is still too expensive for the average earner.* | **wage earner** *Most wage earners are paid by cheque.* **2 a nice little earner** *BrE informal* something that earns you a lot of money: *They're onto a nice little earner with that roadside café.*

**ear·nest¹** /ˈɜːnɪ̣st‖ˈɜːr-/ *adj* **1** very serious and believing that what you say is very important: *such an earnest young man* **2 in earnest** if something starts happening in earnest, it begins properly or as it was planned to happen: *On Monday your training begins in earnest!* **3 be in earnest** to really mean what you are saying, especially when expressing an intention or wish: *I'm sure he was in earnest when he said he wanted to marry her.*|**be in dead/deadly/complete earnest** *I couldn't believe what he was telling me but he was in deadly earnest.* —**earnestly** *adv* —**earnestness** *n* [U]

**earnest²** *n* [singular] **an earnest of** *formal* something that you do or give someone to show that you will do what you have promised to do

**earn·ings** /ˈɜːnɪŋz‖ˈɜːr-/ *n* [plural] **1** the money that you receive for the work that you do: *He has had to pay tax on his earnings since he started at the firm.* **2** the profit that a company makes: *The company's earnings have dropped by 5% in the first quarter.*

**earnings-re·lat·ed** /ˌ·· ·ˈ··◂/ *adj* connected with the amount of money that you earn: *an earnings-related pension scheme*

**ear·phones** /ˈɪəfəʊnz‖ˈɪrfoʊnz/ *n* [plural] electrical equipment that you put over your ears to listen to a radio, RECORD PLAYER etc —see picture at PERSONAL STEREO

**ear·piece** /ˈɪəpiːs‖ˈɪr-/ *n* [C] **1** a piece of electrical equipment that you put into your ear to hear a recording, message etc: *Translations are heard through an earpiece.* **2** [usually plural] one of the two pieces at the side of a pair of glasses that go round your ears —see picture at GLASS¹ **3** the part of a telephone that you listen through

**ear·plug** /ˈɪəplʌg‖ˈɪr-/ *n* [C usually plural] a small piece of rubber put inside your ear to keep out noise etc

**ear·ring** /ˈɪərɪŋ‖ˈɪr-/ *n* [C] a piece of jewellery that you fasten to your ear —see picture at JEWELLERY

**ear·shot** /ˈɪəʃɒt‖ˈɪrʃɑːt/ *n* **1 within earshot** near enough to hear what someone is saying: *Everyone within earshot soon knew her opinion of Reggie.* **2 out of earshot** not near enough to hear what someone is saying: *I waited for her to get out of earshot before laughing.*

**ear-split·ting** /ˈ· ˌ··/ *adj* very loud: *Suddenly an ear-splitting shriek came from behind the door.*

**earth**

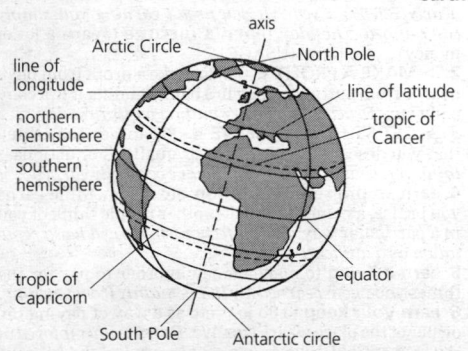

axis
Arctic Circle
North Pole
line of longitude
line of latitude
northern hemisphere
tropic of Cancer
southern hemisphere
tropic of Capricorn
equator
South Pole
Antarctic circle

S2 W2 **earth¹** /ɜːθ‖ɜːrθ/ *n*
**1 ▶WORLD◀** [singular] also **the Earth** the world that we live in: *the planet Earth*|*The earth revolves around the sun.*|*The space shuttle is returning to earth.* —see LAND¹ (USAGE) —see picture at SOLAR SYSTEM
**2 ▶SOIL◀** [U] substance that plants, trees etc grow in: *footprints in the wet earth*|*a lump of earth*
**3 ▶LAND◀** [singular] the hard surface of the world, as opposed to the sea: *After six months at sea, it was good to feel the earth beneath my feet again.* —see LAND¹ (USAGE)
**4 what/why/how etc on earth...?** *spoken* used when you are asking a question about something that you are very surprised or annoyed about: *What on earth did you do that for?*
**5 cost/pay/charge the earth** *informal* to cost etc a very large amount of money: *What a beautiful necklace! It must have cost the earth!*
**6 the biggest/tallest/most expensive etc on earth** the biggest etc example of something that exists
**7 come back/down to earth (with a bump)** to stop behaving or living in a way that is not practical: *When he realized he'd spent all the money he really came back to earth with a bump.*
**8 ▶ELECTRICITY◀** [C usually singular] *BrE* a wire that makes a piece of electrical equipment safe by connecting it with the ground; GROUND¹ (30) *AmE*
**9 ▶ANIMAL'S HOME◀** [C] the hole where a wild animal such as a FOX lives
**10 go to earth** *BrE* to hide in order to escape from someone who is chasing you
**11 nothing on earth** a strong way of saying 'nothing': *Nothing on earth would persuade me to repeat the experience of marriage.*
**12 look/feel etc like nothing on earth** *BrE* to look or feel very strange: *It looks like smoked salmon, but tastes like nothing on earth.*
**13 run sb/sth to earth** *BrE* to find someone, especially by looking in many places: *I finally ran him to earth in the stockroom.* —see also DOWN-TO-EARTH, **move heaven and earth** (HEAVEN (10)), **hell on earth** (HELL¹ (1)), **promise sb the moon/the earth** (PROMISE¹ (3)), **the salt of the earth** (SALT¹ (2))

**earth²** *v* [T] *BrE* to make electrical equipment safe by connecting it to the ground with a wire; GROUND² (5) *AmE*: *The amplifier wasn't properly earthed.*

**earth·bound** /ˈɜːθbaʊnd‖ˈɜːrθ-/ *adj* **1** unable to move away from the surface of the Earth **2** having very little imagination, thinking too much about practical things

**earth·en** /ˈɜːθən, -ðən‖ˈɜːr-/ *adj* [only before noun] **1** an earthen pot, VASE etc is made of baked clay **2** an earthen floor or wall is made of earth

**earth·en·ware** /ˈɜːθənweə, -ðən-‖ˈɜːrθənwer, -ðən-/ *adj* an earthenware cup, plate etc is made of very hard baked clay —**earthenware** *n* [U]

**earth·ling** /ˈɜːθlɪŋ‖ˈɜːrθ-/ *n* [C] a word used, in SCIENCE FICTION stories, by a creature from another world talking about a human

**earth·ly** /ˈɜːθli‖ˈɜːrθli/ *adj* **1 no earthly reason/use/solution etc** no reason, use etc at all: *There seemed to be no earthly reason for his strange behaviour.* **2** [only before noun] *literary* connected with life on Earth rather than in heaven: *our earthly pleasures*

**earth·quake** /ˈɜːθkweɪk‖ˈɜːrθ-/ *n* [C] a sudden shaking of the earth's surface that often causes a lot of damage: *Mexico City was badly hit in the 1985 earthquake.*

**earth-shat·ter·ing** /ˈ· ˌ···/ *adj* surprising or shocking and very important: *the day we heard the earth-shattering news of Kennedy's assassination*

**earth·wards** /ˈɜːθwədz‖ˈɜːrθwərdz/ also **earth·ward** /-wəd‖-wərd/ *adv* in a direction towards the earth's surface: *The missile fell earthwards.* —**earthward** *adj*

**earth·work** /ˈɜːθwɜːk‖ˈɜːrθwɜːrk/ *n* [C usually plural] a large long pile of earth used to stop attacks in the past

**earth·worm** /ˈɜːθwɜːm‖ˈɜːrθwɜːrm/ *n* [C] a common type of long thin brown WORM that lives in soil

**earth·y** /ˈɜːθi‖ˈɜːrθi/ *adj* **1** talking about sex and the human body in a direct and impolite way: *Simon has a very earthy sense of humour.* **2** tasting, smelling, or looking like earth or soil: *a strong earthy smell* —**earthiness** *n* [U]

**ear trum·pet** /ˈ· ˌ··/ *n* [C] a type of tube that is wide at one end, used by old people in the past to help them hear

**ear·wig** /ˈɪəˌwɪɡǁˈɪr-/ *n* [C] a long brown insect with two curved pointed parts at the back of its body

**ease¹** /iːz/ *n* [U] **1 with ease** if you do something with ease, it is very easy for you to do it: *The car travelled smoothly up the hillside, taking the bends with ease.* | *It was the ease with which the burglars got into the house that worried her.* | **with consummate ease** (=easily and gracefully) **2 at ease** feeling relaxed in a situation in which most people might feel a little nervous: **feel/look at ease** *Nurses do all they can to make patients feel at ease.* | **put/set sb at their ease** (=try to make someone feel relaxed) | **ill at ease** (=not relaxed) *You always look ill at ease in a suit.* **3** the ability to feel or behave in a natural or relaxed way: *He had a natural ease which made him very popular.* **4 for ease of application/use etc** *formal* if something is done for ease of use, APPLICATION etc, it is done to make that process easier: *For ease of application there is a special nozzle attached to the tube.* **5 a life of ease** a comfortable life, without problems or worries: *She had a life of ease, having married her boss.* **6 stand at ease** used to tell soldiers to stand in a relaxed way with their feet apart

**ease²** *v*

**1 ▶ MAKE EASIER ◀** [T] to make something, especially a process, happen more easily: *a new drug designed to ease childbirth for women everywhere*

**2 ▶ MOVE STH ◀** [T always + adv/prep] to move something slowly and carefully into another place: **ease sth in/onto etc** *Ease the patient slowly onto the bed.* | *She eased the binoculars out of the box.*

**3 ▶ GET BETTER ◀** [I,T] if something unpleasant eases or you ease it, it gradually gets better: *When the storm eases a little, we'll be able to go out.* | **ease the pain/pressure/stress/tension** *The cream should help ease the pain.* | *an out-of-town shopping project to ease congestion in the city*

**4 ▶ MAKE BETTER ◀** [T] to reduce the amount or the bad effect of something: *a plan designed to ease housing shortages*

**5 ease your grip** to hold something less tightly

**6 ease your mind** to make you feel less worried or nervous about something: *It would ease my mind to know you had arrived safely.*

**ease out** *phr v* [I] if a vehicle eases out, it slowly moves forward into the traffic: *Take your time, ease out slowly and ignore the cars waiting behind you.*

**ease** sb ↔ **out** *phr v* [T] to deliberately try to make someone leave a job, a position of authority etc without officially saying anything

**ease off** also **ease up** *phr v* [I] **1** if something, especially something that annoys you, eases off or eases up, it gets less or better: *The noise didn't ease up for some time.* | *Why don't you wait until the traffic eases off a little?* **2 ease off on sb** to stop being unpleasant to someone, especially because they do not deserve to be treated like this: *Ease off on Roger will you, he's not that bad.*

**ease up** *phr v* [I] **1** to do something more slowly than before, especially because you have been going too fast, working too hard etc: *Dan should ease up or he'll have a nervous breakdown.* **2** [+ **on**] to ease off

**ea·sel** /ˈiːzəl/ *n* [C] a wooden frame that you put a painting on while you paint it

S1 W1 **eas·i·ly** /ˈiːzəli/ *adv* **1** without problems or difficulties: *This recipe can be made quickly and easily.* | *I'll be able to finish that easily by tonight.* **2 easily the best/biggest/most stupid etc** definitely the best etc: *She is easily the most intelligent person in the class.* **3 could/can/might easily** used to say that something is possible or is very likely to happen: *I don't think we should tell her. She could easily forget and say something to Mum.* | **all too easily** (=used to say that a bad event is definitely possible) *The friendly crowd can degenerate, all too easily, into an unruly mob.* **4** in a relaxed way: *His son grinned easily back at him.*

**eas·i·ness** /ˈiːzinəs/ *n* [U] **1** lack of difficulty **2** a feeling of being relaxed and comfortable with someone

**East** /iːst/ *n* **1 the East: a)** the countries in Asia, especially China and Japan: *The martial arts originated in the East.* **b)** the countries in the eastern part of Europe, especially the ones that had Communist governments: *American relations with the East were at their worst in the late 1950s.* **c)** *AmE* the part of the US east of the Mississippi River, especially the states north of Washington DC: *She was born in the East but now lives in Atlanta.* | **back East** *He was born in Minneapolis but he went to college back East.* **2 East-West relations/trade etc** political relations etc between countries in eastern Europe and those in Europe and North America —compare FAR EAST, MIDDLE EAST, NEAR EAST

**east¹** /iːst/ abbreviation **E** *n* **1** [singular, U] the direction from which the sun rises, that is on the right of a person facing north: *The mountains in the east get a lot of snow.* | *Which way is east?* | **to the east (of)** *The sky to the east of the town was already lightening.* **2 the east** the eastern part of a country: *The rain will spread later to the east.* **3 in the east** if there is wind, rain etc in the east, it is coming from the east 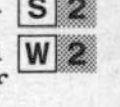

**east²** *adj* **1** in the east or facing the east: *We sailed down the east coast of the island.* **2 east wind** an east wind comes from the east: *a bitterly cold east wind*

**east³** *adv* towards the east: *We zigzagged through the trees, moving east all the time.* | *The road runs east to west.*

**east·bound** /ˈiːstbaʊnd/ *adj* travelling or leading towards the east: *A crash on the eastbound side of the freeway is blocking traffic.*

**East Coast** /ˌ· ˈ·◂/ *n* **the East Coast** the part of the US that is next to the Atlantic Ocean, especially those states north of Washington DC

**East End** /ˌ· ˈ·◂/ *n* **the East End** the eastern part of London, north of the River Thames —**East Ender** *n* [C]

**Eas·ter** /ˈiːstəǁ-ər/ *n* [C, U] **1** a Christian holy day in March or April when Christians remember the death of Christ and his return to life **2** the period of time just before and after this: *We spent the Easter holidays in Wales.*

**Easter Bun·ny** /ˌ·· ˈ··/ *n* [singular] an imaginary rabbit that children believe brings chocolate eggs at Easter

**Easter egg** /ˈ·· ·/ *n* [C] **1** *BrE* a chocolate egg usually given as a present at Easter **2** *AmE* an egg that has been coloured and decorated, usually by a child

**eas·ter·ly¹** /ˈiːstəliǁ-ərli/ *adj* **1** towards or in the east: *an easterly course across the Pacific ocean* **2** easterly winds come from the east: *an easterly breeze*

**easterly²** *n* [C] a wind that blows from the east

**east·ern** /ˈiːstənǁ-ərn/ *adj* **1** in or from the east of a country or area: *There were heavy snows in eastern Minnesota.* | *The eastern sky was just turning pink.* **2** in or from the countries in Asia, especially China and Japan: *Eastern religions* **3** in or from the countries in the east part of Europe, especially the countries that used to have Communist governments: *the Eastern bloc* W2

**East·ern·er** /ˈiːstənəǁ-ərnər/ *n* [C] *AmE* someone who lives in or comes from the eastern US

**east·ern·most** /ˈiːstənməʊstǁ-ərnmoʊst/ *adj* furthest east: *the easternmost part of the island*

**East Side** /ˌ· ˈ·◂/ *n* **the East Side** the south-eastern part of Manhattan in New York, lived in mostly by poor people who have come to the US from other countries

**east·ward** /ˈiːstwədǁ-wərd/ *adj, adv* going or facing towards the east: *The eastward view toward the mountains was spectacular.*

**east·wards** /ˈiːstwədzǁ-wərdz/ also **eastward** *adv* towards the east: *We sailed eastwards.*

**eas·y¹** /ˈiːzi/ *adj* S1 W1

**1 ▶ NOT DIFFICULT ◀** not difficult, and not needing

much physical or mental effort: *The easiest way to get there is through the park.* | *It can't have been easy raising three children all by herself.* | **easy to make/build/do etc** *Are the instructions easy to follow?* | **make things easy (for sb)** *Having a computer will definitely make things a lot easier.* | **easy as pie** (=very easy) | **within easy (walking) distance** (=near enough to walk to)

**2 ▶ NOT WORRIED ◀** not feeling worried or anxious: *Would it make you feel easier if I phoned when I got there?* | **with an easy mind** *I can't go to bed with an easy mind until I know she's safe.* —opposite UNEASY

**3 easy victim/prey etc** someone who cannot easily defend themselves against bad treatment, attack etc: *Elderly and frail, she was easy prey for muggers.*

**4 easy on the eye/ear** pleasant to look at or listen to: *Choose colours that are soft and easy on the eye.*

**5 have an easy time of it** to have no problems or difficulties: *She hasn't had an easy time of it since Jack left.*

**6 take the easy way out** to end a difficult situation in a way that seems easy, but is not the best or most sensible way: *She took the easy way out, and told him she had to visit her mother that afternoon.*

**7 get off easy** *informal* to escape severe punishment for something that you have done wrong: *I thought I was in deep trouble, but I got off easy.*

**8 easy money** money that you do not have to work hard to get

**9 I'm easy** *spoken* used to say that you do not mind what choice is made: *"Would you rather go out for a Chinese or an Indian meal?" "Oh, I'm easy."*

**10 that's easy for you to say** *spoken* used when someone has given you some advice that would be difficult for you to follow

**11 be on easy street** *informal, especially AmE* to be in a situation in which you have plenty of money: *They're on easy street now that he's inherited his aunt's money.*

**12 on easy terms** *BrE* if you buy something on easy terms, you pay for it with several small payments instead of paying the whole amount at once

**13 ▶ SEX ◀** *informal* someone, especially a woman, who is easy has a lot of sexual partners

**14 a woman of easy virtue** *old-fashioned* a woman who has sex with a lot of men

**15 eggs over easy** *AmE* eggs cooked on a hot surface and turned over quickly before serving —see also EASE, EASILY

S2 **easy²** *adv* **1 take it easy a)** also **take things easy** to relax and not do very much: *The doctor says I'm going to have to take it easy for a few weeks.* **b)** *spoken* used to tell someone to become less upset or angry: *Just take it easy and tell us what happened.* **2 go easy on/with sth** to not use too much of something: *Go easy on that whiskey if you're driving!* **3 go easy on sb** to be more gentle and less strict or angry with someone: *Go easy on Peter for a while – he's having a hard time at school.* **4 rest/breathe easy** to stop worrying: *You can rest easy now – they've gone.* **5 easy does it** *spoken* used to tell someone to be careful, especially when they are moving something **6 easier said than done** *especially spoken* used when it would be difficult to actually do what someone has suggested: *I should treat Jim like any other client, but that's easier said than done.* **7 stand easy** a command telling soldiers who are already standing at ease (EASE¹ (6)) to relax more **8 easy come, easy go** *spoken* used when something, especially money, was easily obtained and is quickly used or spent

**easy chair** /ˌ·· ˈ·, ˈ·· ·/ *n* [C] a large comfortable chair

**easy-go·ing** /ˌ·· ˈ··◂/ *adj* not easily upset, annoyed, or worried: *Her easy-going nature made her popular.*

**easy lis·ten·ing** /ˌ·· ˈ···/ *n* [U] music that is relaxing to listen to and has nice tunes, but is not very unusual

**easy-pea·sy** /ˌiːzi ˈpiːzi◂/ *adj BrE* a word meaning very easy, used especially by children

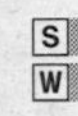

S1 W1 **eat** /iːt/ *v past tense* **ate** /et, eɪt‖eɪt/ *past participle* **eaten** /ˈiːtn/

**1 ▶ FOOD ◀ a)** [I,T] to put food in your mouth and swallow it: *Vegetarians don't eat meat.* | **something to eat** (=some food) *Would you like something to eat?* | **eat like a bird** (=eat very little) | **eat like a horse** (=eat a lot) | **eat right** *AmE* (=eat food that keeps you healthy) | **I couldn't eat another thing** *spoken* (=I am full) **b)** [I] to have a meal: *We usually eat at seven.* | *Do you want to eat at Musso's Restaurant before the movie?* | **eat out** (=have a meal in a restaurant, not at home) *Do you fancy eating out tonight?*

**2 eat your heart out a)** used to compare two things and say that one is much better: *He's the new teen idol – eat your heart out, Michael Jackson!* **b)** *BrE* to be unhappy about something or to want someone or something very much: *She's not coming back so it's no use lying here eating your heart out.*

**3 eat sb alive/eat sb for breakfast** to be very angry with someone, especially someone that you have power over: *You can't tell him that – he'll eat you alive!*

**4 eat sb out of house and home** *humorous* to eat a lot of someone's supply of food, so that they have to buy more

**5 eat crow** *AmE* also **eat humble pie** to be forced to admit that you were wrong and say that you are sorry

**6 have sb eating out of your hand** to have made someone very willing to believe you or do what you want: *The clients were suspicious at first, but he soon had them eating out of his hand.*

**7 what's eating him/her/you?** *spoken* used to ask why someone seems annoyed or upset: *What's eating Sally today? She just yelled at me.*

**8 eat your words** to admit that what you said was wrong: *I had to eat my words when he turned up on time after all.*

**9 I could eat a horse** *spoken* used to say you are very hungry

**10 I'll eat my hat** *spoken old-fashioned* used to say that you think something is not true or will not happen: *If the Democrats win the election, I'll eat my hat!*

**11 ▶ USE/DAMAGE ◀** [I always + adv/prep, T] to damage, destroy, or use a lot of something: *Work alone ate 72 hours of my week.* —see also EATS

**eat** sth ↔ **away** *phr v* [T] to gradually remove or reduce the amount of something: *The wooden parts had been eaten away by damp.*

**eat away at** sth/sb *phr v* [T] **1** to gradually remove or reduce the amount of something: *Rust had eaten away at the metal frame.* **2** to make someone feel very worried over a long period of time: *The thought of mother alone like that was eating away at her.*

**eat into** sth *phr v* [T] **1** to gradually reduce the amount of time, money etc that is available: *All these car expenses are eating into our savings.* **2** to damage or destroy something: *Acid eats into the metal, damaging its surface.*

**eat up** *phr v* **1** [I,T **eat** sth ↔ **up**] *especially spoken* to eat all of something: *Come on, eat it up, there's a good girl.* **2** [T **eat** sth ↔ **up**] *informal* to use all of something until it is gone: *A big car just eats up money.* **3 be eaten up with jealousy/anger/curiosity etc** to be very jealous, angry etc, so that you cannot think about anything else

**eat·a·ble** /ˈiːtəbəl/ *adj* in a good enough condition to be eaten —see also EDIBLE

**eat·er** /ˈiːtə‖-ər/ *n* [C] **big/light/fussy etc eater** someone who eats a lot, not much, only particular things etc: *I've never been a big eater.*

**eat·e·ry** /ˈiːtəri/ *n* [C] *informal especially AmE* a restaurant or other place to eat: *one of the best Knoxville eateries*

**eating ap·ple** /ˈ·· ˌ··/ *n* [C] an apple that you eat raw rather than cooked

**eating dis·or·der** /ˈ·· ·ˌ··/ *n* [C] a medical condition in which you do not eat normal amounts or at normal times

**eats** /iːts/ *n* [plural] *informal* food, especially for a party: *You get the drink, and I'll organize the eats.*

**eau-de-co·logne** /ˌəʊ də kəˈləʊn‖ˌoʊ də kəˈloʊn/ *n* [U] a sweet-smelling liquid used to make you feel fresh and smell nice

**eaves** /iːvz/ *n* [plural] the edges of a roof that stick out beyond the walls: *Birds had nested under the eaves.*

**eaves·drop** /ˈiːvzdrɒp‖-drɑːp/ *v* **eavesdropped, eavesdropping** [I] to listen secretly to other people's conversations: *There was Helena eavesdropping outside the door.* —compare OVERHEAR —**eavesdropper** *n* [C]

eavesdrop

**ebb¹** /eb/ *n* **1** [singular] also **ebb tide** the flow of the sea away from the shore, when the TIDE¹ (1) goes out —opposite FLOOD TIDE **2 be at a low ebb** to be in a bad state or condition: *By March 1933, the economy was at its lowest ebb.* **3 ebb and flow** a situation or state in which something increases and decreases in a kind of pattern: *I relaxed into the ebb and flow of the music.*

**ebb²** *v* [I] **1** if the TIDE ebbs, it flows away from the shore **2** also **ebb away** to gradually decrease: *Linda's enthusiasm began to ebb away.*

**eb·o·ny¹** /ˈebəni/ *n* [U] a hard black wood

**ebony²** *adj literary* black: *Sunlight glinted on her ebony hair.*

**e·bul·li·ent** /ɪˈbʌliənt, ɪˈbʊ-/ *adj formal* very happy and excited: *An ebullient three-year-old bounced around the room.* —**ebullience** *n* [U]

**EC** /ˌiː ˈsiː◂/ *n* **the EC** the European Community; a West European political and trade organization: *EC subsidies*

**ec·cen·tric¹** /ɪkˈsentrɪk/ *adj* **1** behaving or appearing in a way that is unusual and different from most people: *students dressed in eccentric clothing | an eccentric old woman* **2** *technical* eccentric circles do not have the same centre point —compare CONCENTRIC —**eccentrically** /-kli/ *adv* —see picture at CONCENTRIC

**eccentric²** *n* [C] someone who behaves in a way that is different from what is usual or socially accepted: *I was regarded as something of an eccentric.*

**ec·cen·tri·ci·ty** /ˌeksenˈtrɪsɪ̣ti, -sən-/ *n* **1** [U] strange or unusual behaviour: *Kate's mother had a reputation for eccentricity.* **2** [C] an opinion or action that is strange or unusual: *I found his eccentricities amusing rather than irritating.*

**Ec·cles cake** /ˈekəlz keɪk/ *n* [C] *BrE* a round cake filled with CURRANTS (=type of dried fruit)

**ec·cle·si·as·tic** /ɪˌkliːziˈæstɪk◂/ *n* [C] *formal* a priest, usually in the Christian church

**ec·cle·si·as·ti·cal** /ɪˌkliːziˈæstɪkəl/ also **ecclesiastic** *adj* connected with the Christian church or its priests: *ecclesiastical history*

**ECG** /ˌiː siː ˈdʒiː/ *n* [C] *especially BrE* **1** an electrocardiograph; a piece of equipment that records electrical changes in your heart **2** an electrocardiogram; a drawing produced by an electrocardiograph

**ech·e·lon** /ˈeʃəlɒn‖-lɑːn/ *n* [C] **1** also **echelons** a rank or level of responsibility in an organization, business etc, or the people at that level: *the upper echelons of government* **2** *technical* a line of ships, soldiers, planes etc arranged in a pattern that looks like a series of steps

**ech·o¹** /ˈekəʊ‖ˈekoʊ/ *v present tense* **echoes** *past tense and past participle* **echoed** **1** [I often + adv/prep] if a sound echoes, you hear it again because it was made near something such as a wall or hill: *The thunder echoed over the mountains. | Our shouts echoed through the silent streets.* **2** [I] if a place echoes, it is filled with sounds that are repeated or are similar to each other: [+ **with**] *The hall echoed with laughter and stamping feet.* **3** [T] *literary* to repeat what someone else has just said: *"Paula's dead!" "Dead?" echoed Teri, stunned.* **4** [T] to repeat an idea or opinion because you agree with it: *The article simply echoed the NRA's arguments against gun control.*

**echo²** *n plural* **echoes** [C] **1** a sound that you hear again after a loud noise, because it was made near something such as a wall: *The echo of the bells died away, and the valley was quiet again.* **2** something that is very similar to something that has happened or been said before: [+ **of**] *This crash has chilling echoes of the Lockerbie disaster.*

**éclair** /ɪˈkleə, eɪ-‖ɪˈkler, eɪ-/ *n* [C] a long cake covered with chocolate and filled with cream

**é·clat** /eɪˈklɑː/ *n* [U] *literary* **1** praise and admiration: *Miller's new play has been greeted with great éclat.* **2** a way of doing something with a lot of style, especially in order to attract attention

**e·clec·tic¹** /ɪˈklektɪk/ *adj* including a mixture of many different things or people, especially so that you can use the best of all of them: *galleries with an eclectic range of styles and artists* —**eclectically** /-kli/ *adv* —**eclecticism** /-tɪsɪzəm/ *n* [U]

**eclectic²** *n* [C] *formal* someone who chooses the best or most useful parts from many different ideas, methods etc

**e·clipse¹** /ɪˈklɪps/ *n* **1** [C] an occasion when the sun or the moon seems to disappear, because one of them is passing between the other one and the Earth **2** [singular] a situation in which someone loses their power or fame, because someone else has become more powerful or famous: *New movie studios in Hollywood soon led to the eclipse of New York as a film-making center.* **3 in/into eclipse** *formal* less famous or powerful than you should be: *Mary Shelley, the author of Frankenstein, has been too long in eclipse.*

**eclipse²** *v* [T] **1** if the moon eclipses the sun or the earth eclipses the moon, it makes it seem to disappear, by passing in front of it **2** [often passive] to become more important, powerful, famous etc than someone or something else, so that they are no longer noticed: *She felt totally eclipsed by her prettier, brighter, younger sister.*

**e·clip·tic** /ɪˈklɪptɪk/ *n* [singular] *technical* the path along which the sun seems to move

**eco-** /iːkəʊ‖iːkoʊ/ *prefix* concerned with the environment: *eco-warriors* (=people who try to stop damage to the environment)

**e·co-friend·ly** /ˈiːkəʊ ˌfrendli‖ˈiːkoʊ-/ *adj* not harmful to the environment: *eco-friendly products*

**e·co·lo·gi·cal** /ˌiːkəˈlɒdʒɪkəl◂‖-ˈlɑː-/ *adj* [only before noun] **1** connected with the way plants, animals, and people are related to each other and to their environment: *an ecological disaster* **2** interested in preserving the environment: *ecological groups* —**ecologically** /-kli/ *adv*: *an ecologically-sound production process*

**e·col·o·gist** /ɪˈkɒlədʒɪ̣st‖-ˈkɑː-/ *n* [C] a scientist who studies ecology

**e·col·o·gy** /ɪˈkɒlədʒi‖ɪˈkɑː-/ *n* [singular U] the way in which plants, animals, and people are related to each other and to their environment, or the scientific study of this: *the fragile ecology of the tundra*

**ec·o·nom·ic** /ˌekəˈnɒmɪk◂, ˌiː-‖-ˈnɑː-/ *adj* **1** [only before noun] connected with trade, industry, and the management of money: *strategies to promote economic growth | It makes no economic sense at all! |* **economic climate** (=conditions affecting trade, industry, and business) **2** an economic process, activity etc produces enough profit for it to continue; PROFITABLE: *It is no longer economic for us to run the service. | an economic price* —see ECONOMIC (USAGE)

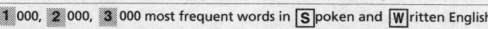

**USAGE NOTE: ECONOMIC**

WORD CHOICE: **economy, economic, economics, economical, cheap, economically**

The adjective of the word **economy** [C], meaning the economy of a country is **economic**: *government measures to boost the economy|the various economies of South America|We are faced with a deepening economic crisis* (NOT *economical*).|*economic growth/benefits/problems/policy*

The study of economies and their money systems is called **economics** (singular): *He's got a degree in Modern History and Economics* (NOT *economic* or *economy*).|*Economics is my favorite subject* (NOT *are my favorite subject*).

The adjective **economical** relates to the word **economy** (sense 2 [U]) meaning the careful use of money, a supply of something, effort etc that avoids any waste: *My new car is quite economical* (=cheap to run).|*She was brought up to be economical with the housekeeping money* (=spend it carefully).

Something that is **economical** is not necessarily **cheap**. For example it may be more economical to buy a packet of soap powder that is twice the usual size, because even though it costs more than the small packet, it does not cost twice the amount. However, sometimes people who sell things call **cheap** things **economical** simply because this word sounds better.

The adverb of both **economic** and **economical** is **economically**: *The country is not economically stable.|You can live here quite economically.*

**ec·o·nom·i·cal** /ˌekəˈnɒmɪkəl, ˌiː-‖-ˈnɑː-/ *adj* using money, time, goods etc carefully and without wasting any: *an economical method of heating*

**ec·o·nom·i·cally** /ˌekəˈnɒmɪkli, ˌiː-‖-ˈnɑː-/ *adv* **1** in a way that is related to systems of money, trade, or business: *In economically advanced countries, childbearing typically begins later in life.*| [sentence adverb] *Economically and politically, they've been disenfranchised.* **2** in a way that uses money, goods, time etc without wasting any: *We'll just have to shop as economically as we can from now on.*

W3 **ec·o·nom·ics** /ˌekəˈnɒmɪks, ˌiː-‖-ˈnɑː-/ *n* **1** [U] the study of the way in which money and goods are produced and used **2** [plural] the way in which money influences whether a plan, business etc will work effectively: *The economics of the scheme will have to be looked at very carefully.* —see also HOME ECONOMICS

**e·con·o·mist** /ɪˈkɒnəmɪst‖ɪˈkɑː-/ *n* [C] someone who studies the way in which money and goods are produced and used and the systems of business and trade

**e·con·o·mize** also **-ise** *BrE* /ɪˈkɒnəmaɪz‖ɪˈkɑː-/ *v* [I] to reduce the amount of money, time, goods etc that you use: [+ **on**] *We can't economize on the central heating because the baby needs a warm house.*

S3 W1 **e·con·o·my¹** /ɪˈkɒnəmi‖ɪˈkɒː-/ *n* **1** [C] the system by which a country's money and goods are produced and used, or a country considered in this way: *a capitalist economy|the burgeoning economies of the Pacific rim* **2** [U] the careful use of money, time, goods etc so that nothing is wasted: *For the sake of economy, I hadn't yet turned on the heating.*|**economy drive** (=a period of time during which you try to spend less money than usual) **3** [C] something that you do in order to spend less money: *One economy would be to take sandwiches instead.*|**make economies** *We're trying to make a few economies this month.*|**false economy** (=something that seems cheaper but costs more in the end) *Buying cheap tyres is a false economy – they wear out much more quickly.* **4 economies of scale** *technical* the financial advantages of producing something in very large quantities —see also BLACK ECONOMY, MARKET ECONOMY, MIXED ECONOMY

**economy²** *adj* [only before noun] **economy size/pack** a product that is cheaper, usually because you are buying a larger amount

**economy class** /ˈ···ˌ·/ *n* [U] the cheapest type of seats in a plane —**economy class** *adv*: *We flew economy class.*

**e·co·sys·tem** /ˈiːkəʊˌsɪstɪm‖-koʊ-/ *n* [C] all the animals and plants in a particular area, and the way in which they are related to each other and to their environment

**ec·sta·sy** /ˈekstəsi/ *n* **1** [C,U] a feeling of extreme happiness: *His expression was one of pure ecstasy.*|**in ecstasy/ecstasies** (=feeling extremely happy)|**go into ecstasies** (=become very happy and excited) **2** [U] a state in which you cannot see or hear what is happening around you, because you are having a powerful religious experience

**Ecstacy** *n* [U] an illegal drug used especially by young people to give a feeling of happiness and energy at parties

**ec·stat·ic** /ɪkˈstætɪk, ek-/ *adj* **1** feeling extremely happy and excited: *an ecstatic welcome from the thousands who lined the streets* **2** in a state in which you are having a powerful religious experience —**ecstatically** /-kli/ *adv*

**ECT** /ˌiː siː ˈtiː/ *n* [U] electro-convulsive therapy; another word for ELECTRIC SHOCK THERAPY

**-ectomy** /ektəmi/ *suffix* [in nouns] *technical* the removing of a particular part of someone's body by an operation: *an appendectomy* (=removing the APPENDIX)

**ECU** /ˈekjuː‖eɪˈkuː/ *n* [C] European Currency Unit; the official unit of money of the EC

**e·cu·men·i·cal** /ˌiːkjʊˈmenɪkəl◂‖ˌek-/ *adj* supporting the idea of uniting the different branches of the Christian religion —**ecumenically** /-kli/ *adv*

**ec·ze·ma** /ˈeksɪmə‖ˈeksɪmə, ˈegzɪmə, ɪgˈziːmə/ *n* [U] a condition in which your skin becomes dry, red, and swollen

**ed** **1** an abbreviation for EDITOR **2** an abbreviation for EDITION

**-ed** /d, ɪd, t/ *suffix* **1** forms the regular past tense and past participle of verbs. The past participle form is often used as an adjective: *I want, I wanted, I have wanted|I show, I showed, I have shown|He walked away.|a sound that echoed through the room|a wanted criminal* **2** [in adjectives] having a particular thing: *a bearded man* (=a man with a beard)|*a kind-hearted woman*

**E·dam** /ˈiːdəm, -dæm/ *n* [U] a type of yellow cheese from the Netherlands

**ed·dy¹** /ˈedi/ *n* [C] a circular movement of water, wind, dust etc: *the racing river caused swirling eddies*

**eddy²** *v* [I] if water, wind, dust etc eddies, it moves around with a circular movement: *The mist eddied round the old house.*

**E·den** /ˈiːdn/ also **the Garden of Eden** *n* [singular] in the Bible story, the garden where Adam and Eve, the first humans lived, often seen as a place of happiness and INNOCENCE

**edge**

on the edge of a cliff

at the water's edge

S2 W2 **edge¹** /edʒ/ *n* [C] **1** the part of an object that is furthest from its centre: *Just leave it on the edge of your plate.* | *Suli stood at the water's edge.* **2** the thin sharp part of a blade or tool that cuts: *Careful – that knife has a very sharp edge!* **3 have the edge on/over** to be slightly better than someone or something, because you have an advantage that they do not have: *Marcia has the edge over the other students, having spent a year in England.* **4 be on edge** to be nervous, especially because you are expecting something unpleasant to happen: *I've been on edge ever since I got her letter.* **5 be on the edge** *informal* to be behaving in a way that makes it seem as if you are going crazy **6 take the edge off** to make something less bad, good, strong etc: *Try this. It should take the edge off the pain.* —see also **the cutting edge of** (CUTTING² (3))

**edge²** *v* **1** [I always + adv/prep, T always + adv/prep] to move gradually with several small movements, or to make something do this: *The car edged forwards at walking pace.* | **edge sth in/across/towards etc** *Hetty edged her chair closer to mine.* | **edge your way in/through/towards etc** (=move somewhere carefully with small movements) *Slowly, we edge our way towards the front of the crowd.* —see picture on page 1262 **2** [T] to put something on the edge or border of something: **edge sth with** *The sleeves were edged with lace.* **3** [I always + adv/prep, T always + adv/prep] to develop gradually, or to make something do this: **edge (sth) in/up/towards** *Prices have been static for months, but are now beginning to edge up.* **4** [T] to cut the edges of an area of grass so that they are tidy and straight

**edge·ways** /ˈedʒweɪz/ also **edge·wise** /-waɪz/ *adv* sideways —see also **get a word in edgeways** (WORD¹ (31))

**edg·ing** /ˈedʒɪŋ/ *n* [C,U] something that forms an edge or border: *a white handkerchief with blue edging*

**edg·y** /ˈedʒi/ *adj* nervous and worried: *She's been edgy lately, waiting for the test results.*

**ed·i·ble** /ˈedɪ̈bəl/ *adj* something that is edible can be eaten: *These berries are edible, but those are poisonous.*

**e·dict** /ˈiːdɪkt/ *n* [C] *formal* **1** an official public order made by someone in a position of power: *The emperor issued an edict forbidding anyone to leave the city.* **2** *especially humorous* any order or command

**ed·i·fice** /ˈedɪ̈fɪ̈s/ *n* [C] *formal* a building, especially a large one: *Their head office was an imposing edifice in Millbank.*

**ed·i·fy** /ˈedɪ̈faɪ/ *v* [T] *formal* to improve someone's mind or character by teaching them something —**edification** /ˌedɪ̈fɪˈkeɪʃən/ *n* [U] *For our edification, the preacher reminded us what 'duty' meant.*

**ed·i·fy·ing** /ˈedɪ̈faɪ-ɪŋ/ *adj formal or humorous* an edifying speech, book etc improves your mind or moral character by teaching you something: *No-one would claim that the film is morally edifying.*

**ed·it** /ˈedɪ̈t/ *v* **1** [I,T] to prepare a book, piece of film etc for printing or broadcasting by deciding what to include, and making sure there are no mistakes: *hours and hours spent editing text* **2** [T] to work as the editor of a newspaper, magazine etc: *She used to edit the Washington Post.* —**edit** *n* [C]

**edit** sth ↔ **out** *phr v* [T] to remove something when you are preparing a book, piece of film etc for printing or broadcasting: *All the swear words were edited out before the film was broadcast.*

W3 **e·di·tion** /ɪˈdɪʃən/ *n* [C] the copies of a book, newspaper etc that are produced and printed at the same time: *Is there a paperback edition?* | **first edition** (=the first copies of a particular book, that are often valuable)

W2 **ed·i·tor** /ˈedɪ̈tə‖-ər/ *n* [C] **1** the person who decides what should be included in a newspaper, magazine etc: *the editor of the Daily Telegraph* **2** someone who prepares a book, film etc for printing or broadcasting by deciding what to include and checking for any mistakes: *a TV script editor* —**editorial** /ˌedɪ̈ˈtɔːriəl◂/ *adj*: *Not screening the program was an editorial decision.*

**ed·i·to·ri·al** /ˌedɪ̈ˈtɔːriəl◂/ *n* [C] a piece of writing in a newspaper that gives the editor's opinion about something, rather than reporting facts

**ed·i·tor·ship** /ˈedɪ̈təʃɪp‖-tər-/ *n* [U] the position of being the editor of a newspaper or magazine

**ed·u·cate** /ˈedjʊkeɪt‖ˈedʒə-/ *v* [T] to teach or train someone, especially at a school, college, or university: *How can our children be educated if schools are not properly funded?* | **educate sb about/on** *a campaign to educate teenagers about the dangers of smoking* —see TEACH (USAGE)

**ed·u·cat·ed** /ˈedjʊkeɪtɪ̈d‖ˈedʒə-/ *adj* **1** intelligent because you have been taught or trained somewhere: *an educated and sensitive woman* | **Harvard-educated/Oxford-educated etc** *a Harvard-educated lawyer* **2** having a high standard of judgement about art, literature etc: *She has very educated tastes.* **3 educated guess** a guess that is likely to be correct because you have enough information

S1 W1 **ed·u·ca·tion** /ˌedjʊˈkeɪʃən‖ˌedʒə-/ *n* **1** [singular, U] the process by which your mind develops through learning at a school, college, or university: *They had worked hard to give their son a good education.* | *adult education classes* **2** [singular, U] the knowledge and skills that you gain from being taught: *a college education* **3** the general area of work or study connected with teaching: *a lecturer in higher education* —see also FURTHER EDUCATION, HIGHER EDUCATION

S2 W2 **ed·u·ca·tion·al** /ˌedjʊˈkeɪʃənəl◂‖ˌedʒə-/ *adj* **1** connected with education: *a fall in educational standards* **2** teaching you something you did not know before: *Work experience is an important educational experience for young people.*

**ed·u·ca·tion·al·ist** /ˌedjʊˈkeɪʃənəlɪ̈st‖ˌedʒə-/ also **ed·u·ca·tion·ist** /-ʃənɪ̈st/ *n* [C] *formal* someone who knows a lot about methods of education

**ed·u·ca·tor** /ˈedjʊkeɪtə‖ˈedʒəkeɪtər/ *n* [C] *formal especially AmE* a teacher

**ed·u·tain·ment** /ˌedjʊˈteɪnmənt‖ˌedʒə-/ *n* [U] films, television programmes, or computer SOFTWARE that educate and entertain at the same time

**Ed·ward·i·an** /edˈwɔːdiən‖-ˈwɔːr-/ *adj* connected with or coming from the time of King Edward VII of Britain (1901–1910): *Edwardian furniture*

**-ee** /iː/ *suffix* [in nouns] **1** someone who is being treated in a particular way: *the payee* (=someone who is paid) | *a trainee* | *an employee* **2** someone who is in a particular state or who is doing something: *an absentee* (=someone who is absent) | *an escapee*

**EEC** /ˌiː iː ˈsiː/ *n* [singular] the European Economic Community; the former name for the EC

**EEG** /ˌiː iː ˈdʒiː/ *n* **1** electroencephalograph; a piece of equipment that records the electrical activity of your brain **2** electroencephalogram; a drawing made by an electroencephalograph

**eek** /iːk/ *interjection* an expression of sudden fear and surprise: *Eek! A mouse!*

**eel** /iːl/ *n* [C] a long thin fish that looks like a snake and can be eaten: *He wriggled like an eel to get free.*

**e'en** /iːn/ *adv poetic* the short form of EVEN¹

**e'er** /eə‖er/ *adv poetic* the short form of EVER

**-eer** /ɪə‖ɪr/ *suffix* [in nouns] someone who does or makes a particular thing, often something bad: *an auctioneer* (=someone who runs AUCTION sales) | *a profiteer* (=someone who makes unfair profits)

**ee·rie** /ˈɪəri‖ˈɪri/ *adj* strange and frightening: *the eerie sound of an owl hooting in the forest at night*

**eff** /ef/ *v* [I] *BrE* **1 effing and blinding** *slang* swearing: *You should have heard him effing and blinding when he hit his thumb with the hammer.* **2 eff off!** *taboo* used to tell someone to go away instead of saying **fuck off** (FUCK¹ (1)) —see also EFFING

**ef·face** /ɪˈfeɪs/ *v* [T] *formal* **1** to prevent you from remembering an unpleasant experience: *Nothing could efface the indignity of being publicly criticized.* **2** to remove a mark or sign, especially by rubbing it **3 efface yourself** to behave in a way that does not make people notice you or look at you —see also SELF-EFFACING

S1 W1 **ef·fect¹** /ɪˈfekt/ *n*

**1 ▶ CHANGE/RESULT ◀** [C,U] the way in which an event, action, or person changes someone or something: [+ **of**] *the harmful effects of smoking* | **have an effect on** *Inflation is having a disastrous effect on the economy.* | **have/achieve the desired effect** (=produce the result you wanted) *The plan failed to achieve the desired effect of diverting traffic from the city.* | **cause and effect** (=something that happens, and the other things that happen as a result of this) —see AFFECT (USAGE)

**2 put/bring sth into effect** to make a plan or idea happen: *It won't be easy to put the changes into effect.*

**3 come into effect/take effect** if a new law, rule, or system comes into effect, it officially starts: *The new tax rates come into effect from April.*

**4 take effect** to start to produce results: *The morphine was starting to take effect and the pain eased.*

**5 in effect** used when you are describing what the real situation is, especially when it is different from the way that it seems to be: *In effect, our wages will fall by 2%.*

**6 to good/little effect** if you do something to good effect, it is successful and does what you want it to: *Pat rubbed the stain frantically with a cloth, but to little effect.*

**7 to this/that effect** used when you are giving the general meaning of what someone says, rather than the exact words: *I thought he was wrong and said something to that effect at dinner.* | **words to that effect** *Jim said he was unhappy at work, or words to that effect.* | **to the effect that** *Karl's memo was to the effect that we all needed to think more about marketing possibilities.*

**8 with immediate effect/with effect from** starting to happen immediately, or from a particular date: *Hoskins is appointed manager, with immediate effect.*

**9 ▶ IDEA/FEELING ◀** [C usually singular] an idea or feeling that an artist, speaker, book etc tries to make you think of or feel: *Turner's paintings give an effect of light.* | **do sth for effect** (=do something deliberately to shock or surprise people)

**10 ▶ PERSONAL THINGS ◀ effects** [plural] *formal* the things that someone owns; BELONGINGS: *Don's few personal effects were in a suitcase under the bed.*

**11 ▶ FILM ◀ effects** [plural] unusual or impressive sounds or images that are artificially produced for a film, play, or radio programme —see also SOUND EFFECTS, SPECIAL EFFECT

**effect²** *v* [T] *formal* to make something happen: *efforts to effect a reconciliation between the warring factions*

S2 W1 **ef·fec·tive** /ɪˈfektɪv/ *adj* **1** producing the result that was wanted or intended: *The ads were simple, but remarkably effective.* **2** impressive or interesting enough to be noticed: *an effective use of colour* **3** [no comparative] if a law, agreement, or system becomes effective, it officially starts: *The cut in interest rates is effective from Monday.* **4** [no comparative] real rather than what is officially intended or generally believed: *The rebels are in effective control of the city.* —**effectiveness** *n* [U]

S2 W2 **ef·fec·tive·ly** /ɪˈfektɪvli/ *adv* **1** in a way that produces the result that was intended: *Children have to learn to communicate effectively.* **2** [sentence adverb] used to describe what the real situation is, especially when it is different from the way that it seems to be: *Effectively, it has become impossible for us to help.*

**ef·fec·tu·al** /ɪˈfektʃuəl/ *adj formal* producing the result that was wanted or intended; EFFECTIVE (1) —opposite INEFFECTUAL —**effectually** *adv*

**ef·fec·tu·ate** /ɪˈfektʃueɪt/ *v* [T] *formal* to make something happen

**ef·fem·i·nate** /ɪˈfemɪ̣nət/ *adj* a man who is effeminate looks or behaves like a woman: *very young and handsome in an effeminate way* —**effeminacy** *n* [U] —**effeminately** *adv*

**ef·fer·vesce** /ˌefəˈves‖ˌefər-/ *v* [I] *technical* a liquid that effervesces produces small bubbles (BUBBLE¹ (1)) of gas

**ef·fer·vesc·ent** /ˌefəˈvesənt◂‖ˌefər-/ *adj* **1** someone who is effervescent is very cheerful and active: *an effervescent personality* **2** a liquid that is effervescent produces small bubbles (BUBBLE¹ (1)) of gas —**effervescence** *n* [U]

**ef·fete** /ɪˈfiːt‖e-/ *adj formal* **1** weak and powerless in a way that you dislike: *an attack against effete intellectuals* **2** looking or behaving like a woman: *an effete, languid young man* —**effetely** *adv*

**ef·fi·ca·cious** /ˌefɪ̣ˈkeɪʃəs◂/ *adj formal* producing the result that was intended, especially when dealing with an illness or a problem: *an equally efficacious method of treatment* —**efficaciously** *adv*

**ef·fi·ca·cy** /ˈefɪ̣kəsi/ *n* [U] *formal* the quality of being able to produce the result that was intended

**ef·fi·cien·cy** /ɪˈfɪʃənsi/ *n* [U] the quality of doing something well and effectively, without wasting time, money, or energy: *The improvements in efficiency have been staggering.* S3 W3

**ef·fi·cient** /ɪˈfɪʃənt/ *adj* a person, machine, or organization that is efficient works well and effectively without wasting time, money, or energy: *an efficient heating system* | *a very efficient secretary* —**efficiently** *adv* S2 W3

**ef·fi·gy** /ˈefɪ̣dʒi/ *n* [C] **1** a figure made of wood, paper, stone etc, that looks like a person, especially one that makes the person look ugly or funny: [+ **of**] *an effigy of the prime minister* **2 burn/hang sb in effigy** to burn or hang a figure of someone at a political DEMONSTRATION (1) because you hate them

**ef·fing** /ˈefɪŋ/ *adj* [only before noun] *BrE spoken* a rude word used to emphasize that you are angry: *She's gone to effing bingo again.* —**effing** *adv* —see also **effing and blinding** (EFF (1))

**ef·flo·res·cence** /ˌefləˈresəns/ *n* [U] *technical* the action of flowers, art etc forming and developing, or the period of time when this happens: *His work represents the efflorescence of a dying culture.*

**ef·flu·ent** /ˈefluənt/ *n* [C,U] liquid waste, especially chemicals or SEWAGE: *The effluent was being discharged straight into the sea.*

**ef·flux** /ˈeflʌks/ *n* [U] *technical* an outward flow of gas or liquid

**ef·fort** /ˈefət‖ˈefərt/ *n* S1 W1

**1 ▶ PHYSICAL/MENTAL ENERGY ◀** [U] the physical or mental energy that is needed to do something: *Lou lifted the box without any apparent effort.* | **take/require effort** *It takes a lot of time and effort to get an exhibition ready.* | **take all the effort out of** (=make something much easier) | **put a lot of effort into** (=work very hard at something) *Frank put a lot of effort into the preparations for the party.*

**2 ▶ ATTEMPT ◀** [C,U] an attempt to do something, especially when this involves a lot of hard work or determination: **effort to do sth** *My efforts to convince Lucy to return failed.* | [+ **at**] *Further efforts at negotiation have broken down.* | **concerted effort** (=a strong sincere attempt) *Jack has made a concerted effort to improve his behaviour.* | **through sb's efforts** (=because of what someone did) *It's only through your efforts that we have managed to raise the money.* | **in an effort to do sth** (=in order to achieve something) *They've been working night and day in an effort to get the bridge ready on time.*

**3 make an effort (to do sth)** to try hard to do something, especially something you do not want to do: *I know you don't like her, but you could make an effort to be polite.* | **make every effort** (=use a lot of effort and try different ways) *Every effort is being made to deal with the issues you raised at the last meeting.*

**4 an effort of will/imagination/concentration** the determination needed to do something: *She dismissed the painful memory with a deliberate effort of will.*

**5 be an effort** to be difficult or painful to do: *I was so*

*weak that even standing up was an effort.* | *Would it be too much effort to get it yourself?*
**6 a good/bad/poor etc effort** something that has been done well, badly etc: *Not a bad effort for a beginner!*

**ef·fort·less** /ˈefətləs‖ˈefərt-/ *adj* something that is effortless is done in a very skilful way that makes it seem easy: *a smooth, effortless volley* —**effortlessly** *adv*: *Her fingers darted effortlessly over the keys.*

**ef·fron·te·ry** /ɪˈfrʌntəri/ *n* [U] *formal* behaviour that you think someone should be ashamed of, although they do not seem to be: *You have the effrontery to ask for a loan!*

**ef·ful·gence** /ɪˈfʌldʒəns/ *n* [U] *literary* brightness of light —**effulgent** *adj*

**ef·fu·sion** /ɪˈfjuːʒən/ *n* [C,U] *formal* an uncontrolled expression of strong feelings: [+ **of**] *effusions of gratitude*

**ef·fu·sive** /ɪˈfjuːsɪv/ *adj* showing strong excited feelings: *Our host gave us an effusive welcome.* —**effusively** *adv*: *"How lovely to see you," she said effusively.* —**effusiveness** *n* [U]

**EFL** /ˌiː ef ˈel/ *n* [U] English as a Foreign Language; the way English is taught to people who do not speak it as their first language

**eg, e.g.** /ˌiː ˈdʒiː/ an abbreviation for 'for example': *citrus fruits, e.g. oranges and grapefruit*

**e·gal·i·tar·i·an** /ɪˌgælɪ̧ˈteəriən‖-ˈter-/ *adj* believing that everyone is equal and should have equal rights: *an egalitarian society* —**egalitarianism** *n* [U]

S1 W2 **egg¹** /eg/ *n*
**1 ▶ BIRDS ◀** [C] a round object with a hard surface, that contains a baby bird, snake, insect etc and which is made by a female bird, snake, or insect: *Blackbirds usually lay their eggs in March.* | *an ostrich egg*
**2 ▶ FOOD ◀** [C,U] an egg, especially one from a chicken, that is used for food: *fried eggs*
**3 ▶ ANIMALS/PEOPLE ◀** [C] a cell produced by a woman or female animal that combines with SPERM (=male cell) to make a baby
**4 have egg on your face** if someone, especially someone in authority, has egg on their face, they look silly because something embarrassing has happened: *The Pentagon's been left with egg on its face.*
**5 put all your eggs in one basket** to depend completely on one thing or one course of action in order to get success
**6 lay an egg** *AmE informal* to fail or be unsuccessful at something that you are trying to do
**7 as sure as eggs is eggs** *BrE old-fashioned* used to tell someone that you are sure that something will happen
**8 good egg** *old-fashioned* someone who you can depend on to be honest, kind etc

**egg²** *v*
**egg** sb ↔ **on** *phr v* [T] to encourage someone to do something, especially something that they should not do: *Joe didn't want to jump but his friends kept egging him on.*

**egg·cup** /ˈeg-kʌp/ *n* [C] a small container that holds a boiled egg while you eat it

**egg·head** /ˈeghed/ *n* [C] *informal* **1** someone who is very intelligent, and only interested in theories and books **2** *AmE* someone who has no hair

**egg·plant** /ˈegplɑːnt‖-plænt/ *n* [C] *especially AmE* a large vegetable with smooth purple skin; AUBERGINE *BrE* —see picture on page 414

**egg roll** /ˌ· ˈ·/ *n* [C] *AmE* a SPRING ROLL

**egg·shell** /ˈegʃel/ *n* [C,U] **1** the hard outside part of a bird's egg **2 eggshell china/paint** a type of CHINA or paint that is thin and hard, like the shell of an egg

**egg-tim·er** /ˈ· ˌ··/ *n* [C] a small glass container with sand in it that runs from one part to the other, used for measuring the time it takes to boil an egg

**e·go** /ˈiːgəʊ, ˈegəʊ‖-goʊ/ *n* [C] **1** the opinion that you have about yourself: *That promotion was a real boost for her ego.* | **have a big ego** (=think that you are very clever or important) *big bikes and equally outsized Hollywood egos* **2 ego trip** *informal* something that you do because it makes you feel important: *This DJ work is just a big ego trip for him!* **3** the part of your mind with which you think and take action, according to Freudian PSYCHOLOGY —compare ID, SUPEREGO

**e·go·cen·tric** /ˌiːgəʊˈsentrɪk◂, ˌe-‖-goʊ-/ *adj* thinking only about yourself and not thinking about what other people might need or want —**egocentrically** /-kli/ *adv* —**egocentricity** /ˌiːgəʊsenˈtrɪsɪ̧ti‖-goʊ-/ *n* [U]

**e·go·is·m** /ˈiːgəʊɪzəm, ˈe-‖-goʊ-/ *n* [U] egotism —**egoist** *n* [C] —**egoistic** /ˌiːgəʊˈɪstɪk◂, ˌe-‖-goʊ-/ *adj*

**e·go·ma·ni·ac** /ˌiːgəʊˈmeɪniæk, ˌe-‖-goʊ-/ *n* [C] someone who thinks that they are very important, and tries to get advantages for themselves without caring about how this affects other people —**egomania** /-niə/ *n* [U]

**e·go·tis·m** /ˈiːgətɪzəm, ˈe-/ *n* [U] the belief that you are much better or more important than other people, or behaviour that shows this

**e·go·tis·tic·al** /iːgəˈtɪstɪkəl/ *adj* believing that you are much better or more important than other people: *He's the most selfish, egotistical individual I have ever met!* —**egotistically** /-kli/ *adv* —**egotist** /ˈɪːgətɪ̧st/ *n* [C]

**e·gre·gious** /ɪˈgriːdʒəs/ *adj formal* an egregious ERROR, failure, problem etc is extremely bad and noticeable: *a most egregious error of judgement* —**egregiously** *adv*

**e·gress** /ˈiːgres/ *n* [U] *formal or law* the act of leaving a building or place, or the right to do this

**e·gret** /ˈiːgrɪ̧t, -et/ *n* [C] a bird that lives near water and has long legs and long white tail feathers

**E·gyp·tian¹** /ɪˈdʒɪpʃən/ *n* [C] someone from Egypt

**Egyptian²** *adj* from or connected with Egypt

**eh** /eɪ/ *interjection spoken BrE, CanE* **1** used when you want someone to repeat something because you did not hear it: *Eh? She's got how many?* **2** used when you want someone to reply to you or agree with something you have said: *Look at these. Smart, eh?* **3** used when you are surprised by something that someone has said

**ei·der·down** /ˈaɪdədaʊn‖-dər-/ *n* [C] a thick warm cover for a bed, filled with duck feathers

**eight** /eɪt/ *number* **1** 8 **2** a team of eight people who row a racing boat **3 have had one over the eight** *BrE old-fashioned* to be drunk —**eighth** *number*

**eigh·teen** /ˌeɪˈtiːn◂/ *number* 18

**eighth** /eɪtθ/ *n* [C] one of eight equal parts of something

**eighth note** /ˈ· ·/ *n* [C] *AmE* a musical note that continues for an eighth of the length of a WHOLE NOTE; QUAVER² (1) *BrE* —see picture at MUSIC

**eigh·ty** /ˈeɪti/ *number* 80

**ei·stedd·fod** /aɪˈstedfəd‖-vɑːd/ *n* [C] a special meeting in Wales at which there are competitions in singing, poetry, and music

**ei·ther¹** /ˈaɪðə‖ˈiːðər/ *conjunction* **1** used to begin a list of two or more possibilities separated by 'or': *You add either one or two stock cubes.* | *She's the kind of person you either love or hate.* | *It was either pink, red, or orange.* —compare OR (1) **2** used to say that if one thing does not happen then something else will have to: *It's your choice! Either she leaves or I will!* | *£75 seems a lot to pay for a starter motor but it's either that or a new car!* S1 W1

**either²** *determiner* **1** one or the other of two things or people: *I've lived in New York and Chicago but don't like either city very much.* | **either way** (=in one way or the other) *You can get to Edinburgh by train or plane but either way it's very expensive.* | *"Shall we have Indian or Chinese?" "I don't mind either way really."* | *The baby's due on the 10th but the doctor said it could be a fortnight either way.* (=it could be born two weeks early or two weeks late) —compare ANY, NEITHER¹ **2** one and the other of two things or people; each: *He sat in the back of the car with a policeman on either side.* | *There are shops at either end of the street.* —compare BOTH **3 an either-or situation** a situation in which you cannot avoid having to make a decision or choice —see ALSO (USAGE) 

**either³** *pron* one or the other of two things or people: *There's tea or coffee – you can have either.* | *Do either of you know where I can buy a zip round here?*

**either⁴** *adv* **1** [only in negatives] also: *I haven't seen the movie and my brother hasn't either.* (=both haven't seen it) | *"I can't swim." "I can't, either."* **2 me either** *AmE spoken* used to say that something is also true about you: *"I don't have any money right now." "Me either."* —compare NEITHER³, TOO (2)

**e·jac·u·late** /ɪˈdʒækjǥleɪt/ *v* [I,T] **1** when a man ejaculates, SPERM comes out of his PENIS **2** *old-fashioned* to suddenly shout or say something, especially because you are surprised —**ejaculation** /ɪˌdʒækjǥˈleɪʃən/ *n* [C,U]

**e·ject** /ɪˈdʒekt/ *v* **1** [T] to make someone leave a place or building by using force: **eject sb from** *The demonstrators were ejected from the hall.* **2** [T] to suddenly send something out: *Ants eject formic acid when another insect tries to attack them.* **3** [I] to jump out of a plane because it is going to crash **4** [I,T] to make something come out of a machine by pressing a button —**ejection** /ɪˈdʒekʃən/ *n* [C,U]

**e·jec·tor seat** /-ˈ·· ˌ·/ also **ejection seat** *AmE* —*n* [C] a special seat that throws the pilot out of a plane when it is going to crash

**eke** /iːk/ *v*

**eke** sth ↔ **out** *phr v* [T] *literary* **1** to make a small supply of something such as food or money last longer by carefully only using small amounts of it: *Today's retired home-owner has to eke out his pension as best he can.* **2 eke out a living/existence** to succeed in getting the things you need to live, even though you have very little money or food: *They eke out a miserable existence in cardboard shacks.*

**EKG** /ˌiː keɪ ˈdʒiː/ *n* [C] an American form of ECG

**e·lab·o·rate¹** /ɪˈlæbərǥt/ *adj* containing a lot of small details or parts that are connected with each other in a complicated way: *an elaborate mosaic consisting of thousands of tiny pieces* | **elaborate plan/notes/excuses etc** (=carefully produced and full of details) —**elaborately** *adv*: *an elaborately carved wooden statue* —**elaborateness** *n* [U]

**e·lab·o·rate²** /ɪˈlæbəreɪt/ *v* [I,T] to give more details or new information about something: *He said he had new evidence, but refused to elaborate any further.* | [+ **on**] *Later chapters simply elaborate on her original theses.* —**elaboration** /ɪˌlæbəˈreɪʃən/ *n* [U]

**é·lan** /ˈeɪlɒn‖eɪˈlɑːn/ *n* [U] *literary* a style that is full of energy and determination: *The attack was planned and led with great élan.*

**e·lapse** /ɪˈlæps/ *v* [I not in progressive] *formal* if a particular period of time elapses, it passes: *Several months were to elapse before his case was brought to trial.*

**e·las·tic¹** /ɪˈlæstɪk/ *n* [U] a type of rubber material that can stretch and then return to its usual length or size: *The ball was attached to the bat with a piece of elastic.*

**elastic²** *adj* **1** made of elastic: *elastic stockings* **2** a material that is elastic can stretch and then go back to its usual length or size: *Children's bones are far more elastic.* **3** a system or plan that is elastic can change or be changed easily: *Language usage is too elastic to be described using just a few simple rules.* —**elasticity** /ˌiːlæˈstɪsǥti/ *n* [U]

**elastic band** /ˌ·ˌ·· ˈ·/ *n* [C] *BrE* a thin circular piece of stretchy rubber used for fastening things together; RUBBER BAND

**E·las·to·plast** /ɪˈlæstəplɑːst‖-plæst/ *n* [C,U] *BrE trademark* a sticky bandage used to cover small cuts; BAND-AID *AmE*

**e·lat·ed** /ɪˈleɪtǥd/ *adj* extremely happy and excited, especially because you have been successful: *Elated by our victory, we sang all the way home.*

**e·la·tion** /ɪˈleɪʃən/ *n* [U] a feeling of extreme happiness and excitement

**el·bow¹** /ˈelbəʊ‖-boʊ/ *n* [C] **1** the joint where your arm bends —see picture at BODY **2** the part of a shirt etc that covers your elbow **3 elbow grease** *informal* hard work and effort, especially when cleaning or polishing something **4 give sb the elbow** *BrE informal* to tell someone that you no longer like them or want them to work for you and that they should leave **5** a curved part of a pipe or CHIMNEY, that is shaped like an elbow

**elbow²** *v* [T] to push someone with your elbows, especially in order to move past them: **elbow your way through** (=move through a group of people by pushing past them) *I began elbowing my way through the crowd.* —see picture on page 1260

**elbow-room** /ˈ·· ·/ *n* [U] enough space in which to move easily: *There's less elbow room in the Ford.*

**el·der¹** /ˈeldə‖-ər/ *adj* **1 elder brother/daughter/sister etc** [only before noun] a brother etc who is older than other brothers etc: *My elder brother looks nothing like me.* —see OLD (USAGE) **2 the elder a)** the older one of two people: *Sarah is the elder of the two.* **b)** used after someone's name to show that they are the older of two people with the same name, usually a father and son: *Pitt the elder* —compare YOUNGER

**elder²** *n* [C] **1** a member of a tribe or other social group who is important and respected because they are old: *a meeting of the village elders* **2** someone who has an official position of responsibility in some Christian churches **3** a small wild tree with white flowers and black berries **4 your elders (and betters)** people who are older than you and who you should respect

**el·der·ber·ry** /ˈeldəbəri‖-dərberi/ *n* [C] the fruit of the elder tree

**el·der·ly** /ˈeldəli‖ˈeldərli/ *adj* **1** old or becoming old: *an elderly lady with white hair* —see OLD (USAGE) **2 the elderly** people who are old, especially people who are too old to look after themselves and need special help S2 W2

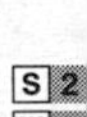

**elder states·man** /ˌ·· ˈ·· ·/ *n* [C] someone old and respected, especially a politician, who people ask for advice because of their knowledge and experience

**el·dest** /ˈeldǥst/ *adj* **1 eldest son/sister/child etc** the oldest son, etc among a group of people, especially brothers and sisters: *Her eldest child is at university now.* **2 the eldest** the oldest one in a group of people, especially brothers and sisters: *I have two brothers – I'm the eldest.*

**e·lect¹** /ɪˈlekt/ *v* **1** [T] to choose someone for an official position by voting: *the country's first democratically elected government* | **elect sb to** *She was elected to Parliament in 1978.* | **elect sb president/mayor etc** *Ronald Reagan was first elected President in 1980.* **2 elect to do sth** *formal* to choose to do something: *Purchasers can elect to pay in monthly instalments.* S2 W3

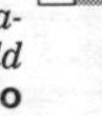

**elect²** *adj* **president/governor/prime minister elect** the person who has been elected as president etc, but who has not yet officially started their job

**e·lec·tion** /ɪˈlekʃən/ *n* **1** [C] an occasion when people vote to choose someone for an official position: *The Socialists won the 1948 election by a huge majority.* **2** [singular] the fact of being elected to an official position: *Within three months of his election he was forced to resign.* —see also GENERAL ELECTION S2 W1

**e·lec·tion·eer·ing** /ɪˌlekʃəˈnɪərɪŋ‖-ˈnɪr-/ *n* [U] speeches and other activities intended to persuade people to vote for a particular person or political party

**e·lec·tive¹** /ɪˈlektɪv/ *adj formal* **1** an elective position or organization is one for which there is an election **2** elective medical treatment is treatment that you choose to have, although you do not have to

**elective²** *n* [C] *AmE* a course that you can choose to study because you are interested in it, while you are studying for a degree in a different subject

**e·lec·tor** /ɪˈlektə‖-tər, -tɔːr/ *n* [C] someone who has the right to vote in an election: *gradually losing the support of the electors*

**e·lec·to·ral** /ɪˈlektərəl/ *adj* [only before noun] connected with elections and voting: *a campaign for electoral reform*

**electoral col·lege** /ˌ·ˌ··· ˈ··/ *n* [singular] a group of people chosen by the votes of the people in each US state, who come together to elect the President

**electoral re·gis·ter** /ˌ··· ˈ···/ also **electoral roll** /ˌ··· ˈ·/ *n* [C] an official list of the people who are allowed to vote in a particular area

**e·lec·to·rate** /ɪˈlektərɪ̣t/ *n* [singular] all the people in a country who have the right to vote

**E·lec·tra com·plex** /ɪˈlektrə ˌkɒmpleks‖-ˌkɑːm-/ *n* [C usually singular] *technical* the unconscious sexual feelings that a girl is supposed to have towards her father —compare OEDIPUS COMPLEX

S2 W3 **e·lec·tric** /ɪˈlektrɪk/ *adj* **1** an electric machine, light etc works using electricity: *an electric heater* **2 electric current** a flow of electricity **3** an electric wire, PLUG[1] (1) etc is used for carrying electricity **4** an electric situation is one in which people are very excited because something important is going to happen: *The atmosphere in the courtroom was electric.*

S3 **e·lec·tri·cal** /ɪˈlektrɪkəl/ *adj* related to or connected with electricity: *I think there's an electrical fault.* | *an electrical engineer* —**electrically** /-kli/ *adv*

**electrical storm** /ˌ··· ˈ·/ also **electric storm** /ˌ·· ˈ·/ *n* [C] a violent storm in which electricity is produced

**electric blan·ket** /ˌ·· ˈ··/ *n* [C] a special BLANKET (=large cloth on a bed) with electric wires in it, used for making the bed warm

**electric chair** /ˌ·· ˈ·/ *n* [C usually singular] a chair in which criminals are killed using electricity, in order to punish them for crimes such as murder; used in the US etc

**electric eel** /ˌ·· ˈ·/ *n* [C] a large South American fish that looks like a snake, and can give an electric shock

**electric eye** /ˌ·· ˈ·/ *n* [C] *informal* a PHOTOELECTRIC CELL

**el·ec·tri·cian** /ɪˌlekˈtrɪʃən, ˌelɪk-/ *n* [C] someone whose job is to deal with or repair electrical equipment

S2 W3 **e·lec·tri·ci·ty** /ɪˌlekˈtrɪsɪ̣ti, ˌelɪk-/ *n* [U] **1** the power that is usually used in modern buildings to provide light and to make machines work **2** the supply of electricity to a particular place: *The electricity was cut off when we didn't pay the bill.* **3** a feeling of excitement: *The electricity seemed to have gone out of their relationship.*

**e·lec·trics** /ɪˈlektrɪks/ *n* [plural] *BrE* the parts of a machine that use electrical power: *The car won't start – I think there's something wrong with the electrics.*

**electric shock** /ˌ·· ˈ·/ *n* [C] a sudden shock to your body, caused by electricity

**electric shock ther·a·py** /ˌ·· ˈ· ˌ···/ *n* [U] a method of treatment for mental illness that involves sending electricity through someone's brain

**e·lec·tri·fi·ca·tion** /ɪˌlektrɪ̣fɪ̣ˈkeɪʃən/ *n* [U] the process of changing a railway so that it uses electrical power, or making electricity available in a particular area

**e·lec·tri·fy** /ɪˈlektrɪ̣faɪ/ *v* [T] **1** to change a railway so that it uses electrical power, or to make electricity available in a particular area **2** if a performance or a speech electrifies the people who are watching it, it makes them feel very interested or excited: *Her words had an electrifying effect.* —**electrifying** *adj* —**electrified** *adj*: *electrified fences*

**electro-** /ɪlektrəʊ, -trə‖-troʊ, -trə/ *prefix technical* **1** concerning or worked by electricity: *to electrocute* (=kill by electricity) | *an electromagnet* **2** electric and: *electro-chemical*

**e·lec·tro·car·di·o·gram** /ɪˌlektrəʊˈkɑːdiəgræm‖-troʊˈkɑːr-/ *n* [C] *technical* an ECG (2)

**e·lec·tro·car·di·o·graph** /ɪˌlektrəʊˈkɑːdiəgrɑːf‖-troʊˈkɑːrdiəgræf/ *n* [C] *technical* an ECG (1)

**electro-con·vuls·ive ther·a·py** /ˌ·· ·ˌ·· ˈ···/ *n* [U] ELECTRIC SHOCK THERAPY

**e·lec·tro·cute** /ɪˈlektrəkjuːt/ *v* [T usually passive] to injure or kill someone by passing electricity through their body: *An employee was electrocuted on the new equipment.* —**electrocution** /ɪˌlektrəˈkjuːʃən/ *n* [U]

**e·lec·trode** /ɪˈlektrəʊd‖-troʊd/ *n* [C] one of the two points at which electricity enters or leaves a BATTERY[1] (1) or other piece of electrical equipment: *fuel cells with two electrodes*

**e·lec·tro·en·ceph·a·lo·gram** /ɪˌlektrəʊɪnˈsefələgræm, -trəʊen-‖-troʊ-/ *n* [C] *technical* an EEG (2)

**e·lec·tro·en·ceph·a·lo·graph** /ɪˌlektrəʊɪnˈsefələgrɑːf, -trəʊen-‖-troʊɪnˈsefələgræf, -troʊen-/ *n* [C] *technical* an EEG (1)

**e·lec·trol·y·sis** /ɪˌlekˈtrɒlɪ̣sɪ̣s, ˌelɪk-‖-ˈtrɑː-/ *n* [U] **1** *technical* the process of separating a liquid into its chemical parts by passing an electric current through it **2** the process of using electricity to destroy hair roots and to remove unwanted hairs from your face etc

**e·lec·tro·lyte** /ɪˈlektrəlaɪt/ *n* [C] a liquid that can be separated into different chemical parts by passing electricity through it

**e·lec·tro·mag·net** /ɪˌlektrəʊˈmægnɪ̣t‖-troʊ-/ *n* [C] a piece of metal that becomes MAGNETIC (=able to attract metal objects) when an electric current is turned on —**electromagnetic** /ɪˌlektrəʊmægˈnetɪk◂‖-troʊ-/ *adj*

**e·lec·tro·mag·ne·tis·m** /ɪˌlektrəʊˈmægnətɪzəm‖-troʊ-/ *n* [U] *technical* a force caused by the movement and exchange of positively and negatively charged PARTICLES (=bits of material) in atoms

**e·lec·tron** /ɪˈlektrɒn‖-trɑːn/ *n* [C] a very small piece of matter that moves around the NUCLEUS (=central part) of an atom: *an electron microscope*

**e·lec·tron·ic** /ɪˌlekˈtrɒnɪk, ˌelɪk-‖-ˈtrɑː-/ *adj* **1** electronic equipment uses things such as chips CHIP[1] (4a), TRANSISTORS, or valves VALVE (3) that have an effect on the electricity going through a piece of equipment such as a television or computer: *'smart' electronic car alarms* **2** using electronic equipment: *electronic music* —**electronically** /-kli/ *adv* S3 W3

**electronic mail** /ˌ···· ˈ·/ *n* [U] E-MAIL

**e·lec·tron·ics** /ɪˌlekˈtrɒnɪks, ˌelɪk-‖-ˈtrɑː-/ *n* [U] **1** the study of making equipment that works electronically **2** the industry connected with making electroinic equipment

**e·lec·tro·plate** /ɪˈlektrəʊpleɪt‖-troʊ-/ *v* [T usually passive] to put a very thin layer of metal onto the surface of an object, using ELECTROLYSIS

**el·e·gant** /ˈelɪ̣gənt/ *adj* **1** very beautiful and graceful: *a tall, elegant woman* | *elegant handwriting* **2** an idea or a plan that is elegant is very clever and simple: *an elegant solution to a problem* —**elegantly** *adv* —**elegance** *n* [U]

**el·e·gi·ac** /ˌelɪ̣ˈdʒaɪək◂/ *adj literary* **1** showing that you feel upset about someone or something that no longer exists: *He spoke of his childhood in elegiac tones.* **2** connected with elegies (ELEGY): *elegiac verse*

**el·e·gy** /ˈelɪ̣dʒi/ *n* [C] a poem or song written to show sadness for someone or something that no longer exists: *an elegy to Lenny's memory*

**el·e·ment** /ˈelɪ̣mənt/ *n* [C] 

**1 ▶ CHEMISTRY ◀** a simple chemical substance such as CARBON or oxygen that consists of atoms of only one kind —compare COMPOUND[1] (1)

**2 an element of surprise/danger/doubt etc** a small amount of a quality or feeling: *There's always an element of risk in this kind of investment.*

**3 ▶ PEOPLE ◀** a group of people who form part of a larger group, especially when the rest of the group does not approve of them: *There is a strong right-wing element in the organization.*

**4 ▶ PART ◀** one part of a whole system, plan, piece of writing etc: *Rhyme is just one of the elements of his poetry.*

**5 ▶ WEATHER ◀ the elements** [plural] the weather, especially bad weather: *battling against the elements*

**6 ▶ HEATING ◀** the heating part of a piece of electrical equipment such as a KETTLE

**7 the elements of sth** the most simple things that you have to learn first about a subject: *I never managed to understand even the elements of calculus.*

**8 ▶ EARTH/AIR/FIRE/WATER ◀** one of the four

substances (earth, air, fire, and water) from which people used to believe that everything was made

**9 be in your element** to be in a situation that you enjoy, because you are good at it: *He's in his element when he's talking to large groups of people.*

**10 be out of your element** to be in a situation that makes you uncomfortable or unhappy: *I felt out of my element surrounded by so much finery.*

**el·e·men·tal** /ˌelɪ̵ˈmentl◂/ *adj* **1** an elemental feeling exists at the simplest and most basic level: *Love and fear are two of the most elemental human emotions.* **2** *technical* existing as a simple chemical element that has not been combined with anything else

**el·e·men·ta·ry** /ˌelɪ̵ˈmentəri◂/ *adj* **1** simple or basic: *You made a very elementary mistake.* **2** [only before noun] concerning the first and easiest part of a subject: *an elementary coursebook for learners of English* **3** [only before noun] *AmE* elementary education is for children between 5 and 11 years old; PRIMARY[1] (2) *BrE*

**elementary par·ti·cle** /ˌ····· ˈ···/ *n* [C] *technical* one of the types of pieces of matter including ELECTRONS, PROTONS, and NEUTRONS that make up atoms

**elementary school** /··ˈ···· ˌ·/ *n* [C] **1** a school in the US where basic subjects are taught for the first six years of a child's education **2** a state school in England or Wales during the late 19th and early 20th century for children aged 5 to 13

**el·e·phant** /ˈelɪ̵fənt/ *n* [C] a very large grey animal with four legs, two TUSKS (=long curved teeth) and a TRUNK (=long nose) that it can use to pick things up —see also WHITE ELEPHANT

**el·e·phan·tine** /ˌelɪ̵ˈfæntaɪn◂‖-tiːn◂/ *adj formal* slow, heavy, and awkward, like an elephant: *She climbed the steps with heavy elephantine movements.*

**el·e·vate** /ˈelɪ̵veɪt/ *v* [T] **1** *formal* to give someone or something a more important rank or position than they had before: [+ **to**] *Both were later elevated to positions of authority.* **2** *formal* to make someone feel happier and more sensitive: *The beautiful countryside was enough to elevate her spirits.* **3** to improve something or make it more important: *in Japan, where just-in-time delivery has been elevated to an art form* **4** *technical* to lift someone or something to a higher position: *Elevate the leg.* **5** *technical* to increase the amount, temperature, pressure etc of something: *These drugs may elevate acid levels in the blood.*

**el·e·vat·ed** /ˈelɪ̵veɪtɪ̵d/ *adj* **1** elevated thoughts, words etc seem to be intelligent or of high moral standard: *elevated philosophical language* **2** [only before noun] an elevated position or rank is very important **3** higher up than other things: *From our elevated vantage point we could see the castle.* **4** *formal* elevated levels, temperatures etc are higher than normal

**elevated rail·way** /ˌ····· ˈ··/ *BrE*, **elevated railroad** *AmE n* [C] a railway that runs on a kind of continuous bridge above the streets in a town

**el·e·vat·ing** /ˈelɪ̵veɪtɪŋ/ *adj formal or humorous* making you feel interested in intelligent or moral subjects: *beach holiday that you would hardly call an elevating experience*

**el·e·va·tion** /ˌelɪ̵ˈveɪʃən/ *n* **1** [singular] a height above the level of the sea: [+ **of**] *The observatory is located on Mt Hopkins at an elevation of 2600m.* **2** [U] *formal* a situation in which someone is given a more important rank or position: *His sudden elevation to the Council surprised everyone.* **3** [C,U] *formal* an increase in the amount or level of something: *a sudden elevation of blood pressure*

**4** [C] *technical* an upright side of a building, as shown in a drawing done by an ARCHITECT (=person who plans buildings) *the front elevation of a house* **5** [C] *technical* the angle made with the HORIZON by pointing a gun: *The cannon was fired at an elevation of 60 degrees.*

**el·e·va·tor** /ˈelɪ̵veɪtə‖-ər/ *n* [C] **1** *AmE* a machine that takes people and goods from one level to another in a building; LIFT[2] (1) *BrE* **2** a machine with a moving belt and containers, used for lifting grain and liquids, or for taking things off ships

**elevator mu·sic** /ˈ···· ˌ··/ *n* [U] *AmE informal* the type of music that is played in shops and public places, and is usually thought to be boring

**e·lev·en** /ɪˈlevən/ *number* **1** 11 **2** a team of eleven players in football or CRICKET (2)

**eleven-plus** /·ˌ·· ˈ·/ *n* **the eleven-plus** an examination which children in Britain aged 11 took in the past in order to decide what type of education they would have

**e·lev·en·ses** /ɪˈlevənzɪ̵z/ *n* [U] *BrE informal* a cup of coffee or tea and a BISCUIT (1), that you have in the middle of the morning

**e·lev·enth** /ɪˈlevənθ/ *n* [C] **1** one of eleven equal parts of something **2 the eleventh hour** the last moment before something important happens: *War was averted at the eleventh hour.*

**elf** /elf/ *n plural* **elves** /elvz/ [C] an imaginary creature like a small person with pointed ears

**el·fin** /ˈelfɪ̵n/ *adj* someone who looks elfin is small and delicate: *dark hair and a white elfin face*

**e·li·cit** /ɪˈlɪsɪ̵t/ *v* [T] to succeed in getting information or a reaction from someone, especially when this is difficult: *My attempts at conversation didn't elicit much response.* | **elicit sth from sb** *By patient questioning we managed to elicit enough information from the witnesses.* —**elicitation** /ɪˌlɪsɪ̵ˈteɪʃən/ *n* [U]

**e·lide** /ɪˈlaɪd/ *v* [T] to leave out the sound of a letter or of a part of a word —**elision** /ɪˈlɪʒən/ *n* [C,U]

**el·i·gi·ble** /ˈelɪ̵dʒɪ̵bəl/ *adj* **1** someone who is eligible for something is able or allowed to do it, for example because they are the right age: [+ **for**] *Are you eligible for social security benefits?* | **eligible to do sth** *Anyone over the age of 18 is eligible to vote.* **2** rich, attractive, and not married, and therefore desirable for marriage: *a rich eligible bachelor* —**eligibility** /ˌelɪ̵dʒɪ̵ˈbɪlɪ̵ti/ *n* [U]

**e·lim·i·nate** /ɪˈlɪmɪ̵neɪt/ *v* [T] **1** to completely get rid of something that is unnecessary or unwanted: *Under the agreement, all trade barriers will be eliminated.* | **eliminate sth from** *Police have eliminated Morris from their enquiries.* **2** [usually passive] to defeat a team or person in a competition, so that they no longer take part in it: *Our team was eliminated in the first round.* **3** to kill someone in order to prevent them from causing trouble: *a ruthless dictator who eliminated all his rivals*

**e·lim·i·na·tion** /ɪˌlɪmɪ̵ˈneɪʃən/ *n* [U]

**1 ▶ REMOVAL OF STH ◀** the removal or destruction of something: [+ **of**] *the elimination of smallpox with worldwide vaccination*

**2 process of elimination** a way of discovering the cause of something by carefully examining each possibility until only one is left: *The identity of the murderer was arrived at by a process of elimination.*

**3 ▶ DEFEAT ◀** the defeat of a team or player in a competition, so that they may no longer take part

**4 ▶ KILLING ◀** a situation in which someone is killed in order to prevent them from causing trouble: [+ **of**] *the elimination of dissidents*

**5 ▶ BODY PROCESS ◀** *technical* the process of getting rid of substances that your body no longer needs

**e·lite** /eɪˈliːt, ɪ-/ *n* [C] **1** a group of people who have a lot of power and influence because they have money, knowledge, or special skills: *a small privileged elite* **2 elite corps/squad/college etc** a group of people that contains the best, most educated etc people of a larger group: *an elite corps of officers*

**e·lit·ist** /eɪˈliːtɪ̵st, ɪ-/ *adj* based on a system in which small groups of people have a lot of power or advantages: *an elitist education system* —**elitism** *n* [U] —**elitist** *n* [C]

**e·lix·ir** /ɪˈlɪksə‖-ər/ *n* **1** [C] *literary* a magical liquid that is supposed to cure people of illness, make them younger etc **2** [C] something that is supposed to solve problems as if by magic: *Don't imagine that lowering inflation is an elixir for all our economic ills.*

**E·liz·a·be·than** /ɪˌlɪzəˈbiːθən◂/ *adj* connected to the period 1558-1603 when Elizabeth I was queen of England: *Elizabethan drama* —**Elizabethan** *n* [C] *The Earl of Essex was a famous Elizabethan.*

**elk** /elk/ *n* [C] a very large European and Asian DEER with big flat horns

**el·lipse** /ɪˈlɪps/ *n* [C] a curved shape like a circle, but with two slightly longer and flatter sides

**el·lip·sis** /ɪˈlɪpsɪ̣s/ *n plural* **ellipses** /-siːz/ [C,U] an occasion when words are deliberately left out of a sentence, though the meaning can still be understood

**el·lip·ti·cal** /ɪˈlɪptɪkəl/ also **el·lip·tic** /-tɪk/ *adj* **1** having the shape of an ellipse: *The earth's orbit is elliptical.* **2** elliptical speech or writing is difficult to understand because more is meant than is actually said: *an elliptical remark*

**elm** /elm/ *n* [C,U] a type of large tree with broad leaves, or the wood from this tree

**el·o·cu·tion** /ˌeləˈkjuːʃən/ *n* [U] good clear speaking in public, involving voice control, pronunciation etc: *elocution lessons* —**elocutionary** *adj* —**elocutionist** *n* [C]

**e·lon·gate** /ˈiːlɒŋgeɪt‖ɪˈlɒːŋ-/ *v* [I,T] to become longer, or make something longer than normal —**elongation** /ˌiːlɒŋˈgeɪʃən‖ɪˌlɒːŋ-/ *n* [C,U]

**e·lon·gat·ed** /ˈiːlɒŋgeɪtɪ̣d‖ɪˈlɒːŋ-/ *adj* longer than normal: *tribeswomen with rings around their elongated necks*

**e·lope** /ɪˈləʊp‖ɪˈloʊp/ *v* [I] to leave your home secretly in order to get married —**elopement** *n* [C,U]

**el·o·quent** /ˈeləkwənt/ *adj* **1** able to express your ideas and opinions well, especially in a way that influences people: *an eloquent appeal for support* **2** showing a feeling or meaning without using words: *The photographs are an eloquent reminder of the horrors of war.* —**eloquently** *adv* —**eloquence** *n* [U]

S1 W1 **else** /els/ *adv* **1 who/what/why etc else** or **anything/someone/anywhere etc else a)** besides or in addition to someone, something etc: *I've said I'm sorry. What else can I do?|Who else was at the party?|Do you want anything else to eat?* **b)** apart from or instead of something, someone etc: *Everyone else but me was invited.|In the end she married somebody else.|It's not in my drawer, where else could it be?* **2 or else** or otherwise: *You must pay £100 or else go to prison.|Your book must be here, or else you've lost it.*

Frequencies of the word **else** in spoken and written English.

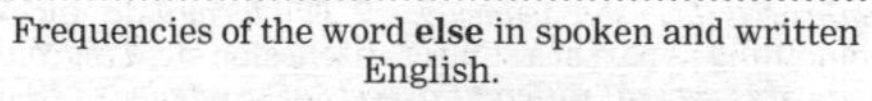

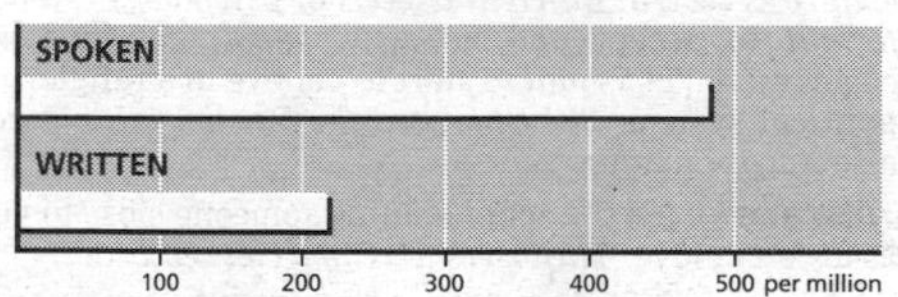


Based on the British National Corpus and the Longman Lancaster Corpus

This graph shows that the word **else** is much more common in spoken English than in written English. This is because it is used a lot in questions and is used in some common spoken phrases.

**else** (*adv*) **SPOKEN PHRASES**

**3 anything else?** used to ask someone if they want to buy another thing, say another thing etc: *"Twenty Marlborough and a box of matches please." "Anything else?" "No, thanks."* **4 there's nothing else** used to say that the thing you have mentioned is the only one that exists, is possible etc: *You'll have to have bread and cheese. There's nothing else, I'm afraid.|It was closed, so we just went home. There was nothing else to do.* **5 what else?/who else?/where else? etc** used to say that it is obvious that the thing, person, place etc that has been mentioned is the only one possible: *"Are you giving him computer games for his birthday?" "Of course, what else?"* **6 what else can you do/say?** used to say that it is impossible to do or say anything apart from what you have mentioned: *I had to give it to her. What else could I do?* **7 or else** used to threaten someone: *You'd better do it, or else!* **8 if nothing else** used to say that something is worth doing, good for you etc for one reason, even if there are no other reasons: *He said that if nothing else, teaching taught him how to deal with people.*

**else·where** /elsˈweə, ˈelsweə‖ˈelswer/ *adv* in or to another place: *outbreaks of rioting elsewhere in the region* S2 W2

**ELT** /ˌiː el ˈtiː/ *n* [U] *especially BrE* English Language Teaching; the teaching of the English language to people whose first language is not English

**e·lu·ci·date** /ɪˈluːsɪ̣deɪt/ *v* [I,T] *formal* to explain something that is difficult to understand very clearly, by providing more information: *His theory is further elucidated in a series of articles published between 1976 and 1980.* —**elucidation** /ɪˌluːsɪ̣ˈdeɪʃən/ *n* [C,U] **elucidatory** /ɪˈluːsɪ̣deɪtəri‖-dətɔːri/ *adv*

**e·lude** /ɪˈluːd/ *v* [T] **1** to escape from someone or something, especially by tricking them: *The fleeing rebels managed to elude their pursuers.* **2** if something that you want eludes you, you fail to find or achieve it: *Success had so far eluded him.* **3** if a fact or the answer to a problem eludes you, you cannot remember or solve it: *The exact terminology eludes me for the moment.*

**e·lu·sive** /ɪˈluːsɪv/ *adj* **1** an elusive person or animal is difficult to find or not often seen: *an elusive man who was never in his office* **2** an elusive result is difficult to achieve: *Success in the business world has so far proved elusive.* **3** an elusive idea or quality is difficult to describe or understand: *The meaning of the poem was somewhat elusive.* —**elusively** *adv* —**elusiveness** *n* [U]

**elves** /elvz/ *n* the plural of ELF

**'em** /əm/ *pron spoken* sometimes used as a short form of 'them': *Go on, Bill, you tell 'em!*

**em-** /ɪm, em/ *prefix* the form used for EN- before b, m, or p: *an embittered man* (=made bitter)|*empowerment*

**e·ma·ci·a·ted** /ɪˈmeɪʃieɪtɪ̣d, -si-/ *adj* extremely thin from lack of food or illness: *The prisoners were ill and emaciated.* —**emaciation** /ɪˌmeɪʃiˈeɪʃən, -si-/ *n* [U] *in an advanced state of emaciation*

**e-mail** /ˈiː meɪl/ *n* [U] a system that allows people to send messages to each other by computer; ELECTRONIC MAIL —**e-mail** *v* [T] *Will you e-mail me about it?* —see picture on page 837

**em·a·nate** /ˈeməneɪt/ *v*

**emanate from** sth *phr v* [T not in passive] to flow or come from: *Delicious smells emanated from the kitchen.* —**emanation** /ˌeməˈneɪʃən/ *n* [C,U]

**e·man·ci·pate** /ɪˈmænsɪ̣peɪt/ *v* [T] *formal* to make someone free from social, political, or legal restrictions that limit what they can do: *Learning will emancipate the oppressed and engender social change.* —**emancipation** /ɪˌmænsɪ̣ˈpeɪʃən/ *n* [U] *the emancipation of slaves*

**e·man·ci·pat·ed** /ɪˈmænsɪ̣peɪtɪ̣d/ *adj* **1** socially, politically, or legally free **2** an emancipated woman is not influenced by old-fashioned ideas about how women should behave

**e·mas·cu·late** /ɪˈmæskjʊ̣leɪt/ *v* [T often passive] **1** to make someone or something weaker or less effective: *The bill has been emasculated by Congress.* **2** to make a man feel less male: *Some men feel emasculated if they work for a woman.* **3** *technical* to remove all or part of a male's sex organs; CASTRATE —**emasculation** /ɪˌmæskjʊ̣ˈleɪʃən/ *n* [U]

**em·balm** /ɪmˈbɑːm‖-ˈbɑːm, -ˈbɑːlm/ *v* [T] to treat a dead body with chemicals, oils etc to prevent it from decaying: *ancient Egyptian embalming techniques* —**embalmer** *n* [C]

**em·bank·ment** /ɪmˈbæŋkmənt/ *n* [C] **1** a wide wall of

stones or earth built to keep the water in a river from flowing over its banks, or to support a road or railway over low ground **2** a slope of earth, stone etc that rises from either side of a railway or road

**em·bar·go¹** /ɪm'bɑːgəʊ‖-'bɑːrgoʊ/ *n plural* **embargoes** [C] an official order stopping trade with another country: **put/impose an embargo on** *an embargo imposed on wheat exports* | **trade/oil/arms etc embargo** *They're accused of trying to break the oil embargo.* | [+ **on**] *an embargo on wheat exports* | *They're accused of trying to break the oil embargo.*

**embargo²** *v* [T] to stop trade with another country by an official order: *a decision to embargo the Southern States*

**em·bark** /ɪm'bɑːk‖-ɑːrk/ *v* [I,T] to get onto a ship or put or take something onto a ship —opposite DISEMBARK (1) —**embarkation** /ˌembɑː'keɪʃən‖-bɑːr-/ *n* [C,U]

**embark on/upon** sth *phr v* [T] to start something, especially something new and difficult that will take a long time: *In the 1950s China embarked on a major program of industrialization.*

**em·bar·rass** /ɪm'bærəs/ *v* [T] **1** to make someone feel anxious, ashamed, or uncomfortable, especially in a social situation: *The old woman's blunt questions embarrassed her, making her momentarily tongue-tied.* **2** to do something that causes problems for a government, political organization, or politician: *a series of revelations that has embarrassed the government*

**em·bar·rassed** /ɪm'bærəst/ *adj* **1** ashamed, nervous, or uncomfortable in a social situation: *I managed to spill water on one of the guests – I was so embarrassed!* | *an embarrassed smile* | [+ **about**] *At about the age of twelve, girls start feeling acutely embarrassed about changing their clothes in front of other people.* —see SHAME¹ (USAGE) **2 financially embarrassed** having no money or having debts

**em·bar·ras·sing** /ɪm'bærəsɪŋ/ *adj* making you feel ashamed, nervous, or uncomfortable: *The firm wants to avoid any embarrassing questions about its finances.* —**embarrassingly** *adv*

**em·bar·rass·ment** /ɪm'bærəsmənt/ *n* **1** [U] the feeling you have when you are embarrassed: [+ **at**] *He could not hide his embarrassment at his children's rudeness.* **2** [C] an event that causes a government, political organization etc problems: *The allegations have been an embarrassment to the administration.* **3** [C] someone who behaves in a way that makes you feel ashamed and uncomfortable: [+**to**] *His mother's boasting was an embarrassment to him.* **4 financial embarrassment** debts or a lack of money that causes problems for you **5 embarrassment of riches** so many good things that it is difficult to decide which one you want

**em·bas·sy** /'embəsi/ *n* [C] **1** a group of officials who represent their government in a foreign country **2** the official building used by these officials: *the American Embassy in Paris*

**em·bat·tled** /ɪm'bætld/ *adj formal* **1** surrounded by enemies, especially in war or fighting: *Their embattled army finally surrendered.* **2** an embattled person, organization, etc has many problems or difficulties: *embattled companies fighting off takeover bids*

**em·bed** /ɪm'bed/ *v* **embedded, embedding** [T usually passive] **1** to fix something firmly and deeply in a surface or solid object: [+ **in**] *Small stones were embedded in the ice.* **2** if ideas, attitudes, or feelings etc are embedded, you believe or feel them very strongly: *deeply embedded feelings of shame*

**em·bel·lish** /ɪm'belɪʃ/ *v* [T] **1** to make a story or statement more interesting by adding details that are not true: *She gave an embellished account of what had happened.* **2** to make something more beautiful by adding decorations: [+ **with**] *The ceiling was embellished with cherubs.* —**embellishment** *n* [C,U]

**em·ber** /'embə‖-ər/ *n* [C usually plural] a piece of wood or coal in a fire that is no longer burning but is still red and very hot: *glowing embers*

**em·bez·zle** /ɪm'bezəl/ *v* [I,T] to steal money from the place where you work: *She had embezzled $10,000 by falsifying the accounts.* —**embezzlement** *n* [U] —**embezzler** *n* [C]

**em·bit·ter** /ɪm'bɪtə‖-ər/ *v* [T] to make someone feel hate and anger for a long time because they think they have been treated unfairly: *The incident had embittered relations between the two countries.* —**embittered** *adj*

**em·bla·zon** /ɪm'bleɪzən/ *v* [T] **1** to put a name, design etc on something so that it can easily be seen: *The manufacturer's name was emblazoned on the packet.* **2** to decorate a SHIELD¹ (2) or flag with a COAT OF ARMS

**em·blem** /'embləm/ *n* [C] **1** a picture or shape that is used to represent a country, group etc: [+ **of**] *The national emblem of England is a rose.* —see picture at SIGN¹ **2** something that represents an idea or principle: [+ **of**] *Expensive cars are seen as an emblem of success.* —compare SYMBOL (3)

**em·ble·mat·ic** /ˌemblə'mætɪk◂/ *adj formal* seeming to represent or be a sign of something —**emblematically** /-kli/ *adv*

**em·bod·i·ment** /ɪm'bɒdɪmənt‖ɪm'bɑː-/ *n* **the embodiment of** someone or something that represents or is very typical of an idea or quality: *He is the embodiment of evil.*

**em·bod·y** /ɪm'bɒdi‖ɪm'bɑːdi/ *v* [T] **1** if a person, thing, or organization embodies an idea or principle it clearly expresses it and shows its importance by the way it behaves or affects behaviour: *The country's constitution embodies the ideals of equality and freedom.* **2** *formal* to include something: *Their latest car model embodies many new improvements.*

**em·bold·en** /ɪm'bəʊldən‖-'boʊl-/ *v* [T] *formal* to give someone more courage: *Emboldened by her smile, he asked her to dance.*

**em·bo·lis·m** /'embəlɪzəm/ *n* [C] *technical* something such as a hard mass of blood or a small amount of air that blocks a tube carrying blood through the body: *a coronary embolism*

**em·boss** /ɪm'bɒs‖ɪm'bɑːs, 'bɒːs/ *v* [T usually passive] to make a raised pattern on the surface of metal, paper, leather etc: **emboss sth with** *The firm's paper is embossed with its name and address.* —**embossed** *adj*

**em·brace¹** /ɪm'breɪs/ *v* **1** [I,T] to put your arms around someone and hold them in a friendly or loving way: *She embraced her son tenderly.* **2** [T] *formal* to include something as part of a subject, discussion etc: *This course embraces several different aspects of psychology.* **3** [T] *formal* to accept and use new ideas, opinions etc eagerly **4** [T] *formal* to start to believe in a religion or political system: *She embraced the Muslim faith.* —see also ALL-EMBRACING

**embrace²** *n* [C] the act of holding someone close to you as a sign of love: *The lovers were in a close embrace.*

**em·bro·ca·tion** /ˌembrə'keɪʃən/ *n* [C,U] *formal* a liquid medicine that you rub on a part of your body that is stiff or ACHING after too much exercise

**em·broi·der** /ɪm'brɔɪdə‖-ər/ *v* **1** [I,T] to make a pattern of stitches on cloth with coloured cotton or silk threads: *The dress was embroidered with flowers.* —see picture on page 839 **2** [T] to make a story or report of events more interesting or exciting by adding details, that you have invented; EMBELLISH (1) —**embroidered** *adj*: *richly embroidered*

**em·broi·der·y** /ɪm'brɔɪdəri/ *n* **1** [C,U] a decoration or pattern made by sewing onto cloth, or the act of making this **2** [U] imaginary details that are added to make a story seem more interesting or exciting: *I just want the truth from you, with no embroidery.*

**embroidery hoop** *n* [C] a circular wooden frame used to hold cloth firmly in place while patterns are being SEWN into it; TAMBOUR

**em·broil** /ɪm'brɔɪl/ *v* [T usually passive] to involve someone in a difficult situation: **embroil sb/sth in** *Soon they were embroiled in a fierce argument.*

**em·bry·o** /'embriəʊ‖-brioʊ/ *n plural* **embryos** [C] **1** an animal or human that has not yet been born, and is in its first state of development in the mother's body —compare FOETUS **2 in embryo** not yet complete, but still developing: *His plans were still in embryo.*

**em·bry·ol·o·gy** /ˌembri'ɒlədʒi‖-'ɑːl-/ *n* [U] the scientific study of embryos —**embryologist** *n* [C]

**em·bry·on·ic** /ˌembri'ɒnɪk◂‖-'ɑːn-/ *adj* in an undeveloped or very early stage of growth: *Britain's embryonic wind energy industry*

**em·cee**, **MC** /ˌem 'siː/ *n* [C] *AmE* someone who is in charge of a social event or programme and introduces various people or performers; MASTER OF CEREMONIES: *She's emcee of her radio show.* —**emcee** *v* [I,T]

**e·mend** /ɪ'mend/ *v* [T] to take the mistakes out of something that has been written, before it is printed —compare AMEND —**emendation** /ˌiːmen'deɪʃən/ *n* [C,U]

**em·e·rald**[1] /'emərəld/ *n* [C] a bright green stone that is valuable and often used in jewellery

W2 **emerald**[2] *adj* bright green —see picture on page 411

**e·merge** /ɪ'mɜːdʒ‖-ɜːrdʒ/ *v* [I] **1** to appear or come out from somewhere: [+ **from**] *The sun emerged from behind the clouds.* **2** if facts emerge, they become known after being hidden or secret: *Eventually the truth emerged.* | **it emerged that** *Later it emerged that the judge had been employing an illegal immigrant.* **3** to come to the end of a difficult experience: [+ **from**] *She emerged from the divorce a stronger person.* **4** to begin to be known or noticed: *a religious sect that emerged in the 1830s* —**emergence** *n* [U] *Japan's emergence as a world leader*

S2 W3 **e·mer·gen·cy** /ɪ'mɜːdʒənsi‖-ɜːr-/ *n* [C] an unexpected and dangerous situation that must be dealt with immediately: *Lifeguards are trained to deal with emergencies.* | **emergency meeting/repairs/exit etc** (=needed to deal with an urgent and unexpected problem) *He called an emergency meeting of the governors.* | *Emergency exits are clearly marked.* —see also STATE OF EMERGENCY

**emergency brake** /·'··· ˌ·/ *n* [C] *AmE* a piece of equipment in a car that you pull up with your hand to stop the car from moving; HANDBRAKE *especially BrE*

**emergency cord** /·'··· ·/ *n* [C] *AmE* a chain that a passenger pulls to stop a train in an emergency; COMMUNICATION CORD *BrE*

**emergency room** /·'··· ˌ·/ *n* [C] *AmE* a place in a hospital where people who have been hurt in accidents are taken for treatment; CASUALTY (3) *BrE*

**emergency services** /·'··· ˌ···/ *n* [plural] *BrE* the official organizations, for example the police, that deal with crime, fires, and injuries

**e·mer·gent** /ɪ'mɜːdʒənt‖-ɜːr-/ *adj* [only before noun] in the early stages of existence or development: *the emergent nations of the world*

**e·mer·ging** /ɪ'mɜːdʒɪŋ‖-ɜːr-/ *adj* [only before noun] in an early state of development: *the emerging Thai auto industry*

**e·mer·i·tus** /ɪ'merɪtəs/ *adj* an emeritus PROFESSOR (=university teacher) is no longer working but still has an official title

**em·e·ry** /'eməri/ *n* [U] a very hard mineral that is used for polishing things and making them smooth

**emery board** /'··· ·/ *n* [C] a long narrow piece of stiff paper with emery on it, used for shaping your nails

**e·met·ic** /ɪ'metɪk/ *n* [C] *technical* something that you eat or drink in order to make yourself VOMIT (=bring up food from your stomach)

**em·i·grant** /'emɪgrənt/ *n* [C] someone who leaves their own country to live in another —compare IMMIGRANT

**em·i·grate** /'emɪgreɪt/ *v* [I] to leave your own country in order to live in another: *Her family emigrated to America in the 1850s.* —**emigration** /ˌemɪ'greɪʃən/ *n* [C,U]

**ém·i·gré** /'emɪgreɪ/ *n* [C] *French* someone who leaves their own country to live in another, usually for political reasons: *Russian émigrés living in Paris*

**em·i·nence** /'emɪnəns/ *n* **1** [U] the quality of being famous and important: *a scientist of great eminence* **2** [C] *formal* a hill or area of high ground **3 Eminence** a title used when talking to or about a CARDINAL (=priest of high rank in the Roman Catholic Church) *Their Eminences are discussing the matter.*

**em·i·nent** /'emɪnənt/ *adj* an eminent person is famous and admired by many people: *an eminent lawyer* —see FAMOUS (USAGE)

**eminent do·main** /ˌ··· ·'·/ *n* [U] *technical* the right of the US government to take private land for public use

**em·i·nent·ly** /'emɪnəntli/ *adv formal approving* to a very high degree; perfectly: *eminently qualified for the job*

**e·mir** /e'mɪə‖e'mɪr/ *n* [C] a Muslim ruler, especially in Asia and parts of Africa: *the emir of Kano in Nigeria*

**e·mir·ate** /'emɪrɪt‖ɪ'mɪrɪt/ *n* [C] the position or country of an emir

**em·is·sa·ry** /'emɪsəri‖-seri/ *n* [C] someone who is sent with an official message or to do special work, often secretly: *a special emissary of the ayatollah*

**e·mis·sion** /ɪ'mɪʃən/ *n* **1** [C] an amount of gas or other substance that a machine or factory produces and sends into the air: *Britain has agreed to cut emissions of nitrogen oxide from power stations.* | *emissions of CFCs* **2** [U] the sending out of light, heat, gas etc

**e·mit** /ɪ'mɪt/ *v* **emitted**, **emitting** [T] **1** to send out heat, light, gas etc: *The chimney emitted clouds of smoke.* **2** to make a particular kind of sound: *recording the whistles emitted by dolphins*

**e·mol·li·ent** /ɪ'mɒliənt‖ɪ'mɑː-/ *n* [C] *formal* **1** a substance that makes your skin softer and reduces pain: *This is a powerful emollient against sunburn.* **2 emollient words/phrases etc** emollient words etc make you feel calmer when you have been angry

**e·mol·u·ment** /ɪ'mɒljʊmənt‖ɪ'mɑːl-/ *n* [C] *formal* money or another form of payment for work you have done

**e·mo·tion** /ɪ'məʊʃən‖ɪ'moʊ-/ *n* [C,U] a strong human feeling such as love, hate, anger etc: *A mixture of emotions welled up inside him as she spoke.* | *The accused man showed little sign of emotion as he was sentenced.* W3

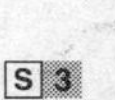

**e·mo·tion·al** /ɪ'məʊʃənəl‖ɪ'moʊ-/ *adj* **1** making people have strong feelings or opinions: *Abortion is a very emotional issue.* **2** showing your feelings to other people, especially by crying when you are upset: *He became very emotional when we had to leave.* **3** [only before noun] connected with your feelings and the way you control them: *We monitor the physical and emotional development of the children.* **4** influenced by your feelings rather than by your thoughts or knowledge: *an emotional response to the problem* —**emotionally** *adv* S3 W3

**e·mo·tion·al·is·m** /ɪ'məʊʃənəlɪzəm‖ɪ'moʊ-/ *n* [U] a tendency to show or feel too much emotion

**e·mo·tive** /ɪ'məʊtɪv‖ɪ'moʊ-/ *adj* making people have strong feelings: **emotive issue/area/word etc** *Child abuse is an emotive subject.* —**emotively** *adv*

**em·pan·el** /ɪm'pænl/ *v* [T] to choose the people to serve on a JURY

**em·pa·thize** also **-ise** *BrE* /'empəθaɪz/ *v* [I] to be able to understand someone else's feelings, problems etc, especially because you have had similar experiences: [+ **with**] *A founder member of the Gay Rights Movement, Mr Smith ensures that the reader empathizes with him.* —compare SYMPATHIZE

**em·pa·thy** /'empəθi/ *n* [U] the ability to understand other people's feelings and problems: [+ **with**] *a doctor who had great empathy with her patients* —compare SYMPATHY

**em·pe·ror** /'empərə‖-ər/ *n* [C] the ruler of an EMPIRE

**em·pha·sis** /'emfəsɪs/ *n plural* **emphases** /-siːz/ [C,U] **1** special importance that is given to one part of something: *In Japan there is a lot of emphasis on politeness.* | **place/put emphasis on** *The course puts an emphasis on practical work.* **2** [C,U] if you put emphasis on a S3 W2

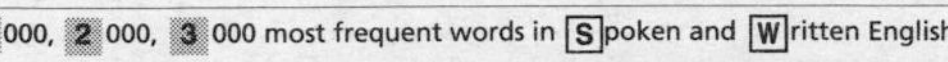

particular word or phrase, you say it slightly louder in order to make it more important: *The emphasis should be on the first syllable.*

S2 W2 **em·pha·size** also **-ise** *BrE* /ˈemfəsaɪz/ *v* [T] to give special or additional importance to something: *Logan made a speech emphasizing the need for more volunteers.* | **emphasize that** *It should be emphasized that flying is a very safe way to travel.*

**em·phat·ic** /ɪmˈfætɪk/ *adj* **1** an emphatic remark, opinion etc is expressed in a clear, strong way to show its importance: *an emphatic denial* **2** clear and undoubted: *an emphatic victory* —**emphatically** /-kli/ *adv*

**em·phy·se·ma** /ˌemfɪ̈ˈsiːmə/ *n* [U] *technical* a disease that affects the lungs, making it difficult to breathe

W3 **em·pire** /ˈempaɪə‖-paɪr/ *n* [C] **1** a group of countries that are all controlled by the ruler or government of one country: *the Roman empire* **2** a group of organizations controlled by one powerful company or person: *an enormous business empire*

**em·pir·i·cal** /ɪmˈpɪrɪkəl/ *adj* [only before noun] based on scientific testing or practical experience, not on ideas from books: *Scientists are hoping to find empirical evidence to confirm their theories.* —**empirically** /-kli/ *adv*

**em·pir·i·cis·m** /ɪmˈpɪrɪ̈sɪzəm/ *n* [U] the belief in basing your ideas on practical experience —**empiricist** *n* [C]

**em·place·ment** /ɪmˈpleɪsmənt/ *n* [C] a special position prepared for a gun or other large piece of military equipment: *a gun emplacement*

S2 W2 **em·ploy**[1] /ɪmˈplɔɪ/ *v* [T] **1** to pay someone to work for you: *The company employs 2000 people worldwide.* | **be employed as sth** *Dave is employed as a baggage handler at the airport.* | **employ sb to do sth** *Freelance consultants have been employed to look at ways of reducing waste.* —see also SELF-EMPLOYED, UNEMPLOYED **2** to use a particular method or skill in order to do something: *The report examines teaching methods employed in the classroom.* **3 be employed in doing sth** to spend your time doing something: *Her days are employed in gardening and voluntary work.*

**employ**[2] *n* [U] **in sb's employ** *formal* if you are in someone's employ, you work for them: *in the Prince's employ*

**em·ploy·a·ble** /ɪmˈplɔɪəbəl/ *adj* suitable to be employed

S2 W2 **em·ploy·ee** /ɪmˈplɔɪ-iː, ˌemplɔɪˈiː/ *n* [C] someone who is paid to work for someone else: *bad employee relations*

S1 W2 **em·ploy·er** /ɪmˈplɔɪə‖-ər/ *n* [C] a person, company, or organization that employs people: *The clothing industry is a large-scale employer of women.* | *a fair employer*

S1 W1 **em·ploy·ment** /ɪmˈplɔɪmənt/ *n* **1** [U] work that you do to earn money: *students seeking employment after college.* | *Are you in full-time employment?* | **in employment** (=doing a job) **2** [U] the situation or condition in which people are employed: *a government inquiry into employment and training* | **full employment** (=a situation in which everyone in society has a job) —opposite UNEMPLOYMENT **3** [U] *formal* the use of a particular method or skill to achieve something: [+ **of**] *Was the employment of force justified?* **4** [C] *formal* a useful activity: *Knitting is a pleasant evening employment.*

**employment a·gen·cy** /ˈ·ˌ·· ˌ···/ *n* [C] a business that makes money by finding jobs for people

**em·po·ri·um** /ɪmˈpɔːriəm/ *n plural* **emporiums** *or* **emporia** [C] *old-fashioned* a large shop

**em·pow·er** /ɪmˈpaʊə‖-ər/ *v* [T] **1** to give someone more control over their own life or situation: *The aim of the course is to empower women.* **2** *formal* to give an organization the power or legal right to do something: **be empowered to do sth** *The college is empowered to grant degrees.* —**empowerment** *n* [U]

**em·press** /ˈemprɪ̈s/ *n* [C] a female ruler of an EMPIRE, or the wife of an EMPEROR: *the empress Josephine*

**emp·ties** /ˈemptiz/ *n* [plural] bottles or glasses that are empty: *We can take the empties to be recycled.*

**emp·ti·ness** /ˈemptinɪ̈s/ *n* [U] **1** a feeling of great unhappiness and loneliness: *She felt an emptiness in her heart when he left.* **2** the state of having nothing in an area or space: [+ **of**] *the silence and emptiness of the desert*

S2 W2 **emp·ty**[1] /ˈempti/ *adj*

**1** ▶ **CONTAINER** ◀ having nothing inside: *an empty box* | *Your glass is empty – can I fill it up?*

**2** ▶ **ROOM/BUILDING** ◀ an empty room, building etc does not have any people in it: *The house had been empty for six months before we moved in.* | *The hall was half-empty.*

**3** ▶ **NOT USED** ◀ not being used by anyone: *I spotted an empty table in the corner.* | **be empty of** *The roads were almost empty of traffic.*

**4** ▶ **PERSON/LIFE** ◀ unhappy because nothing interesting or important happens or because you feel your life has no purpose: *His early death left her empty and despairing.* | *Her days were empty.*

**5 empty words/gestures/promises etc** empty words etc are not sincere or have no effect: *She knew her protest would be nothing more than an empty gesture.*

**6 do sth on an empty stomach** to do something without having eaten any food first: *Children shouldn't go to school on an empty stomach.*

**7 empty nest** *AmE* the situation that parents are in when all their children have left home —**emptily** *adv*

**empty**[2] *v* **1** [T] also **empty out** if you empty a container, you remove everything that is in it: *I had to completely empty out my bag to find my keys.* **2** [T] if you empty the things that are in a container, you take or pour them out of it: *It's your turn to empty the garbage.* | **empty sth onto/into etc** *Kim emptied the candies into a glass jar.* **3** [I] if a place empties, everyone leaves it: *The stores were closing, and the streets began to empty.* **4** [I + **(out) into**] if a river empties into a larger area of water, it flows into it: *The Elbe empties out into the North Sea.*

**empty-hand·ed** /ˌ·· ˈ··◂/ *adj* without getting what you hoped or expected to get: *I spent all morning looking for a suitable present, but came home empty-handed.*

**empty-head·ed** /ˌ·· ˈ··◂/ *adj informal* silly, and unable to think or behave seriously: *an empty-headed blonde*

**EMS** /ˌiː em ˈes/ *n* [singular] European Monetary System; a system for limiting how much the different currencies (CURRENCY) of countries within the European Union can go up and down in value in relation to each other

**e·mu** /ˈiːmjuː/ *n plural* **emus** *or* **emu** [C] a large Australian bird that can run very fast but cannot fly

**em·u·late** /ˈemjɪ̈leɪt/ *v* [T] **1** to try to be like someone else, because you admire them: *The local khans tried to emulate the art, culture, and pageantry of the Persian courts.* **2** if one computer or piece of electronic equipment emulates another, they both perform in the same way —**emulation** /ˌemjɪ̈ˈleɪʃən/ *n* [U]

**e·mul·si·fi·er** /ɪˈmʌlsɪ̈faɪə‖-ər/ *n* [C] something that is added, especially to food, to prevent liquids and solids from separating: *contains sunflower oil, emulsifiers, and lecithin*

**e·mul·si·fy** /ɪˈmʌlsɪ̈faɪ/ *v* [I,T] if two liquids emulsify, they combine to become a smooth mixture

**e·mul·sion** /ɪˈmʌlʃən/ *n* [C,U] **1** a mixture of liquids that do not completely combine, such as oil and water **2** a type of paint used inside buildings on walls or ceilings, that is not shiny when it dries —compare GLOSS PAINT **3** *technical* the substance on the surface of photographic film that makes it react to light

**en-** /ɪn, en/ *prefix* **1** to cause to become; make: *enlarge* **2** to put into a particular condition: *endanger* | *enriched*

**-en** /ən/ *suffix* **1** [in adjectives] made of something: *a golden crown* | *wooden seats* **2** [in verbs] to make something, have a particular quality: *to darken* (=make or become dark) | *ripening fruit* | *This strengthened his resolve.* (=made it stronger)

S3 W1 **en·a·ble** /ɪˈneɪbəl/ *v* [T] **1** to give someone the ability or opportunity to do something: **enable sb to do sth** *Money from her aunt enabled Jan to buy the house.* **2** *formal* to make something possible: *a policy designed to enable the introduction of flexible working hours*

**en·a·bling** /ɪˈneɪblɪŋ/ *adj* [only before noun] *technical* an enabling law is one that makes something possible or gives someone special legal powers

**en·act** /ɪˈnækt/ *v* [T] **1** to make a proposal into law: *Congress refused to enact the bill.* **2** *formal* to act in a play, story etc: *a drama enacted on a darkened stage* —**enactment** *n* [C,U]

**e·nam·el**[1] /ɪˈnæməl/ *n* [U] **1** a glass-like substance that is put onto metal, clay etc for decoration or protection **2** the hard, smooth outer surface of your teeth —see picture at TEETH **3** paint that is usually used on wood, and that produces a shiny surface —**enamel** *adj*

**enamel**[2] *v* [T] to cover or decorate something with enamel

**en·am·oured** *BrE*, **enamored** *AmE* /ɪˈnæməd‖-ərd/ *adj* [not before noun] **1** liking something very much: [+ **of/with**] *You don't seem very enamoured with your job.* **2** *formal* in love with, or very fond of someone: [+ **of/with**] *He was greatly enamoured of Elizabeth.*

**en bloc** /ɒn ˈblɒk‖ɑːn ˈblɑːk/ *adv* all together as a single unit, rather than separately: *You cannot dismiss these stories en bloc.*

**en·camp** /ɪnˈkæmp/ *v* [I,T] *formal* to make a camp or put someone in a camp: *The soldiers were encamped near Damascus.*

**en·camp·ment** /ɪnˈkæmpmənt/ *n* [C] a large temporary camp, especially of soldiers: *a military encampment*

**en·cap·su·late** /ɪnˈkæpsjɡleɪt‖-sə-/ *v* [T] to put the main facts or ideas of something in a short form or a small space: [+ **in**] *Her whole philosophy can be encapsulated in this one sentence.* —**encapsulation** /ɪnˌkæpsjɡˈleɪʃən‖-sə-/ *n* [C,U]

**en·case** /ɪnˈkeɪs/ *v* [T often passive] to cover or surround something completely: [+ **in**] *His broken leg was encased in plaster.* | *her sleek legs encased in sheer black stockings*

**-ence** /əns/ *suffix* [in nouns] another form of the suffix -ANCE: *its existence* (=the fact that it exists) | *reference* | *occurrence*

**en·chant** /ɪnˈtʃɑːnt‖ɪnˈtʃænt/ *v* [T often passive] **1** to make someone feel very interested, happy, and excited: [+ **by/with**] *Venice enchanted me instantly.* **2** *literary* to use magic on something

**en·chant·ed** /ɪnˈtʃɑːntɪ̀d‖ɪnˈtʃæn-/ *adj* an enchanted object or place has been changed by magic, so that it has special powers: *an enchanted castle* —see also DISENCHANTED

**en·chant·er** /ɪnˈtʃɑːntə‖ɪnˈtʃæntər/ *n* [C] *literary* someone who uses magic on people and things

**en·chant·ing** /ɪnˈtʃɑːntɪŋ‖ɪnˈtʃæn-/ *adj* very attractive: *The child looked enchanting in a pale blue dress.* | *an enchanting romantic comedy* —**enchantingly** *adv*

**en·chant·ment** /ɪnˈtʃɑːntmənt‖ɪnˈtʃænt-/ *n* **1** [C,U] a feeling of mystery that strongly interests or attracts you: *The forest had an air of enchantment.* **2** [C] *literary* a change caused by magic; SPELL[2] (1)

**en·chant·ress** /ɪnˈtʃɑːntrɪ̀s‖ɪnˈtʃæn-/ *n* [C] *literary* **1** a woman that men find very attractive and interesting **2** a woman who uses magic on people and things

**en·chi·la·da** /ˌentʃɪ̀ˈlɑːdə/ *n* [C] **1** a Mexican food consisting of a flat piece of bread rolled around meat and covered with a hot-tasting thick liquid **2 the whole enchilada** *AmE informal* the whole situation; everything: *Come on. Let's hear it – the whole enchilada.*

**en·cir·cle** /ɪnˈsɜːkəl‖-ɜːr-/ *v* [T] to surround someone or something completely: *a luscious garden, encircled by walled parkland* —**encirclement** *n* [U]

**en·clave** /ˈenkleɪv, ˈeŋ-/ *n* [C] a place or a group of people that is surrounded by people or areas that are different: *the Italian-American enclave in New York*

**en·close** /ɪnˈkləʊz‖-ˈkloʊz/ *v* [T] **1** to put something inside an envelope as well as a letter: *Please enclose a cheque with your order.* | **please find enclosed** (=used in business letters to say that you are sending something as well as a letter) *Please find enclosed an agenda for the meeting.* **2** [often passive] to surround something, especially with a fence or wall, in order to make it separate: *A high wall enclosed the courtyard.*

**en·clo·sure** /ɪnˈkləʊʒə‖-ˈkloʊʒər/ *n* **1** [C] an area surrounded by a wall or fence, and used for a particular purpose: *the bear enclosure at the zoo* **2** [U] the act of making an area separate by putting a wall or fence around it: *the enclosure of arable land for pasture* **3** [C] something that is put inside an envelope as well as a letter

**en·code** /ɪnˈkəʊd‖-ˈkoʊd/ *v* [T] to put a message or other information into a CODE[1] (4) —opposite DECODE

**en·com·pass** /ɪnˈkʌmpəs/ *v* [T] **1** to include a wide range of ideas, subjects, etc: *The study encompasses social, political, and economic aspects of the situation.* **2** to completely cover or surround something: *The houses encompassed about one hundred square metres.*

**en·core**[1] /ˈɒŋkɔː‖ˈɑːŋkɔːr/ *n* [C] an additional or repeated part of a performance, especially a musical one: *The audience demanded an encore.*

**encore**[2] *interjection* used when you have enjoyed a musical performance very much and want the performer to sing or play more: *Pavarotti's performance, greeted by roars of 'Encore!'*

**en·coun·ter**[1] /ɪnˈkaʊntə‖-ər/ *v* [T] **1** to experience problems, difficulties, or opposition when you are trying to do something: *We encountered a serious setback when two members of the expedition were injured.* **2** to meet someone or experience something unexpectedly: *I first encountered him at summer school.* W3

**encounter**[2] *n* [C] **1** an occasion when you meet someone, especially in an unplanned or unexpected way: *She didn't remember our encounter last summer.* | **chance encounter** (=a meeting caused by luck or chance) **2** a short dangerous struggle or meeting between two people or groups: *one of the bloodiest encounters of the American Civil War* | **close encounter** (=situation that could have been dangerous or unpleasant) *a close encounter with a poisonous snake*

**en·cour·age** /ɪnˈkʌrɪdʒ‖ɪnˈkɜːr-/ *v* [T] **1** to say or do something that helps someone have the courage or confidence to do something: *Haldene encouraged him in his work.* | **encourage sb to do sth** *Patricia encouraged me to apply for the job.* **2** to make something more likely to happen or make people more likely to do something: *a meeting format that will encourage debate* | **encourage sb to do sth** *A good public transport encourages people to leave their cars at home.* —opposite DISCOURAGE —**encouragement** *n* [C,U] S2 W1

**en·cour·aged** /ɪnˈkʌrɪdʒd‖ɪnˈkɜːr-/ *adj* [not before noun] feeling more hopeful and confident: *She felt encouraged by the many letters of support.*

**en·cour·ag·ing** /ɪnˈkʌrɪ̀dʒɪŋ‖ɪnˈkɜːr-/ *adj* giving you hope and confidence: *The results of the survey have been very encouraging.* —**encouragingly** *adv* S3

**en·croach** /ɪnˈkrəʊtʃ‖-ˈkroʊtʃ/ *v*
**encroach on/upon** sth *phr v* [T] **1** to gradually take more control of someone's time, possessions, rights etc than you should: *a government that is encroaching on the rights of individuals* **2** to gradually cover more and more land: *houses encroaching upon farmland* —**encroachment** *n* [C,U]

**en·crust·ed** /ɪnˈkrʌstɪ̀d/ *adj* covered with a thin hard layer of something: [+ **with/in**] *boots thickly encrusted with mud* —**encrustation** /ˌɪnkrʌˈsteɪʃən/ *n* [C,U]

**en·cum·ber** /ɪnˈkʌmbə‖-ər/ *v* [T] *formal* to make it difficult for someone to move easily or for something to happen in the usual way: [+ **by/with**] *I was too encumbered by suitcases to run.* —**encumbrance** *n* [C]

**-ency** /ənsi/ *suffix* [in nouns] another form of the suffix -ANCY: *a tendency*

**en·cyc·li·cal** /ɪnˈsɪklɪkəl/ *n* [C] *technical* a letter sent by the Pope to all Roman Catholic BISHOPS or to members of the Roman Catholic Church

**en·cy·clo·pe·di·a** also **encyclopaedia** *BrE* /ɪnˌsaɪklə'piːdiə/ *n* [C] a book or set of books containing facts about many different subjects, or about one particular subject

**en·cy·clo·pe·dic** also **encyclopaedic** *BrE* /ɪnˌsaɪklə'piːdɪk◂/ *adj* encyclopedic knowledge, memory etc has a very large amount of information in it

S1 W1 **end¹** /end/ *n* [C]

**1 ▶ LAST PART ◀** the last part of something such as a period of time, activity, book, or film: *He's leaving at the end of October.* | *I found the end of the movie very disappointing.* | **from beginning to end** *Her story was a pack of lies from beginning to end.*

**2 ▶ FURTHEST POINT ◀** the furthest point of a place or object: *He sat at one end of the table and I sat at the other.* | *The street is closed off at both ends.* | *a long pole with a hole at one end* | **end to end** (=in a line with the ends touching) *Put the two tables end to end.*

**3 ▶ FINISHED ◀** a situation in which something is finished or no longer exists: *the end of all my dreams* | **be at an end** (=finished) *The long hot summer was at last at an end.* | **come to an end** (=finished and no longer continuing) *That job came to an end last month.* | **put an end to** *Winning the competition put an end to his financial problems.* | **to the end of time** *literary* (=for ever)

**4 ▶ AIM ◀** [usually plural] the result that you hope to achieve: *She'll stop at nothing to achieve her own ends.* | **to that end** *formal*: *Joel wants to buy a car and is saving money to that end.* | **an end in itself** (=something you aim to do because you want to, not in order to get other advantages) *Learning to play the piano was an end in itself for me.* | **the end justifies the means** (=the result you want makes acceptable the bad things you do in order to get it)

**5 in the end** after a period of time; finally: *In the end, I decided that I wouldn't go after all.* —see LASTLY (USAGE)

**6 days/hours/weeks etc on end** for many days, hours etc without stopping: *It snowed for days on end.*

**7 no end** *spoken* very much: *Thanks for the letter – it cheered me up no end.*

**8 no end of** *spoken* a lot of something: *We've had no end of problems with the house since we moved.*

**9 put/stand sth on end** to put something in a position so that its longest edge is upright —see also **make sb's hair stand on end** (HAIR (6))

**10 ▶ PART OF AN ACTIVITY ◀** *informal* the particular part of a job, activity, place etc that you are involved in, or that affects you: *She works in the sales end of things.* | *Let's hope they keep their end of the bargain.* | **at your end** *spoken* (=where you are) *What's the weather like at your end?*

**11 ▶ SPORT ◀** one of the two halves of a sports field that a team defends or attacks: *The teams change ends at half-time.*

**12 ▶ DEATH ◀** [C usually singular] a word meaning death, used because you want to avoid saying this directly: *James was with his father at the end.*

**13 at the end of the day** *spoken* used to give your opinion after you have discussed all the possibilities of a situation or problem: *At the end of the day, it's his responsibility, and there's nothing you can do.*

**14 be at the end of your tether/rope** to have no more PATIENCE or strength to deal with something: *I'm at the end of my tether with their constant arguing.*

**15 it's not the end of the world** *spoken* used to say that a possible problem is not too serious or bad: *After all, it's not the end of the world if you fail this test.*

**16 hold/keep your end up** *BrE informal* to continue to be brave or act effectively in a difficult situation

**17 make (both) ends meet** to have just enough money to buy what you need: *Since Mike lost his job, we can hardly make ends meet.*

**18 the end of the road/line** the end of a process or activity: *I tried to tell him that this defeat was not the end of the road, that football was only a game.*

**19 the (absolute) end** *BrE spoken* used to show disapproval of someone or something in an amused way: *Look at this untidy room – you're the absolute end!*

**20 living end** *AmE spoken* used as an expression of strong approval or disapproval: *What will she do next? She's the living end!*

**21 do sth to the bitter end** to keep doing something until you have tried every possible method: *We'll fight this decision to the bitter end.*

**22 go to the ends of the earth** to do everything you can, even if it is very difficult, in order to have or achieve something: *I'd go to the ends of the earth to be with him.*

**23 get/have your end away** *BrE slang* to have sex —see also **be-all and end all** (BE² (10)), DEAD END, **go off at the deep end** (DEEP¹ (17)), **be at a loose end** LOOSE¹ (14), ODDS AND ENDS, **be on the sharp end of** (SHARP¹ (21)), **come to a sticky end** (STICKY (7)), **the tail end of a queue/meeting etc** (TAIL¹ (9)), **jump/be thrown in at the deep end** (DEEP¹ (16)), **get the wrong end of the stick** (WRONG¹ (12)), **at your wits' end** (WIT¹ (6))

**end²** *v* **1** [I] to finish or stop: *World War II ended in 1945.* | *The film ended with the heroine dying.* **2** [T] to make something finish or stop: *Jane decided it was time to end the relationship with Bob.* **3 end your days/life** if you end your days in a particular place or doing a particular thing, you spend the last part of your life there or doing that **4 end it all** to kill yourself S1 W1

**end in** sth *phr v* [T not in passive] **1** to have in a particular result, or finish in a particular way: *Their marriage ended in divorce.* | **it'll all end in tears** *BrE spoken* (=used to warn that a situation will end in an unpleasant or unhappy way) *This game will end in tears. I know it.* **2** to have a particular shape at one end: *The fine end in a sharp point.*

**end up** *phr v* [I] *informal* **1** to come to be in a particular situation or state, especially when you did not plan it: *He'll end up in prison if he's not careful.* | **end up doing sth** *We were going to go out, but ended up watching videos.* **2** to arrive in a place you did not plan to go to: *We got to Rome okay, but our luggage ended up in Paris.*

**en·dan·ger** /ɪn'deɪndʒə‖-ər/ *v* [T] to put someone or something in a dangerous situation where they can be hurt, damaged, or destroyed: *Smoking during pregnancy can endanger your baby's health.* | *If unemployment continues to rise, social stability may be endangered.*

**endangered spe·cies** /·,·· '··/ *n* [C] a type of animal or plant that may soon no longer exist: *The whale is an endangered species.*

**en·dear** /ɪn'dɪə‖ɪn'dɪr/ *v*

**endear** sb **to** sb *phr v* [T] to make someone popular and liked: *Diana's friendly disposition endears her to everyone she meets.*

**en·dear·ing** /ɪn'dɪərɪŋ‖ɪn'dɪr-/ *adj* making someone love or like you: *an endearing smile* —**endearingly** *adv*

**en·dear·ment** /ɪn'dɪəmənt‖ɪn'dɪr-/ *n* [C] an action or word that expresses your love for someone: *whispering endearments to her* | **term of endearment** (=a way you address someone you love)

**en·deav·our¹** *BrE*, **endeavor** *AmE* /ɪn'devə‖-ər/ *v* [I] *formal* to try very hard: **endeavour to do sth** *We always endeavor to give our customers excellent service.*

**endeavour²** *BrE*, **endeavor** *AmE* *n* [C,U] *formal* an attempt or effort, especially to do something new or difficult: *The expedition was an oustanding example of human endeavour.* | **best endeavours** *Despite our best endeavours, we couldn't get the machine started.*

**en·dem·ic** /en'demɪk, ɪn-/ *adj* an endemic disease is always present in a particular place, or among a particular group of people: *Violent crime is now endemic in parts of Chicago.* —compare PANDEMIC

**end game** /'· ·/ *n* [C] *technical* something that happens at the end of an activity, especially a game of CHESS

**end·ing** /'endɪŋ/ *n* [C] **1** the way in which a story, film, etc finishes: *The story has a happy ending.* **2** the last part of a word: *Verbal nouns have the ending -ing.*

**en·dive** /ˈendɪv‖ˈendaɪv/ *n* [C,U] **1** a plant with curly green leaves that you eat raw **2** *AmE* a plant with bitter tasting leaves that is eaten raw; CHICORY *BrE*

**end·less** /ˈendləs/ *adj* **1** something unpleasant that is endless continues, or seems to continue, for a long time: *the endless round of meetings and interviews* **2** *technical* an endless belt, chain etc is circular with the ends joined —**endlessly** *adv*: *Sue was endlessly patient.*

**en·do·crine gland** /ˈendəʊkrɪn ˌglænd, -kraɪn-‖-doʊ-/ *n* [C] *technical* an organ of your body that puts HORMONES into your blood

**en·dorse** /ɪnˈdɔːs‖-ɔːrs/ *v* [T] **1** to express formal support or approval for someone or something: *The committee has endorsed our proposals.* **2** to sign your name on the back of a cheque **3** to say in an advertisement that you use a particular product and like it: *big names who endorsed American Express* **4** [usually passive] *BrE* to write a driving offence on someone's DRIVING LICENCE: *His licence was endorsed for speeding.* —**endorsement** *n* [C,U]

**en·dow** /ɪnˈdaʊ/ *v* [T] to give a college, hospital etc a large sum of money that will provide it with an income

**endow** sb **with** sth *phr v* [T] **1 be endowed with** to naturally have a good feature or quality: *She was endowed with both looks and brains.* **2** *formal* to give someone something —see also WELL-ENDOWED

**en·dow·ment** /ɪnˈdaʊmənt/ *n* **1** [C,U] a sum of money that is given to a place such as a college or hospital to give it an income, or the giving of this money: *an endowment of land and investments given to the college* **2** [C] a quality or ability that someone has naturally: *Man has already changed dogs' genetic endowments by breeding them selectively.*

**endowment pol·i·cy** /·ˈ·· ˌ···/ *n* [C] *technical* an insurance arrangement that pays you an agreed sum of money after a period of time

**end prod·uct** /ˈ· ˌ··/ *n* [C usually singular] something that is produced by an industrial process, or by a particular activity: *Desk top publishing can produce a very high quality end product.* —compare BY-PRODUCT

**end re·sult** /ˌ· ·ˈ·/ *n* [C usually singular] the final result of a process or activity: *If present trends continue, the end result will inevitably be socialized medicine.*

**en·due** /ɪnˈdjuː‖ɪnˈduː/ *v* [T] *formal*

**endue** sb **with** sth *phr v* [T] to make someone have a lot of a good quality: *endued with a spirit of public service*

**en·dur·ance** /ɪnˈdjʊərəns‖ɪnˈdʊr-/ *n* [U] the ability to suffer difficulties or pain with strength and patience: *The marathon really tested his endurance.*

**en·dure** /ɪnˈdjʊə‖ɪnˈdʊr/ *v* **1** [T] to suffer something painful or deal with a very unpleasant situation for a long time with strength and patience: *There are limits to what the human body can endure.* | *Bosnians have now endured several years of war.* —see graph at BEAR **2** [I] to remain alive or continue to exist: *a city built to endure* —**endurable** *adj*

**en·dur·ing** /ɪˈdjʊərɪŋ‖-ˈdʊr-/ *adj* continuing to exist for a long time: *the enduring appeal of the short story*

**end us·er** /ˈ· ˌ··/ *n* [C] the person who actually uses a particular product: *researching end-users' preferences*

**end·ways** /ˈendweɪz/ also **end·wise** /-waɪz/ *adv AmE* **1** with the end forward: *The box looks narrow when you look at it endways.* **2** with the ends touching each other: *Put the tables together endways.*

**end zone** /ˈ· ·/ *n* [C] the place at the end of an American football field where you take the ball to get points —see picture on page 1263

**en·e·ma** /ˈenɪmə/ *n* [C] a liquid that is put into someone's RECTUM in order to make them empty their BOWELS

W2 **en·e·my** /ˈenəmi/ *n* [C] **1** someone who hates you and wants to harm you: *She's a dangerous enemy to have.* | **be enemies** (=hate and oppose each other) *Jake and Paul have been enemies for years.* | **make an enemy (of sb)** *He's a ruthless businessman and has made a lot of enemies.* | **sworn enemies** (=enemies determined never to end their quarrel) **2** someone who opposes you and wants to prevent you doing something: *political enemies* | *Greenpeace, an enemy of the chemical industry, is pressing for more environmental legislation.* **3** someone you are fighting in a war: *Our enemies were hidden in the trenches.* | **enemy forces** (=the army, navy etc of the country that you are fighting) | **enemy soldiers/aircraft** *Enemy aircraft were spotted overhead.* **4 be your own worst enemy** to behave in a way that causes problems for yourself **5** *literary* something that changes something else or makes it weaker: *Jealousy is the enemy of love.*

**en·er·get·ic** /ˌenəˈdʒetɪk◂‖-ər-/ *adj* very active because you have a lot of energy: *an able and energetic politician* —**energetically** /-kli/ *adv*: *He fought energetically against apartheid.*

**en·er·gize** also **-ise** *BrE* /ˈenədʒaɪz‖-ər-/ *v* [T] **1** to make someone feel more determined and energetic **2** [usually passive] to make a machine work: *electric motors energized by solar cells* —**energizing** *adj*

**en·er·gy** /ˈenədʒi‖-ər-/ *n* [C,U] **1** the physical and mental strength that makes you able to be active: *The task will take an enormous amount of time and energy.* | **be full of energy** *She came back full of energy after her vacation.* | **nervous energy** (=energy that you have because you feel nervous) **2** power that is used to provide heat, drive machines etc such as oil and coal: *the world's energy resources* **3 energies** the effort that you use to do things: **apply/devote your energies to** *She's devoting all her energies to the wedding preparations.* S1 W1

**en·er·vat·ed** /ˈenəveɪtɪ̣d‖-ər-/ *adj formal* having lost energy and feeling weak: *I was utterly enervated by the argument.* | *reclining on the chaise longue, languid and enervated*

**en·er·vat·ing** /ˈenəveɪtɪŋ‖-ər-/ *adj* making you feel weak: *Extreme heat can be very enervating.*

**en·fant ter·ri·ble** /ˌɒnfɒn teˈriːblə‖ˌɑːnfɑːn-/ *n* [C] *French* someone who behaves in a way that shocks and amuses other people: *Ken Russell, the enfant terrible of the British film industry*

**en·fee·ble** /ɪnˈfiːbəl/ *v* [T] *formal* to make someone weak —**enfeebled** *adj*

**en·fold** /ɪnˈfəʊld‖-ˈfoʊld/ *v* [T] *formal* to enclose or surround something: *He enfolded her in his arms.*

**en·force** /ɪnˈfɔːs‖-ɔːrs/ *v* [T] **1** to make people obey a rule or law: *Governments make laws and the police enforce them.* **2** to make something happen, especially by threats or force; IMPOSE: *The unions hope to enforce a closed shop.* —**enforceable** *adj* —**enforcement** *n* [U] *law enforcement agencies in the US*

**en·forced** /ɪnˈfɔːst‖-ɔːrst/ *adj* made to happen or exist by law, or by conditions that you cannot control: *a period of enforced isolation*

**en·fran·chise** /ɪnˈfræntʃaɪz/ *v* [T] **1** to give a group of people the right to vote —opposite DISENFRANCHISE **2** to free a slave —**enfranchisement** /-tʃɪz-‖-tʃaɪz-/ *n* [U]

**en·gage** /ɪnˈgeɪdʒ/ *v formal* **1** [T] to attract someone and keep their interest: *The new toy didn't engage the child's interest for long.* **2** [T] to arrange to employ someone: **engage sb to do sth** *His father engaged a private tutor to improve his maths.* **3** [I,T] to make one part fit into another part of a machine: *She engaged the clutch and the car moved forwards.* | [+ **with**] *The wheel engages with the cog and turns it.* —opposite DISENGAGE (2) **4** [T] to begin to fight with an enemy: *The two armies engaged at dawn.* W3

**engage in** *formal phr v* [T] **1** to take part or become involved in an activity: *a politician engaged in various business activities* **2 engage sb in conversation** to start talking to someone and involve them in a conversation

**engine**

**en·gaged** /ɪnˈgeɪdʒd/ *adj* **1** having agreed to get married: *They've been engaged for six months.* | [+ **to**] *Have you met the man she's engaged to?* | **get engaged** (=agree to marry someone) *Siobhan and Ray have just got engaged.* **2** *BrE* an engaged telephone is being used; BUSY¹ (7) *AmE* | **engaged line/number** *I can't get through – her line's engaged.* | **engaged tone** (=the sound you hear when the telephone is engaged) **3** a public toilet that is engaged is being used —opposite VACANT (1) **4 be otherwise engaged** *formal* to be unable to do something because you have arranged to do something else

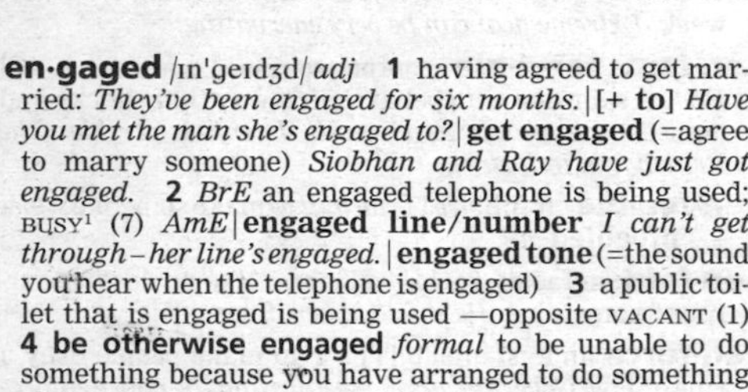

**en·gage·ment** /ɪnˈgeɪdʒmənt/ *n* **1** [C] an agreement to marry someone: *They've officially announced their engagement.* | **break off your engagement** (=say you no longer want to marry someone) **2** [C] an arrangement to do something or meet someone: *He has engagements this month at various clubs.* | **prior/previous engagement** (=an arrangement you have already made) *I won't be able to make it – I have a prior engagement.* **3** [C] *technical* a battle between armies, navies etc **4** [U] the fitting together of the working parts of a machine

**engagement ring** /ˈ· ·· ·/ *n* [C] a ring that a man gives to a woman when they decide to marry

**en·gag·ing** /ɪnˈgeɪdʒɪŋ/ *adj* attracting someone's attention and interest: *an engaging smile* —**engagingly** *adv*

**en·gen·der** /ɪnˈdʒendə‖-ər/ *v* [T] *formal* to be the cause of a situation or feeling: *Racial inequality engenders conflict.*

S1 W2 **en·gine** /ˈendʒɪ̇n/ *n* [C] **1** a piece of machinery with moving parts that changes power from steam, electricity, oil etc, into movement: *the engine of a car* | *a jet engine* **2** a vehicle that pulls a railway train **3 engine of change/destruction etc** *formal* something that causes change etc: *a newspaper that was the engine of cultural change* —see also FIRE ENGINE

**engine driv·er** /ˈ·· ˌ··/ *n* [C] *BrE* someone who drives a train; ENGINEER¹ (5) *AmE*

**en·gi·neer¹** /ˌendʒɪ̇ˈnɪə‖-ˈnɪr/ *n* [C] **1** someone who designs the way roads, bridges, machines etc are built: *Mike's an electrical engineer.* **2** someone who controls the engines on a ship or aircraft **3** *BrE* someone who repairs electrical or mechanical equipment: *The engineer's coming to fix the phone today.* **4** a soldier in the army who designs and builds roads, bridges etc **5** *AmE* someone who drives a train S3 W3

**engineer²** *v* [T] **1** to arrange something by clever secret planning: *He had powerful enemies who engineered his downfall.* **2** [often passive] to design and plan the construction of roads, bridges, machines, etc: *This new jet engine is superbly engineered.*

**en·gi·neer·ing** /ˌendʒɪ̇ˈnɪərɪŋ‖-ˈnɪr-/ *n* [U] the profession and activity of designing the way roads, bridges, machines etc are built —see also CIVIL ENGINEERING W2

**En·glish¹** /ˈɪŋglɪʃ/ *n* [U] **1** the language of Britain, the US, Australia, and some other countries **2** English language and literature as a subject of study: *a professor of English* **3 the English** people from England, or sometimes from all of Britain

**English²** *adj* from or connected with England or Britain

**English break·fast** /ˌ·· ˈ··/ *n* [C] *BrE* a large cooked breakfast consisting of BACON, eggs, TOAST¹ (1) etc —compare CONTINENTAL BREAKFAST

**English horn** /ˌ·· ˈ·/ *especially AmE* COR ANGLAIS

**En·glish·man** /ˈɪŋglɪʃmən/ *n* [C] a man from England

**English muf·fin** /ˌ·· ˈ··/ *n* [C] *AmE* a round flat piece of bread that you TOAST² (2) before eating it; MUFFIN *BrE*

**En·glish·wom·an** /ˈɪŋglɪʃˌwʊmən/ *n* [C] a woman from England

**en·grave** /ɪnˈgreɪv/ *v* [T] **1** to cut words or pictures on metal, wood, glass etc: **engrave sth on** *a silver pocket watch with the initials HTS engraved on the back* | **engrave sth with** *a pendant engraved with a simple geometric design* **2 be engraved in your memory/mind/heart** *formal* to be impossible to forget: *That day would be engraved in his memory for ever.* **3** to prepare a special metal plate for printing **4** to print something using a specially prepared metal plate —**engraver** *n* [C]

**en·grav·ing** /ɪn'greɪvɪŋ/ *n* **1** [C] a picture printed from an engraved metal plate: *an old engraving of London Bridge* **2** [U] the art or work of engraving things

**en·gross** /ɪn'grəʊs‖-'groʊs/ *v* [T] **1** if something engrosses you, you are extremely interested in it: *Their revolutionary talk engrossed him, and he listened intently.* **2 engross yourself in/with** to become very interested in something and spend a lot of time doing it

**en·grossed** /ɪn'grəʊst‖-'groʊst/ *adj* so interested in something that you do not notice anything else: [+ **in/with**] *I tried to attract her attention but she was engrossed in conversation with Stephen.*

**en·gross·ing** /ɪŋ'grəʊsɪŋ‖-'groʊs-/ *adj* so interesting that you do not notice anything else: *an engrossing story*

**en·gulf** /ɪn'gʌlf/ *v* [T] **1** if a feeling, especially an unpleasant one, engulfs you, you feel it extremely strongly: *I knew I was very near death, and a terrifying panic engulfed me.* **2** if a war/social change etc engulfs a place, it affects it so much that it changes completely: *a war that engulfed the whole of Europe* **3** to completely surround or cover something: *Thick white smoke engulfed the courtyard.* **4 be engulfed in flames** if a building is engulfed in flames, the whole building is burning

W3 **en·hance** /ɪn'hɑːns‖ɪn'hæns/ *v* [T] to improve something: *The flavor of most foods can be enhanced by good cooking.* —**enhancement** *n* [C,U] | *much needed enhancements*

**e·nig·ma** /ɪ'nɪgmə/ *n* [C] someone or something that is strange or mysterious and difficult to understand or explain: *The neighbours had come to regard him as something of an enigma.*

**en·ig·mat·ic** /ˌenɪg'mætɪk◂/ *adj* rather mysterious and difficult to understand or explain: *an enigmatic smile* —**enigmatically** /-kli/ *adv*: *"You'll find out soon enough," she said enigmatically.*

**en·join** /ɪn'dʒɔɪn/ *v* [T] **1** *formal* to order someone to do something **2** *AmE law* to legally prevent someone from going near a person or place

S1 W1 **en·joy** /ɪn'dʒɔɪ/ *v* [T] **1** to get pleasure from something: *Did you enjoy the movie?* | **enjoy doing sth** *Young children enjoy helping with household tasks.* **2** to have something good such as success or a particular ability or advantage: *These workers enjoy a high level of job security.* **3 enjoy yourself** to be happy and experience pleasure in a particular situation: *She was determined to enjoy herself at the party, even though her ex-boyfriend would be there.* **4 enjoy!** *AmE spoken* used when you give someone something and you want them to get pleasure from it: *Here's your steak – enjoy!*

> **USAGE NOTE: ENJOY**
> GRAMMAR
> **Enjoy** is nearly always followed by a noun phrase, a pronoun, or by a verb with *-ing*: *Did you enjoy the movie? Yes, I enjoyed it a lot* (NOT *I enjoyed with/of it*). | *I really enjoyed myself last night at the theater* (NOT *I enjoyed at the theater*). | *He enjoys travelling very much* (NOT *He enjoys very much travelling* or *He enjoys to travel*).

S3 **en·joy·a·ble** /ɪn'dʒɔɪəbəl/ *adj* something enjoyable gives you pleasure: *games to make learning more enjoyable* —**enjoyably** *adv*

**en·joy·ment** /ɪn'dʒɔɪmənt/ *n* **1** [U] the pleasure that you get from something: *Acting has brought me enormous enjoyment.* **2** [C] something that you enjoy doing; AMUSEMENT (2): *Golf and bridge were just some of his enjoyments.* **3** [U] *formal* the fact of having something

**en·large** /ɪn'lɑːdʒ‖-ɑːrdʒ/ *v* [I,T] to become bigger or to make something bigger: *We're planning to enlarge the garden.* | *Travel enlarges the mind.*

**enlarge on/upon** sth *phr v* [T] to provide more facts or details about something you have already mentioned: *Mrs Maughan did not enlarge on what she meant by 'unsuitable'.*

**en·large·ment** /ɪn'lɑːdʒmənt‖-ɑːr-/ *n* **1** [C] a photograph that has been printed again in a larger size **2** [C,U] an increase in size or amount

**en·lar·ger** /ɪn'lɑːdʒə‖-'lɑːrdʒər/ *n* [C] a piece of equipment for making photographs larger

**en·light·en** /ɪn'laɪtn/ *v* [T] *formal* to explain something to someone: *Baldwin enlightened her as to the nature of the experiment.* —**enlightening** *adj*: *an enlightening explanation*

**en·light·ened** /ɪn'laɪtənd/ *adj* **1** treating people in a kind and sensible way and understanding their needs and problems: *The more enlightened factory owners built homes for their workers in Britain in the 19th century.* **2** showing a good understanding of something and not believing things about it that are false: *enlightened opinions*

**En·light·en·ment** /ɪn'laɪtnmənt/ *n* **the Enlightenment** a period in the eighteenth century when many writers and scientists believed that science and knowledge, not religion, could improve people's lives

**enlightenment** *n* [U] **1** *formal* the state of understanding something clearly or the act of making someone understand something clearly **2** the state in the BUDDHIST and HINDU religions, of no longer having any human desires, so that you are united spiritually with the universe

**en·list** /ɪn'lɪst/ *v* **1 enlist sb's help** to persuade someone to help you: *I enlisted the help of a local artist to do a painting for her birthday.* **2** [I] to join the army, navy etc: *In the first year of the war a million men enlisted voluntarily.* —see JOIN[1] (USAGE) **3** [T + **in/into**] to persuade people to join your organization —**enlistment** *n* [C,U]

**enlisted man** /·'·· ·/ *n* [C] *AmE* **enlisted man/woman** someone in the army, navy etc whose rank is below that of an officer

**en·liv·en** /ɪn'laɪvən/ *v* [T] to make something more interesting or amusing: *a talk enlivened by photos*

**en masse** /ˌɒn 'mæs‖ˌɑːn-/ *adv French* if a group of people do something en masse, they all do it together: *The senior management resigned en masse.*

**en·meshed** /ɪn'meʃt/ *adj* [not before noun] very involved in an unpleasant or complicated situation: *Congress worried about becoming enmeshed in a foreign war.*

**en·mi·ty** /'enmɪ̣ti/ *n* [C,U] *formal* the feeling of hatred or anger towards someone: *We must try to remove the causes of distrust and enmity between the two communities.*

**en·no·ble** /ɪ'nəʊbəl‖ɪ'noʊ-/ *v* [T] *formal* **1** if something ennobles you it improves your character **2** to make someone a NOBLEMAN (=a member of the part of society that includes princes, DUKES etc) —**ennoblement** *n* [U]

**en·nui** /ɒn'wiː‖ɑːn-/ *n* [U] *French formal* a feeling of being tired and bored, especially as a result of having nothing to do

**e·nor·mi·ty** /ɪ'nɔːmɪ̣ti‖-ɔːr-/ *n* **1** [singular] the enormity of a situation, event etc is how serious it is or how big an effect it will have: *the enormity of his crimes* **2** [U] the enormity of a problem, subject, job etc is how large or difficult it is: *Don't be put off by the enormity of the task.* **3** [C] an extremely serious and cruel act

**e·nor·mous** /ɪ'nɔːməs‖-ɔːr-/ *adj* extremely large in size or in amount: *an enormous bouquet of flowers* | *The amount of paperwork involved is enormous.* —see graph at GREAT —**enormously** *adv*: *enormously fat* —**enormousness** *n* [U] S2 W3

**e·nough[1]** /ɪ'nʌf/ *adv* **1** to the necessary degree: *Her sentence was light because the judge said she had suffered enough already.* | *Are the carrots cooked enough?* **2 tall/kind/fast etc enough** as tall, kind, fast etc as is necessary: *I didn't bring a big enough bag.* | *Is your tea sweet enough?* | [+ **for**] *Is it warm enough for you?* | **mad/tall/silly etc enough to do sth** *Is the water hot enough for a bath?* | *He said he would never see her again and I was gullible enough to believe him.* | *Would you be kind enough to let us know when you are arriving?* | **not good enough** (=not satisfactory or acceptable) *I'm going to go up to that* S1 W1

E

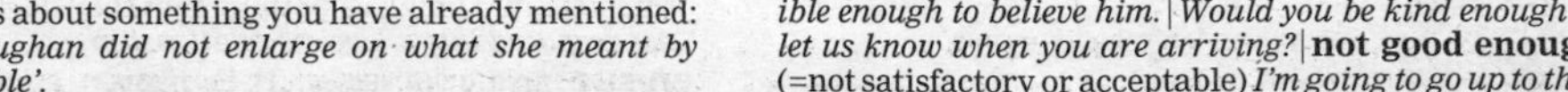

1 000, 2 000, 3 000 most frequent words in Spoken and Written English

*school and tell them it's just not good enough.* **3 difficult/happy/busy etc enough** rather difficult, happy etc: *I was happy enough in Bordeaux, but I missed my family.* | *It's bad enough doing this without you giving me orders all the time.* | *It was natural enough that she should be annoyed.* **4 strangely/oddly/curiously enough** although this is strange, odd etc: *Funnily enough, I bumped into her only yesterday.* **5 near enough** *BrE spoken* nearly: *Your jacket's near enough dry now.* | *This bottle's near enough finished.* | *That's £3000 near enough, isn't it?* —see also **fair enough** (FAIR[1] (17)), **sure enough** (SURE[2] (2))

S1 W2 **enough[2]** *determiner, pron* **1** as much or as many as may be necessary: *Move over, I don't have enough room.* | *Not enough is known about what really happened.* | *Leave the potatoes if you've had enough.* | [+ **for**] *There aren't enough chairs for everyone.* | **enough to do/eat etc** *Erica was worried that the children weren't getting enough to eat.* | **enough sth to do sth** *There's enough material left to make matching pillows.* | **more than enough** (=too much) *No, thank you, I've had more than enough.* | **not nearly enough/nowhere near enough** (=much less than enough) *There was nowhere near enough wine to go round.* | **that's enough** *spoken* (=stop behaving like that) *Now, David, that's quite enough – be a good boy.* | **enough is enough** *spoken* (=there is no need to say or do any more) *I could lend him another $20 but, really, enough's enough.* | **time/food etc enough**: *There'll be time enough to get to know each other later on.* **2 have had enough (of sth)** *spoken* to be thoroughly tired or sick of something and want it to stop: *When I got in from work I just sat down and cried. I'd had enough.* | *I've just about had enough of your sass.* **3 enough said** *spoken* there is no need to say any more, I understand everything: *"I saw her coming out of his room at 6 o'clock this morning." "Enough said."* —see ADEQUATE (USAGE)

**USAGE NOTE: ENOUGH**

GRAMMAR

**Enough** comes after adjectives and adverbs: *She's not old enough* (NOT *She's not enough old*). | *He didn't pack the bowls carefully enough and they broke.* | *Well I've done my best, and I hope it's good enough.*

**Enough** usually comes before a plural or uncountable noun: *enough people/money.* It is only used after the noun in slightly formal or old-fashioned English: *There was money enough for all.* However, *time enough* is still fairly common: *There'll be time enough for that later.*

**enough**

Joel wasn't tall enough to play.

There wasn't enough cake for everyone.

**en pas·sant** /ˌɒn ˈpæsɒn‖ˌɑːn pɑːˈsɑːn/ *adv French formal* if you say or mention something en passant, you say a few words about it while you are talking about something else: *She happened to mention en passant, that she'd seen Joan.*

**en·quire** /ɪnˈkwaɪə‖-ˈkwaɪr/ *v* [I,T] *especially BrE* another spelling of INQUIRE

**en·qui·ry** /ɪnˈkwaɪəri‖ˈɪŋkwəri, ɪnˈkwaɪri, ˈɪŋkwəri/ *n* [C,U] *especially BrE* another spelling of INQUIRY S3 W3

**en·rage** /ɪnˈreɪdʒ/ *v* [T] to make someone extremely angry: *She asked him to leave, enraged by his sexist comments.*

**en·rap·tured** /ɪnˈræptʃəd‖-ərd/ *adj formal* feeling such pleasure and happiness that you can think of nothing else: *The orchestra played before an enraptured audience.*

**en·rich** /ɪnˈrɪtʃ/ *v* [T] **1** to improve the quality of something, especially by adding things to it: *a fertilizer that enriches the soil* | *Education can enrich your life.* **2** to make someone richer —**enrichment** *n* [U]

**en·rol** *BrE*, **enroll** *AmE* /ɪnˈrəʊl‖-ˈroʊl/ *v* **enrolled, enrolling** [I,T] to officially arrange to join a school, university or course, or arrange for someone else to: [+ **on** *BrE*, + **in** *AmE*] *There were 500 people enrolled in the Western Civilization class.* —see JOIN[1] (USAGE) —**enrolment** *n* [C,U]

**Enrolled Nurse** /ˌ·ˌ· ˈ·/ *n* [C] a nurse who has passed an examination in England, Scotland, or Wales

**en route** /ˌɒn ˈruːt‖ˌɑːn-/ *adv French* on the way: *We were going to the Florida Keys but we stopped en route to visit Miami.* | [+ **from/for/to**] *a boat en route to the Bahamas*

**en·sconce** /ɪnˈskɒns‖ɪnˈskɑːns/ *v* [T] to put yourself in a comfortable and safe place: **ensconce yourself** *He ensconced himself in an armchair in front of the fire.* | *safely ensconced in the penthouse suite*

**en·sem·ble** /ɒnˈsɒmbəl‖ɑːnˈsɑːm-/ *n* **1** [C] a small group of musicians who play together regularly: *The ensemble will play an all-Bach program tonight.* **2** [C usually singular] a set of clothes that are worn together: *The leggings combined with a long black tunic made an attractive ensemble.* **3** [C usually singular] a set of things that go together to form a whole

**en·shrine** /ɪnˈʃraɪn/ *v* [T usually passive] *formal* if something such as a law, tradition, or right is enshrined in something, it is preserved, especially in written form, so that people will remember and respect it: **enshrine sth in** *Ancient practices and customs are enshrined in local folk literature.* | *inalienable rights enshrined in the Constitution*

**en·shroud** /ɪnˈʃraʊd/ *v* [T] *formal* **1** if something such as mystery enshrouds something, it makes it difficult to understand or explain: *corn circles and the mystery that enshrouds them* **2** to cover or hide something: *hills enshrouded in mist*

**en·sign** /ˈensaɪn, -sən‖ˈensən/ *n* [C] **1** a flag on a ship that shows what country the ship belongs to **2** a low rank in the US navy, or an officer who has this rank —see table on page B4 **3** an officer of low rank in the British army in the past **4** *AmE* a small piece of metal on your uniform that shows your rank

**en·slave** /ɪnˈsleɪv/ *v* [T usually passive] **1** *formal* to trap someone in a situation that they cannot easily escape from: *enslaved by marriage and trapped by taboos and prejudice* **2** to make someone into a slave —**enslavement** *n* [U]

**en·snare** /ɪnˈsneə‖-ˈsner/ *v* [T] *formal* to force or trick someone into doing something that they do not want to do: *ensnared into a loveless relationship*

**en·sue** /ɪnˈsjuː‖ɪnˈsuː/ *v* [I] to happen as a result of something: *Serious problems will ensue if something is not done about gang rivalry now.*

**en·su·ing** /ɪn'sjuːɪŋ‖-'suː-/ *adj* [only before noun] happening after a particular action or event, especially as a result of it: **the ensuing battle/argument/panic etc** *Japan attacked Port Arthur and in the ensuing Russo-Japanese war the Russians were defeated.* | **the ensuing year/six months/weeks etc** (=the time after an event)

**en suite** /ɒn 'swiːt◂‖ɑːn-/ *adj BrE* an en suite bathroom is joined onto a bedroom: *four bedrooms, two with en suite bathrooms*

S3 W1 **en·sure** *especially BrE* /ɪn'ʃʊə‖-'ʃʊr/ *v* [T] to make it certain that something will happen: *All the necessary steps had been taken to ensure their safety.* | [+ **that**] *His wife ensured that he took all his pills every day.* —compare INSURE —see INSURE (USAGE)

**-ent** /ənt/ *suffix* [in adjectives and nouns] another form of the suffix -ANT: *different* | *residents*

**en·tail** /ɪn'teɪl/ *v* [T] **1** to make it necessary to do something: *Changing the computer system would entail substantial periods of re-training.* | **entail doing sth** *My job entailed being on call 24 hours a day.* **2** *old use* to arrange for your property to become the property of a particular person, especially your son, after your death

**en·tan·gle** /ɪn'tæŋgəl/ *v* [T always + adv/prep] to make something become twisted or caught in a rope, net etc

**en·tan·gled** /ɪn'tæŋgəld/ *adj* **1** involved in an argument, or a situation that is difficult to escape from, or a relationship that causes problems etc: [+ **in**] *Military observers fear that the US could get entangled in another Vietnam.* | [+ **with**] *Sue became romantically entangled with a work colleague.* **2** twisted or caught in something such as a rope or net: [+ **in/with**] *Penguins and seals have been found entangled in lengths of fishing net.*

**en·tan·gle·ment** /ɪn'tæŋgəlmənt/ *n* [C] **1** a difficult situation or relationship that is hard to escape from: *emotional entanglements* **2** [C often plural] a fence made of BARBED WIRE that prevents enemy soldiers from getting too close

**entendre** *n* —see DOUBLE ENTENDRE

**en·tente** /ɒn'tɒnt‖ɑːn'tɑːnt/ *n* [C,U] *French* a situation in which two countries have friendly relations with each other

S1 W1 **en·ter** /'entə‖-ər/ *v*

**1** ▶ **GO INTO** ◀ **a)** [I,T] to go or come into a place: *Silence fell as I entered the room.* | *Adie was one of the few reporters who had dared to enter the war zone.* **b)** [T] if an object enters part of something, it goes inside it: *The bullet had entered his brain through the back of his skull.*

**2** ▶ **START WORKING** ◀ [I,T] to start working in a particular profession or organization: *Andrea is studying law as a preparation for entering politics.* | *He entered the Church as a young man.*

**3** ▶ **START TO TAKE PART IN** ◀ [T] to start to take part in an activity, for example a course or a game: *Her doctor recommended that she enter a drug treatment program.*

**4** ▶ **COMPUTER** ◀ [T] **a)** to put information into a computer by pressing the keys: *If a command is entered incorrectly, the machine will not recognize it.* **b)** if you enter a computer system, you are given permission to use it by the computer

**5** ▶ **WRITE INFORMATION** ◀ [T] to write information on a particular part of a form, document etc: *Enter your name in the space provided.*

**6** ▶ **COMPETITION/EXAMINATION** ◀ [I,T] to arrange to take part in a race, competition, examination etc, or to arrange for someone else to take part: *I've entered you and Dan in the sack race.*

**7** ▶ **PERIOD OF TIME** ◀ [T] **a)** to begin a period of time when something happens: *The economy entered a period of recession in the mid 1980s.* **b) enter its third week/sixth day/second year etc** if something enters its third week, its sixth day etc, it continues for a third week, a sixth day etc: *The talks have now entered their third week.*

**8 it never entered my mind/head** *spoken* used when you are very surprised by what has happened: *It never entered my head that he would have a gun.*

**9** ▶ **CHANGE** ◀ [T] if a particular quality enters something, it starts to exist in it and change it, especially suddenly: *A note of panic entered her voice.*

**10 enter sb's life** if someone or something enters your life, you start to know them or be affected by them: *By the time Angie entered his life, he was almost 30.*

**11** ▶ **START DISCUSSING** ◀ [T] to start to discuss or study a particular subject: *Here we enter a disputed and delicate area of the law.*

**12 enter a plea of guilty/not guilty** *law* to say that you are guilty or not guilty of a particular crime in a court

**13 enter an offer/complaint/objection etc** *formal* to officially make an offer, complaint etc

**enter into sth** *phr v* [T] **1** to start doing something, especially discussing or studying something: *This is not the place to enter into a detailed discussion of economic policy.* **2** to affect a situation and be something that you must consider when you make a choice: *Money doesn't enter into it – it's the principle I object to.* **3 enter into an agreement/contract etc** *formal* to officially make an agreement to do something **4 enter into the spirit of it/things** to take part in a game, party etc in an eager way

**enter upon sth** *phr v* [T] *formal* to start doing something or being involved in it

Frequencies of **enter** and **go/come in** in spoken and written English.

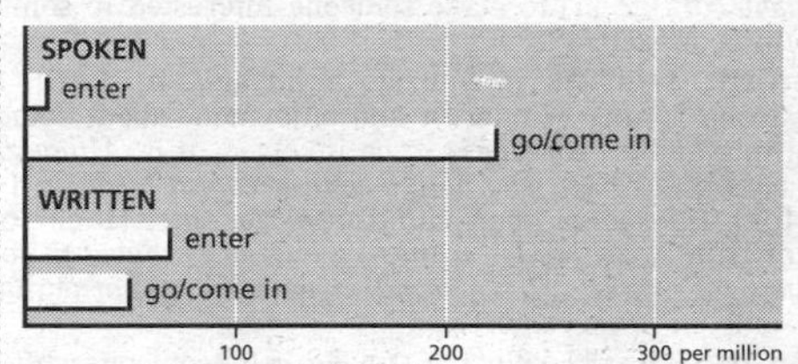


Based on the British National Corpus and the Longman Lancaster Corpus

This graph shows that it is much more usual in spoken English to use the expressions **go in** and **come in**, rather than the word **enter**. This is because **enter** is a formal word when used in this meaning and is more common in written English.

**en·te·ri·tis** /ˌentə'raɪtɪ̈s/ *n* [U] a painful infection in your INTESTINES

**en·ter·prise** /'entəpraɪz‖-ər-/ *n* **1** [C] a large and complicated piece of work, especially one that is done with a group of other people: *a joint scientific enterprise* **2** [U] the ability to think of new activities or ideas and make them work: *a woman with enterprise and creativity* **3** [C] a company, organization, or business: *state-owned enterprises* **4** [U] the practice of starting and running small companies: *a knowledge of American capitalist enterprise* —see also FREE ENTERPRISE, PRIVATE ENTERPRISE W2

**enterprise cul·ture** /'··· ˌ··/ *n* [C,U] a society or attitude in which starting successful businesses is believed to be very important

**en·ter·pris·ing** /'entəpraɪzɪŋ‖-tər-/ *adj* showing the ability to think of new activities or ideas and make them work: *An enterprising young student was selling copies of the answers to the test.* —**enterprisingly** *adv*

**en·ter·tain** /ˌentə'teɪn‖-tər-/ *v* **1** [I,T] to invite people to your home for a meal or party or take your company's customers to have a meal, drinks etc: *The restaurant is mainly used by executives entertaining clients.* **2** [T] to do something that amuses or interests people: **entertain sb with** *He entertained us with a stream of anecdotes about the Yukon.* **3 entertain an idea/hope/doubt**

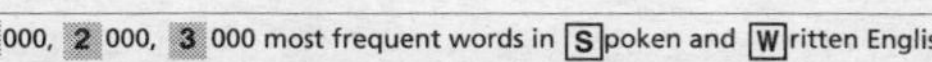
1 000, 2 000, 3 000 most frequent words in S poken and W ritten English

etc to think that something might be true, even for a short period of time

**en·ter·tain·er** /ˌentəˈteɪnə‖-tərˈteɪnər/ *n* [C] someone who tells jokes, sings etc to amuse people: *street entertainers*

**en·ter·tain·ing¹** /ˌentəˈteɪnɪŋ◂‖-tər-/ *adj* amusing and interesting: *very entertaining storyteller|an entertaining evening*

**entertaining²** *n* [U] the practice of inviting people for meals or to parties, especially for business reasons

S3 **en·ter·tain·ment** /ˌentəˈteɪnmənt‖-tər-/ *n* **1** [U] things such as films, television, performances etc that amuse or interest people: *providing entertainment for tourists* **2** [C] a performance or show: *a musical entertainment*

**en·thral** also **enthrall** *especially AmE* /ɪnˈθrɔːl‖-ˈθrɒl/ *v* [T] to make someone so interested and excited that they listen or watch something very carefully

**en·thralled** /ɪnˈθrɔːld‖-ˈθrɒːld/ *adj* so interested that you pay a lot of attention to what you are seeing or hearing: *Richard listened, enthralled by the Captain's stories.*

**en·thrall·ing** /ɪnˈθrɔːlɪŋ‖-ˈθrɒːl-/ *adj* extremely interesting

**en·throne** /ɪnˈθrəʊn‖-ˈθroʊn/ *v* [T usually passive] to have a ceremony to show that a new king or queen is beginning to rule —**enthronement** *n* [C,U]

**en·thuse** /ɪnˈθjuːz‖ɪnˈθuːz/ *v* **1** [I] to talk about something in a very interested or excited way: **[+ about/over]** *Jenny spent the entire evening enthusing about her new car.* **2** [T] to make someone interested in something or excited by it

W3 **en·thu·si·as·m** /ɪnˈθjuːziæzəm‖ɪnˈθuː-/ *n* **1** [U] a strong feeling of interest and enjoyment about something and an eagerness to be involved in it: *Although she's a beginner, she played with great enthusiasm*|**[+ for]** *He shares your enthusiasm for jazz.*|**lack of enthusiasm** *the government's lack of enthusiasm for women's rights* **2** [C] *formal* an activity or subject that someone is very interested in

**en·thu·si·ast** /ɪnˈθjuːziæst‖ɪnˈθuː-/ *n* [C] someone who is very interested in a particular activity or subject: *a golfing enthusiast*

S3 **en·thu·si·as·tic** /ɪnˌθjuːziˈæstɪk◂‖-ˌθuː-/ *adj* showing a lot of interest and excitement about something: *The singer got an enthusiastic reception.*|**[+ about]** *I was less than enthusiastic about the idea of Bob coming to visit.* —**enthusiastically** /-kli/ *adv*

**en·tice** /ɪnˈtaɪs/ *v* [T] to persuade someone to do something by offering them something if they will do it: **entice sb away/across/down etc** *He tried to entice the dog away from its post by the door.*|**entice sb** *Banks are offering low interest rates in an attempt to entice new customers.* —**enticement** *n* [C,U]

**en·ti·cing** /ɪnˈtaɪsɪŋ/ *adj* very pleasant or interesting so that you feel strongly attracted: *It was a hot day and the water looked enticing.* —**enticingly** *adv*

S3 W2 **en·tire** /ɪnˈtaɪə‖-ˈtaɪr/ *adj* [only before noun] the entire group, amount, period of time etc is used when you want to emphasize what you are saying: *the entire staff|We spent the entire afternoon gossiping.*

S2 W2 **en·tire·ly** /ɪnˈtaɪəli‖-ˈtaɪr-/ *adv* completely and in every possible way: *an entirely different matter|She devoted herself entirely to her research.*|**consist/depend entirely etc** *The programme consists entirely of taped interviews with survivors of the Holocaust.*

**en·tir·e·ty** /ɪnˈtaɪərʒti‖-ˈtaɪr-/ *n* [U] **in its/their entirety** *formal* as a whole and including every part: *The correspondence has been published in its entirety for the first time.*

S2 W2 **en·ti·tle** /ɪnˈtaɪtl/ *v* [T] **1** if something entitles you to something, it gives you the official right to have or do it: **be entitled to sth** *Mothers under 16 were entitled to a maternity grant of £25 a week.* **2 be entitled sth** if a book, play etc is entitled something, that is its name: *an autobiography entitled "Myself, My Two Countries"* **3 be entitled to do something** *Ricardo believes his daughter is perfectly entitled to marry whoever she chooses.*

**en·ti·tle·ment** /ɪnˈtaɪtlmənt/ *n* [C,U] the official right to have or receive something, or the amount that you receive: *welfare entitlements*|**[+ to]** *The amount of money you earn does not affect your entitlement to child benefit.*

**en·ti·ty** /ˈentʒti/ *n* [C] *formal* something that exists as a single and complete unit: *The mind and body are seen as separate entities.*

**en·tomb** /ɪnˈtuːm/ *v* [T often in passive] *formal* to bury or trap someone under the ground

**en·to·mol·o·gy** /ˌentəˈmɒlədʒi‖-ˈmɑː-/ *n* [U] the scientific study of insects —**entomologist** *n* [C] —**entomological** /ˌentəməˈlɒdʒɪkəl◂‖-ˈlɑː-/ *adj*

**en·tou·rage** /ˈɒntʊrɑːʒ‖ˈɑːn-/ *n* [C usually singular, also + plural verb *BrE*] a group of people who travel with an important person: *the popstar and her entourage*

**en·trails** /ˈentreɪlz/ *n* [plural] the inside parts of an animal or person's body, especially their BOWELS

**en·trance** /ˈentrəns/ *n* **1** [C] a door, gate etc that you go through to enter a place: **[+ to/of]** *the main entrance to the school* —opposite EXIT¹ **2** [C usually singular] the act of entering a place or room: *Their conversation was interrupted by the entrance of four visitors.* **3** [U] permission to become a member of or become involved in a profession, university, society etc: *entrance examinations*|**gain entrance to** *By some chance he gained entrance to the Indian Civil Service.* **4** [U] the right or ability to go into a place: *entrance fees*|**gain entrance to** *No one is sure how the men gained entrance to the factory.* **5 make your/an entrance a)** to come on to the stage in a play: *The hero doesn't make his entrance until Act II, Scene 2.* **b)** to enter a room, especially in a way that makes everyone notice you: *Lady Elizabeth made a noisy entrance.* S3 W3

**en·tranced** /ɪnˈtrɑːnst‖-ˈtrænst/ *adj* very interested in and pleased with something so that you pay a lot of attention to it: *entranced by the sweetness of her voice* —**entrance** *v* [T]

**en·tran·cing** /ɪnˈtrɑːnsɪŋ‖-ˈtræns-/ *adj* very interesting and attractive

**en·trant** /ˈentrənt/ *n* [C] *formal* someone entering a competition, university, or profession: *The winning entrant will receive a £500 scholarship.*

**en·trap** /ɪnˈtræp/ *v* [T] *formal* to trap someone, especially by tricking or deceiving them: *cunning and devious questions intended to entrap her*

**en·trap·ment** /ɪnˈtræpmənt/ *n* [U] the practice of trapping someone by tricking them, especially to show that they are guilty of a crime

**en·treat** /ɪnˈtriːt/ *v* [T] *formal* to ask someone to do something for you in a way that shows you are very upset

**en·trea·ty** /ɪnˈtriːti/ *n* [C,U] *formal* a serious request in which you ask someone to do something for you

**en·trée** /ˈɒntreɪ‖ˈɑːn-/ *n French* **1** [C] the main dish of a meal **2** [C,U] *formal* the right or freedom to enter a place or to join a group of people: **[+ to/into]** *The letter provided an easy entrée to the court at Turin.*

**en·trenched** /ɪnˈtrentʃt/ *adj* strongly established and not likely to change: **entrenched attitudes/habits/positions etc** *The government's attitude now seems less entrenched.*|**deeply/firmly entrenched** *deeply entrenched racial views*

**en·trench·ment** /ɪnˈtrentʃmənt/ *n* **1** [U] the process in which an attitude, belief etc becomes firmly established **2** [C] a system of TRENCHES (=long deep holes) dug by soldiers for defence or protection

**en·tre nous** /ˌɒntrə ˈnuː‖ˌɑːn-/ *adv French spoken* an expression used to tell someone that what you are going to say is secret and they must not tell anyone else

**en·tre·pre·neur** /ˌɒntrəprəˈnɜː‖ˌɑːntrəprəˈnɜːr/ *n* [C]

someone who starts a company, arranges business deals, and takes risks in order to make a profit —**entrepreneurial** *adj*: *entrepreneurial skills*

**en·tro·py** /ˈentrəpi/ *n* [U] *technical* a measure of the lack of order in a system, that includes the idea that the lack of order increases over a period of time

**en·trust, intrust** /ɪnˈtrʌst/ *v* [T] to make someone responsible for doing something important: **entrust sb with sth** *I was entrusted with the task of looking after the money.* | **entrust sth to sb** *The infant Prince was entrusted to an English nurse, Miss Shaw.*

2 2 **en·try** /ˈentri/ *n*
**1** ▶ **COMPETITION** ◀ [C] **a)** a set of answers, a song or picture etc that is intended to win a competition: *Over a thousand entries were received within the first week of the competition.* **b)** [usually singular] the number of people or things taking part in a competition: *We've attracted a record entry this year.*
**2** ▶ **BECOMING INVOLVED** ◀ [C,U] a situation in which someone starts to take part in a system, a particular kind of work etc, or joins a group of people: *the entry of women into the paid labour force* | **gain entry** (=become involved) *The Eastern European countries hope to gain entry to the European Union by the end of the century.*
**3** ▶ **RIGHT TO ENTER** ◀ [U] the right to enter a place, building etc: *an entry visa* | **no entry** (=a phrase written on signs to show that you are not allowed to go into a place or through a particular door)
**4** ▶ **ACT OF ENTERING** ◀ [C,U] the act of going into something: [+ **into**] *the triumphal entry of the Russian army into the city* | **gain entry** (=get into a place, especially when this is difficult or illegal) *The thieves gained entry through an open kitchen window.*
**5** ▶ **DOOR** ◀ [C] a door, gate, or passage that you go through to enter a place —see also ENTRANCE[1] (1)
**6** ▶ **STH WRITTEN** ◀ [C] a short piece of writing in an ENCYCLOPAEDIA, DIARY etc: *The journal's last few entries described the events vividly.*
**7** ▶ **COMPUTER** ◀ [U] the act of writing of information onto a computer: *data entry*

**en·try·phone** /ˈentrifəʊn‖-foʊn/ *n* [C] a type of telephone outside a building that allows visitors to ask someone inside to open the door

**en·try·way** /ˈentriweɪ/ *n* [C] *AmE* a passage or small room you go through to enter a place

**en·twine** /ɪnˈtwaɪn/ *v* [I,T often passive] **1** to twist two things together or to wind one thing around another: *They walked together with their arms entwined.* **2 be entwined** to be closely connected with each other in a complicated way: *The meaning of art and the meaning of life are almost inextricably entwined.*

**E num·ber** /ˈiː ˌnʌmbə‖-ər/ *n* [C] *BrE* a number representing a chemical that has been added to a food, shown on the outside of a container

**e·nu·me·rate** /ɪˈnjuːməreɪt‖ɪˈnuː-/ *v* [T] *formal* to name a list of things one by one

**e·nun·ci·ate** /ɪˈnʌnsieɪt/ *v* **1** [I,T] to pronounce words clearly and carefully —see also ARTICULATE[2] (2) **2** [T] *formal* to express an idea clearly and exactly: *the theory Darwin was to enunciate decades later* —**enunciation** /ɪˌnʌnsiˈeɪʃən/ *n* [U]

**e·nure** /ɪˈnjʊə‖ɪˈnjʊr/ *v* [T] another spelling of INURE

**en·vel·op** /ɪnˈveləp/ *v* [T] to wrap something up or cover it completely: *mountain peaks enveloped in thick mist* —**enveloping** *adj* —**envelopment** *n* [U]

3 **en·ve·lope** /ˈenvələʊp‖-loʊp/ *n* [C] **1** a thin paper cover in which you put a letter **2** a layer of something that surrounds something else: [+ **of**] *an envelope of gases around the planet*

**en·vi·a·ble** /ˈenviəbəl/ *adj* an enviable quality, position, or possession is good and other people would like to have it: *Now he was in the enviable position of not having to work for a living.* —**enviably** *adv*

**en·vi·ous** /ˈenviəs/ *adj* wanting something that someone else has: *an envious look* | [+ **of**] *Her colleagues were envious of her success.* —see also JEALOUS —**enviously** *adv*

**en·vi·ron·ment** /ɪnˈvaɪərənmənt‖-ˈvaɪr-/ *n* [C,U] **1** all the situations, events, people etc that influence the way in which people live or work: *a helpful learning environment* | *a more competitive economic environment* **2 the environment** the air, water, and land in which people, animals, and plants live: *More legislation is needed to protect the environment.* —see also ECOLOGY S1 W1

**en·vi·ron·ment·al** /ɪnˌvaɪərənˈmentl◂‖-ˌvaɪr-/ *adj* concerning or affecting the air, land, or water on Earth: *the environmental damage caused by the chemical industry* —**environmentally** *adv* S1 W2

**en·vi·ron·men·tal·ist** /ɪnˌvaɪərənˈmentəlɪst‖-ˌvaɪr-/ *n* [C] someone who is concerned about protecting the environment —**environmentalism** *n* [U]

**environmentally friend·ly** /·ˌ····· ˈ··◂/ also **environment friendly** /···ˌ··· ˈ··/ *adj* soaps, containers etc that are environmentally friendly do not harm the environment

**en·vi·rons** /ˈenvɪrənz, ɪnˈvaɪərənz‖ɪnˈvaɪrənz/ *n* [plural] *formal* the area surrounding a place: *Geneva and its immediate environs*

**en·vis·age** /ɪnˈvɪzɪdʒ/ also **en·vi·sion** *AmE* /ɪnˈvɪʒən/ *v* [T] to imagine that something will happen in the future: *I don't envisage any major problems.*

**en·voy** /ˈenvɔɪ/ *n* [C] someone who is sent to another country as an official representative: *A special envoy was sent to try to secure the release of the hostages.*

**en·vy**[1] /ˈenvi/ *v* **envied, envying** [T] to wish that you had someone else's possessions, abilities etc: *Evelyn was good-looking, rich, and intelligent – all the girls envied her.* | **envy sb (for) sth** *He envied Rosalind for her youth and strength.* —compare JEALOUS

**envy**[2] *n* [U] **1** the feeling of wanting something that someone else has: *He stared with envy at Robert's new car.* | **green with envy** (=envying someone a lot) **2 be the envy of** to be something that other people admire and want to have very much: *Britain's National Health Service was once the envy of the world.* —compare JEALOUSY

**en·zyme** /ˈenzaɪm/ *n* [C] *technical* a chemical substance produced by living cells in plants and animals, that causes changes in other chemical substances without being changed itself: *the digestive enzymes in your stomach*

**e·on** /ˈiːən/ *n* [C] another spelling of AEON

**ep·au·let, epaulette** /ˌepəˈlet/ *n* [C] a small piece of cloth decorating the shoulder of a coat or shirt, especially on a uniform

**é·pée** /ˈepeɪ/ *n* [C] *French* a narrow sword with a sharp point, used in the sport of FENCING (1)

**e·phem·e·ra** /ɪˈfemərə/ *n* [plural] things that are only popular or important for a short time: *records, pictures of pop-stars, and other such ephemera*

**e·phem·e·ral** /ɪˈfemərəl/ *adj* popular or important for only a short time: *Fashions are by nature fickle and ephemeral.* —**ephemerally** *adv*

**ep·ic**[1] /ˈepɪk/ *n* [C] **1** a book, poem, or film that tells a long story: *Universal Pictures' dinosaur epic "Jurassic Park"* **2** a long poem that tells the story of what gods or important people did in ancient times: *Homer's epic "Iliad"*

**epic**[2] *adj* **1** epic stories or poems are full of brave actions and events: *Phileas Fogg's epic journey around the world* **2** very big or impressive: **of epic proportions** *They organized a banquet of epic proportions.*

**ep·i·cen·tre** *BrE*, **epicenter** *AmE* /ˈepɪˌsentə‖-ər/ *n* [C] a place on the surface of the Earth that is above the point where an EARTHQUAKE begins inside the Earth

**ep·i·cure** /ˈepɪkjʊə‖-kjʊr/ *n* [C] *formal* someone who enjoys good food and drink; GOURMET

**ep·i·cu·re·an** /ˌepɪkjʊˈriːən◂/ *adj formal* gaining pleasure from the senses, especially through good food and drink —**epicurean** *n* [C]

**ep·i·dem·ic** /ˌepɪ̵ˈdemɪk◂/ *n* [C] **1** a large number of cases of a particular infectious disease occuring at the same time: *a flu epidemic.* **2** a sudden increase in the amount of times that something bad happens: *the recent epidemic of car thefts* —**epidemic** *adj*: *Violence is reaching epidemic proportions in the inner cities.*

**ep·i·der·mis** /ˌepɪ̵ˈdɜːmɪ̵s‖-ɜːr-/ *n* [C,U] *technical* the outside layer of your skin

**ep·i·dur·al** /ˌepɪˈdjuːrəl◂‖-ˈduː-/ *n* [C] a medical process in which a drug is put into your lower back to prevent you feeling pain, especially when you are having a baby

**ep·i·glot·tis** /ˌepɪ̵ˈglɒtɪ̵s‖-ˈglɑː-/ *n* [C] a thin piece of flesh at the back of your throat —see picture at RESPIRATORY

**ep·i·gram** /ˈepɪ̵græm/ *n* [C] a short sentence that expresses an idea in a clever or amusing way

**ep·i·gram·mat·ic** /ˌepɪ̵grəˈmætɪk◂/ *adj* expressed in a way that is short, clever, and amusing —**epigrammatically** /-kli/ *adv*

**ep·i·lep·sy** /ˈepɪ̵lepsi/ *n* [U] a medical condition in the brain that can suddenly make you become unconscious or unable to control your movements

**ep·i·lep·tic**[1] /ˌepɪ̵ˈleptɪk◂/ *adj* caused by epilepsy: *an epileptic fit*

**epileptic**[2] *u* [C] someone who has epilepsy

E

**ep·i·logue** also **epilog** *AmE* /ˈepɪ̵lɒg‖-lɔːg, -lɑːg/ *n* **1** [C] a speech or piece of writing added to the end of a book, film, or play **2** [singular] *literary* something that happens at the end of a series of events —compare PROLOGUE

**E·piph·a·ny** /ɪˈpɪfəni/ *n* [not with *the*] a Christian holy day on January 6th that celebrates the Three Kings coming to see the baby Jesus

**epiphany** *n* [C] *literary* a moment of sudden very strong emotions

**e·pis·co·pa·cy** /ɪˈpɪskəpəsi/ also **e·pis·co·pate** /ɪˈpɪskəpət/ *n* [U] *technical* **1** the rank of a BISHOP (=a priest of high rank in charge of a large area) , or the time during which someone is bishop **2** all the bishops, or the system of the church government by bishops

**e·pis·co·pal** /ɪˈpɪskəpəl/ *adj* **1** connected with a BISHOP **2** an episcopal church is governed by BISHOPS

**Episcopal Church** /·ˌ··· ˈ·/ *n* [singular] a PROTESTANT church in the US that developed from the Anglican Church

**E·pis·co·pa·li·an** /ɪˌpɪskəˈpeɪliən◂/ *n* [C] a member of an episcopal church —**Episcopalian** *adj*

**ep·i·sode** /ˈepɪ̵səud‖-soud/ *n* [C] **1** an event or a short period of time during which something specific happened: *one of the saddest episodes in his tormented life* **2** a television or radio programme that is one of a series of programmes telling one story: *Watch next week's thrilling episode!*

**ep·i·sod·ic** /ˌepɪ̵ˈsɒdɪk◂‖-ˈsɑː-/ *adj formal* **1** happening at times that are not regular: *episodic headaches* **2** consisting of many different parts when different things happen: *an episodic account of how a group of humble people are affected by the war* —**episodically** /-kli/ *adv*

**E·pis·tle** /ɪˈpɪsəl/ *n* [C] one of the letters written by the first Christians which are in the New Testament of the Bible

**epistle** *n* [C] *formal* a long or important letter

**e·pis·to·la·ry** /ɪˈpɪstələri‖-təleri/ *adj formal* written in the form of a series of letters: *an epistolary novel*

**ep·i·taph** /ˈepɪ̵tɑːf‖-tæf/ *n* [C] a short piece of writing on the stone over someone's grave

**ep·i·thet** /ˈepɪ̵θet/ *n* [C] an adjective or short phrase used to describe someone, especially when praising or blaming them: *He hardly deserves the epithet 'fascist'.*

**e·pit·o·me** /ɪˈpɪtəmi/ *n* **the epitome of** the best possible example of something: *Jan's behaviour seemed to me to be the very epitome of selfishness.*

**e·pit·o·mize** also **-ise** *BrE* /ɪˈpɪtəmaɪz/ *v* [T] to be a very typical example of something: *This fiasco epitomizes the lack of regulation in the industry.*

**e·poch** /ˈiːpɒk‖ˈepək/ *n* [C] a period of history, especially one in which important events take place: *the beginning of a new epoch in the history of mankind*

**epoch-mak·ing** /ˈ·· ˌ··/ *adj* very important in changing or developing people's lives

**e·pon·y·mous** /ɪˈpɒnɪ̵məs‖ɪˈpɑː-/ *adj technical* the eponymous character in a book, film, or play is the character whose name forms its title: *Hester, the book's eponymous heroine* —**eponymously** *adv*

**e·pox·y res·in** /ɪˌpɒksi ˈrezɪ̵n‖ɪˌpɑː-/ *n* [U] a type of RESIN used as a glue

**Ep·som salts** /ˌepsəm ˈsɔːlts‖-ˈsɒːlts/ *n* [plural,U] a white powder that can be mixed with water and used as a kind of medicine

**Ep·stein-Barr vi·rus** /ˌepstaɪn ˈbɑː ˌvaɪərəs‖-ˈbɑːr ˌvaɪr-/ also **EBV** *n* [U] *AmE* an illness that makes you feel very tired and weak and can last for a long period of time; ME *BrE*

**eq·ua·ble** /ˈekwəbəl/ *adj* **1** *formal* calm and not easily annoyed: *Mary's equable temperament made her easy to work with.* **2** *technical* having weather or conditions that are neither too hot nor too cold: *an equable climate* —**equably** *adv* —**equability** /ˌekwəˈbɪlɪ̵ti/ *n* [U]

**e·qual**[1] /ˈiːkwəl/ *adj* S W
**1** ▶ **SAME** ◀ the same in size, value, amount, number etc as something else: *Jennifer cut the cake into six equal pieces.* | [+ **to**] *A pound is roughly equal to 500 grams.* | **of equal power/strength/weight** *Choose two stones of roughly equal weight and size.*
**2** ▶ **SAME RIGHTS/CHANCES** ◀ having the same rights, opportunities etc as everyone else, whatever your race, religion, or sex: *Our constitution states that all men are equal.* | **equal opportunities** (=the same chances of employment, pay etc for everyone) *This company is an equal opportunity employer.* | **equal rights** (=the same rights for everyone) *a clear statement guaranteeing equal rights for women*
**3** ▶ **BE ABLE** ◀ **be equal to** to have the ability to deal with a problem, piece of work etc successfully: *I'm sure Barbara's quite equal to the task.*
**4** ▶ **AS GOOD AS** ◀ having as high a standard or quality as something else: *religious architecture equal to any in the world*
**5 on equal terms** with neither side having any advantage over the other: *a new law to enable small businesses to compete on equal terms with large multinational corporations*
**6 all (other) things being equal** *spoken* used when saying what you would normally choose, unless there were special facts to consider: *I'd rather go by train, all other things being equal.*

**equal**[2] *v* **equalled, equalling** *BrE*, **equaled, equaling** *AmE* **1** [linking verb] to be exactly the same in size, number, or amount as something else: *Two plus two equals four.* | *Trade should balance when supply equals demand.* **2** [T] to be as good as or get to the same standard as someone or something else: *Thompson equalled the world record.* **3** [T] to produce a particular result or effect: *A highly-trained workforce equals high productivity.* S

**equal**[3] *n* [C] **1** someone who is as important, intelligent etc as you are, or who has the same rights and opportunities as you do: *It's a relief to find a boss who treats employees as equals.* **2 be without equal** also **have no equal** *formal* to be better than everyone or everything else of the same type: *His paintings are without equal in the Western world.* S

**e·qual·i·ty** /ɪˈkwɒlɪ̵ti‖ɪˈkwɑː-/ *n* [U] a position or situation in which people have the same rights, advantages etc: *Women have yet to achieve full equality with men in the work-place.* | **racial/sexual equality** (=equality between all races or between men and women)

**e·qual·ize** also **-ise** *BrE* /ˈiːkwəlaɪz/ *v* **1** [T] to make two or more things the same in size, value, amount etc **2** [I] *BrE* to get a point in a game, especially football, so that you have the same number of points as your opponent; TIE² (2) *AmE*: *England equalized a few minutes before the end of the game.* —**equalization** /ˌiːkwəlaɪˈzeɪʃən‖-lə-/ *n* [U]

**e·qual·iz·er** /ˈiːkwəlaɪzə‖-ər/ *n* [C] **1** *BrE* a GOAL (2) that makes the points of each team in a game equal **2** *AmE slang* a gun

S2 W2 **e·qual·ly** /ˈiːkwəli/ *adv* **1** [+ adj/adv] to the same degree or amount: *An equally acceptable solution could surely be found elsewhere.* **2** in equal parts or amounts: *We try to divide the work equally.* **3** [sentence adverb] used when introducing a second idea or statement that is as important as your first one: *I want to encourage her to do well, but equally I don't want to make her feel pressurized.*

**equals sign** /ˈ·· ·/ *BrE* **equal sign** *AmE* —*n* [C] a sign used in mathematics to show that two things are the same size, number, or amount: *In the equation x=y, x is to the left of the equals sign.*

**eq·ua·nim·i·ty** /ˌiːkwəˈnɪmɨti, ˌekwə-/ *n* [U] *formal* calmness, especially in the way that you react to things: *He received the news with surprising equanimity.*

**e·quate** /ɪˈkweɪt/ *v* [T] to consider that two or more things are similar or connected: **equate sth with** *Some people equate nationalism with fascism.*

W3 **e·qua·tion** /ɪˈkweɪʒən/ *n* **1** [C] a statement in mathematics, showing that two quantities are equal: *In the equation 2x + 1 = 7, what is x?* **2** [C] **enter into the equation/be part of the equation** to be a fact that affects a particular problem, situation, idea etc: *We hadn't realized that cost would enter into the equation at all.* **3** [singular] the act of equating two things

**e·qua·tor, Equator** /ɪˈkweɪtə‖-ər/ *n* [singular, U] an imaginary line drawn around the middle of the Earth that is exactly the same distance from the North Pole and the South Pole —see picture at EARTH¹

**eq·ua·to·ri·al** /ˌekwəˈtɔːriəl◂/ *adj* **1** connected with or near the equator: *the equatorial rainforest* **2** very hot and wet: *an equatorial climate*

**e·quer·ry** /ɪˈkweri, ˈekwəri‖ˈekwəri/ *n* [C] a male official in a royal court, who serves a member of the royal family

**e·ques·tri·an** /ɪˈkwestriən/ *adj* connected with horse riding: *equestrian events* —**equestrian** *n* [C]

**equi-** /ekwɨ, iːkwɨ/ *prefix* equal or equally: *equidistant* | *an equilateral triangle* (=with equal sides)

**e·qui·dis·tant** /ˌiːkwɨˈdɪstənt◂/ *adj* at an equal distance from or between two places

**e·qui·lat·e·ral tri·an·gle** /ˌiːkwɨlætərəl ˈtraɪæŋgəl/ *n* [C] *technical* a TRIANGLE (1) whose three sides are all the same length —see picture at SHAPE¹

**e·qui·lib·ri·um** /ˌiːkwɨˈlɪbriəm/ *n* [singular, U] **1** a balance between opposing forces or influences: *They were anxious not to upset the trading equilibrium.* **2** a calm balance of emotions, attitudes, feelings etc: *Setting up a home helped to re-establish some kind of equilibrium in her life.*

**eq·uine** /ˈekwaɪn, ˈiː-/ *adj* connected with horses, or looking like a horse

**eq·ui·noc·tial** /ˌiːkwɨˈnɒkʃəl◂, ˌe-‖-ˈnɑːk-/ *adj* connected with the equinox

**eq·ui·nox** /ˈiːkwɨnɒks, ˈe-‖-nɑːks/ *n* [C] one of the two times in a year when all places in the world have a day and night of equal length —compare SOLSTICE

**e·quip** /ɪˈkwɪp/ *v* **equipped, equipping** [T] **1** to provide a person, group, building etc with the things that are needed for a particular kind of activity or work: **equip sb with** *The boys equipped themselves with torches and rope, and set off.* | **be equipped to do sth** *The emergency services are equipped to deal with disasters of this kind.* | **equip sb/sth** *It cost $100,000 to equip the gym.* | **well/poorly/fully etc equipped** *It was a modern, bright, well equipped hospital.* **2** if education or training equips you to do something, it prepares you and makes you able to do it: **equip sb for** *We want our son to have an education that will equip him for later life.*

**e·quip·ment** /ɪˈkwɪpmənt/ *n* **1** [U] all the special tools, machines, clothes etc that you need for a particular activity: *Dentists must take great care in sterilizing all their equipment.* | **office/video/sports etc equipment** *fire-fighting equipment* | **piece of equipment** *a very delicate piece of equipment* **2** [singular] the process of equipping someone or something S2 W2

**eq·ui·poise** /ˈekwɨpɔɪz/ *n* [U] *formal* a balance between different influences, especially mental or emotional influences

**eq·ui·ta·ble** /ˈekwɨtəbəl/ *adj formal* an equitable action, process etc treats everyone in an equal way; fair: *an equitable division of wealth* —**equitably** *adv*

**eq·ui·ty** /ˈekwɨti/ *n* **1** [U] *formal* a situation in which no one has an unfair advantage; fairness: *a society run on the principles of equity and justice* **2** [U] *technical* the value of a piece of property or of a company's shares (SHARE² (6)) after debts have been paid **3 equities** [plural] *technical* business shares (SHARE² (6)) that give you some of the company's profits rather than a fixed regular payment **4** [U] *law* the principle that a fair judgement must be made in a situation where the existing laws do not provide an answer

**e·quiv·a·lent¹** /ɪˈkwɪvələnt/ *adj* having the same value, purpose, job etc as a person or thing of a different kind: **[+ to]** *It's equivalent to the rank of captain in our army.* | *Alternatively, we could give you an equivalent amount in company shares.* —**equivalently** *adv* —**equivalence** *n* [U] 

**equivalent²** *n* [C] something that is equivalent to something else: *Some Japanese words have no English equivalents.* | *It's the French equivalent of the IRS.*

**e·quiv·o·cal** /ɪˈkwɪvəkəl/ *adj* **1** words or statements that are equivocal have more than one possible meaning and are deliberately unclear; AMBIGUOUS: *His answer was evasive and equivocal.* **2** equivocal actions or behaviour are mysterious or difficult to understand —**equivocally** /-kli/ *adv*

**e·quiv·o·cate** /ɪˈkwɪvəkeɪt/ *v* [I] *formal* to say something that has more than one possible meaning, in order to avoid giving a clear or direct answer —**equivocation** /ɪˌkwɪvəˈkeɪʃən/ *n* [C,U]

**er** /ɜː, ə‖ɜːr, ər/ *interjection* a sound you make when you do not know exactly what to say next: *Well, er – I'm not really sure.*

**-er¹** /ə‖ər/ *suffix* forms the comparative of many short adjectives and adverbs: *hot, hotter* | *dry, drier* | *My car is fast, but hers is faster.* | *Her car goes faster than mine.* —see also -EST

**-er²** *suffix* [in nouns] **1** someone who does something or who is doing something: *a dancer* (=someone who dances or is dancing) | *the diners* (=people having dinner) **2** something that does something: *a screwdriver* (=tool for driving in screws) **3** someone who makes a particular kind of thing: *a hatter* (=someone who makes hats) **4** someone who lives in or comes from a particular place: *a Londoner* (=someone from London) | *the villagers* (=people who live in the village) **5** someone skilled in or studying a particular subject: *a geographer* (=someone who studies GEOGRAPHY) **6** something that has something: *a three-wheeler car* (=with three wheels) —see also -AR, -OR

**e·ra** /ˈɪərə‖ˈɪrə/ *n* [C] a long period of time in history that is different in some way from other periods: *In the Victorian era such behaviour was socially unacceptable.*

**e·rad·i·cate** /ɪˈrædɨkeɪt/ *v* [T] to completely get rid of something such as a disease or a social problem: **[+ from]** *Smallpox has now been eradicated from the world.* —**eradication** /ɪˌrædɨˈkeɪʃən/ *n* [U]

**e·rase** /ɪˈreɪz‖ɪˈreɪs/ *v* [T] **1** to remove information from a computer memory or recorded sounds from a tape: *Unfortunately, the tape has been erased.* **2** to remove 

marks or writing so that they can no longer be seen **3** *formal* to get rid of or destroy something so that it no longer exists: *The World Bank has agreed to erase the debt.* | *the 163 villages erased by the eruption of Krakatoa* **4 erase sth from your mind/memory** to make yourself forget something bad that has happened

**e·ras·er** /ɪˈreɪzə‖-sər/ *n* [C] *especially AmE* **1** a rubber object used to remove pencil or pen marks from paper; RUBBER (2a) *BrE* **2** a thing you use for cleaning marks from a BLACKBOARD

**e·ra·sure** /ɪˈreɪʒə‖-ʃər/ *n formal* **1** [C] a mark that is left when words or letters are removed with an eraser **2** [U] the act of completely removing or destroying something

**ere** /eə‖er/ *preposition, conjunction old use or poetic* before: **ere long** (=soon)

**e·rect**[1] /ɪˈrekt/ *adj* **1** in a straight upright position: *She held her head erect.* **2** an erect PENIS or NIPPLE is stiff and bigger than it usually is —**erectly** *adv* —**erectness** *n* [U]

**erect**[2] *v* [T] **1** *formal* to build a building, wall, STATUE etc: *an imposing town hall, erected in 1892* **2** to fix all the pieces of something together, and put it in an upright position: *We had to sleep in hastily erected bunk beds.* **3** to establish something such as a system or institution

**e·rec·tile** /ɪˈrektaɪl‖-tl/ *adj technical* connected with a man's erection

**e·rec·tion** /ɪˈrekʃən/ *n* **1** [C] if a man has an erection, his PENIS increases in size and becomes stiff and upright because he is sexually excited **2** [U] the act of building something or putting it in an upright position: *the erection of a new temple* **3** [C] *formal* something that has been built, especially a large structure

**erg** /ɜːg‖ɜːrg/ *n* [C] *technical* a unit used to measure work or energy

**er·go** /ˈɜːgəʊ‖ˈɜːrgoʊ/ *adv Latin formal* [sentence adverb] therefore

**er·go·nom·ics** /ˌɜːgəˈnɒmɪks‖ˌɜːrgəˈnɑː-/ *n* [U] the study of how the design of equipment affects how well people can do their work: *the ergonomics of computer hardware* —**ergonomic** *adj* —**ergonomically** /-kli/ *adv*

**ERM** /ˌiː ɑːr ˈem/ *n* **1** [U] the abbreviation of EXCHANGE RATE MECHANISM **2** [singular] the abbreviation of the EUROPEAN EXCHANGE RATE MECHANISM

**er·mine** /ˈɜːmɪ̣n‖ˈɜːr-/ *n* **1** [U] an expensive white fur, used especially for the clothes of judges, kings, and queens **2** [C] a small thin animal of the WEASEL[1] family whose fur is white in winter

**e·rode** /ɪˈrəʊd‖ɪˈroʊd/ *v* also **erode away** **1** [I,T] if the wind, rain etc erodes something such as rock or soil, or if they erode, their surface is gradually destroyed: *East-facing cliffs are being constantly eroded by heavy seas.* **2** [I,T] to gradually destroy or reduce something such as someone's power, rights or confidence: *She feels that her personal authority has been eroded.*

**e·ro·ge·nous zone** /ɪˌrɒdʒənəs ˈzəʊn‖ɪˌrɑːdʒənəs ˈzoʊn/ *n* [C] a part of your body that gives you sexual pleasure when it is touched

**e·ro·sion** /ɪˈrəʊʒən‖ɪˈroʊ-/ *n* [U] **1** the process of being gradually destroyed by rain, wind, the sea etc: *soil erosion* | *the erosion of the coastline* **2** the process of gradually destroying or reducing something: *the erosion of civil liberties* —**erosive** /ɪˈrəʊsɪv‖ɪˈroʊ-/ *adj*

**e·rot·ic** /ɪˈrɒtɪk‖ɪˈrɑː-/ *adj* **1** an erotic book, film etc shows people having sex, and is often intended to make people reading or looking at it have feelings of sexual pleasure **2** erotic dreams, experiences, or activities involve feelings of sexual excitement —**erotically** /-kli/ *adv*

**e·rot·i·ca** /ɪˈrɒtɪkə‖ɪˈrɑː-/ *n* [plural] erotic writing, drawings etc —compare PORNOGRAPHY

**e·rot·i·cis·m** /ɪˈrɒtɪ̣sɪzəm‖ɪˈrɑː-/ *n* [U] a style or quality that expresses strong feelings of sexual love and desire, especially in works of art: *the eroticism of Donne's early love poems*

**err** /ɜː‖ɜːr/ *v* [I] **1 err on the side of caution** to be too careful rather than risk making mistakes **2** *formal or old use* a word meaning to make a mistake

**er·rand** /ˈerənd/ *n* [C] **1** a short journey in order to do something for someone, for example delivering or getting something for them: *I have a couple of errands for you.* | **send sb on an errand** *His mother sent him on an errand.* | **run an errand** *Uncle Pio has made me run errands for him all morning.* **2 errand of mercy** *literary or humorous* a journey made in order to help someone who is in a very difficult or dangerous situation —see also **(send sb on) a fool's errand** (FOOL[1] (10))

**er·rant** /ˈerənt/ *adj* [only before noun] *usually humorous* an errant husband, wife, son etc has done something wrong —see also KNIGHT-ERRANT

**er·rat·ic** /ɪˈrætɪk/ *adj* erratic actions, movements etc seem to have no pattern or plan: *The bus service into town was highly erratic.* —**erratically** /-kli/ *adv*: *The car was weaving erratically across the road.*

**er·ra·tum** /eˈrɑːtəm/ *n plural* **errata** /-tə/ [C] *Latin technical* a mistake in a book, shown in a list added after it is printed

**er·ro·ne·ous** /ɪˈrəʊniəs‖ɪˈroʊ-/ *adj formal* erroneous ideas, statements etc are wrong because they are based on information that is not correct —**erroneously** *adv*

**er·ror** /ˈerə‖ˈerər/ *n* **1** [C,U] a mistake, especially a mistake in speaking or writing or a mistake that causes serious problems: *an essay full of spelling errors* | *Heath committed a grave error by making concessions to the right wing of the party.* | **computer/driver etc error** *Mrs Leigh's huge phone bill was the result of a computer error.* | **human error** (=made by a person rather than a machine) | **commit an error** (=make a mistake) *Heath committed an error by making concessions to extremists.* | **a grave error** (=a serious mistake) **2 error of judgment** a mistake in the way that you examine a situation and decide what to do **3 see the error of your ways** *literary or humorous* to realize that you have been behaving badly and decide to stop **4 be in error** to have made a mistake, especially when making an official decision: *The company has admitted that they were in error.* **5 in error** if you do something in error, it is wrong but you did not intend to do it: *The letter was opened in error.* —compare MISTAKE —see also **trial and error** (TRIAL[1] (3)) S2 W2

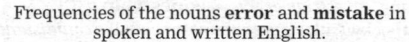

Frequencies of the nouns **error** and **mistake** in spoken and written English.

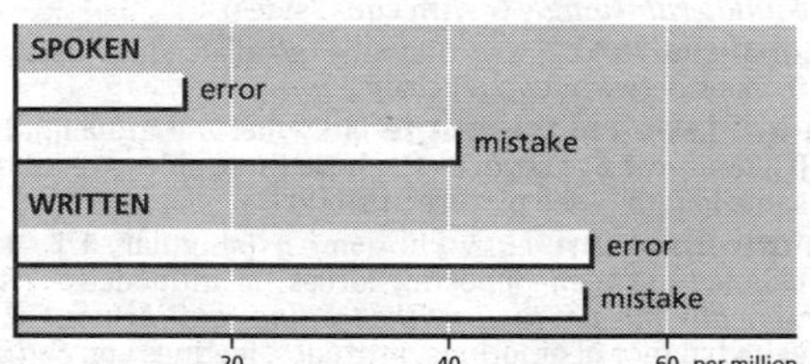


Based on the British National Corpus and the Longman Lancaster Corpus

Thise graph shows that the word **mistake** is more common in spoken English than the word **error**. This is because **error** is not used in a very general way. It is used when describing particular types of mistake, for example in the expressions **computer error** or **error of judgement**, and sounds formal when used on its own. It is therefore more common in written English.

**er·satz** /ˈeəzæts‖ˈerzɑːts/ *adj* [usually before noun] artificial, and not as good as the real thing: *ersatz coffee*

**Erse** /ɜːs‖ɜːrs/ *n* [U] a GAELIC language spoken in Ireland

**erst·while** /ˈɜːstwaɪl‖ˈɜːrst-/ *adj* [only before noun] your erstwhile friends, supporters, enemies etc were your friends etc until recently: *He has won over many of his erstwhile critics.*

**er·u·dite** /ˈerʊ̣daɪt/ *adj* showing a lot of knowledge based on careful study —**eruditely** *adv* —**erudition** /ˌerʊˈdɪʃən/ *n* [U]

**e·rupt** /ɪˈrʌpt/ *v* [I] **1** if a VOLCANO erupts, it explodes and sends smoke, fire, and rock into the sky **2** if fighting, violence, loud noises etc erupt, they start suddenly: *Gang violence can erupt for no apparent reason.* **3 erupt into laughter/shouting etc** to suddenly start laughing or shouting **4** if spots erupt on your body, they suddenly appear on your skin —**eruption** /ɪˈrʌpʃən/ *n* [C,U]

**-ery** /əri/ *suffix* also **-ry** *(in nouns)* **1 a)** the art, behaviour, or condition of something or of being something: *slavery* (=being a slave)|*bravery* (=being brave) **b)** a collection of things of a particular kind: *modern machinery* (=machines)|*in all her finery* (=fine clothes) **2** a place where a particular thing lives or is done, made, or sold: *a rookery* (=where birds called ROOKS live)|*a bakery* (=where bread is baked)|*an oil refinery*

**-es** /ɪ̵z/ *suffix* the form used for -s when it is added to a word ending with s, z, ch, sh, or y: *glasses*|*buzzes*|*watches*|*ladies*

**es·ca·late** /ˈeskəleɪt/ *v* **1** [I,T] if fighting, violence, or an unpleasant situation escalates, or if someone escalates it, it becomes much worse: *They don't want the fighting to escalate into a full-scale war.* **2** [I] if prices or costs escalate, they become much higher —**escalation** /ˌeskəˈleɪʃən/ *n* [C, U]

**es·ca·la·tor** /ˈeskəleɪtə‖-ər/ *n* [C] a set of stairs that move and carry people from one level within a building to another

**escalator**

**es·ca·lope** /ˈeskəlɒp‖ɪsˈkæləp/ *n* [C] *BrE* a thin piece of meat, especially VEAL (=meat from a young cow), cooked in hot fat

**es·ca·pade** /ˈeskəpeɪd/ *n* [C] an adventure or series of events that are exciting or contain some risk: *Have you heard about Jane's latest escapade?*

S3 W2 **es·cape¹** /ɪˈskeɪp/ *v*

**1** ▶ **PERSON/PLACE** ◀ [I,T] to get away from a place when someone is trying to catch you or stop you leaving: *Anyone trying to escape will be shot!*|[+ **from/through/over etc**] *Two men have escaped from Durham jail.*|**escape sb's clutches** (=escape from them) *They managed to escape the clutches of the enemy soldiers and flee to Switzerland.*

**2** ▶ **DANGER** ◀ [I,T] to get away from a dangerous situation that is likely to harm you if you do not leave: *Only four people managed to escape before the roof collapsed.*|**escape from/through/into etc** *The dog escaped through the back window of the bus.*|**escape sth** *refugees escaping war and famine*

**3** ▶ **GAS/LIQUID ETC** ◀ [I] if gas, liquid, light, heat etc escapes from somewhere, it comes out when you do not want it to: *Screw the top back firmly to prevent any fumes escaping.*

**4** ▶ **AVOID** ◀ [I,T] to succeed in avoiding being involved in an unpleasant, difficult, or dangerous situation: *The back seat passengers escaped death by inches.*

**5** ▶ **SOUND** ◀ [I,T] if a sound escapes from someone's mouth, they accidentally make that sound

**6 escape sb's attention/notice** if something escapes your attention or notice, you do not see it or realize that it is there

**7 the name/date/title escapes me** *spoken* used when you cannot remember something: *I've met him before, but his name escapes me.*

**8 there's no escaping (the fact)** used to emphasize that something is definitely important or will definitely happen: *There's no escaping the fact that she did actually lie to you.* —**escaped** *adj* [only before noun] *escaped prisoners*

**escape²** *n* **1** [C,U] the act of getting away from a place where you do not want to be, or from an unpleasant or dangerous situation: *They had been planning their escape for months.*|[+ **from**] *the story of Papillon's daring escape from Devil's Island*|**make your escape** *The party was boring – we couldn't wait to make our escape.*|**a lucky escape** (=a situation in which you were lucky to have avoided something unpleasant) **2** [singular, U] a way of getting away from an unpleasant situation, especially by doing something else to avoid thinking about it: *Teenagers turn to drugs as a form of escape.* **3 an escape of gas/liquid etc** an amount of gas, liquid etc that comes out of the place where it is being kept as a result of an accident: *escapes of radiation from the generating plant* —see also FIRE ESCAPE S3

**es·cap·ee** /ˌeskeɪˈpiː, ɪˌskeɪˈpiː/ *n* [C] *literary* someone who has escaped from somewhere

**escape ve·loc·i·ty** /ˌ·ˈ· ·ˌ···/ *n* [C,U] the speed that a ROCKET¹ (1) must travel at in order to get into space

**es·cap·is·m** /ɪˈskeɪpɪzəm/ *n* [U] something that helps you to forget about your normal life and think of more pleasant things: *It's not intended to be a serious movie – it's sheer escapism.* —**escapist** *adj*

**es·ca·pol·o·gy** /ˌeskəˈpɒlədʒi‖-ˈpɑː-/ *n* [U] the skill of escaping from ropes, chains etc as part of a performance —**escapologist** *n* [C]

**e·scarp·ment** /ɪˈskɑːpmənt‖-ɑːr-/ *n* [C] a high steep slope or cliff that joins two levels on a hill or mountain

**es·chew** /ɪsˈtʃuː/ *v* [T] *formal* to deliberately avoid doing or using something, usually for moral, religious, or practical reasons: *a meek, lamb-like saviour who eschews violence*

**es·cort¹** /ˈeskɔːt‖-ɔːrt/ *n* [C] **1** a person or a group of people or vehicles that go with someone in order to protect or guard them: *a motorcycle escort*|**under escort** (=protected or guarded by an escort) *The suspects arrived under armed escort.* **2** someone, especially a man, who takes someone to a formal social event: *Her escort was a handsome young officer.* **3** someone who is paid to go out with someone socially: *She works for an escort agency.*

**e·scort²** /ɪˈskɔːt‖-ɔːrt/ *v* [T] **1** to go with someone to protect or guard them: *The visitors were escorted by marine guards to the airport.* **2** to go with someone and show them a place: **escort sb round** *BrE*/**around** *The Queen was escorted round the factory by two of the managers.*

**es·cri·toire** /ˌeskrɪ̵ˈtwɑː‖-ˈtwɑːr/ *n* [C] *French* a small writing desk

**es·crow** /ˈeskrəʊ‖-kroʊ/ *n* [U] *law* an object such as a written contract, money etc that is held by someone while an agreement is being fulfilled

**e·scutch·eon** /ɪˈskʌtʃən/ *n* [C] *formal* a SHIELD¹ (2) on which someone's COAT OF ARMS (=FAMILY SIGN) is painted

**-ese** /iːz/ *suffix* **1** [in nouns] the people or language of a particular country or place: *The Viennese* (=people from Vienna) *are so charming*|*learning Japanese* (=the language of Japan) **2** [in adjectives] belonging to a particular country or place: *Chinese music* **3** [in nouns] language or words used by a particular group, especially when it sounds ugly or is difficult to understand: *journalese* (=language used in newspapers)|*officialese* (=language used in office or legal writing)

**Es·ki·mo** /ˈeskɪ̵məʊ‖-moʊ/ *n* [C] a word for a member of a race of people living in the very cold northern areas of North America that many of them consider offensive —compare INUIT

**ESL** /ˌiː es ˈel/ *n* [U] the abbreviation of English as a Second Language; the teaching of English to students living in an English-speaking country

**ESOL** /ˈiːsɒl‖-sɔːl/ the abbreviation of English for Speakers of Other Languages

**e·soph·a·gus** /ɪˈsɒfəgəs‖ɪˈsɑː-/ *n* [C] the American spelling of OESOPHAGUS

**es·o·ter·ic** /ˌesəˈterɪk◂, ˌiːsə-/ *adj* known and understood by only a few people who have special knowledge about

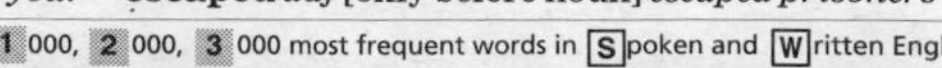

something: *an esoteric form of Buddhism* —**esoterically** /-kli/ *adv*

**ESP** /ˌiː es ˈpiː/ *n* [U] **1** the abbreviation of extra-sensory perception; the ability to know what will happen in the future, or to know what another person is thinking **2** the abbreviation of English for special purposes; the teaching of English to business people, scientists etc

**esp** the written abbreviation of especially

**es·pa·drille** /ˌespəˈdrɪl‖ˈespədrɪl/ *n* [C] *French* a light shoe that is made of cloth and rope —see picture on page 840

**es·pe·cial** /ɪˈspeʃəl/ *adj formal* SPECIAL

S1 W1 **es·pe·cial·ly** /ɪˈspeʃəli/ also **specially** *spoken adv* **1** [sentence adverb] used to emphasize that something is more important or happens more with one particular thing than with others: *Crime is growing at a rapid rate, especially in urban areas.* **2** [+ adj/adv] to a particularly high degree or much more than usual: *I was feeling especially tired that evening.* | *"Do you feel like going out for a drink?" "Not especially, no."* **3** for a particular person, purpose etc: [+ **for**] *I bought these chocolates especially for you.*

**USAGE NOTE: ESPECIALLY**

WORD CHOICE: **especially, specially, special**

**Especially** is most often used to emphasize something, or to say that something is more worth mentioning or more important than the other things you are talking about: *It can be especially difficult for drivers to see cyclists at night. The town is especially crowded in the summer* (=much more than in winter). *I hate interruptions, especially when I'm trying to work* (=I do not mind as much at other times).

**Specially** is usually used when you do something that is different from what you usually do for a particular purpose. It is often used with the passive form of a verb: *a specially made/designed/adapted etc car* | *I bought it specially for you.*

**Special** is the adjective for both **specially** and **especially**.

SPELLING

In spoken English **especially** is often shortened to **specially**, but it is usually written in full.

**Specially** may be written (and heard) as **especially** in slightly formal English. **Special** is hardly ever written **especial**, which is very formal.

GRAMMAR

**Specially** and **especially** are not common at the start of a sentence or clause. You would usually say: *I especially like New York* (NOT *especially I like New York*).

**Es·pe·ran·to** /ˌespəˈræntəʊ‖-ˈrɑːntoʊ/ *n* [U] an artificial language invented in 1871 to help people from different countries in the world speak to each other

**es·pi·o·nage** /ˈespiənɑːʒ/ *n* [U] the activity of secretly finding out a country's or company's secrets: *Some of the embassy staff were certainly involved in espionage.*

**es·pla·nade** /ˌespləˈneɪd‖ˈesplənɑːd/ *n* [C] *especially BrE* a wide street next to the sea in a town

**es·pouse** /ɪˈspaʊz/ *v* [T] *formal* to support an idea, belief etc especially a political one: *This government claims to espouse the principle of freedom of choice.* —**espousal** *n* [singular, U]

**es·pres·so** /eˈspresəʊ, ɪˈspre-‖-soʊ/ *n* [C,U] a strong black Italian coffee

**esprit de corps** /eˌspriː də ˈkɔː‖-ˈkɔːr/ *n* [U] *French* feelings of loyalty towards people who are all involved in the same activity as you

**es·py** /ɪˈspaɪ/ *v* [T] *literary* to suddenly see someone or something

**Esq** *especially BrE* a written abbreviation of esquire

**-esque** /esk/ *suffix* [in adjectives] **1** in the manner or style of a particular person, group, or place: *Kafkaesque* (=in the style of the writer Franz Kafka, or like the situations or characters in his books) **2** like something: *picturesque* (=pleasant to look at)

**es·quire** /ɪˈskwaɪə‖ˈeskwaɪr, ɪˈskwaɪr/ *n* a title that can be written after a man's name, especially on the address of an official letter

**-ess** /es, ɪ̵s/ *suffix* [in nouns] a female: *an actress* (=a female actor) | *a waitress* | *two lionesses*

**es·say¹** /ˈeseɪ/ *n* [C] **1** a short piece of writing by a student as part of a course of study: [+ **on/about**] *an essay on the causes of the French Revolution* **2** a short piece of writing giving someone's ideas about politics, society etc **3** *formal* an attempt to do something S2

**essay²** *v* [T] *formal* to attempt to do something

**es·say·ist** /ˈeseɪ-ɪ̵st/ *n* [C] someone who writes essays, especially as a form of literature

**es·sence** /ˈesəns/ *n* **1** [singular] the most basic and important quality of something: [+ **of**] *In his paintings Picasso tries to capture the essence of his subjects.* **2** [U] a liquid obtained from a plant, flower etc that has a strong smell or taste and is used especially in cooking: *vanilla essence* **3 in essence** used when talking about the most basic and important part of something, especially an idea, belief, or argument: *In essence, you are saying that people do not really have free will.* **4 speed/time is of the essence** used to say that it is important to do something as quickly as possible

**es·sen·tial¹** /ɪˈsenʃəl/ *adj* **1** extremely important and necessary in order to do something correctly or successfully: *If you're going walking in the mountains, strong boots are essential.* | [+ **for/to**] *Good food and plenty of exercise are essential for a healthy life.* | **it is essential (that)** *It is essential that the oil is checked every 10,000 km.* | **it is essential to do sth** *It's essential to read the small print at the bottom of any document.* **2** the essential parts, qualities, or features of something are the most important, typical, or noticeable ones: *The essential character of the village has not changed in over 300 years.* | **essential difference/feature/point etc** *The essential difference between man and apes is intelligence.* S2 W2

**essential²** *n* **1** [C usually plural] something that is important because it is necessary for life or for doing something: *The charity provides homeless people with essentials like food and clothing.* | **bare essentials** (=the most necessary things) *We don't have much room for luggage so we're only taking the bare essentials.* **2 the essentials** [plural] the basic and most important information or facts about a particular subject: *the essentials of English grammar*

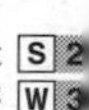

**es·sen·tial·ly** /ɪˈsenʃəli/ *adv* used when stating the most basic facts about something: *Eisenhower was essentially a moderate in politics.* | [sentence adverb] *Essentially, the plan is worthwhile, but some changes will have to be made.* S2 W3

**essential oil** /·ˌ·· ˈ·/ *n* [C] an oil from a plant that has a strong smell and is used for making PERFUME¹ (1) or in AROMATHERAPY

**est** **1** the written abbreviation of established: *H. Perkins and Company, est. 1869* **2** the written abbreviation for ESTIMATED

**-est** /ɪ̵st/ *suffix* **1** forms the SUPERLATIVE of many shorter adjectives and adverbs: *cold, colder, coldest* | *dry, drier, driest* | *Our soap washes whitest.* —see also -ER **2** also **-st** *old use or Biblical* forms the second person singular of verbs: *thou goest*

**es·tab·lish** /ɪˈstæblɪʃ/ *v* [T] **1** to start a company, organization, system, situation etc that is intended to exist or continue for a long time: *My grandfather established the family business in 1938.* **2** to find out facts that will prove that something is true: *Attorneys are trying to establish the validity of his claim.* | **establish that** *It has been firmly established that she was not there at the time of the crime.* | **establish a link/connection** *establishing a link between ozone depletion and the use of CFC* S3 W1 *gases* **3** to make people accept that you can do something, or that you have a particular quality: **establish yourself as/in** *They have established themselves as the most powerful political party in the country.* **4 establish links/contacts/trust etc** to start having a relationship with someone or to start discussions with them: *We decided to try and establish contacts with similar groups in the US.*

3 **es·tab·lished** /ɪˈstæblɪʃt/ *adj* [only before noun] **1** already in use or existing for a long period of time: *established anti-cancer drugs* | **well established** *well-established teaching methods* **2** known to do a particular job well, because you have done it for a long time: *an established political figure*

3 **es·tab·lish·ment** /ɪˈstæblɪʃmənt/ *n* **1** [C] *formal* an
2 institution, especially a business, shop etc: *The hotel is a well-run establishment.* **2 the Establishment** the group of people in a society who have a lot of power and influence and are often opposed to any kind of change or new ideas: *It's no good fighting the Establishment; it will always win in the end.* **3 the medical/legal/military etc establishment** a powerful controlling group within a particular type of activity **4** [U] the act of establishing an organization, relationship, or system: [+ **of**] *Since the establishment of the club three years ago, membership has doubled.*

2 **es·tate** /ɪˈsteɪt/ *n* **1** [C] *BrE* an area where houses or
2 buildings of a similar type have all been built together in a planned way: **council/industrial/housing etc estate** *Rachel was brought up on a bleak post-war council estate in Liverpool.* **2** [singular] *law* all of someone's property and money, especially everything that is left after they die: *She left her estate to her husband.* **3** [C] a large area of land in the country, usually with one large house on it and one owner: *workers on the Osborne estate* **4** [singular] *old-fashioned* a condition or state of life: *the holy estate of matrimony* —see also FOURTH ESTATE, REAL ESTATE

**estate a·gent** /·ˈ· ˌ··/ *n* [C] *BrE* someone whose business is to buy and sell houses or land for people; REAL ESTATE AGENT OR REALTOR *AmE* —**estate agency** *n* [C]

**estate car** /·ˈ· ·/ *n* [C] *BrE* a car with a door at the back, folding back seats, and a lot of room for boxes, cases etc; STATION WAGON *AmE*

**estate tax** /·ˈ· ·/ *n* [C,U] a tax in the US on the money and possessions of a dead person —see also INHERITANCE TAX

**es·teem¹** /ɪˈstiːm/ *n* [U] a feeling of respect and admiration for someone: **hold sb in high/great esteem** *She was an actress who was held in high esteem by everyone who knew her.* | **a token of sb's esteem** (=a sign of their esteem) *Please accept this gift as a small token of our affection and esteem.* —see also SELF-ESTEEM

**esteem²** *v* [T] **1** to respect and admire someone: **highly esteemed** (=greatly respected) *a highly esteemed artist and critic* **2 esteem it an honour/favour/pleasure etc** *old-fashioned* used as a very polite way of saying you think something is an honour etc **3 esteem someone worthy/reliable etc** *old-fashioned* to believe that someone has a particular quality: *He esteemed the assistant trustworthy enough to look after the shop.*

**es·thete** /ˈiːsθiːt‖ˈes-/ *n* [C] an American spelling of AESTHETE —**esthetic** /iːsˈθetɪk‖es-/ *adj* —**esthetical** *adj* —**esthetically** /-kli/ *adv* —**esthetics** *n* [U]

**es·ti·ma·ble** /ˈestɪ̠məbəl/ *adj formal* deserving respect and admiration

3 **es·ti·mate¹** /ˈestɪ̠mɪ̠t/ *n* [C] **1** a calculation of the
2 value, size, amount etc of something: **a rough estimate** (=not very exact) *At a rough estimate I'd say it's about 150 miles.* | **a conservative estimate** (=deliberately rather low) *That seems a conservative estimate to me.* —see also GUESSTIMATE **2** a statement of how much it will probably cost to build or repair something: *We got two or three estimates so we could pick the cheapest.*

**estimate²** /ˈestɪ̠meɪt/ *v* [T] to try to judge the value, size, speed, cost etc of something, partly by calculating and partly by guessing: *The mechanic estimated the cost of repairs at $150.* | *Iraq is estimated to have over 100 such weapons.* | **estimate that** *It is estimated that between 70 and 90 per cent of car crimes occur in the daytime.* | **estimate how many/what etc** *It is difficult to estimate how many deaths are caused by passive smoking each year.* —**estimated** *adj* an estimated number, cost etc has been partly calculated and partly guessed | *The concert was watched on TV by an estimated one billion people.* —**estimator** *n* [C]

**es·ti·ma·tion** /ˌestɪ̠ˈmeɪʃən/ *n* [U] **1** your opinion of the value, nature etc of someone or something: **in my/your etc estimation** *This will simply lead, in our estimation, to further problems.* **2** respect or admiration for someone; ESTEEM¹: **go up/come down in sb's estimation** (=be respected more or less by someone)

**es·tranged** /ɪˈstreɪndʒd/ *adj* **1** an expression used especially in newspaper reports meaning no longer living with your husband or wife: **estranged husband/wife** *She was shot in bed by her estranged husband.* **2** no longer having any connection with a relative or good friend, because of an argument: [+ **from**] *Mollie became increasingly estranged from her son.* **3** no longer feeling any connection with something that used to be important in your life: [+ **from**] *estranged from their religious traditions* —**estrangement** /ɪˈstreɪndʒmənt/ *n* [C,U]

**E**

**es·tro·gen** /ˈiːstrədʒən‖ˈes-/ *n* [U] the usual American spelling of OESTROGEN

**es·tu·a·ry** /ˈestʃuəri, -tʃəri/ *n* [C] the wide part of a river where it goes into the sea: *the Thames estuary*

**estuary En·glish** /ˈ···· ˌ··/ *n* [U] a way of speaking English that is common in the London area and is now starting to spread to other areas of England. In Estuary English the letters 't', 'l', and 'h' are often not pronounced.

**ETA** /ˌiː tiː ˈeɪ/ *n* the abbreviation for estimated time of arrival; the time when a plane, ship etc is expected to arrive: *What's our ETA?*

**et al** /ˌet ˈæl/ *adv Latin* written after a list of names to mean that other people are also involved in something: *'The Human Embryo' by Brodsky, Rosenblum, et al.*

**etc** /et ˈsetərə/ *adv Latin* the written abbreviation for et cetera, used after a list to show that there are many other similar things or people that you could have added: *loans taken out to cover the cost of repairs, new equipment etc* | **etc etc** (=used when you are rather bored or annoyed by the list you are giving) *The letter says pay at once, they've reminded us before etc etc.*

**et cet·e·ra** /etˈsetərə/ *adv Latin* the full form of etc

**etch** /etʃ/ *v* **1** [I,T] to cut lines on a metal plate, piece of glass, stone etc to form a picture **2 be etched on your memory/mind** *literary* if an experience, name etc is etched on your memory or mind, you cannot forget it and you think of it often: *a terrible event that is etched forever on my memory* **3** [T usually passive] if someone's face is etched with pain, sadness etc you can see these feelings from their expression **4** [T] to make lines or patterns appear on something very clearly: *deep furrows etched in the sand* —**etched** *adj*: *etched glass* —**etcher** *n* [C,U]

**etch·ing** /ˈetʃɪŋ/ *n* [C] a picture made by printing from an etched metal plate

**e·ter·nal** /ɪˈtɜːnəl‖-ɜːr-/ *adj* **1** continuing for ever and having no end: *the Christian promise of eternal life* **2** *informal* seeming to continue for ever, especially because of being boring or annoying: *Why can't you stop your eternal complaining!* **3 eternal truths** principles that are always true

**e·ter·nal·ly** /ɪˈtɜːnəl-i‖-ɜːr-/ *adv* **1** for ever **2 eternally grateful** used to say that you are very grateful

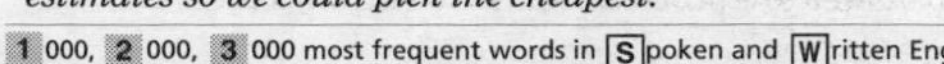

3 *informal* very often: *She seems to be eternally asking me for help.*

**eternal tri·an·gle** /ˌ·· ˈ···/ *n* [singular] the difficult situation that occurs when two people have a sexual relationship with the same person

**e·ter·ni·ty** /ɪˈtɜːnɪ̈ti‖-ɜːr-/ *n* **1 an eternity** a period of time that seems very long because you are annoyed, anxious etc: *Every moment seemed like an eternity.* **2** [U] the whole of time without any end: **for all eternity** *a little animal preserved for all eternity as a fossil* **3** [U] the state of existence after death that some people believe continues for ever

**-eth** /ɪ̈θ/ *suffix* also **-th** *old use or Biblical* forms the third person singular of verbs: *he goeth*

**eth·a·nol** /ˈeθənɒl, ˈiː-‖-noʊl/ *n* [U] *technical* ETHYL ALCOHOL

**e·ther** /ˈiːθə‖-ər/ *n* **1** [U] a clear liquid used in the past as an ANAESTHETIC to make people sleep before an operation **2 the ether** *BrE* **a)** the air through which radio waves travel: *Messages are flying through the ether.* **b)** also **aether** *poetic* the upper part of the sky

**e·the·re·al** /ɪˈθɪəriəl‖ɪˈθɪr-/ *adj* very delicate and light, in a way that does not seem real: *ethereal beauty* —**ethereally** *adv*

**e·ther·net** /ˈiːθənet‖-ər-/ *n* [U] a special system of wires used for connecting computer networks around the world

**eth·ic** /ˈeθɪk/ *n* **1** [C] a general idea or belief that influences people's behaviour and attitudes: *The modern ethic seems to be to get as much money as you can without worrying how you get it.* —see also WORK ETHIC **2 ethics** [plural] moral rules or principles of behaviour for deciding what is right and wrong: *The ethics of his actions are suspect, but technically he is within the law.* | **professional ethics** (=the moral rules relating to a particular profession) | **a code of ethics** (=a set of moral rules)

**eth·i·cal** /ˈeθɪkəl/ *adj* [no comparative] **1** connected with principles of what is right and wrong: *The use of animals in scientific tests raises some difficult ethical questions.* **2** morally good or correct: *Is it ethical to use drugs to control prisoners' behaviour?* —opposite UNETHICAL —**ethically** /-kli/ *adv*

W3 **eth·nic¹** /ˈeθnɪk/ *adj* **1** connected with a particular race, nation, or tribe and their customs and traditions: *The city's population includes a wide range of different ethnic groups.* | *ethnic Turks living in Bulgaria* | **ethnic violence/divisions/unrest** (=violence etc between people from different races, tribes etc) **2 ethnic cooking/fashion/design etc** cooking, fashion etc from countries that are a long way from Britain or the US, which seems very different and unusual: *the delights of ethnic cooking* **3 ethnic cleansing** the action of forcing people to leave their homes because of their RACIAL or national group —**ethnically** /-kli/ *adv*

**ethnic²** *n* [C] *AmE* someone who belongs to a different race from the main group living in a particular country

**ethnic mi·nor·i·ty** /ˌ·· ·ˈ···/ *n* [C] a group of people of a different race from the main group in a country

**eth·no·cen·tric** /ˌeθnəʊˈsentrɪk◂‖-noʊ-/ *adj* based on the idea that your own race, nation, group etc is better than any other: *ethnocentric insensitivity* —**ethnocentrism** *n* [U] —**ethnocentricity** /ˌeθnəʊsenˈtrɪsɪ̈ti‖-noʊ-/ *n* [U]

**eth·nog·ra·pher** /eθˈnɒgrəfə‖eθˈnɑːgrəfər/ *n* [C] someone who studies ethnography

**eth·nog·ra·phy** /eθˈnɒgrəfi‖eθˈnɑː-/ *n* [U] the scientific study of different races of people —**ethnographic** /ˌeθnəˈgræfɪk◂/ *adj* —**ethnographically** /-kli/ *adv*

**eth·nol·o·gy** /eθˈnɒlədʒi‖eθˈnɑː-/ *n* [U] the scientific study and comparison of the origins and organization of different races of people —compare ANTHROPOLOGY, SOCIOLOGY —**ethnologist** *n* [C] —**ethnological** /ˌeθnəˈlɒdʒɪkəl◂‖-ˈlɑː-/ *adj* —**ethnologically** /-kli/ *adv*

**e·thos** /ˈiːθɒs‖ˈiːθɑːs/ *n* [singular] the set of ideas and moral attitudes belonging to a person or group: *the competitive spirit in the American ethos*

**eth·yl al·co·hol** /ˌeθəl ˈælkəhɒl, ˌiːθaɪl-‖-hɒːl/ *n* [U] *technical* the type of alcohol in alcoholic drinks

**e·ti·o·lat·ed** /ˈiːtiəleɪtɪ̈d/ *adj* **1** *literary* pale and weak **2** *technical* a plant that is etiolated is white because it has not received enough light —**etiolation** /ˌiːtiəˈleɪʃən/ *n* [U]

**et·i·ol·o·gy** /ˌetiˈɒlədʒi, ˌiːti-‖-ˈɑːlə-/ *n* [C,U] *technical* the cause of a disease or the scientific study of this —**etiological** /ˌetiəˈlɒdʒɪkəl◂, ˌiːti-‖-ˈlɑː-/ *adj* —**etiologically** /-kli/ *adv*

**et·i·quette** /ˈetɪket‖-kət/ *n* [U] the formal rules for polite behaviour in society or in a particular group: *a breach of professional etiquette*

**-ette** /et/ *suffix* [in nouns] **1** a small thing of a particular type: *a kitchenette* (=small kitchen) | *a snackette* (=a very small meal) **2** a woman who is doing a particular job: *an usherette* (=female USHER) **3** something that is not real, but is IMITATION (2): *flannelette* | *chairs covered with leatherette*

**et·y·mol·o·gy** /ˌetɪ̈ˈmɒlədʒi‖-ˈmɑː-/ *n* **1** [U] the study of the origins, history, and changing meanings of words **2** [C] a description of the history of a particular word —**etymologist** *n* [C] —**etymological** /ˌetɪ̈məˈlɒdʒɪkəl◂‖-ˈlɑː-/ *adj* **etymologically** /-kli/ *adv*

**EU** /ˌiː ˈjuː/ *n* [singular] the abbreviation of the European Union

**eu·ca·lyp·tus** /ˌjuːkəˈlɪptəs/ *n* [C,U] a tall tree that produces an oil with a strong smell, used in medicines

**Eu·cha·rist** /ˈjuːkərɪ̈st/ *n* **the Eucharist** the holy bread and wine, representing Christ's body and blood, used during a Christian ceremony, or the ceremony itself —**Eucharistic** /ˌjuːkəˈrɪstɪk◂/ *adj*

**eu·clid·e·an, Euclidean** /juːˈklɪdiən‖jʊ-/ *adj* related to the GEOMETRY described by Euclid

**eu·gen·ics** /juːˈdʒenɪks/ *n* [plural] the study of methods to improve the mental and physical abilities of human beings by choosing who should become parents

**eu·lo·gize** also **-ise** *BrE* /ˈjuːlədʒaɪz/ *v* [I,T] to praise someone or something very much: *a poem eulogizing the bravery of the nation's warriors* —**eulogist** *n* [C] —**eulogistic** /ˌjuːləˈdʒɪstɪk◂/ *adj* —**eulogistically** /-kli/ *adv*

**eu·lo·gy** /ˈjuːlədʒi/ *n* [C,U] a speech or piece of writing in which you praise someone or something very much, especially at a funeral

**eu·nuch** /ˈjuːnək/ *n* [C] a man who has had his TESTICLES removed, especially someone who guarded a king's wives in some Eastern countries in the past

**eu·phe·mis·m** /ˈjuːfɪ̈mɪzəm/ *n* [C] a polite word or expression that you use instead of a more direct one to avoid shocking or upsetting someone: *'Pass away' is a euphemism for 'die'.*

**eu·phe·mis·tic** /ˌjuːfɪ̈ˈmɪstɪk◂/ *adj* euphemistic language uses polite words and expressions to avoid shocking or upsetting people: *a euphemistic expression such as 'powder room' for 'toilet'* —**euphemistically** /-kli/ *adv*

**eu·pho·ni·ous** /juːˈfəʊniəs‖jʊˈfoʊ-/ *adj formal* words or sounds that are euphonious are pleasant to listen to

**eu·pho·ri·a** /juːˈfɔːriə‖jʊ-/ *n* [U] a short but extremely strong feeling of happiness and excitement: *the current state of euphoria after Ireland's amazing victory over England last Saturday*

**eu·phor·ic** /juːˈfɒrɪk‖jʊˈfɔːrɪk, -ˈfɑː-/ *adj* feeling very happy and excited —**euphorically** /-kli/ *adv*

**Eu·ra·sian¹** /jʊˈreɪʒən, -ʃən/ *adj* concerned with both Europe and Asia

**Eurasian²** *n* [C] *old-fashioned* someone who has one European parent and one Asian parent

**Eu·re·ka** /jʊˈriːkə/ *interjection often humorous* used to show how happy you are that you have discovered the answer to a problem, found something etc

**Eu·ro** /ˈjʊərəʊ‖ˈjʊroʊ/ *adj* [only before noun] European, especially connected with the European Union: *There's some new Euro directive on import regulations.*

**Euro-** /jʊərəʊ‖jʊroʊ/ *prefix* **1 a)** European, especially western European: *Eurocommunism* **b)** European and: *Euro-American relations* **2** of the European Union: *the Europarliament*

**Eu·ro·cheque** /ˈjʊərəʊtʃek‖ˈjʊroʊ-/ *n* [C] *trademark* a special cheque that can be used in different banks or shops, especially in Europe

**Eu·ro·crat** /ˈjʊərəʊkræt‖ˈjʊroʊ-/ *n* [C] *informal* a government official of the European Union, especially one who makes decisions you do not like

**Eu·ro·dol·lar** /ˈjʊərəʊˌdɒlə‖ˈjʊroʊˌdɑːlər/ *n* [C usually plural] *technical* a US dollar that has been put in a European bank or lent to a European customer to help trade and provide an international money system

**Eu·rope** /ˈjʊərəp‖ˈjʊr-/ *n* **1** the large land mass that lies north of the Mediterranean and goes as far east as the Ural Mountains **2** the European Union: *Britain's future lies in Europe.* **3** *BrE* the CONTINENT[1] (1) of Europe not including Britain: *a rail link to Europe through the Channel Tunnel*

**Eu·ro·pe·an**[1] /ˌjʊərəˈpiːən◂‖ˌjʊrə-/ *n* [C] someone from Europe

**European**[2] *adj* from or connected with Europe: *European law*

**European Cur·ren·cy Unit** /ˌ···· ˈ··· ˌ·· / *n* [C] an ECU

**European Ex·change Rate Mech·a·nis·m** /ˌ···· ·ˈ· ·ˌ···/ *n* [singular] the ERM; a system for controlling the EXCHANGE RATE between the money of the different countries of the European Union

**European Mon·e·ta·ry Sys·tem** /ˌ···· ˈ···· ˌ··/ *n* [singular] the EMS; a system for limiting how much the different currencies (CURRENCY (1)) of countries within the European Union can go up or down in value in relation to each other

**European U·nion** /ˌ···· ˈ··/ *n* [singular] a European political and economic organization that encourages trade and friendship between the countries that are members

**Eu·sta·chian tube** /juːˈsteɪʃən ˌtjuːb‖-ˌtuːb/ *n* [C] one of the pair of tubes that join your ears to your throat

**eu·tha·na·si·a** /ˌjuːθəˈneɪziə‖-ˈneɪʒə/ *n* [U] the painless killing of people who are very ill or very old in order to stop them suffering: MERCY KILLING

**e·vac·u·ate** /ɪˈvækjueɪt/ *v* **1** [T] to send people to a safe place from a dangerous place: **evacuate sb from/to** *The villagers were evacuated to the countryside.* **2** [I,T] to empty a place by making all the people leave: *The whole building has been evacuated.* **3** *formal* to empty your BOWELS —**evacuation** /ɪˌvækjuˈeɪʃən/ *n* [C,U]

**e·vac·u·ee** /ɪˌvækjuˈiː/ *n* [C] someone who is sent away from a place because it is dangerous, for example because there is a war

**e·vade** /ɪˈveɪd/ *v* [T] **1 evade the subject/question/issue etc** to avoid talking about something, especially because you are trying to hide something: *Stop trying to evade the issue.* **2** to find a way of not doing something you should do: **evade your responsibilities/duty/problems** *You can't go on evading your responsibilities forever.* **3** to avoid doing something that you should do according to the law such as paying tax: *If you try to evade paying taxes you risk going to prison.* **4** to escape from someone who is trying to catch you: *Williams succeeded in evading capture for several days.* **5** *formal* if success, the truth etc evades you, you cannot achieve it or understand it

**e·val·u·ate** /ɪˈvæljueɪt/ *v* [T] to carefully consider something to see how useful or valuable it is: *evaluating the success of the training scheme*

W3 **e·val·u·a·tion** /ɪˌvæljuˈeɪʃən/ *n* [C,U] the act of considering something to decide how useful or valuable it is, or a document in which this is done: *an intensive evaluation of the health care program*

**e·van·gel·i·cal** /ˌiːvænˈdʒelɪkəl◂/ *adj* **1** evangelical Christians believe that they should persuade as many people as possible to become Christians **2** very eager to persuade people to accept your ideas and beliefs: *Andrew talks about green issues with almost evanglical fervour.*

**e·van·ge·list** /ɪˈvændʒɨlɨst/ *n* [C] **1** someone who travels around speaking at meeting to persuade people to become Christians **2 Evangelist** one of the four writers of the books in the Bible called the Gospels —**evangelism** /ɪˈvændʒɨlɪzəm/ *n* [U] —**evangelistic** /ɪˌvændʒɨˈlɪstɪk◂/ *adj*

**e·van·ge·lize** also **-ise** *BrE* /ɪˈvændʒɨlaɪz/ *v* [I,T] to try to persuade people to become Christians

**e·vap·o·rate** /ɪˈvæpəreɪt/ *v* **1** [I, T] if a liquid evaporates or if something evaporates it, it changes into steam **2** [I] if a feeling evaporates, it slowly disappears: *Hopes of reaching an agreement are beginning to evaporate.* —**evaporation** /ɪˌvæpəˈreɪʃən/ *n* [U]

**evaporated milk** /ˌ···· ˈ·/ *n* [U] milk which has been made thicker by removing some of the water

**e·va·sion** /ɪˈveɪʒən/ *n* [C,U] **1** the act of avoiding doing something that you should do, or an example of this behaviour: *tax evasion* **2** an act of deliberately avoiding talking about something or dealing with something: *His speech was full of lies and evasions.*

**e·va·sive** /ɪˈveɪsɪv/ *adj* **1** not willing to answer questions directly: *Paul's being very evasive about the new contract.* **2 evasive action** action to avoid being injured or harmed —**evasively** *adv* —**evasiveness** *n* [U]

**eve** /iːv/ *n* **1** [C usually singular] the night or day before an important religious day or holiday: **Christmas Eve** (=24th December)|**New Year's Eve** (=31st December) **2 the eve of** the time just before an important event: *on the eve of the election* **3** [C] *poetic* evening: *one summer's eve*

**e·ven**[1] /ˈiːvən/ *adv* **1** used to emphasize something that is unexpected or surprising in what you are saying: *Even the younger children enjoyed the concert.*|*We've all been naughty sometimes – even Mummy!*|**not even** *Henry's a strict vegetarian – he doesn't even eat cheese.*|*I never even saw the kid until I hit him.* **2 even bigger/better/brighter etc** used to emphasize that someone or something is bigger, better etc than before, or than someone or something else you have just mentioned: *New Jet now washes even whiter.*|*Diane knows even less about it than I do.* **3** used to add a stronger, more exact word to what you are saying: *Molly looked depressed, even suicidal.*|*The bride looked beautiful, radiant even.* **4 even so** *spoken* used to introduce something that is the opposite or very different from what you have been saying: *I myself don't believe in ghosts. Even so, I wouldn't like to be alone in that room at night.* **5 even if** no matter if: *Charlie's going to have problems finding a job even if she gets her A levels.* **6 even though** used to emphasize that although something happens or is true, something else also happens or is true: *Even though they loved each other, they decided to part.*|*I can still remember, even though it was so long ago.* **7 even now/then** in spite of what has happened, what you have done, or what is true: *I explained it all to him again, but even then he didn't understand.*|*Even now I find it hard to believe her story.* **8 even as** used to emphasize that something happens at the same moment as something else: *I tried to phone her, but even as I was phoning she was leaving the building.*|*Even as we watched the car skidded out of control.* S1 W1

**even**[2] *adj*

**1 ▶ SURFACE ◀** completely flat with all parts at the same height: *The floor must be completely even before we lay the tiles.*|*an even stretch of road*

**2 ▶ NOT CHANGING ◀** an even rate, temperature etc is steady and does not change much: *We were travelling at an even speed.*|*an even rhythm*

**3 ▶ DIVIDED EQUALLY ◀** divided equally, so that there is the same amount of something in each place, for each person etc: *an even distribution of wealth*

**4 even number** a number that can be divided exactly by

two: *2, 4, 6 and 8 are even numbers* —opposite **odd number** (ODD (6))
**5 ▶ COMPETITION ◀** having teams or competitors that are equally good so that everyone has a chance of winning: *This year's Superbowl was a very even contest.*
**6 ▶ LINE OF THINGS ◀** regularly spaced and neat-looking: *even rows of gleaming white teeth*
**7 be even** *informal* to no longer owe someone something, especially money: *If you give me $5 for the ticket, we'll be even.*
**8 have an even chance (of)** to be just as likely to happen as to not happen: *Derek has an even chance of getting the job.*
**9 get even with** *informal* to harm someone just as much as they have harmed you: *He's not getting away with this, I'll get even with him one day.* —compare UNEVEN —see also EVEN-TEMPERED, **break even** (BREAK[1] (9)) —**evenness** *n* [U]

**even³** *v*
**even out** *phr v* [I,T] if two amounts, levels etc even out, or if you even them out, the differences between them become smaller: *You have to wait until the water level in the pipes evens out.* | **even sth ↔ out** *They even out your payments over the whole year.*
**even up** *phr v* [T **even** sth ↔ **up**] to make a situation or competition more equal

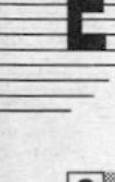

**even⁴** *n* [U] *poetic* evening

**even-hand·ed** /ˌ·· ˈ··◂/ *adj* giving fair and equal treatment to everyone; IMPARTIAL: *even handed justice* —**even-handedly** *adv*

**eve·ning¹** /ˈiːvnɪŋ/ *n* **1** [C,U] the early part of the night between the end of the day and the time you go to bed: *We always go swimming on Friday evenings.* | **in the evening** *Mick often goes to the pub in the evening.* | **for the evening** *I'm going out for the evening.* | **early/late evening** *It happened in the early evening, around half past six.* **2 a musical/poetry etc evening** an event involving music, poetry etc that takes place in the evening **3 the evening of your life** *literary* the last part of your life

**evening²** *interjection informal* used to greet someone when you meet them in the evening: *Evening Joe, everything all right?*

**evening class** /ˈ·· ·/ *n* [C] a course of study for adults in the evening

**evening dress** /ˈ·· ·/ *n* **1** [U] special clothes worn for formal meals, parties etc in the evening **2** also **evening gown** *especially AmE* [C] a dress worn by women to formal meals, parties etc in the evening

**eve·nings** /ˈiːvnɪŋz/ *adv especially AmE* during the evening: *I'm always at home evenings.*

**evening star** /ˌ·· ˈ·/ *n* [singular] the PLANET Venus, seen as a bright star in the western sky in the evening

**e·ven·ly** /ˈiːvənli/ *adv* **1** with equal amounts or numbers of something in every part of a particular area, or divided equally among a group of people: *Support for the Liberals is fairly evenly spread across the country.* | *Spread the butter evenly over the toast.* **2** in a steady or regular way: *breathing deeply and evenly* | **evenly spaced** *rows of evenly spaced desks* **3** dealing with or affecting all parts of something in the same way: *Cook the meat quickly for about 3 minutes, until evenly browned.* **4 evenly matched** if two competitors are evenly matched, they have an equal chance of winning: *The two wrestlers were very evenly matched.* **5** if you say something evenly, you say it in a calm way without getting angry or upset: *"You can do whatever you like," she said evenly*

**e·vens** /ˈiːvənz/ *adj technical* if the ODDS (=probability that a horse will win a race) of a horse in a race are evens, then it is equally likely that it will win or lose: *Black Flag is the evens favourite.*

**e·ven·song** /ˈiːvənsɒŋ‖-sɔːŋ/ *n* [U] the evening religious ceremony in the Church of England

**e·vent** /ɪˈvent/ *n*
**1 ▶ INTERESTING/EXCITING ◀** [C] something that happens, especially something important, interesting or unusual: *the most important events of 1994* | *The article discusses the events which led up to the prime minister's resignation.* | **sequence of events** (=the order in which events happened) *reconstructing the sequence of events on the night of the murder* | **course of events** (=the way that each event caused the next one, without being planned) *Nothing you could have done would have changed the course of events.*
**2 ▶ COMPETITION/PERFORMANCE/PARTY ◀** [C] an important performance, sports competition, party etc which has been arranged for a particular date and time: *the biggest event of the racing season* | **social/sporting/fund-raising etc event** *The Christie Ball soon became the social event of the year.*
**3 ▶ IN A SPORTS COMPETITION ◀** [C] any of the races, competitions etc arranged as part of a day's sports.: *The next event will be the 100 metres.* —see also FIELD EVENT, THREE-DAY EVENT
**4 in any/either event** also **at all events** used just before or after a statement to emphasize that it will happen in spite of anything else that may happen: *I'll probably see you tomorrow but I'll phone in any event.*
**5 in the event** used to emphasize what actually happened in a situation as opposed to what you thought might happen: *We were afraid he would be nervous on stage, but in the event he sang beautifully.*
**6 in the event of rain/ fire/an accident etc** also **in the event that** used to tell people what they should do or what will happen if something else happens: *Britain agreed to support the US in the event of war.*
**7 in the normal course of events** if things happen in the normal way: *In the normal course of events, John will inherit the money from his Uncle.*

**even-tem·pered** /ˌ·· ˈ··◂/ *adj* not becoming angry easily; calm

**e·vent·ful** /ɪˈventfəl/ *adj* full of interesting or important events: *She's led quite an eventful life.* | *an eventful holiday* —**eventfully** *adv*

**e·ven·tide** /ˈiːvəntaɪd/ *n* [U] *poetic* evening

**e·ven·tu·al** /ɪˈventʃuəl/ *adj* [only before noun] happening or achieving something at the end of a process: *Sweden were the eventual winners of the tournament.* | *the eventual outcome*

**e·ven·tu·al·i·ty** /ɪˌventʃuˈæləti/ *n* [C] *formal* a possible event or result, especially an unpleasant one: *We must be prepared for every eventuality.*

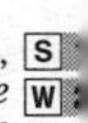

**e·ven·tu·al·ly** /ɪˈventʃuəli, -tʃəli/ *adv* after a long time, especially after a long delay or a lot of problems: *He worked so hard that eventually he made himself ill.* | *She eventually passed her driving test.* | *"Did you manage to contact Roger?" "Well yes, eventually."*

**e·ven·tu·ate** /ɪˈventʃueɪt/ *v formal* to happen as a result of something
**eventuate in** sth *phr v* [T] *formal* to be the final cause of something: *The scandal finally eventuated in the resignation of the prime minister.*

**ev·er** /ˈevə‖ˈevər/ *adv* **1** a word meaning at any time; used mostly in questions, negatives, comparisons, or sentences with 'if': *Nothing ever makes Ted angry.* | *"Do you ever get to the theatre?" "No, never."* | *I don't remember ever seeing him before.* | *If you're ever in Seattle, come and see me.* | **have you ever** *"Have you ever been to Paris?" "Yes, I have."* | *That's the biggest fish I've ever seen.* | **hotter/thinner/taller etc than ever** (=hotter, thinner etc than before) *It's colder than ever today.* | **as friendly/cheerful/boring etc as ever** (=as friendly, cheerful etc as in the past) *Magda was pale and thin, but her eyes were as bright as ever.* | **hardly ever** (=almost never) *I hardly ever see Sara these days.* | **never ever** *spoken* (=used to emphasize that something has never happened or someone has never done something) or: *I never ever said anything like that!* | **rarely, if ever** (=probably never) *Brian rarely, if ever, gets to bed before 3 am.* | **if ever there was one** *spoken* (=used when saying that someone or something is a typical example of something): *Joe's great, a real Northern comic if ever there was one.* **2** a word meaning always; used especially with expressions of time: *Ever optimistic, Gemma decided to give him another chance.*|*His company is making ever larger profits.*|**ever since** (=continuously since) *Paul came here for a holiday several years ago and he's been here ever since.*|**for ever** *He said he would love her for ever.*|**for ever and ever** (=always, used especially in children's stories)|**happily ever after** (=used at the end of children's stories) *The prince and princess got married and lived happily ever after.*|**as ever** *especially BrE* (=as usually happens) *As ever, Kim refused to admit she was wrong.*|**ever-growing/ever-increasing/ever-present etc** (=always growing etc) *the ever-increasing problems of our inner cities* **3 how/what/who etc ever** *BrE old-fashioned* used to add force to a question: *How ever shall we get there?*|*Whatever are you doing?* **4 did you ever!** *old-fashioned* used to show your surprise, disbelief etc: *Did you ever hear of such a thing!* **5 ever so cold/wet/nice etc** *BrE spoken* very cold, wet etc: *The assistant was ever so helpful.*|*Thanks ever so much.* **6 ever such a nice boy/cold day/pretty colour etc** *BrE* a very nice, cold etc person or thing: *You'll like her, she's ever such a nice girl.* **7 Was sb ever** *AmE spoken* used to add force to a statement: *Was he ever mad!* (=he was very angry) **8 Yours ever/Ever yours** *informal* used at the end of a letter above the signature **9 ever and anon** *poetical* from time to time

**ev·er·green**[1] /ˈevəgriːn‖-ər-/ *n* [C] a tree or bush that does not lose its leaves in winter

**evergreen**[2] *adj* **1** an evergreen tree or bush does not lose its leaves in winter **2** an evergreen sportsman, singer etc is very good even though they are fairly old: *the evergreen Perry Como*

**ev·er·last·ing** /ˌevəˈlɑːstɪŋ◂‖ˌevərˈlæ-/ *adj* a word used especially in religious writing, meaning continuing to exist for ever; ETERNAL (1): *life everlasting*|*the Buddhist's search for everlasting peace* —**everlastingly** *adv*

**ev·er·more** /ˌevəˈmɔː‖ˌevərˈmɔːr/ *adv* **for evermore** *literary* if you do something for evermore you continue to do it for ever: *I will love you for evermore.*

**ev·ery** /ˈevri/ *determiner* **1** each one of a group of things or people that make a group or set: *Every student has to fill in a questionnaire.* (=all the students)|**every single** *Unfortunately the President disagreed with every single thing his aides said.* **2** used to emphasize that you are talking about the whole of something: *Victor ate every bit of his meal.*|*What a wonderful movie! I enjoyed every minute of it.*|**every word** (=everything someone says or writes) *I know every word of his songs by heart.* **3 every time** each time; WHENEVER (1): *Every time I see him, he looks miserable.* **4 every day/every 3 weeks/every 10 years etc** used to say that something happens at regular periods of time, after a certain distance etc: *Richard visits his mother every week.*|*You should change the oil every 5,000 miles.*|*Freda had to stop to rest every hundred yards or so.* **5 one in every hundred/two in every thousand etc** used when saying how often something affects a particular group of people or things: *Thirty children in every hundred born in Mali will die before the age of five.* **6 in every way** in all ways: *My new job's better than my old one in every way.* **7 every other** the first, third, fifth etc or the second, fourth, sixth etc of things that can be counted: *Apply the ointment every other day.*|*I see Harold every other Friday.* **8 every bit as** used when saying strongly that someone is just as good, important as someone else: *She was every bit as rude as her sister.* **9 every Tom, Dick, and Harry** *spoken* an expression meaning eveyone or anyone used especially when talking about people you don't approve of: *She didn't want every Tom, Dick, and Harry knowing about her private affairs.* **10 every hope/chance/reason etc** as much hope, chance, reason etc as possible: *There is every chance that you will succeed.* (=you probably will)|*We have every reason to believe that Hodges is telling the truth.*|*The airline takes every possible precaution to ensure the safety of its passengers.* **11 every last drop/bit/scrap etc** *informal* every single drop, piece etc: *Robert had to pick up every last bit of paper from the floor.* **12 every now and then/again** also **every so often** sometimes but not often: *I still see her every now and then.* **13 every which way** *AmE informal* in every direction: *The rain came down and the crowd in the field ran every which way.* —see EACH (USAGE).

**USAGE NOTE: EVERY**

SPELLING

**Everyone** written as one word is only used about people and can never be followed by **of**. **Every one** can be used about anything and is always used with an *of* phrase either stated or suggested: *Every one of your tires needs replacing.*|*There are five thousand people living here and almost every one (of them) has their own car* (=every one of the group mentioned has a car).

**Everybody** is written as one word. **Every body** would mean 'every dead body'.

**Every day** is spelled as two words as an adverb but only one word as an adjective: *She swims every day.*|*the everyday life of Scottish highlanders.* Note that you never say **every days**.

**Everything** and **everywhere** are single words **every time** is two words.

**ev·ery·bod·y** /ˈevribɒdi‖-bɑːdi/ *pron* everyone S1 W3

**ev·ery·day** /ˈevrideɪ/ *adj* [only before noun] ordinary, usual, or happening every day: *The book is written in simple everyday language.*|**everyday life** *Stress is just part of everyday life.*

**Ev·ery·man** /ˈevrimæn/ *n* [singular] *literary* a typical, ordinary person: *This character is a symbol for Everyman.*

**ev·ery·one** /ˈevriwʌn/ *pron* every person; everybody: *If everyone is ready, I'll begin.*|*They gave a prize to everyone who passed the exam.*|*Has everyone finished their drinks?*|*The canteen's almost empty. Where is everyone?* (=the people who are usually here)|**everyone else** (=all the other people) *I usually stay up after everyone else has gone to bed.*|**everyone but Ann/Mark/me etc** (=all of the people except Ann, Mark etc) *Everyone but Peter got there on time*—see EACH[1] (USAGE) S1 W1

**ev·ery·place** /ˈevripleɪs/ *adv AmE* in, at, or to every place; everywhere

**ev·ery·thing** /ˈevriθɪŋ/ *pron* **1** each thing or all things: *Everything is ready for the party.*|*I've forgotten everything I learned at school.*|**everything else** (=all the other things) *There's only bread left; they've eaten everything else.* **2** used when talking in general about your life or about a situation: *I'm OK – how's everything with you?*|*Everything's much better now we're allowed to work at home.* **3 be/mean everything (to sb)** to be the thing that is most important to you and that you care about the most: *Money isn't everything.*|*Her daughter means everything to her now.* **4 and everything** *spoken* and so on: *Tina's worried about her work and everything.* **5 have everything going for you** to have all the qualities that are likely to give you an advantage over other people and make you succeed: *You shouldn't worry so much – you've got everything going for you.* **6 everything but the kitchen sink** *informal* all the equipment that you need and also a lot of things that you do not need: *"What's he got in that bag?" "Everything but the kitchen sink!"* S1 W1

**ev·ery·where** /ˈevriweə‖-wer/ also **everyplace** *AmE adv* **1** in, at, or to every place: *I've looked everywhere but I can't find it.*|*His dog used to follow him everywhere.*|*It must have rained overnight – there are puddles everywhere.*|**everywhere else** (=in, at, or to every other place) *It must be in here – I've looked everywhere else.* **2 be everywhere** to be very common: *Girls with long straight hair were everywhere in the 1960s.* S2 W3

**e·vict** /ɪˈvɪkt/ *v* [T] to legally force someone to leave the house they are living in: *We were evicted for non-payment of rent.* —**eviction** /ɪˈvɪkʃən/ *n* [C,U]

**ev·i·dence**[1] /ˈevɪ̈dəns/ *n* **1** [U] facts, objects, or signs that make you believe that something exists or is true: [+ **of/for**] *evidence of life on other planets*|**evidence that** *There's some evidence that a small amount of alcohol is* S3 W1

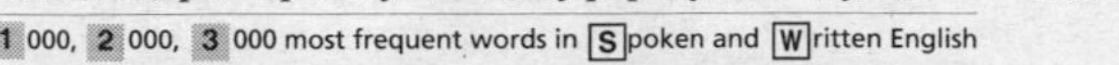

*good for you.* | **medical/scientific/archaeological etc evidence** *Medical evidence shows that men are more likely to have heart attacks than women.* | **not a shred of evidence** (=no evidence at all) *There is not a shred of evidence in support of these outrageous claims.* **2** [U] information given in a court of law in order to prove that someone is guilty: *Murrow's evidence was enough to convict Hayes of murder.* | **give evidence** *Carol was called upon to give evidence.* **3 be in evidence** *formal* to be present and easily seen or noticed: *The army is more in evidence in the cities than in rural areas.* —see also KING'S EVIDENCE, QUEEN'S EVIDENCE, STATE'S EVIDENCE

**evidence²** *v* [T usually passive] *formal* to show that something exists or is true: *The volcano is still active, as evidenced by the recent eruption.*

W3 **ev·i·dent** /ˈevɪ̣dənt/ *adj* easily noticed or understood; OBVIOUS: *Bob began eating his lunch with evident enjoyment.* | **it is evident that** *From the look on Joe's face it was evident that the news came as a complete shock.* —see also SELF-EVIDENT

**ev·i·dent·ly** /ˈevɪ̣dəntli/ *adv* **1** [sentence adverb] used when saying that something seems likely, based on the information that you have: *Evidently she's been bullied at work and is very unhappy.* **2** [+ adj/adv] in a way that is very easy to see and understand: *Mary was evidently upset when she heard about Irene's death.*

W3 **e·vil¹** /ˈiːvəl/ *adj* **1** someone who is evil deliberately does very cruel things to harm other people: *an evil dictator responsible for the deaths of millions* | *An evil glint came into her eye when she picked up the knife.* **2** very unpleasant: *There's an evil smell coming from the drains.* **3** connected with the Devil or having special powers to harm people: *evil spirits* **4** having a very harmful influence on people: *the evil effects of materialism* **5 the evil eye** the power, which some people believe exists, to harm people by looking at them: *traditional symbols to ward off the evil eye* **6 the evil hour/day etc** a time when you expect something unpleasant or difficult to happen: *the evil hour when he would have to face his uncle's anger* —**evilly** *adv*

**evil²** *n* **1** [C] a very harmful or unpleasant influence or effect: *the evils of capitalism* **2** [U] a powerful force that makes people behave in a cruel way, or wicked behaviour in general: *the eternal struggle between good and evil* —see also **the lesser of two evils** (LESSER (2)), **necessary evil** (NECESSARY (3))

**evil-do·er** /ˌ·· ˈ··/ *n* [C] *old-fashioned* someone who does evil things

**e·vince** /ɪˈvɪns/ *v* [T] *formal* to show a feeling or quality very clearly in what you do or say: *His remarks evinced a strong interest in my daughter's financial position.*

**e·vis·ce·rate** /ɪˈvɪsəreɪt/ *v* [T] *formal or technical* to cut the BOWELS or other organs out of a body

**e·voc·a·tive** /ɪˈvɒkətɪv‖ɪˈvɑː-/ *adj* making people remember something by producing a feeling or memory in them: [+ **of**] *a huge scrubbed kitchen evocative of the sun and bright colours of Provence*

**e·voke** /ɪˈvəʊk‖ɪˈvoʊk/ *v* [T] to produce a strong feeling or memory in someone: *a stage set intended to evoke the mood of a brothel* —**evocation** /ˌevəˈkeɪʃən, ˌiːvəʊ-‖ˌevə-, ˌiːvoʊ-/ *n* [C,U]

W3 **ev·o·lu·tion** /ˌiːvəˈluːʃən, ˌevə-‖ˌevə-/ *n* [U] **1** the scientific idea that plants and animals develop gradually from simpler to more complicated forms **2** the gradual change and development of an idea, situation, or object: *the evolution of the computer over the past 30 years*

**ev·o·lu·tion·a·ry** /ˌiːvəˈluːʃənəri◂, ˌevə-‖ˌevəˈluːʃəneri◂/ *adj* **1** connected with scientific evolution: *evolutionary biology* **2** connected with gradual change and development: *an evolutionary process*

**e·volve** /ɪˈvɒlv‖ɪˈvɑːlv/ *v* [I,T] to develop or make something develop by gradually changing: [+ **from/out of etc**] *Darwin believed that we evolved from apes.* | **evolve sth** *evolving a new management style*

**ewe** /juː/ *n* [C] a female sheep

**ew·er** /ˈjuːə‖ˈjuːər/ *n* [C] a large container for water used in the past

**ex** /eks/ *n* [C usually singular] *informal* someone's former wife, husband, GIRLFRIEND, or BOYFRIEND: *Unfortunately, my ex showed up at the dance.*

**ex-** /eks/ *prefix* former and still living: *my ex-wife* | *an ex-England cricketer* —compare LATE¹ (7)

**ex·a·cer·bate** /ɪgˈzæsəbeɪt‖-ər-/ *v* [T] to make a bad situation worse: *Reilly's crass comments just exacerbated the tension.* —**exacerbation** /ɪgˌzæsəˈbeɪʃən‖-sər-/ *n* [U]

**ex·act¹** /ɪgˈzækt/ *adj* **1** correct and including all the necessary details: *exact description of the assassin* | *I don't know the exact terms of the agreement.* | **exact replica/copy etc** *They built an exact replica of the opera house in Naples.* | **to be exact** *spoken* (=used when giving an exact answer, statement etc) *It was more than 20 years ago – to be exact!* **2 the exact colour/moment/type etc** used to emphasize how similar or close two things are: *the exact colour I was looking for* | *He came into the room at the exact moment I mentioned his name.* **3** someone who is exact is very careful and thorough in what they do **4 the exact opposite** someone or something that is as different as possible from another person or thing: *Gina's the exact opposite of her sister in character.* **5** an exact science is based on calculating and measuring things rather than on opinions, guessing etc S3

**exact²** *v* [T] *formal* to demand and get something from someone by using threats, force etc: *exacting payment*

**ex·act·ing** /ɪgˈzæktɪŋ/ *adj* exacting work is hard and involves a high level of skill: *exacting but stimulating work* | *exacting scrutiny of the texts* —**exactingly** *adv*

**ex·act·i·tude** /ɪgˈzæktɪ̣tjuːd‖-tuːd/ *n* [U] *formal* the state of being exact

**ex·act·ly** /ɪgˈzæktli/ *adv* **1** used to emphasize that a particular number, amount, or piece of information is completely correct: *We were wearing exactly the same clothes.* | *It's exactly half past five.* | **exactly where/what/when etc** *Tell me exactly what he said.* | *Exactly where does Petra live?* **2** used to emphasize a statement: *He gave exactly the reply they wanted to hear.* | *That's exactly what we've been trying to tell you.* S1 W2

Frequencies of the adverb **exactly** in spoken and written English.

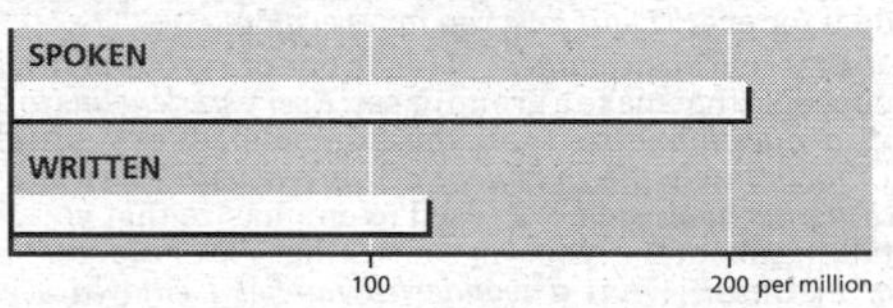


Based on the British National Corpus and the Longman Lancaster Corpus

This graph shows that the adverb **exactly** is much more common in spoken English than in written English. This is because it is used in some common spoken phrases.

**exactly** (*adv*) **SPOKEN PHRASES**

**3 exactly** used as a reply to show that you think what someone has said is completely correct or true: *"So you think we should sell the house and move to the country?" "Exactly."* **4 not exactly a)** used as a reply to show that you think that what someone has said is not completely correct or true: *"You hate Lee, don't you?" "Not exactly. I just think he's a bit annoying that's all."* **b)** used when you say the opposite of what you mean, either as a humorous remark, or to show that you are annoyed: *Imagine calling me fat! I mean, she's not exactly thin herself, is she?* | *I wouldn't bother asking Dave, he's not exactly Einstein, is he?* **5 why/what/where etc exactly...?** used when asking someone to tell you the exact place, reason, thing etc: *Where exactly did you stay in Portugal?* **6 I don't know exactly/I don't exactly know** used to say that you are not sure about something: *"What does he want?" "I don't know exactly, but he said it's really urgent."* **7 that's exactly what....** used to say that what someone has said, done etc is exactly the same as what you or another person said, did etc: *"I don't think he should leave his job." "That's exactly what I told him yesterday."*

**ex·ag·ge·rate** /ɪɡˈzædʒəreɪt/ *v* [I,T] to make something seem better, more important etc than it really is: *Sue says she's seen Jurassic Park twenty times, but I'm sure she's exaggerating.* | **exaggerate sth** *exaggerating the pain to get our sympathy* | **greatly exaggerate** *The extent of the damage was greatly exaggerated by the press.* —**exaggeratedly** /ɪɡˈzædʒəreɪtɪ̵dli/ *adv*

**ex·ag·ge·rat·ed** /ɪɡˈzædʒəreɪtɪ̵d/ *adj* **1** described as better, more important etc than is really true: *exaggerated reports of the army's gains* **2** an exaggerated sound or movement is emphasized to make people notice: *exaggerated movements of his arms*

**ex·ag·ge·ra·tion** /ɪɡˌzædʒəˈreɪʃən/ *n* [C,U] a statement or way of saying something that makes something seem better, more important etc than it really is: *I can say without exaggeration he's the best operator in the business.* | **it is no exaggeration** *It is no exaggeration to say your life will be changed forever.*

**ex·alt** /ɪɡˈzɔːlt‖-ˈzɒːlt/ *v* [T] *formal* **1** to put someone or something into a high rank or position **2** to praise someone, especially God: *Exalt ye the Lord.*

**ex·al·ta·tion** /ˌeɡzɔːlˈteɪʃən, ˌeksɔːl-‖-ɒːl-/ *n formal* **1** [C,U] a very strong feeling of happiness, power etc **2** [U] the state of being put into a high rank or position

**ex·alt·ed** /ɪɡˈzɔːltɪ̵d‖-ɒːl-/ *adj* **1** having a very high rank and highly respected: *I felt shy in such exalted company.* **2** *formal* filled with a great feeling of joy

S1 **ex·am** /ɪɡˈzæm/ *n* [C] **1** a spoken or written test of knowledge, especially an important one: *How did you do in your exams?* | *an oral exam* | **pass/fail an exam** (=succeed/not succeed) *Did you pass the exam?* | **chemistry/French etc exam** (=an exam in a particular subject) | **take/sit an exam** *He failed his English exam and had to take it again* **2** *AmE* a set of medical tests: *an eye exam* **3** *AmE* the paper on which the questions for an exam are written: *Do not open your exams until I tell you.*

S3 W2 **ex·am·i·na·tion** /ɪɡˌzæmɪ̵ˈneɪʃən/ *n* **1** [C] *formal* a spoken or written test of knowledge: *The examination results will be announced in September.* **2** [C,U] the process of looking at something carefully in order to see what it is like: *a detailed examination of population statistics* | **be under examination** *The proposals are still under examination.* | **on closer examination** *On closer examination the vases were seen to be cracked in several places.* **3** a set of medical tests **4** [C,U] the process of asking questions to get specific information, especially in a court of law —see also CROSS-EXAMINATION

**examine**

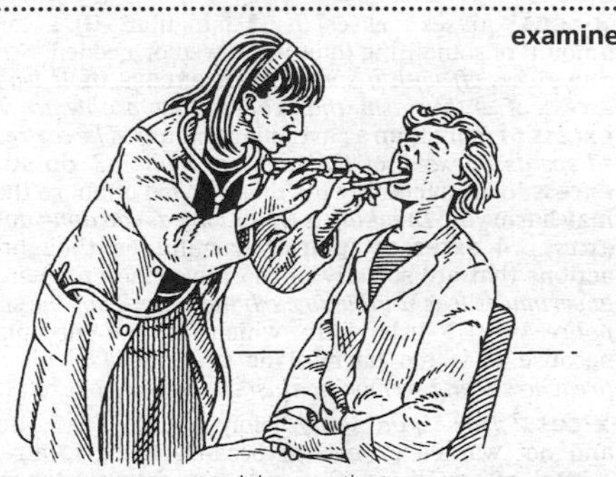

examining a patient

S3 W2 **ex·am·ine** /ɪɡˈzæmɪ̵n/ *v* [T] **1** to look at something carefully, in order to make a decision, find something, check something etc: *After examining the evidence, I can find no truth in these claims.* | **examine sth for** *The police will have to examine the weapon for fingerprints.* **2** if a doctor examines you, they look at your body to check that you are healthy **3** *formal* to ask someone questions to test their knowledge of a subject: **examine sb on** *You will be examined on American history.* **4** *technical* to officially ask someone questions in a law court

Frequencies of the verbs **examine**, **take/have a look at** and **inspect** in spoken and written English.

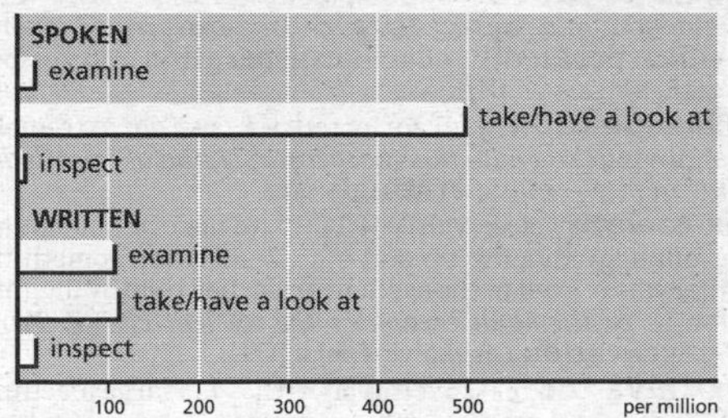


This graph shows that the expressions **have a look at** and **take a look at** are much more common in spoken English than the words **examine** or **inspect**. This is because **have a look at** and **take a look at** are much more general than **examine** or **inspect**, which mean to look at something carefully in order to find out about it or check if it is satisfactory. They are more common in written English.

**ex·am·in·er** /ɪɡˈzæmɪ̵nə‖-ər/ *n* [C] someone from a university, college, or professional institution who tests students' knowledge or ability

**exam pa·per** /ˈ·ˌ··/ *n* [C] **1** *BrE* the paper on which the questions for an EXAM are written **2** *AmE* the papers on which you write the answers to a test or exam

**ex·am·ple** /ɪɡˈzɑːmpəl‖ɪɡˈzæm-/ *n* [C] **1 for example** used before mentioning a specific thing, person, place etc in order to explain what you mean or to support an argument: *Many countries, for example, Mexico and Japan, have a lot of earthquakes.* | *Look at John, for example, now there's someone who's overcome his physical disabilities.* **2** a thing, person, situation etc that you mention to show what you mean or to show that something is true: *The two examples on this page show the behaviour patterns of severely depressed patients.* | [+ of] *a wonderful example of High Gothic architecture* | **give an example** *I don't really understand what you mean, could you give me an example?* | **good example** (=example that shows something clearly) | **classic/typical example** *a classic example of what not to do* | **prime example** (=example of something you do not like or do not approve of) *Franco, a prime example of a man hungry for power* **3 set an example** to behave in a sensible way so that other people will copy you: *It's my duty as an officer to set an example to the troops.* **4 be an example to** if someone's behaviour is an example to you, it is so good that you should copy it: *Her courage is an example to us all.* **5 follow sb's example** to copy someone's behaviour yourself: *I suggest you follow Rosie's example and start doing regular exercize.* **6 make an example of** to punish someone so that other people are afraid to do the same thing

This graph shows some of the words most commonly used with the noun **example**.

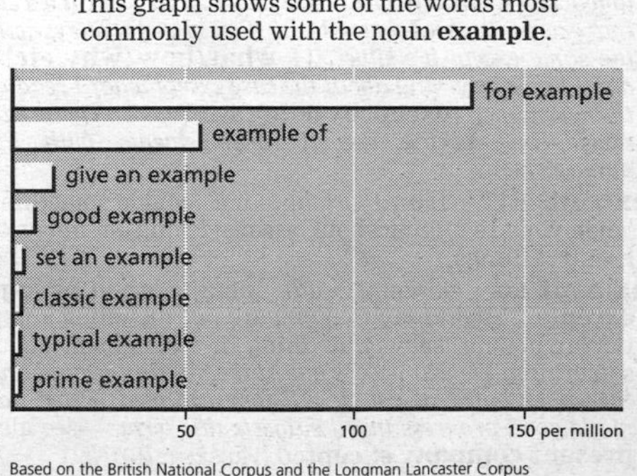


Based on the British National Corpus and the Longman Lancaster Corpus

**ex·as·pe·rate** /ɪg'zɑːspəreɪt‖ɪg'zæ-/ *v* [T usually passive] to make someone very annoyed by continuing to do something that upsets them

**ex·as·pe·rat·ed** /ɪg'zɑːspəreɪtɪ̣d‖-'zæs-/ *adj* very annoyed and upset: *He gave an exasperated snort.* —**exasperatedly** *adv* —**exasperation** /ɪg,zɑːspə'reɪʃən‖-,zæs-/ *n* [U]

**ex·as·pe·rat·ing** /ɪg'zɑːspəreɪtɪŋ‖-'zæs-/ *adj* extremely annoying: *You have this exasperating habit of never looking at me!* —**exasperatingly** *adv*

**ex·ca·vate** /'ekskəveɪt/ *v* [I,T] **1** to make a hole in the ground by digging up soil etc **2** discover something that was buried in the earth in an earlier time by digging for it: *Schliemann excavated the ancient city of Troy.* —**excavation** /,ekskə'veɪʃən/ *n* [C,U]

**ex·ca·va·tor** /'ekskəveɪtə‖-ər/ *n* [C] **1** a large machine that digs and moves earth and soil; STEAM SHOVEL *AmE* **2** someone who digs to find things that have been buried under the ground for a long time

W3 **ex·ceed** /ɪk'siːd/ *v* [T] **1** to be more than a number or amount, especially a fixed number: *Working hours must not exceed 42 hours a week.* **2** to go beyond an official or legal limit: *He was fined for exceeding the speed limit.*

**ex·ceed·ing·ly** /ɪk'siːdɪŋli/ *adv* extremely: *I'd like to say thank you. You've been exceedingly kind.*

E

**ex·cel** /ɪk'sel/ *v* **excelled, excelling** [I, not in progressive] to do something very well, or much better than most people: **[+ at/in]** *I never excelled at sport.* | **excel yourself** (=do better than you usually do) *Dinner was fantastic! Joe's really excelled himself this time.*

**ex·cel·lence** /'eksələns/ *n* [U] the quality of being excellent

**Ex·cel·len·cy** /'eksələnsi/ *n* **your excellency/his excellency** a way of talking to or about people who hold high positions in the state or the church: *His Excellency the Spanish ambassador*

S1 W2 **ex·cel·lent** /'eksələnt/ *adj* extremely good or of very high quality: *Edward made an excellent speech.* | *You've got some excellent CDs here.* —**excellently** *adv*

S2 W2 **ex·cept¹** /ɪk'sept/ *conjunction* **1 except for a)** apart from: *Except for one old lady, the bus was empty.* | *The roads were clear except for a few cars.* **b) except for John/her/me etc** leaving out or not including John, her etc: *The children are all asleep except for Lorna.* **c)** if someone or something had not happened or existed: *Nina would have left him years ago except for the children.* **2 except do sth** apart from doing something: *Tom does everything around the house except cook.* | *a computer that can do everything except talk* **3** *spoken* but: *I'd love to go, except it's too expensive.* | *It doesn't matter that I had to wait, except you did say four o'clock.*

**except²** *prep* used to introduce the only thing or person in a group about which a statement is not true: *Everyone except Adam went to the concert.* | *You can have any of the cakes except this one.* | *We're open every day except Monday.* | **[+ in/to/up etc]** *I can take my vacation at any time except in August.* | *Peter's not going anywhere except to work.* | **[+ (that)]** *The house was just as I left it except that everything was covered with dust.* | *I've got one exactly the same except it's silver.* | **[+ what/how/why etc]** *I don't know anything about the case except what I read in the newspaper.* | **except by doing sth** *You can't get credit except by making special arrangements with the management.*

**except³** *v* [T + **from**] *formal* to not include something when you are talking about or considering a number or group of things

**ex·cept·ed** /ɪk'septɪ̣d/ *adj* **Paul/football/biology excepted** used to say that you are not including a particular person, subject, or thing in a statement about something: *We want every one at the meeting, David and Steven excepted of course.* | *History excepted, Peter has made good progress in all subjects this term.* —see also **present company excepted** (PRESENT³ (5))

**ex·cept·ing** /ɪk'septɪŋ/ *prep* used to introduce the only thing or person in a group about which a statement is not true: *O'Rourke answered all the questions excepting the last one.* | **always excepting** *Dogs are not allowed in here, always excepting guide dogs.*

**ex·cep·tion** /ɪk'sepʃən/ *n* [C,U] **1** something or someone that is not included in a rule, does not follow the expected pattern etc: *With one or two notable exceptions, there are few women conductors.* | **no exception** (=used to emphasize that a law or rule concerns someone or something) *The law applies to all European countries; Britain is no exception.* | **minor exception** (=one that is not very important) | **exception to a rule** *The spelling of this word is an interesting exception to the rule.* | **the exception that proves the rule** (=used to say that the fact that something is not true or does not exist in one situation emphasizes the fact that it is true or exists in general) *Most people here are very dedicated; I'm afraid Rhea's the exception that proves the rule.* **2 make an exception** used to say that on one particular occasion the normal rules or standards do not have to be obeyed: *We don't usually give credit, but as you're a regular customer we'll make an exception this time.* **3 take exception to sth** to be angry or upset because of something: *Tom took great exception to my remark about Americans.* **4 without exception** used to say that something is true of all the people or things in a group: *Every type of plant, without exception, contains some kind of salt.* **5 with the exception of** used to introduce the only thing, person, or place about which a statement is not true: *I think everyone, with the possible exception of Fauzi, will pass the exam.* 

**ex·cep·tion·a·ble** /ɪk'sepʃənəbəl/ *adj formal* making you feel offended and angry: *a highly exceptionable remark*

**ex·cep·tion·al** /ɪk'sepʃənəl/ *adj* **1** unusually good: *Richard is an exceptional student.* | *exceptional bravery* **2** unusual and likely not to happen often: *This is an exceptional case; I've never seen anything like it before.* | **in exceptional circumstances** *Promotion in the first year is only given in exceptional circumstances.*

**ex·cep·tion·al·ly** /ɪk'sepʃənəli/ *adv* [+ adj/adv] used to emphasize a quality that you are describing: *She defended her position exceptionally well.* | *an exceptionally talented player*

**ex·cerpt** /'eksɜːpt‖-ɜːrpt/ *n* [C + **from**] a short piece taken from a book, poem, piece of music etc

**ex·cess¹** /ɪk'ses, 'ekses/ *n* **1** [singular, U] a larger amount of something than is allowed or needed: *Scrape any excess off with a spatula.* | **an excess of** *It was an excess of enthusiasm that caused the problem.* **2 in excess of** more than a particular amount: *The car reached speeds in excess of 100 miles per hour.* **3 do sth to excess** to do something too much or too often, so that it may harm you: *Drinking is OK as long as you don't do it to excess.* **4 excesses** [plural] harmful or thoughtless actions that are socially or morally unacceptable: *The government was unable to curb the excesses of the secret police.* **5** [U] behaviour which is not acceptable because it is too harmful or extreme: *The minister preached a long sermon against the dangers of excess.*

**ex·cess²** /'ekses/ *adj* [only before noun] **1** additional and not wanted or needed because there is already enough of something: *Cut any excess fat from the meat.* **2 excess baggage/luggage** bags or cases that weigh more than the legal limit that you can take on a plane

**ex·ces·sive** /ɪk'sesɪv/ *adj* much more than is reasonable or necessary: *Boyd's wife left him because of his excessive drinking.* | *$15 for two cokes seems a little excessive.*

**ex·change¹** /ɪks'tʃeɪndʒ/ *n* 
**1 ► GIVING/RECEIVING ◄** [C,U] the act of exchanging one thing for another or doing something to someone at the same time as they do it to you: *an exchange of political prisoners* | *an honest exchange of information* | **fair exchange** (=an exchange in which the things given and received are of equal value) *Four of my cassettes for your*

*Madonna CD is a fair exchange.* —see also PART-EXCHANGE
**2 in exchange** if you do or give something in exchange for something else, you do it or give it in order to get that thing: *They have offered to release the hostages, but what do they want in exchange?* | [+ **for**] *I've offered to paint the kitchen in exchange for a week's accommodation.*
**3 ▶ ARGUMENT ◀** [C] a short conversation, usually between two people who are angry with each other: *a quiet exchange between the judge and the clerk* | **heated exchange** (=a very angry conversation) *The DJ was fired after a heated exchange on air with a call-in listener.*
**4 ▶ MONEY ◀** [U] **a)** a process in which you change money from one CURRENCY to another: *Most capital cities have extensive exchange facilities.* **b)** [C] the EXCHANGE RATE
**5 ▶ BETWEEN FAMILIES/SCHOOLS ◀** [C] an arrangement in which someone changes their job, home etc with someone else usually for a short period of time, or in which students from different countries visit each other: *I'm only here for one term, I'm on an exchange with Dr Fisher.*
**6 ▶ WAR ◀** [C,U] an event during a war when armies use weapons against each other: *an exchange of fire*
**7 corn/wool/cotton etc exchange** a large building in a town, that was used in the past for buying and selling corn, wool etc —see also LABOUR EXCHANGE, STOCK EXCHANGE
**8 ▶ SCIENCE ◀** [U] *technical* the movement of one substance into the place where another substance was

**ex·change²** *v* [T] **1** to give someone something and receive the same kind of thing from them at the same time: *We still exchange gifts at Christmas.* | *At the end of the game players traditionally exchange shirts with each other.* | **exchange addresses/telephone numbers** (=give someone your address or telephone number and take theirs) *Did you exchange phone numbers with the guy that hit you?* **2** to give someone something so that they will give you something that is better, more suitable, or more useful for you: *The store will not exchange goods without a receipt.* | **exchange sth for** *Where can I exchange my dollars for pounds?* **3** if two people exchange something, they do something to each other: **exchange looks/glances** (=look at each other) *Sally and I exchange amused glances when we heard this.* | **exchange greetings/insults** (=greet or insult each other) | **exchange words** (=talk to someone) *Until this evening I had never so much as exchanged a word with him.* | **exchange blows** (=fight) *Students exchanged blows with locals, and police were called in.* **4 exchange information/ideas** if two people or a group of people exchange information, ideas etc they discuss something: *We envision an artistic community where people are free to exchange ideas.* **5 exchange houses** to go and live in someone else's house while they come and live in yours, usually for a holiday: *We exchanged houses with an American family for three weeks.* **6 exchange contracts** *especially BrE* to complete the final stage of buying a house by signing a contract with the person you are buying it from —**exchangeable** *adj*

**exchange rate** /·'· ·/ *n* [C] the value of the money of one country compared to the money of another country: *a more favourable exchange rate in the bank than in the hotel*

**exchange rate mech·a·nis·m** /·'· · ˌ···/ *n* [U] a system for controlling the exchange rate between the money of one country and that of another; ERM

**Ex·cheq·uer** /ɪks'tʃekə‖'ekstʃekər/ *n* **the Exchequer** the British government department that is responsible for collecting taxes and paying out public money; TREASURY (1)

**ex·cise¹** /'eksaɪz/ *n* [C,U] the government tax that is put on the goods that are produced and used inside a country: *excises on gasoline and cigarettes* | **excise officer** (=someone who collects excise) | **excise duty** (=the money paid as excise) —see also CUSTOMS AND EXCISE

**ex·cise²** /ɪk'saɪz/ *v* [T] *formal* to remove or get rid of something, especially by cutting it out: *The tumour was excised.* —**excision** /ɪk'sɪʒən/ *n* [C,U]

**ex·ci·ta·ble** /ɪk'saɪtəbəl/ *adj* becoming excited too easily: *A puppy is naturally affectionate and excitable.* —**excitability** /ɪkˌsaɪtə'bɪlɪ̣ti/ *n* [U]

**ex·cite** /ɪk'saɪt/ *v* [T] **1 excite interest/suspicion/jealousy etc** to make someone feel a particular emotion: *The court case has excited a lot of public interest.* **2 excite comment/rumour etc** if something excites comment etc, it makes people talk about it: *The book excited very little comment on this side of the Atlantic.* **3** [not in progressive or passive] to make someone feel happy, interested, or hopeful because something good has happened or is going to happen: *His playing is technically brilliant, but it doesn't excite me.* **4** [not in progressive] to make someone feel nervous so that they cannot relax: *The doctor warned us not to excite Douglas, who had been very ill.* **5** to make someone feel sexual desire **6** *technical* to make an organ, nerve etc in your body react or increase its activity

**ex·cit·ed** /ɪk'saɪtɪ̣d/ *adj* **1** happy, interested, or hopeful because something good has happened or will happen: *Steve's flying home tomorrow – we're all really excited.* | *excited crowds of shoppers* | [+ **about**] *The kids are so excited about Christmas.* | [+ **by**] *We were all excited by the prospect of a party.* | [+ **at**] *He got very excited at finding such perfect specimens.* | **get/feel/look etc excited** *Maria's starting to get pretty excited about the wedding.* **2** very nervous and upset about something so that you cannot relax: *When Thierry gets excited he starts to stutter.* | [+ **about**] *There's no point getting excited about it. We can't change things.* **3** feeling sexual desire **4 nothing to get excited about** *spoken* used to say that a film, book etc is not very good or enjoyable and rather disappointing: *Unfortunately Doyle's latest novel is nothing to get excited about.* —**excitedly** *adv*: *Squirrels chattering excitedly in the branches above.*

**ex·cite·ment** /ɪk'saɪtmənt/ *n* **1** [U] the feeling of being excited: *squeals of excitement* | [+ **of**] *The new job held none of the excitement of her career in the police.* | [+ **at**] *their excitement at the discovery* | *The news that Ms Street had eloped with Jean caused great excitement.* | *his eyes shining with excitement* | **in (sb's) excitement** *In my excitement, I had forgotten to turn off the taps.* | **mounting excitement** (=a feeling of excitement that increases) **2** [C] an exciting event or situation: *I found it difficult to sleep after the excitements of the day.* 

**ex·cit·ing** /ɪk'saɪtɪŋ/ *adj* making you feel excited: *an exciting discovery* | **find sth exciting** *Stuart found the atmosphere of the college enormously exciting.* —**excitingly** *adv*: *excitingly different band* 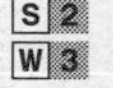

**ex·claim** /ɪk'skleɪm/ *v* [I,T] to say something suddenly and loudly because you are surprised, angry, or excited: *"Look at you!" she exclaimed when we came in, covered in mud.* | [+ **at/over**] *They all exclaimed at his ignorance.*

**ex·cla·ma·tion** /ˌeksklə'meɪʃən/ *n* [C] a sound, word, or short sentence that you say suddenly and loudly because you are surprised, excited, or angry: [+ **of**] *horrified exclamations of disgust*

**exclamation mark** /··'·· ·/ *BrE*, **exclamation point** *AmE n* [C] the mark '!' that you write after a sentence or word that expresses surprise, anger, or excitement —see picture at PUNCTUATION MARK

**ex·clude** /ɪk'sklu:d/ *v* [T] **1** to deliberately not include something, especially a particular group of people or things: *a special diet that excludes dairy products* | **exclude sb/sth from sth** *If we exclude uncompleted projects from the calculations, the total spent is still more than $15 billion.* | **specifically/explicitly exclude sth** *The provisions of the Act specifically excluded minors.* **2** to not allow someone to take part in something or not allow them to enter a place: **exclude sb from (doing) sth** *navigation laws to exclude foreign vessels from trading in English ports* **3** to deliberately not pay attention to someone so that they feel lonely or unwanted: *We're not* 

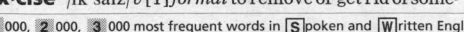

*trying to exclude her, it's just that we have nothing in common with her.* **4** to decide that something is not a possibility: *Social workers have excluded sexual abuse as a reason for the child's disappearance.*|**exclude the possibility of/that** *At this stage we cannot entirely exclude the possibility of staff cuts.* — opposite INCLUDE

**ex·clud·ing** /ɪk'skluːdɪŋ/ *prep* a word meaning not including, used especially when you are making a list or calculating a total: *Television is watched in 97 per cent of American homes (excluding Alaska and Hawaii).*

**ex·clu·sion** /ɪk'skluːʒən/ *n* [U] **1** a situation in which someone or something is not allowed to take part in an activity, be a member of an organization etc: *China's exclusion from the United Nations* **2 to the exclusion of** if you do something to the exclusion of something else, you only do the first thing and do not do the second thing at all: *Your essays tend to concentrate on one theme to the exclusion of everything else.* **3 exclusion zone** an area that the government does not allow people to enter, because it is dangerous or because secret things happen there: *the military exclusion zone*

**ex·clu·sive¹** /ɪk'skluːsɪv/ *adj* **1** exclusive places, organizations, clothes etc are so expensive that not many people can afford to use or buy them: *Bel Air is an exclusive suburb of Los Angeles.*|*an exclusive girls' school* **2** available only to particular people, so that only they can have, do, or use something: **be exclusive to sb** *This offer is exclusive to readers of The Sun.*|**exclusive access/rights/use etc** *Rafferty managed to gain exclusive control of the company.* **3 exclusive report/interview/coverage** a report, interview etc which is only printed in one newspaper or broadcast by one television programme: *Tune in to our exclusive coverage of Wimbledon.* **4 mutually exclusive** if two things are mutually exclusive, you cannot have or do both of them: *Lesbianism and motherhood are not mutually exclusive.* **5 exclusive of** not including: *Our prices are exclusive of sales tax.* —**exclusively** *adv* —**exclusiveness** *n* [U]

**exclusive²** *n* [C] an important or exciting story that is printed in only one newspaper, because that newspaper was the first to find out about it: *a New York Post exclusive about the Kennedy marriage*

**ex·com·mu·ni·cate** /ˌekskə'mjuːnɪ̆keɪt/ *v* [T] to punish someone by no longer allowing them to be a member of the Roman Catholic church —**excommunication** /ˌekskəmjuːnɪ̆'keɪʃən/ *n* [C,U]

**ex·co·ri·ate** /ɪk'skɔːrieɪt/ *v* [T] *formal* to express a very bad opinion of a book, play etc: *an excoriating review in the Times* —**excoriation** /ekˌskɔːri'eɪʃən/ *n* [C,U]

**ex·cre·ment** /'ekskrɪ̆mənt/ *n* [U] *formal* the solid waste material that you get rid of through your BOWELS

**ex·cres·cence** /ɪk'skresəns/ *n* [C] *formal* **1** something such as an ugly building that makes the surrounding area seem less attractive: *The new museum is nothing but an excrescence on the urban landscape.* **2** an ugly growth on an animal or plant

**ex·cre·ta** /ɪk'skriːtə/ *n* [plural] *formal* the solid or liquid waste material that people and animals produce and get rid of from their bodies

**ex·crete** /ɪk'skriːt/ *v* [I,T] *formal* to get rid of waste material from your body through your BOWELS, your skin etc —compare SECRETE (1)

**ex·cre·tion** /ɪk'skriːʃən/ *n* **1** [U] the process of getting rid of waste material from your body **2** [C,U] the waste material that people or animals get rid of from their bodies

**ex·cru·ci·at·ing** /ɪk'skruːʃieɪtɪŋ/ *adj* **1** extremely painful, so that you are unable to move or do something: *When I bend my arm the pain is excruciating.* **2** extremely unpleasant, because it is boring, embarrassing, or sad: *Helena described the events of the night before in excruciating detail.* —**excruciatingly** *adv*

**ex·cul·pate** /'ekskʌlpeɪt/ *v* [T] *formal* to prove that someone is not guilty of something —**exculpation** /ˌeks-kʌl'peɪʃən/ *n* [U]

**ex·cur·sion** /ɪk'skɜːʃən‖ɪk'skɜːrʒən/ *n* [C] **1** a short journey arranged so that a group of people can visit a place, especially while they are on holiday: *a day's excursion to the island* **2** a short journey made for a particular purpose: *a shopping excursion* **3 excursion into sth** *formal* an attempt to experience or learn about something that is new to you: *Neither of his brief excursions into marriage had been a success.*

**ex·cu·sa·ble** /ɪk'skjuːzəbəl/ *adj* behaviour that is excusable can be forgiven: *an excusable reaction of anger*

**ex·cuse¹** /ɪk'skjuːz/ *v* [T] **1 excuse me** *spoken* **S2** **a)** used when you want to get someone's attention politely, especially when you want to ask a question: *Excuse me, can you tell me the way to the museum please?* **b)** used to say that you are sorry for doing something rude or embarrassing: *Oh, excuse me. I didn't know anyone was in here.* **c)** used to ask someone politely to move so that you can walk past: *Excuse me, could I just squeeze past you?* **d)** used when you want to politely tell someone that you are leaving a place: *Excuse me a moment, Mr Jonson. I'll be right back.* **e)** used when you disagree with someone but want to be polite about it: *Excuse me, but I don't think that's what he meant at all.* **f)** *AmE* used to say you are sorry when you hit someone accidentally, make a small mistake etc: *Oh, excuse me, did I spell your name wrong?* **g)** *especially AmE* used to ask someone to repeat something that they have just said: *"What time is it?" "Excuse me?" "I asked you what time it is."* **2** to forgive someone for doing something that is not seriously wrong, such as being rude or careless: *I'll excuse you this time, but try and be prompt in the future.*|*Please excuse my bad handwriting.*|**excuse sb for (doing) sth** *I cannot excuse them for treating their animals so badly.* **3** to allow someone not to do something that they are supposed to do: *Ball was excused guard duty that night.*|**excuse sb from (doing) sth** *Can I be excused from swimming today? I have a cold.* **4** to give reasons for someone's careless or offensive behaviour in order to make it seem more acceptable: *Nothing can excuse that kind of rudeness.*|**sb can be excused for doing sth** (=used to say that you understand why someone has done something and think they should not be blamed for it) *His poetry means a lot to him, so perhaps he can be excused for neglecting his work in order to write.* **5** to give someone permission to leave a place: *May I please be excused from the table?*|**excuse yourself** *Richard politely excused himself, claiming he had too much work to do.* **6 excuse me for living!** *spoken* used when someone has offended you or told you that you have done something wrong

**USAGE NOTE: EXCUSE**

WORD CHOICE: **excuse me, I'm sorry, I beg your pardon, pardon me**

In British English, you say **(I'm) sorry** to a person if you accidentally touch them, or push against them, or get in their way (for example, if you step on someone's foot). You might also hear the rather old-fashioned expression **I beg your pardon**.

In American English you say **Excuse me** or **Pardon me.**

**ex·cuse²** /ɪk'skjuːs/ *n* [C] **1** a reason that you give to **S3** explain careless or offensive behaviour: [+ **for**] *What's your excuse for being late this time?*|**there is no excuse for sth** *There is no excuse for such rudeness.*|**make an excuse** *Fay's always making excuses for his erratic moods.*|**have an excuse** *I'm sure Mike has a good excuse for not repaying the money.* **2** a false reason that you give to explain why you are doing something or not doing something: **excuse to do sth** *She wanted an excuse to be at the bus stop when Billy got off.*|[+ **for**] *The conference is an excellent excuse for a few days' holiday by the sea.*|**find/have an excuse** *Now at last I had an excuse to call* *him.* | **make an excuse** *I made an excuse at the first possible moment, and got up to leave.* | **give sb an excuse** *The arrival of the doctor gave them an excuse to leave.* **3 make your excuses** to explain why you are not able to do something: *Please make my excuses at the meeting tomorrow. I have an appointment with an important client.* **4 a poor/rotten etc excuse for sth** used when you think someone is very bad at something they are doing or at their job: *Derico is a rotten excuse for a lawyer, why on earth did you hire him?* **5** *AmE* a note written by your doctor or one of your parents saying that you were ill on a particular day; SICK NOTE *BrE*

**USAGE NOTE: EXCUSE**

WORD CHOICE: **reason, explanation, excuse, pretext**

If you call something a **reason**, either you believe it, or you are just repeating what someone else has said: *His reason for being late was that his car broke down* (=either you know the car did break down which made him late, or that was simply the reason he gave you).

If you call something an **explanation**, you are just repeating what someone else has said: *His explanation for being late was that his car broke down* (= that was the reason he gave – it may or may not be true). An **explanation** often sounds more like a personal opinion, a **reason** more like a fact.

If you call something an **excuse** it suggests that you may not believe it is true or, if it is true, you do not believe that it really explains what happened: *His excuse for being late was that his car broke down* (=perhaps the car broke down, or perhaps it did not OR you think it did break down, but that is not really a good enough reason for being late). If you say *My excuse is....* you are giving a reason that you know is not really good enough to explain what you did.

If you call something a **pretext**, you definitely do not think that it is true or the real reason: *His pretext for being late was that his car broke down* (=you do not believe it broke down OR it did, but you know there was another reason why he was really late).

**ex·di·rec·to·ry** /ˌ· ·ˈ···◂/ *adj BrE* deliberately not given in the public telephone book; UNLISTED (2) *AmE* | **go ex-directory** *After a number of threatening calls, Amy went ex-directory.*

**ex·ec** /ɪɡˈzek/ *n* [C] *informal* an EXECUTIVE[1] (1)

**ex·e·cra·ble** /ˈeksɨkrəbəl/ *adj formal* extremely bad: *execrable handwriting* —**execrably** *adv*: *execrably bad*

**ex·e·crate** /ˈeksɨkreɪt/ *v* [T] *literary* to express strong disapproval or hatred for someone or something

**ex·e·cute** /ˈeksɨkjuːt/ *v* [T] **1** to kill someone, especially legally as a punishment for a serious crime: **be executed for sth** *He was executed for treason.* —see KILL[1] (USAGE) **2** *formal* to do something that you have carefully planned or that you have agreed to do: *The directors make the decisions, but the managers have to execute them.* **3** *formal* to perform a difficult action or movement: *The skaters' routine was perfectly executed.* **4** *law* to make sure that the instructions in someone's WILL[2] (2) are followed **5** *formal* to make a work of art such as a painting

**ex·e·cu·tion** /ˌeksɨˈkjuːʃən/ *n* **1** [C,U] the act of killing someone, especially as a legal punishment for a serious crime: *a public execution* **2** [U] *formal* a process in whch you do something that has been carefully planned or agreed: [+ **of**] *the formulation and execution of urban policy* **3** [U] *formal* the performance of a difficult action or movement **4** [U] *formal* the act of making a work of art such as a painting

**ex·e·cu·tion·er** /ˌeksɨˈkjuːʃənə‖-ər/ *n* [C] someone who legally kills someone else as a punishment for a serious crime: *a public executioner, also called at that time, the hangman*

**ex·ec·u·tive**[1] /ɪɡˈzekjɡtɪv/ *n* **1** [C] someone who has an important job as a manager in a company or business: *a publishing executive* **2 the executive** the part of a government that is responsible for making sure that new laws and other decisions are done in the way they have been planned —compare JUDICIARY, LEGISLATURE **3** [C] the group of people in a political organization, society etc that makes the rules and makes sure that they work in the way they were planned: *the executive of the union* S3 W2

**executive**[2] *adj* [only before noun] **1** connected with making decisions and organizing, especially within a company or a government: *Clancy has been given full executive powers on this matter.* | **executive body/committee** (=a group of people who make decisions etc) **2** for the use of people who have important jobs in the management of a company or business: *the executive dining-room* **3** expensive and of high quality, so that only someone with a good job can afford it: *an executive car*

**executive priv·i·lege** /ˌ··· ˈ···/ *n* [C] *AmE* the right of a president or other government leader to keep official records and papers secret

**ex·ec·u·tor** /ɪɡˈzekjɡtə‖-ər/ *n* [C] a person, lawyer, or bank that deals with the instructions in someone's WILL[2] (2)

**ex·e·ge·sis** /ˌeksɨˈdʒiːsɨs/ *n* [C,U] *formal* a detailed explanation of a piece of writing, especially one from the Bible

**ex·em·plar** /ɪɡˈzemplə, -plɑː‖-ər, -ɑːr/ *n* [C] *formal* a good or typical example

**ex·em·pla·ry** /ɪɡˈzempləri/ *adj* **1** excellent and providing a good example for people to follow: *praised for their exemplary behaviour* **2** [only before noun] severe and intended to be a warning: *an exemplary punishment*

**ex·em·pli·fy** /ɪɡˈzemplɨfaɪ/ *v* [T] **1** to be a very typical example of something: *Los Angeles exemplifies America's diversity.* **2** to give an example of something —**exemplification** /ɪɡˌzemplɨfɪˈkeɪʃən/ *n* [C,U]

**ex·empt**[1] /ɪɡˈzempt/ *v* [T] to give someone special permission not to do something that they would normally have to do: *a special clause exempting children* | **exempt sb from** *Marty's bad health exempts him from military service.*

**exempt**[2] *adj* having special permission not to do something you would normally have to do: [+ **from**] *The interest is exempt from income tax.*

**ex·emp·tion** /ɪɡˈzempʃən/ *n* **1** [C] *AmE* the amount of money that you are allowed to earn each year before you start to pay tax; PERSONAL ALLOWANCE *BrE* **2** [C,U] permission not to do something you would normally have to do

**ex·er·cise**[1] /ˈeksəsaɪz‖-ər-/ *n* S1 W2

**1 ▶ FOR HEALTH ◀** [U] physical activities that you do in order to stay healthy and become stronger: *I could use some exercise – let's go for a swim.* | **do/take exercise** (=exercise regularly) *Do at least fifteen minutes exercise each day.* | **get exercise** (=do exercise as part of your daily life) *You don't get much exercise sitting at a desk all day like this.*

**2 ▶ MOVEMENT ◀** [C] a movement or set of movements that you do regularly in order to keep a particular part of your body strong and healthy: *The doctor gave me some exercises to help with my back.* | **do exercises** *Jan does her exercises every morning.*

**3 ▶ FOR A SKILL ◀** [C usually plural] an activity or process that helps you practise a particular skill such as playing a musical instrument or singing

**4 ▶ IN A BOOK ◀** [C] a set of questions in a book which test a student's skill or knowledge: *Do Exercises 3 and 4 on page 51 for homework.*

**5 ▶ ARMY/NAVY ETC ◀** [C] an activity that trains soldiers, pilots etc for war when there is still peace: *a naval exercise*

**6 ▶ FOR A RESULT ◀** [singular] an activity that is intended to have a particular result: *Getting everyone to*

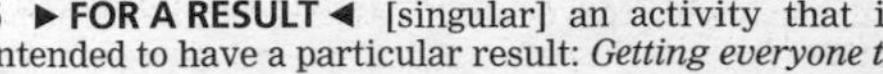

*agree was quite a difficult exercise.* | **an exercise in awareness/self-control etc** (=something that you do in order to gain or develop a particular quality) *The ceremony was an exercise in self-congratulation for a leader desperate to regain popularity.*
**7 the exercise of power/influence/authority etc** *formal* the use of power, influence etc in order to achieve something

S3 W2 **exercise²** *v* **1** [I] to walk, do sports etc in order to stay healthy and become stronger: *It's important to exercise regularly.* **2** [T] to make a particular part of your body move in order to make it stronger: *Swimming exercises all the major muscle groups.* **3 exercise power/influence/caution etc** *formal* to use power, influence etc: *I intend to exercise my right to vote.* **4** [T] to make an animal walk or run in order to keep it healthy and strong: *Don't out exercising the horses.* **5** [T often passive] *formal* to make someone think about a subject or problem and consider how to deal with it: *Scientists continue to be exercised about the ethics of genetic engineering.*

**exercise bike** /'··· ,·/ *n* [C] a bicycle that does not move and is used for indoor exercise

**exercise book** /'··· ,·/ *n* [C] a small book that students write their work in

**ex·ert** /ɪɡ'zɜːt‖-ɜːrt/ *v* [T] **1 exert pressure/control/influence** to use your power, influence etc in order to have a particular effect: *Photography has exerted a profound influence on art in this century.* **2 exert yourself** to make a strong physical or mental effort: *He won both games without even seeming to exert himself.*

**ex·er·tion** /ɪɡ'zɜːʃən‖-ɜːr-/ *n* [C,U] strong physical or mental effort: *The afternoon's exertions had left us feeling exhausted.* | *mental exertion*

**ex·e·unt** /'eksiʌnt/ *v Latin* a word written in the instructions of a play to tell two or more actors to leave the stage

**ex gra·tia** /,eks 'ɡreɪʃə/ *adj Latin* an ex gratia payment is one made to help someone or as a gift, not because you have a legal duty to do it: *an ex gratia payment of £15,000*

**ex·hale** /eks'heɪl/ *v* [I,T] to breathe air, smoke etc out of your mouth: *Take a deep breath, then exhale slowly.* —**exhalation** /,ekshə'leɪʃən/ *n* [U]

**ex·haust¹** /ɪɡ'zɔːst‖-'zɒːst/ *v* [T] **1** to make someone extremely tired so that they have no energy left: *I find a full day's teaching exhausts me.* | **exhaust sb to do sth** *It exhausted him even to talk very long.* **2** to use all of something: *We've nearly exhausted our coal reserves.* **3 exhaust a subject/topic etc** to talk about something so much that you have nothing more to say about it: *Once we'd exhausted the subject of Jill's wedding, we had nothing to say to each other.*

**exhaust²** *n* **1** [C] a pipe on a car or machine through which gas or steam passes; EXHAUST PIPE **2** [U] the gas or steam produced when an engine is working

**ex·haust·ed** /ɪɡ'zɔːstɪ̈d‖-'zɒːs-/ *adj* **1** extremely tired and having no energy: *Man, I'm exhausted!* | [+ **from/by**] *Jill lay on the grass, exhausted by her long run.* | *What's wrong? You look absolutely exhausted.* **2** having or containing no more of a particular thing or substance: *an exhausted coal mine*

**ex·haust·ing** /ɪɡ'zɔːstɪŋ‖-'zɒːs-/ *adj* making you feel extremely tired: *an exhausting journey*

**ex·haus·tion** /ɪɡ'zɔːstʃən‖-'zɒːs-/ *n* [U] **1** extreme tiredness: **nervous exhaustion** (=a medical condition in which you feel very sad or anxious because you have been working too hard or have been very worried) **2** the act of using all the available substances, materials etc so that there are none left: [+ **of**] *the exhaustion of oil supplies*

**ex·haus·tive** /ɪɡ'zɔːstɪv‖-'zɒːs-/ *adj* extremely thorough: *an exhaustive search for the missing boy* —**exhaustively** *adv*: *examined the issue exhaustively without result*

**exhaust pipe** /-'· ·/ *n* [C] a pipe on a car or a machine through which gas or steam passes—see picture on page 409

**ex·hib·it¹** /ɪɡ'zɪbɪ̈t/ *v* **1** [I,T] to put something in a public place so that people can go to see it: *David's going to exhibit his roses at the flower show.* **2** [T] *formal* to show a particular quality, emotion, or ability so that people notice it easily: *Moira's exhibiting classic signs of depression.* **3** [T] *formal* to show someone something: *He rolled up his trouser leg to exhibit his wounded knee.*

**exhibit²** *n* [C] **1** something, for example a painting, that you put in a public place so that people can go to see it: *Many exhibits were donated by local millionaire John Severi.* **2** an object, piece of clothing etc that is used in a court of law to prove that someone is guilty or not guilty: *Exhibit A is the blood-stained hammer found next to the victim's body.* **3** an EXHIBITION (1): *a big exhibit in Milan*

**ex·hi·bi·tion** /,eksɪ̈'bɪʃən/ *n* **1** [C] a public show where you put things so that people can go to see them: [+ **of**] *an exhibition of black and white photographs* **2** [U] the act of showing something such as a painting in a public place: [+ **of**] *She never agreed to the public exhibition of her sculptures while she was still alive.* | **on exhibition** also **on exhibit** (=being shown) *A collection of paintings by David Hockney is on exhibition at the Museum of Contemporary Art.* **3 an exhibition of rudeness/jealousy/temper etc** very rude, embarrassing, or offensive behaviour: *I've never seen such an exhibition of jealousy in my entire life.* **4 make an exhibition of yourself** behave in a silly or embarrassing way: *Sam made a real exhibition of himself, getting drunk and then taking all his clothes off.* **5** [C] *BrE* a small amount of money given as a prize to a student: *Michael won an exhibition at Cambridge.* W2

**ex·hi·bi·tion·is·m** /,eksɪ̈'bɪʃənɪzəm/ *n* [U] **1** behaviour that is intended to make people notice or admire you, but which most people think is silly: *Look at those idiots standing on the statue. It's just pure exhibitionism.* **2** behaviour in which someone shows their PENIS or breasts to people in a public place because they have mental problems —**exhibitionist** *n* [C] —**exhibitionistic** /,eksɪ̈bɪʃə'nɪstɪk/ *adj*

**ex·hib·i·tor** /ɪɡ'zɪbɪ̈tə‖-ər/ *n* [C] someone who is showing something, for example a painting, in a public place so that people can go to see it: *a book exhibitor at TESOL*

**ex·hil·a·rate** /ɪɡ'zɪləreɪt/ *v* [T] to make someone feel very excited and happy —**exhilaration** /ɪɡ,zɪlə'reɪʃən/ *n* [U]

**ex·hil·a·rat·ed** /ɪɡ'zɪləreɪtɪ̈d/ *adj* feeling extremely happy and excited: *I am always exhilarated by the bustle and noise of New York.*

**ex·hil·a·rat·ing** /ɪɡ'zɪləreɪtɪŋ/ *adj* making you feel very excited and happy: *Racing down the ski slope for the first time was an exhilarating experience.* —**exhilaratingly** *adv*

**ex·hort** /ɪɡ'zɔːt‖-ɔːrt/ *v* [T] *formal* to try very hard to persuade someone to do something: **exhort sb to do sth** *He exhorted the troops to prepare for battle.* —**exhortation** /,eksɔː'teɪʃən‖-ɔːr-/ *n* [C,U]

**ex·hume** /ɪɡ'zjuːm, eks'hjuːm‖ɪɡ'zuːm, ɪk'sjuːm/ *v* [T usually passive] *formal* to remove a dead body from a grave, especially in order to check the cause of death —**exhumation** /,ekshjʊ'meɪʃən/ *n* [C,U]

**ex·i·gen·cy** /'eksɪ̈dʒənsi, ɪɡ'zɪ-/ also **ex·i·gence** /'eksɪ̈dʒəns, 'eɡzɪ̈-/ *n* [C usually plural] *formal* something that you must do to deal with an urgent situation: *the exigencies of war*

**ex·i·gent** /'eksɪ̈dʒənt, 'eɡzɪ̈-/ *adj formal* **1** demanding a lot of attention from other people in a way that is unreasonable **2** an exigent situation is urgent, so that you must deal with it very quickly

**ex·ig·u·ous** /ɪɡ'zɪɡuəs/ *adj formal* very small in amount: *exiguous earnings*

**ex·ile¹** /'eksaɪl, 'eɡzaɪl/ *n* **1** [singular, U] a situation in which you are forced to leave your country to live in another country, especially for political reasons: *After a long period of enforced exile he returned to rule his country again.* | **be in exile** *Some of her best works were written while she was in exile.* | **go into exile** *He was forced to go into exile to escape imprisonment after the coup.* | **send sb into exile** (=force someone to leave) **2** [C] someone who has been forced to live in exile —see also TAX EXILE

**exile²** *v* [T usually passive] to force someone to leave their country, especially for political reasons: *After the war he was exiled and the other leaders imprisoned.* | **exile sb to** *After publishing the novel he was arrested and exiled to Siberia.* —**exiled** *adj* [only before noun]

S3 W1 **ex·ist** /ɪg'zɪst/ *v* [I not in progressive] **1** if someone or something exists, that person or thing is real and has not been imagined by someone: *Do fairies really exist?* | *Stop pretending the problem doesn't exist.* | *Tom acts as if I don't exist at times.* **2** to happen or be present in a particular situation or place: *The custom of arranged marriages still exists in many countries.* **3** to stay alive, especially in a difficult situation when you do not have enough money, food etc: [+ **on**] *The hostages existed on bread and water for over 5 months.*

S3 W2 **ex·ist·ence** /ɪg'zɪstəns/ *n* **1** [U] the state of existing: *It is impossible to prove the existence of God.* | **be in existence** (=exist at a particular time) *There are three different versions of his health record currently in existence.* | **come into existence** (=start to exist) *Scientists have many theories about how the universe first came into existence.* **2** [C usually singular] the type of life that someone has, especially when it is bad or unhappy: *Pablo led a lonely existence when he first moved to San Juan.* | *I don't call this a life, it's an existence.* | **eke out an existence** (=get just enough food or money to live on) *Farmers eked out a primitive existence on the dry, stony land.* | **sb's/sth's very existence** (=the fact that something exists at all, especially when something could prevent it from existing) *a drug on which his very existence depended*

**ex·ist·ent** /ɪg'zɪstənt/ *adj formal* existing now: *The existent pension scheme will not change.* —opposite NONEXISTENT

**ex·is·ten·tial** /ˌegzɪ'stenʃəl◂/ *adj* [only before noun] connected with the existence of humans or existentialism: *the existential notion that man is in control of his own life*

**ex·is·ten·tial·is·m** /ˌegzɪ'stenʃəlɪzəm/ *n* [U] the modern belief that people are responsible for their own actions and experiences: *Sartre, the high priest of French existentialism* —**existentialist** *adj* —**existentialist** *n* [C]

S3 W2 **ex·ist·ing** /ɪg'zɪstɪŋ/ *adj* [only before noun] existing systems, situations etc are the present ones being used now: *Changes will be made to the existing laws.*

S3 **ex·it¹** /'egzɪ̵t, 'eksɪ̵t/ *n* [C] **1** a door or space through which you can leave a place, especially a room in a big building: *We made for the nearest exit.* | *an exit sign* | **emergency/fire exit** (=a special door used only when there is a fire etc) **2** [usually singular] the act of leaving a place, especially a room: | **make an exit** (=go out) *They made a swift exit when they saw the police approaching.* **3** a place on a MOTORWAY or FREEWAY where vehicles can leave it: *Take exit 13 into Lynchburg.* **4** [usually singular] an occasion when someone stops being involved in a situation, event, etc, often because they have not been successful or have done something wrong: *Manchester United's early exit from the championship*

**exit²** *v* **1** [I] to leave a place: [+ **from/through**] *I exited through a side window.* **2** [I,T] to stop using a computer PROGRAM¹ (1): *You exit the system by pressing the F3 button.* **3** [I,T] *Latin* a word used in the instructions of a play to tell an actor to leave the stage: *Exit Hamlet, bearing the body of Polonius.*

**exit poll** /'· ·/ *n* [C] a process of asking people how they have voted in an election in order to discover the likely result of the election

**ex·o·dus** /'eksədəs/ *n* [singular] a situation in which a lot of people leave a particular place at the same time: [+ **from/to**] *the exodus of Jews from Eastern Europe* | **mass exodus** *often humorous* (=when everybody goes somewhere) *I joined in the mass exodus to the bar every lunchtime.*

**ex·of·fi·ci·o** /ˌeks ə'fɪʃiəʊ‖-ʃioʊ/ *adj Latin formal* an ex-officio member of an organization is only a member because of their rank or position: *The Mayor is an ex-officio member of the Parish Council.* —**ex officio** *adv*

**ex·on·e·rate** /ɪg'zɒnəreɪt‖ɪg'zɑː-/ *v* [T] to state officially that someone who has been blamed for something is not responsible for it: *The report did not exonerate the social workers involved in the Cleveland child abuse case.* | **exonerate sb from/of** *Recent medical evidence has exonerated Dr Lamont from all blame.* —**exoneration** /ɪgˌzɒnə'reɪʃən‖-ˌzɑː-/ *n* [U]

**ex·or·bi·tant** /ɪg'zɔːbɪ̵tənt‖-ɔːr-/ *adj* an exorbitant price, rate, demand etc is much higher than is reasonable or usual: *It's a good restaurant but the prices are exorbitant.* —**exorbitance** *n* [U] —**exorbitantly** *adv*

**ex·or·cis·m** /'eksɔːsɪzəm‖-ɔːr-/ *n* [C,U] **1** a process during which someone forces evil spirits to leave a place or someone's body by using special words and ceremonies **2** the act of making yourself forget a bad memory or experience

**ex·or·cist** /'eksɔːsɪ̵st‖-ɔːr-/ *n* [C] someone who forces evil spirits to leave a place or someone's body

**ex·or·cize** also **-ise** *BrE* /'eksɔːsaɪz‖-ɔːr-/ *v* [T] to force evil spirits to leave a place or someone's body by using special words and ceremonies: *prayers to exorcize ghosts*

**ex·ot·ic** /ɪg'zɒtɪk‖ɪg'zɑː-/ *adj approving* seeming unusual and exciting because of being connected with a foreign country: *exotic birds* | *Zara is an exotic name. Where's she from?* —**exotically** /-kli/ *adv*

**ex·ot·ic·a** /ɪg'zɒtɪkə‖ɪg'zɑː-/ *n* [plural] unusual and exciting things that come from foreign countries

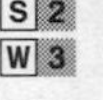

**exotic danc·er** /·ˌ·· '··/ *n* [C] a dancer who takes off their clothes while dancing —see also STRIPTEASE

**ex·pand** /ɪk'spænd/ *v* **1** [I,T] to become larger in size, number, or amount, or to make something become larger: *Water expands as it freezes.* | *The population of the town expanded rapidly in the 1960s.* | **expand sth** *exercises designed to expand the chest muscles* —opposite CONTRACT² (1) **2** [T] to increase the amount or range of an activity: *As children grow older they expand their interests and become more confident.* **3** [I,T] if a company, business etc expands or if someone expands it, they open new shops, factories etc **4** [I] to become more confident or friendly: *After a few whiskies he started to expand a little.* S2 W3

**expand on/upon sth** *phr v* [T] to add more details or information to something that you have already said: *Payne later expanded on his initial statement, saying he hadn't meant it the way it sounded.*

**ex·pand·a·ble** /ɪk'spændəbəl/ *adj* able to be made larger: *an expandable waistband*

**ex·panse** /ɪk'spæns/ *n* [C] a very large area of water, sky, land etc: [+ **of**] *Vast expanses of sand stretched out in front of us.*

**ex·pan·sion** /ɪk'spænʃən/ *n* **1** [U] the act or process of increasing in size, range, amount etc: *the expansion of gases* **2** [U] the act or process of making a company or business larger by opening new shops, factories etc: *The industry has just undergone a period of rapid expansion.* **3** [C] a detailed idea, story etc that is based on one that is simpler or more general: *The novel is an expansion of a short story he wrote about forty years ago.* W3

**ex·pan·sion·is·m** /ɪk'spænʃənɪzəm/ *n* [U] a process in which the amount of land and power that a country has increases —**expansionary** *adj* —**expansionist** *adj* —**expansionist** *n* [C]

**ex·pan·sive** /ɪk'spænsɪv/ *adj* **1** very friendly and willing to talk a lot: *After a couple of drinks she suddenly became more expansive.* **2** very large and wide in area: *a broad expansive valley* **3** expansive behaviour or ideas are confident but not always practical: *He made an expansive gesture and said "Who cares anyway?"* —**expansively** *adv* —**expansiveness** *n* [U]

**ex·pat** /ˌeks'pæt/ *n* [C] *informal* an expatriate

**ex·pa·ti·ate** /ɪk'speɪʃieɪt/ *v*

**expatiate on/upon** sth *phr v* [T] *formal* to speak or write in detail about a particular subject: *He began to expatiate on the topic of the free market economy.*

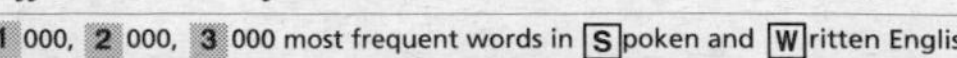

**ex·pat·ri·ate¹** /eks'pætriət, -trieɪt‖eks'peɪ-/ *n* [C] someone who lives in a foreign country: *British expatriates living in Spain* —**expatriate** *adj* [only before noun]

**ex·pat·ri·ate²** /eks'pætrieɪt‖-'peɪ-/ *v* [T] to force someone to leave their own country and go to live in another country, especially because they have broken the law —compare EXILE²

S1 W1 **ex·pect** /ɪk'spekt/ *v* [T]
**1 ▶ THINK STH WILL HAPPEN ◀** to think that something will happen because it seems likely or has been planned: **expect (that)** *The troops expect the attack will come at dawn.* | **expect to do sth** *The rent was much more than we had expected to pay.* | **expect sb/sth to do sth** *He'd been out celebrating and expected his girlfriend to drive him home.* | **fully expect** (=be completely sure something will happen) *Smedley fully expected to be paid for giving me this information.* | **half expect** (=think it is possible that something will happen) *I half expected to see her at the party.* | **as expected** (=in the way that was planned) *The ascent of the mountain is proceeding as expected.* | **is (only) to be expected** (=used to say that you are not surprised that an unpleasant situation or remark etc has happened or been said) *Some resentment of the new baby was only to be expected.*
**2 ▶ BE WAITING FOR ◀** to believe that someone or something is going to arrive: *We're expecting Alison home any minute now.* | *Snow is expected by the weekend.*
**3 ▶ DEMAND ◀** to demand that someone does something because it is a duty or seems reasonable: *The officer expects complete obedience from his troops.* | **expect sb to do sth** *You can't expect kids to be quiet all the time.* | **expect a lot/too much of sb** (=think someone can do more than perhaps is possible) *The school expects a lot of its students.*
**4 ▶ WANT STH TO HAPPEN ◀** to think it is reasonable that something should happen or exist: *A job and somewhere to live – is that too much to expect?* | *We had expected to be consulted at the very least.*
**5 be expecting** if a woman is expecting, she is going to have a baby
**6 What else can/do you expect?** *spoken* used to say that you are not surprised by something unpleasant or disappointing because it has happened before: *Tracey didn't leave a forwarding address, but then what can you expect?*
**7 I expect** *spoken especially BrE* used to introduce or agree with a statement that you think is probably true: *I expect Mum will phone tonight.* | **I expect so** *"Do you think Ruth will get to art college?" "Yes, I expect so."*

This graph shows how common the different grammar patterns of the verb **expect** are.

expect to do sth
expect sth/sb
expect sth to do sth
expect (that)
expect from
expect of
other
10% 20% 30% 40%

Based on the British National Corpus and the Longman Lancaster Corpus

**ex·pec·tan·cy** /ɪk'spektənsi/ *n* [U] the feeling that something pleasant or exciting is going to happen: *I saw the look of expectancy in the children's eyes.* —see also LIFE EXPECTANCY

**ex·pec·tant** /ɪk'spektənt/ *adj* [usually before noun] **1** hopeful that something good or exciting will happen: *a row of expectant faces* —see NERVOUS (USAGE) **2 expectant mother** a woman who is going to have a baby —**expectantly** *adv*

**ex·pec·ta·tion** /ˌekspek'teɪʃən/ *n* [C,U] **1** the belief that something will happen because it is likely or planned: **your expectation is that** *My expectation is that interest rates will go up.* | **against/contrary to (all) expectations** *Against all expectations, Mike finished high school with top grades.* | **in expectation of** (=thinking that something will happen) *They closed the windows in expectation of rain.* **2** [usually plural] a belief that something good will happen in the future: **have high expectations** (=believe that something good will happen or that someone will be successful in the future) *The school has high expectations for his future career.* | **beyond (your) expectations** (=better than you expected) *Paulito has succeeded beyond our expectations.* | **fall short of/not come up to sb's expectations** (=not be as good or as successful as you expected) *If profits fall short of expectations, how will you repay your loan?* | *The film just didn't come up to our expectations.* | **(not) live up to sb's expectations** (=(not) be as good as people expected) *The show lived up to all our expectations — it was wonderful!* | **arouse expectations** (=make you think that something good is going to happen) *The ceasefire has aroused expectations of an end to the war.* **3** the belief that something ought to happen or that someone should behave in a particular way: *Some have totally unrealistic expectations of both medical and nursing staff.* **4 expectation of life** the number of years that someone is likely to live; LIFE EXPECTANCY S2 W2

**ex·pec·ted** /ɪk'spekt̬ɪd/ *adj* [only before noun] an event or person that is expected is one you think will happen or are waiting for: *The expected storm never occurred so we had the barbecue after all.* S3 W2 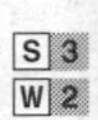

**ex·pec·to·rant** /ɪk'spektərənt/ *n* [U] *formal* a type of cough medicine that you take to help get rid of PHLEGM (=a sticky substance) in your lungs

**ex·pec·to·rate** /ɪk'spektəreɪt/ *v* [I] *formal* to force liquid out of your mouth; SPIT¹ (1)

**ex·pe·di·en·cy** /ɪk'spiːdiənsi/ also **ex·pe·di·ence** /-diəns/ *n* [C,U] what it is useful or necessary to do in a particular situation, even if it is morally wrong: *Not burying the dead soldiers was unfortunately a matter of expediency.*

**ex·pe·di·ent¹** /ɪk'spiːdiənt/ *n* [C] a clever and effective way of dealing with a problem, even though it may be morally wrong: **by the expedient of** *Moore escaped by the simple expedient of lying down in a clump of grass.*

**expedient²** *adj* helping you to deal with a problem quickly and effectively, although sometimes in a way that is morally wrong: **be expedient to do sth** *We have decided it would be expedient to appoint a committee to investigate the problem.* —opposite INEXPEDIENT —**expediently** *adv*

**ex·pe·dite** /'eksp̬ɪdaɪt/ *v* [T] to make a process happen more quickly: *strategies to expedite the decision-making process*

**ex·pe·di·tion** /ˌeksp̬ɪ'dɪʃən/ *n* **1** [C] a long journey, especially one made by a group of people, to a place that is dangerous or that has not been visited before: *Brown led an expedition to the top of Kilimanjaro.* **2** [C] the group of people that make this journey: *He was the youngest member of the British Everest expedition in 1974.* **3** [C] *often humorous* a short journey, usually made for a particular purpose: **a shopping expedition** *a shopping expedition to the mall* **4** [U] the act of doing something more quickly than you would usually

**ex·pe·di·tion·a·ry** /ˌeksp̬ɪ'dɪʃənəri◂‖-neri/ *adj* **expeditionary army/force etc** an army etc that is sent to a battle in another country

**ex·pe·di·tious** /ˌeksp̬ɪ'dɪʃəs◂/ *adj formal* quick and effective —**expeditiously** *adv*: *Complaints must be dealt with expeditiously.*

**ex·pel** /ɪk'spel/ *v* **expelled, expelling** [T] **1** to dismiss someone officially from a school or organization: **expel sb from** *I was expelled from school when I was fourteen.* | **expel sb for doing sth** *Three party members were* *expelled for accepting bribes.* | **get expelled** *You can get expelled for smoking.* **2** to force a foreigner to leave a country, especially because they have broken the law or for political reasons: *The government is trying to expel all journalists.* **3** to force air, water, or gas etc out of your body or out of a container —see also EXPULSION

**ex·pend** /ɪkˈspend/ *v* [T] **expend time/money/resources etc** to use or spend a lot of time etc in order to do something: *Try not to expend more energy than necessary.* | **expend sth in/on (doing) sth** *A great deal of time and money has been expended on creating a pleasant office atmosphere.*

**ex·pen·da·ble** /ɪkˈspendəbəl/ *adj* **1** no longer useful or important so that you can get rid of it: *This government seems to think skilled shipyard workers are expendable.* **2** a soldier who is expendable could be allowed to die

W2 **ex·pen·di·ture** /ɪkˈspendɪtʃə‖-ər/ *n* **1** [C,U] the total amount of money that a government, organization, or person spends during a particular period of time: *welfare expenditures* | **[+ on]** *The total expenditure on defence has dropped since 1989.* | **public expenditure** (=the amount of money a government spends on services for the public) —compare INCOME **2** [U] the act of spending or using time, money, energy etc: *The work should be produced with minimum expenditure of time and money.*

S3 W2 **ex·pense** /ɪkˈspens/ *n* [C,U] **1** the amount of money that you have to spend on something: **household/medical/living etc expenses** (=the money that you spend for a particular purpose) *The students share all the household expenses.* | **go to great expense** also **go to a lot of expense** (=spend a lot of money on something) *We went to a lot of expense to provide the safety equipment so please take care of it.* | **spare no expense** (=spend as much money as is necessary to get the best or most expensive things) *Julie's parents had spared no expense for her wedding.* | **at great/little/no expense** *We were wined and dined at great expense.* | **think of the expense** (=it's too expensive) *I'd love to go to the Caribbean but think of the expense!* **2 expenses** [plural] money that you spend while you are doing your job on things such as travel and food, and which your employer then pays to you: **be on expenses** (=if the cost of something is on expenses, the person that you work for pays for it rather than you) *Come on, have another drink. It's all on expenses, you know.* | **all expenses paid** (=something, especially a holiday or journey that is all paid for by someone else) *The prize is an all expenses paid trip to Rio.* **3 at sb's expense a)** if you do something at someone's expense, they pay for you to do it: *Bill's just been on a computing course, all at the company's expense.* **b)** if you make jokes at someone's expense, you laugh about them: *Louis kept making jokes at his wife's expense.* **4 at the expense of** if something is done at the expense of something else, it is only achieved by harming the other thing: *High production rates are often achieved at the expense of quality of work.*

**expense ac·count** /ˈ·ˈ· ·ˌ·/ *n* [C] a system that allows someone who works for a company to spend the company's money rather than their own on hotels, meals etc

S1 W2 **ex·pen·sive** /ɪkˈspensɪv/ *adj* **1** costing a lot of money: *That's a very expensive camera. Is it insured?* | *the most expensive restaurant in town* | **expensive to produce/run/buy etc** *Cadillacs are beautiful cars but expensive to run.* | **prohibitively expensive** (=so expensive that most people cannot afford it) **2 expensive mistake** a mistake that puts you in a very bad situation: *Losing your temper with the client was a very expensive mistake; we've lost the contract.* —**expensively** *adv*

S1 W1 **ex·pe·ri·ence¹** /ɪkˈspɪəriəns‖-ˈspɪr-/ *n*

**1 ▶ KNOWLEDGE/SKILL ◀** [U] knowledge or skill gained while doing a job: **[+ in]** *Karl has considerable experience in modern methods of diagnosis.* | **political/teaching/computing etc experience** *The job requires no secretarial experience.* | **previous experience** *The interviewer asked if I had any previous experience.* | **lack of experience** *He didn't get the post, due to lack of experience.* | **get/gain experience** *Fran is gaining valuable experience working for her father's firm.* | **practical experience** (=experience gained by actually doing something, rather than knowledge from books etc) *good judgements based on sound practical experience* | **have experience on your side** (=have an advantage over other people because you know more about a particular thing than they do or have been doing it for longer) *Sampras is a skilful player, but Becker has experience on his side.* | **first-hand experience of** (=experience gained by actually doing something) *Kevin has first-hand experience of living in Italy.*

**2 ▶ OF LIFE ◀** [U] the state of knowing, or having learnt a lot, about life and the world from events that have happened to you and people you have met: **in your experience** *In my experience, these things never last very long.* | **past/personal experience** *Past experience told her that none of the students would have prepared the lesson.* | **know from bitter experience** (=know what is likely to happen in a particular situation because you have learned from unpleasant or difficult experiences) *Rita knew from bitter experience not to rely on Martin in a crisis.* | **learn from (your) experience** *There's no point telling teenagers anything – you just have to let them learn from their experience.* | **experience shows that...** *Experience shows that staff respond very well to a more consultative approach.*

**3 ▶ STH THAT HAPPENS ◀** [C] something that happens to you or something you do, especially when this affects or influences you in some way: *childhood experiences* | **[+ of/with]** *This was my first experience of living with other people.* | **[+ for]** *Failing an exam was a new experience for me.* | **a bad/strange/dreadful experience** *It was a strange experience to see my father being taken to hospital on a stretcher.* | **a memorable/unforgettable etc experience** *Reaching the top of Mt Whitney was an unforgettable experience.* | **quite an experience** (=very interesting, exciting etc) *Parachuting is quite an experience, let me tell you.* | **religious experience** (=a situation in which you feel, hear, or see something that affects you strongly and makes you believe in God) *She claimed to have had some sort of religious experience while in Africa.*

**4 the black/female/Russian etc experience** [U] events or knowledge shared by the members of a particular society or group of people: *No writer has ever expressed the black experience with such passion as Toni Morisson.*

**5 work experience a)** a system in which a student can work for a company in order to learn about a job **b)** the period of time during which a student does this: *Ella is about to do work experience with a clothing manufacturer.*

**experience²** *v* [T] **1** if you experience a problem or situation, it happens to you or affects you: *Children need to experience things for themselves in order to learn from them.* | *Germany experienced a period of enormous growth in the 60s.* | **experience sth at first hand** (=know about something because it has affected your directly, rather than just reading or hearing about it) *During the war they experienced at first hand the horror of night bombing raids.* **2** to feel a particular emotion or physical sensation: *Many women experience feelings of nausea during pregnancy.* 

**ex·pe·ri·enced** /ɪkˈspɪəriənst‖-ˈspɪr-/ *adj* possessing skills or knowledge because you have done something often or for a long time: *an experienced pilot* | **[+ in]** *Blake's very experienced in microsurgery.* S3

**ex·per·i·en·tial** /ɪkˌspɪəriˈenʃəl◂‖-ˌspɪr-/ *adj* based on or connected with experience: *experiential approaches to learning*

**ex·per·i·ment¹** /ɪkˈsperɪmənt/ *n* [C, U] **1** a thorough test using scientific methods to discover how someone or something reacts under certain conditions: **[+ in/on/with]** *experiments on sleep deprivation* | **do/conduct/carry out/perform an experiment** (=do an experiment) *Joule carried out a series of simple experiments to* 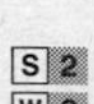

*test his theory.* **2** a process in which a new idea or method is tested to see if it is useful or effective: *an experiment in private enterprise*|**by experiment** *Find out by experiment what foods the baby likes.*

**ex·per·i·ment²** /ɪk'sperɪ̇ment/ *v* [I] **1** to try various ideas, methods etc to see whether they will work or what effect they will have: [+ **with/on**] *I'm seeing children of 6 experiment with drugs.* **2** to test something using scientific methods to see if it is true or to obtain more information about it: [+ **with/on**] *activists protesting against experimenting on animals* —**experimenter** *n* [C]

W3 **ex·per·i·men·tal** /ɪk,sperɪ̇'mentl◂/ *adj* **1** used for, connected with, or resulting from experiments: *experimental animals*|*experimental data* **2** using new ideas or methods: *experimental teaching techniques*

**ex·per·i·men·tal·ly** /ɪk,sperɪ̇'mentl-i/ *adv* **1** in a way that is connected with experiments: *data obtained experimentally* **2** in a way that involves using new ideas or methods: *The Americans experimentally exploded the first nuclear weapon in the history of mankind.* **3** if you do something experimentally you do it in order to see or feel what something is like: *He ran his fingers experimentally over the animal's back.*

**ex·pe·ri·men·ta·tion** /ɪk,sperɪ̇men'teɪʃən/ *n* [U] the process of testing various ideas, methods etc to see whether they will work or what effect they have: *There is often a period of sexual experimentation during adolescence.*|[+ **with/in**] *experimentation with different combinations of chemicals*

S3 W2 **ex·pert¹** /'ekspɜːt‖-ɜːrt/ *n* [C] someone who has a special skill or special knowledge of a subject: [+ **on/in/at**] *He's an expert in electronic music.*

W3 **expert²** *adj* having a special skill or special knowledge of a subject: *Ministers depend on civil servants for expert advice.* —**expertly** *adv* —**expertness** *n* [U]

W3 **ex·per·tise** /,ekspɜː'tiːz‖-ɜːr-/ *n* [U] special skills or knowledge in a particular subject: *trainee engineers with varying degrees of computer expertise*|[+ **in**] *expertise in the field of literary criticism*

**expert sys·tem** /,·· '··/ *n* [C] a computer system containing a lot of information about one particular subject, so that it can help someone find an answer to a problem

**ex·pi·ate** /'ekspieɪt/ *v* [T] *formal* to be sorry for something you have done wrong and accept your punishment willingly, or try to do something to improve what you did —**expiation** /,ekspi'eɪʃən/ *n*: *the expiation of your sins*

**ex·pir·a·tion** /,ekspɪ̇'reɪʃən/ *n* [U] the American form of EXPIRY

**expiration date** /··'·· ,·/ *n* [C] *AmE* the date on which something can no longer be used or is no longer safe to eat—see also **expiry date** (EXPIRY (2)), SELL-BY DATE

**ex·pire** /ɪk'spaɪə‖-'spaɪr/ *v* [I] **1** if an official document expires, the period of time during which it can be used ends: *My passport expires next week.*|[+ **on/in/at**] *Our contracts are due to expire on 20 June.* **2** if a period of time when someone has a particular position of authority expires, it ends: *The chairman's term of office expires at the end of March.* **3** *literary* if someone expires, they die: *Ophelia expires in Act IV of Hamlet.*

**ex·pir·y** /ɪk'spaɪəri‖-'spaɪri/ *n* [U] *BrE* **1** the end of a period of time during which an official document can be used, or of a period of authority; EXPIRATION *AmE* **2 expiry date** the date on which something can no longer be used: *Check the expiry date on your passport.*

S1 W1 **ex·plain** /ɪk'spleɪn/ *v* [I,T] **1** to make something clear or easy to understand: *Our lawyer carefully explained the procedure.*|**explain (to sb) why/how/where etc** *The librarian will explain how to use the catalogue system.*|**explain that** *I explained that I was really a police officer.*|**explain (sth) to sb** *He briefly explained the situation to them.* **2** to give or be a reason for something: *Wait! I can explain everything.*|**explain that** *She explained that she had been ill.*|**explain why/how etc** *Perhaps genetic differences can explain why some women develop breast cancer and others do not.* **3 explain yourself a)** to tell someone who is angry or upset with you the reasons why you did something: *Mr Hennessey tells me you haven't been to school for the last few days; I think you'd better explain yourself.* **b)** to say clearly what you mean: *No, I didn't mean that. I guess I haven't explained myself very well.*

**explain** sth ↔ **away** *phr v* [T] to tell someone the reason why you did something or why something happened in order to make it seem less important or not your fault: *That woman finds more ways to explain away her failures than anyone I've ever met!.*

**ex·pla·na·tion** /,eksplə'neɪʃən/ *n* **1** [C,U] the reasons given for why something happened or why you did something: *I'm waiting to hear your explanation.*|[+ **for**] *He'd better have a good explanation for his behaviour!*|[+ **of**] *Did Valerie give any explanation of why she was late?*|**in explanation of** (=as a reason for) *In explanation of the job cuts, the firm said that orders had been much lower than expected.*|**provide/come up with an explanation** *After failing to come up with an adequate explanation, Smith was arrested for robbery.* —see EXCUSE² (USAGE) **2** [C] a statement or piece of writing intended to describe how something works or make something easier to understand: *Each of the diagrams was accompanied by a simple explanation.*|[+ **of**] *I'll try and give you a quick explanation of how the machine works.* S3 W2

**ex·plan·a·to·ry** /ɪk'splænətəri‖-tɔːri/ *adj* intended to describe how something works or make something easier to understand: *explanatory notes at the end of each chapter* —see also SELF-EXPLANATORY

**ex·ple·tive** /ɪk'spliːtɪv‖'eksplətɪv/ *n* [C] *formal* a rude word that you use when you are angry or in pain: *a mild expletive such as 'damn'*

**ex·pli·ca·ble** /ek'splɪkəbəl/ *adj* [often in negatives] able to be easily understood or explained: *for no explicable reason* —opposite INEXPLICABLE

**ex·pli·cate** /'eksplɪ̇keɪt/ *v* [T] *formal* to explain a work of literature, an idea etc in detail —**explication** /,eksplɪ̇'keɪʃən/ *n* [C,U]

**ex·pli·cit** /ɪk'splɪsɪ̇t/ *adj* **1 explicit instructions/warnings etc** an explicit instruction etc is expressed in a way that is very clear: *There was no explicit mention in the report of Capt Kirk's involvement.*|**make something explicit** *The contrast could not have been made more explicit.* **2 be explicit** to say something very clearly and directly: *I don't quite understand your plan. Could you be a little more explicit, please?*|[+ **about**] *Sadie was very explicit about her reasons for wanting a divorce.* **3** language or pictures that are explicit describe or show sex or violence very clearly: *The film contains some very explicit love scenes.* —compare IMPLICIT —**explicitly** *adv* —**explicitness** *n* [U]

**ex·plode** /ɪk'spləʊd‖-'sploʊd/ *v*

**1** ▶ **BURST** ◀ [I,T] to burst, or to make something burst, into small pieces, usually with a loud noise and in a way that causes damage: *We sat in the bomb shelter listening to the enemy shells exploding.* —compare IMPLODE

**2** ▶ **GET ANGRY** ◀ [I] to suddenly become angry or dangerous: *These guys tend to explode at any moment over the least thing.*|[+ **in/with/into**] *Tensions are running high and police are afraid the situation may explode into violence.*

**3** ▶ **PROVE FALSE** ◀ [T] to prove that something that many people think or believe, is wrong or not true: **explode a myth/rumour etc** *The book explodes many myths about rape.*

**4** ▶ **GET BIGGER** ◀ [I] to increase greatly in numbers or amount: *The population exploded in the early 1970s.*

**5** ▶ **MAKE A LOUD NOISE** ◀ [I] to make a very loud noise: *A clap of thunder exploded overhead.*

**6** ▶ **MOVE SUDDENLY** ◀ [I] to suddenly begin moving or doing something very quickly: [+ **into**] *Nancy exploded into action.*|*The engine suddenly exploded into life.*

**ex·plod·ed** /ɪk'spləʊdɪ̇d‖-'sploʊ-/ *adj technical* an exploded drawing, model etc shows the parts of something separately but in a way that shows how they are related or put together: *an exploded diagram of an engine*

W3 **ex·ploit**[1] /ɪk'splɔɪt/ *v* [T] **1** to treat someone unfairly in order to get money or an advantage for yourself: *People who work at home are more easily exploited by employers.* **2** to use something fully and effectively in order to gain an advantage or profit: *Casey founded a company to exploit the mineral resources in the area.* —**exploitable** *adj* —**exploiter** *n* [C]

**ex·ploit**[2] /'eksplɔɪt/ *n* [C usually plural] brave and exciting actions that people admire: *the exploits of the early explorers of the Canadian forests*

**ex·ploi·ta·tion** /ˌeksplɔɪ'teɪʃən/ *n* [U] **1** a situation in which someone treats someone else unfairly in order to get money or an advantage for themselves: *the exploitation of children in factories in the 1900's* **2** a process in which materials or someone's skills are used effectively in order to gain an advantage or profit: *guidelines on the controlled exploitation of ocean resources*

**ex·ploit·a·tive** /ɪk'splɔɪtətɪv/ *adj* treating people unfairly to get money or an advantage: *exploitative employers*

**ex·plo·ra·tion** /ˌeksplə'reɪʃən/ *n* [C,U] **1** an examination of an area or journey through it in order to find out what is there or what it is like: *The North Sea has been an important centre for oil exploration.* | [+ **of**] *the exploration of space* **2** an examination or discussion of something to find out more about it: [+ **into**] *an exploration into the local records*

**ex·plo·ra·to·ry** /ɪk'splɒrətəri‖ɪk'splɔːrətɔːri/ *adj* done in order to find out more about something: *exploratory surgery*

S3 W2 **ex·plore** /ɪk'splɔː‖-'splɔːr/ *v* **1** [I,T] to travel through or examine an area in order to find out what is there or what it is like: *Lewis and Clark explored the territory from St Louis to the Pacific.* | *exploring for gold* **2** [T] to examine or discuss something carefully in order to find out more about it: *a theme explored by Mrs. Gaskell in her later novels*

**ex·plo·rer** /ɪk'splɔːrə‖-ər/ *n* [C] someone who travels through an area about which little is known or which has not been visited before

**ex·plo·sion** /ɪk'spləʊʒən‖-'sploʊ-/ *n* **1** [C] a loud sound caused by something such as a bomb bursting into small pieces: *a nuclear explosion* | [+ **of**] *The explosion of the space shuttle Challenger shocked the nation.* **2** [C,U] a process in which something such as a bomb is deliberately made to explode: *controlled explosion of the device* **3** [C] a sudden or rapid increase in the number or amount of something: *The population explosion in India caused famine and poverty.* **4** [C] a sudden expression of emotion, especially anger: *His frustration grew, and I expected an explosion at any minute.* **5** [C] a sudden very loud noise: *an explosion of laughter*

**ex·plo·sive**[1] /ɪk'spləʊsɪv‖-'sploʊ-/ *adj* **1** able or likely to explode: *At high temperatures this gas is explosive.* | **explosive device** (=a bomb) **2** an explosive situation is violent or dangerous: *the explosive atmosphere of the inner cities* **3** increasing suddenly or rapidly in amount or number: *the computer industry's explosive growth* **4** tending to show angry violent feelings suddenly: *an explosive temperament* **5** having great force or power, usually as the result of an explosion: *The bullet hit its target with explosive force.* **6** an explosive sound is sudden and loud —**explosively** *adv* —**explosiveness** *n* [U]

**explosive**[2] *n* [C] a substance that can cause an explosion: *Semtex, the explosive used in the Lockerbie airplane disaster* —see also HIGH EXPLOSIVE, PLASTIC EXPLOSIVE

**ex·po** /'ekspəʊ‖-poʊ/ *n* [C] *informal* an EXPOSITION (2)

**ex·po·nent** /ɪk'spəʊnənt‖-'spoʊ-/ *n* [C] **1** someone who supports an idea, belief etc and who tries to explain it and persuade others that it is good or useful: [+ **of**] *a leading exponent of Jungian psychology* **2** someone whose work or methods provide a good example of a particular skill, idea, or activity: [+ **of**] *The poet Goethe is a supreme exponent of the Romantic response to nature.* **3** *technical* a sign written above and to the right of a number or letter to show how many times that quantity is to be multiplied by itself, for example $2^3$

**ex·po·nen·tial** /ˌekspə'nenʃəl◂/ *adj* **1 exponential growth/increase** *technical* a rate of growth that becomes faster as the amount of the thing that is growing increases **2** *technical* using a sign that shows how many times a number is to be multiplied by itself: *$y^n$ is an exponential expression* —**exponentially** *adv*

**ex·port**[1] /'ekspɔːt‖-ɔːrt/ *n* **1** [U] the sale of goods to another country: [+ **of**] *The export of electronic equipment has risen sharply.* | **export market/industry/licence etc** *Export licences for arms are strictly controlled.* **2** [C usually plural] a product that is sold to another country: *Wheat is one of Alberta's chief exports.* | **invisible export** (=something that is sold to another country which is not an industrial product, food etc) *Selling insurance overseas is Britain's largest invisible export.* —opposite IMPORT[2] (1, 2) W2

**ex·port**[2] /ɪk'spɔːt‖-ɔːrt/ *v* **1** [I,T] to sell goods to another country: **export sth to sb** *In 1986 the company exported about 210,000 cases of wine to the UK.* **2** [T] to introduce an activity, idea etc to another place or country: *The influence of African music has been exported to many parts of the western world.* —opposite IMPORT[1] —**exportation** /ˌekspɔː'teɪʃən‖-ɔːr-/ *n* [U]

**ex·port·er** /ɪk'spɔːtə‖-'spɔːrtər/ *n* [C] a person, company, or country that sells goods to another country [+ **of**] *Saudi Arabia, a leading exporter of oil* —opposite IMPORTER

**ex·pose** /ɪk'spəʊz‖-'spoʊz/ *v* [T] W3
**1** ▶ **SHOW** ◀ to show something that is usually covered: *The wolf opened its mouth to expose a row of sharp white teeth.* | **expose sth to sth** *Wounds that are exposed to the air heal more quickly.*
**2** ▶ **TO STH DANGEROUS** ◀ to put someone in a harmful situation, position etc, where they have no protection against something dangerous: **expose sb to sth** *The report revealed that workers had been exposed to unacceptably high levels of radiation.* | **expose yourself to ridicule/criticism etc** (=say or do something that may make people laugh at you, criticize you etc)
**3** ▶ **TELL THE TRUTH** ◀ to tell the truth about something, or show what it is really like, especially because you think it is harmful, illegal etc: *a radical group that works to expose and condemn racism* | **expose sb as sth** *Klaus von Bulow was exposed as a liar and a cheat.*
**4** ▶ **SEE/EXPERIENCE** ◀ to learn about beliefs, ideas etc, especially by seeing things or having new experiences: **expose sb to sth** *Travel abroad exposes children to different languages and cultures.*
**5** ▶ **PHOTOGRAPH** ◀ to allow light onto a piece of film in a camera in order to take a photograph
**6** ▶ **FEELINGS** ◀ to show other people feelings that you usually hide, especially by behaving in a particular way: *Eric broke down and wept, exposing the vulnerable side of his nature.*
**7 expose yourself** if a man exposes himself, he shows his sexual organs to someone he does not know in a public place, usually because he is mentally ill

**ex·po·sé** /ek'spəʊzeɪ‖ˌekspə'zeɪ/ *n* [C] a story in a newspaper or on television that shows people the truth about something, especially something dishonest or illegal: [+ **of**]: *an exposé of corrupt practices by lawyers*

**ex·posed** /ɪk'spəʊzd‖-'spoʊzd/ *adj* **1** not protected from the weather: *an exposed coastline* **2** not protected from attack; VULNERABLE: *Fiorentina's defence looked very exposed in the second half.*

**ex·po·si·tion** /ˌekspə'zɪʃən/ *n* **1** [C,U] a clear and detailed explanation: [+ **of**] *a lucid exposition of educational theories* **2** [C] an important event at which industrial goods are shown

**ex post fac·to law** /ˌeks pəʊst 'fæktəʊ ˌlɔː‖-poʊst

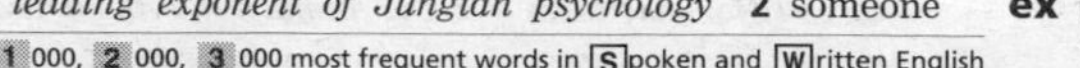

ˈfæktoʊ ˌlɔː/ *n* [C] *law* a law that makes a particular action into a crime, and then punishes people who took that action before it had legally become a crime

**ex·pos·tu·late** /ɪkˈspɒstʃʊ̈leɪt‖-ˈspɑː-/ *v* [I] *formal* to express strong disapproval, disagreement, or annoyance: **expostulate (that)** *"But that's the equivalent of saying that you drank beer but didn't swallow it," expostulated one reporter.* —**expostulation** /ɪkˌspɒstʃʊ̈ˈleɪʃən‖-ˌspɑː-/ *n* [C,U]

W3 **ex·po·sure** /ɪkˈspəʊʒə‖-ˈspoʊʒər/ *n*
**1** ▶**TO DANGER**◀ [C,U] the state of being put into a situation that is harmful because you have no protection from something that is dangerous: **[+ to]** *Skin cancer can be caused by prolonged exposure to the sun.* | *Through TV, kids have regular exposure to sex and violence.*
**2** ▶**TRUTH**◀ [C,U] something that is said or written in order to tell people the truth about something illegal, dishonest, or harmful: *The exposure of George Davis' illicit financial dealings provoked a public outcry.*
**3** ▶**MAKE FACTS KNOWN**◀ [U] things that are said and written on television and in newspapers that make a person or event known to a lot of people: *The failure of their marriage has received a lot of exposure in the press recently.*

**4** ▶**BE VERY COLD**◀ [U] if you have exposure you are extremely cold and ill, especially because you have been outside in very cold weather for too long without protection: *We nearly died of exposure on the mountainside.*
**5** ▶**PHOTOGRAPHY**◀ [C] **a)** a length of film in a camera that is used to take a photograph: *I have three exposures left on this roll.* **b)** the amount of time a piece of film is exposed (EXPOSE (5)) to the light when making a photograph
**6** ▶**SHOW**◀ [C] the act of showing something that is usually hidden
**7** ▶**DIRECTION**◀ [singular] the direction in which a building, hill etc faces: *My bedroom has a southern exposure.* —see also INDECENT EXPOSURE

**ex·pound** /ɪkˈspaʊnd/ *v* [I, T] *formal* to explain or talk about something in detail: **[+ on]** *a philosopher expounding on the illusory nature of the world*

S2 W1 **ex·press¹** /ɪkˈspres/ *v* [T]
**1** ▶**IN WORDS**◀ to tell people what you are feeling or thinking by using words: *Bill's never been afraid to express his opinions.* | **express sympathy/fear/anger etc** *Parents have expressed their concerns about their children's safety.* | **express interest** (=say that you are interested in something) *The public are expressing an increasing interest in green issues.* | **express opposition to** (=say publicly that you do not agree with something) *Managers and players alike expressed opposition to the scheme.* | **express thanks/gratitude** (=thank someone in a speech or by writing a letter) *Finally, I'd like to express my sincere gratitude for your help in this matter.* | **express yourself** (=let people know your thoughts and feelings so that they can understand) *Young children often have difficulty expressing themselves.* | **can't express** *Words can't express how angry we felt.*
**2** ▶**IN ART/MUSIC ETC**◀ to show your feelings or thoughts using art, music, films etc: *Many of Munch's paintings express a deep feeling of despair.* | **express yourself by/through etc** *Alain expresses himself best through his music.*
**3** ▶**IN BEHAVIOUR/LOOK**◀ to let people know what you are feeling or thinking by the look on your face or by your behaviour: *The look on Paul's face expressed his total contempt for them.*
**4** ▶**FEELING**◀ if a feeling expresses itself it can be clearly seen and understood: *Major Hall's frustration expressed itself in occasional bouts of rage.*
**5** ▶**LETTER/PACKAGE**◀ *BrE* to send a letter or package using a special post system so that it arrives very quickly
**6** ▶**MATHEMATICS**◀ *technical* to show a mathematical idea in a particular form: *Express three-quarters as a decimal.*

**express²** *adj* [only before noun] **1** an express command, desire, or aim is deliberately stated for a particular reason: *Matthew left express instructions to keep all doors locked.* | *I came here with the express purpose of seeing you.* **2 express train/coach/service** a train or bus that travels very quickly: *There's an express service between London and Glasgow twice daily.* **3 express post/mail/delivery** a system within the Post Office that delivers letters and packages very quickly **4 express lane** *AmE* a LANE (2) on a FREEWAY used by vehicles that are travelling fast

**express³** *n* **1** [C usually singular] a train or bus that travels from one place to another very quickly: **London-Gatwick Express/Orient Express** (=a fast train or bus which does a particular journey regularly) **2** [U] a post service that delivers letters and packages very quickly: *Send these books by express.*

**express⁴** *adv* **send/deliver sth express** to send or deliver a letter, parcel etc quickly using a special post service

**ex·pres·sion** /ɪkˈspreʃən/ *n* S2 W1
**1** ▶**WORDS**◀ [C] a word or group of words with a particular meaning: *The expression 'in the family way' means 'pregnant'.* | **pardon/forgive/excuse the expression** (=used when you have used a word that you think may offend someone) *He doesn't know his ass from a hole in the ground if you'll pardon the expression.*
**2** ▶**ON SB'S FACE**◀ [C] a look on someone's face that shows what they are thinking or feeling: *a thoughtful expression* | **an expression of surprise/fear/amusement** *Petra looked at her plate with an expression of disgust.*
**3** ▶**SAY/WRITE**◀ [C,U] something you say or write that shows what you think or feel: **an expression of sympathy/thanks etc** *Mrs Mayer received their expressions of sympathy with great dignity.* | **give expression to sth** *The minister gave expression to his anger in an attack on the government last night.* | **freedom of expression** (=the right to express your opinions freely)
**4** ▶**ACTIONS/BEHAVIOUR**◀ [C,U] something you do or make that shows what you think or feel: **[+ of]** *The recent strikes are an expression of the worker's discontent.* | **give expression to** *John gave expression to his love of nature in his paintings.* | **find expression** *Pam's latent artistic talents found their expression in music.*
**5** ▶**EVENTS**◀ [C,U] the way in which feelings and ideas are shown in particular events: **find expression in sth** *The fiscal crisis has found its clearest expression in the poverty of the inner cities.*
**6** ▶**MUSIC**◀ [U] the quality of singing or playing a musical instrument with feeling: *Try to put a bit more expression into the slow passage.*
**7** ▶**MATHEMATICS**◀ [C] *technical* a sign or group of signs that show a mathematical idea in a particular form: *$x^2 + 4$ is an algebraic expression*

**ex·pres·sion·is·m** /ɪkˈspreʃənɪzəm/ *n* [U] a style of painting, writing, or music that expresses feelings rather than describing objects and experiences —**expressionist** *n* [C] —**expressionist** *adj*

**ex·pres·sion·less** /ɪkˈspreʃənləs/ *adj* an expressionless face or voice does not show what someone thinks or feels: *a blank expressionless stare* —**expressionlessly** *adv*

**ex·pres·sive** /ɪkˈspresɪv/ *adj* **1** showing very clearly what someone thinks or feels: *Cath threw up her arms in an expressive gesture.* **2 be expressive of sth** showing a particular feeling or influence: *The sculpture is expressive of Michelangelo's spiritual aspirations.* —**expressively** *adv* —**expressiveness** *n* [U]

**ex·press·ly** /ɪkˈspresli/ *adv formal* **1** if you say something expressly, you say it very clearly and firmly: *I expressly forbade them to bring animals into the house.*

2 deliberately: *The building is expressly designed to conserve energy.*

**express post** /ˌ· ˈ·/ *BrE*, **express mail** *AmE* *n* [U] a post service that delivers letters and parcels very quickly

**ex·press·way** /ɪkˈspreswеɪ/ *n* [C] *AmE* a very wide road, usually in a city, on which cars can travel very quickly without stopping —see also FREEWAY, MOTORWAY

**ex·pro·pri·ate** /ɪkˈsprəʊprieɪt‖-ˈsproʊ-/ *v* [T] *formal* **1** to take away private property for public use **2** to take something from someone illegally in order to use it —**expropriator** *n* [C] —**expropriation** /ɪkˌsprəʊpriˈeɪʃən‖-ˌsproʊ-/ *n* [C, U]

**ex·pul·sion** /ɪkˈspʌlʃən/ *n* [C,U] **1** the process of sending a person or group of people away from a place often by using force: *the expulsion of rebel forces* **2** the act of sending someone away from a school or organization so that they can no longer go there or be a member: *Tina's anti-social behaviour eventually led to her expulsion.* **3** the act of getting rid of a substance from your body or from a container —see also EXPEL

**ex·punge** /ɪkˈspʌndʒ/ *v* [T] *formal* **1** to remove a name from a list, piece of information, or book **2** to make someone forget something unpleasant: *I tried to expunge the whole episode from my memory.*

**ex·pur·gated** /ˈekspəgeɪt‖-ər-/ *adv* an expurgated book, play etc has had some parts removed because they are considered harmful or offensive: *an expurgated version of the writings of de Sade* | —**expurgate** *v* [T] —**expurgation** /ˌekspəˈgeɪʃən‖-pər-/ *n* [C, U]

**ex·qui·site** /ɪkˈskwɪzɪt, ˈekskwɪ-/ *adj* **1** extremely beautiful and very delicately made: *exquisite craftsmanship* **2** very sensitive and delicate in the way you behave or do things: *Darling, you have exquisite taste.* **3** *literary* exquisite pain or pleasure is felt very strongly —**exquisitely** *adv* —**exquisiteness** *n* [U]

**ex-ser·vice·man** /ˌ· ˈ···/ *n plural* **ex-servicemen** [C] *especially BrE* a man who used to be in the army, navy, or AIRFORCE

**ex-ser·vice·wom·an** /ˌ· ˈ····/ *n plural* **ex-servicewomen** [C] *especially BrE* a woman who used to be in the army, navy, or AIRFORCE

**ext.** the written abbreviation of EXTENSION (2): *Contact Alison Lever on Ext. 3945.*

**ex·tant** /ɪkˈstænt/ *adj formal* still existing in spite of being very old: *Few of the manuscripts are extant.*

**ex·tem·po·ra·ne·ous** /ɪkˌstempəˈreɪniəs◂/ *adj* spoken or done without any preparation or practice: *an extemporaneous speech* —**extemporaneously** *adv* —**extemporaneousness** *n* [U]

**ex·tem·po·re** /ɪkˈstempəri/ *adj* spoken or done without any preparation or practice: *an extempore speech* —**extempore** *adv*

**ex·tem·po·rize** also **-ise** *BrE* /ɪkˈstempəraɪz/ *v* [I] *formal* to speak without preparation, especially during a performance; AD-LIB —**extemporization** /ɪkˌstempəraɪˈzeɪʃən‖-rə-/ *n* [C,U]

3 **ex·tend** /ɪkˈstend/ *v*
2 **1 ▶ CONTINUE ◀** [I always + adv/prep] to continue for a particular distance or over a particular area: **across/over/through etc** *The River Nile extends as far as Lake Victoria.* | **extend 100 km/30 yards etc** *Smith Point extends a hundred yards or so into the water.* | *The forest extended in all directions as far as the eye could see.*

**2 ▶ MAKE STH BIGGER ◀** [T] to make a building, road etc bigger or longer: *We extended the kitchen by six feet.*

**3 ▶ HAPPEN/EXIST ◀** [I always + adv/prep] to continue to happen or exist for a certain period of time: [+ **for/into/over etc**] *The hot weather extended well into October.*

**4 ▶ TIME ◀** [T] to increase a period of time that has been agreed, especially in order to finish a job or pay money that you owe: *Management have agreed to extend the deadline.*

**5 ▶ CONTROL/INFLUENCE ◀** [I always + adv/prep, T] if you extend your control, influence etc or if it extends over something, it becomes more powerful: *We hope to extend the effects of sanctions against the regime.* | [+ **into/over/beyond etc**] *My duties at the school extend beyond just teaching.* | *The regulations do not extend to foreign visitors.*

**6 ▶ OFFER HELP/THANKS ◀** [T] *formal* to offer someone help, sympathy, thanks etc: **extend a welcome/greeting/invitation etc** *We'd like to extend a warm welcome to our French visitors.* | **extend thanks to sb** (=thank someone officially) | **extend condolences/sympathies** (=offer sympathy to someone when someone they know or love dies) | **extend credit to sb** (=if a bank extends credit to someone it lends them money)

**7 ▶ ARMS/LEGS ETC ◀** [T] to stretch out a part of your body: *a bird soaring on extended wings*

**8 ▶ STRENGTH/INTELLIGENCE ◀** [T] to make someone use all their strength, intelligence etc, in order to achieve good results: *Olympiakos won the match without ever being fully extended.*

**extended fam·i·ly** /ˌ·ˌ·· ˈ···/ *n* [C] a family group that consists not only of parents and children but also of grandparents, AUNTS etc

**ex·ten·sion** /ɪkˈstenʃən/ *n* S2
**1 ▶ EXTRA ROOMS ◀** [C] another room or rooms W3
which are added to a building: *The extension to the National Museum houses the Picasso collection.*

**2 ▶ TELEPHONE ◀** [C] **a)** one of many telephone lines in a large building which all have different numbers: **extension number** *My extension number is 3821.* **b)** one of two or more telephones, usually in someone's house, which all have the same number: *Can you put an extension in the bedroom?*

**3 ▶ EXTRA TIME ◀** [C usually singular] an additional period of time given to someone in order to finish a job, pay money that they owe etc: *Donald's been given an extension to finish his thesis.* | *The pub's got an extension tonight.* (=it will stay open longer than usual)

**4 ▶ ELECTRIC WIRE ◀** [C] also **extension lead** *BrE*, **extension cord** *AmE* an additional piece of electric wire used when the wire you already have is not long enough: *Use the extension when you cut the grass.*

**5 ▶ CONTROL/INFLUENCE ◀** [singular U] a process in which someone's or something's influence or control increases: [+ **of**] *the extension of the copyright laws to cover recorded material*

**6 ▶ MAKING STH BIGGER ◀** [singular U] the process of making a road, building etc bigger or longer: [+ **of**] *the proposed extension of the London-Cambridge motorway*

**7 by extension** used before mentioning something that is naturally connected to or is a natural result of something else: *My primary responsibility is to the company, and by extension to the people who work for it.*

**8 ▶ UNIVERSITY/COLLEGE ◀** [U] part of a British university or college that offers courses to people who are not full time students: **extension course** (=a course done by people who cannot study full time)

**9 ▶ STRETCH ARM/LEG ◀** [U] **a)** a process in which you stretch a part of the body: *I had physiotherapy to improve the extension of my right hand.* **b)** the position of a part of the body when it is stretched: *Your leg should now be at full extension.*

**ex·ten·sive** /ɪkˈstensɪv/ *adj* **1** covering a large area: W3
*The house stands in extensive grounds.* | **extensive damage/repairs etc** *The storm caused extensive damage.* **2** containing or dealing with a lot of information and details: *The abortion issue has been the subject of extensive debate.* —**extensively** *adv*: *Despite reading extensively, I still failed the exam.* —**extensiveness** *n* [U]

**ex·tent** /ɪkˈstent/ *n* **1** [singular] the limit or degree of S2
something's influence etc: *The success of a marriage* W1
*depends on the extent to which you are prepared to work at it.* | **to a certain extent/to some extent** (=used to say that something is partly, but not completely, true) *To a*

*certain extent it was my fault that we lost the contract.* | **to a great/large extent** (=used to say that something is mainly true) *These policies are to a large extent responsible for the region's economic decline.* | **to a lesser/greater extent** (=used when comparing two things to say that one thing has less or more influence) *These changes will affect all managers and to a lesser extent some shop-floor workers.* | **to such an extent/to the extent that** (=used to say that something has affected or influenced something so much that it causes something else to happen) *Violence increased to the extent that residents were afraid to leave their homes.* | **to what extent...?** (=used to ask how big an amount or influence is) *To what extent can we blame the government for this lack of information?* **2** [U] the size of a large area: **full extent of** *From the top window we could see the full extent of the park.* | **in extent** *The region is over 10,000 square kilometres in extent.* **3** [U] the size or degree of something dangerous or difficult, such as an injury or a problem: *Considering the extent of his injuries he's lucky to be alive.* | *It would be foolish to underestimate the extent of the problem.*

**ex·ten·u·ate** /ɪk'stenjueɪt/ *v* [T] *formal* to make an action, especially a crime, seem less bad or harmful by suggesting reasons for it: **extenuating circumstances** (=facts which explain bad or criminal behaviour) —**extenuation** /ɪkˌstenju'eɪʃən/ *n* [U]

**ex·te·ri·or¹** /ɪk'stɪəriə‖-'tɪriər/ *n* [C] **1** [usually singular] the appearance or outside surface of something: *Sun, rain and frost had damaged the exterior of the building.* **2 a cool/sullen etc exterior** behaviour that seems calm, unfriendly etc but which often hides a different feeling or attitude: *Karl hid his nervousness behind a calm exterior.* **3** a picture, film etc of an outdoor scene —opposite INTERIOR¹

**exterior²** *adj* **1** on the outside or outside surface of something: *The exterior walls need a new coat of paint.* **2 exterior to** separate or divided from something —opposite INTERIOR²

**ex·ter·mi·nate** /ɪk'stɜːmɪ̥neɪt‖-ɜːr-/ *v* [T] to kill large numbers of people or animals of a particular type so that they no longer exist —**exterminator** *n* [C] —**extermination** /ɪkˌstɜːmɪ̥'neɪʃən‖-ɜːr-/ *n* [C,U]

W2 **ex·ter·nal** /ɪk'stɜːnl‖-ɜːr-/ *adj* **1** connected with the outside of a surface or body: *The external walls were in need of repair.* | **for external use** (=medicine that is for external use must be put on your skin and not swallowed) **2** coming from outside a particular place or organization: *Considerable external pressure was put on Congress to override the veto.* | *information from external sources* **3** connected with foreign countries: *China will not tolerate any external interference in its affairs.* **4** *BrE* coming from outside a particular school or university: **external examination** (=not arranged by your own school or university) | **external examiner** (=someone from outside a particular school or university who examines its students) **5 external ear/gill/genitals etc** *technical* a part of an animal's body that is on the outer surface of the body rather than inside it —opposite INTERNAL —**externally** *adv*

**ex·ter·nal·ize** also **-ise** *BrE* /ɪk'stɜːnəlaɪz‖-ɜːr-/ *v* [T] to express inner feelings —**externalization** /ɪkˌstɜːnəlaɪ'zeɪʃən‖-ˌstɜːrnələ-/ *n* [C,U]

**ex·ter·nals** /ɪk'stɜːnlz‖-ɜːr-/ *n* [plural] the outer appearance of a situation

**ex·tinct** /ɪk'stɪŋkt/ *adj* **1** an extinct animal, plant, language etc no longer exists: *Dinosaurs have been extinct for millions of years.* **2** an extinct belief or custom no longer exists **3** an extinct VOLCANO no longer erupts (ERUPT (1))

**ex·tinc·tion** /ɪk'stɪŋkʃən/ *n* [U] **1** a situation in which a particular kind of animal, plant etc no longer exists: *Conservationists are trying to save the whale from extinction.* | **face extinction/be threatened with extinction** *Many endangered species now face extinction.* **2** a process in which a belief, way of life, feeling etc is destroyed or stops existing: *Their traditional way of life seems doomed to extinction.*

**ex·tin·guish** /ɪk'stɪŋgwɪʃ/ *v* [T] *formal* **1** to make a fire or light stop burning or shining: *Please extinguish all cigarettes.* **2** to destroy an idea or feeling or make it stop existing: *All hope was almost extinguished.*

**ex·tin·guish·er** /ɪk'stɪŋgwɪʃə‖-ər/ *n* [C] *informal* a FIRE EXTINGUISHER

**ex·tir·pate** /'ekstɜːpeɪt‖-ɜːr-/ *v* [T] *formal* to completely destroy something that is unpleasant or unwanted —**extirpation** /ˌekstɜː'peɪʃən‖-ɜːr-/ [U]

**ex·tol** /ɪk'stəʊl‖-'stoʊl/ *v* [T] *formal* to praise something very much: **extol the virtues/merits of** *a speech extolling the merits of free enterprise*

**ex·tort** /ɪk'stɔːt‖-ɔːrt/ *v* [T] to illegally force someone to give you money by threatening them: **extort money from/out of sb** *Landlords tried to cover their losses by extorting high rents from tenants.* —**extortion** /ɪk'stɔːʃən‖-ɔːr-/ *n* [U] *Confessions were obtained by extortion.* —**extortioner** *n* [C] —**extortionist** *n* [C]

**ex·tor·tion·ate** /ɪk'stɔːʃənɪ̥t‖-ɔːr-/ *adj* an extortionate price, demand, etc is extremely high: *Most drivers under 25 can only get insurance at extortionate rates.* —**extortionately** *adv*

**extra-** /ekstrə/ *prefix* outside; beyond: *extragalactic* (=outside our GALAXY) | *extramarital sex* (=between people who are not married to each other)

**ex·tra¹** /'ekstrə/ *adj* more of something, in addition to the usual or standard amount or number: *Could you get an extra loaf of bread?* | *Alan had taken extra care with his appearance that evening.* | *Residents can use the gym at no extra cost.* | **extra ten minutes/three metres/five kilos etc** *I asked for an extra day to finish the work.*

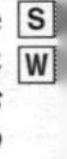

**extra²** *adv* **1 cost/earn/pay extra** to cost, earn, or pay more money than the usual amount: *I earn extra for working on Sunday.* | **be extra** (=cost an additional amount of money) *Dinner costs $15 but wine is extra.* | **ten minutes/three metres/five kilos extra** *I got 2 metres extra to make the curtains.* **2** [+ adj/adv] used to emphasize an adjective or adverb: *You're going to have to work extra hard to pass the exam.*

**extra³** *n* [C] **1** something which is added to a basic product or service which improves it and also costs more: **optional extra** (=something attractive or comfortable that you can choose to have or not) *Tinted windows and a sunroof are optional extras.* **2** something attractive or helpful that you do not get more money for: *Lena did a lot of little extras for him that weren't part of her job description.* **3** an actor in a film who does not say anything but is part of a crowd **4** a special EDITION of a newspaper containing important news: *Extra! Extra! Read all about it!*

**ex·tract¹** /ɪk'strækt/ *v* [T] **1** to remove an object from somewhere, especially by pulling it: *You'll have to have that wisdom tooth extracted.* | **extract sth from sth** *Prue managed to extract the stopper from the bottle.* **2** to carefully remove a substance from another substance which contains it, using a machine, chemical process etc: *47 tonnes of gold have been extracted at the mine.* | **extract sth from sth** *The nuts are crushed to extract the oil from them.* **3** to skilfully remove something which is among a lot of other objects or inside something: **extract sth from sth** *James slowly extracted a £5 note from his wallet.* **4** to find out information or get money from someone who does not want to give it by asking questions or using physical force: **extract sth from sb** *I finally managed to extract the truth from her.*

**ex·tract²** /'ekstrækt/ *n* **1** [C] a short piece of writing, music etc taken from a particular book, piece of music etc, especially in order to show what it is like: **[+ from]** *I've only seen short extracts from the film.* **2** [C,U] a substance taken from another substance by using a special process: **vanilla/malt/yeast extract** *Add one teaspoon of vanilla extract.*

**ex·trac·tion** /ɪk'strækʃən/ *n* **1** [C,U] the process of removing an object or substance from inside something else: [+ **of**] *the extraction of uranium from uranium ore* **2 be of French/Russian/Italian etc extraction** to be from a French, Russian etc family even though you were not born in that country

**ex·trac·tor** /ɪk'stræktə‖-ər/ also **extractor fan** /·'·· ·/ *n* [C] a machine for removing air that is hot or smells unpleasant from a kitchen, factory etc

**ex·tra·cur·ric·u·lar** /ˌekstrəkə'rɪkjʊ̈lə◂‖-ər◂/ *adj* extracurricular activities are not part of the course that a student is doing

**ex·tra·di·ta·ble** /'ekstrədaɪtəbəl/ *adj* an extraditable crime is one for which someone can be sent back to the country where the crime happened to be judged in a court of law: *Terrorism is an extraditable offense.*

**ex·tra·dite** /'ekstrədaɪt/ *v* [T + **from/to**] to use a legal process to send someone who may be guilty of a crime back to the country where the crime happened in order to judge them in a court of law —**extradition** /ˌekstrə'dɪʃən/ *n* [C,U] *an extradition order*

**ex·tra·ju·di·cial** /ˌekstrədʒuː'dɪʃəl◂/ *adj* beyond or outside the ordinary powers of the law

**ex·tra·mar·i·tal** /ˌekstrə'mærɪ̈tl◂/ *adj* an extramarital sexual relationship is one that someone has with a person who is not their husband or wife

**ex·tra·mu·ral** /ˌekstrə'mjʊərəl◂‖-'mjʊr-/ *adj* **1** connected with a place or organization but happening or done outside it: *extramural activities* **2** *especially BrE* extramural courses, studies etc involve students from outside a particular college or university —opposite INTRAMURAL

**ex·tra·ne·ous** /ɪk'streɪniəs/ *adj* **1** not belonging to or directly connected with a particular subject or problem; IRRELEVANT: [+ **to**] *Such details are extraneous to the matter in hand.* **2** coming from outside: *extraneous noises* —**extraneously** *adv*

**ex·tra·or·di·na·ri·ly** /ɪk'strɔːdənərɪ̈li‖ɪkˌstrɔːrdn'erɪ̈li, ˌekstrə'ɔːrdn-erɪ̈li/ *adv especially BrE* **1** [+ adj/adv] extremely: **extraordinarily beautiful/difficult/successful etc** *an extraordinarily beautiful young boy* **2** in a way that seems strange: *I'm afraid Jane can behave quite extraordinarily at times.*

S3 W3 **ex·tra·or·di·na·ry** /ɪk'strɔːdənəri‖ɪk'strɔːrdn-eri, ˌekstrə'ɔːr-/ *adj* **1** very much better, more beautiful, or more impressive than usual: *a woman of extraordinary beauty* **2** very unusual or surprising because it would normally be very unlikely to happen or exist: *the extraordinary landscapes of Cappodocia* | **quite/most extraordinary** *BrE* (=very unusual) *Chris's behaviour that morning was quite extraordinary.* | **extraordinary thing to do/say/happen** *What an extraordinary thing to do!* | **how extraordinary!** *BrE spoken* (=used to express surprise) *"Well then Jim got down on all fours and started barking like a dog." "How extraordinary!"* **3 extraordinary meeting/session etc** a meeting which takes place in addition to the usual ones **4 envoy/ambassador/minister extraordinary** an official employed for a special purpose, in addition to the usual officials

**ex·trap·o·late** /ɪk'stræpəleɪt/ *v* [I,T] **1** to make a guess about something in the future from facts that you already know: **extrapolate sth from sth** *It's my job to extrapolate future developments from contemporary trends.* **2** *technical* to guess a value that you do not know by continuing a curve which is based on values that you already know —**extrapolation** /ɪkˌstræpə'leɪʃən/ *n* [C, U]

**extra sen·so·ry per·cep·tion** /ˌ·· ···· ·'··/ *n* [U] ESP (1)

**ex·tra·ter·res·tri·al**[1] /ˌekstrətə'restriəl◂/ *n* [C] a living creature that people think may exist on another PLANET

**extraterrestrial**[2] *adj* connected with things that exist outside the Earth

**ex·tra·ter·ri·to·ri·al** /ˌekstrəterɪ̈'tɔːriəl◂/ *adj* **1** *formal* outside a particular country **2** *law* extra-territorial rights, powers etc are governed from outside a country or area: *an extraterritorial jurisdiction treaty* —**extraterritoriality** /ˌekstrəterɪ̈tɔːri'ælɪ̈ti/ *n* [U]

**extra time** /ˌ·· '·/ *n* [U] *especially BrE* a period of usually thirty minutes added to the end of football games to give one of the two teams a chance to win; OVERTIME (4) *AmE*

**ex·trav·a·gant** /ɪk'strævəgənt/ *adj* **1** spending a lot of money on things that are not necessary: *It was very extravagant of you to spend £500 on a dress.* **2 extravagant with sth** using too much of something or wasting it: *We mustn't be too extravagant with the electricity.* **3** very impressive because of being very expensive, beautiful etc: *Myra and Paul decided to give an extravagant dinner party.* **4** ideas or behaviour that are extravagant are too extreme and are not sensible: *extravagant claims about the effectiveness of the system* —**extravagantly** *adv* —**extravagance** *n* [C,U]

**ex·trav·a·gan·za** /ɪkˌstrævə'gænzə/ *n* [C] a very large and expensive entertainment

**ex·tra·vert** /'ekstrəvɜːt‖-ɜːrt/ *n* [C] another spelling of EXTROVERT

**ex·treme**[1] /ɪk'striːm/ *adj* **1** [only before noun] very great in degree: *Extreme poverty still exists in many rural areas.* **2 extreme south/point/end/limit etc** the extreme south etc is the place furthest towards the south etc **3** extreme opinions, beliefs, or organizations, especially political ones, are considered by most people to be unacceptable and unreasonable: *extreme right-wing nationalists* **4** very unusual and severe: *Her ideas about raising kids have always been a little extreme.* | **extreme example/case** *Social workers were horrified by this extreme case of cruelty.* 

**extreme**[2] *n* [C] **1** something that goes beyond normal limits, so that it seems very unusual and unacceptable: *We had every extreme of weather that weekend – gales, snow, and sunshine.* | **be driven to extremes** *Driven to extremes by the rioting, the government imposed a six pm curfew.* | **go to extremes/take sth to extremes** (=behave in a way that goes beyond normal limits, especially in order to achieve something) | **go to the opposite extreme/go from one extreme to the other** (=change from being extreme in one way to being extreme in a completely different way) **2 in the extreme** to a very great degree: *My great-aunt had been generous in the extreme over the years.*

**ex·treme·ly** /ɪk'striːmli/ *adv* to a very great degree: *I'm extremely sorry to have troubled you.* S1 W2

**extremis** *n* —see IN EXTREMIS

**ex·trem·is·m** /ɪk'striːmɪzəm/ *n* [U] opinions, ideas, and actions, especially political or religious ones, that most people think are unreasonable and unacceptable

**ex·trem·ist** /ɪk'striːmɪ̈st/ *n* [C] someone who has extreme political opinions and aims, and who is willing to do unusual or illegal things in order to achieve them: *The bomb was planted by right-wing extremists.* —**extremist** *adj*

**ex·trem·i·ty** /ɪk'stremɪ̈ti/ *n* **1** [C often plural] one of the parts of your body that is furthest away from the centre, for example your fingers and toes **2** [U] the degree to which a belief, opinion, situation, or action goes beyond what is usually thought to be acceptable: *The committee was uncomfortable about the extremity of the proposal.* **3** [C] the part that is furthest away from the centre of something: *A land-locked stretch of water formed the western extremity of the Gulf of Tajura.*

**ex·tri·cate** /'ekstrɪ̈keɪt/ *v* [T] **1** to escape from a difficult or embarrassing situation: [+ **from**] *By 1897 his lawyers had managed to extricate him from the contract.* | **extricate yourself** *I desperately tried to think of a way to extricate myself from Mrs. Bedford's questioning.* **2** to remove someone or something from a place in which they are trapped: *Firemen had to extricate the driver from the wreckage.* —**extrication** /ˌekstrɪ̈'keɪʃən/ *n* [U]

**ex·tro·vert, extravert** /'ekstrəvɜːt‖-ɜːrt/ *n* [C] someone

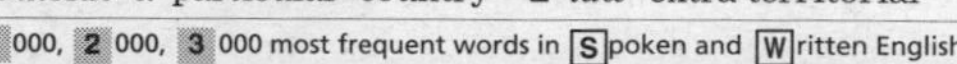

who is active and confident, and who enjoys spending time with other people: *Gini was an extrovert and loved to perform to a crowd.* —**extrovert** *adj* —opposite INTROVERT

**ex·tro·vert·ed** /ˈekstrəvɜːtɪ̯d‖-vɜːr-/ *adj* having a confident character and enjoying the company of other people —**extroversion** /ˌekstrəˈvɜːʃən‖-ˈvɜːrʒən/ *n* [U] —opposite INTROVERTED

**ex·trude** /ɪkˈstruːd/ *v* [T] *formal* **1** to push or force something out through a hole **2** *technical* to force plastic or metal through a hole so that it has a particular shape —**extrusion** /ɪkˈstruːʒən/ *n* [C,U]

**ex·u·be·rant** /ɪgˈzjuːbərənt‖ɪgˈzuː-/ *adj* **1** happy and cheerful, and full of energy and excitement **2** plants that are exuberant are healthy and growing very quickly —**exuberance** *n* [U] —**exuberantly** *adv*

**ex·ude** /ɪgˈzjuːd‖ɪgˈzuːd/ *v* **1 exude confidence/sympathy etc** if you exude a particular quality, it is easy to see that you have a lot of it **2** [I,T] to flow out slowly and steadily, or to make something do this: *Trunkfishes exude a poisonous liquid that can kill other fish.*

**ex·ult** /ɪgˈzʌlt/ *v* [I] *formal* to show that you are very happy and proud, especially because you have succeeded in doing something: [+ **at/in**] *They exulted at their victory.* | [+ **over**] *The people exulted over their fallen enemies.* —**exultation** /ˌegzʌlˈteɪʃən/ *n* [U]

**ex·ul·tant** /ɪgˈzʌltənt/ *adj formal* very happy or proud, especially because you have succeded in doing something: *Exultant crowds were dancing in the streets.* —**exultantly** *adv*

**-ey** /i/ *suffix* [in adjectives] the form used for -Y especially after y: *clayey soil*

S 1 W 1

E

## eye¹ /aɪ/ *n* [C]

① BODY PART
② WATCH/SEE
③ LOOK AT
④ LOOK AFTER
⑤ WATCH FOR
⑥ NOTICE
⑦ DISAGREE/DISBELIEVE
⑧ SURPRISE
⑨ LOVE/SEXUAL ATTRACTION
⑩ JUDGE
⑪ SPOKEN PHRASES
⑫ PURPOSE
⑬ OTHER MEANINGS

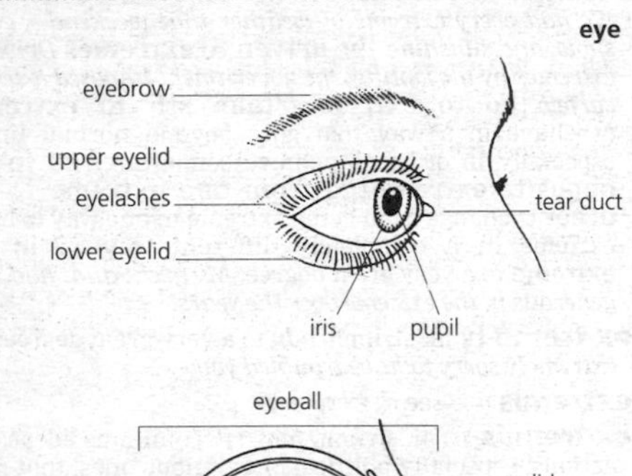


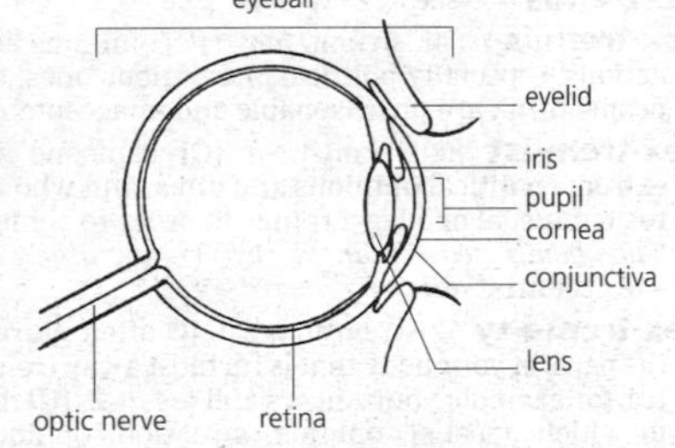


### ① BODY PART

**1** one of the two parts of the body that people and animals use to see: *Annie has blue eyes.* | *Close your eyes and count to ten.*

**2 blue-eyed/one-eyed/bright-eyed/wide-eyed etc** having blue eyes, one eye, bright eyes, eyes that are wide open etc

### ② WATCH/SEE

**3 have/keep your eye on sb** to be carefully watching everything that someone does, especially because you do not trust them to do things properly: *I've got my eye on you now, so you do as you're told!*

**4 clap/lay/set eyes on sb/sth** *spoken* an expression meaning to see someone or something, used especially when you are surprised or shocked: *I'd never clapped eyes on him before in my life!*

**5 the naked eye** if you can see something with the naked eye, you can see it without using any artificial help such as a TELESCOPE or microscope: *On a clear night these stars can be seen with the naked eye.* | **invisible to the naked eye** (=cannot be seen without artificial help)

**6 be all eyes** *especially spoken* to watch carefully what is happening or what someone is doing: *We were all eyes as he slowly drew back the curtain.*

**7 in front of/before your (very) eyes** *especially spoken* an expression meaning happening so that you can clearly see it, used especially when what you see is surprising or shocking: *Ladies and gentlemen, before your very eyes I will now make this rabbit disappear.*

### ③ LOOK AT

**8 catch sb's eye a)** to attract someone's attention and make them look at something: *All of a sudden something red caught his eye.* **b)** to look at someone at the same moment that they are looking at you: *I caught Ben's eye in the rear-view mirror and knew what he was thinking.*

**9 eye contact** if you have eye contact with someone, you look directly at them and they look directly at you: *Always establish eye contact with the customer – it inspires confidence.*

**10 cannot take your eyes off sb/sth** to be unable to stop looking at someone or something, especially because they are very attractive or interesting: *She was so beautiful I simply couldn't take my eyes off her.*

**11 look sb in the eye** [usually in negatives] to look directly and steadily at someone because you are not embarrassed or ashamed: *I couldn't look him in the eye afterwards, knowing that I had lost all that money.*

**12 run/cast your eye over sth** to look at something quickly without reading it in detail: *Could you just cast your eye over this report before I hand it in?*

④ **LOOK AFTER**
**13 keep your eye on sth/sb** to look after someone or something and make sure that they are safe: *Mary offered to keep an eye on the baby while I went out.*

⑤ **WATCH FOR**
**14 keep an eye out for sth** to hope to notice or find something: *Could you keep an eye out for my red pen? I seem to have mislaid it.*
**15 keep your eyes open/peeled** *spoken* to watch carefully for something: *Keep your eyes peeled for a campsite.*

⑥ **NOTICE**
**16 have eyes in the back of your head** to know what is happening all around you, even when this might seem impossible: *You need to have eyes in the back of your head to be a teacher.*
**17 have eyes like a hawk** to notice every small detail or everything that is happening, and therefore to be difficult to deceive: *We never got away with anything in Mrs. Podell's class—she had eyes like a hawk.*
**18 have your eye on sth** to have noticed something that you want to buy or have: *I've got my eye on a nice little sports car that I'm saving up for.*

⑦ **DISAGREE/DISBELIEVE**
**19 not see eye to eye** to always disagree with someone: *Liz never saw eye to eye with her daughter-in-law.*
**20 my eye!** *spoken* used to express surprise or disagreement: *A diamond necklace my eye! That was glass!*
**21 in a pig's eye!** *AmE spoken* used to show that you do not believe what someone is saying: *Dan said he got up early to do all his chores. In a pig's eye he did!*

⑧ **SURPRISE**
**22 not be able to believe your eyes** *spoken* used when you see something very surprising: *I couldn't believe my eyes – there she was, stark naked!*
**23 eyes popping out of your head** also **eyes out on stalks** *BrE especially spoken* used when you are very surprised or shocked by something you see

⑨ **LOVE/SEXUAL ATTRACTION**
**24 make eyes at sb/give sb the eye** to look at someone in a way that shows you find them sexually attractive: *Janet spent the whole evening making eyes at other men.*
**25 only have eyes for sb** if someone only has eyes for someone else, they only love and are interested in that one person: *I knew it was hopeless – Mark only had eyes for his wife.*
**26 have your eye on sb** to notice someone, especially because you think they are attractive: *Mark's got his eye on that new girl in the accounts department.* | *I hear you've got your eye on a new player for the team.*

⑩ **JUDGE**
**27 have a (good) eye for sth** to be good at noticing and recognizing what is attractive, valuable, of good quality etc: *Gail has a good eye for colour.*
**28 in the eyes of the law/the world/the police etc** in the opinion or judgment of the law, the world, the police etc: *In the eyes of the law stealing is an offence, no matter what your motives.*
**29 to my eye** *spoken* used when you want to give your opinion about the way something looks: *To my eye the paint seemed darker than it had done in the shop.*
**30 get/keep your eye in** *BrE* to begin to practise or to continue practising your ability to judge the speed and direction of the ball in games such as CRICKET (2) and tennis

⑪ **SPOKEN PHRASES**
**31 be up to your eyes in sth** to be very busy doing something: *I really can't take on anything else just now – I'm up to my eyes in paperwork as it is.*
**32 with your eyes closed/shut** easily and without any difficulty: *I don't know why you're so worried – you could run that place with your eyes closed!*
**33 have eyes bigger than your stomach** to take more food than you are able to eat: *I can't finish this cake – I must have eyes bigger than my stomach!*
**34 one in the eye for** *BrE* a defeat or disappointment for someone else, usually used when you are pleased about it: *If we win the cup it'll be one in the eye for Martin – he said we wouldn't even make it to the final.*

⑫ **PURPOSE**
**35 with an eye to** if you do something with an eye to something else, you do it in order that the second thing will happen: *Davies bought several houses, with an eye to making a quick profit.*
**36 with an eye to the main chance** an expression meaning wanting to take advantage of any possible chance to succeed, usually used in a disapproving way

⑬ **OTHER MEANINGS**
**37 more to sth/sb than meets the eye** if there is more to a situation, problem, or person than meets the eye, they are more complicated than they seem to be at first: *I reckon there's more to this 'relocation' business than meets the eye.*
**38 with your eyes open** knowing fully what the problems, difficulties, results etc of a situation might be: *You went into this with your eyes open, so it's no use complaining now!*
**39 close/shut your eyes to sth** to ignore something or pretend that you do not know it is happening: *I closed my eyes to the fact that she wasn't supposed to be there, and bought her a drink.*
**40 drop/lower your eyes** to move your eyes so that you are looking at a point lower than where you were looking before, especially because you are shy: *Melissa lowered her eyes demurely as he came into the room.*
**41 for your eyes only** used to say that something is secret and must only be seen by one particular person
**42 an eye for an eye** a system in which you punish someone by hurting them in the same way as they hurt someone else: *An eye for an eye is no way to run a civilized justice system.*
**43 ▶NEEDLE◀** the hole in a needle that you put the thread through —see picture at NEEDLE[1]
**44 ▶CLOTHING◀** a small circle or U-shaped piece of metal used together with a hook for fastening clothes
**45 ▶STORM◀** the calm centre of a storm, especially a CYCLONE
**46 ▶POTATO◀** a dark spot on a potato from which a new plant can grow —see also BLACK EYE, CAT'S EYE, PRIVATE EYE, RED EYE, **the apple of sb's eye** (APPLE (2)), **not bat an eye/eyelid** (BAT[2] (2)), BIRD'S-EYE VIEW, **turn a blind eye (to)** (BLIND[1] (2b)), **see sth out of the corner of your eye** (CORNER[1] (8)), **cry your eyes out** (CRY[1] (1)), **the evil eye** (EVIL[1] (5)), **give sb the glad eye** (GLAD (8)), **in your mind's eye** (MIND[1] (43)), **here's mud in your eye** (MUD (4)), **open sb's eyes (to)** (OPEN[2] (3b)), **in the public eye** (PUBLIC[1] (4)), **make sheep's eyes at** (SHEEP (4)), **a sight for sore eyes** (SIGHT[1] (9)), **in the twinkling of an eye** (TWINKLE[1] (3)), **keep a weather eye on** (WEATHER[1] (5)), **pull the wool over sb's eyes** (WOOL (4))

**eye²** *present participle* **eyeing** *or* **eying** *v* [T] to look at someone or something with interest, especially because you do not trust them or because you want something: *The child eyed me with curiosity.* | *Julian sat there eyeing my brandy.*

**eye** sb ↔ **up** *phr v* [T] *informal* to look at someone in a way that shows you think they are sexually attractive: *They all stood in a corner, eyeing up the local girls.*

**eye·ball¹** /ˈaɪbɔːl‖-bɒːl/ *n* [C] **1** the round ball that forms the whole of your eye, including the part inside your head —see picture at EYE[1] **2 eyeball to eyeball** if two people are eyeball to eyeball, they are directly facing each other, especially in an angry or threatening way: *an eyeball-to-eyeball confrontation*

**eyeball**[2] *v* [T] *informal* to look directly and closely at something: *They eyeballed us suspiciously before speaking.*

**eye·brow** /ˈaɪbraʊ/ *n* [C] **1** the line of hair above your eye —see picture at EYE[1] **2 raise your eyebrows** to move your eyebrows upwards in order to show surprise or disapproval: *"Really?" she said, raising one eyebrow slightly.* **3 be up to your eyebrows in sth** *spoken* to be very busy doing something: *I'm sorry I can't come, but I'm up to my eyebrows in marking exams.*

**eyebrow pen·cil** /ˈ·· ˌ··/ *n* [C,U] a special pencil you can use to make your eyebrows darker

**eye-catch·ing** /ˈ· ˌ··/ *adj* something eye-catching is unusual or attractive in a way that makes you notice it: *an eye-catching new outfit* —**eye-catchingly** *adv*

**eye·ful** /ˈaɪfʊl/ *n* [C] **1** an amount of liquid, dust, or sand that has got into someone's eye **2** *slang* something or someone, especially a woman, who is very attractive to look at: *She's quite an eyeful!* **3 get an eyeful of this/that!** *spoken especially BrE* used to tell someone to look at something because it is interesting or unusual

**eye·glass** /ˈaɪglɑːs‖-glæs/ *n* [C] **1** a LENS (1) for one eye, worn to help you see better with that eye; MONOCLE **2 eyeglasses** *BrE old-fashioned or AmE* a pair of glasses (GLASS[1] (3))

**eye·lash** /ˈaɪlæʃ/ *n* [C] **1** one of the small hairs that grow along the edge of your EYELIDS —see picture at EYE[1] **2 flutter your eyelashes** if a woman flutters her eyelashes, she moves them up and down very quickly, especially in order to look sexually attractive

**eye·less** /ˈaɪləs/ *adj* having no eyes

**eye·let** /ˈaɪlɪ̣t/ *n* [C] a hole surrounded by a metal ring that is put in leather or cloth so that a string can be passed through it —see picture at SHOE[1]

**eye lev·el** /ˈ· ˌ··/ *n* [singular] a height equal to the level of your eyes: *Pictures should be hung at eye level.*

**eye·lid** /ˈaɪlɪd/ *n* [C] the two pieces of skin that cover your eye when it is closed —see also **not bat an eyelid** (BAT[2] (2)), —see picture at EYE[1]

**eye·lin·er** /ˈaɪˌlaɪnə‖-ər/ *n* [C,U] a coloured substance that you put along the edges of your eyelids to make your eyes look bigger or more noticeable —see picture at MAKE-UP

**eye-o·pen·er** /ˈ· ˌ···/ *n* [C] a situation, event etc from which you learn something surprising, or something that you did not know before —see also **open sb's eyes (to)** (OPEN[2] (3b))

**eye patch** /ˈ· ·/ *n* [C] a piece of material worn over one eye, usually because that eye has been damaged

**eye pen·cil** /ˈ· ˌ··/ *n* [C,U] an eyeliner

**eye·piece** /ˈaɪpiːs/ *n* [C] the glass piece that you look through in a MICROSCOPE or TELESCOPE

**eye shad·ow** /ˈ· ˌ··/ *n* [C,U] a coloured substance that you put on your EYELIDS to make your eyes look more attractive —see picture at MAKE-UP

**eye·sight** /ˈaɪsaɪt/ *n* [U] your ability to see

**eye·sore** /ˈaɪsɔː‖-sɔːr/ *n* [C] something that is very ugly, especially a building surrounded by other things that are not ugly: *The tower block was an obvious eyesore in such a rural area.*

**eye strain** /ˈ· ·/ *n* [U] a pain you feel in your eyes, for example because you are tired or have been reading a lot

**eye tooth** /ˈ· ·/ *n* [C] **1** one of the long pointed teeth at the corner of your mouth; CANINE TOOTH **2 give your eye teeth for sth** *spoken* used when you want something very much: *I'd give my eye teeth to be able to play the piano like that.*

**eye wash** /ˈ· ·/ *n* [U] **1** a special liquid used for washing your eyes when they are sore **2** *BrE spoken old-fashioned* something that you do not believe is true: *Don't talk such eyewash!*

**eye·wit·ness** /ˈaɪˌwɪtnɪ̣s/ *n* [C] someone who has seen something such as a crime happen, and is able to describe it afterwards: *According to an eyewitness, the bomb went off at exactly three o'clock.*

**ey·ing** /ˈaɪ-ɪŋ/ the present participle of EYE[2]

**eyot** /eɪt, ˈeɪət/ *n* [C] *BrE* a small island in a river

**ey·rie** also **eyry** *BrE* /ˈɪəri, ˈeəri, ˈaɪəri‖ˈɪri, ˈeri, ˈaɪri/ *n* [C] **1** the NEST of a large bird, especially an EAGLE, that is usually built high up in rocks or trees **2** *informal* a room or building that is very high up

# F,f

**F, f** /ef/ *plural* **F's, f's** *n* [C] the sixth letter of the English alphabet

**f** **1** the written abbreviation of FORTE[2] **2** [plural] **ff** the written abbreviation of 'following', used in a book: *see pages 54ff*

**F[1]** /ef/ *n* **1** also **f** [C,U] the fourth note in the musical scale (SCALE[1] (8)) of C major or the musical key (KEY[1] (4)) based on this note **2** a mark given to a student whose work is not good enough

**F[2]** **1** the written abbreviation of FAHRENHEIT: *Water boils at 212° F* **2** the written abbreviation of FEMALE **3** the written abbreviation of FALSE

**FA** /ˌef ˈeɪ◂/ *n* **1** the Football Association; the organization that is in charge of professional football in England: *the FA Cup* **2** **sweet FA** *BrE slang* nothing

**fa** /fɑː/ *n* [singular] the fourth note in a musical SCALE[1] (8) according to the SOL-FA system

**fab** /fæb/ *adj informal* a word meaning extremely good, used especially in the 1960s

**Fa·bi·an** /ˈfeɪbiən/ *adj* [only before noun] connected with, or based on, the ideas of a British political group that has SOCIALIST[2] ideas and aims —**Fabian** *n* [C]

**fa·ble** /ˈfeɪbəl/ *n* **1** [C] a traditional short story that teaches a moral lesson, especially a story about animals: *the fable of the fox and the crow* **2** [U] such stories considered as a group; LEGEND (2): *monsters of fable and legend*

**fa·bled** /ˈfeɪbəld/ *adj especially literary* famous and often mentioned in traditional stories; LEGENDARY: [+ **for**] *a city fabled for its wealth*

W3 **fab·ric** /ˈfæbrɪk/ *n* **1** [C,U] cloth used to make clothes, curtains etc; material: *man-made fabrics* —see CLOTHES (USAGE) **2** [singular] the basic structure of a society, way of life etc and its relationships and traditions: *The family is the most important unit in the social fabric.* **3** **the fabric of** the basic structure of a building including the walls and the roof

**fab·ri·cate** /ˈfæbrɪkeɪt/ *v* [T] **1** to invent a story, piece of information etc in order to deceive someone: *The police were accused of fabricating evidence.* **2** *technical* to make or produce goods or equipment; MANUFACTURE[1] (1): *The discs are expensive to fabricate.*

**fab·ri·ca·tion** /ˌfæbrɪˈkeɪʃən/ *n* **1** [C,U] a piece of information or story that someone has invented in order to deceive people *Officer: can't you see their story is a complete fabrication?* **2** [U] *technical* the process of making or producing something

**fabric con·di·tion·er** /ˈ·· ˌ···/ *BrE*, **fabric soft·en·er** *AmE* /ˈ·· ˌ···/ *n* [C,U] a chemical that you put in water when washing clothes in order to make them feel softer

**fab·u·lous** /ˈfæbjᵊləs/ *adj* **1** extremely good or impressive: *You look fabulous!*|*a fabulous goal by Maradona* **2** [only before noun] very large in amount or size: *The painting was sold for a fabulous sum.* **3** [only before noun] fabulous creatures, places etc are mentioned in traditional stories, but do not really exist: *dragons and other fabulous creatures*

**fab·u·lous·ly** /ˈfæbjᵊləsli/ *adv* **fabulously expensive/rich/successful etc** extremely expensive etc

**fa·cade, façade** /fəˈsɑːd, fæ-/ *n* [C] **1** the front of a building, especially a large and important one: *A gang of stonemasons were restoring the facade of the cathedral.* **2** [usually singular] a way of behaving that hides your real feelings: *the unpleasant reality lurking behind that facade of respectability*

S1 W1 **face[1]** /feɪs/ *n* [C]
**1** ▶ **FRONT OF YOUR HEAD** ◀ the front part of the head from the chin to the forehead: *She has such a pretty face.*|*Bob's face was covered in cuts and bruises.*|**a sea of faces** (=a lot of faces seen together) *The Principal looked down from the platform at the sea of faces below* —see picture at HEAD[1].
**2** ▶ **EXPRESSION** ◀ an expression on someone's face: *the children's happy faces*|**make/pull a face** (=change your expression to make people laugh, or to show that you are angry, disappointed etc) *Emma was making faces at me through the window.*|**you should have seen his/her face** *spoken* (=used to say how angry, surprised etc someone looked) *You should have seen Steve's face when I told him I was resigning.*|**sb's face was a picture** *spoken* (=used to say that they looked very angry, surprised etc)|**sb's face brightened/lit up** (=they started to smile and look happy) *David's face lit up when I mentioned her name.*|**sb's face fell** (=they started to look disappointed or upset) *His face fell when I told him the news.*|**a face like thunder** (=a very angry expression) *Mr Neeson came striding towards us with a face like thunder.*|**a long face** (=an unhappy or worried expression)
**3** ▶ **PERSON** ◀ **a)** **a famous/well-known face** someone who is famous from television, magazines, films etc **b)** **new/different face** someone who you have not seen before: *There are a few new faces in class this year.* **c)** **the same old faces** people that you see often, especially too often: *It's the same old faces at our meetings every week.*
**4** **pale-faced/round-faced etc** having a face that has a particular shape or colour: *a pale-faced youth* —see also RED-FACED
**5** **serious-faced/grim-faced etc** showing a particular expression on your face: *Negotiators emerged grim-faced after the day's talks.* —see also BAREFACED, PO-FACED, POKER-FACED, STONY-FACED
**6** **face to face** **a)** if two people are face to face, they are very close and in front of each other: **meet sb face to face** *I've never met her face to face. We've only talked on the phone.*|**come face to face with** (=suddenly meet someone who makes you very frightened, surprised etc) *At that moment he came face to face with Sergeant Burke.* **b)** in a situation where you have to accept or deal with something unpleasant: **bring sb face to face with** *He was brought face to face with the truth about his daughter's disappearance.*|**come face to face with** *This was the first time I'd ever come face to face with poverty.* —see also FACE-TO-FACE
**7** **to sb's face** if you say something unpleasant to someone's face you say it to them directly: *I told him to his face just what I thought.*
**8** **face down/downwards** with the face or front towards the ground: *The body was lying face down on the carpet.*
**9** **face up/upwards** with the face or front towards the sky: *She laid the cards out face upwards.*
**10** **in the face of** in a situation where there are many problems, difficulties, or dangers: *bravery in the face of danger*
**11** **on the face of it** used to say that something seems true but that you think there may be other facts about it which are not yet clear: *It looks, on the face of it, like a minor change in the regulations.*|*On the face of it, Norman seems the ideal man for the job.*
**12** **the face of** **a)** the way in which an organization, system etc appears to people: *Recent events that changed the face of the British monarchy* **b)** the general appearance of a particular place: *the changing face of the landscape*
**13** **lose face** to make other people lose their respect for you: *He doesn't want to back down and risk losing face.*
**14** **save face** if you do something to save face, you do it so that people will not lose their respect for you: *Rather than admit defeat, Franklin compromised in order to save face.*
**15** **blow up/go up in sb's face** if a situation blows up or

goes up in your face, it goes wrong, especially in an embarrassing way

**16 disappear/vanish off the face of the earth** to suddenly disappear: *I haven't seen Paul in ages, he seems to have vanished off the face of the earth.*

**17 sb's face doesn't fit** used to say that someone is not the right kind of person for a particular group, organization etc

**18 put a brave face (on)** to make an effort to behave in a happy cheerful way when you are upset or disappointed: *He was shattered, though he put on a brave face.*

**19 set your face against** *especially BrE* to be very determined that something should not happen

**20 ▶ MOUNTAIN/CLIFF ◀** a steep, high side of a mountain, cliff etc: *The cliff face was starting to crumble into the sea.*

**21 ▶ CLOCK ◀** the front of a clock

**22 ▶ MINE ◀** the part of a mine from which coal, stone etc is cut

**23 ▶ OUTSIDE SURFACE ◀** one of the outside surfaces of an object or building: *A cube has six faces.*

**24 ▶ SPORT ◀** the part of a bat (BAT[1] (2)) or racket (RACKET[1] (3)) that you use to hit the ball

**25 in your face/in yer face** *slang* behaviour, criticisms, remarks etc that are in your face are very direct and often shocking or surprising: *Parson's 'in your face' style of interviewing*

**26 what's his face/what's her face** *spoken* used as a way of talking about someone when you cannot remember their name: *I saw old what's his face in school yesterday.*

**27 put your face on** *informal humorous* to put MAKE-UP on —see also **have egg on your face** (EGG[1] (4)), **fly in the face of** (FLY[1] (28)), **a straight face** (STRAIGHT[1] (11)), **laugh in sb's face** (LAUGH[1] (12)), **not just a pretty face** (PRETTY[1] (5)), **show your face** (SHOW[1] (13)), **shut your face** (SHUT[1] (3)), **a slap in the face** (SLAP[2] (2)), **be staring sb in the face** (STARE[1] (2)), **do sth till you're blue in the face** (BLUE[1] (6)), **wipe the smile/grin off sb's face** (WIPE[7]), **have sth written all over your face** (WRITE (5))

S1 W1 **face²** *v* [T]

**1 ▶ DIFFICULT SITUATION ◀** if you face a difficult situation or if it faces you, you must deal with it: *The President faces the difficult task of putting the economy back on its feet.* | *McManus is facing the biggest challenge of his career.* | **be faced with/by** *I was faced with the awful job of breaking the news to the girl's family.*

**2 ▶ ADMIT A PROBLEM EXISTS ◀** to accept that a difficult situation or problem exists, even though you would prefer to ignore it:**face the fact that** *Many couples refuse to face the fact that they have problems with their marriage.* | **face facts** *It's time that we started to face a few hard facts.* | **face the truth** *He had to face the awful truth that she no longer loved him.* |**(let's) face it** *spoken* (=used when saying something that someone may find difficult to accept or admit): *Face it kid, you're never gonna be a rock star.*

**3 can't face** if you cannot face something, you feel unable to do it because it seems too unpleasant or difficult: *I don't want to go back to school again – I just can't face it.* | **can't face doing sth** *He couldn't face driving all the way to Los Angeles.*

**4 ▶ BE OPPOSITE ◀** to be opposite a person, building etc so that you are pointing towards them, or to point in a particular direction: *They stood facing each other for a few minutes.* | *Rita's apartment faces the harbor.* | **face north/east etc** (=point towards the north, east etc) *My bedroom faces south.* | **south-facing/west-facing etc** *a south-facing garden* —see FRONT[1] (USAGE)

**5 ▶ UNPLEASANT POSSIBILITY ◀** to have the possibility that something bad or unpleasant might happen to you: *If he can't pay up, he's faced with losing his home.* | *Evans could face the electric chair.*

**6 ▶ TEAM/OPPONENT ◀** to play against an opponent or team in a game or competition: *Martinez will face Robertson in tomorrow's final.*

**7 ▶ DIFFICULT PERSON ◀** to deal with someone who is difficult to deal with, or talk to someone who you do not want to talk to: *You're going to have to face him sooner or later.*

**8 face the music** *informal* to accept criticism or punishment for something you have done

**9 ▶ BUILDING ◀ be faced with stone/concrete etc** to be covered in stone, CONCRETE[1] etc

**face** sb ↔ **down** *phr v* [T to deal with someone in a strong and confident way: *The police chief faced down reporters who were calling for his resignation.*

**face up to** sth *phr v* [T] to accept and deal with an unpleasant fact or problem: *They'll never offer you another job; you might as well face up to it.*

**face** sb **with** sth *phr v* [T often passive] to show someone evidence that proves they have done something wrong

**face card** /ˈ· ·/ *n* [C] *AmE* the king, queen, or jack (JACK[1] (2)) in a set of playing cards; COURT CARD *BrE*

**facecloth** /ˈ· ·/ *n* [C] *BrE* a small piece of rough cloth used to wash the face or hands; WASHCLOTH *AmE*

**face cream** /ˈ· ·/ *n* [C,U] a thick cream used to clean the face or to keep it soft and smooth

**face·less** /ˈfeɪsləs/ *adj* a faceless person, organization etc consists of a lot of people who you do not know, and who do not seem interested in or to have sympathy for ordinary people: *faceless bureaucrats*

**face·lift** /ˈfeɪslɪft/ *n* [C] **1** a medical operation in which doctors remove loose skin on someone's face in order to make them look younger **2** work or repairs that make a place or object look newer or better: **give sth a facelift** *The new owner had given the pub a face-lift.*

**face-off** /ˈ· ·/ *n* [C] **1** *AmE informal* a fight or argument: *a face-off between police and rioters* **2** a way of starting a game of ICE HOCKEY —**faceoff** *phr v* [T]

**face pack** /ˈ· ·/ *n* [C] a thick cream that you spread over your face in order to clean and improve your skin

**face pow·der** /ˈ· ˌ··/ *n* [U] powder that you put on your face in order to make it look smoother and give it more colour —see picture at MAKE-UP

**face sav·er** /ˈ· ˌ··/ *n* [C] something that helps you not to lose other people's respect

**face-sav·ing** /ˈ· ˌ··/ *adj* [only before noun] a face-saving action or arrangement helps you not to lose other people's respect: *a face-saving compromise*

**fac·et** /ˈfæsɪt/ *n* [C] **1** one of several parts of someone's character, a situation etc; ASPECT (1): **[+ of]** *discussing the many facets of the problem* **2 multi-faceted/many faceted** consisting of many different parts: *a multi-faceted issue* **3** one of the flat sides of a jewel

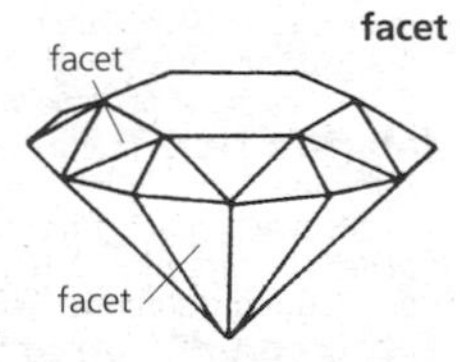


**fa·ce·tious** /fəˈsiːʃəs/ *adj* saying things that are intended to be clever and funny but are really silly and annoying: *Don't be so facetious!* | *facetious comments* —**facetiously** *adv* —**facetiousness** *n* [U]

**face-to-face** /ˌ· · ˈ·◂/ *adj* [only before noun] a face-to-face meeting, conversation etc is one where you are actually with another person and talking to them

**face val·ue** /ˌ· ˈ··/ *n* [U] **1 take sth at face value** to accept a situation or accept what someone says, without thinking there may be a hidden meaning: *You shouldn't always take his remarks at face value.* **2** [C,U] the value or cost shown on the front of something such as a stamp or coin

**fa·cial¹** /ˈfeɪʃəl/ *adj* on your face or connected with your face: *a slight facial resemblance between the two men* | *facial hair* —**facially** *adv*: *Facially the two sisters are very similar.*

**facial²** *n* [C] a process in which creams are rubbed into the skin of your face in order to clean and improve your skin

**facial scrub** /ˌ·· ˈ·/ *n* [C] a thick substance which you use to clean the skin on your face thoroughly

**fa·cile** /ˈfæsaɪl‖ˈfæsəl/ *adj* **1** a facile remark, argument etc is too simple and shows a lack of careful thought or understanding: *facile logic* **2** [only before noun] *formal* a facile achievement or success has been obtained too easily: *a facile victory* —**facilely** *adv* —**facileness** *n* [U]

**fa·cil·i·tate** /fəˈsɪlɪ̵teɪt/ *v* [T] *formal* to make it easier for a process or activity to happen: *Computers can be used to facilitate language learning.* —**facilitation** /fəˌsɪlɪ̵ˈteɪʃən/ *n* [U]

**fa·cil·i·tat·or** /fəˈsɪlɪ̵teɪtə‖-ər/ *n* [C] **1** someone who helps a group of people discuss things with each other or do something effectively **2** *technical* something that helps a process to take place

S3 W1 **fa·cil·i·ty** /fəˈsɪlɪ̵ti/ *n* **1 facilities** [plural] rooms, equipment, or services that are provided for a particular purpose: *a 5-star hotel with fantastic facilities* | *child-care facilities* | *toilet facilities* **2** [usually singular] a special part of a piece of equipment or a system which makes it possible to do something: *Is there a call-back facility on this phone?* | *a bank account with an overdraft facility* **3** [singular] a natural ability to do something easily and well: [+ **for**] *She has an amazing facility for mental arithmetic.* **4** [C] a place or building used for a particular activity or industry, or for providing a particular type of service: *a chlorine-production facility* **5 with great facility** *formal* very easily

**fac·ing** /ˈfeɪsɪŋ/ *n* [C,U] **1** an outer surface of a wall or building made of a different material from the rest in order to make it look attractive **2** material fastened to the inside of a piece of clothing to strengthen it **3 facings** parts of a jacket, coat etc around the neck and wrists which have a different colour from the rest

**fac·sim·i·le** /fækˈsɪmɪ̵li/ *n* [C] **1** an exact copy of a picture, piece of writing etc **2** *formal* a FAX[1](1) —**facsimile** *adj*

S1 W1 **fact** /fækt/ *n*
**1 ▸ TRUE INFORMATION ◂** [C] a piece of information that is known to be true: *First of all, we need to establish the facts of the case.* | [+ **about**] *The book is full of interesting facts about the World Cup.* | **facts and figures** (=the basic details, numbers etc concerning a particular situation or subject) | **it's a fact/that's a fact** (=used to emphasize that something is definitely true or that something definitely happened) *The divorce rate in the US is now twice as high as in the 1950s – that's a fact.* | **it's a fact that** *It's a fact that most deaths from lung cancer are caused by smoking.* | **I know for a fact that** *spoken* (=used to say that you definitely know that something is true) *I know for a fact that she earns more than I do.* | **get your facts right/wrong** (=be right or wrong about something) *We need to be sure we've got our facts right before making wild accusations.* | **stick/keep to the facts** (=only say what you know is true) *Let's just stick to the facts and not jump to any conclusions.* | **the bare facts** (=the basic details of a situation or story) | **hard facts** (=details or pieces of information that can be proved to be true) *We need some hard facts not just theories and suppositions.* | **the facts speak for themselves** (=they show clearly that something is true) *She obviously knows what she's doing—the facts speak for themselves.*
**2 the fact (that)** used when talking about a situation and saying that it is true: *He refused to help me, despite the fact that I asked him several times.* | **given the fact (that)/in view of the fact (that)** (=used when saying that a particular fact influences your judgement about something or someone) *Given the fact that this is their first game, I think they did pretty well.* | **owing to the fact (that)/due to the fact (that)** (=because) *The school's poor exam record is largely due to the fact that it is chronically underfunded.*
**3 ▸ REAL EVENTS/NOT A STORY ◂** [U] situations, events etc that really happened and have not been invented: *Much of the novel is based on fact.*
**4 in fact/in actual fact a)** used to say what the real truth of a situation is, especially when this is different from what people think or say it is: *They told me it would be cheap but in fact it cost me nearly $500.* | *Her teachers said she was a slow learner, whereas in actual fact she was partially deaf.* **b)** used when you are adding something, especially something surprising, to emphasize what you have just said: *We live very close to Lesley's parents, in the same road in actual fact.*
**5 as a matter of fact** *spoken* **a)** used when you are answering someone and telling them what you really think or what the real situation is: *"I didn't think you'd mind me using your office." "Well as a matter of fact I do mind."* **b)** used to add an important fact that increases the effect of what you are saying: *Our ELT department is doing really well. As a matter of fact we've just signed a big new contract in China.*
**6 in point of fact** *spoken* an expression used in discussions and speeches to add another piece of information or disagree with what someone else has said
**7 the fact is/the fact of the matter is** *spoken* used when you are telling someone what is actually true in a particular situation, especially when this is different from what people believe: *The fact of the matter is that the company is unlikely to survive the recession.*
**8 the fact remains** used to emphasize that a situation is true and people must realize this: *The fact remains that the number of homeless people is rising daily.*
**9 sth is a fact of life** used to say that a situation exists and must be accepted: *Mass unemployment seems to be a fact of life nowadays.*
**10 the facts of life a)** the details about sex and how babies are born **b)** the way life really is, with all its problems and difficulties
**11 after the fact** after something has happened or been done, especially after a mistake has been made —see also **as a matter of fact** (MATTER[1] (16))



**fact-find·ing** /ˈ· ˌ··/ *adj* **fact-finding trip/tour/mission etc** a trip during which you try to find out facts and information about something for your organization, government etc

**fac·tion** /ˈfækʃən/ *n* **1** [C] a small group of people within a larger group, who have different ideas from the other members: *warring factions* **2** [U] *formal* disagreement or fighting within a group or a political party **3** [C,U] a story in a film or television programme that is based on real events but is not completely true —**factional** *adj*

**fac·ti·tious** /fækˈtɪʃəs/ *adj formal* made to happen artificially by people rather than happening naturally

**fac·tor¹** /ˈfæktə‖-ər/ *n* [C] 
**1 ▸ CAUSE/INFLUENCE ◂** one of several things that influence or cause a situation: *The rise in crime is mainly due to social and economic factors.* | [+ **in**] *The vaccination program has been a major factor in the improvement of health standards.* | **key/crucial factor** *The weather could be a crucial factor in tomorrow's game.* | **the deciding factor** (=the most important factor) *We liked both houses, but in the end the deciding factor was the location.*
**2 by a factor of five/ten etc** if something increases or decreases by a factor of five, ten etc it increases or decreases by five times, ten times etc
**3 ▸ LEVEL ON A SCALE ◂** a particular level on a scale of measurement of the force or effectiveness of something: *factor 15 suntan oil* | *a wind chill factor of -20*
**4 ▸ MATHEMATICS ◂** a number that divides into another number exactly: *3 is a factor of 15.*
**5 ▸ LAND ◂** *ScotE* someone who looks after another person's land

**factor²** *v* [T] *AmE technical* to divide a number into factors
**factor** sth ↔ **in** *phr v* [T] to include a particular thing

in your calculations about how long something will take, how much it will cost etc

**fac·to·ri·al** /fæk'tɔːriəl/ *n* [C] *technical* the result when you multiply a number by all the numbers below it: *factorial 3 = 3 × 2 × 1*

**fac·tor·ize** also **-ise** *BrE* /'fæktəraɪz/ *v* [T] *technical* to divide a number into factors —**factorization** /,fæktəraɪ'zeɪʃən‖-rə-/ *n* [U]

S2 W2 **fac·to·ry** /'fæktəri/ *n* [C] **1** a building or group of buildings in which goods are produced in large quantities, using machines: *a car factory|factory workers* **2 on the factory floor** among the ordinary workers in a company

**factory farm** /'··· ,·/ *n* [C] *BrE* a farm where animals are kept inside, in small spaces or small CAGES, and made to grow or produce eggs very quickly —**factory farming** *n* [U]

**fac·to·tum** /fæk'təʊtəm‖-'toʊ-/ *n* [C] *formal* a servant or worker who has to do many different kinds of jobs for someone: *He's our general factotum.*

**fact sheet** /'· ·/ *n* [C] a piece of paper giving all the most important information about something

**fac·tu·al** /'fæktʃuəl/ *adj* based on facts: *factual information|Try to keep your account of events as factual as possible.* —**factually** *adv*: *The document is factually correct.*

**fac·ul·ty** /'fækəlti/ *n plural* **faculties** [C] **1** a natural ability, such as the ability to see, hear, or think clearly: [+ **of**] *the faculty of reason*|**in full possession of all your faculties** (=able to see, hear, think etc in the normal way) **2** a particular skill that someone has: [+ **for**] *She had a great faculty for absorbing information.* **3** a department within a university: *the Faculty of Engineering* **4 the faculty** *AmE* all the teachers in a university: *There was a mixed reaction to the proposal among the faculty.*

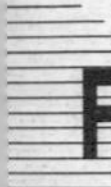

**fad** /fæd/ *n* [C] something that someone likes or does for a short time, or that is fashionable for a short time: *The break-dancing craze soon passed, as most fads do.* —**faddy, faddish** *adj*: *She keeps trying all these faddy diets.* —**faddiness, faddishness** *n* [U]

**fade** /feɪd/ *v* **1** also **fade away** [I] to gradually disappear: *Hopes of a peace settlement are beginning to fade.|Over the years her beauty had faded a little.* **2** [I, T] to lose colour and brightness, or to make something do this: *the fading evening light*|**fade sth** *The sun had faded the curtains.* —see picture on page 1258 **3** also **fade away** [I] to become weaker physically, especially so that you become very ill or die **4** [I] if a team fades, it stops playing as well as it did before: *The Broncos faded in the second half.*

**fade** sth ↔ **in** *phr v* [T] to make a picture or sound appear or be heard gradually —**fade-in** /'· ·/ *n* [C]

**fade** sth ↔ **out** *phr v* [T] to make a picture or sound disappear slowly or become quieter —**fade-out** /'· ·/ *n* [C]

**fae·ces** also **feces** *AmE* /'fiːsiːz/ *n* [plural] *formal* solid waste material from the BOWELS —**faecal** /'fiːkəl/ *adj*

**fae·ry, faerie** /'feəri‖'feri/ *n* [C] *old-use* a FAIRY(1)

**faff** /fæf/ *v*

**faff about/around** *phr v* [I] *BrE informal* to waste time doing unnecessary things: *I wish you'd stop faffing around!*

**fag**[1] /fæg/ *n* [C] **1** *BrE slang* a cigarette **2** *AmE slang* an offensive word for a HOMOSEXUAL **3 be a fag** *BrE informal* to be a boring or difficult thing to do: *I hate ironing – it's such a fag.* **4** a young student in some British PUBLIC SCHOOLS who has to do jobs for an older student

**fag**[2] *v* [I + **for**] to do jobs for an older student at a British PUBLIC SCHOOL —**fagging** *n* [U]

**fag end** /,· '·◂/ *n* [C] *informal* **1** *BrE* the end of a cigarette that someone has finished smoking **2 the fag end of** *especially BrE* the last part of something, especially when it is not as good or interesting as the rest

**fagged** /fægd/ *adj BrE informal* **1** also **fagged out** [not before noun] extremely tired: *I was fagged out after the journey.* **2 I can't be fagged** used to say that you are too tired or bored to do something

**fag·got** /'fægət/ *n* [C] **1** *BrE* a ball made of meat mixed with bread, which is cooked **2** *AmE slang* an offensive word for a HOMOSEXUAL **3** a collection of small sticks for burning on a fire **4** *Br E informal* an impolite word for someone you do not like, especially a woman

**fag-hag** /'· ·/ *n* [C] *slang especially AmE* an offensive word for a woman who spends time with HOMOSEXUAL men

**Fah·ren·heit** /'færənhaɪt/ *n* [U] a scale of temperature in which water freezes at 32° and boils at 212°

**fail**[1] /feɪl/ *v* S2 W1

**1 ► TRY BUT FAIL ◄** [I] to be unsuccessful in something that you want to do: *Peace talks between the two countries have failed.*|**fail to do sth** *Doctors failed to save the girl's life.*|**fail miserably** (=be completely unsuccessful in a way that it is embarrassing): *Millions of people have tried to quit smoking and failed miserably.*

**2 ► NOT DO WHAT IS EXPECTED ◄** [I] to not do what is expected, needed, or wanted: **fail to do sth** *The letter failed to arrive.|The report cleverly fails to mention the real cost of this experiment.*|**fail in your duty/responsibility** *I would be failing in my duty if I didn't warn you of the consequences of your actions.*

**3 ► EXAM/TEST ◄ a)** [I,T] to not pass a test or examination: *I failed my driving test the first time I took it.*|[+ **on**] *I passed the written paper but failed on my oral.* **b)** [T] to decide that someone has not passed a test or examination

**4 I fail to see/understand** *formal* used to show that you are annoyed by something that you do not accept or understand: *I fail to see why you find it so amusing.*

**5 ► COMPANY/BUSINESS ◄** [I] to be unable to continue because of a lack of money: *A large number of small businesses failed in the recession.*

**6 ► MACHINE/BODY PART ◄** [I] if a part of a machine or an organ in your body fails, it stops working: *The rocket's engine failed a few seconds after take-off.|My uncle's kidneys failed two days after the operation.*

**7 never fail to do sth** to do something so regularly that people are sure that you will do it: *My grandson never fails to phone me on my birthday.*

**8 your courage/will/nerve fails (you)** if your courage etc fails, or fails you, you suddenly do not have it when you need it: *At the last moment my nerve failed. I walked away from her door without knocking.*

**9 fail sb** to not do what someone has trusted you to do: *I feel I've failed my children by not spending more time with them.* —see also **words fail me** (WORD[1] (10))

**10 ► CROPS ◄** [I] to not grow or produce food: *If the crops fail again this year, people will starve.*

**11 ► RAINS ◄** [I] to not come at the usual time of year

**12 failing sight/health** sight or health that is becoming worse

**fail**[2] *n* **1 without fail a)** if you do something without fail, you always do it: *Tim visits his mother every day without fail.* **b)** used to tell someone very firmly that they must do something: *I want that work finished by tomorrow, without fail!* **2** [C] an unsuccessful result in a test or examination: *I got a fail in history.*

**failed** /feɪld/ *adj* [only before noun] **a failed actor/writer etc** someone who wanted to be an actor etc but was unsuccessful

**fail·ing**[1] /'feɪlɪŋ/ *n* [C] a fault or weakness: *I love him, despite his failings.*

**failing**[2] *prep* used to say that if your first suggestion is not successful or possible, there is another possibility that you could try: *There are two cheap hotels, but failing either of these, you may as well go back to where you were before.*|failing that *Try to get them to pay for the damage, or failing that, claim on their insurance.*

**fail-safe** /'· ·/ *adj* **1** a fail-safe machine, piece of equipment etc contains a system that makes the machine stop working if one part of it fails **2** a fail-safe plan is certain to succeed

S2 W2 **fail·ure** /ˈfeɪljə‖-ər/ *n*
**1** ▶ **LACK OF SUCCESS** ◀ [C,U] a lack of success in achieving or doing something: *How can we account for the failure of the League of Nations to achieve peace in Europe?* | **end/result in failure** *Harry's ambitious plans ended in failure.*
**2** ▶ **UNSUCCESSFUL PERSON/THING** ◀ [C] someone or something that is not successful: *I always felt a bit of a failure at school.* | **a total/complete failure** *The whole thing was a total failure from start to finish.* | **crop failure** *a series of crop failures*
**3 failure to do sth** an act of not doing something which should be done or which people expect you to do: *Failure to produce proof of identity could result in prosecution.*
**4** ▶ **MACHINE/BODY PART** ◀ [C,U] an occasion when a machine or part of your body stops working properly: *engine failure* | [+ **in**] *a failure in the computer system caused by a mechanical fault* | **heart/kidney/liver failure** *The disease can result in terminal kidney failure.*
**5** ▶ **BUSINESS** ◀ [C,U] a situation in which a business has to close because of a lack of money: *The number of small business failures is growing each year.*

**fain** /feɪn/ *adv old use* **would fain do sth** *old use* if you would fain do something, you would like to do it

**faint¹** /feɪnt/ *adj* **1** difficult to see, hear, smell etc: *a faint noise* | *the faint outline of the cliffs* **2 a faint hope/chance/feeling etc** a very small or slight chance etc: *There's still a faint hope that they might be alive.* | *There was a faint edge of menace in his voice.* **3** feeling weak because you are very ill, tired, or hungry: [+ **with**] *feeling faint with hunger and fatigue* **4 not have the faintest idea** to not know anything at all about something: *They didn't seem to have the faintest idea what I was talking about.* —see also **damn sb/sth with faint praise** (DAMN⁵ (2)), —**faintly** *adv*: *Her name sounds faintly familiar.* | *The sun shone faintly through the clouds.* —**faintness** *n* [U]

**faint²** *v* [I] **1** to suddenly become unconscious for a short time: *Several fans fainted in the blazing heat.* **2 I nearly/almost fainted** *spoken* used to say that you were very surprised by something: *I nearly fainted when they told me the price.*

**faint³** *n* [C] an act of becoming unconscious | **in a (dead) faint**: *She fell down in a faint.*

**faint-heart·ed** /ˌ·ˈ··◂/ *adj* **1** not trying very hard, because you do not want to do something, or you are not confident that you can succeed: *She made a rather faint-hearted attempt to stop him from leaving.* **2 not for the faint-hearted** *humorous* used to say that something is difficult and needs a lot of effort

S1 W2 **fair¹** /feə‖fer/ *adj*
**1** ▶ **REASONABLE AND ACCEPTABLE** ◀ a situation, system, or way of treating people that is fair seems reasonable and acceptable: *a fair wage for the job* | *Who said life was fair?* | *Everyone should have the right to a fair trial.* | **it is fair to do sth** *It seems fair to give them their money back.* | **it's fair to say that** (=used to say that a judgement about something seems reasonable) *I think it's fair to say that she was not to blame for the accident.*
**2** ▶ **TREATING EVERYONE EQUALLY** ◀ a fair situation, judgement, description etc is one in which everyone is treated equally: *Why do you let her stay out late and not me? It's not fair!* | **fair to** *The old law wasn't fair to women.* | **it's only fair (that)** *You pay him $10 an hour – it's only fair that I should get the same.*
**3** ▶ **FAIR PERSON** ◀ someone who treats everyone in a reasonable, equal way: *The boss is a hard man – hard but fair.*
**4** ▶ **QUITE BIG/FAR/A LOT** ◀ **a fair size/number/amount/distance etc** *especially BrE* a fairly large size, number etc: *There's a fair amount of unemployment around here.* | *We had travelled a fair way by lunch time.*
**5** ▶ **SKIN/HAIR** ◀ light in colour: *He had blue eyes and fair hair.* | *Both her children are very fair.*—opposite dark¹ (4) —see picture on page 412.
**6** ▶ **LEVEL OF ABILITY** ◀ neither particularly good nor particularly bad; average: *Her written work is excellent but her practical work is only fair.*
**7** ▶ **ACCORDING TO THE RULES** ◀ a fair fight, game, or election is one that is played or done according to the rules: *free and fair elections*
**8** ▶ **WEATHER** ◀ pleasant and not windy, rainy etc: *That morning the weather was fair, and the air was warm.*
**9 have a fair idea of** to know quite a lot about what something is like: *I think I have a fair idea of what the job involves.*
**10 have had more than your fair share of** to have had more of something, especially something unpleasant, than seems reasonable or fair: *Poor old Alan! He's had more than his fair share of bad luck recently.*
**11 give sb a fair crack of the whip** *BrE informal* to give someone the chance to do something especially to show that they are able to do it
**12 a fair shake** *AmE informal* fair treatment that allows someone the same chances as everyone else: *Inner city kids aren't getting a fair shake in the schools.*
**13 by fair means or foul** using any method to get what you want, including dishonest or illegal methods
**14 fair-to-middling** not feeling very well
**15 all's fair in love and war** used to say that in some situations any method of getting what you want is acceptable
**16** ▶ **PLEASANT/ATTRACTIVE** ◀ *old use* pleasant and attractive: *The fair city of Rome.* | *a fair maiden* —see also FAIRLY, FAIRNESS

Frequencies of the adjective **fair** in spoken and written English.

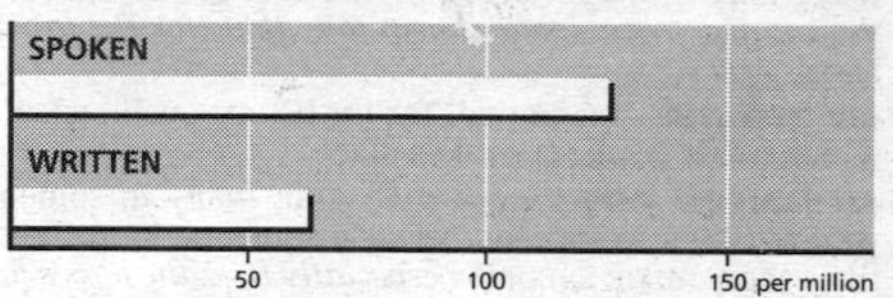


Based on the British National Corpus and the Longman Lancaster Corpus

This graph shows that the adjective **fair** is much more common in spoken English than in written English. This is because it is used in a lot of common spoken phrases.

**fair** (*adj*) **SPOKEN PHRASES**

**17 fair enough** *especially BrE* used to say that you agree with someone's suggestion or that something seems reasonable: *"See you on Tuesday at 8." "Fair enough."* | *Well, if you want to go on your own that's fair enough.*
**18 it's/that's not fair** used when you think that what is happening is unfair: *It's not fair, you never let me borrow your clothes.* | **It's/that's not fair on sb** *You can't just give the clever kids attention because that's not fair on the rest of the class.*
**19 to be fair** used when adding something after someone has been criticized, which helps to explain or excuse what they did: *She should have phoned to tell us what her plans were although, to be fair, she's been very busy.*
**20 fair comment** *BrE* used to say that a remark or criticism seems fair: *"I don't mind doing the work, but you should have asked me." "Fair comment."*
**21 be fair!** used to tell someone not to be unreasonable or criticize someone too much: *Come on, be fair, the poor girl's trying her hardest!*
**22 fair's fair** used when you think it is fair that someone should do something, especially because of something that has happened earlier: *Come on, fair's fair – I paid last time so it's your turn.*
**23 you can't say fairer than that** *BrE* used to say that an offer you are making to someone is the best,

fairest offer they can possibly get: *I'll give you £25 for it – you can't say fairer than that, can you?*
**24 it's a fair cop** *BrE* used in a joking way when someone catches you doing something that you should not be doing: *"I saw you, now give me that back." "All right, it's a fair cop."*
**25 with your own fair hands** *BrE humorous* used to say that you did something by yourself without any help: *"Did you do all the decorating yourself?" "Yes, it's all been done with my own fair hands."*

S2 W3 **fair²** *adv* **1 play fair** to do something in a fair and honest way **2 hit sth fair and square** to hit something directly in a particular place: *I hit him fair and square on the nose.* **3 tell sb fair and square** to tell someone honestly and directly

**fair³** *n* [C] **1** a form of outdoor entertainment, at which there are large machines to ride on and games in which you can win prizes; CARNIVAL (2) *AmE* —see also FUNFAIR **2** *BrE* a market where animals and farm products are sold: *a cattle fair* **3** an event at which farm products and equipment are shown and entered in competitions, and where there are often games and large machines to ride on: **state/county fair** (=a fair for the whole state or county) **4** a regular occasion when companies show their newest products in order to advertise them: *a trade fair | The Frankfurt Book Fair* **5** an outdoor event with games and things to buy, organized to get money; FETE¹(1) *BrE*

**fair cop·y** /ˌ· ˈ··/ *n* [C] a neat copy of a piece of writing

**fair din·kum** /ˌfeə ˈdɪŋkəm‖ˌfer-/ *adj AustrE spoken* real or true

**fair game** /ˌ· ˈ·/ *n* [U] someone or something that is easy to criticize or deserves to be criticized: *The behaviour of the younger royals made them fair game for the tabloid press.*

**fair·ground** /ˈfeəgraʊnd‖ˈfer-/ *n* [C] an open space on which a fair (FAIR ³ (1)) takes place

**fair-haired boy** /ˌ.. ˈ ./ *n* [C] *AmE informal* someone who is likely to succeed because someone in authority likes them; BLUE-EYED BOY *especially BrE*: *the boss's fair-haired boy*

S1 W2 **fair·ly** /ˈfeəli‖ˈferli/ *adv* **1** more than a little, but much less than very: *The house had a fairly large garden. | She speaks English fairly well.* —see RATHER (USAGE) **2** in a way that is fair and not dishonest, unreasonable etc: *I felt I hadn't been treated fairly.* **3** *BrE* used to say that someone did something quickly or a lot: *He fairly raced past us on his motorcycle.*

**fair-mind·ed** /ˌ· ˈ··◂‖ˈ· ˌ··/ *adj* able to understand and judge situations fairly and always considering other people's opinions: *He's a fair-minded man – I'm sure he'll listen to what you have to say.*

**fair·ness** /ˈfeərnəs‖ˈfer-/ *n* [U] **1** the quality of being fair **2 in fairness (to)** used after you have just criticized someone to add something more favourable which explains their behaviour: *Tardelli had a poor match, although in fairness he was playing with a knee injury.*

**fair play** /ˌ· ˈ·/ *n* [U] **1** playing according to the rules of a game without cheating **2** *BrE* fair treatment of people without cheating or dishonesty —see also **turnabout is fair play** (TURNABOUT (2))

**fair sex** /ˌ· ˈ·/ *n* **the fair sex** *old-fashioned* women

**fair·way** /ˈfeəweɪ‖ˈfer-/ *n* [C] the part of a GOLF COURSE that you hit the ball along towards the hole —see picture on page 1264

**fair-weath·er friend** /ˌ· ·· ˈ·/ *n* [C] someone who only wants to be your friend when you are successful

**fai·ry** /ˈfəri‖ˈferi/ *n* [C] **1** a small imaginary creature with magic powers, which looks like a very small person **2** an offensive word for a HOMOSEXUAL man

**fairy god·moth·er** /ˌ·· ˈ···/ *n* [C] a woman with magic powers who saves people from trouble, especially in children's stories

**fai·ry·land** /ˈferilænd‖ˈferi-/ *n* **1** [U] an imaginary place where fairies live **2** [singular] a place that looks very beautiful and special: *At night, the harbor is a fairyland.*

**fairy lights** /ˈ·· ·/ *n* [plural] *BrE* small coloured lights used especially to decorate a Christmas tree

**fairy tale** /ˈ··· ·/ also **fairy sto·ry** /ˈ··· ˌ··/ *BrE* —*n* [C] **1** a children's story in which magical things happen **2** a story that someone has invented and is difficult to believe

**fai·ry·tale** /ˈfeəriteɪl‖ˈferi-/ *adj* [only before noun] extremely happy, lucky etc in a way that usually only happens in children's stories: *a fairytale romance*

**fait ac·com·pli** /ˌfeɪt əˈkɒmpli‖-ˌækɑːmˈpliː/ *n* [singular] *French* something that has already happened or been done and cannot be changed

**faith** /feɪθ/ *n* W2
**1 ▶ TRUST/BELIEF IN SB/STH ◀** [U] a strong belief that someone or something can be trusted to be right or to do the right thing: **have faith in** *I have great faith in her, she won't let me down.* | **destroy/restore sb's faith in** (=take away or give back their faith) *It's really restored my faith in human nature.* | **lose faith in**: *The public has quite simply lost faith in the government.*
**2 ▶ RELIGION ◀ a)** [U] belief and trust in God: *deep religious faith* | [+ **in**] *my faith in God* **b)** [C] one of the main religions in the world: *people from all faiths | the Jewish faith*
**3 break faith with** to stop supporting or believing in a person, organization, or idea: *How could he tell them the truth without breaking faith with the Party?*
**4 keep faith with** to continue to support or believe in a person, organization, or idea
**5 good faith** honest and sincere intentions: *He proposed a second meeting as a sign of his good faith.* | **in good faith** (=without intending to deceive someone) *The woman who sold me the car claimed she had acted in good faith.*
**6 an act of faith** something you do that shows you trust someone completely: *Letting Sammy borrow my new camera was a real act of faith.*

**faith·ful¹** /ˈfeɪθfəl/ *adj* **1** remaining loyal to a person, belief, political party etc and continuing to support them: *years of faithful service* | [+ **to**] *Russell remained faithful to his principles to the last.* **2** representing an event or an image in a way that is exactly true or that looks exactly the same: *a faithful account of what had happened | a faithful reproduction of the original picture* **3** loyal to your wife, boyfriend etc by not having a sexual relationship with anyone else: [+ **to**] *Do you think Bob's always been faithful to you?* —**faithfulness** *n* [U]

**faithful²** *n* **1 the faithful a)** the people who are very loyal to a leader, political party etc and continue to support them **b)** the people who believe in a religion **2** [C] a loyal follower, supporter, or member: *a handful of old faithfuls at the meeting*

**faith·ful·ly** /ˈfeɪθfəl-i/ *adv* **1** in a faithful way: *He had served the family faithfully for 40 years.* **2 promise faithfully** to promise that you will definitely do something: *Ann promised faithfully that she would never tell.* **3 Yours faithfully** *especially BrE* the usual polite way of ending a formal letter, which you have begun with Dear Sir or Dear Madam —compare **Yours sincerely** (SINCERELY (2))

**faith heal·ing** /ˈ· ˌ··/ *n* [U] a method of treating illnesses by praying —**faith healer** *n* [C]

**faith·less** /ˈfeɪθləs/ *adj formal* someone who is faithless cannot be trusted: *a faithless friend* —**faithlessly** *adv* —**faithlessness** *n* [U]

**fake¹** /feɪk/ *n* [C] **1** a copy of a valuable object, painting etc that is intended to deceive people: *We thought it was a genuine antique, but it was only a fake.* **2** someone who is not what they claim to be or does not have the skills they say they have: *He claimed to have natural healing powers, but he turned out to be a fake.*

**fake²** *adj* [usually before noun] **1** made to look like a real material or object in order to deceive people: *fake* *fur* **2** pretending to be something you are not in order to deceive people: *A fake doctor tricked his way into a hospital last night.*

**fake**[3] *v* **1** [T] to make an exact copy of something, or invent figures or results, in order to deceive people: *He faked his father's signature on the cheque.* | *The results of these experiments were faked.* **2** [I,T] to pretend to be ill, interested etc when you are not: fake it *I thought he was really hurt but he was faking it.* **3** [I,T] to pretend to move in one direction, but then move in another, especially when playing sport: *He faked a pass and then handed the ball off to Perry.*

**fake** sb **out** *phr v* [T] *AmE* to deceive someone by making them think you are planning to do something when you are really planning to do something else

**fa·kir** /ˈfeɪkɪə, ˈfæ-, fæˈkɪə‖fəˈkɪr, fæ-/ *n* [C] a travelling Hindu or Muslim holy man

**falafel** /ˌfəˈlæfəl/ *n* [C,U] fried balls of an Arabic food made with CHICKPEAS

**fal·con** /ˈfɔːlkən‖ˈfæl-/ *n* [C] a bird that kills and eats other animals and can be trained to hunt

**fal·con·er** /ˈfɔːlkənə‖ˈfælkənər/ *n* [C] someone who trains falcons to hunt

**fal·con·ry** /ˈfɔːlkənri‖ˈfæl-/ *n* [U] the skill or sport of using falcons to hunt

S1 W1 **fall**[1] *v* /fɛl/ *past tense* **fell** *past participle* **fallen** /ˈfɔːlən‖ˈfɑː-/

**1 ▶ MOVE DOWNWARDS ◀** [I] to move downwards from a higher position to a lower position: *The rain had started falling again.* | [**+out of/from/on** etc *Wyatt fell from a second floor window.* | [**+down**] *I'm always worried that one of the kids will fall down the stairs.* | **sb's trousers/socks etc are falling down** *His shirt was all dirty and his trousers were falling down.* | **rise and fall** *The little boat rose and fell with the movement of the waves.*

**2 ▶ GO DOWN ONTO THE GROUND ◀** [I] to suddenly go down onto the ground after you have been standing, walking, or running, especially without intending to: *I fell and hit my head.* | *Careful you don't fall – the path's very icy.* | [**+ on/into etc**] *One of the horses slipped and fell into a ditch.* | **fall flat on your face** (=fall so that you are lying facing the ground) *She fell flat on her face in the mud.* | **fall to your knees** (=move down from a standing position so that your body is resting on your knees)

**3 ▶ TO A LOWER AMOUNT ETC ◀** [I] to go down to a lower price, amount, level etc, especially a much lower one: *In winter the temperature often falls below zero.* | **fall steeply/sharply(= by a large amount)** *Interest rates fell sharply.* | *falling income levels*

**4 fall asleep/ill/silent/pregnant** to become asleep, ill etc: *I fell asleep halfway through the film.*

**5 fall in love** to start to love someone or something very much: [**+ with**] *As soon as we met, we fell in love with each other.* | *Primmie fell in love with California on sight.*

**6 fall to pieces/bits a)** to break into many pieces: *The vase fell to bits as soon as it hit the floor.* **b)** if something such as a plan or a relationship falls to pieces, it stops working properly

**7 be falling to pieces/bits** to be in very bad condition, especially because of being very old: *The walls were all dirty and the furniture was falling to pieces.*

**8 fall into/out of** to go into or out of a place very quickly because you are in a hurry or very tired: *As soon as she got home she fell into bed.*

**9 fall into decay/disrepair/disrepute etc** to become decayed, in bad condition, no longer respected etc: *Over the years the old palace had fallen into decay.*

**10 fall flat** if a joke, remark, or performance falls flat, it fails to interest or amuse people:

**11 fall short of** to be less than the amount or standard that is needed or that you want: *Unfortunately, the course fell far short of our expectations.*

**12 fall out of fashion/favour** to stop being popular or fashionable

**13 fall from grace/favour** to stop being liked by people in authority: *I don't think she'll get promotion—she's rather fallen from grace recently.*

**14 fall into the hands of/ clutches of** if something or someone falls into the hands of an enemy or dangerous person, the enemy etc gets control or possession of them: *The documents fell into the hands of the KGB.*

**15 fall victim/prey to** to get a very serious illness or be attacked or deceived by someone: *While in Africa she fell victim to a rare blood disorder.*

**16 fall into the habit of** to start doing something, especially something that you should not do: *He soon fell into the habit of having a drink on the way home from work.*

**17 fall into the trap (of)** to make a mistake that many people make: *It's easy to fall into the trap of believing that the threat of nuclear war is over.*

**18 fall back into your old ways** to start doing things or behaving in the way that you used to, especially in a way that other people disapprove of: *I expect she'll soon fall back into her old ways.*

**19 fall into a category/group etc** also **fall under a heading** to be part of a group of things or people that are similar in some way: *A lot of my friends fall into the same category.*

**20 fall into place a)** if parts of a situation that you have been trying to understand fall into place, you start to understand how they are connected with each other: *Gradually the clues started falling into place and it became clear who the murderer was.* **b)** if the parts of something that you want to happen fall into place, they start to happen in the way that you want: *We've found someone who'll lend us the money, and it looks as if things are finally falling into place.*

**21 fall into line** to obey someone or do what other people want you to do, especially when you do not want to do it at first: *If you can persuade her, the others will soon fall into line.*

**22 fall into step with a)** to start doing something in the same way as the other members of a group: *The other countries on the Security Council are expected to fall into step with the US.* **b)** to start to walk next to someone else, at the same speed as them

**23 fall by the wayside a)** to become unsuccessful after being successful at first: *A lot of marriages fall by the wayside because couples cannot talk to each other.* **b)** to stop being important and therefore be forgotten about: *With so many domestic problems, foreign policy issues tended to fall by the wayside.*

**24 night/darkness/dusk falls** *literary* used to say that the night begins and that it starts to become dark: *We arrived at the village just as night was falling.*

**25 ▶ LIGHT/SHADOW ◀** [I always + adv/prep] to shine on a surface or go onto a surface: *The last rays of sunlight were falling on the fields.*

**26 fall down on the job** *informal* to not do your work or duties as well as you should: *I'd be falling down on my job if I didn't take an interest in the welfare of my staff.*

**27 it fell off the back of a lorry** *BrE humorous* used to say that something was stolen

**28 fall foul of** to do something which makes someone angry, or which breaks a rule with the result that you are punished: *Edwards fell foul of the authorities and was ordered to leave the country.*

**29 it's as easy as falling off a log** *spoken* used to say that something is very easy to do

**30 fall on deaf ears** if someone's words fall on deaf ears, no-one pays any attention to them: *His pleas fell on deaf ears.*

**31 fall on hard times** to have problems because you do not have enough money: *middle-class families that have fallen on hard times*

**32 ▶ LOSE POWER ◀** [I] if a leader or a government falls, they lose their position of power: *The previous administration fell after only 6 months in office.*

**33 ▶ BE TAKEN BY AN ENEMY ◀** [I] if a place falls in a war or an election, a group of soldiers or a political party takes control of it: [**+ to**] *The city fell to the advancing Russian armies.*

**34 ▶ BE KILLED ◀** [I] *literary* to be killed in a war

F

35 ▶**HIT**◀ [I always + adv/prep] to hit a particular place or a particular part of someone's body: [+ **on**] *The first punch fell on his nose.*
36 ▶**HANG DOWN**◀ [I always + adv/prep] to hang down loosely: [+ **to/over**] *Her hair fell to her shoulders.*
37 ▶**VOICE/SOUND**◀ [I] if someone's voice or a sound falls, it becomes quieter or lower
38 **fall from sb's lips** *literary* if words fall from someone's lips, they say them
39 **silence/sadness/calm etc falls** *literary* used to say that a group of people or a place becomes quiet, sad etc: [+ **on/upon**] *As she entered the ballroom a great silence fell on the assembled guests.*
40 ▶**SPECIAL EVENT/CELEBRATION**◀ **fall on** to happen on a particular day or date: *Christmas falls on a Saturday this year.*
41 **sb's eyes/gaze/glance fell on** used to say that someone saw something when they were looking at something else: *He was going through some old papers when his eyes fell on a photo of his mother.*
42 **the stress/accent/beat falls on** used to say that a particular part of a word, phrase, or piece of music is emphasized or is played more loudly than the rest: *In the word 'report', the stress falls on the second syllable.*
43 **fall at sb's feet** to kneel in front of someone, especially to ask them to do something or to show your respect
44 **fall between two stools** to be neither one type of thing nor another, or be unable to choose between two ways of doing something: *The movie falls between two stools – it's neither a thriller nor a comedy.*

45 **I almost fell off my chair** *spoken* used to say that you were very surprised when something happened —see also **fall/land on your feet** (FOOT[1] (17)), **let drop/fall** (LET[1] (17)), **sb's face fell** (FACE[1] (2)), **stand or fall by/on** (STAND[1] (47))

**fall about** *phr v* [I] *BrE* to laugh a lot about something **fall about laughing** *The moment she started speaking everyone fell about laughing.*

**fall apart** *phr v* [I] **1** if an organization, system etc falls apart, it stops working effectively and has a lot of problems: **be falling apart at the seams** *The Health Service is falling apart at the seams.* **2 be falling apart** to be in very bad condition: *I'm not riding in your old car—it's falling apart.* **3** if your life, your world etc falls apart, you suddenly have a lot of personal problems: *When his wife left him his world just fell apart .* **4** to break into pieces: *The book fell apart in my hands as soon as I tried to pick it up.*

**fall away** *phr v* [I] **1** if something such as a feeling, a quality, or a noise falls away, it gradually becomes weaker or quieter and disappears: *As confidence fell away consumers kept more of their cash in their pockets.* **2** to slope downwards: *After that the road falls away to the city of Odawara.* **3** to become separated from something after being fixed to it: *A piece of wood had fallen away from the foot of the door.* **4** to stop being able to be seen as you move through an area: *An hour out of London the rows of houses started to fall away and we were surrounded by beautiful countryside.*

**fall back** *phr v* [I] **1** if soldiers fall back, they move back because they are being attacked: *He ordered the men to fall back.* **2** to move backwards because you are very surprised, frightened etc: *They fell back in horror.*

**fall back on** *phr v* [I] **1** to use something or depend on someone's help when dealing with a difficult situation, especially after you have tried using other methods or tried to deal with it yourself: **have sb/sth to fall back on** *Diana always had her father's money to fall back on.* | *In that case we'll have to fall back on our original plan.* **2** to use a particular method, argument etc because it seems simple and easy, not because it is the best one to use: *They tend to fall back on the same tired old arguments.*

**fall behind** *phr v* [I,T] **1** to go more slowly than other people so that they gradually move further ahead of you: *The older walkers soon fell behind* **2** to become less successful than someone else: *The Eisenhower administration allowed the US to fall behind the Soviet Union in the production of nuclear arms.* | [+ **with**] *In secondary school she started falling behind with her schoolwork.* **3** to fail to finish a piece of work or to pay someone money that you owe them at the right time: [+ **with/on**] *We fell behind with the payments on the car and it was repossessed.* | **fall behind schedule** *Preparations for the festival have fallen behind schedule because of technical difficulties.*

**fall down** *phr v* [I] **1** if someone falls down, they fall onto the ground: *Margo fell down and twisted her ankle.* **2** if something such as a wall, building, tree etc falls down, it falls onto the ground: *The bridge fell down with an enormous crash.* **3 be falling down** if a building is falling down, it is in very bad condition **4** if an argument, plan,system etc falls down, it fails to work because of a particular weakness: *That's where the whole argument falls down.*

**fall for** *phr v* [T] *informal* **1** to be tricked into believing something that is not true: *She'll never fall for that one!* | **fall for sth hook, line, and sinker** (=to be completely deceived by a trick) **2** to start to love someone: *That was the summer I worked at the fairground, and met and fell for Lucy.*

**fall in** *phr v* [I] **1** if the roof, ceiling etc falls in, it falls onto the ground **2** if a group of soldiers fall in, they form neat lines behind each other so that an officer can check them

**fall in behind** sb *phr v* [T] to form a line behind someone

**fall into** sth *phr v* **1 fall into conversation/a discussion/an argument** to start talking or arguing with someone: *I fell into conversation with a visiting Japanese professor.* **2** to start to have a particular mood, especially suddenly: *She's liable to fall into sudden fits of rage.* **3** to contain two or more different parts: *The agreement falls into two distinct sections.*

**fall in with** *phr v* [T] to accept someone's suggestions, decisions etc and not disagree with them: *I'm quite happy to fall in with whatever you decide.*

**fall off** *phr v* **1** [I,T] if part of something falls off, it becomes separated from the main part: *The door handle keeps falling off.* **2** [I] if the amount, rate, or quality of something falls off, it becomes less: *Rising prices have caused demand for household goods to fall off dramatically.*

**fall on/upon** *phr v* [I] **1** *literary* to suddenly attack or get hold of someone: *The samurai fell on him and pinned his arms tight.* **2** *literary* to eagerly start eating or using something: *The kids fell on the pizzas as if they hadn't eaten for weeks.* **3** if a duty or responsibility falls on you, you are given that duty or responsibility: *an obligation which may fall upon any citizen*

**fall out** *phr v* [I] **1** to have a quarrel: [+ **with**] *She's fallen out with her boyfriend.* **2** if a group of soldiers who are standing together fall out, they leave and go to different places **3** if something such as a tooth or your hair falls out, it comes out: *My dad's hair fell out when he was only 30.*

**fall over** *phr v* [I] **1** [I,T] if someone falls over or if they fall over something, they fall onto the ground: *Mind you don't fall over.* | *Tommy fell over one of the electric cables.* **2** if something falls over, it falls from an upright position onto its side: *The fence fell over in the wind.* **3 be falling over yourself to do sth** to be very eager to do something, especially something you do not usually do: *Sylvia was falling over herself to be nice to me.*

**fall through** *phr v* [I] if an agreement, plan etc falls through, it is not completed successfully: *The deal fell through at the last minute.*

**fall to** *phr v* [T] **1** if a duty falls to someone, especially an unpleasant one, it is their responsibility to do it: **it fell to sb to do sth** *It fell to me to give her the bad news.* **2** to start doing something with a lot of effort: *They fell to work with a will.* **3 fall to doing something** *especially literary* to start doing something: *When* *things really started to go wrong, they fell to arguing among themselves.*

**fall to sb's lot** *literary* to be something that someone has or must deal with

S2 W2 **fall²** *n*

**1 ▶ MOVEMENT DOWNWARDS ◀** [C, singular] movement downwards towards the ground or towards a lower position: *the constant fall of the rain* | **break sb's fall** (=prevent someone from falling too quickly and hurting themselves badly) *Luckily there were some bushes next to the house and they broke my fall.*

**2 have a fall** to fall onto the ground and hurt yourself: *Grandma had a bad fall and broke her hip.*

**3 ▶ REDUCTION ◀** [C] a reduction in the amount, level, price etc of something: [+ **in**] *the recent fall in house prices* | *a fall in coal output*

**4 ▶ AUTUMN ◀** [singular] *AmE* autumn: **the fall** *We met in the fall of '88.*

**5 ▶ LOSE POWER/BECOME UNSUCCESSFUL ◀** [singular] a situation in which someone or something loses their position of power or becomes unsuccessful: [+ **from**] *Until his fall from power in 1978, the Shah remained a firm ally of the Americans.* | **rise and fall** (=period of success and then failure) *the rise and fall of the British motorcycle industry*

**6 fall from grace** a situation in which someone stops being respected by other people or loses their position of authority, especially because they have done something wrong: *Jackson's spectacular fall from grace*

**7 ▶ DEFEAT ◀** [singular] a situation in which a country, city etc is defeated by an enemy: *the fall of France in 1940*

**8 falls** [plural] a place where a river suddenly goes straight down over a cliff: *Niagara Falls* | **the falls** *We went to see the falls.*

**9 ▶ SPORT ◀** [C] an act of forcing your opponent onto the ground in WRESTLING or JUDO

**10 ▶ AMOUNT OF SNOW ETC ◀** [C] an amount of snow, rocks etc that has fallen onto the ground: *a heavy fall of snow*

**11 the fall** the occasion in the Bible when God punished Adam and Eve by making them leave the Garden of Eden

**fal·la·cious** /fəˈleɪʃəs/ *adj formal* containing or based on false ideas: *Such an argument is misleading, if not wholly fallacious.* —**fallaciously** *adv*

**fal·la·cy** /ˈfæləsi/ *n* **1** [C] a false idea or belief, especially one that a lot of people believe is true: *It's a common fallacy to think that crime is caused by poverty.* **2** [C, U] *formal* a weakness in someone's argument or ideas which is caused by a mistake in their thinking —see also PATHETIC FALLACY

**fall·back** /ˈfɔːlbæk‖ˈfɒːl-/ *n* [C] something that can be used if the usual supply, method etc fails: *It's wise to have an extra video player as a fallback.*

**fall·en¹** /ˈfɔːən‖ˈfɒːl-/ past participle of FALL¹

**fallen²** *adj* **1** on the ground after falling down: *The road was blocked by a fallen tree.* **2 a fallen woman** *old-fashioned* a woman who has had a sexual relationship with someone she is not married to **3 the fallen** *formal* soldiers who have been killed in a war

**fall guy** /ˈ· ·/ *n* [C] *informal, especially AmE* **1** someone who is punished for someone else's crime or mistake; SCAPEGOAT: *I knew what he had in mind. He'd kill Barak and set me up as the fall guy.* **2** someone who is easily tricked or made to seem stupid

**fal·li·ble** /ˈfælɪ̈bəl/ *adj* able to make mistakes or be wrong: *Parents are fallible, Susie, just like everyone else.* | *These surveys are often a rather fallible guide to public opinion.* —**fallibility** /ˌfælɪ̈ˈbɪlɪ̈ti/ *n* [U] —opposite INFALLIBLE

**falling-out** /ˌ·· ˈ·/ *n* **have a falling-out (with)** *informal* to have a bad quarrel with someone

**falling star** /ˌ·· ˈ·/ *n* [C] a SHOOTING STAR

**fall line** /ˈ· ·/ *n* [C] the natural slope of a hill straight down from top to bottom

**fal·lo·pi·an tube** /fəˌləʊpiən ˈtjuːb‖fəˈloʊpiən tuːb/ *n* [C] one of the two tubes in a female through which eggs move to the UTERUS

**fall·out** /ˈfɔːlaʊt‖ˈfɒːl-/ *n* [U] **1** the dangerous RADIOACTIVE dust which is left in the air after a NUCLEAR (3) explosion and which slowly falls to earth *There can be little lasting protection against the effects of radio-active fall out.* **2** the results or effects of a particular event, especially when they are unexpected: *The political fall-out of the Iran-Contra affair cost him his job.*

**fallout shel·ter** /ˈ·· ˌ··/ *n* [C] a building under the ground in which people can shelter from a NUCLEAR (3) attack

**fal·low** /ˈfæləʊ‖-loʊ/ *adj* fallow land is dug or ploughed (PLOUGH² (1)) but is not used for growing crops: *Dig over the plot in autumn and let it lie fallow over winter.*

**fallow deer** /ˈ·· ·/ *n* [C] a small European DEER which is yellowish brown with white spots

**false** /fɔːls‖fɒːls/ *adj* S3 W3

**1 ▶ UNTRUE ◀** a statement, story, etc that is false is completely untrue: *Please decide whether the following statements are true or false.* | *false accusations*

**2 ▶ WRONG ◀** based on incorrect information or ideas: *I don't want to give you any false hopes.* | *We often make false assumptions about people of other cultures.* | **a false sense of security** (=a feeling of being safe when you are not really safe) *It's easy to feel a false sense of security if crime never touches you personally.*

**3 ▶ NOT REAL ◀ a)** not real, but intended to seem real and deceive people: *a suitcase with a false bottom* | *The man had given a false name and address.* **b)** artificial: **false teeth/hair/eyelashes etc** *Oh no! Grandad's lost his false teeth again.*

**4 ▶ NOT SINCERE ◀** not sincere or honest, and pretending to have feelings that you do not really have: *She's very false.* | *a false laugh* | **false modesty** *"You played brilliantly." "Not really," Ian replied with false modesty.*

**5 one false move** used when warning someone that if they disobey you, make a mistake, or move suddenly something very bad will happen to them: *One false move, and I'll shoot!*

**6 under false pretences** if you get something under false pretences, you get it by deceiving people: *He was accused of obtaining money under false pretences.*

**7 false imprisonment/arrest** the illegal act of putting someone in prison or arresting (ARREST²) them for a crime they have not done

**8 false economy** something that you think will save money but which will really cost you more: *It's a false economy not to have travel insurance on your belongings.*

**9 false friend** a word in a foreign language that seems similar to one in your own, so that you wrongly think they both mean the same thing

**10 sail/fly under false colours** to pretend to be something that you are not

**false a·larm** /ˌ· ·ˈ·/ *n* [C] a situation in which people think that something bad is going to happen, but this is a mistake: *We all thought the building was about to go up in smoke, but it was a false alarm.*

**false dawn** /ˌ· ˈ·/ *n* [C] a situation in which something good seems likely to happen, but it does not: *The ceasefire turned out to be another false dawn.*

**false·hood** /ˈfɔːlshʊd‖ˈfɒːls-/ *n formal* **1** [C] a statement that is untrue **2** [U] the practice of telling lies

**false start** /ˌ· ˈ·/ *n* [C] **1** an unsuccessful attempt to begin a process or event: *After several false starts, the concert finally began.* **2** a situation at the beginning of a race when one competitor starts too soon and the race has to start again

**false teeth** /ˌ· ˈ·/ *n* [plural] a set of artificial teeth worn by someone who has lost their natural teeth

**fal·set·to** /fɔːlˈsetəʊ‖fɒːlˈsetoʊ/ *n* [C] a very high male voice —**falsetto** *adv*

**fals·ies** /ˈfɔːlsiz‖ˈfɒːl-/ *n* [plural] *informal* pieces of material inside a BRA used to make a woman's breasts look larger

**fal·si·fy** /ˈfɔːlsɪ̠faɪ‖ˈfɒːl-/ *v* **falsified, falsifying** [T] to change figures, records etc so that they contain false information: *Somebody had been falsifying the accounts.* —**falsification** /ˌfɔːlsɪ̠fɪ̠ˈkeɪʃən‖ˌfɒːl-/ *n* [C, U]

**fal·si·ty** /ˈfɔːlsɪ̠ti‖ˈfɒːl-/ *n* [U] *formal* the quality of being false or not true

**fal·ter** /ˈfɔːltə‖ˈfɒːltər/ *v* [I] **1** to become weaker and unable to continue in an effective way: *The economy is showing signs of faltering.*|*My mother's iron grip upon the household never faltered.* **2** to speak in a voice that sounds weak and uncertain, and keeps stopping: *Laurie's voice faltered as she tried to thank him.* **3** to become less certain and determined that you want to do something: *We must not falter in our resolve.* **4** to move unsteadily because you suddenly feel weak or afraid: *She faltered for a moment.*

**fal·ter·ing** /ˈfɔːltərɪŋ‖ˈfɒːl-/ *adj* nervous and uncertain or unsteady: *a baby's first faltering steps* —**falteringly** *adv*

**fame** /feɪm/ *n* [U] the state of being known about by a lot of people because of your achievements: **win fame/rise to fame** *Streisand first won fame as a singer before she became an actress.*|**at the height of your fame** *The Beatles were at the height of their fame.*|**claim to fame** (=the reason why someone or something is well known) *The town's only claim to fame is that Queen Elizabeth I once visited it.*|**fame and fortune** *He set off to find fame and fortune.*

**famed** /feɪmd/ *adj especially literary* well-known: [+ **for**] *the island of Lontar, famed for its nutmeg and cloves*

**fa·mil·i·al** /fəˈmɪliəl/ *adj* [only before noun] *formal* connected with a family or typical of a family: *economic and familial relationships*

S2 W2 **fa·mil·i·ar¹** /fəˈmɪliə‖-ər/ *adj*
**1** ▶ **EASY TO RECOGNIZE** ◀ someone or something that is familiar is easy to recognize because you have seen or heard them many times before: *a familiar tune*|**vaguely familiar** (=a little familiar) *Her face seems vaguely familiar, but I can't quite place her.*|**look/sound familiar (to sb)** *The voice on the phone sounded familiar to me.*
**2 be familiar with** to know something well because you have seen it, read it, or used it many times before: *Are you familiar with this type of machine?*
**3** ▶ **PLACE/SITUATION** ◀ a familiar place, situation etc is one that you know well: *It was a relief to be back in familiar surroundings.*
**4** ▶ **COMMON** ◀ a familiar sight, problem, story etc is one that you see or hear about too often because it is part of a common social problem: **all-too-familiar** *Beggars on the streets are becoming an all-too-familiar sight.*
**5 be on familiar terms with** to know someone well and be able to talk to them in an informal way: *He's on familiar terms with all the teachers.*
**6** ▶ **TOO FRIENDLY** ◀ talking to someone as if you know them well although you do not: [+ **with**] *I thought he was being a bit familiar with my wife.*
**7** ▶ **INFORMAL STYLE** ◀ informal and friendly in speech, writing, etc: *The novel is written in an easy, familiar style.* —see also FAMILIARLY

**familiar²** *n* [C] **1** a cat or other animal that lives with a WITCH and has magical powers **2 familiars** *old use* close friends or companions

**fa·mil·iar·ise** /fəˈmɪliəraɪz/ *v* a British spelling of FAMILIARIZE

**fa·mil·i·ar·i·ty** /fəˌmɪliˈærɪ̠ti/ *n* **1** [U] a good knowledge of a particular subject or place: + **with** *In fact his familiarity with the Bronx was pretty limited.* **2** [U] a feeling of being relaxed and comfortable because you are in a place you know well or with people you know well: *I miss the familiarity of home.* **3 familiarity breeds contempt** an expression meaning that if you know someone too well, you find out their faults and respect them less

**fa·mil·i·ar·ize** also **-ise** *BrE* /fəˈmɪliəraɪz/ *v* **familiarize yourself with sth/familiarize sb with sth** to learn about something so that you understand it, or teach someone else about something so that they understand it: *Employees must familiarize themselves with the health and safety manual.* —**familiarization** /fəˌmɪliəraɪˈzeɪʃən‖-rə-/ *n* [U]

**fa·mil·i·ar·ly** /fəˈmɪliəli‖-liərli/ *adv* in an informal or friendly way: *Charles, familiarly known as Charlie*

**fam·i·ly** /ˈfæməli/ *n plural* **families** 
**1** ▶ **PEOPLE WHO ARE CLOSELY RELATED** ◀ [U] a group of people who are related to each other, especially a mother, father, and their children: *Ned comes from a big family of eight children.*|*Do you know the family next door?*|[also + plural verb *BrE The family now live in London.*|**family home/business/holiday etc** *He grew up knowing that he would take over the family business one day.*|**nuclear family** (=a family consisting of mother, father, and their children)|**extended family** (=all the people in a family including aunts, uncles, grandparents etc)|**one-parent family/single-parent family** (=a family in which there is only one parent)|**family background** (=the sort of family you come from)|**she's/he's family** *informal* (=used to say that someone is related to you)
**2** ▶ **ALL THE PEOPLE RELATED TO YOU** ◀ [C,U] all the people you are related to, including those who are now dead: *I'm moving to Detroit because I have some family there.*|[also + plural verb *BrE*] *My family come from Scotland originally.*|**be in sb's family** (=be owned by someone's family, especially for a long time) *That painting has been in our family for 200 years.*|**run in the family** (=be a common feature in a particular family) *Asthma runs in the family.*
**3** ▶ **CHILDREN** ◀ [C] children: *Couples with young families wouldn't want to live here.*|**start a family** (=have children) *They're getting married next year, and hope to start a family straight away.*|**bring up/raise a family** *the problems of bringing up a family on a very low income*|**a family film/show/etc** (=suitable for children as well as adults)
**4 family size/pack/ etc** a product sold in a large container packet big enough for a whole family
**5** ▶ **GROUP OF ANIMALS/THINGS** ◀ [C] *technical* a group of related animals, plants, languages etc: *The cat family includes lions and tigers.*|*Spanish and Italian are part of the Romance language family.*
**6 in the family way** *old-fashioned* PREGNANT

**family cred·it** /ˌ··· ˈ··/ *n* [U] money given by the government in Britain to parents who do not earn much money

**family doc·tor** /ˌ··· ˈ··/ *n* [C] a doctor trained in general medicine, who a family visits regularly

**family man** /ˈ··· ˌ·/ *n* [C] **1** a man who enjoys being at home with his wife and children **2** a man with a wife and children

**family name** /ˈ··· ˌ·/ *n* [C] the name someone shares with all the members of their family; SURNAME, LAST NAME

**family plan·ning** /ˌ··· ˈ··/ *n* [U] the practice of controlling the number of children that are born using CONTRACEPTION: *a family planning clinic*

**family prac·tice** /ˌ·· ˈ··/ *n* [U] *AmE* a part of medical practice in the US in which doctors learn to treat general health problems and problems connected with families and people of all ages —**family practitioner** /ˌ··· ˈ···/ *n* [C]

**family room** /ˈ··· ˌ·/ *n* [C] **1** *AmE* a room in a house where the family can play games, watch television etc **2** a room in a PUB in Britain where children are allowed to sit

**family tree** /ˌ··· ˈ·/ *n* [C] a drawing that gives the names of all the members of a family over a long period of time, and shows how they are related to each other

**fam·ine** /ˈfæmɪ̠n/ *n* [C, U] a situation in which a large number of people have little or no food for a long time and many people die

**fam·ished** /ˈfæmɪʃt/ *adj* [not before noun] *informal* extremely hungry: *What's for supper? I'm famished.*

**family**

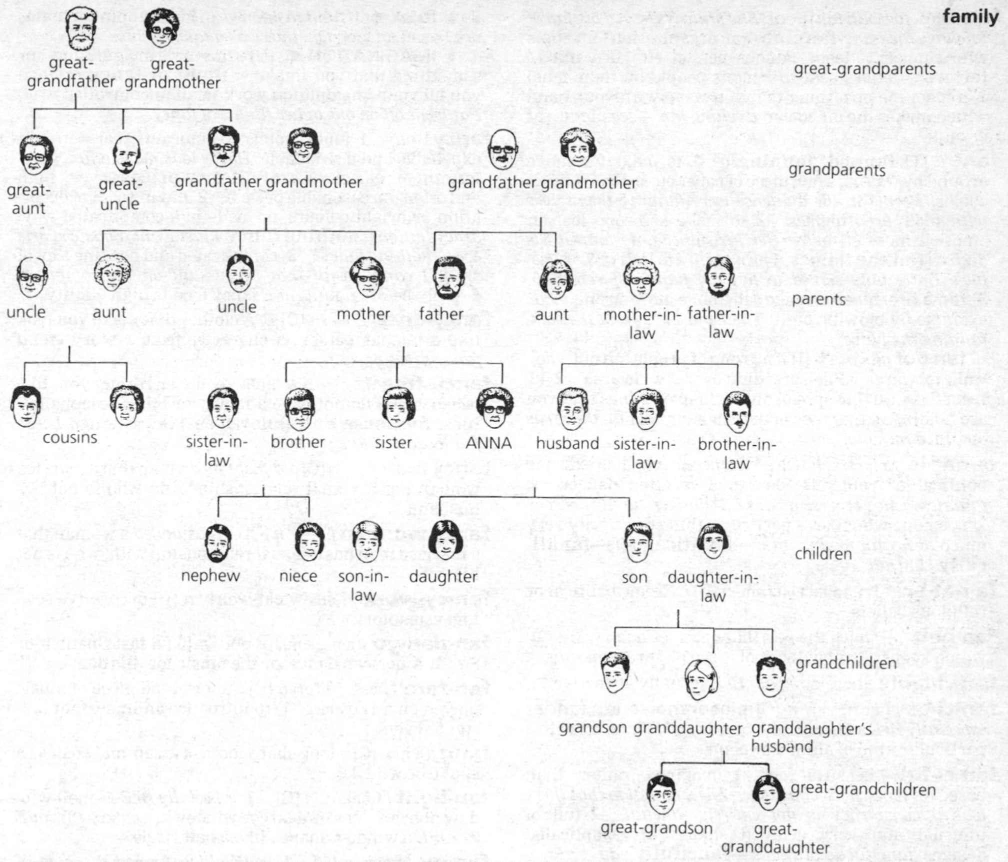

great-grandfather great-grandmother
great-grandparents
great-aunt great-uncle grandfather grandmother grandfather grandmother
grandparents
uncle aunt uncle mother father aunt mother-in-law father-in-law
parents
cousins sister-in-law brother sister ANNA husband sister-in-law brother-in-law
nephew niece son-in-law daughter son daughter-in-law
children
grandchildren
grandson granddaughter granddaughter's husband
great-grandchildren
great-grandson great-granddaughter

S2 W2 **fa·mous** /ˈfeɪməs/ *adj* **1** known about and talked about by many people in many places: *a famous actor* | **[+ for]** *France is famous for its wine.* | **[+ as]** *Virginia is famous as the birthplace of several US presidents.* | **world-famous** (=famous all over the world) *Da Vinci's world-famous portrait of the Mona Lisa.* | **the rich and famous** *a nightclub in LA that caters for the rich and famous* **2** *spoken* [only before noun] used about someone or something who you have heard about but have never met: *Ah, so this is the famous Jill.* **3 famous last words** *spoken* used when someone has said too confidently that they can do something or that something will happen: *"Even I can't get lost around there." "Famous last words."* **4** *old-fashioned* very good; excellent

**USAGE NOTE: FAMOUS**

WORD CHOICE: **famous, well-known, distinguished, eminent, renowned, notorious, infamous**

**Well-known** is like **famous**, but if someone is well-known, it is often with a particular group of people, or for a particular skill, achievement etc: *She's very well-known in the literary world.* If you are **famous**, most people have heard of you, and know who you are: *That big house in Malibu belongs to a famous movie star.*

**Distinguished** and **eminent** are used especially of people who are famous for serious work in science, the arts etc: *a distinguished writer* | *an eminent surgeon.*

Places or people are **renowned** for a particular quality, characteristic, or skill: *Florence is renowned for its beautiful buildings.* | *the renowned cellist, Jacqueline Du Pre.* If someone is **notorious** they are famous for something bad: *the notorious gangster Marco Fellini* | *Many politicians are notorious hypocrites.*

**Infamous** is like **notorious** but slightly literary, and is often used about people, places, and events in the past or when they are a long way away: *The infamous Bastille prison.*

**fa·mous·ly** /ˈfeɪməsli/ *adv* **1 get on/along famously** *old-fashioned* to have a friendly relationship with someone **2** *formal* in a way that is famous

**fan**

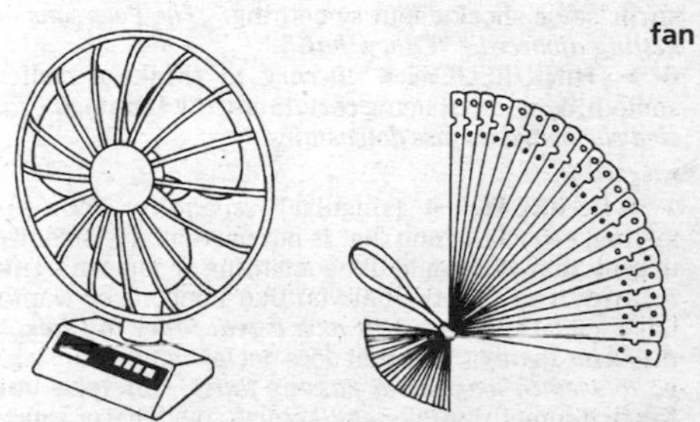

**fan¹** /fæn/ *n* [C] **1** someone who likes a particular sport or performing art very much, or who admires a famous S2 W2 person: *a football fan* | [+ **of**] *She's always been a big fan of Michael Jackson.* | **fan club** (=an organization for people who support a team, famous person etc) | **fan mail/letters** (=letters sent to famous people by their fans) **2** a machine or a thing that you wave with your hand which makes the air cooler: *a ceiling fan* —see picture at ENGINE

**fan²** *v* [T] **fanned, fanning** *v* **1** to make air move around by waving a fan, piece of paper etc so that you feel cooler: *People in the audience were fanning themselves with their programmes.* **2** to make someone feel an emotion more strongly: *Her resistance only fanned his desire.* | **fan the flames** *A provocative article in The People's Daily only served to fan the flames of rebellion.* **3 fan a fire/blaze** to make a fire burn more strongly, for example by blowing on it: *The wind blew from the east, fanning the blaze.*

**fan out** *phr v* **1** [I] if a group of people fan out, they walk forwards while spreading over a wide area **2** [T **fan** sth ↔ **out**] to spread out a group of things that you are holding so that they make a half-circle: *Fan the cards out, then pick one.*

**fa·nat·ic** /fə'nætɪk/ *n* [C] **1** someone who has extreme political or religious ideas and is often dangerous: *fanatics who represent a real danger to democracy* **2** someone who likes a particular thing or activity very much: *a health food fanatic* —**fanatical** *adj* —**fanatically** /-kli/ *adv*

**fa·nat·i·cis·m** /fə'nætɪ̇sɪzəm/ *n* [U] extreme political or religious beliefs

**fan belt** /'· ·/ *n* [C] the belt that operates a fan (FAN¹ (2)) which keeps a car engine cool —see picture at ENGINE

**fan·ci·a·ble** /'fænsiəbəl/ *adj BrE* sexually attractive

**fan·ci·er** /'fænsiə‖-ər/ *n* [C] **pigeon/horse etc fancier** *especially BrE* someone who breeds and is interested in a particular kind of animal or plant

**fan·ci·ful** /'fænsɪfəl/ *adj* **1** imagined rather than based on facts: *a fanciful story* | *The suggestion that there was a conspiracy is not entirely fanciful.* **2** full of unusual and very detailed shapes or complicated designs: *fanciful decorations* —**fancifully** *adv*

S3 **fan·cy¹** /'fænsi/ *v* **fancied, fancying** [T]
**1** ▶ **LIKE/WANT** ◀ *especially BrE* to like or want something, or want to do something: *Fancy a quick drink, Emma?*
**2** ▶ **SEXUAL ATTRACTION** ◀ *BrE informal* to feel sexually attracted to someone: *All the girls fancied him like mad.*
**3 fancy yourself** *BrE informal* to behave in a way that shows you think you are very attractive or clever: *That bloke on the dance-floor really fancies himself.*
**4** ▶ **THINK STH WILL BE SUCCESSFUL** ◀ *BrE* to think someone or something is likely to be successful in something: **fancy sb's chances** *I don't fancy our chances of getting a ticket this late.*
**5 fancy!/fancy that!** *BrE spoken* used to express your surprise or shock about something: *"The Petersons are getting divorced." "Fancy that!"*
**6** ▶ **THINK/BELIEVE** ◀ *literary* to think or believe something without being certain: **fancy (that)** *She fancied she heard a noise downstairs.*

**fancy²** *n*
**1** ▶ **DESIRE FOR** ◀ [singular] *especially BrE* **a)** a feeling, especially one that is not particularly strong or urgent, that you would like something or someone: **take a fancy to** (=decide that you like someone or want to have something) *Mr Hill took a real fancy to Clara.* | **a passing fancy** (=one that does not last long) *Wanting to go to Mexico was just a passing fancy.* **b) take your fancy** if something takes your fancy, you like it or want to have it: *Did anything take your fancy?*
**2 tickle sb's fancy** *informal* to seem attractive or amusing to someone: *The idea of playing a joke on the Sergeant really tickled his fancy.*
**3** ▶ **IDEA** ◀ [C] *old-fashioned* an idea or opinion that is not based on fact: *Oh, that was a fancy of his.*
**4** ▶ **IMAGINATION** ◀ [U] *literary* imagination or something that you imagine: **flight of fancy** (=when you let your imagination work in an uncontrolled way) *Pat went off on one of her flights of fancy.*

**fancy³** *adj* **1** fancy hotels, restaurants, cars etc are expensive and fashionable: *Harry took me to a fancy restaurant for our anniversary.* | **fancy prices** (=very high and often unreasonable prices) **2** having a lot of decoration or bright colours, or made in a complicated way: *fancy buttons* | **nothing fancy** *I just want a basic sports coat – nothing fancy.* **3** complicated and needing a lot of skill: *I can't do all that fancy stuff on the computer.* **4** [only before noun] *AmE* fancy food is high quality S3

**fancy dress** /ˌ·· '·/ *n* [U] *BrE* clothes that make you look like a famous person, a character from a story etc: *a fancy-dress party*

**fancy-free** /ˌ·· '·/ *adj* able to do anything you like because you do not have a family or other responsibilities: **footloose and fancy-free** *Ten years ago I was footloose and fancy-free.*

**fancy man** /'·· ·/ *n* [C] *old-fashioned* a man that a married woman has a sexual relationship with, who is not her husband

**fancy wom·an** /'·· ˌ··/ *n* [C] *old-fashioned* a woman that a married man has a sexual relationship with, who is not his wife

**fan·cy·work** /'fænsiwɜːk‖-wɜːrk/ *n* [U] decorative sewing; EMBROIDERY

**fan·dan·go** /fæn'dæŋgəʊ‖-goʊ/ *n* [C] a fast Spanish or South American dance, or the music for this dance

**fan·fare** /'fænfeə‖-fer/ *n* [C] a short, loud piece of music played on a TRUMPET¹ (1) to introduce an important person or event

**fang** /fæŋ/ *n* [C] a long sharp tooth of an animal such as a snake or wild dog

**fan·light** /'fænlaɪt/ *n* [C] **1** *especially BrE* a small window above a door or a larger window; TRANSOM (3) *AmE* **2** *AmE* a window shaped like a half circle

**fan·ny** /'fæni/ *n* [C] **1** *AmE old-fashioned* the part of your body that you sit on; BOTTOM¹ (7) **2** *BrE taboo* a woman's outer sex organs

**fan·ta·si·a** /fæn'teɪziə, ˌfæntə'zɪə‖fæn'teɪʒə/ *n* [C] **1** a piece of music that does not have a regular form or style **2** a piece of music consisting of a collection of well known tunes

**fan·ta·size** also **-ise** *BrE* /'fæntəsaɪz/ *v* [I,T] to imagine something strange, or very pleasant happening to you: **fantasize (that)** *I used to fantasize that my real parents were famous movie stars.* | [+ **about**] *She would fantasize about her future life with Kyle.*

**fan·tas·tic** /fæn'tæstɪk/ *adj* **1** extremely good, attractive, enjoyable etc: *You look fantastic!* | *Sounds like a fantastic idea to me.* **2** *spoken* used when someone has just told you something good: *"I've passed my driving test." "Fantastic!"* **3** a fantastic amount is extremely large: *Teenagers spend fantastic amounts of money on clothes.* **4** a plan, suggestion etc that is fantastic is not likely to be possible **5** [only before noun] a fantastic story, creature, or place is very strange or unreal: *fantastic tales of dragons and fairy queens* —**fantastically** /-kli/ *adv*: *a fantastically expensive meal* S3

**fan·tas·ti·cal** /fæn'tæstɪkəl/ *adj* strange and unreal: *a fantastical tale*

**fan·ta·sy** /'fæntəsi/ *n plural* **fantasies** **1** [C,U] an exciting and unusual experience or situation you imagine happening to you but which will probably never happen: *He used to indulge in fantasies about being a famous actor.* | *sexual fantasies* | *Young children sometimes can't distinguish between fantasy and reality.* | **live in a fantasy world** *He lived in a fantasy world and never faced up to his problems.* **2** [singular, U] an idea or belief that is based only on imagination, not on real facts: *These claims about being 'the party of law and order' are pure fantasy.*

**fan·zine** /ˈfænziːn/ *n* [C] a magazine written by and for people who admire and support a popular musician, a sports team etc

**far¹** /fɑː‖fɑːr/ *adv comparative* **farther** or **further** *superlative* **farthest** or **furthest**

S 1 W 1

① A LONG DISTANCE
② MUCH/VERY/A LOT
③ GIVING YOUR OPINION
④ NOT AT ALL
⑤ TO A PARTICULAR DEGREE
⑥ PROGRESS/SUCCEED

**① A LONG DISTANCE**

**1** ▶**LONG DISTANCE**◀ a long distance: *Have you driven far?|We walked much further than we had intended.*|**far away** *My parents don't live far away.*|**far above/below/across etc** *The office blocks towered far above them.*|**far from/far away from** *We were sitting too far away from the stage to be able to see very much.*

**2 how far** used when asking or mentioning the distance between two places or the distance someone has travelled: *How far is it to the station?|I wonder how far we've walked today.*

**3 as far as** up to a particular point or distance: *The flood waters had come up as far as the house.*

**4 as far as the eye can see** up to the longest distance away that you can see: *hills sweeping back as far as the eye could see*

**5 far and wide** over or from a large area: **hunt/search far and wide** *He would hunt far and wide for rare medicinal herbs.*|**travel/wander/spread etc far and wide** *Since then I have travelled far and wide.*

**② MUCH/VERY/A LOT**

**6** [+ adj/adv] **far stronger/far more intelligent/far more quickly etc** much stronger, more intelligent etc: *She works far longer hours than I do.|You'll get there far more quickly by car.*

**7 far too much/long/soon etc** much too much, long, soon etc: *It costs far too much money.|It's far too early to tell if she'll be OK.*

**8** to a great degree: **far above/below** *The increase in inflation is far below what experts predicted.*|**far removed** (=very different) *Life on the islands is far removed from the hustle and bustle of life in Manila.*

**9 by far/far and away** used to say that something is much better, worse etc than anything else: *The grass snake is by far the most common snake.*

**③ GIVING YOUR OPINION**

**10 as far as I'm/we're concerned** *spoken* used to give your opinion about something: *As far as I'm concerned, it sounds like a great idea.*

**11 as far as sth is concerned** *spoken* used to give your opinion or to state facts about a particular thing: *This has been a difficult period as far as the German economy is concerned.*

**12 as far as I know/as far as I can remember** *spoken* used to say that you think that something is true, although you do not know all the facts, cannot remember completely etc: *As far as I can tell, the whole thing should cost about £500.*

**13 I wouldn't go as far as to say** *spoken* used to say that you think a particular idea or opinion is too extreme or unlikely to be true: *"Do you think they'll win?" "Oh I wouldn't go as far as to say that, but they're looking pretty good."*

**④ NOT AT ALL**

**14 far from** used to say that the opposite of something is true, or the opposite of what you expect happens: **far from being** *Far from being a reactionary, he's actually quite liberal in his views.*|**far from doing sth** *Far from helping the situation, you've just made it worse.*|**far from pleased/happy etc** *Michael walked in, looking far from happy.*

**15 far from it** *spoken* used to say that the opposite of what someone says is true; certainly not: *"Is he a good driver?" "Far from it!"*

**16 far be it from me to do sth** *spoken* used when you are going to criticize someone or give them advice, and you want to pretend that you do not want to do this: *Far be it from me to try and run your life, but I really think you should leave him.*

**⑤ TO A PARTICULAR DEGREE**

**17 how far** used to ask to what degree something is true: *How far is violence caused by society?|I'm not sure how far this will help the economy.*

**18 as far as it goes** used to say that an idea, suggestion, plan etc is satisfactory, but only to a limited degree: *It's a perfectly good law as far as it goes, but it doesn't deal with the real problems.*

**19 so far** up to a particular point, degree, distance etc: *You can only trust him so far.*|**so far and no further** *They can extend the budget so far and no further.*

**⑥ PROGRESS/SUCCEED**

**20 how far have you got?** used when asking or talking about how much of something someone has done or how much they have achieved: [+ **with**] *How far did you get with the cleaning?*

**21 so far so good** *spoken* used to say that things have been happening successfully until now

**22 sb will/should go far** used to say that you think someone will be successful in the future: *She is an excellent musician and should go far.*

**23** ▶**LONG TIME**◀ a long time in the past or the future, or a long time into a particular period: **far back** (=a long time in the past) *The story takes us far back in the past, to the time of the Pharaohs.*|**far into** *We worked far into the night.* —see also FAR-OFF

**24 so far** until now: *We haven't had any trouble so far.*

**25 as far as possible/so far as possible** as much as possible: *We try to use local materials as far as possible.*

**26 go as far as to do sth** to behave in a way that seems surprising or extreme: *She even went as far as to threaten to kill herself.*

**27 go too far** also **take/carry sth too far** to do something too much or in an extreme way, especially so that people get angry: *That little brat has gone too far this time!|The general view was that the President had gone too far in his support for the Contras.*

**28 not go far** **a)** if money does not go far you cannot buy very much with it: *A dollar doesn't go very far these days.* **b)** if a supply of something does not go far, it is not enough: *That pot of coffee won't go far if everyone wants some.*

**29 not be far off/out/wrong** *informal* used to say that something is almost correct: *The weather forecast wasn't far off, just look at the rain.*

**30 in so far as/in as far as/insofar as** *formal* to the degree that something affects another thing or is connected with it: *The Committee's recommendations, in so far as they affect deaf people, are set out in this document.*

**far²** *adj comparative* **farther** /ˈfɑːðə‖ˈfɑːrðər/ or **further** /ˈfɜːðə‖ˈfɜːrðər/ *superlative* **farthest** /ˈfɑːðǝ̇st‖ˈfɑːr-/ *or* **furthest** /ˈfɜːðǝ̇st‖ˈfɜːr-/ **1** a long way away: *You can see my house from here; it isn't far.* | *In the far distance she could see the outlines of tall, city buildings.* **2 the far end/side etc** the end or side that is furthest from you: *She swam to the far side of the lake.* **3 the far north/south etc** the part of a country or area that is furthest in the direction of north, south etc: *the great plains in the far west of the country* **4 the far left/right** people who have extreme LEFT WING or RIGHT WING political opinions **5 be a far cry from** to be very different from something else: *The current economic situation is a far cry from what was predicted at the election.*

**far·a·way** /ˈfɑːrəweɪ/ *adj* **1** [only before noun] distant: *She was lost and alone in a faraway place.* | *faraway noises* **2 a faraway look** an expression on your face which shows that you are not paying attention but thinking about something very different

**farce** /fɑːs‖fɑːrs/ *n* **1** [singular] an event or a situation that is badly organized or that does not happen in the way that it should: *Blacks were completely shut out of the political process. For them, the right to vote was a farce.* **2** [C] a humorous play in which people are involved in silly situations **3** [U] the style of writing or acting that is concerned with this kind of play

**far·ci·cal** /ˈfɑːsɪkəl‖ˈfɑːr-/ *adj* extremely silly and badly organized: *the farcical effect of period costumes made with polyester fabrics.* —**farcically** /-kli/ *adv*

**fare¹** /feə‖fer/ *n* **1** [C] the price you pay to travel by bus, train, plane etc: **bus/train/air fare** *Air fares have shot up by 20%.* | **half-fare/full-fare** *Children under 4 travel half-fare.* —see COST¹ (USAGE) **2 simple/wholesome/homely etc fare** *old-fashioned* good, healthy, simple food **3** [C] a passenger in a taxi

**fare²** *v* **fare well/badly/better etc** to be successful, unsuccessful etc. *Although Chicago has fared better than some cities, unemployment remains a problem.* **1 how did sb fare?** *He wondered how Paul had fared during the war.*

**Far East** /ˌ· ˈ·◂/ *n* **the Far East** the countries in the east of Asia, such as China, Japan etc —compare MIDDLE EAST, NEAR EAST —**Far Eastern** *adj*

**fare·well** /feəˈwel‖fer-/ *n* **1 farewell party/drink** a party or drink that you have because someone is leaving soon **2** [C,U] *old-fashioned* an act of saying goodbye to someone: **bid farewell to** (=say goodbye to someone) **3** *old-fashioned* used like 'goodbye' when leaving someone for a long time

**far-fetched** /ˌ· ˈ·◂/ *adj* extremely unlikely to be true or to happen: *His explanation sounds pretty far-fetched to me.*

**far-flung** /ˌ· ˈ·◂/ *adj* **1** very distant: *some far-flung corner of Ontario* **2** spread out over a very large area: *far-flung trading posts*

**far gone** /ˌ· ˈ·/ *adj* [not before noun] *informal* very ill, drunk, crazy etc *She's pretty far gone, can you drive her home?*

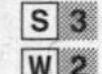
**farm¹** /fɑːm‖fɑːrm/ *n* [C] **1** an area of land, used for growing crops or keeping animals: **live/ work on a farm** *Joe had worked on the farm all his life.* | **chicken/ sheep/pig etc farm**: *He runs a pig farm in Lincolnshire.* **2** the main house on a farm where the farmer lives —see also FACTORY FARM, FISH FARM, FUNNY FARM

**farm²** *v* [I, T] to use land for growing crops, keeping animals etc *The family has farmed there for generations.*

**farm** sth ↔ **out** *phr v* [T] to send work to other people instead of doing it yourself: *farming out work to freelancers*

**farm belt** /ˈ· ·/ *n* [C] an area where there are many farms

**farm·er** /ˈfɑːmə‖ˈfɑːrmər/ *n* [C] someone who owns or manages a farm

**farm·hand** /ˈfɑːmhænd‖ˈfɑːrm-/ *n* [C] someone who works on a farm

**farm·house** /ˈfɑːmhaʊs‖ˈfɑːrm-/ *n* [C] the main house on a farm, where the farmer lives

**farm·ing** /ˈfɑːmɪŋ‖ˈfɑːrmɪŋ/ *n* [U] the practice or business of growing crops or keeping animals on a farm

**farm·land** /ˈfɑːmlænd, -lənd‖ˈfɑːrmlænd/ *n* [U] land used for farming

**farm·stead** /ˈfɑːmsted‖ˈfɑːrm-/ *n* [C] *especially AmE* a farmhouse and the buildings around it

**farm·yard** /ˈfɑːmjɑːd‖ˈfɑːrmjɑːrd/ *n* [C] an area surrounded by farm buildings

**far-off** /ˌ· ˈ·◂/ *adj* **1** a long way from where you are: *a far-off country* **2** a long time ago: *in those far-off days when we were young*

**far-out** /ˌ· ˈ·◂/ *adj* **1** very strange or unusual: *far-out ideas* **2** *old-fashioned* extremely good

**far-reach·ing** /ˌ· ˈ··◂/ *adj* having a great influence or effect: *far-reaching reforms*

**far·ri·er** /ˈfæriə‖-ər/ *n* [C] someone who makes shoes (SHOE¹ (2)) for horses' feet

**Farsi** /ˈfɑːzi‖ˈfɑːr-/ *n* [U] the language of Iran; PERSIAN

**far-sight·ed** /ˌ· ˈ··◂/ *adj* **1** able to realize what will happen in the future and make wise decisions: *a far-sighted economic policy.* **2** *especially AmE* able to see or read things clearly only when they are far away from you; LONGSIGHTED —opposite SHORT-SIGHTED —**far-sightedly** *adv* —**farsightedness** *n* [U]

**fart¹** /fɑːt‖fɑːrt/ *v* [I] *taboo* to make air come out of your BOWELS (1)

**fart about/around** *phr v* [I] *informal* to waste time not doing very much

**fart²** *n* **1** *taboo* an act of making air come out of your BOWELS (1) **2** *slang* a stupid and uninteresting person: *a boring old fart*

**far·ther¹** /ˈfɑːðə‖ˈfɑːrðər/ *adv* **1** a greater distance than before or than something else; further: *We'd better not go any farther today.* | **farther away/apart etc** *The boats were drifting farther and farther apart.* | *He heard a voice farther down the track.* | **farther afield** (=at or to a greater distance away) **farther south/north etc** *I think the state boundary is farther south than here.* **2** if you do something farther, you do it more or to a greater degree; further: *We'd better investigate farther.* | **take sth farther** (=do more about it) *I don't think we should take this subject any farther or we'll be wasting time.*

**farther²** *adj* [only before noun] more distant: *A table was set at the farther end of the kitchen.*

**USAGE NOTE: FARTHER**

WORD CHOICE: **farther, farthest, further, furthest**

When you are talking or writing about real places and distances you can use either **farther, farthest** or **further, furthest** (which are the most usual words in spoken English): *farther/ further down the road* | *What's the farthest/furthest distance you've ever run?*

**Further** (but not **farther**) is also used with the meaning 'more', 'extra', 'additional' etc: *a college of further education* | *For further information write to the above address.*

**far·thest¹** /ˈfɑːðǝ̇st‖ˈfɑːr-/ *adv* at or to the greatest distance away *Who ran farthest?* | **farthest away/apart etc** *She lived farthest away from school of all of us.*

**farthest²** *adj* the most distant: *the farthest corners of the globe*

**far·thing** /ˈfɑːðɪŋ‖ˈfɑːr-/ *n* [C] an old British coin that was worth one quarter of a PENNY

**fa·scia** /ˈfeɪʃə/ *n* [C] a long board above a shop with the shop's name on it

**fas·ci·nate** /ˈfæsɨneɪt/ *v* [T not in progressive] if something fascinates you, it makes you think about it a lot, want to watch it a lot etc: *The idea of travelling through time fascinates me.* | **what fascinates sb is** *What fascinates me most about him is his accent. Where does it come from?*

**fas·ci·nat·ed** /ˈfæsɨneɪtɨd/ *adj* [not before noun] extremely interested by something or someone: [+ **by**] *I was fascinated by her voice.* | **fascinated to discover/hear/learn etc** *Listeners will be fascinated to hear that Oprah has lost more than 50lbs.*

S3 **fas·ci·nat·ing** /ˈfæsɨneɪtɪŋ/ *adj* extremely interesting: *a fascinating book* | **find sb/sth fascinating** *I found his tale of a wild and lawless life fascinating.* —**fascinatingly** *adv*

**fas·ci·na·tion** /ˌfæsɨˈneɪʃən/ *n* **1** [singular, U] the state of being very interested in something, so that you want to look at it, learn about it etc: *The children looked on in fascination.* | **have a fascination for/with** (=be very interested in something) *Ken always had a fascination for stories about undersea exploration.* **2** [C,U] something that interests you very much, or the quality of being very interesting: *the fascinations of the busy street* | **hold/have a fascination for sb** (=interest someone very much) *India will always hold a great fascination for me.*

**fas·cis·m** /ˈfæʃɪzəm/ *n* [U] a RIGHT WING political system in which people's lives are completely controlled by the state and no political opposition is allowed, used in Germany and Italy in the 1930s and 40s

**fas·cist** /ˈfæʃɨst/ *n* [C] **1** someone who supports fascism: *The fascists came to power in 1933.* **2** *informal* someone who is cruel and unfair and does not like people to argue with them: *My last boss was a real fascist.* **3** *informal* someone who has extreme RIGHT WING opinions: *They're just a bunch of fascists.* —**fascist** *adj*: *fascist dictatorship*

**-fashion** /fæʃən/ *suffix* [in adverbs] like something, or in the way that a particular group of people does something: *They ate Indian-fashion, using their fingers.*

S2 W2 **fash·ion¹** /ˈfæʃən/ *n* **1** [singular, U] the popular style of clothes, hair, behaviour etc at a particular time, that is likely to change: **a/the fashion for** *a fashion for alternative therapies* | **be the fashion** *Eastern religions such as Buddhism used to be the fashion in the 60s.* | **be in fashion** *Hats are in fashion again this year.* | **be out of fashion/go out of fashion** (=not be popular) *Maxi skirts went out of fashion years ago.* | **come into fashion** *His ideas are coming back into fashion these days.* | **be all the fashion** (=be very popular) *Psychoanalysis now seems to be all the fashion.* | **fashion conscious** (=always wanting to wear the newest fashions) *Teenage girls are very fashion conscious.* **2** [C] a style of clothes, hair etc that is popular at a particular time: *men's fashions* | *This is a very popular fashion at the moment.* | *High heels are this year's fashion.* | **the latest fashion** *They'll have all the latest fashions.* | **a fashion for doing sth/the fashion of doing sth** *Camilla started the fashion of wearing odd socks.* **3** [U] the business or study of making and selling clothes, shoes etc in new and changing styles: *fashion magazines* | **the fashion industry** *When I leave college I want to work in the fashion industry.* **4 in a ... fashion** in a particular way: *Leave the building in an orderly fashion.* **5 after a fashion** if you do something after a fashion, you can do it, but not very well: *"Can you speak Russian?" "After a fashion."* **6 after the fashion of** in a style that is typical of a particular person: *Her early work is very much after the fashion of Picasso and Braque.* **7 like it's going out of fashion** *informal* if you eat, drink, or use something like it's going out of fashion, you eat, drink, or use a lot of it: *Danny's been spending money like it's going out of fashion.* **8 fashion victim** *BrE informal* someone who always wears or does what is fashionable, even if it does not look good on them —see also **parrot fashion** (PARROT¹ (2))

**fashion²** *v* [T] **1** to shape or make something, using your hands or only a few tools **fashion sth from sth** *He fashioned a box from a few old pieces of wood.* **2** [usually passive] to influence and form someone's ideas and opinions: *Our attitudes to politics are fashioned by the media.*

**fash·ion·a·ble** /ˈfæʃənəbəl/ *adj* **1** popular, especially for a short period of time: *Pastel shades are very fashionable at the moment.* **2** popular with, or used by, rich people: *She desperately wants to move to a more fashionable address.* **3** someone who is fashionable wears good clothes, goes to expensive restaurants etc —opposite UNFASHIONABLE —**fashionably** *adv*: *fashionably dressed*

**fashion house** /ˈ.. ./ *n* [C] a company that produces new and expensive styles of clothes

**fashion plate** /ˈ.. ./ *n* [C] *AmE* someone who likes to wear very fashionable clothes

**fashion show** /ˈ.. ./ *n* [C] an event at which new styles of clothes are shown to the public

**fast¹** /fɑːst‖fæst/ *adj* S2

**1 ▶ MOVING QUICKLY ◀ a)** moving or travelling quickly: *Burell is the fastest runner in the world.* | *The first pitch was fast and hard.* **b)** able to travel or move very quickly: *a fast car.* | *The horse was fast but not a good jumper.* W2

**2 ▶ IN A SHORT TIME ◀ a)** doing something or happening in a short time: *a fast journey* | *IBM is shedding labour at an alarmingly fast rate.* **b)** able to do something in a short time: *Are you a fast reader?* **c)** happening without delay: *This time the response was much faster.*

**3 ▶ CLOCK ◀** [not before noun] a clock that is fast shows a later time than the real time: **five minutes/an hour etc fast** *That can't be the time – my watch must be fast.*

**4 pull a fast one** *informal* to deceive someone by using a clever trick: *Make sure he doesn't try and pull a fast one.*

**5 fast road** a road on which vehicles can travel very quickly —see also FAST LANE

**6 fast film/lens** a film or LENS (2) that can be used when there is little light, or when photographing something that is moving very quickly

**7 ▶ COLOUR ◀** a colour that is fast will not change when clothes are washed —see also COLOURFAST

**8 ▶ SPORTS ◀** a fast surface is one on which a ball moves very quickly

**9 make sth fast** an expression meaning to tie something firmly, used especially on ships: *He made the rope fast to the metal ring.*

**10 fast and furious** done very quickly with a lot of effort and energy, or happening very quickly with a lot of sudden changes: *Political developments in South Africa have been fast and furious.*

**11 He's/she's etc a fast worker** *informal* used to say that someone can get what they want very quickly, especially in starting a sexual relationship with another person

**12 fast talker** someone who talks quickly and easily but is often not honest or sincere: *Nixon quickly gained a reputation as a fast talker.*

**13 the fast set** *old-fashioned* a group of fashionable young people who spend their time doing exciting things

**14 fast friends** *literary* two people who are very friendly for a long time

**15 ▶ WOMAN ◀** *old-fashioned* becoming involved quickly in sexual relationships with men —see also FAST FOOD, FAST FORWARD, FAST LANE **make a fast buck** (BUCK¹ (1))

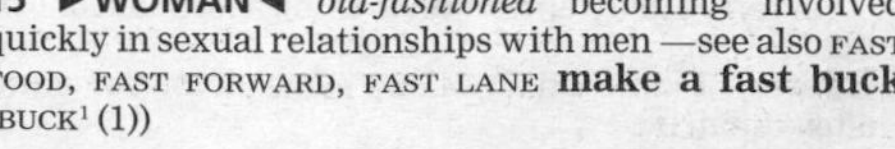

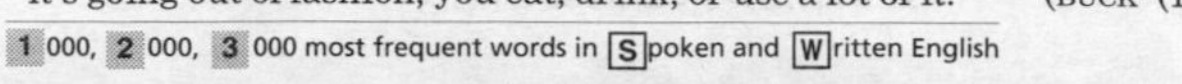

**fast²** *adv*
**1 ▶ QUICKLY ◀** moving quickly: *Slow down – you're going too fast.* | *We ran back to the house as fast as we could.* | **as fast as his legs could carry him** (=running as quickly as he could)
**2 ▶ IN A SHORT TIME ◀ a)** in a short time: *Young kids grow up fast these days.* | **fast becoming/disappearing/developing etc** *Britain is fast becoming a sweat-shop economy based on cheap labour.* **b)** soon and without delay: *The survivors needed help fast.* | *He wanted to know how fast we could get it done.*
**3 fast asleep** sleeping very deeply: *Shh! The baby's fast asleep!*
**4 hold on fast** to hold onto something very tightly: *She held on fast as they went round the bend.*
**5 stick fast/be stuck fast** to become or be firmly fixed and unable to move: *My leg was stuck fast in the mud.*
**6 hold fast to** to continue to believe in or support an idea, principle etc: *Bonhoeffer held fast to his beliefs till the very end.*
**7 be getting/be going nowhere fast** *informal* to not succeed in making progress or achieving something: *I kept asking her the same question, but I was getting nowhere fast.*
**8 not so fast** *spoken* **a)** used to tell someone to do something more slowly or carefully: *Not so fast! You don't want to damage the engine.* **b)** used to say that something has not yet happened or is not yet true: *"Henry will be manager soon." "Not so fast – he's only just been made a team leader."*
**9 fast by** *literary* very close to something: *fast by the river*
**10 play fast and loose with** *old-fashioned* to treat a sexual partner in a careless way: *He felt that Lyn had played fast and loose with his emotions.* —see also **stand fast** (STAND¹ (17)), **thick and fast** (THICK² (2))

**fast³** *v* [I] to eat little or no food for a period of time, especially for religious reasons: *Muslims fast during Ramadan.*

**fast⁴** *n* [C] a period during which someone does not eat for religious reasons: **break a fast** (=eat or drink something to end your fast)

**fast·ball** /ˈfɑːstbɔːl‖ˈfæstbɒːl/ *n* [C] a ball that is thrown very quickly towards the BATTER² (3) in a game of BASEBALL

**fast day** /ˈ· ,·/ *n* [C] a day when you do not eat any food, especially for religious reasons

**fas·ten** /ˈfɑːsən‖ˈfæ-/ *v*
**1 ▶ CLOTHES/BAG ETC ◀** also **fasten up a)** [T] to join together the two sides of a coat, shirt, bag etc so that it is closed: *"I'm going now," she said, fastening her coat.* | *Fasten your seatbelt!* —opposite UNFASTEN **b)** [I] to become joined together with buttons, hooks etc: *I was so fat that my skirt wouldn't fasten.*
**2 ▶ WINDOW/GATE ETC ◀ a)** [T] to firmly close a window, gate etc so that it will not open: *Make sure all the windows are securely fastened before you leave.* —opposite UNFASTEN **b)** [I] to become firmly closed: *This door won't fasten.*
**3 ▶ FIX STH TO STH ◀** [T] to fix something firmly to another object or surface, especially using tape, a metal pin etc: **fasten sth to sth** *Someone had fastened a notice to my door.* | *Chains were fastened round his ankles.*
**4 fasten your teeth/legs/arms etc:** to hold something firmly with your teeth, legs, arms, etc: **[+ around]** *She fastened her arms around his neck.* | **[+ onto/into]** *The snake had fastened its jaws onto his leg.*
**5 fasten your eyes on** to look at someone or something for a long time: *He rose, his eyes still fastened on the piece of paper.*
**6 fasten your attention on** to think a lot about one particular thing
**7 fasten blame on** to blame someone or something, often unfairly

**fasten on/upon** sth *phr v* [T] to decide quickly and eagerly that an idea is the best one: *American companies were quick to fasten on to Japanese business methods.*
**fasten onto** sb *phr v* [T] to follow someone and stay with them, especially when they do not want you to

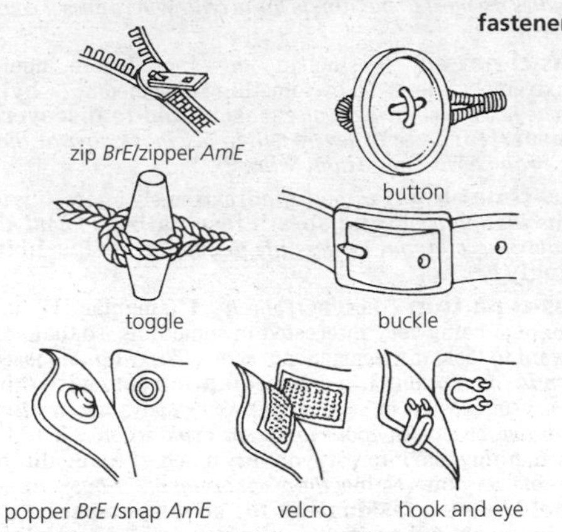


**fas·ten·er** /ˈfɑːsənə‖ˈfæsənər-/ *n* [C] *BrE* something such as a button, ZIP¹ (1) etc that you use to join something together, especially a piece of clothing

**fas·ten·ing** /ˈfɑːsənɪŋ‖ˈfæ-/ *n* [C] something that you use to keep a door, window etc firmly shut

**fast food** /ˈ· ·/ *n* [U] food such as HAMBURGERS which is prepared quickly in a restaurant

**fast for·ward** /,· ˈ··/ *n* [U] a process in which a TAPE or VIDEO is wound forward quickly without being played —**fast-forward** *v* [I,T]

**fas·tid·i·ous** /fæˈstɪdiəs/ *adj* very careful about small details in your appearance, work etc: *dressed with fastidious care* —compare FUSSY (1) —**fastidiously** *adv* —**fastidiousness** *n* [U]

**fast lane** /ˈ· ·/ *n* **1** *BrE* the part of a big road that is used by fast vehicles —see picture on page 415 **2 life in the fast lane** *informal* an exciting way of living that involves dangerous and expensive activities

**fast·ness** /ˈfɑːstnɪ̈s‖ˈfæst-/ *n* [C] *literary* a safe place that is difficult to reach: *mountain fastnesses*

**fast-track** /ˈ· ·/ *adj* [only before noun] someone with a fast-track job will quickly become more important in an organisation

**fat¹** /fæt/ *adj* S2 W3
**1 ▶ FLESH ◀** having a lot of flesh on your body, especially too much flesh: *You'll get fat if you eat all that chocolate.* | *That big fat opera singer – what's his name?* —opposite THIN¹ (2)
**2 ▶ THICK OR WIDE ◀** thick or wide: *Dobbs was smoking a fat cigar.* | *a big fat book*
**3 ▶ MONEY ◀** [only before noun] *informal* containing or worth a large amount of money: *a fat cheque* | *a job in the City with a nice fat salary*
**4 fat chance** *informal* used to say that something is very unlikely to happen: **[+ of]** *What, John get a job? Fat chance of that!*
**5 a fat lot of good/use** *spoken* not at all useful or helpful: *"I don't know much about cars." "Well you're a fat lot of use aren't you?"*
**6 fat cat** *informal* someone who has too much money
**7 in fat city** *AmE informal* having plenty of money: *We'll be in fat city if this deal goes through.*
**8 grow fat on sth** to become rich because of something: *The finance men had grown fat on managing other people's money.* —**fatness** *n* [U]

**USAGE NOTE: FAT**

WORD CHOICE: **fat, overweight, large, heavy, plump, chubby, stout, tubby, obese**

If you want to be polite about someone, do not say that they are **fat. (A little) overweight** or just **large** is a more polite way of saying the same thing. In American English, you can also say that someone is **heavy** when you want to be polite.

**Plump** is most often used of women and children and means slightly (and pleasantly) fat.

**Chubby** is most often used of babies and children and also means pleasantly fat and healthy-looking. When you are describing adults, **stout** means slightly fat and heavy and **tubby** means short and fat, especially around the stomach.

If someone is extremely fat and unhealthy they are **obese. Obese** is also the word used by doctors.

**fat**[2] *n*
**1 ► PERSON OR ANIMAL ◄** [U] a substance that is stored under the skin of people and animals, and helps to keep them warm: *Rolls of fat bulged over his collar.* | *I didn't like the meat – there was too much fat on it.*
**2 ► IN FOOD ◄** [C,U] an oily substance contained in certain foods: *Try to reduce the amount of fat in your diet.*
**3 ► FOR COOKING ◄** [C,U] an oily substance taken from animals or plants and used in cooking: *Skim off all the fat, then add the vegetables.*
**4 the fat is in the fire** used to say that there will be trouble because of something that has happened
**5 live off the fat of the land** to get enough money to live comfortably without doing much work
**6 run to fat** to start to become fat, especially because you are getting older or do not do much exercise —see also **chew the fat** (CHEW[1] (4)), PUPPY FAT

**fa·tal** /ˈfeɪtl/ *adj* **1** resulting in someone's death: *Meningitis is a serious illness, fatal in some cases.* | **fatal accident/illness/injury etc** *a fatal climbing accident* | **prove fatal** (=be fatal) *If it is not treated correctly, the condition can prove fatal.* **2** having a very bad effect, especially making someone fail or stop what they are doing: **it is fatal to do sth** *It's always fatal to stay up late before an exam.* | **fatal mistake/error** *Graf made a fatal mistake halfway through the match.* | **fatal blow** *a fatal blow to the communist system in Eastern Europe* | **fatal flaw** (=a serious weakness in someone or something) *There was one fatal flaw in his argument.*

**fa·tal·is·m** /ˈfeɪtl-ɪzəm/ *n* [U] the belief that there is nothing you can do to prevent events from happening —**fatalist** *n* [C]

**fa·tal·is·tic** /ˌfeɪtlˈɪstɪk◄/ *adj* believing that there is nothing you can do to prevent things from happening: *a fatalistic attitude towards death* —**fatalistically** /-kli/ *adv*

**fa·tal·i·ty** /fəˈtælɪti/ *n* **1** [C] a death in an accident or a violent attack: *a 50% increase in the number of traffic fatalities* **2** [U] the fact that a disease is certain to cause death: *New drugs have reduced the fatality of the disease.* **3** [U] the feeling that you cannot control what happens to you: *Gera looked on her future with a certain degree of fatality.*

**fa·tal·ly** /ˈfeɪtəl-i/ *adv* **1** in a way that causes death: **fatally injured/wounded/stabbed etc** *Two officers were fatally injured in the explosion.* **2** in a way that will make something fail or be unable to continue: **fatally flawed/weakened etc** *Bolton's idea was fatally flawed.*

**fate** /feɪt/ *n* **1** [C] the things that will happen to someone, especially unpleasant events: *I wouldn't wish such a fate on my worst enemy.* | **sb's fate/the fate of sb** *No one knows what the fate of the hostages will be.* | **seal/decide sb's fate** (=make it certain that something unpleasant will happen to someone) *By then our fate had been sealed and we were doomed never to return home.* | **leave sb to their fate** (=leave someone when something terrible could happen to them) *He sailed away from the island, leaving the other men to their fate.* | **suffer a fate** *The rest of Europe was to suffer the same fate.* **2** [U] a power that is believed to control what happens in people's lives: *Fate plays cruel tricks sometimes.* | **by a twist of fate** (=in an unexpected way) *By a strange twist of fate, he died the day before Julia arrived.* **3 a fate worse than death** *often humorous* something terrible that might happen to you: *Toby saw marriage as a fate worse than death.* **4 the Fates** the three goddesses who, according to the ancient Greeks, controlled what happened to people —see also **tempt fate** (TEMPT (3))

**fat·ed** /ˈfeɪtɪd/ *adj* [not before noun] something that is fated to happen seems certain to happen because mysterious force is controlling events: **to be fated to do sth** *She knew that their happiness was fated not to last.* —see also ILL-FATED

**fate·ful** /ˈfeɪtfəl/ *adj* having an important, especially bad, effect on future events: *that fateful day* | *It was a fateful decision which was to change the rest of his life.* —**fatefully** *adv*

**fat farm** /ˈ· ·/ *n* [C] *AmE informal* a place where people who are fat can go to lose weight and improve their health —compare HEALTH FARM

**fat-free** /ˌ· ˈ·◄/ *adj* containing no fat: *fat-free yoghurt*

**fat·head** /ˈfæthed/ *n* [C] *informal* a stupid person —**fatheaded** *adj*

**fa·ther**[1] /ˈfɑːðə‖-ər/ *n* [C] S1 W1
**1 ► PARENT ◄** a male parent *Ask your father to help you.* | *Andrew was very excited about becoming a father.* | **a father of two/three/four etc** (=a man with two, three etc children) *The driver, a father of four, escaped uninjured.* —see picture at FAMILY
**2 ► PRIEST ◄** a priest, especially in the Roman Catholic church: *I have sinned, Father.*
**3 fathers** [plural] people related to you who lived a long time ago; ANCESTORS: *We must honour the customs of our fathers.* —see also FOREFATHERS
**4 ► GOD ◄ Father** a way of addressing or talking about God, used in the Christian religion: *our Heavenly Father*
**5 father figure** an older man who you trust and respect
**6 the father of sth** the man who was responsible for starting something: *Freud is the father of psychoanalysis.*
**7 like father like son** used to say that a boy behaves like his father, especially when this behaviour is bad
**8 a bit of how's your father** *BrE informal humorous* the act of having sex —see also CITY FATHER, PILGRIM FATHERS

**father**[2] *v* [T] **1** to make a woman have a child: *It was rumoured that the bishop had fathered two children.* **2** to start an important new idea or system: *Bevan fathered the concept of the National Health Service.*
**father** sth **on** sb *phr v* [T] *especially BrE* to claim that someone is responsible for inventing or thinking of something: *theories fathered on Freud by his critics*

**Father Christ·mas** /ˌ·· ˈ··/ *n* [singular] *BrE* an imaginary man who wears red clothes, has a long white beard, and is said to bring presents to children at Christmas; SANTA CLAUS

**fa·ther·hood** /ˈfɑːðəhʊd‖-ðər-/ *n* [U] the state of being a father

**father-in-law** /ˈ·· · ˌ·/ *n plural* **father-in-laws** or **fathers-in-law** [C] the father of your husband or wife —see picture at FAMILY

**fa·ther·land** /ˈfɑːðəlænd‖-ðər-/ *n* [singular] a word meaning the place where someone or their family was born, used especially about Germany —see also MOTHER COUNTRY, MOTHERLAND

**fa·ther·ly** /ˈfɑːðəli‖-ðər-/ *adj* kind and gentle in a way that is considered typical of a good father: *Howard put a fatherly arm around her.* | *fatherly advice*

**Fa·ther's Day** /ˈ·· ·/ *n* [C] a day on which people give cards and presents to their father

**fath·om¹** /ˈfæðəm/ *n* [C] a unit for measuring the depth of water, equal to 1.8 metres

**fathom²** *v* [T] also **fathom out** to understand what something means after thinking about it carefully: *I still can't fathom out what she meant.*

**fath·om·less** /ˈfæðəmləs/ *adj literary* **1** too deep to be measured: *the fathomless ocean* **2** too complicated to be understood: *a fathomless mystery*

**fa·tigue¹** /fəˈtiːg/ *n* **1** [U] very great tiredness: *Steve was pale with fatigue after two sleepless nights.* **2** [U] a weakness in metal or wood, caused when it is bent or stretched many times, which is likely to make it break; METAL FATIGUE **3 fatigues** [plural] **a)** loose-fitting army clothes **b)** duties that a soldier has to do such as cleaning and cooking, especially as a punishment

**fatigue²** *v* [T] *formal* to make someone very tired —**fatigued** *adj*: *Fatigued after her long journey, Beth fell into a deep sleep.*

**fat·so** /ˈfætsəʊ‖-soʊ/ *n* [C] *informal* an insulting word for someone who is fat

**fat·ted** /ˈfætɪ̇d/ *adj* —see **kill the fatted calf** (KILL¹ (14))

**fat·ten** /ˈfætn/ *v* [I,T] to make an animal become fatter so that it is ready to eat, or to become fat and ready to eat

**fatten** sb/sth ↔ **up** *phr v* [T] *often humorous* to make a person or animal fatter: *He's too thin – you ought to try fattening him up a bit.*

**fat·ten·ing** /ˈfætn-ɪŋ/ *adj* likely to make you fat: *I don't eat cake – it's far too fattening.*

**fat·ty¹** /ˈfæti/ **fattier, fattiest** *adj* containing a lot of fat: *Avoid fatty foods.* | *fatty tissue*

**fatty²** *n* [C] *informal* an insulting word for someone who is fat

**fatty acid** /ˌ·· ˈ··/ *n* [C] an acid that a cell needs to use food effectively

**fat·u·ous** /ˈfætʃuəs/ *adj* very silly or stupid: *fatuous comments* —**fatuously** *adv* —**fatuousness** *n* [U]

**fat·wa** /ˈfætwɑː/ *n* [C] an official order made by an important Islamic religious leader

**fau·cet** /ˈfɔːsɪ̇t‖ˈfɒː-/ *n* [C] *AmE* the thing that you turn on and off to control the flow of water from a pipe; TAP¹ (1) *BrE* —see picture on page 833

S2 W3 **fault¹** /fɔːlt‖fɒːlt/ *n* [C]

**1 ▶ RESPONSIBLE FOR MISTAKE ◀ be sb's fault** if something bad that has happened is someone's fault, they should be blamed for it, because they made a mistake or failed to do something: *I'm really sorry – it's all my fault.* | **be sb's own fault** *She failed the test but it was her own fault, she didn't do any work.* | **be sb's fault (that)** *It's not my fault that the brakes didn't work properly.* | **be sb's fault for doing sth** *He lost his job, but it was his own fault for telling lies.*

**2 at fault** if a particular person, organization, or system is at fault, they are responsible for something bad that has happened: *The police said that the other driver was at fault – he should have slowed down.*

**3 ▶ STH WRONG WITH STH ◀ a)** something that is wrong with a machine, system, design etc, which prevents it from working properly: *a design fault* | [+ **in**] *It sounds like there's a fault in one of the loudspeakers.* **b)** something that is wrong with something, which could be improved: *I suppose the book's worst fault is its total lack of good taste.* | **for all its faults** (=in spite of its faults) *The treaty was a great achievement for all its faults.* **c)** a mistake in the way that something was made, which spoils its appearance: [+ **in**] *The sweater had a fault in it and I had to take it back.*

**4 ▶ SB'S CHARACTER ◀** a bad or weak part of someone's character: *His worst fault is his arrogance.* | *I really like Sarah, but she does have her faults.* | **for all his/her etc faults** (=in spite of someone's faults) *For all his faults he was a good father.*

**5 find fault with** to criticize someone or something and complain about them: *I wish you'd stop trying to find fault with everything I do.*

**6 through no fault of her/my etc own** used to say that something bad that happened to someone was not caused by them: *Through no fault of her own, Lisa lost her job.*

**7 ▶ CRACK ◀** a large crack in the rocks that form the Earth's surface

**8 generous/kind etc to a fault** extremely generous, kind etc: *Generous to a fault, Mr Samson agreed to provide the necessary equipment free of charge.*

**9 ▶ TENNIS ◀** a mistake made when a player is serving (SERVE¹ (10))

**fault²** *v* [T] to find a mistake in something: **cannot fault sth** *Richards gave a superb performance which could not be faulted.* | **be hard/difficult to fault** *His cooking's excellent – it's hard to fault.*

**fault·less** /ˈfɔːltləs‖ˈfɒːlt-/ *adj* having no mistakes; perfect: *Yasmin spoke faultless French.* —**faultlessly** *adv* —**faultlessness** *n* [U]

**fault·y** /ˈfɔːlti‖ˈfɒːlti/ *adj* **1** something such as a machine that is faulty has something wrong with it that stops it from working properly, or was not made properly: *If the goods are faulty you are entitled to get your money back.* **2** a way of thinking about something that is faulty contains a mistake which results in a wrong decision: *Through neglect or faulty judgment, Meredith had failed to take security measures.* —**faultily** *adv*

**faun** /fɔːn‖fɒːn/ *n* [C] an ancient Roman god with the body of a man and the legs and horns of a goat

**fau·na** /ˈfɔːnə‖ˈfɒː-/ *n* [C, U] *technical* all the animals living in a particular area or period in history —compare FLORA

**fauv·is·m** /ˈfəʊvɪzəm‖ˈfoʊ-/ *n* [U] a style of painting that uses pure bright colours, which was developed in the early 20th century

**faux** /fəʊ‖foʊ/ *adj* [only before noun] *especially AmE* artificial: *a necklace of faux pearls*

**faux pas** /ˌfəʊ ˈpɑː, ˈfəʊ pɑː‖ˌfoʊ/ *n* [C] *French* an embarrassing mistake in a social situation

**fa·va bean** /ˈfɑːvə biːn/ *n* [C] *AmE* a large flat pale green bean; BROAD BEAN *BrE*

**fave** /feɪv/ *n* [C] *informal* a favourite person or thing: *Chocolate ice cream! That's my fave.* —**fave** *adj*

**fa·vor** /ˈfeɪvə‖-ər/ *n,,v* the American spelling of FAVOUR

**fa·vo·ra·ble** /ˈfeɪvərəbəl/ *adj* the American spelling of FAVOURABLE

**fa·vored** /ˈfeɪvəd‖-vərd/ *adj* the American spelling of FAVOURED

**fa·vo·rite** /ˈfeɪvərɪ̇t/ *adj,n* the American spelling of FAVOURITE

**fa·vo·rit·is·m** /ˈfeɪvərɪ̇tɪzəm/ *n* [U] the American spelling of FAVOURITISM

**fa·vour¹** *BrE*, **favor** *AmE* /ˈfeɪvə‖-ər/ *n* S1 W2

**1 ▶ HELP ◀** [C] something that you do for someone in order to help them or be kind to them: **ask a favour (of sb)** *Can I ask a favor of you?* | **do sb a favour** *Could you do me a favour and turn off that light?* | **do sth as a favour** *I'm doing this as a favour, remember, it's not part of my job.* | **owe sb a favour** (=feel that you should help someone because they have helped you) *Of course I'll help you move house; I owe you a favour anyway.* | **return a favour** (=help someone because they have helped you) *Thanks for looking after all my things – I'll return the favor sometime!*

**2 do me/us a favour!** *BrE spoken* used when you are annoyed because someone has asked a silly question or done something to upset people: *Do us a favour, Mike, and shut up!* | *"Did you like it?" "Do me a favour!"*

**3 ▶ SUPPORT/APPROVAL ◀** [U] support or approval for something such as a plan, idea, or system: **find/gain/win/favour** (=be supported by a particular group of people) *The idea may find favor with older people.* | **lose favour** (=stop being supported by people) *Plans to increase taxes have lost favour among party members.* | **look with favour on** *formal* (=use your power to help something to succeed) *We're hoping the President will look with favor upon such a proposal.*

**4 in favour of** if you are in favour of a plan, idea, or system, you agree with it and support it: *Are you in favour of the death penalty?* | *Senior ministers spoke in favour of the bill.* | **in sb's/sth's favour** *The vote was 60-59 in his favour.* | **be all in favour of** (=completely approve of something) *I'm all in favour of people going out and enjoying themselves so long as they don't disturb other people.* | **come down in favour of** (=finally decide to support a plan or action): *The senate has come down in favour of the appointment of Judge Thomas.* | **vote/decide in favour of** (=vote or decide to support something) | **find/rule in favour of sb** *formal* (=make a legal decision that supports someone)
**5 ▶ CHOOSE STH INSTEAD ◀ in favour of** if you decide not to use one plan, idea, or system in favour of another, you choose the other one because you think it is better: *Plans for a tunnel were rejected in favour of the bridge mainly because of the increased costs.*
**6 ▶ UNFAIR SUPPORT ◀** [U] support that is given to one person or group and not to others in a way that seems unfair: **show favour to sb** *Judges have to be careful not to show favour to either party in a dispute.*
**7 ▶ POPULAR/LIKED ◀ in favour** if someone is in favour, people like them and approve of them at the present time: **be in favour with** *She's very much in favour with the management at the moment.* | **back in favour** (=popular again) *Looks like her old boyfriend is back in favor.*
**8 ▶ UNPOPULAR/NOT LIKED ◀ out of favour a)** if someone is out of favour, they are no longer liked, for example by their employers, teachers, or voters: *The boss didn't say 'hello' this morning – I think I must be out of favour.* | **fall out of favour** (=stop being liked) *Once a presidential candidate falls out of favour it is very difficult for them to regain popularity.* **b)** methods, ideas etc that are out of favour are not fashionable or popular any more: **go out of favour** *Grammar-based teaching methods went out of favour in the 60s and 70s.*
**9 ▶ ADVANTAGE ◀ in sb's favour** if something is in someone's favour, it gives them an advantage over someone else: *The fast surface at Wimbledon is very much in Becker's favour.* | *The system operates in favour of the upper classes.* | **the odds are (stacked) in sb's favour** (=someone has a big advantage)
**10 ▶ MONEY ◀ in sb's favour** if a cheque is in someone's favour it should be paid to them: *He made out a cheque for £200 in her favour.*
**11 ▶ GIFT ◀** [C] *AmE* a small gift given to guests at a party
**12 ▶ STH YOU WEAR ◀** [C] something you wear to show that you support a particular political party, football team etc
**13 ▶ SEX ◀ favours** [plural] *old-fashioned* a sexual relationship that a woman agrees to have with a man —see also **curry favour with** (CURRY² (2)), **without fear or favour** (FEAR¹ (6))

W3 **favour²** *BrE*, **favor** *AmE* —*v* [T]
**1 ▶ PREFER ◀ a)** to think that a plan, idea etc is better than other plans, ideas etc: *The president is believed to favor further tax cuts.* **b)** to prefer something and choose it instead of something else: *loose clothing of the type favoured in Arab countries*
**2 ▶ GIVE AN ADVANTAGE ◀** to treat someone much better than someone else, in an unfair way: *a tax cut that favours rich people*
**3 ▶ HELP ◀** to provide suitable conditions for something to happen: *The state of the economy does not favour the development of small businesses.*
**4 ▶ LOOK LIKE ◀** *especially AmE* to look like one of your parents or grandparents: *She favors her Aunt Jen.*
**favour** sb **with** sth *phr v* [T] *formal* to give someone something such as a look or reply: *The Captain favoured her with a salute.*

**fa·vou·ra·ble** *BrE*, **favorable** *AmE* /ˈfeɪvərəbəl/ *adj* **1** a favourable report, comment, or reaction shows that you think that someone or something is good or that you agree with them: *The film received favourable reviews.* | *Her ideas met with a favourable response.* **2** making people like or approve of someone or something: **favourable impression** *The young girl made a most favourable impression on them.* **3** suitable and likely to make something happen or succeed: [+ **for/to**] *The conditions are now favourable for economic recovery.* **4** favourable conditions or terms are reasonable and not too expensive or difficult: *The bank offered to lend us the money on very favourable terms.* —**favourably** *adv*

**fa·voured** *BrE*, **favored** *AmE* /ˈfeɪvəd‖-ərd/ *adj* **1** receiving special attention, help, or treatment, especially in an unfair way: *Foreign aid seems to go mostly to favored governments who are supporters of the US.* **2** chosen by many people: *Brittany is a favoured holiday destination for families.* **3** having desirable qualities: *a house in a favoured position* —see also ILL-FAVOURED, WELL-FAVOURED

**fa·vou·rite¹** *BrE*, **favorite** *AmE* /ˈfeɪvərɪ̣t/ *adj* [only before noun] **1** your favourite person or thing is the one that you like the most: *Who's your favourite actor?* | *I'll take you to my favorite restaurant tomorrow.* S3 W3
**2 favourite son** a politician, sports player etc who is popular with people in the area that they come from

**favourite²** *BrE*, **favorite** *AmE*—*n* [C] **1** something that you like more than other things of the same kind **my/your etc favourite** *I like all her books but this one is my favourite.* | *Which one's your favorite?* | **an old favourite/a special favourite** *This dress is an old favorite of hers.* **2** someone who is liked and treated better than others by a teacher or parent: *You always were Dad's favourite.* —see also FAVOURITISM **3** the horse, runner etc that is expected to win a race or competition: *Italy were favorites to win the World Cup.*

**fa·vou·ri·tis·m** *BrE*, **favoritism** *AmE* /ˈfeɪvərɪ̣tɪzəm/ *n* [U] the act of treating one person or group better than others in an unfair way: *If we give her the job we'll be accused of favouritism.*

**fawn¹** /fɔːn‖fɒːn/ *n* [C] a young DEER

**fawn²** *adj* pale yellow-brown —**fawn** *n* [U]

**fawn³** *v*
**fawn on/over** sb to praise someone and be friendly to them in an insincere way, because you want them to like you or give you something: *When Madonna was in Paris she had the press fawning all over her.*

**fax machine**

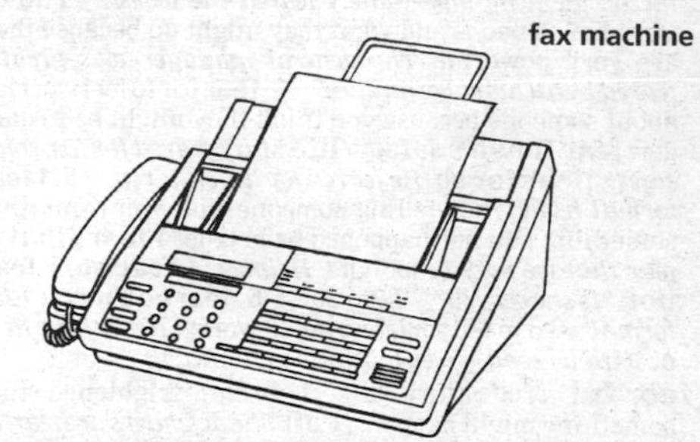

**fax¹** /fæks/ *n* **1** [C] a letter or message that is sent in eletronic form down a telephone line and then printed using a special machine: *Did you get my fax?* **2** [C] also **fax machine** a machine used for sending and receiving faxes: *What's your fax number?* —see picture on page 837 **3** [U] the system of sending letters and messages using a fax machine: *Most of our business is done by fax these days.*

**fax²** *v* [T] to send someone a letter or message using a fax machine: **fax sb sth** *They've agreed to fax us their proposals tomorrow.* | **fax sth (through) to sb** *The order will be faxed through to the manufacturer.*

**fay** /feɪ/ *n* [C] *poetic* a FAIRY (1)

S3 W1 **faze** /feɪz/ *v* [T] *informal* if you are fazed by a new or difficult situation, it makes you feel confused or shocked: *Ned seems rather fazed by the new computer system.*

**FBI** /ˌef biː ˈaɪ/ *n* [U] Federal Bureau of Investigation; the police department in the US that is controlled by the central government, and is concerned with crimes in more than one state —compare CIA

**FC** /ˌef ˈsiː/ an abbreviation of Football Club, used in names of football clubs: *Liverpool FC*

**fe·al·ty** /ˈfiːəlti/ *n* [U] *old-fashioned* loyalty to a king, queen etc

S3 W1 **fear¹** /fɪə‖fɪr/ *n* [C,U] **1** an unpleasant feeling of being frightened or worried that something bad is going to happen: *The boy's eyes were full of fear.* | *McCarthy exploited deep-seated fears about communism among the American people.* | **[+ of]** *fear of flying* | *My fear of dentists dates back to when I was a child.* | **[+ for]** *fears for the future* | **fear that** *fears that his wife might leave him* | **in fear** (=feeling afraid) *He thought he heard something and glanced round in fear.* | **live in fear of** (=always be afraid of) *Ordinary people live in fear of being arrested by the secret police.* | **in fear of your life** (=feeling afraid that you may be killed) | **sb's fears are unfounded** (=there is no reason for someone to feel afraid or worried) *My fears for their safety proved unfounded.* **2 for fear of/for fear that** because you are worried that you will make something happen: *Helen didn't want to get out of bed, for fear of waking her husband.* **3 no fear!** *BrE informal often humorous* used to say that you are definitely not going to do something: *"Are you going to Bill's party tonight?" "No fear!"* **4 put the fear of God into sb** *informal* to make someone feel that they must do something by telling them what will happen if they do not do it: *The Italian manager must have put the fear of God into his team.* **5 there's no fear of** used to say that something will definitely not happen: *There's no fear of him changing his mind.* **6 without fear or favour** *formal* in a fair way: *to enforce the law without fear or favour*

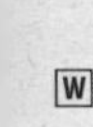
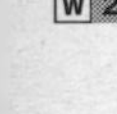

W2 **fear²** *v* [T] **1** a word meaning to feel frightened or worried that something bad may happen: *Fearing another earthquake, local officials ordered an evacuation.* | **fear that** *Einstein feared that other German scientists would build a nuclear bomb first.* | **fear to do sth** *formal* (=be afraid to do something) *Women feared to go out at night.* **2 fear the worst** to think that the worst possible thing has happened or might happen: *When Tom heard about the accident he immediately feared the worst.* **3** to be afraid of someone and what they might do because they are very powerful: *The general manager was greatly feared by all his subordinates.* **4 fear for** to feel worried about someone because you think they might be in danger: **fear for sb's safety/life** *Mary feared for her son's safety.* | **fear for sb** | *He feared for his children.* **5 I fear** *formal* used when telling someone that you think that something bad has happened or is true: **I fear (that)** *I fear that we may be too late, Holmes.* | **I fear so/I fear not**: *"Is she very ill?" "I fear so."* **6 fear not/never fear** *formal* used to tell someone not to worry: *Never fear, he'll be with us soon.* —see also GOD-FEARING

**fear·ful** /ˈfɪəfəl‖ˈfɪr-/ *adj* **1** *formal* frightened that something might happen: **[+ of]** *The defenders are fearful of another attack.* | **fearful that** *fearful that the disease may strike again* **2** *BrE* extremely bad **be in a fearful state/condition/mess** *The room was in a fearful state.* **3** *old use* [only before noun] frightening: *fearful shapes in the darkness* —**fearfulness** *n* [U]

**fear·ful·ly** /ˈfɪəfəli‖ˈfɪr-/ *adv* **1** in a way that shows you are afraid: *She glanced fearfully over her shoulder.* **2** [+ adj/adv] *old-fashioned* extremely: *She's fearfully clever.*

**fear·less** /ˈfɪələs‖ˈfɪr-/ *adj* not afraid of anything: *a fearless warrior* —**fearlessly** *adv* —**fearlessness** *n* [U]

**fear·some** /ˈfɪəsəm‖ˈfɪr-/ *adj* very frightening to look at: *a woman of fearsome dimensions*

**fea·si·ble** /ˈfiːzəbəl/ *adj* a plan, idea, or method that is feasible is possible and is likely to work: *Your plan is not economically feasible.* —**feasibly** *adv* —**feasibility** /ˌfiːzəˈbɪləti/ *n* [U] *a feasibility study*

**feast¹** /fiːst/ *n* [C] **1** a large meal for a lot of people, to celebrate a special occasion: *a wedding feast* | **hold a feast** *A great feast was held in Columbus's honour.* **2** a very good, large meal: *Jane's mother had cooked us a real feast.* | **midnight feast** (=a meal eaten secretly at night by children) **3** an occasion when there are a lot of enjoyable things to see or do: **[+ for]** *Next week's film festival should be a real feast for cinema-goers.* **4** a day or period when there is a religious festival —see also MOVABLE FEAST

**feast²** *v* **1 feast on/upon sth** to eat a lot of a particular food with great enjoyment: *flies feasting on rotting flesh* **2 feast your eyes on** to look at someone or something with great pleasure: *Travellers came to feast their eyes on the natural beauty of the region.* **3** [I] to eat and drink a lot to celebrate something **4** [T usually passive] to be honoured by a special meal

**feat** /fiːt/ *n* [C] something that someone does that is impressive because it needs a lot of skill, strength etc: **[+ of]** *a remarkable feat of engineering* | **perform/accomplish/achieve a feat** *How did they accomplish such an extraordinary feat?* | **sth is no mean feat** (=is difficult to do) *Getting a degree is no mean feat!*

**fea·ther¹** /ˈfeðə‖-ər/ *n* [C] **1** one of the things that cover a bird's body, consisting of a stem with soft hairs growing on either side: *an ostrich feather* | **feather bed/pillow etc** (=a bed etc that is filled with feathers) **2 a feather in your cap** something you have done that you should be proud of —see also **light as a feather** (LIGHT³ (4)), **birds of a feather** (BIRD (4)), **ruffle sb's feathers** (RUFFLE¹ (2))

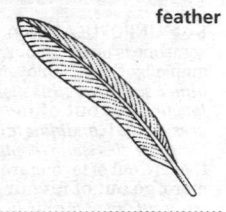

feather

**feather²** *v* [T] **1 feather your nest** to get money by dishonest methods **2 feather the oars** to put the OARS flat on the surface of the water when you are rowing a boat **3** to put feathers on an ARROW —see also **tar and feather sb** (TAR² (3))

**feath·er bed·ding** /ˌfeðəˈbedɪŋ‖-ər-/ *n* [U] the practice of letting workers keep their jobs even if they are not needed or do not work well

**feather bo·a** /ˌ·· ˈ··/ *n* [C] a long SCARF¹ (1) made of feathers and worn around a woman's neck

**feath·er·brained** /ˈfeðəbreɪnd‖-ər-/ *adj* extremely silly

**feather dust·er** /ˌ·· ˈ··/ *n* [C] a stick with feathers on the end used for removing dust

**feath·ered** /ˈfeðəd‖-ərd/ *adj* having feathers, or made from feathers

**feath·er·weight** /ˈfeðəweɪt‖-ər-/ *n* [C] a BOXER (1) who is heavier than a BANTAMWEIGHT but lighter than a LIGHTWEIGHT (2)

**feath·er·y** /ˈfeðəri/ *adj* **1** made of a lot of soft thin pieces: *The plant has feathery leaves.* **2** soft and light

**fea·ture¹** /ˈfiːtʃə‖-ər/ *n* [C] **1** a part of something that you notice because it seems important, interesting, or typical: *The house has many interesting features, including a large Victorian fireplace.* | **[+ of]** *An important feature of Van Gogh's paintings is their bright colours.* | **common feature** *Mass unemployment is a common feature of industrialized societies.* | **geographical feature** (=part of an area such as a hill, river etc) **2** a piece of writing about a subject in a newspaper or a magazine: **[+ on]** *There was a feature on Kevin Costner in last week's Sunday Times.* **3** [usually plural] the parts of someone's face such as their eyes, nose etc: *He had fine delicate features.* **4** a film being shown at a cinema: *There were a couple of short cartoons before the main feature.*  

**feature²** *v* **1** [T] to show a particular person or thing 

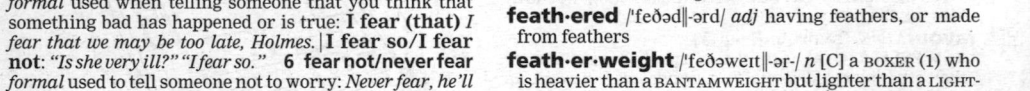

in a film, magazine, show etc: *an exhibition featuring paintings by contemporary artists*|**feature sb as** (=include a famous actor who plays a particular person) *featuring Marlon Brando as the Godfather* **2** [I] to be included in something and be an important part of it: [+ **in**] *Violence seems to feature heavily in all of his books.* **3** [T] a word meaning to include something new or unusual, used especially in advertisements: *The car features an anti-lock braking system.* **4** [T] to show or advertise a particular kind of product: *This week we're featuring a brand new range of frozen foods.* **5** to show a film, play etc: *A popular Berkeley theater featured a porno movie called 'Slaves of Love'*

**feature film** /'·· ˌ·/ *n* [C] a full length film that has a story and is acted by professional actors

**fea·ture·less** /'fiːtʃələs‖-tʃər-/ *adj* a featureless place has no interesting parts: *the flat and rather featureless plains in the south*

**Feb** the written abbreviation of FEBRUARY

**fe·brile** /'fiːbraɪl‖'febrəl/ *adj* **1** *literary* full of nervous excitement or activity: *a febrile imagination* **2** *medical* concerned with or caused by a fever

**Feb·ru·a·ry** /'februəri, 'febjʊri‖'febjueri/ *n* [C,U] the second month of the year between January and March: **in February** *The bridge will open in February 1998.*|**last/next February** *Mum died last February.*|**on February 10th** (also **on 10th February** *BrE*) *The meeting will be on February 10th.* (spoken as *on the tenth of February* or *on February the tenth* or *(AmE) on February tenth*)

**fe·ces** /'fiːsiːz/ *n* [plural] the usual American spelling of FAECES —**fecal** /'fiːkəl/ *adj*

**feck·less** /'fekləs/ *adj* lacking determination, and not achieving anything in your life: *a dull, rather feckless young man* —**fecklessly** *adv* —**fecklessness** *n* [U]

**fec·und** /'fekənd, 'fiːkənd/ *adj formal* able to produce many children, young animals, or crops; FERTILE —**fecundity** /fɪ'kʌndʒti/ *n* [U]

**fed¹** /fed/ the past tense and past participle of FEED¹ —see also FED UP

**fed²** *n* [C] *AmE informal* an agent of the FBI

W3 **fed·e·ral** /'fedərəl/ *adj* **1** a federal country or system of government consists of a group of states which have their own government to decide their own affairs, and are controlled by a single national government which makes decisions on foreign affairs, defence etc: *Switzerland is a federal republic.* **2** concerned with the central government of a country such as the US, rather than the government of one of its states: *federal funding*

**Federal Bu·reau of In·ves·ti·ga·tion** /ˌ··· ˌ··· ···'··/ *n* the FBI

**fed·e·ral·is·m** /'fedərəlɪzəm/ *n* [U] belief in or support for a federal system of government

**federal tax** /ˌ··· '·/ *n* [C, U] *AmE* a tax in the US that is paid to the central government

**fed·e·rate** /'fedəreɪt/ *v* [I + **with**] if a group of states federate, they join together to form a federation

**fed·e·ra·tion** /ˌfedə'reɪʃən/ *n* **1** [C] a group of organizations, clubs, or people that have joined together to form a single group: *the National Federation of Women's Institutes* **2** [C] a group of states that have joined together to form a single group: *the Russian Federation* **3** [U] the act of joining together to form a group

**fed up** /ˌ· '·/ *adj* [not before noun] *informal* annoyed or bored, and wanting something to change: [+ **with**] *I'm really fed up with this weather – why can't it be sunny for a change?*|*You look really fed up – what's the matter?*|**get fed up** *In the end she got fed up with waiting for him to decide.*|*I'm getting fed up with your stupid comments.*|**fed up to the back teeth** (=extremely annoyed)

> **USAGE NOTE: FED UP**
> GRAMMAR
> In British English, you will often hear people say **fed up of,** as well as **fed up with**: *I'm fed up of all this waiting around.* But many people consider this to be wrong.

**fee** /fiː/ *n* [C often plural] **1** an amount of money that you pay to a professional person for their work: **charge a fee** *Some lawyers charge exorbitant fees.*|**legal/medical fee**: *The insurance company paid all my medical fees.* **2** an amount of money that you pay to do something: *school fees*|**entrance fee** *The entrance fees have gone up by 50%.* —see COST¹ (USAGE), PAY² (USAGE) S2 W2

**fee·ble** /'fiːbəl/ *adj* **1** extremely weak: *My grandfather was too feeble to sit up in bed.*|*a feeble attempt* **2** a feeble joke, excuse, argument etc is not very good or effective: *people who come in late with feeble excuses* **3** a feeble manager, teacher etc cannot control the people they are in charge of

**feeble-mind·ed** /ˌ·· '··◂/ *adj* **1** unable to think clearly and decide what to do: *Her husband's so feeble-minded – he won't do a thing unless she tells him to.* **2** *old use* having much less than average intelligence —**feeble-mindedly** *adv* —**feeble-mindedness** *n* [U]

**feed¹** /fiːd/ *past tense and past participle* **fed** /fed/ *v* S1

**1** ▶ **GIVE FOOD** ◀ [T] **a)** to give food to a person or animal: *Have you fed the cat?*|*He's so old and ill he can't feed himself any more.*|**feed sth to sb** *Feed the food to the baby in small pieces.*|**feed sb on sth** *Most people feed parrots on nuts.* **b)** to provide enough food for a group of people: *You can't feed a family of five on $100 a week.* W2

**2** ▶ **PLANT** ◀ [T] to give a special substance to a plant which makes it grow: *Feed the tomatoes once a week.*

**3** ▶ **ANIMAL/BABY** ◀ [I] if a baby or an animal feeds, they eat: *Frogs generally feed at night.* —see also **feed on sth** (FEED¹)

**4** ▶ **SUPPLY STH** ◀ [T] to supply something such as FUEL¹ (1) or information to someone or something: **feed sth with** *The carburettor has to keep feeding the cylinders with petrol.*|**feed sth into** *The data is then fed into a computer.*|**feed sth to sb** *US intelligence had been feeding false information to a KGB agent.*

**5** ▶ **PUSH STH THROUGH** ◀ [T] to gradually push or put something such as a tube or a wire through a small hole: **feed sth into/through** *The tube was fed down through the patient's throat into her stomach.*

**6** [T] **feed sb's guilt/vanity/paranoia etc** to do something that makes someone feel more guilty etc: *You shouldn't say that, you'll only feed his paranoia.*

**7 feed lines/jokes to sb** to say things to another performer so that they can make jokes

**8 well-fed/under-fed/poorly-fed** having plenty of food or not enough food: *exhausted, under-fed children*

**9 feed your face** *informal* to eat a lot of food

**10 feed sb a line** *informal* to tell someone something which is not true so that they will do what you want: *She tried to feed him a line about unexpected expenses.*

**11 feed a meter** to keep putting money into a machine so that you can have electricity, park your car etc —see also BREASTFEED, FORCE-FEED, SPOON-FEED, **mouth to feed** (MOUTH¹ (9))

**feed off** sth *phr v* [T] **1** if an animal feeds off something, it gets food from it: *The pigeons feed off our neighbour's crops.* **2** an insulting way of saying that someone uses something to continue their activities: *The press feeds off gossip and tittle-tattle.*

**feed on** sth *phr v* [T] **1** if an animal feeds on a particular food, it usually eats that food: *Owls feed on mice and other small animals.* **2** if a feeling or process feeds on something, it becomes stronger because of it: *Prejudice feeds on mistrust and ignorance.*

**feed** sb **up** *phr v* [T] to give someone a lot of food to make them more healthy

**feed²** *n*

**1** ▶ **BABY** ◀ [C] one of the times when you give milk to a small baby: *Is it time for Zoe's feed yet?*

**2** ▶ **ANIMAL FOOD** ◀ [U] food for animals: *hen-feed*

**3** ▶ **TUBE** ◀ [3] a tube which supplies a machine with FUEL¹ (1): *There's a blockage in the petrol feed.*

4 ►MEAL◄ [C] *old-fashioned* a big meal
5 ►PERFORMER◄ [C] *BrE* a performer who says things so that another performer can make jokes about them —see also CHICKENFEED

S3 **feed·back** /ˈfiːdbæk/ *n* [U] **1** advice, criticism etc about how successful or useful something is: *Most of the feedback we've received so far has been positive.* **2** an unpleasant high noise heard when a MICROPHONE is too close to an AMPLIFIER

**feed·bag** /ˈfiːdbæg/ *n* [C] *AmE* a bag put around a horse's head containing food; NOSEBAG

**feed·er** /ˈfiːdə‖-ər/ *n* [C] **1 a slow/fussy etc feeder** a baby that eats it's food in a slow, FUSSY etc way **2** a small road or railway line that takes traffic onto a main road or railway line **3** a container with food for animals or birds **4** *old-fashioned* a piece of cloth put under a baby's chin when he or she is eating; BIB (1)

**feeder school** /ˈ·· ˌ·/ *n* [C] a school from which many pupils go to a SECONDARY SCHOOL in the same area

**feeding-bot·tle** /ˈ·· ˌ··/ *n* [C] a plastic bottle used for giving milk to a baby or young animal

**feeding ground** /ˈ·· ·/ *n* [C] a place where a group of animals or birds find food to eat

S1 W1 **feel¹** /fiːl/ *v past tense and past participle* **felt** /felt/
**1** ►FEEL HAPPY/SICK ETC◄ [linking verb, I] to experience a particular feeling or emotion: *You can never tell what he's feeling.* | **feel fine/sick/hungry/guilty etc** *I'm feeling a little better today.* | *I felt a bit awkward having to ask them for money.* | *We felt insulted by their offer.* | **feel as if/as though** *I felt as though I'd won a million dollars.*
**2** ►NOTICE◄ [T not in progressive] to notice something that is happening to you: *He loved feeling the sand between his toes.* | **feel sb/sth do sth** *Terry felt the snake touch his foot.* | **feel yourself doing sth** *I felt myself blushing slightly.*
**3** ►FEEL SMOOTH/DRY ETC◄ [linking verb] if something feels smooth, dry, cold etc, this is the feeling it gives you, especially when you touch it: *Her skin felt cold and rough.* | **feel as if/as though** *My leg feels as if it's broken.*
**4 it feels good/strange etc** if a situation, event etc feels good, strange etc, this is how it makes you feel: *It felt wonderful to be wearing clean clothes again.* | *How does it feel to be 40?*
**5** ►HAVE AN OPINION◄ [T not usually in progressive] to have a particular opinion, especially one that is based on your feelings, not on facts: **feel (that)** *I can't help feeling that he deserved it.* | **[+ about]** *How do you feel about all these changes in the curriculum?* | **feel sure/certain** (=think that something is definitely true) *She felt sure she'd made the right decision.*
**6 feel like a)** to want to have something or do something: *I felt like another glass of wine.* | *He didn't feel like going to work.* **b)** to give you a particular feeling: *It's nice fabric – it feels like velvet.* | *I was only there two days but it felt like a week!* **c)** to feel as if you are a particular kind of person: *They made me feel like one of the family.*
**7** ►TOUCH◄ [T] to touch something with your fingers to find out about it: *She could feel a lump on her breast.* | *Feel the quality of this cloth.* —see picture on page 1260
**8 feel around/on etc sth (for sth)** to search for something with your fingers: *She felt about in her bag for a pencil.*
**9 feel the force/effects/benefits etc of sth** to experience the good or bad results of something: *The company is beginning to feel the effects of the strike.*
**10 feel the need to do sth** to feel that you need to do something: *Sometimes we feel the need to get out of New York and take things easy.*
**11 feel your way a)** to move carefully, with your hands out in front of you because you cannot see properly: *He felt his way across the room, and found the light switch.* **b)** to do things slowly and carefully, because you are unsure about a new situation: *He hasn't been in the job long and he's still feeling his way.*
**12 feel free** *spoken* used to tell someone that you are happy if they want to do something: *"Could I use your phone for a minute?" "Feel free."* | **feel free to do sth** *Please feel free to make suggestions.*
**13 I know (just/exactly) how you feel** *spoken* used to express sympathy with a remark someone has just made: *"Everything I do seems to go wrong!" "I know just how you feel!"*
**14 not feel yourself** *spoken* to not feel as healthy or happy as usual: *Don't take any notice of her – she's not feeling quite herself today.*
**15 feel your age** to realize that you are not as young or active as you used to be: *It was only looking at his son that made him feel his age.*
**16 feel the cold** to suffer because of cold weather: *Old people tend to feel the cold more.*
**17 feel a death/a loss etc** to react very strongly to a bad event, especially someone's death: *Susan felt her grandmother's death more than the others.*

**feel for** sb *phr v* [T] to feel sympathy for someone: *I really feel for the parents of that little boy who was killed.*

**feel** sb ↔ **out** *phr v* [T] *AmE informal* to ask someone's opinions or feelings: *Have you felt out your parents about using the cabin?*

**feel** sb ↔ **up** *phr v* [T] *informal* to touch someone sexually, without their permission

**feel²** *n* [singular] **1** the way that something feels when you touch it: *I like the feel of this cloth.* | *a soft feathery feel* **2** a general idea about something: *The weight adds a feel of quality to these plates.* **3 have a feel for** *informal* to have a natural understanding of something and skill in doing it: *You've got to have a feel for the music.* 

**feel·er** /ˈfiːlə‖-ər/ *n* [C usually plural] **1** one of the two long things on an insect's head which it uses to feel or touch things **2 put out feelers** to start to try to discover what people think about something that you want to do: *They seem to be interested in a peace settlement and have begun putting out feelers.*

**feel-good** /ˈ· ·/ *adj* **feel-good film/programme/music etc** a film etc whose main purpose is to make you feel happy and cheerful

**feel good factor** /ˈ· · ˌ··/ *n* [U] *especially BrE* a feeling among ordinary people that everything is going well, and they need not worry about spending money

**feel·ing¹** /ˈfiːlɪŋ/ *n* 
**1** ►ANGER/SADNESS/JOY ETC◄ [C] something that you feel such as anger, sadness, or happiness: **[+ of]** *She suddenly had a great feeling of relief.* | *Feelings of guilt are common in such cases.* | *It's a wonderful feeling to be back home again.* | **the feeling's mutual** (=used to say that you have the same feeling about someone as they have about you) *"I don't ever want to see you again." "The feeling's mutual."* | **feelings are running high** (=people are very angry or excited) *It was the last game of the season, and feelings were running high.*
**2** ►OPINION◄ [C] what you think and feel about a situation: *My own personal feeling is that we should be very careful.* | **[+ on]** *What are your feelings on the issue of abortion?* | **[+ about]** *I think I've already made my feelings about this perfectly clear.* | **have mixed feelings** (=not be sure what you feel or think) *Parents often have mixed feelings about their children leaving home.*
**3 have/get the feeling (that)** to think that something is probably true, or will probably happen: *Leslie suddenly got the feeling that somebody was watching her.* | *I've got a horrible feeling I forgot to turn off the cooker.*
**4** ►GENERAL ATTITUDE◄ [U] a general attitude among a group of people about a subject: **[+ against/in favour of]** *Johnson underestimated the strength of public feeling against the war in Vietnam.*
**5** ►HEAT/COLD/PAIN ETC◄ [C] something that you feel in your body such as heat, cold, tiredness etc: *I keep getting this funny feeling* (=a strange feeling) *in my neck.* | *feelings of dizziness.*

**6 ▶ ABILITY TO FEEL ◀** [U] the ability to feel pain, heat etc in part of your body: *Herzog had lost all feeling in his toes.*
**7 ▶ EFFECT OF A PLACE/BOOK ETC ◀** [singular] the effect that a place, book, film etc has on people and the way it makes them feel: *Glastonbury has a great feeling of history about it.*
**8 I know the feeling** *spoken* used to say that you understand how someone feels because you have had the same experience: *"It's so embarrassing when you can't remember someone's name." "I know the feeling."*
**9 bad/ill feeling** anger, lack of trust etc between people, especially after an argument or unfair decision: *The recent rail strikes have caused a lot of ill feeling.*
**10 with feeling** in a way that shows you feel very angry, happy etc: *Chang spoke with feeling about the injustices of the regime.*
**11 a feeling (for) a)** an ability to do something or understand a subject, which you get from experience: *It's difficult to explain – you just get this feeling for it.* **b)** a natural ability to do something: *She has a real feeling for the violin.*
**12 ▶ EMOTIONS NOT THOUGHT ◀** [U] a way of reacting to things using your emotions, instead of thinking about them carefully: *The Romantic writers valued feeling above all else.* —see also **no hard feelings** (HARD[1] (26)), **hurt sb's feelings** (HURT[1] (5))

**feeling[2]** *adj* showing strong feelings: *a feeling look* —**feelingly** *adv*

**fee-pay·ing** /ˈ· ˌ··/ *adj BrE* **1 fee-paying school** a school which you have to pay to go to **2 fee-paying student/patient** a student or PATIENT who pays for their education or medical treatment

**feet** /fiːt/ the plural of FOOT —see also **cold feet** COLD[1] (7)) **feet of clay** (FOOT[1] (23)), **have itchy feet** (ITCHY (4))

**feign** /feɪn/ *v* [T] *formal* to pretend to have a particular feeling or to be ill, asleep etc: *Feigning a headache, I went upstairs to my room.|Mattie watched him approach with feigned indifference.*

**feint[1]** /feɪnt/ *n* [C] a movement or an attack that is intended to deceive an opponent, especially in BOXING

**feint[2]** *v* [I,T] to pretend to hit someone in BOXING

**feist·y** /ˈfaɪsti/ *adj approving* having a strong, determined character and being willing to argue with people: *She has the feisty image of the successful entrepreneur.*

**fe·la·fel** /fəˈlɑːfəl/ *n* [C] another spelling of FALAFEL

**feld·spar** /ˈfeldspɑː‖-ɑːr/ also **felspar** *n* [U] a kind of grey or white mineral

**fe·li·ci·ta·tions** /fɪˌlɪsɪ̵ˈteɪʃənz/ *interjection formal* used to wish someone happiness

**fe·li·ci·tous** /fɪˈlɪsɪ̵təs/ *adj formal* well-chosen and suitable: *a felicitous choice of candidate* —**felicitously** *adv*

**fe·li·ci·ty** /fɪˈlɪsɪ̵ti/ *n formal* **1** [U] happiness: *domestic felicity* **2** [U] the quality of being well-chosen or suitable: *the felicity of this arrangement* **3 felicities** [plural] suitable or well-chosen remarks or details

**fe·line[1]** /ˈfiːlaɪn/ *adj* **1** connected with cats or other members of the cat family such as lions **2** looking like or moving like a cat: *She moves with feline grace.*

**feline[2]** *n* [C] *technical* a cat or a member of the cat family such as a tiger

**fell[1]** /fel/ the past tense of FALL[1]

**fell[2]** *n* [C] a mountain or hill in the north of England

**fell[3]** *v* [T] **1** to cut down a tree **2** to knock someone down with great force

**fell[4]** *adj* **at/in one fell swoop** doing a lot of things at the same time, using only one action: *I pressed the wrong button and deleted all the files in one fell swoop.*

S 3 **fel·la** /ˈfelə/ *n* [C] *spoken* **1** a man: *I was talking to this fella I work with.* **2** a boyfriend: *She's fine. her new fella's lovely.*

**fel·la·ti·o** /fəˈleɪʃiəʊ‖-ʃioʊ/ *n* [U] *formal* the practice of touching a man's PENIS with the lips and tongue to give sexual pleasure —compare CUNNILINGUS

**fel·ler** /ˈfelə‖-ər/ *n* [C] *informal* a man

**fel·low[1]** /ˈfeləʊ‖-loʊ/ *n* [C] **1** *old-fashioned* a man: *Paul's an easy-going sort of fellow.* **2** *old-fashioned* a friendly way of addressing a man: *Hello my dear fellow!* **3** *old-fashioned* **your/his etc fellows** the people who you work with, go to school with etc: *He's much more serious than his school fellows.* **4** *especially BrE* a member of an important society or a college: *Fellow of the Royal College of Surgeons.*

**fellow[2]** *adj* **1 fellow workers/students/countrymen etc** people who work, study etc with you: *She ignored her fellow passengers throughout the whole journey.* **2 our fellow man/men** other people in general: *We all have obligations to our fellow men.* **3 fellow feeling** a feeling of sympathy and friendship towards someone because they are like you: *As an only child myself, I had a certain fellow feeling for Laura.* W 3

**fel·low·ship** /ˈfeləʊʃɪp‖-loʊ-/ *n* **1** [C;U] a feeling of friendship resulting from shared interests or experiences: *A close fellowship developed among them.* **2** [C] a group of people who share an interest or belief, especially Christians who have religious ceremonies together **3** [C] *BrE* a job at a university which involves making a detailed study of a particular subject **4** [C] *especially AmE* money given to a student to allow them to continue their studies at an advanced level **5** [C] *AmE* a group of officials who decide which students will receive this money

**fellow trav·ell·er** *BrE*, **fellow traveler** *AmE* /ˌ·· ˈ···/ *n* [C] someone you disapprove of because they agree with the aims of the Communist Party

**fel·on** /ˈfelən/ *n* [C] *law* someone who is guilty of a serious crime

**fel·o·ny** /ˈfeləni/ *n* [C,U] *law* a serious crime such as murder —compare MISDEMEANOUR (2)

**fel·spar** /ˈfelspɑː‖-ɑːr/ *n* [U] another spelling of FELDSPAR

**felt [1]** /felt/ the past tense and past participle of FEEL[1]

**felt[2]** *n* [U] a thick soft material made of wool, hair, or fur that has been pressed flat

**felt-tip** /ˈ· ·/ also **felt-tip pen** /ˌ· · ˈ·/ *n* [C] a pen that has a hard piece of felt at the end that the ink comes through —see picture at PEN[1]

**fem** a written abreviation for FEMININE or FEMALE

**fe·male[1]** /ˈfiːmeɪl/ *adj* **1** belonging to the sex that can have babies or produce eggs: *a female spider* **2** a female plant or flower produces fruit **3** *technical* a female part of a piece of equipment has a hole into which another part fits: *a female plug* —**femaleness** *n* [U] S 3 W 2

**female[2]** *n* [C] **1** a person or animal that belongs to the sex that can have babies or produce eggs **2** a woman or girl: *the prettiest female in Savannah* W 3

**Fem·i·dom** /ˈfemɪdɒm‖-dɑːm/ *n* [C] *trademark* a loose rubber tube with one end closed that fits inside a woman's VAGINA when she is having sex, so that she will not have a baby

**fem·i·nine** /ˈfemɪ̵nɪ̵n/ *adj* **1** having qualities that are considered to be typical of women, especially by being gentle, delicate and pretty: *Dianne loved pretty feminine things.|his slim, feminine hand* **2** a feminine noun, PRONOUN etc belongs to a class of words that have different inflections (INFLECTION[1] (2)) from MASCULINE (4) or NEUTER[1] (2) words

**fem·i·nin·i·ty** /ˌfemɪ̵ˈnɪnɪ̵ti/ *n* [U] qualities that are considered to be typical of women, especially qualities that are gentle, delicate, and pretty: *Different cultures often have different concepts of femininity and masculinity.*

**fem·i·nis·m** /ˈfemɪ̵nɪzəm/ *n* [U] the belief that women should have the same rights and opportunities as men—**feminist** *adj: feminist principles*

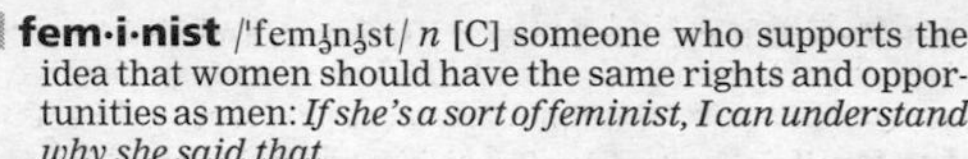

W3 **fem·i·nist** /ˈfemɪnɪst/ *n* [C] someone who supports the idea that women should have the same rights and opportunities as men: *If she's a sort of feminist, I can understand why she said that.*

**femme fa·tale** /ˌfæm fəˈtɑːl‖ˌfem-/ *n* [C] *French* a beautiful woman who men find very attractive, even though she may make them unhappy

**fe·mur** /ˈfiːmə‖-ər/ *n* [C] the THIGH bone —**femoral** /ˈfemərəl/ *adj* —see picture at SKELETON

**fen** /fen/ *n* [C] an area of low flat wet land, especially in Eastern England

S3 **fence**[1] /fens/ *n* [C] **1** a structure made of wood, metal etc that surrounds a piece of land **2** a wall or other structure that horses jump over in a race or competition **3** *slang* someone who buys and sells stolen goods **4 sit on the fence** to avoid saying which side of an argument you support: *The Liberals prefer to sit on the fence while the other parties fight it out.* —see also **mend (your) fences** (MEND[1] (4))

**fence**[2] *v* **1** [T] to put a fence around something **2** [I] to fight with a long thin sword as a sport **3** [I + **with**] to answer someone's questions in a clever way in order to get an advantage in an argument

**fence** sb/sth ↔ **in** *phr v* [T] **1** to surround a place with a fence **2** [often passive] to make someone feel that they cannot leave a place or do what they want: *Mothers with young children often feel fenced in at home.*

**fence** sb/sth ↔ **off** *phr v* [T] to separate one area from another area with a fence: *a planting area fenced off from the main garden*

**fenc·er** /ˈfensə‖-ər/ *n* [C] someone who fights with a long thin sword as a sport

**fenc·ing** /ˈfensɪŋ/ *n* [U] **1** the sport of fighting with a long thin sword **2** fences or the pieces of wood, metal etc used to make them

**fend** /fend/ *v* **fend for yourself** to look after yourself without needing help from other people: *The kids had to fend for themselves while their parents were away.*

**fend** sb/sth **off** *phr v* [T] **1** to defend yourself against someone who is attacking you: *A bag or briefcase can be used to fend off an attacker.*|*fending off the blows with his sword* **2** to deal with difficult questions, especially by avoiding answering them directly: *I did my best to fend off his critical remarks.*

**fend·er** /ˈfendə‖-ər/ *n* [C] **1** *AmE* a bar fixed on the front or back of a car to protect it if it hits something; BUMPER[1] (1) *BrE* —see picture on page 409 **2** *AmE* the side part of a car that covers the wheels; WING[1] (6) *BrE* —see picture on page 409 **3** a low metal wall around a FIREPLACE that prevents burning wood or coal from falling out **4** *AmE* a curved piece of metal over the wheel of a bicycle that prevents water and mud from flying up; MUDGUARD *BrE* —see picture at BICYCLE[1] **5** an object such as an old tyre used to protect the side of a boat

**fender-bend·er** /ˈ·· ˌ··/ *n* [C] *AmE informal* a car accident in which little damage is done

**fen·nel** /ˈfenl/ *n* [U] a pale green plant whose seeds are used to give a special taste to food and which is also used as a vegetable

**fe·ral** /ˈferəl, ˈfɪərəl‖ˈferəl, ˈfɪrəl/ *adj* feral animals used to live with humans but have become wild: *feral cats*

**fer·ment**[1] /fəˈment‖fər-/ *v* [I,T] if fruit, beer, wine etc ferments or if it is fermented, the sugar in it changes to alcohol, especially because of the action of YEAST —**fermented** *adj*: *fermented fruit* —**fermentation** /ˌfɜːmenˈteɪʃən‖ˌfərmən-/ *n* [U]

**fer·ment**[2] /ˈfɜːment‖ˈfɜːr-/ *n* [U] a situation of great excitement or trouble in a country, especially because people disagree strongly with the government: **be in (a state of) ferment** *The whole of Russia was in ferment.*

**fern** /fɜːn‖fɜːrn/ *n* [C] a type of plant which has feathery green leaves, but no flowers —**ferny** *adj*

**fe·ro·cious** /fəˈrəʊʃəs‖-ˈroʊ-/ *adj* **1** violent, dangerous, and frightening: *The battle was long and ferocious.*|*ferocious dogs* **2** very strong, severe, and unpleasant: *a ferocious headache*|*The heat was ferocious.* —**ferociously** *adv* —**ferociousness** *n* [U]

**fe·ro·ci·ty** /fəˈrɒsɪti‖fəˈrɑː-/ *n* [U] violence and cruelty

**fer·ret**[1] /ˈferɪt/ *n* [C] a small animal with a pointed nose used to hunt rats and rabbits

**ferret**[2] *v* [I] **1** [always + adv/prep] *informal* to search for something inside a drawer, box etc by pushing things about: [+ **about/around/for**] *She ferreted about in her desk for a pen.* **2** to hunt rats and rabbits using a ferret

**ferret** sth ↔ **out** *phr v* [T] to succeed in finding a piece of information that is difficult to find: *She managed to ferret out the details of her husband's affair.*

**fer·ris wheel** /ˈferɪs ˌwiːl/ *n* [C] *esecially AmE* a large upright wheel with seats on it for people to ride on in an AMUSEMENT PARK; BIG WHEEL *BrE*

**fer·rous** /ˈferəs/ *adj technical* containing or connected with iron: *Ferrous metals are magnetic.*

**fer·rule** /ˈferuːl, ˈferəl‖ˈferəl/ *n* [C] a piece of metal or rubber put on the end of a stick to make it stronger

**fer·ry**[1] /ˈferi/ *n* [C] a boat that carries people or goods across a river or a narrow part of a sea

**ferry**[2] *v* [T always + adv/prep] to carry people or things a short distance from one place to another in a boat or other vehicle: **ferry sb/sth to/from etc** *The lifeboat ferried the crew and passengers to safety.*|*A small bus ferries tourists from their hotels to the beach.*

**fer·ry·boat** /ˈferibəʊt‖-boʊt/ *n* [C] a FERRY[1]

**fer·ry·man** /ˈferimən/ *n* [C] someone who guides a ferry across a river

**fer·tile** /ˈfɜːtaɪl‖ˈfɜːrtl/ *adj* **1** fertile land or soil produces good crops: *the fertile plains of western Canada* **2** able to produce babies, young animals, or new plants: *Most men remain fertile into old age.* —opposite INFERTILE **3 fertile imagination/mind/brain** *often humorous* an imagination etc that is able to think of interesting and unusual ideas **4 fertile ground** a situation where new ideas, political groups etc can easily develop and succeed: *Poor areas of East London became fertile ground for Mosley's fascist movement.*

**fer·til·i·ty** /fɜːˈtɪlɪti‖fɜːr-/ *n* [U] **1** the ability of the land or soil to produce good crops: *loss of soil fertility* **2** the ability of a person, animal, or plant to produce babies, young animals, or seeds

**fertility drug** /-ˈ··· ˌ·/ *n* [C] a drug given to a woman to help her have a baby

**fer·ti·lize** also **-ise** *BrE* /ˈfɜːtɪlaɪz‖ˈfɜːrtl-aɪz/ *v* [T] **1** to make SPERM join an egg so that a young baby or animal develops, or to join particles of POLLEN so that a new plant develops **2** to put a substance on the soil which makes crops grow —**fertilization** /ˌfɜːtɪlaɪˈzeɪʃən‖ˌfɜːrtl-əˈzeɪ-/ *n* [U]

**fer·ti·liz·er** /ˈfɜːtɪlaɪzə‖ˈfɜːrtl-aɪzər/ *n* [C,U] a substance that is put on the land to make crops grow S3

**fer·vent** /ˈfɜːvənt‖ˈfɜːr-/ *adj* believing or feeling something very strongly and sincerely: *a fervent appeal for peace*|**fervent admirer/believer/supporter etc** *Even her most fervent admirers admit that Thatcher had her faults.* —**fervency** *n* [U] —**fervently** *adv*

**fer·vid** /ˈfɜːvɪd‖ˈfɜːr-/ *adj formal* believing or feeling something too strongly —**fervidly** *adv*

**fer·vour** *BrE*, **fervor** *AmE* /ˈfɜːvə‖ˈfɜːrvər/ *n* [U] very strong belief or feeling: *religious fervour*

**fess** /fes/ *v*

**fess up** [I] *AmE informal* to admit that you have done something wrong but it is not very serious: *Come on, fess up! Who ate that last cookie?*

**fes·ter** /ˈfestə‖-ər/ *v* [I] **1** if an unpleasant feeling or problem festers, it gets more unpleasant: *The insult festered in his mind.* **2** if a wound festers, it becomes infected: *festering sores* **3** if rubbish or dirty objects fester, they decay and smell bad

S3 W3 **fes·ti·val** /ˈfestɪvəl/ *n* [C] **1** an occasion when there are performances of many films, plays, pieces of music etc, which happens in the same place every year: *the Newport Jazz festival* **2** a special occasion when people celebrate something such as a religious event, and there is often a public holiday: *Christmas is one of the main festivals in the Christian Calendar.*

**fes·tive** /ˈfestɪv/ *adj* **1** looking or feeling bright and cheerful in a way that seems suitable for celebrating something: *There was a festive atmosphere in the city.* | *John was obviously in a festive mood.* **2 festive occasion** a day when you celebrate something special such as a birthday **3 the festive season** the period around CHRISTMAS

**fes·tiv·i·ty** /feˈstɪvɪti/ *n* [U] **1 festivities** [plural] things that are done to celebrate a special occasion such as drinking, eating, dancing etc: *The festivities started with a procession through the town.* **2** a happy and cheerful atmosphere that exists when people celebrate something: *There was an air of festivity in the village.*

**fes·toon¹** /feˈstuːn/ *v* [T] to cover something with long pieces of material, especially for decoration: **be festooned with** *Malaga was festooned with banners and flags in honour of the king's visit.*

**festoon²** *n* [C] *formal* a long thin piece of material, used especially for decoration

**fet·a** /ˈfetə/ *n* [U] a white cheese from Greece made from sheep's milk

**fe·tal** /ˈfiːtl/ *adj* the usual American spelling of foetal (FOETUS)

S2 **fetch** /fetʃ/ *v* [T] **1** *BrE* to go to the place where something or someone is and bring them back: *Quick! Go and fetch a doctor.* | **fetch sth from** *Would you mind going to fetch the kids from school?* | **fetch sb sth/fetch sth for sb** *Run upstairs and fetch me my glasses, will you?* —see BRING (USAGE) **2** to be sold for a particular amount of money, especially at a public sale: *The painting is expected to fetch at least $20 million.* **3 fetch sb a blow/clip etc** *BrE informal* to hit someone: *I fetched him a clip round the ear.* **4 fetch and carry** to do simple and boring jobs for someone as if you were their servant: *Am I supposed to fetch and carry for him all day?* **5** *BrE* to make people react in a particular way: *This announcement fetched a huge cheer from the audience.*

**fetch up** *phr v BrE informal* **1** [I always + adv/prep] to arrive somewhere without intending to: **[+ in/at etc]** *I fell asleep on the train and fetched up in Glasgow.* **2** [I,T] to VOMIT¹: *She fetched up all over the blankets.*

**fetch·ing** /ˈfetʃɪŋ/ *adj* attractive, especially because the clothes you are wearing suit you: *Your sister looks very fetching in that dress.* —**fetchingly** *adv*

**fete¹** /feɪt/ *n* [C] **1** *BrE* an outdoor event where there are competitions and things to eat and drink, usually organized to get money: *the church fete* **2** *AmE* a special occasion to celebrate something: *Prom Night is the fete of the year for high school students.*

**fete²** *v* [T usually passive] to honour someone by holding public celebrations for them: *The team was feted from coast to coast.*

**fet·id** /ˈfiːtɪd‖ˈfetɪd/ *adj formal* having a strong, bad smell: *the black fetid water of the lake*

**fet·ish** /ˈfetɪʃ, ˈfiː-‖ˈfetɪʃ/ *n* [C] **1** something you are always thinking about or spending too much time doing: *Physical exercise has become something of a fetish nowadays.* | **have a fetish about** *Sue has a real fetish about keeping everything tidy.* **2** an unusual object or activity which gives someone sexual pleasure: *a leather fetish* **3** an object that is treated like a god and is thought to have magical powers

**fet·ish·ist** /ˈfetɪʃɪst, ˈfiː-‖ˈfet-/ *n* [C] someone who gets sexual pleasure from unusual objects or activities —**fetishism** *n* [U] —**fetishistic** /ˌfetɪˈʃɪstɪk◂, ˌfiː-‖ˌfet-/ *adj*

**fet·lock** /ˈfetlɒk‖-lɑːk/ *n* [C] the back part of a horse's leg, just above the HOOF¹ (1) —see picture at HORSE¹

**fet·ter¹** /ˈfetə‖-ər/ *n* **fetters** [plural] *literary* **a)** the things that prevent someone from being free: *breakingthe fetters of convention* **b)** chains that were put around a prisoner's feet in former times

**fetter²** *v* [T] *literary* **1** to restrict someone's freedom and prevent them from doing what they want: *fettered by family responsibilities* **2** to put chains on a prisoner's hands or feet

**fet·tle** /ˈfetl/ *n* **in fine fettle/in good fettle** *old-fashioned* healthy or working properly

**fet·tuc·ci·ne** /ˌfetʊˈtʃiːni/ *n* [U] *Italian* thin flat pieces of PASTA

**fe·tus** /ˈfiːtəs/ *n* [C] the usual American spelling of FOETUS

**feud¹** /fjuːd/ *n* [C] an angry and often violent quarrel between two people or groups that lasts for a long time: **[+ over]** *a bitter feud over territory*

**feud²** *v* [I] to continue quarrelling for a long time often in a violent way: **feud (with sb) over sth** *the bitter feuding over the leadership of the EC*

**feud·al** /ˈfjuːdl/ *adj* [only before noun] connected with feudalism: *the feudal system* | *feudal society*

**feu·dal·is·m** /ˈfjuːdl-ɪzəm/ *n* [U] a system which existed in the Middle Ages, in which people received land and protection from a lord when they worked and fought for him

**feu·dal·is·tic** /ˌfjuːdl-ˈɪstɪk◂/ *adj* based on a system in which only a few people have all the power in a way that seems very old fashioned

F

**fe·ver** /ˈfiːvə‖-ər/ *n* **1** [C,U] an illness or a medical condition in which you have a very high temperature: *He's in bed with a fever.* | *Take some aspirin – it'll help the fever to go down.* —see also HAY FEVER, SCARLET FEVER, YELLOW FEVER **2** [singular] a situation in which people feel very excited or feel very strongly about something: *a fever of excitement on Wall Street* | **election/carnival fever etc** (=great interest or excitement about a particular activity or event) **3 fever pitch/point/heat** if people's feelings are at fever pitch etc, they are extremely excited: *The children's excitement rose to fever pitch as Christmas approached.*

**fever blis·ter** /ˈ·· ˌ··/ *n* [C] *AmE* a COLD SORE

**fe·vered** /ˈfiːvəd‖-ərd/ *adj* [only before noun] *literary* **1** extremely excited or worried; FEVERISH (2) *fevered cries* **2** suffering from a fever; FEVERISH (1): **fevered brow** (=a hot forehead caused by a fever) *She wiped his fevered brow.* **3 a fevered imagination** someone who has a fevered imagination imagines strange things and cannot control their thoughts: *These stories are merely a product of her fevered imagination.*

**fe·ver·ish** /ˈfiːvərɪʃ/ *adj* **1** suffering from a fever: *feeling feverish* | *Her cheeks looked hot and feverish.* **2** very excited or worried about something: *They waited in a state of feverish anxiety for their mother to come home.* | **feverish activity/preparations/haste** (=activities that are done very quickly because there is not much time) *The show was about to begin and there were signs of feverish activity backstage.* —**feverishly** *adv*

**few** /fjuː/ *quantifier; n* [plural] **1 a few/the few** [no comparative] a small number (of): *I've got a few books on gardening.* | *I'll pop into the supermarket and get a few bits and pieces.* | *only a few hundred yards past the crossroads* | *It's one of the few companies trying to tackle the problem.* | **a few of** *I've read a few of her books.* | **a few more** *There are a few more things I'd like to discuss.* | **a few minutes/the last few days/the next few years etc** *George arrived a few minutes later.* | *Ignore this letter if you have paid in the last few days.* | **a few people** *There were a few people sitting at the back of the hall.* | **only a very few** (=not many) **2 quite a few/a good few/not a few** a S1 W1 fairly large number: *She must have cooked a good few dinners over the years.* **3** not many; not enough: *low-paid jobs that few people want | There may be few options open to you. | The meals are awful, but few complain. | Which one has the fewest mistakes?* | **few of** *Very few of the staff come from the local area.* **4 no fewer than** used to emphasize how surprisingly large a number is; at least: *I tried to contact him no fewer than ten times.* **5 as few as** used to emphasize how surprisingly small a number is: *She can remember all the words accurately after reading it as few as three times* **6 to name but a few** used when you are mentioning only a small number of people or things as examples of a large group: *I've visited many fascinating countries; Japan, India, Turkey, and Russia to name but a few.* **7 the chosen few** the small number of people to be invited or selected: *Such information is made available only to the chosen few.* **8 precious few (of)** a very small number: *Only a small percentage of the seeds germinated and precious few of those survived.* **9 few and far between** rare; not happening or available often: *Jobs are few and far between at the moment.* **10 have a few (too many)** *informal* to have too much alcohol to drink: *He looks as if he's had a few!* —opposite MANY

**USAGE NOTE: FEW**

WORD CHOICE: **few, few, a little, little**

When talking about amounts, you use **(a) few** with plural countable nouns, and **(a) little** with uncountable nouns.

**A few** is positive and means a small number but not a lot: *Yes, I do know a few words of French. | There are a few beers left in the fridge.*

**Few** is negative and means not many: *I'm afraid I know few words of French.* **Few** used alone is fairly formal, and you would most often use it with **very**: *Very few people come here now.*

With words for time, **a few** is almost always used: *after a few minutes | a few years before*

**A little** is positive and means some, but not a lot: *Fortunately he still had a little money left.* In more informal British English, **a bit** means the same thing: *Don't worry, you've got a bit more time to get the work done.*

**Little** is negative and means 'not much': *Unfortunately he now had little money left.* Again, this is fairly formal, and speakers often avoid using **little** on its own. You would normally say **very little**.

**fey** /feɪ/ *adj* very sensitive and behaving or talking in a strange way: *a fey and delicate child*

**fez** /fez/ *n* [C] a round red hat with a flat top and no BRIM[1]

**ff** the written abbreviation for 'and following', meaning the pages after the one you have mentioned: *pages 17ff*

**fi·an·cé** /fiˈɒnseɪ‖ˌfiɑːnˈseɪ/ *n* [C] the man who a woman is going to marry and who she is ENGAGED (1) to

**fi·an·cée** /fiˈɒnseɪ‖ˌfiɑːnˈseɪ/ *n* [C] the woman who a man is going to marry and who he is ENGAGED (1) to

**fi·as·co** /fiˈæskəʊ‖-koʊ/ *n* [C,U] an event that is completely unsuccessful, in a way that is very embarrassing or disappointing: *The first lecture I ever gave was a complete fiasco.*

**fi·at** /ˈfiːæt, ˈfaɪæt/ *n* [C] *formal* an official command given by someone in a position of authority, without considering what other people want: *The matter was settled by presidential fiat.*

**fib**[1] /fɪb/ *n* [C] *spoken* a small unimportant lie: **tell fibs** *Don't tell fibs!*

**fib**[2] *v* **fibbed, fibbing** [I] *spoken* to tell a small unimportant lie: *I think you're fibbing.* —**fibber** *n* [C]

**fi·ber** /ˈfaɪbə‖-ər/ *n* [C] the American spelling of FIBRE

**fi·ber·board** /ˈfaɪbəbɔːd‖-bərbɔːrd/ *n* [U] the American spelling of FIBREBOARD

**fi·ber·fill** /ˈfaɪbəfɪl‖-bər-/ *n* [U] an artificial substance used to fill PILLOWS[1] (1) and DUVETS

**fi·ber·glass** /ˈfaɪbəglɑːs‖-bərglæs/ *n* [U] the American spelling of FIBREGLASS

**fi·bre** *BrE*, **fiber** *AmE* /ˈfaɪbə‖-ər n **1** [U] parts of plants that you eat but cannot DIGEST[1] (1), which help food to move quickly through your body: *Fruit and vegetables are high in fibre content.* **2** [U] a mass of threads used to make rope, cloth etc: *man-made/natural fibre Nylon is a man-made fibre.* **3** [C] a thin thread, or one of the thin parts like threads that form natural materials such as wood **4 nerve/muscle fibres** [plural] the thin pieces of flesh that form the nerves or muscles in your body **5 with every fibre of your being/to the very fibre of your being** *literary* if you feel something with every fibre of your being, you feel it very strongly: *He wanted her with every fibre of his being.* —see also **moral fibre** (MORAL[1] (2))

**fi·bre·board** *BrE*, **fiberboard** *AmE* /ˈfaɪbəbɔːd‖-bər/ *n* [U] board made from wood fibres pressed together

**fi·bre·glass** *BrE*, **fiberglass** *AmE* /ˈfaɪbəglɑːs‖-bər glæs/ *n* [U] a light material made from glass threads, used for making sports cars and small boats

**fibre op·tics** /ˌ·· ˈ··/ *n* [U] the process of using very thin threads of glass or plastic to carry information in the form of light, especially on telephone lines —**fibre optic** *adj*

**fi·brous** /ˈfaɪbrəs/ *adj* consisting of many fibres or looking like fibres: *The coconut has a fibrous outer covering.*

**fib·u·la** /ˈfɪbjʊlə/ *n* [C] *technical* the outer bone of the two bones in your leg below your knee —see picture at SKELETON[1]

**fiche** /fiːʃ/ *n* [C,U] a MICROFICHE

**fick·le** /ˈfɪkəl/ *adj* **1** someone who is fickle is always changing their mind about people or things that they like, so that you cannot depend on them: *an unpredictable and fickle lover* **2** something such as weather that is fickle often changes suddenly —**fickleness** *n* [U] *the fickleness of fame*

**fic·tion** /ˈfɪkʃən/ *n* **1** [U] books and stories about imaginary people and events: *popular fiction* —opposite NON-FICTION **2** [C] something that people want you to believe is true but which is not true: *preserving the fiction of his happy childhood*

**fic·tion·al** /ˈfɪkʃənəl/ *adj* fictional people or descriptions are imaginary and from a book or story: *fictional characters | a fictional description of growing up in Detroit*

**fic·tion·al·ize** also **-ise** *BrE* /ˈfɪkʃənəlaɪz/ *v* [T] to make a film or story about a real event, changing some details and adding some imaginary characters: *a fictionalized account of his life in Berlin* —**fictionalization** /ˌfɪkʃənəlaɪˈzeɪʃən‖-lə-/ *n* [C,U]

**fic·ti·tious** /fɪkˈtɪʃəs/ *adj* invented by someone and not real: *a fictitious address | The author fills this real town with fictitious characters.*

**fic·tive** /ˈfɪktɪv/ *adj AmE* fictive events, people etc are imaginary and not real: *the fictive world of James Bond*

**fid·dle**[1] /ˈfɪdl/ *n* [C] *informal* **1** *BrE* a dishonest way of getting money: *a tax fiddle* | **be on the fiddle** (=be getting money dishonestly or illegally) *They suspected he was on the fiddle all along.* **2** a VIOLIN **3 be a fiddle** to be difficult to do and involve complicated movements of your hands: *This blouse is a bit of a fiddle to do up.* —see also **fit as a fiddle** (FIT[2] (3)), **play second fiddle to sb** (PLAY[1] (15))

**fiddle**[2] *v* **1** [I] to keep moving something or touching it with your fingers, especially because you are bored or nervous: [+ **with**] *She sat for a time, fiddling, with her glass. | Stop fiddling will you!* **2** [T] to give false information about something, in order to avoid paying money or to get extra money: *Bert had been fiddling his income tax for years.* | **fiddle the books** (=give false figures in a company's financial records)

**fiddle around** also **fiddle about** *BrE phr v* [I] to waste time doing unimportant things: *We can't fiddle around here all day – let's move on.*

**fiddle around with** sth also **fiddle about with** sth *BrE phr v* [T] **1** to keep moving the parts of something or making changes to it, especially in a way that is stupid or dangerous: *Why did you let her fiddle around with the remote control?* **2** to keep changing the positions of a group of things until you find the arrangement that you like: *Is it all right if I fiddle around with these figures?*

**fiddle with** sth *phr v* [T] **1** to move part of a machine in order to make it work, without knowing exactly what you should do: *After fiddling with the tuning I finally got JFM.* **2** to move or touch something that does not belong to you, in an annoying way: *Don't let him fiddle with my bag.*

**fiddle-fad·dle** /ˈfɪdl ˌfædl/ *n* [U] *old-fashioned* nonsense

**fid·dler** /ˈfɪdlə‖-ər/ *n* [C] **1** someone who plays the VIOLIN, especially someone who plays FOLK MUSIC **2** someone who gives false information to the government or a company, to pay less money or get more than they should: *tax fiddlers*

**fid·dle·sticks** /ˈfɪdlˌstɪks/ *interjection old-fashioned* nonsense

**fid·dling** /ˈfɪdlɪŋ/ *adj* [only before noun] unimportant, and annoying: *all these fiddling little jobs around the house*

**fid·dly** /ˈfɪdli/ *adj* **1** difficult to do because you have to deal with very small objects: *He managed to fix the television, but it was a fiddly job.* **2** unimportant, slightly difficult, and annoying: *I can't be bothered with all the fiddly details.*

**fi·del·i·ty** /fɪˈdeləti/ *n* [C] **1** loyalty to your husband, girlfriend etc, shown by having sex only with them: **[+ to]** *Tom's fidelity to his wife was never in question.* **2** the quality of not changing something when you are producing it again in a different form, by recording, translating, making a film etc: **[+ to]** *the new translation's fidelity to Proust's great work* **3** the quality of being faithful to your friends, or of not doing anything that is against your beliefs —see also HIGH FIDELITY, FAITHFUL[1]

**fid·get**[1] /ˈfɪdʒət/ *v* [I] to keep moving your hands or feet, especially because you are bored or nervous: *The teacher told them to stop fidgeting.* | **fidget with sth** *Donna began fidgeting with her pencil.*

**fidget**[2] *n* [C] *informal* **1** someone who keeps moving and is unable to sit or stand still: *I wish you'd sit still for a change – you're such a fidget!* **2 get/have the fidgets** *BrE* to be unable to stop moving: *He gets the fidgets if he has to sit in one place for more than ten minutes.*

**fid·get·y** /ˈfɪdʒəti/ *adj informal* tending to fidget a lot: *sitting with three bored, fidgety children*

**fie** /faɪ/ *interjection old use* **fie on sb** used to express anger or disapproval towards someone

**fief** /fiːf/ *n* [C] an area of land that belonged to a lord in former times

S1 **field**[1] /fiːld/ *n* [C]

W1 **1 ▶ FARM ◀** an area of land where crops are grown or animals feed on grass: *a field of wheat*

**2 ▶ SUBJECT ◀** a subject that people study or are involved in as part of their work: **[+ of]** *He's well known in the field of ancient history.* | *improvements in the field of health and safety* | **in his/her field** *Professor Marwick is one of the leading experts in her field.* | **be outside your field** (=not be connected with your work or studies)

**3 ▶ PRACTICAL WORK ◀** work or study that is done in the field is done in the real world rather than in a classroom or LABORATORY: **in the field** *His theories haven't been tested in the field.* | **field trials/testing** *field trials for an anti-cancer drug*

**4 baseball/soccer/sports etc field** an area of ground where a sport is played

**5 take the field** to go onto the area where a sport is played so that you can take part in a game or competition: supporters cheered as the team took the field.

**6 ▶ COMPETITORS ◀ the field a)** all the horses or runners in a race: **lead/be ahead of the field** *Egyptian Prince is leading the field as they come round the final bend.* **b)** all the people, companies, or products who are competing against each other: **lead/be ahead of the field** *Microsoft is already way ahead of the rest of the field.*

**7 snow/ice etc field** a large area covered with snow etc

**8 coal/oil/gas field** a large area where coal, oil, or gas is found

**9 magnetic/gravitational/force field** the area in which a natural force is felt or has an effect

**10 field of vision/view** the whole area that you are able to see without turning your head: *The buildings obstructed our field of vision.*

**11 the field (of battle)** the time or place where there is fighting in a war: **on the field of battle** *It is always better to negotiate than to settle disputes on the field of battle.* | **in the field** *The new tank has yet to be used in the field.*

**12 field of fire** the area that you can hit by shooting from a particular position

**13 ▶ TEAM ◀ the field** the team that is throwing and catching the ball in a game such as CRICKET (2) or BASEBALL, rather than the team that is hitting

**14 ▶ COMPUTERS ◀** an amount of space made available for a particular type of information: *The field for the user's name is 25 characters.* —see also **play the field** (PLAY[1] (25))

**field**[2] *v* **1** [T] if you field a team, group of candidates, or an army, they represent you or fight for you in a competition, election, or war: *The Ecology Party fielded 109 candidates in the 1983 election.* **2 be fielding** the team that is fielding in a game of CRICKET (2) or BASEBALL is the one that is throwing and catching the ball, rather than the one hitting it **3** [T] if you field the ball in a game of CRICKET (2) or BASEBALL, you stop it after it has been hit **4 field a question** to answer a difficult question: *The Senator had to field some tricky questions from reporters.*

**field corn** /ˈ· ·/ *n* [U] *AmE* MAIZE grown to use as grain or to feed to animals, rather than to be eaten —compare SWEET CORN

**field day** /ˈ· ·/ *n* [C] **1 have a field day** *informal* to have a chance to do what you want, especially a chance to criticize someone: *When the scandal finally came out, the press had a field day.* **2** *AmE* a day when pupils at a school have sports competitions and parents watch; SPORTS DAY *BrE*

**field·er** /ˈfiːldə‖-ər/ *n* [C] one of the players who tries to catch the ball in a game of CRICKET (2) or BASEBALL

**field e·vent** /ˈ· ·ˌ·/ *n* [C] a sport such as jumping or throwing the JAVELIN (1) in an ATHLETICS competition —compare TRACK EVENT

**field glass·es** /ˈ· ˌ··/ *n* [plural] BINOCULARS

**field goal** /ˈ. ./ *n* [C] **1** the act of kicking the ball over the bar of the GOAL (3) in American football **2** the act of putting the ball through the circle to get points in BASKETBALL

**field hock·ey** /ˈ· ˌ··/ *n* [U] *AmE* HOCKEY (1) played on grass

**field mar·shal** /ˈ· ˌ··/ *n* [C] an officer of the highest rank in the British army —see table on page B4

**field·mouse** /ˈfiːldmaus/ *n* [C] a mouse that has a long tail and lives in fields

**fields·man** /ˈfiːldzmən/ *n* [C] *BrE* FIELDER

**field sports** /ˈ· ˌ·/ *n* [plural] sports that happen in the countryside, such as hunting, shooting, and fishing

**field test** /ˈ· ·/ *n* [C] a test of a new piece of equipment that is done in the place where it will be used rather than in a LABORATORY —**field-test** *v* [T]

**field trip** /ˈ· ·/ *n* [C] an occasion when students go somewhere to learn about a particular subject: *a geography field trip*

**field·work** /ˈfiːldwɜːk‖-wɜːrk/ *n* [U] the study of scientific or social subjects that is done outside the classroom or LABORATORY —**fieldworker** *n* [C]

**fiend** /fiːnd/ *n* [C] **1 television/fresh-air/sports fiend etc** someone who likes something much more than other people do **2** a very cruel or wicked person **3** an evil spirit

**fiend·ish** /ˈfiːndɪʃ/ *adj* **1** cruel and unpleasant: *Philip had a fiendish instinct for discovering other people's weak spots.* **2** very clever in an unpleasant way: *a fiendish plan to take over the company* **3** extremely difficult or unpleasant: *He set us some fiendish exam questions.* —**fiendishly** *adv*

**fierce** /fɪəs‖fɪrs/ *adj* **1** a fierce person or animal is angry or ready to attack, and looks very frightening: *armed guards accompanied by fierce dogs*|*She turned round, looking fierce.* **2** fierce emotions are very strong and often angry: *Fierce resentment was aroused by this injustice.* **3** done with a lot of energy and strong feelings, and sometimes violent: *a fierce attack on government policy*|*Fighting was fiercest near the town centre.*|**fierce competition** *There is fierce competition for those scholarships.* **4** fierce cold, heat, or weather is much colder, hotter etc than usual: *a fierce wind* **5 something fierce** *AmE spoken* more loudly, strongly etc than usual: *It was snowing something fierce yesterday.* —**fiercely** *adv* —**fierceness** *n* [U]

F

**fi·er·y** /ˈfaɪəri‖ˈfaɪri/ *adj* **1** containing or looking like fire: *a fiery sunset* **2** bright red: *a fiery blush* **3** becoming angry very quickly: *He has a very fiery temper.* **4** showing or encouraging anger: *a fiery speech* **5** fiery foods taste very strong and hot

**fi·es·ta** /fiˈestə/ *n* [C] *Spanish* **1** a religious holiday with dancing, music etc, especially in Spain and South America **2** a party

**fife** /faɪf/ *n* [C] a small musical instrument like a FLUTE, often played in military bands

**fif·teen** /ˌfɪfˈtiːn◂/ *number* 15 —see table on page B3

**fifth** /fɪfθ, fɪftθ/ *n* [C] **1** one of five equal parts of something **2** *AmE* an amount of alcohol equal to 1/5 of an American GALLON (2), sold in bottles: *a fifth of bourbon* **3 fifth wheel** *AmE* someone who is with you when you do not want them to be there: *She said she didn't want to be the fifth wheel.*

**fifth col·umn** /ˌ· ˈ··/ *n* [C] a group of people who work secretly during a war to help the enemies of the country they live in —**fifth columnist** *n* [C]

**fif·ty** /ˈfɪfti/ *number* **1** 50 —see table on page B3 **2 the fifties a)** the years between 1950 and 1959: *Standards of living rose in the fifties.* **b)** the numbers between 50 and 59: especially when used to measure temperature: *sunny, with temperatures in the mid fifties* **3 be in your fifties** to be aged between 50 and 59: **early/mid/late fifties** *He must be in his early fifties by now.* **4** a piece of paper money equal to fifty dollars or fifty pounds

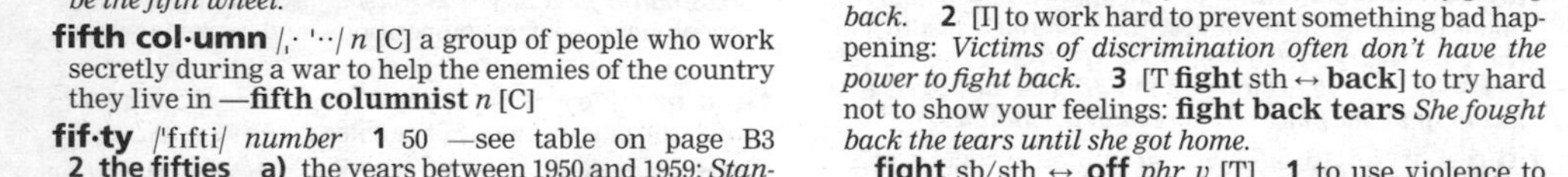

**fifty-fif·ty** /ˌ·· ˈ··◂/ *adj spoken* **1** divided or shared equally between two people: *We should divide the profits on a fifty-fifty basis.*|**go fifty-fifty (on sth)** (=share the cost of something equally): *Let's go fifty-fifty on a new television set.* **2** having an equal chance of happening in one of two ways: *Do you reckon our chances of success are about fifty-fifty?*

**fig¹** /fɪg/ *n* [C] **1** a soft sweet fruit with a lot of small seeds, often eaten dried, or the tree on which this fruit grows —see picture on page 413 **2** *BrE* **not care/not give a fig (for sth)** to not be concerned or interested in something at all **3 not worth a fig** of no value

**fig²** **1** the written abbreviation of FIGURE **2** the written abbreviation of FIGURATIVE

**fight¹** /faɪt/ *past tense and past participle* **fought** /fɔːt‖fɒːt/ *v* S1 W1

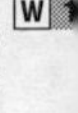

**1 ▶WAR◀** [I,T] to take part in a war or battle: *Did your Uncle fight in the last war?*|**fight sb** *Vietnam fought France and then the US over 30 years.*|[+ **against/with**] *He fought against the Russians on the Eastern Front.*|[+ **about/over/for**] *Britain and Argentina fought for control of the islands.*|**fight a war** *Neither country is capable of fighting a long war.*

**2 ▶HIT PEOPLE◀** [I,T] if someone fights another person, or if two people fight, they hit and kick each other in order to hurt each other: *Two guys were fighting in the street outside the bar.*|**fight sb** *Grant has fought most of the boys in his street.*|[+ **with**] *Phil was fighting with Ryan in the playground.*|[+ **about/over/for**] *two dogs fighting over a bone*

**3 ▶COMPETE◀** [I,T] to compete strongly for something, especially a job or political position or in a sport: **fight sb for sth** *Williams fought several rivals for the leadership of the party.*|[+ **for**] *If you want the job you'll have to fight for it.*|**fight an election** *The mayor has decided against fighting another election.*

**4 ▶ARGUE◀** [I] to argue about something: *The kids fought in the back seat the whole trip.*|[+ **about/over**] *They're fighting about whose turn it is to do the dishes.*

**5 ▶SPORT◀** [I,T] to hit someone as a sport: *Ali fought Foreman for the heavyweight title.*

**6 ▶EMOTION◀** [T] also **fight back/down** to try very hard not to show your feelings or not to do something you want to do: *He fought the impulse to slap her.*

**7 fight your way** to push people away in order to go somewhere: *We fought our way through the crowd.*

**8 fight a losing battle** to work hard when you cannot succeed: *I think they're fighting a losing battle with that libel suit.*

**9 fight shy of doing sth** to try to avoid doing something or being involved in something: *Jane fought shy of participating in the discussions.*

**10 fighting spirit/words** the desire to fight or words which express that desire: *The marches aroused their fighting spirit.*

**11 have a fighting chance** to have a chance to do something or achieve something if you work very hard at it: *Lewis has a fighting chance to win the gold medal.*

**12 fight fire with fire** to use the same methods as your opponents in an argument

**fight back** *phr v* **1** [I] to use violence against someone who has attacked you: *The rebels are fighting back.* **2** [I] to work hard to prevent something bad happening: *Victims of discrimination often don't have the power to fight back.* **3** [T **fight** sth ↔ **back**] to try hard not to show your feelings: **fight back tears** *She fought back the tears until she got home.*

**fight** sb/sth ↔ **off** *phr v* [T] **1** to use violence to keep someone or something away: *The stars had to fight off the crowds to get out of the auditorium.* **2** to try hard to get rid of something: *Elaine's fighting off a cold.*|*Bardot fought off the sex symbol image.*

**fight** sth **out** *phr v* [T] to argue, or use violence until a disagreement is settled: *We left them to fight it out.*

**fight²** *n* S2 W3

**1 ▶HIT◀** [C] an act of fighting in which two people or groups hit, push etc each other: [+ **between**] *a fight between two gangs.*|[+ **over**] *fights over territory*|**get into a fight** *He's always getting into fights with other boys.*|**have a fight** *The cat had a fight last night.*|**start/pick a fight** *Are you trying to start a fight?*

**2 ▶BATTLE◀** [C] a battle between two armies, especially the fighting that happens at one particular place and time: [+ **for**] *the fight for Bunker Hill*

**3 ▶ARGUMENT◀** [C] a quarrel or an argument: **have a fight** *They've had a fight with the neighbours.*

**4 ▶ACHIEVE/PREVENT STH◀** [singular] the work of trying to achieve something, change something, or prevent something: [+ **against**] *the fight against crime*|

[+ **for**] *We will not give up the fight for better conditions.* | **have a fight on your hands** (=have to oppose someone to achieve something) *He'll have a fight on his hands to get Malone acquitted.*
**5** ▶ **SPORT** ◀ [C] an act of fighting as a sport: *Are you going to watch the big fight tonight?*
**6** ▶ **ENERGY** ◀ [U] the energy and desire to keep fighting for something you want to achieve: *There's still plenty of fight left in your grandmother.*
**7 put up a good fight** to work very hard to fight or compete in a difficult situation: *Although our team didn't win, they put up a good fight.*
**8 a fight to the finish** a fight that continues until one side is completely defeated —see also **pick a quarrel/fight** (PICK[1] (9))

**fight·er** /ˈfaɪtə‖-ər/ *n* [C] **1** someone who fights **2** someone who keeps trying to achieve something in difficult situations: *James is a fighter – he'll come through it all right.* **3** also **fighter plane/aircraft** a small, fast military plane that can destroy other planes —see also FREEDOM FIGHTER

**fig leaf** /ˈ· ·/ *n* [C] **1** the large leaf of the FIG[1] (1) tree, sometimes shown in paintings as covering people's sex organs **2** something that is intended to hide embarrassing facts

**fig·ment** /ˈfɪɡmənt/ *n* [C] **a figment of sb's imagination** something that you imagine to be real, but does not exist: *The sinister plot is just a figment of his imagination.*

**fig·u·ra·tive** /ˈfɪɡjʊ̈rətɪv, -ɡə-/ *adj* **1** if a word or phrase is used in a figurative way, it is used about something different from what it normally refers to, to give you a picture in your mind: *I was using the word 'battle' in its figurative sense.* —compare LITERAL[1] (1) **2** *technical* figurative art shows objects, people, or the countryside in the way they really look —compare ABSTRACT[1] (3) —**figuratively** *adv*: *He's up to his eyes in paperwork – figuratively speaking, of course.*

S1 W1 **fig·ure**[1] /ˈfɪɡə‖ˈfɪɡjər/ *n* [C]
**1** ▶ **NUMBER** ◀ **a)** a number representing an amount, especially an officially published number: *keeping unemployment figures down* **b)** a number from 0 to 10, written as a sign rather than a word: **a four/five/six figure number** (=a number in the thousands, ten thousands, hundred thousands etc) | **double figures** (=numbers between 10 and 99): *His score is now well into double figures.*
**2** ▶ **AMOUNT OF MONEY** ◀ a particular amount of money: *an estimated figure of $200 million*
**3 father/mother/authority figure** someone who is considered to be like a father etc, or to represent authority, because of their character or behaviour: *He had always looked upon Sarah as a kind of mother figure.*
**4 figures** [plural] the activity of adding, multiplying etc numbers; ARITHMETIC: **have a head for figures** (=be good at arithmetic)
**5 put a figure on it/give an exact figure** to say exactly how much something is worth, or how much or how many of something you are talking about: *I know it's worth a lot of money but I couldn't put a figure on it.*
**6** ▶ **WOMAN'S BODY** ◀ the shape of someone's body, especially a woman's body: *She has a great figure.* | **keep your figure** (=keep your body in an attractive shape): *How does she manage to keep her figure when she eats so much?* —see BODY (USAGE)
**7** ▶ **KIND OF PERSON** ◀ someone who has a particular type of character or appearance or who is important in a particular way: *He was the outstanding political figure of his time.* | *She stood there, a frail but defiant figure.* —see also **cult figure** (CULT (2))
**8 a fine figure of a man/woman** someone who is tall and has a good body
**9** ▶ **FAR AWAY/DIFFICULT TO SEE** ◀ the shape of a person, especially one that is far away or is difficult to see: *a dark figure in the distance*
**10** ▶ **PAINTING/MODEL** ◀ a person in a painting or model: *an 18th century Maori figure* —see also FIGURINE
**11** ▶ **DRAWING** ◀ a numbered drawing or a DIAGRAM in a book
**12** ▶ **MATHEMATICAL SHAPE** ◀ a GEOMETRIC shape: *a hexagon is a six-sided figure*
**13** ▶ **ON ICE** ◀ a pattern formed in FIGURE SKATING
**14 a figure of fun** someone who people laugh at

**figure**[2] *v* **1** [I] to be important in a process, event, or situation, and be noticed because of this: *Kennedy's descendants were to figure prominently in the country's history.* **2** [T] *informal especially AmE* to form a particular opinion after thinking about a situation: **figure that** *I figured that he was drunk and shouldn't be allowed to drive.* **3 that figures/it figures** *spoken especially AmE* **a)** used when something happens or someone behaves in a way that you expect, but do not like: *"It rained the whole weekend." "Oh, that figures."* **b)** used to say that something is reasonable or makes sense: *If Terry has talked to Lennox, then he knows you are here. It figures.* **4** [T] *AmE* to calculate an amount: *Larry figured his expenses for the past month.* S2 W3

**figure** sth ↔ **out** *phr v* [T] to think about a problem or situation until you find the answer or understand what has happened: [+ **how/what**] *Can you figure out how to do it?* | **figure sth out** *It took me hours to figure those algebra problems out.* | **figure out that** *She figured out that he was leaving on Tuesday.*

**figure** sb **out** *phr v* [T] to understand why someone behaves in the way they do: *Women. I just can't figure them out.*

**fig·ured** /ˈfɪɡəd‖ˈfɪɡjərd/ *adj* [only before noun] decorated with a small pattern: *figured silk*

**fig·ure·head** /ˈfɪɡəhed‖ˈfɪɡjər-/ *n* [C] **1** someone who seems to be the leader of a country or organization but who has no real power: *The Queen is merely a figurehead.* **2** a wooden model of a woman that used to be placed on the front of ships

figure of eight *BrE* /figure eight *AmE*

**figure of eight** /ˌ·· · ˈ·/ *BrE*, **figure eight** *AmE* *n* [C] *BrE* the pattern or shape of a number eight, as seen in a knot, dance etc

**figure of speech** /ˌ·· · ˈ·/ *n* [C] a word or expression that is used in a different way from the normal one, to give you a picture in your mind: *When I said it was a battle to the death it was just a figure of speech.*

**figure skat·ing** /ˈ·· ˌ··/ *n* [C] a kind of SKATING in which you cut patterns in the ice with your SKATES[1] (1) —**figure skater** *n* [C]

**fig·u·rine** /ˌfɪɡjʊ̈ˈriːn, ˈfɪɡjʊ̈riːn‖ˌfɪɡjʊ̈ˈriːn/ *n* [C] a small model of a person made of CHINA (=baked clay), used as a decoration

**fil·a·ment** /ˈfɪləmənt/ *n* [C] a very thin thread, especially the thin wire in a LIGHT BULB

**fil·bert** /ˈfɪlbət‖-bərt/ *n* [C] *especially AmE* a HAZELNUT

**filch** /fɪltʃ/ *v* [T] *informal* to steal something, especially something small or not very expensive: *He was sacked for filching food from the kitchen.*

S1 W2 **file¹** /faɪl/ *n* [C] **1** information about a particular person or subject that is kept by an official organization: [+ **on**] *Mendoza read over the file on the murders again.* | **keep a file on** (=collect and store information) *The government keeps a file on known terrorists.* **2** a box or folded piece of heavy paper that is used to store papers in the proper order: *Fran came in holding a blue file.* **3** a collection of information on a computer that is stored under a particular name: *a spreadsheet file* **4 on file a)** kept in a file so that it can be used later: *We will keep your application on file.* **b)** officially recorded: *The petition has to be on file by March 3rd.* **5** a metal tool with a rough surface used to smooth other surfaces or to cut through wood, metal etc —see also NAIL FILE —see picture at TOOL¹ **6** a line of people one behind the other: **in file** *walking in file* —see also INDIAN FILE, SINGLE FILE, RANK AND FILE

S3 **file²** *v* **1** [I always + adv/prep] to walk in a line of people, one behind the other: [+ **past/into/through etc**] *The mourners filed past the coffin.* **2** [I always + adv/prep,T] *law* to officially record something such as a complaint, law case, official document etc: *Mr Genoa filed a formal complaint against the department.* | [+ **for**] *The Morrisons have filed for divorce.* **3** [T] to keep papers with information on them in a particular place so that you can find them easily: *Contributors' contracts are filed alphabetically.* | **file sth away** *The exam papers will be filed away in my office.* **4** [I always + adv/prep,T] to cut or rub something or make something smooth, using a metal tool with a rough surface: *She was filing her nails.* | [+ **through/away/down etc**] *I need to file down the sharp edges.*

F

**file cab·i·net** /'· ˌ···/ *n* [C] *AmE* a FILING CABINET

**fil·et¹** /'fɪlɪt‖'fɪlɪt, -leɪ, fɪ'leɪ/ *n* [C] the usual American spelling of FILLET ¹ (1)

**filet²** *v* [T] the usual American spelling of FILLET² (1)

**fi·li·al** /'fɪliəl/ *adj formal* concerning the way in which a son or daughter should behave towards their parents: *her filial duty*

**fil·i·bus·ter** /'fɪlɪbʌstə‖-ər/ *v* [I] *especially AmE* to try to delay action in Congress by making very long speeches —**filibuster** *n* [C]

**fil·i·gree** /'fɪlɪgriː/ *n* [U] delicate work made of gold or silver wire, used to decorate things: *silver filigree jewellery*

**filing cab·i·net** /'·· ˌ···/ *n* [C] *BrE* a piece of office furniture that has drawers for storing letters, reports etc

**fil·ings** /'faɪlɪŋz/ *n* [plural] very small sharp bits that come off a piece of metal when it is filed (FILE² (4))

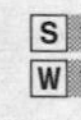
S1 W1 **fill¹** /fɪl/ *v*

**1 ▶ MAKE STH FULL ◀ a)** also **fill up** [T] to put the right amount of a liquid, substance, or material into a container, or put in enough to make it full: *I filled a saucepan and put it on the stove.* | *You've filled the bath too full.* | **fill sth with** *Fill the pots with earth.* | **fill sth to the brim** (=fill something completely) **b) be filled with** if a container is filled with something, it has had as much of something as possible put inside it: *The next drawer was filled with neat piles of shirts.*

**2 ▶ BECOME FULL ◀** also **fill up** [I] if a place, building, or container fills, it gradually becomes full of people, things, or a particular substance: *They opened the doors and the hall quickly started to fill.* | [+ **with**] *The trench is filling up with water.*

**3 ▶ NOT LEAVE ANY SPACE ◀** [T] if a lot of people or things fill a place, there are so many of them that there seems to be no room for anyone or anything else: *Piles of newspapers filled the garage.* | **be filled with** *The streets were filled with cheering crowds.*

**4 ▶ HOLE/CRACK ◀** also **fill in** [T] to put a substance in a hole or crack in order to make a surface smooth again: *Fill any cracks in the wall before you paint it.*

**5 ▶ SOUND/SMELL/LIGHT ◀** [T] if a sound, smell, or light fills a place or space, you notice it because it is very loud or strong: *The smell of freshly baked bread filled the room.* | *The stage filled with light.* | **be filled with** *The air was filled with the sound of happy children.*

**6 ▶ EMOTIONS ◀** [T] if an emotion fills you, you feel it very strongly: *A feeling of bliss filled his body.* | **be filled with** *She was filled with a deep contentment.*

**7 fill a need/demand** to give people something they want but which they have not been able to have until now: *The program helps fill a growing need among teenagers for practical advice about drugs.*

**8** [T] if you fill a period of time with a particular activity you use most of your time doing it: *Our days were filled with talk and music.* | **fill sth doing sth** *Harry filled his spare time reading and writing to friends.*

**9 fill yourself** *informal* to eat so much food that you cannot eat any more: **fill yourself with** *Don't fill yourself up with sweets, we're eating in an hour.*

**10 fill a job/post/position a)** to do a particular job: *Women fill 30% of the senior positions.* **b)** to accept someone's offer of a job: *a shortage of trained secretaries willing to fill permanent office vacancies*

**11 fill a role** be a part of something: *Pop music undoubtedly fills an important role in teenagers' lives.*

**12 fill an order** *especially AmE* to supply the goods requested by a customer

**13 fill the bill** *AmE* to have exactly the right qualities; **fit the bill** FIT¹ (7): *We needed an experienced reporter and Willis fills the bill.*

**14 ▶ TEETH ◀** [T] to put a FILLING² (1) in a tooth

**15 ▶ SAIL ◀** [I,T] if a sail fills or the wind fills a sail, the sail has a rounded shape rather than hanging down loosely

**fill in** *phr v*

**1 ▶ DOCUMENT ◀** [T **fill** sth ↔ **in**] to write all the necessary information on an official document: *Don't forget to fill in your boarding cards.*

**2 ▶ TELL SB NEWS ◀** [T **fill** sb ↔ **in**] to tell someone about things which have happened recently, especially because you have not seen them for a long time: **fill sb in on sth** *Let me fill you in on what's been happening in the office over lunch.*

**3 ▶ CRACK/HOLE ◀** [T **fill** sth ↔ **in**] to put a substance in a hole or crack in order to make a surface smooth again: *filling in the holes in the road*

**4 fill in time** to use your time doing something unimportant, especially when you are waiting for something to happen: *We've got some time to fill in before the show. Let's go for a drink.*

**5 ▶ SPACE ◀** [T **fill** sth ↔ **in**] to paint or draw over the space inside a shape: *Somebody had filled in all the 'o's' on the page.*

**6 ▶ DO SB'S JOB ◀** [I] to do someone's job or work because they are unable to do it: **fill in for sb** *Sally's off sick. Can you fill in for her for a few days?*

**7 ▶ HIT SB ◀** [T **fill** sb **in**] *BrE informal* to hit someone hard and repeatedly all over their body: *One more crack like that and I'll fill you in.*

**fill out** *phr v* **1** [T **fill** sth ↔ **out**] to write all the necessary information on an official document: *You* *haven't filled out the counterfoil.* **2** [I] **a)** if your body fills out it becomes rounded or large in a way that is considered attractive: *Young Kevin has really filled out in the last six months.* **b)** a phrase meaning to become fat, used when you do not want to offend someone: *I think Eric is filling out around the waist.*

**fill up** *phr v*

**1 ► MAKE STH FULL ◄** [T **fill** sth ↔ **up**] to put the right amount of a liquid or substance in a container or enough to make it full: *Brad just kept filling up everyone's glasses with champagne.*

**2 ► BECOME FULL ◄** [I] to gradually become full of people, things, or a substance: *The church was filling up with people who had come to pay their respects.*

**3 ► DOCUMENT ◄** [T **fill** sth ↔ **up**] to write all the necessary information on an official document

**4 fill (yourself) up** *informal* to eat so much food that you cannot eat any more: [+ **with**] *Don't fill yourself up with too many cookies.*

**5 ► STOP SB FEELING HUNGRY ◄** [T **fill** sb **up**] *informal* food that fills you up makes you feel you have eaten a lot when you have only eaten a small amount: *I used to just have a sandwich for lunch, but that doesn't fill me up anymore.*

**fill**[2] *n* **1 have your fill of sth** to no longer be able to accept an unpleasant situation: *I've had my fill of screaming kids for one day.* **2 eat/drink your fill** to eat or drink as much as you want or need **3 a fill of sth** the quantity you need to fill something

**filled gold** /ˌ· ˈ·◂/ *n* [U] *AmE* ROLLED GOLD

**fill·er** /ˈfɪlə‖-ər/ *n* [singular, U] **1** a substance used to fill cracks in wood, walls etc, especially before you paint them **2** *especially AmE* stories, information, drawings etc that are not important but are used to fill a page in a newspaper or magazine

**filler cap** /ˈ·· ·/ *n* [C] *BrE* the lid that fits over the hole in a car that you pour petrol through

**fil·let**[1] /ˈfɪlɪ̣t‖ˈfɪlɪ̣t, -leɪ, fɪˈleɪ/ *n* [C] a piece of meat or fish without bones; FILET *AmE*: *a fillet of sole*

**fillet**[2] *v* [T] to remove the bones from a piece of meat or fish; FILET *AmE*: *filleted sole*

**fill-in** /ˈ· ·/ *n* [singular] *BrE informal* someone who does someone else's job when they are unable to do it: *I'm only here as a fill-in while Robert's away.*

**fill·ing**[1] /ˈfɪlɪŋ/ *adj* food that is filling makes your stomach feel full: *That fruitcake is really filling stuff.*

**filling**[2] *n* **1** [C] a small amount of metal that is put into your tooth to prevent it from decaying **2** [C,U] the food that is put inside a PIE, SANDWICH[1] etc: *cherry pie filling*

**filling sta·tion** /ˈ·· ˌ··/ *n* [C] a place where you can buy petrol for your car; PETROL STATION *BrE*

**fil·lip** /ˈfɪlɪ̣p/ *n* [singular] **give sb/sth a fillip** to do something that adds excitement or interest to something: *All these activities and parties have given a fillip to my self-esteem.*

**fil·ly** /ˈfɪli/ *n* [C] a young female horse

S2 W1 **film**[1] /fɪlm/ *n* **1** [C] *especially BrE* a story that is told using sound and moving pictures, shown at a cinema or on television for entertainment; MOVIE *AmE*: *Have you seen any good films recently?* | *a French film* —see also **silent film** (SILENT (4)) **2** [U] the making of films considered as an art or a business: *I'm interested in photography and film.* | *the film industry* **3** [U] the material used in a camera for taking photographs or recording moving pictures for the cinema | **roll of film** (=film in a metal container) *I shot five rolls of film on vacation.* | **on film** *The whole incident was recorded on film.* **4** [C] *BrE* a metal container with film in it that you put inside a camera to take photographs **5** [singular, U] a very thin layer of something that appears on the surface of something else: *a film of oil on the surface of the water* —see also CLINGFILM

**film**[2] *v* [I,T] to use a camera to record a story or real events so that it can be shown in the cinema or on television: *The explosion had been filmed by an amateur cameraman.* | *filming on location in Prague*

**film over** *phr v* [I] if your eyes film over they become covered with a thin layer of liquid: *The dog's eyes had filmed over, and it was breathing heavily.*

**film fes·ti·val** /ˈ· ˌ···/ *n* [C] an event when a lot of films are shown, and sometimes prizes are given for the best ones

**film star** /ˈ· ·/ *n* [C] a famous actor or actress in cinema films; MOVIE STAR *AmE*

**film·strip** /ˈfɪlmˌstrɪp/ *n* [C] a photographic film that shows photographs, drawings etc, one at a time, not as moving pictures: *an educational filmstrip*

**Fi·lo·fax** /ˈfaɪləfæks/ *n* [C] *trademark* a small book in which you write addresses, things you must do etc, with pages you can add or take out

**fi·lo pas·try** /ˌfiːləʊ ˈpeɪstri‖-loʊ-/ *n* [U] a type of PASTRY (2) with many very thin layers

**fil·ter**[1] /ˈfɪltə‖-ər/ *n* [C] **1** a piece of equipment or a substance that you pass gas or liquid through to remove unwanted substances: *a water filter* **2** a piece of glass or plastic that changes the amount or colour of light allowed into a camera or TELESCOPE[1] **3** a piece of equipment that only allows certain sounds to pass through it **4** *BrE* a light used to tell drivers they can turn right or left

**filter**[2] *v* **1** [T] to clean a liquid or gas by passing it through a special substance or piece of equipment: *You need to filter the drinking water.* **2** [I always + adv/prep] if people filter somewhere, they move gradually in that direction through a door, passage etc: [+ **in/out etc**] *Chattering noisily, the crowd began to filter into the auditorium.* **3** [I always + adv/prep] if news or information filters somewhere, people gradually hear about it from each other: [+ **back/through etc**] *The news slowly filtered through to everyone in the office.* **4** [I always + adv/prep] if light or sound filters into a place, it can be seen or heard only slightly: [+ **in/into/through**] *A few rays of sunshine filtered into the cave.* **5** [I] *BrE* if traffic filters, cars can turn left or right while other vehicles going straight ahead must wait

**filter** sth ↔ **out** *phr v* [T] to remove something by using a filter: *The machine filters out sediment.*

**filter tip** /ˈ·· ·/ *n* [C] the special end of a cigarette that removes some of the harmful substances from the smoke —**filter tipped** *adj*

**filth** /fɪlθ/ *n* [U] **1** an extremely dirty substance: *Go and wash that filth off your hands!* **2** very rude offensive language, stories, or pictures about sex: *I don't know how you can read that filth!*

**filth·y**[1] /ˈfɪlθi/ *adj* **filthier, filthiest** **1** extremely dirty: *Simon never cleans his house – it's absolutely filthy!* **2** showing or describing sexual acts in a very rude or offensive way: *Mitch was just telling us a filthy joke when Kia walked in.* —**filthily** *adv* —**filthiness** *n* [U] S3

**filthy**[2] *adv* **1 filthy dirty** very dirty **2 filthy rich** *informal* an expression meaning extremely rich, used when you think someone has too much money

**fil·tra·tion** /fɪlˈtreɪʃən/ *n* [U] the process of being cleaned by passing through a FILTER[1] (1)

**fin** /fɪn/ *n* [C] **1** one of the thin body parts that a fish uses to swim **2** part of a plane that sticks up at the back and helps it to fly smoothly —see picture at AIRCRAFT **3** *BrE* a large flat rubber shoe that you wear to help you swim better; FLIPPER (2) *AmE* **4** a thin piece of metal that sticks out from something such as a car

**fi·na·gle** /fɪ̣ˈneɪgəl/ *v* [T] **finagled, finagling** *AmE informal* **1** to obtain something that is difficult to get, but not by using the usual or official methods: *How he finagled four front row seats to the game I'll never know.* **2** to trick someone into giving you something, especially money: **finagle sb out of sth** *He finagled me out of ten bucks.* —**finagler** *n* [C]

**fi·nal**[1] /ˈfaɪnl/ *adj* **1** [only before noun] last in a series of actions, events, parts of a story etc: *The final episode of 'Prime Suspect' is on tonight.* | **final stage/moments** S1 W1

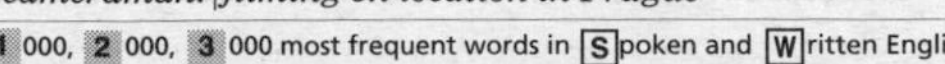

etc *They scored in the final minute of the game.* | **final demand** (=the last time you are sent a bill when you must pay) **2** if a decision, offer, agreement etc is final, it cannot be changed: **be final** *My decision is final. Do not ask me again!* | **final decision/say/approval etc** *We recommended the plan to the chancellor, who had the final say.* | **and that's final!** *spoken* (=used to say that a decision will not be changed) *No more money, and that's final!* **3** [only before noun] happening at or near the end of an event or process: *They fought many battles before their final defeat.* **4** [only before noun] being the result at the end of a process: *the differences between the original script and the final film*

**final²** *n* [C] **1 finals** *BrE* the set of examinations that university students take at the end of their time at university **2** *AmE* an examination taken at the end of each class a student takes at university **3** the last and most important game, race etc in a set of games or races: *He ran well in the heats but came in last in the final.* | **the finals** (=the last few games or races in a competition) *the 1994 World Cup finals*

**fi·na·le** /fɪˈnɑːli‖fɪˈnæli/ *n* [C] the last part of a piece of music or a show: *the finale of a Broadway show* | **grand finale** (=very impressive end to a show) *The fireworks were the grand finale of the closing ceremonies.*

**fi·nal·ist** /ˈfaɪnəl-ɪ̈st/ *n* [C] one of the people or teams that reaches the final game in a competition or set of sports matches

**fi·nal·i·ty** /faɪˈnælɪ̈ti/ *n* [U] the quality or feeling that something has when you know it is over and cannot be changed: *The word 'retirement' has a horrible air of finality about it.*

**fi·nal·ize** also **-ise** *BrE* /ˈfaɪnəl-aɪz/ *v* [T] to finish the last part of a plan, business deal etc: *Jo flew out to Thailand to finalize the details of the deal.* —**finalization** /ˌfaɪnəlaɪˈzeɪʃən‖-nl-ə-/ *n* [U]

S2 W1 **fi·nal·ly** /ˈfaɪnəl-i/ *adv* **1** after a long time: *After several delays we finally took off at six o'clock. Finally, to my relief, Garth brought up the subject of money.* **2** as the last of a series of things: [sentence adverb] *And finally, I'd like to thank the crew.* **3** in a finished state: *It's not finally settled yet.* —see LASTLY (USAGE)

S3 W2 **fi·nance¹** /ˈfaɪnæns, fɪ̈ˈnæns‖fɪ̈ˈnæns, ˈfaɪnæns/ *n* **1** [U] the management of money, especially money controlled by a government, company, or large organization: *the university's finance committee* | **high finance** (=financial activities involving countries or large companies) **2 finances a)** the money that a person, company, organization etc has available: *The committee's finances are very limited.* **b)** the way a person, company, organization etc manages their money: *My finances are in a real mess.* **3** [U] money, especially money provided by a bank, to help run a business or buy something: **[+ for]** *We need to raise finance for further research.*

W3 **finance²** *v* [T] to provide money, especially a large amount of money, to pay for something: *These concerts are financed by the Arts Council.*

**finance com·pa·ny** /ˈ·· ˌ···, ·ˈ· ˌ···/ *n* [C] *AmE* a company that lends money, especially to businesses

S3 W1 **fi·nan·cial** /fɪ̈ˈnænʃəl, faɪ-/ *adj* connected with money or the management of money: *New York is a great financial center.* | *financial assistance for city schools* | **a financial success** (=something that makes a profit) *It was a wonderful film, but not exactly a financial success.* —**financially** *adv*

**financial aid** /·ˌ·· ˈ·/ *n* [U] *AmE* money given or lent to students at college or university to pay for their education

**financial in·cen·tive** /·ˌ·· ·ˈ··/ *n* [C] money given to someone if they work harder or for special jobs

**financial in·sti·tu·tion** /·ˌ·· ··ˈ··/ *n* [C] *technical* a business organization that lends and borrows money, for example a bank: *All the big financial institutions cut their interest rates today.*

**financial mar·kets** /·ˌ·· ˈ··/ *n* [plural] *technical* banks and other financial institutions that make business contracts with each other

**financial year** /·ˌ·· ˈ·/ *n* [singular] the period of a year over which a company's profits and losses are calculated —compare FISCAL YEAR

**fi·nan·cier** /fɪ̈ˈnænsiə, faɪˈnæn-‖ˌfɪnənˈsɪr/ *n* [C] someone who controls or lends large sums of money

**finch** /fɪntʃ/ *n* [C] a small bird with a short beak

**find¹** /faɪnd/ *past tense and past participle* **found** /faʊnd/ *v* [T] S1 W1

**1 ▶ BY SEARCHING ◀** to discover or see something that you have been searching for —see OBTAIN (USAGE): *I can't find the car keys.* | *Let's hope we can find a parking space.* | *No-one has found a solution to this problem.* | **find sb sth** *I found him a nice second-hand car.*

**2 ▶ ARRIVE ◀** to discover that someone or something is in a particular condition or doing a particular thing when you arrive or first see them: *I'm sure we'll find her hard at work when we get home.* | *Michael woke up to find his bedroom ankle-deep in water.* | **find sb doing sth** *Carrie went into the kitchen, where she found them giggling together.* | **[+ (that)]** *When I got to school I found that class was cancelled.*

**3 ▶ BY STUDY ◀** to discover or learn something by study, tests etc: *Will we ever find a cure for the disease?* | *The liquid was found to contain 7.4g of phenylamine.* | **[+ that]** *It was found that 80% of young people borrow money.*

**4 ▶ THINK/FEEL ◀** to have a particular feeling or idea about something: *I hate flying – I find it absolutely terrifying.* | *Lots of women I know find him attractive.*

**5 find sth easy/difficult/impossible** if you find something difficult or easy it seems difficult or easy to you when you do it: *He said that, after Russian, I should find German easy.* | **find it difficult/easy etc to do sth** *He found it almost impossible to express what he wanted to say.*

**6 ▶ BY EXPERIENCE ◀** to learn or know something by experience: **[+ (that)]** *You might find that his work improves now he's going to a new school.* | *One thing I find about living in the big city is that people are more friendly than I expected.* | **find sb/sth doing sth** *You find more women entering the film business now.*

**7 ▶ BY CHANCE ◀** to discover something by chance, especially something useful or interesting: *I found a purse in the street.* | *We found a really good bar near the hotel.*

**8 ▶ STH YOU NEED ◀** to achieve or get something that you need: *Finding accommodation in Berlin can be a nightmare.* | *Two lonely people who managed to find happiness together.*

**9 ▶ REALIZE ◀** to notice or realize a fact, often a fact that is surprising: **[+ (that)]** *He got up to leave and found that the door was jammed.* | *I found I was really looking forward to going back to work.*

**10 ▶ ANIMALS/PLANTS ◀** if something is found somewhere, it lives or exists there: *This species is only found in West Africa.*

**11 ▶ MONEY/TIME/ENERGY ◀** to have enough money, time, energy etc to be able to do something you want to do: *He has to find £1000 to repay the loan.* | *I wouldn't mind learning a language, but I can't find the time right now.* | *David wanted to defend himself, but couldn't find the courage to speak up.*

**12 find your way** to reach a place by discovering the right way to get there: *Will you be able to find your way back to the house?*

**13 find its way** if something finds its way somewhere, it arrives or gets there after some time: *Only one of her inventions has found its way into the shops.*

**14 find yourself doing sth** to gradually realize that you are doing something, although you had not intended or planned to do it: *Peter, who was usually shy, found himself talking to the girls.*

**15 find yourself in/at etc a)** to realize that you are in a particular situation, especially a bad one, that you did not expect: *If you find yourself worrying about things, call*

*me.* | *They suddenly found themselves without a goalkeeper.* **b)** to realize that you have arrived somewhere without intending to: *After wandering around, we found ourselves back at the hotel.*
**16 find yourself** *often humorous* to discover what you are really like and what you want to do: *She went to India to find herself.*
**17 find sb guilty/find sb not guilty** to officially decide that someone is guilty or not guilty of something: *Galbraith was found not guilty and set free.* | [+of] *A clearly innocent man has been found guilty of a serious crime.*
**18 find comfort/pleasure/fulfilment in** to experience a good feeling because of something: *He found great satisfaction in kneading the dough and baking the bread.*
**19 find fault with** to criticize someone or something, often unfairly and frequently: *The teacher would always find fault with our grammar.*
**20 find favour (with)** be liked or approved of by someone: *The recipes rapidly found favour with restaurant owners.*
**21 find in sb's favour/find in favour of sb** to judge that someone is right or not guilty: *The Tribunal found in favour of the defendant.*
**22 find your feet** to get used to a new situation, especially one that is difficult at first: *Matt's only been at the school two weeks and he hasn't found his feet yet.*
**23 find its mark/target** if an ARROW (1), bullet etc finds its target, it hits what it is supposed to
**24 find your tongue** to manage to speak after being too nervous to say anything
**25 be found wanting** *formal* to not be good enough: *Ryan's proposals have been examined, and found wanting by the rest of the team.*
**26 all found** *BrE* used to mean that in addition to your wages you get food and a room: *The cook gets paid £90 a week all found.*

**find out** *phr v* **1 find** sth ↔ **out** [I, T] to learn information, after trying to discover it or by chance: [+ **who/what/how etc**] *He hurried off to find out what the problem was.* | **find out sth** *We never found out her real name.* | [+ **that**] *I found out that he was having an affair with another woman.* | [+ **about**] *I need to find out more about these night courses.* | [+ **if**] *A number of tests have been carried out to find out if these drugs have any effect.* —see KNOW[1] (USAGE) **2 find** sb **out** [T] to discover that someone has been doing something dishonest or illegal: *After years of defrauding the company, he was finally found out.*

**find against** sb *phr v* [T not in passive] *law* to judge that someone is right or not guilty: *The judge found against the plaintiff.*

**find for** sb *phr v* [T not in passive] *law* to judge that someone is wrong or guilty: *The judge found for the plaintiff.*

**find**[2] *n* **a find** something very good or valuable that you discover by chance: *That little Greek restaurant was a real find!*

**find·er** /ˈfaɪndə‖-ər/ *n* [C] someone who finds something

**fin de siè·cle** /ˌfæn də ˈsjeklə◂/ *adj French* typical of the end of the 19th century, especially typical of the art, literature, and attitudes of the time

W2 **find·ing** /ˈfaɪndɪŋ/ *n* [C usually plural] **1** the information that someone has learnt as a result of their studies, work etc: *Surveys conducted in other countries reported similar findings.* **2** *law* a decision made by a judge or jury

S1 W1 **fine**[1] /faɪn/ *adj*
**1 ▶ALL RIGHT◀** *especially spoken* **a)** good enough; all right. *"I could make you some dinner if you like." "It's okay, a sandwich is fine, thanks."* | *This apartment is fine for two, but it gets very cramped with your mother here.* | **I'm fine** *"More coffee?" "No, I'm fine, thanks."* **b)** healthy: *"How are you?" "Fine, thanks."* | *"Is your wife better now?" "Oh, she's fine."*
**2 ▶VERY GOOD◀** of a very high quality or standard: *Many people regard Beethoven's fifth symphony as his finest work.* | *There is some fine architecture in the old city.* | *fine bone china* | *fine wine*
**3 ▶GRAND◀** [usually before a noun] grand, expensive, better than others of the same kind: *A tall woman in fine clothes got out of the carriage.* | *the fine ladies and gentlemen who frequent the elegant restaurants of Paris*
**4 ▶NOT GOOD◀** *informal* used when you really think that something is not good or satisfactory at all: *"Now's a fine time to tell me!" he fumed.* | *That's a fine mess you've got us into!*
**5 ▶WEATHER◀** not raining, perhaps with the sun shining: *If it's fine tomorrow we'll go out.* | *It was a fine evening.*
**6 ▶THIN◀** very thin: *This thread's very fine – it's difficult to see.* | *a fine coating of dust* —see picture at THIN
**7 ▶SMALL◀ a)** involving differences, changes, or details that are difficult to understand or notice: *the finer points of policy detail* | *the fine tuning on the radio* | *Scientists are now able to measure fine distinctions between levels of sleep depth.* **b)** in small grains, pieces, or drops: *fine sugar* | *fine drizzle*
**8 ▶NET◀** having small holes: *a fine mesh*
**9 ▶IDEAS/SPEECHES◀** too grand and probably not true or unlikely to have any effect: *It's all very well politicians making fine speeches, but they never get anything done.*
**10 a fine/woman/person** a good person that you have a lot of respect for: *Your father is a fine man, a real gentleman,*
**11 that's/it's fine by me** used to say that you agree to something: *"I thought we could go out to eat." "That's fine by me."*
**12 fine features** someone with fine features has a small and attractively-shaped nose, mouth etc
**13 finer feelings/qualities etc** feelings, qualities etc such as love, honour, loyalty and kindness
**14 a fine figure of a man/woman** someone who looks big, strong and physically attractive: *Vellios was a fine figure of a man.*
**15 a fine line** if you say that there is a fine line between two different things, you mean that there is a point at which one can easily become the other: *There's a fine line between bravery and recklessness.*
**16 not to put too fine a point on it** *often humorous* used when you are criticizing something in a plain and direct way: *That's a real yobs' pub – not to put too fine a point on it.*
**17 sb's finest hour** an occasion when someone is extremely successful and proud of their achievement

**fine**[2] *interjection* used to agree to a suggestion: *"I'll see you at eight then." "Okay. Fine."*

**fine**[3] *adv* **1** *spoken* in a way that is satisfactory: *"How's it going?" "Fine, thanks."* | *The technician has been to fix it and it works fine now.* **2** if you cut something fine, you cut it very thin or in very small pieces **3 do fine** *spoken* **a)** to be good enough or be satisfactory: *We don't need to get her anything expensive – a calendar will do fine.* **b)** to do something well or in a satisfactory way: *"I can't draw this." "You're doing fine! Don't give up now."* **4 sth will do me/us fine** *BrE spoken* used to say that something is satisfactory or good enough: *Chips'll do me fine, darling.* **5 cut it fine** *informal* to leave yourself only just enough time to do something

**fine**[4] *v* [T] to make someone pay money as a punishment: **fine sb for doing sth** *She was fined $50 for passing a stopped school bus.*

**fine** sth ↔ **down** *BrE* to improve something by making it thinner, smaller, or more exact

**fine**[5] *n* [C] money that you have to pay as a punishment: *I got a £40 fine for speeding* | **heavy fine** (=a fine that costs you a lot of money) *There's a heavy fine for driving drunk.* | **parking/library fines etc** *I forgot to return my books on time and paid $3 in library fines.*

**fine art** /ˌ· ˈ·/ *n* [U] **1** paintings, drawings, music, SCULPTURE etc that is of very good quality: *the question* *of whether photography should be considered fine art* **2 have something down to a fine art** to be extremely good at something after having practised a lot: *Chris and I have got the morning routine of showers, breakfast, kids to school down to a fine art.* **3 the fine arts** [plural] activities such as painting, music, and SCULPTURE that are concerned with producing beautiful rather than useful things: *a student of the fine arts*

**fine·ly** /ˈfaɪnli/ *adv* **1** into very thin or very small pieces: *Add the finely chopped onion to the butter, and fry till golden.* **2** to a very exact degree: *These instruments are very finely tuned.* **3** beautifully and delicately: *She had an oval face with finely formed features.*

**fine print** /ˌ· ˈ·/ *n* [U] SMALL PRINT

**fi·ne·ry** /ˈfaɪnəri/ *n* [U] clothes and jewellery that are beautiful or very expensive, and are worn for a special occasion: *The guests arrived in all their finery.*

**fines herbes** /ˌfiːn ˈeəb‖-ˈeərb/ *n* [U] *French* a mixture of thinly cut plants, added to food to improve its taste

**fi·nesse¹** /fɪ̇ˈnes/ *n* [U] delicate and impressive skill: *Dario played the sonata with finesse.*

**finesse²** *v* [T] **1** *AmE* to do something with style and delicate skill: *The skier finessed the difficulties of the mountain.* **2** to handle a situation well, but in a way that is slightly deceitful: *He finessed the deal, using his charm to cover up his lack of knowledge.*

**fine-tooth comb** /ˌ· ˈ· ·, ˌ· · ˈ·/ *n* [C] **go through/over sth with a fine-tooth comb** to examine something very carefully and thoroughly: *going over the evidence with a fine-tooth comb.*

**fine-tune** /ˌ· ˈ·/ *v* [T] to make very small changes to something, especially a machine or system, so that it works as well as possible —**fine tuning** *n* [U]

S2 W2 **fin·ger¹** /ˈfɪŋɡə‖-ər/ *n* [C]
**1 ▶PART OF YOUR HAND◀** one of the four long thin parts on your hand, not including your thumb: *She let sand run through her fingers.* | *Tim ran his finger along the windowsill.* —see also INDEX FINGER, LITTLE FINGER, MIDDLE FINGER, RING FINGER
**2 not lift/raise a finger** to not make any effort to help someone with their work: *We moved furniture all day long, and Sarah never lifted a finger.*

finger

Keep your fingers crossed.

**3 keep your fingers crossed** to hope that something will happen the way you want: *We're all keeping our fingers crossed that Dan will actually call Megan.*
**4 put your finger on** to realize exactly what is wrong, different, or unusual about a situation: *I couldn't quite put my finger on what was different about Simone.*
**5 not lay a finger on sb** to not hurt someone at all, especially not to hit them: *Don't you dare lay a finger on me, or I'll call the police!*
**6 be all fingers and thumbs** *BrE* to use your hands in an awkward or careless way, so that you drop or break things
**7 pull/take/get your finger out** *BrE spoken* used to tell someone to work harder
**8 be caught with your fingers in the till** to be found stealing money from the place where you work
**9 ▶SHAPED LIKE A FINGER◀** anything that is long and thin, like the shape of a finger, especially a piece of land, an area of water, or a piece of food
**10 ▶DRINK◀** an amount of an alcoholic drink that is as high in the glass as the width of someone's finger: *Gimme three fingers of whiskey, and make it quick!*
**11 have a finger in every pie** an expression meaning to be involved in many activities and have influence over them, used especially when you think someone has too much influence
**12 have/keep your finger on the pulse** to always know about the most recent changes or developments in a situation or organization
**13 twist/wrap sb around your little finger** to be able to persuade someone to do anything that you want
**14 put two fingers up at sb** *BrE informal* to show someone you are angry with them in a very offensive way by holding up your first two fingers with the back of your hand facing them
**15 give sb the finger** *AmE informal* to show someone you are angry with them in a very offensive way by holding up your middle finger with the back of your hand facing them
**16 long-fingered/delicate-fingered etc** having long fingers, delicate fingers etc: *Lee rubbed his stubby-fingered hands together.*
**17 two-fingered/three-fingered etc** using two, three etc fingers to do something: *I've become pretty fast, even with my two-fingered typing.* —see also FISH FINGER, **have green fingers** (GREEN¹ (10)), **burn your fingers** (BURN¹ (18)), **point the finger at sb** (POINT² (7)), **let sth slip through your fingers** (SLIP¹ (7)), **snap your fingers** (SNAP¹ (6)), **have sticky fingers** (STICKY (6)), **work your fingers to the bone** (WORK¹ (27))

**finger²** *v* [T] **1** to touch or handle something with your fingers: *She fingered the beautiful cloth with envy.* **2** *informal especially AmE* if someone, especially a criminal, fingers another criminal, they tell the police what they have done

**finger bowl** /ˈ·· ·/ *n* [C] a small bowl in which you wash your fingers during a meal

**fin·ger·ing** /ˈfɪŋɡərɪŋ/ *n* [U] the positions in which a musician puts his fingers to play a piece of music, or the order in which he uses his fingers

**fin·ger·mark** /ˈfɪŋɡəmɑːk‖-ɡərmɑːrk/ *n* [C] a mark made by dirty fingers on something clean

**fin·ger·nail** /ˈfɪŋɡəneɪl‖-ɡər-/ *n* [C] the hard flat part that covers the top end of your finger

**finger-paints** /ˈ·· ·/ *n* [plural] special paints that children use to paint with, using their fingers —**finger painting** *n* [U]

**fin·ger·plate** /ˈfɪŋɡəpleɪt‖-ɡər-/ *n* [C] a metal or glass plate that is fastened to a door near the handle or key hole

**fin·ger·print¹** /ˈfɪŋɡəˌprɪnt‖-ɡər-/ *n* [C] a mark made by the pattern of lines at the end of a person's finger, which can be used by the police to help find criminals: *His fingerprints were all over the gun.* | **leave (your) fingerprints** *He was careful not to leave any fingerprints.* | **take sb's fingerprints** (=make a picture of someone's fingerprints) *The police questioned Beresford and took his fingerprints.*

fingerprint

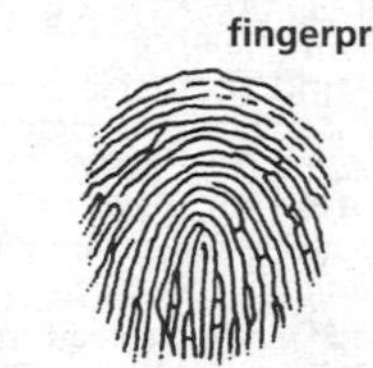

**fingerprint²** *v* [T] to press someone's finger on ink and then press it on paper in order to make a pattern of the lines at the end of the finger

**fin·ger·stall** /ˈfɪŋɡəstɔːl‖-ɡərstɒːl/ *n* [C] *BrE* a cover for your finger that protects it if it is injured

**fin·ger·tip** /ˈfɪŋɡəˌtɪp‖-ɡər-/ *n* [C] **1** the end of a finger **2 have sth at your/their fingertips** to have something, especially knowledge or information, ready and available to use very easily: *We have all the facts and figures at our fingertips.* **3 to your fingertips** *BrE* in all ways: *She's British to her fingertips.*

**fin·i·cky** /ˈfɪnɪki/ *adj* **1** too concerned with unimportant details and small things that you like or dislike; FUSSY: *She's very finicky about what she eats.* **2** needing to be done very carefully, while paying attention to small details: *It was a finicky job, trying to get the spring back into my watch.*

S1 W2 **fin·ish¹** /ˈfɪnɪʃ/ *v*
**1 ▶STOP DOING STH◀** [I,T] to come to the end of doing or making something, so that it is complete: **finish sth** *You can't go anywhere until you finish your homework.* | **finish doing sth** *I finished typing the report just minutes before it was due.* | *"Are they still working on the road by you?" "No, they've finally finished."*
**2 ▶STOP◀** [I] *especially BrE* when an event, activity, or period of time finishes, it ends, especially at a particular time: *The football season finishes in May.* | *What time does school finish?*
**3 ▶EAT◀** also **finish up/off** [T] to eat or drink all the rest of something, so there is none left: *Finish up your peas or you won't get any dessert.* | *Sylvia finished her cigarette.*
**4 ▶END WITH/BY◀** also **finish off** [I,T] to complete an event, performance, piece of work etc by doing one final thing: [+ **with**] *The party finished with a sing-song.* | **finish by doing sth** *She finished off her speech by thanking her sponsors.*
**5 ▶RACE◀** [I,T] to be in a particular position at the end of a race, competition etc: *I finished the 100 meters in sixth place.*
**6 ▶SURFACE◀** [T] to give the surface of something, especially wood, a smooth appearance by painting, polishing, or covering it: *The furniture had been attractively finished in a walnut veneer.*
**7 ▶ALL SB'S STRENGTH ETC◀** **finish sb** to take away all of someone's strength, energy etc: *That last five-mile ride up the hill really finished me.*
**8 ▶USE ALL OF STH◀** *BrE* to use up the entire supply of something, especially food: *The ice cream's finished, can you get some more?*
**9 put/add the finishing touches** to add the final detail or details that make your work complete

**finish off** *phr v* **1** [T **finish** sth ↔ **off**] to use or eat all of something, so there is none left: *Who finished off the cake?* **2** [T **finish** sb/sth ↔ **off**] to kill a person or animal when they are already weak or wounded **3** [T **finish** sb **off**] to take away all of someone's strength, energy etc: *It had already been an exhausting week, and that last argument just finished me off.* **4** [I,T **finish** sth↔ **off**] to end a performance, event etc by doing one final thing: *We finished off the evening by going out for a drink.*

**finish up** *phr v* **1** [linking verb] *especially BrE* to finally be in a particular place, condition etc at the end of a situation or series of events; end up (END²): *We finished up in Rome after a three week tour.* | *I finished up completely broke, tired, and hungry.* **2** [T **finish** sth↔ **up**] to eat or drink all the rest of something **3** to end an event, situation etc by doing one final thing

**finish with** sth/sb *phr v* [T] **1** *especially BrE* to no longer need to use something: **be finished with** *Are you finished with the scissors?* **2** *BrE* to end a relationship with someone: *Michael's finally finished with Teresa after all these years.*

This graph shows how common the different grammar patterns of the verb **finish** are.

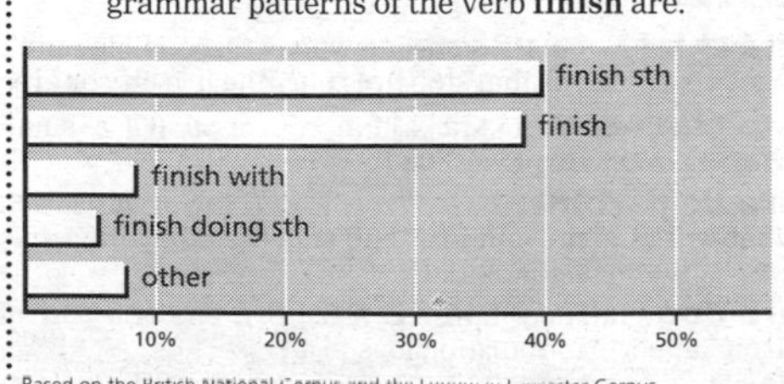


Based on the British National Corpus and the Longman Lancaster Corpus

S3 **finish²** *n* **1** [C] the end or last part of something: *I was watching the race but I didn't get to see the finish.* | **from start to finish** (=from the beginning of something until the end) *The meeting was a disaster from start to finish.* | **a close finish** (=an end of a race where two competitors are very close to each other) **2 fight to the finish** to fight until one side is completely defeated **3** [C,U] the appearance of the surface of an object after it has been painted, polished etc: *That table has a beautiful finish.*

**fin·ished** /ˈfɪnɪʃt/ *adj* **1** [only before noun] fully and properly made or completed: *It took a long time to do, but the finished product was worth it.* —opposite UNFINISHED **2** [not before noun] no longer able to do something successfully: *If the bank refuses to give us money, we're finished!*

**finishing school** /ˈ··· ·/ *n* [C] a private school where rich girls go to learn social skills

**fi·nite** /ˈfaɪnaɪt/ *adj* [I] **1** having an end or a limit: *Earth's resources are finite—opposite* INFINITE. **2** *technical* a finite verb form shows a particular tense or subject. 'Am', 'was', and 'are' are examples of finite verb forms, but 'being' and 'been' are non-finite

**fink¹** /fɪŋk/ *n* [C] *AmE informal old-fashioned* **1** someone who tells the police, a teacher, or a parent when someone else breaks a rule or a law **2** someone you dislike because they do cruel or unkind things

**fink²** *v* [I] *AmE informal old-fashioned* to tell the police, a teacher, or a parent that someone has broken a rule or a law

**fi·ord** /ˈfiːɔːd, fjɔːd‖fiːˈɔːrd, fjɔːrd/ *n* [C] another spelling of FJORD

**fir** /fɜː‖fɜːr/ *n* [C] a tree with leaves like needles that it keeps in the winter

**fire¹** /faɪə‖faɪr/ *n* S1 W1
**1 ▶BURNING◀** [U] the flames, light and heat produced when something burns: *The warehouse was completely destroyed by fire.* | **be on fire** (=be burning) *The house is on fire!* | **catch fire/catch on fire** (=start to burn) *Mary knocked the candle over and the table cloth caught on fire.* | **set sth on fire/set fire to sth** (=make something start burning) *Sparks from the fireplace could easily set the curtains on fire.* | *Rioters set fire to a whole row of stores.*

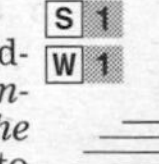

**fire**

Lisa lit the candle.

He set fire to the car.

The curtain caught fire.

**2 ▶ UNCONTROLLED FIRE ◀** [C] burning material that you did not light deliberately and that burns things you do not want to be damaged: *Thirty people died in a fire in downtown Chicago.* | **start a fire** (=deliberately make a fire start burning) | **a fire breaks out** (=a fire starts suddenly) *A fire broke out in the kitchens of the hotel.* | **put out a fire** (=stop a fire burning) *It took firemen several hours to put out the fire.* | **fight a fire** (=try to stop a fire burning) **forest/brush fire** (=a very large fire in the forest or in an area of grass)
**3 ▶ CONTROLLED FIRE ◀** [C] burning material that you have lit to provide heat, cook food etc: *a cheerful fire crackling in the fire place* | **make/build/light a fire** (=start one burning) *You put up the tent and I'll start the fire.* | **put out the fire** (=stop it burning) *Smoke billowed up as he poured sand over the fire.*
**4 ▶ SHOOTING ◀** [U] an act of shooting, especially of many guns at the same time: *You will soon be facing enemy fire.* | **be under fire** (=be shot at) *Our platoon was under fire from a machine gun position.* | **come under fire** (=be shot at) *The planes came under anti-aircraft fire.* | **open fire** (=start shooting) *Troops opened fire on the rebels.* | **hold your fire** (=stop shooting) | **be in the line of fire** (=be where you may be hit if someone shoots)
**5 ▶ HEATING EQUIPMENT ◀** [C] *BrE* a machine that produces heat to warm a room, using gas or electricity as power: *Turn on the fire, I'm cold.* | *a gas fire*
**6 ▶ CRITICISM ◀ under fire** being criticized very strongly for something you have done: *The committee came under fire from fundamentalist church leaders.*
**7 an open fire** a fire that burns coal or wood in a FIREPLACE

**8 gas fired/coal fired etc** *BrE* operated by burning gas, coal etc: *a coal fired power station*
**9 light a fire under sb** *AmE spoken* to do something that makes someone who is being lazy start doing their work
**10 ▶ EMOTION ◀** [U] a very strong emotion that makes you want to think about nothing else: [+ **of**] *the fire of religious fanaticism* | **be on fire with** *Harry was on fire with enthusiasm.*
**11 ▶ INJURY ◀ be on fire** *literary* an injured part of your body that is on fire feels very painful
**12 go through fire (and water) (for sb)** *old-fashioned* to do something very difficult and dangerous for someone
**13 fire and brimstone** a phrase describing Hell, used by some religious people —see also CEASEFIRE, **add fuel to the fire/flames** (FUEL[1] (3)), **fight fire with fire** (FIGHT[1] (12)), **get on like a house on fire** (HOUSE[1] (8)), **hang fire** (HANG[1] (11)), **play with fire** (PLAY[1] (22)), **there's no smoke without fire** (SMOKE[1] (6))

**USAGE NOTE: FIRE**

WORD CHOICE: **light, set fire to, catch fire, put out, go out, extinguish**

If you want something to burn you usually **light** it: *She lit a cigarette./the stove/a match*

You can also **set fire to** things, especially things that are not supposed to be burnt: *Crowds rioted through the street, breaking windows and setting fire to cars.*

When something begins to burn, especially by accident, it **catches fire**: *The blaze started when some oily rags caught fire.*

To stop a fire you **put** it **out**, or else it may **go out** on its own (NOT *go off*).

On official notices and instructions you may see **extinguish**: *Will passengers please extinguish all cigarettes.*

S3 W3 **fire**[2] *v*
**1 ▶ SHOOT ◀** [I,T] to shoot bullets from a gun, or to shoot small bombs: *Roy took careful aim and fired.* | [+ **at/on/into**] *Police fired on the crowd.* | **fire a gun/weapon etc** (=make it shoot) *The pistol has obviously been fired recently.* | **fire a shot/bullet/round etc** *Who fired the bullet that killed the President?* | **fire sth at sb** *The F16 fighter plane fired two missiles at the enemy aircraft.*
**2 ▶ JOB ◀** [T] *especially AmE* to force someone to leave their job; SACK[2] (1) *BrE*: **fire sb for sth** *They fired her for stealing from the company.*
**3 ▶ EXCITE ◀** [T] also **fire up** to make someone feel very excited or interested in something; INSPIRE: **be fired with ambition/longing etc** *After reading Steinbeck, Joel was fired with the ambition to become a writer.* | **fire sb's imagination** *Jill's imagination was fired by Granny's stories.*
**4 ▶ ENGINE ◀** [I] if a vehicle's engine fires, the petrol is lit to make the engine work
**5 ▶ CLAY ◀** [T] to bake clay pots etc in a KILN: *fired earthenware*
**6 fire questions (at)** to ask someone a lot of questions quickly, often in order to criticize them
**7 fire away** also **fire ahead** *spoken* used when you are ready to answer questions: *"I have a few questions." "Fire away."*
**8 not firing on all cylinders** *informal* not thinking sensibly, or acting strangely
**9 fired up** *informal* excited and eager: *We've gotta get fired up for this game or we have no hope of winning!*

**fire back** sth *phr v* [T] to quickly and angrily answer a question or remark: *Claire fired back an angry response.*

**fire off** *phr v* [T] **1** to shoot a weapon, often so that there are no bullets etc left: *Chuck reloaded and fired off both barrels.* **2** to quickly send an angry letter to someone: *I fired off a furious letter to the editor.*

**fire a·larm** /ˈ· ·ˌ·/ *n* [C] a piece of equipment that makes a loud noise to warn people of a fire in a building: *We were in the middle of an exam when the fire alarm went off.*

**fire·arm** /ˈfaɪərɑːm‖ˈfaɪrɑːrm/ *n* [C] a small gun that can be carried

**fire·ball** /ˈfaɪəbɔːl‖ˈfaɪrbɒːl/ *n* [C] a large, hot fire, such as the very hot cloud of burning gases formed by an atomic explosion

**fire·bomb** /ˈfaɪəbɒm‖ˈfaɪrbɑːm/ *n* [C] a bomb that makes a fire start burning when it explodes

**fire·brand** /ˈfaɪəbrænd‖ˈfaɪr-/ *n* [C] **1** someone who tries to make people angry about a law, government etc so that they will try to change it **2** a large burning piece of wood

**fire·break** /ˈfaɪəbreɪk‖ˈfaɪr-/ *n* [C] a narrow piece of land without any plants and trees on it, made to prevent fires from spreading

**fire·brick** /ˈfaɪəˌbrɪk‖ˈfaɪr-/ *n* [C] a brick that is not damaged by heat, used in chimneys

**fire bri·gade** /ˈ· ·ˌ·/ *n* [C] **1** *BrE* an organization that works to prevent fires and stop them burning; FIRE DEPARTMENT *AmE* **2** *AmE* a group of people who are not paid but who work together to stop fires burning

**fire·bug** /ˈfaɪəbʌg‖ˈfaɪr-/ *n* [C] *informal* someone who deliberately starts fires to destroy property; arsonist (ARSON)

**fire chief** /ˈ· ˌ·/ *n* [C] someone who is responsible for all the organizations that stop fires burning in a city or area

**fire·crack·er** /ˈfaɪəˌkrækə‖ˈfaɪrˌkrækər/ *n* [C] a small FIREWORK that explodes loudly

**fire de·part·ment** /ˈ. .ˌ../ *n* [C] *AmE* the organization that works to prevent fires and stop them burning; FIRE SERVICE, FIRE BRIGADE *BrE*

**fire·dog** /ˈfaɪədɒg‖ˈfaɪrdɒːg/ *n* [C] *BrE* one of a pair of iron supports for burning logs in a FIREPLACE

**fire door** /ˈ· ˌ·/ *n* [C] a heavy door in a building that is kept closed to help to prevent a fire from spreading

**fire drill** /ˈ· ·/ *n* [C, U] the act of practising what people must do to leave a burning building safely

**fire-eat·er** /ˈ· ˌ··/ *n* [C] **1** an entertainer who puts burning sticks into his mouth **2** *informal* someone who gets angry and quarrels very easily

**fire en·gine** /ˈ· ˌ··/ *n* [C] a special large vehicle that carries people and equipment to stop fires burning, especially the equipment that shoots water at a fire —compare FIRE TRUCK *AmE*

**fire es·cape** /ˈ· ·ˌ·/ *n* [C] metal stairs or a metal LADDER on the outside of a tall building, that people can use to escape if there is a fire

**fire ex·tin·guish·er** /ˈ· ·ˌ···/ *n* [C] a metal container with water or chemicals in it, used for stopping small fires

**fire extinguisher**

**fire fight** /ˈ· ·/ *n* [C] a short gun battle, involving soldiers or the police

**fire fight·er** /ˈ· ˌ··/ *n* [C] someone who stops fires burning, either as their job or as a special helper during forest fires or wars

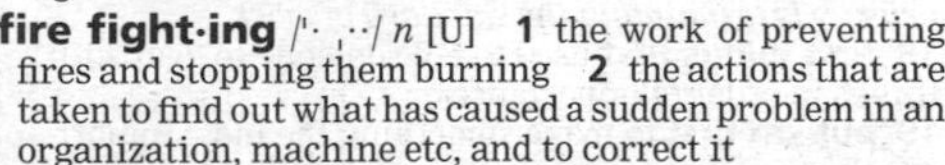

**fire fight·ing** /ˈ· ˌ··/ *n* [U] **1** the work of preventing fires and stopping them burning **2** the actions that are taken to find out what has caused a sudden problem in an organization, machine etc, and to correct it

**fire·fly** /ˈfaɪəflaɪ‖ˈfaɪr-/ *n plural* **fireflies** [C] an insect with a tail that shines in the dark; LIGHTNING BUG

**fire·guard** /ˈfaɪəgɑːd‖ˈfaɪrgɑːrd/ *n* [C] a large frame made of woven wire that is put in front of a FIREPLACE to protect people; FIRESCREEN *AmE*

**fire·house** /ˈfaɪəhaʊs‖ˈfaɪr-/ *n* [C] *AmE* a small FIRE STATION, especially in a small town

**fire hy·drant** /ˈ· ˌ··/ *n* [C] a water pipe in a street used to get water for stopping fires burning; FIREPLUG *AmE*

**fire i·rons** /ˈ· ˌ··/ *n* [plural] the metal tools used for looking after a fire in a FIREPLACE

**fire·light** /ˈfaɪəlaɪt‖ˈfaɪr-/ *n* [U] the light produced by a small fire: *The room glowed cozy and warm in the firelight.*

**fire·light·er** /ˈfaɪəˌlaɪtə‖ˈfaɪrˌlaɪtər/ *n* [C] *BrE* a piece of a substance that burns easily and helps to light a coal fire

**fire·man** /ˈfaɪəmən‖ˈfaɪr-/ *n* [C] **1** a man whose job is to stop fires burning; FIREFIGHTER **2** someone who looks after the fire in a steam railway engine or a FURNACE

**fire·place** /ˈfaɪəpleɪs‖ˈfaɪr-/ *n* [C] the opening in the wall of a room, used for a wood or coal fire to heat the room

**fire·plug** /ˈfaɪəplʌg‖ˈfaɪr-/ *n* [C] *AmE* a FIRE HYDRANT

**fire·pow·er** /ˈfaɪəˌpaʊə‖ˈfaɪrˌpaʊər/ *n* [U] *technical* the number of weapons that an army, military vehicle etc has available

**fire·proof** /ˈfaɪəpruːf‖ˈfaɪr-/ *adj* a building, piece of cloth etc that is fireproof cannot be badly damaged by flames —**fireproof** *v* [T]

**fire-rais·ing** /ˈ· ˌ··/ *n* [U] *BrE* the crime of starting a fire deliberately; ARSON —**fire-raiser** *n* [C]

**fire sale** /ˈ· ·/ *n* [C] a sale of goods that have been slightly damaged by a fire, or of goods that cannot be stored because of a fire

**fire·screen** /ˈfaɪəskriːn‖ˈfaɪr-/ *n* [C] *AmE* a large frame made of woven wire that is put in front of a FIREPLACE to protect people; FIREGUARD *BrE*

**fire ser·vice** /ˈ· ˌ··/ *n* [singular] *BrE* the organization that works to prevent fires and stop them burning; FIRE DEPARTMENT *AmE*

**fire·side** /ˈfaɪəsaɪd‖ˈfaɪr-/ *n* [C usually singular] the area close to or around a small fire, especially in a home: *a cat dozing in the broken armchair by the fireside*

**fire sta·tion** /ˈ· ˌ··/ *n* [C] a building where the equipment used to stop fires burning is kept, and where FIRE FIGHTERS stay until they are needed

**fire·storm** /ˈfaɪəstɔːm‖ˈfaɪrstɔːrm/ *n* [C] a very large fire, usually started by bombs, that is kept burning by the high winds that it causes

**fire·trap** /ˈfaɪətræp‖ˈfaɪr-/ *n* [C] a building that would be very dangerous if a fire started there

**fire truck** /ˈ· ·/ *n* [C] *AmE* a special vehicle that carries people and special equipment to stop fires burning —compare FIRE ENGINE

**fire·watch·er** /ˈfaɪəwɒtʃə‖ˈfaɪrwɑːtʃər, -wɔːtʃ-/ *n* [C] *BrE* someone who watched for FIRE BOMBS in British cities during the Second World War

**fire·wat·er** /ˈfaɪəˌwɔːtə‖ˈfaɪrˌwɔːtər, -ˌwɑː-/ *n* [U] strong alcoholic drink, such as WHISKY

**fire·wood** /ˈfaɪəwʊd‖ˈfaɪr-/ *n* [C] wood cut for burning on fires

**fire·work** /ˈfaɪəwɜːk‖ˈfaɪrwɜːrk/ *n* [C usually plural] **1** a small container filled with powder that burns or explodes to produce coloured lights, noise, and smoke: *a New Year's Eve fireworks display* **2 there will be fireworks** *spoken* used to say that someone will be angry: *There'll be fireworks if I get home late again.*

**firing line** /ˈ·· ·/ *n* **be in the firing line** to be in a position or situation in which you can be attacked or blamed for something, often unfairly

**firing squad** /ˈ·· ˌ·/ *n* [C] a group of soldiers with the duty of killing someone by shooting them as a punishment

**firm**[1] /fɜːm‖fɜːrm/ *n* [C] a business or company, especially a small one: **electronics/advertising/law etc firm** *She works for an electronics firm.* | **a firm of accountants/solicitors etc** *Kevin is with a firm of accountants in Birmingham.* 

**firm**[2] *adj* 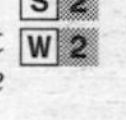

**1** ▶ **HARD** ◀ not completely hard, but not soft and not easy to bend into a different shape: *The sofa cushions are fairly firm.* | *a firm green apple*

**2** ▶ **NOT LIKELY TO MOVE** ◀ strong or fixed in position, and not likely to move or break: *The ladder felt strong and firm.*

**3** ▶ **NOT LIKELY TO CHANGE** ◀ firm decisions, beliefs etc are not likely to change, because you are sure about them: *The client hasn't reached a firm decision on the matter yet.*

**4** ▶ **STRONG AND IN CONTROL** ◀ behaving or speaking in a way that is strong and that shows you are not likely to change your answer, belief etc: *Cal replied with a polite but firm 'no'.* | *The country needs firm leadership.* | **be firm with sb** *You need to be firm with her, or she'll try to take control.*

**5 a firm grip/hold/grasp** if you have something in a firm hold you are holding it tightly and strongly: *He took a firm grip of my arm and marched me towards the door.* | **a firm handshake** (=in which you hold the other person's hand strongly or tightly)

**6 take a firm stand/line** to state your opinion clearly and not be persuaded to change it

**7 stand/hold firm** to not change your actions or opinions: *Gothard is urging Christians to stand firm against divorce.*

**8** ▶ **MONEY** ◀ not falling in value: *The pound was still firm against the dollar this morning.* —see also FIRM OFFER —**firmly** *adv* —**firmness** *n* [U]

**firm**[3] *v* [T] to press down on soil to make it harder or more solid W3

**firm** sth ↔ **up** *phr v* [T] **1** to make arrangements, ideas etc more definite and exact: *We're hoping to firm up the deal later this month.* **2** to make a part of your body have more muscle and less fat by exercising

**fir·ma·ment** /ˈfɜːməmənt‖ˈfɜːr-/ *n* [singular] *literary* the sky or heaven

**firm of·fer** /ˌ· ˈ··/ *n* [C] a price suggested for a service or for goods that becomes legally fixed if it is accepted

**firm·ware** /ˈfɜːmweə‖ˈfɜːrmwer/ *n* [U] *technical* instructions to computers that are stored on chips (CHIP[1] (4a)) so that they can be done much faster, and cannot be changed or lost —compare HARDWARE, SOFTWARE

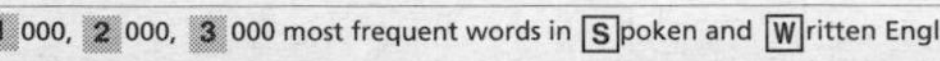

# first /fɜːst‖fɜːrst/ *number*

① BEFORE
② THE FIRST TIME STH HAPPENS OR IS DONE
③ BEGINNING
④ MAIN/IMPORTANT
⑤ THE FIRST REASON/FACT ETC
⑥ BEST
⑦ MORNING
⑧ NOT KNOW
⑨ OTHER MEANINGS

## ① BEFORE

**1** before anything or anyone else: *She reached the top of the hill first.* | *It's mine, I saw it first.* —see FIRSTLY (USAGE)

**2 the first** someone or something that is before other people or things: **be (the) first to do sth** *My sister said I'd be first to get married, but she was wrong.* | **come (in) first** (=win a race) *Lewis came first in the 100m race.*

**3** before doing anything else, or before anything else happens: *I always read the funnies first.* | *First I have to clean up the house, then I'll come shopping with you.* | **first of all** *First of all we'd better make sure we have everything we need.*

**4 make the first move** to be the person who does something when everyone is nervous and uncomfortable about starting to do something: *Barney really likes Hannah, but he's too shy to make the first move.*

**5 do/say sth in the first place** *spoken* used to say that someone said or did something before: *I don't really want to go. . . ." Oh Well, why didn't you say so in the first place?"*

**6 in the first instance** *especially BrE* before you do anything else: *It is important in the first instance to be sure that there is a demand for the product you wish to sell.*

## ② THE FIRST TIME STH HAPPENS OR IS DONE

**7** happening or done before other events or actions of the same kind: *He made his first appearance on the stage in the 1950s.* | *My first reaction was that the story couldn't possibly be true.* | **the first time**: *The first time I flew in a plane I was really nervous.*

**8** done for the first time: *The book was first published in Australia last year.*

**9 the first** someone who does something that has never been done or happened before: *No one had ever settled in the valley before; he was the first.* | **be the first to do sth** *She was the first to see the importance of the nineteenth century writers in this context.*

**10 a first** something that has never been done or happened before: *Roger Bannister's four-minute mile was a notable first in the history of athletics.*

**11 at first glance/sight** the first time that you see something, before you notice much detail: *At first glance the twins look identical.*

**12 first come, first served** used to say that people who arrive, ask etc before other people, will be dealt with or given something before them

## ③ BEGINNING

**13 the first** the people or things at the beginning of a row, line, series, period of time etc: *the first Monday of every month* | *for the first six months of my time in Nepal* | *the first chapter of the book*

**14** at the beginning of a situation or activity: *When we were first married, we lived in Toronto.* | *We first became friends when we were teenagers.*

**15 at first** in the beginning: *Alistair felt tired at first, but soon got used to the long working hours.* —compare **at last** (LAST³ (2)) —see FIRSTLY (USAGE)

**16 from the (very) first** from the beginning: *The relationship was doomed to failure from the first.*

## ④ MAIN/IMPORTANT

**17** being the most important or main thing: *The first priority is to maintain the standard of work.*

**18 first things first** used to tell someone to deal with things in order of importance

**19 put sth first** to make something the most important thing: *Rob seems to put money first, and happiness second in his life.*

**20 come first** to be the most important thing to someone: **[+ with]** *Alma's family will always come first with her.*

**21 first and foremost** as the main reason for or purpose of something: *The aim of the exercise was first and foremost to give confidence to the students.*

**22 first among equals** someone who leads a group of people but is not considered to be more important than them

## ⑤ THE FIRST REASON/FACT ETC

**23** used to give an important fact or reason that will be followed by others: *Well, first, the building is too small, and second, it isn't in a very good location.*

**24 first of all** *spoken* used to introduce the first thing that you are going to talk about: *First of all I'd like to welcome you to the meeting.*

**25 first off** *spoken* used to introduce a fact, reason, or statement that will be followed by others, especially when you are annoyed with someone: *First off, you should have told me where you were going.*

**26 in the first place** *spoken* used to give a fact or reason that proves what you are saying in an argument *Well, in the first place, Quinn would never say any such thing.* —see FIRSTLY (USAGE)

## ⑥ BEST

**27 first choice** the thing or person you like best: *Frances was our first choice as a name for the baby.*

**28 come first/win first prize** to be the best in a competition: *My jam won first prize at the county fair.*

**29 a first** the highest level of university degree you can get in Britain: **get a first (in)** *Helen got a first in Law.*

**30 of the first water** *old-fashioned* of the highest quality: *a jewel of the first water*

## ⑦ MORNING

**31 first thing** as soon as you get up in the morning, or as soon as you start work: *The boss was here first thing, but he's gone to Newcastle now.* | *I'll phone him first thing Monday.*

**32 at first light** very early in the morning: *They left at first light and were in the mountains by nightfall.*

## ⑧ NOT KNOW

**33 not have the first idea about/not know the first thing about** to not know anything about a subject, or not know how to do something: *I wouldn't have the first idea about what to do in an emergency.* | *I don't know the first thing about cars.*

**34 the first I (have) heard/I knew etc of it** *spoken* used when you have just found out about something that other people already know, and are slightly annoyed about it: *Andrew's been promoted? That's the first I've heard about it.*

### ⑨ OTHER MEANINGS

**35 (at) first hand** if you hear or experience something at first hand, you hear etc it directly, not through other people: *The school had to deal first hand with the social problems of the area.*

**36 first a)** first gear; the lowest GEAR[1] (2) in a car, bicycle, or other vehicle, that you use to begin moving: **be in first** *Put the car in first when you park on a hill.* **b)** *AmE* FIRST BASE

**37 I'd die/kill myself etc first** *spoken* used to emphasize how strongly you do not want to do something: *I'll never take him back. I'd die first!*

**first aid** /ˌ· ˈ·/ *n* [U] simple medical treatment that is given as soon as possible to someone who is injured or who suddenly becomes ill: **give first aid** *Being given first aid at the scene of the accident probably saved his life.*

**first aid·er** /ˌ· ˈ··/ *n* [C] *BrE* someone who is trained to give first aid

**first aid kit** /ˌ. ˈ. ˌ./ *n* [C] a special box containing BANDAGES and medicines to treat people who are injured or become ill suddenly

**first base** /ˌ· ˈ·/ *n* [C] **1 a)** the first of the four places in a game of BASEBALL (1) that a player must touch before gaining a point **b)** the position of a defending player near this place: *He plays first base for the Red Sox.* **2** *AmE informal* the first stage of success in an attempt to achieve something: get to/reach first base: *You've gotten to first base if you've landed an interview.* **3 get to first base** *AmE spoken* an expression meaning to kiss or hug someone in a sexual way, used especially by young men

**first·born** /ˈfɜːstbɔːn‖ˈfɜːrstbɔːrn/ *n* [singular] *literary* your first child —**firstborn** *adj*: *her firstborn son*

**first class** /ˌ· ˈ·◂/ *n* **1** [U] the best and most expensive seats or rooooms in a train, boat etc: *We prefer to travel in first class.* —compare BUSINESS CLASS, CABIN CLASS, ECONOMY CLASS, TOURIST CLASS. **2** [U] **a)** a class of mail in Britain, used for letters and parcels, that is quicker and more expensive than second class mail —compare SECOND CLASS (1) **b)** the class of mail used in the US for ordinary business and personal letters **3** [C] the highest standard for a degree from a British university

**first-class** *adj* **1** of very good quality and much better than other things of the same type: *This is a first-class wine.* **2** using the first class of mail **3** using the first class of seats and rooms in a plane, train etc: *a first-class passenger* —**first class** *adv*: *If I send the letter first class it should arrive tomorrow.*

**first cous·in** /ˌ· ˈ··/ *n* [C] a child of your AUNT or UNCLE; COUSIN (1)

**first-de·gree** /ˌ· ·ˈ·◂/ *adj* [always before noun] **1 first-degree murder** *AmE* murder of the most serious type, in which someone deliberately kills someone else —compare MANSLAUGHTER **2 first-degree burn** a burn that is not very serious

**first e·di·tion** /ˌ· ·ˈ··/ *n* [C] one of the copies of a book that was produced the first time the book was printed

**first-ev·er** /ˌ· ˈ··◂/ *adj* [always before noun] happening for the first time: *It was the day that Michael Jackson gave his first-ever televised interview.*

**first fam·i·ly** /ˌ· ˈ···/ *n* [C usually singular] the family of the President of the US

**first floor** /ˌ· ˈ·◂/ *n* [C] **1** *BrE* the floor of a building just above the one at the bottom level **2** *AmE* the floor of a building at the bottom level —compare GROUND FLOOR (1) *BrE* —see FLOOR[1] (USAGE)

**first-foot·ing** /ˌ· ˈ··/ *n* [U] *ScotE* the custom in Scotland of visiting people as soon as the New Year has begun —**first-footer** *n* [C]

**first fruits** /ˌ· ˈ·/ *n* [plural] the first good result of something: *One of the first fruits of Mao's visit to Moscow was a new treaty with the Russians.*

**first gear** /ˌ· ˈ·/ *n* [C] the lowest GEAR[1] (1) in a car or other motor vehicle, used when starting to move or when going up or down a very steep hill

**first gen·e·ra·tion** /ˌ· ··ˈ··◂/ *n* [singular] **1** the children of people who have moved to live in a new country **2** the first type of a machine to be developed: *The first generation of computers were huge and slow.* **3** the first people to do something: *the first generation of environmentalists* —**first-generation** *adj*

**first half** /ˌ· ˈ·/ *n* [C] the first of two equal periods of time that a sports match is divided into

**first-hand** /ˌ· ˈ·◂/ *adj* **first-hand experience/knowledge/account** experience etc that has been learned or gained by doing something yourself: *journalists with first-hand experience of working in war zones* —compare SECOND-HAND —see also **(at) first hand** (FIRST[1] (35))

**first la·dy** /ˌ· ˈ··/ *n* [C usually singular] the wife of the President of the US, or of the GOVERNOR of a US state

**first lan·guage** /ˌ· ˈ··/ *n* [C] the language that you first learn as a child —compare SECOND LANGUAGE

**first lieu·ten·ant** /ˌ· ·ˈ··◂/ *n* [C] a middle rank in the US army, Marines, or Air Force, or someone who has this rank —see table on page B4

**first·ly** /ˈfɜːstli‖-ɜːr-/ *adv* [sentence adverb] used to say that the fact or reason that you are going to mention is the first one and will be followed by others: *Firstly, I would like to thank everyone who has contributed to this success.* S2

**USAGE NOTE: FIRSTLY**

WORD CHOICE: **firstly, first (of all), in the first place, to start/begin with, at first, in the beginning**

**Firstly/first (of all)/in the first place/to start with/to begin with** are often used to introduce a series of reasons, ideas, remarks etc: *There are three reasons why I don't like him: first(ly)/to start with he's rude, second(ly) he's a liar, and third(ly)/finally he owes me money.*

You use **first (of all)** (NOT *firstly*) to introduce a series of actions, often in order of time: *First of all I get dressed, next I bring in the paper, then I fix breakfast.*

**At first** can only be used for a period of time, often when you are comparing it with a later period. **To start/begin with** and **in the beginning** can be used in this way too: *You'll find it difficult at first/to begin with, but later/soon it'll get easier.*

**first mate** /ˌ· ˈ·/ *n* [C] the officer on a non-military ship who has the rank just below captain

**first name** /ˈ· ·/ *n* [C] **1** the name or names that come before your family name: *Her first name's Helen, but I don't know her surname.* **2 be on first name terms (with sb)** *BrE*, **be on a first name basis** *AmE* to know someone well enough to call them by their first name —compare SURNAME

**first night** /ˌ· ˈ·/ *n* [C] the evening when the first public performance of a show, play etc is given

**first of·fend·er** /ˌ· ·ˈ··/ *n* [C] someone who is guilty of breaking the law for the first time

**first of·fi·cer** /ˌ· ˈ···◂/ *n* [C] FIRST MATE

**first per·son** /ˌ· ˈ··◂/ *n* [singular] **1** *technical* a form of a verb or a pronoun that is used to show that you are the speaker. For example, 'I', 'me', 'we', and 'us' are first person pronouns, and 'I am' is the first person singular of the verb 'to be' **2** a way of telling a story in which the writer or speaker tells it as though he were involved in the story: *a first person narrative* —compare SECOND PERSON, THIRD PERSON

**first-rate** /ˌ· ˈ·◂/ *adj* of the very best quality: *He's a first-rate surgeon.*

**first re·fus·al** /ˌ· ·ˈ··/ *n* **have/give sb first refusal on sth** *BrE* to let someone decide whether to buy something before you offer to sell it to other people: *I'll let you have first refusal on the car.*

**first strike** /ˌ· ˈ·◂/ *n* [C] an attack made on your enemy before they attack you

**first-string** /ˌ· ˈ·◂/ *adj* [only before noun] a first-string player in a team plays when the game begins because they are the most skilled —compare SECOND-STRING

**first-time buy·er** /ˌ· · ˈ··/ *n* [C] someone who is buying a house or an apartment for the first time

**First World** /ˌ· ˈ·◂/ *n* [singular] the rich industrial countries of the world —compare THIRD WORLD —**first world** *adj* [always before noun]

**First World War** /ˌ· · ˈ·/ *n* [singular] the big war fought in Europe between 1914 and 1918

**firth** /fɜːθ‖fɜːrθ/ *n* [C] a narrow area of sea between two areas of land, or the place where a river flows into the sea, especially in Scotland: *the Firth of Forth*

**fis·cal**[1] /ˈfɪskəl/ *adj formal* connected with money, taxes, debts, etc owned and managed by the government: *a fiscal crisis* —**fiscally** *adv*

**fiscal**[2] *n* [C] *informal* PROCURATOR FISCAL

**fiscal year** /ˌ·· ˈ·/ *n* [C] the period of a year which the government uses to calculate how much tax a person or business must pay —compare FINANCIAL YEAR

**fish**

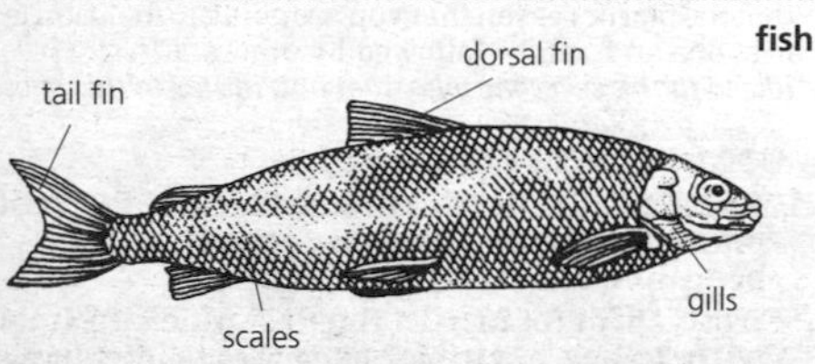


S2 W1 **fish**[1] /fɪʃ/ *n plural* **fish** or **fishes** [C] **1** an animal that lives in water, and uses its FINS (1) and tail to swim: *The lake is well stocked with fish.* | **catch a fish** *Ronny caught three huge fish this afternoon.* **2** [U] the flesh of a fish used as food: *White wine is traditionally drunk with fish.* **3 like a fish out of water** feeling uncomfortable because you are in an unfamiliar place or situation: *I felt like a fish out of water in my new school.* **4 there are plenty more fish in the sea** used to tell someone whose relationship has ended that there are other people they can have a relationship with **5 neither fish nor fowl** neither one thing nor another **6 have other/bigger fish to fry** *informal* to have other things to do, especially more important things: *I can't deal with this now, I've got other fish to fry!* **7 an odd fish/a queer fish** *BrE old-fashioned* someone who is slightly strange or crazy **8 a cold fish** an unfriendly person who seems to have no strong feelings **9 a big fish in a little pond** someone who is important or who has influence over a very small area —see also **drink like a fish** (DRINK[1] (2)), **a fine/pretty kettle of fish** (KETTLE (4))

**fish**[2] *v* **1** [I] to try to catch fish: [+ **for**] *We're fishing for trout.* **2** [T always + adv/prep] also **fish out** to find something after searching through a bag, pocket etc, and take it out: **fish sth ↔out** *Eric fished a peppermint out of the bag.* **3** [I always +adv/prep] *informal* to search for something in a bag, pocket etc: [+ **about/around**] *She fished around in her purse and pulled out a photo.* | [+ **for**] *Chris fished in his pocket for a coin.* **4** [T] to try to catch fish in a particular area of water: *Other nations are forbidden to fish the waters within 200 miles of the coast.* **5** [T] also **fish out** to pull someone or something out of water: **fish sb out** *Police frogmen fished the body out of the East River a week later.* **6 fish for compliments** to try to make someone say something nice about you, usually by asking a question: *It's sickening the way he's always fishing for compliments when she's around.* **7 fish for information/news/gossip etc** to try to find out secret information: *Reporters were hanging around fishing for information on the Congressman's resignation.* **8 fish in troubled waters** to try to gain an advantage from other people's problems **9 fish or cut bait** *AmE spoken* used to tell someone to do what they say they will, or stop talking about it

**fish and chips** /ˌ· · ˈ·/ *n* [U] a meal consisting of fish covered with a mixture of flour and milk and cooked in oil and long, thin pieces of potato cooked in oil

**fish·cake** /ˈfɪʃkeɪk/ *n* [C] a small round flat food consisting of cooked fish mixed with cooked potato

**fish·er·man** /ˈfɪʃəmən‖-ʃər-/ *n plural* **fishermen** /-mən/ [C] someone who catches fish as a sport or as a job —compare ANGLER

**fish·e·ry** /ˈfɪʃəri/ *n* [C] a part of the sea where fish are caught as a business

**fish-eye lens** /ˌ·· ˈ·/ *n* [C] a type of curved LENS (=piece of glass on the front of a camera) that allows you to take photographs of a wide area

**fish farm** /ˈ· ˌ·/ *n* [C] an area of water used for breeding fish as a business —**fish farming** *n* [U]

**fish fin·ger** /ˌ· ˈ··/ *n* [C] *BrE* a long piece of fish covered with small pieces of dried bread and cooked; FISH STICK *AmE*

**fish·ing** /ˈfɪʃɪŋ/ *n* [U] **1** the sport or business of catching fish: *Fishing is one of his hobbies.* | **go fishing** *Terry's going fishing at Lake Arrowhead next weekend.* **2 be on a fishing expedition** *AmE* to try to find out secret information S

**fishing line** /ˈ·· ·/ *n* [U] very long string made of strong material and used to catch fish

**fishing rod** /ˈ·· ·/ *n* [C] a long thin pole with a long string and a hook fixed to it, used for catching fish

**fishing tack·le** /ˈ·· ˌ··/ *n* [U] equipment used for fishing

**fish ket·tle** /ˈ· ˌ··/ *n* [C] a long, deep dish used for cooking whole fish

**fish mar·ket** /ˈ· ˌ··/ *n* [C] a special market that only sells fish

**fish meal** /ˈ· ·/ *n* [U] dried fish crushed into a powder and put on the land to help plants grow

**fish·mon·ger** /ˈfɪʃmʌŋgə‖-mɑːŋgər, -mʌŋ-/ *n* [C] *especially BrE* someone who sells fish

**fish·net stock·ings** /ˌfɪʃnet ˈstɒkɪŋz‖-ˈstɑː-/ also **fishnet tights** /ˌ... ˈ./ *BrE* —*n* [plural] STOCKINGS with a pattern of small holes that make them look like a net

**fish slice** /ˈ· ·/ *n* [C] *BrE* a kitchen tool used especially for turning food when cooking, with a wide flat part and a handle —see picture on page 833

**fish stick** /ˈ· ·/ *n* [C] *AmE* a long piece of fish covered with small pieces of dried bread and cooked; FISH FINGER *BrE*

**fish·tail** /ˈfɪʃteɪl/ *v* [I] *AmE* if a vehicle or aircraft fishtails, it slides from side to side, usually because the tyres are sliding on water or ice

**fish·wife** /ˈfɪʃwaɪf/ *plural* **fishwives** /-waɪvz/ *n* [C] an insulting word for a woman with a loud voice

**fish·y** /ˈfɪʃi/ *adj* **1** *informal* seeming bad or dishonest: *There's something very fishy about his business deals.* **2** tasting or smelling of fish

**fis·sile** /ˈfɪsaɪl‖-səl/ *adj* **1** *technical* able to be split by atomic fission **2** tending to split along natural lines of weakness

**fis·sion** /ˈfɪʃən/ *n* [U] *technical* **1** the process of splitting an atom to produce large amounts of energy or an explosion —compare FUSION (2) **2** the process of dividing a cell into two or more parts

**fis·sure** /ˈfɪʃə‖-ər/ *n* [C] a deep crack, especially in rock or earth

**fist** /fɪst/ *n* [C] **1** the hand when the fingers are curled in towards the PALM, especially in order to express anger or hit someone: *She held the money tightly in her fist.* | **clench your fist** (=hold your fist very tightly closed) *Malcolm clenched his fists angrily.* | **fist fight** (=a fight in which you use your bare hands to hit someone) *The argument quickly turned into an all-out fist fight.* —see also HAM-FISTED, TIGHT-FISTED, **hand over fist** (HAND[1] (37)) —see picture at BODY **2 make a good/bad fist of** *BrE informal* to make a successful or unsuccessful attempt to do something

**fist·ful** /ˈfɪstfʊl/ *n* [C] an amount that is as much as you can hold in your hand: [+ **of**] *a child clutching a fistful of toffees*

**fis·ti·cuffs** /ˈfɪstɪkʌfs/ *n* [plural] *old-fashioned* a fight in which you use your bare hands to hit someone

S1 W2 **fit[1]** /fɪt/ *v past tense* **fitted** also **fit** *AmE past participle* **fit**

**1 ▶ RIGHT SIZE ◀** [I,T not in progressive] to be the right size and shape for someone or something: *The dress fits perfectly.* | **fit sb** *The jacket fitted me pretty well but the trousers were too small.* | **fit (sb) like a glove** (=fit the shape of sb's body perfectly) —see CLOTHES (USAGE)

**2 ▶ FIT A SPACE ◀** [I always + adv/prep, not in progressive] to be the right size and shape for a particular space, and not be too big: [+ **in/into/under etc**] *Will my tennis racket fit in your bag?*

**3 ▶ EQUIPMENT/PART ◀** [T] to put a small piece of equipment into a place, or a new part onto a machine, so that it is ready to be used: **fit sth on/to etc** *Anti-theft devices are fitted to all our cars.* | **fit sth** *The plumber fit the sink this morning.*

**4 ▶ PUT IN PLACE ◀** [I always + adv/prep, T always + adv/prep] to put or join something in a particular place where it is meant to go: [+ **in/over/together**] *The plastic cover fits neatly over the frame.* | **fit sth ↔ in/onto/together etc** *She fit a piece into the jigsaw puzzle.*

**5 ▶ FIND A PLACE FOR ◀** [I always + adv/prep, T always + adv/prep] to find enough space for something in a room, vehicle, container etc: **fit sb/sth ↔ in** *Can you fit in another passenger?*

**6 ▶ MATCH ◀** [I,T not in progressive] if something fits a system, idea etc, it says the same thing or follows the same principles: **fit in with** *Sonny's behaviour didn't fit in with what I knew of him.* | [+ **in/into**] *educational videos designed to fit into the syllabus* | **fit sth** *a phenomenon that didn't fit the expected pattern*

**7 ▶ SUITABLE ◀** [T not in progressive] to have the qualities, experience etc that are suitable for a particular job, situation etc: *The punishment should fit the crime.* | *The music fits the words perfectly.* | **fit sb for sth** *Webb's negotiating skills fitted him for the task.* | **fit the bill** (=have exactly the right qualities) *We wanted an experienced sportscaster, and Waggoner fit the bill.*

**8 ▶ DESCRIPTION ◀** [T not in progressive] if a description fits someone or something, it describes them exactly: *Police said the car fits the description of the stolen vehicle.*

**9 ▶ DECIDE GROUP ◀** [I,T] to belong to a particular group or set of ideas: [+ **into**] *A lot of people didn't fit into the categories the researchers had devised.* —see also **sb's face doesn't fit** (FACE[1] (17)), **if the cap fits** (CAP[1] (4))

**fit in** *phr v* **1** [I] to be accepted by other people in a group because you have the same attitudes and interests: *At first I felt awkward, but I soon learned to fit in.* | [+ **with**] *Larry doesn't seem to fit in with the other children.* **2** [T **fit** sth/sb ↔ **in**] to manage to do something or see someone, even though you have a lot of other things to do: *The doctor said he can fit me in at 4:30.* **3** [T **fit** sth ↔ **in/into**] to find a time when something can happen without causing problems: *How is the extra work going to fit into the schedule?* | [+**with**] *Nancy tried to fit her holidays in with Alex's.*

**fit** sb/sth ↔ **out** *phr v* [T] **1** to provide a room or building with equipment or decorations: *snug mountain cabins fitted out with pine furniture* **2** to dress someone, especially in a particular type of clothing: *Jennifer was fitted out like a Queen.*

**fit** sb/sth ↔ **up** *phr v* [T] **1** to provide a room or building with equipment or decorations: *The bedroom is fitted up as an office.* **2** *BrE spoken* to make someone seem guilty of a crime thay have not done; FRAME[2] (3): **fit sb up for sth** *Watson had been fitted up for the murder.*

**USAGE NOTE: FIT**

WORD CHOICE: **fit, suit, fit in, match, go together/with**

If something is not too big and not too small for a person or other thing, it **fits** (them): *A size 12 dress should fit.* | *You can't put those shelves in there, they won't fit.*

If clothes or other personal things are the right style, colour etc for someone, you say they **suit** them: *Casual clothes really don't suit her.* | *A green dress won't suit me.* | *That new haircut suits you!* Schools, places, times, situations etc may also **suit** people: *A management position would suit him down to the ground.* | *California doesn't suit everyone.* | *Will ten o'clock suit you?*

If people **fit in** they have a good social relationship with the other people in a group, and share the same attitudes, interests etc: *Laura fits in perfectly at the tennis club.*

If things are almost the same in some way and look good together, they **match**: *The curtains don't match the carpet* (= they are not the same pattern/colour).

If things look right together in style, colour etc, they **go together** or **go with** each other: *The curtains don't go with the carpet* (= they are not the same colour and do not look good together either). Things can **go together** in other ways too: *Fish and white wine go particularly well together.*

In British English the usual past form of **fit** is **fitted**, but in the first meaning you can also use **fit** in more informal English: *Two years ago, these pants fit me perfectly.* In American English, the usual past form is **fit**, but you can also use **fitted** for all the meanings.

**fit[2]** *adj* **fitter, fittest** S2 W3

**1** having the qualities that are suitable for a particular job, occasion, purpose etc: [+ **for**] *I don't think Carol is the fittest person for the job.* | **fit to do sth** *She's not fit to look after children.* | **fit to eat/drink** *This food isn't fit to eat.* | **be in a fit state** *We're trying to get the house into a fit state for visitors.* | **fit for a King** (=of the highest quality): *food fit for a King*

**2 ▶ STRONG ◀** *especially BrE* healthy and strong because you exercise regularly: *Sandy's very fit – he runs almost 30 miles a week.* | **keep fit** (=exercise in order to stay strong) *She keeps fit by swimming every morning.* | **physically fit** *AmE*: *Rowers have to be extremely physically fit.* —opposite UNFIT (1)

**3 ▶ HEALTHY ◀** *especially BrE* healthy after having been ill: *I'm glad to see you looking fit again.* | **fit as a fiddle** (=completely healthy) *She's 86, but as fit as a fiddle.* | **fighting fit** (=extremely healthy) | **be in a fit state/condition** (=be healthy enough, after being ill or drunk, to be able to do something) *Brog was in no fit state to drive when he left the party.*

**4 fit to drop** extremely tired after using a lot of effort or energy: *We worked till we were fit to drop.*

**5 fit to be tied** *spoken especially AmE* very angry, anxious, or upset: *The teacher will be fit to be tied when she sees the mess you've made.*

**6 fit to wake the dead** a noise that is fit to wake the dead is extremely loud: *They were screaming fit to wake the dead.*

**7 laughing/coughing fit to burst** *informal* laughing or coughing a lot: *The girls were laughing fit to burst.*

**8 see/think fit (to do sth)** an expression meaning to

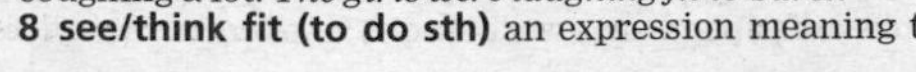

decide that it is right or suitable to do a particular thing, used especially when you do not agree with this decision: *You know the situation best. Do whatever you think fit.*

**fit**³ *n*
**1 ▶ EMOTION ◀** [C] a very strong and uncontrollable emotion: [+ **of**] *In a fit of temper he slammed his hands down on the keyboard.* | *a fit of depression*
**2 be a good/tight/close etc fit** to fit a person or a particular space well, tightly, closely etc: *This jacket is a beautiful fit.*
**3 ▶ LOSE CONSCIOUSNESS ◀** [C] a short period of time when someone loses consciousness and cannot control their body because their brain is not working properly: *an epileptic fit* | **have a fit** *The baby's having a fit! Call the doctor!*
**4 ▶ SUITABLE ◀** [singular] *formal* a relationship between two things or systems in which they match each other or are suitable for each other: [+ **between**] *We must be sure that there's a fit between the needs of the children and the education they receive.*
**5 ▶ LAUGH/COUGH ◀** a period during which you laugh or cough a lot: *a coughing fit* | [+ **of**] *a fit of the giggles* | **in fits (of laughter)** (=laughing a lot) *The show was hilarious – we were all in fits.* | **have sb in fits** (=make someone laugh a lot) *Cyril had us in fits from the minute we walked in the door.*
**6 in/by fits and starts** repeatedly starting and stopping: *The old car moved in fits and starts up the road.* | *Beverley tends to do things in fits and starts.*
**7 have/throw a fit** *informal* to be very angry or shocked: *If your mother finds out about this she'll have a fit.*

**fit·ful** /ˈfɪtfəl/ *adj* happening irregularly for short periods of time: *fitful showers of rain* —**fitfully** *adv*: *She slept fitfully.*

**fit·ment** /ˈfɪtmənt/ *n* [C] *BrE* a piece of furniture that is made especially for a particular space in a room: *bathroom fitments*

**fit·ness** /ˈfɪtnɪ̣s/ *n* [U] **1** the state of being healthy and strong so that you are able to do hard work or sport: *She's following an exercise programme to improve her fitness.* | **physical fitness** *Running marathons requires a high level of physical fitness.* **2** the degree to which someone or something is suitable or good enough for a particular situation or purpose: [+ **for**] *We examine candidates' fitness for the job.* | **fitness to do sth** *The police questioned his fitness to drive.*

**fit·ted** /ˈfɪtɪ̣d/ *adj* **1 be fitted with** to have or include something as a permanent part: *Is your car fitted with automatic locks?* **2** [only before noun] *BrE* made or cut to fit a particular space: *a fitted carpet* | *fitted cupboards* **3** having the right qualities or experience for a particular job: *Elinor is well fitted to be the sales manager.*

**fitted kit·chen** /ˌ·· ˈ··/ *n* [C] *BrE* a kitchen that has cupboards that fit exactly into a particular space

**fitted sheet** /ˌ·· ˈ·/ *n* [C] a sheet that fits exactly over the MATTRESS on a bed

**fit·ter** /ˈfɪtə‖-ər/ *n* [C] *BrE* someone who puts together or repairs machines or electrical equipment: *a gas fitter*

**fit·ting**¹ /ˈfɪtɪŋ/ *n* [C] **1** [usually plural] a piece of furniture that is usually included in a house but can be moved if necessary, such as a COOKER (1) —compare FIXTURE (1) **2** [usually plural] a part of a piece of equipment that makes it possible for you to use it: *a sink with chrome fittings* (=handle and taps) | *the light fittings* **3** an occasion when you put on a piece of clothing that is being made for you, to see if it fits properly

**fitting**² *adj formal* right for a particular situation or occasion; APPROPRIATE¹: *I thought the memorial was a fitting tribute to the President.* | **it is fitting that** *It was not fitting that he remarried so soon after his wife's death.*

**fitting room** /ˈ··· ·/ *n* [C] an area in a shop where you can put on clothes to see how they look

**five** /faɪv/ *number* **1** 5 —see table on page B1 **2** a piece of paper money worth $5 or £5: *Do you have two fives for a ten?* —see also FIVER **3 give sb (a) five** to hit the inside of someone's hand with your hand to show that you are very pleased about something **4 take five** used to tell people to stop working for a few minutes **5 five-day/five-month/five-year** happening or continuing for five days, months, or years: *I've got a five-month contract in Bahrain.* **6 fives** [U] a British ball game in which the ball is hit with the hand against any of three walls —compare HANDBALL (1) —see also HIGH FIVE, NINE-TO-FIVE

**five-and-ten** /ˌ· · ˈ·/ also **five-and-dime** *n* [C] *AmE old-fashioned* a shop that sells many different types of inexpensive goods, especially for the house; DIME STORE

**five o'clock shad·ow** /ˌ· ·· ˈ··/ *n* [singular] the dark colour on a man's chin where the hair has grown a little bit during the day

**fiv·er** /ˈfaɪvə‖-ər/ *n* [C] *BrE* £5 or a five pound note: *It's only a fiver to get in.*

**five-spot** /ˈ· ·/ *n* [C] *AmE old-fashioned* a piece of paper money worth $5: *It only costs a five-spot.*

**five-star** /ˈ· ·/ *adj* [only before noun] a five-star hotel or restaurant is very good

**five star gen·e·ral** /ˈ· · ˈ···/ *n* [C] *AmE* a GENERAL who commands an army

**five-stones** /ˈ· ·/ *n* [U] *BrE* a children's game in which the players try to pick up small objects between throwing one of them into the air and catching it

**fix**¹ /fɪks/ *v* [T] S W
**1 ▶ REPAIR ◀** to repair something that is broken or not working properly; MEND¹ (1b) *BrE*: *Dad's outside fixing the brakes on the Chevy.* —see graph at REPAIR¹
**2 ▶ LIMIT ◀** to decide on a limit for something, especially prices, costs etc, so that they do not change: [+ **at**] *The interest rate has been fixed at 6.5%.*
**3 fix a time/day/place etc** to decide on a particular time etc when something will happen: *Have you fixed a date for the wedding yet?*
**4 ▶ ARRANGE ◀** also **fix up** to make arrangements for something: *If you want to meet the big boss, I can fix it.*
**5 ▶ FASTEN ◀** to fasten something firmly to something else, so that it stays there permanently: **fix sth to/on** *We fixed the shelves to the wall using screws.*
**6 ▶ MAKE FOOD ◀** *informal especially AmE* to prepare a meal or drinks: *I watched the kids while he fixed dinner.* | **fix sb sth** *I'll fix you a whisky sour.*
**7 fix your attention/eyes/mind etc on** to think about or look at someone or something carefully: *Aziz tried to fix his mind on the job at hand.*
**8 ▶ HAIR ETC ◀** *especially AmE* to make your hair or MAKE-UP look neat and attractive: *Who fixed your hair for the wedding?* | **fix your face** (=put make-up on your face) *Hold on. Let me just fix my face before we go out.*
**9 ▶ CAT/DOG ◀** *AmE informal* to do a medical operation on a cat or dog so that it cannot have babies; NEUTER²
**10 ▶ RESULT OF COMPETITION ◀** to arrange an election, game etc dishonestly, so that you get the result you want: *The fight must have been fixed. Nobody goes down that easily!*
**11 ▶ PUNISH ◀** *informal* to punish someone for something they have done: *I'll fix him for taking my car without my permission!*
**12 fix sb with a stare/glare/look etc** to look directly into someone's eyes for a long time: *Rachel fixed him with an icy stare.*
**13 ▶ PAINTINGS/PHOTOGRAPHS ◀** to use a chemical process on paintings, photographs etc that makes the colours or images permanent
**14 be fixing to do sth** *AmE spoken* an expression meaning to prepare to do something, used in some parts of the US: *I'm fixing to go to the store. Do you need anything?*
**15 ▶ CURE ◀** *AmE informal* to make a part of the body that is damaged completely better: *They'll fix your leg for you.*

**fix on** sth/sb *phr v* [T] to choose a suitable thing or

person especially after thinking about it carefully: *We've finally fixed on a place to have the concert.*

**fix** sb/sth ↔ **up** *phr v* [T] **1** to arrange a meeting, event etc, especially by persuading someone to agree to it: *We'll have to fix up a time to meet.* | **fix up to do sth** *BrE I've fixed up to be in Toronto for the next conference.* **2** to improve something or make it suitable: *We fixed up the guest bedroom before my parents came to stay.* **3** to provide someone with something they want: [+ **with**] *Can you fix me up with a bed for the night?* **4** to find a suitable romantic partner for someone: *Bring your brother too. I'm sure we can find someone to fix him up with.*

**fix²** *n* **1 be in a fix** to have a problem that is difficult to solve: *We were in a real fix.* | *The car broke down and there wasn't a phone in sight.* **2** [singular] an amount of something, especially an illegal drug, that you often use and badly want: *addicts looking for a fix* | *I need my fix of caffeine in the morning or I can't think.* **3** [singular] something that has been dishonestly arranged: *The election was a fix!* **4 get a fix on sb/sth a)** to find out exactly where someone or something is: *The search boat can't get a fix on the yacht's position.* **b)** to understand what someone or something is really like: *I sat and stared for a while, trying to get a fix on the situation.*

**fix·a·ted** /fɪk'seɪtɪ̣d/ *adj* **1** always thinking or talking about one particular thing: [+ **on**] *Jeremy seems to be fixated on this idea of travelling around the world.* **2** *technical* having stopped developing emotionally or mentally

**fix·a·tion** /fɪk'seɪʃən/ *n* [C] **1** an unnaturally strong interest in or love for someone or something: [+ **about/with**] *Trevor's got this fixation about cleanliness.* **2** *technical* a kind of mental illness in which someone's mind or emotions stop developing, so that they are like a child

**fix·a·tive** /'fɪksətɪv/ *n* [C,U] **1** a substance used to glue things together or to hold things such as hair or false teeth in place **2** a chemical used on a painting or photograph so that the colours do not change

S3 W3 **fixed** /fɪkst/ *adj* **1** firmly fastened to a particular position: **be fixed to/in/on** *The tables are fixed to the floor.* **2** times, amounts, meanings etc that are fixed cannot be changed: *The classes begin and end at fixed times.* | *fixed prices* **3 have fixed ideas/opinions** to have very definite ideas or opinions which are often unreasonable: [+ **about/on**] *He has very fixed ideas about how a wife should behave.* **4 how are you fixed for** *spoken* used to ask someone how much of something they have: *How are you fixed for cash?* **5 fixed expression/smile/frown etc** a fixed smile, expression etc does not change and does not seem to express real emotions **6 have no fixed abode/address** *law BrE* to not have a permanent place to live

**fixed as·sets** /ˌ· '··/ *n* [plural] *technical* land, buildings, or equipment that a business owns and uses

**fixed cap·i·tal** /ˌ· '···/ *n* [U] *technical* buildings or machines that a business owns and that can be used for a long time to produce goods

**fixed charge** /ˌ· '·/ *n* [C] a cost that does not change for a long time

**fixed costs** /ˌ· '·/ *n* [plural] *technical* costs, such as rent, that a business has to pay even when it is not producing anything

**fix·ed·ly** /'fɪksɪ̣dli/ *adv* looking at, or thinking about only one thing: *Anna stared fixedly ahead, trying to concentrate on the road.*

**fix·er** /'fɪksə‖-ər/ *n* [C] someone who is good at arranging events, situations etc for other people so that they have the results they want, especially by using dishonest or illegal methods

**fix·ings** /'fɪksɪŋz/ *n* **the fixings** *AmE* the vegetables, bread etc that are eaten with meat at a large meal; TRIMMINGS (3) *BrE*: *turkey with all the fixings*

**fix·i·ty** /'fɪksɪ̣ti/ *n* [U] *formal* the state of not changing: *fixity of purpose*

**fix·ture** /'fɪkstʃə‖-ər/ *n* [C] **1** [usually plural] a piece of equipment that is fixed inside a house or building and is sold as part of the house: **the fixtures and fittings** *BrE* (=all the pieces of equipment that are normally included as part of a house or building) **2 be a (permanent) fixture** to be always present and not likely to move or go away: *The dog became a permanent fixture in our lives.* **3** *BrE* a sports match that has been arranged for a particular time and place: *a list of this season's fixtures*

**fizz¹** /fɪz/ *v* [I] if a liquid fizzes, it produces a lot of BUBBLES¹ (1) and makes a continuous sound: *champagne fizzing out of the bottle* —see picture on page 1261

**fizz²** *n* [singular, U] **1** the BUBBLES¹ (1) of gas in some kinds of drinks or the sound that they make **2** *BrE informal* CHAMPAGNE

**fiz·zle** /'fɪzəl/ *v*

**fizzle out** *phr v* [I] *informal* to gradually stop happening, especially because people become less interested in something: *Their romance just fizzled out.*

**fiz·zy** /'fɪzi/ *adj* **1** a fizzy liquid contains BUBBLES¹ (1) of gas —opposite FLAT¹(4) **2 fizzy drink** *BrE* a sweet, non-alcoholic drink with BUBBLES of gas; SOFT DRINK

**fjord**, **fiord** /'fiːɔːd, fjɔːd‖fiː'ɔːrd, fjɔːrd/ *n* [C] a narrow area of sea between high cliffs on the coast of Norway

**flab** /flæb/ *n* [U] *informal* soft, loose fat on a person's body

**flab·ber·gas·ted** /'flæbəgɑːstɪ̣d‖-bərgæs-/ *adj informal* extremely surprised or shocked: *Teachers were flabbergasted at the decision to close down the school.*

**flab·by** /'flæbi/ *adj informal* **1** having soft, loose fat rather than strong muscles: *She's getting old and flabby.* **2** a flabby argument, excuse etc is weak and not effective —**flabbiness** *n* [U]

**flac·cid** /'flæsɪ̣d, 'flæksɪ̣d/ *adj technical* soft and weak instead of firm —**flaccidity** /flæ'sɪdɪ̣ti,flæk-/ *n* [U]

**flack** /flæk/ *n* [U] another spelling of FLAK

**flag¹** /flæg/ *n* [C] **1** a piece of cloth with a coloured pattern or picture on it that represents a country or organization: *The children waved their flags as the Queen went by.* | *the flag of Texas* | **a flag flies** (=a flag is shown on a pole) *Flags were flying at half-mast for the death of the Premier.* **2** a coloured piece of cloth used as a signal: *The flag went down, and the race began.* **3 under the flag of** if a group of people do something under the flag of a particular country or organization, they do it as representatives of that country or organization **4 the flag** an expression meaning a country or organization and its beliefs, values, and people: *loyalty to the flag* **5 keep the flag flying** to achieve success on behalf of your country in a competition **6** a FLAGSTONE —see also **fly the flag** (FLY¹(27))

**flag² flagged, flagging** *v* **1** [T] make a mark against something to show that it is important: *I've flagged the parts I want to comment on.* **2** [I] to become tired or weak: *By ten o'clock I was beginning to flag and went up to bed.*

**flag** sb/sth ↔ **down** *phr v* [T] to make the driver of a vehicle stop by waving at them: *I flagged down a taxi.*

**fla·gel·lant** /'flædʒɪ̣lənt, flə'dʒelənt/ *n* [C] *formal* someone who whips themselves as a religious punishment

**fla·gel·late** /'flædʒɪ̣leɪt/ *v* [T] *formal* to whip yourself or someone else, especially as a religious punishment

**flag foot·ball** /'· ˌ··/ *n* [U] *AmE* a game like American football in which players tear off flags from around other players' waists instead of knocking them down —compare TOUCH FOOTBALL

**flagged** /flægd/ *adj* covered with FLAGSTONES

**flag·ging** /'flægɪŋ/ *adj* becoming tired, weaker, or less interested: *concern for the United States' flagging economy*

**flag·on** /'flægən/ *n* [C] a large container for liquids

**flag·pole** /'flægpəʊl‖-poʊl/ *n* [C] a tall pole on which a flag hangs; FLAGSTAFF

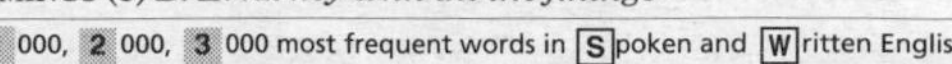

1 000, 2 000, 3 000 most frequent words in Spoken and Written English

**fla·grant** /ˈfleɪgrənt/ *adj* **flagrant abuse/violation etc** a flagrant action is shocking because it is done in a way that is easily noticed and shows no respect for laws, truth etc: *flagrant disregard for human rights* —**flagrantly** *adv*

**flag·ship** /ˈflægʃɪp/ *n* [C] **1** the most important ship in a group of ships belonging to the navy, on which the ADMIRAL sails **2** the best and most important product, building etc that a company owns or produces: *the flagship of the new Ford range*

**flag·staff** /ˈflægstɑːf‖-stæf/ *n* [C] a tall pole on which a flag hangs; FLAGPOLE

**flag·stone** /ˈflægstəʊn‖-stoʊn/ *n* [C] a smooth flat piece of stone used for floors, paths etc

**flag stop** /ˈ· ·/ *n* [C] *AmE* a place where buses stop only if they are asked to do so

**flag-wav·ing** /ˈ· ˌ··/ *n* [U] the expression of strong national feelings, especially when these feelings seem too extreme

**flail[1]** /fleɪl/ *v* **1** [I,T] to wave your arms or legs in an uncontrolled way: *His arms flailed above the surface of the water.* **2** [T] to beat someone or something violently, usually with a stick **3** [I,T] to beat grain with a flail

**flail[2]** *n* [C] a tool consisting of a stick that swings from a long handle, used in the past to separate grain from wheat by beating it

**flair** /fleə‖fler/ *n* **1** [singular] a natural ability to do something very well: **have a flair for** *Carla has an instinctive flair for business.* **2** [U] a way of doing things that is interesting and shows imagination: *Bates's advertising campaigns tended to lack flair.*

**flak, flack** /flæk/ *n* [U] **1** *informal* strong criticism: **get/take flak** *The administration has taken a lot of flak over its decision to pull troops out of Somalia.* **2** bullets or shells (SHELL[1] (3)) that are shot from guns on the ground at enemy aircraft —see also FLAK JACKET

**flake[1]** /fleɪk/ *n* [C + **of**] **1** a very small flat thin piece that breaks away easily from something else: *soap flakes* —see also SNOWFLAKE —see picture on page 416 **2** *AmE informal* someone who seems crazy

**flake[2]** *v* **1** [I] also **flake off** to break off in small thin pieces: *The paint is beginning to flake off.* **2** [I,T] to break fish or another food into small thin pieces, or to break in this way: *Poach the fish until it flakes easily.*

**flake out** *phr v* [I] *informal* to fall asleep because you are extremely tired: *Karl got home at eight o'clock and flaked out on the sofa.*

**flak jack·et** /ˈ· ˌ··/ *n* [C] a special coat made of heavy material with metal inside it to protect soldiers and policemen from bullets

**flak·y** /ˈfleɪki/ *adj* **1** tending to break into small thin pieces: *rich, flaky pastry* **2** *informal especially AmE* slightly crazy: *Carrie's pretty flaky but she's fun to be with.* —**flakiness** *n* [U]

**flam·bé** /ˈflɒmbeɪ‖flɑːmˈbeɪ/ also **flam·béed** /ˈflɒmbeɪd‖flɑːmˈbeɪd/ *adj French* food that is flambéed has an alcoholic drink such as BRANDY poured over it to produce flames —see picture on page 838

**flam·boy·ant** /flæmˈbɔɪənt/ *adj* **1** behaving or dressing in a confident or surprising way that makes people notice you: *his flamboyant stage personality | flamboyant gestures* **2** brightly coloured and easily noticed: *flamboyant clothes* **flamboyantly** *adv* —**flamboyance** *n* [U]

**flame[1]** /fleɪm/ *n* [C,U] **1** hot bright burning gas that you see when something is on fire: *the flame of a candle | Flames poured out of the windows of the building.* —see picture at CANDLE **2 in flames** burning strongly: *The house was in flames by the time we arrived.* **3 go up in flames/burst into flames** to begin burning suddenly and strongly: *I was driving along and the engine just burst into flames.* **4 a flame of passion/desire/vengeance etc** *literary* a strong feeling —see also **old flame** (OLD[1] (13)), **naked flame** (NAKED (3)), **fan the flames** (FAN[2] (2)), **add fuel to the fire/flames** (FUEL[1](3))

**flame[2]** *v* [I] **1** *literary* to become suddenly bright with light or colour, especially red or orange: *Her cheeks flamed for an instant.* **2** also **flame up** to suddenly burn more strongly or brightly

**fla·men·co** /fləˈmeŋkəʊ‖-koʊ/ *n* [C,U] a fast, exciting Spanish dance, or the GUITAR music that is played for this dance

flamenco

**flame·proof** /ˈfleɪmpruːf/ also **flame re·sist·ant** /ˈ· ·ˌ··/ *adj* specially made or treated with chemicals so it does not burn easily

**flame throw·er** /ˈ· ˌ··/ *n* [C] a machine like a gun that shoots flames or burning liquid, used as a weapon or for clearing plants

**flam·ing** /ˈfleɪmɪŋ/ *adj* [only before noun] **1 a flaming argument/row/temper** a very angry argument or temper: *He had had a flaming row with his wife earlier that evening.* **2** *BrE informal* used to emphasize what you are saying, especially when you feel annoyed: *You flaming idiot!* **3** covered with flames

**fla·min·go** /fləˈmɪŋgəʊ‖-goʊ/ *n* [C] a tropical bird that has very long thin legs, pink feathers, and a long neck

**flam·ma·ble** /ˈflæməbəl/ *adj* easily set on fire: *Caution! Highly flammable chemicals.* —opposite NONFLAMMABLE

**flan** /flæn/ *n* [C] *especially BrE* **1** a round PIE (1) or cake that is filled with fruit, cheese etc **2** *AmE* a sweet baked CUSTARD made with eggs —compare PIE, QUICHE

**flange** /flændʒ/ *n* [C] the flat edge that stands out from the main surface of an object such as a railway wheel, to keep it in the right position

**flank[1]** /flæŋk/ *n* [C] **1** the side of an animal's or person's body, between the RIBS[1] (1) and the HIP[1](1) —see picture at HORSE[1] **2** the side of an army in a battle or war: *We were attacked on our left flank.* **3** the side of a hill, mountain, or very large building

**flank[2]** *v* **be flanked by** to have something or someone on both sides: *Yeltsin emerged, flanked by his bodyguards.*

**flan·nel[1]** /ˈflænl/ *n* **1** [U] soft cloth, usually made of cotton or wool, used for making clothes: *a flannel suit* **2** [C] *BrE* a piece of cloth you use to wash yourself; WASHCLOTH *AmE* **3** [U] *BrE informal* something that someone says that has no real meaning or is not sincere **4 flannels** [plural] *especially BrE* men's trousers made of flannel

**flannel[2]** *v* [I] *BrE* to say things that are not sincere to avoid answering a question directly

**flan·nel·ette** /ˌflænəlˈet/ *n* [U] soft cotton cloth used especially for night clothes, sheets etc

**flap[1]** /flæp/ *n* **1** [C] a thin flat piece of cloth, paper, skin etc that is fixed by one edge to a surface, which you can lift up easily: *He lifted the tent flap slowly to see what was making the noise.* —see also CAT FLAP **2** [singular] the noisy movement of something such as cloth in the air: *the flap of the sails* **3** [singular] *informal* a situation in which people feel very excited, angry, or worried about something: **be in a flap** *Rafi's in a bit of a flap over the wedding plans.* —see also UNFLAPPABLE **4** [C] a part of the wing of an aircraft that can be raised or lowered to help the aircraft go up or down

**flap²** *v* **1** [I] if a bird flaps its wings, it moves its wings up and down in order to fly **2** [I,T] if a piece of cloth, paper etc flaps it moves around quickly and noisily: *The flags were flapping in the breeze.* **3** [I] *BrE informal* to behave in an excited, nervous, or angry way: *There's no need to flap!*

**flap·jack** /ˈflæpdʒæk/ *n* [C] **1** *BrE* a cake made of OATS, sugar, SYRUP, and butter **2** *AmE* a thick round unsweetened cake made of flour, milk, and eggs, cooked in a pan and eaten for breakfast; PANCAKE (2)

**flap·per** /ˈflæpə‖-ər/ *n* [C] a fashionable young woman in the late 1920s who wore short dresses, had short hair, and had ideas that were considered very modern

**flare¹** /fleə‖fler/ *v* **1** also **flare up** [I] to suddenly begin to burn, or to burn more brightly for a short time: *The match flared in the darkness.* **2** also **flare up** [I] if strong feelings flare or flare up, people suddenly become angry, violent etc: *Violence has flared up again in the Middle East.* **3** also **flare up** [I] if a disease or illness flares up, it suddenly becomes worse: *My asthma tends to flare up on smoggy days.* **4** [I,T] to become wider towards the bottom end or edge, or to make something do this: [+ **out**] *The dress flared out from the hips.*|*flared trousers*|*The bull flared its nostrils and charged.* —see picture on page 840

**flare out at** sb *phr v* [T] *AmE* to say something suddenly in an angry way: *I said something about the weather and he flared out at me for no reason.*

**flare²** *n* **1** [C] a piece of equipment that produces a bright flame, or the flame itself, used outdoors as a signal: *Flares marked the landing site.* **2** [C usually singular] a sudden bright flame **3 flares** [plural] trousers that become wide below the knee

**flare path** /ˈ· ·/ *n* [C] a path for aircraft to land on that is lit with special lights

**flare-up** /ˈ· ·/ *n* [C] **1** a situation in which someone suddenly becomes angry or violent: *Apart from one or two flare-ups the match went fairly smoothly.* **2** a situation in which someone suddenly has problems because of a disease or illness after not having any problems for a long time: *a flare-up of her arthritis*

S3 **flash¹** /flæʃ/ *v*
**1** ► **SHINE** ◄ [I,T] to shine suddenly and brightly for a short time, or to make something shine in this way: *The lightning flashed.*|**flash sth into/at/towards** *Why is that guy flashing his headlights at me?*|**flash on and off** (=shine for a short time and then stop shining) *Red warning lights flashed on and off.*
**2** ► **MOVE QUICKLY** ◄ [I always + adv/prep] to move very quickly: [+ **by/past/through**] *A couple of police cars flashed past, sirens wailing.*
**3** ► **SHOW STH QUICKLY** ◄ [T] to show something to someone for only a short time: *He flashed his identification card.*
**4** ► **MEMORIES/IMAGES** ◄ [I always + adv/prep] if thoughts, images, memories etc flash through your mind, you suddenly think of them or remember them: [+ **across/through/into**] *The possibility that Frank was lying flashed through my mind.*
**5** ► **TIME** ◄ [I always + adv/prep] if a period of time flashes by, past etc, it seems to end very quickly: [+ **by/past**] *Our vacation seemed to just flash by.*
**6** ► **PICTURES** ◄ [I always + adv/prep] to be shown quickly on television or on a film: [+ **across/onto/past etc**] *Images of the war flashed across the screen.*
**7** ► **EYES** ◄ [I] if your eyes flash, they seem to be very bright for a moment, especially because of a sudden emotion: [+ **with**] *Janet's blue eyes flashed with anger.*
**8** ► **NEWS/INFORMATION** ◄ [T always + adv/prep] to send news or information somewhere quickly by radio, computer, or SATELLITE (1): **flash sth to/throughout/all over etc** *News can be flashed all over the world within seconds of it happening.*
**9 flash a smile/glance/look etc at sb** to smile or look at someone quickly and for a short time
**10** ► **SEX ORGANS** ◄ [I,T] if a man flashes, he shows his sexual organs in public
**11 your life flashes before your eyes** if your life flashes before your eyes, you suddenly remember many events from your life, especially because you are in great danger and might die

**flash** sth **around** *phr v* [T] to show people that you have a lot of money in order to try and make them admire you: *wealthy clients flashing their credit cards around and buying everything in sight*

**flash²** *n*
**1** ► **LIGHT** ◄ [C] a bright light that shines for a short time and then stops shining: *flashes of lightning in the valley*
**2** ► **CAMERA** ◄ [C,U] a special bright light used when taking photographs indoors or when there is not much light: *Did the flash go off?*
**3 in a flash/like a flash/quick as a flash** very quickly: *Just wait here. I'll be back in a flash.*
**4 flash of brilliance/inspiration/intuition/anger** if someone has a flash of brilliance, anger etc, they suddenly have a clever idea or suddenly have a particular feeling: *Her essays show occasional flashes of brilliance.*
**5** ► **BRIGHT COLOUR/STH SHINY** ◄ [C] if there is a flash of something brightly coloured or shiny, it appears suddenly for a short time: [+ **of**] *The bird stood watching for the underwater flash of a turning fish.*
**6** ► **LOOK** ◄ *BrE humorous* a quick look; GLIMPSE² (1)
**7** ► **SIGNAL** ◄ the act of shining a light as a signal: *Two flashes mean danger.*
**8 a flash in the pan** a sudden success that ends quickly and is unlikely to happen again: *Rival record companies assumed the group would be a flash in the pan.*
**9** ► **MILITARY** ◄ a small piece of coloured cloth worn on the shoulder of a military uniform —see also NEWSFLASH

**flash³** *adj* **1** [only before noun] happening very quickly or suddenly, and lasting for only a short time: *Flash fires swept through the Los Angeles foothills last night.* —see also FLASH FLOOD **2** *BrE informal* looking very new, bright, and expensive-looking: *a big flash car* **3** *informal* [not before noun] liking to have expensive clothes and possessions so that other people notice you: *Who was that flash geezer we saw you with last night?*

**flash·back** /ˈflæʃbæk/ *n* **1** [C,U] a scene in a film, play, book etc that shows something that happened before that point in the story: *The events of the hero's childhood are shown as a series of flashbacks.* **2** [C] a sudden very clear memory of something that happened to you in the past **3** [C] *technical* a burning gas or liquid that moves back into a tube or container

**flash bulb** /ˈ· ·/ *n* [C] a small BULB (=a bright light) used when you take photographs indoors or when it is dark outside

**flash burn** /ˈ· ·/ *n* [C] a burn that you get from being near a sudden, very hot flame, for example an explosion

**flash·card** /ˈflæʃkɑːd‖-kɑːrd/ *n* [C] a card with a word or picture on it, used in teaching

**flash·er** /ˈflæʃə‖-ər/ *n* [C] a man who shows his sexual organs to women in public

**flash flood** /ˌ· ˈ·/ *n* [C] a sudden flood that is caused by a lot of rain falling in a short period of time

**flash freeze** /ˌ· ˈ·/ *v* [T] to freeze food quickly so that the quality is not damaged

**flash·gun** /ˈflæʃgʌn/ *n* [C] a piece of equipment that lights a special bright light when you press the button on a camera to take a photograph

**flash·light** /ˈflæʃlaɪt/ *n* [C] a small electric light that you can carry in your hand; TORCH¹(1) *BrE*

**flash·point** /ˈflæʃpɔɪnt/ *n* [C] **1** a place where trouble or violence might easily develop suddenly and be hard to control: *Beirut is one of the flashpoints of the Middle East.* **2** [usually singular] *technical* the lowest temperature at which a liquid such as oil will produce enough gas to burn if a flame is put near it

**flash·y** /ˈflæʃi/ *adj informal* too big, bright, or expensive in a way that other people disapprove of: *Marc always drove large flashy cars.*

**flask** /flɑːsk‖flæsk/ *n* [C] **1** *BrE* a special type of bottle that you use to keep liquids either hot or cold, for example when travelling **2** a flat bottle usually used to carry alcohol **3** a glass bottle with a narrow top, used in a LABORATORY

**flasks**

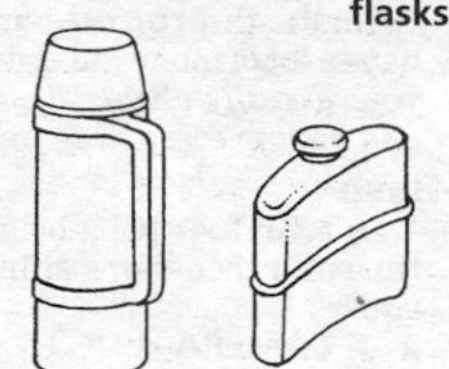

thermos flask hip flask

S2 W2 **flat¹** /flæt/ *adj* **flatter, flattest**
**1** ▶ **SURFACE** ◀ smooth and level, without raised or hollow areas, and not sloping or curving: *a flat-bottomed boat | a perfectly flat sandy beach* | **flat as a pancake** (=very flat) *The countryside near there is flat as a pancake.*
**2 flat rate/price/fee etc** a flat rate, price, amount of money etc is fixed and does not change or have anything added to it: *We charge a flat fee for car hire.*
**3** ▶ **TYRE/BALL** ◀ having no air or not enough air in it
**4** ▶ **DRINK** ◀ having lost its BUBBLES¹ (1) of gas and so not tasting fresh: *This Coke must have been opened ages ago – it's completely flat!* —opposite FIZZY (1)
**5** ▶ **NOT INTERESTING** ◀ [not before noun] a performance, book etc that is flat seems rather boring
**6** ▶ **BATTERY** ◀ *BrE* a flat BATTERY (1) has lost its electrical power: | **go flat** (=become flat) *Have you checked that the batteries haven't gone flat?*
**7** ▶ **BUSINESS/TRADE** ◀ not busy: *The building industry's been completely flat for several years.*
**8 E flat/B flat/A flat etc** a musical note that is one SEMITONE lower than the note E, B, A etc
**9** ▶ **MUSICAL SOUND** ◀ if a musical note is flat, it is played or sung at a slightly lower pitch (PITCH² (3)) than it should be: *The guitar was flat through the whole song.*
**10** ▶ **VOICE** ◀ not showing much emotion, or not changing much in sound as you speak: *"He's dead," she said in a flat voice.*
**11 flat refusal/denial etc** a refusal etc that is definite and which someone will definitely not change: *Our requests were met with a flat refusal.*
**12 and that's flat!** *spoken* used to say that you will definitely not change what you have just said: *I won't go, and that's flat!*
**13 be flat on your back a)** to be lying down so that all of your back is touching the floor: *Arthur was flat on his back under the car.* **b)** to be very ill so that you have to stay in bed for a period of time
**14** ▶ **SHOES** ◀ flat shoes have very low heels —see picture on page 840
**15** ▶ **NOT DEEP** ◀ not very deep, thick, or high, especially in comparison to its width or length: *a round, flat apple tart*
**16** ▶ **LIGHT** ◀ having little variety of light and dark: *Flat lighting is typical of Avedon's portraits.* —**flatness** *n* [U] —see also **fall/go into a flat spin** (SPIN² (4))

S2 W3 **flat²** *n* [C]
**1** ▶ **PLACE TO LIVE** ◀ *BrE* a place for people to live that consists of a set of rooms that are part of a larger building; APARTMENT *AmE*: *They have a flat in Crouch End.* | *a ground-floor flat* | **a block of flats** (=a large building with many flats in it)
**2** ▶ **TYRE** ◀ *especially AmE* a tyre that does not have enough air inside; PUNCTURE *BrE*
**3** ▶ **MUSIC** ◀ **a)** a musical note that is one SEMITONE lower than a particular note **b)** the sign (♭) in written music that shows that a note is one SEMITONE lower than a particular note —compare SHARP³, NATURAL² (2) —see picture at MUSIC
**4** ▶ **LAND** ◀ **flats** [plural] an area of land that is at a low level, especially near water: *mud flats*
**5 the flat of sb's hand/a knife/a sword etc** the flat part or flat side of something
**6 on the flat** *BrE* on ground that is level and does not slope: *It's much easier walking on the flat.*

This graph shows how common the nouns **flat** and **apartment** are in British and American English.



Based on the British National Corpus and the Longman Lancaster Corpus

In British English **flat** is used to mean a place where people live, which has a set of rooms including a kitchen and bathroom, and is part of a larger building. Americans use **apartment** for this meaning. In both British and American English **apartment** can be used to mean a large room with expensive furniture, decorations etc, used especially by an important person such as a president or prince.

**flat³** *adv*
**1** ▶ **FLAT POSITION** ◀ in a position in which the surface of something is against another surface without curving or sloping: **lie flat** *He lay flat on the floor to look for it under the bed.*
**2 three minutes/10 seconds etc flat** *informal* used to emphasize that something happens or is done very quickly: *I was dressed in five minutes flat.*
**3 fall flat** *informal* **a)** if a joke or story falls flat, people are not amused by it: *Oh Dear! My joke about fat people fell completely flat, didn't it?* **b)** if something you have planned falls flat it is unsuccessful
**4** ▶ **MUSIC** ◀ if you sing or play music flat, you sing or play slightly lower than the correct note so that the sound is unpleasant —compare SHARP² (4)
**5 fall flat on your face a)** to fall so that you are lying on your front on the ground **b)** *informal* to not have the result you wanted or expected, especially when this is embarrassing: *It is a wonderful theory, but falls flat on its face when put into practice.*
**6 flat out a)** *informal* as fast as possible: *They were working flat out to get the job done on time.* **b)** *AmE spoken* in a direct way: **ask/tell sb flat out** *She asked him flat out whether he'd been seeing another woman.*
**7 tell sb flat** *BrE spoken* to tell someone something directly and definitely: *I told him flat that I didn't want to see him again.*
**8 go flat against** *BrE spoken* to directly disobey someone or ignore them: *I don't know why you bother to ask – you'll go flat against my advice anyway!* —see also **flat broke** (BROKE² (1))

**flat cap** /ˌ· ˈ·/ *n* [C] *BrE* a cap made of cloth, with a stiff piece that sticks out at the front —see picture at CAP

**flat·car** /ˈflætkɑː‖-kɑːr/ *n* [C] *AmE* a railway carriage without a roof or sides, used for carrying goods

**flat-chest·ed** /ˌ· ˈ··◂/ *adj* a woman who is flat-chested has small breasts

**flat feet** /ˌ· ˈ·/ *n* [plural] a medical condition in which someone's feet rest flat on the ground because the middle of each foot is not as curved as it should be

**flat·fish** /ˈflætˌfɪʃ/ *n* [C] a type of sea fish with a thin flat body such as COD or PLAICE

**flat-foot·ed** /ˌ· ˈ··◂/ *adj* **1** having flat feet **2** *informal* moving in an awkward way; CLUMSY (1) **3** *informal* dealing with situations in a way that is not sensitive to other people's thoughts or feelings: *Her husband's grasp on life is flat-footed and practical.* **4 catch sb flatfooted** *AmE old-fashioned* to find someone not working at a time when they should be

**flat i·ron** /ˈ· ··/ *n* [C] a type of iron used in the past that was not heated by electricity

**flat·let** /ˈflætlɪ̈t/ *n* [C] *BrE* a small apartment

**flat·ly** /ˈflætli/ *adv* **1 flatly refuse/deny/oppose etc** to say something in a direct and definite way that is not likely to change: *She flatly refused to tell us where he was.* **2** without showing any emotion: *"Aunt Alicia has changed her will," she said flatly.*

**flat·mate** /ˈflætmeɪt/ *n* [C] *BrE* someone who shares a flat with one or more other people; ROOMMATE (2) *AmE*

**flat rac·ing** /ˈ· ˌ··/ *n* [U] horse racing without any fences on flat ground —compare STEEPLECHASE (1)

**flat share** /ˈ· ·/ *n* [C] *BrE* an arrangement in which two or more people share an apartment

**flat·ten** /ˈflætn/ *v* **1** [I,T] also **flatten out** to make something flat or flatter or to become flat or flatter: *Noah flattened the cardboard boxes before throwing them away.* | *The land flattened out as we neared the coast.* **2** [T] to destroy a building or town by knocking it down, bombing it etc: *Dresden was flattened in the war.* **3 flatten yourself against** to press your body against something: *I flattened myself against the wall.* **4** [T] *informal* to defeat someone completely and easily in a game, argument etc: *We flattened them 6-0.* **5** [T] *informal* to hit someone very hard

**flat·tened** /ˈflætnd/ *adj* [not before noun] unhappy and embarrassed because of what someone has said about you

**flat·ter** /ˈflætə‖-ər/ *v* [T] **1** to praise someone in an insincere way in order to please them or get something from them: *He flattered her, saying how beautiful her eyes were.* **2 be flattered** to be pleased because someone has shown you that they like or admire you: *I was flattered to be asked to write an article for the magazine.* **3** to make someone look more attractive, thinner, or younger than they really are: *outfits designed to flatter the fuller figure* **4 flatter yourself** if you flatter yourself that something is true about your abilities or achievements, you make yourself believe it is true, although it is not: **flatter yourself that** *She flatters herself that she could have been a model.*

**flat·ter·er** /ˈflætərə‖-tərər/ *n* [C] someone who flatters people

**flat·ter·ing** /ˈflætərɪŋ/ *adj* clothes, pictures etc that are flattering make someone look more attractive than they really are: *You look great! That colour is very flattering on you.*

**flat·ter·y** /ˈflætəri/ *n* [U] insincere praise: *She uses a mixture of charm and flattery to get what she wants.* | **flattery will get you nowhere!** *humorous spoken* (=flattery will not help you get what you want from me)

**flat·top** /ˈflæt-tɒp‖-tɑːp/ *n* [C] a type of hair style that is very short and looks flat on top —see picture at HAIRSTYLE

**flat·u·lence** /ˈflætjɡ̈ləns‖-tʃə-/ *n* [U] too much gas in the stomach —**flatulent** *adj*

**flat·ware** /ˈflætˌweə‖-wer/ *n* [U] *AmE* a word for knives, forks, and spoons; CUTLERY

**flaunt** /flɔːnt‖flɒːnt, flɑːnt/ *v* [T] **1** to show your money, success, beauty etc so that other people notice it: *In New York the rich flaunt their wealth while the poor starve on the streets.* **2 if you've got it, flaunt it** *humorous spoken* used to tell someone not to hide their beauty, wealth, or abilities

**flau·tist** /ˈflɔːtɪ̈st‖ˈflɒː-/ *n* [C] *BrE* someone who plays the FLUTE; FLUTIST *AmE*

**fla·vor·ful** /ˈfleɪvəfʊl‖-vər-/ *adj AmE* having a strong pleasant taste: *a flavorful Mexican dish*

**fla·vour**[1] *BrE*, **flavor** *AmE* /ˈfleɪvə‖-ər/ *n* **1** [C] the particular taste of a food or drink: *Which flavor do you want – chocolate or vanilla?* **2** [U] the quality of tasting good or pleasant: *A pinch of herbs will add flavour to any dish.* **3** [singular] a quality or feature that makes something have a particular style or character: *The stories have a strong regional flavour.* **4** [singular] an idea of what the typical qualities of something are: *Marston's book gives you a flavour of life in the 16th century.* **5 flavour of the month** the idea, person, style etc that is the most popular one for a short time: *Health care reform seems to be the political flavor of the month.*

**flavour**[2] *BrE*, **flavor** *AmE* —*v* [T] to give something a particular taste or more taste

**fla·voured** *BrE*, **flavored** *AmE* /ˈfleɪvəd‖-vərd/ *adj* **1 strawberry-flavoured/chocolate-flavoured etc** tasting of strawberries, chocolate etc **2** having had a flavour added: *flavored milk*

**fla·vour·ing** *BrE*, **flavoring** *AmE* /ˈfleɪvərɪŋ/ *n* [C,U] a substance used to increase the flavour of something: *This yoghurt contains no artificial flavourings.*

**flaw** /flɔː‖flɒː/ *n* [C] **1** a mistake, mark, or weakness that makes something imperfect; DEFECT[1]: *a slight flaw in the glass* **2** a mistake in an argument, plan, or set of ideas: **fundamental flaw** (=a very important mistake or weakness) *The lack of reliable statistics was a fundamental flaw in Walton's argument.* | **fatal flaw** (=a very important weakness that makes something certain to fail) **3** a fault in someone's character: *Jealousy is Othello's major flaw.*

**flawed** /flɔːd‖flɒːd/ *adj* having a mistake or weakness: *In many cases the data was incomplete or flawed.*

**flaw·less** /ˈflɔːləs‖ˈflɒː-/ *adj* having no mistakes, marks, or weaknesses; PERFECT[1] (2): *Peterson's flawless performance as the hero* —**flawlessly** *adv*

**flax** /flæks/ *n* [U] **1** a plant with blue flowers, used for making cloth and oil **2** the thread made from this plant, used for making LINEN (2)

**flax·en** /ˈflæksən/ *adj literary* flaxen hair is light in colour

**flay** /fleɪ/ *v* [T] **1** to criticize someone very severely *I came out of the meeting feeling thoroughly flayed and harassed.* **2** *literary* to whip or beat someone very severely

**flea** /fliː/ *n* [C] **1** a very small insect without wings that jumps and bites animals and people to eat their blood **2 send sb off with a flea in their ear** to talk angrily to someone, especially because they have done something you disapprove of

**flea·bag** /ˈfliːbæɡ/ *n* [C] **1** *BrE* a dirty animal or person that you dislike **2** *AmE* a cheap dirty hotel

**flea·bite** /ˈfliːbaɪt/ *n* [C] the bite of a flea

**flea col·lar** /ˈ· ˌ··/ *n* [C] a special collar, worn by a dog or cat, that contains chemicals to keep fleas away from them

**flea mar·ket** /ˈ· ˌ··/ *n* [C] a market where old or used goods are sold

**flea·pit** /ˈfliːˌpɪt/ *n* [C] *old-fashioned humorous* a cheap dirty cinema or theatre

**fleck** /flek/ *n* [C] a small mark or spot: **[+ of]** *flecks of dust*

**flecked** /flekt/ *adj* having small marks or spots: *red cloth flecked with white*

**fledged** *adj* see FULLY-FLEDGED

**fledg·ling**[1], **fledgeling** /ˈfledʒlɪŋ/ *n* [C] a young bird that is learning to fly

**fledgling**[2], **fledgeling** *adj* [only before noun] a fledgling state, or organization, has only recently been formed and is still developing: *a fledgling republic*

**flee** /fliː/ *past tense and past participle* **fled** /fled/ *v* [I,T] to leave somewhere very quickly in order to escape from danger: *When they saw the police car, his attackers turned and fled.* | **flee the country/city** *We were forced to flee the country.* | **[+ from/to/into]** *The Dalai Lama fled to India after a failed uprising against the Chinese.*

**fleece**[1] /fliːs/ *n* [C] **1** the woolly coat of a sheep **2** an artificial soft material used to make warm coats

**fleece**[2] *v* [T] *informal* to charge someone too much money for something

**fleec·y** /ˈfliːsi/ *adj* soft and woolly, or looking soft and woolly: *fleecy white towels*

**fleet**[1] /fliːt/ *n* [C] **1** a group of ships, or all the ships in a navy: *the US seventh fleet* **2** a group of planes, cars etc that are controlled by one company: *a fleet of taxis*

**fleet**[2] *adj literary* fast, quick: **fleet of foot** (=fast at running)

**fleet ad·mi·ral** /ˈ· ˌ···/ *n* [C] the highest rank in the US navy, or someone who holds this rank —see table on page B4

**fleet·ing** /ˈfliːtɪŋ/ *adj* [usually before noun] lasting for only a short time: **fleeting glimpse/impression/glance etc** *I caught a fleeting glimpse of them as they drove past.* | **fleeting moment** *For one fleeting moment, I thought I recognized her.* —**fleetingly** *adv*

**Fleet Street** /ˈ· ·/ *n* [singular] a street in London where many important newspaper offices used to be, often used as a name for the British newspaper industry

**Flem·ish** /ˈflemɪʃ/ *n* [U] a language like German spoken in northern Belgium

W3 **flesh**[1] /fleʃ/ *n* [U] **1** the soft part of the body of a person or animal that is between the skin and the bones: **flesh wound** (=a slight injury from a knife or bullet) **2** the soft part of a fruit or vegetable that can be eaten: *Cut the melon in half and scoop out the flesh.* **3 in the flesh** if you see or meet someone in the flesh, you see or meet someone who you previously had only seen in pictures or films: *Fans flocked to see their heroes in the flesh.* **4 make sb's flesh creep/crawl** to make someone feel frightened: *The way he always stared at her made her flesh creep.* **5 your own flesh and blood** someone who is part of your family: *I couldn't see my own flesh and blood insulted in this way.* **6 the spirit is willing but the flesh is weak** used to say that you would you like to do something, but are not strong enough, either physically or mentally, to do it **7 the flesh** *literary* the physical human body, as opposed to the mind or spirit: **the pleasures of the flesh** (=things such as drinking, eating a lot, or having sex) **8 put flesh on** to give more details about something to make it clear, more interesting etc: *I'll try to put some flesh on the plan Margaret has outlined.* **9 more than flesh and blood can stand/bear** used to describe something that you find too unpleasant to think about **10 go the way of all flesh** *literary* to die —see also **get your pound of flesh** (POUND[1] (6)), **press the flesh** (PRESS[1] (15))

**flesh**[2] *v*

**flesh** sth↔ **out** *phr v* [T] to add more details to something in order to improve it: *You need to flesh out your argument with a few more examples.*

**flesh-col·oured** *BrE*, **flesh-colored** *AmE* /ˈ· ˌ··/ *adj* having a pinkish colour like that of white people's skin: *flesh-coloured tights*

**flesh·ly** /ˈfleʃli/ *adj* [only before noun] *literary* physical, especially sexual

**flesh·pots** /ˈfleʃpɒts‖-pɑːts/ *n* [plural] *humorous* areas where there are many places that people go to for pleasure, especially sexual pleasure: *the fleshpots of Rio*

**flesh·y** /ˈfleʃi/ *adj* **1** having a lot of flesh: *the fleshy part of your hand* **2** having a soft, thick inner part: *a plant with dark green fleshy leaves*

**flew** /fluː/ the past tense of FLY[1]

**flex**[1] /fleks/ *v* [T] **1** tighten your muscles or bend part of your body **2 flex your muscles** to show your ability to do something, especially your skill or power

**flex**[2] *n* [C] *BrE* an electrical wire covered with plastic, used to connect electrical equipment to an electricity supply; CORD[1] (3) *AmE* —see also LEAD[2] (8)

**flex·ib·il·i·ty** /ˌfleksəˈbɪləti/ *n* [U] **1** the ability to change or be changed easily to suit a different situation **2** the ability to bend or be bent easily

**flex·i·ble** /ˈfleksəbəl/ *adj* **1** a person, plan etc that is flexible can change or be changed easily to suit any new situation: *We can be flexible about your starting date.* —opposite INFLEXIBLE **2** something that is flexible can bend or be bent easily: *shoes with flexible rubber soles* —**flexibly** *adv*

**flex·i·time** /ˈfleksitaɪm/ *BrE*, **flex·time** /ˈflekstaɪm/ *AmE* —*n* [U] a system in which people work a fixed number of hours each week or month, but can change the times at which they start and finish each day

**flick**[1] /flɪk/ *v* **1** [T] to make something move away by hitting or pushing it suddenly or quickly, especially with your thumb and finger: **flick sth from/off etc** *Papa flicked the ash from his cigar.* | **flick sth ↔ away/off etc** *I flicked away the dandruff from his shoulders.* —see picture on page 1259 **2** [I always + adv/prep,T] to move with a sudden, quick movement or to make something move in this way: [+ **from/up/down**] *The cow's tail flicked from side to side.* **3** [T] to make a light, machine etc stop or start working by pressing or moving a button: **flick sth↔ on/off** *Sandra flicked the TV on.* **4** [T] if you flick something such as a whip or rope, you move it so that the end moves quickly away from you: *Ricky flicked a towel at his sister's bare legs.*

**flick through** sth *phr v* [T] to look at a book, magazine, set of photographs etc quickly

**flick**[2] *n* **1** [C] a short, light, sudden movement or hit with a part of your body, whip etc: *With a flick of the wrist, Frye sent the ball into the opposite court.* **2 a flick of a switch** used to emphasize how easy it is to start a machine and use it: *All it takes is a flick of a switch.* **3** [C usually singular] *old-fashioned especially AmE* a film **4 the flicks** *BrE old-fashioned* the cinema **5 have a flick through** to look at a book, magazine, set of pictures etc very quickly: *I had a quick flick through your report.*

**flick·er**[1] /ˈflɪkə‖-ər/ *v* [I] **1** to burn or shine with an unsteady light that goes on and off quickly: *The candle flickered.* **2** [always + adv/prep] if an emotion or expression flickers on someone's face or through their mind, it exists or is shown for only a short time: [+ **across/through/on etc**] *A puzzled smile flickered across the lady's face.* **3** to quickly make a sudden small movement or series of movements: *Polly's eyelids flickered for a moment, then she slept.*

**flicker**[2] *n* [C] **1** an unsteady light that goes on and off quickly: *the flicker of the firelight* **2 a flicker of interest/remorse/guilt etc** a feeling or expression that continues for a very short time **3** a quick sudden movement or series of movements

**flick knife** /ˈ· ·/ *n* [C] *BrE* a knife with a blade inside the handle that moves quickly into position when you press a button; SWITCHBLADE *AmE*

**fli·er** /ˈflaɪə-ər/ *n* another spelling of FLYER

**flies** /flaɪz/ —see FLY[3]

**flight** /flaɪt/ *n* S W

**1 ► TRAVEL ◄** [C] a journey in a plane or space vehicle: *It's an hour's flight to Paris from here.*

**2 ► PLANE ◄** [C] a plane making a particular journey: *TWA Flight 284* | **call a flight** (=tell people the plane is ready to leave) *I've got to run – my flight's been called.* —see also CHARTER FLIGHT

**3 ► FLYING ◄** [U] the act of flying through the air: **in flight** *pelicans in flight*

**4 ► STAIRS ◄** [C] a set of stairs between one floor and the next: *Bert lives two flights down from here.* | **flight of stairs** *She tripped and fell down a whole flight of stairs.*

**5 ► ESCAPE ◄** [U] the act of escaping from a dangerous situation or a difficult problem: [+ **from**] *Donald Wood's hasty flight from South Africa early in 1978*

**6 take (to) flight** to run away in order to try and escape from someone: *The rest of the gang took flight.*

**7 put sb to flight** *old-fashioned* make someone run away in order to try and escape

**8 flight of imagination/fancy/fantasy** thoughts, ideas etc that are full of imagination but that are not practical or sensible

**9 ► BIRDS ◄** [C] a group of birds all flying together: *a flight of swallows* —see also IN-FLIGHT, TOP-FLIGHT

**flight at·tend·ant** /ˈ· ·ˌ··/ *n* [C] someone who looks after the comfort and safety of the passengers on a plane; STEWARD (1) or STEWARDESS

**flight deck** /ˈ· ·/ *n* [C] **1** the flat surface of a ship which military aircraft use to fly into the air from **2** the room in a plane where the pilot sits to control the plane

**flight·less** /ˈflaɪtləs/ *adj* unable to fly: *a flightless bird*

**flight lieu·ten·ant** /ˌ· ·ˈ··◂/ *n* [C] *BrE* a middle rank in the British air force, or someone who holds this rank —see table on page B4

**flight path** /ˈ· ·/ *n* [C] the course that a plane or space vehicle travels along

**flight re·cord·er** /ˈ· ·ˌ··/ *n* [C] a piece of equipment in an aircraft that records details such as the plane's speed and direction; BLACK BOX

**flight ser·geant** /ˈ· ˌ··/ *n* [C] *BrE* a middle rank in the British air force, or someone who holds this rank —see table on page B4

**flight sim·u·la·tor** /ˈ· ˌ····/ *n* [C] a machine that imitates the movements of an aircraft, used to train pilots

**flight·y** /ˈflaɪti/ *adj* a woman who is flighty changes her ideas or activities a lot without finishing them or being serious about them —**flightiness** *n* [U]

**flim·flam** /ˈflɪmflæm/ *n informal* **1** [U] stories, information etc that do not seem serious or true: *all this psychic flimflam* **2** [C usually singular] a trick intended to cheat someone —**flimflam** *v* [T]

**flim·sy** /ˈflɪmzi/ *adj* **1** flimsy cloth or clothing is light and thin, and can tear easily: *a flimsy summer dress* **2** flimsy equipment, buildings etc are not well-made and are easily broken **3** a flimsy argument, excuse etc is not believable: *The evidence against him is extremely flimsy.* —**flimsily** *adv* —**flimsiness** *n* [U]

**flinch** /flɪntʃ/ *v* [I] **1** to make a sudden small backward movement when you are shocked by pain or afraid of something **2 sb didn't (even) flinch** used to say that someone did not seem surprised about something **3** to avoid doing something because you dislike it or are afraid of it: **never flinch from doing sth** *He never flinched from doing his duty.*

**fling**[1] /flɪŋ/ *v past tense and past participle* **flung** /flʌŋ/ [T]
**1** ▶**THROW**◀ [always + adv/prep] to throw something quickly with a lot of force: **fling sth at/into/on etc** *Spectators flung bottles and cans at the marchers.* | **fling sth↔ down** *Sammy flings down his coat and stomps upstairs.*
**2** ▶**BODY**◀ [always + adv/prep] to move yourself or part of your body suddenly and with a lot of force: [+ **down/through/towards etc**] *Ian flung himself down on his bed.* | **fling sth around/towards etc** *Flinging his arms around her, he kissed her.* | **fling sth ↔ back/out etc** *Katie flung back her head and laughed.*
**3 fling yourself into** to begin to do something using a lot of effort: *After the divorce he flung himself into his work and tried to forget her.*
**4 fling a door/window etc open** to quickly and suddenly open a door, window etc: *We flung open all the windows.*
**5 fling sb in prison/jail** to put someone in prison, often without having a good reason: *Opposition leaders were flung into jail.*

**fling** sth ↔ **off** *phr v* to quickly remove a piece of clothing, a sheet, or a cover: *Tom flung off his blanket in the middle of the night.*

**fling** sb/sth ↔ **out** *phr v* [T] *especially BrE* **1** to suddenly make someone leave an organization or place **2** [**fling** sth↔ **out**] to get rid of something you no longer want or need

**fling**[2] *n* [C usually singular] **1** a short and not very serious sexual relationship: **have a fling** *They had a brief fling years ago.* **2** a short period of time during which you enjoy yourself without worrying about anything: **have your fling** *I'm going to have my fling first and see a bit of the world.*

**flint** /flɪnt/ *n* **1** [C,U] a type of smooth hard stone, usually black or grey in colour, or a piece of this stone **2** [C] a piece of this stone or a small piece of metal that makes a small flame when you strike it with steel

**flint·lock** /ˈflɪntlɒk‖-lɑːk/ *n* [C] a gun used in the past

**flint·y** /ˈflɪnti/ *adj* a flinty expression or person does not show emotions: *Duvall gave him a flinty stare.*

**flip**[1] /flɪp/ **flipped, flipping** *v* **1** [T] to turn something over or into a different position with a quick, sudden movement: **flip sth↔ open** *Paula flipped the lid of the printer open.* **2** [T] to make a flat object such as a coin go upwards and turn over in the air; TOSS[1] (4): *We flipped a coin to see who would go first.* **3** [I] *informal* also **flip out** to suddenly become very angry or upset: *Dad flipped when he found out I'd been skipping school.* | **flip your lid** (=suddenly become very angry) **4** [I] *AmE informal* to feel very excited and like something very much: [+ **over**] *Krissy really flipped over our kitten.* **5** *especially AmE* [T] to quickly start or stop electrical equipment by pressing or moving a button: *Who flipped the switch?* | **flip sth↔ on/off** *Josie flipped on the radio.*

**flip** sb ↔ **off** *phr v* [T] *AmE* also **flip sb the bird** to make a rude sign at someone by raising your middle finger and keeping your other fingers down

**flip out** *phr v* [I] *informal* **1** to suddenly become very angry or upset: *Francie will flip out if you get a scratch on her new car.* **2** to suddenly start behaving in a crazy way: *The paper says a veteran flipped out and gunned down a bunch of people.*

**flip over** *phr v* [I,T] to turn something from one side onto the other: *Larry flipped over onto his other side, trying to get comfortable.* | **flip sth↔ over** *Mary flipped over the cushions on the couch.*

**flip through** sth *phr v* [T] to look at a book, magazine etc quickly

**flip**[2] *n* [C] **1** a quick, light hit with your thumb or finger, especially one that makes an object turn over in the air: *a flip of the coin* **2** a movement in which you jump up and turn over in the air, so that your feet go over your head

**flip**[3] *adj informal* FLIPPANT

**flip chart** /ˈ· ·/ *n* [C] large pieces of paper that are connected at the top so that the pages can be turned over to present information to groups of people

**flip-flop**[1] /ˈ· ·/ *n* [C] a type of open shoe, usually made of rubber, with only a V-shaped band across the front to hold your feet; THONGS (2) *AmE* —see picture at SHOE[1]

**flip-flop**[2] *v* [I] *AmE informal* to change your opinion about something

**flip·pant** /ˈflɪpənt/ *adj* not being serious about something that other people think you should be serious about, so that they think you do not care: *A hospital is hardly the place for such flippant remarks.* —**flippantly** *adv* —**flippancy** *n* [U]

**flip·per** /ˈflɪpə‖-ər/ *n* [C] **1** a flat part on the body of some large sea animals such as SEALS, used for swimming **2** a large flat rubber shoe worn to help you swim faster

**flip·ping** /ˈflɪpɪŋ/ *adj BrE spoken* used to emphasize what you are saying when you are annoyed: *I'm not flipping waiting any longer.* —**flipping** *adv*

**flip side** /ˈ· ·/ *n* [singular] **1** the side of a record that has a song on it that is less popular than the one on the other side **2** the bad effects of something, after you have just described the good effects: *The flip side is that it may cause more pollution.*

**flirt**[1] /flɜːt‖flɜːrt/ *v* [I] to behave towards and talk to someone as though you are sexually attracted to them, but not in a very serious way: [+ **with**] *Tony flirted with every woman at the party.*

**flirt with** sth *phr v* [T not in passive] **1** to consider doing something, but not be very serious about it **2** to take an unnecessary risk and not be worried about it: *The Prince has always enjoyed flirting with danger.*

**flirt**[2] *n* [C] someone who often behaves towards and talks to people as though she or he is sexually attracted to them, but not in a very serious way

**flir·ta·tion** /flɜːˈteɪʃən‖flɜːr-/ *n* **1** [C] a short period of time during which you are interested in something: [+ **with**] *a brief flirtation with Eastern religions* **2** [U] behaviour that shows a sexual attraction to someone, though not in a serious way **3** [C] a short sexual relationship which is not serious

**flir·ta·tious** /flɜːˈteɪʃəs‖flɜːr-/ *adj* behaving in a way that deliberately tries to attract sexual attention, but not

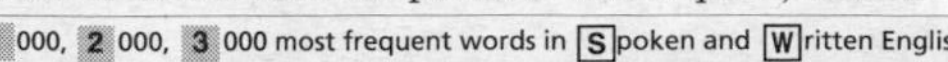

in a serious way: *a flirtatious young girl* —**flirtatiously** *adv* —**flirtatiousness** *n* [U]

**flit** /flɪt/ *v* **flitted, flitting** [I always + adv/prep] to move lightly or quickly and not stay in one place for very long: *birds flitting about from branch to branch* —see also **do a moonlight flit** (MOONLIGHT[1] (2))

**float[1]** /fləʊt‖floʊt/ *v*
**1 ► ON WATER ◄** [I] **a)** to stay or move on the surface of a liquid without sinking: *Wood usually floats.* | *Annie was floating on her back in the pool.* | **along/down/past etc** *The logs floated down the river.* **b)** [T] to put something on the surface of a liquid so that it does not sink: *Pour the coffee and brandy into a mug, then float the cream on top.*
**2 ► IN THE AIR ◄** [I always + adv/prep] if something floats, especially something very light or filled with air, it moves slowly in the air or stays up in the air: [+ **up/down/through etc**] *He watched the balloon float up into the sky.*
**3 ► MUSIC/SOUNDS/SMELLS ETC ◄** [I always + adv/prep] if sounds, smells etc float somewhere, people in another place can hear or smell them: [+ **down/towards/into etc**] *The sound of her voice came floating down from an upstairs window.*
**4 ► MONEY ◄** [I,T] *technical* if a country floats its money or its money floats, the value of the money is allowed to change freely in relation to money from other countries: *Russia floated the ruble on the foreign exchange market.*

**5 ► SUGGEST ◄** [T] to suggest an idea or plan, especially in order to find out what people think about it: *The idea was first floated in a speech given by the President a few months ago.*
**6 ► COMPANY ◄** [T] to sell shares (SHARE[2] (6)) in a company or business to the public for the first time —see also FLOTATION (1)
**7 ► CHEQUE ◄** *AmE* [T] to write a cheque that you do not have enough money in the bank to pay; BOUNCE[1] (3) *BrE*
**8 ► MOVE GRACEFULLY ◄** [I] to move gracefully and lightly: *Rachel floated around the bedroom in a lace nightgown.*
**9 ► NO DEFINITE PURPOSE ◄** [I always + adv/prep] to keep changing what you are doing without having any particular ideas or plans: *Dean seems to float from job to job, never getting anywhere.* —**floater** *n* [C]

**float[2]** *n* [C] **1** a large vehicle that is decorated to be part of a PARADE[1] (1): *a procession of Carnival floats* —see also MILK FLOAT **2** *AmE* a SOFT DRINK[2] (1) that has ice cream floating in it **3** a light object that floats on the surface of the water, used especially for catching fish **4** a light object used when swimming to support your body **5** a small amount of money that someone in a shop keeps so that they have enough money to give change to people

**floa·ta·tion** /fləʊˈteɪʃən‖floʊ-/ *n* [C] a British spelling of FLOTATION

**float·ing** /ˈfləʊtɪŋ‖ˈfloʊ-/ *adj* **1 floating population** if a city has a floating population, the number of people who live there keeps changing because people move into and out of it **2** *technical* an organ or part of your body that is floating is not properly connected or is not in the usual place

**floating vot·er** /ˌ·· ˈ··/ *n* [C] someone who is not sure which political party to vote for at an election

**flock[1]** /flɒk‖flɑːk/ *n* **1** [C] a group of sheep, goats, or birds —compare HERD[1] (1) **2** [C usually singular] a large group of the same kind of people: [+ **of**] *a flock of tourists* **3** [C usually singular] *formal or humorous* a priest's flock is the group of people who regularly attend his church **4** [U] small pieces of wool, cotton etc used for filling CUSHIONS[1] (1) **5** also **flock·ing** /ˈflkIŋ‖ˈflɑː-/ *AmE* a soft substance used to make patterns on the surface of wallpaper, curtains, etc

**flock[2]** *v* [I always + adv/prep] to go to a place in large numbers because something interesting or exciting is happening there: **flock to/into/around etc** *Californians are flocking to enrol in special aerobics classes.*

**floe** /fləʊ‖floʊ/ *n* [C] see ICE FLOE

**flog** /flɒg‖flɑːg/ *v* **flogged, flogging** [T] **1** to beat a person or animal with a whip or stick: *Thieves were flogged in public.* **2** *especially BrE informal* to sell **3 be flogging a dead horse** *spoken* to be wasting time or effort by trying to do something that is impossible **4 flog sth to death** *especially BrE informal* to repeat a story, complaint, idea etc so often that people become bored with it

**flog·ging** /ˈflɒgɪŋ‖ˈflɑːgɪŋ/ *n* [C] a punishment in which someone is severely beaten with a whip or stick

**flood[1]** /flʌd/ *v* S3
**1 ► COVER WITH WATER ◄** [I,T] to make a place become covered, or to become covered with water: *Three days of heavy rain flooded many Eastern cities.* | *The basement flooded and everything got soaked.*
**2 ► GO/ARRIVE IN LARGE AMOUNTS/NUMBERS ◄** [I] to arrive or go somewhere in large numbers: [+ **in/into/out/across etc**] *Letters came flooding in from irate viewers.* | *Refugees flooded across the border.*
**3 be flooded with** to receive so many things such as letters, complaints, or inquiries that you cannot deal with them: *We've been flooded with offers of help.*
**4 ► SEND LARGE AMOUNTS/NUMBERS ◄** [T] to send a large number of things such as letters or complaints to an organization so that it is difficult for people there to deal with them: **flood sth with** *Campaigners flooded Congress with letters of protest.*
**5 flood the market** to sell something in very large numbers or amounts, so that the price goes down: [+ **with**] *Japanese companies were accused of flooding the market with cheap steel.*
**6 ► RIVER ◄** [I,T] if a river floods, it is too full, and spreads water over the land around it
**7 ► ENGINE ◄** [I,T] if an engine floods or you flood it, it has too much petrol in it, so that it will not start
**8 ► LIGHT ◄** [I,T] if light floods a place or floods into it, it makes it very light and bright: *The sunset flooded the canyon with rose-colored light.*
**9 ► FEELING ◄** [I,T] if a feeling or memory floods over someone or floods back, they feel or remember it very strongly: [+ **over/back**] *I felt happiness and relief flooding over me.*
**10 flood with tears** if someone's face floods with tears, they cry a lot

**flood** sb↔ **out** *phr v* **be flooded out** to be forced to leave your home because of floods

**flood[2]** *n* **1** [C,U] a very large amount of water that covers an area that is usually dry: *Floods in Bangladesh caused over 1000 deaths.* —see picture on page 836 **2 flood of** a very large number of things or people that arrive at the same time: *A TV show featuring sexy home videos was halted after a flood of complaints.* **3 in floods of tears** crying a lot **4 the Flood** the great flood described in the Bible story, that covered the world: **before the Flood** (=a very long time ago) **5 be in flood** a river that is in flood has much more water in it than usual —see also FLASH FLOOD S3

**flood·gate** /ˈflʌdgeɪt/ *n* [C usually plural] **1 open the floodgates a)** to suddenly make it possible for a lot of people to do something by removing laws and rules which had previously prevented or controlled it: *worries that a Labour government would open the floodgates to immigration* **b)** to make someone show their true feelings which they have been trying not to show **2** a gate used to control the flow of water from a large lake, river etc

**flood·ing** /ˈflʌdɪŋ/ *n* [U] a situation in which an area of land becomes covered with water, for example because of heavy rain

**flood·light** /ˈflʌdlaɪt/ *n* [C usually plural] a very bright light, used to light the outside of buildings, sports grounds etc at night

**flood·lit** /ˈflʌdlɪt/ *adj* surrounded by floodlights so that people can see at night

**flood plain** /ˈ· ·/ *n* [C] the large area of flat land on either side of a river that is sometimes covered with water

**flood tide** /ˈ· ·/ *n* [C] the flow of the TIDE[1] (1) in towards the land —opposite EBB[1] (1)

S1 W1 **floor**[1] /flɔː‖flɔːr/ *n*

**1 ▶ FLAT SURFACE ◀** [C] the flat surface on which you stand indoors: *Amos ran inside, spreading mud all over the kitchen floor.* —see picture on page 833 —see LAND[1] (USAGE)

**2 ▶ LEVEL IN BUILDING ◀** [C] one of the levels in a building: *Our office is on the top floor.*|*a two-bedroomed ground floor flat*

**3 ▶ OCEAN/FOREST/CAVE FLOOR ETC ◀** [singular] the ground at the bottom of the ocean, the forest etc: *creatures that live on the ocean floor*

**4 the floor a)** the people attending a public meeting: *Are there any questions from the floor?* **b)** the part of a parliament, public meeting place etc where people sit: *The delegates crowded the floor of the House.*

**5 take the floor a)** to begin speaking at an important public meeting **b)** to begin dancing

**6 have the floor** to be speaking or have the right to speak at an important public meeting: *The Senator from Wyoming had the floor.*

**7 ▶ DANCE ◀** an area where people dance: **dance floor** *Couples were already gliding over the dance floor.*

**8 ▶ WHERE PEOPLE WORK ◀** [C] a large area in a building where a lot of people do their jobs: *The stock market floor was wildly busy.*|**shop floor** (=the area in a factory where people work using machines) *The manager's office is above the shop floor.*

**9 ▶ CAR ◀** [C] *BrE* the part of a car that forms its inside floor; FLOORBOARD (2) *AmE*

**10 go through the floor** if a price, amount etc goes through the floor, it becomes very low: *In the past few years share prices have gone through the floor.*

**11 ▶ LIMIT ◀** [singular] an officially agreed limit so that something cannot go below a certain value: **put a floor under** *The French government tried to put a floor under the value of the Franc.* —see also **be/get in on the ground floor** (GROUND FLOOR (2)), **wipe the floor with** (WIPE[1] (5))

**12** [C] *BrE* the area of the stock exchange where people buy and sell shares (SHARE[2] (6))

**USAGE NOTE: FLOOR**

In American English the bottom floor of a building (at ground level) is called the **first floor.** In British English this is called the **ground floor.**

The next level up is called the **second floor** in American English and the **first floor** in British English.

GRAMMAR

People say *He lives on the second/ninth/etc floor* (NOT *at/in the second/ninth etc floor*).

**floor**[2] *v* [T] **1** to surprise or shock someone so much that they do not know what to say or do: *Her last question completely floored me.* **2** to hit someone so hard that they fall down: *The Champion floored Watson with a single punch.* **3 floor it** *AmE informal* to make a car go as fast as possible

**floor·board** /ˈflɔːbɔːd‖ˈflɔːrbɔːrd/ *n* [C] **1** [usually plural] a board in a wooden floor —see picture at BOARD **2** *AmE* the floor in a car

**floor·ing** /ˈflɔːrɪŋ/ *n* [U] material used to make or cover floors

**floor lamp** /ˈ· ·/ *n* [C] *AmE* a lamp at the top of a tall pole on a flat base that stands on the floor of a room; STANDARD LAMP *BrE* —see picture at LIGHT[1]

**floor-length** /ˈ· ·/ *adj* long enough to reach the floor: *a floor-length evening gown*

**floor mod·el** /ˈ· ˌ··/ *n* [C] *AmE* a piece of furniture or equipment for the home, such as a washing machine, that has been in a store for people to look at and is often sold at a cheaper price

**floor plan** /ˈ· ·/ *n* [C] a drawing of the shape of a room or area in a building and the position of things in it, as seen from above

**floor show** /ˈ· ·/ *n* [C] a performance by singers, dancers etc at a NIGHTCLUB

**floo·zy, floozie** /ˈfluːzi/ *n* [C] *old-fashioned* a woman who is sexually immoral and who you disapprove of

**flop**[1] /flɒp‖flɑːp/ *v* **flopped, flopping** [I] **1** [always + adv/prep] also **flop down** to sit or lie down in a relaxed way, by letting all your weight fall heavily onto a chair etc: [+ **in/onto/across etc**] *"I'm exhausted," said Max, flopping into a chair.* **2** [always + adv/prep] to move or fall in an awkward, or uncontrolled way: [+ **around/along/onto etc**] *A bird with an injured wing flopped helplessly along the ground.* **3** *informal* if something such as a product, play, or plan flops, it is not successful because people do not like it: *Despite all the media hype 'Heaven's Gate' flopped at the box office.*

**flop**[2] *n* **1** [C] *informal* a film, play, product etc that is not successful: *The show was a flop and lasted only one night.* **2** [singular] the movement or noise that something makes when it falls heavily: *He fell with a flop into the water.* **3** *AmE* a flophouse —see also BELLY FLOP, FLIP-FLOP

**flop·house** /ˈflɒphaʊs‖ˈflɑːp-/ *n* [C] *AmE slang* a cheap hotel, that often has many beds in one room; DOSS HOUSE *BrE*

**flop·py** /ˈflɒpi‖ˈflɑːpi/ *adj* soft and often hanging loosely downwards: *a dog with long, floppy ears* —**floppiness** *n* [U]

**floppy disk** /ˌ·· ˈ·/ also **floppy** *n* [C] a square piece of plastic on which information for a computer is stored; DISKETTE —compare HARD DISK

**flo·ra** /ˈflɔːrə/ *n* [U] all the plants of a particular place or country: *the flora of the Alps* —compare FAUNA

**flo·ral** /ˈflɔːrəl/ *adj* decorated with or made of flowers: *floral dresses*|**floral tributes** (flowers at a funeral) —see picture on page 839

**flor·id** /ˈflɒrɪ̣d‖ˈflɔː-, ˈflɑː-/ *adj literary* **1** having a red face: *florid cheeks* **2** having a lot of unnecessary decoration or detail: *florid language* —**floridly** *adv*

**flor·in** /ˈflɒrɪ̣n‖ˈflɔː-, ˈflɑː-/ *n* [C] a coin used in Britain before 1971, ten of which made one pound (£1)

**flor·ist** /ˈflɒrɪ̣st‖ˈflɔː-/ *n* [C] **1** someone who owns or works in a shop that sells flowers **2** also **florist's** a shop that sells flowers

**floss**[1] /flɒs‖flɑːs, flɔːs/ *n* [U] **1** thin silk used for sewing **2** DENTAL FLOSS —see also CANDYFLOSS

**floss**[2] *v* [T] to clean between your teeth with DENTAL FLOSS

**flo·ta·tion** /fləʊˈteɪʃən‖floʊ-/ *n* [C,U] **1** the act of offering shares (SHARE[2] (6)) in a company to the public for the first time: *a massive flotation of government bonds* **2 flotation chamber/compartment etc** a container filled with air or gas, fixed to something to make it float

**flo·til·la** /fləˈtɪlə‖floʊ-/ *n* [C] a group of small ships

**flot·sam** /ˈflɒtsəm‖ˈflɑː-/ *n* [U] **1** broken pieces of wood, plastic etc from a wrecked ship floating in the sea or scattered on the shore —compare JETSAM **2** also **flotsam and jet·sam** /ˌ·· · ˈ··/ people who do not have jobs or homes

**flounce**[1] /flaʊns/ *v* [I always + adv/prep] to move in a way that shows that you are angry: [+ **out/off/past etc**] *Sandra flounced out of the room.*

**flounce**[2] *n* **1** [C] a band of cloth on clothing that is stitched into folds as a decoration **2** [singular] a sudden quick movement that shows people that you are annoyed

**flounced** /flaʊnst/ *adj* a flounced skirt or dress is one that is decorated with flounces

**floun·der¹** /ˈflaʊndə‖-ər/ *v* [I] **1** [always + adv/prep] to move awkwardly or with difficulty, especially in water, mud etc **2** to be unable to decide what to say or do so that you find it difficult to continue: *He left his interviewer floundering by answering every question with the word 'no'.* **3** to have a lot of problems and have difficulty continuing: *Brando's career was floundering when he was offered the role.*

**flounder²** *n* [C] a small flat fish, used as food

**flour¹** /flaʊə‖flaʊr/ *n* [U] a powder made by crushing grain, especially wheat, and used for making bread, cakes etc —see also PLAIN FLOUR, SELF-RAISING FLOUR

**flour²** *v* [T] to cover a surface with flour

**flour·ish ¹** /ˈflʌrɪʃ‖ˈflɜːrɪʃ/ *v* **1** [I] to grow well and be very healthy; THRIVE: *The plants flourished in the warm sun.* **2** [I] to develop well and be successful: *Russia's flourishing black market economy* **3** [T] to wave something in your hand in order to make people notice it: *Ellie ran in, flourishing her acceptance letter.*

**flour·ish²** *n* **1 with a flourish** with a large confident movement that makes people notice you: *Mr Darcy swept back his hat with a flourish.* **2** [C] something such as a decoration or detail that is not necessary: *His speech was full of rhetorical flourishes.* **3** [C] a curved line when writing, which is done for decoration **4** [C] a loud part of a piece of music, played especially when an important person enters: *a flourish of trumpets*

**flour·mill** /ˈflaʊəˌmɪl‖/ *n* [C] a place where flour is made from grain

**flour·y** /ˈflaʊəri‖ˈflaʊri/ *adj* covered with or tasting of flour

**flout** /flaʊt/ *v* [T] to deliberately disobey a law, rule etc: *Countries that flout the agreement will have sanctions imposed on them.*

S2 W2 **flow¹** /fləʊ‖floʊ/ *n*

**1 ▶ MOVEMENT OF LIQUID ◀** [C usually singular] a smooth steady movement or supply of liquid: *Smoking affects the flow of blood to the brain.*

**2 ▶ SUPPLY/MOVEMENT ◀** [C usually singular] a continuous supply or movement of something from one place to another: [+ **of**] *the flow of arms into Bosnia*

**3 in full flow** if someone is in full flow, they are busy talking about something and seem likely to continue for a long time

**4 ▶ WORDS/IDEAS ◀** [U] the continuous stream of words or ideas when someone is speaking, writing, or thinking about something: **break/interrupt sb's flow** *You've interrupted my flow now – I don't know what I was going to say next.*

**5 ▶ OF THE SEA ◀** [singular] the movement of the TIDE¹ (1) towards the land: *the ebb and flow of the tide*

**6 go with the flow** to decide to do the same thing as other people, and not ask if you can do something different: *I don't mind, I'll just go with the flow.*

**7 go against the flow** to do something very different from what other people are doing —see also CASH FLOW, **ebb and flow** (EBB¹ (3))

S3 **flow²** *v* [I]

**1 ▶ LIQUID ◀** if a liquids flows, it moves in a steady continuous stream: [+ **over/down/through etc**] *A great river flowed along the valley.*

**2 ▶ GOODS/INFORMATION/PEOPLE ETC ◀** if goods, information, people etc flow, they move or are supplied continuously in large numbers from one place to another:[+ **in/out/through/from etc**] *Money has been flowing into the country from Western aid agencies.*

**3 ▶ TRAFFIC ◀** if traffic flows, it moves easily from one place to another

**4 ▶ ALCOHOL ◀** if alcohol flows at a party, people drink a lot and there is a lot available: **flow freely** *The champagne flowed freely and everyone had a good time.*

**5 ▶ WORDS/IDEAS ◀** if conversation or ideas flow, people talk or have ideas steadily and continuously, without anything stopping or interrupting them: **flow easily/freely** *The wine loosened our tongues, and conversation flowed freely.*

**6 flow from** to come from a particular idea, place, or person: *the political wrangle that has flowed from this decision*

**7 ▶ FEELINGS ◀** if an emotion flows, someone feels it strongly: [+ **through/into/from etc**] *Compassion for Mattie flowed through her.*

**8 ▶ CLOTHES/HAIR ◀** if clothing, hair etc flows, it falls or hangs loosely and gracefully

**9 ▶ SEA ◀** if the TIDE¹ (1) flows, it moves towards the land —compare EBB² (1)

**flow chart** /ˈ· ·/ also **flow di·a·gram** /ˈ· ˌ···/ *n* [C] a drawing that uses shapes and lines to show how a series of actions or parts of a system are connected with each other: *a flow chart of the company's managerial structure*

**flow·er¹** /ˈflaʊə‖-ər/ *n* **1** [C] the coloured part of a plant or tree that produces seeds or fruit: *Fruit trees produce flowers in the spring.* **2** [C] a small plant that is grown for the beauty of this part: *He grows flowers in the front garden.* **3 in flower** a plant or tree that is in flower has flowers on it: **come into flower** (=start to have flowers) *Roses usually come into flower in May or June.* **4 the flower of** *literary* the best part or most perfect part of something: *The flower of the nation's youth was lost in the war.* **5** *BrE old-fashioned* used to address someone in a friendly and informal way S2 W2

**flower²** *v* [I] **1** to produce flowers **2** *formal* to develop and reach a high level of achievement: *English painting flowered briefly during the Renaissance.*

**flower ar·rang·ing** /ˈ·· ˌ··/ *n* [U] the art of arranging flowers in an attractive way

**flow·er·bed** /ˈflaʊəbed‖-ər-/ *n* [C] an area of ground in which flowers are grown

**flower child** /ˈ·· ·/ *n plural* **flower children** [C] a young person in the 1960s and 70s who was against war and wanted peace and love in society

**flow·ered** /ˈflaʊəd‖-ərd/ *adj* decorated with pictures of flowers: *flowered curtains*

**flower girl** /ˈ·· ·/ *n* [C] **1** *BrE* a girl or woman who sells flowers in a street market **2** *AmE* a young girl who carries flowers in a wedding ceremony —compare BRIDESMAID

**flow·er·ing** /ˈflaʊərɪŋ/ *n* **the flowering of** a successful period in the development of something

**flow·er·less** /ˈflaʊələs‖-ərləs/ *adj* not producing flowers

**flower peo·ple** /ˈ·· ˌ··/ *n* [plural] *BrE* young people in the 1960s and 70s who were against war and wanted peace and love in society

**flow·er·pot** /ˈflaʊəpɒt‖-ərpɑːt/ *n* [C] a plastic or clay pot in which you grow plants

**flower pow·er** /ˈ·· ˌ··/ *n* [U] the ideas of young people in the 1960s and 70s who believed that peace and love were the most important things in life

**flower show** /ˈ·· ˌ·/ *n* [C] a show at which people can look at different kinds of flowers and plants

**flow·er·y** /ˈflaʊəri/ *adj* **1** decorated with pictures of flowers: *a flowery pattern* **2** flowery speech or writing uses complicated and rare words instead of simple clear language

**flow·ing** /ˈfləʊɪŋ‖ˈfloʊ-/ *adj* moving, curving, or hanging gracefully: *long flowing white hair*

**flown** /fləʊn‖floʊn/ the past participle of FLY¹

**flow sheet** /ˈ· ·/ *n* [C] an American form of FLOW CHART

**fl. oz.** *n* the written abbreviation of FLUID OUNCE

**flu** /fluː/ *n* [C,U] a common infectious disease which is like a bad COLD² (2) but is more serious; INFLUENZA: **the flu** *Darby's been in bed with the flu.* | **flu** *BrE*: *Kate's got flu.*

**flub** /flʌb/ *v* [I,T] *AmE* to make a stupid mistake, or fail to do something by making a mistake: *He flubbed his first try at the SAT.*

**fluc·tu·ate** /ˈflʌktʃueɪt/ *v* [I] if something such as a price or amount fluctuates, it changes very often from a high level to a low one and back again: [+ **between**] *The present output of oil fluctuates between 3 and 5 million gallons per week.* | **fluctuate wildly** *House prices fluctuated wildly in the 80s.*

**fluc·tu·a·tion** /ˌflʌktʃuˈeɪʃən/ *n* [C,U] sudden changes in something such as the price, amount, or level of something: *price fluctuations*

**flue** /fluː/ *n* [C] a metal pipe or tube, especially in a CHIMNEY, that lets smoke or heat from a fire out of a building

**flu·ent** /ˈfluːənt/ *adj* **1** able to speak a language very well: *"Can she speak Arabic?" "Yes, she's fluent."* **2 fluent French/Japanese etc** someone who speaks fluent French etc speaks it like a person from that country **3** speaking, writing, or playing a musical instrument confidently and without long pauses: —**fluently** *adv* —**fluency** *n* [U]

**fluff**[1] /flʌf/ *n* [U] **1** soft, light bits of thread or wool that have come from wool, cotton, or other materials **2** soft light hair or feathers, especially from a young bird or animal —compare DOWN[5] (2) —see also **bit of fluff** (BIT[1] (19))

**fluff**[2] *v* [T] **1** also **fluff up, fluff out** to make something soft appear larger by shaking or brushing it: *Sue fluffed the pillows for me.* **2** also **fluff up, fluff out** if a bird fluffs its feathers, it raises them and makes itself look bigger **3** *informal* to make a mistake or do something badly: *Rupert fluffed the catch.* | **fluff your lines** (=make a mistake when speaking in a play)

**fluff·y** /ˈflʌfi/ *adj* **1** made of or covered with something soft and light, such as wool, hair or feathers: *a fluffy little kitten* **2** food that is fluffy is made soft and light by shaking, or beating so that air is mixed into it: *Cream the butter and sugar until fluffy.* —**fluffiness** *n* [U]

**flu·id**[1] /ˈfluːɪ̈d/ *n* [C,U] *technical* a liquid: *The doctor told him to drink a litre of fluid a day.*

**fluid**[2] adj **1** fluid movements are relaxed and graceful: *fluid and expressive gestures* **2** [not before noun] a situation or system that is fluid is likely to change often, or is able to change —**fluidity** /fluˈɪdɪ̈ti/ *n* [U]

**fluid ounce** /ˌ·· ˈ·/ *n* [C] a unit for measuring liquids, equal to 0.0284 of a litre —see tables on page B2 and B3

**fluke** /fluːk/ *n* [C] *informal* something that is unlikely or surprising and only happens because of luck *It was a complete fluke, meeting my sister at the airport.* —**fluky, flukey** *adj*

**flum·moxed** /ˈflʌməkst/ *adj* completely confused by something: *I was totally flummoxed by his last question.* —**flummox** *v* [T]

**flung** /flʌŋ/ the past tense and past participle of FLING[1]

**flunk** /flʌŋk/ *v informal especially AmE* **1** [I,T] to fail a test: *Tony flunked chemistry last semester.* **2** [T] to give someone low marks on a test so that they fail it

**flunk out** *phr v* [I] *informal especially AmE* to be forced to leave a school or college because your work is not good enough: *Ben messed around and flunked out of college.*

**flun·key, flunky** /ˈflʌŋki/ *n* [C] someone who is always with an important person and treats them with too much respect: *The Stones were surrounded by the usual flunkeys and hangers-on.*

**flu·o·res·cent** /flʊəˈresənt‖flʊ-, flɔː-/ *adj* **1** fluorescent colours are very bright and easy to see, even in the dark: *a fluorescent pink T-shirt* **2** a fluorescent substance produces a bright white light when electricity or other types of power pass through it —**fluorescence** *n* [U]

**fluorescent light** /·ˌ·· ˈ·/ a fluorescent light produces light when electricity is passed through a gas-filled tube

**flu·o·ri·date** /ˈflʊərɪ̈deɪt‖ˈflʊr-, ˈflɔːr-/ *v* [T] to add fluoride to water in order to protect people's teeth —**fluoridation** /ˌflʊərɪ̈ˈdeɪʃən‖ˌflʊr-, ˌflɔːr-/ *n* [U]

**flu·o·ride** /ˈflʊəraɪd‖ˈflʊraɪd/ *n* [U] a chemical compound of fluorine, especially one that helps to protect teeth against decay

**flu·o·rine** /ˈflʊəriːn‖ˈflʊriːn/ *n* [U] a chemical substance that is usually in the form of a poisonous gas

**fluo·ro·car·bon** /ˌflʊərəʊˈkɑːbən‖ˌflʊroʊˈkɑːr-/ *n* [C] any chemical that contains the substances fluorine and CARBON (1): *damage to the ozone layer caused by fluorocarbons* —see also CFC

**flur·ried** /ˈflʌrid‖ˈflɜːrid/ *adj* confused and nervous or excited: *the flurried activity surrounding the wedding*

**flur·ry** /ˈflʌri‖ˈflɜːri/ *n* **1** [singular] an occasion when there is suddenly a lot of activity within a short period of time: [+ **of**] *After a quiet spell there was a sudden flurry of phone calls.* **2** [C] if there is a flurry of snow, rain, or wind, it suddenly starts snowing etc for a short time: *Snow flurries are expected overnight.*

**flush**[1] /flʌʃ/ *n* **1** [singular] a red colour that appears on your face or body, especially because you are embarrassed, ill, or excited: *"How can you tell?" he said as a flush crept up his neck.* —see also HOT FLUSH **2 a flush of pride/embarrassment etc** a sudden feeling of pride, excitement, or another emotion **3 the first flush of youth/success etc** the beginning of a period of time when you feel excited because you are young, successful etc **4** [C] a set of cards that someone has in a card game that are all of the same suit (SUIT[1] (3)) **5** [C] the part of a toilet that cleans it with a sudden flow of water **6** [C] the act of cleaning something by forcing water through it

**flush**[2] *v* **1** [I,T] if you flush a toilet or if it flushes, you make water go through it to clean it: **flush sth down the toilet** *Mandy accidentally flushed her ring down the toilet.* **2** [I] to become red in the face: *Flushing slightly, Lesley looked away.* **3** also **flush out** [T] to clean something by forcing water or another liquid through it: *Try flushing out the blockage with boiling water.* **4** [T always + adv/prep] to make someone leave the place where they are hiding: **flush sb from/out of** *The police managed to flush the gang from their hideout.*

**flush**[3] *adj* **1** if two surfaces are flush they are at exactly the same level, so that the place where they meet is flat: [+ **with**] *Make sure that the cupboard is flush with the wall.* **2** [not before noun] *informal* if someone is flush they suddenly have plenty of money for a short time

**flush**[4] *adv* fitting together so that the place where two surfaces meet is flat: *The door should fit flush into its frame.*

**flushed** /flʌʃt/ *adj* **1** red in the face: *Nona was hot and flushed.* | [+ **with**] *Her face flushed with pride.* **2 flushed with success/excitement** excited and eager because you have achieved something

**flus·ter** /ˈflʌstə‖-ər/ *v* [T] to make someone nervous and confused by making them hurry or interrupting them —**fluster** *n* [singular] *BrE*

**flus·tered** /ˈflʌstəd‖-ərd/ *adj* confused and nervous: *Elijah got really flustered during the interview.*

**flute** /fluːt/ *n* [C] a musical instrument that you play by holding it across your lips, blowing into it, and pressing keys (KEY[1] (3)) with your fingers to change the notes

**flut·ed** /ˈfluːtɪ̈d/ *adj* decorated with long narrow curves that curve inwards: *fluted columns*

**flut·ist** /ˈfluːtɪ̈st/ *n* [C] *AmE* someone who plays the flute; FLAUTIST *BrE*

**flut·ter**[1] /ˈflʌtə‖-ər/ *v* **1** [I,T] if a bird or insect flutters its wings or if its wings flutter, its wings move quickly and lightly up and down: *butterflies fluttering from flower to flower* **2** [I] to wave or move gently in the air: *Dead leaves fluttered slowly to the ground.* **3** [I,T] if your heart or your stomach flutters, you feel very excited or nervous **4 flutter your eyelashes (at sb)** if a woman flutters her eyelashes at a man, she uses her sexual attractiveness to influence him

**flutter**[2] *n* **1** [singular] the state of being nervous, confused or excited: **in a flutter** *We're all in a flutter of excitement at the moment.* | **cause a flutter** (=make people excited or interested) *News of her arrest caused quite a flutter in the office.* **2 have a flutter** *BrE informal* to risk a small amount of money on the result of a horse race; BET[2] (1) **3** [singular] a fluttering movement: *a flutter of wings* **4** [C] *technical* an irregular heart beat **5** [U] *technical* a shaking movement that stops a machine working properly

**flu·vi·al** /ˈfluːviəl/ *adj technical* relating to or produced by rivers

**flux** /flʌks/ *n* [U] **1 be in (a state of) flux** to be changing a lot so that you cannot be sure what will happen: *The education system is in a state of flux, with new requirements constantly being added.* **2** a substance that is added to a metal to help it melt or when sticking two pieces of metal together; SOLDER[1]

S2 W2

**fly[1]** /flaɪ/ *v past tense* **flew** /fluː/ *past participle* **flown** /fləʊn‖floʊn/

① PLANE
② BIRDS/INSECTS ETC
③ FLOAT HIGH IN THE AIR
④ MOVE FREELY
⑤ MOVE/GO FAST
⑥ TIME GOES QUICKLY
⑦ ANGRY
⑧ ATTACK
⑨ OTHER MEANINGS

**① PLANE**

**1** [I] to travel by plane: *You can fly direct from London to Tokyo in under 12 hours now.* | **fly on** (=continue flying to another place) *The first stop is San Francisco, and from there we're flying on to Hawaii.*

**2** [I] to move through the air in order to go from one place to another: *These planes can fly at incredibly high speeds.*

**3** [T] to carry or send goods or people by plane: **fly sth into/out of** *US planes have been flying food and medical supplies into the area.*

**4** [I,T] to use a particular AIRLINE or use a particular type of ticket when flying: *We usually fly economy class.*

**5** [I,T] to control a plane through the air: *The Prince has his own private jet which he flies himself.*

**6 fly a mission** to fly a plane in a war, especially in order to attack an enemy

**7** [T] to cross an area of water in a plane: *the first woman to fly the Atlantic*

**② BIRDS/INSECTS ETC**

**8** [I] to move through the air using wings: [+ **up/into etc**] *a flock of seagulls flying overhead*

**③ FLOAT**

**9** [I always + adv/prep] to float high in the air: *I watched the balloons fly up into the sky.*

**④ MOVE FREELY**

**10** [I] if your hair, coat etc is flying, it moves freely and loosely in the air: *long hair flying in the wind*

**⑤ MOVE/GO FAST**

**11** [I always + adv/prep] to go somewhere very quickly: [+ **down/across/out of etc**] *She flew down the stairs to find out what had happened.*

**12** [I always + adv/prep] to move suddenly and very quickly: [+ **open/shut/back etc**] *The door suddenly flew open.* | *Sparks were flying everywhere.*

**13 send sb/sth flying** to knock somone or something so that they fall through the air: *He crashed into the table and sent the glasses flying.*

**14 go flying** to suddenly fall through the air after being knocked by something or someone: *The boat rocked to the side and I went flying across the room.*

**15 I must fly** *spoken* used to say that you must leave quickly

**⑥ TIME GOES QUICKLY**

**16 time flies** *spoken* used to say that a period of time passes or something happens in an unexpectedly short time: *Is it August already? How time flies!* | **Time flies when you are having fun!** (=often used humorously to mean that something has been very boring)

**17 fly by/past** if a period of time flies by or past, it passes very quickly without you noticing: *We've been so busy, the week has just flown by.*

**⑦ ANGRY**

**18 fly into a temper/rage** to suddenly become extremely angry: *My father flew into a rage and demanded his money back.*

**19 fly off the handle** *informal* to become very angry suddenly and unexpectedly about something that does not seem very important: *There's no need to fly off the handle like that.*

**20 let fly** to suddenly start shouting at someone because you feel very angry about something: [+ **at**] *The woman let fly a torrent of abuse at him.*

**21 go fly a kite** *spoken* used to say that you think that someone is being very annoying

**⑧ ATTACK**

**22 let fly** to suddenly attack someone: [+ **with**] *The soldiers let fly with a hail of machine-gun fire.*

**⑨ OTHER MEANINGS**

**23 ▶ ESCAPE ◀** [T] to leave somewhere in order to escape: *They were forced to fly the country in 1939.*

**24 fly the coop** *informal especially AmE* to leave or escape: *All my children have flown the coop now.*

**25 fly by the seat of your pants** *informal* to do something by guessing how to do it because you have very little knowledge or experience

**26 ▶ FLAG ◀** [I,T] if a flag flies, or if you fly it, it is fixed to a pole or a building, ship etc: *a ship flying the Dutch flag*

**27 fly the flag** to behave in a way that shows that you are proud of your country, organization etc

**28 fly in the face of** to be the opposite of what most people think is reasonable, sensible, or normal: *Eysenck's claim flies in the face of all the evidence.*

**29 rumours/accusations etc are flying** if RUMOURS, ACCUSATIONS etc are flying about something, a lot of people are saying things about it: *Rumours were flying round the capital about a possible military takeover.*

**30 ▶ PLAN ◀** *AmE* [I] a plan that will fly is good or useful —see also **the bird has flown** (BIRD (7)), **as the crow flies** (CROW[1] (3)), **sparks fly** (SPARK[1] (6))

**fly at sb** also **fly into sb** *AmE phr v* [T] to suddenly rush towards someone because you are very angry with them: *The old man flew at her in rage.*

**fly[2]** *v past tense and past participle* **flied** [I] *AmE* to hit a ball in BASEBALL high into the air, especially so that the ball is caught by the other team

**fly[3]** *n* [C]

**1 ▶ INSECT ◀** a small flying insect with two wings: *The flies kept buzzing around us.*

**2 ▶ TROUSERS ◀** also **flies** *BrE* the part at the front of a pair of trousers which you can open and which consists of a ZIP[1] (1) or a row of buttons: *He did up his fly.*

**3 sb wouldn't hurt a fly/sb wouldn't harm a fly** *spoken* used to say that someone is very gentle and is not likely to hurt anyone

**4 be going down like flies/be dropping like flies** *informal* used to say that a lot of people are becoming ill with a particular disease
**5 fly in the ointment** *informal* the only thing that spoils something and prevents it from being successful
**6 be a fly on the wall** to be able to watch what happens without other people knowing that you are there: *I wish I'd been a fly on the wall during that conversation.* —see also FLY-ON-THE-WALL
**7 there are no flies on sb** *BrE spoken* used to say that someone is not stupid and cannot be tricked
**8 ► FISHING ◄** a hook that is made to look like a fly, used for catching fish
**9 ► BASEBALL ◄** a flyball

**fly**[4] *adj old-fashioned especially BrE* clever and not easily tricked: *He's a fly old bird.*

**fly·a·way** /ˈflaɪəweɪ/ *adj* **flyaway hair** hair that is soft and thin and becomes untidy easily

**fly ball** /ˈ· ·/ *n* [C] a ball that has been hit high into the air in a game of BASEBALL

**fly·blown** /ˈflaɪbləʊn‖-bloʊn/ *adj* **1** *especially BrE* old, dirty, and in bad condition **2** *BrE* meat that is flyblown has flies' eggs in it and is not suitable for eating

**fly·boy** /ˈflaɪbɔɪ/ *n* [C] *AmE informal* a pilot

**fly·by** /ˈflaɪbaɪ/ *AmE n* [C] a group of planes that fly close together on a special occasion for people to watch

**fly-by-night** /ˈ· · ˌ·/ *adj* [only before noun] *informal* a fly-by-night company, businessman is not well established and may only be interested in making quick profits

**fly·catch·er** /ˈflaɪˌkætʃə‖-ər/ *n* [C] a small bird that catches flies in the air

**fly-drive hol·i·day** /ˈ· · ˌ···/ *n* [C] a holiday arranged at a fixed price that includes your flight, a car to drive, and a place to stay

**fly·er** /ˈflaɪə‖-ər/ *n* [C] **1** a sheet of paper advertising something, which is given to people in the street or is pushed through their door **2** *informal* a pilot **3** *informal* a FLYING START

**fly·fish·ing** /ˈflaɪˌfɪʃɪŋ/ *n* [U] the sport of fishing in a river or lake with special hooks that are made to look like flies

**fly half** /ˌ· ˈ·/ *n* [C] a fast-running player in RUGBY whose job is to pass the ball to a line of players

**fly·ing**[1] /ˈflaɪ-ɪŋ/ *adj* **1 with flying colours** if you pass a test with flying colours, you are very successful in it **2 a flying visit** a quick visit because you are in a hurry *They've been down here for a flying visit.* **3 a flying jump/leap** a long high jump made while you are running

**flying**[2] *n* [U] the activity of travelling by plane: *fear of flying*

**flying but·tress** /ˌ·· ˈ··/ *n* [C] a half ARCH[1] (1) joined to the top of the outside wall of a large building such as a church in order to support it

**flying doc·tor** /ˌ·· ˈ··/ *n* [C] a doctor, especially in Australia, who goes by plane to visit sick people who live a long way from the nearest town

**flying fish** /ˌ·· ˈ·/ *n* [C] a tropical sea fish that can jump out of the water

**flying fox** /ˌ·· ˈ·/ *n* [C] a FRUIT BAT

**flying of·fic·er** /ˈ·· ˌ···/ *n* [C] a rank in the British air-force —see table on page B4

**flying pick·et** /ˌ·· ˈ··/ *n* [C] someone who travels to different factories, mines etc during a strike (STRIKE[2] (1)) and tries to persuade workers to stop working, although they do not work there themselves

**flying sau·cer** /ˌ·· ˈ··/ *n* [C] a round-shaped SPACECRAFT carrying creatures from space; UFO

**flying squad** /ˈ·· ·/ *n* [C] a special group of police officers in Britain whose job is to travel quickly to the place where there has been a serious crime

**flying start** /ˌ·· ˈ·/ *n* **1 get off to a flying start** *informal* to begin very well: *He's got off to a flying start in his new job.* **2** a start to a race in which the competitors are already moving very quickly

**flying tack·le** /ˌ·· ˈ··/ *n* [C] a way of stopping someone from running by putting your arms around their legs and making them fall over

**fly leaf** /ˈ· ·/ *n* [C] a page at the beginning or end of a book, on which there is usually no printing

**fly-on-the-wall** /ˌ· · · ˈ·◄/ *adj* [only before noun] a fly-on-the-wall television programme shows people's daily lives in a very natural way, because they forget they are being filmed

**fly·o·ver** /ˈflaɪ-əʊvə‖-oʊvər/ *n* [C] **1** *BrE* a bridge that carries a road over another road; OVERPASS *AmE* —see picture on page 415 **2** *AmE* a flypast

**fly·pa·per** /ˈflaɪˌpeɪpə‖-ər/ *n* [C,U] paper covered with a sticky substance used to catch flies

**fly·past** /ˈflaɪpɑːst‖-pæst/ *n* [C] *BrE* a group of planes that fly close together on a special occasion for people to watch

**fly·sheet** /ˈflaɪʃiːt/ also **fly** *n* [C] a sheet of material that is put over a tent to protect it from the rain

**fly·specked** /ˈflaɪspekt/ *adj especially AmE* covered with small spots of waste matter from flies

**fly·swat·ter** /ˈflaɪˌswɒtə‖-ˌswɑːtər/ *n* [C] a square net fixed to a handle and used for killing flies

**fly·weight** /ˈflaɪweɪt/ *n* [C] a BOXER (1) who belongs to the lightest class of boxers and weighs 51 kilos

**fly·wheel** /ˈflaɪwiːl/ *n* [C] a heavy wheel that keeps a machine working at a steady speed because of its weight

**fly·whisk** /ˈflaɪˌwɪsk/ *n* [C] *BrE* a small brush, used in former times for keeping flies away

**FM** /ˌef ˈem◄/ *n* [U] frequency modulation; a system used for broadcasting radio programmes which produces a very clear sound —compare AM

**fnarr** /fnɑː‖fnɑːr/ *interjection BrE spoken humorous* used to say that what has just been said also has a sexual meaning although this was not intended: *"He's got a big one, hasn't he?" "Fnarr!"*

**foal**[1] /fəʊl‖foʊl/ *n* [C] a very young horse

**foal**[2] *v* [I] to give birth to a foal

**foam**[1] /fəʊm‖foʊm/ *n* [U] **1** a mass of small BUBBLES[1] (1) on the surface of something, such as the sea or coffee, which are formed when air mixes with a liquid **2** a substance used for cleaning or shaving (SHAVE[1] (1)) which consists of a mass of small BUBBLES[1] (1) **3** foam rubber: *a foam mattress* —**foamy** *adj*

**foam**[2] *v* [I] **1** to produce foam: *When he opened the can it foamed all over his hand.* **2 foam at the mouth** to make a mass of small BUBBLES[1] (1) come out of your mouth because you are very angry or ill

**foam rub·ber** /ˌ· ˈ··◄/ *n* [U] soft rubber full of air bubbles used in PILLOWS, chair seats etc

**fob**[1] /fɒb‖fɑːb/ *v* **fobbing, fobbed**

**fob** sb ↔ **off** [T] **1** to try to stop someone complaining or asking questions by giving them explanations, excuses etc that are obviously untrue: **fob sb off with** *He tried to fob her off with some story about losing her telephone number.* **2** to make someone accept something that is not as good as the thing they wanted: **fob sb off with** *Don't let them fob you off with some cheap imported brand.*

**fob** sth ↔ **off on** sb [T] to persuade someone into accepting something by a trick or deceit: *You can't just fob all your difficult jobs off on to me!*

**fob**[2] *n* [C] **1** a small object fixed to a key ring as a decoration **2** a short chain or piece of cloth to which a fob watch is fastened

**fob watch** /ˈ· ·/ *n* [C] a watch that fits into a pocket, or is pinned to a woman's dress

**fo·cal** /ˈfəʊkəl‖ˈfoʊ-/ *adj* [only before noun] **1** the focal point, issue etc is the thing that people pay most attention to **2 focal attention/awareness** the main part of your attention when you are looking at or thinking about something

**focal length** /ˌ·· ˈ·/ *n* [C] *technical* the distance between the centre of a lens and the focal point

**focal point** /ˈ·· ·/ *n* [C] **1** the person or thing that you pay most attention to: *The man on horseback acts as the focal point of the picture.* **2** *technical* the point on a LENS or a mirror where light RAYS (1) meet

**fo'c'sle** /ˈfəʊksəl‖ˈfoʊ-/ *n* [C] *BrE* the front part of a ship, where the sailors live; FORECASTLE *AmE*

W2 **fo·cus¹** /ˈfəʊkəs‖ˈfoʊ-/ *v* **focussing, focussed** or **focused** **1** [I,T] to pay special attention to a particular person or thing instead of others: **[+ on]** *Modern medicine has tended to focus too much on developing highly complicated surgical techniques.* | **focus attention on** *The recent wave of bombings has focussed public attention on the region.* **2** [T] to change the position of the LENS (2) on a camera, TELESCOPE¹ etc, so that you can see something clearly: **focus sth on** *He focused his binoculars on the building opposite.* **3** [I,T] if your eyes focus, or if you focus your eyes, you gradually become able to see something clearly **4** [I,T] if you focus beams of light or if they focus, they pass through a LENS and meet at a point

W2 **focus²** *n* **1** [singular] the subject or situation that people pay special attention to: **[+ of]** *The focus of the conference shifted from population growth to the education of women.* | **the focus is on sth** *The focus of recent legislation has been on environmental issues.* | **the focus of attention** *The war in Bosnia had now become the focus of worldwide media attention.* **2** [U] special attention that is given to one particular subject or situation: **[+ on]** *grammar based teaching, with its focus on accuracy rather than fluency* | **bring/throw sth into focus** (=make people notice something and pay special attention to it) *The case has brought the problem of child abuse sharply into focus.* **3 in focus/out of focus** if a photograph or an instrument such as a TELESCOPE¹ is in focus, the edges of the things you are looking at can be seen clearly, if it is out of focus they cannot be seen clearly **4** [C] *technical plural* **foci** the point where beams of light or waves of sound meet after their direction has been changed

F

**fo·cussed** *BrE*, **focused** *AmE* /ˈfəʊkəst‖ˈfoʊ-/ *adj* paying careful attention to what you are doing, in a way that shows you are determined to succeed: *This year she's a much more focused player.*

**fod·der** /ˈfɒdə‖ˈfɑːdər/ *n* [C,U] food for farm animals —see also CANNON FODDER

**foe** /fəʊ‖foʊ/ *n* [C] *literary* an enemy

**foe·tal**, **fetal** /ˈfiːtl/ *adj* [only before noun] connected with a foetus: *foetal abnormalities*

**foetal po·si·tion** /ˈ·· ·ˌ··/ *n* [C] the body position of an unborn child inside its mother, in which the body is curled, and the legs are pulled up against the chest

**foe·tus, fetus** /ˈfiːtəs/ *n* [C] a young human or animal before birth —compare EMBRYO (1)

**fog¹** /fɒg‖fɑːg, fɒːg/ *n* [C,U] **1** cloudy air near the ground which is difficult to see through: *Thick fog is making driving conditions hazardous.* | **fog bank** (=a large area of fog) —compare MIST¹ (1) **2 in a fog** *informal* confused and unable to think clearly: *Sorry, what did you say? – my mind's in a fog at the moment.*

**fog²** *v* **fogged, fogging** **1** [I,T] if something made of glass fogs up or becomes fogged up, it becomes covered in small drops of water that make it difficult to see through **2 fog the issue** to make a subject, problem etc become unclear and more complicated: *I think we're just fogging the issue by looking at all these details.*

**fog·bound** /ˈfɒgbaʊnd‖ˈfɑːg-, ˈfɒːg-/ *adj* prevented from travelling or working normally because of fog: *Moscow airport was fogbound.*

**fogey, fogy** /ˈfəʊgi‖ˈfoʊ-/ *n plural* **fogeys** or **fogies** [C] someone who has old-fashioned ideas and dislikes change: **old fogey** *Don't be such an old fogey!*

**fog·gy** /ˈfɒgi‖ˈfɑːgi, ˈfɒːgi/ *adj* **1** very misty because of fog: *a foggy day in November* **2 not have the foggiest (idea)** *spoken* to not know at all: *None of us had the foggiest idea about how to put the tent up.* **3 a foggy memory/recollection** an unclear memory of something that happened in the past: *I only have a foggy recollection of my grandmother.* —**foggily** *adv* —**fogginess** *n* [U]

**fog·horn** /ˈfɒghɔːn‖ˈfɑːghɔːrn, ˈfɒːg-/ *n* [C] **1** a piece of equipment that makes a loud noise, which is used by ships in fog to warn other ships of their position **2 a voice like a foghorn** *humorous* a very loud, unpleasant voice

**fog lamp** /ˈ· ·/ *BrE*, **fog light** /ˈ· ·/ *AmE* —*n* [C] a strong light on the front of a car that helps drivers to see in fog

**foi·ble** /ˈfɔɪbəl/ *n* [C] a habit or feature of someone's character which is a little strange or silly: *We all have our little foibles.*

**foie gras** /ˌfwɑː ˈgrɑː/ *n* [U] PATE DE FOIE GRAS (=type of food made from LIVER)

**foil¹** /fɔɪl/ *n* **1** [U] metal sheets that are as thin as paper, used for wrapping food: *Cover the chicken with silver foil and bake in a hot oven.* —see also TINFOIL **2** [U] paper that is covered with very thin sheets of metal: *Cigarettes are wrapped in foil to keep them fresh.* **3 be a foil to** to emphasize another person or thing's good qualities, by being very different from them: *His quiet determination is a perfect foil to Eva's energetic enthusiasm.* **4** [C] a light narrow sword used in FENCING (1)

**foil²** *v* [T often passive] to prevent something bad that someone is planning to do: *A massive arms-smuggling plan has been foiled by the CIA.*

**foist** /fɔɪst/ *v*

**foist** sth **on/upon** sb *phr v* [T] to force someone to accept or have to deal with something that they do not want: *I keep getting work foisted on me at the last minute.*

**-fold** /fəʊld‖foʊld/ *suffix* **1** [in adjectives] of a particular number of kinds: *A window has a twofold purpose – to allow light into the room and let people see out.* | *The value of the house has increased fourfold.* (=it is now worth four times as much as before) **2** [in adverbs] a particular number of times: *The value of the house has increased fourfold.* (=it is now worth four times as much as before)

**fold¹** /fəʊld‖foʊld/ *v*

**1 ► BEND ◄** [T] to bend a piece of paper, cloth etc by laying or pressing one part over another: *Fold the paper along the dotted line.* | **fold sth in two/half** *The woman folded the tickets in two and tore them in half.*

**2 ► MAKE STH SMALLER/NEATER ◄** [T] also **fold up** to fold something several times so that it makes a small neat shape: *I wish you kids would fold up your clothes!*

**3 ► FURNITURE ETC ◄ a)** [I] if something such as a piece of furniture folds in a particular way, it is designed so that part of it can be folded to make it smaller: **[+ away/up/down etc]** *a useful little bed that folds away when you don't need it* **b)** [T] to fold or bend part of something such as a piece of furniture to make it smaller: **fold** sth ↔ **down/up/away etc** *Can you fold up these chairs while I clean the floor?*

**4 fold your arms/legs etc** to bend your arms or legs, especially so that they are resting against your body: *George stood silently with his arms folded.*

**5 ► BUSINESS ◄** [I] also **fold up** if an organization folds or folds up, it closes because it does not have enough money to continue

**6 ► COVER ◄** [T] to cover something, especially by wrapping it in material or putting your hand over it: **fold sth in sth** *a silver dagger folded in a piece of white cloth*

**7 fold sb in your arms** *especially literary* to hold someone closely by putting your arms around them

**fold** sth **in** *phr v* [T] to gently mix another substance into a mixture when you are preparing food: *Fold in the sugar and whisk until stiff.*

**fold²** *n* [C]
**1 ▶ LINE ◀** a line made in paper or material when you fold one part of it over another: *Bend back the card and cut along the fold.*
**2 ▶ LOOSE SKIN/MATERIAL ◀** [usually plural] **a)** a rounded shape made by folded material: *Ahmed had a dagger concealed in the folds of his robe.* **b)** an area of loose folded skin: *The old dog had thick folds of skin around its neck.*
**3 the fold** the group of people that you belong to and share the same beliefs and ideas as: **return/come back to the fold** *Many Democrats who voted Republican in the 80s have now returned to the fold.*|**stray from/leave the fold** *a former advocate of free market economics who had strayed from the fold*
**4 ▶ SHEEP ◀** a small area of a field surrounded by a wall or fence where sheep are kept for safety
**5 ▶ ROCK ◀** *technical* a bend in layers of rock, caused by underground movements in the earth
**6 ▶ VALLEY ◀** *literary* a small narrow valley

**fold·a·way** /ˈfəʊldəweɪ‖ˈfoʊld-/ *adj* [only before noun] a foldaway bed, table etc can be folded up so it uses less space

**fold·er** /ˈfəʊldə‖ˈfoʊldər/ *n* [C] **1** a container for keeping loose papers in, made of folded card **2** a picture of a folder on a computer screen, which shows you where information can be stored

**fold·ing** /ˈfəʊldɪŋ‖ˈfoʊl-/ *adj* [only before noun] a folding bicycle, bed, chair etc has parts that you can bend or fold together to make it easier to carry or store

**fo·li·age** /ˈfəʊli-ɪdʒ‖ˈfoʊ-/ *n* [U] the leaves of a plant

**fo·li·o** /ˈfəʊliəʊ‖ˈfoʊlioʊ/ *n plural* **folios** *technical* **1** [C] a book made with very large sheets of paper **2** [C] a single numbered sheet of paper from a book

2 **folk¹** /fəʊk‖foʊk/ *n* **1 folks** [plural] **a)** *especially AmE* your parents and family: *Is it OK if I call my folks?*|**the folks back home** *Wait till the folks back home hear about this!* **b)** used when addressing a group of people in a friendly way: *That's all for now, folks.* **c)** *AmE* people: *Folks around here don't take too kindly to strangers.* **2 country folk/farming folk/fisher folk etc** [plural] *literary* people who live in a particular area or do a particular kind of work: *simple country folk* **3** [plural] *BrE old-fashioned* people: **young folk/old folk** *Young folk these days don't know the meaning of work.* **4** [U] FOLK MUSIC

**folk²** *adj* [only before noun] **1** folk art, stories, customs etc are traditional and typical of the ordinary people who live in a particular area: *folk tales*|*an old Spanish folk song* **2 folk science/psychology/wisdom etc** science etc that is based on simple ideas that ordinary people can understand and does not involve a high level of technical knowledge **3 folk medicine/remedy** a traditional type of medical treatment that uses plants etc rather than modern scientific methods

**folk dance** /ˈ· ·/ *n* [C] a traditional dance from a particular area, or a piece of music for this dance—**folk dancer** *n* [C]

**folk he·ro** /ˈ· ˌ··/ *n* [C] someone who people in a particular place admire very much because of something they have done: *Casey Jones is a well-known American folk hero.*

**folk·lore** /ˈfəʊklɔː‖ˈfoʊklɔːr/ *n* [U] the traditional stories, customs etc of a particular area or country: *According to local folklore, the cave was once occupied by a witch.*

**folk mu·sic** /ˈ· ˌ··/ *n* [U] **1** traditional music that has been played by ordinary people in a particular area for a long time **2** a style of popular music in which people sing and play GUITARS, without any electronic equipment

**folk·sy** /ˈfəʊksi‖ˈfoʊ-/ *adj informal* **1** *especially AmE* friendly and informal: *The town had a certain folksy charm.* **2** in a style that is typical of traditional countryside styles or customs

**fol·li·cle** /ˈfɒlɪkəl‖ˈfɑː-/ *n* [C] one of the small holes in the skin that hairs grow from

## fol·low /ˈfɒləʊ‖ˈfɑːloʊ/ *v* S1 W1

① GO BEHIND
② AFTER/NEXT
③ OBEY RULES/TEACHINGS ETC
④ UNDERSTAND
⑤ DO THE SAME AS
⑥ BE INTERESTED IN
⑦ OTHER MEANINGS

### ① GO BEHIND

**1** [I,T] to walk, drive, run etc behind someone else, going in the same direction as them: **follow sb/sth** *If you'll just follow me, I'll show you to the office.*|*Tom Selleck walked in, followed by a crowd of photographers.*|**follow** *I knew the way, so I went first, and the others followed.*

**2** [T] to go closely behind someone in order to watch them and find out where they go: *Marlowe looked over his shoulder to make sure no-one was following him.*

### ② AFTER/NEXT

**3** [I,T] to happen directly after an event or period: *There was a major increase in immigration in the years that followed the First World War.*|**be (closely) followed by** *The lightning was followed by a great crash of thunder.*|**in the days/weeks etc that followed** *We saw a lot of each other in the months that followed.*|**there follows** (=after that there is) *There followed a long and embarrassing silence.*|**follow shortly** (=happen soon) *The late night movie will follow shortly.* —see also FOLLOWING¹

**4** [I,T] to come directly after something else, for example in a book or a series of things: *A full report of the results follows this chapter.*|**be followed by** *In English the letter 'Q' is always followed by a 'U'.*|**there follows** (=after that there is) *There follows a long description of the writer's early life.*

**5** [I,T] to do an important job after someone else: **be followed by** *Ivan was followed by a succession of weak rulers.*

**6 a hard act to follow** *spoken* someone who is so good at something that it will be difficult for the next person to be as good or as successful

**7 as follows** used to introduce a list of names, things, instructions etc that come next: *The results are as follows: First was Sweden, then Germany, then Ireland.*

**8 to follow** after the main part of a meal: *We're having the poached salmon, with chocolate mousse to follow.*

### ③ OBEY RULES/TEACHINGS ETC

**9 follow sb's orders/wishes/advice etc** to do something in the way that someone has told you to do it, advised you to do it etc: *If you'd followed my advice, none of this would have happened.*|**follow sb's orders etc to the letter** (=do exactly what someone told you to do)

**10 follow the instructions/a diagram etc** to do something according to the rules or instructions that say how it should be done: *Did you follow the instructions on the package?*

[continued on next page]

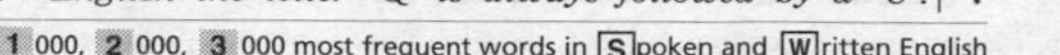

[continued from previous page]

**11 follow the signs/sb's directions** to go in the direction that the signs say you should go or that someone has told you to go: *Follow the signs for the airport, then turn off when you see the hotel.*

**12** [T] to believe in and obey a particular set of religious or political ideas, or a leader who teaches these ideas: *They still follow the teachings of Mahatma Gandhi.*

④ **UNDERSTAND**

**13** [I,T] to understand something such as an explanation or story: *I didn't quite follow what he was saying.* | **easy/hard to follow** *I must admit I found the plot a bit hard to follow.*

⑤ **DO THE SAME AS**

**14** [I,T] to do the same thing as someone else after they have done it: *We all had to follow the teacher.* | **follow sb into** (=do the same job as someone else especially a member of your family) *None of my children seem to want to follow me into journalism.* | **follow sb's example** (=do the same as them because it is a good thing to do) *They have an excellent childcare policy, and we're hoping other companies will follow their example.*

**15 follow suit** to do the same as someone else has just done: *The Russian team pulled out of the Los Angeles Olympics, and several Eastern European countries followed suit.*

**16 follow (in) sb's footsteps** to do the same job as someone else who did it before you: *My father was a jazz player, and I wanted to follow in his footsteps.*

**17 follow the herd/crowd** to do the same thing as other people, without really thinking about what you want to do

⑥ **BE INTERESTED IN**

**18** [T] to be interested in a particular sports team, and be concerned about its performance and results: *The President follows the Red Sox.*

**19** [T] to be interested in the way a situation or set of events develops, and try to find out the latest information about it: *Have you been following that crime series on TV?*

⑦ **OTHER MEANINGS**

**20 follow your instincts/feelings** to do something in the way that you feel is best

**21 follow your nose a)** to do something in the way that you feel is right, without asking or checking **b)** to go straight forward: *Turn left at the bank, then just follow your nose.*

**22 ▶ GO IN A PARTICULAR DIRECTION ◀** [T] **a)** to continue along a particular road, river etc: *Follow the main road until you get to the coast.* **b)** to go in the same direction as something else, especially something that is very close: *The railway follows the road for several miles, and then branches off.*

**23 follow a trend/pattern/course etc** to continue to happen or develop in a particular way: *In Australia, the weather follows a fairly predictable pattern.*

**24 it follows (that)** [I] it must be true as a result of something else that is true: *Just because you're rich, it doesn't necessarily follow that you're happy.*

**25 ▶ WATCH/LISTEN CAREFULLY ◀** [T] to carefully watch someone move or listen to them speaking: **follow sb with your eyes** *The men all followed her with their eyes as she entered the bar.*

**26 ▶ THINK ABOUT/STUDY ◀** [T] to study or think about a particular idea or subject and try to find out more about it: *It turned out we were both following the same line of research.*

**27 ▶ BE ABOUT ◀** [T] to show or describe someone's life or a series of events, for example in a film or book: *The film follows Rocky's career as a boxer from his early days.*

**28 follow a profession/trade/way of life** *formal* to do a particular job or have a particular way of life

**follow** sb **around** also **follow** sb **about** *BrE phr v* [T] to keep following someone everywhere they go: *I wish you'd stop following me around.*

**follow through** *phr v* **1** [I,T] to do what needs to be done after the main part of something is finished, in order to make sure it is complete or successful: **follow sth ↔ through** *The success of any healthcare program depends on how it is followed through.* **2** [I] to continue moving your arm after you have hit the ball in tennis, GOLF etc —see also FOLLOW-THROUGH

**follow up** *phr v* **1** [T **follow** sth ↔ **up**] to do something as a result of something you have found out, someone has suggested etc: *The police were criticized for failing to follow up the complaint.* **2 follow (sth) up with** to do something in addition to what you have already done in order to make sure of success: *The train drivers have voted to follow up their one-day strike with a series of 48-hour stoppages.* —see also FOLLOW-UP[1]

**fol·low·er** /ˈfɒləʊə‖ˈfɑːloʊər/ *n* [C] someone who believes in a particular system of ideas, or who supports a leader who teaches these ideas: *Marx and his followers were convinced that capitalism would destroy itself.* | **[+ of]** *followers of Sun Myung Moon, better known as Moonies* —see also CAMP FOLLOWER

S2 W1 **fol·low·ing¹** /ˈfɒləʊɪŋ‖ˈfɑːloʊ-/ *adj* **1 the following afternoon/month/page/chapter etc** the next afternoon, month etc: *He was sick in the evening, but the following day he was better.* **2 the following example/way etc** the example, way etc that will be mentioned next: *Payment may be made in any of the following ways: cheque, cash, or credit card.* **3 a following wind** a wind that is blowing in the same direction as a ship, and helps it to move faster

**following²** *n* [C] **1** [usually singular] a group of people who support or admire someone: *The band has a big following in Europe.* **2 the following** the people or things that you are going to mention: *The following have been selected to play in tomorrow's game: Louise Carus, Fiona Douglas...* —see also FOLLOWING[1]

**following³** *prep* after an event or as a result of it: *Following the speech, there will be a few minutes for questions.* | *Thousands of refugees left the country following the outbreak of civil war.*

**follow-my-lead·er** /ˌ·· · ˈ··/ *BrE*, **follow-the-leader** *AmE* —*n* [U] a children's game in which one of the players does actions which all the other players must copy

**follow-through** /ˌ·· ˈ·/ *n* [singular] **1** movement of your arm after you have hit the ball in tennis, GOLF etc —see picture on page 1264 **2** the things that someone does in order to complete a plan: *The budget has to cover not only the main project but the follow-through.*

**follow-up¹** /ˈ·· ·/ *adj* [only before noun] a follow-up visit, examination, study etc is done to make sure that an earlier one was effective, or to continue a plan of action that was started earlier: *a follow-up story on the Watergate break-in* —see also **follow up** (FOLLOW[1])

**follow-up²** *n* **1** [C,U] something that is done to make sure that earlier actions have been successful or effective: *preventative treatment and follow-up several weeks later* **2** [C] a book, film, article etc that comes after another one that has the same subject or characters: *Spielberg says he's planning to do a follow-up next year.*

**fol·ly** /ˈfɒli‖ˈfɑːli/ *n* **1** [C,U] *formal* a very stupid thing to do, especially one that is likely to have serious results: **it would be folly to do sth** *It would be sheer folly to reduce spending on health education.* | **the folly of** *a writer who satirized the follies of aristocratic society* **2** [C] an unusual building that was built in former times as a decoration, not to be used or lived in

**fo·ment** /fəʊˈment‖foʊ-/ *v formal* **foment revolution/trouble/discord etc** to cause trouble and make people start fighting each other or opposing the government: *They were accused of fomenting rebellion.* —**fomentation** /ˌfəʊmenˈteɪʃən,-mən-‖ˌfoʊ-/ *n* [U]

**fond** /fɒnd‖fɑːnd/ *adj* **1 be fond of sb** to like someone very much, especially when you have known them for a long time and almost feel love for them: *Joe's quite fond of her, isn't he?* | **grow fond of** *Over the years we've grown very fond of each other.* **2 be fond of sth** to like something, especially something you have liked for a long time: *I'm not very fond of country music.* | **grow fond of** *I'd grown fond of the place and it was difficult to leave.* **3 be fond of doing sth a)** to enjoy doing something very much: *Jilly's very fond of drawing.* **b)** to do something often, especially something that annoys other people: *My Grandfather was very fond of handing out advice to all my friends.* **4** [only before noun] a fond look, smile, action etc shows you like someone very much: *He gave her a fond look.* | **a fond farewell** *As we parted we said a fond farewell.* **5 have fond memories of** to remember something with great pleasure: *Marie still had fond memories of their time together.* **6 a fond belief/hope** a belief or hope that something will happen, which seems silly because it is very unlikely to happen: **in the fond hope/belief that** *They sent him to another school in the fond hope that his behaviour would improve.* —see also FONDLY —**fondness** *n* [U] *His wife had a great fondness for expensive clothes.*

**fon·dant** /ˈfɒndənt‖ˈfɑːn-/ *n* [C,U] a sweet made of small grains of sugar

**fon·dle** /ˈfɒndl‖ˈfɑːndl/ *v* [T] to gently touch and move your fingers over part of someone's body in a way that shows love: *She fondled the puppy's neck.*

**fond·ly** /ˈfɒndli‖ˈfɑːndli/ *adv* **1 fondly imagine/believe/hope etc** to believe something that is untrue, hope for something that will probably not happen etc: *Some people still fondly believe that modern science can solve all the world's problems.* **2** in a way that shows you like someone very much: *He turned to see her smiling fondly at him.*

**fon·due** /ˈfɒndjuː‖fɑːnˈduː/ *n* [C,U] a dish made of small pieces of food that you put in melted cheese or chocolate

**font** /fɒnt‖fɑːnt/ *n* [C] **1** a large stone container in a church, that holds the water used for the ceremony of BAPTISM (1) **2** *technical* a set of letters of a particular size and type, used for printing books, newspapers etc

S1 W1 **food** /fuːd/ *n* **1** [U] things that people and animals eat, such as vegetables or meat: *The food's great and it's not that expensive.* | *There are food shortages in many areas.* **2** [C,U] a particular type of food: **junk food/health food etc** *All he ever eats is junk food.* | *Try to cut down on sweet and fatty foods.* | **dog food/pet food/baby food** (=food for dogs etc) | **be off your food** (=feel ill and not want to eat anything) **3 food for thought** something that makes you think carefully: *The teacher's advice certainly gave me food for thought.*

**food bank** /ˈ· ·/ *n* [C] *AmE* a place that gives food to poor people

**food chain** /ˈ· ·/ *n* **the food chain** all animals and plants considered as a group in which one type of animal eats another and then is eaten by another animal: *Pollution is affecting many creatures lower down the food chain.*

**food cou·pon** /ˈ· ˌ··/ *n* [C] a FOOD STAMP

**food·ie** /ˈfuːdi/ *n* [C] *informal* someone who is very interested in cooking and eating food

**food poi·son·ing** /ˈ· ˌ···/ *n* [U] a painful stomach illness caused by eating food that contains harmful BACTERIA

**food pro·cess·or** /ˈ· ˌ···/ *n* [C] a piece of electrical equipment that helps to prepare food in various ways, such as cutting and mixing —see picture on page 833

**food stamp** /ˈ· ·/ *n* [C] an official piece of paper that the US government gives to poor people so they can buy food

**food·stuff** /ˈfuːdstʌf/ *n* [C usually plural, U] a word meaning food, used especially when talking about the business of producing or selling food: *A wide variety of foodstuffs is available in the local market.*

**fool**[1] /fuːl/ *n*

**1 ▶ STUPID PERSON ◀** [C] a stupid person or someone who has done something stupid: *What a fool she had been to think that he would stay.*

**2 any fool can** *spoken* used to say that it is very easy to do something or to see that something is true: *Any fool can see that the painting's a fake.*

**3 be no fool/nobody's fool** to be difficult to trick or deceive, because you have a lot of experience and knowledge about something: *Katherine was nobody's fool when it came to money.*

**4 make a fool of yourself** to do something stupid that you feel embarrassed about afterwards and that makes you seem silly: *Sorry I made such a fool of myself last night. I must have been drunk.*

**5 ▶ FOOD ◀ gooseberry fool/strawberry fool etc** *BrE* a sweet food made of soft cooked fruit mixed with cream

**6 make a fool of sb** to deliberately try to make someone seem stupid: *I suddenly realised that I was being made a fool of.*

**7 more fool you/him etc** *BrE spoken* used to say that you think someone was stupid to do something and it is their own fault if this causes trouble: *"Jim smashed up my car." "More fool you for letting him borrow it!"*

**8 be living in a fool's paradise** to feel happy and satisfied, and believe there are no problems, when in fact this is not true

**9 play/act the fool** to behave in a silly way, especially in order to make people laugh: *Stop playing the fool! You'll fall.*

**10 (send sb on) a fool's errand** to make someone go somewhere or do something for no good reason

**11 ▶ ENTERTAINER ◀** [C] a man whose job was to entertain a king or other powerful person in former times, by doing tricks, singing funny songs etc —see also APRIL FOOL

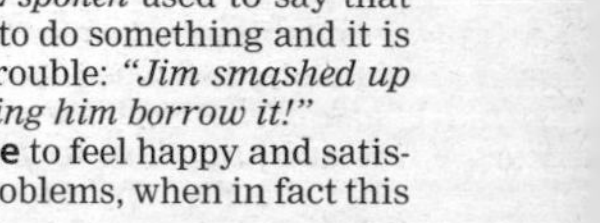


**fool**[2] *v* **1** [T] to trick someone into believing something: *You can't fool me with that old excuse.* | **fool sb into doing sth** *Don't be fooled into believing their promises.* **2 you could have fooled me** *spoken* used to show that you do not believe what someone has told you: *"Look, we're doing our best to fix it." "Well, you could have fooled me."* **3 sb is just fooling** *spoken* used to say that someone is not serious and is only pretending that something is true: *Don't pay any attention to Henry. He's just fooling.*

**fool around** also **fool about** *BrE phr v* [I] **1** to waste time behaving in a silly way: *He spent the whole afternoon just fooling around.* **2** to behave in a careless and irresponsible way: [+ **with**] *Some idiot's been fooling around with the electricity supply!* **3** to have a sexual relationship with someone else's wife, boyfriend etc: *Anthony's been fooling around with one of the secretaries.*

**fool**[3] *adj* [only before noun] *AmE informal* silly or stupid: *What did you say a fool thing like that for?*

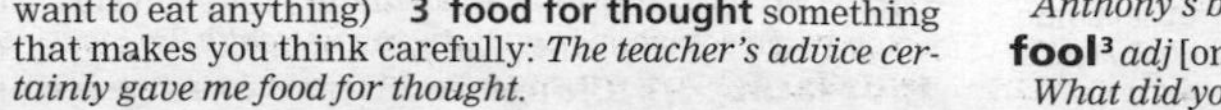

**fool·e·ry** /ˈfuːləri/ *n* [C,U] *BrE old-fashioned* silly or stupid behaviour

**fool·har·dy** /ˈfuːlhɑːdi‖-ɑːr-/ *adj* taking stupid and unnecessary risks: *a foolhardy attempt to capture more territory* —**foolhardiness** *n* [U]

**fool·ish** /ˈfuːlɪʃ/ *adj* **1** a foolish action, remark etc is stupid and shows that someone is not thinking sensibly: *I've never heard anything so foolish in all my life.*|**it is foolish (of sb) to do sth** *It was foolish of them to expect the economy to recover so quickly.* **2** a foolish person behaves in a silly way or looks silly: *I was young and foolish at the time.*|*a foolish grin* —**foolishly** *adv: She foolishly agreed to go with them.* —**foolishness** *n* [U]

**fool·proof** /ˈfuːlpruːf/ *adj* a foolproof method, plan, system etc is certain to be successful: *a foolproof way of preventing credit card fraud*

**fools·cap** /ˈfuːlskæp/ *n* [U] a large size of paper, especially paper for writing on

**fool's gold** /ˌ· ˈ·/ *n* [U] **1** a kind of yellow metal that exists in some rocks and looks like gold **2** something that you think will be very exciting, very attractive etc but in fact is not

S1 W1 **foot¹** /fʊt/ *n plural* **feet** /fiːt/ [C]

**1 ▶ BODY PART ◀** the part of your body that you stand on and walk on: *I have a really bad pain in my foot.*

**2 on foot** if you go somewhere on foot, you walk there: *It takes about 30 minutes on foot, or 10 minutes if you go by car.*

**3 ▶ MEASUREMENT ◀** *written abbreviation* **ft** *plural* **foot** or **feet** a unit for measuring length, equal to 12 inches (INCH¹ (1)) or about 30 centimetres: *He's six feet tall, with blonde hair and a moustache.* —see table on page B2

**4 ▶ BOTTOM PART ◀ the foot of** the lowest part of something such as a mountain, tree, or set of stairs, or the end of a bed where your feet go: *a stunningly beautiful lake at the foot of the mountain*

**5 get/jump/rise to your feet etc** to stand up after you have been sitting: *Mike leapt to his feet and ran towards the window.*

**6 be on your feet a)** to be standing for a long time without having time to sit down: *The worst thing about working in the shop is that you're on your feet all day.* **b)** to stand up: *As soon as the bell rang the class were on their feet and out of the door.* **c)** to feel better again after being ill and in bed: *We'll soon have you on your feet again.*

**7 be rushed off your feet/be run off your feet** to be very busy: *Just before Christmas, most of the salespeople are rushed off their feet.*

**8 set foot in** to go to or enter a place: *She swore she would never set foot in his house ever again.*

**9 be/get under your feet** to annoy you by always being in the same place as you and preventing you from doing what you want: *I hate summer vacation. The kids are under my feet all day long.*

**10 put your foot down a)** to say very firmly that someone must do something or must stop doing something: *You'll just have to put your foot down and tell him he can't stay out on school nights.* **b)** *informal* to make a car go faster

**11 put your feet up** *informal* to relax, especially by sitting with your feet supported on something

**12 put your foot in it** *especially BrE* **put your foot in your mouth** *especially AmE* to say something without thinking carefully, so that you embarrass or upset someone: *I've really put my foot in it this time. I didn't realize that was her husband!*

**13 have two left feet** *informal* to be very CLUMSY (1) *Dan's got two left feet when it comes to dancing.*

**14 get off on the wrong foot** to start a relationship badly, usually by having an argument: *Simon and I got off on the wrong foot but we're good friends now.*

**15 not put a foot wrong** *especially BrE* to do everything right and make no mistakes, especially in your job

**16 have/keep both feet on the ground** to think in a sensible and practical way and not have ideas or aims that will be impossible to achieve

**17 put sth back on its feet** to improve the situation of a country, organization etc: *It was Larry who put the club back on its feet.*

**18 fall/land on your feet** to get into a good situation because you are lucky after being in a difficult situation: *Don't worry about Nina, she always falls on her feet.*

**19 get your foot in the door** to get your first opportunity to work in a particular organization or industry

**20 have a foot in both camps** to be involved with or connected with two opposing groups of people

**21 have one foot in the grave** *humorous* to be very old or very ill

**22 ...my foot!** *BrE old-fashioned* used to show that you do not believe something that someone has just said: *£50 my foot! It'll cost £200 at least.*

**23 leave feet first** *humorous* to die before you leave a place or job

**24 feet of clay** someone that you admire who has feet of clay has faults that you did not realize they had

**25 foot soldier/patrol** a soldier or group of soldiers that walks and does not use a horse or a vehicle

**26 foot passenger** a passenger on a ship who has not brought a car with them

**27 -footed** /fʊtɪ̬d/ **a) left-footed/right-footed** using your left foot or right foot when you kick the ball **b) flat-footed/four-footed** having a particular kind or number of feet

**28 foot pedal/brake/pump etc** a machine or control that you operate using your feet

**29 ▶ SOCK ◀ the foot** the part of a sock that covers your foot: *There's a hole in the foot of my stocking.*

**30 ▶ POETRY ◀** *technical* a part of a line of poetry in which there is one strong BEAT² (3)) and one or two weaker ones —see also **the boot is on the other foot** (BOOT¹ (6)), **get/have cold feet** (COLD¹ (7), UNDERFOOT) **drag your feet/heels** (DRAG¹ (8)), **find your feet** (FIND¹ (22)), **from head to foot** (HEAD¹ (2)), **stand on your own (two) feet** (STAND¹ (32)), **sweep sb off their feet** (SWEEP¹ (12))

**foot²** *v* **foot the bill** to pay for something, especially something expensive that you do not want to pay for: *He ordered a load of drinks and then left me to foot the bill!*

**foot·age** /ˈfʊtɪdʒ/ *n* [U] cinema film showing a particular event: *old footage from the First World War*

**foot and mouth dis·ease** /ˌ· · ˈ· ·ˌ·/ *n* [U] a serious disease that kills cows and sheep

**foot·ball** /ˈfʊtbɔːl‖-bɒːl/ *n* **1** [U] *BrE* a game played by two teams of eleven players who try to kick a round ball into their opponents' GOAL (3); SOCCER: *watching football on TV*|*a football club* **2** [U] *AmE* a game played by two teams of eleven players who carry or kick an OVAL (=egg shaped) ball; AMERICAN FOOTBALL *BrE*: *college football games* **3** [C] a ball used in these games —see also FLAG FOOTBALL, **political football** (POLITICAL (5)) S W

**foot·bal·ler** /ˈfʊtbɔːlə‖-bɒːlər/ *n* [C] *BrE* someone who plays football, especially a professional player

**football pools** /ˈ· · ˌ·/ *n* —see **the pools** (POOL¹ (4))

**foot·bridge** /ˈfʊtˌbrɪdʒ/ *n* [C] a narrow bridge used by people who are walking

**foot·er** /ˈfʊtə‖-ər/ *n* **1 six-footer/eighteen-footer etc** someone or something that measures six feet tall, eighteen feet long etc **2** [U] *BrE* a game of football

**foot·fall** /ˈfʊtfɔːl‖-fɒːl/ *n* [C,U] *literary* the sound of each step when someone is walking: *heavy footfalls*

**foot fault** /ˈ· ·/ *n* [C] a mistake in tennis when the person who is serving (SERVE[1] (10)) is not standing behind the line

**footie** /fʊtiː/ *n* [U] *BrE* a game of football

**foot·hill** /ˈfʊtˌhɪl/ *n* [C usually plural] one of the smaller hills below a group of high mountains: *the foothills of the Himalayas*

**foot·hold** /ˈfʊthəʊld‖-hoʊld/ *n* [C] **1** a position from which you can start to make progress and achieve your aims: **gain/establish a foothold** *Extreme right wing parties gained a foothold in the latest European elections.* **2** a small hole or crack where you can safely put your foot when climbing a steep rock

**foot·ing** /ˈfʊtɪŋ/ *n* [U] **1** the conditions or arrangements under which something exists or operates: **on a legal/scientific/official etc footing** *The article attempts to put their work on a more scientific footing.* | **on a sound/firm/solid footing** *new reforms that will put the country back on a firm financial footing* | **on an equal footing/on the same footing** (=in the same situation or state as someone else) *The new law puts women on an equal footing with men.* | **on a war footing** (=ready to go to war at any time) **2** the position of your feet when you are standing firmly on a SLIPPERY or dangerous surface: *struggling to keep her footing on the slippery path* | **lose/miss your footing** (=fall because you are no longer balanced)

**foo·tle** /ˈfuːtl/ *v* **footle around/about** to waste time doing unimportant things when you should be working

**foot·lights** /ˈfʊtlaɪts/ *n* [plural] a row of lights along the front of the stage in a theatre —see picture at THEATRE

**foot·ling** /ˈfuːtlɪŋ/ *adj* [only before noun] *old-fashioned* unimportant and annoying

**foot lock·er** /ˈ· ˌ··/ *n* [C] *AmE* a strong box that soldiers have at the end of their beds to keep their possessions in

**foot·loose** /ˈfʊtluːs/ *adj* **1** able to move around freely because you have no permanent work or home: *footloose students traveling around Europe* **2 footloose and fancy free** able to do what you want and enjoy yourself because you have no responsibilities

**foot·man** /ˈfʊtmən/ *plural* **footmen** /-mən/ *n* [C] a male servant in former times who opened the front door, announced the names of visitors etc

**foot·mark** /ˈfʊtmɑːk‖-mɑːrk/ *n* [C] a mark made by someone's shoe or foot

**foot·note** /ˈfʊtnəʊt‖-noʊt/ *n* [C] a note at the bottom of the page in a book, which gives more information about something

**foot·path** /ˈfʊtpɑːθ‖-pæθ/ *n* [C] *especially BrE* a narrow path for people to walk along, especially in the countryside; TRAIL[2] (4) *AmE*

**foot·print** /ˈfʊtˌprɪnt/ *n* [C] a mark made by a foot or shoe: *the footprints of a deer*

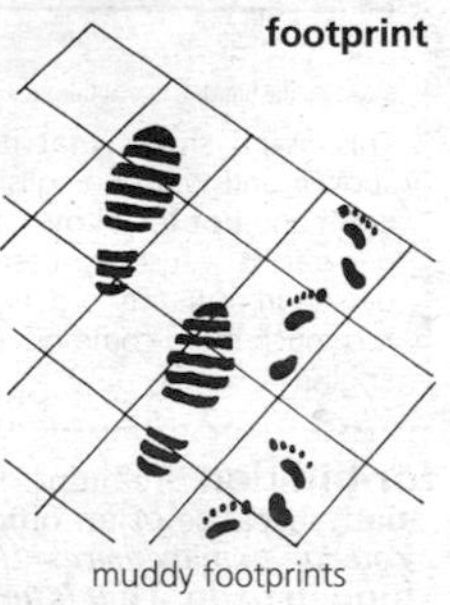

**footprint**

muddy footprints

**foot·rest** /ˈfʊt-rest/ *n* [C] a small piece of furniture that you can rest your feet on when you are sitting down

**foot·sie** /ˈfʊtsi/ *n* **play footsie** *informal* **a)** to secretly touch another person's feet with your feet under a table to show that you find them sexually attractive **b)** *AmE* to work together and help each other in a dishonest way: *politicians playing footsie with each other*

**foot·slog·ging** /ˈfʊtslɒgɪŋ‖-slɑːg-/ *n* [U] *BrE informal* a lot of walking around, which makes you very tired

**foot·sore** /ˈfʊtsɔː‖-sɔːr/ *adj* having feet that hurt because you have walked a long distance

**foot·step** /ˈfʊtstep/ *n* [C] the sound made when someone walks a single step: *heavy footsteps on the stairs* —see also **follow (in) sb's footsteps** (FOLLOW (16))

**foot·stool** /ˈfʊtstuːl/ *n* [C] a low piece of furniture used to support your feet when you are sitting down

**foot·wear** /ˈfʊtweə‖-wer/ *n* [U] things that people wear on their feet, such as shoes or boots

**foot·work** /ˈfʊtwɜːk‖-wɜːrk/ *n* [U] skilful use of your feet when dancing or playing a sport

**fop** /fɒp‖fɑːp/ *n* [C] *old-fashioned* a man who is too interested in his clothes and appearance —**foppish** *adj* —**foppishness** *n* [U]

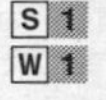

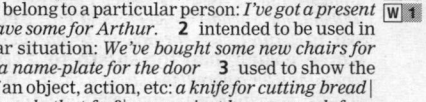

**for**[1] /fə; *strong* fɔː‖fər; *strong* fɔːr/ *prep* **1** intended to be given to or belong to a particular person: *I've got a present for you.* | *Save some for Arthur.* **2** intended to be used in a particular situation: *We've bought some new chairs for the office.* | *a name-plate for the door* **3** used to show the purpose of an object, action, etc: *a knife for cutting bread* | *What did you do that for?* | *a space just large enough for a table and two chairs* | **for sale/hire/rent** (=available to be bought, hired) *House for sale.* | *They have tools and garden equipment for hire.* **4** if you do something for someone, you do it instead of them in order to help them: *I looked after the kids for her.* | *Let me lift that for you.* **5** if something is done for someone, or if they are given something for a problem, they are helped or their situation is improved: *The doctor knew that there was nothing he could do for her.* | *I've found it for you.* | *I'll do what I can for you.* | *What can I do for you?* (=can I help you?) **6** if something is arranged for a particular time, it is planned that it should happen then: *I've invited them for 9 o'clock.* | *I've made an appointment for 18th October.* | *It's time for supper.* **7** if you buy someone something, or arrange an event for their birthday etc, you do it to celebrate that occasion: *What did you get for your birthday?* **8** used to express a length of time: *Bake the cake for 40 minutes.* | *They had been walking for a good half hour.* | *I've been meaning to ask you for ages.* | *He's been off work for a long time.* | **for a while**: *I'm borrowing it for a while.* —see DURING (USAGE), SINCE[3] (USAGE) **9 for now/for the moment** used to say that you are suggesting something as a temporary solution, but it may be changed later: *I think for now we're just going to have to keep the cats in the house.* **10** used to express distance: *We walked for miles.* | *Factories and warehouses stretched for quite a distance along the canal.* **11** used to state where a person, vehicle etc is going: *I set off for work.* | *the night before leaving for New York* | *the train for Manchester* | **I'm for bed/home** *BrE* (=I'm going to bed/going home) **12** used to show a price or amount: *a cheque for a hundred pounds* | *The diamond was insured for two thousand dollars.* **13** in order to have, do, get, or obtain something: *She decided to look for a job.* | *Mother was too ill to get up for dinner.* | *the qualifications necessary for entry to university* | *I paid $3 for it.* | *an expert whom you can rely on for advice* | *For further details, write to this address.* | *Let's go for a walk.* | *We just did it for fun.* | *waiting for the bus* | *legislating for equality* | **run for your life** (=to save your life) **14 now for** *spoken* used to say what you're going to have or do now: *Now for some fun!* **15** because of or as a result of something: *if, for any reason, you cannot attend ...* | *a reward for bravery* | *We could hardly see for the mist.* | *A certain amount must be deducted for depreciation.* | **for doing sth** *He got a ticket for driving through a red light.* **16** as to or concerning something: *I felt sorry for him.* | *He has a talent for upsetting people.* | *I'm sure she's the ideal person for the job.* | *We had pasta for lunch.* | *Fortunately for him, he can swim.* | *The success rates for each task are given in Table 4.* | **too...for me/her etc** (=more than I can deal with) *You're too quick for me!* | **he's a great one for** (=he always wants or is concerned with) *He's a great one for details.* | **Are you all right for money?** (=do you have enough?) | **...is not for me** (=is not suitable or appropriate for me) *City life is not for me.* **17** if you work for a company, play for a team etc, this is the one in which you work, play etc: *surveyors working for property services* | *He writes for a weekly paper.* | *She plays for the A team.* **18** in favour of, supporting, or in agreement with something: *discussing the case for and against nuclear energy | How many people voted for the proposal? | Three cheers for the captain.* | **I'm all for** (=I approve of) *I'm all for people enjoying themselves.* **19** representing, meaning, or as a sign of something: *What's the word for 'happy' in French? | Red is for danger.* **20** used after a comparative form to mean after, as a result of, or because of: *You'll feel better for a break.* **21** used to say that a particular feature of someone or something is surprising when you consider what they are: *It's cold for the time of year. | She looks young for her age.* **22 for sb/sth to do sth a)** used to introduce a phrase that is used instead of a CLAUSE (2): *It is really unusual for Michael to get cross.* | **I can't bear for sb/sth to** *I can't bear for you to be unhappy.* | **nothing worse/easier than for sb/sth to**: *There's nothing worse than for a parent to ill treat a child.* **b)** used when you are describing what someone should do, might do, or has done: *The plan is for us to leave in the morning.* | **a need/desire/chance for sb/sth to** *There is an urgent need for someone to tackle this problem. | There will be another opportunity for them to do it again.* **c)** used when you are explaining a reason for something: *He must have had some bad news for him to be so quiet.* (=as/since he is so quiet) | *I've sent off my coat for it to be cleaned.* (=in order that it may be cleaned) **d)** used when you are saying what someone or something is able to do: *It's easy for a computer to keep a record of this information. | It's impossible for me to get money out of Dorothy.* | **large/difficult/near enough for sb/sth to** *The dolphin was near enough for me to reach out and touch it.* | **too large/difficult/near for sb/sth to** *It's too difficult for me to explain.* **23 for each/every** used to say that each of one kind of thing has or will have something of another kind: *For each mistake, you'll lose half a point. | For every three people who agree, you'll find five who don't.* **24 for all a)** in spite of: *For all his efforts, he still came last. | She still loves him for all that.* **b)** considering how little: *For all the success you've had, you might just as well have not bothered!* **25 for all I know/care** *spoken* used to say that you do not really know or care: *For all I know, he could be dead. | He can jump into the river for all I care!* **26 I wouldn't do it for anything** *informal* used to emphasize that you definitely would not do it: *I would not go through that again for anything.* **27 I for one believe/think that...** *spoken* this is my opinion, even if no one else agrees: *I for one believe that she's making a big mistake.* **28 for one thing... (and for another)** used when you are giving reasons for a statement you have made: *No, I'm not going to buy it; for one thing I don't like the colour, and for another it's far too expensive.* **29 if it weren't for/if it hadn't been for** if a particular thing had not happened, if someone had not done something, or if a situation was different: *If it hadn't been for you, I would not be alive now.* **30 (well,) that's/there's...for you!** *spoken* **a)** used to say that it is typical that something has been a disappointment; you cannot expect anything better of that type of thing: *That's foreign hotels for you!* **b)** used to say that something is the complete opposite of what you were saying: *I gave it to her and she just threw it away; there's gratitude for you!* **31 be (in) for it** to be likely to be blamed or punished: *You'll be in for it if she finds out what you've done!*

S2 W1 **for²** *conjunction formal* used to introduce the reason for something; because: *He found it increasingly difficult to read, for his eyes were failing.*

**for·age¹** /ˈfɒrɪdʒ‖ˈfɑː-, ˈfɔː-/ *v* [I] **1** to go around searching for food or other supplies: [+ **for**] *The children are forced to forage for scraps in the streets.* | **a foraging party** (=group of soldiers searching for food etc) **2** to search for something with your hands in a bag, drawer etc: *She foraged around in her purse, and finally produced her ticket.* —**forager** *n* [C]

**forage²** *n* **1** [singular] an act of searching for food **2** [U] food supplies for horses and cattle

**for·ay¹** /ˈfɒreɪ‖ˈfɔː-, ˈfɑː-/ *n* [C] **1** a short attempt at doing a particular job or activity, especially one that is very different from what you usually do: *After a brief unsuccessful foray into politics, he went back to his law practice.* **2** a short sudden attack by a group of soldiers: *their nightly forays into enemy territory* **3** a short journey somewhere in order to get something or do something: *her twice-weekly foray to the shops*

**foray²** *v* [I + **into**] to go out and make a sudden attack against the enemy, especially in order to get food or supplies

**for·bade** /fəˈbæd, -ˈbeɪd‖fər-/ the past tense of FORBID

**for·bear¹** /fɔːˈbeə, fə-‖fɔːrˈber, fər-/ *past tense* **forbore** /-ˈbɔː‖-ˈbɔːr/ *past participle* **forborne** /-ˈbɔːn‖-ˈbɔːrn/ *v* [I] *formal* to not do something, even though you could do it if you wanted to: [+ **from**] *He forbore from making suggestions for fear of insulting her.* | **forbear to do sth** *Clara forbore to mention that the result was likely to be the same.*

**for·bear²** /ˈfɔːbeə‖ˈfɔːrber/ *n* [C] a FOREBEAR

**for·bear·ance** /fɔːˈbeərəns‖fɔːrˈber-/ *n* [U] *formal* patience, self-control, and willingness to forgive someone: *Higgins accepted the decision with commendable forbearance.*

**for·bear·ing** /fɔːˈbeərɪŋ‖fɔːrˈber-/ *adj formal* patient and willing to forgive

**for·bid** /fəˈbɪd‖fər-/ *past tense* **forbade** /-ˈbæd, -ˈbeɪd/ *past participle* **forbidden** /-ˈbɪdn/ *v* [T] **1** to tell someone that they definitely must not do something: *You may not go to the party – I absolutely forbid it!* | **forbid sb from doing sth** *Women are forbidden from going out without a veil.* | **strictly forbid** *The law strictly forbids racial or sexual discrimination.* | **forbid sb to do sth** *He was forbidden to leave the base as a punishment.* **2 God/Heaven forbid** *spoken* used to emphasize that you hope that something will not happen: *Who would run the business if, God forbid, you were to die?* **3** *formal* to make it impossible for someone to do something: *Lack of space forbids the listing of all those who contributed.*

Frequencies of **forbid**, **say sb can't** and **not let/allow** in spoken and written English.

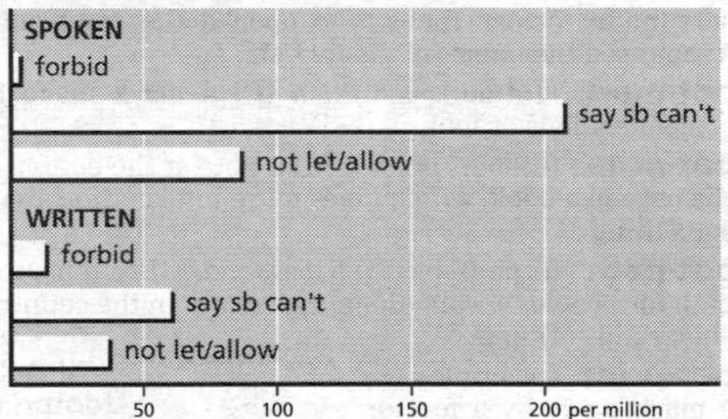


Based on the British National Corpus and the Longman Lancaster Corpus

This graph shows that it is much more usual in both spoken and written English to use the expressions **say sb can't** and **not let/allow**, rather than **forbid**. **Forbid** is less general. It is usually used when a government, law or person in authority orders someone not to do something. It is much more common in written English than in spoken English.

**for·bid·den** /fəˈbɪdn‖fər-/ *adj* **1** not allowed, especially because of an official rule: **strictly forbidden** *You can't smoke here – it's strictly forbidden.* | **it is forbidden to do sth** *It is forbidden to marry someone who is not a member of the same faith.* **2** a forbidden place is one that you are not allowed to go to: *the Great Mosque, whose precincts are forbidden to Christians* **3** a forbidden activity, object etc is one that seems exciting because you are not allowed to do it or have it: *the forbidden sensual pleasures of the old city* | **forbidden fruit** (=something forbidden that gives great pleasure)

**for·bid·ding** /fəˈbɪdɪŋ‖fər-/ *adj* having a frightening or unfriendly appearance: *Despite her forbidding manner she's actually quite a kind person.* —**forbiddingly** *adv*

**for·bore** /fɔːˈbɔː, fə-‖fɔːrˈbɔːr, fər-/ the past tense of FORBEAR

**for·borne** /fɔːˈbɔːn, fə-‖fɔːrˈbɔːrn, fər-/ the past participle of FORBEAR

S 3 W 1 **force¹** /fɔːs‖fɔːrs/ *n*
**1 ▶ MILITARY ◀ a)** [C] a group of people who have been trained to fight in a war: *forces loyal to President Aquino*|*a highly efficient fighting force* **b) the forces** the army, navy, and air force: *Both her sons are in the forces.* **c)** [U] military action used as a way of achieving your aims: *After World War I the use of force to settle conflicts was prohibited.* |**by force (of arms)** *The Serbs were accused of imposing these boundaries by force.*
**2 ▶ VIOLENCE ◀** [U] violent physical action used to get what you want: *The question is whether the police used reasonable force when arresting him.*|**by force** *Her ex-husband tried to get the children back by force.*
**3 ▶ PHYSICAL POWER ◀ a)** [U] the amount of physical power that is used or produced when something moves or hits something else: *waves hitting the rocks with tremendous force*|*The force of the explosion blew out all the windows.*|**brute force** (=simple physical force) *They kicked the door open by sheer brute force.* **b)** [C,U] *technical* power that produces movement in another object, for example by pulling it or pushing it: *the force of gravity*
**4 ▶ STRONG INFLUENCE ◀** [C] something or someone that has a strong influence on the way events develop, on people's lives, or on the way people think: *Mrs Thatcher is no longer the force she once was in British politics.*|**driving force** (=person or thing that has the strongest influence on the way things happen) *The need for short-term profits seems to be the driving force behind these mergers.*|**a force for peace/progress/good etc** (=someone whose actions make peace, progress etc more likely to happen)|**a force to be reckoned with** (=a company, organization etc with a lot of power and influence) *Within just a few months, Microsoft became a force to be reckoned with in the global software market.*|**forces beyond sb's control** *The fall in coffee prices was due to forces beyond their control.*|**the forces of evil/oppression** *the fight against the forces of oppression*
**5 ▶ POWERFUL EFFECT ◀** [U] the powerful effect of what someone says or does: *Even after 30 years, the play has lost none of its force.*|*the force of public opinion*
**6 ▶ ORGANIZED GROUP ◀** [C] a group of people who have been trained and organized for a specific purpose: *the company's sales force*
**7 join/combine forces** to join together so that you can deal with a problem, defend yourselves etc: *Local churches have joined forces to help the homeless.*|**[+ with]** *The Nationalists joined forces with the Communists.*
**8 ▶ LAW/RULE ◀ in force a)** if a law or a rule is in force, it exists and must be obeyed: **come into force** (=start to operate) *The new law on drink-driving comes into force next month.* **b)** in a large group, especially in order to protest about something: *Villagers turned out in force to protest about the new road.*
**9 by/from force of habit** if you do something by force of habit, you do it because you have always done the same thing in the past
**10 force of circumstance(s)** the effect of a situation on what you do or decide: *Force of circumstance compelled him to leave Italy.*
**11 the forces of nature** natural forces such as wind, rain, or EARTHQUAKES
**12 ▶ WIND ◀ a) force 8/9/10 etc** a unit for measuring the strength of the wind **b) gale/hurricane force wind** extremely strong wind that does a lot of damage
**13 ▶ POLICE ◀ the force** a word meaning the police force, used especially by police officers: *He resigned after 17 years in the force.* —see also LABOUR FORCE, TASK FORCE, TOUR DE FORCE

S 2 W 1 **force²** *v* [T]
**1 ▶ MAKE SB DO STH ◀ a)** to make someone do something that they do not want to do, especially by threatening them: **force sb to do sth** *Government troops have forced the rebels to surrender.* |**force sb** *Nobody forced me – it was my own decision.*|**force sb/sth (into) doing sth** *These women are forced into accepting low-paid jobs.* **b)** if a situation forces you to do something, it makes you do it, even though you do not want to: **force sb to do sth** *The high cost of borrowing is forcing many companies to close.*|**force sb into (doing) sth** *Bad health forced her into taking early retirement.*
**2 force yourself (to do sth) a)** to make yourself do something that you do not want to do: *I forced myself to get out of bed.* **b)** *BrE spoken* used when trying to persuade someone to do something that they seem unwilling to do, because you know they will enjoy it: *"I couldn't eat another thing!" "Go on! Force yourself!"*
**3 ▶ MAKE SB/STH MOVE ◀** to make someone or something move in a particular direction or into a different position, especially using physical force: **force sth into/out of** *Firemen attempted to enter the building but were forced back by the flames.*
**4 force your way in/out/through etc** to push and use physical force to get into, out of, or through something: *The doctor forced his way through the crowd.*
**5 ▶ OPEN STH ◀** to use physical force to open something: **force sth ↔ open** *Robbers forced open the safe in the manager's office.* |**force the lock/window/door** (=open it using force, often causing damage)
**6 force sb's hand** to make someone do something unwillingly or earlier than they had intended: *We didn't want to raise our prices but the fall in the dollar forced our hand.*
**7 force the issue** to do something that makes it necessary for someone to make decisions or take action, instead of waiting for the situation to develop: *Rather than trying to force the issue, we gave them another day to decide.*
**8 force a smile/laugh etc** to make yourself smile, laugh etc even though you feel upset or annoyed
**9 force the pace** to make the other runners in a race have to run faster by running ahead of them
**force** sth ↔ **back** *phr v* [T] to try hard to stop yourself from showing your emotions: *Janet forced back her tears.*
**force** sth ↔ **down** *phr v* [T] **1** to make yourself swallow something that you do not want to eat or drink: *I managed to force down a piece of stale bread.* **2** to make a plane have to land by threatening to attack it
**force** sth **on/upon** sb *phr v* [T] to make someone accept something even though they do not want it: *children with piano lessons forced upon them*
**force** sth ↔ **out of** sb *phr v* [T] to make someone tell you something by asking them many times, threatening them etc: *I wasn't going to tell him, but he forced it out of me.*

**forced** /fɔːst‖fɔːrst/ *adj* **1** done unwillingly and with effort, not because of any sincere feeling: *Their smiles seemed rather forced.* **2** done suddenly and quickly, because the situation makes it necessary: *a forced march back to base*|**a forced landing** (=when an aircraft has to land quickly because of an unexpected problem)

**force-feed** /ˈ· ·/ *v* [T] to force someone to eat by putting food or liquid down their throat

**force·ful** /ˈfɔːsfəl‖ˈfɔːrs-/ *adj* **1** a forceful person expresses their opinions very strongly and clearly and people are easily persuaded by them: *She has a strong character, very forceful and determined.* **2** forceful arguments, reasons etc are strongly and clearly expressed, and help persuade you that something is true —**forcefully** *adv*: *Dole spoke out forcefully against the plan.* —**forcefulness** *n* [U]

**force ma·jeure** /ˌfɔːs mæˈʒɜː‖ˌfɔːrs mɑːˈʒɜːr/ *n* [U] *French formal* unexpected events that prevent you from doing what you intended or promised: *The company tried to escape its obligations by claiming force majeure.*

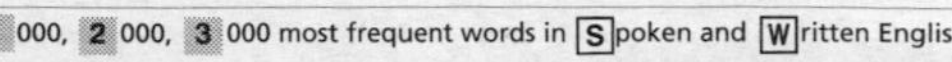

**for·ceps** /ˈfɔːseps, -sɪ̈ps‖ˈfɔːr-/ *n* [plural] a medical instrument used for picking up and holding things

**for·ci·ble** /ˈfɔːsɪ̈bəl‖ˈfɔːr-/ *adj* done using physical force, especially as a result of an official order: *forcible seizure of their assets* —**forcibly** *adv*: *Police threatened to have the protesters forcibly removed.*

**ford**[1] /fɔːd‖fɔːrd/ *n* [C] a place where a river is not deep, so that you can walk or drive across it

**ford**[2] *v* [T] to walk or drive across a river at a place where the water is not deep

**fore-** /fɔː‖fɔːr/ *prefix* **1** before: *to forewarn* **2** placed at the front: *her forenames|a horse's forelegs* **3** the front part of something: *his strong forearms*

**fore**[1] /fɔː‖fɔːr/ *n* **come to the fore** to become important or influential: *Yeltsin first came to the fore when he was the Party Chief in Moscow.*

**fore**[2] *adj* [only before noun] *technical* the fore parts of a ship, plane, or animal are the parts at the front —opposite AFT

**fore·arm** /ˈfɔːrɑːm‖-ɑːrm/ *n* [C] the lower part of the arm, between the hand and the elbow —see also **forewarned is forearmed** (FOREWARN (2)) —see picture at BODY

**fore·bear** /ˈfɔːbeə‖ˈfɔːrber/ *n* [C usually plural] *formal* someone who was a member of your family a long time in the past

**fore·bod·ing** /fɔːˈbəʊdɪŋ‖fɔːrˈboʊ-/ *n* [U] a feeling that something very unpleasant is going to happen soon: *She waited for news from the hospital with a grim sense of foreboding.*

**fore·cast**[1] /ˈfɔːkɑːst‖ˈfɔːrkæst/ *n* [C] a description of what is likely to happen in the future, based on information that is available now: *the company's annual sales forecast|the weather forecast*

**forecast**[2] *past tense & past participle* **forecast** *or* **forecasted** *v* [T] to make a statement saying what is likely to happen in the future, based on information that is available now: *Bad weather had been forecast for the day of the race.*|**forecast (that)** *The Federal Reserve Bank has forecast that the economy will grow by 2% this year.* —**forecaster** *n* [C]

**fore·castle** /ˈfəʊksəl‖ˈfoʊk-/ *n* [C] *AmE* the front part of a ship, where the sailors live; FO'C'SLE *BrE*

**fore·close** /fɔːˈkləʊz‖fɔːrˈkloʊz/ *v* [I + **on**, T] *technical* to take away someone's property because they have failed to pay back the money that they borrowed to buy it —**foreclosure** /-ˈkləʊʒə‖-ˈkloʊʒər/ *n* [U]

**fore·court** /ˈfɔːkɔːt‖ˈfɔːrkɔːrt/ *n* [C] a large open area in front of a building such as a garage, or hotel

**fore·doomed** /fɔːˈduːmd‖fɔːr-/ *adj formal* intended by FATE (2) to be unsuccessful or unhappy

**fore·fa·thers** /ˈfɔːˌfɑːðəz‖ˈfɔːrˌfɑːθərz/ *n* [plural] the people, especially men, who were part of the same family as you a long time in the past

**fore·fin·ger** /ˈfɔːˌfɪŋgə‖ˈfɔːrˌfɪŋgər/ *n* [C] the finger next to your thumb; INDEX FINGER

**fore·foot** /ˈfɔːfʊt‖ˈfɔːr-/ *n* [C] one of the two front feet of a four-legged animal

**fore·front** /ˈfɔːfrʌnt‖ˈfɔːr-/ *n* **1 be in/at the forefront (of)** to have an important and leading position among a group of people, organizations etc that are trying to achieve something or are developing new ideas: *The Pasteur Institute has been at the forefront of research into the AIDS virus.* **2 be in/at the forefront of sb's mind** to be thought about by someone and seem important to them

**fore·gath·er** /fɔːˈgæðə‖fɔːrˈgæðər/ *v* [I] to FORGATHER

**fore·go, forgo** /fɔːˈgəʊ‖fɔːrˈgoʊ/ *v past tense* **forewent** /-ˈwent/ *past participle* **foregone** /-ˈgɒn‖-ˈgɔːn/ [T] *formal* to decide to not do or have something, especially something enjoyable: *The monks have to forego earthly pleasures.*

**fore·go·ing** /fɔːˈgəʊɪŋ‖ˈfɔːrˈgoʊ-/ *adj* **the foregoing** *formal* the things that have just been mentioned

**fore·gone con·clu·sion** /ˌ‥ ·ˈ‥/ *n* **be a foregone conclusion** if something is a foregone conclusion, the result of it is certain, even though it has not yet happened or been decided: *The election result was a foregone conclusion.*

**fore·ground** /ˈfɔːgraʊnd‖ˈfɔːr-/ *n* **1 the foreground** the nearest part of a scene in a picture or a photograph **2 be in the foreground** to be regarded as important and receive a lot of attention: *Education and health were very much in the foreground during the post-war years.*

**fore·hand** /ˈfɔːhænd‖ˈfɔːr-/ *n* [singular] a way of hitting the ball in tennis, with the flat part of your hand facing the direction of the ball —**forehand** *adj* —see picture on page 1264

**fore·head** /ˈfɒrɪ̈d, ˈfɔːhed‖ˈfɔːrɪ̈d, ˈfɑːrɪ̈d, ˈfɔːrhed/ *n* [C] the part of your face above your eyes and below your hair —see picture at HEAD[1]

**for·eign** /ˈfɒrɪ̈n‖ˈfɔː-, ˈfɑː-/ *adj* **1** not from your own country or the country you are talking about: *Can you speak any foreign languages?|foreign tourists|I thought she sounded foreign.* **2** [only before noun] involving or dealing with other countries: *America's foreign policy* **3 foreign body/matter/object** *formal* something that has come into something else, and that should not be there: *Make sure you remove all foreign matter from the wound.* **4 foreign to** *formal* **a)** not typical of someone's usual character: *Any form of cruelty is foreign to his nature.* **b)** seeming strange and unfamiliar: *The idea of doing something just for pleasure is quite foreign to them.* —**foreignness** *n* [U] S3 W1

**foreign af·fairs** /ˌ‥ ·ˈ·/ *n* [plural] politics, business matters etc that affect or concern the relationship between your country and other countries

**for·eign·er** /ˈfɒrɪ̈nə‖ˈfɔːrɪ̈nər, ˈfɑː-/ *n* [C] someone who comes from a different country: *Foreigners are not allowed to own land.*

**foreign ex·change** /ˌ‥ ·ˈ·/ *n* [U] **1** the system of buying and selling foreign money: *The foreign exchange markets reacted quickly to the cut in German interest rates.* **2** foreign money, especially money obtained by selling goods to a foreign country: *Coffee is a valuable source of foreign exchange for Uganda.*

**Foreign Of·fice** /ˈ‥ ˌ‥/ *n* the British government department that is responsible for dealing with foreign affairs

**fore·knowl·edge** /fɔːˈnɒlɪdʒ‖fɔːrˈnɑːl-/ *n* [U] *formal* knowledge that something is going to happen before it actually does: [+ **of**] *The senator denied having any foreknowledge of the affair.*

**fore·leg** /ˈfɔːleg‖ˈfɔːr-/ *n* [C] one of the two front legs of a four-legged animal

**fore·lock** /ˈfɔːlɒk‖ˈfɔːrlɑːk/ *n* [C] **1** a piece of hair that falls over someone's forehead —see picture at HORSE[1] **2 forelock-tugging/touching** *BrE* showing too much respect towards people in authority

**fore·man** /ˈfɔːmən‖ˈfɔːr-/ *n plural* **foremen** /-mən/ [C] **1** a skilled worker who is in charge of a group of builders or factory workers **2** the leader of a JURY (=the group of 12 people who decide whether someone is guilty in a court of law)

**fore·most** /ˈfɔːməʊst‖ˈfɔːrmoʊst/ *adj* **foremost scientist/expert/writer etc** the most important and respected scientist, writer etc: *one of Europe's foremost authorities on childhood diseases* —see also **first and foremost** (FIRST (21))

**fore·name** /ˈfɔːneɪm‖ˈfɔːr-/ *n* [C] *formal* someone's FIRST NAME

**fo·ren·sic** /fəˈrensɪk, -zɪk/ *adj* [only before noun] connected with the methods used for finding out who is guilty of a crime: **forensic science/medicine etc** *A specialist in forensic science was called as a witness.*|**forensic evidence** (=blood, hair, FINGERPRINTS etc, used to prove that someone is guilty)

**fore·or·dain** /ˌfɔːrɔːˈdeɪn‖ˌfɔːrɔːr-/ *v* [T] *formal* to decide or arrange how something will happen before it actually happens: *Their love seemed foreordained.*

**fore·play** /ˈfɔːpleɪ‖ˈfɔːr-/ *n* [U] sexual activity, such as kissing and touching the sexual organs, done before having sex

**fore·run·ner** /ˈfɔːˌrʌnə‖-ər/ *n* [C] **1** a person, organization, machine etc which existed a long time before a similar one that exists now, and which the present one is based upon: [+ **of**] *The suffragettes were forerunners of the modern women's movement.* **2** a sign or warning that something is going to happen

**fore·see** /fɔːˈsiː‖fɔːr-/ *past* **foresaw** /-ˈfɔː‖-ˈsɒː/ *past participle* **foreseen** /-ˈsiːn/ *v* [T] to know that something is going to happen before it actually happens: *The method was used in ways that could not have been foreseen by its inventors.* | **foresee that** *Few analysts foresaw that oil prices would rise so steeply.*

**fore·see·a·ble** /fɔːˈsiːəbəl‖fɔːr-/ *adj* **1 in the foreseeable future** fairly soon: *There is a possibility of severe water shortages in the foreseeable future.* **2 for the foreseeable future** continuing in the future for as long as you can imagine: *Their dependence on oil exports is likely to continue for the foreseeable future.* **3** foreseeable difficulties, events etc are ones that you can imagine happening in the future: *planning for any foreseeable financial losses*

**fore·shad·ow** /fɔːˈʃædəʊ‖fɔːrˈʃædoʊ/ *v* [T] to be a sign of something that will happen in the future: *The events in Spain in the 1930s foreshadowed the rise of Nazi Germany.*

**fore·shore** /ˈfɔːʃɔː‖ˈfɔːrʃɔːr/ *n* [singular] **1** the part of the shore between the highest and lowest levels that the sea reaches **2** the part of the shore between the edge of the sea and the part of the land that has houses, grass etc

**fore·short·ened** /fɔːˈʃɔːtnd‖fɔːrˈʃɔːrtnd/ *adj* objects, places etc that are foreshortened appear to be smaller, shorter, or closer together than they really are: *Some of the figures are oddly foreshortened, giving the picture a disturbing quality.* —**foreshorten** *v* [T]

**fore·sight** /ˈfɔːsaɪt‖ˈfɔːr-/ *n* [U] the ability to imagine what is likely to happen and to consider this when planning for the future: *The report blames the accident on lack of foresight by the original planners.* | **have the foresight to do sth** *Luckily she had had the foresight to destroy the incriminating documents.*

**fore·skin** /ˈfɔːˌskɪn‖ˈfɔːr-/ *n* [C] a loose fold of skin covering the end of a man's PENIS

S2 W2 **for·est** /ˈfɒrɪ̣st‖ˈfɔː-, ˈfɑː-/ *n* [C] a large area of land that is thickly covered with trees: *Much of Scandinavia is covered in dense pine forest.* | *a forest fire*

**fore·stall** /fɔːˈstɔːl‖fɔːrˈstɒːl/ *v* [T] to prevent something from happening or prevent someone from doing something by doing something first: *Gero urged reforms in order to forestall trouble.*

**for·est·er** /ˈfɒrɪ̣stə‖ˈfɔːrɪ̣stər, ˈfɑː-/ *n* [C] someone who works in a forest taking care of, planting, and cutting down the trees

**for·est·ry** /ˈfɒrɪ̣stri‖ˈfɔː-, ˈfɑː-/ *n* [U] the science or skill of looking after large areas of trees

**fore·taste** /ˈfɔːteɪst‖ˈfɔːr-/ *n* **be a foretaste of** to be a sign of something more important, more impressive etc that will happen in the future: *Two spectacular wins at the start of the season were a foretaste of things to come.*

**fore·tell** /fɔːˈtel‖fɔːr-/ *v past tense and past participle* **foretold** /-ˈtəʊld‖-ˈtoʊld/ [T] to say what will happen in the future, especially by using special magical powers: *the birth of Christ, foretold by prophets*

**fore·thought** /ˈfɔːθɔːt‖ˈfɔːrθɒːt-/ *n* [U] careful thought about what needs to be done in order to make sure things happen well in the future: *No one had had the forethought to bring a corkscrew.*

**fore·told** /fɔːˈtəʊld‖fɔːrˈtoʊld/ the past tense and past participle of FORETELL

S3 **for·ev·er, for ever** /fərˈevə‖-ər/ *adv* **1** continuing or lasting for all future time: *Our love will last forever.* | *These valuable works of art have been lost forever.* **2** *especially spoken* for a very long time: *We'll be stuck here forever if the car won't start.* | **take forever** (=take a long time) *It took forever to clean up after the party.* **3 be forever doing sth** *spoken* to do something many times, especially in a way that annoys people: *He's forever making comments about my weight.* **4 forever and a day** *spoken* a very long time: *It's going to take me forever and a day to pay for it.* **5 forever and ever** a phrase meaning forever, used especially in stories

**fore·warn** /fɔːˈwɔːn‖fɔːrˈwɔːrn/ *v* [T often passive] **1** to warn someone about something dangerous, unpleasant, or unexpected before it happens: [+ **of/about/against**] *She had been forewarned of the discomforts of travelling by train in the Soviet Union.* **2 forewarned is forearmed** used to say that if you know about something in advance, you can be properly prepared for it —**forewarning** *n* [C,U]

**fore·went, forwent** /fɔːˈwent‖fɔːr-/ past tense of FORGO

**fore·wom·an** /ˈfɔːˌwʊmən‖ˈfɔːr-/ *n* [C] **1** a female worker who is in charge of a group of other workers, especially in a factory **2** a woman who is the leader of a JURY (=a group of 12 people who decide if someone is guilty in a court of law)

**fore·word** /ˈfɔːwɜːd‖ˈfɔːrwɜːrd/ *n* [C] a short piece of writing at the beginning of a book

**for·feit**[1] /ˈfɔːfɪ̣t‖ˈfɔːr-/ *v* [T] to lose something valuable by having it taken away from you, either as a punishment or because of a law or rule: *By becoming a German citizen he forfeited his right to live in the US.* —**forfeiture** /-fɪ̣tʃə‖-əʀ/ *n* [U]

**forfeit**[2] *n* [C] something that is taken away from you or something that you have to do, because you have broken a rule or made a mistake

**forfeit**[3] *adj* **be forfeit** *formal* to be legally or officially taken away from you as a punishment: *Unless he returns with the prisoners as he promised, his life shall be forfeit.*

**for·gath·er, foregather** /fɔːˈgæðə‖fɔːr, ˈgæðər/ *v* [I] *formal* to meet as a group

**for·gave** /fəˈgeɪv‖fər-/ the past tense of FORGIVE

**forge**[1] /fɔːdʒ‖fɔːrdʒ/ *v* [T] **1** to illegally copy something, especially something printed or written on paper, to make people think that it is real: *Someone stole my credit card and forged my signature.* | *a forged passport* **2 forge a relationship/alliance/links etc** to develop a strong relationship, with other groups or other countries: *Gorbachev was able to forge new links between Russia and the West.* **3** to make something from a piece of metal by heating the metal and shaping it

**forge ahead** *phr v* [I] **1** to make progress and become more and more successful: *individuals who have forged ahead in this competitive field* **2** to move forward in a strong and powerful way

**forge**[2] *n* [C] **1** a place where metal is heated and shaped into objects **2** a large piece of equipment that produces high temperatures and is used for heating and shaping metal objects

**forg·er** /ˈfɔːdʒə‖ˈfɔːrdʒər/ *n* [C] someone who illegally copies documents, money, paintings etc, to try to make people think they are real

**for·ge·ry** /ˈfɔːdʒəri‖ˈfɔːr-/ *n* **1** [C] a document, painting, or piece of paper money that has been forged: *The painting was actually a very clever forgery.* **2** [U] the crime of forging official documents, money etc

**for·get** /fəˈget‖fər-/ *past tense* **forgot** /-ˈgɒt‖-ˈgɑːt/ *past participle* **forgotten** /-ˈgɒtn‖-ˈgɑːtn/ *v* S1 W1
**1** ▶ **FACTS/INFORMATION** ◀ [I,T] to be unable to remember facts, information, or something that happened in the past: *I'm sorry, I've forgotten your name.* | [+ **(that)**] *Don't forget that it's Sarah's birthday on Tuesday.* | [+ **about**] *Charles seems to have forgotten about what happened.* | [+ **how/what/when/why etc**] *Natalie managed to forget where she'd parked the car.*
**2** ▶ **STH YOU MUST DO** ◀ to not remember to do something that you have to do: *"Did you remember to post*

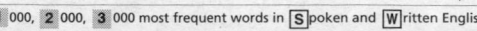

F

*that letter?" "Oh, sorry, I forgot."* | **forget to do sth** *Someone's forgotten to turn off their headlights.* | **forget (that)** *I forgot that I was supposed to come in early this morning.* | **clean forget** (=completely forget) *He meant to invite Monica to the party but he clean forgot.*

**3 ▶ NOT BRING ◀** [I,T] to not bring something that you need, because you did not remember to bring it: *Don't forget your passport.* | *I didn't forget the torch.*

**4 ▶ STOP THINKING ABOUT ◀** [I,T] to try to stop thinking and worrying about someone or something that makes you unhappy: *Years after their divorce Olivia still could not forget John.* | [+ **about**] *I'd forget about it if I were you.*

**5 ▶ NOT CARE ABOUT ◀** [I,T] to not care about or give attention to someone or something: [+ **about**] *Don't go off to college and forget about your old friends, okay?*

**6 ▶ STOP A PLAN ◀** [I, T] to stop trying to do something because it no longer seems possible: [+ **about**] *We'll have to forget about going on holiday.* | *If we can't get any funding we might as well forget the whole thing.*

**7 not forgetting** used to add something to a list of things: *Bear in mind that we have to pay for all the packaging and transportation costs, not forgetting airport taxes.*

**8 forget yourself** to do something stupid or embarrassing, especially by losing control of your emotions

Frequencies of the verb **forget** in spoken and written English.

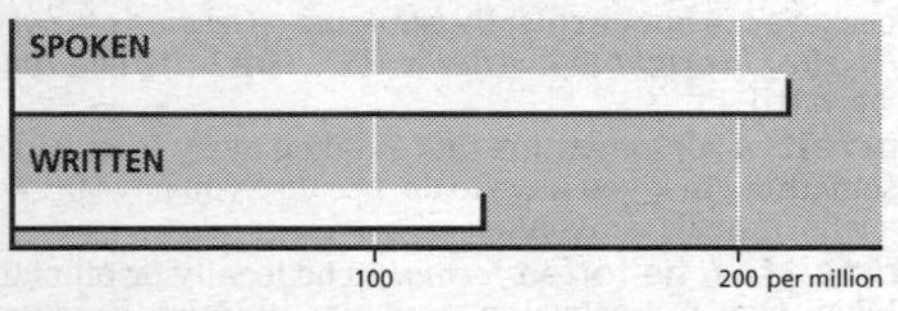


Based on the British National Corpus and the Longman Lancaster Corpus

This graph shows that the verb **forget** is much more common in spoken English than in written English. This is because it is used in a lot of common spoken phrases.

**forget** (*v*) **SPOKEN PHRASES**

**9 don't forget a)** used to remind someone to do something: *We need bread, milk, and eggs. Don't forget now, will you?* | **don't forget to do sth** *Don't forget to lock the place up when you leave.* **b)** used to remind someone about an important fact or detail that they should consider: *The kids won't be home until late, don't forget, so we'll be eating on our own.* | **don't forget (that)** *But don't forget you have to pay interest on the loan.*

**10 forget it a)** used when someone asks you what you just said and you do not want to repeat it: *"What was that? I didn't hear." "Nothing, forget it."* **b)** used to tell someone that something is not important and they do not need to worry about it: *"I'm really sorry, I'll get you another one." "Forget it, I've got lots of bowls."* **c)** used to tell someone that you refuse to do something or that it will be impossible for them to do something: *"Lend me $10." "Forget it, no way."* | *If you're thinking of getting Roy to help, you can forget it!* **d)** used to tell someone to stop asking or talking about something, because it is annoying you: *Look, just forget it will you. I'm not coming and that's that.*

**11 I'll never forget** used to say that you will always remember something from the past, because it was sad, funny, enjoyable etc: *I'll never forget the look on his face when I said I'd marry him.*

**12 I forget** used to say that you can not remember a particular detail about something you are talking about: **I forget what/where/how etc** *I forget what he said exactly, but it was very rude.* | **I forget the name/details etc** *You go down Weir Road then turn left into, I forget the name of it, but it's first left after the bank.*

**13 forget that** used to tell someone to ignore what you have just said because it is not correct, important etc: *Then mix the flour with 500 cls of milk, no, forget that, 50 cls of milk.*

**14 and don't you forget it** used to remind someone angrily about an important fact that should make them behave differently: *Listen, I'm the boss around here, and don't you forget it!*

**15 aren't you forgetting...?/haven't you forgotten...?** used to tell someone that they have forgotten to consider something important: *"Wait a minute – aren't you forgetting something? No? Well what about saying 'thank you'?"*

**for·get·ful** /fəˈgetfəl‖fər-/ *adj* often forgetting things —**forgetfulness** *n* [U] —**forgetfully** *adv*

**forget-me-not** /-ˈ- · ,-/ *n* [C] a small plant with pale blue flowers

**for·get·ta·ble** /fəˈgetəbəl‖fər-/ *adj often humorous* not very interesting or good: *a completely forgettable movie*

**for·giv·a·ble** /fəˈgɪvəbəl‖fər-/ *adj* bad behaviour that is forgivable is not seriously bad and you can easily forgive it: *I suppose a little over-excitement is forgivable under the circumstances.*

**for·give** /fəˈgɪv‖fər-/ *v past tense* **forgave** /-ˈgeɪv/ *past participle* **forgiven** /-ˈgɪvən/ [I,T] **1** to decide not to blame someone or be angry with them although they have done something wrong: *Can you ever forgive me?* | **forgive sb for sth** *I can't forgive him for what he did to my sister.* | **forgive sb sth** *forgive us our sins* | **I'd never forgive myself** *If anything happened to the kids I'd never forgive myself.* | **forgive and forget** (=forgive someone for something and behave as if they had never done it) **2 forgive me** *spoken* used when you are going to say something or ask something that might seem rude or offensive: *Forgive me, Mr Lewis, but I don't think that is relevant.* | **forgive me for asking/saying etc** *Forgive me for saying so, but I think that's nonsense.* **3 sb could be forgiven for thinking/wondering/believing etc sth** used to say that it is easy to understand why someone would think or believe something: *A foreign visitor could be forgiven for thinking football is a religion in this country.* S3

**for·give·ness** /fəˈgɪvnɪ̀s‖fər-/ *n* [U] the act of forgiving someone: **ask for/beg for forgiveness** (=ask someone to forgive you)

**for·giv·ing** /fəˈgɪvɪŋ‖fər-/ *adj* willing to forgive: *My father was a kind and forgiving man.*

**for·go** /fɔːˈgəʊ‖fɔːrˈgoʊ/ *v* [T] to FOREGO

**for·got** /fəˈgɒt‖fərˈgɑːt/ the past tense of FORGET

**for·got·ten**[1] /fəˈgɒtn‖fərˈgɑːtn/ the past participle of FORGET

**forgotten**[2] *adj* [usually before noun] that people have forgotten about or no longer pay much attention to: *a rare plant growing in a forgotten corner of the churchyard*

**forks**

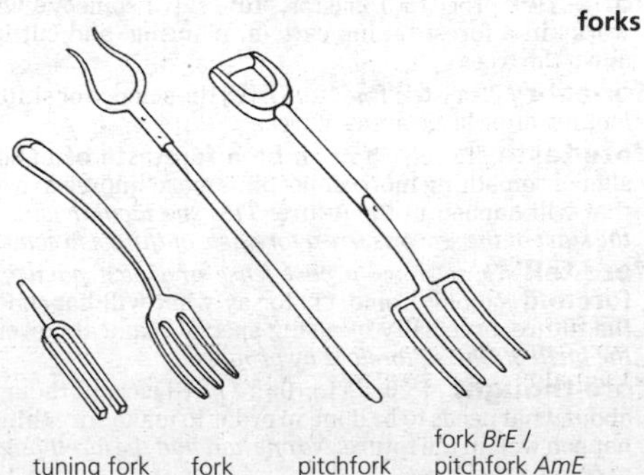


**fork**[1] /fɔːk‖fɔːrk/ *n* [C] **1** a tool used for picking up and eating food, with a handle and three or four points: *knives and forks* **2** a garden tool used for digging, with a handle and three or four points —compare PITCHFORK **3** a place where a road or river divides into two parts, or one of the parts it divides into: *Take the left fork then go straight on for two miles.* **4 the forks** the parallel metal bars between which the front wheel of a bicycle or MOTORCYCLE is fixed —see also TUNING FORK —see picture at BICYCLE

**fork²** *v* **1** [I] if a road, path, or river forks, it divides into two parts **2 fork left/right** to travel towards the left or right part of a road when it divides into two parts: *Fork left at the bottom of the hill.* **3** [T] to pick up, carry, or turn something over using a fork: *He forked some bacon onto a piece of bread.*

**fork out** (sth) *phr v* [I,T] *informal* to spend a lot of money on something, not because you want to but because you have to: [+ **for/on**] *I had to fork out over £600 on my car when I had it serviced.*

**forked** /fɔːkt‖fɔːrkt/ *adj* having one end divided into two or more parts: *Snakes have forked tongues.*

**forked light·ning** /ˌ· ˈ··/ *n* [U] lightning that is in the form of a line of light that divides into several smaller lines near the bottom —compare SHEET LIGHTNING —see picture on page 836

**fork-lift truck** /ˌ· · ˈ·/ also **fork-lift** /ˈ· ·/ *n* [C] a small vehicle with special equipment on the front for lifting and moving heavy things

**for·lorn** /fəˈlɔːn‖fərˈlɔːrn/ *adj* **1** seeming lonely and unhappy: *a forlorn little figure sitting outside the station* **2** a place that is forlorn seems empty and sad, and is often in bad condition: *The house looked old and forlorn.* **3 a forlorn hope** something you hope for that is very unlikely to happen: *We continued negotiating in the forlorn hope of finding a peace formula.*

S1 W1 **form¹** /fɔːm‖fɔːrm/ *n*

**1** ► **TYPE** ◄ [C] a type of something, that exists in many different types: [+ **of**] *Trains are a very cost-effective form of transport.* | *She dislikes any form of exercise.*

**2** ► **WAY STH IS/APPEARS** ◄ [C] the way in which something exists, is presented, or appears: *We oppose racism in all its forms.* | **take a form/take the form of** (=happen or exist in a particular way or as a particular type) *The assignment can take any form you like – a written essay, a piece of recorded music, or whatever.*

**3** ► **SHAPE** ◄ [C] a shape, especially one that you cannot see very clearly: [+ **of**] *the shadowy forms of the divers*

**4** ► **DOCUMENT** ◄ [C] an official document with spaces where you have to answer questions and provide information: *I was interested in the job and sent off for an application form.* | **fill in/out a form** (=write the answers to the questions on a form) *Fill in the form and send it back with your cheque.* —see picture at FILL

**5 in the form of a)** having the shape of: *The main staircase was in the form of a big 'S'.* **b)** existing in a particular form: *People are bombarded with information in the form of magazines and TV advertising.*

**6** ► **ART/LITERATURE** ◄ [U] the structure of a work of art or piece of writing, rather than the ideas it expresses, events it describes etc: *Writers like Henry James place a lot of emphasis on form as well as content.*

**7** ► **LEVEL OR PERFORMANCE** ◄ [U] **a)** how well a sports person, team or race horse is performing, or has performed recently: *Judging by her most recent form, she should easily win a medal at the Olympics.* **b) on present/current/past etc form** based on how well a person, team, organization etc is performing or achieving their aims: *On current form, the Democrats could lose control of the Senate in the mid-term elections.*

**8** ► **SCHOOL** ◄ [C] *BrE* a class in a school: *We stopped doing Art in the fourth form.* —see also SIXTH FORM

**9** ► **GRAMMAR** ◄ [C] a way of writing or saying a word, for example one that shows it is in the past or the plural: *'Was' is a past form of the verb 'to be'.*

**10** ► **SEAT** ◄ [C] a long low wooden seat without a back

**11 bad form** *BrE old-fashioned* behaviour that is considered to be socially unacceptable: *It is considered rather bad form to arrive early at a dinner party.*

**12 be in good/great etc form** also **be on good/great etc form** *BrE* to be full of confidence and energy, so that you do something well or talk in an interesting or amusing way etc: *Michelle was in great form at last week's conference.* —see also FORM TEACHER

**form²** *v* S1 W1

**1** ► **START TO EXIST** ◄ [I,T often passive] to start to exist, or make something start to exist, especially as the result of a natural process: *The rocks were formed more than 4000 million years ago.* | *Ice was beginning to form around the edges of the windows.*

**2** ► **BE PART OF** ◄ [linking verb] to be part of something, or be the thing that something is based on: *Newton's theories form the basis of modern mathematics.*

**3** ► **BE OR ACT AS STH** ◄ [linking verb] if something forms something, it acts as or works in a particular way: *The river formed a natural boundary between the two countries.*

**4** ► **MAKE/PRODUCE** ◄ [T] **a)** to make something, especially by combining two or more parts: *In English the past tense is usually formed by adding 'ed'.* **b)** to make something so that it has a particular shape: *Cut off the corners of the square to form a diamond.*

**5** ► **ESTABLISH/MAKE** ◄ [T] **a)** to establish an organization, committee, government etc: *The United Nations was formed in 1945.* **b) form a relationship/alliance/attachment** to establish a relationship with someone: *She has difficulty forming long-term relationships with men.*

**6 form an opinion/impression/idea** to use available information to develop or reach an opinion or idea: *Police are trying to form an idea of what kind of person the killer is.*

**7** ► **DEVELOP** ◄ [T] to make someone develop into a particular type of person: *Events in early childhood often help to form our personalities in later life.*

**8** ► **LINE** ◄ [I,T] to come together and make a group or a line: *Film-goers began to form a line outside the cinema.*

**form·al¹** /ˈfɔːməl‖ˈfɔːr-/ *adj* **1** formal behaviour is very polite, and is used with people you do not know well, or in official situations or at important social occasions: *Our boss is very formal, she doesn't call anyone by their first name.* **2** formal language is used in speeches, in serious or official writing, or at official meetings or important social occasions: *You shouldn't use 'Yours faithfully' in a letter to a friend – it sounds too formal.* **3** a formal occasion is serious and important, and people who go to it wear good clothes and behave according to strict social rules: *I only wear this suit for formal dinners.* **4** a formal decision or action is made or done officially or publicly: *On July 19th a formal declaration of war was made in Berlin.* **5 formal education/training/qualification** education etc in a subject or skill gained in a school, college etc rather than practical experience of it: *Many of the health workers had no formal medical training.* —see also FORMALLY

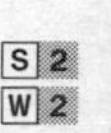

**formal²** *n* [C] *AmE* **1** a formal social event such as a dance, at which you have to wear formal clothes **2** an expensive and usually long dress that women wear at a formal occasion

**for·mal·de·hyde** /fɔːˈmældəhaɪd‖fɔːr-/ *n* [U] a strong-smelling gas that can be mixed with water and used for preserving things: *frogs preserved in formaldehyde*

**formal dress** /ˌ·· ˈ·/ *n* [U] clothes worn for formal social occasions, especially a black JACKET (1), black trousers, and a BOW TIE for men, or a long dress for women

**for·ma·lin** /ˈfɔːmələn‖ˈfɔːr-/ *n* [U] a liquid made by mixing formaldehyde and water, used for preserving things

**for·ma·lise** /ˈfɔːməlaɪz‖ˈfɔːr-/ *v* a British spelling of FORMALIZE

**form·al·is·m** /ˈfɔːməlɪzəm‖ˈfɔːr-/ *n* [U] a style or method in art, religion, or science that pays too much attention to established rules —**formalist** *n, adj*

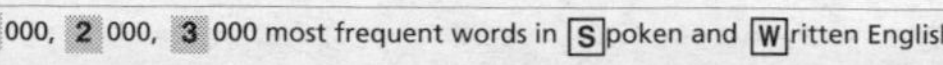

**for·mal·i·ty** /fɔːˈmælǝ̇ti‖fɔːr-/ *n* **1** [C usually plural] something that you must do as a formal or official part of an activity or process: *There are a few formalities to settle before you become legal owner of the car.* **2 be a formality** to be something that you must do even though it has no practical importance or effects: *The physical exam is just a formality.* **3** [U] polite and formal behaviour: *The following morning, Mr Harrison greeted her with stiff formality.*

**for·mal·ize** also **-ise** *BrE* /ˈfɔːməlaɪz‖ˈfɔːr-/ *v* [T] to make a plan, decision, or idea official, especially by deciding and clearly describing all the details: *Final arrangements for the takeover have yet to be formalized.* —**formalization** /ˌfɔːməlaɪˈzeɪʃən‖ˌfɔːrmələ-/ *n* [U]

**for·mal·ly** /ˈfɔːməli‖ˈfɔːr-/ *adv* **1** officially: *Mr Wright has formally accepted the job.* **2** in a polite way: *He bowed formally to each guest in turn.*

W3 **for·mat¹** /ˈfɔːmæt‖ˈfɔːr-/ *n* [C] **1** the way in which something is organized or arranged: *I'd like to change the format of the meetings a little.* **2** the size, shape, design etc, in which something such as a book or magazine is produced: *a travel show with a music video type format*

**format²** *v* **formatted, formatting** [T] **1** to arrange a book, page etc according to a particular design or plan **2** *technical* to organize the space on a computer DISK so that information can be stored on it —**formatting** *n* [U] —**formatted** *adj*

W2 **for·ma·tion** /fɔːˈmeɪʃən‖fɔːr-/ *n* **1** [U] the process by which something develops into a particular thing or shape: *Damp conditions are needed for the formation of mould.* **2** the process of starting a new organization or group: *the formation of a new government* **3** the way in which a group of things are arranged to form a pattern or shape: *The flowers had been planted in a star formation.* **4 in formation** if a group of planes, ships, soldiers etc are moving in formation, they are marching, flying etc in a particular order or pattern **5** [C,U] something, especially a rock or cloud, that is formed in a particular shape, or the shape in which it is formed: *rock formations*

**for·ma·tive** /ˈfɔːmətɪv‖ˈfɔːr-/ *adj* [only before noun] having an important influence on the way someone's character develops: **formative influence/effect etc** *Parents have the greatest formative effect on their childrens' behaviour.* | **formative years/period/stages etc** (=the period when someone's character develops)

**for·mer¹** /ˈfɔːmə‖ˈfɔːrmər/ *adj* [only before noun] **1** happening or existing before, but not now: *The coal industry is now barely half its former size.* | *civil war in the former Yugoslavia* | **former president/soldier/wife etc** (=someone who was a president etc, but who is not now) *a former principal of the school* **2 your former self** what you were like before you were changed by age, illness, trouble etc: *She seems more like her former self.* | **be a shadow of your former self** (=be much less confident, healthy, energetic etc than you used to be)

**former²** *n* **1 the former** *formal* the first of two people or things that you have just mentioned: *Of the two possibilities, the former seems more likely.* —opposite LATTER¹ **2 first/fourth/sixth former** *BrE* used in some schools to show which class a student is in, according to how many years they have been in school

**for·mer·ly** /ˈfɔːməli‖ˈfɔːrmərli/ *adv* in earlier times: *Peru was formerly ruled by the Spanish.* —compare LATTERLY

**for·mi·ca** /fɔːˈmaɪkə‖fɔːr-/ *n* [U] *trademark* strong plastic made in thin sheets, used especially for covering the surfaces of tables: *formica tabletops*

**for·mic ac·id** /ˌfɔːmɪk ˈæsǝ̇d‖ˌfɔːr-/ *n* [U] an acid used especially for colouring cloth and in treating leather

**for·mi·da·ble** /ˈfɔːmǝ̇dəbəl, fəˈmɪd-‖ˈfɔːr-/ *adj* **1** a formidable person etc is one that you feel respect for because they are very powerful, or impressive: *With her management skills and his marketing expertise, they make a formidable combination.* | *The Pentium machines have formidable processing power.* **2** difficult to deal with and needing a lot of effort or skill: *The rally is a formidable test of both car and driver.* | **formidable problem/task** *the formidable task of creating a new filing system* —**formidably** *adv*

**form·less** /ˈfɔːmləs‖ˈfɔːrm-/ *adj* **1** without a definite shape: *Figures emerged out of the mist, dull and formless at first.* **2** ideas or feelings that are formless are not clear or definite: *A formless melancholy overcame her.* —**formlessly** *adv* —**formlessness** *n* [U]

**form let·ter** /ˈ· ˌ··/ *n* [C] a standard letter that is sent to a number of people

**form teach·er** /ˈ· ˌ··/ *n* [C] *BrE* the teacher who is responsible for all the students in the same class at a school

**for·mu·la** /ˈfɔːmjǝ̇lə‖ˈfɔːr-/ *n plural* **formulas** *or* **formulae** /-liː/ **1** [singular] a method or set of principles that you use to solve a problem or to make sure that something is successful: *We're still searching for a peace formula.* | [+ **for**] *The two sides worked out an acceptable formula for settling the strike.* | **magic formula** (=a method that is certain to be successful) *There's no magic formula for a happy marriage.* **2** [C] a series of numbers or letters that represent a mathematical or scientific rule: *the formula for calculating distance* **3** [C] a list of the substances used to make a medicine, FUEL¹ (1), drink etc, showing the amounts of each substance that should be used: *Coca-Cola's patented formula* **4 Formula One/Two/Three etc** a type of car racing, in which the different types are based on the size of the cars' engines: *a Formula One car* **5** [C,U] *AmE* a type of liquid food for babies that is similar to milk **6** [C] a fixed and familiar series of words that seems meaningless or insincere: *a speech full of the usual formulas and cliches* W3

**for·mu·la·ic** /ˌfɔːmjǝ̇ˈleɪ-ɪk◂‖ˌfɔːr-/ *adj formal* containing or made from ideas or expressions that have been used many times before and are therefore not very imaginative: *formulaic verse*

**for·mu·late** /ˈfɔːmjǝ̇leɪt‖ˈfɔːr-/ *v* [T] **1 formulate a plan/policy/program etc** to develop a plan or proposal, and decide all the details of how it will be done: *The government is formulating a new education policy.* **2** to choose particular words to express your thoughts or feelings: *He paused, trying to formulate an answer that would satisfy them.* —**formulation** /ˌfɔːmjǝ̇ˈleɪʃən‖ˌfɔːr-/ *n* [C,U]

**for·ni·cate** /ˈfɔːnǝ̇keɪt‖ˈfɔːr-/ *v* [I] a word meaning to have sex with someone who you are not married to, used to show strong disapproval —**fornication** /ˌfɔːnǝ̇ˈkeɪʃən‖ˌfɔːr-/ *n* [U]

**for·sake** /fəˈseɪk‖fər-/ *v past tense* **forsook** /-ˈsʊk/ *past participle* **forsaken** /-ˈseɪkən/ [T] *literary* **1** to leave someone, especially when you should stay because they need you: *God will never forsake you.* **2** to stop doing or leave something that you have or enjoy: *We had to forsake the comfort of our hotel room and spend the night waiting at the airport.* —see also GODFORSAKEN

**for·sooth** /fəˈsuːθ‖fər-/ *adv old use* certainly

**for·swear** /fɔːˈsweə‖fɔːrˈswer-/ *v past* **forswore** /-ˈswɔː‖-ˈswɔːr/ *past participle* **forsworn** /-ˈswɔːn‖ˈswɔːrn/ [T] *literary* to promise that you will not do or possess something: *a monk forswearing all possessions*

**for·sy·thi·a** /fɔːˈsaɪθiə‖fərˈsɪ-/ *n* [C,U] a bush that is covered with bright yellow flowers in the spring

**fort** /fɔːt‖fɔːrt/ *n* [C] a strong building or group of buildings used by soldiers or an army for defending an important place —see also **hold the fort** (HOLD¹ (19))

**for·te¹** /ˈfɔːteɪ‖fɔːrt/ *n* **1 be your/their forte** to be something that you do well or are skilled at: *Cooking has never been her forte.* **2** [C] a note or line of music played or sung loudly

**for·te²** /ˈfɔːteɪ‖ˈfɔːr-/ *adj, adv music* played or sung loudly

**forth** /fɔːθ‖fɔːrθ/ *adv literary* **1 and so forth** used to represent other things of the type you have already mentioned without actually naming them: *She started telling me about her bad back, her migraines, and so forth.* S2

**2 from that day/time/moment forth** *literary* beginning on that day or at that time: *From that moment forth they became close friends.* **3** [only after verb] *literary* going out from a place or point, and moving forwards or outwards: *factory chimneys that belched forth thick smoke* **4** *literary* towards a place that is in front of you; forwards: *She stretched forth her hand.* —see also **back and forth** (BACK² (11)), **hold forth** (HOLD¹), **put forth** (PUT)

**forth·com·ing** /ˌfɔːθˈkʌmɪŋ◂‖ˌfɔːrθ-◂/ *adj* **1** a forthcoming event, meeting etc is one that has been planned to happen soon: *a potential vote-winner in the forthcoming election* **2 be forthcoming** to be willing to give information about something: [+ **about**] *Jarvis was never very forthcoming about his love life.* **3** [not before noun] not given or offered when needed: *When no reply was forthcoming, she wrote again.*

**forth·right** /ˈfɔːθraɪt‖ˈfɔːrθ-/ *adj* saying honestly what you think, in a way that sometimes seems rude: *She answered in her usual forthright manner.*

**forth·with** /fɔːθˈwɪð, -ˈwɪθ‖fɔːrθ-/ *adv formal* immediately: *These instructions must be carried out forthwith.*

**for·ti·eth** /ˈfɔːtiəθ‖ˈfɔːr-/ *n* [C] one of forty equal parts of something

**for·ti·fi·ca·tion** /ˌfɔːtɪ̣fɪ̣ˈkeɪʃən‖ˌfɔːr-/ *n* [U] the process of making something stronger

**for·ti·fi·ca·tions** /ˌfɔːtɪ̣fɪ̣ˈkeɪʃənz‖ˌfɔːr-/ *n* [plural] towers, walls etc built around a place in order to protect it or defend it: *The army destroyed most of the town's fortifications.*

**fortified wine** /ˌ··· ˈ·/ *n* [C,U] wine such as SHERRY or PORT (3) that has strong alcohol added

**for·ti·fy** /ˈfɔːtɪ̣faɪ‖ˈfɔːr-/ *v* [T] **1** to build towers, walls etc around an area or city in order to defend it: *a fortified city* **2** to encourage an attitude or feeling and make it stronger: *Recent successes had fortified the team spirit.* **3** [often passive] to make someone feel physically or mentally stronger: **fortify yourself** *We had some coffee to fortify ourselves for the journey.* **4** [usually passive] to make food or drinks more healthy by adding VITAMINS to them: *fortified milk products*

**for·tis·si·mo** /fɔːˈtɪsɪ̣məʊ‖fɔːrˈtɪsɪ̣moʊ/ *adj, adv music* played or sung very loudly —**fortissimo** *adj* —compare FORTE²

**for·ti·tude** /ˈfɔːtɪ̣tjuːd‖ˈfɔːrtɪ̣tuːd/ *n* [U] courage shown when you are in great pain or experiencing a lot of trouble: *She bore her illness with great fortitude.*

S3 **fort·night** /ˈfɔːtnaɪt‖ˈfɔːrt-/ *n* [C usually singular] *BrE* two weeks: *I'm going away for a fortnight's holiday.*

**fort·night·ly** /ˈfɔːtnaɪtli‖ˈfɔːrt-/ *adj, adv BrE* happening every fortnight or once a fortnight: *We used to dread my uncle's fortnightly visits.*

**for·tress** /ˈfɔːtrɪ̣s‖ˈfɔːr-/ *n* [C] a large, strong building used for defending an important place

**for·tu·i·tous** /fɔːˈtjuːɪ̣təs‖fɔːrˈtuː-/ *adj formal* happening by chance, especially in a way that has a good result: *a fortuitous meeting* —**fortuitously** *adv*

S3 **for·tu·nate** /ˈfɔːtʃənət‖ˈfɔːr-/ *adj* **1** someone who is fortunate has something good happen to them, or is in a good situation; lucky: *Think of others less fortunate than yourselves.* | **fortunate to do sth** *He was fortunate enough to escape unharmed.* | **fortunate that** *You're fortunate that you've still got a job.* | **fortunate in having** *I was fortunate in having such supportive parents.* **2** a fortunate event is one in which something good happens by chance, especially when this saves you from trouble or danger: *By a fortunate coincidence, a passer-by heard her cries for help.*

**for·tu·nate·ly** /ˈfɔːtʃənətli‖ˈfɔːr-/ *adv* [sentence adverb] happening because of good luck: *Fortunately the fire was discovered soon after it started.*

S3 **for·tune** /ˈfɔːtʃən‖ˈfɔːr-/ *n*
W3 **1 ▶ MONEY ◀** [C] a very large amount of money: *He inherited his fortune from his father.* | **cost/spend/be worth a fortune** *They must have spent a fortune on that house.* | **a small fortune** (=a lot of money) *She won a small fortune on the horses.* | **make a/your fortune** (=make a lot of money in business) *The guy who invented Post-It notes must have made a fortune by now.*
**2 ▶ CHANCE ◀** [U] chance, and the good or bad influence that it has on your life: *I felt it was useless to struggle against fortune.* | **ill fortune** (=bad luck) *We were stoical, and did not complain of ill-fortune.* | **have the good fortune to do sth** *I had the good fortune to be invited to stay in Rome.*
**3 ▶ WHAT HAPPENS TO YOU ◀** [C usually plural] the good or bad things that happen in life: *This defeat marked a change in the team's fortunes.* | **the fortunes of war** (=things that can happen to people during a war)
**4 tell sb's fortune** to tell someone what will happen to them in the future by looking at their hands, using cards etc: *She paid £5 to have her fortune told.*
**5 fortune smiles on sth/sb** *literary* used to say that someone or something is lucky —see also SOLDIER OF FORTUNE, **fame and fortune** (FAME), **give hostages to fortune** (HOSTAGE (2)), **seek your fortune** (SEEK (4))

**fortune cook·ie** /ˈ·· ˌ··/ *n* [C] a Chinese BISCUIT that contains a piece of paper that says what will happen to you in the future

**fortune hunt·er** /ˈ·· ˌ··/ *n* [C] someone who wants to marry another person only to get their money

**fortune-tell·er** /ˈ·· ˌ··/ *n* [C] someone who uses magical methods to tell people what will happen to them in the future —**fortune telling** *n* [U]

**for·ty** /ˈfɔːti‖ˈfɔːrti/ *number* 40

**forty-five** /ˌ·· ˈ·◂/ *n* [C] *informal* **1** also **45** a small record with one song on each side **2** also **.45, Colt 45** *trademark* a small gun

**forty winks** /ˌ·· ˈ·/ *n* [U] *informal* a very short sleep: *Mr. Carey lay down on the sofa for forty winks.*

**for·um** /ˈfɔːrəm/ *n* [C] **1** an organization, meeting, TV programme etc where people have a chance to publicly discuss an important subject: [+ **for**] *The committee provided a useful forum for exposing the extent of discrimination.* | [+ **on**] *an international forum on the environment* **2** a large outdoor public place in ancient Rome used for business and discussion

**for·ward¹** /ˈfɔːwəd‖ˈfɔːrwərd/ *adv* **1** also **forwards** /-wədz‖-wərdz/ —towards a place or position that is in front of you: *He leaned forward slightly to try and hear what they were saying.* | *The crowd surged forwards.* **2** towards greater progress, improvement, or development: *The building of the new sports stadium is going forward.* | *trying to find a way forward in the peace talks* **3** towards the future in a way that is hopeful: *This is just the moment at which companies should be looking forward.* **4 from that day/time/moment etc forward** beginning on that day or at that time: *They never met again from that day forward.* **5** in or towards the front part of a ship —compare AFT, BACKWARDS —see also FAST FORWARD, **look forward to** (LOOK¹), **backwards and forwards** (BACKWARDS (4)) S1 W1

**forward²** *adj* **1** [only before noun] directed towards a place or position that is in front of you: *Army roadblocks prevented any further forward movement.* **2 forward planning/thinking** the act of making plans so that you will be prepared for what will happen in the future: *Forward planning is essential if you want the venture to succeed.* **3 no further forward** not having made much progress, especially compared to what was expected: *We've been trying to find a solution for weeks but we're no further forward.* **4** [only before noun] situated at or near the front of a ship, vehicle, building etc: *We sat in one of the forward sections of the train.* **5** *formal* too confident and friendly in dealing with people you do not know very well: *She was careful in what she said, having no wish to sound forward.* —compare BACKWARD S2 W3

**forward³** *v* **1** [T] to send letters, goods etc to someone, especially when they have moved to a new address: *We*

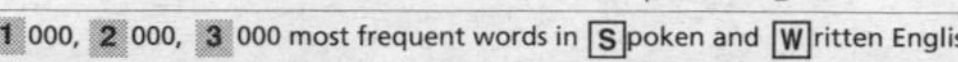
1 000, 2 000, 3 000 most frequent words in Spoken and Written English

*will forward the goods on receipt of your cheque.* | **forward sth to sb** *Can you forward my mail to me, please?* **2** [T] *formal* to help something to develop so that it becomes successful: *I see this new responsibility as a good chance to forward my career.*

**forward**[4] *n* [C] an attacking player on a team in sports such as football, BASKETBALL etc

**forwarding ad·dress** /'··· ,·‖'··· ,··/ *n* [C] an address that you leave for someone when you move to a new place so that they can send your mail to you

**forward-look·ing** /'·· ,··/ *adj* planning for and thinking about the future in a positive way, especially by being willing to use modern methods or ideas: *forward-looking companies able to spot the trends*

**forward mar·ket** /'·· ,··/ *n* [C] *technical* a market on the STOCK EXCHANGE that buys and sells products at an agreed price on a fixed date in the future; FUTURES MARKET

**for·ward·ness** /'fɔːwədnɪ̥s‖'fɔːrwərd-/ *n* [U] behaviour that is too confident or friendly

**forward roll** /,·· '·/ *n* [C] a movement in GYMNASTICS in which you roll over forwards onto your back so that your feet go over your head

**for·wards** /'fɔːwədz‖'fɔːrwərdz/ *adv* FORWARD

**fos·sil** /'fɒsəl‖'fɑː-/ *n* [C] **1** an animal or plant that died many thousands of years ago and that has been preserved in rock: *fossils of early reptiles* —see also LIVING FOSSIL **2** *informal* an insulting word for an old person

**fossil fu·el** /'·· ,··/ *n* [C,U] a FUEL[1] (1) such as coal or oil that is produced by the very gradual decaying of animals or plants over millions of years: *Environmentalists would like to see fossil fuels replaced by renewable energy sources.*

**fos·sil·ize** also **-ise** *BrE* /'fɒsɪ̥laɪz‖'fɑː-/ *v* **1 be fossilized** people, ideas, systems etc that are fossilized are very old-fashioned and never change or develop: *The valley's government was a fossilized specimen of feudal rule.* **2** [I,T] to become or form a FOSSIL by being preserved in rock —**fossilization** /,fɒsɪ̥laɪ'zeɪʃən‖,fɑːsɪ̥lə-/ *n* [U]

**foster-** /fɒstə‖fɒːstər, fɑː-/ *prefix* giving or receiving parental care although not of the same family: *a foster-mother* | *a foster-son* | *a foster-home* | *Danny is my foster-brother.* (=we have different parents, but he is being brought up with me in my family)

**fos·ter**[1] /'fɒstə‖'fɑːstər/ *v* **1** [I,T] to take someone else's child into your family for a period of time but without becoming their legal parent: *They fostered a little Romanian boy for a few months.* —compare ADOPT (1) **2** [T] to help a skill, feeling, idea etc develop over a period of time: *These sessions are designed to foster better working relationships.*

**foster**[2] *adj* **1 foster mother/father/parents** the people who foster a child: *It is sometimes difficult to find suitable foster parents.* **2 foster child** a child who is fostered **3 foster home** a private home where a child is fostered

**fought** /fɔːt‖fɒːt/ the past tense and past participle of FIGHT[1]

**foul**[1] /faʊl/ *adj*

**1** ▶ **SMELL/TASTE** ◀ a foul smell or taste is very unpleasant: *I gulped down some water to take the foul taste out of my mouth.* | **foul-tasting/foul-smelling** *The bags of garbage had been piled up in a foul-smelling heap.*

**2 in a foul mood/temper** *especially BrE* in a very bad mood and likely to get angry: *He's in a foul mood today, isn't he?*

**3** ▶ **UNPLEASANT** ◀ *especially BrE* very unpleasant: *I've had an absolutely foul day.*

**4** ▶ **AIR/WATER** ◀ very dirty: *The water in the harbour was foul with oil.*

**5 foul language** rude and offensive words: *I've never heard such foul language in all my life!*

**6** ▶ **WEATHER** ◀ *especially BrE* if the weather is foul, it is stormy and windy, with a lot of rain or snow

**7** ▶ **EVIL** ◀ *especially literary* evil or cruel: *foul deeds* —see also **by fair means or foul** (FAIR[1] (13)), **fall foul of** (FALL[1] (29)) —**foully** *adv* —**foulness** *n* [U]

**foul**[2] *v* **1** [I,T] **a)** if a player fouls in a game of sport, or fouls another player, they do something that is not allowed by the rules: *An Everton player had been fouled in the penalty area.* **b)** to hit a ball outside the limit of the playing area in BASEBALL: *On average, most batters foul at least one ball in each at bat.* **2** *formal* to make something very dirty, especially with waste: *A thick column of black smoke rose from the wreck, fouling the air.* **3** also **foul up** [I,T] if a rope, chain, or part of a machine fouls or if something fouls it, it twists or cannot move properly: *Check that nothing can foul the moving parts.*

**foul up** *phr v informal* **1** [T **foul** sth ↔ **up**] to spoil something: *The weather really fouled up our vacation plans.* **2** [I,T **foul** sth ↔ **up**] to do something wrong or spoil something by making mistakes: *Glen completely fouled up the seating arrangements.*

**foul**[3] *n* [C] an action in a sport that is against the rules: *That was a foul – he touched the ball with his hand!*

**foul line** /'· ·/ *n* [C] a line marked on a sports field outside of which a ball cannot be legally played

**foul-mouthed** /,· '·◂/ *adj* swearing too much: *a foul-mouthed little boy* —**foul mouth** /'· ·/ *n* [C]

**foul play** /,· '·/ *n* [U] **1** if the police think someone's death was caused by foul play, they think that person was murdered: *The police said they had no reason to suspect foul play.* **2** actions that are dishonest or unfair: *He will use any amount of foul play to get what he wants.*

**foul-up** /'· ·/ *n* [C] *informal* a problem caused by a stupid or careless mistake: *There was a foul-up on my charter flight home and several people didn't get seats.*

**found**[1] /faʊnd/ the past tense and past participle of FIND[1]

**found**[2] *v* [T] **1** to start something such as an organization, company, or city: *Founded in 1935 in Ohio, Alcoholics Anonymous is now a world-wide organization.* **2** to start something such as a school or hospital, by providing money for it: *Eton College was founded by Henry VI in 1440.* **3 be founded on a)** to be the main idea, belief etc that something else develops from: *Racism is not founded on rational thought, but on fear.* **b)** to be the solid layer of cement, stones etc that a building is built on: *The castle is founded on solid rock.* **4** *technical* to melt metal and pour it into a MOULD (=a hollow shape), to make things such as tools, parts for machines etc —**founding** *n* [U]: *the founding of the University of Chicago* —see also FOUNDATION, WELL-FOUNDED W3

**foun·da·tion** /faʊn'deɪʃən/ *n* W2

**1** ▶ **BUILDING** ◀ [C] *AmE* also **foundations** [plural] *especially BrE* the solid layer of cement, bricks, stones etc that is under a building to support it: **lay the foundations** (=build them) *It should take us about three weeks to lay the foundations.*

**2** ▶ **BASIC IDEA** ◀ [C] a basic idea, principle, situation etc that something develops from: [+ **of**] *All theories should be built on a foundation of factual knowledge.* | **a solid/firm foundation** *He hoped that this job would serve as a firm foundation for his chosen career.*

**3** ▶ **ORGANIZATION** ◀ [C] an organization that gives money to a CHARITY (2), for research etc: *the Carnegie Foundation*

**4** ▶ **ESTABLISHMENT** ◀ [C,U] the establishment of an organization, business, school etc: *Since its foundation in 1835, this school has served the community.*

**5 lay/provide the foundation(s) for** to provide the conditions that will make it possible for something to be successful: *Good planning after the war laid the foundations for the nation's economic miracle.*

**6 be without foundation/have no foundation** if a statement, idea etc is without foundation, there is no proof that it is true: *Your accusations are completely without foundation.*

**7** ▶ **SKIN** ◀ [U] a cream the same colour as your skin that you put on before the rest of your MAKE-UP —see picture at MAKE-UP

**8 shake/rock sth to its foundations** to completely change the way something is done or the way people think by having a completely new idea: *Darwin's theory rocked the scientific establishment to its foundations.*

**foundation course** /ˈ·· ˌ·/ *n* [C] *BrE* a course of study including several different subjects, taught in the first year at some universities in Britain

**foundation gar·ment** /ˈ·· ˌ··/ *n* [C] a piece of clothing worn in the past by women under their clothes

**foundation stone** /·ˈ·· ·/ *n* [C] **1** a large stone placed at the bottom of an important building to show when it was built, usually as part of a ceremony **2** the facts, ideas, principles etc that form the base from which something else develops or begins: *Greek and Latin were once viewed as the foundation stones of a good education.*

**found·er**[1] /ˈfaʊndə‖-ər/ *n* [C] someone who establishes a business, organization, school etc

**founder**[2] *v* [I] *formal* **1** to fail after a period of time because something has gone wrong or a new problem has caused difficulties: *Their marriage began to founder soon after the honeymoon.* **2** if a ship or boat founders, it fills with water and sinks

**founder mem·ber** /ˌ·· ˈ··/ *n* [C] *BrE* someone who has helped to establish a new organization, club etc and is one of its first members; CHARTER MEMBER *AmE*

**founding fa·ther** /ˌ·· ˈ··/ *n* [C often plural] **1** someone who begins something such as a new way of thinking, or a new organization: *L. Threlkeld, one of the founding fathers of anthropology in Australia* **2 Founding Fathers** the group of men who wrote the American Constitution and Bill of Rights and started the US as a country

**found·ling** /ˈfaʊndlɪŋ/ *n* [C] *old use* a baby who has been left by its parents, and is found and looked after by other people

**foun·dry** /ˈfaʊndri/ *n* [C] a place where metals are melted and poured into MOULDS (=hollow shapes) to make parts for machines, tools etc: *an iron foundry*

**fount** /faʊnt/ *n* [C] **1 the fount of all knowledge/wisdom etc** *literary or humorous* the place, person, idea etc that all knowledge, WISDOM etc comes from; SOURCE[1] (1) **2** *BrE technical* a complete set of letters of one kind and size used to print books, newspapers etc; FONT (2) *AmE*

**foun·tain** /ˈfaʊntɪn‖ˈfaʊntn/ *n* [C] **1** a structure from which water is sent up into the air, which is often in a small pool **2** a flow of liquid, or of something bright and colourful that goes straight up into the air: **[+ of]** *A fountain of sparks shot high into the night sky.* —see also DRINKING FOUNTAIN, SODA FOUNTAIN

**foun·tain·head** /ˈfaʊntɪnhed‖ˈfaʊntn-/ *n* [singular + **of**] the origin of something; SOURCE[1] (1)

**fountain pen** /ˈ·· ·/ *n* [C] a pen that you fill with ink —see picture at PEN[1]

**four** /fɔː‖fɔːr/ *number* **1** 4 **2** four o'clock: *I'll meet you just after four, okay?* **3** a group of four people or things: *The boxes were stacked in fours.* | **make up a four** (=complete a group of 4 people) *Will you make up a four for a game of cards?* —compare FOURSOME **4 on all fours** supporting your body with your hands and knees: *Billy was down on all fours on the ice.* **5 from the four corners of the earth/world** from places or countries that are very far away from each other: *People gathered from the four corners of the earth for the ecology convention.* **6 four on the floor** *AmE* if a car has four on the floor, it has four GEARS worked by a GEAR LEVER **7** a long narrow boat rowed in races by four people **8 a coach and four** a carriage pulled by four horses —see also **four ply** (PLY[2]), **be scattered to the four winds** (SCATTER[1] (3)) —**fourth** *number*

**four-eyes** /ˈ· ·/ *n* [singular] a rude way of addressing someone who wears glasses —**four-eyed** *adj*

**four-flush·er** /ˈ· ˌ··/ *n* [C] *AmE informal* someone who cheats or tries to deceive people

**four-leaved clo·ver** /ˌ· · ˈ··/ also **four-leaf clover** *n* [C] a CLOVER plant that has four leaves instead of the usual three, and is considered to be lucky

**four-let·ter word** /ˌ· ·· ˈ·/ *n* [C] a word that is considered very rude and offensive: *complaints about the use of four-letter words on TV*

**four-post·er** /ˌ· ˈ··/ also **four-poster bed** /ˌ· ·· ˈ·/ *n* [C] a bed with four tall posts at the corners, a cover fixed at the top of the posts, and curtains around the sides

**four·some** /ˈfɔːsəm‖ˈfɔːr-/ *n* [C] a group of four people, especially two men and two women, who are together for a social occasion: **make up a foursome** (=complete a group of four people) *make up a foursome for bridge*

**four-square**[1] /ˌ· ˈ·◂/ *adj* **1** a building that is four-square is solidly and plainly built, and square in shape **2** *especially BrE* firm and determined

**four-square**[2] *adv* firmly: *standing four-square in the hallway*

**four-star**[1] /ˈ· ·/ *n* [U] *BrE* a type of petrol with LEAD[3] (1) in it

**four-star**[2] *adj* of a high standard or quality: *four-star restaurants*

**four-star gen·e·ral** /ˌ· · ˈ···/ *n* [C] *AmE* a GENERAL[2] of a high rank in the US army

**four-stroke** /ˈ· ·/ *adj* a four-stroke engine works with two up and down movements of a PISTON

**four·teen** /ˌfɔːˈtiːn◂‖ˌfɔːr-/ *number* 14 —**fourteenth** *n* [C]

**fourth** /fɔːθ‖fɔːrθ/ *number* [C] one of four equal parts of something; QUARTER[1] (1)

**fourth di·men·sion** /ˌ· ·ˈ··/ *n* **the fourth dimension a)** an expression meaning time, used especially by scientists and writers of SCIENCE FICTION **b)** a type of experience that is outside normal human experience: *ghosts, ESP, and other aspects of the fourth dimension*

**fourth es·tate** /ˌ· ·ˈ·/ *n* [singular] newspapers, news magazines, radio, and television, the people who work for them, and the political influence that they have; the PRESS[2]

**fourth-gen·e·ra·tion lan·guage** /ˌ· ···· ˈ··/ also **4GL** /ˌfɔː dʒiː ˈel‖ˌfɔːr-/ *n* [singular] a computer language that is easy to use, and contains easier and faster ways of doing things

**Fourth of Ju·ly** /ˌ· · · ˈ·/ *n* [singular] a national holiday in the US that celebrates the beginning of the United States as a nation; INDEPENDENCE DAY: *a Fourth of July picnic*

**four-wheel drive** /ˌ· · ˈ·/ also **4WD** /ˈfɔː dʌbəljuː ˈdiː‖ˈfɔːr-/ *n* [C,U] a system in a car or other vehicle by which the power of the engine is given to all four wheels to make it easier to drive —**four-wheel drive** *adj*: *a four-wheel drive Toyota*

**fowl** /faʊl/ *n plural* **fowls** *or* **fowl** [C] **1** a bird, especially a chicken, that is kept for its meat and eggs **2** *old use* a bird —see also **neither fish nor fowl** (FISH[1] (5))

**fowl pest** /ˈ· ·/ *n* [U] an illness that spreads quickly among chickens and some other birds

**fox**[1] /fɒks‖fɑːks/ *n* **1** [C] a wild animal like a dog with reddish-brown fur, a pointed face, and a thick tail **2** [C] *informal* someone who is clever and deceitful: *He was a sly old fox.* **3** [U] the skin and fur of a fox, used to make clothes **4** [C] *AmE informal* someone who is sexually attractive: *She's such a fox!*

**fox**[2] *v* [T] **1** *BrE informal* to be too difficult for someone to do or understand: *Those childproof containers always fox me.* **2** *especially BrE* to confuse or deceive someone in a clever way

**fox·glove** /ˈfɒksglʌv‖ˈfɑːks-/ *n* [C] a tall plant with many bell-shaped flowers

**fox·hole** /ˈfɒkshəʊl‖ˈfɑːkshoʊl/ *n* [C] **1** a hole in the ground that soldiers use to fire from or hide from the enemy **2** a hole in the ground where a fox lives

**fox·hound** /ˈfɒkshaʊnd‖ˈfɑːks-/ *n* [C] a dog with a very good sense of smell, trained to hunt and kill foxes

**fox·hunt·er** /ˈfɒkshʌntə‖ˈfɑːkshʌntər/ *n* [C] a horse used in the sport of foxhunting

**fox·hunt·ing** /ˈfɒkshʌntɪŋ‖ˈfɑːks-/ *n* [U] the sport of hunting foxes (FOX¹ (1)) with dogs while riding on a horse —**fox-hunting** *adj* —**foxhunt** *n* [C]

**fox ter·ri·er** /ˌ· ˈ···/ *n* [C] a small dog with short hair

**fox·trot** /ˈfɒkstrɒt‖ˈfɑːkstrɑːt/ *n* [C] a type of formal dance with short, quick steps, or a piece of music for this dance —**foxtrot** *v* [I]

**fox·y** /ˈfɒksi‖ˈfɑːksi/ *adj* **1** like a FOX¹ (1) in appearance: *He was a tall, thin man with a rather foxy face.* **2** clever and deceitful: *That foxy bastard. How did he get away with it?* **3** *AmE informal* sexually attractive: *a foxy lady*

**foy·er** /ˈfɔɪeɪ‖ˈfɔɪər/ *n* [C] **1** a room or hall at the entrance to a public building; LOBBY¹ (1): *We met in the theatre foyer.* **2** *AmE* a small room or hall at the entrance to a private house or flat

**FPO** /ˌef piː ˈəʊ‖-ˈoʊ/ an abbreviation of 'fleet post office' or 'field post office', used as part of the address of someone in the American navy or army

**Fr** **1** a written abbreviation of Father, used in front of the name of a priest **2** a written abbreviation of FRANC (=a unit of French money) **3** a written abbreviation of French or France

**frac·as** /ˈfrækɑː‖ˈfreɪkəs/ *n plural* **fracas** *or* **fracases** *AmE* [C] a short, noisy fight involving several people: *There was a fracas outside the courtroom as the suspect emerged.*

**frac·tion** /ˈfrækʃən/ *n* [C] **1** a very small amount of something: [+ **of**] *Gwen carefully opened the door a fraction.* **2** a division or a part of a whole number in mathematics: *¾ and ½ are fractions* —see also COMMON FRACTION, IMPROPER FRACTION, PROPER FRACTION, VULGAR FRACTION

**frac·tion·al** /ˈfrækʃənəl/ *adj* **1** very small in amount: *She made a fractional alteration to the floral centerpiece.* **2** connected with fractions, in mathematics —**fractionally** *adv*

**frac·tious** /ˈfrækʃəs/ *adj* if a baby or child is fractious, they are angry or upset: *Babies tend to be fractious when they are teething.* —**fractiousness** *n* [U]

**frac·ture¹** /ˈfræktʃə‖-ər/ *v* [I, T] if a bone or other hard substance fractures or is fractured, it breaks or cracks: *He fractured a leg in pre-season training.* | *Under such pressure, rock will begin to fracture.* | *a fractured rib*

**fracture²** *n* [C] a crack or broken part in a bone or other hard substance: *Check all the parts to be sure there are no fractures in the metal.*

**fra·gile** /ˈfrædʒaɪl‖-dʒəl/ *adj* **1** not strong, and therefore easily broken or damaged: *The parcel was marked FRAGILE – HANDLE WITH CARE.* **2** easily damaged, spoilt, or destroyed: *The country's fragile economy is threatened by the continued drought.* **3** a fragile person looks thin and delicate and is often weak or likely to become ill **4** *BrE* if someone feels fragile they feel ill, especially because they have drunk too much alcohol —**fragility** /frəˈdʒɪləti/ *n* [U] —compare FRAIL

W3 **frag·ment¹** /ˈfrægmənt/ *n* [C] a small piece of something that has broken off or that comes from something larger: *Roger examined the few words remaining on the charred fragment of paper.* | *a fragment of poetry*

**frag·ment²** /frægˈment‖ˈfrægment, frægˈment/ *v* [I,T often passive] to break something, or be broken into a lot of small, separate parts: *His day was fragmented by interruptions and phone calls.* —**fragmented** *adj*: *a rapidly changing and fragmented society* —**fragmentation** /ˌfrægmənˈteɪʃən, -men-/ *n* [U]

**frag·ment·ary** /ˈfrægməntəri‖-teri/ *adj* made of many different pieces: *We have received only fragmentary accounts of the incident.*

**fra·grance** /ˈfreɪgrəns/ *n* **1** [C,U] a pleasant smell: *This soup has a delicate fragrance and a slightly sweet taste.* —compare AROMA, SMELL² (1) **2** [C] a liquid that you put on your body to make it smell pleasant: *They make soaps and fragrances based on natural ingredients.*

**fra·grant** /ˈfreɪgrənt/ *adj* having a pleasant smell: *The damask rose is extremely fragrant.* —**fragrantly** *adv*

**fraid·y cat** /ˈfreɪdi kæt/ *AmE informal n* [C] a word meaning someone who is too frightened to do something, used especially by children; SCAREDY-CAT

**frail** /freɪl/ *adj* **1** someone who is frail is thin and weak, especially because they are old: *He was a man of about sixty, frail and bent.* **2** not strongly made or built and therefore easily damaged: *It seemed impossible that these frail boats could survive in such a storm.* —compare FRAGILE

**frail·ty** /ˈfreɪlti/ *n* **1** [U] lacking in strength or health: *He noticed with shock the frailty of her thin body.* | *the frailty of the urban economy* **2** [C] something bad or weak in your character: *human frailties*

**frame¹** /freɪm/ *n* S3 W3

**1 ▶ BORDER ◀** [C] a firm structure that holds something such as a picture or window, and provides a border for it: *Stretch the embroidery on a frame before starting to sew.* | **door/window/picture frame** *He leaned against the door frame.*

**2 ▶ STRUCTURE ◀** [C] the structure or main supporting parts of a piece of furniture, vehicle, or other object: *a bicycle frame* | *There was nothing wrong with the frame of the chair, just the upholstery.*

**3 ▶ BODY ◀** [C] the structure formed by the bones of someone's body: *Louise's slight frame*

**4 ▶ MAIN FACTS/IDEAS ◀** [singular] the main ideas, facts etc that something is based on: *A clear explanation of the subject provides a frame on which a deeper understanding can be built.*

**5 ▶ GLASSES ◀** the metal or plastic part of a pair of glasses (GLASS¹ (3)) that holds the lenses (LENS (1)) —see picture at GLASS¹

**6 be in a . . . frame of mind** to have an attitude at a particular time that helps you to do something: *Philip, I don't think you're in a proper frame of mind to enter the House of God.*

**7 ▶ BOX ◀** [C] a large wooden box covered with glass or plastic in which young plants are grown outdoors: *cucumber frames*

**8 ▶ SPORT ◀** [C] a complete part in the games of SNOOKER or BOWLING: *I won the next three frames.*

**9 ▶ PHOTOGRAPH ◀** [C] an area of a photographic film that contains one photograph, or many of these which together make a cinema or VIDEO film —see also CLIMBING FRAME, COLD FRAME

**frame²** *v* [T] **1** to surround something with a border so that it looks pleasant or so that you can see it clearly: *Sarah's long, dark hair framed her face.* | **be framed by** *a courtyard framed by a rectangle of tightly clipped grass* **2** to put a picture in a structure that will hold it firmly **3** to deliberately make someone seem guilty of a crime, by providing things that seem like proof: *I'm convinced Murphy's been framed.* | **frame sb for** *He told the court that the police had tried to frame him for assault.* **4** to organize and develop a plan, system etc: *a theory originally framed by Marx* **5 gilt-framed/wood-framed etc** having a frame or frames of a particular colour or material: *a red-framed mirror* | *wire-framed spectacles* —see also FRAME-UP

**frame of ref·er·ence** /ˌ· · ˈ···/ *n* [C usually singular] the knowledge, experiences, or beliefs that someone uses to understand something

**frame-up** /ˈ· ·/ *n* [C] a plan to make someone seem guilty of a crime when they are not

**frame·work** /ˈfreɪmwɜːk‖-wɜːrk/ *n* [C] **1** the main supporting parts of a building, vehicle, or object: *airships with a rigid metal framework* **2** a set of facts, ideas etc from which more complicated ideas are developed, or on which decisions are based: [+ **of**] *a framework of Marxist theory* | [+ **for**] *This paper seeks to provide a framework* W3 *for future research.* **3 social/political/legal etc framework** the structure of a society, a legal or political system etc: *a legal and political framework favourable to trade*

**franc** /fræŋk/ *n* [C] the standard unit of money in France and some other countries

**fran·chise¹** /ˈfræntʃaɪz/ *n* **1** [C] permission to sell a company's goods or service, that is given or sold to a business person: *a Benetton franchise* **2** [U] the legal right to vote in your country's elections: *universal franchise*

**franchise²** *v* [T] to give or sell a franchise to someone

**fran·chi·see** /ˌfræntʃaɪˈziː/ *n* [C] someone who is given or sold a franchise

**Franco-** /fræŋkəʊ‖-koʊ/ *prefix* **1** of France: *a Francophile* (=someone who loves France) **2** French and: *the Franco-Belgian border*

**fran·co·phone** /ˈfræŋkəʊfəʊn‖-kəfoʊn/ *adj* **1** having a French-speaking population: *francophone countries* **2** from a French-speaking country or population: *francophone African literature*

**fran·glais** /ˈfrɒŋgleɪ‖ˌfrɑːŋˈgleɪ/ *n* [U] a mixture of the French and English languages

**frank¹** /fræŋk/ *adj* **1** honest and truthful in what you say: *a frank exchange of ideas* | **be frank with sb** *He was completely frank with her about what happened.* **2 to be frank** used when you are saying something true that other people may not like: *To be perfectly frank, I think that's a crazy idea.* —**frankness** *n* [U]

**frank²** *v* [T] to print a sign on an envelope showing that the cost of sending it has been paid

**frank·fur·ter** /ˈfræŋkfɜːtə‖-fɜːrtər/ also **frank** *AmE* —*n* [C] a long reddish smoked SAUSAGE; HOT DOG¹ *AmE*

**frank·in·cense** /ˈfræŋkənsens/ *n* [U] a substance that is burnt to give a sweet smell, especially at religious ceremonies

**franking ma·chine** /ˈ·· ·ˌ·/ *n* [C] a machine that prints signs on envelopes to show that the charge for sending them has been paid

S3 **frank·ly** /ˈfræŋkli/ *adv* **1** honestly and directly, especially in speech: *I stated my views frankly.* **2** [sentence adverb] used to show that you are saying something direct and honest: *Frankly, I'm not very interested.*

**fran·tic** /ˈfræntɪk/ *adj* **1** extremely hurried and using a lot of energy but not very organized: *I couldn't understand her frantic signalling.* | **frantic activity/search/rush etc** *Before the game there was a frantic rush to get the last few seats.* **2** extremely worried and frightened about a situation, so that you cannot control your feelings: *A frantic note had crept into Jane's voice.* | **get/become/grow frantic**: *There was still no news of Jill, and her parents were getting frantic.* | **frantic with worry/grief etc** *Your mother's been frantic with worry wondering where you've been.* —**frantically** /-kli/ *adv* —see also FRENETIC

**frap·pé** /ˈfræpeɪ‖fræˈpeɪ/ *n* [C,U] **1** *AmE* a thick kind of MILK SHAKE **2** a strong alcoholic drink poured over very thin pieces of ice —**frappé** *adj*

**frat** /fræt/ *n* [C] *AmE informal* FRATERNITY (2)

**fra·ter·nal** /frəˈtɜːnl‖-ɜːr-/ *adj* **1** showing a special friendliness to other people because you share interests or ideas with them: *fraternal sympathy with the workers out on strike* **2** of or belonging to brothers: *fraternal loyalty* —**fraternally** *adv*

**fra·ter·ni·ty** /frəˈtɜːnəti‖-ɜːr-/ *n* **1 the racing/teaching/scientific fraternity** all the people who work in a particular profession: *He's a member of the medical fraternity.* **2** [C] a club of male students at an American university, usually living in the same building: *a fraternity brother* —compare SORORITY **3** [U] a feeling of friendship between members of a group: *the Revolutionary ideas of fraternity and equality*

**frat·er·nize** also **-ise** *BrE* /ˈfrætənaɪz‖-ər-/ *v* [I] to show friendliness towards people who you are not supposed to be friendly with: [+ **with**] *The soldiers fraternized with the enemy on Christmas Day.* —**fraternization** /ˌfrætənaɪˈzeɪʃən‖-tərnə-/ *n* [U]

**frat·ri·cide** /ˈfrætrəsaɪd/ *n* [C,U] **1** the crime of murdering your brother or sister **2** the murder of people from your country or local area

**fraud** /frɔːd‖frɒːd/ *n* **1** [C,U] a method of illegally getting money from someone, often by using clever and complicated methods: *financial losses due to theft or fraud* | **tax/share/bankruptcy etc fraud** (=fraud in a particular financial area) **2** [C] someone who deceives people to gain money, friendship etc: *She realized later that the insurance salesman had been a fraud.*

**Fraud Squad** /ˈ· ·/ *n* [singular] the department in the British police force that examines fraud in business

**fraud·u·lent** /ˈfrɔːdjələnt‖ˈfrɒːdʒə-/ *adj* fraudulent actions or words are intended to deceive: *fraudulent banking practices* | *fraudulent statements* —**fraudulently** *adv* —**fraudulence** *n* [U]

**fraught** /frɔːt‖frɒːt/ *adj* **1** an activity or situation that is fraught is full of problems and is very difficult to deal with: *After the argument, relations between them were fraught.* | **fraught with problems/difficulties/danger** *Any program of sudden change is likely to be fraught with pitfalls.* **2** full of anxiety or worry: *Julie was unhappy, fraught and depressed.* **3 fraught with meaning** showing strong feelings that are not expressed in words: *She gave me a long look, fraught with meaning.*

**fray¹** /freɪ/ *v* [I] **1** if cloth or other material frays, the threads become loose because the material is old: *That sleeve will fray if you don't darn it.* —see picture on page 1258 **2** if someone's temper or nerves fray, they become annoyed: *It was only three o'clock and tempers were already beginning to fray.* —**frayed** *adj*: *The carpet was badly frayed.*

**fray²** *n* **the fray** a quarrel, argument, or fight: **join/enter the fray** *It wasn't long before all the demonstrators had joined in the fray.*

**fraz·zle** /ˈfræzəl/ *n* [singular] *BrE informal* **be burnt to a frazzle etc** to be so burnt that there is almost nothing left

**fraz·zled** /ˈfræzəld/ *adj informal* annoyed and unable to deal with problems or difficulties, especially because you have been very busy: *I felt tired and frazzled.*

**freak¹** /friːk/ *n* [C] **1 bike/fitness/film etc freak** *informal* someone who is so interested in bikes, fitness etc that other people think they are strange or unusual: *Carrot juice is a favourite with health-food freaks.* **2** someone who looks very strange or behaves in a very unusual way: *Women who were good at physics used to be considered freaks.* **3** something in nature, such as a strangely-shaped plant or animal, that is very unusual: *One of the lambs was a freak – it had two tails.* | **a freak of nature** (=something physically strange or unusual) *By some freak of nature there was a snowstorm in June.* **4 control freak** someone who always wants to control situations and other people

**freak²** *adj* [only before noun] **freak accident/storm/conditions etc** an accident, storm etc that is unexpected and very unusual: *A freak wave wrecked most of the seafront.*

**freak³** *v* [I] *informal especially AmE* to become suddenly angry or frightened, especially so that you cannot control your behaviour: *She freaked when she heard he was coming to the party.*

**freak out** *phr v* [I,T] *informal* to become very anxious, upset, or frightened, or make someone very anxious, upset or frightened: **freak sb out** *It freaked me out to see him so depressed.*

**freak·ish** /ˈfriːkɪʃ/ *adj* very unusual and strange: *freakish behaviour* —**freakishly** *adv* —**freakishness** *n* [U]

**freak·y** /ˈfriːki/ *adj spoken* strange and slightly frightening: *That science fiction film was really freaky!*

**freck·le** /ˈfrekəl/ *n* [C usually plural] a small brown spot on your skin, caused by the sun —see picture on page 412

**freck·led** /ˈfrekəld/ *adj* having freckles: *a lightly freckled face*

# free[1] /friː/ *adj*

① ALLOWED TO DO WHAT YOU WANT
② COSTING NOTHING
③ NOT A PRISONER
④ NOT BUSY
⑤ NOT BEING USED
⑥ WITHOUT/NOT HAVE
⑦ NOT FIXED/ABLE TO MOVE
⑧ OTHER MEANINGS

## ① ALLOWED TO DO WHAT YOU WANT

**1** allowed to do whatever you want, without being controlled or restricted: **free to do sth** *The children are free to decide which activity they would like to do.*
**2 feel free** *spoken* used to tell someone that they can do something: *Feel free to ask questions.* | *"Can I make myself some tea?" "Feel free."*
**3** without restrictions or controls: *We had a free and open discussion about religion.* | *a free exchange of information* | **free access/passage/movement etc** *free movement of people and goods between the towns* | **free speech** (=being able to say whatever you want)
**4 free election/society/press** an election etc that is not controlled by the government so that people can vote, live etc how they want to
**5 give sb a free hand/rein** to let someone do whatever they want or need to do in a particular situation: *She gave the producer a free rein with the script.*
**6 free and easy** relaxed, friendly, and without many rules: *a free and easy discussion*
**7 a free spirit** someone who lives as they want to rather than in the way that society considers normal
**8 free agent** someone who can do what they want to, and who is not controlled by anyone else: *You're a free agent – you don't owe them anything.*

## ② COSTING NOTHING

**9** costing nothing: *We were given a free lunch with lots of wine.* | *The soft drinks are free, but you have to pay for the beer.* | **a free gift** (=something you are given by a shop or company)
**10 a free ride** something that you do not have to pay for, because someone else is paying for it: *Government employees are getting a free ride on taxpayers' money.*

## ③ NOT A PRISONER

**11** not a prisoner: *The rapist could be free in as little as three years.* | **set sb free** (=give someone their freedom) *Mandela was finally set free in 1993.* | **a free man** (=a man who was a prisoner)

## ④ NOT BUSY

**12** if you are free, or have some free time, you have no work, and nothing else that you must do: *Are you free next weekend?* | **a free day/morning/half-hour etc** *If you have a free afternoon, go and see this movie.* | **free time** *I don't have enough free time during the week.*

## ⑤ NOT BEING USED

**13** something that you want to use is free if no one else is using it: *There's a washing machine free, but you may have to wait for a dryer.*

## ⑥ WITHOUT/NOT HAVE

**14 tax-free/duty-free etc** without tax etc: *duty-free wine*
**15 lead-free/salt-free etc** not containing lead, salt etc: *lead-free petrol*
**16 free from/of sth** without something that you do not want to have: *free of obligations* | *free from disease*
**17 free of sth/sb** away from something or someone you are glad to be without: *I'm free of that place at last.*

## ⑦ NOT FIXED/ABLE TO MOVE

**18** an action or movement that is free is graceful and not restricted: *a free swing of the arm*
**19** loose and not fixed to anything: *The free end of the flag has been torn by the wind.*
**20 free hand/arm/leg etc** the arm, leg etc that you are not already using: *With her free hand, she clung to the rope.*
**21** *technical* not combined with any other simple chemical substance; pure: *free oxygen*

## ⑧ OTHER MEANINGS

**22** *old-fashioned* too friendly, in a way that does not show enough respect: *Your son's manner is rather free.*
**23 be free with** to be generous with something: *Mr. Leath is free with his money.* | *free with criticism*
**24 make free with** to use something that belongs to someone else when you should not: *I wonder if he knows that Jenny is making free with his money?*
**25** a translation that is free gives a general idea of a piece of writing rather than exactly translating every word

W3 **free[2]** *v* [T] **1** to allow someone to leave prison or somewhere they have been kept by force; RELEASE[1] (1): *Lincoln freed the slaves.* | *persuading the terrorists to free the hostages* **2** to move or loosen something or someone that is fixed or trapped: *After three hours the firemen freed her from the wreckage.* **3** also **free up** to make something available so that it can be used: *This would free resources that are badly needed.* **4** to help someone by removing something unpleasant: [+ **from**] *They aim to free the country from its enormous debts.* **5** to make someone no longer be restricted by unfair rules, a cruel government etc: [+ **from**] *marching to free the capital city from the rebels* **6** to help someone to do something, by removing restrictions or making them responsible for fewer things: **free sb to do sth** *freeing teachers to concentrate on particular subjects* | **free sth** *Writing frees the imagination.*

**free[3]** *adv* **1** without payment: *This card allows you to travel free for a month.* | **for free** *They let me have these chillies for free.* | **free of charge** *You may park here free of charge after 6 p.m.* **2** not fixed or held in a particular place or position: *The window had swung free in the wind.* | **pull/struggle free** (=move to get away from somewhere) *Ken grabbed her around the waist, but she managed to struggle free.* **3 break free** to escape from a place or a situation: *At last he's broken free and started a new life in New York.* **4 run free** if an animal runs free it is allowed to go where it wants to, without being controlled: *a zoo where the animals can run free* **5 walk free** if a criminal walks free, they are not put in prison **6 I'll tell you that for free** *spoken* used to emphasize what you are saying, in an angry way: *I'm not going to offer to help you out again, I'll tell you that for free!* —compare FREELY —see also SCOT-FREE

**-free** /friː/ *suffix* [in adjectives and adverbs] without something that you do not want: *a salt-free diet* | *a trouble-free journey* | *We bought the cigarettes duty-free.* | *They live in the house rent-free.*

**free as·so·ci·a·tion** /ˌ· ···'··/ *n* [U] *technical* a method of finding out about someone's mind by asking them to say the first word they think of when you say a particular word

**free·bie, freebee** /ˈfriːbiː/ *n* [C] *informal* something that you are given free, usually something small and not expensive

**free·boot·er** /ˈfriːbuːtə‖-ər/ *n* [C] someone who joins in a war in order to steal other people's goods and money —**freeboot** *v* [I]

**free·born** /ˌfriːˈbɔːn◂‖-ɔːrn◂/ *adj* not born as a slave

**free col·lec·tive bar·gain·ing** /ˌ· ··· ˈ···/ *n* [U] *BrE* talks between TRADE UNIONS and employers about pay or working conditions that are not controlled by law

S 2 W 2 **free·dom** /ˈfriːdəm/ *n* **1** [C,U] the right to do what you want without being controlled or restricted by anyone: *The protest is about the infringement of our democratic freedoms.* | **freedom of speech/expression/choice etc** (=the legal right to choose, express yourself etc) *The journalists claimed they were being denied the right to freedom of expression.* **2** [U] the state of being free and allowed to do what you want: *Kids have too much freedom these days.* | **freedom to do sth** *Women have gained the freedom to decide whether or not to marry.* | **complete freedom** *The teachers are given complete freedom in their choice of teaching methods.* **3** [U] the state of being free because you are not in prison: *One of the escaped prisoners was arrested again after only 48 hours of freedom.* **4 freedom from** the state of not being affected by something that makes you worried, unhappy, afraid etc: *The new supplies will ensure temporary freedom from starvation and disease.* | *freedom from worry* **5 freedom of information** the availability to everyone of information that a government has about people and organizations **6 freedom of the city** an honour in Britain that gives someone the right to be a full member of a city —compare LIBERTY

**freedom fight·er** /ˈ·· ˌ··/ *n* [C] someone who fights in a war against an unfair or dishonest government, army etc —compare GUERRILLA, TERRORIST

**free en·ter·prise** /ˌ· ˈ···/ *n* [U] the principle and practice of allowing private business to operate without much government control —see also PRIVATE ENTERPRISE

**free-fall** /ˈ· ·/ *n* [U] **1** part of a jump or fall from an aircraft that is made before the PARACHUTE[1] is opened **2** a very fast and uncontrolled fall in the value of something: **in free-fall** *The pound sterling was in free fall.* —**free-falling** *adj*

**free-float·ing** /ˌ· ˈ··◂/ *adj* not connected to or influenced by anything: *free-floating anxiety*

**free-for-all** /ˌ· · ˈ·/ *n* [singular] *informal* a noisy quarrel or fight that a lot of people join: *Once a few people had been noticed stealing the supplies, there was a free-for-all.*

**free·hand** /ˈfriːhænd/ *adj* drawn with your hand and a pen or pencil: *a freehand sketch* —**freehand** *adv*

**free·hold** /ˈfriːhəʊld‖-hoʊld/ *n* [C,U] complete ownership of a building for an unlimited time: *They've bought the freehold of their house.* —**freehold** *adj*: *The flat is a freehold property.* —**freehold** *adv* —compare LEASEHOLD

**free·hold·er** /ˈfriːhəʊldə‖-hoʊldər/ *n* [C] an owner of freehold land or property

**free house** /ˌ· ˈ·, ˈ· ·/ *n* [C] *BrE* a PUB that can buy beer from different companies, rather than being controlled by one company —compare TIED HOUSE *BrE*

**free kick** /ˌ· ˈ·/ *n* [C] a chance for one football team to kick the ball, when the other team has done something wrong

**free·lance** /ˈfriːlɑːns‖-læns/ *adj, adv* working independently for several different companies or organizations rather than being directly employed by one: *a freelance journalist* | *She's working freelance.* —**freelance** *v* [I] *He's freelancing for the BBC.* —**freelance** also **freelancer** *n* [C]

**free·loader** /ˈfriːləʊdər‖-loʊdər/ *n* [C] *informal* someone who takes food, drink, etc from other people, without giving anything in return —**freeload** *v* [I]

**free love** /ˌ· ˈ·/ *n* [U] an expression meaning the practice or principle of having sex with people without being faithful to one person or without being married, used especially in the 1960s and 1970s

**free·ly** /ˈfriːli/ *adv* **1** if you can travel, speak, operate etc freely, you can do it as much as you like and in whatever way you like: *In France he could write freely, without fear of arrest.* **2** without any restrictions on movement: *breathing freely* | *She shook the pen so that the ink flowed more freely.* **3 freely admit/acknowledge** to agree that something is true, especially when this is difficult: *I freely admit I made many mistakes.* **4** if a piece of writing is translated freely, the translation does not attempt to translate the original words exactly, but gives a general meaning **5 freely available** very easy to obtain: *The two research groups are making their findings freely available to each other.* **6** generously, or in large quantities: *Promises were freely given that prices would be low.*

**free·man** /ˈfriːmən/ *n* [C] someone who is not a slave

**free mar·ket** /ˌ· ˈ··/ *n* [C] **1** *technical* a market on the STOCK EXCHANGE in business shares (SHARE[2] (6)) in which the prices are not controlled or fixed **2** a situation in which prices are not controlled or limited in any way

**free mar·ket e·con·o·my** /ˌ· ˌ·· ·ˈ···/ *n* [C] a system of trade in which prices are allowed to rise and fall without being restricted by the government

**free mar·ket·eer** /ˌ· ··ˈ·/ *n* [C] someone who thinks that prices should be allowed to rise and fall naturally and should not be fixed by the government

**Free·ma·son** /ˈfriːˌmeɪsən, ˌfriːˈmeɪsən/ *n* [C] a man who belongs to a secret society, in which each member helps the other members to become successful

**Free·ma·son·ry** /ˈfriːmeɪsənri, ˌfriːˈmeɪ-/ *n* [U] the system and practices of Freemasons

**free par·don** /ˌ· ˈ··/ *n* [C] *law* the official act of forgiving someone for a crime

**free pe·ri·od** /ˌ· ˈ···/ *n* [C] a period of time in a school day when a student does not have a class

**free·phone** /ˈfriːfəʊn‖-foʊn/ *n* [U] *BrE* an arrangement by which a company or organization pays the cost of telephone calls made to it

**free port** /ˌ· ˈ·/ *n* [C] a port where goods from all countries can be brought in and taken out without being taxed

**free·post** /ˈfriːpəʊst‖-poʊst/ *n* [U] *BrE* an arrangement by which a company or organization pays the cost of letters that you send to it by post

**free-range** /ˌ· ˈ·◂/ *adj* **1** farm animals that are free-range are not kept in small CAGES but are allowed to move around in a large enclosed area: *free-range hens* **2** food that is free-range comes from these farm animals: *free-range eggs* —compare BATTERY (2)

**free·si·a** /ˈfriːziə‖-ʒə/ *n* [C] a plant with pleasant smelling flowers

**free·stand·ing** /ˌfriːˈstændɪŋ◂/ *adj* standing alone without being fixed to a frame, wall, or other support

**free·style** /ˈfriːstaɪl/ *n* [U] a competition in which swimmers use the CRAWL[2] (2) method of swimming: *the 100m freestyle*

**free·think·er** /ˌfriːˈθɪŋkə‖-ər/ *n* [C] someone who has their own opinions, ideas, and beliefs, rather than accepting other people's —**freethinking** *adj*

**free trade** /ˌ· ˈ·◂/ *n* [U] a situation in which the goods coming into or going out of a country are not controlled or taxed

**free verse** /ˌ· ˈ·/ *n* [U] poetry that does not have a fixed structure —compare BLANK VERSE

S2 W3 **free·way** /ˈfriːweɪ/ *n* [C] *AmE* a very wide road in the US, usually in cities, built for fast travel: *the Ventura freeway* —compare MOTORWAY, EXPRESSWAY, HIGHWAY (1)

**free·wheel** /ˌfriːˈwiːl/ *v* [I] to ride a bicycle or drive a vehicle downhill, without using power from your legs or the engine

**free·wheel·ing** /ˌfriːˈwiːlɪŋ◂/ *adj informal* not worried about rules or what will happen in the future: *A lot of the girls envied me my independent, freewheeling life.*

**free will** /ˌ· ˈ·/ *n* [U] **1 do sth of your own free will** to do something because you want to, not because someone else has forced you to: *He went of his own free will.* **2** the belief that human effort rather than God or FATE (2) can affect what happens in life

**freeze¹** /friːz/ *v past* **froze** /frəʊz‖froʊz/ *past participle* **frozen** /ˈfrəʊzən‖ˈfroʊ-/

**1 ▶ LIQUID ◀** [I,T] if a liquid freezes, or something freezes it, it becomes hard and solid because the temperature is very cold: *The water at the edge of the lake froze last night.* | **freeze sth** *The cold weather can even freeze petrol in car engines.* —compare MELT¹ (1), THAW¹ (1)

**2 ▶ EARTH ◀** [I,T] if something such as earth that contains liquid freezes, or something freezes it, it becomes hard because of cold temperatures: *The ground was frozen under the thin snow.*

**3 ▶ MACHINE/ENGINE ◀** also **freeze up** [I,T] if a machine, engine, pipe etc freezes, or something freezes it, the liquid inside it becomes solid with cold, so that it does not work properly: *The water pipes have frozen up.*

**4 ▶ FOOD ◀** [I,T] to make food extremely cold so that you can preserve it for a long time, or to be able to be preserved in this way: *I'm going to freeze some of these beans.* | *Tomatoes don't freeze well.*

**5 it's freezing** *spoken* used to say that the temperature is extremely cold: *It's freezing in here – can't we shut a few windows?* —see COLD¹ (USAGE)

**6 ▶ FEEL COLD ◀** [I] *spoken* if someone freezes, they feel very cold: *You'll freeze if you don't put a coat on.* | **freeze to death** *spoken* (=feel extremely cold) *Come inside, you must be freezing to death.*

**7 ▶ WAGES/PRICES ◀** [T] if a government or company freezes wages, prices etc, they do not increase them, and keep them at a particular level: *Student grants were frozen at 1989 levels.*

**8 ▶ MONEY/PROPERTY ◀** [T] to legally prevent money in a bank from being spent, property from being sold etc: *The court froze their assets.*

**9 ▶ STOP MOVING ◀** [I] to stop moving suddenly and stay completely still and quiet: *I froze and listened; someone was in my apartment.* | *"Freeze! Drop your weapons!" shouted Officer Greer.*

**10 freeze to death** to become so cold that you die

**freeze** sb **out** *phr v* [T] to deliberately prevent someone from being involved in something, by making it difficult for them, being unkind to them etc: *You've got to stop freezing me out of the decision-making.*

**freeze over** *phr v* [I] if an area or pool of water freezes over, its surface turns into ice: *We'll go skating if the lake has frozen over.*

**freeze²** *n* **1** [C] a fixing of wages, prices etc at a particular level: *pay freezes* **2** [C] a stopping of some activity: [+ **on**] *a freeze on production* **3** *BrE* [singular] a period of extremely cold weather **4** *AmE* a short period of time, especially at night, when the temperature is extremely low —see also DEEP FREEZE

**freeze-dry** /ˌ· ˈ·◂/ *v* [T] to preserve food or drink by freezing and drying it very quickly: *freeze-dried coffee*

**freeze-frame** /ˈ· ˌ·/ *n* [U] the process of stopping the action on a moving film at one particular place: *Press the freeze-frame button on the video.* —**freeze-frame** *v* [T]

**freez·er** /ˈfriːzə‖-ər/ *n* [C] **1** a large machine in which food can be stored at very low temperatures for a long time; DEEP FREEZE —see picture on page 833 **2** *AmE* a part of a FRIDGE in which food can be stored at very low temperatures for a long time —compare FRIDGE

**freez·ing** /ˈfriːzɪŋ/ *n* [U] **above/below freezing** above or below the temperature at which water freezes: *It was well below freezing when we left.*

**freezing com·part·ment** /ˈ·· ·ˌ··/ *n* [C] a part of a FRIDGE in which food can be stored at very low temperatures for a long time

**freez·ing point** /ˈ·· ·/ *n* **1** [U] the temperature at which water turns into ice **2** [C usually singular] the temperature at which a particular liquid freezes: *Alcohol has a lower freezing point than water.* —compare BOILING POINT

**freight¹** /freɪt/ *n* **1** [U] goods that are carried by ship, train, or aircraft: *freight containers* **2** [C] *AmE* a FREIGHT TRAIN

**freight²** *v* [T] to send goods by air, sea, or train

**freight·er** /ˈfreɪtə‖-ər/ *n* [C] a ship or aircraft that carries goods

**freight·lin·er** /ˈfreɪtˌlaɪnə‖-ər/ *n* [C] *especially BrE* a train that carries large amounts of goods in special containers

**freight train** /ˈ· ·/ *n* [C] a train that carries goods

**French¹** /frentʃ/ *n* **1** the language of France, and some other countries: *How do you ask for directions in French?* **2** the language and literature of France as a subject of study: *She's studying French at London University.* **3 the French** the people of France: *The French celebrate 14th July.*

**French²** *adj* **1** belonging to or involved with France or its people: *an excellent French wine* **2** belonging to or involved with the French language: *an introduction to French grammar* **3 take French leave** to leave your job without permission **4 pardon/excuse my French** *spoken* used to say sorry for swearing

**French bean** /ˌ· ˈ·/ *n* [C] *BrE* a bean with a long green case that is picked when it is young and soft; GREEN BEAN —see picture on page 414

**French bread** /ˌ· ˈ·/ *n* [U] white bread in the shape of a thick stick

**French chalk** /ˌ· ˈ·/ *n* [U] CHALK¹ (2) used for drawing lines on cloth when making clothes

**French doors** /ˈ· ˌ·/ *n* [plural] *especially AmE* FRENCH WINDOWS

**French dress·ing** /ˌ· ˈ··/ *n* [U] a mixture of oil and VINEGAR that is put on raw vegetables

**French fry** /ˌ· ˈ·/ *n* [C usually plural] *especially AmE* a long thin piece of potato cooked in fat; CHIP¹ (3a) *BrE*

**French horn** /ˌ· ˈ·/ *n* [C] a HORN¹ (4), that is shaped like a circle, with a wide bell-like opening

**French kiss** /ˌ· ˈ·/ *n* [C] a kiss made with your mouths open and with your tongues touching

**French let·ter** /ˌ· ˈ··/ *n* [C] *informal old-fashioned* a CONDOM

**French loaf** /ˌ· ˈ·/ *n* [C] *BrE* a long thin white LOAF of bread; FRENCH STICK

**French·man** /ˈfrentʃmən/ *n plural* **Frenchmen** /-mən/ [C] a man born in France or one who has French parents

**French pol·ish** /ˌ· ˈ··/ *n* [U] a clear liquid put on wooden furniture to protect it and make it shine

**French seam** /ˌ· ˈ·/ *n* [C] a double SEAM (1) used when making clothes, which hides the edges that have been cut

**French stick** /ˌ· ˈ·/ *n* [C] a long thin white LOAF of bread

**French toast** /ˌ· ˈ·/ *n* [U] pieces of bread put into a mixture of egg and milk and then cooked in hot oil

**French win·dows** /ˌ· ˈ··/ *n* [plural] a pair of light doors made of glass in a frame, usually opening out on to a garden or BALCONY (1)

**French·wom·an** /ˈfrentʃˌwʊmən/ *n plural* **Frenchwomen** /-ˌwɪmɪn/ [C] a woman born in France or one who has French parents

**fre·net·ic** /frəˈnetɪk/ *adj* frenetic actions are very fast, uncontrolled and excited: *a frenetic departure*

**fren·zied** /ˈfrenzid/ *adj* frenzied activity is done with a lot of anxiety or excitement and not much organization or control: *frenzied efforts to find a solution* —**frenziedly** *adv*

**fren·zy** /ˈfrenzi/ *n* [C,U] **1** a state of uncontrolled excitement or emotion: *religious frenzies* | **in a frenzy** *She pleaded with them in a frenzy to release her son.* | **a frenzy of passion/remorse etc** *They fell into a frenzy of helpless alarm at the news.* **2 a frenzy of preparation/activity etc** a period of sudden energetic activity: *The house was in a frenzy of activity as my aunts prepared for the wedding.*

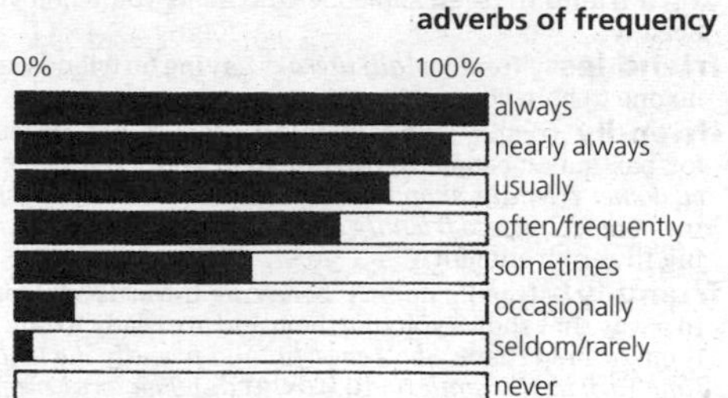


W3 **fre·quen·cy** /ˈfriːkwənsi/ *n* **1** [U] the number of times that something happens: **[+ of]** *The frequency of mining accidents has steadily decreased over the past 20 years.* | **high/low frequency** (=happening very often or not often) *The high frequency of cases of diarrhoea is because of poor hygiene.* | **with increasing frequency** (=more and more often) **2** [U] the fact that something happens a lot: *We are concerned about the frequency of crime in the area.* **3** [C] *technical* the number of radio waves for every second that a radio signal is broadcast: *This station broadcasts on three different frequencies.* **4** [C,U] the rate at which a sound WAVE² (4) moves up and down: **high/low frequency** (=sounding high or low) *The whistle is of such a high frequency the human ear cannot detect it.*

W3 **fre·quent¹** /ˈfriːkwənt/ *adj* happening often: *I try to maintain frequent contact with my children.* | *Her headaches are becoming less frequent.* | **a frequent visitor/user/correspondent etc** (=someone who often visits, uses something etc) *The Governor became a frequent visitor.* —opposite INFREQUENT adv —see picture at FREQUENCY

**fre·quent²** /frɪˈkwent‖frɪˈkwent, ˈfriːkwənt/ *v* [T] *formal* to go to a particular place often: *The bar was frequented by actors from the nearby theatre.*

S3 W2 **frequently** /ˈfrikwəntli/ *adv* very often or many times: *Sperm whales frequently dive to search for squid.*

**fres·co** /ˈfreskəʊ‖-koʊ/ *n* [C] a painting made on a wall by using WATERCOLOUR paint on a surface of wet PLASTER¹ (1) —compare MURAL

S2 W2 **fresh** /freʃ/ *adj*

**1 ▶NEW◀** new or recently made, added etc to replace something or add to it: *I'll just make some fresh coffee.* | *There's been no fresh news of the fighting since yesterday.* | **a fresh attempt/look/approach etc** (=done again in a new way) *We need to have a fresh look at the problem.* | **fresh information/ evidence/facts** (=new facts etc that change a situation): *This fresh evidence may prove his innocence.* | **a fresh sheet/copy/page/towel etc** (=clean, new, and not used before) *You'll have to start again on a fresh sheet of paper.*

**2 ▶FOOD/FLOWERS◀ a)** fresh food is good because it was very recently produced, picked, or prepared: *Let's eat the bread while it's still fresh.* | *Did you get fresh or frozen peas?* | **fresh from the oven/sea/garden etc** *The beans are picked fresh from the garden.* **b)** fresh flowers have recently been picked

**3 ▶COOL/CLEAN◀** looking, feeling or tasting pleasantly clean or cool: *the fresh coolness of the air after rain* | *a fresh clean taste*

**4 ▶NOT TIRED◀** full of energy because you are not tired: *Somehow she managed to seem fresh and lively even at the end of the day.*

**5 fresh air** air that is outside a building or town, and is cleaner: *Let's open the windows and have some fresh air in here!*

**6 fresh from/fresh out of sth** having just finished your education or training, and not having a lot of experience: *a pleasant young man, fresh from university*

**7 ▶WEATHER◀** wind or weather that is fresh is cold: *It's a bit fresh today.*

**8 ▶WATER◀** fresh water contains no salt

**9 be fresh out of sth** *AmE spoken* to have just used your last supplies of something: *I'm fresh out of cough drops – I'll have to stop at the drug store.*

**10 a fresh complexion** healthy-looking skin on your face

**11 fresh-made/fresh-cut/fresh-grated** *especially AmE* having just been made, cut etc: *fresh-ground coffee* —see also FRESHLY

**12 fresh as a daisy** *informal* not tired and ready to do things

**13 fresh in your/their mind** recent enough to be remembered clearly: *She wants to write about her visit while it's still fresh in her mind.*

**14 make a fresh start** to start something again in a completely new and different way after being unsuccessful: *After the accident, they decided to make a fresh start in another town.*

**15 get/be fresh with sb a)** to behave or speak rudely or without respect for someone: *Don't you get fresh with me, son!* **b)** to show someone in a rudely confident way that you think they are sexually attractive: *He started getting fresh with me.* —**freshness** *n* [U]

**fresh·en** /ˈfreʃən/ *v* **1** [T] also **freshen up** to make something look clean, new, and attractive, or smell pleasant: *I think I'll freshen up the paintwork in the bathroom.* **2** to make something feel cool: *Freshen your skin with avocado body lotion.* **3** [I] if wind or the weather freshens, it gets colder

**freshen** (sb ↔) **up** *phr v* [I,T] to wash your hands and face in order to feel clean and comfortable: *He hurried into the bathroom to freshen up before the meeting.*

**fresh·er** /ˈfreʃə‖-ər/ *n* [C] *BrE* a student who has just started at a college or university: *a freshers' party*

**fresh-faced** /ˌ· ˈ·/ *adj* having a young, healthy-looking face: *a fresh-faced youth*

**fresh·ly** /ˈfreʃli/ *adv* **freshly ground/picked/made etc** recently ground, picked, made etc: *freshly ground pepper*

**fresh·man** /ˈfreʃmən/ *n* [C] *AmE* a student in the first year of HIGH SCHOOL or university

**fresh·wa·ter** /ˈfreʃwɔːtə‖-wɔːtər, -wɑː-/ *adj* **1** having water that contains no salt: *freshwater lakes* **2** living in water that contains no salt: *freshwater crabs* —compare SALTWATER

**fret¹** /fret/ *v* **fretted, fretting 1** [I,T] *especially spoken* to feel worried about small or unimportant things, or to make someone feel like this: *Don't you fret – everything will be all right.* | **[+ about/over]** *Nicki was always fretting over something or other.* **2** [T] to make something gradually smaller and weaker by rubbing it over a long period of time

**fret²** *n* **1** [C] one of the raised lines on the NECK (=long straight part) of a VIOLIN, GUITAR etc **2 be/get in a fret** *BrE informal* to become worried or anxious about something: *Aunt Joan always gets in a fret if we're late.*

**fret·ful** /ˈfretfəl/ *adj* anxious and complaining, especially about small or unimportant things: *The child was tired and fretful.* —**fretfully** *adv* —**fretfulness** *n* [U]

**fret·ted** /ˈfretɪ̣d/ *adj* cut or shaped into complicated patterns as decoration

**fret·work** /ˈfretwɜːk‖-wɜːrk/ *n* [U] patterns cut into thin wood, or the activity of making these patterns

**Freud·i·an** /ˈfrɔɪdiən/ *adj* **1** connected with or according to Sigmund Freud's ideas about the way the mind works, and the way it can be studied **2** a Freudian remark or action is connected with the ideas about sex that people have in their minds but do not usually talk about

**Freudian slip** /ˌ... ˈ.ˌ/ *n* [C] something you say that is different from what you intended to say, and shows your true thoughts

**Fri** the written abbreviation of FRIDAY

**fri·a·ble** /ˈfraɪəbəl/ *adj technical* friable rocks or soil are easily broken into very small pieces or into powder

**fri·ar** /ˈfraɪə‖-ər/ *n* [C] a man who belongs to a Christian group, whose members in the past travelled around teaching about Christianity and asking for money and food —compare MONK

**fric·as·see** /ˈfrɪkəseɪ‖ˌfrɪkəˈsiː/ *n* [C,U] a dish made of small pieces of meat in a thick white SAUCE (1)

**fric·a·tive** /ˈfrɪkətɪv/ *n* [C] a sound, such as /f/ or /z/, made by forcing your breath through a narrow opening between your lips, or between your tongue and your lips or teeth

**fric·tion** /ˈfrɪkʃən/ *n* [U] **1** disagreement, angry feelings, or unfriendliness between people: **cause/create friction** *Restrictions on trade have caused friction between these two nations.* **2** the rubbing of one surface against another: *Check your rope frequently, as friction against the rock can wear it down.* **3** in science, friction is the natural law that prevents one surface from sliding easily over another surface: *Heat can be produced by chemical reactions or friction.*

F

**Fri·day** /ˈfraɪdi/ written abbreviation **Fri** *n* [C,U] the day between Thursday and Saturday. In Britain, Friday is considered the fifth day of the week, and in the US it is considered the sixth day of the week: *Mom said she mailed the letter last Friday.* | **on Friday** *The committee meeting is on Friday.* | **on a Friday** *My birthday is on a Friday this year.* | **Friday morning/evening etc** *Can you meet me Friday morning?* | **on Fridays** (=each Friday) | **the Friday** *BrE* (=the Friday of the week being mentioned) *Mr Jones flew in on the Friday and left on the following Wednesday.*

S2 **fridge** /frɪdʒ/ *n* [C] a special cupboard for keeping food cold; REFRIGERATOR —see picture on page 833

**fridge-freez·er** /ˌ. ˈ../ *n* [C] *BrE* a large fridge with a part that keeps food frozen

S1 W1 **friend** /frend/ *n* [C]

**1** ▶ **PERSON YOU LIKE** ◀ someone who you like very much and like to spend time with: *Jerry, I'd like to introduce you to my friend Lucinda.* | **be friends with sb** *My parents have been friends with the Murkets for twenty years.* | **friend of mine/yours/Billy's etc** *A friend of mine told me this joke yesterday.* | **best friend** (=the friend you like best) *One of Tricia's best friends is getting married tomorrow.* | **good/close friend** (=one of the friends you like most) *One of my good friends just had a baby.* | **old friend** (=one you have known a long time) *Bruce is an old friend of mine.* | **friend of a friend** *I met Stephano through a friend of a friend.*

**2 make friends** to meet people and become friendly with them: *Jenny has always found it easy to make friends at school.* | [+ **with**] *Have you made friends with your neighbors yet?*

**3 be just (good) friends** used to say that you are not having a romantic relationship with someone: *Ben's not her boyfriend, I think they're just good friends.*

**4** ▶ **SUPPORTER** ◀ someone who supports a theatre, arts organization, CHARITY (2) etc by giving money or help: *We would like to invite you to become a friend of the orchestra.*

**5** ▶ **NOT AN ENEMY** ◀ someone who is not an enemy and will not harm you or cause trouble for you: *Who goes there? Friend or foe?* | *Don't worry, you're among friends.*

**6 be no friend of/to** to oppose someone or something: *I'm no friend of socialism, as you know.*

**7** ▶ **AT PUBLIC OCCASION** ◀ used to address someone or a group of people in a parliament, meeting, or other formal public occasion: *Friends, we are gathered here today to witness the marriage of Nick and Jo.*

**8 Friend** a member of the Society of Friends; a QUAKER

**9 our/your friend** used to talk about someone you do not know, who has done something annoying: *Our friend with the loud voice is back.*

**10 have friends in high places** to know important people who can help you

**11 a friend in need** someone who helps you when you need it

**friend·less** /ˈfrendləs/ *adj literary* having no friends and no one to help you

**-friendly** /frendli/ *suffix* [in adjectives] **1** not difficult for particular people to use: *a user-friendly computer* | *a customer-friendly shopping environment* **2** not harming something: *eco-friendly washing powder* (=not harming the environment)

**friend·ly¹** /ˈfrendli/ *adj* **1** behaving towards someone in a way that shows you like them and are ready to talk to them or help them: *She's cheerful and friendly the whole time.* | *a friendly smile* | [**+to/towards**] *The local people are always friendly to visitors.* **2 be friendly with sb** to be friends with someone: *Betty's very friendly with the Jacksons.* **3** not at war with your own country, or not opposing you: *friendly nations* **4** *BrE* a friendly game is played for pleasure or practice, and not because it is important to win: *a friendly match against AC Milan* **5 environmentally friendly/ozone friendly etc** not damaging to the environment etc: *environmentally friendly washing powders* **6 friendly fire** bombs, bullets etc that accidentally kill people who are fighting on the same side —see also USER FRIENDLY —**friendliness** *n* [U] S2 W3

**friendly²** *n* [C] *BrE* a game played for pleasure or practice, and not because it is important to win

**friendly so·ci·e·ty** /ˈ... ˌ.../ *n* [C] an association in Britain that people regularly pay small amounts of money to, which then provides them with money when they become old or ill

**friend·ship** /ˈfrendʃɪp/ *n* **1** [C] a relationship between friends: *Our friendship developed quickly over the weeks that followed.* | **form a friendship** (=make friends with someone) *The two boys formed a deep and lasting friendship.* | **strike up a friendship** (=begin to be friends with someone you have just met) **2** [U] the feelings and behaviour that exist between friends: *I could always rely on Gary for friendship and support.* W3

**fri·er** /ˈfraɪə‖-ər/ *n* [C] another spelling of FRYER

**fries** /fraɪz/ *n* [plural] *especially AmE* pieces of potato cut into pieces, usually long and thin, and then cooked in hot fat

**Frie·si·an** /ˈfriːziən‖-ʒən/ *n* [C] *especially BrE* a type of cow that is black and white; HOLSTEIN *AmE*

**frieze** /friːz/ *n* [C] a thin border along the top of the wall of a building or in a room, usually decorated with pictures, patterns etc

**frig** /frɪg/ *v*

**frig about/around** *phr v taboo especially BrE* **1** [I] to waste time doing unnecessary or unimportant things: *Stop frigging about and help!* **2** [T **frig** sb/sth **around/about**] to treat someone badly or unfairly

**frig·ate** /ˈfrɪgɪt/ *n* [C] a small, fast warship used especially for protecting other ships

**frig·ging** /ˈfrɪgɪŋ/ *adj* [only before noun] *adv taboo spoken* used to emphasize something you are saying when you are angry, annoyed etc: *I can't open the frigging door!*

**fright** /fraɪt/ *n* **1** [singular] the feeling you have when something frightens you: **give sb a fright** (=do something that makes someone feel afraid) *You gave me such a fright creeping up on me like that!* | **get/have a fright** *I got an awful fright when your dog rushed out at me.* | **get/have the fright of your life** (=to feel extremely afraid) **2** [U] a feeling of fear: *The child was wild with fright and began to scream.* **3 take fright** to be very afraid of something, especially so that you run away from it: *The bird took fright and flew away.* **4 look a fright** *old-fashioned* to look untidy or unattractive —see also STAGE FRIGHT

**fright·en** /ˈfraɪtn/ *v* [T] **1** to make someone feel afraid: *Don't stand so near the edge, you're frightening me!* | **frighten sb to death/frighten sb out of their wits** (=make someone feel extremely afraid) *She'll be frightened to death when she sees the way you drive.* **2 frighten sb into/out of (doing) sth** to force someone to do something or not to do something by making them afraid: *The lawyers frightened the old lady into signing the paper.*

**frighten** sb ↔ **away** *phr v* [T] to make a person or animal go away by making them feel afraid: *Terrorist activity in the area has frightened most tourists away.*

**frighten** sb/sth ↔ **off** *phr v* [T] to make a person or animal so nervous or afraid that they go away or do not do something they were going to do: *The investors were frightened off by the company's low profits that year.*

S 2 **fright·ened** /ˈfraɪtnd/ *adj* feeling afraid: *a frightened animal* | **[+ of]** *I was frightened of being left by myself in the house.* | **frightened to do sth** *I'll be frightened to look out of the airplane window.* | **[+ that]** *She's frightened that her ex-husband will find her.*

**fright·en·ers** /ˈfraɪtn-əz‖-ərz/ *n* [plural] *BrE slang* **put the frighteners on** sb to make someone do what you want by threatening them

**fright·en·ing** /ˈfraɪtn-ɪŋ/ *adj* making you feel afraid or nervous: *That's a frightening thought.* | **it is frightening (to do sth)** *It's frightening to think how easily children can be hurt.* —**frighteningly** *adv*

**fright·ful** /ˈfraɪtfəl/ *adj* **1** *especially BrE* unpleasant or bad: *There's been a frightful accident on the motorway.* **2** *BrE old-fashioned* used to emphasize how bad something is: *a frightful mess.* —**frightfulness** *n* [U]

**fright·ful·ly** /ˈfraɪtfəli/ *adv BrE old-fashioned* very

**fri·gid** /ˈfrɪdʒɪ̣d/ *adj* **1** a woman who is frigid does not like having sex **2** not friendly or kind: *The guard looked at us with a frigid stare.* **3** a place that is frigid is very cold —**frigidly** *adv* —**frigidity** /frɪˈdʒɪdɪ̣ti/ *n* [U]

**frill** /frɪl/ *n* [C] **1** a decorative edge on a piece of cloth made by another piece of cloth with many small folds in it: *a frill on the bottom of the skirt* **2 without frills/with no frills** without attractive but unnecessary details or decorations: *a no-frills deal*

**frill·y** /ˈfrɪli/ *adj* having many decorative folds of cloth: *a little girl's frilly dress*

**fringe¹** /frɪndʒ/ *n* [C] **1** *BrE* the part of your hair that hangs over your forehead; bangs (BANG² (3)) *AmE* —see picture on page 412 **2** a decorative edge of hanging threads on a curtain, piece of clothing etc **3 on the fringe of a)** at the part of something that is farthest from the centre: *It was easier to move around on the fringe of the crowd.* **b)** not quite belonging to or accepted by a group of people who share the same job, activities etc: *a small group on the fringes of the art world* **4 the right wing/nationalist/radical etc fringe** a group of people within an organization or political party who have extreme ideas that most people do not agree with: *The terrorist fringe condemned the decision.* **5 the fringe,** also **fringe theatre** the performance of plays that are unusual or that try to make people think differently —see also **the lunatic fringe** (LUNATIC (3))

**fringe²** *adj* [only before noun] different from the most usual or accepted way of thinking or doing things: *The environment is no longer a fringe issue in Europe.*

**fringe³** *v* [T] to be around the edge of something; BORDER: *A line of trees fringed the pool.*

**fringe ben·e·fit** /ˈ· ˌ···/ *n* [C usually plural] an additional service or advantage given with a job besides wages; PERK¹: *The pay is awful but there are several fringe benefits.*

**fringe thea·tre** /ˌ· ˈ··/ *n* [U] *BrE* plays by new writers, often on difficult subjects or written in unusual ways, that are not performed in the main theatres

**frip·pe·ry** /ˈfrɪpəri/ *n* [C] an unnecessary and useless object or decoration: *She spends all her money on fripperies.*

**fris·bee** /ˈfrɪzbi/ *n* [C,U] *trademark* a piece of plastic shaped like a plate that you throw to someone else to catch as a game

**frisk** /frɪsk/ *v* **1** [T] also **frisk down** *AmE* to search someone for hidden weapons, drugs etc by feeling their body with your hands: *We were frisked at the airport, can you believe it?* —see picture on page 1260 **2** [I] to run and jump playfully: *The lambs were frisking around the pen.*

**frisk·y** /ˈfrɪski/ *adj* full of energy, fun, and cheerfulness: *a frisky colt* | *He's still frisky, even at eighty years old!* —**friskily** *adv* —**friskiness** *n* [U]

**fris·son** /ˈfriːsɒn‖friːˈsoʊn/ *n* [C] a sudden feeling of excitement or fear: *a frisson of alarm*

**frit** /frɪt/ *adj BrE dialect* frightened

**frit·ter¹** /ˈfrɪtə‖-ər/ *n* [C] a thin piece of fruit, vegetable, or meat covered with a mixture of eggs and flour and cooked in hot fat: **apple/corn/banana fritter** (=made of apple, corn etc)

**fritter²**

**fritter** sth ↔ **away** *phr v* [T] to waste time, money, or effort on something small or unimportant: **[+ on]** *They frittered their pocket-money away on sweets.*

**fritz** /frɪts/ *n* [singular] *AmE informal* **be on the fritz** if something electrical is on the fritz, it is not working properly

**fri·vol·i·ty** /frɪˈvɒlɪ̣ti‖-ˈvɑː-/ *n* **1** [U] lack of serious or sensible thought or behaviour: *Your frivolity is out of place on such a solemn occasion.* **2 frivolities** [plural] **a)** silly or amusing actions or words, especially in a situation where you should be serious or sensible **b)** unimportant or unnecessary things: *Student life should be more than parties and other frivolities.*

**friv·o·lous** /ˈfrɪvələs/ *adj* **1** not serious or sensible, especially in a way that is not suitable for a particular occasion: *The court discourages frivolous law suits.* **2** a frivolous person likes having fun rather than doing serious or sensible things —**frivolously** *adv*

**frizz** /frɪz/ *v* [T] *informal* to make your hair curl very tightly —**frizz** *n* [U]

**friz·zle** /ˈfrɪzəl/ *v* [I,T] *informal* also **frizzle up** to dry or burn something, or to be dried or burnt, especially into a curly shape

**frizz·y** /ˈfrɪzi/ *adj* frizzy hair is tightly curled

**fro** /frəʊ‖froʊ/ *adv* see TO AND FRO

**frock** /frɒk‖frɑːk/ *n* [C] **1** *old-fashioned* a woman's or girl's dress: *a party frock* **2** a long loose piece of clothing worn by some Christian MONKS

**frock coat** /ˌ· ˈ·‖ˈ· ·/ *n* [C] a knee-length coat for men, worn in the 19th century

**frog** /frɒg‖frɑːg, frɒːg/ *n* [C] **1** a small green animal that lives near water and has long legs for jumping —compare TOAD **2 have a frog in your throat** *informal* to have difficulty in speaking because of a sore throat **3 Frog** *informal* an offensive word for a French person

frog

**frog·man** /ˈfrɒgmən‖ˈfrɑːg-, ˈfrɒːg-/ *n* [C] someone who swims under water using special equipment to help them breathe, especially as a job

**frog·march** /ˈfrɒgmɑːtʃ‖ˈfrɑːgmɑːrtʃ, ˈfrɒːg-/ *v* [T] *BrE* to force someone to walk somewhere by having two people on either side of them who hold their arms very tightly

**frog·spawn** /ˈfrɒgspɔːn‖ˈfrɑːgspɒːn, ˈfrɒːg-/ *n* [U] frog's eggs

**frol·ic¹** /ˈfrɒlɪk‖ˈfrɑː-/ *v* [I] to play in an active, happy way; FRISK (2): [+ **around/about/over**] *The kids spent all day frolicking around in the surf.*

**frolic²** *n* [C often plural] a cheerful, enjoyable game or activity: *Everyone joined in the Saturday night frolics.*

**frol·ic·some** /ˈfrɒlɪksəm‖ˈfrɑː-/ *adj especially literary* active and liking to play: *frolicsome kittens*

S1 W1 **from** /frəm; *strong*frɒm‖frəm· frʌm; *strong* frɑːm/ *prep* **1** starting at a particular place, position, or condition: *How do you get from here to Colchester?|running from one side of the building to the other|The hotel is on the main road from Caernarfon.|dropped from a height of six feet|translating from French into English*|**go from A to B** (=go from one point or situation to another) *People will choose different methods of going from A to B.*|**go from bad to worse** (=get worse) *When she arrived, things just went from bad to worse!* **2 from house to house/shop to shop/place to place etc a)** calling at every house, shop, etc: *She went from house to house asking if anyone had seen him.* **b)** in different houses, places etc: *From office to office things work differently.|It will vary from time to time and from place to place.|Everything goes wrong from time to time.* (=sometimes) **3** starting at a particular time: *He'll be here tomorrow from about seven o'clock onwards.|in a week from now*|**from morning to night** (=without stopping) *housewives who work from morning to night*|**from now on** (=from this time onwards) *From now on, I will only be working in the mornings.* —see SINCE³ (USAGE) **4** beginning at a particular limit or price: *The sizes range from a hundred down to twenty.|The yield from this type of investment can be anything from five to ten percent.* **5** if you see, watch, or do something from a place, this is where you are when you see, watch, or do it: *From the top of the hill, you can see for miles.|There's a man watching us from behind that fence.* **6** used to express a distance: *We live about five km from Boston.|a large Victorian house only fifty yards from my workplace.|It's about an hour and a half from Scarborough.* **7** if something is moved or taken from a place or person, it is removed, taken away or taken out: *She pulled her chair away from her desk.|I had to take that new toy away from him.|Subtract three from 15.|He took a knife from his pocket.|His absence from class has been noted.* **8** used to say what the origin of something is: *He gets his good looks from his mother.|I'll show you a short extract from one of our training videos.|Do you know where the information came from?|an infectious disease which he got from another sick dog|Members are chosen from a list drawn up by the Home Secretary.|I bought it from a shop in the market.|I got this from Colin.* **9** sent or given by someone: *I've received a bill for nineteen dollars from the hospital.|I had a phone call from John.|You need to get permission from the owner.|with lots of love from Elaine and Martin* **10 you can tell him from me...** *spoken* used to ask someone to tell another person something, when you are annoyed or determined: *Well, you can tell him from me that I'll be making an official complaint.* **11** someone who comes from a particular place lives, works, or belongs there: *We invited speakers from all the regions.|Students from all faculties will have access to the machines.|Alison from the Job Centre is on the phone.*|**I'm from/I come from Devon/New York etc** (=born in Devon, New York etc) **12** used to state the cause of something: *mothers who are exhausted from all the sleepless nights|Death rates from accidents have declined.*|**suffer from** (=be affected by; have) *Mum suffers from migraines.* **13** used to introduce the reason for, or origin of, an opinion or judgement: *From what I've read, the company seems to be in difficulties.|It's obvious from a quick glance that the plan has changed dramatically.*|**from my point of view** (=how something affects you) *These changes are ideal from my point of view.|From Clarisse's point of view, it's very distressing indeed.*|**from memory** (=according to what I can remember) *From memory, the film wasn't as good as the book.* **14** used to state the substance that is used to make something: *Bread is made from flour, water, and yeast.* **15** used after words such as 'protect', 'prevent', or 'keep', to introduce the situation or action that is stopped, avoided, or prevented: *These problems have prevented me from completing the work.|people who have been disqualified from driving* **16** used when you are comparing things, and saying how they are similar or different: *She's quite different from her sister.|Our two cats are so alike, I can never tell one from the other.*

**from·age frais** /ˌfrɒmɑːʒ ˈfreɪ‖frəˌmɑːʒ-/ *n* [U] *French* a soft white mild cheese you can eat with a spoon

**frond** /frɒnd‖frɑːnd/ *n* [C] a leaf of a FERN or PALM¹ (2)

**front**

Sue ran in front of the bus.

Sue got a seat at the front of the bus /in the front of the bus.

S1 W1 **front¹** /frʌnt/ *n*

**1 ▶ GROUP/LINE ◀ the front** the front of a group or line of people or things is the position that is furthest forward in the direction that they are facing or moving: [+ **of**] *She always sits at the front of the class.*|**in/at the front** *I think I can see them, they're right at the front.*|**the front of the line/queue/crowd** *TV reporters shoved their way to the front of the crowd.*

**2 ▶ FORWARD SIDE/SURFACE ◀ the front** the side or surface of something that is in the direction that it faces or moves: [+ **of**] *Where did that scratch on the front of my car come from?* —compare REAR¹ (1)

**3 the front** the most important side or surface of something, that you look at first: **on the front** *Get a postcard with a picture of our hotel on the front of it.*|[+ **of**] *She's on the front of the Radio Times.* —opposite BACK¹ (2) —compare REAR¹ (1)

**4 ▶ BUILDINGS ◀ the front** the most important side, where you go in

**5 ▶ BOOK ◀ the front** the first pages

**6 in front of sth a)** near the side of something that is in the direction that it faces or moves: *right in front of the car* —opposite BEHIND¹ (1) —see picture on page 1257 **b)** near the side of a building where you go in: *She parked in front of the office.*

**7 in front of sb a)** ahead of someone, in the direction that they are facing or moving: *Come out here in front of the class.* **b)** if you say or do something in front of someone you do it where they can see or hear you: *Don't swear in front of the children!* **c)** if you have problems or difficulties in front of you, you will soon need to deal with them

**8 in front a)** in the most forward or leading position; ahead: *Mrs Ramsay's horse was well in front.|He drove straight into the car in front.* —compare BEHIND¹ (1) **b)** in the area nearest the most forward part of something, or the entrance to a building

**9 out front** also **out the front/out in front** *BrE* the area near the entrance to a building: *Hurry up! The taxi is out front.*

**10 in/up front** also **in the front** *especially BrE* in the part of a car where the driver sits: *"Get in the car, kids." "Can I sit in front, Mom?"*

**11 be brought/called/hauled in front of sb** to have to see someone in authority about something you have done

wrong: *My whole section was called in front of the manager.*
**12 sit in front of** to spend time using or watching something such as a computer or television: *You've spent all day just sitting in front of the television.*
**13 ▶WEATHER◀** [C] *technical* the place where two areas of air of different temperatures meet, often shown as a line on weather maps: **warm/cold front** (=an area of warm or cold air)
**14 on the publicity/money/health front etc** in a particular area: *Constant effort is needed on the publicity front.*
**15 up front** *informal* **a)** money that is paid up front is paid before work is done, or goods are supplied *We need two hundred pounds up front.* **b)** directly and clearly from the start: *Jorge wanted to help her, but she'd told him up front she did not need it.* —see also UPFRONT
**16 ▶SEA◀ the front** *especially BrE* the part of a town next to the sea, between the beach and the shops, hotels etc; SEAFRONT
**17 ▶BODY◀** your chest, or the part of your body that faces forward: *I've spilled some soup down my front.*
**18 on all fronts** in every area of the activity that you are involved in: *We're making rapid progress on all fronts.*
**19 be a front for** *informal* to be used for hiding a secret or illegal activity: *Could his business be a front for drug smuggling?*
**20 put on/show a front** to behave in a way that is braver or happier than you feel: *I know you're scared, but you've got to put on a brave front.*
**21 ▶ORGANIZATION◀** [singular] used in the name of a political party or unofficial military organization: *the People's Liberation Front*
**22 ▶WAR◀** [C] a line along which fighting takes place during a war; FRONT LINE: *trucks heading towards the Western Front* —see also HOME FRONT
**23 ▶CHURCH◀** [C] a side of a large, important church building: *the west front*

**USAGE NOTE: FRONT**
WORD CHOICE: **in front of, behind, at/in the front of, at/in the back of, face, opposite, before**
**In front of** (opposite **behind**) is used when one thing is separate from the other: *A child ran out in front of the bus* (=in the road outside the bus).
**At/in the front of** (opposite **at/in the back of**) is used when one thing is inside or part of the other: *The child took a seat at/in the front of the bus* (=in the front part of the bus).
If a building is in front of something, it **faces** it: *The hotel faced the Mediterranean.*
A person or place that faces another one exactly, with a space between, is **opposite** it. If the bus stop is *opposite the station* it is not *in front of the station* but on the other side of the road. *I live opposite Greg.*
One event may happen **before** another: *Let's have a drink before dinner* (NOT *in front of dinner*).

**front²** *adj* [only before noun] **1** at, on, or in the front of something: *Your front teeth are going to have to be straightened.* | **front door/room/garden** (=at the front of a house) | **front seat/row** *Good news! I got us front row seats!* —opposite BACK⁴ (1) **2** *informal* a front man or organization acts lawfully in business as a way of hiding a secret or illegal activity: *a front organization for importing heroin* **3** *technical* a front vowel sound is made by raising your tongue at the front of your mouth —opposite BACK⁴ (7)

**front³** *v* **1** [I,T] if a building fronts onto the sea, a road etc, the front of the building faces it: [+ **onto**] *Our hotel fronts onto a main road.* | **front sth** *houses fronting the lake* **2 be fronted by/with** to be covered or decorated at the front with something: *Victor led us into a large building fronted with marble.* **3** [T] to lead something such as a group or television programme by being the person that the public see most: *She's fronting a weekly current affairs program.*
**front for** sb/sth *phr v* [T] *informal* to act as the person or organization used for hiding the real nature of a secret or illegal activity: *Police suspected her of fronting for a gang of forgers.*

**front·age** /ˈfrʌntɪdʒ/ *n* [U] the part of a building or piece of land that is along a road, river, etc

**front·al** /ˈfrʌntl/ *adj* [only before noun] *formal* **1** at or connected with the front part of something: *the frontal area of the brain* **2** towards the front of something: *From the frontal approach, the house looks grand and imposing.* **3 full frontal** showing people with no clothes on, from the front: *full frontal nudity* —**front·ally** *adv*

**frontal sys·tem** /ˈ‥ ˌ‥/ *n* [C] *technical* a weather FRONT¹ (13)

**front-and-center** /ˌ‥ ˈ‥◂/ *adj AmE* very important and needing attention: *Prayer in schools has become a front-and-center issue for the White House.*

**frontbench** /ˌ· ˈ·◂/ *n* [C] the front row of seats on each side of the British parliament, on which the leaders of the political parties sit —compare BACKBENCH

**front·bench·er** /ˌfrʌntˈbentʃə◂‖-ər◂/ *n* [C] someone who sits on a front bench in the British parliament —compare BACKBENCHER

**front door** /ˌ· ˈ·/ *n* [C usually singular] the main entrance door to a house, at the front —compare BACK DOOR¹ (1)

**fron·tier** /ˈfrʌntɪə‖frʌnˈtɪr/ *n* **1 the frontier** an area where people have never lived before, that not much is known about, especially in the western US before the 20th century: *the settlement of the Oklahoma frontier* | *space, the final frontier* **2** [C] *especially BrE* the border of a country, where people cross from one country to another: [+ **between/with**] *Lille is close to the frontier between France and Belgium.* | **on/at the frontier** *Troops established a road block on the frontier.* **3 the frontiers of knowledge/physics etc** the limit of what is known about something: **push back the frontiers** (=discover new things) **4 roll back the frontiers** to make something such as government power smaller

**fron·tiers·man** /ˈfrʌntɪəzmən‖frʌnˈtɪrz-/ *n* [C] a man who lived in the American frontier

**fron·tis·piece** /ˈfrʌntɪ̣spiːs/ *n* [C] a picture or photograph at the beginning of a book, usually opposite the page with the title on it

**front line** /ˌ· ˈ·◂/ *n* **1 be the front line** the place where fighting happens in a war; FRONT¹ (22): *troops in the front line* **2 in the front line a)** doing something that has not been done before: *in the front line of the fight against cancer* **b)** likely to be blamed for an organization's mistakes —**front-line** *adj* [only before noun]: *front-line conditions*

**front man** /ˈ· ·/ *n* [C usually singular] a person who speaks for an organization, for example an illegal one, but is not the leader of it

**front mat·ter** /ˈ· ˌ‥/ *n* [U] all the pages at the very beginning of a book, including the page with the title on it

**front money** /ˈ· ˌ‥/ *n* [singular] money that is paid for something before you get it

**front of·fice** /ˌ· ˈ‥/ *n* [singular] *AmE* the managers of a company

**front page** /ˌ· ˈ·/ *n* [C] the first page of a newspaper

**front-page** /ˈ· ·/ *adj* [only before noun] *informal* interesting, important, or exciting enough to be printed on the front page of a newspaper: *a front-page story*

**front room** /ˌ· ˈ·/ *n* [C] the main room in a house where you usually sit; LIVING ROOM

**front-run·ner** /ˌ· ˈ‥/ *n* [C] the person or thing that is most likely to succeed in a competition: *Thomson and Palmer are the front-runners for promotion.*

**frost¹** /frɒst‖frɒːst/ *n* **1** [U] ice that looks white and powdery and covers things that are outside when the temperature is very cold: *The grass and trees were white with frost.* **2** [C] very cold weather, when water freezes: **late/early frost** *Even in May we can sometimes get a late frost.* | **hard frost** (=extremely cold weather) *Our pipes burst in the hard frost.* —see also FROSTY, FROSTED

**frost²** *v* [T] *especially AmE* to cover a cake with a mixture of powdery sugar and liquid; ICE²

**frost up** also **frost over** *phr v* [I] to become covered in frost: *The car door's all frosted up and I can't get it open.*

**frost·bite** /ˈfrɒstbaɪt‖ˈfrɒːst-/ *n* [U] a condition caused by extreme cold, that makes your fingers, toes etc swell, become darker and sometimes drop off —**frostbitten** /-bɪtn/ *adj*

**frost·ed** /ˈfrɒstɪd‖ˈfrɒːstɪd/ *adj* covered with FROST¹ (1), or with something that looks like frost

**frosted glass** /ˌ·· ˈ·◂/ *n* [U] glass that is not transparent: *a frosted glass screen*

**frost·ing** /ˈfrɒstɪŋ‖ˈfrɒːstɪŋ/ *n* [U] **1** *especially AmE* a sweet substance put on cakes and made from powdery sugar and liquid; ICING **2** a rough surface that is not shiny

**frost·y** /ˈfrɒsti‖ˈfrɒːsti/ *adj* **1 a)** extremely cold: *frosty air* **b)** covered with FROST¹ (1): *She stumbled, falling heavily on the frosty ground.* **2** unfriendly: *"This is a members-only club," said the doorman with frosty politeness.* | **frosty smile/expression/stare** *He gave me a frosty stare.* —**frostily** *adv*

**froth¹** /frɒθ‖frɒːθ/ *n* **1** [singular, U] small BUBBLES¹ (1) that form on top of a liquid that has air mixed in it: *He carefully wiped the froth from his moustache.* **2** [singular, U] small, white BUBBLES¹ (1) of SALIVA around a person's or animal's mouth **3** [U] talk or ideas that are attractive but have no real value or meaning: *The book has too much froth and not enough fact.*

**froth²** *v* [I] **1** also **froth up** if a liquid froths it produces or contains BUBBLES¹ (1) on top: *When you first open the bottle the beer will froth for a few seconds.* **2** if someone's mouth froths, SALIVA comes out as small white BUBBLES¹ (1) **3 froth at the mouth a)** *informal* to be extremely angry: *By the time I got out of the traffic jam I was frothing at the mouth.* **b)** to have SALIVA coming out of your mouth as small white BUBBLES¹ (1)

**froth·y** /ˈfrɒθi‖ˈfrɒːθi/ *adj* **1** a liquid that is frothy has lots of small BUBBLES¹ (1) on top: *a cup of hot frothy capuccino* **2** a frothy book, film etc is enjoyable but not serious or important —**frothily** *adv*

**frown¹** /fraʊn/ *v* [I] to make an angry, unhappy, or confused expression, moving your EYEBROWS together: *She saw him frown as he read the letter.* | [+ at] *Mattie frowned at him disapprovingly.*

**frown on/upon** sb/sth *phr v* [T usually passive] to disapprove of something, especially someone's behaviour: *Even though divorce is legal it is still frowned upon.*

**frown²** *n* [C usually singular] the expression on your face when you frown: **with a frown** *He looked at her with a puzzled frown.*

**frow·zy** /ˈfraʊzi/ also **frowsty** /ˈfraʊsti/ *BrE* —*adj* **1** someone who is frowzy is not very clean or tidy and smells bad: *a frowzy old woman who kept cats* **2** a house or room that is frowzy has no fresh air in it and smells bad: *The air in the room had become stale and frowzy.*

**froze** /frəʊz‖froʊz/ the past tense of FREEZE¹

**fro·zen¹** /ˈfrəʊzən‖ˈfroʊ-/ the past participle of FREEZE¹

**frozen²** *adj* **1** frozen food has been stored at a very low temperature in order to preserve it: *frozen meat* **2 be frozen (stiff)** *spoken* to feel very cold: *I'm frozen! Put the fire on.* **3** earth that is frozen is so cold it has become very hard: *The ground was frozen beneath our feet.* **4** a river, lake etc that is frozen has a layer of ice on the surface **5 be frozen with fear/terror/fright** to be so afraid, shocked etc that you cannot move

**fruc·ti·fy** /ˈfrʌktɪfaɪ/ *v* [I,T] *technical* to produce fruit or to make a plant produce fruit —**fructification** /ˌfrʌktɪfɪˈkeɪʃən/ *n* [U]

**fruc·tose** /ˈfrʌktəʊs‖-toʊs/ *n* [U] a kind of natural sugar in fruit juices and HONEY (1)

**fru·gal** /ˈfruːgəl/ *adj* **1** careful to only buy what is necessary: *As children we were taught to be frugal and hard-working.* **2** a frugal meal is a small meal of plain food: *We sat down to a frugal breakfast.* —**frugally** *adv* —**frugality** /fruːˈgælɪti/ *n* [U]

**fruit¹** /fruːt/ *n plural* **fruit** or **fruits** **1** [C,U] something such as an apple, BANANA, or STRAWBERRY that grows on a tree or other plant, and tastes sweet: *fresh fruit and vegetables* | *a bowl of fruit* —see also DRIED FRUIT, SOFT FRUIT —see picture on page 413 **2** [C,U] *technical* the part of a plant, bush, or tree that contains the seeds **3 the fruit/fruits of sth** the good results that you have from something, after you have worked very hard **4 bear fruit** if a plan or activity bears fruit, it produces the good results that you intended **5 in fruit** *technical* trees, plants etc that are in fruit are producing their fruit **6 the fruits of the earth/nature** all the natural things that the earth produces, such as fruit, vegetables, or minerals **7** [C] *old-fashioned slang* an insulting way of talking to or about a man who is a HOMOSEXUAL **8 old fruit** *old-fashioned slang BrE* used by men as a way of addressing a man that they know well S2 W2

**fruit²** *v* [I] *technical* if a tree or a plant fruits, it produces fruit

**fruit bat** /ˈ· ·/ *n* [C] a large BAT¹ (1) that lives in hot countries and eats fruit

**fruit·cake** /ˈfruːtkeɪk/ *n* **1** [C,U] a cake that has dried fruit in it **2** [C] *informal* someone who seems to be mentally ill or behaves in a strange way: *She's a bit of a fruitcake.* —see also **nutty as a fruitcake** (NUTTY (3))

**fruit·er·er** /ˈfruːtərə‖-tərər/ *n* [C] *BrE old-fashioned* someone who sells fruit

**fruit fly** /ˈ· ·/ *n* [C] a small fly that eats fruit or decaying plants

**fruit·ful** /ˈfruːtfəl/ *adj* **1** something you do that is fruitful has good results: *Today's meeting proved more fruitful than last week's.* —opposite FRUITLESS **2** *literary* land that is fruitful produces a lot of corn, vegetables, fruit etc —**fruitfully** *adv* —**fruitfulness** *n* [U]

**fru·i·tion** /fruˈɪʃən/ *n* [U] *formal* the successful result of a plan, idea etc: **come to fruition/be brought to fruition** *All his plans had come to fruition.*

**fruit·less** /ˈfruːtləs/ *adj* failing to achieve what was wanted, especially after much effort: | **fruitless attempt/search/journey** *a fruitless attempt to settle the dispute* | *So far, their search has been fruitless.* —opposite FRUITFUL (1) —**fruitlessly** *adv* —**fruitlessness** *n* [U]

**fruit ma·chine** /ˈ· ·ˌ·/ *n* [C] *BrE* a machine in which you put a coin, that gives money back if you make three pictures of the same thing appear; SLOT MACHINE *AmE*

**fruit sal·ad** /ˌ· ˈ··/ *n* [C,U] a dish of many different types of fruit cut into small pieces

**fruit·y** /ˈfruːti/ *adj* **1** tasting or smelling strongly of fruit: *a very fruity wine* **2** a voice or laugh that is fruity sounds low and pleasant **3** *BrE informal* a remark, story etc that is fruity is about sex and slightly shocking or offensive

**frump** /frʌmp/ *n* [C] a woman who is frumpy

**frump·y** /ˈfrʌmpi/ also **frump·ish** /ˈfrʌmpɪʃ/ *adj* a woman who is frumpy looks unattractive because she dresses in old-fashioned clothes

**frus·trate** /frʌˈstreɪt‖ˈfrʌstreɪt/ *v* [T] **1** if something frustrates you it makes you feel annoyed or angry because you are unable to do what you want: *I think the fact that he's working with amateurs really frustrates him.* **2** to prevent someone's plans, efforts or attempts from succeeding: *Their attempts to speak to him were frustrated by the guards.* —compare THWART¹

**frus·trat·ed** /frʌˈstreɪtɪd‖ˈfrʌstreɪtɪd/ *adj* **1** feeling annoyed, upset, and impatient, because you cannot control or change a situation, or achieve something: **get frustrated** *He gets frustrated when he can't win.* |

[+ **with/at**] *I can't understand this. I just get frustrated with it.*| **sexually frustrated** (=feeling dissatisfied because you cannot have sex) **2 a frustrated poet/actor/dancer etc** someone who wants to develop a particular skill but has not been able to do this

**frus·trat·ing** /frʌˈstreɪtɪŋ‖ˈfrʌstreɪtɪŋ/ *adj* making you feel annoyed, upset, or impatient because you cannot do what you want to do

**frus·tra·tion** /frʌˈstreɪʃən/ *n* **1** [C,U] the feeling of being annoyed, upset, or impatient, because you cannot control or change a situation, or achieve something: *It wasn't what he said that made me cry—it was sheer frustration.*| **in/with frustration** *Souness watched in frustration as his team lost yet again.* **2** [U] the fact of being prevented from achieving what you are trying to achieve: [+ **of**] *The frustration of his ambitions made him a bitter man.*

S3 **fry**[1] /fraɪ/ *v past and past participle* **fried** **1** [I,T] to cook something in hot fat or oil, or to be cooked in hot fat or oil: *Fry the onions until they are golden.* —see picture on page 833 **2** [I,T] *AmE slang* to kill someone, or to be killed, as a punishment in the ELECTRIC CHAIR —see also DEEP FRY, FRIES, STIR-FRY —**fried** *adj*

**fry**[2] *n* [plural] **1** very young fish —see also **small fry** (SMALL[1] (12)) **2 fries** [plural] *AmE* long thin pieces of potato that have been cooked in fat; chips (CHIP[1] (3a)) *BrE*

**fry·er, frier** /ˈfraɪə‖-ər/ *n* [C] **1 deep fat fryer/deep fryer** *AmE* a big deep pan for frying food **2** *AmE* a chicken that has been specially bred to be fried

**frying pan** /ˈ·· ˌ·/ *n* [C] **1** a round flat pan with a long handle, used for frying food; SKILLET *AmE* —see picture at PAN[1] **2 out of the frying pan and into the fire** to go from a bad situation to one that is even worse

**fry-up** /ˈ· ·/ *n* [C] *informal BrE* a meal of fried food such as eggs, BACON, potatoes etc

**ft** **1** the written abbreviation of FOOT[1] (3): *a board 6ft x 4ft* **2 Ft** the written abbreviation of FORT, used in names of places: *Ft. Lauderdale*

**fuch·sia** /ˈfjuːʃə/ *n* **1** [C,U] a garden bush with hanging bell-shaped flowers in two colours of red, pink, or white **2** [U] a bright pink colour

S3 **fuck**[1] /fʌk/ *v taboo spoken* **1 Fuck off!** an offensive way of telling someone to go away: *Fuck off you stupid bastard!* **2** [I,T] to have sex with someone **3 fuck it/you/her/John!** used to emphasize that you are annoyed or angry at someone or something: *Oh fuck it! I'm going home early!*

**fuck around** also **fuck about** *BrE phr v* [I] *taboo spoken* to waste time or behave in a silly or careless way

**fuck** sb **around** also **fuck** sb **about** *BrE phr v* [I] *taboo spoken* to make someone angry or annoyed by wasting their time: *The telephone company has been fucking me around all week.*

**fuck** sb ↔ **off** *phr v* [T] *taboo spoken* to make someone feel annoyed or angry: *Steve really fucks me off when he doesn't write down my phone messages.*

**fuck** sb ↔ **over** *phr v* [T] *AmE taboo* to treat someone very badly: *Bev had been fucked over so many times she no longer expected life to be fair.*

**fuck** sb ↔ **up** *phr v* [T] *taboo spoken* to make someone very unhappy and confused so that they cannot control their life: *Heroin fucks you up.*

**fuck up** *phr v taboo spoken* [I,T **fuck** sth ↔ **up**] to make a mistake or do something badly: *You really fucked up this time.*

**fuck with sb** *phr v* [T] *taboo spoken* to annoy someone or make them angry: *I wouldn't fuck with Alfie if I were you.*

**fuck**[2] *interjection taboo* used when you are annoyed about something: *Fuck! I forgot my keys!*

**fuck**[3] *n taboo spoken* **1** [C usually singular] the act of having sex **2 the fuck** used when you are angry to emphasize what you are saying: *Get the fuck out of here!*| **who/why/what etc the fuck** *What the fuck do you think you're doing?* **3 not care/give a fuck** to not care at all what happens

**fuck all** /ˈ· ·, ˌ· ˈ·/ *n* [U] *BrE taboo spoken* nothing: *I don't know why they employ him. He does fuck all anyway.*

**fucked up** /ˌ· ˈ·/ *adj taboo* very unhappy and confused, so that you cannot control your life properly: *She's pretty fucked up.*

**fuck·er** /ˈfʌkə‖-ər/ also **fuck** *BrE* —*n* [C] *taboo spoken* someone who you dislike very much, think is stupid etc

**fuck·head** /ˈfʌkhed/ *n* [C] *AmE taboo spoken* someone you dislike or think is stupid: *Get lost, fuckhead.*

**fuck·ing** /ˈfʌkɪŋ/ *adj* [only before noun] *taboo spoken* S1 **1** used to emphasize that you are angry or annoyed: *I wish that fucking parrot would shut up!* **2** used to emphasize your opinion of something: *He's a fucking good football player.*

**fuck·ing A** /ˌfʌkɪŋ ˈeɪ/ *interjection AmE taboo* used when you are very surprised, shocked etc by something: *Fucking A! I never thought L.A. would be this hot.*

**fuck-up** /ˈ· ·/ *n* [C] *taboo spoken* a situation that has been dealt with very badly: *Relations with the staff were bad, so any change in the schedule was seen as 'yet another fuck-up by the management'.*

**fud·dle**[1] /ˈfʌdl/ *v* [T] *BrE informal* if something, especially alcohol or drugs, fuddles you or your mind, it makes you unable to think clearly: *Too much drink fuddles your brain.*

**fuddle**[2] *n* [singular] *informal* **in a fuddle** feeling very confused and unable to think clearly: *Poor old Tom. Since his wife died he's been in a terrible fuddle.*

**fud·dled** /ˈfʌdld/ *adj* unable to think clearly, especially because you are drunk or old

**fud·dy-dud·dy** /ˈfʌdi ˌdʌdi/ *n* [C] someone who has old-fashioned ideas and attitudes: *You're such an old fuddy-duddy. Most women wear trousers these days!* —**fuddy-duddy** *adj*

**fudge**[1] /fʌdʒ/ *n* **1** [U] a soft creamy light brown sweet food **2 a fudge** *especially BrE* an attempt to deal with a situation that does not solve its problems completely, or only makes it seem better

**fudge**[2] *v* **1** [I,T] to avoid giving exact details or a clear answer about something **fudge the issue** (=avoid a particular subject) *politicians fudging the issue of arms sales* **2** [T] to change important figures or facts to deceive people: *Sibley has been fudging his data for years now.*

**fudge**[3] *interjection* used when you are angry or annoyed, instead of saying a more offensive word: *Oh fudge! I've left my wallet at home!*

**fudg·y** /ˈfʌdʒi/ *adj AmE* slightly sticky with a strong sweet chocolate taste

**fu·el**[1] /ˈfjuːəl/ *n* **1** [C,U] a substance such as coal, gas, or oil that can be burned to produce heat or energy: *Don't leave the engine switched on. It wastes fuel.*| *Coal is one of the cheapest fuels.* **2** [U] something that makes someone's anger, hatred etc worse: **fuel to sth** *His behaviour was only fuel to her jealousy.* **3 add fuel to the fire/flames** to make a situation a lot worse than it was already S2 W2

**fuel**[2] *v past tense* **fuelled** *BrE*, **fueled** *AmE* **1** [T] to make a situation worse or make someone's feelings stronger: *The attempts to stop the strike only fuelled the workers' resentment.* **2** [T] to put oil, petrol etc in a vehicle **3** also **fuel up** [I] if a vehicle fuels up, fuel is put into it: *It's amazing that some planes can fuel up in mid air.*

**fuel in·jec·tion** /ˈ·· ·ˌ··/ *n* [U] a method of putting liquid fuel directly into an engine, which allows a car to ACCELERATE more quickly

**fug** /fʌg/ *n* [singular] *BrE informal* air inside a room that feels heavy and unpleasant because of smoke, heat, or too many people: *There's a terrible fug in here. Let's open a window.* —**fuggy** *adj*



F

**fu·gi·tive¹** /ˈfjuːdʒɪtɪv/ *n* [C] someone who is hiding, especially from the police, and is trying to avoid being caught: [+ **from**] *a fugitive from Stalin's oppressive regime*

**fugitive²** *adj* [only before noun] **1** trying to escape **2** *literary* lasting for a very short time: *rare and fugitive visits*

**fugue** /fjuːg/ *n* [C,U] a way of writing music using a tune that is repeated regularly in different keys (KEY¹ (4)) by different voices, instruments etc, or a piece of music written this way

**-ful¹** /fəl/ *suffix* [in adjectives] **1** full of something: *an eventful day* **2** having the quality of something or causing something: *restful colours* | *Is it painful?* —**fully** /fəli/ [in adverbs] *shouting cheerfully*

**-ful²** /fʊl/ *suffix* [in nouns] **1** the amount of a substance needed to fill a particular container: *two cupfuls of milk* **2** as much as can be carried by or contained in a particular part of the body: *carrying an armful of flowers*

**ful·crum** /ˈfʊlkrəm, ˈfʌl-/ *n plural* **fulcrums** *or* **fulcra** /-krə/ [C] the point on which a LEVER (=bar) turns, balances, or is supported in turning or lifting something

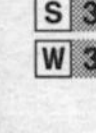

**ful·fil** *BrE*, **fulfill** *AmE* /fʊlˈfɪl/ *v* [T] **1** if a hope, promise, wish etc is fulfilled, the thing that you had hoped, promised, wanted etc happens or is done: *Visiting Disneyland has fulfilled a boyhood dream.* | *Eisenhower finally fulfilled his election pledge to end the war in Korea.* **2 fulfil a need** to provide something that someone needs **3 fulfil a requirement/condition** to reach a standard that is necessary, especially one that has been officially decided: *Much of the electrical equipment failed to fulfill safety requirements.* **4 fulfil a role/function/duty etc** to do the things you are supposed or expected to do because of your job, position in society etc: *Does the established Church fulfil any useful function in modern society?* **5** if your work fulfils you, it makes you feel satisfied because you are using all your skills, qualities etc **6 fulfil yourself** to feel satisfied because you are using all your skills, qualities etc: *She succeeded in fulfilling herself both as an actress and as a mother.* **7 fulfil your potential** to be as successful as you possibly could be: *While he is very competent, he is not really fulfilling his potential.* **8 fulfil a prediction/prophecy** to happen in a way someone has said something would happen

**ful·filled** /fʊlˈfɪld/ *adj* satisfied with your life, job etc because you feel that it is interesting, useful, or important, and you are using all your skills: *I'm sure I'd feel more fulfilled if I had a job that involved working with people, caring for people.*

**ful·fil·ling** /fʊlˈfɪlɪŋ/ *adj* a job, relationship etc that is fulfilling makes you feel satisfied because it allows you to use all your skills and qualities: *A career in nursing still provides one on the most fulfilling of jobs.*

**ful·fil·ment** *BrE*, **fulfillment** *AmE* /fʊlˈfɪlmənt/ *n* [U] **1** the feeling of being satisfied, especially in your job, because you are using all your skills and qualities: **sense/feeling of fulfilment** *Being responsible for so many people gave her a tremendous sense of fulfilment.* | **seek fulfillment** (=try to find it) **2 fulfilment of a wish/need etc** an occasion when something that is wanted, needed etc happens or is given **3 fulfilment of a promise/duty/condition etc** the action of doing what you have promised, your duty, what you have been asked to do etc: *The offer of this contract is subject to the fulfilment of certain conditions.*

S1 W1 **full¹** /fʊl/ *adj*

**1** ▶ **CONTAINER/ROOM/PLACE ETC** ◀ also **full up** if something such as a container, room, or place is full, no more things or people can go in it: *a full box of cereal* | *The class is full, but you can register now for next term.* | [+ **of**] *We walked in to find the kitchen full of smoke.* | **full to the brim** (=filled to the top of something) *a cup full to the brim with water* | **full to bursting** *BrE* (=very full) *the room was full to bursting*

**2** ▶ **COMPLETE/TOTAL** ◀ **a)** including all parts or details: *Please write your full name and address on the form.* | *We have a full range of new cars.* | **the full story** (=everything someone knows about something) *I still don't think he's telling us the full story.* **b)** the highest level or greatest amount of something: *Weissman and I are in full agreement on this issue.*

**3 be full of a)** to feel or express a strong emotion: *children full of excitement at Christmas* | *He's full of guilt about the death of his daughter.* **b)** to think or talk about one thing all the time: *He was full of his plans for travelling around the world.* | **be full of yourself** (=only think about yourself) *Brad's all right, but he's a little too full of himself.* **c)** to contain many things of the same kind: *a sky full of stars* | *His essay is full of mistakes.*

**4** ▶ **TIME** ◀ **a)** lasting the whole time: *My father spent three full hours trying to explain one problem in my math book.* **b)** filled with many things to do: *I've had a full week. I'm looking forward to staying home tonight.*

**5** ▶ **FOOD** ◀ *informal* also **full up** *BrE* having eaten so much food that you cannot eat any more: *No more, thanks. I'm full.* | **do sth on a full stomach** (=do physical activity just after a meal)

**6 at full speed** as fast as possible: *Parker was driving at full speed when he hit the wall.*

**7 rise to your full height/draw yourself up to your full height** to stand up very straight

**8 fall/lie full length** to fall or lie flat, with your body stretched out

**9** ▶ **CLOTHING** ◀ a full skirt, pair of trousers etc is made with a lot of material and fits loosely: *full sleeves* | *a dress with a full skirt*

**10 full marks** *BrE* the highest number of points that you can get for school work

**11** ▶ **BODY** ◀ **a)** a full face, figure, etc is rounded or large in an attractive way **b)** used to mean fat when you do not want to offend someone: *clothes for the fuller figure*

**12 in full view of sb** so that everybody watching can see everything: *The argument happened on stage in full view of the audience.*

**13 have/lead a full life** to do many different and interesting things

**14 full flavour** *BrE*, **full flavor** *AmE* a pleasantly strong taste: *This wine has a wonderful full flavour.* —see also FULL-BODIED

**15** ▶ **SOUND** ◀ a full sound is pleasantly loud or strong: *the full sound of the cello section* —opposite THIN¹ (7)

**16 be full of crap/shit** *taboo spoken* used to say that you think what someone is saying is wrong or stupid: *Don't listen to Jerry. He's full of crap.*

**17 in full a)** if you pay an amount of money in full, you pay the whole amount: *The debt must be paid in full by 31 January 1998.* **b)** if you write or copy something in full, you write it in its complete form

**18 to the full** in the best or most complete way: *To appreciate this opera to the full, you should read the story first.* —see also FULLY, **come/turn full circle** (CIRCLE¹ (7)), **be full of beans** (BEAN¹ (4)), **at full belt** (BELT¹ (6)), **(at) full blast** (BLAST¹ (4)), **in full cry** (CRY¹ (8)), **full member** (MEMBER (1)), **(at) full pelt** (PELT² (3)), **be in full swing** (SWING² (7)), **(at) full tilt** (TILT² (1)), **have your hands full** (HAND¹ (32))

**full²** *adv* directly: [+ **on/in**] *The ball struck him full on the chest.* —see also **know full well** (KNOW¹ (19))

**full·back** /ˈfʊlbæk/ *n* [C] a player in a football team who plays in a particular position, or the position that they play in

**full beam** /ˌ· ˈ·/ *n* [U] *BrE* lights at the front of a car that are on as brightly as possible; HIGH BEAM *AmE*

**full-blood·ed** /ˌ· ˈ··◂/ *adj* [only before noun] **1** involving very strong feelings or emotions: **full-blooded argument/fight etc** (=an angry or violent argument etc) *The argument ended up as a full-blooded screaming match.* **2** having parent, grandparents etc from only one race of people: *There are very few full-blooded Cherokee Indians left.*

**full blown** /ˈ· ·/ *adj* **1** having all of the qualities of something in its most complete or advanced stage: *The border fighting has turned into a full blown war.|full-blown AIDS* **2** *often literary* a full-blown flower is completely open

**full board** /ˌ· ˈ·/ *n* [U] a hotel that offers full board provides people with three meals a day *A two night break costs £125 full board* —compare HALF BOARD

**full-bod·ied** /ˌ· ˈ··◂/ *adj* tasting strong and rich: *a full-bodied red wine*

**full-court press** /ˌ· · ˈ·/ *n* [singular] **1** a method of attacking in the game of BASKETBALL **2** *AmE informal* the use of pressure or influence by one group on another: *The DEA and the Justice Department put a full court press on the drug baron.*

**full-cream** /ˌ· ˈ·◂/ *adj BrE* full-cream milk has not had the cream removed

**full dress** /ˌ· ˈ·/ *n* [U] special clothes worn for official occasions and ceremonies: *officers in full battle dress* —**full-dress** *adj* —see also EVENING DRESS, MORNING DRESS

**ful·ler's earth** /ˌfʊləz ˈɜːθ‖-ərz ˈɜːrθ/ *n* [U] dried clay made into a powder and used to make oil clearer and cleaner

**full-face** /ˌ· ˈ·◂/ *adj* a full-face photograph or picture of someone shows the whole of their face —compare PROFILE[1] (1)

**full-fat** /ˌ· ˈ·◂/ *adj BrE* full-fat milk or cheese has not had any of the fat taken out

**full-fledged** /ˌ· ˈ·◂/ *adj especially AmE* **1** completely developed, trained, or established; FULLY-FLEDGED (1) *BrE*: *a full-fledged lawyer* **2** a young bird is full-fledged when it has grown all its feathers and can fly; FULLY-FLEDGED (2) *BrE*

**full-grown** /ˌ· ˈ·◂/ *adj AmE* a full-grown animal, plant, or person has developed to their full size and will not grow any bigger; FULLY-GROWN *BrE*: *A full-grown male elephant may weigh 2,000 pounds.*

**full house** /ˌ· ˈ·/ *n* [C usually singular] **1** an occasion at a cinema, concert hall, sports field etc when someone is sitting in every seat: *Speaking to a full house at the auditorium, he outlined his plan.* **2** three cards of one kind and a pair of another kind in a game of cards

**full-length**[1] /ˌ· ˈ·◂/ *adj* **1 full-length mirror/photograph/portrait** a mirror etc that shows all of a person, from their head to their feet: *a full-length portrait of the queen* **2 full-length skirt/dress/coat** a full length skirt etc reaches the ground, or is the longest possible for that particular type of clothing: *a full-length evening dress* **3 full-length play/book/film** a play, book etc of the normal length

**full-length**[2] *adv* [only after verb] someone who is lying full-length is lying flat with their legs straight out: *Alison was stretched out full-length on the couch.*

**full lock** /ˌ· ˈ·◂/ *adv BrE* if you turn a car's STEERING WHEEL full lock, you turn it as far as it can be turned

**full moon** /ˌ· ˈ·/ *n* [singular] the moon when it looks completely round —compare NEW MOON, HALF MOON

**ful·lness** also **fulness** *BrE* /ˈfʊlnɪs/ *n* [U] **1 in the fullness of time** when the right time comes; EVENTUALLY: *I'm sure he'll tell us what's bothering him in the fullness of time.* **2** satisfaction: *the human search for fullness in life* **3** the condition of being full

**full-page** /ˌ· ˈ·◂/ *adj* [only before noun] covering all of one page, especially in a newspaper or magazine: *a full-page advertisement*

**full pro·fes·sor** /ˌ· ·ˈ··/ *n* [C] *AmE* a teacher at an American university who has reached the highest position and has gained TENURE (=the right to keep the job as long as they want it) —see also ASSISTANT PROFESSOR, ASSOCIATE PROFESSOR

**full-scale** /ˌ· ˈ·◂/ *adj* [only before noun] **1** to the fullest amount or degree possible: *a full-scale inquiry into the train crash* **2** a drawing, model, copy etc of something that is full-scale is the same size as the thing it represents

**full-size** /ˌ· ˈ·◂/ *adj* of the largest possible size: *I need a full-size wrench to loosen this.*

**full stop**[1] /ˌ· ˈ·/ *n* **1** [C] *BrE* a point (.) that marks the end of a sentence or the shortened form of a word; PERIOD[1] (5) *AmE* —see picture at PUNCTUATION MARK **2** *AmE* [singular] the state of being completely stopped, usually in a car: *The car can accelerate from a full stop to 60 mph in five seconds.* **3 come to a full stop** to stop completely, especially because of a problem or difficulty: *Production came to a full stop when the generator blew up.*

**full stop**[2] *interjection BrE* used to say that you have definitely decided something, and you will not change your decision; PERIOD[1] (6): *I don't have a reason. I just don't want to go, full stop.*

**full-term** /ˌ· ˈ·◂/ *adj* born after a PREGNANCY of a normal length: *a full-term baby* —compare PREMATURE (2)

**full time** /ˌ· ˈ·/ *n* [U] *BrE* the end of the normal period of playing time in a sports game, especially football: *At full time neither team had scored.* —see also HALF TIME

**full-time** /ˌ· ˈ·◂/ *adj, adv* **1** working or studying for the number of hours that work is usually done: *She works full-time, and has two kids.*|**full-time staff/student** *They're looking for full-time staff at the library.* **2 full-time job a)** a job that you do for all the normal working hours in a week **b)** hard work that you are not being paid for that takes a lot of your time: *Looking after three children all day is a full-time job.* —compare PART-TIME S3

**ful·ly** /ˈfʊli/ *adv* **1** completely: *We are fully committed to the idea of political reform.* **2** used to emphasize how big, far away etc something is: *The nearest big town is fully 300 miles away.* 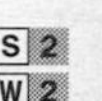 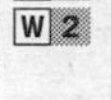

**fully-fash·ioned** /ˌ·· ˈ··◂/ *BrE adj* clothing that is fully fashioned is made to fit the shape of the body exactly

**fully-fledged** /ˌ·· ˈ·◂/ *adj especially BrE* **1** completely developed, trained, or established; FULL-FLEDGED (1) *AmE*: *After seven years of training she's now a fully-fledged doctor.* **2** a young bird is fully-fledged when it has grown all its feathers and can fly; FULL-FLEDGED (2) *AmE*

**fully-grown** /ˌ·· ˈ·◂/ *adj* a fully-grown animal, plant, or person has developed to their full size and will not grow any bigger; FULL-GROWN *AmE*

**ful·mi·nate** /ˈfʊlmɪneɪt, ˈfʌl-/ *v* [I + **against/at**] *formal* to speak angrily against something: *an article fulminating against American Imperialism* —**fulmination** /ˌfʊlmɪˈneɪʃən, ˌfʌl-/ *n* [C,U]

**ful·ness** /ˈfʊlnɪs/ *n* [U] another spelling of FULLNESS

**ful·some** /ˈfʊlsəm/ *adj formal* a fulsome piece of writing, speech etc gives too much praise to be sincere: *His speech was packed with fulsome praise for the managing director.* —**fulsomely** *adv* —**fulsomeness** *n* [U]

**fum·ble** /ˈfʌmbəl/ *v* **1** [I] to hold or try and move something with your hands carelessly or awkwardly: [+ **for/with**] *Steve fumbled drunkenly with the keys, dropping them on the floor.* **2** [I + **for/with**] if you fumble with your words when you are speaking, you have difficulty saying something **3** [I,T] *AmE* to drop a ball after catching it —**fumble** *n* [C]

**fume** /fjuːm/ *v* [I] **1** to be angry, usually without saying anything: *She sat in the car, fuming about what she had heard.*|[+ **at**] *AmE* (=show you are angry by saying a lot of things to someone) **2** to give off smoke or gases

**fumes** /fjuːmz/ *n* [plural] strong-smelling gas or smoke that is unpleasant to breathe in: *strong smell of paint fumes* S3

**fu·mi·gate** /ˈfjuːmɪ̵geɪt/ *v* [T] to clear disease, BACTERIA, insects etc from somewhere using chemicals, smoke, or gas —**fumigation** /ˌfjuːmɪ̵ˈgeɪʃən/ *n* [U]

S2 W3 **fun**[1] /fʌn/ *adj* **1** [only before noun] a fun activity or experience is enjoyable: *It was a fun night out – we'll have to do it again sometime.* **2** someone who is fun is enjoyable to be with because they are cheerful and amusing: **a fun person/girl/guy etc** *especially AmE*: *She's a fun person to be around.* | **good/great fun** *BrE*: *The O'Brian boys were great fun.*

S2 **fun**[2] *n* [U] **1** an experience or activity that is very enjoyable and exciting: *It's no fun to be working inside when the weather's nice.* | **good/great fun** *BrE*: *Why don't you come with us? It'll be great fun.* | **have fun** (=to have an enjoyable time) *The children were having so much fun, I hated to call them inside.* | **What fun!** (=that sounds very enjoyable!) **2 for fun** also **for the fun of it** if you do something for fun, you do it because you enjoy it and not for any other reason: *We drove all the way to the beach, just for fun.* **3 full of fun** playful and liking amusement: *Jan's always so cheerful and full of fun.* **4 fun and games** playful activites: *My job isn't all fun and games you know—I work hard as well.* **5 not be my idea of fun** used to talk about an activity, situation etc that is exciting or interesting to other people but is not for you: *Digging up old bones in a hot desert is not my idea of fun.* **6 in fun** if you make a joke or say something about someone in fun, you do not intend it to be insulting: *Don't get upset Chris, she only said it in fun.* **7 make fun of sb/sth** to make a joke about someone that is insulting or makes them feel bad: *The kids at school always made fun of Jill's clothes.* **8 like fun** *AmE spoken* used when you think something will not happen, or when something is not true: *"I'm going to Barbara's house." "Like fun you are! Come and finish your chores first."* —see also FUNNY, **figure of fun** (FIGURE[1] (14)), **poke fun at** (POKE[1] (5))

S3 W1 **func·tion**[1] /ˈfʌŋkʃən/ *n* **1** [C] the purpose that something is made for, or the job that someone does: *The function of a cash-machine is to provide people with cash when the bank is shut.* | **perform a function** *In your new job you will be expected to perform many different functions.* **2** [C] a large party or ceremonial event, especially for an important or official occasion: *This room may be hired for weddings and other functions.* **3** [U] the way in which something works or the way in which it is used: *Bauhaus architects thought that function was more important than form.* **4 a function of a)** if one thing is a function of another, it is produced by or varies according to the other thing **b)** *technical* a mathematical quantity that changes according to how another mathematical quantity changes: *in $x = 5y$, $x$ is a function of $y$* **5** [C] one of the basic operations performed by a computer

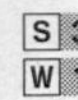

**function**[2] *v* [I] **1** if something functions, it works in the way it is supposed to: *When the camera is functioning properly the green light comes on.* **2** if something functions in a particular way, it works in that way: *Can you explain exactly how this new system will function?* **3 not function** if someone cannot function, they cannot do the activities that people normally do: *She nurses people in their homes who are too ill to function alone.*

**function as** sth *phr v* [T] to be or work as something: *Athens functioned as a centre of trade in the thirteenth century.*

**func·tion·al** /ˈfʌŋkʃənəl/ *adj* **1** designed to be useful rather than beautiful or decorative: *It's not fast – it's just a solid, functional car.* **2** working in the way that something is supposed to: *With a few minor adjustments the filter will be functional again.* **3** having a useful purpose —**functionally** *adv*

**func·tion·al·is·m** /ˈfʌŋkʃənəlɪzəm/ *n* [U] the idea that the most important thing about a building, piece of furniture etc is that it is useful —**functionalist** *n* [C] —**functionalist** *adj*

**func·tion·a·ry** /ˈfʌŋkʃənəri‖-neri/ *n* [C] someone who has a job doing unimportant or boring official duties

**function key** /ˈ·· ·/ *n* [C] *technical* a key on the KEYBOARD[1] (1) of a computer that tells the machine to do something

**function word** /ˈ·· ·/ *n* [C] a word such as a PRONOUN or PREPOSITION that is used in place of another word or shows the relationship between two words. For example, in the sentences 'The cat is hungry. It hasn't been fed yet,' 'it' is a function word.

**fund**[1] /fʌnd/ *n* [C] **1** an amount of money that is collected and kept for a particular purpose: *The school's funds for sports and music have been seriously depleted.* | **set up a fund** (=begin to collect money) *His grandparents set up a fund for his college education.* —see also FUNDING, TRUST FUND —see MONEY (USAGE) **2** an organization that is responsible for collecting and spending an amount of money: *We give to the Children's Fund every Christmas.* —compare CHARITY (2) **3 a fund of** a large supply of something: *He was a large man with a strong Texan drawl and a fund of stories.* **4 be short of funds** to have little or no money: *The Museum is so short of funds it may sell the painting.* **5 in funds** having enough money to do what is necessary S3 W1

**fund**[2] *v* [T] **1** to provide money for an activity, organization, event etc: *The project is jointly funded by several local companies.* **2** *technical* to change the arrangements for paying a debt, so that you have more time to pay S3 W3

**fun·da·men·tal**[1] /ˌfʌndəˈmentl◂/ *adj* **1** affecting the simplest and most important parts of something: *She's not just in a bad mood, she must have a fundamental psychological problem.* | **fundamental change/difference** *a fundamental difference in opinion* | **fundamental mistake/error** *His fundamental mistake was to rely too much on other people.* **2** very necessary and important as a part of something from which everything else develops: [+ **to**] *Water is fundamental to survival.* S2 W2

**fundamental**[2] *n* **the fundamentals of** the most important ideas, rules etc that something is based upon: *I couldn't even grasp the fundamentals of mechanics.*

**fun·da·men·tal·is·m** /ˌfʌndəˈmentəlɪzəm/ *n* [U] **1** the practice of following religious laws very strictly **2** a belief that some Christians have that everything in the Bible is completely true

**fun·da·men·tal·ist** /ˌfʌndəˈmentəlɪ̵st/ *n* [C] **1** someone who follows religious laws very strictly: *Muslim fundamentalists* **2** a Christian who believes that everything in the Bible is completely true —**fundamentalist** *adj*: *a fundamentalist doctrine*

**fun·da·men·tal·ly** /ˌfʌndəˈmentəli/ *adv* in every way that is important or basic: *They are good friends even though their views on many things are fundamentally different.*

**fund·ing** /ˈfʌndɪŋ/ *n* [U] an amount of money used for a specific purpose: *Funding may be available from the UN.*

**fund rais·er** /ˈ· ··/ *n* [C] a person or event that collects money for a specific purpose

**fu·ne·ral** /ˈfjuːnərəl/ *n* [C] **1** a religious ceremony for burying or burning a dead person: *The funeral will be held at St. Martin's church.* | **funeral procession/car/service etc** *The mayor gave the funeral oration.* **2 it's your funeral** *spoken* used to warn someone that they, and no one else, must deal with the result of their actions: *If you show up late again, it's your funeral.*

**funeral di·rec·tor** /ˈ··· ·ˌ··/ *n* [C] someone who is paid to organize a funeral; UNDERTAKER *BrE*

**funeral home** /ˈ··· ˌ·/ also **funeral par·lour** /ˈ··· ˌ··/ *especially AmE* *n* [C] the place where a body is kept before a funeral

**fu·ne·ra·ry** /ˈfjuːnərəri‖-nəreri/ *adj* [only before noun] related to a funeral or a grave: *a funerary urn*

**fu·ne·re·al** /fjʊˈnɪəriəl‖-ˈnɪr-/ *adj* sad, slow, and suitable for a funeral: *funereal music* —**funereally** *adv*

**fun·fair** /ˈfʌnfeə‖-fer/ *n* [C] *BrE* a noisy outdoor event where you can ride on machines, play games to win prizes etc; FAIR[3] (1)

**fun·gal** /ˈfʌŋgəl/ also **fun·gous** /ˈfʌŋgəs/ *adj technical* connected with or caused by a fungus: *a fungal infection*

**fun·gi·cide** /ˈfʌndʒɨsaɪd, ˈfʌŋgɨ-/ *n* [C,U] a chemical used for destroying fungus

**fun·goid** /ˈfʌŋgɔɪd/ *adj technical* like a fungus: *fungoid growths*

**fun·gus** /ˈfʌŋgəs/ *n plural* **fungi** /-dʒaɪ, -gaɪ/ *or* **funguses** **1** [C,U] a simple fast-growing type of plant, such as a MUSHROOM[1] or MOULD[1] (1) **2** [U] this type of plant, especially considered as a disease

**fun house** /ˈ· ·/ *n* [C] *AmE* a building at a FUNFAIR in which there are things that amuse or shock people

**fu·nic·u·lar** /fjʊˈnɪkjɡlə‖-ər/ *n* [C] a small railway that goes up a hill or a mountain, pulled by a thick metal rope

**funk**[1] /fʌŋk/ *n* [U] **1** a style of music with a strong RHYTHM that is based on JAZZ and African music **2 in a (blue) funk** *informal* very unhappy, worried, or afraid about something: *She's been in a funk ever since she failed that exam.* **3** *AmE informal* a strong smell that comes from someone's body

**funk**[2] *v* [T] *BrE old-fashioned* to avoid doing something because it is difficult, or because you are afraid to do it

**funk·y** /ˈfʌŋki/ *adj informal* **1** modern, fashionable, and interesting: *We found some really funky shoes at the market yesterday.* **2** funky music is simple with a strong RHYTHM that is easy to dance to

**fun·nel**[1] /ˈfʌnl/ *n* [C] **1** a tube used for pouring liquids or powders into a container with a narrow opening: *Use a funnel to pour the oil into the bottle.* —see picture at LABORATORY **2** *BrE* a metal CHIMNEY for letting smoke out from a steam engine or steam ship —compare SMOKESTACK

**funnel**[2] *v* **funnelled, funnelling** *BrE*, **funneled, funneling** *AmE* [I,T] to pass or be passed through a narrow opening, especially to pass a large amount of something through it: [+ **through/into**] *The crowd funnelled through the narrow streets.* | **funnel sth into sth** *He funneled the petrol into the can.*

**fun·nies** /ˈfʌniz/ *n* **the funnies** *AmE informal* a number of different CARTOONS (1) in newspapers or magazines

**fun·ni·ly** /ˈfʌnɨli/ *adv* **1** in an odd or unusual way: *She's been behaving funnily lately.* **2 funnily enough** *spoken* used to say that something is unexpected or strange: *Funnily enough, I was just about to call you when you called me.* **3** in an amusing way

S1 **fun·ny** /ˈfʌni/ *adj*
W3 **1** ▶ **AMUSING** ◀ making you laugh: *He was telling funny anecdotes about Hollywood.* | **hysterically/hilariously funny** *Everyone except me seemed to find her mistakes hilariously funny.*
**2** ▶ **STRANGE** ◀ unusual and difficult to explain: *I had a funny feeling that something was going to happen.* | *It was a funny sort of day, hot but with huge rain clouds.*
**3** ▶ **DISHONEST** ◀ seeming to be illegal or dishonest, although you are not exactly sure why: *There's something funny going on here.* | **funny business** (=activities that are illegal or dishonest) *When I checked the accounts I realized that there was some funny business going on.*
**4 go funny** *informal* if something goes funny it stops working properly: *I just turned it on and the picture went all funny.*
**5** ▶ **ILL** ◀ feeling slightly ill: *I always feel funny after a long ride in the car.*
**6** ▶ **CRAZY** ◀ *BrE* slightly crazy: *After his wife died he went a bit funny.*
**7 see the funny side of sth** to be able to laugh in a difficult or bad situation: *Fortunately, the patient saw the funny side of the mix up and decided not to take us to court.*

Frequencies of the adjective **funny** in spoken and written English.

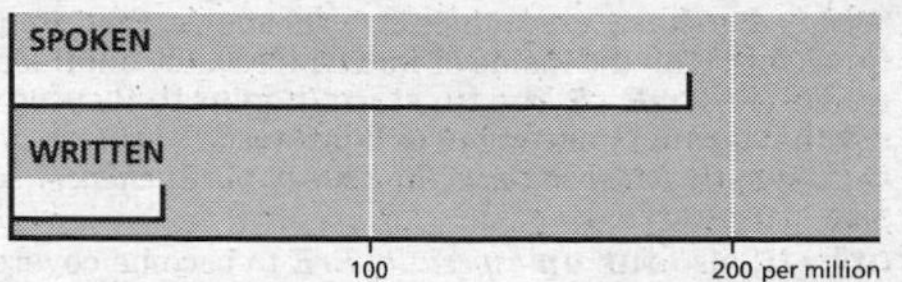


Based on the British National Corpus and the Longman Lancaster Corpus

This graph shows that the adjective **funny** is much more common in spoken English than in written English. This is because it is used in a lot of common spoken phrases.

**funny** (*adj*) **SPOKEN PHRASES**

**8 it's funny** used to say that you do not really understand why something happens, but it does and you think it is strange, interesting, worrying etc: *It's funny, but I've known her for years and I don't even know her name.* | **it's funny (that)** *It's funny Jack didn't come. I hope he's ok.* | **it's funny how** *It's funny how you remember the words of songs, even ones you don't really like.*
**9 that's funny** used when you are surprised by something that has happened and you can not explain it: *That's funny! I'm sure I put my wallet down there, and now it's gone.*
**10 the funny thing is** used to say what the strangest or most amusing part of a story or situation is: *But the funny thing is, after they'd argued for ages about where to go, the car wouldn't start.* | *The funny thing is, I sort of knew this would happen.*
**11 it's not funny** used to tell someone not to laugh at or make jokes about something you think is very serious: *It's not funny! I'm the one who's going to get blamed for this, you know.*
**12 very funny!** used when someone is laughing at you or making a joke and you do not think it is funny: *Oh very funny! Instead of laughing you could try and help.* | *Very funny! Who's hidden my car keys?*
**13 what's so funny?** used when someone is laughing and you want to know why: *Hey, what's so funny. Did I say something stupid?*
**14 funny little** used to describe something or someone that is small and unusual: *I got it in that funny little shop in Market Street.*
**15 funny old** used to describe something or someone that is strange but that you like or think is interesting: *Yes, he's a funny old man – you never know what he's going to say.*
**16 I'm not being funny, but...** used when you are going to say something that may seem strange or amusing but is actually serious: *I'm not being funny, but I quite liked it in hospital.*
**17 funny peculiar or funny ha-ha?** *BrE* used when someone has described something as funny and you want to know if they mean that it is strange or amusing: *"You are funny, Albert." "How do you mean? Funny peculiar or funny ha-ha?"*

**funny bone** /ˈ·· ·/ *n* [singular] the soft part of your elbow that particularly hurts when you hit it hard

**funny farm** /ˈ·· ·/ *n* [C] *informal humorous* an expression meaning a PSYCHIATRIC HOSPITAL that some people consider offensive

**funny mon·ey** /ˈ·· ˌ··/ *n* [U] *informal* money that has been printed illegally —see also COUNTERFEIT[1]

**funny pa·pers** /ˈ·· ˌ··/ *n* [plural] *AmE informal* another expression meaning FUNNIES

**fun run** /ˈ· ˌ·/ *n* [C] an event in which people run a long distance in order to collect money, usually for CHARITY

**fur**[1] /fɜː‖fɜːr/ *n* **1** [U] the thick soft hair that covers the bodies of some types of animal, for example cats or

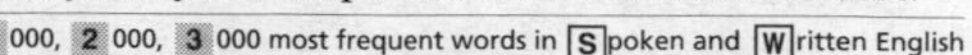

dogs **2** [C,U] the fur-covered skin of an animal, especially used for making clothes: *Traders exchanged whiskey for furs.* | *a fur coat* **3** [C] a coat or piece of clothing made of fur: *She wore a small fur wrapped around her neck.* **4** a hard grey chemical substance that sometimes forms on the inside of water-pipes and containers; SCALE[1] (11) *AmE* **5 the fur starts/begins to fly** used to say that an angry argument or fight starts: *The fur really started to fly when she saw the state of the kitchen.* —see also FURRY

**fur²** *v* [I] also **fur up** *especially BrE* to become covered with FUR[1] (4)

**fur·bish** /ˈfɜːbɪʃ‖ˈfɜːr-/ *v* [T] also **furbish up** to improve the appearance of, or decorate something old —compare REFURBISH (1)

**fu·ri·ous** /ˈfjʊəriəs‖ˈfjʊr-/ *adj* **1** [not before noun] extremely angry: *I've never been so furious in my whole life.* | [+ **with/at/about etc**] *He was furious with himself for not standing up to Gillman.* **2** [only before noun] done with a lot of energy, effort, or anger: *There was a sudden furious barking from the backyard.* | **furious debate/argument** *a furious debate in Parliament over the new tax* —**furiously** *adv*

**furl** /fɜːl‖fɜːrl/ *v* [T] to roll or fold something such as a flag, umbrella, or sail —**furled** *adj*: *a furled newspaper*

**fur·long** /ˈfɜːlɒŋ‖ˈfɜːrlɔːŋ/ *n* [C] a unit for measuring length, equal to 201 metres and used in horse racing —see table on page B2

**fur·lough** /ˈfɜːləʊ‖ˈfɜːrloʊ/ *n* [C,U] a period of time when a soldier or someone working in another country can return to their own country: **on furlough** *a young soldier home on furlough*

F

**fur·nace** /ˈfɜːnəs‖ˈfɜːr-/ *n* [C] **1** a large container in which a very hot fire is made, to produce power or heat, or to melt metals —see also BLAST FURNACE **2 be like a furnace** *spoken* to be extremely hot: *Let's open a window, it's like a furnace in here!*

**fur·nish** /ˈfɜːnɪʃ‖ˈfɜːr-/ *v* [T] **1** to put furniture and other things into a house or room: *The apartment was furnished in Art Deco style.* | **furnish sth with sth** *a room furnished with a desk and swivel chair* **2** to supply or provide something: *They were asked to furnish capital for the new enterprise.* | **furnish sb/sth with** *The gardener furnished me with the necessary information.* —**furnished** *adj*: *a furnished flat*

**fur·nish·ings** /ˈfɜːnɪʃɪŋz‖ˈfɜːr-/ *n* [plural] the furniture and other things in a room, such as curtains, baths etc

S2 W3 **fur·ni·ture** /ˈfɜːnɪtʃə‖ˈfɜːrnɪtʃər/ *n* [U] large movable objects such as chairs, tables, and beds that you use in a room to make it comfortable to live or work in: *The small room was crammed with furniture.* | *office furniture*

**fu·ro·re** /fjʊˈrɔːri, ˈfjʊrɔː‖ˈfjʊərɔːr/ *BrE*, **fu·ror** /ˈfjʊərɔː‖ˈfjʊrɔːr/ *AmE* —*n* [singular] a sudden expression of anger or excitement among a large group of people about something that has happened: *The security leaks have caused a considerable furore within government circles.*

**fur·ri·er** /ˈfʌriə‖ˈfɜːriər/ *n* [C] someone who makes or sells fur clothing

**fur·row¹** /ˈfʌrəʊ‖ˈfɜːroʊ/ *n* [C] **1** a deep line or fold in the skin of someone's face, especially on the forehead **2** a long, narrow cut or hollow area in the surface of something: *There were furrows in the tarmac to drain off the rainwater.* **3** a long narrow cut made in the ground with a PLOUGH[1] (1)

**furrow²** *v* **1** [I,T] to make the skin on your face form deep lines or folds, especially because you are worried or angry: *Her husband's brows were furrowed in concentration.* **2** [T] to make a deep cut or hollow area in something —**furrowed** *adj*: *a furrowed brow*

**fur·ry** /ˈfɜːri/ *adj* covered with fur, or looking or feeling as if covered with fur: *furry little kittens* | *a large furry towel*

S1 W1 **fur·ther¹** /ˈfɜːðə‖ˈfɜːrðər/ *adv*

**1 ▶MORE◀** if you do something further you do it more, or to a greater degree: *I will develop this point further next week.* | *Things were further complicated by the fact that she did not speak Spanish.* | [+ **into/away etc**] *Marcus sank further into debt.* | **delay/detain sth/sb further** (=make you wait) *After we've finished this I won't detain you any further.*

**2 ▶DISTANCE◀** *especially BrE* used to say that a place is a long way from or more distant than another place; FARTHER: *I don't think I can move a step further.* | [+ **up/away/along etc**] *A little further up Main Street is an old house that's being restored.* —see FARTHER[1] (USAGE)

**3 take sth further** to do something at a more serious or higher level, especially by talking about it: *Would you be willing to take this research further?* | **take the matter further** (=discuss a subject at a higher level and with more important people) *I'm going to take the matter further and discuss this with your parents.*

**4 ▶TIME◀ further back/on/ahead etc** used to say how much more distant something is in the past or future: *Five years further on, a cure has still not been found.* | *The records don't go any further back than 1960.* | **further down the road** (=in the future) *Further down the road we're looking at using up our timber resources.*

**5 go (one step) further** to do or say more than before: *Some argued that we should go one step further and get rid of him altogether.*

**6 ▶IN ADDITION◀** [sentence adverb] *formal* used to introduce something additional that you want to talk about; FURTHERMORE: *He promised not to identify his informant, and further, not to quote him directly.*

**7 further to** *formal* used in letters or in formal speech to mention a previous subject you want to discuss more: *Further to your letter of February 5th, we can confirm your order.*

**8 nothing can be further from the truth** used when you want to say that something is totally untrue

**9 sth must not go any further** used to say that something you are telling someone is secret or private

**10 nothing is further from sb's mind** *spoken* used to say that you have not been thinking about something, especially when you really have been thinking about it: *"Did you come here to see Peter?" "No, nothing could be further from my mind!"*

**further²** *adj* [only before noun] **1** more or additional: *Are there any further questions?* | **a further 10 miles/5 minutes/£500 etc** *Cook gently for a further ten minutes.* **2 until further notice** until you are told that something has changed: *Lacunza ordered the suspension of the elections until further notice.*

**further³** *v* [T] to help something succeed or become successful: *He dedicated his life to furthering the cause of world peace.* | **further sb's career** *Alan had been using her to further his career.*

**fur·ther·ance** /ˈfɜːðərəns‖ˈfɜːr-/ *n* [U] *formal* **1 the furtherance of** the development or progress of something: *the furtherance of science* **2 in furtherance of** in order to help something progress or become complete

**further ed·u·ca·tion** /ˌ·· ··ˈ··/ *n* [U] *BrE* education for adults after leaving school that is not at a university —compare HIGHER EDUCATION

**fur·ther·more** /ˌfɜːðəˈmɔː‖ˈfɜːrðərmɔːr/ *adv* [sentence adverb] *formal* in addition to what has already been said: *Furthermore, my aim is to provide the best service possible under these difficult circumstances.* W3

**fur·ther·most** /ˈfɜːðəməʊst‖ˈfɜːrðərmoʊst/ *adj formal* most distant: *In the furthermost corner sat a tall thin man.* | [+ **from**] *in the corner furthermost from the door*

**fur·thest** /ˈfɜːðəst‖ˈfɜːr-/ *adj, adv* **1** at the greatest distance from a place or point in time; FARTHEST: *There was a huge tapestry on the furthest wall.* | [+ **away/from**] *He walked slowly toward the end of the jury box furthest from the judge.* —see FARTHER[1] (USAGE) **2** to the greatest degree or amount or more than before: *Maltby's book has probably gone furthest in explaining these events.*

**fur·tive** /ˈfɜːtɪv‖ˈfɜːr-/ *adj* behaving as if you want to keep something secret: *There was something furtive about his appearance.* | **furtive glances/looks** *Christine kept* *stealing furtive glances at me.* —**furtively** *adv* —**furtiveness** *n* [U]

**fu·ry** /ˈfjʊəri‖ˈfjʊri/ *n* **1** [U] extreme, often uncontrolled anger: *I was shaking with fury.* **2** [C] a feeling of extreme anger: **in a fury** *"Go on then!" shouted Jamie in a fury. "See if I care!"* | **fly into a fury** (=quickly become very angry) *Paul flew into one of his furies.* **3 much to sb's fury/ to the fury of sb** if something is done much to someone's fury, it makes them very angry: *The report was leaked to the press, much to the president's fury.* **4 a fury of** a state of very busy activity or strong feeling: *She was listening with such a fury of concentration that she did not notice Arthur had left.* **5 like fury** *informal* with great effort or energy: *We went out and played like fury.* **6 the fury of the wind/sea/waves etc** used to describe bad weather conditions: *At last the fury of the storm lessened.* **7** [C] **Fury** one of the three snake-haired goddesses in ancient Greek stories, who punished crime

**furze** /fɜːz‖fɜːrz/ *n* [U] a wild bush with PRICKLY stems and bright yellow flowers

**fuse**[1] /fjuːz/ *n* [C] **1** a short thin piece of wire that is inside electrical equipment and prevents damage by melting and stopping the electricity when there is too much power: *two 13 amp fuses* | **blow a fuse** (=make it melt by putting too much electricity through it) **2** also **fuze** *AmE* a thing that delays a bomb, FIREWORK etc from exploding until you are a safe distance away or makes it explode at a particular time: *The fuse was set to go off at 6 p.m.* **3 a short fuse** if someone has a short fuse, they get angry very easily —see also **blow a fuse** (BLOW[1] (23))

**fuse**[2] *v* [I,T] **1** to join together, or to make something join together, to become a single thing: [+ **together**] *The egg and sperm fuse together as one cell.* **2** *BrE* if an electrical system or electrical equipment fuses or you fuse them, it stops working because a fuse has melted: *The lights have fused again.* **3** if metals, rocks etc fuse or you fuse them, they become joined together by being heated **4** *technical* if a rock or metal fuses or you fuse it, it becomes liquid by being heated: *Lead fuses at quite a low temperature.*

**fuse box** /ˈ· ·/ *n* [C] a box that contains the fuses of the electrical system of a house or other building

**fused** /fjuːzd/ *adj BrE* if a piece of electrical equipment is fused, it is fitted with a fuse

**fu·se·lage** /ˈfjuːzəlɑːʒ‖-sə-/ *n* [C] the main part of a plane, in which people sit or goods are carried —see picture at AIRCRAFT

**fu·si·lier** /ˌfjuːzɪ̈ˈlɪə‖-ˈlɪr/ *n* [C] a soldier in the past who carried a light gun called a MUSKET

**fu·sil·lade** /ˌfjuːzɪ̈ˈlɑːd‖-sɪ̈-/ *n* [singular] **1** a rapid series of loud noises, especially shots from a gun **2** a rapid series of questions or remarks

**fu·sion** /ˈfjuːʒən/ *n* [U] **1** the combination or joining together of separate things, ideas, or groups: *Her work is a fusion of several different styles of music.* **2** a joining together of separate things by heating them —compare FISSION —see also NUCLEAR FUSION

**fusion bomb** /ˈ·· ˌ·/ *n* [C] another word for a HYDROGEN BOMB

S3 **fuss**[1] /fʌs/ *n* **1** [singular] nervous or anxious behaviour that is usually about unimportant things: **be a fuss** *James said he'd better be getting back or there'd be a fuss.* | **get/be in a fuss** *She gets in such a fuss before people come to dinner.* **2** [singular, U] attention or excitement that is unnecessary or unwelcome: *They wanted a quiet wedding without any fuss.* **3 make/kick up a fuss (about)** to complain or become angry about something, especially when this is not necessary: *Josie kicked up a fuss because she thought the soup she ordered was too salty.* **4 make a fuss of** *BrE* **make a fuss over** *AmE* to pay a lot of attention to someone, to show that you are pleased with them or like them: *Make a fuss of your dog when he behaves properly.*

**fuss**[2] *v* **1** [I] to worry a lot about things that may not be very important: *I wish you'd stop fussing – I'll be perfectly all right.* **2** [I] to pay too much attention to small, unimportant details: [+ **with/around/about**] *Paul was fussing with his clothes, trying to get his tie straight.* **3 be fussed (about)** *BrE spoken* used when you do not think it matters what happens or is done: *"Where do you want to go?" "I'm not fussed."* **4** [I] *AmE* to behave in an unhappy or angry way: *The baby woke up and started to fuss.*

**fuss over** sb/sth *phr v* [T] to pay a lot of or too much attention to someone, especially to show that you are pleased with them or like them

**fuss·pot** /ˈfʌs-pɒt‖-pɑːt/ *BrE*, **fuss·bud·get** /ˈfʌsˌbʌdʒɪ̈t/ *AmE* —*n* [C] someone who is very fussy

**fuss·y** /ˈfʌsi/ *adj* **1** too concerned or worried about small, usually unimportant details, and difficult to please: *Leonora was fussy about her looks.* | **fussy eater** (=someone who dislikes many types of food) —compare FASTIDIOUS **2 not be fussy** *spoken* used when you do not mind what decision is made, where you go etc: *"Do you want to go out or just rent a movie?" "I'm not fussy."* | [+ **who/what/how etc**] *Geese are not fussy whose grass they eat.* **3** fussy clothes, objects, buildings etc are too detailed and decorated: *The furniture looked comfortable, nothing fussy or too elaborate.* **4** with small, exact, and careful actions, sometimes showing nervousness: *She patted her hair with small fussy movements.* —**fussily** *adv* —**fussiness** *n* [U]

**fus·ti·an** /ˈfʌstiən‖-tʃən/ *n* [U] **1** a type of rough heavy cotton cloth, worn especially in the past **2** *literary* words that sound important but have very little meaning —**fustian** *adj*

**fus·ty** /ˈfʌsti/ *adj* **1** if rooms, clothes, buildings etc are fusty, they have an unpleasant smell, because they have not been used for a long time **2** *informal* ideas or people that are fusty are old-fashioned: *These fusty ideas about education should be brought up-to-date.* —**fustiness** *n* [U]

**fu·tile** /ˈfjuːtaɪl‖-tl/ *adj* actions that are futile are useless because they have no chance of being successful: *a futile attempt to save the paintings from the flames* | **be futile to do sth** *It was futile to continue the negotiations.* —**futility** /fjuːˈtɪlɪ̈ti/ *n* [U]

**fu·ton** /ˈfuːtɒn‖-tɑːn/ *n* [C] a flat soft CUSHION used for sleeping on, especially in Japan —see picture at BED[1]

**fu·ture**[1] /ˈfjuːtʃə‖-ər/ *adj* [only before noun] **1** likely to happen, become, or exist at a time after the present: *Careful accounting may help to predict future costs.* | **future wife/husband etc** (=someone who will be your wife, husband etc) **2** *technical* in grammar, being the form of a verb used to show a future act or state: *the future tense* **3 for future reference** something kept for future reference is kept in order to be used or looked at in the future S1 W1

**future**[2] *n* S1 W2

**1 the future** the time after the present: *Write an essay of 500 words describing your plans for the future.* | *Most science fiction stories are set in the future.*

**2 in future** also **in the future a)** at some time in the future: *In the future we will be using a much more sophisticated computer system.* | **in the near/immediate future** (=soon) *The recession shows no signs of easing in the immediate future.* | **in/for the forseeable future** (=for as long as you can imagine or plan for) *We will not be hiring anyone else in the forseeable future.* | **in the distant future** (=a very long time ahead in the future) *Space travel to other planets may be possible in the distant future.* **b)** from now until a much later time: *I'll sleep in her room in future to prevent her sleepwalking.*

**3 ▶ WHAT WILL HAPPEN TO YOU ◀** [C] what someone or something will do or what will happen to them in the future: *The islands should have the right to decide their own future.* | **sth/sb's future is uncertain** *For young adults in the inner cities, the future is uncertain.*

**4 ▶ POSSIBILITY OF SUCCESS ◀** [singular, U] a chance or possibility of success at a later time: *I'd like to discuss my future in the company.* | **the future of sth** *Ferguson is optimistic about the future of the business.* | **a**

**future in sth** *He felt there was no future in farming these days.* | **have a great/promising/bright future** (=to seem likely to do well in a job, sport etc)
**5 the future** *technical* in grammar, the form of a verb that shows that the act or state that has been described will happen or exist at a later time: *In the sentence, "I will leave tomorrow", the verb "will" indicates the future.*
**6 futures** [plural] *technical* goods, money, land etc that will be supplied or exchanged in the future at a time and price that has already been agreed
**7 look to the future** to plan for what will happen or think about what could happen in the future

**future per·fect** /ˌ·· ˈ··/ *n technical* **the future perfect** in grammar, the form of a verb that shows that the action described by the verb will be complete before a particular time in the future, formed in English by 'will have' or 'shall have' —**future perfect** *adj*

**futures mar·ket** /ˈ·· ˌ··/ *n* [C] *technical* the buying and selling of futures (FUTURE[1] (6)); FORWARD MARKET

**fu·tur·is·m** /ˈfjuːtʃərɪzəm/ *n* [C] a style of painting, music, and literature in the early 20th century that express the violent, active qualities of modern life, machines, science etc —**futurist** *n* [C]

**fu·tur·is·tic** /ˌfjuːtʃəˈrɪstɪk◂/ *adj* **1 futuristic design/building/film etc** a building, film etc that is so unusual and modern in appearance that it looks as if it belongs in the future instead of the present: *The futuristic sports stadium is the pride of the city.* **2** futuristic ideas, books etc imagine what may happen in the future, especially through scientific developments: *Orwell's disturbing futuristic novel, '1984'.*

**fu·tu·ri·ty** /fjʊˈtjʊərɟti‖-ˈtʊr-/ *n formal* **1** [U] the time after the present; FUTURE[1] (1) **2** [C] an event or possibility that may happen in the future

**futz** /fʌts/ *v*
**futz around** *phr v* [I] *AmE informal* to waste time, especially by doing small, unimportant jobs slowly: *I spent the entire day just futzing around.*

**fuzz**[1] /fʌz/ *n* [U] **1** thin soft hair or a hairlike substance that covers something: *When Jack was born he had a fuzz of black hair on his head.* **2** a small amount of soft material that has come from clothing etc; *AmE* LINT (1) **3 the fuzz** an insulting way of talking to or about the police, used especially in the 1960s and 1970s

**fuzz**[2] *v* [T] to make something fuzzy

**fuzz·y** /ˈfʌzi/ *adj* **1** unclear or confused and lacking details: **fuzzy account/description etc** *She gave a rather fuzzy account of what had happened.* **2** if a sound or picture is fuzzy, it is unclear: *Some of the photos were so fuzzy it was hard to tell who was who.* **3** having short soft hair, fur etc that stands upright: *I stroked the kitten's fuzzy back.* —**fuzzily** *adv* —**fuzziness** *n* [U]

**f-word** /ˈef wɜːd‖-wɜːrd/ *n* [singular] a word used when you are talking about the word FUCK but do not want to say it because it is rude. It is not used instead of the word 'fuck': *Mommy, Billy said the f-word.*

**fwy** *AmE* the written abbreviation for FREEWAY

**FX** /ˌef ˈeks/ **1** an abbreviation for FOREIGN EXCHANGE **2** an abbreviation for SPECIAL EFFECTS

**FY** *AmE* the abbreviation for FISCAL YEAR

**-fy** /faɪ/ *suffix* [in verbs] another form of the suffix -IFY

# G,g

**G, g** /dʒiː/ *plural* **G's, g's** the seventh letter of the English alphabet

**g** the written abbreviation of GRAM

**G**[1] *n* **1** also **g** [C,U] the fifth note in the musical SCALE[1] (8) of C MAJOR[1] (4), or the musical KEY based on this note **2** [C] *technical* the amount of force caused by GRAVITY (1) on an object that is lying on the Earth: *Astronauts endure a force of several G's during take-off.* **3** [U] *AmE informal* a GRAND (=$1000)

**G**[2] *adj AmE* a film that is G has been officially approved as suitable for people of any age; U *BrE* —compare PG

**G & T** /ˌdʒiː ən ˈtiː/ *n* [C,U] gin and tonic; a popular alcoholic drink served with ice and a thin piece of LEMON (1)

**G7** /ˌdʒiː ˈsevən/ *n* **the G7** the Group of Seven; the seven richest industrial nations in the world: Canada, France, Germany, Britain, Italy, Japan, and the US

**gab** /gæb/ *v* **gabbed, gabbing** [I + **about**] *informal* to talk continuously, usually about things that are not important: *You two were gabbing so much you didn't even see me!* —see also **the gift of the gab** (GIFT (4)), —**gab** *n* [U] —**gabby** *adj*

**gab·ar·dine, gaberdine** /ˈgæbədiːn, ˌgæbəˈdiːn‖ˈgæbərdiːn/ *n* **1** [U] a strong material which does not allow water to go through and is often used for making coats **2** [C] a coat made from gabardine

**gab·ble**[1] /ˈgæbəl/ *v* **gabbled, gabbling** [I,T] to say something so quickly that people cannot hear you or understand you properly: *Just calm down, stop gabbling, and tell me what has happened.* | **gabble away/on** *Gina tends to gabble away when she's excited.*

**gabble**[2] *n* [singular, U] a lot of talking that is difficult to understand, when several people are talking at the same time: *A gabble of voices came from the next room.*

**gab·er·dine** /ˈgæbədiːn, ˌgæbəˈdiːn‖ˈgæbərdiːn/ *n* another spelling of GABARDINE

**ga·ble** /ˈgeɪbəl/ *n* [C] the upper end of a house wall where it joins with a sloping roof and makes a shape like a TRIANGLE (2): *the gable end of the barn*

**ga·bled** /ˈgeɪbəld/ *adj* having one or more gables: *a gabled cottage*

**gad** /gæd/ *v* **gadded, gadding**

**gad about/around** *phr v* [I] *informal* to go out and enjoy yourself, going to many different places, especially when you should be doing something else: *While I'm at home cooking, he's gadding about with his friends.*

**gad·a·bout** /ˈgædəbaʊt/ *n* [C] *informal* someone who goes out a lot or travels a lot in order to enjoy themselves

**gad·fly** /ˈgædflaɪ/ *n* [C] **1** a fly that bites cattle and HORSES **2** someone who annoys other people by criticizing them

**gad·get** /ˈgædʒɪ̈t/ *n* [C] a small, useful, and cleverly-designed machine or tool: *a clever gadget for sharpening knives* —see MACHINE[1] (USAGE)

**gad·get·ry** /ˈgædʒɪ̈tri/ *n* [U] modern gadgets in general: *I don't understand how all this electronic gadgetry works.*

**Gae·lic**[1] /ˈgeɪlɪk, ˈgælɪk/ *n* [U] one of the Celtic languages, especially spoken in parts of Scotland and in Ireland

**Gaelic**[2] *adj* speaking Gaelic, or connected with Gaelic

**Gaelic foot·ball** /ˌ·· ˈ··/ *n* [U] a game played in Ireland between two teams of 15 players, using a round ball that can be kicked or hit with the hands

**gaff** /gæf/ *n* [C] **1** a stick with a hook at the end, used to pull big fish out of the water **2** *British slang* someone's house —see also **blow the gaff** (BLOW[1] (14))

**gaffe** /gæf/ *n* [C] an embarrassing mistake made in a social situation or in public; FAUX PAS: *The consul's comments were a major diplomatic gaffe.*

**gaf·fer** /ˈgæfə‖-ər/ *n* [C] **1** the person who is charge of the lighting in making a cinema film **2** *informal humorous* an old man **3** *BrE informal* a man who is in charge of people, especially in a factory

**gag**[1] /gæg/ *v* **gagged, gagging** **1** [I] to be unable to swallow and seem about to bring up food from your stomach: *The foul stench made her gag.* | [+ **on**] *He almost gagged on his first mouthful of food.* **2** [T] to put a piece of cloth over someone's mouth to stop them making a noise: *Thugs gagged her and tied her to a chair* | **bound and gagged** (=tied and gagged) **3** [T] to stop people saying what they want to say and expressing their opinions: *an attempt to gag political activists* | **gagging clause/writ/order** (=a legal agreement or official order that stops you from speaking about something in public) **4 gag me with a spoon!** *AmE spoken* used especially by older children to express a strong feeling of dislike

**gag**[2] *n* [C] **1** *informal* a joke or funny story: *the same old gags* **2** a piece of cloth put over someone's mouth to stop them making a noise **3 gag order** an order made by the court to prevent any public reporting of a case which is still being considered by a court of law

**ga·ga** /ˈgɑːgɑː/ *adj* [not before noun] *informal* **1** an insulting word used to describe someone who is confused because they are old: *Sid keeps forgetting my name. I think he's going a bit gaga.* **2** having a strong but often temporary feeling of love for someone; INFATUATED: [+ **about/over**] *fans go gaga over the the pretty-baby looks of Sridevi*

**gag·gle** /ˈgægəl/ *n* **1 a gaggle of tourists/children etc** a noisy group of people: *a gaggle of teenage girls* **2 a gaggle of geese** a number of geese (GOOSE[1] (1)) together

**gai·e·ty** /ˈgeɪɪ̈ti/ *n old-fashioned* **1** [U] the fact that someone or something is cheerful and fun: *Lars enjoyed the warmth and gaiety of these occasions.* **2 gaieties** enjoyable events or activities: *Elaine missed the gaieties of life in Paris.* —see also GAY[1]

**gai·ly** /ˈgeɪli/ *adv* **1** in a happy cheerful way: *He walked past whistling gaily.* **2** in a way that shows you do not care about, or do not realize, the effects of your actions: *They gaily went on talking after the film had started.* **3 gaily coloured/painted/decorated etc** having bright cheerful colours: *gaily coloured tropical birds*

**gain**[1] /geɪn/ *v* S2 W2

**1 ▶GET STH◀** [T] to obtain or achieve something important or valuable: *She gained high grades in English and Math.* | *After gaining independence in 1957, it was renamed 'Ghana'.* | *when radical left parties gained control of local authorities*

**2 ▶GET GRADUALLY◀** [I,T] to gradually get more and more of a useful or valuable quality, skill etc: **gain experience/support/a reputation etc** *The Greens are gaining more and more support.* | *You'll gain useful experience in working with computers.* | **gain in popularity/confidence etc** (=become more popular, more confident etc) | **gain currency** (=when an idea becomes more popular): *These ideas have gained currency in recent years.*

**3 ▶GET AN ADVANTAGE◀** [I,T] to get an advantage from a situation, opportunity, or event: **gain (sth) from** *It was the better-educated women who gained most from this expansion of opportunities.* | **stand to gain** (=or likely to get an advantage): *Who is it who really stands to gain from these tax cuts?* | **there's nothing to be gained** (=it will not help you): *There's nothing to be gained by losing your temper.*

**4 gain weight/speed/height** to increase in weight, speed, or height: *Carrie's gained a lot of weight recently.*

**5 gain access (to sth)** **a)** to manage to enter a building: *New ramps will help the disabled gain better access.* **b)** to manage to see someone or use something: *People*

*should be able to gain easy access to this sort of information.*
**6 gain entrance/entry a)** to enter a building that is locked: *Thieves gained entry through the skylight.* **b)** to join or become part of a system or organization: *At the age of 48 she gained entrance to the Civil Service.*
**7 gain ground** make steady progress and become more popular, more successful etc: *The anti-smoking lobby has steadily gained ground in the last decade.*
**8 gain time** to deliberately do something to give yourself more time to think: *Maybe if we said you were sick we could gain some time.* —opposite LOSE (12)
**9 ▶ CLOCK ◀** [I,T] if a clock or watch gains or gains time, it goes too fast —opposite LOSE (15)
**10 ▶ ARRIVE ◀** [T] *formal or literary* to reach a place after a lot of effort or difficulty: *The swimmer finally gained the river bank.* —see also **nothing ventured, nothing gained** (VENTURE[1] (4))
**gain on/upon** sb/sth *phr v* [T] to gradually get closer to a person, car etc that you are chasing: *Quick – they're gaining on us!*

**USAGE NOTE: GAIN**
WORD CHOICE: **gain, get, win, earn, make**
You can **gain** something useful or necessary whether or not you deserve it. Though you may **gain** weight, strength, a scholarship, a fortune, etc usually people speak of **gaining**, or less formally **getting**, things that you cannot touch such as experience, knowledge, education, and satisfaction. You especially **gain** (or **get**) things of this sort that other people give you, for example: support, recognition, popularity and respect.
If you **win** something solid like a television or money, you get it partly by chance: *Carla won $1,000 in Las Vegas!*
If you **win** something you cannot touch, such as support, recognition, popularity, favour, or respect, you gain it by your own effort or abilities, usually from someone else: *People disliked him at first, but his reliability soon won their approval.* You can also **win** new friends.
If you say that someone wins *a scholarship/a place at university* etc, it means they did something to get it, and probably that other people tried to get it as well (compare *gained*). *She won a prize* could mean either that she got it by luck (eg in a game), or by her own efforts.
You **earn** (or less formally **get**) money for work you do: *He earns/gets £400 a week* (NOT *gains*). You can also **earn** something that you deserve such as support, recognition, popularity, or respect: *The newspaper quickly gained a reputation for fair, impartial reporting.* | *Take a break, now you've earned it!*
You can also **make** money, especially from your own business or in a way that does not involve working: *He made a profit of $50,000 on Wall Street last month.*

W3 **gain²** *n* **1** [C,U] an increase in the amount or level of something: *a gain in weekly output* | *weight gain* **2** [C] an advantage or improvement, especially one achieved by planning or effort: *The new machinery has produced big efficiency gains.* | *a policy that brought Japan considerable gains in the post-war period* **3** [U] financial profit, when this seems to be the only thing you are interested in: *companies that care only about short-term gain* | **for gain** *Some of these tribes used to sell their women for gain.* **4 ill-gotten gains** *humorous* money or advantages obtained dishonestly —see also CAPITAL GAINS
**gain·ful** /ˈɡeɪnfəl/ *adj* **gainful employment/work/activity** *formal* work or activity for which you are paid —**gainfully** *adv: gainfully employed*
**gain·say** /ˌɡeɪnˈseɪ/ *v past tense and past participle* **gainsaid** /ˈsed/ [T usually in negatives] *formal* to say that something is not true, or to disagree with someone: *It may be very difficult to gainsay the claim.*
**gait** /ɡeɪt/ *n* [singular] the way someone walks: *He moved off again with a slow shuffling gait.*
**gai·ter** /ˈɡeɪtə‖-ər/ *n* [C usually plural] a cloth or leather covering worn below the knee by men in past times
**gal** /ɡæl/ *n* [C] **1** *AmE informal* a girl or woman: *She's a great gal.* **2** *BrE old-fashioned* an UPPER-CLASS pronunciation of girl
**gal.** the written abbreviation of GALLON
**ga·la** /ˈɡɑːlə‖ˈɡeɪlə, ˈɡælə/ *n* [C] **1** a public entertainment or performance to celebrate a special occasion: **gala night/event etc** *a gala night at the opera* **2** *BrE* a sports competition, especially in swimming
**ga·lac·tic** /ɡəˈlæktɪk/ *adj* related to a galaxy
**gal·ax·y** /ˈɡæləksi/ *n* [C] **1** one of the large groups of stars that make up the universe **2 the Galaxy** the large group of stars in which our sun and its PLANETS are **3** [singular] a large number of things that are similar: *A whole galaxy of pills and tablets was lined up on the table.*
**gale** /ɡeɪl/ *n* [C] **1** a very strong wind: *The fence was blown down in the gale.* | **it is blowing a gale** *BrE* (=it is very windy) —see picture on page 836 **2 a gale/gales of laughter** a sudden loud sound of laughter: *Gales of laughter came from the next room.*
**gale-force** /ˈ· ·/ *adj* a gale-force wind is strong enough to be dangerous or cause damage —**gale-force** *adv: blowing gale-force*
**gall¹** /ɡɔːl‖ɡɒːl/ *n* **1 have the gall to do sth** to do something rude and unreasonable that most people would be too embarrassed to do: *Being a Tory politician, he still had the gall to be interviewed on TV and claim all the credit.* **2** [U] *old-fashioned* anger and hate that will not go away **3** [U] *old use* BILE **4** [C] a swelling on a tree or plant caused by damage from insects or infection **5** [C] a painful place on an animal's skin, caused by something rubbing against it
**gall²** *v* [T] to make someone feel upset and angry because of something that is unfair: **it galls sb (that)** *It really galls me they could blame my Vicky for their own screw-up.*
**gal·lant¹** /ˈɡələnt, ˈɡælənt‖ɡəˈlænt, ˈɡæləːnt/ *adj old-fashioned* a man who is gallant is kind and polite towards women
**gal·lant²** /ˈɡælənt/ *adj old use* brave: *gallant deeds* —**gallantly**
**gal·lant³** /ˈɡælənt, ɡəˈlænt‖ɡəˈlænt, ɡəˈlɑːnt/ *n* [C] *old use* a well-dressed young man who is kind and polite towards women
**gal·lan·try** /ˈɡæləntri/ *n* [U] *formal* **1** courage, especially in a battle: *a medal for gallantry* **2** polite attention given by men to women
**gall blad·der** /ˈ· ˌ··/ *n* [C] the organ in your body in which BILE is stored —see picture at DIGESTIVE SYSTEM
**gal·le·on** /ˈɡæliən/ *n* [C] a sailing ship used mainly by the Spanish from the 15th to the 17th century
**gal·le·ry** /ˈɡæləri/ *n* [C] **1 a)** a large building where people can see famous pieces of art: *an exhibition of African art at the Hayward Gallery* **b)** [C] a small privately owned shop or STUDIO (3) where you can see and buy pieces of art **2 a)** [C] an upper floor or BALCONY built out from an inner wall of a hall, theatre, or church, from which people can watch a performance, DEBATE[1] (1, 2) etc: *the public gallery in Congress* —see picture at THEATRE **b) the gallery** the people sitting in a gallery **3 play to the gallery** to do or say something just because you think it will please people and make you popular **4** [C] a level passage under the ground in a mine or CAVE[1] —see also PRESS GALLERY, SHOOTING GALLERY W3
**gal·ley** /ˈɡæli/ *n* [C] **1** a long low Greek or Roman ship with sails which was rowed by SLAVES in the past **2** a kitchen on a ship: *The fire extinguishers are stored in the galley.* **3 a)** a TRAY used by printers which holds

TYPE[1] (3) **b)** also **galley proof** a sheet of paper on which a PRINTER (2) prints a book so that mistakes can be put right before it is divided into pages

**Gal·lic** /ˈgælɪk/ *adj* typical of France or French people: *Gallic charm*

**gal·ling** /ˈgɔːlɪŋ‖ˈgɒː-/ *adj* making you feel upset and angry because of something that is unfair: *The most galling thing is that the guy who got promoted is less qualified than me.*

**gal·li·vant** /ˈgælɪvænt/ *v* [I] *informal or humorous* to spend time enjoying yourself and going from place to place for pleasure: **gallivant about/around** *She spent six months gallivanting around Europe.*

**gal·lon** /ˈgælən/ *n* [C] **1** *BrE* a unit for measuring liquids, equal to 4.5435 litres **2** *AmE* a unit for measuring liquids, equal to 3.785 litres —see table on page B2

**gal·lop**[1] /ˈgæləp/ *v* **1** [I] if a horse gallops, it moves very fast with all its feet leaving the ground together [+ **along/across/towards etc**] *wild horses galloping over the sand* **2** [I,T] if you gallop, you ride very fast on a horse or you make it go very fast [+ **along/across/towards etc**] *I watched as Jan galloped away.* **3** [I always + adv/prep] to move very quickly: *Ian came galloping down the stairs.*

**gallop through** sth *phr v* [T] *informal* to do a job, some work etc very quickly: *Neil galloped through his homework*.

**gallop**[2] *n* **1 a)** [singular] the movement of a horse at its fastest speed when all four feet leave the ground together: **break into a gallop** (=begin to go very fast) **b)** [C] a ride on a horse when it is galloping **2 at a gallop a)** at the fastest speed possible when riding a horse: *Rogers set off at a gallop.* **b)** *informal* very quickly

**gal·lop·ing** /ˈgæləpɪŋ/ *adj* [only before noun] rapidly increasing or developing: **galloping inflation** *galloping inflation of 20 to 30%*

**gal·lows** /ˈgæləʊz‖-loʊz/ *n plural* **gallows** [C] a structure used for killing criminals by hanging them from a rope

**gallows hu·mour** *BrE*, **gallows humor** *AmE* /ˈ·· ˌ··/ *n* [U] humour which makes very unpleasant or dangerous things seem funny

**gall·stone** /ˈgɔːlstəʊn‖ˈgɒːlstoʊn/ *n* [C] a hard stone which can form in your GALL BLADDER

**Gal·lup poll** /ˈgæləp pəʊl‖-poʊl/ *n* [C] *trademark* a count of people's opinions on a subject, especially to find out how they will vote in an election

**ga·loot** /gəˈluːt/ *n* [C] *AmE informal* someone who is not at all graceful and does not dress neatly: *You clumsy galoot!*

**ga·lore** /gəˈlɔː‖-ˈlɔːr/ *adj* [only after noun] in large amounts or numbers: *There are bargains galore in the sales this year.*

**ga·losh·es** /gəˈlɒʃɪz‖-ˈlɑː-/ *n* [plural] *old-fashioned* rubber shoes worn over ordinary shoes when it rains or snows

**ga·lumph** /gəˈlʌmf/ *v* [I always + adv/prep] *informal* to move in a noisy, heavy, and awkward way

**gal·van·ic** /gælˈvænɪk/ *adj* **1** *formal* making people react suddenly with strong feelings or actions: *The bomb warning had a galvanic effect.* **2** *technical* connected with the production of electricity by the action of acid on metal

**gal·va·nise** /ˈgælvənaɪz/ *v* a British spelling of GALVANIZE

**gal·va·nis·m** /ˈgælvənɪzəm/ *n* [U] *technical* the production of electricity by the use of chemicals, especially as in a BATTERY (1)

**gal·va·nize** also **-ise** *BrE* /ˈgælvənaɪz/ *v* [T] to shock or surprise someone so that they do something to solve a problem, improve a situation etc: **galvanize sb into (doing) sth** *The possibility of defeat finally galvanized us into action.*

**gal·va·nized** also **-ise** *BrE* /ˈgælvanaɪzd/ *adj* **galvanised iron/metal etc** metal with a covering of ZINC made using electricity

**gam·bit** /ˈgæmbɪt/ *n* [C] **1** something that you do or say which is intended to give you an advantage in an argument: *a clever debating gambit*|**opening gambit** (=the thing you say first) **2** a planned series of moves at the beginning of a game of CHESS

**gam·ble**[1] /ˈgæmbəl/ *v* **1** [I] to risk money or possessions on the result of something uncertain, such as a card game, a race or a horse: *We're forbidden to drink or gamble.*|**gamble on sth** *Jack loves gambling on the horses.*|**gamble heavily** (=gamble often, using a lot of money) **2** [I,T] to do something that involves a lot of risk, and that will not succeed unless things happen the way you would like them to: **gamble on** *They're gambling on Johnson being fit for Saturday's game.*|**gamble sth on sth** *Potter gambled everything on his new play being a hit.*|**gamble with** *We can't relax our safety standards – we'd be gambling with people's lives.* —**gambler** *n* [C]

**gamble** sth ↔ **away** *phr v* [T] to lose money by gambling: *Nielsen gambled his inheritance away.*

**gamble**[2] *n* [singular] an action or plan that involves a risk but that you hope will succeed: *We've never used this agency before, so it's a bit of a gamble.*|**take a gamble** *I think she's taking a gamble setting up her own business like that.*|**a gamble pays off** (=brings success) *Ellen had to admit the gamble had paid off.*

**gam·bling** /ˈgæmblɪŋ/ *n* [U] **1** the practice of risking money or possessions on the result of something uncertain, such as a card game, or a horse race: *They had always strongly disapproved of gambling.* **2 gambling den** a place where people go to gamble illegally

**gam·bol** /ˈgæmbəl/ *v* [I always + adv/prep] to jump or run around in a lively active way: *lambs gambolling in a field* —**gambol** *n* [C]

**game**[1] /geɪm/ *n* S1 W1

**1 ► ACTIVITY OR SPORT ◄** [C] **a)** an activity or sport in which people compete with each other according to agreed rules: *What's your favorite game?*|*Dan's never liked card games.* **b)** an occasion when a game is played: *Did you see the game on TV last night?*|*Let's have a game of chess.* **c) your game** how well you play a particular game: **raise/improve your game** *Liam's taking lessons to improve his game.* **d) games** a large organized sports event: *the Olympic Games* **e)** *BrE* organized sports as a school subject or lesson: *We have games on Thursdays.* —compare MATCH[1] (2) —see also BALL GAME, BOARD GAME, WAR GAME

**2 ► PART OF A MATCH ◄** [C] one of the parts into which a single competition is divided, for example in tennis or BRIDGE[1] (4): *Graf leads, two games to one.*

**3 ► CHILDREN'S GAME ◄** [C] a children's activity in which they play with toys, pretend to be someone else etc: *a game of hide-and-seek*|*Look! Now you've spoilt our game!*

**4 ► BE A GAME ◄** [C] to be something that you do to enjoy yourself rather than for a serious purpose: *Some of those kids think life's just a game.*

**5 play games/silly games (with)** to behave in a dishonest or unfair way in order to get what you want: *Are you sure he's really interested, and not just playing silly games with you?*

**6 give the game away** to spoil a surprise or secret by doing or saying something that lets someone guess what the secret is: *Lynn gave the game away by laughing when Kim walked in.*

**7 ► ANIMALS/BIRDS ◄** [U] wild animals, birds, and fish that are hunted for food, especially as a sport —see also BIG GAME

**8 beat/play sb at their own game** to beat someone or fight back against them by using the same methods that they use: *Jackie decided to play Dean at his own game and left without paying the bill.*

**9 what's her game/your game etc?** *spoken* used to ask what the true reason for someone's behaviour is: *Reg is being very nice all of a sudden. What's his game?*
**10 advertising/public relations etc game** *informal* the profession of advertising etc
**11 a game of chance** a game in which you risk money on the result: *Poker is a game of chance.*
**12 the game's up** *spoken* used to tell someone that something wrong or dishonest that they have done has been discovered: *Come on, Don. The game's up. I know where you've hidden it.*
**13 be on the game** *slang* to be a PROSTITUTE
**14 make game of** *old-fashioned* to make fun of someone —see also FAIR GAME, **away game/match** (AWAY[2]), **fun and games** (FUN[1] (4)), **the name of the game** (NAME[1] (13))

**game[2]** *adj* **1** willing to try something dangerous, new, or difficult: *If you're game, we can do it now.* | [+ **for**] *We're game for a change.* | **game to do sth** *"Who's game to have a try?"* **2 game leg** *old-fashioned* an injured or painful leg —**gamely** *adv*

**gamekeep·er** /ˈ· ··/ *n* [C] someone whose job is to look after wild animals and birds that are kept to be hunted on private land

**game park** /ˈ· ·/ *n* [C] a GAME RESERVE

**game plan** /ˈ· ·/ *n* [C] a plan for achieving success, especially in business or sports: *The former coach blamed the defeat on no game plan and no inspiration.*

**game point** /ˈ· ·/ *n* [C,U] the situation in a game such as tennis in which one player will win the game if they win the next point —compare MATCH POINT

**game re·serve** /ˈ· ·ˌ·/ *n* [C] a large area of land that is designed for wild animals to live in safely

**game show** /ˈ· ·/ *n* [C] a television programme in which people play games or answer questions to win prizes

G

**games·man·ship** /ˈgeɪmzmənʃɪp/ *n* [U] the ability to succeed by using the rules of a game to your own advantage

**gam·ete** /ˈgæmiːt/ *n* [C] a type of cell which joins with another cell, starting the development of a baby or other young creature

**game war·den** /ˈ· ˌ··/ *n* [C] someone whose job is to look after wild animals in a GAME RESERVE

**gam·ey, gamy** /ˈgeɪmi/ *adj* having the strong taste of wild animals that are hunted for food

**ga·mine** /ˈgæmiːn/ *n* [C] a small thin girl or woman who looks like a boy —**gamine** *adj*: *a gamine hairstyle*

**gam·ing** /ˈgeɪmɪŋ/ *n* [U] *old-fashioned* playing cards or other games of chance for money; GAMBLING: *gaming tables*

**gam·ma** /ˈgæmə/ *n* [C] the third letter of the Greek alphabet

**gamma glob·u·lin** /ˌgæmə ˈglɒbjʊlɪn‖-ˈglɑː-/ *n* [U] a natural substance in your body which is a type of ANTIBODY and gives protection against some diseases

**gamma ray** /ˈ·· ·/ *n* [C usually plural] a beam of light with a short WAVELENGTH (2), that can pass through solid objects

**gam·mon** /ˈgæmən/ *n* [U] *BrE* meat from a pig's leg which has been preserved using salt: *gammon steak*

**gam·my** /ˈgæmi/ *adj BrE old-fashioned* a gammy leg or knee is injured or painful

**gam·ut** /ˈgæmət/ *n* [singular] the complete range of possibilities: [+ **of**] *College life opened up a whole gamut of new experiences.* | **run the (whole) gamut** (=include or experience all the possibilities between two extremes) *Her feelings that day ran the whole gamut of emotions.*

**gam·y** /ˈgeɪmi/ *adj* another spelling of GAMEY

**-gamy** /gəmi/ *suffix* [in U nouns] marriage to a particular number or kind of people: *bigamy* (=being married to two people) | *monogamy* —**gamous** *suffix* [in adjectives]

**gan·der** /ˈgændə‖-ər/ *n* [C] **1** a male GOOSE[1] (1b) **2 have/take a gander at** *spoken* to look at something

**gang[1]** /gæŋ/ *n* **1** a group of young people who spend time together, and often cause trouble and fight against other groups: *a skinhead gang* | *members of a notorious gang* | [+ **of**] *a gang of kids hanging around the mall* **2** [C] a group of criminals who work together: *Several gangs were operating in the area.* | [+ **of**] *a gang of smugglers* **3** *humorous* a group of friends, especially young people: *The whole gang will be there next weekend.* **4** a group of workers or prisoners doing physical work together —see also CHAIN GANG S3

**gang[2]** *v*
**gang up on** sb *phr v* [T] to join together into a group to attack someone or oppose them: *I hate school! They all gang up on me!*

**gang-bang** /ˈ· ˌ·/ *n* [C] **1** *informal* an occasion when several people have sex with each other at the same time **2** a GANG RAPE —**gang-bang** *v* [I,T]

**gang·bust·ers** /ˈgæŋˌbʌstəz‖-ərz/ *n* **come on like gangbusters** *AmE informal* to begin to do something very eagerly and with a lot of energy: *You can't come on like gangbusters with women – be more subtle!*

**gang·land** /ˈgæŋlænd, -lənd/ *adj* **a gangland killing/murder/shooting etc** a killing etc connected with the world of organized and violent crime: *Sharp may have been the victim of a gangland revenge killing.*

**gan·gling** /ˈgæŋglɪŋ/ *adj* unusually tall and thin, and not at all graceful in the way you move: *an awkward gangling teenager*

**gan·gli·on** /ˈgæŋgliən/ *n* [C] *technical* **1** a painful raised area of skin that is full of liquid, often on the back of your wrist **2** a mass of nerve cells

**gan·gly** /ˈgæŋgli/ *adj* another form of GANGLING

**gang·plank** /ˈgæŋplæŋk/ *n* [C] a board for walking on between a boat and the shore, or between one boat and another

**gang rape** /ˈ· ·/ *n* [C] an occasion when several men attack a woman to force her to have sex with them

**gan·grene** /ˈgæŋgriːn/ *n* [U] the decay of the flesh of part of your body because blood has stopped flowing there as a result of illness or injury —**gangrenous** *adj*

**gang·ster** /ˈgæŋstə‖-ər/ *n* [C] a member of a violent group of criminals: *a gangster movie*

**gang·way** /ˈgæŋweɪ/ *n* [C] **1** a space between two rows of seats in a theatre, bus, or train; AISLE (1) **2** a large GANGPLANK **3 gangway!** *spoken* used to tell people in a crowd to let someone go through

**gan·ja** /ˈgændʒə/ *n* [U] *slang* MARIJUANA

**gan·net** /ˈgænɪt/ *n* [C] **1** a large sea bird that lives in large groups on cliffs **2** *BrE* someone who eats a lot

**gan·try** /ˈgæntri/ *n* [C] a large metal frame which is used to support heavy machinery or railway signals

**gaol** /dʒeɪl/ *n, v* a British spelling of JAIL

**gaol·bird** /ˈdʒeɪlbɜːd‖-bɜːrd/ *n* [C] a British spelling of JAILBIRD

**gaol·er** /ˈdʒeɪlə‖-ər/ *n* [C] a British spelling of JAILER

**gap**

Ken squeezed through a gap in the fence.

**gap** /gæp/ *n* [C] S2
**1 ► A SPACE ◄** a space between two objects or two

W2

parts of an object because of something that is missing: [+ **in**] *The neighbors' dog got in through a gap in the hedge.* | [+ **between**] *Lou has big gaps between her front teeth.*
**2** ▶ **DIFFERENCE** ◀ a big difference between two situations, amounts, groups of people etc: [+ **between**] *the widening gap between the rich and the poor* | **fill the gap** *Donors will be asked to fill the gap between state funding and actual costs.* | **bridge the gap** (=reduce the amount or importance of a difference) *His films attempt to bridge the gap between tradition and modernity.* —see also **the generation gap** (GENERATION)
**3** ▶ **STH MISSING** ◀ something that is missing that stops something else from being good or complete [+ **in**] *There are huge gaps in my knowledge of history.* | *Frank's death has left a big gap in my life.*
**4** ▶ **IN A MOUNTAIN** ◀ a low place between two higher parts of a mountain
**5** ▶ **IN TIME** ◀ a period of time between two periods of time when nothing is happening: *an awkward gap in the conversation*
**6 gap in the market** an opportunity to develop a particular product and sell it because it has not been developed yet

**gape** /geɪp/ *v* [I] **1** to look at something for a long time, especially with your mouth open, because you are very surprised or shocked: *What are all these people gaping at?* —see GAZE[1] (USAGE) **2** also **gape open** to come apart or open widely: *Dan stood at the door, his shirt gaping open.* —**gape** *n* [C]

**gap·ing** /ˈgeɪpɪŋ/ *adj* [only before noun] a gaping hole, wound, or mouth is very wide and open

**gap-toothed** /ˌ· ˈ·◂/ *adj* having wide spaces between your teeth

S2 **gar·age[1]** /ˈgærɑːʒ, -ɪdʒ‖gəˈrɑːʒ/ *n* [C] **1** a building for keeping a car in, usually next to a house —compare CARPORT —see picture on page 410 **2** a place where motor vehicles are repaired: *My car's at the garage.* **3** *BrE* a place where you buy petrol; PETROL STATION

**garage[2]** *v* [T] to put or keep a vehicle in a garage

**garage sale** /ˈ·· ˌ·‖·ˈ· ˌ·/ *n* [C] *AmE* a sale of used furniture, clothes etc from people's houses, usually held in someone's garage

**gar·am ma·sa·la** /ˌgɑːrəm məˈsɑːlə, -mɑː-/ *n* [U] a mixture of SPICES which gives a hot taste to food, used especially in Indian cooking

**garb[1]** /gɑːb‖gɑːrb/ *n* [U] *formal or literary* a particular style of clothing, especially clothes that show your type of work or look unusual: *clothed in priestly garb*

**garb[2]** *v* **be garbed in** *literary* to be dressed in a particular type of clothes: *singers garbed in costumes of gold*

S3 **gar·bage** /ˈgɑːbɪdʒ‖ˈgɑːr-/ *n* [U] **1** *especially AmE* waste material, such as paper, empty containers, and food thrown away; RUBBISH[1] (1) *BrE*: *Can you take the garbage out when you go?* **2** stupid words, ideas etc: *You're talking garbage.* **3 garbage in, garbage out** used to say that if you put bad information into a computer, you will get bad results —see graph at RUBBISH[1]

**garbage can** /ˈ·· ˌ·/ *n* [C] *AmE* a container with a lid for holding waste until it can be taken away; DUSTBIN *BrE* —see picture on page 410

**garbage col·lec·tor** /ˈ·· ·ˌ··/ *n* [C] *AmE* someone whose job is to remove waste from garbage cans; DUSTMAN *BrE*

**garbage dis·po·sal** /ˈ·· ·ˌ··/ *n* [C] *AmE* a small machine in the kitchen SINK which breaks vegetable waste into small pieces; WASTE DISPOSAL (1) *BrE*

**garbage man** /ˈ·· ˌ·/ *n* [C] *AmE* a garbage collector

**garbage truck** /ˈ·· ˌ·/ *n* [C] *AmE* a large vehicle which goes from house to house to collect the contents of garbage cans; DUST CART *BrE*

**gar·ban·zo** /gɑːˈbænzəʊ‖gɑːrˈbɑːnzoʊ/ also **garbanzo bean** /·ˈ·· ˌ·/ *n* [C] another word for CHICK-PEA, used especially in the western US

**gar·bled** /ˈgɑːbəld‖ˈgɑːr-/ *adj* a garbled statement or report is very unclear and confusing: *The papers had some garbled version of the story.* | *a garbled phone message.*

**gar·çon** /ˈgɑːsɒn‖gɑːrˈsoʊn/ *n* [C] *French* a waiter, especially in a French restaurant

**gar·den[1]** /ˈgɑːdn‖ˈgɑːr-/ *n* **1** [C] *especially BrE* a piece of land around or next to your house where there is usually lawn (=area of grass) and an area where you grow flowers, plants, or vegetables; YARD (3) *AmE Grace is out in the garden mowing the lawn.* | **rose garden/herb garden etc** (=where a particular type of plant is grown) —see picture on page 410: **2** [C] *AmE* the part of a garden that has flowers and plants in it: *We're thinking of planting a little garden in our yard.* **3 gardens** [plural] a large area of land where plants and flowers are grown so that the public can go and see them: *the Botanic Gardens at Kew* **4 Gardens** *BrE* used in the name of streets: *number 211 Roland Gardens* —see also KITCHEN GARDEN, MARKET GARDEN, **lead sb up the garden path** (LEAD[1] (18)) S1 W1

**garden[2]** *v* [I] to work in a garden, keeping it clean, making plants grow etc —**gardening** *n* [U]: *Since he's retired he's become very interested in gardening.*

**garden cen·tre** /ˈ·· ˌ··/ *n* [C] *BrE* a place that sells plants, flowers and equipment for gardens; NURSERY (4)

**garden cit·y** /ˌ·· ˈ··/ *n* [C] *BrE* a town that has been designed to have a lot of trees, areas of grass, and open spaces —compare NEW TOWN

**gar·den·er** /ˈgɑːdnə‖ˈgɑːrdnər/ *n* [C] **1** someone who enjoys growing flowers and plants: *Mom has always been a good gardener.* **2** someone whose job is to work in gardens

**garden flat** /ˈ·· ˌ·/ *n* [C] *BrE* an apartment on the lowest floor of a house, which has a door leading to the garden

**gar·de·ni·a** /gɑːˈdiːniə‖gɑːr-/ *n* [C] a large white pleasant-smelling flower that grows on a bush

**garden par·ty** /ˈ·· ˌ··/ *n* [C] *BrE* a formal party for a lot of people which is held in a large garden; LAWN PARTY *AmE*

**garden-va·ri·e·ty** /ˈ·· ·ˌ···/ *adj* [only before noun] *AmE* very ordinary and not very interesting: *He's just one of your garden-variety singers.*

**gar·gan·tu·an** /gɑːˈgæntʃuən‖gɑːr-/ *adj* extremely large; GIGANTIC: *What a gargantuan bed!*

**gar·gle[1]** /ˈgɑːgəl‖ˈgɑːr-/ *v* [I + **with**] to clean the inside of your mouth and throat by blowing air through water or medicine in the back of your throat: *Gargling with salt water may help your sore throat.*

**gargle[2]** *n* **1** [C,U] liquid that you gargle with **2** [singular] the act of gargling

**gar·goyle** /ˈgɑːgɔɪl‖ˈgɑːr-/ *n* [C] an ugly stone figure of a person or animal that carries rain water from the roof of an old building, especially a church

**gar·ish** /ˈgeərɪʃ‖ˈger-/ *adj* very brightly coloured in a way that is unpleasant to look at: *Many of the rugs are too garish for my taste.* —**garishly** *adv* —**garishness** *n* [U]

**gar·land[1]** /ˈgɑːlənd‖ˈgɑːr-/ *n* [C] a ring of flowers or leaves that is given to someone to wear around their neck

**garland[2]** *v* [T] *literary* to decorate someone or something, especially with flowers

**gar·lic** /ˈgɑːlɪk‖ˈgɑːr-/ *n* [U] a plant like a small onion, used in cooking to give a strong taste: *a clove of garlic* (=single section of it) | *a garlic press* (=tool used to crush garlic) —**garlicky** *adj*: *his garlicky breath* —see picture on page 414 S3

**gar·ment** /ˈgɑːmənt‖ˈgɑːr-/ *n* [C] *formal or technical* a piece of clothing —see picture at CLOTHES

**gar·ner** /ˈgɑːnə‖ˈgɑːrnər/ *v* [T] *formal* to take or collect something, especially information

**gar·net** /ˈgɑːnɪt‖ˈgɑːr-/ *n* **1** [C] a dark red stone used as a jewel **2** [U] a dark red colour

**gar·nish[1]** /ˈgɑːnɪʃ‖ˈgɑːr-/ *n* [C] something that you add to food to decorate it

**garnish[2]** *v* [T] **1** to add something to food in order to decorate it: **garnish sth with** *Garnish each dish with a* *slice of lemon.* **2** also **garnishee** *technical* to take money from someone's wages because they have not paid their debts

**gar·ret** /ˈgærȷ̊t/ *n* [C] a small uncomfortable room at the top of a house —compare ATTIC

**gar·ri·son¹** /ˈgærȷ̊sən/ *n* [C] a group of soldiers living in a town or FORT and defending it: *The garrison was called out when news of the enemy's advance was received.* | *a garrison town*

**garrison²** *v* [T] to send a group of soldiers to defend or guard a place: *Our regiment will garrison a coastal town.*

**gar·rotte** /gəˈrɒt‖gəˈrɑːt/ *v* [T] to kill someone using a metal collar or wire which is pulled tightly around their neck —**garrotte** *n* [C]

**gar·ru·lous** /ˈgærələs/ *adj* always talking a lot: *Ian isn't normally this garrulous!* —**garrulously** *adv* —**garrulousness** *n* [U]

**gar·ter** /ˈgɑːtə‖ˈgɑːrtər/ *n* [C] **1** a band of ELASTIC (=material that stretches) worn around your leg to keep a sock or STOCKING up **2** *AmE* one of four pieces of elastic fixed to a woman's underwear and to her stockings to hold them up; SUSPENDER (1) *BrE*

**garter belt** /ˈ·· ˌ·/ *n* [C] *AmE* a piece of women's underwear with garters hanging down from it which fasten onto STOCKINGS (1) and hold them up; SUSPENDER BELT *BrE*

**garter snake** /ˈ·· ˌ·/ *n* [C] a harmless American snake with lines of colour along its back

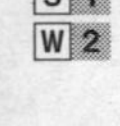

**gas¹** /gæs/ *n plural* **gases** also **gasses** **1** [C,U] a substance like air, which is not solid or liquid, and usually cannot be seen: *hydrogen gas* | **a gas cylinder** (=for storing gas) **2** [U] a substance of this type which is burnt for heating or cooking: *a gas oven* | *Can you light the gas for me?* **3** [U] a substance of this type used to poison people or to control them: *Police fired tear gas into the crowd.* **4** [U] *AmE* [U] GASOLINE **5 gas mark 4,5,6 etc** *BrE* a measurement of the temperature of a gas OVEN **6** *AmE slang* the condition of having gas in your stomach; WIND¹ (9) *BrE* **7** [singular] *AmE* something that is fun and makes you laugh a lot: *The state fair was a real gas.*

**gas²** *v* **1** [T] to poison or kill someone with gas **2** [I] *informal* to talk for a long time about unimportant or boring things *They were just standing there gassing away.*

**gas** sth ↔ **up** *phr v* [I,T] *AmE* to put petrol in a car: *We'd better gas up before we go.*

**gas·bag** /ˈgæsbæg/ *n* [C] *informal* someone who talks too much; WINDBAG

**gas cham·ber** /ˈ· ˌ··/ *n* [C] a large room in which people or animals are killed with poisonous gas

**gas·e·ous** /ˈgæsiəs/ *adj* like gas or in the form of gas

**gas-fired** /ˌ· ˈ·◂/ *adj especially BrE* using gas as a fuel: *a gas-fired central heating system*

**gas-guz·zler** /ˈ· ˌ··/ *n* [C] *AmE informal* a car that uses a lot of petrol —**gas-guzzling** *adj*

**gash** /gæʃ/ *n* [C] **1** a large deep wound from a cut *a deep gash on his leg* **2** a long deep hole in something: *The trench cut a brown gash through the green lawn.* —**gash** *v* [T]

**gas·hold·er** /ˈgæsˌhəʊldə‖-ˌhoʊldər/ *n* [C] a very large round metal container or building from which gas is carried in pipes to buildings

**gas·i·fy** /ˈgæsȷ̊faɪ/ *v* [I,T] to change into a gas, or to make something do this —**gasification** /ˌgæsȷ̊fȷ̊ˈkeɪʃən/ *n* [U]

**gas·ket** /ˈgæskȷ̊t/ *n* [C] **1** a flat piece of material, often rubber, placed between two surfaces so that steam, oil, gas etc cannot escape **2 blow a gasket** **a)** if a vehicle blows a gasket, steam or gas escapes from the engine **b)** *informal* to become very angry

**gas·light** /ˈgæs-laɪt/ *n* **1** [U] the light produced from burning gas **2** [C] also **gas lamp** a lamp in a house or on the street which gives light from burning gas

**gas·man** /ˈgæsmæn/ *n* [C] *BrE* someone who comes to your home to see how much gas you have used or to repair your gas system

**gas mask** /ˈ· ·/ *n* [C] a piece of equipment worn over your face to protect you from poisonous gases —see picture at MASK¹

**gas me·ter** /ˈ· ˌ··/ *n* [C] a piece of equipment that measures how much gas is used in a building

**gas·o·hol** /ˈgæsəhɒl‖-hɔːl/ *n* [U] *AmE* petrol with a small amount of alcohol in it, which can be used in cars and is cheaper than petrol

**gas·o·line, gasolene** /ˈgæsəliːn/ *n* [U] *AmE* a liquid obtained from PETROLEUM, used mainly for producing power in the engines of cars; PETROL *BrE*

**gas·om·e·ter** /gæˈsɒmȷ̊tə‖-ˈsɑːmȷ̊tər/ *n* [C] a GASHOLDER

**gasp¹** /gɑːsp‖gæsp/ *v* [I,T] **1** to breathe in suddenly, quickly, and in a way that can be heard, especially because you are surprised or afraid: *"My leg! My leg!" he gasped. "I think it's broken!"* | [+ **with**] *Ollie gasped with pain and slumped forward.* | [+ **at**] *The audience gasped at the splendour of the costumes.* **2** [I] to breathe quickly and deeply because you are having difficulty breathing: **gasp for air/breath** *Brendan climbed slowly, gasping for breath.* **3 be gasping** *BrE spoken* to be very thirsty: *Put the kettle on, love, I'm gasping.* **4 be gasping for** *BrE spoken* to feel that you urgently need something such as a drink or cigarette: *I'm gasping for a pint!*

**gasp²** *n* [C] **1** an act of taking in your breath suddenly in a way that can be heard, especially because you are surprised or afraid: [+ **of**] *With a gasp of pure horror, Stormgren jumped up and ran.* | **give a gasp** *She gave a little gasp and clutched George's hand.* **2** an act of taking in air quickly because you are having difficulty breathing: *Between gasps Michael said that he was allergic to cats.* **3 at your last gasp** about to die: *He rolled his eyes as though at his last gasp.*

**gas pedal** /ˈ· ˌ··/ *n* [C] *AmE* the thing that you press with your foot to make a car go faster; ACCELERATOR (1) —see picture on page 409

**gas per·me·a·ble lens** /ˌ· ···· ˈ·/ *n* [C] a kind of CONTACT LENS that allows oxygen to reach your eyes

**gas ring** /ˈ· ·/ *BrE n* [C] a metal ring that gets hot when gas passes through it, used for cooking food; BURNER (2) *AmE*

**gas sta·tion** /ˈ· ˌ··/ *n* [C] *AmE* a place where you can buy petrol and oil for motor vehicles; PETROL STATION *BrE*

**gas·sy** /ˈgæsi/ *adj BrE* a gassy drink has too much gas in it: *This beer is really gassy.* —**gassiness** *n* [U]

**gas·tric** /ˈgæstrɪk/ *adj* [only before noun] *technical* **1** related to your stomach: *gastric ulcers* **2 gastric juices** the acids in your stomach that break food into smaller parts **3 gastric flu** an illness that makes you VOMIT¹ and gives you DIARRHOEA

**gas·tri·tis** /gæˈstraɪtȷ̊s/ *n* [U] an illness which makes the inside of your stomach become swollen, so that you feel a burning pain

**gas·tro·en·te·ri·tis** /ˌgæstrəʊ-entəˈraɪtȷ̊s‖-troʊ-/ *n* [U] an illness which makes your stomach and INTESTINE become swollen

**gas·tro·nom·ic** /ˌgæstrəˈnɒmɪk◂‖-ˈnɑː-/ *adj* [only before noun] connected with the art of cooking good food or the pleasure of eating it: *sampling the gastronomic delights of Thailand* —**gastronomically** /-kli/ *adv*

**gas·tron·o·my** /gæˈstrɒnəmi‖gæˈstrɑː-/ *n* [U] the art and science of cooking and eating good food

**gas tur·bine** /ˌ· ˈ··/ *n* [C] an engine in which a wheel of special blades is driven round at high speed by hot gases

**gas·works** /ˈgæswɜːks‖-wɜːrks/ *n plural* **gasworks** [C] a place where gas is made from coal

**gate¹** /geɪt/ *n* [C] **1** a frame that you can open and close to get through a fence, wall etc at the entrance to a place: *a garden gate* | *In front of him were the wrought-iron gates of the palace.* —compare DOOR (1) —see picture on page 410 **2** the place where you leave an airport building to get on a plane: *Air France flight 76 leaves from gate 6A.* **3 Irangate/Watergate/Contragate etc** used with the name of a place or a person to give a name to an event involving dishonest behaviour by a politician or other S2 W2 public official **4** *BrE* **a)** the number of people who go in to see a sports event, especially a football match **b)** the amount of money that these people pay

**gate**[2] *v* [T] *BrE* to prevent a student from leaving a school as a punishment for behaving badly

**gâ·teau** /ˈgætəʊ‖gɑːˈtoʊ/ *n plural* **gâteaux** /-təʊz‖-ˈtoʊz/ [C,U] *BrE* a large sweet cake, often filled and decorated with cream, fruit, chocolate etc

**gate·crash** /ˈgeɪtkræʃ/ *v* [I,T] to go to a party that you have not been invited to —**gatecrasher** *n* [U]

**gated com·mu·ni·ty** /ˌ·· ·ˈ···/ *n* [C] *AmE* an area of shops, houses etc with a fence or wall around it and an entrance that is guarded

**gate·house** /ˈgeɪthaʊs/ *n* [C] a small building next to the gate of a park or at the entrance to the land surrounding a big house

**gate·keep·er** /ˈgeɪtˌkiːpə‖-ər/ *n* [C] someone whose job is to open and close a gate

**gate-leg ta·ble** /ˌ· · ˈ··/ *n* [C] a table that can be made larger by moving a leg out to support a folding part

**gate·post** /ˈgeɪtpəʊst‖-poʊst/ *n* [C] **1** one of two strong upright poles fixed to the ground to support a gate —see picture on page 410 **2 between you, me and the gatepost** *BrE spoken* used to say that you are going to tell someone your opinion, but you want it to be a secret

**gate·way** /ˈgeɪt-weɪ/ *n* **1** [C] the opening in a fence, wall etc that can be closed by a gate **2 the gateway to a)** a place, especially a city, that you can go through in order to reach another much bigger place: *St. Louis is the gateway to the West.* **b)** a way of achieving something: *Hard work is the gateway to success.* **3** [C] a way of connecting two computer networks (NETWORK[1] (4)) that would otherwise not be able to be connected

S2 W2 **gath·er**[1] /ˈgæðə‖-ər/ *v*

**1 ▶ COME TOGETHER ◀** [I] to come together and form a group: *On Fridays the men gather together at the mosque.* | *Tens of thousands of people had gathered outside the US embassy.* | **gather around/round** *I'd like everyone to gather round so I can demonstrate how the system works.* | **gather together** *Could the bride's family all gather together for a photo?* | **be gathered** *Dozens of photographers were gathered outside Jagger's villa.*

**2 ▶ KNOW/THINK ◀** [T not in progressive] to know something or think something is true, because of something that you have heard or seen: *You two know each other, I gather.* | **gather (that)** *I gather you've had some problems with our sales department.* | **from what I can gather/as far as I can gather** (=this is what I believe to be true) *She's his niece, from what I can gather.*

**3 ▶ COLLECT ◀** [T] **a)** to search for things of the same type in several different places and collect them together: *Thelma went along the lane gathering blackberries.* **b)** to collect information, ideas etc for example in order to write a book or a report | *Floyd's gathering ideas for his new novel.*

**4 gather speed/force** to move faster or become stronger: *The cart gathered speed as it coasted down the hill.*

**5 gather dust** if something useful gathers dust, it is not being used: *You may as well take these books – they're just gathering dust.*

**6 gather momentum a)** to gradually move faster, especially because of going down a hill **b)** if a plan or process gathers momentum, it develops quickly and affects more and more people: *A major anti-corruption campaign was gathering momentum.*

**7 ▶ CLOTH ◀** [T] **a)** to pull material into small folds: *The skirt is gathered at the waist.* **b)** to pull material or a piece of clothing closer to you: *Moira gathered her skirts round her and climbed the steps.*

**8 gather yourself/gather your strength** to prepare yourself for something you are going to do, especially something difficult: *I need to rest and gather my strength for the exam.*

**9 ▶ CLOUDS ◀** [I] to gradually increase in number: *Storm clouds were gathering so we hurried home.*

**10 the gathering darkness/dusk/shadows etc** *literary* the time in the evening when it is getting dark: *the evening's gathering shadows*

**11 gather sb to you/gather sb up** *old-fashioned* to take someone into your arms and hold them in order to protect them or show them love

**gather** sth ↔ **in** *phr v* [T] to collect crops together: *gathering in the harvest*

**gather** sth ↔ **together/up** *phr v* [T] to pick up lots of things from different places: *Paul gathered up his papers and left the room.* | *She gathered up some of the children's clothes and stuffed them in a bag.*

**gather**[2] *n* [C] a small fold produced by pulling cloth together

**gath·er·ing** /ˈgæðərɪŋ/ *n* [C] **1** a meeting of a group of people: *a select gathering of 20 or 30 people* **2** a fold or group of folds in cloth

**gauche** /gəʊʃ‖goʊʃ/ *adj* lacking confidence and experience in social situations, so that you often say or do the wrong thing: *a mature, successful businesswoman, not a gauche teenager, flushing with girlish embarrassment* —**gauchely** *adv* —**gaucheness** *n* [U]

**gau·cho** /ˈgaʊtʃəʊ‖-tʃoʊ/ *n* [C] a South American COWBOY (1)

**gau·dy** /ˈgɔːdi‖ˈgɒːdi/ *adj* clothes, colours etc that are gaudy are too bright and look cheap: *gaudy jewelry* —**gaudily** *adv* —**gaudiness** *n* [U]

**gauge**[1] also **gage** *AmE* /geɪdʒ/ *n* [C]

**1 ▶ INSTRUMENT ◀** an instrument for measuring the size or amount of something: *a rain gauge* | *the fuel gauge in a car*

**2 ▶ WIDTH ◀ a)** the width of thin metal objects such as wire, or screws: *a narrow-gauge screw* **b)** the width of thin material such as metal or plastic sheets: *heavy gauge black polythene*

**3 ▶ RAILWAY ◀** the distance between the lines of a railway or between the wheels of a train: **broad/narrow gauge** (=with more/less than the standard distance between the rails)

**4 ▶ GUN ◀** the width of the BARREL[1] (3) of a gun: *a 12-gauge shotgun*

**5 ▶ MEASURE ◀** a standard measure of weight, size etc to which objects can be compared

**gauge**[2] *v* [T] **1** form a correct idea of how people feel about something or what they are likely to do: *The city council failed to gauge the strength of local feeling on this issue.* | [+ **what/how etc**] *It is difficult to gauge what the other party's next move will be.* **2** to calculate something by using a particular instrument or method: *The thermostat will gauge the temperature and control the heat.*

**gaunt** /gɔːnt‖gɒːnt/ *adj* **1** very thin and pale, especially because of illness or continued worry: *I looked into her face and it was gaunt with exhaustion.* **2** a building, mountain etc that is gaunt looks very plain and unpleasant: *a gaunt cathedral* —**gauntness** *n* [U]

**gaunt·let** /ˈgɔːntlɪt‖ˈgɒːnt-/ *n* **1** [C] a long GLOVE (1) that covers someone's wrist and protects their hand, for example in a factory **2** [C] a GLOVE (1) covered in metal, used for protection by soldiers in past times **3 throw down the gauntlet** to invite someone to fight or compete over a disagreement **4 pick up/take up the gauntlet** to accept the invitation to fight or compete over a disagreement **5 run the gauntlet** to be criticized or attacked by a lot of people: *Once again Clinton had to run the gauntlet of the press.*

**gauze** /gɔːz‖gɒːz/ *n* [U] **1** very thin transparent material with very small holes in it, often used for curtains **2** also **gauze bandage** *AmE* thin cotton with very small holes in it that is used for tying around a wound —**gauzy** *adj*

**gave** /geɪv/ the past tense of GIVE[1]

**gav·el** /ˈgævəl/ *n* [C] a small hammer that the person in charge of a meeting, law court, AUCTION[1] etc hits on a table in order to get people's attention

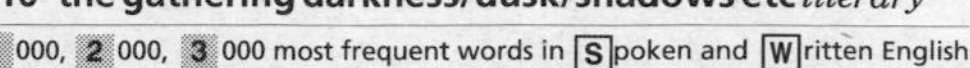

**ga·votte** /gəˈvɒt‖gəˈvɑːt/ *n* [C] a fast, cheerful French dance, or the music for this dance

**gawd** /gɔːd‖gɒːd/ *interjection* used to represent the word 'god' when it is said in this way as an expression of surprise, fear etc

**gawk** /gɔːk‖gɒːk/ *v* [I] to look at something for a long time, in a way that looks stupid: [+ **at**] *Don't just stand there gawking at those girls!*

**gaw·ky** /ˈgɔːki‖ˈgɒːki/ *adj* moving in a nervous and awkward way, as if you cannot control your arms and legs: *a gawky, long-legged teenager* —**gawkiness** *n* [U]

**gawp** /gɔːp‖gɒːp/ *v* [I] *BrE* to look at something for a long time, especially with your mouth open because you are surprised: *tourists gawping at Buckingham Palace*

S3 **gay**[1] /geɪ/ *adj* **1** sexually attracted to people of the same sex as yourself; HOMOSEXUAL: **gay rights/community etc** (=the rights etc of gay people): *a gay rights demonstration* **2** *old-fashioned* bright or attractive: *gay colours* **3** *old-fashioned* cheerful and excited: *She felt excited and quite gay.* **4 with gay abandon** in a careless and thoughtless way —see also GAILY, GAIETY —**gayness** *n* [U]

**gay**[2] *n* [C] someone who is HOMOSEXUAL, especially a man

**gaze**[1] /geɪz/ *v* [I always + adv/prep] to look at someone or something for a long time, giving it all your attention often without realizing you are doing so: [+ **into/at etc**] *Patrick was gazing into the fire.* | *We gazed up at the stars.*

**USAGE NOTE: GAZE**

WORD CHOICE: **look, gaze, stare, gape**

These words all describe **looking** at someone or something for a long time.

You may **gaze** at something interesting or beautiful without realizing you are doing it: *He stood gazing at Helen./at the breathtaking landscape.*

If you **stare** at someone or something, you look directly at them for a long time without moving your eyes, for example because you are angry, very interested, or are thinking hard about something: *She stared at the page for several minutes, uncertain what to write.* | *Why are you staring at me like that?*

You **gape** at something with your mouth open when you are very surprised or shocked: *He just stood and gaped as the building began to crumble.*

**gaze**[2] *n* [singular] a long steady look: *a curious gaze* | **lower your gaze** *Ellen smiled uncomfortably and lowered her gaze.* | **meet sb's gaze** (=look directly at someone who is looking at you): *He didn't dare to meet her gaze.*

**ga·ze·bo** /gəˈziːbəʊ‖-ˈzeɪboʊ, -ˈziː-/ *n* [C] a small building in a garden, where you can sit and look at the view

**ga·zelle** /gəˈzel/ *n* [C] a type of small DEER, which jumps very gracefully and has large beautiful eyes

**ga·zette**[1] /gəˈzet/ *n* [C] **1** *BrE* an official newspaper, especially one from the government giving important lists of people who have been employed by them etc **2** *AmE* a newspaper

**gazette**[2] *v* [T] *BrE* **1 be gazetted** *formal* to be officially given a specific military job **2** to give someone an official job, especially in the military forces

**gaz·et·teer** /ˌgæzəˈtɪə‖-ˈtɪr/ *n* [C] a list of names of places, printed as a dictionary or as a list at the end of a book of maps

**gaz·pa·cho** /gæzˈpætʃəʊ‖gəˈspɑːtʃoʊ/ *n* [U] a cold Spanish soup made from TOMATO, GREEN PEPPER, CUCUMBER, and onion

**ga·zump** /gəˈzʌmp/ *v* [T] *BrE informal* to sell a house to another person who offers you more money than someone that you have already agreed to sell it to: *We were gazumped at the last minute.*

**GB** /ˌdʒiː ˈbiː/ the written abbreviation of Great Britain

**Gb** the written abbreviation of GIGABYTE

**GBH** /ˌdʒiː biː ˈeɪtʃ/ *n* [U] *BrE* grievous bodily harm; the serious crime of attacking someone and injuring them

**GCE** /ˌdʒiː siː ˈiː◂/ *n* [C] General Certificate of Education; a school examination in one of a range of subjects, taken in England and Wales before 1988 by students aged 15 or over

**GCSE** /ˌdʒiː siː es ˈiː/ *n* [C] General Certificate of Secondary Education; a school examination in one of a range of subjects that is taken by students aged 15 or over in Britain

**g'day** /gəˈdeɪ/ *interjection AustrE & NZE* an informal way of saying 'hello'

**GDP** /ˌdʒiː diː ˈpiː/ gross domestic product; the total value of all goods and services produced in a country, in one year, except for income received from abroad —compare GNP

**gear**[1] /gɪə‖gɪr/ *n* S3

**1** ▶ **IN CARS ETC** ◀ [C,U] the machinery in a vehicle that turns power from the engine into movement: *The new model has five forward gears.* | *driving cautiously along in third gear* | **bottom gear** *BrE*, **low gear** *AmE* (=the gear used for driving slowly) | **in gear** (=with a gear connecting the engine to the wheels, and therefore ready to move) *Don't turn off the engine while you're still in gear.*

**2** ▶ **MACHINERY** ◀ a piece of machinery that performs a particular job: *the landing gear of a plane* | *heavy lifting gear*

**3** ▶ **EQUIPMENT** ◀ a set of equipment or tools you need for a particular activity: *He's crazy about photography – he's got all the gear.* | *We'll need camping gear when we go away.*

**4** ▶ **CLOTHES** ◀ a set of clothes that you wear for a particular occasion or activity: *Bring your rain gear.* | *You have to wear protective gear for this.*

**5 change gear** *BrE*, **shift gear** *AmE* **a)** to move a vehicle into a different gear —see picture on page 415 **b)** to start something in a different way, especially in the amount of energy or effort you use: *The boss expects us to be able to change gear just like that.*

**6 in top gear** *BrE*, **in high gear** *AmE* **a)** the gear used at high speeds **b)** doing something with the greatest possible effort and energy: *During this period, Japan's export industries were in top gear.* | *The Republican's propaganda machine moved into high gear.*

**7 be thrown out of gear** if a process is thrown out of gear, something prevents it from happening in the way that was planned

**8** ▶ **DRUGS** ◀ [U] *slang* a word meaning illegal drugs, used by people who take drugs

**gear**[2] *v* [T] **1 be geared to** to be organized in a way that is suitable for a particular purpose or situation: *The typical career pattern was geared to men whose wives didn't work.* | **be geared to do sth** *The course curriculum is geared to span three years.* **2 be geared up** to be well prepared for something you have to do [**+for**] *The party is all geared up for the election.* | *We need to be geared up to deal with this sort of emergency.*

**gear·box** /ˈgɪəbɒks‖ˈgɪrbɑːks/ *n* [C] a metal box containing the gears of a vehicle

**gear·ing** /ˈgɪərɪŋ‖ˈgɪr-/ *n* [U] *technical* the relationship between the amount of money that a company is worth and the amount that it owes in debts

**gear le·ver** /ˈ· ˌ··/ *n* [C] a metal rod that you move in order to control the gears of a vehicle —see picture at BICYCLE[1]

**gear shift** /ˈ· ·/ *n* [C] *AmE* a gear lever —see picture on page 409

**gear stick** /ˈ· ·/ *n* [C] *BrE* a gear lever —see picture on page 409

**geck·o** /ˈgekəʊ‖-koʊ/ *n* [C] a type of small LIZARD

**gee**[1] /dʒiː/ *interjection especially AmE* used to show that you are surprised or annoyed: *Aw, gee, Mom, do we have to go?*

**gee**[2] *v*

**gee up** *phr v* **1** [T] *BrE informal* to encourage someone to try harder: **gee** sb ↔**up** *The team needs a captain who can gee them up a bit.* **2 gee up!** used to tell a horse to go faster

**gee·gaw** /ˈdʒiːgɔː, ˈgiː-‖-gɒː/ *n* [C] another spelling of GEWGAW

**gee-gee** /ˈ· ·/ *n* [C] *BrE* a word meaning a horse, used by or to children, or when talking about HORSE RACING

**geek** /giːk/ *n* [C] *slang especially AmE* someone who is boring and wears clothes that are unfashionable —**geeky** *adj*

**geese** /giːs/ the plural of GOOSE[1] (1)

**gee whiz** /ˌ· ˈ·/ *interjection AmE old-fashioned* used to show that you are surprised or annoyed

**geez** /dʒiːz/ *interjection* another spelling of JEEZ

**gee·zer** /ˈgiːzə‖-ər/ *n* [C] *informal* a man: *a funny old geezer | Some stupid geezer had moved my bags.*

**Gei·ger count·er** /ˈgaɪgə ˌkaʊntə‖-gər ˌkaʊntər/ *n* [C] an instrument for finding and measuring RADIOACTIVITY

**gei·sha** /ˈgeɪʃə/ also **geisha girl** /ˈ·· ·/ *n* [C] a Japanese woman who is trained in the art of dancing, singing, and providing entertainment, especially for men

**gel[1]** /dʒel/ *n* [C,U] a thick, wet substance that is used in various bath or beauty products: *hair gel*

**gel[2]** *v* **gelled, gelling** [I] **1** if a liquid gels it becomes firmer or thicker; JELL (2) **2** if an idea or plan gels it becomes clearer or more definite: *My ideas gelled as I talked the problem over.* **3** if two or more people gel, they start working well together as a group

**gel[3]** /gel/ *n* [C] *old-fashioned* used to represent the word 'girl', when it is said in this way

**gel·a·tine** /ˈdʒelətiːn‖-tn/ also **gel·a·tin** /-tɪn‖-tn/ *AmE*— *n* **1** [U] a clear substance obtained from boiled animal bones, used for making JELLY **2** [C] a piece of coloured plastic that is put over a light to change its colour

**ge·lat·i·nous** /dʒɪˈlætɪnəs‖-ˈlætn-əs/ *adj* in a state between solid and liquid, like a JELLY (4)

**geld** /geld/ *v* [T] to remove the TESTICLES of a horse

**geld·ing** /ˈgeldɪŋ/ *n* [C] a horse that has been gelded

**gel·ig·nite** /ˈdʒelɪgnaɪt/ *n* [U] a very powerful explosive

**gem** /dʒem/ *n* [C] **1** a beautiful stone that has been cut into a special shape; jewel: *precious gems* **2** something that is very special or beautiful: *The capital, Tallin, is an architectural gem.* **3** a very helpful or useful person: *Ben, you're a real gem!*

**Gem·i·ni** /ˈdʒemɪnaɪ‖-ni/ *n* **1** [singular] the third sign of the ZODIAC, represented by TWINS[1] and believed to affect the character and life of people born between May 21 and June 21 **2** [C] someone who was born between May 21 and June 21

**Gen.** a written abbreviation of General

**gen[1]** /dʒen/ *n* [U] *BrE informal* information: **[+ on]** *She has all the gen on cheap flights.*

**gen[2]** *v* **genned, genning**

**gen up** *phr v* [T] *BrE informal* to learn a lot of information about something for a particular purpose **[+ on]** *It's a good idea to gen up on the company's product before the interview.*

**-ge·nar·i·an** /dʒəneəriən‖ -ner-/ *suffix* [in nouns and adjectives] someone who is a particular number of DECADES (=periods of 10 years) old: *an octogenarian* (=between 80 and 89 years old) | *a septuagenarian ex-judge*

**gen·darme** /ˈʒɒndɑːm‖ˈʒɑːndɑːrm/ *n* [C] a French policeman

**gen·der** /ˈdʒendə‖-ər/ *n* **1** [C,U] *formal* the fact of being male or female: *Discrimination on grounds of race or gender is forbidden.* **2 a)** [U] the system in some languages of marking words such as nouns, adjectives, and PRONOUNS as being MASCULINE (4), FEMININE (2), or NEUTER[1] (2) **b)** [C] a group such as FEMININE (2) into which words are divided in this system

**gender bend·er** /ˈ·· ˌ··/ *n* [C] *informal* someone, often a popular singer or entertainer, who behaves or dresses in a way typical of someone of the opposite sex

**gender-spe·cif·ic** /ˈ···ˌ··/ *adj* for males only, or females only: *This law is gender-specific, singling out women.*

**gene** /dʒiːn/ *n* [C] a small part of the material inside the NUCLEUS of a cell, that controls the development of the qualities that have been passed on to a living thing from its parents S2 W2

**ge·ne·al·o·gy** /ˌdʒiːniˈælədʒi/ *n* **1** [U] the study of the history of families **2** [C] an account of the history of a family, especially when shown in a drawing that shows how each person is related to the others —**genealogist** *n* [C] —**genealogical** /ˌdʒiːniəˈlɒdʒɪkəl◂‖-ˈlɑː-/ *adj* —**genealogically** /-kli/ *adv*

**gene pool** /ˈ· ·/ *n* [C] all of the genes available to a particular SPECIES

**gen·e·ra** /ˈdʒenərə/ the plural of GENUS

**gen·e·ral[1]** /ˈdʒenərəl/ *adj* S1 W1

**1** ▶ **NOT DETAILED** ◀ describing only the main features of something, not the details: *a general introduction to computing* | **general idea** *I've got a general idea of how I want the new room to look.* | **in general terms** (=without considering specific details) *The minister talked in general terms about the need for fairer taxation.*

**2 in general a)** usually or in most situations: *In general, about 10% of the candidates are eventually offered positions.* **b)** as a broad subject: *We're trying to raise awareness about the environment in general and air pollution in particular.*

**3** ▶ **AS A WHOLE** ◀ considered in terms of a whole situation, group, etc, not of the specific parts that it consists of; OVERALL[1]: *There are a few intelligent ones, but the general standard isn't very high.* | *We were impressed by the quality of their work and the general air of professionalism.* | **a general anaesthetic** (=for the whole body, not one part of it)

**4** ▶ **ORDINARY/NOT SPECIFIC** ◀ of an ordinary kind, not one particular kind: *I spend about 10 hours a week doing general cooking and cleaning.* | *How widespread is AIDS in the general population?* | *It's a good general fertilizer.*

**5** ▶ **MOST PEOPLE** ◀ shared by or affecting most people, or most of the people in a group: *Keynes' view of economics gained general acceptance in the 1930's.* | *How soon can the drug be made available for general use?*

**6 the general area/neighbourhood/location** not the exact place or direction, but somewhere near: *Several bombs landed in the same general area.*

**7** ▶ **JOB** ◀ used in the name of a job to show that the person who does this job has complete responsibility: *the general manager* | *the Attorney General*

**8 as a general rule** used to say what happens in most cases: *He doesn't give interviews as a general rule, but he's prepared to make an exception in this case.*

**9 the general public** ordinary people, who do not have important positions or belong to specific groups: *Health education is aimed at the general public as well as at high-risk groups.* | *The doors opened to the general public last night at the Klondyke Building.*

**10 in the general interest** in a way that helps or brings advantage to most people: *It's in the general interest to invest in public transportation.* —see also GENERALLY

**general[2]** *n* [C] an officer of very high rank in the army or air force —see table on page B4

**general coun·sel** /ˌ··· ˈ··/ *n* [C] **1** the chief legal officer of a US company **2** a firm of US lawyers that gives general technical advice

**general de·liv·er·y** /ˌ··· ·ˈ···/ *n* [U] *AmE* a post office department to which you can send letters for someone who is travelling and which will keep them until they are collected; POSTE RESTANTE *BrE*

**general e·lec·tion** /ˌ··· ·ˈ··/ *n* [C] an election in which all the people voting in a country vote at the same time to choose a government

**general head·quar·ters** /ˌ··· ·ˈ··/ *n* [plural] the place from which the actions of an organization, especially a military one, are controlled

**gen·e·ral·ise** /ˈdʒenərəlaɪz/ *v* a British spelling of GENERALIZE

G

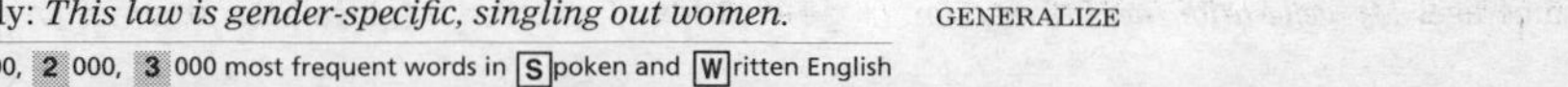

**gen·e·ral·i·ty** /ˌdʒenəˈrælᶟti/ *n* **1** [C often plural] a very general statement that avoids mentioning details or specific cases: *Can we stop dealing in generalities and start suggesting practical steps to take?* **2 the generality of** most of; the MAJORITY (1) of: *Temporary workers are considerably younger than the generality of workers.* **3** [U] *formal* the quality of being true or useful in most situations

**gen·e·ral·i·za·tion** also **-isation** *BrE* /ˌdʒenərəlaɪˈzeɪʃən‖-lə-/ *n* **1** [C] a general statement or opinion that is only partly true because it is based on only a few cases or incomplete knowledge: *You're making too many generalizations about an issue that you don't really understand.* | **sweeping generalization** (=saying that something is true in every case or situation): *Please! No sweeping generalizations like "all women are bad drivers".* **2** [U] the act of making generalizations

**gen·e·ral·ize** also **-ise** *BrE* /ˈdʒenərəlaɪz/ *v* **1** [I] to make a general statement about a number of different things or people without mentioning any details: *It's difficult to generalize about the typical Republican voter.* **2** [I] to form a general principle or opinion after considering only a small number of facts or examples: *It's stupid to generalize and say that all young people are rude.* | [+ **from**] *We can generalize from the samples and conclude that nitrogen levels have increased.* **3** [T] *formal* to put a principle, statement, or rule into a more general form so that it covers a larger number of examples: *I will first illustrate it by a simple example and then generalize it.*

**general knowl·edge** /ˌ··· ˈ··/ *n* [U] knowledge of facts about many different subjects: *a general knowledge quiz*

S1 W1 **gen·er·al·ly** /ˈdʒenərəli/ *adv* **1** in a general way, considering without details or specific cases: *The system has generally been found very easy to use.* | *She's not really ill, just generally run-down.* **2** by or to most people: *The plants are generally regarded as weeds.* | *So, is the plan generally acceptable?* **3** usually or most of the time: *Jonathan says he generally gets in to work by 8.00.* **4 generally speaking** used to introduce a statement that is true in most cases but not always: *Generally speaking, the more expensive the stereo, the better it is.*

G

**general prac·tice** /ˌ··· ˈ··/ *n* **1** [U] the work of a doctor or lawyer who deals with all the ordinary types of illness or legal case, rather than one specific type **2** [C] a group of lawyers or doctors who do all kinds of work

**general prac·ti·tion·er** /ˌ··· ˈ···/ *n* [C] a doctor who is trained in general medicine and treats people in a particular area or town; GP

**general-pur·pose** /ˌ··· ˈ··◂/ *adj* [only before noun] a general-purpose product, vehicle etc is suitable for most situations or jobs that such things are normally used for: *general-purpose glue*

**gen·er·al·ship** /ˈdʒenərəlʃɪp/ *n* [U] the skill of leading an army, developing plans for battle etc

**general staff** /ˌ··· ˈ·/ *n* **the general staff** the group of military officers who work for a commanding officer

**general store** /ˈ··· ˌ·/ *n* [C] *AmE* a shop that sells a wide variety of goods, especially one in a small town

**general strike** /ˌ··· ˈ·/ *n* [C] a time when most of the workers in a country refuse to work in order to protest about working conditions, wages, etc

W2 **gen·e·rate** /ˈdʒenəreɪt/ *v* [T] **1** to produce or create something: *a useful technique for generating new ideas* | *The program would generate a lot of new jobs.* | **generate sales/profits/income etc** *What sales volume would be required to generate an income of $96,000?* **2 generate excitement/interest/ill-feeling** to produce strong feelings among a large number of people: *News of the Queen's visit is generating a lot of excitement.* **3** to produce heat, electricity, or another form of energy: *The flowing water is used to drive turbines, which generate electricity.*

**gen·e·ra·tion** /ˌdʒenəˈreɪʃən/ *n* **1** [C] **a)** all people of about the same age: *My generation never knew an America before Vietnam.* | [also + plural verb *BrE*] *The younger generation don't know what hard work is.* **b)** all the members of a family of about the same age: *We're the fourth generation of Carters to live in this house.* | *a second-generation Canadian* (=whose parents are Canadian but whose grandparents were not) | **the generation gap** (=the lack of understanding between generations caused by their different attitudes and experiences) **2** [C] the average period of time between the birth of a person and the birth of that person's children: *Within a generation Japan regained the status of a great power.* **3** [C] all the members of a group of things which have been developed from a previous group: *the latest generation of anti-tank missiles* **4** [U] the process of producing something or making something happen: *the generation of electricity*

**gen·e·ra·tive** /ˈdʒenərətɪv/ *adj especially technical* able to produce something

**generative gram·mar** /ˌ···· ˈ··/ *n* [C,U] the description of a language using rules that produce all the sentences of the language that are correct according to the rules of grammar

**gen·e·ra·tor** /ˈdʒenəreɪtə‖-ər/ *n* [C] a machine that produces electricity: *a coal-powered generator*

**ge·ner·ic** /dʒᶟˈnerɪk/ *adj* **1 generic name/term/label etc** a word that describes a whole class of things: *Misogyny is the generic term for all hostile feelings and actions towards women.* **2** *technical* belonging to or typical of a GENUS **3** *especially AmE* a generic product does not have a TRADEMARK (1) —**generically** /-kli/ *adv*

**gen·e·ros·i·ty** /ˌdʒenəˈrɒsᶟti‖-ˈrɑː-/ *n* **1** [U] willingness to give money, time etc in order to help or please someone: *an act of great generosity* **2** [C] an act of being generous

**gen·e·rous** /ˈdʒenərəs/ *adj* **1** willing to give money, spend time etc, in order to help people or give them pleasure: [+ **to**] *She's always very generous to the kids.* | **it is generous of sb (to do sth)** *What lovely presents – it's very generous of you!* | **generous with your help/time/money etc** *I'd like to thank Simon, who's been very generous with his time.* **2** larger than the usual or expected amount: *a generous glass of port* | *We offer a generous salary and benefits package.* | *generous welfare payments* **3** sympathetic in the way you deal with people, and tending not to criticize them, get angry, or treat them unkindly: *She was generous enough to overlook my little mistake.* | *not a very generous attitude* —**generously** *adv*: *Please give generously to the refugee fund.*

**gen·e·sis** /ˈdʒenᶟsᶟs/ *n formal* **the genesis of** the beginning or origin of something: *a discovery that was to be a genesis of modern physics*

**gene ther·a·py** /ˈ· ˌ···/ *n* [U] a way of treating certain diseases by adding to the body a GENE that it does not have

**ge·net·ic** /dʒᶟˈnetɪk/ *adj* connected with GENES or GENETICS: *genetic defects* | *These abnormalities may have a genetic basis.*

**ge·net·ic·ally** /dʒəˈnetɪkli/ *adv* **1** in a way that is connected with GENETICS **2 genetically engineered** a vegetable, VIRUS etc that is genetically engineered has been produced by a method that involves changing the structure of its GENES

**genetic code** /·ˌ·· ˈ·/ *n* [C] the arrangement of GENES that controls the way a living thing develops

**genetic en·gin·eer·ing** /·ˌ·· ··ˈ··/ *n* [U] the science of changing the GENETIC structure of an animal, plant, or human in order to affect the way it develops —**genetic engineer** *n* [C]

**genetic fin·ger·print** /·ˌ·· ˈ···/ *n* [C] the pattern of GENETIC information which is different for each person or animal

**genetic fin·ger·print·ing** /·ˌ·· ˈ····/ *n* [U] the process of examining someone's GENETIC structure, especially in order to find out if they are guilty of a crime

**ge·net·ics** /dʒᶟˈnetɪks/ *n* [plural] the study of how the nature and development of living things is affected by their GENES (=the parts of their cells that pass on characteristics from their parents) —see also GENE, HEREDITY —**geneticist** /-tɪ̣sɪ̣st/ *n* [C]

**ge·ni·al** /ˈdʒiːniəl/ *adj* having a cheerful and friendly character or manner —**genially** *adv* [U] —**geniality** /ˌdʒiːniˈælɪ̣ti/ *n* [C]

**ge·nie** /ˈdʒiːni/ *n* [C] a magical spirit in old Arabian stories

**gen·i·tal** /ˈdʒenɪ̣tl/ *adj* connected with or affecting the outer sex organs: *genital herpes|genital mutilation* —**genitally** *adv*

**gen·i·tals** /ˈdʒenɪ̣tlz/ also **gen·i·ta·li·a** /ˌdʒenɪ̣ˈteɪliə/ *technical n* [plural] the outer sex organs

**gen·i·tive** /ˈdʒenɪ̣tɪv/ *n* [C] *technical* a form of the noun in some languages, which shows a relationship of possession or origin between one thing and another —**genitive** *adj*

**ge·ni·us** /ˈdʒiːniəs/ *n* **1** [U] a very high level of intelligence, mental skill, or artistic ability, which only a few people have: **a writer/work/woman etc of genius** *an imaginative novelist of great genius|The film reveals Fellini's genius.*|**a stroke of genius** (=a very clever idea) **2** [C] someone who has an unusually high level of intelligence, mental skill or artistic ability: *a musical genius|You can't compare him with a true genius like Einstein.*|**be a genius at sth** *Watch your money – Lou's a genius at cards.* **3 have a genius for (doing) sth** to be especially good at doing something: *Bernard had a genius for bringing out the best in his students.|Warhol's genius for publicity* **4** [U] the special quality of a particular group of people, period of time etc: *the French artistic genius*

**genius lo·ci** /ˌdʒiːniəs ˈləʊsaɪ‖-ˈloʊ-/ *n* [singular] *Latin* the typical character of a place and the feelings it produces in people

**gen·o·cide** /ˈdʒenəsaɪd/ *n* [U] the deliberate murder of a whole group or race of people: *the genocide of the Jews during the Holocaust* —**genocidal** /ˌdʒenəˈsaɪdl◂/ *adj*

**ge·nome** /ˈdʒiːnəʊm‖-noʊm/ *n* [C] *technical* the total of all the GENES that are found in one type of living thing: *the human genome*

**gen·re** /ˈʒɒnrə‖ˈʒɑːnrə/ *n* [C] *formal* a particular type of art, writing, music etc, which has certain characteristics that all examples of this type share: *Science fiction as a genre is relatively new.|Leon's movies are outstanding examples of the genre.*

**gent** /dʒent/ *n* [C] **1** *informal especially BrE* a GENTLEMAN: *Quite the gent, he was – in a dress shirt, top hat, and black overcoat.* **2 the gents** [singular] *BrE* a public toilet for men; MEN'S ROOM *AmE*

**gen·teel** /dʒenˈtiːl/ *adj* **1** behaving and speaking in an unnatural and very polite way, because you want people to think you belong to a high social class **2** *old-fashioned* of a high social class: *a genteel neighbourhood* —**genteelly** *adv*

**gen·tian** /ˈdʒenʃən/ *n* [C] a small plant with blue flowers that grows in mountain areas

**gentian vi·o·let** /ˌ·· ˈ···/ *n* [U] a purple ANTISEPTIC² (1) liquid that is used to treat burns or stings

**gen·tile** /ˈdʒentaɪl/ *n* [C] someone who is not Jewish —**gentile** *adj*

**gen·til·i·ty** /dʒenˈtɪlɪ̣ti/ *n* [U] *formal* the quality of appearing to belong to a high social class: *her pretensions to gentility*

S3 W3 **gen·tle** /ˈdʒentl/ *adj* **1** kind and careful in your character or behaviour and not at all violent or unpleasant: *Be gentle when you brush the baby's hair.|Lynne was a sweet, gentle girl.|a little gentle mockery*|[+ **with**] *He was incredibly gentle with her during her illness.* **2** not strong, loud, forceful, or extreme: *Take a little gentle exercise.|Mother's gentle laughter|the gentle warmth of the evening sun* **3** a gentle wind or rain is soft and light: *a gentle breeze clearing the mist* **4** a gentle hill or slope is not steep or sharp: *the gentle contours of the South Downs* —see also GENTLY —**gentleness** *n* [U]

**gen·tle·folk** /ˈdʒentlfəʊk‖-foʊk/ *n* [plural] *old use* people belonging to the higher social classes

**gen·tle·man** /ˈdʒentlmən/ *n* [C] **1** a man who always behaves towards other people in a polite and honourable way and who can be trusted to keep his promises: *a real gentleman|Martin – always the perfect gentleman – got to his feet when my mother walked in.* **2** a polite word for a man, used especially when talking to or about a man you do not know: *Could you serve this gentleman please, Ms Bath?*|**ladies and gentlemen** (=used at the beginning of a speech) **3** *old-fashioned* a man from a high social class, especially one whose family owns a lot of property S3 W2

**gentleman farm·er** /ˌ··· ˈ··/ *n* [C] *BrE* a man belonging to a high social class who owns and runs a farm for pleasure rather than profit

**gen·tle·man·ly** /ˈdʒentlmənli/ *adj* a man who is gentlemanly is polite, honourable, and always careful to consider other people's feelings

**gentleman's a·gree·ment** /ˌ··· ·ˈ··/ *n* [C] an agreement that is not written down, made between people who trust each other

**gen·tle·wo·man** /ˈdʒentlˌwʊmən/ *n* [C] *old use* a woman who belongs to a high social class

**gent·ly** /ˈdʒentli/ *adv* **1** in a gentle way: *I patted her gently on the shoulder.|The road curved gently upwards.* **2 gently!** *BrE spoken* used to tell someone to be careful when they are handling something, moving something etc: *Gently, Sammy, you don't want to break it.*|**gently does it** *Careful when you lift that desk – gently does it!* W3

**gen·tri·fic·ation** /ˌdʒentrɪ̣fɪ̣ˈkeɪʃən/ *n* [U] the process by which a street that poor people used to live in is changed when people with more money go to live there —**gentrify** /ˈdʒentrɪ̣faɪ/ *v* [T usually passive]

**gen·try** /ˈdʒentri/ *n* [plural] *old-fashioned* people who belong to a high social class: **the landed gentry** (=the gentry who own land)

**gen·u·flect** /ˈdʒenjʊ̣flekt/ *v* [I] to bend your knee when in church or a holy place as a sign of respect —**genuflection** /ˌdʒenjʊ̣ˈflekʃən/ *n* [C,U]

**gen·u·ine** /ˈdʒenjuɪ̣n/ *adj* **1** a genuine feeling, desire etc is one that you really feel, not one you pretend to feel in order to deceive people; sincere: *The reforms are motivated by a genuine concern for the disabled.* **2** something genuine really is what it seems to be; real: *It's either a genuine diamond or a very good fake.* **3** someone who is genuine is honest and friendly and you feel you can trust them: *Dan's a real genuine guy.* **4 the genuine article** *informal* a person, or sometimes a thing, that is a true example of their type: *If you want to meet a real Southerner, Jake is the genuine article.* —**genuinely** *adv: He genuinely believes in what he sells.* —**genuineness** *n* [U] S3 W3

**ge·nus** /ˈdʒiːnəs, ˈdʒen-/ *n plural* **genera** /ˈdʒenərə/ [C] *technical* one of the groups into which scientists divide animals or plants, below a FAMILY (5) and above a SPECIES —see also GENERIC

**ge·o-** /dʒiːəʊ, dʒɪə‖dʒioʊ, dʒɪə/ *prefix technical* concerning the Earth or its surface: *geophysics|geopolitical*

**ge·o·cen·tric** /ˌdʒiːəʊˈsentrɪk◂‖ˌdʒiːoʊ-/ *adj* having the Earth as the central point, or measured from the centre of the Earth: *Ptolemy's geocentric model of the universe*

**ge·o·de·sic dome** /ˈdʒiːəʊdiːsɪk ˈdəʊm‖-ədiːsɪk ˈdoʊm/ *n* [C] *technical* a large building shaped like a ball, made from small flat pieces that are connected together to form POLYGONS

**ge·og·ra·phy** /dʒiˈɒgrəfi, ˈdʒɒgrəfi‖dʒiˈɑːg-/ *n* [U] **1** the study of the countries, seas, rivers, towns etc of the world: *a geography lesson* —see also PHYSICAL GEOGRAPHY, POLITICAL GEOGRAPHY **2 the geography of** the way all the parts of a building, city etc are arranged: *The geography of the old section of Boston is really complicated.* —**geographer** *n* [C] —**geographical** /ˌdʒiːəˈgræfɪkəl◂/ *adj: a geographical area* —**geographically** /-kli/ *adv*

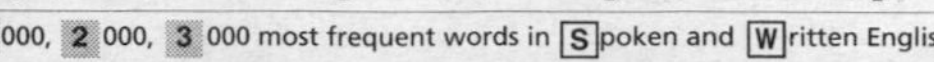

**ge·ol·o·gy** /dʒi'ɒlədʒi‖-'ɑːlə-/ *n* [U] the study of the rocks, soil etc that make up the Earth, and of the way they have changed since the Earth was formed —**geologist** *n* [C] —**geological** /ˌdʒiːə'lɒdʒɪkəl◂‖-'lɑː-/ *adj*: *geological periods* —**geologically** /-kli/ *adv*

**ge·o·met·ric** /ˌdʒiːə'metrɪk◂/ also **ge·o·met·ri·cal** /-trɪkəl/ *adj* **1** like the shapes and lines in GEOMETRY, especially in having regular patterns: *a geometric design* **2** related to GEOMETRY —**geometrically** /-kli/ *adv*

**geometric pro·gres·sion** /ˌ····'··/ *n* [U] a set of numbers in order, in which each is multiplied by a specific number to produce the next number in the series (as in 1, 2, 4, 8, 16,...) —compare ARITHMETIC PROGRESSION

**ge·om·e·try** /dʒi'ɒmɪ̈tri‖-'ɑːm-/ *n* [U] the study in MATHEMATICS of the angles and shapes formed by the relationships of lines, surfaces, and solid objects in space

**ge·o·phys·ics** /ˌdʒiːəʊ'fɪzɪks‖ˌdʒiːoʊ-/ *n* [U] the study of the movements of parts of the Earth, and the forces involved with it, including the weather, the sea beds etc —**geophysical** *adj* —**geophysicist** *n* [C]

**ge·o·pol·i·tics** /ˌdʒiːəʊ'pɒlɪ̈tɪks‖ˌdʒiːoʊ'pɑː-/ *n* [U] the study of the effects of a country's position, population etc on its political character and development —**geopolitical** /ˌdʒiːəʊpə'lɪtɪkəl◂‖ˌdʒiːoʊ-/ *adj*

**Geor·die** /'dʒɔːdi‖'dʒɔːr-/ *n BrE* **1** [C] someone from Tyneside in NE England **2** [U] a way of speaking typical of people from Tyneside —**Geordie** *adj*

**George** /dʒɔːdʒ‖dʒɔːrdʒ/ *n* **by George!** *old-fashioned spoken* used when you are pleasantly surprised: *By George, I think you're right!*

**geor·gette** /dʒɔː'dʒet‖dʒɔːr-/ *n* [U] a light strong material, used for making clothes

**Geor·gian** /'dʒɔːdʒən, -dʒiən‖'dʒɔːrdʒən/ *adj* **1** Georgian buildings, furniture etc come from the 18th century, when Britain was ruled by the Kings George the First, Second, and Third: *an elegant Georgian townhouse* **2** connected with the country of Georgia, in the Caucasus

G

**ge·o·sta·tion·ar·y** /ˌdʒiːəʊ'steɪʃənəri◂‖-oʊ'steɪ-ʃəneri◂/ also **geosynchronous** *adj* a geostationary spacecraft or SATELLITE (1) goes around the Earth at the same speed as the Earth moves, so that it is always above the same place on the Earth

**ge·ra·ni·um** /dʒə'reɪniəm/ *n* [C] a plant with red, pink, or white flowers and round leaves

**ger·bil** /'dʒɜːbəl‖'dʒɜːr-/ *n* [C] a small animal with fur, a tail and long back legs that is often kept as a pet

**ge·ri·at·ric** /ˌdʒeri'ætrɪk◂/ *adj* **1** [only before noun] connected with the medical care and treatment of old people: *The geriatric ward at the hospital is under threat of closure.* **2** *informal* too old to work properly or effectively: *geriatric judges|another of those geriatric 1960s rock bands*

**ge·ri·at·rics** /ˌdʒeri'ætrɪks/ *n* [U] the medical treatment and care of old people —compare GERONTOLOGY —**geriatrician** /ˌdʒeriə'trɪʃən/ *n* [C]

**germ** /dʒɜːm‖dʒɜːrm/ *n* [C] **1** *not technical* a bacterium (BACTERIA) that can make you ill: *This disinfectant kills all known germs.* **2 the germ of an idea/theory/feeling etc** the early stage of an idea, feeling etc that may develop into something bigger and more important: *This doctrine contains the germ of Hegel's later philosophy.* —see also WHEATGERM, GERM WARFARE

**Ger·man** /'dʒɜːmən‖'dʒɜːr-/ *n* **1** [C] someone who comes from Germany **2** [U] the language of Germany, Austria, and parts of Switzerland —**German** *adj*

**ger·mane** /dʒɜː'meɪn‖dʒɜːr-/ *adj formal* an idea, remark etc that is germane to something is connected with it in an important and suitable way; RELEVANT: [+ **to**] *It's an interesting idea, but not really germane to the main argument.|economic solutions germane to the present-day environment*

**Ger·man·ic** /dʒɜː'mænɪk‖dʒɜːr-/ *adj* **1** connected with the language family that includes German, Dutch, Swedish and English **2** typical of Germany or the Germans

**German mea·sles** /ˌ·· '··/ *n* [U] an infectious disease that causes red spots on your body, and can damage an unborn child; RUBELLA

**German shep·herd** /ˌ·· '··/ *n* [C] a large dog rather like a WOLF that is often used by the police, for guarding property etc; ALSATIAN *BrE* —see picture at DOG[1]

**ger·mi·cide** /'dʒɜːmɪ̈saɪd‖'dʒɜːr-/ *n* [C,U] a substance that kills BACTERIA

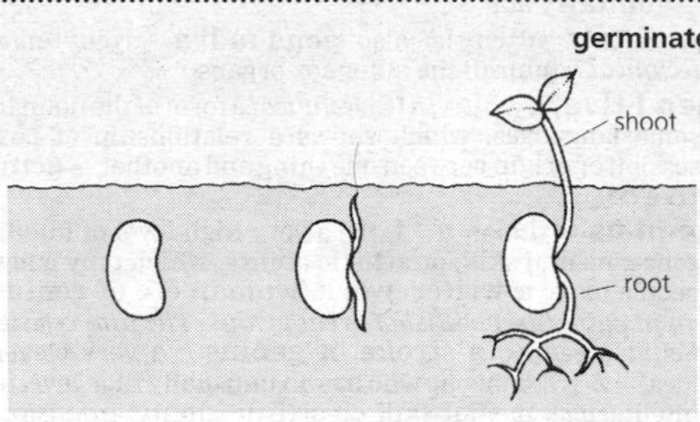


**ger·mi·nate** /'dʒɜːmɪ̈neɪt‖'dʒɜːr-/ *v* **1** [I,T] if a seed germinates or if it is germinated, it begins to grow: *Carnation seeds will germinate at a low temperature.* **2** [I] if an idea, feeling etc germinates, it begins to develop: *The idea of forming a business partnership began to germinate in his mind.* —**germination** /ˌdʒɜːmɪ̈'neɪʃən‖ˌdʒɜːr-/ *n* [U]

**germ war·fare** /ˌ· '··/ *n* [U] the use of harmful BACTERIA in war to cause illness and death among the enemy

**ge·ron·i·mo** /dʒə'rɒnɪ̈məʊ‖-'rɑːnɪ̈moʊ/ *interjection* a shout used by children when jumping off a high place

**ger·on·toc·ra·cy** /ˌdʒerɒn'tɒkrəsi‖ˌdʒerən'tɑː-/ *n* [C,U] government by old people, or a government that consists of old people

**ger·on·tol·o·gy** /ˌdʒerɒn'tɒlədʒi‖ˌdʒerən'tɑː-/ *n* [U] the scientific study of old age and the changes it causes in the body —compare GERIATRICS —**gerontologist** *n* [C] —**gerontological** /dʒəˌrɒntə'lɒdʒɪkəl◂‖-ˌrɑːntə'lɑː-/ *adj*

**ger·ry·man·der·ing** /'dʒerimændərɪŋ/ *n* [U] the practice of changing the size and borders of an area for election purposes, to deliberately give one group or party an unfair advantage over the others

**ger·und** /'dʒerənd/ *n* [C] *technical* a noun in the form of a PRESENT PARTICIPLE, that describes an action or experience, such as 'shopping', in the sentence 'I like shopping'; VERBAL NOUN

**ge·stalt** /gə'ʃtɑːlt/ *n* [C] *technical* a whole thing that is different from all its parts put together and has qualities that are not present in any of its parts: *gestalt psychology*

**ge·sta·po** /ge'stɑːpəʊ‖-poʊ/ *n* [C] the secret police force used by the state in Germany during the NAZI period

**ges·ta·tion** /dʒe'steɪʃən/ *n* **1** [U] *technical* the process by which a child or young animal develops inside its mother's body before birth **2** also **gestation period** [singular] **a)** *technical* the time during which a child or young animal develops inside its mother's body **b)** the time it takes to develop an idea, plan etc before it is made known

**ges·tic·u·late** /dʒe'stɪkjɪ̈leɪt/ *v* [I] to make movements with your arms and hands, usually while speaking, because you are excited, angry, or cannot think of the right words to use: *Jane gesticulated wildly and shouted "Stop! Stop!"* —**gesticulation** /dʒeˌstɪkjɪ̈'leɪʃən/ *n* [C,U] *Wild gesticulations of the hands accompanied his speech.*

**ges·ture[1]** /'dʒestʃə‖-ər/ *n* **1** [C,U] a movement of part of your body, especially your hands or head, to show what you mean or how you feel: *Jim raised his hands in a*  W3 *despairing gesture.* | *This form of sign language is rich in gesture.* **2** [C] something that you say or do, often something small, to show your feelings or intentions: *It was a kind gesture to offer to drive me home.* | **a gesture of friendship/goodwill/support etc** *The miners went on strike too, as a gesture of solidarity with the railway workers.* —**gestural** *adj*

**gesture**[2] *v* [I always + adv/prep] to use a movement of your hand to tell someone something, or show them what you mean: [+ **to/towards etc**] *"It's somewhere over there." He gestured vaguely at a group of buildings.* | **gesture for sb to do sth** *The lieutenant gestured for Cook to enter his office.*

**ge·sund·heit** /gəˈzʊndhaɪt/ *interjection AmE* used to wish someone good health when they have just sneezed (SNEEZE[1] (1))

**get** /get/ *v past tense* **got** /gɒt‖gɑːt/ *past participle* **got** *especially BrE* **gotten** /ˈgɒtn‖ˈgɑːtn/ *especially AmE, present participle* **getting** S1 W1

① RECEIVE/OBTAIN
② MOVE/GO/TRAVEL
③ HAVE/OWN
④ BECOME/MAKE STH BECOME
⑤ UNDERSTAND
⑥ OTHER MEANINGS

### ① RECEIVE/OBTAIN

**1 ▶RECEIVE◀** [T not in passive] to be given or receive something: *Sharon always seems to get loads of mail.* | *Why do I always get socks for Christmas?* | **get sth from/off sb** *Jordan says he got the drugs off a friend.* | **get a shock/surprise/thrill etc** *He'll get a real shock when he sees the bill.* —see graph at RECEIVE

**2 ▶OBTAIN◀** [T] to obtain something: *Where did you get that painting?* | *There's no place in town you can get a good haircut.* | **get sb sth** *He's just popped out to get me some stamps.* | **get sth for sb** *Gerrard was sent to get help for his sister.* —see OBTAIN (USAGE)

**3 ▶GET BY BUYING◀** [T] to buy something: *That cat-basket? I got it on Harlow Market.* | **get sth for $20/£100/50p etc** *You can't get a decent CD player for under $500.* | **get sth free/cheap etc** *Dee gets all her clothes cheap from charity shops.* | **get sb sth** *While you're out, could you get me a newspaper?* | **get sth for sb** *She got a ticket for Bobby as well.* —see graph at BUY

**4 ▶GET MONEY BY SELLING◀** [T] to receive a particular amount of money for something when you sell it: *How much are you expecting to get for your house?* | **get £10/50p/$100 etc for** *Ian got $500 for that old car of his.*

**5 ▶GET AN ILLNESS◀** [T not in passive] to catch an illness, especially one that is not very serious: *It's fairly unusual for adults to get measles.* | **get sth off/from** *He seems to have got a cold off one of the kids at playgroup.*

**6 ▶JOB◀** [T] to be given or offered a new job or position, especially because of your own efforts: *Why don't you get yourself a job instead of lazing around all day?* | **get promotion** (=be offered a more important, better paid job than the one you are already doing) *Some people have been here for years and have never got promotion.*

**7 ▶EARN MONEY◀** [T not in passive] to be earning a particular amount of money: *How much do you think Stewart gets?* | **get £3,000/£5/$100,000 etc a day/hour/year etc** *Tracey gets five dollars an hour canning fruit.*

### ② MOVE/GO/TRAVEL

**8 ▶ARRIVE◀** [I always + adv/prep] to arrive somewhere: *What time will we get there?* | **get to/as far as/up to etc** *Next day they got to the camp, tired and hungry.*

**9 get the train/bus/ferry etc** to travel somewhere on a train, bus etc: *I'm getting the train home tonight.*

**10 ▶MOVE◀** [I always +adv/prep] to move to or go somewhere: [+ **out of/over/into etc**] *Get out of my house!* | *Somehow, water had gotten in through the lining.*

**11 ▶MAKE STH MOVE◀** [T] to make something move to a different place or position, especially with some difficulty: **get sth out/through/off etc** *How on earth are they going to get that piano down the stairs?*

### ③ HAVE/OWN

**12 have got** *especially BrE* [T] to possess or own something: *What kind of car has she got?* | *Darren's got a Master's Degree in Linguistics.*

**13** [T] to have particular features or characteristics: *She's got an awful temper.* | *Mr Williams is about 80, and he's got a shiny bald head.*

### ④ BECOME/MAKE STH BECOME

**14** [linking verb] to change from one state, feeling etc to another; become: **get angry/cold/upset etc** *When I tried to talk to him about it, he just got really angry.* | *This is getting silly.* | **get lost/trapped/caught etc** (=to become lost, trapped etc) *Just think of all those people getting killed out there.* | *Nick's getting married in September.* | **get hot/cold/warm etc** *It's getting quite chilly out there.* | *Eat your dinner before it gets cold.* —see BECOME (USAGE)

**15** [T not in passive] to make someone or something do something: **get sb/sth to do sth** *Get Chris to wash his jeans occasionally.* | **get sth doing sth** *I wonder if Frankie could get this video working.*

**16 get going/moving/cracking etc** to make yourself do something or move somewhere more quickly: *What are we all waiting for? Let's get moving!*

**17 get to see/know/understand etc** to gradually begin to see, know, understand etc: *I'm sure the kids will soon get to like each other.*

**18 get to do sth** to be able to do something, especially when this is difficult or unusual: *Since the divorce, he hardly ever gets to see Jenny.*

### ⑤ UNDERSTAND

**19** [T not in passive or progressive] *informal* to understand something: **get the message/hint** (=to finally understand what someone has been trying to tell you, in an indirect way) *I get the message – you just don't want me to come with you.* | **get what/how/who etc** *She still doesn't get what the movie's about.*

**20 get it** *spoken* to understand something, especially after it has been explained to you several times: *Oh, the paper's supposed to go in this way up. I get it.*

**21 not get it** *spoken* to not understand something, especially a joke: *He just didn't get it.*

### ⑥ OTHER MEANINGS

**22 ▶BRING◀** [T] to bring someone or something back from somewhere; FETCH (1): *Run upstairs and get a pillow.* | **get sb/sth from** *She's just gone to get the kids from Mary-Ann's house.* | **go and get (sb) sb/sth** *Go and get me a cloth, would you?*

**23 ▶REACH A POINT◀** [I always + adv/prep] to reach a particular point or stage of something: **get to/**

[continued on next page]

[continued from previous page]
**as far as/up to etc** *He's already got up to page 200.*| *When you get to the end of the test paper, read it through.*
**24 ▶ CLOTHES ◀ get sth on/off etc** to put a piece of clothing on or take it off: *You'd better get those wet things off.*
**25 ▶ COOK ◀** [T not in passive] to prepare a meal: *Who's going to get the dinner tonight?*| **get sb dinner/lunch etc** *He expects her to get him his dinner every night.*
**26 you get** *spoken* used to say that something happens or exists: *I didn't know you got tigers in Europe.*
**27 get the door/phone etc** *spoken* to answer the door, a telephone etc *Can you get the door for me? I'm in the bath!*
**28 you've got me there** *spoken* used to say you do not know the answer to something: *"So how do you spell 'rhythm' then?" "You've got me there."*
**29 ▶ RADIO/TELEVISION ◀** [T not in passive or progressive] to be able to receive a particular radio signal, television station etc: *Can you get satellite TV here?*
**30 ▶ PUNISH ◀** [T not in passive or progressive] *spoken* to do something to harm or hurt someone who has harmed or hurt you: **get sb for sth** *I'm going to get you for that!*
**31 ▶ ATTACK ◀** [T not in passive or progressive] to attack or harm someone: *Good luck with the diving – and mind the sharks don't get you!*
**32 get sth fixed/done/mended etc** to spend time and effort fixing something, finishing a job etc: *It's about time we got the kitchen repainted.*
**33 it (really) gets me** *spoken* used to say that something really annoys you: *It really gets me the way he leaves wet towels on the bathroom floor.*
**34 get you/him/her** *spoken humorous* used to say that someone is trying to seem more important, clever etc than they really are: *Get you, talking about going on a luxury cruise!*

**get about** *BrE phr v* [I] **1** to be able to go or travel to different places: *She's eighty now, and doesn't get about much any more.* **2** if news or information gets about, it is told to a lot of people: *I don't mind you knowing, but I don't really want it to get about.* **3** *informal* if someone gets about, they have sexual relationships with a lot of different people

**get** sth ↔ **across** *phr v* [T not in passive] to succeed in communicating ideas, information etc to someone else: **get sth across to sb** *How can I get it across to you people how important this is?*

**get along** *phr v* [I] **1** if two or more people get along,they have a friendly relationship: *If you two are going to share a room, you'd better learn how to get along.*| [+ **with**] *I've always found him a bit difficult to get along with.* **2** to progress in something you are doing: *How's your granddaughter getting along at university?* **3** *spoken* to continue with something that you were doing before: *I'd like to stay and chat, but I really must be getting along.*

**get around** *phr v* **1** [I] to be able to go or travel to different places **2** [I] if news or information gets around or gets round, a lot of people come to hear about it: *It quickly got around that Joshua was back in town.* **3** [T **get around** sb] to gently persuade someone to do what you want by being nice to them: *Freddie knows exactly how to get around his mother.* **4** [T **get around** sth] to find a way of dealing with a problem, especially by trying to avoid it: *Bill's rather stupidly promised her a week in Paris – I don't know how he's going to get around that one.*

**get around to** *phr v* [T not in passive] to finally do something that you have been intending to do for some time: *I don't know when we'll get around to doing any more decorating.*

**get at** sb/sth *phr v* [T] **1** *informal* to criticize someone repeatedly in an annoying way: *She can't think why Moira's always getting at her.* **2** [not in passive] to seem to be saying something that other people do not completely understand: *What exactly are you getting at, Helen?* **3** to be able to reach something: *You have to use a ladder to get at the jars on the top shelves.* **4** to use threats to influence the decision of people who are involved in a court case: *At least eight members of the jury had been got at.* **5** to find something out, especially the truth about a situation: **get at the truth/facts/information etc** *They're prepared to use any means possible to get at the truth.*

**get away** *phr v* [I] **1** to succeed in leaving a place, especially when this is not easy: *There's a meeting after work, but I should be able to get away by seven.* **2** to escape from someone who is chasing you or trying to catch you: *The three men got away in a stolen car.*| [+ **from**] *Gillie managed to get away from the man and call the police.* **3** *informal* to take a holiday away from the place you normally live: *Will you manage to get away this summer?* **4 get away!** *BrE spoken* used to say you are very surprised by something or do not believe it: *"He's been invited to a garden party at Buckingham Palace." "Get away!"* **5 the one that got away** something good that you nearly had or that nearly happened, but did not

**get away from** *phr v* [T not in passive] **1** to begin to talk about other things rather than the subject you are supposed to be discussing: *I think we're getting away from the main issue.* **2 there's no getting away from** *spoken* used to say that a fact must be dealt with or considered: *There's no getting away from it – we just can't afford to move house at the moment.* **3 get away from it all** an expression used especially in advertisements meaning to have a relaxing holiday: *get away from it all in sunny Barbados.*

**get away with** *phr v* [T not in passive] **a)** to not be caught or punished for something you have done wrong: *I don't know how they manage to get away with paying such low wages.*| **get away with murder** *informal* (=repeatedly do something wrong, and not get caught or punished) *Just because he's been working here a long time, he thinks he can get away with murder.* **b)** *spoken* to be able to do something, even though it is not the best thing to do: *I think you could just about get away with wearing navy shoes with that dress.*

**get back** *phr v* **1** [I] to return to a place: *We'll probably get back at about nine.* **2** [I + **to**] to start doing something again or talking about something again: *Let's get back to the main point of the discussion.* **3** [T **get** sth ↔ **back**] to have something returned to you: *Did you get your books back?* **4** [T **get** sb **back**] *informal* to do something to hurt or harm someone who has hurt or harmed you: *Don't worry. I'll get her back for this!*

**get back at** sb *phr v* [T not in passive] to do something to hurt or harm someone who has hurt or harmed you: *He only asked Jean for a date to get back at his ex-girlfriend.*

**get back to** sb *phr v* [T] *especially spoken* used to say that you will try to talk to someone again later, especially on the telephone: *I'm a bit busy at the moment – can I get back to you?*

**get behind** *phr v* [I + **with**] if you get behind with a job, payments, rent etc, you have not done or paid as much of it as you should have done by now: *Try not to get too far behind with your work.*

**get by** *phr v* [I] to have enough money to buy the things you need, but no more: *Her old age pension gives her barely enough to get by.*| **get by on £5/$20/$100 etc** *With four kids to feed, Josie gets by on just $75 a week.*

**get down** *phr v* **1** [T not in passive **get** sb **down**] to gradually make someone feel unhappy and tired: *All this waiting and delay is really getting her down.* **2** [T **get** sth ↔ **down**] **a)** to write something, especially something that someone is saying: *a group of reporters trying to get down every word he said* **3** [T] to succeed in swallowing something **4** [I] *BrE* an expression used especially by children meaning to leave the table after a meal

**get down to** sth *phr v* [T] to finally start doing something that needs a lot of time or energy: *After Christmas I'm going to get down to some serious job-hunting.* | **get down to doing sth** *Isn't it time you got down to marking those papers?*

**get in** *phr v* **1** [I] to succeed in entering a place: *They arrived at the stadium in good time, but they still couldn't get in.* **2** [I] if a train, plane etc gets in at a particular time, that is the time it arrives: *What time does the bus get in?* **3** [I] to be elected to a position of political power: *It's unlikely the Liberal Democrats will get in again.* **4** [I] to arrive home: *I'll phone her as soon as I get in.* **5** [T **get** sth ↔ **in**] to gather together something such as crops and bring them to a sheltered place: *The whole village was involved with getting the harvest in.* **6** [T **get** sb ↔ **in**] to ask someone to come to your home or workplace to do a job, especially to repair something: *We'll have to get the engineer in.* **7** [T **get** sth **in**] to send something to a particular place or give it to a particular person: *Please can you get your assignments in by Thursday.* | *We have to get an insurance claim in as quickly as possible.* **8** [I] to succeed in getting a place at a university, college etc: *How many of your students got in this year?*

**get in on** *phr v* [T not in passive] *informal* to become involved in something that other people are doing or planning: **get in on the act** (=get involved in something exciting, interesting, important etc): *Now the Republicans are hoping to get in on the act.*

**get in with** sb *phr v* [T] *informal* to become friendly with someone, especially someone who could be helpful to you in some way: *He spends all his time trying to get in with the boss.*

**get into** **1 what's got into sb** *spoken* used to express surprise that someone is behaving very differently from the way they usually behave: *I don't know what's got into Danny – he's suddenly started doing all the cooking and cleaning.* **2 get (sb) into a temper/state etc** to become angry or make someone angry, become upset or make someone upset etc: *Don't get into a mood about it.* **3 get (sb) into trouble/difficulties etc** to do something that causes trouble for yourself or for someone else: *That's another fine mess you've got me into.* **4** [T not in passive] to start doing something habitually: **get into the habit/way/routine etc of** *He had gotten into the habit of walking home through the park.* **5** [T not in passive] *informal* to begin to be interested in an activity or subject: *Lots of my friends are getting into Green politics.* **6 cannot get into** *informal* if you cannot get into clothes, they are too small for you

**get off** *phr v* **1** [I] to start a journey: *They're planning to get off by midday.* **2** [T **get** sth **off**] to send a letter, parcel etc by mail: *I'll have to get this letter off by tonight.* **3** [I] if a criminal gets off, they get little or no official punishment for their crime: *Financial fraudsters often get off because the details of the case are too complex to be understood by juries.* **4** [T **get** sb **off** sth] to help someone avoid being punished for a crime or something they have done wrong: *I'll pay anything you ask if you manage to get her off.* **5** [I **get** sb **off**] to succeed in making someone, especially a baby, go to sleep: *Guy's upstairs trying to get the baby off.* | **get sb off to sleep** *Has she got the baby off to sleep yet?* **6** [I] *AmE informal* to have an ORGASM **7** [I,T] to finish work and leave your workplace at the end of the day: *What time do you get off work?* | [+ **at**] *Shelley gets off at five-thirty.* **8 Get off!** *spoken* used to tell someone to stop touching you or to keep away from something **9 tell sb where to get off** *spoken* to tell someone that they are asking you for too much or are behaving in a way you will not accept: *"She expects me to look after her kids all the time." "If I were you I'd tell her where to get off."*

**get off on** sth *phr v* [T not in passive] *informal* to become excited by something, especially sexually excited

**get off to** *phr v* [T not in passive] to start to do something in a particular way: **get off to a good/bad start** *As far as school goes, Johnnie has got off to an extremely good start.*

**get off with** *phr v* [T not in passive] *informal* to start a sexual relationship with someone: *She spent the whole evening trying to get off with Phil.*

**get on** *phr v*
**1** [I] *especially BrE* if two or more people get on, they have a friendly relationship with each other: [+ **with**] *How does Gina get on with her colleagues?*
**2 ▶ PROGRESS ◀** [I] to make progress in something you are doing; GET ALONG (2): *He's new here, but he seems to be getting on fine.*
**3 be getting on a)** if time is getting on, it is getting late: *Tell Rea to hurry – it's getting on.* **b)** *informal* if someone is getting on, they are getting old: *We're both getting on now.*
**4 ▶ CONTINUE DOING STH ◀** [I] to continue with something you were doing before [+ **with**] *Get on with your work!*
**5 ▶ ABLE TO DO STH ◀** [I] to be able to do something, in spite of problems or difficulties: *I don't know how we'll manage to get on without you.*
**6 get it on** *AmE* to have sex: *Do you think those two have got it on yet?*
**7 Get on with it!** *spoken* used to tell someone to hurry: *Will you lot stop messing around and get on with it!*
**8 let sb get on with it a)** *spoken* used to say that you do not care what someone does, even though it might have bad results: *Well, if she wants to go ahead and ruin her career, let her get on with it.* **b)** to let someone do something without your help or advice: *Why can't my parents ever just let me get on with it?*
**9 Get on/along with you!** *old-fashioned spoken* used to say you do not believe what someone has said

**be getting on for** *phr v* [T not in passive] **be getting on for 90/10 o'clock/2,000 etc** to be almost that age, time, number etc: *Mrs McIntyre must be getting on for 90 by now.* | *They paid getting on for $100,000 for it.*

**get onto** *phr v* [T not in passive] **1** to speak or write to someone, especially someone you want to help you: *I'm afraid I can't help you – you'd better get onto the Foreign Office.* **2** to find out about someone who has been doing something wrong: *Why did the police fail to get onto this gang earlier?* **3** to be elected as a member of a committee, a political organization etc: *Very few women ever get onto industry's controlling bodies.* **4** to begin to talk about a subject after you have been discussing something else: *After a few minutes they got onto the subject of the election.*

**get out** *phr v* **1** [I] to escape from somewhere: *How on earth did the dog manage to get out?* | [+ **of**] *No-one's ever gotten out of this jail.* **2** [T **get** sb **out**] to help someone escape from or leave somewhere: *Asylum seekers have appealed to the President to help get them out.* **3** [I] if information gets out, a lot of people know about it though it is meant to be secret: *We have to make absolutely certain that none of this gets out.* | **get out that** *It's bound to get out that he's retiring soon.* **4** [T **get** sth ↔ **out**] to succeed in producing or publishing PUBLISH something: *They said they'd try and get the catalog out by the end of the month.* **5** [T **get** sth ↔ **out**] to succeed in saying something, especially when this is very difficult: *I wanted to tell him I loved him, but couldn't get the words out.*

**get out of** *phr v* [T not in passive] **1** to avoid doing something you have promised to do or are supposed to do: *See if you can get out of that meeting tomorrow.* | **get out of doing sth** *Danny's always trying to get out of taking the kids to school.* **2** [**get** sb **out of**] to help someone to avoid doing something they are supposed to do: *Wendy wants you to try and get her out of classes tomorrow.* | **get sb out of doing sth** *OK, I'll see if I can get you out of having to testify.* **3** [ **get** sth **out of** sb] to force or persuade someone to tell you

[continued on next page]

[continued from previous page]
something or give you something **4** [**get** sth **out of** sth] to gain pleasure or enjoyment from something: *I don't know what people get out of listening to deafeningly loud music.*

**get over 1 a)** [T not in passive] to get well again after an illness: *She's still trying to get over that bout of flu she had.* **b)** to begin to feel better after an upsetting emotional experience: *Some people never really get over the early death of a parent.* **2** [T **get** sth ↔ **over**] to succeed in communicating ideas, information etc to other people: *There's no point in having brilliant ideas unless you can get them over.* **3** [T **get** sth **over**] to do and finish something difficult that you have to do: *Angela says she'll be in touch when she gets her exams over.* | **get sth over with** *I'll speak first if you like – I'd rather get it over with quickly.* **4** [**get over** sth] to successfully deal with problems, difficulties etc: *Once we've got over the first few months, we should be making a reasonable profit.* **5 can't/couldn't get over** *spoken* used to say that you are very surprised, shocked, or amused by something: *Carrie couldn't get over how thin and pale he looked.* | **I just can't/couldn't get over it** *They suddenly fired all the company directors. I just can't get over it.*

**get round** *phr v BrE* **1** [I] if news or information gets round, it is told to a lot of people: **get round that** *It wasn't long before it got round that Tracey was going out with James.* **2** [T **get round** sth] to find a way of dealing with a problem, especially by trying to avoid it: *There's no way your mother can stay here – we'll just have to get round it somehow.* **3** [T **get round** sb] to gently persuade someone to do what you want by being nice to them: *He's determined he won't give in – see if you can get round him.*

**get round to** *phr v* [T not in passive] *BrE* to finally do something that you have been intending to do for some time, but have not because you were too busy, too lazy etc *I haven't even got around to unpacking from my holiday yet!*

**get through** *phr v* **1** [T not in passive] to come to the end of a difficult or unpleasant experience or period of time: *It's going to be hard to get through the next couple of days.* **2** [I,T] to pass a test, examination etc: *I'm afraid your daughter failed to get through her mid-term exams.* **3** [T **get** sb/sth **through** sth] to make sure someone or something passes an examination, test etc: *You'll never get that old car through its smog test.* **4** [T **get** ↔sth **through**] to succeed in having a plan, new law etc approved by an official group: *Once again we failed to get the Bill through Parliament.* **5** [I] to succeed in reaching someone by telephone: [+ **to**] *At last I managed to get through to one of the managers.* **6** [T **get through** sth] to use a lot of something or spend a lot of money: *He gets through at least $500 every weekend.*

**get through to** *phr v* [I,T **get** sth **through to** sb] to succeed in making someone understand something, especially when this is difficult: **get it through to sb (that)** *You must try and get it through to them that this is no joke.*

**get to sb** *phr v* [T] *informal* to make you feel very annoyed or upset: *I know they're being unfair, but don't let them get to you.* —see REACH (USAGE)

**get together** *phr v* **1** [I] if two or more people get together, they meet each other: *We must get together some time for a drink.* | [+ **with**] *It's ages since I got together with the gang from school.* **2** [I] if two people get together, they start a romantic or sexual relationship: *Those two should get together – they have a lot in common.* **3 get yourself together** to begin to be in control of your life, your emotions etc: *She needs a bit of time to get herself together.* **4 get it together** *spoken* **a)** [I] to begin to be in control of your life, your emotions etc: *If this team doesn't get it together by next month, we'll all be fired.* **b)** if two people get it together, they begin to develop a romantic or sexual relationship with each other

**get up** *phr v* **1** [I] to wake up and get out of your bed after sleeping, especially in the morning: *What time did you get up this morning?* **2** [T **get** sb **up**] to make someone wake up and get out of their bed, especially in the morning: *Get me up at seven, would you?* **3** [I] to stand up: *No, please don't get up.* **4** [I] if a wind or storm gets up, it starts and gets stronger **5** [T **get** sth **up**] to organize something: *She's getting a collection up for Sue's birthday.* **6 get sb up as** *BrE* to dress someone as someone or something else: *He arrived at the party got up as Count Dracula.* **7 get it up** *informal* to get an ERECTION (1) **8 get up speed/steam** to begin to move or travel faster

**get up to** *phr v* [T] to do something, especially something slightly bad: *Go upstairs and see what the kids are getting up to.*

**get·a·way** /ˈgetəweɪ/ *n* [C] **make a getaway** to escape from somewhere after doing something criminal, or to get away from an unpleasant situation: *The thieves made a getaway through a downstairs window.* | **getaway car** (=a car used by criminals to escape after a crime)

**get-go** /ˈ· ·/ *n* **from the get-go** *AmE informal* from the beginning: *From the get-go, I knew these tapes were special.*

**get-to·geth·er** /ˈ· ·,··/ *n* [C] a friendly informal meeting or party: *a family get-together*

**get·up** /ˈgetʌp/ *n* [C] *informal* a set of clothes, especially strange or unusual clothes: *I hardly recognized him in that getup!*

**get-up-and-go** /,· · · ˈ·/ *n* [U] *informal* energy, and determination to do things *He was the only candidate who had some get-up-and-go.*

**gew·gaw** /ˈgjuːgɔː, ˈguː-‖-gɒː/ *n* [C] a cheap brightly coloured piece of jewellery or decoration

**gey·ser** /ˈgiːzə‖ˈgaɪzər/ *n* [C] **1** a natural spring of hot water that sometimes rises suddenly into the air **2** a machine fixed to a wall over a bath or SINK and used for heating water in some British houses

**ghast·ly** /ˈgɑːstli‖ˈgæstli/ *adj* **1** a ghastly situation, person, experience etc is one that you do not like or enjoy at all: *What ghastly weather!* | *I hope they don't bring their ghastly children with them.* | *It was absolutely ghastly.* **2** making you very frightened, upset or shocked: *a ghastly accident* **3 look/feel ghastly** to look or feel ill, upset, or unhappy: *Are you alright? You look ghastly!* —**ghastliness** *n* [U]

**ghat** /gɔːt‖gɒːt/ *n* [C] *IndE & PakE* **1** a set of steps leading down to a river or lake **2** a place where dead bodies are burnt in a ceremony

**ghee** /giː/ *n* [U] melted butter made from the milk of a cow or BUFFALO, used in Indian cooking

**gher·kin** /ˈgɜːkɪn‖ˈgɜːr-/ *n* [C] a small type of CUCUMBER that has been preserved in VINEGAR

**ghet·to** /ˈgetəʊ‖-toʊ/ *n plural* **ghettos** *or* **ghettoes** [C] **1** a part of a city where people of a particular race or class live separately from the main population, usually in bad conditions **2** a part of a city where Jews were forced to live in former times: *She was born in a Polish ghetto.*

**ghetto blast·er** /ˈ·· ,··/ *n* [C] *informal* a large radio and TAPE RECORDER that can be carried around, and is often played very loudly in public places; BOOM BOX *AmE*

**ghet·to·ize** *v* also **-ise** *BrE* /ˈgetəʊaɪz‖-toʊ-/ [T] **1** to force people to live in a ghetto **2** to make part of a town become a ghetto

**ghi** /giː/ *n* [U] another spelling of GHEE

**ghost**[1] /gəʊst‖goʊst/ *n* [C] **1** the spirit of a dead person that some people think they can feel or see in a place: *The ghosts of past landlords are said to haunt this pub.* | **ghost story** *We used to scare each other by telling ghost stories at night.* —see also HOLY GHOST **2 the ghost of a smile/sound etc** a smile etc that is so slight you are not sure it happened: *He had the ghost of a smile on his lips.* **3** a GHOST WRITER **4** a second image that is not clear, especially on a television picture **5 give up the ghost** *humorous* **a)** to die **b)** if a machine gives up the ghost, it does not work any more and cannot be repaired: *My car's finally given up the ghost – I'm selling it for scrap.* **6 not a ghost of a chance** not even a slight chance of doing something, or of something happening: *There's not a ghost of a chance of finding the missing child now.*

**ghost[2]** *v* [T] to write something as a GHOST WRITER

**ghost·ly** /ˈgəʊstli‖ˈgoʊst-/ *adj* slightly frightening and seeming to be connected with ghosts or spirits: *a ghostly stare* —**ghostly** *adv*: *ghostly pale* —**ghostliness** *n* [U]

**ghost town** /ˈ· ·/ *n* [C] a town that used to have a lot of people living and working in it, but now has very few

**ghost train** /ˈ· ·/ *n* [C] a small train ride at a British FUNFAIR, that is designed to frighten you by taking you through a dark place full of SKELETONS (1) and things that jump out at you

**ghost writ·er** /ˈ· ˌ··/ *n* [C] someone who writes a book or story for another person who then says it is their own work —**ghost-write** *v* [T]

**ghoul** /guːl/ *n* [C] **1** an evil spirit in stories that takes bodies from graves and eats them **2** someone who gets pleasure from unpleasant things such as accidents that shock other people —**ghoulish** *adj* —**ghoulishness** *n* [U]

**GHQ** /ˌdʒiː eɪtʃ ˈkjuː/ *n* [U] General Headquarters; the place that a large military operation is controlled from

**GI** /ˌdʒiː ˈaɪ/ *n* [C] a soldier in the US army, especially during the Second World War

**gi·ant[1]** /ˈdʒaɪənt/ *adj* [only before noun] extremely big and much bigger than other things of the same type: *a giant sized box of detergent* | *a giant supermarket just outside town*

**giant[2]** *n* [C] **1** a very tall, strong man in children's stories who is often bad and cruel **2** a very large, successful company: *the German chemicals giant, BASF* **3** a very big man **4** someone who is very good at doing something: *Scorcese is a giant of the American cinema.*

**gi·ant·ess** /ˈdʒaɪəntes/ *n* [C] an extremely tall strong woman in children's stories who is often bad and cruel

**giant kil·ler** /ˈ·· ˌ··/ *n* [C] *BrE* a person, sports team etc that defeats a much stronger opponent

**giant pan·da** /ˌ·· ˈ··/ *n* [C] a PANDA (1)

**gib·ber** /ˈdʒɪbə‖-ər/ *v* [I] to speak quickly in a way that no one can understand, especially because you are very frightened or shocked: *The little boy was soaking wet and gibbering with agitation.*

**gib·ber·ing** /ˈdʒɪbərɪŋ/ *adj BrE* so frightened, shocked, or excited that you speak quickly in a way that no one can understand: **a gibbering wreck** (=someone who is very shocked or frightened)

**gib·ber·ish** /ˈdʒɪbərɪʃ/ *n* [U] something you write or say that has no meaning, or is very difficult to understand: *You're talking gibberish!*

**gib·bet** /ˈdʒɪbɪ̈t/ *n* [C] a wooden frame on which criminals were hanged (HANG[1] (3)) in the past with a rope around their neck

**gib·bon** /ˈgɪbən/ *n* [C] a small animal like a monkey, with long arms and no tail, that lives in trees in Asia

**gibe** /dʒaɪb/ *n* [C] another spelling of JIBE

**gib·lets** /ˈdʒɪblɪ̈ts/ *n* [plural] the inside parts of a bird that can be eaten, and are taken out before the bird is cooked

**gid·dy[1]** /ˈgɪdi/ *adj* **1** feeling slightly sick and unable to balance, because everything seems to be moving; DIZZY (1): *Just watching those kids spinning makes me feel giddy.* **2 be giddy with sth** to be very happy because something good has happened: *Amanda was giddy with success.* **3** [only before noun] making you feel as if you may fall: *a giddy height* **4** *old-fashioned* silly and not interested in serious things: *Fiona's very pretty but a bit giddy.* —**giddily** *adv* —**giddiness** *n* [U]

**giddy[2]** *v*
**giddy up** [I] used to command a horse to go faster

**gift** /gɪft/ *n* [C] S2 W2
**1** ▶ **OBJECT** ◀ something that you give someone on a special occasion or to thank them: *The earrings were a gift from my aunt.* | **make sb a gift of sth** *Grandma made me a gift of her silver.* | **free gift** *Enjoy a free gift with any purchase of $20 or more.*
**2** ▶ **ABILITY** ◀ a natural ability; TALENT (1): *Donne's poetic gift* | [+ **for**] *Dee has a gift for making everyone feel at ease.* —see also GIFTED
**3 a gift** *BrE informal* something that is easier or cheaper than you expected: *The exam paper was a gift.*
**4 the gift of the gab** *informal* an ability to speak confidently and to persuade people to do what you want
**5 be in someone's gift** *BrE informal* to be in someone's power to give a favour to someone they choose: *The chairmanship of this committee is in the gift of the minister.*
**6 never/don't look a gift horse in the mouth** *informal* used to tell someone to be grateful for something that has been given to them, instead of asking questions about it or finding something wrong with it —see also **God's gift to women/men etc** (GOD (15))

**gift cer·tif·i·cate** /ˈ· ·ˌ···/ *n* [C] *AmE* a special piece of paper that is worth a particular amount of money when it is exchanged for goods in a shop; GIFT TOKEN *BrE*

**gift·ed** /ˈgɪftɪ̈d/ *adj* having a natural ability to do one or more things extremely well: *a gifted pianist* | **gifted child** (=one who is extremely intelligent)

**gift shop** /ˈ· ·/ *n* [C] a shop that sells small things that are suitable for giving as presents

**gift to·ken** /ˈ· ˌ··/ *n* [C] a special piece of paper that is worth a particular amount of money when it is exchanged for goods in a shop; GIFT CERTIFICATE *AmE*

**gift vou·cher** /ˈ· ˌ··/ *n* [C] a gift token

**gift-wrap** /ˈ· ·/ *v* [T] to wrap a present with attractive coloured paper: *Would you like it gift-wrapped?*

**gig[1]** /gɪg/ *n* [C] **1** a performance by a musician or a group of musicians playing modern popular music or JAZZ[1] (1) **2** a small carriage with two wheels and pulled by one horse

**gig[2]** **gigged, gigging** *v* [I] to give a performance of modern popular music or JAZZ[1] (1)

**gig·a·byte** /ˈgɪgəbaɪt/ *n* [C] *technical* one BILLION BYTES

**gi·gan·tic** /dʒaɪˈgæntɪk/ *adj* extremely big: *a gigantic skyscraper* —**gigantically** /-kli/ *adv*

**gig·gle[1]** /ˈgɪgəl/ **giggled, giggling** *v* [I] to laugh quietly and often like a child, because something is funny, or because you are nervous or embarrassed: *If you can't stop giggling you'll have to leave the classroom.* —**giggly** *adj*

**giggle[2]** *n* **1** [C] a quiet, repeated laugh: *She broke into a nervous giggle whenever the manager spoke to her.* **2 have (a fit of) the giggles** *informal* to be unable to stop giggling **3 give sb the giggles** *informal* to make someone unable to stop giggling **4 a giggle** *especially BrE informal* something that you think is fun to do that will not hurt anyone or anything: *We used to hide Mum's keys for a giggle.*

**gig·o·lo** /ˈʒɪgələʊ, ˈdʒɪ-‖-loʊ/ *n plural* **gigolos** [C] a man who has sex with women for money

**gild** /gɪld/ *v* [T] **1** to cover something with a thin layer of gold or with something that looks like gold: *an ornate gilded mirror* **2** *literary* to make something look as if it is covered in gold: *The autumn sun gilded the lake.* **3 gild the lily** *BrE* to spoil something by trying to improve it when it is already good enough

**gill[1]** /gɪl/ *n* [C] **1** one of the organs on the sides of a fish through which it breathes —see picture at FISH[1] **2** one of the thin pale lines on the bottom of a MUSHROOM[1] **3 green/pale about the gills** *informal* looking sick because you are shocked, afraid, or ill

**gill[2]** /dʒɪl/ *n* [C] a measure of liquid equal to 0.142 litres —see table on page B2

**gil·lie** /ˈgɪli/ *n* [C] a man who acts as a guide to someone who is fishing or shooting for sport in Scotland

G

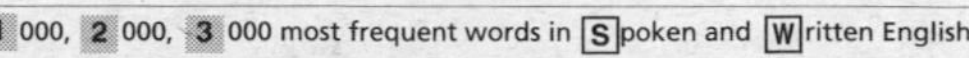

**gilt[1]** /gɪlt/ *n* **1** [U] a thin shiny material, such as gold or something similar, used to cover objects for decoration **2** [C] a SHARE[2] (6) that is GILT-EDGED **3** [C] *especially AmE* a young female pig

**gilt[2]** *adj* [only before noun] covered with gilt: *gilt lettering*

**gilt-edged** /ˌ· ˈ·◂/ *adj technical* gilt-edged stocks (STOCK[1] (3)) or shares (SHARE[2] (6)) do not give you much INTEREST (=additional money) but are considered very safe as they are sold mainly by governments

**gim·crack** /ˈdʒɪmkræk/ *adj* [only before noun] cheap and badly made

**gim·let** /ˈgɪmlɪ̈t/ *n* [C] **1** a tool that is used to make small holes in wood so that you can put screws in easily **2 gimlet-eyed/gimlet eyes** if someone is gimlet-eyed, or has gimlet eyes, they look at things very hard and notice every detail **3** an alcoholic drink made with GIN (1) or VODKA and LIME[1] (1)

**gim·me** /ˈgɪmi/ *spoken* a short form of 'give me' that many people think is incorrect: *Gimme that! It's mine!*

**gim·mick** /ˈgɪmɪk/ *n* [C] *informal* **1** a trick or an object that makes you notice a product and want to buy it: *advertising gimmicks* **2** something unusual that someone does to make people notice them —**gimmicky** *adj* —**gimmickry** *n* [U]

**gin** /dʒɪn/ *n* **1** [C,U] a strong alcoholic drink made mainly from grain —see also PINK GIN, GIN AND TONIC **2** [C] a trap for catching small animals or birds —see also COTTON GIN

**gin and ton·ic** /ˌ· · ˈ··/ *n* [C,U] a popular alcoholic drink served with ice and a thin piece of LEMON (1) or LIME[1] (1)

**gin·ger[1]** /ˈdʒɪndʒə‖-ər/ *n* [U] a root with a very strong hot taste that is used in cooking, or the plant that has this root —see picture on page 414

**ginger[2]** *adj* **1** *BrE* hair or fur that is ginger is bright orange-brown in colour —see picture on page 412 **2** [only before noun] flavoured with ginger

**ginger[3]** *v BrE*
  **ginger** sth ↔ **up** *phr v* [T] to make something more exciting

**ginger ale** /ˌ·· ˈ·‖ˈ·· ·/ *n* [C,U] a non-alcoholic drink that tastes of ginger and is often mixed with alcohol

**ginger beer** /ˌ·· ˈ·‖ˈ·· ·/ *n* [C,U] a non-alcoholic drink with a strong taste of ginger

**gin·ger·bread** /ˈdʒɪndʒəbred‖-dʒər-/ *n* **1** [U] a sweet cake or BISCUIT (1) with ginger in it **2 gingerbread man** a piece of gingerbread in the shape of a person

**ginger group** /ˈ·· ·/ *n* [C] *BrE* a group of people within a political party or organization that tries to persuade the other members to support their ideas —compare LOBBY[1] (2)

**gin·ger·ly** /ˈdʒɪndʒəli‖-ər-/ *adv, adj* if you move gingerly or touch something gingerly you do it in a careful way because you are afraid it will be dangerous or painful: *He gingerly felt his way along the dark tunnel.*

**ginger nut** /ˈ·· ·/ *BrE* **ginger snap** *AmE n* [C] a hard BISCUIT (1) with ginger in it

**ging·ham** /ˈgɪŋəm/ *n* [U] cotton cloth that has a pattern of small squares in white and one dark colour: *a red and white gingham tablecloth* —see picture on page 839

**gin·gi·vi·tis** /ˌdʒɪndʒɪ̈ˈvaɪtɪ̈s/ *n* [U] a medical condition in which your GUMS are red, swollen, and painful

**gi·nor·mous** /dʒaɪˈnɔːməs‖-ˈnɔːr-/ *adj BrE informal* extremely large: *Look Mum! It's ginormous!* —**ginormously** *adv*

**gin rum·my** /ˌ· ˈ··/ *n* [U] a type of RUMMY (=card game for two people)

**gin·seng** /ˈdʒɪnseŋ‖-sæŋ, -seŋ/ *n* [U] medicine made from the root of a Chinese plant, that some people think keeps you young and healthy

**gin sling** /ˌ· ˈ·/ *n* [C] a drink made from GIN (1) mixed with water, sugar, and LEMON or LIME juice

**gin trap** /ˈ· ·/ *n* [C] a GIN (2)

**gip·sy** /ˈdʒɪpsi/ *n* [C] a British spelling of GYPSY

**gi·raffe** /dʒɪ̈ˈrɑːf‖-ˈræf/ *n* [C] an extremely tall African animal with a very long neck and legs and pale brown fur with dark spots

**gird** /gɜːd‖gɜːrd/ *v past tense and past participle* **girded** *or* **girt** /gɜːt‖gɜːrt/ [T] *literary* **1 gird (up) your loins** *biblical or humorous* to get ready to do something **2** to fasten something around you

**gir·der** /ˈgɜːdə‖ˈgɜːrdər/ *n* [C] a strong beam, made of iron or steel, that supports a floor, roof, or bridge

**gir·dle** /ˈgɜːdl‖ˈgɜːr-/ *n* [C] **1** a piece of women's underwear which fits tightly around her stomach, bottom, and HIPS[1] (1) and makes her look thinner **2** *ScotE* a GRIDDLE

**girl** /gɜːl‖gɜːrl/ *n* [C] **S W**

**1 ► CHILD ◄** a female child: *Don't do that, you naughty girl!* | **little girl** *spoken*: *I used to go there on vacation when I was a little girl.*

**2 ► DAUGHTER ◄** a daughter: *They have two girls and a boy.*

**3 ► WOMAN ◄** a word meaning a woman, which is sometimes considered offensive by women: *the office girls*

**4 girls** [plural] used by a woman to address a group of other women that she knows well: *Come on girls!*

**5 the girls** *informal* a woman's female friends: *a night out with the girls*

**6 old girl a)** *informal* an old woman: *Surely the old girl's dead by now?* **b)** *old-fashioned* used to address a woman you know well: *Listen, old girl, I think you need some rest.* —see also OLD GIRL

**7 factory girl/shop girl/office girl** *old-fashioned* a young woman who works in a factory, shop, office etc

**8 my girl** *old-fashioned* used by an older person to address a girl or woman who is younger than they are, or when they are annoyed: *Just remember who you're talking to, my girl!*

**9** *old-fashioned* a woman who you are having a romantic relationship with

**10 ► SERVANT ◄** *old-fashioned* a woman servant

**girl Fri·day** /ˌ· ˈ··/ *n* [C] a girl or woman worker who does several different jobs in an office

**girl·friend** /ˈgɜːlfrend‖ˈgɜːrl-/ *n* [C] **1** a girl or woman that you have a friendly, loving relationship with, usually over a fairly long period of time: *Shirley was his first serious girlfriend.* | **ex-girlfriend** (=a former girlfriend) **2** a woman who you are having a romantic relationship with **3** *especially AmE* a woman's female friend: *She's out with one of her girlfriends.* —see also BOYFRIEND

**girl·hood** /ˈgɜːlhʊd‖ˈgɜːrl-/ *n* [U] the period of her life when a woman is a girl —see also BOYHOOD

**girl·ie[1]**, **girly** /ˈgɜːli‖ˈgɜːrli/ *adj informal* **1 girlie magazine/calendar etc** a magazine etc with pictures of women with no clothes on **2** a woman who is girly behaves in a silly way, for example by pretending to be shy or always thinking about how she looks **3** *spoken* suitable only for girls rather than men or boys: *Pink's a girlie color!*

**girlie[2]** *n* [C] an offensive word used by men to address a woman who they think is less sensible or intelligent than a man

**girl·ish** /ˈgɜːlɪʃ‖ˈgɜːr-/ *adj* behaving like a girl, or looking like a girl: *a peal of girlish laughter* —**girlishly** *adv*

**girl scout** /ˌ· ˈ·/ *n* [C] a SCOUT (=member of the Girl Scouts Association in the US) —see also BOY SCOUT

**girl·y** /ˈgɜːli‖ˈgɜːrli/ *adj* another spelling of GIRLIE[1]

**gi·ro** /ˈdʒaɪərəʊ‖ˈdʒaɪroʊ/ *n BrE* **1** [C] a cheque paid by the government to someone who is unemployed **2** [U] a system of BANKING in Britain in which a central computer can send money from one BANK ACCOUNT to another electronically

**girt** /gɜːt‖gɜːrt/ the past participle of GIRD

**girth** /gɜːθ‖gɜːrθ/ *n* **1** [C] the size of something or someone large when they are measured around their middle: *the enormous girth of the tree* | *Maxwell heaved his considerable girth into the long, sleek car.* **2** [C] a band of leather which is passed tightly around the middle of a horse to keep a SADDLE[1] (1) or load firmly in position —see picture at HORSE[1]

**gis·mo** /ˈgɪzməʊ‖-moʊ/ *n* [C] another spelling of GIZMO

**gist** /dʒɪst/ *n* **the gist** the main idea and meaning of what someone has said or written: [+ **of**] *The gist of his argument is that full employment is impossible.* | **get the gist** (=understand the main meaning of something) *Don't worry about all the details—as long as you get the gist of it.*

**git** /gɪt/ *n* [C] *BrE slang* an unpleasant and annoying person, especially a man: *You miserable git!*

**gite** /ʒiːt/ *n* [C] *French or BrE* a holiday house in France

## give[1] *v past tense* gave /geɪv/ *past participle* given /ˈgɪvən/

S1 W1

① PROVIDE/SUPPLY
② TELL SB STH/PROVIDE INFORMATION
③ DO STH
④ PRODUCE A FEELING/ILLNESS/RESULT
⑤ ALLOW
⑥ JUDGE
⑦ TIME
⑧ THINK ABOUT STH
⑨ LIKE STH
⑩ BEND/BREAK
⑪ OTHER MEANINGS

### ① PROVIDE/SUPPLY

**1** [T] to provide or supply someone with something: **give sb sth** *Researchers were given a £10,000 grant to continue their work.* | *Can you give me a ride to the office on Tuesday?* | *He went to Las Vegas. He has a friend there who will give him a job.* | *The doctor gave him something for the pain.* | **give sth to sb** *The firm gives a generous discount to companies that place large orders.*

**2** [T] to give something to someone by putting it near them or in their hand: **give sb sth** *A policeman gave me a ticket for speeding.* | **give sth to sb** *Why don't you give those packages to me while you find out about the train?*

**3** [T] to provide someone with something as a present: **give sb sth** *Jon always gives her flowers on her birthday.*

**4** [I,T] to give money, food etc in order to help people who are poor: *He gives generously to the church.* | **give sth to sb** *They regularly give 5% of their income to charity.*

### ② TELL SB STH/PROVIDE INFORMATION

**5** [T] to tell someone information or details about something: *a brochure giving holiday details* | *The first chapter gives a broad outline of the topic.* | *You will be asked to give evidence when the case is brought to trial.* | **give sb sth** *When will you be able to give us your answer?* | **give (sb) information/a description/an example etc** *Dad gave me some information on buying a new car.* | **give (sb) advice/instructions/a warning etc** *The instructions the manufacturer gave aren't very clear.* | **give (sb) an account/report/message etc** *The newspaper gave a disturbing account of the murder.* —see SAY[1] (USAGE)

**6 give sb your word/promise** to promise to do something: *I gave him my word not to repeat anything of what he'd told me.*

**7 give sb to understand/believe** *formal* to make someone believe that something will happen or is true: *I was given to understand that the contract would be approved by the end of the week.*

**8 give it to me straight** *spoken* used when you want someone to tell you something unpleasant directly

### ③ DO STH

**9 give (sb/sth) a smile/laugh/shout/push etc** to smile, laugh, shout etc: *He gave me a quick smile and a hug.* | *Ooh, the baby just gave a kick!*

**10 give (sb/sth) assistance/help/support etc** to do something to help someone or something be successful: *Committee members agreed to give the policy of increasing wheel-chair access their full support.*

**11 give (sb) a hand** *spoken* to help someone do something, especially something that involves physical work: *Can you give me a hand? I need to move this box.*

**12 give sb a call/ring** *BrE*/**bell** *BrE*/**buzz** to call someone on the telephone: *I'll give you a call about seven, okay?*

**13 give a speech/concert/performance etc** to talk, play an instrument etc in front of a group of people: *Seamus Heaney is giving a poetry reading Thursday evening.* | *She gave a performance of great beauty and sweetness.*

**14 give a party/dance etc** to be the person who organizes a party etc, especially at your own home: *Julie is giving a wedding shower for Lori next Saturday.*

**15 give sth a try/shot/go** *BrE*/**whirl** to be willing to attempt to do something: *I'm not usually much good at these sorts of games, but I'll give it a go.*

**16 ►JOB◄** [T] to ask someone to do a job or task: *My algebra teacher always gives us a lot of homework.* | *Give Mike something to do – he's just sitting there.*

**17 give (sb) trouble/a hard time/problems etc** to do something that causes problems or makes a situation difficult for someone: *This new computer program is giving us a little bit of trouble.* | *She's always giving her mother a hard time these days.*

**18 give (sb) a signal/alarm/sign etc** to say or do something that tells someone what to do in a particular situation: *The man who was controlling the traffic gave me the signal to move forward.*

### ④ PRODUCE A FEELING/ILLNESS/RESULT

**19** [T] to produce a particular emotional or physical feeling: **give sb sth** *He gave us quite a shock, appearing suddenly like that.* | *The heat gave me a real headache.* | *Targets help give workers a sense of achievement.*

**20** [T] to infect someone with the same illness you have: **give sb sth** *Don't come too close – I don't want to give you my cold!* | **give sth to sb** *It's very unlikely a doctor could give hepatitis to a patient.*

**21** [T] to produce a particular effect, solution, result etc: *The fields that had not been fertilized gave surprisingly high yields.* | *The camera's focus should be set to give maximum resolution.*

### ⑤ ALLOW

**22** [T] to allow something or someone to do something: *Women were given the vote in the early 1900's.* | *I gave the students the freedom to choose their own topics.* | **give (sb) permission/consent** *Her father finally gave his consent to her marriage.* | **give sb a chance/opportunity to do sth** *These meetings give everyone a chance to express their opinions.*

**23 give sb authority/responsibility/control etc** to allow someone to have power or control over something: *Schools have recently been given responsibility for their own budgets.*

**24** [I] to be willing to change what you think or do in a

[continued on next page]

[continued from previous page]
situation according to what else happens: *If only he'd give a little, we'd have this whole thing settled by now.*

### ⑥ JUDGE

**25** [T] to decide how much time a criminal will have to spend in prison: **give sb sth** *The judge gave her two years.* | *He was given life for murdering three women.*
**26 give sth out/offside etc** *BrE* to decide that a player or a ball is playing against the rules: *The linesman gave the ball out.*

### ⑦ TIME

**27 give sb time/a few weeks/all day etc** to allow someone or a situation to have enough time to develop, do something etc: *Give him time. It's always hard to adjust to a new place.* | **give sb time to do sth** *Flexible working hours could give working parents more time to spend with their children.*
**28 I give it six weeks/a month etc** *spoken* used when you think that something is not going to continue successfully for very long: *Steve and Celia are going to get married? I give it six weeks.*

### ⑧ THINK ABOUT STH

**29 give (sth) thought/attention/consideration etc** to spend some time thinking about something carefully: *Congress has been giving the crime bill serious consideration.* | *I'll give the matter some thought and let you know my decision next week.* | **not give sth a second thought/another thought** (=not think or worry about something): *Don't give it a second thought. I'll take care of the whole thing.*
**30 give (sb) the impression/sense/idea etc** to make someone think about something in a particular way: **give (sb) the impression that** *Paul didn't want to give Mr Bergman the impression that he was avoiding him.*

### ⑨ LIKE STH

**31 give me sth (any day/time)** *spoken* used to say that you like something much more than something else: *I don't like spicy food much. Give me meat and potatoes any day.*
**32 give anything/a lot/your right arm etc** *spoken* used when you want something very much: *I'd give my right arm for a complexion like that.*

### ⑩ BEND/BREAK

**33** [I] if a material gives, it bends or stretches when you put pressure on it: *The leather will give a little after you've worn the shoes a while.*
**34** [I] if something such as a chair or shelf gives, it breaks suddenly: *The branch suddenly gave beneath him.*

### ⑪ OTHER MEANINGS

**35 not give a damn/toss** *BrE*/**shit etc** *spoken* used when you do not care at all about something: *I don't give a damn what you think.*
**36 ▶ MAKE STH HAVE A PARTICULAR QUALITY ◀** [T not in progressive] to add a quality or characteristic to a person, place, thing etc: *The new sponsor gives the theatre some respectability.* | **give a smell/taste/look etc** *Rub the salad bowl with a clove of garlic to give a delicate tang.* | *Her tan gave her a healthy look.*
**37 give (sth) coherence/form/shape etc** to organize something, especially something such as an idea or situation: *The painter takes his emotions and gives them artistic form.*
**38 give (sb/sth) credit/respect/priority etc** to treat something or someone in a way that shows it is important or has value: *You have to give him credit for trying to learn the language.* | *Top priority should be given to finishing on schedule.*
**39 don't give me that** *spoken* used when you do not believe someone's excuse or explanation: *"I'm sorry I'm late. My car broke down." "Oh, don't give me that."*
**40 give sb what for** *informal* to tell someone angrily that you are annoyed with them
**41 ▶ PAY ◀** [T] to be willing to pay a particular amount of money for something: **give sb sth for** *He said he'd give us £700 for our old Ford.*
**42 give as good as you get** to fight or argue with someone using the same amount of skill or force that they are using
**43 give or take a few minutes/a penny/a mile etc** if a number, time, or amount is correct give or take a few minutes etc, it is approximately correct: *You can usually predict how tall a child will be as an adult, give or take a couple of inches.*
**44 I'll give you that** *spoken* used when you accept that something is true, even though you do not like it or disagree with other parts of it: *Yes, he's handsome, I'll give you that, but he's really arrogant.*
**45 I give you the chairman/prime minister/groom etc** *BrE spoken* used at the end of a speech to invite people to cheer or APPLAUD (1) a special guest
**46 What gives?** *spoken* used when you want to ask what is happening
**47 ▶ SEX ◀** [T] *old-fashioned* if a woman gives herself to a man, she has sex with him —see also **give way** (way[1] (31))

**give away** *phr v* [T] **1** [**give** sth ↔ **away**] to give something to another person because you do not want it any longer or because they need it more than you: *I need to give away some of these old baby clothes.* | **give sth away to** *He gave away immense amounts of money to charity.* **2** [**give** sth ↔ **away**] if a company gives away something, they give things to people in order to persuade them to buy that company's products: *They're giving a compact disc away with every copy of the magazine.* **3** [**give** sth ↔ **away**] to do something that shows what you really think or what is really true: *Katheryn studied the juror's faces, but they gave away no clues as to the verdict.* **4** [**give** sb **away**] to show that someone is doing something wrong: **give yourself away** *Most shoplifters give themselves away by constantly looking around for cameras.* **5** [**give** sth ↔ **away**] to tell someone something that you should keep secret: *I was afraid the kids would give the whole thing away.* | **give the game away** (=tell someone a secret plan, idea etc) **6** [**give** sth ↔ **away**] to lose something by doing something silly or stupid: *The goalkeeper gave away two goals.* | *I swear the Democrats are just giving this election away.* **7** [**give away** sth↔] to give someone something such as a prize in a ceremony: *The university chancellor gave away our diplomas.* **8** [**give** sb ↔ **away**] when a man, especially the BRIDE's father, gives the bride away, he walks with her to the front of the church and formally gives permission for her to marry: *She asked her eldest brother to give her away.*

**give** sth ↔ **back** *phr v* [T] **1** to return something to the person who owned it before: **give sth↔ back to sb** *She read the letter, signed it, and gave it back to Rae.* | **give sb back sth** *I need to give Jack back the money he lent me.* | **give sb sth back** *Mom! Tell Josh to give me my pens back!* **2** if you give someone back a quality, ability, or characteristic, you make them have it again after they had lost it; RESTORE (5): *The operation gave him back his sight.*

**give in** *phr v* **1** [I] to unwillingly agree to someone's demands after they have spent a lot of time arguing with you, trying to persuade you etc: *They argued back and forth until finally Buzz gave in.* | [**+ to**] *O'Neill was giving in to pressure from London to hurry the reforms.* **2** [I] to stop playing, fighting etc and accept that you will be defeated: *They weren't a particularly good team, but they refused to give in and accept defeat.* **3** [T **give** sth ↔ **in**] *BrE* to give something such as an official paper or piece of work to someone; **hand in** (HAND[2]) *AmE*: *Rosa decided to give in her notice.* | *You were supposed to give this work in four days ago.*

**give in to** *phr v* [T] to no longer control a strong emotion or desire: *If you feel the urge for a cigarette, try not to give in to it.*

**give of** sth *phr v* [T] if you give of yourself, your time or money, or your best, you do things for other people without expecting them to do anything for you: *professionals who give of their free time to help underprivileged youngsters*

**give off** sth *phr v* [T] to produce a smell, light, heat, a sound etc: *Chives give off a delicate oniony scent.*

**give off**

The milk gave off a bad smell.

**give on/onto** sth *phr v* [T not in passive] if a window, door, building etc gives on or onto a particular place, it leads to that place or you can see that place from it: *a gate giving on to the main road | a small window giving onto fields*

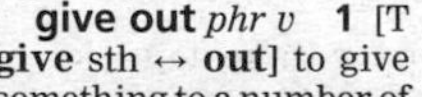

**give out** *phr v* **1** [T **give** sth ↔ **out**] to give something to a number of different people, especially to give information to people: *Students were giving out leaflets to everyone on the street. | You had no right to give my telephone number out.* **2** [I] if a part of your body gives out, it stops working properly: *I am so frightened that my legs give out, and I reach for the railing.* **3** [I] if a supply of something gives out, there is none left: *My money began to give out. | predictions that the world's oil supply would soon give out* **4** [T **give out** sth] to produce light, heat, a sound, a gas etc: *A palm-oil lamp gave out yellowish light.* **5** [T **give** sth ↔ **out**] *BrE formal* to announce something, especially officially: *Mr Banks gave out the last verse of the hymn.* | **give out that** *It was given out that the prime minister was to undergo minor surgery.* **6** [I] *especially AmE* to end: *She parked near the spot where the blacktop gave out.*

**give over** *phr v* [I,T] *BrE spoken* used to tell someone angrily to stop doing something or to be quiet: *"We're going to thrash you lot five-nil." "Oh, give over!"* | **give over doing sth** *Oh, give over complaining, we're nearly there.*

**give over to** *phr v* [T] **1 be given over to** to be used for a particular purpose: *The best land near the village was given over to vineyards. | Two days were given over to the celebrations.* **2** [**give** sb/sth ↔ **over to**] to allow yourself or your life to be completely controlled by another person, a feeling, or an activity: *a life given over to sexual excess* | **give yourself over to** *After her husband's death, she gave herself over to her work.* **3** [**give** sth/sb ↔ **over to**] to give the responsibility for something or someone to someone else: *His mother gave him over to his uncle's care when he was very small.*

**give up** *phr v* **1** [I,T **give** sth ↔ **up**] to stop doing something or having something, especially something that you do regularly: *Shaun's giving up his karate, he's bored with it. | When Ed left, she gave up hope of ever marrying.* | **give up doing sth** *I've given up expecting him to change.* | **give up a job/career/work etc**: *Peter had given up a promising career in law to become a teacher.* | **give up smoking/drinking/alcohol/cigarettes etc** (=stop doing something that is unhealthy): *I gave up smoking when I got pregnant.* **2** [I,T **give** sth ↔ **up**] to stop attempting to do something, especially something difficult, without completing it: *They searched for the ball for a while, but eventually gave up and went home.* | **give up doing sth** *I gave up trying to persuade him to get a degree.* | **give it/that up** *"Give it up," Anna advised me. "You'll never get him to agree."* | **I give up** *spoken* (=used when you do not know the answer to a question or joke): *"Why did the chicken cross the road?" "I give up. Why?"* **3** [T **give** sb **up**] to allow yourself or someone else to be caught by the police or enemy soldiers: **give yourself up** *The police issued a statement urging the fugitive to give himself up.* **4** [T **give up** sth] to agree to do something during the time you would normally spend doing things you enjoy: *The club secretary will need to give up an hour or two a week to do the correspondence.* **5** [T **give** sth/sb ↔ **up**] to give someone else possession of something you have: *thoughts that Israel might give up some of the occupied territory* | **give sth ↔ up to sb** *John gave up his seat to an elderly lady on the bus.* | **give sb up for adoption** (=allow your child to become legally part of someone else's family) **6** [T **give** sb ↔ **up**] to end a relationship with someone, especially a romantic relationship: *He's started going out with Emma, but he doesn't want to give up this other girl!* **7 give sb up for dead/lost etc** to believe that someone is dead and stop looking for them: *The ship sank and the crew were given up for dead.* —see also **give up the ghost** (GHOST[1] (5))

**give up on** sb *phr v* [T] to stop hoping that someone will change, do something etc: *He'd been in a coma for six months, and doctors had almost given up on him.*

**give** yourself **up to** sth *phr v* [T] to allow yourself to feel some emotion completely, without trying to control it: *He gave himself up to despair.*

**give**[2] *n* [U] the ability to bend or stretch when put under pressure: *The rope has quite a bit of give in it.*

**give-and-take** /ˌ· · ˈ·/ *n* [U] a willingness between two people or groups to understand each other, and to let both of them have some of the things they want: *In any relationship there always has to be some give-and-take.*

**give·a·way**[1] /ˈgɪvəweɪ/ *n* **1** [singular] something that makes it easy for you to guess something: **be a clear/dead giveaway** *He'd been smoking dope; his glazed eyes were a dead giveaway.* **2** [C] something that a shop gives you when you buy a product

**giveaway**[2] *adj* [only before noun] giveaway prices are extremely cheap

**give·back** /ˈgɪvbæk/ *n* [C] *AmE* an amount of money or goods that you receive from some companies if you buy a product from them

**giv·en**[1] /ˈgɪvən/ *adj* [only before noun] **1** a given time, date etc is one that has been previously arranged: *At a given time we'll all start shouting and cheering.* **2 at any given time/point etc** at any particular time, point etc: *The distance from the centre of a circle to the edge is the same at any given point.* **3 be given to (doing) sth** to tend to do something, especially something that you should not do: *She is given to making wild accusations.* **4 take sth as given** to base your argument on the belief that something is clearly true

**given**[2] *prep* used to say that something is not surprising when you consider the situation it happened in; CONSIDERING[2]: *Given the circumstances, you've coped well.* | [+ **that**] *Given that there was so little time, I think they've done a good job.*

**given**[3] *n* [C] *formal* a basic fact that you accept as being true

**given**[4] the past participle of GIVE

**given name** /ˈ·· ·/ *n* [C] *AmE* your FIRST NAME

**giz·mo** /ˈgɪzməʊ‖-moʊ/ *n* [C] *informal* a word meaning a small piece of equipment, used when you cannot remember or do not know its correct name

**giz·zard** /ˈgɪzəd‖-ərd/ *n* [C] the stomach of a bird

**gla·cé** /ˈglæseɪ‖glæˈseɪ/ *adj* [only before noun] glacé fruits, especially cherries (CHERRY), have been covered in sugary liquid

**glacé i·cing** /ˌ··ˈ··‖·ˌ·ˈ··/ *n* [U] *BrE* a type of ICING used to decorate cakes

**gla·cial** /ˈgleɪʃəl/ *adj* **1** involving ice and glaciers, or formed by glaciers: *a glacial valley* **2** a glacial look or expression is extremely unfriendly **3** extremely cold: *a glacial wind* —**glacially** *adv*

**gla·ci·a·tion** /ˌgleɪsiˈeɪʃən/ *n* [U] *technical* the process in which land is covered by glaciers, or the effect this process has

**gla·ci·er** /ˈglæsiə‖ˈgleɪʃər/ *n* [C] a large mass of ice which moves slowly down a mountain valley —see picture on page 835

S2 W3 **glad** /glæd/ *adj* **gladder, gladdest** **1** pleased and happy about something: *"The doctor says she'll be well again soon." "I'm so glad."* | [+ **(that)**] *I'm really glad I don't have to go back there again.* | [+ **about**] *Deep down he felt glad about the news.* | **glad to know/see/hear** *We were all glad to hear you passed your exams.* | **be/feel glad for sb** *When I heard they were getting married I felt genuinely glad for them both.* **2 be glad of sth** to be grateful for something: *Thanks Marge, I'll be glad of the help.* **3 be glad to do sth** to be very willing and eager to do something: *"Would you give me a hand?" "I'd be glad to."* | **be only too glad to** (=extremely willing): *I'd be only too glad to let you take the kids today.* **4 I would be glad if** used to say you would be pleased if someone would do something for you: *I would be glad if you could arrange it for me.* **5** making people feel happy: *a glad day for everyone* **6 glad rags** *informal* your best clothes that you wear for special occasions **7 glad tidings** *old-fashioned* good news **8 give sb the glad eye** *BrE old-fashioned* to look at someone in a way that shows you are sexually attracted to them —see also GLAD-HAND, GLADLY —**gladness** *n* [U]

This graph shows how common the different grammar patterns of the adjective **glad** are.

| Pattern | Approx. frequency |
|---|---|
| glad (that) | ~47% |
| glad to do sth | ~33% |
| be glad | ~8% |
| glad when | ~4% |
| glad of | ~3% |
| other | ~4% |

10% 20% 30% 40% 50%

Based on the British National Corpus and the Longman Lancaster Corpus

**glad·den** /ˈglædn/ *v* [T] **gladden sb's heart** *old-fashioned* to make someone feel pleased and happy: *It gladdened the old man's heart to see his grandchildren playing in the yard.*

**glade** /gleɪd/ *n* [C] *literary* an open space in a wood or forest

**glad-hand** /ˌ· ˈ·,ˈ· ·/ *v* [I, T] to give someone a very friendly welcome or be nice to them in order to get what you want: *politicians gladhanding in the crowds*

**glad·i·a·tor** /ˈglædieɪtə‖-ər/ *n* [C] a soldier who fought against other men or wild animals in a public place in Roman times in order to entertain people —**gladiatorial** /ˌglædiəˈtɔːriəl◂/ *adj*

**glad·i·o·lus** /ˌglædiˈəʊləs‖-ˈoʊ-/ *plural* **gladioli** /-laɪ/ *n* [C] a garden plant with long leaves and brightly-coloured flowers

**glad·ly** /ˈglædli/ *adv* **1** willingly or eagerly: *I would gladly have done it for him.* **2** happily: *"Here's Michelle!" he said gladly.*

**glam·or** /ˈglæmə‖-ər/ *n* [U] an American spelling of GLAMOUR

**glam·o·rize** also **-ise** *BrE* /ˈglæməraɪz/ *v* [T] to make something seem more attractive than it really is: *a widespread perception that Hollywood movies tend to glamorize war* —**glamorization** /ˌglæməraɪˈzeɪʃən‖-rə-/ *n* [U]

**glam·or·ous** /ˈglæmərəs/ *adj* a person, place, or activity that is glamorous seems very attractive and exciting, because it is beautiful or is connected with wealth and success: *a glamorous film star* | *glamorous couples in chauffeur-driven limousines* | *Tatiana's glamorous lifestyle* —**glamorously** *adv*

**glam·our** *usually* **glamor** *AmE* /ˈglæmə‖-ər/ *n* [U] **1** the attractive and exciting quality that something has because it is connected with wealth and success: *Young actors are often dazzled by the glamor of Hollywood.* **2** strong personal attractiveness **3 glamour girl** an actress who is beautiful but is not very good at acting

**glance¹** /glɑːns‖glæns/ *v* [I always + adv/prep] **1** to quickly look at someone or something once: [+ **at/towards/up etc**] *He glanced nervously at his watch.* | *Nadine glanced round to see if there was anyone that she knew.* **2** to read something very quickly [+ **at/over/etc**] *Can you glance through these figures and tell me what you think of them?* **3** to flash: *light glancing on the water* W

**glance off** *phr v* [I,T] to hit a surface at an angle and then move away from it in another direction: *The bullet glanced off the side of the car.*

**USAGE NOTE: GLANCE**

WORD CHOICE: **glance, have/take a quick look, glimpse, catch/get a glimpse of**

If you **glance** at something, you look at it quickly: *After the first ten minutes the interviewer started yawning and glancing at his watch.*

In spoken English you often use **have/take a (quick) look**, especially to check if something is correct or working properly: *Could you just have a quick look at the engine for me?*

If you **glimpse** (or more commonly **catch/get a glimpse of**) someone or something, you see them by chance, for a very short time: *I can't describe him well, I only caught a glimpse of him as he drove off.*

**glance²** *n* [C] **1** a quick look: **give/take/shoot/throw a glance (at)** (=look at someone or something quickly) *He gave her a quick glance as she walked into the room.* | **exchange glances** (=look at each other quickly) **2 at a glance** if you know something at a glance, you know it as soon as you see it: *He'll be able to tell if the diamonds are genuine at a glance.* **3 at first glance** when you first look at something: *At first glance the place seemed deserted.* W

**glanc·ing** /ˈglɑːnsɪŋ‖ˈglæn-/ *adj* **a glancing blow** a hit that partly misses so that it does not have its full force —**glancingly** *adv*

**gland** /glænd/ *n* [C] an organ of the body which produces a substance that the body needs, such as SWEAT² (1) or SALIVA: *Mumps make your glands swell up.* | *the pituitary gland*

**glan·du·lar** /ˈglændjʊ̆lə‖-dʒələr-/ *adj* related to the glands, or produced by the glands

**glandular fe·ver** /ˌ··· ˈ··/ *n* [U] *BrE* an infectious disease which makes your LYMPH GLANDS swell up and makes you feel weak for a long time afterwards; MONONUCLEOSIS *AmE*

**glare¹** /gleə‖gler/ *v* [I] **1** to look angrily at someone for a long time: **glare at sb** *She glared at him accusingly.* **2** [always + adv/prep] to shine with a very strong bright light which hurts your eyes: [+ **through/in**] *The sun glared through the car windscreen.*

**glare²** *n* **1** [singular] a bright unpleasant light which hurts your eyes: *the harsh glare of the desert sun* **2** [C] a long angry look: *She gave him an icy glare.* **3 the glare of publicity** the full attention of newspapers, television etc, especially when you do not want it

**glar·ing** /ˈgleərɪŋ‖ˈgler-/ *adj* **1** very bad and very noticeable: *the glaring injustices of the Soviet legal system* | **glaring error/mistake** *The report contained a number of glaring errors.* **2** too bright and difficult to look at: *the glaring light of the headlamps* —**glaringly** *adv*

**glas·nost** /ˈglæznɒst‖ˈglɑːsnoʊst/ *n* [U] *Russian* a word meaning the willingness of a country or organization to show what it is doing and discuss its decisions, used especially about the government of the former USSR

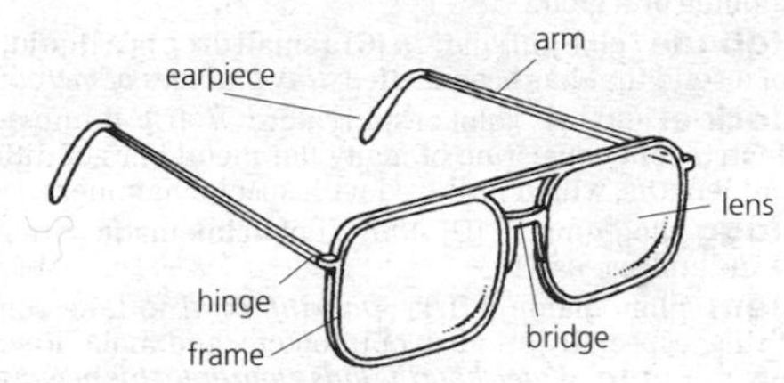


S1 W1 **glass**[1] /glɑːs‖glæs/ *n*
**1 ▶ TRANSPARENT ◀** [U] a transparent solid substance, for example used for making windows and bottles: *a glass bowl* | *Polly cut herself on a piece of broken glass.*
**2 ▶ FOR DRINKING ◀** [C] a container used for drinking made of glass, or the drink in it: *a wine glass* | **[+ of]** *a glass of red wine*
**3 ▶ FOR EYES ◀ glasses** [plural] a set of two pieces of specially cut glass in a frame, which you wear in order to see more clearly: *I hate wearing glasses.* | *I need a new pair of glasses.* —see also OPERA GLASSES, FIELD GLASSES
**4 ▶ GLASS OBJECTS ◀** [U] objects which are made of glass, especially ones used for drinking and eating; GLASSWARE: *a priceless collection of Venetian glass*
**5 people in glass houses shouldn't throw stones** used to say that you should not criticize someone for having a fault if you have the same fault yourself
**6 under glass** plants that are grown under glass are protected from the cold by a glass cover: *tomatoes grown all year round under glass*
**7 glass ceiling** an imaginary limit that prevents women from being successful, even though there are no actual laws or rules to stop them
**8 ▶ MIRROR ◀** *old-fashioned* a mirror
**9 the glass** *old-fashioned* a BAROMETER (1) —see also CUT GLASS, GROUND GLASS, LOOKING GLASS, MAGNIFYING GLASS, PLATE GLASS, **raise your glasses** (RAISE[1] (12)), STAINED GLASS

**glass**[2] *v*
**glass** sth ↔ **in** *phr v* [T] to cover something with glass, or to build a glass structure around something

**glass·blow·er** /ˈglɑːsˌbləʊə‖ˈglæsˌbloʊər/ *n* [C] someone who shapes hot glass by blowing air through a tube

**glass fi·bre** /ˌ· ˈ··◂/ *n* [U] FIBREGLASS

**glass·ful** /ˈglɑːsfʊl‖ˈglæs-/ *n* [C] the amount of liquid a glass will hold

**glass·house** /ˈglɑːshaʊs‖ˈglæs-/ *n* [C] *BrE* **1** a building which is used for growing plants and is made of glass; GREENHOUSE **2 the glasshouse** *slang* a military prison

**glass·ware** /ˈglɑːsweə‖ˈglæswer/ *n* [U] glass objects, especially ones used for drinking and eating

**glass wool** /ˌ· ˈ·/ *n* [U] *BrE* FIBREGLASS

**glass·y** /ˈglɑːsi‖ˈglæsi/ *adj* **1** smooth and shining, like glass: *the glassy green waters of the Hudson River* **2 glassy eyes/stare** eyes that show no feeling or understanding, and do not move

**glassy-eyed** /ˌ·· ˈ·◂/ *adj* having still eyes and an expression that shows no feeling or understanding: *They had him doped-up. He was sort of glassy-eyed.*

**glau·co·ma** /glɔːˈkəʊmə‖glɒːˈkoʊ-/ *n* [U] an eye disease in which increased pressure inside your eye gradually makes you lose your sight

**glau·cous** /ˈglɔːkəs‖ˈglɒː-/ *adj technical* a glaucous leaf or plant has a fine white powdery surface

**glaze**[1] /gleɪz/ *v* **1** [I] also **glaze over** if your eyes glaze over, they show no expression because you are very bored or tired **2** [T] to cover plates, cups etc made of clay with a thin liquid that gives them a shiny surface **3** [T] to cover fruit, cake, or meat with a liquid which gives it an attractive shiny surface **4** [T] to fit glass into window frames in a house, door etc

**glaze**[2] *n* **1** [C] a liquid that is used to cover plates, cups etc made of clay and give them a shiny surface **2** [U] liquid which is put onto fruit, cake, or meat to give it an attractive shiny surface **3** [U] a transparent covering of oil paint spread over a painting

**glazed** /gleɪzd/ *adj* **glazed look/eyes/expression etc** if you have a glazed look etc your eyes show no expression because you are very bored or tired

**gla·zi·er** /ˈgleɪziə‖-ʒər/ *n* [C] someone whose job is to fit glass into window frames

**glaz·ing** /ˈgleɪzɪŋ/ *n* [U] glass that has been used to fill windows —see also DOUBLE-GLAZING

**gleam**[1] /gliːm/ *v* [I] **1** to shine softly: *The spire of the Golden Temple gleamed in the autumn sun.* | **[+ with]** *the table's surface gleaming with wax polish* **2 gleam with happiness/joy etc** if your eyes or face gleam with a feeling, they show it: *His face gleamed with amusement.* —**gleaming** *adj*: *gleaming glass skyscrapers*

**gleam**[2] *n* [C] **1** a small pale light, especially one that shines for a short time: **[+ of]** *They saw the gleam of a lamp ahead.* **2** the brightness of something that shines: **[+ of]** *the sudden gleam of white teeth* **3** a sudden expression that appears for a moment on someone's face or in their eyes: **[+ of]** *A gleam of satisfaction crossed her face.*

**glean** /gliːn/ *v* **1** [T] to find out facts and information slowly and with difficulty: **glean sth from** *I've managed to glean a few details about him from his friends.* **2** [I,T] to collect grain that has been left behind after the crops have been cut

**glean·ings** /ˈgliːnɪŋz/ *n* [plural] small pieces of information that you have found out with difficulty

**glebe** /gliːb/ *n* [U] **1** *poetic* earth or soil **2** *BrE* land given to a priest to provide part of his income

**glee** /gliː/ *n* **1** [U] a feeling of satisfaction and excitement because something good has happened to you or something bad has happened to someone else: *The kids watched with glee as I tried to catch the hamster.* **2** [C] a song for three or four voices together

**glee club** /ˈ· ·/ *n* [C] *AmE* a group of people who sing together for enjoyment

**glee·ful** /ˈgliːfəl/ *adj* really enjoying the fact that something good has happened to you or that something bad

has happened to someone else —**gleefully** *adv* —**gleefulness** *n* [U]

**glen** /glen/ *n* [C] a deep narrow valley in Scotland or Ireland

**glib** /glɪb/ *adj* **1** glib remarks, explanations etc are difficult to believe because they are said easily and without thinking: *glib generalizations about the problem of racism* **2** someone who is glib says things to persuade people without being certain that they are true: *glib politicians with their easy solutions* —**glibly** *adv* —**glibness** *n* [U]

**glide[1]** /glaɪd/ *v* [I always + adv/prep] to move smoothly and quietly, as if no effort was being made: [+ **across/over etc**] *a snake gliding across the path*| *The plane glided to a halt just short of the control tower.*

**glide[2]** *n* [C] **1** a smooth, quiet movement that seems to take no effort **2** the act of moving from one musical note to another without a break in sound **3** *technical* a vowel which is made by moving your tongue from one position to another one —see also DIPHTHONG

**glid·er** /ˈglaɪdə‖-ər/ *n* [C] a light plane without an engine

**glid·ing** /ˈglaɪdɪŋ/ *n* [U] the sport of flying in a glider —see also HANG GLIDING

**glim·mer[1]** /ˈglɪmə‖-ər/ *n* [U] **1 a glimmer of hope/doubt/recognition** a small sign of hope, doubt etc **2** a light that is not very bright: *the glimmer of a candle*

**glimmer[2]** *v* [I] to shine with a light that is not very bright: *A light glimmered at the end of the hall.*

**glim·mer·ing** /ˈglɪmərɪŋ/ *n* [C often plural] a small sign of thought or feeling: *glimmerings of interest*

**glimpse[1]** /glɪmps/ *v* [T] **1** to see someone or something for a moment without getting a complete view of them: *I glimpsed her face in the crowd, but then she was gone* —see GLANCE[2] (USAGE) **2** to begin to understand something for a moment: *He glimpsed the despair that she must have felt.*

**glimpse[2]** *n* [C] **1** a sight of someone or something that you only have for a short time and that is not complete: **get/catch a glimpse of** *I caught only a glimpse of the president's car.*| **fleeting glimpse** (=a very short one) —see GLANCE[2] (USAGE) **2** a short experience of something that helps you begin to understand it: *a glimpse of what life might be like in the future*

**glint[1]** /glɪnt/ *v* [I] **1** if a shiny surface glints, it gives out small flashes of light: *Her gold bracelet glinted in the morning sunlight.* **2** if your eyes glint, they shine and show an unfriendly feeling: *Derek's eyes glinted when he saw the money.*

**glint[2]** *n* [C] **1** a look in someone's eyes which shows an unfriendly feeling: *There was an evil glint in her eyes.* **2** a flash of light from a shiny surface

**glis·ten** /ˈglɪsən/ *v* [I] to shine and look wet or oily: *Her dark hair glistened in the moonlight.*| [+ **with**] *The boy's back was glistening with sweat.*

**glitch** /glɪtʃ/ *n* [C] **1** a small fault in the working of something **2** a false electronic signal caused by a sudden increase in the supply of electric power

**glit·ter[1]** /ˈglɪtə‖-ər/ *v* [I] to shine brightly with flashing points of light: *The blades of their swords glittered in the sunlight.*

**glitter[2]** *n* [U] **1** brightness consisting of many flashing points of light: *the glitter of his gold cigarette case* **2** the attractiveness of a place or a way of living which is connected with rich or famous people; GLAMOUR (1): *Jersey City is a world away from the glitter of Manhattan.* **3** very small pieces of shiny paper that are used for decoration —**glittery** *adj*

**glit·te·ra·ti** /ˌglɪtəˈrɑːti/ *n* [plural] rich, famous, and fashionable people whose activities are often reported in newspapers and magazines

**glit·ter·ing** /ˈglɪtərɪŋ/ *adj* **1** giving off many small flashes of light: *glittering jewels* **2** very successful, and connected with rich and famous people: *a glittering career in the diplomatic service* —**glitteringly** *adv*

**glitz** /glɪts/ *n* [U] the exciting, attractive quality which is connected with rich, famous and fashionable people; GLAMOUR (1): *show business glitz* —**glitzy** *adj*

**gloam·ing** /ˈgləʊmɪŋ‖ˈgloʊ-/ *n* [U] **the gloaming** *poetic* the time in the early evening when it is becoming dark; DUSK

**gloat** /gləʊt‖gloʊt/ *v* [I] to show in an unpleasant way that you are happy about your own success or about someone else's failure: [+ **over**] *Dick was still gloating over Scotland's 5-0 defeat.* —**gloat** *n* [singular] *I bet Sam's having a gloat over that one.* —**gloatingly** *adv*

**glob** /glɒb‖glɑːb/ *n* [C] *informal* a small amount of something soft or liquid that has a round shape: *globs of mud sticking to the cat's fur*

**glo·bal** /ˈgləʊbəl‖ˈgloʊ-/ *adj* **1** affecting or including the whole world: *AIDS is a global problem which needs a global response.* **2** considering all parts of a problem or a situation together: *The report takes a global view of the company's problems.* —**globally** *adv* W3

**global warm·ing** /ˌ·· ˈ··/ *n* [U] a general increase in world temperatures caused by increased amounts of CARBON DIOXIDE around the Earth

**globe** /gləʊb‖gloʊb/ *n* [C] **1** a round object with a map of the Earth drawn on it **2 the globe** the world: *We export our goods all over the globe.* **3** an object shaped like a ball; SPHERE (1)

**globe·trot·ter** /ˈgləʊbtrɒtə‖ˈgloʊbtrɑːtər/ *n* [C] *informal* someone who travels to many different countries —**globe-trotting** *adj*

**glob·u·lar** /ˈglɒbjʊlə‖ˈglɑːbjʊlər/ *adj* in the shape of a globule or a globe

**glob·ule** /ˈglɒbjuːl‖ˈglɑː-/ *n* [C] a small drop of a liquid, or of a solid that has been melted: *tiny globules of mercury*

**glock·en·spiel** /ˈglɒkənspiːl‖ˈglɑː-/ *n* [C] a musical instrument consisting of many flat metal bars of different lengths, which is played with special hammers

**glogg** /glɒg‖glɒːg/ *n* [U] *AmE* a hot drink made with red wine and SPICES[1] (1)

**glom** /glɒm‖glɑːm/ *v* [I,T] *AmE informal* to take something, especially an idea, opinion etc, and make it your own: [+ **onto**] *Watch how the kids glom onto this new style.*

**gloom** /gluːm/ *n* [singular, U] **1** *especially literary* almost complete darkness: *A tall figure appeared in the canyon's gloom.* **2** a feeling of great sadness and lack of hope: *The officers sat sunk in gloom.*

**gloom·y** /ˈgluːmi/ *adj* **1** sad because you think the situation will not improve: *When I saw their gloomy faces, I knew something was wrong.* **2** making you feel that things will not improve: *a gloomy economic forecast* **3** dark, especially in a way that seems sad: *Ezra Pound's daughter visited him in his gloomy study in Carlyle Mansions.* —**gloomily** *adv* —**gloominess** *n* [U]

**glop** /glɒp‖glɑːp/ *n* [U] *AmE informal* a thick soft wet mass, especially of food that looks too unpleasant to eat —**gloppy** *adj*

**glo·ri·fied** /ˈglɔːrɪfaɪd/ *adj* [only before noun] made to seem like something more important: *The so-called college was no more than a glorified school.*

**glo·ri·fy** /ˈglɔːrɪfaɪ/ *v* [T] **1** to make someone or something seem more important or better than they really are: *films which glorify violence* **2 glorify God/the Lord etc** to give praise and thanks to God —**glorification** /ˌglɔːrɪfɪˈkeɪʃən/ *n* [+ **of**] *the glorification of war*

**glo·ri·ous** /ˈglɔːriəs/ *adj* **1** having or deserving great fame, praise, and honour: *It was a glorious political career while it lasted.*| *a glorious victory* **2** very beautiful, attractive, or impressive: *glorious colors*| *a glorious sight* **3** extremely enjoyable; WONDERFUL: *We spent three glorious weeks in Hawaii.* **4 glorious day/summer/weather** weather etc that is very nice because it is sunny and clear —**gloriously** *adv*

**glo·ry[1]** /ˈglɔːri/ *n* **1** [U] the importance, honour, and praise that people give someone or something they admire a lot: *As a child he dreamt of future glory as an*

*Olympic champion.* | **covered in/with glory** *The team finished the season covered with glory.* **2** [C] something that is especially beautiful, or makes you feel proud: *the glories of Roman architecture* | **crowning glory** (=the final completion of something successful) *The Oscar was the crowning glory of her career.* **3** [U] a beautiful and impressive appearance: *After years of neglect the palace has been restored to its former glory.* | **in all its/their etc glory** *Wild flowers in all their glory carpeted the meadow.* **4 bask/bathe in sb's reflected glory** to share some of the importance and praise that belongs to someone close to you **5 Glory (be) to God/Jesus etc** *spoken* used to say that God deserves praise, honour, and thanks **6 glory days** a time in the past when someone was admired: *his glory days on the high school football team* **7 to the (greater) glory of** *formal* in order to increase the honour that is given to someone or something: *Bach composed to the greater glory of God.* **8 go to glory** *old use* to die

**glory²** *v*

**glory in** sth *phr v* [T not in passive] to enjoy something very much such as praise or people's attention

**gloss¹** /glɒs‖glɒːs, glɑːs/ *n* **1** [singular, U] shiny brightness on a surface: *shoes shined to a high gloss* | *The gloss had gone from her dark hair.* **2** [singular, U] a pleasant appearance of something, which is better than the truth: *The General's image soon lost its gloss.* **3** [C] an explanation of a piece of writing, especially in a note at the end of a page or book **4 gloss finish/print** a surface or photograph that has been made shiny —compare MATT

**gloss²** *v* [T] to provide an explanation of a piece of writing, especially in a note at the end of a page or book

**gloss over** sth *phr v* [T] to deliberately avoid talking about unpleasant facts or say as little as possible about them: *She glossed over the details of her divorce and changed the subject.*

**glos·sa·ry** /ˈglɒsəri‖ˈglɒː-, ˈglɑː-/ *n* [C] a list of explanations of words, especially unusual ones, at the end of a book

**gloss paint** /ˌ· ˈ·/ *n* [C,U] paint which looks shiny after it dries —compare EMULSION (2)

**gloss·y¹** /ˈglɒsi‖ˈglɒːsi, ˈglɑːsi/ *adj* **1** shiny and smooth: *the cat's glossy fur* **2** *AmE* trying too hard to be attractive or perfect: *He may have glossy manners, but Gordon's no gentleman.* —**glossiness** *n* [U]

**glossy²** *n* [C] **1** *BrE* also **glossy magazine** a fashion magazine printed on good quality, shiny paper, usually with lots of colour pictures **2** a photograph printed on shiny paper

**glot·tal stop** /ˌ·· ˈ·/ *n* [C] *technical* a speech sound made by completely closing and then opening your glottis, which in English may take the place of a /t/ between vowel sounds or may be used before a vowel sound

**glot·tis** /ˈglɒtɪ̱s‖ˈglɑː-/ *n* [C] the space between your VOCAL CORDS, which produce the sound of your voice by movements in which this space is opened and closed —**glottal** *adj* —see picture at RESPIRATORY

**gloves**

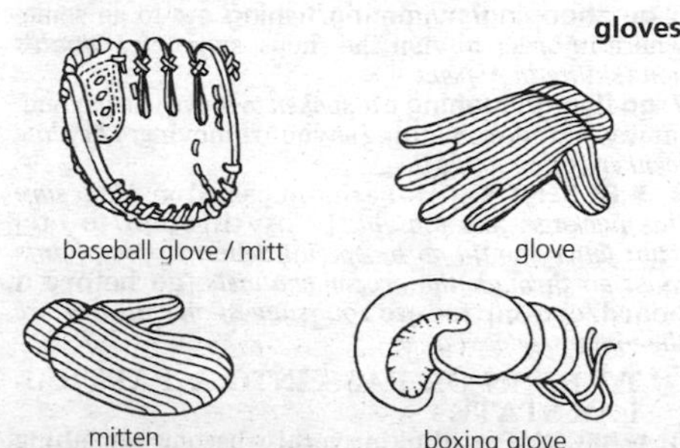


**glove** /glʌv/ *n* [C] **1** a piece of clothing which covers your hand, especially one which has separate parts for each finger —compare MITTEN **2** a large leather glove used in BOXING **3** a large leather glove used to catch the ball in BASEBALL —see also **fit (sb) like a glove** (FIT¹ (1))

**glove com·part·ment** /ˈ· ·ˌ··/ also **glove box** /ˈ· ·/ *n* [C] a small shelf in a car in front of the passenger seat where small things such as maps can be kept —see picture on page 409

**gloved** /glʌvd/ *adj* wearing a glove

**glove pup·pet** /ˈ· ˌ··/ *n* [C] a PUPPET (1) that you put over your hand

**glow¹** /gləʊ‖gloʊ/ *n* [singular] **1** a soft steady light, especially from something that is burning without flames: *The glow from the dying fire lit his face.* | *the glow of city lights on the horizon* **2** brightness of colour, especially colours like red and orange: *the glow of copper pans hanging in the kitchen* **3** the bright colour your face or body has after exercise or when you are very pleased and excited: *a healthy rosy glow in her cheeks* **4 a glow of pleasure/satisfaction/happiness etc** a strong feeling of pleasure etc

**glow²** *v* [I] **1** to shine with a soft, steady light: *We saw a lamp glowing in the garden.* **2** to produce a red light and heat without flames: *His cigarette glowed in the dark.* **3** if your face or body glows, it is red or hot as a result of exercise or strong emotion **4 glow with pride/pleasure/triumph etc** to look very happy because you feel proud etc: *The boys emerged scrubbed and glowing with happiness.*

**glow·er** /ˈglaʊə‖-ər/ *v* [I + at] to look angrily at someone —**gloweringly** *adv*

**glow·ing** /ˈgləʊɪŋ‖ˈgloʊ-/ *adj* **1 glowing report/account/description etc** a report etc full of praise: *Her supervisor gave her a glowing reference.* **2 in glowing terms** using a lot of praise: *He speaks of you in glowing terms.* —**glowingly** *adv*

**glow-worm** /ˈ· ·/ *n* [C] an insect which gives out light from its body

**glu·cose** /ˈgluːkəʊs‖-koʊs/ *n* [U] a natural form of sugar that exists in fruit

**glue¹** /gluː/ *n* [C,U] a sticky substance used for joining things together S3

**glue²** *v present participle* **gluing** *or* **glueing** [T] **1** to join two things together using a special sticky substance: **glue sth together** *I managed to glue the pieces back together.* **2 be glued to** *informal* to look at something with all your attention: *Those kids are glued to the TV all day.* **3 glued to the spot** unable to move because you are very surprised, frightened, interested etc

**glue-snif·fing** /ˈ· ˌ··/ *n* [U] the habit of breathing in gases from glues or similar substances in order to produce an artificial state of excitement: SOLVENT ABUSE —**glue sniffer** *n* [C]

**glue·y** /ˈgluːi/ *adj* **1** sticky like glue **2** covered with glue

**glum** /glʌm/ **glummer, glummest** *adj* sad and not talking much; GLOOMY: *Hey, don't look so glum. Everything will be OK!* —**glumly** *adv* —**glumness** *n* [U]

**glut¹** /glʌt/ *n* [C usually singular] a supply of something that is more than you need: [+ of] *a glut of oil on the market*

**glut²** *v* **glutted, glutting** [T] **1 be glutted with** to be supplied with too much of something: *The shops are glutted with oranges.* **2 glut yourself on sth** to eat too much

**glu·ten** /ˈgluːtn/ *n* [U] a sticky PROTEIN substance that is found in flour made of wheat

**glu·ti·nous** /ˈgluːtɪ̱nəs‖-tn-əs/ *adj* very sticky

**glut·ton** /ˈglʌtn/ *n* [C] **1** someone who eats too much **2 a glutton for punishment** someone who seems to enjoy working hard or doing something unpleasant —**gluttonous** *adj* —**gluttonously** *adv*

**glut·ton·y** /ˈglʌtəni/ *n* [U] *formal* the bad habit of eating and drinking too much

**gly·ce·rine** /ˈglɪsərɪn/ *n* [U] a thick sweet transparent liquid made from fats and used in medicines, explosives, and foods

**gm** the written abbreviation of GRAM

**GMT** /ˌdʒiː em ˈtiː/ *n* [U] Greenwich Mean Time; the time as measured at Greenwich in London, that is used as an international standard for measuring time

**gnarled** /nɑːld‖nɑːrld/ *adj* **1** a gnarled tree or branch is rough and twisted with hard lumps **2** gnarled hands or fingers are twisted, rough, and difficult to move, usually because they are old

**gnarl·y** /ˈnɑːli‖ˈnɑːr-/ *adj AmE slang* **1** a word meaning very good or excellent, used by young people: *"My mom said I can go out tonight!" "Gnarly, man! Let's go."* **2** a word meaning not good enough, used by young people

**gnash** /næʃ/ *v* [T] **gnash your teeth** to move your teeth against each other so that they make a noise, especially because you are unhappy or angry —**gnash** *n* [C]

**gnash·ers** /ˈnæʃəz‖-ərs/ *n* [plural] *BrE informal* teeth

**gnat** /næt/ *n* [C] a small flying insect that bites

**gnaw** /nɔː‖nɒː/ *v* [I always + adv/prep, T] to keep biting something hard: **[+ away/at/on]** *Val gnawed at her fingernails.* | **gnaw sth** *a dog gnawing a bone* | **gnaw a hole in sth** *A rat had gnawed a hole in the box.*

**gnaw at** sb *phr v* [T] to make someone feel worried or frightened: *Something's gnawing at Celia – she's been very moody.*

**gnaw·ing** /ˈnɔːɪŋ‖ˈnɒː-/ *adj* [only before noun] painful or worrying, especially only slightly but for a long time: *gnawing doubts about her own abilities*

**gnome** /nəʊm‖noʊm/ *n* [C] **1** a creature in children's stories like a little old man with a pointed hat who lives under the ground and guards gold, jewels etc **2** a stone or plastic figure representing one of these creatures: *a garden gnome*

**gno·mic** /ˈnəʊmɪk‖ˈnoʊ-/ *adj* gnomic remarks are short, clever, and difficult to understand: *gnomic predictions about the future of the economy* —**gnomically** /-kli/ *adv*

**GNP** /ˌdʒiː en ˈpiː/ *n* [singular] Gross National Product; the total value of all the goods and services produced in a country, usually in a single year

**gnu** /nuː/ *n* [C] a large southern African animal with a tail and curved horns; WILDEBEEST

**go**

Nick's gone to Paris for the weekend.

Derek's been to Paris three times.

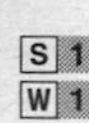

S1 W1

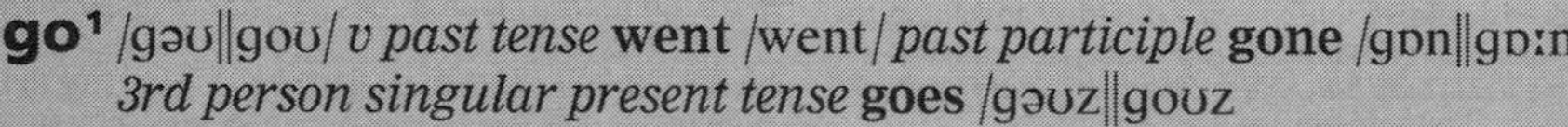

## go¹ /gəʊ‖goʊ/ *v past tense* **went** /went/ *past participle* **gone** /gɒn‖gɒːn/ *3rd person singular present tense* **goes** /gəʊz‖goʊz

① TO MOVE AWAY FROM THE SPEAKER
② TO BE IN OR PASS INTO A PARTICULAR STATE
③ TO START TO DO SOMETHING OR TO DO SOMETHING
④ POSITION
⑤ SOUND
⑥ TO FINISH OR STOP
⑦ OTHER MEANINGS

### ① TO MOVE AWAY FROM THE SPEAKER

**1 ▶ LEAVE SOMEWHERE ◀** [I] to leave a place to go somewhere else; DEPART: *I wanted to go, but Anna wanted to stay.* | *It's late; I must be going.* | *What time does the last train go?* | *The doctor hasn't gone yet.*

**2 go and do sth** to go somewhere in order to do something: *I'll just go and get my coat.* | *It's time you went and saw the doctor.*

**3 ▶ VISIT ◀** *past participle* also **been** [I] to visit a place or go to a place and then leave it: *Nancy has gone to Paris.* (=she is in Paris now) | *Nancy has been to Paris.* (=she has visited Paris in the past) | *The doctor hasn't been here yet.* —see VISIT (USAGE)

**4 ▶ MOVE/TRAVEL ◀** [I always + adv/prep] to travel or move in a particular way, in a particular direction or a particular distance: **[+ by/up/to etc]** *We went by bus.* | *I want to go home.* | *Where are you going?* | *They all went away and left me alone.* | **be going somewhere** (=intend to go somewhere) *We're going to my parents' for Christmas.* | **go to hospital/prison etc** (=go to hospital in order to get medical treatment, to prison as a punishment etc)

**5 go for sth** to go somewhere in order to take part in a particular activity: *Let's go for a swim before lunch.*

**6 go shopping/swimming/fishing etc** to go somewhere in order to visit the shops, swim etc: *Dinah's gone skiing in Aspen.*

**7 go flying/laughing etc** *spoken* to move in a particular way or to do something as you are moving: *The plate went crashing to the floor.*

**8 ▶ BE SENT ◀** [I] to be sent or passed on: *Make sure this package goes tonight.* | **[+ by/through/to etc]** *That letter should go by special delivery.* | *Complaints must go through the proper channels.* | **go before a board/committee etc** *Your suggestion will go before the committee next week.*

### ② TO BE IN OR PASS INTO A PARTICULAR STATE

**9 ▶ BECOME ◀** [linking verb] to become something different and often not so good, either naturally or by

changing deliberately: *The company went bankrupt last year.* | **go bad/sour etc** *The milk went sour.* | **go grey/white etc** *Jessica went bright red with shame.* | **go mad/deaf/bald etc**: *I think you're going crazy.* | **go wild/mad/white etc with sth** *The crowd was going wild with excitement.* —see BECOME (USAGE)
**10 ▶ BE IN A PARTICULAR STATE ◀** [linking verb] to be or remain in a particular, usually bad, state: *All her complaints went unheard.* | *After these attacks he went in fear of his life.* | **go hungry** (=have nothing to eat) *When food is short it's often the mother who goes hungry.*

## ③ TO START TO DO SOMETHING OR TO DO SOMETHING

**11 ▶ START STH ◀** [I] to start doing something: *The signal to begin a race is 'Ready, get set, go!'* | *The preparations have been completed and we're ready to go.* | **get going (on sth)** *You'd better get going on this contract if you want to finish on time.*
**12 ▶ OPERATE ◀** [I] if a machine goes it works properly: *My watch isn't going.*
**13 go to church/school etc** to regularly attend church, school etc: *Joey's too young to go to Cubs.* | *Iain didn't go to university.* —see graph at ATTEND —see JOIN[1] (USAGE)
**14 ▶ HAPPEN ◀** [I always + adv/prep] to happen or develop in a particular way: **go well/smoothly/swimmingly etc**: *The party went well.* | *Everything's going fine at the moment.* | **how are things going/how's it going/how goes it?** *How are things going at school, Joanna?* | **the way things are going** (=used before you give your opinion of what is going to happen next) *The way things are going, we're going to miss the bus.*
**15 be going to do sth a)** to intend to do something: *Wendi's going to ring us from the station.* **b)** to be certain or expected to happen in the future: *Do you think it's going to rain?* —see also GONNA
**16 ▶ MAKE A MOVEMENT ◀** [I always + adv/prep] to make a particular movement: [+ **like/up/down etc**] *While he was describing her, he went like this with his hands.*
**17 don't go doing sth** *spoken* used to tell someone not to do something, especially something that is wrong or bad: *It's a secret, so don't go telling everyone.*
**18 have gone and done sth** *spoken* used when you are surprised by what someone has done: *Kay's gone and lost the car keys!* | **have gone and done it** (=have really made a big mistake) *Tom's really gone and done it this time.*
**19 go it alone** to do something, especially start a business, alone: *Hamish decided to go it alone and set up his own company.*
**20 go one better** to do something better than someone else had done it, or get something better than they have: *We went one better and got a colour printer.*
**21 go far** to succeed in whatever you choose to do: *Ginny's a smart girl, and I'm sure she'll go far.*
**22 go too far** to go beyond the limits of what is reasonable or acceptable: *I think he went too far when he called you a fat idiot!*
**23 go do sth** *spoken* used to tell someone to go away when you are angry: *Go jump in the lake!*
**24 here goes/here we go** *spoken* used just before you do something that is exciting, dangerous etc: *Well, here goes. Wish me luck!*

## ④ POSITION

**25 ▶ BE PLACED ◀** [I always + adv/prep, not in progressive] if something goes somewhere, that is its usual position: [+ **in/under/on etc**] *Where do these plates go?* | *The sofa can go against the wall.*
**26 ▶ FIT ◀** [I not in progressive] to fit or be contained in something: *All that food won't go in this little cupboard.*
**27 ▶ COLOUR ◀** [I] if two colours go, they look good together: *Pink and orange don't go.*
**28 ▶ DIVIDE ◀** [I not in progressive] to divide a number, especially so as to get a whole number in the answer: *Three into two won't go.* | **go into** *Two goes into ten five times.*

## ⑤ SOUND

**29 ▶ SONG/STORY ◀** [I always + adv/prep, T, not in progressive] to be said or sung in a particular way: *How does the story go?* | *The tune goes something like this.* | **go that** *The story goes that he was poisoned by his wife.*
**30 ▶ MAKE A SOUND ◀** [T] to make a particular sound: *Ducks go 'Quack'.* | *The cannon suddenly went boom.*
**31 ▶ WHISTLE/BELL ◀** [I] to make a noise as a warning or signal: *A bell goes to mark the end of each class.*
**32 ▶ SAY ◀** [T] *spoken* to say something: *She goes to me: "I hope you've got a licence for that thing!"*
**33 here/there sb goes again** *spoken* used when someone has annoyed you by continuing to do something they know you do not like: *There she goes again – complaining about the way things are run around here.*

## ⑥ TO FINISH OR STOP

**34 ▶ DISAPPEAR ◀** [I] to no longer exist; disappear: *Has your headache gone yet?* | *My pen's gone; who's taken it?*
**35 have to/must/can go** if someone or something has to go, you have to get rid of them: *That secretary will have to go; she can't even type.*
**36 ▶ GET WORSE ◀** [I] to get worse or be lost altogether: *Dad's sight is starting to go.*
**37 ▶ DIE ◀** [I] used to mean to die when you do not want to say this directly: *Now that his wife's gone, he's all on his own.* | **dead and gone** (=dead)
**38 ▶ BECOME DAMAGED ◀** [I] to become weak, damaged etc or stop working properly: *My old sweater had started to go at the elbows.* | *The bulb's gone in the bathroom.*
**39 ▶ BE SPENT ◀** [I] to be spent or used up: *I don't know where all my money goes!* | [+ **on**] *Half her salary goes on the rent.* | **not go far** *$20 doesn't go far these days.*
**40 ▶ BE SOLD ◀** [I] to be sold: **go for sth** *That lovely house went for £30,000.* | **go to sb** *Each lot will go to the highest bidder.* | **Going, going, gone** (=used to say something has been sold) *"Any more bids?" said the auctioneer; "Going ... going ... gone – to the man in the grey hat."* | **be going cheap** (=not cost very much) *I bought some mugs because they were going cheap.*
**41 ▶ TIME ◀** [I always + adv/prep] to pass: [+ **slowly/quickly etc**] *The summer is going fast.*
**42 there goes sth** *spoken* used to show your disappointment when something stops you doing what you wanted to do: *Well, there goes my chance of stardom!*

## ⑦ OTHER MEANINGS

**43 ▶ REACH ◀** [I always + adv/prep, not in progressive] to reach as far as is stated: [+ **to/from/down etc**] *Does this road go to the station?* | *The valley goes from east to west.* | *This belt won't go around my waist.*
**44 what sb says goes** *informal* someone is in authority and other people must do as they say: *You might not like it, but Phil's in charge, and what he says goes.*
**45 anything goes** used to say that anything someone says or does is acceptable: *With this season's fashions, anything goes.*
**46 ▶ HELP ◀** [I] to help to make, prove, or show something: *Which qualities go to make a good teacher?* | **go to show** *It just goes to show, you never know what's going to happen next.*
**47 be going** *informal* to be available to be used: *Are*

[continued on next page]

[continued from previous page]
*there any jobs going in your firm?* | **be going spare** *I'll have that cupcake if it's going spare.*
**48 to go** **a)** still remaining before something happens: *Only ten days to go to Christmas!* **b)** still to be dealt with before you have finished what you are doing: *Laura's sat six exams and has two more to go.* **c)** still to travel before you reach the place you are going to: *Only another five miles left to go.* **d)** *AmE* if you buy food from a restaurant to go, you buy it to take away and eat at home or somewhere else: *Two chicken dinners with corn to go.* —compare TAKE-OUT (1)
**49 as someone/something goes** compared with the average person or thing of that type: *He's not bad, as politicians go.* | **as things go** *£100,000 for a four-bedroomed house isn't bad as things go these days.*
**50 there you go** *spoken* used to say that something that has happened cannot be changed or was what you expected: *Well, there you go, better luck next time.*
**51 churchgoer/theatregoer etc** someone who regularly goes to church, the theatre etc
**52 theatregoing/churchgoing etc** the act of regularly going to the theatre, to church etc
**53 go it** *BrE old-fashioned* **a)** to go very fast **b)** to behave very excitedly or carelessly —see also GOING[1], GOING[2], GONE[2], GONE[3], **as far as it goes** (FAR[1] (19)), **go as far as to** (FAR[1] (27)), **go halves on (sth)** (HALF[1] (12))

**go about** *phr v* **1** [T **go about** sth] also **set about** to begin working at something; TACKLE[1] (1): *I don't know what is the best way to go about it.* | **go about doing sth** *I wouldn't have the faintest idea how to go about writing a novel.* **2** [T **go about** sth] to do something that you usually do: *The townspeople were going about their business as usual.* **3** [I] *BrE* if a ship goes about, it turns to go in the opposite direction **4 go about with sb** to go around with someone

**go after** sth/sb *phr v* [T not in passive] to try to get or catch something or someone: *I've decided to go after that job in Ohio.*

**go against** sb/sth *phr v* [T not in passive] **1** if you go against someone's wishes or ideas, you do the opposite of what they want: *She went against her counsel's advice.* **2** if a decision, judgment etc goes against you, it is unfavourable to you and you lose: *José's lawyer intimated the case might go against him.* | *The vote went against the government.* **3** to not be in agreement with something: *Such ideas went against his Calvinist upbringing.* | **go against the grain** (=be hard for someone to do because it does not agree with their beliefs, ideas etc until then) *It just went against the grain for men to salute a woman officer.*

**go ahead** *phr v* [I] **1** to begin: *Go ahead, we're all listening.* | *"Do you mind if I smoke?" "No, go right ahead."* | **go ahead with (doing) sth** *Their solicitor is asking if you want to go ahead with the deal?* | **go ahead and do sth** *The newspaper decided to go ahead and publish the story.* **2** also **go on ahead** to go somewhere before the other people in your group: *You go ahead and we'll catch you up later.* | **go ahead of sb** *Kemp went ahead of the convoy to take a look.* **3** to take place: *The sale went ahead as planned.* —see also GO-AHEAD[1]

**go along** *phr v* [I] to continue with a plan, activity etc: *I'm sure she was making her speech up as she went along.*

**go along with** sb/sth *phr v* [T] **1** to agree with or support someone or something: *They were happy to go along with our suggestions.* | **not go along with sth** *informal* (=disapprove of particular behaviour or ideas) **2 go along with you!** *BrE informal* used to say that you do not believe what someone is saying to you

**go around** also **go round** *phr v* **1 go around doing sth** if you go around doing something, especially something people do not approve of, you often do it: *You can't go around accusing people like that.* **2** [I,T **go around** sth] to usually dress or behave in a particular way: *She often goes around the house naked.* | **go around with your eyes shut** (=not notice what is happening around you) **3** [I, T, usually in progressive] if an illness, some news etc is going around it is being passed from one person to another: *There's a rumor going around that Eddie's broke.* | **go around the school/office etc** *A new flu bug's going around the office.* **4 go around with sb/go around together** also **go about** to often go out with someone: *I used to go around with a really bad crowd.* **5** [I] to be enough for everyone to have some: *Is there enough ice-cream to go around?* | *There were never enough text-books to go around.* **6** [I] to move in a circular way: *The wheels went around faster and faster.* | **go around and around** (=go round in a circular way many times) —see also **go around in circles** (CIRCLE[1] (6)) **7 what goes around comes around** an expression meaning that your chance will come again if you are patient

**go at** sth/sb *phr v* [T not in passive] *informal* **1** to start to do something with a lot of energy; TACKLE[1] (1): *Harry went at the problem like a bull at a barn door.* **2** to attack someone or start to fight: *The two girls went at each other like animals.* | **go at it** *The boxers went at it until officials pulled them apart.*

**go away** *phr v* [I] **1** to leave a place or a person: *Go away! Leave me alone!* **2** to spend some time somewhere else, especially on holiday: *Are you going away this year?* **3** if a problem, unpleasant feeling etc goes away, it disappears: *His stutter went away once his mother was home.*

**go back** *phr v* [I] **1** to return to a place you have been to before or to something you were doing before: *I think we ought to go back now.* | *Once you've made the decision I'm afraid there's no going back.* | **go back for sth** (=go back to get something) *I had to go back for my passport.* | **go back to (doing) sth** *Melissa's decided to go back to teaching now Timmy's at school.* | **go back out/inside/downstairs etc** *It's cold out here – let's go back into the kitchen.* **2** [always + adv/prep] to have been made, built, or started at some time in the past: *The old dairy goes back to Tudor times.*

**go back on** sth *phr v* [T] to break or not succeed in keeping to an agreement or promise: **go back on your word/promise etc** *You can rely on Sarah; she won't go back on her word.*

**go by** *phr v* **1** [I] to pass: *Two years went by.* | *Never let a good opportunity go by.* **2** [T not in passive **go by** sth] to use the information or advice you get from a person, a book, a set of rules etc: *Don't go by that old map; it's out of date.* | **go by the book** (=obey rules very strictly) **3** [T not in passive **go by** sth] to form an opinion or judgment of someone or something from something else: *You can't always go by appearances.*

**go down** *phr v* [I]
**1 ▶ GO DOWNSTAIRS ◀** to go to a lower floor of a building: *We went down for dinner at nine o'clock.* | *The elevator was going down.*
**2 ▶ BECOME LOWER ◀** to not be so expensive, high etc: *Your temperature seems to be going down.* | *Tomatoes have gone down.* (=they cost less than before)
**3 ▶ STANDARD ◀** if something goes down, its quality or standard gets worse: *This neighbourhood has really gone down in the last few years.* (=more poor people have moved there) | **go down in sb's opinion/estimation** (=respect someone less) *Fiona's gone down in my estimation since I found out her political views.*
**4 go down well/badly etc** to get a particular sort of reaction from someone: *Matt's joke went down like a lead balloon.*
**5 ▶ SINK ◀** to disappear from sight or below a surface: *Ten men died when the ship went down.* | *The sun was going down behind the mountains.*
**6 ▶ BECOME FLATTER ◀** to become less swollen or lose air: *The swelling will go down if you rest your foot.*
**7 ▶ FOOD/DRINK ◀** to pass down your throat: *I*

*couldn't get the pill to go down.* | *That meringue went down very nicely.*
**8 ▶ BE REMEMBERED ◀** [always + adv/prep] to be recorded or remembered in a particular way: [**+ as/in**] *The talks went down as a landmark in the peace process.* | **go down in history** (=be remembered for many years) *Her work will go down in history.*
**9 ▶ REACH ◀** [always + adv/prep] to reach as far as a particular place: *Some steps went down to the beach.*
**10 ▶ GO SOUTH ◀** to go further south in a country or go from a city to somewhere less important: [**+ to**] *We're going down to the country for the weekend.*
**11 ▶ SPORT ◀ a)** to lose a match or competition: *Chang went down to Sampras in the third set.* **b)** to move down to a lower position in an official list of teams or players: [**+ to**] *United went down to the second division.*
**12 ▶ COMPUTER ◀** to stop working for a short time: *Overloading caused all the computers to go down.*
**13 go down on your knees** to bend your body so that your knees are on the ground, supporting your weight: *Nick went down on one knee to ask her to marry him.*
**14 go down on all fours** to bend your body so that your knees and your hands are on the ground, supporting your weight
**15 ▶ LIGHTS ◀** *literary* if lights go down, they become less bright: *The lights went down and the curtain rose on an empty stage.*
**16 ▶ FROM UNIVERSITY ◀** *BrE* to leave a university after doing a degree or at the end of each TERM[1] (9): [**+ from**] *Emily went down from Oxford with a first class degree.*
**17 ▶ TO PRISON ◀** *slang* to be sent to prison: *Bert went down for five years.*

**go down with** sth *phr v* [T not in passive] *informal* to become ill, especially with an infectious disease: *The children have gone down with mumps.*

**go for** sb/sth *phr v* [T not in passive] **1** to attack someone physically or with words: *Lorna really went for me when I disagreed.* **2** to try to get or win something: *Oona's going for that job in sales.* | *Jackson is going for his second gold medal here.* | **go for it** *informal* (=do everything you can to get something) *If you really want the job, go for it!* —see also **go for broke** (BROKE[2] (3)) **3** to choose or take something: *In a small garden, go for dwarf varieties to maximize space.* **4** *informal* to like something or find something or someone attractive: *Annie tends to go for older men.* **5** *spoken* to also be true about someone or something else: *I told him to work harder, and that goes for you, too.* (=you have to work harder, too) **6** to be sold for a particular price: *How much did that Alpha Romeo go for?* **7 go for nothing** to be wasted: *All that hard work went for nothing when the project was dropped.* —see also **have a lot going for you/not have much going for you** (GOING[2] (4))

**go in** *phr v* [I] **1** to enter a building: *Dad wants me to go in before it gets dark.* **2** when the sun or the moon goes in, it becomes covered with cloud **3** to join someone in order to start a business etc: [**+ with**] *They want me to go in with them on the new venture.*

**go in for** sth *phr v* [T] **1** to do an exam or take part in a competition: *Are you going in for the Proficiency exam?* **2** to like something or do something often because you enjoy it: *I don't go in for garden gnomes.* | **go in for doing sth** *Maggie goes in for improving her mind.* **3** to choose something as your job: *Have you thought of going in for nursing?*

**go into** sth *phr v* [T]
**1 ▶ JOB ◀** [not in passive] to enter a particular profession or business: *Sophie wants to go into the army.* | **go into partnership** *Frank's going into partnership with a friend.*
**2 ▶ TIME/MONEY/EFFORT ◀** [not in passive] to be spent or used to get, make, or do something: *Years of research have gone into this book.*
**3 ▶ EXPLAIN/DESCRIBE ◀** to explain or describe something in detail: *I don't want to go into the matter now.* | **go into details** *Clare wouldn't go into details about her problems.*
**4 ▶ CONSIDER ◀** to examine something thoroughly: *My broker is going into the question of long-term cover.*
**5 ▶ HIT ◀** [not in passive] if a vehicle goes into a tree, wall, or another vehicle, it hits it: *His car went into a lamppost in the high street.*
**6 ▶ DIVIDE ◀** [not in passive] *informal* if a number goes into another number, the second number can be divided by the first: *12 goes into 60 five times.*
**7 ▶ BEGIN A MOVEMENT ◀** [not in passive] if a vehicle or its driver goes into a particular movement, it starts to do it: *The plane had gone into a nosedive and crashed.*
**8 ▶ SPEECH ◀** [not in passive] to begin a long speech, often when it is not necessary: *Norman went into a long monologue about crime.*

**go off** *phr v*
**1 ▶ EXPLODE ◀** [I] to explode: *The bomb went off at 6.30 this morning.*
**2 ▶ MAKE A NOISE ◀** [I] to make a loud noise: *Our neighbor's car alarm is always going off in the middle of the night.*
**3 ▶ STOP WORKING ◀** [I] if a machine goes off, it stops working: *The central heating goes off at 9 o'clock.* | *Suddenly, all the lights went off.*
**4 go off well/badly etc** to happen in a particular way: *The party went off swimmingly.*
**5 ▶ FOOD ◀** [I] *BrE* if food goes off, it goes bad: *The milk's gone off.*
**6 ▶ STOP ◀** [I] *BrE* if a pain goes off, you stop feeling it
**7 ▶ STOP LIKING SB/STH ◀** [T **go off** sb/sth] *BrE informal* to stop liking something or someone: *Val went off coffee when she was pregnant.* | **go off doing sth** *I've gone off cooking lately.*
**8 ▶ SLEEP ◀** [I] *informal* to go to sleep: **go off to sleep** *Has the baby gone off to sleep yet?*
**9 ▶ GET WORSE ◀** [I] *BrE informal* to get worse: *The service in this restaurant has really gone off.*

**go off with** sth/sb *phr v* [T] *informal* **1** to leave your husband, wife, partner etc in order to have a relationship with someone else: *She's gone off with her husband's best friend.* **2** to take something away from a place without having permission: *Who's gone off with my pen?*

**go on** *phr v*
**1 ▶ CONTINUE AN ACTION ◀** [I] to continue without stopping or changing: *We can't go on like this; I want a divorce!* | **go on with sth** *Go on with your work until I come back.* | **go on doing sth** *You can't go on drinking so much – you're not doing yourself any good.* | **go on and on** (=continue for a long time) *The noise seemed to go on and on.*
**2 ▶ DO STH NEXT ◀** [I] to do something after you have finished doing something else: **go on to sth** *Let's go on to the next item on the agenda.* | **go on to do sth** *She went on to become a successful surgeon.*
**3 ▶ HAPPEN ◀** to take place or happen: *What's going on in the kitchen?* | *There's something fishy going on here.* —see also GOINGS-ON
**4 ▶ USE AS PROOF ◀** [T not in passive **go on** sth] to base an opinion or judgment on something: *Police haven't much to go on in their hunt for the killer.*
**5 ▶ BEGIN TO WORK ◀** [I] if a machine goes on, it begins to operate: *The heat goes on automatically at 6 o'clock.*
**6 ▶ TIME ◀** [I] to pass: *As time went on, I grew very fond of him.*
**7 ▶ CONTINUE WITH A STORY/EXPLANATION ETC ◀** [I] to continue talking, especially after stopping or changing to a different subject: *Go on, I'm listening.* | [**+ with**] *After a short pause Maria went on*

[continued on next page]

[continued from previous page]
*with her story.* | **go on to do sth** *The councillor went on to explain where the new supermarket would be.*
**8 ▶ BEHAVE IN THE SAME WAY ◀** [I always + adv/prep] to often behave in a particular way: *The way she's going on she'll have a nervous breakdown.*
**9 ▶ COMPLAIN ◀** [I] *BrE* to continue to complain or ask someone to do something: **go on at sb about sth** *I wish you'd stop going on at me about my weight!* | **go on at sb to do sth** *Mum kept going on at him to tidy his room.*
**10 be going on (for)** to be nearly a time, age, number etc: *Nancy must be going on for 60, you know. Jenny's one of those wise teenagers who's 16 going on 70* (=she seems older than she is, or thinks she is)
**11 ▶ MEDICINE ◀** [T not in passive **go on** sth] to begin to take a type of medicine: **go on the pill** *Dani's too young to go on the pill.*
**12 ▶ GO IN FRONT OF ◀** [I] to go somewhere before the other people you are with: *Bill went on in the car and I followed on foot.*
**13 ▶ TALK TOO MUCH ◀** [I] *informal* to talk too much: *You don't half go on!* | **go on and on** *They went on and on about the importance of safety belts.*
**14 ▶ DEVELOP ◀** [I] *BrE informal* to develop or make progress: *How's the work going on?*
**15 go on a)** used to encourage someone to do something: *Go on, have another cookie.* **b)** also **go on with you** *BrE spoken* used to tell someone that you do not believe them: *I told her she had the most beautiful eyes I'd ever seen. "Oh, go on with you!" she said, blushing with pleasure.*
**16 to be going on with/to go on with** *informal, BrE* if you have enough of something to be going on with, you have enough to use at present until the situation improves: *Have you got enough money to be going on with?*

**17 go on the dole** *BrE informal* to begin to claim money from the government because you are not working

**go out** *phr v* [I]
**1 ▶ FOR ENTERTAINMENT ◀** to leave your house, especially in order to enjoy yourself: *Are you going out tonight?* | *Let's go out for a walk.* | **go out doing sth** *Liam goes out drinking every Friday.* | **go out to do sth** *Can I go out to play now?* | **go out and do sth** *You should go out and get some fresh air.*
**2 ▶ WITH BOY/GIRL ◀** to spend a lot of time with someone and have a romantic relationship with them: **go out with sb** *Jean used to go out with my brother.* | **go out together** *How long have you been going out together?*
**3 ▶ FIRE/LIGHT ◀** to stop burning or shining: *The candle spluttered and went out.* —see FIRE[1] (USAGE)
**4 ▶ ON TV/RADIO ◀** to be broadcast on television or radio: *The program goes out live at 5 o'clock on Mondays.*
**5 ▶ MOVE ABROAD ◀** to travel to a place far away, often in order to live there: *They've gone out to Australia.*
**6 ▶ STRIKE ◀** *BrE* also **go out on strike** to stop working because of a disagreement
**7 go out like a light** *informal* to go to sleep very quickly: *As soon as his head touched the pillow, he went out like a light.*
**8 ▶ NOT BE FASHIONABLE/USED ◀** to stop being fashionable or used: *Flared trousers are going out again.* —opposite **come in** (COME[1])
**9 ▶ SEA ◀** to go back to its lower level: *The tide's going out.* —opposite **come in** (COME [1])
**10 ▶ MAKE PUBLIC ◀** to let everyone know about something: *Word went out that the President was dead.*
**11 heart/thoughts go out to sb** to have a lot of sympathy for someone: *Our hearts go out to the victim's family.*
**12 ▶ TIME ◀** [always + adv/prep] *literary* to end: *March went out with high winds and rain.*

**go over** *phr v*
**1 ▶ GO NEAR SB/STH ◀** [I] to go nearer to someone or something: *Blake went over and sat on the bed.* | [+ **to**] *Chiara went over to the bar.* | **go over to do sth** *He had gone over to say goodbye.*
**2 ▶ EXAMINE ◀** [T, **go over** sth] to look at something or think about something carefully: *I had gone over and over what happened in my mind.*
**3 ▶ SEARCH ◀** [T, **go over** sth] to search something very carefully: *The police have been over the apartment with a fine-tooth comb.*
**4 ▶ VISIT ◀** [T, **go over** sth] to visit a building etc to decide whether to buy or rent it: *We'd been over several houses before finding this one.*
**5 ▶ REPEAT ◀** [T, **go over** sth] to repeat something in order to learn it or understand it: *Maybe if I went over it all again I would see what she meant.*
**6 go over well/badly etc** if a speech, performance etc goes over well, the people listening like it: [+ **with**] *His speech went over well with the Left of the party.*
**7 ▶ CHANGE ◀** [I] to change your beliefs, religion, habits etc: **go over from sth to sth** *Lloyd George went over to Labour in 1951.* | **go over to doing sth** *I've gone over to drinking black coffee.*
**8 ▶ TV/RADIO ◀** [I] to change to a broadcast from another place: [+ **to**] *We're going over to the White House for an important announcement.*
**9 ▶ CLEAN ◀** [T] to clean something: *Liz went over the carpet with the hoover.*

**go round** also **go around** *phr v* [I]
**1 ▶ BE ENOUGH ◀** to be enough for everyone: *Are there enough chairs to go around?*
**2 ▶ ILLNESS/NEWS ETC ◀** if an illness, news etc goes around, it is passed from one person to another: *There's a lot of flu going around at the moment.*
**3 go round in your head** if words, sounds etc go round in your head, you continue to hear them for a long time: *That stupid song kept going around in my head.*
**4 ▶ DRESS/BEHAVE ◀** to usually dress or behave in a particular way: *These shoplifters go round in pairs.* | **go around doing sth** *You can't go around telling people what to do all the time!*
**5 go around with sb/go round together** to often go out with someone —see also **go round in circles** (CIRCLE[1] (6))

**go slow** *phr v* [I] *BrE* to put as little effort as possible into your work, as a form of STRIKE[2] (1) —see also GO-SLOW

**go through** *phr v* **1** [T, **go through** sth] to suffer or experience something bad: *How does she keep smiling after all she's been through?* **2** [T, **go through** sth] to use something and have none left; **get through** (GET): *Austria was so expensive – we went through all our money in one week.* **3** [I,T, **go through** sth] if a law goes through, or goes through Parliament, it is officially accepted: *The Bill went through Parliament without a vote.* **4** [I] if a deal or agreement goes through, it is officially accepted: *Your application for a loan has gone through.* **5** [T, **go through** sth] *BrE* to slowly make a hole in something: *My toe has gone through my sock.* **6** [T, **go through** sth] to practise something, for example a performance: *Let's go through the whole thing again, from the beginning.* **7** [T, **go through** sth] to look at or for something carefully: *Dave went through his pockets looking for the keys.* **8** [T, **go through** sth] to read a document from beginning to end: *Could you just go through this file and mark anything that's relevant?*

**go through with** sth *phr v* [T] to do something you had promised or planned to do, even though it causes problems or you are no longer sure you want to do it: *Jenny felt she couldn't go through with the abortion.*

**go to** sth *phr v* [T, not in passive] **1 go to great lengths/go to a lot of trouble** to take a lot of trouble to do something: *They went to great lengths to make sure I felt at home.* **2 go to great expense** to spend a lot of money to do something **3** to begin to experience or do something: *Shh! Daddy's trying to go to sleep.*| *Britain and Germany went to war in 1939.* **4** to be given to someone: *All the money raised will go to local charities.*

**go together** *phr v* [I] **1** if two things go together, they look, taste etc good together: *Pork and apple go well together* — see FIT[1] (USAGE) **2** if two people are going together, they are having a romantic relationship: *I didn't know Sharon and Les were going together.*

**go under** *phr v* [I] **1** if a business goes under, it has serious problems and fails: *Many restaurants go under in the first year.* **2** if a ship or something that is floating goes under, it sinks beneath the surface: *The Titanic finally went under, watched by those survivors who had found a place in the lifeboats.*

**go up** *phr v* [I]
**1 ▶ INCREASE ◀** *spoken* to increase in number or amount: *I see cigarettes are going up again.* (=are getting more expensive)
**2 ▶ BE BUILT ◀** *spoken* to be built: *New houses are going up all around the town.*
**3 ▶ EXPLODE/BURN ◀** *spoken* to explode or be destroyed in a fire: *The whole building went up in flames.* —see also **go up in smoke** (SMOKE[1] (5))
**4 ▶ SHOUT ◀** if a shout or a CHEER goes up, people start to shout or CHEER
**5 ▶ THEATRE ◀** if the curtain goes up at a theatre, it opens for the performance to start: *The curtain went up on an empty stage.*
**6 ▶ REACH ◀** to reach as far as a particular place: [+ **to**] *The trees go right up to the beach.*
**7 ▶ TO UNIVERSITY ◀** *BrE* to go to a university to begin a course of study: [+ **to**] *She went up to Oxford in 1975.*
**8 ▶ TO TOWN ◀** *BrE* to go to a town or city from a smaller place: [+ **to**] *I like to go up to town for Christmas shopping.*

**go with** *phr v* [T not in passive]
**1 ▶ MATCH/SUIT ◀** if one thing goes with another, they look, taste etc good together: *That shade of blue goes with your eyes.* —see FIT[1] (USAGE)
**2 ▶ BE PART OF STH ◀** to be included as part of something: *The house goes with the job.*| **go with doing sth** *Responsibility goes with becoming a father.*
**3 ▶ EXIST TOGETHER ◀** to often exist with something else: *Ill health often goes with poverty.*
**4 ▶ BOY/GIRL ◀** *informal* to have someone as your boyfriend or girlfriend or to have a sexual relationship with someone: *Is Martin still going with Jane?*
**5 ▶ AGREE ◀** to accept someone's idea or plan: *Let's go with John's original proposal.*

**go without** *phr v* [I,T] **1** to be able to live without something or without doing something: *We can't afford a holiday, so we'll just have to go without.*| **go without sth** *She had gone without food to feed the children.* **2 it goes without saying** used to say that something is so obvious that it does not need to be said: *It goes without saying that young doctors should work fewer hours.*

1 **go²** *n plural* **goes**
**1 ▶ TRY ◀** [C] an attempt to do something **have a go** *"I can't open this jar." "Let me have a go."*| **have a go at (doing) sth** *Daisy had six goes at her driving-test before she passed.*| **at one go** *Ruby blew out all her candles at one go.*| **give sth a go** (=try to do sth even though you do not think you will succeed) *I don't think I can make him change his mind, but I'll give it a go.*
**2 ▶ IN A GAME ◀** [C] someone's turn in a game etc: *Whose go is it?*| *If you throw a two you miss a go.*| **have a go on sth** *Can I have a go on your computer?*| **3p/5p/10p a go** *Guess the weight of the cake, 10 pence a go.*
**3 make a go of sth** *informal* to make a business, marriage etc succeed: **make a go of it** *Do you think they'll make a go of it with this restaurant?*
**4 on the go** *informal* very busy or working all the time: *I'm on the go all day and then collapse into bed at about 10 o'clock.*
**5 it's no go** *spoken* used to say that something has not happened or that it will not happen *I went and asked for a rise but it was no go, I'm afraid.* —see also NO-GO AREA (2)
**6 all the go** *old-fashioned* very fashionable
**7 it's all go** *BrE spoken* it is very busy: *It's all go in the toy department in December.*
**8 have a go at sb** *spoken, especially BrE* to complain: *Mark's bound to have a go at me for spending all this money.*
**9 have a go** *spoken, especially BrE* **a)** to attack someone physically: *A whole gang of yobs were standing around, just waiting to have a go.* **b)** to try to catch someone who you see doing something wrong, rather than waiting for the police: *The public should not be encouraged to have a go.*
**10 ▶ ENERGY ◀** [U] *BrE* liveliness and energy: *The children are full of go this morning.* —see also GET-UP-AND-GO

**goad¹** /gəʊd‖goʊd/ *v* [T] **1** to make someone do something by annoying them or encouraging them until they do it: **goad sb into (doing) sth** *Kathy goaded him into telling her what he had done.*| **goad sb on** *Duval was goaded on by the need for more money.* **2** to push animals ahead of you with a sharp stick

**goad²** *n* [C] **1** a sharp stick for making cattle move forward **2** something that forces someone to do something

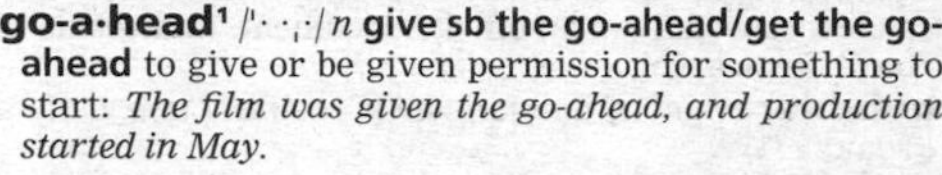

**go·a·head¹** /ˈ· ·ˌ·/ *n* **give sb the go-ahead/get the go-ahead** to give or be given permission for something to start: *The film was given the go-ahead, and production started in May.*

**go-ahead²** *adj BrE* using or encouraging new methods or ideas and therefore likely to succeed; PROGRESSIVE[1] (1): *This go-ahead company introduced profit-sharing.*

**goal** /gəʊl‖goʊl/ *n* [C] **1** something that you hope to achieve in the future; aim: **achieve a goal** *We've achieved our goal of building a shelter for the homeless.*| **long-term goal/short-term goal** (=that you hope to achieve after a long or short time) **2** the action of making the ball go into the scoring (SCORE[2] (1)) area in games such as football or HOCKEY, or the point won by doing this: **score a goal** *Baggio scored the first goal for Italy.* **3** the area between two posts where the ball must go for a point to be won: **keep goal** (=be the goalkeeper) —see picture on page 1264 S2 W1

**goal·ie** /ˈgəʊli‖ˈgoʊ-/ *n* [C] *informal* a goalkeeper —see picture on page 1264

**goal·keep·er** /ˈgəʊlˌkiːpə‖ˈgoʊlˌkiːpər/ *n* [C] the player in a sports team who has to try to stop the ball going into his team's goal —see picture on page 1264

**goal·less** /ˈgəʊl-ləs‖ˈgoʊl-/ *adj* **a goalless draw** a match where no goals are scored (SCORE[2] (1))

**goal line** /ˈ· ·/ *n* [C] a line that marks the end of a playing area, where the goal is placed

**goal·mouth** /ˈgəʊlmaʊθ‖ˈgoʊl-/ *n* [C] the area directly in front of the GOAL (3)

**goal·post** /ˈgəʊlpəʊst‖ˈgoʊlpoʊst/ *n* [C usually plural] **1** one of the two posts, with a bar along the top or across the middle, that form the GOAL (3) in games like football and HOCKEY **2 move the goalposts** *BrE informal* to change the rules, limits etc while someone is trying to do something, and make it more difficult for them

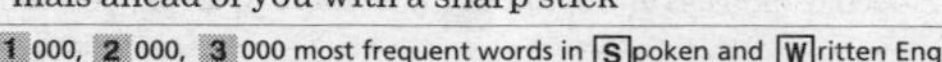

**goal·ten·der** /ˈgəʊlˌtendə‖ˈgoʊlˌtendər/ *n* [C] *AmE* a GOALKEEPER

**goat** /gəʊt‖goʊt/ *n* [C] **1** an animal a little like a sheep that can climb steep hills and rocks **2 get sb's goat** *spoken* to make someone extremely annoyed: *I'll tell you another thing that really got my goat.* **3 act/play the goat** *BrE informal* to behave in a silly way **4 old goat** an unpleasant old man, especially one who annoys women in a sexual way —see also BILLY GOAT

goat

**goa·tee** /gəʊˈtiː‖goʊ-/ *n* [C] a small pointed BEARD on the end of a man's chin —see picture on page 412

**goat·herd** /ˈgəʊthɜːd‖ˈgoʊthɜːrd/ *n* [C] someone who looks after a group of goats

**goat·skin** /ˈgəʊtˌskɪn‖ˈgoʊt-/ *n* **1** [C,U] leather made from the skin of a goat, or a wine container made from this **2** [C] the skin of a goat

**gob**[1] /gɒb‖gɑːb/ *n* [C] *informal* **1** *BrE* an impolite word meaning your mouth: *Shut your gob!* **2** a mass of something wet and sticky: [+ **of**] *a gob of spit* **3 gobs** *AmE informal* a large amount of something: *gobs of money*

**gob**[2] *v* [I] *BrE informal* to blow a small amount of liquid out of your mouth; SPIT[1] (1)

**gob·bet** /ˈgɒbɪ̣t‖ˈgɑː-/ *n* [C] a small piece of something, especially food

**gob·ble** /ˈgɒbəl‖ˈgɑː-/ *v informal* **1** [I,T] also **gobble up** to eat something very quickly or in a way people do not consider polite: *Don't gobble your food!* **2** [T] also **gobble up** to finish a supply of something quickly: *Inflation has gobbled up our wage increases.* **3** [I] to make a sound like a TURKEY (1) —**gobble** *n* [C]

**gob·ble·dy·gook, gobbledegook** /ˈgɒbəldiguːk‖ˈgɑːbəldigʊk, -guːk/ *n* [U] *informal* complicated language, especially in an official document, that seems to have no meaning

**gob·bler** /ˈgɒblə‖ˈgɑːblər/ *n* [C] *AmE informal* a TURKEY (1)

**go-be·tween** /ˈ· ·ˌ·/ *n* [C] someone who takes messages from one person or group to another, because the two sides cannot meet or do not wish to meet: *Martin acted as a go-between in the negotiations.*

**gob·let** /ˈgɒblɪ̣t‖ˈgɑːb-/ *n* [C] a cup made of glass or metal, with a base and a stem but no handles —see picture at GLASS[1]

**gob·lin** /ˈgɒblɪ̣n‖ˈgɑːb-/ *n* [C] a small, often ugly creature in children's stories that likes to trick people

**gob·smacked** /ˈgɒbsmækt‖ˈgɑːb-/ *adj BrE spoken* very surprised, pleased, or disappointed

**gob·stop·per** /ˈgɒbˌstɒpə‖ˈgɑːbˌstɑːpər/ *n* [C] *BrE* a large round hard sweet; JAWBREAKER (1) *AmE*

**go-cart** /ˈ· ·/ *n* [C] an American spelling of GO-KART

**God** /gɒd‖gɑːd/ *n* [singular, not with *the*] **1** the BEING[2] (1) who Christians, Jews, and Muslims pray to —see also **act of God** (ACT[2] (10)) **2 God/oh God/my God/good God** *spoken* used to add force to what you are saying, when you are surprised, annoyed, or amused: *Oh God, how embarrassing!* **3 I swear/hope/wish etc to God** used to emphasize that you promise, hope or wish that something is true: *I hope to God nothing goes wrong.* **4 God knows** *spoken* **a)** used to show that you are annoyed because you do not know something, or because you think that something is unreasonable: **God knows who/what/how etc** *God knows what she's doing in there.* | **God only knows** *It'll cost God only knows how much.* **b)** used to add force to what you are saying: *God knows, it hasn't been easy.* **5 what/how/where/who in God's name** *spoken* used to add force to a question when you are angry or surprised: *Where in God's name have you been?* **6 God forbid** *spoken* used to say that you very much hope that something will not happen: [+ **(that)**] *God forbid that she should ever hurt you.* **7 honest to God** *spoken* used to emphasize that you are not lying or joking: *Honest to God, I didn't tell her!* **8 God almighty** *spoken* used to express surprise, shock, annoyance, or anger **9 God help you/him etc** *spoken* used to warn someone: *God help you if Tom comes home and you're still here!* **10 God help us** *spoken, usually humorous* used when you think that something bad is going to happen: *"Simon's doing the cooking." "God help us!"* **11 God bless** *spoken* used to show your affection for someone: *Goodnight, Jenny – God bless.* **12 God willing** *spoken* used to say that you hope there will be no problems: *We'll be moving next month, God willing.* **13 God-given** received from God: *a God-given talent for singing* | **a God-given right** (=the right to do something without asking anyone else's opinion) **14 God give me strength!** *spoken* used when you are becoming annoyed **15 God's gift to women/men etc** someone who thinks they are perfect or extremely attractive: *Paul thinks he's God's gift to the film industry.* **16 God rest his/her soul** also **God rest him/her** *old-fashioned* used to show respect when speaking about someone who is dead **17 play God** to behave as though you have the power to do whatever you like: *scientists who think they can play God with their genetic experiments* **18 by God** *old-fashioned* used to add force when you are expressing determination or surprise —see also **there but for the grace of God** (GRACE[1] (6)), **in the lap of the gods** (LAP[1] (5)), **thank God/goodness/heavens** (THANK (2))

**USAGE NOTE: GOD**

FORMALITY AND POLITENESS

In informal spoken English the following expressions are very common. They are used in a non-religious way, but some people would consider them to be offensive. **Oh (my) God/My God/Good God/God!** are all used to show strong surprise, fear, excitement or annoyance, or to emphasize what is said: *Oh God, what's that?* | *My God, I forgot to lock the door.* | *God he was sexy!* | *Good God no!*

**For God's sake** is used to draw attention strongly to a particular point: *How can she do that, she's only seven for God's sake!* It is also used with orders to make them stronger, or to show annoyance: *For God's sake shut up!*

**Thank God** shows you are happy and pleased about something: *Thank God you're here!* | *Thank God for that!*

**God (only) knows** is a strong way of saying 'I don't know'.

SPELLING

**God** is always written with a capital letter in these expressions.

GRAMMAR

**God** is not used with *the*: *I pray to God every night* (NOT *the God*).

**god** /gɒd‖gɑːd/ *n* [C] **1** a male BEING who is believed to control the world or part of it, or represents a particular quality: *Mars, the god of war* **2** [C] someone or something to which you give too much importance or respect: *material wealth became their god* **3 the gods a)** *informal* the seats high up and at the back of a theatre **b)** the force that some people believe controls their lives, bringing them good or bad luck: *The gods are against me!*

**god-aw·ful** /ˌ· ˈ··◂/ *adj* [only before noun] *informal* very bad or unpleasant

**god·child** /ˈgɒdtʃaɪld‖ˈgɑːd-/ *plural* **godchildren** /-ˌtʃɪldrən/ *n* [C] the child that a GODPARENT promises to help and to teach Christian values to

**god·dam·mit** /gɒˈdæmɪ̣t‖ˌgɑːdˈdæm-/ *interjection especially AmE* used to express annoyance, anger etc

**god·damn, goddam** /ˈgɒdæm‖ˌgɑːdˈdæm◂/ also **god-damned** /-dæmd/ *adj* [only before noun] *spoken* a word used to express annoyance or give force to an expression:

*Where's the goddamn key?* —**goddamn**, **goddam**, **goddamned** *adv*: *I just did something so goddamned stupid.*

**god·daugh·ter** /ˈgɒdˌdɔːtə‖ˈgɑːdˌdɒːtər/ *n* [C] a girl that a GODPARENT promises to help and to teach Christian values to

**god·dess** /ˈgɒdɪ̣s‖ˈgɑː-/ *n* [C] a female BEING³ (1) who is believed to control the world or part of it, or represents a particular quality: *Aphrodite, goddess of love*

**god·fa·ther** /ˈgɒdˌfɑːðə‖ˈgɑːdˌfɑːðər/ *n* [C] **1** a man who promises to help a child and to teach him or her Christian values **2** *slang* the head of a criminal organization or MAFIA group

**god-fear·ing** /ˈ· ˌ··/ *adj old-fashioned* leading a good life following the rules of the Christian religion

**god·for·sak·en** /ˈgɒdfəseɪkən‖ˈgɑːdfər-/ *adj* a godforsaken place is far away from where people live and contains nothing interesting, attractive, or cheerful: *Do you really enjoy living in this godforsaken dump?*

**god·head** /ˈgɒdhed‖ˈgɑːd-/ *n* **the Godhead** *formal* a word meaning God, used by Christians to mean the Father, the Son, and the Holy Spirit

**god·less** /ˈgɒdləs‖ˈgɑːd-/ *adj old-fashioned* not showing respect for God or belief in a god —**godlessly** *adv*

**god·like** /ˈgɒdlaɪk‖ˈgɑːd-/ *adj* like a god or with a quality suitable for a god: *surveying the world with godlike calm*

**god·ly** /ˈgɒdli‖ˈgɑːdli/ *adj old-fashioned* obeying God and leading a good life —**godliness** *n* [U]

**god·moth·er** /ˈgɒdˌmʌðə‖ˈgɑːdˌmʌðər/ *n* [C] a woman who promises to help a child, and to teach him or her Christian values

**god·pa·rent** /ˈgɒdˌpeərənt‖ˈgɑːdˌper-/ *n* [C] someone who promises to help a child, and to teach him or her Christian values

**god·send** /ˈgɒdsend‖ˈgɑːd-/ *n* [singular] something good that happens to you when you really need it: *That cheque from Sandy was a real godsend.*

**god·son** /ˈgɒdsʌn‖ˈgɑːd-/ *n* [C] a boy that a godparent promises to help and to teach Christian values to

**god·speed** /ˌgɒdˈspiːd‖ˈgɑːdspiːd, ˌgɑːdˈspiːd/ *n* [U] *old use* used to wish someone good luck especially before a journey

**God squad** /ˈ· ·/ *n slang* an insulting way of describing Christians who try to persuade other people to become Christians

**go·er** /ˈgəʊə‖ˈgoʊər/ *n* [C] **1 cinema-/concert-/theatre-goer** someone who regularly goes to theatres etc **2** *BrE spoken* a woman who often has sex with different men: *one of my mum's friends who's a bit of a goer*

**go·fer** /ˈgəʊfə‖ˈgoʊfər/ *n* [C] *informal* someone who carries messages or gets or takes things for their employer

**go-get·ter** /ˌ· ˈ··, ˈ· ˌ··‖ˈ· ˌ··/ *n* [C] someone who is likely to be successful because they are very determined and have a lot of energy: *She's a real go-getter.*

**gog·gle** /ˈgɒgəl‖ˈgɑː-/ *v* [I] to look at something with your eyes wide open in surprise or shock: [+ **at**] *They were goggling at us as if we were freaks.*

**goggle box** /ˈ·· ·/ *n* [C usually singular] *BrE informal* a television

**goggle-eyed** /ˌ·· ˈ·◂/ *adj* with your eyes wide open and looking directly at something: *staring goggle-eyed at the women*

**gog·gles** /ˈgɒgəlz‖ˈgɑː-/ *n* [plural] something that protects your eyes, made of two round pieces of glass or plastic with an edge that fits against your skin

**go-go danc·er** /ˈ· · ˌ··/ *n* [C] a woman who dances with sexy movements in a bar or NIGHTCLUB —**go-go dancing** *n* [U]

**go·ing¹** /ˈgəʊɪŋ‖ˈgoʊ-/ *n* [U]
**1 ▶LEAVING◀** the act of leaving a place: *His going will be no great loss to the company.*
**2 ▶SPEED◀** the speed at which you travel or work: *We climbed the mountain in three hours, which wasn't bad going.* | **hard/rough/slow going** *I'm getting the work done, but it's slow going.*
**3 heavy going** if a book, play etc is heavy going, it is boring and difficult to understand
**4 while the going's good** *especially BrE* before someone stops you from doing what you want: *Let's get out while the going's good.*
**5 ▶GROUND◀** the condition of the ground, especially for a horse race —see also **comings and goings** (COMING¹ (2))

**going²** *adj* **1** [not before noun] *informal* available: *Are there any jobs going where you work?* **2 the biggest/best/nicest ... going** the biggest, best etc of a particular thing: *Jim's the biggest fool going.* **3 the going rate** the usual cost of a service or job: *£15 per hour is the going rate for tuition.* **4 have a lot going for you/not have much going for you** to have or not have many advantages and good qualities that will bring success: *Stop being so depressed. You have a lot going for you.* **5 a going concern** a business which is making a profit and is expected to continue to do so

**going-o·ver** /ˌ·· ˈ··/ *n* **1** a thorough examination of something to make sure it is all right: *The car needs a good going-over.* **2 give sb a going-over** *especially BrE* to hit someone and hurt them

**goings-on** /ˌ·· ˈ·/ *n* [plural] activities or events that are strange, especially ones that involve sex or make you think something dishonest may be happening: *There are certainly some strange goings-on at that house, I reckon.*

**goi·tre** *BrE*, **goiter** *AmE* /ˈgɔɪtə‖-ər/ *n* [C,U] a disease of the THYROID GLAND that makes your neck very swollen

**go-kart** also **go-cart** *AmE* /ˈgəʊ kɑːt‖ˈgoʊ kɑːrt/ *n* [C] a small vehicle with an engine, made of an open frame on four wheels and used in races —**go-karting** *n* [U]

**gold¹** /gəʊld‖goʊld/ *n* **1** [U] a valuable soft yellow metal that is an ELEMENT (=simple substance) and is used for making coins, jewellery etc: **strike gold** (=find it in the ground) **2** [U] coins, jewellery etc made of this metal: *Vanessa wore so much gold it's no wonder she was mugged.* **3** [C,U] the colour of this metal: *The room was decorated in golds and blues.* **4** [C] *informal* a GOLD MEDAL **5 gold digger** *old-fashioned slang* a woman who tries to attract rich men —see also **have a heart of gold** (HEART (13))

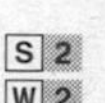

**gold²** *adj* **1** made of gold: *a gold chain* **2** having the colour of gold: *gold buttons* | *gold velvet curtains* —compare GOLDEN

**gold·brick** /ˈgəʊldbrɪk‖ˈgoʊld-/ also **gold·brick·er** /-brɪkə‖-ər/ *n* [C] *AmE informal* someone who stays away from their work, especially with the false excuse that they are ill —**goldbrick** *v* [I]

**gold card** /ˌ· ˈ·/ *n* [C] a special CREDIT CARD that gives you additional advantages or services, such as a high spending limit

**gold dust** /ˈ· ·/ *n* [U] **1** gold in the form of a fine powder **2 be like gold dust** to be very valuable and difficult to find: *Good secretaries are like gold dust.*

**gold·en** /ˈgəʊldən‖ˈgoʊl-/ *adj* **1** having a bright, rich, yellow colour, like gold: *golden sunlight* | *golden hair* —see picture on page 411 **2** made of gold: *a golden crown* **3 a golden opportunity** a good chance to get something valuable or to be very successful: *Don't turn the job down – it's a golden opportunity.* **4 golden boy/girl** someone who is popular and successful: *the golden girl of US tennis* **5** [only before noun] a golden period of time is one of great happiness or success: *the golden summers of childhood* **6 golden oldie** a popular song written several years ago that people still enjoy listening to  W 3

**golden age** /ˈ·· ·/ *n* [usually singular] an unusually good time of great achievement and happiness, especially in the past: *the golden age of film*

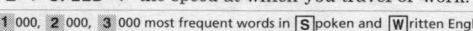

**golden an·ni·ver·sa·ry** /ˌ·· ··ˈ···/ *n* [C] *AmE* a GOLDEN WEDDING

**golden brown** /ˌ·· ˈ·◂/ *adj* a light brown colour: *Bake the biscuits until golden brown.*

**golden ea·gle** /ˌ·· ˈ··/ *n* [C] a large light brown bird that lives in northern parts of the world

**golden hand·shake** /ˌ·· ˈ··/ *n* [C] *BrE* a large amount of money given to someone when they leave their job

**golden ju·bi·lee** /ˌ·· ˈ···/ *n* [C] *BrE* the date that is exactly 50 years after some important event, especially of becoming king or queen —compare DIAMOND JUBILEE, SILVER JUBILEE

**golden par·a·chute** /ˌ·· ˈ···/ *n* [C] *BrE informal* part of a business person's contract which states that they will be paid a large sum of money when the contract ends

**golden rai·sin** /ˌ·· ˈ··/ *n* [C] *AmE* a small pale RAISIN (=dried fruit) used in baking; SULTANA *BrE*

**golden re·triev·er** /ˌ·· ·ˈ··/ *n* [C] a fairly large dog with silky light brown fur

**golden rule** /ˌ·· ˈ·/ *n* [usually singular] a very important principle, way of behaving etc that should be remembered

**golden syr·up** /ˌ·· ˈ··/ *n* [U] *BrE* a sweet, thick liquid made from sugar that is used in cooking

**golden wed·ding** /ˌ·· ˈ··/ also **golden wedding an·niver·sa·ry** /ˌ·· ˈ·· ··ˌ···/ *BrE informal n* [C] the date that is exactly 50 years after a wedding; GOLDEN ANNIVERSARY *AmE* —compare DIAMOND WEDDING, SILVER WEDDING

**gold·field** /ˈgəʊldfiːld‖ˈgoʊld-/ *n* [C] also **goldfields** *plural* an area of land where gold can be found

**gold·finch** /ˈgəʊldˌfɪntʃ‖ˈgoʊld-/ *n* [C] a small singing bird with yellow feathers on its wings

**gold·fish** /ˈgəʊldˌfɪʃ‖ˈgoʊld-/ *n* [C] a small shiny orange fish often kept as a pet

**goldfish bowl** /ˈ·· ˌ·/ *n* [C] **1** a round glass bowl in which fish are kept as pets **2** **live in a goldfish bowl** to be in a situation in which people can know everything about your life

**gold leaf** /ˌ· ˈ·/ *n* [U] gold which has been beaten into extremely thin sheets for use in decoration

**gold med·al** /ˌ· ˈ··/ *n* [C] a round, flat piece of gold given to someone for a special achievement, especially for winning a race or competition —see also BRONZE MEDAL, SILVER MEDAL

**gold med·al·list** *BrE*, **gold medalist** *AmE* /ˌ· ˈ···/ *n* [C] someone who wins a gold medal

**gold·mine** /ˈgəʊldmaɪn‖ˈgoʊld-/ *n* [C] **1** *informal* a business or activity that produces large profits: *I bet that shop's a real goldmine.* **2** a deep hole or system of holes underground from which rock containing gold is taken **3** **be sitting on a goldmine** to own something very valuable, especially without realizing this

**gold plate** /ˌ· ˈ·/ *n* [U] **1** a layer of gold on top of another metal **2** dishes, spoons etc made of gold —**gold-plated** *adj*: *Is it solid gold or gold-plated?*

**gold-rimmed** /ˌ· ˈ·◂/ *adj* having a gold edge or border: *gold-rimmed glasses*

**gold rush** /ˈ· ·/ *n* [C] a situation when a lot of people hurry to a place where gold has just been discovered

**gold·smith** /ˈgəʊldˌsmɪθ‖ˈgoʊld-/ *n* [C] someone who makes things out of gold

**gold stan·dard** /ˈ· ˌ··/ *n* **the gold standard** the use of the value of gold as a fixed standard on which to base the value of money

**go·lem** /ˈgəʊləm‖ˈgoʊ-/ *n* [C] *AmE informal* a stupid person

S2 W3 **golf** /gɒlf‖gɑːlf, gɒːlf/ *n* [U] a game in which the players hit a small white ball into holes in the ground with a set of golf clubs using as few hits as possible: **a round of golf** (=a game of golf) —**golfer** *n* [C]

**golf ball** /ˈ· ·/ *n* [C] **1** a small hard white ball used in the game of golf **2** a small ball in an electric TYPEWRITER that has the letters of the alphabet on it, and that moves to print them onto paper **3** an electric TYPEWRITER that operates in this way —compare DAISYWHEEL PRINTER

**golf club** /ˈ· ·/ *n* [C] **1** an organization of people who play golf, or the land and buildings they use **2** a long wooden or metal stick used for hitting the ball in the game of golf —see picture on page 1264

**golf course** /ˈ· ·/ *n* [C] an area of land that golf is played on

**golf·ing** /ˈgɒlfɪŋ‖ˈgɑː-, ˈgɒː-/ *n* [U] the activity of playing golf: *Ian goes golfing on Sundays.*

**golf links** /ˈ· ·/ *plural* **golf links** *n* [C] a golf course, especially by the sea

**go·li·ath** /gəˈlaɪəθ/ *n* [C] a person or company that is very large, strong, and powerful; GIANT²: *How can a small computer company compete with the goliaths of the industry?*

**gol·li·wog** /ˈgɒliwɒg‖ˈgɑːliwɑːg/ *n* [C] a child's DOLL¹ (1) made of cloth, like a man with a black face, white eyes, and short black hair

**gol·ly¹** /ˈgɒli‖ˈgɑːli/ *interjection old-fashioned* used to express surprise

**golly²** *n* [C] *informal* a golliwog

**-gon** /gən, *strong* gɒn‖gən, *strong* gɑːn/ *suffix* [in nouns] a shape with a particular number of sides and angles: *a hexagon* (=with six sides) | *a polygon* (=with many sides)

**go·nad** /ˈgəʊnæd‖ˈgoʊ-/ *n* [C] *technical* the male or female sex organ in which the SPERM (1) or eggs (EGG¹ (3)) are produced

**gon·do·la** /ˈgɒndələ‖ˈgɑːn-, gɑːnˈdoʊlə/ *n* [C] **1** a long narrow boat with a flat bottom and high points at each end, used on the CANALS in Venice in Italy **2** the place where passengers sit that hangs beneath an AIRSHIP or BALLOON¹ (2) **3** the enclosed part of a CABLE CAR where the passengers sit

**gon·do·lier** /ˌgɒndəˈlɪə‖ˌgɑːndəˈlɪr/ *n* [C] a man who rows a gondola in Venice

**gone¹** /gɒn‖gɒːn/ the past participle of go —see GO¹ (USAGE)

**gone²** *adj informal* **1** **be gone** to be showing the effects of taking drugs or drinking alcohol: *Look at Michelle – she's totally gone!* **2** **be gone on sb** to be very fond of someone and think they are very attractive: *Our Kate's really gone on that boy next door.* **3** **be five/six/seven etc months gone** *BrE informal* to have been PREGNANT for a particular length of time

**gone³** *prep BrE informal* used like 'past', to mean later than a particular time or older than a particular age: *When we got home it was gone midnight.*

**gon·er** /ˈgɒnə‖ˈgɒːnər/ *n informal* **be a goner** someone who will soon die, or is in an impossible situation: *If Mark's still inside the plane, he's a goner.*

**gong** /gɒŋ‖gɒːŋ, gɑːŋ/ *n* [C] a round piece of metal that hangs in a frame and that you hit with a stick to give a deep ringing sound, used for example to call people somewhere, often to announce that a meal is ready

**gon·na** /ˈgɒnə, gənə‖ˈgɒːnə, gənə/ a way of saying 'going to', which many people think is incorrect: *This isn't gonna be easy.*

**gon·or·rhe·a, gonorrhoea** /ˌgɒnəˈriːə‖ˌgɑː-/ *n* [U] a disease of the sex organs that is passed on during sex; VD

**gon·zo jour·nal·is·m** /ˈgɒnzəʊ ˌdʒɜːnəlɪzəm‖-zoʊ ˌdʒɜːr-/ *n* [U] *AmE informal* reporting in newspapers which is concerned with shocking or exciting the reader and not with giving true information —**gonzo journalist** *n* [C]

**goo** /guː/ *n* [U] *informal* **1** an unpleasantly sticky substance: *What's all this goo at the bottom of the bag?* **2** words or feelings that are too emotional or romantic —see also GOOEY

**good¹** /gʊd/ *adj comparative* **better** /ˈbetə‖-ər/ *superlative* **best** /best/ S W

**1** ▶ **OF A HIGH STANDARD** ◀ of a high standard: *a good reputation* | *a good quality cloth* | *a good Muslim* | *This book is not as good as her last one.* | *His test scores were good, but hers were even better.* | *We received the best medical treatment.* | **very/extremely/pretty etc good** *Mike's done an extremely good job of painting the* *windows.* | **(not) good enough** *Your work's simply not good enough.* | **be too good for sb** *informal*: *David doesn't deserve to have a girlfriend like Kate – she's much too good for him!* —opposites BAD[1] (2), POOR (3)

**2 ▶ OF THE RIGHT KIND ◀** having qualities that are worth praising: *He is a good husband.* | *$50 is a very good price.* | *That's good news!* | *They've had a really good idea.* | **any good** *"Is your new doctor any good?" – "Yes, she's OK."* – opposite BAD[1] (1)

**3 no good/not much good/not any good a)** not very useful: *This radio's not much good, is it?* | **it is no good doing sth** *It's no good talking to him – he never listens.* | **no good for sth** *These glasses are no good for champagne.* | **no good to sb** *A car's not much good to me, since I can't drive!* **b)** bad: *The movie wasn't much good.*

**4 ▶ SKILFUL ◀ a)** clever or skilful: *She's a good skier.* | **good at sth/doing sth** *Alfred is very good at languages.* | **good with sth/sb** (=skilful at using something or dealing with someone) *My receptionist is very good with people.* —opposites BAD[1] (2), POOR (5)

**5 be no good at/not be much good at/not be very good at** not to be skilful at something or doing something: *You're not very good at reading maps, are you?*

**6 ▶ STRONG ◀** strong; likely to be successful, to persuade people etc: *I want an explanation, and it had better be good!* | *That's a good point.* | *You have a fairly good chance of winning.* —opposites POOR (3), WEAK (5)

**7 ▶ ENJOYABLE ◀** enjoyable; pleasant: *It's good to see you again.* | *That was good fun.* | **have a good time/day/weekend etc** *The kids had a very good time at the zoo.* | **too much of a good thing** (=something which stops being pleasant because you have too much of it or it continues for too long) —see also **the good old days** (OLD (16))

**8 ▶ SUITABLE ◀ a) good for sth** | **good for doing sth** suitable for something: *It's a good day for a trip to the mountains.* | *This is the best knife for cutting vegetables.* | *Those cards would be good for the invitations.* **b) good for sb** *especially AmE* convenient for someone: *Ten o'clock is good for me.* | *So we're all meeting at the beach? That's good for me.*

**9 ▶ HELPFUL ◀** helpful: *good advice* | *That's a very good example.* | *She'll be a good influence on him.* | **be good for sth** (=help it to develop or be produced): *This weather is very good for business.* | *It's been a good year for apples.* —opposites BAD[1] (2), POOR (3)

**10 ▶ IN A GOOD CONDITION ◀** in a satisfactory condition for use; not broken, damaged, decayed, OUT-OF-DATE etc: *You need good shoes for hiking.* | **good for three days/a week etc** (=to be used during that time) *This ticket is good for one month.* | **as good as new** (=in perfect condition, especially after being cleaned or repaired) *They've fixed the car, and it's as good as new.* —see also **pay good money for** (MONEY (5))

**11 ▶ HEALTHY ◀** healthy: *This water isn't good to drink.* | **feel good** *I don't feel too good.* | *He's feeling better today.* | **be good for sb** *Milk is good for you.* | *It isn't good for children to watch too much TV.*

**12 ▶ SHOWING APPROVAL ◀** *Good spoken* **a)** used to show that you are pleased about something: *Good, I'm glad you've got it under control.* | "Seven minus two is five". "Good". **b)** used when something has been decided or agreed: *Good. We'll use the new one, then.*

**13 ▶ CHILD ◀** a word meaning well-behaved, used especially about a child: *She's such a good baby.* | *Be a good girl, now.* | **as good as gold** (=extremely well-behaved)

**14 ▶ KIND ◀** kind: **good about** *I had some time off work when my mother was ill, but my boss was very good about it.* | **good of sb (to do sth)** *formal*: *It was good of you to come to the funeral.* | **good to sb** (=an expression meaning kind to someone, used especially to defend someone) *Mr Hawkins has always been very good to me.*

**15 ▶ LARGE ◀** large in amount, area, or range: *They stock a good range of furniture.* | *a good crop of mangoes* | *I've travelled a good distance.* | **a good while** *informal* (=quite a long time) *We'd waited a good while by now.* —see also GOODISH

**16 ▶ MORALLY RIGHT ◀** morally right: *a good man* | *I still think it was a good thing to do.* | **my/his etc good deed for the day** *informal* (=something you do that helps someone else, especially something boring or unimportant) | **the good guys** *informal* (=the people who represent morally right behaviour, especially in films) | **be no good** *informal* (=be a morally bad person) *Stay away from Gerry. He's no good.* —opposite BAD[1] (3)

**17 ▶ COMPLETE ◀** complete; thorough: *Take a good look at it.* | *She had a good cry.* | *That needs a good washing.* | **good and ...** *informal* very or completely: *Don't rush me; I'll do it when I'm good and ready.*

**18 a good deal** a lot: *They went out a good deal.* | **a good deal of trouble/time etc** *I went to a good deal of trouble to get this ticket.*

**19 a good deal larger/better etc** also **a good bit larger/better etc** *BrE* much larger, better etc: *Their kitchen is a good deal wider than ours.*

**20 a good friend** someone who you know very well and like very much

**21 hold good** if a law, rule, reason etc holds good it is or remains effective or true: *theories that hold good for all countries* | *These words, uttered in 1848, still hold good today.*

**22 the good** good people generally; those who do what is right: *Christians believe that the good go to heaven when they die.* —see also **the great and the good** (GREAT[1] (21))

**23 be too good to be true/to last** *informal* to seem to be so good that you think something must be wrong, or expect something bad to happen: *She found out he was married – I knew he was too good to be true!*

**24 in good time (for sth/to do sth)** if you arrive somewhere in good time to do something, you arrive early enough to do it

**25 in her/their etc own good time** *informal* someone who does something in their own good time does not do it when other people want them to, but only when they are completely ready to do it

**26 as good a time/place etc as any** *usually spoken* used to say that although a time etc is not perfect, there will not be a better one: *Well, I suppose this is as good a spot as any to set up camp.*

**27 good for nothing** *informal* someone who is good for nothing is completely useless and worthless —see also GOOD-FOR-NOTHING

**28 to be good for a meal/a few drinks etc** *informal* be likely to give you something: *My uncle should be good for a few bucks.*

**29 good offices** [plural] *formal* services provided, especially by someone in a position of power, that help someone out of a difficulty: *Through the good offices of the ambassador we were given special permission to travel.*

**30 be in sb's good books** *informal* if you are in someone's good books, they like you or approve of you more than they usually do: *I'll ask my boss for the day off – I'm in her good books at the moment.*

**31 the good book** *old-fashioned, sometimes humorous* the Bible

**32 good Samaritan** someone who gives help to people in trouble: *Mrs Hoare was the good Samaritan who came to our rescue.*

**33 in good faith** *formal* sincerely: *I promised you that in good faith, but I can't do it, I'm afraid.*

**34 a good three miles/ten years etc** at least three miles, ten years etc, and probably more: *It's a good mile away.* | *He's a good ten years younger than her.*

**35 be good for another three years/hundred miles etc** something that is good for a particular length of time is not in good condition but will probably last for that length of time: *Nonsense, my bike's good for a few miles yet!*

**36 a good few/many** *informal* quite a lot of something: *I've done this a good few times now.* | *"How many people were there?" "Oh, a good many."*

**37 as good as done/finished/yours etc** used to say

that something is almost done etc, or definitely will be soon: *The work is as good as finished.*

**38 as good as dead/ruined/useless etc** in a state that is not much better than being dead, ruined etc: *If he finds out, I'm as good as dead!*

**39 give as good as you get** *BrE informal* to react to someone who attacks or harms you by doing equal damage to them

**40 have a good thing going** to be doing something that is and will continue to be successful: *They've got a good thing going with that little business of theirs.*

**41 be as good as your word** to keep your promise: *He said he'd see what he could do, and he was as good as his word.*

**42 a good word for sb/sth** a favourable remark about someone or something: | **have a good word (to say) for sb/sth** *I'm afraid no one had a good word to say for her.* | **put in a good word for sb** *When you see the CEO, put in a good word for me.*

**43 be onto a good thing** *informal* to have found a way of getting a lot without paying money or working hard

**44 make good** also **make it good** an expression meaning to become successful and rich after being poor, used especially in newspapers: *a boy from a hick town who made good in New York*

**45 make good a debt/loss etc** an expression meaning to pay someone money that you owe, or provide money instead of what has been lost, used especially in business: *The loss to the company was made good by contributions from its subsidiaries.*

**46 make good your escape** *literary* to succeed in escaping

**47 the good life** a simple, natural way of living —see also **so far so good** (FAR[1] (22)), **while the going's good** (GOING[1] (4)), **for good measure** (MEASURE[2] (9)), **bad/good sailor** (SAILOR (2)), **that's/it's all well and good** (WELL[3] (5))

Frequencies of the adjective **good** in spoken and written English.

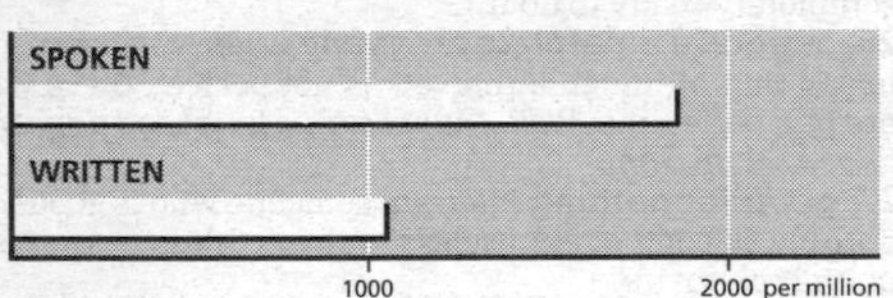


Based on the British National Corpus and the Longman Lancaster Corpus

This graph shows that the adjective **good** is much more common in spoken English than in written English. This is because it has special uses in spoken English and is used in some common spoken phrases.

**good** *(adj)* **SPOKEN PHRASES**

**48 good** used to say that you are pleased that something happens or is done *"I could do it tomorrow if you want." "Good."* used to tell someone that you think their work or what they are doing is good: *Good, that's the way, keep going.* **49 oh good** used to say that you are pleased that something you didn't know about happens or is done *"I've invited Danny and Marilyn to dinner tonight." "Oh good."* **50 good morning/afternoon/evening** used to say hello to someone in the morning, afternoon or evening: *Good afternoon everyone. Sorry I'm late.* **51 what a good girl/boy/dog etc** used to tell a child or animal that it has behaved well or done something well: *What a good girl! Mummy's going to give you a nice chocolate.* **52 good idea/point/question** used when someone says or suggests something interesting or important that you had not thought of before: *"But tomorrow's Sunday, the bank will be closed." "Yes, good point."* **53 that's no good** used to say that something is not suitable or convenient: *"I could do it next week." "That's no good. I'll be away."* **54 that's/it's not good enough** used to say that you are not satisfied with something and you are annoyed about it: *Look, it's just not good enough. I've been waiting an hour!* **55 good luck** used to say that you hope that someone is successful or that something good happens to them: *"When's the exam?" "Next week." "Well, good luck and stay calm."* **56 good luck to him/them** used to say that you hope someone is successful, although you think it is very unlikely that they will be: *Good luck to them. You've got to respect them for trying.* **57 good for you/her** also **good on you/her** *BrE, AusE* used to say that you approve of or are pleased with what someone has done or decided: *"I told him to go away and leave me alone." "Good for you."* **58 it's a good thing** also **it's a good job** *BrE* used to say that you are glad something happened, because there would have been problems if it had not happened: *It's a good thing you were in. I lost my keys.* | **and a good thing/job too** *BrE She's gone, and a good thing too.* **59 good old John/Karen etc** used to praise someone, especially because they have behaved in the way that you would expect them to: *Good old Roger! I knew he wouldn't let us down.* **60 good grief/god/lord/heavens/gracious!** used to express surprise, anger, or other strong feelings: *"It's going to cost us £500 to repair it." "Good grief!"* **61 be a good laugh** *BrE* to be enjoyable or amusing: *You should come to the club with us some time, it's always a good laugh.* **62 be good for a laugh** to be enjoyable, or amusing to do, although not useful, important etc: *Let's go watch the guys trying to skate. That should be good for a laugh.* **63 that's a good one** used to tell someone that you do not believe something they have said and think it is a joke or a trick: *You won $50,000? Very funny, that's a good one!* **64 all in good time** used when someone wants you to hurry but you are not going to: *"When are we going to open our presents, Mom?" "All in good time, Billy, all in good time."* **65 if you know what's good for you** used to threaten someone that something bad will happen to them if they don't do something: *Do as he says, if you know what's good for you!* **66 would you be good enough to/be so good as to...?** *formal* used to ask someone very politely to do something: *Would you be good enough to help me with my bags.* **67 good day** *BrE old-fashioned* used to say 'hello' or 'goodbye' **68 very good** *BrE old-fashioned* used to tell someone in a position of authority over you that you will do what they have told you to: *"Tell the men to come in." "Very good, sir."* **69 (jolly) good show** *old-fashioned BrE* used to express your satisfaction with something

**good**[2] *n*

**1 ▶ADVANTAGE◀** gain or advantage: **do sb (a power of/the world of) good** (=to bring someone (a lot of) advantages or improvement) *It'll do you good to have a vacation.* | *That little talk with the boss certainly did him the world of good!* | **for the good of** (=to help something) *I hate swimming – I only go for the good of my health.* | **for your/his/their own good** *Come on, drink up the medicine – it's for your own good!* | **do more harm than good** *I don't think you should go – it's bound to do more harm than good.* | **the common/general good** *formal* (=the advantage of everyone in society or in a group)

**2 do no good/not do any good** to not have any useful effect: *Try and persuade her if you like, but I don't think it'll do any good!*

**3 What's the good of...?/What good is...?** *informal* used to say that having or doing something brings you no advantage: *What's the good of buying a boat if you're too busy to use it?* | *What good is money when you haven't any friends?*

**4 ▶GOOD BEHAVIOUR◀** [U] actions or behaviour that are morally right or that follow religious principles: *She is definitely an influence for good on those boys.* | *There's good in him, in spite of his violent behaviour.* | **good and evil** *the eternal struggle between good and evil* — see also DO-GOODER

**5 be up to no good** *informal* to be doing or planning something wrong or dishonest: *Anyone waiting around on street corners at night must be up to no good.*
**6 for good** also **for good and all** *informal* if someone closes something, leaves, stays etc for good, they close it, leave etc permanently: *We've separated from each other before, but I think it's for good this time.*
**7 be £10, $50 etc to the good** to have made a profit of £10, $50 etc
**8** [singular] *technical* a particular article that is produced in order to be sold: *a good that could have been obtained more cheaply elsewhere* — see also GOODS (1)

**good**[3] *adv AmE* a word meaning well, which some people think is incorrect: *Listen to me good!*

**good af·ter·noon** /· ˌ··'·/ *interjection, n* [C] an expression meaning hello, used when you are greeting someone in the afternoon

**good·bye** /gʊd'baɪ/ *interjection, n* [C] used when you are leaving or being left by someone: *"Goodbye, John, see you tomorrow."* | **say goodbye** *I just have to say goodbye to Fred* | **say your goodbyes** *We said our goodbyes and left.*

**good day** /· '·/ *interjection, n* [C] **1** *especially AustrE, NZE* an expression meaning hello, used when you are greeting someone especially in the morning or afternoon **2** *especially BrE, old fashioned* an expression used to say hello or goodbye

**good eve·ning** /· '··/ *interjection, n* [C] an expression meaning hello used when you are greeting someone in the evening —compare GOOD NIGHT

**good faith** /ˌ· '·/ *n* **in good faith** if an agreement, deal etc is made in good faith, it is made honestly with no intention to deceive anyone: *a contract drawn up in good faith*

**good-for-noth·ing** /ˌ· · '··◂/ *n* [C] someone who is lazy or has no skills —**good-for-nothing** *adj* [only before noun]

**Good Fri·day** /ˌ· '··/ *n* [C,U] the Friday before the Christian holiday of EASTER

**good-heart·ed** /ˌ· '··◂/ *adj* kind and generous

**good-hu·moured** *BrE*, **good-humored** *AmE* /ˌ· '··◂/ *adj* naturally cheerful and friendly: *Jo is always remarkably good-humoured whatever happens.* —**good-humouredly** *adv*

**good·ie** /'gʊdi/ also **goody** *n* [C] *informal humorous* someone in a book or film who is good and does things you approve of

**good·ish** /'gʊdɪʃ/ *adj* [only before noun] *BrE informal* **1 a goodish distance/number etc** quite a long way, quite a lot etc **2** fairly good but not very good

**good-look·ing** /ˌ· '··◂/ *adj* someone who is good-looking has an attractive face —see BEAUTIFUL (USAGE) —**good-looker** *n* [C]

**good looks** /ˌ· '·/ *n* [plural] the attractive appearance of someone's face: *the young actor's romantic good looks* | **keep your good looks** (=still be attractive) *She's certainly kept her good looks.*

**good·ly** /'gʊdli/ *adj* [only before noun] **1 a goodly number/sum/amount etc** *old-fashioned* a large amount: *a goodly number of people* **2** *old use* pleasant in appearance or good in quality

S2 **good mor·ning** /· '··/ *interjection, n* [C] an expression meaning hello, used when you are greeting someone in the morning

**good-na·tured** /ˌ· '··◂/ *adj* naturally kind and helpful and not easily made angry —**good-naturedly** *adv* —**good-naturedness** *n* [U]

S2 **good·ness** /'gʊdnɪ̆s/ *n* [U]
**1 my goodness!/goodness (gracious) me!** *spoken* used to when you are surprised or sometimes angry: *My goodness, you did buy a lot!*
**2 have the goodness to do sth** *formal* used to show extreme politeness when asking someone to do something: *Will you have the goodness to excuse me?*
**3 for goodness' sake** *spoken* used when you are annoyed or surprised: *For goodness' sake stop arguing!*
**4 goodness (only) knows** *spoken* used to emphasize that you are not sure about something or to make a statement stronger: *That bar's been closed for goodness knows how long.* | *Goodness knows, I tried to help him!*
**5 ▶ BEING GOOD ◀** the quality of being good: *Claire has an essential goodness of character.*
**6 ▶ BEST PART ◀** the best part, especially the part of food which is good for your health: *All the goodness of an egg is in the yolk.*

**good night** /ˌ·'·/ *interjection, n* [C] an expression used when you are leaving or being left by someone at night, especially before going to bed or to sleep: *Good night. Sleep well.* —compare GOOD EVENING —see also **kiss sb goodbye/goodnight etc** (KISS[1] (1)) S3

**goods** *n* [plural] **1** things that are produced in order to be sold: *The demand for goods and services is lower this year.* | *electrical goods* | **consumer goods** (=televisions, washing machines etc) **2 come up with the goods/deliver the goods** to do what other people need or expect: *Tony makes a lot of promises but rarely comes up with the goods.* **3** possessions which can be moved, as opposed to houses, land etc | **sb's worldly goods** (=everything someone owns) **4 have/get the goods on sb** *especially AmE* to have or find proof that someone is guilty of a crime: *Face it, Bukowski, we got the goods on you!* **5** *BrE* heavy things which can be carried by road, train etc; FREIGHT[1] (2) *especially AmE*: *a goods train* **6 he's/she's/it's the goods** *spoken* used to say that you really like someone or something: *Emma thinks he's the goods!* —see also DRY GOODS S2 W2

**goods and chattels** *n* [plural] *law* personal possessions

**good-tempered** *adj* cheerful and not easily made angry

**goodwill** *n* [U] **1** kind feelings towards or between people and a willingness to be helpful **2** the success of a company, and its good relationship with its customers, calculated as part of its value when it is sold: *We paid £60,000 for the store, plus £5,000 for goodwill.*

**good·y**[1] /'gʊdi/ *n plural* **goodies** [C usually plural] *informal* **1** something that is nice to eat: *We brought lots of goodies for the picnic.* **2** something attractive, pleasant, or desirable: *The CD is given away as an extra goody when you buy the CD player.* **3** a GOODIE

**goody**[2] *interjection* a word used especially by children to express pleasure

**goody-good·y** /'·· ˌ··/ also **goody-two-shoes** /ˌ·· '· ·/ *AmE n* [C] someone who likes to seem very good and helpful in order to please their parents, teachers etc

**goo·ey** /'gu:i/ *adj informal* **1** sticky, soft and often sweet: *gooey cakes* **2** expressing your love for someone in a way that other people think is silly; SENTIMENTAL: *Babies make her go all gooey.*

**goof**[1] /gu:f/ also **goof up** *v* [I] *especially AmE* to make a silly mistake: *The restaurant totally goofed up our reservations.* —**goof-off** /'· ·/ *n* [C] —**goof-up** /'· ·/ *n* [C]
**goof around** *phr v* [I] *AmE informal* to spend time doing silly things; MESS ABOUT *BrE*
**goof off** *phr v* [I] *AmE informal* to waste time or avoid doing any work: *Wayne's been goofing off at school and his report card shows it.*

**goof**[2] *n* [C] *informal especially AmE* **1** someone who is silly **2** a silly mistake: *a goof on the spelling test*

**goof·y** /'gu:fi/ *adj informal* stupid or silly: *a goofy grin* —**goofily** *adv* —**goofiness** *n* [U]

**goo·gly** /'gu:gli/ *n* **1** [C] a ball bowled (BOWL[2] (2)) in CRICKET (2) in such a way that it looks as if it will go in one direction but goes in the other **2 bowl sb a googly** *BrE* to ask someone a question that is intended to trick them

**goo-goo eyes** /ˌ· · '·/ *n* [plural] *AmE humorous* a silly look that shows you love someone: **make goo-goo eyes at sb** *Look at them, making goo-goo eyes at each other.* —**goo-goo eyed** *adj*

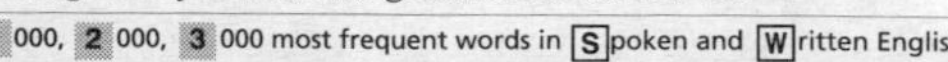

**gook** /guːk/ *n* [C] *AmE* a very offensive word for someone from a country in the Far East

**goo·ly, goolie** /ˈguːli/ *n* [C usually plural] *BrE slang* an impolite word meaning a TESTICLE

**goon** /guːn/ *n* [C] *informal* **1** *especially BrE* a silly or stupid person **2** *especially AmE* a violent criminal that is paid to frighten or attack people

**goop** /guːp/ *n* [U] *AmE informal* a thick, slightly sticky substance: *What's that goop you're putting on your hair?*

**goose¹** /guːs/ *n* **1 a)** [C] *plural* **geese** /giːs/ a bird that is similar to a duck but larger and makes a hissing (HISS (1)) or honking (HONK¹ (2)) noise **b)** a female goose —compare GANDER (1) **2** [U] the cooked meat of this bird **3** *old-fashioned* a silly person **4 kill the goose that lays the golden egg** to destroy the thing that brings you profit or success —see also WILD-GOOSE CHASE, **wouldn't say boo to a goose** (BOO² (3)), **cook someone's goose** (COOK¹ (6))

**goose²** *v* [T] *AmE informal* to touch or press someone on their bottom as a rude joke

**goose·ber·ry** /ˈgʊzbəri, ˈguːz-, ˈguːs-‖ˈguːsberi/ *n* [C] **1** a small round green fruit with a sour taste that grows on a bush —see picture on page 413 **2 play gooseberry** *BrE informal* to be the unwanted third person who is with two people who are having a romantic relationship and want to be alone together

**goose·bumps** /ˈguːsbʌmps/ *n* [plural] *AmE* goose pimples

**goose·flesh** /ˈguːsfleʃ/ *n* [U] *especially BrE* goose pimples

**goose pim·ples** /ˈ· ˌ··/ *n* [plural] a condition in which your skin is raised up in small points because you are cold or frightened

**goose·step** /ˈguːs-step/ *n* **the goosestep** a way of marching, used by soldiers in some countries, in which each step is taken without bending your knee —**goosestep** *v* [I]

**GOP** /ˌdʒiː əʊ ˈpiː‖-oʊ-/ *n* **the GOP** *AmE* Grand Old Party; the Republican Party in US politics

**go·pher** /ˈgəʊfə‖ˈgoʊfər/ *n* [C] a North and Central American animal like a large rat that lives in holes in the ground

**Gor·di·an knot** /ˌgɔːdiən ˈnɒt‖ˌgɔːrdiən ˈnɑːt/ *n* **cut the Gordian knot** to quickly solve a difficult problem by determined action

**gore¹** /gɔː‖gɔːr/ *v* [T] if an animal gores someone, it wounds them with its horns or TUSKS

**gore²** *n* **1** [U] *literary* blood that has flowed from a wound and become thicker and darker **2** [C] a piece of material that gets wider towards the bottom, used in making a skirt —see also GORY

**gorge¹** /gɔːdʒ‖gɔːrdʒ/ *n* [C] **1** a deep narrow valley with steep sides **2 make sb's gorge rise** to make someone feel sick or very angry about something: *When they saw the burned-out homes it made their gorge rise.*

**gorge²** *v* **1 gorge yourself on/with** to eat until you are too full to eat any more: *We gorged ourselves on ripe plums.* **2 be gorged with** to have eaten so much of something that you are completely full

S3 **gor·geous** /ˈgɔːdʒəs‖ˈgɔːr-/ *adj informal* **1** extremely beautiful or attractive: *a gorgeous blonde | gorgeous silks* **2** extremely pleasant or enjoyable: *What a gorgeous afternoon!* (=warm and sunny) —**gorgeously** *adv* —**gorgeousness** *n* [U]

**gor·gon** /ˈgɔːgən‖ˈgɔːr-/ *n* [C] **1** *informal* an ugly frightening woman **2 Gorgon** one of the three sisters in ancient Greek stories with snakes on their heads that made anyone who looked at them change into stone

**go·ril·la** /gəˈrɪlə/ *n* [C] **1** a very large African monkey that is the largest of the APES¹ (1) **2** *slang* an ugly, strong man who is employed to protect an important person

**gorm·less** /ˈgɔːmləs‖ˈgɔːrm-/ *adj BrE informal* stupid, especially in appearance: *a gormless grin* —**gormlessly** *adv* —**gormlessness** *n* [U]

**gorse** /gɔːs‖gɔːrs/ *n* [U] a PRICKLY bush with bright yellow flowers, which grows in the countryside

**gor·y** /ˈgɔːri/ *adj* **1** *informal* clearly describing or showing violence, blood, and killing: *That film was too gory for me.* **2 all the gory details** *often humorous* all the interesting details about an unpleasant event: *Come on, I want to hear all the gory details.* **3** *literary* covered in blood —see also GORE² —**gorily** *adv* —**goriness** *n* [U]

**gosh** /gɒʃ‖gɑːʃ/ *interjection* used to express surprise: *Gosh, it's cold.* S2

**gos·ling** /ˈgɒzlɪŋ‖ˈgɑːz-, ˈgɒːz-/ *n* [C] a young GOOSE¹ (1)

**go-slow** /ˌ· ˈ·◂/ *n* [C] **1** *BrE* a way of protesting against an employer by working as slowly as possible; SLOWDOWN² (2) *AmE* —compare WORK-TO-RULE **2** *WAfrE* a TRAFFIC JAM

**gos·pel** /ˈgɒspəl‖ˈgɑːs-/ *n* **1 Gospel** [C] one of the four stories of Christ's life in the Bible **2** [C usually singular] a particular set of ideas that someone believes in very strongly and tries to persuade other people to accept: **spread/preach the gospel** *spreading the gospel of monetarism* **3** also **gospel truth** /ˌ·· ˈ·/ [U] something that is completely true: **take sth as gospel** *Don't take everything she says as gospel.* **4** also **gospel mu·sic** /ˈ·· ˌ··/ [U] a style of Christian music usually performed by Black singers in which religious songs are sung strongly and loudly: *a gospel choir*

**gos·sa·mer** /ˈgɒsəmə‖ˈgɑːsəmər/ *n* [U] **1** *literary* a very light thin material **2** light silky thread which SPIDERS leave on grass and bushes

**gos·sip¹** /ˈgɒsɨp‖ˈgɑː-/ *n* **1** [C,U] conversation or information about other people's behaviour and private lives, often including unkind or untrue remarks: *What's the latest gossip?* | **have a gossip** *Phil's in there having a gossip with Maggie.* | **idle gossip** (=gossip not based on facts) **2** [C] someone who likes talking about other people's private lives

**gossip²** *v* [I] to spend time talking to someone about other people's behaviour and private lives or about other things that do not concern you: [+ **about**] *Julie was gossiping about Jane and Mick's affair.*

**gossip col·umn** /ˈ·· ˌ··/ *n* [C] a regular article in a newspaper or magazine about the behaviour and private lives of famous people —**gossip columnist** *n* [C]

**gos·sip·y** /ˈgɒsɨpi‖ˈgɑː-/ *adj informal* **1** a gossipy person likes to gossip **2** talk or writing that is gossipy, is informal and full of gossip: *a long, gossipy letter*

**got** /gɒt‖gɑːt/ the past tense and a participle of GET —see GOTTEN (USAGE)

**got·cha** /ˈgɒtʃə‖ˈgɑː-/ *interjection* **1** a word meaning 'I've got you' that is used to surprise someone, or to show them that you have gained a sudden advantage over them **2** a word meaning 'I understand': *"Yeah, okay, 5 o'clock, gotcha."*

**Goth·ic** /ˈgɒθɪk‖ˈgɑː-/ *adj* **1** the Gothic style of building was common in Western Europe between the 12th and 16th centuries. Its main features were pointed ARCHES¹ (1, 2), tall PILLARS (1), and tall thin pointed windows. **2** a Gothic story, film etc is about frightening things that happen in mysterious old buildings, and lonely places, and was popular in the early 19th century **3** Gothic writing, printing etc has thick decorated letters

**got·ta** /ˈgɒtə‖ˈgɑːtə/ *spoken* a short form of 'have got to', 'has got to', 'have got a', or 'has got a', which most people think is incorrect: *We gotta go now.*

**got·ten** /ˈgɒtn‖ˈgɑːtn/ *AmE* the past participle of GET: *You've gotten us into a lot of trouble.* —see also ILL-GOTTEN

**USAGE NOTE: GOTTEN**

GRAMMAR

In British English, **got** is the past participle of **get**, but in American English, **gotten** is more commonly used as the past participle: *Kim's gotten engaged!* | *He'd gotten up early that day.* **Got** is used in British English to mean 'possess': *We've got two cars.* It may also be used this way in American English, though Americans usually use 'have': *We have two cars.* **Got** is also used in British English to mean 'buy' or 'receive': *Tim has just got a new bicycle.* In American English, you can say either: *Tim has just gotten a new bicycle or Tim just got a new bicycle.*

**Got** is used in both British and American English to mean 'must': *I've got to talk to him.* In American English, if you say *I've gotten to talk to him*, you mean you have succeeded in talking to him, but in both British and American English you would usually say: *I got to talk him.* **Gotten** is not used in British English.

**gou·ache** /gʊˈɑːʃ, gwɑːʃ/ *n* **1** [U] a method of painting using colours that are mixed with water and made thicker with a type of GUM[1] (3) **2** [C] a picture produced by this method

**Gou·da** /ˈgaʊdə, ˈguːdə/ *n* [U] a yellow Dutch cheese that does not have a very strong taste

**gouge¹** /gaʊdʒ/ *v* [T] to make a deep hole or cut in the surface of something: *the desks were scratched and gouged*

**gouge** sth ↔ **out** *phr v* [T] **1** to make a hole in something such as rock etc by removing material that is on the surface: *Glaciers gouged out narrow valleys during the Ice Age.* **2 gouge sb's eyes out** to remove someone's eyes with a pointed weapon

**gouge²** *n* [C] a hole or cut made in something, usually by a sharp tool or weapon

**gou·lash** /ˈguːlæʃ‖-lɑːʃ, -læʃ/ *n* [C,U] a dish from Hungary made of meat cooked in liquid with a hot tasting pepper

**gourd** /gʊəd‖gɔːrd, gʊrd/ *n* [C] a round fruit whose outer shell can be used as a container **2** the round fruit whose shell can be used in this way

**gour·mand** /ˈgʊəmənd‖ˈgʊr-/ *n* [C] someone who is too interested in eating and drinking

**gour·met¹** /ˈgʊəmeɪ‖ˈgʊr-, gʊrˈmeɪ/ *adj* [only before noun] producing or connected with very good food and drink: *a gourmet cook*

**gourmet²** *n* [C] someone who knows a lot about food and wine and who enjoys good food and wine

**gout** /gaʊt/ *n* [U] a disease that makes your toes, fingers, and knees swollen and painful —**gouty** *adj*

W3 **gov·ern** /ˈgʌvən‖-ərn/ *v* **1** [I,T] to officially and legally control a country and make all the decisions about taxes, laws, public services etc: *The country was governed by a small military élite.* **2** [T] if rules, principles etc govern the way a system or situation works, they control how it happens or what happens: *rules governing the export of live animals*|*the laws that govern the universe* **3** [T] to affect the grammar of another word and make it have a particular form **4** [T] *old-fashioned* to control a strong or dangerous emotion

**gov·ern·ess** /ˈgʌvənɪs‖-ər-/ *n* [C] a female teacher who lives with a rich family and teaches their children at home

**gov·ern·ing** /ˈgʌvənɪŋ‖-ər-/ *adj* **1** [only before noun] having the power to control an organization, country etc: **governing body** (=the group of people controlling an institution) *the university's governing body*|**governing party** (=the political party that is governing a country) **2 governing principle** a principle that has the most important influence on something: *Freedom of speech for all is one of the governing principles in a democracy.* —see also SELF-GOVERNING

S2 W1 **gov·ern·ment** /ˈgʌvəmənt, ˈgʌvənmənt‖ˈgʌvərn-/ *n* **1** also **Government** [C] the group of people who govern a country or state: *The new military government does not have popular support.*|[also + plural verb *BrE*] *The Government are planning further cuts in public spending.*|**government policy/funding/statistics** *Government statistics show an increase in unemployment.*|**form a government** (=become the government after an election in a parliamentary system) *Which party will form the next goverment?*|**under a government** (=during the period of a government) *changes in policy under the last Labour government* **2** [U] a form or system of government: *the return to democratic government*|**local government** (=the government of towns, cities etc)|**central government** (=the government of a whole country) **3** [U] the act or process of governing: *Government has been entrusted to the elected politicians.*|**be in government** (=be governing a country) *How long have the Christian Democrats been in government?* **4** [U] *especially AmE* the degree to which the government controls economic and social activities: *a pledge of less government and greater personal freedom*

**government health warn·ing** /ˌ··· ˈ· ˌ··/ *n* [C] *BrE* a notice that, by law, must be put on some products, for example cigarettes, to warn people that they are dangerous to their health

**gov·er·nor** /ˈgʌvənə‖-nər/ *n* [C] **1** also **Governor** W3 **a)** the person in charge of governing a state in the US **b)** the person in charge of governing a country that is under the political control of another country **2** *especially BrE* a member of a committee that controls an organization or institution: *a school governor* **3** *BrE* the person in charge of a prison; WARDEN (2) *AmE*: *After the riot the prison governor resigned.* **4** a part of a machine that controls how the machine works, especially by limiting it in some way **5** *BrE* a GUVNOR —see also GUBERNATORIAL

**Governor-Gen·e·ral** /ˌ··· ˈ···/ *n* [C] someone who represents the King or Queen of Britain in other Commonwealth countries which are not REPUBLICS: *the Governor-General of Australia*

**gov·ern·or·ship** /ˈgʌvənəʃɪp‖-nər-/ *n* [U] the position of being governor, or the period during which someone is governor

**govt** a written abbreviation of GOVERNMENT

**gown** /gaʊn/ *n* [C] **1** a long dress worn by a woman on formal occasions: *Arabella wore a blue silk evening gown.* **2** a long loose piece of clothing worn for special ceremonies by judges, teachers, lawyers, and members of universities **3** a long loose piece of clothing worn in a hospital by someone doing or having an operation —see also DRESSING GOWN

**GP** /ˌdʒiː ˈpiː/ *n* [C] *especially BrE* general practitioner; a doctor who is trained in general medicine and treats people in a particular area or town

**GPA** /ˌdʒiː piː ˈeɪ/ *n* [C] grade point average; the average of a student's marks over a period of time in the US education system

**grab¹** /græb/ *v* **grabbed, grabbing** [T] S3

**1** ▶ **WITH YOUR HAND** ◀ to take hold of someone or W3 something with a sudden or violent movement: *The policeman grabbed his shoulder.*|**grab sth from sb** *I managed to grab the gun from Bowen.*|**grab hold of** *Kay grabbed hold of my arm to stop herself falling.*

**2** ▶ **FOOD/SLEEP** ◀ *informal* to get some food or sleep quickly because you are busy: *I managed to grab an hour's sleep this afternoon.*|**grab a bite to eat** *Let's grab a bite to eat before we go.*

**3** ▶ **GET STH FOR YOURSELF** ◀ to take something for yourself, especially in an unfair way: *Bob tried to grab the profit for himself.*|*Try to get there early and grab a seat.*

**4 how does sth grab you?** *spoken* used to ask someone if they would be interested in doing a particular thing: *How does the idea of a trip to Spain grab you?*

**5 grab a chance/opportunity** *informal* to take the opportunity to do or have something immediately: *Grab your chance to travel while you're still young!*

**grab at** *phr v* [T] **1** to quickly and suddenly put out your hand in order to take hold of something: *Donny hid behind his mother, grabbing at her skirt.* **2** to immediately try to take an opportunity that someone offers you: *Melanie grabs at every invitation that comes her way.*

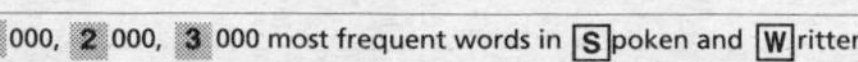

**grab²** *n* **1 make a grab for/at** to suddenly try to take hold of something: *I made a grab for the revolver.* **2 be up for grabs** *informal* if a job, prize, opportunity etc is up for grabs, it is available for anyone who wants to try to have it **3** [C] a piece of machinery used for taking hold of things

**grab bag** /ˈ· ˌ·/ *n AmE* **1** [C] a container filled with small presents that you put your hand in to to pick one out; LUCKY DIP (1) *BrE* **2** [singular] *informal* a situation in which things are decided by chance **3** [singular] a mixture of different things or styles; RAGBAG: *A grab bag of different kinds of music accompanies the film.*

**grace¹** /greɪs/ *n*
**1 ▶ WAY OF MOVING ◀** [U] a smooth controlled way of moving that is attractive to look at, especially because it seems natural and relaxed: *Lena had the grace and poise of a model.*
**2 ▶ BEHAVIOUR ◀ a)** [U] polite and pleasant behaviour: *Jenny answered their questions with grace and dignity.* | **have the (good) grace to do sth** (=be polite enough to do something) *Meg didn't even have the grace to apologize.* **b) graces** [plural] the skills needed to behave in a way that is considered polite and socially acceptable: *social graces*
**3 ▶ MORE TIME ◀** [U] more time that is added to the period you are allowed for finishing a piece of work, paying a debt etc: **a day's/week's etc grace** *I got a day's grace to finish my essay.*
**4 with (a) good/bad grace** willingly and cheerfully, or in an unwilling and angry way: *Kevin smiled and accepted his defeat with good grace.*
**5 ▶ GOD'S KINDNESS ◀** [U] God's kindness shown to people because he loves them: **by/through the grace of God** (=because of God's kindness) *By the grace of God, Alan wasn't hurt.*
**6 there but for the grace of God (go I)** used to say how lucky you feel that you are not in the same bad situation as someone else

**7 ▶ PRAYER ◀** [C,U] a prayer thanking God, said before a meal: **say grace** *Who will say grace?*
**8 be in sb's good graces** to be liked and approved by someone at a particular time
**9 ▶ SOUL ◀** [U] the state of someone's soul when it has been freed from evil, according to Christian belief: **be in a state of grace** (=to have been forgiven for what you have done wrong when you die)
**10 Your/His etc Grace** used as a title for talking to or about a DUKE, DUCHESS, or ARCHBISHOP
**11 the Graces** three beautiful Greek goddesses who often appear in art —see also **fall from grace** (FALL¹ (14)), **saving grace** (SAVING¹ (13))

**grace²** *v* [T] **1 grace sth/sb with your presence** an expression meaning to bring honour to an occasion or group of people by being present, often used jokingly when someone comes late or does not often come to meetings etc: *Ah so you've decided to grace us with your presence!* **2** to make a place or an object look more beautiful or attractive: *His portrait now graces the wall of the drawing room.*

**grace·ful** /ˈgreɪsfəl/ *adj* **1** moving in a smooth and attractive way, or having an attractive shape: *a slim graceful figure* **2** behaving in a polite and pleasant way: *a graceful apology* —**gracefully** *adv*: *When I am no longer needed, I shall retire gracefully.* —**gracefulness** *n* [U]

**grace·less** /ˈgreɪsləs/ *adj* **1** not being polite, especially when someone has been kind to you: *She was utterly graceless, showing no gratitude for all we had done.* **2** moving or doing something in a way that seems awkward **3** something that is graceless is unattractive and unpleasant to look at: *graceless architecture* —**gracelessly** *adv* —**gracelessness** *n* [U]

**gra·cious** /ˈgreɪʃəs/ *adj* **1** behaving in a polite, kind, and generous way, especially to people of a lower class: *Thank you for your gracious hospitality.* **2** having the kind of expensive style, comfort, and beauty that only rich people can afford: *gracious colonial houses* | *the gracious ease of the hotel foyer* | **gracious living** (=an easy way of life enjoyed by rich people) **3** a word meaning kind and forgiving, used to describe God —**graciously** *adv* —**graciousness** *n* [U]

**gracious!** *interjection old-fashioned* used to express surprise or to emphasize 'yes' or 'no': **good gracious!/gracious me!/goodness gracious!** *Good gracious! What have you done to your hair?* | *"You aren't disappointed are you?" "Good gracious, no, of course not."*

**grad** /græd/ *n* [C] *AmE informal* a GRADUATE¹

**grad·a·ble** /ˈgreɪdəbəl/ *adj* an adjective which is gradable can be used in the COMPARATIVE¹ (4) or SUPERLATIVE¹ (2) forms, or with words such as 'very', 'fairly', and 'almost' —**gradability** /ˌgreɪdəˈbɪlɪti/ *n* [U]

**gra·da·tion** /grəˈdeɪʃən/ *n* [C] *formal* a small change, or a stage in a set of changes or degrees of development: *There are many gradations of colour between light and dark blue.*

**grade¹** /greɪd/ *n* S3 W3
**1 ▶ STANDARD ◀** [C,U] a particular standard or level of quality that a product, material etc has: *Grade A eggs* | *low-grade steel*
**2 ▶ COMPANY ◀** [C] the level of importance you have or the level of pay you receive in a company or organization: *Wilma has a lot of responsibility but she's still on a secretarial grade.*
**3 make the grade** to succeed or reach the necessary standard: *Nina'll never make the grade as a professional tennis player.*
**4 ▶ SCHOOL YEAR ◀** [C] a particular year of a school course in the American school system: *Bobby's in the second grade.*
**5 ▶ MARK IN SCHOOL ◀** [C] *especially AmE* a mark given for a particular piece of work in school, or for your work during all or part of a year: *You need good grades to go to college.*
**6 ▶ SLOPE ◀** [C] *AmE* degree of slope, especially in a road or railway; GRADIENT *BrE*

**grade²** *v* [T] **1** to separate things, or arrange them in order according to their quality or rank: *potatoes graded according to size* **2** *especially AmE* to give a mark to an examination paper or to a piece of school work: *Matt's busy at home grading papers.* **3** to give a particular rank and level of pay to a job

**grade cross·ing** /ˈ· ˌ··/ *n* [C] *AmE* a place where a road and railway cross each other, usually with gates that shut the road while the train passes; LEVEL CROSSING *BrE*

**grad·ed** /ˈgreɪdɪd/ *adj* designed to suit different levels of learning: *graded coursebooks*

**grade point av·e·rage** /ˈ· · ˌ···/ *n* [C] GPA

**grade school** /ˈ· ˌ·/ *n* [C] *AmE* an ELEMENTARY SCHOOL

**gra·di·ent** /ˈgreɪdiənt/ *n* [C] a degree of slope, especially in a road or railway; GRADE¹ (6) *AmE*: *a steep gradient*

**grad school** /ˈ· ·/ *n* [C] *AmE informal* a GRADUATE SCHOOL

**grad·u·al** /ˈgrædʒuəl/ *adj* **1** happening, developing, or changing slowly over a long period of time: *Computerization has resulted in the gradual disappearance of many manual jobs.* | *I noticed a gradual change in her behaviour.* **2** a gradual slope is not steep —**gradualness** *n* [U]

**grad·u·a·lly** /ˈgræˌdʒəli/ *adv* in a way that happens or develops slowly over a long period of time: *The rock gradually wears away due to the action of the water.* S2 W3

**grad·u·ate¹** /ˈgrædʒuɪt/ *n* [C] **1** someone who has completed a university degree course, especially for a first degree: *a history graduate* | [+ **of**] *a graduate of Birmingham University* —compare UNDERGRADUATE **2** *AmE* someone who has completed a course at a college, school etc: *a high-school graduate*

**graduate²** /ˈgrædʒueɪt/ *adj* **1** [only before noun] *AmE* a graduate student is studying for a MASTER'S or a

DOCTORATE degree after receiving their first degree; POSTGRADUATE[2] (1) *BrE* **2** graduate studies or courses are done after receiving your first degree

**graduate³** *v* **1** [I] to obtain a degree, especially a first degree, from a college or university: [+ **from**] *Mitch graduated from Stanford with a degree in Law.* **2** [I] *AmE* to complete your education at HIGH SCHOOL: [+ **from**] *Jerry graduated from high school last year.* **3 graduate (from sth) to** to start doing something that is bigger, better or more important: *Bob played college baseball but never graduated to the Majors.* **4** [T] *especially AmE* to give a degree or DIPLOMA to someone who has completed a course

**grad·u·at·ed** /ˈɡrædʒueɪtɪ̣d/ *adj* **1** divided into different levels or GRADES[1] (1): *graduated rates of taxation* **2** a tool or container that is graduated has small marks on it showing measurements

**graduate school** /ˈ··· ˌ·/ *n* [C] *AmE* a college or university where you can study for a MASTER's or a DOCTORATE degree after receiving your first degree, or the period of time when you study for these degrees

**grad·u·a·tion** /ˌɡrædʒuˈeɪʃən/ *n* **1** [U] the time when you complete a university degree course or your education at an American HIGH SCHOOL: *After graduation Helen went into accountancy.* **2** [U] a ceremony at which you receive a university degree or a DIPLOMA from an American HIGH SCHOOL: *graduation day* **3** [C] a mark showing measurement on an instrument or container for measuring

**Grae·co-** /ɡriːkəʊ, ɡrekəʊ‖-koʊ/ *prefix* another spelling of GRECO

**graf·fi·ti** /ɡræˈfiːti, ɡrə-/ *n* [U] rude, humorous, or political writing and pictures on the walls of buildings, trains etc

**graft¹** /ɡrɑːft‖ɡræft/ *n* **1** [C] a piece of healthy skin or bone taken from someone's body and put in or on another part of their body that has been damaged: *Her severe burns were treated with skin grafts.* **2** [C] a piece cut from one plant and tied to or put inside a cut in another, so that it grows there **3** [U] *informal especially BrE* hard work *I was too tired to talk after a hard day's graft.* **4** [U] *especially AmE* the practice of obtaining money or advantage by the dishonest use of influence, especially political influence: *Theo rose to power through graft and corruption.*

**graft²** *v* **1** [I,T] to put a piece of skin or bone from one part of someone's body onto another part that has been damaged: **graft sth onto** *They grafted skin from his thigh onto his badly burned face.* **2** [I,T + **on/onto**] to join a part of a flower, plant, or tree onto another flower, plant, or tree **3 graft sth onto** to try to combine an idea, style etc with another idea or style: *modern institutions grafted onto medieval traditions* **4** [I] *informal especially BrE* to work hard

**graft off** sb ↔ *phr v* [T] *especially AmE* to get money or advantages from someone by the dishonest use of influence, especially political influence: *politicians who graft off each other*

**Grail** /ɡreɪl/ *n* **the Grail** —see HOLY GRAIL

**grain** /ɡreɪn/ *n*
**1** ▶ **FOOD** ◀ **a)** [U] the seeds of crops such as corn, wheat, or rice that are gathered for use as food, or these crops themselves **b)** [C] a single seed of corn, wheat etc —see picture on page 416
**2** ▶ **OF WOOD ETC** ◀ **the grain** the natural arrangement of the threads or FIBRES (3) in wood, flesh, rock, and cloth, or the pattern you see as a result of this: *Cut the wood in the direction of the grain.* —see picture at KNOT[1]
**3 a grain of sympathy/truth/doubt etc** a small amount of truth etc: *They don't have a grain of common sense between them.*
**4** ▶ **SMALL PIECE** ◀ [C] a single, very small piece of a substance such as sand, salt etc
**5 go against the grain** if something that you have to do goes against the grain, you do not like doing it, because it is not what you would naturally do: *It went against the grain for her to be so strict*
**6** ▶ **MEASURE** ◀ [C] the smallest measure of weight, used for medicines, equal to .0648 gram —see table on page B2 —see also **take sth with a pinch/grain of salt** (SALT[1] (4))

**grain·y** /ˈɡreɪni/ *adj* a photograph that is grainy has a rough appearance, as if the images are made up of spots

**gram, gramme** /ɡræm/ written abbreviation **g** or **gm** *n* [C] the basic unit for measuring weight in the METRIC system —see table on page B2 S3

**-gram** /ɡræm/ *suffix* [in nouns] a message delivered as an amusing surprise: *On his birthday we sent him a kissagram* (=a girl who was paid to give him a message and kiss him).

**gram·mar** /ˈɡræmə‖-ər/ *n* **1** [U] the rules by which words change their forms and are combined into sentences, or the study or use of these rules: *I find German grammar very difficult.|I often have to correct his grammar.* **2** [C] a particular description of grammar or a book that describes grammar rules: *Have you seen that new French grammar?* S3 W3

**gram·mar·i·an** /ɡrəˈmeəriən‖-ˈmer-/ *n* [C] someone who studies and knows about grammar

**grammar school** /ˈ·· ˌ·/ *n* [C] **1** a school in Britain for children over the age of 11 who have to pass a special examination to go there —compare COMPREHENSIVE SCHOOL **2** *AmE old-fashioned* an ELEMENTARY SCHOOL

**gram·mat·i·cal** /ɡrəˈmætɪkəl/ *adj* **1** [only before noun] concerning grammar: *grammatical rules* **2** correct according to the rules of grammar —**grammatically** /-kli/ *adv*

**gramme** /ɡræm/ *n* [C] another spelling of GRAM

**gram·o·phone** /ˈɡræməfəʊn‖-foʊn/ *n* [C] *old-fashioned* a RECORD PLAYER

**gram·pus** /ˈɡræmpəs/ *n* [C] a sea animal like a WHALE

**gran** /ɡræn/ *n* [C] *BrE informal* grandmother

**gra·na·ry¹** /ˈɡrænəri‖ˈɡreɪ-, ˈɡræ-/ *n* [C] a place where grain, especially wheat, is stored

**granary²** *adj* [only before noun] *BrE* granary bread is bread which contains whole grains of wheat

**grand¹** /ɡrænd/ *adj* **1** a grand building, occasion etc is very impressive: *We attended a grand ceremony at the Palace.* | **on a grand scale** *Preparations for the wedding are taking place on a grand scale.* **2** a grand plan or idea aims to achieve something very impressive: *As a young minister he was full of grand ideas for social reform.* **3** people who are grand are rich and important but often too proud: *A very grand-looking gentleman entered the room.* **4** *informal or dialect* very good, pleasant, or enjoyable: *We had a grand day out at the seaside.* | *Wasn't it grand to see Ted again?* **5 grand total** the final total you get when you add up several numbers or amounts **6 the Grand Old Man of** a man who has been involved in an activity or a profession for a long time and is highly respected: *the Grand Old Man of British theatre* —**grandly** *adv* —**grandness** *n* [U] S2 W3

**grand²** *n* [C] **1** *plural* **grand** *informal* a thousand pounds or dollars: *That new car of his cost him fifteen grand.* **2** *informal* a GRAND PIANO

**gran·dad** *especially BrE*, **granddad** *especially AmE* /ˈɡrændæd/ *n* [C] **1** *informal* grandfather **2** *BrE informal* an impolite way of addressing an old man: *Hurry up, grandad!* S2

**gran·dad·dy, granddaddy** /ˈɡrændædi/ *n* [C] *AmE informal* **1** grandfather **2 the grandaddy of** the first or greatest example of something: *Louis Armstrong, the grandaddy of all jazz trumpeters*

**grandad shirt** /ˈ·· ˌ·/ *n* [C] a shirt without a collar —see picture on page 840

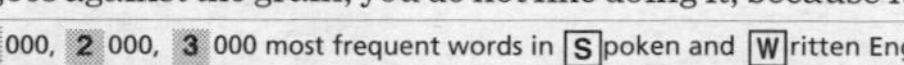

S3 **grand·child** /ˈgræntʃaɪld/ *plural* **grandchildren** /-ˌtʃɪldrən/ *n* [C] the child of your son or daughter —see picture at FAMILY

**grand·dad** /ˈgrændæd/ *n* [C] the usual American spelling of GRANDAD

**grand·dad·dy** /ˈgrændædi/ *n* [C] another spelling of GRANDADDY

**grand·daugh·ter** /ˈgrænˌdɔːtə‖-ˌdɒːtər/ *n* [C] the daughter of your son or daughter —see picture at FAMILY

**gran·dee** /grænˈdiː/ *n* [C] **1** a Spanish or Portuguese NOBLEMAN of the highest rank in former times **2** a politician of the highest social class who has a lot of influence

**gran·deur** /ˈgrændʒə‖-ər/ *n* [U] impressive beauty, power, or size: *the grandeur of the mountains* —see also **delusions of grandeur** (DELUSION (2))

S3 **grand·fa·ther** /ˈgrændˌfɑːðə‖-ər/ *n* [C] the father of your father or mother —see picture at FAMILY

**grandfather clock** /ˈ··· ˌ·/ *n* [C] an old-fashioned tall clock which stands on the floor

**grand fi·na·le** /ˌ· ·ˈ··/ *n* [C] the last and most impressive or exciting part of a show or performance

**gran·dil·o·quent** /grænˈdɪləkwənt/ *adj formal* using words that are too long and formal in order to sound important; POMPOUS —**grandiloquence** *n* [U]

**gran·di·ose** /ˈgrændiəʊs‖-oʊs/ *adj* grandiose plans sound very important or impressive, but will never really happen because they are not practical: *It's just another of Wheeler's grandiose schemes.*

**grand ju·ry** /ˌ· ˈ··/ *n* [C] *law* a group of people in the US who decide whether someone charged with a crime should be judged in a court of law —**grand juror** *n* [C]

**grand lar·ce·ny** /ˌ· ˈ···/ *n* [U] *AmE law* the crime of stealing very valuable goods

S1 **grand·ma** /ˈgrænmɑː/ *n* [C] *informal* grandmother

**grand mal** /ˌgrɒn ˈmæl‖ˌgrɑːn-/ *n* [U] *technical* a serious form of EPILEPSY

**grand mas·ter** /ˌ· ˈ··/ *n* [C] a CHESS player of a very high standard

S3 **grand·moth·er** /ˈgrænˌmʌðə‖-ər/ *n* [C] the mother of your mother or father —see picture at FAMILY

**grand op·e·ra** /ˌ· ˈ···/ *n* [C,U] an OPERA with a serious subject in which all the words are sung

S1 **grand·pa** /ˈgrænpɑː/ *n* [C] *informal* grandfather

**grand·par·ent** /ˈgrænˌpeərənt‖-ˌper-/ *n* [C usually plural] one of the parents of your mother or father *My grandparents live in Sussex.* —see picture at FAMILY

**grand pi·an·o** /ˌ· ·ˈ··/ *n* [C] the type of large piano often used in concerts —compare UPRIGHT PIANO

**grand prix** /ˌgrɒn ˈpriː‖ˌgrɑːn-/ *n* [C] one of a set of international races, especially a car race

**grand slam** /ˌ· ˈ·/ *n* [C] **1** the winning of all of a set of important sports competitions in the same year **2** a hit in BASEBALL which gets four runs (RUN² (17)) because it is a HOME RUN and there are players on all the bases (BASE¹ (8)) **3** the winning of all of the tricks (TRICK² (11)) possible in one game of cards, especially in BRIDGE¹ (4)

**grand·son** /ˈgrænsʌn/ *n* [C] the son of your son or daughter —see picture at FAMILY

**grand·stand** /ˈgrændstænd/ *n* [C] a large structure that has many rows of seats where people sit and watch sports competitions, games, or races

**grand·stand·ing** /ˈgrædstændɪŋ/ *n* [U] *AmE* an action that is intended to make people notice and admire you: *His opening the new school is just a piece of political grandstanding.*

**grand tour** /ˌ· ˈ·/ *n* [C] **1** *humorous* an occasion when someone takes you around a building to show it to you: *They took us on a grand tour of their new house.* **2 the grand tour** a trip round Europe made in former times by young English or American people from rich families as part of their education

**grange** /greɪndʒ/ *n* [C] a large country house with farm buildings

**gran·ite** /ˈgrænɪ̵t/ *n* [U] a very hard grey rock, often used in building

**gran·ny¹, grannie** /ˈgræni/ *n* [C] *informal* grandmother: *Look what granny's bought you!* S3

**granny², grannie** *adj* [only before noun] *BrE* of a style typically used by old women: *granny shoes*

**granny flat** /ˈ·· ·/ *n* [C] *BrE* a separate place inside or next to someone's house, that is designed for an old relative to live in

**granny knot** /ˈ·· ˌ·/ *n* [C] a REEF KNOT in which the two pieces of string are crossed in the wrong way

**gra·no·la** /grəˈnəʊlə‖-ˈnoʊ-/ *n* [U] *AmE* breakfast food made from mixed nuts, grains, and seeds

**grant¹** /grɑːnt‖grænt/ *n* [C] an amount of money given to someone, especially by the government for a particular purpose: *We're hoping to get a grant from the local council for the project.* | **student grant** (=a grant to pay for a student's education at university) S1 W2

**grant²** *v* [T] **1** *formal* to give someone something that they have asked for, especially official permission to do something: **grant sb sth** *The Norton consortium has been granted permission to build a shopping mall.* | **grant sb's request** *Your request for housing benefit has been granted.* **2** to admit that something is true although it does not make much difference to your opinion: **I grant you** *Darren's not an intellectual, I grant you, but he does work hard.* | **granted** (=used when you admit that what someone has said is true) *Granted, we don't want to scare them, but it's time we applied some pressure.* **3 take it for granted (that)** to believe that something is true without making sure: *Sorry! I just took it for granted that you'd want to come.* **4 take sb/sth for granted** to expect that someone will always be there when you need them and never show them any special attention or thank them: *I'm sick and tired of my husband taking me for granted!* S2 W2

**grant-main·tained** /ˌ· ·ˈ·◂/ *adj* a grant-maintained school in Britain receives its money directly from the central government rather than from the local government

**gran·u·lar** /ˈgrænjʊ̵lə‖-ər/ *adj* consisting of or covered with granules

**gran·u·lat·ed** /ˈgrænjʊ̵leɪtɪ̵d/ *adj* granulated sugar is in the form of small white grains rather than powder

**gran·ule** /ˈgrænjuːl/ *n* [C] a small hard piece of something: *coffee granules*

**grape** /greɪp/ *n* [C] a small round juicy fruit that grows on a VINE and is often used for making wine: *a bunch of grapes* —see picture on page 413

**grape·fruit** /ˈgreɪpfruːt/ *n* [C] a round yellow CITRUS fruit with a thick skin, like a large orange —see picture on page 413

**grape·vine** /ˈgreɪpvaɪn/ *n* [C] **1 hear sth on the grapevine** to hear about something because the information has been passed from one person to another in conversation: *I heard about his resignation on the grapevine.* **2** a climbing plant on which grapes grow; VINE (1)

**graph** /græf, grɑːf‖græf/ *n* [C] a drawing that uses a line or lines to show how two or more sets of measurements are related to each other: *Martin showed me a graph of their recent sales.* —see picture at CHART¹

**graph·ic** /ˈgræfɪk/ *adj* **1 a graphic account/description etc** a very clear description of an event that gives a lot of details, especially unpleasant ones: *Cookson gives a graphic account of her unhappiness as a child.*

2 [only before noun] connected with or including drawing, printing, or designing: *a graphic artist|the graphic arts*

**graph·i·cally** /'græfɪkli/ *adv* **1** if you describe something graphically, you describe it very clearly with a lot of detail: *Stella described the scene so graphically that I could almost imagine I was there.* **2** *formal* using a graph: *statistics represented graphically*

**graphic de·sign** /,·· ·'·/ *n* [U] the art of combining pictures, words, and decoration in the production of books, magazines etc —**graphic designer** *n* [C]

**graph·ics** /'græfɪks/ *n* [plural] drawings or images that are designed to represent objects or facts, especially in a computer program —see also COMPUTER GRAPHICS

**graph·ite** /'græfaɪt/ *n* [U] a soft black substance that is a kind of carbon, used in pencils, paints, and electrical equipment

**gra·phol·o·gy** /græ'fɒlədʒi‖-'fɑː-/ *n* [U] the study of HANDWRITING in order to understand people's characters —**graphologist** *n* [C]

**graph pa·per** /'· ,··/ *n* [U] paper with many squares printed on it, used for drawing GRAPHS

**-gra·phy** /grəfi/ *suffix* used in nouns to mean the making of a copy or picture of something: *radiography|photography*

**grap·ple** /'græpəl/ *v* [I] to fight or struggle with someone, holding them tightly: [+ **with**] *Two men grappled with a guard at the door.*

**grapple with** sth *phr v* [T] to try hard to deal with a difficult problem: *The Government is grappling with major areas of social policy.*

**grap·pling i·ron** /'··· ,··/ also **grappling hook** /'··· ·/ *n* [C] an iron tool with several hooks that you tie to a rope and use to hold a boat still, look for objects on the bottom of a river etc

**grasp¹** /grɑːsp‖græsp/ *v* [T] **1** to take and hold something firmly: *Make sure you grasp the rope with both hands.*|**grasp hold of sth** *Paula grasped hold of my arm.* **2** [not in progressive] to completely understand a fact or an idea, especially a complicated one: *They failed to grasp the full significance of his remarks.* **3 grasp a chance/opportunity** to eagerly and quickly use an opportunity to do something **4 grasp the nettle** *BrE* to deal with an unpleasant situation firmly and without delay

**grasp at** sth *phr v* [T] **1** to eagerly try to use an opportunity: *He was ready to grasp at any excuse, however flimsy.* **2** to try to hold on to something

**grasp²** *n* [singular] **1** the way you hold something or your ability to hold it: *The book slipped from his grasp and fell to the floor.*|*Take a firm grasp on the rope.* **2** your ability to understand a complicated idea or situation: **a good/poor grasp of** *You seem to have a good grasp of the subject.*|**beyond sb's grasp** (=too difficult for them to understand) **3** your ability to achieve or gain something: **within sb's grasp** *Success is now within our grasp.* **4** *especially literary* control or power

**grasp·ing** /'grɑːspɪŋ‖'græs-/ *adj* too eager to get money and unwilling to give any of it away or spend it: *Hanson was a hard, grasping man.*

S2 W2 **grass¹** /grɑːs‖græs/ *n*
**1 ► IN FIELDS ◄ a)** [U] a very common plant with thin green leaves that grows in fields and is often eaten by animals: *a blade of grass|Please keep off the grass.* **b)** [C] a particular kind of grass: *sea grasses*
**2 ► DRUG ◄** [U] *slang* MARIJUANA
**3 ► CRIMINAL ◄** [C] *BrE informal* someone, usually a criminal, who gives information about other criminals to the police; INFORMER; STOOLPIGEON *AmE* —see also SUPERGRASS
**4 not let the grass grow under your feet** to not waste time or delay starting something
**5 put sb out to grass** *informal* to make someone leave their job because they are too old to do it effectively: *an old judge being put out to grass* —see also GRASS ROOTS, **snake in the grass** (SNAKE¹ (3))

**grass²** *v* [I] *BrE informal* if a criminal grasses on other criminals, he tells the police about their activities: [+ **on**] *That bastard must have grassed on us!*|**grass sb up** *BrE*: *I wonder who grassed us up?*

**grass** sth ↔ **over** *phr v* [T] to cover land with grass

**grass·hop·per** /'grɑːs,hɒpə‖'græs,hɑːpər/ *n* [C] an insect that has long back legs for jumping and that makes short loud noises —see also **knee-high to a grasshopper** (KNEE-HIGH (2))

**grass·land** /'grɑːslænd‖'græs-/ also **grasslands** [plural] *n* [U] a large area of land covered with wild grass

**grass roots** /,· '·/ *n* **the grass roots** the ordinary people in an organization, rather than the leaders —**grass roots** *adj*: *We are hoping for full participation at grass roots level.*

**grass snake** /'· ·/ *n* [C] a common snake that is not poisonous

**gras·sy** /'grɑːsi‖'græsi/ *adj* covered with grass: *sitting on a grassy bank*

**grate¹** /greɪt/ *n* [C] the metal bars and frame that hold the wood, coal etc in a FIREPLACE

**grate²** *v* **1** [T] to rub cheese, fruit etc against a rough or sharp surface in order to break them into small pieces: *grated carrot* —see picture on page 834 **2** [I] to make an unpleasant sound: [+**on/against**] *the sound of chalk grating against the blackboard* **3** [I] to have an annoying effect on someone's nerves: [+ **on**] *Hardy's constant questions were beginning to grate on me.* —see also GRATING²

**grate·ful** /'greɪtfəl/ *adj* **1** feeling that you want to thank someone because of something kind that they have done: *Dr Cameron has received hundreds of letters from grateful patients.*|[+ **for**] *I'm so grateful for all your help.*|**be grateful to sb for sth** *He was extremely grateful to Gladstone for his support.*|**be grateful that** *I'm very grateful that you didn't tell my husband about this.*|**deeply/eternally grateful** (=extremely grateful) **2 be grateful for small mercies** used in a bad situation to say that things could be worse than they are: *Well, be grateful for small mercies – at least you've still got a job!* **3 I would be grateful if you could/would ...** *formal* used to make requests in formal situations or letters: *We would be most grateful if you could confirm these arrangements immediately.* —opposite UNGRATEFUL —**gratefully** *adv*: *We gratefully accepted their offer.* —**gratefulness** *n* [U] W3

**grat·er** /'greɪtə‖-ər/ *n* [C] a tool used for grating food: *a cheese grater*

**grat·i·fy** /'grætɪ̣faɪ/ *v* [T] *formal* **1 be gratified** to feel pleased and satisfied: *I was very gratified to hear how much they liked my work.* **2** to satisfy a desire: *Hoping to gratify my curiosity, I opened the door.* —**gratification** /,grætɪ̣fɪ̣'keɪʃən/ *n* [C,U]

**grat·i·fy·ing** /'grætɪ̣faɪ-ɪŋ/ *adj* pleasing and satisfying: *It's gratifying to know they liked our project.* —**gratifyingly** *adv*

**grat·ing¹** /'greɪtɪŋ/ *n* [C] a metal frame with bars across it, used to cover a window or hole: *Leaves clogged the grating over the drain.*

**grating²** *adj* a grating sound is hard and unpleasant: *a harsh grating laugh* —**gratingly** *adv*

**grat·is** /'grætɪ̣s, 'greɪtɪ̣s/ *adj, adv* provided without payment; free *Medical advice was provided gratis.*

**grat·i·tude** /'grætɪ̣tjuːd‖-tuːd/ *n* [U] the feeling of being grateful: *Tears of gratitude filled her eyes.*|*I couldn't adequately express my gratitude to Francis.*|[+ **for**] *I* *didn't get a single word of gratitude for all my trouble.* | **deepest gratitude** (=very great gratitude) —opposite INGRATITUDE —see also **owe a debt of gratitude to sb** (DEBT (4))

**gra·tu·i·tous** /grəˈtjuːɟtəs‖-ˈtuː-/ *adj* **gratuitous violence/insults/cruelty etc** violence etc that is done for no reason and causes unnecessary harm or offence —**gratuitously** *adv* —**gratuitousness** *n* [U]

**gra·tu·i·ty** /grəˈtjuːɟti‖-ˈtuː-/ *n* [C] *formal* **1** a small gift of money given to someone for a service they provided; TIP[1] (2) **2** *especially BrE* a large gift of money given to someone when they leave their job, especially in the army, navy etc

**grave[1]** /greɪv/ *n* [C] **1** the place in the ground where a dead body is buried —compare TOMB **2 the grave** *especially literary* death: *Had his spirit returned from the grave to haunt them?* **3 sb would turn/spin in their grave** used to say that someone who is dead would strongly disapprove of something happening now: *The way Bill plays that piece would have Mozart turning in his grave.* —see also **dig your own grave** (DIG[1] (4)), **from (the) cradle to (the) grave** (CRADLE[1] (4)), **have one foot in the grave** (FOOT[1] (20)), **silent as the grave** (SILENT (6)), **a watery grave** (WATERY (5))

**grave[2]** *adj* **1** very serious and worrying: *This decision may have very grave consequences.* | *I have grave doubts about his ability.* **2** looking or sounding quiet and serious, especially because something important or worrying has happened: *Turnbull's face was grave as he told them about the accident.* —**gravely** *adv*: *Adam nodded gravely.* —see also GRAVITY (2, 3)

**grave[3]** /grɑːv/ *adj* a grave ACCENT[1] (4) is a mark put above a letter in some languages such as French to show the pronunciation, for example è —compare ACUTE (7), CIRCUMFLEX

**grave·dig·ger** /ˈgreɪvˌdɪgə‖-ər/ *n* [C] someone whose job is to dig graves

**grav·el** /ˈgrævəl/ *n* [U] small stones, used to make a surface for paths, roads etc: *a gravel path* | *a gravel pit* (=a place where gravel is dug out of the ground)

**grav·elled** /ˈgrævəld/ *adj* a gravelled path or road has a surface made of gravel

**grav·el·ly** /ˈgrævəli/ *adj* **1** a gravelly voice has a low, rough sound **2** covered with or mixed with gravel: *gravelly soil*

**gra·ven** /ˈgreɪvən/ *adj* **graven image** *literary* an image or figure that has been made out of stone, wood, or metal

**grave·side** /ˈgreɪvsaɪd/ *n* [singular] **at the graveside** beside a grave, especially when someone is being buried there

**grave·stone** /ˈgreɪvstəun‖-stoun/ *n* [C] a stone above a grave showing details of the person buried there; HEADSTONE

**grave·yard** /ˈgreɪvjɑːd‖-jɑːrd/ *n* [C] **1** an area of ground where people are buried, often next to a church —compare CEMETERY, CHURCHYARD **2** a place where things that are no longer wanted or useful are left: *a graveyard for old cars*

**graveyard shift** /ˈ·· ˌ·/ *n* [C] *especially AmE* a regular period of working time at night

**grav·i·tas** /ˈgrævɪtæs/ *n* [U] *formal* a seriousness of manner that people respect

**grav·i·tate** /ˈgrævɟteɪt/ *v* [I always + adv/prep] *formal* to be attracted to something and therefore move towards it or become involved with it: [**+ to/towards**] *Very sporty students tended to gravitate towards others with similar interests.*

**grav·i·ta·tion** /ˌgrævɟˈteɪʃən/ *n* [U] **1** *technical* the force that causes two objects to move towards each other because of their MASS[1] (6) **2** the act of gravitating towards something

**grav·i·ta·tion·al** /ˌgrævɟˈteɪʃənəl◂/ *adj* connected with or resulting from the force of gravity: *the planet's gravitational field*

**grav·i·ty** /ˈgrævɟti/ *n* [U] **1** *technical* the force that causes something to fall to the ground or to be attracted to another PLANET **2** *formal* the extreme and worrying seriousness of a situation: *Carl did not seem to understand the gravity of this situation.* **3** an extremely serious way of behaving, speaking etc: *The Consul spoke slowly and with great gravity.* —see also CENTRE OF GRAVITY

**gra·vy** /ˈgreɪvi/ *n* [U] **1** a SAUCE made from the juice that comes from meat as it cooks, mixed with flour **2** *slang, especially AmE* money, profit, or something that you like that is gained when you do not expect it

**gravy boat** /ˈ·· ·/ *n* [C] a long JUG (1) that you pour gravy from

**gravy train** /ˈ·· ˌ·/ *n* **the gravy train** *informal* an organization, activity, or business from which many people can make money or profit without much effort

**gray** /greɪ/ *adj, n, v* the usual American spelling of GREY

**graze[1]** /greɪz/ *v*

**1** ▶ **EAT GRASS** ◀ **a)** [I] if an animal grazes, it eats grass that is growing: *The sheep continued to graze.* **b)** [T] to let animals eat grass: *fields where they used to graze their sheep*

**2** ▶ **INJURE YOURSELF** ◀ [T] to break the surface of your skin by rubbing it against something: *Oliver grazed his knee when he fell over.*

**3** ▶ **TOUCH STH** ◀ [T] to touch something lightly while passing it: *As the plane climbed away, its wing seemed to graze the treetops.*

**4** ▶ **EAT** ◀ [I] to eat small amounts of food all through the day instead of having regular meals

**5** ▶ **TELEVISION** ◀ [I] to keep changing television CHANNELS, watching only a little of each programme

**graze[2]** *n* [C] a wound caused by rubbing that slightly breaks the surface of your skin

**GRE** /ˌdʒiː ɑːr ˈiː/ *n* [C] Graduate Record Examination; an examination taken by students in the US who have done a first degree and want to go to GRADUATE SCHOOL

**grease[1]** /griːs/ *n* [U] **1** animal fat that is soft after being melted **2** any thick oily substance, especially one used to make parts of machines work smoothly

**grease[2]** *v* [T] **1** to put grease on something: *Grease the pan before you pour the batter in.* **2 grease sb's palm** to give someone money in a secret or dishonest way in order to persuade them to do something **3 like greased lightning** *informal* extremely fast: *He disappeared like greased lightning when the police arrived.*

**grease gun** /ˈ· ·/ *n* [C] a tool for forcing grease into machinery

**grease mon·key** /ˈ· ˌ··/ *n* [C] *slang* someone who repairs car engines or other machinery; MECHANIC

**grease·paint** /ˈgriːs-peɪnt/ *n* [U] a thick soft kind of paint that actors use on their face or body

**grease·proof pa·per** /ˌgriːs-pruːf ˈpeɪpə‖-ər/ *n* [U] *BrE* a kind of paper that GREASE[1] (1) cannot pass through, used in cooking and for wrapping food; WAXED PAPER *AmE*

**greas·er** /ˈgriːsə, -zə‖-ər/ *n* [C] **1** someone who puts GREASE on machinery to make it run smoothly **2** *AmE slang* a very offensive word for someone from Latin America, especially Mexico

**greas·y** /ˈgriːsi, -zi/ *adj* **1** covered in grease or oil: *greasy food* | *greasy hair* **2** slippery: *The roads are greasy after the rain.* **3** too polite and friendly in a way that seems insincere or unpleasant; SMARMY —**greasily** *adv* —**greasiness** *n* [U]

**greasy spoon** /ˌ·· ˈ·/ *n* [C] a small cheap restaurant that mainly serves fried (FRY[1] (1)) food

# **great** /greɪt/ *adj* S1 W1

① VERY GOOD
② A LOT/VERY MUCH
③ LARGE
④ IMPORTANT
⑤ FAMILY
⑥ OTHER MEANINGS

## ① VERY GOOD

**1** *spoken* **a)** very good; excellent: *We had a great time at the fair.* | *You can come after all? Great!* | *It's great to see you again!* **b)** used when you really think that something is not good, satisfactory or enjoyable at all: *"Daniel's cancelled the party." "Oh great!"*
**2 ▶ IN GOOD HEALTH ◀** feeling well and happy: *I feel great this morning!*
**3 ▶ SKILFUL/SUCCESSFUL ◀ a)** considered to be one of the best in the world and therefore admired by many people: *a great work of art* | *one of the greatest boxers of all time* **b)** able to do something well: [+ **at**] *Joanna's great at chess.*
**4 the greats** the most famous and successful performers, especially in sport or entertainment: **the all-time greats**: *Charlie Chaplin is one of the all-time cinema greats.*
**5 be no great shakes** to not be very good or skilful: *Alex thinks he's an ace at tennis, but he's no great shakes.*
**6 ▶ VERY SUITABLE ◀** *informal* to be very useful or suitable for something: [+ **for**] *This knife's great for peeling vegetables.*
**7 go great guns** *informal* to do something very fast and successfully: *Their campaign began slowly, but now they're going great guns.*

## ② A LOT/VERY MUCH

**8 great care/pleasure/strength etc** a lot of care etc: *Take great care with those glasses.* | *It gives me great pleasure to introduce tonight's speaker.*
**9 a great deal** a lot: *I've travelled a great deal.* | [+ **of**] *I have a great deal of work right now.*
**10 a great number/quantity/extent etc** a very large number etc: *Agnes survived the accident and went on to live to a great age* (=she was very old when she died). | **the great many** (=very many) | **the great majority** (=almost all) *a proposal supported by the great majority of members*
**11 great friend/admirer etc** a very good friend, a very keen admirer etc
**12 be a great one for writing/sailing/football etc** *BrE* to enjoy writing, sailing, football etc very much: *Adam's a great one for football – he never misses a match.*
**13 a great talker/reader etc** someone who enjoys doing a lot of talking, reading etc

## ③ LARGE

**14 ▶ VERY LARGE ◀** very large and impressive: *The great northern plain is divided by two rivers.* | *a great herd of buffalo* —see BIG (USAGE)
**15 great big/stupid/fat etc** *spoken* used to emphasize how big, stupid etc something or someone is: *They live in a great big house.*
**16 huge/enormous great** *BrE spoken* used to emphasize how big something is: *There's a huge great spider in the bath.*

## ④ IMPORTANT

**17 ▶ IMPORTANT ◀** [only before noun] especially important or serious: *a great state occasion* | *the great political issues of our time*
**18 the great advantage of/the great thing about** the most important advantage of something: *The great thing about nylon is that it's extremely tough.*
**19 ▶ HAVING INFLUENCE ◀** having a lot of influence or power as a result of what you have achieved: *We must strive to make our country great again.* | *the great man himself*
**20 the Great** used in the name or title of someone or something to show their importance: *King Alfred the Great*
**21 the great and the good** *formal or humorous* people who are considered important

## ⑤ FAMILY

**22 great-grandmother/great-grandfather etc** the grandmother etc of one of your parents —see picture at FAMILY
**23 great-granddaughter/great-nephew etc** the GRANDDAUGHTER, NEPHEW etc of your child —see picture at FAMILY

## ⑥ OTHER MEANINGS

**24 Great Scott/Great Heavens!** *old-fashioned* used to express surprise
**25 Greater** used before the name of a city to mean the city and its outer areas: *Greater Manchester*
**26 be great with child** *biblical* to be PREGNANT —**greatness** *n* [U]

**great-grand·child** /· '··/ *n* [C] the GRANCHILD of your child

**great·coat** /'greɪtkəʊt‖-koʊt/ *n* [C] a long heavy coat

W3 **great·ly** /'greɪtli/ *adv formal* [usually before verb or participle] extremely or very much: *We greatly regret the trouble we have caused.* | *a greatly improved design*

**grebe** /gri:b/ *n* [C] a bird similar to a duck

**Gre·cian** /'gri:ʃən/ *adj literary* from ancient Greece, or having a style or appearance that is considered typical of ancient Greece

**Gre·co-, Graeco-** /gri:kəʊ, grekəʊ‖-koʊ/ *prefix* **1** of ancient Greece; Greek **2** ancient Greek and *Greco-Roman art*

**greed** /gri:d/ *n* [U] **1** a strong desire for more food or drink than you need: **pure greed** *It's pure greed but I'd love some more of that cake.* **2** a strong desire for more money, power, possessions etc than you need: *a man driven by greed and envy*

**greed·y** /'gri:di/ *adj* **1** wanting more food or drink than you need: *Don't be greedy – leave some cake for us.* | You greedy pig! **2** always wanting more money, possessions etc: **greedy for profit/power/fame etc** *The company had become too greedy for profit.* —**greedily** *adv* —**greediness** *n* [U]

**Greek¹** /gri:k/ *n* **1** [U] the language of modern or ancient Greece **2** [C] someone from Greece **3** [C] *AmE* a member of a SORORITY or FRATERNITY (2) at an American college or university **4 it's all Greek to me** *informal* used to say that you cannot understand something

**Greek²** *adj* **1** from or connected with Greece **2 Greek god** *informal* a very attractive man



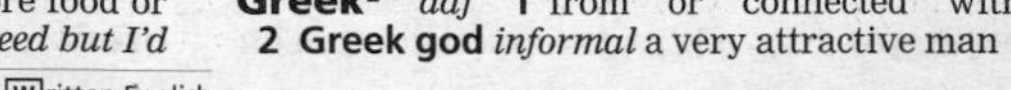

S1 W2 **green¹** /griːn/ *adj*
**1 ▶ COLOUR ◀** having the colour of grass or leaves: *Go on – the traffic lights have turned green!* | *green eyes* —see picture on page 411
**2 ▶ GRASSY ◀** covered with green grass: *green fields*
**3 ▶ FRUIT/PLANT ◀** very young, or not yet ready to be eaten: *The bananas are still green.* | *new green shoots on the roses*
**4 ▶ WITHOUT EXPERIENCE ◀** *informal* young and lacking experience: *a new batch of very green recruits*
**5 ▶ ILL ◀** *informal* looking pale and unhealthy because you are ill: *George looked a bit green the next morning.* | **green around/about the gills** (=looking ill or frightened)
**6 ▶ ENVIRONMENT ◀** connected with the environment: *green issues*
**7 ▶ POLITICS ◀** belonging to the Green political party
**8 green with envy** wishing very much that you had something that someone else has
**9 the green-eyed monster** *humorous or literary* jealousy
**10 have green fingers** *BrE*, **have a green thumb** *AmE* to be good at making plants grow
**11 the green stuff** *AmE informal* money

S2 W3 **green²** *n* **1** [C,U] the colour of grass and leaves: *a room decorated in pale blues and greens* **2 greens** [plural] **a)** *informal* vegetables with large green leaves: *Eat your greens.* **b)** *AmE* leaves and branches used for decoration, especially at Christmas —compare GREENERY **3** [C] a level area of grass, especially in the middle of a village: *playing cricket on the green* —see also BOWLING GREEN, VILLAGE GREEN **4** [C] a smooth flat area of grass around each hole on a GOLF COURSE —see picture on page 1264 **5 Green** [C] someone who supports the Green political party

**green³** *v* **1** to fill an area with growing plants in order to make it more attractive: *the challenge of greening the city* **2** to make a person or organization realize the importance of environmental problems: *the greening of public opinion*

**green·back** /ˈgriːnbæk/ *n* [C] *AmE informal* an American BANKNOTE

**green bean** /ˌ· ˈ·/ *n* [C] a long thin green vegetable which is picked before the beans inside it grow; FRENCH BEAN *BrE* —see picture on page 414

**green belt** /ˈ· ·/ *n* [C,U] an area of land around a city where building is not allowed, in order to protect fields and woods

**green card** /ˌ· ˈ·/ *n* [C] **1** a British motor insurance document that you need when you drive abroad **2** a document that a foreigner must have in order to work legally in the US

**green·e·ry** /ˈgriːnəri/ *n* [U] green leaves and plants

**green·field site** /ˈgriːnfiːld ˌsaɪt/ *n* [C] a piece of land that has never been built on before

**green·fly** /ˈgriːnflaɪ/ *n plural* **greenflies** [C] a very small green insect that feeds on and damages young plants

**green·gage** /ˈgriːngeɪdʒ/ *n* [C] a juicy greenish-yellow PLUM¹ (1)

**green·gro·cer** /ˈgriːnˌgrəʊsə‖-ˌgroʊsər/ *n* [C] *especially BrE* **1** someone who owns or works in a shop selling fruit and vegetables **2 greengrocer's** a greengrocer's shop

**green·horn** /ˈgriːnhɔːn‖-hɔːrn/ *n* [C] *informal* someone who lacks experience and can be easily deceived

**green·house** /ˈgriːnhaʊs/ *n* [C] a glass building used for growing plants that need warmth, light, and protection

**greenhouse ef·fect** /ˈ·· ·ˌ·/ *n* [singular] the gradual warming of the air surrounding the Earth as a result of heat being trapped by POLLUTION —see also GLOBAL WARMING

**greenhouse gas** /ˈ·· ˌ·/ *n* [C] a gas, especially CARBON DIOXIDE or METHANE, that is thought to trap heat above the Earth and cause the greenhouse effect

**green·ish** /ˈgriːnɪʃ/ *adj* slightly green: *a greenish tinge*

**green light** /ˈ· ·/ *n* [C] **1** the colour of a TRAFFIC LIGHT that shows cars they can go forward **2 give sb the green light** to allow a project, plan etc to begin: *The government has given the green light to Sunday trading.*

**green·light** /ˈgriːnlaɪt/ *v* [T] to give official permission for something to be started

**green on·ion** /ˌ· ˈ··/ *n* [C] *AmE* an onion with a small white round part and a long green stem, usually eaten raw; SPRING ONION *BrE*

**green pa·per** /ˌ· ˈ··/ *n* [C] a document produced by the British government containing proposals to be discussed, that may later be used in making laws —compare WHITE PAPER, BILL¹ (2)

**green pep·per** /ˌ· ˈ··/ *n* [C] a vegetable with green flesh and white seeds that you can cook or eat raw in SALADS

**green pound** /ˌ· ˈ·/ *n* [C,U] the value of the pound STERLING when exchanged for farm products in the EC

**green rev·o·lu·tion** /ˌ· ··ˈ··/ *n* [singular] **1** an increase in the amount that is produced by crops, such as wheat, due to improved scientific methods of farming **2** the new interest in protecting the environment that has developed in many parts of the world

**green sal·ad** /ˌ· ˈ··/ *n* [C] a SALAD made with LETTUCE and other raw green vegetables

**green tea** /ˌ· ˈ·/ *n* [U] light-coloured tea made from leaves that have been heated with steam

**Green·wich Mean Time** /ˌgrenɪtʃ ˈmiːn taɪm, ˌgrɪ-, -nɪdʒ-/ abbreviation **GMT** *n* [U] the time as measured at Greenwich in London

**greet** /griːt/ *v* [T] **1** to say hello to someone or welcome them: *Mr Grimshaw got up from behind his desk to greet me.* | **greet sb with a smile/kiss etc** *Billie greeted us with a cheerful grin.* **2** [always + adv/prep] to react to something in a particular way: **be greeted with** *The proposal was greeted with bursts of laughter.* **3** to be the first thing you see or hear when you arrive somewhere: *As we entered, complete chaos greeted us.*

**greet·ing** /ˈgriːtɪŋ/ *n* [C] **1** words you use or something you do when you meet someone: *I said good morning to Diane, but she didn't return my greeting.* | **exchange greetings** (=greet each other) **2** [usually plural] a message saying that you hope someone will be happy, healthy etc: *birthday greetings* **3 greetings!** *formal or humorous* used to say hello to someone

**greet·ings card** /ˈ·· ˌ·/ *n* [C] a card that you send to someone on their birthday, at Christmas etc

**gre·gar·i·ous** /grɪˈgeəriəs‖-ˈger-/ *adj* **1** friendly and preferring to be with others rather than alone; SOCIABLE¹ **2** *technical* gregarious animals tend to live in a group —**gregariously** *adv* —**gregariousness** *n* [U]

**Gre·go·ri·an cal·en·dar** /grɪˌgɔːriən ˈkælɪ̈ndə‖-dər/ *n* [singular] the system of arranging the 365 days of the year in months and giving numbers to the years from the birth of Christ, used in the West since 1582

**Gregorian chant** /·ˌ··· ˈ·/ *n* [C,U] a kind of church music for voices alone

**grem·lin** /ˈgremlɪ̈n/ *n* [C] an imaginary evil spirit that is blamed for problems in machinery, especially when no scientific explanation can be found

**gre·nade** /grɪ̈ˈneɪd/ *n* [C] a small bomb that can be thrown by hand or fired from a gun: *a hand grenade*

**gren·a·dier** /ˌgrenəˈdɪə◂‖-ˈdɪr◂/ *n* [C] a soldier in a famous REGIMENT¹ (1) of the British army

**gren·a·dine** /ˈgrenədiːn, ˌgrenəˈdiːn/ *n* [U] a sweet liquid made from POMEGRANATES that is used in drinks

**grew** /gruː/ *v* the past tense of GROW

S2 W2 **grey¹** usually **gray** *AmE* /greɪ/ *adj*
**1** ▶ **COLOUR** ◀ having a colour of black mixed with white, like the colour of ash: *an old lady with grey hair* | *a grey sky*
**2** ▶ **HAIR** ◀ having grey hair: **go grey** *My brother went grey in his forties.* —see picture on page 412.
**3** ▶ **FACE** ◀ looking pale because you are tired, frightened, or ill: *Noel's face was gray with fatigue.*
**4** ▶ **BORING** ◀ boring and unattractive; GLOOMY: *the grey anonymous men in government offices*
**5** ▶ **OF OLD PEOPLE** ◀ *BrE* connected with old people: *the grey vote*
**6 grey area** an area of law or science that cannot be dealt with in a definite way because it is outside those areas that have clear rules and limits

**grey²** usually **gray** *AmE n* [C,U] the colour of smoke and rain clouds: *dull greys and browns* —see picture on page 411

**grey³** usually **gray** *AmE v* [I] if someone greys, their hair becomes grey: *Jim's beginning to gray at the temples.*

**grey·hound** /ˈgreɪhaʊnd/ *n* [C] a type of thin dog that can run very fast and is used in races —see picture at DOG¹

**grey·ish** usually **grayish** *AmE* /ˈgreɪ-ɪʃ/ *adj* slightly grey

**grey mat·ter** /ˈ· ˌ··/ *n* [U] *informal* your intelligence

**grid** /grɪd/ *n* **1** [C] a metal frame with bars across it —see also CATTLE GRID **2** [C] a pattern of straight lines that cross each other and form squares **3 the grid** *BrE* the network of electricity supply wires that connects POWER STATIONS: *the national grid* **4** [C] a system of numbered squares printed on a map so that the exact position of any place can be found **5** [C] a set of starting positions for all the cars in a motor race

**grid·dle** /ˈgrɪdl/ *n* [C] a round iron plate that is used for cooking flat cakes on top of a STOVE¹ (2) or over a fire

**grid·dle·cake** /ˈgrɪdlˌkeɪk/ *n* [C] *AmE* a PANCAKE (2)

**grid·i·ron** /ˈgrɪdaɪən‖-ərn/ *n* [C] **1** an open frame of metal bars for cooking meat or fish over a very hot fire **2** *AmE* a field marked in white lines for American football

**grid·lock** /ˈgrɪdlɒk‖-lɑːk/ *n* [U] *especially AmE* **1** a situation in which streets in a city are so full of cars that they cannot move **2** a situation in which nothing can happen, usually because people disagree strongly: *Clinton is in gridlock with the Congress.* —**gridlocked** *adj*

**grief** /griːf/ *n* **1** [U] extreme sadness, especially because someone you love has died: [+ **over/at**] *The grief she felt over Helen's death was almost unbearable.* **2** [C] something that makes you feel extremely sad: *It was a grief to him that he had never had any children.* **3 good grief!** *spoken* used when you are slightly surprised or annoyed: *Good grief! This must have cost you a fortune! Where did you get the money?* **4 come to grief** to fail, or to be harmed or destroyed in an accident: *The expedition shortly came to grief on Vanikoro Reef.* **5 give sb grief** *informal* to criticize someone in an annoying way: *I'd better go home now – my Mum'll give me grief if I'm not back for dinner.*

**grief-strick·en** /ˈ· ˌ··/ also **grief-struck** /ˈ· ·/ *adj* feeling very sad because of something that has happened

**griev·ance** /ˈgriːvəns/ *n* [C, U] something that you complain about because you feel you have been treated unfairly: [+ **against**] *Anyone who has a legitimate grievance against the company can take it to the committee.* | **air your grievances** (=tell other people you feel you have been treated unfairly) *The meetings provide employees with an opportunity to air their grievances.* | **nurse a grievance** (=think about it continuously) | **sense of grievance** (=a feeling that you have been treated unfairly) *Grant's deep sense of grievance at not being promoted*

**grieve** /griːv/ *v* **1** [I,T] to feel extremely sad, especially because someone you love has died: *People need time to grieve after the death of a loved one.* | **grieve sth** *The family grieved the loss of its only son.* **2** [T] if something grieves you, it makes you feel very unhappy: **it grieves sb to think/say/see etc** *It grieves me to think of all the money we've spent on that ungrateful brat.*

**grieved** /griːvd/ *adj literary* very sad and upset: **be grieved (at)** *I am deeply grieved at this sad news.*

**griev·ous** /ˈgriːvəs/ *adj* **1** *formal* very serious and likely to be very harmful: *a grievous error* | *a grievous shortage of hospital beds* **2** *especially literary* a grievous wound or pain is severe and hurts a lot —**grievously** *adv* —**grievousness** *n* [U]

**grievous bod·i·ly harm** /ˌ·· ˌ··· ˈ·/ *n* [U] *BrE law* serious injury caused by a criminal attack; GBH

**grif·fin, gryphon** /ˈgrɪfən/ *n* [C] an imaginary animal in stories that has a lion's body and an EAGLE's wings and head

**grif·ter** /ˈgrɪftə‖-ər/ *n* [C] *AmE informal* someone who dishonestly obtains something, especially money —**grift** *v* [T]

**grill¹** /grɪl/ *v* **1** [I,T] if you grill something, or if it grills, you cook it by putting it close to very strong direct heat: *Grill the burgers for eight minutes each side.* **2** [T] to ask someone a lot of difficult questions in order to make them explain their actions, opinions etc: *I was grilled by customs officers for several hours.*

**grill²** *n* [C] **1** *BrE* a part of a COOKER (1) in which very strong heat from above cooks food on a metal shelf below; BROILER (1) *AmE*: *Pop it under the grill for five minutes.* **2** a flat frame with metal bars across it that can be put over a fire, so that food can be cooked quickly on it **3** a place where you can buy and eat grilled food: *Henry J. Bean's Bar and Grill* —see also MIXED GRILL **4** a grille

**grille, grill** /grɪl/ *n* [C] **1** a frame with metal bars or wire across it that is put in front of a window or door for protection **2** the metal bars at the front of a car that protect the RADIATOR (2)

**grill·ing** /ˈgrɪlɪŋ/ *n* **give sb a grilling** to ask someone a lot of difficult questions in order to make them explain their actions or opinions

**grill pan** /ˈ· ·/ *n* [C] a square flat pan, used under a GRILL² (1) —see picture at PAN¹

**grim** /grɪm/ *adj* **grimmer, grimmest**
**1** ▶ **SITUATION/NEWS** ◀ making you feel worried and unhappy: *There's more grim news from the war zone.* | **things look grim (for)** *Things look pretty grim for farmers right now.* | **grim prospect** (=something bad that will probably happen)
**2** ▶ **PLACE/BUILDING ETC** ◀ unpleasant and unattractive: *a grim industrial town*
**3** ▶ **PERSON** ◀ looking or sounding very serious because the situation is very bad: *The grim-faced judge sentenced Burke to life-imprisonment.* | **grim determination** (=serious determination in spite of difficulties or dangers)
**4 feel grim** *informal* to feel ill: *I felt a bit grim the morning after the party.*
**5** ▶ **OF BAD QUALITY** ◀ *BrE informal* very bad in quality: *You should see some of her recent essays – they're pretty grim.*
**6 hold/hang on for grim death** *BrE informal* to hold something very tightly because you are afraid —**grimly** *adv*: *Arnold smiled grimly.* —**grimness** *n* [U]

**gri·mace¹** /grɪˈmeɪs, ˈgrɪməs/ *v* [I] to twist your face in an ugly way because you do not like something, because you are feeling pain, or because you are trying to be funny: *Toni muttered and grimaced at each tug of the comb.* | [+ **with**] *Baggio lay grimacing with pain.*

**grimace²** *n* [C] an expression you make by twisting your face because you do not like something or because you are feeling pain: *Bernie gave a grimace of disgust and left the room.*

**grime** /graɪm/ *n* [U] dirt that forms a black layer on surfaces: *black with grime*

**grim·y** /ˈgraɪmi/ *adj* covered with dirt: *grimy windows*

**grin¹** /grɪn/ *v* [I] **grinned, grinning** **1** to smile widely: *Grinning sheepishly, James admitted he was seeing Sue.* | [+ **at**] *Stop grinning at me, you stupid jackass!* | [+ **with**] *grinning with delight* | **grin from ear to ear** (=grin very widely) **2 grin and bear it** to accept and bear an unpleasant or difficult situation without complaining, usually because you realize there is nothing you can do to make it better

**grin²** *n* [C] a wide smile: *a broad grin* | *Take that cheeky grin off your face!* —see also **wipe the smile/grin off sb's face** (WIPE¹ (7))

**grind¹** /graɪnd/ *v past tense and past participle* **ground** /graʊnd/

**1 ▶ INTO SMALL PIECES ◀** [T] **a)** also **grind up** [T] to break something such as corn or coffee beans into small pieces or powder, either in a machine or between two hard surfaces **b)** *AmE* to cut food, especially raw meat, into very small pieces by putting it through a machine: MINCE¹ (1) *BrE*

**2 ▶ SMOOTH/SHARP ◀** [T] to make something smooth or sharp by rubbing it on a hard surface or by using a machine: *a stone for grinding knives and scissors* | *The lenses are ground to a high standard of precision.*

**3 ▶ PRESS STH DOWN ◀** [T always + adv/prep] to press something down into a surface and rub it with a strong twisting movement: **grind sth into/in** *He dropped a cigar butt and ground it into the carpet with his heel.*

**4 grind your teeth** to rub your upper and lower teeth together making a noise

**5 grind to a halt a)** if a vehicle grinds to a halt, it stops gradually: *Traffic ground to a halt as it approached the accident site.* **b)** if a country, organization, or process grinds to a halt, it gradually stops working: *As more and more workers joined the strike, Britain's economy was grinding to a halt.*

**6 grind the faces of the poor** to make poor people work very hard and give them almost nothing in return —see also **have an axe to grind** (AXE¹ (4))

**grind** sb ↔ **down** *phr v* [T] to treat someone in a cruel way for such a long time that they lose all courage and hope; OPPRESS: *Years of dictatorship had ground the people down.*

**grind on** *phr v* [I] to continue for an unpleasantly long time: *Winter grinds on until March.*

**grind** sth ↔ **out** *phr v* [T] to produce information, writing, music etc in such large amounts that it becomes boring: *Frank just keeps grinding out detective stories.*

**grind²** *n* **1** [singular] something that is hard work and physically or mentally tiring: *I find the journey to work a real grind.* | **the daily grind** (=things that you have to do every day that are boring) **2** [C] *AmE informal* a student who never does anything except study; SWOT¹

**grind·er** /ˈgraɪndə‖-ər/ *n* [C] a machine for crushing coffee beans, PEPPERCORNS etc into powder: *a pepper grinder*

**grind·ing** /ˈgraɪndɪŋ/ *adj* [only before noun] **1 grinding poverty/misery** a situation that makes your life very difficult and unhappy, and never seems to improve **2** a grinding noise is the continuous unpleasant noise of machinery parts rubbing together

**grind·stone** /ˈgraɪndstəʊn‖-stoʊn/ *n* [C] a large round stone that is turned like a wheel while tools, knives etc are rubbed against it to make them sharp —see also **keep your nose to the grindstone** (NOSE¹ (15))

**grin·go** /ˈgrɪŋgəʊ‖-goʊ/ *n plural* **gringos** [C] an offensive word for someone from North America, used by people in Latin American countries

**grip¹** /grɪp/ *n*

**1 ▶ FIRM HOLD ◀** [C usually singular] the way you hold something tightly or your ability to do this: *Don't loosen your grip on the rope or you'll fall.*

**2 ▶ POWER ◀** [singular] power and control over someone or something: **have a grip on sth** *The chancellor doesn't seem to have a very firm grip on the economy.*

**3 come/get to grips with** to understand and deal with a difficult problem or situation: *I've never really got to grips with this new technology.*

**4 lose your grip** to become less confident and less able to deal with a situation: *I handled that interview very badly – I must be losing my grip.*

**5 get/keep a grip on yourself** to start controlling your emotions when you have been very upset: *Stop being hysterical and get a grip on yourself.*

**6 be in the grip of** to be experiencing a very unpleasant situation that cannot be controlled or stopped: *a country in the grip of famine*

**7 ▶ STOP STH SLIPPING ◀** [C] **a)** a special part of a handle that has a rough surface so that you can hold it firmly without it slipping: *a racquet with a rubber grip* —see picture on page 1264 **b)** the ability of something to stay on a surface without slipping: *I want some tennis shoes with a good grip.*

**8 ▶ FOR HAIR ◀** [C] *BrE* a HAIRGRIP

**9 ▶ CAMERAMAN ◀** [C] someone whose job is to move the cameras around while a television show or film is being made

**10 ▶ BAG ◀** [C] *old-fashioned* a bag or case used for travelling

**grip²** *v* **gripped, gripping 1** [I,T] to hold something very tightly: *I gripped the handrail tightly and tried not to look down.* **2** [T] to have a strong effect on someone or something: *a country gripped by economic problems* | *Panic suddenly gripped me when it was my turn to speak.* **3** [T] to hold someone's attention and interest: *a story that really grips you* **4** [T] if something grips a surface, it stays on it without slipping: *Radial tires grip the road well.* —see also GRIPPING

**gripe¹** /graɪp/ *v* [I] to complain about something continuously and in an annoying way: [+ **about**] *Joe came in griping about how cold it was outside.*

**gripe²** *n informal* **1** [C] something unimportant that you complain about: *My main gripe was the price of refreshments.* **2 the gripes** *old-fashioned* sudden bad stomach pains

**gripe wa·ter** /ˈ· ˌ··/ *n* [U] *BrE* a liquid medicine given to babies when they have stomach pains

**grip·ing** /ˈgraɪpɪŋ/ *adj* a griping pain is a sudden severe pain in the stomach

**grip·ping** /ˈgrɪpɪŋ/ *adj* a gripping film, story etc is very exciting and interesting —**grippingly** *adv*

**gris·ly** /ˈgrɪzli/ *adj* extremely unpleasant, usually because death, decay, or destruction is involved: *the grisly discovery of human remains in the cellar*

**grist** /grɪst/ *n* **(all) grist to the mill** something additional that can be used for your advantage in a particular situation: *Any publicity is good – it's all grist to the mill.*

**gris·tle** /ˈgrɪsəl/ *n* [U] the part of meat that is not soft enough to eat —**gristly** *adj*

**grit¹** /grɪt/ *n* [U] **1** very small pieces of stone or sand that are scattered on frozen roads to make them less slippery **2** *informal* determination and courage **3 grits** *AmE* HOMINY grain that is roughly crushed before cooking, often eaten for breakfast —**gritty** *adj*

**grit²** *v* [T] **gritted, gritting 1** to scatter grit on a frozen road to make it less slippery **2 grit your teeth** to use all your determination to continue in spite of difficulties: *Just grit your teeth and hang on – it will be over soon.*

**grit·ter** /ˈgrɪtə‖-ər/ *n* [C] *BrE* a large vehicle that puts salt or sand on the roads in winter to make then less icy; SALT TRUCK *AmE*

**griz·zle** /ˈgrɪzəl/ *v* [I] *BrE informal* **1** if a baby or child grizzles, they cry quietly and continuously **2** to complain continuously in an annoying way

**griz·zled** /ˈgrɪzəld/ *adj literary* having grey or greyish hair

**griz·zly bear** /ˌ·· ˈ·‖ˈ·· ·/ also **grizzly** *n* [C] a very large brownish-grey bear that lives in the Rocky Mountains of North America

**groan¹** /grəʊn‖groʊn/ *v* [I] **1** to make a long deep sound because you are in pain, upset, or disappointed: *The kids all groaned when I swtiched off the TV.* | **moan and**

groan (=complain a lot) *I'm tired of him moaning and groaning all the time.* **2** to make a sound similar to someone groaning: *The old tree groaned in the wind.* **3** if a table groans with food there is a very large amount of food on it

**groan²** *n* [C] **1** a long deep sound that you make when you are in pain or do not want to do something: *Casey let out a groan of protest at having to go to bed.* **2** *literary* a long low sound like someone groaning: *The door opened with a groan.*

**groat** /grəʊt‖groʊt/ *n* **1 groats** [plural] grain, especially OATS with the outer shell removed **2** [C] a former British coin that had a low value

**gro·bag, growbag** /'grəʊbæg‖'groʊ-/ *n* [C] *BrE* a large plastic bag containing specially prepared earth for growing vegetables

**gro·cer** /'grəʊsə‖'groʊsər/ *n* [C] **1** someone who owns or works in a shop that sells food such as flour, sugar, food in cans, and other things used in the home **2 grocer's** a grocer's shop

**gro·cer·y** /'grəʊsəri‖'groʊ-/ *n* **1 groceries** [plural] goods sold by a grocer or a SUPERMARKET **2** also **grocery store** /'···· ·/ [C] *AmE* a SUPERMARKET

**gro·dy** /'grəʊdi‖'groʊ-/ *adj AmE slang* a word meaning very unpleasant or offensive, used especially by children

**grog** /grɒg‖grɑːg/ *n* [U] **1** a mixture of strong alcoholic drink, especially RUM¹, and water **2** *informal* any alcoholic drink

**grog·gy** /'grɒgi‖'grɑːgi/ *adj* weak and unable to walk steadily or think clearly because you are ill or very tired: *I felt really groggy after 15 hours on the plane.* —**groggily** *adv*

**groin** /grɔɪn/ *n* [C] **1** the place where the tops of your legs meet the front of your body —see picture at BODY **2** a GROYNE

**grom·met** /'grɒmɪ̣t‖'grɑː-/ *n* [C] **1** a small metal ring used to make a hole in cloth or leather stronger **2** a small piece of plastic put into a child's ear in order to remove liquid from it

**groom¹** /gruːm, grʊm/ *v* **1** [T] to take care of animals, especially horses, by cleaning and brushing them **2** [I,T] to take care of your own appearance by keeping your hair and clothes clean and tidy: *a well-groomed woman in her twenties* **3** [T] to prepare someone for an important job or position in society by training them over a long period: **groom sb for sth** *Tim was being groomed for a managerial position.* | **groom sb to do sth** *Clare's father is grooming her to take his place when he retires.* **4** [I,T] if an animal grooms itself or another animal, it cleans its own fur and skin or that of the other animal —**grooming** *n* [U] —see also WELL-GROOMED

**groom²** *n* [C] **1** a BRIDEGROOM **2** someone whose job is to feed, clean, and take care of horses

**grooms·man** /'gruːmzmən, 'grʊms-/ *n* [C] *AmE* a friend of a BRIDEGROOM who has special duties at a wedding; USHER¹ (1) *BrE*

**groove¹** /gruːv/ *n* [C] **1** a thin line cut into a surface, especially to guide the movement of something: *The bolt slid easily into the groove.* **2 be in a groove** to be living or working in a situation that has been the same for a long time and that is unlikely to change

**groove²** *v* [T] to make a long narrow track in something —**grooved** *adj*

**groov·y** /'gruːvi/ *adj* a word meaning fashionable, modern, and fun, used especially in the 1960s

**grope¹** /grəʊp‖groʊp/ *v* **1** [I always + adv/prep] to try to find something that you cannot see by feeling with your hands: [+ **for/through/around etc**] *Ginny groped for her glasses on the bedside table.* | *groping around in the dark* **2 grope your way along/across etc** to go somewhere by feeling the way with your hands because you cannot see: *I groped my way along the wall to the door.* **3** [I] to try hard to find the right words to say, or the right solution to a problem but without any real idea of how to do this: [+ **for**] *Accusations of misconduct left Keeler groping for a response.* **4** [T] *informal* to move your hands over someone's body to get sexual pleasure, especially when they do not want you to do this

**grope²** *n* [C] *informal* an act of groping (GROPE¹ (4))

**gross¹** /grəʊs‖groʊs/ *adj* S3
**1 ▶TOTAL◀ a)** a gross amount of money is the total amount before any tax or costs have been taken away: *a gross profit of $15 million* | *gross receipts* (=the gross amount of money received) —compare NET³ (1) **b)** a gross weight is the total weight of something, including its wrapping
**2 gross negligence/misconduct/injustice etc** behaviour that is clearly wrong and unacceptable: *a gross exaggeration of the truth*
**3 ▶RUDE◀** behaviour that is gross is extremely rude and completely unacceptable
**4 ▶NASTY◀** *spoken* very unpleasant to look at or think about: *Ooh, gross! I hate spinach!*
**5 ▶FAT◀** extremely fat and unattractive —**grossly** *adv*: *grossly overweight* —**grossness** *n* [U]

**gross²** *adv* **earn £20,000/$30,000 etc gross** to earn £20,000 etc before tax has been taken away: *a junior executive earning more than $30,000 gross*

**gross³** *v* [T] to gain an amount as a total profit, or earn it as a total amount, before tax has been taken away: *This type of store may gross $8 million or more annually.*

**gross** sb **out** *phr v* [T] *spoken AmE* to make someone wish they had not seen or been told about something because it is so unpleasant

**gross⁴** *determiner n plural* **gross** [C] a quantity of 144 things: *a gross of candles*

**gross do·mes·tic prod·uct** /,· ··· '··/ *n* [singular] *technical* the GDP; the total value of all the goods and services produced in a country, except for income received from abroad —compare GROSS NATIONAL PRODUCT

**gross mar·gin** /,· '··/ *n* [C] the financial difference between what something costs to produce and what it is sold for

**gross na·tion·al prod·uct** /,· ··· '··/ *n technical* [singular] the GNP; the total value of all the goods and services produced in a country, including income from abroad —compare GROSS DOMESTIC PRODUCT

**gross prof·it** /,· '··/ *n* [C] GROSS MARGIN

**gro·tesque¹** /grəʊ'tesk‖groʊ-/ *adj* **1** strange or unusual in a way that is shocking or offensive: *The idea of my best friend becoming my stepmother was too grotesque to contemplate.* **2** extremely ugly in a strange or unnatural way: *a grotesque figure with a huge head* —**grotesquely** *adv*

**grotesque²** *n* **1** [C] an image of someone who is strangely ugly **2 the grotesque** a grotesque style in art

**grot·to** /'grɒtəʊ‖'grɑːtoʊ/ *n* [C] a small natural CAVE¹, or one that someone has made in their garden

**grot·ty** /'grɒti‖'grɑːti/ *adj BrE informal* nasty, dirty, or unpleasant: *a grotty little bedsit* —**grottily** *adv* —**grottiness** *n* [U]

**grouch¹** /graʊtʃ/ *n informal* **1** [C] someone who is always complaining: *My grandad is such an old grouch.* **2** [C] something unimportant that you complain about: *One of his main grouches is that they never put the top back on the toothpaste.*

**grouch²** *v* [I + **about**] *informal* to complain in an angry way; GRUMBLE¹ (1)

**grouch·y** /'graʊtʃi/ *adj* in a bad temper, especially because you are tired —**grouchiness** *n* [U]

G

# ground[1] /graʊnd/ *n*

① EARTH SURFACE
② AREA
③ SUBJECT
④ OPINION/ATTITUDE
⑤ REASON
⑥ SUCCESS/ADVANTAGE
⑦ HIDE/FIND
⑧ COLOUR/PAINT
⑨ OTHER MEANINGS

## ① EARTH SURFACE

**1** [U] the surface of the earth: *The leaf slowly fluttered to the ground.* | *The air raids were followed by military action on the ground.* | **below/above ground** *miners working 10-hour shifts below ground* —compare FLOOR[1] (1) —see LAND[1] (USAGE)

**2 ▶SOIL◀** [U] the soil on and under the surface of the earth: *Dig the ground over in autumn.* | *marshy ground*

**3 ▶UNDER THE SEA◀** [U] the bottom of the sea: *Our ship touched ground.*

## ② AREA

**4 ▶OPEN LAND◀** [U] an area of land without buildings or trees: *a view across open ground* | *They're building a car lot on some waste ground across the street.*

**5 grounds** [plural] **a)** a large area of land or sea that is used for a particular activity or sport: *hunting grounds* | *fishing grounds* **b)** the land or gardens around a large house, hospital etc

**6 parade/recreation/burial etc ground** an area of land that is used for a particular purpose —see also PLAYGROUND

**7 ▶SPORTS◀** [C] *BrE* the place where a sport such as football or CRICKET (2) is played; STADIUM: *the team's home ground* (=where they usually play)

**8 cover a lot of ground** to travel a very long distance: *You certainly covered a lot of ground on your travels.*

## ③ SUBJECT

**9 ▶AREA OF KNOWLEDGE◀** [U] an area of knowledge, ideas, experience etc: **go over the same ground** (=talk about the same things again) *The article says nothing new – it just goes over the same old ground.* | **be on familiar ground/be on your own ground** (=be talking about or dealing with a subject you know a lot about) *Keith's on familiar ground. He's worked with this type of computer before.*

**10 be on dangerous/safe ground** to be expressing ideas that are likely or unlikely to offend or embarrass someone

**11 cover a lot of ground** to give information about many different parts of a subject: *It's absurd to try to cover so much ground in such a short lecture.*

## ④ OPINION/ATTITUDE

**12 the middle ground** the area of political opinion that most people agree about: *the middle ground between two passionately opposed views*

**13 common ground** an area of opinion that two people or groups share: *We hope to find some common ground as a basis for agreement.*

**14 shift/change your ground** to begin to use different reasons or ideas to support your opinions

**15 hold your ground** to continue to support a particular opinion in spite of opposition

**16 the moral high ground** an opinion that is regarded as morally better than others

## ⑤ REASON

**17 ▶REASON◀** [C usually plural] a reason, especially one that makes you think that something is true or correct: **grounds for (doing) sth** *Jim has strong grounds for asking for more money.* | **on moral/legal etc grounds** *He refused to sign the contract on moral grounds.* | **on grounds of** *The divorce was granted on ground of adultery.* | **on the grounds that** *Zoe was awarded compensation on the grounds that the doctor had been negligent.*

## ⑥ SUCCESS/ADVANTAGE

**18 get off the ground** if a plan, a business idea etc gets off the ground, or if you get it off the ground, it starts to be successful: *It took a while for the business to get off the ground, but it's making a profit now.*

**19 gain ground a)** to get an advantage and become more successful: *The Republicans have been gaining ground in the opinion polls.* **b)** if an idea, belief etc gains ground, it starts to become accepted or believed by more people: *a theory gaining ground among academics*

**20 lose ground** to lose an advantage and become less successful

## ⑦ HIDE/FIND

**21 go to ground** *BrE* to hide from someone, especially the police

**22 run sb to ground** *BrE* to succeed in finding someone after a long search: *I finally ran Luke to ground in the basement store room.*

## ⑧ COLOUR/PAINT

**23 ▶BACKGROUND◀** [C] the colour that is the background for a design: *white flowers on a blue ground*

**24 ▶PAINT◀** [C] the first covering of paint on a painting

## ⑨ OTHER MEANINGS

**25 fertile ground/breeding ground** a situation in which it is easy for something to develop: *The universities were a fertile ground for left-wing radicalism.* | *a breeding ground for germs*

**26 on the ground** in the actual place where something, especially a war, is happening, rather than in another place where it is being discussed: *While the politicians talked of peace, the situation on the ground remained tense.*

**27 on your own ground/on home ground** in the place or situation that is most familiar to you: *I wouldn't dream of meeting my ex-husband again unless I was on home ground.*

**28 work/drive yourself into the ground** to work so hard that you become extremely tired: *Kay's working herself into the ground trying to meet her deadlines.*

**29 grounds** *plural* the small pieces of something such as coffee which sink to the bottom of a liquid: *coffee grounds*

**30 ▶ELECTRICAL◀** [singular] *AmE* a wire that connects a piece of electrical equipment to the ground for safety; EARTH[1] (8) *BrE* —see also **break new ground** (BREAK[1] (33)), **cut the ground from under sb's feet** (CUT[1] (25)), **have/keep both feet on the ground** (FOOT[1] (16)), **stand your ground** (STAND[1] (8)), **stand/hold your ground** (STAND[1] (17)), **suit sb down to the ground** (SUIT[2] (1)), **be thin on the ground** (THIN[1] (12)), **hit the ground running** (HIT[1] (22))

**ground²** *v* **1** [T usually passive] to stop an aircraft or pilot from flying: *All planes are grounded until the fog clears.* **2** [I,T] if you ground a boat or if it grounds, it hits the bottom of the sea so that it cannot move **3 be grounded in/on** to be based on something: *David's values are grounded in a Protestant work ethic.* **4** [T] *informal* to stop a child going out with their friends as a punishment for behaving badly: *I got home at 2 am and Dad grounded me on the spot.* **5** [T] *AmE* to make a piece of electrical equipment safe by connecting it to the ground with a wire; EARTH² *BrE* —see also WELL-GROUNDED

**ground** sb **in** sth *phr v* [T usually passive] to teach someone the basic things they should know in order to be able to do something: *The recruits were grounded in combat techniques.*

**ground³** *adj* [only before noun] ground coffee or nuts have been broken up into powder or very small pieces, using a special machine

**ground⁴** the past tense and past participle of GRIND¹

**ground bait** /ˈ· ·/ *n* [U] food that you throw onto a river, lake etc when you are fishing in order to attract fish

**ground beef** /ˌ· ˈ·/ *n* [U] *AmE* BEEF¹ (1) that has been cut up into very small pieces, often used to make HAMBURGERS; MINCE² *BrE*

**ground·break·ing** /ˈgraʊndˌbreɪkɪŋ/ *adj* groundbreaking work involves making new discoveries, using new methods etc

**ground cloth** /ˈ· ·/ *n* [C] *AmE* a piece of material that water cannot pass through which people sleep on when they are camping; GROUNDSHEET *BrE*

**ground con·trol** /ˈ· ·ˌ·/ *n* [U] the people on the ground who are responsible for guiding the flight of SPACECRAFT or aircraft

**ground cov·er** /ˈ· ˌ··/ *n* [U] plants that cover the soil

**ground crew** /ˈ· ·/ *n* [C] the group of people who work at an airport looking after the aircraft; GROUND STAFF *BrE*

**ground·er** /ˈgraʊndə‖-ər/ *n* [C] a ball hit along the ground in BASEBALL

**ground floor** /ˌ· ˈ·◂/ *n* **1** [C] *especially BrE* the floor of a building that is at ground level; FIRST FLOOR (2) *AmE* —see FLOOR¹ (USAGE) **2 be/get in on the ground floor** to become involved in a plan, business activity etc from the beginning

**ground for·ces** /ˈ· ˌ··/ *n* [plural] military groups that fight on the ground rather than at sea or in the air

**ground glass** /ˌ· ˈ·◂/ *n* [U] **1** glass that has been made into a powder **2** glass that has been rubbed on the surface so that you cannot see through it, but light passes through it

**ground·hog** /ˈgraʊndhɒg‖-hɑːg, -hɔːg/ *n* [C] a small North American animal that has thick brown fur and lives in holes in the ground; WOODCHUCK

**ground·ing** /ˈgraʊndɪŋ/ *n* **1** [singular] a training in the basic parts of a subject or skill: [+ **in**] *A thorough grounding in mathematics is essential for the economics course.* **2** [C] *AmE* a punishment for a child's bad behaviour in which they are not allowed go out with their friends for a period of time

**ground·less** /ˈgraʊndləs/ *adj* groundless fears, worries etc are unnecessary because there are no facts to base them on: *Fortunately my suspicions proved groundless.*

**ground lev·el** /ˈ· ˌ··/ *n* [singular] the same level as the surface of the earth, rather than above it or below it

**ground·nut** /ˈgraʊndnʌt/ *n* [C] *BrE technical* a PEANUT or peanut plant

**ground plan** /ˈ· ·/ *n* [C] **1** a drawing of how a building is arranged at ground level, showing the size, position, and shape of walls, rooms etc **2** a plan of how something will happen in the future

**ground rent** /ˈ· ·/ *n* [C,U] rent paid to the person who owns the land that your house is built on

**ground rules** /ˈ· ·/ *n* [plural] the basic rules or principles on which future actions or behaviour should be based

**ground·sheet** /ˈgraʊndʃiːt/ *n* [C] *BrE* a piece of material that water cannot pass through which people sleep on when they are camping; GROUND CLOTH *AmE*

**grounds·man** /ˈgraʊndzmən/ *plural* **groundsmen** /-mən/ *n* [C] *especially BrE* a man whose job is to take care of large gardens or a sports field

**ground squir·rel** /ˈ· ˌ··/ *n* [C] a North American animal that lives in the ground and often damages crops; GOPHER

**ground staff** /ˈ· ·/ *n* [C] *BrE* **1** the people who take care of the grass and sports equipment at a sports ground **2** the group of people who work at an airport looking after the aircraft; GROUND CREW

**ground stroke** /ˈ· ·/ *n* [C] a way of hitting the ball after it has hit the ground in tennis and similar games

**ground·swell** /ˈgraʊndswel/ *n* **1 groundswell of support/opinion etc** a sudden increase in how strongly people feel about something **2** [singular, U] the strong movement of the sea that continues after a storm or strong winds

**ground·work** /ˈgraʊndwɜːk‖-wɜːrk/ *n* [U] important work that has to take place before another activity, plan etc can be successful: *The groundwork for the peace summit was laid during last month's conference.*

**group¹** /gruːp/ *n* [C] **1** several people or things that are all together in the same place: [+ **of**] *a group of tall trees* | *Get into groups of four.* | [also + plural verb *BrE*] *A group of us are going to London for the concert.* **2** several people or things that are connected with each other in some way: [+ **of**] *A group of animal rights activists claimed responsibility for the bomb.* | *the Germanic group of languages* | **income/ethnic etc group** (=people with the same income level, same race etc) **3** several companies that all have the same owner: *a giant textiles group* **4** a number of musicians or singers who perform together, usually playing popular music: *a rock group* —see also AGE GROUP, BLOOD GROUP, INTEREST GROUP, PLAYGROUP S1 W1

**group²** *v* **1** [I,T] to come together to make a group or to arrange people or things in a group: [+ **on/in/together etc**] *Can you all group around the piano?* **2** [T always + adv/prep] to divide people or things into groups or types according to a system: *The soils can be broadly grouped according to their acidity.*

**group cap·tain** /ˌ· ˈ··◂/ *n* [C] a fairly high rank in the British airforce, or someone who has this rank —see table on page B4

**group·ie** /ˈgruːpi/ *n* [C] someone, especially a young woman, who follows POP muscians to their concerts, hoping to meet them

**group·ing** /ˈgruːpɪŋ/ *n* [C] a set of people, things, or organizations that have the same interests, qualities, or features: *The unemployed form the largest single grouping of the electorate.*

**group prac·tice** /ˌ· ˈ··/ *n* [C,U] a group of doctors who work together, in the same building

**group ther·a·py** /ˌ· ˈ···/ *n* [U] a method of treating people with emotional or PSYCHOLOGICAL problems by bringing them together in groups to talk about their problems

**grouse¹** /graʊs/ *n* **1** [C] *informal* a complaint, especially an unreasonable one **2** [C,U] a small fat bird that is hunted and shot for food and sport, or the meat of this bird

**grouse²** *v* [I + **about**] *informal* to complain about something in an angry way: GRUMBLE¹ (1)

**grove** /grəʊv‖groʊv/ *n* **1** [C] an area of land planted with a particular type of fruit tree: *an orange grove* —compare ORCHARD **2** [C] *literary* a small group of trees **3 Grove** used in the names of roads: *Lisson Grove*

**grov·el** /ˈgrɒvəl‖ˈgrɑː-, ˈgrʌ-/ *v* **grovelled, grovelling** *BrE*, **groveled, groveling** *AmE* [I] **1** to behave with

G

too much respect towards someone, because you are asking them to help or forgive you: *There's nothing worse than seeing a man grovel just to keep his job.* **2** to lie or move flat on the ground because you are afraid of someone, or as a way of showing obedience: *That dog grovels every time you shout.*

S1 W1 **grow** /grəʊ||groʊ/ *v past tense* **grew** /gruː/ *past participle* **grown** /grəʊn||groʊn/
**1 ▶ PERSON/ANIMAL ◀** [I] to become bigger and develop over a period of time: *How you've grown since the last time I saw you!*| **grow 2 inches/5cm etc** *Stan grew two inches in six months.*| **growing boy/girl** *Of course he eats a lot – he's a growing boy!*
**2 ▶ PLANTS/CROPS ◀ a)** [I] to exist and develop somewhere in a natural way: *There's corn growing in that field.*| *It's too cold for orchids to grow here.* **b)** [T] to make plants or crops grow by taking care of them: *We grow all our own vegetables.* —see RAISE[1] (USAGE)

**grow out of**

He's grown out of his clothes.

**3 ▶ HAIR/NAILS ◀ a)** [I] if hair, nails etc grow, they become longer **b)** [T] if you grow your hair, nails, you do not cut them
**4 ▶ INCREASE ◀** [I] to increase in amount, size, or degree: *De Niro's reputation continues to grow.*| *Fears are growing for the safety of the crew.*| **growing concern/interest/disbelief etc** *Scientists view the hole in the ozone layer with growing concern.*| **a growing number** *A growing number of people are taking part-time jobs.*| **grow in strength/confidence** (=become stronger, more confident)
**5 grow old/hot/worse etc** to become old etc over a period of time: *She grew impatient with his constant excuses.*| *I'm scared of growing old.*
**6 grow to like/fear/respect etc** to gradually start to like etc someone or something: *After a while the kids grew to like Mr Cox.*
**7 ▶ IMPROVE ◀** [I] to improve in ability or character: *She's grown tremendously as a musician since Pallino took her on.*
**8 ▶ BUSINESS ◀** [T] to make something increase in size or importance: *We want to grow the export side of the business.*
**9 it doesn't grow on trees** *spoken* used about money, to mean that you should not waste it

**grow apart** *phr v* [I] if two people grow apart, their relationship becomes less close: *He said the couple had been growing apart for at least a year.*

**grow away from** sb *phr v* [T not in passive] to begin gradually to have a less close relationship with someone that you loved: *While at university she had grown away from her family.*

**grow into** sb/sth *phr v* [T not in passive] **1** to develop over a period of time and become a particular kind of person or thing: *Susan's grown into a lovely young woman.* **2** if a child grows into clothes, they become big enough to wear them: *His new jacket's a bit big for him now but he'll soon grow into it.* **3** to gradually learn how to do a job or deal with a situation successfully

**grow on** sb *phr v* [T] if someone or something grows on you, you like them more and more: *His music is difficult to listen to, but after a while it grows on you.*

**grow out of** sth *phr v* [T] **1** if a child grows out of clothes, they become too big to wear them **2** if a child grows out of a habit, they stop doing it as they get older: *She used to bite her nails but seems to have grown out of it.* **3** to develop from something small or simple into something bigger or more complicated: *The dispute grew out of an argument between a worker and the foreman.*

**grow up** *phr v* [I] **1** develop from being a child to being an adult: *What do you want to be when you grow up?*| *I grew up on a farm.* **2 grow up!** *spoken* used to tell someone to behave more like an adult, especially when they have been behaving in a silly way **3** to start to exist and become bigger or more important: *Trading settlements grew up along the river.*

**grow·bag** /ˈgrəʊbæg||ˈgroʊ-/ *n* [C] another spelling of GROBAG

**grow·er** /ˈgrəʊə||ˈgroʊər/ *n* [C] a person or company that grows fruit, vegetables etc in order to sell them: *apple growers*

**grow·ing pains** /ˈ·· ˌ·/ *n* [plural] **1** aches and pains that children can sometimes feel in their arms and legs when they are growing **2** problems and difficulties that are experienced at the beginning of a new activity

**growl** /graʊl/ *v* **1** [I] if an animal growls it makes a long deep angry sound: *The dog growled at any stranger who came close.* **2** [I,T] to say something in a low angry voice: *'Get out of my way,' he growled.* —**growl** *n* [C] *The bear gave a sudden growl.*

**grown[1]** /grəʊn||groʊn/ *adj* [only before noun] **grown man/woman** an expression meaning an adult man or woman, used especially when you think someone is not behaving as an adult should: *A grown man should know better than to shout and scream.* —compare FULL-GROWN, HOMEGROWN

**grown[2]** the past participle of GROW

**grown-up[1]** /ˌ· ˈ·◂/ *adj* **1** fully developed as an adult: *Before you know it, they'll be all grown-up and leaving home.* **2** behaving like an adult or typical of an adult: *I expect more grown-up behaviour of you now.*

**grown-up[2]** /ˈ· ·/ *n* [C] a word meaning an adult person, used especially by or to children: *If you're frightened, tell one of the grown-ups.*

**growth** /grəʊθ||groʊθ/ *n* W2
**1 ▶ INCREASE IN AMOUNT ◀** [U] an increase in amount, size, or degree: *efforts to control population growth*| [**+ in**] *During the 1970's there was rapid growth in oil production and consumption.*| **growth rate** (=the speed at which something increases or grows) *Japan's economic growth rate*| **growth area/industry** (=an area of business that is growing very quickly)
**2 ▶ PERSON/ANIMAL/PLANT ◀** [U] the development of the physical size, strength etc of a person, animal or plant over a period of time: *Vitamins are essential for healthy growth.*
**3 ▶ INCREASE IN IMPORTANCE ◀** [singular, U] the gradual development and increase of a particular feeling, idea, or way of living: [**+ of**] *the growth of capitalism*| *Currently there is a growth of interest in African music.*
**4 ▶ PERSONAL DEVELOPMENT ◀** [U] the development of someone's character, intelligence or emotions: **emotional/intellectual/personal etc growth** *A loving home environment is essential for a child's personal growth.*
**5 ▶ SWELLING ◀** [C] a swelling on your body or under your skin, caused by disease: *a cancerous growth*
**6 ▶ GROWING THING ◀** [C,U] something which has grown: *I thought the tree was dead, but there are signs of new growth.*

**groyne, groin** /grɔɪn/ *n* [C] a low wall built out into the sea to prevent the sea from removing sand and stones from the shore —see picture on page 835

**grub[1]** /grʌb/ *n* **1** [U] *informal* food: *Let's get some grub.* **2** [C] an insect when it is in the form of a small soft white worm

**grub[2]** [I always + adv/prep] *informal* to look for something, especially by moving things, looking under them etc: [**+ around/about**] *The dog was grubbing around under a bush looking for a bone.*

**grub** sth ↔ **up/out** *phr v* [T] to dig around something and then pull it out of the ground: *Farmers were encouraged to grub up hedgerows.*

**grub·by** /ˈgrʌbi/ *adj* **1** fairly dirty: *a grubby handkerchief* **2** grubby behaviour or activity is morally unpleasant: *the grubby details of Harper's financial dealings* —**grubbiness** *n* [U]

**grub·stake** /ˈgrʌbˌsteɪk/ *n* [U] *AmE informal* money provided to develop a new business in return for a share of the profits

**grudge¹** /grʌdʒ/ *n* [C] **1** a feeling of anger or dislike you have for someone because you cannot forget that they harmed you: [+ **against**] *He's had a grudge against Bob ever since he was promoted.* | **bear (sb) a grudge** (=continue to have a grudge) **2 grudge fight/match** a fight or competition in sport between two people who dislike each other a lot

**grudge²** *v* [T] **1** to do or give something very unwillingly; BEGRUDGE: **grudge doing sth** *I really grudge paying so much money for such poor service.* **2 grudge sb sth** to not want someone to have something: *I don't grudge him his success.*

**grudg·ing** /ˈgrʌdʒɪŋ/ *adj* done or given very unwillingly: *He was looking at Nick with a certain grudging respect.* —**grudgingly** *adv*: *He grudgingly admitted that he'd been wrong.*

**gru·el** /ˈgruːəl/ *n* [U] a thin liquid food made of crushed OATS that was eaten in the past by poor or sick people

**gru·el·ling** *BrE*, **grueling** *AmE* /ˈgruːəlɪŋ/ *adj* very tiring because you have to use a lot of effort for a long time: *a gruelling 6 hour mountain hike* —**gruellingly** *adv*

**grue·some** /ˈgruːsəm/ *adj* very unpleasant and shocking, and usually connected with death or injury; GRISLY: *Spare me all the gruesome details.* —**gruesomely** *adv*

**gruff** /grʌf/ *adj* **1** unfriendly or annoyed, especially in the way you speak: *a gruff reply* **2** a gruff voice sounds low and rough as if the speaker does not want to talk —**gruffly** *adv* —**gruffness** *n* [U]

**grum·ble¹** /ˈgrʌmbəl/ *v* [I] **1** to keep complaining in an unhappy way: [+ **about/at etc**] *The farmers are always grumbling about the weather.* **2** to make a very low sound that gets quieter then louder continuously; RUMBLE¹ (1): *Is that your tummy grumbling?* **3 mustn't grumble** *BrE spoken* used to say that you are fairly well or that you have no serious problems: *"How are you today?" "Mustn't grumble."* —**grumbler** *n* [C]

**grumble²** *n* [C] **1** something that you feel dissatisfied about and keep complaining about: *Take your grumbles to the boss – don't bother me with them.* **2 have a grumble** to complain about something

**grum·bling ap·pen·dix** /ˌ·· ·ˈ··/ *n* [singular] *BrE not technical* a condition in which your APPENDIX (1) causes you pain from time to time

**grump·y** /ˈgrʌmpi/ *adj* bad-tempered and tending to complain —**grumpily** *adv* **grumpiness** *n* [U]

**grunge** /grʌndʒ/ *n* [U] **1** *AmE informal* dirt; GRIME: *What's all that grunge in the bathtub?* **2** a style of fashion popular with young people in the early 1990s, in which they wear clothes that look dirty and untidy **3** a type of loud music played with electric GUITARS popular during this period

**grung·y** /ˈgrʌndʒi/ *adj AmE informal* dirty and sometimes smelling bad in an offensive way: *grungy jeans*

**grunt¹** /grʌnt/ *v* **1** [I,T] to make short sounds or say a few words in a low rough voice, showing that you do not want to have a conversation: *I tried to cheer him up but he only grunted.* **2** [I] if an animal grunts, especially a pig, it makes short low sounds deep in its throat

**grunt²** *n* [C] **1** a short low sound made deep in your throat like the sound a pig makes: *Chris just gave a grunt and went back to sleep.* **2** *AmE slang* an INFANTRY soldier

**grunt work** /ˈ· ·/ *n* [U] *AmE informal* the hard uninteresting part of a piece of work; DONKEYWORK

**Gru·yère** /ˈgruːjeə‖gruːˈjer/ *n* [U] a kind of hard cheese with holes in it, from Switzerland

**gryph·on** /ˈgrɪfən/ *n* [C] another spelling of GRIFFIN

**g-spot** /ˈdʒiː spɒt‖-spɑːt/ *n* [C] a centre of sexual feeling in a woman's VAGINA

**G-string** /ˈdʒiː ˌstrɪŋ/ *n* [C] a very small piece of cloth, leather etc worn to cover your sexual organs

**GTI** /ˌdʒiː tiː ˈaɪ/ *adj* a GTI car has a special FUEL system which helps it to go at high speeds —compare FUEL INJECTION

**gua·ca·mo·le** /ˌgwɑːkəˈməʊli‖-ˈmoʊ-/ *n* [U] a Mexican dish made with crushed AVOCADOS

**gua·no** /ˈgwɑːnəʊ‖-noʊ/ *n* [U] solid waste passed from the stomachs of sea birds that is often put on soil to help plants grow

**guar·an·tee¹** /ˌgærənˈtiː/ *v* [T] S2 W3

**1 ▶ PROMISE STH WILL HAPPEN ◀** to promise that something will certainly happen or be done: **guarantee (that)** *Take this opportunity, and I guarantee you won't regret it.* | **guarantee sth** *The authorities could not guarantee the safety of the UN observers.* | **guarantee sb sth** *Even if you complete your training I can't guarantee you a job.*

**2 ▶ A PRODUCT ◀** to make a formal written promise to repair or replace a product if it has a fault within a specific period of time after you buy it: **guarantee sth against** *a toaster guaranteed for one year against failure of parts*

**3 ▶ LEGAL ◀** to make yourself legally responsible for the payment of money

**4 ▶ MAKE STH CERTAIN ◀** to make it certain that something will happen: *She soon learned that marriage does not guarantee happiness.*

**5 ▶ CERTAIN TO DO STH ◀ be guaranteed to do sth** to be certain to behave, work, or happen in a particular way: *If you yell at him, he's guaranteed to do the opposite of what you want.*

**6 ▶ PROTECT ◀ guarantee sth against** *AmE* to provide complete protection against harm or damage: *Rustshield guarantees your car against corrosion.*

**guarantee²** *n* [C] S2

**1** a formal written promise to repair or replace a product without charging, if it has a fault within a specific time after you buy it: *The television comes with a two-year guarantee.* | **be under guarantee** (=be protected by a guarantee) *Your watch will be repaired free if it's still under guarantee.* **2** a formal and firm promise that something will be done or will happen: [+ **of**] *Is there a guarantee of work after training?* | **give sb a guarantee (that)** *Can you give me a guarantee that the work will be finished on time?* **3 a)** an agreement to be responsible for someone else's promise, especially a promise to pay a debt **b)** something valuable given to someone to keep until the owner has kept their a promise, especially to pay a debt —compare SECURITY (4), WARRANTY

**guar·an·tor** /ˌgærənˈtɔː‖-ˈtɔːr/ *n* [C] *law* someone who promises that they will pay for something if the person who should pay for it does not

**guar·an·ty** /ˈgærənti/ *n* [C] *AmE law* a formal promise, especially of payment —see also WARRANTY

**guard¹** /gɑːd‖gɑːrd/ *n* S3 W3

**1 ▶ PERSON ◀** [C] **a)** someone whose job is to guard a place, person, or object in order to protect them from attack or from thieves: *The guards stopped us at the gate.* —see also SECURITY GUARD **b)** someone whose job is to guard prisoners and prevent them from escaping

**2 be on guard** to be responsible for guarding a place or person for a specific period of time: *Who was on guard when the fire broke out?*

**3 keep/stand/mount guard (over)** to guard a person or place: *Catherine kept guard over the horses while we looked for water.*

**4 ▶ GROUP ◀** [singular] a group of people, especially soldiers, who guard someone or something

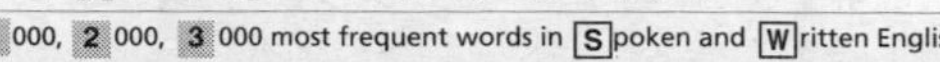

**5 be under (armed) guard** to be guarded by a group of people with weapons
**6 ▶ THING ◀** [C] something that is fitted to a machine or worn on a part of your body to protect you against damage or injury: *a football player's mouth guard*
**7 catch/throw/take sb off guard** to surprise someone by doing or saying something that they are not ready to deal with: *Senator O'Hare was caught off guard by the reporter's question.*
**8 be on your guard** to pay careful attention to what is happening so that you avoid being tricked or getting into danger: *Be on your guard – they always try to cheat tourists.* | **lower your guard/let your guard down** (=forget to be careful)
**9 ▶ ON A TRAIN ◀** [C] *BrE* an official in charge of a train; CONDUCTOR (4) *AmE*
**10 ▶ BOXING ◀** [singular] the position of your hands in BOXING when you are holding them up to defend yourself
**11 the Guards** special groups of soldiers in the British army whose original duty was to guard the king or queen

**guard²** *v* [T] **1** to protect a person, place, or valuable object by staying near them and watching them: *The Sergeant told Swift to guard the entrance to the building.* | **guard sb/sth against** *There is no one to guard these isolated farms against possible attack.* **2** to watch a prisoner and prevent them from escaping **3 guard your tongue** *old-fashioned* used to tell someone to be careful of what they say so that they do not tell a secret

**guard against** sth *phr v* [T] to try to prevent something from happening by being careful: *Nurses should guard against becoming too emotionally attached to their patients.*

**guard dog** /ˈ· ·/ *n* [C] a dog often used by soldiers, police officers etc that is trained to guard a place

**guard·ed** /ˈgɑːdɪ̣d‖ˈgɑːr-/ *adj* a guarded statement, remark etc deliberately does not give much information about your thoughts and feelings: *"What do you want?" Her tone was guarded and hesitant.* —**guardedly** *adv*

**guard·house** /ˈgɑːdhaʊs‖ˈgɑːr-/ *n* [C] a building for soldiers who are guarding the entrance to a military camp

**guard·i·an** /ˈgɑːdiən‖ˈgɑːr-/ *n* [C] **1** someone who is legally responsible for looking after someone else's child, especially after the child's parents have died **2** *formal* someone who guards or protects something, especially an institution or moral principle: [+ **of**] *The US has represented itself as the guardian of democracy.*

**guardian an·gel** /ˌ··· ˈ··/ *n* [C] **1** a good spirit who is believed to protect a person or place **2** someone who helps or protects someone else when they are in trouble

**guard·i·an·ship** /ˈgɑːdiənʃɪp‖ˈgɑːr-/ *n* [U] *law* the position of being legally responsible for someone else's child, or the period during which you have this position

**guard·rail** /ˈgɑːd-reɪl‖ˈgɑːrd-/ *n* [C] **1** a bar or RAIL that is intended to prevent people from falling from a bridge or stairs **2** *especially AmE* a bar or RAIL¹ (1) intended to prevent drivers from going off the road in a car accident

**guard·room** /ˈgɑːd-rʊm, -ruːm‖ˈgɑːrd-/ *n* [C] a room, especially in a GUARDHOUSE, for soldiers who are guarding a military camp

**guards·man** /ˈgɑːdzmən‖ˈgɑːr-/ *n* [C] **1** a British soldier in the Guards (GUARD¹ (11)) **2** a member of the US National Guard

**guard's van** /ˈ· ·/ *n* [C] *BrE* the part of a train where the official in charge of it travels, usually at the back; CABOOSE *AmE*

**gua·va** /ˈgwɑːvə/ *n* [C] a small tropical fruit with pink flesh and many seeds inside

**gu·ber·na·to·ri·al** /ˌguːbənəˈtɔːriəl◂‖-bər-/ *adj formal* connected with the position of being a GOVERNOR

**gue·ril·la** /gəˈrɪlə/ *n* [C] another spelling of guerrilla

**guern·sey** /ˈgɜːnzi‖ˈgɜːrn-/ *n* [C] a SWEATER made of wool with a special pattern of raised stitches across the shoulder

**guer·ril·la** /gəˈrɪlə/ *n* [C] a member of an unofficial military group, especially one fighting to remove a government from power, that attacks its enemies in small groups unexpectedly: *guerrilla warfare* —compare FREEDOM FIGHTER, TERRORIST

**guess¹** /ges/ *v* S1 W3
**1 ▶ WITHOUT BEING SURE ◀** [I,T] to try to answer a question or make a judgment about something without having all the necessary facts, so that you are not sure whether you are correct: *I'd say he's around 50, but I'm only guessing.* | **guess what/who/how etc** *Guess how much I had to pay – 3,000 pounds!* | **guess at** *We can only guess at what caused the crash.*
**2 ▶ GUESS CORRECTLY ◀** [I,T] to guess something correctly: [+ **from**] *"How did you know I won?" "I just guessed from the look on your face."* | **guess that** *I'd never have guessed that you two were brothers.* | **guess sth** *You've guessed my secret.* | **have guessed as much** (=have guessed something before someone tells you) *He told me he was leaving, but I had already guessed as much.*
**3 I guess** *spoken especially AmE* used to mean that you suppose something is true or likely: *I guess I never married because I just didn't find the right girl.* | **I guess so/not** *"She wasn't happy?" "I guess not."*
**4 keep sb guessing** to not tell someone what is going to happen next
**5 guess what/you'll never guess** *spoken* used when you are about to tell someone something that will surprise them: *Guess what! Bradley's resigned.* | *You'll never guess who I saw today.*

**guess²** *n* [C] S2 **1** an attempt to guess something: *If you're not sure of the answer give us your best guess.* | *I'll give you three guesses.* | **make a guess (at)** *I don't know the exact figure but I'll make a guess at it.* | **rough guess** (=one that is unlikely to be exact) *I'd say she's about 35, but that's only a rough guess.* | **wild guess** (=one that is made without much thought) | **have a guess at** *BrE*/**take a guess at** *AmE* (=try to guess something) *Take a guess at what's in the third box and you could win a trip to Hawaii.* | **at a guess** *spoken* (=used to mean that what you are saying is just a guess) *The girl was twelve years old at a guess.* **2** an opinion formed by guessing: **my guess is** *My guess is that there won't be many people there today.* **3 be anybody's guess** to be something that no one knows: *What she's going to do with her life now is anybody's guess.* **4 your guess is as good as mine** *spoken* used to tell someone that you do not know any more than they do about something

**guess·ti·mate** /ˈgestɪ̣mɪ̣t/ *n* [C] *informal* an attempt to judge a quantity by guessing it —**guesstimate** /-tɪ̣meɪt/ *v* [I,T]

**guess·work** /ˈgeswɜːk‖-wɜːrk/ *n* [U] the method of trying to find the answer to something by guessing: *In this study, scientific methods seem to have been replaced by guesswork.*

**guest¹** /gest/ *n* [C] S2 W2
**1 ▶ AT YOUR HOUSE ◀** someone who is staying in someone else's home because they have been invited: *We have guests staying with us.*
**2 ▶ AT A HOTEL ◀** someone who is paying to stay in a hotel, GUESTHOUSE etc: *The hotel takes very good care of its guests.*
**3 ▶ AT A RESTAURANT/CLUB ◀** someone who is invited to a restaurant, theatre, club etc by another person who pays for them: *I'd like you to be my guest for dinner tonight.*
**4 ▶ ON A SHOW ◀** someone famous who is invited to take part in a show, concert etc, in addition to those who usually take part: **make a guest appearance** *She is making her first guest appearance on the show.*
**5 be my guest** *spoken* used to politely give someone permission to do what they have asked to do: *"Do you mind if I look at your notes?" "Of course not. Be my guest."*
**6 guest of honour** *BrE*/**honor** *AmE* the most important person who has been invited to a special occasion, especially a celebration that is given for them

**7 guest speaker** someone who has been invited to make a speech at a meeting —compare HOST[1] (1)

**guest**[2] *v* [I] to take part in a show, concert etc as a guest performer

**guest book** /ˈ· ·/ *n* [C] a book in which everyone who comes to a formal occasion or stays at a hotel writes their name

**guest·house** /ˈgesthaʊs/ *n* [C] a private house where people can pay to stay and have meals

**guest·room** /ˈgest-rʊm, -ruːm/ *n* [C] a room in a private house that is kept for visitors to sleep in

**guest work·er** /ˈ· ˌ··/ *n* [C] a foreign worker, usually from a poor country, working in another country for a limited period

**guff** /gʌf/ *n* [U] *informal* nonsense: *Don't give me any of that guff.*

**guf·faw** /gəˈfɔː‖-ˈfɒː/ *v* [I] to laugh loudly —**guffaw** *n* [C] *A loud guffaw came from the back of the room.*

W3 **guid·ance** /ˈgaɪdəns/ *n* [U] **1** help and advice given to someone about their work, education, personal life etc: [+ **on/about**] *I went to a career counselor for guidanceon how to start my job search.* **2** the process of directing a MISSILE (1) in flight: *electronic guidance systems*

**guidance coun·sel·or** /ˈ·· ˌ···/ *n* [C] *AmE* someone employed in a school to give advice to students about what subjects to study and to help them with personal problems —see also MARRIAGE GUIDANCE

S2 W2 **guide**[1] /gaɪd/ *n* [C]
**1** ▶ **PERSON** ◀ **a)** someone who shows you the way to a place, especially someone whose job is to show a place to tourists: *a tour guide* **b)** someone who advises you and influences the way you live and behave: *The medicine man was the tribe's spiritual guide.*
**2** ▶ **FOR JUDGING STH** ◀ something that provides information on which you can base your judgement, or your method of doing something: [+ **to**] *The opinion polls are not a very reliable guide to how people will vote.*
**3** ▶ **BOOK** ◀ **a)** a book that provides information on a particular subject or explains how to do something; HANDBOOK: [+ **to**] *a guide to North American birds* **b)** a guidebook
**4** ▶ **GIRL** ◀ *BrE* **a) the Guides** the Guides Association, which trains girls in practical skills and tries to develop their character **b)** a member of the Guides Association

**guide**[2] *v* [T] **1** to take someone through or to a place that you know very well, showing them the way: [+ **along/through/to etc**] *He guided us through the narrow streets to the central mosque.* **2** to help someone to move in a particular direction: *She took her friend's arm to guide her.* **3** to strongly influence someone's behaviour, thoughts etc: *He let himself be guided by his mother's opinion.* **4** to show someone the right way to do something, especially something difficult or complicated: **guide sb through** *We need a lawyer to guide us through the procedure.* —see also GUIDING —see LEAD[1] (USAGE)

**guide·book** /ˈgaɪdbʊk/ *n* [C] a special book about a city, area etc that gives details about the place and its history

**guided mis·sile** /ˌ·· ˈ··/ *n* [C] a MISSILE (1) that can be controlled electronically while it is flying

**guide dog** /ˈ· ·/ *n* [C] *BrE* a dog trained to guide a blind person; SEEING EYE DOG *AmE*

**guided tour** /ˌ·· ˈ·/ *n* [C] a trip around a city, building etc led by someone who tells people about the place: *a guided tour of the palace*

**guide·lines** /ˈgaɪdlaɪnz/ *n* [plural] official instructions about the best way to do something, especially something that could be difficult or dangerous: [+ **for/on**] *Staff have been issued with new guidelines for dealing with infectious patients.*

**guid·ing** /ˈgaɪdɪŋ/ *adj* **guiding principle/star/light** a principle, idea, or person that you follow in order to help you decide what you should do in a difficult situation

**guild** /gɪld/ *n* [C] **1** an organization of people who do the same job, who joined together in the past to help each other improve their businesses **2** a group of people with the same interest: *the Women's Guild*

**guil·der** /ˈgɪldə‖-ər/ *n* [C] the standard unit of money in the Netherlands; GULDEN

**guild·hall** /ˌgɪldˈhɔːl, ˈgɪldhɔːl‖ˈgɪldhɒːl/ *n* [C] a large building in which members of a guild met in the past

**guile** /gaɪl/ *n* [U] *formal* the use of clever dishonest methods to deceive someone —**guileful** *adj*

**guile·less** /ˈgaɪl-ləs/ *adj* behaving in an honest way, without trying to hide anything or deceive people —**guilelessly** *adv* —**guilelessness** *n* [U]

**guil·le·mot** /ˈgɪlɪ̥mɒt‖-mɑːt/ *n* [C] a black and white sea bird with a narrow beak

**guil·lo·tine**[1] /ˈgɪlətiːn/ *n* [C] **1** a piece of equipment used to cut off the heads of criminals, especially in France in the past **2** a piece of equipment used to cut large sheets of paper **3** *BrE* the setting of a time limit on the discussion about a proposed law in the British parliament

**guillotine**[2] *v* [T] **1** to cut off someone's head using a guillotine **2** *BrE* to limit the period of time allowed for the discussion of a proposed law in the British parliament

**guilt** /gɪlt/ *n* [U] **1** a strong feeling of shame and sadness because you have done something that you know is wrong: [+ **about/at**] *Don't you have any feelings of guilt about leaving David?* | **sense of guilt** *He felt an enormous sense of guilt when he thought about how he'd treated her.* **2** the fact of having broken an official law or moral rule: *an admission of guilt* | *It is up to the prosecution to establish the defendant's guilt.* **3** responsibility and blame for something bad that has happened: *The teacher said Sonia was impossible to control and that the guilt lay with her parents.* **4 guilt trip** a feeling of guilt about something: **lay/put a guilt trip on sb** *AmE informal* (=make someone feel guilty about something)

**guilt·less** /ˈgɪltləs/ *adj* not responsible for a crime or for having done something wrong; INNOCENT[1] (1) —**guiltlessly** *adv*

**guilt-rid·den** /ˈ· ˌ··/ *adj* feeling so guilty about something that you cannot think about anything else

**guilt·y** /ˈgɪlti/ *adj* **guiltier, guiltiest** S2 W3
**1** ▶ **ASHAMED** ◀ feeling very ashamed and sad because you have done something that you know is wrong: [+ **about**] *I feel really guilty about forgetting her birthday again.* | **guilty conscience** *My guilty conscience got the better of me, and I went back to apologize.*
**2** ▶ **OF A CRIME** ◀ having done something that is a crime: **guilty of** *The jury found her guilty of murder.* | **plead guilty** *law* (=admit in a court of law that you are guilty) | **not guilty** *law* (=not guilty of the offence you are charged with in a court of law) —opposite INNOCENT[1] (1)
**3** responsible for behaviour that is morally or socially unacceptable: **guilty of doing sth** *Lately the press has been guilty of reporting scandal in order to sell papers.*
**4 guilty party** *formal* the person who has done something illegal or wrong —**guiltily** *adv* —**guiltiness** *n* [U]

This graph shows some of the words most commonly used with the adjective **guilty**.

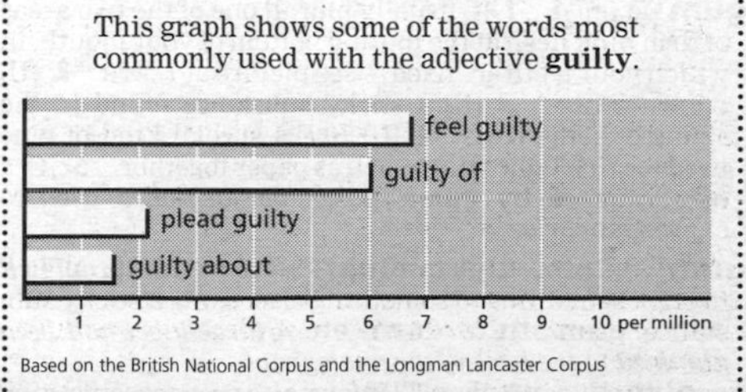


Based on the British National Corpus and the Longman Lancaster Corpus

**guin·ea** /ˈgɪni/ *n* [C] a British gold coin or unit of money used in the past, worth £1.05

**guinea fowl** /ˈ··· ˌ·/ *n* [C] a grey African bird that is often used for food

**guinea pig** /ˈ··· ·/ *n* [C] **1** a small round animal that has fur, short ears, and no tail, which is kept as a pet **2** someone who is used in a scientific test to see how successful or safe a new product, system etc is

**guise** /gaɪz/ *n* [C] *formal* the appearance of something that makes it seem different from how it really is, especially in order to deceive someone: **in/under the guise of** *Advertising material was given to us under the guise of information.* | **in a different guise** *It's just the same set of ideas in a diffferent guise.*

W3 **gui·tar** /gɪˈtɑː‖-ˈtɑːr/ *n* [C] a musical instrument that has six strings and is played by plucking (PLUCK[1] (5)) the strings —**guitarist** *n* [C]

**gu·lag** /ˈguːlæg‖-lɑːg/ *n* [C] one of a group of prison camps in the former USSR, where conditions were very bad

**gulch** /gʌltʃ/ *n* [C] *AmE* a narrow deep valley formed by flowing water, but usually dry

**gul·den** /ˈgʊldən‖ˈguːl-/ *n* [C] a GUILDER

W3 **gulf** /gʌlf/ *n* [C] **1** a large area of sea partly enclosed by land: *the Gulf of Mexico* **2** a great difference and lack of understanding between two groups of people, especially in their beliefs, opinions, and way of life: [+ **between**] *The gulf between management and unions is as wide as ever.* **3** a deep hollow place in the Earth's surface; CHASM (1)

**Gulf Stream** /ˈ· ·/ *n* [singular] a current of warm water that flows northeastward in the Atlantic Ocean from the Gulf of Mexico towards Europe

**gull[1]** /gʌl/ *n* [C] **1** a large common black and white sea bird that lives near the sea; SEAGULL **2** *literary* someone who is easily deceived

**gull[2]** *v* [T] *old use* to cheat or deceive someone

**gul·let** /ˈgʌlɪ̣t/ *n* [C] the tube through which food goes down your throat

**gul·ley** /ˈgʌli/ *n* [C] another spelling of gully

**gul·li·ble** /ˈgʌlɪ̣bəl/ *adj* too ready to believe what other people tell you, so that you are easily deceived: *Plastic replicas were sold to gullible tourists as ancient relics.* —**gullibly** *adv* —**gullibility** /ˌgʌlɪ̣ˈbɪlɪ̣ti/ *n* [U]

**gul·ly** /ˈgʌli/ *n* [C] **1** a small narrow valley, usually formed by a lot of rain flowing down the side of a hill **2** a deep DITCH[1]

**gulp[1]** /gʌlp/ *v* **1** [T] also **gulp** sth ↔ **down** to swallow something quickly: *She gulped down the rest of her coffee and left.* **2** [T] also **gulp** sth ↔ **in** to take in quick large breaths of air: *We rushed outside and gulped in the sweet fresh air.* **3** [I] to swallow suddenly because you are surprised or nervous: *I gulped when I saw the bill.*

**gulp** sth ↔ **back** *phr v* [T] to stop yourself from expressing your feelings: *Sandra tried to gulp back her tears.*

**gulp[2]** *n* [C] an act of gulping: **take a gulp** *He took a gulp and handed the cup back to Rachel.* | **in one gulp/at a gulp** *I've seen him swallow a whole glass of vodka in one gulp.*

**gum[1]** /gʌm/ *n* **1** [C usually plural] one of the two areas of firm pink flesh at the top and bottom of your mouth, in which your teeth are fixed —see picture at TEETH **2** [U] CHEWING GUM **3** [U] a sticky substance found in the stems of some trees **4** [U] *BrE* a special kind of glue used to stick light things such as paper together **5** [C] a GUM TREE **6 by gum!** *spoken old-fashioned* used to express surprise

**gum[2]** *v* **gummed, gumming** [T always + adv/prep] *BrE* to stick something to something else, using a sticky substance: **gum sth to/down etc** *A large label had been gummed to the back of the photograph.*

**gum** sth ↔ **up** *phr v* [T] *informal* to prevent something from working properly by covering it with a sticky substance: *Dirt had got inside the watch and gummed up the works.*

**gum·ball** /ˈgʌmbɔːl‖-bɒːl/ *n* [C] *AmE* CHEWING GUM in the form of a small round brightly coloured sweet

**gum·bo** /ˈgʌmbəʊ‖-boʊ/ *n* [U] **1** a thick soup made with meat, fish, and OKRA (=a small green vegetable) **2** a word used in some parts of the US for OKRA

**gum·boil** /ˈgʌmbɔɪl/ *n* [C] a painful swelling on your GUM[1] (1); ABSCESS

**gum·boot** /ˈgʌmbuːt/ *n* [C] *BrE old-fashioned* a tall boot made of rubber worn to keep your feet dry

**gum·drop** /ˈgʌmdrɒp‖-drɑːp/ *n* [C] a firm transparent sweet that is like JELLY

**gum·my** /ˈgʌmi/ *adj* **1** sticky or covered in GUM[1] (3) **2** a gummy smile shows the gums (GUM[1] (1)) in your mouth

**gump·tion** /ˈgʌmpʃən/ *n* [U] the ability and determination to decide what needs doing and to do it: *He probably didn't even have enough gumption to propose to her.*

**gum·shoe** /ˈgʌmˌʃuː/ *n* [C] *AmE old-fashioned* a DETECTIVE

**gum tree** /ˈ· ·/ *n* [C] **1** a tall tree which produces a strong-smelling oil used in medicine; EUCALYPTUS **2 be up a gum tree** *BrE informal* to be in a very difficult situation

S2 W2 **gun[1]** /gʌn/ *n* [C] **1** a weapon from which bullets or SHELLS[1] (3) are fired **2** a tool used to send out a liquid, such as paint, GREASE[1] (2), or glue, by pressure —see also FLASHGUN, SPRAY GUN **3** *AmE informal* someone who is temporarily put in a position to do a particular job: *He was the sixth gun on the job.* **4 hired gun** *AmE informal* someone who is paid to shoot someone else —see also SON OF A GUN, **stick to your guns** (STICK[1]), **jump the gun** (JUMP[1] (11)), **go great guns** (GREAT[1] (7)), **spike sb's guns** (SPIKE[2] (4))

**gun[2]** *v* **1** [T] *AmE informal* to make the engine of a car go very fast by pressing the ACCELERATOR (1) very hard: **gun it** (=make a car go fast) **2 be gunning for sb** *BrE informal* to be trying to find an opportunity to criticize or harm someone: *Ever since I proved he'd made a mistake in the accounts he's been gunning for me.*

**gun** sb ↔ **down** *phr v* [T] to shoot someone and badly injure or kill them, especially someone who cannot defend themselves: *Innocent civilians were gunned down in the street.*

**gun·boat** /ˈgʌnbəʊt‖-boʊt/ *n* [C] **1** a small military ship that is used near a coast **2 gunboat diplomacy** the practice of threatening to use force against another country to make them agree to your demands

**gun car·riage** /ˈ· ˌ··/ *n* [C] a frame with wheels on which a heavy gun is moved around

**gun con·trol** /ˈ· ·ˌ·/ *n* [U] laws that restrict the possession and use of guns

**gun dog** /ˈ· ·/ *n* [C] a dog trained to find and bring back dead birds shot for sport; BIRD DOG *AmE*

**gun·fight** /ˈgʌnfaɪt/ *n* [C] a fight between people using guns —**gunfighter** *n* [C]

**gun·fire** /ˈgʌnfaɪə‖-faɪr/ *n* [U] the repeated firing of guns, or the noise made by this: *enemy gunfire*

**gunge¹** /gʌndʒ/ *n* [U] *BrE informal* any substance that is dirty, sticky, or unpleasant; GUNK¹ —**gungy** *adj*

**gunge²** *v* **be gunged up with sth** *BrE informal* to be blocked with a dirty sticky substance

**gung-ho** /ˌgʌŋ ˈhəʊ‖-ˈhoʊ/ *adj informal* very eager to do something, especially too eager: *His gung-ho attitude was not appropriate for such delicate negotiations.*

**gunk¹** /gʌŋk/ *n* [U] *informal* any substance that is dirty, sticky, or unpleasant; GUNGE *BrE*: *The milk congealed into a black gunk on the stove.* —**gunky** *adj*

**gunk²** *v* **be gunked up (with)** *AmE informal* to be blocked with a dirty sticky substance: *Here's your problem. The fuel line's all gunked up.*

**gun·man** /ˈgʌnmən/ *n* [C] a criminal or TERRORIST who uses a gun

**gun·met·al** /ˈgʌnˌmetl/ *n* [U] a dull grey coloured metal which is a mixture of COPPER (1), TIN¹ (1), and ZINC

**gun·nel** /ˈgʌnl/ *n* [C] a GUNWALE

**gun·ner** /ˈgʌnə‖-ər/ *n* [C] **1** a soldier, sailor etc whose job is to aim or fire a large gun **2** a soldier in the British ARTILLERY (=part of the army which uses heavy guns): *Gunner Smith*

**gun·ner·y** /ˈgʌnəri/ *n* [U] the science and practice of shooting with heavy guns: *a gunnery officer*

**gun·ny·sack** /ˈgʌnisæk/ *n* [C] *AmE* a large bag made from HEMP, in which coal, potatoes etc are stored

**gun·point** /ˈgʌnpɔɪnt/ *n* **at gunpoint** while threatening or being threatened with a gun: *The frightened clerk was forced at gunpoint to hand over all the money.*

**gun·pow·der** /ˈgʌnˌpaʊdə‖-ər/ *n* [U] an explosive substance in the form of a powder

**gun·run·ning** /ˈ· ˌ··/ *n* [U] the activity of taking guns into a country secretly and illegally, especially so that they can be used by people who want to fight against their government —**gun-runnner** *n* [C]

**gun·ship** /ˈgʌnʃɪp/ *n* [C] a military HELICOPTER used to protect other helicopters and to destroy enemy guns

**gun·shot** /ˈgʌnʃɒt‖-ʃɑːt/ *n* **1** [C] the sound made when a gun is fired **2** [U] the bullets fired from a gun: **gunshot wound** (=a wound caused by a bullet) **3 out of/within gunshot** beyond or within the distance that can be reached by a shot fired from a gun

**gun-shy** /ˈ· ·/ *adj* **1** a GUN DOG that is gun-shy is easily frightened by the noise of a gun **2** *AmE* very careful or frightened about doing something, because of a bad experience in the past

**gun·sling·er** /ˈgʌnˌslɪŋə‖-ər/ *n* [C] *AmE* someone who is very skilful at using guns, especially a criminal

**gun·smith** /ˈgʌnˌsmɪθ/ *n* [C] someone who makes and repairs guns

**gun·wale** /ˈgʌnl/ *n* [C] *technical* the upper edge of the side of a boat or small ship

**gup·py** /ˈgʌpi/ *n plural* **guppies** [C] a small brightly-coloured tropical fish

**gur·gle¹** /ˈgɜːgəl‖ˈgɜːr-/ *v* [I] **1** if something such as a stream gurgles, it makes a low sound, like water flowing through a pipe **2** if a baby gurgles, it makes this kind of sound in its throat —**gurgling** *adj*: *a gurgling stream*

**gurgle²** *n* [C] the sound of gurgling

**gur·ney** /ˈgɜːni‖ˈgɜːr-/ *n* [C] *AmE* a long narrow table with wheels used for moving sick people in a hospital

**gu·ru** /ˈgʊruː/ *n* [C] **1** *informal* someone who knows a lot about a particular subject, and to whom people go for advice: *one of the president's foreign policy gurus* **2** a Hindu religious teacher or leader

**gush¹** /gʌʃ/ *v* **1** [I always + adv/prep] if a liquid gushes from something, such as a hole or cut, it comes out in large quantities: [+ **out/from/down etc**] *The blood began to gush out, red and frightening.* | *oil gushing from the broken pipe* **2** [T] if something gushes a liquid, large quantities of that liquid come out of it: *The wound gushed blood.* **3** [I,T] to express your admiration, pleasure etc too strongly so that people do not think you are sincere: *"I simply loved your book," she gushed.* **4** [I] if words or emotions gush out, you suddenly express them very strongly: [+ **out**] *All that pent up frustration gushed out in a torrent of abuse.*

**gush²** *n* **1** a large quantity of liquid that suddenly flows from somewhere: *Gushes of water sprayed out of the pipe.* **2 a gush of relief/anxiety etc** a sudden feeling or expression of emotion

**gush·er** /ˈgʌʃə‖-ər/ *n* [C] an OIL WELL where the natural flow of oil is very strong, so that a pump is not needed

**gush·ing** /ˈgʌʃɪŋ/ also **gush·y** /ˈgʌʃi/ *adj informal* expressing admiration, pleasure etc strongly, so that people may think you are not sincere —**gushingly** *adv*

**gus·set** /ˈgʌsɪ̈t/ *n* [C] a small piece of material stitched into a piece of clothing to make it stronger, wider, or more comfortable in a particular place

**gus·sy** /ˈgʌsi/ *v*

**gussy up** *phr v* [I,T] *AmE informal* to make yourself look attractive by wearing your best clothes etc: **gussy yourself up** *Jolene gussied herself up for the party.*

**gust¹** /gʌst/ *n* [C] **1** a sudden strong movement of wind: *A sudden gust of wind blew the door shut.* **2** a sudden strong feeling of anger, excitement etc: *A gust of rage swept through him.*

**gust²** *v* [I] if the wind gusts, it blows strongly with sudden short movements: *wind gusting at up to 45 miles per hour*

**gus·to** /ˈgʌstəʊ‖-toʊ/ *n* [U] **with gusto** if you do something with gusto, you do it with a lot of eagerness and energy: *Brendon always sang hymns with great gusto.*

**gust·y** /ˈgʌsti/ *adj* with wind blowing in strong sudden movements: *a cold, gusty October night*

**gut¹** /gʌt/ *n*

**1 ▶ COURAGE ◀ guts** [plural] *informal* the courage and determination you need to do something difficult or unpleasant: *Sonia succeeded through sheer guts and determination.* | **have the guts to do sth** *No one had the guts to tell Paul what a mistake he was making.*

**2 ▶ BODY PARTS ◀ a) guts** [plural] the organs inside your body **b)** the tube through which food passes from your stomach

**3 gut reaction/feeling/instinct etc** *informal* a reaction or feeling that you are sure is right, although you cannot give a reason for it: *He had a gut feeling that Sarah was lying.*

**4 hate sb's guts** *informal* to hate someone very much

**5 sweat/slog your guts out** *informal* to work very hard

**6 at gut level** if you know something at gut level, you feel sure about it, though you could not give a reason: *She knew at gut level that he was guilty.*

**7 ▶ STRING ◀** [U] a type of strong string made from the INTESTINE of an animal —see also CATGUT

**8 I'll have sb's guts for garters** *BrE informal* used to say that you would like to punish someone severely for something they have done —see also BEER BELLY, **bust a gut** (BUST¹ (3)), GREEDY-GUTS, **spill your guts** (SPILL¹ (4))

**gut²** *v* **gutted, gutting** [T] **1** [usually passive] to completely destroy the inside of a building, especially by fire: *The kitchen was completely gutted.* **2** to remove the organs from inside a fish or animal in order to prepare it for cooking **3** to change something by removing some of the most important or central parts: *gutting the system from the inside so as to restructure it completely* —see also GUTTED

**gut·less** /ˈgʌtləs/ *adj informal* lacking courage or determination —**gutlessly** *adv* **gutlessness** *n* [U]

**guts·y** /ˈgʌtsi/ *adj informal* brave and determined: *a gutsy young fighter*

**gut·ted** /ˈgʌtɪ̈d/ *adj* **1** seriously damaged or completely destroyed **2** *BrE spoken* very shocked or disappointed: *"And how did you feel when Arsenal scored?" "Totally gutted."* **3** *BrE spoken* very tired; EXHAUSTED: *I was gutted by the end of the week!*

**gut·ter¹** /ˈgʌtə‖-ər/ *n* **1** [C] the edge of a road next to the

G

path, where water collects and flows away **2** [C] an open pipe or CHANNEL[1] (4), fixed to the edge of a roof to collect and carry away rain water —see picture on page 410 **3 the gutter** the bad social conditions of the lowest and poorest level of society: *Men like him usually ended up in jail – or the gutter.* **4 the gutter press** *BrE* the newspapers that print shocking stories about people's personal lives —compare TABLOID

**gutter**[2] *v* [I] *literary* if a CANDLE gutters it burns with an unsteady flame

**gutter out** *phr v* [I] *AmE* to become gradually weaker and then stop completely: *What had been a promising film career in the end just guttered out.*

**gut·ter·ing** /ˈgʌtərɪŋ/ *n* [U] the open pipes that are fixed to the edge of the roof of a house to collect and carry away rain water —see also GUTTER[1] (2)

**gut·ter·snipe** /ˈgʌtəsnaɪp‖-ər-/ *n* [C] *old-fashioned* a dirty, untidy, badly-behaved child from a poor home

**gut·tur·al** /ˈgʌtərəl/ *adj* a guttural voice or sound is or seems to be produced deep in the throat

**guv** /gʌv/ *n BrE spoken* used by men, as a way of addressing a male customer in a shop, taxi etc: *Where to, guv?*

**guv·nor, guv'nor** /ˈgʌvnə‖-ər/ *n BrE spoken* **1** a man who is in a position of authority over you, usually your employer: *You'll have to speak to the guvnor about that.* **2** *old-fashioned* used as a way of addressing a man of a higher social class than you

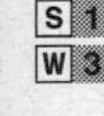

**guy**[1] /gaɪ/ *n* [C] **1** *informal* a man: *Dave's a nice guy when you get to know him.* **2** a figure of a man burnt every year on Guy Fawkes' Night, in Britain **3** also **guy rope** a rope that stretches from the top or side of a tent or pole to the ground to keep it in the right position **4 guys** [plural] *AmE spoken* used when talking to or about a group of people, male or female: *Hey you guys! Where are you going?* **5 no more Mr Nice Guy!** used to say that you will stop trying to behave honestly and fairly —see also **wise guy** (WISE[1] (6))

**guy**[2] *v* [T] *old-fashioned* to copy how someone talks or behaves in a way that makes people laugh

**Guy Fawkes' Night** /ˌgaɪ ˈfɔːks naɪt‖-ˈfɒːks-/ *n* [singular] November 5th, when in Britain people light FIREWORKS and burn a GUY[1] (2) on a fire

**guz·zle** /ˈgʌzəl/ *v* [I,T] *informal* to eat or drink a lot of something, eagerly and quickly: *They've been guzzling beer all evening.* —see also GAS-GUZZLER

**gym** /dʒɪm/ *n informal* **1** [C] a special hall or room that has equipment for doing physical exercise; GYMNASIUM **2** [U] exercises done indoors for physical development and as a sport, especially as a school subject: **gym kit/shoes etc** *Do not wear your gym kit outdoors.*

**gym·kha·na** /dʒɪmˈkɑːnə/ *n* [C] **1** *BrE* a sporting event at which people on horses compete in races and jumping competitions **2** *AmE* a car race that involves difficult driving

**gym·na·si·um** /dʒɪmˈneɪziəm/ *n* [C] a special hall or room that has equipment for doing physical exercise

**gym·nast** /ˈdʒɪmnæst, -nəst/ *n* [C] someone who is very good at doing physical exercises, especially someone who competes against other people in gymnastic competitions

**gym·nas·tics** /dʒɪmˈnæstɪks/ *n* [U] **1** a sport involving skilled and controlled physical exercises and movements, often performed in competitions **2 mental/intellectual/moral gymnastics** very clever thinking **3 verbal gymnastics** using words in a very clever way —**gymnastic** *adj*: *gymnastic skills*

**gym shoe** /ˈ· ·/ *n* [C] a light shoe with a cloth top and a flat rubber bottom used for games and sport, especially at school; PLIMSOLL *BrE*

**gym·slip** /ˈdʒɪmˌslɪp/ *n* [C] *BrE* **1** a type of dress without sleeves that girls used to wear over a shirt as a part of their school uniform **2 gymslip mother** a girl who has a baby while she is still at school

**gyn-** /gaɪn/ *prefix technical* concerning women: *gynaecology* (=treatment of women's diseases)

**gy·nae·col·o·gy** *BrE*, **gynecology** *AmE* /ˌgaɪnɪ̵ˈkɒlədʒi‖-ˈkɑː-/ *n* [U] the study and treatment of medical conditions and illnesses affecting only women —**gynaecologist** *n* [C] —**gynaecological** /ˌgaɪnɪ̵kəˈlɒdʒɪkəl◂‖-ˈlɑː-/ *adj*

**gyp**[1] /dʒɪp/ *n informal* **1 give sb gyp** *BrE* **a)** to be painful: *My bad leg is really giving me gyp today.* **b)** to punish someone or be angry with them because of something they have done **2** [singular] *AmE* **a)** something that you were tricked into buying **b)** a situation in which you feel you have been cheated: *What a gyp!*

**gyp**[2] *v* **gypped, gypping** [T] *informal* to cheat someone: *Ten quid? You've been gypped!*

**gyp·sum** /ˈdʒɪpsəm/ *n* [U] a soft white substance that is used to make PLASTER OF PARIS

**gyp·sy** also **gipsy** *BrE* /ˈdʒɪpsi/ *n* [C] **1** a member of a dark-haired race that is thought to be of Indian origin, who usually live and travel around in CARAVANS **2** someone who does not like to stay in the same place for a long time; TRAVELLER (2)

**gy·rate** /dʒaɪˈreɪt‖ˈdʒaɪreɪt/ *v* [I] *literary* to turn around fast in circles: *The dancers gyrated wildly to the beat of the music.* —**gyration** /dʒaɪˈreɪʃən/ *n*

**gy·ro** /ˈdʒaɪrəʊ‖-roʊ/ *n* [C] *informal* a gyroscope

**gy·ro·scope** /ˈdʒaɪrəskəʊp‖-skoʊp/ *n* [C] a wheel that spins inside a frame and is used for keeping ships and aircraft steady or as a child's toy —**gyroscopic** /ˌdʒaɪrəˈskɒpɪk◂‖-ˈskɑː-/ *adj*

**H, h** /eɪtʃ/ *plural* **H's h's** the 8th letter of the English alphabet —see also H-BOMB

**H²O** /ˌeɪtʃ tuː ˈəʊ‖-ˈoʊ/ *n* [U] *technical* the chemical sign for water

**ha¹** /hɑː/ *interjection* used when you are surprised or have discovered something interesting: *Ha! I thought it might be you hiding there!* —see also AHA, HA-HA

**ha²** the written abbreviation of HECTARE(S)

**ha·be·as cor·pus** /ˌheɪbiəs ˈkɔːpəs‖-ˈkɔːr-/ *n* [U] *law* the right of someone in prison to come to a court of law so that the court can decide whether they should stay in prison

**hab·er·dash·er** /ˈhæbədæʃə‖-bədæʃər/ *n* [C] *old-fashioned* a shopkeeper who sells haberdashery

**hab·er·dash·er·y** /ˈhæbədæʃəri‖-bər-/ *n* **1** [C] *BrE* a shop or part of a large store where things used for making clothes are sold **2** [C] *AmE old-fashioned* a shop or part of a large store where men's clothes, especially hats, are sold **3** [U] the goods sold in these shops

S3 W3 **hab·it** /ˈhæbɪ̵t/ *n*

**1 ► STH YOU DO REGULARLY ◄** [C,U] something that you do regularly, often without thinking about it because you have done it so many times before: *Dalton was a man of regular habits.* | **out of habit/from habit** (=because it is a habit) *After we moved I kept driving to the old house out of habit.* | **be in the habit of doing sth** *Jeff was in the habit of taking a walk after dinner.* | **get into/get in/out of the habit** (=start/stop doing something regularly) *Since I stopped taking lessons, I've gotten out of the habit of practising my saxophone.* | *She got in the habit of having a drink with us on Fridays.* | **eating/drinking habits** (=how often, how much, and what you eat or drink) *When she is busy, her eating habits become erratic.*

**2 ► ANNOYING BEHAVIOUR ◄** [C] something that someone does regularly and that other people find annoying: **have a habit of doing sth** *Glenna has an annoying habit of talking to herself while she's working.* | **a bad/filthy/disgusting habit** *Don't bite your fingernails – it's a disgusting habit.*

**3 ► DRUGS ◄** a strong physical need to keep taking a drug regularly: *Many of them get into petty crime to support their habit.* | **heroin/cocaine etc habit** *His cocaine habit ruined him physically and financially.* | **kick the habit** (=stop taking a drug regularly)

**4 break the habit** to stop doing something that is annoying or bad for your health: *a new system that's supposed to help you break the smoking habit*

**5 don't make a habit of (doing) sth** *spoken* used to tell someone who has done something bad or wrong that they should not do it again: *You're ten minutes late. I hope you're not going to make a habit of this.*

**6 I'm not in the habit of doing sth** *spoken* used when you are offended because someone has suggested that you have done something that you have not done: *I'm not in the habit of lying to my friends.*

**7 old habits die hard** used to say that it is difficult to make people change their attitudes or behaviour

**8 ► CLOTHES ◄** [C] a long loose piece of clothing worn by people in some religious groups: *a nun's habit*

**9 habit of thought/mind** the way someone usually thinks about something, or the attitudes they usually have —see also **a creature of habit** (CREATURE (5)), **by/from force of habit** (FORCE¹ (9))

**USAGE NOTE: HABIT**

WORD CHOICE: **habit, custom, tradition, practice, convention**

A **habit** is usually something someone does again and again, perhaps without them realizing it: *He has an annoying habit of biting his nails.*

A **custom** is usually something which has been done for a long time by a group —for example, a school, company, or society, perhaps every year: *the custom of holding exams in June* | *a local custom*

A **tradition** is similar to a **custom**, but may be older and passed down from parents to their children: *the tradition of eating turkey at Thanksgiving* | *a family tradition*

A **practice** is the usual way of doing things in business, law etc: *The normal practice in this company is to send the bill as soon as the job is done.*

The **conventions** of a society are its generally accepted rules of behaviour: *It is a matter of convention for people attending funerals to wear dark clothes.*

**hab·i·ta·ble** /ˈhæbɪ̵təbəl/ *adj* good enough for people to live in: *It would cost a fortune to make the place habitable.* —**habitability** /ˌhæbɪ̵təˈbɪlɪ̵ti/ *n* [U]

**hab·i·tat** /ˈhæbɪ̵tæt/ *n* [C] the natural home of a plant or animal: *The polar bear's habitat is the icy wastes of the Arctic.* | **natural habitat** *Mountain areas are the natural habitat of the golden eagle.*

**hab·i·ta·tion** /ˌhæbɪ̵ˈteɪʃən/ *n formal* **1 unfit for human habitation** a building that is unfit for human habitation is not safe or healthy for people to live in **2** [U] the act of living in a place: *There was no sign of habitation as far as the eye could see.* **3** [C] a house or place to live in

**habit-form·ing** /ˈ·· ˌ··/ *adj* a drug or activity that is habit-forming makes you want to keep taking it, keep doing it etc

**ha·bit·u·al** /həˈbɪtʃuəl/ *adj* **1** done as a habit or doing something from habit: *My father was a habitual gambler.* | *habitual drinking* **2** [only before noun] usual or typical of someone: *James took his habitual morning walk around the garden.* —**habitually** *adv*: *habitually violent behaviour*

**ha·bit·u·ate** /həˈbɪtʃueɪt/ *v* **be/become habituated to (doing sth)** *formal* to be or gradually become used to something: *Over the centuries, these animals have become habituated to living in such a dry environment.*

**ha·bit·u·é** /həˈbɪtʃueɪ/ *n* [C **+of**] *formal* someone who regularly goes to a particular place or event

**ha·ci·en·da** /ˌhæsiˈendə/ *n* [C] a large farm in Spanish-speaking countries

**hack¹** /hæk/ *v* **1** [I always + adv/prep, T always + adv prep] to cut something into pieces roughly or violently: **hack away/at etc** *She hacked away at the ice, trying to make a hole.* | **hack sth into/through etc** *We had to hack a path through the jungle.* **2 can't hack sth** *informal* to feel that you cannot do something that is difficult or boring: *I've been doing this job for years, but I just can't hack it anymore.* **3** [I] *AmE* to drive a taxi **4** [I,T always + adv/prep] *BrE* to ride a horse along roads or through the country

**hack into** *phr v* [T] *informal* to secretly find a way to get into the information on someone else's computer system so that you can use or change it

**hack²** /hæk/ *n* [C] **1** a writer who does a lot of low quality work, especially writing newspaper articles: *hack journalism* —see also HACKWORK **2** an unimportant politician: *The meeting was attended by the usual old party hacks.* **3** *AmE informal* a taxi, or a taxi driver **4** an act of hitting something roughly with a cutting tool: *Just give it a hack with the axe.* **5** an old, tired horse **6** a horse you can pay money to ride on **7** *BrE* a ride on a horse

**hacked-off** /ˌ· ˈ·/ *adj BrE informal* extremely annoyed: *I'm really hacked-off; I left my coat on the bus.*

**hack·er** /ˈhækə‖-ər/ *n* [C] *informal* someone who secretly uses or changes the information in other people's computer systems —**hacking** *n* [U]

H

**hacking cough** /ˌ·· ˈ·/ *n* [usually singular] a repeated painful cough with an unpleasant sound

**hacking jacket** /ˈ·· ˌ··/ *n* [C] *BrE* a woollen JACKET (1) worn when riding a horse

**hack·les** /ˈhækəlz/ *n* [plural] **1 sb's hackles rise** if someones hackles rise they begin to feel very angry, because someone's behaviour or attitude offends them: *Laura saw the insolent look on his face, and felt her hackles rising.* | **raise sb's hackles** (=make someone angry) *tactless remarks that were enough to raise anyone's hackles* **2** the long feathers or hairs on the back of the neck of some animals and birds, which stand up straight when they are in danger

**hack·ney car·riage** /ˈhækni ˌkærɪdʒ/ *n* [C] *BrE* **1** also **hackney coach** /ˈ·· ·/ *AmE* a carriage pulled by a horse, used in the past like a taxi **2** also **hackney cab** /ˈ·· ·/ *formal* a taxi

**hack·neyed** /ˈhæknid/ *adj* a hackneyed phrase, statement, etc is boring and does not have much meaning because it has been used so often; TRITE

**hack·saw** /ˈhæksɔː‖sɒː/ *n* [C] a cutting tool with small teeth on its blade, used especially for cutting metal —see picture at TOOL[1]

**hack·work** /ˈhækwɜːk‖-wɜːrk/ *n* [U] uninteresting work, especially writing, done to earn money rather than because you enjoy it

**had** /d, əd, həd; *strong* hæd/ **1** the past tense and past participle of HAVE **2 be had** *informal* to be tricked or be made to look stupid: *I'm afraid you've been had! This watch is a fake!*

**had·dock** /ˈhædək/ *n plural* **haddock** [C,U] a common fish that lives in northern seas and is often used as food

**Ha·des** /ˈheɪdiːz/ *n* [U] the land of the dead in the stories of ancient Greece; HELL[1] (3)

**hadj** /hædʒ/ *n* [C] another spelling of HAJ

**had·ji** /ˈhædʒi/ *n* [C] another spelling of HAJJI

**had·n't** /ˈhædnt/ short for 'had not': *If I hadn't seen it myself, I'd never have believed it.*

**hae·ma·tol·o·gy** *BrE*, **hematology** *AmE* /ˌhiːməˈtɒl ədʒi‖-ˈtɑː-/ *n* [U] the scientific study of blood

**haemo-** *BrE*, **hemo-** *AmE* /hiːməʊ, -mə, hemə‖-moʊ, -mə, hemə/ *prefix technical* concerning the blood: *a haemorrhage* (=bleeding)

**hae·mo·glo·bin** *BrE*, **hemoglobin** *AmE* /ˌhiːməˈgləʊ bɪ̈n‖-ˌgloʊ-/ *n* [U] a red substance in the blood that contains iron and carries oxygen

**hae·mo·phil·i·a** *BrE*, **hemophilia** *AmE* /ˌhiːməˈfɪliə/ *n* [U] a serious disease that prevents the blood from becoming thick, so that a person loses a lot of blood easily

**hae·mo·phil·i·ac** *BrE*, **hemophiliac** *AmE* /ˌhiːmə ˈfɪliæk/ *n* [C] a person who suffers from haemophilia

**hae·mor·rhage**[1] *BrE*, **hemorrhage** *AmE* /ˈhemərɪdʒ/ *n* [C,U] a serious medical condition in which a person BLEEDS a lot, often inside the body

**haemorrhage**[2] *BrE*, **hemorrhage** *AmE* —*v* [I] to have a haemorrhage

**hae·mor·rhoids** *BrE*, **hemorrhoids** *AmE* /ˈhemə rɔɪdz/ *n* [plural] painfully swollen BLOOD VESSELS at the ANUS

**haft** /hɑːft‖hæft/ *n* [C] *technical* a long handle on an AXE[1] (1) or on other weapons

**hag** /hæg/ *n* [C] an ugly or unpleasant woman, especially one who is old or looks like a WITCH (1)

**hag·gard** /ˈhægəd‖-ərd/ *adj* having lines on your face and dark marks around your eyes, especially because you are ill, worried, or have not had enough sleep: *Suddenly, he was looking much older, his face haggard and unshaven.*

**hag·gis** /ˈhægɪ̈s/ *n* [C,U] a food eaten in Scotland, made from the heart and other organs of a sheep, cut up and boiled in a skin made from the sheep's stomach

**hag·gle** /ˈhægəl/ *v* [I] to argue, especially when trying to agree about the price of something: **haggle with sb over/about** *I had to haggle with the taxi driver over the fare.* —**haggling** *n* [U]

**hag·i·og·ra·phy** /ˌhægiˈɒgrəfi‖-ˈɑːg-/ *n* [C,U] **1** a book about the lives of SAINTS **2** a book about someone that describes them as better than they really are

**hag-rid·den** /ˈ· ˌ··/ *adj literary* always worried by problems in your life

**ha-ha**[1] /ˌ· ˈ·/ *interjection* **1** used in writing to represent a shout of laughter **2** *spoken* used, sometimes angrily, to show that you do not think something is funny: *Oh, very funny, John, ha ha.*

**ha-ha**[2] /ˈ· ·/ *n* [C] a wall or fence set in a hole in the ground which divides parts of a park etc without spoiling the view

**hai·ku** /ˈhaɪkuː/ *n* [C] *plural* **haiku** a type of Japanese poem with three lines consisting of five, seven, and five SYLLABLES

**hail**[1] /heɪl/ *n* **1** [U] frozen rain drops which fall as hard balls of ice **2 a hail of bullets/stones** a large number of bullets, stones etc thrown or fired at someone **3 a hail of criticism/abuse** a lot of criticism etc

**hail**[2] *v* [T] to call to someone in order to greet them or try to attract their attention: *She leaned out of the window and hailed the first passerby.* | **hail a cab/taxi** *The hotel doorman will hail a cab for you.*

**hail** sb/sth **as** sth *phr v* [T often passive] to describe someone or something as being very good, especially in newspapers, magazines etc: *Lang's first film was immediately hailed as a masterpiece.*

**hail from** sth *phr v* [T not in passive] *especially humorous* to have been born in a particular place: *What part of the world do you hail from?*

**hail-fel·low-well-met** /ˌ· ·· · ˈ·/ *adj old-fashioned* very friendly and cheerful, sometimes in a way that you do not trust: *very cheerful and noisy in a hail-fellow-well-met sort of way*

**Hail Ma·ry** /ˌheɪlˈmeəri‖-ˈmeri/ *n* [C] a special Roman Catholic prayer to Mary, the mother of Jesus

**hail·stone** /ˈheɪlstəʊn‖-stoʊn/ *n* [C] a small ball of frozen rain

**hail·storm** /ˈheɪlstɔːm‖-ɔːrm/ *n* [C] a storm when a lot of HAIL[1] (1) falls

**hair** /heə‖her/ *n* **1** [U] the mass of things like fine threads that grows on your head: *She brushed her hair.* | *I must get my hair cut – it's getting too long.* | **blond/red/dark hair** *Emma's the one with the red hair.* | **short/long/shoulder-length hair** *Jane has long blond hair.* | **straight/curly/wavy/thick hair** *Her long wavy hair was tied back with a bow.* | **dark-haired/fair-haired/short-haired etc** *He's a tall, fair-haired guy.* —see picture at HEAD[1] **2** [C] one of the long fine things like thread that grows on people's heads and on other parts of their bodies, or similar things that grow on animals: *The cat has left white hairs all over the sofa.* **3 get in sb's hair** *informal* to annoy someone, especially by always being near them **4 keep your hair on** *spoken* used to tell someone to keep calm and not get annoyed **5 let your hair down** *informal* to enjoy yourself and start to relax, especially after working very hard: *The party gave us all a chance to really let our hair down.* **6 make sb's hair stand on end** to make someone very frightened **7 not have a hair out of place** to have a very neat appearance **8 not turn a hair** to remain completely calm when something bad or surprising suddenly happens **9 not harm/touch a hair of sb's head** to not harm someone in any way **10 the hair of the dog (that bit you)** *humorous* an alcoholic drink that you drink to cure a headache caused by drinking too much alcohol the night before —see also **have a good/fine head of hair** (HEAD[1] (4)), —see also **not see hide nor hair of** (HIDE[2] (4)), **split hairs** (SPLIT[1] (7)), **tear your hair (out)** (TEAR[2] (11)) S1 W1

**hairstyles**

**hair·breadth** /ˈheəbredθ, -bretθ‖ˈher-/ *n* [singular] another spelling of HAIR'S BREADTH

**hair·brush** /ˈheəbrʌʃ‖ˈher-/ *n* [C] a brush you use on your hair to make it smooth —see picture at BRUSH[1]

**hair·cloth** /ˈheəklɒθ‖ˈherklɒːθ/ *n* [U] rough material made from animal hair, especially from horses or CAMELS

**hair·cut** /ˈheəkʌt‖ˈher-/ *n* [C] **1** the act of having your hair cut by someone: *I'm going for a haircut.* **2** the style your hair is cut in: *Do you like my new haircut?*

**hair·do** /ˈheəduː‖ˈher-/ *n plural* **hairdos** [C] *informal* a woman's haircut

**hair·dress·er** /ˈheəˌdresə‖ˈherˌdresər/ *n* [C] **1** a person who cuts, washes, and arranges people's hair in particular styles **2 the hairdresser's** the hairdresser's shop —compare BARBER —**hairdressing** *n* [U]

**hair·dry·er, hairdrier** /ˈheəˌdraɪə‖ˈherˌdraɪər/ *n* [C] a machine that blows out hot air for drying hair

**hair·grip** /ˈheəgrɪp‖ˈher-/ *n* [C] *BrE* a very small thin piece of metal folded in half and used to hold a woman's hair in place; BOBBY PIN *AmE* —see picture at PIN[1]

**hair·less** /ˈheələs‖ˈher-/ *adj* with no hair

**hair·line** /ˈheəlaɪn‖ˈher-/ *n* [C] **1** the line around your head, especially at the front, where your hair starts growing: *a receding hairline.* **2 a hairline crack/fracture** a very thin crack: *a hairline fracture in a bone*

**hair·net** /ˈheənet‖ˈher-/ *n* [C] a very thin net that stretches over your hair to keep it in place

**hair·piece** /ˈheəpiːs‖ˈher-/ *n* [C] a piece of false hair used to make your own hair look thicker

**hair·pin** /ˈheəˌpɪn‖ˈher-/ *n* [C] a pin made of wire bent into a U- shape to hold long hair in position —see picture at PIN[1]

**hairpin bend** /ˌ·· ˈ·/ *n* [C] a very sharp U-shaped curve in a road, especially on a steep hill

**hair-rais·ing** /ˈ· ˌ··/ *adj* frightening in a way that is exciting: *a hair-raising car chase*

**hair re·stor·er** /ˈ· ·ˌ··/ *n* [C,U] a substance or liquid that is supposed to make hair grow again

**hair's breadth** /ˈ· ·/ *n* [singular] a very small amount or distance: *The bullet missed me by a hair's breadth.*

**hair shirt** /ˌ· ˈ·/ *n* [C] a shirt made of rough uncomfortable cloth containing hair, worn in the past by some religious people to punish themselves

**hair slide** /ˈ· ·/ *n* [C] *BrE* a small attractive metal or plastic object used to fasten a woman's hair in place; BARRETTE *AmE*

**hair-split·ting** /ˈ· ˌ··/ *n* [U] the act of paying too much attention to small differences and unimportant details, especially in an argument —see also **split hairs** (SPLIT[1] (7))

**hair spray** /ˈ· ·/ *n* [U] a sticky substance that is sprayed (SPRAY[1] (1)) from a container and used to keep hair in place

**hair·spring** /ˈheəsprɪŋ‖ˈher-/ *n* [C] a very small spring inside a watch that helps the watch work correctly

**hair·style** /ˈheəstaɪl‖ˈher-/ *n* [C] the style in which someone's hair has been cut or shaped

**hair trig·ger** /ˌ· ˈ··◂/ *n* [C] **1** a TRIGGER[1] (1) on a gun that needs very little pressure to fire the gun **2 hair trigger temper** someone who has a hair trigger temper gets very angry easily

**hair·y** /ˈheəri‖ˈheri/ *adj* **1** having a lot of body hair: *He's a skinny guy with hairy legs.* | *a hairy chest* **2** *informal* dangerous or frightening, often in a way that is exciting: *We had to climb down the cliff, and that was pretty hairy.* —**hairiness** *n* [U]

**haj, hadj** /hædʒ/ *n* [C] a journey to Mecca for religious reasons, that all Muslims try to make at least once in their life

**haj·ji, hadji** /ˈhædʒi/ *n* [C] used as a title for a Muslim who has made a haj

**hake** /heɪk/ *n* [C,U] a sea fish, used as food

**ha·kim** /hɑːˈkiːm/ *n* [C] a Muslim doctor

**ha·lal, hallal** /hɑːˈlɑːl/ *adj* halal meat is meat from an animal that has been killed in a way that is approved by Muslim law

**hal·berd** /ˈhælbəd‖-ərd/ *n* [C] a weapon with a blade on a long handle, used in past times

**hal·cy·on days** /ˌhælsiən ˈdeɪz/ *n* [plural] *especially literary* a time when you are very happy: *She often recalled the halcyon days of her youth.*

**hale** /heɪl/ *adj* **hale and hearty** someone, especially an old person, who is hale and hearty is very healthy and active: *still hale and hearty at 74*

**half**[1] /hɑːf‖hæf/ *predeterminer, adj* [only before noun]  S1 W1
**1** being half of an amount, time, distance, number etc: *events that happened over half a century ago* | *Only half the guests had arrived by seven o'clock.* | *The studio is only half a block away.* | **half a mile/pound/hour etc** (=half of a unit of measurement) *half a pound of butter* | *It's about half a mile down the road.* | **a half hour/mile etc** *You can't just waltz in a half hour late—we need you here on*

*time.* **2** if something is half one thing and half something else, it is a combination of those two things: *A Minotaur is a monster that is half man, half bull.* **3 half one/two/three etc** *BrE informal* thirty minutes after the hour mentioned: *I rang at about half six.* **4 half a dozen a)** six: *half a dozen eggs* **b)** several or many: *The children seemed to be singing 'Happy Birthday' to half a dozen different tunes.* **5 be half the battle** *spoken* used to say that when you have done the most difficult part of an activity, the rest is easy: *Getting Jimmy dressed in the mornings is half the battle.* **6 half the fun/time/trouble etc** the largest part of something: *Half the trouble with John is that he never really listens to what you say.* | *Kids seem to think that climbing up a slide is half the fun.* **7 half a minute/moment/second etc** *spoken* a very short time: *Hold on, this will only take half a second.* **8 have half a mind to do sth** *spoken* **a)** to say that you would like to do something but you probably will not do it, especially when you want to show your disapproval of what someone has done: *I have half a mind to tell him what an idiot he is.* **b)** used as a not very serious threat to show your disapproval of what someone has done: *I have half a mind to tell your mother about this.* **9 only half the story** an explanation that is not complete, used especially to say that someone is trying to keep something secret: *Journalists are convinced that the Congressman was only telling them half the story.* **10 half measures** actions or methods that are not effective in dealing with a difficult problem: *The opposition accused the government of being satisfied with half measures.* **11 go off at half cock/half cocked** to happen without enough preparation being done, with the result that it is not successful

**half²** *n, pron plural* **halves** /hɑːvz‖hævz/ [C]
**1 ▶50%◀** either of the two equal parts into which something is divided or can be divided; ½: *Half of 50 is 25.* | *An hour and a half later I was still waiting for him to arrive.* | *"How old is Samantha now?" "She's five and a half."* | *The trade figures improved in the second half of last year.* | *Half of the class was working on math problems while the other half divided into reading groups.* | *Scott gave her a piece of chocolate and kept the other half for himself.* | **reduce/cut sth by half** (=make something 50% smaller) *The new policy could cut the world oil production by half.* | **break/cut sth in half** (=cut something into two equal parts) *He cut the cake in half.*

**2 ▶NUMBER◀** the number ½: *Three halves make 1½.*
**3 half past** *especially BrE* thirty minutes after the hour mentioned: **half past one/two/three etc** *Bill came home about half past one.* | *She said she'd be home by six or half past.*
**4 ▶SPORTS EVENT◀** either of the two parts into which a sports event is divided: *The Minnesota Vikings pulled ahead to win by seven points in the second half.*
**5 ▶FOOTBALL ETC◀** a player who plays in the middle part of the field
**6 ▶BEER◀** *BrE* a half of a PINT of beer: *Fancy a quick half down the pub?* | *two halves of bitter*
**7 ▶TICKET◀** *BrE* a child's ticket, for example on a bus or train, that is cheaper than an adult's ticket: *One and a half to Waterloo, please.*
**8 and a half** *informal* used when you think that something is very unusual or surprising, or very good: *That was a meal and a half!*
**9 your better half/other half** *humorous* your husband or wife: *Let me introduce you to my better half.*
**10 not do sth by halves** to do something very eagerly and using a lot of care and effort: *I'm sure it will be a fantastic wedding. Eva never does anything by halves.*
**11 you don't know the half of it** *spoken* used to emphasize that a situation is more difficult, complicated, or unpleasant than people realize: *"I know it was a dreadful time, just after the war." "You don't know the half of it."*
**12 go halves (on sth)** to share something, especially the cost of something, equally between two people: *Do you want to go halves on a pizza?*
**13 how the other half lives** how people who are much richer or much poorer than you manage their lives, work, money etc: *He's working for a millionaire, so he's getting a taste of how the other half lives.*
**14 too clever/rich/virtuous etc by half** *BrE informal* clever, rich etc in an annoying way: *That boy's too arrogant by half.*

**half³** *adv* **1** partly, but not completely: *I was half in love with her by the end of the evening.* | *She was standing there half-dressed, putting on her makeup in front of the mirror.* | *He seemed to half expect her to come back and apologize.* | **half-finished/half-empty/half full** *Cups of half-finished tea were on the floor beside the bed.* **2** used to emphasize something, especially when a situation is extremely bad: *I had been driven half out of my mind with worry.* | *The kitten looked half starved.* **3 half as much/big etc again** larger by an amount that is equal to half the original size: *Roy invested his savings in a new store that was half as big again as the old one.* **4 not half as good/interesting etc (as)** much less good, less interesting etc than someone or something else: *The movie wasn't half as entertaining as the book.* | *She can't love you half as much as I do.* **5 not half** *BrE spoken* used when you want to emphasize an opinion or statement: *She doesn't half talk once she gets started.* | *"Did you enjoy it, then?" "Not half!"* **6 not half bad** an expression meaning good, used especially when you are rather surprised that something is good: *Actually, the party wasn't half bad.* **7 half and half** partly one thing and partly another: *"What is she, then, a psychiatrist or a social worker?" "Sort of half and half."* S2

**half-and-half** /ˌ· · ˈ·/ *n* [U] *AmE* a mixture that is half milk and half cream, used in coffee or tea

**half-arsed** /ˌhɑːf ˈɑːst◂‖ˌhæf ˈɑːrst◂/ *BrE*, **half-assed** *AmE* /ˌhɑːf ˈæst◂‖ˌhæf-/ *adj informal* **1** done without enough attention or effort: *He made a half-arsed attempt to clean up after the party.* **2** completely stupid: *What a half-assed idea!*

**half·back** /ˈhɑːfbæk‖ˈhæf-/ *n* [C] **1** a player in football, RUGBY, HOCKEY etc who plays in the middle part of the field **2** a player in American football who, at the start of play, is behind the front line of players and next to the FULLBACK

**half-baked** /ˌ· ˈ·◂/ *adj* a half-baked idea, suggestion, plan etc has not been properly planned: *Education has been damaged by the half-baked notions of theorists who've never been in a classroom.*

**half board** /ˌ· ˈ·/ *n* [U] *especially BrE* the price of a room in a hotel that includes breakfast and dinner —compare FULL BOARD

**half-breed** /ˈ· ·/ *n* [C] a word which is now considered offensive meaning someone whose parents are of different races, especially one white parent and one Native American parent —**half-breed** *adj*

**half broth·er** /ˈ· ˌ··/ *n* [C] a brother who is the son of only one of your parents

**half-caste** /ˈ· ·/ *n* [C] a word which is now considered offensive, meaning someone whose parents are of different races —**half-caste** *adj*

**half cock** /ˌ· ˈ·/ —see **go off at half cock** (HALF¹ (11))

**half-crazed** /ˌ· ˈ·◂/ *adj* behaving in a slightly crazy, uncontrolled way: *half-crazed with pain*

**half crown** /ˌ· ˈ·◂/ *n* [C] a coin used in Britain before 1971. There were eight half crowns in £1

**half-cup** /ˈ· ·/ *n* [C] *AmE* a small container used to measure an amount of food when cooking, or the amount that this holds: *Add a half-cup of sugar.*

**half-cut** /ˌ· ˈ·/ *adj BrE old-fashioned* drunk

**half-day** /ˈ· ·/ *n* [C] a day when you work or go to school either in the morning or the afternoon, but not all day

**half dol·lar** /ˌ· ˈ··/ *n* [C] an American or Canadian coin worth 50 cents

**half-heart·ed** /ˌ· ˈ··◂‖ˈ· ˌ··/ *adj* a half-hearted attempt to do something is done without much effort and without much interest in the result: *She made a half-hearted* *attempt to be friendly.* —**half-heartedly** *adv* —**half-heartedness** *n* [U]

**half-hol·i·day** /ˌ· ˈ···/ *n*[C] *BrE* a morning or afternoon in which you do not have to go to work or school; HALF DAY

**half-hour·ly** /ˌ· ˈ··◂/ *adj, adv* done or happening every half hour: *the half-hourly chimes of the clock*

**half-length** /ˌ· ˈ·◂‖ˈ· ·/ *adj* **1** a half-length coat reaches to just above the knee **2** a half-length painting or picture shows the top half of someone's body

**half-life** /ˈ· ·/ *n* [C] the half life of a RADIOACTIVE substance is the length of time it takes to lose half of its RADIOACTIVITY

**half-light** /ˈ· ·/ *n* [U] the dull grey light you see when it is almost dark but not completely dark: *Briggs heard the commotion but in the half-light of dawn could not see anyone clearly.*

**half-mast** /ˌ· ˈ·/ *n* **at half-mast a)** a flag that is at half mast has been put at the middle of the pole in order to show respect and sadness for someone important who has died **b)** *BrE humorous* if someone's trousers are at half-mast, they are too short

**half moon** /ˌ· ˈ·/ *n* [C] the shape of the moon when only half of it is showing —compare FULL MOON, NEW MOON —see picture on page 412

**half nel·son** /ˌhɑːf ˈnelsən‖ˌhæf-/ *n* [C] a way of holding your opponent's arm behind their back in the sport of WRESTLING

**half note** /ˈ· ·/ *n* [C] *AmE* a musical note which continues for half the length of a WHOLE NOTE; MINIM *BrE* —see picture at MUSIC

**half·penny** /ˈheɪpni/ *n* [C] a small coin worth half of one penny, used in Britain in the past —see also **not have two halfpennies to rub together** (RUB[1] (11))

**half price** /ˌ· ˈ·◂/ *adv* at half the usual price: *Do you like the new carpet? We got it half price in the sale.* —**half-price** *adj*: *half-price sale items*

**half-sis·ter** /ˈ· ˌ··/ *n* [C] a sister who is the daughter of only one of your parents

**half step** /ˈ· ·/ *n* [C] *AmE* the difference in PITCH[2] (3) between any two notes that are next to each other on a piano; SEMITONE *BrE*

**half-term** /ˌ· ˈ·◂/ *n* [C] *BrE* a short holiday from school in the middle of a TERM[1] (9) —compare MIDTERM[2]

**half-tim·bered** /ˌ· ˈ··◂/ *adj* a half-timbered house is usually old and shows the wooden structure of the building on the outside walls

**half time** /ˌ· ˈ·◂‖ˈ· ·/ *n* [U] a short period of rest between two parts of a game, such as football or BASKETBALL: *The score at half time was 34-7.* —see also FULL TIME

**half·tone** /ˌhɑːfˈtəʊn◂‖ˈhæftoʊn/ *n* **1** [U] a method of printing black and white photographs that shows different shades of grey by changing the number of black DOTS in an area of the photograph **2** [C] a photograph printed by this method **3** [C] *AmE* a HALF STEP

**half-truth** /ˈ· ·/ *n* [C] a statement that is only partly true, especially one that is intended to keep something secret: *His replies were full of evasions and half-truths.*

**half vol·ley** /ˌ· ˈ··/ *n* [C] **1** an action in tennis in which the ball is hit just after it hits the ground **2** in CRICKET, a ball that can easily be hit by the BATSMAN just after it hits the ground

**half·way** /ˌhɑːfˈweɪ◂‖ˌhæf-/ *adj, adv* **1** at a middle point in space or time between two things: *We reached the halfway point ten miles into our walk.* | *Grease the muffin tins and fill them halfway with batter.* | [+ **up/along etc**] *He chased Kevin halfway up the stairs.* | *It was a terrible film – I left halfway through.* | **be halfway there** (=be halfway to achieving something) *If we can just finish this section we'll be halfway there.* **2 halfway respectable/decent/civil etc** reasonably RESPECTABLE etc: *It's the only halfway decent hotel around here.* **3 go halfway towards doing sth** to achieve something partly but not completely: *These measures only go halfway towards solving the problem.* —see also **meet sb halfway** (MEET[1] (17))

**halfway house** /ˌ·· ˈ·/ *n* **1** [singular] something which is a combination of the qualities of two things, but may not be as good as either of those two things by themselves: *His clarinet solos are a kind of halfway house between the styles of Dodds and Russell.* **2** [C] a place for former prisoners or people who have had mental illnesses, where they can live until they are ready to live on their own

**half-wit** /ˈ· ·/ *n* [C] *informal* a stupid person or someone who has done something stupid —**half-witted** *adj*: *a burly half-witted fellow with one eye* —**half-wittedly** *adv*

**half-year·ly** /ˌ· ˈ··/ *adj, adv* done or happening every six months: *half-yearly meetings in June and December*

**hal·i·but** /ˈhæləbət/ *n* [C] a large flat sea fish used as food

**hal·i·to·sis** /ˌhæləˈtəʊsəs‖ˈtoʊ-/ *n* [U] a condition in which someone's breath smells very bad

**hall** /hɔːl‖hɒːl/ *n* [C] **1** the area just inside the door of a house or other building that leads to other rooms; HALLWAY (1): *We hung our coats on a rack in the entrance hall.* **2** a passage in a building or house that leads to many of the rooms; CORRIDOR (1): *Each floor of the dorm had ten rooms on both sides of the hall.* **3** a building or large room for public events such as meetings or dances: *Five hundred people filled the lecture hall.* | *Carnegie Hall* **4 Hall** *especially BrE* part of the name of some large houses in the country: *Haddon Hall* **5** *BrE* a place provided by a college or university for students to live in; HALL OF RESIDENCE —see also CITY HALL, MUSIC HALL, TOWN HALL S1 W2

**hal·lal** /hɑːˈlɑːl/ *adj* another spelling of HALAL

**hal·le·lu·jah** /ˌhæləˈluːjə◂/ *interjection* **1** used as an expression of thanks, JOY, or praise to God **2** used when something has finally happened that you think should have happened before: *"The bus is here!" "Well, hallelujah."* —**hallelujah** *n* [C]

**hal·liard** /ˈhæljəd‖-ərd/ *n* [C] another spelling of HALYARD

**hall·mark[1]** /ˈhɔːlmɑːk‖ˈhɒːlmɑːrk/ *n* [C] **1** an idea, method, or quality that is typical of a particular person or thing: [+ **of**] *Non-violence and simplicity were the hallmarks of Gandhi's philosophy.* | **have all the hallmarks of** *The explosion had all the hallmarks of a terrorist attack.* **2** a mark put on silver, gold, or PLATINUM that shows the quality of the metal, and where and when it was made

**hallmark[2]** *v* [T] to put a hallmark on silver, gold, or PLATINUM

**hal·lo** /həˈləʊ, he-, hæ-‖-ˈloʊ/ *interjection old-fashioned* a British form of HELLO

**Hall of Fame** /ˌ· · ˈ·/ *n* [C] a place in the US where people can go to learn about a particular sport or activity and the famous people connected with it

**hall of res·i·dence** /ˌ· · ˈ···/ *n* [C] *BrE* a college or university building where students live; DORMITORY[1] (2) *AmE*

**hal·lowed** /ˈhæləʊd‖-loʊd/ *adj* **1** made holy: **hallowed ground** (=land, especially around a church, that has been made holy) **2** *sometimes humorous* important and respected: *a hallowed tradition* | *the hallowed portals* (=doors) *of Broadcasting House*

**Hal·low·een, Hallowe'en** /ˌhæləʊˈiːn◂‖-loʊ-/ *n* [U] the night of October 31st, when it was believed that the spirits of dead people appeared, and which is now celebrated by children, who dress as WITCHes, GHOSTs etc

**hal·lu·ci·nate** /həˈluːsəneɪt/ *v* [I] to see or hear things that are not really there

**hal·lu·ci·na·tion** /həˌluːsəˈneɪʃən/ *n* **1** [C, U] the experience of seeing or feeling something that is not really there **2** [C] something which you imagine you can see or hear, but which is not really there: *drug-induced hallucinations*

**hal·lu·ci·na·to·ry** /həˈluːsənətəri‖-tɔːri/ *adj formal* **1** causing hallucinations or resulting from hallucinations: *hallucinatory drugs* **2** using strange images,

H

sounds etc like those experienced in a hallucination: *a hallucinatory collage of images*

**hal·lu·ci·no·gen·ic** /həˌluːsənəˈdʒenɪk◂/ *adj* hallucinogenic drugs make people experience hallucinations

**hall·way** /ˈhɔːlweɪ‖ˈhɒːl-/ *n* [C] **1** the area just inside the door of a house or other building that leads to other rooms; HALL (1) **2** a passage in a building or house that leads to many of the rooms; CORRIDOR (1)

**ha·lo** /ˈheɪləʊ‖-loʊ/ *n* [C] **1** a bright circle that is often shown above or around the heads of holy people in religious art **2** a bright circle of light

**hal·o·gen** /ˈhælədʒen/ *n* [U] one of a group of five simple chemical substances that make compounds easily

**halt[1]** /hɔːlt‖hɒːlt/ *n* [singular] a stop or pause: **bring sth to a halt** (=make something stop moving or continuing) *Heavy snowfalls brought traffic to a halt on the Brenner Pass.* | *fuel shortages that have brought the industry to a grinding halt* | **come/grind/crash etc to a halt** (=stop moving or continuing) *The whole peace process seems to have ground to a halt.* | *Joe slammed on the brakes and the car skidded to a halt.* | **call a halt (to)** (=officially stop an activity from continuing) *The IRA leadership has called a halt to its campaign of violence.*

**halt[2]** *v* **1** [I] to stop moving: *The parade halted by a busy corner.* **2 halt!** used as a military command to order someone to stop moving or soldiers to stop marching: *Company halt!* | *Halt! Who goes there?* **3** [T] to prevent someone or something from continuing with something: *There were calls to halt the hunting of seals.*

**hal·ter** /ˈhɔːltə‖ˈhɒːltər/ *n* [C] **1** a rope or leather band that fastens around a horse's head, usually used to lead the horse **2** also **halter top** a type of clothing for women that ties behind the neck and across the back, so that the arms and back are not covered **3** *literary* a piece of rope used to hang (HANG (3)) criminals

**hal·ter·neck** /ˈhɔːltənek‖ˈhɒːltər-/ *adj* a halterneck shirt ties around the neck and behind the back, so that the arms and back are not covered —**halterneck** *n* [C]

**halt·ing** /ˈhɔːltɪŋ‖ˈhɒːl-/ *adj* if your speech or movements are halting, you stop for a moment between words or movements, especially because you are not confident: *We carried on a halting conversation in our imperfect German.* —**haltingly** *adv*

**halve** /hɑːv‖hæv/ *v* [T] **1** to cut or divide something into two equal pieces: *Halve the eggplant lengthwise and hollow out the center.* **2** to reduce something by a half: *The European Union plans to halve production of CFCs by the end of the decade.*

**halves** /hɑːvz‖hævz/ the plural of HALF

**hal·yard, halliard** /ˈhæljəd‖-ərd/ *n* [C] *technical* a rope used to raise or lower a flag or sail

**ham[1]** /hæm/ *n* **1** [C,U] the upper part of a pig's leg that has been preserved with salt or smoke, or the meat from this: *a ham sandwich* | *a seven-pound ham* **2** [C] *informal* an actor who performs with too much false emotion **3** [C] someone who receives and sends radio messages for fun rather than as their job **4 hams** [plural] the upper part of a person's or animal's legs

**ham[2]** *v* **ham it up** *informal* to perform with too much false emotion when acting

**ham·burg·er** /ˈhæmbɜːgə‖-bɜːrgər/ *n* **1** [C] very small pieces of BEEF pressed together, cooked, and eaten between two round pieces of bread **2** [U] *AmE* beef that has been cut into very small pieces; MINCE[2] *BrE*

**ham-fist·ed** /ˌ· ˈ··◂/ also **ham-handed** *adj informal* **1** not at all skilful with your hands; CLUMSY (1) **2** not at all skilful or careful in the way that you deal with people: *the government's ham-fisted approach towards the disabled* —**ham-fistedly, ham-handedly** *adv*

**ham·let** /ˈhæmlət/ *n* [C] a very small village

**ham·mer[1]** /ˈhæmə‖-ər/ *n* [C]
**1** ▶ **TOOL** ◀ **a)** a tool with a heavy metal part on a long handle, used for hitting nails into wood —see picture at TOOL[1] **b)** a tool like this with a wooden head used to make something flat, make a noise etc: *an auctioneer's hammer*
**2 come/go under the hammer** to be offered for sale at an AUCTION[1]
**3 be/go at it hammer and tongs** *informal* to fight or argue very loudly
**4** ▶ **PIANO** ◀ a wooden part of a PIANO that hits the strings inside to make a musical sound
**5** ▶ **GUN** ◀ the part of a gun that hits the explosive CHARGE[1] (8) that fires a bullet —see picture at GUN[1]
**6** ▶ **SPORT** ◀ a heavy metal ball on a wire with a handle that is thrown as far as possible, as a sport

**hammer[2]** *v*
**1** ▶ **HIT STH WITH A HAMMER** ◀ [I,T] to hit something with a hammer in order to force it into a particular position or shape: **hammer sth into/onto** *He hammered the door into its frame.* | *The blacksmith then hammers the horseshoe into its final shape.*
**2** ▶ **HIT REPEATEDLY** ◀ [I] to hit something many times, especially making a loud noise: [+ **against/on**] *The rain was hammering against the window.*
**3** ▶ **DEFEAT** ◀ [T] *informal* to defeat someone completely at a sport: *Arsenal hammered Manchester United in yesterday's game.*
**4** ▶ **HIT HARD** ◀ *informal* [T] to hit or kick something very hard: *Robinson hammered the ball into the goal.*
**5 hammer away at a)** to work hard and continuously at something: *I kept hammering away at the essay until it was done.* **b)** to repeat something continuously until you are sure that people understand or accept what you are saying: *Petersen kept hammering away at his demand for a public inquiry.*
**6 hammer sth home** to make sure that people understand what you want to say by speaking in a determined way: *an important point that needs to be hammered home*
**7** ▶ **HEART** ◀ [I] if your heart hammers, you feel it beating strongly and quickly: *She stood outside the door, her heart hammering.*

**hammer** ↔ sth **in, hammer** sth **into** sb/sth *phr v* [T] to repeat something continuously until people completely understand it: *The coach hammered his message into the team.*

**hammer out** sth *phr v* [T] to decide on an agreement, contract, etc after a lot of discussion and disagreement: *The UN is trying to force the warring factions to get together and hammer out a solution.*

**hammer and sick·le** /ˌ·· · ˈ··/ *n* [singular] **1** the sign of a hammer crossing a SICKLE on a red background, used as a sign of COMMUNISM **2** the flag of the former Soviet Union

**ham·mered** /ˈhæməd‖-ərd/ *adj* [only before noun] **1** hammered silver, gold etc has a pattern of small hollow areas on its surface **2** *informal* very drunk

**ham·mer·ing** /ˈhæmərɪŋ/ *n* [singular] **1 give/take a hammering** to attack or be attacked very severely: *Dresden took a real hammering during the war.* **2** the sound of someone hitting something with a hammer or with their FISTS (=closed hands) *There was a hammering at the door.*

**ham·mock** /ˈhæmək/ *n* [C] a thing for sleeping in, consisting of a long piece of cloth or a net that is hung between two trees

**ham·per[1]** /ˈhæmpə‖-ər/ *v* [T] to restrict someone's movements, activities, or achievements by causing difficulties for them: *Women's progress in the workplace is still hampered by male attitudes.*

**hamper[2]** *n* [C] **1** a basket with a lid, often used for carrying food: *a picnic hamper* —see picture at BASKET **2** *AmE* a large basket that you put dirty clothes in until they can be washed; LAUNDRY BASKET *BrE*

**ham·ster** /ˈhæmstə‖-ər/ *n* [C] a small animal like a mouse, often kept as a pet

**ham·string¹** /ˈhæmˌstrɪŋ/ *n* [C] a TENDON behind your knee

**hamstring²** *v past tense and past participle* **hamstrung** /-strʌŋ/ [T often passive] to restrict someone's activities or development so much that they cannot do the job they are supposed to do: *Police officers claim that they are hamstrung by regulations and paperwork.*

## hand¹ /hænd/ *n*

S1 W1

① PART OF THE BODY
② HELP/WORK
③ SKILFUL
④ CONTROL
⑤ DEAL WITH/BE INVOLVED IN
⑥ CLOSE
⑦ DIRECTLY/NOT DIRECTLY
⑧ OTHER MEANINGS

### ① PART OF THE BODY

**1** [C] the part at the the end of a person's arm, including the fingers and thumb, used to pick up or keep hold of things: *He held the pencil in his right hand.* | *Go wash your hands.* | **hold hands** *They kissed and held hands.* | **take sb by the hand** (=hold sb's hand in order to take them somewhere) *Marika took the child by the hand and led her away.* —see picture at BODY

**2 hand in hand** holding each other's hand, especially to show love: *They strolled hand in hand through the flower garden.*

**3 right-handed/left-handed** using the right hand for most actions rather than the left, or the left hand rather than the right: *a left-handed tennis player*

**4 right/left hander** a player who uses mainly the right hand or mainly the left hand

### ② HELP/WORK

**5 a hand** help with something you are doing, especially something that involves physical work: **give/lend sb a hand** *It's really heavy – can you give me a hand?* | **need a hand** *Tell me if you need a hand.* —see HELP¹ (USAGE)

**6 ▶WORKER◀** [C] someone who does physical work on a farm, in a factory etc

**7 not do a hand's turn** *BrE informal* to do no work at all: *He never does a hand's turn to help me.*

### ③ SKILFUL

**8 a dab hand** someone who is very good at doing something: *She's a dab hand at making pastry.*

**9 good with your hands** skilful at making things

**10 turn your hand to** to start doing something new or practising a new skill: *Larry can turn his hand to anything.*

**11 keep your hand in** to keep practising something so you do not lose your skill: *You should work part-time, just to keep your hand in.*

### ④ CONTROL

**12 in the hands of/in sb's hands** controlled by someone: *The area is already in rebel hands.*

**13 a firm hand** strict control of someone: *That child is a little monster. She obviously needs a firm hand.*

**14 get out of hand** to become impossible to control: *Deal with the problem before it gets completely out of hand.*

**15 take sb/sth in hand** to bring someone or something under control: *It's time these young offenders were taken in hand.*

### ⑤ DEAL WITH/BE INVOLVED IN

**16 in hand** being dealt with: *Don't worry – all the arrangements are in hand.* | **have sth in hand** *Give them a call to let them know we have the matter in hand.*

**17 have a hand in** to influence or be involved in something: *I suspect John had a hand in this.*

**18 in the hands of/in sb's hands** being dealt with by someone: *The whole affair is now in the hands of the police.*

**19 in good/safe/capable hands** being dealt with or looked after by someone who can be trusted: *We left the project in the capable hands of our deputy manager.*

**20 off your hands** if something or someone is off your hands, you are not responsible for them any more: *We have more free time now the kids are off our hands.*

**21 have sth/sb on your hands** to have a difficult job, problem, or responsibility that you must deal with: *They'll have a battle on their hands if they try to build a road here.*

### ⑥ CLOSE

**22 at hand** *formal* near in time or space: *The great day was almost at hand.* | **near/close at hand** *There are shops and buses close at hand.*

**23 have/keep sth to hand** to have or keep something where you can easily reach it

**24 on hand** close by and ready when needed: *The nurse will be on hand if you need her.*

### ⑦ DIRECTLY/NOT DIRECTLY

**25 first hand/at first hand** by direct personal experience: *She stayed there to experience village life at first hand.* | *first hand eyewitness accounts of the riot*

**26 at second/third/fourth hand** passed from the first person who actually saw or heard something to a second, third, or fourth person: *I may have the story wrong as I heard it at second hand.* —see also SECOND HAND

**27 by hand a)** by a person, not a machine: *Every buttonhole is made by hand.* **b)** delivered from one person to another, not sent through the post

### ⑧ OTHER MEANINGS

**28 go hand in hand** to be closely connected: *High unemployment and high crime often go hand in hand.*

**29 get your hands on a)** to obtain something: *They all want to get their hands on my money.* **b)** to catch someone you are angry with: *Wait until I get my hands on her, she's borrowed my best skirt.*

**30 lay your hands on** to find or obtain something: *I'll bring some tapes if I can lay my hands on them.*

**31 have time on your hands** to have a lot of time because you have no work to do

**32 have your hands full** to be very busy or too busy: *I'm sorry I can't help – I have my hands full with problems at home.*

**33 out of hand** if you refuse something out of hand, you refuse immediately and completely

**34 hand in glove** closely connected with someone, especially in a bad or illegal activity: *They suspect the politicians are hand in glove with the mafia.*

**35 right/left hand side** the side on your right or left: *Keep to the left hand side of the road.*

**36 on the one hand...on the other hand** used when comparing different or opposite facts or ideas: *On the one hand I want to sell the house, but on the other hand I can't bear the thought of moving.*

**37 make/lose/spend hand over fist** *informal* to gain, lose, or spend money very quickly and in large amounts

**38 give sb a (big) hand** to CLAP¹ (1) loudly in order to show your approval of a performer or speaker

[continued on next page]

[continued from previous page]
**39 ▶ CARD GAMES ◀ a)** [C] a set of playing cards held by one person in a game: *a winning hand* **b)** a game of cards: *We played a couple of hands of poker.*
**40 ▶ ON A CLOCK ◀** [C] a long, thin piece of metal that points at the numbers on a clock: *the hour hand*
**41 time/money in hand** time or money that is available to be used: *We still have a couple of weeks in hand before the deadline.*
**42 at the hands of** if you suffer at the hands of someone, they treat you badly: *They suffered terribly at the hands of the secret police.*
**43 tie/bind sb hand and foot a)** to tie someone's hands and feet **b)** to severely restrict someone's freedom to make decisions: *We're bound hand and foot by all these safety regulations.*
**44 sb's hand (in marriage)** *old-fashioned* permission or agreement for a man to marry a particular woman: *He asked for her hand in marriage.*
**45 ▶ WRITING ◀** [singular] the way you write; HANDWRITING: *a letter written in a neat hand*
**46 ▶ HORSE ◀** [C] a unit for measuring the height of a horse, equal to about 10 centimetres —see also FREEHAND, HANDS-ON, HANDS UP, **be an old hand at** (OLD (31)), **bite the hand that feeds you** (BITE[1] (14)), **force sb's hand** (FORCE[2] (6)), **overplay your hand** (OVERPLAY (2)), **shake hands (with)** (SHAKE[1] (5)), **wash your hands of** (WASH[1] (5)), **win hands down** (WIN[1] (1))

S2 W2 **hand²** *v* [T] **1** to pass something to someone else: **hand sb sth** *Can you hand me that book, please?* | **hand sth to sb** *She handed her ticket to the ticket collector.* **2 you have to hand it to sb** *spoken* used to say that you admire someone: *You have to hand it to her. She's really made a success of that company.*

**hand** sth ↔ **around** also **hand** sth ↔ **round** *BrE phr v* [T] to offer something to all the people in a group: *She was busy handing around cups of coffee.*

**hand** sth ↔ **back** *phr v* [T] **1** to pass something back to someone: *Kurt examined the document and handed it back to her.* **2** to give something back to someone it used to belong to: *The land was handed back to its original owner.*

**hand** sth ↔ **down** *phr v* [T] **1** to give or leave something to people who are younger than you or live after you: *stories that were handed down from generation to generation* | *a ring which was handed down from her grandmother* —see also HAND-ME-DOWN **2** to pass something to someone who is below you: *The truck driver handed down her rucksack.* **3 hand down a decision/ruling/sentence etc** to officially announce a decision, a punishment etc

**hand** sth ↔ **in** *phr v* [T] to give something to a person in authority: *Hand your papers in at the end of the exam.*

**hand** sth ↔ **on** *phr v* [T] to give something you have finished dealing with to someone who is waiting for it

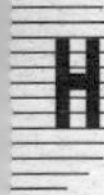

**hand** sth ↔ **out** *phr v* [T] **1** to give something to each member of a group of people; DISTRIBUTE: *Could you start handing these books out.* **2 hand out advice** to give advice, even if people do not want to hear it —see also HANDOUT

**hand over** *phr v* **1** [T **hand** sb/sth ↔ **over**] to give someone or something to someone else to take care of or to control: *The resistance fighters agreed to hand over the hostages.* **2** [I,T **hand** sth ↔ **over**] to give power or responsibility to someone else: *The captain was unwilling to hand over the command of his ship.* | *Before handing over to Jim, I'd like to thank you all for your support.*

S3 **hand·bag** /ˈhændbæg/ *n* [C] a small bag, used by women to carry money and personal things; PURSE[1] (3) *AmE* —see picture at BAG[1]

**hand·ball** /ˈhændbɔːl‖-bɒːl/ *n* **1** [U] a game, played especially in the US, in which you hit a ball against a wall with your hand **2** [C] the ball used in this game **3** [C,U] the offence, in football, of touching the ball with your hands

**hand·bas·ket** /ˈhændˌbɑːskɪ̈t‖-ˌbæs-/ *n* —see **go to hell in a handbasket** (HELL[1] (23))

**hand·bill** /ˈhændˌbɪl/ *n* [C] a small printed notice or advertisement

**hand·book** /ˈhændbʊk/ *n* [C] a short book giving information or instructions

**hand·brake** /ˈhændbreɪk/ *n* [C] *BrE* a piece of equipment in a car that you pull up with your hand to stop the car from moving; EMERGENCY BRAKE *AmE* —see picture on page 409

**hand·car** /ˈhændkɑː‖-kɑːr/ *n* [C] *AmE* a small railway vehicle operated by pushing large handles up and down

**hand·cart** /ˈhændkɑːt‖-kɑːrt/ *n* [C] a small vehicle used for carrying goods, that is pushed or pulled by hand

**hand·craft·ed** /ˈhændˌkrɑːftɪ̈d‖-kræft-/ *adj* skilfully made by hand, not by machine

**hand·cuff** /ˈhændkʌf/ *v* [T] to put handcuffs on someone

**hand·cuffs** /ˈhændkʌfs/ *n* [plural] a pair of metal rings joined by a chain for holding a prisoner's wrists together

**hand-eye co·or·di·na·tion** /ˌ· ˈ· ···ˌ··/ *n* [U] the way in which your hands and eyes work together, especially in sport

**hand·ful** /ˈhændfʊl/ *n* **1** [C] an amount that you can hold in your hand: [+ **of**] *a handful of nuts* **2 a handful of** a very small number of people or things: *Only a handful of countries have implemented these regulations.* **3 a handful** *informal* someone, especially a child, who is difficult to control

**hand gre·nade** /ˈ· ·ˌ·/ *n* [C] a small bomb which is thrown by hand

**hand·gun** /ˈhændgʌn/ *n* [C] a small gun that you hold in one hand when you fire it

**hand-held** /ˌ· ˈ·◂/ *adj* a hand-held machine or piece of electronic equipment is small enough to hold in your hand when you use it: *a hand-held TV camera*

**hand·i·cap** /ˈhændikæp/ *n* [C] **1** an inability to use part of your body or mind because it has been damaged: *a mental or physical handicap* **2** a condition or situation that makes it difficult for someone to do what they want: *Not speaking the language is a real handicap.* **3** a disadvantage given to the stronger competitors in a race or competition, in order to make it fair: *She had a handicap of 7 in golf.*

**hand·i·capped** /ˈhændikæpt/ *adj* **1** having serious difficulty using part of your body or mind fully because of injury or damage: **physically/mentally handicapped** *mentally handicapped children* | **visually handicapped** (=blind or partly blind) **2 the handicapped** people who are physically or mentally handicapped: *meeting the needs of the handicapped* **3 be handicapped by** to have difficulties in doing what you want to do, because of a particular problem: *Rescue efforts were handicapped by the darkness.* —compare DISABLED

**hand·i·craft** /ˈhændikrɑːft‖-kræft/ also **craft** *n* [C usually plural] a skill needing careful use of your hands, such as SEWING, making baskets etc

**handily** —see HANDY

**hand·i·work** /ˈhændiwɜːk‖-wɜːrk/ *n* [U] **1** work that needs skill in using your hands: *When he'd cut the hedge he stood back and admired his handiwork.* **2 the handiwork of** something, especially something bad, that has been done by a particular person or group: *The explosion looks like the handiwork of terrorists.*

**hand job** /ˈ· ·/ *n* [C] *taboo slang* the act of exciting a man's sex organs by touching or rubbing them

**hand·ker·chief** /ˈhæŋkətʃɪ̈f‖-kər-/ *n* [C] a piece of cloth or thin soft paper for drying your nose or eyes

**han·dle¹** /ˈhændl/ *v* 
**1 ▶ DEAL WITH STH ◀** [T] **a) to deal with a difficult situation or problem:** *She couldn't handle the pressures of her new job.* **b)** to deal with something by doing what is necessary: *My secretary will handle all the details.*

2 ▶ **DEAL WITH SB** ◀ [T] to deal with people or behave towards them in a particular way, especially to get what you want: *She's very good at handling difficult customers.* | **handle yourself** (=control your behaviour) *advice on how to handle yourself in an interview*
3 ▶ **HOLD** ◀ [T] to pick up, touch, or feel something with your hands: *When the children handle the kittens it makes the mother cat restless.*
4 ▶ **CONTROL WITH YOUR HANDS** ◀ **a)** [T] to control the movement of a vehicle, tool etc: *The windsurfer handled her board with great skill.* **b) handle well/badly etc** to be easy or difficult to drive or control: *The car handles well, even on wet roads.*
5 ▶ **IN CHARGE OF** ◀ [T] to be in charge of: *Ms Brown handles the company's accounts.*
6 ▶ **MACHINES/SYSTEMS** ◀ [T] to have the power, equipment, or systems that are necessary to deal with a particular amount of work, number of people etc: *The computers are capable of handling massive amounts of data.*
7 ▶ **BUY/SELL** ◀ [T] to buy, sell, or deal with goods or services in business or trade: *Bennet was charged with handling stolen goods.*

S3 **handle**[2] *n* [C] **1** the part of a door, drawer, window etc that you use for opening it **2** the part of an object that you use for holding it: *a knife with an ivory handle* —see pictures at GUN[1] and TOOL[1] **3 get a handle on** [T] to start to understand a person, situation etc: *It's difficult to get a handle on exactly how this law will affect us.* **4** *informal* a name used by someone, especially by a user of CB RADIOS —see also **fly off the handle** (FLY[1] (19))

**han·dle·bar mous·tache** /ˌhændlbɑː məˈstɑːʃ‖-bɑːr ˈmʌstæʃ/ *n* [C] a long thick MOUSTACHE which curves upwards at both ends

**han·dle·bars** /ˈhændlbɑːz‖-bɑːrz/ *n* [plural] the bar above the front wheel of a bicycle or MOTORCYCLE that you turn to control the direction it goes in —see picture at BICYCLE[1]

**han·dler** /ˈhændlə‖-ər/ *n* [C] someone who trains an animal, especially a dog

**hand·ling** /ˈhændlɪŋ/ *n* [U] **1** the way in which a problem or person is treated or dealt with: *The President has been much criticized for his handling of health policy.* **2** the act of picking something up, or touching or feeling it with your hands: *his gentle handling of the baby*

**handling charge** /ˈ·· ˌ·/ *n* [C] the amount charged for dealing with goods or moving them from one place to another

**hand·loom** /ˈhændluːm/ *n* [C] a small machine for weaving by hand

**hand lug·gage** /ˈ· ˌ··/ *n* [U] the small bags that you carry when you are travelling, especially on a plane

**hand·made** /ˌhændˈmeɪd◂/ *adj* made by hand, not by machine: *expensive handmade shoes*

**hand·maid·en** /ˈhændˌmeɪdn/ also **hand·maid** /ˈhændmeɪd/ *n* [C] **1** *old use* a female servant **2** *formal* an idea, principle etc that has an important part in supporting or helping another idea etc: [+ **of**] *Militarism, Ross wrote, is the handmaiden of imperialism.*

**hand-me-down** /ˈ· · ˌ·/ *n* [C usually plural] a piece of clothing which has been used by someone and then given to another person in the family: *I always had to wear my sister's hand-me-downs.*

**hand·out** /ˈhændaʊt/ *n* [C] **1** money or goods that are given to someone, for example because they are poor: *They only want a helping hand from the government, not a handout.* **2** a piece of paper with information given to people who are attending a lesson, meeting etc: *You'll find a full list of references on the last page of the handout.*

**hand·o·ver** /ˈhændəʊvə‖-oʊvər/ *n* [C] the act of making someone else responsible for something: *Arrangements for the handover of prisoners have been made.* —see also **hand over** (HAND[2])

**hand·picked** /ˌhændˈpɪkt◂/ *adj* someone who is handpicked has been carefully chosen for a special purpose: *volunteers handpicked for their ability to speak Spanish*

**hand·rail** /ˈhænd-reɪl/ *n* [C] a long bar fixed to the side of a passage or stairs for people to hold while they walk

**hand·saw** /ˈhændsɔː‖-sɒː/ *n* [C] a small tool for cutting wood etc that has a flat blade and sharp V shaped teeth

**hands·free** /ˈhændzfriː/ *adj* [only before noun] a handsfree machine is one that you operate without using your hands

**hand·shake** /ˈhændʃeɪk/ *n* [C] **a)** the act of taking someone's right hand and shaking it, which people do when they meet or leave each other or when they have made an agreement **b)** the way that someone does this: *a nice firm handshake* —see also GOLDEN HANDSHAKE

**hands off**[1] /ˌ· ˈ·/ *interjection* used to warn someone not to touch something: *Hands off, that's my candy bar!*

**hands off**[2] /ˈ· ·/ *adj* [only before noun] letting other people do what they want and make decisions, without telling them what to do: *a hands-off style of management*

**hand·some** /ˈhænsəm/ *adj* **1 a)** a man who is handsome is attractive; GOOD-LOOKING **b)** a woman who is handsome is attractive in a strong healthy way —see BEAUTIFUL (USAGE) **2** an object, building etc that is handsome is attractive in an impressive way **3 a handsome profit/fee/sum etc** a large amount of money: *He sold the stocks and made a handsome profit for himself.* **4 a handsome gift/offer etc** a generous or valuable gift etc: *She received a handsome gift of money from her aunt.* —**handsomely** *adv*

**hands-on** /ˈ· ·/ *adj* [only before noun] providing practical experience of something by letting people do it themselves: *The computer course includes plenty of hands-on training.*

**hand·spring** /ˈhændsprɪŋ/ *n* [C] a movement in which you turn yourself over completely, first with your hands on the floor and then your feet again

**hand·stand** /ˈhændstænd/ *n* [C] a movement in which you put your hands on the ground and your legs into the air

**hands up** /ˌ· ˈ·/ *interjection* **1** used to tell people to put one of their hands in the air if they want something or if they know the answer to a question: *Hands up everyone who wants a cup of tea.* **2** used when threatening someone with a gun

**hand to hand** /ˌ· · ˈ·◂/ *adj, adv* **hand to hand fighting/combat** a way of fighting in a war using hands, knives etc rather than guns

**hand to mouth** /ˌ· · ˈ·◂/ *adv* with only just enough money and food to live and nothing for the future: *living hand to mouth* —**hand-to-mouth** *adj*: *a hand-to-mouth existence*

**hand tow·el** /ˈ· ˌ··/ *n* [C] a small TOWEL[1] for drying your hands

**hand·writ·ing** /ˈhændˌraɪtɪŋ/ *n* [U] the style of someone's writing: *I recognised her handwriting on the envelope.*

**hand·writ·ten** /ˌhændˈrɪtn◂/ *adj* written by hand, not printed

**hand·y** /ˈhændi/ *adj* **1** useful and simple to use: *a handy little gadget for peeling potatoes* **2** *informal* near and easy to reach: *If there's a pen and paper handy, I'll make a shopping list.* | **be handy for** *BrE*: *Theo's flat is handy for the shops.* **3 come in handy** to be useful: *Take a sleeping bag with you – it might come in handy.* **4** good at using something, especially a tool: [+ **with**] *He's handy with a screwdriver.* —**handily** *adv* —**handiness** *n* [U] S3

**hand·y·man** /ˈhændimæn/ *n* [C] someone who is good at doing repairs and practical jobs in the house

**hang**[1] /hæŋ/ *v past tense and past participle* **hung** /hʌŋ/ S1
**1** ▶ **HANG FROM ABOVE** ◀ **a)** [T] to fix or put something in a position so that the bottom part is free to move and does not touch the ground: *Hang your coat on the hook.* **b)** [I always + adv/prep] to be fixed in position at the top so that the bottom part is free to move and does not touch the ground: [+ **on/from/out of etc**] *A large handbag hung from her shoulder.* | *She sat there with a cigarette hanging out of her mouth.* W2

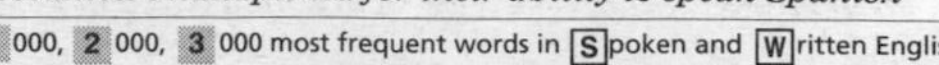

**2 ▶ PICTURES ETC ◀ a)** [I always + adv/prep, T] to fix a picture, photograph etc to a wall, or to be fixed this way: [+ **on**] *A photograph of a handsome soldier hung on the wall.* **b)** [I always + adv/prep, T] to show a picture publicly or be shown publicly: *Her portrait now hangs in the National Gallery.* **c) be hung with** if the walls of a room are hung with pictures or decorations, the pictures etc are on the walls: *rooms hung with rich tapestries*
**3 ▶ KILL/BE KILLED ◀** *past tense and past participle* **hanged** [I,T] to kill someone by dropping them with a rope around their neck, or to die in this way, especially as a punishment for a serious crime: [+ **for**] *They were convicted of genocide and hanged for their crimes.* | *Corey hanged himself in his prison cell.*
**4 hang in the balance** to be in a situation in which the end is not certain, and something bad may happen: *The future of the airline hangs in the balance.*
**5 hang by a thread** to be in a very dangerous situation: *For weeks after the accident, her life hung by a thread.*
**6 ▶ PAPER ◀** [T] to fix WALLPAPER[1] on a wall
**7 ▶ DOOR ◀** [T] to fix a door in position
**8 ▶ MIST/SMOKE/SMELL ◀** [T] to stay in the air in the same place for a long time: *The smoke from the bonfires hung in the air.*
**9 hang in there** also **hang tough** *informal, especially AmE* to remain brave and determined when you are in a difficult situation: *You're innocent and you'll win, so hang in there!*
**10 hang your head** to look ashamed and embarrassed: *He hung his head and didn't answer her questions.*
**11 hang fire** to be delayed or prevented from happening or continuing: *The whole project is hanging fire until next week's meeting.*
**12 leave sth hanging in the air** to fail to make a definite decision about a question: *important issues left hanging in the air*
**13 hang a right/left** *AmE spoken* used to tell the driver of a car to turn right or left
**14 hang up your hat** *informal* to leave your job, especially at the end of your working life
**15 hang loose** *old-fashioned* used to tell someone to stay calm and relaxed
**16 I'll be hanged/I'm hanged if** *BrE old-fashioned* used to express annoyance or to say that you will not allow something to happen: *I'll be hanged if I'll let these people order me around!*
**17 hang it/hang it all** *BrE old-fashioned* used to say that you are disappointed or annoyed about something
**18 hang sth** *BrE old-fashioned* used to say that you are not going to do something: *Oh hang the ironing, let's go for a drink.*

**hang about** *phr v BrE* **1** [I] *spoken* to move slowly or take too long doing something: *Don't hang about, we've got a train to catch!* **2** [I] to spend time somewhere without any real purpose: *There are always kids hanging about down by the shops.* **3 hang about with** to spend a lot of time with someone: *I don't know what he's doing, hanging about with that bunch.* **4 hang about!** *spoken* used to ask someone to wait or stop what they are doing: *Hang about – I'm nearly ready.*

**hang around** *phr v* [I,T] *informal* **1** to wait or stay somewhere with no real purpose: *I hung around the station for an hour but he never showed up.* **2 hang around with** to spend a lot of time with someone: *He hangs around with Luke and Callum.*

**hang back** *phr v* [I] to be unwilling to speak or do something because you are shy: *Don't hang back – go and introduce yourself.*

**hang on** *phr v* **1** [I] to hold something tightly: *We all hung on as the bus swung around a sharp bend.* | [+ **to**] *Hang on to the rail or you'll fall.* **2 hang on!** *BrE spoken* used to ask or tell someone to wait: *Hang on! I'll be back in a minute.* **3** [I] to continue doing something in spite of difficulties: *I know you're tired, but try to hang on a bit longer.* **4** [T] **hang on** sth to depend on: *The team's survival in the league hangs on the result of this game.* **5 hang on sb's words/every word** to pay close attention to everything someone is saying

**hang on to** sth/sb *phr v* [T] to keep something: *I'd hang on to that letter. You might need it later.*

**hang out** *phr v* **1** [I always + adv/prep] *informal* to spend a lot of time in a particular place or with particular people: *She hangs out with a pretty wild crowd.* | *That's the corner where all the junkies hang out.* —see also HANGOUT **2** [T **hang** sth ↔ **out**] to hang clothes on a piece of string outside in order to dry them: *I've hung out the washing.* **3 let it all hang out** *slang* to relax and do what you like

**hang over** sth/sb *phr v* [I] if something unpleasant hangs over you, you are worried because it is likely to happen soon: *The prospect of famine hangs over the whole area.* | **be hanging over sb's head** *With the exams hanging over her head she can't sleep at night.*

**hang round** *phr v* [I,T] to **hang around** (HANG[1])

**hang together** *phr v* [I] **1** to help each other and work together to achieve an aim: *We must hang together if we're going to get out of this mess.* **2** if a plan, story, set of ideas etc hangs together, it is well-organized and makes sense: *The case for the defence just doesn't hang together.*

**hang up**

Paula is hanging up her suit.

After arguing for ten minutes she hung up.

**hang up** *phr v* **1** [I,T] to finish a phone conversation by putting the telephone down: *After I hung up I realized I forgot to ask him his telephone number.* | **hang up on sb** (=put the phone down before they have finished speaking) *I was so angry, that I hung up on her.* **2** [T **hang** sth ↔ **up**] to hang clothes on a hook etc **3 be hung up on/about** *informal* to be anxious about something when there is no reason to be: *She's hung up about people knowing she didn't go to college.* —see also HANG-UP

**hang²** *n* **get/have the hang of something** *informal* to learn how to do something or use something: *Using the computer isn't difficult once you get the hang of it.*

**hang·ar** /ˈhæŋə‖-ər/ *n* [C] a very large building where aircraft are kept

**hang·dog** /ˈhæŋdɒg‖-dɔːg/ *adj* a hang dog expression on your face shows you feel sorry or ashamed about something

**hang·er** /ˈhæŋə‖-ər/ *n* [C] a thing for hanging clothes on, consisting of a curved piece of wood or metal with a hook on it

**hanger-on** /ˌ·· ˈ·/ *n* [C] someone who spends a lot of time with a person who is important, famous, or rich, because they hope to get some advantage: *Hollywood celebrities and their hangers-on*

**hang glid·er** /ˈ· ˌ··/ *n* [C] a large frame covered with cloth that you hold on to and fly slowly through the air on, without an engine

**hang glid·ing** /ˈ· ˌ··/ *n* [U] the sport of flying using a hang glider

**hang·ing** /ˈhæŋɪŋ/ *n* [C,U] **1** the practice or act of punishing someone by putting a rope around their neck and hanging them until they are dead: *public hangings | right-wingers who want to bring back hanging* **2 it's/that's no hanging matter** used to say that a problem or mistake is not as bad as someone thinks it is **3** a large piece of cloth hung on a wall as a decoration: *wall hangings*

**hang·man** /ˈhæŋmən/ *n* [C] someone whose job is to kill criminals by hanging them

**hang·nail** /ˈhæŋneɪl/ *n* [C] a piece of skin that has become loose near the bottom of the fingernail

**hang·out** /ˈhæŋaʊt/ *n* [C] *informal* a place someone likes to go to often: *a favourite hangout for artists*

**hang·o·ver** /ˈhæŋəʊvə‖-oʊvər/ *n* [C] **1** the HEADACHE and sickness that you get the day after you have drunk too much alcohol **2 a hangover from** *BrE* an attitude, habit etc from the past, that is not suitable or practical any more; HOLDOVER *AmE*: *a hangover from her schooldays*

**hang-up** /ˈ· ·/ *n* [C] *informal* if you have a hang-up about something you feel unreasonably worried or embarrassed about it: *She's got a real hang-up about her nose.* —see also **hang up** (HANG[1])

**hank** /hæŋk/ *n* [C] an amount of wool, cotton, or thread that has been wound into a loose ball

**han·ker** /ˈhæŋkə‖-ər/ *v*

**hanker after/for** *phr v* [T] to secretly feel that you want something, over a long period: *Lucy had always hankered after a place of her own.*

**han·ker·ing** /ˈhæŋkərɪŋ/ *n* [singular] a strong wish to have something

**han·kie, hanky** /ˈhæŋki/ *n* [C] *informal* HANDKERCHIEF

**hank·y-pank·y** /ˌhæŋki ˈpæŋki/ *n* [U] *humorous* sexual activity that is not very serious

**Han·sard** /ˈhænsɑːd‖-sərd/ *n* [singular] the official written record of what happens in the British Parliament

**han·som** /ˈhænsəm/ also **hansom cab** /ˈ·· ·/ *n* [C] a two-wheeled vehicle pulled by a horse, used in the past as a taxi

**Ha·nuk·kah, Chanukah** /ˈhɑːnʊkə‖ˈkɑːnəkə, ˈhɑː-/ *n* an eight-day Jewish holiday in December

**ha'penny** /ˈheɪpni/ *n* [C] another spelling of HALFPENNY

**hap·haz·ard** /ˌhæpˈhæzəd◂‖-ərd◂/ *adj* happening or done in a way that is not planned or recognized: *The training was carried out in a haphazard fashion.* —**haphazardly** *adv*

**hap·less** /ˈhæpləs/ *adj* [only before noun] *literary* unlucky: *Hapless passers-by could be dragged into the argument.*

**hap·ly** /ˈhæpli/ *adv old use* perhaps

**hap'orth** /ˈheɪpəθ‖-ərθ/ *n* [singular + **of**] *old-fashioned BrE* an amount that is worth half of one penny

S1 W1 **hap·pen** /ˈhæpən/ *v* [I] **1** if an event or situation happens, it exists and continues for a period of time, especially without being planned first: *The accident happened early on Tuesday morning. | No one knew who had fired the gun – it all happened so quickly. | It's impossible to predict what will happen in Cambodia in the next few months.* | **sth is bound to happen** (=something is certain to happen) | **sth happens all the time** (=something happens often) *This kind of thing happens all the time.* | **whatever happens** *I'll look after you whatever happens.* —see OCCUR[1] (USAGE) —see also **happen to** **2** to be caused as the result of an event or action: *She pressed hard on the brake pedal, but nothing happened. | What would happen if your parents found out?* **3** to do or have something by chance: **happen to do sth** *I happened to meet her on my way home.* | **it happens that** (=by chance, it is true that) *It happened that the new person in the office was the woman he had met at Gail's party.* **4 sb/sth happens to be** used when telling someone something in an angry way, especially because you are annoyed by something they have just said: *That woman you're talking about just happens to be my wife!* —see also **accidents will happen** (ACCIDENT (5))

**happen by** *phr v* [I,T] *AmE* to find a place by chance

**happen on** sb/sth, **happen upon** sb/sth *phr v* [T] to find something or meet someone by chance: *They were strolling through the old part of the town when they happened on a tiny Greek restaurant.*

**happen to** sb/sth *phr v* [T] **1** if an event happens to someone or something, they are involved in it and affected by it: *A funny thing happened to me on my way home last night.* **2 whatever happened to a)** used when you want to know where someone is and what they are doing, because it is a long time since you saw them: *Whatever happened to Kate Scott?* **b)** used when saying that something such as an idea, quality, or custom seems to have disappeared or been forgotten about: *Whatever happened to the idea of the paperless office?*

Frequencies of the verb **happen** in spoken and written English.

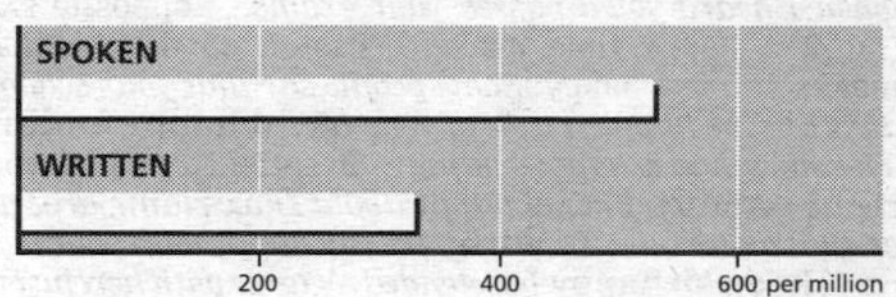


Based on the British National Corpus and the Longman Lancaster Corpus

This graph shows that the verb **happen** is much more common in spoken English than in written English. This is because it is used in a lot of common spoken phrases.

**happen** (*v*) **SPOKEN PHRASES**

**5 what's happening? a)** used to ask what people are doing, or what the situation is, especially when you are worried or annoyed about this: *Hey, what's happening? Why has the light gone out? | What's happening here, then? You'd better stop that!* **b)** *AmE* used when you meet someone you know well, to ask them how they are and what they have been doing: *Hey Carl, what's happening, man?* **6 what's going to happen/what happens/what will happen...?** used to ask what the result of something will be: *What happens if you push this button? | What's going to happen when she finds out?* **7 whatever happens** used to say that no matter what else happens, one thing will certainly happen: *Whatever happens in the future, we wish you well.* **8 as it happens** used to tell someone something that you think will be useful for them, and is connected with what they have just been talking about: *As it happens I know someone who might be able to give you some advice.* **9 it (just) so happens that** used to tell someone about something interesting that is connected with what you have just been talking about: *Now, it just so happens that he had been to the same school as me.* **10 these things happen** used to tell someone not to worry about a mistake they have made, an accident they have caused etc: *These things happen: don't give it another thought.* **11 anything can happen** used to say that it is impossible to know what will happen: *Anything can happen in a race like that.* **12 see what happens** used to say that if someone does not know what the result of doing something will be, they

H

should try it and find out: *Just turn the switch and see what happens. Is it working?* **13 what usually happens is/what tends to happen is** used to say what usually happens in a particular situation: *What tends to happen is we meet up for a drink, then go for something to eat.* **14 you don't/do you happen to...?** used politely to ask someone if they have or know something: *You don't happen to know his address, do you?*

S2 **hap·pen·ing¹** /ˈhæpənɪŋ/ *n* [C] something that happens, especially a strange event: *recent mysterious happenings on the island*

**happening²** *adj slang* fashionable and exciting

**hap·pen·stance** /ˈhæpənstæns/ *n* [U] *AmE* something good that happens by chance: *It was just happenstance that we met.*

**hap·pi·ly** /ˈhæpɪ̈li/ *adv* **1** in a happy way: *a happily married couple* **2** [sentence adverb] fortunately: *Happily, his injuries were not serious.* **3** very willingly: *I'd happily go for you.*

**hap·pi·ness** /ˈhæpinɪ̈s/ *n* [U] the state of being happy: *She believes she's finally found true happiness.*

S1 W1 **hap·py** /ˈhæpi/ *adj* **1** having feelings of pleasure, for example because something good has happened to you: *Larry looked really happy when we gave him his present.* | *He was a happy child who rarely cried.* | **be happy to be doing sth** *They felt happy to be going home.* | **happy that** *I'm happy that everything worked out well in the end.* | **be/feel happy for sb** *I felt really happy for you when I heard you'd passed your exams.* —opposite SAD (1) **2** a happy time, place, occasion etc is one that makes you feel happy: *Some people say that your schooldays are the happiest time of your life.* | **a happy ending** *The story has a happy ending.* **3** satisfied or not worried: [+ **about**] *I'm not happy about Dave riding around on that motorbike.* | [+ **with**] *Are you happy with your new car?* | **keep sb happy** *I pretended to agree with her, just to keep her happy.* **4 be happy to do sth** to be very willing to do something, especially to help someone: *I'd be happy to take you in my car.* **5 Happy Birthday/Christmas/Anniversary etc** used when greeting someone on their birthday, at Christmas etc **6 the happy event** the time when a baby is born or when two people get married **7 a happy medium** a way of doing something that is somewhere between two possible choices and that satisfies everyone **8 happy as a lark** very happy **9 not a happy bunny** *BrE*/**not a happy camper** *AmE humorous* someone who is not pleased about a situation **10** *formal* suitable: *His choice of words was not a very happy one.*

**happy-go-luck·y** /ˌ·· · ˈ··◂/ *adj* not caring or worrying about what happens: *a happy-go-lucky kind of person*

**happy hour** /ˈ·· ˌ·/ *n* [singular] a special time in a bar when alcoholic drinks are sold at lower prices

This graph shows how common the different grammar patterns of the adjective **happy** are.

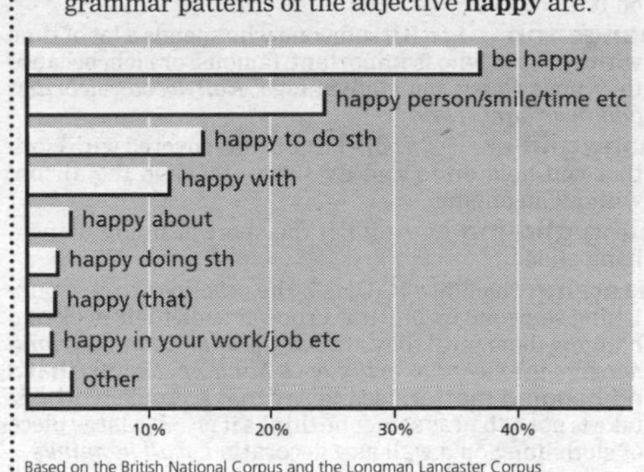


Based on the British National Corpus and the Longman Lancaster Corpus

**har·a·kiri** /ˌhærəˈkɪri/ *n* [U] a way of killing yourself by cutting open your stomach, used in former times in Japan to avoid losing your honour

**ha·rangue¹** /həˈræŋ/ *v* [T] to make a loud speech that criticizes or blames someone or tries to persuade people about something: *Mr Major was harangued by reporters.*

**harangue²** *n* [C] a loud long angry speech that criticizes or blames people, or tries to persuade them: *The principal launched into his usual harangue about standards of behaviour.*

**har·ass** /ˈhærəs, həˈræs/ *v* [T] **1** to treat someone unfairly by threatening them or being continuously unpleasant to them: *Black teenagers are being constantly harassed by the police.* **2** to annoy someone by continually interrupting them: *Stop harassing me will you! I'm trying to work!* **3** to continually attack an enemy

**har·assed** /ˈhærəst, həˈræst/ *adj* anxious and tired because you have too many problems or things to do: *The waiter looked harassed so I didn't bother him.*

**har·ass·ment** /ˈhærəsmənt, həˈræsmənt/ *n* [U] **1** unpleasant and often threatening behaviour, or offensive remarks: **sexual/racial harassment** (=towards someone of a different sex or race) *sexual harassment in the workplace* **2** a feeling of anxiety and tiredness because you have too many problems or things to do

**har·bin·ger** /ˈhɑːbɪndʒə‖ˈhɑːrbɪndʒər/ *n* [C + **of**] *literary* a sign that something is going to happen soon

**har·bour¹** *BrE*, **harbor** *AmE* /ˈhɑːbə‖ˈhɑːrbər/ *n* [C] an area of water next to the land where the water is calm, so that ships are safe when they are inside it

**harbour²** *BrE*, **harbor** *AmE* *v* [T] **1** to protect and hide criminals that the police are searching for **2** to keep bad thoughts, fears, or hopes in your mind for a long time: **harbour a grudge** *I think he's harbouring some sort of grudge against me.*

S1 W1

## hard¹ /hɑːd‖hɑːrd/ *adj*

① FIRM TO TOUCH
② DIFFICULT
③ INVOLVING WORK AND EFFORT
④ FULL OF PROBLEMS
⑤ UNKIND
⑥ USING FORCE
⑦ UNFORTUNATE
⑧ OTHER MEANINGS

### ① FIRM TO TOUCH

**1** firm and stiff, and difficult to press down, break, or cut: *Diamond is the hardest substance known to man.* | *The plums are much too hard to be eaten now.* | *The chairs in the waiting room felt hard and uncomfortable.* —opposite SOFT (1)

### ② DIFFICULT

**2** difficult to do or understand: *This year's exam was much harder than last year's.* | **be hard for sb** *It must be hard for her, bringing up three kids on her own.* | **be hard to come by** (=be difficult to get or find) *Good jobs are hard to come by these days.* | **the hardest**

**thing is** *The hardest thing is going to be telling her parents.* —opposite EASY[1] (1)
**3 hard to tell/say** difficult to know: *It was hard to tell whether Katie really wanted to go.*
**4 find sth hard to believe** to think that something is probably not true: *I find it extremely hard to believe that he didn't know.*
**5 hard to take** difficult to accept or believe: *She found all this sudden concern for her welfare rather hard to take.*

### ③ INVOLVING WORK AND EFFORT
**6 ▶ A LOT OF EFFORT ◀** using or involving a lot of mental or physical effort: *It's been a long hard day.* | **hard work** *It's not easy running a business – it takes a great deal of hard work.*
**7 hard going a)** difficult to do and needing a lot of effort **b)** boring: *I find most of Sartre pretty hard going.*
**8 too much like hard work** used to say that you do not want to do something because it will be too much effort
**9 make hard work of** to make something you are trying to do seem more difficult than it really is
**10 hard-earned/hard-won** achieved after a lot of effort
**11 be hard at it** *informal* to be very busy doing something: *Sarah was hard at it on her computer.*

### ④ FULL OF PROBLEMS
**12** a period of time that is hard is one when you do not have enough money and have a lot of problems: **times are hard** *Times were hard and we were forced to sell our home.*
**13 have a hard life** to have many problems and not have much money or comfort: *Miners used to have a very hard life.*
**14 it's hard on/for sb** used to say that a situation causes a lot of problems and difficulties for someone: *It's hard on the kids having their father in hospital.*

### ⑤ UNKIND
**15** showing no feelings or sympathy: *He had a hard face and cold blue eyes.* | *I'm afraid I said some very hard things to her.* | *You're a hard man, Mr Dawson.*
**16 be hard on** to treat someone in a way that that is unfair, unkind, or too strict: *You mustn't be too hard on David – he's been under a lot of pressure lately.*
**17 a hard taskmaster/master** someone who makes people work too hard
**18 ▶ STRONG/NOT AFRAID ◀** *informal* strong, ready to fight, and not afraid of anyone or anything: *I suppose you think you're really hard, don't you!*
**19 a hard case** *informal* a strong and violent person

### ⑥ USING FORCE
**20** using force: *Jane gave the door a good hard push.*

### ⑦ UNFORTUNATE
**21 ▶ FEEL SORRY FOR SB ◀ hard luck** also **hard lines** *BrE spoken* used to tell someone that you feel sorry for them
**22 hard cheese** *especially BrE spoken* used to tell someone that you do not feel sorry for them
**23 hard-luck story** a story you tell someone to make them feel sorry for you

### ⑧ OTHER MEANINGS
**24 give sb a hard time** *informal* **a)** to deliberately make someone feel uncomfortable or embarrassed: *Come on guys – stop giving me such a hard time!* **b)** to criticize someone a lot: *My boss has been giving me a really hard time.*
**25 be hard on sth** to have a bad effect on something: *Running 50 miles a week is really hard on the knee joints.*
**26 no hard feelings** *spoken* used to tell someone who you have been arguing with that you do not feel anger towards them any more
**27 as hard as nails** not feeling any emotions, especially fear or sympathy
**28 learn/do sth the hard way** to learn about something by a bad experience or by making mistakes
**29 hard winter** a very cold winter —opposite MILD[1] (1)
**30 ▶ WATER ◀** hard water contains a lot of minerals and does not mix easily with soap
**31 hard facts/information/evidence etc** facts, information etc that are definitely true and can be proved: *Police have several theories, but no hard evidence.*
**32 take a (long) hard look at** to think about something without being influenced by your feelings: *We need to take a long hard look at the whole system of welfare payments.*
**33 take a hard line on/over** to deal with something in a very strict way: *They've promised to take a hard line on law and order.*
**34 the hard stuff** *informal* strong alcohol or illegal drugs
**35 a hard left/right** a sharp turn to the left or right
**36 ▶ PRONUNCIATION ◀** a hard 'c' is pronounced /k/ rather than /s/; a hard 'g' is pronounced /g/ rather than /dʒ/ —**hardness** *n* [U] *a material that would combine the flexibility of rubber with the hardness of glass* —see also **drive a hard bargain** (DRIVE[1] (9))

S1 W2 **hard**[2] *adv*
**1 ▶ USING ENERGY/EFFORT ◀** using a lot of effort, energy, or attention: *She had been working hard all morning.* | *I tried as hard as I could to remember his name.*
**2 ▶ WITH FORCE ◀** with a lot of force: *Tyson hit him so hard that he fell back on the ropes.* | *The boys pressed their noses hard against the window.* | *It's raining hard.*
**3 be hard hit/be hit hard** to be badly affected by something that has happened: *The Italian economy has been particularly hard hit by the world recession.*
**4 be hard put/pressed/pushed (to do sth)** *informal* to have difficulty doing something: *We'd be hard pushed to get there by 7 o'clock.*
**5 be hard done by** *informal* to be unfairly treated: *The other children felt hard done by because they didn't get any chocolates.*
**6 take sth hard** *informal* to feel upset about something, especially bad news: *She's taking it very hard.*
**7 laugh hard/cry hard etc** to laugh, cry etc a lot: *He laughed so hard he had tears in his eyes*
**8 hard on the heels of** happening soon after something: *Hard on the heels of the last week's defeat comes news of yet another disaster.*
**9 be hard on sb's heels** to follow close behind or soon after someone: *They fled in panic with the enemy hard on their heels.*
**10 baked/set hard** made firm and stiff by being heated, glued etc —see also HARD BY, HARD UP, HARD UPON **play hard to get** (PLAY[1] (10))

**hard-and-fast** /ˌ· · ˈ·◂/ *adj* **hard and fast rules/regulations** rules that are fixed and that you cannot change

**hard·back** /ˈhɑːdbæk‖ˈhɑːrd-/ *n* [C] a book that has a strong stiff cover: *a hardback edition* | **in hardback** *The book sold more than a million copies in hardback.* —compare PAPERBACK

**hard·ball** /ˈhɑːdbɔːl‖ˈhɑːrdbɔːl-/ *n* [U] *AmE* **1** the game of BASEBALL rather than SOFTBALL **2 play hardball** *informal* to be very determined to get what you want, especially in business or politics

**hard·bit·ten** /ˌ· ˈ··◂/ *adj* not easily shocked or upset, because you have had a lot of experience: *a hard-bitten journalist*

**hard·board** /ˈhɑːdbɔːd‖ˈhɑːrdbɔːrd/ *n* [U] a material made from small pieces of wood pressed together

**hard-boiled** /ˌ· ˈ·◂/ *adj* **1** a hard-boiled egg has been boiled until it becomes solid —compare SOFT-BOILED[1] (4) **2** *informal* not showing your emotions and not influenced by your feelings; TOUGH

**hard·bound** /ˈhɑːdbaʊnd‖ˈhɑːrd-/ *adj* HARDCOVER

**hard by** /ˌ· ˈ·/ *adv, prep old use* very near: *in a house hard by the city gate*

**hard can·dy** /ˌ· ˈ··/ *n* [C] *AmE* a hard piece of sweet food, which often tastes of fruit; BOILED SWEET *BrE*

**hard cash** /ˌ· ˈ·/ *n* [U] money that consists of notes and coins, not cheques or CREDIT CARDS

**hard ci·der** /ˌ· ˈ··/ *n* [U] *AmE* an alcoholic drink made from apples; CIDER (1) *BrE*

**hard cop·y** /ˈ· ˌ··/ *n* [U] information from a computer that is printed out onto paper —compare SOFT COPY

**hard core** /ˌ· ˈ·/ *n BrE* **a) the hard core** the small central group that is most active within a group or organization: *the hard core of the Communist party* **b)** [singular] *BrE* a group of people who cannot be persuaded to change their behaviour or beliefs: *a hard core of young offenders*

**hard-core** /ˌ· ˈ·◂/ *adj* **1 hard-core pornography** magazines, films etc that show the details of sexual behaviour, often in an unpleasant way **2** [only before noun] having an extremely strong belief or opinion that is unlikely to change: *hard-core opposition to the government's educational policies*

**hard court** /ˌ· ˈ·/ *n* [C] an area for playing tennis which has a hard surface, not grass

**hard·cov·er** /ˈhɑːdˌkʌvə‖ˈhɑːrdˌkʌvər/ *adj* a hardcover book has a strong stiff cover

**hard cur·ren·cy** /ˌ· ˈ···/ *n* [C,U] money that will not lose value because it is from a country that has a strong ECONOMY and can be used in other countries to buy things

**hard disk** /ˌ· ˈ·/ *n* [C] a part that is fixed inside a computer and is used for permanently storing information —compare FLOPPY DISK

**hard-drink·ing** /ˈ· ˌ··/ *adj* drinking a lot of alcohol: *a hard-drinking man*

**hard drugs** /ˌ· ˈ·/ *n* [plural] very strong illegal drugs such as HEROIN and COCAINE —compare SOFT DRUG

**hard-edged** /ˌ· ˈ·◂/ *adj* a hard-edged report, article etc deals with unpleasant subjects or criticizes someone severely in a way that may offend some people

**hard·en** /ˈhɑːdn‖ˈhɑːrdn/ *v* **1** [I,T] to become firm or stiff, or to make something firm or stiff: *Make sure you give the paint enough time to dry and harden.* **2** [I] to become more strict and determined and less sympathetic: *Opposition to the military regime has hardened since the massacres.* | *a hardening of attitudes* | *His face hardened.* —compare SOFTEN (4) **3** [T] if an experience hardens someone, it makes them stronger and more able to deal with difficult or unpleasant situations **4 hardened criminal/police officer etc** a criminal, etc who has had a lot of experience of things that are shocking and is therefore less affected by them **5 become hardened towards/to** to become used to something shocking because you have seen it many times **6 harden your heart** to make yourself not feel pity or sympathy for someone

**hard hat** /ˌ· ˈ·/ *n* [C] a protective hat, worn especially by workers in places where buildings are being built —see picture at HAT

**hard-head·ed** /ˌ· ˈ··◂/ *adj* practical and able to make difficult decisions without letting your emotions affect your judgment: *a hard-headed business tycoon* —**hard-headedness** *n* [U]

**hard-heart·ed** /ˌ· ˈ··◂/ *adj* not caring about other people's feelings —**hard-heartedness** *n* [U]

**hard-hit·ting** /ˌ· ˈ··◂/ *adj* criticizing someone or something in a strong and effective way: *a hard-hitting report*

**har·di·ness** /ˈhɑːdinǝs‖ˈhɑːr-/ *n* [U] the ability to bear difficult or severe conditions

**hard la·bour** *BrE*, hard labor *AmE* /ˌ· ˈ··/ *n* [U] punishment in prison which consists of hard physical work

**hard land·ing** /ˌ· ˈ··/ *n* [singular] *technical* a sudden fall in economic activity coming after a successful period

**hard left** /ˌ· ˈ·◂/ *n* [singular] the part of a political party that believes strongly in SOCIALISM

**hard-line** /ˌ· ˈ·◂/ *adj* having extreme political beliefs, and refusing to change them: *a hard-line Marxist* —see also **take a hard line on /over** (HARD[1] (33))

**hard·lin·er** /ˌhɑːdˈlaɪnǝ, ˈhɑːdlaɪnǝ‖ˌhɑːrdˈlaɪnǝr◂/ *n* [C] a politician who wants political problems to be dealt with in a strong and extreme way: *Communist hardliners*

**hard liq·uor** /ˌ· ˈ··/ *especially AmE n* [U] strong alcohol such as WHISKY

**hard·ly** /ˈhɑːdli‖ˈhɑːrdli/ *adv* S2 W2 **1** almost not: *I hadn't seen him for years but he had hardly changed at all.* | **can/could hardly do sth** *The children were so excited they could hardly speak.* | *I can hardly believe it.* | **hardly anyone/anything** (=almost no one or almost nothing) *Hardly anyone writes to me these days.* | **hardly any** (=very few) *There are hardly any cookies left.* | **hardly ever** (=almost never) *She hardly ever wore a hat.* | **hardly a day goes by when/without** (=used to say that something happens almost every day or every week) *Hardly a day goes by when I don't think of her.* —see ALMOST (USAGE) **2** used to say that something had only just happened or someone had only just done something: *The day had hardly begun, and he felt exhausted already.* **3** used to say that something is not at all true, possible, correct etc: *It's hardly what I'd call the perfect relationship.* | **hardly surprising** *It was hardly surprising you didn't pass your exam.* | **hardly the time/place/person** (=a very unsuitable time, place, person) *This is hardly the place to talk about our marriage problems.* | **you can/could hardly do sth** (=it would not be sensible to do it) *You could hardly blame Jane for being nervous.* | **could hardly be** *The message could hardly be clearer.* | **hardly a child/beginner etc** *He was fifteen – hardly a kid.*

**USAGE NOTE: HARDLY**

GRAMMAR

**Hardly** is a negative word, so it is not used with another negative word: *hardly any pollution* (NOT *hardly no pollution*) | *We could hardly believe our eyes* (NOT *We couldn't hardly believe our eyes...*).

**Hardly** usually comes just before the main verb: *He could hardly hear her* (NOT *He hardly could hear her*).

**Hardly** is used at the beginning of sentences only in very formal or old-fashioned writing. People would say, and usually write: *The game had hardly begun when it started to rain* (compare the formal: *Hardly had the game begun when it started to rain...*).

**Hardly** is not the adverb of *hard*: You say: *I tried hard to remember.* | *She works very hard* (NOT hardly).

**hard-nosed** /ˌ· ˈ·◂/ *adj* [usually before noun] not affected by emotions, and determined to get what you want: *a hard-nosed approach to business negotiations*

**hard nut** /ˌ· ˈ·/ *n* [C] **1** *informal* someone who is physically or mentally very strong, or thinks that they are strong **2 a hard nut to crack** someone or something that is difficult to deal with

**hard of hear·ing** /ˌ· · ˈ··/ *adj* [not before noun] **1** unable to hear very well **2 the hard of hearing** people who are unable to hear very well

**hard-on** /ˈ· ·/ *n* [C] *taboo* an ERECTION (1)

**hard pal·ate** /ˌ· ˈ··/ *n* [C] the hard part of the top of your mouth that is at the front behind your teeth —compare SOFT PALATE

**hard porn** /ˌ· ˈ·/ *n* [U] *informal* magazines, films etc that show sexual behaviour in an unacceptable, sometimes violent way: *sales of hard-porn videos* —compare SOFT PORN

**hard-pressed** /ˌ· ˈ·◂/ *adj* **1** having a lot of problems and not enough money or time: *Hard-pressed local authorities are finding it difficult to pay for essential services.* **2 sb would be hard pressed to do sth** used to say that it would be difficult for someone to do something: *They'd be hard-pressed to find a better editor.*

**hard right** /ˌ· ˈ·◂/ *n* [singular] the part of a political party that believes strongly in RIGHT WING political ideas

**hard rock** /ˌ· ˈ·/ *n* [U] a type of ROCK MUSIC that has loud electric GUITARS and a strong beat

**hard-scrab·ble** /ˌ· ˈ··/ *adj AmE* hard-scrabble land is difficult to grow crops on

**hard sell** /ˌ· ˈ·◂/ *n* [singular] a way of selling something in which there is a lot of pressure on you to buy —compare SOFT SELL

**hard·ship** /ˈhɑːdʃɪp‖ˈhɑːrd-/ *n* [C,U] the condition of having very little money so that life is very difficult: *a time of great economic hardship*

**hard shoul·der** /ˌ· ˈ··/ *n* [singular] *BrE* the area at the side of a big road where you are allowed to stop if you have a problem with your car; SHOULDER[1] (9) *AmE* —see picture on page 415

**hard·top** /ˈhɑːdtɒp‖ˈhɑːrdtɑːp/ *n* [C] a car that has a metal roof which cannot be removed —compare CONVERTIBLE[2]

**hard up** /ˌ· ˈ·◂/ *adj* not having enough money to buy the things you need, especially for a short period of time: *We were too hard up to afford new clothes.*

**hard up·on** /ˈ· ·ˌ·/ also **hard on** *prep literary* **1** soon after **2** close behind

**hard·ware** /ˈhɑːdweə‖ˈhɑːrdwer/ *n* [U] **1** computer machinery and equipment, as opposed to the programmes that make computers work —compare SOFTWARE **2** equipment and tools for your home and garden **3** the machinery and equipment that is needed to do something: *tanks and other military hardware*

**hard-wearing** /ˌ· ˈ··◂/ *adj BrE* clothes, materials etc that are hard-wearing will remain in good condition for a long time; LONGWEARING *AmE*

**hard-wired** /ˌ· ˈ·◂/ *adj technical* computer systems that are hard-wired are controlled by HARDWARE rather than SOFTWARE and therefore cannot be easily changed by the user

**hard·wood** /ˈhɑːdwʊd‖ˈhɑːrd-/ *n* **1** [C,U] strong heavy wood from trees such as OAK that take a long time to grow, used for making furniture **2** [C] a tree that produces this kind of wood —compare SOFTWOOD

**hard-working** /ˌ·ˈ··/ *adj* working with a lot of effort: *a hard-working teacher*

**har·dy** /ˈhɑːdi‖ˈhɑːrdi/ *adj* **1** strong and healthy and able to bear difficult living conditions: *the hardy fishermen who turned out in these arctic conditions* **2** a hardy plant is able to live through the winter

**hardy pe·ren·ni·al** /ˌ·· ·ˈ···/ *n* [C] **1** a hardy plant that produces flowers for several years —see also PERENNIAL[2] **2** an idea that is often suggested or discussed

**hare[1]** /heə‖her/ *n plural* **hare** or **hares** [C] **1** an animal like a rabbit but larger, that can run very quickly —see picture at RABBIT[1] **2 run with the hare and hunt with the hounds** *old-fashioned* to try to support both sides in an argument

**hare[2]** *v* [I always + adv/prep] *BrE informal* to run or go very fast: [+ **off/away**] *He hared off down the road.*

**hare·bell** /ˈheəbel‖ˈher-/ *n* [C] a wild plant with bell-shaped blue flowers on a thin stem

**hare·brained** /ˈheəbreɪnd‖ˈher-/ *adj* a harebrained person, plan etc is very silly and unlikely to succeed: *wasting public money on hairbrained schemes*

**hare cours·ing** /ˈ· ˌ··/ *n* [U] the sport of chasing a HARE with dogs

**hare·lip** /ˌheəˈlɪp‖ˌher-/ *n* [singular, U] the condition of having your top lip divided into two parts because it did not develop properly before birth —**harelipped** *adj*

**har·em** /ˈhɑːrim, hɑːˈriːm‖ˈhæːrəm,ˈher-/ *n* [C] **1** the group of wives or women who lived with a rich or powerful man in some Muslim societies in the past **2** part of a Muslim house that is separate from the rest of the house, where only women live

**harem pants** /ˈ·· ˌ·,·ˈ· ˌ·‖ˈ·· ˌ·/ *n* [plural] loose-fitting women's trousers made from thin cloth

**har·i·cot** /ˈhærɪkəʊ‖-koʊ/ also **haricot bean** /ˌ··· ˈ·/ *n* [C] a small white bean

**hark** /hɑːk‖hɑːrk/ *v* **1 hark at him/her!** *BrE spoken* used when you think someone is saying something stupid or unreasonable: *Hark at him! I bet he couldn't do any better.* **2 hark!** *old use* used to tell someone to listen

**hark back** *phr v* [I] **1** to remember and talk about things that happened in the past **2** to be similar to something in the past: [+ **to**] *music that harks back to the early age of jazz*

**har·ken** /ˈhɑːkən‖ˈhɑːr-/ *v* [I] another spelling of HEARKEN

**har·le·quin** /ˈhɑːlɪ̣kwɪ̣n‖ˈhɑːr-/ *n* [C] **1** a character in some traditional plays who wears brightly coloured clothes and plays tricks **2** a harlequin pattern is made up of DIAMOND shapes in many different colours

**har·lot** /ˈhɑːlət‖ˈhɑːr-/ *n* [C] *old use* a PROSTITUTE

**harm[1]** /hɑːm‖hɑːrm/ *n* [U] **1** damage, injury, or trouble caused by someone's actions or by an event: **do harm to** *Modern farming methods have done considerable harm to the countryside.* | **do more harm than good** (=cause even more problems rather than improving the situation) *Criticizing people's work often does more harm than good.* | **where's the harm in that?** *spoken* (=used when you think that something seems a reasonable thing to do) | **no harm done** *spoken* (=used to tell someone not to worry about something they have done) **2 come to no harm/not come to any harm** to not be hurt or damaged: *She was relieved to see the children had come to no harm.* **3 mean no harm/not mean any harm** to have no intention of hurting or upsetting anyone: *He doesn't mean any harm – he's only joking.* **4 it does no harm to do sth/there's no harm in doing sth** used to suggest that someone should do something: *It does no harm to ask.* | *There's no harm in trying.* **5 it wouldn't do sb any harm to do sth** used to suggest that someone should do something that may be helpful or useful: *It would do you no harm to get some experience first.* **6 out of harm's way a)** in a safe place **b)** if something dangerous is out of harm's way, it is in a place where it is unable to hurt anyone or damage anything —compare HURT[3] —see also GRIEVOUS BODILY HARM S3

**harm[2]** *v* [T] **1** to damage something: *Too much direct sunlight will harm the plant.* **2 harm sb's image/reputation** to make people have a worse opinion of a person or group **3** to hurt someone: *The dogs look fierce, but they wouldn't harm anyone.*

**harm·ful** /ˈhɑːmfəl‖ˈhɑːrm-/ *adj* causing or likely to cause harm: *the harmful effects of smoking* | [+ **to**] *chemicals that are harmful to the environment* —**harmfully** *adv* —**harmfulness** *n* [U]

**harm·less** /ˈhɑːmləs‖ˈhɑːrm-/ *adj* **1** unable or unlikely to hurt anyone or cause damage: *The dog seems fierce, but actually he's harmless.* **2** not likely to upset or offend anyone: **harmless fun** *It was just a bit of harmless fun.* —**harmlessly** *adv* —**harmlessness** *n* [U]

**har·mon·ic** /hɑˈmɒnɪk‖hɑːrˈmɑː-/ *adj technical* concerned with the way notes are played or sung together to give a pleasing sound: *harmonic scales*

**har·mon·i·ca** /hɑːˈmɒnɪkə‖hɑːrˈmɑː-/ *n* [C] a small musical instrument that you play by blowing into it and moving it from side to side; MOUTH ORGAN

**har·mo·ni·ous** /hɑːˈməʊniəs‖hɑːrˈmoʊ-/ *adj* **1** harmonious relationships, agreements etc are ones in which people are friendly and helpful to one another **2** sounds that are harmonious are very pleasant **3** parts, colours etc that are harmonious look good or work well together: *The decor is a harmonious blend of traditional and modern.* —**harmoniously** *adv* —**harmoniousness** *n* [U]

**har·mo·ni·um** /hɑːˈməʊniəm‖hɑːrˈmoʊ-/ *n* [C] a musical instrument like a small piano worked by pumped air

**harmonize** also **-ise** *BrE* /ˈhɑːmənaɪz‖ˈhɑːr-/ *v* **1** [I] if two or more things harmonize, they work well together or look good together: [+ **with**] *colours that don't seem to harmonize with each other* **2** [T] to make two or more sets of rules, taxes etc the same: *harmonizing Europe's widely varying immigration procedures* **3** [I] to sing or play music in HARMONY

**har·mo·ny** /ˈhɑːməni‖ˈhɑːr-/ *n* **1** [C usually plural, U] notes of music combined together in a pleasant way: **in harmony** *a choir singing in perfect harmony* **2 be in harmony with** *formal* to agree with another idea, feeling etc, or look good with other things: *Your suggestions are not in harmony with the aims of this project.* **3 live/work in (perfect) harmony** to live or work together without fighting or disagreeing with each other **4** [U] the pleasant effect made by different things that form an attractive whole: *the harmony of sea and sky* —compare DISCORD (2)

**har·ness¹** /ˈhɑːnɪ̤s‖ˈhɑːr-/ *n* [C,U] **1** a piece of equipment for controlling a horse, consisting of long pieces of leather held together by metal and worn over the horse's head and shoulders **2** a piece of equipment used to fasten someone in a place or to stop them from falling: *a safety harness* **3 be back in harness** *informal* to have come back to do your usual work **4 in harness with** working closely with another group

**harness²** *v* [T] **1** to control and use the natural force or power of something: *harnessing the power of the wind to generate electricity* **2** to fasten two animals together, or to fasten an animal to something using a harness **3** to put a harness on a horse

**harp¹** /hɑːp‖hɑːrp/ *n* [C] a large musical instrument with strings that are stretched from top to bottom of a frame with three corners —**harpist** *n* [C]

**harp²** *v*

**harp on** *informal* [I *BrE*, T *AmE*] to talk about something continuously, especially in a way that is annoying or boring: [+ **about**] *My grandfather harps on about the war all the time.*

**har·poon** /hɑːˈpuːn‖hɑːr-/ *n* [C] a weapon used for hunting WHALES —**harpoon** *v* [T]

**harp·si·chord** /ˈhɑːpsɪkɔːd‖ˈhɑːrpsɪkɔːrd/ *n* [C] a musical instrument like a PIANO, used in former times

**har·py** /ˈhɑːpi‖ˈhɑːrpi/ *n* [C] *literary* a cruel or nasty woman

**har·ri·dan** /ˈhærɪdən/ *n* [C] *old-fashioned* a bad-tempered, unpleasant woman

**har·row** /ˈhærəʊ‖-roʊ/ *n* [C] a farming machine with sharp metal blades, used to break up the earth before planting crops —**harrow** *v* [I,T]

**har·rowed** /ˈhærəʊd‖-roʊd/ *adj* a harrowed look or expression shows that you are very worried or afraid

**har·row·ing** /ˈhærəʊɪŋ‖-roʊ-/ *adj* very frightening or shocking and making you feel very upset: *a harrowing experience | harrowing video tapes of torture*

**har·ry** /ˈhæri/ *v* **harried, harrying** [T] **1** to keep asking someone for something in a way that is upsetting or annoying **2** to attack an enemy repeatedly

**harsh** /hɑːʃ‖hɑːrʃ/ *adj*

**1 ▶CONDITIONS/WEATHER◀** difficult to live in and very uncomfortable, cold etc: *The prisoners had to endure harsh living conditions and near starvation. | the harsh winters of northern China* | **harsh reality** *experiencing the harsh realities of adult life*

**2 ▶SOUND/LIGHT/COLOUR◀** unpleasant and too loud or bright: *a harsh, croaking voice | They stepped out into the harsh sunlight.*

**3 ▶CRUEL/STRICT◀** criticizing, punishing, or treating people in a very cruel or strict way: **harsh criticism** *Brando has had to endure some harsh criticism from the press. | a harsh, authoritarian regime*

**4 ▶LINES/SHAPES ETC◀** ugly and unpleasant to look at: *the harsh outline of the factories against the sky*

**5 ▶CLEANING SUBSTANCE◀** too strong and likely to damage the thing you are cleaning —**harshly** *adv* —**harshness** *n* [U]

**hart** /hɑːt‖hɑːrt/ *n* [C] *especially BrE* a male DEER

**har·um-scar·um** /ˌheərəm ˈskeərəm‖ˌherəm ˈsker-/ *adv old-fashioned* in an uncontrolled way and without thinking —**harum-scarum** *adj*

**har·vest¹** /ˈhɑːvɪ̤st‖ˈhɑːr-/ *n* **1** [C,U] the time when crops are gathered from the fields, or the act of gathering them: *harvest time* **2** [C] the size or quality of the crops that have been gathered: **a poor/bumper harvest** (=a harvest that produces few crops or a lot of crops) **3 reap a harvest** to get good or bad results: *The company is now reaping the harvest of careful planning.*

**harvest²** *v* [I,T] to gather crops from the fields

**har·vest·er** /ˈhɑːvɪ̤stə‖ˈhɑːrvɪ̤stər/ *n* [C] someone who gathers crops —see also **combine harvester** (COMBINE² (1))

**harvest fes·ti·val** /ˌ·· ˈ···/ *n* [C] *especially BrE* an occasion in the Christian religion when people thank God for the harvest —compare THANKSGIVING

**harvest moon** /ˌ·· ˈ·/ *n* [usually singular] the FULL MOON in autumn

**has** /z, əz, həz; *strong* hæz/ the third person singular of the present tense of HAVE¹

**has-been** /ˈ· ·/ *n* [C] *informal* someone who was important or popular but who has now been forgotten

**hash¹** /hæʃ/ *n* **1 make a hash of** *informal* to do something very badly: *I made a real hash of my exams.* **2** [U] *informal* HASHISH **3** [C,U] a dish made with cooked meat and potatoes

**hash²** *v*

**hash** sth ↔ **up** *phr v* [T] *informal* to do something very badly: *She was so nervous at the interview that she completely hashed it up.* —**hash-up** *n* [C]

**hash browns** /ˌ· ˈ·/ *n* [plural] potatoes that are cut into very small pieces, pressed together, and cooked in oil

**hash·ish** /ˈhæʃɪʃ, -iːʃ/ *n* [U] the strongest form of the drug CANNABIS

**has·n't** /ˈhæzənt/ the short form of 'has not': *Hasn't she finished yet?*

**hasp** /hɑːsp‖hæsp/ *n* [C] a flat metal thing used to fasten a door, lid etc

**has·sle¹** /ˈhæsəl/ *n* **1** [C,U] *spoken* something that is annoying, because it causes problems or is difficult to do: *I don't feel like cooking tonight, it's too much hassle. | It's such a hassle not having a washing machine.* **2** [C] *AmE informal* an argument between two people or groups: *hassles with the management*

**hassle²** *v* **hassled, hassling** *informal* **1** [T] to be continuously asking someone to do something in a way that annoys them: *I wish you'd stop hassling me.* **2** [I + **with**] to argue with someone

**has·sock** /ˈhæsək/ *n* [C] **1** a small CUSHION¹ (1) for kneeling on in a church **2** *AmE* a soft round piece of furniture used as a seat or for resting your feet on; POUF (1) *BrE*

**hast** /hæst/ **thou hast** *old use* a way of saying you have

**haste** /heɪst/ *n* [U] **1** great speed in doing something, especially because you do not have enough time: *I soon regretted my haste.* | **in your haste to do sth** *In his haste to leave he forgot his briefcase.* **2 in haste** quickly or in a hurry: *They left in haste, without even saying goodbye.* **3 make haste** *old use* to hurry or do something quickly **4 more haste less speed** *BrE* used to say that it is useless to do something too quickly

**has·ten** /ˈheɪsən/ *v* **1** [T] to make something happen faster or sooner: *Her death had been hastened by large doses of pain-killing drugs.* **2** [I] to do or say something quickly or without delay: **hasten to do sth** *I hastened to assure her that there was no danger.* **3** [I always + adv/prep] *formal* to go somewhere quickly **4 I hasten to add** used when you realize that what you have said may not have been understood correctly: *an exhausting course, which, I hasten to add, was also great fun*

**hast·y** /ˈheɪsti/ *adj* done in a hurry, especially with bad results: *He soon regretted his hasty decision.* | *a hasty breakfast* —**hastily** *adv* —**hastiness** *n* [U]

S2 W3 **hat** /hæt/ *n* [C] **1** a piece of clothing that you wear on your head: **straw/bowler/woolly etc hat** *She wore an enormous flowery hat.* **2 keep something under your hat** *informal* to keep something secret **3 be wearing your manager's/teacher's etc hat** *informal* to be doing your duty as a manager etc, which is not your only duty **4 I take my hat off to** *informal* used to say you admire someone very much because of what they have done **5 pass the hat round** *BrE* **/pass the hat (around)** *AmE* to collect money from a group of people, especially in order to buy someone a present **6 bowler-hatted/top-hatted etc** wearing a BOWLER hat, etc **7 my hat!** *old-fashioned* used to express great surprise —see also HARD HAT, **at the drop of a hat** (DROP² (5)), **hang up your hat** (HANG¹ (14)), **I'll eat my hat** (EAT (10)), OLD HAT, **be talking through your hat** (TALK¹ (47)), **throw your hat into the ring** (THROW¹ (33))

**hat·band** /ˈhætbænd/ *n* [C] a band of cloth or leather fastened around a hat

**hat box** /ˈ· ·/ *n* [C] a special box used for carrying a hat in

**hatch¹** /hætʃ/ *v* **1** also **hatch out** [I,T] if an egg hatches or is hatched, it breaks letting the young bird, insect etc come out: *The eggs take three days to hatch.* **2** also **hatch out** [I,T] if a young bird, insect etc hatches or is hatched, it comes out of its egg: *All the chicks have hatched out.* **3 hatch a plot/plan/deal etc** to form a plan etc secretly

**hatch²** *n* [C] **1** a hole in a ship or aircraft, used for loading goods, or the door that covers it —see picture at AIRCRAFT **2** also **hatchway** a small hole in the wall or floor between two rooms, or the door that covers it: *the hatch between the kitchen and the dining room* **3** the act of hatching eggs

**hatch·back** /ˈhætʃbæk/ *n* [C] a car with a door at the back that opens upwards

**hat·check** /ˈhæt-tʃek/ *n* [C] *AmE old-fashioned* the place in a restaurant, theatre etc where you can leave your coat

**hatch·er·y** /ˈhætʃəri/ *n* [C] a place for hatching eggs, especially fish eggs

**hatch·et** /ˈhætʃɪ̇t/ *n* [C] a small AXE with a short handle —see also **bury the hatchet** (BURY (8))

**hatchet-faced** /ˈ·· ˌ·/ *adj* having an unpleasantly thin face with sharp features

**hatchet job** /ˈ·· ˌ·/ *n* **do a hatchet job on** *informal* to criticize someone severely and unfairly in a newspaper, on television etc: *Republican columnists did a hatchet job on Dukakis.*

**hatchet man** /ˈ·· ˌ·/ *n* [C] *informal* someone who is employed to make unpopular changes in an organization

**hatch·ing** /ˈhætʃɪŋ/ *n* [U] fine lines drawn on or cut into a surface

**hatch·way** /ˈhætʃweɪ/ *n* [C] a HATCH² (2)

**hate¹** /heɪt/ *v* [T not in progressive] **1** to dislike someone very much and feel angry towards them: *Jill really hates her stepfather.* | **hate sb's guts** *informal* (=hate someone very much) **2** *informal* to dislike something very much: *I hate housework.* | *Liz won't eat that, she hates bananas.* | **hate doing sth** *Paul hates having his photo taken.* | **hate to do sth** *I hate to see you making a fool of yourself.* | **hate sb doing sth** *Jenny's mother hates her staying out late.* | **hate it when** *I hate it when people ask me for money.* **3 I'd hate (sb) to do sth** *spoken* used to emphasize that you really do not want something to happen: *I'd hate you to go.* **4 I hate to think what/how** *spoken* used when you feel sure that something would have a bad result: *I hate to think what would have happened, if you hadn't called the police.* **5 I hate to ask/interrupt/disturb etc** *spoken* used to say that you are sorry that you have to ask etc: *I hate to ask, but would you be able to give me a lift home tonight?* **6 I hate to (have to) say this, but...** *spoken* used when saying something that you do not want to say, for example because it is embarrassing —**hated** *adj*: *the hated dictator* —opposite LOVE S1 W3

This graph shows how common the different grammar patterns of the verb **hate** are.

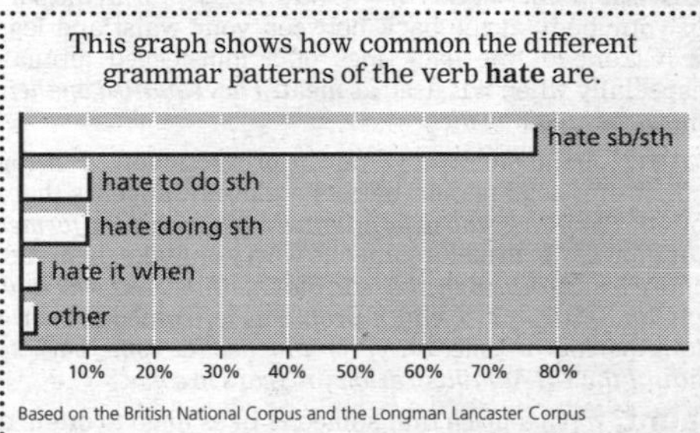


Based on the British National Corpus and the Longman Lancaster Corpus

**hate²** *n* [U] an angry unpleasant feeling that someone has when they hate someone and want to harm them: *Their minds were poisoned with envy and hate.* —opposite LOVE² (1) —see also PET HATE

**hate·ful** /ˈheɪtfəl/ *adj old-fashioned* very bad, unpleasant, or unkind —**hatefully** *adv*

**hath** /hæθ/ *old use* has

**hat·pin** /ˈhætˌpɪn/ *n* [C] a long pin that is used to make a woman's hat stay on her head —see picture at PIN¹

**ha·tred** /ˈheɪtrɪ̇d/ *n* [U] an angry feeling of extreme dislike for someone or something: *Her voice was full of hatred and contempt.* | [+ **of**] *Tom's hatred of authority* | [+ **for/towards**] *Strangely, the murderer said he never felt hatred for any of his victims.* | **deep hatred** *This experience left him with a deep hatred of politicians.*

**hat stand** /ˈhætstænd/ *n* [C] a tall pole with hooks at the top used to hang coats and hats on —see picture on page 838

**hat·ter** /ˈhætə‖-ər/ *n* [C] someone who makes or sells hats —see also **as mad as a hatter** (MAD (14))

**hat-trick** /ˈ· ·/ *n* [C] a series of three successes, especially in sports such as football when the same person scores (SCORE² (1)) three times: *Saunders scored a hat-trick in the final game of the series.*

**haugh·ty** /ˈhɔːti‖ˈhɒː-/ *adj* **haughtier, haughtiest** behaving in a proud unfriendly way: *a haughty laugh* —**haughtily** *adv* —**haughtiness** *n* [U]

**haul¹** /hɔːl‖hɒːl/ *v* **1** [I always + adv/prep,T] to pull something heavy with a continuous, steady movement: **haul sth along/in/across etc** *The fishermen were hauling in their nets.* **2 haul sb over the coals** to speak to someone angrily and severely because they have done something wrong **3** to carry goods in a vehicle **4 haul yourself up/out of etc a)** to succeed in achieving a higher position in society, in a competition etc: *He hauled himself out of the gutter and became the world heavyweight champion.* **b)** to pull yourself up, out of etc: *I see you've managed to haul yourself out of bed.* **5 haul off and hit/punch sb** *AmE informal* to hit someone very hard **6 haul ass** *AmE slang* to hurry

**haul** sb **up** *phr v* [T usually passive] *informal* to officially bring someone to a court of law to be judged: *Campbell was hauled up in front of the magistrate.*

**haul²** *n* [C] **1** a large amount of goods that has been stolen, or found by the police: *The robbers' haul included a very valuable diamond ring.* | *Police announced a drugs haul worth two million pounds.* **2 long/slow haul** something that takes a lot of time and effort: **it's been a long haul** *At last we've won our freedom but it's been a long bitter haul.* **3** the amount of fish caught when fishing with a net —see also LONG-HAUL, SHORT-HAUL

**haul·age** /ˈhɔːlɪdʒ‖ˈhɒːl-/ *n* [U] **1** the business of carrying goods by road or railway **2** the charge for this

**haul·i·er** /ˈhɔːliə‖ˈhɒːliər/ *BrE,* **hau·ler** *AmE* /ˈhɔːlə‖ˈhɒːlər/ *n* [C] someone who owns or manages a haulage business

**haunch** /hɔːntʃ‖hɒːntʃ/ *n* **1 haunches** [plural] the part of your body at the back between your waist and legs **2** [C] one of the back legs of a four-legged animal, especially when it is used as meat: *They squatted on their haunches playing dice.*

**haunt¹** /hɔːnt‖hɒːnt/ *v* [T not in progressive] **1** if the spirit of a dead person haunts a place, it appears there often: *The pub is said to be haunted by the ghost of a former landlord.* **2** to make someone worry or make them sad: *Clare was haunted by the fear that her husband was having an affair.* **3** to cause problems for someone over a long period of time: *an error that would come back to haunt the US Administration for years to come*

**haunt²** *n* [C] a place that someone likes to go to often: **a favourite haunt** *The Café Vienna was a favourite haunt of journalists and actors.*

**haunt·ed** /ˈhɔːntɪ̌d‖ˈhɒːn-/ *adj* **1** a haunted building is believed to be visited regularly by the spirit of a dead person: *a haunted house* **2 haunted expression/look** a worried or frightened expression etc

**haunt·ing** /ˈhɔːntɪŋ‖ˈhɒːn-/ *adj* sad but also beautiful and staying in your thoughts for a long time: *a haunting melody* —**hauntingly** *adv*

**haute cou·ture** /ˌəʊt kuːˈtjʊə‖ˌoʊt kuːˈtʊr/ *n* [U] *French* the business of making and selling very expensive and fashionable clothes for women —**haute couturier** *n* [C]

**haute cui·sine** /ˌəʊt kwɪˈziːn‖ˌoʊt-/ *n* [U] *French* cooking of a very high standard, especially French cooking

**hau·teur** /əʊˈtɜːʳ‖hɒːˈtɜːr/ *n* [U] *formal* a proud, very unfriendly manner

**Ha·van·a** /həˈvænə/ *n* [C] a type of CIGAR made in Cuba

S1 W1 **have¹** /v, əv, həv; *strong* hæv/ *auxiliary verb past tense* **had** /d, əd, həd; *strong* hæd/ *third person singular present tense* **has** /z, əz, həz; *strong* hæz/ *negative short forms* **haven't** /ˈhævənt/, **hadn't** /ˈhædnt/, **hasn't** /ˈhæzənt/ **1** used with the past participle of another verb to make the perfect tense of that verb: *We have finished the decorating.* | *Have you read that book yet?* | *We have been spending too much money.* **2 had better/best** used when telling someone what they should do: *You'd better phone to say you'll be late.* | *We'd better not tell Jim about our plans just yet.* **3 have had it** *spoken* **a)** used to say that someone will be in serious trouble for something they have done: *Press the wrong button and you've had it!* **b)** used to say that someone is tired: *We'll have to stop for the night – the kids have just about had it.* **c)** used to say that something is so old or damaged that it cannot be used any more: *It looks as if your stereo's had it.* **d) have had it with** used to say you do not want to waste any more time on someone or something that has annoyed you **4 had sb done sth** if someone had done something: *Had we known about the plans for the factory, we would never have bought the house.*

**have²** *v* [T not usually in passive] S1

**1** ▶ **HAVE AN APPEARANCE/QUALITY/FEATURE** ◀ [not in progressive] also **have got** *especially BrE* used when saying what someone or something looks like, what qualities or features they possess etc: *She has dark hair and brown eyes.* | *I think the idea does have some good points.* | *You need to have a lot of patience to be a teacher.*

**2** ▶ **INCLUDE/CONTAIN** ◀ [not in progressive] also **have got** *especially BrE* to include or contain something or a particular number of things or people: *Japan has a population of over 120 million.* | *Our old apartment had a huge kitchen.* | *How many pages has it got?*

**3** ▶ **OWN/BE ABLE TO USE** ◀ [not in progressive] also **have got** *spoken BrE* **a)** to own something or have been given it to use: *They used to have a Mercedes Benz.* | *Has she got a fax machine?* | *Have you ever had your own business?* **b)** to own a pet or animal: *He's a lovely dog – How long have you had him?*

**4** ▶ **DO STH** ◀ *BrE* a word meaning to do something, used in certain phrases: **have a look/walk/sleep/talk/think etc** *Do you mind if I have a look at what's on television?* | **have a holiday/bath/shower etc** *It's about time she had a holiday.*

**5** ▶ **EAT/DRINK/SMOKE** ◀ to eat, drink, or smoke: *She sat down and had another drink.* | **have lunch/a meal etc** *I usually have breakfast at about 8 o'clock.*

**6** ▶ **HAVE AN IDEA/FEELING** ◀ [not in progressive] also **have got** *especially BrE* to think of an idea or experience a particular feeling: *If you have any good ideas for presents, let me know.* | *I have lots of happy memories of my time in Japan.* | **have a shock/surprise etc** *When the waiter brought the bill they had a nasty shock.*

**7** ▶ **HAVE A DISEASE/INJURY/PAIN** ◀ [not in progressive] also **have got** *especially BrE* to suffer from a disease, injury, or pain: *Sarah's got a cold.* | *The doctor said he had a broken leg.*

**8** ▶ **EXPERIENCE STH** ◀ to experience something or be affected by something: **have problems/difficulties/troubles etc** *We've been having a lot of difficulties with our new computer system.* | **have an accident/crash** *I'm afraid your son has had a serious accident.* | **have a good/terrible etc time** *Thanks for everything – we had a great time.*

**9 have sth stolen/broken/taken etc** if you have something stolen, broken etc, someone steals it etc: *She had all her jewellery stolen.*

**10 have your hair cut/your car repaired/your house painted etc** to pay a professional person to cut your hair etc for you: *Where do you normally have your hair done?* | *We'd only just had a new engine put in.*

**11 have sth ready/done/finished etc** to have made something ready to be used, or have finished doing something: [+ **by**] *I should have the car ready by Monday.*

**12 have sth going/working/on** to make a machine operate: *She always has the TV going at full blast.*

**13** ▶ **KEEP/PUT STH IN A PARTICULAR POSITION** ◀ [not in progressive] also **have got** *especially BrE* to keep or have put something in a particular position: **have sth open/closed/out/in/over etc** *I had my eyes half-closed.* | *Janice likes to have the window open at night.*

**14** ▶ **RECEIVE** ◀ also **have got** *especially BrE* to receive something: **have a letter/phone call/**

**message** *I had lots of phone calls.* | **have news/information** *Have you had any news yet from Graham?* | **have help/advice etc** *I expect he had some help from his father.*
**15 can/could/may I have** used when politely asking someone to give you something: *Can I have the bill please?* | *Could we have our ball back?*
**16 I'll have/we'll have** *spoken* used to ask for what you want especially to eat or drink: *I'll have one vegetable curry and two chapatis please.*
**17 have a brother/grandmother etc** [not in progressive] also **have got** *especially BrE* if you have a brother, grandmother etc, they are part of your family: *She has an uncle who lives in Wisconsin.*
**18 ▶ KNOW SB ◀** [not in progressive] also **have got** *especially BrE* to know someone because you have a relationship with them, work with them etc: *I have a friend who looks like you.*
**19 have a duty/responsibility etc** also **have got** *especially BrE* if you have a particular duty, responsibility etc, it is yours and you must do it
**20 have a job/position/role etc** also **have got** *especially BrE* if you have a particular job, position etc, it is yours and you are the one who does it
**21 ▶ EMPLOY/BE IN CHARGE OF ◀** [not in progressive] to employ or be in charge of a group of workers: *She had more than 20 servants who took care of her every need.*
**22 ▶ HAVE AN AMOUNT OF TIME ◀** [not in progressive] also **have got** *especially BrE* if you have a particular amount of time, it is available for you to do something: *You have 30 seconds to answer the question.* | *I wish I had more time to talk to you.*
**23 ▶ HAVE GOODS/ROOMS AVAILABLE ◀** [not in progressive] also **have got** *especially BrE* if a shop or a hotel has goods or rooms, they are available to you to buy or use: *Do you have any single rooms?* | *They didn't have any sweaters in my size.*
**24 ▶ HAVE BROUGHT STH WITH YOU ◀** [not in progressive] also **have got** *especially BrE* to have brought something with you or keep something near you: *Have you got your pen?* | **have sth with you** *I'm afraid I don't have my address book with me.* | **have sth on you** *How much money do you have on you?*
**25 have sb with you** also **have got** *especially BrE* if you have someone with you, they are present with you: *Luckily I had a friend with me who spoke German.*
**26 ▶ HOLD SB ◀ have sb by sth** also **have got** *especially BrE* to hold someone violently by a part of their body: *They had him by the throat.*
**27 have visitors/guests** if you have visitors or guests, they have to come to your home, office etc: *Sorry, I didn't realize you had visitors.*
**28 have a meeting/party/concert etc** to hold an event such as a meeting: *We're having a party on Saturday – you're very welcome to come.*
**29 have an effect/influence/result etc** to cause a particular result: *This could have a disastrous effect on the world economy.*
**30 have the chance/opportunity/honour etc to do sth/of doing sth** to be able to do something: *If you have the chance you should go and see it – it's a really good film.* | *I had the honour of meeting the Duke of Edinburgh.*
**31 have a baby/twins etc** if a woman has a baby, it is born from her body: *Anna insisted on having the baby at home.*
**32 have an operation/treatment etc** to be given an operation, treatment etc for a medical problem
**33 ▶ MAKE SB DO STH ◀** [not in progressive] **a)** make someone start doing something: **have sb laughing/crying etc** *Within minutes he had the whole audience laughing and clapping.* **b)** to persuade or order someone to do something: **have sb doing sth** *She had me doing all kinds of jobs for her.* | **have sb do sth** *AmE I'll have Hudson show you to your room.*
**34 ▶ SEX ◀** [not in progressive] *informal* to have sex with someone: *I expect she's had lots of men.*
**35 ▶ NOT ALLOW ◀ I won't have/we can't have** *spoken* used to say that you do not want or you refuse to allow something to happen: *I won't have you walking home on your own – let me call you a taxi.*
**36 have it coming** also **have got it coming** *spoken* used to say that you are not sorry that something bad has happened to someone, because they deserve it: *I'm not surprised his wife left him – he's had it coming for years.*
**37 I've got it** *spoken* used to say you have suddenly thought of the solution to a problem or understand
**38 you have me there** also **you've got me there** *spoken* used to say that you do not know the answer to a question
**39 I'll have you know** *spoken* used to start to tell someone something when you are annoyed with them
**40 have sb doing sth** *especially in questions or negatives* to allow someone to do something or agree that they should do it: *I wouldn't have you walking home all by yourself.*
**41 have done with** to finish or settle an argument or a difficult situation: *Let's get this sorted out and have done with it.*
**42 have it (that) a)** to say that something is true: **rumour has it** (=a lot of people are saying) *Rumour has it he's going out with Michele.* **b)** to be told that something is true: **have it on good authority** (=to have been told by someone you can trust)
**43 have it in for** *spoken* to want to harm someone: *Dean thinks his teachers have it in for him.*
**44 have (got) it in you** to have a particular quality, skill, or ability: *You should have seen the way Dad was dancing – I didn't know he had it in him!*
**45 have (got) something against sb** to dislike someone for something they have done: *I don't know what she's got against me.*
**46 have (got) nothing against sb** *especially spoken* used to say that you do not dislike the person you are talking about: *I've got nothing against Gary, but I wish he'd show a little more initiative.*
**47 be not having any (of that)** *spoken* to refuse to agree to something, listen to someone etc: *I tried to explain to her, but she just wasn't having any.*
**48 you've been had** *spoken* used to say that someone has been deceived, for example, by being tricked into paying too much money: *You paid £200? You've been had!*
**49 have sth/sb/(all) to yourself** to be the only person or people in a place, using something, talking to someone else etc: *He couldn't wait to have Beth all to himself.*

**have sb/sth in** also **have got sb/sth in** *BrE phr v* [T] **a)** to have someone in your home in order to do building work etc: *She won't go to work while she's got the builders in.* **b)** to have something in your home that you can use, eat etc

**have it off** *phr v* [I + **with**] *BrE slang* to have sex with someone

**have on** also **have got on** *especially BrE* [T] **1** [**have** sth **on**] to be wearing a piece of clothing or type of clothing: *She had on lime-green slacks and a purple nylon shirt.* | **have nothing on** (=have no clothes on) *Jimmy had nothing on except his socks.* **2 have the TV/radio/washing machine etc on** to have your television, radio etc switched on and working: *Billie has his walkman on all day long.* **3 be having sb on** *especially BrE* to make someone believe something that is not true, especially as a joke: *He told you he's a Managing Director? He's having you on!* **4** [**have** sth **on**] to have arranged to do something, go somewhere etc, especially when this means you cannot do something else: *Sorry, I can't do any overtime this weekend – I've got too much on already.* **5** [**have** sth **on** sb] to know about something bad that someone has done: *What do the police have on him?* **6** [**have nothing on sb/sth**] to not be nearly as good as someone or something else: *Supermarket vodkas are fine, but they have nothing on brands like Stolichnaya.*

**have sth out** *phr v* [T] **1** [**have** sth **out**] **have a tooth/your tonsils etc out** to have a tooth etc removed by a medical operation **2 have it out with sb** *informal* to settle a disagreement or difficult situation by talking to the person involved, especially when you are angry with them

**have** sb **up** *phr v* [T] *BrE informal* to take someone to court, especially to prove they are guilty of a crime: *Last year he was had up for drunken driving.*

S1 **have³** *v* [**have to do sth** also **have got to do sth** *especially BrE*] **1** if you have to do something, you must do it because your situation forces you to do it, because you have arranged to do it, or because someone makes you do it: *In the end she had to go into a mental hospital.* | *I hate having to get up early in the morning.* | *We had to do Latin every day.* **2** used when saying that it is important that something happens, or that something must happen if something else is to happen: *There has to be an end to the violence.* | *You have to believe me!* | *There will have to be a complete ceasefire before the Government will agree to talks.* **3** used when telling someone how to do something: *First of all you have to mix the flour and the butter.* **4** used when saying that you are sure that something will happen, or you are sure that something is true: *The price of houses has to go up sooner or later.* | *None of the others could have done the murder, so it had to be the husband.* **5** *spoken* used when talking about an annoying event which caused you problems: *Of course it had to happen on a Sunday, when all the dentists are shut.* **6** *spoken* used when talking about something annoying or surprising that someone does: *She has to go to Marks and Spencers – nowhere else is good enough for her.* | **do you have to do sth?** (=used to ask someone to stop doing something that annoys you) *Lieutenant, do you have to keep repeating everything I've just said?* **7 I have to say/admit/confess** *spoken* used when speaking honestly about something awkward or embarrassing: *I have to say I don't know the first thing about computers.* —see also MUST¹

**ha·ven** /ˈheɪvən/ *n* [C] a place where people go to be safe: *The border region was a natural haven for fugitives.*

**have-nots** /ˌ· ˈ·/ *n* **the have-nots** the poor people in a country or society —see also HAVES

**have·n't** /ˈhævənt/ the short form of 'have not'

**hav·er·sack** /ˈhævəsæk‖-ər-/ *n* [C] *BrE old-fashioned* a bag that you carry on your back

**haves** /hævz/ *n* **the haves** the rich people in a country or society: *the widening gap between the haves and the have-nots* —see also HAVE-NOTS

**hav·oc** /ˈhævək/ *n* [U] a situation in which there is a lot of confusion or damage: **cause/create havoc** *The Wall Street Crash created havoc and ruin.* | **wreak havoc (on)/play havoc with** (=to cause great harm by causing a confusing situation)

**haw** /hɔː‖hɒː/ *v* —see **hum and haw** (HUM¹ (4))

**hawk¹** /hɔːk‖hɒːk/ *n* [C] **1** a large bird that hunts and eats small birds and animals **2** a politician who believes in using military force: *Meese and other hawks in the Reaganite administration* —opposite DOVE¹ (2) **3 watch sb like a hawk** to watch someone very carefully **4 have eyes like a hawk** to be quick to notice things, especially small details

**hawk²** *v* **1** [T] to try to sell goods by carrying them around **2** [I] to cough up PHLEGM

**hawk·er** /ˈhɔːkə‖ˈhɒːkər/ *n* [C] someone who carries goods from place to place and tries to sell them

**hawk-eyed** /ˈ· ·/ *adj* quick to notice small details: *hawk-eyed customs officers*

**hawk·ish** /ˈhɔːkɪʃ‖ˈhɒːk-/ *adj* supporting the use of military force —**hawkishness** *n* [U]

**haw·ser** /ˈhɔːzə‖ˈhɒːzər/ *n* [C] a thick rope or steel CABLE¹ (2) used on a ship

**haw·thorn** /ˈhɔːθɔːn‖ˈhɒːθɔːrn/ *n* [C, U] a small tree that has small white flowers and red berries

**hay** /heɪ/ *n* [U] **1** long grass that has been cut and dried, often used as food for cattle **2 hit the hay** *slang* to go to bed **3 make hay while the sun shines** do something while the conditions are favourable —see also **a roll in the hay** (ROLL² (10))

**hay·cock** /ˈheɪkɒk‖-kɑːk/ *n* [C] a small round pile of hay left in a field to dry

**hay fe·ver** /ˈ· ˌ··/ *n* [U] a medical condition, like a bad cold (COLD² (2)), that is caused by POLLEN (=dust from plants)

**hay·loft** /ˈheɪlɒft‖-lɒːft/ *n* [C] the top part of a farm building where hay is stored

**hay·mak·ing** /ˈheɪˌmeɪkɪŋ/ *n* [U] the process of cutting and drying hay

**hay·rick** /ˈheɪrɪk/ *n* [C] a haystack

**hay·ride** /ˈheɪraɪd/ *n* [C] *AmE* an organized ride in a CART filled with hay, usually as part of a social event for young people

**hay·stack** /ˈheɪstæk/ *n* [C] a large firmly built pile of hay —see also **like looking for a needle in a haystack** (NEEDLE¹ (6))

**hay·wire** /ˈheɪwaɪə‖-waɪr/ *adj* **go haywire** *informal* to start working in completely the wrong way: *The computer went haywire and started printing numbers at random.*

**haz·ard¹** /ˈhæzəd‖-ərd/ *n* [C] **1** something that may be dangerous, cause accidents etc: *Ice on the road is a major hazard at this time of the year.* | **be a hazard to** *Polluted water sources are a hazard to wildlife.* | **fire hazard** (=something that may cause a fire) | **health hazard** (=something that is likely to harm your health) **2** a risk that cannot be avoided **hazard of doing sth** *the economic hazards of running a small farm* | **occupational hazard** (=a danger that always exists in a job) *Divorce seems to be an occupational hazard for politicians.*

**hazard²** *v* [T] **1** to say something that is only a suggestion or guess and so might not be correct: **hazard a guess** *Would you like to hazard a guess as to how much he earns?* **2** *formal* to risk losing your money, property etc in an attempt to gain something

**hazard light** /ˈ·· ·/ *n* [C usually plural] a special light on a vehicle that flashes to warn other drivers of danger

**haz·ard·ous** /ˈhæzədəs‖-zər-/ *adj* **1 hazardous chemicals/waste/substances etc** *technical* chemicals etc that are dangerous and likely to harm people's health **2 hazardous journey/operation/undertaking etc** a journey etc that involves danger

**haze¹** /heɪz/ *n* [singular, U] **1** smoke, dust, or MOISTURE in the air which makes it difficult to see through: [+ **of**] *a haze of cigarette smoke* | **heat haze** (=a haze that forms in hot weather) **2** the feeling of being very confused and unable to think clearly

**haze²** *v* [T] *AmE* to play tricks on a new college student as part of the ceremony of joining a club

**haze over** *phr v* [I] to become HAZY (1): *The sky hazed over.*

**ha·zel¹** /ˈheɪzəl/ *n* [C, U] a small tree that produces nuts

**hazel²** *adj* light brown: *hazel eyes* —**hazel** *n* [U] —see picture on page 412

**ha·zel·nut** /ˈheɪzəlnʌt/ *n* [C] the nut of the HAZEL¹ tree

**haz·y** /ˈheɪzi/ *adj* **1** not clear because of a slight mist that is caused by heat, smoke etc: *The tower looked dim in the hazy English air.* **2** an idea, memory etc that is hazy is not clear or exact: *My memories of the holiday are rather hazy.* **3 be hazy about** to not know or understand very much about something: *Most people are pretty hazy about Clinton's economic program.* —**hazily** *adv* —**haziness** *n* [U]

**H-bomb** /ˈeɪtʃ bɒm‖-bɑːm/ *n* [C] a powerful NUCLEAR bomb

**HCF** /ˌeɪtʃ siː ˈef/ the abbreviation of HIGHEST COMMON FACTOR

**H.E.** the abbreviation of His Excellency or Her Excellency, used in the title of an AMBASSADOR

**he** /hiː/ *pron* [used as subject of a verb] **1** used to talk about a male person or animal that has already been mentioned or is already known about: *"Where's Paul?" "He's gone to the cinema."* | *Be careful of that dog. He sometimes bites.* **2** used to talk about anyone, everyone, or S1 W1 an unknown person who may be either male or female: *Everyone should do what he considers best.* **3 He** used when writing about God

**USAGE NOTE: HE**
POLITENESS
Some people, especially women, do not like the use of **he** to include both men and women in a sentence like: *Everyone should do what he thinks best.* Instead they use **he or she, she or he,** or **they**: *Everyone should do what they think best.*
In writing **he/she** is often used, or simply **s/he**. Often you can write what you want to say in a different way in order to avoid the problem. For example say: *People should all do what they think best.*

**he-** /hiː/ *prefix* a male animal: *a he-goat*

**-head** /hed/ *suffix* [in nouns] **1** the top of something: *a pithead* (=the top of a coalmine) **2** the place where something begins; SOURCE[1] (1): *a fountainhead*

## head[1] /hed/ *n*

S1 W1

① TOP OF BODY
② MIND
③ UNDERSTAND
④ TOP PERSON
⑤ TOP/FRONT/MOST IMPORTANT PART
⑥ CALM
⑦ CRAZY
⑧ INTELLIGENT/SENSIBLE
⑨ TOO PROUD
⑩ ALCOHOL/DRUGS
⑪ FOR EACH PERSON
⑫ OTHER MEANINGS

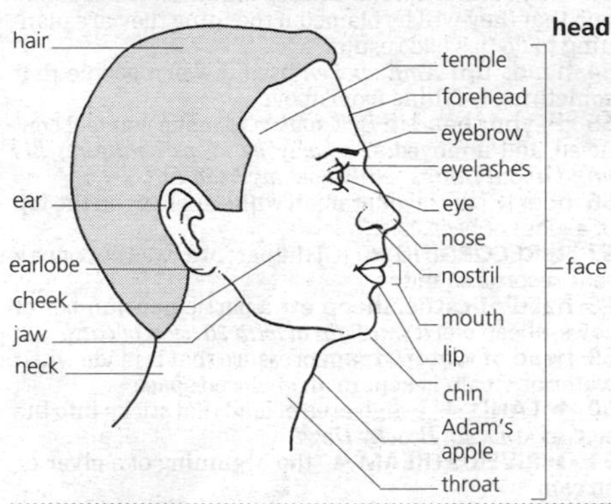


### ① TOP OF BODY
**1** [C] the top part of your body which has your eyes, mouth, brain etc in it: *My head aches.|He turned his head and looked at me.|severe head injuries*
**2 from head to foot/toe** over your whole body: *He was shaking from head to foot.|dressed in black from head to toe*
**3 a bad/sore head** *informal* a pain in your head: *I woke up with a bad head the next morning.*
**4 have a good/fine head of hair** to have a lot of hair on your head

### ② MIND
**5** [C] your mind: *My head was full of strange thoughts.*| **in/inside sb's head** *All the details are in my head.*| **do sth in your head** (=calculate something in your mind) *I can do the figures in my head.*
**6 sth never entered sb's head** used to say that you never thought of something: *"Do you think she's crazy?" "The thought never entered my head!"*
**7 don't bother/trouble your head about it** *spoken* used to tell someone not to worry about something
**8 put sth out of your head** *spoken* to stop worrying about something
**9 can't get something out of your head** to be unable to stop thinking about something
**10 put your heads together** *informal* to discuss a difficult problem together: *We'll gave to put our heads together and see if we can come up with some ideas.*
**11 have your head in the clouds** to spend too much time thinking about things that you would like to do

### ③ UNDERSTAND
**12 get your head round** *BrE informal* to understand something difficult
**13 can't make head nor tail of** to be completely unable to understand something: *I can't make head nor tail of this letter – does it mean anything to you?*
**14 go over your head** to be too difficult for you to understand: *The discussions went completely over my head.*
**15 get sth into your head** *informal* to understand and realize something: *I wish he'd get it into his head that I don't want to go out.*|**get sth into sb's head** (=make someone understand and realize something)

### ④ TOP PERSON
**16** [C] the leader or person in charge of a group or organization: [+ **of**] *Eileen is head of the family now.|the former head of the FBI, J Edgar Hoover*
**17 head waiter/chef/gardener etc** the most senior waiter etc
**18 ▶ OF A SCHOOL ◀** [C] *BrE informal* the teacher who is in charge of a school: **head teacher|the head** *We'll have to ask the head for permission.*

### ⑤ TOP/FRONT/MOST IMPORTANT PART
**19 the head of** the top or front of something, or the most important part of it: **at the head of** *Write your name clearly at the head of each page.*|**the head of the table** (=the part where the most important people sit) *Frank sat proudly at the head of the table.*
**20** [singular] the large or wide end of a long thin object such as a tool: [+ **of**] *the head of a hammer*
**21 ▶ PLANT ◀** [C] the top of a plant where its leaves and flowers grow

### ⑥ CALM
**22 keep your head** to remain calm in a difficult or dangerous situation: *a leader with a steady nerve and the ability to keep her head in a crisis*
**23 lose your head** to become too anxious to think or behave calmly: *When the engine caught fire, I just lost my head.*
**24 a clear/cool head** the ability to think clearly or calmly in a difficult or dangerous situation: *You need to approach this kind of emergency with a cool head.*

[continued on next page]

[continued from previous page]

⑦ **CRAZY**
**25 be out of your head/off your head** *BrE spoken* to be crazy
**26 not be right in the head** *spoken* to be mentally ill or crazy
**27 need your head examined** *spoken* to be crazy: *If you ask me, anyone who believes in UFO's needs their head examined!*

⑧ **INTELLIGENT/SENSIBLE**
**28 have your head screwed on (straight)** *informal* to be sensible
**29 have a good head on your shoulders** to be sensible or intelligent
**30 use your head** to think about something sensibly

⑨ **TOO PROUD**
**31 have a bighead** also **have a swollen head** *BrE informal* to think you are much better, more important, more skilful etc than you are
**32 go to sb's head** *informal* if success goes to someone's head, it makes them feel more important than they really are

⑩ **ALCOHOL/DRUGS**
**33 go to sb's head** to make someone quickly feel slightly drunk: *The wine went straight to my head.*
**34 be out of your head** *informal* to not know what you are doing because you have taken illegal drugs or drunk too much alcohol

⑪ **FOR EACH PERSON**
**35 a head/per head** for each person: **$5/£10 etc a head** *The meal worked out at $50 a head.*

⑫ **OTHER MEANINGS**
**36 ▶COIN◀ heads** the side of a coin which has the king's or queen's head on it—opposite **tails** (TAIL[1] (5a))
**37 keep your head above water** to only just manage to continue to live on your income or keep your business working inspite of money problems
**38 keep/get your head down** to work steadily and quietly: *He promised he would get his head down and work for his exams.*

**39 laugh/shout/scream your head off** *informal* to laugh, shout etc very loudly
**40 be banging your head against a brick wall** to keep trying to do something which seems impossible: *I feel as if I'm banging my head against a brick wall.*
**41 take it into your head to do sth** to suddenly decide to do something that does not seem sensible: *They suddenly took it into their heads to go off without telling anyone.*
**42 turn/stand sth on its head** to consider a statement or idea in the opposite way from the way in which it was intended
**43 give sb their head** to give someone the freedom to do what they want to do
**44 go head to head with** *AmE* to deal with someone in a very direct and determined way
**45 come/bring sth to a head** if a problem or difficult situation comes to a head, or if something brings it to a head, it suddenly becomes very bad: *The crisis came to a head when the bank refused to accept our cheques.*
**46 go over sb's head** to ask a more important person than the one you would normally ask: *My boss was angry because I went over his head to the department manager.*
**47 be over your head in debt** *AmE* to owe so much money that there is no possibility of paying it all back
**48 have a head for figures/facts/business etc** to be good at doing calculations, remembering facts etc
**49 have no head for heights** to be unable to look down from high places without feeling nervous
**50 head and shoulders above the rest/others** much better at something than everyone else
**51 head over heels in love** loving someone very much: *Sam was obviously head over heels in love with his new bride.*
**52 heads will roll** *spoken* used to say that some people will be punished severely for something that has happened
**53 on your own head be it** *spoken* used to tell someone that they will be blamed if the thing they are planning to do has bad results
**54 heads up!** *AmE spoken* used to warn people that something is falling from above
**55 do your head in** *BrE spoken* to make you feel confused and annoyed: *The way he keeps changing his mind about things really does my head in.*
**56 beer** [C] the layer of small white BUBBLES on the top of a glass of beer
**57 ▶RECORDING◀** [C] the part of a TAPE RECORDER that records sound
**58 head of cattle/sheep etc** a particular number of cows, sheep etc: *a small farm with 20 head of cattle*
**59 head of water/steam** pressure that is made when water or steam is kept in an enclosed space
**60 ▶LAND◀** a high area of land that sticks into the sea; HEADLAND: *Beachy Head*
**61 ▶RIVER/STREAM◀** the beginning of a river or stream
**62 ▶INFECTION◀** [C] the white centre of a swollen spot on your skin —see also **bite sb's head off** (BITE[1] (9)), **bury your head in the sand** (BURY (11)), **hold your head high/hold up your head** (HOLD[1] (38)), **nod your head** (NOD[1] (1)), **off the top of your head** (TOP[1] (16)), **shake your head** (SHAKE[1] (4)), **turn sb's head** (TURN[1] (21)), **standing on your head** (STAND[1] (38))

S2 W2 **head**[2] *v*
**1 ▶GO TOWARDS◀** [I] to go or make something go in a particular direction: **[+ for/towards/across etc]** *The ship was heading for Cuba.* | *It's about time we were heading home.* | **head north/south etc** *We headed south towards the capital.* | **be headed (for)** *especially AmE*: *Where are you guys headed?*
**2 ▶BE IN CHARGE◀** also **head up** [T] to be in charge of a government, organization, or group of people: *a delegation headed by former President Jimmy Carter*
**3 be heading for** also **be headed for** *especially AmE* if you are heading for a situation, it is likely to happen to you: *They're heading for disaster.*
**4 ▶BE AT THE TOP◀** [T] **a)** to be at the top of a list or group of people or things: *The movie heads the list of Oscar nominations.* **b) be headed** if a page is headed with a particular word or sentence, it has it on the top: *The page was headed 'Expenses'.*
**5 ▶BE AT THE FRONT◀** to be at the front of a line of people: *a procession headed by the Reverend Martin Luther King*
**6 ▶FOOTBALL◀** [T] to hit the ball with your head, especially in football —see picture on page 1264

**head off** *phr v* **1** [T **head** sth ↔ **off**] to prevent something from happening: *They've headed off several crises since they took charge.* **2** [T **head** sth ↔ **off**] to stop someone moving in a particular direction by moving in front of them: *Soldiers headed them off at the border.* **3** [I] to leave to go to another place: *I'm heading off now.*

**head·ache** /ˈhedeɪk/ *n* [C] **1** a pain in your head: **splitting headache** (=a very bad headache) **2** *informal* an annoying or worrying problem: *Censorship was a constant headache for Soviet newspapers.* —**headachy** *adj*: *a headachy feeling*

**head·band** /ˈhedbænd/ *n* [C] **1** a band that you wear around your head to keep your hair off your face **2** a similar band around a horse's head —see picture at HORSE[1]

**head·bang·er** /'hedbæŋə‖-ər/ *n* [C] **1** *informal* someone who enjoys HEAVY METAL music and moves their head around violently to the beat of the music **2** someone who behaves in a stupid or crazy way

**head·board** /'hedbɔːd‖-bɔːrd/ *n* [C] the upright wooden board at the end of a bed where your head is

**head boy** /ˌ· '·/ *n* [C] the boy who is chosen in a British school each year to represent the school

**head·butt** /'hedbʌt/ *v* [T] to deliberately hit someone in the stomach with your head

**head·case** /'hedkeɪs/ *n* [C] *slang* a crazy person

**head·cheese** /'hedtʃiːz/ *n* [U] *AmE* meat from the head of a pig boiled and pressed, BRAWN (2) *BrE*

**head count** /'· ·/ *n* **do a head count** to count how many people are present

**head·dress** /'hed-dres/ *n* [C] something that someone wears on their head for decoration on a special occasion: *a feathered headdress*

**head·ed** /'hedʒd/ *adj* **1 two-headed/three-headed etc** having two heads etc **2 headed notepaper** paper for writing letters that has your name and address printed at the top **3 red-headed/grey-headed etc** having red hair etc

**head·er** /'hedə‖-ər/ *n* [C] **1** a shot in football made by hitting the ball with your head **2** the top of a page, especially on a computer **3 take a header** to jump or fall into water with your head going in first

**head-first** /ˌ· '·◂/ *adv* **1** moving forward with the rest of your body following your head: **fall/plunge head-first** *I fell head-first down the stairs.* **2** if you rush into something head-first, you start doing it too quickly without thinking carefully

**head·gear** /'hedgɪə‖-ər/ *n* [U] *informal* hats and other things that you wear on your head

**head girl** /ˌ· '·/ *n* [C] the girl who is chosen in a British school each year to represent the school

**head-hunt·er** /'· ˌ··/ *n* [C] **1** someone who finds people with the right skills and experience to do a particular job, and persuades them to leave their present jobs **2** a member of a tribe of people who cut off and keep the heads of their enemies —**headhunt** *v* [T]

**head·ing** /'hedɪŋ/ *n* [C] the title written at the top of a piece of writing

**head·lamp** /'hedlæmp/ *n* [C usually plural] a HEADLIGHT

**head·land** /'hedlənd/ *n* [C] an area of land that sticks out from the coast into the sea —see picture on page 835

**head·less** /'hedləs/ *adj* without a head: *a headless corpse*

**head·light** /'hedlaɪt/ *n* [C usually plural] one of the large lights at the front of a vehicle —see picture on page 409

S3 **head·line**[1] /'hedlaɪn/ *n* [C usually plural] **1** the title of a newspaper report, which is printed in large letters above the report: *an eye-catching headline* **2 the headlines** the important points of the main news stories that are read at the beginning of a news programme **3 hit the headlines/make the headlines** to be reported in newspapers or on radio and television: *Computer crime first hit the headlines in 1983.*

**headline**[2] *v* [T] **1** [usually passive] to give a headline to an article or story **2** *AmE* to appear as the main performer in a show: *Frank Sinatra headlines this month's production.*

**head·lock** /'hedlɒk‖-lɑːk/ *n* [C] a way of holding someone around their neck so that they cannot move

**head·long** /'hedlɒŋ‖-lɔːŋ/ *adv* **1** if you rush headlong into something, you start doing it too quickly without thinking carefully: **rush headlong into** *Martin just isn't the type to rush headlong into marriage.* **2** falling with your head first and the rest of your body following **3** running very quickly without looking where you are going: *He fled headlong down a narrow passageway.* —**headlong** *adj*: *a headlong dash for the frontier*

**head·man** /'hedmən/ *n plural* **headmen** /-mən/ [C] a chief of a village where a tribe lives

**head·mas·ter** /ˌhed'mɑːstə‖'hedˌmæstər/ *n* [C] *BrE* a male teacher who is in charge of a school

**head·mis·tress** /ˌhed'mɪstrɪ̆s‖'hedˌmɪs-/ *n* [C] *BrE* a female teacher who is in charge of a school

**head of·fice** /ˌ· '··/ *n* **1** [C] the main office of a company **2** [singular] the managers who work there

**head of state** /ˌ· ·'·/ *n* [C] the main representative of a country, such as a queen, king, or president

**head-on** /ˌ· '·◂/ *adv* **1 meet/crash etc head-on** if two vehicles meet head-on, the front part of one vehicle hits the front part of the other: *Their car collided head-on with a van.* **2** if someone deals with a problem head-on, they deal with it in a direct and determined way: *It would be best to tackle the situation head-on.* —**head-on** *adj*: *a head-on collision*

**head·phones** /'hedfəʊnz‖-foʊnz/ *n* [plural] a piece of equipment that you wear over your ears to listen to a radio or recording

**head·piece** /'hedpiːs/ *n* [C] **1** something you wear on your head for protection **2** a decorated title at the top of a page or piece of writing

**head·quar·tered** /'hedˌkwɔːtəd, hed'kwɔːtəd‖-ɔːrtərd/ *adj* having your headquarters at a particular place: *Many top companies are headquartered here.* —**headquarter** *v* [T]

**head·quar·ters** /'hedˌkwɔːtəz, ˌhed'kwɔːtəz‖-ɔːrtərz/ *n* *plural* **headquarters** [C] **1** the main building or offices used by a large organization **2** *abbreviation* **HQ** the place from which military operations are controlled W3

**head·rest** /'hed-rest/ *n* [C] the top part of a chair or of the front seat in a car that supports the back of your head —see picture on page 409

**head·room** /'hed-rʊm, -ruːm/ *n* [U] **1** the amount of space above your head, especially when you are in a car **2** the amount of space above a vehicle when it is under a bridge

**head·scarf** /'hedskɑːf‖-skɑːrf/ *n* [C] a square piece of cloth that women wear on their heads, tied under their chin —see picture at SCARF[1]

**head·set** /'hedset/ *n* [C] a set of HEADPHONES

**head·ship** /'hedʃɪp/ *n* [C] **1** a position of being in charge of an organization **2** *BrE* the job of being in charge of a school

**head·shrink·er** /'hedˌʃrɪŋkə‖-ər/ *n* [C] *informal* a PSYCHIATRIST or PSYCHOANALYST

**head·square** /'hedskweə‖-skwer/ *n* [C] a HEADSCARF

**head·stand** /'hedstænd/ *n* [C] a position in which you turn your body upside down, with your head and hands on the floor and your legs and feet in the air

**head start** /'· ·/ *n* [C] **1** an advantage that helps you to be successful: *Give your children a head start by sending them to nursery school.* **2** a start in a race in which you begin earlier or further ahead than someone else

**head·stone** /'hedstəʊn‖-stoʊn/ *n* [C] a piece of stone on a grave on which the dead person's name is written; GRAVESTONE, TOMBSTONE

**head·strong** /'hedstrɒŋ‖-strɒːŋ/ *adj* very determined to do what you want, even when other people advise you not to do it: *an impuslive headstrong child*

**head ta·ble** /ˌ· '··/ *n* [C] *AmE* a table at a formal meal where the most important people or those giving speeches sit; TOP TABLE *BrE*

**head teach·er** /ˌ· '··/ *n* [C] *BrE* the teacher who is in charge of a school; PRINCIPAL[2] (2) *AmE*

**head wait·er** /ˌ· '··/ *n* [C] the WAITER who is in charge of the other waiters in a restaurant —see picture on page 838

**head·wa·ters** /'hedwɔːtəz‖-wɒːtərz,-wɑː-/ *n* [plural] the part where a stream starts before it flows into a river

**head·way** /'hedweɪ/ *n* **make headway a)** to make progress towards achieving something in spite of difficulties: [+ **towards/in/with etc**] *They had made no headway towards finding a solution.* **b)** to move forwards

H

**head·wind** /ˈhedˌwɪnd/ *n* [C,U] a wind that blows directly towards you when you are moving

**head·word** /ˈhedwɜːd‖-wɜːrd/ *n* [C] one of the words whose meaning is explained in a dictionary

**head·y** /ˈhedi/ *adj* [usually before noun] **1** a heady smell, drink, etc is pleasantly strong and seems to affect your senses: *a heady aroma*|*a heady combination of wine and brandy* **2** very exciting in a way that makes you feel as if you can do anything you want to: *the heady atmosphere of the early sixties*

**heal** /hiːl/ *v* **1** [I] also **heal up** if a wound or a broken bone heals, the flesh, skin, bone etc grows back together and becomes healthy again: *It took three months for my arm to heal properly.* **2** [T] to cure someone who is ill or make a wound heal **3 heal the wounds/breach/divisions** to make people stop being angry with each other —see also FAITH HEALING

**heal over** *phr v* [I] **1** if a wound or an area of broken skin heals over, new skin grows over it and it becomes healthy again **2** [I,T] if an argument heals over or is healed over, it is forgotten

**heal·er** /ˈhiːlə‖-ər/ *n* [C] someone who is believed to have the natural ability to cure people

S1 W1 **health** /helθ/ *n* [U] **1** your physical condition and how healthy you are: *Betty's anxious about her husband's health.*|*Smoking can seriously damage your health.*|**be in good/excellent/poor health** (=be generally healthy or unhealthy)|**be good/bad for your health** *A low-fat diet is better for your health.* **2** the state of being healthy: *Even if you haven't got much money, at least you've got your health.*|**sb is a picture of health** (=used to say that someone looks very healthy) **3** the work of providing medical services to keep people healthy: *The government has promised to spend more on health and education.* **4** how successful an economy or organization is: *The monthly trade figures are seen as an indicator of the health of the economy.* **5 drink (to) sb's health** to say that you wish someone will be healthy and happy, and then have a drink of alcohol

**health and safe·ty** /ˌ· · ˈ··/ *n* [U] an area of government and law concerned with people's health and safety, especially at work

**health care** /ˈ· ·/ *n* [U] the service of looking after the health of all the people in a country or an area

**health cen·ter** /ˈ· ˌ··/ *n* [C] *AmE* a building where students go to get medical help or advice

**health cen·tre** /ˈ· ˌ··/ *n* [C] *BrE* a building where several doctors have offices

**health club** /ˈ· ·/ *n* [C] a private club where people can go to exercise in order to become physically stronger and more attractive

**health farm** /ˈ· ·/ *n* [C] a place where people pay to stay so that they can lose weight

**health food** /ˈ· ·/ *n* [C,U] food that contains only natural substances

**health·ful** /ˈhelθfəl/ *adj AmE* likely to make you healthy: *healthful mountain air*

**health vis·it·or** /ˈ· ˌ···/ *n* [C] a nurse in Britain who visits people in their homes

S3 W3 **health·y** /ˈhelθi/ *adj*

**1 ▶ PERSON/ANIMAL ◀** physically strong and not likely to become ill: *a healthy baby boy*|*I've always been perfectly healthy until now.*

**2 ▶ MAKING YOU HEALTHY ◀** likely to make you healthy: *a healthy diet*

**3 ▶ GOOD FOR YOUR CHARACTER ◀** [usually in questions or negatives] good for someone's mind or character: *I don't think it's healthy for her to spend so much time alone.*

**4 ▶ SHOWING GOOD HEALTH ◀** showing that you are healthy: *Her face had a healthy glow.*|*a healthy skin*|**a healthy appetite** (=a desire to eat a lot)

**5 ▶ COMPANY/SOCIETY ETC ◀** a healthy company, society, economic system etc is working effectively and successfully: *The economy is looking quite healthy now.*

**6 a healthy respect/contempt/curiosity etc** a natural and sensible feeling: *a healthy contempt for silly regulations*

**7 ▶ AMOUNT ◀** large and showing that someone is successful: *By the end of the year we should make a healthy profit.* —**healthily** *adv* —**healthiness** *n* [U]

**heap¹** /hiːp/ *n* [C] **1** a large untidy pile of things: *a rubbish heap*|**[+ of]** *heaps of dead leaves*|**in heaps** *Dirty clothes lay in heaps on the floor.* **2 heaps of** *informal* a lot of something: *Don't worry, we've got heaps of time.* **3** *humorous* an old car that is in bad condition **4 fall/collapse in a heap** to fall down and lie without moving **5 be struck/knocked all of a heap** *BrE old-fashioned informal* to be suddenly very surprised or confused

**heap²** *v* [T] **1** also **heap up** to put a lot of things on top of each other in an untidy way: *The ashes from the fire were heaped in a huge pile.*|**heap sth on/onto** *They had heaped all the rubbish onto the back of the truck.* **2 be heaped with** if a plate is heaped with food, it has a lot on it **3 heap praises/insults etc on** to praise, insult etc someone a lot

**heaped** /hiːpt/ *adj* **heaped teaspoon/tablespoon etc** an amount of something that is as much as a spoon can hold: *Add 3 heaped teaspoons of sugar.*

**heaps** /hiːps/ *adv* **heaps better/bigger etc** *informal* much better, bigger etc

**hear**

Joe can't hear the phone ringing because he's listening to music.

**hear** /hɪə‖hɪr/ *v past tense and past participle* **heard** /hɜːd‖hɜːrd/ S1 W1

**1 ▶ HEAR SOUNDS/WORDS ETC ◀** [I,T not in progressive] to know that a sound is being made, using your ears: *Did you hear that noise?*|*I called his name, but he pretended not to hear.*|**hear sb/sth doing sth** *I think I can hear someone knocking.*|**hear sb/sth do sth** *Dixon's going to resign – I heard him say so.*|**hear what** *I'm sorry, I didn't hear what you said.*|**be heard to say/ask/remark etc** *One delegate was heard to remark that the conference had been a waste of time.*

**2 ▶ LISTEN TO SB/STH ◀** [T not usually in progressive] to listen to what someone is saying, the music they are playing etc: *Without waiting to hear her answer, he stood up and walked away.*|*You can hear that broadcast again on Monday at 9.00.*|**hear sb do sth** *Pavarotti is amazing – you should hear him sing 'Nessun dorma'.*|**hear what** *Let's hear what he's got to say.*|**I hear what you're saying** *spoken* (=used to tell someone that you have listened to their opinion) *I hear what you're saying, but we can't ignore the facts.*

**3 ▶ BE TOLD STH ◀** [I,T not usually in progressive] to be told or find out a piece of information: **hear (that)** *I hear you've been selected to play for the A team.*|**[+ about]** *Did you hear about the fire?*|**be glad/pleased to hear (that)** *I'm glad to hear your sister's feeling better.*|**so I've heard** *spoken* (=used to say that you already know about something) *"Nina's quit her job." "Yes, so I've heard."*|**hear sth** *We've heard such a lot about you.*|**hear what/how/who etc** *When the authorities heard what we were planning, they tried to stop us.*|**hear anything of** (=receive any news about) *Have you heard anything of Bob lately?*|**hear sth on the grapevine** (=find out

about something in conversation)|**I've heard it said** *spoken* also **I've heard tell** *old-fashioned* (=used when you are repeating something that someone else has told you) *I've heard it said she's a tough businesswoman.*
**4 ▶ IN COURT ◀ hear a case** if a court or a committee hears a case, they listen to all the evidence in order to make a decision: *The case was heard at Teeside Crown Court on April 10.*
**5 I won't hear of it** *spoken* used to say that someone should not do something, especially because you want to help them: *I've offered to pay Simon for fixing my car, but he won't hear of it.*
**6 I/we haven't heard the last of** *spoken* used to say that someone or something will cause more problems for you: *I'm sure we haven't heard the last of that woman.*
**7 I'll/he'll etc never hear the end of it** *spoken* used to say that someone will criticize or make jokes about something you have done: *If my Mum finds out, I'll never hear the end of it.*
**8 be hearing things** to imagine you can hear a sound when really there is no sound: **I must be hearing things** *I must be hearing things, I could have sworn you just called my name.*
**9 (do) you hear me?** *spoken* used when you are giving someone an order and want to be certain that they will obey you: *Now you go straight home. You hear me?*
**10 now hear this!** *AmE old use* used to introduce an important official announcement
**11 you could hear a pin drop** used to say that a place was extremely quiet: *After she finished telling her story you could have heard a pin drop.*
**12 I can't hear myself think** *spoken* used to say that the place where you are is too noisy
**13 have you heard the one about...** used when asking someone if they know a joke: *Have you heard the one about the turtle and the elephant?*
**14 I've heard that one before** *spoken* used when you do not believe someone's excuse or explanation: *Kept late at the office, were you? I've heard that one before.*

**hear from** sb *phr v* [T not in progressive] **1** to receive news from someone, usually by letter: *Have you heard from Sarah lately?*|**I look forward to hearing from you** (=used at the end of a letter) **2** to listen to someone giving their opinion in a radio or television discussion programme: *And now we are going to hear from some of the victims of violent crime.*

**hear of** sb/sth *phr v* [T] **1 have heard of** to know that someone or something exists because you have been told about them: *I've never heard of him!* **2** [not in progressive] to get news or information about someone or something: **she/he was last heard of** (=the last time people say they saw someone) *He was last heard of in Lansing, Michigan in 1935.* —compare **hear from** (HEAR) —see also UNHEARD-OF

**hear** sb **out** *phr v* [T not in passive] to listen to all of what someone wants to tell you without interrupting them: *Look, I know you're angry but you could at least hear me out.*

**Hear! Hear!** /ˌ· ˈ·/ *interjection especially BrE* used in parliament or in a meeting to say that you agree with the person who is speaking

**hear·er** /ˈhɪərə‖ˈhɪrər/ *n* [C] someone who hears something

S3 W2 **hear·ing** /ˈhɪərɪŋ‖ˈhɪr-/ *n* **1** [U] the sense which you use to hear sounds: *Speak up, please. My hearing is not too good.* —see also HARD OF HEARING **2** [C] a meeting of a court or special committee to find out the facts about a case **3 give sb a (fair) hearing** to give someone an opportunity to explain their actions, ideas, or opinions **4 in/within sb's hearing** if you say something in someone's hearing, you say it where they can hear you: *Don't mention that in John's hearing or he'll go crazy.*

**hearing aid** /ˈ·· ·/ *n* [C] a small thing which fits into or behind your ear to make sounds louder, worn by people who cannot hear well

**hear·ken, harken** /ˈhɑːkən‖ˈhɑːr-/ *v* [I + **to**] *literary* to listen

**hear·say** /ˈhɪəseɪ‖ˈhɪr-/ *n* [U] something that you have heard about from other people but do not know to be definitely true or correct: *I wouldn't take any notice of it, it's just hearsay.*

**hearse** /hɜːs‖hɜːrs/ *n* [C] a large car used to carry a dead body in a COFFIN at a funeral

**heart** /hɑːt‖hɑːrt/ *n* S1 W1
**1 ▶ BODY ORGAN ◀** [C] the organ in your chest which pumps blood through your body: *Eating too many fatty foods is bad for the heart.*|*My heart was beating so fast I thought it would burst.*|**have heart trouble/have a heart condition** (=have problems with your heart)|**a weak heart** (=an unhealthy heart) —see picture at RESPIRATORY
**2 ▶ EMOTIONS/LOVE ◀** [C] *especially literary* the part of your body that feels strong emotions and feelings: *My head said no, but my heart kept saying yes.*|**affairs of the heart** (=matters connected with love)|**(deep) in your heart** (=used when saying what someone really feels) *She still loved him, deep down in her heart.*|**heart and soul** (=completely) *You love the boy heart and soul, don't you?*|**break sb's heart** (=to make someone extremely sad, especially by ending a romantic relationship with them)
**3 ▶ YOUR CHEST ◀** [C usually singular] the part of your chest near your heart: *He put his hand across his heart to show where the pain was.*
**4 ▶ SHAPE ◀** [C] a shape used to represent a heart —see picture at SHAPE[1]
**5 from the heart** if you say or mean something from the heart, you really mean it or feel it very strongly: *He spoke simply but from the heart.*|**from the bottom of my heart** *I want to thank you from the bottom of my heart.*|**straight from the heart** *What she said came straight from the heart.*
**6 in your heart of hearts** if you know, feel, or believe something in your heart of hearts, you are secretly sure about it although you may not admit it: *Claire knew in her heart of hearts that she would never go back there.*
**7 ▶ IMPORTANT PART OF STH ◀** the most important part of a problem, question etc: **get to the heart of the matter/problem/question etc** *The new book gets to the heart of the controversy over nuclear power.*
**8 ▶ THE MIDDLE PART OF AN AREA ◀** [C] the middle of an area: **in the heart of** *somewhere deep in the heart of Texas*
**9 know/learn something by heart** to know or learn something so that you can remember all of it: *You have to know all the music by heart.*
**10 set your heart on** to want something very much: *The coach had set his heart on winning.*
**11 a)** [C] **▶ CARD GAMES ◀** a heart shape printed in red on a playing card **b) hearts** [plural] the SUIT (=set) of playing cards that have these shapes on them: *the ace of hearts* **c)** [C] one of the cards in this set: *Have you got any hearts?*
**12 kind-hearted/cold-hearted/hard-hearted etc** having a kind, unkind, cruel etc character
**13 have a heart of gold** to be very kind
**14 have a heart of stone** to be very cruel or unsympathetic
**15 a man/woman after my own heart** someone who likes the same things or behaves in the same way that you do: *Geoff was clear-thinking and decisive – a man after my own heart.*
**16 at heart** if you are a particular kind of person at heart, that is the kind of person that you really are: *I've always been a country boy at heart.* —see also **have sb's (best) interests at heart** (INTEREST[1] (5)), **young at heart** (YOUNG[1] (4))
**17 close/dear to sb's heart** very important to someone
**18 my/his/her heart leapt** *literary* used to say that someone suddenly felt happy and full of hope
**19 my/his etc heart sank** used to say that someone

suddenly lost hope and began to feel sad: *Our hearts sank when we heard the results of the voting.*
**20 my heart was in my mouth** used to say that you suddenly felt very afraid
**21 my heart bleeds (for sb)** used to say that you do not really feel any sympathy towards someone: *"He's had to sell his Ferrari." "My heart bleeds for him."*
**22 my/his/her heart goes out to sb** used to say that someone feels a lot of sympathy towards another person
**23 my/his/her heart isn't in it** used to say that someone does not really want to do something: *I tried to join in the fun, but somehow my heart wasn't in it.*
**24 not have the heart to do something** to be unable to do something because it will make someone unhappy: *I didn't have the heart to tell my daughter we couldn't keep the puppy.*
**25 be in good heart** *formal* to feel cheerful and confident: *Our troops are in good heart and ready for action.*
**26 take heart** to feel encouraged: *We took heart when we saw the sign, knowing that we were close to home.*
**27 take sth to heart** to be very upset by something that someone says or does to you: *Don't take her criticisms so much to heart.*
**28 do sth to your heart's content** to do something as much as you want: *After I leave, Joe can sing in the shower to his heart's content.*
**29 it does your heart good to see/hear** used to say that something makes you feel happy: *It does my heart good to see him running around again.*
**30 have a heart!** *often humorous* used to tell someone not to be too strict or unkind
**31 with all your heart** with all your strength, energy or emotion: *Ben hated school with all his heart.*
**32 have your heart's desire/have everything your heart could desire** to get everything that you could possibly want
**33 know the way to sb's heart** *humorous* to know the way to please someone: *What a great meal!You certainly know the way to a man's heart!*
**34 ► VEGETABLE ◄** [C] the firm middle part of some vegetables: *artichoke hearts*
**35 his/her heart is in the right place** *informal* used to say that someone is really a kind person, even though they may not appear to be: *He's a little grouchy sometimes, but his heart's in the right place.* —see also **a broken heart** (BROKEN² (10)), **cross my heart** (CROSS¹ (9)), **eat your heart out** (EAT (2)), **have a change of heart** (CHANGE² (1)), **sick at heart** (SICK¹ (9)), **strike at the heart of** (STRIKE¹ (9)), **wear your heart on your sleeve** (WEAR¹ (10)), **win sb's heart** (WIN¹ (3)), **with a heavy heart** (HEAVY¹ (25))

**heart·ache** /ˈhɑːteɪk‖ˈhɑːrt-/ *n* [U] a strong feeling of great sadness and anxiety

**heart at·tack** /ˈ· ·ˌ·/ *n* [C] a sudden serious medical condition in which someone's heart stops working, causing them great pain

**heart·beat** /ˈhɑːtbiːt‖ˈhɑːrt-/ *n* [C,U] the action or sound of your heart as it pumps blood through your body: *the amount of blood pumped by each heartbeat*

**heart·break** /ˈhɑːtbreɪk‖ˈhɑːrt-/ *n* [U] great sadness or disappointment

**heart·break·ing** /ˈhɑːtˌbreɪkɪŋ‖ˈhɑːrt-/ *adj* making you feel extremely sad or disappointed: *heartbreaking pictures of starving children* —**heartbreakingly** *adv*

**heart·brok·en** /ˈhɑːtˌbrəʊkən‖ˈhɑːrtˌbroʊ-/ *adj* extremely sad because of something that has happened: *When her parents split up she was heartbroken.*

**heart·burn** /ˈhɑːtbɜːn‖ˈhɑːrtbɜːrn/ *n* [U] an unpleasant burning feeling in your stomach or chest caused by INDIGESTION

**heart dis·ease** /ˈ· ·ˌ·/ *n* [C,U] an illness which prevents someone's heart from working normally

**heart·en** /ˈhɑːtn‖ˈhɑːr-/ *v* [T usually passive] to make someone feel happier and more hopeful: *I was heartened by the news that the operation had been a success.* —**heartening** *adj* —**hearteningly** *adv* —opposite DISHEARTEN

**heart fail·ure** /ˈ· ˌ··/ *n* [U] a serious medical condition in which someone's heart stops, often resulting in death

**heart·felt** /ˈhɑːtfelt‖ˈhɑːrt-/ *adj* very strongly felt and sincere: *a heartfelt apology*

**hearth** /hɑːθ‖hɑːrθ/ *n* [C] **1** the area of floor around a FIREPLACE in a house **2 hearth and home** *literary* your home and family: *the joys of hearth and home*

**heart·i·ly** /ˈhɑːtɪ̮li‖ˈhɑːr-/ *adv* **1** loudly and cheerfully: *He laughed heartily and embraced his brother.* **2** completely or very much: **heartily agree/approve of/support etc** *a sentiment with which she heartily agreed* | **heartily fed up with/sick of** *By the end we were heartily fed up with the whole thing.* **3 eat/drink heartily** to eat or drink a large amount

**heart·land** /ˈhɑːtlənd‖ˈhɑːrt-/ *n* [C] **1 the heartland** the central part of a country or area of land: *in the Russian heartland* **2** the most important part of a country or area for a particular activity, or the part where a political group has most support: *the Democratic heartlands of the Deep South*

**heart·less** /ˈhɑːtləs‖ˈhɑːrt-/ *adj* not feeling any pity: *How can you be so heartless?* —**heartlessly** *adv* —**heartlessness** *n* [U]

**heart-lung ma·chine** /ˌ· ˈ· ·ˌ·/ *n* [C] a machine that pumps blood and oxgyen around someone's body during a medical operation

**heart·rend·ing** /ˈhɑːtˌrendɪŋ‖ˈhɑːrt-/ *adj* making you feel great pity: *heartrending stories of children being taken from their parents*

**heart-search·ing** /ˈ· ˌ··/ *n* [U] the process of examining very carefully your feelings about something or your reasons for doing something

**heart·sick** /ˈhɑːtˌsɪk‖ˈhɑːrt-/ *adj* very unhappy or disappointed

**heart·strings** /ˈhɑːtˌstrɪŋz‖ˈhɑːrt-/ *n* [plural] **tug/tear at sb's heartstrings** to make someone feel strong love or sympathy

**heart·throb** /ˈhɑːtθrɒb‖ˈhɑːrtθrɑːb/ *n* [C] a famous actor, singer etc who is very attractive to women: *teenage heartthrobs 'Take That'*

**heart-to-heart** /ˌ· · ˈ·◂/ *n* [C] a conversation in which two people say honestly and sincerely what they really feel about something: *Why don't you have a heart-to-heart with him and sort out your problems?* —**heart-to-heart** *adj*

**heart·warm·ing** /ˈhɑːtˌwɔːmɪŋ‖ˈhɑːrtˌwɔːr-/ *adj* making you feel happy because you see other people being happy or kind to each other: *a heartwarming sight* —**heartwarmingly** *adv*

**heart·wood** /ˈhɑːtwʊd‖ˈhɑːrt-/ *n* [U] the older harder wood at the centre of a tree

**heart·y** /ˈhɑːti‖ˈhɑːrti/ *adj* **1** cheerfully friendly: *a hearty laugh* **2** *old-fashioned* strong and healthy —see also **hale and hearty** (HALE) **3** a hearty meal is very large **4** *especially BrE* with a friendly, noisy and cheerful manner that is not sincere —**heartiness** *n* [U] —see also HEARTILY

**heat¹** /hiːt/ *n* S W
**1** [U] warmth or hotness: *The heat of the water caused the glass to shatter.* | *Black surfaces absorb heat from the sun.*
**2 the heat a)** very hot weather: *I couldn't stand the heat.* | **the heat of the day** (=the hottest part of the day) **b)** *AmE* the system in a house that keeps it warm in the winter; HEATING *BrE*
**3** [C usually singular] the hot temperature of an OVEN or a heating system: *When the oven reaches the correct heat, the light goes off.* | **turn up/turn down the heat** *She turned up the heat on the cooker.*
**4 in the heat of the moment/argument/battle etc** while feeling angry or excited: *In the heat of the argument I said a few things I regret now.*

**5 take the heat out of the situation** to make a situation calmer and make people less angry and excited
**6 the heat is on/off** *spoken* used to say that a situation is very difficult, or that a difficult situation has now ended and you can relax
**7 on heat** also **in heat** *AmE* if a female animal is on heat, her body is ready to have sex with a male
**8 ►IN A RACE◄** [C] a part of a race or competition whose winners then compete against each other in the next part —see also DEAD HEAT, WHITE HEAT

**heat²** *v* [I,T] to make something become warm or hot: *Heat the milk until it boils.*
**heat up** *phr v* **1** [I,T] to become warm or hot or to make something become warm or hot: **heat sth ↔ up** *I heated up the remains of last night's supper.* | **heat up** *The stove takes a while to heat up.* **2** [I] if a situation heats up, it becomes dangerous or full of problems
**heat** sth **through** *phr v* [T] to heat food thoroughly

**heat·ed** /ˈhiːtɪ̈d/ *adj* **1** a heated SWIMMING POOL, room etc is made warm using a heater **2 heated argument/debate/discussion etc** an argument etc that is full of angry and excited feelings —**heatedly** *adv*

**heat·er** /ˈhiːtə‖-ər/ *n* [C] a machine for making air or water hotter: *Did you turn the heater off?* —see picture on page 409

**heat ex·haus·tion** /ˈ· ·ˌ··/ *n* [U] weakness and sickness caused by doing too much work, exercise etc when it is hot

**heath** /hiːθ/ *n* [C] an area of open land where grass, bushes, and other small plants grow

**hea·then¹** /ˈhiːðən/ *adj old-fashioned* not connected with or belonging to the Christian religion or any of the large established religions

**heathen²** *n old use* **1 the heathen** *old-fashioned* people who are heathen **2** [C] *old-fashioned* someone who is heathen **3** [singular] *often humorous* someone who refuses to believe in something

**heath·er** /ˈheðə‖-ər/ *n* [U] a low plant with small purple, pink, or white flowers which grows on hills

**Heath Rob·in·son** /ˌhiːθ ˈrɒbɪ̈nsən‖-ˈrɑː-/ *adj BrE* a Heath Robinson machine, system etc is very complicated in an amusing way but not at all practical; RUBE GOLDBERG *AmE*

S2 **heat·ing** /ˈhiːtɪŋ/ *n* [U] *BrE* a system for heating a room or building warm; the heat *AmE*: *a huge heating bill* —see also CENTRAL HEATING

**heat light·ning** /ˈ· ˌ··/ *n* [U] *especially AmE* LIGHTNING¹ (1) without THUNDER or rain

**heat·proof** /ˈhiːtpruːf/ *adj* heatproof material cannot be damaged by heat

**heat pump** /ˈ· ·/ *n* [C] part of a machine that takes heat from one place to another

**heat rash** /ˈ· ·/ *n* [C,U] painful or ITCHY red spots on someone's skin caused by heat

**heat-re·sist·ant** /ˈ· ·ˌ··/ *adj* not easily damaged by heat

**heat-seek·ing** /ˈ· ··/ *adj* a heat-seeking weapon is able to find and move towards the hot gases from an aircraft or ROCKET and destroy it

**heat·stroke** /ˈhiːtstrəʊk‖-stroʊk/ *n* [U] fever and weakness caused by being outside in the heat of the sun for too long —compare SUNSTROKE

**heat wave** /ˈ· ·/ *n* [C] a period of unusually hot weather, especially one that continues for a long time

**heave¹** /hiːv/ *v* **1** [I,T] to pull or lift something very heavy with one great effort: **heave sth onto/into/towards etc** *He heaved the pack up onto his back.* | *We heaved with all our strength but couldn't shift the old piano.* | **heave at/on sth** *He heaved on the rope with all his strength.* **2** [T] to throw something heavy using a lot of effort **3 heave a sigh** to breathe out noisily and slowly once, because you are pleased or disappointed: *She heard him heave a great sigh and then saw that he was crying.* | **heave a sigh of relief** *Paolo heaved a great sigh of relief when he heard that she had returned.* **4** [I] if the sea or someone's chest heaves, it moves up and down with very strong movements: *Brigg's chest was heaving with exhaustion.* **5** [I] *informal* to VOMIT (1) **6 heave into sight/view** *past tense and past participle* **hove** to appear, especially by getting closer from a distance: *A few moments later a barge hove into view.* —see also HEAVING
**heave to** *phr v past tense* **hove to** /ˌhəʊv ˈtuː‖ˌhoʊv-/ [I] *technical* if a ship heaves to, it stops moving

**heave²** *n* **1** [C] a strong pulling, pushing, or lifting movement: *He gave the door a good heave.* **2** [U] *literary* a strong rising or falling movement

**heave-ho** /ˌ· ˈ·/ *interjection* **1** *old-fashioned* used as an encouragement to a person or group of people who are pulling something, especially on ships **2 give someone the (old) heave-ho** *informal* to end a relationship with someone, or to make someone leave their job

**heav·en** /ˈhevən/ *n* **1** also **Heaven** [singular] the place where God is believed to live and where good people are believed to go when they die **2** [U] *informal* a very good situation or place: **sheer heaven** (=perfect heaven) *It was sheer heaven being able to stay in bed all day!* | **heaven on earth** *I had imagined that being married to Max would be heaven on earth.* **3 for heaven's sake** *spoken* **a)** used to show that you are annoyed or angry: *Oh, for Heaven's sake! Do they have to make so much noise?* **b)** used to emphasize a question or request: *For heaven's sake don't tell Simon about this!* **4 heaven forbid** *spoken* used to say that you very much hope something will not happen: *"Will your parents be coming to the party?" "Heaven forbid!"* **5 heaven help** *spoken* **a)** used to say that you will be very angry with someone if they do something: *Heaven help him if he ever comes back here again!* **b)** used to say that it is dangerous to do something: *Heaven help anyone who goes in there at night.* **6 heaven (only) knows** *spoken* **a)** used to say that you do not know and cannot imagine what is happening or what will happen: *We used to keep in touch, but Heaven knows what they're all doing now.* **b)** used to emphasize what you are saying: *I just couldn't get him to stop gambling although heaven knows I tried hard enough.* **7 what/how/why etc in heaven's name** *spoken* used when asking a surprised and angry question: *What in heaven's name did you think you were doing?* **8 the heavens** *literary* the sky **9 the heavens opened** *especially literary* it started to rain very hard **10 move heaven and earth** to try very hard to achieve something —see also **be in seventh heaven** (SEVENTH (2)), **thank heaven(s)** (THANK (2)) S3

**heav·en·ly** /ˈhevənli/ *adj* **1** *old-fashioned* very beautiful, pleasant, or enjoyable: *What heavenly weather!* **2** [only before noun] *biblical* existing in or belonging to heaven: *a heavenly choir of angels* | **heavenly Father** (=God) | **the Heavenly Host** (=all the angels) **3** *literary* existing in or connected with the sky or stars

**heavenly bod·y** /ˌ··· ˈ··/ *n* [C] a star, PLANET or the moon

**Heav·ens!** /ˈhevənz/ also **Good Heavens!, Heavens a·bove!**, /ˌ·· ·ˈ·/ also **Heavens to Bet·sy!** /ˌhevənz tə ˈbetsi/ *AmE* —*interjection* used to express surprise, especially when you are annoyed: *Good Heavens what a mess!*

**heaven-sent** /ˌ·· ˈ·◂‖ˈ·· ·/ *adj* happening fortunately at exactly the right time: *a heaven-sent opportunity*

**heav·en·ward** /ˈhevənwəd‖-wərd/ also **heav·en·wards** /-wədz‖-wərdz/ *adv literary* towards the sky

**heav·ily** /ˈhevɪ̈li/ *adv* W3
**1 ►A LOT/IN LARGE AMOUNTS◄** a lot or in large amounts: *It's been raining heavily all day.* | **drink/smoke heavily** *Paul was drinking heavily by this time.*
**2 ►VERY◄** very or very much: **heavily dependent/reliant/influenced** *Japan is heavily dependent on imported oil from the Middle East.*
**3 ►SLEEP◄** if you sleep heavily, you cannot be woken easily: *Joe slept heavily for eight hours.*
**4 breathe heavily** to breathe slowly and loudly
**5 heavily built** having a large broad body that looks strong

H

**6 be heavily into** *informal* to do something a lot or be very interested in it: *Brenda's heavily into motorbikes.*
**7 ▶ SLOWLY ◀** if you do or say something heavily, you do it slowly, especially because you are sad or bored: *He was walking heavily, his head down.*

**hea·ving** /ˈhiːvɪŋ/ *adj BrE informal* very busy or full of people: [+ **with**] *The place was heaving with showbiz types.*

S1 W1 **heav·y**[1] /ˈhevi/ *adj* **heavier, heaviest**
**1 ▶ WEIGHT ◀** weighing a lot: *I can't lift this case – it's too heavy.* | *The baby seemed to be getting heavier and heavier in her arms.* | **how heavy?** (=how much does it weigh) *How heavy is the parcel?* —opposite LIGHT[3] (4)
**2 ▶ A LOT ◀ a)** a lot or in very large amounts: *The traffic was heavier than normal and I was late for work.* | **heavy rain/snow** *flooding caused by heavy rain over the weekend* | **heavy use/consumption** *the film's heavy use of special effects*
**3 heavy smoker/drinker** someone who smokes a lot or drinks a lot of alcohol
**4 ▶ SERIOUS/SEVERE ◀** serious or severe: *heavy winter storms* | *a heavy burden of responsibility* | **heavy fine/penalty** *heavy fines for possession of hard drugs* | **a heavy cold** (=a very bad cold) *She's in bed with a heavy cold.* | **heavy losses** *Most insurance companies suffered heavy losses last year.*
**5 ▶ NEEDING PHYSICAL EFFORT ◀** needing a lot of physical strength and effort: *heavy manual work*
**6 ▶ NEEDING MENTAL EFFORT ◀** not easy or entertaining and needing a lot of mental effort: *I want something to read on holiday – nothing too heavy.*
**7 heavy going** difficult to understand or deal with: **find sth heavy going** *I found Balzac's books pretty heavy going.*
**8 be heavy on** *informal* to use a lot or too much of something: *The car's rather heavy on oil.*
**9 heavy schedule/timetable/day etc** one in which you have a lot to do in a short time: *I'd had a heavy day at the office.*
**10 heavy sleeper** someone who does not wake easily
**11 heavy breathing** breathing that is slow and loud —see also HEAVY BREATHER
**12 make heavy weather of sth** *BrE* to make something that you are doing seem more difficult or complicated than it really is: *All Nick had to do was reorganize the files but he was making heavy weather of it.*

**13 ▶ CLOTHES ETC ◀** clothes, jewellery, or shoes that are heavy are large, thick, and solid: *a heavy winter coat*
**14 ▶ BODY/FACE ◀** having a large, broad, or thick appearance that is unattractive: *a large, heavy-featured woman* | **heavy build** (=a large broad body)
**15 ▶ WITH FORCE ◀** hitting something or falling with a lot of force or weight: *the sound of heavy footsteps in the hall* | *Ali caught him with a heavy blow to the jaw.*
**16 heavy silence/atmosphere** a situation in which people feel sad, anxious, or embarrassed: *A heavy silence fell upon the room.*
**17 heavy sky/clouds** looking dark and grey as though it will soon rain
**18 heavy seas** sea with big waves: *The ship went down in heavy seas off the coast of Scotland.*
**19 ▶ FOOD ◀** solid and making your stomach feel full and uncomfortable: *a heavy meal* | *heavy fruitcake*
**20 ▶ GROUND ◀ a)** soil that is heavy is thick and solid **b)** a sports ground or race track that is heavy is muddy: *The going is heavy at Epsom today.*
**21 ▶ SMELL ◀** strong and usually sweet: *a heavy fragrance* | **be heavy with a scent/fragrance/smell** *The garden was heavy with the scent of summer.*
**22 be heavy with fruit/blossom etc** *literary* if trees are heavy with fruit etc they have a lot of fruit etc on them
**23 ▶ AIR ◀** unpleasantly warm and not at all fresh because there is no wind: *the damp heavy atmosphere of the rainforest*
**24 heavy irony/sarcasm** remarks that very clearly say the opposite of what you really feel
**25 with a heavy heart** *literary* feeling very sad: *It was with a heavy heart that Kate kissed her children goodbye.*
**26 ▶ RELATIONSHIP ◀** *informal* involving serious or strong emotions: *She didn't want things to get too heavy at such an early stage in their relationship.*
**27 heavy date** *AmE usually humorous* a very important DATE with a BOYFRIEND or GIRLFRIEND
**28 ▶ SERIOUS/WORRYING ◀** *slang* a situation that is heavy makes you feel that people are very angry or have very strong feelings
**29 ▶ GUNS/WEAPONS ◀** [only before noun] large and powerful: *tanks and heavy weaponry*
**30 have a heavy foot** *AmE informal* to drive too fast —**heaviness** *n* [U]

**heavy**[2] *adv* **time hangs/lies heavy on your hands** if time hangs or lies heavy on your hands, it seems to pass slowly because you are bored or have nothing to do

**heavy**[3] *n* [C] **1** *informal* [usually plural] a large strong man who is paid to protect someone or to threaten other people **2** a serious male character in a play or film, especially a bad character; VILLAIN (1) **3 the heavies** *BrE* large, serious newspapers

**heavy breath·er** /ˌ·· ˈ··/ *n* [C] a man who calls a woman on the telephone and does not speak, but breathes loudly, in order to get sexual pleasure —**heavy breathing** *n* [U]

**heavy cream** /ˌ·· ˈ·/ *n* [U] *AmE* thick cream; DOUBLE CREAM *BrE*

**heavy-du·ty** /ˌ·· ˈ··◂/ *adj* **1** heavy duty materials are strong and thick and not easily damaged: *heavy-duty canvas* **2** heavy-duty machines or equipment are designed to be used for very hard work **3** *especially AmE informal* very serious, complicated, or involving strong emotions: *a heavy-duty affair*

**heavy goods ve·hi·cle** /ˌ·· ˈ· ˌ···/ *n* [C] an HGV

**heavy-hand·ed** /ˌ·· ˈ··◂/ *adj* done without thinking about other people's feelings: *a heavy-handed style of management* —**heavy-handedly** *adv* —**heavy-handedness** *n* [U]

**heavy-heart·ed** /ˌ·· ˈ··◂/ *adj literary* very sad

**heavy hit·ter** /ˌ·· ˈ··/ *n* [C] *AmE* **1** someone who has a lot of power, especially in business or politics **2** a BASEBALL player who hits the ball very hard

**heavy in·dus·try** /ˌ·· ˈ···/ *n* [U] industry that produces large goods such as cars and machines, or materials such as coal, steel, or chemicals —compare LIGHT INDUSTRY

**heavy-lad·en** /ˌ·· ˈ··◂/ *adj literary* **1** carrying or supporting something very heavy **2** having many worries or problems

**heavy met·al** /ˌ·· ˈ··◂/ *n* [U] **1** a type of ROCK[1] (2) music with a strong beat, played very loudly on electric GUITARS **2** *technical* a metal that has a high SPECIFIC GRAVITY, such as gold, MERCURY, and LEAD[3] (1)

**heavy pet·ting** /ˌ·· ˈ··/ *n* [U] sexual activities without actually having sex: *teenagers who indulge in heavy petting*

**heavy-set** /ˌ·· ˈ·◂/ *adj* someone who is heavy-set is large or broad and looks strong or fat

**heav·y·weight** /ˈheviweɪt/ *n* [C] **1** someone or something that is very important or has a lot of influence: *one of the heavyweights of the movie industry* **2** a BOXER (1) in the heaviest weight group

**He·bra·ic** /hɪˈbreɪ-ɪk/ *adj* connected with the Hebrew language or people: *Hebraic literature*

**He·brew** /ˈhiːbruː/ *n* **1** [U] the language traditionally used by the Jewish people **2** [C] a member of the Jewish people, especially in ancient times —**Hebrew** *adj*

**heck** /hek/ *interjection informal* **1** used to show that you are annoyed or to emphasize something you are saying: *Oh heck! I've lost my keys!* | **a heck of a lot** *a heck of a lot of money* | **where/how/who etc the heck** *Where the heck are we?* **2 what the heck!** *spoken* used to say that you will do something even though you really should not do it: *It's rather expensive, but what the heck!*

**heck·le** /ˈhekəl/ *v* [I,T] to interrupt a speaker at a public meeting —**heckler** *n* [C] —**heckling** *n* [U] *The speaker's voice was drowned by constant heckling.*

**heck·u·va** /ˈhekəvə/ *adj spoken* an abbreviation of 'heck of a'; used to emphasize that something is very big, very good etc: *That was a heckuva storm last night.*

**hec·tare** /ˈhektɑː, -teə‖-ter/ *n* [C] a unit for measuring area, equal to 10,000 square metres —see table on page B2

**hec·tic** /ˈhektɪk/ *adj* very busy or full of activity: *I've had a pretty hectic day at the office.* | *a hectic social life* —**hectically** /-kli/ *adv*

**hecto-** /hektəʊ‖-toʊ/ *prefix* 100 times a particular unit: *a hectometre* (=100 metres) —see table on page B2

**hec·tor** /ˈhektə‖-ər/ *v* [I,T] to speak to someone in an angry, threatening way: *a hectoring, bullying tone of voice*

**he'd** /id, hid, hiːd/ *strong* **1** the short form of 'he had': *By the time I got there he'd gone.* **2** the short form for 'he would': *I'm sure he'd help if he could.*

**hedge**[1] /hedʒ/ *n* [C] **1** a row of small bushes or trees growing close together, usually dividing one field or garden from another **2** something that gives you protection in case you lose money: *Buying a house will be a hedge against inflation.*

**hedge**[2] *v* **hedged, hedging** **1** [I] to avoid giving a direct answer to a question: *You're hedging again – have you got the money or haven't you?* **2 hedge your bets** to reduce your chances of failure or loss by having several choices available to you: *It's a good idea to hedge your bets by applying to more than one college.* **3** [T] to make a hedge around an area of land

**hedge** sb/sth **in** *phr v* **be hedged in a)** to be surrounded or enclosed by something: *The building was hedged in with trees.* **b)** if you feel hedged in by something, you feel that your freedom is restricted by it

**hedge against** sth *phr v* [T] to try to protect yourself against possible problems, especially financial loss: *Any well-managed business will hedge against price increases.*

**hedge·hog** /ˈhedʒhɒg‖-hɔːg/ *n* [C] a small brown European animal whose body is round and covered with sharp SPINES (=sharp needles)

**hedge·row** /ˈhedʒrəʊ‖-roʊ/ *n* [C] *especially BrE* a line of bushes or small trees growing along the edge of a field or road

**hedge spar·row** /ˈ· ˌ··/ *n* [C] a small common bird that lives in Europe and America

**he·don·ist** /ˈhiːdən-ɪst/ *n* [C] someone who believes that pleasure is the most important thing in life —**hedonism** *n* [U] —**hedonistic** /ˌhiːdənˈɪstɪk◂/ *adj*

**hee·bie-jee·bies** /ˌhiːbi ˈdʒiːbiz/ *n* **give sb the heebie-jeebies** *informal* to make someone feel nervous

**heed**[1] /hiːd/ *v* [T] *formal* to pay attention to someone's advice or warning: *If she had only heeded my warnings, none of this would have happened.*

**heed**[2] *n* [U] *formal* **pay/give heed to sth** also **take heed of sth** to pay attention to something and seriously consider it: **pay no heed to** *Tom paid no heed to her warning.*

**heed·less** /ˈhiːdləs/ *adj* **heedless of** not paying attention to something: *O'Hara rode on, heedless of danger.*

**hee-haw** /ˈhiː ˌhɔː‖ˌhɒː/ *n* [C] the noise made by a DONKEY

**heel**[1] /hiːl/ *n* [C]
**1 ► OF YOUR FOOT ◄** the back part of your foot —see pictures at BODY and FOOT[1]
**2 ► OF A SHOE ◄** the raised part of a shoe that is under the back of your foot —see picture at SHOE[1]
**3 high-heeled/low-heeled etc** high-heeled or low-heeled shoes have high or low heels
**4 ► OF A SOCK ◄** the part of a sock that covers your heel
**5 ► OF YOUR HAND ◄** the raised part of your hand near your wrist: *I pressed the paper down firmly with the heel of my hand.*
**6 heels** [plural] a pair of women's shoes with high heels
**7 be on/at sb's heels** to be following closely behind someone, especially in order to catch or attack them: *The gang were at his heels.*
**8 on the heels of** very soon after something: *Kinnock's resignation came on the heels of the party's fourth defeat.*
**9 bring sb to heel** to force someone to behave in the way that you want them to
**10 call sth to heel a)** if you call a dog to heel, you tell it to come back to you **b)** if someone comes to heel they obey you again
**11 come to heel** if a dog comes to heel, it comes back to its owner when the owner calls it
**12 take to your heels** to start running as fast as possible: *As soon as he saw me he took to his heels.*
**13 turn/spin on your heel** to suddenly turn away from someone, especially in an angry or rude way
**14 under the heel of** completely controlled by a government or group: *The whole country was under the heel of a tyrannical dictatorship.*
**15 ► BAD MAN ◄** *old-fashioned* a man who behaves badly towards other people —see also WELL-HEELED, ACHILLES' HEEL **click your heels** (CLICK[1] (1)), **cool your heels** (COOL[2] (4)), **dig your heels in** (DIG (1)), DOWN AT HEEL, **drag your heels** (DRAG[1] (8)), **hard on sb's heels** (HARD[2] (9)), **head over heels (in love)** (HEAD[1] (51)), **hot on sb's heels** (HOT[1] (15)), **kick your heels** (KICK[1] (11))

**heel**[2] *v* **1** [T] to put a heel on a shoe **2 heel!** *spoken* used when telling a dog to walk next to you **3** [T] to send the ball backwards in RUGBY by hitting it with your heel

**heel over** *phr v* [I] if something heels over, it leans to one side as if it is going to fall: *The ship was heeling over in the wind.*

**hef·ty** /ˈhefti/ *adj* **1** a hefty person, book etc is big and heavy: *a hefty volume containing over 1200 pages* **2** a hefty amount of something such as money is very large: *a hefty fine* **3** a hefty blow, kick etc is done using a lot of force: *a hefty punch* —**heftily** *adv*

H

**he·gem·o·ny** /hɪˈgeməni, ˈhedʒɪ̈məni‖hɪˈdʒeməni, ˈhedʒɪ̈moʊni/ *n* [U] *formal* a situation in which one state or country controls others

**He·gi·ra, Hejira** /ˈhedʒɪ̈rə, hɪˈdʒaɪrə/ *n* [singular] the journey of Muhammad from Mecca to Medina in AD 622

**Hegira cal·en·dar** /ˌ··· ˈ···, ·ˌ·· ˈ···/ *n* [singular] the Muslim system of dividing a year of 354 days into 12 months and starting to count the years from the Hegira

**heif·er** /ˈhefə‖-ər/ *n* [C] a young cow that has not yet given birth to a CALF (=baby cow) —compare BULLOCK, OX, STEER

**heigh-ho** /ˌheɪ ˈhəʊ‖-ˈhoʊ/ *interjection old-fashioned* used when you have to accept something that is boring or unpleasant

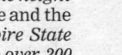

**height** /haɪt/ *n* 
**1 ► TALL ◄ a)** [U] how tall someone is: **sb's height** *State your age, height, and weight.* | **be the same/right etc height** *My daughter's already about the same height as I am.* **b)** [C,U] the distance between the base and the top of something: *What's the height of the Empire State Building?* | **in height** *Some of the pyramids are over 200 feet in height.* —see picture at LENGTH
**2 ► DISTANCE ABOVE THE GROUND ◄** [C] a particular distance above the ground: *It's a miracle she didn't break her neck falling from that height.* | *at a height of 10,000 feet*
**3 gain/lose height** if an aircraft gains height or loses height, it moves higher in the sky or it drops lower in the sky: *The plane was rapidly losing height.*
**4 ► HIGH PLACE ◄ heights** *plural* **a)** places that are a long way above the ground: *Rachel had always been*

*scared of heights.* | **have a head for heights** (=not be afraid of heights) **b)** a particular high place: *the Golan Heights*
**5 reach/attain/rise to new heights a)** to reach a very high level of achievement or success: *Her career rose to new heights.* | **take sth to new heights** *Torville and Dean took ice dancing to new heights.* **b)** to reach a very great level or degree: *War fever had reached new heights.*
**6 the height of** the part of a period of time that is the busiest, hottest etc, or when there is the most activity: *the height of the tourist season*
**7 be at the height of your success/fame/powers etc** to be at the time when you are most successful, famous etc: *The Beatles were at the height of their fame.*
**8 be the height of fashion/stupidity/luxury etc** to be extremely fashionable, stupid etc: *Flared trousers were considered to be the height of fashion in those days.*

**height·en** /ˈhaɪtn/ *v* [I,T] if something heightens a feeling, effect etc, or if a feeling etc heightens, it becomes stronger or increases; INTENSIFY: *Lemon helps to heighten the flavour.* | *Berg uses music to heighten tension in the scene.* | **heighten awareness** (=make people realize something more clearly) *an attempt to heighten their awareness of political issues*

**hei·nous** /ˈheɪnəs/ *adj formal* very shocking and immoral: *a heinous crime* —**heinously** *adv* —**heinousness** *n* [U]

**heir** /eə‖er/ *n* [C] **1** the person who has the legal right to receive the property or title of another person when they die: [+ **to**] *John was the sole heir to a vast estate.* | **the heir to the throne** (=the person who will become king or queen) **2** the person who will take over a position or job after you: *Jonson was his political heir as leader of the Nationalist Party.*

**heir ap·par·ent** /ˌ· ·ˈ··/ *n* [C] an heir whose right to receive the family property, money, or title cannot be taken away —compare HEIR PRESUMPTIVE

**heir·ess** /ˈeərɨs, ˈeəres‖ˈer-/ *n* [C] a woman who will receive a lot of money, property, or a title when an older member of her family dies

**heir·loom** /ˈeəluːm‖ˈer-/ *n* [C] a valuable object that has been owned by a family for many years and that is passed from the older members to the younger members

**heir pre·sump·tive** /ˌ· ·ˈ··/ *n* [C] an HEIR whose right to receive the family property, money, or title can be taken away if someone else with a better claim is born —compare HEIR APPARENT

**heist** /haɪst/ *n* [C] *AmE informal* an act of robbing something very valuable from a shop, bank etc: *a jewelry heist* —**heist** *v* [T]

**He·ji·ra** /ˈhedʒɨrə, hɪˈdʒaɪrə/ *n* another spelling of the HEGIRA

**held** /held/ past tense and past participle of HOLD[1]

**hel·i·cop·ter** /ˈhelɨkɒptə‖-kɑːptər/ *n* [C] a type of aircraft with large metal blades on top which turn around very quickly to make it fly

**helicopter pad** /ˈ···· ˌ·/ *n* [C] an area where helicopters can land

**he·li·o·graph** /ˈhiːliəgrɑːf‖-græf/ *n* [C] an instrument that sends messages by directing flashes of light with a mirror

**he·li·o·trope** /ˈhiːliətrəʊp, ˈhe-‖ˈhiːliətroʊp/ *n* **1** [C] a garden plant that has pleasant-smelling pale purple flowers **2** [U] the colour of this flower

**hel·i·pad** /ˈhelipæd/ *n* [C] a helicopter pad

**hel·i·port** /ˈhelipɔːt‖-pɔːrt/ *n* [C] a small airport for HELICOPTERS

**he·li·um** /ˈhiːliəm/ *n* [U] a gas that is lighter than air, often used in BALLOONS

**he·lix** /ˈhiːlɪks/ *n* [C] *technical* a line that curves and rises around a central line; SPIRAL —see also DOUBLE HELIX

**he'll** /il, hil· *strong* hiːl/ *strong* **1** the short form of 'he will' **2** the short form of 'he shall'

**hell**[1] /hel/ *n* S1 W3
**1 ▶ UNPLEASANT SITUATION ◀** [singular, U] *informal* a situation, experience, or place that is very unpleasant: *Central London was hell the Saturday before Christmas.* | **sheer hell** (=extremely unpleasant) *"How was your exam?" "Sheer hell!"* | **hell on earth** *This town is my idea of hell on earth.*
**2 ▶ SUFFERING ◀** a place or situation in which people suffer very much, either physically or emotionally: *the hell of the battlefield* | **make sb's life hell** *He'll make my life hell if I don't do what he wants.* | **living hell** *Josh felt trapped in a living hell.*
**3 ▶ WHEN YOU DIE ◀** also **Hell** [singular] the place where the souls of bad people are believed to be punished after death, especially in the Christian and Muslim religions
**4 how/what/where etc the hell?** *spoken* used to show that you are very surprised or angry: *What the hell does he think he's doing?* | *Where the hell have you been?*
**5 a/one hell of a** *spoken* used to emphasize the idea that something is very big, very good, very bad etc: *He's one hell of a good actor.* | *a hell of a lot of money* | **have one hell of a time** *We had one hell of a time trying to get here.*
**6 go to hell!** *spoken* used to tell someone that you do not care about them or about what they think: *If John doesn't like it, he can go to hell!*
**7 feel/look like hell** *spoken* to feel or look very ill or tired: *I've been feeling like hell all week.*
**8 beat/irritate/scare etc the hell out of sb** *informal* to beat, irritate etc someone very much
**9 (just) for the hell of it** *spoken* for no serious reason, or only for fun: *We decided to go for a midnight swim, just for the hell of it.*
**10 what the hell!** *spoken* used to say that you will do something and not worry about any problems it causes: *What the hell, let's go with them.*
**11 to hell with** *spoken* used to say that you do not care about something any more: *To hell with school! I'm going to leave and get a job.*
**12 run/work/hurt etc like hell** *informal* to run, work etc very quickly or very much: *We ran like hell and didn't stop until we were safely home.*
**13 like hell/the hell** *spoken* used to say that you do not believe what someone has said, or that you disagree with it: *"Like hell you'd pay it back", Wade said wearily.*
**14 from hell** *informal* the worst you can imagine: *It was disaster after disaster – the holiday from hell!*
**15 mad/weird/ugly etc as hell** *especially AmE spoken* very angry, strange etc: *I wouldn't ask him now, he's mad as hell.*
**16 give sb hell** *informal* to blame someone angrily: *My dad gave me hell when he found out that I'd borrowed the car.*
**17 get the hell out (of somewhere)** *informal* to leave a place quickly and suddenly: *Let's get the hell out of here!*
**18 there'll be hell to pay** *spoken* used to say that people will be very angry: *There'll be hell to pay when the boss finds out.*
**19 catch hell** *AmE spoken* to be blamed or punished: *You'll catch hell when your Mom comes home!*
**20 all hell broke loose** *informal* used to say that people suddenly become very noisy or angry: *The rival gang arrived and all hell broke loose.*
**21 hell's bells** *spoken* also **hell's teeth** *BrE* used to express great annoyance or surprise
**22 come hell or high water** *informal* in spite of any problems or difficulties: *I decided I would get the job done by Friday, come hell or high water.*
**23 go to hell in a handbasket** *AmE informal* if a system or organization has gone to hell in a handbasket, it has stopped working properly: *The education system in this state has gone to hell in a handbasket.*
**24 run/go hell for leather** *informal* to run away as fast as possible
**25 hell on wheels** *AmE informal* someone who does exactly what they want and does not care what happens as a result

**26 play (merry) hell with** *informal* to make something stop working or happening as it should: *The cold weather played hell with the weekend sports schedule.*
**27 when hell freezes over** *informal* used to say that something will never happen —see also **not a hope in hell** (HOPE[1] (5))

**hell²** *interjection* **1** *especially BrE* used to express anger or annoyance: *Oh hell! I've left my purse at home.* **2** *AmE* used to emphasize something you are saying: *Hell, I don't know!*

**hell-bent** /ˌ· ˈ·◂/ *adj* [not before noun] very determined to do something, especially something that other people do not approve of: **hell-bent on (doing) sth** *They seemed hell-bent on creating a scandal.*

**hell·cat** /ˈhelkæt/ *n* [C] *informal* a woman who has a violent temper

**Hel·lene** /ˈheliːn/ *n* [C] *formal* a Greek, especially an ancient Greek

**Hel·len·ic** /heˈlenɪk/ *adj* connected with the history, society, or art of the ancient Greeks

**hell-hole** /ˈ· ·/ *n* [C] a very unpleasant place: *His last apartment was a real hell-hole.*

**hell·ish** /ˈhelɪʃ/ *adj informal* extremely unpleasant: *I've had a hellish day at work.* —**hellishly** *adv*: *a hellishly difficult exam*

S1 **hel·lo** /həˈləʊ, he-‖-ˈloʊ-/ also **hallo, hullo** *BrE interjection* **1** used as a usual greeting: *Hello, John! How are you?* | **say hello to sb** *She always says hello to me in the street.* | **hello there** *Well, hello there! I haven't seen you for ages.* **2** used when answering the telephone or starting a telephone conversation: *Hello, is Rachel there please?* **3** used when calling to get someone's attention: *Hello! Is there anybody home?* **4** *BrE* used to show that you are surprised or confused by something: *Hello! What's happened here?*

**helm** /helm/ *n* **1** [C] the wheel or TILLER which guides a ship or boat **2 at the helm a)** in charge of something: *The company flourished with David Finch at the helm.* **b)** guiding a ship or boat **3** *old use* a helmet

**hel·met** /ˈhelmɪ̈t/ *n* [C] a strong hard hat worn for protection by soldiers, MOTORCYCLE riders, the police etc —see also CRASH HELMET, PITH HELMET

**helmets**

crash helmet

pith helmet

see also picture at **hat** and **cap**

**hel·met·ed** /ˈhelmɪ̈tɪ̈d/ *adj* wearing a helmet

**helms·man** /ˈhelmzmən/ *n plural* **helmsmen** /-mən/ [C] someone who guides a ship or boat

S1 W1 **help¹** /help/ *v*
**1 ▶MAKE POSSIBLE OR EASIER◀** [I,T] to make it possible or easier for someone to do something by doing part of their work or by giving them something they need: *If there's anything I can do to help, just give me a call.* | *She devoted her life to helping the poor and sick.* | **help sb (to) do sth** *We all helped him fill out the application form.* | *Andy said he would help us to move the furniture.* | **help sb with sth** *Do you mind helping me with this a minute?* | **help (to) do sth** *Part of my job is to help organize conferences.* | **help sb into/out of/across etc** (=help someone move to a particular place) *He was so drunk we had to help him into the taxi.* | **help sb on/off with sth** (=help someone put on or take off a piece of clothing) *Here, let me help you on with your coat.*
**2 ▶BE GOOD FOR◀** [T] to make it easier for something to develop or be improved: *The fall in oil prices should help economic development.* | **help sb (to) do sth** *All this arguing isn't going to help us win the election.*
**3 ▶MAKE BETTER◀** [I,T] to make a situation better, easier, or less painful: *Crying won't help.* | *It helped a lot to know that someone understood how I felt.* | **help sth** *A couple of aspirin might help your headache.*
**4 Help!** *spoken* used to call people and ask them to help you when you are in danger
**5 can't help it a)** to not be responsible for something unpleasant or annoying: *I can't help it if she's late, can I?* **b)** to be unable to stop doing something, or change the way that you behave: *I always get angry with him, I just can't help it.*
**6 can't/couldn't help doing sth** to be unable to stop yourself from doing something: *I can't help thinking that we've made a big mistake.* | *I couldn't help hearing what you just said.*
**7 can't/couldn't help but do sth** if you cannot help but do something, it is impossible for you not to do it: *I couldn't help but notice the bruise she had under her eye.*
**8 can't help yourself** to be unable to stop yourself from doing something you should not do: *Sue doesn't always mean to be so rude but sometimes she just can't help herself.*
**9 help yourself (to sth) a)** to take something that you want, such as food, without asking permission: *Please help yourself to more; there's plenty of everything.* **b)** *informal* to steal something: *Obviously he had been helping himself to the money.*
**10 help sb to sth** to serve someone food or drink: *Can I help you to some dessert?*
**11 God help him/them etc** *spoken* used to say that something bad may happen to someone: *If you trust that man with a secret, God help you.*
**12 a helping hand** help and support: **give sb a helping hand** *She's been giving me a helping hand with the children.*
**13 it can't be helped** *spoken* used to say that there is nothing you can do to change an unpleasant situation: *It's going to make a terrible noise, but never mind. It can't be helped.*
**14 not if I can help it** *spoken* used to say that you are not going to do something: *"Are you going to the meeting this afternoon?" "Not if I can help it."*
**15 so help me (God)** used when making a serious promise, especially in a court of law

**help out** *phr v* **1** [I,T] to help someone who is busy by doing some of their work for them: *Is there anything I can do to help out?* | **help sb out** *If you haven't got time to finish I'll help you out.* **2** [T] to give help and support to someone who has problems: *He was obviously in some kind of trouble, but I didn't know how I could help him out.*

H

**USAGE NOTE: HELP**

WORD CHOICE: **help, assist, give/lend a hand, help out, come to somebody's aid/assistance, aid, give/send aid**

**Help** and **assist** can both describe people or institutions helping each other do a job. However, **assist** is more formal and often suggests that the person assisting is doing a simple or unimportant part of what has to be done: *My company assists businesses in all their office cleaning requirements.* | *You will assist the administrative officer with day-to-day organization* (Note that **assist** can never mean 'attend' or 'be present at').

In more informal English people often use **give/lend a hand** or **help out**, especially where there is something practical to do and not enough people to do it: *Can you give me a hand with the drinks?* | *I sometimes lend a hand/help out at the old folk's home.*

If someone is in danger or trouble, you may **help** them or more formally **come to their aid/assistance**: *My car's broken down, can you help?* | *If you get into difficulties, the lifeguard will come to your assistance.*

If a person, charity, or government helps with money or other necessary things, **aid** (formal) or often **give/send aid** may be used: *Many projects are aided by Oxfam.* | *Aid will be sent to the area as* *soon as possible.* Informally **help** would be used: *Please help the homeless.*

GRAMMAR

**Help** (but not **assist**) is often followed by a verb in the *to* or basic form: *He helped me (to) pass my exam* (=I passed NOT *He helped me passing...*). But note that the expression **can't help...** meaning 'cannot stop yourself...' is only followed by the *-ing* form of a verb: *I couldn't help laughing.*

You **help/assist/aid** someone, not *to* them.

S1 W1 **help²** *n* **1** [U] the action of helping someone by doing part of their work or by showing them how to do it: *If I need any help, I'll call you.* | [+ **with**] *Do you want any help with that?* **2** [U] the fact of being useful or making something easier to do: *That map isn't much help.* | **with the help of** *We got it open with the help of a knife.* | **be of great/little/no help** *I'm sorry I haven't been of much help to you.* **3 be a (big/great/real) help** also **be a lot of help a)** to be very useful, or give a lot of help: *Thanks. You've been a big help.* **b)** often used jokingly to say that something is not useful, or someone is not helping you: *A lot of help you've been! Why did you bother to come?* **4** [U] help which people can give to save someone from danger or difficulty: *She screamed at them to go and get help.* **5** [U] advice, treatment, information, or money which is given to people who need it: *A lot of these children need professional help.* | [+ **with**] *You may be able to get help with the rent.* | **beyond help** (=no longer able to be helped or saved) *I'm afraid the patient is beyond help.* **6 the help** *AmE* someone's servant or servants

**help·er** /ˈhelpə‖-ər/ *n* [C] **1** someone who helps another person: *She's the cook's helper.* **2** *AmE* someone who is employed to do some of the work in someone else's home

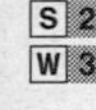

S2 W3 **help·ful** /ˈhelpfəl/ *adj* **1** useful in making a situation better or easier: **it is helpful (for sb) to do sth** *Sometimes it's helpful to make a list of everything you have to do.* | *It'd be helpful for me to know what your plans for the week are.* | **helpful in doing sth** *Any information would be helpful in determining what happened.* | **helpful suggestions/hints/ideas etc** *Has anybody got any helpful suggestions?* **2** always willing to help people: *She's a helpful child.* —**helpfully** *adv* —**helpfulness** *n* [U]

**help·ing** /ˈhelpɪŋ/ *n* [C] the amount of food that someone gives you or that you take; SERVING: *a huge helping of potatoes*

**help·less** /ˈhelpləs/ *adj* **1** unable to look after yourself or to do anything to help yourself: *Without proper defences we'd be helpless against an enemy attack.* | *Why is he so helpless?* **2** unable to control a strong feeling that you have: [+ **with**] *We rolled on the floor, helpless with laughter.* | **helpless rage/despair/laughter etc** *fits of helpless laughter* —**helplessly** *adv* —**helplessness** *n* [U]

**help·line** /ˈhelplaɪn/ *n* [C] a telephone number that you can ring if you need advice or information

**help·mate** /ˈhelpmeɪt/ also **help·meet** /-miːt/ *n* [C] *biblical* a helpful partner, usually a wife

**hel·ter-skel·ter¹** /ˌheltə ˈskeltə‖ˌheltər ˈskeltər/ *adv* quickly and without order or organization: *He ran off helter-skelter down the slope.*

**helter-skelter²** *n* [C] *BrE* a tall structure in a FAIRGROUND which you sit on at the top and slide round and round to the bottom

**hem¹** /hem/ *n* [C] the edge of a piece of a cloth that is turned under and stitched down, especially the lower edge of a skirt, trousers etc —see picture on page 840

**hem² hemmed, hemming** *v* **1** [T] to turn under the edge of a piece of material or clothing and stitch it in place **2 hem and haw** *AmE* to keep pausing before saying something, and avoid saying it directly

**hem** sb **in** *phr v* [T usually passive] **1** to surround someone closely, in a way that prevents them from moving: *They were hemmed in by steep mountains on all sides.* **2** to make someone feel that they are not free to do what they want to do: *She felt hemmed-in by the daily routine.*

**he-man** /ˈ· ·/ *n* [C] *humorous* a strong man with powerful muscles

**hem·i·sphere** /ˈhemɪ̇sfɪə‖-fɪr/ *n* [C] **1** a half of the earth, especially one of the northern and southern halves above and below the EQUATOR **2** one of the two halves of your brain **3** half of a SPHERE (=an object which is round like a ball)

**hem·line** /ˈhemlaɪn/ *n* [C] the length of a dress, skirt etc: *Short hemlines are in this spring.*

**hem·lock** /ˈhemlɒk‖-lɑːk/ *n* [C,U] a very poisonous plant, or the poison that is made from it

**hemo-** /hiːməʊ,-mə, hemə‖-moʊ, -mə, hemə/ the American spelling of HAEMO-

**he·mo·glo·bin** /ˌhiːməˈgləʊbɪ̇n‖ˈhiːməˌgloʊbɪ̇n/ *n* [U] the American spelling of HAEMOGLOBIN

**he·mo·phil·i·a** /ˌhiːməˈfɪliə/ *n* [U] the American spelling of HAEMOPHILIA

**he·mo·phil·i·ac** /ˌhiːməˈfɪliæk/ *n* [C] the American spelling of HAEMOPHILIAC

**hem·or·rhage** /ˈhemərɪdʒ/ *n* [C,U] the American spelling of HAEMORRHAGE

**hem·or·rhoids** /ˈhemərɔɪdz/ *n* [plural] the American spelling of HAEMORRHOIDS

**hemp** /hemp/ *n* [U] a type of plant that is used to make rope and sometimes to produce the drug CANNABIS

**hen** /hen/ *n* [C] **1** an adult female chicken **2** any female bird of which the male is the COCK¹ (5)

**hence** /hens/ *adv formal* **1** [sentence adverb] for this reason: *He's an extremely private person; hence his reluctance to give interviews.* **2 ten days hence/five months hence etc** ten days from now, five months from now etc W2

**hence·forth** /ˌhensˈfɔːθ, ˈhensfɔːθ‖-ɔːrθ/ also **hence·for·ward** /ˌhensˈfɔːwəd‖-ˈfɔːrwərd/ *adv formal* from this time on: *The company will henceforth be known as "Johnson and Brown."*

**hench·man** /ˈhentʃmən/ *n plural* **henchmen** /-mən/ [C] a faithful supporter, especially of a political leader or a criminal

**hen house** /ˈ· ·/ *n* [C] a small building where chickens are kept

**hen·na** /ˈhenə/ *n* [U] a reddish-brown substance used to change the colour of hair —**henna** *v* [T]

**hen par·ty** /ˈ· ˌ··/ *n* [C] *informal BrE* a party for women only, that happens just before one of them gets married —compare STAG PARTY

**hen·pecked** /ˈhenpekt/ *adj* a man who is henpecked is always being told what to do by his wife, and is afraid to disagree with her: *a henpecked husband*

**hep·a·ti·tis** /ˌhepəˈtaɪtɪ̇s◂/ *n* [U] a disease of the LIVER (1) that causes fever and yellow colour in your skin

**hepatitis A** /ˌ···· ˈ·/ *n* [U] a usually less severe form of hepatitis, caused by infected food or water

**hepatitis B** *n* [U] a severe form of hepatitis passed from one person to another in infected blood

**hep·ta·gon** /ˈheptəgən‖-gɑːn/ *n* [C] a shape with seven sides —**heptagonal** /hepˈtægənəl/ *adj*

**her¹** /ə, hə; *strong* hɜː‖ər, hər; *strong* hɜːr/ *determiner* [possessive form of 'she'] **1** belonging to or connected with a woman, girl, or female animal that has been mentioned or is known about: *Maria starts her swimming lessons on Friday.* | *It's her first child.* **2** connected with a country, ship, car etc that has been mentioned: *Her top speed is about 110 miles an hour.* S1 W1

**her²** *pron* [object form of 'she'] **1** a woman, girl, or female animal that has been mentioned or is known about: *Janet? I've not seen her for a long time.* | *Give her the keys.* | *Is that her over there?* —see ME (USAGE) **2** a country, ship, car etc that has been mentioned: *God bless this ship and all who sail in her.* S1 W1

**her·ald¹** /ˈherəld/ *v* [T] **1** to be a sign of something that is going to happen: *The talks herald a new era in East-West relations.* **2** to say publicly that someone or something will be good or important: *She has been heralded as one of the country's finest musicians.*

**herald²** *n* **1** [C] someone who carried messages from a ruler in the past **2 herald of** a sign that something is soon going to happen: *primroses, the first herald of spring*

**he·ral·dic** /he'rældɪk/ *adj* connected with heraldry

**her·ald·ry** /'herəldri/ *n* [U] the skill of making or the study of coats of arms (COAT OF ARMS)

**herb** /hɜːb‖ɜːrb, hɜːrb/ *n* [C] a small plant that is used to improve the taste of food, or to make medicine

**her·ba·ceous** /hə'beɪʃəs‖hɜːr'beɪ-, ɜːr'beɪ-/ *adj technical* plants that are herbaceous have soft stems rather than wood stems

**herbaceous bor·der** /·,·· '··/ *n* [C] part of a garden where plants are grown that live for many years and do not need to be replaced

**herb·al** /'hɜːbəl‖'ɜːr-, 'hɜːr-/ *adj* made of herbs: *herbal tea | herbal remedies*

**herb·al·ist** /'hɜːbəlɪ̈st‖'ɜːr-, 'hɜːr-/ *n* [C] someone who grows, sells, or uses HERBS, especially to treat illness

**herbal medi·cine** /,·· '··‖,·· '···/ *n* **1** [U] the practice of treating illness using plants **2** [C,U] medicine made from plants

**herb gar·den** /'· ,··/ *n* [C] a garden in which only HERBS are grown

**herb·i·cide** /'hɜːbɪ̈saɪd‖'hɜːr-,'ɜːr-/ *n* [C,U] *technical* a substance used to kill unwanted plants

**her·bi·vore** /'hɜːbɪ̈vɔː‖'hɜːrbɪ̈vɔːr, 'ɜːr-/ *n* [C] an animal that only eats plants —**herbivorous** /hɜː'bɪvərəs‖hɜːr-, ɜːr-/ *adj* —compare CARNIVORE, OMNIVORE

**her·cu·le·an** /,hɜːkjʊ'liːən◂,hɜː'kjuːliən‖-ɜːr-/ *adj* needing great strength or determination: *a herculean task*

**herd¹** /hɜːd‖hɜːrd/ *n* **1** [C] a group of animals of one kind that lives and feeds together: [+ **of**] *a herd of cattle* | [also + plural verb in *BrE*] *A herd of cows were descending into the valley.* —compare FLOCK¹ (1) **2 the herd** people generally, especially when thought of as being easily influenced: *She's never been the sort of person to follow the herd.* | **the herd instinct** (=the need to behave in the same way as everyone else)

**herd²** *v* **1** [I always + adv/prep, T] to come together or bring people together in a large group, especially roughly: [+ **into/through etc**] *The waiting tourists were herded onto the bus.* **2** [T] to make animals move together in a group: *herding sheep*

**herds·man** /'hɜːdzmən‖-ɜːr-/ *plural* **herdsmen** /-mən/ *n* [C] a man who looks after a herd of animals

S1 W1 **here¹** /hɪə‖hɪr/ *adv* **1** in this place: *Is George here?* | *Kabul is four hundred miles west of here.* | *I knew there would be no one here in this room.* | *Shall we eat here?* | **here and now** (=used to emphasize what you are saying) *I'll tell you here and now that I am not going to resign.* | **on here/out here/down here/over here etc** *It's very cold out here.* | *We're over here!* —compare THERE¹ (1) **2** happening now: *I'll be glad when the summer vacation is here.* **3** at this point in a discussion: *There are many reasons for this decline, which we cannot discuss here.* **4 here's/here is/here are/here comes etc** used when introducing something or someone, or showing them to someone: *Here comes Michael now.* | *Here's the shop I was telling you about.* **5 here/here is/here's/here we are etc** used when you have just found something that you have been looking for: *Ah, here we are, here's my address book.* **6 here's/here/here you are etc** used when you are giving something to someone: *Here's some money for you.* | *Here are your keys back.* **7 neither here nor there** not important: *The hospital needs this machine. The fact that it costs a lot of money is neither here nor there.* **8 here and there** scattered around in several different places: *Windows were shattered and there was minor damage to buildings here and there.* **9 here, there, and everywhere** *informal* in many different places: *We've been looking for you here, there, and everywhere.* **10 here goes!** used when you are going to try to do something difficult: *I've never ridden a motorbike before, so here goes!* **11 here we go (again)** *informal* used when something unpleasant is beginning to happen again: *Janet stormed off in a temper. "Here we go again," Matt thought.* **12 Here's to** used when you are going to drink something to wish someone good luck, show your respect for them etc: *Here's to the happy couple.* | *Here's to your new job.* **13 here to stay** if something is here to stay, it has become a part of life and will continue to be so

Frequencies of the word **here** in spoken and written English.

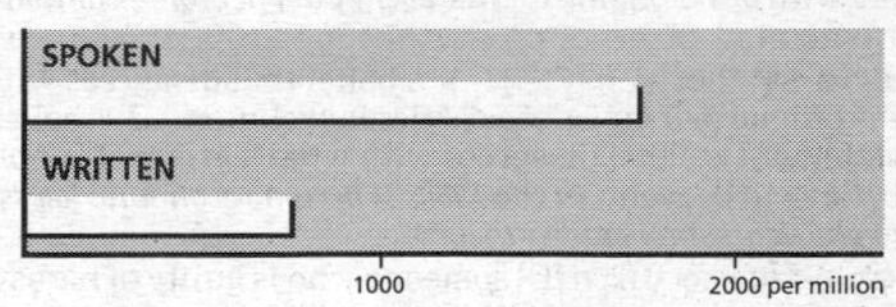


Based on the British National Corpus and the Longman Lancaster Corpus

This graph shows that the word **here** is much more common in spoken English than in written English. This is because it has special uses in spoken English and is used in a lot of common spoken phrases.

**here** ( *adv*) **SPOKEN PHRASES**

**14 a)** used when you are giving or offering something to someone: *Here, have my chair. I don't mind standing.* **b)** *BrE* used to get someone's attention or to show that you are annoyed: *Here! Just what do you think you're doing?* **15 here is a)** used when you are giving something to someone: *Here's some money. Have a good time.* **b)** used to say that someone or something is arriving: *Ah, look – here's the mailman.* | **here it is/they are** *Here they are, late as usual.* **c)** used to tell someone that you have found something, or to say where something is: *Oh, here's the knife, it was under these dishes.* | **here it is/they are** *Here she is, hiding behind the curtains.* **16 here you are/here you go** used when you are giving something to someone: *Here you are John, have some cake.* **17 here we go** used when you are starting to do something or when something is starting to happen: *Right, here we go, the game's starting.* **18 here goes** used when you are going to try something and you do not know what will happen: *O.K. Here goes. Stand back everyone.* **19 here comes** used when you can see something or someone arriving: *Quick, here comes the bus. Have you got the right money?*

**here²** *interjection* **1** used when you are giving or offering something to someone: *Here, have my chair. I don't mind standing.* **2** *BrE* used to attract someone's attention or to express annoyance: *Here! Just what do you think you're doing?*

**here·a·bouts** /,hɪərə'baʊts, 'hɪərəbaʊts‖,hɪr-,'hɪr-/ also **hereabout** *AmE adv* somewhere near the place where you are: *There must be a public telephone hereabouts.*

**here·af·ter¹** /,hɪər'ɑːftə‖,hɪr'æftər/ *adv* **1** [sentence adverb] *formal* from this time **2** *formal* after death **3** *law* in a later part of a legal document

**hereafter²** *n* **the hereafter** a life after death: *Do you believe in the hereafter?*

**here·by** /,hɪə'baɪ, 'hɪəbaɪ‖,hɪr-,'hɪr-/ *adv law* a word meaning 'by this statement', used in official documents or statements: *I hereby declare that James Lowe is elected to serve as MP for this constituency.*

**he·red·i·ta·ry** /hɪ̈'redɪ̈təri‖-teri/ *adj* **1** mental or physical qualities, abilities, or illnesses etc that are hereditary are passed from parent to child in the cells of the body

**2** **a)** *BrE* a position, rank, or title that is hereditary can be passed from an older to a younger person in the same family, usually when the older one dies **b)** having a legal right to receive a position, rank, or title in this way: *a hereditary peer*

**he·red·i·ty** /hɪ̈ˈredɪ̈ti/ *n* [U] the process by which mental or physical qualities, abilities, or illnesses pass from parents to children in the cells of the body

**here·in** /ˌhɪərˈɪn‖ˌhɪr-/ *adv formal* in this place, situation, document etc: *the conditions stated herein* —compare THEREIN

**here·in·af·ter** /ˌhɪərɪnˈɑːftə‖ˌhɪrɪnˈæftər/ *adv law* later in this official statement, document etc: *Messrs Wilson and Cartwright, hereinafter referred to as "the insurers"...*

**here·of** /ˌhɪərˈɒv‖hɪrˈʌv, -ˈɑːv/ *adv formal or law* connected with or belonging to this: *every part hereof* —compare THEREOF

**her·e·sy** /ˈherɪ̈si/ *n* [C,U] **1** a belief that disagrees with the official principles of a particular religion **2** a belief, statement etc that disagrees with what a group of people believe to be right: *In the 1980s it became economic heresy to challenge monetarist theory.*

**her·e·tic** /ˈherɪ̈tɪk/ *n* [C] someone who is guilty of heresy: *Cranmer was put to death as a heretic.* —**heretical** /hɪ̈ˈretɪkəl/ *adj*

**here·to** /ˌhɪəˈtuː‖ˌhɪrˈtuː/ *adv formal* to this: *my signature hereto appended*

**here·to·fore** /ˌhɪətʊˈfɔː‖ˈhɪrtʊfɔːr/ *adv formal* before this time

**here·up·on** /ˌhɪərəˈpɒn‖ˌhɪrəˈpɑːn/ *adv formal* at or after this moment

**here·with** /ˌhɪəˈwɪð, -ˈwɪθ‖ˌhɪr-/ *adv formal* with this letter or document: *I enclose herewith two copies of the contract.*

**her·i·ta·ble** /ˈherɪ̈təbəl/ *adj law* property that is heritable can be passed from the older members of a family to the younger ones; HEREDITARY (2)

**her·i·tage** /ˈherɪ̈tɪdʒ/ *n* [singular, U] important qualities, customs, and TRADITIONS that have been in a society for a long time: *the cultural heritage of Italy* —compare INHERITANCE

**her·maph·ro·dite** /hɜːˈmæfrədaɪt‖hɜːr-/ *n* [C] a living thing that has the organs of both male and female —**hermaphrodite** *adj* —**hermaphroditic** /hɜːˌmæfrəˈdɪtɪk◂‖hɜːr-/ *adj*

**her·met·ic** /hɜːˈmetɪk‖hɜːr-/ *adj technical* very tightly closed so that air cannot get in or out; AIRTIGHT —**hermetically** /-kli/ *adv*: *stored in hermetically sealed containers.*

**her·mit** /ˈhɜːmɪ̈t‖ˈhɜːr-/ *n* [C] someone who lives alone and has a simple way of life, usually for religious reasons —compare RECLUSE

**her·mit·age** /ˈhɜːmɪ̈tɪdʒ‖ˈhɜːr-/ *n* [C] a place where a hermit lives or has lived

**hermit crab** /ˈ‥ ˌ·/ *n* [C] a kind of CRAB[1] (1) that lives in the empty shells of other sea creatures

**her·ni·a** /ˈhɜːniə‖ˈhɜːr-/ *n* [C,U] a medical condition in which an organ pushes through the muscles that are supposed to contain it; RUPTURE[1] (3)

W3 **he·ro** /ˈhɪərəʊ‖ˈhɪroʊ/ *n plural* **heroes** [C] **1** a man who is admired for doing something extremely brave: *He had dared to speak out against injustice, and overnight he became a national hero.* | **war hero** (=a soldier who was very brave in a war) **2** the man or boy who is the main character in a book, film, play etc: *Indiana Jones is the hero of the film.* **3** someone you admire very much for their intelligence, skill etc: **sb's hero** *My hero as a boy was the great Di Maggio.* **4** *AmE* a SANDWICH made of a long LOAF of bread filled with meat, cheese etc —see also HEROINE

**he·ro·ic** /hɪˈrəʊɪk‖-ˈroʊ-/ *adj* **1** extremely brave or determined and admired by many people: *her heroic efforts to save her family* **2** a heroic story, poem etc involves a hero **3 on a heroic scale/of heroic proportions** very large or great: *a battle on a heroic scale* —**heroically** /-kli/ *adv*

**heroic coup·let** /ˌ·‥ ˈ‥/ *n* [C] a pair of lines in poetry which end with the same sound and that have five beats in each line

**he·ro·ics** /hɪˈrəʊɪks‖-ˈroʊ-/ *n* [plural] language or behaviour that is too brave for a particular situation: *America's present need is not heroics, but calm diplomacy.*

**her·o·in** /ˈherəʊɪn‖-roʊ-/ *n* [U] a powerful and illegal drug made from MORPHINE: *a heroin addict*

**her·o·ine** /ˈherəʊɪn‖-roʊ-/ *n* [C] **1** the woman or girl who is the main character in a book, film, play etc: *the tragic heroine of Sophocles' play.* **2** a woman who is extremely brave and is admired by many people: *a heroine of the French Resistance* **3** a woman you admire very much for her intelligence, skill etc —see also HERO

**her·o·is·m** /ˈherəʊɪzəm‖-roʊ-/ *n* [U] very great courage: *stories of heroism and self-sacrifice*

**her·on** /ˈherən/ *n* [C] a large bird with very long legs and a long beak, that lives near water

**hero wor·ship** /ˈ‥ ˌ‥/ *n* [U] great admiration for someone you think is very brave, good, skilful etc —**hero-worship** *v* [T]

**her·pes** /ˈhɜːpiːz‖ˈhɜːr-/ *n* [U] a very infectious disease that causes spots on the skin, especially on the face or GENITALS

**her·ring** /ˈherɪŋ/ *n plural* **herrings** or **herring** [C] a long thin silver sea fish that can be eaten —see also RED HERRING

**her·ring·bone** /ˈherɪŋbəʊn‖-boʊn/ *n* [U] a pattern consisting of a continuous line of V shapes, used in cloth etc —see picture on page 839

**herring gull** /ˈ‥ ·/ *n* [C] a large white bird that lives near the sea in Britain

**hers** /hɜːz‖hɜːrz/ *pron* the possessive form of 'she'; of or belonging to a female person or animal already mentioned: *This is my coat. Hers* (=her coat) *is over there.* | *My shoes are brown and hers are red.* | *Paul's a friend of hers.* S3

**her·self** /əˈself, hə-; *strong* ˈhɜː-‖ər-, hər-; *strong* ˈhɜːr-/ *pron* **1** reflexive form of 'she': *She hurt herself.* | *She made herself a cup of coffee.* **2** the strong form of 'she' used to emphasize the subject or object of a sentence: *It must be true that she's leaving because she told me so herself.* | *She herself told me.* **3** *informal* in her usual state of mind or body: *She's feeling much more herself today.* **4 (all) by herself a)** alone: *She lives by herself.* **b)** without help from anyone else: *The little girl wrote the letter all by herself.* **5 (all) to herself** for her own use; not having to share: *She had the house to herself while her parents were gone.* S2 W1

**hertz** /hɜːts‖hɜːrts/ *n plural* **hertz** [C] a measurement meaning one time each second, used to measure SOUND WAVES

**he's** /iz, hiz; *strong* hiːz/ **1** the short form of 'he is': *He's a writer.* | *He's reading.* **2** the short form of 'he has': *He's bought a new car.*

**hes·i·tan·cy** /ˈhezɪ̈tənsi/ also **hes·i·tance** /-təns/ *n* [U] the quality of being uncertain or slow in doing or saying something

**hes·i·tant** /ˈhezɪ̈tənt/ *adj* uncertain about what to do or say because you are nervous or unwilling: *Gail gave me a hesitant little smile.* | **hesitant to do sth** *The economist was hesitant to comment on government policy.* —**hesitantly** *adv*

**hes·i·tate** /ˈhezɪ̈teɪt/ *v* **1** [I] to pause before saying or doing something because you are not sure or nervous: *Harriet hesitated a moment before replying.* **2 hesitate to do sth** to be unwilling to do something because you are not sure that it is right: *Don't hesitate to contact me if you need any more information.* —**hesitatingly** *adv*

**hes·i·ta·tion** /ˌhezɪ̈ˈteɪʃən/ *n* [C,U] the action of hesitating: *After some hesitation one of them began to speak.* | **have no hesitation in** *I would have no hesitation in declining the post.* | **after/without a moment's hesitation** *Without a moment's hesitation she kissed him.*

**hes·si·an** /ˈhesiən‖ˈheʃən/ *n* [U] *BrE* thick rough cloth sometimes used for making sacks (SACK[1] (1)); BURLAP *AmE*

**het** /het/ —see HET UP

**hetero-** /het ərəʊ, -rə‖-roʊ, -rə/ *prefix formal or technical* other; opposite; different: *heterosexual* (=attracted to the opposite sex)

**het·e·ro·dox** /ˈhet ərədɒks‖-dɑːks/ *adj formal* heterodox beliefs, practices etc are not approved of by a particular group, especially a religious one —compare UNORTHODOX

**het·e·ro·ge·ne·ous** /ˌhet ərəʊˈdʒiːniəs‖-roʊ-/ also **het·e·roge·nous** /ˌhetəˈrodʒənəs◂‖-ˈrɑː-/ *AmE* —*adj formal* consisting of parts or members that are very different from each other: *a heterogeneous collection of buildings* —**heterogeneity** /ˌhet ərəʊdʒə̇ˈniːə̇ti‖-roʊ-/ *n* [U] —**heterogeneously** *adv*

**het·e·ro·sex·u·al** /ˌhet ərəˈsekʃuəl◂/ *adj* sexually attracted to people of the opposite sex —compare BISEXUAL[1] (1), HOMOSEXUAL —**heterosexual** *n* [C] —**heterosexuality** /ˌhet ərəsekʃuˈælə̇ti/ *n* [U] —**heterosexually** *adv*

**het up** /ˌhet ˈʌp/ *adj* [not before a noun] *informal* anxious, upset, or slightly angry: *Why's Andy so het up?* | [+ **about**] *Mike's very het up about his exams.*

**heu·ris·tic** /hjʊˈrɪstɪk/ *adj formal* **1** heuristic education is based on discovering and experiencing things for yourself **2** helping you in the process of learning or discovery —**heuristically** /-kli/ *adv*

**heu·ris·tics** /hjʊˈrɪstɪks/ *n* [plural, U] the study of how people use their experience to find answers to questions or to improve performance

**hew** /hjuː/ *v past tense* **hewed** *past participle* **hewed** or **hewn** /hjuːn/ *literary* **1** [I,T] to cut something with a cutting tool: *hewn stone* **2 hew a path/channel etc** to cut a path etc through something —see also ROUGH-HEWN —**hewer** *n* [C]

**hewn** /hjuːn/ the past participle of hew

**hex[1]** /heks/ *n* [C] *especially AmE* an evil CURSE[2] (2) that brings trouble

**hex[2]** *v* [T] *especially AmE* to use magic powers to make bad things happen to someone; CURSE[1] (3)

**hex·a·de·ci·mal** /ˌheksəˈdesə̇məl◂/ also **hex** *adj technical* hexadecimal numbers are based on the number 16 and are mainly used on computers

**hex·a·gon** /ˈheksəgən‖-gɑːn/ *n* [C] a shape with six sides —**hexagonal** /hekˈsægənəl/ *adj*

**hex·a·gram** /ˈheksəgræm/ *n* [C] a star shape with six points, made from two TRIANGLES

**hex·am·e·ter** /hekˈsæmə̇tə‖-ər/ *n* [C] a line of poetry with six main beats

**hey** /heɪ/ *interjection* a shout used to get someone's attention or to express surprise, interest, or annoyance

**hey·day** /ˈheɪdeɪ/ *n* **sb's/sth's heyday** the time when someone or something was most popular, successful, or powerful: *a picture of Greta Garbo in her heyday*

**hey pres·to** /ˌheɪ ˈprestəʊ‖-toʊ/ *interjection especially BrE* used to say that something happens so easily that it seems to be magic

**HGV** /ˌeɪtʃ dʒiː ˈviː/ *n* [C] *BrE* a HEAVY GOODS VEHICLE; a large road vehicle used for moving goods

S 1 **hi** /haɪ/ *interjection informal* hello: *Hi! How are you?* | **hi there!** *Hi there! I haven't seen you for ages.*

**hi·a·tus** /haɪˈeɪtəs/ *n* [C usually singular] **1** *formal* a break or INTERRUPTION in an activity: *Talks between the two countries have resumed after a six year hiatus.* **2** a space where something is missing, especially in a piece of writing **3** *technical* a pause between two vowel sounds

**hi·ber·nate** /ˈhaɪbəneɪt‖-ər-/ *v* [I] if an animal hibernates, it sleeps for the whole winter —**hibernation** /ˌhaɪbəˈneɪʃən‖-bər-/ *n* [U]

**hi·bis·cus** /haɪˈbɪskəs/ *n* [C,U] a tropical plant with large brightly coloured flowers

**hic·cup[1], hiccough** /ˈhɪkʌp, -kəp/ *n* [C] **1** [usually plural] a sudden, quick, movement of your DIAPHRAGM (1) that happens repeatedly and uncontrollably for a short time: **get/have hiccups** *Don't drink so fast – you'll get hiccups.* **2** a small problem or delay: *Fortunately, the computer problem was only a hiccup.*

**hiccup[2]** *v* **hicupped, hiccupping** [I] to have hiccups

**hick** /hɪk/ *n* [C] *AmE informal* an insulting word for someone who lives in the countryside, and is considered to be less educated than people who live in the city

**hick·ey** /ˈhɪki/ *n* [C] *AmE* a red mark on someone's skin caused by someone else sucking it as a sexual act; LOVEBITE *BrE*

**hick·o·ry** /ˈhɪkəri/ *n* [C,U] a North American tree that produces nuts, or the wood that comes from this tree

**hid** /hɪd/ the past tense of HIDE[1]

**hid·den[1]** /ˈhɪdn/ the past participle of HIDE[1]

**hidden[2]** *adj* **1** difficult to see or find: *hidden passages and hidden staircases* **2** not easy to notice or realize: *hidden problems*

**hidden a·gen·da** /ˌ·· ·ˈ··/ *n* [C] an intended result of a plan or activity that you do not tell other people about: *Voters suspected a hidden political agenda.*

**hide[1]** /haɪd/ *v past tense* **hid** *past participle* **hidden** /ˈhɪdn/ **1** [T] to deliberately put or keep something in a place where it cannot easily be seen or found: *My girlfriend keeps hiding my cigarettes.* | **hide sth from sb** *The bushes hid Dave's bike completely from the passers-by.* | **keep sth hidden** *Confidential documents are kept hidden in a secret vault.* | **hide sth in/under/behind etc** *She hides his letters under her pillow.* **2** [I] to go or stay in a place where you hope no one will find you: *Quick – she's coming – we'd better hide!* | [+ **under/behind/in etc**] *Harry hid under the bed until they had gone.* | **hide from** *Kylie tried to hide from the stranger.* **3** [T] to keep someone in a place where other people will not find them: **hide sb from** *an attempt to hide her children from their violent father* **4** [T] to not show your feelings to people: *Paul struggled to hide his disappointment at not getting the job.* **5** [T] to deliberately not tell people facts or information: *He took off his ring to hide the fact that he was married.* | **hide sth from** *Don't try to hide anything from me.* **6 have nothing to hide** to be willing to tell people about everything you have done, because you have done nothing dishonest, illegal, or immoral: *The company claimed that the deal was legal and that they had nothing to hide.* **7 hide your light under a bushel** to not tell anyone that you are very good at something

S 2 W 2

**hide**

**hide[2]** *n* [C] **1** *BrE* a place from which you can watch animals or birds without being seen by them; BLIND[3] (3) *AmE* **2** an animal's skin, especially when it has been removed to be used for leather: *ox hide gloves* **3 have/tan sb's hide** *spoken humorous* to punish someone severely **4 not see hide nor hair of** *spoken* to have not seen someone at all recently: *I haven't seen hide nor hair of him for ages.*

**hide-and-seek** /ˌ· · ˈ·/ also **hide-and-go-seek** /ˌ· · · ˈ·/ *AmE* —*n* [U] a children's game in which one player shuts their eyes while the others hide, and then goes to look for them

**hide·a·way** /ˈhaɪdəweɪ/ *n* [C] a place where you can go when you want to be alone

**hide·bound** /ˈhaɪdbaʊnd/ *adj* having old-fashioned attitudes and ideas; NARROW-MINDED: *hidebound reactionaries*

H

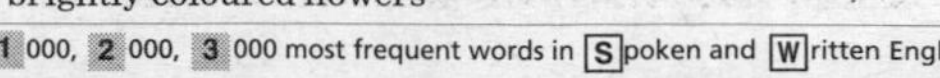

**hid·e·ous** /ˈhɪdiəs/ *adj* extremely unpleasant or ugly: *a hideous dress* —**hideously** *adv* —**hideousness** *n* [U]

**hide-out** /ˈ· ·/ *n* [C] a place where someone goes because they do not want anyone to find them

**hid·ing** /ˈhaɪdɪŋ/ *n* **1 be/go into hiding** to hide somewhere because you have done something illegal or are in danger: *The gang spent weeks in hiding before they were finally caught.* **2 give sb/get a good hiding** *spoken informal* **a)** used to say that you will physically punish someone: *Any more cheek from you and you'll get a good hiding.* **b)** to defeat someone or be defeated very seriously, especially in a sports game **3 be on a hiding to nothing** *BrE informal* to be completely wasting your time trying to do something

**hiding place** /ˈ·· ˌ·/ *n* [C] a place where you can hide or where you can hide something

**hie** /haɪ/ *v* [I,T] *old use* to make yourself hurry, or go quickly

**hi·er·ar·chy** /ˈhaɪrɑːki‖-ɑːr-/ *n* **1** [C,U] a system within an organization in which people have authority and control over the people in the rank below them, who then have authority over the people below them: *a rigid hierarchy* **2** [C] the group of people in an organization who have power or control: *All policy decisions were made by the communist hierarchy.* —**hierarchical** /haɪˈrɑːkɪkəl‖-ɑːr-/ *adj* —**hierarchically** /-kli/ *adv*

**hi·e·ro·glyph·ics** /ˌhaɪrəˈglɪfɪks/ *n* [U] a system of writing that uses pictures to represent words —**hieroglyphic** *adj*: *hieroglyphic script*

**hi-fi** /ˈhaɪ faɪ, ˌhaɪ ˈfaɪ/ *n plural* **hi-fis** **1** [C] a piece of high quality electronic equipment for playing recorded music **2** [U] a way of playing recorded music that is very clear and of very good quality

**hig·gle·dy-pig·gle·dy** /ˌhɪgəldi ˈpɪgəldi/ *adj* things that are higgledy-piggledy are mixed together in an untidy way —**higgledy-piggledy** *adv*

**-high** /haɪ/ *suffix* [in adjectives] of a particular height: *The wall was about chest-high.* (=as high as your chest) | *a 7000 metre-high mountain*

S1 W1

## high¹ /haɪ/ *adj*

① MEASUREMENT/DISTANCE
② LARGE AMOUNT/NUMBER
③ IMPORTANT
④ SOUND
⑤ VERY GOOD
⑥ DRUGS/ALCOHOL
⑦ HAPPY
⑧ PROUD
⑨ OTHER MEANINGS

a high shelf

a tall building

### ① MEASUREMENT/DISTANCE

**1 ▶FROM BOTTOM TO TOP◀** something that is high measures a long distance from its bottom to its top: *the highest mountain in Japan* | *a castle surrounded by high walls* | **100 feet/30 metres etc high** *a building 20 stories high* | *How high is the Eiffel tower?* | *a ten-foot high wall* | **chest/waist/knee etc high** (=as high as your chest etc) *The grass was knee-high.*

**2 ▶ABOVE THE GROUND◀** being a long way, or a longer way than usual, above the ground: *a spacious room with a high ceiling* | *a high shelf* | *high in the sky* | **high up** *High up among the clouds, we could just see the summit of Everest.*

**3 ▶SEA/RIVER ETC◀** having risen to a higher level than usual: *The river was unusually high.* | *high tide*

### ② LARGE AMOUNT/NUMBER

**4** a high amount, number, or level is greater than normal: *high blood pressure* | *high levels of radiation* | *high temperatures* | **high rent/price/tax etc** *the high cost of insurance* | **at high speed** (=very fast) *A car was approaching at high speed.* | **high proportion/percentage** (=a very large part of an amount) *A high proportion of married women have part-time jobs.*

**5 ▶CONTAINING A LOT◀** containing a lot of a particular substance or quality: *an alloy with a high carbon content* | **high in fat/sugar/salt etc** *Beer is high in calories.*

### ③ IMPORTANT

**6 ▶IN SOCIETY/ORGANIZATION◀** having an important or powerful position in society or in an organization: *the highest rank in the US Navy* | *the City's highest honour* | **high up** (=in a powerful position) *someone high up in in the civil service* | **high office** *With men like Gould in high office, it was easy for the military to influence policy.* | **high society** (=rich people of the highest social class) —see also HIGH-UP, HIGH-RANKING, **have friends in high places** (FRIEND (10))

**7 be high on the list/agenda** to be important and need to be dealt with quickly

### ④ SOUND

**8** near the top of the range of sounds that humans can hear: *Dogs respond to sounds that are too high for the human ear.* —see also HIGH-PITCHED

### ⑤ VERY GOOD

**9 high quality/standard/calibre etc** very good quality etc: *high quality goods* | *a high standard of workmanship*

**10 high opinion/praise/regard etc** strong approval,

or an expression of strong approval: **have a high opinion of** *I have a high opinion of Miss Boyce's work.* | **hold sb/sth in high esteem/regard** (=respect them very much) *As an educationalist, he was held in high esteem.*
**11 high standards/principles** rules of personal behaviour based on the the belief that everyone should always be very good and honest: *a man of high moral principles*
**12 have high hopes/expectations** to hope for or expect very good results or great success: *parents who have such high hopes for their children*
**13 high point/spot** the best part of an activity or occasion: *Our visit to the Grand Canyon was definitely the high point of our vacation.*

⑥ **DRUGS/ALCOHOL**
**14** [not before noun] behaving in an unusually excited way because of taking drugs: [+ **on**] *They were high on cocaine.* | **get high** (=take a drug to make yourself high) | **high as a kite** (=very high)

⑦ **HAPPY**
**15 high spirits** feelings of happiness and energy, especially when you are having fun: *I know the kids are a bit noisy but it's just high spirits.* | **in high spirits** *It was a bright sunny day and we set off in high spirits.*
**16 ▶ HAPPY/EXCITED ◀** happy and excited: [+**on**] *We were still high on our victory over the champions.*
**17 have a high old time** *old-fashioned* to enjoy an occasion very much

⑧ **PROUD**
**18 be/get on your high horse** to behave or talk as if you are better than other people
**19 high and mighty** talking or behaving as if you think you are more important than other people

⑨ **OTHER MEANINGS**
**20 it is high time** used to mean that something should have been done already: *It's high time you got a job and settled down.*
**21 ▶ FOOD ◀** cheese, meat etc that is high is not fresh and has a strong smell or taste
**22 high wind** a strong wind
**23 high complexion/colouring** a naturally pink or red face
**24 high drama/adventure** events or situations that are very exciting: *a life with moments of high drama*
**25 ▶ TIME ◀** the middle or the most important part of a particular period of time: *high summer* | *the high renaissance* | **high noon** (=12 o'clock in the middle of the day) —see also HIGH SEASON
**26 high life/living** the enjoyable life that rich people and fashionable people have: *the high life of a capital city*
**27 high finance** the business of dealing with very large sums of money
**28 high style/register** the style of language used in literature —see also HIGHLY, **in high dudgeon** (DUDGEON), **stink to high heaven** (STINK[1] (1))

**USAGE NOTE: HIGH**
WORD CHOICE: **high, higher, advanced, tall**
**High** (opposite **low**) is used of most things, especially when you are thinking only of how far something, or its top, is from the ground: *a high shelf* | *a high mountain* | *The shelf's too high, I can't reach it.*
Many things you cannot touch may also be **high**: *a high standard* | *a high degree of sophistication* | *high technology*. However, with some words related to education **higher** (or **advanced**) must be used instead: *higher education* | *advanced teaching/techniques* | *a higher degree/diploma* (but do not confuse this with *High School diploma* etc).
**Tall** (opposite **short**) is used for people and animals: *Your son's getting tall, isn't he?*
**Tall** is also used for things that are high and narrow, especially when you are thinking of the complete distance from top to bottom: *a tall building like the Sears Tower* | *a tall tree/column/vase/fridge/bottle*

**high**[2] *adv*
**1 ▶ ABOVE THE GROUND ◀** at or to a level high above the ground: [+ **into/above etc**] *Paula threw the ball high into the air.* | *flying high in the sky*
**2 ▶ VALUE/COST/AMOUNT ◀** at or to a high value, cost, amount etc: *The dollar stayed high after a busy day on the foreign exchanges.* | *He scored higher than anyone else in the class.*
**3 ▶ SOUND ◀** with a high sound: *boy's voices, ringing high above everyone else's*
**4 ▶ ACHIEVEMENT ◀** to a high rank or level of achievement, especially in an organization, business etc: *Don't set your goals too low. You should always aim high.*
**5 be left high and dry** *informal* to be left without any help or without the things that you need
**6 look/search high and low** to try to find someone or something by looking everywhere: *We looked high and low for Sandy but couldn't find her.*
**7 hold your head high** to behave in a proud confident way, especially in a difficult situation: *You've kept the family together, I think you can hold your head high.*
**8 live high on the hog** *AmE informal* to enjoy expensive food, clothes etc without worrying about the cost: *They've been living high on the hog since Jim got the money from his aunt.* —see also **be riding high** (RIDE[1] (7)), **be running high** (RUN[1] (28))

**high**[3] *n* [C]
**1 ▶ NUMBER/AMOUNT ◀** the highest price, number, temperature etc that has ever been recorded: *The price of oil reached a new high this week.*
**2 ▶ WEATHER ◀ a)** the highest temperature in a particular day, week, month etc: *Highs today were in the mid 20's.* **b)** an area of HIGH PRESSURE[2] that affects the weather
**3 ▶ DRUGS ◀** a feeling of pleasure or excitement produced by some drugs: *The high she got from cocaine never lasted.*
**4 ▶ EXCITEMENT ◀** a feeling of happiness or excitement you get from doing something you enjoy: **be on a high** *I've been on a high ever since we won the game last week.*
**5 ▶ SCHOOL ◀** a short form of HIGH SCHOOL, used in the name of a school: *She graduated from Reseda High in 1979.*
**6 on high** *biblical* in, to, or from heaven or a high place
**7 from on high** *humorous* from someone in a position of authority: *an order from on high*

**high·ball** /ˈhaɪbɔːl‖-bɔːl/ *n* [C] *especially AmE* an alcoholic drink, especially WHISKY or BRANDY mixed with water or SODA
**high beam** /ˌ· ˈ·/ *n* [U] *AmE* lights at the front of a car that are on as brightly as possible —see also BRIGHTS
**high-born** /ˌ· ˈ·◂/ *adj formal* born into the highest social class
**high·boy** /ˈhaɪbɔɪ/ *n* [C] *AmE* a piece of tall wooden furniture with many drawers; TALLBOY *BrE*
**high·brow** /ˈhaɪbraʊ/ *adj* **1** a highbrow book, film etc is intended for very intelligent people who like serious subjects **2** someone who is highbrow is interested in serious or complicated ideas and subjects; INTELLECTUAL —**highbrow** *n* [C] —compare LOWBROW
**high·chair** /ˌhaɪˈtʃeə‖ˈhaɪtʃer/ *n* [C] a special tall chair that a young child sits in to eat —see picture at CHAIR[1]

**High Church** /ˌ· ˈ·◂/ *n* [U] the part of the Church of England that is closest in its beliefs to the Roman Catholic Church —compare LOW CHURCH —**High Church** *adj*

**high-class** /ˌ· ˈ·◂/ *adj* [usually before noun] of good quality and style, and usually expensive: *a high-class restaurant* —compare LOW-CLASS

**high com·mand** /ˌ· ·ˈ·/ *n* [singular] the most important leaders of a country's army, navy etc: *the German High Command*

**high com·mis·sion** /ˌ· ·ˈ··/ *n* [C] **1** a group of people working for a government or an international organization to deal with a specific problem **2** a group of people with official duties concerning the relationship of one Commonwealth country with another —**High Commissioner** *n* [C]

**high court** /ˌ· ˈ·◂/ *n* [C usually singular] a court of law in Britain that is at a higher level than ordinary courts and that can be asked to change the decisions of a lower court

**high-def·i·ni·tion** /ˌ· ··ˈ··◂/ *adj* [only before noun] a high-definition television or computer shows images very clearly

**higher¹** /ˈhaɪə‖-ər/ *adj* [the comparative of *high*] **1** [only before noun] more advanced in development or organization: *the higher forms of mammals, such as the primates and big cats* **2** at a more advanced level of knowledge: *higher mathematics* —see HIGH (USAGE)

**high·er²** *n* [C] the higher level of the Scottish Certificate of Education

**higher ed·u·ca·tion** /ˌ·· ··ˈ··/ *n* [U] college or university education as opposed to school or HIGH SCHOOL —compare FURTHER EDUCATION

**higher-up** /ˌ·· ˈ·◂/ *n* [C] *informal* someone who has a high rank in an organization: *Rumour has it that the higher-ups want to push the schedule forward.*

**highest com·mon fac·tor** /ˌ···· ˈ··/ *n* [C] *technical* the largest number that a set of numbers can be divided by exactly: *the highest common factor of 12, 24 and 30 is 6.*

**high ex·plo·sive** /ˌ· ·ˈ··◂/ *n* [C,U] a substance that explodes with great power and violence

**high·fa·lu·tin** /ˌhaɪfəˈluːtɪn◂‖-tn◂/ *adj informal* highfalutin language or behaviour seems silly although it is intended to be impressive

**high fi·del·i·ty** /ˌ· ·ˈ···◂/ *adj* [usually before noun] high fidelity recording equipment produces sound that is very clear —see also HI-FI

**high five** /ˌ· ˈ·/ *n* [singular] *especially AmE* the action of hitting someone's open hand with your own above your heads to show that you are pleased about something

**high-fli·er** /ˌ· ˈ··/ *n* [C] someone who is extremely successful in their job or in school: *a young businessman pegged as a high-flier by the media* —**high-flying** *adj*

**high-flown** /ˌ· ˈ·◂/ *adj* high-flown language sounds impressive but does not have much real meaning

**high-grade** /ˌ· ˈ·◂/ *adj* [only before noun] of the best quality: *high-grade beef*

**high-hand·ed** /ˌ· ˈ··◂/ *adj* using your authority in an unreasonable way: *high-handed and insensitive management decisions* —**high-handedly** *adv* —**high-handedness** *n* [U]

**high heels** /ˌ· ˈ·/ *n* [plural] women's shoes with high heels —**high-heeled** *adj* —see picture on page 840

**high jinks** also **hi·jinks** /ˈhaɪdʒɪŋks/ *AmE n* [U] *old-fashioned* noisy or excited behaviour when people are having fun: *youthful high jinks*

**high jump** /ˈ· ·/ *n* **1 the high jump** a sports event in which someone runs and jumps over a bar that is raised higher each time they jump **2 be (in) for the high jump** *BrE informal* if someone is for the high jump, they will be punished for something they have done wrong —**high jumper** *n* [C]

**high·land** /ˈhaɪlənd/ *adj* [only before noun] **1** coming from or connected to the Scottish Highlands: *Highland pipers* **2** from or about an area with a lot of mountains: *workers in highland Ecuador*

**High·land·er** /ˈhaɪləndə‖-ər/ *n* [C] someone from the Scottish Highlands

**Highland fling** /ˌ·· ˈ·/ *n* [C] a fast Scottish dance, danced by one person

**high·lands** /ˈhaɪləndz/ *n* [plural] **1 the Highlands** an area in the north of Scotland where there are a lot of mountains **2** an area of a country where there are a lot of mountains: *forested highlands* —compare LOWLANDS

**high-lev·el** /ˌ· ˈ··◂/ *adj* [only before noun] **1** done by or involving people who are in powerful positions, for example the government: *officials attending a high-level conference on arms control* **2** at a high level or degree: *high-level anxiety* **3** high-level words or language are very formal or technical **4** a high-level computer language is similar to human language rather than machine language —compare LOW-LEVEL

**high life** /ˈ· ·/ *n* **the high life** a way of life that involves a lot of parties, and expensive food, wine, travel etc

**high·light¹** /ˈhaɪlaɪt/ *v* [T] **1** to make a problem or subject easy to notice so that people pay attention to it: *a test to highlight students' strengths and weaknesses* **2** to mark written words with a special coloured pen, or in a different colour on a computer, so that you can see them easily **3** to make some parts of your hair a lighter colour than the rest —**highlighting** *n* [U]

**highlight²** *n* **1** [C] the most important, interesting, or enjoyable part of something such as a holiday, performance, or sports competition: *That weekend in Venice was definitely the highlight of our trip.* **2 highlights** [plural] areas of hair that have been made a lighter colour than the rest **3** [C] *technical* a light, bright area on a painting or photograph

**high·light·er** /ˈhaɪlaɪtə‖-ər/ *n* [C] a special light coloured pen used for marking words in a book, article etc

**high·ly** /ˈhaɪli/ *adv* **1** [+ adj, adv] very: *highly successful* | *highly skilled* **2** [+ adj, adv] to a high level or standard: *She is a highly educated woman.* | *highly paid experts* **3 highly placed** in an important or powerful position: *a highly placed government official.* **4 speak/think highly of** to tell other people how good someone is at something or to think they are very good at something

**highly strung** /ˌ·· ˈ·◂/ *especially BrE,* also **high-strung** /ˌ· ˈ·◂/ *AmE* —*adj* nervous, and easily upset or excited: *a highly strung child*

**High Mass** /ˌ· ˈ·/ *n* [C, U] a very formal church ceremony in the Roman Catholic Church

**high-mind·ed** /ˌ· ˈ··◂/ *adj* having very high moral standards or principles: *a high-minded sermon on charity* —**high-mindedly** *adv* —**high-mindedness** *n* [U]

**High·ness** /ˈhaɪnɪs/ *n* [C] **Your/Her/His Highness** used to speak to or about a king, queen, prince etc

**high-oc·tane** /ˌ· ˈ··◂/ *adj* high-octane petrol is of a very high quality

**high-pitched** /ˌ· ˈ·◂/ *adj* a high-pitched voice or sound is higher than usual

**high-pow·ered** /ˌ· ˈ··◂/ *adj* [usually before noun] **1** a high-powered machine, vehicle, or piece of equipment is very powerful: *a high-powered automobile* **2** having a powerful and important job: *a high-powered publisher*

**high-pres·sure¹** /ˌ· ˈ··◂/ *adj* [only before noun] **1** a high-pressure job or situation is one in which you need to work very hard; STRESSFUL **2 high-pressure sales/selling methods etc** very direct and often successful ways of persuading people to buy something: *high-pressure sales techniques* **3** containing or using a very high pressure or force of water, gas, air etc

**high-pressure²** *n* [U] a condition of the air over a large area that affects the weather

**high priest** /ˌ· ˈ·/ *n* [C] **1** *informal* someone who is famous for being the best at something such as a type of art or music: *the high priest of modern jazz* **2** a chief PRIEST in some religions

**high-prin·ci·pled** /ˌ· ˈ···◂/ *adj* having high moral standards

**high-pro·file** /ˌ· ˈ··◂/ *adj* [only before noun] attracting a lot of public attention, usually deliberately: *a high-profile public figure* —**high profile** *n* [singular]

**high-rank·ing** /ˌ· ˈ··◂/ *adj* [only before noun] having a high position in a government or other organization

**high re·lief** /ˌ· ·ˈ·/ *n* [U] **1** a form of art in which figures cut in stone or wood stand out from the surface —compare BAS-RELIEF **2 throw sth into high relief** to make something very clear and easy to notice

**high-rise** /ˈ· ·/ *adj* [only before noun] high-rise buildings are tall buildings with many levels —compare LOW-RISE —**high rise** *n* [C] *They live in a high rise on the East Side.*

**high-risk** /ˌ· ˈ·◂/ *adj* [only before noun] involving a risk of death, injury, failure etc: *high-risk investments | cancer screening for women over 55 and other high-risk groups*

**high road** /ˈ· ·/ *n* [C] *BrE old use* a main road

**high rol·ler** /ˌ· ˈ··/ *n* [C] *AmE informal* someone who spends a lot of money carelessly or risks a lot of money on games, races etc

**high school** /ˈ· ·/ *n* **1** [C,U] a school in the US and Canada for children of 14 or 15 to 18 years old **2** used in the names of some schools in Britain for children from 11 to 18 years old: *Leytonstone High School for Girls* —*compare* SECONDARY SCHOOL

**high seas** /ˌ· ˈ·/ *n* **the high seas a)** the areas of ocean around the world that do not belong to any particular country **b)** *literary* the sea

**high sea·son** /ˌ· ˈ··/ *n* [singular, U] *especially BrE* the time of year when businesses make a lot of money and prices are high, especially in the tourist industry; PEAK SEASON —compare LOW SEASON

**high-sound·ing** /ˌ· ˈ··◂/ *adj* [only before noun] high-sounding statements, principles etc seem very impressive but are often insincere

**high-speed** /ˌ· ˈ·◂/ *adj* [only before noun] designed to travel or operate very fast: *a high-speed train*

**high-spir·it·ed** /ˌ· ˈ···◂/ *adj* **1** someone who is high-spirited has a lot of energy and enjoys fun and adventure **2** a horse that is high-spirited is nervous and difficult to control

**high street** /ˈ· ·/ *n* [C] *BrE* the main street of a town where most of the shops and businesses are: *Camden High Street | peak sales on the high street at Christmas |* **high street banks/shops etc** (=the shops etc that most people use) —compare MAIN STREET (1)

**high-strung** /ˌ· ˈ·◂/ *adj* an American form of HIGHLY STRUNG

**high ta·ble** /ˌ· ˈ··/ *n* [U] *BrE* the table where the most important people at a formal occasion sit

**high·tail** /ˈhaɪteɪl/ *v* **hightail it** *informal* to leave a place quickly: *kids hightailing it down the street on their bikes*

**high tea** /ˌ· ˈ·/ *n* [C,U] *BrE* a meal of cold food, cakes etc eaten in the early evening

**high-tech** /ˌhaɪˈtek◂/ *adj* [usually before noun] **1** using high technology: *high-tech industries* —compare LOW TECH **2** furniture, designs etc that are high-tech are made in a very modern style —**high tech** *n* [U]

**high tech·nol·o·gy** /ˌ· ·ˈ···/ *n* [U] the use of the most modern machines and methods in industry, business etc

**high-ten·sion** /ˌ· ˈ··◂/ *adj* **high-tension wires/cables etc** wires etc that have a powerful electric current going through them

**high tide** /ˌ· ˈ·/ *n* **1** [C,U] the point or time at which the sea reaches its highest level **2** [singular] the time when something is at its best or most successful: *The election victory marked the high tide in the party's fortunes.*

**high-toned** /ˌ· ˈ·◂/ *adj* seeming to be concerned with high moral principles

**high trea·son** /ˌ· ˈ··/ *n* [U] the crime of putting your country in great danger, for example by giving military secrets to the enemy

**high-up** /ˈ· ·/ *n* [C] *BrE* someone who has a high rank in an organization; HIGHER-UP

**high wa·ter** /ˌ· ˈ··/ *n* [U] the period of time during which the water in a river or the sea is at its highest level because of the TIDE[1] (1) —compare LOW WATER —see also **come hell or high water** (HELL[1] (22))

**high water mark** /ˌ· ˈ·· ·/ *n* [singular] **1** the mark that shows the highest level that the the sea or a river reaches **2** the time when someone or something is most successful: *the high water mark of Herrera's presidency*

**high·way** /ˈhaɪweɪ/ *n* [C] **1** *especially AmE* a broad main road that joins one town to another —compare FREEWAY, EXPRESSWAY, MOTORWAY **2** *BrE* **a)** *old-fashioned* any road or street **b) the public highway** an expression used in legal documents meaning roads **3 highway robbery** *AmE informal* a situation in which something costs you a lot more than it should: *It's highway robbery, charging that much for gas!* S2

**Highway Code** /ˌ·· ˈ·/ *n* [singular] the set of official rules and laws about driving and using roads in Britain

**high·way·man** /ˈhaɪweɪmən/ *n plural* **highwaymen** /-mən/ [C] someone who stopped people and carriages on the roads and robbed them especially in the 17th and 18th centuries

**highway pa·trol** /ˈ·· ·ˌ·/ *n* [singular] the police who make sure that people obey the rules on main roads in the US

**high wire** /ˈ· ·/ *n* [C] a tightly stretched rope or wire high above the ground that someone walks along, usually as part of a CIRCUS performance

**hi·jack[1]** /ˈhaɪdʒæk/ *v* [T] **1** to use violence or threats to take control of a plane, vehicle, or ship **2** to take control of something and use it for your own purposes: *Some people think the party has been hijacked by right-wing extremists.* —**hijacker** *n* [C]

**hijack[2]** *n* [C] *BrE* an act of hijacking a plane, vehicle etc

**hi·jack·ing** /ˈhaɪdʒækɪŋ/ *n* **1** [C,U] the use of violence or threats to take control of a plane: *the recent series of airplane hijackings* **2** [U] the act of stealing goods from vehicles

**hi·jinks** /ˈhaɪdʒɪŋks/ *n* [plural] an American spelling of HIGH JINKS

**hike[1]** /haɪk/ *n* [C] **1** a long walk in the mountains or countryside: *a hike in the woods* **2** *especially AmE informal* a large increase in prices, wages, taxes etc: *a petition against the proposed tax hikes* **3 take a hike** *AmE spoken* used to tell someone rudely to go away

**hike[2]** *v* **1** [I, T] to walk a long way in the mountains or countryside: **hike sth** *AmE*: *He wants to hike the Himalayas.* | **go hiking** *The kids often go hiking at weekends.* —compare WALKING[1] (1) **2** also **hike** sth ↔ **up** [T] *especially AmE* to increase prices, taxes, fees etc, especially by a large amount

**hike** sth ↔ **up** **1** *especially AmE informal* to lift up a piece of your clothing: *She hiked her skirt up to climb the stairs.* **2** HIKE[2] (2)

**hik·er** /ˈhaɪkə‖-ər/ *n* [C] someone who walks long distances in the mountains or country for pleasure; WALKER (1)

**hi·lar·i·ous** /hɪˈleəriəs‖-ˈler-/ *adj* extremely funny: *You should have seen that program last night – it was hilarious!* —**hilariously** *adv*

**hi·lar·i·ty** /hɪˈlærɪ̣ti/ *n* [U] laughter, or a feeling of fun: *Gloria's costume caused a good deal of hilarity.*

**hill** /hɪl/ *n* [C] **1** an area of land that is higher than the land around it, like a mountain but smaller **2** a slope on a road: *There's a steep hill ahead – get into low gear.* **3 on the Hill** *AmE* on CAPITOL HILL or in the US government **4 over the hill** no longer young, and therefore no longer attractive or good at doing things: *Kathleen thinks she's over the hill, but she's only 32.* **5 it doesn't amount to a hill of beans** *AmE spoken* it is not important S2 W2

**hill·bil·ly** /ˈhɪlbɪli/ *n* [C] *AmE* an insulting word meaning an uneducated person who lives in the mountains

**hill·ock** /ˈhɪlək/ *n* [C] a little hill

**hill·side** /ˈhɪlsaɪd/ *n* [C] the sloping side of a hill

**hill sta·tion** /ˈ· ˌ··/ *n* [C] a town in the hills, especially in South Asia, where people go to escape the hot weather

**hill·y** /ˈhɪli/ *adj* having a lot of hills: *a hilly region*

**hilt** /hɪlt/ *n* [C] **1** the handle of a sword or knife that is used as a weapon —see picture at SWORD **2** **(up) to the hilt** completely, or as much as possible: *mortgaged up to the hilt | I'd back him to the hilt any day.*

S1 W1 **him** /ɪm· *strong* hɪm/ *strong pron* object form of 'he': *I don't know why he left early, I'll have to ask him about it. | It's a great movie, with Sylvester Stallone as we've never seen him before! | Imagine Ian becoming a pilot, and him so scared of flying too.* —see ME (USAGE)

**himbo** /ˈhɪmbəʊ‖-boʊ/ *n* [C] *humorous* a young man who is sexually attractive but is not very intelligent

S1 W1 **him·self** /ɪmˈself·hɪm-/ *strong pron* **1** used to emphasize the pronoum 'he', a male name etc: *To her surprise it was the President himself who opened the door. | It must be true, he said so himself. | How can he criticise her work when he has been judged so harshly himself.* **2** **not be/feel etc himself** if a man, boy etc is not himself, he does not feel or behave in the way that he usually does because he is nervous or upset: *I think there's something on his mind – he hasn't really seemed himself lately.* **3** **(all) by himself** **a)** alone: *He said he would prefer to spend some time by himself for a while.* **b)** without help: *My son was about 2 years old before he could walk by himself.* **4** **(all) to himself** if a man, boy etc has something to himself, he does not have to share it with anyone: *When his brother got married, John finally had a bedroom to himself.* **5** **a)** the reflexive form of HE: *I don't think he hurt himself when he fell | His name is James but he usually calls himself Jim. | He spends all day by the fire, talking to himself.* **b)** the reflexive form of HE used after words like EVERYONE, ANYONE, NO ONE etc: *Everyone should learn to respect himself.* —see also YOURSELF

**hind¹** /haɪnd/ *adj* **hind legs/feet** the back legs or feet of an animal with four legs —see also **talk the hind legs off a donkey** (TALK¹ (11))

**hind²** *n* [C] a female DEER

**hin·der** /ˈhɪndə‖-ər/ *v* [T] to make it difficult for someone to do something or for something to develop: *High interest rates will hinder economic growth.*

**Hin·di** /ˈhɪndi/ *n* [U] one of the official languages of India

**hind·most** /ˈhaɪndməʊst‖-moʊst/ *adj old use* furthest behind —see also **devil take the hindmost** (DEVIL (14))

**hind·quar·ters** /ˈhaɪndˌkwɔːtəz‖-ˌkwɔːrtərz/ *n* [plural] the back part of an animal, including the back legs —see picture at HORSE¹

**hin·drance** /ˈhɪndrəns/ *n* **1** [C] something or someone that makes it difficult for you to do something successfully: **be a hindrance to** *Lack of funding was a serious hindrance to the progress of our research.* | **be more of a hindrance than a help** (=try to help but cause more problems) **2** [U] *formal* the act of making it difficult for someone to do something —see also **without let or hindrance** (LET² (2))

**hind·sight** /ˈhaɪndsaɪt/ *n* [U] the ability to understand facts about a situation only after it has happened: **with the benefit/wisdom of hindsight** (=when hindsight makes it possible to realize what mistakes were made) *With the benefit of hindsight it's easy to criticize Lyndon Johnson's fateful decision.*

**Hin·du** /ˈhɪnduː, ˌhɪnˈduː◂/ *n plural* **Hindus** [C] someone who believes in Hinduism —**Hindu** *adj*: *a Hindu temple*

**Hin·du·is·m** /ˈhɪndu-ɪzəm/ *n* [U] the main religion in India, which includes belief in DESTINY and REINCARNATION

**hinge¹** /hɪndʒ/ *n* [C] a metal part used to fasten a door to its frame, a lid to a box etc, so that can swing open and shut —see picture at GLASS¹

**hinge²** *v*

**hinge on/upon** sth *phr v* [T not in progressive] if a result hinges on something happening, it depends on it completely: *The future prospects of a student hinge on his performance in these examinations*

**hinged** /hɪndʒd/ *adj* joined by a hinge

**hint¹** /hɪnt/ *n* [C] **1** something that you say or do in order to tell someone something in an indirect way, so that they can guess what you mean: **drop a hint (that)** (=give a hint) *Harry was dropping hints that he wanted to be invited to the party.* | **a broad hint** (=one that is deliberately easy to understand) | **take a/the hint** (=understand someone's hint) *I kept looking at my watch, but Laura wouldn't take the hint – she didn't leave till midnight.* **2** a very small amount or sign of something: **[+ of]** *There was a hint of anger in his voice. | a sauce with a hint of garlic* | **give no hint of/that** *literary*: *a blue sky that gave no hint of the storm to come* **3** a useful piece of advice about how to do something: **[+ on]** *helpful hints on looking after house plants*

**hint²** *v* [I,T] to say something in an indirect way, but so that someone can guess what you mean: **[+ at]** *What are you hinting at?* | **hint (that)** *I think she was hinting that I might be offered a contract.*

**hin·ter·land** /ˈhɪntəlænd‖-ər-/ *n* [singular] an area of land beyond a coast or large river

**hip¹** /hɪp/ *n* [C] **1** one of the two parts on each side of your body between the top of your leg and your waist —see picture at BODY **2** [usually plural] the red fruit of some kinds of ROSE bushes; ROSE HIP

**hip²** *interjection* **hip, hip, hooray!** used as a shout of approval

**hip³** *adj informal* doing things or done according to the latest fashion

**hip·bath** /ˈhɪpbɑːθ‖-bæθ/ *n* [C] a bath you can sit but not lie down in

**hip flask** /ˈ· ·/ *n* [C] a small container for strong alcoholic drinks, made to fit in your pocket —see picture at FLASK

**hip hop** /ˈ· ·/ *n* [U] a kind of popular dance music with a regular heavy BEAT and spoken words

**hip·hug·gers** /ˈhɪphʌgəz‖-ərz/ *n* [plural] *AmE* HIPSTERS

**hip·pie, hippy** /ˈhɪpi/ *n* [C] someone opposed to the traditional standards of society who wears unusual clothes, has long hair, and takes drugs for pleasure

hippie

**hip·po** /ˈhɪpəʊ‖-poʊ/ *n* [C] *informal* a hippopotamus

**hip pock·et** /ˌ· ˈ··/ *n* [C] a back pocket in a pair of trousers or a skirt

**Hip·po·crat·ic oath** /ˌhɪpəkrætɪk ˈəʊθ‖-ˈoʊθ/ *n* [singular] the promise made by doctors that they will keep to the principles of the medical profession

**hip·po·pot·a·mus** /ˌhɪpəˈpɒtəməs‖-ˈpɑː-/ *n* [C] a large African animal with a large head, a wide mouth, and thick grey skin, that lives in and near water

**hip·py** /ˈhɪpi/ *n* [C] another spelling of HIPPIE

**hip·sters** /ˈhɪpstəz‖-ərz/ *n* [plural] *BrE* trousers that fit tightly over your HIPS and do not cover your waist; HIPHUGGERS *AmE*

**hire¹** /haɪə‖haɪr/ *v* [T] **1** *BrE* to pay money to borrow something for a period of hours or days; LET¹ (11), RENT¹ (3) *AmE*: *Let's hire a car for the weekend.* —see BORROW (USAGE) **2** **a)** to employ someone for a short time to do a job for you: *I'm hiring a private detective to trace my ex-husband.* **b)** *especially AmE* to employ someone: **hire and fire** (=employ and dismiss people) S

**hire** sth ↔ **out** *phr v* [T] *BrE* **1** to allow someone to use something for a short time in exchange for money; RENT¹ (3) *AmE*: *a little company that hires out boats to tourists* **2** **hire yourself out** to arrange to work for someone

**USAGE NOTE: HIRE**

WORD CHOICE: **hire, hire out, rent, rent out, let out, employ, take on, appoint, charter**

In British English you **hire** things for just a short time and the owner **hires** them **out** to you: *Let's hire a car for the weekend.* | *I'll have to hire a suit for the wedding.*

You **rent** things for a longer period: *Is that your own fax or do you rent it?* You **rent** a house, room etc and the owner **lets** it **(out)** to you.

In American English, however, you **rent** all of these things, and the owner **rents** them **out**. This is now starting to be used in British English as well.

In American English you **hire** people for any job, but in British English you only **hire** people for a particular purpose for a short time. Otherwise you **employ** them or **take** them **on** (or, more formally, **appoint** them): *We hired a caterer for the wedding reception.* | *Business is good – we'll have to take on more workers.*

In both American English and British English groups, companies etc may **charter** buses, ships, or planes for a special purpose: *UNICEF has chartered a plane to carry supplies to the disaster area.*

**hire²** *n* [U] **1** *BrE* an arrangement by which you borrow something for a short time in exchange for money: *a car hire company* | **for hire** (=available to hire) *boats for hire* | **on hire from** (=being hired) *The crane is on hire from a construction company.* **2** *old use* wages —see also **ply for hire** (PLY[1] (4))

**hired hand** /ˌ· ˈ·/ *n* [C] *AmE* someone who is employed to help on a farm

**hire·ling** /ˈhaɪəlɪŋ‖ˈhaɪr-/ *n* [C] someone who will work for anyone who is willing to pay

**hire pur·chase** /ˌ· ˈ··/ *n* [U] *BrE* a way of buying expensive goods by regularly paying small amounts over a period of time; INSTALLMENT PLAN *AmE*

**hir·sute** /ˈhɜːsjuːt, hɜːˈsjuːt‖ˈhɜːrsuːt, hɜːrˈsuːt/ *adj literary or humorous* having a lot of hair especially on your body and face

S1 W1 **his¹** /ɪz; *strong* hɪz/ *determiner* [possessive form of 'he'] **1** used to talk about something that belongs to or is connected with someone who has already been mentioned or who the person you are talking to already knows about: *He broke his arm while playing football with his children.* | *A man of his age shouldn't be running about like that.* **2** used especially after words like 'everyone', 'anyone', 'no one' etc when you mean 'their': *Who cares what everyone else is doing – each to his own, I say.* —compare THEIR

S1 W2 **his²** *pron* [possessive form of 'he'] **1** used to talk about something that belongs to or is connected with someone who has already been mentioned or who the person you are talking to already knows about: *That's not Philip's wife – his is a tall blonde woman.* | **sb/sth of his** *That stupid brother of his ran into my car.* **2** used after words like 'everyone', 'anyone', 'no one' etc when you mean 'theirs': *Everyone only wants what is his by right.* —compare THEIRS

**His·pan·ic** /hɪˈspænɪk/ *adj* from or connected with a country where Spanish or Portuguese is spoken —**Hispanic** *n* [C]

**hiss** /hɪs/ *v* **1** [I] to make a noise which sounds like 'ssss': *The snake slowly uncoiled, making a loud hissing noise.* **2** [T] to say something in a loud whisper: *"Be quiet," she hissed.* **3** [T] to hiss at a performer or speaker that you do not like —**hiss** *n* [C] —see picture on page 1261

**hist** /hɪst/ *interjection old use* a sound used to get someone's attention or to ask someone to be quiet

**his·ta·mine** /ˈhɪstəmiːn/ *n* [C] a chemical compound that can increase the flow of blood in your body

**his·to·gram** /ˈhɪstəgræm/ *n* [C] a BAR CHART

**his·to·ri·an** /hɪˈstɔːriən/ *n* [C] someone who studies or writes about history W3

**his·tor·ic** /hɪˈstɒrɪk‖-ˈstɔː-, -ˈstɑː-/ *adj* **1** a historic event or place is important because it is, or will be, remembered as part of history: *an historic building* | *a historic meeting between two great leaders* **2** historic times are the periods of time whose history has been recorded —compare PREHISTORIC

**his·tor·i·cal** /hɪˈstɒrɪkəl‖-ˈstɔː-, -ˈstɑː-/ *adj* **1** connected with the study of history: *historical research* **2** historical events, facts, people etc happened or existed in the past: *Was King Arthur a real historical figure?* **3** describing or based on events in the past: *a historical novel* —**historically** /-kli/ *adv* W2

**historic pres·ent** /ˌ·ˌ·· ˈ··/ *n* [singular] the present tense, used in some languages to describe events in the past to make them seem more real

**his·to·ry** /ˈhɪstəri/ *n* S2 W1

**1 ▶ PAST EVENTS ◀** [U] all the things that happened in the past, especially the political, social, or economic development of a nation: *India has been invaded several times during its history.* | *Throughout history the achievements of women have been largely ignored.* | **change the course of history** *Those decisions made at the Yalta Conference changed the course of history.*

**2 ▶ SUBJECT OF STUDY ◀** [U] the study of history, especially as a subject in school or university: *a degree in European history*

**3 ▶ DEVELOPMENT OF STH ◀** [singular, U] the development of a subject, activity, institution etc since it started: *the worst disaster in the history of space travel*

**4 ▶ BOOK ◀** [C] a book about past events: *a history of World War II*

**5 ▶ PAST LIFE ◀** **a history of** if someone has a history of illness, problems, or criminal activity, these things have happened to them or been done by them in the past: *The defendant had a history of violent assaults against women.*

**6 make history** to do something important that will be recorded and remembered: *Lindbergh made history when he flew across the Atlantic in 1927.*

**7 will go down in history** something that will go down in history, is important enough to be remembered and recorded: *This day will go down in history as the start of a new era in South Africa.*

**8 ...and the rest is history** used to say that everyone knows the rest of a story you have been telling

**9 that's past/ancient history** *spoken* used to say that something is not important any more

**10 history repeats itself** used to say that things often happen in the same way as they happened before —see also NATURAL HISTORY, CASE HISTORY

**his·tri·on·ics** /ˌhɪstriˈɒnɪks‖-ˈɑːn-/ *n* [plural] loud, extremely emotional behaviour that is intended to get people's sympathy and attention —**histrionic** *adj*

**hit¹** /hɪt/ *v past tense and past participle* **hit** *present participle* **hitting** S1 W2

**1 ▶ TOUCH SB/STH HARD ◀** [T] to touch someone or something quickly and usually hard with your hand, a stick etc: **hit sth with** *Billy was hitting a tin can with a spoon.* | **hit sb on the nose/in the stomach/over the head etc** *She hit him playfully over the head with her newspaper.* | **get hit** *Stand back you lot, or you'll get hit.* —compare PUNCH[1] (1), SLAP[1] (1)

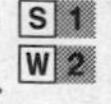

**2 ▶ HIT/CRASH INTO STH ◀** [T] to move into something quickly and hard: *The football hit the trash can with a bang.* | *The driver was drunk and hit three stationary cars.*

**3 ▶ ACCIDENTALLY ◀** [T] to move a part of your body quickly and hard against something so that it hurts you: **hit sth on/against etc** *I fell and hit my head on the table.*

**4 ▶ IN SPORT ◀** [T] **a)** to make something such as a ball move by hitting it with a bat, stick etc: *He hit the shuttlecock gently this time.* **b)** to get a point or some points by hitting a ball etc: **hit two goals/a six etc** *The batter hit a home run.*

**5 ▶ WORK A MACHINE ETC ◀** [T] to press a part in a machine, car, etc to make it work: *Hit the brakes!*

6 ▶ **HURT SB** ◀ [T] to deliberately move your hand, a stick, etc against someone and hurt them: *Mom, she keeps hitting me!* | **hit sb with sth** *They used to hit the kids with a leather belt.* | **hit sb over the head/in the stomach etc** *She hit him as hard as she could around his face.*
7 ▶ **BULLETS/BOMBS ETC** ◀ [T often passive] to wound someone or damage something with a bullet, bomb etc: **hit sb/sth in/on etc** *A second shot hit her in the back.* | **be badly hit** *Our ship was badly hit and sank within minutes.*
8 ▶ **ATTACK** ◀ [I,T usually passive] to attack someone suddenly: *The convoy was hit by Afghan government troops.*
9 ▶ **HURT, BUT NOT PHYSICALLY** ◀ [T] *informal* to do something that harms someone: **hit sb where it hurts** (=in the way you think will be most upsetting for them) *You should hit your husband where it hurts most – in his wallet!* | **hit sb when they are down** (=harm someone even though they are already defeated or very weak)
10 ▶ **BAD LUCK ETC** ◀ [I,T] if something such as bad luck, illness, bad weather etc hits or hits someone, it suddenly affects them: *The storm finally hit.* | *The guilt hit him like a lead weight.* | **be badly/severely/hard hit** *The company has been badly hit by the drop in prices.* | **the worst/hardest hit** *the areas of the country hardest hit by the recession*
11 ▶ **REACH A LEVEL/NUMBER** ◀ [T] to reach a particular level or number: *Youth unemployment has hit the one million mark.* | **hit rock-bottom/hit an all-time low** (=reach an extremely low level) *World oil prices have hit rock-bottom.*
12 ▶ **PROBLEM/TROUBLE** ◀ [T] to experience trouble, a problem etc: *I had hit a few snags in my work.* | **hit a bad patch** *spoken* (=have a short period of difficulty)
13 ▶ **REALIZE** ◀ [T] if a fact hits you, you suddenly realize its importance and feel surprised or shocked: *The full meaning of the night's events hit me and I started crying.* | **it hits sb** *Suddenly it hit me. He was trying to ask me to marry him.*
14 **not know what hit you** *informal* to be so surprised or shocked by something that you cannot think clearly
15 ▶ **ARRIVE** ◀ [T] *informal* to arrive or go somewhere: *They hit the main road two kilometres further on.* | **hit town** *especially AmE*: *I'll look for work as soon as I hit town.*

16 **hit the road** *informal* to start on a journey
17 ▶ **TELL SB STH** ◀ [T] *informal* if you hit someone with some information or news, you tell them something surprising or entertaining: *Once you've hit the customer with the price you want to close the deal quickly.*
18 **hit it off (with sb)** *informal* if two people hit it off with each other, they like each other as soon as they meet: *I knew you'd hit it off with Mike.*
19 **hit the big time** *informal* to suddenly become very famous, successful and rich
20 **hit the bottle** *informal* to start to drink a lot of alcohol
21 **hit the dirt/the deck** *informal* to fall to the ground because of danger
22 **hit the ground running** to start doing something successfully without any delay
23 **hit the jackpot a)** to win a lot of money **b)** *informal* to have a big success
24 **hit the nail on the head** *especially spoken* used to say that what someone has said is exactly right
25 **hit the roof/the ceiling** [I] *spoken* to become extremely angry: *Dad hit the roof when I got home at 2 am.*
26 **hit the sack** *informal* to go to bed
27 **hit the spot** *informal* if food hits the spot, it stops you being hungry and tastes good —see also **the shit will hit the fan** (SHIT[1] (12))

**hit back** *phr v* [I] to attack or criticize a person or group that has attacked or criticized you: **hit back (at sb/sth)** *Stung by Maria's contempt, Philip hit back with a few well-chosen words.*

**hit on** *phr v* [T] **1** [**hit on** sth] also **hit upon** to have a good idea after thinking about a problem for a long time: *He hit upon this ingenious method of freezing food.* **2** [**hit on** sth] also **hit upon** to discover something by a lucky chance: *I think you may have hit upon the only error in the whole program.* **3** [**hit on** sb] *AmE informal* to talk to someone in a way that shows you are sexually attracted to them: *Don spent the whole night hitting on anything that moved.*

**hit out** *phr v* [I] **1** to express strong disapproval of someone or something: [+ **at/against**] *The bishop has hit out at the govenment's policy on homeless people.* **2** to try to hit someone [+ **at**] *He hit out at me without thinking.*

**hit** sb **up for** sth *phr v* [T] *AmE spoken* to ask someone for something: *Can I hit you up for a loan till Thursday?*

**hit²** *n* [C usually singular] **1** a quick, hard touch with your hand or something you are holding: *That was a hard hit!* **2** an occasion when something that is aimed at something else touches it, reaches it, or damages it: *I scored a hit with my first shot.* | **a direct hit** *Our ship took a direct hit and sank.* **3** something such as a piece of music, a film, or a play that is extremely popular: **a hit single/show etc** *The latest Broadway hit musical, "The Mask"* | **a big/smash hit** *Chris de Burgh had a smash hit with "Lady in Red".* **4 be/make a hit with sb** to be liked very much by someone: *Your husband was a big hit with the kids.* **5 a hit at sb** a remark that is intended to hurt someone **6** *slang* the action of deliberately breathing in the smoke of an illegal drug **7** *AmE slang* a murder —see also HIT MAN

**hit-and-miss** /ˌ· · ˈ·/ *adj* done in a way that is not planned or organized

**hit-and-run** /ˌ· · ˈ·◂/ *adj* [only before noun] **1** a hit-and-run accident is one in which the driver of a car hits a person or another car and then drives away without stopping to help: **hit-and-run driver** (=one who does not stop after an accident) **2** a hit and run military attack is one in which the attackers arrive suddenly and unexpectedly and leave quickly

**hitch¹** /hɪtʃ/ *v* **1** [I,T] *informal* to ask for a free ride from the drivers of passing cars by putting your hand out with your thumb raised; HITCHHIKE: [+ **across/around/to**] *They hitched all the way across Europe.* | **hitch a ride with sb** *We hitched a ride with a trucker from New York to Montreal.* **2 get hitched** *spoken informal* to get married **3** [T always + adv/prep] to fasten something such as a TRAILER (1) to the back of a car so that it can be pulled **4** [T always + adv/prep] to tie a horse to something

**hitch** sth ↔ **up** *phr v* [T] **1** to pull, especially a piece of clothing, upwards: *He hitched up his trousers and started to work.* **2 hitch up a horse/wagon/team etc** to tie a horse to something, so that the horse can pull it: *He hitched up his wagon and headed west.*

**hitch²** *n* [C] **1** a problem that delays something for a short time: *Except for a few technical hitches the show went very well.* | **without a hitch** *The Miss Universe pageant went off without a hitch.* **2** a short, sudden pull upwards: *He gave his belt a hitch.*

**hitchhike**

**hitch·hike** /ˈhɪtʃhaɪk/ also **hitch** *v* [I] to travel by asking drivers of passing cars for free rides —**hitchhiker** *n*

**hi-tech** /ˌhaɪ ˈtek◂/ another spelling of HIGH-TECH

**hith·er** /ˈhɪðə‖-ər/ *adj old use* here: **hither and thither** (=in many directions) *A little girl was running hither and thither.*

**hith·er·to** /ˌhɪðəˈtuː◂‖-ər-/ *adv formal* up to this time: *The printing press made books available to people hitherto unable to afford them.*

**hit list** /ˈ· ·/ *n* [C] *informal* the names of people, organizations etc who you plan to do bad things to: *The company has a hit list of factories it wants to close down.*

**hit man** /ˈ· ·/ *n* [C] a criminal who is employed to kill someone

**hit pa·rade** /ˈ· ·ˌ·/ **the hit parade** *n old-fashioned* a list of popular records, usually songs, showing which records have sold the most copies

**HIV** /ˌeɪtʃ aɪ ˈviː◂/ *n* [U] a kind of VIRUS (=very small living thing that causes disease) that enters the body through blood or sexual activity, and can cause AIDS: **be HIV positive** (=have the HIV virus in your body)

**hive**[1] /haɪv/ *n* **1** [C] **a)** also **beehive** a small box where BEES are kept **b)** the group of bees who live together in a hive **2 a hive of industry/activity etc** *BrE* a place that is full of people who are very busy **3 hives** [U] a skin disease in which a person's skin becomes red and painful

**hive**[2] *v*
 **hive** sth ↔ **off** *phr v* to separate one part of a business from the rest, usually by selling it

**hi·ya** /ˈhaɪjə/ *interjection spoken* used to say hello

**HM** *BrE* the abbreviation for His or Her Majesty

**h'm, hmm** /m, hm/ *interjection* a sound that you make to express doubt, a pause, or disagreement

**HMS** /ˈ· · ·/ His/Her Majesty's ship; a title for a ship in the British Navy, and for places on the land that are used by the navy: *HMS Belfast*

**hoard**[1] /hɔːd‖hɔːrd/ *n* [C] a collection of things that someone keeps hidden because they like them or consider them to be valuable: [+ **of**] *He kept a little hoard of chocolates in his top drawer.*

**hoard**[2] *v* also **hoard up** [T] to collect and save large amounts of food, money, etc

**hoard·er** /ˈhɔːdə‖ˈhɔːrdər/ *n* [C] someone who likes to keep things

**hoard·ing** /ˈhɔːdɪŋ‖ˈhɔːr-/ *n* [C] *BrE* **1** a high fence around a piece of land where something is being built **2** a high fence or board on which large advertisements are stuck; BILLBOARD *AmE*

**hoar·frost** /ˈhɔːfrɒst‖ˈhɔːrfrɒːst/ *n* [U] FROST[1] (1)

**hoarse** /hɔːs‖hɔːrs/ *adj* **1** a hoarse voice sounds rough, as if the speaker has a sore throat: *His voice was hoarse from laughing.* **2** a person who is hoarse has a hoarse voice —**hoarsely** *adv* —**hoarseness** *n* [U]

**hoar·y** /ˈhɔːri/ *old-fashioned adj* **1** very old: *a hoary old joke* **2** hoary hair is grey or white **3** having grey or white hair —**hoariness** *n* [U]

**hoax**[1] /həʊks‖hoʊks/ *n* [C] **1** a false warning about something dangerous or bad: *a bomb hoax*|**hoax call** (=a telephone call that gives false information) **2** an attempt to make people believe something that is not true: *The Hitler Diaries were an elaborate hoax.*

**hoax**[2] *v* [T] to trick someone by means of a hoax —**hoaxer** *n* [C]

**hob** /hɒb‖hɑːb/ *n* [C] *BrE* **1** the flat top of a COOKER (1) that you cook on **2** *old use* a metal shelf next to a fire

**hob·ble** /ˈhɒbəl‖ˈhɑː-/ *v* **1** [I] to walk with difficulty, especially as a result of an injury to your legs or feet: *an old man hobbling along the street* **2** [T] to loosely fasten two of an animal's legs together, to stop it from running away **3** [T] to deliberately make sure that a plan, system etc cannot work successfully

**hob·ble·de·hoy** /ˈhɒbəldihɔɪ‖ˈhɑː-/ *n* [C] *old-fashioned* a rude young person

**hob·by** /ˈhɒbi‖ˈhɑː-/ *n* [C] an activity that you enjoy doing in your free time: *One of her hobbies is horse-riding.* S3

**hob·by·horse** /ˈhɒbihɔːs‖ˈhɑːbihɔːrs/ *n* **1** [C] a child's toy like a horse's head on a stick, which the child pretends to ride on **2 be on your hobbyhorse** to talk for a long time about a subject you think is very interesting

**hob·gob·lin** /hɒbˈgɒblɪn, ˈhɒbgɒb-‖ˈhɑːbgɑːb-/ *n* [C] a GOBLIN that plays tricks on people

**hob·nail** /ˈhɒbneɪl‖ˈhɑːb-/ *n* [C] a large nail with a big, flat top, used to make the bottom part of heavy boots and shoes stronger —**hobnailed** *adj*

**hob·nob** /ˈhɒbnɒb‖ˈhɑːbnɑːb/ *v* [I] *informal* to spend time talking to people who are in a higher social position than you: [+ **with**] *hobnobbing with the bosses at the sports club*

**ho·bo** /ˈhəʊbəʊ‖ˈhoʊboʊ/ *n* [C] *plural* **hobos** *AmE* someone, especially in the 1920s, who travelled from place to place because they had no home or job; TRAMP[1] (1)

**Hob·son's choice** /ˌhɒbsənz ˈtʃɔɪs‖ˌhɑːb-/ *n* [U] a situation in which there is only one thing you can do

**hock**[1] /hɒk‖hɑːk/ *n* **1** [U] *especially BrE* a German white wine **2** [C] the middle joint of an animal's back leg —see picture at HORSE[1] **3 be in hock** *informal* **a)** something that is in hock has been sold temporarily because you need money; pawned (PAWN[2]) **b)** to be in debt: *in hock to the big banks* **4** [C] *especially AmE* a piece of meat from above the foot of an animal, especially a pig: *pork hocks*

**hock**[2] *v* [T] *informal* to sell something temporarily because you are poor and need the money; PAWN[2]

**hock·ey** /ˈhɒki‖ˈhɑːki/ *n* [U] **1** *especially BrE* a game played on grass by two teams of 11 players each, with sticks and a ball; FIELD HOCKEY *AmE* **2** *especially AmE* also **ice hockey** a team game similar to HOCKEY, but played on ice

**ho·cus-po·cus** /ˌhəʊkəs ˈpəʊkəs‖ˌhoʊkəs ˈpoʊ-/ *n* [U] a method or belief that you think is based on false ideas: *He thinks psychology is a load of hocus-pocus.*

**hod** /hɒd‖hɑːd/ *n* [C] a container shaped like a box with a long handle, used for carrying bricks

**hodge-podge** /ˈhɒdʒ pɒdʒ‖ˈhɑːdʒ pɑːdʒ/ *n* [singular] the American form of the word HOTCHPOTCH

**hoe**[1] /həʊ‖hoʊ/ *n* [C] a garden tool with a long handle used for breaking up the soil

**hoe**[2] *v* **hoed, hoeing** [I,T] to break up soil with a hoe

**hog**[1] /hɒg‖hɑːg, hɒːg/ *n* [C] **1** *especially AmE* a pig, especially a fat one for eating **2** a male pig that is kept for meat —compare BOAR, SOW[2] **3** *informal* a person who eats too much: *You greedy hog!* **4 go the whole hog** to do something thoroughly: *Why don't we go the whole hog and get wine?* **5 go hog wild** *AmE informal* to suddenly do a lot of some activity that you do not usually do —see also ROAD HOG —**hoggish** *adj*

**hog**[2] *v* **hogged, hogging** [T] *informal* to keep or use all of something: *Keith's been hogging the bathroom all morning.*|**hog the road** (=drive badly so that you take up too much space)

**Hog·ma·nay** /ˈhɒgməneɪ‖ˌhɑːgməˈneɪ/ *n* [U] New Year's Eve and the parties that take place at that time in Scotland

**hogs·head** /ˈhɒgzhed‖ˈhɑːgz-, ˈhɒːgz-/ *n* [C] a large container for holding beer, or the amount that it holds

**hog·wash** /ˈhɒgwɒʃ‖ˈhɑːgwɑːʃ, ˈhɒːg-, -wɒːʃ/ *n* [U] stupid talk: *That's a load of hogwash!*

**ho ho** /ˌhəʊ ˈhəʊ‖ˌhoʊ ˈhoʊ/ *interjection* used to represent the sound of laughter

**ho-hum** /ˌhəʊ ˈhʌm‖ˌhoʊ-/ *adj informal* boring and ordinary: *It was a ho-hum sort of day.*

**hoick** /hɔɪk/ *v* [T] also **hoick up** *BrE informal* to lift or pull something up especially with a sudden movement: *She hoicked up her skirt and began to dance.*

H

**hoi pol·loi** /ˌhɔɪ pəˈlɔɪ/ *n* **the hoi polloi** an insulting word for ordinary people

**hoist¹** /hɔɪst/ also **hoist up** *v* [T] **1** to raise, lift, or pull up something, especially using ropes: *The sailors hoisted the cargo onto the deck.*|*hoist the flag* **2 be hoist with your own petard** to be harmed or embarassed by something that you planned yourself

**hoist²** *n* [C] **1** a piece of equipment for lifting heavy objects with ropes **2** [usually singular] an upward pull

**hoi·ty-toi·ty** /ˌhɔɪti ˈtɔɪti/ *adj old-fashioned* behaving in a proud way, as if you are important

**ho·key** /ˈhəʊki‖ˈhoʊ-/ *adj AmE* expressing emotions in a way that is too simple, old-fashioned, or silly: *a hokey song*

**ho·kum** /ˈhəʊkəm‖ˈhoʊ-/ *n* [U] *slang especially AmE* stupid talk, especially talk used to deceive someone or make them admire you: *All that talk about improving schools is just a bunch of hokum.*

S1 W1

## hold¹ /həʊld‖hoʊld/ *v past and past participle* held /held/ *v*

① IN YOUR HANDS/ARMS
② HAVE/POSSESS
③ KEEP/CONTROL
④ SAVE/STORE
⑤ KEEP STH IN A POSITION
⑥ SUPPORT/NOT BREAK
⑦ NOT CHANGE/CONTINUE
⑧ RESPONSIBILITY
⑨ OPINION/BELIEF
⑩ STOP/DELAY STH
⑪ CONTAIN/INCLUDE
⑫ OTHER MEANINGS

### ① IN YOUR HANDS/ARMS

**1 a)** [T] to have something firmly in your hand or arms: *He was holding a knife in one hand.*|*Can you hold the groceries for me while I open the door?*|*I held the baby in my arms.*|**hold hands** (=hold each other's hands) *The couple sat, holding hands under a tree.* **b)** [T always + adv/prep] to move something that you have in your hands into a particular position: **hold sth out/up/towards etc** *Hold the negative up to the light so we can see.*

**2 ▶HOLD SB CLOSE◀** [T] to put your arms around someone in order to comfort them, show you love them etc: *She held him tightly, wiping away his tears.*

### ② HAVE/POSSESS

**3 hold a position/rank/job** to have a particular job or position, especially an important or powerful one: *Most of the senior positions are held by men.*

**4 ▶OWN STH◀** [T] to own or possess something, especially money or land: *He holds a half share in the company.*

### ③ KEEP/CONTROL

**5 ▶ARMY◀** [T] if an army holds a place, it either defends it from attack, or controls it by using force: *The French army held the town for three days.*

**6 ▶KEEP SB SOMEWHERE◀** [T] to keep a person or animal somewhere, and not allow them to leave: *Police are holding two men in connection with the jewel robbery.*|**hold sb prisoner/hostage/captive** (=to keep someone in a room, prison etc and not allow them to leave

### ④ SAVE/STORE

**7 ▶KEEP TO BE USED◀** [T] to keep something to be used when it is needed: *Our computer holds all the records of births and deaths in Britain since 1950.*

**8 hold a place/seat/room etc** [T] save a room, place etc for someone until they want to use it: *They're holding a table for us.*

### ⑤ KEEP STH IN A POSITION

**9** [T always + adv/prep] to make something stay in a particular position: **hold sth down/up/in place etc** *Ted held the ladder firmly in place.*|*Can you hold the lid down so I can lock the suitcase?*|*It's only held on with a couple of screws.*|**hold sth open** *Mark held open the door as she came up behind him.*

**10 ▶ARM/LEG/BACK ETC◀** [T always + adv/prep] to put or keep a part of your body in a particular position: **hold sth up/out/straight etc** *Hold out your hand and I'll give you a present!*

### ⑥ SUPPORT/NOT BREAK

**11 ▶BE STRONG ENOUGH◀ a)** [T] to support the weight of something: *Be careful, I don't think that branch will hold you.* **b)** [I] to continue to be able to support the weight of something: *I don't think this shelf will hold if we put any more on it.*

### ⑦ NOT CHANGE/CONTINUE

**12 ▶AMOUNT/LEVEL◀** [T] to make something continue at a particular rate, level, or number: *hold spending to $10.2 billion*|*Make sure you hold your speed at 30 mph in this area.*

**13 hold sb's interest/attention** to make someone continue being interested in something: *Colourful pictures hold the students' interest.*

**14 ▶WEATHER/LUCK◀** also **hold out** [I] if good weather or good luck holds, it continues unchanged for a long time: *If our luck holds we could reach the final.*

**15 ▶MUSIC◀** [T] to make a musical note continue for a long time

**16 hold a course** if an aircraft, ship etc holds a course, it continues to move in a particular direction: *The ship held a northwesterly course.*

**17** [I] to still be true or continue to have an effect: *What I said yesterday still holds.*

**18 hold good/hold true** to still be true in several different situations: *This advice will hold good throughout your life.*

### ⑧ RESPONSIBILITY

**19 hold the fort** to be responsible for looking after something while the person usually responsible is not there: *She's holding the fort while the manager's on holiday.*

**20 be left holding the baby** *BrE*/**the bag** *AmE* to become responsible for something that someone else has started

**21 hold sb responsible/accountable (for sth)** to consider someone to be responsible for something, so that they will be blamed if anything bad happens: *I'll hold you personally responsible if anything happens to the boy.*

### ⑨ OPINION/BELIEF

**22** [T not in progressive, usually passive] *formal* to believe something to be true: [+ **that**] *It is widely held that the council will decide to take military action.*|**hold sb/sth to be sth** *It is held to be his most important novel.*

**23 ▶OPINIONS◀ hold an opinion/view/belief etc** to have a particular opinion about something: *She*

*holds extreme political views.* | **commonly held belief** (=something that many people believe to be true)

**24 hold sth dear** to think that something is very important: *a threat to everything that I hold dear*

**25 hold fast to sth** *formal* to keep believing in an idea or principles: *They held fast to their faith in spite of their suffering.*

### ⑩ STOP/DELAY STH

**26 hold it!** *spoken* **a)** used to interrupt someone: *Hold it a minute! I've just had a really good idea.* **b)** used to tell someone to wait or to stop what they are doing

**27 hold everything!** *spoken* used to tell someone to immediately stop what they are doing: *Hold everything! We have to change it all back again!*

**28 hold your fire!** a military order to tell soldiers to stop shooting

**29 hold your horses!** *spoken* used to tell someone to stop and think about something

### ⑪ CONTAIN/INCLUDE

**30 ▶ HAVE SPACE FOR ◀** [T, not in progressive] to have the space to contain a particular amount of something: *This pan holds three gallons of water.* | *The movie theater holds 500 people.*

**31** [T] *formal* if the future or a future situation holds something, that may be part of it: *Who knows what the future holds?*

### ⑫ OTHER MEANINGS

**32 hold a meeting/election/party etc** [T] to arrange for an event, meeting, election, party etc to happen: *The meeting will be held in the Town Hall.*

**33** [I] also **hold the line** to wait until the person you have telephoned is ready to answer: *Mr Stevenson's busy at the moment – would you like to hold?*

**34 ▶ HAVE A QUALITY ◀** [T] *formal* to have a particular quality: *Such an emphasis on religion may hold little appeal for modern tastes.*

**35 hold a conversation** to have a conversation

**36 not hold a candle to** *informal* to be much worse than someone or something else

**37 hold all the cards** to have a strong advantage in a situation

**38 hold up your head** to show pride or confidence in a difficult situation: *I'll never be able to hold up my head in this town again.*

**39 hold your own** to defend yourself, or to succeed, in a difficult situation: *Although he is the youngest competitor, he seems to be holding his own.*

**40 hold the road** if a car holds the road well you can drive it quickly around bends without losing control

**41 not hold water** if an argument, statement etc does not hold water, it does not seem to be true or reasonable: *His explanation of where the money came from just doesn't hold water.*

**42 hold your drink/liquor/alcohol etc** if someone can hold their drink, they are able to drink a lot of alcohol without becoming drunk

**43 there's no holding sb** *spoken* used when someone is so keen to do something you cannot prevent them from doing it: *When he starts talking about football there's no holding him.* —see also **hold your breath** (BREATH (7)), **hold court** (COURT[1] (5)), **hold your tongue** (TONGUE[1] (16)), **hold your head high** (HIGH[2] (7))

**hold** sth **against** sb *phr v* [T] to allow something bad that someone has done to make you dislike them or want to harm them: *It all happened years ago. You can't still hold it against him, surely?*

**hold back** *phr v* **1** [T **hold** sb/sth ↔ **back**] to make someone or something stop moving forward: *They had erected the barriers to hold back the flood.* **2** [T **hold back** sth] to stop yourself from feeling or showing a particular emotion: *We struggled to hold back our laughter.* **3** [T **hold** sb ↔ **back**] to prevent someone from developing or improving: *Spending so much time playing sport is holding him back at school.* **4** [I] to be slow or unwilling to do something especially because you are being careful: *The tone of his voice made Steven hold back.* **5** [I,T **hold** sth ↔ **back**] to keep something secret: *Tell me about it – don't hold anything back!*

**hold** sth/sb ↔ **down** *phr v* [T] **1** to prevent something such as prices from rising: *We shall hold down prices until the new year.* | *the best way to hold down inflation* **2** to keep people under control or limit their freedom: *held down for centuries by their Ottoman conquerors* **3 hold down a job** to succeed in keeping a job for a period of time: *He's never held down a job for longer than a few weeks.*

**hold forth** *phr v* [I] give your opinion on a subject, especially for a long time: [+ **on**] *Archer was holding forth on the collapse of society.*

**hold off** *phr v* **1** [I,T] to delay something: *Buyers have been holding off until the price falls.* | **hold off doing sth** *We will hold off making our decision until Monday.* **2** [T **hold** sb ↔ **off**] to prevent someone who is attacking you from coming any closer: *We managed to hold off the gang until the police arrived.* **3** [I] if rain or snow holds off, none of it falls, although you thought it would: *The rain held off until after the game.*

**hold on** *phr v* [I] **1 hold on!** *spoken* **a)** used to tell someone to wait for a short time: *Hold on, I'll just get my coat.* **b)** used when you have just noticed something surprising: *Hold on! Isn't that your brother's car over there?* **2** to wait for a short period of time: *I'll hold on for another few minutes if you like.* | *It's coming soon, just hold on for it.* **3** to continue doing something when it is very difficult to do so: *They didn't know if they would be able to hold on until help arrived.*

**hold on to** sb/sth *phr v* [T] **1** to keep your hands or arms tightly around something so that it cannot move or you cannot fall: *Hold on to the rail or you'll slip!* **2** to keep something by not losing it, selling it, or having it taken from you: *Despite the attacks we held on to the bridge for three more days.* | *I think I'll hold on to the records, but you can have the tapes.*

**hold out** *phr v* **1** [I] if something such as a supply of something holds out it has not all yet been finished or used: *Will the water supply hold out through the summer?* **2** [I] to continue to defend a place that is being attacked: *They'll have to surrender – they can't hold out forever.* **3 not hold out much hope/prospect of** to not think that something is possible or likely to have a good result: *Negotiators are no longer holding out much hope of a peaceful settlement*

**hold out for** sth *phr v* [T] to not accept anything less than what you have asked for: *The kidnappers are still holding out for the release of all political prisoners.*

**hold out on** sb *phr v* [T] *informal* to refuse to give someone information or an answer that they need: *Why didn't you tell me straight away instead of holding out on me?*

**hold over** *phr v* **1** [T **hold** sth **over**] to do or deal with something at a later date: *The game was held over until the following week because of the bad weather.* —see also HOLDOVER **2** [**hold** sth **over** sb] to use knowledge about someone to threaten them: *He knows I've been in prison and is holding it over me.* **3 be held over** *AmE* if a play, film, concert etc is held over, it is shown for longer than planned, because it is very good

**hold** sb **to** sth *phr v* [T] **1** to make someone do what they have promised: *"I'll ask him tomorrow." "All right, but I'm going to hold you to that."* **2** to prevent your opponent in a sports game from getting more than a particular number of points: *We held them to 2-2.*

**hold together** *phr v* **1** [I,T **hold** sth **together**] if a group or organization holds together or you hold it together it stays strong and does not break apart: *The party was held together by personal loyalty to the leader.* **2** [I] to remain good enough to be used: *I hope*

[continued on next page]

H

[continued from previous page]
*the washing machine holds together – I can't afford a new one.*

**hold up** *phr v* **1** [T **hold** sth ↔ **up**] to support something and prevent it from falling down: *The roof is held up by pillars.* **2** [**hold** sb/sth ↔ **up** often passive] to delay someone or something: *The building work has been held up by bad weather.* | *Sorry we're late – we were held up at work.* **3** [**hold up** sth] to rob or try to rob a place by using violence: *His brother tried to hold up the drugstore and was sent to jail.* —see also HOLD-UP **4** [I] to remain strong and not become weaker: *His physical condition held up remarkably well.*

**hold** sb/sth **up as** *phr v* [T] to use someone or something as an example: *The school is being held up as a model for other inner-city secondary schools.*

**hold with** sth *phr v* [T, usually in negatives] to approve of or agree with something: *We don't hold with physical violence in this school* | **hold with doing sth** *I don't hold with letting people smoke in public places.*

S2 W3 **hold**[2] *n*
**1** ▶ **ACTION OF HOLDING STH** ◀ [singular] the action of holding something tightly; GRIP[2] (1): *She tightened her hold on the rope.* | **have/keep hold of** *Make sure you keep hold of my hand when we cross the road.*
**2 get/take/grab/seize hold of sth** to take something and hold it with your hands: *Grab hold of the rope and pull yourself up.* | *I took hold of her hand and gently led her away.*
**3 get hold of a)** to find or borrow something so that you can use it: *I need to get hold of a car.* **b)** to find someone for a particular reason: *I must get hold of Vanessa to see if she can babysit for me.*
**4 on hold** waiting to speak or be spoken to on the telephone: **put sb on hold** *Do you mind if I put you on hold?*
**5 put sth on hold** to delay doing or starting something
**6 take hold** to start to have an effect: *The fever was beginning to take hold.*
**7** ▶ **SPORT** ◀ [C] a particular position that you hold an opponent in, in a sport such as WRESTLING or JUDO
**8** ▶ **CLIMBING** ◀ [C] somewhere you can put your hands or feet when you are climbing: *The cliff is steep and it's difficult to find a hold.*
**9** ▶ **SHIP** ◀ [C] the part of a ship below the DECK[1] (1) where goods are stored
**10 have a good hold of sth** to understand something well
**11 get hold of an idea/impression/story etc** to learn or begin to believe something: *Where on earth did you get hold of that idea?*
**12 have a hold over/on sb** to have power or influence over someone: *Ever since he found out about her past, he's had a frightening hold on her.*
**13 no holds barred** no rules or limits: *There are no holds barred when it comes to making a profit.*

**hold·all** /ˈhəʊld-ɔːl‖ˈhoʊld-ɒːl/ *n* [C] *BrE* a large bag for carrying clothes —see picture at BAG

S3 W2 **hold·er** /ˈhəʊldə‖ˈhoʊldər/ *n* [C] **1** someone who possesses or has control of a place, land, tickets etc: *Season-ticket holders are furious at the rise in rail fares.* **2 candle/cigarette holder etc** a thing which is used to hold a CANDLE etc

W3 **hold·ing** /ˈhəʊldɪŋ‖ˈhoʊl-/ *n* [C] something which a person possesses, especially land or shares (SHARE[2] (5)) in a company —see also SMALLHOLDING

**holding com·pa·ny** /ˈ·· ˌ···/ *n* [C] a company that holds a controlling number of the shares (SHARE[2] (5)) in other companies

**holding pat·tern** /ˈ·· ˌ··/ *n* [C] the line of travel that an aircraft follows as it flies over a landing place while it is waiting for permission to land

**hold·o·ver** /ˈhəʊldˌəʊvə‖ˈhoʊldˌoʊvər/ *n* [C] *especially AmE* an action, feeling, or idea that has continued from the past into the present; HANGOVER (2): [+ **from**] *Her fear of dogs is a holdover from her childhood.* —see also **hold over** (HOLD[1])

**hold-up** /ˈ· ·/ *n* [C] **1** a situation that stops something from happening for a short time; DELAY[1] (2): *An unexpected hold-up meant we had fallen 3 weeks behind schedule.* **2** a situation in which traffic stops or can only move very slowly: *There was a hold-up on the*

hold-up

*highway this morning.* **3** *informal* an attempt to rob someone by threatening them with a gun —see also **hold up** (HOLD[1])

S1 W2 **hole**[1] /həʊl‖hoʊl/ *n* [C]
**1** ▶ **SPACE IN STH SOLID** ◀ an empty space in something solid: [+ **in**] *We'll just dig a big hole in the ground and bury the box in it.*
**2** ▶ **SPACE STH CAN GO THROUGH** ◀ a space in something that allows things, light etc to get through to the other side; GAP (1): [+ **in**] *The dog got out of the yard through a hole in the fence.*
**3** ▶ **ANIMAL'S HOME** ◀ the home of a small animal: *a rabbit hole*
**4** ▶ **UNPLEASANT PLACE** ◀ *informal* an unpleasant place for living in, working in, etc: *I've got to get out of this hole.*
**5 be in a hole** to be in a difficult situation
**6 be full of holes** an idea or plan that is full of holes can easily be proved wrong or has many faults
**7** ▶ **GOLF** ◀ **a)** a hole in the ground that you try to get the ball into in the game of GOLF —see picture on page 1264 **b)** one part of a GOLF COURSE with this kind of hole at one end: *an 18 hole golf course*
**8 hole in one** an act of hitting the ball in GOLF from the starting place into the hole with only one hit
**9 make a hole in sth** *informal* to use a large part of an amount of money, food etc: *The cost of the house repairs made a big hole in my savings.*
**10 need something like a hole in the head** *spoken* used to say that you definitely do not need or want something
**11 hole-and-corner** secret or hidden, especially in a dishonest way: *hole-and-corner meetings* —see also BLACK HOLE, WATERING HOLE

**hole**[2] *v* [T] **1 be holed** if a ship or boat is holed, it has a hole in it **2** also **hole out** [I] to hit the ball into the hole in GOLF

**hole up** *phr v* [I always + adv/prep] *informal* to hide somewhere for a period of time: [+ **with/in**] *He escaped on his way to prison and holed up with his girlfriend.*

**hole in the heart** /ˌ· · · ˈ·/ *n* [singular, U] a medical condition, where the two sides of someone's heart are not properly separated

**hole-in-the-wall** /ˌ· · · ˈ·/ *n* [C] **1** *BrE informal* CASH DISPENSER **2** *AmE* a small dark store or restaurant

**hol·i·day**[1] /ˈhɒlɪ̈di‖ˈhɑːlɪ̈deɪ/ *n* **1** *BrE* also **holidays** a time of rest from work, school etc; VACATION[1] (1) *AmE*: *Everyone at work is ready for a holiday.* | *The school holidays start on Wednesday.* | **on (your) holiday** *Jackie's*   S2 W2

*been on holiday for the last two weeks.* **2** *BrE* also **holidays** a period of time when you travel to another place for pleasure: *We're going to Spain for our holidays.* | **have a holiday** *I didn't have a proper holiday this year.* **3** a day fixed by law on which people do not have to go to work or school: **public holiday** *Martin Luther King Day is now a public holiday in most states.* | **national holiday** *The 4th of July is a national holiday in the US.* | **bank holiday** *BrE*: *We're going to Devon for the Bank holiday weekend.*

This graph shows how common the nouns **holiday** and **vacation** are in British and American English.

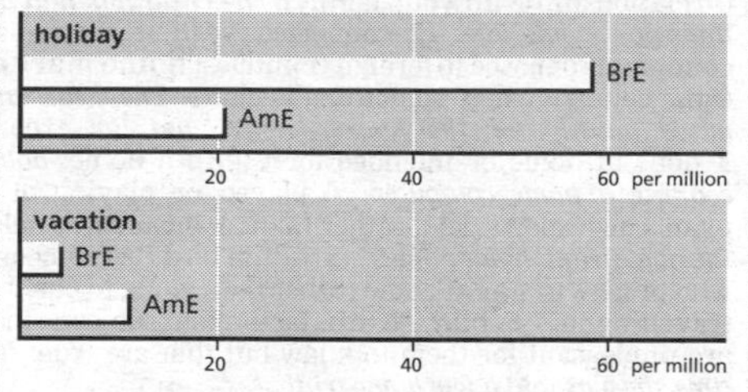


Based on the British National Corpus and the Longman Lancaster Corpus

In British English the word **holiday** is used to mean a time of rest from work, school etc, or a period of time when you travel to another place for pleasure. Americans use **vacation** for this meaning. In both American and British English **holiday** is used to mean a day fixed by law on which people do not have to go to work or school. In both American and British English **vacation** is used to mean one of the periods of time each year when universities are closed.

**holiday²** *v* [I] *BrE* to spend your holiday in a place; VACATION² *AmE*: [+ **in/at**] *They're holidaying in Majorca.*

**holiday camp** /'··· ˌ·/ *n* [C] *BrE* a place where people go for their holidays and where activities are organized for them

**holiday home** /'···ˌ·/ *n* [C] *BrE* a house that someone owns where they go during their holidays

**hol·i·day·mak·er** /'hɒlədiˌmeɪkə‖'hɑːlədeɪˌmeɪkər/ *n* [C] *BrE* someone who has travelled to another place for a holiday; VACATIONER *AmE* —**holidaymaking** *n* [U]

**hol·i·er-than-thou** /ˌ··· · '·/ *adj* behaving in a way that shows that you think you are morally better than other people

**hol·i·ness** /'həʊlinəs‖'hoʊ-/ *n* **1** [U] the quality of being pure and good in a religious way: *God's holiness* **2 Your/His Holiness** used as a title for addressing or talking about the Pope

**ho·lis·tic** /həʊ'lɪstɪk‖hoʊ-/ *adj* **1** based on the principle that a person or thing is more than just their many small parts added together: *a holistic approach to education* **2 holistic medicine** medical treatment based on the belief that the whole person must be treated, not just the part of their body that has a disease —**holistically** /-kli/ *adv*

**hol·ler** /'hɒlə‖'hɑːlər/ *v* [I,T] *especially AmE informal* to shout loudly: *The kid just kept hollering until she got her way.* | **holler at sb** *Stop hollering at me! I'll be there in a second!* —**holler** *n* [C]

**hol·low¹** /'hɒləʊ‖'hɑː-/ *adj* **1** having an empty space inside: *The children hid in the hollow tree.* **2 hollow face/eyes etc** eyes etc that sink inwards: *I could feel her appraising me with those hollow, dead eyes.* **3** a sound that is hollow is low and clear like the sound made when you hit something empty **4** feelings or words that are hollow are not sincere: *hollow promises made by corrupt politicians* **5 hollow laugh/voice etc** a hollow laugh or voice is one that makes a weak sound and is without emotion: *He gave a little hollow laugh and didn't reply.* —**hollowly** *adv* —**hollowness** *n* [U]

**hollow**

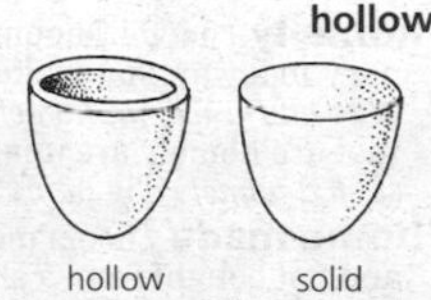


**hollow²** *n* a place in something that is at a slightly lower level than its surface: *The cat had tried to hide in a hollow in the ground.*

**hollow³** *v*
**hollow** sth ↔ **out** *phr v* [T] to make a hole or empty space by removing the inside part of something

**hol·ly** /'hɒli‖'hɑːli/ *n* [U] a small tree with dark green sharp leaves and red berries (BERRY), or the leaves and berries of this tree used as a decoration at Christmas

**hol·ly·hock** /'hɒlihɒk‖'hɑːlihɑːk/ *n* [C] a tall thin garden plant with many flowers growing together

**Hol·ly·wood** /'hɒliwʊd‖'hɑː-/ *n* [singular] a city in California where films are made and many famous actors live

**hol·o·caust** /'hɒləkɔːst‖'hɑːləkɒːst/ *n* [C] **1** a situation in which there is great destruction and a lot of people die: *a nuclear holocaust* **2 the Holocaust** the killing of millions of Jews by the Nazis in the 1930s and 1940s

**hol·o·gram** /'hɒləgræm‖'hoʊl-,'hɑːl-/ *n* [C] a kind of photograph made with a LASER that looks as if it is not flat when you look at it from an angle

**hols** /hɒlz‖hɑːlz/ *n* [plural] *BrE old-fashioned spoken* holidays

**Hol·stein** /'hɒlstən, 'hɒlstiːn‖'hɑːl-/ *n* [C] *especially AmE* a black and white cow; FRIESIAN *BrE*

**hol·ster** /'həʊlstə‖'hoʊlstər/ *n* [C] a leather object worn on a belt for carrying a small gun

**ho·ly** /'həʊli‖'hoʊ-/ *adj* **1** connected with God and religion; SACRED: *the holy city of Benares* | *anointed with holy water* **2** very religious: *a holy man* **3 holy cow/cats/shit/mackerel etc** *spoken especially AmE* used to express surprise, admiration, or fear **4 a holy terror** *informal* a child who causes trouble —see also **take (holy) orders** (ORDER¹ (20)) W3

**Holy Bi·ble** /ˌ·· '··/ *n* [singular] the BIBLE (1)

**Holy Com·mu·nion** /ˌ·· ·'··/ *n* [U] COMMUNION (2)

**Holy Fam·i·ly** /ˌ·· '···/ *n* [singular] Jesus, his mother Mary, and her husband Joseph

**Holy Fa·ther** /ˌ·· '··/ *n* [singular] used to address the Pope

**Holy Ghost** /ˌ·· '·/ *n* [singular] the HOLY SPIRIT

**Holy Grail** /ˌ·· '·/ *n* [singular] **1** something that you try very hard to get or achieve but never can **2** the cup believed to have been used by Christ before his death

**Holy Land** /'·· ·/ *n* [singular] the parts of the Middle East where most of the events mentioned in the Bible happened

**holy of ho·lies** /ˌ·· · '··/ *n* [singular] **1** *humorous* a room in a building where only important people are allowed to go **2** the most holy part of a Jewish temple

**Holy See** /ˌ·· '·/ *n* [singular] *formal* the office of the Pope

**Holy Spir·it** /ˌ·· '··/ *n* [singular] God in the form of a spirit according to the Christian religion

**holy war** /'·· ˌ·/ *n* [C] a war that is fought to defend the beliefs of a religion

**Holy Week** /'·· ·/ *n* [singular] the week before Easter in the Christian church

**Holy Writ** /ˌ·· '·/ *n* [U] **1** a piece of writing that people treat as if it were completely true in every detail **2** *old-fashioned* the Bible

**hom·age** /'hɒmɪdʒ‖'hɑː-/ *n* [singular] *formal* something you do to show respect and honour for an important person: **pay homage to sb** (=show respect and honour for someone) *The film pays homage to Woody Allen, using some of his best comic lines.*

**hom·burg** /'hɒmbɜːg‖'hɑːm-/ *n* [C] a soft hat for men, with a wide edge around it

H

S1 W1 **home¹** /həʊm‖hoʊm/ *n*
**1 ▶PLACE WHERE YOU LIVE◀** [C,U] the house, apartment, or place where you live: *They have a comfortable home on the outskirts of the town.* | **at home** *Her daughter lives at college during the week and at home on the weekends.* | **work from home** *BrE* (=do your work at home instead of at a company) | **make your home somewhere** *A family of swallows had made their home under the roof.*
**2 ▶WHERE YOU CAME FROM/BELONG◀** [C,U] the place where you came from or where you usually live, especially when this is the place where you feel happy and comfortable: **make somewhere your home** *She was born in Italy, but she's made Charleston her home.* | **back home** (=used to talk about the place where your family and friends live) *Sherri said she misses friends and family back home.*
**3 be/feel at home a)** to feel comfortable in a place or with a person: [+ **in**] *I'm already feeling at home in the new apartment.* | [+ **with**] *Penny is very much at home with Roger's family.* **b)** to feel happy or confident about doing or using something: [+ **with/in**] *I've never felt particularly at home with computers.*
**4 ▶IN YOUR COUNTRY◀ at home** in the country where you live, as opposed to foreign countries: *improved sales of trucks both at home and abroad* | *I miss the hot weather we have at home in India.*
**5 ▶FAMILY◀** [C,U] the place where a child and his or her family live: **leave home** *He didn't leave home until he was 21.* | **come from a broken home** *old-fashioned* (=come from a family in which one parent has left the home)
**6 ▶PROPERTY◀** [C] a house, apartment etc considered as property which you can buy or sell: *Attractive, modern homes for sale.*
**7 ▶FOR TAKING CARE OF SB◀** [C] a place where people who are very old or sick, or children who have no family are looked after: *an old people's home* | *They had to put her mother in a home.* —see also REST HOME
**8 dogs'/cats' home** a place where animals with no owners are looked after
**9 make yourself at home** *spoken* used to tell someone who is visiting you that they should relax: *Make yourself at home while I get some coffee.*

**10 make sb feel at home** to make someone feel relaxed by being friendly towards them: *I'd like to thank everyone again for making me feel so much at home.*
**11 find a home for** *BrE* to find a place where something can be kept: *I'll have to find a home for the new wine glasses.*
**12 the home of a)** the place where something was first discovered, made, or developed: *America is the home of baseball.* **b)** the place where a plant or animal grows or lives: *India is the home of elephants and tigers.*
**13 ▶SPORTS TEAM◀ at home** if a sports team plays at home, they play at their own sports field
**14 home from home** *BrE,* **home away from home** *AmE* a place that you think is as pleasant and comfortable as your own house
**15 what's that when it's at home?** *BrE spoken humorous* used to ask what someone means when they use a long or unusual word
**16 home sweet home** used to say how pleasant it is to be in your home
**17 ▶GAMES◀** [U] a place in some games or sports which a player must try to reach in order to win a point —see also HOME PLATE, HOME RUN

S1 W1 **home²** *adv* **1** to or at the place where you live: *Is Sue home from work yet?* | *He stayed home for a week to finish writing his book.* | **go home** *I'm going home now. See you tomorrow.* | **get home** (=arrive at your home) *By the time we got home the programme had finished.* | **return home** *After three months touring Europe they returned home to Boston.* **2 take home** to earn a certain amount of money after tax has been taken off: *The average store worker takes home around $300 a week.* **3 hit/drive/hammer etc sth home a)** to hit or push something firmly into the correct position **b)** to make sure that someone understands what you mean by saying it in an extremely direct and determined way: *a powerful film with imagery that really drives its message home* **4 bring sth home to sb** to make you realize how serious, difficult or dangerous something is **5 be home and dry** *informal especially BrE* to have succeeded in doing something **6 be home free** *AmE informal* to have succeeded in doing the most difficult part of something: *Only one more page of the hard stuff and we're home free.* —see also **close to home** (CLOSE² (20))

**home³** *adj* [only before noun] **1** connected with or belonging to your home or family: **home address** *Make sure to give us your full home address.* | **home life** (=relationship with your family) *The child has had an unhappy home life.* **2** connected with a particular country, as opposed to foreign countries: **home market** (=the country where something is made) *These cars are made mainly for the home market, not for export.* **3** done at home or intended for use in a home: *home cooking* | *a home computer* **4** played or playing at a team's own sports field, rather than an opponent's field: *the home team* | *home games* **5 home bird** *BrE* someone who prefers to stay at home rather than going to parties, travelling etc **6 home truths** facts about someone that are unpleasant for them to know but that are true: *It's time she was told a few home truths!*

**home⁴** *v*
**home in on** *phr v* [T] **1** to aim exactly at an object or place and move directly to it: *The bat can home in on insects using a kind of 'radar'.* **2** to direct your efforts or attention towards a particular fault or problem: *We homed in on the fault in the system and fixed it quickly.*

**home base** /ˈ· ·/ *n* [U] [singular] *AmE* HOME PLATE

**home·bod·y** /ˈhəʊmˌbɒdi‖ˈhoʊmˌbɑːdi/ *n* [C] *informal* someone who enjoys being at home

**homeboy** /ˈhəʊmbɔɪ‖ˈhoʊm-/ *n* [C] *AmE slang* a friend or someone from the same area or GANG¹ (1) as you

**home brew** /ˌ· ˈ·/ *n* [U] beer made at home —**home brewed** *adj*

**home·com·ing** /ˈhəʊmˌkʌmɪŋ‖ˈhoʊm-/ *n* [C] **1** an occasion when someone comes back to their home after a long absence **2** *AmE* an occasion when former students return to their high school or college

**Home Coun·ties** /ˌ· ˈ··/ *n* [plural] the counties (COUNTY¹) around London

**home e·co·nom·ics** /ˌ· ··ˈ··/ *n* [U] the study of cooking, SEWING, and other skills used at home, taught as a subject at school

**home front** /ˌ· ˈ·/ *n* [singular] the people who stay and work in their own country while others go abroad to fight in a war

**home·grown** /ˌhəʊmˈgrəʊn◂‖ˌhoʊmˈgroʊn◂/ *adj* **1** vegetables that are homegrown are grown in your own garden **2** made or produced in your own country, town etc: *homegrown entertainment*

**home help** /ˌ· ˈ·/ *n* [C] *BrE* someone who helps ill or old people in their homes with cleaning, cooking etc

**home·land** /ˈhəʊmlænd, -lənd‖ˈhoʊm-/ *n* [C] **1** the country where someone was born **2** a large area of land in South Africa where part of the black population lived, under the APARTHEID system

**home·less** /ˈhəʊmləs‖ˈhoʊm-/ *adj* **1** without a home: *homeless children* **2 the homeless** people who have nowhere to live, and who often live on the streets —**homelessness** *n* [U]

**home·ly** /ˈhəʊmli‖ˈhoʊm-/ *adj* **1** *BrE* simple and ordinary in a way that makes you feel comfortable: *The cottage had a warm, homely feel.* **2** *AmE* people or faces that are homely are unattractive or ugly: *I've never seen such a homely dog in my life!*

**home·made** /ˌhəʊmˈmeɪd◂‖ˌhoʊm-/ *adj* made at home and not bought from a shop: *homemade cake*

**home·mak·er** /ˈhəʊmˌmeɪkə‖ˈhoʊmˌmeɪkər/ *n* [C]

*especially AmE* a woman who works at home cleaning and cooking etc and does not have another job; HOUSEWIFE

**home mov·ie** /ˌ· '··/ *n* [C] a filmyou make, often of a family occasion, that is intended to be shown at home, not in a cinema

**Home Of·fice** /'· ˌ··/ *n* [singular] the British government department which deals with keeping order inside the country, controlling who enters the country etc

**ho·me·o·path** /'həumiəˌpæθ‖'hou-/ *n* [C] someone who treats diseases using homeopathy

**ho·me·op·a·thy** /ˌhəumi'ɒpəθi‖ˌhoumi'ɑːp-/ *n* [U] a system of medicine in which a disease is treated by giving extremely small amounts of a substance that has the same effect as the disease —**homeopathic** /ˌhəumiə'pæθɪk◂‖ˌhou-/ *adj* —**homeopathically** /-kli/ *adv*

**home·own·er** /'həumˌəunə‖'houmˌounər/ *n* [C] someone who owns their home

**home plate** /'· ·/ *n* [singular] the place where you stand to hit the ball in BASEBALL and the last place the player who is running must touch in order to get a point —see picture on page 1263

**hom·er** /'həumə‖'houmər/ *n* [C] *AmE informal* a home run —**homer** *v* [I]

**home room** /'· ·/ *n* [C] *AmE* a classroom where students have to go at the beginning of every school day

**home rule** /ˌ· '·/ *n* [U] the right of the people in a country to control their own affairs, after previously being controlled by another country

**home run** /ˌ· '·/ *n* [C] a long hit in BASEBALL which allows the player who hits the ball to run around all the bases (BASE[1] (8)) and get a point

**Home Sec·re·ta·ry** /ˌ· '····/ *n* [C,U] the British Government minister who is in charge of the HOME OFFICE

**home·sick** /'həumˌsɪk‖'houm-/ *adj* feeling unhappy because you are a long way from your home —**homesickness** *n* [U]

**home·spun** /'həumspʌn‖'houm-/ *adj* **1** homespun ideas are simple and ordinary: *homespun philosophy* **2** homespun cloth is woven at home

**home·stead**[1] /'həumsted, -stɪ̈d‖'houm-/ *n* [C] **1** a farm and the area of land around it **2** *AmE old use* a piece of land given by the government

**homestead**[2] *v* [I,T] *AmE old use* to live and work on a homestead —**homesteader** *n* [C]

**home stretch** /ˌ· '·/ *n* [singular] **1** also **home straight** *BrE* the last part of a race where there is a straight line to the finish **2** the last part of an activity or journey

**home time** /'· ·/ *n* [U] *BrE* the time at the end of the school day when you can go home

**home town** /ˌ· '·/ *n* [C] the place where you were born and spent your childhood

**home·wards** /'həumwədz‖'houmwərdz/ also **home·ward** *especially AmE adv* **1** towards home: *The children were heading homewards.* **2 homeward bound** *literary* going towards home —**homeward** *adj*: *homeward journey* —opposite OUTWARD (2)

S2 **home·work** /'həumwɜːk‖'houmwɜːrk/ *n* [U] **1** work that a student at school is asked to do at home —compare CLASSWORK **2** something you do to prepare for an important activity: **sb has done their homework** (=someone has prepared something well) *You could tell that she'd really done her homework.*

**home·work·er** /'həumˌwɜːkə‖'houmˌwɜːrkər/ *n* [C] someone who works from their home —**homeworking** *n* [U]

**hom·ey**[1], **homy** /'həumi‖'hou-/ *adj AmE* pleasant, like home: *Flora liked the homey atmosphere of Aunt Fran's farm.* —compare HOMELY (1)

**homey**[2], **homie** *n* [singular] *AmE* a HOMEBOY

**hom·i·cid·al** /ˌhɒmɪ̈'saɪdl◂‖ˌhɑː-/ *adj* likely to murder someone: *a homicidal maniac*

**hom·i·cide** /'hɒmɪ̈saɪd‖'hɑː-/ *n* **1** [C,U] *especially AmE* murder **2** [U] *AmE* the police department that deals with murder

**hom·i·ly** /'hɒmɪ̈li‖'hɑː-/ *n* [C] *formal* **1** advice about how to behave that is often unwanted **2** *literary* a speech given as part of a Christian church ceremony

**hom·ing** /'həumɪŋ‖'houm-/ *adj* a bird or animal that has a homing instinct has a special ability that helps it find its way home over long distances

**homing de·vice** /'·· ·ˌ·/ *n* [C usually singular] a special part of a weapon that helps it to find the place that it is aimed at

**homing pi·geon** /'·· ˌ··/ *n* [C] a PIGEON that is able to find its way home over long distances

**hom·i·ny** /'hɒmɪ̈ni‖'hɑː-/ *n* [U] a food made from crushed SWEET CORN

**homo-** /həuməu, -mə, hɒmə‖houmou, -mə, hɑːmə/ *prefix formal or technical* same: *homosexual* (=attracted to the same sex) | *homographs* (=words spelt the same way)

**ho·moe·o·path** /'həumiəˌpæθ‖'hou-/ *n* [C] a British spelling of HOMEOPATH

**ho·moe·op·athy** /ˌhəumi'ɒpəθi‖ˌhoumi'ɑːp-/ *n* [U] a British spelling of HOMEOPATHY

**ho·mo·ge·ne·ous** /ˌhəumə'dʒiːniəs◂‖ˌhou-/ also **ho·mo·ge·nous** /hə'mɒdʒɪ̈nəs‖-'mɑː-/ *adj* consisting of people or things that are all of the same kind: *a homogeneous community* —compare HETEROGENEOUS —**homogeneously** *adv*

**ho·mo·ge·nize** also **-ise** *BrE* /hə'mɒdʒənaɪz‖-'mɑː-/ *v* [T] to change something so that its parts become similar or the same: *plans to homogenize the various school systems*

**ho·mo·ge·nized** /hə'mɒdʒɪ̈naɪzd‖-'mɑː-/ *adj* homogenized milk has had the cream on top mixed with the milk

**hom·o·graph** /'hɒməgrɑːf, 'həu-‖'hɑːməgræf, 'hou-/ *n* [C] a word that is spelt the same as another, but is different in meaning, origin, grammar, or pronunciation: *The noun 'record' and the verb 'record' are homographs of each other.*

**hom·o·nym** /'hɒmənɪm, 'həu-‖'hɑː-, 'hou-/ *n* [C] a word that is spelt the same and sounds the same as another, but is different in meaning or origin. The noun 'bear' and the verb 'bear' are homonyms

**ho·mo·pho·bia** /ˌhəumə'fəubiə‖ˌhoumə'fou-/ *n* [U] hatred and fear of HOMOSEXUALS —**homophobic** *adj*

**hom·o·phone** /'hɒməfəun, 'həu-‖'hɑːməfoun, 'hou-/ *n* [C] a word that sounds the same as another but is different in spelling, meaning or origin: *'Knew' and 'new' are homophones.*

**Ho·mo sa·pi·ens** /ˌhəuməu 'sæpienz‖ˌhoumou 'seɪpiənz/ *n* [U] the type of human being that exists now

**ho·mo·sex·u·al** /ˌhəumə'sekʃuəl◂, ˌhɒ-‖ˌhou-/ *n* [C] someone, especially a man, who is sexually attracted to people of the same sex —compare BISEXUAL[1] (1), HETEROSEXUAL —see also GAY[1] (1) —**homosexual** *adj* —**homosexuality** /ˌhəuməsekʃu'ælɪ̈ti,ˌhɒ-‖ˌhou-/ *n* [U]

**Hon** /ɒn‖ɑːn/ **1** the written abbreviation of HONOURABLE (1), used in the titles of British NOBLES and Members of Parliament: *the Hon Arthur Cobbett* **2** the written abbreviation of HONORARY (2) used in official job titles: *Hon Sec* (=honorary secretary)

**hon** *pron AmE spoken* an abbreviation of HONEY, used to address someone you love: *Come here, hon, let me tie your shoes.*

**hon·cho** /'hɒntʃəu‖'hɑːntʃou/ *n* **the head honcho** *informal especially AmE* the person who is in charge

**hone** /həun‖houn/ *v* [T] **1** to improve your skill at doing something, especially when you are already very good at it: *He set about honing his skills as a draughtsman.* | **finely honed** (=extremely well-developed) *finely honed intuition* **2** to make knives, swords etc sharp

**hon·est** /'ɒnɪ̈st‖'ɑːn-/ *adj* 
**1 ► CHARACTER ◄** someone who is honest does not lie or steal etc: *It was very honest of him to give them the*

*money back.* | *an old woman with a plain, honest face you could trust* | **scrupulously honest** (=always very honest) *She is scrupulously honest in all her business dealings.*
**2 ▶ STATEMENT/ANSWER ETC ◀** not hiding the truth or the facts about something: *an honest answer* | **let's be honest** *Let's be honest – the only reason she married him was for his money.* | **be honest with sb** *I'm not sure if Joe was being completely honest with me when he said he'd never met them before.* | **be honest about sth** *At least he's been honest about it.*
**3 to be honest** *spoken* used when you tell someone what you really think: *To be honest, I don't like him very much.*
**4 honest!** *spoken* used to try to make someone believe you: *I didn't mean to hurt him, honest!*
**5 honest to God** *spoken* used to emphasize that something you say is really true
**6 ▶ WORK ◀** honest work is done without cheating, using your own efforts: *I bet he's never done an honest day's work in his life!* | **earn an honest living** *Young families struggling even to earn an honest living.*
**7 ▶ ORDINARY/GOOD PEOPLE ◀** honest people are not famous or special, but behave in a good, socially acceptable way: *She came from a good, honest, working-class background.*
**8 make an honest woman (out) of** *old-fashioned* to marry a woman because she is going to have a baby

S 2 **hon·est·ly** /ˈɒnəstli‖ˈɑːn-/ *adv* **1** in an honest way: *"I don't know," she answered honestly.* | *Did he come by the money honestly, or was it stolen?* **2** used to say that you really think that something is true, especially when it seems surprising: *Does he honestly expect me to believe his story?* **3** *spoken* used when you are shocked or annoyed by something someone has said or done: *Honestly! Can't you think of something better to do with your time?* **4** *spoken* used to try to make someone believe that what you have just said is true: *It wasn't me, honestly!*

**honest-to-good·ness** /ˌ··· ˈ··/ *adj* [only before noun] simple and good: *plain honest-to-goodness home cooking*

**hon·es·ty** /ˈɒnəsti‖ˈɑːn-/ *n* [U] **1** the quality of being honest: *a politician of rare honesty and courage* **2 in all honesty** *spoken* used when telling someone that what you are saying is what you really think: *I must add, in all honesty, that I think the task ahead of us will be difficult.*

**hon·ey** /ˈhʌni/ *n* [U] **1** a sweet sticky substance produced by BEES, used as food **2** *especially AmE spoken* used to address someone you love

**hon·ey·bee** /ˈhʌnibiː/ *n* [C] a BEE that makes honey

**hon·ey·comb** /ˈhʌnikəʊm‖-koʊm/ *n* [C] **1** a structure made by BEES, which consists of many six-sided cells in which honey is stored **2** something that is arranged or shaped in this pattern

**hon·ey·combed** /ˈhʌnikəʊmd‖-koʊmd/ *adj* [+ **with**] filled with many holes, hollow passages etc

**hon·ey·dew mel·on** /ˌhʌnidjuː ˈmelən‖-duː-/ *n* [C] a type of MELON —see picture on page 413

**hon·eyed** /ˈhʌnid/ *adj literary* honeyed words or honeyed voices sound soft and pleasant, but are often insincere: *"How kind you are," Brett said in a honeyed voice.*

**hon·ey·moon¹** /ˈhʌnimuːn/ *n* [C] **1** a holiday taken by two people who have just got married: **on your honeymoon** *We're going to Hawaii on our honeymoon.* **2** also **honeymoon period** the period of time when a new government, leader etc has just started and no one criticizes them

**honeymoon²** *v* [I always + adv/prep] to go somewhere for your honeymoon —**honeymooner** *n* [C]

**hon·ey·pot** /ˈhʌnipɒt‖-pɑːt/ *n* [C] something that is attractive to a lot of people

**hon·ey·suck·le** /ˈhʌniˌsʌkəl/ *n* [C] a climbing plant with pleasant-smelling yellow or pink flowers

**honk¹** /hɒŋk‖hɑːŋk, hɒːŋk/ *n* **1** a loud noise made by a car horn —see picture on page 1261 **2** a loud noise made by a GOOSE¹ (1)

**honk²** *v* **1** [I,T] if a car horn or a GOOSE¹ (1) honks, it makes a loud noise **2** [I] also **honk up** *slang* to VOMIT¹

**hon·ky, honkie** /ˈhɒŋki‖ˈhɑːŋ-, ˈhɒːŋ-/ *n* [C] *AmE slang* an insulting word for a white person

**hon·ky-tonk¹** /ˈhɒŋki tɒŋk‖ˈhɑːŋki tɑːŋk, ˈhɒːŋki tɒːŋk/ *n* [C] *AmE* a cheap bar where COUNTRY MUSIC is played

**honky-tonk²** *adj* [only before a noun] **1 honky-tonk music/piano** a type of piano music which is played in a cheerful way **2** *AmE* cheap, brightly-coloured, and not good quality

**hon·or** /ˈɒnə‖ˈɑːnər/ *n* [C,U] the American spelling of HONOUR

**hon·or·a·ble** /ˈɒnərəbəl‖ˈɑːn-/ *adj* the American spelling of HONOURABLE

**hon·o·rar·i·um** /ˌɒnəˈreəriəm‖ˌɑːnəˈrer-/ *n* [C] *formal* a sum of money offered to someone for professional services

**hon·or·ar·y** /ˈɒnərəri‖ˈɑːnəreri/ *adj* **1** an honorary title, rank, or university degree is given to someone as an honour **2** an honorary position in an organization is held without receiving any payment **3** an honorary member of a group is treated like a member of that group but does not belong to it: *They regard her as a kind of honorary man.*

**hon·or·if·ic** /ˌɒnəˈrɪfɪk◂‖ˌɑːnə-/ *n* [C] an expression or title that is used to show respect for the person you are speaking to

**honor roll** /ˈ·· ·/ *n* [C] *AmE* a list of the best students in a school or college

**hon·ors** /ˈɒnəz‖ˈɑːnərz/ *n* [plural] the American spelling of HONOURS —see also **with honours** (HONOUR¹ (12))

**honor sys·tem** /ˈ·· ˌ··/ *n* [C] *AmE* **1** an agreement between members of a group to obey rules: *the school's honor system* **2** a way of recording the fact that a student has achieved a high standard of work

**hon·our¹** *BrE*, **honor** *AmE* /ˈɒnə‖ˈɑːnər/ *n* W 3
**1 ▶ RESPECT ◀** [U] the respect that you, your family, your country etc receive from other people, which makes you feel proud: *For the French team, winning tomorrow's game is a matter of national honour.* | **sb's honour is at stake** (=someone's honour could be badly affected if they do not succeed) *This can't get to the media. The company's honor is at stake here!*
**2 ▶ STH THAT MAKES YOU PROUD ◀** [singular] *formal* something that makes you feel very proud: **it is an honour to do sth** (=used when saying politely that you are pleased to do something, especially at a formal occasion) | **have the honour of doing sth** *formal*: *Earlier this year I had the honor of meeting the President and Mrs Clinton.* | **do sb the honour of doing sth** (=make someone proud and happy by doing something for them) | **a rare honour** (=a very special honour)
**3 in honour of** in order to show how much you admire and respect someone: *a memorial in honour of those who died for their country*
**4 ▶ GIVEN BY A GOVERNMENT ◀** [C] something such as a special title or MEDAL given to someone to show how much people respect them for what they have achieved: **highest honour** (=most important honour) *Churchill received many of his country's highest honours.*
**5 the place/seat of honour** the place which is given to the most important guest
**6 be an honour to** to bring admiration and respect to your country, school, family etc because of your behaviour or achievements: *a young man who was a great athlete and an honour to his college*
**7 with full military honours** if someone is buried with full military honours, there is a military ceremony at their funeral
**8 ▶ MORAL PRINCIPLES ◀** [U] strong moral beliefs and standards of behaviour that make people respect and trust you: **a matter/point/question of honour** (=something that you feel you must do because of your moral principles) *It is a point of honour with me to repay all my debts promptly.* | **man of honour** *old-fashioned*

(=a man who always behaves in a way that is based on high moral standards)
**9 be/feel honour bound** to feel that it is your moral duty to do something: *Don't tell Kit either, because she'd feel honor bound to do something about it.*
**10 on your honour a)** if you swear on your honour to do something, you promise very seriously to do it **b)** *old-fashioned* if you are on your honour to do something, you are being trusted to do it
**11 do the honours** *spoken* to pour the drinks, serve food etc at a social occasion
**12 ► UNIVERSITY ◄** *BrE* **a) with honours** if you pass a university degree with honours, you pass it at a level that is higher than the most basic level **b) First Class/Second Class Honours** the highest or second highest level of degree at a British university
**13 Your Honour** used when speaking to a judge
**14 ► SEX ◄** *old use* if a woman loses her honour, she has sex with a man she is not married to —see also **guest of honour** (GUEST[1] (6)), MAID OF HONOUR

**honour²** *BrE*, **honor** *AmE* —*v* [T] **1 be/feel honoured** to feel very proud and pleased: **be/feel honoured to do sth** *I felt deeply honored to be playing against the former Wimbledon Champion.* **2** to treat someone with special respect: *our honoured guests this evening* **3** *formal* to show publicly that someone is respected and admired, especially by praising them or giving them a special title **4 honour a contract/agreement etc** to do what you have agreed to do in a contract etc **5 honour a cheque/voucher etc** to accept a cheque etc as payment **6 sb has decided to honour us with their presence** *humorous* used when someone arrives late, or to someone who rarely comes to a meeting, class etc

**Hon·our·a·ble** /ˈɒnərəbəl‖ˈɑːn-/ *written abbreviation* **Hon** *adj* **1** used in Britain in the titles of children whose father is a lord and in the titles of judges and members of parliament **2 Honourable Member** used by British members of parliament when talking to or about each other in the House of Commons —compare RIGHT HONOURABLE

**honourable** *BrE*, **honorable** *AmE* —*adj* **1** an honourable action or activity deserves respect and admiration: *My father doesn't think acting is an honorable profession.* **2** behaving in a way that is morally correct and shows you have high moral standards: *a principled and honourable man* **3** an honourable arrangement or agreement is fair to everyone who is involved in it —**honourably** *adv*

**honourable men·tion** *BrE*, **honorable mention** *AmE* /ˌ····ˈ··/ *n* [C] a special honour in a competition for work that was of high quality but did not get a prize

**honours de·gree** /ˈ··ˌ·/ *n* [C] a university degree that is above the basic level in one or two particular subjects at a British university: *an honours degree in German* | **joint honours degree** (=a degree in two main subjects)

**honours list** /ˈ··ˌ·/ *n* [singular] a list of important people in Britain to whom titles are given as a sign of respect

**hooch, hootch** /huːtʃ/ *n* [U] *especially AmE* strong alcoholic drink that has been made illegally

**hood** /hʊd/ *n* [C] **1** a part of a coat that you can pull up to cover your head: *a fur-lined hood* **2** a cover fitted above a COOKER[1] (1) to remove the smell of cooking **3** *AmE* the metal covering over the engine on a car: *Check under the hood and see what that noise is.* **4** *BrE* a folding cover on a car or PRAM, which gives protection from the rain **5** a cover that someone puts over their head to prevent them from being recognized **6** *slang originally AmE* a hoodlum: *gangs of hoods roaming the streets*

**-hood** /hʊd/ *suffix* [in nouns] the state or time of being something: *a happy childhood* | *growing to manhood* | *There's not much likelihood*

**hood·ed** /ˈhʊdɪ̣d/ *adj* having or wearing a hood: *a hooded cape*

**hood·lum** /ˈhuːdləm/ *n* [C] *informal* a violent criminal

**hoo·doo** /ˈhuːduː/ *n* [U] a type of VOODOO

**hood·wink** /ˈhʊdˌwɪŋk/ *v* [T + **into**] to trick someone in a clever way so that you can get an advantage for yourself

**hoo·ey** /ˈhuːi/ *n* [U] *AmE* stupid talk; nonsense

**hoof¹** /huːf‖hʊf, huːf/ *n* [C] *plural* **hoofs** *or* **hooves** /huːvz‖huːvz, hʊvz/ **1** the hard foot of an animal such as a horse, cow etc —see picture at HORSE[1] **2 on the hoof** *BrE* if you make decisions on the hoof, you make them while you are doing other things, without stopping to think

**hoof²** *v* **hoof it** *slang* to run away quickly

**hoof·er** /ˈhuːfə‖ˈhʊfər, ˈhuː-/ *n* [C] *AmE slang* a dancer

**hoo-ha** /ˈhuː hɑː/ *n* [U] *BrE* noisy talk or excitement about something unimportant: *What's all the hoo-ha about?*

**hooks**

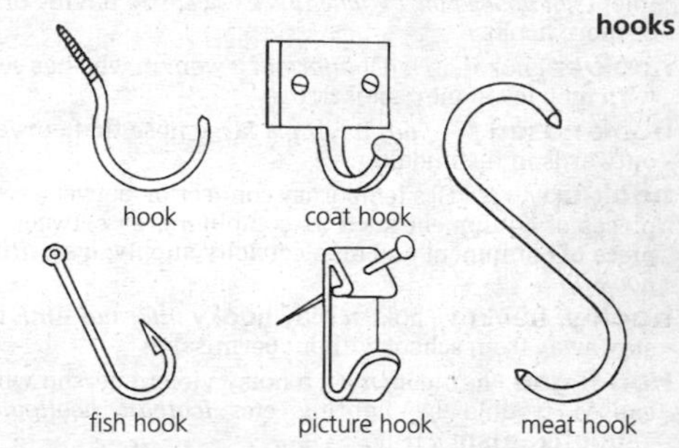


**hook¹** /hʊk/ *n* [C] S3
**1 ► FOR HANGING THINGS ON ◄** a curved piece of metal or plastic that you use for hanging things on: *Put your coat on the hook.*
**2 ► FOR CATCHING FISH ◄** a curved piece of thin metal with a sharp point for catching fish: *a fish hook*
**3 by hook or by crook** if you are going to do something by hook or by crook, you are determined to do it: *In the old days if you had a deadline, you met it by hook or by crook.*
**4 let/get sb off the hook** to allow someone or help someone to get out of a difficult situation: *We almost sued the magazine for libel, but in the end we let them off the hook.*
**5 leave/take the phone off the hook** to leave or take the telephone RECEIVER (=the part you speak into) off the part where it is usually placed so that no one can call you
**6 ► WAY OF HITTING SB ◄** a way of hitting your opponent in BOXING, in which your elbow is bent
**7 hook, line, and sinker** if someone believes something hook, line, and sinker, they believe a lie completely: *She swallowed the whole story hook, line, and sinker.*
**8 ► A TUNE ◄** a part of the tune in a song that makes it very easy to remember —see also BOAT HOOK, **sling your hook** (SLING[1] (4))

**hook²** *v* [T]
**1 ► FISH ◄** to catch a fish with a hook: *I hooked a 20 pound salmon last week.*
**2 ► FASTEN ◄** [always + adv/prep] to fasten or hang something onto something else: **hook sth over/around/onto etc** *He managed to hook his leg over the branch.* | **get hooked on/onto** *My jacket got hooked on a rosebush.*
**3 ► BEND YOUR FINGER/ARM ETC ◄** [always + adv/prep] to bend your finger, arm, or leg, especially so that you can pull or hold something else: **hook sth around/over etc** *Jack hooked his arm around the other man's neck.*
**4 ► ATTRACT ◄** *AmE informal* to succeed in attracting someone

**hook** sth ↔ **up** *phr v* [T] *especially AmE* to connect a piece of electronic equipment to another piece of equipment or to an electricity supply: *Is the video hooked up to the TV?*

**hook up with** *phr v* [T] *especially AmE* **a)** to meet someone and become friendly with them: *I'll give you a few names of people to hook up with out there.* **b)** to agree to work together with another organization for a particular purpose

**hook·ah** /ˈhʊkə/ *n* [C] a pipe for smoking drugs that consists of a long tube and a container of water

**hook and eye** /ˌ· · ˈ·/ *n* [U] a small metal hook and ring used for fastening clothes —see picture at FASTENER

**hook and lad·der** /ˌ· · ˈ··/ *n* [C] *AmE* a FIRE ENGINE with long LADDERS fixed to it

**hooked** /hʊkt/ *adj* **1** curved outwards or shaped like a hook: *hooked claws | a hooked nose* **2** [not before noun] *informal* if you are hooked on a drug, you feel a strong need for it and you cannot stop taking it; ADDICTED[1] **3** [not before noun] if you are hooked on something, you enjoy it very much and you want to do it as often as possible: *I got hooked on TV when I was sick* **4** having one or more hooks

**hook·er** /ˈhʊkə‖-ər/ *n* [C] *informal* a woman who has sex with men for money; PROSTITUTE

**hook-nosed** /ˈ· ˌ·/ *adj* having a large nose that curves outwards in the middle

**hook-up** /ˈ· ·/ *n* [C] a temporary connection between two pieces of equipment such as computers, or between a piece of equipment and an electricity supply: *a satellite hook-up*

**hook·y, hookey** /ˈhʊki/ *n* **play hooky** *informal AmE* to stay away from school without permission

**hoo·li·gan** /ˈhuːlɪ̥gən/ *n* [C] a noisy violent person who causes trouble by fighting etc: *football hooligans* —**hooliganism** *n* [U]

**hoop** /huːp‖hʊp, huːp/ *n* [C] **1 jump/go through hoops** to have to do a lot of difficult things as a test of how suitable you are for something **2** one of the circular bands of metal or wood around a BARREL[1] (1) **3** a curved piece of wood or metal that is stuck into the ground and used in the game of CROQUET **4** a large ring that CIRCUS (1) animals are made to jump through or that children used to play with in the past —see also COCK-A-HOOP, HULA HOOP —**hoop** *v* [T]

**hoop-la** /ˈhuːp lɑː‖ˈhuːp-, ˈhʊp-/ *n* [U] **1** *especially AmE* excitement about something which attracts a lot of public attention: *all the hoopla that surrounded the trial* **2** *BrE* a game in which prizes can be won by throwing a ring over an object from a distance

**hoo·ray** /hʊˈreɪ, ˌhuːˈreɪ◂/ *interjection* shouted when you are very glad about something —see also **hip hip hooray** (HIP[2]), —**hooray** *n* [C]

**hoose·gow** /ˈhuːsgaʊ/ *n* [C] *AmE old use* a prison

**hoot[1]** /huːt/ *n* [C] **1** a shout or laugh that shows you think something is funny or stupid: **hoots of laughter/derision** *a speech that was greeted with hoots of derision* **2** a sound that an OWL makes **3** a short clear sound made by a vehicle or ship, as a warning **4 be a hoot** *spoken* to be very funny or amusing **5 don't give a hoot/don't care two hoots** *spoken* used when saying that you do not care about something at all: *I don't give a hoot for her opinion!*

**hoot[2]** *v* **1** [I,T] if a vehicle or ship hoots, it makes a loud clear noise as a warning: [+ **at**] *The car behind was hooting at me.* **2** [I] if an OWL hoots, it makes a long 'oo' sound **3** [I,T] to laugh loudly because you think something is funny or stupid: [+ **with**] *hooting with laughter*

**hoot·er** /ˈhuːtə‖-ər/ *n* [C] **1** *BrE* a piece of equipment that makes a loud noise and is used on cars, ships, or in factories **2** *BrE slang* your nose **3 hooters** [plural] *AmE* an offensive word for a woman's breasts

**hoo·ver[1]** /ˈhuːvə‖-ər/ *n* [C] *BrE trademark* VACUUM CLEANER

**hoover[2]** *v* [I,T] *BrE* to clean a floor, CARPET etc using a VACUUM CLEANER (=a machine that sucks up dirt) —see picture at CLEAN[2]

**hooves** /huːvz‖huːvz, hʊvz/ the plural of HOOF

**hop[1]** /hɒp‖hɑːp/ *v* **hopped, hopping**

**1 ▶JUMP◀** [I] to move by jumping on one foot: *a child hopping up and down the stairs*

**2** [I] if a bird, an insect, or a small animal hops, it moves by making quick short jumps

**3** [I always + adv/prep] *informal* to get into, onto, or out of something, especially a vehicle: [+ **in/out/on etc**] *Hop in – I'll drive you to the bus stop.*

**4 hop a plane/bus/train etc** *AmE informal* to get on a plane, bus, train etc, especially after suddenly deciding to do so: *So we hopped a bus to Phoenix that night.*

**5 hop it!** *BrE spoken* used to tell someone to go away

**6 hopping mad** *informal* very angry: *Mrs C's going to be hopping mad when she hears!*

**hop[2]** *n* [C]

**1 keep sb on the hop** *informal* to make someone very busy: *The children keep me on the hop all day.*

**2 catch sb on the hop** to do something when someone is not expecting it and is not ready

**3 ▶JUMP◀** a short jump

**4 ▶PLANT◀** [usually plural] part of a flower that is used for making beer, or the tall plant on which it grows

**5 ▶FLIGHT◀** a single short journey by plane: *crossing Australia in a series of hops*

**6 ▶DANCE◀** a social event at which people dance

**hop, step, and jump** /ˌ· ˌ· · ˈ·/ *n* [singular] *informal* the TRIPLE JUMP

**hope[1]** /həʊp‖hoʊp/ *v* [I,T] **1** to want something to happen or be true, and to believe it is possible: **hope (that)** *I hope you have a lovely birthday.* | *I hope I'm not disturbing you.* | *Let's just hope we can find somewhere to park.* | **hope to do sth** *Joan's hoping to study Law at Harvard.* | [+ **for**] *We were hoping for good weather* | **hope for the best** (=hope that a situation will end well when there is a risk of things going wrong) *All we can do is hope for the best and wait.* | **hope against hope** (=continue to hope for something even when it is unlikely to happen) *Daniel waited all day, hoping against hope that Annie would change her mind.* S1 W1

Frequencies of the verb **hope** in spoken and written English.

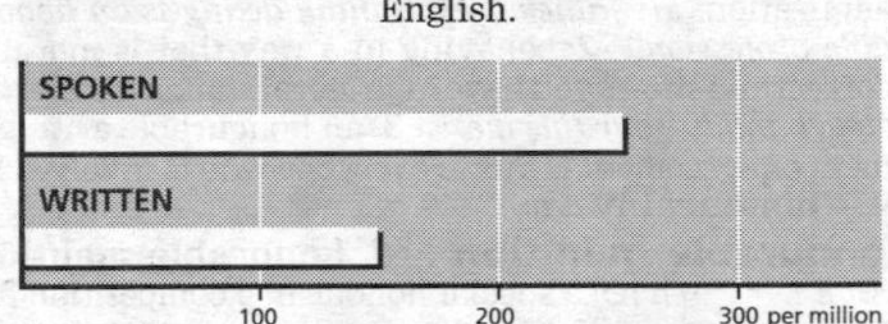


Based on the British National Corpus and the Longman Lancaster Corpus

This graph shows that the verb **hope** is much more common in spoken English than in written English. This is because it is used in a lot of common spoken phrases.

**hope** (*v*) **SPOKEN PHRASES**

**2 I hope (that)** used to say that you hope something will happen: *I hope you're coming to the party.* | **I do hope (that)** *BrE* (=a polite way of saying that you hope something will happen) *It was great to see you and I do hope that we'll meet up again soon.* **3 I hope so** used to say that you hope something that has been mentioned happens or is true: *"Do we get paid this week?" "I certainly hope so!"* **4 I hope not** used to say that you hope something that has been mentioned does not happen or is not true: *I don't think I'm busy that day, at least I hope not anyway.* **5 I am hoping** used to say that you hope something will happen, especially because you are depending on it: **I am hoping (that)** *I'm hoping he's going to do my car for me because I can't afford to take it to the garage.* | **I'm hoping to do sth** *Oh what a shame! We were hoping to see you today.* **6 let's hope (that)** used to tell someone that you hope something will happen or will not happen: *Let's just hope someone finds her bag and hands it in.* **7 I should hope so (too)** *BrE* used to say that you feel very strongly that something should happen: *"Well, they should get their money back." "I should hope so too, after being treated like that."* **8 I hope to God (that)** used to say that you hope very much that something will happen or will not happen, because otherwise there will be serious problems: *I hope to God I haven't left the car window open.*

W2 **hope²** *n* [U]
**1 ▶ FEELING ◀** a feeling of wanting something to happen, and a belief that it is likely to happen: **[+ for]** *The people are full of hope for the future.* | **give/offer hope to sb** (=make it possible for people to have hope) *This new treatment may offer hope to thousands of cancer patients.* | **lose hope/give up hope** (=stop hoping) *Michael's parents had almost given up hope of ever seeing him again.* | **in the hope that** (=because you hope that something will happen) *He showed me a picture of the missing girl in the hope that I might recognize her.* | **glimmer/ray of hope** (=something that gives you a little hope) *The union's offer to negotiate offered a ray of hope.* | **live in hope** (=keep hoping for something) *We haven't had any success yet, but we live in hope.* | **not hold out any hope** (=not give someone any reason to hope for something) *I'm afraid the doctors didn't hold out much hope.*
**2 ▶ STH YOU HOPE FOR ◀** [C] something that you hope will happen: *She told me all her secret hopes and fears.* | **[+ of]** *hopes of fame and fortune* | **have hopes of doing sth** (=hope to do it) *At one time he had hopes of playing at Wimbledon* | **my one hope is...** *My one hope was that I would see my family again.* | **have high hopes for** (=hope that someone or something will be successful) *the high hopes parents have for their children* | **hopes are fading** (=people are beginning to lose hope) *The search for survivors continues, but hopes are fading fast.* | **pin your hopes on** (=hope that something will happen because all your plans depend on it) *I can't pin my hopes on getting this job.* —see WISH (USAGE)
**3 raise/dash sb's hopes** to make someone's hopes seem more likely, or make them seem impossible: *Sally's hopes of meeting someone nice were dashed again.*
**4 get/build sb's hopes up** to make someone's hopes seem more likely, or to feel that your hopes are more likely to happen: *I don't want to get your hopes up, but I know you're a favorite for the part.*
**5 ▶ CHANCE ◀** [C,U] a chance of succeeding or of something good happening: **[+ of]** *there was no hope of escape* | **hope that** *There is some hope that we'll find a solution to our problems.* | **not a hope!** *spoken* (=used to mean that there is no chance of something happening) *"Do you think they'll refund our money?" "Not a hope!"* | **not a hope in hell** *spoken* (=not even the smallest chance of success) *They don't have a hope in hell of winning this game.* | **some hope/what a hope!** *BrE spoken humorous* (=used to say that there is no chance that something will happen) *"Your dad might lend you the car." "Some hope!"*
**6 there's hope for you yet !** *spoken* used to say that someone could still be successful, often in a joking way
**7 be sb's last/only hope** to be someone's last or only chance of getting the result they want: *For many people who couldn't find work, the colonies were the last hope.*
**8 be beyond hope** if a situation is beyond hope it is so bad that there is no chance of any improvement: **[+ of]** *Some of these patients are beyond hope of recovery.*

**hope chest** /ˈ· ·/ *n* [C] *AmE* things needed for starting a home that young women used to collect before getting married; BOTTOM DRAWER *BrE*

**hope·ful¹** /ˈhəʊpfəl‖ˈhoʊp-/ *adj* **1** believing that what you hope for is likely to happen: **[+ about]** *Everyone's feeling pretty hopeful about the future.* | **hopeful that** *We're hopeful that the team will be fit for next Saturday's game.* | **be hopeful of doing sth** *BrE*: *The police are hopeful of finding more clues to the murder.* **2** *informal* making you feel that what you hope for is likely to happen: *Things might get better, but it doesn't look very hopeful right now.* —**hopefulness** *n* [U]

**hopeful²** *n* [C] someone who is hoping to be successful, especially in acting, music etc: **young hopefuls** *hundreds of young hopefuls waiting to be auditioned*

**hope·ful·ly** /ˈhəʊpfəli‖ˈhoʊp-/ *adv* **1** [sentence adverb] used when you are saying what you hope will happen: *Hopefully we can solve the problem.* **2** in a way that shows that you are hopeful: *"Will there be any food left over?" he asked hopefully.* S1

**hope·less** /ˈhəʊpləs‖ˈhoʊp-/ *adj* **1** a hopeless situation is so bad that there is no chance of success or improvement: **be in a hopeless mess/state/condition** *The economy is in a hopeless mess.* **2** if something that you try to do is hopeless, there is no possibility of it being successful: **it is hopeless** *We tried to stop the flames from spreading, but we knew it was hopeless* | *a hopeless task* **3** *informal* very bad at doing something: *a hopeless cook* | **be hopeless (at doing sth)** *I've always been hopeless at spelling.* | *Oh, Dan you forgot the potatoes – you're hopeless.* **4** feeling no hope: *hopeless looks on the faces of the refugees.* **5 hopeless case** *often humorous* someone who cannot be helped: *He had power to cure even hopeless cases.* —**hopelessness** *n* [U] S3

**hope·less·ly** /ˈhəʊpləsli‖ˈhoʊp-/ *adv* **1** used when emphasizing how bad a situation is, and saying that it will not get better: *We found ourselves hopelessly outnumbered by the enemy.* **2 be hopelessly in love** to have very strong feelings of love for someone **3** feeling that you have no hope: *staring hopelessly into space*

**hopped-up** /ˌ· ˈ·◂/ *adj AmE slang* **1** happy and excited, especially because of the effects of drugs **2** a hopped-up car, engine etc has been made much more powerful: *a hopped-up Mustang*

**hop·per** /ˈhɒpə‖ˈhɑːpər/ *n* [C] a large FUNNEL¹ (1)

**hop·scotch** /ˈhɒpskɒtʃ‖ˈhɑːpskɑːtʃ/ *n* [U] a children's game using squares marked on the ground in which each child has to jump from one square to another

**horde** /hɔːd‖hɔːrd/ *n* [C] a large crowd moving in a noisy uncontrolled way: **[+ of]** *hordes of people milling around the station*

**ho·ri·zon** /həˈraɪzən/ *n* **1 the horizon** the line far away where the land or sea seems to meet the sky: *We could see a ship on the horizon.* **2 horizons** [plural] the limit of your ideas, knowledge, experience: *narrow political horizons* | **broaden/expand sb's horizons** *a course of study that will broaden your horizons* **3 be on the horizon** to seem likely to happen in the future: *Business is good now, but there are a few problems on the horizon.*

**hor·i·zon·tal¹** /ˌhɒrɪˈzɒntl◂‖ˌhɑːrɪˈzɑːntl◂/ *adj* flat and level: *a horizontal surface* —**horizontally** *adv* —opposite VERTICAL¹ —compare DIAGONAL —see picture at VERTICAL¹

**horizontal²** *n* **1** [C] a horizontal line or surface **2 the horizontal** a horizontal position

**hor·mone** /ˈhɔːməʊn‖ˈhɔːrmoʊn/ *n* [C] a chemical substance produced by your body that influences your body's growth, development and condition —**hormonal** /hɔːˈməʊnəl‖-ˈmoʊ-/ *adj*

**hormone re·place·ment ther·a·py** /ˌ·· ·ˈ·· ˈ···/ *n* [U] a treatment for women during or after the MENOPAUSE, that adds hormones to the body

**horn¹** /hɔːn‖hɔːrn/ *n*
**1 ▶ OF AN ANIMAL ◀** [C] one of the pair of hard pointed parts that grow on the heads of cows, goats, and other animals
**2 ▶ SUBSTANCE ◀** [U] **a)** the substance that animals' horns are made of: *a knife with a horn handle* **b)** [C] a part of an animal's head that stands out like a horn, for example on a SNAIL
**3 ▶ ON A CAR ◀** [C] the thing in a vehicle that is used to make a loud sound as a signal or warning: **blow/sound your horn** (=make a noise with your horn) —see picture on page 409
**4 ▶ MUSICAL INSTRUMENT ◀** [C] **a)** one of several

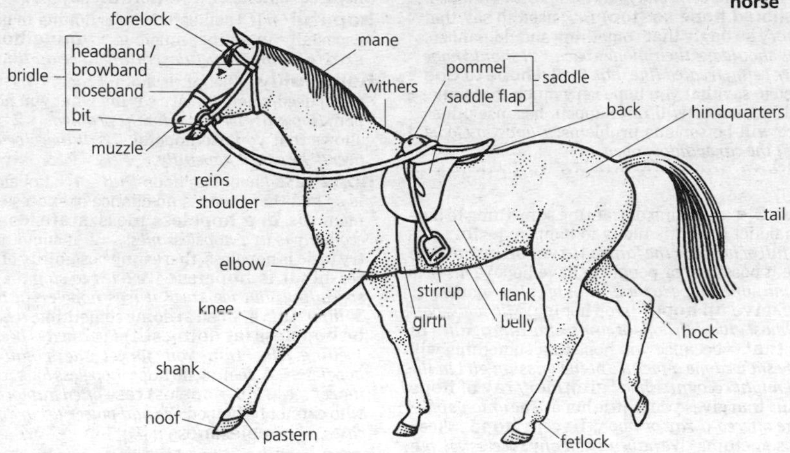


musical instruments that consist of a long metal tube, wide at one end, that you play by blowing **b)** a musical instrument made from an animal's horn —see also FRENCH HORN, ENGLISH HORN, POST HORN
**5 drinking horn/powder horn etc** a container in the shape of an animal's horn, used in the past for drinking from, carrying GUNPOWDER etc
**6 draw/pull in your horns** to reduce the amount of money you spend
**7 be on the horns of a dilemma** to be in a situation in which you have to choose between two unpleasant or difficult situations —see also **blow your own trumpet/horn** (BLOW[1] (21)), **lock horns** (LOCK[1] (6)), **take the bull by the horns** (BULL[1] (3))

**horn²** *v AmE*
**horn in** *phr v* [I] *AmE* to interrupt or try to take part in something when you are not wanted: **[+ on]** *He horned in on my date.*

**horn·bill** /ˈhɔːnˌbɪl‖ˈhɔːrn-/ *n* [C] a tropical bird with a very large beak

**horned** /hɔːnd‖hɔːrnd/ *adj* having horns or something that looks like horns: *horned cattle*

**hor·net** /ˈhɔːnɪ̈t‖ˈhɔːr-/ *n* [C] **1** a large black and yellow insect that can sting **2 stir up a hornets' nest** to cause a lot of trouble and quarrelling without intending to

**horn of plen·ty** /ˌ· · ˈ··/ *n* [C] a CORNUCOPIA (1)

**horn·pipe** /ˈhɔːnpaɪp‖ˈhɔːrn-/ *n* [C] a traditional dance performed by SAILORS or the music for this dance

**horn-rimmed** /ˌ· ˈ·◂/ *adj* horn-rimmed SPECTACLES have frames made of plastic that is made to look like horn

**horn·y** /ˈhɔːni‖ˈhɔːrni/ *adj* **1** made of a hard substance, such as horn **2** skin that is horny is hard and rough **3** *informal* sexually excited: *feeling horny* **4** *informal* sexually attractive: *I think he's horny.*

**hor·o·scope** /ˈhɒrəskəʊp‖ˈhɑːrəskoʊp, ˈhɔː-/ *n* [C] a description of your character and the things that will happen to you, based on the position of the stars or PLANETS at the time of your birth

**hor·ren·dous** /hɒˈrendəs, hə-‖hɑː-, hɔː-/ *adj* **1** frightening and terrible: *a horrendous experience.* **2** *spoken* extremely unreasonable or unpleasant: *horrendous prices* —**horrendously** *adv*

S2 **hor·ri·ble** /ˈhɒrɪ̈bəl‖ˈhɔː-, ˈhɑː-/ *adj* **1** very unpleasant and often frightening or upsetting: *a horrible murder* **2** *spoken* very bad or unpleasant: *horrible weather|I have a horrible feeling we're going to miss the plane.* **3** *spoken* rude and unfriendly: *What a horrible man.* —**horribly** *adv*: *Her face was horribly scarred.*

**hor·rid** /ˈhɒrɪ̈d‖ˈhɔː-, ˈhɑː-/ *adj informal especially BrE* **1** very unpleasant: *a horrid smell* **2** behaving in a nasty unkind way: *Don't be so horrid!* —**horridly** *adv*

**hor·rif·ic** /hɒˈrɪfɪk, hə-‖hɔː-, hɑː-/ *adj* extremely bad, especially in a way that is frightening or upsetting: *horrific accidents* —**horrifically** /-kli/ *adv*

**hor·ri·fy** /ˈhɒrɪ̈faɪ‖ˈhɔː-, ˈhɑː-/ *v* [T] to make someone feel very shocked and upset or afraid: **horrified to see/hear etc** *We were horrified to see children living in such terrible conditions.* —**horrifying** *adj*: *horrifying news* —**horrifyingly** *adv*

**hor·ror** /ˈhɒrə‖ˈhɔːrər, ˈhɑː-/ *n* **1** [U] a strong feeling of shock and fear: *The crowd gasped in horror as Senna's car crashed.* | **to sb's horror** (=making someone shocked or afraid) *To her horror, Rachel realized her savings account had been cleaned out.* **2** [C] something that is very terrible, shocking, or frightening: *the horrors of modern warfare* **3 have a horror of** to be very frightened of something or dislike it very much: *He has a horror of snakes.* **4 give sb the horrors** to make someone feel unreasonably frightened or nervous **5 little horror** *especially BrE* a young child who behaves badly **6** [C] something that is extremely ugly W3

**horror film** /ˈ·· ˌ·/ *BrE*, **horror mov·ie** /ˈ·· ˌ··/ *AmE* —*n* [C] a film in which strange and frightening things happen, for example Dracula or Frankenstein

**horror sto·ry** /ˈ·· ˌ··/ *n* [C] **1** *informal* a report about bad experiences, bad conditions etc: *horror stories about patients being given the wrong drugs* **2** a story in which strange and frightening things happen

**horror-struck** /ˈ·· ·/ also **horror-strick·en** /ˈ·· ˌ··/ *adj* suddenly very shocked and frightened: *He stared horror-struck as the car moved towards the edge of the cliff.*

**hors de com·bat** /ˌɔː də ˈkɒmbɑː‖ˌɔːr də ˈkɑːmbɑː/ *adj French formal* unable to fight because you are wounded

**hors d'oeu·vre** /ˌɔː ˈdɜːv‖ˌɔːr ˈdɜːrv/ *plural* **hors d'oeuvres** /-ˈdɜːvz‖-ˈdɜːrvz/ *n* [C] food that is served in small amounts before the main part of the meal

**horse¹** /hɔːs‖hɔːrs/ *n* **1** a large strong animal that people ride on and use for pulling heavy things **2 the horses** *informal* horse races **3 straight from the horse's mouth** if you hear something straight from the horse's mouth, you are told it by someone who has direct knowledge of it **4** [C] a piece of sports equipment in a GYMNASIUM used for jumping over; VAULTING HORSE **5 horse sense** *old-fashioned* sensible judgement gained from experience; COMMON SENSE **6** the process of trying to reach an agreement by offering each other things in exchange for other things. **7** [U] *old-fashioned slang* S3 W1

HEROIN —see also **dark horse** (DARK[1] (9)), **never/don't look a gift horse in the mouth** (GIFT (6)), **be flogging a dead horse** (FLOG (3)), **hold your horses** (HOLD[1] (29)), **put the cart before the horse** (CART[1] (4)), STALKING HORSE, WHITE HORSES

**horse**[2] *v*
**horse around/about** *phr v* [I] *informal* to play roughly: *Stop horsing around, you'll break something!*

**horse·back** /ˈhɔːsbæk‖ˈhɔːrs-/ *n* **on horseback** riding a horse —**horseback** *adj*

**horse·box** /ˈhɔːsbɒks‖ˈhɔːrsbɑːks/ *n* [C] *BrE* a large vehicle for carrying horses, often pulled by another vehicle; HORSE TRAILER *AmE*

**horse chest·nut** /ˌ· ˈ··‖ˈ· ˌ··/ *n* [C] **1** a large tree which produces shiney brown nuts and has white and pink flowers **2** a nut from this tree

**horse-drawn** /ˈ· ·/ *adj* [only before a noun] pulled by a horse

**horse·fly** /ˈhɔːsflaɪ‖ˈhɔːrs-/ *n* [C] a large fly that bites horses and cattle

**horse·hair** /ˈhɔːsheə‖ˈhɔːrsher/ *n* [U] the hair from a horse's MANE and tail, sometimes used to fill the inside of furniture

**horse·man** /ˈhɔːsmən‖ˈhɔːrs-/ *n plural* **horsemen** /-mən/ [C] someone who rides horses

**horse·man·ship** /ˈhɔːsmənʃɪp‖ˈhɔːrs-/ *n* [U] the practice or skill of riding horses

**horse·play** /ˈhɔːspleɪ‖ˈhɔːrs-/ *n* [U] *old-fashioned* rough, noisy behaviour in which older children play by pushing or hitting each other for fun

**horse·pow·er** /ˈhɔːsˌpaʊə‖ˈhɔːrsˌpaʊər/ written abbreviation **hp** *n* [U] a unit for measuring the power of an engine

**horse rac·ing** /ˈ· ˌ··/ *n* [U] a sport in which horses race against each other

**horse·rad·ish** /ˈhɔːsˌrædɪʃ‖ˈhɔːrs-/ *n* [C,U] a plant whose root has a very strong hot taste and is eaten with meat

**horse-rid·ing** /ˈ· ··/ *n* [U] the activity of riding horses —**horse-riding** *adj*

**horseshit** /ˈ· ·/ *AmE taboo* nonsense; BULLSHIT: *That's total horseshit!*

**horse·shoe** /ˈhɔːʃ-ʃuː, ˈhɔːs-‖ˈhɔːr-/ *n* [C] **1** a curved piece of iron that is nailed on to the bottom of a horse's foot **2** a sign of good luck in the shape of a horseshoe

**horse·shoes** /ˈhɔːʃ-ʃuːz, ˈhɔːs-‖ˈhɔːr-/ *n* [U] an American outdoor game in which horseshoes are thrown at a post

**horse show** /ˈ· ·/ *n* [C] a sports event in which people riding horses compete to show their skill in riding

**horse trail·er** /ˈ· ˌ··/ *n* [C] *AmE* a large vehicle for carrying horses, pulled by another vehicle; HORSEBOX *BrE*

**horse·whip** /ˈhɔːsˌwɪp‖ˈhɔːrs-/ *v* [T] to beat someone hard with a whip

**horse·wom·an** /ˈhɔːsˌwʊmən‖ˈhɔːrs-/ *n* [C] *plural* **horsewomen** /-ˌwɪmɪn/ a woman who rides horses

**hors·ey, horsy** /ˈhɔːsi‖ˈhɔːrsi/ *adj* **1** very interested in horses and fond of riding horses **2 horsey face/appearance/smell etc** a face etc that is like a horse's

**hor·ti·cul·ture** /ˈhɔːtɪ̈ˌkʌltʃə‖ˈhɔːrtɪ̈ˌkʌltʃər/ *n* [U] the practice or science of growing flowers, fruit and vegetables —**horticultural** /ˌhɔːtɪ̈ˈkʌltʃərəl◂‖ˌhɔːr-/ *adj* —**horticulturalist** *n* [C] —compare AGRICULTURE

**ho·san·na** /həʊˈzænə‖hoʊ-/ *n* [C] *biblical* a shout of praise to God —**hosanna** *interjection*

**hose**[1] /həʊz‖hoʊz/ *n* [C,U] **1** *BrE* a long rubber or plastic tube which can be moved and bent to put water onto fires, gardens etc; HOSEPIPE *BrE* **2** a word meaning TIGHTS, STOCKINGS (1), or socks, used especially in shops **3** tight-fitting trousers worn by men in past times

**hose**[2] *v* [T] **1** to cover something with water using a hose **2** *AmE slang* to cheat or deceive someone
**hose** sth/sb ↔ **down** *phr v* [T] to wash something or someone using a hose: *Would you hose down the car for me?*

**hose·pipe** /ˈhəʊzpaɪp‖ˈhoʊz-/ *n* [C] *BrE* a long hose

**ho·sier** /ˈhəʊziə‖ˈhoʊʒər/ *n* [C] *old-fashioned* someone who sells socks and men's underwear

**ho·sier·y** /ˈhəʊzjəri‖ˈhoʊʒəri/ *n* [U] a general word for TIGHTS, STOCKINGS (1), or socks, used in shops and in the clothing industry

**hos·pice** /ˈhɒspɪ̈s‖ˈhɑː-/ *n* [C] **1** a special hospital where people who are dying are looked after **2** *old use* a house for people who are travelling to stay and rest in

**hos·pi·ta·ble** /ˈhɒspɪtəbəl, hɒˈspɪ-‖hɑːˈspɪ-, ˈhɑːspɪ-/ *adj* friendly, welcoming, and generous to visitors: *The local people were very kind and hospitable.* —**hospitably** *adv*

**hos·pi·tal** /ˈhɒspɪtl‖ˈhɑː-/ *n* [C,U] a large building where sick or injured people are looked after and receive medical treatment: **in/to/from hospital** *BrE*: *He's in hospital, recovering from an operation.* | **in/to/from the hospital** *AmE*: *After the accident Jane was rushed to the hospital.* | **be admitted to (the) hospital** (=be brought into a hospital for treatment) *A man has been admitted to hospital with gunshot wounds.* | **hospital bed** (=a place in a hospital for a sick person) S2 W1

**hos·pi·tal·i·ty** /ˌhɒspɪ̈ˈtælɪ̈ti‖ˌhɑː-/ *n* [U] friendly behaviour towards visitors: *Thanks for your hospitality over the past few weeks.* —see also **corporate hospitality** (CORPORATE (4))

**hos·pi·tal·ize** also **-ise** *BrE* /ˈhɒspɪtl-aɪz‖ˈhɑː-/ *v* [T] **be hospitalized** to be taken into a hospital for treatment —**hospitalization** /ˌhɒspɪtl-aɪˈzeɪʃən‖ˌhɑːspɪtlə ˈzeɪ-/ *n* [U]

**host**[1] /həʊst‖hoʊst/ *n* [C] W3
**1** ▶ **AT A PARTY** ◀ someone at a party, meal etc who has invited the guests and who provides them with food, drink etc —see also HOSTESS (1): *Our host brought in some more wine.*
**2** ▶ **ON TELEVISION** ◀ someone who introduces the guests on a television or radio programme; COMPÈRE: *a game show host* —see also HOSTESS (2)
**3** ▶ **COUNTRY/GOVERNMENT** ◀ a country, government or organization that provides the necessary space, equipment etc for a special event: **host country/government/city etc** *the host city for the next Olympic Games* | **play host (to)** (=provide the place, food etc for a special meeting or event) *Japan played host to the first World Championship Grand Prix.*
**4 a (whole) host of** a large number of: *a host of possibilities*
**5** ▶ **IN CHURCH** ◀ **the Host** *technical* the bread that is used in the Christian ceremony of Communion
**6** ▶ **ANIMAL/PLANT** ◀ *technical* an animal or plant on which a smaller animal or plant is living as a PARASITE
**7** ▶ **ARMY** ◀ *old use* an army: *the approaching host*
**8** *old use* a man in charge of a hotel

**host**[2] *v* [T] **1** to provide the place and everything that is needed for an organized event: *Which country is going to host the next World Cup?* **2** to be the host on a radio or television programme: *a chat show hosted by Oprah Winfrey*

**hos·tage** /ˈhɒstɪdʒ‖ˈhɑː-/ *n* [C] **1** someone who is kept as a prisoner by an enemy so that the other side will do what the enemy demands: **hold sb hostage** (=keep someone as a hostage) *The group are holding three western tourists hostage.* | **take sb hostage** (=seize someone and use them as a hostage) *the aid-worker who was taken hostage by a rebel militia* **2 give hostages to fortune** to take a risk that may bring trouble in the future, especially by making promises

**hos·tel** /ˈhɒstl‖ˈhɑː-/ *n* [C] **1** somewhere where people, especially people living away from home, can stay and eat fairly cheaply **2** a YOUTH HOSTEL **3** a place where people who have no homes can stay

**hos·tel·ler** also **hosteler** *AmE* /ˈhɒst ələ‖ˈhɑːst ələr/ *n* [C] someone travelling from one YOUTH HOSTEL to another

**hos·tel·ry** /ˈhɒst əlri‖ˈhɑː-/ *n* [C] **1** *old use* a hotel **2** *BrE humorous* a PUB

**host·ess** /ˈhəʊstɪ̈s‖ˈhoʊ-/ *n* [C] **1** a woman at a party, meal etc who has invited all the guests and provides them with food, drink etc **2** a woman who introduces the guests on a television or radio show **3** a woman who shows people to seats in a restaurant in the US

**hos·tile** /ˈhɒstaɪl‖ˈhɑːstl, ˈhɑːstaɪl/ *adj* **1** angry and deliberately unfriendly towards someone and ready to argue with them: *The President was given a hostile reception by a crowd of angry farmers.* **2** opposing a plan or idea very strongly: [+ **to/towards**] *Senator Lydon was openly hostile to our proposals.* **3** belonging to an enemy: *hostile territory* **4 hostile environment** conditions that are difficult to live in or exist in

**hos·til·i·ty** /hɒˈstɪlɪ̆ti‖hɑː-/ *n* **1** [U] a feeling or attitude that is extremely unfriendly: [+ **towards/between**] *hostility towards foreigners*|**open hostility** (=hostility that is clearly shown) **2** [U] strong or angry opposition to a plan or idea: *The reform program was greeted with hostility by conservatives* **3 hostilities** [plural] *formal* acts of fighting: *a cessation of hostilities.*

**hos·tler** /ˈɒslə‖ˈhɑːstðər-/ *n* [C] the usual American spelling of OSTLER

S1 W2

## hot¹ /hɒt‖hɑːt/ *adj* **hotter, hottest**

① HIGH TEMPERATURE
② HOT TASTE
③ DIFFICULT TO DEAL WITH
④ ANGRY
⑤ POPULAR
⑥ FOLLOWING CLOSELY
⑦ OTHER SENSES

**hot**

| cold → hot | |
|---|---|
| ████████ | hot |
| ██████ | warm |
| ████ | tepid / lukewarm |
| | cold |

### ① HIGH TEMPERATURE

**1 ▶ WEATHER/FOOD/LIQUID ETC ◀** having a high temperature: *It's too hot in here – shall I open a window?*|*a nice hot bath*|*How hot is the water?*|*the hottest summer I can remember*|*hot countries*|**red hot** (=used to describe an object or surface that is very hot)|**white hot** (=used to describe metal that is extremely hot)|**boiling/broiling/scorching/baking/roasting hot** (=used to describe weather that is extremely hot) *a scorching hot day in August*|**boiling/scalding hot** (=used to describe liquid that is extremely hot)|**piping hot** (=used to describe food or water that is nice and hot) *Pour the sauce over the pasta and serve piping hot.*|**burning hot** (=used to describe the sun or a surface when it is extremely hot) *the burning hot sands of the desert*|**stifling/sweltering hot** *informal* (=used to describe weather or places that are uncomfortably hot)|**be hot as hell** *informal* (=used to describe a place that is extremely hot)

**2 ▶ FEELING HOT ◀** [not before a noun] feeling hot in a way that is uncomfortable: *I was hot and tired at the end of the day.* —see COLD (USAGE)

### ② HOT TASTE

**3** food that tastes hot contains pepper etc and has a burning taste

### ③ DIFFICULT TO DEAL WITH

**4 hot issue/topic etc** a subject that people disagree strongly about: *Abortion is a hot issue on both sides of the Atlantic.*

**5 be too hot to handle** if a problem or situation is too hot to handle it is impossible to deal with because it is causing too much trouble and anger: *The Watergate investigation eventually became too hot to handle.*

**6 be a hot potato** *informal* if a subject or problem is a hot potato, it is difficult to deal with

**7 ▶ DIFFICULT/UNPLEASANT SITUATION ◀** [not before noun] *informal* if a situation or place becomes too hot for someone, it is because other people are angry with them: *When things got too hot for him he sold up and left town.*|**make it hot for** (=cause a lot of trouble for someone)

**8 get into hot water** to get into a difficult situation by doing something wrong

### ④ ANGRY

**9 hot temper** someone who has a hot temper becomes angry very easily —see also HOT-TEMPERED

**10 get hot under the collar** *spoken* to become angry and ready to quarrel

### ⑤ POPULAR

**11** *informal* popular at a particular point in time: *Bros was a really hot group a few years ago.*|**hot property** (=an actor, singer etc that many theatre or film companies want) *Michael Jackson soon became the hottest property in show business.*

**12 be a hot ticket** *AmE* to be a very popular and fashionable person whom everyone wants to see: *Jodie Foster seems to be this year's hot ticket.*

### ⑥ FOLLOWING CLOSELY

**13 in hot pursuit** following someone quickly, and closely because you want to catch them: *The car sped away with the police in hot pursuit.*

**14 be hot on sb's trail/track** to be close to and likely to catch someone you have been chasing

**15 be hot on sb's heels** to be very close behind someone: *Jake came sprinting towards me with Mrs Bass's dog hot on his heels.*

**16 come hot on the heels of** to happen very soon after another event

### ⑦ OTHER SENSES

**17 ▶ GOOD AT STH ◀** *informal* very good at doing something: *a hot new guitar player*

**18 be hot stuff** *spoken* **a)** to be very good at a particular activity: *You should see him on the tennis court – he's really hot stuff.* **b)** to be sexually attractive

**19 not so hot** *spoken* not very good: *"How are you feeling?" "Not so hot; I'm really tired."*

**20 be in the hot seat** to have the job of making difficult and sometimes unpleasant decisions

**21 be hot on sth** *informal* **a)** to know a lot about something: *I'm not very hot on European history.* **b)** to be very strict about something: *They're really hot on punctuality here.*

**22 be hot on sb** to be sexually attracted to someone

**23 be hot at sth** *informal* to be very good at doing something: *I'm not too hot at basketball.*

**24 ▶ COMPETITION ◀** competition that is hot is between people or companies that are trying very hard to win or succeed: *Competition for the best jobs is getting hotter all the time.*

**25 ▶ NEWS ◀** hot news is about very recent events and therefore interesting or exciting: *a hot news item*

**26 be hot off the press** if a newspaper, report etc is hot off the press, it has only just been printed

**27 hot favourite** *BrE*, **hot favorite** *AmE* a competitor that most people expect to win a race or competition

**28 hot tip** a very good piece of advice about which horse is likely to win a race
**29 hot air** if someone talks hot air, they make statements which sound impressive, but are really meaningless: *It's all just hot air – he hasn't the money to pay for it.*
**30 hot spot** **a)** a place where there is likely to be trouble, fighting etc **b)** an area that is popular for a particular activity or type of entertainment
**31 go hot and cold** **a)** to suddenly feel very worried or frightened by something: *When I saw a police car outside, I went hot and cold all over.* **b)** to experience sudden changes in the temperature of your body because you are ill —see also **blow hot and cold** (BLOW[1] (15))
**32 be hot and bothered** *informal* to be so worried and confused by things going wrong that you cannot think clearly
**33 ► STOLEN ◄** *slang* goods that are hot have been stolen: *He was caught trying to sell hot video recorders.*
**34 hot money** money that is frequently moved from one country to another in order to make a quick profit
**35 ► MUSIC ◄** having a strong exciting RHYTHM
**36 ► SEXUALLY EXCITING ◄** a film, book, etc that is hot is sexually exciting —see also RED-HOT, HOTLY, HOTS

**hot**[2] *v* **hotted, hotting**
**hot up** *phr v* [I] *informal especially BrE* to become more exciting or dangerous with a lot more activity; INTENSIFY: *The election campaign is hotting up.*

**hot-air bal·loon** /ˈ· · ˌ/ *n* [C] a large BALLOON filled with hot air used for carrying people up into the sky

**hot·bed** /ˈhɒtbed‖ˈhɑːt-/ *n* **be a hotbed of** a place where a lot a particular kind of activity, especially bad or violent activity, happens: *Bavaria was a hotbed of extremist politics in the 20s and 30s.*

**hot-blood·ed** /ˌ· ˈ··◂/ *adj* having very strong emotions such as anger or love, that are difficult to control; PASSIONATE

**hot cake** /ˌ· ˈ·/ *n* [C] **be selling/going like hot cakes** *spoken* to be sold very quickly and in large amounts

**hot choco·late** /ˌ· ˈ··/ *n* [C,U] a hot drink made with chocolate powder and milk or water

**hotch·potch** /ˈhɒtʃpɒtʃ‖ˈhɑːtʃpɑːtʃ/ *especially BrE*, usually **hodgepodge** *AmE* —*n* [singular] *informal* a number of things mixed up without any sensible order or arrangement; MISHMASH

**hot-cross bun** /ˌ· · ˈ·/ *n* [C] a small round sweet cake, with a cross-shaped mark on top, that is eaten just before Easter

**hot dish** /ˌ· ˈ·/ *n* [C,U] *AmE* hot food cooked and served in a deep covered dish

**hot dog**[1] /ˌ· ˈ·‖ˈ· ·/ *n* [C] a cooked SAUSAGE in a long round piece of bread

**hot dog**[2] /ˌ· ˈ·/ *interjection AmE* used to express pleasure or surprise

**hot dog**[3] /ˈ· ·/ *v* [I] *AmE informal* to do a fast and exciting sport, especially skiing (SKI[2]), in a way that will attract a lot of attention and admiration: *skiers hot dogging down the slopes*

S2 W1 **ho·tel** /həʊˈtel‖hoʊ-/ *n* [C] a building where people pay to stay and eat meals

**ho·tel·i·er** /həʊˈtelier, -liər‖hoʊ/ *n* [C] someone who owns or manages a hotel

**hot flush** /ˌ· ˈ·/ *especially BrE*, usually **hot flash** *AmE* —*n* [C] a sudden hot feeling, which women have during their MENOPAUSE

**hot·foot**[1] /ˌhɒtˈfʊt◂‖ˈhɑːtfʊt/ *adv informal* moving fast and eagerly: *We ran hotfoot to the scene of the accident.*

**hotfoot**[2] *v* **hotfoot it** *informal* to walk or run quickly

**hot·head** /ˈhɒthed‖ˈhɑːt-/ *n* [C] someone who does things too quickly without thinking —**hotheaded** /ˌhɒtˈhedɪd◂‖ˌhɑːt-/ *adj* —**hotheadedly** *adv*

**hot·house** /ˈhɒthaʊs‖ˈhɑːt-/ *n* [C] **1** a heated building, usually made of glass, where flowers and delicate plants can grow —compare GREENHOUSE **2** a place or situation where a lot of people are interested in particular ideas or activities: *Vienna was a hothouse of artistic activity.* **3 hothouse atmosphere/environment etc** conditions in which strong attitudes and emotions develop among a group of people who are separated from ordinary people: *the hothouse atmosphere of a girls boarding school*

**hot line** /ˈ· ·/ *n* [C] **1** a direct telephone line between government leaders in different countries, which is only used in serious situations: *the hot line between Washington and Moscow* **2** a special telephone line for people to find out about or talk about something: *Call our crime hot line today.*

**hot·ly** /ˈhɒtli‖ˈhɑːtli/ *adv* **1 hotly debated/disputed/denied etc** discussed etc very angrily or with very strong feelings: *The rumor has been hotly denied.* **2 hotly pursued** chased closely by someone: *The man ran out of the store hotly pursued by two security guards.*

**hot pants** /ˈ· ·/ *n* [plural] very short tight women's shorts (SHORT[3] (2a))

**hot·plate** /ˈhɒtpleɪt‖ˈhɑːt-/ *n* [C] a metal surface, usually on a COOKER, that can be heated so that you can cook a pan of food on it

**hot·pot** /ˈhɒtpɒt‖ˈhɑːtpɑːt/ *n* [C,U] *BrE* a mixture of meat, potatoes and onions, cooked slowly together

**hot rod** /ˈ· ·/ *n* [C] *informal especially AmE* an old car that has been fitted with a more powerful engine to make it go very fast

**hots** /hɒts‖hɑːts/ *n* **have/get the hots for sb** *informal* to be sexually attracted to someone

**hot·shot** /ˈhɒtʃɒt‖ˈhɑːtʃɑːt/ *n* [C] *informal* someone who is very successful and confident —**hotshot** *adj*: *a hotshot lawyer*

**hot spring** /ˌ· ˈ·/ *n* [C] a place where hot water comes up naturally from the ground

**hot-tem·pered** /ˌ· ˈ··◂/ *adj* having a tendency to become angry easily

**hot tub** /ˌ· ˈ·/ *n* [C] a heated bath that several people can sit in —compare JACUZZI

**hot-water bot·tle** /ˌ· ˈ·· ˌ··/ *n* [C] a rubber container full of hot water used to make a bed warm —see picture at BOTTLE[1]

**hot-wire** /ˈ· ·/ *v* [T] *slang* to start the engine of a vehicle, by using the wires of the IGNITION system

**hou·mous, houmus** /ˈhuːməs, ˈhʊ-/ *n* [U] other spellings of HUMMUS

**hound**[1] /haʊnd/ *n* [C] **1** a dog used for hunting: **ride to hounds** *BrE old-fashioned* (=go FOXHUNTING) **2** *informal* a dog

**hound**[2] *v* [T] **1** to keep following someone and asking them questions in an annoying or threatening way; HARASS (1): *after the court case Lee was hounded relentlessly by the Press.* **2 hound sb out (of)** to make things so unpleasant for someone that they are forced to leave

**hour** /aʊə‖aʊr/ *n* [C] S1 W1
**1 ► 60 MINUTES ◄** a period of 60 minutes. There are 24 hours in a day: *The flight to Moscow takes just over three hours.* | *Karen is paid $10 an hour.* | **in an hour/in an hour's time** (=an hour from now) *I'll be back in an hour.* | **an hour's work/wait etc** *The system crashed and I lost three hours' work* | **pay/charge by the hour** (=pay or charge someone according to the number of hours it takes to do something)

**2 ▶ DISTANCE ◀** the distance you can travel in an hour: **be an hour from** *We're only an hour by car from New York.* | **an hour's drive/walk etc** (=a distance that takes an hour to drive, walk etc) *It's only about an hour's drive from here, isn't it?*
**3 ▶ TIMES FOR BUSINESS/WORK ETC ◀ hours** [plural] a fixed period of time in the day when a particular activity, business etc happens: *hours of business 9.00 – 5.00* | **office/opening hours** (=when an office or shop is working or open) | **visiting hours** (=when you can visit someone in hospital) | **out of hours** *BrE* (=before or after the usual working or business hours) | **after hours** (=after the time when a business, especially a bar, is supposed to close) | **lunch/dinner hour** (=the period in the middle of the day when people stop work for a meal) —see also RUSH HOUR, HAPPY HOUR
**4 work long/regular etc hours** if you work long, regular etc hours, the period that you work is longer than usual, always the same etc: *the long hours worked by hospital doctors* | **work unsocial hours** (=work in the evenings so that you cannot spend time with family or friends) | **work all the hours that God sends** (=work all the time that you can)
**5 ▶ TIME OF DAY ◀** *often plural* a particular period or point of time during the day or night: **the small hours** (=the period between midnight and two or three o'clock in the morning) *The celebrations went on into the small hours.* | **the hours of darkness/daylight** *literary*: *Few people dared to venture out during the hours of darkness.* | **at this hour** *spoken* (=used when you are surprised or annoyed by something happening too late at night or too early in the morning) *Who can be calling at this late hour?* | **unearthly/ungodly hour** *spoken* (=used when you are complaining about how early or late something is) *We had to get up at some ungodly hour to catch a plane.* | **at all hours (of the day or night)** *spoken* (=at any time) *Our neighbours play loud music at all hours.* | **till all hours** *spoken* (=until an unreasonably late time at night) *She's up till all hours studying.* | **keep late/regular etc hours** (=go to bed and get up at late, regular etc times) —see also **waking hours/life/day etc** (WAKING)

**6 ▶ LONG TIME ◀ a) hours** [plural] *informal* a long time or a time that seems long: *We had to spend hours filling in forms.* | *I've been waiting here for hours.* | **hours and hours** (=a very long time) *a really boring lecture – and it just went on for hours and hours* **b) hour after hour** continuously for many hours
**7 within hours of** only a few hours after doing something or after something happening: *Within hours of landing, troops had started to advance inland.*
**8 ▶ O'CLOCK ◀** the time of the day when a new hour starts, for example one o'clock, two o'clock etc: **strike the hour** (=if a clock strikes the hour, it rings, to show that it is one o'clock, seven o'clock etc) | **(every hour) on the hour** (=every hour at six o'clock, seven o'clock etc) *There are flights to Boston every hour on the hour.*
**9 1300/1530/1805 hours** used to give the time in official or military reports and orders
**10 by the hour/from hour to hour** if a situation is changing by the hour or from hour to hour, it is changing very quickly and very often: *This financial crisis is growing more serious by the hour.*
**11 ▶ POINT IN HISTORY OR SB'S LIFE ◀** an important moment or period in history or in your life: **finest hour** *This was our country's finest hour.* | **sb's hour of need/glory etc** (=a time when someone needs help, is very successful etc) *Don't desert me in my hour of need.*
**12 of the hour** of a particular time, especially the present time: *one of the burning questions of the hour* | **the hero/man of the hour** (=someone who does something very brave, is very successful etc at a particular time) —see also **the eleventh hour** (ELEVENTH (2)), HOURLY, ZERO HOUR

**hour·glass** /ˈaʊəɡlɑːs‖ˈaʊrɡlæs/ *n* [C] **1** a glass container for measuring time in which sand moves slowly from the top half to the bottom in exactly one hour **2 hourglass figure** a woman who has an hourglass figure has a narrow waist in comparison with her chest and HIPS

**hour hand** /ˈ· ,·/ *n* [C] the shorter of the two pieces on a clock or watch that show you what time it is

**hour·ly** /ˈaʊəli‖ˈaʊrli/ *adj* **1** happening or done every hour: *hourly news broadcasts* **2 hourly pay/earnings/fees etc** the amount you earn or charge for every hour you work —**hourly** *adv*: *The database is updated hourly.*

**house¹** /haʊs/ *plural* **houses** /ˈhaʊzɪ̈z/ *n* [C] S1 W1
**1 ▶ WHERE YOU LIVE ◀ a)** a building that you live in, especially one that has more than one level and is intended to be used by one family: *a four bedroom house* | *Why don't you all come over to our house for coffee?* | **set up house** (=start to live in a house, especially with another person) | **move house** *BrE* (=leave your house and go to live in another one) —see picture on page 410 **b)** all the people who live in a house: *He gets up at six and disturbs the whole house.*
**2 keep house** to do all the cooking, cleaning etc in a house
**3 ▶ LARGE BUILDING ◀ a) opera house/court house etc** a large public building used for a particular purpose **b) House** used in the names of office buildings: *Longman House, Harlow, Essex*
**4 hen house/coach house/storehouse etc** a building used for keeping animals, goods, equipment etc in
**5 ▶ COMPANY ◀** a company, especially one that produces books, lends money, or designs clothes: *America's oldest publishing house* | *the House of Dior*
**6 in house** if you work in house, you work at the offices of a company or organization, not at home
**7 put/set your own house in order** if someone should put or set their own house in order, they should improve the way they behave before criticizing other people
**8 get on like a house on fire** *informal* to quickly have a very friendly relationship with someone
**9 ▶ PARLIAMENT ◀** a group of people who make the laws of a country: *The President will address both houses of Congress.* | **the house** (=the house of Commons or Lords in Britain, or the house of representatives in the US) —see also LOWER HOUSE, UPPER HOUSE
**10 this house** *formal* used to mean the people who are voting in a formal DEBATE when you are stating the proposal that is being discussed
**11 ▶ IN A SCHOOL ◀** a group of children of different ages at the same school which competes against other groups in the school, for example in sports competitions
**12 ▶ THEATRE ◀ a)** the part of a theatre, cinema etc where people sit: **full/packed/empty house** (=a large or small AUDIENCE) *The show has been playing to packed houses since it opened.* —see also HOUSE LIGHTS **b)** the people who have come to watch a performance; AUDIENCE **c)** a performance that is one of a series during the day
**13 be on the house** if drinks or meals are on the house you do not have to pay for them because they are provided free by the owner of the bar, restaurant etc
**14 house wine** ordinary wine that is provided by a restaurant to be drunk with meals: *A glass of house red, please.*
**15 go all round the houses** *BrE* to go through an unnecessarily complicated process in order to do something or answer something
**16 ▶ ROYAL FAMILY ◀** an important family, especially a royal family: *the House of Windsor* —see also COUNCIL HOUSE, **eat sb out of house and home** (EAT (4)), OPEN HOUSE, PUBLIC HOUSE, **(as) safe as houses** (SAFE¹ (5))
**17 bring the house down** to make a lot of people laugh, especially when you are acting in a theatre

**house²** /haʊz/ *v* [T] **1** to provide someone with a place to live: *The refugees are being housed in temporary accommodation.* **2** if a building houses something, it is kept there: *The library is currently housed in the British Museum.*

**house ar·rest** /ˈ· ·ˌ·/ *n* **be under house arrest** to be told that you must stay inside your house by the government

**house·boat** /ˈhaʊsbəʊt‖-boʊt/ *n* [C] a boat that you can live in

**house·bound** /ˈhaʊsbaʊnd/ *adj* unable to leave your house, especially because you are ill or old

**house·boy** /ˈhaʊsbɔɪ/ *n* [C] *old use* a word which is now considered offensive, meaning a man who is employed to do general work at someone's house

**house·break·er** /ˈhaʊsˌbreɪkə‖-ər/ *n* [C] a thief who enters someone else's house by breaking locks, windows etc; BURGLAR —**housebreaking** *n* [U]

**house·bro·ken** /ˈhaʊsˌbrəʊkən‖-ˌbroʊ-/ *adj AmE* an animal that is housebroken has been trained not to make the house dirty with its URINE and FAECES; HOUSE-TRAINED *BrE*

**house·coat** /ˈhaʊs-kəʊt‖-koʊt/ *n* [C] a long, loose coat worn at home to protect clothes while cleaning etc

**house·craft** /ˈhaʊs-krɑːft‖-kræft/ *n* [U] *BrE old-fashioned* DOMESTIC SCIENCE

**house·fly** /ˈhaʊsflaɪ/ *n plural* **houseflies** [C] a common type of fly that lives in houses

**house·ful** /ˈhaʊsfʊl/ *n* **a houseful of** a large number of people or things in your house: *We had a houseful of guests last weekend.*

**house guest** /ˈ· ˌ·/ *n* [C] a friend or relative who is staying in your house for a short time

S2 W2 **house·hold**[1] /ˈhaʊshəʊld‖-hoʊld/ *n* [C] *BrE* all the people who live together in one house

**household**[2] *adj* [only before a noun] **1** connected with looking after a house and the people in it; DOMESTIC: **household goods/products/items** *washing powder and other household products | household chores* **2 be a household name/word** to be very well known: *Coca Cola is a household name around the world.*

**house·hold·er** /ˈhaʊsˌhəʊldə‖-ˌhoʊldər/ *n* [C] *formal* someone who owns or is in charge of a house

**house hus·band** /ˈ· ˌ··/ *n* [C] a husband who stays at home and does the cooking, cleaning etc

**house·keep·er** /ˈhaʊsˌkiːpə‖-ər/ *n* [C] someone who is employed to manage the cleaning, cooking etc in a house or hotel

**house·keep·ing** /ˈhaʊsˌkiːpɪŋ/ *n* [U] **1** the work and organization of things that need to be done in a house, for example cooking and buying food **2** also **housekeeping money** an amount of money that is kept and used to pay for food and other things needed in the home **3** jobs that need to be done to keep a system working properly

**house lights** /ˈ· ·/ *n* [plural] the lights in the part of a cinema or theatre where people sit

**house·maid** /ˈhaʊsmeɪd/ *n* [C] *old-fashioned* a female servant who cleans someone's house

**house·man** /ˈhaʊsmən/ *n plural* **housemen** /-mən/ *BrE* [C] someone who has nearly finished training as a doctor and is working in a hospital; INTERN *AmE*

**house mar·tin** /ˈ· ˌ··/ *n* [C] a small black and white European bird of the SWALLOW[2] (1) family

**house·mas·ter** /ˈhaʊsˌmɑːstə‖-ˌmæstər/ *n* [C] *especially BrE* a male teacher who is in charge of one of the houses (HOUSE[1] (11)) in a school

**house·mis·tress** /ˈhaʊsˌmɪstrɪ̣s/ *n* [C] *especially BrE* a female teacher who is in charge of one of the houses (HOUSE[1] (11)) in a school

**house mu·sic** /ˈ· ˌ··/ *n* [U] a type of popular music

**house of cards** /ˌ· · ˈ·/ *n* [singular] **1** a plan that is so badly arranged that is likely to fail **2** an arrangement of PLAYING CARDS built carefully but easily knocked over

**House of Com·mons** /ˌ· · ˈ··/ *n* [singular] the part of the British or Canadian parliament whose members are elected by the people

**house of God** /ˌ· · ˈ·/ *n* [singular] *literary* a church

**House of Lords** /ˌ· · ˈ·/ *n* [singular] the part of the British parliament whose members are not elected but have positions because of their rank or title

**House of Rep·re·sen·ta·tives** /ˌ· · ··ˈ···/ *n* [singular] the larger of the two parts of the US Congress or of the parliament of Australia or New Zealand — compare SENATE (1)

**house of wor·ship** /ˌ· · ˈ··/ *n* [C] *especially AmE* a church

**house·par·ent** /ˈhaʊsˌpeərənt‖-ˌper-/ *n* [C] someone who looks after a group of children who live together in a special home because they have no families or need special care

**house par·ty** /ˈ· ˌ··/ *n* [C] a group of people who stay as guests in a large country house

**house·phone** /ˈhaʊsfəʊn‖-foʊn/ *n* [C] a telephone that can only be used to make calls within a building, especially a hotel

**house·plant** /ˈhaʊsplɑːnt‖-plænt/ *n* [C] a plant that you grow indoors for decoration

**house·proud** /ˈhaʊspraʊd/ *adj* spending a lot of time on keeping your house clean and tidy

**house·room** /ˈhaʊsruːm, -rʊm/ *n* [U] *especially BrE* **1 not give sth houseroom** to not like something and not want it **2** space in a house for a person or thing

**house-sit** /ˈ· ·/ *v* [I] to look after someone's house while they are away

**Houses of Par·lia·ment** /ˌ·· · ˈ···/ *n* [singular] the buildings where the British parliament meets, or the parliament itself

**house-to-house** /ˌ· · ˈ·◂/ *adj* **house-to-house inquiries/survey/search etc** inquiries etc that are made by visiting each house in a particular area: *The abduction sparked a house-to-house search in the Willenhall area.*

**house·tops** /ˈhaʊs-tɒps‖-tɑːps/ *n* **shout/broadcast/proclaim sth from the housetops** to say something publicly so that everyone will hear or know about it

**house-trained** /ˈ· ·/ *adj BrE* a pet that is house-trained has been trained not to make the house dirty with its URINE and FAECES; HOUSEBROKEN *AmE* —**housetrain** *v* [T]

**house·wares** /ˈhaʊsweəz‖-werz/ *n* [plural] *AmE* small things used in the home, for example plates, lamps etc, or the department of a large shop that sells these things

**house-warm·ing** /ˈ· ˌ··/ *n* [C] a party that you give to celebrate moving into a new house: *Are you coming to Jo's housewarming on Friday?*

**house·wife** /ˈhaʊs-waɪf/ *n plural* **housewives** /-waɪvz/ [C] a married woman who works at home doing the cooking, cleaning etc, but does not have a job outside the house; HOMEMAKER —**housewifely** *adj*

**house·work** /ˈhaʊswɜːk‖-wɜːrk/ *n* [U] work that you do to take care of a house such as washing, cleaning etc: *I spent all morning doing the housework.*

**hous·ing** /ˈhaʊzɪŋ/ *n* **1** [U] the houses or conditions that people live in: *health problems caused by bad housing* **2** [U] the work of providing houses for people to live in: *government housing policy* **3** [C] a protective cover for a machine: *the engine housing* W2

**housing as·so·ci·a·tion** /ˈ·· ··ˌ··/ *n* [C] an association in Britain, formed by a group of people so that they can build homes for themselves, or can buy homes of their own

**housing es·tate** /ˈ·· ·ˌ·/ *BrE*, **housing de·vel·opment** /ˈ·· ·ˌ···/ *AmE* —*n* [C] a large number of houses that have been built together in a planned way

**housing pro·ject** /ˈ·· ˌ··/ *n* [C] *especially AmE* a group of houses or apartments, usually built with government money, for poor families

**hove** /həʊv‖hoʊv/ *v* [I] the past tense and past participle of HEAVE[1] (6)

**hov·el** /ˈhɒvəl‖ˈhʌ-, ˈhɑː-/ *n* [C] a small dirty place where someone lives, especially a very poor person

**hov·er** /ˈhɒvə‖ˈhʌvər, ˈhɑː-/ *v* [I] **1** if a bird, insect, or HELICOPTER hovers, it stays in one place in the air **2** to stay nervously in the same place especially because you are waiting for something or are uncertain what to do: [+ **around/about**] *I noticed several reporters hovering around outside the courtroom.* **3** [always + adv/prep] to be in an uncertain state: [+ **around/between etc**] *The dollar has been hovering around the 110 yen level.*

**hov·er·craft** /ˈhɒvəkrɑːft‖ˈhʌvərkræft, ˈhɑː-/ *n plural* **hovercraft** or **hovercrafts** [C] a vehicle that travels just above the surface of land or water by means of a strong current of air forced out beneath it —compare HYDROFOIL

**hover mow·er** /ˈ·· ,··/ *n* [C] a machine for cutting grass that moves just above the ground

S1 W1 **how¹** /haʊ/ *adv*

**1 ▶ QUESTIONS ◀ a)** used to ask about what way or what method you should use to do something, find out about something, go somewhere etc: *How do you spell foyer?|How should I dress for this job interview?|How on earth do you manage to afford so many holidays?|I want to know how you say 'good luck' in Japanese.* **b)** used to ask about the amount, size, degree etc of something: *How big is the state of Louisiana compared to England?|How many kids do they have now?|How long did you live in Manchester for?|* **how much?** (=used to ask the price of something) *How much is that sweater, the blue one?* **c)** used to ask about someone's health or about their feelings: *How's your ankle this morning? Has the swelling gone down?* **d)** used to ask about someone's opinion of something or about their experience of something: *How did your exams go?|How was the play?* **e)** used to ask about the way something looks, behaves, or is expressed: *How does that speech of Macbeth's end, the one about 'a tale told by an idiot'?|How does that song go, anyway?*

**2 ▶ EMPHASIZE ◀** used before an adjective or adverb to emphasize the quality you are mentioning: *He was impressed at how well she could read.|"John's been in an accident." "Oh, how awful!"|It depends on how busy they are whether they'll be able to go or not.*

Frequencies of the word **how** in spoken and written English.

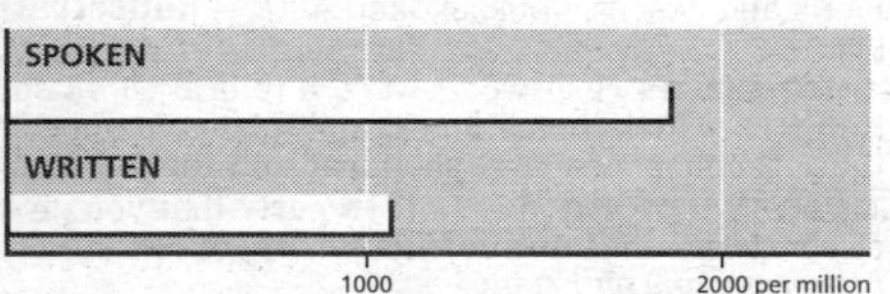


Based on the British National Corpus and the Longman Lancaster Corpus

This graph shows that the word **how** is much more common in spoken English than in written English. This is because it is used a lot to ask questions, is used to emphasize what you are saying, and is used in a lot of common spoken phrases.

**how** (*adv*) **SPOKEN PHRASES**

**3 how are you?** used when you meet someone, to ask if they are well: *"Hi Francie, how are you?" "Fine, thanks, how are you?"*

**4 how's it going?/how are you doing? a)** used when you meet someone, to ask if they are well, happy etc: *"Hey, how's it going?" "OK."* **b)** used to ask if someone is happy with what they are doing: *So how's it going at work these days? Still enjoying it?*

**5 how about...? a)** used to make a suggestion about what to do: *No, I'm busy on Monday. How about Tuesday at seven?|* **how about doing sth** *How about putting the sofa closer to the window?|* **how's about** *informal especially AmE*: *How's about going to the beach this afternoon?* **b)** used to introduce a new idea, fact etc that has not yet been discussed: *"Mary and Ken are still away." "And how about Billy?"*

**6 how about you?** used to ask someone what they want or what their opinion is, after you have said what you want or what your opinion is: *I can't stand opera, how about you?*

**7 how do you mean?** used to ask someone to explain something they have just said: *"What's your family situation?" "How do you mean?" "Are you married?"*

**8 how's that?** used to ask someone whether something is satisfactory: *How's that? Can you see now?*

**9 how come?** used to ask why something has happened or been said, especially when you are surprised by it: *How come Dave's home? Isn't he feeling well?*

**10 how do you do?** a polite expression used when you meet someone for the first time

**11 how are things?** used when you meet someone, to ask if they are well, happy etc: *"Hello Peter, how are things?" "Oh, not too bad."*

**12 how do you know?** used to ask how someone found out about something or why they are sure about something: *"Better bring an umbrella. It's going to rain later." "How do you know?"*

**13 how can you/how could you...?** used when you are very surprised by or disapprove strongly of something: *William! How could you say such a thing!*

**14 how about that!/how do you like that!** used to ask what someone thinks of something that you think is surprising, rude, very good etc: *He lost 15 pounds in a month! How about that!*

**15 how so?** used to ask someone to explain an opinion they have given: *"Rick's parents are a little strange, I think." "How so?"*

**16 and how!** *AmE old-fashioned* an expression meaning 'yes, very much,' used to strongly emphasize your reply to a question: *"Was Matt drunk?" "And how!"*

**how²** *conjunction* **1** used at the beginning of a CLAUSE (2) in which you explain the method of doing something: *He has to understand that this is how we do things in this household, even if his mother does them differently.|* **how to do sth** *The class teaches students how to plan a budget.* **2** used at the beginning of a CLAUSE (2) in which you introduce a fact or statement: *We were both traveling across Europe, and that's how we first met.|Okay, do you remember how we discussed yesterday the Roman rule of Britain?* **3** *spoken* in whatever way: *In your own house you can act how you want.*

**how·dah** /ˈhaʊdə/ *n* [C] a covered seat used for riding an elephant

**how·dy** /ˈhaʊdi/ *interjection AmE* used to say hello in an informal, usually humorous way

**how·ev·er¹** /haʊˈevə‖-ər/ *adv* **1** used when you are adding a fact or piece of information that seems surprising, or seems to disagree with what you have just said: *People like this are usually harmless. They can, however, be a nuisance.|This method has been widely adopted. However, it is not yet clear that it is the best method.* —see BUT¹ (USAGE) **2 however hard/serious/long/carefully etc** it makes no difference how hard, serious, long, carefully etc: *You should report any incident, however serious or minor it is.|We'll have to finish the job, however long it takes.|* **however much/many** (=it makes no difference, how much or how many) *I really want the car, however much it costs.* **3** used to mean how, when you want to show that you find something very surprising: *However did he get that job?* S2 W1

**however²** *conjunction* in whatever way: *You can do it however you like.|If we win the match we'll be delighted however it happens.*

**how·it·zer** /ˈhaʊɪtsə‖-ər/ *n* [C] a heavy gun which fires shells (SHELL¹ (2)) high into the air so that they travel a short distance

**howl¹** /haʊl/ *v* **1** [I] if a dog, WOLF, or other animal howls, it makes a long loud sound: *The dogs howled all night.* **2** [I] to make a long loud cry because you are unhappy, in pain, or angry: *the constant howling from the baby upstairs.* **3** [I,T] to shout or demand something angrily: [+ **for**] *Right wing Republicans have been howling for military intervention.* **4** [I] if the wind howls, it makes a loud high sound as it blows: *wind howling in the trees* **5 howl with laughter** to laugh very loudly **6 be a howling success** to be extremely successful

**howl** sb/sth ↔ **down** *phr v* [T] to prevent someone or something from being heard by shouting loudly and angrily

**howl²** *n* [C] **1** a long loud sound made by a dog, WOLF, or other animal **2** a loud cry of pain or anger **3 howl of laughter** a very loud laugh

**howl·er** /ˈhaʊlə‖-ər/ *n* [C] *BrE informal* a stupid mistake that makes people laugh

**how·so·ev·er** /ˌhaʊsəʊˈevə‖-soʊˈevər/ *adv literary* HOWEVER

**how·zat** /ˌhaʊˈzæt/ *interjection* used in CRICKET when claiming that a player is OUT[1] (37)

**HP** /ˌ· ˈ·/ **1** an abbreviation of HORSEPOWER **2** *BrE* an abbreviation of HIRE PURCHASE: **on HP** *We bought it on HP.*

**HQ** /ˌeɪtʃ ˈkjuː/ an abbreviation of HEADQUARTERS

**hr** *plural* **hrs** a written abbreviation of HOUR

**HRH** an abbreviation of His or Her Royal Highness

**HRT** /ˌeɪtʃ ɑː ˈtiː‖-ɑːr-/ *n* [U] an abbreviation of HORMONE REPLACEMENT THERAPY

**ht** the written abbreviation of HEIGHT

**hub** /hʌb/ *n* [C] **1** the central and most important part of an area, system etc, which all the other parts are connected to: [+ **of**] *York used to be the hub of a vast rail network.* **2** the central part of a wheel to which the AXLE is joined —see picture at BICYCLE[1]

**hub·bub** /ˈhʌbʌb/ *n* [singular, U] a mixture of loud noises, especially the noise of a lot of people talking at the same time

**hub·by** /ˈhʌbi/ *n* [C] *informal* husband

**hub·cap** /ˈhʌbkæp/ *n* [C] a metal cover for the centre of a wheel on a vehicle —see picture on page 409

**hu·bris** /ˈhjuːbrɪs/ *n* [U] *literary* great and unreasonable pride

**huck·le·ber·ry** /ˈhʌkəlbəri‖-beri/ *n* [C] a small dark-blue North American fruit that grows on a bush

**huck·ster** /ˈhʌkstə‖-ər/ *n* [C] **1** *AmE* someone who uses very strong, direct selling methods, sometimes dishonestly **2** *old-fashioned* someone who sells small things in the street or to people in their houses

**hud·dle¹** /ˈhʌdl/ *v* **huddled, huddling 1** [I,T] also **huddle together/up** if a group of people huddle together, they gather closely together in a group, especially because they are cold or frightened: *A few die-hard football fans huddled together in the rain waiting for tickets* **2** [I always + adv/prep] to lie or sit with your arms and legs close to your body because you are cold or frightened: *I jumped in bed and huddled under the blankets.*

**huddle²** *n* [C] **1** a group of people standing or sitting close together, or a group of things placed together in a confused way: [+ **of**] *a huddle of straw huts* **2** a group of players in American football who gather around one player who tells them the plan for the next part of the game **3 get/go into a huddle** to form a small group away from other people in order to discuss something

**hue** /hjuː/ *n* [C] *especially literary* **1** a colour or kind of colour: *Her hair turned a deep golden hue in the light of the sun.* **2** a type of opinion, belief etc: **of every hue** (=of many kinds) *Political opinions of every hue were represented at the conference.*

**hue and cry** /ˌ· · ˈ·/ *n* [singular] angry protests about something

**huff¹** /hʌf/ *v* [I] *informal* **1 huff and puff** to breathe out noisily, especially because you are tired: *By the time he got to the top he was huffing and puffing.* **2 huffing and puffing** behaviour that shows that someone disagrees strongly with something such as an official plan

**huff²** *n* **in a huff** feeling angry or bad-tempered, especially because someone has offended you: **go off/walk off/leave in a huff** *I told her she was always late and now she's gone off in a huff.*

**huff·y** /ˈhʌfi/ *adj informal* in a bad temper: *It's no use getting all huffy about it.* —**huffily** *adv*

**hug¹** /hʌg/ *v* **hugged, hugging** [T] **1** to put your arms around someone and hold them tightly to show love or friendship: *Jane threw her arms around him and hugged him tight.* —see picture on page 1260 **2** to hold something in your arms close to your chest: *He was hugging a big pile of books.* **3** to move along the side, edge, top etc of something, staying very close to it: *The boat hugged the coast.* **4 hug yourself with joy/delight etc** to feel very pleased with yourself

**hug²** *n* [C] the action of putting your arms around someone and holding them tightly to show love or friendship: **give sb a hug** *Paul gave me a big hug and smiled.* —see also BEAR HUG

**huge** /hjuːdʒ/ *adj* **1** extremely large: *huge sums of money | Your room's positively huge compared to mine.* **2** to a very great degree: **a huge success/disappointment etc** *The play was a huge success.* —**hugely** *adv*: *hugely successful* —**hugeness** *n* [U] S2 W2

**huh** /hʌh, hʌ/ *interjection spoken* **1** *especially AmE* used at the end of a question, often to ask for agreement: *Not a bad little place, huh?* **2** used to show that you have not heard or understood a question: *"Carly, are you listening to me?" "Huh?"* **3** used to show disagreement or surprise, or to show that you do not find something impressive: *"She looks nice." "Huh! Too much make-up, if you ask me."*

**hu·la** /ˈhuːlə/ *n* [singular] a Polynesian dance done by women using gentle movements of the HIPS —**hula** *adj*: *hula skirts*

**hula hoop** /ˈ·· ·/ *n* [C] a large ring which you make swing around your waist by moving your HIPS

**hulk** /hʌlk/ *n* [C] **1** a large heavy person or thing: *a hulk of a man* **2** the main part of an old ship that is not used any more

**hulk·ing** /ˈhʌlkɪŋ/ *adj* [only before a noun] very big and often awkward: *a hulking great figure of a man*

**hull¹** /hʌl/ *n* [C] the main part of a ship: **wooden-hulled/steel-hulled etc** (=having a wood, steel etc hull) —see picture at YACHT

**hull²** *v* [T] to take off the outer part of vegetables, rice, grain etc

**hul·la·ba·loo** /ˌhʌləbəˈluː, ˈhʌləbəluː/ *n* [C usually singular] **1** excited talk, newspaper stories etc, especially when something surprising or shocking is happening; UPROAR: *the huge hullabaloo over the film in the press* **2** a lot of noise, especially made by people shouting

**hul·lo** /hʌˈləʊ‖-loʊ/ *interjection spoken* [C] *especially BrE* another spelling of HELLO

**hum¹** /hʌm/ *v* **hummed, humming 1** [I,T] to sing a tune by making a continuous sound with your lips closed: *Carol hummed quietly to herself as she worked.* **2** [I] to make a low, continuous sound: *insects humming in the hot summer air* **3** [I] to be very busy and full of activity: [+ **with**] *Wall Street was humming with rumours.* **4 hum and haw** *BrE* to take a long time to say something etc because you are not sure what to say —see also **hem and haw** (HEM[2] (2))

**hum²** *n* [singular] a low continuous sound: *the hum of bees | the distant hum of traffic*

**hu·man¹** /ˈhjuːmən/ *adj* **1** belonging to or concerning people, especially as opposed to animals or machines: *theories of human behaviour | The cat's eyes looked almost human.* **2** human weaknesses, emotions etc are typical of ordinary people: *common human failings such as greed and envy* **3 sb is only human** used to say that someone should not be blamed for what they have done **4** someone who seems human shows that they have the same feelings and emotions as ordinary people: *He's really not so bad. When you get to know him he seems quite human.* —opposite INHUMAN **5 the human touch** someone, especially someone in authority, who has the human touch deals with people in a kind, friendly way: *Senior managers have been accused of lacking the human touch.* **6** mistakes made by a person, rather than by a machine **7** a quality that makes a story interesting because it is about people's feelings, relationships etc —see MAN[1] (USAGE) W1

**human²** also **human be·ing** /ˌ·· ˈ··/ *n* [C] a man, woman, or child —see also MAN[1] (3) 

**hu·mane** /hjuːˈmeɪn/ *adj* treating people or animals in a way that is not cruel and causes them as little pain or suffering as possible: *Farmers will be asked to consider more humane ways of transporting livestock.* —**humanely** *adv* —opposite INHUMANE

**hu·man·is·m** /ˈhjuːmənɪzəm/ *n* [U] **1** a system of beliefs concerned with the needs of people and not with religious ideas **2** the study in the Renaissance of the ideas of the ancient Greeks and Romans —**humanist** *n* [C] —**humanistic** /ˌhjuːməˈnɪstɪk◂/ *adj*

**hu·man·i·tar·i·an** /hjuːˌmænəˈteəriən‖-ˈter-/ *adj* concerned with improving bad living conditions and preventing unfair treatment of people: *humanitarian aid to the refugees* —**humanitarian** *n* [C] —**humanitarianism** *n* [U]

**hu·man·i·ties** /hjuːˈmænətiz/ *n* **the humanities** subjects of study such as literature, history, PHILOSOPHY etc

**hu·man·i·ty** /hjuːˈmænəti/ *n* [U] **1** people in general: *30% of humanity lives in conditions of terrible poverty.* **2** the state of being human and having qualities and rights that all people have: *We must never forget our common humanity.* **3** kindness, respect, and sympathy towards other people

**hu·man·ize** also **-ise** *BrE* /ˈhjuːmənaɪz/ *v* [T] to make a system more pleasant or more suitable for people: *an attempt to humanize the huge governmental bureaucracy*

**hu·man·kind** /ˌhjuːmənˈkaɪnd/ *n* [U] people in general

**hu·man·ly** /ˈhjuːmənli/ *adv* **be humanly possible a)** to do as much as anyone could possibly do: *Doctors did everything humanly possible to save the child's life.* **b)** if something is humanly possible, it can be done using a great deal of effort: *I'm not sure it will be humanly possible to prevent the disease from spreading.*

**human na·ture** /ˌ·· ˈ··/ *n* [U] **1** the qualities or ways of behaving that are natural and common to most people **2 it's (only) human nature** used to say that a particular feeling or way of behaving is normal and natural

**hu·man·oid** /ˈhjuːmənɔɪd/ *adj* something, especially a machine, that is humanoid has a human shape and qualities: *a humanoid robot* —**humanoid** *n* [C]

**human race** /ˌ·· ˈ·/ *n* **the human race** all people, considered together as a single group —see also MAN[1] (3)

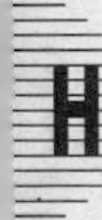

**human re·sourc·es** /ˌ·· ·ˈ··‖ˌ·· ˈ···/ *n* **1** [plural] the abilities and skills of people **2** the department in a company that deals with employing, training, and helping people; PERSONNEL (2)

**human rights** /ˌ··ˈ·/ *n* [plural] the basic rights which every person has to be treated in a fair, equal way without cruelty, especially by their government: *flagrant human rights violations*

**hum·ble**[1] /ˈhʌmbəl/ *adj* **1** having a low social class or position: **humble background/origins etc** *Lacocca rose from humble beginnings to become boss of Ford.* | *a humble country parson* **2** not considering yourself or your ideas to be as important as other people's: *He thanked us again with a humble smile.* —opposite PROUD (2) **3 my humble apologies** *spoken* used to say you are sorry, but not in a very serious way **4 in my humble opinion** *spoken* used to give your opinion about something in a slightly humorous way **5** simple and not advanced, but useful or effective: **the humble** *high-priced successor to the humble pocket calculator* **6 eat humble pie** to admit that you were wrong about something **7 your humble servant** a formal way of ending a letter, used in the past —**humbly** *adv* —see also HUMILITY

**humble**[2] *v* **humbled, humbling 1 be humbled** if you are humbled, you realize that you are not as important, good, kind etc as you thought you were: *He felt humbled by their offer.* **2** [T] to easily defeat someone who is much stronger than you are: *The mighty US army was humbled by a small South East Asian country.* **3 humble yourself** to show that you are not too proud to ask for something, admit you are wrong etc —**humbling** *adj*: *a humbling experience*

**hum·bug** /ˈhʌmbʌg/ *n* **1** [U] insincere words or behaviour, especially pretending to feel shocked or disapprove of something **2** [U] *old-fashioned* someone who pretends to be someone they are not, or to have qualities or opinions they do not have **3** [C] *BrE* a sweet made of hard boiled sugar, usually tasting of mint (MINT[1] (2))

**hum·ding·er** /hʌmˈdɪŋə‖-ər/ *n* [singular] *informal* a very exciting or impressive game, performance, or event: **a real humdinger** *Foreman's next match promises to be a real humdinger.*

**hum·drum** /ˈhʌmdrʌm/ *adj* boring and ordinary, and having very little variety or interest: **a humdrum existence/job** *a humdrum office job*

**humerus** /ˈhjuːmərəs/ [C] *n technical* the bone between your shoulder and elbow

**hu·mid** /ˈhjuːmədd/ *adj* weather that is humid makes you feel uncomfortable because the air feels very hot and wet: *Tokyo is extremely humid in mid-summer.* —compare DRY[1] (2)

**hu·mid·i·fi·er** /hjuːˈmɪdəfaɪə‖-ər/ *n* [C] a machine that makes the air in a room, container etc less dry

**hu·mid·i·fy** /hjuːˈmɪdəfaɪ/ *v* [T] to add very small drops of water to the air in a room etc because the air is too dry

**hu·mid·i·ty** /hjuːˈmɪdəti/ *n* [U] **1** the amount of water contained in the air: *90% humidity* **2** air or weather that is uncomfortably warm and wet

**hu·mil·i·ate** /hjuːˈmɪlieɪt/ *v* [T] to make someone feel ashamed and upset, especially by making them seem stupid or weak: *Her boss humiliated her in front of all her colleagues.* —**humiliated** *adj*: *I've never felt so humiliated in all my life!*

**hu·mil·i·at·ing** /hjuːˈmɪlieɪtɪŋ/ *adj* making you feel ashamed, embarrassed, and angry because you have been made to look weak or stupid: *a humiliating defeat*

**hu·mil·i·a·tion** /hjuːˌmɪliˈeɪʃən/ *n* **1** [U] a feeling of shame and great embarrassment, because you have been made to look stupid or weak: *She would do anything rather than suffer the humiliation of asking her parents for money.* **2** [C usually singular] a situation that makes you feel humiliated

**hu·mil·i·ty** /hjuːˈmɪləti/ *n* [U] the quality of not being too proud about yourself —see also HUMBLE[1]

**humming bird** /ˈ·· ·/ *n* [C] a very small brightly-coloured tropical bird whose wings move very quickly

**hum·mock** /ˈhʌmək/ *n* [C] a very small hill; HILLOCK

**hum·mus, humus** /ˈhuːməs, ˈhʊ-/ *n* [U] a type of Greek food made from a soft mixture of CHICK PEAS, oil and GARLIC

**hu·mor·ist** /ˈhjuːmərəst‖ˈhjuː-, ˈjuː-/ *n* [C] someone, especially a writer, who tells funny stories

**hu·mor·ous** /ˈhjuːmərəs‖ˈhjuː-, ˈjuː-/ *adj* deliberately funny and entertaining, especially in a clever way: *a humorous account of her travels in South America* —**humorously** *adv*

**hu·mour**[1] *BrE*, **humor** *AmE* /ˈhjuːmə‖ˈhjuːmər, ˈjuː-/ *n* **1** [U] the quality in something that makes it funny: *Mr Thorne failed to see the humour in the situation.* **2** [U] the way that a particular person or group find certain things amusing: *English humour* | **sense of humour** *Ackroyd's often bizarre sense of humor* **3** [U] the ability to understand and enjoy amusing situations or to laugh at things: *Paul radiated humour and charm.* | **sense of humour** *It's vital to have a sense of humor in this job.* **4 good humour** the ability to remain cheerful, especially in situations that would make some people upset or angry: *Danny reacted to these criticisms with his usual good humour.* **5 in a good humour/in a bad humour etc** in a good or bad temper —see also GOOD-HUMOURED **6** [C] one of the four liquids that in the past were thought to be present in the body and to influence someone's character **7 out of humour** *old-fashioned* in a bad temper

**humour**[2] *BrE*, **humor** *AmE* *v* [T] to agree with someone even though you know they are wrong: *I decided I'd better try and humour him, as I couldn't face another argument.*

**hu·mour·less** /ˈhjuːmələs‖ˈhjuːmər-, ˈjuː-/ *adj* too serious and not able to laugh at things that other people think are amusing —**humourlessly** *adv* —**humourlessness** *n* [U]

**hump¹** /hʌmp/ *n* **1** [C] a large round shape that rises above the surface of the ground or a surface: *I could just make out the hump of a hill in the distance.* **2** [C] one of the two raised parts on the back of a CAMEL **3** [C] a raised part on someone's back that is caused by an unusually curved SPINE (1) **4 be over the hump** to have succeeded in doing the most difficult part of something **5 give sb the hump/get the hump** *BrE spoken* to make someone feel angry or upset, or to feel angry or upset: *He'll get the right hump when he finds out you've drunk all his Scotch.*

**hump²** *v* **1** [T always + adv/prep] *BrE informal* to carry something heavy somewhere, especially with difficulty: **hump sth down/along/across etc** *I just about managed to hump the suitcases upstairs.* **2** [I,T] *slang* to have sex with someone

**hump·back** /ˈhʌmpbæk/ *n* [C] another form of HUNCHBACK

**hump-backed bridge** /ˌ· · ˈ·/ also **hump-back bridge** *n* [C] *especially BrE* a short steep bridge

**humpback whale** /ˌ·· ˈ·/ *n* [C] a large WHALE

**humph** /hʌmf, hmh, hm/ *interjection* used to show that you do not believe something or do not approve of something

**hu·mus** /ˈhjuːməs/ *n* [U] soil made of decayed plants, leaves etc which is good for growing plants

**Hun** /hʌn/ *n* **the Hun** *slang* an insulting word for German people, used especially during the First and Second World Wars

**hunch¹** /hʌntʃ/ *n* [C] a feeling that something is true or that something is happening, even though you have very little information about it: *"How did you know that Campbell was a murderer?" "Oh, it was just a hunch."* | **have a hunch (that)** *I had a hunch that something like this would happen.*

**hunch²** *v* **1** [I always + adv/prep] to bend down and forwards so that your back forms a curve: [+ **over**] *She hunched nervously over her drink.* **2 hunch your shoulders** to raise your shoulders into a rounded shape, especially because you are cold, anxious etc —**hunched** *adj*

**hunch·back** /ˈhʌntʃbæk/ *n* [C] an offensive word for someone whose back has a large raised part on it because their SPINE (1) curves in an unusual way

**hun·dred** /ˈhʌndrɪ̈d/ *number* **1** 100: *a hundred years* | *two hundred miles* **2 a hundred times** many times: *I've told you a hundred times not to do that!* **3 a hundred per cent** *spoken* **a)** completely: *I agree with you a hundred per cent.* **b)** well: *I'm still not really feeling a hundred per cent.*

**USAGE NOTE: HUNDRED**

GRAMMAR

Singular and plural forms of the number words **dozen, hundred, thousand, million** and **billion** are all used in the same ways.

When one of these words follows a word showing number or amount, it is not put in the plural and does not have *of* after it: *a/three/several hundred years* (NOT *three hundreds of years*) | *ten million people* | *a few dozen eggs* | *about fifty thousand miles*

Where there is no other word showing a number or amount, the plural is used: *He has hundreds of books* (NOT *He has hundred of books.*) *It will cost thousands of dollars* (=I do not know how many thousand exactly).

**hundreds and thou·sands** /ˌ·· · ˈ··/ *BrE n* [plural] small thin pieces of coloured sugar used to decorate cakes

**hun·dredth** /ˈhʌndrɪ̈dθ/ *n* [C] **1** one of the hundred equal parts of something **2** 100th

**hun·dred·weight** /ˈhʌndrɪ̈dweɪt/ written abbreviation **cwt** *n* [C] a unit for measuring weight equal to 112 pounds or 50.8 kilograms —see table on page B2

**hung** /hʌŋ/ past tense and past participle of HANG

**Hun·gar·ian¹** /hʌŋˈgeəriən‖-ˈger-/ *n* **1** [U] the language of Hungary **2** [C] someone from Hungary

**Hungarian²** *adj* from or connected with Hungary

**hun·ger¹** /ˈhʌŋgə‖-ər/ *n* **1** [U] lack of food, especially for a long period of time, that can cause illness or death; STARVATION: *Thousands of people are dying from hunger every day.* **2** [U] the feeling that you need to eat: *Babies often cry from hunger.* | **hunger pangs** (=sudden feelings of being hungry) **3 hunger for** a strong need or desire for something: *the West's hunger for material wealth*

**hunger²** *v* [I] *literary* to want something very much: [+ **for/after**] *a nation hungering for change*

**hunger strike** /ˈ·· ·/ *n* [C] a situation in which someone refuses to eat for a long time in order to protest about something —**hunger striker** *n* [C]

**hung ju·ry** /ˌ· ˈ··/ *n* [singular] a JURY (1) that cannot agree about whether someone is guilty of a crime

**hung·o·ver** /hʌŋˈəʊvə‖-ˈoʊvər/ *adj* feeling ill because you have drunk too much alcohol the previous evening —see also HANGOVER

**hung par·lia·ment** /ˌ· ˈ···/ *n* [C] *BrE* a parliament in which no one political party has more elected representatives than the others added together

**hun·gri·ly** /ˈhʌŋgrɪ̈li/ *adv* **1** in a way that shows you want to eat someting very much: *J.D. ate hungrily, covering the french fries with layers of catsup.* **2** in a way that shows you very much want something: *Her gaze fell hungrily on my diamond ring.*

**hun·gry** /ˈhʌŋgri/ *adj* **1** wanting to eat something: *There's tons of food – I hope you're all hungry!* | **get hungry** *If you get hungry between meals, have a piece of fruit.* **2** ill or weak as a result of not having enough to eat for a long time: *We can't justify wasting food when half the world is hungry.* **3 the hungry** people who do not have enough food to eat **4 go hungry** to not have enough to eat: *Thousands of families go hungry every day in this country.* **5 be hungry for** to want or need something very much: *young people hungry for excitement and adventure* **6 power-hungry/news-hungry etc** wanting power, news etc very much S3

**hung-up** /ˌ· ˈ·/ *adj informal* very anxious and unhappy about a situation: [+ **about**] *She's really hung-up about her parents.*

**hunk** /hʌŋk/ *n* [C] **1** a thick piece of something, especially food, that has been cut or torn from a bigger piece: [+ **of**] *a hunk of bread.* —see picture on page 416 **2** [C] *informal* a man who is attractive because he is big and strong

**hun·ker** /ˈhʌŋkə‖-ər/ *v* [I] *AmE* to sit on your heels with your knees bent up in front of you; SQUAT: [+ **down**] *They hunkered down by the fire.*

**hunker down** *phr v* [I,T often passive] *AmE* to work hard to completely prepare yourself for a difficult situation

**hun·kers** /ˈhʌŋkəz‖-ərz/ *n* **on your hunkers** sitting on your heels with your knees bent up in front of you: *The little boy was squatting on his hunkers, completely absorbed in his game.*

**hunk·y** /ˈhʌŋki/ *adj* a man who is hunky is attractive and strong-looking

**hun·ky-dor·y** /ˌhʌŋki ˈdɔːri/ *adj* [not before noun] *informal* a situation that is hunky-dory is one in which everyone feels happy and there are no problems

**hunt¹** /hʌnt/ *v* **1** [I,T] to chase animals and birds in order to catch and kill them: *At one time man had to hunt to survive.* | **hunt sth** *hunting big game in Kenya* **2** [I] to look hard for something you have lost: *We've been hunting for the car keys for the last half-hour.* **3** [I,T] *BrE* to hunt foxes (FOX¹ (1)) as a sport, riding on horses and using dogs **4** [T] to search for and try to catch someone, especially a criminal: *Police are hunting the killer.*

**hunt** sb/sth ↔ **down** *phr v* [T] to catch someone in order to kill, hurt, or punish them, after chasing them or trying very hard to catch them

**hunt** sb/sth ↔ **out** *phr v* [T] **1** to search for someone in order to catch or get rid of them: *Military Police were ordered to hunt out subversives.* **2** to look for something that you have not used or seen for a long time: *I must try and hunt out that old tennis racket*

**hunt²** *n* **1** [C] an occasion when people chase animals in order to catch and kill them: *a tiger hunt* **2** [singular] a search for someone or something that is difficult to find: **the hunt for** *the hunt for the remains of the Titanic* | **the hunt is on** (=used to say that people have started looking for someone or something) | **have a hunt around for** *informal* (=look for something) *I'll have a hunt around for it in my desk.* **3** [C] an organized sporting event in Britain in which people riding on horses hunt foxes (FOX¹ (1)) using dogs **4** [C] *BrE* a group of people who regularly hunt foxes (FOX¹ (1)) together

**hunt·er** /ˈhʌntə‖-ər/ *n* **1** [C] a person or animal that hunts wild animals **2 souvenir/autograph/bargain etc hunter** someone who looks for or collects a particular type of thing **3** [C] a strong horse used in Britain for hunting foxes (FOX¹ (1)) —see also BOUNTY HUNTER, FORTUNE HUNTER

**hunt·ing** /ˈhʌntɪŋ/ *n* [U] **1** the act of chasing and killing animals for food or for sport **2** the sport of hunting foxes (FOX¹ (1)) in Britain **3 job-hunting/house-hunting etc** the activity of looking for a job, house etc **4 go hunting** to hunt for animals, especially as a sport —**hunting** *adj*: *a hunting rifle*

**hunting ground** /ˈ·· ·/ *n* **1** [C] a place where animals are hunted **2 a happy/good hunting ground for** a place where people who are interested in a particular thing can easily find what they want

**hunt·ress** /ˈhʌntrɨs/ *n* [C] *literary* a female hunter

**hunt sab·o·teur** /ˌ· ··ˈ·/ *n* [C] *BrE* member of a group that tries to stop people from hunting foxes (FOX¹ (1))

**hunts·man** /ˈhʌntsmən/ *n* [C] *especially BrE* **1** a man who hunts animals **2** the person in charge of the dogs in FOXHUNTING

**hur·dle¹** /ˈhɜːdl‖ˈhɜːr-/ *n* **1** [C] a frame that a person or horse has to jump over during a race: **clear a hurdle** (=successfully jump over a hurdle) **2** [C] a problem or difficulty that you must deal with before you can achieve something: *Finding enough money was the first hurdle.* | **clear a hurdle** (=deal successfully with a problem) **3 the 100 metres/400 metres hurdles** a race in which the runners have to jump over hurdles **4** [C] a moveable part of a temporary fence around animals or land

**hurdle²** *v* **1** [T] to jump over something while you are running: *Barrett hurdled the fence and ran off down the street.* **2** [I] to run in hurdle races —**hurdler** *n* [C] —**hurdling** *n* [U]

**hur·dy-gur·dy** /ˈhɜːdi ˌgɜːdi‖ˌhɜːrdi ˈgɜːrdi/ *n* [C] a small musical instrument that you operate by turning a handle

**hurl** /hɜːl‖hɜːrl/ *v* **1** [T always + adv/prep] to throw something violently and with a lot of force, especially because you are angry: **hurl sth through/across/over etc** *Demonstrators were hurling bricks through the windows.* **2 hurl abuse/insults/accusations etc at sb** to shout at someone in a loud and angry way **3 hurl yourself at/against** to throw yourself at someone or something with a lot of force

**hurl·ing** /ˈhɜːlɪŋ‖ˈhɜːr-/ *n* [U] an Irish ball game played between two teams of 15 players

**hur·ly-bur·ly** /ˈhɜːli ˌbɜːli‖ˌhɜːrli ˈbɜːrli/ *n* [U] a lot of busy, noisy activity: *the hurly-burly of city life*

**hur·ray** /hʊˈreɪ/ also **hur·rah** /hʊˈrɑː/ *interjection old-fashioned* a shout that shows you are pleased —see also **hip, hip, hurray!** (HIP²)

**hur·ri·cane** /ˈhʌrɨkən‖ˈhɜːrɨkeɪn/ *n* [C] a violent storm, especially in the western Atlantic ocean —compare CYCLONE, TYPHOON, TORNADO —see picture on page 836

**hurricane lamp** /ˈ··· ·/ *n* [C] a lamp that has a strong cover to protect the flame inside from the wind

**hur·ried** /ˈhʌrid‖ˈhɜːrid/ *adj* [usually before noun] done very quickly, often too quickly, because you are in a hurry; RUSHED: *We just caught the plane after several hurried phone calls from the airport.* —**hurriedly** *adv*

**hur·ry¹** /ˈhʌri‖ˈhɜːri/ *v* **1** [I,T] to do something or go somewhere more quickly than usual, especially because there is not much time: *The movie begins as six – we'll have to hurry.* | **hurry through/along/down etc** *She hurried down the corridor as fast as she could.* | **hurry after sb** *John went hurrying off after his girlfriend.* | **hurry to do sth** *They were hurrying to catch their train.* | **hurry sth** *I don't want to have to hurry my meal.* **2** [T] to make someone do something more quickly: *Don't hurry me; I'm working as fast as I can.* **3 hurry up!** *spoken* used to tell someone to do something more quickly: *Hurry up, we're late!* | **hurry up with** *Hurry up with the accounts – the boss is waiting for them.* **4** [T always + adv/prep] to take someone or something quickly to a place: **hurry sth to/through/across etc** *Emergency supplies have been hurried to the areas worst hit by the famine.*

**hurry** sb/sth **up** *phr v* [T] to make someone do something more quickly or to make something happen more quickly

**hurry²** *n* **1 be in a hurry** to do something, go somewhere, need something etc more quickly than usual, often too quickly: *Sorry, I can't stop, I'm in a hurry.* | *You'll make mistakes if you do things in too much of a hurry.* | **be in a hurry to do sth** *Why are you in such a hurry to leave?* **2 will not be doing sth (again) in a hurry** *spoken* used to say that you do not want to do something again: *We won't be going back there again in a hurry, I can tell you.* **3 in your hurry to do sth** while you are trying to do something too quickly: *In his hurry to leave the room he tripped over a chair.* **4 be in no hurry/not be in any hurry** to be able to wait because you have plenty of time in which to do something: *I'll wait till you've closed up – I'm not in any hurry.* **5 be in no hurry to do sth/not be in any hurry to do sth** to be unwilling to do something or not want to do it soon: *I'm in no particular hurry to leave* **6 (there's) no hurry** *spoken* used to tell someone that they do not have to do something soon: *You can give me the money back next month. There's no great hurry.* **7 what's (all) the hurry?/why (all) the hurry?** *spoken* used to say that someone is doing something too quickly: *We've got plenty of time – what's all the hurry?* S3

**hurt¹** /hɜːt‖hɜːrt/ *v past tense and past participle* **hurt** **1** [I,T] if a part of your body hurts, you feel pain in it: *My back hurts.* | **it hurts** *Where does it hurt?* | **hurt sb** *My shoulder's really hurting me.* | **hurt like hell** (=hurt very much) **2** [T] if you hurt part of your body you injure it or make it feel painful, especially in an accident: *Several people were seriously hurt in the accident.* | **hurt your arm/leg/nose etc** *I hurt my finger in the door* | **hurt yourself** (=injure yourself) *Careful you don't hurt yourself – it's very sharp.* **3** [I,T] if something hurts part of your body, it makes it feel painful: *The sun's hurting my eyes* **4** [T] to cause physical pain to someone: *Put that thing down – you might hurt someone with it.* **5** [I,T] to make someone feel very upset, unhappy, sad etc: **hurt sb's feelings** *I'm really sorry, I didn't mean to hurt your feelings.* | **what hurts is that** *What really hurts is that he never even said goodbye.* | **hurt sb** *The last thing I want to do is to hurt you.* **6 be hurting yourself** to be making yourself feel even more unhappy, upset, sad, etc **7** [T] to have a bad effect on someone or something, especially by making them less successful or powerful: *Foreign competition has definitely hurt the firm's position in the market.* **8 be hurting a)** *AmE informal* to feel very upset, unhappy, sad etc **b)** if a group, organization etc is hurting, they do not have something important that they need, for example money: [+ **for**] *Our division in Salem is hurting for competent staff right now.* **9 it won't/doesn't hurt (sb) to do sth** *spoken* used to say that there is no reason why someone cannot or should not do something: *It won't hurt Julia to get up early for once.* **10 one more won't hurt** *spoken* used to encourage someone to have another drink, piece of chocolate etc —compare HARM² S2 W3

**hurt²** *adj* **1** [not usually before noun] physically injured: **badly/seriously hurt** *This man needs a doctor – he's badly hurt.* **2** very upset or unhappy because someone has said or done something unkind, dishonest, or unfair: *a hurt expression* | **deeply hurt** *I was feeling deeply hurt by what she had just said.*

**hurt³** *n* [C,U] a feeling of great unhappiness because someone, especially someone you trust, has treated you unkindly or unfairly: *the hurt caused by the breakup of his marriage* —compare HARM¹

**hurt·ful** /ˈhɜːtfəl‖ˈhɜːrt-/ *adj* making you feel very upset or offended: *a hurtful remark* —**hurtfully** *adv* —**hurtfulness** *n* [U]

**hur·tle** /ˈhɜːtl‖ˈhɜːr-/ *v* [I always + adv/prep] if something, especially something big or heavy, hurtles somewhere, it moves or falls very fast: **hurtle down/through/along etc** *Huge pieces of rock went hurtling down the mountainside.*

S1 W1 **hus·band**[1] /ˈhʌzbənd/ *n* **1** [C] the man that a woman is married to: *Have you met her husband?*| **ex-husband** (=a man that a woman used to be married to) —see picture at FAMILY **2 husband and wife** a man and woman who are married

**husband**[2] *v* [T] *formal* to be very careful in the way you use your money, supplies etc and not waste any: *carefully husbanded resources*

**hus·band·man** /ˈhʌzbəndmən/ *n* [C] *old use* a farmer

**hus·band·ry** /ˈhʌzbəndri/ *n* **1** [U] *technical* farming: *animal husbandry* **2** [U] *old-fashioned* careful management of money and supplies

**hush**[1] /hʌʃ/ *v* **1 hush!** *spoken* used to tell people to be quiet or to comfort a child who is crying or upset: *Hush, now. Try to get to sleep.* **2** [T] to make someone stop shouting, talking, crying etc **3** [I] to stop shouting, talking etc

**hush** sth ↔ **up** *phr v* [T] to prevent the public from knowing about something dishonest or immoral: *The whole affair has been hushed up by school officials.*

**hush**[2] *n* **1** [singular] a period of silence that comes after there has been a lot of noise, shouting etc, especially because people are expecting something to happen: **a hush falls/descends** (=everyone becomes quiet) *A sudden hush descended on the crowd.* **2 can we have/let's have a bit of hush** *BrE spoken* used to ask people, especially noisy children, to be quiet

**hushed** /hʌʃt/ *adj* [usually before noun] quiet because people are listening, waiting to hear something, or talking quietly: *A hushed courtroom awaited the verdict.*| **hushed tones/voice/whispers etc** (=quiet speech)

**hush-hush** /ˌ· ˈ·◂‖ˈ· ·/ *adj informal* an official operation etc that is hush-hush is very secret

**hush mon·ey** /ˈ· ˌ··/ *n* [U] money that is paid to someone not to tell other people about something embarrassing

**hush pup·py** /ˈ· ˌ··/ *n* [C] a small fried cake made of MAIZE flour eaten in the southern states of the US

**husk**[1] /hʌsk/ *n* [C,U] the dry outer part of grains, seeds etc and some types of nut

**husk**[2] *v* [T] to remove the husks from grains, seeds etc

**hus·ky**[1] /ˈhʌski/ *adj* **1** a husky voice is deep, quiet, and rough-sounding, often in an attractive way: *"Come quickly" she said in a husky whisper.* **2** *especially AmE* a man who is husky is big and strong —**huskily** *adv* —**huskiness** *n* [U]

**husky**[2] *n* [C] a dog with thick hair used in Canada and Alaska to pull SLEDGES over the snow

**hus·sar** /hʊˈzɑː‖-ɑːr/ *n* [C] a British CAVALRY (2) soldier

**hus·sy** /ˈhʌsi, ˈhʌzi/ *n* [C] *old-fashioned* a woman who is sexually immoral: *The shameless hussy!*

**hus·tings** /ˈhʌstɪŋz/ *n* **the hustings** *BrE* the process of trying to persuade people to vote for you by making speeches etc: **be at/on the hustings** *All the candidates are out on the hustings.*

**hus·tle**[1] /ˈhʌsəl/ *v* **hustled, hustling** **1** [T] to make someone move quickly, especially by pushing them roughly: **hustle sb out/into/through etc** *I was hustled out of the building by a couple of security men.*| **hustle sb off somewhere** *She hustled the kids off to school.* **2** [I,T] *AmE* to sell or obtain things, especially unofficially or illegally: *small time thieves hustling stolen goods on the street* **3** [I] *AmE* to do something with a lot of energy and determination: *C'mon kids, let's hustle!* **4** [I] *AmE slang* to work as a PROSTITUTE

**hustle**[2] *n* [U] **1** busy and noisy activity: **hustle and bustle** *the hustle and bustle of the market place* **2** *AmE* dishonest and illegal ways of getting money

**hus·tler** /ˈhʌslə‖-ər/ *n* **1** [C] *especially AmE* someone who tries to trick people into giving them money **2** [C] *AmE* a PROSTITUTE

**hut** /hʌt/ *n* [C] a small, simple building with only one or two rooms: *a wooden hut*

**hutch** /hʌtʃ/ *n* [C] **1** a small wooden CAGE used for keeping small animals in, especially rabbits **2** [C] *AmE* a piece of furniture used for storing and showing dishes; WELSH DRESSER *BrE*

**hy·a·cinth** /ˈhaɪəsɪ̇nθ/ *n* [C] a garden plant with blue, pink, or white bell-shaped flowers and a sweet smell

**hy·ae·na** /haɪˈiːnə/ another spelling of HYENA

**hy·brid** /ˈhaɪbrɪ̇d/ *n* **1** [C] an animal or plant produced from parents of different breeds or types: *Most modern roses are hybrids.* **2** [C] something that consists of or comes from a mixture of two or more other things

**hy·dra** /ˈhaɪdrə/ *n plural* **hydrae** /-dri/ [C] **1** a snake in ancient Greek stories with many heads that grow again when they are cut off **2** something that is evil and very difficult to get rid of

**hy·drant** /ˈhaɪdrənt/ *n* [C] a water pipe in a street where you can get water to put on fires that are burning

**hy·drate** /ˈhaɪdreɪt/ *n* [C] *technical* a chemical substance that contains water

**hy·draul·ic** /haɪˈdrɒlɪk, -ˈdrɔː-‖-ˈdrɒː-/ *adj* [usually before noun] moved or operated by the pressure of water on other liquid: *a hydraulic pump*| *hydraulic brakes* —**hydraulically** /-kli/ *adv*

**hy·draul·ics** /haɪˈdrɒlɪks, -ˈdrɔː-‖-ˈdrɒː-/ *n* [plural] the scientific study of the use of moving liquids

**hydro-** /haɪdrəʊ, -drə‖-droʊ, -drə/ *prefix* **1** concerning or using water: *hydroelectricity* (=produced by water power)| *hydrotherapy* (=treatment of disease using water) **2** concerning or containing HYDROGEN: *hydrocarbons*

**hy·dro·car·bon** /ˌhaɪdrəˈkɑːbən‖-ˈkɑːr-/ *n* [C] *technical* a chemical compound that consists of HYDROGEN and CARBON (1), such as coal or gas

**hy·dro·chlor·ic ac·id** /ˌhaɪdrəklɒrɪk ˈæsɪ̇d‖-klɔː-/ *n* [U] a strong acid used especially in industry

**hy·dro·e·lec·tric** /ˌhaɪdrəʊ-ɪˈlektrɪk◂‖-droʊ-/ *adj* using water power to produce electricity: *a hydroelectric power station* —**hydroelectrically** /-kli/ *adv* —**hydroelectricity** /ˌhaɪdrəʊɪlekˈtrɪsɪ̇ti‖-droʊ-/ *n* [U]

**hy·dro·foil** /ˈhaɪdrəfɔɪl/ *n* [C] a large boat that raises itself above the surface of the water when it travels at high speeds —compare HOVERCRAFT

**hy·dro·gen** /ˈhaɪdrədʒən/ *n* [U] a simple chemical substance that is found in water, and also exists as a gas which is lighter than air

**hydrogen bomb** /ˈ··· ˌ·/ *n* [C] a very powerful NUCLEAR bomb

**hydrogen per·ox·ide** /ˌ··· ·ˈ··/ *n* [U] a chemical liquid used for killing BACTERIA and making hair lighter; PEROXIDE

**hy·dro·pho·bi·a** /ˌhaɪdrəˈfəʊbiə‖-ˈfoʊ-/ *n* **1** [U] *technical* RABIES **2** fear of water

**hy·dro·plane**[1] /ˈhaɪdrəpleɪn/ *n* **1** [C] a HYDROFOIL **2** [C] *AmE* a plane that can take off from and land on water; SEAPLANE

**hydroplane**[2] *v* [I] **1** *AmE* if a car hydroplanes, it slides uncontrollably on a wet road; AQUAPLANE[2] (2) *BrE* **2** if a boat hydroplanes, it travels very quickly just touching the surface of the water

**hy·e·na, hyaena** /haɪˈiːnə/ *n* [C] a wild animal like a dog that feeds on the meat of dead animals

**hy·giene** /ˈhaɪdʒiːn/ *n* **1** [U] the study and practice of preventing illness or stopping it from spreading by keeping things clean: *public hygiene* **2** [U] the practice of keeping your body clean

**hy·gien·ic** /haɪˈdʒiːnɪk‖-ˈdʒe-, -ˈdʒiː-/ *adj* clean and likely to prevent bacteria, infections, or disease from spreading: *food processed in hygienic conditions*| *That's not very hygienic.* —**hygienically** /-kli/ *adv*

**hy·gien·ist** /ˈhaɪdʒiːnɪ̇st, haɪˈdʒiːnɪ̇st/ *n* [C] *BrE* someone who helps a DENTIST by cleaning patients' teeth and giving advice about keeping teeth healthy; DENTAL HYGIENIST *AmE*

H

**hy·men** /'haɪmən/ *n* [C] a piece of skin that partly covers the entrance to the VAGINA of some girls or women who have not had sex

**hymn** /hɪm/ *n* [C] a song of praise to God: *a hymn book*

**hymn book** /'· ·/ also **hym·nal** /'hɪmnəl/ *technical n* [C] a book containing Christian songs of praise to God

**hype¹** /haɪp/ *n* [U] attempts to make the public interested in a product, film etc by saying how good it is on television, radio etc: **media hype** *Despite all the media hype, I found the film very disappointing.*

**hype²** *v* [T] to try to get a lot of public attention for something by saying how good it is on television, radio etc

**hype** sth ↔ **up** *phr v* [T] to make an event, thing, or person seem better or more important than it is

**hyped up** /ˌ· '·/ *adj* [not before noun] *informal* excited or nervous about something that is going to happen: [+ **about**] *Jerry is really hyped up about his exams.*

**hy·per** /'haɪpə‖-ər/ *adj informal* extremely excited or nervous about something

**hyper-** /haɪpə‖-pər/ *prefix* more than usual; especially too much: *hypersensitive* (=too sensitive) | *hyperinflation*

**hy·per·ac·tive** /ˌhaɪpər'æktɪv◂/ *adj technical* a hyperactive child is too active and can only keep still or quiet for very short periods of time —**hyperactivity** /ˌhaɪpəræk'tɪvɪ̵ti/ *n* [U]

**hy·per·bo·le** /haɪ'pɜːbəli‖-ɜːr-/ *n* [U] a way of describing something by saying it is much bigger, smaller, worse etc than it actually is: *To say 'This chair weighs a ton' is an example of hyperbole.* —see also EXAGGERATE —**hyperbolic** /ˌhaɪpə'bɒlɪk◂‖-pər'bɑː-/ *adj*

**hy·per·crit·i·cal** /ˌhaɪpə'krɪtɪkəl◂‖-pər-/ *adj* too eager to criticize other people and things, especially about small details —**hypercritically** /-kli/ *adv*

**hy·per·in·fla·tion** /ˌhaɪpərɪn'fleɪʃən/ *n* [U] a rapid rise in prices that seriously damages a country's economy

**hy·per·mar·ket** /'haɪpəˌmɑːkɪ̵t‖-pərˌmɑːr-/ *n* [C] *BrE* a very large SUPERMARKET, usually built outside a town

**hy·per·sen·si·tive** /ˌhaɪpə'sensɪ̵tɪv◂‖-pər-/ *adj* **1** [+ **to**] extremely sensitive to any change in conditions, to pain, to certain chemicals, drugs etc **2** too easily hurt or upset by unimportant things: [+ **to/about**] *She's hypersensitive to any form of criticism.* —**hypersensitivity** /ˌhaɪpəsensɪ̵'tɪvɪ̵ti‖-pər-/ *n* [U]

**hy·per·ten·sion** /ˌhaɪpə'tenʃən‖-pər-/ *n* [U] *technical* a medical condition in which your BLOOD PRESSURE is too high

**hy·phen** /'haɪfən/ *n* [C] a short written or printed line (-) that joins words or SYLLABLES: *'Co-operate' can be written with or without a hyphen.* —compare DASH² (1)

**hy·phen·ate** /'haɪfəneɪt/ *v* [T] to join words or SYLLABLES with a HYPHEN —**hyphenation** /ˌhaɪfə'neɪʃən/ *n* [U]

**hy·phen·a·ted** /'haɪfəneɪtɪ̵d/ *adj* containing a hyphen

**hyp·no·sis** /hɪp'nəʊsɪ̵s‖-'noʊ-/ *n* **1** [U] a sleep-like state of the brain in which someone's thoughts and actions can be influenced by the person who caused this state: **under hypnosis** (=in a state of hypnosis) *describing details of your early childhood while under hypnosis* **2** [U] the act of hypnotizing (HYPNOTIZE) someone

**hyp·no·ther·a·py** /ˌhɪpnəʊ'θerəpi‖-noʊ-/ *n* [U] the use of hypnosis to treat emotional or physical problems —**hypnotherapist** *n* [C]

**hyp·not·ic¹** /hɪp'nɒtɪk‖-'nɑː-/ *adj* **1** making you feel tired or unable to think clearly, especially because of a regularly repeated sound or movement: *The steady ticking of the clock had a hypnotic effect.* **2** [only before noun] connected with HYPNOSIS: *a hypnotic trance* —**hypnotically** /-kli/ *adv*

**hypnotic²** *n* [C] *technical* a drug that helps you to sleep; SLEEPING PILL

**hyp·no·tise** /'hɪpnətaɪz/ *v* [T] the British spelling of hypnotize

**hyp·no·tis·m** /'hɪpnətɪzəm/ *n* [U] the practice of hypnotizing people

**hyp·no·tist** /'hɪpnətɪ̵st/ *n* [C] someone who hypnotizes people, especially in public for entertainment

**hyp·no·tize** also **-ise** *BrE* /'hɪpnətaɪz/ *v* [T] **1** to make someone be in a sleep-like state in which their thoughts and actions can be influenced by your suggestions **2 be hypnotized** to be so interested or excited when seeing or listening to something that you cannot think of anything else: *We were completely hypnotized by Bylsma's performance of the Haydn.*

**hy·po** /'haɪpəʊ‖-poʊ/ *n* [C] *informal* a HYPODERMIC

**hypo-** /haɪpəʊ, -pə‖-poʊ, -pə/ *prefix technical* less than usual, especially too little: *dying of hypothermia* (=too low body temperature)

**hy·po·chon·dri·a** /ˌhaɪpə'kɒndriə‖-'kɑːn-/ *n* [U] a state in which you continuously worry that there is something wrong with your health, even when you are not ill

**hy·po·chon·dri·ac** /ˌhaɪpə'kɒndriæk‖-'kɑːn-/ *n* [C] someone who always worries about their health, even when they are not ill —**hypochondriac** *adj*

**hy·poc·ri·sy** /hɪ'pɒkrɪ̵si‖-'pɑː-/ *n* [U] a way of behaving in which you pretend to have better moral principles than you actually do: **sheer hypocrisy** *It's sheer hypocrisy for politicians to preach about family values when so many of them are having affairs.*

**hyp·o·crite** /'hɪpəkrɪt/ *n* [C] someone who pretends to be morally good

**hyp·o·crit·i·cal** /ˌhɪpə'krɪtɪkəl◂/ *adj* behaving in a way that is intended to make people believe that you are morally better than you really are: *hypocritical concern for the less privileged members of society.*

**hy·po·der·mic¹** /ˌhaɪpə'dɜːmɪk◂‖-ɜːr-/ *n* [C] an instrument with a very thin hollow needle used for putting drugs directly into the body through the skin; a SYRINGE

**hypodermic²** *adj* used in an INJECTION (1) beneath the skin: *a hypodermic needle* —**hypodermically** /-kli/ *adv*

**hy·pot·e·nuse** /haɪ'pɒtɪ̵njuːz‖-'pɑːtənuːs, -nuːz/ *n* [C] *technical* the longest side of a TRIANGLE that has a RIGHT ANGLE —see picture at SHAPE¹

**hy·po·ther·mi·a** /ˌhaɪpəʊ'θɜːmiə‖-poʊ'θ-ɜːr-/ *n* [U] a serious medical condition caused by extreme cold

**hy·poth·e·sis** /haɪ'pɒθɪ̵sɪ̵s‖-'pɑː-/ *n plural* **hypotheses** /-siːz/ **1** [C] an idea that is suggested as a possible way of explaining a situation, proving an idea etc, which has not yet been shown to be true: **put forward a hypothesis** (=suggest a hypothesis) *A number of hypotheses have been put forward concerning the possible origins of mankind.* **2** [U] ideas or guesses rather than facts: *All this is mere hypothesis.*

**hy·po·thet·i·cal** /ˌhaɪpə'θetɪkəl◂/ *adj* based only on an idea or suggestion about what might happen or might be true and not on a real situation: *Let's consider a hypothetical case.* | **purely hypothetical** (=completely hypothetical) *The question is purely hypothetical.* —compare IMAGINARY —**hypothetically** /-kli/ *adv*

**hys·ter·ec·to·my** /ˌhɪstə'rektəmi/ *n* [C,U] a medical operation to remove a woman's WOMB

**hys·te·ri·a** /hɪ'stɪəriə‖-'steriə/ *n* **1** [U] extreme excitement that makes people cry, laugh, shout etc uncontrollably: *an outbreak of hysteria among the group's fans* **2** [U] a situation in which a lot of people are affected by the same extreme emotion such as fear or anger which often makes them behave in an unreasonable way: *anti-communist hysteria* | **mass hysteria** *Since the General's death, the population has been gripped by mass hysteria.* **3** *technical* a medical condition which upsets someone's emotions and makes them suddenly feel very nervous, excited, anxious etc —**hysteric** /hɪ'sterɪk/ *adj*

**hys·ter·i·cal** /hɪ'sterɪkəl/ *adj* **1** behaving in a wild, uncontrollable way, especially by shouting or crying because you are extremely excited: *Hysterical fans tried to stop Madonna's car at the airport.* **2** *spoken* extremely funny —**hysterically** /-kli/ *adv*

**hys·ter·ics** /hɪ'sterɪks/ *n spoken* **1 have hysterics** to be extremely upset or angry: *Mum'd have hysterics if she knew what you'd done.* **2 be in hysterics/have sb in hysterics** to be laughing uncontrollably or to make someone laugh uncontrollably

**Hz** *n* [C] the written abbreviation for HERTZ

# I, i

**I, i¹** /aɪ/ **1** *plural* **I's, i's** *n* [C] the ninth letter of the English alphabet **2** the ROMAN NUMERAL representing the number one

S1 W1 **I²** /aɪ/ *pron* used as the subject of a verb when you are the person speaking: *I've just seen a strange man in your garden.* | *I'm not late again, am I?* —see ME (USAGE)

**I³** *AmE* the abbreviation of INTERSTATE (=an important road between states in the US): *the point where I95 meets I40*

**-i** /-i/ *p* **-is** *suffix* **1** [in nouns] a person or the language of a particular place or country, especially in Asia: *two Pakistanis* | *speakers of Nepali* **2** [in adjectives] of a particular place or country: *Bengali food* | *the Israeli army*

**-ial** /iəl/ *suffix* another form of the suffix -AL: *a managerial job* (=with the duties of a manager)

**i·amb** /ˈaɪæm‖ˈaɪæm, ˈaɪæmb/ also **i·am·bus** /aɪˈæmbəs/ *n* [C] *technical* a unit of RHYTHM (1) in poetry, that has one short or weak beat followed by a long or strong beat, as in the word 'alive' —**iambic** /aɪˈæmbɪk/ *adj*

**iambic pen·tam·e·ter** /ˌ· ˌ·· ˈ···/ *n* [C,U] a common pattern of beats in English poetry, in which each line consists of five iambs

**-ian** /iən/ *suffix* [in adjectives and nouns] another form of the suffix -AN: *Dickensian characters* (=like those in Dickens' books) | *a librarian* (=someone who works in a library)

**-iana** /iɑːnə‖iænə/ *suffix* also **-ana** [in nouns] a collection of objects, papers, etc, connected with someone or something: *Churchilliana* | *Shakespeariana*

**I·be·ri·an** /aɪˈbɪəriən‖-ˈbɪr-/ *adj* connected with Spain or Portugal: *the Iberian peninsula*

**i·bex** /ˈaɪbeks/ *plural* **ibexes** or **ibex** *n* [C] a wild goat that lives in the mountains of Europe, Asia, and North Africa

**ib·id** /ˈɪbɪd/ also **ib·i·dem** /ˈɪbɪdem, ɪˈbaɪdem/ *adv Latin* from the same book, writer, or article as the one that has just been mentioned

**-ibility** /ɪ̯bɪlɪ̯ti/ *suffix* [in nouns] another form of the suffix -ABILITY: *invincibility*

**-ible** /ɪ̯bəl/ *suffix* [in adjectives] another form of the suffix -ABLE: *irresistible*

**IBM-com·pat·i·ble** /ˌaɪ biː em kəmˈpætɪ̯bəl/ *adj* an IBM-compatible computer is designed to work in the same way as a type of computer made by the IBM company, and can use the same computer PROGRAMS¹ (1) —**IBM-compatible** *n* [C]

**-ic** /ɪk/ *suffix* [in adjectives] **1** of, like, or connected with a particular thing: *photographic* (=of photography) | *an alcoholic drink* (=containing alcohol) | *polysyllabic* (=containing several SYLLABLES) | *pelvic* (=of the PELVIS) | *Byronic* (=like or connected with the poet Byron) **2** [in nouns] someone who is affected by a particular unusual condition, a mental illness for example: *an alcoholic* (=someone who cannot stop drinking alcohol) —**ically** /ɪkli/ [in adverbs] *photographically*

**-ical** /ɪkəl/ *suffix* [in adjectives] another form of the suffix -ic (1): *historical* (=of history) | *satirical* —**ically** /ɪkli/ [in adverbs]: *historically*

**ICBM** /ˌaɪ siː biː ˈem/ *n* [C] Intercontinental Ballistic Missile; a MISSILE (1) that can travel very long distances

S2 W3 **ice¹** /aɪs/ *n* **1** [U] water that has frozen into a solid state: *Would you like some ice in your drink?* | *The wind blew the snow across the ice on the lake.* | *Her hands were as cold as ice.* **2 keep/put something on ice** to do nothing about a plan or suggestion for a period of time: *Opposition to Irish home rule was put on ice for the duration of the war.* **3 be (skating) on thin ice** to be in a situation in which you are likely to upset someone or cause trouble: *Don't question him too closely about where he got the money – you'd be on very thin ice.* **4** [C] **a)** a cold sweet food like ICE CREAM, made with fruit juice instead of milk or cream; SORBET **b)** *old-fashioned, especially BrE* an ICE CREAM **5** [U] *AmE old-fashioned* diamonds —see also ICY, BLACK ICE, DRY ICE, **break the ice** (BREAK¹ (30)), **cut no ice** (CUT¹ (35))

**ice²** *v* [T] *especially BrE* to cover a cake with ICING (=a mixture made of liquid and powdery sugar) —compare FROST²

**ice** sth ↔ **down** *phr v* [T] *AmE* to cover an injury in ice to stop it from swelling: *Make sure you ice that ankle down as soon as you get inside.*

**ice over/up** also **be iced over/up** *phr v* [I] to become covered with ice: *The lake was iced over by morning.* | *The plane's engines had iced up.*

**Ice Age** /ˈ· ·/ *n* [C] one of the long periods of time, thousands of years ago, when ice covered many northern countries

**ice axe** also **ice ax** *AmE* /ˈ· ·/ *n* [C] a metal tool, used by mountain climbers to cut into ice —see also ICE PICK

**ice·berg** /ˈaɪsbɜːg‖-bɜːrg/ *n* [C] a very large mass of ice floating in the sea, most of which is under the surface of the water —see also **the tip of the iceberg** (TIP¹ (7))

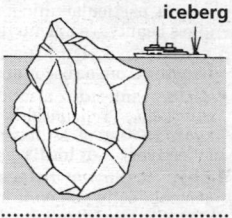

iceberg

**iceberg let·tuce** /ˌ·· ˈ··/ *n* [C,U] a firm round, pale green LETTUCE

**ice·bound** /ˈaɪsbaʊnd/ *adj* surrounded by ice, especially so that it is impossible to move: *The Russian Fleet was icebound.*

**ice·box** /ˈaɪsbɒks‖-bɑːks/ *n* [C] **1** *AmE old-fashioned* a REFRIGERATOR **2** a box where food is kept cold with blocks of ice

**ice·break·er** /ˈaɪsˌbreɪkə‖-ər/ *n* [C] **1** a ship that cuts a passage through floating ice **2** something that you say or do to make people less nervous when they first meet: *This game is an effective icebreaker at the beginning of a semester.* —see also **break the ice** (BREAK¹ (30))

**ice buck·et** /ˈ· ˌ··/ *n* [C] **1** a container filled with ice to keep bottles of wine cold **2** a container in which pieces of ice are kept for putting in drinks

**ice cap** /ˈ· ·/ *n* [C] an area of ice that permanently covers land or sea, such as that on the North or South Poles

**ice-cold** /ˌ· ˈ·◂/ *adj* extremely cold: *ice-cold drinks* | *Her hands were ice-cold.*

**ice cream** /ˌ· ˈ·◂‖ˈ· ·/ *n* **1** [U] a frozen sweet food made of milk or cream, sugar etc, with an added taste of fruit, nuts, chocolate etc: *vanilla ice cream* **2** [C] *BrE* a small amount of this food for one person: *"Mummy, can I have an ice cream?"* S2

**ice-cream so·da** /ˌ· · ˈ··/ *n* [C] a mixture of ice cream, sweet SYRUP, and SODA WATER, served in a tall glass

**ice cube** /ˈ· ·/ *n* [C] a small block of ice used to make drinks cold

**iced cof·fee** /ˌ· ˈ··/ *n* [C,U] cold coffee with ice and milk, or a glass of this drink

**iced tea** /ˌ· ˈ·/ *n* [C,U] cold tea with ice, lemon, and sugar, or a glass of this drink

**ice floe** /ˈ· ·/ *n* [C] an area of ice floating in the sea, that has broken off from a larger mass

**ice hock·ey** /ˈ· ˌ··/ *n* [U] a sport played on ice, in which players try to hit a hard flat round object into the other team's GOAL (3) with special sticks

**Ice·land·er** /ˈaɪsləndə‖-ər/ *n* [C] someone from Iceland

**Ice·lan·dic** /aɪsˈlændɪk/ *adj* connected with Iceland, its people, or their language

**ice lol·ly** /ˈ· ˌ··/ *plural* **ice lollies** *n* [C] *BrE* a piece of sweet tasting ice on a stick, that you suck; POPSICLE *AmE*

**ice·man** /ˈaɪs-mæn/ *n plural* **icemen** /-men/ [C] *AmE* a man who delivered ice to people's houses in the past, so that they could keep food cold

**ice pack** /ˈ· ·/ *n* [C] **1** a bag containing ice, used to keep injured or painful parts of your body cold **2** a large area of crushed ice floating in the sea —compare PACK ICE

**ice pick** /ˈ· ·/ *n* [C] a sharp tool used for cutting or breaking ice

**ice rink** /ˈ· ·/ *n* [C] a specially prepared surface of ice where you can ICE-SKATE

**ice sheet** /ˈ· ·/ *n* [C] an ICE CAP

**ice-skate** /ˈ· ·/ *v* [I] to slide on ice wearing ice skates —**ice-skater** *n* [C] —**ice-skating** *n* [U]

**ice skate** /ˈ· ·/ *n* [C usually plural] a special boot with thin metal blades on the bottom, that allows you to move quickly on ice —compare ROLLER SKATE

**ice wa·ter** /ˈ· ˌ··/ *n* [C,U] very cold water with pieces of ice in it, or a glass of this

**ich·neu·mon fly** /ɪkˈnjuːmən flaɪ‖-ˈnuː-/ *n* [C] an insect that lays eggs on or inside the LARVA of another insect

**-ician** /ɪʃən/ *suffix* [in nouns] a skilled worker who deals with a particular thing: *a beautician* (=someone who gives beauty treatments) | *a technician*

**i·ci·cle** /ˈaɪsɪkəl/ *n* [C] a long thin pointed piece of ice hanging from a roof or other surface

**-icide** /ɪsaɪd/ *suffix* also **-cide** [in nouns] killer; killing: *insecticide* (=chemical substance for killing insects) | *suicide* (=act of killing oneself) —**-icidal** /ɪsaɪdl/ [in adjectives] —**-icidally** /ɪsaɪdl-i/ [in adverbs]

**i·ci·ly** /ˈaɪsəli/ *adv* if you say something icily or look at someone icily you do it in an angry or very unfriendly way: *She started talking, but he glared at her icily.*

**ic·ing** /ˈaɪsɪŋ/ *n* [U] **1** a mixture made from powdery sugar and liquid, used to cover cakes; FROSTING (1) *AmE* **2** **the icing on the cake** something that makes a very good experience perfect: *It was a great evening but meeting you here was just the icing on the cake!*

**icing sug·ar** /ˈ·· ˌ··/ *n* [U] *BrE* powdery sugar that is mixed with liquid to make icing; CONFECTIONER'S SUGAR *AmE*

**ick·y** /ˈɪki/ *adj informal* very unpleasant, especially to look at, taste, or feel: *Those dumplings look really icky!*

**i·con** /ˈaɪkɒn‖-kɑːn/ *n* [C] **1** a small sign or picture on a computer SCREEN[1] (1) that is used to start a particular operation: *To open a new file, click on the icon at the top of the screen.* **2** someone famous who is admired by many people and is thought to represent an important idea: *Anita Roddick has been feted as some kind of environmentally conscious feminist icon.* **3** also **ikon** a picture or figure of a holy person that is used in worship in the Greek or Russian Orthodox Church —**iconic** /aɪˈkɒnɪk‖-ˈkɑː-/ *adj*

**i·con·o·clast** /aɪˈkɒnəklæst‖-ˈkɑː-/ *n* [C] someone who attacks established ideas and customs

**i·con·o·clas·tic** /aɪˌkɒnəˈklæstɪk◂‖-ˌkɑːn-/ *adj* iconoclastic ideas, opinions, writings etc attack established beliefs and customs: *Wolfe's theories were revolutionary and iconoclastic.*

**i·co·nog·ra·phy** /ˌaɪkəˈnɒgrəfi‖-ˈnɑː-/ *n* [U] the way that a particular people, religious or political group etc represent ideas in pictures or images: *Crocodiles and hippopotami are both symbols of evil in the iconography of ancient Egypt.*

**-ics** /ɪks/ *suffix* [in nouns] **1** the scientific study or use of something: *linguistics* (=the study of language) | *electronics* (=the study or making of electronic apparatus) | *acoustics* **2** the actions typically done by a particular type of people: *athletics* (=running, jumping, throwing, etc) | *acrobatics* **3** qualities or events connected with something: *the acoustics* (=sound qualities) *of the hall*

**ic·y** /ˈaɪsi/ *adj* **1** extremely cold: *An icy wind blew from the north.* | *The bath water was icy cold.* **2** covered in ice: *The roads will be icy tonight.* **3** an icy comment, look etc shows that you feel annoyed with or unfriendly towards someone: *Jo fixed the other woman with an icy stare.* —see also ICILY —**iciness** *n* [U]

**I'd** /aɪd/ **1** the short form of 'I had': *I wish I'd been there.* **2** the short form of 'I would': *I'd leave now if I were you.*

**ID** /ˌaɪ ˈdiː/ *n* [C,U] a document that shows your name and date of birth, usually with a photograph: *Do you have any ID, sir?*

**id** /ɪd/ *n* [U] *technical* according to Freudian PSYCHOLOGY (1), the part of your mind that is completely unconscious but has hidden needs and desires —compare EGO (3), SUPEREGO

**ID card** /ˌaɪ ˈdiː kɑːd‖-kɑːrd/ *n* [C] an IDENTITY CARD

**-ide** /aɪd/ *suffix* [in nouns] *technical* a chemical compound: *cyanide* | *sulphide*

**i·dea** /aɪˈdɪə/ *n* S1 W1

**1** ▶ **PLAN/SUGGESTION** ◀ [C] a plan or suggestion for a possible course of action, especially one that you think of suddenly: **[+ for]** *What gave you the idea for the book?* | **[+ of]** *What do you think about John's idea of recruiting two new people?* | **idea that** *What do you think of this idea that we should all wear uniforms?* | **it is sb's idea to do sth** *It was Mary's idea to hold the party outside.* | **good/great idea** *What a good idea!* | **have an idea** (=think of an idea) *George has had a brilliant idea – let's hire the church hall.* | **hit on/come up with an idea** (=to think of an idea) | **new idea** *These meetings are intended to pool knowledge and inspire new ideas.* | **toy with the idea of doing sth** (=think about a plan or suggestion, but not very seriously) *We toyed with the idea of going to Paris.* | **entertain an idea** (=consider it as a possibility) *formal*: *There is evidence to show that she entertained the idea of suicide long before this.* | **bright idea** (=a very clever idea, often used jokingly to mean a very stupid idea or action) *Whose bright idea was it to turn the fridge off, then?*

**2** ▶ **KNOWLEDGE** ◀ [C,U] **a)** a general understanding of something, based on knowing something about it: *Before I undertake this work, I need an idea of the problems involved.* | **some idea** (=at least a little knowledge about something) *You must have some idea of where they went.* | **general/rough idea** (=a not very exact idea) *Can you give me a rough idea of how much the repairs will cost?* **b)** to not know at all: **have no idea** *I've no idea where she's gone.* | *"When are they arriving?" "No idea."* | **not have the faintest/slightest/foggiest idea** *spoken*: *I don't have the foggiest idea how much he earns.*

**3** ▶ **AIM/INTENTION** ◀ [C,U] the aim, intention, or purpose of doing something: *The idea was to buy a new dress, but we only got as far as the supermarket!* | **[+ of]** *The idea of the game is get the ball past your opponent.* | **big ideas** (=plans to become important, successful etc) *He was a man with big ideas – he even dreamed of becoming president.* | **have other ideas** (=have different plans from the ones that someone else has for you) *They wanted Mike to go to law school, but he had other ideas.*

**4** ▶ **IMAGE** ◀ [C,U] an image in your mind of what something is like or should be like: **[+ of]** *Chefs differ in their idea of what makes a good dessert.* | **not my idea of fun/a good time etc** *Walking up a mountain in the pouring rain isn't my idea of fun.*

**5** ▶ **BELIEF** ◀ [C usually plural] an opinion or belief:

*Jack has some pretty strange ideas.* | [+ **about**] *traditional ideas about women*
**6 have an idea (that)** to be fairly sure that something is true, without being completely sure: *I'm not certain where she is, but I've a pretty good idea.* | *Benson? Yes, I have an idea he works in the library.*
**7 ► PRINCIPLE ◄** [C] a principle or belief about how something is or should be: [+ **of**] *The whole idea of democracy was something strange and new to most people.* | **idea that** *It's based on the idea that all people are created equal.*
**8 it is a (good) idea to do sth** *spoken* used to give someone advice about what to do: *It'd be a good idea to call and let them know you're coming.*
**9 get the idea** *informal* to begin to understand something or be able to do something: *Just read through the instructions – you'll get the idea.*
**10 get the wrong idea** to think that something is true when it is not: *Don't get the wrong idea about Dan and Helen – they're just friends.*
**11 have the right idea** to be using the right kind of method or general principle in something that you are trying to do: *He still makes a few mistakes but I reckon he's got the right idea.*
**12 where did you get that idea?** *spoken* used to say that what someone thinks is in fact completely wrong: *No, I'm not seeing Jane. Where did you get that idea?*
**13 put ideas into sb's head** to make someone think of doing something that they had not thought of before, especially something stupid or impossible: *Nick tells me he wants a motorbike. Have you been putting ideas into his head?*
**14 that's an idea!** *spoken* used to say that you like what someone has just suggested: *"We could hire a car when we get there." "That's an idea!"*
**15 that's the idea** *spoken* used to tell someone who is learning to do something that they are doing it the right way, in order to encourage them
**16 sb's idea of a joke** *informal* something that is intended to be a joke but makes you angry: *I suppose hiding the car keys was his idea of a joke!*
**17 you have no idea** *spoken* used when you are telling someone that something is extremely good, bad etc: *You have no idea how worried I was.*
**18 the idea!** *old-fashioned* used to express surprise or disapproval when someone has said something stupid or strange —see also **buck up your ideas** (BUCK)

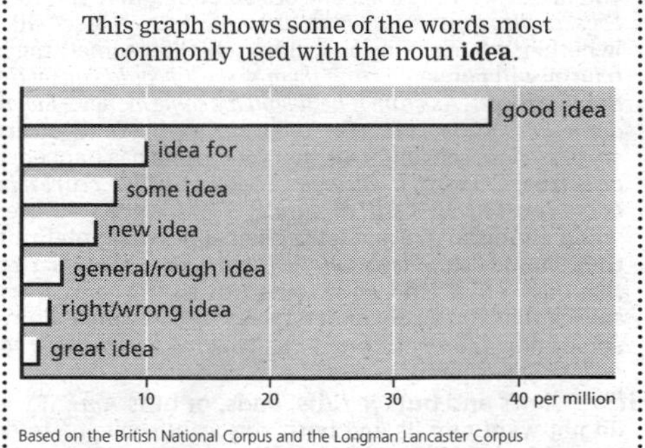


S2 W2 **i·deal¹** /ˌaɪˈdɪəl◂/ *adj* **1** the best that something could possibly be: *advice on how to reach your ideal weight* | *an ideal place for a picnic* **2** [only before noun] an ideal world, job, system etc is one that you imagine to be perfect, but that is not likely to really exist: *In an ideal world there would be no need for a police force.*

**ideal²** *n* [C] **1** a principle or perfect standard that you hope to achieve: *Social justice and equality, like many ideals, are difficult to realise.* **2** an idea of what something would be like if it had no faults or problems: [+ **of**] *the democratic ideal of government*

**i·deal·ise** /aɪˈdɪəlaɪz/ *v* [T] a British spelling of IDEALIZE

**i·deal·is·m** /aɪˈdɪəlɪzəm/ *n* [U] **1** strong belief in principles or perfect standards, even when they are very difficult to achieve in real life: *youthful idealism* | *The movement appealed to their idealism.* **2** *technical* a way of using art to show the world as a perfect place, even though it is not —compare REALISM (2), NATURALISM

**i·deal·ist** /aɪˈdɪəlɪst/ *n* [C] someone who tries to live according to principles or perfect standards, especially in a way that is not practical or possible

**i·deal·is·tic** /aɪˌdɪəˈlɪstɪk◂/ *adj* believing in principles or perfect standards that cannot really be achieved: *We were young and idealistic and anything seemed possible.* —**idealistically** /-kli/ *adv*

**i·deal·ize** also **-ise** *BrE* /aɪˈdɪəlaɪz/ *v* [T] to imagine or represent something or someone as being perfect or better than they really are: *Boys often idealize their fathers.* —**idealization** /aɪˌdɪəlaɪˈzeɪʃən‖-lə-/ *n* [U]

**i·deal·ly** /aɪˈdɪəli/ *adv* **1** [sentence adverb] used to describe the way you would like things to be, even though this may not be possible: *How many orders are you hoping for, ideally?* | *Ideally I'd like a job where I can work from home.* **2 ideally suited/placed/qualified etc** having very suitable qualities etc for a particular situation: *He was ideally suited for the job.* S3

**id·em** /ˈɪdem, ˈaɪdem/ *Latin* from the same book, author etc as the one that has just been mentioned

**i·den·ti·cal** /aɪˈdentɪkəl/ *adj* exactly the same: *four identical houses* | [+ **to**] *This system is identical to the one used in France* —**identically** /-kli/ *adv*

**identical twin** /·ˌ···ˈ·/ *n* [C usually plural] one of a pair of brothers or sisters born at the same time, who look almost exactly alike

**i·den·ti·fi·a·ble** /aɪˈdentɪfaɪəbəl/ *adj* someone or something that is identifiable can be recognized: *Only three people in the photograph are identifiable.*

**i·den·ti·fi·ca·tion** /aɪˌdentɪfɪˈkeɪʃən/ *n* [U] **1** official papers or cards, such as your PASSPORT, that prove who you are: *Do you have any identification?* | **means of identification** *My only means of identification was my driver's licence.* —see also ID **2** your ability to say who someone is because you have seen them before: *procedures for the identification of suspects* **3** the act or process of recognizing something: *Correct identification of needs is vital.* **4** a strong feeling of sympathy with someone that makes you able to share their feelings: *identification with the heroine of the play*

**identification pa·rade** /·ˌ···ˈ·· ·ˌ·/ *n* [C] *BrE* a process in which a WITNESS to a crime looks at a group of people to see if they can recognize the criminal; LINE-UP (4) *AmE*

**i·den·ti·fy** /aɪˈdentɪfaɪ/ *v* [T] **1** to recognize and correctly name someone or something: *I agreed to try and identify the body.* | **identify sb/sth** *The aircraft were identified as American.* **2** to recognize something or discover exactly what it is, what its nature or origin is, etc: *The first task is to identify local crime problems.* | *Scientists have identified the gene that causes abnormal growth.* **3** to make it clear to other people who someone is: **identify sb as sb** *His accent identified him as a Frenchman.* W1

**identify with** *phr v* [T] **1** [**identify with** sb] to feel able to share or understand the feelings of another person: *I didn't enjoy the movie because I couldn't identify with any of the characters.* **2 be identified with** to be closely connected or involved with something such as a political group: *She has always been identified with the radical left.* **3** [**identify** sth **with** sb/sth] to think that something is the same as, or closely connected with, something else: *It is a mistake to identify art with life.*

**i·den·ti·kit** /aɪˈdentɪˌkɪt/ *n* [C] *BrE* **1** a method used by the police for producing a picture of a possible criminal from descriptions given by a WITNESS or witnesses; COMPOSITE¹ (2) *AmE*: *an identikit portrait* **2 identikit**

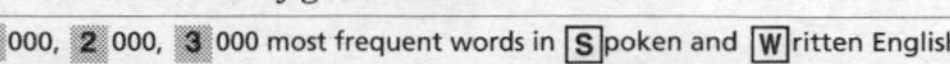

**houses/popstars etc** all exactly the same, and with no interesting or unusual features

W2 **i·den·ti·ty** /aɪˈdentɪti/ *n* **1** [C,U] **sb's identity** who someone is; someone's name: *The identity of the killer is still unknown.* | **mistaken identity** (=when someone is mistaken for someone else) *He was chased and shot by the police in a case of mistaken identity.* **2** [U] the qualities and attitudes you have that make you feel you have your own character and are different from other people: **sense of identity** *He has no sense of his own identity.* | **cultural/ethnic/social identity** (=a strong feeling of belonging to a particular group, race etc) | **identity crisis** (=a feeling of uncertainty about who you really are and what your purpose in life is) **3** [U] *formal* exact SIMILARITY between two things

**identity card** /ˈ·'··· ·/ *n* [C] a card with your name, date of birth, photograph, and SIGNATURE on it, that proves who you are; ID CARD

**id·e·o·gram** /ˈɪdiəgræm/ also **id·e·o·graph** /-grɑːf‖-græf/ *n* [C] a written sign, for example in Chinese, that represents an idea rather than the sound of a word

**i·de·o·lo·gic·al** /ˌaɪdiəˈlɒdʒɪkəl◂‖-ˈlɑː-/ *adj* based on strong beliefs or ideas, especially political or economic ideas, that may not be practical in real life: *an ideological commitment to privatization* —**ideologically** /-kli/ *adv*

W3 **i·de·ol·o·gy** /ˌaɪdiˈɒlədʒi‖-ˈɑːl-/ *n* [C,U] **1** a set of ideas on which a political or economic system is based: *the ideologies of fascism and communism* **2** a set of ideas and attitudes that strongly influence the way people behave: *an ideology that views women as 'the weaker sex'*

**ides** /aɪdz/ *n* [plural] a date or period of time around the middle of the month in the ancient Roman calendar

**id·i·o·cy** /ˈɪdiəsi/ *n* **1** [U] extreme stupidity or silliness: *the idiocy of our rulers* **2** [C] a very stupid remark or action

**id·i·o·lect** /ˈɪdiəlekt/ *n* [C,U] *technical* the way in which a particular person uses language —compare DIALECT

**id·i·om** /ˈɪdiəm/ *n* **1** [C] a group of words with a meaning of its own that is different from the meanings of each separate word put together: *'Under the weather' is an idiom meaning 'ill'.* **2** [C,U] *literary* a style of expression in writing, speech, or music, that is typical of a particular group of people

**id·i·o·mat·ic** /ˌɪdiəˈmætɪk◂/ *adj* **1 idiomatic phrase/expression** an idiom: *an idiomatic phrase* **2** typical of the natural way in which someone using their own language speaks or writes: *After a year in Madrid, her Spanish was fluent and idiomatic.* —**idiomatically** /-kli/ *adv*

**id·i·o·syn·cra·sy** /ˌɪdiəˈsɪŋkrəsi/ *n* [C] **1** an unusual habit or way of behaving that someone has: *Her idiosyncrasies included talking to her plants.* **2** an unusual or unexpected feature that something has: *one of the many idiosyncrasies of English spelling* —**idiosyncratic** /ˌɪdiəsɪnˈkrætɪk◂/ *adj*

**id·i·ot** /ˈɪdiət/ *n* [C] **1** a stupid person or someone who has done something stupid: *Some idiot drove into the back of my car.* **2** *old use* someone who is mentally ill or has a very low level of intelligence —**idiotic** /ˌɪdiˈɒtɪk◂‖-ˈɑːt-/ *adj* —**idiotically** /-kli/ *adv*

**idle¹** /ˈaɪdl/ *adj* **1** not working or producing anything: **lie/stand idle** *We can't leave this expensive machinery lying idle.* | *The whole team stood idle, waiting for the mechanic.* **2** lazy: *a crowd of idle students* | *Come on, you idle lot!* **3** not serious, or not done with any definite intention: *The doctor hated wasting time on idle chatter.* | *If you say 'no', mean it. Never make idle threats.* **4 the idle rich** rich people who do not have to work

**idle²** *v* **idled, idling** **1** [I always + adv/prep] to spend time doing nothing: *Tom was idling at the corner when a well-dressed businessman came up to him.* **2** [I,T] if an engine idles or if you idle it, it runs slowly while it is not connected to the system that makes parts move **3** [T] to stop using a factory or stop providing work for your workers, especially temporarily

**idle** sth ↔ **away** *phr v* [T] to spend time in a relaxed way, doing nothing: *We were just idling away the time by the river.*

**id·ler** /ˈaɪdlə‖-ər/ *n* [C] *old-fashioned* someone who is lazy and does not work

**i·dol** /ˈaɪdl/ *n* [C] **1** someone or something that you love or admire very much: **be the idol of** *a football player who was the idol of the younger boys* | **TV/pop idol** (=a famous actor or performer that many people admire) *the chance to meet your favorite TV idol* **2** a picture or STATUE that is worshipped as a god

**i·dol·a·ter** /aɪˈdɒlətə‖-ˈdɑːlətər/ *n* [C] *formal* someone who worships a picture or STATUE of a god

**i·dol·a·tress** /aɪˈdɒlətrɪs‖-ˈdɑː-/ *n* [C] *formal* a woman who worships a picture or STATUE as a god

**i·dol·a·try** /aɪˈdɒlətri‖-ˈdɑː-/ *n* [U] **1** the practice of worshipping IDOLS **2** too much admiration for someone or something: *idolatry of power* —**idolatrous** *adj*

**i·dol·ize** also **-ise** *BrE* /ˈaɪdəl-aɪz/ *v* [T] to admire and love someone so much that you think they are perfect: *They had one child, a girl whom they idolized.*

**id·yll** /ˈɪdəl, ˈɪdɪl‖ˈaɪdl/ *n* [singular] *literary* a place or experience in which everything is peaceful and everyone is perfectly happy: *the rural idyll of peace and plenty*

**i·dyl·lic** /ɪˈdɪlɪk, aɪ-‖aɪ-/ *adj* very happy and peaceful, with no problems or dangers: *an idyllic setting on the shores of a lake* —**idyllically** /-kli/ *adv*: *idyllically happy*

**i.e.** /ˌaɪ ˈiː/ *Latin* used to explain the exact meaning of something that you have just said: *The film is only open to adults, i.e. people over 18.*

**-ie** /i/ *suffix* [in nouns] *informal* another form of the suffix -y² (1): *dearie*

**if¹** /ɪf/ *conjunction* **1** used to talk about something that might happen: *What can you do if your child behaves badly in a public place?* | *If you don't leave now I'm calling the police.* | *We can always get a taxi if there's a problem with the car.* | **if by any chance** *If by any chance Peter should phone, can you tell him I'll talk to him later?* | **if not** *I think there's a train at midday. If not you'll have to wait till 12.30.* **2** used when you are talking about something that always happens in a particular situation: *If I go to bed late I feel dreadful in the morning.* | *Plastic will melt if it gets too hot.* **3 even if** although something is true or something happens: *Even if I did lose a stone, I still wouldn't look skinny.* **4** used to mean 'though', when you are describing someone or something that you like: *He's a pleasant child, if a little spoiled.* **5** used like 'whether' when asking or deciding whether something is true or will happen: *I rang them to see if I could cancel the appointment.* | *Ask him if he'll lend me some money.* | *I wonder if John's home yet.* **6** used when saying that you are surprised, upset, angry etc that something has happened or is true: *I'm sorry if you took it that way.* | *I don't care if he is my brother. He's still an idiot.* **7 if I were you** used when giving advice and telling someone what you think they should do: *If I were you I'd jump at the chance of a job like that.* **8 it isn't as if.../it's not as if...** used when saying that you do not understand why someone is doing something: *I can't think why they're being so mean. It's not as if they're short of money.* S1 W1

**if²** *n* **1 ifs and buts** *BrE*/**ifs, ands, or buts** *AmE* if you do not want any ifs and buts, you want someone to do something quickly without arguing: *No ifs and buts – just make sure the job is done by tomorrow!* **2 and it's a big if** used to say that something is not likely to happen: *We can do it if, and it's a big if, we get the money.*

**if·fy** /ˈɪfi/ *adj informal* full of uncertainty: *The whole plan is beginning to look pretty iffy.* | *I'm a bit iffy about having a party here.*

**-iform** /ɪfɔːm‖ɪfɔːrm/ *suffix* [in adjectives] *technical* like or in the shape of something: *cruciform* (=cross-shaped)

**-ify** /ɪfaɪ/ *suffix* [in verbs] also **-fy** **1** to affect something in a particular way, or become something: *to purify* (=make or become pure) | *to clarify the situation* (=make it clear) **2** to fill someone with a particular feeling: *They* *terrify me.* (=fill me with terror) **3 a)** *informal* to do something in a silly or annoying way: *to speechify* (=make speeches, use important sounding words) **b)** to make something or someone be like or typical of a person or group: *Frenchified* (=like the French)

**ig·loo** /ˈɪgluː/ *n* [C] a house made from blocks of hard snow or ice

**ig·ne·ous** /ˈɪgniəs/ *adj technical* igneous rocks are formed from LAVA (=hot liquid rock under the ground)

**ig·nite** /ɪgˈnaɪt/ *v* **1** [I,T] *formal* to start burning or to make something start burning: *The fuel is ignited by a high voltage spark.* **2 ignite controversy/resentment etc** to make people suddenly feel very angry or upset about something

**ig·ni·tion** /ɪgˈnɪʃən/ *n* **1** [singular] the electrical part of a vehicle's engine that makes it start working —see picture on page 409 **2** [U] *formal* the act of starting to burn, or making something do this

**ig·no·ble** /ɪgˈnəʊbəl‖-ˈnoʊ-/ *adj formal* ignoble thoughts, feelings, or actions are ones that you should feel ashamed or embarrassed about —**ignobly** *adv*

**ig·no·min·i·ous** /ˌɪgnəˈmɪniəs/ *adj formal* making you feel ashamed, especially because you seem stupid, unimportant, or dishonest: *an ignominious departure* | *another ignominious failure* —**ignominiously** *adv*

**ig·no·mi·ny** /ˈɪgnəmɪni/ *n formal* **1** [C] an event or situation that makes you feel ashamed: *He came last, an ignominy he could hardly bear.* **2** [U] shame and public dishonour: *the ignominy of defeat*

**ig·no·ra·mus** /ˌɪgnəˈreɪməs/ *n* [C] *plural* **ignoramuses** someone who does not know about things that most people know about

**ig·no·rance** /ˈɪgnərəns/ *n* [U] **1** lack of knowledge or information about something: *My mistake was caused by ignorance, not malice.* | **keep sb in ignorance** (=not tell someone about something that they should know about) *Adopted children shouldn't be kept in ignorance about their true origins.* **2 ignorance is bliss** used to say that if you do not know about a problem, you cannot worry about it

**ig·no·rant** /ˈɪgnərənt/ *adj* **1** not knowing facts or information that you ought to know: *an ignorant and uneducated man* | [+ **of**] *They were ignorant of any events outside their own town.* | [+ **about**] *I'm very ignorant about politics.* —see IGNORE (USAGE) **2** caused by a lack of knowledge and understanding: *What an ignorant thing to say!* | *ignorant opinions* **3** *BrE spoken* rude or impolite; ILL-MANNERED

S 2 W 2 **ig·nore** /ɪgˈnɔː‖-ˈnɔːr/ *v* [T] **1** to behave as if you had not heard or seen someone or something: *Either she didn't see me wave or she deliberately ignored me.* | *Sam rudely ignored the question.* **2** to deliberately pay no attention to something that you have been told or that you know about: *As far as homelessness goes, the vast majority of people just sit back and ignore it.*

**USAGE NOTE: IGNORE**

WORD CHOICE: **ignore, be ignorant of, not know**

If you **ignore** something, you know about it or have seen or heard it, but choose not to take notice of it: *Some drivers simply ignore speed limits.*

If you are **ignorant of** something, you do not know about it: *No driver can pretend to be ignorant of speed limits.*

**i·gua·na** /ɪˈgwɑːnə/ *n* [C] a large tropical American LIZARD

**i·kon** /ˈaɪkɒn‖-kɑːn/ *n* [C] another spelling of ICON (3)

**il-** /ɪl/ *prefix* the form used for IN- before l: *illogical* (=not logical)

**i·lex** /ˈaɪleks/ *n* [C,U] **1** a type of OAK tree with leaves that are always green **2** *technical* one of a family of trees and bushes including HOLLY

**ilk** /ɪlk/ *n* **of that/his/their ilk** of that type, his type etc: *Irving Berlin and composers of his ilk*

**I'll** /aɪl/ the short form of 'I will' or 'I shall'

**ill¹** /ɪl/ *adj* **1** [not usually before noun] *especially BrE* suffering from a disease or not feeling well; sick: *Bridget can't come – she's ill.* | **feel ill** *I was feeling ill that day, and decided to stay at home.* | **be taken ill/fall ill** (=become ill) *She was suddenly taken ill at school.* | **seriously ill** (=very ill) *seriously ill in hospital* | **mentally ill** (=with a disease of the mind) | **terminally ill** (=with an illness that you will die from) *a hospice for the terminally ill* | **ill health** *He had to resign due to ill health.* —see also ILLNESS —see SICK¹ (USAGE) **2** [not before noun] *BrE* suffering from the effects of an injury: *The two policemen are still seriously ill with gunshot wounds.* **3** [only before noun] bad or harmful: *She seemed to have suffered no ill effects from her ordeal.* | *accusations of ill treatment by the police* **4 ill at ease** nervous, uncomfortable, or embarrassed: *He always felt shy and ill at ease at parties.* **5 it's an ill wind (that blows nobody any good)** *spoken* used to say that every problem brings an advantage for someone —see also ILL FEELING, ILL WILL S 3 W 3

This graph shows how common the adjectives **ill** and **sick** are in British and American English.

ill
BrE
AmE
20 40 60 per million

sick
BrE
AmE
20 40 60 per million

Based on the British National Corpus and the Longman Lancaster Corpus

In British English the word **ill** means not healthy. Americans usually use **sick** for this meaning. In British English **sick** can be used in this way, but is more commonly used in expressions such as **be sick** or **feel sick** meaning to VOMIT or feel that you are going to VOMIT.

**ill²** *adv* **1 be ill treated/ill used etc** to be treated badly, unpleasantly, or cruelly: *Most of our clients have been ill-treated as children.* **2** not well or not enough; badly: *She was ill prepared for the ordeal ahead.* | *"I see one third of a nation ill-housed, ill-clad, ill-nourished." (F.D. Roosevelt)* **3 can ill afford (to do) sth** to be unable to do something without making the situation you are in very difficult: *I was wasting time I could ill afford to lose.* **4 think/speak ill of** *formal* to think or say unpleasant things about someone: *She really believes you should never speak ill of the dead.*

**ill³** *n* **1** [plural] problems and difficulties: *Free-market economics was seen as the cure for all our ills.* **2** [U] *formal* harm, evil, or bad luck: *She did not like Matthew but she would never wish him ill.*

**ill-ad·vised** /ˌ· ·ˈ·◂/ *adj* not sensible or not wise and likely to cause problems in the future: *an ill-advised response to the crisis* | **you would be ill-advised to do sth** (=used to advise someone not to do something stupid) *You would be ill-advised to lend him any money.* —**ill-advisedly** *adv*: *Scott ill-advisedly took matters into his own hands.*

**ill-as·sort·ed** /ˌ· ·ˈ··◂/ *adj* an ill-assorted group of people or things do not seem to belong together in a group

**ill-bred** /ˌ· ˈ·◂/ *adj* rude or behaving badly, especially because your parents did not teach you to behave well: *an ill-bred upstart criticizing everyone else*

**ill-con·sid·ered** /ˌ· ·ˈ··◂/ *adj* decisions, actions, ideas etc that are ill-considered have not been carefully thought about: *The program is ill-considered and a waste of everyone's time.*

**ill-de·fined** /ˌ· ·ˈ·◂/ *adj* **1** not described clearly

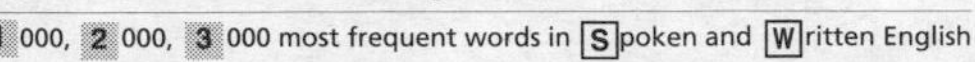

enough: *The party's policies were often vague and ill-defined.* **2** not clearly marked, or not having a clear shape; INDISTINCT: *an ill-defined track between the two lakes*

**ill-dis·posed** /ˌ· ·'··/ *adj formal* unfriendly or unsympathetic: [+ **towards**] *I was feeling generally ill-disposed toward my fellow man.*

**il·le·gal¹** /ɪ'liːgəl/ *adj* not allowed by the law: *They were caught selling illegal drugs.* | **it is illegal to do sth** *It's illegal to drive without a licence.* —opposite LEGAL (1) —illegally *adv*

**illegal²** *n* [C] *AmE spoken* an illegal immigrant: *We don't want illegals coming for welfare dollars!*

**illegal im·mi·grant** /·ˌ·· '···/ also **illegal a·li·en** *AmE* /·ˌ·· '···/ *n* [C] someone who comes to live in a country from abroad, without official permission

**il·le·gal·i·ty** /ˌɪlɪ'gæləti/ *n* **1** [U] the state of being illegal **2** [C] an action that is illegal

**il·le·gi·ble** /ɪ'ledʒəbəl/ *adj* difficult or impossible to read: *I'm not sure what this note says – Dad's writing is almost illegible!* —opposite LEGIBLE —**illegibly** *adv* —**illegibility** /ɪˌledʒə'bɪləti/ *n* [U]

**il·le·git·i·mate** /ˌɪlə'dʒɪtəmət◂/ *adj* **1** born to parents who are not married **2** not allowed or acceptable according to established rules or agreements: *illegitimate use of public funds* —**illegitimately** *adv* —**illegitimacy** *n* [U]

**ill-e·quipped** /ˌ· ·'·◂/ *adj* not having the necessary equipment or skills for a particular situation or activity: *They were ill-equipped for the journey.* | **ill-equipped to do sth** *an inexperienced teacher who was ill-equipped to deal with such children*

**ill-fat·ed** /ˌ· '··◂/ *adj literary* unlucky and leading to serious problems or death: *One of the group was killed on the ill-fated expedition.*

**ill-fa·voured** *BrE*, **ill-favored** *AmE* /ˌ· '··◂/ *adj literary or old-fashioned* having an unattractive face; ugly

**ill feel·ing** /ˌ· '··/ *n* [U] angry feelings towards someone: *Whatever ill feeling there had been between them had vanished by now.*

**ill-found·ed** /ˌ· '··/ *adj formal* not based on true facts: *Unfortunately her faith in British justice proved ill-founded.*

**ill-got·ten** /ˌ· '··◂/ *adj* **ill-gotten gains/wealth etc** *especially humorous* money that was obtained in an unfair or dishonest way: *They rushed home to gloat over their ill-gotten gains.*

**il·lib·e·ral** /ɪ'lɪbərəl/ *adj formal* **1** not supporting freedom of expression or of personal behaviour: *illiberal and undemocratic policies* **2** not generous —**illiberally** *adv* —**illiberality** /ɪˌlɪbə'ræləti/ *n* [U]

**il·li·cit** /ɪ'lɪsət/ *adj* not allowed by laws or rules, or strongly disapproved of by society: *an illicit love affair* | *illicit diamond trading* —**illicitly** *adv*

**il·lit·e·rate** /ɪ'lɪtərət/ *adj* **1** someone who is illiterate has not learned to read or write **2** badly written, in an uneducated way: *It was an illiterate letter, full of mistakes.* **3 politically/scientifically etc illiterate** knowing very little about politics, science etc —**illiteracy** *n* [U]

**ill-judged** /ˌ· '·◂/ *adj formal* an action that is ill-judged has not been thought about carefully enough: *an ill-judged decision*

**ill-man·nered** /ˌ· '··◂/ *adj formal* not polite; behaving badly in social situations —opposite WELL-MANNERED

**ill-na·tured** /ˌ· '··◂/ *adj formal* unpleasant or unkind: *ill-natured gossip*

S2 W3 **ill·ness** /'ɪlnəs/ *n* [C,U] a disease of the body or mind: *She had all the normal childhood illnesses.* | *mental illness* | **serious illness** *an insurance policy that guarantees an income in the event of serious illness* | **minor illness** (=one that is not very serious) *people who go to the doctor even for the most minor illnesses* —see also DISEASE

**il·lo·gi·cal** /ɪ'lɒdʒɪkəl‖ɪ'lɑː-/ *adj* **1** not sensible or reasonable: *erratic and illogical behaviour* —opposite LOGICAL (1) **2** not based on the principles of LOGIC: *an illogical conclusion* —**illogically** /-kli/ *adv* —**illogicality** /ɪˌlɒdʒə'kæləti‖ɪˌlɑː-/ *n* [U]

**ill-o·mened** /ˌ· '··◂/ *adj literary* likely to bring a lot of problems or suffering in the future: *an ill-omened business venture*

**ill-starred** /ˌ· '·◂/ *adj literary* unlucky and likely to cause or experience a lot of problems or unhappiness: *an ill-starred love affair*

**ill-tem·pered** /ˌ· '··◂/ *adj formal* **1** easily made angry or impatient **2** an ill-tempered meeting, argument etc is one in which people are angry and often rude to each other: *ill-tempered exchanges in the presidential debate*

**ill-timed** /ˌ· '·◂/ *adj* happening, done, or said at the wrong time: *His remarks are ill-timed and inappropriate.*

**ill-treat** /ˌ· '·/ *v* [T] to be cruel to someone, especially to a child or animal —**ill-treatment** *n* [U]

**il·lu·mi·nate** /ɪ'luːməneɪt, ɪ'ljuː-‖ɪ'luː-/ *v* [T] **1** to make a light shine on something, or fill a place with light: *The room was illuminated by the glow of the fire.* **2** *formal* to make something much clearer and easier to understand: *His lecture illuminated and explained many scientific phenomena.* **3** to decorate buildings, streets, etc with lights for a special occasion **4** *literary* to make someone look happy or excited: *A sudden smile illuminated her face.*

**il·lu·mi·nat·ed** /ɪ'luːməneɪtəd, -'ljuː-‖-'luː-/ *adj* **1** lit up by lights: *a big illuminated sign over the entrance* **2 an illuminated book/bible/manuscript etc** a book of a type produced by hand in the Middle Ages, whose pages are decorated with gold paint and other bright colours

**il·lu·mi·nat·ing** /ɪ'luːməneɪtɪŋ, ɪ'ljuː-‖ɪ'luː-/ *adj* making things much clearer and easier to understand: *I didn't find his reply very illuminating.*

**il·lu·mi·na·tion** /ɪˌluːmə'neɪʃən, ɪˌljuː-‖ɪˌluː-/ *n* **1** [U] lighting provided by a lamp, light etc: *An electric light bulb provided the only illumination.* | *The illumination is too weak to show the detail of the painting.* **2** [C usually plural] a picture or pattern painted on a page of a book, especially in former times: *valuable manuscripts with many illuminations* **3 illuminations** *especially BrE* a show of coloured lights used to make a town bright and colourful: *the famous Blackpool illuminations* **4** [U] *formal* clear explanation of a particular subject: *illumination of a previously unexplored topic*

**ill-use** /ˌɪl 'juːz/ *v* [T usually passive] *formal* to treat someone badly or unfairly: *She's been ill-used by her colleagues.* —**ill-usage** /-'juːsɪdʒ/ *n* [U]

**il·lu·sion** /ɪ'luːʒən/ *n* [C] **1** an idea or opinion that is wrong, especially about yourself: **illusion that** *He cherished the illusion that she loved him.* | **be/labour under an illusion** (=believe something that is not true) | **have no illusions about** (=realize the unpleasant truth about something) *He has no illusions about the harsh realities of the economic climate.* **2** something that seems to be different from the way it really is: *The mirrors in the room gave an illusion of greater space.* —see also OPTICAL ILLUSION

**il·lu·sion·ist** /ɪ'luːʒənəst/ *n* [C] someone who does surprising tricks that make things seem to appear or happen

**il·lu·so·ry** /ɪ'luːsəri/ also **il·lu·sive** /ɪ'luːsɪv/ *adj formal* false but seeming to be real or true: *the apparent but illusory successes of the last 15 years*

**il·lus·trate** /'ɪləstreɪt/ *v* [T] **1** to make the meaning of something clearer by giving examples: *To illustrate the point, Dr Fisher told a story.* **2** to be an example which shows that something is true or that a fact exists: *Nixon's downfall illustrates the immense power of the media.* **3** [usually passive] to put pictures in a book, article etc: *a beautifully illustrated book* W2

**il·lus·tra·tion** /ˌɪlə'streɪʃən/ *n* **1** [C] a picture in a book, article etc, especially one that helps you to understand it: *Children like books with lots of illustrations.* **2** [C,U] a story, event, action etc that shows the truth or existence of something very clearly: [+ **of**] *a striking illustration of 19th century attitudes to women* | **by way of illustration** (=as an example) *By way of illustration, I should like to mention a recent case.* **3** [U] the act or process of illustrating something

**il·lus·tra·tive** /ˈɪləstreɪtɪv, -strət-‖ɪˈlʌstrətɪv/ *adj* helping to explain the meaning of something: *an illustrative example* —see also ILLUSTRATE (2)

**il·lus·tra·tor** /ˈɪləstreɪtə‖-ər/ *n* [C] someone who draws pictures, especially for books

**il·lus·tri·ous** /ɪˈlʌstriəs/ *adj formal* famous and admired because of what you have achieved in the past: *I would like to introduce our illustrious guest, Professor Brookes.*

**ill will** /ˌ· ˈ·/ *n* [U] strong dislike; HOSTILITY: *At first there was a lot of suspicion and ill will among the team.* | **bear sb no ill will** (=feel no dislike or anger towards someone)

**I'm** /aɪm/ the short form of 'I am': *I'm a student.*

**im-** /ɪm/ *prefix* the form used for IN- before b, m, or p: *immobilize* | *impossible*

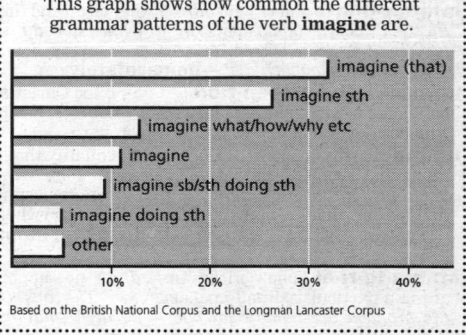

S3 W1 **im·age** /ˈɪmɪdʒ/ *n* [C]

**1 ▶ PUBLIC OPINION ◀** the general opinion that most people have of a person, organization, product etc: *The party is seeking to improve its image with women voters.* | **project an image** (=make an image) *The princess aimed to project an image of herself as serious and hard-working.*

**2 ▶ IDEA IN MIND ◀** a picture that you have in your mind, especially about what someone or something is like or the way they look: *She had a clear image of how she would look in twenty years' time.* | *He didn't really conform to the hard-drinking, hard-living image of the political journalist.*

**3 ▶ PICTURE/WHAT YOU SEE ◀ a)** a picture of an object in a mirror or in the LENS (2) of a camera: *She gazed at her image in the glass.* **b)** a picture on the SCREEN[1] (1,2) of a television, cinema, or computer: *The image on a computer screen is made up of thousands of pixels.* **c)** a copy of the shape of a person or thing, especially cut in wood, stone etc: *carved images in the rocks*

**4 ▶ DESCRIPTION ◀** a phrase or word that describes something in a poetic way: *the image of man as a prisoner of the gods*

**5 be the (very/living/spitting) image of** to look exactly like someone or something else: *He's the very image of his father.*

**6 in the image of** *literary* in the same form or shape as someone or something else: *According to the Bible, man was made in the image of God.* —see also MIRROR IMAGE

**im·ag·e·ry** /ˈɪmɪdʒəri/ *n* [U] **1** the use of poetic phrases and images to describe something in literature: *the symbolic imagery of Dylan Thomas* **2** the representation of ideas in paintings, films etc: *the romantic imagery of the Pre-Raphaelite painters*

**i·ma·gi·na·ble** /ɪˈmædʒɪ̇nəbəl/ *adj* **the best/worst/kindest etc imaginable** used to emphasize that something is the best, worst etc example of something that it is possible to imagine: *He was defeated in the most humiliating circumstances imaginable.* | **every imaginable** *Posters were plastered on every imaginable surface.*

**i·ma·gi·na·ry** /ɪˈmædʒɪ̇nəri‖-neri/ *adj* not real, but produced from pictures or ideas in your mind: *All the characters in this book are imaginary.* —compare IMAGINATIVE

S3 W3 **i·ma·gi·na·tion** /ɪˌmædʒɪ̇ˈneɪʃən/ *n* **1** [C,U] the ability to form pictures or ideas in your mind: *Children often have very vivid imaginations.* | *With a little imagination, he could visualize the old house as a luxury hotel.* **2** [U] something that is caused only by your mind, and does not really exist or did not really happen: *Did you hear that noise, or was it my imagination?* **3 in your imagination** only existing or happening in your mind, not in real life: *The difficulties are all in your imagination.* **4 capture/catch sb's imagination** to make people feel very interested and excited: *His music captured the imagination of a whole generation of young people.* **5 leave sth to sb's imagination** to deliberately not describe something because you think someone can guess or imagine it: *I'll leave the details of the affair to your imagination.* **6 use your imagination!** *spoken* used to tell someone that they can easily guess the answer to a question, so you should not need to tell them —see also **not by any stretch of the imagination** (STRETCH[2] (5))

**i·ma·gi·na·tive** /ɪˈmædʒɪ̇nətɪv/ *adj* **1** someone who is imaginative is good at thinking of new, interesting ideas, and at forming pictures in their mind: *an imaginative child* **2** something that is imaginative contains new and interesting ideas used in a clever way: *imaginative writing* | *an imaginative solution to the problem* —compare IMAGINARY —**imaginatively** *adv*

S2 W2 **i·ma·gine** /ɪˈmædʒɪ̇n/ *v* [T]

**1 ▶ MENTAL PICTURE ◀** [not usually in progressive] to form a picture or idea in your mind about what something could be like: **imagine (that)** *Try to imagine that you are a tourist arriving in London for the first time.* | *Close your eyes and imagine a tropical island.* | **imagine what/how/why etc** *I can just imagine what the place is going to look like in a few years' time.* | **imagine sb doing sth** *I can just imagine Sarah running her own business.* | **imagine doing sth** *It's hard to imagine working in a place like that.* | **imagine sb/sth as** *I never knew my grandmother but I always imagine her as a kind, gentle person.* | **imagine sb in/with/without etc** *Somehow I can't imagine him without a beard.*

**2 ▶ WRONG IDEA ◀** to have a false or wrong idea about something: *She doesn't love him, he's just imagining it.* | *imagined dangers* | **imagine (that)** *He imagines that people don't like him but they do.* | **imagine sb/sth to be sth** *I was surprised when I saw the farm. I had imagined it to be much bigger.*

**3 ▶ THINK STH ◀** [not in progressive] to think that something is true, but without being sure or having proof: *You must miss him, I imagine.* | **imagine (that)** *I imagine she's home by now if you want to phone her.*

**4 you can't imagine** *BrE spoken* used to emphasize how good, bad etc something is: *You can't imagine what a terrible week we had.*

**5 ▶ SURPRISED ◀ (just) imagine!** *spoken old-fashioned* used to show surprise, shock, or disapproval: *He dyed his hair bright yellow! Just imagine!* | **imagine doing sth** *Imagine going all that way for nothing!*

This graph shows how common the different grammar patterns of the verb **imagine** are.



Based on the British National Corpus and the Longman Lancaster Corpus

**i·ma·gin·ings** /ɪˈmædʒɪ̇nɪŋz/ *n* [plural] *literary* situations or ideas that you imagine, but which are not real or true

**im·am** /ˈɪmɑːm, ˈɪmæm/ *n* [C] a Muslim religious leader or priest

**im·bal·ance** /ɪmˈbæləns/ *n* [C,U] a lack of a fair or correct balance between two things, which results in problems or unfairness: *a hormonal imbalance* | **redress an imbalance** (=put it right) *an attempt to redress the imbalance between rich and poor*

**im·be·cile** /ˈɪmbəsiːl‖-səl/ *n* [C] **1** someone who is very

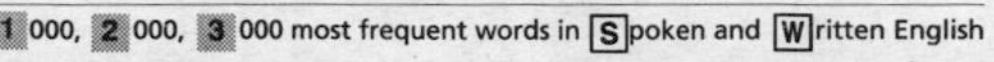

stupid or behaves very stupidly: *He looked at me as if I was a complete imbecile.* **2** *old-fashioned* a word meaning someone who is mentally ill, now considered offensive —**imbecilic** /ˌɪmbɪ̵ˈsɪlɪk◂/ *adj*

**im·be·cil·i·ty** /ˌɪmbɪ̵ˈsɪlɪ̵ti/ *n* **1** [C,U] very stupid behaviour or an action that is very stupid **2** [U] the condition of being an imbecile

**im·bed** /ɪmˈbed/ *v* **imbedded, imbedding** [T] another spelling of EMBED

**im·bibe** /ɪmˈbaɪb/ *v* [I,T] *formal or humorous* **1** to drink something, especially alcohol: *Having imbibed rather too freely, he fell forward against the table.* **2** to accept and be influenced by qualities, ideas, values etc: *imbibing radical political ideas*

**im·bro·gli·o** /ɪmˈbrəʊliəʊ‖ɪmˈbroʊlioʊ/ *n plural* **imbroglios** [C] a difficult, embarrassing, or confusing situation, especially in politics or public life: *He found himself in the greatest imbroglio of his tenure at the UN.*

**im·bue** /ɪmˈbjuː/ *v*
**imbue** sb **with** sth *phr v* [T usually passive] to make someone feel an emotion very strongly: *a people deeply imbued with national pride*

**IMF** /ˌaɪ em ˈef/ *n* **the IMF** the International Monetary Fund; an international organization that tries to encourage trade between countries and to help poorer countries develop economically

**im·i·tate** /ˈɪmɪ̵teɪt/ *v* [T] **1** to copy something because you think it is good: *Do kids really imitate the violence they see on TV?* | *Our methods have been imitated all over the world.* **2** to copy the way someone behaves, speaks, moves etc, especially in order to make people laugh: *"Give that back!" she screeched, imitating Jess's high-pitched squeal.* —**imitator** *n* [C]

**im·i·ta·tion** /ˌɪmɪ̵ˈteɪʃən◂/ *n* **1** [C,U] an attempt to imitate someone or something, or the act of doing this: *Bill can do a passable imitation of an American accent.* | *Children learn a lot by imitation.* | **a pale imitation** (=something that is much less good than the thing it imitates) *The remake of 'Casablanca' was a pale imitation of the original movie.* **2** [C] a copy of something: *The table is a genuine antique not a cheap imitation.* | **imitation leather/wood/ivory etc** (=something that looks like an expensive material but is a copy of it)

**im·i·ta·tive** /ˈɪmɪ̵tətɪv‖-teɪtɪv/ *adj formal* copying someone or something, especially in a way that shows you do not have any ideas of your own —**imitatively** *adv* —**imitativeness** *n* [U]

**im·mac·u·late** /ɪˈmækjʊ̵lɪ̵t/ *adj* **1** very clean and tidy: *Richard looked immaculate in a white silk dinner jacket.* **2** exactly correct or perfect in every detail: *Your timing is immaculate!* —**immaculately** *adv*

**Immaculate Con·cep·tion** /·ˌ··· ·ˈ··/ *n* the Christian belief that Christ's mother Mary was a VIRGIN (=someone who has never had sex) when Christ was born

**im·ma·nent** /ˈɪmənənt/ *adj formal* **1** a quality that is immanent seems to be naturally present: *Hope seems immanent in human nature.* **2** God or another spiritual power that is immanent is present everywhere —compare EMINENT, IMMINENT —**immanence, immanency** *n* [U]

**im·ma·te·ri·al** /ˌɪməˈtɪəriəl◂‖-ˈtɪr-/ *adj* **1** not important in a particular situation; IRRELEVANT: *The causes of the problem are immaterial now – we need solutions.* **2** *formal* not having a real physical form

**im·ma·ture** /ˌɪməˈtʃʊə‖-ˈtʃʊr/ *adj* **1** someone who is immature behaves or thinks in a way that is typical of someone much younger: *I married much too young – I was very immature.* **2** not fully formed or developed: *The immature plants are susceptible to frost.* —**immaturity** *n* [U]

**im·mea·su·ra·ble** /ɪˈmeʒərəbəl/ *adj* too big or too extreme to be measured: *This latest scandal has done immeasurable damage to his reputation.* —**immeasurably** *adv*: *The company's position has improved immeasurably since last year.*

**im·me·di·a·cy** /ɪˈmiːdiəsi/ *n* [U] the quality of seeming to happen right now that makes something seem more important or urgent to you: *Television brings a new immediacy to world events.*

**im·me·di·ate** /ɪˈmiːdiət/ *adj* S2 W2
**1** ▶ **NO DELAY** ◀ happening or done at once and without delay: *The police response to the situation was forceful and immediate.* | *seek immediate medical attention*
**2** ▶ **NOW** ◀ [only before noun] existing now, and needing to be dealt with quickly: *Our immediate concern was to stop the fire from spreading.* | *I have no immediate plans to leave.*
**3** ▶ **AFTER/BEFORE** ◀ [only before noun] happening just before or just after someone or something else: *My immediate predecessor went to work for a rival firm.* | *the immediate future*
**4** ▶ **NEAR** ◀ [only before noun] next to, or very near to, a particular place: *The immediate area was sealed off after the bomb.*
**5 immediate family/kin** people who are very closely related to you, such as your parents, children, brothers, and sisters

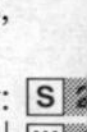

**im·me·di·ate·ly¹** /ɪˈmiːdiətli/ *adv* **1** without delay: *Cook the mixture for ten minutes and serve immediately.* | *As soon as I got their fax, I wrote back immediately.* **2** [+ adj/adv] very soon before or after something: *The baby was given up for adoption immediately after birth.* **3** [+ adj/adv] very near to something: *Charles lives in the apartment immediately above ours.* **4 immediately involved/concerned/affected etc** very closely involved etc in a particular situation: *All those immediately involved will be informed of the decision.*

**immediately²** *conjunction BrE formal* as soon as: *Make sure the property you are buying is insured immediately you exchange contracts.*

**im·me·mo·ri·al** /ˌɪmɪ̵ˈmɔːriəl◂/ *adj* **1 since/from time immemorial** for longer than people can remember: *The tribe had inhabited the area since time immemorial.* **2** *formal* starting longer ago than people can remember, or than written history shows: *an immemorial custom*

**im·mense** /ɪˈmens/ *adj* extremely large: *An immense amount of money and time has been put into finding a cure.*

**im·mense·ly** /ɪˈmensli/ *adv* very much; extremely: *We enjoyed the play immensely.* | *immensely popular*

**im·men·si·ty** /ɪˈmensɪ̵ti/ *n* [U] **1** the great size and seriousness of something such as a problem you have to deal with or a job you have to do: *the immensity of the task before us* **2** also **immensities** [plural] the great size of something, especially something that cannot be measured: *the immensities of outer space*

**im·merse** /ɪˈmɜːs‖-ɜːrs/ *v* [T] **1** *especially technical* to put someone or something deep into a liquid so that it is completely covered: **immerse sb/sth in** *Immerse your foot in ice cold water to reduce the swelling.* **2 immerse yourself in** to become completely involved in an activity: *Jane was determined to immerse herself in the African way of life.* —**immersed** *adj*: *completely immersed in his job*

**im·mer·sion** /ɪˈmɜːʃən, -ʒən‖ɪˈmɜːrʒən/ *n* [U] **1** the fact of being completely involved in something you are doing: *He was well respected, despite his immersion in the murkier side of politics.* **2 a)** the action of immersing something in liquid, or the state of being immersed **b)** BAPTISM (=a ceremony to introduce someone into a church) in which someone's whole body is put into water **3** the language teaching method in which people are put in situations where they have to use the new language **4** *BrE informal* an immersion heater

**immersion heat·er** /·ˈ·· ˌ··/ *n* [C] *BrE* an electric water heater that provides hot water for a house

**im·mi·grant** /ˈɪmɪ̵grənt/ *n* [C] someone who comes from abroad to live permanently in another country —compare EMIGRANT

**im·mi·grate** /ˈɪmɪ̵greɪt/ *v* [I] to come into a country in order to live there permanently —see also EMIGRATE

**im·mi·gra·tion** /ˌɪmɪ̣ˈɡreɪʃən/ *n* [U] **1** the process of entering another country in order to live there: *normal immigration procedures* **2** the total number of people who do this: *Immigration fell in the 1980s.* **3** also **immigration control** the place at an airport, sea port etc where officials check the documents of everyone entering the country

**im·mi·nent** /ˈɪmɪ̣nənt/ *adj* an event that is imminent will happen very soon: *A declaration of war now seemed imminent.* | *The company is now in imminent danger of collapse.* —compare IMMANENT —**imminence** *n* [U] —**imminently** *adv*

**im·mo·bile** /ɪˈməʊbaɪl‖ɪˈmoʊbəl/ *adj* **1** not moving at all: *A few soldiers were lounging around on two immobile tanks.* **2** unable to move or walk normally: *Kim's illness had rendered her completely immobile.* —**immobility** /ˌɪməˈbɪlɪ̣ti/ *n* [U]

**im·mo·bi·lize** also **-ise** *BrE* /ɪˈməʊbɪ̣laɪz‖ɪˈmoʊ-/ *v* [T] **1** to prevent someone or something from moving: *The broken limb must be immobilized immediately.* **2** to stop something from working: *The car's security device will immobilize the ignition system.* —**immobilization** /ɪˌməʊbɪ̣laɪˈzeɪʃən‖ɪˌmoʊbələ-/ *n* [U]

**im·mod·e·rate** /ɪˈmɒdərɪ̣t‖ɪˈmɑː-/ *adj formal* not within reasonable and sensible limits; EXCESSIVE: *immoderate wage demands* | *immoderate drinking* —**immoderately** *adv*

**im·mod·est** /ɪˈmɒdɪ̣st‖ɪˈmɑː-/ *adj* **1** having a very high opinion of yourself and your abilities, and not embarrassed about telling people how clever you are etc —opposite MODEST (1) **2** *old-fashioned* behaviour or clothes that are immodest may embarrass or offend people because they do not follow the usual social rules concerning sexual behaviour —**immodestly** *adv* —**immodesty** *n* [U]

**im·mo·late** /ˈɪməleɪt/ *v* [T] *formal* to kill someone or something by burning them —**immolation** /ˌɪməˈleɪʃən/ *n* [U]

**im·mor·al** /ɪˈmɒrəl‖ɪˈmɔː-/ *adj* **1** morally wrong: *They condemned slavery as immoral.* **2** not following accepted standards of sexual behaviour —compare AMORAL —**immorally** *adv*

**im·mo·ral·i·ty** /ˌɪməˈrælɪ̣ti/ *n* [U] behaviour that is morally wrong: *the immorality of bombing civilians*

**im·mor·tal** /ɪˈmɔːtl‖-ɔːr-/ *adj* **1** living or continuing forever: *Plato believed that the soul is immortal.* **2** an immortal line, play, song etc is so famous that it will never be forgotten: *Shakespeare's immortal lines* —**immortal** *n* [C]

**im·mor·tal·i·ty** /ˌɪmɔːˈtælɪ̣ti‖-ɔːr-/ *n* [U] the condition of living forever or being remembered forever

**im·mor·tal·ize** also **-ise** *BrE* /ɪˈmɔːtəlaɪz‖-ɔːr-/ *v* [T] to make someone or something famous for a long time, especially by writing about them, painting a picture of them etc: *Dickens' father was immortalized as Mr Micawber in 'David Copperfield'.*

**im·mo·va·ble** /ɪˈmuːvəbəl/ *adj* **1** impossible to move: *Lock your bike to something immovable like a railing or lamp-post.* **2** impossible to change or persuade: *The president is immovable on this issue.* —**immovably** *adv*

**im·mune** /ɪˈmjuːn/ *adj* **1** someone who is immune to a particular disease cannot catch it **2** not affected by something such as criticism, bad treatment etc: **[+ to]** *They're always so rude that I've almost become immune to it.* **3** specially protected from something unpleasant: **[+ from]** *Peterson was told he would be immune from prosecution if he co-operated with the police.*

**immune sys·tem** /ˈ·ˌ··/ *n* [C] the system by which your body protects itself against disease

**im·mu·nise** /ˈɪmjɪ̣naɪz/ *v* a British spelling of IMMUNIZE

**im·mu·ni·ty** /ɪˈmjuːnɪ̣ti/ *n* [U] the fact of not being affected by a disease or harmed by something unpleasant: **[+ to]** *immunity to infection* | **[+ from]** *They were granted immunity from prosecution.*

**im·mu·nize** also **-ise** *BrE* /ˈɪmjɪ̣naɪz/ *v* [T] to protect someone from a particular illness, especially by putting a substance into their body by INJECTION (1): **immunize sb against sth** *All girls are routinely immunized against German measles.* —compare VACCINATE —**immunization** /ˌɪmjɪ̣naɪˈzeɪʃən‖-nə-/ *n* [C,U]

**im·mu·no·de·fi·cien·cy** /ˌɪmjɪ̣nəʊdɪˈfɪʃənsi, ɪˌmjuːnəʊ-‖-noʊ-/ *n* [C,U] a medical condition in which your body is unable to fight infection in the usual way —**immunodeficient** *adj*

**im·mu·nol·o·gy** /ˌɪmjɪ̣ˈnɒlədʒi‖-ˈnɑː-/ *n* [U] the scientific study of the prevention of disease and how the body reacts to disease

**im·mure** /ɪˈmjʊə‖ɪˈmjʊr/ *v* [T] *formal or literary* to shut someone in somewhere so that they cannot get out

**im·mu·ta·ble** /ɪˈmjuːtəbəl/ *adj formal* never changing or impossible to change: *the immutable principles of liberty and justice* —**immutably** *adv* —**immutability** /ɪˌmjuːtəˈbɪlɪ̣ti/ *n* [U]

**imp** /ɪmp/ *n* [C] **1** a small creature in stories who has magic powers and behaves very badly **2** a child who behaves badly, but in a way that amuses people rather than annoying them —see also IMPISH

**im·pact¹** /ˈɪmpækt/ *n* [C] **1** the effect or influence that an event, situation etc has on someone or something: *the environmental impact of increased road traffic* | **have an impact (on)** *Warnings about the dangers of smoking seem to have little impact on this age group.* **2** the force of one object hitting another: *The impact pushed the engine backwards and crushed my legs.* **3 on impact** at the moment when one things hits another: *a missile which explodes on impact* 

**im·pact²** /ɪmˈpækt/ *v* [I + **on**, T] *especially AmE* to have an important or noticeable effect on someone or something: *How will this program impact on the local community?*

**im·pact·ed** /ɪmˈpæktɪ̣d/ *adj* a tooth that is impacted is growing under another tooth so that it cannot develop properly

**im·pair** /ɪmˈpeə‖-ˈper/ *v* [T] to make something less good than it usually is or less good than it should be: *Do not boil the sauce as this can impair the flavor.* —**impairment** *n* [U]

**im·paired** /ɪmˈpeəd‖-ˈperd/ *adj* not as good as before or not as good as it should be: *A special device for viewers with impaired hearing.* | *TV reception may be impaired in some areas.*

**im·pa·la** /ɪmˈpɑːlə/ *n* [C] a large brown graceful African animal; ANTELOPE

**im·pale** /ɪmˈpeɪl/ *v* [T often passive] to push a sharp pointed object through something or someone: *Gregson fell to a horrible death, impaled on the railings below.* —**impalement** *n* [U]

**im·pal·pa·ble** /ɪmˈpælpəbəl/ *adj formal* **1** impossible to touch or feel physically —opposite PALPABLE (2) **2** very difficult to understand

**im·pan·el** /ɪmˈpænl/ *v* [T] another spelling of EMPANEL

**im·part** /ɪmˈpɑːt‖-ɑːrt/ *v* [T] *formal* **1** to give information, knowledge, wisdom etc to someone **2** to give a particular quality to something: *Oregano imparts a delicious flavour to the stew.*

**im·par·tial** /ɪmˈpɑːʃəl‖-ɑːr-/ *adj* not giving special favour or support to any one person or group; fair: *We offer impartial advice on pensions and investments.* | *an impartial observer* —**impartially** *adv* —**impartiality** /ɪmˌpɑːʃiˈælɪ̣ti‖-ɑːr-/ *n* [U]

**im·pass·a·ble** /ɪmˈpɑːsəbəl‖ɪmˈpæ-/ *adj* a road, path, or area that is impassable is impossible to travel along or through: *The road is impassable due to snow.*

**im·passe** /æmˈpɑːs‖ˈɪmpæs/ *n* [singular] a situation in which it is impossible to continue with a discussion or plan because the people involved cannot agree: **reach an impasse** *Negotiations seemed to have reached an impasse.*

**im·pas·sioned** /ɪmˈpæʃənd/ *adj* an impassioned speech,

request, argument etc is full of strong feeling and emotion: *She appeared on television to make an impassioned appeal to the kidnappers.*

**im·pas·sive** /ɪm'pæsɪv/ *adj* not showing any emotion or feeling: *Oscar's face remained impassive throughout the trial.* —**impassively** *adv* —**impassivity** /ˌɪmpæ'sɪvɪ̈ti/ *n* [U]

**im·pa·tience** /ɪm'peɪʃəns/ *n* [U] **1** annoyance at having to accept delays, other people's weaknesses etc: *Fiona's impatience with her slower students was beginning to show.* **2** great eagerness for something to happen, especially something that is going to happen soon

**im·pa·tient** /ɪm'peɪʃənt/ *adj* **1** annoyed because of a situation you cannot control, especially when you have to wait for something: *After an hour's delay, passengers were becoming impatient.*|*I'm coming – don't be so impatient!* **2** very eager for something to happen and not wanting to wait: [+ **for**] *The woman stood there, impatient for me to be gone.*|**impatient to do sth** *Glen was clearly impatient to be off.* —**impatiently** *adv*

**im·peach** /ɪm'piːtʃ/ *v* [T] *law* **1** to charge a public official with a serious crime, especially in the US: *The House Judiciary Committee voted that President Nixon should be impeached.* **2** to say that someone is guilty of a serious crime, especially a crime against the state —**impeachment** *n* [U]

**im·pec·ca·ble** /ɪm'pekəbəl/ *adj* completely perfect and without any mistakes: *Eliza had impeccable manners.*|*an impeccable performance* —**impeccably** *adv*: *impeccably dressed*

**im·pe·cu·ni·ous** /ˌɪmpɪ'kjuːniəs◂/ *adj formal or humorous* having very little money, especially over a long period: *a gifted but impecunious painter* —**impecuniously** *adv* —**impecuniousness** *n* [U]

**im·ped·ance** /ɪm'piːdəns/ *n* [singular, U] *technical* a measure of the power of a piece of electrical equipment to stop the flow of an ALTERNATING CURRENT

**im·pede** /ɪm'piːd/ *v* [T] to prevent something from happening in the normal way, or make it happen more slowly: *Storms at sea impeded our progress.*

**im·ped·i·ment** /ɪm'pedɪ̈mənt/ *n* [C] **1** a physical or nervous problem that makes it difficult for someone to speak or move normally: *a speech impediment* **2** a situation or event that makes it difficult or impossible for someone or something to succeed or make progress: [+ **to**] *The main impediment to development is the country's huge foreign debt.*

**im·ped·i·men·ta** /ɪmˌpedɪ̈'mentə/ *n* [plural] *often humorous* bags, animals, supplies etc that you take with you on a journey, and that may slow you down

**im·pel** /ɪm'pel/ *v* [T] an idea, emotion etc that impels you to do something makes you feel very strongly that you must do it: **impel sb to do sth** *Donnelly felt impelled to write and complain.* —compare COMPEL

**im·pend·ing** /ɪm'pendɪŋ/ *adj* an impending event or situation, especially an unpleasant one, is going to happen very soon: *I had a sense of impending doom.*|*an impending ecological crisis*

**im·pen·e·tra·ble** /ɪm'penɪ̈trəbəl/ *adj* **1** impossible to get through, see through, or get into: *an impenetrable barrier of thorn bushes*|*impenetrable darkness* **2** very difficult or impossible to understand: *The document was written in impenetrable lawyer's jargon.* —**impenetrably** *adv* —**impenetrability** /ɪmˌpenɪ̈trə'bɪlɪ̈ti/ *n* [U]

**im·pen·i·tent** /ɪm'penɪ̈tənt/ *adj formal* not feeling sorry for something bad or wrong that you have done —**impenitently** *adv* —**impenitence** *n* [U]

**im·per·a·tive¹** /ɪm'perətɪv/ *adj* **1** extremely important and needing to be done or dealt with immediately: **it is imperative (that)** *It is absolutely imperative that these safety measures are implemented immediately.*|**it is imperative to do sth** *By now, it had become imperative to evacuate the area.* **2** a voice, manner etc that is imperative is very firm and has a feeling of authority **3** *technical* an imperative verb is one that expresses a command —**imperatively** *adv*

**imperative²** *n* [C] **1** something that must be done urgently: *Reducing unemployment has become an imperative for the government.* **2** *technical* the form of a verb that expresses a command: *In 'Come here!' the verb 'come' is in the imperative.* **3** *formal* an idea, belief, or emotion that strongly influences people to behave in a particular way: *the sexual imperative*

**im·per·cep·ti·ble** /ˌɪmpə'septɪ̈bəl‖-pər-/ *adj* an imperceptible change, movement etc is difficult to see or notice because it is very small: *an almost imperceptible change of speed* —**imperceptibly** *adv*: *The daylight faded almost imperceptibly into night.* —**imperceptibility** /ˌɪmpəseptɪ̈'bɪlɪ̈ti‖-pər-/ *n* [U]

**im·per·fect¹** /ɪm'pɜːfɪkt‖-ɜːr-/ *adj* not completely correct or perfect: *an imperfect knowledge of German*|*I got it cheap because it's slightly imperfect.* —**imperfectly** *adv* —**imperfection** /ˌɪmpə'fekʃən‖-pər-/ *n* [C,U]

**imperfect²** also **imperfect tense** *n* [singular] *technical* the form of a verb that shows an incomplete action in the past

**im·pe·ri·al** /ɪm'pɪəriəl‖-'pɪr-/ *adj* **1** connected with an EMPIRE or with the person who rules it: *Britain's imperial expansion in the 19th century*|*a major imperial power* **2** [only before noun] connected with the system of weights and measurements based on INCHes, miles etc —compare METRIC

**im·pe·ri·al·is·m** /ɪm'pɪəriəlɪzəm‖-'pɪr-/ *n* [U] **1** a political system in which one country rules a lot of other countries, and tries to find more that it can defeat and govern **2** methods by which a rich or powerful country can get political or trade advantages over poorer countries —compare COLONIALISM —**imperialist** *n* —**imperialist, imperialistic** /ɪmˌpɪəriə'lɪstɪk◂‖-ˌpɪr-/ *adj*

**im·per·il** /ɪm'perɪ̈l/ *v formal* **imperilled** *BrE*, **imperiled** *AmE* [T] to put something in danger: *The whole project was imperilled by a lack of funds.*

**im·pe·ri·ous** /ɪm'pɪəriəs‖-'pɪr-/ *adj* giving orders and expecting to be obeyed, in a way that seems too proud: *She had an imperious domineering manner which Tim did not like.*|*an imperious voice* —**imperiously** *adv* —**imperiousness** *n* [U]

**im·per·ish·a·ble** /ɪm'perɪʃəbəl/ *adj formal* formed or made in a way that will exist for a long time or for ever: *The manufacturers claim that the material is imperishable.*|*imperishable memories* —opposite PERISHABLE

**im·per·ma·nent** /ɪm'pɜːmənənt‖-ɜːr-/ *adj formal* not staying the same forever; TEMPORARY: *A row of precarious and impermanent wooden huts clung to the hillside.* —**impermanence** *n* [U]: *The impermanence of the situation worried him.*

**im·per·me·a·ble** /ɪm'pɜːmiəbəl‖-ɜːr-/ *adj technical* not allowing liquids or gases to pass through: *an impermeable shell membrane*

**im·per·mis·si·ble** /ˌɪmpɜː'mɪsɪ̈bəl‖-ɜːr-/ *adj formal* something that is impermissible cannot be allowed: *an impermissible infringement of the rules*

**im·per·son·al** /ɪm'pɜːsənəl‖-ɜːr-/ *adj* **1** not showing any feelings of sympathy, friendliness etc: *She left a short impersonal note, saying that she was leaving.* **2** a place or situation that is impersonal does not make people feel that they are important or valued: *a large impersonal city*|*Health care has become increasingly bureaucratic and impersonal.* **3** *technical* in grammar, an impersonal sentence or verb is one where the subject is represented by a word such as 'it', as in the sentence 'It rained all day' —compare PERSONAL¹ —**impersonally** *adv*

**im·per·so·nate** /ɪm'pɜːsəneɪt‖-ɜːr-/ *v* [T] **1** to pretend to be someone else by copying their appearance, voice, and behaviour, especially in order to deceive people: *He gained access to the building by impersonating a police* *officer.* **2** to copy someone's voice and behaviour, especially in order to make people laugh: *Eddie was standing on the table, trying to impersonate John Wayne.* —**impersonation** /ɪmˌpɜːsəˈneɪʃən‖-ɜːr-/ *n* [C,U]: *On the club circuit, he's renowned for his Elvis impersonations.*

**im·per·so·nat·or** /ɪmˈpɜːsəneɪtə‖-ˈpɜːrsəneɪtər/ *n* [C] someone who copies the way that other people look, speak, and behave, as part of a performance

**im·per·ti·nent** /ɪmˈpɜːtɪ̣nənt‖-ɜːr-/ *adj* rude and not respectful, especially to someone who is older or more important: *The question about her age was very impertinent.* —**impertinently** *adv* —**impertinence** *n* [U]

**im·per·tur·ba·ble** /ˌɪmpəˈtɜːbəbəl‖-pərˈtɜːr-/ *adj* remaining calm and unworried in spite of problems or difficulties: *His steady, imperturbable nature reassured me.* —**imperturbably** *adv* —**imperturbability** /ˌɪmpətɜːbəˈbɪlɪ̣ti‖-pərtɜːr-/ *n* [U]

**im·per·vi·ous** /ɪmˈpɜːviəs‖-ɜːr-/ *adj* **1** not affected or influenced by something and seeming not to notice it: [+ **to**] *Janet carried on reading, impervious to the row going on around her.* | *He seems to be impervious to criticism.* **2** not allowing anything to enter or pass through: *impervious volcanic rock*

**im·pe·ti·go** /ˌɪmpɪ̣ˈtaɪgəʊ‖-goʊ/ *n* [U] an infectious skin disease

**im·pet·u·ous** /ɪmˈpetʃuəs/ *adj* tending to do things very quickly, without thinking carefully first: *It was an impetuous decision which she soon regretted.* —**impetuously** *adv* —**impetuousness** *n* [U] —**impetuosity** /ɪmˌpetʃuˈɒsɪ̣ti‖-ˈɑː-/ *n* [U]

**im·pe·tus** /ˈɪmpɪ̣təs/ *n* [U] **1** feeling an influence that makes people or helps something to develop or continue doing something: **gain/lose impetus** *The campaign is already gaining impetus.* | *As a result of this failure, a lot of the initial impetus was lost.* | [+ **for**] *Einstein's work provided the impetus for a major shift in the study of physics.* **2** *technical* the force that makes an object start moving, or keeps it moving once it has started

**im·pi·e·ty** /ɪmˈpaɪɪ̣ti/ *n formal* **1** [U] lack of respect for religion or God **2** [C usually plural] an action that shows a lack of respect for religion or God —see also IMPIOUS

**im·pinge** /ɪmˈpɪndʒ/ *v*

**impinge on/upon** *phr v* [T] *formal* to have an effect on someone or something; influence: *The change of government scarcely impinged on ordinary people's lives.* | *We were discussing the way welfare policies impinge on women.* —**impingement** *n* [U]

**im·pi·ous** /ˈɪmpiəs/ *adj formal* lacking respect for religion or God —**impiously** *adv* —**impiousness** *n* [U] —see also IMPIETY

**imp·ish** /ˈɪmpɪʃ/ *adj* behaving badly and causing trouble, but in a way that is amusing rather than serious or annoying; MISCHIEVOUS —**impishly** *adv*: *Tony grinned impishly at her.* —**impishness** *n* [U]

**im·plac·a·ble** /ɪmˈplækəbəl/ *adj* very determined to continue opposing someone or something: *an implacable enemy* | *The tabloid newspapers remained implacable in their opposition.* —**implacably** *adv*: *A few organizations remain implacably opposed to Sunday trading.* —**implacability** /ɪmˌplækəˈbɪlɪ̣ti/ *n* [U]

**im·plant¹** /ɪmˈplɑːnt‖ɪmˈplænt/ *v* **1** [T] to strongly fix an idea, feeling, or way of behaving in someone's mind, so that it becomes part of their character: *a deep sense of patriotism that had been implanted in him by his father* | *The phrase implanted itself in my memory.* **2** [T] to put something into someone's body by doing a medical operation: *Surgeons successfully implanted an artificial knee-joint.* —**implantation** /ˌɪmplɑːnˈteɪʃən‖-plæn-/ *n* [U]

**im·plant²** /ˈɪmplɑːnt‖-plænt/ *n* [C] something that has been implanted in someone's body in a medical operation: *silicon implants* —compare TRANSPLANT²

**im·plau·si·ble** /ɪmˈplɔːzɪ̣bəl‖-ˈplɒː-/ *adj* difficult to believe and therefore unlikely to be true: *an implausible explanation* | *His excuses were totally implausible.* —**implausibly** *adv* —**implausibility** /ɪmˌplɔːzɪ̣ˈbɪlɪ̣ti‖-ˌplɒː-/ *n* [U]

**im·ple·ment¹** /ˈɪmplɪ̣ment/ *v* [T] **implement a plan/policy/proposal etc** to take action or make changes that you have officially decided should happen: *We have decided to implement the committee's suggestions in full.* W3

**im·ple·ment²** /ˈɪmplɪ̣mənt/ *n* [C] a tool or instrument, especially a fairly large one with no motor: *ploughs, hoes, and other farming implements*

**im·ple·men·ta·tion** /ˌɪmplɪ̣menˈteɪʃən/ *n* [U] the act of implementing a plan, policy etc: *implementation of the peace plan*

**im·pli·cate** /ˈɪmplɪ̣keɪt/ *v* [T] **1** to show or seem to show that someone is involved in something wrong or criminal: **implicate sb in sth** *The letter seemed to implicate Mitchell in the robbery.* **2** to show or seem to show that something is the cause of something bad or harmful: *Tobacco has already been implicated as one of the causes of the disease.*

**im·pli·ca·tion** /ˌɪmplɪ̣ˈkeɪʃən/ *n* **1** [C usually plural] a possible future effect or result of a plan, action, or event, which must be considered or discussed: [+**of**] *What are the implications of these proposals?* | **have implications for** *This could have serious implications for the company's future.* | *You can't just close reactors down – there are all sorts of safety implications.* **2** [C,U] something that you do not say directly but that you seem to want people to believe: [+ **that**] *I resent the implication that I would have lied to you.* | **by implication** *The law bans organized protests and, by implication, any form of opposition.* —see also IMPLY (1) **3** [U] a situation in which someone is shown to be involved in something wrong or criminal: [+ **of**] *the implication of the former Chief of Staff in a major scandal* **4** something that you believe to be shown by a particular situation, action etc: [+ **in**] *The implication in this case is that he's innocent.* —see also IMPLICATE W2

**im·pli·cit** /ɪmˈplɪsɪ̣t/ *adj* **1** **implicit criticism/threat/approval** criticism etc that is suggested or understood without being stated directly: *Her words contained an implicit threat.* | *implicit criticism* —compare EXPLICIT **2** **be implicit in** *formal* to form a central part of something, but without being openly stated: *Confidentiality is implicit in your relationship with a counsellor.* **3** **implicit trust/faith** trust etc that is complete and contains no doubts: *They had an implicit faith in his powers.* —**implicitly** *adv*: *We trusted Lopez implicitly.*

**im·plode** /ɪmˈpləʊd‖-ˈploʊd/ *v* [I] to explode inwards —compare EXPLODE (1) —**implosion** /ɪmˈpləʊʒən‖-ˈploʊ-/ *n* [C,U]

**im·plore** /ɪmˈplɔː‖-ɔːr/ *v* [T] *formal* to ask for something in an emotional way; PLEAD (1): *John, I implore you, stop now before it's too late.* | **implore sb to do sth** *She implored the soldiers to save her child.*

**im·ply** /ɪmˈplaɪ/ *v* [T] **1** to suggest that something is true without saying this directly: **imply (that)** *She managed to imply she'd contributed the money without actually saying so.* | *an implied threat* —see INFER (USAGE) **2** if a fact, event etc implies something, it shows that it is likely to be true: *The high level of radiation in the rocks implies that they are volcanic in origin.* **3** if a principle, action, idea etc implies something, it makes other actions or conditions necessary: *Democracy implies a respect for individual liberties.* W2

**im·po·lite** /ˌɪmpəˈlaɪt◂/ *adj* not polite; rude: *It was very impolite not to write and thank them.* —**impolitely** *adv* —**impoliteness** *n* [C,U]

**im·pol·i·tic** /ɪmˈpɒlɪ̣tɪk‖-ˈpɑː-/ *adj formal* not sensible or not behaving in a way that is likely to bring you advantage: *It was considered impolitic for him to spend too much time with the radicals in the party.*

**im·pon·de·ra·ble¹** /ɪm'pɒndərəbəl‖-'pɑːn-/ *adj formal* something that is imponderable cannot be exactly measured, judged, or calculated

**imponderable²** *n* [C usually plural] *formal* something that cannot be exactly measured, judged, or calculated: *There are so many imponderables that it is impossible to make an accurate prediction.*

**im·port¹** /ɪm'pɔːt‖-ɔːrt/ *n* **1** [C] something that is brought into one country from another in order to be sold: *cheap imports of grain* **2** [U] the process or business of bringing goods into one country from another: *The government eventually banned the import of all electrical goods.* —opposite EXPORT¹ **3** [U] *formal* importance or meaning: *a matter of no great import*

**import²** /'ɪmpɔːt‖-ɔːrt/ *v* [T] **1** to bring something into a country from abroad in order to sell it: *imported oil* **2** *technical* to move information from one computer into another —opposite EXPORT²

S2 W1 **im·por·tance** /ɪm'pɔːtəns‖-ɔːr-/ *n* [U] **1** the quality of being important: *The doctor stressed the importance of regular exercise.* | **attach importance to** (=treat something as if it is important) *Much greater importance is now attached to environmental concerns.* | **of great/vital/crucial importance** (=very important) *This is an issue of great importance to all disabled people.* **2** the reason why something is important: *The real importance of this law is the protection it gives to female workers.*

S1 W1 **im·por·tant** /ɪm'pɔːtənt‖-ɔːr-/ *adj* **1** an important event, decision, problem etc has a big effect or influence on people's lives or on events in the future: *a very important meeting* | *Listen everyone, I've got some important news!* | **it is important to do sth** *It is important to explain to the patient what is happening.* | **it is important that** *It's vitally important that you understand the danger.* | **be important to sb/sth** *Money was the only thing that was important to Carson.* **2** people who are important have a lot of power or influence: *a very important customer* | *an important client*

**im·por·tant·ly** /ɪm'pɔːtəntli‖-ɔːr-/ *adv* **1 more/equally/less importantly** [sentence adverb] used to show that the next statement or question is more, equally etc important than what you said before it: *Most importantly, you must keep a record of everything you do.* **2** in a way that shows you think that what you are saying or doing is important: *"I've got to look after his books," the youngest boy said importantly.* | *striding importantly into the room*

**im·por·ta·tion** /ˌɪmpɔː'teɪʃən‖-ɔːr-/ *n* **1** [U] the business of buying goods from another country and having them sent to your country to be sold there **2 a)** [U] the act of bringing into a country something new or different such as a new plant, custom, or idea **b)** [C] something that is brought into a country in this way —compare IMPORT²

**import du·ty** /'·· ˌ··/ *n* [C,U] a tax on goods that are brought into one country from another country

**im·port·er** /ɪm'pɔːtə‖-'pɔːrtər/ *n* [C] a person, company, or country that buys goods from another country, to be sold or used in their own country: *Japan is one of the world's largest importers of tropical timber.* —opposite EXPORTER

**import li·cence** /'·· ˌ··/ *n* [C] a document that gives permission for goods to be brought into one country from another

**im·por·tu·nate** /ɪm'pɔːtʃʊnɪt‖-ɔːr-/ *adj formal* always asking for things in an annoying or unreasonable way: *importunate demands* —**importunately** *adv* —**importunity** /ˌɪmpə'tjuːnɪti‖-pər'tuː-/ *n* [U]

**im·por·tune** /ˌɪmpə'tjuːn‖ˌɪmpər'tuːn/ *v* [T] *formal* to ask someone for something repeatedly, especially in an annoying or unreasonable way; beg: [+ **for**] *importuning passers-by for money*

W2 **im·pose** /ɪm'pəʊz‖-'poʊz/ *v* **1 impose a ban/tax/fine etc (on)** to officially order that something should be forbidden, restricted, taxed etc, or that someone should be punished: *The government imposed a ban on the sale of ivory.* | *We have decided to impose sanctions on countries that break the agreement.* **2 impose a burden/strain etc (on/upon)** to have a bad effect on something or someone by causing them problems: *The President's health care proposals would not impose any great burden on the state's finances.* **3** [T] to force someone to have the same ideas or beliefs as you: **impose sth on sb** *parents who impose their own moral values on their children* **4** [I] to unreasonably expect or ask someone to do something for you when this is inconvenient for them: [+ **on/upon**] *We could ask them to let us stay the night, but I don't want to impose on them.*

**im·pos·ing** /ɪm'pəʊzɪŋ‖-'poʊ-/ *adj* large, important-looking, and impressive: *an imposing building*

**im·po·si·tion** /ˌɪmpə'zɪʃən/ *n* **1** [C usually singular] something that someone unreasonably expects or asks you to do for them, which is inconvenient: *I regarded his request for a loan as something of an imposition.* **2** [U] the introduction of something such as a rule, tax, or restriction: *the imposition of martial law*

S2 W2 **im·pos·si·ble** /ɪm'pɒsɪbəl‖ɪm'pɑː-/ *adj*

**1 ▶ CAN'T BE DONE ◀** something that is impossible cannot happen or be done: *Further research is impossible without more money.* | *This crossword's absolutely impossible!* | *Impossible! It can't be true.* | **find it impossible to do sth** *Members with young children often found it impossible to attend evening meetings.* | **ask the impossible** (=ask for something that cannot be done) *Expecting the project to be completed by October was really asking the impossible.* | **do the impossible** (=succeed in doing something that seems impossible) *Somehow, Jen had done the impossible and got us all tickets.* | **impossible demands/requests etc** (=demands etc for something that is impossible)

**2 ▶ SITUATION ◀** a situation that is impossible is extremely difficult to deal with: *Helen's refusal to cooperate has put me in an impossible position.* | *His bad temper is making life impossible for the rest of the family.*

**3 ▶ PERSON ◀** someone who is impossible behaves in a very unreasonable and annoying way: *You're impossible! Yesterday you said you didn't like carrots, and today you won't eat potatoes!* —**impossibly** *adv: impossibly difficult* | *They were asking an impossibly high price.* —**impossibility** /ɪmˌpɒsɪ'bɪlɪti‖-ˌpɑː-/ *n* [C,U] *To walk there would have been a virtual impossibility.*

**im·pos·tor** also **imposter** *AmE* /ɪm'pɒstə‖ɪm'pɑːstər/ *n* [C] someone who pretends to be someone else in order to trick people

**im·pos·ture** /ɪm'pɒstʃə‖ɪm'pɑːstʃər/ *n* [U] *formal* a situation in which someone tricks people by pretending to be someone else

**im·po·tent** /'ɪmpətənt/ *adj* **1** unable to take effective action because you do not have enough power, strength, or control: *Emergency services seem almost impotent in the face of such a disaster.* | *impotent rage* **2** a man who is impotent is unable to have sex because he cannot get an ERECTION (1) —**impotently** *adv* —**impotence** *n* [U]

**im·pound** /ɪm'paʊnd/ *v* [T] *law* if the police or law courts impound your possessions they take them and keep them until you claim them: *Last time I went to Rome my car was impounded.*

**im·pov·e·rish** /ɪm'pɒvərɪʃ‖ɪm'pɑː-/ *v* [T] **1** [often passive] to make someone very poor: *Many peasants were impoverished by the land tax.* **2** to make something worse in quality: *Crop rotation has not impoverished the soil.* —**impoverishment** *n* [U]

**im·pov·e·rished** /ɪm'pɒvərɪʃt‖-'pɑː-/ *adj* **a)** very poor: *an impoverished student* **b)** worse in quality: *Our lives would be impoverished without music.*

**im·prac·ti·ca·ble** /ɪm'præktɪkəbəl/ *adj* something that is impracticable cannot be done even though it seems a good idea: *It was an appealing plan but quite impracticable.* —**impracticably** *adv* —**impracticability** /ɪmˌpræktɪkəˈbɪləti/ *n* [U]

**im·prac·ti·cal** /ɪmˈpræktɪkəl/ *adj* **1** an idea, suggestion, or action that is impractical is not sensible because it would be too difficult, too expensive etc: *A 24-hour service would be impractical for a small organization like this.* **2** someone who is impractical is not good at dealing with ordinary practical matters, such as making or repairing things: *a hopelessly impractical man, who couldn't even boil an egg* —**impractically** /-kli/ *adv* —**impracticality** /ɪmˌpræktɪˈkæləti/ *n* [U]: *the sheer impracticality of such a large scale screening program*

**im·pre·ca·tion** /ˌɪmprɪˈkeɪʃən/ *n* [C] *formal* an offensive word or phrase that you say when you are very angry; a CURSE² (2)

**im·pre·cise** /ˌɪmprɪˈsaɪs◂/ *adj* not exact; INACCURATE: *a very imprecise method of measurement | an imprecise term* —**imprecisely** *adv* —**imprecision** /-ˈsɪʒən/ *n* [U]

**im·preg·na·ble** /ɪmˈpregnəbəl/ *adj* **1** a building that is impregnable is so strong that no one can get into it by force: *an impregnable fortress* **2** *formal* attitudes, opinions etc that are impregnable cannot be changed or influenced: *her impregnable obstinacy* —**impregnably** *adv* —**impregnability** /ɪmˌpregnəˈbɪləti/ *n* [U]

**im·preg·nate** /ˈɪmpregneɪt‖ɪmˈpreg-/ *v* [T] **1** to make a substance spread completely through something, or to spread completely through something: [+ **with**] *The material has been impregnated with disinfectant.* **2** to make a woman or female animal PREGNANT

**im·pre·sa·ri·o** /ˌɪmprəˈsɑːriəʊ‖-rioʊ/ *n* [C] someone who organizes performances in theatres, concert halls etc

W3 **im·press¹** /ɪmˈpres/ *v* [T] **1** [not in progressive] if something or someone impresses you, you admire them because you notice how good, clever, successful etc they are: *What impressed us most about the book was its vivid language. | Steve borrowed his dad's sports car to impress his girlfriend.* | **be impressed with/by** *We're very impressed with the standard of the children's work.* | **be favourably impressed** *I think the boss was favourably impressed by your presentation.* | **be suitably impressed** (=be as impressed as you should be) **2** to make the importance of something clear to someone: **impress sth on sb** *Father impressed on me the value of hard work.* **3** to press something into a soft surface so as to make a mark or pattern as a result of this pressure: **be impressed in/on** *patterns impressed in the clay*

**impress²** /ˈɪmpres/ *n* [C] *formal or literary* a mark or pattern made by pressing something into a surface

**impression**

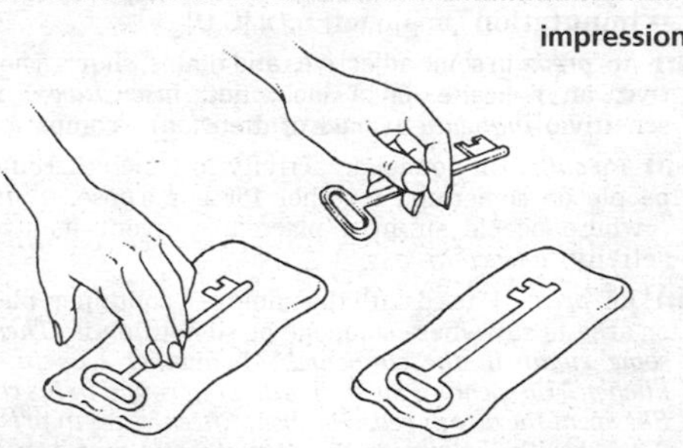

He took an impression of the key.

S3 W2 **im·pres·sion** /ɪmˈpreʃən/ *n*

**1 ▶ OPINION ◀** [C] the opinion or feeling you have about someone or something because of the way they seem: [+ **of**] *What's your impression of Frank as a boss? | Now I have a very different impression of England.* | **first impression** *First impressions can be deceptive.* | **create a good/bad impression** *Arriving late won't create a very favourable impression.* | **make an impression (on)** (=make someone admire you) *It was their first meeting, and Richard was determined to make an impression.* | **have/get the impression (that)** (=think that something is a fact because of the way the situation seems) *I get the distinct impression that we're not wanted here.* | **be under the impression (that)** (=wrongly believe that something is a fact because of the way the situation seems) *I'm sorry, I was under the impression that you were the manager.*

**2 ▶ COPYING SB ◀** [C] the act of copying the speech or behaviour of a famous person in order to make people laugh: **do an impression (of)** *Jean does a great impression of Tina Turner.*

**3 ▶ MARK ◀** [C] a mark left by pressing something into a soft surface: *An impression of a heel was left in the mud.*

**4 ▶ BOOK ◀** [C] all the copies of a book printed at one time —compare EDITION

**im·pres·sio·na·ble** /ɪmˈpreʃənəbəl/ *adj* easy to influence, especially because you are young: **at an impressionable age** *It's damaging to criticize kids when they're at an impressionable age.* —**impressionability** /ɪmˌpreʃənəˈbɪləti/ *n* [U]

**im·pres·sion·is·m** /ɪmˈpreʃənɪzəm/ *n* [U] **1** a style of painting used especially in France in the 19th century which uses colour instead of details of form to produce effects of light or feeling **2** a style of music from the late 19th and early 20th centuries that produces feelings and images by the quality of sounds rather than by a pattern of notes —**impressionist** *adj*: *impressionist painters*

**im·pres·sion·ist** /ɪmˈpreʃənəst/ *n* [C] **1** someone who uses impressionism in the paintings or music that they produce **2** someone who copies the speech or behaviour of famous people in order to entertain other people

**im·pres·sion·is·tic** /ɪmˌpreʃəˈnɪstɪk◂/ *adj* based on a general feeling of what something is like, rather than on specific facts or details: *an impressionistic account of what happened* —**impressionistically** /-kli/ *adv*

**im·pres·sive** /ɪmˈpresɪv/ *adj* something that is impressive seems very good, large, important etc so that you admire it: *Among the guests was an impressive array of authors and critics. | the remains of an impressive Roman villa* —**impressively** *adv* —**impressiveness** *n* [U] 

**im·pri·ma·tur** /ˌɪmprəˈmeɪtə, -ˈmɑː-‖-ər/ *n* [singular] **1** *usually humorous* approval of something, especially from an important person **2** official permission to print a book, especially when this is given by the Roman Catholic Church

**im·print¹** /ˈɪmprɪnt/ *n* [C] **1** the mark left by an object being pressed into or onto something: [+ **of**] *the imprint of her hand on the soft sand* **2** *technical* the name of a PUBLISHER as it appears on a book: *This dictionary is published under the Longman imprint.*

**imprint²** /ɪmˈprɪnt/ *v* **1 be imprinted on your mind/memory** if something is imprinted on your mind or memory, you can never forget it: *The sight of her waving from the window was forever imprinted on my mind.* **2** [T] to print or press the mark of an object on something: **be imprinted with** *notepaper imprinted with the Duke's monogram*

**im·pris·on** /ɪmˈprɪzən/ *v* [T] **1** to put someone in prison or to keep them somewhere and prevent them from leaving: *The government imprisoned or exiled all opposition leaders.* **2** if a situation or feeling imprisons people it restricts what they can do: *Many elderly people felt imprisoned in their own homes.*

**im·pris·on·ment** /ɪmˈprɪzənmənt/ *n* [U] the state of being in prison, or the time someone spends there: *sentenced to a long term of imprisonment* | **life imprisonment** (=imprisonment for the rest of your life, or for a long time) *life imprisonment for murder*

**im·prob·a·ble** /ɪmˈprɒbəbəl‖-ˈprɑː-/ *adj* **1** not likely to happen or to be true: **it is improbable that** *It seems improbable that he could have driven home in less than an hour.* | **highly improbable** *a highly improbable explanation.* **2** surprising and slightly strange: *Theirs was an improbable partnership.* —**improbably** *adv* —**improbability** /ɪmˌprɒbəˈbɪlɪ̈ti‖-ˌprɑː-/ *n* [C,U]

**im·promp·tu** /ɪmˈprɒmptjuː‖ɪmˈprɑːmptuː/ *adj* done or said without any preparation or planning: *an impromptu party* —**impromptu** *adv: He insists he was speaking impromptu.*

**im·prop·er** /ɪmˈprɒpə‖-ˈprɑːpər/ *adj* **1** unacceptable according to the normal standards of moral, social, or professional behaviour: *It is quite improper for you to have an affair with one of your students.* | **an improper suggestion** (=about sex) **2** illegal or dishonest: *allegations of improper banking practices* **3** not correct according to a set of rules: *the improper use of a singular verb with a plural subject* —**improperly** *adv: If you are improperly dressed, you will not be admitted.*

**improper frac·tion** /·ˌ·· ˈ··/ *n* [C] *technical* a FRACTION (2) such as 107/8 in which the top number is larger than the bottom number —compare PROPER FRACTION

**im·pro·pri·e·ty** /ˌɪmprəˈpraɪɪ̈ti/ *n formal* [C] behaviour or a particular action that is unacceptable according to moral, social, or professional standards: *Accusations of impropriety were made against the company's directors.*

S2 W1 **im·prove** /ɪmˈpruːv/ *v* **1** [T] to make something better: *a course for students wishing to improve their English* | *Many dishes are greatly improved by adding fresh herbs.* **2** [I] become better: *Let's hope the weather improves before Saturday.* | *Some wines improve with age.* —see RAISE[1] (USAGE)

**improve on/ upon** sth *phr v* [T] to do something better than before or make it better than before: *Bertorelli has scored 165 points, and I don't think anyone will improve on that.*

**im·proved** /ɪmˈpruːvd/ *adj* better than before: *improved performance throughout the company* | *New improved formula!*

W2 **im·prove·ment** /ɪmˈpruːvmənt/ *n* **1** [C,U] an act of improving or a state of being improved: **[+ in]** *There's certainly been an improvement in the children's behaviour.* | **[+to]** *We need to carry out some improvements to the computer system.* | **show an improvement** *This month's trading figures show some improvement.* | **room for improvement** (=the possibility of improving even more) *Your English is much better but there's still room for improvement.* **2** [C] a change or addition that improves something: *Power steering is just one of the improvements to be found in the new 160cc model.* **3 be an improvement on** to be better than something similar that existed before: *The new electronic controls are a big improvement on the old system.*

**im·prov·i·dent** /ɪmˈprɒvɪ̈dənt‖-ˈprɑː-/ *adj formal* too careless to save any money or to plan for the future: *the generous but improvident welfare provision of the 1960s* —**improvidence** *n* [U] —**improvidently** *adv*

**im·pro·vise** /ˈɪmprəvaɪz/ *v* **1** [I] to do something without any preparation, because you are forced to do this by unexpected events: *I forgot to bring the notes for my speech, so I just had to improvise.* **2** [T] to make something by using whatever you can find because you do not have the equipment or materials that you need: *We improvised a crude shelter using branches.* **3** [I] to perform music, DRAMA or COMEDY that comes straight from your imagination and has never been performed before: *You can't be a good jazz musician if you can't improvise.* —**improvisation** /ˌɪmprəvaɪˈzeɪʃən‖ɪmˌprɑːvə-/ *n* [C,U]

**im·pru·dent** /ɪmˈpruːdənt/ *adj formal* not sensible or wise: *It would be rather imprudent to invest in an arms company at the moment.* —**imprudently** *adv* —**imprudence** *n* [C,U]

**im·pugn** /ɪmˈpjuːn/ *v* [T] *formal* to express doubts about someone's honesty, courage, ability etc: *The honour of our country has been grossly impugned!*

**im·pulse** /ˈɪmpʌls/ *n* **1** [C,U] a sudden strong desire to do something before thinking whether it is a sensible thing to do: **impulse to do sth** *Gerry couldn't resist the impulse to skip work and go down to the beach.* | **on impulse** (=because of an impulse) *She had invited Joseph on a sudden impulse but was now regretting it.* | **impulse buying** (=buying things without planning or choosing carefully) **2** [C] an aim or reason that causes a particular kind of activity or behaviour: *The prime impulse of capitalism is the making of money.* **3** [C] *technical* a single push or force moving for a short time in one direction along a nerve or electric wire

**im·pul·sion** /ɪmˈpʌlʃən/ *n* [U] a sudden strong desire to do something

**im·pul·sive** /ɪmˈpʌlsɪv/ *adj* tending to do things as soon as you think of them, without considering the possible dangers or problems: *Arthur Morel was a quick, careless, impulsive boy.* | *In a burst of impulsive generosity I offered to pay.* —**impulsively** *adv* —**impulsiveness** *n* [U]

**im·pu·ni·ty** /ɪmˈpjuːnɪ̈ti/ *n* **do sth with impunity** if you do something wrong or immoral with impunity, there is no risk that you will be punished for it: *Men used to be able to violently abuse their wives with almost total impunity.*

**im·pure** /ɪmˈpjʊə‖-ˈpjʊr/ *adj* **1** an impure substance has something else mixed with it, especially something of a lower quality: *An added danger was that the group was using impure sodium chlorate in their bombs.* —opposite PURE (1) **2** *old-fashioned or humorous* impure thoughts, feelings etc are morally bad, especially because they are about sex: *He tried, without success, to rid his mind of any impure thoughts about Julia.* —opposite PURE (4)

**im·pu·ri·ty** /ɪmˈpjʊərɪ̈ti‖-ˈpjʊr-/ *n* **1** [C usually plural] part of an almost pure substance that is of a lower quality: *All natural minerals contain impurities.* **2** [U] the state of being impure

**im·pu·ta·tion** /ˌɪmpjʊ̈ˈteɪʃən/ *n formal* **1** [C] a statement that someone is guilty of a crime or of doing something bad: *It was the first time she had confronted him with such direct imputations.* **2** [U] **[+ of]** the act of imputing something

**im·pute** /ɪmˈpjuːt/ *v*

**impute** sth **to** sb/sth *phr v* [T] *formal* to say, often unfairly, that someone or something is responsible for something that has happened: *The police were not guilty of the violence imputed to them.* —**imputable** *adj* —**imputation** /ˌɪmpjʊˈteɪʃən/ *n* [C,U]

**in-** /ɪn/ *prefix* in some adjectives and nouns, shows a negative, an opposite, or a lack; not: *insensitive* (=not sensitive) | *inattention* (=lack of attention) —compare UN-

**-in** /ɪn/ *suffix* [in nouns] an activity in which a group of people do something together for a purpose: *a sit-in* (=where people sit in a place to prevent its usual activity) | *a teach-in*

**in**[1] /ɪn/ *prep* **1** used with the name of a container, place, or area to say where someone or something is: *There's some sugar in the cupboard.* | *My mother was in the kitchen.* | *He spends a lot of time driving round in his car.* | *She spent the day in bed.* | *He spent fifteen years in prison.* **2** used with the names of countries and towns to say where someone or something is: *Mr Fisher is in Boston this week.* | *The taxi man got lost in Manchester.* | *My parents live in New Zealand now.* **3** used with the names of months, years, seasons etc to say when something happens: *He first visited Russia in 1937.* | *These changes first started in the 1840s.* | *He retired in October.* **4** during a period of time: *It was amazing how much we managed to do in a day.* **5** at the end of a period of time: *I'll be with*

*you in a minute.|I think he'll be a millionaire in a year or two.* **6** if you have not done something in several weeks, years etc you have not done it for that period of time: *I haven't enjoyed myself so much in years.* **7** included as part of something: *She said all this in her speech.|Your shouldn't believe everything you read in the newspapers.* **8** working at a particular kind of job: *She used to be a teacher, but she's in marketing now.|He's been in politics for fifteen years.* **9** wearing something: *He looked very handsome in his uniform.|She was dressed in a blue linen suit.* **10** using a particular way of talking or writing: *Her parents always talk to her in German|She shouted my name in a harsh voice.|The children are only allowed to write in pencil.* **11** arranged so as to form a particular shape or group: *The soldiers stood in a line and waited for orders.|People were sitting in small groups chatting.|Arrange the words in alphabetical order.* **12** used with numbers or amounts to show a proportion: *One in every 10 children now suffers from asthma* **13** used to show a connection between two things: *We need a further increase in investment.|Milk is very rich in calcium.|She never showed any interest in music.|an expert in human biology* **14** used to show the feelings you have when you do something: *She looked at me in horror.|It was all done purely in fun.* **15** used to say how one person should consider another: *You've got a very good friend in Pat.|We have a very good candidate in Peter Dobrowski* **16 in that** because: *The situation is rather complicated in that we have two managing directors.* **17 in all** used when giving a total amount: *There were about 800 people in all.* **18 in doing sth** when or by doing something: *In raising money to support her work, Baker made contact with many organisations that were sympathetic to her ideas.*

**in²** *adv* **1** so as to be contained inside something or surrounded by it: *She opened the cupboard and put the tins in.|He picked up a glass and poured some water in.* **2** inside a building, especially the building where you live or work: *I'm afraid Mr Stewart won't be in until tomorrow morning.|She's never in when I call.|We're staying in this evening.* **3** if a train, boat, or plane is in, it has arrived at a station, aiport etc: *Our train's not in yet.|When's her flight due in?* **4** if you send something in, you send it to an organization, where it will be dealt with: *All entries must be in by next week.|Letters have been pouring in from all over the country.* **5** if you write, paint, or draw something in, you add it: *Fill in your name and address on the form provided.|The information is typed in by trained keyboarders.* **6** if clothes, colours etc are in, they are fashionable: *Stripes are definitely in this summer.* **7** if a person or team is in, they are batting (BAT² (1)) in a game such as CRICKET (2): *Surrey have chosen to go in first.* **8** if a ball is in during a game, it is inside the area where the game is being played: *Her second serve was just in.* **9 be in for sth** if someone is in for something unpleasant, it is going to happen to them: *I'm afraid he's in for a bit of a disappointment.* **10 be in for it** *informal* if someone is in for it, they are going to be punished: *We're really in for it now.* **11 be/get in on sth** to be involved in something that is happening: *I think you ought to be in on this discussion, Ted.* **12 have (got) it in for sb** *informal* if someone has got it in for you, they do not like you and want to cause problems or difficulties for you: *I think the teacher's really got it in for me.* **13** if something falls or turns in, it falls or turns towards the centre: *The map had started to curl in at the edges.* **14** if a boat or the TIDE¹ (I) comes in, it comes towards the shore: *The tide was coming in.|The boat drifted in to the shore.* **15 be in with sb** *informal* to be friendly with someone: *She's in with the theatrical crowd.* **16 be in at sth** to be present when something happens: *I was lucky enough to be in at the start of the research project.*

**in³** *adj* **1** *informal* clothes or colours that are in are fashionable: *Red is definitely the in colour this year.|Long skirts are in at the moment.* **2** [only before a noun] an in joke is a private joke that is understood by only a small group of people

**in·a·bil·i·ty** /ˌɪnəˈbɪlᵻti/ *n* [singular, U] the fact of being unable to do something: *the government's inability to control inflation*

**in·ac·ces·si·ble** /ˌɪnəkˈsesᵻbəl◂/ *adj* **1** difficult or impossible to reach: *These mountain villages are completely inaccessible in winter.* **2** difficult or impossible to understand or afford: *an inaccessible subject such as theoretical nuclear physics* —**inaccessibly** *adv* —**inaccessibility** /ˌɪnəksesᵻˈbɪlᵻti/ *n* [U]

**in·ac·cu·ra·cy** /ɪnˈækjᵿrəsi/ *n* **1** [C] a statement that is not completely correct: *I think your report contained various inaccuracies and half-truths.* **2** [U] a lack of correctness: *As a journalist you simply cannot tolerate inaccuracy.*

**in·ac·cu·rate** /ɪnˈækjᵿrᵻt/ *adj* not completely correct: *an inaccurate translation of the French* —**inaccurately** *adv*

**in·ac·tion** /ɪnˈækʃən/ *n* [U] the fact that someone is not doing anything: *Several newspapers have criticized the President for his inaction.*

**in·ac·tive** /ɪnˈæktɪv/ *adj* not doing anything or not working —**inactivity** /ˌɪnækˈtɪvᵻti/ *n* [U]

**in·ad·e·qua·cy** /ɪnˈædᵻkwᵻsi/ *n* **1** [U] a feeling that you are unable to deal with situations because you are not as good as other people: *Unemployment can often cause feelings of inadequacy and low self-esteem.* **2** [U] the fact of not being good enough in quality, ability, size etc for a particular purpose: [+ **of**] *the inadequacy of local health care* **3** [C] a fault or weakness in your character: *I'm quite aware of my own inadequacies.*

**in·ad·e·quate** /ɪnˈædᵻkwᵻt/ *adj* **1** not good enough, big enough, skilled enough etc for a particular purpose: *An inadequate supply of vitamin A can lead to blindness.|* [+ **for**] *The parking facilities are inadequate for such a busy shopping centre.* **2** someone who feels inadequate feels unable to deal with situations because they think they are not as good as other people: *The teacher made us feel inadequate and stupid if we made mistakes.* —**inadequately** *adv*

**in·ad·mis·si·ble** /ˌɪnədˈmɪsᵻbəl◂/ *adj formal* **inadmissible evidence** information that is not allowed to be used in a court of law —**inadmissibly** *adj* —**inadmissibility** /ˌɪnədmɪsᵻˈbɪlᵻti/ *n* [U]

**in·ad·vert·ent·ly** /ˌɪnədˈvɜːtəntli‖-ɜːr-/ *adv* without realizing what you are doing: *I inadvertently stepped on his toe.* —**inadvertent** *adj: the inadvertent disclosure of sensitive information* —**inadvertence** *n* [C,U]

**in·ad·vis·a·ble** /ˌɪnədˈvaɪzəbəl◂/ *adj* an action that is inadvisable is not sensible; unwise: *It is inadvisable to climb in these mountains on your own.*

**in·a·li·e·na·ble** /ɪnˈeɪliənəbəl/ *adj formal* an inalienable right cannot be taken away from you

**i·nam·o·ra·ta** /ɪˌnæməˈrɑːtə/ *n* [C] *literary or humorous* the woman that a man loves

**i·nane** /ɪˈneɪn/ *adj* extremely stupid or without much meaning: *inane remarks|an inane conversation* —**inanely** *adv* —**inanity** /ɪˈnænᵻti/ *n* [C,U]

**in·an·i·mate** /ɪnˈænᵻmᵻt/ *adj* not living: *A rock is an inanimate object.*

**in·ap·pli·ca·ble** /ˌɪnəˈplɪkəbəl, ɪnˈæplɪkəbəl‖ɪnˈæplɪ-/ *adj* a description, question, or rule that is inapplicable to a particular subject cannot sensibly be used about it: [+ **to**] *These new regulations are inapplicable to us.* —**inapplicability** /ˌɪnəplɪkəˈbɪlᵻti, ɪnˌæplɪkə-‖ɪnˌæplɪkə-/ *n* [U]

**in·ap·pro·pri·ate** /ˌɪnəˈprəʊpri-ᵻt‖-ˈproʊ-/ *adj* **1** not suitable for a particular purpose or situation: *I thought his comments were wholly inappropriate on such a solemn occasion.|*[+ **for**] *an inappropriate gift for a child* **2** not correct according to generally accepted rules of social, moral, or professional behaviour: *It would be* *inappropriate for me to discuss her case at this meeting.* —**inappropriately** *adv: inappropriately dressed* —**inappropriateness** also **inappropriacy** *n* [U]

**in·apt** /ɪn'æpt/ *adj formal* an inapt phrase, statement etc is not right for a particular situation: *a very inapt comment* —compare INEPT —**inaptly** *adv* —**inaptness** *n* [U]

**in·ar·tic·u·late** /ˌɪnɑː'tɪkjələt◂‖-ɑːr-/ *adj* **1** not able to express yourself clearly when you speak **2** speech that is inarticulate is not clearly expressed or pronounced: *inarticulate mutterings* —**inarticulately** *adv* —**inarticulateness** also **inarticulacy** *n* [C,U]

**in·as·much** /ˌɪnəz'mʌtʃ/ *adv formal* **inasmuch as** used to introduce an additional phrase that explains the rest of your sentence or says in what limited way it is true: *Anne is also guilty, inasmuch as she knew what the others were planning.*

**in·at·ten·tion** /ˌɪnə'tenʃən/ *n* [U] lack of attention: [+ **to**] *inattention to detail*

**in·at·ten·tive** /ˌɪnə'tentɪv◂/ *adj* not giving enough attention to someone or something: *an inattentive student* —**inattentively** *adv* —**inattentiveness** *n* [U]

**in·au·di·ble** /ɪn'ɔːdəbəl‖-'ɒː-/ *adj* too quiet to be heard: *inaudible muttering* —**inaudibly** *adv* —**inaudibility** /ɪnˌɔːdə'bɪləti‖-ˌɒː-/ *n* [U]

**in·au·gu·ral** /ɪ'nɔːgjərəl‖ɪ'nɒː-/ *adj* [only before noun] **1 inaugural speech/lecture** the first speech given by someone starting an important job, such as a president or a university PROFESSOR **2 inaugural meeting/concert etc** the first in a series of meetings, concerts etc

**in·au·gu·rate** /ɪ'nɔːgjəreɪt‖-'nɒː-/ *v* [T] **1** if an event inaugurates an important change or period of time, it comes at the beginning of it: *The International Trade Agreement inaugurated a period of high economic growth.* **2** to introduce a new person into an important job such as that of president, by holding a special ceremony **3** to open a building or service for the first time or to start a public event with a ceremony —**inauguration** /ɪˌnɔːgjə'reɪʃən‖ɪˌnɒː-/ *n* [C,U] *Eight months after Hoover's inauguration came the Wall Street Crash.*

**in·aus·pi·cious** /ˌɪnɔː'spɪʃəs◂‖ˌɪnɒː-/ *adj formal* seeming to show that future success is unlikely: *an inauspicious start to the journey* —**inauspiciously** *adv*

**in-be·tween** /ˌ· ·'·◂/ *adj informal* in the middle between two points, sizes, periods of time etc: *Neither the 12 nor the 14 fits properly – I must be an in-between size.*

**in·board** /'ɪnbɔːd‖-bɔːrd/ *n* [C] a motor inside a boat —compare OUTBOARD MOTOR

**in·born** /ˌɪn'bɔːn◂‖-ɔːrn◂/ *adj* an inborn quality or ability is one that you have had naturally since birth: *Lincoln had an inborn sense of the truth.*

**in·bound** /'ɪnbaʊnd/ *adj AmE* an inbound flight or train is coming towards the place where you are

**in-bounds** /ˌ· '·◂/ *adj AmE* if the ball is in-bounds in a sport, it is in the playing area

**in·bred** /ˌɪn'bred◂/ *adj* **1** having developed as a natural part of your character: *an inbred responsiveness to music* **2** produced by INBREEDING

**in·breed·ing** /'ɪnbriːdɪŋ/ *n* [U] the producing of children, animals, or new plants from closely related members of the same family

**in·built** /'ɪnbɪlt/ *adj especially BrE* an inbuilt quality, feature etc is part of the character of someone or something and cannot be removed: *an organization with an inbuilt tendency to expand*

**Inc** /ɪŋk; *formal* ɪn'kɔːpəreɪtəd‖-ɔːr-/ the written abbreviation of INCORPORATED; used in the US after the name of a company to show that it has become a CORPORATION (1): *General Motors Inc* —compare LTD, PLC

**in·cal·cu·la·ble** /ɪn'kælkjələbəl/ *adj* too many or too great to be calculated: *A scandal of this nature would do the school incalculable harm.* —**incalculably** *adv*

**in·can·des·cent** /ˌɪnkæn'desənt◂‖-kən-/ *adj* **1** giving a bright light when heated **2 incandescent with rage** *BrE* extremely angry —**incandescence** *n* [U]

**in·can·ta·tion** /ˌɪnkæn'teɪʃən/ *n* [C, U] the set of special words that someone uses in magic, or the act of saying these words

**in·ca·pa·ble** /ɪn'keɪpəbəl/ *adj* **1** [not before noun] unable to do something or to feel a particular emotion: [+ **of**] *incapable of understanding even the simplest instructions*|*incapable of pity* **2** weak and unable to care for yourself —**incapably** *adv* —**incapability** /ɪnˌkeɪpə'bɪləti/ *n* [U]

**in·ca·pa·ci·tate** /ˌɪnkə'pæsəteɪt/ *v* [T often passive] if something such as an illness or accident incapacitates you, it makes you too ill or weak to live and work normally: *He was permanently incapacitated after the accident.* —**incapacitation** /ˌɪnkəpæsə'teɪʃən/ *n* [U]

**in·ca·pa·ci·ty** /ˌɪnkə'pæsəti/ *n* [singular, U] **1** the condition of being too ill or weak to live and work normally: *temporary incapacity through illness* **2** the inability to do something: *the author's incapacity to convey his ideas*

**in·car·ce·rate** /ɪn'kɑːsəreɪt‖-ɑːr-/ *v* [T usually passive] *formal* to keep someone in a place, especially a prison —**incarceration** /ɪnˌkɑːsə'reɪʃən‖-ˌkɑːr-/ *n* [U]

**in·car·nate¹** /ɪn'kɑːnət‖-ɑːr-/ *adj* [only after noun] **evil/wisdom/the devil etc incarnate** someone who is considered to be the human form of evil, wisdom etc

**incarnate²** /'ɪnkɑːneɪt‖-ɑːr-/ *v* [T] *formal* **1** to be the human form of a particular quality **2** to make something appear in a human form

**in·car·na·tion** /ˌɪnkɑː'neɪʃən‖-ɑːr-/ *n* **1** [C] the period of time, according to some religions, during which someone is alive in the form of a particular person or animal: *She believed that in a previous incarnation she had been an Egyptian queen.* **2 be the incarnation of goodness/evil/sweetness** to perfectly represent goodness etc in human form: *She was the incarnation of perfect wisdom.* **3 the Incarnation** the act of God coming to Earth in the human form of Jesus Christ, according to the Christian religion

**in·cau·tious** /ɪn'kɔːʃəs‖-'kɒː-/ *adj* done or said without thinking about the possible effects, and therefore causing problems: *incautious remarks* —**incautiously** *adv*

**in·cen·di·a·ry¹** /ɪn'sendiəri‖-dieri/ *adj* [only before noun] **1 incendiary bomb/device/attack etc** designed to cause a fire **2** an incendiary speech or piece of writing is intended to make people angry and is likely to cause trouble

**incendiary²** *n* [C] a bomb designed to cause a fire

**in·cense¹** /'ɪnsens/ *n* [U] a substance which has a pleasant smell when you burn it, and which is used in religious ceremonies

**incense²** /ɪn'sens/ *v* [T] to make someone extremely angry: *Spectators, incensed by the referee's decision, ran onto the field.*

**in·censed** /ɪn'senst/ *adj* extremely angry: *When I reported the matter to Stalin, he became incensed.*

**in·cen·tive** /ɪn'sentɪv/ *n* [C,U] something which encourages you to work harder, start new activities etc: *With prices so low there is little incentive for the farmers.*| **incentive to do sth** *The chance of a higher salary gives young people the incentive to work harder.*|**tax incentives** (=offers of reduced taxes) S3

**in·cep·tion** /ɪn'sepʃən/ *n* [singular] *formal* the start of an organization or institution: *a history of the Labour Party from its inception to the present day*

**in·ces·sant** /ɪn'sesənt/ *adj* an incessant activity, noise etc continues without stopping, in an annoying way: *The child's incessant talking started to irritate her.* —**incessantly** *adv*

**in·cest** /'ɪnsest/ *n* [U] illegal sex between people who are closely related, for example between a brother and sister, or father and daughter

**in·ces·tu·ous** /ɪnˈsestʃuəs/ *adj* **1** an incestuous relationship is a sexual relationship between people who are closely related in a family **2** an incestuous relationship is one in which a small group of people or organizations only help each other, in a way that is unfair to other people: *the incestuous relationship between sport and television* —**incestuously** *adv* —**incestuousness** *n* [U]

S2 W3 **inch¹** /ɪntʃ/ *n* [C] **1** a unit for measuring length, equal to 2.54 centimetres —see tables on pages B2 and B3 **2** a very small distance: *A bullet thudded into the wall only inches from where I was standing.* | *The bus missed our car by inches.* (=almost hit it) **3** enough rain or snow to cover an area an inch deep: *Over five inches of rain has fallen in the last week.* **4 every inch a)** completely or in every way: *He looked every inch a gentleman.* **b)** the whole of an area: [+ **of**] *They're determined to defend every inch of their territory.* **5 give sb an inch and they'll take a yard/mile** used to say that if you allow someone a little freedom or power, they'll try to take a lot more **6 inch by inch** moving very gradually and slowly: *Inch by inch the soldiers were driven back.* **7 not give/budge an inch** to refuse to change your opinion even slightly about something in spite of attempts to persuade you: *Neither side is prepared to give an inch in the negotiations.* **8 beat/thrash sb within an inch of their life** to hit someone so hard and so many times that you almost kill them

**inch²** *v* [I always + adv/prep, T always + adv/prep] to move very slowly in a particular direction, or make something do this: [+ **along/towards/around etc**] *I started inching forward along the ledge towards the open window.* | **inch sth along/towards etc** *He slowly inched the box forward, unable to lift it.*

**in·cho·ate** /ɪnˈkəʊɪ̈t‖-ˈkoʊ-/ *adj formal* inchoate ideas, plans, attitudes etc are only just starting to develop

**in·ci·dence** /ˈɪnsɪ̈dəns/ *n* [singular] *formal* the number of times something bad happens, for example how many people have a particular illness or how many crimes there are: *a survey to determine the incidence of heart defects among premature babies* | *the high incidence of alcoholism among the unemployed*

W2 **in·ci·dent** /ˈɪnsɪ̈dənt/ *n* [C] **1** something that happens, especially something that is unusual: *After the children had been punished, nobody mentioned the incident again.* | **without incident** (=without anything unusual or unpleasant happening) *Despite my fears the meal passed without incident.* **2** a serious or violent event that causes disagreement: *a major diplomatic incident*

**in·ci·den·tal¹** /ˌɪnsɪ̈ˈdentl◂/ *adj* **1** happening or existing in connection with something else that is more important: *minor incidental details* | **incidental expenses** (=small expenses connected with a particular activity): *Keep a record of any incidental expenses on your trip.* **2** [not before noun] happening as a result of something in a way that can be expected: [+ **to**] *Drinking too much is almost incidental to bartending.*

**incidental²** *n* [C usually plural] something that you have to do, buy etc which you had not planned to do or buy: *It's useful to carry extra cash for taxis, tips and other incidentals.*

S3 **in·ci·den·tal·ly** /ˌɪnsɪ̈ˈdentəli/ *adv* **1** [sentence adverb] used when adding more information to what was said before, or when you want to talk about something else you have just thought of: *a beautiful town which, incidentally, is where they filmed 'The French Lieutenant's Woman'* | *Incidentally, this wine goes particularly well with cheese.* **2** happening in a way that was not planned, but as a result of something else: *Quite incidentally, I found out some very useful information at the party.*

**incidental mu·sic** /ˌ····ˈ··/ *n* [U] music played during a play, film etc in order to give the right feeling

**in·cin·e·rate** /ɪnˈsɪnəreɪt/ *v* [T usually passive] to burn something completely in order to destroy it: *All the infected clothing was incinerated.* —**incineration** /ɪnˌsɪnəˈreɪʃən/ *n* [U]

**in·cin·e·ra·tor** /ɪnˈsɪnəreɪtə‖-ər/ *n* [C] a machine designed to burn things at a very high temperature in order to destroy them

**in·cip·i·ent** /ɪnˈsɪpiənt/ *adj* [only before noun] *formal* starting to happen or exist: *those tiny yawns that are sure signs of incipient boredom* —**incipiently** *adv*

**in·cise** /ɪnˈsaɪz/ *v technical* **1** [T + **in/into**] to cut a pattern or mark into a surface **2** [T] to cut carefully into something with a sharp knife

**in·ci·sion** /ɪnˈsɪʒən/ *n* [C,U] a cut into something, especially into someone's body using a special knife during a medical operation, or the act of making this kind of cut: *The incision was carefully stitched and bandaged.*

**in·ci·sive** /ɪnˈsaɪsɪv/ *adj* words, remarks etc that are incisive are very clear and direct and deal immediately with the most important part of a subject: *Her questions were well-formulated and incisive.* —**incisively** *adv* —**incisiveness** *n* [U]

**in·ci·sor** /ɪnˈsaɪzə‖-ər/ *n* [C] one of the teeth at the front of your mouth which have a sharp edge —compare CANINE TOOTH, MOLAR —see picture at TEETH

**in·cite** /ɪnˈsaɪt/ *v* [T] to deliberately encourage people to cause trouble, fight, argue etc: **incite sb to do sth** *He was charged with inciting the students to riot.* | **incite sb to sth** *inflammatory articles that incited people to violence and hatred* —**incitement** *n* [U]

**in·ci·vil·i·ty** /ˌɪnsɪ̈ˈvɪlɪ̈ti/ *n* [U] *formal* impolite behaviour

**in·clem·ent** /ɪnˈklemənt/ *adj formal* inclement weather is unpleasant because it is cold, rainy etc —**inclemency** *n* [U]

**in·cli·na·tion** /ˌɪŋklɪ̈ˈneɪʃən/ *n*
**1 ▶ DESIRE ◀** [C,U] a feeling that makes you want to do something: *You always follow your own inclinations instead of considering other people's feelings.* | **inclination to do sth** *I have not the slightest inclination to take unnecessary risks.*
**2 ▶ TENDENCY ◀** [C,U] tendency to think or behave in a particular way: **inclination to do sth** *an inclination to see everything in political terms*
**3 inclination of the head** the movement of bending your neck so that your head is lowered: *With a slight inclination of the head she showed her approval.*
**4 ▶ SLOPE ◀** [C,U] *formal* a slope or the angle at which something slopes

**in·cline¹** /ɪnˈklaɪn/ *v* [not in progressive] *formal*
**1 ▶ TEND TO DO STH ◀ a)** to think that a particular belief or opinion is most likely to be right: [+ **to/towards**] *He has always inclined to the belief that all men are capable of great evil.* | **incline to do sth** *I incline to accept the official version of events.* **b)** to tend to behave in a particular way or to show a particular quality: [+ **to/towards**] *The child has always inclined towards laziness.*

**2 ▶ INFLUENCE ◀** [T] if a situation, fact etc inclines you to do or think something, it influences you towards a particular action or opinion: **incline sb to do sth** *I know that you acted hastily, but that does not incline me to forgive you.*
**3 incline your head** to bend your neck so that your head is lowered
**4 ▶ TO SLOPE ◀** [I,T] to be sloping at a particular angle or to make something do this

**in·cline²** /ˈɪnklaɪn/ *n* [C] a slope: *a steep incline*

**in·clined** /ɪnˈklaɪnd/ *adj* S3
**1 ▶ TENDING TO DO STH ◀** [not before noun] tending to behave in a particular way: **be inclined to do sth** *She's inclined to tell lies.*
**2 be inclined to agree/think/believe etc** to have a particular opinion but not to hold it very strongly: *Arthur has some strange ideas, but on this occasion I'm inclined to agree with him.*
**3 ▶ WISHING TO DO SOMETHING ◀** [not before noun] wanting to do something: **inclined to do sth** *You can even swim in the lake – if you feel inclined to.*
**4 mathematically/linguistically/musically inclined** naturally interested in or good at something such as

mathematics or languages: *We sent her to the Arts school because she's very musically inclined.* **5 ▸ SLOPING ◂** sloping or leaning in a particular direction

**in·close** /ɪnˈkləʊz‖-ˈkloʊz/ *v* [T] another spelling of ENCLOSE

**in·clos·ure** /ɪnˈkləʊʒə‖-ˈkloʊʒər/ *n* [C,U] another spelling of ENCLOSURE

S2 W1 **in·clude** /ɪnˈkluːd/ *v* [T] **1** [not in progressive] if a group or a set includes something or someone, it has that thing or person as one of its parts: *Our tour party included several retired couples.* | *The price includes postage charges.* —see COMPRISE (USAGE) **2** to make someone or something part of a larger group or set: *The team is looking strong, especially now they have included Roscoe.* | **include sth in/on etc** *Teachers must include attendance figures in their monthly reports.* | *Is service included in the bill?* **3 include me out** *spoken* a humorous way of saying you do not want to be included in a group —opposite EXCLUDE

**in·clud·ed** /ɪnˈkluːdɪ̵d/ *adj* [only after noun] **myself/John etc included** including myself, John etc: *Everyone has to go to the dentist's, you included.*

S2 W1 **in·clud·ing** /ɪnˈkluːdɪŋ/ *prep* used to introduce something or someone that is included in the larger group or amount you have just mentioned: *There were twelve of us, including me and Tom.* | *£25.50 including postage and packing* —opposite EXCLUDING

**in·clu·sion** /ɪnˈkluːʒən/ *n* **1** [U] the act of including someone or something in a larger group or set, or the fact of being included in one: *His inclusion in the team has caused a lot of controversy.* **2** [C] someone or something that has been included in a larger group or set: *With the recent inclusions there will be 28 delegates in all.*

**in·clu·sive** /ɪnˈkluːsɪv/ *adj* **1** an inclusive price or cost includes everything: *an all-inclusive charge* | [+ **of**] *The rent is £50 a week, inclusive of heating and lighting.* **2 April to June inclusive/15 to 20 inclusive, etc** including April, June and all the months between them, 15 and 20 and all the numbers between them etc

**USAGE NOTE: INCLUSIVE**

AmE-BrE DIFFERENCE

Where British English speakers might use **inclusive** in this way: *Monday to Friday inclusive*, American speakers may use **through**: *Monday through Friday*

**in·cog·ni·to** /ˌɪnkɒgˈniːtəʊ‖ˌɪnkɑːgˈniːtoʊ/ *adv* if a famous person travels incognito, they travel without letting people know who they are

**in·co·her·ent** /ˌɪnkəʊˈhɪərənt◂‖-koʊˈhɪr-/ *adj* **1** thoughts, ideas etc that are incoherent are very badly expressed or badly arranged and are difficult to understand: *At times the narrative is completely incoherent.* **2** speaking unclearly: *As the child's temperature soared she became incoherent.* —**incoherently** *adv* —**incoherence** *n* [U]

S2 W1 **in·come** /ˈɪŋkʌm, ˈɪn-/ *n* [C,U] the money that you earn from your work or that you receive from INVESTMENTS: *Most of my income goes on my rent.* | **be on a high/low income**: *It's only reasonable that people on a high income should pay more tax.* | **live within your income** (=to not spend more than you earn) | **unearned income** (=income from property, INVESTMENTS etc) —compare EXPENDITURE (1) —see PAY[1] (USAGE)

**income tax** /ˈ·· ·/ *n* [U] tax paid on the money that you earn

**in·com·ing** /ˈɪnkʌmɪŋ/ *adj* [only before noun] **1** arriving or coming in: *incoming flights* | *the incoming tide* **2** an incoming president, government etc has just been elected or chosen: *It is hoped that the incoming administration will inject some life into Capitol Hill.*

**in·com·mode** /ˌɪnkəˈməʊd‖-ˈmoʊd/ *v* [T] *formal* to make a situation difficult for someone

**in·com·mo·di·ous** /ˌɪnkəˈməʊdiəs◂‖-ˈmoʊ-/ *adj formal* inconvenient, difficult, or uncomfortable

**in·com·mu·ni·ca·do** /ˌɪnkəmjuːnɪˈkɑːdəʊ‖-doʊ/ *adv* if you are kept incommunicado, you are kept in a place where you cannot see or talk to anyone else: *The men were arrested and held incommunicado in prison camps.*

**in·com·pa·ra·ble** /ɪnˈkɒmpərəbəl‖-ˈkɑːm-/ *adj* so good, beautiful etc that nothing else can even be compared to it: *a writer of incomparable prose* | *the incomparable view of San Marco* —**incomparably** *adv*

**in·com·pat·i·ble** /ˌɪnkəmˈpætɪ̵bəl◂/ *adj* **1** two people who are incompatible have completely different characters so that it is difficult for them to have a good relationship: *God knows why they ever got married. They're totally incompatible!* **2** two beliefs, statements, actions etc that are incompatible cannot exist or be accepted together because they are completely different: [+ **with**] *His business interests are incompatible with his presidential responsibilities.* **3** two things that are incompatible are of different types so that they cannot be used together: *Their blood groups were incompatible.* —**incompatibly** *adv* —**incompatibility** /ˌɪnkəmpætɪ̵ˈbɪlɪ̵ti/ *n* [U]

**in·com·pe·tence** /ɪnˈkɒmpɪ̵təns‖-ˈkɑːm-/ *n* [U] lack of the ability or skill to do your job properly: *The manager in charge was fired for incompetence.*

**in·com·pe·tent** /ɪnˈkɒmpɪ̵tənt‖-ˈkɑːm-/ *adj* not having the ability or skill to do your job properly: *an incompetent teacher* —**incompetent** *n* [C] —**incompetently** *adv*

**in·com·plete** /ˌɪnkəmˈpliːt◂/ *adj* **1** not having all its parts: *Unfortunately I do not have the information because our records are incomplete.* **2** not completely finished: *an incomplete process* —**incompletely** *adv* —**incompleteness** *n* [U]

**in·com·pre·hen·si·ble** /ɪnˌkɒmprɪˈhensɪ̵bəl‖-ˌkɑːm-/ *adj* difficult or impossible to understand: *Legal documents are full of incomprehensible jargon.* | *I find your whole attitude quite incomprehensible.* —**incomprehensibly** *adv* —**incomprehensibility** /ɪnˌkɒmprɪhensɪ̵ˈbɪlɪ̵ti‖-ˌkɑːm-/ *n* [U]

**in·com·pre·hen·sion** /ɪnˌkɒmprɪˈhenʃən‖-ˌkɑːm-/ *n* [U] the state of not being able to understand something: *"Are you leaving me?" she cried, her face full of incomprehension and rage.*

**in·con·cei·va·ble** /ˌɪnkənˈsiːvəbəl/ *adj* too strange or unusual to be thought real or possible: *A few years ago a car fuelled by solar energy would have been inconceivable.* | **it is inconceivable that** *It seemed inconceivable that a man in such a powerful position could be so stupid.* —**inconceivably** *adv* —**inconceivability** /ˌɪnkənsiːvəˈbɪlɪ̵ti/ *n* [U]

**in·con·clu·sive** /ˌɪnkənˈkluːsɪv◂/ *adj* not leading to a clear decision or result: *The evidence against the two men was inconclusive.* | *The talks were inconclusive and both parties agreed to further meetings.* —**inconclusively** *adv* —**inconclusiveness** *n* [U]

**in·con·gru·i·ty** /ˌɪnkənˈgruːɪ̵ti/ *n* **1** [U] strangeness, especially in being unsuitable, unusual, or unexpected in relation to the things around: *He was suddenly struck by the incongruity of drinking champagne out of plastic glasses.* **2** [C] an act or event which seems strange or unsuitable because it seems very different from what is happening around it

**in·con·gru·ous** /ɪnˈkɒŋgruəs‖-ˈkɑːŋ-/ *adj* something that is incongruous seems strange and unsuitable because it is so unexpected in a particular situation and so different from everything around it: *The modern building looked incongruous in such a quaint old village.* —**incongruously** *adv* —**incongruousness** *n* [U]

**in·con·se·quen·tial** /ɪnˌkɒnsɪ̵ˈkwenʃəl◂‖-ˌkɑːn-/ *adj* not important; INSIGNIFICANT: *He made a few inconsequential remarks before moving on to the next guests.* —**inconsequentially** *adv*

**in·con·sid·e·ra·ble** /ˌɪnkənˈsɪdərəbəl◂/ *adj* **not inconsiderable** *formal* fairly large or important: *He has built up a not inconsiderable business empire.*

**in·con·sid·er·ate** /ˌɪnkənˈsɪdərɪ̈t◂/ *adj* not caring about the feelings, needs or comfort of other people: *It was inconsiderate of him to keep us waiting like that.* —**inconsiderately** *adv*

**in·con·sis·ten·cy** /ˌɪnkənˈsɪstənsi/ *n* **1** [U] changes in someone's behaviour or reactions that make their ideas, wishes etc unclear: *Inconsistency in management creates unnecessary anxieties among the workforce.* **2** [C usually plural] two statements that cannot both be true because they each state the facts differently: *There were several inconsistencies in his report.*

**in·con·sis·tent** /ˌɪnkənˈsɪstənt◂/ *adj* **1** ideas or statements that are inconsistent cannot be accepted or believed together because they each state the facts differently: *The accounts of the witnesses are inconsistent.* | [+ **with**] *What the Government says now is inconsistent with its election promises.* **2 be inconsistent with** behaviour that is inconsistent with a particular set of principles or standards is not right according to those principles etc: [+ **with**] *conduct inconsistent with what is expected of a congressman* **3** inconsistent behaviour, work etc changes too often from good to bad or from situation to situation: *The team's performance has been highly inconsistent this season.* | *an inconsistant approach to discipline*

**in·con·so·la·ble** /ˌɪnkənˈsəʊləbəl◂‖-ˈsoʊ-/ *adj* so sad that it is impossible for anyone to comfort you: *The boy was inconsolable after the death of his dog.* —**inconsolably** *adv*: *weeping inconsolably*

**in·con·spic·u·ous** /ˌɪnkənˈspɪkjuəs◂/ *adj* not easily seen or noticed: *She put on an inconspicuous grey dress, hoping she wouldn't be seen in the crowd.* —**inconspicuously** *adv* —**inconspicuousness** *n* [U]

**in·con·stant** /ɪnˈkɒnstənt‖-ˈkɑːn-/ *adj formal* unfaithful in love or friendship: *She was charming, but an inconstant and unreliable friend.* —**inconstancy** *n* [U]

**in·con·tes·ta·ble** /ˌɪnkənˈtestəbəl◂/ *adj* clearly true and impossible to disagree with; INDISPUTABLE: *incontestable evidence of her innocence* —**incontestably** *adv* —**incontestability** /ˌɪnkəntestəˈbɪlɪ̈ti/ *n* [U]

**in·con·ti·nent** /ɪnˈkɒntɪ̈nənt‖-ˈkɑːn-/ *adj* **1** unable to control the passing of food waste from your body **2** *old use* unable to control your sexual urges —**incontinence** *n* [U]

**in·con·tro·ver·ti·ble** /ɪnˌkɒntrəˈvɜːtɪ̈bəl‖ɪnˌkɑːntrəˈvɜːr-/ *adj* a fact that is incontrovertible is definitely true and no one can prove it to be false; INDISPUTABLE: *The photograph provides incontrovertible evidence that Martin was at the scene of the crime.* —**incontrovertibly** *adv* —**incontrovertability** /ɪnˌkɒntrəvɜːtəˈbɪlɪ̈ti‖-ˌkɑːntrəvɜːr-/ *n* [U]

**in·con·ve·ni·ence**[1] /ˌɪnkənˈviːniəns/ *n* **1** [C] something that causes you problems or difficulty: *Compared to the trouble we've had in the past, this is only a minor inconvenience.* **2** [U] the state of having problems or difficulty: *We hope the delay has not caused any inconvenience to our customers.*

**inconvenience**[2] *v* [T] to cause someone problems or difficulty: *I hope it won't inconvenience you to drive me to the station.*

**in·con·ve·ni·ent** /ˌɪnkənˈviːnjənt◂/ *adj* causing problems or difficulty, often in a way that is annoying; not CONVENIENT: *It's a bit inconvenient for me to get to the centre of town. Can we meet somewhere else?* | *an inconvenient time* —**inconveniently** *adv*

3 **in·cor·po·rate** /ɪnˈkɔːpəreɪt‖-ɔːr-/ *v* [T] to include something as part of a group, system, plan etc: **incorporate sth into/in** *We've incorporated many environmentally-friendly features into the design of the building.* | *Our original proposals were not incorporated in the new legislation.* —**incorporation** /ɪnˌkɔːpəˈreɪʃən‖-ɔːr-/ *n* [U]

**in·cor·po·rat·ed** /ɪnˈkɔːpəreɪtɪ̈d‖-ɔːr-/ *written abbreviation* **Inc** *adj* used after the name of a company in the US to show that it has become a CORPORATION (1)

**in·cor·po·re·al** /ˌɪnkɔːˈpɔːriəl‖-kɔːr-/ *adj formal* not existing in any physical form but only as a spirit —**incorporeally** *adv*

**in·cor·rect** /ˌɪnkəˈrekt◂/ *adj* **1** not correct or true: *incorrect spelling* **2** not following the rules of polite behaviour —**incorrectly** *adv* —**incorrectness** *n* [U]

**in·cor·ri·gi·ble** /ɪnˈkɒrɪ̈dʒɪ̈bəl‖-ˈkɔː-/ *adj often humorous* someone who is incorrigible is bad in a way that cannot be changed or improved: **an incorrigible liar/gambler/rogue etc** *Peter, you are an incorrigible flirt!* —**incorrigibly** *adv*

**in·cor·rup·ti·ble** /ˌɪnkəˈrʌptɪ̈bəl◂/ *adj* **1** too honest to be influenced by anything that is illegal or morally wrong: *A good judge must be incorruptible.* **2** *formal* material that is incorruptible will never decay and cannot be destroyed: *Gold was precious because it was incorruptible.* —**incorruptibly** *adv*: *incorruptibly honest* —**incorruptibility** /ˌɪnkərʌptɪ̈ˈbɪlɪ̈ti/ *n* [U] —see also CORRUPT[1]

**in·crease**[1] /ɪnˈkriːs/ *v* **1** [I] to become larger in amount, number, or degree: *The population of London increased dramatically in the first half of the century.* | *The pain increased steadily until I could think of nothing else.* | **increase in value/price/importance etc** *Investments are certain to increase in value.* | [+ **by**] *Food prices increased by 10% in less than a year.* —see RAISE[1] (USAGE) **2** [T] to make something larger in amount, number, or degree: *Now they want to increase our rents!* | *Political tensions that might increase the likelihood of a nuclear war.* —**increasing** *adj*: *There is increasing difficulty in finding trained staff.* —opposite DECREASE[1] —compare REDUCE 

**in·crease**[2] /ˈɪnkriːs/ *n* [C,U] a rise in amount, number, or degree: [+ **in**] *an increase in the crime rate* | **pay/price/tax increase** *Recent tax increases have affected the poor more than the rich.* | **be on the increase** (=be increasing) *Diseases like TB and pneumonia are on the increase.* 

**in·creased** /ɪnˈkriːst/ *adj* larger than before: *an increased awareness of the risks involved* 

**in·creas·ing·ly** /ɪnˈkriːsɪŋli/ *adv* more and more all the time [+ adj/adv]: *The classes at the college have become increasingly full over the past five years.* [sentence adverb]: *Increasingly, it is the industrial power of Japan and South East Asia that dominates world markets.* 

**in·cred·i·ble** /ɪnˈkredɪ̈bəl/ *adj* **1** too strange to be believed or very difficult to believe: *She told us the incredible story of her 134 days lost in the desert.* | *It's incredible how much Tom has changed since he met Sally.* **2** extremely good or extremely large: *Tony has an incredible singing voice.* | *They stock an incredible range of goods.* —**incredibility** /ɪnˌkredɪ̈ˈbɪlɪ̈ti/ *n* [U]

**in·cred·i·bly** /ɪnˈkredɪ̈bli/ *adv* **1** [+adj/adv] extremely: *I'm sorry I haven't phoned. I've been incredibly busy this week.* **2** [sentence adverb] in a way that is hard to believe: *Incredibly, even though the car was a write-off, he wasn't hurt at all.* 

**in·cre·du·li·ty** /ˌɪnkrɪ̈ˈdjuːlɪ̈ti‖-ˈduː-/ *n* [U] a feeling that you cannot believe something; DISBELIEF: *Matt's comment brought a look of complete incredulity to Jill's face.*

**in·cred·u·lous** /ɪnˈkredjʊ̈ləs‖-dʒə-/ *adj* unable or unwilling to believe something: *He raised his eyebrows and gave me an incredulous look.* —**incredulously** *adv*

**in·cre·ment** /ˈɪŋkrɪ̈mənt/ *n* [C] **1** an amount that is regularly added to the amount that someone is paid each year: *The starting salary is £10,000, but with increments it can rise to £16,500.* **2** the amount by which a number, value, or amount increases —**incremental** *adj*

**in·crim·i·nate** /ɪnˈkrɪmɪ̈neɪt/ *v* [T] to make someone seem guilty of a crime: *He refused to speak because he was worried that he would incriminate himself.* | *incriminating evidence* —**incrimination** /ɪnˌkrɪmɪ̈ˈneɪʃən/ *n* [U]

**in·crim·i·na·to·ry** /ɪnˈkrɪmɪ̈nətəri‖-nətɔːri/ *adj* making someone seem to be guilty

**in·crowd** /ˈ· ·/ *n* **the in-crowd** a small group of people who are admired by other people, for example because they are very fashionable, and who do not let many other people join them: *I was never one of the in-crowd at school.*

**in·crus·ta·tion** /ˌɪnkrʌsˈteɪʃən/ *n* [C] an amount of dirt, salt etc which forms a hard layer on a surface: [+ **of**] *an incrustation of salt on the bottom of the boat*

**in·cu·bate** /ˈɪŋkjɡ̈beɪt/ *v* [I,T] **1** if a bird incubates its eggs or if they incubate, they are kept warm by the bird until the young birds come out **2** [I,T] *technical* if a disease incubates, or if you incubate it, it develops in your body until you show physical signs of it

**in·cu·ba·tion** /ˌɪŋkjɡ̈ˈbeɪʃən/ *n* [U] the period between becoming infected with a disease and showing the first physical signs of it

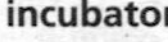

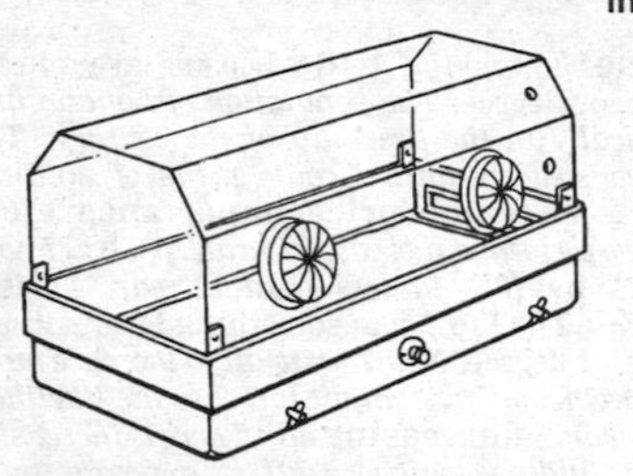

**incubator**

**in·cu·ba·tor** /ˈɪŋkjɡ̈beɪtə‖-ər/ *n* [C] **a)** a heated container for keeping eggs warm until the young birds etc come out **b)** a piece of hospital equipment used for keeping very small or weak babies alive

**in·cu·bus** /ˈɪŋkjɡ̈bəs/ *n* [C] **1** someone or something that causes a lot of worries **2** *literary* a male DEVIL that has sex with a sleeping woman —compare SUCCUBUS **3** *literary* a bad dream; NIGHTMARE (1)

**in·cul·cate** /ˈɪŋkʌlkeɪt‖ɪnˈkʌl-/ *v* [T] *formal* to fix ideas, principles etc in someone's mind: **inculcate sth in/into** *She tries very hard to inculcate traditional values into her students.* | **inculcate sb with sth** *Schools inculcate children with patriotic ideas from an early age.* —**inculcation** /ˌɪŋkʌlˈkeɪʃən/ *n* [U]

**in·cul·pate** /ˈɪŋkʌlpeɪt‖ɪnˈkʌl-/ *v* [T] *formal* to show that someone is guilty of a crime

**in·cum·ben·cy** /ɪnˈkʌmbənsi/ *n* [C] *formal* the period of time during which someone is an incumbent

**in·cum·bent**[1] /ɪnˈkʌmbənt/ *n* [C] *formal* **1** someone in an official position, especially a political one: *Castillo was to be the new incumbent at the City Controller's office.* **2** a priest who is in charge of a church

**incumbent**[2] *adj formal* **1 it is incumbent upon sb to do sth** if it is incumbent upon you to do something, it is your duty or responsibility to do it: *It is incumbent upon the teacher to maintain discipline.* **2 the incumbent president/priest/Senator etc** the president etc at the present time

**in·cur** /ɪnˈkɜː‖-ˈkɜːr/ *v* **incurred, incurring** [T] **1** to put yourself in an unpleasant situation by your own actions, so that you lose something, get punished etc: **incur losses/debts etc** *Milton incurred debts of over $300,000.* | **incur sb's anger/disapproval etc** *We incurred her displeasure.* **2 incur expenses** to have to spend money on something

**in·cur·a·ble** /ɪnˈkjʊərəbəl‖-ˈkjʊr-/ *adj* **1** impossible to cure: *an incurable disease* **2** impossible to change: *My mother is an incurable optimist.* —**incurably** *adv*: *incurably romantic* —**incurable** *n* [C]

**in·cu·ri·ous** /ɪnˈkjʊəriəs‖-ˈkjʊr-/ *adj formal* not naturally interested in finding out about the things around you: *The child watched with an incurious gaze.*

**in·cur·sion** /ɪnˈkɜːʃən, -ʒən‖ɪnˈkɜːrʒən/ *n* [C] *formal* **1** a sudden attack into an area that belongs to other people: *a British and French incursion into China in 1857* **2** the unwanted arrival of something in a place where it does not belong: *the incursion of tabloid-style reporting into such a famous newspaper*

**in·debt·ed** /ɪnˈdetɪ̈d/ *adj* **be indebted to** to be very grateful to someone for the help they have given you: **greatly/deeply indebted** *I am deeply indebted to my husband for helping me edit the book.* —**indebtedness** *n* [U]

**in·de·cen·cy** /ɪnˈdiːsənsi/ *n* [U] *law* behaviour that is sexually offensive, especially INDECENT EXPOSURE: *gross indecency*

**in·de·cent** /ɪnˈdiːsənt/ *adj* **1** indecent behaviour, movements, clothes etc are likely to shock or offend people, because they involve sex or because they show parts of the body that are usually covered: *You can't go to a dinner party in that dress – it's positively indecent!* **2** not acceptable: *The funeral formalities were performed with almost indecent haste.* —**indecently** *adv*: *indecently dressed*

**indecent as·sault** /ˌ·· ·ˈ·/ *n* [C,U] *law* an attack on a person which includes sexual violence

**indecent ex·po·sure** /ˌ·· ·ˈ··/ *n* [U] *law* the criminal offence of deliberately showing your sex organs in a place where this is likely to offend people —see also FLASHER

**in·de·ci·pher·a·ble** /ˌɪndɪˈsaɪfərəbəl◂/ *adj* impossible to read or understand: *an indecipherable signature*

**in·de·ci·sion** /ˌɪndɪˈsɪʒən/ *n* [U] the state of being unable to decide what to do: *tortured by doubt and indecision*

**in·de·ci·sive** /ˌɪndɪˈsaɪsɪv◂/ *adj* **1** unable to make clear decisions or choices: *an indecisive leader* **2** having an unclear result; INCONCLUSIVE: *a confused indecisive battle* —**indecisively** *adv* —**indecisiveness** *n* [U]

**in·dec·o·rous** /ɪnˈdekərəs/ *adj formal* behaving in a way that is not polite or socially acceptable —**indecorously** *adv*

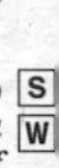

**in·deed** /ɪnˈdiːd/ *adv* **1** [sentence adverb] used to emphasize a statement or answer: *"Would it help if you had an assistant?" "It would, indeed."* | *There are few, if indeed any, authors with such a gift for dialogue.* **2** *formal* used to introduce additional information that emphasizes what you have just said: *I didn't mind at all. Indeed, I was pleased.* **3** *especially BrE* used to emphasize the word 'very' in expressions such as 'very good indeed' and 'very much indeed': *I am very sorry indeed for my foolish behaviour.* | *Thank you very much indeed.* **4** *especially BrE spoken* used to express disbelief, surprise, or annoyance at something you have been told: *"He's taken a three hour lunch break." "Has he, indeed?"* | *"Why would anyone say such a horrible thing?" "Why, indeed?"*

**in·de·fat·i·ga·ble** /ˌɪndɪˈfætɪgəbəl/ *adj formal* determined and never becoming tired: *an indefatigable campaigner for human rights* —**indefatigably** *adv*

**in·de·fen·si·ble** /ˌɪndɪˈfensɪ̈bəl◂/ *adj* **1** too bad to be excused or defended: *indefensible behaviour* **2** impossible or very difficult to defend from military attack —**indefensibly** *adv*

**in·de·fi·na·ble** /ˌɪndɪˈfaɪnəbəl◂/ *adj* an indefinable feeling, quality etc is difficult to describe or explain: *She felt a sudden indefinable sadness.* —**indefinably** *adv*

**in·def·i·nite** /ɪnˈdefənɪ̈t/ *adj* **1** an indefinite action or period of time has no definite end arranged for it: *an indefinite ban on imports of gold* **2** not clear or definite; VAGUE: *indefinite opinions* —**indefiniteness** *n* [U]

**indefinite ar·ti·cle** /ˌ··· ˈ···/ *n* [C] the word 'a' or 'an' in the English language or a word in another language that is used like 'a' or 'an' —compare DEFINITE ARTICLE —see also ARTICLE[1] (4)

**in·def·i·nit·ely** /ɪnˈdefənɪ̈tli/ *adv* **1** for a period of time for which no definite end has been arranged: *Negotiations have been suspended indefinitely.* **2** without giving clear or exact details

**in·del·i·ble** /ɪnˈdelɪ̈bəl/ *adj* **1** impossible to remove or forget; permanent: *The teacher's words left an indelible* *impression on me for years to come.* **2 indelible ink/pencil/marker etc** ink etc that makes a permanent mark which cannot be removed —**indelibly** *adv*: *a moment indelibly imprinted on my mind*

**in·del·i·cate** /ɪnˈdelɪ̣kɪ̣t/ *adj* likely to embarrass or shock people: *He made an indelicate remark at the dinner table.* —**indelicately** *adv* —**indelicacy** *n* [U]

**in·dem·ni·fi·ca·tion** /ɪnˌdemnɪ̣fɪ̣ˈkeɪʃən/ *n law* **1** [U + **for/against**] the act of paying, or promising to pay, someone for loss, injury, or damage **2** [C,U + **for**] a payment made to someone for loss, injury or damage

**in·dem·ni·fy** /ɪnˈdemnɪ̣faɪ/ *v* **indemnified, indemnifying** [T] *law* **1** [+ **against/for**] to promise to pay someone if something they possess is damaged or lost **2** [+ **for**] to pay someone money because of loss, injury, or damage that they have suffered

**in·dem·ni·ty** /ɪnˈdemnɪ̣ti/ *n law* **1** [U] protection against loss or damage, especially in the form of a promise to pay for any losses or damage **2** [C] a payment for the loss of money, goods etc

**in·dent**[1] /ɪnˈdent/ *v* **1** [T] to start a line of writing further towards the middle of the page than other lines **2** [I + **for**] *especially BrE* to order goods by writing on an official form

**indent**[2] /ˈɪndent/ *n* [C + **for**] *especially BrE* **1** an order for goods to be sent abroad, or for supplies for an army **2** an official written order for goods

**in·den·ta·tion** /ˌɪndenˈteɪʃən/ *n* [C] **1** a cut into the surface or edge of something: *The bite left deep indentations.* **2** a space at the beginning of a line of writing **3** [C,U] *especially BrE* the act of indenting

**in·dent·ed** /ɪnˈdentɪ̣d/ *adj* an indented edge or surface has cuts or marks in it: *a deeply indented coastline*

**in·den·ture** /ɪnˈdentʃə‖-ər/ also **indentures** *plural* — *n* [C] a formal contract, especially in former times, between an APPRENTICE[1] and his master

2 **in·de·pen·dence** /ˌɪndɪ̣ˈpendəns/ *n* [U] **1** political freedom from control by the government of another country: [+ **from**] *Nigeria gained independence from Britain in 1960.*|*minority groups striving for political independence* **2** the time when a country becomes politically independent: *The country has made great advances since independence.* **3** the freedom and ability to make your own decisions in life, without having to ask other people for permission, help, or money: *financial independence*|*I was enjoying a new feeling of independence.*

**Independence Day** /·ˈ·· ˌ·/ *n* [singular] the FOURTH OF JULY

2 **in·de·pen·dent** /ˌɪndɪ̣ˈpendənt◂/ *adj*

**1** ► **COUNTRY/ORGANIZATION** ◄ [no comparative] not governed or controlled by another country or organization: *India became independent in 1947.*|*The independent role of the Police Commission must never be compromised.*|**independent school/broadcasting etc** *especially BrE* (=not owned or paid for by the government)

**2** ► **PERSON** ◄ **a)** confident and able to do things by yourself in your own way, without wanting help or advice from other people: *I quite like living alone, it's made me more independent.*|[+ **of**] *study material that helps the student to be independent of the teacher* **b)** [no comparative] having enough money to live so that you do not have to depend on other people: *financially independent*|[+ **of**] *Robert aimed to be independent of his parents by the time he was twenty.*

**3 of independent means** having your own income from property, INVESTMENTS etc: *a woman of independent means*

**4 independent inquiry/opinion/advice etc** something that is done or given by people who are not involved in a particular situation and who can therefore be trusted to be fair in judging it: *There have been demands for an independent inquiry into allegations of police misconduct.*

**5** ► **SEPARATE** ◄ existing separately and not connected with or influenced by any others: *Three independent studies in three different countries all arrived at the same conclusion.*|[+ **of**] *reports from two separate sources entirely independent of one another* —**independently** *adv*: *two systems that operate independently of each other*

**Independent** *n* [C] a politician who does not belong to a political party

**independent clause** /ˌ····ˈ·/ *n* [C] *technical* a CLAUSE (2) which can make a sentence by itself, for example 'she went home' in the sentence 'She went home because she was tired.'; MAIN CLAUSE

**in-depth** /ˈ· ·/ *adj* [only before noun] **in-depth study/investigation/report etc** an examination or description of something that is thorough and complete so that all the details are considered: *scientists doing an in-depth study of the causes of lung cancer*

**in·de·scri·ba·ble** /ˌɪndɪsˈkraɪbəbəl◂/ *adj* something that is indescribable is so terrible, so good, so strange etc that you cannot describe it, or it is too difficult to describe: *a feeling of indescribable joy*|*There was an indescribable tension in the room.* —**indescribably** *adv*: *indescribably squalid conditions*

**in·de·struc·ti·ble** /ˌɪndɪˈstrʌktɪ̣bəl◂/ *adj* too strong to be destroyed: *indestructible optimism*|*These toys are great because they're practically indestructible.* —**indestructibly** *adv* —**indestructibility** /ˌɪndɪsˌtrʌktɪ̣ˈbɪlɪ̣ti/ *n* [U]

**in·de·ter·mi·na·ble** /ˌɪndɪˈtɜːmɪ̣nəbəl◂‖-ɜːr-/ *adj* impossible to find out or calculate exactly: *water of indeterminable depth* —**indeterminably** *adv*

**in·de·ter·mi·nate** /ˌɪndɪˈtɜːmɪ̣nɪ̣t◂‖-ɜːr-/ *adj* impossible to know about definitely or exactly: *a girl of indeterminate age* —**indeterminately** *adv* —**indeterminacy** *n* [U]

**in·dex**[1] /ˈɪndeks/ *n plural* **indices** /-dɪ̣siːz/ or **indexes** W3
[C] **1** an alphabetical list of names, subjects etc at the back of a book, with the numbers of the pages where they can be found **2** a set of cards, each with a name or piece of information on it, arranged in alphabetical order, as used in a library; CARD INDEX **3** a sign by which the level of something can be judged or measured: *This may be taken as an index of economic growth.* **4** *technical* a system by which prices, costs etc can be compared to those of a previous date

**index**[2] *v* [T] **1** to make an index for something **2** [+ **to**] to arrange for the level of wages, PENSIONS etc to increase or decrease according to the level of prices —**indexation** *n* [C]

**index card** /ˈ·· ·/ *n* [C] one of the cards in an index

**index fin·ger** /ˈ·· ˌ··/ *n* [C] the finger next to your thumb; FOREFINGER

**index-linked** /ˌ·· ˈ·◂/ *adj technical BrE* index-linked wages, PENSIONS etc, increase or decrease according to the rise or fall of prices

**In·di·a ink** /ˈɪndiə ˌɪŋk/ *n* [U] black ink used especially for Chinese or Japanese writing with a brush

**In·di·an**[1] /ˈɪndiən/ *n* **1** [C] someone from India **2** [C] someone from one of the races that lived in North, South, and Central America before Europeans arrived

**Indian**[2] *adj* **1** from or connected with India **2** connected with Indians

**Indian corn** /ˌ··· ˈ·/ *n* [U] *especially AmE* MAIZE that is several different colours and is only used for decoration

**Indian file** /ˈ···· ·/ *n* [U] if people walk in Indian file, they walk one behind another; SINGLE FILE

**Indian giv·er** /ˌ··· ˈ··/ *n* [C] *AmE informal* an expression that is now considered offensive meaning someone who gives you something and then takes it back —**Indian giving** *n* [U]

**Indian ink** /ˌ··· ˈ·/ *n* [U] *BrE* black ink used especially for Chinese or Japanese writing with a brush

**Indian sum·mer** /ˌ··· ˈ··/ *n* [C] **1** a period of warm weather in autumn **2** a happy or successful time, especially near the end of your life or CAREER[1] (1)

**Indian wrest·ling** /ˌ··· ˈ··/ *n* [U] *AmE* a game in which you stand facing someone with your foot touching theirs, and try to push them over by pushing their hand

**india rub·ber** /ˌ··· ˈ··◂/ *n old-fashioned* **1** [U] rubber used for making toys, removing pencil marks etc: *an india rubber ball* **2** [C] *BrE* a piece of rubber used for removing pencil marks; ERASER

W1 **in·di·cate** /ˈɪndʒkeɪt/ *v*

**1 ▶ FACTS ◀** [T] to show that a particular situation exists or that something is likely to be true: *The survey results seem to indicate a connection between poor housing conditions and bad health.* | **indicate that** *This indicates that rape is more widespread than people believe.*

**2 ▶ POINT AT ◀** [T] to direct someone's attention to something, for example by pointing: *"She's the one I was tellng you about," whispered Toby, indicating a girl in a cheap cotton dress.*

**3 ▶ YOUR WISHES/INTENTIONS ◀** [T] to say or do something to make your wishes, intentions etc clear: *The Russians have already indicated their willingness to co-operate.* | **indicate that** *Ralph patted the sofa to indicate that she should join him.*

**4 ▶ A SIGN FOR ◀** [T] to be a sign for something; REPRESENT: *The symbols indicate different groups of sounds.*

**5 ▶ IN A CAR ◀** [I,T] *BrE* to show the direction in which you intend to turn in a vehicle, using lights or your hands; signal: *Don't forget to indicate before you pull out.* —see picture on page 415

**6 ▶ TREATMENT ◀ be indicated** *formal* if a particular kind of treatment is indicated, the need for it is shown

Frequencies of **indicate** and **show** in spoken and written English.

SPOKEN
indicate
show
WRITTEN
indicate
show
100 200 300 400 per million

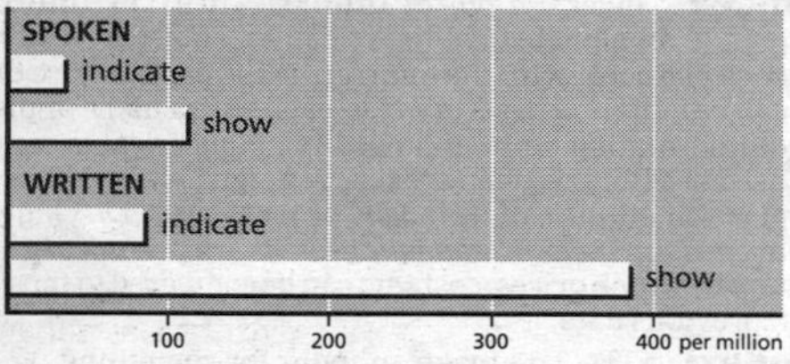

Based on the British National Corpus and the Longman Lancaster Corpus

This graph shows that **show** is much more common than **indicate** in both spoken and written English. This is because **show** is much more general in meaning and is more commonly used in informal English than **indicate**.

W3 **in·di·ca·tion** /ˌɪndʒˈkeɪʃən/ *n* [C,U] a sign that something is probably happening or that something is probably true: **[+ of]** *He gave no indication of his own feelings at all.* | **[+ that]** *a clear indication that they were in financial difficulty* | **every indication** (=very clear signs) *The two leaders greeted each other with every indication of good feeling.*

**in·dic·a·tive¹** /ɪnˈdɪkətɪv/ *adj* **1 be indicative of** to be a clear sign that a particular situation exists or that something is likely to be true: *This behaviour is indicative of her whole attitude, I'm afraid.* **2** *technical* an indicative verb form is used for making statements

**indicative²** *n* [C,U] *technical* the form of a verb that is used to make statements. For example, in the sentences 'Penny passed her test', and 'Michael likes cake', the verbs 'passed' and 'like' are in the indicative.

**in·di·ca·tor** /ˈɪndʒkeɪtə‖-ər/ *n* [C] **1** something that can be regarded as a sign which shows you in what way a situation is changing: *All the main economic indicators suggest that trade is improving.* **2** *BrE* one of the lights on a car that flash to show which way the car is turning; TURN SIGNAL *AmE* **3** a POINTER (1) on a machine that shows the temperature, pressure, speed etc —see picture on page 409

**in·di·ces** /ˈɪndʒsiːz/ the plural of INDEX

**in·dict** /ɪnˈdaɪt/ *v* [I,T] *law especially AmE* to officially charge someone with a criminal offence: **indict sb for sth** *He was indicted for fraud before a grand jury.* —**indictment** *n* [C,U]

**in·dict·a·ble** /ɪnˈdaɪtəbəl/ *adj law especially AmE* an indictable offence is one for which you can be indicted

**in·dict·ment** /ɪnˈdaɪtmənt/ *n* **1 be an indictment of** to be a very clear sign that a system, method etc is very bad or very wrong: *The fact that these children cannot read is a damning indictment of our education system.* **2** [C] *law especially AmE* an official written statement charging someone with a criminal offence **3** [U] *law especially AmE* the act of officially charging someone with a criminal offence

**in·die** /ˈɪndi/ *n* [C] a small independent company, especially one that produces records of popular music or television programmes

**indie mu·sic** /ˈ·· ˌ··/ *n* [U] records of popular music produced by a small independent company

**in·dif·fer·ence** /ɪnˈdɪfərəns/ *n* [U] lack of interest or concern: *He always treats Jane with complete indifference.* | **be a matter of indifference to** (=be something that someone does not care about) *Whether you stay or leave is a matter of total indifference to me.*

**in·dif·fer·ent** /ɪnˈdɪfərənt/ *adj* **1** not caring about what is happening, especially about other people's problems or feelings: **[+ to]** *Customs officials were indifferent to their plight.* **2** not particularly good; MEDIOCRE: *an indifferent cook* —**indifferently** *adv*

**in·di·ge·nous** /ɪnˈdɪdʒənəs/ *adj* indigenous animals, plants etc have always lived or grown naturally in the place where they are, as opposed to others that were brought there: **[+ to]** *There were no snakes indigenous to the islands.* —**indigenously** *adv*

**in·di·gent** /ˈɪndɪdʒənt/ *adj formal* not having much money or many possessions; POOR (1) —indigence *n* [U] indigent *n* [C]

**in·di·ges·ti·ble** /ˌɪndɪˈdʒestʒbəl◂/ *adj* **1** food that is indigestible cannot easily be broken down in the stomach into substances that the body can use —opposite DIGESTIBLE **2** facts that are indigestible are not easy to understand: *indigestible statistics* —**indigestibly** *adv*

**in·di·ges·tion** /ˌɪndɪˈdʒestʃən/ *n* [U] pain that you get when your stomach cannot deal with food that you have eaten: *You'll get indigestion eating that fast!*

**in·dig·nant** /ɪnˈdɪgnənt/ *adj* expressing anger and surprise, because you feel insulted or unfairly treated: *Harriet was indignant at the suggestion that she might need help.* | *anger expressed by an indignant snort* —**indignantly** *adv*: *"Of course I didn't tell her!" Sasha said indignantly.*

**in·dig·na·tion** /ˌɪndɪgˈneɪʃən/ *n* [U] feelings of anger and surprise because you feel insulted or unfairly treated: *Chamberlain found, to his great indignation, that he was not to be included in the team.* | *anger fuelled by righteous indignation* | **[+ at]** *Her indignation at such rough treatment was understandable.*

**in·dig·ni·ty** /ɪnˈdɪgnʒti/ *n* [C,U] a situation that makes you feel very ashamed, unimportant, and not respected: *She suffered many such indignities during her years with their family.* | **the indignity of** *At least the general was spared the indignity of a public trial.*

**in·di·go** /ˈɪndɪgəʊ‖-goʊ/ *n* [U] a dark purplish blue colour —**indigo** *adj*

**in·di·rect** /ˌɪndʒˈrekt◂/ *adj* **1** not by the fastest, easiest, or straightest way: *They took an indirect route, avoiding the town centre.* **2** not said in a clear direct way: *It was an indirect way of asking me to leave.* **3** the indirect result of an action is not caused directly by it, but by something else which that action caused: *The accident was an indirect result of the bus being late.* —opposite DIRECT¹ —**indirectly** *adv*: *Perhaps I was indirectly to blame for the misunderstanding.*

**indirect dis·course** /ˌ··· ˈ··/ *n* [U] *AmE technical* INDIRECT SPEECH

**indirect ob·ject** /ˌ··· ˈ··/ *n* [C] *technical* the second OBJECT[1] (6) of a verb in a sentence, which is the person or thing that the DIRECT OBJECT is given to, said to, made for etc. For example, in the sentence 'I asked him a question', the indirect object is 'him'.

**indirect speech** /ˌ··· ˈ·/ *BrE* **indirect discourse** *AmE* *n* [U] *technical* the style used to report what someone said without repeating their actual words. For example, in the sentence 'Julia said that she didn't want to go', the clause 'that she didn't want to go' is indirect speech. Her actual words were 'I don't want to go'.

**indirect tax·a·tion** /ˌ··· ·ˈ··/ *n* [U] a system of collecting taxes by adding an amount to the price of goods and services that people buy

**in·dis·cer·ni·ble** /ˌɪndɪˈsɜːnɪbəl◂‖-ɜːr-/ *adj* very difficult to see, hear, or notice: *The path was almost indiscernible in the mist.*

**in·dis·ci·pline** /ɪnˈdɪsɪplɪn/ *n* [U] a lack of control with the result that people behave badly: *Indiscipline among the troops eventually led to a riot.* —see also DISCIPLINE[1] (1)

**in·dis·creet** /ˌɪndɪˈskriːt◂/ *adj* careless about what you say or do, especially by talking about things which should be kept secret: *It was very indiscreet of Colin to tell them about our plan.* —**indiscreetly** *adv*

**in·dis·cre·tion** /ˌɪndɪˈskreʃən/ *n* **1** [U] a lack of careful thought or good judgment in the things that you say or do: *the startling indiscretion of her statement to the press* **2** [C] an action or remark that shows a lack of careful thought or good judgment **3** [C] something you do that is morally or socially unacceptable: *The indiscretions of his youth were not entirely forgotten.*

**in·dis·crim·i·nate** /ˌɪndɪˈskrɪmɪnɪt◂/ *adj* **1** indiscriminate killing, violence, damage etc is done without any thought about who is harmed or what is damaged: *the indiscriminate slaughter of innocent civilians* **2** not thinking carefully before you make a choice —**indiscriminately** *adv*

**in·di·spen·sa·ble** /ˌɪndɪˈspensəbəl◂/ *adj* someone or something that is indispensable is so important or useful that it is impossible to manage without them: *a piece of equipment that modern divers regard as indispensable* —**indispensably** *adv* —**indispensability** /ˌɪndɪspensəˈbɪlɪti/ *n* [U]

**in·dis·posed** /ˌɪndɪˈspəʊzd‖-ˈspoʊzd/ *adj* [not before noun] *formal* **1** ill and therefore unable to be present: *Mrs Rawlins regrets that she is temporarily indisposed.* **2 indisposed to do sth** not willing to do something

**in·dis·po·si·tion** /ɪnˌdɪspəˈzɪʃən/ *n formal* **1** [C,U] a slight illness: *his wife's sudden indisposition* **2** [U] an unwilling attitude

**in·dis·pu·ta·ble** /ˌɪndɪˈspjuːtəbəl/ *adj* an indisputable fact is so certain that it must be true: *The evidence was indisputable.* —**indisputably** *adv*: *He was indisputably in the wrong.*

**in·dis·so·lu·ble** /ˌɪndɪˈsɒljʊbəl◂‖-ˈsɑː-/ *adj formal* an indissoluble relationship cannot be destroyed: *an indissoluble union* —**indissolubly** *adv* —**indissolubility** /ˌɪndɪsɒljʊˈbɪlɪti‖-sɑː-/ *n* [U]

**in·dis·tinct** /ˌɪndɪˈstɪŋkt◂/ *adj* an indistinct sound, image, or memory cannot be seen, heard, or remembered clearly: *She muttered something indistinct.* —**indistinctly** *adv* —**indistinctness** *n* [U]

**in·dis·tin·guish·a·ble** /ˌɪndɪˈstɪŋgwɪʃəbəl/ *adj* things that are indistinguishable are so similar that you cannot see any difference between them: [+ **from**] *an artificial material that is almost indistinguishable from real silk* —**indistinguishably** *adv*

S3 W1 **in·di·vid·u·al**[1] /ˌɪndɪˈvɪdʒuəl◂/ *adj* **1** [only before noun] considered separately from other people or things in the same group: *Each individual leaf on the tree is different.* | *the needs of the individual customer* **2** [only before noun] belonging to or intended for one person rather than a group: *Everyone has their own individual opinions.* | *The children get far more individual attention in these small classes.* | *individual portions of butter* **3** an individual style, way of doing things etc is different from anyone else's; DISTINCTIVE: *a tennis player with a very individual style* | *a very individual way of dressing*

**individual**[2] *n* [C] **1** one person, considered separately from the rest of the group or society that they live in: *the rights of the individual* | *It is important to know the HIV test can vary from individual to individual.* **2** a person with thoughts, feelings, and ideas of their own: *With adequate support, any child will grow into a fully developed individual.* **3** *informal* a person of a particular kind, especially one who is unusual in some way: *a strange-looking individual in a green jacket* W1

**in·di·vid·u·al·is·m** /ˌɪndɪˈvɪdʒuəlɪzəm/ *n* [U] **1** the belief that the rights and freedom of individual people are the most important rights in a society: *capitalism, which encouraged competition and individualism* **2** the behaviour or attitude of someone who does things in their own way without being influenced by other people —**individualist** *adj*

**in·di·vid·u·al·ist** /ˌɪndɪˈvɪdʒuəlɪst/ *n* [C] someone who does things in their own way and has different opinions from most other people: *a rebel and an individualist* —**individualistic** /ˌɪndɪvɪdʒuəˈlɪstɪk◂/ *adj* —**individualistically** /-kli/ *adv*

**in·di·vid·u·al·i·ty** /ˌɪndɪvɪdʒuˈælɪti/ *n* [U] the quality that makes someone or something different from all other things or people: *a strict regime, that left little room for individuality*

**in·di·vid·u·al·ize** also **-ise** *BrE* /ˌɪndɪˈvɪdʒuəlaɪz/ *v* [T] to make something different so that it fits the special needs of a particular person or place: *an individualized learner program*

**in·di·vid·u·al·ly** /ˌɪndɪˈvɪdʒuəli/ *adv* separately, not together in a group: *The bridegroom thanked them all individually.* | [sentence adverb] *Individually, they're nice kids, but in a group they can be a nightmare!*

**in·di·vid·u·ate** /ˌɪndɪˈvɪdʒueɪt/ *v* **1** [T] to make someone or something clearly different from others of the same kind: *The characters are beautifully individuated in the play.* **2** [I] *AmE* to have an idea of yourself as an independent person, separate from other people

**in·di·vis·i·ble** /ˌɪndɪˈvɪzɪbəl◂/ *adj* something that is indivisible cannot be separated or divided into parts —**indivisibly** *adv* —**indivisibility** /ˌɪndɪvɪzɪˈbɪlɪti/ *n* [U]

**Indo-** /ɪndəʊ‖-doʊ/ *prefix* **1** of India; Indian **2** Indian and: *the Indo-Pakistani border*

**in·doc·tri·nate** /ɪnˈdɒktrɪneɪt‖ɪnˈdɑːk-/ *v* [T] to train someone to accept a particular set of political or religious beliefs and not consider any others: *People were indoctrinated not to question their leaders.* —**indoctrination** /ɪnˌdɒktrɪˈneɪʃən‖-ˌdɑːk-/ *n* [U] *objective discussion, free from propaganda and indoctrination*

**Indo-Eu·ro·pe·an** /ˌ·· ··ˈ··◂/ *adj* the Indo-European group of languages includes English, French, Hindi, Russian, and most of the languages of Europe and N India

**in·do·lent** /ˈɪndələnt/ *adj formal* lazy —**indolently** *adv* —**indolence** *n* [U] *a life of luxury and indolence*

**in·dom·i·ta·ble** /ɪnˈdɒmɪtəbəl‖ɪnˈdɑː-/ *adj* **indomitable spirit/courage etc** determination or courage that can never be defeated: *a woman of indomitable strength* —**indomitably** *adv*

**in·door** /ˈɪndɔː‖-ɔːr/ *adj* [only before noun] used or happening inside a building: *an indoor swimming pool* | *indoor shoes* —opposite OUTDOOR

**in·doors** /ˌɪnˈdɔːz◂‖-ɔːrz◂/ *adv* into or inside a building: *Let's go indoors and have something to eat.* | *It rained all afternoon, so we had to stay indoors.* —opposite OUTDOORS

**in·dorse** /ɪnˈdɔːs‖-ɔːrs/ *v* another spelling of ENDORSE

**in·du·bi·ta·ble** /ɪnˈdjuːbɪtəbəl‖ɪnˈduː-/ *adj formal* definitely true without any possible doubt —**indubitably** *adv*: *"Are you sure we can rely on you?" "Indubitably."*

**in·duce** /ɪnˈdjuːs‖ɪnˈduːs/ *v* [T] **1** to make someone decide to do something, especially something that seems unwise: **induce sb to do sth** *Nothing would induce me to vote for him again.*|*What could have induced you to do such a ridiculous thing?* **2** to make a woman give birth to her baby, by giving her a special drug: *She had to be induced because the baby was four weeks late.* **3** *formal* to cause a particular physical condition: *This drug may induce drowsiness.*

**in·duce·ment** /ɪnˈdjuːsmənt‖ɪnˈduːs-/ *n* [C,U] something such as money or a gift that you are offered to persuade you to do something: **inducement to do sth** *They offered her a share in the business as an inducement to stay.*

**in·duct** /ɪnˈdʌkt/ *v* [T often passive] *formal* **1** [+ **into**] to officially place someone, especially a priest, in their new job, rank, position etc in a special ceremony **2** *AmE* to officially introduce someone into a group or organization, especially the army

**in·duc·tee** /ˌɪndʌkˈtiː/ *n* [C] *AmE* someone who is being or has just been introduced into the army

**in·duc·tion** /ɪnˈdʌkʃən/ *n* **1** [C,U] the introduction of someone into a new job, company, official position etc: *an induction course* **2** [C] a ceremony in which someone is officially introduced into an official position or an organization **3** [C,U] the process of making a woman give birth to her baby by giving her a special drug **4** [U] *technical* the production of electricity in one object by another that already has electrical or MAGNETIC power **5** [U] *technical* a process of thought that uses known facts to produce general rules or principles —compare DEDUCTION (1)

**induction coil** /-ˈ-- -/ *n* [C] *technical* a piece of electrical equipment that changes a low VOLTAGE to a higher one

**in·duc·tive** /ɪnˈdʌktɪv/ *adj technical* **1** using known facts to produce general principles **2** connected with electrical or MAGNETIC induction

**in·due** /ɪnˈdjuː‖ɪnˈduː/ *v* [T] another spelling of ENDUE

**in·dulge** /ɪnˈdʌldʒ/ *v* **1** [I,T] to let yourself do or have something that you enjoy, especially something that is considered bad for you: [+ **in**] *Most of us were too busy to indulge in heavy lunchtime drinking.*|*Eva had never been one to indulge in self pity.*|**indulge yourself** *I haven't had strawberries and cream for a long time, so I'm really going to indulge myself.* (=eat a lot)|**indulge sth** *Ray has enough money to indulge his taste for expensive wines.* **2** [T] to let someone have or do whatever they want, even if it is bad for them: **indulge sb's every whim** *His mother pampered and spoiled him, indulging his every whim.*

**in·dul·gence** /ɪnˈdʌldʒəns/ *n* **1** [U] the habit of eating too much, drinking too much etc —see also SELF-INDULGENCE **2** [C] something that you do or have for pleasure, not because you need it: *An occasional glass of sherry was his only indulgence.* **3** [C,U] freedom from punishment by God, or a promise of this, which was sold by priests in the Middle Ages **4** [U] *old use* permission

**in·dul·gent** /ɪnˈdʌldʒənt/ *adj* willing to allow someone, especially a child, to do what they want, even if this is not good for them: *a camping trip paid for by their indulgent grandparents* —**indulgently** *adv*

W1 **in·dus·tri·al** /ɪnˈdʌstriəl/ *adj* **1** connected with industry or the people working in it: *industrial pollution*|*industrial output*|**industrial accident/injury** (=happening at work) **2** having many industries, or industries that are well developed: *an industrial nation* **3** of the type used in industry: *industrial detergents* —compare INDUSTRIOUS —**industrially** *adv*

**industrial ac·tion** /-ˌ-- ˈ--/ *n* [U] *BrE* a protest such as a STRIKE (=stopping work) used by workers in a disagreement with their employer

**industrial ar·chae·ol·o·gy** /-ˌ--- --ˈ---/ *n* [U] the study of the history of old factories, machines etc

**industrial art** /-ˌ--- ˈ-/ *AmE n* [U] a subject taught in school about how to use tools, machinery etc

**industrial dis·pute** /-ˌ--- -ˈ-, -ˌ--- ˈ--/ *n* [C] a disagreement between a group of workers and their employer

**industrial es·pi·o·nage** /-ˌ--- ˈ----/ *n* [U] attempts to steal secret information from another company in order to help your own company

**industrial es·tate** /-ˌ--- -ˈ-/ *BrE* a piece of land on the edge of a town planned as a place for factories and small businesses

**in·dus·tri·al·is·m** /ɪnˈdʌstriəlɪzəm/ *n* [U] the system by which a society gets its wealth through industries and machinery

**in·dus·tri·al·ist** /ɪnˈdʌstriəlɪst/ *n* [C] the owner or manager of a factory, industrial company etc

**in·dus·tri·al·ize** also **-ise** *BrE* /ɪnˈdʌstriəlaɪz/ *v* [I, T] if a country or place is industrialized or if it industrializes, it develops a lot of industry

**in·dus·tri·a·lized** /ɪnˈdʌstriəlaɪzd/ *adj* having a lot of factories, mines, industrial companies etc: *the industrialized nations of the West*

**industrial re·la·tions** /-ˌ--- -ˈ--/ *n* [plural] the relationship between workers and employers

**industrial rev·o·lu·tion** /-ˌ--- --ˈ--/ *n* [singular] the period, especially in the 18th and 19th centuries in Europe, when machines were invented and the first factories were established

**industrial tri·bu·nal** /-ˌ--- -ˈ--/ *n* [C] a type of court in Britain to which individual workers can take complaints against their employers

**in·dus·tri·ous** /ɪnˈdʌstriəs/ *adj* tending to work hard —**industriously** *adv* —**industriousness** *n* [U] —compare INDUSTRIAL

**in·dus·try** /ˈɪndəstri/ *n* **1** [U] the production of goods, especially in factories: *a decline in manufacturing industry*|**heavy industry** (=the production of large goods such as aircraft, cars etc)|**light industry** (=the production of small goods) **2** [singular] the people and organizations that work in industry: *an agreement that will be welcomed by both sides of industry* (=employers and workers) **3** [C] a particular type of industry, trade, or service: *the coal industry*|*Italy's thriving tourist industry*|**service industries** (=businesses that provide services, such as hotels and banks) **4** [singular] an area of work which is not really an industry but which has grown too large: *another book from the Shakespeare industry*

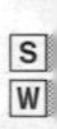

**-ine** /aɪn/ *suffix formal or technical* **1** of or concerning something: *equine* (=of horses) **2** made of or like something: *crystalline*

**i·ne·bri·ate** /ɪˈniːbriɪt, -brieɪt/ *n* [C] *old-fashioned* someone who is often drunk —**inebriate** *adj*

**i·ne·bri·a·ted** /ɪˈniːbrieɪtɪd/ *adj formal* drunk —**inebriation** /ɪˌniːbriˈeɪʃən/ *n* [U]

**in·ed·i·ble** /ɪnˈedɪbəl/ *adj* not suitable for eating: *The food was so burnt as to be inedible.*

**in·ed·u·ca·ble** /ɪnˈedjʊkəbəl‖-dʒə-/ *adj formal* impossible or very difficult to educate

**in·ef·fa·ble** /ɪnˈefəbəl/ *adj formal* too great or beautiful to be described in words: *ineffable joy* —**ineffably** *adv* —**ineffability** /ɪnˌefəˈbɪlɪti/ *n* [U]

**in·ef·fec·tive** /ˌɪnɪˈfektɪv◂/ *adj* something that is ineffective does not achieve what it is intended to achieve: *The various treatments for AIDS have so far proved ineffective.* —**ineffectively** *adv* —**ineffectiveness** *n* [U]

**in·ef·fec·tu·al** /ˌɪnɪˈfektʃuəl◂/ *adj* not having the ability, confidence, or personal authority to get things done: *an ineffectual leader*|*an ineffectual attempt* —**ineffectually** *adv*

**in·ef·fi·cient** /ˌɪnɪˈfɪʃənt◂/ *adj* a worker, organization, or system that is inefficient does not work well and wastes time, money, or energy: *an inefficient heating* *system|Local government was inefficient and corrupt.* —**inefficiently** *adv* —**inefficiency** *n* [C,U] *the inefficiency of the postal service*

**in·el·e·gant** /ɪn'elɪgənt/ *adj* not graceful: *an inelegant belly-flop into the water* —**inelegantly** *adv* —**inelegance** *n* [U]

**in·el·i·gi·ble** /ɪn'eləd͡ʒəbəl/ *adj* not being able to have or do something: [+ **for**] *Temporary workers are ineligible for the staff discount scheme.*|**ineligible to do sth** *ineligible to vote in the election* —**ineligibility** /ɪn,eləd͡ʒə'bɪləti/ *n* [U]

**in·e·luc·ta·ble** /,ɪnɪ'lʌktəbəl◂/ *adj literary* impossible to escape from; unavoidable —**ineluctably** *adv*

**in·ept** /ɪ'nept/ *adj* having no skill: *an inept driver|Blake was intellectually able but politically inept.|He made some inept sexist comment.* —**ineptly** *adv* —**ineptitude, ineptness** *n* [U] —compare INAPT

**in·e·qual·i·ty** /,ɪnɪ'kwɒləti‖-'kwɑː-/ *n plural* **inequalities** [C,U] an unfair situation, in which some groups in society have less money, influence, or opportunity than others: *the inequalities still suffered by disabled people*

**in·eq·ui·ta·ble** /ɪn'ekwətəbəl/ *adj formal* not equally fair to everyone; UNJUST: *an inequitable financial settlement after the divorce* —**inequitably** *adv*

**in·eq·ui·ty** /ɪn'ekwəti/ *n plural* **inequities** [C,U] *formal* unfairness, or something that is unfair: *gross inequities of income and wealth*

**in·e·rad·i·ca·ble** /,ɪnɪ'rædɪkəbəl◂/ *adj formal* an attitude or quality of character that is ineradicable can never be completely removed —**ineradicably** *adv*

**in·ert** /ɪ'nɜːt‖-ɜːrt/ *adj* **1** not having the strength or power to move: *an inert form lying on the bed* **2** very slow and unwilling to take any action: *Congress remained inert and skeptical about the proposal.* **3** *technical* not producing a chemical reaction when combined with other substances: *inert gases* —**inertly** *adv* —**inertness** *n* [U]

**in·er·tia** /ɪ'nɜːʃə‖-ɜːr-/ *n* [U] **1** a tendency for a situation to stay unchanged for a long time: *The government's wish to avoid conflict resulted in political inertia.* **2** lack of energy and a feeling that you do not want to do anything **3** *technical* the force that keeps an object in the same position or state of movement until it is moved or stopped by another force —**inertial** *adj*

**inertia reel seat·belt** /·,·· · '··/ *n* [C] a type of SEAT BELT that will unwind if it is pulled normally but not if it is pulled suddenly

**inertia sel·ling** /·,·· '··/ *n* [U] *especially BrE* the practice of sending goods to people who have not asked for them, and then demanding payment if the goods are not returned

**in·es·ca·pa·ble** /,ɪnɪ'skeɪpəbəl◂/ *adj* impossible to avoid: *The inescapable conclusion is that Pamela stole the money.* —**inescapably** *adv*

**in·es·sen·tial** /,ɪnə'senʃəl◂/ *adj formal* not needed; unnecessary: *He lived very simply with few inessential items in his apartment.* —**inessentials** *n* [plural]

**in·es·ti·ma·ble** /ɪn'estəməbəl/ *adj formal* too much or too great to be calculated: *The legal case has done inestimable damage to his reputation.* —**inestimably** *adv*

3 **in·ev·i·ta·ble** /ɪ'nevətəbəl/ *adj* **1** certain to happen and impossible to avoid: *A further escalation of the crisis now seems inevitable.* **2 the inevitable** a situation that is certain to happen: *One day the inevitable happened and I was caught sneaking in late.* **3** [only before noun] happening so regularly that you know it will happen again: *the inevitable bouts of travel sickness on school trips* —**inevitability** /ɪ,nevətə'bɪləti/ *n* [U]

3 **in·ev·i·ta·bly** /ɪn'evətəbli/ *adv* as was certain to happen and could not be prevented: *Inevitably, we had overlooked a few points.*

**in·ex·act** /,ɪnɪg'zækt◂/ *adj* not exact: *Sociology is an inexact science.* —**inexactness** *n* [U]

**in·ex·cu·sa·ble** /,ɪnɪk'skjuːzəbəl◂/ *adj* inexcusable behaviour is too bad to be excused: *Such rudeness is inexcusable!* —**inexcusably** *adv*

**in·ex·haus·ti·ble** /,ɪnɪg'zɔːstəbəl◂‖-'zɒːs-/ *adj* existing in such large amounts that it can never be finished or used up: *a man of inexhaustible energy|an inexhaustible supply of firewood* —**inexhaustibly** *adv*

**in·ex·o·ra·ble** /ɪn'eksərəbəl/ *adj formal* an inexorable process cannot be stopped: *the inexorable decline of Britain's manufacturing industry* —**inexorably** *adv*: *The story moves inexorably towards its tragic conclusion.* —**inexorability** /ɪn,eksərə'bɪləti/ *n* [U]

**in·ex·pe·di·ent** /,ɪnɪk'spiːdiənt◂/ *adj formal* a plan or action that is inexpedient is not useful because it is not likely to achieve the result you want —**inexpedience, inexpediency** *n* [U]

**in·ex·pen·sive** /,ɪnɪk'spensɪv◂/ *adj* cheap and of good quality for the price you pay: *clean and inexpensive accommodation in the centre of town* —**inexpensively** *adv* —**inexpensiveness** *n* [U]

**in·ex·pe·ri·ence** /,ɪnɪk'spɪəriəns‖-'spɪr-/ *n* [U] lack of experience: *youthful inexperience*

**in·ex·pe·ri·enced** /,ɪnɪk'spɪəriənst◂‖-'spɪr-/ *adj* not having had much experience: *Lyn is still too young and inexperienced to go abroad on her own.*

**in·ex·pert** /ɪn'ekspɜːt‖-ɜːrt/ *adj* not good at doing something —**inexpertly** *adv* —**inexpertness** *n* [U]

**in·ex·plic·a·ble** /,ɪnɪk'splɪkəbəl◂‖ɪn'eksplɪkəbəl, ,ɪnɪk'splɪk-/ *adj* too unusual or strange to be explained or understood: *the inexplicable disappearance of a young woman* —**inexplicably** *adv* —**inexplicability** /,ɪnɪksplɪkə'bɪləti/ *n* [U]

**in·ex·pres·si·ble** /,ɪnɪk'spresəbəl◂/ *adj* **inexpressible joy/sorrow/relief etc** a feeling or condition that is too strong to be described in words —**inexpressibly** *adv*: *He looked inexpressibly sad.*

**in·ex·press·ive** /,ɪnɪk'spresɪv◂/ *adj* a face that is inexpressive shows no emotion at all

**in·ex·tin·guish·a·ble** /,ɪnɪk'stɪŋgwɪʃəbəl◂/ *adj literary* **inextinguishable hope/love/spirit etc** hope etc that is so strong that it cannot be destroyed —**inextinguishably** *adv*

**in ex·tre·mis** /,ɪn ɪk'striːmɪs/ *adv Latin formal* **1** in a very difficult and urgent situation when very strong action is needed **2** at the moment of death

**in·ex·tric·a·ble** /,ɪnɪk'strɪkəbəl◂, ɪn'ekstrɪk-/ *adj formal* two or more things that are inextricable cannot be separated from each other: *Character development is an inextricable part of the novel.*

**in·ex·tric·a·bly** /,ɪnɪk'strɪkəbli, ɪn'ekstrɪk-/ *adv* **be inextricably linked/connected/mixed etc** if two or more things are inextricably linked etc, they are very closely connected and cannot be separated: *Poor health and bad housing conditions are inextricably linked.*

**in·fal·li·ble** /ɪn'fæləbəl/ *adj* **1** always right and never making mistakes: *I'm only human, I'm not infallible.|an infallible memory* **2** something that is infallible always works or has the intended effect: *He had an infallible cure for a hangover.* —**infallibly** *adv* —**infallibility** /ɪn,fælə'bɪləti/ *n* [U]

**in·fa·mous** /'ɪnfəməs/ *adj* **1** well known for being bad or morally evil: *an infamous traitor|plans to deal with Los Angeles' infamous smog* —see FAMOUS (USAGE) **2** *literary* evil: *infamous behaviour* —**infamously** *adv*

**in·fa·my** /'ɪnfəmi/ *n* **1** [U] the state of being evil or well known for evil things **2** [C usually plural] an evil action

**in·fan·cy** /'ɪnfənsi/ *n* [singular, U] **1** the period of a child's life before it can walk or talk: *She had five children, but four of them died in infancy.* **2 in its infancy** something that is in its infancy is just starting to be developed: *Agricultural research is still in its infancy in parts of the Third World.*

**in·fant**[1] /'ɪnfənt/ *n* [C] **1** *literary or technical* a very young child or baby: *The infant, cradled in Miriam's arms, began to cry.* —see picture at CHILD **2 infants** [plural] children in school in Britain between the ages of four and eight **3 infant school/teacher/class etc** a W3 school etc for children aged between four and eight in Britain

**infant²** *adj* [only before noun] an infant company, organization etc has just started to exist or be developed: *The plan was designed to protect infant industries in Mexico.*

**in·fan·ti·cide** /ɪnˈfæntɪ̵saɪd/ *n* [U] *technical* the crime of killing a child

**in·fan·tile** /ˈɪnfəntaɪl/ *adj* **1** infantile behaviour seems silly in an adult because it is typical of a child: *I was sick of his infantile jokes.* **2** *technical* affecting very young children: *infantile colic*

**infantile pa·ral·y·sis** /ˌ··· ·ˈ···/ *n* [U] *old-fashioned* POLIO

**infant mor·tal·i·ty rate** /ˌ·· ·ˈ···· ·/ written abbreviation **IMR** *n* [C] the number of deaths of babies under one year old, expressed as the number out of each 1000 babies born alive in a year

**infant prod·i·gy** /ˌ·· ˈ···/ *n* [C] a child with an extremely high level of ability in music, art, mathematics etc: *Mozart, the most famous infant prodigy of all*

**in·fan·try** /ˈɪnfəntri/ *n* [U] soldiers who fight on foot —compare CAVALRY

**in·fan·try·man** /ˈɪnfəntrimən/ *n plural* **infantrymen** /-mən/ [C] a soldier who fights on foot

**in·fat·u·at·ed** /ɪnˈfætʃueɪtɪ̵d/ *adj* having unreasonably strong feelings of love, but only for a short time and especially for someone that you do not know very well: [+ **with**] *John had become infatuated with the French teacher.*

**in·fat·u·a·tion** /ɪnˌfætʃuˈeɪʃən/ *n* [C,U] unreasonably strong feelings of love that you only have for a short time, especially for someone that you do not know very well: *As I thought, it was another passing infatuation.*

**in·fect** /ɪnˈfekt/ *v* [T] **1** to give someone a disease: *People with the virus may feel perfectly well, but they can still infect others.* **2** to put something that spreads disease into food, water, the air etc **3** if your excitement, eagerness etc infects other people, it makes them begin to feel the same way: *Lucy's enthusiasm soon infected the rest of the class.*

**in·fect·ed** /ɪnˈfektɪ̵d/ *adj* **1** a part of your body or a wound that is infected, has harmful BACTERIA in it which prevent it from healing (HEAL (1)): *It was only a small cut, but it became infected.* **2** food, water etc that is infected contains BACTERIA that spread disease

W3 **in·fec·tion** /ɪnˈfekʃən/ *n* [C,U] **1** a disease caused by BACTERIA or a VIRUS (1) that affects a particular part of your body: *You ought to get some antibiotics for that ear infection.* **2** the act or result of infecting someone: *Always sterilize the needle to prevent infection.*

**in·fec·tious** /ɪnˈfekʃəs/ *adj* **1** an infectious illness can be passed from one person to another, especially through the air you breathe: **highly infectious** *There seems to be a highly infectious type of flu going around.* **2** someone who is infectious has an illness and could pass it to other people **3** infectious feelings or laughter spread quickly from one person to another: *Her giggles were infectious and soon we were all laughing.* —**infectiously** *adv* —**infectiousness** *n* [U]

**in·fer** /ɪnˈfɜː‖-ɜːr/ *v* **inferred, inferring** [T] to form an opinion that something is probably true because of other information that you already know: **infer sth from** *facts that can be inferred from archaeological data* | **infer that** *It would be wrong to infer that people who are overweight are just greedy.*

**USAGE NOTE: INFER**

WORD CHOICE: **infer, imply**

In formal English the speaker or writer **implies** something, and the listener or reader **infers** it. *His report implied* (=suggested indirectly) *that the building was unsafe. I inferred from his report that the building was unsafe* means that this is what I thought the report meant.

**Infer** is now often used to mean **imply** but some people think that this is not correct: *Are you inferring I'm drunk* (=are you trying to tell me I'm drunk?)

**in·fer·ence** /ˈɪnfərəns/ *n* **1** [C] something that you think is true, based on information that you already know: **draw inferences** *What inferences have you drawn from this evidence?* **2** [U] the act of inferring something: **by inference** *measures directed against the enemies of National Socialism, including by inference all radicals and communists* —**inferential** /ˌɪnfəˈrenʃəl◂/ *adj*: *inferential evidence* —**inferentially** *adv*

**in·fe·ri·or¹** /ɪnˈfɪəriə‖-ˈfɪriər/ *adj* **1** not good, or less good in quality, value, or skill than someone or something else: *I felt very inferior among all those academics.* | *Pay less, and you get an inferior product.* | [+ **to**] *This machine is technically inferior to Western models.* **2** *formal* lower in rank: *an inferior court of law* —compare SUPERIOR¹ —**inferiority** /ɪnˌfɪəriˈɒrɪ̵ti‖-ˌfɪriˈɔːr-/ *n* [U]

**inferior²** *n* [C] someone who has a lower position or rank than you in an organization —compare SUPERIOR²

**inferiority com·plex** /·ˌ··ˈ··· ˌ··/ *n* [C] a continuous worrying feeling that you are much less important, clever etc than other people

**in·fer·nal** /ɪnˈfɜːnl‖-ɜːr-/ *adj* **1** [only before noun] *old-fashioned* used to express anger or annoyance about something: *I wish the children would stop that infernal noise.* **2** *literary* connected with HELL: *the infernal powers of darkness* —**infernally** *adv*

**in·fer·no** /ɪnˈfɜːnəʊ‖-ɜːrnoʊ/ *n* [C] *literary* an extremely large and dangerous fire: **raging inferno** (=an extremely violent fire) *Within minutes the oilrig had become a raging inferno.*

**in·fer·tile** /ɪnˈfɜːtaɪl‖-ˈfɜːrtl/ *adj* **1** infertile land or soil is not good enough to grow plants in **2** an infertile person or animal cannot have babies —**infertility** /ˌɪnfəˈtɪlɪ̵ti‖-fər-/ *n* [U]

**in·fest** /ɪnˈfest/ *v* [T] if insects, rats etc infest a place, they appear in large numbers and usually cause damage: [+ **with**] *hair infested with lice* | *shark-infested waters* —**infestation** /ˌɪnfeˈsteɪʃən/ *n* [C,U]: *an infestation of cockroaches*

**in·fi·del** /ˈɪnfɪ̵dəl/ *n* [C] *old use* an insulting word for someone who does not believe what you consider to be the true religion

**in·fi·del·i·ty** /ˌɪnfɪ̵ˈdelɪ̵ti/ *n* [C,U] an act of being unfaithful to your wife, husband etc by having sex with someone else: *Paul sometimes suspected her of infidelity.*

**in·field** /ˈɪnfiːld/ *n* [singular] **1** the part of a CRICKET (2) field nearest to the player who hits the ball **2** the part of a BASEBALL field inside the four bases —see picture on page 1263 **3** the group of players in the CRICKET (2) or BASEBALL infield —compare OUTFIELD —**infielder** *n* [C]

**in·fight·ing** /ˈɪnfaɪtɪŋ/ *n* [U] unfriendly competition and disagreement between members of the same group or organization: *political infighting*

**in·fil·trate** /ˈɪnfɪltreɪt‖ɪnˈfɪltreɪt, ˈɪnfɪl-/ *v* **1** [I always + adv/prep,T] to secretly join an organization or enter a place in order to find out information about them or harm them: *Police attempts to infiltrate neo-Nazi groups were largely unsuccessful.* | [+ **into**] *Enemy forces have been infiltrating into our territory.* **2** [+ **into**] to secretly introduce someone or something into an organization or place: *plans to infiltrate sabotage agents into the UK* —**infiltrator** *n* [C] —**infiltration** /ˌɪnfɪlˈtreɪʃən/ *n* [U]

**in·fi·nite** /ˈɪnfɪ̵nɪ̵t/ *adj* **1** very great: *Hilary takes infinite care over her work.* **2** without limits in space or time: *The universe is infinite.* —compare INFINITE (1), NON-INFINITE (2)

**in·fi·nite·ly** /ˈɪnfɪ̵nɪ̵tli/ *adv* [+ adj/adv] very much: *Living in the country is infinitely preferable to living in London.*

**in·fin·i·tes·i·mal** /ˌɪnfɪnɪ̵ˈtesɪ̵məl◂/ *adj* extremely small: *infinitesimal changes in temperature* —**infinitesimally** *adv*

**in·fin·i·tive** /ɪn'fɪnɨtɪv/ *n* [C] *technical* the basic form of a verb, such as 'be', 'make' or 'go', usually used with 'to' in the form 'to be', 'to make', 'to go' etc —see also SPLIT INFINITIVE

**in·fin·i·tude** /ɪn'fɪnɨtjuːd‖-tuːd/ *n* [singular, U] *formal* a number or amount without limit; INFINITY: *the vast infinitude of space*

**in·fin·i·ty** /ɪn'fɪnɨti/ *n* **1** [U] a space or distance without limits or an end: *The universe stretches away into infinity.* **2** [singular] a number that is too large to be calculated: **an infinity of** *An infinity of interpretations have been put on the novel.*

**in·firm** /ɪn'fɜːm‖-ɜːrm/ *adj* **1** weak or ill, especially because you are old: *Her grandmother is now old and infirm.* **2 the infirm** all the people who are weak or ill

**in·fir·ma·ry** /ɪn'fɜːməri‖-ɜːr-/ *n* [C] **1** a hospital **2** a room in a school or other institution where people can go if they are ill

**in·fir·mi·ty** /ɪn'fɜːmɨti‖-ɜːr-/ *n* [C,U] bad health or a particular illness: *She blamed her infirmity on the damp climate.*

**in fla·gran·te de·lic·to** /ɪn flə,grænteɪ dɪ'lɪktəʊ‖-toʊ/ *adv Latin, technical or humorous* in the act of having sex, especially with someone else's husband or wife

**in·flame** /ɪn'fleɪm/ *v* [T] *literary* to make someone's feelings of anger, excitement etc much stronger: *Seeing her again inflamed all his old desire.*

**in·flamed** /ɪn'fleɪmd/ *adj* a part of your body that is inflamed is red and swollen, because it is hurt or infected

**in·flam·ma·ble** /ɪn'flæməbəl/ *adj* **1** *BrE* inflammable materials or substances will start to burn very easily: *Petrol is highly inflammable.* —opposite NONFLAMMABLE —see FLAMMABLE (USAGE) **2** an inflammable temper easily becomes angry or violent

**in·flam·ma·tion** /,ɪnflə'meɪʃən/ *n* [C,U] swelling and soreness on or in part of your body, which is often red and hot to touch: *an inflammation of the eye*

**in·flam·ma·to·ry** /ɪn'flæmətəri‖-tɔːri/ *adj* **1** an inflammatory speech, piece of writing etc is likely to make people feel angry: *His inflammatory remarks about the homeless were seized on by the press.* **2** *technical* an inflammatory disease, condition etc causes inflammation

**in·fla·ta·ble**[1] /ɪn'fleɪtəbəl/ *adj* an inflatable object has to be filled with air before you can use it: *an inflatable mattress*

**inflatable**[2] *n* [C] a rubber boat filled with air

**inflate**

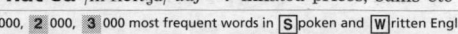

**in·flate** /ɪn'fleɪt/ *v* **1** [I,T] if you inflate something, or if it inflates, it fills with air or gas so that it becomes larger: *It took us half an hour to inflate the dinghy.* | *Her life jacket failed to inflate.* **2** [T] to make something seem more important or impressive than it is: *Our egos were already inflated by success.* **3** [T] *technical* to make prices increase: *The sudden influx of Westerners has inflated house prices out of all proportion.*

**in·flat·ed** /ɪn'fleɪtɨd/ *adj* **1** inflated prices, sums etc are unreasonably high: *These company directors are paid grossly inflated salaries.* **2** inflated ideas, opinions etc about something make it seem more important than it really is: *people with an inflated idea of their own importance* **3** filled with air or gas

**in·fla·tion** /ɪn'fleɪʃən/ *n* [U] **1** a continuing increase in prices or the rate at which prices increase: *Inflation is now running at over 16%.* **2** the process of filling something with air —compare DEFLATION 

**in·fla·tion·a·ry** /ɪn'fleɪʃənəri‖-ʃəneri/ *adj* relating to or causing price increases: *inflationary wage increases* | **inflationary spiral** (=the continuing rise in wages and prices because an increase in one causes an increase in the other)

**inflation-proof** /·'·· ·/ *adj* protected against price increases: *inflation-proof pensions*

**in·flect** /ɪn'flekt/ *v* **1** [I] if a word inflects, its form changes according to its meaning or use **2** [I,T] if your voice inflects or if you inflect it, the sound of it becomes higher or lower as you are speaking

**in·flect·ed** /ɪn'flektɨd/ *adj* an inflected language contains many words which change their form according to their meaning or use: *German is an inflected language.*

**in·flec·tion, inflexion** /ɪn'flekʃən/ *n* **1** [U] the way in which a word changes its form to show difference in its meaning or use **2** [C] one of the forms of a word that changes in this way, or one of the parts that is added to it **3** [C,U] the way the sound of your voice goes up and down when you are speaking —**inflectional** *adj*

**in·flex·i·ble** /ɪn'fleksɨbəl/ *adj* **1** inflexible rules, arrangements etc are impossible to change **2** unwilling to make even the slightest change in your attitudes or plans etc: *an arrogant man with an inflexible will* **3** inflexible material is stiff and will not bend —**inflexibly** *adv* —**inflexibility** /ɪn,fleksɨ'bɪlɨti/ *n* [U]

**in·fle·xion** /ɪn'flekʃən/ *n* [C,U] another spelling of INFLECTION

**in·flict** /ɪn'flɪkt/ *v* **1** [T] to make someone suffer something unpleasant: *The judge inflicted the severest possible penalty.* | **inflict sth on/upon sb** *He inflicted a great deal of suffering on his wife and children.* —see graph at PAIN[1] **2 inflict yourself on** *humorous* to visit or be with someone when they do not want you: *Frank's in-laws are inflicting themselves on us for the weekend.* —**infliction** /ɪn'flɪkʃən/ *n* [U]

**in-flight** /'· ·/ *adj* [only before a noun] provided during a plane journey: *in-flight entertainment*

**in·flow** /'ɪnfləʊ‖-floʊ/ *n* **1** [C] the movement of people, money, goods etc into a place: *the inflow of migrants* **2** [singular, U] the flow of water into a place —opposite OUTFLOW

**in·flu·ence**[1] /'ɪnfluəns/ *n* **1** [C,U] power to have an effect on the way someone or something develops, behaves, or thinks without using direct force or commands: **[+ with]** *She used her influence with the chairman to get me the job.* | **have an influence on** *Claude's work had a major influence on generations of musicians.* | **under the influence of** (=controlled by the influence of) *They had come under the influence of a strange religious sect.* **2** [C] someone or something that has an influence on other people or things: **be a bad/good influence (on)** *Gaye's mother said I was a bad influence on her daughter.* | **outside influences** (=influences from beyond your own group) *The tribe remains untouched by outside influences.* **3 under the influence** *informal* drunk S2 W1

**influence**[2] *v* [T] to have an effect on the way someone or something develops, behaves, thinks etc without directly forcing or commanding them: *Bruckner was much influenced by Wagner's orchestral music.* | *Don't let me influence your decision.* | **influence sb to do sth** *What influenced you to take the job?* 

**in·flu·en·tial** /,ɪnflu'enʃəl◂/ *adj* having a lot of influence and therefore changing the way people think and behave: *an influential politician* | **influential in doing sth**

*Dewey was influential in shaping economic policy.* | **highly influential** *a highly influential art magazine*

**in·flu·en·za** /ˌɪnfluˈenzə/ *n* [U] *technical* an infectious disease that is like a very bad cold; usually shortened to FLU

**in·flux** /ˈɪnflʌks/ *n* [C] the arrival of large numbers of people or large amounts of money, goods etc especially suddenly: [+ **of**] *Tourism has brought a huge influx of wealth into the region.*

**in·fo** /ˈɪnfəʊ‖-foʊ/ *n* [U] *informal* information

**in·fo·mer·cial** /ˈɪnfəʊmɜːʃəl‖-foʊmɜːr-/ *n* [C] *AmE* a long television advertisement that provides a lot of information and seems like a normal programme

S2 W2 **in·form** /ɪnˈfɔːm‖-ɔːrm/ *v* [T] **1** to formally or officially tell someone about something or give them information: *They thought it better to inform the police.* | **inform sb about/of** *Please inform us of any change of address as soon as possible.* | **inform sb (that)** *We regret to inform you that your application has been rejected.* | **inform sb who/why/how etc** *Could you please inform us what books you have in stock?* **2** *formal* to influence someone's attitude or opinion: *Her experience as a refugee informs the content of her latest novel.*

**inform against/on** sb *phr v* [T] to tell the police or an enemy information about someone that will harm them: *Treachery intervened when German sympathisers informed on them.*

W3 **in·for·mal** /ɪnˈfɔːməl‖-ɔːr-/ *adj* **1** relaxed and friendly without being restricted by rules of correct behaviour: *The atmosphere at work is fairly informal.* | *The two groups met for informal talks.* **2** an informal style of writing or speaking is suitable for ordinary conversations or letters to friends **3** informal clothes are suitable for wearing at home or in ordinary situations: *Students and teachers shared a taste for informal dress.* —**informally** *adv* —**informality** /ˌɪnfɔːˈmæləti‖-fɔːr-/ *n* [U]

**in·for·mant** /ɪnˈfɔːmənt‖-ɔːr-/ *n* [C] **1** someone who gives secret information about someone else, especially to the police: *The FBI were warned about the spy ring by a paid informant.* —compare INFORMER **2** *technical* someone who gives information about their language, social customs etc to someone who is studying them

S1 W1 **in·for·ma·tion** /ˌɪnfəˈmeɪʃən‖-fər-/ *n* **1** [U] facts or details that tell you something about a situation, person, event etc: *For further information phone the number below.* | **information that** *We have received information that Grant may have left the country.* | [+ **about/on**] *The book contains information about a wide variety of subjects.* | **provide information** *The guide will provide you with information about the area.* | **additional/further information** *For further information, please ask at Reception.* | **gather/collect information** *The survey didn't collect any information about temporary workers.* | **relevant/necessary/useful information** *There is a severe lack of relevant information and research about this disease.* | **detailed information** *Readers requiring more detailed information should consult Herman and McCure.* | **piece of information** *I've one or two useful pieces of information to pass on to you.* | **my/our information is** (=used when officially stating what you know about a situation) *Our information is that troops have already invaded the city.* **2 for your information** *spoken* used when you are telling someone that they are wrong about a particular fact: *For your information, I've worked as a journalist for six years.* **3 for information only** written on copies of letters and documents that are sent to someone who needs to know about them but does not have to deal with them —see also **inside information** (INSIDE[4] (2)) **4** [U] *AmE* the telephone service which provides telephone numbers to people who ask for them; DIRECTORY ENQUIRIES *BrE* —**informational** *adj*

This graph shows some of the words most commonly used with the noun **information**.

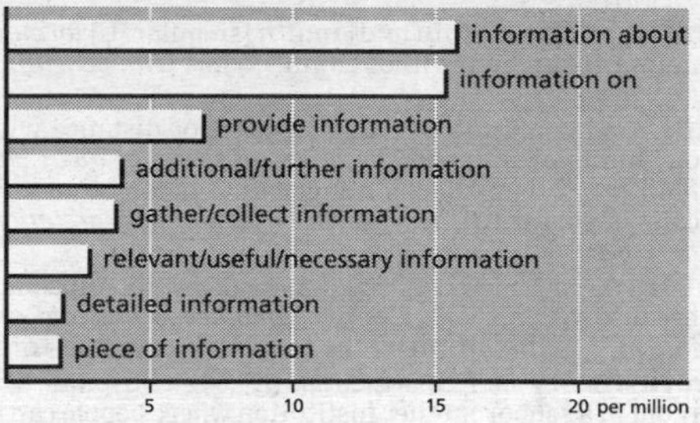

information about
information on
provide information
additional/further information
gather/collect information
relevant/useful/necessary information
detailed information
piece of information

5 10 15 20 per million

Based on the British National Corpus and the Longman Lancaster Corpus

**information cen·tre** /ˈ··ˌ·· ˌ··/ *n* [C] a place where you can get information about an area, event etc

**information re·triev·al** /··ˈ·· ·ˌ··/ *n* [U] the process of finding stored information, especially on a computer

**information sci·ence** /ˌ···· ˈ··/ *n* [U] the science of collecting, arranging, storing, and sending out information

**information su·per·high·way** /ˌɪnfəmeɪʃən ˌsuːpə ˈhaɪweɪ, -ˌsjuː‖-fərmeɪʃən ˌsuːpər-/ *n* [singular] the various systems that can be used to send or obtain information, pictures, films etc by electronic means, for example from a computer in one place to a computer in a different place

**information tech·nol·o·gy** /··ˈ·· ·ˌ···/ *n* [U] the study or use of electronic processes for storing information and making it available; IT

**information the·o·ry** /··ˈ·· ˌ···/ *n* [U] *technical* the mathematical principles related to sending and storing information

**in·for·ma·tive** /ɪnˈfɔːmətɪv‖-ɔːr-/ *adj* providing many useful facts or ideas: *She gave an informative talk on various aspects of child care.* —**informatively** *adv* —**informativeness** *n* [U]

**in·formed** /ɪnˈfɔːmd‖-ɔːr-/ *adj* **1** having a lot of knowledge or information about a particular subject or situation: *Informed sources have denied that the President was involved at all.* **2 well-informed/ill-informed/badly-informed** knowing a lot or not knowing much about what is happening in the world: *She seemed to be fairly well-informed about the underlying economic issues.* **3 informed guess/estimate/judgment etc** a guess etc that is based on knowledge of a subject or situation **4 keep sb informed** to give someone the latest news and details about a situation: *Please keep me fully informed of any developments.*

**in·form·er** /ɪnˈfɔːmə‖-ɔːrmər/ *n* [C] someone who is involved in an organization, especially a criminal organization, but who secretly tells the police, the army etc about its activities in return for money —compare INFORMANT (1)

**in·fo·tain·ment** /ˈɪnfəʊˌteɪnmənt‖-foʊ-/ *n* [U] *AmE* television programmes that deal with important subjects in a way that people can enjoy

**infra-** /ɪnfrə/ *prefix technical* below something in a range; beyond: *the infrared end of the spectrum* —compare ULTRA- (1)

**in·frac·tion** /ɪnˈfrækʃən/ *n* [C,U + **of**] *formal* an act of breaking a rule or law

**infra dig** /ˌɪnfrə ˈdɪg/ *adj* [not before noun] *informal BrE* below the standard of social behaviour that is suitable for a person of your class or rank: *It's a bit infra dig for her to wear jeans on such a formal occasion.*

**infra-red** /ˌɪnfrə ˈred◂/ *adj* infra-red light gives out heat but cannot be seen —compare ULTRAVIOLET

**in·fra·struc·ture** /ˈɪnfrəˌstrʌktʃə‖-ər/ *n* [C] the basic systems and structures that a country or organization needs in order to work properly, for example transport, communications, and banking systems: *the country's economic infrastructure* —**infrastructural** *adj*

**in·fre·quent** /ɪn'friːkwənt/ *adj* not happening often; rare: *They would make infrequent visits to the house.* —**infrequently** *adv*: *We see them only very infrequently.* —**infrequency** *n* [U] —see RARE (USAGE)

**in·fringe** /ɪn'frɪndʒ/ *v* [T] to do something that is against a law or someone's legal rights: *Increasing care must be taken not to infringe copyright.* —**infringement** *n* [C,U] *a minor infringement of the rules*

**infringe on/upon** sth *phr v* [T] to limit someone's freedom in some way: *He found that all the media attention was infringing upon his private life.*

**in·fu·ri·ate** /ɪn'fjʊərieɪt‖-'fjʊr-/ *v* [T] to make someone extremely angry: *It infuriates me to think of all the money we've wasted.*

**in·fu·ri·a·ting** /ɪn'fjʊərieɪtɪŋ‖-'fjʊr-/ *adj* very annoying: *It was infuriating to be so close and yet unable to contact them.* —**infuriatingly** *adv*

**in·fuse** /ɪn'fjuːz/ *v* **1** *formal* [T] to fill something or someone with a particular feeling or quality: **infuse sth/sb with** *She managed to infuse the situation with humour.* | **infuse sth into** *Hannah wanted desperately to infuse some vitality into their dull marriage.* **2** [I,T] if you infuse tea or HERBS or if they infuse, you leave them in very hot water while their taste passes into the water

**in·fu·sion** /ɪn'fjuːʒən/ *n* **1** [C,U] the act of putting a new feeling or quality into something: *What the department needs is an infusion of new ideas.* **2** [C] a drink made with HERBS in hot water that is usually taken as a medicine

**-ing** /ɪŋ/ *suffix* **1** forms the present participle of verbs: *They're dancing.* | *to go dancing* | *a dancing bear* **2** [in U nouns] the action or process of doing something: *She hates swimming.* | *No parking.* (=do not park here) **3** [in U nouns] **a)** a case or example of doing something: *to hold a meeting* **b)** a product or result of doing something: *a beautiful painting* **4** [in nouns] something used to do something or used for making something: *a silk lining* | *ten metres of shirting* (=cloth for shirts)

**in·ge·ni·ous** /ɪn'dʒiːnjəs/ *adj* **1** an ingenious plan, idea, INVENTION etc is the result of clever thinking and new ideas, and works well: *an ingenious way of making money* | *an ingenious gadget* **2** someone who is ingenious is very good at inventing things or thinking of new ideas —**ingeniously** *adv*

**in·gé·nue** /'ænʒeɪnjuː‖'ændʒənuː/ *n* [C] *French* a young inexperienced girl, especially in a film or play

**in·ge·nu·i·ty** /ˌɪndʒə'njuːɪ̈ti‖-'nuː-/ *n* [U] cleverness of inventing things and thinking of new ideas

**in·gen·u·ous** /ɪn'dʒenjuəs/ *adj* inexperienced, simple, trusting, and honest —**ingenuously** *adv* —**ingenuousness** *n* [U] —opposite DISINGENUOUS

**in·gest** /ɪn'dʒest/ *v* [T] *technical* to take food into your body —compare DIGEST[1] —**ingestion** /ɪn'dʒestʃən/ *n* [U]

**in·gle·nook** /'ɪŋgəlnʊk/ *n* [C] *especially BrE* a seat by the side of a large open fireplace, or the space that it is in

**in·glo·ri·ous** /ɪn'glɔːriəs/ *adj literary* causing shame and dishonour: *an inglorious defeat* —**ingloriously** *adv*

**in·got** /'ɪŋgət/ *n* [C] a lump of pure metal in a regular shape, usually shaped like a brick

**in·grained** /ɪn'greɪnd/ *adj* **1** ingrained attitudes or behaviour are firmly established and therefore difficult to change: *an ingrained prejudice against all foreigners* **2** ingrained dirt is under the surface of something and very difficult to remove

**in·grate** /ɪn'greɪt, 'ɪŋgreɪt‖'ɪŋgreɪt/ *n* [C] *formal* an ungrateful person

**in·gra·ti·ate** /ɪn'greɪʃieɪt/ *v* **ingratiate yourself (with)** to try hard to get someone's approval, by doing things to please them, expressing admiration etc: *The child glared so fiercely that I tried to ingratiate myself with her by offering candy.*

**in·gra·ti·at·ing** /ɪn'greɪʃieɪtɪŋ/ *adj* trying too hard to get someone's approval: *I can't stand that ingratiating manner of his.* —**ingratiatingly** *adv*

**in·grat·i·tude** /ɪn'grætɪ̈tjuːd‖-tuːd/ *n* [U] ungratefulness: *I've never seen such ingratitude in all my life!*

**in·gre·di·ent** /ɪn'griːdiənt/ *n* [C] **1** one of the types of food you use to make a particular dish: *Have we got all the ingredients for a casserole?* **2** a quality you need to achieve something: *Imagination and hard work are the ingredients of success.*

**in·gress** /'ɪngres/ *n* [U] *literary* the right to enter a place or the act of entering it

**in-group** /'· ·/ *n* [C] a small group of people in an organization or activity who like the same things and are friendly with each other, but do not want other people to join them; CLIQUE —**in-group** *adj*

**in·growing** /ˌɪn'grəʊɪŋ◂‖-'groʊ-/ *BrE,* **in·grown** /ˌɪn'grəʊn◂‖-'groʊn◂/ *AmE adj* [no comparative] an ingrowing TOENAIL grows inwards, cutting into the surrounding skin

**in·hab·it** /ɪn'hæbɪ̈t/ *v* [T] if animals or people inhabit an area or place, they live there: *The island is mainly inhabited by sheep.* —**inhabitable** *adj*

**in·hab·i·tant** /ɪn'hæbɪ̈tənt/ *n* [C] one of the people who live in a particular place: *a city of six million inhabitants*

**in·ha·lant** /ɪn'heɪlənt/ *n* [C,U] a medicine or drug that you breathe in, for example when you have a cold

**in·hale** /ɪn'heɪl/ *v* [I, T] *especially technical* to breathe in air, smoke, or gas: *It is dangerous to inhale ammonia fumes.* | **inhale deeply** (=inhale a lot of air or smoke) *Myra lit another cigarette and inhaled deeply.* —opposite EXHALE —**inhalation** /ˌɪnhə'leɪʃən/ *n* [C,U]

**in·hal·er** /ɪn'heɪlə‖-ər/ *n* [C] a small plastic tube containing medicine that you breathe in in order to make breathing easier

**in·here** /ɪn'hɪə‖-'hɪr/ *v*

**inhere in** sth *phr v* [T] *technical* to be a natural part of something

**in·her·ent** /ɪn'hɪərənt, -'her-‖-'hɪr-, -'her-/ *adj* a quality that is inherent in something is a natural part of it and cannot be separated from it: [+ **in**] *I'm afraid the problems you mention are inherent in the system.* —**inherently** *adv*: *Nuclear power is inherently dangerous and wasteful.*

**in·her·it** /ɪn'herɪ̈t/ *v* **1** [I,T] to receive money, property etc from someone after they have died: **inherit sth from** *She inherited the land from her grandfather.* **2** [T] to have a problem caused by mistakes that other people have made in the past: **inherit sth from** *The government claims to have inherited all of its problems from the previous administration.* **3** [T] to have the same character or appearance as your parents: **inherit sth from** *Gordon's inherited his father's bad temper.* **4** [T] *informal* to get something that someone else does not want any more: **inherit sth from** *We inherited the furniture from the previous tenants.* —see also DISINHERIT

**in·her·i·tance** /ɪn'herɪ̈təns/ *n* **1** [C,U] money, property etc that you receive from someone who has died: *She had squandered and gambled away her inheritance within a year.* **2** [U] *formal* ideas, beliefs, skills, literature, music etc from the past that influence people in the present: *our literary inheritance*

**inheritance tax** /'·⋯ ˌ·/ *n* [U] a tax on the money or property that you give to someone else after you die

**in·he·r·itor** /ɪn'herɪ̈tə‖-ər/ *n* [C] someone who receives money, property etc from someone who has just died

**in·hib·it** /ɪn'hɪbɪ̈t/ *v* [T] **1** to prevent something from growing or developing as much as it might have done otherwise: *Failure to set up a good transport network inhibited the expansion of trade.* **2** to make someone feel embarrassed or less confident so that they cannot do or say what they want to: **inhibit sb from doing sth** *Being too critical may inhibit a child from asking you things he needs to know.* | *an inhibiting influence*

**in·hib·it·ed** /ɪn'hɪbɪ̣tɪ̣d/ *adj* not confident or relaxed enough to do or say what you want to: **feel inhibited** *When discussing sexual matters many people feel very inhibited.* —**inhibitedly** *adv*

**in·hi·bi·tion** /ˌɪnhɪ̣'bɪʃən/ *n* [C,U] a feeling of worry or embarrassment that stops you doing or saying what you really want to: **lose your inhibitions** (=stop feeling worried etc) *That night she finally lost her inhibitions and told him how she felt.*

**in·hos·pi·ta·ble** /ˌɪnhɒ'spɪtəbəl‖ˌɪnhɑː-/ *adj* **1** an inhospitable place is difficult to live or stay in because of severe weather conditions or lack of shelter: *inhospitable desert regions* **2** unfriendly to a visitor, especially by not welcoming them, offering them food etc

**in-house** /ˌ· '·◂/ *adj, adv* within a company or organization rather than outside it: *We have an in-house training unit.* | *The keyboarding is done in-house.*

**in·hu·man** /ɪn'hjuːmən/ **1** very cruel without any normal feelings of pity: *an inhuman tyrant* | *The slaves were subjected to inhuman discipline.* **2** lacking any human qualities in a way that seems strange or frightening: *a fear of modern technology as something inhuman and threatening* | *The interviewer had a cold, almost inhuman, manner.* —**inhumanly** *adv*

**in·hu·mane** /ˌɪnhjuː'meɪn/ *adj* causing too much suffering and therefore considered cruel and unacceptable: **inhumane treatment/conditions/laws etc** *the inhumane treatment of political prisoners* —**inhumanely** *adv*

**in·hu·man·i·ty** /ˌɪnhjuː'mænɪ̣ti/ *n* [C usually plural, U] cruel behaviour or acts: *The book focuses on the inhumanity of the labour camps.*

**in·im·i·cal** /ɪ'nɪmɪkəl/ *adj formal* very unfavourable for something: *a cold, inimical climate* | [+ **to**] *conditions inimical to economic development* —**inimically** /-kli/ *adv*

**in·im·i·ta·ble** /ɪ'nɪmɪ̣təbəl/ *adj* too good or skilful for anyone else to copy with the same high standard: *the inimitable Billie Holliday* | *singing in his own inimitable style* —**inimitably** *adv* —compare IMITATE

**in·iq·ui·tous** /ɪ'nɪkwɪ̣təs/ *adj formal* very unfair and morally wrong: *an iniquitous system of taxes that victimizes the poor* —**iniquitously** *adv*

**in·iq·ui·ty** /ɪ'nɪkwɪ̣ti/ *n* [C, U] *formal* **1** the quality of being very unfair or evil, or something that is very unfair **2 den of iniquity** *humorous* a place where there is a lot of immoral behaviour: *Our mother regarded the pub as a den of iniquity.*

W2 **i·ni·tial¹** /ɪ'nɪʃəl/ *adj* [only before noun] happening at the beginning; first: *She overcame her initial shyness and really enjoyed the evening.* | *an initial investment of £5000*

**initial²** *n* [C] **1** the first letter of someone's first name: *"Can I have your initial, Mr Davies?" "It's G, Mr G Davies."* **2 initials** [plural] the first letters of all your names in order: *His initials are DPH: they stand for David Perry Hallworth.*

**initial³** *v* **initialled, initialling** *BrE,* **initialed, initialing** *AmE* [T] to write your initials on a document to make it official or to show that you agree with something: *You have to initial any corrections on a cheque.*

W3 **i·ni·tial·ly** /ɪ'nɪʃəli/ *adv* at the beginning: *The president initially appeared to endorse the idea.*

**i·ni·ti·ate¹** /ɪ'nɪʃieɪt/ *v* [T] **1** *formal* to arrange for something important to start, such as an official process or a new plan: *The plaintiffs initiated court proceedings in order to recover their debts.* **2** to introduce someone to special knowlege or skills that they did not know about before: *During that summer he was initiated into the mysteries of sex.* **3** to introduce someone into an organization, club, group etc, usually with a special ceremony: *In August Ivan was initiated into the Oakland chapter of the Hell's Angels.*

**initiate²** *n* [C] someone who has been allowed to join a particular group and has been taught its secrets

**i·ni·ti·a·tion** /ɪˌnɪʃi'eɪʃən/ *n* [C,U] **1** the process of officially introducing someone into a club or group, or of introducing a young person to adult life, often with a special ceremony: *The initiation ceremony involves elaborate dances.* **2** the act of starting something such as an official process, a new plan etc

**i·ni·tia·tive** /ɪ'nɪʃətɪv/ *n* W2

**1** ▶ **YOUR OWN DECISIONS** ◀ [U] the ability to make decisions and take action without waiting for someone to tell you what to do: *I wish my son would show a bit more initiative.* | **use your (own) initiative** *Don't keep asking me for advice. Use your initiative.* | **on your own initiative** (=without being told what to do) *Lieutenant Carlos was not obeying orders. He acted on his own initiative.*

**2** ▶ **PLAN** ◀ [C] an important new plan or process that has been started in order to achieve a particular aim or to solve a particular problem: *a government initiative to help exporters*

**3** ▶ **ADVANTAGE** ◀ **the initiative** the power to gain an advantage by taking actions that will influence events: **seize/hold/lose the initiative** *Zhukov was quick to seize the initiative and launched a massive counter attack.*

**4 take the initiative** to be the first one to take action to improve a situation or relationship, especially when other people are waiting for someone else to do something: *Why don't you take the initiative and arrange a meeting?*

**5** ▶ **TO CHANGE A LAW** ◀ [C] *law* a process by which ordinary citizens can propose a change in the law by signing a PETITION¹ (1)

**in·ject** /ɪn'dʒekt/ *v* [T] **1** to put liquid, especially a drug, into someone's body by using a special needle: **inject sth into** *The drug is injected directly into the base of the spine.* | **inject sb with** *The patient had been injected with a narcotic drug.* **2** to improve something by adding excitement, interest etc to it: *They hoped that the adoption of a child would inject new life into their marriage.* **3** [+ **into**] to provide more money, equipment etc for something

**in·jec·tion** /ɪn'dʒekʃən/ *n* **1** [C,U] an act of giving a drug by using a special needle: **give sb an injection** *The nurse gave me a tetanus injection.* **2** [C,U] the act of forcing a liquid into something: *a fuel injection system* **3** [C] an addition of money to something in order to improve it: [+ **of**] *a massive injection of public funds* S3

**in-joke** /'· ·/ *n* [C] a joke that is only understood by a particular group of people

**in·ju·di·cious** /ˌɪndʒuː'dɪʃəs/ *adj formal* an injudicious action, remark etc is not sensible and is likely to have bad results: *I thought his choice of words injudicious, to say the least.* —**injudiciously** *adv* —**injudiciousness** *n* [U]

**In·jun** /'ɪndʒən/ *n* **honest Injun** *spoken especially AmE* used especially by children to make someone believe they are telling the truth

**in·junc·tion** /ɪn'dʒʌŋkʃən/ *n* [C] **1** *law* an order given by a court which forbids someone to do something: [+ **against**] *The company is seeking an injunction against the strike.* | **take out an injunction against** (=get an injunction from a court) *Johnson took out an injunction to prevent the publication going ahead.* **2** *formal* a piece of advice or a command from someone in authority

**in·jure** /'ɪndʒə‖-ər/ *v* [T] **1** to cause physical harm to someone or to yourself, for example in an accident or an attack: *One of the players injured his knee and had to be carried off.* | **be badly/seriously/critically injured** *Two people have been critically injured in a road accident.* **2 injure sb's pride/self-esteem etc** to upset someone by damaging their confidence —compare WOUND³

**in·jured** /'ɪndʒəd‖-ərd/ *adj* **1** having an injury: *He isn't injured – just shocked.* **2 the injured** injured people:

*Firefighters had to cut open the wreckage in order to get the injured out.* **3 an injured look/expression etc** a look that shows you feel you have been treated unfairly **4 injured pride/feelings etc** a feeling of being upset or offended because you think you have been unfairly treated **5 the injured party** *formal* the person who has been unfairly treated in a particular situation

**in·ju·ri·ous** /ɪn'dʒʊəriəs‖-'dʒʊr-/ *adj formal* causing injury, harm, or damage: *Smoking is injurious to health.*

W2 **in·ju·ry** /'ɪndʒəri/ *n* **1** [C] a wound or damage to part of your body caused by an accident or attack: **sustain injuries** *formal* (=be injured) *The driver of the lorry sustained only minor injuries to legs and arms.* | **internal injuries** (=injuries inside your body) **2** [U] physical harm that is caused by an accident or attack: *insurance against injury at work* **3 do yourself an injury** *BrE humorous* to accidentally hurt yourself: *Don't lift that tool-box – you'll do yourself an injury!* —see also **add insult to injury** (ADD[1] (8))

**injury time** /'··· ,·/ *n* [U] *BrE* playing time added on to a game such as football because of time lost when players are injured

**in·jus·tice** /ɪn'dʒʌstɪ̇s/ *n* **1** [C,U] a situation in which people are treated very unfairly and not given their rights: *the injustice of slavery* | *innumerable injustices against the black population* **2 do sb an injustice** to judge someone's character unfairly: *It would be doing Brett an injustice to say that he didn't care about other people.*

**ink**[1] /ɪŋk/ *n* **1** [C,U] coloured liquid used for writing, printing or drawing **2** [U] the black liquid in sea creatures such as OCTOPUS and SQUID

**ink**[2] *v* [T] **1** to put ink on something **2** *AmE* to write something in ink, especially your SIGNATURE on a contract etc: *Just ink your name on the bottom line.*

**ink** sth ↔ **in** *phr v* [T] to complete something done in pencil by drawing over it in ink

**ink·jet print·er** /'ɪŋkdʒet ,prɪntə‖-ər/ *n* [C] an electronic printer, usually connected to a small computer —see picture on page 837

**ink·ling** /'ɪŋklɪŋ/ *n* **have an inkling** to have a slight idea about something: *We had no inkling that he was leaving.* | *No one gave me the slightest inkling of what they were planning.*

**ink pad** /'· ·/ *n* [C] a small box containing ink on a thick piece of cloth, used for putting ink onto a stamp (STAMP[2] (2)) that is pressed onto paper

**ink·stand** /'ɪŋkstænd/ *n* [C] a container for pens and pots of ink, kept on a desk

**ink·well** /'ɪŋk-wel/ *n* [C] a container for ink which fits into a hole in a desk

**ink·y** /'ɪŋki/ *adj* **1** marked with ink: *inky fingers* **2** *poetic* very dark: *I stared out into the inky blackness of the night.* —**inkiness** *n* [U]

**in·laid** /,ɪn'leɪd◂/ *adj* **1** an inlaid box, table, floor etc has a thin layer of another material set into its surface for decoration: [+ **with**] *a wooden jewellery box inlaid with ivory* **2** [+ **in/into**] metal, stone etc that is inlaid into the surface of another material is set into its surface as decoration

**in·land**[1] /'ɪnlənd/ *adj* [only before noun] an inland area, city etc is not near the coast

**inland**[2] /ɪn'lænd/ *adv* in a direction away from the coast and towards the centre of a country: *The mountains are five miles inland.*

**Inland Rev·e·nue** /,·· '···/ *n* [singular] the government department which collects national taxes in Britain

**in-laws** /'· ·/ *n* [plural] *informal* your relatives by marriage, especially the father and mother of your husband or wife: *We have to spend Christmas with the in-laws.*

**in·lay** /'ɪnleɪ/ *n* **1** [C,U] a material which has been set into the surface of furniture, floors etc for decoration, or the pattern made by this: *a cedarwood casket with gold inlay* **2** [C] a substance used by a DENTIST to fill a hole in a decayed tooth

**in·let** /'ɪnlet, 'ɪnlɪ̇t/ *n* [C] **1** a narrow area of water reaching from the sea or a lake into the land or between islands: *bays and sheltered inlets along the coast* **2** the part of a machine through which liquid or gas flows in: *a fuel inlet*

**in lo·co pa·ren·tis** /ɪn ,ləʊkəʊ pə'rentɪs‖-,loʊkoʊ-/ *adv Latin, formal or law* having the responsibilities of a parent for someone else's child: *As a teacher, you should regard yourself as being in loco parentis.*

**in·mate** /'ɪnmeɪt/ *n* [C] someone who is kept in a prison or MENTAL HOSPITAL: *One of the inmates has escaped.*

**in me·mo·ri·am** /ɪn mɪ̇'mɔːriəm/ *prep Latin* an expression meaning 'in memory of', used especially on the stone above a grave

**in·most** /'ɪnməʊst‖-moʊst/ *adj* [only before noun] **1** your inmost feelings, desires etc are the ones you feel most strongly and keep private **2** *formal* furthest inside: *She consigned the letter to the inmost recesses of her desk.* —opposite OUTERMOST

**inn** /ɪn/ *n* [C] **1** *especially BrE* a small PUB or hotel, especially one in the countryside, built in an old-fashioned style **2** a word used in the names of some PUBS and hotels: *We're staying at the Holiday Inn.*

**in·nards** /'ɪnədz‖-ərdz/ *n* [plural] **1** *informal* the parts inside your body, especially your stomach **2** the parts inside a machine

**in·nate** /ɪ'neɪt◂/ *adj* an innate quality has been part of your character since you were born: *Donna had an innate ability to sense when someone was unhappy.* —**innately** *adv*: *the army's innately conservative values*

**in·ner** /'ɪnə‖-ər/ *adj* [only before noun] **1** on the inside or close to the centre of something: *an inner room* | *Dial 0171 for inner London.* | *the inner ear* —opposite OUTER **2** connected with your soul or deepest feelings: *I really enjoy yoga – it gives me a sense of inner calm.* **3 inner meanings/thoughts etc** meanings or thoughts that are secret and not expressed: *Sarah suspected that his comment had an inner meaning.* **4 inner circle** the few people in an organization, political party etc who control it or share power with its leader: *The invasion plans were only divulged to the President's inner circle.* **5 the inner man/woman a)** the soul **b)** *humorous* the desire for food; APPETITE (1) W2

**inner cit·y** /,·· '··◂/ *n* [C] the part near the middle of a city where the buildings are in a bad condition and the people are poor: *the problem of deprivation in our inner cities* —**inner city** *adj*: *squalor in inner-city areas*

**in·ner·most** /'ɪnəməʊst‖-nərmoʊst/ *adj* [only before noun] **1** your innermost feelings, desires etc are the ones you feel most strongly about and do not talk about **2** *formal* furthest inside: *the innermost depths of the cave*

**inner tube** /'·· ·/ *n* [C] **1** the air-filled rubber tube inside a tyre **2 go inner-tubing** *AmE* to ride on an inner tube either on water or down a snow-covered hill

**in·ning** /'ɪnɪŋ/ *n* [C] one of the nine playing periods in a game of BASEBALL or SOFTBALL

**in·nings** /'ɪnɪŋz/ *n plural* **innings** **1** [C] the period of time when a cricket team or player bats (BAT[2] (1)) **2 he/she had a good innings** *BrE informal* used about someone who has died to say that they had a long life: *It's sad. Still, she was 89 – she had a good innings.*

**inn·keep·er** /'ɪn,kiːpə‖-ər/ *n* [C] *old use* someone who owns or manages an INN

**in·no·cence** /'ɪnəsəns/ *n* [U] **1** the fact of being not guilty of a crime: *Can you prove your innocence?* | **protest your innocence** (=say repeatedly that you are not guilty) *The prisoners continued to protest their innocence.* **2** the state of not having much experience of life or knowledge about evil in the world, especially so that you are easily deceived: *In our innocence we believed everything we were told.* | *the innocence of childhood* **3 in**

**all innocence** if you do or say something in all innocence, you have no intention of doing harm or of offending anyone

**in·no·cent¹** /ˈɪnəsənt/ *adj* **1** not guilty of a crime: *Nobody would believe that I was innocent.*|[+ **of**] *He's innocent of murder.* **2 innocent victims/bystanders/people etc** people who get hurt or killed in a war or as a result of a crime though they are not involved in it: *innocent victims of ruthless terrorism* **3** done or said without intending to harm or offend anyone: *He was startled by their angry reaction to his innocent remark.* **4** not having much experience of life, so that you are easily deceived; NAIVE: *I was thirteen years old and very innocent.* —**innocently** *adv*

**innocent²** *n* [C] someone who does not have much experience of life or knowledge about evil in the world

**in·noc·u·ous** /ɪˈnɒkjuəs‖ɪˈnɑːk-/ *adj* not offensive, dangerous, or harmful: *an innocuous remark*|*Those innocuous-looking cases contain enough explosive to destroy this building.* —**innocuously** *adv* —**innocuousness** *n* [U]

**in·no·vate** /ˈɪnəveɪt/ *v* [I] to start to use new ideas, methods, or inventions

W3 **in·no·va·tion** /ˌɪnəˈveɪʃən/ *n* **1** [C] a new idea, method, or invention: *recent technological innovations* **2** [U] the introduction of new ideas or methods: *We must encourage innovation if the company is to remain competitive.*

**in·nov·at·ive** /ˈɪnəˌveɪtɪv/ *adj* **1** an innovative process, method, plan etc is new, different, and better than those that existed before **2** using clever new ideas and methods: *a young innovative company*

**in·no·vat·or** /ˈɪnəveɪtə‖-ər/ *n* [C] someone who introduces changes and new ideas

**in·nu·en·do** /ˌɪnjuˈendəʊ‖-doʊ/ *n plural* **innuendoes** or **innuendos** **1** [C] an indirect remark about sex or about something bad that someone has done: *lies and innuendoes* **2** [U] the act of making such unpleasant remarks: *a despicable smear campaign based on rumour, innuendo, and gossip*

**in·nu·it** /ˈɪnjuɪt, ˈɪnuɪt/ *n* [U] *adj* INUIT

**in·nu·me·ra·ble** /ɪˈnjuːmərəbəl‖ɪˈnjuː-, ɪˈnuː-/ *adj* very many, or too many to be counted: *They received innumerable letters of complaint about the programme.*

**in·nu·mer·ate** /ɪˈnjuːmərɪt‖ɪˈnjuː-, ɪˈnuː-/ *adj* unable to do calculations or understand basic mathematics —**innumeracy** *n* [U]

**i·noc·u·late** /ɪˈnɒkjʊleɪt‖ɪˈnɑː-/ *v* [T] to protect someone against a disease, usually by injecting (INJECT (1)) them with a weak form of it: [+ **against**] *All the children had been inoculated against hepatitis.* —compare IMMUNIZE, VACCINATE —**inoculation** /ɪˌnɒkjʊˈleɪʃən‖-ˌnɑːk-/ *n* [C,U]

**in·of·fen·sive** /ˌɪnəˈfensɪv◂/ *adj* unlikely to offend anyone: *Her husband was a small, inoffensive-looking man.* —**inoffensively** *adv* —**inoffensiveness** *n* [U]

**in·op·e·ra·ble** /ɪnˈɒpərəbəl‖ɪnˈɑː-/ *adj* **1** an inoperable illness or TUMOUR (=lump) cannot be treated or removed by a medical operation: *an inoperable spinal tumour* **2** an inoperable system or method is not practical and therefore cannot be used

**in·op·e·ra·tive** /ɪnˈɒpərətɪv‖ɪnˈɑː-/ *adj formal* **1** a machine that is inoperative is not working, or is not in working condition **2** a system or a law that is inoperative is not working or cannot be made to work

**in·op·por·tune** /ɪnˈɒpətjuːn‖ˌɪnɑːpərˈtuːn◂/ *adj formal* **1** an inopportune moment or time is not suitable or good for something: *I'm afraid you've called at rather an inopportune moment.* **2** happening at an unsuitable or bad time: *an inopportune visit* —**inopportunely** *adv* —**inopportuneness** *n* [U]

**in·or·di·nate** /ɪˈnɔːdənɪt‖-ɔːr-/ *adj* far more than you would reasonably or normally expect: *Testing is taking up an inordinate amount of teachers' time.* —**inordinately** *adv*: *She's inordinately fond of her parrot.*

**in·or·gan·ic** /ˌɪnɔːˈgænɪk◂‖-ɔːr-/ *adj* **1** not consisting of anything that is living: *inorganic matter* **2** not produced or allowed to develop in a natural way —opposite ORGANIC (1, 5) —**inorganically** /-kli/ *adv*

**inorganic chem·is·try** /ˌ····ˈ···/ *n* [U] *technical* the part of chemistry concerning the study of substances that do not contain CARBON —compare ORGANIC CHEMISTRY

**in·pa·tient** /ˈɪnpeɪʃənt/ *n* [C] someone who stays in a hospital for treatment, rather than coming in for treatment from outside —compare OUTPATIENT

**in·put¹** /ˈɪnpʊt/ *n* [singular, U] **1** ideas, advice, money, or effort that you put into a job, meeting etc in order to help it succeed: *The conference would not have been such a success without your valuable input.* **2** *technical* **a)** electrical power that is put into a machine for it to use **b)** information that is put into a computer —compare OUTPUT¹ W3

**input²** *v past tense and participle* **inputted** or **input** [T] to put information into a computer

**in·quest** /ˈɪŋkwest/ *n* [C] **1** a legal process to find out the cause of someone's death: **hold an inquest (into)** *An inquest will be held into the death of the actor, Tom Barnard.* **2** an unofficial discussion about the reasons for someone's defeat or failure to do something

**in·qui·e·tude** /ɪnˈkwaɪɪtjuːd‖-tuːd/ *n* [U] *literary* anxiety

**in·quire, enquire** /ɪnˈkwaɪə‖-ər/ *v* [I,T] **1** to ask someone for information: *"Are you getting married?" the television interviewer inquired.*|[+ **about**] *I am writing to inquire about your advertisement in The Times.*|**inquire whether/why/how etc** *The waiter inquired whether we would like to sit near the window.* —see ASK (USAGE) **2 inquire within** used on notices, especially in shop windows, to mean that you can find out more about something inside: *Vacancies – inquire within.* —**inquirer** *n* [C]

**inquire after** sb/sth *phr v* [T] to ask someone about someone else, about how they are and what they are doing: *He called me aside to inquire after my daughter.*

**inquire into** sth *phr v* [T] to ask questions in order to get more information about something: *The investigation will inquire into the exact circumstances of the sale.*

**inquire** sth **of** sb *phr v* [T] *formal* to ask someone a question about something: *He nervously inquired of his host whether he could light a cigarette.*

**in·quir·ing, enquiring** /ɪnˈkwaɪərɪŋ‖-ˈkwaɪr-/ *adj* [only before noun] **1** an inquiring look or expression shows that you want to ask about something **2 an inquiring mind** someone who has an inquiring mind is very interested in finding out more about everything: *As a child he had a lively inquiring mind.* —**inquiringly** *adv*: *Victor raised an eyebrow inquiringly.*

**in·quir·y, enquiry** /ɪnˈkwaɪəri‖ɪnˈkwaɪri, ˈɪŋkwəri/ *n* W3 **1** [C] a question you ask in order to get information: [+ **about**] *We're getting a lot of inquiries from travel companies about our new London-Rio service.*|**make inquiries** *I don't know who sent the gift, but I'll make discreet inquiries.*|**be helping the police with their inquiries** *BrE* (=be answering questions about a crime) **2** [U] the act of asking questions in order to get information: *On further inquiry, it emerged that Malcolm had not been involved in the campaign.*|**line of inquiry** (=method of inquiry) *No definite information yet – but we're following up a most promising line of inquiry.* **3 enquiries** the name of a service or office from which you can get information **4** [C] an official process, in the form of a series of meetings, intended to find out why something happened: [+ **into**] *Local residents are calling for a public inquiry into the accident.*|**hold/conduct an inquiry** *complaints that the inquiry is being conducted behind closed doors* **5 scientific inquiry** a process of trying to discover facts by scientific methods

**inquiry a·gent** /·'···‖·'··ˌ··, '··· ˌ··/ *n* [C] *BrE old-fashioned* a PRIVATE DETECTIVE

**in·qui·si·tion** /ˌɪŋkwɪˈzɪʃən/ *n* **1 the Inquisition** the Roman Catholic organization in former times whose aim was to find and punish people who had unacceptable religious beliefs **2** [singular] a series of questions that someone asks you in a threatening or unpleasant way:

*When I got home I had to face a two hour inquisition from my parents about where I'd been.*

**in·quis·i·tive** /ɪnˈkwɪzɪ̍tɪv/ *adj* **1** asking too many questions and trying to find out too many details about something or someone: *Don't be so inquisitive – it makes people uncomfortable.* **2** interested in a lot of different things and wanting to find out more about them: *a cheerful, inquisitive little boy* —**inquisitively** *adv*: *He peeped inquisitively into the drawer.* —**inquisitiveness** *n* [U]

**in·quis·i·tor** /ɪnˈkwɪzɪ̍tə‖-ər/ *n* [C] **1** someone who is asking you a lot of difficult questions and making you feel very uncomfortable **2** an official of the INQUISITION —**inquisitorial** /ɪnˌkwɪzɪ̍ˈtɔːriəl◂/ *adj* —**inquisitorially** *adv*

**in·quo·rate** /ɪnˈkwɔːrɪ̍t/ *adj formal* an inquorate meeting does not have enough people to make decisions or vote

**in re** /ɪn ˈriː/ *prep* an expression used especially in business letters that means 'concerning'

**in·roads** /ˈɪnrəudz‖-roudz/ also **inroad** *n* **make inroads into/on a)** to become more and more successful, powerful, or popular and so take away power, trade, votes etc from a competitor or enemy: *Video is making huge inroads into attendance figures at movie theaters.* **b)** to use more and more of something such as space, time, money, or energy so that there is less available: *The administrative workload is making massive inroads into our working day.*

**in·sa·lu·bri·ous** /ˌɪnsəˈluːbriəs◂/ *adj formal* insalubrious conditions or places are unpleasant and bad for your health

**ins and outs** /ˌ· · ˈ·/ *n* [plural] all the exact details of a complicated situation, problem, system etc: *I don't really know all the ins and outs of the matter.*

**in·sane** /ɪnˈseɪn/ *adj* **1** *informal* completely stupid or crazy, often in a way that is dangerous: *I don't know what made Sarah marry him – she must have been totally insane.* | *The whole idea sounds absolutely insane to me.* **2** *especially law* someone who is insane is permanently and seriously mentally ill so that they cannot live in normal society: *The killer was declared criminally insane.* **3 drive sb insane** *informal* to make someone feel more and more annoyed or angry, usually over a long period of time: *I had to give up teaching – it was driving me insane.* —**insanely** *adv*: *insanely jealous*

**in·san·i·ta·ry** /ɪnˈsænɪ̍təri‖-teri/ *adj*: insanitary conditions or places are very dirty and likely to cause disease; UNSANITARY *especially AmE*

**in·san·i·ty** /ɪnˈsænɪ̍ti/ *n* [U] **1** very stupid actions that may cause you serious harm: *It was sheer insanity to drive across the mountains in the dark.* **2** *especially law* the state of being seriously mentally ill, so that you cannot live normally in society: *The court acquitted Campbell on the grounds of temporary insanity.*

**in·sa·tia·ble** /ɪnˈseɪʃəbəl/ *adj* always wanting more and more of something: **insatiable appetite/desire/demand etc** *an insatiable demand for Western consumer goods* —**insatiably** *adv*

**in·scribe** /ɪnˈskraɪb/ *v* [T] to carefully cut, print, or write words on something, especially on the surface of a stone or coin: **inscribe sth in/on etc** *Inside the cover someone had inscribed the words 'To Thomas, with love'.* | **inscribe sth with** *The tomb was inscribed with a short epitaph.*

**in·scrip·tion** /ɪnˈskrɪpʃən/ *n* [C] a piece of writing inscribed on a stone, in the front of a book etc

**in·scru·ta·ble** /ɪnˈskruːtəbəl/ *adj* someone who is inscrutable shows no emotion or reaction in the expression on their face so that it is impossible to know what they are feeling or thinking: *an inscrutable smile* —**inscrutably** *adv* —**inscrutability** /ɪnˌskruːtəˈbɪlɪ̍ti/ *n* [U]

**in·sect** /ˈɪnsekt/ *n* [C] a small creature such as a fly or ANT, that has six legs, and sometimes wings: *an insect bite* | *mosquitoes and other flying insects*

**in·sec·ti·cide** /ɪnˈsektɪ̍saɪd/ *n* [U] a chemical substance used for killing insects —compare PESTICIDE —**insecticidal** /ɪnˌsektɪ̍ˈsaɪdl◂/ *adj*

**in·sec·ti·vore** /ɪnˈsektɪ̍vɔː‖-vɔːr/ *n* [C] a creature that eats insects for food —**insectivorous** *adj*

**in·se·cure** /ˌɪnsɪˈkjuə◂‖-ˈkjur◂/ *adj* **1** not feeling at all confident about yourself, your abilities, your relationships etc: *I'd only just started at university and I still felt very shy and insecure.* **2** a job, INVESTMENT etc that is insecure does not give you a feeling of safety, because it is likely to be taken away or lost at any time: *Running a small business is a very insecure occupation.* **3** a building or structure that is insecure is not safe, because it is likely to fall down —**insecurity** *n* [U] *Student teachers often suffer from a great sense of insecurity.* —**insecurely** *adv*

**in·sem·i·nate** /ɪnˈsemɪ̍neɪt/ *v* [T] to put SPERM into a female animal in order to make her have a baby —**insemination** /ɪnˌsemɪ̍ˈneɪʃən/ *n* [U] —see also ARTIFICIAL INSEMINATION

**in·sen·sate** /ɪnˈsenseɪt/ *adj formal* **1** not able to feel things; INANIMATE **2** unreasonable and crazy: *insensate rage*

**in·sen·si·bil·i·ty** /ɪnˌsensɪ̍ˈbɪlɪ̍ti/ *n* [U] **1** *formal* the state of being unconscious **2** *old use* inability to experience feelings such as love, sympathy, anger etc

**in·sen·si·ble** /ɪnˈsensɪ̍bəl/ *adj formal* **1** not knowing about something that could happen to you; UNAWARE: [+ **of**] *She remained insensible of the dangers that lay ahead.* **2** unable to feel something or be affected by it: [+ **to/of**] *insensible to the cold* **3** *old use* not conscious: *He fell to the ground, insensible.* —**insensibly** *adv*

**in·sen·si·tive** /ɪnˈsensɪ̍tɪv/ *adj* **1** not noticing other people's feelings, and not realizing when they are upset or when something that you do will upset them: *One insensitive official insisted on seeing her husband's death certificate.* | [+ **to**] *She's totally insensitive to Jack's feelings.* **2** not paying attention to what is happening or to what people are saying, and therefore not changing your behaviour because of it: [+ **to**] *Companies that are insensitive to global changes will lose sales.* | *Outwardly he seems insensitive to criticism.* **3** not affected by physical effects or changes: [+ **to**] *insensitive to pain* | *insensitive to light* —**insensitively** *adv* —**insensitivity** /ɪnˌsensɪ̍ˈtɪvɪ̍ti/ *n* [U]

**in·sep·a·ra·ble** /ɪnˈsepərəbəl/ *adj* **1** people who are inseparable are always together and are very friendly with each other: *Jane and Sarah soon became inseparable companions.* **2** things that are inseparable cannot be separated or cannot be considered separately: [+ **from**] *In poetry meaning is inseparable from form.* —**inseparably** *adv* —**inseparability** /ɪnˌsepərəˈbɪlɪ̍ti/ *n* [U]

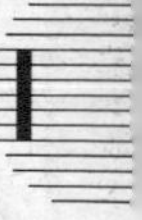

**in·sert¹** /ɪnˈsɜːt‖-ɜːrt/ *v* [T] **1** to put something inside or into something else: **insert sth in/into/between** *He inserted a sheet of paper into the printer.* | *Insert one 20p coin.* **2** to add something to the middle of a document or piece of writing: *The manager wanted to insert a clause giving him 30% of any future earnings.*

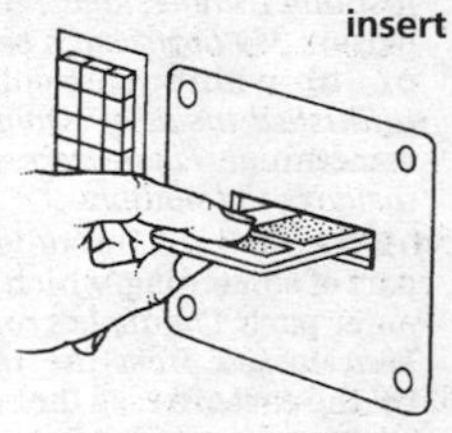
insert

**in·sert²** /ˈɪnsɜːt‖-ɜːrt/ *n* [C] **1** printed pages that are put inside a newspaper or magazine in order to advertise something: *a six-page insert on computer software* **2** something that is designed to be put inside something else: *He wore special inserts in his shoes to make him look taller.*

**in·ser·tion** /ɪnˈsɜːʃən‖-ɜːr-/ *n* **1** [U] the act of putting something inside something else **2** [C] something that is added to the middle of a document or piece of writing

**in-ser·vice** /ˌ· ˈ··◂/ *adj* **in-service training/courses etc** training etc that you do while you are working in a job

**in·set**[1] /ˈɪnset/ *n* [C] a small picture, map etc in the corner of a page or larger picture etc, which shows more detail or information: *See inset for a comparison of world grain exporters.*

**inset**[2] /ɪnˈset/ *v past tense and past participle* **inset** *or* **insetted** [T] **1** to put something in as an inset on a printed page **2 be inset with** if something is inset with decorations, jewels etc, it has them set in its surface

**in·shore** /ˌɪnˈʃɔː◂‖-ˈʃɔːr/ *adv* near, towards, or to the shore: *The fishing boats usually stay close inshore.* —**inshore** *adj*: *an inshore lifeboat*

S2 W2 **in·side**[1] /ɪnˈsaɪd/ *prep*
**1 ▶ CONTAINER ◀** in a container or other closed space so that it is completely covered or surrounded: *I'll leave the keys inside an envelope.* | *The jewels were locked away inside the safe.*
**2 ▶ BUILDING/ROOM ◀** in a room or building, especially when you are looking at it from the outside: *Mail was piled up just inside the doorway.*
**3 ▶ COUNTRY ◀** a word meaning in a country or area, used when you want to emphasize that something is happening there and not outside it: *Very little is known of events inside Albania.* | *The guerrillas were said to be operating from bases inside the war zone.*
**4 ▶ ORGANIZATION ◀** a word meaning in an organization or company, used when you want to emphasize that something is happening or known about there, but not outside it: *women's influence inside the Party* | *There have been rumours of bitter disputes inside the company.*
**5 ▶ FEELING ◀** if you have a feeling inside you, you feel it but do not express it or tell other people about it: *It's no good bottling all the anger up inside you – you've got to let it out.*
**6 ▶ HEAD/MIND ◀** if something happens inside you, or inside your head or mind, it is part of what you think and feel: *Something inside of me told me not to trust him.* | *Steve's a strange guy – you never know what's going on inside his head.*
**7 ▶ BODY ◀** in your body: *She could feel the baby kicking inside her.* | *You'll feel better once you've got a good meal inside you* (=after you have eaten something).
**8 ▶ TIME ◀** *especially spoken* if you do something inside a particular amount of time, it takes you slightly less than that amount of time to do it: *Jonson's time of 9.3 seconds was just inside the world record.* | **inside (of) two hours/inside (of) fifteen minutes etc** *We did the return trip to Birmingham in just inside three hours.*

S2 W3 **inside**[2] /ɪnˈsaɪd/ *adv* **1** in something: *The car was locked and the keys were inside.* | *The purse had £50 inside.* **2** in a house or other building: *It's raining. We'll have to go inside.* | *She could hear voices inside, but no-one came to the door.* **3** if you have a feeling inside, you have the feeling but do not show it to other people: *You just don't understand how I feel inside!* **4** *informal* in prison: *My boyfriend's been inside for a year.* **5 inside of a)** within a particular period of time: *We should get it finished inside of a month.* **b)** *AmE* on the inside of something: *There were now about a thousand people inside of the stadium.*

**inside**[3] /ɪnˈsaɪd, ˈɪnsaɪd/ *n* **1 the inside a)** the inner part of something, which is surrounded or hidden by the outer part: *The apple's rotten on the inside.* | *The door had been locked from the inside.* —opposite OUTSIDE[1] (1) **b)** the part of a road that is nearest to the edge on the side where you are driving: *He tried to overtake me on the inside.* **2 inside out** with the usual outside parts on the inside: *You've got that jumper inside out.* | *Turn cushion covers inside out to wash them.* **3 on the inside** someone who is on the inside is a member of a group or an organization: *Someone on the inside must have helped with the robbery.* **4 sb's inside/insides** *informal* someone's stomach: *My insides are beginning to complain about the lack of food.* **5 turn sth inside out** to search a place very thoroughly by moving everything that is in it: *The drug squad turned the apartment inside out.* **6 know sth inside out** to know something in great detail: *She knows her subject inside out.*

**inside**[4] /ˈɪnsaɪd/ *adj* **1** on or facing the inside of something: *the inside pages of the newspaper* **2 inside information/the inside story etc** information that is available only to people who are part of a particular group or organization: *Police believe the robbers may have had inside information.*

**inside lane** /ˌ·· ˈ·/ *n* [C] **1** the part of a road that is closest to the edge, usually used by slow vehicles —see picture on page 415 **2** the part of a circular track for racing that is nearest to the centre of the circle and is therefore shorter

**in·sid·er** /ɪnˈsaɪdə‖-ər/ *n* [C] someone who has a special knowledge of a particular organization because they are part of it: *an insider's view of the way that a Japanese company works* —compare OUTSIDER (3)

**insider trad·ing** /ˌ·· ˈ··/ also **insider dealing** *n* [U] illegal buying and selling of a company's shares (SHARE[2] (5)) involving the use of secret information known only by people connected with the company

**inside track** /ˌ·· ˈ·/ *n* [C] **1** the part of a circular track for racing that is nearest to the centre of the circle and is therefore shorter **2** *AmE* a position that gives someone an advantage over the people they are competing against: *the inside track to success in business*

**in·sid·i·ous** /ɪnˈsɪdiəs/ *adj* an insidious danger or problem spreads gradually without being noticed, and causes serious harm: *an insidious trend towards censorship of the press* —**insidiously** *adv* —**insidiousness** *n* [U]

**in·sight** /ˈɪnsaɪt/ *n* **1** [U] the ability to understand and realize what people or situations are really like: *a woman of great insight* **2** [C] a sudden clear understanding of something, especially something complicated: **[+ into]** *The article gives us a real insight into the causes of the present economic crisis.*

**in·sig·ni·a** /ɪnˈsɪgniə/ *n plural* **insignia** [C] a BADGE (1) or sign that shows what official or military rank someone has, or which group or organization they belong to: *the royal insignia* | *military insignia*

**in·sig·nif·i·cant** /ˌɪnsɪgˈnɪfɪkənt◂/ *adj* too small or unimportant to consider or worry about: *Looking at the Earth from space makes you realize how small and insignificant we all are.* | *an insignificant difference* —**insignificantly** *adv* —**insignificance** *n* [U]

**in·sin·cere** /ˌɪnsɪnˈsɪə◂‖-ˈsɪr◂/ *adj* pretending to be pleased, sympathetic etc, especially by saying nice things, but not really meaning what you say: *insincere praise* | *an insincere smile* —**insincerely** *adv* —**insincerity** /ˌɪnsɪnˈserʒti/ *n* [U]

**in·sin·u·ate** /ɪnˈsɪnjueɪt/ *v* [T] **1** to say something which seems to mean something unpleasant without saying it directly, for example saying indirectly that someone is being dishonest: **insinuate that** *Are you insinuating that the money was stolen?* **2 insinuate yourself into** to gradually gain someone's love, trust etc by pretending to be friendly and sincere: *He managed to insinuate his way into her affections.*

**in·sin·u·a·tion** /ɪnˌsɪnjuˈeɪʃən/ *n* **1** [C] something that someone insinuates: *the insinuation that they did not know how to run their own business* **2** [U] the act of insinuating something

**in·sip·id** /ɪnˈsɪpʒd/ *adj* **1** food or drink that is insipid does not have much taste: *an insipid pasta dish* **2** not interesting, exciting, or attractive: *an insipid young man* —**insipidly** *adv* —**insipidness, insipidity** /ˌɪnsʒˈpɪdʒti/ *n* [U]

**in·sist** /ɪnˈsɪst/ *v* [I] **1** to say firmly and repeatedly that something is true, especially when other people think it may not be true: **insist that** *Mike insisted that he was right.* | **[+ on]** *She kept insisting on her innocence.* **2** to demand that something should happen and refuse to let anyone say no: **[+ on]** *Her parents insisted on speaking to the headmistress.* | *Stay for supper – I insist!* | **insist that** *They insisted that everyone should come to the party.*

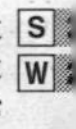

**3 if you insist** *spoken* used when agreeing to do something that you do not really want to do: *"Why don't you call them up today?" "Oh, if you insist!"*

**insist on** sth *phr v* [T] **1** to think that something is very important, and demand that you have it: *We insist on the highest standards of cleanliness in the hotel.* **2** to keep doing something, especially something that is inconvenient or annoying: *She will insist on washing her hair just when I want to have a bath.*

**in·sis·tence** /ɪn'sɪst əns/ *n* [U] an act of demanding that something should happen and refusing to let anyone say no: **insistence that** *his insistence that they discuss the problem* | [+ **on**] *an insistence on punctuality* | **at sb's insistence** (=because someone insisted) *At her father's insistence, she joined them for a drink.*

**in·sis·tent** /ɪn'sɪst ənt/ *adj* **1** demanding firmly and repeatedly that something should happen: **insistent that** *She was insistent that they should all meet for dinner.* | [+ **on**] *insistent on good manners* **2** making a continuous loud sound that is difficult to ignore: *the insistent pounding of drums* —**insistently** *adv*

**in si·tu** /ɪn 'sɪtjuː‖ɪn 'saɪtuː/ *adv Latin* if something remains in situ, it remains in its usual place

**in·so·far** /ˌɪnsə'fɑː‖-'fɑːr/ *adv* —see **in so far as/in as far as/insofar as** (FAR[1] (31))

**in·sole** /'ɪnsəʊl‖-soʊl/ *n* [C] a foot-shaped piece of cloth, leather etc that you put inside your shoe

**in·so·lent** /'ɪnsələnt/ *adj* rude and not showing any respect: *an insolent tone of voice* | *You insolent child!* —**insolently** *adv* —**insolence** *n* [U]

**in·sol·u·ble** /ɪn'sɒljəbəl‖ɪn'sɑːl-/ *adj* **1** an insoluble problem is or seems impossible to solve: *insoluble conflicts within the department* **2** an insoluble substance does not become a liquid when you put it into a liquid —compare DISSOLVE (1)

**in·sol·va·ble** /ɪn'sɒlvəbəl‖ɪn'sɑːl-/ *adj especially AmE* an insolvable problem is or seems impossible to solve; INSOLUBLE (1) —**insolvably** *adv*

**in·sol·vent** /ɪn'sɒlvənt‖ɪn'sɑːl-/ *adj* not having enough money to pay what you owe; BANKRUPT: *insolvent private companies* —**insolvency** *n* [U]

**in·som·ni·a** /ɪn'sɒmniə‖-'sɑːm-/ *n* [U] the condition of not being able to sleep

**in·som·ni·ac** /ɪn'sɒmniæk‖ɪn'sɑːm-/ *n* [C] someone who cannot sleep easily —**insomniac** *adj*

**in·so·much** /ˌɪnsəʊ'mʌtʃ‖-soʊ-/ *adv formal* **1 insomuch that** *especially AmE* to such a degree that **2** another form of the word INASMUCH

**in·sou·ci·ance** /ɪn'suːsiəns/ *n* [U] *formal* a cheerful feeling of not caring or worrying about anything: *He strolled through the house with an air of insouciance.* —**insouciant** *adj* —**insouciantly** *adv*

**in·spect** /ɪn'spekt/ *v* [T] **1** to examine something carefully in order to find out more about it or that it is not satisfactory: *I got out of the car to inspect the damage.* | **inspect sth for cracks/faults etc** (=in order to check that there are no cracks etc) *He carefully inspected the china for cracks.* —see graph at EXAMINE **2** to make an official visit to a building, organization etc to check that everything is satisfactory and that rules are being obeyed: *The building is regularly inspected by the fire-safety officer.* | *General Allenby arrived to inspect the troops.*

S3 **in·spec·tion** /ɪn'spekʃən/ *n* [C, U] **1** an official visit to a building or organization to check that everything is satisfactory and that rules are being obeyed: [+ **of**] *regular inspections of the prison* | **carry out an inspection** *An inspection was carried out at the school.* | **tour of inspection** (=an official journey or visit to inspect something) **2** a careful examination of something to find out more about it: **on closer inspection** (=when looked at more closely) *On closer inspection, the scrap of paper turned out to be a £20 note.*

**in·spec·tor** /ɪn'spektə‖-ər/ *n* [C] **1** an official whose job is to check that something is satisfactory and that rules are being obeyed: *ticket inspectors* | *a Health and Safety inspector* **2** a police officer of middle rank: *Inspector Blake* —see also CHIEF INSPECTOR **3** *BrE* someone whose job is to visit schools and judge the quality of the teaching

**in·spec·tor·ate** /ɪn'spektərɪ̈t/ *n* [C] the group of INSPECTORS who officially inspect schools, factories etc

**inspector of tax·es** /ˌ·ˌ··· · '··/ *n* [C] *BrE* a government official who calculates what tax each person should pay

**in·spi·ra·tion** /ˌɪnspɪ̈'reɪʃən/ *n* [C,U] **1** a sudden good idea about what you should do or say: *I haven't started writing the article yet – I'm still waiting for inspiration.* **2** the state of being given encouragement or good ideas about what you should do: **divine inspiration** (=inspiration from God or gods) **3** a person, experience, place, etc that you get inspiration from: *The seascapes of Cape Cod were her inspiration.* **4 be an inspiration to sb** to make someone feel encouraged to be as good, successful etc as possible: *Maya, who bears her illness with such patience, is an inspiration to us all.*

**in·spi·ra·tion·al** /ˌɪnspɪ̈'reɪʃənəl◂/ *adj* providing inspiration: *Jones proved an inspirational figure in Welsh rugby.*

**in·spire** /ɪn'spaɪə‖-'spaɪr/ *v* [T] **1** to encourage someone by making them feel confident and eager to achieve something great: *We need a new captain – someone who can inspire the team.* | **inspire sb to sth** *I hope this success will inspire you to greater efforts.* **2** to make someone have a particular feeling or react in a particular way: *Gandhi's quiet dignity inspired respect even among his enemies.* | **not inspire confidence** (=make people feel anxious because they do not trust your ability): *His driving hardly inspires confidence.* **3** to give someone the idea for a story, painting, poem etc: *The story was inspired by a chance meeting with an old Russian duke.* **4** *technical* to breathe in

**in·spired** /ɪn'spaɪəd‖-'spaɪrd/ *adj* **1** having very exciting special qualities that are better than anyone or anything else: *an inspired leader* | *Wordsworth's most inspired poems* **2 inspired guess** a correct guess that is based on feelings rather than facts **3 politically inspired** started for political reasons: *We suspect that the violence was politically inspired.*

**in·spir·ing** /ɪn'spaɪərɪŋ‖-'spaɪr-/ *adj* giving people energy, a feeling of excitement, and a desire to do something great: *inspiring music* | *King, 27 years old, was a great orator and an inspiring leader.*

**inst** /ɪnst/ *adj BrE formal old-fashioned* used after a date in business letters to mean 'of the present month': *Thank you for your letter of the 21st inst.*

**in·sta·bil·i·ty** /ˌɪnstə'bɪlɪ̈ti/ *n* [U] **1** uncertainty in a situation that is caused by the possibility of sudden change: *the instability of the market* | *political instability* **2** mental problems that are likely to cause sudden changes of behaviour: *nervous instability*

**in·stall, instal** /ɪn'stɔːl‖-'stɒːl/ *v* [T] **1** to put a piece of equipment somewhere and connect it so that it is ready to be used: *They've installed the new network at last.* **2** to put someone in an important job or position, especially with a ceremony: *Churchill was installed as Chancellor of the university.* **3 install yourself in/at etc** to settle somewhere as if you are going to stay for a long time W3

**in·stal·la·tion** /ˌɪnstə'leɪʃən/ *n* **1** [C] a piece of equipment that has been fitted in its place: *The whole computer installation was nearly new.* **2** [U] the act of fitting a piece of equipment somewhere: *the installation of a new washing machine* **3** [C] a place where industrial or military equipment, machinery etc has been put: *nuclear installations* **4** [U] *formal* the ceremony of putting someone in an important job or position: *the installation of the new bishop*

**in·stall·ment plan** /·'·· ·/ *n* [singular, U] *AmE* a system of paying for goods by a series of small regular payments; HIRE PURCHASE *BrE*

**in·stal·ment** also **installment** *AmE* /ɪn'stɔːlmənt/ *n*

[C] **1** one of a series of regular payments, that you make until you have paid all the money you owe: *the second instalment of a loan* | **pay by instalments** *They're letting me pay for the washing machine by instalments.* **2** one of the parts of a story that appears as a series of parts in a magazine, newspaper etc; EPISODE (2)

S3 W2 **in·stance¹** /ˈɪnstəns/ *n* **1 for instance** for example: *You can't rely on her. For instance, she arrived an hour late for an important meeting yesterday.* **2** [C] an example of a particular kind of situation: [+ **of**] *instances of injustice* | **in this instance** *Hilary is right about most things, but in this instance I think she was mistaken.* **3 at sb's instance** *formal* because of someone's wish or request **4 in the first instance** at the beginning of a series of actions: *Anyone wishing to join the society should apply in the first instance to the secretary.*

**instance²** *v* [T] *formal* to give something as an example: *She instanced the first chapter as proof of his skill in constructing scenes.*

S3 **in·stant¹** /ˈɪnstənt/ *adj* **1** happening or produced immediately: *The women took an instant dislike to one another.* | *a system that provides instant hot water* **2** [only before noun] instant food, coffee etc is in the form of powder and prepared by adding hot water: *instant coffee*

**instant²** *n* **1** [C usually singular] a moment: *She caught his eye for an instant.* | **in an instant** (=immediately) *When the rain started, the crowd vanished in an instant.* **2 the instant (that)** as soon as something happens: *The instant I saw him, I knew he was the man the police were looking for.* **3 this instant** *spoken* used when telling someone, especially a child, to do something immediately: *Come here this instant!*

**in·stan·ta·ne·ous** /ˌɪnstənˈteɪniəs◂/ *adj* happening immediately: *The computer gives an instantaneous response.* —**instantaneously** *adv* —**instantaneousness** *n* [U]

**in·stant·ly** /ˈɪnstəntli/ *adv* immediately: *They recognised him instantly.* | *All four victims died instantly.*

**instant re·play** /ˌ·· ˈ··/ *n* [C] an important moment in a sports game on television that is shown again immediately after it happens; ACTION REPLAY *BrE*

S1 W1 **in·stead** /ɪnˈsted/ *adv* **1 instead of** in place of something or someone: *We should do something instead of just talking about it.* | *You must have picked up my keys instead of yours.* | *Could I have tuna instead of ham?* **2** in place of something that has just been mentioned: *If Joe can't attend the meeting, I could go instead.* | *We didn't have enough money for a movie, so we went to the park instead.* | [sentence adverb] *Cardew did not join the navy. Instead, he decided to become an actor.*

**in·step** /ˈɪnstep/ *n* [C] **1** the raised part of your foot between your toes and your ANKLE —see picture at FOOT¹ **2** the part of a shoe or sock that covers this part —see picture at SHOE¹

**in·sti·gate** /ˈɪnstɪ̇geɪt/ *v* [T] **1** to start something such as a legal process or an official inquiry: *Without evidence it would be impossible to instigate an official investigation.* **2** to start trouble by persuading someone to do something bad: *A foreign government was accused of having instigated the bloodshed.* —**instigator** *n* [C]

**in·sti·ga·tion** /ˌɪnstɪˈgeɪʃən/ *n* **1 at sb's instigation** *formal* because of someone's suggestion, request or demand: *At Canham's instigation, a clerk brought in an electric fan.* **2** [U] the act of starting something

**in·stil** *BrE*, **instill** *AmE* /ɪnˈstɪl/ *v* [T] to teach someone a way of thinking or behaving over a long period of time: **instil sth in/into sb** *They instilled good manners into their children at an early age.* —**instillation** /ˌɪnstɪˈleɪʃən/ *n* [U]

**in·stinct** /ˈɪnstɪŋkt/ *n* [C,U] a natural tendency or ability to behave or react in a particular way without having to learn it or think about it: [+ **for**] *an instinct for self-preservation* | **instinct to do sth** *a lion's instinct to hunt* | *My instinct would be to wait and see.* —compare INTUITION

**in·stinc·tive** /ɪnˈstɪŋktɪv/ *adj* based on instinct: *instinctive behaviour* | *an instinctive sympathy with the younger boys* —**instinctively** *adv*: *Instinctively, we dived for cover.*

**in·sti·tute¹** /ˈɪnstɪ̇tjuːt‖-tuːt/ *n* [C] an organization that has a particular purpose such as scientific or educational work, or the building where this organization is based: *The Institute for Contemporary Arts* | *research institutes* W2

**institute²** *v* [T] *formal* to introduce or start a system, rule, legal process etc: *institute divorce proceedings*

**in·sti·tu·tion** /ˌɪnstɪ̇ˈtjuːʃən‖-ˈtuː-/ *n* [C] W1

**1** ▶ **FOR SCIENCE/BUSINESS** ◀ a large establishment or organization that has a particular kind of work or purpose: *the most advanced medical institution in the world* | *a financial institution*

**2** ▶ **HOSPITAL ETC** ◀ **a)** a large building where old people or ORPHANS live and are looked after by an official organization: *The atmosphere of the institution was rather impersonal.* **b)** a word meaning a mental hospital, used when you want to avoid saying this directly

**3** ▶ **CUSTOM** ◀ an established system or custom in society: *the institution of marriage*

**4** ▶ **STARTING STH** ◀ the act of starting or introducing a system, rule etc: [+ **of**] *They approved the institution of a new law.*

**5** ▶ **PERSON** ◀ **be an institution** *humorous* to be so well known in a place that you seem to be a permanent part of it: *Bill Tucker has been the postman in our village for 40 years. He's become something of an institution.* —**institutional** *adj*

**in·sti·tu·tion·al·ize** also **-ise** *BrE* /ˌɪnstɪ̇ˈtjuːʃənəlaɪz‖-ˈtuː-/ *v* [T] *old-fashioned* to put someone in a mental hospital or institution for old people etc

**in·sti·tu·tion·al·ized** also **-ised** *BrE* /ˌɪnstɪ̇tjuːʃənəlaɪzd‖-ˈtuː-/ *adj* **1 institutionalized violence/racism/corruption** violence etc that has happened for so long in an organization or society that it has become accepted as normal **2** *formal* someone who has become institutionalized has lived for a long time in a prison, mental hospital etc and now cannot easily live outside one

**in-store** /ˌ· ˈ·◂/ *adj* happening within a large shop or DEPARTMENT STORE: *in-store sales demonstrations*

**in·struct** /ɪnˈstrʌkt/ *v* [T] **1** to officially tell someone what to do: **instruct sb to do sth** *Our staff have been instructed to offer you every assistance.* | **as instructed** (=in the way that you have been instructed) *We returned the questionnaire as instructed.* **2** to teach or show someone how to do something: **instruct sb in sth** *Mr. Anderson was instructing them in the art of screen printing.* —see TEACH (USAGE) **3** [usually passive] *formal* to officially inform someone about something: **instruct sb that** *We were instructed that the assembly would not vote until noon.* **4** *law* to employ a lawyer to deal with your case in court: *Once you have decided to proceed with a case, you should instruct a good solicitor.*

**in·struc·tion** /ɪnˈstrʌkʃən/ *n* **1 instructions** [plural] the printed information that tells you how to use a piece of equipment etc: *We forgot to read the instructions.* | **follow the instructions** *Follow the instructions on the back of the box.* **2** [C, usually plural] a statement telling someone what they must do: **instructions to do sth** *He had explicit instructions to check everyone's identity card at the door.* | **instructions that** *Mrs Edwards left strict instructions that she was not to be disturbed.* | **on sb's instructions** (=because you have been officially told to do it) *On his instructions, the luggage had been sent on.* | **my instructions are** (=used to tell someone what you have been officially told to do) *My instructions are to give the package to him personally.* **3** [U] *formal* teaching that you are given in a particular skill or subject: *religious instruction* | *driving instruction* | [+ **in**] *You will receive basic instruction in navigation.* | **under (sb's)** S3 W2

**instruction** (=while being taught by someone) *Under Stewart's instruction, I slowly mastered the art of glass blowing.*

**in·struc·tion·al** /ɪnˈstrʌkʃənəl/ *adj formal* providing instruction: *instructional materials*

**instruction ma·nu·al** /·ˈ·· ˌ···/ *n* [C] a book that gives you instructions on how to use or look after a machine

**in·struc·tive** /ɪnˈstrʌktɪv/ *adj* providing a lot of useful information, explanations, and knowledge about something: *an instructive book on photography | a very instructive experience* —**instructively** *adv*

**in·struc·tor** /ɪnˈstrʌktə‖-ər/ *n* [C] **1** someone who teaches a sport or practical skill: *a driving instructor | ski instructors* **2** *AmE* someone who teaches in an American college or university before they have finished being trained: *a social studies instructor*

W 2 **in·stru·ment** /ˈɪnstrʊmənt/ *n* [C]

**1** ▶ **TOOL** ◀ a small tool used in work such as science or medicine where very careful movements are necessary: *surgical instruments*

**2** ▶ **MUSIC** ◀ an object such as a piano, horn, VIOLIN etc, used for producing musical sounds; MUSICAL INSTRUMENT: *stringed instruments*

**3** ▶ **FOR MEASURING** ◀ a piece of equipment for measuring and showing distance, speed, temperature etc: *The pilot studied his instruments anxiously.* | **instrument flying/landing** (=flying or bringing down an aircraft using only instruments)

**4** ▶ **METHOD** ◀ [usually singular] a system, method, or law that is used by people in power to get a particular result: *Sometimes military force can become an instrument of government policy.*

**5** ▶ **DOCUMENT** ◀ *formal* a legal document

**6** *literary* **instrument of fate/God** someone or something that is used by an unseen power which is beyond our control

**7** **instrument of torture** a piece of equipment used to make people suffer pain

**in·stru·men·tal**[1] /ˌɪnstrʊˈmentl◂/ *adj* **1** **be instrumental in** *formal* to be important in making something possible: *Wilson was instrumental in introducing new methods of production.* **2** instrumental music is for instruments, not for voices —**instrumentally** *adv* —**instrumentality** /ˌɪnstrʊmenˈtælɪti/ *n* [U]

**instrumental**[2] *n* [C] a piece of music or a part of a piece of music where no voices are used, only instruments

**in·stru·men·tal·ist** /ˌɪnstrʊˈmentəlɪst/ *n* [C] someone who plays a musical instrument —compare VOCALIST

**in·stru·men·ta·tion** /ˌɪnstrʊmenˈteɪʃən/ *n* [U] **1** the way in which a piece of music is arranged to be played by several different instruments **2** the set of instruments (INSTRUMENT (3)) used to help in controlling a machine: *the complex instrumentation in an aircraft's cockpit*

**instrument pan·el** /ˈ··· ˌ··/ *n* [C] the board in front of the pilot of an aircraft, where all the instruments (INSTRUMENT (3)) are

**in·sub·or·di·nate** /ˌɪnsəˈbɔːdənɪt◂‖-ɔːr-/ *adj* refusing to obey someone who has a higher rank than you in the army, navy etc —**insubordination** /ˌɪnsəbɔːdʒˈneɪʃən‖-ɔːr-/ *n* [U]: *Howell was dismissed for gross insubordination.*

**in·sub·stan·tial** /ˌɪnsəbˈstænʃəl◂/ *adj* **1** *formal* something that is insubstantial is much too small or weak and does not look solid enough: *a slender rope bridge, terrifyingly insubstantial* **2** *literary* not existing as a real object or person: *Pale figures, like insubstantial ghosts, moved through the mist.* —**insubstantiality** /ˌɪnsəbstænʃiˈælɪti/ *n* [U]

**in·suf·fe·ra·ble** /ɪnˈsʌfərəbəl/ *adj* extremely annoying or unpleasant: *the insufferable heat | Lou can be pretty insufferable at times.* —**insufferably** *adv*: *insufferably arrogant*

**in·suf·fi·cient** /ˌɪnsəˈfɪʃənt◂/ *adj* not enough: *insufficient supplies* | [+ **for**] *There were insufficient funds for a research project.* | **insufficient to do sth** *The evidence is quite insufficient to convict him.* —**insufficiently** *adv* —**insufficiency** *n* [singular, U] *an insufficiency of capital*

**in·su·lar** /ˈɪnsjʊlə‖ˈɪnsələr, ˈɪnʃə-/ *adj* **1** not interested in anything except your own group, country, way of life etc: *In today's small world, we must guard against an insular outlook.* **2** *formal* like or connected with an island —**insularity** /ˌɪnsjʊˈlærɪti‖-sə-, -ʃə-/ *n* [U] *the insularity of the British*

**in·su·late** /ˈɪnsjʊleɪt‖ˈɪnsə-, ˈɪnʃə-/ *v* [T] **1** to cover or protect something so that electricity, sound, heat etc cannot get in or out: *insulated cables* | **insulate sth from/against** *A bird fluffs up its feathers to insulate itself against the cold.* **2** to protect someone from unpleasant experiences or unwanted influences: **insulate sb from sth** *students insulated from the experiences of real life*

**in·su·lat·ing tape** /ˈ···· ˌ·/ *n* [U] narrow material used for wrapping around electric wires to insulate them

**in·su·la·tion** /ˌɪnsjʊˈleɪʃən‖ˌɪnsə-/ *n* [U] **1** material used to insulate something, especially a building **2** the act of insulating something or the state of being insulated: *Good insulation can save you lots of money on heating bills.*

**in·su·la·tor** /ˈɪnsjʊleɪtə‖ˈɪnsəleɪtər/ *n* [C] an object or material that insulates, especially one which does not allow electricity to pass through it

**in·su·lin** /ˈɪnsjʊlɪn‖ˈɪnsə-/ *n* [U] a substance produced naturally by your body which allows sugar to be used for energy —see also DIABETES

**in·sult**[1] /ɪnˈsʌlt/ *v* [T] to say or do something that is rude and offensive to someone: *Nobody insults my family and gets away with it!* | *I hope Andy won't feel insulted if I turn down his invitation.* | **insult sb by doing sth** *Please don't insult me by offering me money.*

**in·sult**[2] /ˈɪnsʌlt/ *n* [C] **1** a rude or offensive remark or action: *She was shouting insults at her boyfriend.* | *$200 for all that work? It's an insult.* | **take sth as an insult** *Carol will take it as an insult if you don't come to the party.* **2** **be an insult to sb's intelligence** if something such as a book, lesson, or television programme is an insult to your intelligence, it offends you by being too simple or stupid —see also **add insult to injury** (ADD (8))

**in·sult·ing** /ɪnˈsʌltɪŋ/ *adj* very rude and offensive to someone: *insulting remarks*

**in·su·pe·ra·ble** /ɪnˈsjuːpərəbəl◂‖ɪnˈsuː-/ *adj formal* an insuperable difficulty or problem is impossible to deal with: *Getting an agreement between the two leaders proved to be an insuperable obstacle.* —**insuperably** *adv*

**in·sup·por·ta·ble** /ˌɪnsəˈpɔːtəbəl◂‖-ˈpɔːr-/ *adj formal* too unpleasant for you to bear: *insupportable behaviour | insupportable pain*

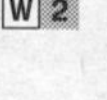

**in·sur·ance** /ɪnˈʃʊərəns‖-ˈʃʊr-/ *n* **1** [U] an arrangement with a company in which you pay them money each year and they pay the costs if anything bad happens to you, such as an illness or an accident: *health insurance | life insurance* (=so that your family receive money if you die) | [+ **against**] *insurance against permanent disability* | [+ **on**] *Do you have insurance on your household contents?* | **claim for sth on your insurance** (=get an insurance company to pay for something) *We can probably claim for the damage on the insurance.* | **take out insurance** (=start paying for insurance protection) **2** [U] the money that you pay regularly to an insurance company; INSURANCE PREMIUM: [+ **on**] *Insurance on my house is very high.* **3** [U] the business of providing insurance: *He works in insurance.* **4** [singular, U] protection against something bad happening: [+ **against**] *I put an extra lock on the door as an added insurance against burglars.* —see also ASSURANCE, (3) NATIONAL INSURANCE

**insurance ad·just·er** /·ˈ··· ˌ··/ *n* [C] *AmE* someone who is employed by an insurance company to decide how much to pay people who have had an accident, had something stolen etc; LOSS ADJUSTER *BrE*

**insurance bro·ker** /ˈ·· ˌ··/ also **insurance agent** *n* [C] someone who arranges and sells insurance as their job

**insurance pol·i·cy** /ˈ··· ˌ···/ *n* [C] a written agreement with an insurance company

**insurance pre·mi·um** /ˈ··· ˌ···/ *n* [C] the money that you pay regularly to an insurance company

**in·sure** /ɪnˈʃʊə‖-ˈʃʊr/ *v* **1** [I,T] to buy insurance to protect yourself against something bad happening to you, your family, your possessions etc: *Have you insured the contents of your home?* | **insure (sth/sb) against sth** *It would be wise to insure your property against storm damage.* | **insure sth for £1000/$2000 etc** *I would advise you to insure the painting for at least £100,000.* **2** [T] to provide insurance for something or someone: *Many companies won't insure young drivers.* **3** an American spelling of ENSURE

**insure against** sth *phr v* [T] to protect yourself against the risk of something bad happening by planning or preparing: *No matter what precautions you may take, you cannot insure against every eventuality.*

**USAGE NOTE: INSURE**

WORD CHOICE: **assure, reassure, insure, ensure, make sure**

If you **assure** someone of something, you tell them that it is really true or will happen: *The receptionist assured me that I would not have to wait long.* | *Christianity assures us there is life after death.*

You **reassure** someone who is worried by telling them that there is nothing to worry about: *The doctor reassured me that there would be no pain.*

You may **insure** something against something bad happening to it by paying money to an insurance company: *Is the house insured against fire?* | *Julia Roberts' legs are insured for a large amount of money.* It is also possible to **insure** your life against death, though where something is certain to happen one day the technical British English word is **assure**.

If you **ensure** (usually **insure** in American English) that something happens, that means you make certain or **make sure** (more informal) it does happen: *Please ensure that the lights are switched off before leaving the building.* In some situations **assure** can be used in this meaning too where the object is reflexive or what is ensured is something such as success, safety, comfort etc: *I assured myself of a seat at the front* (=I made sure I got one). | *The band's latest release has assured their success in the rock world* (=ensured that they will be successful).

**in·sured** /ɪnˈʃʊəd‖-ˈʃʊrd/ *adj* **1** having insurance: *Mike's bike was stolen and it wasn't insured.* | **insured to do sth** *You wouldn't be insured to drive Anne's car.* | [+ **against**] *Is your house insured against fire?* **2 the insured** *law* the person or people who are insured

**in·sur·er** /ɪnˈʃʊərə‖-ˈʃʊrər/ *n* [C] a person or company that provides insurance: *The insurer will pay the full cost of storm damage.*

**in·sur·gent** /ɪnˈsɜːdʒənt‖-ɜːr-/ *n* [C often plural] one of a group of people fighting against the government of their own country —**insurgency** *n* [U] —**insurgent** *adj*: *the insurgent forces* —see also COUNTERINSURGENCY

**in·sur·moun·ta·ble** /ˌɪnsəˈmaʊntəbəl◂‖-sər-/ *adj* a difficulty or problem that is insurmountable is too large or too difficult to deal with: *The language barrier proved an insurmountable barrier to their relationship.*

**in·sur·rec·tion** /ˌɪnsəˈrekʃən/ *n* [C,U] an attempt by a large group of people within a country to take control using force and violence: *an armed insurrection against the party in power* —**insurrectionist** *n*

**in·tact** /ɪnˈtækt/ *adj* [not before noun] not broken, damaged, or spoiled, usually after something bad has happened: *The fireplace was the only thing that remained intact after the tornado.* | *Somehow his reputation survived the scandal intact.*

**in·ta·gli·o** /ɪnˈtɑːliəʊ‖-lioʊ/ *n* [C,U] the art of cutting patterns into a hard substance or the pattern that you get by doing this

**in·take** /ˈɪnteɪk/ *n* **1** [singular] the amount of food, drink etc that you take into your body: *Lower your intake of fat and alcohol to improve your health.* **2** the number of people allowed to enter a school, profession etc: *an increase in the intake of foreign students* **3** [C] a tube, pipe, etc through which air, gas, or liquid is taken in: *air intakes on a jet engine* **4 an intake of breath** a sudden act of breathing in, showing that you are shocked etc

**in·tan·gi·ble** /ɪnˈtændʒəbəl/ *adj* an intangible quality or feeling cannot be clearly felt or described, although you know it exists; INDEFINABLE: *The island of Iona has an intangible quality of holiness.* | *Customer goodwill is an important and intangible asset of a business.* —**intangibly** *adv* —**intangibility** /ɪnˌtændʒəˈbɪləti/ *n* [U]

**in·te·ger** /ˈɪntədʒə‖-ər/ *n* [C] *technical* a whole number: *6 is an integer, but 6.4 is not.*

**in·te·gral** /ˈɪntəgrəl/ *adj* forming a necessary part of something: *Effective communication is an integral part of being a teacher.* | [+ **to**] *Her talents are integral to the team's good performance.* —**integrally** *adv*

**integral cal·cu·lus** /ˌ··· ˈ···/ *n* [U] *technical* a method of measuring the distance a moving object has moved at a particular moment, by using your knowledge of its speed until then

**in·te·grate** /ˈɪntəgreɪt/ *v* **1** [I,T] to join in the life and customs of the group or society that you live in so that you are accepted by them, or to help someone do this: [+ **into/with**] *The child was only adopted a year ago, but she has completely integrated into the family's life.* | *Attempts to integrate the new immigrants have failed.* **2** [T] to combine things that work well together in order to make an effective system: *Train and bus services have been fully integrated.* | **integrate sth with sth** *The school integrates maths lessons with computer studies.* **3** [I,T] to end the separation of races in a place or institution, usually by making separation illegal; DESEGREGATE: *Laws were passed in the US in order to integrate all schools.* —compare SEGREGATE

**in·te·grat·ed** /ˈɪntəgreɪtəd/ *adj* an integrated system, institution etc combines many different groups, ideas, or parts in a way that works well: *an integrated public transport system* | *A fully integrated school with children from many races and classes.* —compare SEGREGATED

**integrated cir·cuit** /ˌ···· ˈ··/ *n* [C] *technical* a very small set of electronic connections printed on a single piece of SEMICONDUCTOR material instead of being made from separate parts

**in·te·gra·tion** /ˌɪntəˈgreɪʃən/ *n* [U] **1** the combining of two or more things so that they work together effectively: *the closer integration of the countries' economies* **2** the acceptance of people in a group or society: *complete integration of racial groups* **3** the ending of laws that make people of different races live, work etc separately W3

**in·teg·ri·ty** /ɪnˈtegrəti/ *n* [U] **1** the quality of being honest and of always having high moral principles: *a man of absolute integrity, with the highest moral standards* **2** *formal* the state of being united as one complete thing: *Removing the chapter destroys the integrity of the book.*

**in·teg·u·ment** /ɪnˈtegjəmənt/ *n* [C] *technical* something such as a shell which covers something else

**in·tel·lect** /ˈɪntəlekt/ *n* **1** [C,U] the ability to understand things and to think intelligently: *new scientific ideas that are a challenge to the human intellect* | *a woman of superior intellect* **2** [C] someone who is very intelligent: *some of the greatest intellects in the world of science*

**in·tel·lec·tual**[1] /ˌɪntəˈlektʃuəl◂/ *adj* **1** an intellectual activity, quality etc involves intelligent thinking in order to understand or enjoy something: *an intellectual film* | *The student showed enormous intellectual ability.* **2** an intellectual person is well-educated and interested in serious ideas and subjects such as science, literature etc: *an intellectual family* —**intellectually** *adv*: *intellectually stimulating* —**intellectualize** *v* [I,T] W3

**intellectual**[2] *n* [C] an intelligent, well-educated person who spends a lot of their time thinking about complicated ideas and discussing them: *He likes to think of himself as an intellectual.* —see INTELLIGENT (USAGE)

**intellectual prop·er·ty** /ˌ····ˈ···/ *n* [U] *law* something which someone has invented or has the right to make or sell, especially something protected by a PATENT[1] (1), TRADEMARK, or COPYRIGHT

S3 W3 **in·tel·li·gence** /ɪnˈteləd͡ʒəns/ *n* [U] **1 a)** the ability to learn, understand, and think about things: *a child of low intelligence | Don't act like such an idiot – use your intelligence!* **b)** a high level of this ability: *a woman of beauty, charm, and intelligence* **2 a)** information about the secret activities of foreign governments, the military plans of an enemy etc: *intelligence gathering* **b)** a group of people or an organization that gathers this information for their government: *He works for British Intelligence. | reports from Military Intelligence*

**intelligence quo·tient** /ˈ··· ˌ··/ *n* [C] IQ

S3 **in·tel·li·gent** /ɪnˈteləd͡ʒənt/ *adj* **1** having a high level of mental ability so that you are good at understanding ideas and thinking quickly and clearly: *If you're reasonably intelligent the maths involved should present no problems.* **2** an intelligent animal is able to think and understand: *Are there intelligent forms of life on other planets?* —**intelligently** *adv*

> **USAGE NOTE: INTELLIGENT**
> WORD CHOICE: **intelligent, intellectual**
> An **intelligent** person is someone with a quick and clever mind, but an **intellectual** person is someone who is well-educated and interested in subjects that need long periods of study. A small child, or even a dog, can be **intelligent** but cannot be called **intellectual**.
> **Intelligent** and **intellectual** are both adjectives, but **intellectual** can also be a noun: *There are too many intellectuals in the government.*

**in·tel·li·gent·si·a** /ɪnˌteləˈd͡ʒentsiə/ *n* **the intelligentsia** the people in a society who are most highly educated and who are most interested in new ideas and developments, especially in art, literature, or politics

**in·tel·li·gi·ble** /ɪnˈteləd͡ʒəbəl/ *adj* intelligible speech, writing, or ideas can be easily understood: *He was so drunk that his speech was barely intelligible.* | [+ **to**] *Newspapers must be intelligible to all levels of readers.* —**intelligibly** *adv* —**intelligibility** /ɪnˌteləd͡ʒəˈbɪləti/ *n* [U] —opposite UNINTELLIGIBLE

**in·tem·per·ate** /ɪnˈtempərət/ *adj formal* **1** not having enough control over your feelings so that you behave in a way that is unacceptable to other people: *an intemperate outburst* **2** regularly drinking too much alcohol —**intemperately** *adv* —**intemperance** *n* [U]

S3 W1 **in·tend** /ɪnˈtend/ *v* [T] **1** to have something in your mind as a plan or purpose: **intend to do sth** *I intend to get there as soon after 5 as I can.* | **intend sb/sth to do sth** *I didn't intend her to see the painting until it was finished.* | *He was insulted by my remark, but I hadn't intended it to be offensive.* | **it is intended that** *It is intended that all new employees will receive appropriate training.* | **fully intend** (=definitely intend) *Kate had fully intended returning home on Sunday but she couldn't get a flight.* —see PROPOSE (USAGE) **2 be intended for sb/sth** to be provided or designed for a particular purpose or person: *a book intended for young children* **3 intended target/victim/destination etc** the person, thing, result etc that an action is intended to affect or reach: *It seems likely that General Rocha was the intended victim.*

**in·tend·ed** /ɪnˈtendəd/ *n* **sb's intended** *old-fashioned or humorous* the person that you are going to marry: *Meet my intended, Miss Robinson.*

W3 **in·tense** /ɪnˈtens/ *adj* **1** having a very strong effect or felt very strongly: *intense pain | The heat was intense.* **2** there is intense activity, effort etc when people are working, trying, or thinking extremely hard: *a period of intense concentration and study* **3** having feelings or opinions that are extremely strong, serious etc: *She can be so intense, it makes me exhausted. | an intense young man* —**intensely** *adv*: *intensely exciting* —**intensity** *n* [U]

**in·ten·si·fi·er** /ɪnˈtensəfaɪə‖-ər/ *n* [C] *technical* a word, usually an adverb, that is used to emphasize an adjective, adverb, or verb, for example the word 'absolutely' in the phrase 'that's absolutely wonderful'

**in·ten·si·fy** /ɪnˈtensəfaɪ/ *v* [I,T] if an activity, effort, feeling etc intensifies, or if you intensify it, it increases in degree or strength: *Police have now intensified the search for the lost child.* —**intensification** /ɪnˌtensəfəˈkeɪʃən/ *n* [U] *the intensification of the conflict in Bosnia*

**in·ten·sive** /ɪnˈtensɪv/ *adj* **1** involving a lot of activity, effort, or careful attention in a short period of time: *a one-week intensive course in English | a period of intensive fighting* **2 intensive farming/agriculture** farming which produces a lot of food from a small area of land: *Most of lowland Britain is intensively cultivated.* —**intensively** *adv* —see also LABOUR-INTENSIVE

**intensive care** /·ˌ·· ˈ·/ *n* [U] a department in a hospital that gives special attention and treatment to people who are very seriously ill or badly injured

**in·tent**[1] /ɪnˈtent/ *n* [U] **1 to all intents (and purposes)** *especially spoken* almost completely: *To all intents and purposes, their marriage is over.* **2** *formal* what you intend to do; intention: *She behaved foolishly but with good intent.* **3** *law* the intention to do something illegal: *arrested for loitering with intent* | **intent to do sth** *Jefferson was charged with intent to damage property.*

**intent**[2] *adj* **1** giving careful attention to something so that you think about nothing else: *watching the game with an intent stare* | [+ **on/upon**] *Intent upon her work, she ignored the cold.* **2 be intent on (doing) sth** to be determined to do something or achieve something, especially something that may cause damage: *Pete seems intent on stirring up trouble.* —**intently** *adv*: *I noticed her gazing intently at one of the photographs.* —**intentness** *n* [U]

**in·ten·tion** /ɪnˈtenʃən/ *n* [C,U] something that you intend to do: **have no intention of doing sth** *I have no intention of helping him after what he said to me.* | **with the intention of doing sth** *They went into town with the intention of visiting the library.* | **intention to do sth** *It is our intention to be the number one distributor of health products.* | **good intentions/the best intentions** (=intentions to do something good or kind especially when you do not succeed in doing) *So much for all our good intentions!* —see also WELL-INTENTIONED 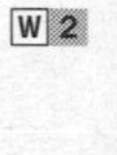

**in·ten·tion·al** /ɪnˈtenʃənəl/ *adj* done deliberately and usually intended to cause harm: *I did trip him, but it wasn't intentional.* —**intentionally** *adv*: *intentionally vague promises* —opposite UNINTENTIONAL

**in·ter** /ɪnˈtɜː‖-ˈtɜːr/ *v* **interred, interring** [T] *formal* to bury a dead person —opposite DISINTER

**inter-** /ɪntə‖-tər/ *prefix* between; among a group: *intermarry* (=marry someone of another race, religion, etc)

**in·ter·act** /ˌɪntərˈækt/ *v* [I] **1** if people interact with each other, they talk to each other and understand each other: [+ **with**] *Vanessa interacts well with other children in the class.* **2** if two or more things interact, they have an effect on each other and work together: *social and economic factors interacting to produce a recession | hormones interacting in the body*

W3 **in·ter·ac·tion** /ˌɪntərˈækʃən/ *n* [C,U] **1** a process by which two or more things have an effect on each other and work together: [+ **of**] *the interaction of the tones of demand and supply* | [+ **with/between**] *complex interaction between mind and body* **2** the activity of talking to other people and understanding them: [+ **with/between**] *the degree of interaction between teacher and student*

**in·ter·act·ive** /ˌɪntərˈæktɪv◂/ *adj* **1** interactive teaching methods, processes etc involve people working together and discussing what they do **2 interactive**

programs computer programs etc involving communication between a computer and the person using it: *interactive educational software* —**interactively** *adv* —**interactivity** /ˌɪntəræk'tɪvɪ̇ti/ *n* [U]

**in·ter a·li·a** /ˌɪntər 'eɪliə, -'ɑːliə/ *adv Latin formal* among other things: *The paper discussed, inter alia, political, economic, and judicial issues.*

**in·ter·breed** /ˌɪntə'briːd‖-ər-/ *v past tense and past participle* **interbred** /-'bred/ [I + **with** , T] to produce young animals from parents of different breeds or groups —compare CROSSBREED², INBREEDING

**in·ter·cede** /ˌɪntə'siːd‖-ər-/ *v* [I] to speak in support of someone, especially in order to try to prevent them from being punished: [+ **with**] *My good friend, Senator Bowie, interceded with the authorities on my behalf.* —see also INTERCESSION

intercept

**in·ter·cept** /ˌɪntə'sept‖-ər-/ *v* [T] to stop or catch something or someone that is going from one place to another: *We rely on the coastguard to intercept boats running drugs from the island.*|*Harker's phone calls had been intercepted.* —**interception** /-'sepʃən/ *n* [C,U]

**in·ter·cep·tor** /ˌɪntə'septəʳ‖-tər'septər/ *n* [C] a light fast military aircraft

**in·ter·ces·sion** /ˌɪntə'seʃən‖-tər-/ *n* **1** [U + **with**] an act of interceding **2** [C,U] a prayer asking for someone to be helped or cured

**in·ter·change¹** /'ɪntətʃeɪndʒ‖-ər-/ *n* **1** [singular, U] an exchange, especially of ideas or thoughts: *the interchange of ideas between students and staff* **2** [C] a point where a MOTORWAY and a main road join and are connected by several smaller roads

I

**interchange²** /ˌɪntə'tʃeɪndʒ‖-ər-/ *v* [I,T] to put each of two things in the place of the other or to be exchanged in this way

**in·ter·chan·gea·ble** /ˌɪntə'tʃeɪndʒəbəl‖-tər-/ *adj* things that are interchangeable can be used instead of each other: *interchangeable parts*|*These two words are almost interchangeable.* —**interchangeably** *adv* —**interchangeability** /ˌɪntətʃeɪndʒə'bɪlɪ̇ti‖-tər-/ *n* [U]

**in·ter·cit·y** /ˌɪntə'sɪti◂‖-tər-/ *adj* [only before noun] happening between two or more cities, or going from one city to another: *an intercity train service*|*intercity rivalry*

**in·ter·col·le·giate** /ˌɪntəkə'liːdʒɪ̇t‖-tər-/ *adj* intercollegiate competitions are between members of different colleges: *an intercollegiate football game*

**in·ter·com** /'ɪntəkɒm‖'ɪntərkɑːm/ *n* [C] a communication system by which people in different parts of a building, aircraft etc to speak to each other: *The pilot spoke to the passengers over the intercom.*

**in·ter·com·mu·ni·cate** /ˌɪntəkə'mjuːnɪ̇keɪt‖-tər-/ *v* [I + **with**] **1** *formal* to communicate with each other and exchange information **2** if two rooms intercommunicate, there is a door leading from one to the other —**intercommunication** /ˌɪntəkəmjuːnɪ̇'keɪʃən‖-tər-/ *n* [U]

**in·ter·con·nect** /ˌɪntəkə'nekt‖-tər-/ *v* [I + **with**] if two systems interconnect, they are connected to each other: *a set of interconnecting pipes* —**interconnected** *adj*

**in·ter·con·ti·nen·tal** /ˌɪntəkɒntɪ̇'nentl◂‖-tər'kɑːn-/ *adj* happening between two CONTINENTS (=for example Africa and Asia) or going from one continent to another: *intercontinental trade*|*an intercontinental flight*

**in·ter·course** /'ɪntəkɔːs‖'ɪntərkɔːrs/ *n* [U] *formal* **1** the act of having sex; SEXUAL INTERCOURSE **2** an exchange of ideas, feelings etc which make people or groups understand each other better: *social intercourse*

**in·ter·de·nom·i·na·tio·nal** /ˌɪntədɪ̇nɒmɪ̇'neɪʃənəl‖ˌɪntərdɪ̇nɑː-/ *adj* between or involving Christians from different groups

**in·ter·de·part·men·tal** /ˌɪntəˌdiːpɑːt'mentl‖ˌɪntərdɪˌpɑːrt'mentl/ *adj* between or involving different departments of a company, government etc: *intense interdepartmental rivalry*

**in·ter·de·pen·dence** /ˌɪntədɪ'pendəns‖-tər-/ *n* [U] a situation in which people or things depend on each other

**in·ter·de·pen·dent** /ˌɪntədɪ'pendənt◂‖-tər-/ *adj* depending on or necessary to each other: *countries with interdependent economies* —**interdependently** *adv*

**in·ter·dict** /'ɪntədɪkt‖tər-/ *n* [C] **1** *law* an official order from a court telling someone not to do something **2** *technical* a punishment in the Roman Catholic Church, by which someone is not allowed to take part in church ceremonies —**interdict** /ˌɪntə'dɪkt‖-ər-/ *v* [T]

**in·ter·dis·ci·plin·ary** /ˌɪntəˌdɪsɪ̇'plɪnəri‖ˌɪntər'dɪsəpləneri/ *adj* an interdisciplinary course of study includes two or more subjects: *an interdisciplinary course*

**in·terest¹** /'ɪntrɪ̇st/ *n*

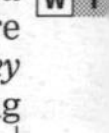
S2 W1

**1 ▶ FEELING ◀** [singular, U] a feeling that makes you want to pay attention to something or to find out more about it: *Ruth listened with evident interest.*|[+ **in**] *They share an interest in poetry.*|**lose interest** (=stop being interested): *The older ones soon lost interest in the game.*|**take an interest (in)** (=be interested in something): *Babies soon begin to take an interest in the world around them.*|**show/express interest** (=say you are interested in something or want to buy it): *Ben has shown an interst in learning French.*|*Several football clubs have expressed an interest in Giggs.*

**2 ▶ QUALITY ◀** [U] a quality or feature of something that attracts your attention or makes you want to know more about it: *Add interest to your decor with a patterned border.*|**of interest** (=interesting): *Tourist information will give you a list of local places of interest.*|**of general interest** (=that everyone wants to know about): *a subject of general interest*|**of special/particular interest**: *This book will be of particular interest to those studying British Politics since 1900.*|**be of no interest (to)** (=not be interesting to someone): *Your private problems are of no interest to me.*

**3 ▶ ACTIVITY ◀** [C] something that you enjoy doing or a subject that you enjoy studying when you are not working: *Her main interest in life is tennis.*|*List your leisure time interests on the back of the form.*

**4 ▶ MONEY ◀** [U] **a)** a charge made for borrowing money: *competitive rates of interest*|[+ **on**] *The interest on the loan is 16.5% per year.* **b)** money paid to you by a bank or financial institution when you keep money in an account there —see also COMPOUND INTEREST, SIMPLE INTEREST

**5 ▶ ADVANTAGE ◀** [C,U] the things that bring advantages to someone or something|**be in your (best) interest(s)** (=be helpful for you): *It would be in your interests to do as he says.*|**look after/protect/safeguard your interests**: *The company is endeavouring to protect its own interests.*|*the national interest*|**have sb's (best) interests at heart** (=care about someone and want to improve their situation): *Private employment agencies may not have your best interests at heart.*

**6 be in the public/national interest** be good or necessary for the safety or success of a country and its people: *The documents were kept secret 'in the public interest'.*

**7 in the interest(s) of justice/efficiency etc** in order to make a situation or system fair, efficient etc: *In the interest of justice, I must speak the truth.*

**8 (just) out of interest/as a matter of interest** *spoken* used to say that you are asking a question only because you are interested and not because you need to know: *Just out of interest, how much did they offer you?*|*As a matter of interest, where did you meet him?*
**9 have no interest in doing sth** not to want to do something: *I have no interest in continuing this conversation.*
**10 declare an interest (in sth)** to state that you are connected with something or someone, and so cannot be completely fair and independent when making a decision involving them: *I must declare an interest here, the second candidate is a friend of mine.*
**11 human interest/love interest** the part of a story or film which is interesting because it is about people's lives or romantic relationships
**12 pay sb back with interest** *informal* to harm or offend someone in an even worse way than they have harmed you
**13 ► SHARE IN COMPANY ◄** [C] *technical* a share in a company, business etc: *She's sold all her interests in the company.*|**controlling interest** (=enough shares to control what decisions are taken) *Müller has a controlling interest in the factory.*
**14 ► POWERFUL GROUP ◄** [C] *technical* a group of people in the same business who share aims or ideas: *landed interests*|*shipping interests* —see also SELF-INTEREST, VESTED INTEREST

This graph shows some of the words most commonly used with the noun **interest**.

interest in
of interest
public/national interest
lose interest
special interest
particular interest
best interests
general interest
10 20 30 40 per million

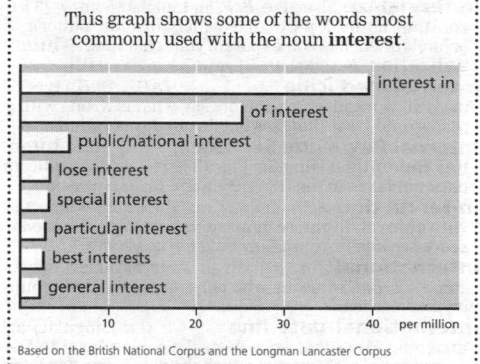

Based on the British National Corpus and the Longman Lancaster Corpus

**interest²** *v* [T] **1** to make someone feel interested: *Here's an article which might interest you.*|*What interests me is all the history of these places.*|**it may interest you to know** *spoken* (=used to introduce a fact which you think may surprise someone) *It may interest you to know that she is now head of a major company.* **2 could I interest you in a drink/a meal etc?** *spoken* used as a polite way of offering someone something

S1 W2 **in·terest·ed** /ˈɪntrɪ̣stɪ̣d/ *adj* **1** giving a lot of attention to something because you want to find out more about it: [+ **in**] *I'm not really interested in politics.*|*Carrie's fourteen now, and all she's interested in is clothes.*|**be interested to hear/know/see etc** *I'd be very interested to hear your opinion.* —opposite UNINTERESTED **2** *informal* eager to do or have something: *I offered to help but they weren't interested.*|**to be interested in doing sth** *Sheila's interested in starting her own business.*|[+ **in**] *Would you be interested in a secondhand Volvo?* **3 interested party/group** a person or group that is directly or personally conerned with a situation and is likely to be affected by its results: *All interested parties should write to the chairman of the inquiry.* —**interestedly** *adv* —see also DISINTERESTED

**interest-free** /ˌ·· ˈ·◂/ *adj* an interest-free LOAN¹ (1) has no interest charged on it: *interest-free credit*

**interest group** /ˈ·· ˌ·/ *n* [C] a group of people who join together to try to influence the government in order to protect their own particular rights, advantages etc

S1 W2 **in·terest·ing** /ˈɪntrɪ̣stɪŋ/ *adj* unusual or exciting in a way that keeps your attention: *an interesting film*|*I found his talk very interesting.*|**it is interesting to see/know etc** *It would be interesting to see figures supporting this argument.*|**it is interesting that** *It's interesting that no one remembers seeing the car.* —see BORING (USAGE)

**in·terest·ing·ly** /ˈɪntrɪ̣stɪŋli/ *adv* **1** [sentence adverb] used to introduce a fact that you think is interesting: *Interestingly enough, Pearson made no attempt to deny the rumour.* **2** in an interesting way

**interest rate** /ˈ·· ˌ·/ *n* [C] the PERCENTAGE amount charged by a bank etc when you borrow money or paid to you by a bank when you keep money in an account there: *The government intends to keep interest rates low.*

**in·ter·face¹** /ˈɪntəfeɪs‖-ər-/ *n* [C] **1** *technical* the part of a computer system through which two different machines are connected **2** the way in which two subjects, events etc affect each other **3** *technical* the surface where two things touch each other

**interface²** *v* [I, T + **with**] *technical* if you interface two parts of a computer system, or if they interface, you connect them

**in·ter·fere** /ˌɪntəˈfɪə‖-tərˈfɪr/ *v* [I] to deliberately get involved in a situation that does not concern you, and try to influence what happens in a way that annoys people: *I wish you'd stop interfering – you've caused enough problems already.*|*the interfering old busybody*|[+ **in**] *Some people believe it's not the church's job to interfere in politics.*

**interfere with** sth/sb *phr v* [T] **1** to prevent something from succeeding or from happening in the way that was planned: *Anxiety can interfere with children's performance at school.* **2** if something interferes with a radio or television broadcast, it spoils the sound or picture that you receive **3** to touch a child sexually: *He was arrested for interfering with young boys.*

**in·ter·fer·ence** /ˌɪntəˈfɪərəns‖-tərˈfɪr-/ *n* [U] **1** an act of interfering: *I resent his interference in my work.*|*Industrial relations should be free from state interference.* **2** unwanted noise on radio or television or on the telephone, or faults in the television picture: *The bad weather's causing a lot of television interference.* **3** *especially AmE* the act of blocking another player in ICE HOCKEY, American football etc by standing in front of them; OBSTRUCTION (4) *BrE* **4 run interference** *AmE* **a)** the act of protecting a player who has the ball in American football by blocking players from the opposing team **b)** the act of helping someone to achieve something by dealing with people or problems that might cause trouble

**in·ter·fer·on** /ˌɪntəˈfɪərɒn‖ˌɪntərˈfɪrɑːn/ *n* [U] a chemical substance that is produced by your body to fight against VIRUSes that cause disease

**in·ter·ga·lac·tic** /ˌɪntəgəˈlæktɪk◂‖-tər-/ *adj* between the large groups of stars in space: *intergalactic travel*

**in·ter·im¹** /ˈɪntərɪm/ *adj* [only before noun] an interim arrangement, report, payment etc is used or accepted temorarily, until a final or complete one is made; PROVISIONAL: *an interim report*|*He received an interim payment of £10,000.*

**interim²** *n* **in the interim** in the period of time between two events; MEANWHILE: *The child will be adopted but a relative is looking after him in the interim.*

**in·te·ri·or¹** /ɪnˈtɪəriə‖-ˈtɪriər/ *n* **1** [C usually singular] the inner part or inside of something: *His new Porsche has red bodywork with a black leather interior.* —opposite EXTERIOR¹ (1) **2 the interior** the part of a country that is farthest away from the coast: *The interior of the country is mainly desert.* **3 Minister/Department of the Interior** the minister or department that deals with matters within a country rather than abroad

**interior²** *adj* [only before noun] inside or indoors: *The interior walls are all painted white.* —opposite EXTERIOR² (1)

**interior de·co·ra·tor** /ˌ·,·· ˈ····/ also **interior de·sign·er** /ˌ·,··· ·ˈ··/ *n* [C] someone whose job is to plan and choose the colours, materials, furniture etc for the inside of people's houses

**in·ter·ject** /ˌɪntəˈdʒekt‖-tər-/ *v* [I,T] to interrupt what someone else is saying with a sudden remark: *"That's absolute rubbish!" he interjected.*

**in·ter·jec·tion** /ˌɪntəˈdʒekʃən‖-tər-/ *n* **1** [C] a word or phrase used to express a strong feeling such as shock, pain, or pleasure; EXCLAMATION **2** [C,U] an INTERRUPTION or the act of interrupting

**in·ter·lace** /ˌɪntəˈleɪs‖-ər-/ *v* [I, T] to join things together by weaving and twisting them over and under each other, or to be joined in this way: *The threads were interlaced with strands of gold.*

**in·ter·lard** /ˌɪntəˈlɑːd‖ˌɪntərˈlɑːrd/ *v* [T + **with**] *literary* to add things that are not necessary to a speech or piece of writing, such as foreign phrases

**in·ter·link** /ˌɪntəˈlɪŋk‖-ər-/ *v* [I, T] to connect or be connected with something else: *a chain of interlinking loops*

**in·ter·lock¹** /ˌɪntəˈlɒk‖ˌɪntərˈlɑːk/ *v* [I, T] if two or more things interlock or are interlocked, they fit firmly together: *a puzzle with 500 fully interlocking pieces*

**interlock²** /ˈɪntəlɒk‖-tərlɑːk/ *n* [C] *technical* a special part of a computer that prevents particular operations happening unless other operations have already happened

**in·ter·loc·u·tor** /ˌɪntəˈlɒkjʊtə‖ˌɪntərˈlɑːkjʊtər/ *n* [C] *formal* the person who is speaking to you

**in·ter·lop·er** /ˈɪntələʊpə‖-tərloʊpər/ *n* [C] someone who enters a place or group where they should not be: *The village women stared at the interloper with curiosity.*

**in·ter·lude** /ˈɪntəluːd‖-ər-/ *n* [C] **1** a period of time or an event that is different from what happens before and afterwards: *a brief interlude of peace before a return to the battlefield* **2** a short period of time between the parts of a play, concert etc **3** a short piece of music, talk etc used to fill such a period

**in·ter·mar·riage** /ˌɪntəˈmærɪdʒ‖-ər-/ *n* [U] **1** marriage between members of different races, families, or social groups: *intermarriage between black and white* **2** marriage within your own family or within a small group of relatives: *intermarriage between cousins*

**in·ter·mar·ry** /ˌɪntəˈmæri‖-ər-/ *v* [I + **with**] **1** if two groups or races intermarry, people from each group marry people from the other **2** to marry someone within your own group or family: *It is not unusual for royal cousins to intermarry.*

**in·ter·me·di·a·ry** /ˌɪntəˈmiːdiəri‖ˌɪntərˈmiːdieri/ *n* [C] a person or organization that tries to help two other people or groups to agree with each other: *Jackson acted as an intermediary between the two parties.* —**intermediary** *adj*: *an intermediary role in the negotiations*

**in·ter·me·di·ate** /ˌɪntəˈmiːdiət◂‖-tər-/ *adj* **1** an intermediate stage in a process of development is between two other stages: *an intermediate stage during which the disease is dormant* **2** an intermediate class, course etc is at a level between the first level and advanced level

**intermediate school** /ˌ..ˈ... ˌ./ *n* [C] *AmE* a JUNIOR HIGH SCHOOL or MIDDLE SCHOOL

**intermediate tech·no·lo·gy** /ˌ.... .ˈ.../ *n* [C,U] a practical science which is suitable for use in developing countries because it is cheap and simple

**in·ter·ment** /ɪnˈtɜːmənt‖-ɜːr-/ *n* [C, U] *formal* the act of burying a dead body

**in·ter·mez·zo** /ˌɪntəˈmetsəʊ‖-tərˈmetsoʊ/ *n* [C] a short piece of music, especially one that is played between the main parts of a concert, OPERA etc

**in·ter·mi·na·ble** /ɪnˈtɜːmɪnəbəl‖-ɜːr-/ *adj* very long and boring: *interminable delays* —**interminably** *adv*: *an interminably long speech*

**in·ter·min·gle** /ˌɪntəˈmɪŋgəl‖-tər-/ *v* [I, T usually passive] to mix together or mix something with something else: [+ **with**] *reds and oranges intermingled with pink*

**in·ter·mis·sion** /ˌɪntəˈmɪʃən‖-tər-/ *n* [C] *especially AmE* a short period of time between the parts of a play, concert etc; INTERVAL (5) *BrE*

**in·ter·mit·tent** /ˌɪntəˈmɪtənt◂‖-tər-/ *adj* happening repeatedly for short periods, but not regularly or continuously: *The weather forecast is for sun, with intermittent showers.* —**intermittently** *adv*

**in·ter·mix** /ˌɪntəˈmɪks‖-ər-/ *v* [I,T] to mix together, or mix things together

**in·tern¹** /ɪnˈtɜːn‖-ɜːrn/ *v* [T] to put someone in prison or limit their movements for political reasons or during a war, without charging them with a crime: *Seven hundred men were interned in the camps.*

**intern²** /ˈɪntɜːn‖-ɜːrn/ *AmE* someone who has nearly finished training as a doctor and is working in a hospital; HOUSEMAN *BrE*

**in·ter·nal** /ɪnˈtɜːnl‖-ɜːr-/ *adj* **1** [only before noun] inside something rather than outside: *They've knocked down a couple of internal walls.* | *the internal measurements of the car* **2** inside your body: *The X-rays showed there were no internal injuries.* | *an internal examination* **3** within an organization, place etc rather than outside it: *There's to be an internal inquiry into the whole affair.* | *the internal mail* **4** within a particular country: *internal trade* | *Internal security became a priority after the bomb attack.* **5** existing in your mind: *internal doubts* —**internally** *adv*: *The matter will be dealt with internally.* | *This medicine must not be taken internally.* —opposite EXTERNAL W2

**internal com·bus·tion en·gine** /ˌ.. .ˈ.. ˌ../ *n* [C] an engine that produces power by burning petrol

**in·ter·nal·ize** also **-ise** *BrE* /ɪnˈtɜːnəlaɪz‖-ɜːr-/ *v* [T] if you internalize a particular belief, attitude, pattern of behaviour etc it becomes part of your character —**internalization** /ɪnˌtɜːnəlaɪˈzeɪʃən‖ɪnˌtɜːrnələ-/ *n* [U]

**internal med·icine** /ˌ.. ˈ..‖ˌ.. ˈ.../ *n* [U] *AmE* a type of medical work in which doctors say what is wrong with a person and treat illnesses but do not do operations

**Internal Rev·e·nue Ser·vice** /ˌ.. ˈ... ˌ../ also **Internal Revenue** *n* [singular] the department that collects national taxes in the US — compare INLAND REVENUE

**in·ter·na·tion·al¹** /ˌɪntəˈnæʃənəl◂‖-tər-/ *adj* connected with or involving more than one nation: *an international peace-keeping force* | *an international conference* 

**international²** *n* [C] **1** an international sports game **2** *BrE* someone who plays for one of their country's sports teams

**international date line** /ˌ..... ˈ. ./ *n* [singular] an imaginary line that goes from the NORTH POLE to the SOUTH POLE, to the east of which the date is one day later than it is to the west

**In·ter·na·tion·ale** /ˌɪntənæʃəˈnæl‖-tər-/ *n* **the Internationale** the international SOCIALIST² (1) song

**in·ter·na·tion·al·is·m** /ˌɪntəˈnæʃənəlɪzəm‖-tər-/ *n* [U] the belief that nations should work together and help each other —**internationalist** *n*

**in·ter·na·tion·al·ize** also **-ise** *BrE* /ˌɪntəˈnæʃənəlaɪz‖-tər-/ *v* [T] to make something international or bring it under international control —**internationalization** /ˌɪntənæʃənəlaɪˈzeɪʃən‖ˌɪntərnæʃənələ-/ *n*

**in·ter·na·tion·al·ly** /ˌɪntəˈnæʃənəli‖-tər-/ *adv* in many different parts of the world: *A recent investment boom should help firms to compete internationally.* | **internationally famous/recognized/celebrated etc**: *Callas quickly became internationally famous.*

**International Mon·e·ta·ry Fund** /ˌ..... ˈ.... ./ *n* the IMF

**in·ter·ne·cine** /ˌɪntəˈniːsaɪn◂‖ˌɪntərˈniːsən◂, -ˈnesiːn◂/ *adj formal* internecine fighting, disputes etc happen between members of the same group or nation: *bitter internecine strife*

**in·tern·ee** /ˌɪntɜːˈniː‖-ɜːr-/ *n* [C] someone who is put into prison during a war or for political reasons, usually without a TRIAL¹ (1): *a call for the release of all internees*

**In·ter·net** /ˈɪntənet‖-tər-/ *n* **the Internet** a computer system that allows millions of computer users around the world to exchange information

**in·tern·ist** /ˈɪntɜːnɪst‖-tɜːr-/ *n* [C] *AmE* a doctor who has a general knowledge about all illnesses and medical conditions but who does not do operations

**in·tern·ment** /ɪnˈtɜːnmənt‖-ɜːr-/ *n* **1** [U] the act of keeping people in prison or in special camps for political reasons, without charging them with a crime **2** [C] the period of time during which someone is kept in this way

**in·ter·pen·e·trate** /ˌɪntəˈpenɪ̵treɪt‖-tər-/ *v* [I, T] *formal* to spread through something or spread through each other —**interpenetration** /ˌɪntəpenɪ̵ˈtreɪʃən‖-tər-/ *n* [C, U]

**in·ter·per·son·al** /ˌɪntəˈpɜːsənəl◂‖-tərˈpɜːr-/ *adj* involving relations between people: *interpersonal skills*

**in·ter·plan·e·ta·ry** /ˌɪntəˈplænɪ̵təri◂‖ˌɪntərˈplænɪ̵teri◂/ *adj* [only before noun] between the PLANETS: *interplanetary travel*

**in·ter·play** /ˈɪntəpleɪ‖-tər-/ *n* [U] the way in which two people or things react with one another or affect each other

**In·ter·pol** /ˈɪntəpɒl‖ˈ-tərpoʊl/ *n* [singular] an international police organization that helps national police forces to catch criminals

**in·ter·po·late** /ɪnˈtɜːpəleɪt‖-ɜːr-/ *v* [T] *formal* **1** to put additional words into a piece of text **2** to interrupt someone by saying something —**interpolation** /ɪnˌtɜːpəˈleɪʃən‖-ˌtɜːr-/ *n* [C,U]

**in·ter·pose** /ˌɪntəˈpəʊz‖-tərˈpoʊz-/ *v* [T] *formal* **1** to put yourself or something else between two other things: *Local activists interposed between party leaders and the people.* **2** to introduce something between the parts of a conversation or argument: *"That might be difficult," interposed Regina.*

W3 **in·ter·pret** /ɪnˈtɜːprɪ̵t‖-ɜːr-/ *v* **1** [T] to believe that someone's actions or behaviour or an event as having a particular meaning: **interpret sth as** *The EC's refusal to intervene in Bosnia should not be interpreted as a sign of weakness.* **2** [I,T] to change words spoken in one language into another: *They spoke good Spanish, and promised to interpret for me.* —see also TRANSLATE (1) **3** [T] to explain the meaning of something: *Freud's attempts to interpret the meaning of dreams* **4** [T] to perform a part in a play, a piece of music etc in a way that shows your feelings about it or what you think it means

W2 **in·ter·pre·ta·tion** /ɪnˌtɜːprɪ̵ˈteɪʃən‖-ɜːr-/ *n* [C, U] **1** an attempt to explain the reason for an event, a result, someone's actions etc: *One possible interpretation is that they want you to resign.* | **put an interpretation on** (=explain something in a particular way) *It's difficult to put an accurate interpretation on the survey results.* **2** the way in which someone performs a play, a piece of music etc and shows what they think and feel about it: *Laurence Olivier's brilliant interpretation of Henry V*

**in·ter·pre·ta·tive** /ɪnˈtɜːprɪ̵tətɪv‖ɪnˈtɜːrprəteɪtɪv/ *adj* concerned with explaining the reasons for something or with the way someone performs a play, piece of music etc: *an interpretative framework* | *interpretative skills*

**in·ter·pret·er** /ɪnˈtɜːprɪ̵tə‖-ˈtɜːrprɪ̵tər/ *n* [C] **1** someone who changes spoken words from one language into another, especially as their job —see also TRANSLATOR **2** a computer PROGRAM[1] (1) that changes an instruction into a form that can be understood directly by the computer

**in·ter·pre·tive** /ɪnˈtɜːprɪ̵tɪv‖ɜːr-/ *adj* interpretative

**interpretive cen·ter** /·ˈ··· ˌ··/ *n* [C] *AmE* a room or building where visitors and tourists can receive historical information about the place they are visiting

**in·ter·ra·cial** /ˌɪntəˈreɪʃəl◂/ *adj* between different races of people: *interracial harmony* —**interracially** *adv*

**in·ter·reg·num** /ˌɪntəˈregnəm/ *n plural* **interregnums** or **interregna** /-nə/ [C] **1** a period of time when a country has no king or queen, because the new ruler has not yet started to rule **2** a period of time when a company, organization etc has no leader, because the new leader has not started their job

**in·ter·re·late** /ˌɪntərɪˈleɪt/ *v* [I,T] if two things interrelate or you interrelate them, they are connected and have an effect on each other: *a model interrelating population, capital, and natural resources*

**in·ter·re·lat·ed** /ˌɪntərɪˈleɪtɪ̵d◂/ *adj* things that are interrelated are connected and have an effect on each other: *Unemployment and inflation are interrelated.* | *Many interrelated factors are at work here.*

**in·ter·re·la·tionship** /ˌɪntərɪˈleɪʃənʃɪp/ also **interrelation** /-rɪˈleɪʃən/ *n* [C,U] a connection between two things that makes them affect each other

**in·ter·ro·gate** /ɪnˈterəgeɪt/ *v* [T] **1** to ask someone a lot of questions for a long time in order to get information, sometimes using threats: *The police interrogated the suspect for several hours.* **2** *technical* to try to get information directly from a part of a computer: *We're having trouble in interrogating the database.* —**interrogator** *n* [C] *He refused to tell his interrogators anything.* —**interrogation** *n* [C,U]

**in·ter·ro·ga·tion mark** /···ˈ·· ˌ·/ *n* [C] *formal* a QUESTION MARK

**in·ter·rog·a·tive**[1] /ˌɪntəˈrɒgətɪv◂‖-ˈrɑː-/ *adj technical* an interrogative sentence, PRONOUN etc, asks a question or has the form of a question: *'Who' and 'what' are interrogative pronouns.* —**interrogatively** *adv*

**interrogative**[2] *n technical* **1 the interrogative** the form of a sentence or verb that is used for asking questions: *Put this statement into the interrogative.* **2** [C] a word such as 'who', or 'what' that is used in asking questions

**in·ter·rupt** /ˌɪntəˈrʌpt/ *v* **1** [I,T] to stop someone from continuing what they are saying or doing by suddenly speaking to them, making a noise etc: *Don't interrupt – I haven't finished yet.* | **interrupt sb** *She began to explain but I interrupted her.* **2** [T] to make a process or activity stop temporarily: *My studies were interrupted by the war.* **3** [T] *literary* if something interrupts a line, surface, view etc it stops it from being continuous —**interruption** /-ˈrʌpʃən/ *n* [C,U] *Let's go somewhere where we can talk without interruption.*

**in·ter·sect** /ˌɪntəˈsekt‖-ər-/ *v* **1** [I,T] if two lines or roads intersect, they meet or go across each other **2** [T usually passive] to divide an area with several lines, roads etc: *The plain is intersected by a network of canals.*

**in·ter·sec·tion** /ˌɪntəˈsekʃən,ˈɪntəsekʃən‖-ər-/ *n* [C] **1** a place where roads, lines etc cross each other, especially where two roads meet **2** [U] the act of intersecting something

**in·ter·sperse** /ˌɪntəˈspɜːs‖ˌ-tərˈspɜːrs/ *v* [T usually passive] **1 be interspersed with** if something is interspersed with a particular kind of thing, it has a lot of them in it: *sunny periods interspersed with occasional showers* **2 intersperse sth with** to put something in between pieces of speech or writing, parts of a film etc

**in·ter·state**[1] /ˌɪntəˈsteɪt◂‖-tər-/ *n* [C] *AmE* a very wide road for long distance travel

**interstate**[2] *adj* [only before noun] involving different states, especially in the US: *interstate commerce* —**interstate** *adv*: *travelling interstate on company business*

**in·ter·stel·lar** /ˌɪntəˈstelə◂‖-tərstelər◂/ *adj* [only before noun] happening or existing between the stars

**in·ter·stice** /ɪnˈtɜːstɪ̵s‖-ɜːr-/ *n* [C usually plural] *formal* a small space or crack between things placed close together: *small plants in the interstices of the rock*

**in·ter·twine** /ˌɪntəˈtwaɪn‖-tər-/ *v* [I,T] **1** if two things intertwine or are intertwined, they are twisted together: *intertwining stems* **2 be (closely) intertwined** if two situations, ideas etc are intertwined, they are closely connected with each other: *The problems of crime and unemployment are closely intertwined.*

**in·ter·val** /ˈɪntəvəl‖-tər-/ *n* [C] **1** the period of time between two events, activities etc: *He left the room, returning after a short interval with a message.* | [+ **between**] *The interval between arrest and trial can be up to six months.* **2 sunny/bright intervals** short periods of fine weather between cloudy, rainy weather etc **3 at weekly/20 minute etc intervals** every week, 20 minutes etc: *The bell rang at half-hourly intervals.* **4 at regular intervals a)** something that happens at regular intervals happens often: *The phone rang at regular intervals all afternoon.* **b)** objects that are placed at regular intervals have all been placed at the same distance from each other: *Trees had been planted at regular intervals.* W3

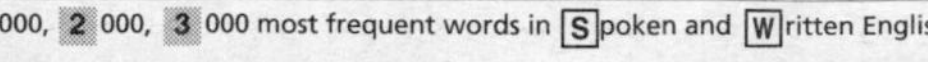

5 *BrE* a short period of time between the parts of a play, concert etc; INTERMISSION *especially AmE*: *We can get some drinks in the interval.* 6 *technical* the amount of difference in PITCH[1] (6) between two musical notes

**in·ter·vene** /ˌɪntəˈviːn‖-tər-/ *v* [I] 1 to do something to try and stop a quarrel, or a war, or to deal with a problem, especially one that you are not directly involved in: [+ **in**] *The police don't usually like to intervene in disputes between husbands and wives.* | *The Federal Reserve Bank had to intervene to protect the value of the dollar.* 2 if an event intervenes it happens in a way that prevents or interrupts something else: *He was just establishing his career when the war intervened.* 3 if a period of time intervenes, it comes between two events

**in·ter·ven·ing** /ˌɪntəˈviːnɪŋ◂‖-ər-/ *adj* **the intervening years/months/decades etc** the amount of time between two events: *I hadn't seen him since 1980, and he had aged a lot in the intervening years.*

W3 **in·ter·ven·tion** /ˌɪntəˈvenʃən‖-tər-/ *n* [C,U] the act of intervening in something such as an argument or activity to influence what happens: *government intervention to regulate prices*

**in·ter·ven·tion·is·m** /ˌɪntəˈvenʃənɪzm‖-tər-/ *n* [U] 1 the belief that a government should try to influence trade by spending government money 2 the belief that a government should try to influence what happens in foreign countries —**interventionist** *adj*

S3 W2 **in·ter·view**[1] /ˈɪntəvjuː‖-ər-/ *n* 1 [C,U] a formal meeting at which someone is asked questions in order to find out whether they are suitable for a job, course of study etc: [+ **for**] *He has an interview next Thursday for a job on the Los Angeles Times.* 2 [C] an occasion when a famous person is asked questions about their life, experiences, or ideas for a newspaper, magazine, TV programme etc: [+ **with**] *an interview with the President* | **give an interview**: *Mellor gave an off-the-cuff interview to reporters outside his home.* 3 [C] an official meeting with someone who asks you questions: *a police interview*

S2 **interview**[2] *v* [T] 1 to ask someone questions in order to find out if they are good enough for a job, course of study etc: *We're interviewing six candidates this afternoon.* 2 to ask a famous person questions about their life or ideas 3 to ask someone questions officially

**in·ter·view·ee** /ˌɪntəvjuˈiː‖-tər-/ *n* [C] the person who answers the questions in an interview

**in·ter·view·er** /ˈɪntəvjuːə‖-tərvjuːər/ *n* [C] the person who asks the questions in an interview

**in·ter·war** /ˌɪntəˈwɔː◂‖-tərˈwɔːr◂/ *adj* happening or connected to the period between the First and the Second World Wars: *the interwar years*

**in·ter·weave** /ˌɪntəˈwiːv‖-ər-/ *v past tense* **interwove** /-ˈwəʊv‖-ˈwoʊv/ *past participle* **interwoven** /-ˈwəʊvən‖-ˈwoʊ-/ 1 **be interwoven** if two lives, problems etc are interwoven they are closely connected in a complicated way: *The histories of our two families are closely interwoven.* 2 [T] to weave two or more things together: *silk interwoven with gold and silver threads* 3 [T] to mix together different styles or methods

**in·tes·tate** /ɪnˈtesteɪt, -stɪ̈t/ *adj law* **die intestate** to die without having made a WILL (=an official statement about who you want to have your property after you die)

**in·tes·tine** /ɪnˈtestɪ̈n/ *n* [C] the long tube that takes food from your stomach out of your body —**intestinal** *adj*: *intestinal bacteria* —see also LARGE INTESTINE, SMALL INTESTINE

**in-thing** /ˌ· ˈ·/ *n* **be the in-thing** *informal* to be very fashionable at the moment

**in·ti·ma·cy** /ˈɪntɪ̈məsi/ *n* 1 [U] a state of having a close personal relationship with someone: *the intimacy and friendliness of family life* | [+ **between**] *a surprising lack of intimacy between parents and children* 2 **intimacies** *plural* remarks or actions of a type that happen only between people who know each other very well: *The women often met to exchange initimacies about their social life.* 3 [U] a word meaning sex, used especially by lawyers and police when they want to avoid using the word 'sex': *Intimacy took place on several occasions.*

**in·ti·mate**[1] /ˈɪntɪ̈mɪ̈t/ *adj*

1 ▶ **FRIENDS** ◀ having an extremely close relationship: *intimate friends* | **be on intimate terms with**: *She's on intimate terms with a big star.*

2 ▶ **PRIVATE** ◀ connected with very private or personal matters: *Valerie always tells me about the most intimate details of their relationship.*

3 **an intimate knowledge of sth** very detailed knowledge of something as a result of study experience

4 ▶ **RESTAURANT/MEAL/PLACE** ◀ private and friendly so that you feel comfortable: *The Wisteria café has a pleasant intimate atmosphere.* | *an intimate meal for two*

5 ▶ **CONNECTION** ◀ **intimate link/connection etc** a very close connection between two things

6 ▶ **SEXUAL** ◀ **a)** connected with sex | **intimate relations/contact**: *The virus can only be transmitted through intimate contact.* **b) be intimate with** *formal* to have sex with someone —**intimately** *adv*

**intimate**[2] /ˈɪntɪ̈meɪt/ *v* [T] *formal* to make people understand what you mean without saying it directly **intimate that** *He intimated, politely but firmly, that we were not welcome.*

**intimate**[3] /ˈɪntɪ̈mɪ̈t/ *n* [C] a close personal friend

**in·ti·ma·tion** /ˌɪntɪ̈ˈmeɪʃən/ *n* [C,U] *formal* an indirect or unclear sign that something may happen: *the first intimations of the approaching conflict*

**in·tim·i·date** /ɪnˈtɪmɪ̈deɪt/ *v* [T] to frighten someone by behaving in a threatening way, especially in order to make them do what you want: *Buildings were bombed in an attempt to intimidate the opposition.* —**intimidation** *n* [U] *allegations of police intimidation*

**in·tim·i·dat·ed** /ɪnˈtɪmɪ̈deɪtɪ̈d/ *adj* [not before noun] feeling worried and less confident, for example because you are in a difficult situation or other people seem better than you: *I was shy, and felt intimidated by the older students.*

**in·tim·i·dat·ing** /ɪˈtɪmɪ̈deɪtɪŋ/ *adj* making you feel worried and less confident: *Some people find interview situations very intimidating.*

**in·to** /ˈɪntə; *before vowels* ˈɪntʊ; *strong* ˈɪntuː/ *prep* S1 W1

1 ▶ **INSIDE CONTAINER, PLACE, AREA** ◀ in order to be inside something or to be in a place or area: *I saw Jim this morning; he was going into the paper shop.* | *Sue got back into bed and pulled the quilt over her head.* | *I've got to go into town this morning and do some shopping.* | *They decided to put £1000 into an investment account.*

2 ▶ **INVOLVED IN STH** ◀ becoming involved in a situation or activity: *At the age of 16, I went into the printing trade as an apprentice.* | *Sorry, I haven't time to go into all these details now.* | *She puts a lot of time and effort into her work.* | *You'll get into trouble if you're not careful.*

3 ▶ **DIFFERENT APPEARANCE, SITUATION** ◀ in a different situation or a different physical form: *They're going to move Ian into a different class.* | *You'll have to eat your vegetables if you want to grow into a big strong boy.* | *Put the car into reverse.* | *Cut the cake into pieces.*

4 ▶ **HIT, TOUCH, MEET** ◀ coming near, or hitting someone or something in a sudden or violent way: *Fred bumped into her knocking her over.* | *He lost control of the car and it crashed into the wall.* | *I ran into Brad* (=met him) *at the Bluebird last night.*

5 **be into sth** *spoken* to like and be interested in something: *I've really got into French films lately.*

6 *spoken* used when you are dividing one number by another: *Eight into twenty four is three.*

7 ▶ **TIME** ◀ at or until a certain time: *Andy and I talked well into the night.* | *John was well into his forties before he got married.*

8 ▶ **DIRECTION** ◀ in a particular direction: *Sue stared straight into the camera.* | *Make sure you're speaking directly into the microphone.*

**in·tol·e·ra·ble** /ɪnˈtɒlərəbəl‖-ˈtɑː-/ *adj* too difficult, unpleasant, annoying etc for you to bear: *The arms race was placing an intolerable strain on the Russian economy.* —**intolerably** *adv*

**in·tol·e·rant** /ɪnˈtɒlərənt‖-ˈtɑː-/ *adj* not willing to accept ways of thinking and behaving that are different from your own: [+ **of**] *intolerant of other people's political beliefs* —**intolerantly** *adv* —**intolerance** *n* [U] *nationalistic rivalry and racial intolerance*

**in·to·na·tion** /ˌɪntəˈneɪʃən/ *n* **1** [C,U] the way in which the level of your voice changes in order to add meaning to what you are saying, for example by going up at the end of a question **2** [U] the act of intoning something

**in·tone** /ɪnˈtəʊn‖-ˈtoʊn/ *v* [T] say something slowly and clearly without making your voice rise and fall much as you speak: *The priest intoned the blessing.*

**in to·to** /ˌɪn ˈtəʊtəʊ‖-ˈtoʊtoʊ/ *adv Latin* as a whole; totally: *They accepted the plan in toto.*

**in·tox·i·cant** /-ˈtɒksɪ̇kənt‖ɪnˈtɑːk-/ *n* [C] *technical* something that makes you drunk, especially an alcoholic drink

**in·tox·i·cat·ed** /ɪnˈtɒksɪ̇keɪtɪ̇d‖-ˈtɑːk-/ *adj* **1** drunk: *The driver was clearly intoxicated.* **2** happy, excited, and unable to think clearly, especially as a result of love, success, power etc: *intoxicated with the experience of freedom* —**intoxicate** *v* [T]

**in·tox·i·cat·ing** /ɪnˈtɒksɪ̇keɪtɪŋ‖-ˈtɑːk-/ *adj* **1** intoxicating drinks can make you drunk **2** making you feel happy, excited, and unable to think clearly: *the intoxicating combination of her beauty, wit and charm*

**in·tox·i·ca·tion** /ɪnˌtɒksɪ̇ˈkeɪʃən‖-ˌtɑːk-/ *n* [U] the state of being drunk

**in·tra-** /ɪntrə/ *prefix formal or technical* **1** inside; within: *intra-departmental* (=within a department) | *intracranial pressure* (=inside the head) **2** into: *an intravenous injection* (=into a VEIN)

**in·trac·ta·ble** /ɪnˈtræktəbəl/ *adj formal* **1** an intractable problem is very difficult to deal with or find an answer to: *the seemingly intractable problem of human greed* **2** having a strong will and difficult to control: *They found the islanders intractable, resisting their offers of gifts.* —**intractably** *adv* —**intractability** /ɪnˌtræktɪ̇ˈbɪlɪ̇ti/ *n* [U]

**in·tra·mu·ral** /ˌɪntrəˈmjʊərəl◂‖-ˈmjʊr-/ *adj especially AmE* intramural courses, competitions etc happen within a school or college and are intended for the students of the school or college —opposite EXTRAMURAL

**in·tran·si·gent** /ɪnˈtrænsɪ̇dʒənt/ *adj formal* unwilling to change your ideas or behaviour in a way that seems unreasonable: *an intransigent attitude* —**intransigence** *n* [U] —**intransigently** *adv*

**in·tran·si·tive** /ɪnˈtrænsɪ̇tɪv/ *adj technical* an intransitive verb has a subject but no object. For example, in the sentence 'my cup broke', 'break' is intransitive. Intransitive verbs are marked [I] in this dictionary. —**intransitive** *n* [C] —**intransitively** *adv* —opposite TRANSITIVE

**in·tra·state** /ˌɪntrəˈsteɪt◂/ *adj AmE* within one state, especially in the US: *intrastate commerce* —compare INTERSTATE²

**in·tra·ve·nous** /ˌɪntrəˈviːnəs◂/ *adj* **1 intravenous injection** an INJECTION that is done into a VEIN (=tube in the body taking blood back to the heart) **2 intravenous drugs/fluids etc** drugs etc that are put directly into a vein —**intravenously** *adv*

**in tray** /ˈ· ·/ *n* [C] a container on your desk in which you keep work and letters that need to be dealt with —compare OUT TRAY —see picture at TRAY

**in·trench** /ɪnˈtrentʃ/ *v* [T] another spelling of ENTRENCH

**in·trep·id** /ɪnˈtrepɪ̇d/ *adj especially literary* willing to do dangerous things or go to dangerous places: *intrepid explorers*

**in·tri·ca·cy** /ˈɪntrɪkəsi/ *n* **1** [C usually plural] one of the small parts or details that together form a pattern, system, method etc: **the intricacies of** *I still haven't mastered the intricacies of the filing system.* **2** [U] the state of containing a large number of parts or details: *designs of amazing intricacy and sophistication*

**in·tri·cate** /ˈɪntrɪkɪ̇t/ *adj* containing many small parts or details that all work or fit together: *intricate patterns*

**in·trigue¹** /ɪnˈtriːg/ *v* **1** [T] if something intrigues you, you are very interested by it, especially because it seems strange or mysterious: *I was intrigued by his request.* **2** [I] *literary* to make secret plans to harm someone or make them lose their position of power: *While King Richard was abroad, the barons had been intriguing against him.*

**in·trigue²** /ˈɪntriːg/ *n* **1** [U] the act or practice of secretly planning to harm someone or make them lose their position of power: *It's an exciting story of political intrigue and murder.* | *a web of intrigue* **2** [C] a secret plan to harm someone or make them lose their position of power

**in·tri·guing** /ɪnˈtriːgɪŋ/ *adj* something that is intriguing is very interesting because it is strange, mysterious, or unexpected: *an intriguing discovery* —**intriguingly** *adv*: *The book is intriguingly titled 'The Revenge of The Goldfish'!*

**in·trin·sic** /ɪnˈtrɪnsɪk, -zɪk/ *adj* being part of the nature or character of someone or something: *The job is of little intrinsic interest.* | *intrinsic goodness* | [+ **to**] *problems that are intrinsic to the situation* —**intrinsically** /-kli/ *adv*

**in·tro** /ˈɪntrəʊ‖-troʊ/ *n* [C] *informal* the introduction to a song, piece of writing etc

**in·tro-** /ɪntrə/ *prefix* into, especially into the inside: *introspection* (=examining your own feelings)

**in·tro·duce** /ˌɪntrəˈdjuːs‖-ˈduːs/ *v* [T] S3 W1

**1** ▶ **WHEN PEOPLE MEET** ◀ if you introduce someone to another person, you formally tell them each other's names, for example at a party or meeting: *"Have you two been introduced? Tom, this is Greg."* | **introduce sb to sb** *I was introduced to Mrs Myers.* | **introduce yourself** (=formally tell someone who you are): *Let me introduce myself; my name is Melody Johnson.*

**2** ▶ **MAKE STH HAPPEN/EXIST** ◀ to make a change, plan, system etc happen or exist for the first time: *plans to introduce a new system of welfare payments* | *The teachers' association wanted to introduce a new kind of test.*

**3** ▶ **BRING TO A PLACE** ◀ to take or bring something to a place for the first time from somewhere else: **introduce sth to/into** *The grey squirrel was introduced into Britain from North America.*

**4** ▶ **NEW EXPERIENCE** ◀ **introduce sb to sth** to show someone something or tell them about it for the first time: *Malcolm introduced me to the joys of wine-tasting.*

**5** ▶ **TELEVISION/RADIO** ◀ to speak at the beginning of a TV or radio programme and say what is going to happen: *Tonight's programme will be introduced by James Adams.*

**6** ▶ **BE THE START OF** ◀ if an event introduces a particular period or change, it is the beginning of it: *The death of Pericles in 429 BC introduced a darker period in Athenian history.*

**7** ▶ **LAW** ◀ to formally present a new law to be discussed and voted on, especially in the British parliament

**8** ▶ **PUT STH INTO** ◀ *technical* to put something carefully into something else: *Fuel was introduced into the jet pipe.*

**in·tro·duc·tion** /ˌɪntrəˈdʌkʃən/ *n* W2

**1** ▶ **START TO USE** ◀ [U] the act of making something start to be used or exist for the first time: [+ **of**] *the introduction of new working methods* | *Since their introduction, compact discs have taken over from records.*

**2** ▶ **BRING STH TO A PLACE** ◀ **a)** [U] the act of bringing something to a place for the first time from somewhere else: [+ **of**] *the introduction of Buddhism to China nearly 2000 years ago* **b)** [C] something that is brought into a place for the first time from somewhere else: *The potato was a sixteenth century introduction.*

**3** ▶ **WHEN MEETING SB** ◀ [C often plural] the act of formally telling two people each other's names when they first meet: *There isn't time for formal introductions.*

**4** ▶ **BOOK/SPEECH** ◀ [C] a written or spoken explanation at the beginning of a book or speech: *In the introduction there's a brief account of Lawrence's life.*

**5** ▶ **EXPLANATION** ◀ [C] something that provides a

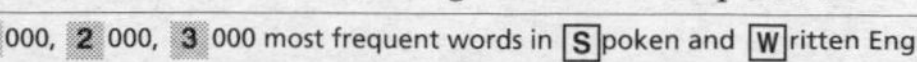

way of learning about something for the first time: [+ to] *This little book is a very good introduction to geometry.* **6** ▶ **LETTER** ◀ [C] an official letter that explains who you are, given to someone you have not met before **7** ▶ **PUT STH INTO STH** ◀ [U] *technical* the act of putting something into something else: [+ of] *the introduction of air into the heating system*

**in·tro·duc·to·ry** /ˌɪntrəˈdʌktəri◂/ *adj* **1 introductory remarks/paragraph etc** things that someone says or writes at the beginning of a book, speech etc in order to explain what it is about **2 introductory course/lesson etc** a course, lesson etc that is intended for people who have never done a particular activity before **3 introductory offer** a special low price to encourage people to buy a new product: *Don't miss our introductory offer!*

**in·tro·spec·tion** /ˌɪntrəˈspekʃən/ *n* [U] the process of thinking deeply about your own thoughts and feelings to find out their real meaning: *He stopped his introspection to listen.*

**in·tro·spec·tive** /ˌɪntrəˈspektɪv◂/ *adj* tending to think deeply about your own thoughts, feelings etc: *a shy and introspective person* —**introspectively** *adv*

**in·tro·vert** /ˈɪntrəvɜːt‖-ɜːrt/ *n* [C] someone who thinks mainly about their own thoughts and personal life and does not enjoy spending time with other people —opposite EXTROVERT

**in·tro·vert·ed** /ˈɪntrəvɜːtɪ̣d‖-ɜːr-/ *adj* someone who is introverted spends a lot of time thinking about their own problems and interests and finds it difficult to talk to other people: *The young girl had become nervous and introverted.* —opposite EXTROVERTED —**introversion** /ˌɪntrəˈvɜːʃən‖-ˈvɜːrʒən/ *n* [U]

**in·trude** /ɪnˈtruːd/ *v* **1** [I] to interrupt someone or become involved in their private affairs in an annoying and unwanted way, especially with the result that you upset or offend them: *Would I be intruding if I came with you?*|[+ **into/on/upon**] *It would be very insensitive to intrude on their private grief.* **2** [I + **on**] to have an unwanted effect on a situation

**in·trud·er** /ɪnˈtruːdə‖-ər/ *n* [C] **1** someone who illegally enters a building or area, usually in order to steal something: *The police think the intruder got in through an unlocked window.* **2** someone who is in a place where they are not wanted: *They had always regarded me as an unwelcome intruder.*

**in·tru·sion** /ɪnˈtruːʒən/ *n* [C,U] **1** an unwanted event or person in a situation that is private: *She considered Pam's presence in the kitchen an intrusion.*|[+ **into/on/upon**] *I resented this intrusion into my domestic affairs.* **2** something that has an unwanted effect on a situation, on people's lives etc: *the intrusion of Western values on a culture that has existed for centuries*

**in·tru·sive** /ɪnˈtruːsɪv/ *adj* affecting someone's private life or interrupting them in an unwanted and annoying way: *They found the television cameras too intrusive.*

**in·trust** /ɪnˈtrʌst/ *v* another spelling of ENTRUST

**in·tu·it** /ɪnˈtjuːɪ̣t‖-ˈtuː-, -ˈtjuː-/ *v* [I,T] *formal* to understand that something is true through your feelings rather than your thoughts

**in·tu·i·tion** /ˌɪntjuˈɪʃən‖-tu-, -tju-/ *n* **1** [U] the ability to understand or know something by using your feelings rather than by carefully considering the facts: *women's intuition*|*Imagination and intuition are vital to good science.* **2** [C] an idea about what is true in a particular situation based on strong feelings rather than facts: *He had an intuition there was trouble brewing.*

**in·tu·i·tive** /ɪnˈtjuːɪ̣tɪv‖-ˈtuː-, -ˈtjuː-/ *adj* **1** an intuitive idea is based on feelings rather than on knowledge or facts: *He seemed to have an intuitive awareness of how I felt.* **2** someone who is intuitive is able to understand situations using their feelings without being told or having any proof —**intuitively** *adv* —**intuitiveness** *n* [U]

**In·u·it** /ˈɪnjuɪ̣t, ˈɪnuɪ̣t/ *n* [C] a member of a race of people living in the very cold northern areas of North America —compare ESKIMO —**Inuit** *adj*

**in·un·date** /ˈɪnəndeɪt/ *v* [T] **be inundated a)** to receive so much of something that you cannot easily deal with it all: *After the broadcast, we were inundated with requests for more information.* **b)** *formal* to be covered with water —**inundation** /ˌɪnənˈdeɪʃən/ *n* [C,U]

**in·ure** /ɪˈnjʊə‖ɪˈnjʊr/ *v*

**inure** sb **to** sth *phr v* [T usually passive] to make someone become used to something unpleasant, so that they are no longer upset by it: *Nurses soon became inured to the sight of suffering.*

**in·vade** /ɪnˈveɪd/ *v* **1** [I,T] to enter a country, town, or area using military force, in order to take control of it: *Hitler invaded Poland in 1939.* **2** [T] to go into a place in large numbers, especially when you are not wanted: *Every summer the town is invaded by tourists.*|*Fans invaded the pitch at half-time.* **3** [T] to affect someone in an unwanted and annoying way: *Her image invaded his mind with immense power.*|**invade sb's privacy**: *Does that give you an excuse to invade my privacy?*|**invade sb's territory** (=start to deal with things that they think they should deal with) —see also INVASION

**in·vad·er** /ɪnˈveɪdə‖-ər/ *n* [C] someone in an army that enters a country or town by force in order to take control of it: *Invaders from the south ransacked the town.*

**in·val·id**[1] /ɪnˈvælɪ̣d/ *adj* **1** a contract, ticket, claim etc that is invalid is not legally or officially acceptable: *Without the right date stamped on it, your ticket will be invalid.* **2** reasons, opinions etc that are invalid are not based on clear thoughts or accurate facts: *Their argument was manifestly invalid.* —opposite VALID (1)

**in·va·lid**[2] /ˈɪnvəliːd, -lɪ̣d‖-lɪ̣d/ *n* [C] someone who cannot look after themselves because of illness, old age, or injury: *I resented being treated as an invalid.* —**invalid** *adj*

**in·va·lid**[3] *v*

**invalid** sb **out** *phr v* **be invalided out** to have to leave the army, navy etc because you are ill or injured

**in·val·i·date** /ɪnˈvælɪ̣deɪt/ *v* [T] **1** to show that something such as a belief or explanation is wrong: *The theory was invalidated by later findings.* **2** to make a document, ticket, claim etc no longer legally or officially acceptable

**invalid chair** /ˈ··· ˌ·/ *n* [C] *BrE old-fashioned* a WHEELCHAIR

**in·va·lid·it·y** /ˌɪnvəˈlɪdɪ̣ti/ *n* [U] **1** the state of being too ill, old, or injured to work: *invalidity benefit* **2** the state of being not legally or officially acceptable: *How is the validity of an agreement to be decided?*

**in·val·u·a·ble** /ɪnˈvæljuəbəl, -jɪ̣bəl‖-ˈvæljɪ̣bəl/ *adj* extremely useful: *Your advice has been invaluable to us.*

**in·var·i·a·ble** /ɪnˈveəriəbəl‖-ˈver-/ *adj* **1** always happening in the same way, at the same time etc: *His invariable answer was "Wait and see."* **2** *technical* never changing: *Mass, unlike weight, is invariable.*

**in·var·i·a·bly** /ɪnˈveəriəbli‖-ˈver-/ *adv* if something invariably happens or is invariably true, it almost always happens or is true, so that you expect it: *It invariably rains when I go there.*|*The security guards were invariably ex-servicemen.*

**in·va·sion** /ɪnˈveɪʒən/ *n* **1** [C,U] an occasion when one country's army enters another country by force, in order to take control of it: *the invasion of Normandy* **2** [C] the arrival in a place of a lot of people or things, often where they are not wanted: *the annual invasion of teenagers and hippies for the Glastonbury Pop Festival* **3 invasion of privacy** a situation in which someone tries to find out personal details about another person's private affairs in a way that is upsetting and often illegal

**in·va·sive** /ɪnˈveɪsɪv/ *adj* invasive medical treatment involves cutting into someone's body: *invasive surgery*

**in·vec·tive** /ɪnˈvektɪv/ *n* [U] *formal* rude and insulting words that someone says when they are very angry: *a stream of invective*

**in·veigh** /ɪnˈveɪ/ *v*
**inveigh against** sb/sth *phr v* [T] *formal* to criticize someone or something strongly

**in·vei·gle** /ɪnˈveɪɡəl, ɪnˈviː-‖ɪnˈveɪ-/ *v*
**inveigle** sb **into** sth *phr v* [T] *formal* to persuade someone to do what you want, especially in a dishonest way: *She had inveigled me into taking messages to her lover.*

**in·vent** /ɪnˈvent/ *v* [T] **1** to make, design, or produce something new for the first time: *Alexander Bell invented the telephone in 1876.* **2** to think of an idea, story etc that is not true, usually in order to deceive people: *They invented a very convincing alibi.*

**USAGE NOTE: INVENT**
WORD CHOICE: **invent, discover**
You **invent** something that did not exist before, such as a machine or a method: *Who invented the computer?*
You **discover** something that existed before but was not known, such as a place, thing, or fact: *In the sixties, oil was discovered under the North Sea.*

**in·ven·tion** /ɪnˈvenʃən/ *n* **1** [C] a useful machine, tool, instrument etc that has been invented: *The dishwasher is a wonderful invention.* **2** [U] the act of inventing something: *The invention of the computer has revolutionized the business world.* **3** [C,U] a story, explanation etc that is not true: *They subsequently admitted that the story was pure invention.* **4** [U] the ability to think of new and clever ideas: *They accused the painter of a total lack of invention.*

**in·ven·tive** /ɪnˈventɪv/ *adj* able to think of new, different, or interesting ideas: *one of the most talented and inventive drummers in modern music* —**inventively** *adv* —**inventiveness** *n* [U] *mechanical inventiveness*

**in·ven·tor** /ɪnˈventə‖-ər/ *n* [C] someone who has invented something, or whose job is to invent things: *the inventor of the vacuum cleaner*

**in·ven·tory** /ˈɪnvəntri‖-tɔːri/ *n* **1** [C] a list of all the things in a place **2** [U] *AmE* all the goods in a shop; STOCK[1] (2): *We made a complete inventory of everything in the apartment.*

**in·verse**[1] /ˌɪnˈvɜːs◂‖-ɜːrs◂/ *adj* [only before noun] **1 in inverse proportion/relation to** getting bigger at the same rate as something else gets smaller, or getting smaller at the same rate as something else gets bigger: *Clearly, the amount of money people save increases in inverse proportion to the amount they spend.* **2** *technical* exactly opposite, especially in order or position: *an inverse correlation* —**inversely** *adv*

**inverse**[2] *n* [C] *technical* the complete opposite of something

**in·ver·sion** /ɪnˈvɜːʃən‖-ˈvɜːrʒən/ *n* [C,U] **1** *formal* the changing of something so that it is the opposite of what it was before, or of turning something upside down **2** *technical* a kind of weather condition in which the air nearest the ground is cooler than the air above it

**in·vert** /ɪnˈvɜːt‖-ɜːrt/ *v* [T] *formal* to put something in the opposite position to the one it was in before, especially by turning it upside down

**in·ver·te·brate** /ɪnˈvɜːtɪbrɪt, -breɪt‖-ɜːr-/ *n* [C] a living creature that does not have a BACKBONE (1) —compare VERTEBRATE —**invertebrate** *adj*

**inverted com·ma** /ˌ··· ˈ··/ *n* [C usually plural] *BrE* **1** one of a pair of marks (“ ”) or (‘ ’) that are put at the beginning and end of a written word, sentence etc to show that someone said it or wrote it, or when writing the title of a book, song etc; QUOTATION MARK —see picture at PUNCTUATION MARK **2 in inverted commas** *spoken* used to show that a word you are using to describe something is only what it is usually called, and not what you think it really is: *Her friends, in inverted commas, all disappeared when she was in trouble.*

**inverted snob·ber·y** /ˌ··· ˈ···/ *n* [U] *BrE* the idea that everything that is typical of the upper classes must be bad

**in·vest** /ɪnˈvest/ *v* **1** [I,T] to give money to a company, business, or bank, in order to get a profit: **invest (sth) in sth** *Jones invested $7 million in an ultra-modern video studio.* | **invest heavily** (=invest a lot of money) *Maxwell had invested heavily in the bond market.* **2** [T] to use a lot of time, effort etc in order to make something succeed: **invest sth in sth** *I've invested a lot of time and effort in this project, and I don't want it to fail.* W3
**invest in** sth *phr v* [T] **1** to buy something in order to sell it again when the value increases and so make a profit: *Oliver made a fortune by investing in antique furniture.* **2** to buy something because it will be useful for you: *It's about time you invested in a new shirt!*
**invest** sb/sth **with** sth *phr v* [T often passive] *formal* **1** to officially give someone power to do something: *invested with the authority to enforce his recommendations* **2** to make someone or something seem to have a particular quality or character: *Richard's heavy-rimmed glasses invested him with an air of dignity.*

**in·ves·ti·gate** /ɪnˈvestɪɡeɪt/ *v* **1** [I,T] to try to find out the truth about something such as a crime, accident, or scientific problem: *The allegations were investigated, and found to be untrue.* | *I heard a noise and went downstairs to investigate.* **2** [T] to try to find out more about someone's character, actions etc, because you think they may have been involved in a crime: *Penney was already being investigated by the police on suspicion of murder.* W2

**in·ves·ti·ga·tion** /ɪnˌvestɪˈɡeɪʃən/ *n* **1** [C] an official attempt to find out the reasons for something such as a crime, accident, or scientific problem: *a criminal investigation* | [+ **into**] *The authorities are planning to launch a full-scale investigation into the crash which claimed over 200 lives.* **2** [U] the act of investigating something: *the investigation of computer fraud* | **under investigation** (=being investigated) *The whole issue is still under investigation.* W2

**in·ves·ti·ga·tive** /ɪnˈvestɪɡətɪv‖-ɡeɪtɪv/ *adj* **investigative journalism/report/work** work or activities that involve investigating something

**in·ves·ti·gat·or** /ɪnˈvestɪɡeɪtə‖-ər/ *n* [C] someone who investigates things, especially crimes: *Government investigators are going through the financial records.*

**in·ves·ti·ga·to·ry** /ɪnˈvestɪɡətəri‖-ɡətɔːri/ *adj* connected with investigating something

**in·ves·ti·ture** /ɪnˈvestɪtʃə‖-tʃʊr/ *n* [C] *formal* a ceremony at which someone is given an official title: *the investiture of the Prince of Wales*

**in·vest·ment** /ɪnˈvestmənt/ *n* **1** [C,U] the money that people or organizations have put into a company, business, or bank in order to get a profit, or to make a business activity successful: [+ **in**] *Wellings made a number of high-risk investments in the property market during the late 80s.* | *new measures aimed at attracting foreign investment into South Africa* **2** [C] something that you buy or do because it will be useful later: **a good/sound investment** *The lessons cost me over $500, but I consider them a good investment.* **3** [C,U] a large amount of time, energy, emotion etc that you spend on something: *a huge investment of time and effort* W1

**in·vest·or** /ɪnˈvestə‖-ər/ *n* [C] someone who gives money to a company, business, or bank in order to get a profit W3

**in·vet·e·rate** /ɪnˈvetərɪt/ *adj* [only before noun] **1 inveterate liar/smoker/womanizer etc** someone who smokes a lot, lies a lot etc and cannot stop: *a voracious reader and inveterate talker* **2 inveterate fondness/distrust/hatred etc** an attitude or feeling that you have had for a long time and cannot change —**inveterately** *adv*

**in·vid·i·ous** /ɪnˈvɪdiəs/ *adj* unpleasant, especially because it is likely to offend people or make you unpopular: *an invidious task* —**invidiously** *adv* —**invidiousness** *n* [U]

**in·vi·gi·late** /ɪnˈvɪdʒɪleɪt/ *BrE v* [I,T] to watch the people who are taking an examination and make sure that they do not cheat; PROCTOR[2] *AmE* —**invigilator** *n* [C] —**invigilation** /ɪnˌvɪdʒɪˈleɪʃən/ *n* [U]

**in·vig·o·rat·ed** /ɪnˈvɪɡəreɪtɪ̣d/ *adj* feeling healthier, stronger, and having more energy than you did before: *He felt invigorated after his day in the country.* —**invigorate** *v* [T]

**in·vig·o·ra·ting** /ɪnˈvɪɡəreɪtɪŋ/ *adj* making you feel more active, and healthy: *an invigorating swim before breakfast* —**invigoratingly** *adv*

**in·vin·ci·ble** /ɪnˈvɪnsɪ̣bəl/ *adj* **1** an invincible team, army etc is too strong to be destroyed or defeated: *the once invincible East German athletics team* **2** an invincible belief, attitude etc is extremely strong and cannot be changed: *her invincible determination* —**invincibly** *adv* —**invincibility** /ɪnˌvɪnsɪ̣ˈbɪlɪ̣ti/ *n* [U]

**in·vi·o·la·ble** /ɪnˈvaɪələbəl/ *adj formal* an inviolable right, law, principle etc is extremely important and should be not got rid of —**inviolably** *adv* —**inviolability** /ɪnˌvaɪələˈbɪlɪ̣ti/ *n* [U]

**in·vi·o·late** /ɪnˈvaɪəlɪ̣t/ *adj formal* something that is inviolate cannot be attacked, changed, or destroyed

**in·vis·i·ble** /ɪnˈvɪzɪ̣bəl/ *adj* **1** something that is invisible cannot be seen: *The house was surrounded by trees and invisible from the road.* | [+ **to**] *germs that are invisible to all but the most powerful microscopes* **2 invisible earnings/exports/trade etc** earnings etc that are connected with services rather than products: *Insurance is one of Britain's largest invisible exports.* —**invisibly** *adv* —**invisibility** /ɪnˌvɪzɪ̣ˈbɪlɪ̣ti/ *n* [U]

**invisible ink** /·ˌ··· ˈ·/ *n* [U] secret ink that cannot be seen on paper until it is heated

**in·vi·ta·tion** /ˌɪnvɪ̣ˈteɪʃən/ *n* **1** [C] a written or spoken request to someone, inviting them to go somewhere or do something: [+ **to**] *Did you get an invitation to the party?* | **invitation to do sth** *Shortly afterwards, Dawson received an invitation to speak at a scientific conference.* | **accept an invitation** *President Yeltsin has accepted an invitation to visit the White House in June.* | **decline an invitation** *formal* (=to not accept an invitation) | **by invitation only** (=only those people who have been invited can attend) **2** [C] a card inviting someone to attend a party, wedding etc: *Have you sent out all the wedding invitations yet?* **3 without invitation** without having been invited: *They were always dropping by to visit, usually without invitation.* **4** [singular, U] encouragement to do something: **take sth as an invitation to do sth** *He seemed to take my silence as an invitation to talk.* **5 at sb's invitation** also **at the invitation of sb** if you go somewhere or do something at someone's invitation, you go there or do it because they have invited you to **6 open/standing invitation** an invitation to do something, especially to visit someone, at any time you like: *My cousin Diana is living in China, and I have an open invitation to visit her.* **7 be an open invitation for/to sb** to make it very easy for someone to rob you or harm you: *Leaving the car unlocked like that is just an open invitation to thieves.*

**in·vite¹** /ɪnˈvaɪt/ *v* [T] **1** to ask someone to come to a party, wedding, meal etc: **invite sb to sth** *Who should we invite to the party?* | **invite sb to do sth** *I'm thinking of inviting them to spend the summer with me in Italy.* | **invite sb for a drink/meal etc** *Why don't you invite her for a drink at the club one evening?* | **be invited** *I'm afraid I wasn't invited.* **2** *formal* to politely ask someone to do something: **invite sb to do sth** *The interviewer invited Senator Axelmann to comment on recent events.* **3** to encourage something bad such as trouble or criticism to happen to you, especially without intending to: *Any government that sells arms to these dictators is inviting trouble.*

**invite** sb **along** *phr v* [T] to ask someone if they would like to come with you when you are going somewhere: *We were going to the beach and I decided to invite her along.*

**invite** sb **back** *phr v* [T] to ask someone to come to your home, hotel etc after you have been out somewhere together: *Richard often used to invite me back for coffee after the show.*

**invite** sb **in** *phr v* [T] to ask someone to come into your home: *Mr Vosset came to the door but didn't invite me in.*

**invite** sb **over** *phr v* [T] to ask someone to come to your home, usually for a drink or a meal: *Max has invited me over for dinner.*

**in·vite²** /ˈɪnvaɪt/ *n* [C] *informal* an invitation to a party, meal etc

**in·vit·ing** /ɪnˈvaɪtɪŋ/ *adj* an inviting sight, smell, offer etc is very attractive and makes you want to go somewhere or do something: *The log fire looked warm and inviting.* —**invitingly** *adv*: *She smiled invitingly.*

**in vi·tro fer·ti·li·za·tion** /ɪn ˌviːtrəʊ fɜːtɪ̣laɪˈzeɪʃən‖-troʊ fɜːrtələ-/ *n* [U] *technical* a process in which a human egg is fertilized (FERTILIZE) outside a woman's body; IVF

**in·vo·ca·tion** /ˌɪnvəˈkeɪʃən/ *n literary* [C,U] a request for help, especially from a god: [+ **to**] *an invocation to Zeus*

**in·voice¹** /ˈɪnvɔɪs/ *n* [C] a list of goods that have been supplied or work that has been done, showing how much you owe for them

**invoice²** *v* [T] **1** to send someone an invoice **2** to prepare an invoice for goods that have been supplied or work that has been done

**in·voke** /ɪnˈvəʊk‖-ˈvoʊk/ *v* [T] *formal* **1** to use a law, principle, or THEORY to support your views: *Such legislation has frequently been invoked to silence political opposition.* **2** to make a particular idea, image or feeling appear in people's minds: *His earlier novels invoke a romanticized picture of life in the countryside.* **3** to ask for help from someone more powerful than you, especially a god: *Isagoras invoked the aid of King Cleomenes.* **4** to make spirits appear by using magic: *invoking the spirits of their dead ancestors*

**in·vol·un·ta·ry** /ɪnˈvɒləntəri‖ɪnˈvɑːlənteri/ *adj* an involuntary movement, sound, reaction etc is one that you make suddenly and without intending to because you cannot control yourself: *an involuntary cry of shock* —**involuntarily** *adv* —**involuntariness** *n* [U]

**in·volve** /ɪnˈvɒlv‖ɪnˈvɑːlv/ *v* [T] **1** to include something as a necessary part or result: *What will the job involve?* | *I didn't realize putting on a play involved so much work.* | **involve doing sth** *Every day each of us makes decisions that involve taking a chance.* **2** to include or affect someone or something: *These changes will involve everyone on the staff.* | *an accident involving a coach and two cars* | *charges involving accusations of widespread corruption* **3** to ask or allow someone to take part in something: **involve sb in sth** *Try to involve as many children as possible in the game.* | *We want to involve the workforce at all stages of the decision-making process.* **4 involve yourself** to take part actively in a particular activity: [+ **in**] *The US has so far been extremely unwilling to involve itself in the crisis in Bosnia.* S2 W1

**in·volved** /ɪnˈvɒlvd‖ɪnˈvɑːlvd/ *adj* **1 be involved** to take part in an activity or event, or be connected with it in some way: [+ **in**] *More than 30 software firms were involved in the project.* | **deeply/heavily involved** (=be involved a lot) *At law school Hilary became heavily involved in student politics.* | **get involved in an argument/discussion/fight etc** *I don't want to get involved in some lengthy argument about who is to blame.* | *The Mafia could well be involved.* **2 be involved in an accident/fight/crash etc** to be one of the people in an accident, crash etc: *I'm afraid your son's been involved in an accident.* **3 work/effort etc involved in doing sth** [not before noun] the work, money, effort, risk etc that is involved in doing something is the amount that is needed in order to succeed in doing it: *Most people don't realize the amount of effort that is involved in writing a novel.* | *I would never go climbing on my own – there's too much risk involved.* **4 be involved with sb** to be having a sexual relationship with someone, especially someone you should not have a relationship with: *Matt's involved with a married woman at work.* **5** having so many different parts that it is difficult to understand; complicated: *The plot was so involved that very few people knew what was going on.*

W3 **in·volve·ment** /ɪnˈvɒlvmənt‖-ˈvɑːlv-/ *n* [U] **1** the act of taking part in an activity or event, or the way in which you take part in it: [+ **in**] *President Clinton defended US involvement in Haiti's domestic affairs.* | *What exactly was his involvement in the murder?* **2** the feeling of excitement and satisfaction that you get from an activity: *a student's emotional involvement in the learning experience*

**in·vul·ne·ra·ble** /ɪnˈvʌlnərəbəl/ *adj* someone or something that is invulnerable cannot be harmed or damaged if you attack or criticize them: *Gerry's confidence seemed to make him invulnerable.* | [+ **to**] *The castle was invulnerable to attack.* —**invulnerably** *adv* —**invulnerability** /ɪnˌvʌlnərəˈbɪlɪti/ *n* [U] —compare VULNERABLE

**in·ward** /ˈɪnwəd‖-wərd/ *adj* **1** [only before noun] felt or experienced in your own mind but not expressed to other people: *a feeling of inward satisfaction* | *inward panic* **2** moving towards the inside or centre of something —**inwardly** *adv*: *I managed to smile, but inwardly I was furious.* —opposite OUTWARD

**inward-look·ing** /ˈ·· ˌ··/ *adj* an inward-looking person or group is more interested in themselves than in other people: *an inward-looking and isolated country community*

**in·wards** /ˈɪnwədz‖-wərdz/ *especially BrE*, **inward** *especially AmE adv* towards the inside of something: *A breeze blew the curtains inwards for a moment.* —opposite OUTWARDS

**i·o·dine** /ˈaɪədiːn‖-daɪn/ *n* [U] a dark blue chemical substance used on wounds to prevent infection

**i·on** /ˈaɪən‖ˈaɪən, ˈaɪɑːn/ *n* [C] *technical* an atom which has been given a positive or negative force by adding or taking away an ELECTRON

**-ion** /ən/ *suffix* [in nouns] the act, state, or result of doing something: *the completion* (=completing) *of the task* | *his election* (=he was elected) *to the post* | *several volcanic eruptions*

**I·on·ic** /aɪˈɒnɪk‖aɪˈɑː-/ *adj* made in the simply decorated style of ancient Greek building: *an ionic column*

**i·on·ize** also **-ise** *BrE* /ˈaɪənaɪz/ *v* [I,T] to form ions or make them form —**ionization** /ˌaɪənaɪˈzeɪʃən‖-nə-/ *n* [U]

**i·on·i·zer** also **-iser** *BrE* /ˈaɪənaɪzə‖-ər/ *n* [C] a machine used to make the air in a room more healthy by producing negative IONS

**i·on·o·sphere** /aɪˈɒnəsfɪə‖aɪˈɑːnəsfɪr/ *n* **the ionosphere** the part of the ATMOSPHERE (1) which is used to help send radio waves around the Earth

**i·o·ta** /aɪˈəʊtə‖-ˈoʊtə/ *n* [singular] **1 not one iota** not even a small amount: *It's no use talking to him – it won't make an iota of difference.* **2** the Greek letter 'I'

**IOU** /ˌaɪ əʊ ˈjuː‖-oʊ-/ *n* [C] *informal* a note that you sign to say that you owe someone some money

**IPA** /ˌaɪ piː ˈeɪ◂/ *n* [singular] the International Phonetic Alphabet; a system of special signs, used to represent the sounds made in speech

**ip·so fac·to** /ˌɪpsəʊ ˈfæktəʊ‖-soʊ ˈfæktoʊ/ *adv Latin formal* used to show that something is known from or proved by the facts

**IQ** /ˌaɪ ˈkjuː/ *n* [C] intelligence quotient; your level of intelligence, measured by a special test, with 100 being the average result: *an IQ of 130*

**ir-** /ɪ/ *prefix* the form used for -IN before r; not: *irregular* (=not regular)

**IRA** /ˌaɪ ɑːr ˈeɪ/ *n* the Irish Republican Army; an illegal organization that wants to unite Northern Ireland and the Republic of Ireland —see also SINN FEIN

**i·ras·ci·ble** /ɪˈræsɪbəl/ *adj formal* easily becoming angry: *He was an irascible, energetic little man.* —**irascibly** *adv* —**irascibility** /ɪˌræsɪˈbɪlɪti/ *n* [U]

**i·rate** /ˌaɪˈreɪt◂/ *adj* extremely angry, especially because you think you have been treated unfairly: *The company received several complaints from irate customers.* —**irately** *adv*

**ire** /aɪə‖aɪr/ *n* [U] *literary* anger: *the ire of angry enemies*

**ir·i·des·cent** /ˌɪrɪˈdesənt◂/ *adj* showing colours that seem to change in different lights: *The painting has a shimmering iridescent quality.* —**iridescence** *n* [U]

**i·rid·i·um** /ɪˈrɪdiəm/ *n* [U] a rare metal used in medicine

**i·ris** /ˈaɪərɪs‖ˈaɪrɪs/ *n* [C] **1** a tall plant with long, thin leaves and large purple, yellow, or white flowers **2** the round coloured part of your eye, that surrounds the black PUPIL (2) —see picture at EYE[1]

**I·rish**[1] /ˈaɪərɪʃ‖ˈaɪrɪʃ/ *n* **the Irish** people from Ireland

**Irish**[2] *adj* from or connected with Ireland

**Irish cof·fee** /ˌ·· ˈ··/ *n* [C,U] coffee with cream and WHISKY added

**I·rish·man** /ˈaɪərɪʃmən‖ˈaɪr-/ *n* [C] a man from Ireland

**Irish Set·ter** /ˌ·· ˈ··/ *n* [C] a type of large dog with long hair

**Irish stew** /ˌ·· ˈ·/ *n* [C,U] a dish of meat, potatoes, and onions boiled together

**I·rish·wom·an** /ˈaɪərɪʃˌwʊmən‖ˈaɪr-/ *n* [C] a woman from Ireland

**irk** /ɜːk‖ɜːrk/ *v* [T] if something irks you, it makes you feel annoyed, especially because you feel you cannot change the situation: *Luna never told me what irked her that Sunday morning.*

**irk·some** /ˈɜːksəm‖ˈɜːrk-/ *adj formal* annoying: *an irksome journey*

S3 W2 **i·ron**[1] /ˈaɪən‖ˈaɪərn/ *n*
**1** ▶ **METAL** ◀ [U] a common hard metal that is used to make steel, is MAGNETIC and is found in very small quantities in food and blood: *There were huge iron gates in front of the mansion.* | *iron ore* | *Spinach is full of iron.*
**2** ▶ **FOR CLOTHES** ◀ [C] a thing that you use for making clothes smooth, which has a heated flat metal base
**3 have several irons in the fire** to be involved in several different activities or have several plans
**4** ▶ **SPORT** ◀ [C] a GOLF CLUB (2) made of metal rather than wood —see picture on page 1264
**5** ▶ **CHAINS** ◀ **irons** [plural] *especially literary* a chain used to prevent a prisoner from moving: **clap sb in irons** *old use* (=put chains on them)
**6 have a will of iron/an iron will** to have an extremely strong and determined character —see also **pump iron** (PUMP[2] (8)), **rule sb/sth with a rod of iron** (RULE[2] (6)), **strike while the iron's hot** (STRIKE[1] (24))

iron

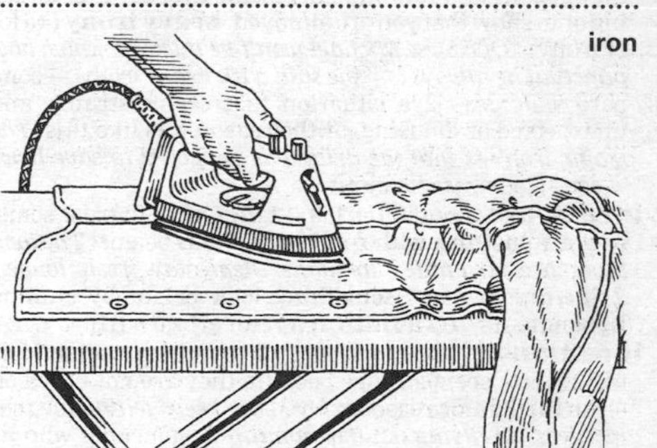

S3 **iron**[2] *v* [T] to make clothes smooth using an iron: *Have you ironed my shirt?* —see also IRONING
**iron** sth **out** *phr v* [T] **1** to solve or get rid of problems or difficulties, especially small ones: *We need to iron out a few operating problems first.* | **iron out the kinks** *AmE* (=deal with small problems so that you can succeed) *You'll need to iron out the kinks in your routine before you go on stage.* **2** to remove folds from your clothes by ironing them

**iron³** *adj* [only before noun] very firm and strong or determined: *iron discipline*

**Iron Age** /ˈ·· ·/ **the Iron Age** the period of time about 3000 years ago when iron was first used for making tools, weapons etc —compare BRONZE AGE, STONE AGE

**Iron Cur·tain** /ˌ·· ˈ··/ **the Iron Curtain** the name that was used for the border between the Communist countries of Eastern Europe and the rest of Europe

**iron-grey** *BrE*, **iron-gray** *AmE* /ˌ·· ˈ·◂/ *adj* iron-grey hair is a dark grey colour

**i·ron·ic** /aɪˈrɒnɪk‖aɪˈrɑː-/ also **i·ron·i·cal** /-ɪkəl/ *adj* **1** using words that are the opposite of what you really mean, especially in a joking way, or to show that you are annoyed: *As the rain lashed down, my mother's one ironic comment was: "An ideal day for a wedding."* —compare SARCASTIC **2** an ironic situation is one in which something strange and unexpected happens, especially in a way that seems amusing: *Your car was stolen at the police station! How ironic!*

**i·ron·i·cal·ly** /aɪˈrɒnɪkli‖aɪˈrɑː-/ *adv* **1** [sentence adverb] used when talking about a situation that seems strange, unexpected, and often amusing: *Ironically, his cold got better on the last day of his holiday.* **2** in an ironic way: *"Oh, no problem!" said Terry, ironically.*

**i·ron·ing** /ˈaɪənɪŋ‖-ər-/ *n* [U] **1** the activity of making clothes smooth with an iron: **do the ironing** *I hate doing the ironing.* **2** clothes that are waiting to be ironed or have just been ironed

**ironing board** /ˈ···· ·/ *n* [C] a small narrow table used for making clothes smooth with an iron

**iron lung** /ˌ·· ˈ·/ *n* [C] a large machine with a metal case that fits round your body and helps you to breathe

**i·ron·mon·ger's** /ˈaɪənˌmʌŋgəz‖ˈaɪərnˌmʌŋgərz, -ˌmɑːŋ/ *n* [singular] *BrE old-fashioned* a shop that sells equipment and tools for your home and garden —**ironmongery** *n* [U]

**iron-on** /ˈ·· ·/ *adj* labels that you can stick to your clothes using a hot iron

**iron ra·tions** /ˌ·· ˈ··/ *n* [plural] small amounts of high energy food, carried by soldiers, climbers etc

**i·ron·stone** /ˈaɪənstəʊn‖ˈaɪərnstoʊn/ *n* [U] a type of rock that contains a lot of iron

**i·ron·ware** /ˈaɪənweə‖ˈaɪərnwer/ *n* [U] articles made of iron

**i·ron·work** /ˈaɪənwɜːk‖ˈaɪərnwɜːrk/ *n* [U] fences, gates and other parts of buildings made of iron bent into attractive shapes

**i·ron·y** /ˈaɪərəni‖ˈaɪrə-/ *n* [U] **1** the use of words that are the opposite of what you really mean, in order to be amusing or to show that you are annoyed: **heavy irony** (=a lot of irony) *"Of course Michael won't be late: you know how punctual he always is," she said with heavy irony.* —compare SARCASM **2** a situation that seems strange and unexpected or amusing, or the reason it is like this: *The tragic irony is that the drug was supposed to save lives.* —see also DRAMATIC IRONY

**ir·ra·di·ate** /ɪˈreɪdieɪt/ *v* [T] **1** *technical* to treat someone or something with X-RAYS or similar beams: *The tomatoes are irradiated to make them stay fresh longer.* **2** *literary* to make something look bright by shining light onto it —**irradiation** /ɪˌreɪdiˈeɪʃən/ *n* [U]

**ir·ra·tion·al** /ɪˈræʃənəl/ *adj* **1** irrational behaviour, feelings etc seem strange because they are not based on clear thought or reasons: *My sister keeps telling me that my fear of flying is irrational.* **2** someone who is irrational tends to behave or do things without thinking clearly or without good reasons: *He's becoming increasingly irrational.* —**irrationally** *adv* —**irrationality** /ɪˌræʃəˈnælɪ̣ti/ *n* [U]

**ir·rec·on·ci·la·ble** /ɪˌrekənˈsaɪləbəl◂/ *adj* irreconcilable opinions, positions etc are so strongly opposed to each other that it is not possible for them to reach an agreement: *The differences between the Israelis and the Palestinians seemed completely irreconcilable.* | [+ **with**] *This belief was irreconcilable with the Church's doctrine of salvation.* —**irreconcilably** *adv*

**ir·re·cov·e·ra·ble** /ˌɪrɪˈkʌvərəbəl◂/ *adj* something that is irrecoverable is lost or has gone and you cannot get it back: *irrecoverable costs* —**irrecoverably** *adv*

**ir·re·dee·ma·ble** /ˌɪrɪˈdiːməbəl◂/ *adj* **1** *especially literary* too bad to be corrected or repaired **2** *technical* irredeemable STOCK¹ (3) cannot be exchanged for money —**irredeemably** *adv*: *irredeemably wicked*

**ir·re·du·ci·ble** /ˌɪrɪˈdjuːsɪ̣bəl◂‖-ˈduː-/ *adj* an irreducible sum, level etc cannot be made smaller or simpler —**irreducibly** *adv*

**ir·re·fu·ta·ble** /ˌɪrɪˈfjuːtəbəl◂/ *adj* an irrefutable statement, argument etc cannot be disproved and must be accepted: *irrefutable evidence* —**irrefutably** *adv*

**ir·re·gard·less** /ˌɪrɪˈgɑːdləs‖-ˈgɑːrd-/ *adv* **irregardless of** *AmE non-standard* a word meaning REGARDLESS, that many people consider to be incorrect

**ir·reg·u·lar¹** /ɪˈregjɣlə‖-ər/ *adj* **1** having a shape, surface, pattern etc that is not even, smooth, or balanced: *a face with irregular features* | *irregular handwriting* **2** not happening at points in time that are at an equal distance from each other: *His heartbeat sounded irregular.* **3** not doing something at the expected time every day, week etc when you should do it or when something normally happens: *Jason's attendance at school has been somewhat irregular.* | *irregular meals* **4** *formal* not obeying the usually accepted legal or moral rules: **highly irregular** (=extremely irregular) *It would be highly irregular for a minister to accept payments of this kind.* **5 irregular word/verb/plural etc** a word etc that does not follow the usual pattern of grammar: *'Go' is an irregular verb.* **6** *AmE* a word meaning CONSTIPATED (=unable to pass food waste from your body) used when you want to avoid saying this directly —**irregularly** *adv* —**irregularity** /ɪˌregjɣˈlærɪ̣ti/ *n* [C,U] *He lived a life of complete irregularity.*

**irregular²** *n* [C] a soldier who is not an official member of a country's army

**ir·rel·e·vance** /ɪˈrelɪ̣vəns/ also **ir·rel·e·van·cy** /-vənsi/ *n* **1** [U] a lack of importance in a particular situation: *The irrelevance of his remark irritated her.* **2** [C] someone or something that is not important in a particular situation

**ir·rel·e·vant** /ɪˈrelɪ̣vənt/ *adj* **1** something that is irrelevant is not important because it is not connected with the situation or subject that you are dealing with, or it has no effect or influence on a situation: *Age is irrelevant if he can do the job.* | [+ **to**] *Her comments seemed irrelevant to the real issue.* **2** having no real or useful purpose: *Students viewed Latin as boring and irrelevant.* —**irrelevantly** *adv*

**ir·re·li·gious** /ˌɪrɪˈlɪdʒəs◂/ *adj formal* opposed to religion or not having any religious feeling

**ir·re·me·di·a·ble** /ˌɪrɪˈmiːdiəbəl◂/ *adj formal* so bad that it is impossible to make it better —**irremediably** *adv*

**ir·rep·a·ra·ble** /ɪˈrepərəbəl/ *adj* irreparable damage, harm etc is so bad that it can never be repaired or made better: *irreparable damage to his heart* —**irreparably** *adv*

**ir·re·place·a·ble** /ˌɪrɪˈpleɪsəbəl◂/ *adj* too special, valuable, or unusual to be replaced by anything else: *the loss of several great works of art, many of them irreplaceable*

**ir·re·pres·si·ble** /ˌɪrɪˈpresɪ̣bəl◂/ *adj* full of energy, confidence, and happiness so that you never seem unhappy: *an irrepressible optimist* —**irrepressibly** *adv*

**ir·re·proa·cha·ble** /ˌɪrɪˈprəʊtʃəbəl◂‖-ˈproʊtʃ-/ *adj formal* something such as someone's behaviour that is irreproachable is so good that you cannot criticize it —**irreproachably** *adv*

**ir·re·sis·ti·ble** /ˌɪrɪˈzɪstɪ̣bəl◂/ *adj* **1** so attractive, desirable etc that you cannot prevent yourself from wanting it: *Chocolate is irresistible for a lot of people.* | **find sb/sth irrestible** *Men find Natalie irresistible.* **2** too strong or powerful to be stopped or prevented: *I had an irresistible urge to kiss him!* —**irresistibly** *adv*

**ir·res·o·lute** /ɪˈrezəluːt/ *adj formal* unable to decide what to do; uncertain —**irresolutely** *adv* —**irresolution** /ɪˌrezəˈluːʃən/ *n* [U]

**ir·re·spec·tive** /ˌɪrɪˈspektɪv/ *adv* **irrespective of** used when saying that a particular fact such as someone's age or race, something's size etc has no effect on a situation and is not important: *The course is open to anyone irrespective of age.*

**ir·re·spon·si·ble** /ˌɪrɪˈspɒnsəbəl◂‖-ˈspɑːn-/ *adj* doing careless things without thinking or worrying about the possible bad results: **be (highly) irresponsible of sb to do sth** *It was highly irresponsible of him to leave the children on their own in the pool.* —**irresponsibly** *adv* —**irresponsibility** /ˌɪrɪspɒnsəˈbɪləti‖-spɑːn-/ *n* [U]

**ir·re·trie·va·ble** /ˌɪrɪˈtriːvəbəl◂/ *adj formal* **1** an irretrievable situation cannot be made right again: *the irretrievable breakdown of their marriage* **2 irretrievable loss** the loss of something that you can never get back —**irretrievably** *adv*: *irretrievably lost*

**ir·rev·e·rent** /ɪˈrevərənt/ *adj* having a lack of respect for organizations, customs, beliefs etc: *an irreverent laugh* —**irreverently** *adv* —**irreverence** *n* [U]

**ir·re·ver·si·ble** /ˌɪrɪˈvɜːsəbəl◂‖-ɜːr-/ *adj* **irreversible damage/change/decline etc** damage, change etc that is so serious or so great that you cannot change something back to how it was before —**irreversibly** *adv*

**ir·rev·o·ca·ble** /ɪˈrevəkəbəl/ *adj* an irrevocable decision, action etc cannot be changed or stopped —**irrevocably** *adv*: *machines that irrevocably changed the pattern of rural life*

**ir·ri·gate** /ˈɪrəgeɪt/ *v* [T] **1** to supply land or crops with water **2** *technical* to wash a wound with a flow of liquid —**irrigation** /ˌɪrəˈgeɪʃən/ *n* [U]

**ir·ri·ta·ble** /ˈɪrətəbəl/ *adj* **1** getting annoyed quickly or easily: *Jo was tired, irritable, and depressed.* **2** *technical* very sensitive and sore: *irritable skin* —**irritably** *adv* —**irritability** /ˌɪrətəˈbɪləti/ *n* [U]

**ir·ri·tant** /ˈɪrətənt/ *n* [C] **1** something that makes you feel annoyed over a period of time: *Low flying aircraft are a constant irritant in this area.* **2** a substance that can make a part of your body painful and sore

**ir·ri·tate** /ˈɪrəteɪt/ *v* [T] **1** to make someone feel annoyed or impatient over a long period, especially by repeatedly doing something **2** to make a part of your body painful and sore: *This cream may irritate sensitive skin.*

**ir·ri·tat·ed** /ˈɪrəteɪtəd/ *adj* **1** feeling annoyed and impatient about something: [+ **about/at/with/by**] *John was irritated by the necessity for polite conversation.* **2** painful and sore

**ir·ri·tat·ing** /ˈɪrəteɪtɪŋ/ *adj* an irritating habit, situation etc is annoying: *She has an irritating habit of interrupting everything you say.* —**irritatingly** *adv*

**ir·ri·ta·tion** /ˌɪrəˈteɪʃən/ *n* **1** [U] the feeling of being annoyed about something, especially something annoying that happens repeatedly or for a long time: *Newspaper reports of yet more scandals are a constant source of irritation for the government.* **2** [C] something that makes you annoyed: *The children are just an irritation for him when he's trying to work.* **3** [U] a painful, sore feeling on a part of your body: *irritation of the skin*

**ir·rup·tion** /ɪˈrʌpʃən/ *n* [C] *formal* a sudden rush of people into a place: *an irruption of the audience onto the stage*

**is** /s, z, əz; *strong* ɪz/ the third person singular of the present tense of BE

**-i·sa·tion** /aɪzeɪʃən/ *suffix* a British spelling of -IZATION

**ISBN** /ˌaɪ es biː ˈen/ *n* a number that is given to every book

**-ise** /aɪz/ *suffix* [in verbs] a British spelling of -IZE

**-ish** /ɪʃ/ *suffix* **1** [in nouns] the people or language of a particular country or place: *Are the British unfriendly?* | *learning to speak Turkish* | *She's Swedish.* **2** [in adjectives] of a particular place: *Spanish food* (=from Spain) **3** [in adjectives] typical of or like a particular type of person: *foolish behaviour* (=typical of a fool) | *Don't be so childish!* (=don't behave like a child) | *snobbish* **4** [in adjectives] the ending of some adjectives that show disapproval: *selfish* | *raffish* **5** [in adjectives] rather; quite: *youngish* (=not very young, but not old either) | *tallish* | *reddish hair* **6** [in adjectives] *spoken* about; **approximately** (APPROXIMATE[1]): *We'll expect you eightish.* (=at about 8 o'clock) | *He's fortyish.* (=about 40 years old)

**Is·lam** /ˈɪslɑːm, ˈɪz-, ɪsˈlɑːm/ *n* [U] **1** the Muslim religion, which was started by Muhammad and whose holy book is the Koran **2** the people and countries that follow this religion —**Islamist** *n* [C] —**Islamic** /ɪzˈlæmɪk, ɪs-/ *adj*

**is·land** /ˈaɪlənd/ *n* [C] **W2** **1** a piece of land completely surrounded by water: *a small island in the middle of the lake* | *The Hawaiian Islands* —see also DESERT ISLAND **2** a place that is different in some way from the area that surrounds it: **an island of peace/calm etc** *The park is an island of peace in the noisy city.*

**is·land·er** /ˈaɪləndə‖-ər/ *n* [C] someone who lives on an island

**isle** /aɪl/ *n* [C] a word for an island, used in poetry or in names of islands: *the Scilly Isles*

**is·let** /ˈaɪlət/ *n* [C] a very small island

**is·m** /ˈɪzəm/ *n* [C] *informal* used to describe a set of ideas or beliefs whose name ends in 'ism', especially when you think that they are not sensible or practical

**-ism** /ɪzəm/ *suffix* [in nouns] **1** a political belief or religion based on a particular principle or the teachings of a particular person: *socialism* | *Buddhism* **2** the action or process of doing something: *his criticism of my work* (=he CRITICIZES it) **3** an action or remark that has a particular quality: *her witticisms* (=funny or WITTY remarks) **4** the state of being like something or someone, or having a particular quality: *heroism* (=being a HERO; bravery) | *magnetism* (=being MAGNETIC) **5** illness caused by too much of something: *alcoholism* **6** the practice of treating people unfairly because of something: *sexism* (=making unfair differences between men and women) | *racism* | *heightism* (=against people who are very tall or short)

**is·n't** /ˈɪzənt/ the short form of 'is not'

**i·so-** /aɪsəʊ, -sə‖-soʊ, -sə/ *prefix technical* the same all through or in every part; equal: *an isotherm* (=line joining places of equal temperature)

**i·so·bar** /ˈaɪsəbɑː‖-bɑːr/ *n technical* a line on a weather map joining places where the air pressure is the same

**i·so·late** /ˈaɪsəleɪt/ *v* [T] **1** to prevent a country, political group etc from getting support from other countries or groups etc, so that it becomes weaker: *The US has sought to isolate Cuba both economically and politically.* **2** *technical* to separate a substance, disease etc from other substances so that it can be studied: [+ **from**] *The hepatitis B virus has been isolated from breast milk.* **3** to separate an idea, word, problem etc so that it can be examined or dealt with by itself: **isolate sth from** *It is impossible to isolate political responsibility from moral responsibility.* **4** to make someone feel separate from other people in a society or group, and make them feel lonely or unhappy: **isolate sb from** *Presley's phenomenal early success isolated him from his friends.* **5** to make a place separate from other places so that people cannot enter it: *villages which have been isolated by recent flooding* **6** to keep someone separate from other people, especially because they have a disease: **isolate sb from** *New-born babies must be isolated from possible contamination.*

**i·so·lat·ed** /ˈaɪsəleɪtəd/ *adj* **W3** **1** an isolated building, village etc is far away from any others: *Not many people visit this isolated spot.* **2** feeling alone and unable to meet or speak to other people: *Young mothers often feel isolated and cut off from the rest of the world.* **3** an isolated action, event, example etc happens only once, and is not likely to happen again: **an isolated incident/episode** *Police say that last week's protest was an isolated incident.*

**i·so·la·tion** /ˌaɪsəˈleɪʃən/ *n* [U] **1** the state of being completely separate from any other place, group etc: *Because of its geographical isolation, the area developed its own unique culture.* **2** a feeling of being lonely and unable to meet or speak to other people: *Retirement can often cause feelings of isolation.* **3 in isolation** if

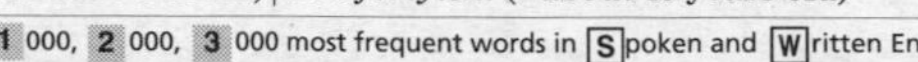

something exists or is considered in isolation, it exists or is considered separately from other things that are connected with it: *Taken in isolation, these events have no particular significance, but there is, in fact, an underlying pattern.* **4** the act of deliberately separating one group, person, or thing from others: *isolation of political prisoners*

**i·so·la·tion·is·m** /ˌaɪsəˈleɪʃənɪzəm/ *n* [U] a disapproving word for beliefs or actions that are based on the political principle that your country should not be involved in the affairs of other countries —**isolationist** *n* [C] —**isolationist** *adj*

**isolation pe·ri·od** /ˈ‥ˌ‥ ˌ‥/ *n* [C] the period of time that someone with an infectious illness needs to be kept apart from other people

**i·so·met·rics** /ˌaɪsəˈmetrɪks/ *n* [plural] exercises that make your muscles stronger by pushing against each other

**i·sos·ce·les tri·an·gle** /aɪˌsɒsəliːz ˈtraɪæŋgəl‖-ˌsɑː-/ *n* [C] a three-sided shape in which two of the sides are the same length —compare EQUILATERAL TRIANGLE, SCALENE TRIANGLE —see picture at SHAPE[1]

**i·so·therm** /ˈaɪsəθɜːm‖-ɜːrm/ *n* [C] *technical* a line on a weather map joining places where the temperature is the same

**i·so·tope** /ˈaɪsətəʊp‖-toʊp/ *n* [C] *technical* one of the possible different forms of an atom of a particular ELEMENT (=simple chemical substance)

**Is·rae·li** /ɪzˈreɪli/ *n* [C] someone from Israel

**Is·rael·ite** /ˈɪzrəlaɪt‖ˈɪzriə-/ *n, adj* (in the Bible) (a person) of the ancient kingdom of Israel

S3 W1 **is·sue[1]** /ˈɪʃuː, ˈɪsjuː‖ˈɪʃuː/ *n*

**1 ▶ SUBJECT/PROBLEM ◀** [C] a problem or subject that people discuss: *Drugs testing of employees is a sensitive issue.* | *the immigration issue* | **raise the issue** (=say that a problem should be discussed) *We should raise the issue of discrimination with the council.* | **sth is not the issue** *spoken* (=used to say that something is not the important part of what you are discussing) *Unemployment is not the issue – the real problem is the decline in public morality.* | **not be an issue** (=not be a problem) *I just got a raise, so money's no longer an issue.* | **avoid/dodge/duck/evade the issue** (=avoid discussing a problem or subject) *When asked about the bill, the senator tried to duck the issue.* | **confuse/cloud the issue** (=make a problem or subject more difficult by talking about things that are not directly connected with it) *clouding the issue with uninformed judgements* | **what's the big issue?** *spoken* (=used when you do not think that something is a problem and you cannot understand why people are worried or arguing)

**2 ▶ MAGAZINE ◀** [C] a magazine or newspaper printed for a particular day, week, or month: *the latest issue of Vogue*

**3 at issue** the problem or subject at issue is the most important part of what you are discussing or considering: *What is at issue is the extent to which exam results reflect a student's ability.*

**4 take issue with** to disagree or argue with someone about something: *It is difficult to take issue with his analysis.*

**5 make an issue (out) of sth** to argue about something, especially in a way that annoys other people because they do not think it is important: *I was upset by Eleanor's remarks, but decided not to make an issue of it.*

**6 ▶ SET OF THINGS FOR SALE ◀** [C] a new set of something such as shares (SHARE[2] (5)) or stamps, made available for people to buy: *a new issue of bonds*

**7 ▶ ACT OF GIVING STH ◀** [singular] the act of officially giving people something to use: *the issue of identity cards to all non-residents*

**8 die without issue** *old use and law* to die without having any children

W2 **issue[2]** *v* [T] **1** to officially make a statement, give an order, warning etc: *Silva issued a statement denying all knowledge of the affair.* | *a warning issued by the Surgeon General* **2** to provide something for each member of a group: **issue sb with** *All the workers were issued with protective clothing.* **3** to officially produce something such as new stamps, coins, or shares (SHARE[2] (5)) and make them available for people to buy

**issue forth** *phr v* [I] *literary* to go or come out of a place: *A low grunt issued forth from his throat.*

**issue from** *phr v* [T] *formal* if something, especially a sound or liquid, issues from somewhere, it comes out of it: *Smoke issued from the factory chimneys.*

**-ist** /ɪ̆st/ *suffix* **1** [in nouns] someone who believes in a particular religion or set of principles or ideas: *a Buddhist* | *a Scottish Nationalist* **2** [in adjectives] connected with or showing a particular political or religious belief: *her socialist views* | *He's very rightist.* (=supports the political RIGHT[3] (4b)) **3** [in nouns] someone who studies a particular subject, plays a particular instrument or does a particular type of work: *a linguist* (=someone who studies or learns languages) | *a novelist* (=someone who writes NOVELS) | *a guitarist* (=someone who plays the GUITAR) | *a machinist* (=someone who operates a machine) —see also -OLOGIST **4** [in adjectives] treating people unfairly because of something: *a very sexist remark* (=making unfair differences between men and women) **5** [in nouns] someone who treats people unfairly because of something: *They're a bunch of racists.*

**isth·mus** /ˈɪsməs/ *n* [C] a narrow piece of land with water on both sides, that connects two larger areas of land: *the Isthmus of Panama*

**IT** /ˌaɪ ˈtiː/ *n* [U] the study or use of electronic processes for storing information and making it available; INFORMATION TECHNOLOGY

**it** /ɪt/ *pron* [used as subject or object] **1** used to talk about the thing, situation, idea etc that has already been mentioned or that the person you are talking to already knows about: *"What should I do with the key?" "Oh just leave it on the table."* | *There were people crying, buildings on fire. It was terrible!* | *She complained about the food so much that I was sorry I mentioned it in the end.* **2** the situation that someone is in now: *I can't stand it any longer. I'm resigning.* | *How's it going Bob? I haven't seen you for ages.* | *And the worst of it is the car isn't even paid for yet.* **3** used as the subject or object of a verb when the real subject or object is later in the sentence: *It makes me sick the way she thinks everyone's in love with her.* | *What's it like being a sailor?* | *Apparently it's cheaper to fly than go by train.* | *It's a pity you couldn't come.* **4** used with the verb 'be' to make statements about the weather, the time, distances etc: *It's over 200 miles from London to Manchester.* | *It was 4 o'clock and the mail still hadn't come.* | *It had obviously been snowing but none of it stuck to the ground.* | *Can you believe she's forgotten it's my birthday today?* **5** used to emphasize that one piece of information in a sentence is more important than the rest: *It was Jane who paid for the meal yesterday.* (=it was Jane and not another person) | *It was the meal that Jane paid for yesterday.* (=it was a meal and not something else) | *It was yesterday that Jane paid for the meal.* (=it was yesterday and not at another time) **6** used as the subject of 'seem', 'appear', 'look' and 'happen': *It seems that no one really knows where he's gone.* | *Since it happened to be such a nice day they thought they'd go to the beach.* **7** used to talk about a child or an animal when you do not know what sex they are: *What will you call it if it's a boy?* **8 a) it's me/John/a car etc** used to give the name of a person or thing when it is not already known: *"Who was that at the door?" "It was a man selling house insurance."* | *"I can't quite make out what it's a photograph of." "Oh, it's our new boat."* **b) it's me/John etc** used to say who is speaking on a telephone: *Hello, it's Carmel here. Is Polly there, please?* —see THERE (USAGE) **9 if it weren't for/if it hadn't been for** if something had not happened: *We would have arrived much earlier if it hadn't been for the snow.* **10 a)** *informal* a particular ability or quality: *In a job like advertising, you've either got it or you haven't!* **b)** *slang* SEXUAL INTERCOURSE: *Have you done it with him yet?* **11 this is it!** *spoken* used to say that something you expected to happen is actually going to happen **12 That's it!** *spoken* **a)** used to say that a particular situation has finished: *You can have one more cookie and then that's it!* **b)** used to praise someone because they

have done something correctly **13 think you're it** *informal* to think you are more important than you are: *Just because he got a higher mark he really thinks he's it.*

**I·tal·i·an**[1] /ɪ'tæliən/ *n* [U] **1** the language of Italy **2** someone from Italy

**Italian**[2] *adj* from or connected with Italy

**I·tal·i·a·nate** /ɪ'tæliəneɪt/ *adj literary* with an Italian style or appearance

**i·tal·i·cize** also **-ise** *BrE* /ɪ'tæləsaɪz/ *v* [T] to put or print something in italics —**italicized** *adj*

**i·tal·ics** /ɪ'tælɪks/ *n* [plural] a type of printed letters that lean to the right, often used to emphasize particular words: **in italics** *This example is written in italics.* —compare ROMAN —**italic** *adj*: *italic script*

**Italo-** /ɪtæləʊ‖-loʊ/ *prefix* Italian: *the Italo-Austrian border*

**itch**[1] /ɪtʃ/ *v* **1** [I,T] if part of your body or your clothes itch, you have an unpleasant feeling on your skin that makes you want to rub it with your nails: *My feet were itching terribly.* | **itch sb** *AmE*: *The label on this shirt itches me.* **2 be itching to do sth** *informal* to want to do something very much as soon as possible: *You could tell they were itching to leave.*

**itch**[2] *n* [singular] **1** an uncomfortable feeling on your skin that makes you want to rub it with your nails **2** *informal* a strong desire to do or have something: [+ **for**] *an itch for adventure*

**itch·y** /'ɪtʃi/ *adj* **1** part of your body that is itchy has an unpleasant feeling that makes you want to rub it with your nails: *My eyes sometimes get red and itchy in the summer.* **2** clothes that are itchy make you have this feeling on your skin: *These tights are all itchy.* **3** wanting to go somewhere new or do something different: *He's had that job now for about eight years, and he's starting to get itchy.* **4 have itchy feet** *especially BrE informal* to want to travel or go somewhere new: *I've only been back home for a few months and I've already got itchy feet.* **5 itchy fingers** *informal* someone with itchy fingers is likely to steal things: *I tucked the bills deep into my pocket, away from itchy fingers.* **6 itching palm** *informal* an official who has an itchy palm is willing to dishonestly accept money —**itchiness** *n* [U]

**it'd** /'ɪtəd/ *usually spoken* the short form of 'it would' or 'it had': *I'd do it if I thought it'd help.*

**-ite** /aɪt/ *suffix* **1** [in nouns] a follower or supporter of a particular idea or person: *a group of Trotskyites* (=followers of Trotsky's political ideas) | *the Pre-Raphaelites* **2** [in adjectives] connected with a particular set of religious or political ideas, or with the ideas of a particular person: *his Reaganite opinions* **3** someone who lives in a particular place or belongs to a particular group: *a Brooklynite* (=someone from Brooklyn) | *the Israelites* (=in the Bible)

W1 **i·tem** /'aɪtəm/ *n* **1** [C] a single thing, especially part of a list, group, or set: *The professor wanted to see item 15, the Egyptian pot.* | [+ **of**] *an item of furniture* **2** [C] a single, usually short, piece of news in a newspaper or magazine, or on TV: *He sat at the kitchen table with the paper reading each item aloud.* **3 be an item** *informal* if two people are an item, they have a sexual relationship: *They're not an item any more.*

**i·tem·ize** also **-ise** *BrE* /'aɪtəmaɪz/ *v* [T] to make a list and give details about each thing on the list —**itemized** *adj*: *an itemized bill*

**i·tin·e·rant** /aɪ'tɪnərənt/ *adj* [only before noun] *formal* travelling from place to place, especially to work: *itinerant labourers*

**i·tin·e·ra·ry** /aɪ'tɪnərəri‖-nəreri/ *n* [C] a plan or list of the places you will visit on a journey: *His itinerary would take him from Bordeaux to Budapest.*

**-itis** /aɪtəs/ *suffix* [in U nouns] **1** an illness or infection that effects a particular part of your body: *tonsillitis* (=infection of the TONSILS) **2** *humorous* the condition of having too much of something or liking something too much: *televisionitis* (=watching too much television)

**it'll** /'ɪtl/ *usually spoken* the short form of 'it will': *It'll be dark before they get back.*

**it's** /ɪts/ **1** the short form of 'it is': *It's raining.* **2** a short form of 'it has': *It's been cloudy all day.*

**its** /ɪts/ *determiner* the possessive form of IT: *The baby had fallen out of its crib.* | *I must admit the plan does have its merits.* S1 W1

**it·self** /ɪt'self/ *pron* **1** the reflexive form of IT: *The cat lay on the sofa, washing itself.* | *It is generally felt that the government has made an idiot of itself.* **2** used to emphasize the pronoun 'it': *We've checked the wiring and the aerial so the problem maybe the television itself.* **3 in itself** considered without other related ideas or situation: *There is a little infection in the lung which in itself is not important.* **4 (all) by itself a)** alone: *Will the dog be safe left in the car by itself?* **b)** without help: *The door seemed to open all by itself.* **5 (all) to itself** if something has something else to itself, it does not have to share that thing with others: *This idea deserves a chapter to itself.* S1 W1

**it·sy-bit·sy** /ˌɪtsi 'bɪtsi◂/ also **it·ty-bit·ty** /ˌɪti 'bɪti◂/ *adj* [only before noun] *spoken humorous* very small

**-i·tude** /ətjuːd‖ətuːd/ also **-tude** [in nouns] *suffix formal* the state of having a particular quality: *certitude* (=being certain) | *exactitude*

**ITV** /ˌaɪ tiː 'viː/ *n* [U] Independent Television; a group of British television companies that are paid for by advertising

**-ity** /əti/ also **-ty** *suffix* [in nouns] the state of having a particular quality, or something that has that quality: *with great regularity* (=regularly) | *such stupidities* (=stupid actions or remarks)

**IUD** /ˌaɪ juː 'diː/ *n* [C] a small plastic or metal object used inside a woman's UTERUS (=place where a baby develops) to prevent a baby being born; COIL[2] (4)

**IV** /ˌaɪ 'viː/ *n* [C] *AmE* medical equipment that is used to put liquid directly into your blood; DRIP[2] (3) *BrE*

**I've** /aɪv/ *usually spoken* the short form of 'I have': *I've never been here before.*

**-ive** /ɪv/ *suffix* [in nouns and adjectives] someone or something that does something or can do something: *an explosive* (=substance that can explode) | *a detective* (=someone who tries to discover facts about crimes) | *the adoptive parents* (=who ADOPT a child)

**IVF** /ˌaɪ viː 'ef/ *technical* a process in which a human egg is fertilized (FERTILIZE (1)) outside the woman's body; IN VITRO FERTILIZATION

**i·vied** /'aɪvid/ *adj literary* covered with ivy

**i·vo·ry** /'aɪvəri/ *n* **1** [U] the hard smooth yellowish-white substance from the TUSKS (=long teeth) of an ELEPHANT: *an ivory chess set* **2** [U] a yellowish white colour **3** [C often plural] something made of ivory, especially a small figure of a person or animal: *a collection of Chinese ivories* **4 the ivories** [plural] *informal* the KEYS (=parts you press down) of a piano —see also **tickle the ivories** (TICKLE[1] (5)) **5** *AmE humorous* someone's teeth **6 ivory tower** a place or situation where you are separated from the difficulties of ordinary life and so are unable to understand them: *ivory tower linguists*

**i·vy** /'aɪvi/ *n* [C, U] a climbing plant with dark green shiny leaves —see also POISON IVY

**Ivy League** /ˌ·· '·◂/ *adj* connected with a group of old and respected universities in the eastern US: *an Ivy League college*

**-ization** /aɪzeɪʃən/ *suffix* makes nouns from verbs ending in -IZE: *civilization* | *crystallization*

**-ize** also **-ise** *BrE* /aɪz/ *suffix* [in verbs] **1** to make something have more of a particular quality: *We need to modernize our procedures.* (=make them more modern) | *Americanized spelling* (=spelling made more American) | *privatized transport systems* (=put back into private ownership) **2** to change something to something else, or be changed to something else: *The liquid crystallized.* (=turned into CRYSTALS) **3** to speak in a particular way: *to soliloquize* (=speak a SOLILOQUY, to yourself) | *I sat and listened to him sermonizing.* (=speaking solemnly, as if in a SERMON) **4** to put into a particular place: *She was hospitalized after the accident.*

**iz·zat·so** /ɪˌzæt'səʊ‖-'soʊ/ *interjection AmE* used to show that you do not believe something that someone has just said

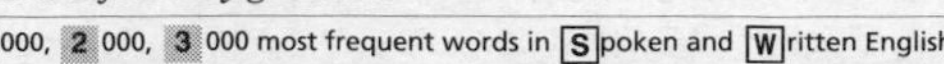

# J,j

**J, j** /dʒeɪ/ *plural* **J's, j's** *n* [C] the tenth letter of the English alphabet

**J** the written abbreviation of JOULE

**jab¹** /dʒæb/ *v* **jabbed, jabbing** [I,T] to push something into or towards something else with short quick movements: **jab sb with sth** *stop jabbing me with your elbow!* | [+ **at**] *She jabbed at the elevator buttons.*

**jab²** *n* [C] **1** a sudden hard push, especially with a pointed object or your FIST (=closed hand) | **right/left jab** (=with your right or left hand) **2** *BrE informal* an INJECTION (1) given to prevent you from catching a disease; SHOT¹ (15): *a typhoid jab*

**jab·ber** /ˈdʒæbə‖-ər/ *v* [I,T] to talk quickly, excitedly, and not very clearly —**jabber** *n* [singular, U]

**jack¹** /dʒæk/ *n* [C]
**1** ▶ **TOOL FOR LIFTING** ◀ a piece of equipment used to lift a heavy weight off the ground, such as a car, and support it while it is in the air: *a hydraulic jack*
**2** ▶ **CARD GAMES** ◀ a card used in card games that has a man's picture on it and is worth less than a queen and more than a ten: *a pair of jacks*
**3** ▶ **ELECTRICAL** ◀ an electronic connection for a telephone or other electric machine
**4** ▶ **CHILDREN'S GAME** ◀ **a) jacks** [plural] a children's game in which the players try to pick up small objects while bouncing (BOUNCE) and catching a ball **b)** a small metal or plastic object that has six points, used in this game
**5** ▶ **BALL** ◀ a small white ball at which players aim larger balls in the game of bowls (BOWL¹ (3a))
**6 I'm all right, Jack** *BrE usually spoken* someone with an I'm all right Jack attitude is happy with their life and does not care about other people
**7** ▶ **PERSON** ◀ **every man jack** *BrE old-fashioned* every single person; everyone: *Every man jack of them is without a job.*
**8 jack shit/diddly** *AmE spoken* an impolite expression meaning nothing at all: *He knows jack shit about cars.* —see also JUMPING JACK, UNION JACK

**jack²** *v*
**jack** sb **around** *phr v* [T] *AmE slang* to waste someone's time by deliberately making things difficult for them: *Stop jacking me around and make up your mind!*
**jack** sth ↔ **in** *phr v* [T] *BrE informal* to stop doing something: *I'd love to jack in my job and go live in the Bahamas.*
**jack off** *phr v* [I, T] *AmE taboo* to MASTURBATE
**jack** sb/sth ↔ **up** *phr v* [T] **1** to lift something heavy off the ground using a jack: *Jack the car up higher – I can't get the tire off.* **2** *informal* to increase prices, sales etc by a large amount: *jacking up their profit margins* **3 be jacked up** *AmE informal* to be excited and nervous

**jack·al** /ˈdʒækɔːl, -kəl‖-kəl/ *n* [C] a wild animal like a dog that lives in Asia and Africa and eats the remaining parts of dead animals

**jack·ass** /ˈdʒæk-æs/ *n* [C] **1** *BrE old-fashioned or AmE informal* an annoying stupid person **2** a male ASS (=animal similar to a horse)

**jack·boot** /ˈdʒækbuːt/ *n* [C] a boot worn by soldiers that covers their leg up to the knee —**jackbooted** *adj*

**jack·daw** /ˈdʒækdɔː‖-dɒː/ *n* [C] a black bird like a CROW¹ (1) that sometimes steals small, bright objects

S2 W3 **jack·et** /ˈdʒækɪ̵t/ *n* [C] **1** a short, light coat: *a denim jacket* | *Gene has to wear a jacket and tie to work.* —see also DINNER JACKET, LIFE JACKET —see picture on page 840 **2** a stiff piece of folded paper that fits over the cover of a book to protect it; DUST JACKET **3** *AmE* a stiff paper cover that protects a record; SLEEVE (4) *BrE* **4** a cover that surrounds and protects some types of machines

**jacket po·ta·to** /ˈ·· ·ˌ··/ *n* [C] *BrE* a potato baked with its skin on

**Jack Frost** /ˌ· ˈ·/ *n* [singular] a way of describing FROST¹ (1) as a person, used especially when talking to children

**jack·ham·mer** /ˈdʒækˌhæmə‖-ər/ *n* [C] *AmE* a large powerful tool used to break hard materials such as the surface of a road; PNEUMATIC DRILL *BrE*

**jack-in-the-box** /ˈ· · · ˌ·/ *n* [C] a children's toy shaped like a box with a figure inside that springs out when the box is opened

**jack-knife¹** /ˈ· ·/ *n plural* **jack-knives** /-naɪvz/ [C] **1** a knife with a blade that folds into its handle **2** a DIVE² (1) in which you bend at the waist when you are in the air

**jack-knife²** *v* **jack-knifing, jack-knifed** [I] if a large vehicle with two parts jack-knifes, the back part swings towards the front part: *The truck skidded and jack-knifed.*

**jack-of-all-trades** /ˌ· · ˈ· ·/ *n* [singular] someone who can do many different types of work, but who often is not very skilled at any of them

**jack-o'-lan·tern** /ˌdʒæk ə ˈlæntən‖-ərn/ *n* [C] a PUMPKIN (1) that has a face cut into it and a CANDLE put inside to shine through the holes

**jack·pot** /ˈdʒækpɒt‖-pɑːt/ *n* [C] a large amount of money that you can win in a game that is decided by chance —see also **hit the jackpot** (HIT¹ (23))

**jack·rab·bit** /ˈdʒækˌræbɪ̵t/ *n* [C] a large North American HARE (=animal like a large rabbit) with very long ears

**Jack Rob·in·son** /ˌdʒæk ˈrɒbɪ̵nsən‖-ˈrɑː-/ *n* **before you can say Jack Robinson** *old-fashioned* very quickly or suddenly

**Jack the Lad** /ˌ· · ˈ·/ *n* [singular] *BrE spoken* a young man who enjoys drinking beer and going out with his male friends, and who thinks he is sexually attractive

**Jac·o·be·an** /ˌdʒækəˈbiːən◂/ *adj* belonging to or typical of the period between 1603 and 1623 in Britain, when James I was king of England: *Jacobean drama*

**Jac·o·bite** /ˈdʒækəbaɪt/ *n* [C] someone in the 17th or 18th centuries who supported King James II of England and wanted one of his DESCENDANTS to rule England —**Jacobite** *adj*

**Jacuzzi**

**Ja·cuz·zi** /dʒəˈkuːzi/ *n* [C] *trademark* a large indoor bath that makes hot water move in strong currents around your body —compare HOT TUB, SPA (2)

**jade** /dʒeɪd/ *n* **1** [U] a hard, usually green stone often used to make jewellery **2** [U] the light green colour of this stone —see picture on page 411 **3** [C] *old use* a woman, especially a rude or immoral woman

**ja·ded** /ˈdʒeɪdɪ̵d/ *adj* someone who is jaded is no longer interested in or excited by life, especially because they have experienced too many things: *magnificent meals to tempt the most jaded appetites*

**Jaf·fa** /ˈdʒæfə/ *n* [C] *BrE* a large orange, especially one that comes from Israel

**jag** /dʒæg/ *n* [C] *informal* **crying/shopping/talking etc jag** a short period of time when you suddenly cry etc without controlling how much you do it

**jag·ged** /ˈdʒægɪ̣d/ *adj* having a rough, uneven edge or surface, often with sharp points on it: *the jagged rocks of St. Saviour's Point* —**jaggedly** *adv*

**jag·u·ar** /ˈdʒægjuə‖ˈdʒægwɑːr/ *n* [C] a large South American wild cat with brown and yellow fur with black spots

**jai a·lai** /ˌhaɪ əˈlaɪ‖ˈhaɪ laɪ/ *n* [U] a game played by two, four, or six people in which they use an object like a basket on a stick to throw a ball

**jail**[1] also **gaol** *BrE* /dʒeɪl/ *n* [C,U] a place where criminals are kept as part of their punishment, or where people who have been charged with a crime are kept before they are judged in a law court; PRISON (1)

**jail**[2] also **gaol** *BrE* —*v* [T] to put someone in jail: *They ought to jail him for life.*

**jail·bird** also **gaolbird** *BrE* /ˈdʒeɪlbɜːd‖-bɜːrd/ *n* [C] *informal* someone who has spent a lot of time in prison

**jail·break** also **gaolbreak** *BrE* /ˈdʒeɪlbreɪk/ *n* [C] an escape or an attempt to escape from prison, especially by several people

**jail·er** also **gaoler** *BrE* /ˈdʒeɪlə‖-ər/ *n* [C] *old-fashioned* someone who is in charge of guarding a prison or prisoners

**Jain** /dʒaɪn/ *n* [C] someone whose religion is Jainism —**Jain** *adj*

**Jain·is·m** /ˈdʒaɪnɪzəm/ *n* [C] a religion of India that is against violence towards any living things

**jal·a·pe·ño** /ˌhæləˈpeɪnjəʊ‖ˌhɑːləˈpeɪnjoʊ/ *n* [C] a small, very hot green PEPPER used especially in Mexican food

**ja·lop·y** /dʒəˈlɒpi‖-ˈlɑːpi/ *n* [C] *old-fashioned* a very old car in bad condition —see also BANGER (2)

**jam**[1] /dʒæm/ *n* **1** [C,U] a very thick sweet substance made from boiled fruit and sugar and eaten especially on bread; CONSERVE: *strawberry jam* **2** [C] a situation in which it is difficult or impossible to move because there are so many people, things, cars etc close together: **traffic jam** *Sorry we're late. We got stuck in a traffic jam.* **3 be in a jam** *informal* to be in a difficult or uncomfortable situation **4 jams** [plural] *AmE* brightly coloured trousers that stop above your knee **5 jam tomorrow** *BrE informal* good things that you are promised if you are patient enough to wait for them —see also JAM SESSION

**jam**[2] *v*

**1 ▶ PUSH HARD ◀** [T] to push something somewhere using a lot of force, or to push too many things into a small place: **jam sth into/under/on** *I'll never jam all my clothes into one suitcase.* | **be jammed (up) against sth** (=pushed tightly against something)

**2 ▶ MACHINE ◀** also **jam up** [I,T] if a lock or a moving part of a machine jams, or if you jam it, it no longer works properly because something is preventing it from moving: *The front roller has jammed on the photocopier.*

**3 ▶ BLOCK ◀** also **jam up** [T] if a lot of people or vehicles jam a place, they block it so that it is difficult to move: *Crowds jammed the entrance to the stadium.* — see also JAMMED (2)

**4 ▶ MUSIC ◀** [I] to play music informally with others without practising first — see also JAM SESSION

**5 jam on the brakes** to slow down a car suddenly by putting your foot down hard on the BRAKE[1] (1)

**6 jam the switchboard** if telephone calls jam the switchboard, so many people are telephoning the same organization that its telephone system cannot work properly

**7 ▶ RADIO ◀** [T] to deliberately prevent broadcasts or other electronic signals from being received by sending out noise on the same WAVELENGTH

**8 sb is jamming** *AmE spoken* used to say that someone is doing something well

**jamb** /dʒæm/ *n* [C] a side post of a door or window

**jam·ba·la·ya** /ˌdʒæmbəˈlaɪə/ *n* [U] a dish from the southern US containing rice, and SEAFOOD

**jam·bo·ree** /ˌdʒæmbəˈriː/ *n* [C] **1** a big noisy party or celebration, usually outdoors **2** a large meeting of scouts (SCOUTS[1] (1)) or guides (GUIDE[1] (4))

**jammed** /dʒæmd/ *adj* **1** [not before noun] impossible to move because of being stuck between two or more surfaces: *The child had got his finger jammed in the door.* **2** *AmE* full of people or things; jam-packed: *The place is jammed. We'll never get in.*

**jam·mies** /ˈdʒæmiz/ *n* [plural] *informal* PYJAMAS

**jam·my** /ˈdʒæmi/ *adj BrE slang* **1 jammy bastard/cow/bugger etc** an impolite expression meaning someone who has been very lucky **2** very easy

**jam-packed** /ˌ· ˈ·◂/ *adj informal* full of people or things that are very close together: **[+ with]** *The square was jam-packed with revelers celebrating the New Year.*

**jam ses·sion** /ˈ· ˌ··/ *n* [C] an occasion when JAZZ[1] (1) or ROCK[1] (2) musicians play music together informally

**Jan** /dʒæn/ the written abbreviation of January

**Jane Doe** /ˌdʒeɪn ˈdəʊ‖-ˈdoʊ/ *n* [singular] *AmE* a woman whose name is not known, especially one who is involved in a law case —compare JOHN DOE

**jan·gle** /ˈdʒæŋgəl/ *v* **1** [I,T] if metal objects or bells jangle or if you jangle them, they make a sharp sound when they hit each other: *jangling bracelets* **2** also **jangle on** [T usually passive] to make someone feel nervous or upset: *jangled nerves* —**jangle** *n* [singular]

**jan·i·tor** /ˈdʒænɪ̣tə‖-ər/ *n* [C] *AmE or ScotE* someone who looks after a school or other large building; CARETAKER (1) *BrE*

**Jan·u·a·ry** /ˈdʒænjuəri, -njʊri‖njueri/ written abbreviation **Jan** *n* [C,U] the first month of the year, between December and February: **in January** *Our new office is opening in January 2000.* | **last/next January** *I haven't heard from him since last January.* | **on January 29th** (also **on 29th January** *BrE*) *Rosie's party was on January 29th.* (spoken as: *on January the twenty-ninth* or *on the twenty-ninth of January* or *(AmE) on January twenty-ninth*)

**Jap·a·nese**[1] /ˌdʒæpəˈniːz◂/ *n* **1** [U] the language of Japan **2 the Japanese** people from Japan

**Japanese**[2] *adj* from or connected with Japan

**Japanese lan·tern** /ˌ··· ˈ··/ *n* [C] a paper decoration, usually with a light inside

**jape** /dʒeɪp/ *n* [C] *old-fashioned* a trick or joke

**jar**[1] /dʒɑː‖dʒɑːr/ *n* [C] **1** a round glass container with a wide lid, used for storing food such as JAM[1] (1) and HONEY (1) **2** the amount of food, drink, etc contained in a jar: *half a jar of peanut butter* **3** [singular] the shock of two things hitting each other, or a sudden pain from something hitting you: *It must have been the jar of the impact that broke her ankle.* **4** a round container made of clay, stone etc used especially in the past for keeping food or drink in **5** *BrE informal* a glass of beer: *We'd had a few jars down the pub.*

**jar**[2] *v* **jarred, jarring** **1** [T] to slightly hurt a part of your body by hitting it against something: *Alice landed badly, jarring her ankle.* **2** [I,T] if you jar something or if two things jar, they are suddenly shaken or hit: *Oops, sorry, did I jar your elbow?* **3** [I,T] also **jar on** to make someone feel slightly annoyed or uncomfortable: **jar on sb's nerves** *The baby's screaming was starting to jar on my nerves.* **4** to be different in style or appearance from something else and therefore look strange: **[+ with]** *a modernistic lamp that jarred with the rest of the room* —**jarring** *adj*

**jar·gon** /ˈdʒɑːgən‖ˈdʒɑːrgən, -gɑːn/ *n* [U] technical words and expressions that are used mainly by people who belong to the same professional group and are difficult to understand: *documents full of legal jargon*

**jas·mine** /ˈdʒæzmɪ̣n/ *n* [C,U] a climbing plant with sweet-smelling small white or yellow flowers

**jas·per** /ˈdʒæspə‖-ər/ *n* [U] a red, yellow, or brown stone that is not very valuable

**jaun·dice** /ˈdʒɔːndɪs‖ˈdʒɒːn-, ˈdʒɑːn-/ *n* [U] a medical condition in which your skin and the white part of your eyes become yellow

**jaun·diced** /ˈdʒɔːndɪst‖ˈdʒɒːn-, ˈdʒɑːn-/ *adj* **1** tending to judge people and things unfavourably, often because you have had disappointing experiences yourself: *a jaundiced view of life* | **with a jaundiced eye** (=thinking of people and situations in a jaundiced way) **2** suffering from jaundice

**jaunt** /dʒɔːnt‖dʒɒːnt, dʒɑːnt/ *n* [C] a short journey for pleasure —**jaunt** *v* [I]

**jaun·ty** /ˈdʒɔːnti‖ˈdʒɒːnti, ˈdʒɑːnti/ *adj* jaunty actions, clothes etc show that you are confident and cheerful: **at a jaunty angle** *His hat was tilted at a jaunty angle.* —**jauntily** *adv* —**jauntiness** *n* [U]

**jav·e·lin** /ˈdʒævəlɪn/ *n* [C] **1** a light SPEAR for throwing, now used mostly in sport **2 the javelin** a sporting event in which competitors throw a javelin

**jaw**[1] /dʒɔː‖dʒɒː/ *n* **1** [C] the lower part of your face that moves when you eat: *Tyson punched his opponent on the jaw.* —see picture at HEAD[1] **2 sb's jaw dropped** used to say that someone looked surprised or shocked: *Her jaw dropped when I told her Jean had left her husband.* **3 jaws** [plural] **a)** the mouth of a person or animal, especially a dangerous animal: *a crocodile snapping its jaws* **b)** the two parts of a machine or tool that move together to hold something tightly **4** [C usually singular] the shape of someone's jaw, especially when it shows something about their character: *She's got a very determined jaw.* **5 the jaws of death/defeat/despair** *literary* a situation in which you almost die, are almost defeated etc **6 the jaws of a cave/tunnel etc** the entrance to a place which is dark and dangerous **7 have a jaw** *old-fashioned* to have a conversation

**jaw**[2] *v* [I] *informal* to talk

**jaw·bone** /ˈdʒɔːbəʊn‖ˈdʒɒːboʊn/ *n* [C] one of the two big bones of the jaw, especially the lower jaw —see picture at SKELETON

**jaw·break·er** /ˈdʒɔːˌbreɪkə‖ˈdʒɒːˌbreɪkər/ *n* [C] *AmE* a round hard sweet; GOBSTOPPER *BrE*

**jay** /dʒeɪ/ *n* [C] a noisy brightly-coloured European bird of the CROW[1] (1) family —see also BLUEJAY

**jay·walk·ing** /ˈdʒeɪˌwɔːkɪŋ‖-ˌwɒː-/ *n* [U] the act of crossing streets with traffic in a careless and dangerous way —**jaywalker** *n* [C]

**jazz**[1] /dʒæz/ *n* [U] **1** music originally played by black Americans with a strong beat and parts in which performers can play alone: *a jazz band* **2 and all that jazz** *spoken* and things like that: *I'm fed up with rules, responsibilities and all that jazz.*

**jazz**[2] *v*

**jazz** sth ↔ **up** *phr v* [T] *informal* to make something more attractive or exciting: *Jazz up your everyday meals with our new range of seasonings.* —**jazzed-up** *adj*

**jazz·y** /ˈdʒæzi/ *adj informal* **1** bright, colourful or very modern in appearance: *jazzy writing paper* **2** in the style of jazz music

**jct** the written abbreviation of JUNCTION

**jeal·ous** /ˈdʒeləs/ *adj* **1** feeling angry and unhappy because someone has something that you would like; ENVIOUS: **[+ of]** *Why are you so jealous of his success?* | **make sb jealous** *It makes me jealous, seeing all these women with babies.* **2** feeling angry and unhappy because someone you like or love is showing interest in another person, or another person is showing interest in them: *She gets jealous if I even look at another woman.* | **jealous husband/wife/lover** *You're acting like a jealous husband.* **3 jealous of** wanting to keep or protect something that you have because you are proud of it: *a country jealous of its heritage* —**jealously** *adv*: *a jealously guarded secret*

**jeal·ous·y** /ˈdʒeləsi/ *n* [C,U] a feeling of being jealous

**jeans** /dʒiːnz/ *n* [plural] trousers made of DENIM (=a strong, usually blue cotton cloth)

**jeep, Jeep** *trademark* /dʒiːp/ *n* [C] a type of car made for travelling over rough ground

**jeer** /dʒɪə‖dʒɪr/ *v* [I,T] to laugh unkindly at someone to show that you strongly disapprove of them: **[+ at]** *of course they jeered at you – you lost the game, right?* —**jeer** *n* [C] *hurtful jeers*

**jeer·ing** /ˈdʒɪərɪŋ‖ˈdʒɪr-/ *adj* a jeering remark or sound is unkind and shows disapproval: *jeering laughter* —**jeering** *n* [U] —**jeeringly** *adv*

**jeez** /dʒiːz/ *interjection AmE* used to strongly express feelings such as surprise, anger, etc

**Je·ho·vah** /dʒɪˈhəʊvə‖-ˈhoʊ-/ *n* a name given to God in the OLD TESTAMENT (=first part of the Bible)

**Jehovah's Wit·ness** /ˌ·,·· ˈ··/ *n* [C] a member of a religious organization that believes the end of the world will happen soon and sends its members to people's houses to try to make them join

**je·june** /dʒɪˈdʒuːn/ *adj formal* **1** ideas that are jejune are too simple: *jejune political opinions* **2** writing or speech that is jejune is boring

**Jek·yll and Hyde** /ˌdʒekɪl ənd ˈhaɪd/ *n* [C] someone who is sometimes nice but at other times is unpleasant

**jell** /dʒel/ *v* [I] **1** also **gel** *BrE* if a thought, plan etc jells, it becomes clearer or more definite: *Things were confused before, but they are really starting to jell now.* **2** also **gel** if a liquid jells it becomes firmer, or thicker

**jel·lied** /ˈdʒelid/ *adj* [only before noun] *especially BrE* cooked or served in jelly: *jellied eels*

**Jell-o, jello** /ˈdʒeləʊ‖-loʊ/ *n* [U] *AmE trademark* JELLY (1)

**jel·ly** /ˈdʒeli/ *n* **1** [C,U] *BrE* a soft solid substance made with sweetened fruit juice and GELATINE; JELLO *AmE*: *raspberry jelly* **2** [U] *AmE* a very thick sweet substance made from boiled fruit and sugar with no pieces of fruit in it; clear JAM[1] (1): *a peanut butter and jelly sandwich* **3** [U] *especially BrE* a soft solid substance made from meat juices and GELATINE; ASPIC **4** [U] substance that is solid but very soft, and moves easily when you touch it: *frogs' eggs floating in a protective jelly* **5 feel like/turn to jelly** if your legs, knees etc feel like jelly, they start to shake because you are frightened or nervous

**jelly ba·by** /ˈ·· ˌ··/ *n* [C] *BrE trademark* a small soft sweet made in the shape of a baby in a variety of colours

**jelly bean** /ˈ·· ·/ *n* [C] a small soft sweet with different tastes and colours that is shaped like a bean

**jel·ly·fish** /ˈdʒelifɪʃ/ *n* [C] a round transparent sea animal that sometimes stings people

**jelly roll** /ˈ·· ˌ·/ *n* [C] *AmE* a long thin cake that is rolled up with JAM[1] (1) or cream inside; SWISS ROLL *BrE*

**jem·my** /ˈdʒemi/ *BrE*, **jimmy** *AmE* *n* [C] a metal bar used especially by thieves to break open locked doors, windows etc —**jemmy** *v* [T + **open**]

**je ne sais quoi** /ˌʒə nə seɪ ˈkwɑː/ *n French, often humorous* **a certain je ne sais quoi** a good quality that you cannot easily describe: *The place looks pretty old and crumbly, but it does have a certain je ne sais quoi.*

**jen·ny** /ˈdʒeni/ *n* [C] a SPINNING JENNY

**jeop·ar·dize** also **-ise** *BrE* /ˈdʒepədaɪz‖-ər-/ *v* [T] to risk losing or spoiling something important or valuable

**jeop·ar·dy** /ˈdʒepədi‖-ər-/ *n* **in jeopardy** in danger of being lost or harmed: **put/place sth in jeopardy** *The killings could put the whole peace process in jeopardy.*

**jerk**[1] /dʒɜːk‖dʒɜːrk/ *v* **1** [I,T] to pull something suddenly and roughly: **[+ at/on]** *Don't keep jerking at the drawer, it won't open.* **2** [I,T] to move or make something move in short, sudden movements: **jerk to a stop/halt** *Suddenly the train jerked to a halt.*

**jerk** sb **around** *phr v* [T] *AmE informal* to waste someone's time or deliberately make things difficult for them

**jerk off** *phr v* [I,T] *taboo especially AmE* to MASTURBATE

**jerk out** *phr v* [I,T] to say something quickly and nervously: *I jerked out some stupid remark.*

**jerk**[2] *n* **1** [C] a sudden quick movement: **with a jerk**

*The train moved off with a jerk.* | **give sth a jerk** (=pull something suddenly) —see also PHYSICAL JERKS **2** [C] *informal* a stupid man who does not care about the effects of his actions: *Tim's such a jerk! He always says the wrong thing.*

**jer·kin** /ˈdʒɜːkɪn‖-ɜːr-/ *n* [C] a short jacket that covers your body but not your arms

**jerk·wa·ter** /ˈdʒɜːkwɔːtə‖ˈdʒɜːrkwɒːtər, -wɑː-/ *adj* [only before noun] *AmE spoken* a jerkwater place, organization etc is small and uninteresting

**jerk·y¹** /ˈdʒɜːki‖-ɜːr-/ *adj* movements that are jerky are rough, with many start and stops: *The bus came to a jerky halt.* —**jerkily** *adv* —**jerkiness** *n* [U]

**jerky²** *n* [U] *AmE* meat that has been cut into thin pieces and dried in the sun or with smoke

**jer·o·bo·am** /ˌdʒerəˈbəʊəm‖-ˈboʊ-/ *n* [C] a very large wine bottle

**Jer·ry** /ˈdʒeri/ *n plural* **Jerries** [C] *especially BrE* an insulting word meaning a German

**jer·ry-built** /ˈdʒeribɪlt/ *adj* built cheaply, quickly, and badly

**Jer·sey** /ˈdʒɜːzi‖-ɜːr-/ *n* [C] a light brown cow

**jer·sey** /ˈdʒɜːzi‖-ɜːr-/ *n* **1** [C] a shirt made of soft material worn by players of sports such as football and RUGBY **2** [C] a piece of clothing made of wool that covers the upper part of your body and your arms; SWEATER **3** [U] a soft material made of cotton or wool

**Je·ru·sa·lem ar·ti·choke** /dʒəˌruːsələm ˈɑːtɪtʃəʊk‖-ˈɑːrtɪtʃoʊk/ *n* [C] an ARTICHOKE (2) —see picture on page 414

**jest¹** /dʒest/ *n* **1 in jest** something you say in jest is intended to be funny, not serious **2** [C] *old-fashioned* something that you say or do to amuse people; joke

**jest²** *v* [I + **about**] *old-use* to say things that you do not really mean in order to amuse people: **I jest!** *spoken* (=used to say that you are joking) —**jestingly** *adv*

**jest·er** /ˈdʒestə‖-ər/ *n* [C] a man employed in the past by a king or ruler to entertain people with jokes, stories etc

**Je·su·it** /ˈdʒezjuɪt‖ˈdʒeʒuɪt, ˈdʒezuɪt/ *n* [C] a man who is a member of the Roman Catholic religious Society of Jesus

**Je·sus¹** /ˈdʒiːzəs/ also **Jesus Christ** /ˌ·· ˈ·/ *n* the person who Christians believe was the son of God, and whose life and teachings Christianity is based on

**Jesus²** *interjection slang* used to express anger or surprise: *Oh Jesus! What are we going to do?*

> **USAGE NOTE: JESUS**
>
> FORMALITY AND POLITENESS
>
> **Jesus!**, **Christ!** and **Jesus Christ!** are all used in a non-religious way in very informal spoken English. They have the same uses as **God!**, but are even stronger: *Jesus, that hurts.* | *Jesus! What are you going to live on?*
>
> Some people, especially those who believe in the Christian religion, are offended by these uses of these words.

**jet¹** /dʒet/ *n* **1** [C] an aircraft with a jet engine: **jet fighter/aircraft** *British jet fighters have joined the UN forces.* **2** [C] a narrow stream of liquid or gas that comes quickly out of a small hole, or the hole itself: *a water jet* **3** [U] a hard black stone that is used for making jewellery

**jet²** *v* **jetted, jetting** [I always + adv/prep] **1** *informal* to travel by plane, especially when you go to many different places: *business executives jetting around the world* **2** if a liquid or gas jets out from somewhere, it comes quickly out of a small hole

**jet-black** /ˌ· ˈ·◂/ *adj* very dark black: *jet-black hair*

**jet en·gine** /ˌ· ˈ··/ *n* [C] an engine that pushes out a stream of hot air and gases behind it, used in aircraft —see picture at AIRCRAFT

**jet foil** /ˈ· ·/ *n* [C] a boat that rises out of the water on structures that look like legs when it is travelling fast

**jet lag** /ˈ· ·/ *n* [U] the tired and confused feeling that you can get after flying a very long distance —**jet-lagged** *adj*

**jet-pro·pelled** /ˌ· ·ˈ·◂/ *adj* using a jet engine for power

**jet pro·pul·sion** /ˌ· ·ˈ··/ *n* [U] the use of a JET ENGINE for power

**jet·sam** /ˈdʒetsəm/ *n* [U] things that are thrown from a ship and float on the sea towards the shore —see also **flotsam and jetsam** (FLOTSAM (2))

**jet set** /ˈ· ·/ *n* **the jet set** *old-fashioned* rich and fashionable people who travel a lot —**jet-setter** *n* [C]

**jet-ski** /ˈ· ·/ *n* [C] a small fast boat that one or two people can ride on for fun

**jet stream** /ˈ· ·/ *n* [singular, U] a current of very strong winds high above the Earth's surface

**jet·ti·son** /ˈdʒetɪsən, -zən/ *v* [T] **1** to get rid of methods, ideas, or ways of doing things: *The new President quickly jettisoned most of the previous economic policies.* **2** to throw things away, especially from a moving plane or ship

**jet·ty** /ˈdʒeti/ *n* [C] a wide wall or flat area built out into the water, used for getting on and off ships —compare PIER (1) —see picture on page 835

**Jew** /dʒuː/ *n* [C] a member of the group of people whose religion is Judaism, who lived in ancient times in the land of Israel, some of whom now live in the modern state of Israel and others in various countires throughout the world —**Jewish** *adj*: *the Jewish religion* | *My husband is Jewish.*

**jew·el** /ˈdʒuːəl/ *n* [C] **1** a small valuable stone, such as a diamond **2 jewels** [plural] jewellery or decorative objects made with valuable stones **3** a very small stone used in the machinery of a watch **4** *informal* someone who is very important to you, or the best thing in a group of things: *The Matisse was the jewel of her art collection.* **5 the jewel in the crown** the best or most valuable part of something —see also CROWN JEWELS

**jew·elled** *BrE*, **jeweled** *AmE* /ˈdʒuːəld/ *adj* decorated with jewels: *the famous jewelled eggs of Fabergé*

**jew·el·ler** *BrE*, jeweler *AmE* /ˈdʒuːələ‖-ər/ *n* [C] **1** someone who owns or works in a shop that sells jewellery **2** someone who makes or repairs jewellery

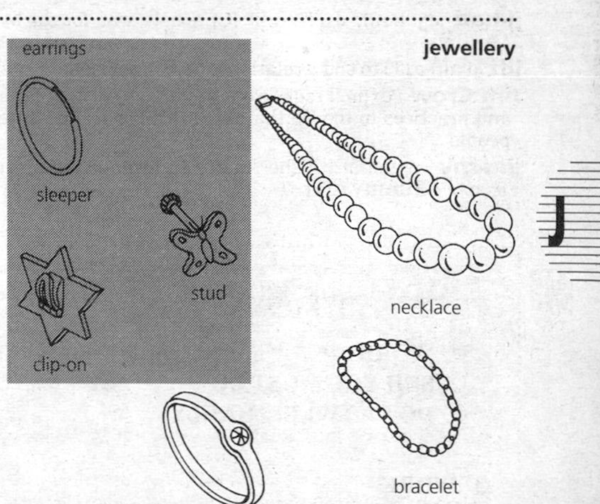


**jew·el·lery** *BrE*, **jewelry** *AmE* /ˈdʒuːəlri/ *n* [U] small things that you wear for decoration, such as rings or NECKLACES: *a piece of jewellery* —see also COSTUME JEWELLERY S3

J

**Jew·ess** /ˈdʒuːɨs/ *n* [C] *old-fashioned* a word meaning a Jewish woman, now usually considered offensive

**Jew·ry** /ˈdʒuːri/ *n* [U] *old-use* the Jewish people

**Jez·e·bel** /ˈdʒezəbəl, -bel/ *n* [C] *old use* a sexually immoral woman

**jib**[1] /dʒɪb/ *n* [C] **1** a small sail —compare MAINSAIL —see picture at YACHT (1) **2** the long part of a CRANE[1] (1)

**jib**[2] *v* **jibbed, jibbing** [I] if a horse jibs, it stops suddenly and will not move

**jib at** sth *phr v* [T] *especially BrE informal* to become suddenly unwilling to do or accept something: *If he jibbed at five hundred pounds, he'll hardly pay four thousand!*

**jibe**[1], **gibe** /dʒaɪb/ *n* [C] an unkind remark intended to make someone seem silly: *She was tired of his constant jibes.*

**jibe**[2] *v* [I + **with**] *AmE* if two statements, reports etc jibe, the information in them matches

**jibe at** sb/sth *phr v* [T] to say something that is intended to make someone seem silly

**jif·fy** /ˈdʒɪfi/ also **jiff** /dʒɪf/ *n* [singular] *spoken* **in a jiffy** very soon: *I'll be with you in a jiffy.*

**Jiffy bag** /ˈ·· ·/ *n* [C] *BrE trademark* a thick soft envelope, used for posting things that might break

**jig**[1] /dʒɪg/ *n* [C] a type of quick dance, or piece of music for this dance

**jig**[2] *v* **jigged, jigging** **1** [I] to dance a jig **2** [I always + adv/prep] to move up and down with quick short movements

**jig·ger** /ˈdʒɪgə‖-ər/ *n* [C] a small amount of alcoholic drink, or the cup this is measured with

**jig·gered** /ˈdʒɪgəd‖-ərd/ *adj* [not before noun] *BrE old-fashioned* **I'll be jiggered!** used when you are very surprised

**jig·ger·y-po·ker·y** /ˌdʒɪgəri ˈpəʊkəri‖-ˈpoʊ-/ *n* [U] *BrE informal* secret dishonest activity to make something seem what it is not: *social jiggery-pokery behind the scenes*

**jig·gle** /ˈdʒɪgəl/ *v* **jiggled, jiggling** [I,T] to move or make something move from side to side with short quick movements

**jig·saw** /ˈdʒɪgsɔː‖-sɒː/ *n* [C] **1** also **jigsaw puz·zle** /ˈ·· ˌ··/ a picture cut up into many pieces that you try to fit together **2** a special SAW (=cutting tool) for cutting out shapes in thin pieces of wood —see picture at TOOL[1]

**ji·had** /dʒɪˈhɑːd, dʒɪˈhæd/ *n* [C] a holy war fought by Muslims

**jilt** /dʒɪlt/ *v* [T] to end a relationship with someone

**Jim Crow** /ˌdʒɪm ˈkrəʊ‖-ˈkroʊ/ *n AmE* a system of laws and practices in the US that separated black and white people

**jim·my** /ˈdʒɪmi/ *n* [C] the American form of the word JEMMY —**jimmy** *v* [T]

jigsaw

**jin·gle**[1] /ˈdʒɪŋgəl/ *v* **jingled, jingling** [I,T] to shake metal things together so that they make a sound like small bells: *Stop jingling those coins in your pocket.*

**jingle**[2] *n* **1** [C] a short song used in advertisements **2** [singular] the sound of small metal objects being shaken together —see picture on page 1261

**jin·go·is·m** /ˈdʒɪŋgəʊɪzəm‖-goʊ-/ *n* [U] a strong belief that your own country is better than others: *a mood of warlike jingoism* —**jingoistic** /ˌdʒɪŋgəʊˈɪstɪk◂‖-goʊ-/ *adj*

**jinks** /dʒɪŋks/ *n* —see HIGH JINKS

**jinn** /dʒɪn/ *n* [C] a GENIE

**jinx** /dʒɪŋks/ *n* [singular] a strange power that brings bad luck: [+ **on**] *So many things have gone wrong, we're beginning to think there's a jinx on the whole wedding.*

**jinxed** /dʒɪŋkst/ *adj* often having bad luck, or making people have bad luck

**jit·ter·bug** /ˈdʒɪtəbʌg‖-ər-/ *n* [singular] a popular fast JAZZ dance in the 1940s

**jit·ters** /ˈdʒɪtəz‖-ərz/ *n* **get the jitters** *informal* to feel anxious, especially before an important event or before something difficult: *It's my driving test next week, and I've got the jitters already.*

**jit·ter·y** /ˈdʒɪtəri/ *adj informal* anxious or nervous

**jive**[1] /dʒaɪv/ *n* [C] **1** a very fast dance, popular especially in the 1930s and 40s, performed to SWING[2] (5) music **2** [U] *AmE informal* statements that you do not believe are true: *Don't give me any of that jive!*

**jive**[2] *v* **1** [I] to dance a jive **2** [T] *AmE informal* to try to make someone believe something that is not true, as a joke

**Jnr** *adj BrE* the written abbreviation of JUNIOR

**Job** /dʒəʊb‖dʒoʊb/ *n* **1 Job's comforter** someone who tries to make you feel more cheerful, but actually makes you feel worse **2 have the patience of Job** to be extremely patient

S1 W1

## job /dʒɒb‖dʒɑːb/ *n*

① WORK
② STH YOU MUST DO
③ DO STH WELL/BADLY
④ COMPUTERS
⑤ CRIME
⑥ OTHER MEANINGS

① WORK

**1** [C] the regular paid work that you do for an employer: **get/find a job (as sth)** *Eventually, Mary got a job as a waitress.* | **take a job** (=accept a job that is offered to you) *I was so desperate that I took the first job that came along.* | **lose a job** *At least there's no danger of you losing your job.* | **temporary/permanent job** *It's a temporary job, but I'm hoping it'll be made permanent.* | **offer (sb) a job** *Well, Ms Taylor, we'd like to offer you the job.* | **part-time/full-time job** (=a job you do for only part of the day or week, or all of the day or week) | **apply for a job** (=try to get a job) *I've applied for a job at the university.* | **job satisfaction** (=the enjoyment that you get from doing your job) | **leave/quit a job** *Oh Rick, you didn't quit your job, did you?* | **change jobs** (=get a different job) | **hold down a job** (=keep a job) | **job security** (=how permanent your job is likely to be) | **Saturday/summer/**

**holiday job** (=a job that you only do on Saturdays etc)|**steady job** (=a job that is likely to continue)|**be out of a job** (=not have a job) *If the project fails we'll all be out of a job.*|**know your job** (=be very experienced at the work you do)|**job losses** *Four hundred more job losses were announced this week.* —see also JOB DESCRIPTION
**2 on the job a)** as part of a particular job: *Most clerical training is done on the job.* **b)** doing a particular job: *We'll put our best people on the job.* **c)** *BrE spoken* having sex
**3 I'm only doing my job** *spoken* used to say that it is not your fault if you have to do something in your work that other people do not like
**4 it's more than my job's worth** *BrE spoken* used to tell someone that you cannot do what they want because it is against your company's rules
**5 jobs for the boys** *BrE* work that someone in power has given to their friends, especially work that is not necessary

### ② STH YOU MUST DO

**6** [C] something that you have to do which involves working or making an effort: *Fixing the roof is going to be the biggest job.*|**odd jobs** (=small things that need to be done, especially in the house or garden)|**get on with a job** (=continue doing a job)|**the job in hand** (=the work that you are doing now)
**7 ▶DUTY◀** [singular] if it is your job to do something, it is your duty to do it: *Leave the dishes – that's my job.*|**it is sb's job (to do sth)** *It's my job to make sure that the work's finished on time.*
**8 fall down on the job** to fail to do something you were supposed to do
**9 a job of work** *BrE old-fashioned* something that you have to do, whether you enjoy it or not

### ③ DO STH WELL/BADLY

**10 do a good/great/marvellous job (with)** to do something very well: *You've done a great job raising your kids.*
**11 make a good/bad job of sth** *BrE* to do something well or badly: *Sarah made a really good job of that presentation.*
**12 do the job** *informal* if something does the job, it is effective in doing what you want it to do: *That little screwdriver should do the job.*
**13 Good job!** *AmE spoken* used to tell someone they have done something well

### ④ COMPUTERS

**14** [C] an action done by a computer

### ⑤ CRIME

**15** [C] *informal* a crime in which money is stolen from a bank, company etc: *a bank job*|**an inside job** (=one done by a member of the organization in which it happens)

### ⑥ OTHER MEANINGS

**16 it's a good job** *BrE spoken* used to say that it is lucky that something happened: *It's a good job you had your safety belt on.*
**17 have a job doing/to do sth** *BrE spoken* to have difficulty doing something: *I had an awful job getting that stain out.*
**18 make the best of a bad job** *especially BrE* to do the best that you can in a situation that you do not like but cannot change
**19 give sth up as a bad job** *BrE* to accept that something is not going to succeed and stop trying to do it
**20 just the job** *BrE spoken* exactly what is needed for a particular situation: *That table you gave us was just the job!*
**21 ▶KIND OF THING◀** *spoken* used to say that something is of a particular type: *Jack's got a new car – a red two-seater job.*
**22 a job lot** *BrE* a mixed group of things that are sold together: *a job lot of furniture* —see also BLOW JOB, HAND JOB, NOSE JOB

**USAGE NOTE: JOB**

WORD CHOICE: **job, work, post, position, line of work/business, do, occupation, trade, profession, vocation, career**

What you do to earn your living is your **job** [C], especially if you work for someone else: *I need a part-time job.*|*a boring job delivering pizzas*

**Work** [U] is something you are paid for doing, especially regularly – *She wants to return to work after having the baby* – but it can also be used where there is no payment or you are not working for someone else: *voluntary work*|*housework*|*her work as a self-employed trainer*

**Post** and **position** are more formal words for a particular job in a company etc: *He was appointed to the post/position of professor of English at Stanford University.*

In spoken English, the kind of work or job someone does may be called their **line of work/business**, or the verb **do** is often used, especially in questions: *What do you do?*|*I'd like to get into that line of work!*

More formally, your kind of work or job is your **occupation** [C]. On a form you might see: *Please state your name and occupation.*

A **trade** is a skilled kind of work in which you make or do things with your hands: *She's an electrician by trade.*

A **profession** is a kind of work such as that of a doctor or lawyer, for which you need special training and a good education. Some **professions,** such as teaching and nursing, are also called **vocations,** which suggests that people do them in order to help others rather than to earn a lot of money.

A **career** is a type of work that you do or hope to do for most of your life: *Her political career began 20 years ago.*

This graph shows some of the words most commonly used with the noun **job**.

get a job
take a job
lose a job
temporary/permanent job
offer (sb) a job
part-time/full-time job
apply for a job
job satisfaction

10 20 30 40 per million

Based on the British National Corpus and the Longman Lancaster Corpus

**job·ber** /ˈdʒɒbə‖ˈdʒɑːbər/ *n* [C] *especially BrE* someone whose job is buying and selling stocks (STOCK[1] (3)) and shares (SHARE[2] (5))

**job·bing** /ˈdʒɒbɪŋ‖ˈdʒɑː-/ *adj BrE* **jobbing gardener/painter etc** someone who does small pieces of work for different people

**job cen·tre** /'· ,··/ *n* [C] a British government service where jobs are advertised and training courses are provided for people who are looking for work

**job de·scrip·tion** /'· ·,··/ *n* [C] an official list of the work and responsibilities that you have in your job

**job·less** /'dʒɒbləs‖'dʒɑːb-/ *adj* without a job; UNEMPLOYED[1]

**job-shar·ing** /'· ··/ *n* [U] an arrangement by which two people both work PART-TIME doing the same job —**job-share** *n* [C]

**jobs·worth** /'dʒɒbzwɜːθ‖'dʒɑːbzwɜːrθ/ *n* [C] *BrE informal* someone who follows the rules of their job too exactly without using any imagination

**jock** /dʒɒk‖dʒɑːk/ *n* [C] **1** *BrE informal* an insulting word for someone from Scotland **2** *AmE informal* an insulting word for someone who does a lot of sport

**jock·ey¹** /'dʒɒki‖'dʒɑːki/ *n* [C] someone who rides horses in races

**jockey²** *v* **1 jockey for position** to try to get into the best position or situation: *businessmen jockeying for position at the bar* **2** [T] to gradually persuade someone to do something: **jockey sb into doing sth** *Do you think you can jockey them into accepting our offer?*

**jockey shorts** /'·· ·/ *n* [plural] *trademark* a type of men's cotton underwear that fits very tightly

**jock·strap** /'dʒɒkstræp‖'dʒɑːk-/ *n* [C] a piece of men's underwear that supports their sex organs during sport

**jo·cose** /dʒə'kəʊs, dʒəʊ-‖dʒə'koʊs, dʒoʊ-/ *adj literary* joking —**jocosely** *adv* —**jocoseness, jocosity** /dʒəkɒsɪ̈ti, dʒəʊ-‖dʒə'kɑː-, dʒoʊ-/ *n* [U]

**joc·u·lar** /'dʒɒkjʊ̈lə‖'dʒɑːkjʊ̈lər/ *adj formal* joking or humorous: *jocular remarks* —**jocularly** *adv* —**jocularity** /,dʒɒkjʊ̈'lærɪ̈ti‖,dʒɑː-/ *n* [U]

**joc·und** /'dʒɒkənd‖'dʒɑː-/ *adj literary* cheerful and happy —**jocundly** *adv* —**jocundity** /dʒəʊ'kʌndɪ̈ti, dʒə-‖dʒoʊ-, dʒə-/ *n* [U]

**jodh·purs** /'dʒɒdpəz‖'dʒɑːdpərz/ *n* [plural] a special type of trousers that you wear when riding horses

**Joe Bloggs** /,dʒəʊ 'blɒgz‖,dʒoʊ 'blɑːgz/ *BrE*, **Joe Blow/Schmo** /-'bləʊ‖-'bloʊ -'ʃməʊ‖'ʃmoʊ/ *AmE n spoken* [singular] the ordinary average person

**jog¹** /dʒɒg‖dʒɑːg/ *v* **jogged, jogging 1** [I] to run slowly and steadily, especially as a way of exercising: *two figures jogging along the beach* **2** [T] to knock or push something lightly by mistake: *You jogged my elbow.* **3 jog sb's memory** to make someone remember something: *Perhaps this photo will help to jog your memory.*

**jog along** *phr v* [I] *informal* to continue in the same way as usual

**jog²** *n* [singular] **1** a slow steady run, especially done as a way of exercising: **go for a jog** *Mike goes for a two-mile jog every morning.* **2** a light knock or push done by accident

**jog·ger** /'dʒɒgə‖'dʒɑːgər/ *n* [C] someone who runs slowly and steadily as a way of exercising

**jog·ging** /'dʒɒgɪŋ‖'dʒɑː-/ *n* [U] the activity of running slowly and steadily as a way of exercising

J

**jogging suit** /'·· ·/ *n* [C] loose thick cotton clothes that you wear when you are running for exercise

**jog·gle** /'dʒɒgəl‖'dʒɑː-/ *v* [I,T] *informal* to shake or move up and down slightly

**jog trot** /'· ·/ *n* [singular] a slow steady run —**jog-trot** *v* [I]

**john** /dʒɒn‖dʒɑːn/ *n* [C] *AmE* **1** *informal* a toilet **2** *AmE slang* the customer of a PROSTITUTE

**John Bull** /,· '·/ *n old-fashioned* **1** [U] England or the English people **2** [C] an insulting word for an Englishman, especially one who does not like foreigners

**John Doe** /,· '·/ *n* [singular] *AmE* a man whose name is not known, especially one who is involved in a law case —compare JANE DOE

**John Han·cock** /,dʒɒn 'hænkɒk‖,dʒɑːn 'hænkɑːk/ *n* [C] *AmE informal* your signature

**john·ny** /'dʒɒni‖'dʒɑːni/ *n* [C] **1** *BrE slang* a CONDOM **2** *old-fashioned* a man **3** *AmE slang* a PENIS

**Johnny-on-the-spot** /,·· · · '·/ *n* [singular] *AmE informal* someone who immediately offers to help, takes an opportunity etc

**johns** /dʒɒnz‖dʒɑːnz/ *n* [plural] — see LONG JOHNS

**john thom·as** /,dʒɒn 'tɒməs‖,dʒɑːn 'tɑː-/ *n* [C] *slang* a PENIS

**joie de viv·re** /,ʒwɑː də 'viːvrə/ *n* [U] *French* a feeling of pleasure and excitement because you are alive

**join¹** /dʒɔɪn/ *v*  S1 W1

**1 ▶CONNECT◀ a)** [T] to connect or fasten things together: *Join the two pieces of wood with strong glue.* | *The hip bone is joined to the thigh bone.* **b)** [I,T] to come together and become connected: *Where does the river join the sea?*

**2 ▶GROUP/ORGANIZATION◀** [T] to become a member of an organization, society, or group: *When did you join the Labour party?* | *Woods joined the Daily Dispatch as a reporter in 1960.*

**3 ▶ACTIVITY◀** [T] to begin to take part in an activity that other people are involved in: **join a course/class/scheme etc** *I joined the class halfway through the second term.* | *Church leaders have joined the campaign to end fox-hunting.*

**4 join a queue/line/row etc** to go and stand at the end of a line of people: *Meanwhile, Carl joined the queue for tickets.*

**5 join sb (for sth)** to meet someone in order to do something together: *I'm going to the theatre tonight. Would you care to join me?*

**6 join sb in doing sth** to do or say something together with someone else: *I'm sure you'll all join me in thanking today's speaker.*

**7 join hands** if people join hands, they hold each other's hands

**8 join the club!** *spoken* used to say that you and a lot of other people are in the same situation: *"I can't find a job at all." "Yeah? Join the club!"*

**9 join battle** *formal* to begin fighting

**10 be joined in marriage/holy matrimony** *formal* to be married —see also **join/combine forces** (FORCE[1] (7)), **if you can't beat 'em, join 'em** (BEAT[1] (20))

**join in** *phr v* [I,T] to take part in an activity as one of a group of people: *Come on, Ian, join in! You can sing!* | **join in the fun/party** *We couldn't wait to join in the fun.*

**join up** *phr v* [I] to become a member of the army, navy, or airforce

**join up with** sb/sth *phr v* [T] *informal* to combine with other people in order to do something: *We joined up with a couple from Derbyshire to make a quiz team.*

**join with** sb *phr v* [T] *formal* to do or say something together, as a group: **join with sb in doing sth** *Please join with me in praying for Sarah's recovery.*

**USAGE NOTE: JOIN**

WORD CHOICE: **join, enrol(l) in/at, enlist in, go to, come to, attend, join in, participate in**

If you go to be with someone, you **join** them: *He was looking forward to joining his wife/family in Detroit* (NOT *joining with them*).

You may also **join** (=become a member of) many kinds of groups of people, such as a club, a team, a political party, a tour group, a company, a church, or a congregation (NOT *join in*). A country may **join** the EU the UN, or another international organization.

You may **join** the army, navy etc or more formally **enlist in** it. You **go to** war (NOT *join* it).

You may **join** a class, course, or university at the beginning, but the more official word is **enrol in/at** (*AmE* **enroll**): *I want to enrol in/join the linguistics class* (NOT *join to*). | *Diane has enrolled at the University of Essex.* When you **go** regularly **to** a class, school etc, you formally **attend** it (NOT *attend to* it).

You usually **go/come to** or more formally **attend** an event such as a meeting, football game, wedding, church service or official dinner (NOT *join*). *Are you coming to my birthday party?*

If you actively take part in something that a group is doing, you **join in** or more formally **participate in** what it does: *I hope you will participate in all our club activities.|Chris joined in the class discussion enthusiastically.*
You **go to**, **attend**, or more actively **participate in** a conference.

**join²** *n* [C] a place where two parts of an object are connected or fastened together: **you can hardly see the join** *It's been glued back together so well, you can hardly see the join.*

**join·er** /ˈdʒɔɪnə‖-ər/ *n* [C] someone who makes wooden doors, window frames etc —compare CARPENTER

**join·er·y** /ˈdʒɔɪnəri/ *n* [U] the trade and work of a joiner —compare CARPENTRY

W2 **joint¹** /dʒɔɪnt/ *adj* [only before noun] **1** shared, owned by, or involving two or more people or groups: *a joint bank account|joint first prize|joint army and airforce operations* **2 joint effort** a situation in which two or more people work together: *"Who cooked the meal?" "Well it was a joint effort really."* **3 joint venture** a business activity begun by two or more people or companies working together **4 joint resolution** *law* a decision or law agreed by both houses of the US Congress and signed by the President —**jointly** *adv*: *tenants who are jointly responsible for their rent*

**joint²** *n* [C] **1** a part of your body where two bones meet: *knee joint* **2** *BrE* a large piece of meat for cooking, usually containing a bone: *a joint of beef* **3** a place where two things or parts of an object are joined together: *Rain penetrates the joints between the concrete panels.* **4 out of joint a)** if a bone in your body is out of joint, it has been pushed out of its correct position **b)** if a system, group etc is out of joint, it is not working properly: *Something is out of joint in our society.* —see also **put sb's nose out of joint** (NOSE¹ (18)) **5** *informal* a cheap bar, club, or restaurant: *a hamburger joint* —see also CLIP JOINT **6** *slang* a cigarette containing CANNABIS —see also **case the joint** (CASE² (2))

**joint³** *v* [T] to cut meat into joints (JOINT² (2))

**joint·ed** /ˈdʒɔɪntɪd/ *adj* having joints and able to move and bend: *a jointed puppet*

**joint hon·ours** /ˌ· ˈ··/ *n* [U] a university degree course in Britain in which two main subjects are studied —compare SINGLE HONOURS

**joint-stock com·pa·ny** /ˌ· ˈ· ˌ···/ *n* [C] *AmE technical* a company that is owned by all the people with shares (SHARE² (5)) in it

**joist** /dʒɔɪst/ *n* [C] one of the beams that support a floor or ceiling

S2 W3 **joke¹** /dʒəʊk‖dʒoʊk/ *n* [C]
**1 ► STH FUNNY ◄** something that you say or do to make people laugh, especially a funny story or trick: *Do you know any good jokes?|Don't get mad – it was only a joke!*|**crack/make a joke** (=say something funny)|**tell a joke** (=tell a short funny story)|**get the joke** *informal* (=understand why a joke is funny)|**play a joke on sb** (=trick them)|**dirty joke** (=about sex)|**sick joke** (=about something unpleasant)|**have a joke** (=not mean something seriously) *I was only having a joke!*
**2 ► STH ANNOYING ◄** *informal* a situation which is so silly or unreasonable that it makes you angry: *The whole meeting was a complete joke.*
**3 go/get beyond a joke** a situation that gets beyond a joke has become serious and worrying: *I haven't heard from them for three weeks now – it's gone beyond a joke.*
**4 be no joke** used to emphasize that a situation is serious or that someone really means what they say: *These rail strikes every week are no joke.*|**it's no joke** *It's no joke, I think she really means to kill herself.*
**5 take a joke** to be able to laugh at a joke about yourself: *Your problem is you just can't take a joke!*
**6 make a joke of** to treat something serious as if it was intended to be funny: *Sure, he made a joke of it but he was clearly hurt.*
**7 not get the joke** to not understand why someone thinks a situation is funny: *"Is that a proposition?" I asked, but she didn't get the joke.*
**8 sb's idea of a joke** *spoken* a situation that someone else thinks is funny but you do not: *I suppose hiding the car key was his idea of a joke.*
**9 the joke's on you/her etc** used to say that the person who was trying to make other people seem silly now seems silly themselves —see also IN-JOKE, PRACTICAL JOKE; **standing joke** (STANDING¹ (4))

**joke²** *v* [I] **1** to say things that are intended to be funny: [+ **about/with**] *It's serious, Donny, don't joke about it!* **2 you're joking!/you must be joking!** *spoken* used to tell someone that what they are suggesting is so strange or silly that you cannot believe that they are serious: *What! Buy a house on my salary? You must be joking!* **3 only joking** *BrE spoken* used to say that you did not really mean what you just said: *Only joking, darling – I love you really!* **4 joking apart/aside** *BrE* used before you say something serious after you have been joking: *Joking apart, she is a very talented painter.* —**jokingly** *adv* S3

**jok·er** /ˈdʒəʊkə‖ˈdʒoʊkər/ *n* [C] **1** *informal* someone who behaves in a way you think is stupid: *Some joker had nailed it to the floor.* **2** a PLAYING CARD that has no fixed value and is only used in some card games **3** someone who makes a lot of jokes **4 the joker in the pack** something or someone whose effect on future events cannot be known

**jok·ey, joky** /ˈdʒəʊki‖ˈdʒoʊ-/ *adj BrE* not serious and tending to make people laugh: *Her jokey manner put us at ease.* —**jokily** *adv* —**jokiness** *n* [U]

**jol·li·fi·ca·tion** /ˌdʒɒlɪfɪˈkeɪʃən‖ˌdʒɑː-/ *n* [C,U] *old-fashioned* fun and enjoyment

**jol·ly¹** /ˈdʒɒli‖ˈdʒɑːli/ *adj* **jollier, jolliest** *especially BrE* **1** happy and cheerful: *Everybody was in a very relaxed and jolly mood.* **2** *old-fashioned* very pleasant and enjoyable: *a very jolly occasion*

**jolly²** *adv BrE old-fashioned* **1** very: *Sounds like a jolly good idea to me.* **2 jolly well** used to emphasize that you are annoyed: *I wish he'd jolly well hurry up.* **3 jolly good!** *spoken* used to say that you are pleased by what someone has just said

**jolly³** *v* [T] **jolly sb into doing sth** *BrE informal* to gently persuade someone to do something
**jolly** sb **along** *phr v* [T] *BrE* to try to make someone do something faster by encouraging them: *You'll have to jolly people along if you want to get this work finished.*
**jolly** sth ↔ **up** *v* [T] *BrE* to make a place brighter and more cheerful

**jolly⁴** *n* [C] **1 get your jollies** *AmE spoken* to get pleasure from a particular experience or activity **2** *BrE old-fashioned* an informal event at which people have fun and enjoy themselves

**Jolly Ro·ger** /ˌ·· ˈ··/ *n* a black flag with a picture of bones on it, used in former times by PIRATES; SKULL AND CROSSBONES (1)

**jolt¹** /dʒəʊlt‖dʒoʊlt/ *v* **1** [I, T] to move suddenly and roughly, or to make someone or something move in this way: *The car jolted and Rachel was thrown backwards.* **2** [T] to give someone a sudden shock

**jolt²** *n* [C] **1** a sudden rough shaking movement: *I felt every jolt of the bus.* **2** a sudden shock: **with a jolt** *I realized with a jolt that they must have gone without me.*

**Jo·nah** /ˈdʒəʊnə‖ˈdʒoʊ-/ *n* [C] someone who seems to bring bad luck

**Jones·es** /ˈdʒəʊnzɪz‖ˈdʒoʊn-/ *n* —see **keep up with the Joneses** (KEEP¹)

**josh** /dʒɒʃ‖dʒɑːʃ/ *v AmE old-fashioned* **1** [I + **with**] to talk to someone in a joking way **2** [T] to laugh at someone in a friendly way: *The guys josh him and call him an egghead.*

**joss stick** /ˈdʒɒs ˌstɪk‖ˈdʒɑːs-/ *n* [C] a stick of INCENSE¹

**jos·tle** /ˈdʒɒsəl‖ˈdʒɑː-/ *v* [I,T] to push or knock against someone in a crowd, especially so that you can get somewhere or do something before other people: *The couple were shoved and jostled by reporters as they left the courtroom.*

**jot**[1] /dʒɒt‖dʒɑːt/ *v* **jotted, jotting**
**jot** sth ↔ **down** *phr v* [T] to write something quickly: *Let me jot down your number and I'll call you tomorrow.*

**jot**[2] *n* **not a jot** *BrE old-fashioned* not at all or none at all: *It doesn't make a jot of difference.*

**jot·ter** /ˈdʒɒtə‖ˈdʒɑːtər/ *n* [C] *BrE* a small book for writing notes in

**jot·tings** /ˈdʒɒtɪŋz‖ˈdʒɑː-/ *n* [plural] *informal* short notes, usually written to remind yourself about something

**joule** /dʒuːl‖dʒuːl, dʒaʊl/ *n* [C] *technical* a measure of energy or work

**jour·nal** /ˈdʒɜːnl‖-ɜːr-/ *n* [C] **1** a serious magazine produced for professional people or those with a particular interest: *the British Medical Journal* **2** *literary* a written record that you make of the things that happen to you each day; DIARY (1)

**jour·nal·ese** /ˌdʒɜːnəlˈiːz‖-ɜːr-/ *n* [U] language that is typical of newspapers

**jour·nal·is·m** /ˈdʒɜːnəl-ɪzəm‖-ɜːr-/ *n* [U] the job or activity of writing news reports for newspapers, magazines, television or radio

W3 **jour·nal·ist** /ˈdʒɜːnəl-ɪst‖-ɜːr-/ *n* [C] someone who writes news reports for newspapers, magazines, television, or radio —compare REPORTER

S3 W2 **jour·ney**[1] /ˈdʒɜːni‖-ɜːr-/ *n* [C] **1** *especially BrE* a trip from one place to another, especially over a long distance: *a train journey across Europe*|*I have a 25-minute journey to work.*|**break your journey** (=stop somewhere for a time to rest) **2** *literary* the process by which something gradually changes and develops: *our journey through life* —see TRAVEL (USAGE)

**journey**[2] *v* [I always + adv/prep] *literary* to travel

**jour·ney·man** /ˈdʒɜːnimən‖-ɜːr-/ *n* [C] *old-fashioned* **1** a trained worker who works for someone else **2** an experienced worker whose work is reasonable but not excellent

**jour·no** /ˈdʒɜːnəʊ‖ˈdʒɜːrnoʊ/ *n* [C] *informal* a JOURNALIST

**joust** /dʒaʊst/ *v* [I] to fight with LANCES (=long sticks) while riding a horse —**joust** *n* [C]

**Jove** /dʒəʊv‖dʒoʊv/ *n* **by Jove!** *BrE old-fashioned* used to express surprise or to emphasize something: *By Jove, you're right!*

**jo·vi·al** /ˈdʒəʊviəl‖ˈdʒoʊ-/ *adj* friendly and cheerful: *a jovial smile* —**jovially** *adv* —**joviality** /ˌdʒəʊviˈælɪti‖ˌdʒoʊ-/ *n* [U]

**jowl** /dʒaʊl/ *n* [C] **1** [usually plural] the skin that covers your lower jaw on either side of your face **2 heavy-jowled** having large jowls that hang down slightly —see also **cheek by jowl** (CHEEK[1] (4))

W3 **joy**[1] /dʒɔɪ/ *n* **1** [U] great happiness and pleasure: **to sb's joy** *To Beth's surprise and joy, she was awarded first prize.*|**jump for joy** (=be very pleased) **2** [C] something or someone that gives you happiness and pleasure: *the joys and sorrows of bringing up a family*|**be a joy to use/drive etc** (=be very pleasant to use/drive etc) *The new Merc's a joy to drive.* **3** [U only in questions or negatives] *BrE spoken* success in doing what you are trying to do: *You could ask the library to trace the book, but I doubt you'll get any joy.*

**joy**[2] *v*
**joy in** sth *phr v* [T] *literary* to be happy because of something

**joy·ful** /ˈdʒɔɪfəl/ *adj* very happy, or likely to make people very happy: *the joyful news* —**joyfully** *adv* —**joyfulness** *n* [U]

**joy·less** /ˈdʒɔɪləs/ *adj* without any happiness at all: *a joyless marriage* —**joylessly** *adv* —**joylessness** *n* [U]

**joy·ous** /ˈdʒɔɪəs/ *adj literary* very happy, or likely to make people very happy: *a joyous occasion* —**joyously** *adv* —**joyousness** *n* [U]

**joy·rid·ing** /ˈdʒɔɪˌraɪdɪŋ/ *n* [U] the crime of stealing a car and driving it in a fast and dangerous way for fun —**joyride** *v* [I] —**joyrider** *n* [C]

**joy·stick** /ˈdʒɔɪˌstɪk/ *n* [C] an upright handle that you use to change the direction in which something such as a plane moves

**JP** /ˌdʒeɪ ˈpiː/ *n* [C] a JUSTICE OF THE PEACE; a MAGISTRATE in Britain

**Jr** *AmE* the written abbreviation of JUNIOR; used after the name of a man who has the same name as his father: *Alan Parks, Jr.*

**jub·i·lant** /ˈdʒuːbɪlənt/ *adj* extremely happy and pleased because you have been successful, or full of people who feel this way: *jubilant celebrations* —**jubilantly** *adv*

**ju·bi·la·tion** /ˌdʒuːbɪˈleɪʃən/ *n* [U] *formal* happiness and pleasure because you have been successful: *shouts of jubilation from the crowd*

**ju·bi·lee** /ˈdʒuːbɪliː, ˌdʒuːbɪˈliː/ *n* [C] a date that is celebrated because it is exactly 25 years, 50 years etc after an important event —see also DIAMOND JUBILEE, GOLDEN JUBILEE, SILVER JUBILEE

**Ju·da·is·m** /ˈdʒuːdeɪ-ɪzəm, ˈdʒuːdə-‖ˈdʒuːdə-, ˈdʒuːdi-/ *n* [U] the Jewish religion based on the Old Testament of the Bible, the Talmud, and the later teachings of the RABBIS —**Judaic** /dʒuːˈdeɪ-ɪk/ *adj*

**Ju·das** /ˈdʒuːdəs/ *n* [C] someone who is disloyal to a friend; TRAITOR

**jud·der** /ˈdʒʌdə‖-ər/ *v* [I] if a vehicle or machine judders, it shakes violently: *The engine juddered to life.* —**judder** *n* [C]

**judge**[1] /dʒʌdʒ/ *n* [C] **1** the official in control of a court who decides how criminals should be punished: **federal judge/high court judge** (=a judge in a particular court) **2** someone who decides on the result of a competition: *The panel of judges included several well-known writers.* **3 be no judge** *informal* to not have enough skill or knowledge to be able to give an opinion on a particular subject: *I don't like this wine – not that I'm any judge of these things.* **4 a good/bad judge of** someone whose opinion on something is usually right or wrong: *Sandra's a very good judge of character.* **5 let me be the judge of that** *spoken* used to tell someone angrily that you do not need their advice —see also **as sober as a judge** (SOBER[1] (1)) W2

**judge**[2] *v* **judged, judging** S2 W3
**1** ▶ **OPINION** ◀ [I,T] to form or give an opinion about someone or something after thinking carefully about all the information you know about them: *It seems a good idea, but without all the facts it's hard to judge.*|**judge sb/sth by sth** *Teachers tend to be judged by their students' exam grades.*|**judge sb/sth on sth** *Why can't they judge me on my brains, not my looks?*|**judge that** *I judged that Williams was a spy.*|**judge sb/sth (to be) sth** *Their reunion was judged to be a great success.*|**judge who/what/how etc** *Well, Sam, can you judge where they might go next?*|**judge sth/sb (to be) good/bad/fair etc** *The headmaster was judged incompetent by school inspectors.*|**judge it unwise/expedient/inappropriate etc to do sth** *At that point we judged it wise to leave them alone.*
**2** ▶ **GUESS** ◀ [I,T] to guess an amount, distance, height, weight etc; ESTIMATE: *"How long will it take?" "It's impossible to judge."*|**judge sb/sth to be sth** *Trevor judged the distance to be about 30 yards.*|**judge how far/long/wide etc sth is** *In this fog, we can't judge how far it is to the other side of the river.*
**3 judging by/from** used to say that you are making a guess based on what you have just seen, heard or learned: *Judging by the look on Adam's face, the news must have been terrible.*
**4** ▶ **COMPETITION** ◀ [I,T] to decide on the result of a competition: *Who's judging the talent contest?*|**judge sb on sth** *Competitors will be judged on speed and accuracy.*
**5** ▶ **CRITICIZE** ◀ [I,T] to form an opinion about someone, especially in an unfair or criticizing way: *What right have you to judge the way they live?*
**6** ▶ **LAW** ◀ [T] to decide whether someone is guilty of a crime in court
**7 It's not for me to judge** *spoken* used to say that you do

not think you have the right to give your opinion about something
**8 as far as I can judge** used to say that you think what you are saying is true, but you are not sure
**9 don't judge a book by its cover** used to say that you should not form an opinion based only on the way something looks

W2 **judg·ment** also **judgement** *BrE* /ˈdʒʌdʒmənt/ *n*
**1 ▶ OPINION ◀** [C,U] an opinion that you form after thinking carefully about something: **in sb's judgment** *In my judgment, we should accept his offer.* | **pass judgment** (=give your opinion or criticism) | **reserve judgment** (=refuse to decide before you have all the facts)
**2 ▶ ABILITY TO DECIDE ◀** [U] the ability to make decisions about situations or people: *The minister's remarks show a lack of political judgement.* | **sound judgment** (=good judgment) *sound editorial judgment*
**3 ▶ LAW ◀** [C,U] an official decision given by a judge or a court of law: *a judgment delivered by the European court*
**4 against your better judgment** if you do something against your better judgment, you do it even though you do not think it is the right thing to do: *In the end I agreed to lend her the money, but it was against my better judgment.*
**5 a judgment** something unpleasant that happens which seems like a punishment for the things you have done wrong
**6 sit in judgment over sb** to criticize someone's behaviour, especially unfairly
**7 judgment call** *AmE* a decision you have to make yourself because there are no fixed rules in a situation —see also LAST JUDGMENT, VALUE JUDGMENT

**judg·ment·al** also **judgemental** *BrE* /dʒʌdʒˈmentl/ *adj* too quick and willing to criticize people

**judgment day** /ˈ··· ·/ also **day of judgment** *n* [singular, not with *the*] the time after death when everyone is judged by God for what they have done in life, according to Christianity and some other religions

**ju·di·ca·ture** /ˈdʒuːdɪkətʃə‖-ər/ *n* **the judicature** *formal* judges and the organization, power etc of the law

**ju·di·cial** /dʒuːˈdɪʃəl/ *adj* **1** connected with a court of law, judges, or their decisions: *the judicial system* —compare EXECUTIVE² (1), LEGISLATIVE (2) **2** behaviour that is judicial is sensible and shows good judgment —**judicially** *adv*

**ju·di·cia·ry** /dʒuːˈdɪʃəri‖-ʃieri, -ʃəri/ *n* **the judiciary** *formal* all the judges in a country who, as a group, form part of the system of government

**ju·di·cious** /dʒuːˈdɪʃəs/ *adj formal* done in a sensible and careful way: *a judicious choice* —**judiciously** *adv* —**judiciousness** *n* [U]

**ju·do** /ˈdʒuːdəʊ‖-doʊ/ *n* [U] a sport from the Far East, in which you try to throw your opponent onto the ground

**jugs**
measuring jug *BrE* / measuring cup *AmE*
jug *AmE*
jug *BrE* / pitcher *AmE*

**jug** /dʒʌg/ *n* [C] **1** *BrE* a container for liquids with a handle and a SPOUT (=for pouring); PITCHER (1) *AmE* **2** also **jug·ful** /ˈdʒʌgfʊl/ the amount of liquid that a jug will hold: *a jug of milk* **3 in (the) jug** *BrE old-fashioned* in prison

**jug-eared** /ˈdʒʌg ˌiːəd‖-ərd/ *adj* having large ears that stick out

**jugged hare** /ˌ· ˈ·/ *n* [U] *BrE* a dish made of HARE that has been cooked in liquid

**jug·ger·naut** /ˈdʒʌgənɔːt‖-ərnɒːt/ *n* [C] **1** *BrE* a very large vehicle, that carries goods over long distances; SEMI (3) *AmE* **2** something large and powerful that destroys everything it meets

**jug·gle** /ˈdʒʌgəl/ *v* **1** [I,T] to keep three or more objects moving through the air by throwing and catching them very quickly: [+ **with**] *juggling with plates* **2** [I,T] if you juggle two or more jobs, activities etc, you try to fit all of them into your life: *juggling the needs of your family with the demands of the job* **3** [T] to arrange numbers, information etc in the way that you want: *No amount of financial juggling could hide the fraud.* —**juggler** *n* [C] —see also **juggling act** (ACT² (12))

**jug·u·lar** /ˈdʒʌgjʊlə‖-ər/ *n* [C] **1** a jugular vein **2 go for the jugular** *informal* to criticize or attack someone very strongly, especially in order to harm them

**jugular vein** /ˌ··· ˈ·/ *n* [C usually singular] the large VEIN (=tube) in your neck that takes blood from your head back to your heart

**juice¹** /dʒuːs/ *n* **1** [C,U] the liquid that comes from fruit and vegetables, or a drink that is made from this *A carton of orange juice.* **2** [U] the liquid that comes out of meat when it is cooked **3 gastric/digestive juice(s)** the liquid inside your stomach that helps you to DIGEST¹ (1) food **4** [U] *informal* something that produces power, such as petrol or electricity —see also **stew in your own juice** (STEW² (2))

**juice²** *v* [T] to get the juice out of fruit or vegetables; SQUEEZE¹ (2)
**juice** sth ↔ **up** *phr v* [T] *AmE informal* to make something more interesting or exciting

**juiced** /dʒuːst/ *adj AmE old-fashioned* drunk

**juic·er** /ˈdʒuːsə‖-ər/ *n* [C] **a)** *AmE* a small kitchen tool used for getting juice out of fruit; LEMON SQUEEZER *BrE* **b)** an electric machine for doing this

**juic·y** /ˈdʒuːsi/ *adj* **1** containing a lot of juice: *a juicy steak* **2 juicy stories/gossip/details** *informal* stories etc that contain interesting or shocking information, especially about people's sexual behaviour **3** *informal* involving a lot of money: *a big fat juicy cheque* **4** *informal* giving you work to do that will lead to a feeling of satisfaction: *a juicy part in 'Moby Dick'* —**juiciness** *n* [U]

**ju·jit·su** /ˌdʒuːˈdʒɪtsuː/ *n* [U] a type of fighting from Japan, in which you hold, throw, and hit your opponent

**ju·ju** /ˈdʒuːdʒuː/ *n* [C,U] a type of West African magic involving objects with special powers, or one of these objects

**juke-box** /ˈdʒuːk bɒks‖-bɑːks/ *n* [C] a machine in public bars that plays music when you put money in

**ju·lep** /ˈdʒuːlɪp/ *n* —see MINT JULEP

**Ju·ly** /dʒʊˈlaɪ/ written abbreviation **Jul** *n* [C,U] the seventh month of the year, between June and August: **in July** *a society founded in July 1890* | **last/next July** *Anne's starting work next July.* | **on July 12th** (also **on 12th July** *BrE*) *"When's the concert?" "On 12th July."* (spoken as: *on the twelfth of July* or *on July the twelfth* or *(AmE) on July twelfth*)

**jum·ble¹** /ˈdʒʌmbəl/ *n* **1** [singular] an untidy mixture of things: [+ **of**] *a jumble of thoughts and feelings* **2** [U] *BrE* things to be sold at a jumble sale; RUMMAGE² (2) *AmE*

**jumble²** also **jumble up** *v* [T often passive] to mix things together so that they are not in a neat order: *In his excitement Ben's words became jumbled.*

**jumble sale** /ˈ·· ·/ *n* [C] *BrE* a sale of used clothes, books etc in order to get money to help a local church, school etc; RUMMAGE SALE

**jum·bo** /ˈdʒʌmbəʊ‖-boʊ/ *adj* [only before noun] *informal* larger than other things of the same type: *jumbo-sized hot dogs*

**jumbo jet** /ˈ·· ·/ also **jumbo** *n* [C] a very large aircraft for carrying passengers

**jump¹** /dʒʌmp/ *v*
**1 ▶ UPWARDS ◀ a)** [I] to push yourself suddenly up in the air using your legs: [+ **over/across/onto etc**] *He jumped over the wall and ran off.* | **jump up and down** *The kids love jumping up and down on their beds.* | **jump clear** (=jump out of danger) *We managed to jump clear of the car before it hit the wall.* **b)** [T] to go over or across something by jumping: *They jumped the barriers to avoid paying for tickets.*
**2 ▶ DOWNWARDS ◀** [I] to let yourself drop from a place that is above the ground: [+ **out/down etc**] *Three people saved themselves by jumping from the window.*
**3 ▶ MOVE FAST ◀** [I always + adv/prep] to move quickly or suddenly in a particular direction: [+ **out/away/up etc**] *Matt jumped up to fetch the TV guide.*
**4 ▶ IN FEAR/SURPRISE ◀** [I] to make a quick sudden movement because you are surprised or frightened: *Sorry, I didn't mean to make you jump.* | **jump out of your skin** (=move suddenly because you are very surprised)
**5 ▶ MACHINE ◀** [I] if a machine jumps, it makes a wrong movement: *The typewriter jumps every time you press 'a'.*
**6 ▶ KEEP CHANGING ◀** [I] to change quickly from one place, position, idea etc to another, often missing something that comes in between: **jump from sth to sth** *Cathy's conversation jumped wildly from one topic to another.* | **jump ahead** *I can't resist jumping ahead when I read crime novels.*
**7 ▶ INCREASE ◀** [I] to increase suddenly and by a large amount: [+ **to**] *ICA's profits jumped to £20 million last year.*
**8 ▶ ATTACK ◀** [T] *informal* to attack someone suddenly: *Somebody jumped him in the park last night.*
**9 jump down sb's throat** *informal* to suddenly speak angrily to someone: *You don't have to jump down my throat! I was only asking how you were.*
**10 jump to conclusions** to form an opinion about something before you have all the facts: *Don't jump to conclusions – he may just want to be friends.*
**11 jump the gun** to start doing something too soon, especially without thinking about it properly
**12 jump for joy** to be extremely happy and pleased: *You don't have to jump for joy, but at least smile!*
**13 (go) jump in a lake!** *spoken* used to tell someone rudely to go away
**14 jump to it!** *spoken* used to order someone to do something immediately
**15 jump bail** to leave a town, city, or country where a court of law has ordered you to stay until your TRIAL¹ (1)
**16 jump rope** *AmE* to jump over a rope as you pass it over you head and under your feet as a game; SKIP *BrE* —see also JUMP ROPE
**17 jump the queue** *BrE*, **jump in line** *AmE* to join a line of people in front of others who were already waiting; cut (CUT¹ (17)) in line *AmE* —see also QUEUE-JUMP
**18 jump a light** to drive past red TRAFFIC LIGHTS
**19 jump a claim** *AmE old-fashioned* to claim someone else's land as your own
**20 jump a train** *especially AmE* to travel on a train, especially a goods train, without paying
**21 jump ship** to leave a ship on which you are working as a sailor, without permission
**22 ▶ SEX ◀** [I,T] *AmE taboo* to have sex with someone
**23 ▶ CAR ◀** [T] *AmE* to start a car in which the BATTERY¹ (1) has lost power by connecting it to the BATTERY of another car; JUMP-START (1)

**jump at** sth *phr v* [T] to eagerly accept the chance to do something: *Yvonne jumped at the chance of a trip to Asia.*

**jump in** *phr v* [I] to interrupt someone or suddenly join a conversation

**jump on** sb *phr v* [T] *informal* to criticize or punish someone, especially unfairly: [+ **for**] *Ryder used to jump on me for every little mistake.*

**jump out at** sb *phr v* [T] if something jumps out at you, it is extremely easy to notice

**jump²** *n* [C]
**1 ▶ UP ◀** an act of pushing yourself suddenly up into the air using your legs: *That was his best jump of the competition.*
**2 ▶ DOWN ◀** an act of letting yourself drop from a place that is above the ground: *a parachute jump*
**3 ▶ STH YOU JUMP OVER ◀** a fence, gate, or wall for jumping over in a race or competition: *Her horse cleared all the jumps in the first round.*
**4 ▶ INCREASE ◀** a sudden large increase in an amount or value: [+ **in**] *a jump in inflation rates*
**5 ▶ PROGRESS ◀** a large or sudden change, especially when it improves things: *a great jump forward for human rights*
**6 stay one jump ahead of sb** *informal* to keep your advantage over the people you are competing with by always being the first to do something new or better
**7 have the jump on sb** *informal especially AmE* to have an advantage because you started doing what was necessary before your competitor —see also RUNNING JUMP, HIGH JUMP, LONG JUMP

**jump ball** /ˈ· ·/ *n* [C] the act of throwing the ball up in a game of BASKETBALL, so that one player from each team can try to gain control of it —see picture on page 1263

**jumped-up** /ˌ· ˈ·◂/ *adj* [only before noun] *BrE* believing that you are more important than you really are, because you have improved your social position: *some jumped-up little bureaucrat*

**jump·er** /ˈdʒʌmpə‖-ər/ *n* [C] **1** *BrE* a piece of clothing made of wool that covers the upper part of your body and arms; SWEATER **2** *AmE* a dress without SLEEVES usually worn over a shirt; PINAFORE *BrE* **3** a person or animal that jumps S3

**jump·er ca·bles** /ˈ·· ˌ··/ *n* [plural] *AmE* JUMP LEADS

**jump·ing jack** /ˌ·· ˈ·/ *n* [C] a jump that is done from a standing position with your arms and legs pointing out to the side; STAR JUMP

**jumping-off point** /ˌ·· ˈ· ˌ·/ *n* [C] a place to start from, especially at the beginning of a journey

**jump jet** /ˈ· ·/ *n* [C] *especially BrE* an aircraft that can take off and land by going straight up and down

**jump-leads** /ˈdʒʌmp liːdz/ *n* [plural] *BrE* thick wires used to connect the batteries (BATTERY¹ (1)) of two cars in order to start one that has lost power

**jump rope** /ˈ· ·/ *n* [C] *AmE* a long piece of rope that children use for jumping over; SKIPPING ROPE *BrE*

**jump shot** /ˈ· ·/ *n* [C] the action in BASKETBALL in which you throw the ball towards the basket as you jump in the air —see picture on page 1263

**jump-start** /ˌ· ˈ·/ *v* [T] **1** to start a car whose BATTERY¹ (1) has lost power by connecting it to the battery of another car **2** to help a process or activity start or become more successful: *lowering taxes to jump-start the economy* —**jump start** *n* [C]

**jump·suit** /ˈdʒʌmpsuːt, -sjuːt‖-suːt/ *n* [C] a piece of clothing like a shirt and a pair of trousers joined together, worn by women

**jump·y** /ˈdʒʌmpi/ *adj* worried or excited especially because you are expecting something bad to happen —**jumpily** *adv* —**jumpiness** *n* [U]

**junc·tion** /ˈdʒʌŋkʃən/ *n* [C] a place where one road, track etc joins another: *the junction of Abbot's Road and Church Street* S3

**junc·ture** /ˈdʒʌŋktʃə‖-ər/ *n* **at this juncture** *spoken formal* at this point in an activity or period of time: *At this juncture I'd like to suggest we take a short break.*

**June** /dʒuːn/ written abbreviation **Jun** *n* [C,U] the sixth month of the year, between May and July: **in June** *My birthday is in June.* | **last/next June** *I finished school last June.* | **on June 1st** (also **on 1st June** *BrE*) *We met on June 1st.* (spoken as: *on June the first* or *on the first of June* or *(AmE) on June first*)

**jun·gle** /ˈdʒʌŋgəl/ *n* **1** [C,U] a thick tropical forest with many large plants growing very close together

2 [singular] a place that is very untidy and where a lot of things have been placed close together: *This place is turning into a jungle already.* 3 [singular] a situation in which it is difficult to become successful or get what you want, especially because a lot of people are competing with each other: *You've got to be tough – it's a jungle out there.* —see also CONCRETE JUNGLE, **law of the jungle** (LAW (10))

**jungle gym** /'·· ,·/ *n* [C] *AmE* a large frame made of metal bars for children to climb on; CLIMBING FRAME *BrE*

W3 **Ju·ni·or** /'dʒuːniə‖-ər/ written abbreviation **Jr** *AmE,* **Jnr** *BrE* [only after noun] used after the name of a man who has the same name as his father: *John J. Wallace, Jr.*

**junior**[1] *adj* 1 [only before noun] having a low rank in an organization or profession: *a junior doctor* —opposite SENIOR[2] 2 **be junior to sb** to have a lower rank than someone —see also SENIOR[2]

**junior**[2] *n* 1 **be two/five/ten etc years sb's junior** to be two, five, ten etc years younger than someone: *She married a man seven years her junior.* 2 [C] *especially BrE* someone who has a low rank in an organization or profession: *an office junior* 3 [C] *BrE* a pupil in a JUNIOR SCHOOL 4 [C] *AmE* a student in the year before the final year of HIGH SCHOOL or university —compare FRESHMAN, SENIOR[1] (2), SOPHOMORE 5 [singular] *AmE especially humorous* a way of speaking to or about your son: *What are we going to do about junior if we go out tonight?* —see also SENIOR[1]

**junior col·lege** /,··· '··/ *n* [C,U] a college in the US or Canada where students take a course of study that continues for two years; COMMUNITY COLLEGE

**junior high school** /,··· '· ·/ also **junior high** *n* [C,U] a school in the US and other countries for children aged 12 to 13 or 14 —compare MIDDLE SCHOOL, SENIOR HIGH SCHOOL

**junior school** /'··· ,·/ *n* [C,U] a school in Britain for children aged 7 to 11

**junior var·si·ty** /,··· '···/ *n* [C,U] *AmE* a team of younger or less experienced sports players who represent a school or college — compare VARSITY (1)

**ju·ni·per** /'dʒuːnɪ̈pə‖-ər/ *n* [C,U] a small bush that produces berries (BERRY) and has leaves that are green all year

**junk**[1] /dʒʌŋk/ *n* 1 [U] old or unwanted objects that have no use or value: *I must get rid of all this junk.* 2 [C] a Chinese sailing boat 3 [U] *slang* a dangerous drug, especially HEROIN 4 *spoken* JUNK FOOD

**junk**[2] *v* [T] to get rid of something because it is old or useless

**junk bond** /'· ·/ *n* [C] a BOND[1] (1) which has a high risk and is often sold to pay for a TAKEOVER

**jun·ket** /'dʒʌŋkɪ̈t/ *n* 1 [U] a sweet dish made from thickened milk 2 [C] *informal especially AmE* a free trip that is paid for by government money

**junk food** /'· ·/ *n* [U] *informal* food that is not healthy because it contains a lot of fat, sugar, or CARBOHYDRATE

**junk·ie, junky** /'dʒʌŋki/ *n* [C] *slang* 1 someone who takes dangerous drugs and is dependent on them 2 **television/soap opera etc junkie** *humorous* someone who likes something so much that they seem to be dependent on it: *a television junkie*

**junk mail** /'· ·/ *n* [U] letters that advertisers send to people

**junk shop** /'· ·/ *n* [C] a shop that buys and sells old things

**junk·y** /'dʒʌŋki/ *n* [C] another spelling of JUNKIE

**junk yard** /'· ·/ *n* [C] *AmE* a place where old or unwanted things can be left, bought, and sold —compare DUMP[2] (1), TIP[1] (4)

**jun·ta** /'dʒʌntə, 'hʊntə/ *n* [C] a military government that has gained power by using force

**Ju·pi·ter** /'dʒuːpɪ̈tə‖-ər/ *n* [singular] a large PLANET that moves around the sun —see picture at SOLAR SYSTEM

**ju·rid·i·cal** /dʒʊ'rɪdɪkəl/ *adj formal* connected with judges or the law

**jur·is·dic·tion** /,dʒʊərɪ̈s'dɪkʃən‖,dʒʊr-/ *n* [U] the right to use an official power to make legal decisions: *That area is not within the State Police's jurisdiction.*

**ju·ris·pru·dence** /,dʒʊərɪ̈s'pruːdəns‖,dʒʊr-/ *n* [U] *formal* the science or study of law

**ju·rist** /'dʒʊərɪ̈st‖'dʒʊr-/ *n* [C] *formal* someone who has a very detailed knowledge of law

**ju·ror** /'dʒʊərə‖'dʒʊrər/ *n* [C] a member of a JURY

**ju·ry** /'dʒʊəri‖'dʒʊri/ *n* [C] 1 a group of 12 ordinary people who listen to details of a case in court and decide whether someone is guilty or not: *The jury finds the defendant not guilty.* | **sit on a jury** (=be part of a jury) 2 a group of people chosen to judge a competition 3 **the jury is out on sth** used to say that something is still not yet certain: *The jury is still out as to the overall impact of the programme.* — see also GRAND JURY

**jury box** /'·· ·/ *n* [C usually singular] the place where the jury sits in a court

**jury du·ty** /'·· ,··/ *n* [U] *AmE* a period of time during which you must be part of a jury; JURY SERVICE *BrE*

**ju·ry·man** /'dʒʊərimən‖'dʒʊr-/ *n* [C] a male member of a jury

**jury serv·ice** /'·· ,··/ *n* [U] *BrE* a period of time during which you must be part of a jury; JURY DUTY *AmE*

**jur·y·wom·an** /'dʒʊəri,wʊmən‖'dʒʊr-/ *n* [C] a female member of a jury

**just**[1] /dʒəst; *strong* dʒʌst/ *adv* 1 exactly: *Thank you. That's just what I need.* | *The house was large and roomy; just right for us.* | *She looks just like her mother.* 2 only: *He's not a thief, just a little boy who likes biscuits.* | *It'll just take a few minutes.* 3 if something has just happened, it happened only a short time ago: *John's just told me that he's getting married.* | *I've just been out shopping.* 4 if you are just doing something, or just about to do something you are starting to do it or going to do it soon: *He was just leaving when the phone rang.* | *I'll just change my clothes, if you don't mind waiting a minute.* 5 used to emphasize something you are saying: *I needed some fresh air, so work would just have to wait.* | *He just got in his car and drove off.* 6 **just before/after/over etc** only a short time before, after etc: *We moved here just after our son was born.* | *I saw her just before she died.* | *It's just under three centimeters long.* 7 **(only) just** if something just happens or is just possible, it does happen or is possible, but it almost did not happen or was not possible: *He just managed to get home before dark.* | *Those pants only just fit you now.* 8 **just about** almost: *The plums are just about ripe now.* | *Just about everybody will be affected by the tax increases.* 9 **just as** equally as: *Brad is just as good as the others.* 10 **just then** at exactly that moment: *Just then there was a sound in the hall.* 11 **just the thing** *informal* exactly the right thing: *This soup is just the thing for a cold winter's day.* 12 *informal* completely: *She was just horrified at my choice of husband.* —see also **just my luck** (LUCK[1] (7))

Frequencies of the adverb **just** in spoken and written English.

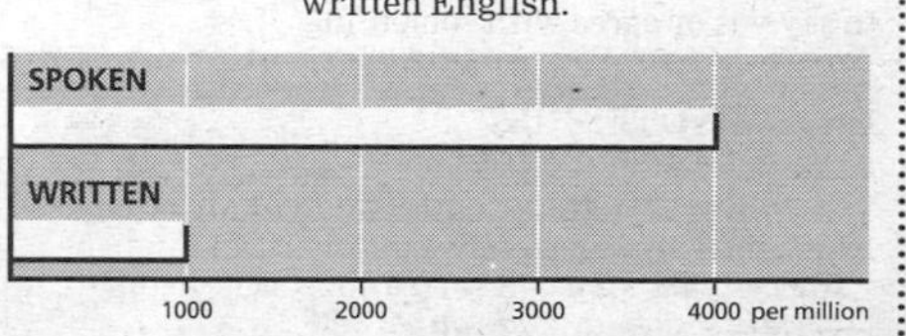


Based on the British National Corpus and the Longman Lancaster Corpus

This graph shows that the adverb **just** is much more common in spoken English than in written English. This is because it is very commonly used in spoken English to mean 'exactly' or to mean 'a short time before or after'. It also has special uses in spoken English and is used in a lot of common spoken phrases.

**just** (*adv*) **SPOKEN USES AND PHRASES**
**13 just a)** used to pause while you think what to say next or think how to describe something: *When I told him the news he just...he just sat there and didn't say a word.|It wasn't an argument, it was just, it was more like a discussion.* **b)** used when politely asking something or telling someone to do something: *Could I just say a few words before we start?* **c)** used when firmly telling someone to do something: *Look, just shut up for a minute!* **14 just a minute/second/moment a)** used to ask someone to wait for a short time while you do something: *Just a minute, I'll see if I can find it for you.* **b)** used to interrupt someone in order to ask them something, disagree with them etc: *Just a minute, I'm not sure I agree with your last point.*
**15 just now a)** a moment ago or a very short time ago: *Where have my glasses gone? I had them just now.* **b)** *especially BrE* at the moment: *We're busy just now, can you come back later?* **16 would just as soon** if you would just as soon do something, you would prefer to do it: *I'd just as soon not be here when she comes.* **17 may just/might just** might possibly: *You could try Renee; she might just know where they live now.* **18 not just yet** not quite yet: *I can't leave just yet. I've still got a couple of letters to write.* **19 it's just that** used when explaining the reason for something, especially when someone thinks there is a different reason: *No, I do like Chinese food, it's just that I'm not hungry.* **20 just think/look/listen** used to tell someone to imagine, look at or listen to the same thing that you are imagining, looking at, or listening to: *Just think – in a week we'll be lying on a beach in the sun!* **21 be just looking** to be looking at things in a shop without intending to buy anything: *"Can I help you?" "No thanks, I'm just looking."* **22 just because ...doesn't mean** used to say that although one thing is true, another thing is not necessarily true: *Just because you're older than me doesn't mean you can tell me what to do.* **23 it's/that's just as well** used to say that it is lucky that something happens because otherwise there would be problems: *It's just as well Kathy didn't come to the film. She'd have hated it.* **24 might just as well** if you might just as well do something, it would be sensible, or a good idea to do it: *There's no point in waiting here. We might just as well go home.* **25 just the same** used to say that your opinion is the same about something, although someone has said something to try to change your opinion: *"The new model is a lot better." "Just the same, I'd rather have the old one I'm used to."* **26 isn't she just/aren't they just** *old-fashioned* used to strongly agree with something someone has said about a person or thing: *"He's a selfish, rude, ignorant man!" "Isn't he just!"* **27 just testing a)** used to tell someone that you only asked them something to check if they knew the answer: *"What's the capital of France?" "Paris, of course!" "Just testing."* **b)** used when you have made a mistake, to pretend that you only did it to see if someone would notice: *"That isn't how you spell 'receive'!" "I know, just testing!"* **28 just on** *BrE* almost exactly: *It's just on three o'clock.* **29 just so a)** with everything arranged neatly and tidily: *Her house always has to be just so.* **b)** *old-fashioned* used to say yes or agree with something

**USAGE NOTE: JUST**
AmE-BrE DIFFERENCE
Time adverbs **just, already,** and **yet** are often used with the simple past tense in American English: *The bell just rang* (=it rang a short time ago).|*I already saw him.*|*Did you eat yet?*
This use is also fairly common now in British English, but it is still considered more correct to say: *The bell has just rung.*|*I've already seen him.*|*Have you eaten yet?*

S 3 W 3 **just²** /dʒʌst/ *adj* **1** morally right and fair: *A medal of honour was his just reward.|I think this is a just punishment bearing in mind the seriousness of the crime.* **2 get your just deserts** to be punished or suffer in a way that other people think you deserve: *I hope that he's caught and gets his just deserts.* —**justly** *adv*: *These men are criminals, but they must be dealt with justly.*

**jus·tice** /ˈdʒʌstɪ̠s/ *n* **1** [U] fairness in the way people are treated: *Sometimes I wonder if there's any justice in this world.* —opposite INJUSTICE —see also POETIC JUSTICE **2** [U] the system by which people are judged in courts of law and criminals are punished: *This has restored my faith in British justice.*|**escape justice** (=avoid being punished for a crime) **3 bring sb to justice** to catch someone who you think is guilty of a crime and arrange for them to go to court: *We will not rest until her killer is brought to justice.* **4 justice has been done/served** used to say that someone has been treated fairly or has been given a punishment they deserve **5 do justice to sb/sth** also **do sb/sth justice** to treat or represent someone or something in a way that is fair and shows their best qualities: *The photo doesn't do her justice – she was really beautiful.|It's impossible to do justice to Mahler's music without a full orchestra.* **6 do yourself justice** to do something such as a test well enough to show your real ability: *Sara panicked in the exam and didn't do herself justice.* **7** also **Justice a)** [C] *AmE* a judge in a law court **b)** [C] *BrE* the title of a judge in the High Court **8** [U] the quality of being right and deserving fair treatment: *No one doubts the justice of our cause.* —see also **rough justice** (ROUGH¹ (14)) W 2

**Justice of the Peace** /ˌ·· · · ˈ·/ abbreviation **JP** *n* [C] someone who judges less serious cases in small law courts and, in the US, can perform marriage ceremonies

**jus·ti·fi·a·ble** /ˈdʒʌstɪ̠faɪəbəl/ *adj* actions, reactions, decisions etc that are justifiable are done for good reasons: *justifiable anger* —**justifiably** *adv*

**justifiable hom·i·cide** /ˌ····· ˈ···/ *n* [U] *law* a situation in which you are not punished for killing someone, usually because you did it to defend yourself

**jus·ti·fi·ca·tion** /ˌdʒʌstɪ̠fɪ̠ˈkeɪʃən/ *n* [C,U] **1** a good and acceptable reason for doing something: *The committee could see no justification for a pay rise.* **2 in justification (of)** to explain why an idea or action is right

**jus·ti·fied** /ˈdʒʌstɪ̠faɪd/ *adj* **1** having an acceptable explanation or reason: *I think your conclusions were fully justified.*|**be justified in doing sth** *Under the circumstances, the principal was justified in expelling this student.* **2 right/left justified** *technical* printed material that is right or left justified has a straight edge where all the words line up on the left or right of a page

**jus·ti·fy** /ˈdʒʌstɪ̠faɪ/ *v* [T] **1** to give an acceptable explanation for something that other people think is unreasonable: *How can you justify the expense?*|**justify doing sth** *It's hard to justify making everyone wait for so long.* **2 justify yourself (to sb)** to prove that what you are doing is reasonable: *I'm in charge here; I don't have to justify myself to you.* **3** to be a good and acceptable reason for something: *Nothing justifies murdering another human being.* S 2 W 3

**jut** /dʒʌt/ *v* **jutted, jutting** [I always + adv/prep] also **jut out** something that juts up or out sticks up or out further than the other things around it: *Tall jagged rocks jutted out over the beach.*

**jute** /dʒuːt/ *n* [U] a natural substance that is used for making rope and rough cloth

**ju·ve·nile** /ˈdʒuːvənaɪl‖-nəl, -naɪl/ *adj* **1** [only before noun] *especially law* connected with young people who are not yet adults: *juvenile crime* **2** silly and typical of a child rather than an adult: *a very juvenile sense of humour* —**juvenile** *n* [C]

**juvenile de·lin·quent** /ˌ··· ·ˈ··/ *n* [C] a child or young person who behaves in a criminal way —**juvenile delinquency** *n* [U]

**jux·ta·pose** /ˌdʒʌkstəˈpəʊz‖ˈdʒʌkstəpoʊz/ *v* [T] *formal* to put things together, especially things that are not normally together, in order to compare them or to make something new —**juxtaposition** /ˌdʒʌkstəpəˈzɪʃən/ *n* [C,U]

**K, k** /keɪ/ *plural* **K's, k's** *n* [C] the eleventh letter of the alphabet

**K, k** **1** *informal* an abbreviation of one thousand: *salary of £30k a year* **2** an abbreviation of KILOBYTE (=a measurement of computer information)

**ka·bob** /kəˈbɑːb/ *n* [C] an American spelling of KEBAB

**kaf·fee·klatch** /ˈkæfeɪklætʃ/ *n* [C] *AmE* an informal social situation when people drink coffee and talk

**kaf·fir** /ˈkæfə‖-ər/ *n* [C] *SAfrE taboo* an offensive word for a black African, used only by white people

**kaf·tan** /ˈkæftæn‖kæfˈtæn/ *n* [C] another spelling of CAFTAN

**Ka·lash·ni·kov** /kəˈlæʃnɪkɒf‖-kɒːf/ *n* [C] a type of RIFLE (=long gun) that can fire very quickly

**kale** /keɪl/ *n* [C,U] a dark green CABBAGE (=type of vegetable)

**ka·lei·do·scope** /kəˈlaɪdəskəʊp‖-skoʊp/ *n* [C] **1** a pattern, situation, or scene that is always changing and has many details or bright colours: [+ **of**] *the kaleidoscope of American ethnic groups* **2** a tube with mirrors and pieces of coloured glass at one end, that shows coloured patterns when you turn it

**ka·lei·do·scop·ic** /kəˌlaɪdəˈskɒpɪk◂‖-ˈskɑː-/ *adj* kaleidoscopic scenes, colours, or patterns change often and quickly —**kaleidoscopically** /-kli/ *adv*

**kam·i·ka·ze** /ˌkæmɪˈkɑːzi◂/ *adj* **1 kamikaze pilot** a pilot who deliberately crashes his plane on enemy camps, ships, etc knowing he will be killed **2 kamikaze attitude/behaviour** willingness to take risks, without caring about your safety: *kamikaze lorry drivers*

**kan·ga** /ˈkæŋgə/ *n* [C] a woman's dress from Africa, consisting of a long piece of cloth wound around the body

**kan·ga·roo** /ˌkæŋgəˈruː◂/ *n* [C] an Australian animal that moves by jumping and carries its babies in a POUCH (=a special pocket of skin)

**kangaroo court** /ˌ··· ˈ·/ *n* [C] an unofficial court that punishes people unfairly

**ka·o·lin** /ˈkeɪələ̇n/ *n* [U] a type of white clay used for making cups, plates etc, and also in medicine

**ka·pok** /ˈkeɪpɒk‖-pɑːk/ *n* [U] a very light material like cotton used for filling soft things like cushions (CUSHION[1] (1))

**ka·put** /kəˈpʊt/ *adj* [not before noun] *spoken* broken: **go kaput** (=become broken)

**kar·a·o·ke** /ˌkæriˈəʊki‖ˌkɑːrəˈoʊ-/ *n* **1** [U] the activity of singing to recorded music for entertainment **2** [C] a machine that plays recorded music which people can sing to

**kar·at** /ˈkærət/ *n* [C] an American spelling of CARAT

**ka·ra·te** /kəˈrɑːti/ *n* [U] a style of fighting from the Far East, in which you kick and hit with your hands

**kar·ma** /ˈkɑːmə‖-ɑːr-/ *n* [U] **1** the force that is produced by the things you do in your life and that will influence you in the future, according to the Hindu and Buddhist religions **2** *informal* luck resulting from your actions; FATE —**karmic** *adj*

**ka·ty·did** /ˈkeɪtidɪd/ *n* [C] *AmE* a type of large GRASSHOPPER that makes a noise like the sound of the words 'katy did'

**kay·ak** /ˈkaɪæk/ *n* [C] a type of light CANOE[1]

**ka·zoo** /kəˈzuː/ *n* [C] a simple musical instrument that you play by holding it to your lips and making sounds into it

**Kb** an abbreviation of KILOBYTE

**KC** /ˌkeɪ ˈsiː/ *n BrE* King's Counsel; the highest level of BARRISTER (=lawyer who speaks in court) when the ruler is a king —compare QC

**ke·bab** /kə̇ˈbæb‖kə̇ˈbɑːb/ also **kabob** *AmE n* [C] small pieces of meat and vegetables cooked on a stick

**kedg·e·ree** /ˈkedʒəriː/ *n* [U] a cooked dish of fish, rice, and eggs mixed together

**keel[1]** /kiːl/ *n* **1** a bar along the bottom of a boat that keeps it steady in the water —see picture at YACHT **2 on an even keel** steady without any sudden changes: *Now that the crisis is over, we must try to get things back on an even keel.*

**keel[2]** *v*

**keel over** *phr v* [I] to fall over sideways: *Several soldiers keeled over in the hot sun.*

**keel·haul** /ˈkiːlhɔːl‖-hɒːl/ *v* [T] **1** *usually humorous* to punish someone severely **2** to pull someone under the keel of a ship with a rope as a punishment

**keen[1]** /kiːn/ *adj* S3 W3

**1 ▶ INTERESTED/EAGER ◀** *especially BrE* someone who is keen is very interested in something or is eager to do it: *a keen photographer* | [+ **on**] *Daniel's very keen on tennis.* | **keen to do something** *She's out of hospital and keen to get back to work.*

**2 ▶ ATTRACTED ◀** *especially BrE* **be keen on sb** to be very attracted to someone: *He must be pretty keen on her – they've been dancing all night.*

**3 ▶ CLEVER ◀** someone with a keen mind is quick to understand things

**4 ▶ COMPETITION ◀ keen competition** a situation in which people compete strongly: *We won the contest in the face of keen competition.*

**5 ▶ SIGHT/SMELL/HEARING ◀** a keen sense of smell or keen sight or hearing is an extremely good ability to smell etc: *Dogs have a very keen sense of smell.*

**6 ▶ SHARP ◀** *literary* a keen knife or blade is extremely sharp

**7 ▶ WIND ◀** *old-fashioned* a keen wind is cold and strong

**8 keen as mustard** *BrE informal* **a)** extremely eager **b)** very quick to understand things —**keenly** *adj* —**keenness** *n* [U]

**keen[2]** *v* [I] *old use* to sing a loud, sad song for someone who has died

**keep[1]** /kiːp/ *v past tense and past participle* **kept** /kept/ S1 W1

**1 ▶ NOT GIVE BACK ◀** [T] to have something and not need to give it back: *You can keep it. I don't need it.* | *Try it for a week and we guarantee you'll want to keep it.*

**2 ▶ NOT LOSE ◀** [T] to continue to have something and not lose it or get rid of it: *No, we're going to keep the house in Vermont and rent it out.* | *It's not getting a job that's the problem – it's keeping it!*

**3 ▶ NOT CHANGE/MOVE ◀** [I, linking verb] to continue to be in a particular state, condition, or place and not change or move: *I'm trying to cut his hair but he won't keep still.* | **keep warm/safe/dry etc** *With this wind it's so difficult to keep warm!* | **keep left/right** (=stay to the left or right of a path or road as you move)

**4 ▶ MAKE SB/STH NOT CHANGE/MOVE ◀** [T] **a)** to make someone stay in a place: *How long are they going to keep her in the hospital?* **b)** to make someone or something continue being in a particular state or situation: **keep sb warm/safe etc** *Take my overcoat. It'll keep you warm.* | *some toys to keep the kids busy* | **keep sth clean/open etc** *We try to keep the major roads open right through winter.* | **keep sb/sth doing sth** *I'll try not to keep you waiting.* | *Keep the engine running.* | **keep sb in suspense** (=keep someone waiting anxiously to know a result) *How much longer are you going to keep us in suspense?* | **keep on the right side of sb** (=not do anything to annoy them) *Keep on the right side of Mrs Salazar, she's very strict.*

**5 ▶ DO STH REPEATEDLY ◀** [I] to continue doing an activity or repeat the same action several times: **keep (on) doing sth** *I keep forgetting to mail this letter.* | *Daddy! Melanie keeps on hitting me!*

**6 ▶ DELAY SB ◀** [T] to delay someone: *He should be here by now. What's keeping him?*

**7 ▶ STORE STH ◀** [T always + adv/prep] to leave

something in one particular place so that you can find it easily: **keep sth in/on/under etc** *I always keep a first aid box in the car, in case we have an accident.*
**8 keep a record/account/diary etc** to regularly record written information somewhere
**9 keep your promise/word etc** to do what you have promised to do: *How do I know you'll keep your word?*
**10 keep a secret** to not tell anyone about a secret that you know: *Can I trust all of you to keep a secret?*
**11 keep to yourself** also **keep yourself to yourself** *BrE* to live a very quiet private life and not do many things that involve other people
**12 keep guard/watch** to guard a place or watch around you all the time
**13 ▶ FOOD ◀** [I] if food keeps, it stays fresh enough to still be eaten: *Eat the salmon because it won't keep till tomorrow.*
**14 keep your head** to stay calm in a difficult situation or an EMERGENCY: *Just keep your head and try to steer in the direction of the skid.*
**15 ▶ ANIMALS ◀** [T] to own and look after animals: *We keep chickens and a couple of pigs.*
**16 ▶ SHOP ◀** [T] *BrE old-fashioned* to own a small business and work in it: *Frank used to keep a butcher's on Park Road.*
**17 ▶ LOOK AFTER ◀** [T] to take care of someone, providing them with money, food etc: **keep sb in sth** *There's enough money there to keep you in silk stockings for a year!*
**18 ▶ PROTECT ◀** [T] *formal* to guard or protect someone: **keep sb (from harm)** *The Lord bless you and keep you.*
**19 ▶ CELEBRATE STH ◀** [T] *old-fashioned* to do the things that are traditionally done to celebrate something such as Christmas: *People don't keep Christmas the way they used to do.* — see also **keep in touch** (TOUCH[2] (6)), **home/keep your eye on sb** (EYE[1] (3)), **keep house** (HOUSE[1] (2)), **keep pace with** (PACE[1] (5)), **keep sb company** (COMPANY (2)), **keep the peace** (PEACE (5)), **keep time** (TIME[1] (61, 62)), **keep your hand in** (HAND[1] (11)), **keep/lose track of** (TRACK[1] (8))

Frequencies of the verb **keep** in spoken and written English.

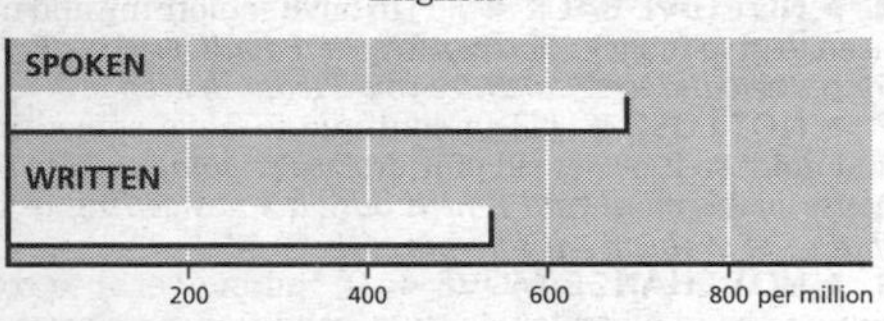


Based on the British National Corpus and the Longman Lancaster Corpus

This graph shows that the verb **keep** is more common in spoken English than in written English. This is because the expression **keep doing sth** is very commonly used in spoken English to mean 'continue to do something' or 'do something repeatedly'. **Keep** is also used in a lot of common spoken phrases.

**keep** (*v*) **SPOKEN PHRASES**

**20 keep going** used to encourage someone who is doing something and to tell them to continue: *"Well done, that's it, keep going!"*
**21 keep it** used to tell someone that they can keep something you have given them or lent them: *Keep it. I've got plenty more at home.*
**22 keep quiet** used to tell someone not to say anything or make any noise: *Keep quiet! I'm trying to watch the game.*
**23 keep away/back!** used to tell someone not to go near something or to move away from something: *Keep back everyone – this is dangerous!*
**24 keep down!** used to tell someone to keep near the ground so they cannot be seen, shot etc
**25 keep it down** used to tell someone to be quieter: *Keep it down, will you. We're trying to sleep.*
**26 how are you keeping?** used to ask if someone is well: *"Hi, Mark! How are you keeping?" "Oh, not so bad."*
**27 keep the change** used when paying someone, to tell them they can keep the extra money you have given them: *"That's $18." "Here's $20. Keep the change."*
**28 keep your hair/shirt on!** used to tell someone to be more calm, patient etc: *Keep your hair on! We've got plenty of time.*
**29 it'll keep** used to say that you can tell someone something or do something later: *"I'd love to hear about it but I've got to go." "Don't worry, it'll keep."*
**30 that'll keep you going** used to tell someone that what you are giving them will last for some time: *Here's £50 – that'll keep you going for a while.*

**keep at** *phr v* [T] **1** [**keep** sb **at** sth] to force someone to continue to work hard: *She kept us at it until eight o'clock!* **2** [**keep at** sth] to continue working hard at something: *Let's just keep at it until we're finished.*

**keep away** *phr v* [I,T **keep** sb/sth **away**] to avoid going somewhere or seeing someone, or to make someone or something do this: *You keep away from my daughter!*

**keep back** *phr v* **1** [T **keep** sth ↔ **back**] to not tell someone something that you know: *I got the feeling he was keeping something back.* **2** [T **keep** sth ↔ **back**] *especially BrE* to not give or pay something that you were going to give: *They kept back some of his wages to pay for the damage.*

**keep** sb/sth ↔ **down** *phr v* [T] **1** to control something and prevent it from increasing: *You can use herbicides to keep down the weeds.* **2** to be able to not VOMIT something (=pass it back up from your stomach) after you have eaten or drunk it: *I could hardly keep anything down for about three days.*

**keep from** *phr v* [T] **1** [**keep** sth **from** sb] to not tell someone something that you know: *You won't be able to keep the truth from her father.* **2** [**keep** sb/sth **from** sth] to prevent someone from doing something or prevent something happening: **keep sb from doing sth** *Mulligan was the only person who kept us from running amok completely.* | **keep (yourself) from doing sth** *I could hardly keep from laughing, it was so funny.* | **keep sth from doing sth** *You put the potatoes in salted water to keep them from turning black.*

**keep** sb **in** *phr v* [T] *BrE* to force someone to stay inside, especially as a punishment in school

**keep in with** sb *phr v* [T] *BrE* to try to stay friendly with someone, especially because this helps you: *You should try to keep in with Benson – he has a lot of influence around here.*

**keep off** *phr v* **1** [T **keep** sth ↔ **off**] to prevent something affecting something else: *They have these transparent covers to keep the dust off.* **2** [I] if rain keeps off, it does not fall

**keep on** *phr v* **1 keep on doing sth** to continue doing something: *I've told him to stop but he keeps on scratching it!* **2** [T **keep** sb **on**] to continue to employ someone: *If you're good they might keep you on after Christmas.* **3** [I] *informal* to talk continuously in an annoying way: [**+ at/about**] *Do you have to keep on about your medical problems the whole time?*

**keep out** *phr v* **1 keep out!** used on signs to tell people to stay away from a place or not enter it **2** [T **keep** sth ↔ **out**] to prevent someone or something getting into a place: *Take this. It should at least keep the rain out.*

**keep out of** sth *phr v* [T] to try not to become involved in something: *We've always tried to keep out of local politics.*

**keep to** *phr v* [T] **1** [**keep to** sth] to stay on a particular road, course, piece of ground etc: *It's best to keep to the paved roads.* **2** [**keep to** sth] to do what you have promised or agreed to do: *Keep strictly to the terms of the contract.* **3 keep sth to yourself** to keep something secret: *It's official. We're leaving, but do me a favour and keep it to yourself will you.* **4 keep to the point/subject etc** to talk or write only about the subject you are supposed to be talking about **5** [**keep** sth **to** sth] to prevent an amount, degree, or level from going higher than it should:

*Can you please keep costs to a minimum?* **6 keep to your room/bed** to stay in your room or bed because you are ill or upset

**keep up** *phr v* **1** [T **keep** sth ↔ **up**] to prevent something from falling or going to a lower level: *The shortage of supplies is keeping the price up.* **2** [I,T **keep** sth ↔ **up**] to continue doing something, or to make something continue: *Keep up the good work!* | *I don't think I can keep this up any longer.* **3** [I] to manage to go or learn as fast as someone: *Slow down, Davey can't keep up.* | [+ **with**] *I'm having trouble keeping up with the rest of the class.* **4** [I] to continue to read and learn about a particular subject: [+ **with**] *It's hard to keep up with the changes in computer technology.* **5 keep your spirits/strength/morale etc up** to try to stay happy, strong, confident etc: *We sang as we marched, to keep our spirits up.* **6** [T **keep** sb **up**] *informal* to prevent someone from going to bed: *I hope I'm not keeping you up.* **7 keep up appearances** to pretend that everything in your life is normal and happy even though you are in trouble, especially financial trouble **8 keep up with the Joneses** to try to have all the possessions that your friends have because you want people to think that you are as good as them

**keep²** *n* [C] **1** [U] all the things such as food, clothing etc that you need to keep you alive, or the cost of providing this: **earn your keep** (=do things in return for the things that are provided for you) *It's time you got a job and started earning your keep.* **2 for keeps** *informal* for ever: *I'm going to settle this argument for keeps!* | *Marriage ought to be for keeps.* **3** [C] a large strong tower, usually in the centre of a castle

**keep·a·way** /ˈ· ··/ *n* [U] *AmE* a children's game in which you try to catch a ball that is being thrown between two other people; **piggy in the middle** (PIGGY¹ (2)) *BrE*

**keep·er** /ˈkiːpə‖-ər/ *n* [C] **1** someone whose job is to look after a particular place: *a lighthouse keeper* | **shopkeeper/storekeeper** (=who owns and works in a shop) **2** someone who cares for or protects animals: **zookeeper/gamekeeper** *The zoo keeper ordered the public away from the lion house.* —see also GAMEKEEPER **3** also **goalkeeper** someone who guards the GOAL (3) in a sport

**keep fit** /ˌ· ˈ·◂/ *n* [U] *BrE* a class in which you do exercises to keep yourself healthy —**keep-fit** *adj*

**keep·ing** /ˈkiːpɪŋ/ *n* [U] **1 in sb's keeping** being looked after or guarded by someone **2 in safe keeping** being carefully guarded somewhere **3 in keeping/out of keeping (with sth)** suitable or not suitable for a particular occasion or purpose: *Please ensure your remarks are in keeping with the seriousness of the occasion.*

**keep·sake** /ˈkiːpseɪk/ *n* [C] a small object that reminds you of someone

**keg** /keg/ *n* [C] a round wooden container with a flat top and bottom, used especially for storing beer; (BARREL¹ (1)); **keg beer/bitter** (=beer etc served from a keg)

**keg·ger** /ˈkegə‖-ər/ *n* [C] *AmE slang* a big party, usually outside, where beer is served from KEGS

**keis·ter** /ˈkaɪstə‖kiːstər/ *n* [C] *AmE old-fashioned* BUTTOCKS (=part of your body that you sit on)

**kelp** /kelp/ *n* [U] a type of large brown SEAWEED

**kel·vin** /ˈkelvɪn/ *n* [C] a unit for measuring temperature

**ken¹** /ken/ *n* **beyond your ken** outside your knowledge or understanding

**ken²** *v* [I,T] *ScotE* to know: *D'ye ken John Peel?*

**ken·nel** /ˈkenl/ *n* [C] **1** a small HUT where a dog sleeps **2** also **kennels** *BrE* a place where dogs are bred (BREED¹ (1, 2)) or can stay while their owners are away

**kept** the past tense and past participle of KEEP¹

**kept wom·an** /ˌ· ˈ··/ *n* [C] *old-fashioned* a woman who is given a place to live, money and clothes by a man who visits her regularly for sex

**kerb** *BrE*, **curb** *AmE* /kɜːb‖kɜːrb/ *n* [C] the edge of the PAVEMENT (=raised path) at the side of a street —see picture on page 410

**kerb craw·ler** *BrE*, **curb crawler** *AmE* /ˈ· ˌ··/ *n* [C] a man who drives his car slowly along the road looking for a PROSTITUTE (=woman who has sex for money) —**kerb crawling** *n* [U]

**ker·chief** /ˈkɜːtʃɪf‖ˈkɜːr-/ *n* [C] **1** a square piece of cloth, worn especially by women in former times around their head or neck **2** *old-fashioned* a handkerchief

**ker·fuf·fle** /kəˈfʌfəl‖kər-/ *n* [C,U] *BrE informal* unnecessary noise and activity; FUSS¹ (2)

**ker·nel** /ˈkɜːnl‖ˈkɜːr-/ *n* [C] **1** the centre part of a nut or seed, usually the part you can eat **2** something that forms the most important part of a statement, idea, plan etc: *There may be a kernel of truth in what he says.*

**ker·o·sene, kerosine** /ˈkerəsiːn/ *n* [U] *AmE, AustrE, NzE* an oil that is burnt for heat and used in lamps for lighting; PARAFFIN (1) *BrE*

**kes·trel** /ˈkestrəl/ *n* [C] a type of small FALCON

**ketch** /ketʃ/ *n* [C] a small sailing ship with two masts (MAST (1))

**ketch·up** /ˈketʃəp/ also **catsup** *especially AmE* —*n* [U] a thick red liquid made from tomatoes (TOMATO) that you eat with food

**ket·tle** /ˈketl/ *n* [C] **1** a metal or plastic container with a lid, a handle, and a SPOUT (=for pouring) , used to boil water —see picture on page 833 **2 put the kettle on** to boil water in a kettle: *I'll put the kettle on for tea.* **3 another/a different kettle of fish** *informal* used to say that a situation that is very different from one that you have just mentioned: *She enjoys public speaking but being on TV is a different kettle of fish.* **4 a fine/pretty kettle of fish** a situation that will cause you problems

**ket·tle·drum** /ˈketldrʌm/ *n* [C] a large metal drum with a round bottom, used in an ORCHESTRA —see also TIMPANI

**kew·pie doll** /ˈkjuːpi dɒl‖-dɑːl/ also **kewpie** *n* [C] a type of American plastic DOLL ¹ (1) with a fat body and a curl of hair on its head

**key¹** /kiː/ *adj* very important and necessary for success or to understand something: *Put your most experienced players in the key positions.* | **key points/questions/issues etc** (=most important) *You can summarize the key points of his speech in a few lines.* | **key mover/player** (=most important person in achieving a result, change etc) S2 W1

**key²** *n* [C] 

**1 ► LOCK ◄** a small specially shaped piece of metal which you put into a lock and turn in order to lock or unlock a door, start a car etc

**2 ► IMPORTANT PART ◄ the key** the part of a plan, action, etc, that everything else depends on: [+ **to**] *Concentration is the key to effective study.*

**3 ► MACHINE/MUSICAL INSTRUMENT ◄** the part of a machine, computer, or musical instrument that you press with your fingers to make it work: *Press the ESCAPE key to exit.* | *She ran her fingers over the piano keys.*

**4 ► MUSICAL NOTES ◄** a set of musical notes with a particular base note, and the quality of sound that they have: *a tune played in the key of C*

**5 ► MAP/DRAWING ◄** the part of a map, technical drawing etc that explains the signs etc on it

**6 ► ISLAND ◄** a small flat island, especially one near the coast of Florida: *the Florida Keys*

**7 ► TEST ANSWERS ◄** the printed answers to a test or to the questions in a TEXTBOOK¹ that are used to check your work —see also LOW-KEY

**key³** *v* [T] *especially BrE* to prepare a surface so that a covering such as paint will stick to it

**key** sth ↔ **in** *phr v* [T] to put information into a computer by using a KEYBOARD¹ (1) —see also KEYED UP

**key** sth **to** sth *phr v* [T usually passive] *especially AmE* to slightly change a system, plan etc so that it works well with something else: **be keyed to the needs of** (=match the needs of) *The daycare hours are keyed to the needs of working parents.*

S3 **key·board¹** /ˈkiːbɔːd‖-bɔːrd/ *n* [C] **1** a row or several rows of keys (KEY¹ (3)) on a musical instrument like a piano or a machine like a computer: *a computer keyboard* —see picture on page 837 **2** also **keyboards** [plural] a musical instrument with a keyboard that can sound like a piano, drums etc

**keyboard²** *v* **1** [I] to use the KEYBOARD¹ (1) of a computer, printing machine etc **2** [T] to put information into a computer by using a KEYBOARD¹ (1)—**keyboarder** *n* [C]

**key card** /ˈ· ·/ *n* [C] a special plastic card that you put in an electronic lock to open a door etc

**keyed up** /ˌ· ˈ·/ *adj* [not before noun] worried or excited: [+ **about**] *Don't get all keyed up about the exam.*

**key·hole** /ˈkiːhəʊl‖-hoʊl/ *n* [C] the hole containing a lock that you use a key in

**keyhole sur·ge·ry** /ˌ·· ˈ···/ *n* [U] a medical operation that is done through a very small hole in the body

**key·note** /ˈkiːnəʊt‖-noʊt/ *n* [C] **1** the main point in a piece of writing, system of beliefs, activity etc, that influences everything else; THEME (1): [+ **of**] *Stability was the keynote of the reign of Queen Mary I.* **2 keynote address/speech** a speech that introduces a formal meeting **3** the note on which a musical key is based

**key·pad** /ˈkiːpæd/ *n* [C] **1** a small KEYBOARD¹ (1) which you hold in your hand, such as the REMOTE CONTROL for a television **2** the part of a computer KEYBOARD¹ (1) that has the number and command keys on it

**key ring** /ˈ· ·/ *n* [C] a metal ring that you keep keys on

**key sig·na·ture** /ˈ· ˌ···/ *n* [C] a set of marks at the beginning of a line of written music to show which KEY¹ (4) it is in

**key·stone** /ˈkiːstəʊn‖-stoʊn/ *n* [C usually singular] **1** the large central stone in an ARCH¹ (1) that keeps the other stones in position —see picture at ARCH¹ **2** the most important part of an idea, belief etc: [+ **of**] *Social justice is the keystone of our policies.*

**key·stroke** /ˈkiːstrəʊk‖-stroʊk/ *n* [C] the action of pressing a key on a TYPEWRITER or computer KEYBOARD¹ (1)

**kg** the written abbreviation of KILOGRAM or KILOGRAMS

**KGB** /ˌkeɪ dʒiː ˈbiː/ *n* **the KGB** the secret police of the former USSR

**kha·ki** /ˈkɑːki‖ˈkæki, ˈkɑːki/ *n* [U] **1** a dull green-brown or yellow-brown colour —see picture on page 411 **2** cloth of this colour, especially when worn by soldiers —**khaki** *adj*

**kha·kis** /ˈkɑːkiz‖ˈkækiz, ˈkɑː-/ *n* [plural] *AmE* trousers made of KHAKI (2) cloth

**kha·lif** /ˈkeɪlɪ̣f, kɑːˈliːf/ *n* [C] another spelling of CALIPH

**kha·li·fate** /ˈkeɪlɪ̣feɪt/ *n* [C] another spelling of CALIPHATE

**khan** /kɑːn/ *n* [C] a ruler or official in Asia, or their title

**kHz** the written abbreviation of KILOHERTZ

**kib·ble¹** /ˈkɪbəl/ *n* [U] *especially AmE* small round pieces of dry dog food

**kibble²** *v* [T] *especially BrE* to crush grain into small pieces

**kib·butz** /kɪˈbʊts/ *n* [C] a type of farm in Israel where many people live and work together

**kib·itz** /ˈkɪbɪts/ *v* [I] *AmE* to make unhelpful comments while someone is doing something —**kibitzer** *n* [C]

**ki·bosh** /ˈkaɪbɒʃ‖-bɑːʃ/ *n* **put the kibosh on sth** *old-fashioned informal* to stop a plan, idea etc from developing; RUIN²

S2 W3 **kick¹** /kɪk/ *v*

**1 ▶ HIT WITH YOUR FOOT ◀** [I,T] to hit something with your foot: *She kicked me under the table.* | *Joe, stop kicking!* | **kick sth down/over etc** *The police kicked the door down.* | **kick sth around/towards etc** *Billy was kicking a ball around the yard.* | **kick sb in the head/face/stomach etc** *I got kicked in the face playing rugby.*

**2 ▶ MOVE YOUR LEGS ◀** [I,T] to move your legs as if you were kicking something: *The cow may kick a bit when you milk her.* | **kick your legs** *They danced and sang and kicked their legs high in the air.*

**3 ▶ KICK A GOAL ◀** [T] to SCORE² (1) by kicking: **kick a goal** *He kicked two penalty goals in the last ten minutes.*

**4 kick a habit** to stop doing something that is a harmful habit: *Some smokers find it surprisingly easy to kick the habit.*

**5 be kicking yourself/will kick yourself/could have kicked yourself** *spoken* used to say that someone is annoyed with themselves because they realize that they have made a mistake or missed a chance: *I could have kicked myself for getting her name wrong.* | *You'll kick yourself when I tell you the answer.* | *I bet they are kicking themselves now.*

**6 kick sb when they are down** to criticize or attack someone who is already in a weak position or having difficulties: *The newspapers cannot resist kicking a man when he is down.*

**7 kick sb in the teeth** *informal* to disappoint or DISCOURAGE someone very much, especially when they need support or hope: *Why is it that whenever I ask you for help you kick me in the teeth?*

**8 kick (sb's) ass** *AmE slang* **a)** to punish or defeat someone: *We really kicked their ass today, didn't we?* **b)** to have fun in a noisy violent way: *Come on, let's kick some ass!*

**9 kick over the traces** *BrE* to free yourself from control and start to behave as if there are no moral restrictions: *Haven't you ever felt you must go out and kick over the traces?*

**10 kick sb upstairs** to move someone to a job that seems to be more important than their present one but actually means that they have less influence

**11 kick your heels** to waste time waiting for something: *We were sitting around kicking our heels for half the day.*

**12 kick the bucket** *humorous informal* to die

**kick about/around** *phr v* **1 be kicking about/around (sth) a)** to be lying somewhere untidily, especially when forgotten: *You should find a copy of the report kicking around somewhere.* | *Goodness knows how many bottles he has kicking about his flat.* **b)** to be travelling around a place with no fixed plan: *He's been kicking around Australia for eight months.* **2** [T] **kick sth ↔ about/around** to discuss an idea with a group of people in order to decide whether it is good or not: *Perhaps we could kick one or two of these ideas around for a while.* **3** [T] **kick sb about/around** to treat someone badly and unfairly: *She was tired of being kicked around by her boss.*

**kick (out) against** *phr v* [T] to react strongly against something: *She has kicked out against authority all her life.*

**kick in** *phr v* **1** [I] *informal* to begin to have an effect or come into opertation: *I could feel the painkillers kick in.* | *Other benefits kick in at a certain level of income.* **2** [I,T] *AmE* to join with others in giving money or help; CONTRIBUTE: *He doesn't really want to kick in and help.* | *We're going to buy Bob a present – do you want to kick in something?* **3 kick sb's face/sb's head in** to severely wound someone by kicking them: *He threatened to kick my head in.* **4** [T] to kick a door so hard that it breaks open: *We had to get the police to kick the door in.*

**kick off** *phr v* **1** [I] when a game of football kicks off, it starts: *The match kicks off at 3 o'clock.* **2** [I,T] if you kick off a meeting, event etc, or if it kicks off, it starts: *The meeting kicked off at 11.00.* | *Right, who would like to kick off?* | **kick sth ↔ off (with)** *I'm going to kick off today's proceedings with a few remarks about next year's budget.* **3** [T] **kick your shoes ↔ off** to remove your shoes by shaking them off your feet: *I slumped into the armchair and kicked off my shoes.*

**kick** sb **↔ out** *phr v* [T] to make someone leave or dismiss them: *Bernard's wife had kicked him out.* | [+ **of**] *He's been kicked out of the golf club.*

**kick up** sth **↔** *phr v* [T] **1 kick up a fuss/row** to loudly complain and show you are annoyed about something: *He was kicking up an awful fuss about his cold* *meal.* **2** to make something, especially dust, go up into the air while you are walking: *As they marched, the soldiers kicked up clouds of dust.*

**kick²** *n* **1** [C] an act of hitting something with your foot: *Brazil scored with the last kick of the match.* | **give sb/sth a good kick** (=to kick them hard) *If the outer door won't open just give it a good kick.* **2** [C] an opportunity, allowed by the referee, for one team in a game of football or RUGBY to kick the ball without being stopped by the other team: *a free kick* | **take a kick** *Pearce came forward to take the kick.* **3 a kick up the arse/backside etc** *informal* severe criticism or punishment for something you have done wrong: *Phil needs a good kick up the arse.* **4 be a kick in the teeth** *informal* to be very disappointing or discouraging, especially when you need support or hope: *Her refusal to see me was a real kick in the teeth.* **5 get a kick out of sth/get a kick from sth** to really enjoy doing something: *Alan gets a real kick out of his job.* **6 give sb a kick** to give someone a strong feeling of pleasure: *It gives her a kick to get you into trouble.* **7 do sth for kicks/get your kicks from sth** *informal* to do something, especially something dangerous or harmful, in order to get a feeling of excitment: *Apparently she steals from supermarkets just for kicks.* **8 have a kick (to it)** *informal* to have a strong effect or taste, especially alcohol **9 be on a health/decorating/Italian food etc kick** *informal* to have a strong new interest: *I'm on a health kick at the moment.*

**kick-ass** /ˈ· ·/ *adj AmE slang* strong, powerful, and sometimes violent: *a kick-ass attitude that will get him into trouble*

**kick·back** /ˈkɪkbæk/ *n* [C,U] *slang* money that you pay secretly or dishonestly for someone's help; BRIBE

**kick·ball** /ˈkɪkbɔːl‖-bɒːl/ *n* [U] an American children's game, similar to BASEBALL, in which you kick the ball rather than hit it

**kick·box·ing** /ˈkɪkˌbɒksɪŋ‖-ˌbɑːks-/ *n* [U] a form of BOXING in which you kick as well as PUNCH (=hit)

**kick·off** /ˈkɪk-ɒf‖-ɒːf/ *n* [C usually singular] **1** the time when a game of football starts, or the first kick: *Kickoff is at 3.00.* **2** *informal* the beginning of a new activity

**kick·stand** /ˈkɪkstænd/ *n* [C] a thing that supports a bicycle or MOTORCYCLE when it is not moving, and keeps it in an upright position

**kick-start¹** /ˈ· ·/ *v* [T] **1** to do something to help a process or activity start or develop more quickly: *lowering interest rates to kick-start the economy* **2** to start a MOTORCYCLE using your foot

**kick-start²** also **kick-start·er** /ˈ· ˌ··/ *n* [C] the part of a MOTORCYCLE that you press with your foot to start it

S1 W2 **kid¹** /kɪd/ *n* **1** [C] *informal* a child: **the kids** (=children that you are responsible for) *I'm taking the kids to the zoo today.* —see CHILD (USAGE) **2** [C] *informal* a young person: *college kids* **3** [C] *informal* a son or daughter **4 kid's stuff** *BrE*/**kid stuff** *AmE* something that is very easy or boring **5** [C,U] a young goat, or the leather made from its skin **6 treat/handle someone with kid gloves** to treat someone very carefully because they easily become upset

**kid²** *v* **kidded, kidding** *informal* **1** [I,T] to say something that is not true, especially as a joke: **just/only kidding** *spoken*: *Don't get mad, I was only kidding.* | **you're kidding (me)** *spoken*: *You won $5000? You're kidding!* **2** [T] to make yourself believe something untrue or unlikely: **not kid yourself (that)** *Don't kid yourself he'll ever change.* **3 no kidding a)** *spoken* used when you do not completely believe someone, or are surprised by what they say: *Carlotta's 39? No kidding?* **b)** used to warn someone that you mean what you say **4 I kid you not** *spoken* used to emphasize that you are telling the truth —**kidder** *n* [C] *AmE*

**kid around** *phr v* [I] to behave in a silly way: *Stop kidding around and listen to me.* —**kidding** *n* [U]

**kid³** *adj informal especially AmE* **kid sister/brother** your kid sister or brother is younger than you are

**kid·die, kiddy** /ˈkɪdi/ *n* [C] *especially BrE informal* a young child —**kiddie** *adj*: *a kiddie seat*

**kid·do** /ˈkɪdəʊ‖-doʊ/ *n* [C usually singular] *especially AmE spoken* a way of addressing someone you know, usually a young person: *Come on kiddo, let's go.*

**kid·nap** /ˈkɪdnæp/ *v* **kidnapped, kidnapping** also **kidnaped, kidnaping** *AmE* [T] to take someone away illegally, usually by force, in order to get money for returning them —**kidnapper** *n* [C]

**kid·nap·ping** /ˈkɪdnæpɪŋ/ also **kidnap** *especially BrE* [C,U] the crime of kidnapping someone: *the recent series of kidnappings* | *a kidnap attempt*

**kid·ney** /ˈkɪdni/ *n* **1** [C] one of the two organs in your lower back that separate waste liquid from your blood and make URINE **2** [C,U] one or more of these organs from an animal, used as food: *steak and kidney pie* S3

**kidney bean** /ˈ·· ·/ *n* [C] a dark red bean that is shaped like a KIDNEY —see picture on page 414

**kill¹** /kɪl/ *v* S1 W1

**1 ► MAKE SB/STH DIE ◄** [I,T] to make a living thing die: *His parents were killed in a plane crash.* | *What's the best way to kill weeds?* | *Drug abuse can kill.* | **kill yourself** *You're going to kill yourself on that motorcycle.* | *The jury returned a verdict that he killed himself with an overdose.*

**2 ► MAKE STH STOP/FAIL ◄** [T] to make something stop or fail, or turn off the power to something: *Nothing that the doctor gives me kills the pain.* | *Quick! Kill the lights.* | *You've got to kill that story before it gets printed.* (=prevent it being printed) | **kill the conversation** (=stop people talking) | **kill a beer/bottle of wine etc** *AmE spoken* (=finish drinking) *Let's kill these beers and go.* | **kill the ball** (=completely stop a fast moving ball) | **kill your speed** (=drive slowly)

**3 ► BE ANGRY WITH SB ◄** [T] *informal* to be very angry with someone: *Maria will kill me if I'm late again.*

**4 ► MAKE SB TIRED/SAD ◄** [T] to make someone feel extremely tired, unhappy etc: **it kills me/her/them** *It kills me to see him working so hard for nothing.*

**5 the suspense is killing me** *spoken* used to say you are impatient to know the result of something

**6 my head is/feet are etc killing me** *spoken* used to say that a part of your body is hurting a lot: *I've walked miles and my feet are killing me.*

**7 ► MAKE SB LAUGH ◄** [T] to make someone laugh a lot at something: *You really killed them tonight, Frenchie!* | **kill yourself laughing** (=laugh a lot)

**8 it won't kill sb (to do something)** *spoken* used when saying that someone could easily do something, and ought to do it: *It wouldn't kill you to give me a bit of help.*

**9 kill time** to do something that is not very useful or interesting while you are waiting for something to happen

**10 kill two birds with one stone** to achieve two things with one action

**11 kill someone with kindness** to be too kind to someone

**12 ► SPOIL STH'S APPEARANCE ◄** [T] if something kills the way something else looks, the two things look wrong together: *That hat kills her whole outfit.*

**13 it will kill or cure** used to say that what you plan to do will either work very well or fail completely

**14 kill the fatted calf** to welcome someone home with a big meal etc after they have been away for a long time —see also **dressed to kill** (DRESSED (4)), **kill the goose that lays the golden egg** (GOOSE¹ (2))

**kill** sth ↔ **off** *phr v* [T] to cause the death of a lot of living things: *Pollution is rapidly killing off plant life.*

**USAGE NOTE: KILL**

WORD CHOICE: **kill, murder, execute, put to death, kill oneself, commit suicide, slaughter, assassinate, massacre**

**Kill** is the general word meaning to make someone or something die: *My uncle was killed in a plane crash.* | *A sharp frost can kill young plants.*

**Murder** means to kill a someone deliberately and illegally: *Davies is accused of murdering his wife and their three young children.*

If someone is killed legally as a punishment for a crime, they are **executed** or **put to death**. *Should serial killers be executed?| Thousands of revolutionaries were put to death after the coup.*

If someone **kills himself or herself**, they **commit suicide**.

**Slaughter** is the technical word for killing animals for food, leather etc but it is also used to describe the violent and unnecessary killing of a large number of people: *Thousands of people are slaughtered every year in road accidents.*

To **assassinate** someone means to murder an important, famous, and usually powerful person for political reasons: *Who really assassinated President Kennedy?*

To **massacre** means to kill large numbers of ordinary people, especially people who cannot defend themselves: *Hundreds of men, women, and children were massacred in the attack.*

**kill**[2] *n* **1** the act of killing a hunted animal: *The hawk's talons grip tight as it makes its kill.* **2 move in/close in for the kill** to come nearer to something and prepare to kill, defeat, or destroy: *Enemy submarines were moving in for the kill.* | **be in at the kill** (=watch something being killed, someone being defeated etc) **3** [singular] an animal killed by another animal, especially for food

**kill·er** /ˈkɪlə‖-ər/ *n* [C] **1** a person, animal, or thing that kills: *Heart disease is America's number one killer.* —see also SERIAL KILLER **2** *AmE slang* something or someone that is very attractive or very good: *a killer movie* —see also LADY-KILLER **3 a/the killer instinct** a desire to succeed that is so strong that you are willing to harm other people —**killer** *adj*: *a killer disease*

**killer whale** /ˈ·· ·/ *n* [C] a black and white WHALE that eats meat

**kill·ing**[1] /ˈkɪlɪŋ/ *n* [C] **1** a murder: *a series of gangland killings* **2 make a killing** *informal* to make a lot of money in a short time

**killing**[2] *adj informal* **1** extremely tiring: *a killing work load* **2** *old-fashioned* very funny —**killingly** *adv*

**kill·joy** /ˈkɪldʒɔɪ/ *n* [C] someone who spoils other people's pleasure

**kiln** /kɪln/ *n* [C] a special OVEN for baking clay pots, bricks etc

**ki·lo** /ˈkiːləʊ‖-loʊ/ *n plural* **kilos** [C] an informal word for KILOGRAM: *The box weighs 6 kilos.*

**kilo-** /kɪlə/ *prefix* 1000 times a particular unit: *a kilogram* (=1000 grams) —see table on page B2

**kil·o·byte** /ˈkɪləbaɪt/ also **K** *n* [C] a unit for measuring computer information equal to 1024 BYTES

**kil·o·gram** /ˈkɪləgræm/ *n* [C] a unit for measuring weight equal to 1000 grams —see table on page B2

**kil·o·hertz** /ˈkɪləhɜːts‖-ɜːr-/ written abbreviation **kHz** *n* [C] a unit for measuring wave lengths, especially of radio signals, equal to 1000 HERTZ

S3 **kil·o·me·tre** *BrE*, **kilometer** *AmE* /ˈkɪləˌmiːtə, kɪˈlɒmɪ̠tə‖kɪˈlɑːmɪ̠tər/ *n* [C] a unit for measuring length, equal to 1000 metres —see table on page B2

**kil·o·watt** /ˈkɪləwɒt‖-wɑːt/ *n* [C] a unit for measuring electrical power equal to 1000 WATTS —see table on page B2

**kilowatt hour** /ˌ··· ˈ·/ *n* [C] the amount of ENERGY produced by a KILOWATT in one hour

**kilt** /kɪlt/ *n* [C] a type of thick skirt, traditionally worn by Scottish men —**kilted** *adj*

**kil·ter** /ˈkɪltə‖-ər/ *n* **out of kilter** not working as well as usual: *Things in my life seem all out of kilter lately.*

**ki·mo·no** /kɪˈməʊnəʊ‖-ˈmoʊnoʊ/ *n* [C] **1** a traditional piece of Japanese clothing like a long coat, that is worn at special ceremonies **2** *especially AmE* a long, loose piece of clothing worn informally indoors, especially by women

**kin** /kɪn/ *n* [plural] **1** *informal* also **kinfolk** your family **2 next of kin** *formal* your most closely related family: *We'll have to notify the next of kin of his death.* —compare KINDRED[1] (1) —see also KITH AND KIN

**-kin** /kɪn/ also **-kins** /kɪnz/ *suffix* [in nouns] a word meaning something small, used especially to children: *a lambkin*

**kind**[1] /kaɪnd/ *n* **1** [C] a type or sort or person or thing: [+ **of**] *What kind of fish is this?| Are you in some kind of trouble?| victimization of the worst kind* | **all kinds of** *They sell all kinds of different things.* | **of this kind** *Operations of this kind always carry risks.* | **of its kind** *the best wine of its kind* **2 kind of** also **kinda** *AmE spoken* **a)** slightly or in some ways: *I'm kind of glad I didn't win.* **b)** used when you are explaining something and want to avoid giving the details: *I kind of made it look like the post office had lost his letter.* **3 a kind of (a)** *especially spoken* used to say that your description of something is not exact: *a kind of a reddish-brown* **4 something of the/that kind** *spoken* something similar to what has been mentioned: *"Are you sure he was wearing jeans?" "Well, something of the kind."* **5 nothing/anything of the kind** used to emphasize what you are saying when you disagree with someone: *I never said anything of the kind!* **6** [U] people or things that are similar in some way or belong to the same group: **sb's (own) kind** *Grace only made friends among her own kind.* **7 be the kind** to be a person of a particular type: *She may not be the marrying kind.* | **be the kind to do sth** *He's not the kind to get excited about money.* **8 two/three etc of a kind** two or three people or things that are of the same type: *You and your brother are two of a kind.* **9 one of a kind** the only one of a particular type of something; UNIQUE: *Each plate is handpainted and one of a kind.* **10 of a kind** used to say that something is not as good as it should be: *Elections of a kind are held, but there is only one party to vote for.* **11 payment in kind** a method of paying someone with goods or services instead of money **12 respond/retaliate etc in kind** to react by doing the same thing as someone else has just done: *If other papers cut their prices, we'll have to respond in kind.* S1 W1

**USAGE NOTE: KIND**

FORMALITY

Remember that **would you be kind enough to/would you be so kind as to...?** are formally polite. When you are speaking or writing informally they may sound unfriendly and it would be better to say, for example: **Please could you .../Could you possibly...?**

On the other hand, **kind of** and **sort of** meaning that something is uncertain or partly true (mainly before adjectives and verbs) are used only in informal contexts: *I kinda like that color.* | *"Did he help you?" "Well, kind of"* (=not as much as I hoped). In very informal speech you sometimes use **kind of** and **sort of** to make a serious statement sound weaker or amusing: *He sort of came up to me and pushed me. So I kind of hit him in the face.* Some people do not consider this to be good English.

GRAMMAR

**Kind(s) of** or **sort(s) of** is regularly used in the singular or plural before singular and uncountable nouns: *one kind of flower/person/bread* | *many kinds of car/person/cheese/attraction* | *several sorts of paint*

The plural **kinds of/sorts of** is also used before plural nouns in more informal English: *these/many kinds of flowers/programs/people* (but NOT *this kind/sort of programs*, though you can more formally say *programs of this kind/sort*).

Remember that whether **kind or sort** itself is singular or plural also relates to the word used just before: *this/one/each/every kind of...|another sort of cheese* but you say *these/ten/many/all/a few kinds of ...|in other kinds of school|shops of all sorts.* In informal spoken English people do say things like: *Those kind/sort of questions are very difficult,* but some people think this is incorrect.

S3 **kind²** *adj* **1** saying or doing things that show that you care about other people and want to help them or make them happy: *It's really kind of you to let us use your pool.|Ms Jarvis is unable to accept your kind invitation.|*[+ **to**] *He's been very kind to me.* —see KINDLY² (USAGE) **2** not causing harm or suffering: *Life has been very kind to me.|I need a soap that's kinder to my skin.* **3 would you be kind enough to do sth/be so kind as to do sth** *formal* used to make a polite request: *Would you be kind enough to close the door, please?* —opposite UNKIND —see also KINDLY², KINDNESS

**kin·der·gar·ten** /ˈkɪndəɡɑːtn‖-dərɡɑːrtn/ *n* [C,U] **1** *AmE* a school or class for young children, usually aged five, that prepares them for normal school **2** *BrE* a school for children aged two to five —compare NURSERY

**kind-heart·ed** /ˌ· ˈ··◂‖ˈ· ˌ··/ *adj* kind and generous —**kind-heartedly** *adv* —**kind-heartedness** *n* [U]

**kin·dle** /ˈkɪndl/ *v* [I,T] **1** to start burning, or to make something start burning: **kindle a fire** (=make a fire using small pieces of wood etc) **2 kindle excitement/interest etc** to make someone interested, excited etc: *The love of poetry was kindled in him by her teaching.*

**kin·dling** /ˈkɪndlɪŋ/ *n* [U] small pieces of dry wood, leaves etc that you use for starting a fire

**kind·ly¹** /ˈkaɪndli/ *adv* **1** in a kind way; generously: *Mr Nunn has kindly agreed to let us use his barn for the dance.* **2** *spoken formal* a word meaning 'please', which is often used when you are annoyed: *Will you kindly put that book back?* **3 not take kindly to** to be unwilling to accept a situation because it annoys you: *Eddie would not take kindly to her working.* **4 look kindly on** to approve of someone or something: *He hoped the committee would look kindly on his request.* **5 think kindly of** to have fond thoughts about someone: *Think kindly of me when I'm gone.*

**kindly²** *adj* kind and caring for other people: *Mrs Gardiner was a kindly old soul.* —**kindliness** *n* [C]

USAGE NOTE: KINDLY

FORMALITY

A request like **would you kindly...?** or **kindly shut the door!** is formally polite. In informal contexts it sounds as though you are annoyed and **could you possibly...?** would be more usual.

WORD CHOICE: **kindly, kind**

**Kindly** is either the adverb of **kind**: *He kindly opened the door for me,* or an adjective with a slightly different meaning from **kind** which is much less common: *She is a kindly person.*

The adjective **kindly** describes a person's general character. **Kind** may also do this, but often describes someone's behaviour at one particular moment: *It was kind of you to help me.|She's often kind to me* (NOT *kindly*).

**kind·ness** /ˈkaɪndnɪ̇s/ *n* **1** [U] kind behaviour towards someone: *I can't thank you enough for your kindness.* **2** [C] a kind action: **do sb a kindness** *It would be doing him a kindness to tell him the truth.* —see also **kill sb with kindness** (KILL¹ (11))

**kin·dred¹** /ˈkɪndrɪ̇d/ *n* [U] **1** *old use* your family —compare KIN **2** [+ **with**] *formal* a family relationship; KINSHIP

**kindred²** *adj* [only before noun] **1 a kindred spirit** someone who thinks and feels the way you do **2** *formal* belonging to the same group or family

**ki·net·ic** /kɪˈnetɪk, kaɪ-/ *adj technical* connected with movement

**kinetic art** /ˌ·ˌ·· ˈ·/ *n* [U] art, such as SCULPTURE, that has moving parts

**kinetic en·er·gy** /ˌ·ˌ·· ˈ···/ *n* [U] *technical* the power of something moving, such as running water

**ki·net·ics** /kɪˈnetɪks, kaɪ-/ *n* [U] *technical* the science that studies the action or force of movement

**kin·folk** /ˈkɪnfəʊk‖-foʊk/ *n* [plural] an American form of KINSFOLK

**king** /kɪŋ/ *n* [C] W1

**1 ▶ RULER ◀** a man who is ruler of a country because he is from a royal family: *He became king on the death of his father.|*[+ **of**] *Henry VIII, King of England*

**2 ▶ THE BEST ◀ a)** someone that you think does a particular thing the best: [+ **of**] *the King of Rock 'n' Roll* **b)** something that is the best of its type: [+ **of**] *the king of Swiss cheeses*

**3 ▶ CHESS ◀** the most important piece in a game of CHESS

**4 ▶ CARDS ◀** a playing card with a picture of a king on it

**5 ▶ IMPORTANT ◀ be king** if something is king at a particular time, it has a big influence on people: *back in the days when jazz was king*

**6 king of the jungle/of beasts** the most important male animal: *The lion is king of the jungle.*

**7 a king's ransom** an extremely large amount of money

**8 live like a king** to have a very good quality of life —see also QUEEN¹

**king·dom** /ˈkɪŋdəm/ *n* [C] **1** a country governed by a king or queen: *the kingdom of Thailand* **2 the kingdom of** an imaginary place where a particular thing or quality has the greatest influence: *the kingdom of love* **3 the animal/plant/mineral kingdom** one of the three parts into which the natural world is divided **4 the kingdom of heaven/God** heaven **5 blow sb/sth to kingdom come** *informal* to completely destroy someone or something **6 wait till kingdom come** to wait for ever W3

**king·fish·er** /ˈkɪŋˌfɪʃə‖-ər/ *n* [C] a small brightly-coloured bird with a blue body that eats fish in rivers

**king·ly** /ˈkɪŋli/ *adj* good enough for a king, or typical of a king: *a kingly feast*

**king·mak·er** /ˈkɪŋˌmeɪkə‖-ər/ *n* [C] someone who influences the choice of people for important jobs

**king·pin** /ˈkɪŋˌpɪn/ *n* [C usually singular] **1** the most important person or thing in a group **2** *technical* a thin strong piece of metal used in hinges (HINGE¹)

**King's Coun·sel** /ˌ· ˈ··/ *n* a KC

**King's Eng·lish** /ˌ· ˈ··/ *n* **the King's English** *old-fashioned* correct English, as it is spoken in Britain —see also QUEEN'S ENGLISH

**king's ev·i·dence** /ˌ· ˈ···/ *n* **turn King's evidence** *BrE* to give information about other criminals in order to get a less severe punishment; STATE'S EVIDENCE *AmE* —see also QUEEN'S EVIDENCE

**king·ship** /ˈkɪŋʃɪp/ *n* [U] the official position or condition of being a king: *the responsibilities of kingship*

**king-size** /ˈ· ·/ also **king-sized** *adj* **1** very large, and usually the largest size of something: *a king-size bed* **2** *informal* very big or strong: *a king-size thirst*

**kink¹** /kɪŋk/ *n* [C] **1** a twist in something that is normally straight: [+ **in**] *The water hose had a kink in it.* **2** something strange or dangerous in your character

**kink²** *v* [I,T] to get or give something a kink

**kink·y** /ˈkɪŋki/ *adj* **1** *informal* someone who is kinky, or does kinky things, has strange ways of getting sexual excitement **2** kinky hair has a lot of small curves —**kinkiness** *n* [U] —**kinkily** *adv*

**kins·folk** /ˈkɪnzfəʊk‖-foʊk/ also **kinfolk** *AmE* *n* [plural] *old-fashioned* your family

**kin·ship** /ˈkɪnʃɪp/ *n* **1** [U + **with**] *literary* a family relationship: *the ties of kinship* **2** [singular, U] a strong connection between people: [+ **with/between**] *Poe shows his kinship with his literary ancestors.*

**kins·man** /ˈkɪnzmən/ *n* [C] *old use* a male relative

**kin·swom·an** /ˈkɪnzˌwʊmən/ *n* [C] *old use* a female relative

**ki·osk** /ˈkiːɒsk‖-ɑːsk/ *n* [C] **1** a small building in the street where newspapers, sweets etc are sold **2** *BrE old-fashioned* a public telephone box

**kip¹** /kɪp/ *n* [singular, U] *BrE informal* a period of sleep: **have a kip** (=sleep for a short time)| **get some kip** *I'm going to lie down and try to get some kip.*

**kip²** *v* **kipped, kipping** [I] *BrE informal* **1** to sleep **2** to lie down in order to sleep: [+ **down**] *kipping down for the night*

**kip·per** /ˈkɪpə‖-ər/ *n* [C] a type of fish that has been preserved using smoke and salt —**kippered** *adj*: *kippered herring*

**kirk** /kɜːk‖kɜːrk/ *n ScotE* **1** [C] a church **2 the Kirk** the Church of Scotland

**kirsch** /kɪəʃ‖kɪərʃ/ *n* [U] a strong alcoholic drink made from CHERRY (1) juice

**kis·met** /ˈkɪzmet, ˈkɪs-/ *n* [U] *literary* the things that will happen to you in your life; FATE (1)

S3 W3 **kiss¹** /kɪs/ *v* **1** [I,T] to touch someone with your lips as a greeting or to show them love: *They kissed again, passionately.*| **kiss sb on** *Did he kiss you on the cheek or on the mouth?*| **kiss sb goodbye/goodnight etc** *Kiss Daddy goodnight.* **2** [T] to touch something with your lips as a sign of respect: *She raised the Crucifix to her lips and kissed it.* **3 sb can kiss goodbye to sth/kiss sth goodbye** *informal* used when you think it is certain that someone will lose their chance of getting or doing something: *If you don't work harder you can kiss goodbye to your chances of going to university.* **4 kiss sth away/better** *spoken* an expression meaning to take away the pain of something by kissing someone, used especially with children: *Here, let Mommy kiss it better.* **5 kiss my ass** *AmE taboo slang* an insulting expression used to show that you do not respect someone **6 kiss (sb's) ass** *AmE taboo slang* to be too nice to someone who can give you something you want —compare KISS-ASS **7** [T] *literary* if the wind, sun etc kisses something, it gently moves or touches it

**kiss up to** sb *phr v* [T] *AmE informal* to try to please someone in order to get them to do something for you: *That guy got his promotion by kissing up to the boss.*

**kiss²** *n* [C] **1** an act of kissing: *Do you remember your first kiss?*| **give sb a kiss** *Come and give your old Grandma a kiss.* **2 the kiss of death** *informal* something that spoils or ruins a plan, activity etc —see also FRENCH KISS, KISS OF LIFE, **blow sb a kiss** (BLOW¹ (16))

**kiss·a·gram** *n* [C] another spelling of KISSOGRAM

**kiss-ass** /ˈ· ·/ *adj* [only before noun] *AmE slang* a very impolite word used to describe the behaviour of someone who tries too hard to please other people

**kiss·ing cous·in** /ˌ·· ˈ··/ *n* [C] *AmE old-fashioned* someone you are not closely related to, but whom you know well

**kiss of life** /ˌ· · ˈ·/ *n* **1 give sb the kiss of life** *especially BrE* to make someone start breathing again by blowing air into their lungs when they have almost DROWNED etc **2** something that helps you continue an activity that you thought would fail: *a grant that was a kiss of life to the project*

**kiss·o·gram, kissagram** /ˈkɪsəgræm/ *n* [C] a humorous greeting for your BIRTHDAY etc that is delivered by someone in a special COSTUME, or the person who delivers it and kisses you

**kit¹** /kɪt/ *n* **1 shaving/sewing/repair kit** [C] a set of tools, equipment etc that you use for a particular purpose or activity **2** [C] something such as furniture that you buy in parts and put together yourself: *He made the model from a kit.* **3** *BrE* [U] a set of clothes and equipment that you use when playing a sport: *football kit* **4** [U] a set of clothes and equipment used by soldiers, SAILORS etc: *survival kit* **5 the whole kit and caboodle** *old-fashioned* everything —see also FIRST AID KIT, TOOL KIT

**kit²** *v* **kitting, kitted** *especially BrE*

**kit** sb **out** *phr v* [T] **1** to provide someone with the clothes and equipment they need for an activity **2 be kitted out/up** to have the correct clothes and equipment to do a particular activity: *all kitted out in waterproof clothes*

**kit bag, kitbag** /ˈkɪtbæg/ *n* [C] *especially BrE* a long narrow bag used by soldiers, SAILORS etc, for carrying their clothes and other possessions

**kitch·en** /ˈkɪtʃɪn/ *n* [C] **1** the room where you prepare and cook food: *Can you help me carry these dishes into the kitchen?*| *the kitchen table* **2 everything but the kitchen sink** *humorous* used when someone has brought too many things with them S1 W2

**kitchen cab·i·net** /ˌ·· ˈ···/ *n* [C] an informal group of people who advise the leader of the government

**kitchen gar·den** /ˌ·· ˈ··/ *n* [C] a part of a garden where you grow your own fruit and vegetables

**kitchen roll** /ˈ·· ·/ *BrE* also **kitchen tow·el** /ˈ·· ˌ··/ *n* [U] thick paper used for cleaning up small amounts of liquid, food etc

**kitchen sink dra·ma** /ˌ·· ˈ· ˌ··/ *n* [C] *BrE* a serious play or film about problems that families have at home

**kite¹** /kaɪt/ *n* [C] **1** a light frame covered in coloured paper or plastic that you let fly in the air on the end of one or two long strings **2** a type of HAWK (=bird that eats small animals) **3** *AmE informal* an illegal cheque **4 fly a kite** to make a suggestion to see what people will think of it —see also **go fly a kite** (FLY¹ (21)), **high as a kite** (HIGH¹ (14))

**kite²** *v* **kited, kiting** [I,T] *AmE informal* **1** also **kite up** to raise the cost of something: *Soaring medical costs keep kiting up insurance premiums.* **2** to obtain money using an illegal cheque

**kite-fly·ing** /ˈ· ˌ··/ *n* [U] **1** the game or sport of flying a kite **2** the act of telling people about an idea, plan etc in order to get their opinion

**kith and kin** /ˌkɪθ ən ˈkɪn/ *n* [plural] *old-fashioned* family and friends

**kitsch** /kɪtʃ/ *n* [U] kitsch decorations, films etc that are made without much serious thought and are SENTIMENTAL and often amuse people because of this —**kitsch** *adj*

**kit·ten** /ˈkɪtn/ *n* [C] **1** a young cat **2 have kittens** *informal* to be very anxious or upset about something

**kit·ten·ish** /ˈkɪtn-ɪʃ/ *adj old-fashioned* a kittenish woman behaves in a silly way in order to attract men

**kit·ty** /ˈkɪti/ *n* **1** [C usually singular] the money that people have collected for a particular purpose: *How much money is there left in the kitty?* **2** [C usually singular] the money that the winner of a game of cards receives **3** [C] a word for a cat, used especially by children

**kitty-cor·ner** /ˌ·· ˈ··/ *adv AmE informal* on the opposite corner of a street from a particular place: [+ **from/to**] *The drugstore is kitty-corner from the bank.*

**ki·wi** /ˈkiːwiː/ *n* [C] **1** a New Zealand bird that has very short wings and cannot fly **2** *informal* someone from New Zealand

**kiwi fruit** /ˈ·· ·/ *n* [C] a small sweet fruit with a brown skin, which is green inside —see picture on page 413

**KKK** /ˌkeɪ keɪ ˈkeɪ/ *n* the abbreviation of Ku Klux Klan

**klans·man** /ˈklænzmən/ *n* [C] *AmE* a member of the Ku Klux Klan

**klax·on** /ˈklæksən/ *n* [C] a loud horn that was fixed onto police cars and other official vehicles in the past

**Kleen·ex** /ˈkliːneks/ *n* [C, U] *trademark* a TISSUE (1)

**klep·to·ma·ni·a** /ˌkleptəˈmeɪniə/ *n* [U] a mental illness in which you have a desire to steal things

**klep·to·ma·ni·ac** /ˌkleptəˈmeɪniæk/ also **klep·to** /ˈkleptəʊ‖-toʊ/ *informal n* [C] someone suffering from kleptomania

**klutz, clutz** /klʌts/ *n* [C] *AmE* someone who drops things and falls easily —**klutzy** *adj*

**km** *n* the written abbreviation of KILOMETRE

**knack** /næk/ *n informal* **1** [singular] a special skill or ability that you usually gain by practice: *There's a knack to starting our lawn mower.* **2 have a knack of doing sth** to have a tendency to do something: *He has a knack of saying the wrong thing.*

**knack·er** /ˈnækə‖-ər/ also **knacker out** *v* [T] *BrE spoken* **1** to become extremely tired: **knacker yourself out** *Slow down – you'll knacker yourself out!* **2 knacker your elbow/hand etc** to hurt your elbow etc so that you cannot use it

**knack·ered** /ˈnækəd‖-ərd/ *adj BrE spoken* **1** extremely tired **2** too old or broken to use: *a knackered old bike*

**knackers' yard** /ˈ·· ,·/ also **knacker's** *n* [C] *BrE* **1** a place where horses are killed **2 ready for the knacker's yard** too old to be useful or work properly

**knap·sack** /ˈnæpsæk/ *n* [C] a bag that you carry on your shoulders

**knave** /neɪv/ *n* [C] **1** *BrE* the playing card with a value between the ten and queen; JACK[1] (2) —see also **cards** (CARD[1] (7)) **2** *old-fashioned* a dishonest boy or man —**knavish** *adj* —**knavishly** *adv*

**knav·e·ry** /ˈneɪvəri/ *n* [C,U] *old use* dishonest behaviour

**knead** /niːd/ *v* [T] **1** to press a mixture of flour and water many times with your hands: *Knead the dough for three minutes.* —see picture on page 834 **2** to press someone's muscles many times in order to help cure pain

S 2 W 2 **knee[1]** /niː/ *n* [C] **1** the joint that bends in the middle of your leg: *Lift using your knees, not your back.* —see picture at BODY **2** the part of your clothes that covers your knee: *holes in both knees* **3 on sb's knee** on the top part of your legs when you are sitting down: *Daddy, can I sit on your knee?* **4 with your knees knocking (together)** feeling very afraid or very cold **5 on your knees** in a way that shows you have no power or are very sorry: *He begged me, on his knees, to forgive him.* **6 bring sb/sth to their knees a)** to defeat a country or group of people in a war **b)** to have such a bad effect on an organization, activity etc that it cannot continue: *The recession has brought many companies to their knees.* **7 put sb over your knee** *old-fashioned* to punish a child by hitting them **8 on bended knee(s)** *old-fashioned* in a way that shows great respect for someone: *worshipping on bended knee* —see also **knee/elbow pad** (PAD[1] (1)), **learn/be taught sth at your mother's knee** (MOTHER[1] (5)), **the bee's knees** (BEE (4)), **weak at the knees** (WEAK (11))

**knee[2]** *v* [T + **in**] to hit someone with your knee: *I kneed him in the groin.*

**knee breech·es** /ˈ· ,··/ *n* [plural] tight trousers that end at your knee, worn especially in the past

**knee cap** /ˈ· ·/ *n* [C] the bone at the front of your knee —see picture at SKELETON

**knee·cap** /ˈniːkæp/ *v* **kneecapped, kneecapping** [T] to shoot someone's kneecaps as an unofficial punishment

**knee-deep** /,· ˈ·◂/ *adj* **1** deep enough to reach your knees: [+ **in**] *knee deep in mud* **2** *informal* having a lot of something: [+ **in**] *knee deep in work*

**knee-high[1]** /,· ˈ·◂/ *adj* **1** tall enough to reach your knees: *knee-high grass* **2 knee-high to a grasshopper** *old-fashioned* used when talking about the past to say that someone was a very small child then

**knee-high[2]** *n* [C] a sock that ends just below your knee

**knee-jerk** /ˈ· ·/ *adj* a knee-jerk reaction, opinion etc is what you feel or say about a situation from habit, without thinking about it

**kneel** /niːl/ also **kneel down** *v past tense and past participle* **knelt** /nelt/ also **kneeled** *AmE* [I] to be in or move into a position where your body is resting on your knees: *a statue of a kneeling figure* | [+ **on**] *We knelt on the floor to have a good look at the map.*

**knee-length** /ˈ· ·/ *adj* long or tall enough to reach your knees: *a knee-length skirt*

**knees-up** /ˈ· ·/ *n* [C] *BrE informal* a noisy party: *After the wedding there was a bit of a knees-up.*

**knell** /nel/ *n* [C] *literary* the sound of a bell being rung slowly because someone has died —see also DEATH KNELL

**knew** /njuː‖nuː/ *v* the past tense of KNOW[1]

**knick·er·bock·ers** /ˈnɪkə,bɒkəz‖ˈnɪkər,bɑːkərz/ *n* [plural] short loose trousers that fit tightly at your knees, worn especially in the past

**knick·ers** /ˈnɪkəz‖-ərz/ *n* [plural] *BrE informal* **1** a piece of women's underwear worn between your waist and the top of your legs; PANTIES: *a pair of frilly knickers* —see picture at UNDERWEAR **2** *AmE* KNICKERBOCKERS **3 get your knickers in a twist** *BrE spoken* to get upset

**knick-knack** /ˈnɪk næk/ *n* [C] a small object used as a decoration: *They had knick-knacks on the top of the bookcase.*

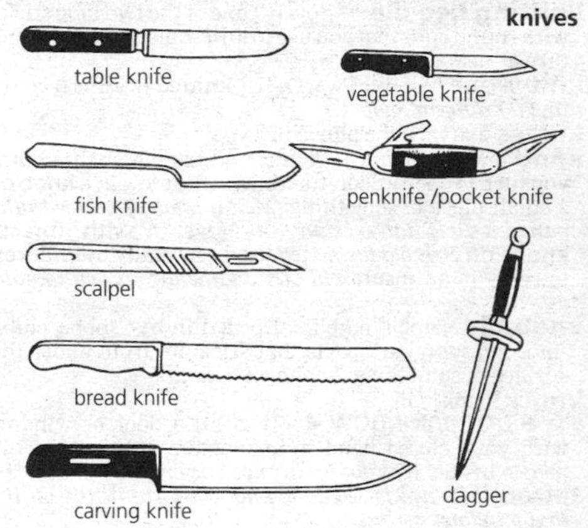


**knife[1]** /naɪf/ *n plural* **knives** /naɪvz/ [C] **1** a metal blade fixed into a handle, used for cutting or as a weapon: *knife and fork* | *He had been stabbed with a knife.* | **kitchen/bread/vegetable etc knife** (=knife used in the kitchen, for cutting bread etc) —see picture on page 834 **2 the knives are out** *informal* used to say that people are being extremely unfriendly to each other **3 have/get your knife into someone** *informal* to dislike someone and be very unfriendly towards them **4 twist/turn the knife** to say something that makes someone more upset about a subject they are already unhappy about **5 under the knife** *humorous* having a medical operation **6 you could cut the atmosphere/air with a knife** used to say that you felt the people in a room were angry with each other —see also PAPER KNIFE  S 3 W 3

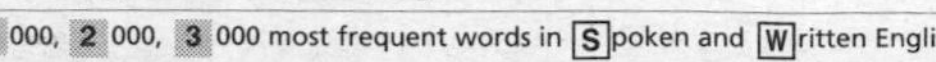

**knife²** *v* [T + **in**] to put a knife into someone's body; STAB¹ (1)

**knife-edge** /ˈ· ·/ *n* **1 be on a knife-edge a)** to be in a situation in which the result is extremely uncertain: *Success or failure is balanced on a knife-edge.* **b)** very anxious about the future result of something: *She is on a knife-edge about her promotion.* **2** [singular] something that is narrow or sharp: *The cliff narrowed down to a knife-edge.*

**knight¹** /naɪt/ *n* [C] **1** a man with a high rank in former times who was trained to fight while riding a horse: *knights in armour* —see also WHITE KNIGHT **2** a man who has received a knighthood and has the title 'SIR' (4) before his name **3** the CHESS piece with a horse's head on it **4 a knight in shining armour** a brave man who saves someone from a dangerous situation

**knight²** *v* [T] to give someone the rank of knight

**knight-er·rant** /ˌ· ˈ··/ *n* [C] a knight in former times who travelled looking for adventure

**knight·hood** /ˈnaɪthʊd/ *n* [C,U] a special rank or title that is given to someone by the King or Queen in Britain

**knight·ly** /ˈnaɪtli/ *adj literary* connected with being a knight or typical of a knight, especially by behaving with courage and honour: *knightly deeds of chivalry*

**knit** /nɪt/ *v past tense and past participle* **knitted** *or* **knitting** [I,T] **1** also **knit up** to make clothing out of wool using two KNITTING NEEDLES: **knit sb sth** *She's knitting me a sweater.* —compare CROCHET **2** *technical* to use a PLAIN (=basic) knitting stitch: *Knit one, purl one.* **3** to join people, things or ideas more closely, or to be closely connected: [+ **together**] *Wherever they live, the Jewish people are knit together by a common faith.*| **well/closely/tightly etc knit** (=with all the parts joined closely) *a closely knit community* **4** [+ **together**] a bone that knits after being broken grows into one piece again **5 knit your brows** to show you are worried, thinking hard etc by moving your EYEBROWS together —**knitter** *n* [C] —see also CLOSE-KNIT

**knit·ting** /ˈnɪtɪŋ/ *n* [U] something that is being knitted

**knitting nee·dle** /ˈ·· ˌ··/ *n* [C] one of the two long sticks with round ends that you use to knit something —see picture at NEEDLE¹

**knit·wear** /ˈnɪt-weə‖-wer/ *n* [U] knitted (KNIT (1)) clothing: *a knitwear shop*

**knives** /naɪvz/ *n* the plural of KNIFE¹

**knob** /nɒb‖nɑːb/ *n* [C] **1** a round handle or thing that you turn to open a door, turn on a radio etc **2 a knob of** a small piece of something: *Melt a knob of butter in the pan.* **3** *BrE taboo slang* a PENIS **4 with (brass) knobs on** *BrE old-fashioned* used especially by children to reply to an insult: *"Idiot!" "Same to you, with knobs on!"*

**knob·bly** /ˈnɒbli‖ˈnɑːbli/ also **knob·by** /ˈnɒbi‖ˈnɑːbi/ *AmE adj* with hard parts that stick out from under the surface of something: *knobbly knees*

**knock¹** /nɒk‖nɑːk/ *v*

**1 ▶DOOR/WINDOW◀** [I] to hit a door or window with your closed hand to attract the attention of the people inside: *Why don't you knock before you come in?*| [+ **at/on**] *I turned to see Jane knocking frantically on the taxi window.*

**2 ▶HIT/MAKE STH MOVE◀** [I always + adv/prep, T] to hit someone or something with a short quick action, so that it moves, falls down etc: *Don't knock the camera, the picture will be blurry.*| **knock sth ↔ down/off/over etc** *The dog managed to knock over a table.*| **knock sth ↔ against/into/in** *I need a hammer to knock these tent pegs in.*| **knock sb/sth flying** *BrE informal* (=hit something or someone so that they move a long distance) *Holly ran through the crowd, knocking people flying.*| **knock a hole in** (=make a hole in something)

**3 ▶HIT SB HARD◀ a) knock sb flat/knock sb to the ground** to hit someone so hard that they fall down: *His assailant knocked him to the ground and ran off with his briefcase.* **b) knock sb unconscious/senseless** to hit someone so hard that they fall unconscious: *The blast from the explosion knocked him unconscious.* **c) knock the living daylights out of/hell out of** *informal* to hit someone many times or very hard

**4 I'll knock your block off** *spoken* used when threatening to hit someone very hard: *If you touch her, I'll knock your block off!*

**5 knock it off** *spoken* used to tell someone to stop doing something, because it is annoying you: *"Hey, knock it off!" Jesse shouted furiously.*

**6 ▶CRITICIZE◀** [T] to criticize someone or their work, especially in an unfair or annoying way: *Some movie reviewers seem to knock every picture they see.*| **don't knock it** *spoken* (=used to tell someone not to criticize something) *"Bungee jumping! You must be crazy!" "Don't knock it till you've tried it."*

**7 knock sb/sth into shape** *informal* to make changes to something in order to make it good enough: *We've only got until Thursday to knock this play into shape.*

**8 ▶MAKE A NOISE◀** [I] if an engine or pipes etc knock, they make a noise like something hard being hit, usually because something is wrong with them

**9 ▶BALL◀** [T always + adv/prep] to kick or hit a ball somewhere: **knock sth about/past/back etc** *We were just knocking a ball about in the yard.*

**10 knock the stuffing out of** *informal* to make someone lose their confidence: *Getting such low grades this semester seems to have knocked the stuffing out of him.*

**11 knock sb's socks off** also **knock 'em dead** *spoken* to surprise and please someone by being very impressive: *Go out there and knock 'em dead, kid.*

**12 knock some sense into sb/into sb's head** *informal* to make someone learn to behave in a more sensible way: *Who knows. Maybe getting arrested will knock some sense into him.*

**13 knock spots off** *BrE spoken* to be much better than someone or something: *Our new computer system knocks spots off the old one.*

**14 knock sth on the head** *BrE informal* to prevent you from doing something you have planned: *I wanted to go for a picnic, but the rain's knocked that on the head.*

**15 knock (sb's) heads together** *informal* to talk angrily to people who are quarrelling or behaving stupidly: *If you kids don't settle down I'm going to come up and knock your heads together!*

**16 you could have knocked me down with a feather** *old-fashioned* used to emphasize how surprised you were by something: *When I heard I'd won, you could have knocked me down with a feather.*

**17 knock the bottom out of** *informal* to make something, such as a price much lower or weaker: *A rise in interest rates would completely knock the bottom out of the property market.* —see also **with your knees knocking (together)** (KNEE¹ (4))

**knock around** also **knock about** *BrE phr v informal*

**1 ▶HIT SB◀** [T **knock** sb **about/around**] to hit someone several times: *My father used to knock me and my brother around a lot.*

**2 ▶RELAX◀** [I,T] to spend time in a relaxing way, without doing anything very important: **knock around town/the house etc** *We spent the weekend just knocking around the house.*

**3 ▶TRAVEL◀** [I,T **knock around** sth] to travel to different places: *I've knocked around a few places in my life.*

**4 ▶IDEAS◀** [T **knock** sth ↔ **around**] to discuss and think about an idea, plan etc with other people: *We've been knocking around a few ideas.*

**5 ▶BALL◀** [T **knock** sth **about**] *BrE* to play a game with a ball, but not in a serious way

**6 ▶BE SOMEWHERE◀** [I] *BrE* if something or someone is knocking around a place, it is somewhere in that place but you are not sure exactly where: *Is there a screwdriver knocking about anywhere?*

**knock back** *phr v* [T] *informal* **1** [**knock** sth ↔ **back**] to quickly drink large quantities of an alcoholic drink: **knock it/them back** *spoken*: *Steve can really knock it back – he's drunk five pints already.* **2** [**knock** sb **back** sth] to cost you a lot of money: *Our summer holiday knocked us back £600 this year.* **3** [**knock** sb **back**] *BrE* to surprise or shock someone: *The news of her death really knocked him back.*

**knock down** *phr v* [T]
**1 ▶ DRIVING A CAR ◀** [**knock** sb **down**] to hit someone with a car while you are driving, so that they are hurt or killed: *He was knocked down by a drunk driver.* | **get knocked down** *Someone said a kid got knocked down by a truck.*
**2 ▶ DESTROY ◀** [**knock** sth ↔ **down**] to destroy a building or part of a building: *We knocked down one of the walls to make a bigger kitchen.*
**3 ▶ REDUCE PRICE ◀** [**knock** sth ↔ **down**] *informal* to reduce the price of something by a large amount: *The new stove we bought was knocked down from $800 to $550.* —see also KNOCKDOWN
**4 ▶ ASK SB TO REDUCE PRICE ◀** [**knock** sb **down to**] *informal* to persuade someone to reduce the price of something they are selling you: *I tried to knock him down to £50.*
**5 ▶ DRINK ◀** [**knock** sth ↔ **down**] *AmE informal* to quickly drink large quantities of an alcoholic drink
**6 ▶ PROVE STH WRONG ◀** [**knock** sth ↔ **down**] *BrE informal* to prove that an idea, plan etc is not good or right: *They knocked the proposal down on the grounds that it was impractical.*

**knock** sth **into** sth *phr v* [T] to make two rooms into one room by taking away the wall that divides them: *We knocked the sitting room and the dining room into one.*

**knock off** *phr v informal*
**1 ▶ STOP WORK ◀** [I] to stop working at the end of the day, before lunch etc: *What time do you knock off for lunch?* | **knock off early** *Is it okay if I knock off a little early today?* | **knock off work** *Alex usually knocks off work about 5:30.* | **knock off for the day** *We knocked off for the day at eight.*
**2 ▶ REDUCE A PRICE ◀** [T **knock** sth ↔ **off**] to reduce the price of something by a particular amount: *He said he'd knock off a couple of pounds if I bought two.*
**3 ▶ REDUCE AMOUNT ◀** [T **knock** sth ↔ **off**] to take a particular amount away from a total: *We're knocking off one mark for each mistake.*
**4 ▶ PRODUCE ◀** [T **knock** sth ↔ **off**] to produce something quickly and easily: *Roland makes huge amounts of money knocking off copies of famous paintings.*
**5 ▶ MURDER ◀** [T **knock** sb **off**] to murder someone
**6 ▶ STEAL ◀** [T **knock** sth ↔ **off**] *BrE* to steal something, especially easily
**7 ▶ SEX ◀** [T **knock** sb **off**] *BrE slang* to have sex with someone

**knock out** *phr v* [T]
**1 ▶ UNCONSCIOUS ◀** [**knock** sb/sth **out**] to make someone become unconscious: *Tyson knocked out his opponent in Round 5.* | *The shock from an electric eel is powerful enough to knock a man out.* —see also KNOCKOUT[1] (2)
**2 ▶ DEFEAT ◀** [**knock** sb/sth **out**] to defeat a person or team in a competition so that they can no longer take part: **knock sb out of** *Indiana knocked Purdue out of the semifinals.* —see also KNOCKOUT[4] (4)
**3 ▶ ADMIRE ◀** [**knock** sb **out**] *informal* to make you feel surprised and full of admiration: *The music was just brilliant – it really knocked me out.*
**4 ▶ SHOCK ◀** [**knock** sb **out**] *informal* to shock someone so much that they do not know what to say or do: *When she told me the real truth it just totally knocked me out.*
**5 ▶ PRODUCE WITH DIFFICULTY ◀** [**knock** sth ↔ **out**] *BrE informal* to produce something, especially when you find this difficult: *It took him several years to knock out a book on the subject.* | **knock sth ↔ out of** *Let's see if we can knock a decent sound out of this old piano.*
**6 ▶ PRODUCE EASILY ◀** [**knock** sth ↔ **out**] *AmE informal* to produce something easily and quickly, especially so that it is not of very good quality: *We can knock out about 50 dresses in a day.*
**7 knock yourself out** *informal* to work very hard in order to do something well: *The Nelsons really knocked themselves out to give Amy a nice wedding.*

**knock over** *phr v* [T] **1** [**knock** sb **over**] to hit someone with a car while you are driving, so that they are hurt or killed: *Beth was knocked over by a motorcyclist when she was crossing the street.* **2** [**knock** sth ↔ **over**] *AmE informal* to rob a place such as a shop or bank and threaten or attack the people who work there

**knock** sth ↔ **together** *phr v* [T] *informal* to make something quickly, using whatever you have available: *We should be able to knock something together with what's in the fridge.*

**knock up** *phr v* [T] **1** [**knock** sth ↔ **up**] *informal* to make something quickly and without using much effort: *A local carpenter knocked up some kitchen units for us out of old pine.* **2** [**knock** sb ↔ **up**] *BrE informal* to wake someone up by knocking on their door: *What time do you want me to knock you up in the morning?* **3** [**knock** sb **up**] *informal* to make a woman PREGNANT

**knock**[2] *n* **1** [C] the sound of something hard hitting a hard surface: *a loud knock at the door* | *a knock in the engine* **2** [C] the action of something hard hitting your body: *He got a knock on the head when he fell.* **3 take a knock** *informal* to have some bad luck or trouble: *Clive's taken quite a few hard knocks lately.*

**knock·a·bout** /ˈnɒkəbaʊt‖ˈnɑːk-/ *adj BrE* knockabout entertainers make people laugh with their silly behaviour, for example by falling over things and pushing each other around

**knock·down** /ˈnɒkdaʊn‖ˈnɑːk-/ *adj* [only before noun] a knockdown price is very cheap —see also **knock down** (KNOCK[1])

**knock-down-drag-out** /ˌ· · ˌ· ·/ *adj AmE* using the most extreme methods to win: *a knock-down-drag-out political campaign*

**knock·er** /ˈnɒkə‖ˈnɑːkər/ *n* **1** [C] a piece of metal on an outside door that you use to knock loudly **2 knockers** [plural] *slang* an offensive word meaning a woman's breasts **3** [C] someone who is always criticizing

**knock-kneed** /ˌ· ˈ·◂‖ˈ· ·/ *adj* having knees that point inwards slightly

**knock·off** /ˈnɒkɒf‖ˈnɑːkɔːf/ *n* [C] *AmE informal* a cheap copy of something expensive

**knock-on** /ˈ· ·/ *adj* **have a knock-on effect** to start a process in which each part is directly influenced by the one before it: *These price rises will have a knock-on effect throughout the economy.*

**knock·out**[1] /ˈnɒk-aʊt‖ˈnɑːk-/ *n* [C] **1** an act of knocking your opponent down in BOXING so that he cannot get up again: *The fight ended in a knockout.* **2 knockout punch/blow a)** a hard hit that knocks someone down so that they cannot get up again —see also **knock out** (KNOCK[1]) **b)** an action or event that causes defeat or failure: *High interest rates have been a knockout blow to the business.* **3** *informal* someone or something that is very attractive or successful: *Baby, you're a knockout.* **4** *BrE* a competition in which winning players or teams continue playing until there is only one winner

**knockout**[2] *adj informal* making someone unconscious: *knockout pills* | *the knockout punch*

**knock-up** /ˈ· ·/ *n* [C] *BrE* a short time before a game when the players practise, especially in tennis

**knoll** /nəʊl‖noʊl/ *n* [C] a small round hill

**knot**[1] /nɒt‖nɑːt/ *n* [C]
**1 ▶ TIED STRING ◀** a join made by tying together two ends of rope, cloth, string etc: *Here, let me fix the knot in your tie.* | *Can you help me undo this knot?*
**2 ▶ HAIR ◀ a)** a mass of hairs, threads etc accidentally twisted together: *I can't get the knots out of my hair.* **b)** a way of arranging your hair into a tight round shape at the back of your head
**3 ▶ SHIP'S SPEED ◀** written abbreviation KT a measure of speed used for ships and aircraft that is about 1853 metres per hour
**4 ▶ PEOPLE ◀** a small group of people standing close together
**5 ▶ HARD MASS ◀** a hard mass that is formed by a lot of things that are close together: *a knot of muscles*
**6 ▶ WOOD ◀** a hard round place in a piece of wood where a branch once joined the tree

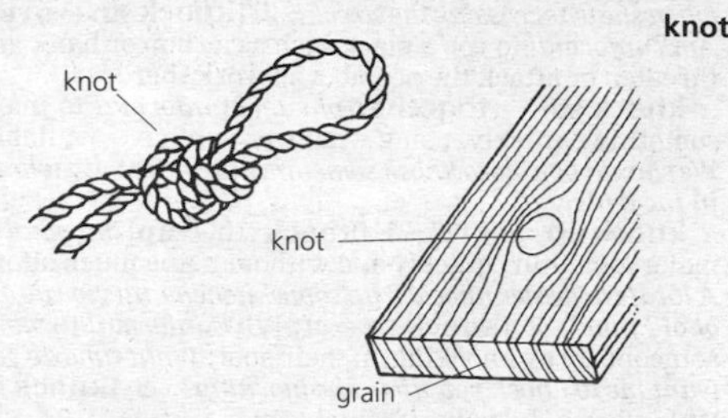


**7 a knot in your stomach/throat etc** a hard uncomfortable feeling in your stomach etc caused by a strong emotion such as fear or anger —see also GORDIAN KNOT, **at a rate of knots** (RATE[1] (7)), **tie the knot** (TIE[2] (4)), **tie yourself (up) in knots** (TIE[2] (5))

**knot[2]** *v* **knotted, knotting** **1** [T] to tie together two ends of rope, cloth, string etc **2** [I,T] **a)** if hair or threads knot they become twisted together **b) knot your hair** to arrange and fasten your hair into a tight round shape at the back of your head **3** [I,T] if a muscle or other part of your body knots, or is knotted it feels hard and uncomfortable: *Fear and anxiety knotted her stomach.*

**knot·ted** /ˈnɒtɪ̮d‖ˈnɑː-/ *adj*
**1** ► **FULL OF KNOTS** ◄ [only before noun] containing a lot of knots: *pieces of knotted string*
**2** ► **MUSCLE** ◄ if a muscle or other part of your body is knotted, it feels hard and uncomfortable: *knotted shoulder muscles*
**3 Get knotted!** *BrE spoken* used to tell someone rudely to go away or that you do not agree with them
**4** ► **HANDS** ◄ knotted hands or fingers are twisted because of old age or too much work

**knot·ty** /ˈnɒti‖ˈnɑːti/ *adj* **1** difficult to solve: *a knotty problem* **2** knotty wood contains a lot of KNOTS (=hard round places)

S1 W1

## know[1] /nəʊ‖noʊ/ *v past tense* knew /njuː‖nuː/ *past participle* known /nəʊn‖noʊn/

① INFORMATION
② I KNOW
③ I DON'T KNOW
④ YOU KNOW
⑤ BE CERTAIN
⑥ SKILL/EXPERIENCE
⑦ PERSON/PLACE
⑧ LANGUAGE/MUSIC ETC
⑨ REALIZE
⑩ RECOGNIZE
⑪ EXPERIENCE
⑫ SPOKEN PHRASES
⑬ OTHER MEANINGS

### ① INFORMATION

**1** [I,T not in progressive] to have information about something: *Who knows the answer?| Do you happen to know the time?| When are they arriving? Maybe Mrs. Mott knows.| instructions telling you everything you need to know| Marriage cancels a will, didn't you know that?| I had spoken without knowing all the facts.|* **know what/where/when etc** *Do you know what I'm supposed to be doing?| I don't know where to go.|* **know about** *The council has known about the leak for six months.|* **know all about** *spoken*: *We know all about David and what he's been up to!|* **know (that)** *She knew that her father was sick, but not how serious it was.|* **knowing that** (=because you know) *I went to bed early knowing that I had to get up at six a.m.|* **want to know** (=want to be told) *I want to know what happened.| I thought you'd want to know immediately.| "When do I start?" Carlos wanted to know.|* **I'm dying to know** *spoken* (=I am very eager to find out) *I'm dying to know who won!|* **without sb knowing** (=secretly, privately, or without someone being told) *You can't do anything without the whole town knowing.|* **know to do sth** (=know that you should do it) *She knows not to tell anyone about it.|* **know sth/sb to be sth** (=know that something is true about them) *a story which he knew to be true| I know him to be a good worker.|* **how do you know?** *spoken* (=how did you find out or what makes you think that?) *How did he know our names?| "Jason won't want to be involved." "How do you know?"|* **as you/we know** *spoken*: *As you know, there's been a tremendous revival of interest in the project.|* **as/so far as I know** (=I believe that it is true, but I am not certain) *No other athlete, so far as I know, has won so many medals.|* **know for certain/sure** *I think she's going but I don't know for sure.|* **know from experience** *I know from experience that he's got a foul temper.|* **I wouldn't know** *spoken* (=I do not know, and I am not the person you should ask) *"When is he coming back?" "I wouldn't know."|* **know the way** (=know how to get to a place) *Does he know the way to your house?*

**2 let sb know** to tell someone about something: *When it stops, let me know.| Give him this medicine, and let us know if he's not better in two days.| Thank you for your application; we'll let you know.* (=we will tell you soon whether you have been successful)| **let it be known (that)** (=let other people know what your opinions or intentions are): *The Prince has let it be known that he does not approve of his son's behaviour.*
**3 know sth inside out** also **know sth backwards** to know something extremely well: *We expect you to know these codes inside out, men.*

### ② I KNOW

**4 I know** *spoken* **a)** used to say that you have suddenly had an idea, thought of a solution to a problem, etc: *"What should we do?" "I know, we could ask Anne to help."* **b)** used to agree with someone or to say that you feel the same way: *"I'm so worn out!" "Yeah, I know."* **c)** used to prevent someone from objecting to what you say by saying the objection first: *It sounds silly, I know, but try it anyway.| I know, I know, I should have had the car checked out before now.*

### ③ I DON'T KNOW

**5 I don't know** *spoken* **a)** used to say that you do not have the answer to a question: *"When did they arrive?" "I don't know."| "Why did you do that?" "I don't know."* **b)** used to show that you disagree slightly with what has just been said: *"I couldn't live there." "Oh, I don't know. It might not be so bad."* **c)** used when you are not sure about something: *Oh, I don't know, sixty, seventy?|* [+ **if/whether/that**] *I don't know if I would want to teach.* **d)** used to show that you are slightly annoyed: *Oh, I don't know! You're hopeless!*
**6 I don't know how/why etc** used to criticize someone: *I don't know how people could treat a child like that.*

**7 I don't know whether you want to...?** *spoken* used to ask someone politely to do something: *I don't know whether you want to respond to that?*
**8 I don't know about you but...** *spoken* used to give an opinion, suggestion, or decision of your own which might be different from that of the person listening: *I don't know about you, but I'm going home.*
**9 I don't know how to thank you/repay you** *spoken formal* used to thank someone

④ **YOU KNOW**
**10 you know** *spoken* **a)** used to emphasize a statement: *There'll be trouble, you know.*|*I don't like to brag but, you know, I did do pretty well.* **b)** used when you need to keep someone's attention, but cannot think of what to say next: *I was just, you know, looking through my slides before you came.* **c)** used when you are explaining or describing something and want to give more information: *That padding that you put on the car, you know, that stuff on the doors.*
**11 you know/do you know** *spoken* used to start talking about something, or make someone listen: *You know your cousin? You'll never guess what she did!*|*You know, it's a sad thing about this guy.*|*Do you know, when I went out this morning that man was still there.*| **(do) you know what/something?** *But do you know what? He got fired.*

⑤ **BE CERTAIN**
**12** [I,T not in progressive] to be sure about something: *I just know I won't get the job.*|*I knew you'd say that.*|*The boy stared at him uncertainly, not knowing whether to believe him.*|**how do you know?** (=what makes you feel certain?) *How do you know he won't do it again?*

⑥ **SKILL/EXPERIENCE**
**13** [T not in progressive] to have learned a lot about something or be skilful and experienced at doing something: *I don't know enough history to make a comparison.*|*I taught him everything he knows.*| **know how to** *Do you know how to change a fuse?*| **know about** *I have a friend who knows about antiques.*|**know all about** *Politicians know all about the power of language.*|**know what you are doing** (=have enough skill and experience to deal with something properly)|**know what you are talking about** *You listen to Aunt Kate, she knows what she's talking about.*|**know your job/subject** also **know your stuff** (=be good at and know all you should know about a job or subject)
**14 think you know everything/think you know all the answers** to behave in a way that is too confident, always trying to give people advice
**15 know a thing or two** *informal* to have a lot of useful information gained from experience

⑦ **PERSON/PLACE**
**16** [T] to be familiar with a person, place, etc: *I've known her for twenty years.*|*Are you really thinking of leaving Kevin for a guy you barely know?*|*Anyone who knows his work and who knows Wales will see the connection.*|*Do you know the Boy's Club in Claremont?*| **know sb well** *We did not know each other well enough to talk freely.*|**get to know** *I'm getting to know the neighbors.*|*You need time to get to know a new instrument.*|**as we know it** (=in the form that we are familiar with) *That will mean an end to the Tory Party as we know it.*|**know sb/sth inside out** (=be very familiar with them) *We need someone who knows the area inside out.*|*That's the thing about Mom, she knows me inside out.*|**know sb by sight** (=often see them, but not know them well) *I know her by sight, but I don't think I've ever spoken to her.*|**knowing him/if I know him** (=I know what he is like and expect him to do a particular thing) *Knowing Sumi, my note's probably still in her pocket.*|*He'll be chatting up the women, if I know Ron!*

⑧ **LANGUAGE/MUSIC ETC**
**17 know a language** to be able to speak, read, and understand a foreign language: *I know some French.*
**18 know a song/a tune/a poem etc** to be able to sing a song, play a tune, say a poem etc because you have learned it: *Do you know all the words to 'As Time Goes By'?*|**know sth (off) by heart** (=to have learned it and be able to repeat it from memory)

⑨ **REALIZE**
**19** [I,T] to realize, find out about, or understand something: *Miss Brown knew as soon as she came in that something was wrong.*|*Hardly knowing what he was doing, Nick pulled out a cigarette.*|*I know I have been avoiding the issue.*|**(do/if) you know what I mean?** *spoken* (=used to ask if someone has understood you) *It's nice to have a change sometimes. Know what I mean?*|**I/she etc should have known** *spoken* (=used to say that someone ought to have realized something) *I should have known it would take this long.*|**I might have known** *BrE spoken* (=I should not be surprised that something has happened, but I am annoyed) *I might have known you'd be mixed up in this mess!*|**know exactly/precisely** *I know exactly how you feel.*|**know perfectly well/full well/only too well** *You know perfectly well what I mean.*|**sb will never know/no one will ever know** (=no one will realize that something has happened) *Just take it, no one will ever know.*|**and you know it** *spoken*: *This has nothing to do with gratitude and you know it.*|**if I had known/if I'd have known** *If I had known they were in trouble, I'd have gone to help.*|**little did she know** *literary*: *As she closed the door, she little knew that this was the last time she would leave this house.*

⑩ **RECOGNIZE**
**20** [T] to be able to recognize someone or something: *Honestly, it had been so long, I hardly knew her.*|[+ **by**] *He looked very different, but I knew him by his voice.*
**21 know sth from sth** to understand the difference between one thing and another: *Lloyd doesn't even know his right from his left.*|*She knows right from wrong: she can't claim she was insane.*
**22 not know sb from Adam** *informal* to not know who someone is at all

⑪ **EXPERIENCE**
**23** [T] to live through an experience: *I never knew an American before Vietnam.*|[+ **about**] *I know all about being poor, so don't think I don't.*
**24 I've never known** used to say that you have never heard of or experienced something as surprising as the thing you are decribing: *This weather is amazing. I've never known anything like it!*
**25 I've never known sb to do sth** used to say that someone never does something: *I've never known him to iron anything.*
**26 sb/sth is not known to be sth** also **sb/sth has never been known to do sth** used to say that there is no information that says that a person or animal behaves in a particular way: *This species is not known to be vicious.*
**27 I've known sb to do sth** also **sb has been known to do sth** used to say that someone does something sometimes, even if it is unusual: *Watch it. He's been known to eat a whole pizza himself!*

⑫ **SPOKEN PHRASES**
**28 you never know** used to say that it is possible that something good may happen: *I might be able to catch the earlier train, you never know.*
**29 how should I know?/how am I to know?/how do I know?** used to say that it is not reasonable to expect that you should know something: *"What's it like?" "I haven't seen it, so how should I know?"*
**30 how was I to know?/how did I know?** used as an excuse or to say that you are sorry: *It's not my fault – how was I to know it would rain!*
**31 I ought to know** used to emphasize that you know about something because you made it, experienced it etc: *"Are you sure there's no sugar in it?" "Of course. I ought to know, I made it!"*
**32 not that I know of** used when answering a question to say that you believe that the answer is 'no', but

[continued on next page]

[continued from previous page]
there may be facts that you do not know about: *"Andrew didn't phone today, did he?" "Not that I know of."*
**33 if you must know** used when you are annoyed at having to give information to someone: *"Where is it?" "In an envelope, if you must know," said James impatiently.*
**34 for all I know** used to say that you do not know about something and it does not really matter because you are not involved or affected: *It cost millions. It could be billions for all I know.*
**35 there's no knowing** it is impossible to know: *There is no knowing what she will do next.*
**36 (I'm/I'll be) damned if I know!** used to emphasize that you do not know something, and are annoyed or think something is hopeless: *"Whatever are we going to do?" "Damned if I know."*
**37 Heaven/God/who/goodness knows! a)** used to say that you do not have any idea what an answer might be, and do not expect to know: *"Where do you think he's disappeared to this time?" "God knows!"* **b)** used to emphasize a statement: *I haven't seen her for goodness knows how long.* | *It might make us more efficient, which heaven knows we need.*
**38 not want to know** *informal* to refuse to listen to a complaint or a problem: *We phoned the council about the damage, but they just didn't want to know.*
**39 knowing my luck** used to say that you expect something bad will happen because you are usually unlucky: *Knowing his luck, he'll get hit with a golf ball or something.*
**40 (well,) what do you know!** used to express surprise: *Well, what do you know – look who's arrived!*
**41 the next thing you know** used to say that something happens suddenly and unexpectedly: *One minute everybody's laughing and the next thing you know, they're all arguing!*
**42 I will (want to) know the reason why** an expression meaning you will want an explanation, used in a threatening way: *It had better be right this time, or I'll know the reason why.*
**43 if you know what's good for you** used to tell someone that they should do something, or you will harm them in some way: *You'll just keep your mouth shut about this if you know what's good for you!*
**44 you know who/what** used to talk about someone or something without mentioning their name: *I saw you know who yesterday.*

**⑬ OTHER MEANINGS**
**45 be known as** to also be called something: *Chicago is known as 'the windy city'.*
**46 know better a)** to be wise or experienced enough to avoid making mistakes: **know better than to...** *She ought to know better than to expect any help from Roger.* **b)** to know or think you know more than someone else: *They said it was gold, but Sharon knew better.*
**47 know best** used to say that someone should be obeyed or that their way of doing things should be accepted because they are experienced: *I think I know best how to deal with my own staff!* | **Mother/Father etc knows best** *Don't argue. Daddy knows best!*
**48 know your own mind** to be confident and have firm ideas about what you want and like
**49 you will be delighted/pleased to know that** *formal* used before you give someone information that they will be pleased to hear: *You will be pleased to know that we have accepted your offer.* — see also **know no bounds** (BOUND[4] (6)), **know the ropes** (ROPE[1] (2)), **know the score** (SCORE[1] (5)), **know your place** (PLACE[1] (31)), **not know what hit you** (HIT[1] (14))
**know of** sb/sth *phr v* [T] to have been told or to have read that something exists, but not know much about it: *I know of one company that makes these things.*

**USAGE NOTE: KNOW**

WORD CHOICE: **know, find out, hear/read about, get to know, learn, study**

If you **know** a fact, person, or place, or how to speak a language, drive a car etc, you have information about it in your mind, or the skills to do it.

Often you **know** something only after you have **heard or read about** it, or if you have **found it out** (especially deliberately) or **got to know** about it (especially by chance): *When he heard about the affair he became extremely angry.* | *I use my dictionary to find out the correct pronunciation* (NOT *know*). | *During the visit we got to know something about the American way of life.* You also **get to know** a person.

If you **learn** something, that may mean that you **find it out**, but this is a formal use of the word: *He learnt the news/that he had won a prize.* Usually to **learn** means to make an effort to remember something you have found out or been taught, or to practise a skill, so that you then **know** it: *I'm trying to learn the names of all the students in my class* (NOT *know*). | *She is learning English/learning to drive.*

If you spend time learning about something, especially in a school, university etc you **study** it: *Gina is studying engineering at London University.*

Frequencies of the verb **know** in spoken and written English.

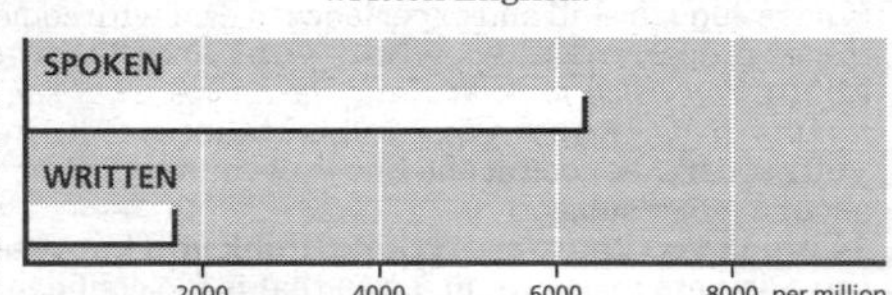


Based on the British National Corpus and the Longman Lancaster Corpus

This graph shows that the verb **know** is much more common in spoken English than in written English. This is because it is used in a lot of common spoken phrases. These are marked *spoken* in the entry.

**know²** *n* **in the know** *informal* having more information about something than most people: *People in the know say that interest rates will have to rise again soon.*

**know-all** /ˈ· ·/ *n* [C] *BrE informal* someone who behaves as if they know everything; KNOW-IT-ALL *AmE*

**know-how** /ˈ· ·/ *n* [U] *informal* practical ability or skill: *Jeff needs more technical know-how to do his new job.*

**know·ing** /ˈnəʊɪŋ‖ˈnoʊ-/ *adj* showing that you know all about something: *He said nothing but gave us a knowing look.*

**know·ing·ly** /ˈnəʊɪŋli‖ˈnoʊ-/ *adv* **1** in a way that shows you know about something secret or embarrassing: *She smiled knowingly at us.* **2** deliberately: *He would never knowingly upset people.*

**know-it-all** /ˈ· · ·/ *n* [C] *informal especially AmE* someone who behaves as if they know everything; KNOW-ALL *BrE*

**knowl·edge** /ˈnɒlɪdʒ‖ˈnɑː-/ *n* [U] **1** the facts, skills, and understanding that you have gained through learning or experience: *You need specialist knowledge to do this job.* | [+ **of**] *His knowledge of ancient civilizations is unrivalled.* | [+ **about**] *We now have greater knowledge about the risks of using these chemicals.* **2 in the knowledge that** knowing that something has happened or is true: *Kay smiled, secure in the knowledge that she was right.* **3 not to your knowledge** *spoken* used to say that something is not true, based on what you know: *"Is it true that she's leaving the company?" "Not to my*

knowledge." **4** information that you have about a particular situation, event etc: **in full knowledge of** (=knowing all the details of a situation) *He acted in full knowledge of the possible consequences.* | **deny all knowledge of sth** (=say that you do not know anything about it) *Evans denied all knowledge of the robbery.* | **come to sb's knowledge** *formal* (=become known about) *The incident first came to our knowledge about a fortnight ago.* | **bring sth to sb's knowledge** *formal* (=give someone information they did not know) **5 to the best of your knowledge** used to say that you think something is true, although you may not have all the facts: *To the best of my knowledge the new project will be starting in June.* **6 without your knowledge** without knowing what is happening: *He was annoyed to find the contract had been signed without his knowledge.* —see also GENERAL KNOWLEDGE, **common knowledge** (COMMON[1] (3)), **working knowledge** (WORKING[1] (5))

**knowl·edge·a·ble** /ˈnɒlɪdʒəbəl‖ˈnɑː-/ *adj* knowing a lot: [+ **about**] *Graham's very knowledgeable about wines.* —**knowledgeably** *adv*

**known[1]** /nəʊn‖noʊn/ the past participle of KNOW[1]

W3 **known[2]** *adj* [only before noun] known about, especially by many people: *a known crack dealer* | *Yes, yes, it's a known problem.* | **be known for** (=be famous for) *The Saumar region is known for its sparkling wines.* —see also **little-known, well-known**

**knuck·le[1]** /ˈnʌkəl/ *n* **1** [C] the joints in your fingers including the ones where your fingers join your hands **2** [C] a piece of meat around the lowest leg joint: *a knuckle of pork* **3 near the knuckle** *BrE informal* rude, or likely to give offence: *Some of his jokes are a bit near the knuckle.* —see also **a rap on/over the knuckles** (RAP[2] (4))

**knuckle[2]** *v*

**knuckle down** *phr v* [I] *informal* to suddenly start working or studying hard: *If he doesn't knuckle down soon, he'll never get through those exams.*

**knuckle under** *phr v* [I] *informal* to accept someone's authority or orders without wanting to

**knuckle-dust·er** /ˈ·· ˌ··/ *n* [C] a metal covering for the backs of the fingers, used as a weapon

**knuck·le·head** /ˈnʌkəlhed/ *n* [C] *AmE spoken* used to address someone who you like who has done something stupid: *You knucklehead, you can't go around saying things like that!*

**ko·a·la** /kəʊˈɑːlə‖koʊ-/ also **koala bear** /·ˌ·· ˈ·/ *n* [C] an Australian animal like a small bear with no tail that climbs trees

**kohl** /kəʊl‖koʊl/ *n* [U] a black pencil used around women's eyes to make them more attractive

**kook** /kuːk/ *n* [C] *AmE informal* someone who is silly or crazy —**kooky** *adj*

**kook·a·bur·ra** /ˈkʊkəbʌrə/ *n* [C] an Australian bird whose song sounds like laughter

**Ko·ran, Qur'an** /kɔːˈrɑːn, kə-‖kəˈræn, -ˈrɑːn/ *n* **the Koran** the holy book of the Muslims —**Koranic** *adj*

**kor·ma** /ˈkɔːmə‖ˈkɔːr-/ *n* [U] an Indian dish made with meat and cream: *chicken korma*

**ko·sher** /ˈkəʊʃə‖ˈkoʊʃər/ *adj* **1 a)** kosher food is prepared according to Jewish law **b)** kosher restaurants or shops sell food prepared in this way **2** *informal* honest or lawful; actually being what is claimed: *Are you sure this offer is kosher?*

**kow·tow** /ˌkaʊˈtaʊ/ *v* [I + **to**] *informal* to be too eager to obey or be polite to someone in authority

**KP** /ˌkeɪ ˈpiː/ *n* [U] *AmE* work that soldiers or children at a camp have to do in a kitchen

**kph** the written abbreviation of kilometres per hour

**kraal** /krɑːl/ *n* [C] **1** a village in South Africa with a fence around it **2** *SAfrE* an enclosed piece of ground in which cows, sheep, etc are kept at night

**kraut** /kraʊt/ *n* [C] *slang* an insulting word for someone from Germany

**Krem·lin** /ˈkremlən/ *n* **the Kremlin a)** the government of Russia and the former USSR **b)** the government buildings of Russia and the former USSR in Moscow

**krill** /krɪl/ *n* [U] small SHELLFISH

**Kriss Krin·gle** /ˌkrɪs ˈkrɪŋgəl/ *n* [singular] *AmE* another name for SANTA CLAUS

**kro·na** /ˈkrəʊnə‖ˈkroʊ-/ *n plural* **kronor** /-nɔː‖-nɔːr/ or **kronur** /-nə‖-nər/ the standard unit of money in Sweden and Iceland

**kro·ne** /ˈkrəʊnə‖ˈkroʊ-/ *n plural* **kroner** /-nə‖-nər/ [C] the standard unit of money in Denmark and Norway

**Kru·ger·rand** /ˈkruːgəˌrænd/ *n* [C] a South African gold coin

**kryp·ton** /ˈkrɪptɒn‖-tɑːn/ *n* [U] a gas that is an ELEMENT (=basic substance), found in the air

**Kt** the written abbreviation of KNIGHT

**kt** the written abbreviation of KNOT[1] (3)

**ku·dos** /ˈkjuːdɒs‖ˈkuːdɑːs/ *n* [U] admiration and respect that you get for being important or doing something important

**Ku Klux Klan** /ˌkuː klʌks ˈklæn/ *n* **the Ku Klux Klan** a secret American political organization of Protestant white men who oppose people of other races or religions

**kum·quat** /ˈkʌmkwɒt‖-kwɑːt/ *n* [C] the American spelling of CUMQUAT

**kung fu** /ˌkʌŋ ˈfuː/ *n* [U] an ancient Chinese fighting art in which you attack people with your hands and feet

**Kurd** /kɜːd‖kɜːrd/ *n* [C] a member of a people living in countries such as Iran, Iraq, and Turkey

**kvetch** /kvetʃ/ *v* [I] *AmE informal* to continually complain about something —**kvetch** *n* [C]

**kw** the written abbreviation of KILOWATT

**kwe·la** /ˈkweɪlə/ *n* [U] a kind of dance music popular among black South African people

**kwh** the written abbreviation of KILOWATTS per hour

**L, l** /el/ *plural* **L's, l's** *n* [C] **1** the 12th letter of the English alphabet **2** the number 50 in the system of ROMAN NUMERALS

**l** **1** the written abbreviation of LITRE **2** the written abbreviation of line **3** also **L** the written abbreviation of lake

**la** /lɑː/ *n* [singular] the sixth note in a musical SCALE[1] (8), according to the SOL-FA system

**Lab** the written abbreviation of LABOUR PARTY

**lab** /læb/ *n* [C] *informal* a LABORATORY

W3 **la·bel**[1] /ˈleɪbəl/ *n* [C] **1** a piece of paper or other material that is stuck onto something and gives information about it: *a luggage label* **2** the name of a record company: *their new release on the Ace Sounds label* **3** a word or phrase which is used to describe a person, group, or thing, but which is unfair or not correct: *Men tend to accept these arrangements in order to avoid attracting the 'sexist' label.*

**label**[2] *v* **labelled, labelling** *BrE,* **labeled, labeling** *AmE* [T] **1** to fix a label onto something or write information on something: *Label the diagram as shown.* | **label sth poison/secret etc** *The file was labelled 'Top Secret'.* **2** to use a word or phrase to describe someone or something, but often unfairly or incorrectly: **label sb/sth (as) sth** *The newspapers had unjustly labelled him a troublemaker.*

**la·bi·a** /ˈleɪbiə/ *n* [plural] the outer folds of the female sex organ

**la·bi·al** /ˈleɪbiəl/ *n* [C] *technical* a speech sound made using one or both lips —**labial** *adj* —see also BILABIAL

**la·bor** /ˈleɪbə‖-ər/ *n* [U] the American spelling of LABOUR

**la·bor·a·to·ry** /ləˈbɒrətri‖ˈlæbrətɔːri/ *n* [C] a special room or building in which a scientist tests and prepares substances: *a research laboratory* | **laboratory experiments/animals etc** *tests on laboratory animals* —see also LANGUAGE LABORATORY W

**Labor Day** /ˈ‥ ˌ‥/ *n AmE* a public holiday in the US on the first Monday in September

**la·bored** /ˈleɪbəd‖-bərd/ *adj* the American spelling of LABOURED

**la·bor·er** /ˈleɪbərə‖-bərər/ *n* [C] the American spelling of LABOURER

**labor-in·ten·sive** /ˌ‥ ·ˈ‥◂/ *adj* the American spelling of LABOUR-INTENSIVE

**la·bo·ri·ous** /ləˈbɔːriəs/ *adj* **1 laborious task/process/method etc** a job or piece of work that is difficult and needs a lot of effort: *the laborious task of collating all the evidence* **2** seeming to be done slowly and with difficulty: *laborious progress through the work* —**laboriously** *adv* | *Selina was laboriously copying out her homework.* —**laboriousness** *n* [U]

**labor-sav·ing** /ˈ‥ ˌ‥/ *adj* the American spelling of LABOUR-SAVING

**labor u·nion** /ˈ‥ ˌ‥/ *n* [C] *AmE* an organization that represents the ordinary workers in a particular trade or profession, especially in meetings with employers; TRADE UNION *BrE*

**laboratory**

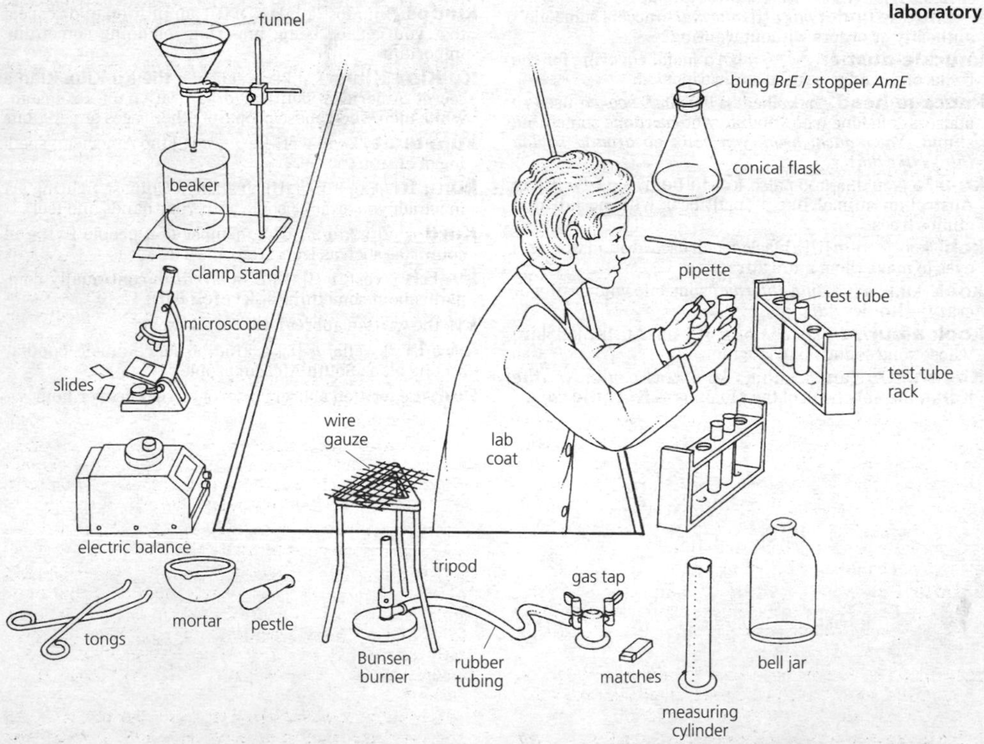

funnel
beaker
clamp stand
microscope
slides
electric balance
tongs
mortar
pestle
wire gauze
tripod
Bunsen burner
rubber tubing
lab coat
gas tap
matches
measuring cylinder
bell jar
bung *BrE* / stopper *AmE*
conical flask
pipette
test tube
test tube rack

S3 W1 **la·bour¹** *BrE*, **labor** *AmE* /ˈleɪbə‖-ər/ *n*
**1 ▶ WORK ◀** [U] effort or work, especially physical work: *The garage charges £30 an hour for labour.* | **manual labour** (=work with tools you hold in your hands) *Building still involves a lot of manual labour.* | **withdraw your labour** (=protest by stopping work) *Workers withdrew their labour for twenty-four hours.* —see also HARD LABOUR
**2 ▶ WORKERS ◀** [U] all the people who work for a company or in a country: *Organized labour banded together to fight the anti-union laws.* | **skilled/unskilled labour** *a shortage of skilled labor* | **cheap labour** (=people who are paid very low wages) | **labour costs/shortages etc** *Immigrants may help to solve labour shortages.* —see also LABOUR FORCE
**3 ▶ BABY ◀** [singular, U] the process in which a baby is born by being pushed from its mother's body, or the period of time during which this happens: **be in labour** *Meg was in labour for 6 hours.* | **go into labour** *Diane went into labour at 2 o'clock.* | **labour pains/ward/room** *No men were allowed in the labour room.*
**4 a labour of love** something that is hard work but that you do because you want to
**5 my/your labours** *formal* a period of hard work: *We sat down to rest after our labours.*

**labour²** *BrE*, **labor** *AmE* —*v* **1** [I] to try very hard to do something; struggle: [**+ over**] *I've been labouring over this report all morning.* | **labour to do sth** *Ray had little talent but labored to acquire the skills of a writer.* **2** [I] to work hard: *Marina had laboured late into the night to finish her essay.* **3 labour under a delusion/misconception/misapprehension etc** to believe something that is not true **4 labour the point** to describe or explain something in too much detail or when people have already understood it **5** [I] if an engine labours it turns too slowly and with difficulty

**Labour¹** *n* [U, not with *the*] the British LABOUR PARTY: *We all vote Labour in this house.*

**Labour²** *adj* supporting or connected with the British LABOUR PARTY: *a Labour MP* | *Labour policies*

**labour camp** *BrE*, **labor camp** *AmE* /ˈ· · ·/ *n* [C] a prison camp where prisoners have to do hard physical work

**la·boured** *BrE*, **labored** *AmE* /ˈleɪbəd‖-bərd/ *adj* showing signs of effort and difficulty: *laboured breathing*

**la·bour·er** *BrE*, **laborer** *AmE* /ˈleɪbərə‖-ər/ *n* [C] someone whose work needs strength rather than skill, especially someone who works outdoors: *a farm labourer*

**labour ex·change** /ˈ· · ˌ·/ *n* [C] a former British government office where people went to find jobs —compare JOB CENTRE

**labour force** *BrE*, **labor force** *AmE* /ˈ· · ·/ *n* **the labour force** all the people who work for a company or in a country

**labour-in·ten·sive** *BrE*, **labor-intensive** *AmE* /ˌ·· ·ˈ··◂/ *adj* an industry or type of work that is labour-intensive needs a lot of workers: *labour-intensive farming methods* —see also CAPITAL INTENSIVE

**labour mar·ket** *BrE*, **labor market** *AmE* /ˈ·· ˌ··/ *n* **the labour market** the combination of workers available and jobs available in one place at one time: *married women re-entering the labor market*

**labour move·ment** *BrE*, **labor movement** *AmE* /ˈ·· ˌ··/ *n* **the labour movement** the political parties representing working people, and all other organizations which have the same beliefs and aims

**Labour Par·ty** /ˈ·· ˌ··/ *n* **the Labour Party** a political party in Britain and some other countries that aims to improve social conditions for ordinary working people and poorer people

**labour re·la·tions** *BrE*, **labor relations** *AmE* /ˈ·· ·ˌ··/ *n* [plural] the relationship between employers and workers: *a company with good labour relations*

**labour-sav·ing** *BrE*, **labor-saving** *AmE* /ˈ·· ˌ··/ *adj* [only before noun] **labour-saving device/gadget/equipment etc** something that makes it easier for you to do a particular job

**Lab·ra·dor** /ˈlæbrədɔː‖-ɔːr/ *n* [C] a large dog with fairly short black or yellow hair —see picture at DOG¹

**la·bur·num** /ləˈbɜːnəm‖-ɜːr-/ *n* [C,U] a small tree with long hanging stems of yellow flowers and poisonous seeds

**lab·y·rinth** /ˈlæbərɪnθ/ *n* [C] **1** a large network of paths or passages which cross each other, making it very difficult to find your way; MAZE (3): [**+ of**] *a labyrinth of long corridors* **2** something that is very complicated and difficult to understand: [**+ of**] *a labyrinth of EC directives* —**labyrinthine** /ˌlæbəˈrɪnθaɪn◂/ *adj*: *the labyrinthine complexity of bureaucracy*

**lace¹** /leɪs/ *n* **1** [U] a fine cloth made with patterns of many very small holes: *a handkerchief trimmed with lace* | *lace curtains* —see also LACY —see picture on page 839 **2** [C] a string that is pulled through special holes in shoes or clothing to pull the edges together and fasten them —see picture at SHOE¹

**lace²** *v* [T] **1** also **lace up** to pull something together or fasten something by tying a LACE¹ (2): *Lace up your shoes or you'll trip over.* | **lace sth to** *The canvas was laced to a steel frame.* **2** to pass a string or LACE¹ (2) through holes in something such as a pair of shoes **3** to add a small amount of alcohol or a drug to a drink: **lace sth with** *coffee laced with Irish whiskey* **4 be laced with** if a book, lesson, speech etc is laced with something, it has a lot of a particular quality all through it: *The novel is laced with sexual imagery.* **5** *literary* to weave or twist something together: *Hannah laced her fingers together.*

**la·ce·rate** /ˈlæsəreɪt/ *v* [T] to tear skin or flesh with something sharp: *badly lacerated by bomb fragments*

**la·ce·ra·tion** /ˌlæsəˈreɪʃən/ *n* [C,U] *technical* serious cuts in your skin or flesh: [**+ to**] *multiple lacerations to the upper arms*

**lace-up** /ˈ· ·/ *n* [C usually plural] *especially BrE* shoes fastened with laces (LACE¹ (2)) —**lace-up** *adj*: *shiny black lace-up shoes*

**lach·ry·mal** /ˈlækrɪməl/ *adj technical* connected with tears: *lachrymal glands*

**lach·ry·mose** /ˈlækrɪməʊs‖-moʊs/ *adj formal* **1** often crying; TEARFUL: *Avril was feeling tired and lachrymose.* **2** making you feel sad: *lachrymose drama*

**lack¹** /læk/ *n* [singular, U] the state of not having something, or of not having enough of it: [**+ of**] *Lack of vitamin B can produce a variety of symptoms.* | **a complete/distinct/marked/total lack of** *Rosie was showing a marked lack of interest in her school work.* | **for/through lack of** (=because there is a lack of) *new mums, exhausted through lack of sleep* | **no lack of** (=used when there is a lot of something) *There was no lack of willing helpers.* S3 W2

**lack²** *v* **1** [T] to not have something that you need, or not have enough of it: *Alex's real problem is that he lacks confidence.* **2 lack for nothing** *formal* to have everything that you need: *Russell's parents made sure that he lacked for nothing.* W3

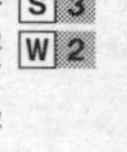

**lack·a·dai·si·cal** /ˌlækəˈdeɪzɪkəl◂/ *adj* not showing enough interest in something or not putting enough effort into it: *David has a rather lackadaisical approach to his work.* —**lackadaisically** /-kli/ *adv*

**lack·ey** /ˈlæki/ *n* [C] someone who behaves like a servant by always doing what someone else tells them to

**lack·ing** /ˈlækɪŋ/ *adj* [not before noun] **1 be lacking in** to not have enough of something such as a quality or skill: *She seems to be sadly lacking in tact.* **2** if something that you need is lacking, you do not have it: *Financial backing for the project is still lacking.* **3** *old-fashioned* not very intelligent: *The poor lad's a bit lacking.*

**lack·lus·tre** *BrE*, **lackluster** *AmE* /ˈlækˌlʌstə‖-ər/ *adj* not very exciting, impressive etc; dull: *a lacklustre performance* | *lacklustre hair*

**la·con·ic** /lə'kɒnɪk‖-'kɑː-/ *adj* using only a few words to say something **—laconically** /-kli/ *adv*

**lac·quer¹** /'lækə‖-ər/ *n* [U] **1** a liquid painted onto metal or wood to form a hard shiny surface **2** *old-fashioned* a transparent liquid that you put on your hair so that it keeps its shape

**lacquer²** *v* [T] **1** to cover something with LACQUER¹ (1): *a black lacquered box* **2** to use LACQUER¹ (2) on your hair

**la·crosse** /lə'krɒs‖lə'krɔːs/ *n* [U] a game played on a field by two teams of ten players, in which each player has a long stick with a net on the end of it and uses this to throw, catch and carry a small ball

**lac·tate** /læk'teɪt‖'lækteɪt/ *v* [I] *technical* to produce milk in your breasts

**lac·ta·tion** /læk'teɪʃən/ *n* [U] *technical* the production of milk in a mother's breasts for her baby, or the period during which this milk is produced

**lac·tic** /'læktɪk/ *adj technical* connected with milk

**lactic a·cid** /ˌ·· '··/ *n* [U] an acid found in sour milk and used to help keep food fresh

**lac·tose** /'læktəʊs‖-toʊs/ *n* [U] a type of sugar found in milk, sometimes used as a food for babies and sick people

**la·cu·na** /lə'kjuːnə‖-'kuː-/ *n plural* **lacunae** /-niː/ or **lacunas** [C] *formal* an empty space in a piece of writing, where something is missing

**lac·y** /'leɪsi/ *adj* made of LACE¹ (1) or looking like lace: *lacy underwear | a plant with delicate, lacy leaves*

S3 W3 **lad** /læd/ *n* [C] *old-fashioned or literary* **1** a boy or young man: *Things were different when I was a lad.* **2 the lads** *BrE spoken* a group of men you know and work with or spend your free time with: *a night out with the lads* | **one of the lads** (=a member of your group of friends) **3** a boy or man who works with horses; STABLE BOY **4 a bit of a lad** *BrE spoken* a man that people like even though he behaves rather badly: *That Charlie's a bit of a lad, isn't he?* —compare LASS —see also JACK THE LAD

S3 **lad·der¹** /'lædə‖-ər/ *n* [C] **1** a piece of equipment for climbing a wall, the side of a building etc, consisting of two long pieces of wood, metal, or rope, joined to each other by RUNGS (=steps) —see also ROPE LADDER, STEPLADDER **2** a series of jobs by which you gradually become more important within an organization: *clerical workers on the bottom rung of the ladder* **3** *BrE* a long thin hole in knitted (KNIT (1)) clothing, STOCKINGS or TIGHTS where stitches have broken; RUN² (19) *AmE* **4** a list of players of a game such as SQUASH or tennis who play each other regularly in order to decide who is the best —see also SNAKES AND LADDERS

**ladder²** *v* [I,T] *BrE* if a STOCKING (1) or a pair of TIGHTS ladders or is laddered, a long thin hole is made in them; RUN² (19) *AmE*

**lad·die, laddy** /'lædi/ *n* [C] *informal especially BrE* a boy

**la·den** /'leɪdn/ *adj literary* **1** heavily loaded with something: **[+ with]** *a Christmas tree laden with presents* | **fully/heavily laden** *The lorry was fully laden.* **2 laden with troubles/problems etc** full of troubles etc: *Antonia was laden with doubts about the affair.*

**ladies' man** /'·· ·/ *n* [C] a man who likes to spend time with women and thinks they enjoy being with him

**ladies' room** /'·· ·/ *n* [C] *AmE* a women's toilet; the ladies *BrE*

**la·ding** /'leɪdɪŋ/ *n* [C,U] see BILL OF LADING

**la·dle¹** /'leɪdl/ *n* [C] a large deep spoon with a long handle, used for lifting liquid out of a container: *a soup ladle* —see picture at SPOON¹

**ladle²** *v* [T] to serve soup or other food onto plates or bowls, especially using a ladle

**ladle** sth ↔ **out** *phr v* [T] to give someone too much of something such as advice or praise, without thinking carefully about it: *ladling out compliments*

S2 W2 **la·dy** /'leɪdi/ *n plural* **ladies** [C]
**1 ▶ WOMAN ◀ a)** a word meaning woman, used because people think it is a more polite word: *Give your coat to the lady over there. | The young lady at reception sent me up here. | the ladies' darts team* | **tea lady/cleaning lady etc** (=a woman who does a particular job) | **lady doctor/councillor etc** (=a polite word, which many women find offensive, for a woman doctor, councillor, etc) —see also DINNER LADY **b)** *approving especially AmE* a woman, especially one with a strong character: *She's a real smart lady.*
**2 ▶ POLITE WOMAN ◀** a woman who is always polite and behaves very well: *Sheila always tries to be a lady.*
**3 ▶ WOMAN OF HIGH CLASS ◀** a woman born into a high social class in Britain: *a lady of noble birth*
**4 ▶ WIFE/GIRL FRIEND ◀** *old-fashioned or literary* a man's wife or female friend: *the captain and his lady*
**5 ▶ WHEN SPEAKING TO A WOMAN ◀** *AmE* a way of addressing a woman, which many women consider to be offensive: *Hey, lady, watch where you're going!*
**6 the ladies** *BrE* a women's toilet; LADIES ROOM *AmE* —compare **the gents** (GENT (2))
**7 Lady a)** used as the title of the wife or daughter of a British NOBLEMAN or the wife of a KNIGHT¹ (2): *Lady Diana* **b)** *BrE* used in the title of women with a high official position: *Lady President*
**8 the lady of the house** *old-fashioned* the most important woman in a house, usually the mother of a family
**9 lady of leisure** *often humorous* a woman who does not work and has a lot of free time: *So you're a lady of leisure now that the kids are at school?*
**10 lady friend** *often humorous* a man's female friend; GIRLFRIEND: *I saw him with his new lady friend.* —see also BAG LADY, FIRST LADY, OLD LADY, OUR LADY

**la·dy·bird** /'leɪdibɜːd‖-bɜːrd/ *BrE*, **la·dy·bug** /'leɪdibʌg/ *n* [C] *AmE* a small round BEETLE (=a type of insect) that is usually red with black spots

**la·dy·fin·ger** /'leɪdiˌfɪŋgə‖-ər/ *n* [C] *AmE* a small cake shaped like a finger, used to make DESSERTS

**lady-in-wait·ing** /ˌ··· '··/ *n* [C] a woman who looks after and serves a queen or PRINCESS

**lady-kill·er** /'·· ˌ··/ *n* [C] *informal* a man who is very attractive to women but treats them badly: *Matt thinks he's such a lady-killer.*

**la·dy·like** /'leɪdilaɪk/ *adj old-fashioned* behaving in the polite, quiet way that was once supposed to be typical of or suitable for women: *scratching herself in a way that was certainly not ladylike*

**Lady Muck** /ˌ·· '·/ *n* [C] *humorous* a woman who has a very high opinion of her own importance: *Look at Lady Muck over there with her parasol.*

**la·dy's fin·gers** /'·· ˌ··/ *n* [plural] OKRA

**la·dy·ship** /'leɪdiʃɪp/ *n* **1 your ladyship/her ladyship** used as a way of speaking to or talking about a woman with the title of Lady: *Her ladyship is waiting for you in the drawing-room.* **2** *BrE spoken* a humorous way of talking about a woman who thinks she is very important: *Do you think her ladyship will be joining us?*

**lag¹** /læg/ **lagged, lagging** *v* **1** [I] to move or develop more slowly than others: *Britain was still lagging in the space race.* | **[+ behind]** *Jessica always lags behind, looking in shop windows.* **2** [T] *BrE* to cover water pipes etc with a special material to prevent heat from being lost: *We've had the hot-water tank lagged.*

**lag²** *n* [C] a delay or period of waiting between one event and a second event; TIME LAG —see also JET LAG, OLD LAG

**la·ger** /'lɑːgə‖-ər/ *n BrE* **1** [C,U] a light-coloured beer or a glass of that beer: *Two halves of lager, please.* **2 lager lout** a young man who drinks too much and then behaves violently or rudely S

**lag·gard** /'lægəd‖-ərd/ *n* [C] *old-fashioned* someone or something that is very slow or late **—laggardly** *adj*

**lag·ging** /'lægɪŋ/ *n* [U] the material used to protect a water pipe or container from heat or cold

**la·goon** /lə'guːn/ *n* [C] **1** a lake of sea water partly or completely separated from the sea by sand, rock etc *a* *tropical lagoon* —see picture on page 835 **2** *AmE* a small lake which is not very deep, near a larger lake or river

**lah-di-dah** /ˌlɑː diː ˈdɑː/ *adj spoken* talking and behaving as if you think you are better or from a higher class than you really are

**laid** /leɪd/ past tense and past participle of LAY[2]

**laid-back** /ˌ· ˈ·◂/ *adj* relaxed and seeming not to be worried about anything: *I don't know how you can be so laid-back about your exams.*

**lain** /leɪn/ the past participle of LIE[1]

**lair** /leə‖ler/ *n* [C] **1** the place where a wild animal hides and sleeps **2** a place where you go to hide or to be alone: *The police tracked the rapist to his lair.*

**laird** /leəd‖lerd/ *n* [C] a Scottish landowner —compare SQUIRE(1)

**lais·sez-faire, laisser-faire** /ˌleseɪ ˈfeə, ˌleɪ-‖-ˈfer/ *n* [U] *French* the principle of allowing private businesses to develop without any state control: *laissez-faire policies*

**la·i·ty** /ˈleɪǝti/ *n* **the laity** all the members of a religious group apart from the priests

S3 W3 **lake** /leɪk/ *n* **1** [C] a large area of water surrounded by land: *boating on the lake* | *Lake Michigan* **2 wine lake/milk lake etc** a very large amount of wine, milk etc that is not needed or used —see also MOUNTAIN (3)

**lake·side** /ˈleɪksaɪd/ *adj* beside a lake: *a lakeside restaurant* —**lakeside** *n* [singular]

**lakh** /læk/ *number IndE & PakE* a hundred thousand

**lam**[1] /læm/ *v*

**lam into** sb *phr v* [T] *BrE informal* to hit someone or speak angrily to them

**lam**[2] *n* **on the lam** *AmE informal* escaping from someone, especially the police: *Sykes was recaptured after three weeks on the lam.*

**la·ma** /ˈlɑːmə/ *n* [C] a Buddhist priest in Tibet, Mongolia etc

**La·ma·is·m** /ˈlɑːmə-ɪzəm/ *n* [U] a form of the Buddhist religion common in Tibet, Mongolia etc

**lamb**[1] /læm/ *n* **1** [C] a young sheep **2** [U] the meat of a young sheep: *roast lamb with mint sauce* **3** [C] *spoken* someone gentle and loveable, especially a child: *Benny's asleep now, the little lamb.* **4 like a lamb** quietly and without any argument: *Suzie went off to school like a lamb today.* **5 like a lamb to the slaughter** used when someone is going to do something dangerous but does not realize it

**lamb**[2] *v* [I] *technical* to give birth to lambs: *The ewes are lambing this week.*

**lam·ba·da** /læmˈbɑːdə‖lɑːm, ləm-/ *n* [singular, U] a sexy DISCO dance from Brazil

**lam·baste** /læmˈbeɪst/ also **lam·bast** /-ˈbæst/ *v* [T] to attack or criticize someone very strongly: *Her new play was really lambasted by the critics.*

**lam·bent** /ˈlæmbənt/ *adj literary* **1** clever in a gentle and amusing way: *lambent wit* **2** a lambent light or flame shines softly and pleasantly

**lamb·skin** /ˈlæmˌskɪn/ *n* **1** [C,U] the skin of a lamb, with the wool still on it: *lambskin gloves* **2** [U] leather made from the skin of lambs

**la·mé** /ˈlɑːmeɪ‖lɑːˈmeɪ/ *n* [U] cloth containing gold or silver threads: *a gold lamé evening skirt*

**lame**[1] /leɪm/ *adj* **1** unable to walk properly because your leg or foot is injured or weak: **go lame** (=become lame) **2** a lame explanation or excuse does not sound very believable: *Nancy came out with some lame excuse about missing the bus again.* —see also LAMELY **3 lame duck** a person, business etc that is experiencing difficulties and needs to be helped **4 lame duck president/administration etc** *especially AmE informal* a president, government etc whose period in office will soon end —**lameness** *n* [U]

**lame**[2] *v* [T usually passive] to make a person or animal unable to walk properly

**lame·brain** /ˈleɪmbreɪn/ *n* [C] *AmE informal* a stupid person: *Don't do it that way, lamebrain; you'll break it.*

**lame·ly** /ˈleɪmli/ *adv* if you say something lamely, you do not sound confident and other people find it difficult to believe you: *"But I still love you," he added rather lamely.*

**la·ment**[1] /ləˈment/ *v* **1** [I,T] to express feelings of great sadness about something: *The nation lamented the death of its great war leader.* | [+ **over**] *lamenting over her luck in love* **2** [T] to express annoyance or disappointment about something you think is unsatisfactory or unfair: *another article lamenting the decline of popular television*

**lament**[2] *n* [C] a song, piece of music, or something that you say, that expresses a feeling of sadness: *A lone piper played a lament.*

**lam·en·ta·ble** /ˈlæməntəbəl, ləˈmentəbəl/ *adj formal* very unsatisfactory or disappointing: *Riley showed a lamentable lack of tact.* —**lamentably** *adv*

**lam·en·ta·tion** /ˌlæmənˈteɪʃən/ *n* [C,U] *formal* deep sadness or something that expresses it: *There was lamentation throughout the land at the news of the defeat.*

**lam·i·nar flow** /ˌlæmǝnə ˈfləʊ‖-nər ˈfloʊ/ *n* [U] *technical* a smooth flow of liquid or gas over a solid surface

**lam·i·nate** /ˈlæmǝnǝt/ *n* [C,U] laminated material

**lam·i·nated** /ˈlæmǝneɪtɪd/ *adj* **1** laminated material has several thin sheets joined on top of each other: *laminated glass* **2** covered with a layer of thin plastic or metal: *wood laminated with plastic* —**laminate** *v* [T]

**lamp** /læmp/ *n* [C] **1** an object that produces light by using electricity, oil, or gas: *a table lamp* —see also HEADLAMP, STANDARD LAMP, STREETLAMP, SAFETY LAMP —see picture at LIGHT[1] **2** a piece of electrical equipment used to provide a special kind of heat, especially as medical treatment: *an infrared lamp* —see also SUNLAMP, BLOWLAMP S3

**lamp·black** /ˈ· ·/ *n* [U] a fine black colouring material made from SOOT (=the black powder produced by smoke)

**lamp·light** /ˈlæmp-laɪt/ *n* [U] the soft light produced by a lamp: *Her eyes shone in the lamplight.*

**lamp·light·er** /ˈlæmpˌlaɪtə‖-ər/ *n* [C] someone whose job was to light lamps in the street in the past

**lam·poon** /læmˈpuːn/ *v* [T] to write about someone, especially a politician, in a way that makes them seem stupid —**lampoon** *n* [C]

**lamp·post** /ˈ· ·/ *n* [C] **1** *especially BrE* a tall pole supporting a lamp that lights a street or public area —see picture on page 410 **2** *AmE* a pole supporting an old-fashioned type of lamp

**lamp·shade** /ˈlæmpʃeɪd/ *n* [C] a decorative cover fixed over a lamp to reduce or direct its light —see picture at LIGHT[1]

**LAN** /læn/ *n* [C] *technical* local area network; a system for communicating by computer in a large place such as an office building

**lance**[1] /lɑːns‖læns/ *n* [C] a long thin pointed weapon that was used in the past by soldiers on horses

**lance**[2] *v* [T] to cut a small hole in someone's flesh with a sharp instrument to let out PUS (=yellow liquid produced by infection): *to lance a boil*

**lance cor·po·ral** /ˌ· ˈ···◂/ *n* [C] a low level rank in the Marines or the British army, or someone who has this rank —see table on page B4

**lanc·er** /ˈlɑːnsə‖ˈlænsər/ *n* [C] a soldier belonging to a REGIMENT (=part of the army) that used to be armed with lances

**lan·cet** /ˈlɑːnsǝt‖ˈlæn-/ *n* [C] **1** a small very sharp pointed knife with two cutting edges, used by doctors to cut flesh **2 lancet arch/window** *technical* a tall narrow ARCH[1] (1) or window that is pointed at the top

**land**[1] /lænd/ *n* S1 W1

**1** ► **NOT SEA** ◄ [U] the solid dry part of the Earth's surface: *After 21 days at sea we sighted land.* | **by land** *It's quicker by land than sea.* | **on land** *The crocodile lays its eggs on land.*

**2** ► **GROUND** ◄ [U] ground, especially when used for farming or building on: *the use and management of land* | *fertile land* | *high land prices*

**3 ► COUNTRY ◄** [C] *especially literary* a country: *people of many lands*|**native land** (=the land where you were born) *She returned at last to her native land.*
**4 ► NOT CITY ◄ the land** the countryside thought of as a place that is quiet and peaceful, or as a place where people grow food: *We want to leave London and get back to the land.*|**live off the land** (=grow or catch all the food you need)
**5 ► PROPERTY ◄** [U] also **lands** *plural* the area of land that someone owns: *Get off my land!*|*The Duke's lands lay south of the mountains.*
**6 see/find out how the land lies** to try to discover what the situation really is before you make a decision
**7 in the land of the living** *spoken humorous* awake: *Now you're back in the land of the living you can put the kettle on.*
**8 land of milk and honey** an imaginary place where life is easy and pleasant
**9 the land of nod** *old-fashioned* an expression meaning sleep, used especially when talking to children —see also **be/live in cloud-cuckoo-land** (CLOUD[1] (6)), DRY LAND, **the lie of the land** (LIE[3] (3))

**USAGE NOTE: LAND**
WORD CHOICE: **world, earth, land, ground, floor, soil, country**
When you are talking about **the world** as a whole, compared with other planets, you often call it **the Earth** (or **the earth**): *From space, the earth looks like a shining blue ball.* But in some phrases *the* is not usually used: *Billions of people live on earth* (NOT usually *on the earth* and definitely NOT *in the earth*).
The hard surface of the world, when it is compared with the area covered by sea, is called **land** [U], but when you are comparing it with the air you say **the ground** or, on a larger scale, **(the) earth**: *After a week adrift at sea, we spotted land.*|*The horse fell to the ground.*|*I won't relax until we're safely back on the ground.*|*Once a meteor from outer space fell to earth here.*|*The earth shook and huge cracks appeared.*
Inside a building the surface you walk on is usually called the **floor** (but it is called **the ground** outside): *The dishes crashed to the kitchen floor.*|*The ground's too wet for camping.*
An area thought of as property is a piece of **land** [U]: *the high price of land in Tokyo*|*He owns a lot of land in New Mexico* (NOT **earth** or **ground** or **big land**). Also when you are talking about large areas, especially when it is used for a particular purpose, you say **land**: *The land isn't much good for raising corn.*|*Much of the land here is used for industry.*
A smaller area is likely to be called a piece of **ground** [U]: *a small piece of ground where I could plant potatoes*|*a patch of waste ground behind the house*
The substance that plants grow in is **soil** [U] or **earth** [U] or (*AmE*) **dirt** [U]: *The soil/earth is pretty good here.*|*The kids were playing on a mound of dirt in the yard.* But when you are talking about its quality, type, or condition, you usually use **soil**: *soil erosion*|*To improve clay soil, dig in as much sand as you can.*
Land that is not covered in buildings is **the country**, often compared with the town or city: *Why don't we take a trip to the country and get some fresh air?* (NOT *land*).
You call a country a **land** [C] only if you want to communicate a particular meaning. In a story, perhaps, or to show your feelings about a country you might say: *My homeland/native land is India* (= that is the country I feel I belong to).|*He visited many foreign lands* (= strange and mysterious countries). Compare this with the following, which is a report of simple facts: *I come from India.*|*He visited many foreign countries.*

**land**[2] *v* S W
**1 ► PLANE ◄** [I,T] if an aircraft lands or if a pilot lands it, it moves down onto the ground: *We are due to land at Heathrow at 12.50.*
**2 ► ARRIVE BY BOAT/PLANE ◄** [I] to arrive somewhere in an aircraft, boat etc: *1969, when the first men landed on the moon*
**3 ► GOODS/PEOPLE ◄** [T] to put something or someone on land from an aircraft or boat: *Troops were landed by helicopter.*|*Trawlers were landing their catch at the harbour.*
**4 ► FALL/COME DOWN ◄** [I always + adv/prep] to come down through the air onto something: [+ **in/on/under etc**] *Louis fell out of the tree and landed in a holly bush.*|*I felt a few drops of rain landing on my head.*
**5 ► PROBLEMS ◄** [I always + adv/prep] to be given to someone unexpectedly, and cause problems that they will have to deal with: [+ **in/on/under etc**] *Just when I thought my problems were over, this letter landed on my desk.*
**6 ► JOB/CONTRACT ETC ◄** [T] *informal* to succeed in getting a job, contract etc that was difficult to get: *Fay landed a plum job with the BBC.*|**land yourself sth** *Bill's just landed himself a part in a Broadway show.*
**7 ► FISH ◄** [T] to catch a large fish
**8 land a punch/blow** to succeed in hitting someone —see also **fall/land on your feet** (FOOT[1] (17))

**land** sb **in** sth *phr v* [T] **1 land sb in trouble/hospital/court etc** to cause serious problems for someone: *We all knew his drinking would land him in court one day.* **2 land sb in it** *spoken* to get someone into trouble by saying that they did something wrong: *Micky landed me in it by saying I was the last one to use the photocopier.*

**land on** sb *phr v* [T] *AmE informal* to speak angrily to someone: *Dale landed on him for forgetting the documents.*

**land up** *phr v* [I always + adv/prep] *informal* to finally get into a particular place, situation, or position after a lot of things have happened to you: **land up in/on etc** *We landed up in a bar at 3 am.*|*Be careful that you don't land up in serious debt.*

**land** sb **with** sth *phr v* [T usually passive] *informal* to give someone something unpleasant to do, because no one else wants to do it: *Maria's been landed with all the tidying up as usual.*

**land a·gent** /ˈ· ˌ··/ *n* [C] someone who looks after land, cattle, farms etc that belong to someone else

**lan·dau** /ˈlændɔː‖-daʊ/ *n* [C] a four-wheeled carriage that is pulled by horses and has two seats and a top that folds back in two parts

**land·ed** /ˈlændɪd/ *adj* [only before noun] **1 landed gentry/family/nobility** a family or group that has owned a lot of land for a long time **2** including a lot of land: *landed estates*

**land·fall** /ˈlændfɔːl‖-fɒːl/ *n* [C usually singular] the first land that you see or arrive at after a long journey by sea or air: *We made our landfall just south of Stornoway.*

**land·fill** /ˈlændfɪl/ *n* **1** [U] the practice of burying waste under the soil, or the waste buried in this way **2** [C] a place where this waste is buried

**land·ing** /ˈlændɪŋ/ *n* [C] **1** the floor at the top of a set of stairs or between two sets of stairs —see picture on page 410 **2** an act of arriving on land or of bringing something onto land from the sea or air: *troop landings in Normandy in 1944*|**crash landing/emergency landing** (=an aircraft's sudden landing because of trouble with the engine etc)

**landing charge** /ˈ·· ˌ·/ *n* [C] *technical* money that you have to pay when goods are unloaded at a port

**landing craft** /ˈ·· ˌ·/ *n* [C] a flat-bottomed boat that opens at one end to allow soldiers and equipment to land directly onto a shore

**landing field** /ˈ·· ·/ *n* [C] a LANDING STRIP

**landing gear** /ˈ·· ·/ *n* [U] an aircraft's wheels and wheel supports —see picture at AIRCRAFT

**landing net** /ˈ·· ·/ *n* [C] a net on a long handle used for lifting a fish out of the water after you have caught it

**landing stage** /ˈ·· ·/ *n* [C] a wooden structure onto which passengers and goods are landed from boats

**landing strip** /ˈ·· ·/ *n* [C] a level piece of ground that has been prepared for aircraft to use; AIRSTRIP

**land·la·dy** /ˈlændˌleɪdi/ *n* [C] **1** the woman that you rent a room, building, or piece of land from **2** a woman who owns or is in charge of a PUB

**land·less** /ˈlændləs/ *adj* owning no land

**land·locked** /ˈlændlɒkt‖-lɑːkt/ *adj* a landlocked country is surrounded by other countries and has no coast

3 **land·lord** /ˈlændlɔːd‖-lɔːrd/ *n* [C] **1** the man that you rent a room, building, or piece of land from **2** a man who owns or is in charge of a PUB

**land·lub·ber** /ˈlændˌlʌbə‖-ər/ *n* [C] *old-fashioned* someone who does not have much experience of the sea or ships

**land·mark** /ˈlændmɑːk‖-mɑːrk/ *n* [C] **1** an event, idea, or discovery that marks an important part of someone's life, of the development of knowledge etc: *The discovery of penicillin was a landmark in the history of medicine.*| **landmark discovery/decision etc** *the landmark decision to join NATO* **2** something that is easy to recognize, such as a tall tree or building, and will help you know where you are

**land·mass** /ˈlændmæs/ *n* [C] *technical* a large area of land

**land·mine** /ˈlændmaɪn/ *n* [C] a kind of bomb hidden in the ground that explodes when someone walks or drives over it

**land of·fice** /ˈ· ˌ··/ *n* [C] a government office in the US that records the sales of all public land

**land·own·er** /ˈlændˌəʊnə‖-ˌoʊnər/ *n* [C] someone who owns a large amount of land —**landowning** *adj*: *the landowning aristocracy* —**landownership** *n* [U]

**land re·form** /ˈ· ·ˌ·/ *n* [C,U] the political principle of sharing farm land so that more people own some of it

**land re·gis·try** /ˈ· ˌ···/ *n* [C] a government office in Britain that keeps records about the sales and ownership of land

**Land Rov·er** /ˈ·ˌ··/ *n* [C] *BrE trademark* a type of strong car made for travelling over rough ground

3 **land·scape**[1] /ˈlændskeɪp/ *n* **1** [C] an area of countryside or land, considered in terms of how attractive it is to look at: *the beauty of the New England landscape in autumn*|*a desolate urban landscape* **2** [C] a picture showing an area of countryside or land: *Cézanne's landscapes* **3** [U] the painting or drawing of landscapes in art **4 the political/intellectual etc landscape** the general situation in which a particular activity takes place: *She dominated the intellectual landscape of Paris.* **5** [U] *technical* LANDSCAPE MODE —see also **a blot on the landscape** (BLOT[2] (2))

**landscape**[2] *v* [T often passive] to make a park, garden etc look attractive and interesting by planting trees and bushes, making different levels etc

**landscape ar·chi·tec·ture** /ˌ·· ˈ····/ *n* [U] the profession or art of planning the way an area of land looks, including roads, buildings, and planted areas —**landscape architect** *n* [C]

**landscape gar·den·ing** /ˌ·· ˈ···/ *n* [U] the profession or art of arranging gardens and parks so that they look attractive and interesting —**landscape gardener** *n* [C]

**landscape mode** /ˈ·· ˌ·/ *n* [C] *technical* a piece of paper, picture, etc that has its longer edge at the top and bottom —opposite PORTRAIT MODE

**land·scap·er** /ˈlændskeɪpə‖-ər/ *n* [C] *AmE* someone whose job is to arrange plants, paths etc in gardens and parks

**land·slide** /ˈlændslaɪd/ *n* [C] **1** a sudden fall of a lot of earth or rocks down a hill, cliff etc **2** a victory in an election in which one person or party gets a lot more votes than all the others: **by a landslide** *The SNP candidate won by a landslide.*|*a landslide victory*

**land·slip** /ˈlændslɪp/ *n* [C] a small landslide

**land·ward** /ˈlændwəd‖-wərd/ *adj* facing towards the land and away from the sea: *the landward side of the hill* —**land·wards** /ˈlændwədz‖-wərdz/ *adv*

**lane** /leɪn/ *n* [C] **1** a narrow road between fields or houses, especially in the countryside: *a dusty lane leading to some cottages* **2** the two or three parallel areas on a main road which are divided by painted lines to keep fast and slow traffic apart: **the inside/outside lane** *Use the outside lane for overtaking only.*|**the fast lane** (=the lane for going past other vehicles) **3** used in the names of roads: *a hotel in Park Lane* **4** one of the narrow parallel areas marked for each competitor in a running or swimming race: *The champion is running in lane five.* **5** a line or course along which ships or aircraft regularly travel between ports or airports: *busy shipping lanes* —see also **life in the fast lane** (FAST LANE (2)) S3 W3

**lan·guage** /ˈlæŋgwɪdʒ/ *n* S2 W1

**1 ▶ ENGLISH/FRENCH/ARABIC ETC ◀** [C,U] a system of communication by written or spoken words, which is used by the people of a particular country or area: *the Japanese language*|*How many languages do you speak?*| **native language** (=the first language you learned) *Andrea's native language is German.*|**modern language** (=a language that is still spoken today)|**dead language** (=a language that is no longer spoken)|**the language barrier** (=the difficulty of communicating with people who speak a different language)

**2 ▶ COMMUNICATION ◀** [U] the ability to use words to communicate: *the origins of language*

**3 ▶ COMPUTERS ◀** [C,U] *technical* a system of instructions and commands for operating a computer: *a programming language such as BASIC or Pascal*

**4 ▶ STYLE/TYPE OF WORDS ◀** [U] the kind of words and style used in one kind of writing or by people in a particular job or activity: *medical language*|*poetic language*

**5 ▶ SOUNDS/SIGNS/ACTIONS ◀** [U] a way of expressing meaning or giving information through sounds, signs, movements etc: *the language of music*

**6 ▶ SWEARING ◀** [U] *informal* words that most people think are offensive: *You never heard such language! It was disgusting.*|**mind/watch your language** (=stop swearing)

**7 strong language a)** angry words used to tell people exactly what you mean **b)** words that most people think are offensive; swearing

**8 speak the same language** if two people speak the same language, they have similar attitudes and opinions —see also BODY LANGUAGE, SIGN LANGUAGE

**language la·bor·a·tory** /ˈ··· ·ˌ···‖ˈ··· ˌ····/ *n* [C] a room in a school or college where you can learn to speak a foreign language by listening to TAPES and recording your own voice

**lan·guid** /ˈlæŋgwɪd/ *adj* **1** moving slowly and making very little effort, but in an attractive way: *Sebastian left with a languid wave of the hand.* **2** lazily slow and peaceful: *a languid afternoon by the river* —**languidly** *adv*

**lan·guish** /ˈlæŋgwɪʃ/ *v* [I] **1** to be forced to stay somewhere where you are unhappy: *Shaw languished in a Mexican jail for fifteen years.* **2** to become weaker or less successful: *Local food production languished through lack of government support.*|*The conversation was languishing.* **3** [+ for] to become ill and unhappy because you want someone or something very much

**lan·guor** /ˈlæŋgə‖-ər/ *n especially literary* **1** [C,U] a pleasant feeling of tiredness or lack of strength **2** [U] pleasant or heavy stillness of the air: *the languor of a hot afternoon* **3** [C] a feeling of sadness because you want someone or something very much —**languourous** *adj* —**languorously** *adv*

**lank** /læŋk/ *adj* lank hair is thin, straight and unattractive —**lankly** *adv* —**lankness** *n* [U] —see picture on page 412

**lank·y** /ˈlæŋki/ *adj* unattractively tall and thin: *long lanky legs* —**lankiness** *n* [U]

**lan·o·lin** /ˈlænəl-ɨn/ *n* [U] an oil that is in sheep's wool and is used in skin creams

**lan·tern** /ˈlæntən‖-ərn/ *n* [C] **1** a lamp that you can carry consisting of a metal or glass container surrounding a flame or light —see picture at LIGHT[1] **2** *technical* a structure at the top of a tower or LIGHTHOUSE, that has windows on all sides —see also CHINESE LANTERN, MAGIC LANTERN

**lantern-jawed** /ˌ·· ˈ·◂‖ˈ·· ·/ *adj* having a long narrow jaw and cheeks that sink inwards

**lan·yard** /ˈlænjəd‖-ərd/ *n* [C] **1** a short piece of rope, used on a ship to tie things **2** a thick string with a knife or whistle on it, that sailors wear around their necks

**lap[1]** /læp/ *n*
**1** ▶ **LEGS** ◀ [C] the upper part of your legs when you are sitting down: *Come and sit on my lap, Ginny.*
**2** ▶ **RACE** ◀ [C] one journey around or along a running track, race course etc: *Hill finished a lap ahead of his team-mate.* | **do/run/swim a lap** *Come on, let's do a few laps in the pool.* | **lap of honour** *BrE*, | **victory lap** *AmE* (=a lap that you do after winning)
**3** ▶ **PART OF JOURNEY** ◀ [singular] a part of a long journey: *The last lap of their journey was by ship.*
**4 in the lap of luxury** having an easy, comfortable life with plenty of money, possessions etc
**5 in the lap of the gods** if the result of something is in the lap of the gods, you do not know what will happen
**6 drop/dump sth in sb's lap** *spoken* to make someone responsible for dealing with something difficult: *Ben just dumped all this work in my lap and told me to get on with it.*

**lap[2]** *v*
**1** ▶ **SEA/LAKE/RIVER** ◀ [I,T] if water laps something or laps against something such as the shore or a boat, it moves against it or hits it in small waves: [+ **against**] *The water of the lake lapped gently against the rocks.*
**2** ▶ **DRINK** ◀ [I, T] if an animal laps something, it drinks it by making small tongue movements
**3** ▶ **IN A RACE** ◀ **a)** [T] to pass a competitor in a race after having completed a whole lap more than they have: *Casey gave up after being lapped twice.* **b)** [I] to make a single journey around a track, race course etc in a particular time
**4** ▶ **PARTLY COVER** ◀ [I,T] *technical* if one thing laps another, a part of one covers part of the other; OVERLAP[1]
**5** ▶ **FOLD/WRAP** ◀ [T always + adv/prep] *literary* to fold or wrap something around something else —**lapping** *n* [U]

**lap** ↔ sth **up** *phr v* [T] **1** to get a lot of pleasure and enjoyment from something, without worrying about whether it is good, true etc: *She seems to be lapping up all the attention she's getting.* | *They sat listening to his story, spellbound, lapping it up.* **2** to drink all of something eagerly

**lap·a·ra·scope** /ˈlæpərəskəʊp‖-skoʊp/ *n* [C] *technical* a piece of equipment with a lighted tube that a doctor uses to look inside someone's body

**lap·a·ros·cop·y** /ˌlæpəˈrɒskəpi‖-ˈrɑː-/ *n* [C,U] *technical* an examination or medical operation on the inside of someone's body, using a laparoscope

**lap belt** /ˈ· ·/ *n* [C] a type of safety belt that fits across your waist when you are sitting in the back of a car

**lap·dog** /ˈlæpdɒg‖-dɔːg/ *n* [C] **1** a small pet dog **2** someone who is completely under the control of someone else and will do anything they say

**la·pel** /ləˈpel/ *n* [C] the part of the front of a coat or JACKET (1) that is joined to the collar and folded back on each side

**lap·i·da·ry[1]** /ˈlæpɨdəri‖-deri/ *adj* [only before noun] *technical* connected with the cutting or polishing of valuable stones or jewels

**lapidary[2]** *n* [C] someone who is skilled in cutting and polishing jewels and valuable stones

**lap·is laz·u·li** /ˌlæpɨs ˈlæzjʊli‖-ˈlæzəli/ *n* **1** [C,U] a valuable bright blue stone **2** [U] a bright blue colour

**lap robe** /ˈ· ·/ *n* [C] *AmE* a small thick BLANKET[1] (1) used to cover your legs when your are travelling

**lapse[1]** /læps/ *n* [C] **1** a short time when someone is careless or forgetful: [+ **in**] *There haven't been any lapses in security recently.* | [+ **of**] *A single lapse of concentration cost Becker the game.* | **a memory lapse** (=when you cannot remember something for a short time) **2** [C] a failure to do something you should do, especially to behave correctly: *He didn't offer Darren a drink and Marie did not appear to notice the lapse.* **3** [C usually singular] a period of time between two events: *The usual time lapse between request and delivery is two days.* | [+ **of**] *a lapse of about ten seconds*

**lapse[2]** *v* [I] **1** to gradually come to an end or to stop for a period of time: *I let the conversation lapse and Kelly finally spoke up.* **2** if a contract, agreement, legal right etc lapses, it comes to an end, for example because an agreed time limit has passed

**lapse into** sth *phr v* [T] **1 lapse into silence/sleep/a daydream etc** to go into a quiet or less active state: *The girl lapsed into a sulky silence.* | *He lapsed into a coma and died two days later.* **2** to start behaving or speaking in a different and usually less good or acceptable way: *Following his death, the Empire lapsed into chaos.* | *She would sometimes deliberately lapse into another dialect.*

**lapsed** /læpst/ *adj* [only before noun] **1** no longer having the beliefs you had, especially religious beliefs: *a lapsed Catholic* **2** *law* not used any more

**lap·top** /ˈ· ·/ *n* [C] a small computer that you can carry with you: *executives with their laptops* —**lap-top** *adj*

**lap·wing** /ˈlæpˌwɪŋ/ *n* [C] a small black and white European bird with raised feathers on its head; PEEWIT

**lar·board** /ˈlɑːbəd‖ˈlɑːrbərd/ *n* [U] *old-fashioned* the left side of a ship; PORT (4)

**lar·ce·nist** /ˈlɑːsənɨst‖ˈlɑːr-/ *n* [C] *law* a thief

**lar·ce·ny** /ˈlɑːsəni‖ˈlɑːr-/ *n* [C, U] *law* the act or crime of stealing —see also PETTY LARCENY

**larch** /lɑːtʃ‖lɑːrtʃ/ *n* [C,U] a tree that looks like a PINE tree but drops its leaves in winter

**lard[1]** /lɑːd‖lɑːrd/ *n* [U] white fat from pigs that is used in cooking

**lard[2]** *v* [T] **1 be larded with sth** if a speech, piece of writing etc is larded with particular types of words or phrases, there are a lot of them in it: *a speech larded with Biblical quotations* **2** to put small pieces of BACON onto meat before cooking it

**lard-ass** /ˈ· ·/ *n* [C] *AmE spoken* an insulting word for someone who is fat

**lar·der** /ˈlɑːdə‖ˈlɑːrdər/ *n* [C] a small room or large cupboard for storing food in a house

**large** /lɑːdʒ‖lɑːrdʒ/ *adj* S W
**1** ▶ **BIG** ◀ bigger or more than usual in number, amount, or size: *Los Angeles is the second largest city in the US.* | *The T-shirt comes in Small, Medium and Large.* | *This could create a large number of new jobs.* | *The town has a large population of elderly people.* —see WIDE (USAGE), BIG (USAGE)
**2** ▶ **PERSON** ◀ a large person is very tall and wide: *A large man with a shotgun blocked our path.* —see FAT[1] (USAGE)
**3 be at large** if a dangerous person or animal is at large, they have escaped from somewhere and may cause harm or damage: *Two of the escaped prisoners are still at large.*
**4 the world/country/public at large** people in general: *The organization provides information on health issues to the public at large.*
**5** ▶ **MORE GENERAL** ◀ **the larger issues/view/picture** the important general facts and questions about a situation, problem etc: *a useful book about the conflict, which helps to explain the larger picture*
**6 (as) large as life** *spoken* used when someone has appeared or is present in a place where you did not expect

to see them: *I turned a corner and there was Joe, as large as life.*
**7 larger than life** someone who is larger than life attracts a lot of attention because they are more amusing, attractive, or exciting than most people
**8 in large part/measure** *formal* mostly —see also **by and large** (BY² (5)), **loom large** (LOOM² (3)), **writ large** (WRIT²) —**largeness** *n* [U]

**large in·tes·tine** /ˌ· ·ˈ··/ *n* [C] the lower part of your BOWELS, where food is changed into solid waste matter —compare SMALL INTESTINE

S3 W2 **large·ly** /ˈlɑːdʒli‖ˈlɑːr-/ *adv* mostly or mainly: *The state of Nevada is largely desert.*|*Kevin's success is largely due to sheer hard work.*

**large-scale** /ˌ· ˈ·◂/ *adj* [only before noun] **1** using or involving a lot of effort, people, supplies etc: *a large-scale rescue operation* **2** a large-scale map, model etc is drawn or made bigger than usual, so that more details can be shown

**lar·gesse, largess** /lɑːˈʒes‖lɑːrˈdʒes/ *n* [U] *formal* the quality or act of being generous and giving money or gifts to people who have less than you, or the money or gifts that you give

**larg·ish** /ˈlɑːdʒɪʃ‖ˈlɑːr-/ *adj informal* fairly big

**lar·go¹** /ˈlɑːgəʊ‖ˈlɑːrgoʊ/ *adj, adv technical* played or sung slowly and seriously

**largo²** *n* [C] *technical* a piece of music played or sung slowly and seriously

**lar·i·at** /ˈlæriət/ *n* [C] *AmE* a LASSO¹

**lark¹** /lɑːk‖lɑːrk/ *n* [C]
**1** a small brown singing bird with long pointed wings; SKYLARK **2** *informal* something that you do to amuse yourself or as a joke, especially something bad: **do sth for a lark** *They hid her passport for a lark.* **3 blow/sod etc that for a lark** *BrE spoken* used when you stop doing something or refuse to do something because it needs too much effort: *Paint the whole room? Sod that for a lark!* **4 this dieting/exercise/gardening lark** *BrE spoken* used to describe an activity that you think is silly or unpleasant: *Salad again? How long are you going to keep up this healthy eating lark?* **5 be up with the lark** to get up very early —see also **happy as a lark** (HAPPY (8))

**lark²** *v*
**lark about/around** *phr v* [I] *BrE informal* to have fun by behaving in a silly way: *A group of kids was larking about near the shops.*

**lar·va** /ˈlɑːvə‖ˈlɑːrvə/ *n plural* **larvae** /-viː/ [C] a creature like a fat WORM that is a young insect which has left the egg and has not yet changed into an insect with wings —**larval** *adj*

**lar·yn·gi·tis** /ˌlærənˈdʒaɪtəs/ *n* [U] an illness which makes talking difficult because your larynx and throat are swollen

**lar·ynx** /ˈlærɪŋks/ *n plural* **larynges** /ləˈrɪndʒiːz/ or **larynxes** [C] *technical* the hollow box-like part in your throat where you make voice sounds —see picture at RESPIRATORY

**la·sa·gne** *BrE*, **lasagna** *AmE* /ləˈsænjə, -ˈzæn‖-ˈzɑːn-/ *n* [C, U] a type of Italian food made with flat pieces of PASTA, meat or vegetables, cheese and a SAUCE made with milk

**las·civ·i·ous** /ləˈsɪviəs/ *adj* showing strong sexual desire: *Mandy gave him a lascivious wink.* —**lasciviously** *adv* —**lasciviousness** *n* [U]

**la·ser** /ˈleɪzə‖-ər/ *n* [C] a piece of equipment that produces a powerful narrow beam of light that can be used in medical operations, to cut metals, or to make patterns of light for entertainment: *laser surgery*

**laser disk** /ˈ·· ˌ·/ *n* [C] a computer DISK that can be read by laser light

**laser print·er** /ˈ·· ˌ··/ *n* [C] a machine connected to a computer system that prints by using laser light —see picture on page 837

**lash¹** /læʃ/ *v*
**1 ▶TIE◀** [T always + adv/prep] to tie something tightly to something else with a rope, or tie two things together: **lash sth to/onto etc** *The oars were lashed to the sides of the boat.*
**2 ▶WIND/RAIN ETC◀** [I always + adv/prep, T] to hit against something with violent force: *The rain lashed her face.*|*waves lashing the shore*|[+ **against/down/across**] *The wind lashed violently against the door.*
**3 ▶HIT◀** [T] to hit someone very hard with a whip, stick etc: *The guards would lash any of the prisoners who fell behind.*
**4 ▶TAIL◀** [I, T] if an animal lashes its tail or its tail lashes, it moves it from side to side quickly and strongly, especially because it is angry
**5 ▶CRITICIZE◀** [T] a word meaning to criticize someone angrily, used especially in newspapers: *Judge lashes drug-dealers.*
**6 lash sb into a fury/rage/frenzy etc** to deliberately make a group of people have strong violent feelings: *The crowd was being lashed into a frenzy by the speaker.*
**lash out** *phr v* [I] **1** to suddenly speak angrily to someone: [+ **at**] *I used to lash out at my children for no reason.* **2** to try to hit someone, with a series of violent, uncontrolled movements: *In its panic, the bear started to lash out.*

**lash²** *n* [C] **1** a hit with a whip, especially as a punishment: *They were each given fifty lashes.* **2** [usually plural] one of the hairs that grow around the edge of your eyes; EYELASH **3** a sudden or violent movement like that of a whip: *With a lash of its tail, the lion sprang at its prey.* **4** the thin piece of leather at the end of a whip

**lash·ing** /ˈlæʃɪŋ/ *n* [C] **1 lashings of** *BrE old-fashioned* a large amount of food or drink: *apple pie with lashings of cream* **2** a punishment of hitting someone with a whip **3** a rope that fastens something tightly to something else

**lash-up** /ˈ· ·/ *n* [C] *BrE informal* an arrangement of things, for example electrical equipment or wires, put together quickly to be used for only a short time

**lass** /læs/ also **las·sie** /ˈlæsi/ *n* [C] *ScotE & NEngE* **1** a girl or young woman **2** a girlfriend —compare LAD

**las·si·tude** /ˈlæsətjuːd‖ˈlæsətjuːd, -tuːd/ *n* [U] *formal* **1** tiredness and lack of energy **2** laziness or lack of interest: *Cheam was accused of moral lassitude.*

**las·so¹** /ləˈsuː, ˈlæsəʊ‖-soʊ/ *n* [C] a rope with one end tied in a circle, used to catch cattle and horses, especially in the western US

**lasso²** *v* [T] to catch an animal using a lasso

**last**

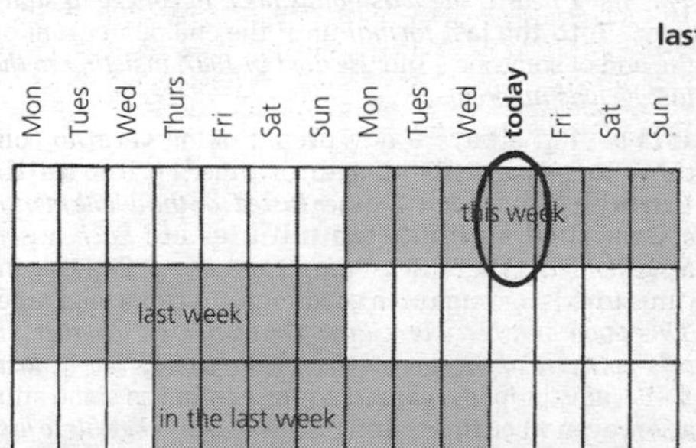

**last¹** /lɑːst‖læst/ *determiner* **1** most recent; the nearest one to the present time: *I haven't seen you since the last meeting.*|**last night/week/year etc** *Did you watch the game on TV last night?*|*Fashion has changed in the last twenty years.*|**(the) last time** (=the most recent S1 W1

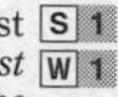

occasion)|*The last time I spoke to Bob he seemed happy enough.* —compare NEXT[1] (2) **2** happening or existing at the end, with no others after: *I didn't read the last chapter of the book.*|*Anna was the last person to see him alive.* **3** remaining after all others have gone, been used etc: *Is this your last cigarette?*|*These are the last four birds of their kind still in existence.* **4 the last person/thing a)** one that you did not expect at all: *She's the last person I'd expect to meet in a disco.* **b)** one that you do not want at all, that is most unsuitable etc: *The last thing we wanted was for the newspapers to find out what was going on.* **5 last thing (at night)** at the very end of the day: *Take a couple of these pills last thing at night to help you get to sleep.* **6 on your last legs** *informal* **a)** very tired: *Sarah looks as if she's on her last legs.* **b)** very ill and likely to die soon **7 on its last legs** *informal* old or in bad condition, and likely to stop working soon: *We'll have to get a new lawn mower this year – the old one is really on its last legs.* **8 have the last word a)** to make the last statement in an argument, which gives you an advantage **b)** to be the person who makes the final decision on something: *The finance committee always has the last word on expenditure.* **9 be the last word in** to be the best, most modern, or most comfortable example of something: *It's the last word in luxury holidays.*

**last²** *adv* **1** most recently before now: *When I last saw her, she was working in New York.* **2** after everything or everyone else: *They told me I'd be interviewed last.*|*Mix together flour, butter, and sugar, and add the eggs last.*| **last of all** (=used when giving a final point or piece of information) *Last of all, I'd like to thank the catering staff for a splendid meal.* **3 last but not least** used when mentioning the last person or thing in a list, to emphasize that they are still important: *Last but not least, let me introduce Jane, our new secretary.*

**last³** *n, pron* **1 the last** the person or thing that comes after all the others: *He was the first to arrive and the last to leave.*|*I think this box is the last.* **2 at (long) last** if something happens at last, it happens after you have waited a long time: *I'm so pleased that Jane's managed to get a job at last.* —see LASTLY (USAGE) **3 the day/week/year etc before last** the day, week etc before the one that has just finished: *I sent the letter off the week before last.* **4 the last of** the remaining parts of something: *Joan took the last of the meat from the dish and passed it to her mother.* **5 haven't heard the last of** if you have not heard the last of a problem, it has not yet finished and it may cause problems for you in the future: *I have a nasty feeling we haven't heard the last of this.*
**6 the last I heard** *spoken* used to tell someone the most recent news that you know about a person or situation: *The last I heard, she was going back to college to study law.* **7 to the last** *formal* until the end of an event or the end of someone's life: *He died in 1987, insisting to the last he was innocent.*

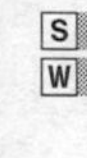
**last⁴** *v* **1** [I always + adv/prep, linking verb] to continue for a particular length of time: [+ **for/until/through etc**] *The hot weather lasted for the whole month of June.*|**last an hour/ten minutes etc** *Each lesson lasts an hour.*|*The ceasefire didn't last long.* **2** [I] to continue to exist or remain in good condition for a long time: *This good weather won't last.*|*We wondered whether all this concern about the environment would really last.* **3** [I + adv/prep] to manage to remain in the same situation, even when this is difficult: *They won't be able to last much longer without fresh supplies.*|*The new manager is very inexperienced – I doubt if he'll last long.* **4** [linking verb] to be enough for someone to use **last (sb) two days/three weeks etc**: *The water supply should last another 48 hours.*|*We only had $50 to last us the rest of the month.*

**last⁵** *n* [C] a piece of wood or metal shaped like a human foot, used by a shoemaker

**last call** /ˌ· ˈ·/ *n* [C] *AmE* the words used by the person who is in charge of a bar when it is going to close and people can order just one more drink; LAST ORDERS *BrE*

**last-ditch** /ˌ· ˈ·◂/ *adj* **a last-ditch attempt/effort etc** a final attempt to achieve something before it is too late: *The negotiators made a last-ditch effort to reach an agreement.*

**last hur·rah** /ˌ· ·ˈ·/ *n* [C usually singular] *AmE* a final effort, event etc at the end of a long period of work etc

**last·ing** /ˈlɑːstɪŋ‖ˈlæs-/ *adj* strong enough, well enough planned etc to last for a very long time: *The reforms will bring lasting benefits.*|*a lasting peace settlement*|**leave a lasting impression** *Our first meeting left a lasting impression on me.*

**last judg·ment** /ˌ· ˈ··/ *n* **the last judgment** the time after death when everyone is judged by God for what they have done in life, according to Christianity and some other religions; JUDGMENT DAY

**last·ly** /ˈlɑːstli‖ˈlæst-/ *adv* [sentence adverb] used when you want to say one more thing at the end of a list: *Lastly, could I ask all of you to keep this information secret.*

**USAGE NOTE: LASTLY**

WORD CHOICE: **lastly, last of all, finally, in the end, at last**

**Lastly, last of all** and **finally** are often used to end a set of points where time is not involved: *There are three reasons why I hate him: first(ly) he's rude, second(ly) he's a liar, and lastly/last of all/finally he owes me money* (NOT *at last*).

**Last (of all)** and **finally** also end a set of actions, often at points of time: *First I get dressed, next I bring in the paper, then I feed the cat, and last/finally I fix my breakfast* (NOT *at last*).

**Finally** is also used, like **in the end**, just to mark something as happening after a long period of time: *I tried hard and finally/in the end I managed it.*|*He fell ill and finally died/in the end he died.*

**At last** has a similar use, but only when something good happens after a period of time: *I tried and at last I managed it.*|*At last I have a good dictionary!* (=I have waited a long time to find one).

**last-minu·te** /ˌ· ˈ··◂/ *adj* [only before noun] happening or done as late as possible within a process, event, or activity: *last-minute changes to the script*

**last name** /ˌ· ˈ·/ *n* [C] *especially AmE* a SURNAME

**last or·ders** /ˌ· ˈ··/ *n* [plural] *BrE* the words used by the person who is in charge of a bar or PUB when it is going to close and people can order just one more drink; LAST CALL *AmE*

**last post** /ˌ· ˈ·/ *n* **the last post** the tune played on a BUGLE at British military funerals, or to call soldiers back to camp for the night

**last rites** /ˌ· ˈ·/ *n* [plural] the ceremony performed in some religions, especially the Catholic religion, for people who are dying

**lat** the written abbreviation of LATITUDE

**latch¹** /lætʃ/ *n* [C] **1** a small metal bar that drops into a U-shaped object to keep doors, gates, windows etc closed: *Gwen lifted the latch and opened the gate.* **2** *especially BrE* a kind of lock for a door that you can open from the inside by turning a handle but that you need a key to open from the outside: **on the latch** (=shut but not locked) *Ray went out, leaving the door on the latch.*

**latch²** *v* [T] to fasten a door, window etc with a latch

**latch on** *phr v* [I] *BrE informal* to understand: *He's so thick it took him ages to latch on.*

**latch onto** sb/sth *phr v* [T] *informal* **1** to follow someone and keep trying to talk to them, get their attention etc, especially when they would prefer to be left alone: *He latched onto Sandy at the party and wouldn't go away.* **2** get very interested in something so that you spend a lot of time thinking about it or discussing it: *It's the kind of issue that the media really latch on to.*

**latch·key** /ˈlætʃkiː/ *n* [C] **1** a key that opens a lock on an outside door of a house or apartment **2 latchkey kid** *old-fashioned* a child whose parents both work and who spends time alone in the house after school

S1 W1 **late¹** /leɪt/ *adj*
**1 ▶AFTER EXPECTED TIME◀** arriving, happening, or done after the time that was expected, agreed, or arranged: *Sorry I'm late – I overslept.* | *The train was late.* | *We apologize for the late departure of flight AZ709.* | *Are we too late to get tickets?* | [+ **for**] *Cheryl overslept and was late for school.*
**2 ▶AFTER USUAL TIME◀** happening or done after the usual or normal time: *a late breakfast* | *The harvest was rather late this year.*
**3 ▶NEAR THE END◀** [only before noun] near to the end of a period of time: | *the late eighteenth century* | *Paul's in his late forties.*
**4 as late as** used to express surprise that something considered old-fashioned was still happening so recently: *Capital punishment was still used in Britain as late as the 1950s.*
**5 ▶PAYMENTS ETC◀ a)** paid, given back etc after the agreed date: *There are strict penalties if repayments on the loan are late.* **b) be late with** to pay something, bring something back etc after the agreed date: *We try never to be late with the rent.*
**6 ▶EVENING◀** [only before noun] near the end of the day: *the late movie* | *We stopped by for a late drink.*
**7 her late husband/the late president etc** used to talk about someone who has died
**8 a late developer** a child whose physical size or character develops slowly
**9 it's (a little) late in the day** used to show disapproval because someone has done something too late for it to be effective: *It's a little late in the day to say you're sorry!*
**10 late of** *formal* having lived in a place until fairly recently: *Billy Hicks, late of this parish*

S2 W3 **late²** *adv* **1** after or later than the usual time: *The stores are open late on Thursdays.* | *Ellen has to work late tonight.* **2** after the arranged or expected time: *The bus came ten minutes late.* **3** near to the end of a period of time or an event: **late in August/the evening/1995** *The wedding took place late in May.* **4 of late** *formal* recently: *Maureen hasn't been feeling too well of late.* **5 late in life** if you do something late in life, you do it at an older age than most people do it **6 better late than never** used to say that you are glad someone has done something, or that they should do something, although they are late —see also **be running late** (RUN¹ (48))

**late-break·ing** /ˈ· ˌ··/ *adj* late-breaking news concerns events that happen just before a news broadcast or just before a newspaper is printed

**late·com·er** /ˈleɪtˌkʌmə‖-ər/ *n* [C] someone who arrives late

**late·ly** /ˈleɪtli/ *adv* recently: *I've been feeling ill just lately.*

**late-night** /ˈ· ·/ *adj* [only before noun] happening late at night: *late-night television* | *late-night shopping*

**la·tent** /ˈleɪtənt/ *adj* something that is latent is present but hidden, and may develop or become more noticeable in the future: *The virus remains latent in the body for many years.* | *latent aggression* —**latency** *n* [U]

**latent heat** /ˌ·· ˈ·/ *n* [U] *technical* the additional heat necessary to change a solid into a liquid, or a liquid into a gas

S1 W1 **lat·er¹** /ˈleɪtə‖-ər/ *adv* **1** after the time you are talking about or after the present time: *I'm going out for a bit – I'll see you later.* | **two years later/three weeks later etc** *He became Senator two years later.* | **later that day/morning/week** *The baby died later that night.* | **later in the day/week/year** *The dentist could fit you in later in the week.* —see LASTLY (USAGE) **2 later on** at some time later or in the future: *I can't eat all of this – I'll finish it later on.* **3 not later than** used when saying that something must be done by a particular time in the future: *Completed entry forms should arrive not later than 31st July.*

**later²** *adj* [only before noun] **1** coming in the future or after something else: *The role of marketing is dealt with in a later chapter.* | *The launch was postponed to a later date.* **2** more recent: *The engine has been greatly improved in later models.* **3 in later years/life** when someone is older: *Using a sunscreen when you are young helps you to have healthy skin in later years.*

**lat·e·ral¹** /ˈlætərəl/ *adj technical* connected with the sides of something, or movement to the side: *The wall is weak and requires lateral support.* —**laterally** *adv*

**lateral²** *n* [C] *technical* something that is at the side or comes from the side

**lateral think·ing** /ˌ··· ˈ··/ *n* [U] a way of thinking in which you use your imagination to make connections between things that are not normally thought of together

**lat·est¹** /ˈleɪtɪst/ *adj* [only before noun] the most recent or the newest: *all the latest gossip* | *Metallica's latest album*

**latest²** *n* **1 the latest** *informal* the most recent news, fashion, or technical improvement: *the latest in computer software* **2 at the latest** no later than the time mentioned: *I should be back by 11 o'clock at the latest.*

**la·tex** /ˈleɪteks/ *n* [U] **1** a thick whitish liquid produced by some plants, especially the rubber tree **2** an artificial substance similar to this, used in making paint, glue etc

**lath** /lɑːθ‖læθ/ *n* [C] /lɑːðz, lɑːθs‖læθs, læðz/ a long flat narrow piece of wood used in building to support PLASTER (=material used to cover walls)

**lathe** /leɪð/ *n* [C] a machine that shapes wood or metal, by turning it round and round against a sharp tool

**la·ther¹** /ˈlɑːðə‖ˈlæðər/ *n* [singular, U] **1** a white mass of BUBBLES produced by mixing soap in water **2** a white mass that forms on a horse's skin when it has been sweating (SWEAT¹ (1)) **3 in a lather** *BrE informal* very anxious, especially because you do not have enough time —**lathery** *adv*

**lather²** *v* **1** [I] to produce a lather: *This soap lathers really well.* **2** [T] to cover something with lather **3** [T] *informal* to hit someone violently

**Lat·in¹** /ˈlætɪn‖ˈlætn/ *n* **1** [U] the language of the ancient Romans **2** [C] someone who comes from Southern Europe

**Latin²** *adj* **1** written in Latin: *a Latin text* **2** connected with a nation that speaks a language such as Italian, Spanish, or Portuguese that developed from Latin

**Latin A·mer·i·can** /ˌ·· ·ˈ···◂/ *adj* connected with South or Central America

**La·ti·no** /læˈtiːnəʊ‖-noʊ/ *n* [C] *AmE* someone living in the US whose family came from a Central or South American country —**Latino** *adj*: *Latino culture*

**lat·i·tude** /ˈlætɪtjuːd‖-tuːd/ *n* **1** [C,U] *technical* the distance north or south of the EQUATOR (=the imaginary line around the middle of the world) measured in degrees —compare LONGITUDE —see picture at EARTH¹ **2 latitudes** [plural] an area at a particular latitude: *At these latitudes you often get strong winds.* **3** [U] *formal* freedom to choose what you do or say: *Pupils enjoy considerable latitude in deciding what they want to study.* —**latitudinal** /ˌlætɪˈtjuːdɪnəl‖-ˈtuːdn-əl/ *adj*

**lat·i·tu·di·na·ri·an** /ˌlætɪtjuːdɪˈneəriən‖-tuːdnˈer-/ *n* [C] *formal* someone who is willing to accept other people's beliefs and behaviour —**latitudinarian** *adj*

**lat·ke** /ˈlɑːtkə/ *n* [C] a Jewish food like a round flat PANCAKE made from raw potato

**la·trine** /ləˈtriːn/ *n* [C] a toilet that is outdoors in a camp or military area

**lat·ter¹** /ˈlætə‖-ər/ *n* **the latter** *formal* the second of two W2 people or things just mentioned: *The system brings both financial and environmental benefits, the latter being especially welcome.* —opposite FORMER² (1)

**latter²** *adj* [only before noun] *formal* **1** being the second of two people or things, or the last in a list just mentioned: *In the latter case, buyers pay a 15% commission.* **2** the latter part of a period of time is nearest to the end of it: *Celebrations are planned for the latter part of November.*

**latter-day** /ˈ·· ·/ *adj* [only before noun] **a latter-day Versailles/Tsar/Robin Hood etc** something or someone that exists now but is like a famous thing or person that existed in the past: *ruling his business empire like a latter-day Tsar*

**Latter-Day Saints** /ˌ··· ˈ·/ *n* [plural] the MORMONS

**lat·ter·ly** /ˈlætəli‖-ər-/ *adv formal* **1** recently: *Jim's behaviour has been a little strange latterly.* **2** towards the end of a period of time: *O'Rourke retired after a 15-year career with Bisons, latterly as chief executive.* —compare FORMERLY

**lat·tice** /ˈlætɪ̞s/ *n* [C] **1** also **lat·tice·work** /ˈlætɪ̞swɜːk‖-wɜːrk/ a pattern or structure made of long flat narrow pieces of wood, plastic etc that are arranged so that they cross each other and the spaces between them are shaped like diamonds (DIAMOND (2)) **2 lattice window** a type of window made of a pattern of many small pieces of glass shaped like diamonds (DIAMOND (2)) **3** *technical* a regular arrangement of objects over an area or in space

**laud** /lɔːd‖lɒːd/ *v* [T] *formal* to praise someone or something

**lau·da·ble** /ˈlɔːdəbəl‖ˈlɒːd-/ *adj formal* deserving praise or admiration, even if not completely successful: *a laudable attempt* —**laudably** *adv*

**lau·da·num** /ˈlɔːdənəm‖ˈlɒː-/ *n* [U] a substance containing the drug OPIUM, used in the past to control pain and help people to sleep

**lau·da·to·ry** /ˈlɔːdətəri‖ˈlɒːdətɔːri/ *adj formal* expressing praise or admiration: *a laudatory biography*

S2 W2 **laugh¹** /lɑːf‖læf/ *v*

**1 ▶MAKE SOUND◀** [I] to make the sounds and movements of the face that people make when they think something is funny: *Jonathan kept pulling funny faces at me, and I couldn't stop laughing.* | [**+ at/about**] *I couldn't understand why they were all laughing at me.* | **burst out laughing** (=suddenly start laughing) *When we saw what had happened to the cake we burst out laughing.* | **laugh your head off** (=laugh loudly and a lot) | **laugh out loud** (=suddenly laugh loudly)

**2 ▶SPEAK◀** [T] to say something in a voice that shows you are amused: *"You look ridiculous!" Nick laughed.*

**3 be laughing** *spoken* to be happy or in a good situation, for example because something has had a successful result for you: *Well they paid me, didn't they, so I'm laughing.*

**4 don't make me laugh** *spoken* used when someone has just told you something that is completely untrue, asked for something impossible etc: *"Do you think we'll finish this today?" "Don't make me laugh."*

**5 no laughing matter** *informal* something serious that should not be joked about: *Losing your job is no laughing matter.*

**6 be laughing all the way to the bank** *informal* to be in a good situation because you have made a lot of money without making much effort

**7 be laughed out of court** *especially BrE* if a person or idea is laughed out of court, the idea is not accepted because people think it is completely stupid: *We can't propose that! We'd be laughed out of court!*

**8 sb will be laughing on the other side of their face** *spoken* used unkindly to mean that although someone is happy or confident now, they will be in trouble or in difficulty later

**9 laughing stock** someone who has done something so stupid that everyone laughs at them: *He was the laughing stock of the school!*

**10 not know whether to laugh or cry** to feel upset or annoyed by something bad or unlucky that has happened: *And when I couldn't find the passports – honestly, I didn't know whether to laugh or cry!*

**11 you have to laugh** *spoken* used to say that, even though a situation is annoying or disappointing, you can also see that there is something funny about it

**12 laugh in sb's face** to behave towards someone in a way that shows that you do not respect them or care about what they think: *I asked them not to park in front of my garage, but they just laughed in my face.*

**13 laugh up your sleeve** to be secretly happy, especially because you have played a trick on someone or criticized them without them knowing

**laugh at** sb/sth *phr v* [T] **1** to treat someone or something as if they are stupid, by laughing or making funny and unkind remarks about them: *I can't go to school wearing that – everyone'll laugh at me.* **2** to seem not to care about something that most people would worry about: *Young offenders just laugh at this sort of sentence.*

**laugh** sth ↔ **off** *phr v* [T] to pretend that something is less serious than it really is by laughing or joking about it: *I tried to tell him he was drinking too much but he just laughed it off.*

**laugh²** *n* [C] **1** the sound you make when you laugh: *a nervous laugh* | **give a laugh** *She gave a little laugh and squeezed my arm.* **2 have a (good) laugh** *BrE* **a)** *informal* to have fun and enjoy yourself: *We always have a good laugh when Kevin comes to stay.* **b)** to laugh about something in a happy way with other people: *It was a nightmare at the time, but afterwards we all had a good laugh about it.* **3 be a (good) laugh** *BrE informal* **a)** to be amusing and fun to be with: *I hope Sarah comes – she's a real laugh.* **b)** if an occasion, activity etc is a good laugh, you enjoy yourself and have fun: *We all went to the beach last night – it was a really good laugh.* **4 do sth for a laugh** *BrE informal* to do something because you think it will be fun, not for a serious reason **5 have the last laugh** to be successful, win an argument etc in the end, after other people have criticized you, defeated you etc earlier **6 be a laugh a minute** *informal* to be very funny, cheerful, and amusing; sometimes used humorously to mean the opposite S3

**laugh·a·ble** /ˈlɑːfəbəl‖ˈlæf-/ *adj* so bad, silly, or unbelievable that it makes you want to laugh: *The profit figures are laughable!* —**laughably** *adv*

**laugh·ing gas** /ˈ·· ·/ *n* [U] *informal* a gas that is sometimes used to stop you feeling pain during an operation

**laughing jack·ass** /ˌ·· ˈ··/ *n* [C] *informal* a KOOKABURRA

**laugh·ing·ly** /ˈlɑːfɪŋli‖ˈlæ-/ *adv* **1** if something is laughingly called something or described in a particular way, you think it is so bad that the name or description seems stupid: *This room is laughingly referred to as the 'Quality Control Centre'.* **2** if you do something laughingly, you are laughing while you do it

**laugh lines** /ˈ· ·/ *n* [plural] *AmE* the American form of LAUGHTER LINES

**laugh·ter** /ˈlɑːftə‖ˈlæftər/ *n* [U] the act of laughing or sound of people laughing: *We could hear riotous laughter from next door.* | **roar/howl/shriek with laughter** (=laugh very loudly) | **dissolve into laughter** (=start to laugh when you have been trying not to)

**laughter lines** /ˈ·· ·/ *n* [plural] *BrE* lines on your skin around your eyes which can be seen when you laugh; LAUGH LINES *AmE*

**launch¹** /lɔːntʃ‖lɒːntʃ/ *v* [T] W2

**1 ▶START STH◀** to start something, especially an official, public, or military activity that has been carefully planned: **launch a campaign/appeal/inquiry** *Police have launched a murder enquiry following the* *discovery of a woman's body.* | **launch an attack/assault/offensive** *The press launched a vicious attack on the President.*

**2 ▶ PRODUCT ◀** to make a new product, book etc available for sale for the first time: *It was a party to launch her new novel.*

**3 ▶ BOAT ◀** to put a boat or ship into the water

**4 ▶ SKY/SPACE ◀** to send a weapon or SPACECRAFT into the sky or into space: *A test satellite was launched from Cape Canaveral.*

**5 launch yourself forwards/up/from etc** to jump up and forwards into the air with a lot of energy

**launch into** sth *phr v* [T] to suddenly start a description or story, or suddenly start criticizing something: *The preacher launched into an attack on adultery.*

**launch out** *phr v* [I always + adv/prep] to start something new, especially something that involves risk: [+ **into**] *Dickson left his father's firm and launched out into business on his own.*

**launch²** *n* [C] **1** an occasion at which a new product, book etc is made available or made known: *the launch of our new hatchback* **2** a large boat with a motor

**launch·er** /ˈlɔːntʃə‖ˈlɒːntʃər/ *n* [C] a structure from which a weapon, ROCKET, or SPACECRAFT is sent into the sky

**launch pad** /ˈ· ·/ also **launching pad** /ˈ·· ·/ *n* [C] a base from which a ROCKET or MISSILE is sent up into the sky

**laun·der** /ˈlɔːndə‖ˈlɒːndər/ *v* [T] **1** to put money which has been obtained illegally into legal businesses and bank accounts, so that you can hide it or use it **2** *formal* to wash and IRON² clothes, sheets etc —**laundered** *adj*

**laun·der·ette** /ˌlɔːndəˈret‖ˌlɒːn-/ also **laundrette** /lɔːnˈdret‖lɒːn-/ *BrE n* [C] a place where you can go to wash your clothes in machines that work when you put coins in them

**laun·dry** /ˈlɔːndri‖ˈlɒːn-/ *n* **1** [C] a place or business where clothes etc are washed and ironed (IRON²) **2** [U] clothes, sheets etc that need to be washed or have just been washed

**laundry bas·ket** /ˈ·· ˌ··/ *n* [C] **1** *BrE* a large basket that you put dirty clothes in until you wash them; HAMPER² (2) *AmE* —see picture at BASKET **2** a basket used for carrying wet clothes that have been washed

**laundry list** /ˈ·· ·/ *n* [C] *AmE* a list you write to remind you of things you have to do or buy

**laur·e·ate** /ˈlɔːriɪt/ *n* [C] someone who has won an important prize, especially the NOBEL PRIZE: *Nigeria's Nobel laureate, Wole Soyinka* —see also POET LAUREATE

**laur·el** /ˈlɒrəl‖ˈlɔː-, ˈlɑː-/ *n* **1** [C,U] a small tree with smooth shiny dark green leaves that do not fall in winter **2 rest/sit on your laurels** to be satisfied with what you have achieved and therefore stop trying to achieve anything new **3 look to your laurels** to work hard in order not to lose the success that you have achieved

**lav** /læv/ *n* [C] *BrE spoken* a lavatory

**la·va** /ˈlɑːvə/ *n* [U] **1** hot liquid rock that flows from a VOLCANO **2** this rock when it has become cold and solid

**lav·a·to·ri·al** /ˌlævəˈtɔːriəl◂/ *adj* lavatorial humour or jokes are about going to the toilet or about sex

**lav·a·to·ry** /ˈlævətəri‖-tɔːri/ *n* [C] *formal* a toilet or the room a toilet is in

**lav·en·der** /ˈlævɪndə‖-ər/ *n* **1** [C,U] a plant that has purple flowers with a strong pleasant smell **2** [U] the dried flowers of this plant, often used to make things smell nice **3** [U] a pale purple colour

**lavender bag** /ˈ··· ˌ·/ *n* [C] a small bag containing dried lavender that you put in a drawer to make your clothes smell nice

**lavender wa·ter** /ˈ··· ˌ··/ *n* [U] a PERFUME¹ (1) made from lavender oil and alcohol

**la·ver** /ˈlɑːvə‖-ər/ *n* [U] a type of sea plant that you can eat

**laver bread** /ˈ·· ·/ *n* [U] a dish made from laver that is boiled and then cooked in butter

**lav·ish¹** /ˈlævɪʃ/ *adj* **1** lavish gifts, meals etc are large and generous, and look as if they have cost a lot of money: *They would organize lavish dinners for potential customers.* | *a lavish production of 'Tosca', with fine costumes and elaborate stage sets* **2 be lavish with** to give something very generously: *He's never very lavish with his praises.* —**lavishly** *adv*: *lavishly decorated with fruit and flowers* —**lavishness** *n* [U]

**lavish²** *v*

**lavish** sth **on/upon** sb *phr v* [T] to give someone a lot of something such as expensive presents, love, or praise: *Roberta lavished attention on the children.*

**law** /lɔː‖lɒː/ *n* S1 W1

**1 ▶ SYSTEM OF RULES ◀** [singular, U] the whole system of rules that citizens of a country or place must obey: **against the law** (=illegal) *Sex discrimination is against the law.* | **break the law** (=do something illegal) *There were easy profits for businessmen who were prepared to break the law.* | **against the law (for sb) to do sth** *It is against the law for children to work before they are fifteen.* | **become law** (=be officially made a law) *The Criminal Justice Bill became law amidst much controversy.* | **by law** (=according to the law) *Seatbelts must, by law, be worn by all passengers.* | **keep/stay/remain/operate within the law** (=make sure that what you do is legal) *They make tough business deals, but are always careful to operate within the law.* | **tax law/divorce law/libel law etc** (=all the laws relating to tax etc) *a specialist in company law* | *She's a partner in a major New York law firm.* —see also CRIMINAL LAW, LAW FIRM

**2 ▶ A RULE ◀** [C] a rule that people in a particular country, city or local area must obey: *Under the new law, any gathering of over 10 people is considered a crime.* | [+ **on**] *European laws on equal opportunities.* | [+ **against**] *There ought to be a law against cutting down trees.*

**3 there's no law against (it)** *spoken* used to tell someone who is criticizing you that you are not doing anything wrong

**4 ▶ POLICE ◀ the law** the police: *I think she may be in trouble with the law.* | **I'll have the law on you** *spoken* (=used to threaten someone that you will call the police) *Get away from my car or I'll have the law on you!*

**5 law and order** a situation in which people respect the law, and crime is controlled by the police, the prison system etc: *The soldiers were brought in to restore law and order after the riots.*

**6 have the law on your side** to be legally right in what you are doing

**7 ▶ SPORT ◀** [C] one of the rules that say how a sport should be played: *the laws of football.*

**8 ▶ BUSINESS/ART ◀** [C] a way in which things happen in an activity such business or art, which is thought of as a rule because it seems impossible to change: *the law of supply and demand* | *the law of perspective*

**9 ▶ NATURAL LAW ◀** [C] a statement that describes and explains how nature works: *the laws of nature* | *the Second Law of Thermodynamics.* | *the law of gravity*

**10 the law of the jungle a)** the idea that people should only look after themselves and not care about other people, if they want to succeed **b)** the principle that only the strongest creatures will stay alive

**11 the law of averages** the PROBABILITY that one result will happen as often as another if you try something often enough: *By the law of averages you'll have to throw a six eventually.*

**12 be a law unto himself/herself etc** to behave in an independent way and not worry about the usual rules of behaviour or what other people do or think

**13 take the law into your own hands** to do something illegal in order to put right something that you think is unjust, for example by violently punishing someone instead of informing the police: *vigilantes who take the law into their own hands*

**14 go to law** to go to court in order to settle a problem

—see also CIVIL LAW, COMMON LAW, **lay down the law** (LAY[2]), POOR LAW, ROMAN LAW, SOD'S LAW, **unwritten law** (UNWRITTEN)

**law-a·bid·ing** /ˈ· ·ˌ··/ *adj* **law abiding citizens/people/neighbours etc** people who respect and obey the law

**law·break·er** /ˈ· ˌ··/ *n* [C] someone who does something illegal —**law-breaking** *n* [U]

**law·court** /ˈlɔːkɔːt‖ˈlɒːkɔːrt/ *n* [C] a room or building where legal cases are judged

**law en·force·ment** /ˈ· ·ˌ··/ *n* [U] the job of making sure that the law is obeyed

**law enforcement a·gent** /ˈ· ···ˌ··/ *n* [C] *AmE* a policeman or policewoman

**law firm** /ˈ· ·/ *n* [C] *especially AmE* a company that provides legal services and employs many lawyers

**law·ful** /ˈlɔːfəl‖ˈlɒː-/ *adj formal or law* **1** considered by the government or law courts to be legal and correct: *a lawful marriage* **2** allowed by law: *doubts as to whether these dealings were lawful | lawful forms of protest* —**lawfully** *adv* —**lawfulness** *n* [U]

**law·less** /ˈlɔːləs‖ˈlɒː-/ *adj* not obeying the law, or not controlled by the law: *lawless terrorists | a lawless frontier town* —**lawlessly** *adv* —**lawlessness** *n* [U]

**Law Lords** /ˈ· ·/ *n* **the Law Lords** the members of the British House of Lords holding high positions in the legal profession, and who form the highest court in the British legal system

**law·mak·er** /ˈlɔːmeɪkə‖ˈlɒːmeɪkər/ *n* [C] *especially AmE* any elected official responsible for making laws

**law·man** /ˈlɔːmæn‖ˈlɒː-/ *n plural* **lawmen** /-men/ [C] *AmE* any professional officer who is responsible for making sure that the law is obeyed

**lawn** /lɔːn‖lɒːn/ *n* **1** [C] an area of ground in a garden or park that is covered with short grass: **mow the lawn** (=cut the grass) **2** [U] a fine cloth made from cotton or LINEN

**lawn chair** /ˈ· ·/ *n* [C] *AmE* a light chair like a folding bed, that you can sit or lie on outside when the sun is shining; SUN LOUNGER *BrE* —see picture at CHAIR[1]

**lawn mow·er** /ˈ· ˌ··/ *n* [C] a machine that you use to cut grass

**lawn par·ty** /ˈ· ˌ··/ *n* [C] *AmE* a formal party held outside in the afternoon, especially in a large garden; GARDEN PARTY *BrE*

**lawn sign** /ˈ· ·/ *n* [C] *AmE* a sign that you put in front of your house before an election to say which person or political party you support

**lawn ten·nis** /ˌ· ˈ··‖ˈ· ˌ··/ *n* [U] *formal* TENNIS

**law school** /ˈ· ·/ *n* [C,U] a school in the US where you study to become a lawyer after your BACHELOR'S DEGREE

**law·suit** /ˈlɔːsuːt, -sjuːt‖ˈlɒːsuːt/ *n* [C] a charge, claim, or complaint against someone that is made in a court of law by a private person or company, not by the police or state; SUIT[1] (4): **file a lawsuit** *Local people filed a private lawsuit against the oil company over water contamination.*

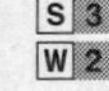

S3 W2 **law·yer** /ˈlɔːjə‖ˈlɒːjər/ *n* [C] someone whose job is to advise people about laws, write formal agreements, or represent people in court —see also ADVOCATE[2], ATTORNEY, BARRISTER, SOLICITOR

**USAGE NOTE: LAWYER**

WORD CHOICE: **lawyer, counsellor/counselor, attorney, barrister, solicitor**

In American English a **lawyer** is often called a **counsellor** (also spelt **counselor**) or, especially if he or she speaks in court, an **attorney**.

In British English a **lawyer** who speaks in court is called a **barrister**, while a **solicitor** works mainly from an office, but may also appear in the less formal and important courts.

**lax** /læks/ *adj* **1** not strict or careful enough about standards of behaviour, work, safety etc; SLACK[1] (1): *lax security* **2** muscles or arms or legs that are lax are not firm or strong and therefore tend to hang loosely —**laxly** *adv* —**laxity** *n* [U] —**laxness** *n* [U]

**lax·a·tive** /ˈlæksətɪv/ *n* [C] a medicine or something that you eat which makes your BOWELS empty easily —**laxative** *adj*

**lay**[1] /leɪ/ *v* the past tense of LIE[1] S1 W2

lay

laying a dress on the bed lying on the bed

**lay**[2] *v past tense and past participle* **laid** /leɪd/

**1** ▶ **PUT SB/STH DOWN** ◀ [T always + adv/prep] to put someone or something down carefully into a flat position: **lay sth in/on/under etc** *Laying my coat carefully on the bed, I crept towards the door. | The bodies were laid under the trees to await burial. | Sharon laid her hand on my arm.*

**2 lay bricks/carpet/concrete/cables etc** to put or fix bricks, a carpet etc in the correct place, especially on the ground or floor: *The man's coming to lay the carpet on Saturday. | laying an oil pipeline across the desert*

**3** ▶ **EGGS** ◀ [I,T] if a bird, insect etc lays eggs, it produces them from its body: *The flies lay their eggs on decaying meat.*

**4** ▶ **RISK MONEY** ◀ [T] to risk an amount of money on the result of a race, sports game etc; BET[2] (1): **lay £5/$10 etc on** *She laid £5 on the favourite, Golden Boy.*

**5 lay the blame on** to blame someone for something that has happened: *Then both sides start trying to lay the blame on each other!*

**6 lay a charge/proposal etc** *formal* to make a statement, suggestion etc in an official or public way: *Your employer has laid a serious charge against you. | Several proposals have been laid before the committee.*

**7 lay sth open/bare** to remove what covers, hides, or shelters something

**8 lay sth ↔ waste** to destroy or damage everything in a place, especially in a war

**9 lay stress/emphasis on** to emphasize something because you regard it as very important: *a political philosophy that lays great stress on individual responsibility*

**10 lay plans/a trap etc** to carefully prepare something, especially something that will harm someone else

**11 lay the table** to put the cloth, plates, knives, forks etc on a table, ready for a meal

**12** ▶ **HAVE SEX** ◀ [T] *slang* to have sex with someone: **get laid** (=find someone to have sex with)

**13 lay sb/sth flat** to hit someone or something and knock them down: *Laid him flat with a single punch!*

**14 lay yourself open to blame/criticism/ridicule etc** to do something that makes it possible that you will be blamed, criticized etc: *I don't want to lay myself open to charges of nepotism.*

**15 lay sth on the line a)** to state something, especially a threat, demand, or criticism, in a very clear way **b)** to risk losing your life, your job etc, especially in order to help someone

**16 lay sb low a)** [usually passive] if an illness lays

someone low, they are unable to do their normal activities for a period of time: *She's been laid low with flu for a week.* **b)** *literary* to knock someone down or injure them seriously
**17 lay the ghost (of)** to finally get rid of something from your past that has been worrying you —see also **lay your hands on** (HAND[1] (30)), **lay/provide the foundation(s) for** (FOUNDATION (5)), **not lay a finger on** (FINGER[1] (5)), **put/lay your cards on the table** (CARD[1] (12))

**lay about** sb *phr v* [T] *literary or old-fashioned* to attack someone violently: *He laid about his attackers with his stick.*

**lay** sth ↔ **aside** *phr v* [T] **1** to store something to use in the future: *She'd managed to lay aside a few pounds each week from her wages.* **2** to stop using, doing, or preparing something, for a short time: *The building plans may have to be laid aside till things improve.*

**lay** sth ↔ **down** *phr v* [T]
**1 ▶TOOLS/WEAPONS◀** to put down your tools, weapons etc as a sign that you will stop using them: *Lay down your weapons and walk slowly towards the door!*
**2 ▶OFFICIALLY STATE◀** [usually passive] to officially state rules that must be obeyed, systems that must be used etc or state something officially or firmly: *The regulations lay down a rigid procedure for checking safety equipment.* | **lay down that** *It is laid down in the regulations that all members must carry their membership cards at all times.*
**3 lay down your life** *formal* to lose your life, for example in a war, in order to help other people: *prepared to lay down his life for his comrades*
**4 lay down the law** to tell other people what to do, how they should think etc, in an unpleasant or rude way
**5 ▶START◀** to start building or making something by doing the first part of the work: *Crick and Watson laid down the foundations of modern genetic research.*
**6 ▶WINE ETC◀** to store something, especially wine, to use in the future

**lay** sth ↔ **in** *phr v* [T] to obtain and store a large supply of something to use in the future

**lay into** sb *phr v* [T] to attack someone physically or with words: *You should have heard her laying into Tommy!*

**lay off** *phr v* **1** [T **lay** sb ↔ **off**] to stop employing a worker, especially for a period in which there is not much work to do: *Harry was laid off for six months during the recession.* **2** [I,T **lay off** sth] *informal* to stop doing, having, or using something: *I think you'd better lay off alcohol for a while.* | **lay off doing sth** *Just lay off hassling me, would you!*

**lay on** *phr v* [T] **1** [**lay** sth ↔ **on**] to provide food, entrtainment etc in a very generous way: *The organizers have laid on a huge meal for us.* | *It's great! – transportation, hotel, food, it's all laid on.* **2** [**lay** sth **on** sb] to give someone something such as a responsibility or problem that is hard to deal with: *Sorry to lay this on you, but we need someone to go to Italy next week.* **3 lay it on (a bit thick)** *informal* **a)** to praise or admire someone or something too much, especially in order to please someone **b)** to state or describe something in a way that goes beyond the truth; EXAGGERATE

**lay** sb/sth **out** *phr v* [T]
**1 ▶SPREAD◀** to spread something out: *Lay out the map on the table and let's have a look.*
**2 ▶ARRANGE◀** to arrange or plan a building, town, garden etc: *The garden is laid out in a formal pattern.*
**3 ▶SPEND◀** *informal* to spend money, especially a lot of money: **lay out sth on** *We've just laid out £500 on car repairs.* —see also OUTLAY[2]
**4 ▶HIT◀** to knock someone down, especially hard enough to make them unconscious: *One of the guards had been laid out and the other was missing.*
**5 ▶BODY◀** to prepare a dead body so that it can be buried

**lay over** *phr v* [I] *AmE* to stay somewhere for a short time before continuing your journey

**lay to** *phr v* [I,T **lay** sth **to**] *technical* if a ship lays to or if you lay it to, it stops moving

**lay** sb/sth ↔ **up** *phr v* [T] **1 be laid up (with)** to have to stay in bed because you are ill or injured: *laid up for a week with flu.* **2 lay up problems/difficulties etc** to do something that will cause problems in the future: *I tell you, she's just laying up trouble for herself, she really is.* **3** *old-fashioned* to collect and store something to use in the future: *laying up firewood for the winter*

**USAGE NOTE: LAY**
GRAMMAR
You **lay** [T] something somewhere, but you **lie** [I] somewhere: *He laid his things on the bed* but *He lay on the bed* (NOT *lied*). In spoken British English you will also sometimes hear things like: *I want to lay down* (instead of *I want to lie down*) but some people consider this to be incorrect.
A third verb **lie** [I] **(lying, lied, lied)** means 'to tell a lie'. **Lied** should not be confused with **lived**: *She lied when she said she lived in Beverley Hills.*

**lay[3]** *n* [C] **1 the lay of the land** *especially AmE* **a)** the situation that exists at a particular time: *I'll go in and get the lay of the land – see if Pam's in a better mood.* **b)** the appearance of an area of land, the way it slopes etc **2 be a great/good lay** *slang* to be good to have sex with **3** *literary* a poem or song

**lay[4]** *adj* [only before noun] **a)** not trained or knowing much about a particular profession or subject: *To the lay observer, these technical terms are incomprehensible.* **b)** not in an official position in the church: *a lay preacher*

**lay·a·bout** /ˈleɪəbaʊt/ *n* [C] *BrE informal* a lazy person who avoids work, responsibility etc

**lay·a·way** /ˈleɪəweɪ/ *n* [U] *AmE* a method of buying goods in which the goods are kept by the seller for a small amount of money until the full price is paid: *I've put the dress on layaway.* —**layaway** *adj*: *a layaway plan*

**lay-by** /ˈ· ·/ *n* [C] *BrE* a space next to a road where vehicles can stop

**layer**

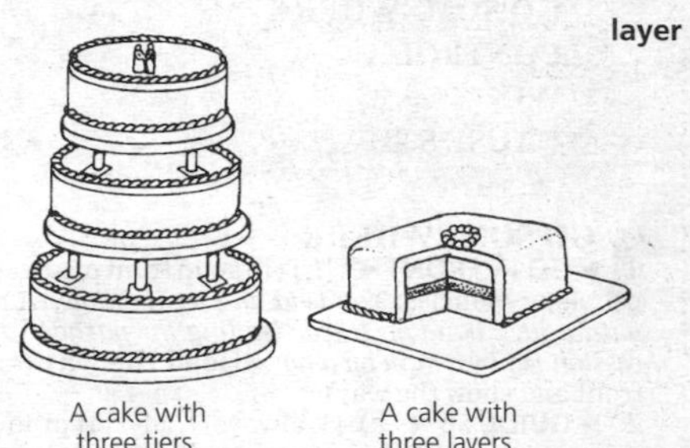

A cake with three tiers.   A cake with three layers.

**lay·er[1]** /ˈleɪə‖-ər/ *n* [C] **1** an amount of a substance that covers all of a surface: [+ **of**] *A thick layer of dust lay on the furniture.* **2** one of several levels of substances lying one on top of another: [+ **of**] *a thin layer of coal between two layers of rock* | *He pulled off layer upon layer of clothing.* —see also OZONE LAYER **3** one of several different levels in a complicated organization, system, set of ideas etc: [+ **of**] *There are many layers of meaning to be discovered in the poem.* | *major changes that have eliminated two layers of management* **4 multi-layered/single-layered etc** having a lot of layers, one layer etc S3 W3

**layer[2]** *v* [T] **1** to make a layer of something or put something down in layers: *potatoes layered with cheese* **2** to cut someone's hair in layers rather than all to the same length

**lay·ette** /leɪˈet/ *n* [C] a complete set of clothing and other things a new baby needs

**lay fig·ure** /ˌ· ˈ··/ *n* [C] a model of the human body used in painting or drawing

**lay·man** /ˈleɪmən/ *n plural* **laymen** /-mən/ [C] **1** someone who is not trained in a particular subject or type of work, especially when they are being compared with someone who is: **the layman** (=laymen in general) *technical terms not easily understood by the layman* | **in layman's terms** (=used when explaining something in simple language) *the GNP or, in layman's terms, the amount of goods produced by a country* **2** someone who is not a priest but is a member of a church

**lay-off** /ˈ· ·/ *n* [C] the act of stopping a worker's employment because there is not enough work: *more lay-offs in the car industry* —see also **lay off** (LAY²)

**lay·out** /ˈleɪaʊt/ *n* [C] **1** the way in which something such as a town, garden, or building is arranged **2** the way in which writing and pictures are arranged on a page —see also **lay sb/sth out** (LAY²)

**lay·o·ver** /ˈleɪəʊvə‖-oʊvər/ *n* [C] *AmE* a short stay between parts of a journey, especially a long plane journey; STOPOVER *BrE*

**lay·per·son** /ˈleɪˌpɜːsən‖-pɜːr-/ *n plural* **laypersons** [C] a word for a LAYMAN used when the person could be a woman or a man

**lay read·er** /ˌ· ˈ··/ *n* [C] someone in Christian churches who is not a priest but who has been given authority to lead a religious service and PREACH (1)

**lay-up** /ˈ· ·/ *n* [C] a throw in BASKETBALL made from very close to the basket or from under it

**lay·wom·an** /ˈleɪˌwʊmən/ *n plural* **laywomen** /-ˌwɪmɪn/ [C] **1** a woman not trained in a particular subject or type of work, especially when she is being compared with someone who is **2** a woman who is not a priest but is a member of a church

**laze** /leɪz/ *v* [I always + adv/prep] to relax and enjoy yourself in a lazy way: *Warren spent the afternoon lazing in the sun.* | **laze about/around** *lazing around when they should have been working* —**laze** *n* [singular]

**la·zy** /ˈleɪzi/ *adj* **1** disliking work and physical activity, and never making any effort: *the laziest boy in the class* | *I was feeling lazy so I called a taxi.* **2** a lazy period of time is spent doing nothing except relaxing: *a lazy Sunday* **3** moving slowly: *a lazy river* —**lazily** *adv* —**laziness** *n* [U]

**la·zy·bones** /ˈleɪzibəʊnz‖-boʊnz/ *n* [C] *informal* a word for a lazy person, often used in a friendly way to someone you like: *Come on, lazybones! Get out of bed.*

**lb** *plural* **lbs** the written abbreviation of pound, a unit of weight equal to 0.454 kilograms: *a 3lb bag of flour*

**lbw** /ˌel biː ˈdʌbəljuː/ *adv* leg before wicket; a way in which your INNINGS can end in CRICKET (2), when the ball hits your leg that is in front of your WICKET

**LCD** /ˌel siː ˈdiː/ *n* [C] **1** liquid crystal display; the part of a watch, CALCULATOR, or small computer where numbers and letters are shown by means of an electric current that is passed through a special liquid —see picture on page 837 **2** the written abbreviation of LOWEST COMMON DENOMINATOR

**LCM** the written abbreviation of LOWEST COMMON MULTIPLE

**lea** /liː/ *n* [C] *poetical* an area of land with grass

**leach** /liːtʃ/ also **leach out** *v* [I,T] *technical* if a substance leaches or is leached from a larger mass such as the soil, it is removed from it by water passing through the larger mass: *Nitrates from agricultural fertilizers leached into the rivers.*

S1 W1

## lead¹ /liːd/ *v past tense and past participle* **led** /led/

① GO SOMEWHERE
② CONTROL
③ WIN
④ CAUSE STH
⑤ LIVE
⑥ BE BEST/FIRST
⑦ OTHER MEANINGS

### ① GO SOMEWHERE

**1 ▶GO IN FRONT◀** [I,T] to go in front of a group of people or vehicles: *You lead and we'll follow.* | *A truck with a jazz band on it was leading the parade.* | *a procession led by a man on a horse* | **lead the way** (=go in front and show the way)

**2 ▶GUIDE SB◀ a)** [T always + adv/prep] to take someone to a place by going with them: **lead sb through/to/along etc** *An official led me along the corridor to a large office.* **b)** [T] to take a person or animal somewhere while holding the person's arm or pulling a rope tied to the animal: **lead sb up/down/through etc sth** *The hostages were blindfolded and led to a waiting car.* | *A groom was leading a racehorse out of the stable.*

**3 ▶ROAD/WIRE◀** [I] if something such as a path, pipe, or wire leads somewhere or leads in a particular direction, it goes there or goes in that direction: [+**down/into/towards etc**] *a flight of steps leading down to the beach* | *animal tracks that led into the woods* | *The thieves cut the wires leading to the surveillance cameras.* | *Where does this road lead?*

**4 ▶DOOR◀** [I] if a door or passage leads to a particular room or place, you can get there by going through it: [+ **to/into**] *a door leading to the conference room*

### ② CONTROL

**5 ▶BE IN CHARGE◀** [T] to be in charge of something such as an important activity, a group of people, or an organization, especially a political party: *a communist-led strike* | *Major will lead the Conservative Party at the next election.* | *Inspector Roberts is leading the investigation into Susan Carr's murder.*

**6 lead sb astray** to encourage someone to do bad or immoral things that they would not normally do: *We think Harry was led astray by some of the older boys.*

**7 ▶CONVERSATION◀** [I,T] to direct a conversation or discussion, especially so that it develops in the way you want: *Mary led the conversation around to the topic of salaries.*

**8 lead sb by the nose** *informal* to make someone do anything you want them to

### ③ WIN

**9** [I,T] to be winning a game or competition: **lead by ten points/two sets/four frames etc** *Agassi was leading by two sets when rain stopped play.* | **lead sb/sth** *Brazil led Germany 1 – 0.* | *Schumacher led the race from start to finish.* | *With two minutes to play the Lakers are still leading.*

### ④ CAUSE STH

**10** [T] to be the thing that makes someone decide to do something: **lead sb to do sth** *What led you to take up acting as a career?* | *Ian's death led me to rethink what I wanted out of life.*

**11 lead sb to believe/expect/understand** *formal* to make someone think something is true, especially when it is not: *We were led to believe that all the money from the concert was going to charity.*

**⑤ LIVE**

**12 lead a normal/exciting/dull etc life** to have a particular kind of life: *We lead a very quiet life since Ralph retired.*

**⑥ BE BEST/FIRST**

**13** [I,T] to be more successful than other people, companies, or countries in a particular activity or area of business or study: *US companies lead the world in biotechnology.* | *Asian-American students under 12 lead in literacy and numeracy.* | **lead the field** (=be the most successful person etc in a particular area of business or study) *a company that leads the field in software applications*

**14 lead the way** to be the first to do something, especially something good or successful, which is likely to encourage others to do the same thing: *The Japanese led the way in using industrial robots.*

**⑦ OTHER MEANINGS**

**15 market-led/demand-led/service-led etc** in which the market, demand etc is the most important influence on the way something happens: *a demand-led recovery*

**16 this leads me to ...** *spoken* used in a speech or discussion to introduce a new subject and connect it with what you have just said: *This leads me to our sales targets for next year.*

**17 lead sb a dance** *informal* to make someone feel worried and confused, especially because they do not know what you are going to do next: *Once they were married, Gwen led her poor husband a hell of a dance.*

**18 lead sb up the garden path** *informal* to deceive someone

**19** [I + **with**, T] to play a particular card as your first card in one part of a game of cards: *He led with the eight of hearts.*

**20 lead with your left/right** to hit someone mainly with your left or right hand in BOXING

**lead into** sth *phr v* [T not in passive] if one subject, discussion etc leads into another, the second one follows naturally from the first because there is a clear connection between them: *Fox mentioned the Korean deal, which led into a general discussion on our prospects in Asia.*

**lead off** *phr v* **1** [I,T] to start something such as a meeting, discussion, or performance by saying or doing something: *I'd like to lead off by thanking Rick Jones for finding the time to be with us today.* | **lead off with** *John, would you lead off with your views on the merger?* | **lead sth ↔ off** *Hal led off the evening with some folk songs.* **2** [I,T] if a road, room etc leads off a place, it connects directly with that place: **lead off from sth** *Go on for about 100 yards and you'll see a path leading off from the main road.* | **lead off sth** *a dining room leading off the hall corridor* **3** [I] *AmE* to be the first player to try to hit the ball in an INNING (=period of play) in a game of BASEBALL

**lead to** sth *phr v* [T not in passive] to make something happen or exist as a result: *an investment program that will lead to the creation of hundreds of new jobs* | *The bank has offered a reward for any information leading to the arrest of the men.*

**lead up to** sth *phr v* [T not in passive] **1** if events lead up to something important that happens, they come before it, and often cause it: *The book describes the trial and the events leading up to it.* **2** to gradually introduce a subject into a conversation, especially a subject that may be embarrassing or upsetting for you or the person you are talking to: *I suppose all this talk about "business opportunities" is leading up to a request for money?*

**USAGE NOTE: LEAD**

WORD CHOICE: **lead, show the way, take, bring, guide, see, direct, tell the way**

To **lead** is to **show the way** by going first: *You lead and we'll follow.* | *She led them down the mountain.*

More usually to show someone the way you just **take or bring** them somewhere: *Please pick him up and take him to the hotel/bring him to my house* (NOT usually *lead*).

Roads, tunnels, corridors etc. may **lead** to places, but cars, planes etc usually **take** you there: *This road leads to/takes you to Chicago* but *The train took me to Grand Central Station* (NOT *led*, unless you were following behind the train!).

If someone needs a lot of help you **guide** them somewhere in order to show them the way and explain things: *We'll need someone to guide us through the hills.* | *He guides tourists around the castle.*

**See someone somewhere** may be used especially if you go with someone to a place because there may be some danger rather than because they do not know the way: *It's very late – Do you want me to see you home?*

To **direct** (slightly formal) is to explain to someone how to get to a place, but not to go with them: *Could you direct me to the station, please?* Less formally you **tell** someone **the way**: *Can you tell me the way to the station, please?*

GRAMMAR

Remember the past tense and past participle of **lead** are both **led**: *She's led an interesting life* (NOT *lead*).

**lead**

Number 4 is in the lead.

S 2 W 2 **lead²** *n*

**1 ► RACES ETC ◄ the lead** the position in front of everyone else in a race or competition: **be in the lead** *Le Mond was in the lead after the third lap.*

**2 take the lead a)** to go ahead of the other competitors in a race or competition: *Korea has taken the lead in ship-building.* **b)** to take the responsibility for organizing something: *It's up to the older members to take the lead and explain things to the newcomers.* **c)** to be the first to do something, hoping that others will copy you: *The Americans have taken the lead in banning nuclear tests.*

**3 ► WINNING AMOUNT ◄** [singular] the distance, number of points etc by which one competitor is ahead of another: [+ **over**] *The Bulls had a 17 point lead over the Celtics by halftime.* | [+ **of**] *The latest polls give the Republicans a lead of 32%.*

**4 ► EXAMPLE ◄** [C] a suggestion or example for people to copy: **give (sb) a lead** *It's up to you to give a moral lead.* | **follow sb's lead** *You say what you think is best. I'll follow your lead.*

**5 ► INFORMATION ◄** [C] a piece of information that may help you to make a discovery or help find the answer to a problem; CLUE[1] (1): *The police have several leads as to the location of the stolen goods.*

**6 ▶ PERFORMER ◀ a)** [C] the main acting part in a play, film etc: *playing the lead in an amateur production of 'Hamlet'* **b) lead singer/guitarist etc** the main singer, GUITAR player etc in a musical group
**7 ▶ FOR DOG ◀** [C] *BrE* a piece of rope, leather etc fastened to a dog's collar in order to control it; LEASH[1] (1)
**8 ▶ ELECTRIC WIRE ◀** [C] *BrE* an electric wire used to connect a piece of electrical equipment to the power supply; CORD[1] (3) *AmE*
**9 be your lead** if it is your lead in a game of cards, you have the right to play your card first

**lead³** /led/ *n* **1** [U] a soft heavy easily melted greyish-blue metal, used for water pipes, covering roofs etc: *lead piping* **2** [C,U] the central part of a pencil **3 go down like a lead balloon** if a suggestion or joke goes down like a lead balloon, people do not like it at all **4** [U] *AmE old-fashioned* bullets: *They filled him full of lead.* **5 leads** [plural] **a)** sheets of lead used for covering a roof **b)** narrow pieces of lead used for holding small pieces of glass together to form a window —see also BLACK LEAD, WHITE LEAD

**lead·ed gas** /ˌledɪ̣d ˈgæs/ *n* also **leaded gasoline** /ˌ·· ˈ···/ [U] *AmE* petrol containing lead; LEADED PETROL *BrE*

**leaded lights** /ˌledɪ̣d ˈlaɪts/ *n* [plural] *BrE* windows with thin narrow pieces of lead (LEAD³ (1)) separating small pieces of glass shaped like squares or diamonds (DIAMOND (2))

**leaded pet·rol** /ˌledɪ̣d ˈpetrəl/ *n* [U] *BrE* petrol containing lead (LEAD³ (1)); LEADED GAS *AmE*

**leaded win·dows** /ˌledɪ̣d ˈwɪndəʊz‖-doʊz/ *n* [plural] LEADED LIGHTS

**lead·en** /ˈledn/ *adj* **1** *literary* dark grey: *a leaden sky* **2** without happiness, excitement, or energy: *a leaden performance*

S3 W1 **lead·er** /ˈliːdə‖-ər/ *n* [C]
**1 ▶ IN CONTROL ◀** the person who directs or controls a team, organization, country etc: *The prize was awarded to President de Klerk and the ANC leader Nelson Mandela.* | *a born leader* | [+ **of**] *the leader of the local black community*
**2 ▶ RACE ◀** the person, organization etc that is in front of all the others in a race or competition: *Schumacher was now catching up and challenging the leaders.* | [+ **in**] *leaders in the field of information technology* —see also MARKET LEADER
**3 ▶ NEWSPAPER ◀** *BrE* a piece of writing in a newspaper giving the paper's opinion on a subject; EDITORIAL
**4 ▶ MUSICIAN ◀** *BrE* the main VIOLIN player in an ORCHESTRA; CONCERTMASTER *AmE*
**5 ▶ TAPE ◀** *technical* the part at the beginning of a film or recording tape which has nothing on it
**6 ▶ BRANCH ◀** *technical* a long thin branch that grows from the stem of a bush or tree beyond other branches
**7 ▶ FISHING ◀** *technical* a short piece of a special string used to tie the hook onto the end of a fishing line (LINE¹ (16))

S3 W2 **lead·er·ship** /ˈliːdəʃɪp‖-ər-/ *n* **1** [U] the position of being the leader of a team, organization etc: *Burns took over the leadership of the party.* | **under sb's leadership** (=while a particular person is leader) **2** [U] the quality of being good at leading a team, organization, country etc: *someone with vision and leadership* **3** [C] all the people who lead a group, organization etc [also + plural verb *BrE*]: *The party leadership are in agreement on this matter.* **4** [U] the position of being in front of others in a competition: *the company's leadership in robot technology*

L

**lead-free** /ˌled ˈfriː◂/ *adj* lead-free petrol contains no LEAD³ (1); UNLEADED

**lead-in** /ˈliːd ɪn/ *n* [C] remarks made by someone to introduce a radio or television show

W2 **lead·ing¹** /ˈliːdɪŋ/ *adj* [only before noun]
**1 ▶ MOST IMPORTANT/BEST ◀** best, most important, or most successful: *the leading software provider in the domestic PC markets* | *a leading heart specialist*
**2 leading edge a)** *technical* the front edge of something **b)** the area of an activity where the most modern and advanced equipment and methods are used: *working at the leading edge of genetic engineering* —see also LEADING-EDGE
**3 leading light** a respected person who leads a group or organization, or is important in a particular area of knowledge or activity
**4 leading question** a question that deliberately tricks someone into giving the answer you want
**5 leading lady/man** the woman or man who acts the most important female or male part in a film, play etc —see also LEADING ARTICLE

**lead·ing²** /ˈledɪŋ/ *n* [U] *technical* **1** lead (LEAD³ (1)) used for covering roofs, for window frames etc **2** the space left between lines of print on a page

**leading ar·ti·cle** /ˌliːdɪŋ ˈɑːtɪkəl‖-ˈɑːr-/ *n* [C] *BrE* a piece of writing in a newspaper giving the paper's opinion on a subject; EDITORIAL

**leading-edge** /ˌliːdɪŋ ˈedʒ/ *adj* [only before noun] leading-edge machines, systems etc are the most modern and advanced ones that exist: *It uses leading-edge voice-recognition software.*

**lead-off** /ˈliːd ɒf‖-ɔːf/ *adj AmE* happening or going first or before others

S2 W2 **leaf¹** /liːf/ *n plural* **leaves** /liːvz/
**1 ▶ PLANT ◀** [C] one of the flat green parts of a plant that are joined to its stem or branches: *a flowering bush with large shiny leaves* | **be in leaf/come into leaf** *The forest was just coming into leaf.*
**2 take a leaf out of sb's book** to copy the way someone else behaves because you admire them
**3 turn over a new leaf** to decide you will change the way you behave and become a better person
**4 ▶ PAPER ◀** [C] *technical* a thin sheet of paper, especially a page in a book —see also LOOSE-LEAF, OVERLEAF
**5 ▶ OF TABLE ◀** [C] a part of the top of a table that can be taken out to make the table smaller
**6 ▶ METAL ◀** [U] metal, especially gold or silver, in a very thin sheet; GOLD LEAF —see also **shake like a leaf** (SHAKE¹ (1))

**leaf²** *v*
**leaf through** sth *phr v* [T] to turn the pages of a book quickly, without reading it properly: *I was leafing through an old school magazine when I came across your photo.*

**leaf·age** /ˈliːfɪdʒ/ *n* [U] the leaves on a tree or plant; FOLIAGE

**leaf·let¹** /ˈliːflɪ̣t/ *n* [C] a small piece of printed paper giving information or advertising: *a leaflet on skin cancer*

**leaflet²** *v* [I,T] to give out leaflets in a particular area: *He's leafleting the neighborhood.*

**leaf mould** *BrE*, **leaf mold** *AmE* /ˈ· ·/ *n* [U] dead decaying leaves that form a rich surface on soil

**leaf·y** /ˈliːfi/ *adj* **1** having a lot of leaves: *leafy green vegetables such as spinach* **2** having a lot of trees and plants: *a leafy suburb*

W2 **league¹** /liːg/ *n* [C] **1** a group of sports teams or players who play games against each other to see who is best: *Spurs finished fourth in the league this season.* —compare CONFERENCE (3) **2 be in a different league from/not be in the same league as** to be much better, or much worse, than someone or something else: *They're not in the same league as the French at making wine.* **3 be in league** to be working together secretly, especially for a bad purpose: [+ **with**] *Union leaders were accused of being in league with the Mafia.* **4** a group of people or countries who have joined together because they have similar aims, political beliefs etc: *the Young Communist League* **5** an old unit for measuring, equal to about five kilometres

**league²** *v* [I, T] *formal* to join together with other people, especially in order to fight for or against something

**league ta·ble** /'· ,··/ *n* [C] *especially BrE* a list that shows the positions of people, teams, or organizations that are competing against each other

S3 **leak¹** /li:k/ *v* **1** [I,T] if a container, pipe, roof etc leaks, or if it leaks gas, liquid etc, there is a small hole or crack in it that lets the gas or liquid flow out or flow through: *The roof always leaks when it rains.* | **leak sth** *My car seems to be leaking oil.* **2** [I] if a gas or liquid leaks, it gets in or through a hole in something: **[+ into/through/out of etc]** *Gas was leaking out of the pipes.* **3** [T] to deliberately give secret information to a newspaper, television company etc: **leak sth to** *Details of his business dealings were leaked to the press.* **4 leak like a sieve** to leak very badly

**leak out** *phr v* [I] if secret information leaks out, a lot of people find out about it: *News of his dismissal soon leaked out.*

**leak²** *n* [C] **1** a small hole that lets liquid or gas flow into or out of something: *There's a leak in the car radiator.* **2 a gas/oil/water leak** an escape of gas or liquid through a hole in something **3** a situation in which secret information is deliberately given to a newspaper, television company etc: *a leak suggesting that the hospital is to be closed* **4 take/have a leak** *slang* to pass water from your body; URINATE —see also **spring a leak** (SPRING¹ (9))

**leak·age** /'li:kɪdʒ/ *n* [C,U] **1** an example of gas, water etc leaking, or the amount of gas or liquid that has leaked **2** the deliberate spreading of information that should be kept secret

**leak·y** /'li:ki/ *adj* having a hole or other fault so that liquid or gas passes through a container, roof, pipe etc: *the constant dripping of a leaky tap* —**leakiness** *n* [U] —see picture on page 1258

S3 **lean¹** /li:n/ *v past tense and past participle* **leaned** or **leant** /lent/ *especially BrE* **1** [I always + adv/prep] to move or bend your body in a particular direction: **[+ forward/back etc]** *Robert was leaning forward, talking to the people in front.* | *They were leaning over her, trying to wake her up.* **2** [I] to slope or bend from an upright position: *trees leaning in the wind* **3** [I always + adv/prep] to support yourself or be supported in a sloping position against a wall or other surface: **[+ on/against]** *He was leaning on the bar with a drink in his hand.* | *There was a ladder leaning against the wall.* **4** [T always + adv/prep] to put something in a sloping position where it is supported: **lean sth on/against sth** *Gail leant her head on his shoulder.*

**lean on** sb/sth *phr v* [T] **1** to depend on someone or something for support and encouragement, especially at a difficult time: *It's good to know you've got friends to lean on.* **2** *informal* to try to influence someone, especially by threatening them: **lean on sb to do sth** *Lean on them to pay up.*

**lean towards** sth *phr v* [T] to tend to support, or begin to support, a particular set of opinions, beliefs etc: *My wife is voting Democrat but I'm leaning towards the Republicans.*

**lean²** *adj* **1** thin in a healthy and attractive way: *lean and athletic looking* —see THIN (USAGE) **2** lean meat does not have much fat on it **3** a lean organization, company etc uses only as much money and as many people as it needs, so that nothing is wasted **4** a lean period is a very difficult time because there is not enough money, business etc: *a lean year for business* —**leanness** *n* [U]

**lean³** *n* [U] the fleshy part of meat and not the bone or fat

**lean·ing** /'li:nɪŋ/ *n* [C] a tendency to prefer or agree with a particular set of beliefs, opinions etc; INCLINATION (2): *Fran has Communist leanings.* | **[+ towards]** *a leaning towards the Right*

**leant** /lent/ the past tense and past participle of LEAN¹

**lean-to** /'· ·/ *n* [C] a small roughly made building that rests against the side of a larger building

**leap¹** /li:p/ *v past tense and past participle* **leapt** /lept/ *especially BrE*, **leaped** *especially AmE*

**1 ▶ JUMP ◀ a)** [I always + adv/prep] to jump high into the air or to jump in order to land in a different place: *Jen leapt across the stream.* **b)** [T] *literary* to jump over something: *Brenda leaped the gate and ran across the field.*

**2 ▶ MOVE FAST ◀** [I always + adv/prep] to move very quickly and with a lot of energy: **[+ up/out/into etc]** *I leapt up the stairs three at a time.* | **leap to your feet** *Morgan leapt to his feet and started shouting.* | **leap to sb's assistance/defence etc** *Wendi leaped to his assistance.*

**3 ▶ INCREASE ◀** [I] to increase quickly and by a large amount: *The price of gas leapt 15% overnight.*

**4 leap at the chance/opportunity/offer** to accept a chance, opportunity, or offer very eagerly: *They were offering a free holiday in the Algarve, so naturally I leapt at the chance.*

**5 leap out at you** if something you are looking at leaps out at you, it is very easy for you to notice because it is unusual or unexpected

**6 ▶ HEART ◀** [I] *especially literary* if your heart leaps, you feel a sudden surprise, happiness, or excitement: *My heart leaped when I saw Paul at the airport.* —see also **look before you leap** (LOOK (10))

**leap²** *n* [C] **1** a big jump: *Bill cleared the ditch with a single leap.* **2 by/in leaps and bounds** if someone or something increases, develops, grows etc by leaps and bounds, they increase etc very quickly: *Andrew's German is improving by leaps and bounds.* **3** a sudden large increase in the number or amount of something: **[+ in]** *a leap in prices* **4** a mental process that is needed to understand something difficult or see the connection between two very different ideas: **a leap of imagination** *It takes a great leap of imagination to see John as a teacher.* **5 a leap in the dark** something you do, or a risk that you take, without knowing what will happen as a result

**leap·frog¹** /'li:pfrɒg‖-frɔ:g, -frɑ:g/ *n* [U] a children's game in which someone bends over and someone else jumps over them

leapfrog

**leapfrog²** *v* [I,T] to achieve something more quickly than usual by missing some of the usual stages: *Nigel leapfrogged two ranks and was made a colonel.*

**leapt** /lept/ the past tense and past participle of LEAP¹

**leap year** /'· ·/ *n* [C] a year, which happens every fourth year, when February has 29 days instead of 28

**learn** /lɜ:n‖lɜ:rn/ *v past tense and past participle* **learned** or **learnt** /lɜ:nt‖lɜ:rnt/ *especially BrE* S1 W1

**1 ▶ SUBJECT/SKILL ◀** [I,T] to gain knowledge of a subject, or skill in an activity, by experience, by studying it, or by being taught: *What's the best way to learn a language?* | *Children are usually very quick at learning.* | **[+ about]** *I am very keen to learn about the town's history.* | **learn (how) to do sth** *I learnt to drive when I was 17.* | **learn how/what/who etc** *In the first lesson we'll learn how to format a text file.* —compare TEACH, see KNOW¹ (USAGE)

**2 ▶ FIND OUT ◀** [I,T] *formal* to find out information, news etc by hearing it from someone else: **[+ of/about]** *We were all saddened to learn of her death.* | **learn sth** *Where did you learn the news?* | **learn (that)** *May was pleased to learn that he had arrived safely.* | **learn who/what/whether etc** *We have yet to learn who will be the new manager.*

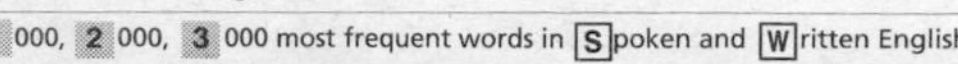

**3 ▶ REMEMBER ◀** [T] to get to know something so well that you can easily remember it; MEMORIZE: *The actor was busy learning her lines.*
**4 ▶ CHANGE YOUR BEHAVIOUR ◀** [T] to gradually understand a situation and start behaving in the way that people expect you to behave: **learn (that)** *They have to learn that they can't just do whatever they like.* | **learn to do sth** *gamblers who had learned to modify their behaviour*
**5 learn from your mistakes** to improve the way you do things because of mistakes you have made
**6 learn (sth) the hard way** to understand a situation or develop a skill by learning from your mistakes and bad experiences
**7 learn your lesson** to suffer so much because you did something wrong or stupid, that you will not do it again: *I really learned my lesson when I got sunburned last year on vacation.* —see also **live and learn** (LIVE (27))

This graph shows how common the different grammar patterns of the verb **learn** are.

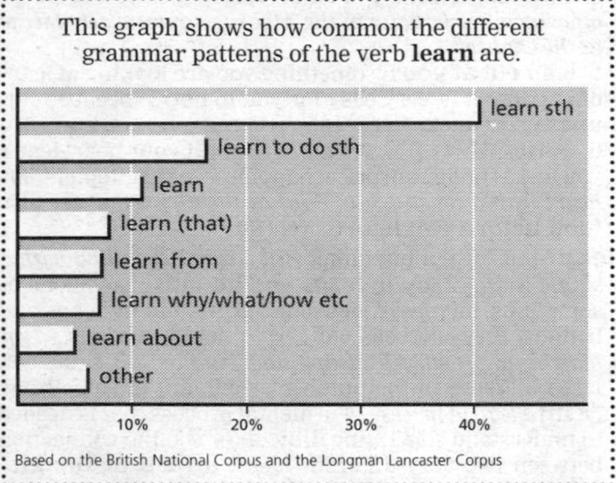


Based on the British National Corpus and the Longman Lancaster Corpus

**learn·ed** /ˈlɜːnɪ̣d‖ˈlɜːr-/ *adj formal* **1** having a lot of knowledge because you have read and studied a lot **2 learned books/works etc** books etc to be used by advanced students —**learnedly** *adv*

**learn·er** /ˈlɜːnə‖ˈlɜːrnər/ *n* [C] **1** someone who is learning to do something: *Jill's a very quick learner.* | [+ **of**] *a grammar book for learners of English* **2** also **learner driver** *BrE* someone who is learning to drive a car

**learner's per·mit** /ˈ‥ ˌ‥/ *n* [C] *AmE* an official document that gives you permission to learn to drive; PROVISIONAL LICENCE *BrE*

S3 W2 **learn·ing** /ˈlɜːnɪŋ‖ˈlɜːr-/ *n* [U] knowledge gained through reading and study: *a man of great learning*

**learning curve** /ˈ‥ ˌ/ *n* [C] the rate at which you learn a new skill

**learning dis·a·bil·i·ty** /ˈ‥ ‥ˌ‥/ *n* [C] a mental problem that affects a child's ability to learn things

**learnt** /lɜːnt‖lɜːrnt/ the past tense and past participle of LEARN

W3 **lease¹** /liːs/ *n* [C] **1** a legal agreement which allows you to use a car, building etc for a period of time, in return for rent: **take out a lease** (=sign a lease so that you can rent something) *We've taken out a lease on an office building.* **2 a new lease of life** *especially BrE*, **a new lease on life** *AmE* **a)** if someone has a new lease of life, they become healthy, active, or happy again after being weak, ill, or tired: *The vacation has given me a new lease of life.* **b)** if something has a new lease of life, improvements are made that mean it will last longer: *Give dirty rugs a new lease of life with our super steam cleaner!*

**lease²** *v* [T] **1** also **lease out** to use or let someone use buildings, property etc on a lease: **lease sb sth/lease sth to sb** *They decided to lease the building to another company.* **2** to pay to use expensive machinery or equipment for a long period, instead of buying it: *We lease all our computers.*

**lease·back** /ˈliːsbæk/ *n* [C,U] *technical* an arrangement in which you sell or give something to someone, but continue to use it by paying them rent

**lease·hold** /ˈliːshəʊld‖-hoʊld/ *adj especially BrE* leasehold property is owned only for as long as is stated in a lease —compare FREEHOLD —**leasehold** *adv*: *Buying leasehold is cheaper.*

**lease·hold·er** /ˈliːshəʊldə‖-hoʊldər/ *n* [C] someone who lives in a leasehold house, apartment etc

**leash¹** /liːʃ/ *n* [C] *especially AmE* **1** a piece of rope, leather etc fastened to a dog's collar in order to control it; LEAD² (7) *BrE*: **be on leash** *All dogs must be on a leash by order of the Parks Department.* **2 have sb on a leash** *humorous* to be able to control someone: *Jerry's wife has him on a tight leash.*

**leash²** *v* [T] *AmE* to put a leash on a dog

**least¹** /liːst/ *determiner, pron* **1 at least a)** not less than a particular number or amount: *It will take you at least 20 minutes to get there.* | *He had been dead for at least a fortnight.* | **at the very least** (=not less than and probably much more than) *It would cost $1 million at the very least.* **b) at least** even if nothing else is true, or even if nothing else happens: *I think you should at least consider his offer.* | *Well, at least I don't spend all my money on drink like some people.* **c)** used when you are mentioning an advantage that makes certain problems or disadvantages seem less serious: *At least he was safe now.* | *The film wasn't very interesting, but at least it filled the time.* **d)** used when you are correcting or changing something that you have just said: *Mary was depressed all evening. Or at least it seemed that way.* | *She has no plans to return to England yet, at least as far as I know.* **2** the smallest in number, amount, or importance: *It's not always wise to buy the one that costs the least.* | *Those with the least money pay the least in taxes.* **3 not the least/not in the least/not the least bit** none at all, or not at all: *It doesn't matter in the least if you're a bit late.* | *She didn't seem the least bit worried.* | *He came up without the least hesitation and asked me what I was doing there.* **4 the least sb could do** used when saying what you think someone should or could do to help someone else: *The least he could do is give them some money towards the rent.* **5 to say the least** used to show that something is worse or more serious than you are actually saying: *He was rather offended, to say the least.* **6 the least of your worries** something you are not worried about because there are other more important problems: *Deciding what to wear for the trial is the least of my worries.* S1 W1

**least²** *adv* **1** less than anything or anyone else: *It happened when we least expected it.* | *He was the least experienced of the teachers* | *The tax hits those who can least afford it.* **2 least of all** especially not a particular person: *No one knew where he was, least of all his family.* **3 not least** *formal* especially: *The president's speeches were alarming, not least to the country's allies.*

**least com·mon mul·ti·ple** /ˌ‥ ‥ ˈ‥‥/ LOWEST COMMON MULTIPLE

**least·wise** /ˈliːstwaɪz/ also **least·ways** /-weɪz/ *adv AmE informal* at least; anyway: *He was there a minute ago, leastwise that's what Sue said.*

**leath·er¹** /ˈleðə‖-ər/ *n* [U] **1** animal skin that has been treated to preserve it, and is used for making shoes, bags etc: *a book bound in leather* —see picture on page 839 **2 leathers** [plural] special leather clothes worn for protection by someone riding a MOTORCYCLE —see also **run/go hell for leather** (HELL¹ (24)) W3

**leather²** *adj* made of leather: *a leather jacket*

**leath·er·ette** /ˌleðəˈret/ *n* [U] a cheap material made to look like leather; NAUGAHYDE *AmE*

**leath·er·y** /ˈleðəri/ *adj* hard and stiff like leather rather than soft or smooth: *leathery skin*

S 1 W 1

**leave**[1] /liːv/ *v past tense and past participle* **left** /left/

① LEAVE A PLACE, VEHICLE
② LEAVE YOUR JOB, HOME, WIFE ETC
③ LEAVE STH SOMEWHERE
④ REMAIN
⑤ NOT DO STH
⑥ STATE/POSITION
⑦ DECIDE/CHOOSE
⑧ DEATH
⑨ OTHER MEANINGS

### ① LEAVE A PLACE, VEHICLE

**1** ▶ **LEAVE** ◀ [I,T] to go away from a place or a person: *What time did you leave the office?* | *They were so noisy that the manager asked them to leave.* | [+ **for**] *They're leaving for Rome in the morning.* | **leave to do sth** *Franca left early to meet her mother.* | **leave sb doing sth** *Ann left Keith dozing in the chair.*

**2** ▶ **TRAIN/SHIP ETC** ◀ [T] to get off a train, ship etc: *Make sure to check the overhead luggage compartments before you leave the plane.*

**3 leave sb to sth** to go away and let someone continue what they are doing: *I'll leave you to your work.*

**4 leave him to himself/leave her to herself etc** to go away from someone so that they are alone

### ② LEAVE YOUR JOB, HOME, WIFE ETC

**5** ▶ **HOME/SCHOOL ETC** ◀ [I,T] to stop living at your parents' home, stop going to school etc: *Zoe wants to be a hairdresser when she leaves school.* | *Tom wants to leave home.*

**6** ▶ **HUSBAND/WIFE ETC** ◀ [I,T] to stop living with someone you had a close relationship with: **leave sb for sb** (=leave in order to live with someone else) *Jan's husband's left her for another woman.*

**7** ▶ **COUNTRY/PLACE** ◀ [I,T] to stop living in a country, town etc and go somewhere else: *They're leaving Minneapolis to live in Santa Fe.*

**8** ▶ **JOB/COMPANY** ◀ [I,T] to stop working for a particular organization or being a member of a group: *Bill's leaving the company after 25 years' service.* | *We are concerned about the number of young people leaving the church.* | *a leaving present* (=for someone who is leaving)

**9 leave sb alone** to stop annoying or upsetting someone: *Why can't you just leave her alone?*

**10 leave sth alone** to stop touching something: *Will you leave that piano alone?* | **leave it/this alone** *Leave it alone or you'll break it!*

**11 leave go of/leave hold of** *BrE* to stop holding something: *Leave go of me!*

**12 leave it at that** used to say that you have said or done enough about something: *Let's leave it at that for today.*

### ③ LEAVE STH SOMEWHERE

**13** ▶ **LET STH REMAIN** ◀ [T always + adv/prep] to let something or someone stay where they are when you go away: **leave sth in/on etc** *Someone's left their car in the middle of the driveway.* | *If you leave that on the floor, it'll get trodden on and broken.* | *I've left the kids with Sandra.*

**14** ▶ **FORGET STH** ◀ [T always + adv/prep] to forget to take something with you when you leave a place: **leave sth behind/in/on etc** *Oh no! I've left the paperwork in my office.*

**15** ▶ **FOR SB TO FIND** ◀ [T] to put something in a place where someone else can find it: *Miriam always leaves a spare key under the plant.* | *I'll leave you some milk in the fridge.*

**16** ▶ **LETTER/MESSAGE** ◀ [T] to leave a letter, package, message etc somewhere for someone: *If you'd care to leave your name and number, he'll call you right back.* | **leave sth for sb/leave sb sth** *Lucy left a note for you.* | *Who left me this message?* | **leave word with sb** (=leave a message with someone) *Could you leave word with my secretary if you can't make it?*

### ④ REMAIN

**17** ▶ **BE LEFT** ◀ [T] to remain after everything else has been taken away or used: *I'll have another brandy if there's any left.* | *By 5 o'clock there was hardly anyone left in the office.* | **have sth left** *How much time do we have left to finish this?* | **be left over** (=remain after you have used or spent all the rest) *If there's any money left over, you can keep it for yourself.*

### ⑤ NOT DO STH

**18** ▶ **DELAY** ◀ [T] to not do something until later: *Let's leave the dishes for tomorrow.* | *Leave it another week, then tell him he'll have to decide.* | *Leave the batter to stand for 15 minutes.* | **leave sth for now** *Leave the filing for now. You can do it later.*

**19** ▶ **NOT DO STH** ◀ [T] to not do something that you ought to do: *I couldn't face the ironing so I just left it.*

**20** ▶ **NOT EAT/DRINK** ◀ [T] if you leave food or drink, you do not eat it because you do not like it or you have had enough: *If you don't like the stew, just leave it.*

**21 leave sb/sth be** to not disturb or annoy someone, or not touch or move something: *Just leave Jenny be and she'll sort things out for herself.*

**22 leave well (enough) alone** to not try to change a situation in case you make it worse than it was before: *If I were you I would leave well alone.*

**23 leave sb to their own devices** to not tell someone what to do or offer them help, but let them do what they decide to do

### ⑥ STATE/POSITION

**24** [T] **a)** to make something stay, or let something stay in a particular state or position: *How did you leave things after the meeting?* | *Leave the batter to stand for 15 minutes.* | **leave sth open/empty/untidy etc** *I wish you'd stop leaving the door open.* | *The trial left a lot of questions unanswered.* | **leave sth on/off/out etc** *Leave the television on, will you?* | **leave sth doing sth** *I'll just leave the engine running while I pop in.* **b)** if something leaves you in a particular condition, you are in that condition as a result of it: *Paying for the repairs left Jim without a cent.* | *Frankly, their rudeness left me speechless.* | **leave sb doing sth** *Carla's narrow escape left her shaking with terror.*

### ⑦ DECIDE/CHOOSE

**25** ▶ **LET SB DECIDE/TAKE RESPONSIBILITY** ◀ [T] to let someone decide something or take responsibility for something: **leave sth with sb** *Leave it with me and I'll fix it for you.* | **leave sth to sb** (=let someone choose or decide) *I've always left financial decisions to my wife.* | **leave doing sth to sb** *I'll leave buying the tickets to you.* | **leave sb to do sth** *BrE*: *I'll leave you to choose which film we see.* | **leave it to me** (=I'll take responsibility for it) *Leave it to me. I'll make sure it gets posted.* | **leave it (up) to sb to do sth** *We left it to Dad to get the packing done.* | *I'll leave it up to you to decide.* | **leave sth to chance** (=take no action and just wait and see what happens)

**26 leave sb with no choice/option** to force someone

[continued on next page]

[continued from previous page]
to do something because there is nothing else they can do: *You leave me with no option but to resign.*

⑧ DEATH

**27 ▶WHEN YOU DIE◀** [T] **a)** to give something to someone after you die: *The old lady left $5 million.* | **leave sth to sb/sth** *He had left all his money to charity.* | **leave sb sth** *Hugo left me his mother's ring.* **b)** to have members of your family still alive when you die: *Collins leaves a wife and three children.*

⑨ OTHER MEANINGS

**28 leave a space/gap etc** to deliberately make a space etc when you are doing something: *Leave a 10 centimetre gap between the young plants.* | **leave room** *Drivers should always leave plenty of room for cyclists.*

**29 leave a mark/stain/scar etc** to make a mark etc that remains afterwards: *The cut was deep and left a terrible scar.* | *William had left a trail of muddy footprints across the floor.*

**30 leave sb cold** to not interest or excite someone at all: *Modern Jazz leaves me cold, I'm afraid.*

**31 leave sb/sth standing** *informal* to be much better, quicker etc than someone or something else: *Anna leaves all her classmates standing.*

**32 leave a lot to be desired** to be very unsatisfactory: *Your conduct this term has left a lot to be desired.*

**33 leave a bad taste in your mouth** if an experience leaves a bad taste in your mouth, remembering it upsets you or makes you feel uncomfortable: *The things she said really left a nasty taste in my mouth.*

**34 leave no stone unturned** to do everything that you can in order to find something or solve a problem: *Jarvis left no stone unturned in his search for the manuscript.*

**35 leave sth aside/leave sth to one side** to not think about or consider something for a time, so that you can think about something else: **leaving aside** (=used to say that you do not want to consider something for a time) *Leaving aside the question of expense, what's your opinion?* —see also **take it or leave it** (TAKE[1] (18a))

**leave** sb/sth **behind** *phr v* [T] **1** to forget to take something with you when you leave a place: *I think I left my credit card behind at the restaurant.* **2** to move far ahead of someone who cannot run, walk, or drive as fast as you can: **leave sb far behind** *BrE* / **leave sb way behind** *especially AmE*: *I was soon left far behind.* **3** to let something or someone stay in a place when you go away, especially permanently: *Sooner or later we have to leave our parents behind.* **4 be/get left behind** to not work as well or as quickly as someone else, so that you make less progress than they do: *You'll have to put in some extra work at night if you don't want to get left behind.*

**leave off** *phr v* [I,T] *informal* to stop doing something: *I wish the rain would leave off for five minutes.* | *Let's start again from where we left off.* | **leave off (doing) sth** *BrE*: *Leave off shouting! I can't hear myself think in here.*

**leave** sb/sth **out** *phr v* [T] **1** to not include someone or something in a group, list, activity etc: *You've left out a zero in this phone number.* | **leave sb/sth out of sth** *Kidd has been left out of the team.* **2 be/feel left out** to feel as if you are not accepted or welcome in a social group: *All the others seemed to know each other and I began to feel left out.* **3 leave it out!** *BrE spoken* used to tell someone to stop lying, pretending, or being annoying

S3 W2 **leave**[2] *n*
**1 ▶HOLIDAY◀** [U] time that you are allowed to spend away from your work, especially in the armed forces: *I've applied for three days' leave.* | **be on leave** *I'm in command while Farringdon is on leave.*
**2 sick/maternity/compassionate leave** time that you are allowed to spend away from work because you are ill, because you have had a baby, or because of a personal problem such as the death of a relative
**3 leave of absence** a period of time that you are allowed to spend away from work for a particular purpose: *She's been given leave of absence to attend a computer course.*
**4 take leave of your senses** to become crazy and behave in a strange way: *You want to marry him? Have you taken leave of your senses?*
**5 ▶PERMISSION◀** [U] *formal* permission to do something, especially something you would not normally be allowed to do: *All this was done entirely without my leave.* | **leave to do sth** *Julia had special leave to do her exams at home.* | **ask leave** *He asked leave to speak to her in private.*
**6 without so much as a by your leave** *old-fashioned* without asking permission, in a way that seems very rude: *How dare you come marching into my office without so much as a by your leave?*
**7 take leave of sb/take your leave** *formal* to say goodbye to someone
**8 by your leave** *old use* used when asking permission to do something —see also **take French leave** (FRENCH[2] (3))

**leav·en**[1] /ˈlevən/ also **leav·en·ing** /ˈlevənɪŋ/ *n* **1** [U] a substance, especially YEAST, that is added to a mixture of flour and water so that it will swell and can be baked into bread **2** [C,U] *literary* a small amount of a quality that makes an event or situation less boring and more interesting or cheerful

**leaven**[2] *v* [T] **1** *formal* to make something less boring and more interesting or cheerful **2** *old-fashioned* to add leaven to a mixture of flour and water —see also UNLEAVENED

**leaves** /liːvz/ the plural of LEAF

**leave-tak·ing** /ˈ· ··/ *n* [C] *literary* an act of saying goodbye when you go away

**leav·ings** /ˈliːvɪŋz/ *n* [plural] *old-fashioned* things that are left because they are not wanted, especially food —compare **leftovers** (LEFTOVER[2] (1))

**lech**[1], **letch** /letʃ/ *n* [C] *BrE informal* a lecher

**lech**[2], **letch** *v*
**lech after/over** sb *phr v* [T] *BrE informal* to show sexual desire for a woman in a way that is unpleasant or annoying: *a middle-aged man leching after young girls*

**lech·er** /ˈletʃə‖-ər/ *n* [C] an insulting word for a man who is always thinking about sex or trying to get sexual pleasure

**lech·er·ous** /ˈletʃərəs/ *adj* a lecherous man is always thinking about sex or trying to get sexual pleasure —**lecherously** *adv*

**lech·er·y** /ˈletʃəri/ *n* [U] too much interest in or desire for sex

**lec·tern** /ˈlektən‖-ərn/ *n* [C] a high, sloping surface for putting an open book or notes on while you are giving a lecture, SERMON etc

**lec·ture**[1] /ˈlektʃə‖-ər/ *n* [C] **1** a long talk given to a group of people on a particular subject, especially as a method of teaching in universities: [+ **on/about**] *a lecture on medieval art* | **give a lecture** *She's giving a series of lectures on molecular biology.* **2** an act of criticizing someone or warning them about something in a long, serious talk, in a way that they think is unfair or unnecessary: [+ **on/about**] *My aunt gave me a long lecture about the dangers of drink.* S3 W3

**lecture**[2] *v* **1** [T] to talk angrily or seriously to someone in order to criticize or warn them, in a way that they think is unfair or unnecessary: *I wish you'd stop lecturing me!* | **lecture sb about/on** *Mrs Reed was continually lecturing her children about their behaviour.* **2** [I] to talk to a group of people on a particular subject, especially as a method of teaching at a university

**lec·tur·er** /ˈlektʃərə‖-ər/ *n* [C] **1** someone who gives a lecture (LECTURE[1] (1)): *a brilliant lecturer* **2** someone who has the lowest teaching rank at a British university or college —see PROFESSOR (USAGE) **3** *AmE* someone who makes speeches in different places on a subject they know well

**lec·ture·ship** /ˈlektʃəʃɪp‖-ər-/ *n* [C] the lowest teaching rank at a British university or college: **[+ in]** *a lectureship in mathematics*

**LED** /ˌel iː ˈdiː/ *n* [C] *technical* light emitting diode; a small piece of equipment on a watch, computer screen etc that produces light when electricity passes through it

**led** /led/ the past tense and past participle of LEAD[1]

**-led** /led/ *suffix* [in adjectives] having a particular thing as the most important or effective cause, influence etc: *an export-led economic recovery*

**ledge** /ledʒ/ *n* [C] **1** a narrow flat surface of rock that is parallel to the ground **2** a narrow flat shelf or surface, fixed to a wall: **window ledge** (=narrow shelf below a window)

**led·ger** /ˈledʒə‖-ər/ *n* [C] **1** a book recording the money received and spent by a business, bank etc **2** a ledger line

**ledger line** /ˈ··· ·/ *n* [C] a line on which you write musical notes that are too high or low to be recorded on a STAVE[1] (1)

**lee** /liː/ *n* [singular] **1 the lee of a wall/hedge etc** the part of a wall etc that provides shelter from the wind **2** the side of something, especially a ship, that is away from the wind **3 the lees** the thick substance that collects at the bottom of a bottle of wine; SEDIMENT —compare DREGS —see also LEE SHORE

**leech** /liːtʃ/ *n* [C] **1** a small soft creature that fixes itself to the skin of animals in order to drink their blood **2** someone who takes advantage of other people, usually by taking their money, food etc **3** *old use* a doctor

**leek** /liːk/ *n* [C] a vegetable with a long white stem and long flat green leaves, which tastes a little like an onion —see picture on page 414

**leer** /lɪə‖lɪr/ *v* [I] to look at someone in an unpleasant way that shows that you find them sexually attractive: **[+ at]** *Stop leering at those girls!* **—leer** *n* [C] *a disgusting leer*

**leer·y** /ˈlɪəri‖ˈlɪri/ *adj informal* careful in the way that you deal with something or someone because you do not trust them; WARY: **[+ of]** *I was very leery of him after I found out he had lied to Jennifer.*

**lee shore** /ˌ· ˈ·/ *n* [singular] *technical* a shore which the wind from the sea is blowing onto

**lee·ward** /ˈliːwəd, ˈluːəd‖-ərd/ *adj technical* **1** the leeward side of something is the side that is sheltered from the wind **2** a leeward direction is the same direction as the wind is blowing: **to leeward** *The ship cruised slowly to leeward.* **—leeward** *adv* —opposite WINDWARD[1]

**lee·way** /ˈliːweɪ/ *n* [U] **1** freedom to do things in the way you want to: *Our reporters have a lot of leeway in what they write.* **2** *BrE* time that you have lost that means you are at a disadvantage: *Janet's got a lot of leeway to make up in her studies after her illness.* **3** *technical* the sideways movement of a ship caused by strong wind

S1 W1 **left**[1] /left/ *adj* [only before noun] **1** on the side of your body that contains your heart: *She held out her left hand.* —opposite RIGHT[1] (4a) **2** on, by, or in the direction of your left side: *Hank had scribbled notes in the left margin.* | *Take a left turn at the crossroads.* **3 have two left feet** *informal* to be very awkward in the way you move; be CLUMSY (1) **4 the left hand doesn't know what the right hand is doing** used to say that one part of a group or organization does not know what the other parts are doing —opposite RIGHT[1] —see also LEFT-OF-CENTRE, LEFT-WING[1]

**left**[2] *adv* towards the left side: *Turn left after the gas station.* —opposite RIGHT[2] (4)

**left**[3] *n* **1** [singular] the left side or direction: *Take the next road on the left.* | *On your left you can see the Houses of Parliament.* | *Our house is just to the left of the school.* **2 the left/the Left** political parties or groups, such as Socialists and Communists, that want money and property to be divided equally, and generally support workers rather than employers **3** [C] a hit made with your left hand: *I caught him on the chin with a straight left.*

**left**[4] the past tense and past participle of LEAVE[1]

**left field** /ˈ· ·/ *n* [singular] **1** a position in BASEBALL in the left side of the OUTFIELD **2 (way) out in left field** *AmE informal* strange or unusual: *Some of his ideas are way out in left field.* **3 come from out in left field** *AmE informal* to be very surprising or unexpected: *His comment about Kia's hair came from out in left field.*

**left field·er** /ˈ· ··/ *n* [C] someone who plays on the left side of a BASEBALL field

**left-hand** /ˌ· ˈ·◂/ *adj* [only before noun] **1** on the left side of something: *We live about halfway down the street on the left-hand side.* **2** curving to the left: *a left-hand bend* **3** always using your left hand to do a particular thing: *David was a left-hand bowler.* —opposite RIGHT-HAND

**left-hand drive** /ˌ· · ˈ·/ *adj* a left-hand drive vehicle has the STEERING WHEEL on the left side **—left-hand drive** *n* [singular]

**left-handed**

Dad is left-handed.

She caught the ball one-handed.

**left-hand·ed** /ˌ· ˈ··◂/ *adj* **1** someone who is left-handed uses their left hand for most things, especially writing **2** done with the left hand: *a left-handed shot* **3** made to be used by left-handed people: *left-handed scissors* **4 left-handed compliment** *AmE* a statement that seems to express admiration or praise, but at the same time is insulting **—left-handed** *adv* **—left-handedness** *n* [U] —opposite RIGHT-HANDED

**left-hand·er** /ˌ· ˈ··/ *n* [C] **1** someone who uses their left hand, especially for throwing a ball **2** a hit made with your left hand —opposite RIGHT-HANDER

**left·ie** /ˈlefti/ another spelling of LEFTY

**left·ist** /ˈleftɪst/ *adj* supporting LEFT-WING politics, groups, or ideas: *leftist views* | *a prominent leftist student group* **—leftism** *n* [U] **—leftist** *n* [C]

**left lug·gage of·fice** /ˌ· ˈ·· ˌ··/ *n* [C] *BrE* a place in a station, airport etc where you can pay to leave your bags and get them later

**left-of-cen·tre** *BrE*, **left-of-center** *AmE* /ˌ· · ˈ··◂/ *adj* having ideas or opinions that agree more with the LEFT[3] (2) in politics than with the RIGHT[3] (4b)

**left·o·ver**[1] /ˈleftəʊvə‖-oʊvər/ *adj* [only before noun] remaining after all the rest has been used, eaten etc: *Any leftover vegetables can be used to make a soup.*

**leftover**[2] *n* **1 leftovers** [plural] food that has not been eaten at the end of a meal: *Give the leftovers to the dog.* **2** [singular] an object, habit, method etc that remains from an earlier time, even though you would expect it to have gone: *They still slept with the lights on, a leftover from more dangerous times.*

**left·ward** /ˈleftwəd‖-wərd/ *adj* on or towards the left: *a leftward bend* —opposite RIGHTWARD **—leftward/leftwards** *adv*

**left-wing**[1] /ˌ· ˈ·◂/ *adj* supporting the political aims of groups such as Socialists and Communists, such as the idea that money and property should be divided more fairly: *She's very left-wing.* | *a left-wing newspaper* —opposite RIGHT-WING **—left-winger** *n* [C]

**left wing²** /ˌ·ˈ·/ *n* [singular] the group of people, within a larger political group, whose ideas are more left-wing than those of other members of the group: *He's on the left wing of the Conservative Party.* | *The party has a small but powerful left wing.*

**left·y, leftie** /ˈlefti/ *n* [C] **1** *informal especially BrE* a humorous or slightly insulting way of talking about someone who has left-wing political ideas **2** *informal especially AmE* someone who uses their left hand to write, throw etc —**lefty** *adj*: *My lefty friends keep telling me I'm a fascist.*

S1 W1 **leg¹** /leg/ *n*
**1** ▶ **BODY PART** ◀ [C] either of the two long parts of your body that your feet are joined to, or a similar part on an animal or insect: *Angie broke her leg skiing.* | *A spider has 8 legs.* | *She's got long skinny legs.* —see picture at BODY
**2** ▶ **FOOD** ◀ [C,U] the leg of an animal when eaten as food: *roast leg of lamb*
**3** ▶ **FURNITURE** ◀ [C] one of the upright parts that supports a piece of furniture: *a chair leg*
**4** ▶ **CLOTHING** ◀ [C] the part of your trousers that covers your leg: *The legs of my jeans were covered in mud.*
**5** ▶ **JOURNEY/RACE** ◀ [C] a part of a long journey, race, process etc that is done one part at a time: *the final leg of the Tour de France*
**6 four-legged/two-legged etc** having four legs, two legs etc: *four-legged animals* —see also CROSS-LEGGED, BOW-LEGGED
**7 leg room** space in which to put your legs comfortably when you are sitting in a car, theatre etc
**8 not have a leg to stand on** *informal* to be in a situation where you cannot prove or legally support what you say: *If you didn't sign a contract, you won't have a leg to stand on.*
**9 pull sb's leg** *informal* to make a joke by telling someone something that is not actually true
**10 be on its last legs** *informal* to be in very bad condition and about to stop working: *The Chevy really is on its last legs now.*
**11 get your leg over** *BrE slang* to have sex with someone
**12** ▶ **SPORT** ◀ [C] *BrE* one of the parts of a special football competition that is played in two parts
**13 have legs** *informal especially AmE* if a piece of news has legs, people continue to be interested in it and talk about it: *These allegations don't have legs – they'll be forgotten by next week.* —see also **break a leg** (BREAK¹ (46)), LEG-PULL, LEG-UP, PEG LEG, SEA LEGS, **shake a leg** (SHAKE¹ (11)), **show a leg** (SHOW¹ (22)), SQUARE LEG, **stretch your legs** (STRETCH¹ (12))

**leg²** *v* **leg it** *BrE informal* to run in order to escape from someone or something: *We saw him coming, and legged it out of the house.*

**leg·a·cy** /ˈlegəsi/ *n* [C] **1** a situation that exists as a result of things that happened at an earlier time: **[+ of]** *The civil wars in the region are largely a legacy of apartheid.* **2** money or property that you receive from someone after they die: *a legacy from her aunt*

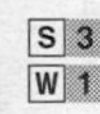

S3 W1 **le·gal** /ˈliːgəl/ *adj* **1** allowed, ordered, or approved by law: *He had twice the legal limit of alcohol in his bloodstream.* | *plans to make the carrying of identity cards a legal requirement* | **the legal age for** *the legal age for voting* **2** [only before noun] concerned with or connected with the law: *free legal advice* | *a costly legal dispute* **3 take legal action/proceedings** to use the legal system to settle an argument, put right an unfair situation etc: *Unless the money is paid immediately we shall be forced to take legal action.* —opposite ILLEGAL¹ —see also LEGALLY

**le·gal·ese** /ˌliːgəlˈiːz/ *n* [U] *informal* language used by lawyers that is difficult for most people to understand

**le·gal·ise** /ˈliːgəlaɪz/ *v* [T] a British spelling of LEGALIZE

**le·gal·ist·ic** /ˌliːgəˈlɪstɪk◂/ *adj* too concerned about small legal details, and not concerned enough about what is really important —**legalistically** /-kli/ *adv* —**legalism** /ˈliːgəlɪzəm/ *n* [U]

**le·gal·i·ty** /lɪˈgæləti/ *n* [U] the fact of being allowed by law: *Some people questioned the legality of the US's attack on Baghdad.*

**le·gal·ize** also **-ise** *BrE* /ˈliːgəlaɪz/ *v* [T] to make a law that allows people to do something that was not allowed before: *the campaign to legalize cannabis* —**legalization** /ˌliːgəlaɪˈzeɪʃən‖-lə-/ *n* [U]

**le·gal·ly** /ˈliːgəli/ *adv* **1** according to the law: *Legally he's still my husband.* | *The ship was legally authorized to carry 200 passengers.* | *Which of them is legally responsible for the accident?* **2 legally binding** an agreement or document that is legally binding must be obeyed by law

**legal pad** /ˈ·· ·/ *n* [C] a PAD¹ (2) of yellow writing paper with lines, of a type sold in the US

**legal pro·fes·sion** /ˈ·· ·ˌ··/ *n* **the legal profession** lawyers, judges, and other people who work in courts of law or advise people about legal problems

**legal-size** /ˈ·· ·/ *adj AmE* legal-size paper is 14 inches (INCH¹ (1)) long and 8 inches wide

**legal sys·tem** /ˈ·· ˌ··/ *n* [C] the laws and the way they work in a particular country

**legal ten·der** /ˌ·· ˈ··/ *n* [U] coins or bank notes that are officially allowed to be used as money

**leg·ate** /ˈlegət/ *n* [C] an important official representative

**leg·a·tee** /ˌlegəˈtiː/ *n* [C] *law* someone who is given money or property after another person dies

**le·ga·tion** /lɪˈgeɪʃən/ *n* [C] **1** an office that represents a government in a foreign country but is lower in rank than an EMBASSY: *the Cuban legation* **2** the people who work in this office

**le·ga·to** /lɪˈgɑːtəʊ‖-toʊ/ *adj, adv technical* played or sung so that each note connects to the next one without pauses between them

**le·gend** /ˈledʒənd/ *n* **1** [C] an old, well-known story, often about brave people, adventures, or magical events: *the legend of Rip Van Winkle who slept for 100 years* **2** [U] all stories of this kind: *Celtic legend* **3** [C] someone who is famous and admired for being extremely good at doing something: *Pele, Maradona, and other footballing legends* —see also LIVING LEGEND **4** [C usually singular] **a)** *literary* words that have been written somewhere, for example on a sign: *A sign above the door bore the legend 'patience is a virtue'.* **b)** *old-fashioned* the words that explain a picture, map etc

**le·gen·da·ry** /ˈledʒəndəri‖-deri/ *adj* **1** famous and admired: *the legendary Babe Ruth, one of the greatest baseball players of all time* **2** talked or read about in legends: *legendary sea monsters*

**le·ger·de·main** /ˌledʒədəˈmeɪn‖-dʒər-/ *n* [U] *old-fashioned* skilful use of your hands when performing tricks

**-legged** /legəd, legd/ *suffix* [in adjectives] having legs of a particular type or number: *four-legged animals* | *a long-legged runner*

**leg·gings** /ˈlegɪŋz/ *n* [plural] **1** women's tight trousers without a ZIP¹ (1), which stretch to fit the shape of your body **2** trousers worn to protect your legs

**leg·gy** /ˈlegi/ *adj* a woman or child who is leggy has long legs: *a leggy blonde* —**legginess** *n* [U]

**le·gi·ble** /ˈledʒəbəl/ *adj* written or printed clearly enough for you to read: *Her handwriting was so tiny it was barely legible.* —**legibly** *adv* —**legibility** /ˌledʒəˈbɪləti/ *n* [U] —opposite ILLEGIBLE

**le·gion¹** /ˈliːdʒən/ *n* [C] **1** a large group of soldiers, especially in ancient Rome **2** *literary* a large number of people

**legion²** *adj* [not before noun] *literary* very many; NUMEROUS: *The stories of her adventures were legion.*

**le·gion·a·ry** /ˈliːdʒənəri‖-neri/ *n* [C] a member of a legion

**le·gion·naire** /ˌliːdʒəˈneə‖-ˈner/ *n* [C] a member of a legion, especially the French Foreign Legion

**legionnaire's dis·ease** /ˌ··ˈ· ·ˌ·/ *n* [U] a serious lung disease

**leg i·rons** /ˈ· ··/ *n* [plural] metal circles or chains that are put around a prisoner's legs

**le·gis·late** /ˈledʒɪ̇sleɪt/ *v* [I] to make a law about something: **[+ against/for/on]** *There are plans to legislate against computer-related crime.*

W2 **le·gis·la·tion** /ˌledʒɪ̇ˈsleɪʃən/ *n* [U] **1** a law or set of laws: *an important piece of human rights legislation|legislation governing minimum wage rates* **2** the act of making laws

**le·gis·la·tive** /ˈledʒɪ̇slətɪv‖-leɪtɪv/ *adj* **1** a legislative institution has the power to make laws: *a legislative assembly* **2** concerned with laws or with making laws: *new legislative measures to stem the flow of drugs into the US* —compare EXECUTIVE² (1), JUDICIAL (1)

**le·gis·la·tor** /ˈledʒɪ̇sleɪtə‖-ər/ *n* [C] someone who has the power to make laws or belongs to an institution that makes laws

**le·gis·la·ture** /ˈledʒɪ̇sleɪtʃə, -lətʃə‖-ər/ *n* [C] an institution that has the power to make or change laws: *the Iowa state legislature* —compare EXECUTIVE¹ (2), JUDICIARY

**le·git** /lɪ̇ˈdʒɪt/ *adj* [not before noun] *spoken* **1** legal or following official rules; LEGITIMATE¹ (1): *Don't worry, the deal's strictly legit.* **2** honest and not trying to deceive people: *Are you sure he's legit?*

**le·git·i·mate¹** /lɪˈdʒɪtɪ̇mɪ̇t/ *adj* **1** correct, allowable, or operating according to the law: *The Mafia uses legitimate business operations as a front.* **2** fair, correct, or reasonable according to accepted standards of behaviour: *Is this a legitimate use of taxpayers' money?|I think that's a perfectly legitimate question.* **3** legitimate children are born to parents who are legally married to each other —**legitimately** *adv* —**legitimacy** *n* [U]

**le·git·i·mate²** /lɪˈdʒɪtɪ̇meɪt/ *v* [T] the usual American form of LEGITIMIZE

**le·git·i·mize** also **-ise** *BrE* /lɪˈdʒɪtɪ̇maɪz/ *v* [T] **1** to make something that is unfair or morally wrong seem acceptable and right: *Mussolini's use of symbols from ancient Rome to try to legitimize Fascist policies* **2** to make something official or legal that had not been before **3** to make a child LEGITIMATE¹ (3)

**leg·less** /ˈlegləs/ *adj BrE informal* drunk

**leg·o** /ˈlegəʊ‖-goʊ/ *n* [U] *trademark* a toy consisting of plastic pieces of various sizes that can be fitted together to build things

**leg-pull** /ˈ· ·/ *n* [C usually singular] *BrE* a joke in which you make someone believe something that is not true —see also **pull sb's leg** (LEG ¹ (9))

**leg room** /ˈ· ·/ *n* [U] space for your legs in front of the seats in a car, theatre etc

**leg·ume** /ˈlegjuːm, lɪˈgjuːm/ *n* [C] **1** a plant of the bean family that has seeds in a POD (=a long thin case) **2** *especially AmE* a bean, PEA, LENTIL etc, used as food —**leguminous** /lɪˈgjuːmɪ̇nəs/ *adj*

**leg-up** /ˈ· ·/ *n* **give sb a leg-up** *informal* **a)** to help someone to get up to a high place by joining your hands together so they can use them as a step **b)** *especially BrE* to help someone to succeed in their job

**leg-warm·er** /ˈ· ˌ··/ *n* [C] a piece of clothing made from wool, which covers the lower part of your leg

**leg·work** /ˈlegwɜːk‖-wɜːrk/ *n* [U] *informal* the hard boring work that has to be done in order to achieve something

**lei** /leɪ/ *n* [C] a circle made of flowers you put around someone's neck as a greeting, especially in Hawaii

W3 **lei·sure** /ˈleʒə‖ˈliːʒər/ *n* [U] **1** time when you are not working or studying and can relax and do things you enjoy: *gardening, sailing, and other leisure pursuits|* **leisure time** *In her leisure time she visits museums and galleries.|* **the leisure industry** (=the business of providing leisure activities) **2 at your leisure** as slowly as you want and when you want: *Take the leaflets home and read them at your leisure.* **3 gentleman/lady of leisure** *humorous* someone who does not have to work

**leisure cen·tre** /ˈ·· ˌ··/ *n* [C] *BrE* a place where you can do many different sports activities, exercise classes etc

**lei·sured** /ˈleʒəd‖ˈliːʒərd/ *adj* **1** having no regular work and a lot of leisure time, especially because you are rich **2** leisurely

**lei·sure·ly** /ˈleʒəli‖ˈliːʒərli/ *adj* moving or done in a relaxed way, without hurrying: *a leisurely stroll|working at a leisurely pace* —**leisurely** *adv*: *The great ship sailed leisurely across the bay.* —**leisureliness** *n* [U]

**leisure suit** /ˈ·· ·/ *n* [C] *AmE* an informal suit popular during the 1970s, consisting of a shirt-like JACKET and trousers made of the same material

**lei·sure·wear** /ˈleʒəweə‖ˈliːʒərwer/ *n* [U] a word meaning clothes that are made to be worn when relaxing or playing sport, used especially by shops or by the companies that make these clothes

**leit·mo·tif, leitmotiv** /ˈlaɪtməʊˌtiːf‖-moʊ-/ *n* [C] **1** a musical phrase that is played at various times during an OPERA or similar musical work to represent a particular character or idea —compare MOTIF (3) **2** a feature that appears often in something such as a book, a speech, or an artist's work

**lem·ming** /ˈlemɪŋ/ *n* [C] **1** a small rat-like animal that is known for killing itself by following other lemmings and jumping into the sea in large numbers **2** someone who copies other people's actions and ideas without thinking about it

**lem·on** /ˈlemən/ *n* **1** [C, U] a fruit with a hard yellow skin and sour juice: *fish served with slices of lemon* —see picture on page 413 **2** [U] *BrE* a drink made from this fruit **3** [U] a pale yellow colour —see picture on page 411 **4** [C] *AmE informal* something that is useless because it fails to work or work properly: *He has an old Dodge that's a real lemon.* **5** [C] *BrE informal* a silly person: *I felt such a lemon when I realized I'd gone on the wrong day.*

**lem·on·ade** /ˌleməˈneɪd◂/ *n* [U] **1** a drink made from lemons, sugar, and water **2** *BrE* a sweet colourless FIZZY drink S3

**lemon curd** /ˌ·· ˈ·/ *n* [U] *BrE* a sweet food made of eggs, butter, and lemon juice, eaten on bread

**lemon sole** /ˌ·· ˈ·/ *n* [C] a flat fish used as food

**lemon squeez·er** /ˈ·· ˌ··/ *n* [C] a small kitchen tool for getting the juice out of a lemon

**lend**

My friend lent me $20.
I borrowed $20.

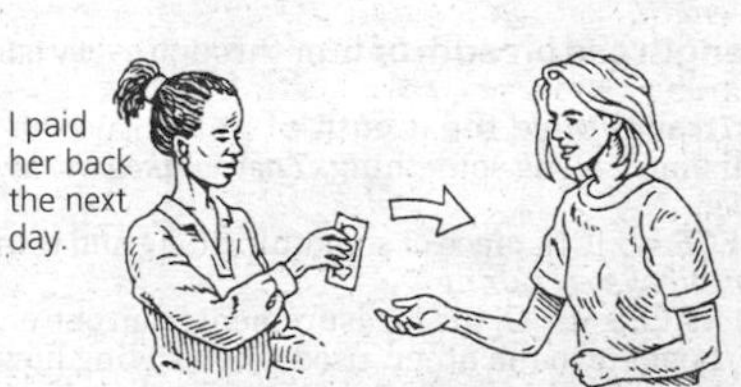
I paid her back the next day.

**lend** /lend/ *v past tense and past participle* **lent** /lent/ S3 W3
**1 ▶ MONEY/CAR/BOOK ETC ◀ a)** [T] to let someone borrow money from you or use something that you own, which they will give you back later: **lend sb sth** *I wish I'd never lent him my car.|Can you lend me $20 till Friday?|* **lend sth to sb** *Reluctantly, I agreed to lend it to her.* **b)** [I,T] if a bank or financial institution lends money, it lets someone borrow it on condition that they pay it back, often gradually, with an additional amount

as interest: *We aim to lend money at reasonable rates of interest.* | **lend sth to sb** *US banks lent billions of dollars to Third World countries in the 1970s.* —see BORROW (USAGE)
**2 lend (sb) a hand** to help someone do something, especially something that needs physical effort
**3 lend an ear** to listen to someone, especially in a sympathetic way
**4 lend itself to** to be suitable for being used in a particular way: *None of her books really lends itself to being made into a film.*
**5 ▶ GIVE A QUALITY ◀** [T] *formal* to give a situation, event etc a particular quality: *The Duke's presence lent the occasion a certain air of dignity.* | **lend sth to sth** *His soft accent lends a kind of warmth to his words.*
**6 lend support/assistance** to support or help someone
**7 lend weight to** to make an opinion, belief etc seem more likely to be correct: *The new evidence lends weight to the theory that the killer was a man.*
**8 lend your name/voice to** to announce publicly that you support something someone is trying to do —**lender** *n* [C]

**lend·ing li·bra·ry** /ˈ·· ˌ···/ *n* [C] a library that lends books, records etc for people to use at home —compare REFERENCE LIBRARY

**lending rate** /ˈ·· ·/ *n* [C] the rate of INTEREST[1] (4) that you have to pay to a bank or other financial institution when you borrow money from them; INTEREST RATE

S2 W2 **length** /leŋθ/ *n*
**1 ▶ SIZE ◀** [C,U] the measurement of something from one end to the other: [+ **of**] *The fish can grow to a length of four feet.* | **2 feet in length/10 metres in length etc** *Vehicles of over 3 metres in length pay an additional toll.* | *pieces of string of different lengths* —compare BREADTH, WIDTH

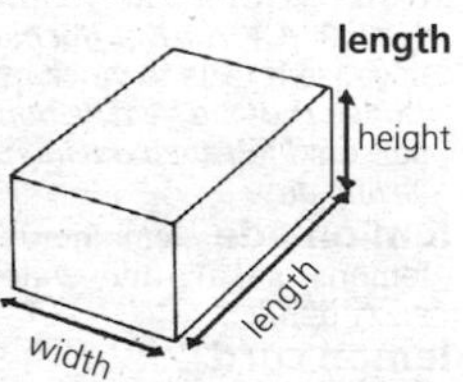


**2 ▶ TIME ◀** [C,U] the amount of time that you spend doing something or that something continues for: *reducing the average length of stay in hospital* | **not for any length of time** (=not for very long) *I didn't want to be left alone with him for any length of time.*
**3 ▶ BOOKS/FILMS ETC ◀** [C, U] the amount of writing in a book, or the amount of time that a film, play etc continues for: *We had to cut the length of the book by two-thirds.* | *Films of this length are pretty unusual.*
**4 go to any lengths/great lengths to do sth** to be willing to use any methods to achieve something that you are very determined to achieve: *Gerald is prepared to go to any lengths to get his daughter back.*
**5 at length a)** if you talk at length about something, you talk about it for a long time: *We've already discussed the subject at great length in previous meetings.* **b)** *literary* after a long time: *"How have you been?" she said at length.*
**6 the length and breadth of** in or through every part of a large area
**7 walk/travel/drive the length of** walk, travel etc the whole distance along something: *They walked the length of the pier.*
**8 ▶ PIECE ◀** [C] a piece of something long and thin: [+ **of**] *a length of steel tubing*
**9 ▶ IN RACES ◀** [C] the measurement from one end of a horse, boat etc to the other, used when saying how far one is ahead of another: *The horse won by three lengths.*
**10 ▶ SWIMMING ◀** [C] the distance from one end of a swimming pool to the other: *I was really bad at swimming – I could barely do a length.* —see also **at arm's length** (ARM[1] (11)), FULL-LENGTH, **measure your length** (MEASURE[1] (5)), SHOULDER-LENGTH

**length·en** /ˈleŋθən/ *v* [I,T] to make something longer or to become longer: *Can you lengthen this skirt for me?* | *The days lengthened as summer approached.* —opposite SHORTEN

**length·ways** /ˈleŋθweɪz/ also **length·wise** /-waɪz/ *adv* in the direction or position of the longest side; LONGWAYS *AmE*: *Lay the bricks lengthways.*

**length·y** /ˈleŋθi/ *adj* **1** continuing for a long time, often too long: *a lengthy court trial* **2** a speech, piece of writing etc that is lengthy is long and often contains too many details —**lengthiness** *n* [U] —**lengthily** *adv*

**le·ni·ent** /ˈliːniənt/ *adj* not strict in the way you punish someone or control their behaviour: *Judges have been accused of being far too lenient in rape cases.* | *a very lenient sentence* —**leniently** *adv* —**leniency** also **lenience** *n* [U]

**lens** /lenz/ *n* [C] **1** a piece of curved glass or plastic which makes things look bigger or smaller, for example in a pair of GLASSES or in a TELESCOPE[1] (3): *Jan wears glasses with thick lenses.* —see picture at GLASS[1] **2** the part of a camera through which the light travels before it hits the film: *a standard 50mm lens* —see picture at CAMERA **3** the clear part inside your eye that focuses (FOCUS[1] (3)) so you can see things clearly —see picture at EYE[1] **4** one of a pair of small curved pieces of plastic that fit closely to your eyes to help you see better; CONTACT LENS

**Lent** /lent/ *n* [U] the period before Easter during which Christians traditionally eat less food or stop doing something that they enjoy —**Lenten** *adj*

**lent** the past tense and past participle of LEND

**len·til** /ˈlentl, -tɪ̥l/ *n* [C] a small round seed like a bean, dried and used for food

**len·to** /ˈlentəʊ‖-toʊ/ *adj, adv technical* music that is played lento is played slowly

**Le·o** /ˈliːəʊ‖ˈliːoʊ/ *n* **1** [singular] the sign of the ZODIAC represented by a lion and believed to affect the character and life of people born between 23 July and 22 August **2** [C] someone who was born between 23 July and 22 August

**le·o·nine** /ˈliːənaɪn/ *adj* connected with lions, or like a lion in character or appearance

**leop·ard** /ˈlepəd‖-ərd/ *n* [C] **1** a large animal of the cat family, with yellow fur and black spots, which lives in Africa and South Asia **2 a leopard can't change its spots** used to say that people cannot change their character

**le·o·tard** /ˈliːətɑːd‖-ɑːrd/ *n* [C] a tight-fitting piece of women's clothing that covers your whole body from your neck to the top of your legs and is worn for exercise or dancing —see picture at UNDERWEAR

**lep·er** /ˈlepə‖-ər/ *n* [C] **1** someone who suffers fom the disease of leprosy **2** someone that people avoid because they have done something that people disapprove of: *They treated me as if I was some kind of leper.*

**lep·re·chaun** /ˈleprɪ̥kɔːn‖-kɑːn, -kɒːn/ *n* [C] an imaginary creature in the form of a little old man, in old Irish stories

**lep·ro·sy** /ˈleprəsi/ *n* [U] a very serious infectious disease in which the flesh and nerves are gradually destroyed —**leprous** *adj*

**ler·gy** /ˈlɜːgi‖ˈlɜːr-/ *n* [C] another spelling of LURGY

**les·bi·an** /ˈlezbiən/ *n* [C] a woman who is sexually attracted to other women —**lesbian** *adj*: *lesbian writers* —**lesbianism** *n* [U]

**lese-ma·jes·ty** /ˌliːz ˈmædʒɪ̥sti, ˌleɪz-/ *n* [U] **1** *humorous* behaviour that shows a lack of respect towards an important person **2** *law* a crime against a king or government

**le·sion** /ˈliːʒən/ *n* [C] *technical* **1** a wound: *multiple lesions to the skin* **2** a dangerous change in part of someone's body such as their lungs or brain, caused by injury or illness: *cerebral lesions*

**-less** /ləs/ *suffix* [in adjectives] **1** without something: *a childless couple* (=who have no children) | *It's quite harmless.* (=will not harm you) | *He was hatless.* (=wore no hat) | *endless complaints* (=that never end) **2** never doing something: *a tireless helper* (=who never gets tired) **3** unable to be treated in a particular way: *on countless occasions* (=too many to be counted)

S1 W1 **less**[1] /les/ *adv* **1** not so much; to a smaller degree: *I found the second half of the play less interesting than the first.* | *We go to Paris less frequently now.* | *You ought to smoke less.* —opposite MORE[1] (1) **2 less and less** gradually becoming smaller in amount or degree: *Our trips became less and less frequent.* **3 much/still less** *formal* certainly not: *They did not intend even to tell the authorities about the experiments, still less seek their approval.*

S1 W1 **less**[2] *determiner, pron* **1 a)** not as much: *You ought to eat less salt.* | *Most of the workers were paid £5 per day, but some received even less.* | *Give him less of the medicine if it seems to upset him.* | *a distance of less than 100 metres* **b)** used to mean fewer or not as many, but often considered incorrect in this meaning: *There were less people there than we expected.* **2 no less than** used when you are giving a number, to emphasize that it is surprisingly large: *The book has been translated into no less than 40 languages.* **3 less than helpful/perfect etc** not at all helpful, perfect etc: *Doctors have been less than successful in treating this condition.* **4 in less than no time** very quickly or very soon: *The debts increased alarmingly, and in less than no time they found that they owed over $10,000.* **5 nothing less than** used to emphasize how important or serious something really is: *His appearance in the show was nothing less than a sensation.* **6 no less** used to emphasize that the person or thing you are talking about is very important: *The building was opened by no less a person than the Prince of Wales.* | *His case is supported by the Police Complaints Committee no less.* **7 less of** *spoken* used to tell someone, usually a child, to stop doing something: *Less of that noise, please!* **8 not ... any the less** just as much: *I know he's done a dreadful thing, but I don't love him any the less.*

**less**[3] *prep* taking away or not counting a particular amount: *What is 121 less 36?* | *He gave us our money back less the $2 service charge.*

**les·see** /le'siː/ *n* [C] *law* someone who is legally allowed to use a house, building, land etc agreement for a fixed period of time in return for payment to the owner —compare LESSOR

**less·en** /'lesən/ *v* [I,T] to become smaller in size, importance, or value, or make something do this: *Garlic is supposed to lessen the risk of heart disease.* | *International tensions lessened after the end of the Cold War.*

**less·er** /'lesə‖-ər/ *adj* [only before noun] **1** *formal* not as large, as important, or as much as something else: *They originally asked for $5 million, but finally settled for a lesser sum.* | **to a lesser extent/degree** *the growing influence of Tokyo, and to a lesser extent Frankfurt, as financial centers* —see also **lesser mortals** (MORTAL[2] (1)) **2 the lesser of two evils** the less unpleasant or harmful of two unpleasant choices **3 lesser known** not well known or not as well known as others: *a lesser known French poet* **4** used in the names of some types of animal, bird, or plant that are slightly smaller than the main type

S2 W3 **les·son** /'lesən/ *n* [C]

**1** ▶ **LEARNING A SKILL** ◀ a period of time in which someone is taught a particular skill, for example how to play a musical instrument or drive a car: *piano lessons* | **take lessons** *She's started taking driving lessons.* | [+ **on/in**] *lessons in social etiquette*

**2** ▶ **IN SCHOOL** ◀ *BrE* a period of time in which students in a school are taught a particular subject; CLASS[1](3) *AmE*: *What did you do last lesson?* | *boring Maths lessons* | [+ **in/on**] *lessons on eight different subjects every week*

**3** ▶ **WARNING** ◀ an experience, especially an unpleasant one, that makes you more careful in the future: *Pearl Harbor was a painful lesson for the US.*

**4 let that be a lesson to you** *spoken* used to warn someone that they must be more careful in order to avoid the same bad experience happening to them again

**5** ▶ **BOOK** ◀ a part of a book that is used for learning a particular subject, especially in school: *Turn to lesson 25.*

**6** ▶ **CHURCH** ◀ a short piece that is read from the Bible during a religious ceremony —see also **learn your lesson** (LEARN[1] (7)), **teach sb a lesson** (TEACH (6))

**les·sor** /le'sɔː‖-'sɔːr/ *n* [C] *law* someone who allows someone else to use their house, building, land etc for a period of time for payment —compare LESSEE

**lest** /lest/ *conjunction formal* **1** in order to make sure that something will not happen: *She pulled away from the window lest anyone see them.* **2** used to show that someone is afraid or worried that a particular thing might happen: *The child watched them, nervous lest they hurt themselves.* | *He paused, afraid lest he say too much.*

**-let** /lɪ̣t/ *suffix* [in nouns] **1** a small kind of something: *a booklet* (=small paper-covered book) | *a piglet* (=young pig) **2** a band worn on a particular part of your body: *an anklet* (=worn on the ankle) S1 W1

**let**[1] /let/ *v past tense and past participle* **let** *present participle* **letting**

**1** ▶ **ALLOW** ◀ [T not in passive] **a)** to allow someone to do something: *I wanted to go out but my Dad wouldn't let me.* | **let sb do sth** *She won't let her children play by the river.* | *Don't let your boss hear you say that.* | **let sb have sth** (=give something to someone) *I can let you have a copy of the report.* —see graph at PERMIT[1] —see graph at FORBID **b)** to allow something to happen: **let sth do sth** *Max let the door swing open.* | *She didn't let her anger show.* | *It'll drive you crazy if you let it.* —see CAN (USAGE) —see graph at PERMIT

**2 let go** to stop holding something: *Let go! You're hurting me.* | **let go of** *She wouldn't let go of the rope.*

**3 let sb go a)** to allow a person or animal to leave a place where they have been kept: *They said they wouldn't let her go until her family paid the ransom.* **b)** a phrase meaning to dismiss someone from their job, used to avoid saying this directly: *I'm afraid we're going to have to let you go.*

**4 let yourself go a)** to allow yourself to relax completely in a social situation, and not worry about what other people think **b)** to take less care of your appearance than usual: *She's really let herself go since her husband died.*

**5 let sth go for £2/$150 etc** *informal* to sell something for a low price

**6 let sb know** to tell someone something: *I'd appreciate it if you'd let me know as soon as possible.* | **let sb know if/whether** *Let us know if you need any more information.*

**7 let alone** used to say that because one thing does not happen or is not true etc, another thing cannot possibly happen or be true: *The baby can't even crawl yet, let alone walk!*

**8** ▶ **WISH** ◀ *literary* used to express a wish that something will happen or will not happen: **(not) let sb/sth do sth** *Don't let him be the one who died, she prayed.* | **let there be** *Let there be roses and sparkling champagne.*

**9 let yourself be bullied/imposed on etc** to allow other people to treat you badly: *Don't let yourself be pushed around.*

**10 never let a day/week go by without ...** to do something every day or every week: *I never let a day go by without phoning my mother.*

**11** ▶ **ROOM/BUILDING** ◀ [T] to allow someone to use a room or building in return for money every week or month; LEASE[2] (1): *Interhome has over 20,000 houses to let across Europe.* | **let sth to sb** *I've let my spare room to a Japanese student.* | **To Let** *BrE*/**For Let** *AmE* (=words on a sign outside a building to show that it is empty and can be rented) —compare HIRE[1] (1), RENT[1] (3)

**12** ▶ **IMAGINE** ◀ *formal* **a) let us suppose/say/imagine** used to ask a reader or listener to imagine that something is true, as a way of helping them understand what you are talking about: *Let us suppose that interest rates go up again. What effect will this have on the property market?* **b) let sth be/equal/represent** used in mathematics or science to mean that one thing can be imagined as representing another: *Let angle A be 45°.*

**13 let sb alone** also **let sb be** to stop annoying someone, or asking them things: *Your mother's tired – let her alone!*

**14 let sth drop/rest** to stop discussing something or trying to deal with something that has been annoying you or worrying you: *He's apologized, so I think you should let it drop now.*

**15 let sth go/pass** to decide not to react to something bad or annoying that someone has done or said: *I know you didn't mean to offend her, so we'll let it pass this time.*

**16 let sth ride** **a)** if you let a situation ride, you let it continue for a time before deciding whether to take any action **b)** if you let a remark that has annoyed you ride, you do not say anything about it
**17 let drop/fall** to say a piece of information as though by accident, although really you want someone to know about it: *She decided that she would casually let drop the news about having the baby.*
**18 let slip** to accidentally say a piece of information that you did not want someone to know
**19 let yourself in for** *informal* to do something that will cause you a lot of trouble: *I don't think Carol realizes what she's letting herself in for.*
**20 let sb have it** *informal* **a)** to shout at someone because you are angry with them: *Mrs Bates really let him have it for leaving the classroom early.* **b)** to hit or shoot someone —see also **let fly** (FLY[1] (20)), **let your hair down** (HAIR (5)), **let it all hang out** (HANG[1]), **live and let live** (LIVE[1] (28)), **let sth rip** (RIP[1] (5))

Frequencies of the verb let **in** spoken and written English.

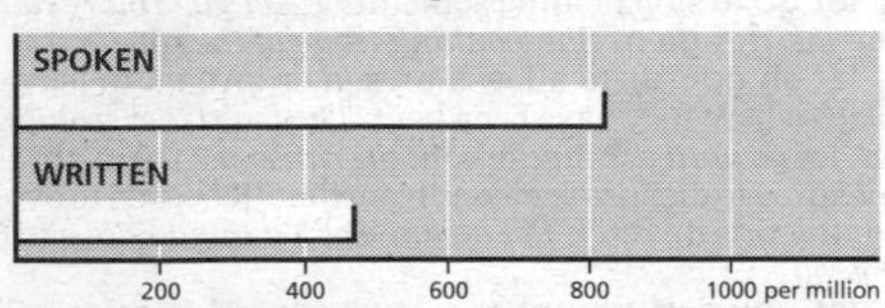


Based on the British National Corpus and the Longman Lancaster Corpus

This graph shows that the verb **let** is much more common in spoken English than in written English. This is because it is more commonly used in spoken English than **allow**, which is more formal and is more common in written English. **Let** is also used in a lot of common spoken phrases.

**let** (*v*) **SPOKEN PHRASES**

**21 let's** used to suggest to someone that you and they should do something together: *Come on, let's dance!* | *Right, let's get these plates washed.* | *Let's move on to the report itself: any comments?* | **let's not** *Let's not talk about work now.* | **don't let's** *BrE*: *Don't let's quarrel.* —see PROPOSE (USAGE)
**22 let's see** **a)** used to say that you are going to try to do something: **let's see if/whether** *Let's see if I can get the car to start.* **b)** used when pausing to remember something or find a piece of information: *Now, let's see ... here it is: "Video recorder, good condition, £75".* | *Let's see, oh, I wanted to ask what you are doing next Wednesday.* **c)** used to ask someone to show you something: *"Come on, let's see." "No, it's a secret!"* | *Let's see your new dress.* | *Right, let's see what you can do with that guitar!*
**23 let me see/think** used when pausing to think of some information or think what to do next: *You sent it to, um, let me see, ... Mike Toghill.*
**24 let me do sth** **a)** used to politely offer to do something for someone: *Here, let me help you with those bags.* **b)** used to tell someone what you are going to do next: *Let me just take your blood pressure.* | *Let me finish this typing then I'll make us some coffee.*
**25 let's say** used to ask someone to imagine something in order to discuss it or understand it better: *OK, you buy an object – let's say a bicycle – for $100. How much interest would you have to pay?* | **let's say (that)** *Let's say you did fail your exams, you could retake them, couldn't you?*
**26 let's just say** used to say that you are not going to tell someone all the details about something: *"So who did it?" "Let's just say it wasn't anyone in this family."*
**27 let him/them etc** **a)** used to say that you do not care whether someone does something or not: *Let her tell everyone, then – I don't care.* | *Well, if he wants to go and kill himself, let him!* **b)** used to say that someone else should do something instead of you: *Let them clear up the mess, it's their fault.*
**28 let's hope** used to say that you hope something will happen, so that there will not be problems: *Let's just hope he got your letter in time.*
**29 let's face it/let's be honest** used to say that you must accept an unpleasant fact: *Let's face it, Ben, no one's going to lend us any more money.*
**30 let well (enough) alone** to not try to change a situation, because you may make it worse: *He's happier now – I'd let well enough alone if I were you.*
**31 let me tell you!** used to emphasize that a feeling you had was very strong: *I was pretty surprised, let me tell you!*
**32 I'll/we'll let it go at that** used to tell someone that you will not punish or criticize them any more for something bad they have done: *Well you've missed your favorite program so we'll let it go at that.*

**let** sb/sth ↔ **down** *phr v* [T] **1** to make someone feel disappointed because you have not behaved well or not done what you said you would do: *I'm counting on you to support me – don't let me down!* | **let sb down badly** *She felt badly let down by her friends.* **2 a)** to give something to someone who is in a lower place than you are: *Let down a rope so that I can climb up.* **b)** to move something that is on a string, rope etc downwards: *Let the basket down gently.* **3 let your hair down** *informal* to relax and enjoy yourself, especially after working hard: *The Christmas party gives everyone a chance to let their hair down.* **4** *BrE* to allow the air to escape from something so that it loses its shape and firmness: *Someone's let my tyres down!* **5 let the side down** *BrE informal* to cause embarrassment or disappointment to your friends, family, team etc, for example by not behaving as they expect you to behave **6 let sb down lightly** to give someone bad news in a way that will not upset them too much **7** to make a piece of clothing longer: *I'm going to let down this old dress for my daughter.*

**let** sb/sth ↔ **in** *phr v* [T] **1** to open the door of a room, building etc so that someone can come in: *I unlocked the door and let him in.* | *My mother let herself in.* **2** to allow light, water, air etc to enter a place: *The windows don't let in much light.* **3 let sb in on** to tell someone about a secret plan, idea etc, and trust them not to tell other people

**let** sb/sth **into** sth *phr v* [T] **1** to allow someone to come into a room or building: *Who let you into my office?* **2 let sb into a secret** to tell someone something secret or private **3 be let into** *technical* if something such as a window or a decoration is let into a wall, brick etc, it is placed so that it is level with the surface it is in

**let** sb/sth **off** *phr v* [T] **1** to not make someone do a piece of work which they should be doing: *Since you practiced the piano yesterday, I'll let you off today.* | **let sb off sth** *She let her son off his chores.* **2** to not punish someone: *I'll let you off this time, but don't do it again.* | **let sb off with sth** *The judge let two of the three prisoners off with only a reprimand.* | **let sb off lightly** (=give someone a less serious punishment than they deserve) **3 a)** to fire a gun **b)** to make a bomb or FIREWORK explode —see also **let sb off the hook** (HOOK[1] (4)), **let off steam** (STEAM[1] (4))

**let on** *phr v* [I,T] *informal* to tell someone something that was meant to be a secret: *I think he knows more about it than he's letting on.* | **let on (that)** *Don't let on that I told you.* | **let on who/why/how etc** *You mustn't let on who gave it to us.*

**let out** *phr v* **1** [T **let** sb ↔ **out**] to allow someone to leave a room, building etc: *Let the dog out, will you?* | *He was in a high-security jail and would probably never be let out.* | **let sb out of sth** *Quietly, I let myself out of her apartment.* **2** [T **let** sth ↔ **out**] to allow light, water, air etc to leave a place: *Close the door, you're letting all the heat out.* **3 let out a scream/cry/roar etc** to make a sound, especially a loud sound: *She let out a sudden scream.* **4** [T **let** sth ↔ **out**] to make a piece of clothing wider or looser, especially because the person it belongs to has become fatter **5** [T **let** sth ↔ **out**] *especially BrE* to allow someone to use a room, building etc in exchange for money —see HIRE[1] (USAGE) **6** [I] *AmE* if a school, film etc lets

out, it ends, so that the people attending it can leave: *What time does the play let out?* —see also **let the cat out of the bag** (CAT (2))

**let up** *phr v* [I] **1** if something, such as bad weather or an unpleasant situation, lets up, it stops or becomes less serious: *When do you think this rain will let up?* **2 not let up** if someone does something without letting up, they do it continuously, especially in an annoying way: *I wish you'd stop nagging! You just never let up, do you?*

**let²** *n* **1** [C] *BrE* **a)** a period during which a house or flat is rented to someone; RENT¹ (1): *a long let* **b)** a house or flat that can be rented **2 without let or hindrance** *law* happening freely without being prevented in any way

**letch** /letʃ/ another spelling of LECH

**let·down** /ˈletdaʊn/ *n* [singular] *informal* an event, performance etc that is not as good as you expected it to be; disappointment: *The ending of the book was a real letdown.* —see also **let down** (LET¹)

**le·thal** /ˈliːθəl/ *adj* **1** causing death, or having the power to cause death: *a lethal dose of a drug* **2** *often humorous* likely to be dangerous or dangerously effective: *That cocktail looks pretty lethal.* **3 a lethal combination** a very bad or dangerous combination of two or more things: *Alcohol and tranquillizers are a lethal combination.*

**le·thar·gic** /lɪ̵ˈθɑːdʒɪk‖-ˈθɑːr-/ *adj* feeling as if you have no energy and no interest in doing anything: *The hot weather was making us all lethargic.* —**lethargically** /-kli/ *adv*

**leth·ar·gy** /ˈleθədʒi‖-ər-/ *n* [U] the feeling of being lethargic: *New mothers often complain of tiredness, lethargy and mild depression.*

**let's** /lets/ the short form of 'let us': *C'mon, let's go!* —see PROPOSE (USAGE)

S1 W1 **let·ter¹** /ˈletə‖-ər/ *n* [C] **1** a written or printed message that is usually put in an envelope and sent by mail: *Bart's writing a letter to his parents.* | *I got a long letter from Melanie today.* | **mail a letter** *AmE*: *Can you mail this letter for me on your way out?* | **post a letter** *BrE*: *I'm just going to post a letter.* **2** any of the signs in writing or printing that represent a speech sound: *'B' is a capital letter, 'b' is a small letter.* **3 do sth to the letter** to pay exact attention to the details of an agreement, rule, set of instructions etc: *He kept his promise to the letter.* | *I followed all the instructions to the letter, but it still wouldn't work.* **4 the letter of the law** the exact words of a law or agreement rather than the intended or general meaning: *various methods of avoiding taxes while adhering to the letter of the law* **5** *AmE* a large cloth letter to put on to clothes, given as a reward for playing in a school or college sports team: *She got her letter in track.* **6 English/American/German letters** [plural] *formal* the study of the literature of a particular country or language: *a major figure in English letters at the turn of the century* —see also CHAIN LETTER, DEAD LETTER, DEAR JOHN LETTER, LETTER OF CREDIT, MAN OF LETTERS, OPEN LETTER

**letter²** *v* [I] *AmE* to earn a LETTER¹ (5) in a sport: [+ **in**] *He lettered in basketball at Brandeis.*

**letter³** *adj AmE* LETTER-SIZE

**letter bomb** /ˈ·· ˌ·/ *n* [C] a small bomb hidden in a package and sent to someone in order to kill or harm them

**let·ter·box** /ˈletəbɒks‖ˈletərbɑːks/ *n* [C] **1** a narrow hole in a door, or a special box where letters, packages etc are delivered **2** *BrE* a box in a post office or street, in which letters can be posted; MAILBOX *AmE*

**let·tered** /ˈletəd‖-ərd/ *adj formal* **1** well educated **2 badly lettered/carefully lettered** with badly drawn, beautifully drawn etc letters or words: *a brightly lettered sign on the boy's door*

**let·ter·head** /ˈletəhed‖-ər-/ *n* [C] the name and address printed at the top of a sheet of writing paper

**let·ter·ing** /ˈletərɪŋ/ *n* [U] **1** written or drawn letters, especially of a particular type, size, colour etc: *a yellow board with black lettering* **2** the art of writing or drawing letters or words

**letter of cred·it** /ˌ·· · ˈ··/ *n* [C] an official letter from a bank allowing a particular person to take money from another bank

**letter-per·fect** /ˌ·· ˈ··◂/ *adj AmE* correct in every detail: *The District Attorney's case was letter-perfect.*

**letter-qual·i·ty** /ˈ·· ˌ···/ *adj* a letter-quality PRINTER (1) produces print that is good enough to be used for business letters, reports etc

**letter-size** /ˈ·· ·/ also **letter** *adj AmE* paper that is letter-size is 8½ inches (INCH¹ (1)) wide and 11 inches long

**let·ting** /ˈletɪŋ/ *n* [C] *BrE* a house or apartment that can be rented: *a holiday letting*

**let·tuce** /ˈletɪ̵s/ *n* [C,U] a round vegetable with thin green leaves used in SALADS —see picture on page 414

**let·up** /ˈletʌp/ *n* [singular, U] a pause or a reduction in a difficult, dangerous, or tiring activity: *There is no sign of a letup in the fighting.* | *We were working seven days a week with no letup.* —see also **let up** (LET¹)

**leu·co·cyte** /ˈluːkəsaɪt/ *n* [C] *technical* another spelling of LEUKOCYTE

**leu·cot·o·my** /luːˈkɒtəmi‖-ˈkɑː-/ *n* [C] *BrE* a LOBOTOMY

**leu·ke·mi·a** also **leukaemia** *BrE* /luːˈkiːmiə/ *n* [U] a type of CANCER in which the blood contains too many WHITE BLOOD CELLS, causing weakness and sometimes death

**leu·ko·cyte** /ˈluːkəsaɪt/ *n* [C] *technical* one of the cells in your blood which fights against infection; WHITE BLOOD CELL

**lev·ee¹** /ˈlevi/ *n* [C] a special wall built to stop a river flooding

**lev·ee²** /ˈlevi, ləˈveɪ/ *n* [C] *old use* a meeting in which a king receives visits from important people

**lev·el¹** /ˈlevəl/ *n* [C] S1 W1

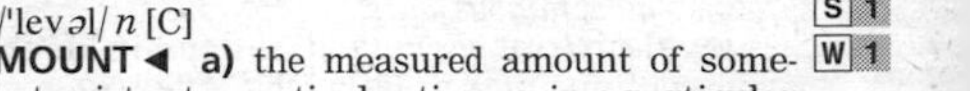

**1 ▶AMOUNT◀ a)** the measured amount of something that exists at a particular time or in a particular place: *Inflation had dropped to its lowest level in 30 years.* | [+ **of**] *concern about the level of carbon monoxide in the air* | **high/low levels** *High levels of radiation were found in the sea.* **b)** the amount of a quality that someone has or that exists in a situation: *a very high level of commitment among the workforce* | *These simple exercises can dramatically reduce stress levels.*

**2 ▶HEIGHT◀** the height of something in relation to the ground or to another object: *Hold out your arm at the same level as your shoulder.* | **at eye level** (=at the same height as your eyes)

**3 ▶LIQUID◀** the height of the surface of a liquid from the ground or from the bottom of a container: *Check the water level in the car radiator.* —see also SEA LEVEL, WATER LEVEL

**4 ▶STANDARD◀** a particular standard of skill or ability, for example in education or sport: *Students at this level tend to have a lot of problems with grammar.* | *By 21, she was regularly playing at international level.* | *an advanced level coursebook*

**5 ▶FLOOR/GROUND◀** a floor or piece of ground, especially when considered in relation to another floor or piece of ground that is higher or lower: *The town is built on different levels.* | *The medical center should be on one level for the convenience of patients.*

**6 ▶RANK OF JOB◀** all the people or jobs within an organization, industry etc that have similar amounts of importance and responsibility: *Training was offered at each level in the department.* | *Decisions like this can only be made at board level.*

**7 at local level/at national level** happening within a small area or the whole area of a country: *Decisions are made at local and not national level.*

**8 on/at one level ... on/at another level** used when you are considering something in one way and then in another way: *At one level I really enjoy the work, but at another level I feel I should be doing something more challenging.*

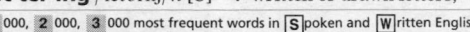

**9 on a practical level/on a personal level etc** used to talk about something, considering it in a practical, personal etc way: *On a more practical level, we should consider how we are going to find the money.*
**10 be on the level** *informal* to be honest: *I'd like to buy that bloke's car, but I'm not sure he's on the level.*
**11 ▶TOOL◀** *especially AmE* a tool used for checking that a surface is flat; SPIRIT-LEVEL

S1 W2 **level²** *adj* **1** a surface, piece of land etc that is level is flat and does not slope in any direction: *Make sure the ground is completely level before you lay the turf.* **2 be level a)** two things that are level are at the same height as each other: [+ **with**] *The top of the tree was level with the roof of the house.* **b)** *BrE* two sports teams, competitors etc that are level have the same number of points: **draw level** (=get enough points to be level) *Faldo has drawn level with Ballesteros on twelve under par.* | **finish level** *The two teams finished level, with 10 points each.* —see also LEVEL-PEGGING **3 do your level best** to try as hard as possible to do something: *I'll do my level best to help you.* **4 a level voice/look/gaze** a steady voice, look etc, that shows you are calm or determined **5 level spoon(ful)/cup** an amount of a substance, that is just enough to fill a spoon or cup, used as a measure in cooking

**level³** *v* **levelled, levelling** *BrE,* **leveled, leveling** *AmE* [T] **1** to make something flat and even: *Pat leveled the wet concrete with a piece of wood.* **2** to knock down or destroy a building or area completely: *The bombing raid levelled a large part of the town.* **3 level the score** *BrE* to make the score in a game or competition equal

**level** sth **at** *phr v* [T] **1** to aim something such as a weapon at someone or something **2 level a charge/accusation/criticism at** to publicly criticize someone or say they are responsible for a crime, mistake etc: *Outrageous accusations were levelled against some of Hollywood's most famous stars.*

**level off/out** *phr v* **1** [I] to stop climbing or falling, and continue at a fixed height: *After climbing steeply through woodland the path levelled off.* | *The plane levelled out at 30,000 feet.* **2** [I] to become steady in development or growth: *Inflation has begun to level off.* **3** [T **level** sth ↔ **off/out**] to make something flat and smooth

**level with** sb *phr v* [T] *informal* to speak honestly to someone, not hiding any unpleasant facts from them: *He asked Ron to level with him about what people were saying about him.* —see also **be on the level** (LEVEL¹ (10))

**level cross·ing** /ˌ·· ˈ··/ *n* [C] *BrE* a place where a road and railway cross each other, usually protected by gates

**level-head·ed** /ˌ·· ˈ··◂/ *adj* calm and sensible in making judgments or decisions

**lev·el·ler** *BrE,* **leveler** *AmE* /ˈlevələ‖-ər/ *n* [C] something, especially death or illness, that makes people of all classes and ranks seem equal

**level-peg·ging** /ˌ·· ˈ··/ *n* **be level-pegging** *BrE* if competitors in a race, election etc are level-pegging, they are equal and it is difficult to know who will win

**level play·ing-field** /ˌ·· ˈ··ˌ·/ *n* [singular] a situation in which different companies, countries etc can all compete fairly with each other because no one has special advantages: *It's not really a level playing-field when one country is subsidizing its car industry with massive government grants.*

**le·ver¹** /ˈliːvə‖ˈlevər, ˈli-/ *n* [C] **1** a long thin piece of metal that you use to lift something heavy by putting one end under the object and pushing the other end down **2** a stick or handle fixed to a machine, that you move to make the machine work —see also GEAR LEVER **3** something you use to influence a situation to get the result that you want

**lever²** *v* [T] **1** to move something with a lever: **lever sth off/up/out etc** *Marc grunted as he levered the stone into place.* **2** to make someone leave a particular job, situation etc: [+ **out**] *They're trying to lever him out of his job as CEO.*

**le·ver·age¹** /ˈliːvərɪdʒ‖ˈle-, ˈliː-/ *n* [U] **1** influence that you can use to make people do what you want: *Diplomatic leverage by the US persuaded several governments to cooperate.* **2** the action, power, or use of a lever

**leverage²** *v* [T] *AmE technical* to make money available, using a particular method: *using public funds to leverage private investment*

**lev·e·ret** /ˈlevərɪ̇t/ *n* [C] a young HARE¹ (1)

**le·vi·a·than** /lɪˈvaɪəθən/ *n* [C] **1** something very large and strong: *a leviathan of a ship* **2** a very large and frightening sea animal

**lev·i·tate** /ˈlevɪ̇teɪt/ *v* [I] to rise and float in the air by magic —**levitation** /ˌlevɪ̇ˈteɪʃən/ *n* [U]

**lev·i·ty** /ˈlevɪ̇ti/ *n* [U] *formal* lack of respect or seriousness when you are dealing with something serious

**lev·y¹** /ˈlevi/ *v* [T] **levy a tax/charge etc** to officially make someone pay a tax etc: [+ **on**] *A new tax has just been levied on all electrical goods.*

**levy²** *n* [C] an additional sum of money, usually paid as a tax

**lewd** /luːd/ *adj* using rude words or movements that make you think of sex: *lewd comments* —**lewdly** *adv* —**lewdness** *n* [U]

**lex·i·cal** /ˈleksɪkəl/ *adj technical* dealing with words, or related to words

**lex·i·cog·ra·phy** /ˌleksɪˈkɒgrəfi‖-ˈkɑː-/ *n* [U] the skill, practice, or profession of writing dictionaries —**lexicographer** *n* [C] —**lexicographical** /ˌlek-sɪkəˈgræfɪkəl◂/ *adj*

**lex·i·col·o·gy** /ˌleksɪˈkɒlədʒi‖-ˈkɑː-/ *n* [U] *technical* the study of the meaning and uses of words

**lex·i·con** /ˈleksɪkən‖-kɑːn, -kən/ *n* **1 the lexicon** *technical* all the words and phrases used in a language or that a particular person knows **2** [C] a book containing an alphabetical list of words with their meanings

**lex·is** /ˈleksɪ̇s/ *n* [U] *technical* all the words in a language

**ley line** /ˈleɪ laɪn/ *n* [C] an imaginary line connecting old buildings, places etc that is believed to follow an ancient track that has special power

**li·a·bil·i·ty** /ˌlaɪəˈbɪlɪ̇ti/ *n* **1** [U] legal responsibility for something, especially for paying money that is owed, or for damage or injury: [+ **for**] *Tenants have legal liability for any damage they cause.* **2 liabilities** *technical* the amount of debt that must be paid **3** [singular] someone or something that is likely to cause problems for someone: *A kid like Tom would be a liability in any classroom.* **4 liability to sth** the amount that something is likely to be affected by a particular kind of problem, illness etc: *The patient may suffer greater liability to bacterial diseases.* —see also LIMITED LIABILITY W2

**li·a·ble** /ˈlaɪəbəl/ *adj* **1 be liable to do sth** to be likely to do or say something or to behave in a particular way, especially because of a fault or natural tendency: *The car is liable to overheat on long trips.* **2** [not before noun] legally responsible for the cost of something: [+ **for**] *Manufacturers are liable for any defects in the equipment.* **3** likely to be affected by a particular kind of problem, illness etc: [+ **to**] *You're more liable to injury when you don't get regular exercise.* **4** *law* likely to be legally punished or forced to do something by law: [+ **to**] *Anyone found trespassing is liable to a maximum fine of $100.* | [+ **for**] *All males between 18 and 60 are liable for military service.*

**li·aise** /liˈeɪz/ *v* [I + **with**] to exchange information with someone who works in another organization or department so that you can both be more effective: *Part of Anne's job as a librarian is to liaise with local schools.*

**li·ai·son** /liˈeɪzən‖ˈliːəzɑːn, liˈeɪ-/ *n* **1** [singular, U] the regular exchange of information between groups of people, especially at work, so that each group knows what the other is doing: [+ **between**] *close liaison between army and police* | **in liaison with** *The project has been set up in liaison with the art department.* **2** [C] a word meaning a sexual relationship between a man and a woman who are not married to each other, used to avoid saying this directly

**liaison of·fi·cer** /'··· ˌ··· ‖'··· ˌ··/ *n* [C] someone whose job is to talk to different departments or groups and to tell each of them about what the others are doing

**li·ar** /'laɪə‖-ər/ *n* [C] someone who tells lies

**Lib** *BrE* the written abbreviation of LIBERAL[3] —**Lib** *adj*

**lib** /lɪb/ *n* see AD LIB, WOMEN'S LIB

**li·ba·tion** /laɪ'beɪʃən/ *n* [C] a gift of wine to a god

**lib·ber** /'lɪbə‖-ər/ *n* **women's libber** see WOMEN'S LIB

**Lib Dem** /ˌlɪb 'dem◂/ *n* [C] *BrE* LIBERAL DEMOCRAT —**Lib Dem** *adj*

**li·bel**[1] /'laɪbəl/ *n* [C,U] an act of writing or printing untrue statements about someone so that other people are likely to have a bad opinion of them: *Holt sued the newspaper for libel.* | *a libel action* (=a court case against someone for libel) —compare SLANDER[1] (2)

**libel**[2] *v* **libelled, libelling** *BrE,* **libeled, libeling** *AmE* [T] to write or print a libel against someone

**li·bel·lous** *BrE,* **libelous** *AmE* /'laɪbələs/ *adj* containing untrue written statements about someone which could make other people have a bad opinion of them: *libellous gossip*

W2 **lib·e·ral**[1] /'lɪbərəl/ *adj* **1** willing to understand and respect other people's ideas, opinions, and feelings: *Young people nowadays take a more liberal attitude towards sexuality.* **2** supporting or allowing gradual political and social changes: *a more liberal policy on issues of crime and punishment* **3** given in large amounts: *a liberal supply of drinks* **4** generous with your money **5** not exact: *a liberal interpretation of the original play* **6 liberal education** a kind of education which encourages you to develop a large range of interests and knowledge and respect for other people's opinions

**liberal**[2] *n* [C] someone with liberal opinions or principles: *a society dominated by white bourgeois liberals*

**Liberal**[3] *n* [C] someone who supports or belongs to the former LIBERAL PARTY or the LIBERAL DEMOCRATS in Britain —**Liberal** *adj*

**liberal arts** /ˌ··· '·/ *n* [plural] the areas of learning which develop someone's ability to think and increase their general knowledge, rather than developing technical skills

**Liberal Dem·o·crats** /ˌ··· '···/ *n* [plural] a British political party of the centre —**Liberal Democrat** *adj*

**lib·e·ral·is·m** /'lɪbərəlɪzəm/ *n* [U] liberal opinions and principles, especially on social and political subjects

**lib·e·ral·i·ty** /ˌlɪbə'ræləti/ *n* [U] *formal* **1** understanding of, and respect for, other people's opinions: *a spirit of liberality and fairness* **2** the quality of being generous

**lib·e·ral·ize** also **-ise** *BrE* /'lɪbərəlaɪz/ *v* [T] to make a system, laws, or moral attitudes less strict —**liberalization** /ˌlɪbərəlaɪ'zeɪʃən‖-rələ-/ *n* [U]

**Liberal Par·ty** /'··· ˌ··/ *n* [singular] a former British political party of the centre

**liberal stud·ies** /ˌ··· '··/ *n* [plural] *especially BrE* subjects that are taught in order to increase student's general knowledge and their ability to write, speak, and study more effectively —compare LIBERAL ARTS

**lib·e·rate** /'lɪbəreɪt/ *v* [T] **1** to free someone from feelings or conditions that make their life unhappy or difficult: [+ **from**] *liberated from shame* | *the liberating power of education* **2** to free prisoners, a city, a country etc from someone's control —**liberator** *n* [C] —**liberation** /ˌlɪbə'reɪʃən/ *n* [U]

**lib·e·rat·ed** /'lɪbəreɪtəd/ *adj* free to behave in the way you want, and not restricted by old rules of social and sexual behaviour: *the magazine for the liberated woman*

**lib·er·tar·i·an** /ˌlɪbə'teəriən‖-bər'ter-/ *n* [C] someone who believes strongly that people should be free to do and think what they want to —**libertarian** *adj*

**lib·er·tine** /'lɪbətiːn‖-ər-/ *n* [C] someone who leads an immoral life and always looks for pleasure, especially sexual pleasure —**libertine** *adj*

**lib·er·ty** /'lɪbəti‖-ər-/ *n*

**1** ▶ **FREEDOM** ◀ [U] the freedom and the right to do whatever you want without asking permission or being afraid of authority: *People will resent these restrictions on their liberty.*

**2** ▶ **LEGAL RIGHT** ◀ [C usually plural] a particular legal right: *liberties such as freedom of speech that we take for granted*

**3** ▶ **WITHOUT PERMISSION** ◀ [singular] something you do without asking permission, which may offend or upset someone else: *What a diabolical liberty!* | **take the liberty of doing sth** *I took the liberty of cancelling the reservation for you.*

**4 be at liberty to do sth** *formal* to have the right or permission to do something: *I'm afraid that I am not at liberty to discuss these matters.*

**5 take liberties with sb/sth** **a)** to make unreasonable changes in something such as a piece of writing: *The film-makers took too many liberties with the original novel.* **b)** *old-fashioned* to treat someone without respect by being too friendly too quickly, especially in a sexual way: *He's been taking liberties with our female staff.*

**6 at liberty** if a prisoner or an animal is at liberty, they are no longer in prison or enclosed in a small place

**li·bi·do** /lɪ'biːdəʊ‖-doʊ/ *n* [C,U] *technical* someone's desire to have sex —**libidinous** /lɪ'bɪdɪnəs/ *adj*

**Li·bra** /'liːbrə/ *n* **1** [singular] the seventh sign of the ZODIAC, represented by a pair of SCALES, and believed to affect the character and life of people born between September 23rd and October 23rd **2** [C] someone who was born between September 23rd and October 23rd

**li·brar·i·an** /laɪ'breəriən‖-'brer-/ *n* [C] someone who works in a library —**librarianship** *n* [U]

**li·bra·ry** /'laɪbrəri, -bri‖-breri/ *n* [C] **1** a room or building containing books that can be looked at or borrowed: *a public library* | *the college library* | *a library book* —compare BOOKSHOP **2** a group of books, records etc, collected by one person **3** a set of books, records etc that are produced by the same company and have the same general appearance: *a library of modern classics* S2 W1

**library pic·tures** /'··· ˌ··/ *n* [plural] *BrE* pictures shown in a television programme that were made at a previous time

**li·bret·tist** /lɪ'bretəst/ *n* [C] someone who writes librettos

**li·bret·to** /lɪ'bretəʊ‖-toʊ/ *plural* **librettos** *n* [C] the words of an OPERA or musical play

**lice** /laɪs/ *n* the plural of LOUSE[1] (1)

**li·cence** *BrE,* **license** *AmE* /'laɪsəns/ *n* S3 W2

**1** ▶ **DOCUMENT** ◀ [C] an official document giving you permission to own or do something for a period of time: *a firearms license* | *How much is the licence fee?* | **lose your licence** (=have your driving licence taken by the police as punishment)

**2** ▶ **FREEDOM** ◀ [U] **a)** freedom to do or say what you think is best: *Headteachers should be allowed greater licence in the exercise of their power.* **b)** freedom to behave in a way that is sexually immoral

**3 artistic/poetic licence** the way in which a writer or painter changes the facts of the real world to make their story, description, or picture of events more interesting or more beautiful

**4** ▶ **RIGHT TO DO STH** ◀ [C] official permission to do something, which seems to give someone the right to do something that is wrong: [+ **for**] *Church groups see the new laws as a licence for promiscuity.* | **licence to print money** (=an officially approved plan in which there is no control over how much money is spent)

**5 under licence** if something is sold, made etc under licence it is sold etc with the permission of a company or organization

**li·cense** also **licence** *BrE* /'laɪsəns/ *v* [T usually passive] to give official permission for someone to do something or for an activity to take place: **be licensed to do sth** *The restaurant is now licensed to sell alcohol.*

**li·censed** also **licenced** /ˈlaɪsənst/ *adj* **1** *BrE* having a licence to sell alcoholic drinks: *a licensed restaurant* **2** a car, gun etc that is licensed is one that someone has official permission to own or use **3** having been given official permission to do a particular job: *a licensed private investigator*

**licensed vict·ual·ler** /ˌ·· ˈ···/ *n* [C] *BrE technical* an owner of a shop or PUB who is allowed to sell alcoholic drink

**li·cen·see** /ˌlaɪsənˈsiː/ *n* [C] someone who has official permission to do something

**license plate** /ˈ·· ·/ *n* [C] *AmE* one of the signs with numbers on it at the front and back of a car; NUMBER PLATE *BrE* —see picture on page 409

**licens·ing hours** /ˈ··· ˌ·/ *n* [plural] the hours during which it is legal to sell alcohol in Britain

**licensing laws** /ˈ··· ˌ·/ *n* [plural] *BrE* the laws that say when and where you can sell alcohol

**li·cen·ti·ate** /laɪˈsenʃiət/ *n* [C] someone who has been given official permission to practise a particular art or profession: *a licentiate of the Royal College of Music*

**li·cen·tious** /laɪˈsenʃəs/ *adj formal* behaving in a sexually immoral or uncontrolled way —**licentiously** *adv* —**licentiousness** *n* [U]

**li·chee** /ˈlaɪtʃiː/ *n* [C] another spelling of LYCHEE

**li·chen** /ˈlaɪkən, ˈlɪtʃən/ *n* [U] a grey, green, or yellow plant that spreads over the surface of stones and trees —compare MOSS

S3 **lick**[1] /lɪk/ *v*
**1** ► **TONGUE** ◄ [T] to move your tongue across the surface of something in order to eat it, clean it etc: *The dog jumped up and licked her face.*
**2** ► **SPORT** ◄ [T] *informal* to defeat an opponent: *I reckon we could lick the best teams in Georgia.*
**3** ► **FLAMES/WAVES** ◄ [I,T] *literary* if flames or waves lick something, they touch it again and again with quick movements: [+ **at/against**] *Soon the flames were licking at the curtains.*
**4 have (got) sth licked** *informal* to have succeeded in dealing with a difficult problem
**5 lick your lips** to feel eager and excited because you are expecting to get something good
**6 lick your wounds** to quietly think about the defeat or disappointment you have just suffered
**7 lick sb's boots** to obey someone completely because you fear them or want to please them —see also BOOTLICKING, **knock/lick sth into shape** (SHAPE[1] (7))
**lick** sth ↔ **up** *phr v* [T] to drink or eat something by licking it

**lick**

**lick**[2] *n* **1** [C usually singular] an act of licking something with your tongue: *Can I have a lick of your ice cream?* **2 a lick of paint/colour/etc** a small amount of paint etc put onto the surface of something to improve its appearance **3 give sth a lick and a promise** **a)** *BrE* to wash or clean something quickly and carelessly **b)** *AmE* to do a job quickly and carelessly **4 at a great lick/at a hell of a lick** *informal especially BrE* very fast **5** [C] *informal* an act of hitting someone

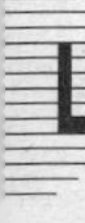

**lick·e·ty-split** /ˌlɪkəti ˈsplɪt/ *adv AmE old-fashioned* very quickly

**lick·ing** /ˈlɪkɪŋ/ *n* [singular] *informal* **1** a defeat in a sports competition or match: *We got a real licking in the final.* **2** a severe beating as a punishment

**lic·o·rice** /ˈlɪkərɪs, -rɪʃ/ *n* [U] the American spelling of LIQUORICE

**lid** /lɪd/ *n*
**1** ► **COVER** ◄ [C] a cover for the open part of a pot, box, or other container: *Can you get the lid off this jar for me?* | *a dustbin lid* —see picture at TOP[1]
**2 keep the lid on** to control a situation so that it does not become worse: *keeping the lid on inflation* | *She was trying to keep the lid on her simmering anger.*
**3** ► **EYE** ◄ [C] an EYELID
**4 put the lid on** *informal* to do something that finally ruins or ends someone's plans or hopes
**5 take the lid off sth/lift the lid on sth** to let people know the true facts about a bad or shocking situation: *Their latest documentary takes the lid off the world of organized crime.*

**lid·ded** /ˈlɪdɪd/ *adj* **1 heavy-lidded eyes** eyes with large EYELIDS **2** a lidded container, pot etc has a lid

**li·do** /ˈliːdəʊ, ˈlaɪ-‖ˈliːdoʊ/ *n* [C] *especially BrE* an outdoor public area, often at a beach, lake etc, for swimming and lying in the sun

**lie**[1] /laɪ/ *v present participle* **lying** *past tense* **lay** /leɪ/ *past participle* **lain** /leɪn/ S2 W1
**1** ► **FLAT POSITION** ◄ **a)** [I always + adv/prep] to be in a position in which your body is flat on the floor, on a bed etc: [+ **on/in/there etc**] *He was lying on the bed smoking a cigarette.* | *Don't lie in the sun for too long.* | **lie still/awake/dead etc** *She would lie awake at nights worrying.* **b)** also **lie down** [I always + adv/prep] to put yourself in a position in which your body is flat on the floor or on a bed: [+ **on/in/there etc**] *Lie on the floor and stretch your legs upwards.* **c)** [I always + adv/prep] to be in a flat position on a surface: [+ **on/in/there etc**] *The papers were lying neatly on his desk, waiting to be signed.*
**2** ► **EXIST** ◄ [I always + adv/prep] if an idea or a quality lies in a particular action, person etc, it exists or is expressed in that action, person, etc: [+ **in/with/outside etc**] *The answer must lie in finding alternative sources of power.* | **the future lies in** (=something will be very important in the future) *The future lies in multimedia.*
**3** ► **BE IN A PLACE** ◄ [I always + adv/prep] if a town, village, etc lies in a particular place, it is in that place: [+ **in/on/below**] *The town lies in a small wooded valley.*
**4 lie ahead/lie before you/lie in store** if something lies ahead of you etc, it is going to happen to you in the future: *How will we cope with the difficulties that lie ahead?* | *I was wondering what lay in store for us.*
**5 lie open/empty/undisturbed etc** to be open etc: *The book lay open on the table.* | *The town now lay in ruins.*
**6 lie in wait (for)** **a)** to remain hidden in a place and wait for someone so that you can attack them: [+ **for**] *a giant crocodile lying in wait for its prey* **b)** if something unpleasant lies in wait for you, it is going to happen to you
**7 lie low** to remain hidden because someone is trying to find you or catch you: *We'll have to lie low until tonight.*
**8 lie at the heart of** *formal* to be the most important part of something: *the issue that lies at the heart of the present conflict*
**9 lie heavy on** *formal* if something lies heavy on you, it makes you feel unhappy: *The feelings of guilt lay heavy on him.*
**10 lie second/third/fourth etc** *BrE* to be in second, third etc position in a competition: *Liverpool are lying third in the football championship.*
**11** ► **DEAD PERSON** ◄ [I always + adv/prep] if someone lies in a particular place, they are buried there: **here lies ...** (=written on a gravestone) *Here lies Percival Smythe.*
**12 lie in state** if an important person who has died lies in state, their body is put in a public place so that people can go and show their respect for them
**13** ► **STAY** ◄ [I always + adv/prep] *old use* to spend the night somewhere: *He was to lie that night at a neighbour's.* —see also **let sleeping dogs lie** (SLEEP[2] (6))
**lie about/around** *phr v* **1** [I,T] if something is

lying around, it has been left somewhere untidily, rather than being in its proper place: *If you leave your shoes lying around like that, you'll trip over them.* | **lie around/about sth** *Papers and books lay around the room in complete chaos.* **2** [I] if you lie around, you spend time lying down and not doing anything: *I felt so lazy just lying around on the beach all day.*

**lie behind** sth *phr v* [T] if something lies behind an action, it is the real reason for the action even though it may be hidden: *I knew that something else lay behind his sudden interest in football.*

**lie down** *phr v* **1** [I] to put yourself in a position in which your body is flat on the floor or on a bed: *You must lie down and rest.* **2 take sth lying down** *informal* to accept bad treatment without complaining: *I'm not going to take this lying down! You'll be hearing from my lawyer.*

**lie in** *phr v BrE* [I] to remain in bed in the morning for longer than usual: *I can't wait to be able to lie in this weekend!*

**lie with sb** *phr v* [T] **1** if a power, duty etc lies with someone, they have that power etc: *The responsibility for this problem lies firmly within the government.* **2** *old use* to have sex with someone

S3 **lie²** *v past tense* **lied** *past participle* **lying** **1** [I] to deliberately tell someone something that is not true: *I could tell from her face that she was lying.* | **lie to sb** *I would never lie to you.* | **lie through your teeth** (=say something that is completely untrue) **2** [I] if a picture, account etc lies, it does not show the true facts or the true situation: *Statistics can often lie.* | *The camera never lies.*

**lie³** *n* **1** [C] something that you say or write that you know is untrue: *There's no truth in her story. It's all lies!* | **tell a lie** *I always know when he's telling lies.* | **tell sb a lie** *Of course it's true. I wouldn't tell you a lie.* | **pack of lies** (=a story or set of statements that is completely untrue) *Their whole account of the event was a pack of lies.* | **barefaced lie** (=a shocking lie) | **white lie** (=a lie that is not serious, or one that is told to avoid upsetting someone) **2 give the lie to** *formal* to show that something is untrue: *This report gives the lie to the company's claim that there has been no pollution.* **3 the lie of the land/ the way the land lies** the way that a situation is developing at a particular time: *I want to see how the land lies before I decide whether or not to take the job.* **4 (I) tell a lie** *BrE spoken* used when you realize that something you have just said is not correct: *It was £25, no, tell a lie, £35.*

**lie de·tec·tor** /'· ·,··/ *n* [C] a piece of equipment used especially by the police to check whether someone is lying, by measuring sudden changes in their heart rate

**lie down** /'laɪdaʊn/ *n* [singular] *BrE* a short rest, usually on a bed: *I'm going upstairs to have a lie down.*

**lief** /liːf/ *adv old use* willingly or gladly

**liege** /liːdʒ/ *n* [C] **1** also **liege lord** a lord who was served and obeyed in the Middle Ages **2** also **leigeman** someone who had to serve and obey a lord in the Middle Ages

**lie-in** /'· ·, · '·/ *n* [singular] *BrE* an occasion when you stay in bed longer than usual in the morning

**li·en** /'liːən, liːn/ *n* [C + **on**] *law* the legal right to keep something that belongs to someone who owes you money, until the debt has been paid

**lieu** /ljuː, luː‖luː/ *n* **in lieu (of)** instead of: *extra time off in lieu of payment*

**Lieut** the written abbreviation of LIEUTENANT

**lieu·ten·ant** /lef'tenənt‖luː'ten-/ *n* **1 a)** [C] a fairly low rank of an officer in the army, navy, or air force, or a fairly high rank in the US police **b)** an officer who has this rank **2 lieutenant colonel/general/Governor etc** an officer or official with the rank below COLONEL, GENERAL², GOVERNOR etc **3** [C] someone who does work for, or in place of, someone in a higher position; DEPUTY (1) —see table on page B4

## life /laɪf/ *n plural* lives /laɪvz/

S1 W1

① PERIOD OF LIVING
② HUMAN EXPERIENCES
③ LIFE AND DEATH
④ LIVING THINGS
⑤ REAL/TRUE
⑥ HOW LONG STH CONTINUES
⑦ ACTIVITY/EXCITEMENT
⑧ OTHER MEANINGS

### ① PERIOD OF LIVING

**1** [C,U] the period between a person's birth and death during which they are alive: *Learning goes on throughout life.* | *You have your whole life ahead of you.* | **in your life** *I'd never seen the woman before in my life.* | **spend your life** *She spent her life moving from one town to another.* | **all your life** (=for the whole of your life) *I've lived in Mayo all my life.* | **early life** (=the part of your life when you were young) *We don't know much about the poet's early life.* | **in later life** (=in the later part of your life) *My grandfather was troubled with illness in later life.* | **late in life** (=when you are older than the usual age) *She had her children late in life.* | **for life** (=not changing for the rest of your life) *As far as I'm concerned, when you get married it's for life.* | **working life** (=the part of your life when you are working) *Norman had started his working life in the shipyards.*

### ② HUMAN EXPERIENCES

**2 ▶ A PERSON'S EXPERIENCES ◀** [C usually singular] the kind of experience that someone has during their life: *a life spent at sea* | **lead a happy/exciting/normal etc life** *Maria led a full and happy life.* | **a hard life** (=a life full of difficulty and trouble) **live a life of crime/sacrifice etc** *Marc dreamed of getting rich and living a life of luxury.* —see also LIFE STORY

**3 ▶ TYPICAL EXPERIENCES ◀** [C,U] all the experiences and activities that are typical of a particular way of living: **army/city/country etc life** *Isobel was bored with country life and longed for London.* | **the life of a soldier/film star etc** *According to his book, the life of a rock star is not a happy one.* | **married life** *after 25 years of married life*

**4 private/social/sex etc life** activities in your life that are private, done with friends, concerned with sex etc: *She enjoys a very active social life.*

**5 ▶ ALL HUMAN EXPERIENCE ◀** [U] all human existence considered as a variety of activities and experiences: *My Aunt Julia had very little experience of life.* | *life's rich pattern* | *Life was hard in the mining communities.*

**6 way of life** the way someone chooses to live their life: *a traditional way of life* | *the American way of life*

**7 quality of life** the level of health, comfort, and pleasure in someone's life

**8 be sb's (whole) life** to be the most important thing or person in someone's life: *Music is Laura's whole life.*

**9 start/make a new life** to completely change your life, for example by moving to another place: *They emigrated to Australia to start a new life there.*

[continued on next page]

[continued from previous page]

③ **LIFE AND DEATH**

**10 ▶ ALIVE NOT DEAD ◀** [C,U] the state of being alive: *Miss Byatt thinks her life is in danger.*|*Smoke detectors protect life and property.*|**save sb's life** *A seatbelt could save your life.*|**risk your life** *Two fire-fighters risked their lives to rescue the children.*|**risk life and limb** (=do something that is very dangerous)|**lose your life** (=die) *Thousands lost their lives in the earthquake.*|**take your own life** (=deliberately kill yourself)|**give your life/lay down your life** (=die in order to save other people or because of a strong belief)|**take sb's life** (=kill someone)|**take your life in your (own) hands** (=put yourself in danger of death) *Every time you cross these busy roads you take your life in your hands.*

**11 a matter of life and death** a serious situation in which someone might die

④ **LIVING THINGS**

**12** [U] **a)** the quality that animals and plants have and that rocks, machines, and dead bodies do not have: *the seeds of life*|**bring sth to life** (=make something live) *In the story the artist brings the statue to life.* **b)** living things, such as people, animals, or plants: *Is there is life on other planets?*|**animal/plant/bird life** *The island is rich in bird life.*

⑤ **REAL/TRUE**

**13 real life** what really happens as opposed to what happens in people's imaginations or in stories: *a real life drama*|**in real life** *In real life crimes are never solved by amateur detectives.*

**14 paint/draw from life** to paint or draw something real, not from another picture

**15 be true to life** to represent life as it really is: *I prefer stories that are true to life.*

⑥ **HOW LONG STH CONTINUES**

**16** [singular] **a)** the period of time during which something takes place or exists: [+ **of**] *during the life of the present parliament* **b)** the period of time during which something is still good enough to use or fresh enough eat: [+ **of**] *What's the average life of a passenger aircraft?* —see also SHELF LIFE

⑦ **ACTIVITY/EXCITEMENT**

**17** [U] activity or movement: **sign of life** *The door was open but there was no sign of life.*

**18 come to life** to start to become exciting or interesting: *The game really came to life in the second half.*

**19 bring sth to life** to make something more exciting or interesting: *Her songs bring our history to life again.*

**20 full of life** very cheerful and active: *Katie seemed young and full of life.*

**21 come to life/roar into life/splutter into life etc** to suddenly start working: *Finally the car spluttered into life.*

**22 be the life and soul of the party** to be the person who brings fun and excitement to a social group or occasion

⑧ **OTHER MEANINGS**

**23 get a life!** *spoken* used to tell someone you think they are boring

**24 that's life** *spoken* used when you are disappointed or upset that something has happened but realize that you must accept it: *Oh well, that's life!*

**25 have the time of your life** to have a very enjoyable time: *The kids had the time of their lives at the waterslide.*

**26 make life difficult/easier etc** to make it difficult, easier etc to do something: *This constant complaining isn't going to make life any easier!*

**27 for dear life** with the greatest possible effort and strength, especially in order to avoid harm: *Vera was clinging onto the branch for dear life.*

**28 cannot for the life of me** *spoken* used to say that you cannot remember or understand something even when you try hard: *I cannot for the life of me see why you are so annoyed.*

**29 not on your life** *spoken* used to say that you definitely will not do something

**30 ▶ PRISON ◀** [U] also **life imprisonment** the punishment of being put in prison for the rest of your life: *He was sentenced to life imprisonment for the murder.* —see also LIFE SENTENCE

**31 the race/game/fright etc of your life** the best race you have ever run, the best game you have ever played

**32 be the life and soul of the party** to make people feel happy by talking a lot, telling jokes etc

**33 ▶ BOOK/FILM ◀** [U] the story of someone's life; BIOGRAPHY: *Boswell's Life of Johnson*

**34 the next life/the life to come** a continued existence that is expected after death

**35 the woman/man in your life** the woman or man with whom you have a sexual or romantic relationship —see also HIGH LIFE, LOW LIFE, CHANGE OF LIFE, **as large as life** (LARGE (6)), **lease of life** (LEASE[1] (2))

**USAGE NOTE: LIFE**

WORD CHOICE: **life, living**

In general, the word **life** relates to the whole experience of living while the word **living** is more about the physical needs of living, for example, how much money you need, etc: *He had a good life* means that he had a lot of good experiences and enjoyed it but *They have a pretty good living* means they have enough food, money etc.

If you **make or earn a living** doing something, the work you do means you can provide yourself with the things that are necessary for life: *Joanne earns a living as a dancer in a nightclub.*

If you **make a life** for yourself somewhere, you go there and find work, establish a home etc: *thousands of refugees, seeking a new life across the border*

The way in which someone or a group of people generally lives is their **way of life**, or less often their **way of living**.

If you are thinking more of the sort of rooms people live in, whether they have things like water, heating etc, you talk about their **living** conditions (NOT *life conditions*): *the appalling living conditions of millions of old people*

If you are thinking of the level of comfort of someone's life, and how much money they have to spend on things that are not necessary, you talk about their **standard of living**: *Most Americans have a higher standard of living than Europeans.*

The **cost of living** is how much people need to spend in order to buy necessary things: *The cost of living keeps rising, but my salary stays the same* (NOT *the cost of life*).

If you are thinking more of the type of food that someone enjoys eating, the exercise they take, and what they do when they are not working, you talk about their **lifestyle**: *The typical lifestyle of a 60s rock star included lots of alcohol, sex and drugs.*

If you are talking about how enjoyable someone's life is, you call it their **quality of life**: *Having a decent washing machine would improve the quality of my life no end!*

GRAMMAR

When talking about **life** [U] in general, you never use *the*: *Life is hard* (NOT *The life...*)|*She loves life in the city.*

**life as·sur·ance** /ˈ· ·ˌ··/ *n* [U] *BrE* LIFE INSURANCE

**life belt** /ˈ· ·/ *n* [C] **1** *BrE* a LIFE BUOY **2** *AmE* a special belt you wear in the water to prevent you from sinking

**life-blood** /ˈ· ·/ *n* [U] **1** the most important thing needed by an organization, relationship etc to continue to exist or develop successfully: *Communication is the life-blood of a good marriage.* **2** *literary* your blood

**life·boat** /ˈlaɪfbəʊt‖-boʊt/ *n* [C] **1** a boat that is sent out to help people who are in danger at sea **2** a small boat carried by ships in order to save people if the ship sinks

**life buoy** /ˈ· ·‖ˈ· ˌ··, · ·/ *n* [C] a large ring made out of material that floats, which you throw to someone who has fallen in the water, to prevent them from drowning

**life cy·cle** /ˈ· ˌ··/ *n* [C] all the different levels of development that an animal or plant goes through during its life

**life ex·pec·tan·cy** /ˌ· ·ˈ···/ *n* [C] **1** the length of time that a person or animal is expected to live **2** the length of time that something is expected to continue to work, be useful etc

**life form** /ˈ· ·/ *n* [C] a living thing such as a plant or animal: *life forms on other planets*

**life guard** /ˈ· ·/ *n* [C] someone who works at a beach or swimming pool to help swimmers who are in danger

**life his·to·ry** /ˌ· ˈ···/ *n* [C] all the events and changes that happen during the life of a living thing

**life in·sur·ance** /ˈ· ·ˌ··/ *n* [U] a type of insurance that someone makes regular payments into so that when they die their family will receive money

**life jack·et** /ˈ· ˌ··/ *n* [C] a piece of clothing that can be filled with air and worn around your upper body to stop you from sinking in the water

**life·less** /ˈlaɪfləs/ *adj* **1** *especially literary* dead or appearing to be dead **2** lacking the positive qualities that make something or someone interesting, exciting, or active: *The actors' performances were lifeless.* **3** not living, or not having living things on it: *The surface of the moon is arid and lifeless.* —**lifelessly** *adv* —**lifelessness** *n* [U]

**life·like** /ˈlaɪflaɪk/ *adj* a lifelike picture, model etc looks exactly like a real person or thing: *a very lifelike statue*

**life·line** /ˈlaɪflaɪn/ *n* [C] **1** something which someone depends on completely: *The telephone is her lifeline to the rest of the world.* **2** a rope used for saving people in danger, especially at sea

**life·long** /ˈlaɪflɒŋ‖-lɔːŋ/ *adj* [only before noun] continuing or existing all through your life: *a lifelong friend*

**life peer** /ˌ· ˈ·/ *n* [C] someone who has the rank of a British PEER[1] (2) but who cannot pass it on to their children

**life peer·ess** /ˌ· ˈ··/ *n* [C] a woman who has the rank of a British PEER but cannot pass it on to her children

**life pre·serv·er** /ˈ· ·ˌ··/ *n* [C] *AmE* something such as a LIFE BELT or LIFE JACKET that can be worn in the water to prevent you from sinking

**lif·er** /ˈlaɪfə‖-ər/ *n* [C] *informal* someone who has been sent to prison for life

**life raft** /ˈ· ·/ *n* [C] a small rubber boat that can be filled with air and used by passengers on a sinking ship

**life·sav·er** /ˈlaɪfseɪvə‖-ər/ *n* [C] **1** someone or something that helps you avoid a difficult or unpleasant situation: *Thanks for all your help, Carrie, you've been a real lifesaver!* **2** a LIFE GUARD

**life·sav·ing** /ˈlaɪfseɪvɪŋ/ *n* [U] the skills necessary to save a person from drowning: *She has a bronze medal in lifesaving.*

**life sci·en·ces** /ˌ· ˈ···/ *n* [plural] subjects such as BIOLOGY that are concerned with the study of humans, plants and animals

**life sen·tence** /ˌ· ˈ··/ *n* [C] the punishment of sending someone to prison for life

**life-size** /ˈ· ·/ also **life-sized** *adj* a picture or model of something or someone that is life-size is the same size as they are in real life: *a life-sized statue of the president*

W3 **life·span** /ˈlaɪfspæn/ *n* [C] the average length of time that someone will live or that something will continue to work: *Men have a shorter lifespan than women.* —compare LIFETIME

**life story** /ˈ· ˌ··/ *n* [C] the story of someone's whole life: *For some reason, she insisted on telling me her whole life story.*

**life·style** /ˈlaɪfstaɪl/ *n* [C] the way someone lives, including the place they live in, the things they own, the kind of job they do, and the activities they enjoy: *a luxurious lifestyle*

**life sup·port sys·tem** /ˈ· ·· ˌ··/ *n* [C] **1** a piece of equipment that keeps someone alive when they are extremely ill **2** a piece of equipment that keeps people alive in conditions where they would not normally be able to live, such as in space **3** a natural system that is necessary for life to continue, for example the process that produces oxygen for people to breathe

**life·time** /ˈlaɪftaɪm/ *n* [C usually singular] **1** the period of time during which someone is alive or something exists: *During her lifetime she had witnessed two world wars.* **2 the chance/experience etc of a lifetime** the best opportunity, experience etc that you will ever have —compare LIFESPAN

**life vest** /ˈ· ·/ *n* [C] *AmE* a LIFE JACKET

**lift**[1] /lɪft/ *v* S2

**1** ▶ **MOVE STH WITH YOUR HANDS** ◀ [T] to take something in your hands and raise it, move it, or carry it somewhere: *He tried to lift the sleeping girl, but she was too heavy.* | **lift sth onto/out of/off etc** *I lifted down my suitcase and opened it.* —see RAISE[1] (USAGE) W2

**2** ▶ **RAISE** ◀ also **lift up** [I,T] to move something upwards, into the air, or to move upwards into the air: *He lifted both hands in a gesture of despair.* | *At high speeds the front of the boat would lift out of the water.*

**3** ▶ **HEAD/EYES** ◀ [T] to move your head or eyes upwards so that you can look at someone or something: *Brig lifted his head as the others came into the room.* | *She lifted her gaze from her book for a minute.*

**4** ▶ **CONTROLS/LAWS** ◀ [T] to remove a rule or a law that says that something is not allowed: *the lifting of sanctions*

**5** ▶ **CLOUDS/MIST** ◀ [I] if cloud or mist lifts, it disappears

**6** ▶ **BY PLANE** ◀ [T] to take people or things to or from a place by aircraft: *More troops are being lifted into the area as the fighting spreads.*

**7 not lift a finger** *informal* to do nothing to help

**8 lift sb's spirits** to make someone feel more cheerful and hopeful

**9** ▶ **SAD FEELINGS** ◀ [I] if feelings of sadness lift, they disappear: *Jan's depression seemed to be lifting at last.*

**10** ▶ **USE SB'S IDEAS/WORDS** ◀ [T] to copy words, ideas, music etc that someone else has written: *The words were lifted from an article in a medical journal.*

**11** ▶ **STEAL** ◀ [T] *informal* to steal something

**12** ▶ **VOICE** ◀ also **lift up** [T] *literary* if you lift your voice, you speak, shout, or sing more loudly

**13** ▶ **INCREASE** ◀ [T] to increase the amount or level of something: *This policy lifted Canadian exports of wheat and flour.*

**14** ▶ **VEGETABLES** ◀ [T] to dig up vegetables that grow under the ground: *lifting potatoes*

**lift off** *phr v* [T] if an aircraft or space vehicle lifts off, it leaves the ground and rises into the air

**lift**[2] *n* S3

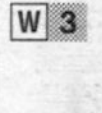

**1** ▶ **IN A BUILDING** ◀ [C] *BrE* a machine that you can ride in, that moves up and down between the floors in a tall building; ELEVATOR (1) *AmE*: *She pressed the button to call the lift.* | **take the lift** *They took the lift down to the bar.* W3

**2** ▶ **IN A CAR** ◀ [C] *BrE* If you give someone a lift, you take them somewhere in your car; RIDE[2] (1) *AmE*: *Do you want a lift into town?* | **give sb a lift** *I'll give you a lift back to London.*

**3** ▶ **MAKE SB HAPPIER** ◀ **give sb a lift** to make someone feel more cheerful and more hopeful

**4** ▶ **LIFTING MOVEMENT** ◀ a movement in which

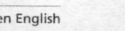

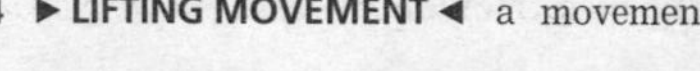

something is lifted or raised up: *the gentle lift and sway of the dinghy*
**5 ▶ WIND/AIRCRAFT ◀** [U] the pressure of air that keeps something up in the air or lifts it higher —see also CHAIRLIFT, SKI LIFT

**lift-off** /ˈ· ·/ *n* [C,U] the moment when a vehicle that is about to travel in space leaves the ground: *Ten seconds to lift-off!* —compare TAKE-OFF (1)

**lig·a·ment** /ˈlɪgəmənt/ *n* [C] a band of strong material in your body, similar to muscle, that joins bones or holds an organ in its place

**lig·a·ture** /ˈlɪgətʃə‖-ər/ *n* [C] *technical* something such as a thread used for tying a BLOOD VESSEL to stop someone bleeding

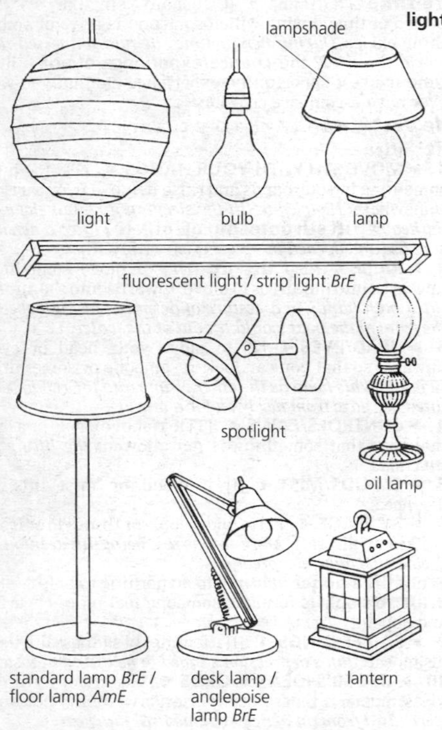


S1 W1 **light**[1] /laɪt/ *n*
**1 ▶ NATURAL/AFTIFICIAL LIGHT ◀ a)** [U] the energy from the sun, a flame, a lamp etc that allows you to see things: *the morning light streaming in through the windows* | *We could see a tiny glimmer of light in the distance.* | **good/strong/bright light** *The light isn't good enough to take a photograph.* | **poor/dim/fading light** *In the fading light she could just make out the shape of a tractor.* | **by/in the light of** (=using the light produced by something) *She was trying to read by the light of a flickering candle.* | **in/into the light** (=out of the shadows where there is light) *Come into the light where I can see you.* | **soft/warm light** *The valley was bathed in the soft light of dawn.* | **cold/harsh light** *The cold blue light of the Arctic.* | **blinding/dazzling light** (=extremely bright light) *a sudden flash of blinding light.* | **a beam/ray of light** (=a thin line of light) *the beam of light from her flashlight* **b)** [C] a particular type of light, with its own particular colour, level of brightness etc: *Monet painted a series of river views in different lights.* —see also NORTHERN LIGHTS, **a trick of the light** (TRICK[2] (10))

**2 the light** the light produced by the sun during the day: *We worked for as long as the light lasted.*
**3 first light** *literary* the first light that appears in the morning sky; DAWN[1] (1): **at first light** *The search continued at first light next morning.*
**4 ▶ LAMP/ELECTRIC LIGHT ETC ◀** [C] **a)** an electric light: *the neon lights of the city* | *lights from the hotel shining on the wet sidewalk* | **turn/switch/put on ↔ the light** *Please turn the light on.* | **turn/switch/put off ↔ the light** also **turn etc the light out** *Alan switched the overhead light off.* | **the light is/comes/goes/on** *The street lights are coming on now.* | **the light goes off/out** *Suddenly all the lights in the house went out.* | **turn the lights down/dim the lights** (=make lights less bright) *Sarah turned the lights down low to add a touch of romance.* | **the house lights** (=the lights in a cinema, theatre etc) —see also **the bright lights** (BRIGHT (13)), **b)** something such as a lamp or a TORCH[1] (1): *Shine a light over here, will you?*
**5 ▶ TRAFFIC CONTROL ◀** [C usually plural] one of a set of red, green and yellow lights used for controlling traffic; TRAFFIC LIGHTS: *We waited for the lights to change.* | *The driver had failed to stop at a red light.* —see also GREEN LIGHT, RED LIGHT DISTRICT, **jump a light** (JUMP[1] (18))
**6 ▶ ON A VEHICLE ◀** [C, usually plural] one of the lights on a car, bicycle etc, especially a HEADLIGHT: *You've left your lights on.* —see also BRAKE LIGHT, PARKING LIGHT
**7 be/stand in sb's light** to prevent someone from getting all the light they need to see or do something: *Could you move to the left a little – you're standing in my light.*
**8 ▶ FOR A CIGARETTE ◀ a light** a match or CIGARETTE LIGHTER to light a cigarette: **have you got a light?** *BrE*/**do you have a light?** *AmE*
**9 set light to** to make something start burning: *The candle fell over and set light to the barn.*
**10 in a new/different/bad etc light** if someone or something is seen or shown in a new, different etc light, you begin to understand them in a particular way or make someone else do this: *There was Brian, pushing the pram, and I suddenly saw him in a new light.* | *an incident that presented the company in the worst possible light*
**11 in the light of** *BrE*/**in light of** *AmE* if you do or decide something in the light of something else, you do it after considering that thing: *In light of the tragic news about our chairman, we have cancelled the 4th of July celebrations.* | **in (the) light of experience** (=as a result of your experience of something)
**12 come to light/be brought to light** if new information comes to light, it becomes known
**13 throw/shed/cast light on** to provide new information that makes a difficult subject or problem easier to understand: *These discoveries may throw some new light on the origins of the universe.*
**14 see the light a)** to suddenly understand something **b)** to begin to believe in a religion very strongly
**15 see the light (of day) a)** if an object sees the light of day, it is taken from the place where it has been hidden, and becomes publicly known: *Some of the Pentagon papers will never see the light of day.* **b)** if a law, decision etc sees the light of day, it comes into existence for the first time
**16 ▶ IN YOUR EYES ◀** [singular, U] *literary* an expression in your eyes that shows an emotion or intention: *There was a murderous light in his eyes.*
**17 light and shade** brightness and darkness in a painting
**18 light at the end of the tunnel** something that gives you hope for the future after a long and difficult period: *It's been a hard few months, but we're finally beginning to see the light at the end of the tunnel.*
**19 have your name in lights** *informal* to be successful and famous in theatre or films
**20 go/be out like a light** *informal* to go to sleep very quickly because you are very tired
**21 a leading light in/of** *informal* someone who is important in a particular group: *She's one of the leading lights of the local dramatic society.*

**22 according to your own lights** *formal* according to your own personal opinions or ideas of right and wrong
**23 ▶ WINDOW ◀** [C] *technical* a window or other opening in a roof or wall that allows light into a room
**24 ▶ FOOD ◀ lights** [plural] *old-fashioned* the lungs of sheep, pigs etc used as food —see also **hide your light under a bushel** (HIDE[1] (7)), **be all sweetness and light** (SWEETNESS (2)), **in the cold light of day** (COLD[1] (14))

S1 W1

## light² *adj*

① NOT DARK
② NOT HEAVY
③ WITHOUT MUCH FORCE
④ NOT DIFFICULT/SEVERE
⑤ SMALL AMOUNT
⑥ FOOD AND DRINK
⑦ NOT VERY SERIOUS
⑧ OTHER MEANINGS

### ① NOT DARK

**1 ▶ COLOUR ◀** a light colour or light skin is pale and not dark: *the lightest shade of blue* | **light orange/grey etc** *light green curtains* —compare DARK[1] (2): DEEP[1] (7)
**2 ▶ DAYLIGHT ◀ it is light** if it is light, there is the natural light of day: **it gets light** (=it becomes light) *It gets light at about 4.00 in the summer.*
**3 ▶ ROOM ◀** a room that is light has plenty of light in it, especially from the sun: *The studio was light and spacious.* —opposite DARK[1] (1)

### ② NOT HEAVY

**4** not weighing very much, or weighing less than you expect: *You can carry this bag – it's fairly light.* | **as light as air/as light as a feather** (=extremely light) —opposite HEAVY[1] (1) —see also LIGHTEN, LIGHTWEIGHT
**5 be a kilo/pound etc (too) light** if something is a kilo etc light, it weighs that amount less than it should weigh
**6** light clothes are thin and not very warm: *She took a light sweater in case the evening was cool.* —opposite THICK[1] (12)

### ③ WITHOUT MUCH FORCE

**7 ▶ WIND ◀** blowing without much force: *a light breeze* —opposite STRONG (17)
**8 ▶ SOUND ◀** very quiet: *There was a light tap at the door.* —opposite LOUD[1] (1)
**9 ▶ TOUCH ◀** very gentle and soft: *She gave him a light kiss on the cheek.* —see also LIGHTLY (1)

### ④ NOT DIFFICULT/SEVERE

**10 ▶ WORK/EXERCISE ◀** not very tiring: *She only has a few light duties around the house.*
**11 ▶ PUNISHMENT ◀** not very severe: *I thought the sentence was too light.* —opposite HARSH (3)
**12 make light work of** to finish a job quickly and easily

### ⑤ SMALL AMOUNT

**13** small in amount, or less than you expected: *The traffic seems very light today.* | **a light meal/lunch etc** (=a meal in which you only eat a small amount)
**14 a light smoker/drinker/eater etc** someone who does not smoke etc very much

### ⑥ FOOD AND DRINK

**15 a)** food or alcoholic drink that is light either does not have a strong flavour or is easy to DIGEST[1] (1): *a light white wine* | *a light dessert* —compare FULL-BODIED, HEAVY[1] (19) **b)** not containing much fat: *a new light cheese spread with only half the fat*

### ⑦ NOT VERY SERIOUS

**16** not serious in meaning, style, or manner, and only intended for entertainment: *an evening of light music* | **light reading** *Christie bought a woman's magazine for a little light reading.* | **a light touch** (=a relaxed and pleasant style) *Your writing style is very formal; you should aim for a lighter touch.* | **on a lighter note/in a lighter vein** (=used when you are introducing a joke, funny story etc after you have been speaking about something serious) —see also LIGHTLY (4)
**17 light relief** something that is pleasant and amusing after something sad or serious: *I'm glad you've arrived – we could all do with a little light relief!*
**18 make light of** to joke about something or treat it as not being very serious, especially when it is important: *He makes light of getting fired, but I know how angry he is.*

### ⑧ OTHER MEANINGS

**19 be light on your feet** to be able to move quickly and gracefully
**20 light sleep** sleep from which you wake up easily
**21 a light sleeper** someone who wakes up easily if there is any noise etc
**22 ▶ SOIL ◀** easy to break into small pieces —opposite HEAVY[1] (20a)
**23 light head** someone who has a light head feels unsteady, for example because they are ill or have drunk too much alcohol —see also LIGHT-HEADED
**24 ▶ HEART ◀** *literary* someone who has a light heart feels happy and not worried —see also LIGHT-HEARTED —**lightness** *n* [U] *a lightness of touch*

S3 W3 **light³** *v past tense and past participle* **lit** /lɪt/ or **lighted**
**1** [T] to deliberately make something start to burn: *I lit another cigarette.* | **put a lighted match/candle to sth** *Martin put a lighted match to the papers.* —see also FIRE (USAGE) **2** [I] to start to burn: *The fire won't light.* **3** [T usually passive] to give light to something: *His bedroom was lit by a bare electric bulb.* | **well/poorly etc lit** also **well/poorly etc lighted** *The room was brightly lit.* —see also LIGHTEN **4 light sb into/along etc** also **light sb's way** *old-fashioned* to provide light for someone while they are going somewhere

**light on/upon sth** *phr v* [T] *literary* **1** to fly to something and sit on it; ALIGHT **2** to find something pleasant by accident: *His eye lit on a ruby ring.*

**light out** *phr v* [I] *AmE informal* to run away because you are afraid

**light up** *phr v* **1** [T **light** sth ↔ **up**] to give light to a place or to shine light on something: *A flare lit up the night sky.* —see also LIGHTING UP TIME **2 a)** [I] if someone's face or eyes light up, they show pleasure, excitement etc: **light up with joy/pride etc:** *His face lit up with glee.* **b)** [T **light** sth ↔ **up**] to make someone's face or eyes show pleasure or excitement: *Suddenly a smile lit up her face.* **3** [I] to become bright with light or colour: *As the screen lit up, he typed in a code.* **4** [I] *informal* to light a cigarette

**light⁴** *adv* **travel light** to travel without much luggage

**light air·craft** /ˌ· ˈ··/ *n* [C] a small plane

**light ale** /ˌ· ˈ·/ *n* [U] a type of fairly weak pale beer

**light bulb** /ˈ· ·/ *n* [C] the glass object inside a lamp that produces light and has to be replaced regularly

**light·en** /ˈlaɪtn/ *v* **1** [T] to reduce the amount of work, worry, debt etc that someone has: *Maybe we should hire another secretary to lighten Barbara's workload.* **2** [I] if someone's face or expression lightens, they begin to look more cheerful: *His whole face would lighten when anyone mentioned Nancy.* **3** [I,T] to become brighter or less dark, or to make something brighter etc: *As the sky lightened we were able to see where we were.* —compare DARKEN **4** [I,T] to reduce the weight of something or become less heavy **5 lighten up!** *AmE spoken* used to tell someone not to be so serious about something: *It was a joke, Kath – lighten up!*

**light·er** /ˈlaɪtə‖-ər/ *n* [C] **1** a small object that produces a flame for lighting cigarettes etc **2** a large, open, low boat used for loading and unloading ships

**light·er·age** /ˈlaɪtərɪdʒ/ *n* [U] the service of moving goods on a lighter, or the charge made for this service

**light-fin·gered** /ˌ· ˈ··◂/ *adj* **1** likely to steal things **2** able to move your fingers easily and quickly, especially when you play a musical instrument

**light-foot·ed** /ˌ· ˈ··◂/ *adj* able to move quickly and gracefully

**light-head·ed** /ˌ· ˈ··◂/ *adj* unable to think clearly or move steadily, for example during a fever or after drinking alcohol; DIZZY (1): *The sun and the wine had made him a little light-headed.* —**light-headedness** *n* [U]

**light-heart·ed** /ˌ· ˈ··◂/ *adj* **1** not intended to be serious: *a lighthearted comedy* **2** cheerful and not worried about anything: *I found her in a light-hearted mood.* —**light-heartedly** *adv* —**light-heartedness** *n* [U]

**light heav·y·weight** /ˌ· ˈ···/ *n* [C] a BOXER (1) who weighs between 72.5 and 79.5 kilograms —**light heavyweight** *adj*

**light·house** /ˈlaɪthaʊs/ *n* [C] a tower with a powerful flashing light that guides ships away from danger

**light in·dus·try** /ˌ· ˈ···/ *n* [U] the part of industry which produces small goods, such as things used in the house

S3 **light·ing** /ˈlaɪtɪŋ/ *n* [U] the lights that light a room, building, or street, or the quality of the light produced: *Better street lighting might help to reduce crime.*

**lighting up time** /ˌ·· ˈ· ˌ·/ *n* [U] *BrE* the time of the evening when the street lights come on and you must put your car lights on

**light·ly** /ˈlaɪtli/ *adv* **1** with only a small amount of weight or force; gently: *Martin kissed his bride lightly on the cheek.* **2** using or having only a small amount of something: *Rub a casserole lightly with olive oil.* | *lightly armed soldiers* **3** without worrying, or without appearing to be worried: *Ma chuckled lightly and went back upstairs.* **4** done without serious thought: **take sth lightly** *Divorce is not a matter you can afford to take lightly.* **5 escape/get off lightly** to be punished in a way that is less severe than you deserve

**light me·ter** /ˈ· ˌ··/ *n* [C] an instrument used by a photographer to measure how much light there is

**light·ning¹** /ˈlaɪtnɪŋ/ *n* [U] **1** a powerful flash of light in the sky caused by electricity and usually followed by thunder: **be struck by lightning** (=be hit by lightning)—see picture on page 836 **2 like lightning** extremely quickly: *The horse streaked like lightning down the track.*

**lightning²** *adj* very fast, and often without warning: *a lightning attack* | **at/with lightning speed** (=extremely quickly)

**lightning bug** /ˈ·· ·/ *n* [C] *AmE* an insect with a tail that shines in the dark; FIREFLY

**lightning con·duc·tor** /ˈ·· ·ˌ··/ *BrE*, **lightning rod** /ˈ·· ·/ *AmE* —*n* [C] a metal wire or bar connecting the highest point of a building to the ground to protect the building from lightning

**lightning strike** /ˌ·· ˈ·/ *n* [C] *BrE* a STRIKE (=act of stopping work) without any warning

**light pen** /ˈ· ·/ *n* [C] a piece of equipment like a pen used to draw lines on a computer screen

**light rail·way** /ˌ· ˈ··/ *BrE*, **light rail** /ˌ· ˈ·/ *AmE* —*n* [C] an electric railway system that uses light trains and usually carries only passengers, not goods

**light·ship** /ˈlaɪtˌʃɪp/ *n* [C] a small ship that stays near a dangerous place at sea and guides other ships using a powerful flashing light

**light show** /ˈ· ·/ *n* [C] a series of moving coloured lights, especially at a POP concert

**lights-out** /ˌ· ˈ·, ˈ· ·/ *n* [U] the time at night when a group of people who are in a school, the army etc must put the lights out and go to sleep

**light·weight¹** /ˈlaɪt-weɪt/ *n* [C] **1** someone who has no importance or influence, or who does not have the ability to think deeply: *an intellectual lightweight* **2** a BOXER (1) who weighs between 59 and 61 kilograms **3** someone or something of less than average weight

**lightweight²** *adj* **1** weighing less than average: *special lightweight fabric* **2** showing a lack of serious thought: *She's written nothing but lightweight novels.*

**light year** /ˈ· ·/ *n* [C] **1** the distance that light travels in one year, about 9,500,000,000,000 kilometres, used for measuring distances between stars **2** also **light years** *plural informal* a very long time: *It all seems light years ago now.*

**lig·ne·ous** /ˈlɪgniəs/ *adj technical* like wood

**lig·nite** /ˈlɪgnaɪt/ *n* [U] a soft substance like coal, used as FUEL¹ (1)

**lik·a·ble**, **likeable** /ˈlaɪkəbəl/ *adj* likable people are nice and easy to like: *a friendly likeable little boy*

**like¹** /laɪk/ *prep* **1** similar in some way to something else: *My mother has a car like yours.* | *He crawled out of the hut on his belly, like a snake.* | **very like** *He's very like his brother.* | **look/sound/feel/taste/seem like** *The building looked like a church.* | *At last he felt like a real soldier.* | **just like** (=exactly like) *She was just like all the other girls.* | **like new** (=in perfect condition) *The carpet just needs a good clean and it'll be like new.* **2 nothing like/anything like** used to say that something is not at all similar to something else, or to ask whether it is similar: *The course was nothing like what I'd expected.* | *Was the film anything like the book?* **3 like this/like so** *spoken* used when you are showing someone how to do something: *You have to fold the corners back, like so.* **4** typical of a particular person: *It's not like Steven to be late.* **5 what is sb/sth like?** used when asking someone to describe or give their opinion of a person or thing: *Have you met the new boss? What's he like?* **6** for example: *far-off countries like Australia and China* | *nutritious foods like eggs and fish* **7 something like** not much more or less than a particular amount; about: *The machinery alone will cost something like thirty thousand pounds.* **8 more like** used when giving an amount or number that you think is more accurate than one that has been mentioned: *The builders say they'll be finished in three months, but I think it'll be more like six.* **9 there's nothing like** *spoken* used to say that a particular thing is the best: *There's nothing like a nice cup of tea!* **10 that's more like it** *spoken* used to tell someone that what they are doing or suggesting is more satisfactory than what they did or suggested before S1 W1

**like²** *v* [T not usually in progressive] **1** to enjoy something or think that it is nice: *I like your new dress.* | *Bill doesn't like Chinese food.* | **like sth best** (=prefer it) *Which of these colours do you like best?* | **like doing sth** *I like swimming, playing tennis, and things like that.* | **like to do sth** *I like to see the children enjoying themselves.* | S1 W1 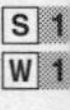

**like sth about sth/sb** *What I like about this job is the flexibility.* | **like it** *I don't like it when you look at me like that!* | *It was a great place for a vacation. You'd have liked it there.* | **like the idea/thought of (doing) sth** *Sandra didn't like the idea of being so far from home.* | **like the look/sound of** *I don't like the look of that black cloud over there. We'd better go in.* | **get to like sth** *informal* (=begin to like it) *I don't think I'll ever get to like modern art.* **2** to think that someone is nice or enjoy being with them: *I don't think he likes me – he never talks to me.* **3** to prefer that something is done in one particular way or at one particular time rather than another: **like sth** *"How do you like your coffee?" "Black, please."* | *I like films with action in them. None of this boring romantic stuff.* **4** to think that it is good to do something, so that you do it regularly or want other people to do it regularly: **like to do sth** *I always like to get up early in the summer.* | **like sb to do sth** *We like our students to take a full part in college social and sports activities.* **5 not like to do sth/not like doing sth** *especially BrE* to not want to do something because you do not feel it is polite, fair, nice etc: *I don't like bothering him when he's busy.* **6** to approve of something or have a good opinion of it: *I really didn't like the way he avoided giving us direct answers.* | **like sb doing sth** *Claus doesn't like anyone arguing with him.* | **like sb to do sth** *I'd like you to be honest with me.*

Frequencies of the verb **like** in spoken and written English.

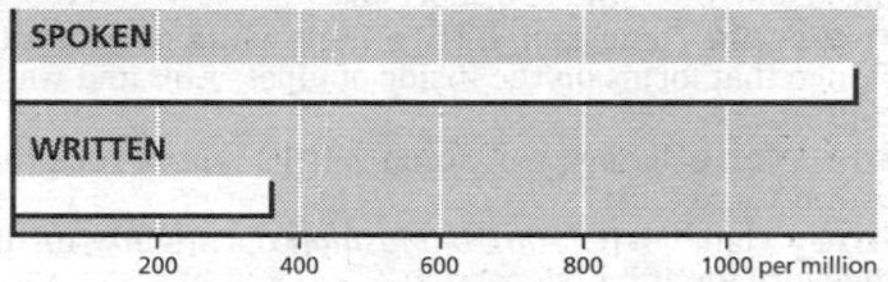


Based on the British National Corpus and the Longman Lancaster Corpus

This graph shows that the verb **like** is much more common in spoken English than in written English. This is because it is used in a lot of common spoken phrases.

**like** (*v*) **SPOKEN PHRASES**

**7 I'd like** used to say what you want: **I'd like sth** *I'd like a cheeseburger.* | **I'd like you/John etc to do sth** *I'd like her to be at tomorrow's meeting.* **8 would you like ...?** **a)** used to ask someone if they want something: **would you like sth** *Would you like some more cake?* | **would you like to do sth?** *Well, would you like to come shopping with me?* | **would you like me/her etc to do sth?** *Would you like me to pick you up in the morning?* **b)** also **How would you like ...?** used to offer someone something that someone does not expect, but that you know they will like: **(How) would you like to do sth?** *How would you like to go to the camp in the mountains this summer?* **9 would like** used to express politely what you want to happen or do: *We'd really like a holiday in Italy, but it's so expensive.* | **would like to do** *I'd just like to comment on a few things that were said.* | **would like sb to do** *We'd like you to come in for a second interview on Monday, if possible.* | **would like (to have) sth done** *I'd like to have the report finished by tomorrow.* **10 if you like** *especially BrE* **a)** used to suggest or offer something: *If you like, I could go with you to the doctor's.* **b)** used to agree to something, even if it is not what you want yourself: *"Can we have spaghetti tonight?" "If you like."* **c)** used to suggest one possible way of describing something or someone: *This experience was, if you like, a door that opened up a whole new world.* **11 whatever/anything etc you like** *especially BrE* whatever you want: *"Which play shall we go to see?" "Oh, whichever you like."* | *Come and stay with us for as long as you like.* **12 I like that!** **a)** used to say that you like what someone has said, shown you etc: *"That's a great story!" he said, roaring with laughter, "I really like that!"* **b)** *especially BrE* used to say that what someone has said or done is rude and unfair: *"I thought you were older than her." "Well, I like that!"* **13 how would you like ...?** **a)** used to ask someone if they want something, especially when you already know they want it: **how would you like sth?** *How would you like a cup of coffee?* | **how would you like to do sth?** *Say, how would you like to go to Italy next summer?* **b)** used to ask someone to imagine how they would feel if something bad happened to them instead of to you or someone else: **how would you like it if?** *How would you like it if you got home to find you'd been burgled?* | **How would you like sb doing sth?** *How would you like your boss calling you an idiot?* **14 how do you like?** **a)** used to ask someone for their opinion of something: *How do you like my new jacket?* **b) how do you like that?** used to ask someone what they think after you have done something or told them something surprising, unpleasant etc **15 (whether you) like it or not** used to emphasize that something unpleasant is true or will happen and cannot be changed: *You're coming to your grandparents' today whether you like it or not!* **16 I'd like to see you/him do sth** used to say that you do not believe someone can do something: *I'd like to see you run as fast as that!* **17 I'd like to think/believe (that)** **a)** used to say that you wish or hope something is true, when you are not sure that it is: *I'd like to believe that one day he'll be well enough to lead a normal life.* **b)** used to say that you think you do something well, especially when you do not want to make yourself seem better than other people: *I'd like to think that my work is as good as anybody's here.*

**like³** *n* **1 sb's likes and dislikes** all the things you like and do not like: *All the children have their likes and dislikes when it comes to food.* **2 and the like** and similar things: *He was interested in natural disasters, such as volcanoes, earthquakes and the like.* **3 the like of sb/sth** also **sb's/sth's like** something similar to someone or a particular person or thing, or of equal importance or value: *He gave a superb performance, the like of which has never been seen since.* | *The man was a genius. We shall not see his like again.* **4 the likes of** *spoken* **a)** used to talk about someone you do not like: *I'd never vote for the likes of him!* **b)** used to talk about people of a particular type or social class: *Those expensive restaurants with fancy food aren't for the likes of us.*

**like⁴** *adj* [only before a noun] *formal* **1** similar in some way: *They understand each other because they are of like mind.* **2 be like to do sth** *old use* to be likely to do something S1 W3

**like⁵** *conjunction especially spoken* **1** in the same way as: *Don't talk to me like you talk to a child.* **2 like I say/said** used when you are repeating something that you have already said: *Like I said, I don't mind helping out on the day.* **3** as if: *I acted like I couldn't see them.* S1

**like⁶** *adv spoken* **1** used in speech to fill a pause while you are thinking what to say next: *This bloke will look at it for me, like, and he'll tell me what it needs.* **2 as like as not/like enough** probably: *The car will be written off as like as not.* S1

**-like** /laɪk/ *suffix* [in adjectives] typical of, or suitable to something: *a jelly-like substance* | *childlike simplicity* | *ladylike behaviour*

**like·a·ble** /ˈlaɪkəbəl/ *adj* another spelling of LIKABLE

**like·li·hood** /ˈlaɪklihʊd/ *n* [singular, U] **1** the degree to which something can reasonably be expected to happen; PROBABILITY: [+ **of**] *taking steps to reduce the likelihood of disease* | [+ **(that)**] *a greater likelihood that you will make* *a profit* **2 in all likelihood** almost certainly: *If I refused, it would in all likelihood mean I'd lose my job.*

S1 W1 **like·ly¹** /ˈlaɪkli/ *adj* **likelier, likeliest 1** something that is likely will probably happen or is probably true: *Snow showers are likely in the next 24 hours.*|*the likely cost of the operation*|*the likeliest outcome of the talks*| **likely to do sth** *remarks that are likely to offend some war veterans*| **more than likely (that)** (=almost certain) *Ian had been sick too, so it's more than likely you caught it from him.* **2** [only before noun] as suitable or almost certain to produce good results: *a likely candidate*|*Search all the most likely places first – maybe he's hiding in the cellar.*| **likely-looking** (=seeming likely to produce results) **3 a likely story** *spoken* used to tell someone you do not believe what they have just said

**likely²** *adv* **1** probably: *I'd very likely have done the same thing in your situation.*| **likely as not** *spoken* (=probably) *Likely as not, we'll never be told what really happened.* **2 not likely!** *spoken especially BrE* used to disagree strongly, or to say that something will not happen: *"He said you'd be giving them a lift." "Not likely!"*

**like-mind·ed** /ˌ· ˈ··◂/ *adj* having similar interests and opinions —**like-mindedness** *n* [U]

**lik·en** /ˈlaɪkən/ *v*

**liken** sb/sth **to** sb/sth *phr v* [T usually passive] *formal* to describe something or someone as being similar to another person or thing: *Critics have likened the new theater to a supermarket.*

**like·ness** /ˈlaɪknɪs/ *n* **1** [C,U] similarity in appearance between people; RESEMBLANCE: [+ **to**] *Hugh's uncanny likeness to his father* **2** [C] a painting or photograph of a person, especially one that looks very like the person; PORTRAIT¹ (1): *That's a remarkable likeness of Julia.*

**like·wise** /ˈlaɪk-waɪz/ *adv* **1** *formal* in the same way; similarly: *I was up at dawn, and my host likewise.*| **do likewise**| *Nanny put on a shawl and told the girls to do likewise.*|[sentence adverb] *There has been an upsurge of interest in chamber music. Likewise opera is receiving a boost from increased record sales.* **2 likewise** *spoken* used to return someone's greeting or polite comment: *"You're always welcome at our house." "Likewise."*

**lik·ing** /ˈlaɪkɪŋ/ *n* **1 have a liking for sth** *formal* to like something: *a liking for chocolate* **2 take a liking to sb** to like someone you have just met **3 to your liking** *formal* being just what you wanted: *I hope everything in the suite was to your liking, Sir.*

**li·lac** /ˈlaɪlək/ *n* **1** [C] a small tree with pale purple or white flowers **2** [U] a pale purple colour —**lilac** *adj*: *a lilac dress* —see picture on page 411

**lil·li·pu·tian** /ˌlɪlɪˈpjuːʃən◂/ *adj* extremely small compared to the normal size of things

**Li·lo** /ˈlaɪləʊ‖-loʊ/ *n* [C] *BrE trademark* a rubber MATTRESS filled with air and used as a bed or for floating on water

**lilt** /lɪlt/ *n* [singular] a pleasant pattern of rising and falling sound in someone's voice or in music —**lilting** *adj*: *a lilting melody*

**lil·y** /ˈlɪli/ *n* [C] one of several types of plant with large bell-shaped flowers of various colours, especially white —see also **gild the lily** (GILD (3)), WATER LILY

**lily-liv·ered** /ˌ·· ˈ··◂/ *adj old-fashioned* lacking courage

**lily of the val·ley** /ˌ·· · · ˈ··/ *n* [C] a plant with several small white bell-shaped flowers

**lily pad** /ˈ·· ·/ *n* [C] the leaf of the WATER LILY that floats on the surface of the water

**lily-white** /ˌ·· ˈ·◂/ *adj* **1** *literary* pure white: *lily-white skin* **2** *informal* morally perfect: *You're not so lily-white yourself!*

**li·ma bean** /ˈliːmə biːn‖ˈlaɪ-/ *n* [C] a flat bean that grows in tropical America, or the plant that produces it

**limb** /lɪm/ *n* [C] **1 out on a limb** alone and without help or support: *All the other EU governments have signed the agreement, leaving Britain out on a limb.*| **go out on a limb** (=take a risk) **2** an arm or leg **3** a large branch of a tree **4 strong-limbed/long-limbed etc** having strong, long etc arms and legs —see also **tear sb limb from limb** (TEAR² (10))

**lim·ber¹** /ˈlɪmbə‖-ər/ *v*

**limber up** *phr v* [I] to do gentle exercises in order to make your muscles stretch and move easily, especially when preparing for a race, competition etc

**limber²** *adj* able to move and bend easily; SUPPLE

**lim·bo** /ˈlɪmbəʊ‖-boʊ/ *n* **1 be in limbo** to be in an uncertain situation in which it is difficult to know what to do: *I'm in limbo now until I know whether I've got the job.* **2 the limbo** a West Indian dance in which the dancer leans backwards and goes under a stick that is lowered gradually

**lime¹** /laɪm/ *n* **1** [C] a small juicy green fruit with a sour taste, or the tree this grows on —see picture on page 413 **2** [C] a tree with pleasant-smelling yellow flowers; LINDEN **3** [U] a white substance obtained by burning LIMESTONE, used for making cement, marking sports fields etc; QUICKLIME —see also BIRDLIME

**lime²** *v* [T] *technical* to add lime to soil to control acid

**lime·ade** /ˌlaɪmˈeɪd/ *n* [U] a drink made from the juice of limes

**lime green** /ˌ· ˈ·◂/ *n* [U] a light yellowish green colour —**lime-green** *adj* —see picture on page 411

**lime·light** /ˈlaɪmlaɪt/ *n* [singular] a situation in which someone receives a lot of attention, especially from newspapers, television etc: **be in the limelight** *Tad loves being in the limelight.*| **steal the limelight** *She's afraid this new actor will steal the limelight from her.*

**lim·e·rick** /ˈlɪmərɪk/ *n* [C] a humorous short poem, with three long lines and two short ones

**lime·scale** /ˈlaɪmskeɪl/ *n* [U] a hard white or grey substance that forms on the inside of pipes, TAPS and water containers

**lime·stone** /ˈlaɪmstəʊn‖-stoʊn/ *n* [U] a type of rock that contains CALCIUM

**li·mey** /ˈlaɪmi/ *n* [C] *AmE old-fashioned* a slightly insulting word for a British person

**lim·it¹** /ˈlɪmɪt/ *n* S2 W2

**1 ▶ GREATEST AMOUNT ALLOWED ◀** [C] the greatest amount, number, speed etc that is allowed: *a 55 mph speed limit*|[+ **to/on**] *Is there any limit to the amount of time we have?*| **set a limit (on)** *attempts to set limits on consumer waste*| **lower/upper limit** (=lowest or highest point something is allowed to reach) *an upper limit for pollution levels*

**2 ▶ GREATEST AMOUNT POSSIBLE ◀** also **limits** [C] the greatest possible amount of something that can exist or be obtained: [+ **of**] *the limits of human knowledge*| **to the limit** *Our finances are already stretched to the limit.*| **there is no limit (to)** *There's no limit to what you can do if you try.*

**3 ▶ PLACE ◀** [C] the furthest point or edge of a place, that must not be passed: *The public is not allowed within a 2-mile limit of the missile site.*

**4 within limits** within the time, level, amount etc considered acceptable: *You can come and go when you want – within limits.*

**5 know your limits** *informal* to know what you are good at doing and what you are not good at: *I know my limits. I'm not an administrator.*

**6 have your limits** *informal* to have a set of ideas about what is reasonable to do, and to not accept behaviour that does not follow those ideas: *You cannot smoke pot in this house. Even I have my limits!*

**7 there are limits!** *spoken* used to express shock or disapproval of someone's behaviour —see also **the sky's the limit** (SKY (3))

**8 be the limit** *spoken* to be so annoying that you upset someone: *Have you lost your glasses again? You really are the limit!*

**9 be over the limit** to have drunk more alcohol than is legal or safe for driving

**10 off limits** *especially AmE* beyond the area where someone is allowed to go: *That area of beach was off limits to us 'city kids'.*

S3 W2 **limit²** *v* **1** [T] to stop an amount or number from increasing beyond a particular point: *a decision to limit imports of foreign cars* | **limit sth to** *Seating is limited to 500.* **2** [T] to stop someone from using as much of something as they want or from behaving in the way they want: *Obviously I'm limited by my pension situation.* | **limit yourself to sth** *We must limit ourselves to one gallon of water per day.* **3 be limited to** to exist or happen only in a particular place, group, or area of activity: *Her traveling has been limited to a few French resorts.*

W3 **lim·i·ta·tion** /ˌlɪmə̯ˈteɪʃən/ *n* **1** [U] the act of limiting something: [+ **of**] *the limitation of armaments* —see also **damage limitation** (DAMAGE¹ (7)) **2** [C usually plural] a limit on how good someone or something can be, what they are able to do etc: **have your limitations** *It's a good little car, but it has its limitations.*

W2 **lim·it·ed** /ˈlɪmə̯tə̯d/ *adj* **1** not very great in amount, number, ability etc, and impossible to improve or increase: *My time is more limited now that I have a baby.* | *families on limited incomes* | *a student of limited intelligence* **2 Limited** written abbreviation **Ltd** used after the name of British business companies that have LIMITED LIABILITY —compare INCORPORATED

**limited com·pa·ny** /ˌ··· ˈ···/ *n* [C] a company whose owners only have to pay a limited amount if the company gets into debt —compare PUBLIC LIMITED COMPANY

**limited e·di·tion** /ˌ··· ·ˈ··/ *n* [C] a fixed number of copies of a book, picture etc produced at one time

**limited li·a·bil·i·ty** /ˌ··· ··ˈ···/ *n* [U] *technical* the legal position of being responsible for paying only a limited amount of debt if something bad happens to yourself or your company

**limited liability com·pa·ny** /ˌ··· ··ˈ··· ˌ···/ *n* [C] *technical* a LIMITED COMPANY

**lim·it·ing** /ˈlɪmə̯tɪŋ/ *adj* **1** preventing any improvement or increase in something: **limiting factor** *A limiting factor in health care is the way resources are distributed.* **2** *informal* preventing someone from developing and doing what they are interested in: *The job's OK, but it's sort of limiting.*

**lim·it·less** /ˈlɪmə̯tləs/ *adj* without a limit or end: *limitless possibilities* —**limitlessly** *adv* —**limitlessness** *n* [U]

**lim·o** /ˈlɪməʊ‖-moʊ/ *n* [C] *informal* a limousine

**lim·ou·sine** /ˈlɪməziːn, ˌlɪməˈziːn/ *n* [C] **1** a big expensive comfortable car **2** a small comfortable bus that people take to and from airports in the US

**limp¹** /lɪmp/ *adj* not firm or strong: *a limp handshake* | *His limp body collapsed forward.* —**limply** *adv* —**limpness** *n* [U]

**limp²** *v* [I] **1** to walk slowly and with difficulty because one leg is hurt or injured —see picture on page 1262 **2** if a ship or aircraft limps somewhere, it goes there slowly, because it has been damaged

**limp³** *n* [C] the way someone walks when they are limping: *Young walked with a slight limp.*

**lim·pet** /ˈlɪmpə̯t/ *n* [C] a small sea animal with a shell, which holds tightly onto the rock where it lives —see picture at SHELL¹

**lim·pid** /ˈlɪmpə̯d/ *adj literary* clear or transparent: *limpid blue eyes* —**limpidly** *adv* —**limpidness** *n* [U] —**limpidity** /lɪmˈpɪdə̯ti/ *n* [U]

**limp-wrist·ed** /ˌ· ˈ··◂/ *adj* a man who is limp-wristed is considered to lack strong, traditionally male qualities

**lim·y** /ˈlaɪmi/ *adj* containing or covered in LIME¹ (3): *limy particles*

**linch·pin, lynchpin** /ˈlɪntʃˌpɪn/ *n* **the linchpin of** the person or thing in a group, system etc that is most important, because everything depends on them

**linc·tus** /ˈlɪŋktəs/ *n* [U] *BrE* a liquid medicine used for curing coughs

**lin·dane** /ˈlɪndeɪn/ *n* [U] a chemical for killing insects, that is dangerous to people

**lin·den** /ˈlɪndən/ *n* [C] *AmE or poetic* a LIME¹ (2) tree

## line¹ /laɪn/ *n*

S1 W1

① LONG THIN MARK
② SHAPE/EDGE
③ OPINION/ATTITUDE
④ WAY/METHOD
⑤ TELEPHONE LINE
⑥ STRING
⑦ WRITING/WORDS
⑧ ROW OF PEOPLE/THINGS
⑨ LIES/EXCUSES
⑩ RAILWAY LINE
⑪ DIRECTION/DISTANCE
⑫ WORK/INTEREST
⑬ OBEY
⑭ WAR
⑮ DO THE SAME
⑯ OTHER MEANINGS

### ① LONG THIN MARK

**1** [C] a long thin, usually continuous mark on a surface: *A wiggly line showed where the river was.* | **straight line** *Can you draw a straight line?* | **dotted line** (=a broken straight line drawn or printed on paper) *Sign your name on the dotted line.*

**2** [C] a long thin mark used to show a limit or border: *a broken white line in the middle of the road* | *If the ball goes over the line, it's out of play.*

**3** [C] an imaginary line, for example one that shows the limits of an area of land: *the line that divides northern and southern Ireland* | *lines of longitude*

**4 county line/state line** *AmE* a border between two counties, states etc

**5 ▶ON SB'S FACE◀** [C] a line on the skin of someone's face or skin; WRINKLE¹ (1): *a forehead etched with deep lines*

**6 the line** *technical* the EQUATOR

### ② SHAPE/EDGE

**7** [C usually plural] the outer shape of something long or tall: *a dress that follows the lines of the body* | *I admired the ship's clean elegant lines.*

### ③ OPINION/ATTITUDE

**8** [C usually singular] an attitude or belief, especially one that is stated publicly: [+ **on**] *What's the candidate's line on abortion?* | **the party line** (=the official opinion of a political party) *By supporting Robertson, she's going directly against the party line.*

**9 take a firm/hard/strict etc line on** to have a very strict attitude towards something: *a judge notorious for taking a tough line on drug users*

### ④ WAY/METHOD

**10 line of action/thought/reasoning etc** a way or method of doing something or thinking about something: **line of inquiry** (=a way of trying to find out

[continued on next page]

[continued from previous page]
about something) *Police are following several lines of inquiry.* | **line of argument** (=a way of persuading someone about something) *Which line of argument is Clarke likely to take?*
**11 along those/similar/different etc lines** done or doing something in that way, a similar way etc: *We've both been thinking along the same lines.* | **something along those lines** (=something like that) *They're organizing a trip to the beach or something along those lines.* | **along the lines of** (=in a particular way) *We'll probably end up doing something along the lines of what you're suggesting.*
**12 on the right lines** done or doing something in the right kind of way: *These new proposals are certainly on the right lines.*

### ⑤ TELEPHONE LINE
**13** [C usually singular] a telephone wire or connection: *We rent the line from British Telecom.* | **on the line** *There's a fault on the line.* | **bad line** (=a line that is not working properly so that you cannot easily hear the other person talking)
**14 hold the line** *spoken* used to politely ask the person who is on the telephone to wait for a short time: *Hold the line, please. I'll put you through to Mr Bork.*

### ⑥ STRING
**15 ▶ DRYING CLOTHES ◀** [C] a piece of string or rope that you hang wet clothes etc on in order to dry them; CLOTHESLINE, WASHING LINE: **the line** *You'd better get your washing off the line – it's raining.*
**16 ▶ FISHING ◀** [C] a strong thin string with a hook on the end, used for catching fish

### ⑦ WRITING/WORDS
**17** [C] a line of words on a page, for example in a poem or a report: *a few lines from Shakespeare*
**18 ▶ ACTOR'S SPEECH ◀** [plural] the words of a play or performance that an actor learns: *After 30 years on the stage, I still forget my lines.*
**19 ▶ PUNISHMENT ◀ lines** [plural] *BrE* a punishment given to school children that consists of writing the same thing a lot of times: *Take a hundred lines!*
**20 drop sb a line** *informal* to write a short letter to someone: *Drop me a line and let me know how you're getting on.*

### ⑧ ROW OF PEOPLE/THINGS
**21** [C] a row of people or things next to each other: [+ **of**] *a line of poplar trees beside the road* | **in a line** *four little boys standing in a line*
**22** [C] *AmE* a row of people standing one behind the other while waiting for something; QUEUE[1] (1) *BrE*: *I was talking with Karen in the lunch line.* —see picture at PUSH[1]

### ⑨ LIES/EXCUSES
**23 shoot a line/spin (sb) a line** to tell someone things that are not true in order to persuade them or to make them admire you
**24 don't give me that line** *spoken* used to tell someone that you do not believe their excuse: *"We just haven't had enough time to ..." "Oh, don't give me that line."*

### ⑩ RAILWAY LINE
**25** a track that a train travels along: **the line** *A train had broken down further along the line.* | **railway line** *a bridge over the railway line* | **the Brighton/Manchester/Cambridge etc line** (=a line that goes to Brighton etc) | **Piccadilly/Victoria/Central etc line** (=a line on London's UNDERGROUND system)

### ⑪ DIRECTION
**26** [C usually singular] the direction or imaginary line along which something travels between two points in space: **in a straight line** *Light travels in a straight line.* | **line of fire/attack/movement etc** (=the direction in which someone shoots, attacks, moves etc) *I was directly in the animal's line of attack.* | **line of vision** *the direction in which you are looking*

### ⑫ WORK/INTEREST
**27 ▶ JOB ◀** [C usually singular] the kind of work someone does: **line of business** *What line of business is he in?* | **be in the building/retail etc line** —see JOB (USAGE)
**28 in the line of duty** if you do something in the line of duty, you do it as part of your job: *Don't thank me, madam – it's all in the line of duty.*
**29 be in sb's line** to be the type of thing that someone is interested in or good at: *I'm afraid cookery isn't really in my line.*

### ⑬ OBEY
**30 fall into line** *informal* to start to do something in the way that a company, organization etc wants you to: *Don't worry, I'm sure he'll soon fall into line and sign with the rest of us.*
**31 bring sb into line** *informal* to make someone behave the way you want them to: *The right wing of the party has got to be brought into line.*
**32 be out of line** *AmE* if someone's behaviour is out of line, it is unacceptable

### ⑭ WAR
**33 ▶ WAR ◀** [C often plural] a row of military defences in front of the area that an army controls during a war: **behind the line(s)** (=in the area where your enemy is) *Parachutists dropped behind the lines.* | **enemy lines** *The base was stationed 100 miles inside enemy lines.*
**34** [C] the line of positions that an army has when it is fighting a battle: *the line of battle*

### ⑮ DO THE SAME
**35 in line with** if something changes in line with something else, it changes in the same way and at the same rate: *Pensions will be increased in line with inflation.*
**36 bring sth into line with** to make something work or happen according to a particular system or set of rules: *British law will have to be changed to bring it into line with the latest European ruling.*
**37 along religious/party/ethnic lines** if people divide along religious, party etc lines they divide according to which religion, political party, or other group they belong to

### ⑯ OTHER MEANINGS
**38 a thin/fine line between** only a slight difference between two things, one of which is something bad: *There's a very fine line between tax evasion and fraud.*
**39 be in line for sth** to be very likely to get or be given something: *Ted's in line for the chairmanship.* | **first/second etc in line for** *She's about second in line for the management job.*
**40 be on the line** *informal* if your job, position etc is on the line, there is a possibility you might lose it: *From now on, all our jobs are on the line.*
**41 somewhere along the line** *informal* during the time that you are involved in an activity or process: *Somewhere along the line, Errol seemed to have lost interest in their marriage.*
**42 ▶ PRODUCT ◀** [C] a type of goods for sale in a shop: *this season's new lines from Paris* | **discontinue a line** (=stop selling a type of goods)
**43 on line** communicating with or by means of a computer: [+ **to**] *The system is on line to the bank's mainframe computer.* | *We need to bring the network back on line.* —see also ON-LINE
**44 ▶ COMPANY ◀** [C usually singular] a company that provides a system for moving goods by sea, air, road etc: *a shipping line* | *the Cunard line*
**45 be in the firing line/in the line of fire a)** to be one of the people who could be criticized or blamed for

something: *As one of the President's chief advisers, he's bound to be in the firing line.* **b)** to be in a place where a bullet etc might hit you
**46** ▶ **SPORT** ◀ [C] a row of players in a game such as American football or RUGBY that is formed when they move into position before play starts again
**47 get a line on** *informal* to get information about someone or something: *Have we got any kind of line on that guy Marston?*
**48** ▶ **DRUG** ◀ [C] *informal* an amount of an illegal drug in powder form, arranged in a line before it is taken: [+ **of**] *a line of coke*
**49** ▶ **FAMILY** ◀ [singular] the people that came or existed before you in your family: *She comes from a long line of actors.* | **be of sb's line** (=be their GRANDCHILD, GREAT-GRANDCHILD etc) *There was no-one directly of James's line to succeed to the throne.* —see also **draw the line at** (DRAW[1] (35)), **hard lines** (HARD[1] (21)), **hook, line and sinker** (HOOK[1] (7)), **lay sth on the line** (LAY[2] (14)), **picket line** (PICKET[1] (1)), **the poverty line/level** (POVERTY (2)), **read between the lines** (READ[1] (11)), **spin a story/yarn/ line** (SPIN[1] (6))

**line²** *v* [T] **1** to cover the inside of a piece of material with another material: *Are those curtains lined?* | **line sth with** *a coat lined with silk* **2** to form a layer over the inner surface of something: *the mucus that lines the stomach* | **line sth with** *The bird lined its nest with feathers.* **3** [usually passive] to form rows along something: *tree-lined avenues* | *Crowds lined the route to the palace.* **4 line your own pockets** to make yourself richer, especially by doing something dishonest

**line up** *phr v* **1** [I,T] to form a row or arrange people or things in a row: *Line up, everybody!* | **line sb/sth ↔ up** *The men were being lined up for an inspection.* **2** [T] to make arrangements so that something will happen or that someone will be available for an event: **line sb/sth up** *Sue's lined up some excellent speakers for tonight.* —see also LINE-UP

**lin·e·age** /ˈlɪni-ɪdʒ/ *n* [C,U] *formal* the way in which members of a family are descended (DESCEND) from other members: *a family of ancient lineage*

**lin·e·al** /ˈlɪniəl/ *adj* **1** *formal* related directly to someone who lived a long time before you: *lineal descendants* **2** another form of LINEAR —**lineally** *adv*

**lin·e·a·ment** /ˈlɪniəmənt/ *n* [C usually plural] *formal* **1** a feature of your face **2** a typical quality

**lin·e·ar** /ˈlɪniə‖-ər/ *adj* **1** consisting of lines, or in the form of a straight line: *a linear diagram* **2** [only before noun] concerning length: *linear measurements* **3** involving a series of directly connected events, ideas etc: *linear thinking* —compare LATERAL THINKING —**linearly** *adv* —**linearity** /ˌlɪniˈærəti/ *n* [U]

**linear ac·cel·e·ra·tor** /ˌ···· ·ˈ····/ *n* [C] *technical* a piece of equipment that makes PARTICLES (=small pieces of atoms) travel in a straight line at increasing speed

**linear per·spec·tive** /ˌ···· ·ˈ··/ *n* [U] a way of drawing and painting that gives the appearance of distance or depth

**line·back·er** /ˈlaɪnˌbækə‖-ər/ *n* [C] a player in American football who tries to TACKLE[1] (3) members of the other team

**lined** /laɪnd/ *adj* **1** a coat, skirt etc that is lined has a piece of thin material covering the inside: *a fleece-lined jacket* **2** paper that is lined has straight lines printed or drawn across it **3** skin that is lined has WRINKLES on it

**line draw·ing** /ˈ· ˌ··/ *n* [C] a DRAWING consisting only of lines

**line drive** /ˈ· ·/ *n* [C] a BASEBALL hit with great force in a straight line fairly near the ground

**line·man** /ˈlaɪnmən/ *n plural* **linemen** /-mən/ [C] **1** *especially AmE* someone whose job is to take care of railway lines or telephone wires; LINESMAN (2) *especially BrE* **2** *AmE* a player in the front line of a sports team

**line man·age·ment** /ˈ· ˌ···/ *n* [U] **1** the system of passing information and instructions in an organization by which each person tells the one immediately higher or lower than them in rank **2** the group of managers in a company who are responsible for its main activities, such as production and sales

**line man·a·ger** /ˈ· ˌ···/ *n* [C] **1** a manager in a company who is responsible for the main activities of production, sales etc **2 sb's line manager** someone who is one level higher in rank than you in a company and is in charge of your work

**lin·en** /ˈlɪnən/ *n* [U] **1** sheets, TABLECLOTHS etc: *bed linen* | *table linen* **2** cloth made from the FLAX plant, used to make high quality clothes, home decorations etc: *a linen jacket* **3** *old use* underwear

**linen bas·ket** /ˈ·· ˌ··/ *n* [C] a LAUNDRY BASKET —see picture at BASKET

**linen cup·board** /ˈ·· ˌ··/ *n* [C] a special cupboard in which sheets, TOWELS etc are kept

**line of scrim·mage** /ˌ· · ˈ··/ *n* [C] a line in American football where the ball is placed at the beginning of a particular PLAY[2] (3)

**line-out** /ˈ· ·/ *n* [C] the way of starting play again in a RUGBY UNION game, when the ball has gone off the field

**line print·er** /ˈ· ˌ··/ *n* [C] a machine that prints information from a computer at a very high speed —**line printing** *n* [U]

**lin·er** /ˈlaɪnə‖-ər/ *n* **1** [C] a piece of material used inside something in order to protect it: *a trash can liner* | *nappy liners* **2** [C] a large passenger ship, especially one of several owned by a company: *an ocean liner* —see also AIRLINER, CRUISE LINER **3** [C,U] *informal* EYELINER

**liner notes** /ˈ·· ·/ *n* [plural] *AmE* printed information about a record that appears on its cover

**lines·man** /ˈlaɪnzmən/ *n plural* **linesmen** /-mən/ [C] **1** an official in a sport who decides when a ball has gone out of the playing area —see picture on page 1264 **2** *especially BrE* someone whose job is to take care of railway lines and telephone wires; LINEMAN (1) *especially AmE*

**line-up** /ˈ· ·/ *n* [C usually singular] **1** a group of people, especially performers, who have agreed to be involved in an event: *Tonight's line-up includes Suzanne Vega.* **2** the players in a sports team who play in a particular game: **starting line-up** (=the first ones to play in a game) **3** a set of events or programmes arranged to follow each other: *the best line-up of radio entertainment in the world* **4** *especially AmE* a row of people examined by a WITNESS to a crime in order to try to recognize a criminal; IDENTIFICATION PARADE *BrE*

**ling** /lɪŋ/ *n* [U] a plant very like HEATHER

**-ling** /lɪŋ/ *suffix* [in nouns] a small, young, or unimportant kind of something: *a duckling* (=young duck) | *minor Prussian princelings* (=unimportant princes)

**lin·ger** /ˈlɪŋgə‖-ər/ *v* [I] **1** to stay somewhere a little longer, especially because you do not want to leave: [+ **over/on etc**] *They lingered over coffee and missed the last bus.* **2** [always + adv/prep] to continue looking at or dealing with something for longer than is usual: [+ **on/over etc**] *Mike couldn't help letting his eyes linger on her face.* **3** also **linger on** to be slow to disappear: *The taste lingers in your mouth.* **4** also **linger on** to be dying slowly so that you stay alive for a long time although you are extremely weak: *Horribly wounded he lingered on to die two years later.* —**lingerer** *n* [C]

**lin·ge·rie** /ˈlænʒəri‖ˌlɑːnʒəˈreɪ, ˈlænʒəri/ *n* [U] women's underwear

**lin·ger·ing** /ˈlɪŋgərɪŋ/ *adj* slow to finish or disappear:

*lingering doubts about the need for reform* | **a lingering death** (=slow and often painful) —**lingeringly** *adv*

**lin·go** /ˈlɪŋgəʊ‖-goʊ/ *n* [C usually singular] *informal* **1** a language, especially a foreign one: *I'd like to go to Greece, but I don't speak the lingo.* **2** words used only by a group of people who do a particular job or activity: *the estate agent's baffling lingo*

**lin·gua fran·ca** /ˌlɪŋgwə ˈfræŋkə/ *n* [C] a language used between people whose main languages are different: *English serves as a lingua franca in many countries.*

**lin·gual** /ˈlɪŋgwəl/ *adj* **1** related to the tongue **2** a lingual sound is made by the movement of the tongue —see also BILINGUAL

**lin·gui·ni** /lɪŋˈgwiːni/ *n* [plural] long thin flat pieces of PASTA

**lin·guist** /ˈlɪŋgwɪ̈st/ *n* [C] **1** someone who studies and is good at foreign languages **2** someone who studies or teaches linguistics

W3 **lin·guis·tic** /lɪŋˈgwɪstɪk/ *adj* related to language, words, or linguistics: *a child's linguistic development* —**linguistically** /-kli/ *adv*

**lin·guis·ti·cian** /ˌlɪŋgwɪ̈ˈstɪʃən/ *n* [C] a LINGUIST (2)

**lin·guis·tics** /lɪŋˈgwɪstɪks/ *n* [U] the study of language in general and of particular languages, their structure, grammar, and history —compare PHILOLOGY

**lin·i·ment** /ˈlɪnɪ̈mənt/ *n* [U] a liquid containing oil that you rub on your skin to cure soreness and stiffness

**lin·ing** /ˈlaɪnɪŋ/ *n* [C,U] a piece of material covering the inside of a box, piece of clothing etc: *The coat has a silk lining.* | *brake linings* —see picture at SHOE[1]

W2 **link**[1] /lɪŋk/ *v* **1 be linked** if people or events are linked, they are connected in some way: *Police think the murders are linked.* | **[+ with/to]** *They believe that this illness is linked to the use of chemical pesticides.* **2** [T] to connect computers, broadcast systems etc, so that electronic messages can be sent between them: **link sth to** *You can link your TV to your stereo for better sound.* | **link sth with** *We'll link your PC with our network via modem.* **3** [T] to connect two or more things together: *These traditional stories link the past and the present.* **4** [T] to believe that one fact or situation is connected with or caused by another: **link sth to/with** *There are compelling reasons for linking crimes like burglary and car theft with poverty.* **5** [T] to join one place to another: *the coastal highway linking Saigon and Hanoi* **6 link arms** to bend your arm and put it through someone else's bent arm

**link up** *phr v* [I] to make a connection with something: **[+ with]** *The train links up with the ferry at Holyhead.* | *My work links up with previous research.* —see also LINKUP

**link**

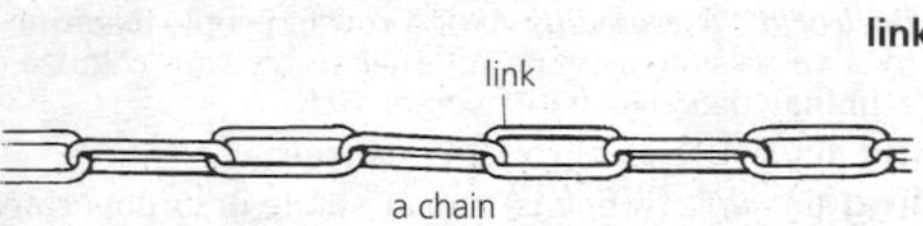


S3 W2 **link**[2] *n* [C] **1** a relationship between two things or ideas, in which one is caused or affected by the other: **[+ between]** *the link between smoking and cancer* **2** a relationship between two or more people, countries, organizations etc: **[+ with/between]** *They have severed all political links with the Left.* **3** one of the rings in a chain **4 rail/road/telephone link** something that joins two places and allows you to travel or communicate between them: *a transatlantic conference via satellite link* **5 link in the chain** one of the steps involved in a process **6 weak link** the weakest part of a plan or the weakest member of a team —see also CUFF LINK, LINKS, MISSING LINK

**link·age** /ˈlɪŋkɪdʒ/ *n* **1** [singular, U] a condition in a political or business agreement, by which one country or company agrees to do something, only if the other promises to do something in return **2** [singular, U] a LINK[2] (1) **3** [C] a system of links or connections

**link·man** /ˈlɪŋkmæn/ *n* [C] a man whose job is to introduce all the separate parts of a radio or television broadcast

**links** /lɪŋks/ *plural* **links** *n* a piece of ground near the sea on which GOLF is played

**link·up** /ˈlɪŋk-ʌp/ *n* [C] a connection between computers, broadcasting systems etc that sends electronic messages between them

**link·wom·an** /ˈlɪŋkˌwʊmən/ *n* [C] a woman whose job is to introduce all the separate parts of a radio or television broadcast

**lin·net** /ˈlɪnɪ̈t/ *n* [C] a small brown singing bird

**li·no** /ˈlaɪnəʊ‖-noʊ/ *n* [U] *BrE informal* linoleum

**li·no·cut** /ˈlaɪnəʊkʌt‖-noʊ-/ *n* **1** [U] the art of cutting a pattern on a block of linoleum **2** [C] a picture printed from such a block

**li·no·le·um** /lɪ̈ˈnəʊliəm‖-ˈnoʊ-/ *n* [U] smooth shiny material in flat sheets used to cover a floor

**Li·no·type** /ˈlaɪnəʊtaɪp‖-noʊ-/ *n* [U] *trademark* a system for arranging TYPE[1] (3) in the form of solid metal lines

**lin·seed** /ˈlɪnsiːd/ *n* [U] the seed of the FLAX (1) plant

**linseed oil** /ˌ·· ˈ·/ *n* [U] the oil from linseed used in some paints, inks etc

**lint** /lɪnt/ *n* [U] **1** *especially AmE* soft light pieces of thread or wool that come off cotton, wool, or other material; FLUFF *BrE* **2** *BrE* soft material used for protecting wounds

**lin·tel** /ˈlɪntl/ *n* [C] a piece of stone or wood across the top of a window or door, forming part of the frame

**li·on** /ˈlaɪən/ *n* [C] **1** a large yellowish-brown animal of the cat family that eats meat, and lives in Africa and parts of Southern Asia: *the lion's roar* —see also LIONESS **2** *especially literary* someone who is very important, powerful, or famous **3 the lion's share (of)** the largest part of something: *The Department of Defense will tke the lion's share of the federal budget.* **4 in the lion's den** among people who are your enemies **5 be thrown/tossed to the lions** to be put in a dangerous or unpleasant situation

**li·on·ess** /ˈlaɪənes, -nɪ̈s/ *n* [C] a female lion

**lion-heart·ed** /ˌ·· ˈ··◂/ *adj literary* very brave

**li·on·ize** also **-ise** *BrE* /ˈlaɪənaɪz/ *v* [T] to treat someone as being important or famous —**lionization** /ˌlaɪənaɪˈzeɪʃən‖-nə-/ *n* [U]

**lip** /lɪp/ *n* **1** [C] one of the two edges of your mouth where your skin is redder or darker: *Marty kissed me right on the lips!* —see picture at HEAD[1] **2** [U] *informal* a word meaning rude, angry talk, used especially by adults to children: **give sb lip** *Don't give me any of your lip!* **3 thin-lipped/full-lipped etc** with lips that are thin, round etc **4** [C usually singular] the edge of something you use to pour liquid from: *There's a crack in the lip of that jug.* **5** [C] the edge of a hollow or deep place in the land, usually one made out of rock: *the lip of the canyon* **6 my lips are sealed** *spoken* used to say that you will keep a secret **7 sth will not pass my lips** used to say that you will not talk about something that is secret: *Don't worry, not a word of this shall pass my lips!* **8 on everyone's lips** being talked about by everyone: *a name that will soon be on everyone's lips* **9** [C] *BrE spoken* an angry expression: *Look at the lip on her!* —see also **lick your lips** (LICK[1] (5)), **read sb's lips** (READ[1] (15)), **keep a stiff upper lip** (STIFF[1] (9)) W2

**lip balm** /ˈ· ·/ *n* [C,U] *AmE* a substance used to protect dry lips

**lip gloss** /ˈ· ·/ *n* [C,U] a substance used to make lips look very shiny

**lip·id** /ˈlɪpɪ̈d/ *n* [C] *technical* one of several types of FATTY substances in living things, such as fat, oil, or WAX[1] (1)

**lip·o·suc·tion** /ˈlɪpəʊˌsʌkʃən‖-poʊ-/ *n* [U] a way of removing fat from someone's body using SUCTION

**lip·py** /ˈlɪpi/ *adj BrE informal* not showing respect in the way that you speak to someone

**lip-read** /ˈlɪp riːd/ *v* [I,T] to understand what someone is saying by watching the way their lips move, especially because you cannot hear —**lip-reading** *n* [U]

**lip salve** /ˈ· ·/ *n* [C,U] *especially BrE* a substance used to make sore lips feel better

**lip ser·vice** /ˈ· ˌ··/ *n* **pay lip service to** to say that you support or agree with something without doing anything to prove your support: *They're only paying lip service to women's rights.*

**lip·stick** /ˈlɪpˌstɪk/ *n* [C,U] a piece of a substance shaped like a small stick, used for adding colour to your lips —see picture at MAKE-UP

**lip synch** /ˈlɪp sɪŋk/ *n* [U] the action of moving your lips at the same time as a recording is being played, to give the appearance that you are singing —**lip-synch** *v* [I]

**liq·ue·fac·tion** /ˌlɪkwǝ̇ˈfækʃǝn/ *n* [U] *technical* the act of making something a liquid or of becoming a liquid

**liq·ue·fy** /ˈlɪkwǝ̇faɪ/ *v* [I,T] *formal* to become liquid, or make something become liquid: *Some gases liquefy at cold temperatures.*

**li·ques·cent** /lɪˈkwesǝnt/ *adj technical* becoming or tending to become liquid

**li·queur** /lɪˈkjʊǝ‖lɪˈkɜːr/ *n* [C,U] a sweet and very strong alcoholic drink, drunk in small quantities after a meal —compare LIQUOR

**liq·uid¹** /ˈlɪkwǝ̇d/ *n* **1** [C,U] a substance that is not a solid or a gas, which flows, is wet, and has no fixed shape: *Water is a liquid.* **2** [C] *technical* either of the CONSONANT sounds /l/ and /r/ —see also WASHING-UP LIQUID

**liquid²** *adj* **1 liquid oxygen/soap etc** oxygen etc in the form of a liquid, instead of its usual gas or solid form **2** clear and shiny, like water: *liquid green eyes* **3** *literary* liquid sounds are clear and pure **4** easily exchanged or sold to pay debts: *liquid funds* —see also LIQUID ASSETS **5 liquid refreshment** *humorous* drink, especially alcoholic drink

**liquid as·sets** /ˌ·· ˈ··/ *n* [plural] *technical* the money that a company or person has, and the property they can easily exchange for money

**liq·ui·date** /ˈlɪkwǝ̇deɪt/ *v* **1** [I,T] to close a business or company in order to pay its debts **2** [T] *technical* to pay a debt: *The stock will be sold to liquidate the loan.* **3** [T] *informal* to kill someone

**liq·ui·da·tion** /ˌlɪkwǝ̇ˈdeɪʃǝn/ *n* [C,U] **1** the act of closing down a company in order to pay its debts by selling its assets (ASSET (1)): **go into liquidation** *land being sold off because the builder has gone into liquidation* **2** the act of paying a debt

**liq·ui·da·tor** /ˈlɪkwǝ̇deɪtǝ‖-ǝr/ *n* [C] an official who ends the trade of a company, so that its debts can be paid

**liquid gas** /ˌ·· ˈ·/ *n* [U] gas changed to liquid by extreme cold

**li·quid·i·ty** /lɪˈkwɪdǝ̇ti/ *n* [U] *technical* **1** a situation in which you have money or goods that can be sold to pay debts **2** the state of being LIQUID¹ (1)

**liq·uid·ize** also **-ise** *BrE* /ˈlɪkwǝ̇daɪz/ *v* [T] to crush fruit or vegetables into a thick liquid

**liq·uid·iz·er** also **-iser** *BrE* /ˈlɪkwǝ̇daɪzǝ‖-ǝr/ *n* [C] *BrE* a small electric machine that makes solid foods into liquids; BLENDER

**liquid lunch** /ˌ·· ˈ·/ *n* [C] *humorous* a LUNCH in which you mainly have alcoholic drinks rather than eating food

**liq·uor** /ˈlɪkǝ‖-ǝr/ *n* [U] **1** *AmE* a strong alcoholic drink, such as WHISKY —compare LIQUEUR **2** *BrE technical* alcoholic drink

**liq·uo·rice** *BrE*, **licorice** *especially AmE* /ˈlɪkǝrɪs, -rɪʃ/ *n* **1** [U] a black substance produced from the root of a plant, used in medicine and sweets **2** [C,U] a sweet or sweets made from this substance

**liquorice all·sorts** /ˌlɪkǝrɪs ˈɔːlsɔːts, -rɪʃ-‖-ˈɒːlsɔːrts/ *n* [plural] *BrE* a mixture of differently shaped brightly coloured sweets containing liquorice

**liquor store** /ˈ·· ·/ *n* [C] *AmE* a shop where alcohol is sold; OFF-LICENCE *BrE*

**lir·a** /ˈlɪǝrǝ‖ˈlɪrǝ/ *n plural* **lire** /-reɪ/ *or* **liras** [C] the standard unit of money in Italy, Syria, and Turkey

**lisle** /laɪl/ *n* [U] cotton material, used in the past for GLOVES and STOCKINGS

**lisp¹** /lɪsp/ *v* [I,T] to speak, pronouncing 's' sounds as 'th'

**lisp²** *n* [singular] if someone has a lisp, they lisp when they speak: *She speaks with a slight lisp.*

**lis·som, lissome** /ˈlɪsǝm/ *adj literary* a body that is lissom is thin and graceful: *her slender lissom figure*

**list¹** /lɪst/ *n* [C] **1** a set of words, numbers etc written one below the other, for example so that you can remember them: *a shopping list*|*an alphabetical list*|[+ **of**] *Make a list of the things you have to do.*|**at the top/bottom of the list** (=regarded as most or least important) **2 enter the lists** *BrE* to become involved in an argument, competition, etc —see also CIVIL LIST, **be on the danger list** (DANGER (4)), HIT LIST, MAILING LIST, SHORT LIST, WAITING LIST S1 W1

**list²** *v* **1** [T] to write a list, or mention things one after the other: *The guidebook lists 1000 hotels and restaurants.* **2** [I] if a ship lists, it leans to one side **3** [I] *old use* to listen S2 W3

**list·ed build·ing** /ˌ·· ˈ··/ *n* [C] a building of historical interest in Britain, that is protected by a government order

**lis·ten¹** /ˈlɪsǝn/ *v* [I] **1** to pay attention to what someone is saying or to a sound that you can hear: *listening to music*|*Listen! There's a strange noise in the engine.*|[+ **to**] *I like listening to the radio.*|**listen hard** (=try to hear something that is very quiet)|**listen intently** (=very carefully and with interest) **2** *spoken* used to tell someone to pay attention to what you are about to say: *Listen, I'm sure we can work this out, if everybody calms down.* **3** to consider carefully what someone says to you: *I told him not to go, but he just wouldn't listen.*|[+ **to**] *I wish I'd listened to your advice.* S1 W1

**listen for** sth/sb *phr v* [T] to pay attention so that you are sure you will hear a sound: *Listen for the moment when the music changes.*

**listen in** *phr v* [I] **1** to listen to a broadcast on the radio: [+ **to**] *I must remember to listen in to the news at noon.* —see also **tune in** (TUNE²) **2** to listen to someone's conversation without them knowing it: [+ **on**] *It sounded like someone was listening in on the extension.*

**listen out** *phr v* [I] *BrE informal* to listen carefully, especially for an unexpected sound: **listen out for** *Listen out for the baby in case she wakes up.*

**listen up** *phr v* [I] *especially AmE spoken* used to get people's attention so they can hear what you are going to say: *Hey everybody, listen up!*

**USAGE NOTE: LISTEN**

GRAMMAR

Remember you can only **listen to** (or sometimes **for**) something: *He's listening to music* (NOT *He's listening music*).

**listen²** *n* [singular] *BrE informal* an act of listening: *Have a listen to this new album!*

**lis·ten·a·ble** /ˈlɪsǝnǝbǝl/ *adj informal* pleasant to hear

**lis·ten·er** /ˈlɪsǝnǝ‖-ǝr/ *n* [C] **1** someone who listens, especially to the radio: *Some of our regular listeners have complained about the new program schedule.* —compare VIEWER (1) **2 a good listener** someone who listens patiently and sympathetically to other people

**lis·ten·ing de·vice** /ˈ··· ·ˌ·/ *n* [C] a piece of equipment that allows you to listen secretly to other people's conversations; a BUG¹ (5) —compare HEARING AID

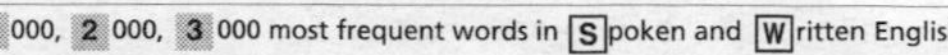

**lis·te·ri·a** /lɪˈstɪəriə‖-ˈstɪr-/ *n* [U] a type of BACTERIA that makes you sick

**list·ing** /ˈlɪstɪŋ/ *n* **1** [C] something that is on a list **2 listings** [plural] lists of films, plays, and other events with the times and places at which they will happen

**list·less** /ˈlɪstləs/ *adj* feeling tired and not interested in things: *The heat was making me listless.* —**listlessly** *adv* —**listlessness** *n* [U]

**list price** /ˈ· ·/ *n* [C] a price that is suggested for a product by the people who make it

**lit¹** /lɪt/ the past tense and past participle of LIGHT²

**lit²** an abbreviation of LITERATURE or LITERARY

**lit·a·ny** /ˈlɪtəni/ *n* [C] **1** a long prayer in the Christian church in which the priest says a sentence and the people reply **2** something that takes a long time to say that repeats phrases, or sounds like a list: *a long litany of complaints*

**li·tchi** /ˈlaɪtʃiː‖ˈliː-/ *n* [C] another spelling of LYCHEE

**lite beer** /ˌlaɪt bɪə‖-ˈbɪr/ *n* [U] *AmE* beer that has fewer CALORIES than normal beer

**li·ter** /ˈliːtə‖-ər/ *n* [C] the American spelling of LITRE

**lit·e·ra·cy** /ˈlɪtərəsi/ *n* [U] **1** the state of being able to read and write: *a new adult literacy campaign* **2 computer literacy** the ability to understand and use computers

**lit·e·ral¹** /ˈlɪtərəl/ *adj* **1** the literal meaning of a word or expression is its basic or original meaning: **literal meaning/sense/interpretation etc** *A trade war is not a war in the literal sense.* —compare FIGURATIVE (1) **2 literal translation** a translation that gives a single word for each original word instead of giving the meaning of the whole sentence in a natural way **3 literal-minded** not showing much imagination; PROSAIC —**literalness** *n* [U]

**literal²** *n* [C] *BrE technical* a printing mistake, especially in the spelling of a word; TYPO

S2 **lit·e·ral·ly** /ˈlɪtərəli/ *adv* **1** according to the most basic or original meaning of a word or expression: *'Inspire' literally meant 'to breathe into'.*| **mean sth literally** (=mean exactly what you say) *I know I said I felt like quitting, but I didn't mean it literally!* **2 take sb/sth literally** to only understand the most basic meaning of words, phrases etc, often with the result that you do not understand what someone really means: *Christians who take the Bible literally* **3** used to emphasize that something is actually true: *The Olympic Games were watched by literally billions of people.* **4** *spoken* used to emphasize something you say that is already expressed strongly: *Dad was literally blazing with anger.*

W2 **lit·e·ra·ry** /ˈlɪtərəri‖ˈlɪtəreri/ *adj* **1** connected with LITERATURE: *a literary prize*| *literary criticism* **2** typical of the style of writing used in literature rather than in ordinary writing and talking: *a very literary style of writing* **3** liking literature very much, and studying or producing it: *a literary woman* —**literariness** *n* [U]

**lit·e·rate** /ˈlɪtərɪ̣t/ *adj* **1** able to read and write —compare NUMERATE **2 computer literate/musically literate etc** having enough knowledge to use a computer, play a musical instrument etc **3** well educated —opposite ILLITERATE (1) —see also LITERACY —**literately** *adv* —**literateness** *n* [U]

**lit·e·ra·ti** /ˌlɪtəˈrɑːti/ *n* **the literati** *formal* a small group of people in a society who know a lot about literature

W2 **lit·e·ra·ture** /ˈlɪtərətʃə‖-tʃʊr/ *n* [U] **1** books, plays, poems etc that people think have value: *one of the great works of English literature* **2** works such as these that are studied as a subject: *a course in modern African literature* **3** all the books, articles, etc on a particular subject: *literature on the history of science* **4** printed information produced by organizations that want to sell something or tell people about something: *Do you have any sales literature available?*

**lithe** /laɪð/ *adj* having a body that moves easily and gracefully: *the dancer's lithe long-limbed body* —**lithely** *adv*

**lith·i·um** /ˈlɪθiəm/ *n* [U] a soft silvery ELEMENT (=simple substance) that is the lightest known metal

**lith·o·graph¹** /ˈlɪθəgrɑːf‖-græf/ *n* [C] a printed picture made by lithography

**lithograph²** *v* [T] to print a picture by lithography

**li·thog·ra·phy** /lɪˈθɒgrəfi‖lɪˈθɑː-/ *n* [U] a process for printing patterns, pictures, etc from something that has been cut into a piece of stone or metal —**lithographic** /ˌlɪθəˈgræfɪk◂/ *adj*

**lit·i·gant** /ˈlɪtɪ̣gənt/ *n* [C] *law* someone who is making a claim against someone or defending themselves against a claim in a court of law

**lit·i·gate** /ˈlɪtɪ̣geɪt/ *v* [I,T] *law* to take a claim or complaint against someone to a court of law

**lit·i·ga·tion** /ˌlɪtɪ̣ˈgeɪʃən/ *n* [U] *law* the process of taking claims to a court of law, in a non-criminal case

**li·ti·gious** /lɪˈtɪdʒəs/ *adj formal* too willing to take any disagreements to a court of law —**litigiousness** *n* [U]

**lit·mus** /ˈlɪtməs/ *n* [U] a chemical that turns red when touched by acid, and blue when touched by an ALKALI

**litmus pa·per** /ˈ·· ˌ··/ *n* [U] paper containing litmus used to test whether a chemical is an acid or an ALKALI

**litmus test** /ˈ·· ˌ·/ *n* [singular] **1** something that makes it clear what someone's attitude, intentions etc are: *The election will be an interesting litmus test on the 'greening' of politics.* **2** a test using litmus paper

**li·to·tes** /ˈlaɪtətiːz, laɪˈtəʊtiːz‖-ˈtoʊ-/ *n* [U] *technical* a way of expressing your meaning by using a word that has the opposite meaning with a negative word such as 'not', for example by saying 'not bad' when you mean 'good'

**li·tre** *BrE*, **liter** *AmE* /ˈliːtə‖-ər/ *n* [C] **1** the basic unit for measuring an amount of liquid, in the METRIC system —see table on page B2 **2 1.3/2.4 etc litre engine** a measurement that shows the size and power of a vehicle's engine

**lit·ter¹** /ˈlɪtə‖-ər/ *n* **1** [U] bits of waste paper, containers etc that people have thrown away and left on the ground in a public place: *Please take your litter away with you.* —compare GARBAGE, RUBBISH, TRASH **2** [C] a group of baby animals such as dogs or cats which one mother gives birth to at the same time **3 cat/kitty litter** [U] small grains of a special substance that you put in a container where your cat gets rid of its solid and liquid waste: *a litter tray* **4** [U] STRAW (12) that a farm animal sleeps on **5 a litter of** a group of things arranged in a very untidy way: *a litter of notes, papers and textbooks* **6** [C] a very low bed for carrying important people on, used in former times

**litter²** *v* **1** also **litter up** [T] if things litter an area there are a lot of them in that place, scattered in an untidy way: *Clothes littered the floor.*| **be littered with** *The road was littered with debris.* **2 be littered with** if something is littered with things, there are a lot of those things in it: *History is littered with examples of failed colonialism.* **3** [I,T] to leave bits of waste paper etc on the ground in a public place **4** [I] *technical* if an animal such as a dog or cat litters, it gives birth to babies

**lit·te·ra·teur** /ˌlɪtərəˈtɜː‖-ˈtɜːr/ *n* [C] someone who is interested in literature, especially a writer whose work is not considered to be very good

**litter bin** /ˈ·· ·/ also **litter bas·ket** /ˈ·· ˌ··/ *BrE* *n* [C] a container in a public place for people to put things in that they are throwing away, such as papers or cans

**lit·ter·bug** /ˈlɪtəbʌg‖-ər-/ also **litter lout** *BrE* *n* [C] someone who leaves waste on the ground in public places

**lit·tle¹** /ˈlɪtl/ *adj* S1 W1

**1 ▶ SIZE ◀** small in size: *a little house*| *their little group of supporters*| **a little bit of** *especially BrE* (=a small piece of something) *little bits of paper all over the floor*| **little tiny** *spoken* (=extremely small) *a little tiny puppy*| **a little something** *informal* (=a small present) *I promised the kids a little something if they ate all their dinner.* **2** used about something or someone that is small to show that you like or dislike them, or that you feel sorry for them: **nice little/clever little etc** *a nice little house*| *a*

*clever little gadget* | *It wasn't a bad little car.* | **nasty little/silly little etc** *another of her silly little jokes* | *a boring little man* | **poor little/pathetic little** (=used when you feel sympathetic) *her sad little face looking up at me* | *a poor little bird with a broken wing*
**3** done in a way that is not very strong or noticeable; slight: *a wry little smile*
**4 ▶ TIME/DISTANCE ◀** short in time or distance: *I can have a nice little nap in the car.* | *You'll find it a little way along this path.* | **a little while** (=a short period of time) *He arrived a little while ago.* | *We sat there for a little while longer.*
**5 ▶ YOUNG ◀** young and small: *a cute little puppy* | *We didn't have toys like this when I was little.* | **a little boy/girl** *two little boys playing in the street* | **your little girl/boy** (=your son or daughter who is still a child) *Mum, I'm 17 – I'm not your little girl any longer.* | **little brother/sister** (=a younger brother or sister who is still a child)
**6 ▶ UNIMPORTANT ◀ a)** not important: *I'm too busy to worry about little things like broken windows.* **b)** used jokingly when you really think that something is important: *There's just that little matter of the £5000 you owe me.*
**7 a little bird told me** *humorous spoken* used to say that someone who you are not going to name has told you something about another person: *A little bird told me you're getting married soon.*
**8 the little woman** *spoken* an expression meaning someone's wife, often considered offensive especially by women

Frequencies of **a little** and **a bit** in spoken and written English.

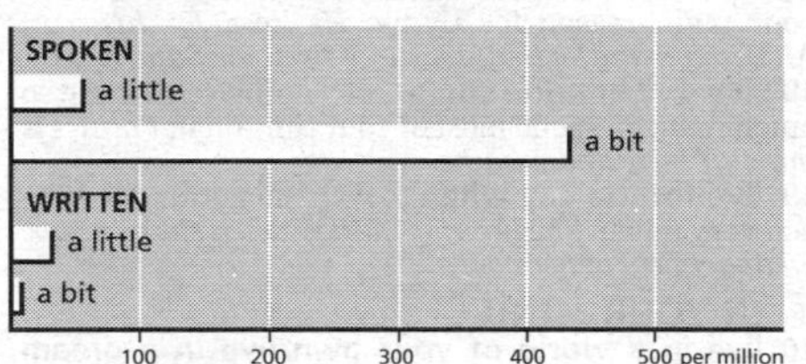


Based on the British National Corpus and the Longman Lancaster Corpus

This graph shows that **a bit** is much more common in spoken English than **a little**. This is because **a bit** is informal and is therefore more commonly used in ordinary conversation. However, in written English **a little** is more common than **a bit**.

**USAGE NOTE: LITTLE**

WORD CHOICE: **little, small**

**Little** often suggests that you are talking about someone or something small that you are fond of or feel sympathetic towards: *What a sweet little dog!* | *A little old lady lived in the house opposite.*

**Small** simply describes the size of something: *My daughter's room is smaller than mine.* | *He packed his things into a small bag.* You also use **small** when you are giving information and facts: *There has been a small increase in production.*

**Little** can also suggest that someone or something is unimportant: *What a silly little man!* When you are speaking it often sounds more friendly or polite to say something is **little** rather than **small**: *I have a little problem, can you help?* makes the problem sound less serious or urgent than: *I have a small problem* and *We're going to have a little test* sounds a little less frightening than: *We're going to have a small test.*

**little²** *quantifier* S1 W1
**1** only a small amount or hardly any of something: *Little is known about these areas of the moon.* | *There's little to be gained from an official complaint.* | *I paid little atttention to what the others were saying.* | **very little** *During that period I ate very little and slept even less* | *There's very little money left.* | *There seems very little point in continuing this discussion.* | **little or no** *peasants who have little or no land* | **little of** *Little of their wealth now remains.* | **do little to help/benefit etc** *The new filing system has done little to improve efficiency.* | **as little as possible** (=the smallest amount that you can have or do) *He always writes as little as possible.* | **little real effect/importance etc** (=used to emphasize that there is hardly any effect etc) *The laboratory tests are of little real value.* | **precious little** (=very little) *There's precious little good news.* —see FEW (USAGE)
**2 a little** also **a little bit** a small amount: *I told him a little bit about it.* | *Fortunately I had a little time to spare.* | *She speaks a little French.* | *A little over half the class can swim.* | **a little more/less** *He poured me out a little more wine.* | *"Would you like some more coffee?" " Just a little, thanks."* | **a little of** *The city is regaining a little of its former splendour.*
**3 ▶ TIME/DISTANCE ◀** a short time or distance: *a little over 60 years ago* | *We walked on a little and then turned back.*
**4 what little** the small amount that there is, that is possible etc: *We did what little we could to help.* | *The firemen recovered what little remained of the bodies.*

**little³** *adv* S1 W1 **1 a little** also **a little bit** to a small degree: *She trembled a little as she spoke.* | *I was a little bit disappointed with my test results.* | **a little more/better/further etc** *We shall have to wait a little longer to see what happens.* **2** not much or only slightly: *The pattern of life here has changed little since I was a boy.* | **little known/understood etc** (=not known etc by many people) *a little known corner of the world* | **little more/better etc (than)** *His voice was little more than a whisper.* | **very little** *The situation has improved very little, in spite of all our efforts.* | **as little as possible** *I try to disturb her as little as possible when she's working.* **3 little did sb think/realize** also **sb little thought/realized** used to mean that someone did not think or realize that something was true: *Little did he realize that we were watching his every move.* **4 little by little** gradually: *Little by little things returned to normal.* **5 more than a little/not a little** *formal* extremely: *Graham was more than a little frightened by what he had seen.* **6 (just) that little bit extra/harder/better etc** more, harder etc by a small amount that will have an important effect: *people who work just that little bit harder than anyone else*

**Little Bear** /ˌ·· ˈ·/ *especially BrE*, **Little Dip·per** /ˌ·· ˈ··/ *especially AmE n* **the Little Bear** a group of stars

**little fin·ger** /ˌ·· ˈ··/ *n* [C] the smallest finger on your hand

**Little League** /ˈ·· ˌ·/ *n* a BASEBALL LEAGUE for children in the US

**little peo·ple** /ˈ·· ˌ··/ *n* [plural] **1** all the people in a country or organization who have no power: *It's the little people who bear the brunt of taxation.* **2 the little people** fairies (FAIRY (1)), especially Irish LEPRECHAUNS

**lit·to·ral** /ˈlɪtərəl/ *n* [C] *technical* an area of land near the coast —**littoral** *adj*

**li·tur·gi·cal** /lɪˈtɜːdʒɪkəl‖-ɜːr-/ *adj* [only before noun] related to church services and ceremonies —**liturgically** /-kli/ *adv*

**lit·ur·gy** /ˈlɪtədʒi‖-ər-/ *n* **1** [C,U] a way of praying in a religious service using a fixed order of words, prayers etc **2 the Liturgy** the written form of these services

**liv·a·ble, liveable** /ˈlɪvəbəl/ *adj* **1** also **livable in** *BrE* a place that is livable in is suitable to live in; HABITABLE **2** if your life is livable, you can bear it; ENDURABLE

S1 W1

# live¹ /lɪv/ *v*

① IN A PLACE/TIME
② LIVE IN A PARTICULAR WAY
③ BE ALIVE
④ SEXUAL RELATIONSHIP
⑤ LIVE FOR A REASON
⑥ IN YOUR MIND
⑦ OTHER MEANINGS

## ① IN A PLACE/TIME

**1 ► IN A PLACE/HOME ◄** [I always + adv/prep] to have your home in a particular place: **live in/at/with/near etc** *Where do you live?* | *We used to live in Bakersfield.* | *They have one daughter who still lives with them.* | **live at home** (=live with your parents) | **look for a place to live** (=look for a house to live in) | **live rough** *BrE* (=have no home and sleep outdoors)

**2 ► PLANT/ANIMAL ◄** [I always + adv/prep] a plant or animal that lives in a particular place grows there or has its home there: **live in/on/near etc** *The birds live only on this island.*

**3 ► AT A PARTICULAR TIME ◄** [I always + adv/prep] to be alive at a particular time or when particular events happen: [+ **before/in/at**] *Pythagoras lived a century before Socrates.* | *He lived during the time of the plague.*

**4 ► TO BE KEPT SOMEWHERE ◄** [I always + adv/prep] *informal especially BrE* to be kept in a particular place: **live in/on etc** *Where does this dish live?*

## ② LIVE IN A PARTICULAR WAY

**5** [I always + adv/prep, T] to have a particular type of life, or live in a particular way: **live in/under/like etc** *These people are living in appalling conditions.* | *He lived like a king.* | **live well** (=have plenty of money, food etc) | **live a quiet/active/healthy life** *Ben has to live a quiet life.* | **live the life of** *She lived the life of an aristocrat.* | **live a life of crime/luxury** *a movie star living a life of luxury* | **live in fear (of)** *Colin lives in fear of having a heart attack.* | **live from day to day** (=deal with each day as it comes without making plans) | **be living on the breadline** (=be very poor) | **live out of a suitcase** (=travel a lot, especially as part of your work)

**6 ► LIVE BY DOING STH ◄** [I] to keep yourself alive by working, eating etc: *They earn barely enough to live.* | **live by doing sth** *They live by hunting and killing deer.* | **live on beans/potatoes/grass etc** (=eat only a particular type of food) *living on a diet of bread and cheese* | **live out of tins/cans** (=eat mainly food from cans, not fresh food) | **live on benefit/welfare/£40 a week etc** (=have only a small amount of money with which to buy food, pay bills etc) *I challenge anyone to try to live on the state pension.*

**7 live it up** *informal* to do things that you enjoy and spend a lot of money: *living it up at the Hotel California*

**8 ► LIVE BY A PRINCIPLE/RULE ETC ◄** [I] to always behave according to a particular set of rules or ideas: *people who live by the Bible*

**9 live by your wits** to get money by being clever or dishonest, and not by doing an ordinary job

**10 live a lie** to pretend all the time that you feel or believe something when actually you do not: *I had to divorce him, I couldn't go on living a lie.*

**11 ► EXCITING LIFE ◄** [I] to have an exciting life: *We're beginning to live at last!*

## ③ BE ALIVE

**12 ► BE/STAY ALIVE ◄** [I] to be alive or be able to stay alive: *Without light, plants couldn't live.* | *He is extremely ill and not expected to live.* | *The baby only lived a few hours.* | *Females live longer on average than males.* | **give sb six months/a year etc to live** (=expect someone who is ill to only live for six months etc) | **live to see/witness sth** (=live long enough to see it) *I'm glad she did not live to witness the break-up of her daughter's marriage.*

**13 the best/greatest/worst ... that ever lived** someone who was better,greater etc at doing something than anyone else in the past or present: *I think Jimi Hendrix was definitely the greatest guitarist that ever lived.*

**14 be living on borrowed time** to be still alive after the time that you were expected to die

## ④ SEXUAL RELATIONSHIP

**15 live with/together** [I] if two people live together, they live with each other in a sexual relationship without getting married: *We wanted to live together and have a child.* | *the man she's been living with for the last four years*

**16 live in sin** *old-fashioned* to live together and have a sexual relationship without being married

## ⑤ LIVE FOR A REASON

**17 live for sb/sth** if you live for someone or something, they are so important to you that they seem to be your main reason for living: *He lived for his art.* | *All through the football season, I lived for Saturdays.*

**18 live and breathe sth** to enjoy doing something so much that you spend most of your time on it: *Politics is the stuff I live and breathe.*

**19 live for the day when** to want something to happen very much: *She lives for the day when she can have an apartment of her own.*

## ⑥ IN YOUR MIND

**20 live in a world of your own/live in a dream world** to have strange ideas about life that are not like those of other people

**21 live in the past** to have old-fashioned ideas and attitudes: *You can't go on living in the past.*

**22 live in sb's memory/live with sb** to continue to exist in someone's memory: *The expression of terror on my son's face lived with me for years.*

**23 ► IMAGINE STH ◄** [I always + adv/prep] to imagine that you are experiencing something: [+ **in/through etc**] *an old actress living in her past glory*

## ⑦ OTHER MEANINGS

**24 ► STILL HAVE INFLUENCE ◄** [I] if someone's idea or work lives, it continues to influence people: *Glasnost lives!* | *Shakespeare's words live with us still.*

**25 as long as I live** used to emphasize that you will always do or feel something: *I'll never forget it as long as I live.*

**26 not live sth down** if you cannot live down something bad that you have done, people do not forget about it: *I was tempted to admit defeat, but I would never have lived it down.*

**27 you live and learn** used to say that you have just heard or learnt something surprising

**28 live and let live** used to say that you should accept other people's behaviour, even if it seems strange

**29 you haven't lived** used to say that someone's life will be boring if they do not have a particular experience: *You haven't lived until you've tasted champagne.*

**30 sb will live to regret it** used to say that someone will wish that they had not done something: *If you marry him, you'll live to regret it.*

**31 if I live to be 100/1000 etc** used to say that you will

never understand something: *If I live to be a thousand years old, I'll never see why she does these things!*
**32 live to fight/see another day** to continue to live or work after a failure or after you have dealt with a difficult situation: *A lot of stores like ours have closed down, but we'll live to see another day.*
**33 long live the King/Queen! etc** *spoken* used as an expression of loyal support
**34 long live democracy/America/the people etc** used to show support for an idea, principle, or nation

**live in** *phr v* [I] if someone who does paid work in a place lives in, they live at that place —see also LIVE-IN

**live off** sth/sb *phr v* [T] to get your income or food from a supply of money or from another person: *Mom used to live off the interest from her savings.* | *Rick disapproves of people who are living off the welfare.* | **live off the land** (=get food from growing vegetables, hunting etc)

**live on** *phr v* [I] to continue to exist: *Alice's memory will live on.* —see also LIVE[1] (24)

**live out** *phr v* **1** [I] when someone who does paid work in a place lives out, they do not live in that place **2** [T] **live out sth** to experience or do something that you have planned or hoped for: *The money enabled them to live out their dreams.* **3 live out your life in/on/along etc** to continue to live in a particular way or place until you die: *He lived out his life in solitude.*

**live through** sth *phr v* [T] to experience difficult or dangerous conditions: *It was hard to describe the nightmare she had lived through.*

**live up to** sth *phr v* [T] if something or someone lives up to a standard, reputation, or promise, they do as well as they were expected to, do what they promised etc: *The bank is insolvent and will be unable to live up to its obligations.* | **live up to your expectations** *The book certainly lived up to his expectations.*

**live with** sth *phr v* [T] to accept a difficult situation that is likely to continue for a long time: *You have to learn to live with stress.*

S3 W3 **live**[2] /laɪv/ *adj*
**1 ► LIVING ◄** [only before noun] not dead or artificial; living: *They are campaigning against experiments on live animals.* —compare DEAD[1] (1)
**2 live broadcast/programme etc** a programme that is seen or heard on television or radio at the same time as it is being made
**3 live performance/act/music etc** a performance in which the entertainer performs for people who are watching rather than for a film, record, etc: *Did the introduction of CDs affect the interest in live music?* | *Madonna live in concert.* | **live recording** (=a recording made of a live performance) | **live audience** (=the people who watch a live performance) *It's always different singing in front of a live audience.*
**4 ► ELECTRIC ◄** a wire or equipment that is live has electricity flowing through it —see also LIVE WIRE (2)
**5 ► BULLETS/BOMBS ◄** a live bullet, bomb etc still has the power to explode because it has not been used: *live ammunition*
**6 live match** a match that has not yet been used to produce a flame
**7 live coals** pieces of coal that are burning
**8 live issue/concern** an issue that still interests or worries people
**9 ► COMPUTER ◄** when a computer system is put into live use, it is used in a real situation by ordinary people instead of just being tested by the people who designed it
**10 live yoghurt** yoghurt containing BACTERIA that are still alive
**11 a real live ...** *spoken* an expression used to emphasize that something surprising has been seen or exists, used especially to or by children: *We saw a real live elephant!*

**live**[3] *adv* **1 broadcast a programme/show/speech etc live** to broadcast something at the same time as it actually happens: *We will be broadcasting the program live from Austin.* **2 perform live** to perform in front of people who have come to watch, rather than for a film, record etc

**live·a·ble** /ˈlɪvəbəl/ *adj* another spelling of livable

**-lived** /lɪvd/ *suffix* [in adjectives] lasting or living for a particular length of time: *Her enthusiasm was short-lived.* (=did not last long) | *to come from a long-lived family*

**lived-in** /ˈ· ·/ *adj* a place that looks lived-in has been used often by people so that it does not seem too new: **have a lived-in look** *often humorous*: *Jared's apartment has that lived-in look.*

**live-in** /ˈlɪv ɪn/ *adj* [only before noun] **1 live-in maid/nanny etc** a worker who lives in the house where they work **2 live-in lover/boyfriend etc** a phrase meaning someone who lives with their sexual partner without being married to them, used especially by people who do not approve of this

**live·li·hood** /ˈlaɪvlihʊd/ *n* [C,U] the way you earn money in order to live: *New fishing regulations will threaten our livelihood.*

**live·long** /ˈlɪvlɒŋ‖-lɔːŋ/ *adj AmE old-fashioned* **all the livelong day** a phrase meaning all day, used when this seems like a long time to you

**live·ly** /ˈlaɪvli/ *adj* S3
**1 ► FULL OF ENERGY ◄** somone who is lively has a lot of energy and is very active: *He'd always been a bright and lively child.*
**2 ► FULL OF INTEREST ◄** something that is lively is exciting and involves quick, intelligent thinking: *That was a pretty lively debate!* | **a lively interest** (=strong interest) *Eric has a lively interest in Eastern cuisine.*
**3 ► EXCITING ◄** a place or situation that is lively is exciting because a lot of things are happening: *Not exactly a lively vacation, was it?*
**4 ► COLOUR ◄** very bright: *a dress of lively reds and yellows*
**5 lively imagination** someone with a lively imagination tends to invent stories, descriptions etc that are not true
**6 make things lively (for sb)** to make a situation more exciting or more difficult for someone: *Our trainer was threatening to make life lively for us if we didn't improve.*
**7 Look/step lively!** *spoken* used to tell someone to hurry —**liveliness** *n* [U]

**liv·en** /ˈlaɪvən/ *v*

**liven up** *phr v* **1** [I,T] to become more exciting, or to make an event become more exciting: *The party really livened up when Mattie arrived.* | **liven sth ↔ up** *Why don't we play some games? That'll liven things up!* **2** [T] to make something look, taste etc more interesting or colourful: **liven sth ↔ up** *Why not liven up the room with some flowers?* **3** [I,T] to become more interested or excited, or to make someone feel like this: *I'm sure she'll liven up when she sees Malcolm.*

**liv·er** /ˈlɪvə‖-ər/ *n* **1** [C] a large organ in your body which produces BILE (1) and cleans your blood —see picture at DIGESTIVE SYSTEM **2** [U] the livers of animals used as food **3 a clean/fast etc liver** someone who lives their life in a morally good, exciting etc way

**live rail** /ˌlaɪv ˈreɪl/ *n* [C] a thick metal bar along a railway track that supplies electricity to trains

**liv·e·ried** /ˈlɪvərid/ *adj* wearing LIVERY (1): *a liveried servant*

**liv·er·ish** /ˈlɪvərɪʃ/ *adj BrE informal* slightly ill, especially after eating or drinking too much

**liver saus·age** /ˈ·· ˌ··/ *n* [U] *BrE* a type of cooked soft SAUSAGE made mainly of LIVER (2); liverwurst *AmE*

**liv·er·wort** /ˈlɪvəwɜːrt‖-vərwɜːrt/ *n* [C,U] a small flat green plant without flowers that grows in wet places

**liv·er·wurst** /ˈlɪvəwɜːst‖-vərwɜːrst/ *n* [U] *AmE* a type of cooked soft SAUSAGE made mainly of LIVER (2); liver sausage *BrE*

**liv·e·ry** /ˈlɪvəri/ *n* **1** [C,U] a type of old-fashioned, expensive-looking uniform for servants **2** [U] *poetic* natural bright colours that cover something **3** [C,U] *BrE* a set of colours and designs used by a company on its property and vehicles —see also LIVERIED

**livery com·pa·ny** /ˈ··· ˌ···/ *n* [C] one of the GUILDS (=ancient trade associations) of London

**liv·e·ry·man** /ˈlɪvərimən/ *n plural* **liverymen** /-mən/ [C] someone who works in a LIVERY COMPANY

**livery sta·ble** /ˈ··· ˌ··/ *n* [C] a place where people pay to have their horses kept, fed etc or where horses can be hired

**lives** /laɪvz/ the plural of LIFE

**live·stock** /ˈlaɪvstɒk‖-stɑːk/ *n* [plural, U] the animals that are kept on a farm

**live wire** /ˌlaɪv ˈwaɪə‖-ˈwaɪr/ *n* [C] **1** *informal* someone who is very active and has a lot of energy **2** a wire that has electricity passing through it

**liv·id** /ˈlɪvɪ̈d/ *adj* **1** extremely angry; FURIOUS: *Mom will be livid if she finds out.* **2** a mark on your skin that is livid is dark blue and grey: *livid bruises* **3** *literary* a face that is livid is very pale —**lividly** *adv*

**liv·ing¹** /ˈlɪvɪŋ/ *adj* **1** alive now: *one of the greatest living composers* **2 living proof** if someone is living proof of a particular fact, they are a good example of how true it is: *I'm living proof that you don't need a college degree to be successful.* **3 in living memory** for as long as anyone can remember: *the worst storm in living memory* **4 in/within living memory** a long time ago but within the lives of people who are still alive: *the worst recession in living memory* **5 living things** anything that lives, such as plants, animals or people **6 living language** a language that is still spoken today

S2 **living²** *n* **1** [C usually singular] the way that you earn money or the money that you earn: *It's not a great job, but it's a living.* | **do sth for a living** (=as your job) *So what do you do for a living?* | **earn/make a living** *It's hard to make a decent living as a musician.* | **scrape/scratch a living** (=get just enough to eat or live) —see LIFE (USAGE) **2 the living** all the people who are alive as opposed to dead people **3** [U] the way in which someone lives their life: *the stresses of city living* **4** [C] the position or income of a PARISH priest; BENEFICE —see also **cost of living** (COST¹ (1)), STANDARD OF LIVING **the land of the living** (LAND¹ (7))

**living death** /ˌ·· ˈ·/ *n* [singular] a life that is so unpleasant, it would seem better to be dead

**living fos·sil** /ˌ·· ˈ··/ *n* [C] *technical* an animal or plant of a very ancient type, that has not changed and still exists

**living hell** /ˌ·· ˈ·/ *n* [singular] a situation that causes you a lot of suffering for a long time: *Walter made my life a living hell.*

**living le·gend** /ˌ·· ˈ··/ *n* [C] someone who is famous for being extremely good at something: *John Lee Hooker isn't just a great blues player – he's a living legend.*

**living quar·ters** /ˈ·· ˌ··/ *n* [plural] the part of an army or industrial camp etc where the soldiers or workers live and sleep

**living room** /ˈ·· ·/ *n* [C] the main room in a house where people relax, watch television etc —compare DRAWING ROOM, FRONT ROOM, LOUNGE¹ (3), PARLOUR

**living stan·dard** /ˈ·· ˌ··/ *n* [C usually plural] the level of comfort and wealth that people have; STANDARD OF LIVING: *a decline in the country's living standards*

**living wage** /ˌ·· ˈ·/ *n* [singular] wages high enough to allow you to buy the things that you need to live

**living will** /ˌ·· ˈ·/ *n* [C] *AmE* a document explaining what medical or legal decisions should be made if you become so ill that you cannot make those decisions yourself

**liz·ard** /ˈlɪzəd‖-ərd/ *n* [C] a type of REPTILE that has four legs, and a long tail

lizard

**ll** the written abbreviation of 'lines', used in books

**lla·ma** /ˈlɑːmə/ *n* [C] a South American animal with thick woolly hair, rather like a camel without a hump

**LLB** *n* [C] Bachelor of Laws; a first university degree in law

**LLD** *n* [C] Doctor of Laws; a DOCTORATE in law

**LLM** *n* [C] Master of Laws; a MASTER's degree in law

**lo** /ləʊ‖loʊ/ *interjection old use* look; used to tell someone to pay attention to something that is surprising —see also LO AND BEHOLD

**load¹** /ləʊd‖loʊd/ *n* [C]

**1 ▶AMOUNT OF STH◀** a large quantity of something that is carried by a vehicle, person etc: *Take this load of wood over to the barn.* —see also **shed its load** (SHED² (8))

**2 a load/loads (of sth)** *informal especially BrE* a lot of something —see graph at MANY: *We got a load of complaints about the loud music.* | *Don't worry, there's loads of time.* | **loads to do/see/eat etc** *There was loads to eat at the party.* —see graph at MANY

**3 truckload/carload etc** the biggest amount or number of something that a vehicle can carry: *a busload of tourists*

**4 a load of crap/rubbish/bull etc** *spoken especially BrE* used to say that something is complete nonsense or stupid: *I never heard such a load of crap in all my life!*

**5 ▶WORK◀** the amount of work that a person or machine has to do: *The computer couldn't handle the load and crashed.* | **a light/heavy load** (=not much work, or a lot of work) *Hans has a heavy teaching load this semester.* | **work load** *My work load has doubled since Mandy left.*

**6 a heavy/difficult load to bear** a responsibility or worry that is difficult to deal with: *Coping with her mother's long illness was a heavy load to bear.* —see also **be a load/weight off your mind** (MIND¹ (15))

**7 ▶WASHING◀** a quantity of clothes etc that are washed together in a washing machine: *Do all the whites in one load.*

**8 get a load of** *spoken* used to tell someone to look at or listen to something surprising or funny: *Get a load of that weird hairdo!*

**9 ▶WEIGHT◀** the amount of weight that the frame of a building or structure can support: *a load-bearing wall*

**10 ▶ELECTRICITY◀** an amount of electrical power

**load²** *v* **1** also **load up** [I,T] to put a load of something on or into a vehicle: *Have you finished loading up?* | [+ **with**] *The boat called at Lerwick to load up with fresh vegetables.* | **load sth** *It took an hour to load the van.* | **load sth into/onto** *Be careful loading that piano into the truck!* **2** [T] to put bullets into a gun, a film into a camera etc: **load sth with** *Did you load it with 200 or 400 film?* | **load sth into** *Can you load the CD into the player, please?* **3** [T] to put a PROGRAM¹ (1) into a computer: **load sth into/from** *You have to load it from the A drive.* **4 load sb with** to give someone a lot of things to carry: *Em always loaded the kids with groceries to carry.*

**load** sb/sth **down** *phr v* [T usually passive] **1** [usually passive] to give someone more responsibility, work etc than they can deal with: *Jane felt loaded down*

cupboard
fridge
microwave
cooker BrE/ stove AmE
FRY
(electric) ring BrE/
burner AmE
oven glove
BAKE
ROAST
oven
freezer
tap BrE/
faucet AmE
breadbin BrE/
breadbox AmE
fire extinguisher
washing-up liquid BrE/
dishwashing liquid AmE
scouring pad
sink
draining
board
funnel
washing
machine
dishwasher
kettle
baking tray BrE/
cookie sheet AmE
floor
scales BrE/ scale AmE
measuring jug
fish slice BrE/
spatula AmE
BURN
measuring
spoons
toaster
cake tin BrE/
muffin tin AmE
cloth
corkscrew
cutlery BrE/
silverware AmE
food
processor
drawer
tin opener BrE/
can opener AmE
worktop BrE/
counter AmE
bin BrE/
wastebasket AmE
breadboard
napkin
tea towel BrE/
dishcloth AmE

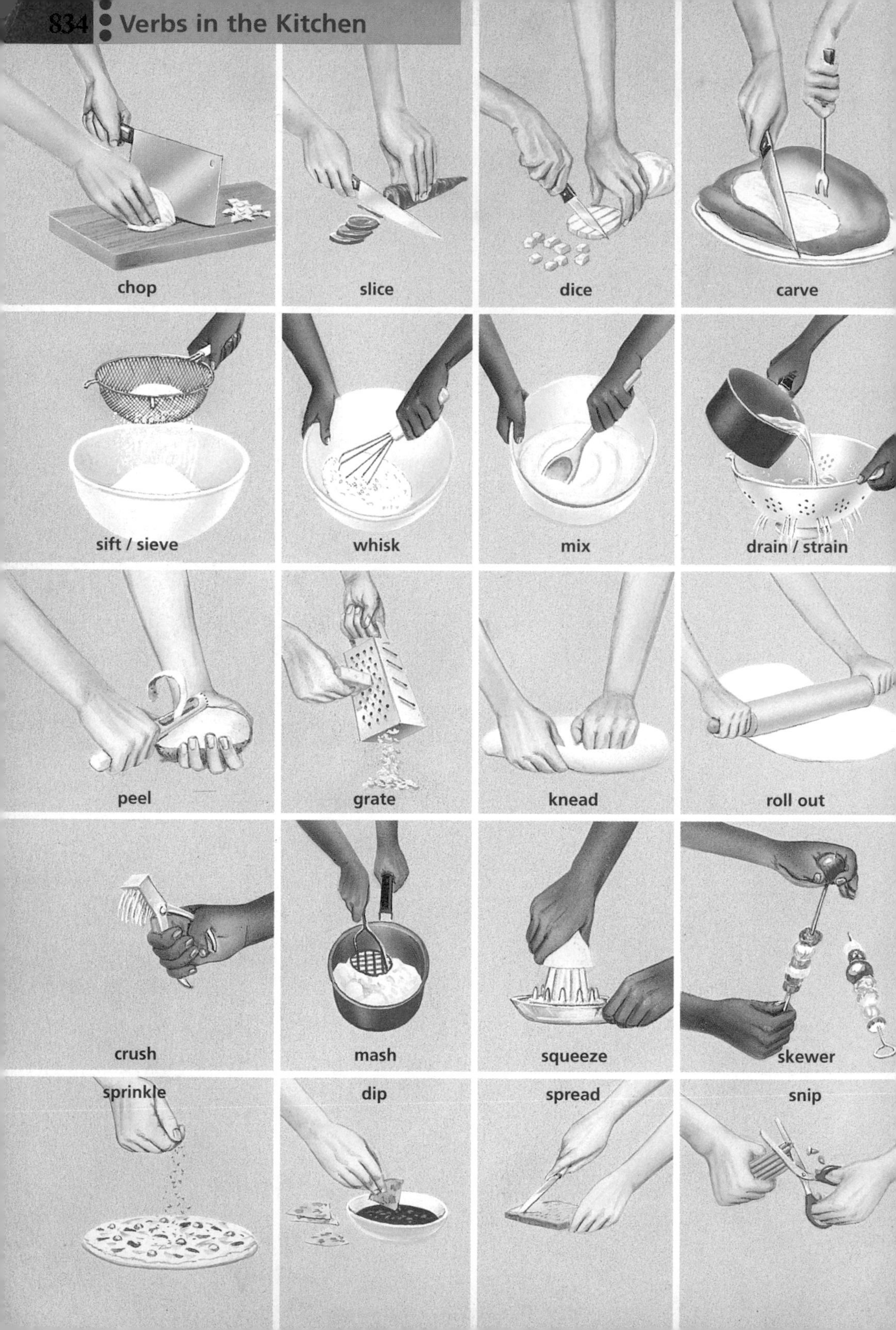
chop
slice
dice
carve
sift / sieve
whisk
mix
drain / strain
peel
grate
knead
roll out
crush
mash
squeeze
skewer
sprinkle
dip
spread
snip

mountainous
peak / summit
ridge / arête
cirque / corrie
corrie glacier
snow line
icefall
tributary glacier
plateau
hanging valley
mountain pass
main valley glacier
bare rock
waterfall
crevasses
scree
glacial meltwater stream
moraine
coastal
headland / promontory
cliff
bay
sand dune
sandy beach
jetty
spit
cave
river mouth
delta
gorge
lagoon
crest
sediment
arch
wash
shingle beach
groyne

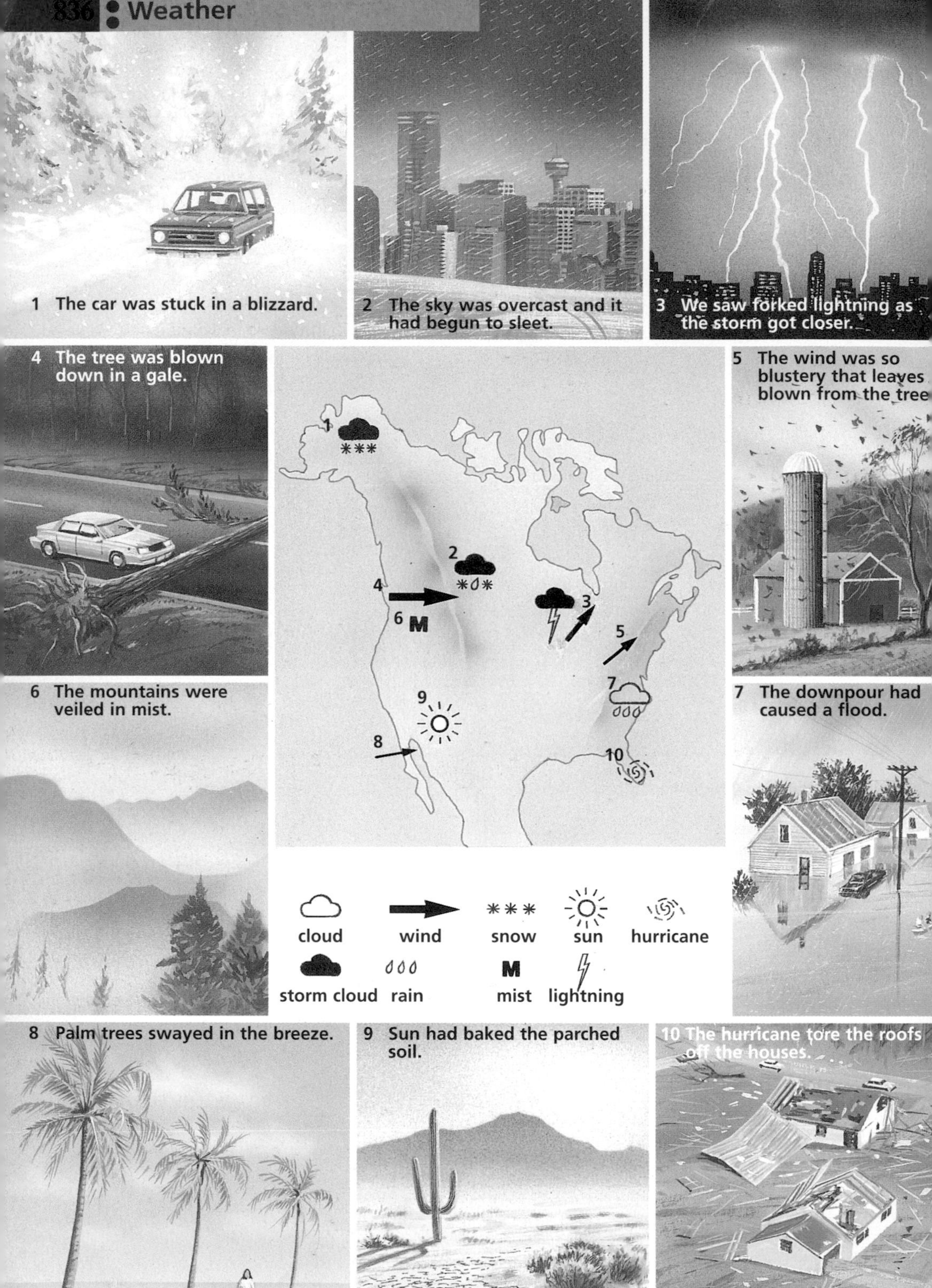


1 The car was stuck in a blizzard.

2 The sky was overcast and it had begun to sleet.

3 We saw forked lightning as the storm got closer.

4 The tree was blown down in a gale.

5 The wind was so blustery that leaves blown from the tree

6 The mountains were veiled in mist.

7 The downpour had caused a flood.

8 Palm trees swayed in the breeze.

9 Sun had baked the parched soil.

10 The hurricane tore the roofs off the houses.

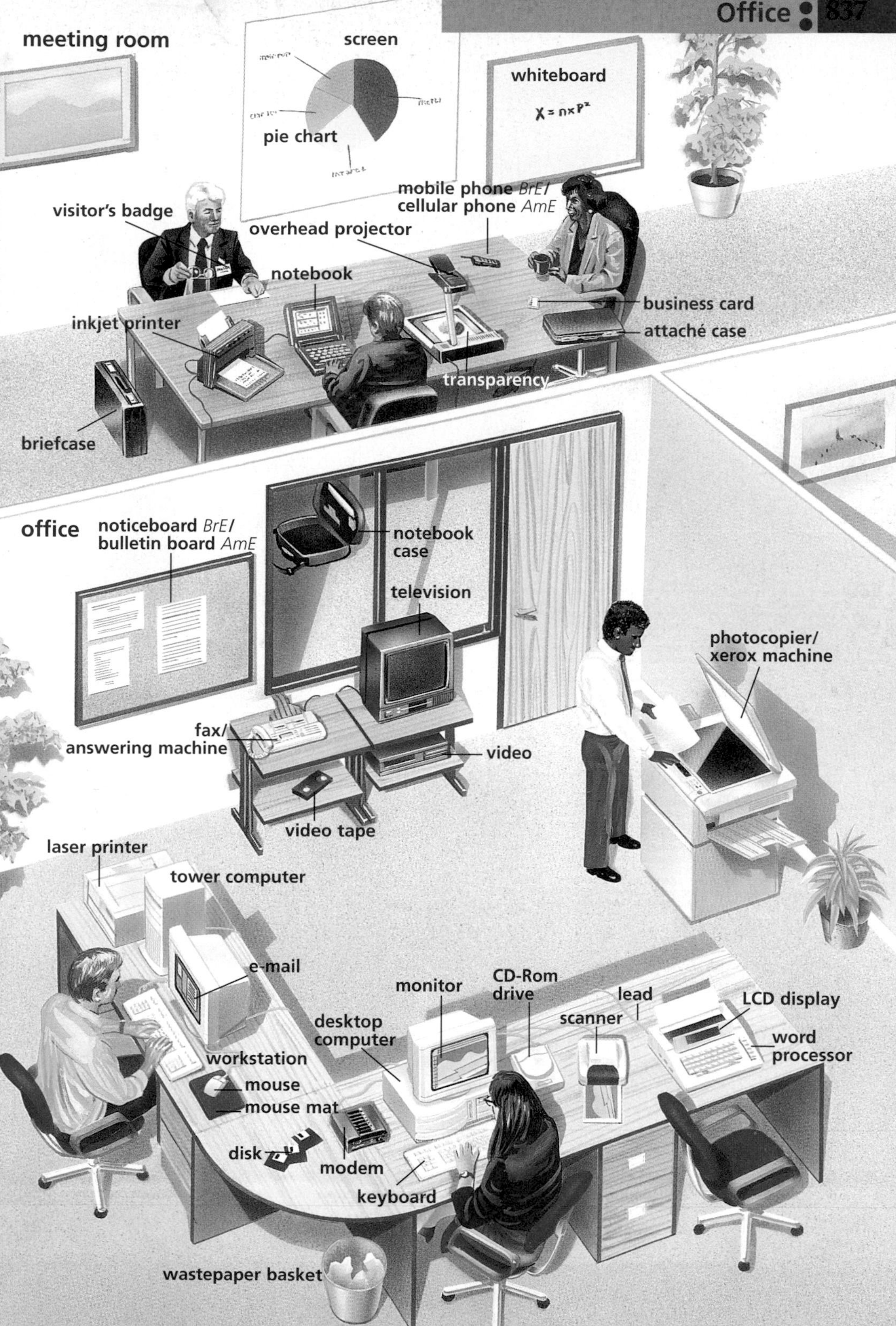

meeting room
screen
whiteboard
pie chart
visitor's badge
mobile phone BrE/
cellular phone AmE
overhead projector
notebook
business card
inkjet printer
attaché case
transparency
briefcase
office
noticeboard BrE/
bulletin board AmE
notebook
case
television
photocopier/
xerox machine
fax/
answering machine
video
video tape
laser printer
tower computer
e-mail
monitor
CD-Rom
drive
lead
LCD display
scanner
desktop
computer
word
processor
workstation
mouse
mouse mat
disk
modem
keyboard
wastepaper basket

hat stand BrE/
coat stand AmE
board
SPECIALS
Rainbow
Trout.
coat rack
swing door
customer
POUR
waiter
corkscrew
UNCORK
SERVE
maitre d'/
head waiter
bow tie
chef
FLAMBÉ
napkin/ serviette BrE
ashtray
RESERVED
SEAT
tablecloth
waitress
espresso cup
dessert trolley BrE/
dessert cart AmE
TAKE THE
ORDER
apron
menu
crudités
TIP
cheeseboard
dip
bill BrE/
check AmE
table mat
cutlery/ silverware AmE

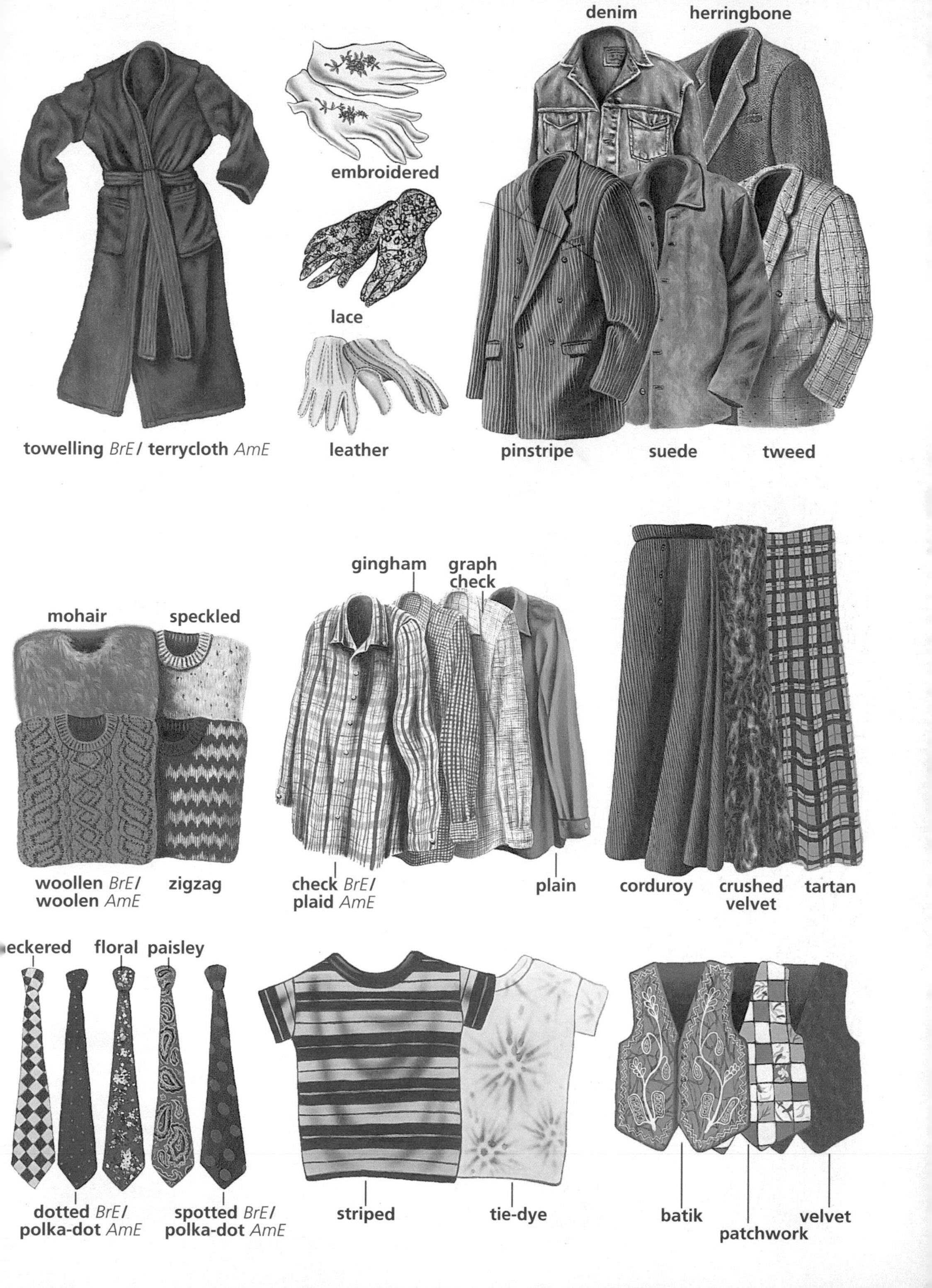

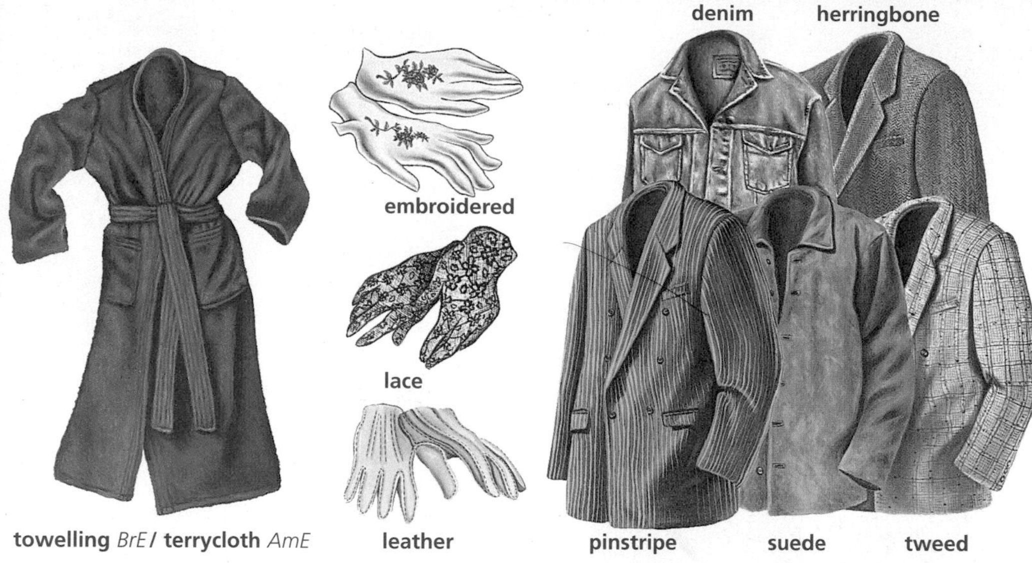


mohair
speckled
woollen *BrE* / woolen *AmE*
zigzag

gingham
graph check
check *BrE* / plaid *AmE*
plain

corduroy
crushed velvet
tartan

eckered
floral
paisley
dotted *BrE* / polka-dot *AmE*
spotted *BrE* / polka-dot *AmE*

striped
tie-dye

batik
patchwork
velvet

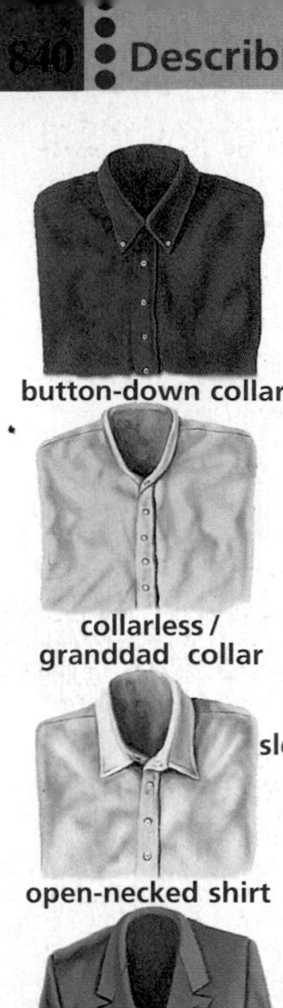
button-down collar
collarless / granddad collar
open-necked shirt
double-breasted jacket

single-breasted jacket
capped sleeves

single cuff
double cuff
bow tie
buttonhole
collar
seam
sleeve
shirt
top pocket
cuff
jacket
cufflinks
trousers BrE/ pants AmE
laces
neck
waistcoat
belt
pencil skirt
hem
tights

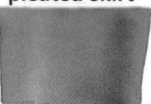

drawstring waistline
waistband
crew neck
polo neck BrE/ turtle neck AmE
scooped neck
turtle neck BrE/ mock turtle AmE
v-neck
pleated skirt
straight skirt
wrap-over skirt

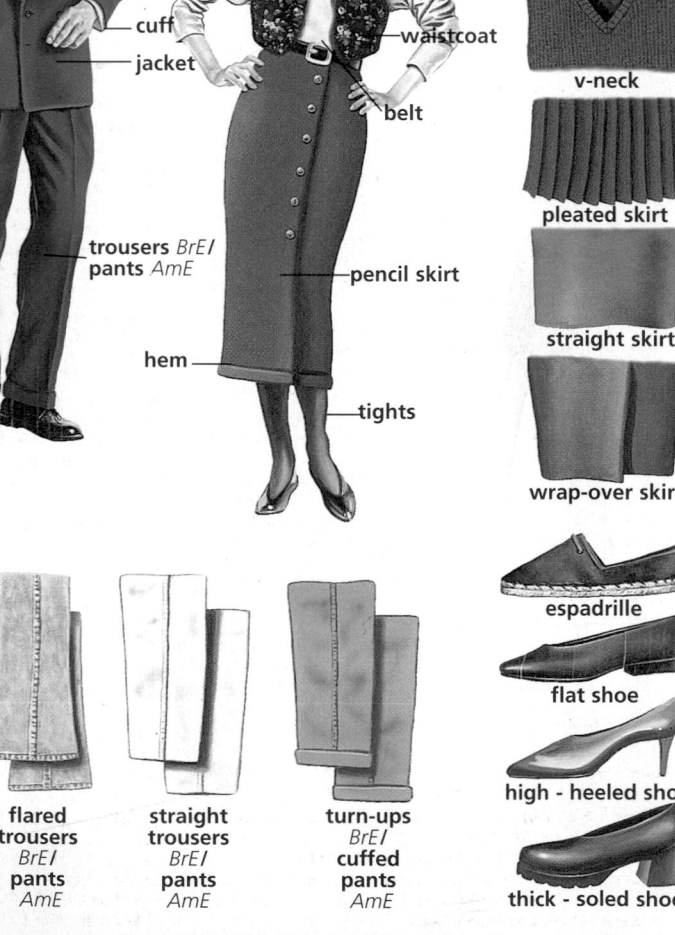

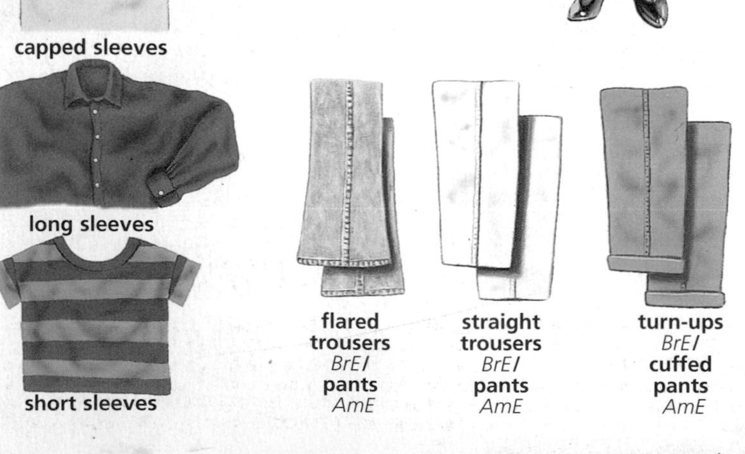
long sleeves
short sleeves
flared trousers BrE/ pants AmE
straight trousers BrE/ pants AmE
turn-ups BrE/ cuffed pants AmE
espadrille
flat shoe
high - heeled shoe
thick - soled shoe

*with money worries.* **2** to make someone carry too many things: *She staggered home loaded down with shopping bags.*

**load·ed** /ˈləʊdɪ̆d‖ˈloʊ-/ *adj*
**1** ▶ **VEHICLE** ◀ carrying a load of something: *a loaded truck*
**2** ▶ **GUN/CAMERA** ◀ containing bullets, film etc: *a loaded pistol*
**3** ▶ **RICH** ◀ [not before noun] *informal* very rich: *Giles can afford it – he's loaded.*
**4** ▶ **FULL** ◀ **be loaded with** *informal* to be full of a particular quality, attitude etc, or contain a lot of something, especially something bad: *Your paper's loaded with spelling mistakes.* | *a voice loaded with menace*
**5** ▶ **WORD/STATEMENT** ◀ a loaded word, statement etc has more meaning, especially a negative meaning, than you first think: *He 'deserved' it? That's a loaded word.*
**6** **loaded question** a question that is unfair because it makes you answer in a particular way —compare **leading question** (LEADING[1] (4))
**7** ▶ **DRUNK** ◀ *informal* very drunk
**8** **the dice/odds are loaded against sb/sth** used to say that someone or something is not likely to succeed or win
**9** **loaded dice** DICE[1] (1) that have weights in them so that they always fall with the same side on top

**load·ing** /ˈləʊdɪŋ‖ˈloʊ-/ *n* [U] an amount added to the cost of an insurance agreement because of special risks, profits etc

**load·sa** /ˈləʊdzə‖ˈloʊ-/ *adj spoken* a lot of: *He gets to shoot loadsa bad guys and snog the girlies.*

**load·star** /ˈləʊdstɑː‖ˈloʊdstɑːr/ *n* [C] another spelling of LODESTAR

**load·stone** /ˈləʊdstəʊn‖ˈloʊdstoʊn/ *n* [C] another spelling of LODESTONE

**loaf[1]** /ləʊf‖loʊf/ *n plural* **loaves** /ləʊvz‖loʊvz/ [C] **1** bread that is shaped and baked in one piece and can be cut into SLICES: *a loaf of bread* **2** **meat/nut loaf** meat or nuts that have been cut very finely, pressed together, and baked **3** **use your loaf** *BrE old-fashioned* used to tell someone to be more sensible or think harder

**loaf[2]** *v* [I] *informal* to waste time in a lazy way when you should be working: **loaf around/about** *They spend all day loafing around on street corners.*

**loaf·er** /ˈləʊfə‖ˈloʊfər/ *n* [C] **1** a flat leather shoe that does not need to be fastened onto your foot —see picture at SHOE[1] **2** someone who loafs around

**loam** /ləʊm‖loʊm/ *n* [U] good quality soil consisting of sand, clay, and decayed plants —**loamy** *adj*

S2 W2 **loan[1]** /ləʊn‖loʊn/ *n* **1** [C] an amount of money that you borrow from a bank etc: **take out a loan** (=borrow money) | **repay a loan** *We're repaying the loan over a three-year period.* | **bank loan** (=money lent by a bank) | **student loan** (=money lent to students) **2** [singular] the act of lending something: [**+ of**] *Thanks for the loan of your camera.* | **give sb the loan of sth** (=lend someone something) **3** **on loan** if something such as a painting or book is on loan, someone is borrowing it: *The book I wanted was out on loan.* | *pictures on loan from the Louvre.*

**loan[2]** *v* [T] **1** *especially AmE* to lend someone something, especially money: **loan sb sth/loan sth to sb** *Can you loan me $5?* **2** *BrE* to lend something valuable, such as a painting, to an organization: *The family loaned their collection of paintings for the exhibition.* —see BORROW (USAGE)

**loan cap·i·tal** /ˈ· ˌ···/ *n* [U] the part of a company's money that was borrowed to help start it

**lo and be·hold** /ˌ· · ·ˈ·/ *interjection humorous* used to make someone pay attention when you are going to mention something surprising that has happened

**loan shark** /ˈ· ·/ *n* [C] someone who lends money at very high rates of INTEREST[1] (4) and will often use threats or violence to get the money back

**loan·word** /ˈləʊnwɜːd‖ˈloʊnwɜːrd/ *n* [C] a word taken into one language from another —see also BORROWING (1)

**loath** /ləʊθ‖loʊθ/ *adj* **be loath to do sth** *formal* to be unwilling to do something: *Sarah was loath to tell her mother all that had happened.*

**loathe** /ləʊð‖loʊð/ *v* [T not in progressive] to hate someone or something very much: *Lucinda loathes spiders.* | **loathe doing sth** *I absolutely loathe travelling.*

**loath·ing** /ˈləʊðɪŋ‖ˈloʊð-/ *n* [singular, U] a very strong feeling of hatred: [**+ for**] *The more he called me 'Sugar', the more my loathing for him increased.*

**loath·some** /ˈləʊðsəm‖ˈloʊð-/ *adj* very unpleasant or cruel; DISGUSTING: *How I detest you, you loathsome creature!* —**loathsomeness** *n* [U]

**loaves** /ləʊvz‖loʊvz/ the plural of LOAF

**lob** /lɒb‖lɑːb/ *v* **lobbed, lobbing** [T] **1** *informal* to throw something somewhere, especially over a wall, fence etc: **lob sth into/at/over etc** *The kids were lobbing pine cones into the neighbor's yard.* **2** to throw or hit a ball in a slow high curve, especially in a game of tennis or CRICKET (2): *Martinez lobbed the ball high over Graf's head.* —**lob** *n* [C] —see picture on page 1263

**lob·by[1]** /ˈlɒbi‖ˈlɑːbi/ *n* [C] **1** a wide passage or large hall just inside the entrance to a public building: *a hotel lobby* —compare FOYER (1) **2** a group of people who try to persuade a government that a particular law or situation should be changed: *The tobacco lobby is trying to change the no smoking laws.* —see also LOBBY[2] **3** an attempt to persuade a government to change a law, make a new law etc: [**+ of**] *a mass lobby of Parliament by women's organizations* —see also LOBBY[2] **4 a)** a hall in the British Parliament where members of parliament and the public meet **b)** one of the two passages in the British Parliament where members go to vote for or against a BILL[1] (2)

**lobby[2]** *v* [I,T] to try to persuade the government or someone with political power that a law or situation should be changed: [**+ for/against**] *The group is lobbying for a reduction in defense spending.* | **lobby sb to do sth** *We've been lobbying our State Representative to support the new health plan.* —**lobbyist** *n* [C]

**lobby** sth **through** *phr v* [T] to get a law officially approved by the government by lobbying: *After months of debate the bill was finally lobbied through Parliament.*

**lobe** /ləʊb‖loʊb/ *n* [C] **1** the soft piece of flesh at the bottom of your ear; EARLOBE **2** *technical* a round part of an organ in your body, especially in your brain or lungs —**lobed** *adj*

**lo·bot·o·my** /ləʊˈbɒtəmi, lə-‖loʊˈbɑː-, lə-/ *n* [C] a medical operation to remove part of someone's brain in order to make them less violent, rarely done now LEUCOTOMY *BrE* —**lobotomize** also **-ise** *BrE v* [T]

**lob·ster** /ˈlɒbstə‖ˈlɑːbstər/ *n* **1** [C] a sea animal with eight legs, a shell, and two large CLAWS **2** [U] the meat of this animal used for food

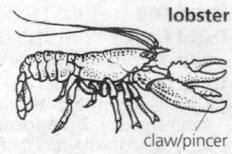

**lobster**

claw/pincer

**lob·ster·pot** /ˈlɒbstəpɒt‖ˈlɑːbstərpɑːt/ *n* [C] a trap shaped like a basket in which lobsters are caught

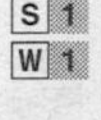

**lo·cal[1]** /ˈləʊkəl‖ˈloʊ-/ *adj* **1** connected with a particular place or area, especially the place you live in: *the local hospital* | *members of the local community* **2** *technical* affecting or limited to one part of your body: *a local infection* | **local anaesthetic** *The tooth was removed under local anaesthetic.* S1 W1

**local[2]** *n* [C] **1** [often plural] someone who lives in the place where you are or the place that you are talking about: *We asked one of the locals to recommend a hotel.* **2** *BrE* a pub near where you live, especially one where you often drink: *I usually have a pint or two at my local on Friday nights.* **3** *AmE* a bus, train etc that stops at all S3

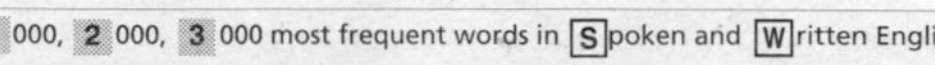

regular stopping places **4** *AmE* a branch of a TRADE UNION

**lo·cal** /ˌləʊ ˈkæl◂‖ˌloʊ-/ *adj* another spelling of LOW-CAL

**local ar·e·a net·work** /ˌ·· ˌ··· ˈ··/ *n* [C] *technical* LAN

**local au·thor·i·ty** /ˌ·· ·ˈ···/ *n* [C] *BrE* the group of people elected or paid to be the government of a particular area, town, or city in Britain: *The local authority are considering his grant application.*

**local call** /ˈ·· ˌ·/ *n* [C] a telephone call to a place near you that does not cost much money

**local col·our** *BrE*, **local color** *AmE* /ˌ·· ˈ··/ *n* [U] additional details in a story or picture that give you a better idea of what a place is really like: *His description of the smells from the market added a touch of local color.*

**local coun·cil** /ˌ·· ˈ··/ *n* [C] the group of people responsible for providing houses, schools, parks etc in a small area such as a town or DISTRICT

**lo·cale** /ləʊˈkɑːl‖loʊ-/ *n* [C] the place where something happens or where the action takes place in a book or a film: *We need a tropical locale for this scene.*

**local gov·ern·ment** /ˌ·· ˈ···/ *n* [C,U] the government of cities, towns etc by elected representatives of the people living in them

**local his·to·ry** /ˌ·· ˈ···/ *n* [U] the history of a particular area —**local historian** /ˌ·· ·ˈ···/ *n* [C]

**lo·cal·i·ty** /ləʊˈkæləti‖loʊ-/ *n* [C] a small area of a country, city etc: **in the locality** (=near to the place you are talking about) *What kind of leisure facilities are there in the locality?*

**lo·cal·ize** also **-ise** *BrE* /ˈləʊkəlaɪz‖ˈloʊ-/ *v* [T] *formal* **1** to find out exactly where something is: *A mechanic is trying to localize the fault.* **2** to limit the effect that something has, or the size of area it covers —**localization** /ˌləʊkəlaɪˈzeɪʃən‖ˌloʊkələ-/ *n* [U]

**lo·cal·ized** also **-ised** *BrE* /ˈləʊkəlaɪzd‖ˈloʊ-/ *adj formal* a word meaning within one small area, used especially to talk about something unpleasant or unwanted: *localized flooding | a localized infection*

S2 **lo·cal·ly** /ˈləʊkəli‖ˈloʊ-/ *adv* **1** near the area where you are or the area you are talking about: *I live locally, so it's easy to get to the office.* **2** in particular small areas: *Most of the country will be dry, but there will be some rain locally.*

**local pa·per** /ˌ·· ˈ··/ *n* [C] **1** a newspaper that gives mainly local news **2** *AmE* a newspaper printed in a town which contains local, national, and international news

**local ra·di·o** /ˌ·· ˈ···/ *n* [U] a radio service that broadcasts programmes for a particular area of the country

**local rag** /ˌ·· ˈ·/ *n* [C] *BrE informal* a local newspaper

**local time** /ˈ·· ·/ *n* [U] the time of day in a particular part of the world: *We'll arrive in Boston at 4:00 local time.*

S3 W3 **lo·cate** /ləʊˈkeɪt‖ˈloʊkeɪt/ *v* **1** [T] to find the exact position of something: *We couldn't locate the source of the radio signal.* **2 be located in/by/near etc** to be in a particular position: *The business is located right in the center of town.* **3** [I always + adv/prep] *AmE* to come to a place and start a business, company etc there: [+ **in/at etc**] *We are offering incentives for companies to locate in our city.*

S3 W2 **lo·ca·tion** /ləʊˈkeɪʃən‖loʊ-/ *n* **1** [C] a particular place or position, especially in relation to other areas, buildings etc: *Could you give me your precise location?* —see POSITION[1] (USAGE) **2** [C,U] a place outside or away from a film STUDIO where scenes are filmed: *It was hard to find a suitable location for the desert scenes.* | **on location** *Most of the movie was shot on location in Africa.* **3** [U] the act of finding the position of something: *The main problem for engineers was the location of underground rivers in the area.*

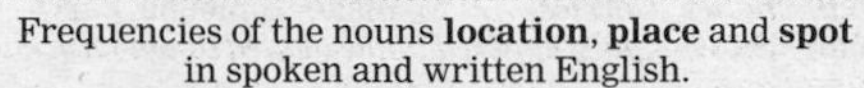
Frequencies of the nouns **location**, **place** and **spot** in spoken and written English.

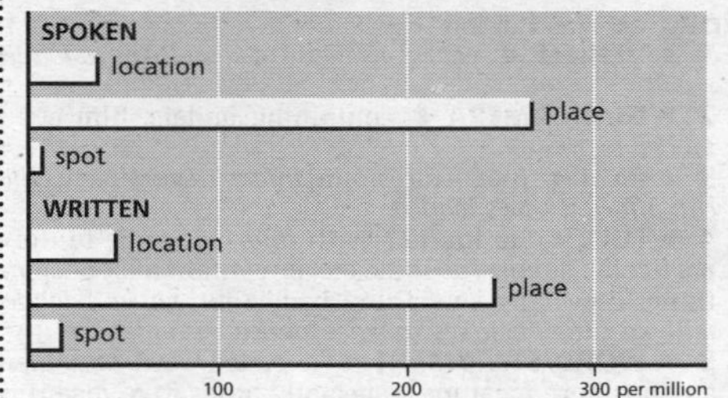


Based on the British National Corpus and the Longman Lancaster Corpus

This graph shows that **place** is much more common than **location** or **spot** in both spoken and written English. This is because **place** is the most general of the three words. **Location** is used to mean a particular place or position, especially in relation to other buildings, areas etc. **Spot** is used to mean a pleasant place or area where you spend time or do something.

**loch** /lɒx, lɒk‖lɑːk, lɑːx/ *n* [C] *ScotE* a lake or a part of the sea partly enclosed by land: *Loch Ness*

**lo·ci** /ˈləʊsaɪ‖ˈloʊ-/ —the plural of LOCUS

**lock[1]** /lɒk‖lɑːk/ *v* S2 W3

**1 ▶ FASTEN SOMETHING ◀** [I,T] to fasten something with a lock or be fastened with a lock: *Did you lock the car? I can't get the door to lock.*

**2 ▶ PUT STH IN A SAFE PLACE ◀** [T always + adv/prep] to put something in a safe place and lock the door, lid etc: **lock sth up/away/in etc** *Joe locked the money in the safe.*

**3 be locked together/in an embrace** if two people are locked together or locked in an embrace, they are holding each other very tightly: *The fighters were locked together. | lovers locked in a deep embrace*

**4 lock arms** to join your arms tightly together with someone else: *The police locked arms to form a barrier against the protesters.*

**5 be locked in battle/combat/dispute etc** to be involved in a serious argument, fight etc with someone: *We found ourselves locked in a costly legal battle.*

**6 lock horns with sb (over sth)** to argue or fight with someone

**7 ▶ WHEEL/PART OF A MACHINE ◀** [I] to become fixed in one position and impossible to move: *The wheels suddenly locked.* —**lockable** *adj*

**lock** sb/sth **away** *phr v* [T] **1** to put something in a safe place and lock the door, lid etc: *We locked all our valuables away before we went on vacation.* **2** to put someone in prison

**lock** sb **in** *phr v* [T] to prevent someone from leaving a room or building by locking the door: *Help me, somebody – I'm locked in.*

**lock onto** sth *phr v* [T] if a MISSILE locks onto a TARGET, it finds it and follows it closely

**lock** sb **out** *phr v* [T] **1** to keep someone out of a place by locking the door: *Oh no, I've locked myself out!* **2** if employers lock workers out, they do not let them enter their place of work until they accept the employers' conditions for settling a disagreement —see also LOCKOUT

**lock up** *phr v* **1** [I,T] to make a building safe by locking the doors, especially at night: **lock sth up** *Don't forget to lock up the warehouse.* **2** [T **lock** sth **up**] to put something in a safe place and lock its door, lid etc **3** [T **lock** sb **up**] *informal* **a)** to put someone in prison: *Rapists should be locked up.* **b)** *often humorous* to put someone in a hospital for people who are mentally ill **4 be locked up (in sth)** if your money is locked up, you have put it into a business, INVESTMENT etc and cannot easily move it or change it into CASH[1]

S 2 **lock**[2] *n*
1 ▶ **ON A DOOR** ◀ [C] a thing for fastening a door, drawer etc, that you can only open with a key: *The rear doors are fitted with childproof locks.* | **pick a lock** (=use something like a pin to open a lock, especially for an illegal purpose)
**2 under lock and key** **a)** kept safely in a box, cupboard etc that is locked: *Dad keeps all his liquor under lock and key.* **b)** kept in a place such as a prison
**3 lock, stock, and barrel** including every part of something: *He moved the whole company, lock, stock, and barrel, to Mexico.*
4 ▶ **HAIR** ◀ **a)** [C] a small BUNCH of the hair on your head: *a stray lock of hair* **b) locks** *[plural] poetic* your hair: *long flowing locks*
5 ▶ **ON A RIVER ETC** ◀ [C] a part of a CANAL (1) or river that is closed off by gates so that the water level can be raised or lowered to move boats up or down a slope
6 ▶ **IN A FIGHT** ◀ [C] a HOLD[2] (7) which WRESTLERS use to prevent their opponent from moving: *a head lock*
7 ▶ **VEHICLE** ◀ [C, U] *especially BrE* the degree to which a vehicle's STEERING WHEEL can be turned in order to turn the vehicle: **on full lock** (=turned as far as possible)
8 ▶ **MACHINE** ◀ [U] the state of a machine when it is stopped in such a way that it cannot be operated: *in the lock position*

**lock·er** /ˈlɒkə‖ˈlɑːkər/ *n* [C] **1** a small cupboard where you leave your outdoor clothes, bags etc while you work or play sports **2** *AmE* a very cold room used for storing food in a restaurant or factory: *a meat locker*

**locker room** /ˈ·· ·/ *n* [C] a room in a sports building, school etc where people change their clothes and leave them in lockers

**lock·et** /ˈlɒkɪt‖ˈlɑː-/ *n* [C] a piece of jewellery that you wear around your neck on a chain, with a small metal case in which you can put a picture, a piece of hair etc

**lock·jaw** /ˈlɒkdʒɔː‖ˈlɑːkdʒɒː/ *n* [U] *not technical* TETANUS

**lock keep·er** /ˈ· ˌ··/ *n* or [C] someone whose job is to open and close the gates of a LOCK[2] (5) or a CANAL (1)

**lock·out** /ˈlɒk-aʊt‖ˈlɑːk-/ *n* [C] a period of time when a company does not allow workers to go back to work, especially in a factory, until they accept its working conditions —see also **lock out** (LOCK[1]), compare STRIKE[2] (1)

**lock·smith** /ˈlɒkˌsmɪθ‖ˈlɑːk-/ *n* [C] someone who makes and repairs locks

**lock·step** /ˈlɒkstep‖ˈlɑːk-/ *n* **in lockstep** *especially AmE* following rules and accepted ideas without thinking

**lock·up** /ˈlɒk-ʌp‖ˈlɑːk-/ *n* [C] a small prison where a criminal can be kept for a short time, often in a village or small town

**lock-up gar·age** /ˌ· · ˈ··‖ˌ· · ·ˈ·/ *n* [C] *BrE* a garage that you can rent to keep cars, goods etc in

**lo·co** /ˈləʊkəʊ‖ˈloʊkoʊ/ *adj AmE informal* crazy: **go loco** *That guy's going loco!* —see also IN LOCO PARENTIS

**lo·co·mo·tion** /ˌləʊkəˈməʊʃən‖ˌloʊkəˈmoʊ-/ *n* [U] *formal or technical* movement or the ability to move

**lo·co·mo·tive**[1] /ˌləʊkəˈməʊtɪv‖ˌloʊkəˈmoʊ-/ *n* [C] *technical or AmE* a railway engine

**locomotive**[2] *adj technical* connected with movement

**lo·co·weed** /ˈləʊkəʊwiːd‖ˈloʊkoʊ-/ *n* [C] a plant that grows in America and makes animals ill if they eat it

**lo·cum** /ˈləʊkəm‖ˈloʊ-/ *n* [C] *BrE* a doctor or priest who does another doctor's or priest's work while they are on holiday, ill etc

**lo·cus** /ˈləʊkəs‖ˈloʊ-/ *n plural* **loci** /ˈləʊsaɪ‖ˈloʊ-/ [C] **1 locus of** *formal* a place or position where something is particularly known to exist or happen: *areas identified as the locus of poverty and deprivation* **2** *technical* the set of all points given by a particular rule in mathematics

**lo·cust** /ˈləʊkəst‖ˈloʊ-/ *n* [C] an insect that lives mainly in Asia and Africa and flies in a very large group, eating and destroying crops: *a swarm of locusts*

**lo·cu·tion** /ləʊˈkjuːʃən‖loʊ-/ *n technical* **1** [U] a style of speaking **2** [C] a phrase, especially one used in a particular area or by a particular group of people

**lode** /ləʊd‖loʊd/ *n* [C usually singular] an amount of ORE (=metal in its natural form) —see also MOTHER LODE

**lode·star, loadstar** /ˈləʊdstɑː‖ˈloʊdstɑːr/ *n especially literary* **1** [singular] a principle or fact that guides someone: *the economic lodestar for achieving low interest rates* **2** the POLE STAR, used as a guide by sailors:

**lode·stone, loadstone** /ˈləʊdstəʊn‖ˈloʊdstoʊn/ *n* [C,U] *old use* iron, or a piece of iron that acts as a MAGNET (1)

**lodge**[1] /lɒdʒ‖lɑːdʒ/ *v*
1 ▶ **STAY SOMEWHERE** ◀ [I always + adv/prep] to pay someone rent so you can live in a room in their house: [+ **at/with etc**] *Paul lodged with a family in Bristol when he first started work.*
**2 lodge a complaint/protest/appeal etc** *BrE* to make a formal or official complaint, protest etc: *They lodged a complaint against the doctor for negligence.*
3 ▶ **BE STUCK** ◀ [I always + adv/prep, T usually passive] to become firmly stuck somewhere, or make something become stuck: [+ **in/down etc**] *The fishbone lodged in her throat.* | **be lodged in/down etc** *The bullet was lodged in his spine.*
4 ▶ **PUT SB SOMEWHERE** ◀ [T] to give or find someone a place to stay for a short time, usually for payment: *a building used to lodge prisoners of war* | **lodge sb in/at etc** *The refugees were lodged in old army barracks.*
5 ▶ **IN A SAFE PLACE** ◀ *formal* to put something in an official place so that it is safe: **lodge sth with sb** *Be sure to lodge a copy of the contract with your solicitor.*

**lodge**[2] *n* [C] **1** a small house built on the land of a large country house **2** a room for someone whose job is to see who enters a building or around a building: *the porter's lodge* **3** a small house in country or mountain areas, used by hunters, skiers (SKI[2]) etc **4 a)** an organisation of FREEMASONS: *a Masonic lodge* **b)** the building where this group meets **5** a BEAVER's home **6** *AmE* a hotel in the mountains **7** *AmE* a WIGWAM

**lodg·er** /ˈlɒdʒə‖ˈlɑːdʒer/ *n* [C] *especially BrE* someone who pays rent to live in a house with its owner; ROOMER *AmE*: **take in a lodger** (=start having a paying guest in your home)

**lodg·ing** /ˈlɒdʒɪŋ‖ˈlɑː-/ *n* [singular, U] **1** a place to stay: **board and lodging** *BrE*: *It's £70 a week for board and lodging.* —compare BOARD[1] (9) ROOM AND BOARD **2 lodgings** *plural* a house where you pay rent to the owner so you can live in one of their rooms

**lodging house** /ˈ·· ·/ *n* [C] *BrE* a building where rooms can be rented for a few days or weeks; ROOMING HOUSE *AmE*

**loft**[1] /lɒft‖lɒːft/ *n*
1 ▶ **ON A FARM** ◀ [C] a raised area in a BARN used for keeping HAY (1) or other crops: *a hayloft*
2 ▶ **UNDER A ROOF** ◀ [C] *BrE* a room or space under the roof of a building; ATTIC
3 ▶ **TYPE OF ROOM/BUILDING** ◀ [C] *especially AmE* **a)** a room that is on a raised level within another room **b)** a building that has this feature: *a loft apartment*
4 ▶ **FOR BIRDS** ◀ [C] a set of CAGES used to keep PIGEONS in
5 ▶ **IN A CHURCH** ◀ the place where a church ORGAN (2) is: *the organ loft*

**loft**[2] *v* [T] to hit a ball very high in GOLF or CRICKET

**loft·y** /ˈlɒfti‖ˈlɒːfti/ *adj* **1** seeming to think you are better than other people: *a lofty manner* **2** lofty ideas, beliefs, attitudes etc are of an unusually high moral quality: *lofty ideals of equality and social justice* **3** *literary* lofty mountains, buildings etc are very high —**loftily** *adv* —**loftiness** *n* [U]

**log**[1] /lɒg‖lɒːg, lɑːg/ *n* [C] **1** a thick piece of wood cut from a tree **2** an official written record of something, especially a journey in a ship or plane **3** a S 3

LOGARITHM —see also **it's as easy as falling off a log** (FALL[1] (30)), **sleep like a log/top** (SLEEP[2] (1))

**log**[2] *v* **logged, logging** **1** [T] to make an official record of events, facts etc **2** [T] to travel a particular distance or for a particular length of time, especially in a plane or ship: *The pilot has logged 1200 flying hours.* **3** [I,T] to cut down trees

**log in/on** *phr v* [I] to do the necessary actions on a computer system that will allow you to begin using it

**log off/out** *phr v* [I] to do the actions that are necessary when you finish using a computer system

**lo·gan·ber·ry** /ˈləʊɡənbəri‖ˈloʊɡənberi/ *n* [C] a soft dark red fruit similar to a RASPBERRY —see picture on page 413

**log·a·rith·m** /ˈlɒɡərɪðəm‖ˈlɒː-, ˈlɑː-/ *n* [C] *technical* a number representing another number in a mathematical system so that complicated multiplying may be done as simple addition; LOG[1] (3)

**log book** /ˈ· ·/ *n* [C] **1** *BrE* an official document containing details about a vehicle and the name of its owner **2** a LOG[1] (2)

**log cab·in** /ˌ· ˈ··/ *n* [C] a small house made of logs (LOG[1] (1))

**loge** /ləʊʒ‖loʊʒ/ *n* [C] *AmE* a set of seats at the side of the lower BALCONY in a theatre or concert hall

**log·ger** /ˈlɒɡə‖ˈlɒːɡər, ˈlɑː-/ *n* [C] someone whose job is to cut down trees; LUMBERJACK

**log·ger·heads** /ˈlɒɡəhedz‖ˈlɒːɡər-, ˈlɑː-/ *n* **be at loggerheads (with sb)** if two people or groups are at loggerheads, they disagree very strongly: *Clare's at loggerheads with her boss over the new working hours.*

**log·ging** /ˈlɒɡɪŋ‖ˈlɒː-, ˈlɑː-/ *n* [U] the work of cutting down trees in a forest: *the logging industry*

**lo·gic** /ˈlɒdʒɪk‖ˈlɑː-/ *n* **1** [U] the science or study of careful reasoning using formal methods **2** [U] a set of reasons someone uses in order to reach an opinion: *I couldn't follow Pete's logic.* **3** [singular, U] sensible reasons or reasonable thinking: **there is a (certain) logic in/to** *There is a certain logic in bringing Simon with us because he does know the area.* | **logic behind an idea/statement etc** *I fail to see the logic behind that idea.* **4** [U] *technical* a set of choices that a computer uses to solve a problem

S3 **lo·gic·al** /ˈlɒdʒɪkəl‖ˈlɑː-/ *adj* **1** seeming reasonable and sensible: *It's a logical site for a new supermarket, with the housing development nearby.* | *a logical conclusion* —opposite ILLOGICAL (1) **2** based on a series of facts, reasons, and ideas that are connected in a correct and intelligent way: *The detective has to discover the murderer by logical deduction.* —**logically** /-kli/ *adv* —**logicality** /ˌlɒdʒɪˈkæləti‖ˌlɑː-/ *n* [U]

**lo·gi·cian** /ləˈdʒɪʃən‖loʊ-/ *n* [C] someone who studies or is skilled in logic

**-logist** /lədʒəst/ *suffix* [in nouns] another form of the suffix -OLOGIST

**lo·gis·tics** /ləˈdʒɪstɪks‖loʊ-/ *n* **1 the logistics of** the practical arrangements that are needed in order to make a plan or activity successful: *the complex logistics of supplying food to the famine areas* **2** [U] the study or skill of moving soldiers, supplying them with food etc —**logistic** also **logistical** *adj* —**logistically** /-kli/ *adv*

**log·jam** /ˈlɒɡdʒæm‖ˈlɒːɡ-, ˈlɑːɡ-/ *n* [C] **1** a problem or difficult situation that must be dealt with: *There's a logjam of bills before Congress.* **2** a tightly packed mass of floating LOGS on a river

**LOGO** /ˈləʊɡəʊ‖ˈloʊɡoʊ/ *n* [U] an easy computer language that is often used in schools

**lo·go** /ˈləʊɡəʊ/ *n plural* **logos** [C] a small design that is the official sign of a company or organization

**log·roll·ing** /ˈlɒɡˌrəʊlɪŋ‖ˈlɒːɡˌroʊ-, ˈlɑːɡ-/ *n* [U] **1** *AmE informal* the practice in the US Congress of helping a member to pass a bill, so that they will do the same for you later **2** *AmE* the practice of praising or helping someone, so that they will do the same for you later **3** a sport in which two people stand on and roll a log floating on water, each person trying to make the other fall off

**-logue** also **-log** *AmE* /lɒɡ‖lɒːɡ, lɑːɡ/ *suffix* [in nouns] something spoken; talk: *a monologue* (=speech by one person)

**-logy** /lədʒi/ *suffix* [in nouns] another form of the suffix -OLOGY: *genealogy*

**loin** /lɔɪn/ *n* **1** [C,U] a piece of meat from the lower part of an animal's back **2 loins** [plural] *especially literary* **a)** the part of your body below your waist and above your legs **b)** the area directly around your sexual organs **3 the fruit of your loins** *biblical or humorous* your children —see also **gird (up) your loins** (GIRD (1))

**loin·cloth** /ˈlɔɪnklɒθ‖-klɒːθ/ *n* [C] a piece of cloth that men in some hot countries wear around their loins

**loi·ter** /ˈlɔɪtə‖-ər/ *v* [I] **1** to stand or wait somewhere, especially in a public place, without any clear reason: *Watch out for any strangers loitering in residential streets.* **2** to move or travel slowly, or to keep stopping when you should keep moving: *Don't loiter on the way home, there's heavy snow forecast.* —**loiterer** *n* [C]

**loi·ter·ing** /ˈlɔɪtərɪŋ/ *AmE*, **loitering with in·tent** /ˌ··· ··ˈ·/ *BrE n* [U] *law* the offence of staying in a place for a long time without having any reason to be there, so that it seems as if you are going to do something illegal

**loll** /lɒl‖lɑːl/ *v* **1** [I always + adv/prep] to sit or lie in a very lazy and relaxed way: [**+ around/about/beside etc**] *We spent our vacation lolling around beside the pool.* **2** [I,T] if your head or tongue lolls or if you loll your head, you allow it to hang in a relaxed uncontrolled way

**lol·li·pop** also **lollypop** *AmE* /ˈlɒlipɒp‖ˈlɑːlipɑːp/ *n* [C] **1** *BrE* frozen juice or ICE CREAM on a stick; POPSICLE *AmE* **2** a hard sweet made of boiled sugar on a stick

**lollipop la·dy** /ˈ··· ˌ··/ *n* [C] *BrE* a woman whose job is to help school children cross a road safely

**lollipop man** /ˈ··· ˌ·/ *n* [C] *BrE* a man whose job is to help school children cross a road safely

**lol·lop** /ˈlɒləp‖ˈlɑː-/ *v* [I + **around/across/about**] *informal* to run with long awkward steps: *Simon's dog came lolloping up the beach.*

**lol·ly** /ˈlɒli‖ˈlɑːli/ *n BrE informal* **1** [C] **a)** frozen juice or ICE CREAM on a stick; LOLLIPOP (1) **b)** a hard sweet made of boiled sugar on a stick; LOLLIPOP (2) **2** [U] *old-fashioned* money

**lol·ly·pop** /ˈlɒlipɒp‖ˈlɑːlipɑːp/ *n* [C] an American spelling of LOLLIPOP

**lone** /ləʊn‖loʊn/ *adj* [only before noun] *especially literary* **1** completely alone, and sometimes seeming sad: *a lone figure standing at the bus stop* —see ALONE (USAGE) **2 lone mother/father/parent** someone who is looking after their children on their own

**lone·ly** /ˈləʊnli‖ˈloʊn-/ *adj* **1** unhappy because you are alone and feel that you do not have anyone to talk to: *Don't you get lonely being on your own all day?* **2** *especially literary* a place that is lonely is a long way from where people live and very few people go there: *a lonely beach* —see also LONESOME, ALONE (USAGE) —**loneliness** *n* [U] S3

**lonely hearts** /ˌ·· ˈ·/ *n* **lonely hearts club/page/column** a club or an advertisement page of a newspaper that is used by people who want to meet a friend or a lover

**lon·er** /ˈləʊnə‖ˈloʊnər/ *n* [C] someone who prefers to be alone or someone who has no friends: *Ken's always been a bit of a loner, even at school.*

**lone·some** /ˈləʊnsəm‖ˈloʊn-/ *adj especially AmE* **1** feeling very unhappy because you are alone or have no friends: *Beth is lonesome without the children.* **2** a lonesome place is one that is a long way from where people live and very few people go there: *a lonesome spot near the canyon* **3 on/by your lonesome (self)** *informal* alone: *What are you doing sitting there all on your lonesome?*

**lone wolf** /ˌ· ˈ·/ *n* [C] a loner

S1 W1 **long**[1] /lɒŋ‖lɔːŋ/ *adj*
**1 ▶ OBJECT/LINE ◀** measuring a great length or a greater length than usual from one end to the other: *Cher used to have really long hair.* | *The line to get into the movie was so long we gave up.* | *The Aleutian Islands form the longest archipelago in the world.* —opposite SHORT[1] (1) —see picture on page 412
**2 ▶ TIME ◀** continuing for a large amount of time: *I thought the play was a little too long.* | *recovering from a long illness* | *People who exercise regularly generally live longer, healthier lives.* | **a long time** *They've been married a long time.* | **get longer** *The days are beginning to get longer.* | **for the longest time** *AmE spoken* (=for a very long time) *I thought for the longest time that his name was Don, but it's really Ron.* —opposite SHORT[1] (4)
**3 ▶ DISTANCE ◀** continuing or travelling a great distance from one place to another: *a long distance runner* | **long walk/flight/drive** *It's a long walk to the shops from here.* | **a long way** *We're still a long way from Aberdeen.* —opposite SHORT[1] (4)
**4 ▶ HOW LONG ◀** [usually after noun] having a particular length or continuing for a particular amount of time: *How long is the concert going to be?* | **an hour/two metres/three pages etc long** *The room is about 10 metres long and 5 metres wide.* | *The article should be about 1500 words long.*
**5 ▶ BOOKS/NAMES/LISTS ETC ◀** books, lists etc that are long contain a lot of pages, details etc: *War and Peace is one of the longest novels I've ever read.* | *He has a long, unpronounceable last name.* —opposite SHORT[1] (16)
**6 ▶ CLOTHING ◀** long dresses, trousers, sleeves etc cover your body to the ANKLES or wrists: *a long ballgown*
**7 all day/year/summer etc long** during all of the day etc
**8 ▶ SEEMING TOO LONG ◀** *spoken* seeming to continue for a longer time or distance than is usual, especially because you are bored, tired etc: *It's been a long week and all I want to do is go home.*
**9 ▶ WORK ◀** if you work long hours or a long day, you work for more time than is usual: *Doctors often work long hours.*
**10 go a long way/have come a long way** to be likely to be successful and achieve things, or to have been successful and achieved things: *Genetic research has come a long way in the last few years.*
**11 go a long way towards doing sth** to help greatly in achieving something: *Your contributions will go a long way towards helping children in need.*
**12 a little of sth goes a long way** *spoken* used to say you do not need much of something: *A little ketchup goes a long way.*
**13 at long last** after a long period of time; finally: *The house sold, at long last, in September.*
**14 long time no see** *spoken* used to say hello when you have not seen someone for a long time
**15 the long and the short of it** *spoken* used when you are trying to tell someone something complicated in only a few words: *Well, the long and the short of it is that we missed the train.*
**16 not by a long chalk/shot** *informal* not at all or not nearly: *Oh, I've not finished yet – no, not by a long chalk.*
**17 how long is a piece of string?** *BrE spoken* used when you think there is no certain answer to a question: *"How long will it take to finish?" "How long is a piece of string?"*
**18 a long memory** an ability to remember things that happened a long time ago: *Those of you with long memories may recall Cooper's fight with Muhammad Ali.*
**19 ▶ VOWEL ◀** a long vowel in a word is pronounced for a longer time than a short vowel with the same sound
**20 long odds** if there are long odds against something happening, it is very unlikely that it will happen
**21 long drink a)** a large cold drink, containing little or no alcohol, served in a tall glass **b)** if you take a long drink, you drink a large amount of liquid at one time
**22 long in the tooth** *informal* too old: *Some of our vehicles are getting a bit long in the tooth.* —see also **as long as your arm** (ARM[1] (10)), **a long face** (FACE[1] (2)), **long/slow haul** (HAUL[2] (2)), **in the long run** (RUN[2] (4)), **a long shot** (SHOT[1] (12)), **it's a long story** (STORY (8)), **cut a long story short** (STORY (11)), **in the long/short/medium term** (TERM[1] (10)), **take the long view (of sth)** (VIEW[1] (10))

**long**[2] *adv* **1** for a long time: *Have you been waiting long?* | *It took me longer than I thought it would to paint the kitchen.* | *How long have you lived in New Jersey?* **2** at a time that is a long time before or after a particular time: **long before/after** *This all happened long before you were born.* | **long ago/since** *If they'd stayed out of the war it would have been over long ago.* | **sth won't be long** *especially spoken* (=used when something is going to happen soon) *Dinner won't be long – only five minutes.* | **sb won't be long** *spoken* (=used to say that someone will be ready, back etc soon) *Wait here, I won't be long.* | **it wasn't long before** (=used when something happens very soon after a particular event) *It wasn't long before we realized Dan had left.* **3 no longer/not any longer** used when something used to happen in the past but does not happen now: *The extra workers won't be needed any longer.* **4 for long** [usually in questions and negatives] for a long time: *I haven't known them for very long.* **5 before long** soon: *It looks like it's going to rain before long.* **6 as/so long as** used to say that one thing can happen or be true only if another thing happens or is true: *You can go out to play as long as you stay in the back yard.* **7 so long** *spoken especially AmE* goodbye S1 W1

**long**[3] *v* [I] to want something very much, especially when it seems unlikely to happen soon: **long to do/have sth** *I long to see her again.* | **long for sth** *Patsy longed for some excitement, something new.* | **long for sb to do sth** *I was longing for him to go.* | **longed-for** *the birth of a longed-for daughter* —see also LONGING

**long**[4] the written abbreviation of LONGITUDE

**long-a·wait·ed** /ˌ· ˈ··◂/ *adj* [only before noun] a long-awaited event, moment etc is one that you have been expecting for a long time: *We finally got our long-awaited pay rise.*

**long·boat** /ˈlɒŋbəʊt‖ˈlɔːŋboʊt/ *n* [C] a type of big rowing boat used especially for travelling on the sea

**long·bow** /ˈlɒŋbəʊ‖ˈlɔːŋboʊ/ *n* [C] a large BOW[3] (1) made from a long thin curved piece of wood, used in former times for hunting or fighting

**long-dis·tance** /ˌ· ˈ··◂/ *adj* [only before noun] **1 long-distance runner/driver etc** someone who runs, travels etc a long distance **2 long-distance call** a telephone call to a place that is far away —**long-distance** *adv*

**long di·vi·sion** /ˌ· ·ˈ··/ *n* [C,U] a method of dividing one large number by another

**long-drawn-out** /ˌ· · ˈ·◂/ *adj* continuing for a longer time than necessary: *The official enquiry was a long-drawn-out process.*

**lon·gev·i·ty** /lɒnˈdʒevɪ̣ti‖lɑːn-, lɔːn-/ *n* [U] **1** *formal* long life: *The inhabitants enjoy good health and longevity.* **2** *technical* the length of a person or animal's life

**long·hand** /ˈlɒŋhænd‖ˈlɔːŋ-/ *n* [U] ordinary writing by hand, as opposed to SHORTHAND, TYPING etc

**long-haul** /ˈ· ·/ *adj* a long-haul aircraft or flight goes a very long distance without stopping —compare SHORT-HAUL —see also **long/slow haul** (HAUL[2] (2))

**long·horn** /ˈlɒŋhɔːn‖ˈlɔːŋhɔːrn/ *n* [C] a cow with long horns, kept for meat

**long·house** /ˈlɒŋhaʊs‖ˈlɔːŋ-/ *n* [C] a kind of house, about a hundred feet long, that was used by some NATIVE AMERICAN tribes

**long·ing**[1] /ˈlɒŋɪŋ‖ˈlɔːŋɪŋ/ *n* [singular, U] a strong feeling of wanting something or someone; YEARNING: *an expression of heartfelt longing* | [+ **for**] *a longing for peace*

**longing**[2] *adj* [only before noun] wanting something very much: *a longing glance* —**longingly** *adv*: *Inez was gazing longingly at him.*

**long·ish** /ˈlɒŋɪʃ‖ˈlɔːŋɪʃ/ *adj informal* fairly long

**lon·gi·tude** /ˈlɒndʒɪ̇tjuːd‖ˈlɑːndʒɪ̇tuːd/ *n* [C,U] a position on the Earth that is measured in degrees east or west of a MERIDIAN (=an imaginary line drawn from the top point of the Earth to the bottom): *The town is at longitude 21° east.* —compare LATITUDE (1) —see picture at EARTH[1]

**lon·gi·tu·di·nal** /ˌlɒndʒɪ̇ˈtjuːdɪ̇nəl◂‖ˌlɑːndʒɪ̇ˈtuː-/ *adj* **1** going from top to bottom, not across: *longitudinal muscles* **2** *formal* related to the development of something over a period of time: *longitudinal research on populations* **3** *technical* measured according to longitude —**longitudinally** *adv*

**long johns** /ˈlɒŋ dʒɒnz‖ˈlɔːŋ dʒɑːnz/ *n* [plural] warm underwear with long legs

**long jump** /ˈ· ·/ *n* **the long jump** a sport in which each competitor tries to jump further than anyone else —**long jumper** *n* [C]

**long-last·ing** /ˌ· ˈ··◂/ *adj* continuing for a long time: *long-lasting effects*

**long-life** /ˌ· ˈ·◂/ *adj BrE* long-life milk, batteries etc are treated so that they stay fresh or continue working for a long time

**long-lived** /ˌlɒŋ ˈlɪvd◂‖ˌlɔːŋ ˈlaɪvd/ *adj* living or existing a long time: *He comes from a long-lived family.* | *long-lived discontent* —compare SHORT-LIVED

**long-lost** /ˌ· ˈ·◂/ *adj* [only before noun] lost or not seen for a long time: *long-lost treasures* | **long-lost relative/uncle/friend etc** *a long-lost cousin*

**long-play·ing rec·ord** /ˌ· ·· ˈ··/ also **long-play·er** /ˌ· ˈ··/ *n* [C] an LP

**long-range** /ˌ· ˈ·◂/ *adj* [only before noun] **1** a long-range decision, plan etc is about a period far in the future: *long-range weather forecast* **2** a long-range missile, bomb etc is able to hit something that is a long way away

**long-run·ning** /ˌ· ˈ··◂/ *adj* [only before noun] a long-running battle, show etc has been happening for a long time: *the long-running dispute over farm subsidies*

**long·ship** /ˈlɒŋˌʃɪp‖ˈlɔːŋ-/ *n* [C] a long narrow open ship used by the Vikings

**long·shore·man** /ˈlɒŋʃɔːmən‖ˈlɔːŋʃɔːr-/ *n* [C] someone whose job is to load and unload ships at a DOCK[1] (1); DOCKER *BrE*

**long·sight·ed** /ˌlɒŋˈsaɪtɪ̇d◂‖ˌlɔːŋ-/ *adj especially BrE* able to see objects or read things clearly only when they are far from your eyes; FAR-SIGHTED (2) *AmE* —opposite SHORT-SIGHTED (1)

**long-stand·ing** /ˌ· ˈ··◂/ *adj* having continued or existed for a long time: **long-standing argument/debate etc** *a long-standing feud between the two families* | **long-standing arrangement/offer/relationship etc** *We have a long-standing tradition of hunting every fall.*

**long-suf·fer·ing** /ˌlɒŋˈsʌfərɪŋ◂‖ˌlɔːŋ-/ *adj* patient in spite of problems and other people's annoying behaviour: *Tom goes out drinking every night, leaving his long-suffering wife to look after the children.*

W3 **long-term** /ˌ· ˈ·◂/ *adj* continuing for a long period of time into the future, or connected with what will happen in the distant future: *long-term loans* | *the long-term implications of the crisis* —see also **in the long/short/medium term** (TERM[1] (10))

**long-time** /ˌ· ˈ·◂/ *adj* [only before noun] having existed or continued to be a particular thing for a long time: *a long-time supporter of civil rights*

**long ton** /ˌ· ˈ·/ *n technical* a British unit of weight equal to 2240 pounds

**lon·gueur** /lɒŋˈgɜː‖lɔːŋˈgɜːr/ *n* [C usually plural] *literary* a very boring part of a book or period of time

**long va·ca·tion** /ˌ· ·ˈ··/ also **long vac** /ˌ· ˈ·/ *informal* —*n* [C] *BrE* the period of three months in the summer when university students have holidays; SUMMER VACATION *AmE*

**long wave** /ˌ· ˈ·◂/ written abbreviation **LW** *n* [U] radio broadcasting or receiving on waves of 1000 metres or more in length —compare MEDIUM WAVE, SHORT WAVE

**long·ways** /ˈlɒŋweɪz‖ˈlɔːŋ-/ also **long·wise** /-waɪz/ *AmE adv* in the direction of the longest side; LENGTHWAYS

**long·wear·ing** /ˌlɒŋˈweərɪŋ◂‖ˌlɔːŋˈwer-/ *adj AmE* long-wearing clothes, shoes etc remain in good condition for a long time even when they are used a lot; HARD-WEARING *BrE*

**long·wind·ed** /ˌlɒŋˈwɪndɪ̇d◂‖ˌlɔːŋ-/ *adj* continuing for too long or using too many words in a way that is boring: *Bray's explanation was unnecessarily long-winded.* —**longwindedly** *adv* —**longwindedness** *n* [U]

**long·wise** /ˈlɒŋwaɪz‖ˈlɔːŋ-/ *adv* the usual American form of LONGWAYS; LENGTHWAYS

**loo** /luː/ *n plural* **loos** [C] *BrE informal* a toilet

**loo·fah, loofa** /ˈluːfə/ *n* [C] a rough kind of SPONGE[1] (1), made from the dried inner part of a tropical fruit

**look up**

He looked up the word in his dictionary.

**look**[1] /lʊk/ *v* S1 W1

**1 ▶ SEE ◀** [I] to turn your eyes towards something, so that you can see it: *Sorry, I didn't see – I wasn't looking.* | *If you look carefully you can see that the painting represents a naked man.* | **[+ at]** *"It's time we left," Ian said, looking at his watch.* | *Look at me when I'm talking to you!* | **[+ away/over/down etc]** *Dad looked up from his paper and smiled.* | *I saw you, I was looking through the window.* —see GAZE[1] (USAGE)

**2 ▶ SEARCH ◀** [I] to try and find something using your eyes: *We looked everywhere but we couldn't find it.* | **look in/under/between etc** *Try looking under the bed.*

**3 ▶ SEEM ◀** [linking verb] to seem to be something, especially by having a particular appearance: *How do I look in this dress?* | **look like** *The intruder was holding what looked like a shotgun.* | **look as if** *You look as if you haven't slept all night.* | **it looks as if** (=seems likely) *The cause of death seems clear – it looks as if he was poisoned.* | **look good/impressive etc** *The plan looks good at the moment, but none of the details have been thought of.* | **look happy/pale/tired etc** *I thought Reg was looking very tired.*

**4 be looking to do sth** *informal* to be planning or expecting to do something: *We're looking to buy a new car early next year.*

**5 look daggers at** *informal* to look at someone with a very angry expression on your face

**6 look sb up and down** to look at someone examining them carefully from their head to their feet, as if you are judging their appearance

**7 look sb in the eye/face** to look directly at someone when you are speaking to them, especially to show that you are not afraid of them or that you are telling the truth: *Owen was burning with humiliation. He dared not look his father in the eye.*

**8 look down your nose at** *informal* to behave as if you think that someone or something is not good enough for you: *He looks down his nose at anyone or anything foreign.*

**9 ▶ FACE A DIRECTION ◀** if a building looks in a particular direction, it faces that direction: *The cabin looks east, so we get the sun first thing in the morning.*

**10 look before you leap** used to say that it is wise to think about possible dangers or difficulties before doing something

**look after** sb/sth *phr v* [T] *especially BrE* **1** to take care of someone by helping them, giving them what they need, or keeping them safe: *Don't worry, I'll look after the kids tomorrow.* | *Susan looked after us very well, she's an excellent cook.* | **be well looked after** *You could tell just by looking at the horse that it had been well looked after.* **2** to be responsible for dealing with something: *I'm leaving you here to look after the business until I get back.* **3 look after yourself** *spoken especially BrE* used when you are saying goodbye to someone in a friendly way **4 be able to look after yourself** to not need anyone else to take care of you: *Don't worry about Maisie – she can look after herself.*

**look ahead** *phr v* [I] to plan future situations, events etc, or to think about the future: *Looking ahead, we must expect radical changes to be made in our system of government.*

**look around/round** *BrE phr v* **1** [I] to search: [+ **for**] *Jason's going to start looking around for a new job.* **2** [I,T] to look at what is in a place such as a building, shop, town etc, especially when you are walking: *Do we have to pay to look around the castle?* | *Let's look round the shops.*

**look at** sb/sth *phr v* [T] **1** to turn your eyes towards something, so that you can see it: *The twins looked at each other and smiled.* **2** to read something quickly, but not thoroughly, in order to form an opinion of it: *I really can't comment on the report – you see, I've not had time to look at it yet.* **3** if someone with a special skill, such as a doctor, looks at something that is damaged or broken, they examine it and try to find out what is wrong with it: *You should get the doctor to look at that cut.* | *Can you look at my car? There's a strange noise coming from the front wheel.* **4** to study and consider something, especially in order to decide what to do: *We need to look very carefully at ways of improving our efficiency.* **5 look at ...!** *spoken* used when you are talking about something as an example of a situation: *Look at Mrs Godfrey, smoking killed her!* **6** to think about something in a particular way: *I'd like to be friends again, but Richard doesn't look at it that way.* **7 not much to look at** *informal* if someone is not much to look at, they are not attractive

**look back** *phr v* [I] **1** to think about something that happened in the past: + **on/to** *When I look back on those days I realize I was desperately unhappy.* | **looking back on it** *informal*: *Looking back on it, I still can't figure out what went wrong.* **2 never look back** to become more and more successful, especially after a particular event: *After winning the scholarship he never looked back.*

**look down on** sb/sth *phr v* [T] to think that you are better than someone else, for example because you are more successful, or of a higher social class than they are: *Mr Garcia looks down on anyone who hasn't had a college education.*

**look for** sb/sth *phr v* [T] **1** to try to find something that you have lost, or someone who is not where they should be: *I'm looking for Steve – have you seen him?* | *Detectives are still looking for the prisoner who escaped three days ago.* —see graph at SEARCH[1] **2 be looking for** to be trying to find a particular kind of thing or person that you need or want: *I'm sorry, we're really looking for someone with no family commitments.* | **be what/who you are looking for** *Salubrious! That's just the word I was looking for.* **3 be looking for trouble** *informal* to be behaving in a way that makes it likely that problems will happen: *You're looking for trouble if you say things like that to me!*

**look forward to** *phr v* [T] to be excited and pleased about something that is going to happen: *I'm really looking forward to our vacation.* | **look forward to doing sth** *My mother says she's looking forward to meeting you.* —see WAIT (USAGE)

**look in** *phr v* [I] *informal* to make a short visit to someone, while you are going somewhere else, especially if they are ill or need help: [+ **on**] *I promised to look in on Dad and see if he's feeling any better.*

**look into** sth *phr v* [T] to try to find out the truth about a problem, crime etc in order to solve it: *Police are looking into the disappearance of two children.*

**look on** *phr v* **1** [I] to watch something happening, without being involved in it or trying to stop it: *Only one man tried to help us, the rest just looked on in silence.* **2** also **look upon** [T **look on** sb/sth] to consider something in a particular way, or as a particular thing: [+ **as**] *I look on him as a good friend.* | [+ **with**] *I look upon all my nephews and nieces with equal affection.*

**look** sth ↔ **out** *phr v* [T] to search for and find a particular thing amongst your possessions: *I'll look out some of my old books for you to read.*

**look out for** sth *phr v* [T] **1** [T] to pay attention to what is happening around you, so that you will notice a particular person or thing if you see them: *Look out for your Aunt while you're at the station.* | *He's looking out for a nice apartment downtown.* **2 look out for yourself/for number one** to think only about what will bring you an advantage, and not think about other people

**look** sth/sb ↔ **over** *phr v* [T] to examine something quickly, without paying much attention to detail: *Do you have a few minutes to look these samples over?* —see also OVERLOOK

**look round** *phr v* [I,T] *especially BrE* to LOOK AROUND

**look through** sb/sth *phr v* [T] **1** to look for something among a pile of papers, in a drawer, in someone's pockets etc: *I've looked through all my papers but I still can't find the contract.* **2** to not notice or pretend not to notice someone you know, even though you see them: **look straight/right through sb** *I saw Fiona in the street yesterday and she looked straight through me.*

**look to** sb/sth *phr v* [T] **1** to depend on someone to provide help, advice etc: [+ **for**] *We look to you for support.* | **look to sb to do sth** *They're looking to the new manager to make the company profitable.* **2** to pay attention to something, especially in order to improve it: *We must look to ways of encouraging new ideas.*

**look up** *phr v* **1** [I] if a situation is looking up, it is improving: **things are looking up** *Now the summer's here things are looking up!* **2** [T **look** sth ↔ **up**] if you look up information in a book, on a computer etc, you try to find a particular bit of information there: *Look up the word in the dictionary.* | *I'll just look up the train times.* **3** [T **look** sb ↔ **up**] to visit someone you know, especially when you are in the place where they live for a different reason: *Don't forget to look me up when you come to Atlanta.*

**look up to** sb *phr v* [T] **1** to admire or respect someone: *I've always looked up to Bill for his courage and determination.*

Frequencies of the verb **look** in spoken and written English.

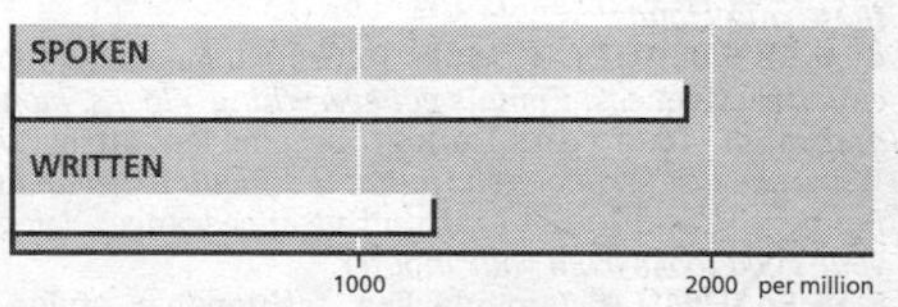


Based on the British National Corpus and the Longman Lancaster Corpus

This graph shows that the verb **look** is much more common in spoken English than in written English. This is because it has special uses in spoken English and is used in a lot of common spoken phrases.

**look** (*v*) **SPOKEN USES AND PHRASES**

**11 look a)** used to tell someone to look at something that you think is interesting, surprising etc: *Look! There's a fox!* **b)** used to get someone's attention so that you can tell them something: *Look. Why don't you think about it and give me your answer tomorrow?* | *Look, I've had enough of this. I'm going home.* **12 it looks like/it looks as if** used to say that something seems to be likely or true: *There are no buses so it looks like we'll be walking home.* **13 look**

**out!** used to warn someone that they are in danger: *Look out! There's a car coming.* **14 Look at that!** used to tell someone to look at something that you think is interesting, bad etc: *Look at that! What a horrible mess!* **15 Look who's here!** used when someone arrives unexpectedly: *Well, look who's here! It's Jill and Paul!* **16 don't look now** used when you see someone you want to avoid: *Oh no! Don't look now but here comes Tony.* **17 look what you're doing/look where you're going etc** used to tell someone to be careful: *Look where you're putting your feet, there's mud all over the carpet.* **18 not be looking yourself** to appear tired, unhappy, ill etc, when you are not usually: *She should take a break – she hasn't been looking herself lately.* **19 look what you've done!** used to angrily tell someone to look at the result of a mistake they have made or something bad they have done: *Look what you've done – my jacket's ruined!* **20 look here** *old-fashioned* used to get someone's attention in order to tell them something, especially when you are annoyed with them: *Look here, you can't say things like that to me!* **21 (I'm) just looking** used when you are in a shop, to say that you are only looking at things, but do not intend to buy anything now: *"Can I help you?" "No, thank you. I'm just looking."*

S1 W1 **look**[2] *n*
**1 ▶ LOOKING AT STH ◀** [C usually singular] an act of looking at something: **have/take a look at** *Let me have a look at that – I think it's mine.* | **have a good/close look** (=look carefully) *If you have a good look you can just see the lighthouse.* | **take one look** *I took one look at the coat and then decided it wasn't worth £50.* —see GLANCE[2] (USAGE) | **have/take a look around** also **have/take a look round** *BrE* (=look at all the things in a particular place) *I have a special interest in old houses. Do you mind if I take a look around?*
**2 ▶ EXPRESSION ◀** [C] an expression that you make with your eyes or face, especially to show someone that you are angry, or that you do not like them: **give sb a look**: *Mike gave him such a severe look he didn't dare argue.* | **dirty look** (=unfriendly look) *Why has Jake been giving me dirty looks all morning?*
**3 ▶ APPEARANCE ◀** [C usually singular] the appearance of something or someone: *The whole area has a very seedy look to it.* | *Mr Flynn had a tired, ill look in his eyes.* | **by the look(s) of it/him** (=it seems that) *The doctor's back from holiday by the looks of it.* | **not like the look of** (=think that something bad has happened or will happen because of something's appearance) *We should turn back now, it's getting dark and I don't like the look of those rain clouds.*
**4 ▶ SB'S BEAUTY ◀ looks** [plural] someone's physical attractiveness: *Fiona's got everything – looks, money and youth.* | **lose your looks** (=become less attractive) *When she lost her looks she found it difficult to get an acting part.* | **good looks** (=attractive appearance) *You get your good looks from your mother.*
**5 ▶ FASHION ◀** [singular] a fashionable style in clothes, hair, furniture etc: *The hippy look is back again.*

**look·a·like** /ˈlʊkəlaɪk/ *n* [C] *informal* someone who looks very similar to someone who is famous: *a Marilyn Monroe lookalike*

**look·er** /ˈlʊkə‖-ər/ *n* [singular] *informal* someone who is attractive, usually a woman: *She's a real looker!*

**looker-on** /ˌ·· ˈ·/ *n plural* **lookers-on** [C] someone who watches something happening without taking part in it; ONLOOKER

**look-in** /ˈ· ·/ *n* [singular] *informal* **1 get/have a look-in** to have a chance to take part in or succeed in something: *Their team was so good that we barely got a look-in.* **2** a short visit —see also **look in** (LOOK[1])

**look·ing glass** /ˈ·· ·/ *n* [C] *old-fashioned* a MIRROR[1] (1)

**look·out** /ˈlʊk-aʊt/ *n*
**1 be on the lookout for** to watch a place or situation continuously in order to find something you want or to be ready for problems or opportunities: *Police were on the lookout for anyone behaving suspiciously.* | *We're always on the lookout for new business opportunities.*
**2 keep a lookout** to keep watching carefully for something or someone, especially for danger: **keep a sharp/special lookout** *When you're driving keep a sharp lookout for cyclists.*
**3 ▶ PERSON ◀** [C] someone whose duty is to watch carefully for something, especially danger: *A lookout reported an enemy plane approaching.*
**4 ▶ PLACE ◀** [C] a place for a lookout to watch from: *a coastguard lookout on the clifftop*
**5 it's your/their own lookout** *BrE spoken* used to say that what someone has chosen to do is their own problem or risk, and no one else's: *If he wants to ruin his health with all these drugs, that's his own lookout.*
**6 be a poor/bad lookout for sb** *BrE spoken* used to say that something bad or unsatisfactory is likely to happen: *It'll be a poor lookout for James if she finds that letter.*

**look-see** /ˌ· ˈ·/ *n* [C] *AmE informal* a quick look at something: **have a look-see** *Can you wait a minute? I just want to have a look-see.*

**loom**[1] /luːm/ *n* [C] a frame or machine on which thread is woven into cloth

**loom**[2] *v* [I] **1** [always + adv/prep] to appear as a large, unclear shape, especially in a threatening way: [**+ up/out/ahead etc**] *A tall figure loomed up out of the mist.* **2** if a problem or difficulty looms, it is likely to happen very soon: *I must start revising – final exams are looming.* **3 loom large** to seem important, worrying, and difficult to avoid: *Fear of failure loomed large in his mind.*

**loon** /luːn/ *n* [C] **1** a large North American bird that eats fish and that makes a long wild sound **2** a silly or strange person —see also **crazy as a loon** (CRAZY[1] (7))

**loon·y** /ˈluːni/ *n* [C] *informal* someone who is crazy or strange: *Her brother's a complete loony.* —**loony** *adj*: *loony ideas*

**loony bin** /ˈ·· ·/ *n* [C] *humorous* a hospital for people who are mentally ill

**loony tune** /ˈ·· ·/ *n* [C] *AmE* a loony

**loop**[1] /luːp/ *n* [C]
**1 ▶ SHAPE OR LINE ◀** a shape like a curve or a circle made by a line curving back towards itself: *The road formed a loop around the peninsula.*
**2 ▶ TO FASTEN STH ◀** something that has this curved shape, especially when used as a handle or to hold something in place: *a belt loop* | *The best bicycle locks are made of a loop of solid metal.*
**3 ▶ IN WOMAN'S BODY ◀** a curved metal or plastic object that is put inside a woman's UTERUS (=place where a baby develops) to prevent her from becoming PREGNANT
**4 ▶ COMPUTER ◀** a set of commands in a computer PROGRAM[1] (1) that are intended to be followed repeatedly
**5 ▶ PLANE ◀** a pattern like a circle made by a plane flying upwards, backwards, and then downwards
**6 ▶ FILM/TAPE ◀** a film or TAPE[1] (1a) loop contains images or sounds that are repeated again and again
**7 ▶ RAILWAY ◀** a railway line that leaves the main track and then joins it again further on
**8 in the loop/out of the loop** *AmE informal* part of a group of people who make decisions about important subjects, or not part of this group: *White House officials insist the Secretary of State is still in the loop.*
**9 knock/throw sb for a loop** *AmE informal* to surprise and upset someone: *Yeah, the news really knocked me for a loop.*

**loop**[2] *v* **1** [T always + adv/prep] to fasten or join something with a loop: **loop sth over/around/together etc** *Loop the wire over the gate to keep it shut.* **2** [I,T] to make a loop or make something into a loop: *a rug with looped threads* **3** [I] to move in a circular direction that forms the shape of a loop: *little streams that loop through the valley* **4 loop the loop** to fly a plane in a loop

**loop·hole** /ˈluːphəʊl‖-hoʊl/ *n* [C] a small mistake in a law that makes it possible to avoid doing something that the law is supposed to make you do: *tax loopholes*

**loop·y** /ˈluːpi/ *adj informal* **1** crazy or strange **2 go loopy** *spoken* **a)** *BrE* to become extremely angry **b)** to become mentally ill

S3 W3 **loose¹** /luːs/ *adj*
**1 ▶ NOT FIXED ◀** not firmly fixed in place: *One of my buttons is loose.*| *a loose floorboard*| **come/work loose** (=become loose) *A piece of stair carpet had come loose.*
**2 ▶ ROPE/CHAIN ETC ◀** a rope, chain etc that is loose is not fastened as firmly or pulled as tight as it should be
**3 ▶ CLOTHES ◀** clothes that are loose are big and do not fit your body tightly: *a loose sweatshirt*
**4 ▶ FREE ◀** an animal or person that is loose is free to move around and not tied to anything or shut in anywhere: **break/get loose** (=get free) *Somehow the horses had broken loose during the night.*| **turn/let sth loose** (=let something go free) *Don't let your dog loose if there are any sheep around.*
**5 ▶ NOT TOGETHER ◀** not tied together, fastened to anything else, or put together in one package: *Do they sell these olives loose?*| *Do you like loose tea, or teabags?*| *Her hair fell loose around her shoulders.*
**6 ▶ CLOTH/A KNOT ETC ◀** tied or woven in a way that is not tight: *a loose knot*| *a loose weave*
**7 ▶ NOT EXACT ◀** [usually before noun] not exact or thoroughly done: **loose translation/interpretation etc** *This is only a loose translation of the original paper.*
**8 ▶ NOT CONTROLLED ◀** not strictly controlled or organized: *a loose, informal trading system*
**9 ▶ IMMORAL ◀** *old-fashioned* behaving in a way that is considered to be sexually immoral: *a loose woman*
**10 ▶ TALK ◀** *old-fashioned* not careful about what you say or who is listening: *There's been a bit of loose talk about it.*
**11 ▶ BODY WASTE ◀** *not technical* having a problem in which the waste from your BOWELS has too much liquid in it: *loose motions*| *He's a bit loose in the mornings.*
**12 cut loose a)** to free yourself from the influence of someone or something: *Anna had finally managed to cut loose from her father's domineering influence.* **b)** *AmE informal* to start enjoying yourself in a happy, noisy way after a period of controlled behaviour: *After the exams we'll really have a chance to cut loose.*
**13 let sb loose on sth** to allow someone to deal with something in the way they want to: *Whatever you do, don't let Derek loose on the garden!*
**14 be at a loose end** also **be at loose ends** *AmE* to have nothing to do: *I was at a loose end so I decided to go see an old movie.*
**15 loose ends** parts of something that have not been completed or properly done: **tie up the loose ends** (=complete something, or deal with any remaining problems) *It's a good report but there are still a few loose ends to be tied up.*
**16 loose change** coins that you have in your bag or pocket: *I've got twenty quid and a bit of loose change as well.*
**17 hang/stay loose** *AmE spoken* used to tell someone to stay calm, or not to worry about something: **—loosely** *adv*: *Just tie it loosely.*| *Loosely translated it means 'watch out'.* **—looseness** *n* [U]

**loose²** *v* [T] **1** to untie someone or something, especially an animal **2** *literary* to fire an ARROW (1), a shot from a gun etc **3** to make something unpleasant begin: *The recent court case has loosed a spate of racist attacks.*
**loose** sth **on/upon** *phr v* [T] to allow something dangerous or destructive to begin to affect a situation or other people: *A potentially lethal drug has been loosed upon unsuspecting kids looking for a quick high.*

**loose³** *adv* loosely —see also **play fast and loose with** (FAST² (10))

**loose⁴** *n* **be on the loose** if a criminal or dangerous animal is on the loose, they have escaped from prison or from their cage

**loose-fit·ting** /ˌ· ˈ··◂/ *adj* loose-fitting clothes are loose on your body, so that they are comfortable: *wearing jeans and a loose-fitting jacket*

**loose-leaf** /ˌ· ˈ·◂/ *adj* having pages that can be put in and removed easily: *a loose-leaf binder*

**loos·en** /ˈluːsən/ *v* **1** [I,T] to make something less tight or less firmly fixed, or to become less tight or less firmly fixed: *You'll need a spanner to loosen that bolt.*| *Check the plug – there may be a loosened connection.* **2** [T] to unfasten something, especially something you are wearing: *Harry loosened his tie.* **3** [T] to make laws, rules etc less strict: *It was time to loosen economic constraints.* **4 loosen your grip/hold a)** to reduce the control or power you have over someone or something: *as communism began to loosen its hold on eastern Europe* **b)** to start holding someone less tightly than you were before: [+ **on**] *The policeman loosened his grip on my arm.* **5 loosen sb's tongue** to make someone talk more freely than usual, for example by making them drunk
**loosen up** *phr v* **1** [I, T **loosen** sth ↔ **up**] to exercise your muscles and joints to make them work more easily, especially before playing a sport or running; WARM-UP (1) **2** [I] to stop worrying and become more relaxed: *Try and loosen up a bit!*

**loot¹** /luːt/ *n* [U] **1** *informal old-fashioned* goods or money that have been stolen **2** goods taken by soldiers from a place where they have won a battle **3** *AmE informal humorous* things that you have bought or been given in large amounts: *Jodie came home from the mall with sacks of loot.*

**loot²** *v* [I, T] to steal things, especially from shops or homes that have been damaged in a war or RIOT²: *Shops were looted and burned down.* **—looting** *n* [U] **—looter** *n* [C]

**lop** /lɒp‖lɑːp/ *v* **lopped, lopping** [T] to cut branches from a tree, especially with a single strong movement
**lop** sth **off** *phr v* [T] **1** to cut a part of something off, especially a branch of a tree **2** to remove a particular amount from a price or charge: *They lopped $15 off the price.*

**lope** /ləʊp‖loʊp/ *v* [I always + adv/prep] to run easily with long steps: [+ **along/across/up etc**] *Brad loped across the field towards home.* **—lope** *n* [singular]

**lop-eared** /ˌ· ˈ·◂/ *adj* a lop-eared animal such as a rabbit has long ears that hang down

**lop·sid·ed** /ˌ· ˈ··◂/ *adj* **1** having one side that is lower or heavier than the other: *a lopsided grin* **2** unequal or uneven in a way that seems unfair: *a lopsided ratio of men to women*

**lo·qua·cious** /ləʊˈkweɪʃəs‖loʊ-/ *adj formal* liking to talk a lot, sometimes too much **—loquaciously** *adv* **—loquacity** /ləʊˈkwæsɪ̣ti‖loʊ-/ *n* [U]

**lo·quat** /ˈləʊkwɒt‖ˈloʊkwɑːt/ *n* [C] the small yellowish fruit of a tree that grows mostly in China and Japan

**Lord** /lɔːd‖lɔːrd/ *n* [singular] **1** also **the Lord** a title of God or Jesus Christ: *Thank you, Lord, for your blessings.* **2 the Lords a)** the members of the British House of Lords considered as a group **b)** the House of Lords **3 Lord (only) knows** *spoken* used when you do not know the answer to something: *Lord knows where I left that bag.* **4 (good) Lord!/Oh Lord!** *spoken* used when you are suddenly surprised, annoyed or worried about something: *Good Lord! Is that the time?* **5 Lord willing** *spoken* used to say that you hope nothing will prevent something from happening: *We'll finally be able to take that trip this year, Lord willing.* **6 the Lord's Day** Sunday, considered as the holy day of the Christian religion **7** *BrE* the title of someone who has a particular type of official job: *Lord Mayor of London*

**lord¹** *n* **1** [C] a man who has a rank in the ARISTOCRACY, especially in Britain, or his title: *Lord Hailsham* —compare LADY (7) **2** [C] a man in medieval Europe who was very powerful and owned a lot of land: *the feudal lords*

**3 my lord** used to address a judge or BISHOP (1) in Britain, and in the past to address a lord **4 your lord and master** *humorous* someone who must be obeyed because they have power over you

**lord²** *v* **lord it over sb** to behave in a way that shows you think you are better or more powerful than someone else: *the outer office where Carol lorded it over her assistants*

**lord·ly** /ˈlɔːdli‖-ɔːr-/ *adj* **1** behaving in a way that shows you think you are better or more important than other people: *Sebastian has a lordly disdain for such everyday affairs.* **2** very grand or impressive: *a lordly feast* —**lordliness** *n* [U]

**lord·ship** /ˈlɔːdʃɪp‖-ɔːr-/ *n* [C] **1 your/his lordship** used when talking to or talking about a LORD¹ (1), or when addressing a British judge or BISHOP (1) **2 his lordship** *BrE spoken* a humorous way of talking about a man who thinks he is very important: *So when will his lordship be back?* **3** [U + **over**] the power of a lord or the period of time when he rules —compare LADYSHIP (1)

**Lord's Prayer** /ˌ· ˈ·/ *n* **the Lord's Prayer** the most important prayer of the Christian religion

**lore** /lɔː‖lɔːr/ *n* [U] knowledge or information about a subject, for example nature or magic, that is not written down but is passed from person to person: *This story has become part of the county lore of Ayrshire.*

**lor·gnette** /lɔːˈnjet‖-lɔːr-/ *n* [C] a pair of GLASSES with a long handle at the side that you hold in front of your eyes

**lorn** /lɔːn‖lɔːrn/ *adj poetical* sad and lonely; FORLORN —see also LOVELORN

S3 **lor·ry** /ˈlɒri‖ˈlɔːri, ˈlɑːri/ *n* [C] *BrE* **1** a large vehicle for carrying heavy goods; TRUCK¹ (1) **2 it fell off the back of a lorry** *spoken humorous* used to say that something was probably stolen

S1 W1 **lose** /luːz/ *v past tense and past participle* **lost** /lɒst‖lɔːst/

**1 ▶NOT HAVE ANY MORE◀** [T] to stop having something that is important to you or that you need: *I can't afford to lose my job, I have a family to support.* | *I lost a lot of money on that deal.* | *We're going to lose five teachers when the schools are merged.* | **lose everything** *If they're lucky they'll make a fortune, if they're unlucky they stand to lose everything.*

**2 ▶NOT WIN◀** [I,T] to not win a game, argument, war etc: *I'm not playing tennis with her any more – I always lose.* | **lose to/against** *Cuba lost to Canada in the world volleyball championships.* | **lose a game/fight/election etc** *Are they in danger of losing this battle?* | **lose by 1 goal/10 votes/20 points etc** *Smithson lost by 7,008 votes.* | **lose sb sth** (=be the reason why someone does not win something) *Allegations of corruption lost him the election.* —opposite WIN¹ (1)

**3 ▶CANNOT FIND◀** [T] to be unable to find someone or something: *Whatever you do, don't lose those keys.* | *Make sure you don't lose each other in the crowd.*

**4 lose your memory/sight/voice etc** to stop having a particular ability or sense: *She lost her sight in a car accident.* | **lose your voice** (=temporarily not be able to speak) *A few days before our first concert I got a cold and lost my voice.*

**5 lose an arm/leg etc** to have an arm, leg etc cut off after injury in an accident or in war: *He lost his right arm in a motorbike accident.*

**6 lose your temper/head/nerve etc** to become angry, nervous etc: *It is vital that you do not lose your head* (=that you manage to stay calm) *even in the most serious crisis.* | *I really wanted to do the jump, but lost my nerve* (=stopped feeling brave and confident) *at the last minute.*

**7 lose your way/bearings** to not know where you are or which direction you should go: *It's very easy to lose your way in the forest.*

**8 lose your balance/footing** to become unsteady or fall: *Sam lost his footing on the snowy bank.*

**9 lose interest/hope/heart etc** to stop being interested in something, having hope etc: *Don't lose heart —there are plenty of other jobs you could apply for.*

**10 lose your mother/father/wife etc** used to say that someone's mother etc has died: *Paul's been very depressed since losing his mother.* | **lose the baby** (=used when a woman's baby dies before it is born)

**11 lose weight** to become thinner: *Kay's lost a lot of weight.* | **lose 20lbs/3st/5kg** *I'd like to lose at least 7 pounds before I go on vacation.*

**12 lose your mind** to become crazy or to stop behaving sensibly: *Have you lost your mind? It's really dangerous to go climbing there without a guide.*

**13 lose your life** to die: *His grandfather lost his life in a mining accident.*

**14 ▶TIME◀** [T] to waste time because of delays, INTERRUPTIONS etc: **lose time/2days/3hours etc** *We lost a lot of valuable time waiting for the others to arrive.* | **there's no time to lose** (=it is neccessary to hurry) *Hurry, there's no time to lose.* | **lose no time in doing sth** (=do something immediately) *George could see how serious it was and lost no time in calling the doctor.* —opposite GAIN¹ (8)

**15 ▶CLOCK/WATCH◀** [T] if a clock or watch loses time, it works too slowly: **lose time/5 minutes/1 hour** *This old watch loses about 2 minutes in every hour.* —opposite GAIN¹ (9)

**16 ▶CONFUSE◀** to confuse someone when you are trying to explain something to them: *I'm sorry, you've lost me now – could you start again?*

**17 ▶ESCAPE FROM◀** to escape from someone who is chasing or following you: *His car was much faster but I eventually managed to lose him.*

**18 lose yourself in sth** to be so involved in something that you do not notice anything else: *It's easy to lose yourself in the magic of this film.*

**19 have nothing to lose** to be in a situation in which you should attempt to do something, because you may be successful, and it will not make things worse if you are not: *You might as well apply for the job – you've got nothing to lose.*

**20 have a lot to lose/have too much to lose** to be in a situation in which you will suffer very much if you do not succeed in doing something

**21 lose sight of a)** to stop being able to see someone or something: *Soon we had lost sight of the boat as it sailed off downstream.* **b)** to forget to consider something important: *She was enjoying herself so much, she'd almost lost sight of the purpose of her visit.*

**22 lose touch (with) a)** to not speak to, write to, or see someone for a long time, so that you do not know where they are: *I've lost touch with all my old school friends.* **b)** to not know the most recent information about something and therefore be unable to understand it properly: *When you're living abroad it's so easy to lose touch with what's happening back home.*

**23 lose it** *spoken* **a)** to become crazy: *I reckon Jack's losing it – he was walking the dog in his pyjamas.* **b)** be unable to stop yourself laughing, crying, shouting etc: *Then she started doing this funny little dance and I just lost it completely.*

**24 lose face** to do something that makes people not trust or respect you any more, especially in a public situation

**25 lose height** if an aircraft loses height it falls to a lower height in the sky

**lose out** *phr v* [I] to not get something such as a job, business contract, or profit because someone else gets it instead: *On this occasion both the dealer and the client lost out.* | **lose out to sb** *We lost out to a French company as they could do the job more cheaply.* | **lose out on sth** *Why is it that women always seem to lose out on career opportunities?*

**los·er** /ˈluːzə‖-ər/ *n* [C] **1** someone who has lost a competition or game: *The losers walked dejectedly off the field.* | **good/bad loser** (=someone who behaves well or badly after losing) **2** someone who is in a worse situation than they were, because of something that has happened: *The real losers if Bailey died would be his kids.* **3** someone who is never successful in life, work, or relationships: **a born loser** *I swear Joe's a born loser.*

S2 W1 **loss** /lɒs‖lɔːs/ *n*
**1** ▶ **NO LONGER HAVING STH** ◀ [C, U] the fact of no longer having something you used to have: *Job losses were common in the 1980s.*|[+ **of**] *a temporary loss of memory*|**weight/blood etc loss**|*rapid hair loss*
**2** ▶ **MONEY** ◀ [C,U] money that has been lost by a business, person, government etc: *losses amounting to £12,000*|*profit and loss*|**make a loss** *The company made a loss of $250,000 in its first year.*|**sell/operate sth at a loss** (=sell something or do something with the result that you have less money than you had in the beginning)
**3** ▶ **LIFE** ◀ [C, U] the death of someone: *My sympathy for your loss.* (=of someone you love)|**suffer heavy losses** *The US forces withdrew after suffering heavy losses.*|**loss of life** *formal*: *The blaze was overcome without loss of life.*
**4 be at a loss** to be confused and uncertain about what to do or say: *I was at a complete loss as to how to find the money in time.*|**be at a loss for words** (=be unable to think what to say)
**5** ▶ **FEELING** ◀ [U] a feeling of being sad or lonely because someone or something is not there any more: **sense of loss** *I still feel an aching sense of loss, even though Allen died four years ago.*
**6** ▶ **PROBLEM** ◀ [singular] a disadvantage caused by someone or something leaving or being removed: **a great loss** *We see your going as a great loss to the company.*
**7 that's your/their loss** *spoken* used to say that something will affect someone in a much worse way than it will affect you: *Well, if he doesn't want to come it's his loss.*
**8** ▶ **GAME** ◀ [C] an occasion on which a competition or game is lost; DEFEAT[2]: [+ **to**] *The loss to the Lions meant we were out of the playoffs.* —see also **cut your losses** (CUT[1] (31)), **a dead loss** (DEAD[1] (13))

**loss ad·just·er** /ˈ· ·ˌ··/ *n* [C] *BrE* someone who is employed by an insurance company to decide how much should be paid to people who make CLAIMS on their insurance; INSURANCE ADJUSTER *AmE*

**loss lead·er** /ˈ· ˌ··/ *n* [C] something that is sold at a very low price to make people go into a shop

S2 W3 **lost¹** /lɒst‖lɔːst/ *adj*
**1** ▶ **CANNOT BE FOUND** ◀ something that is lost is something you had but cannot now find; MISSING: *The lost file eventually turned up among Branson's papers.*
**2** ▶ **CANNOT FIND YOUR WAY** ◀ unable to find your way or not knowing where you are: *Police are generally happy to give directions to lost tourists.*|**get lost** (=become lost) *I got thoroughly lost on the way here.*
**3** ▶ **WASTED** ◀ [only before noun] not used properly; wasted: *It'll be impossible to make up the lost time.*|**lost opportunities/chances etc** *lost market opportunities*
**4 feel/be lost (in the crowd)** to not feel confident about what to do or how to behave, especially among people you do not know: *Will your child feel lost at a nursery?*
**5 Get lost!** *spoken* used to tell someone rudely to go away
**6** ▶ **IN THOUGHT ETC** ◀ [not before noun] thinking so hard about something or being so interested in something that you do not notice what is happening around you: [+ **in**] *I was lost in the beauty of the scenery.*|**lost in thought** *Poirot remained lost in thought.*|**lost to the world** *Alex sat reading, lost to the world.*
**7 get lost (in sth)** to be forgotten or not noticed in a complicated process or busy time: *It's easy for your main points to get lost in a long speech.*
**8** ▶ **NOT UNDERSTAND** ◀ **be lost** to be completely confused by a complicated explanation: *"Did you understand the instructions?" "No, I'm totally lost."*
**9 be lost on sb** if something is lost on someone, they do not understand or want to accept it: *All my warnings were completely lost on Beth.*
**10 be lost for words** to be unable to say anything because you are very surprised, upset etc: *It's not often Glenda's lost for words.*
**11** ▶ **NOT EXISTING** ◀ not existing or owned any more: *the lost dreams of her youth*
**12** ▶ **DESTROYED/KILLED** ◀ destroyed, ruined, or killed: **lost at sea/lost in battle etc** *The whole crew was lost at sea.*
**13 a lost cause** something that has no chance of succeeding: *Trying to interest my son in classical music is a lost cause.*
**14 lost soul** *often humorous* someone who does not seem know where they are or what to do —see also **give sb up for dead/lost etc** (GIVE[1]), **make up for lost time** (MAKE[1]), **there is no love lost between** (LOVE[2] (11))

**lost²** the past tense and past participle of LOSE

**lost-and-found** /ˌ· · ˈ·/ *n* **the lost-and-found** a place where things that are lost are kept until someone comes to claim them; LOST PROPERTY *BrE*

**lost prop·er·ty** /ˌ· ˈ···/ *n BrE* **1** [U] things that have been found in public places because people have lost or forgotten them **2** [C] also **lost property office** *BrE* a place where these things are kept until someone comes to claim them; LOST-AND-FOUND

**lot** /lɒt‖lɑːt/ *n* S1 W1
**1** ▶ **LARGE AMOUNT** ◀ **a lot** also **lots** *informal* a large quantity or number: *The stereo cost a lot, but it was worth it.*|*"How much ice cream do you want?" "Lots, please."*|[+ **of**] *There were lots of people at the party.*|**a lot to do/see/eat etc** *There's a lot to do before the wedding.*|**an awful lot** (=a very large amount) —see graph at MANY
**2** ▶ **MUCH** ◀ [+ comparative] if something is a lot or lots better, easier etc, it is much better, easier etc: *Benny can run lots faster than me.*|*Andrea always had a lot more money than I had.*
**3 have a lot on** *BrE*/**have a lot going on** *AmE* to be very busy, with a lot of things to do in a short time
**4 have a lot on your mind** to have a lot of problems that you are worried about
**5 thanks a lot** *spoken* **a)** thank you very much **b)** used when you are annoyed about something and do not really mean thank you at all: *"I forgot to bring your money." "Well, thanks a lot!"*
**6** ▶ **TO BE SOLD** ◀ [C] something that is sold, especially at an AUCTION[1]: *Lot fifteen was a box of old books.*
**7 have a lot to answer for** to be responsible for a bad situation: *Jerry's got a lot to answer for. If it weren't for him, Ann would never have left Denver.*
**8 the lot** *especially BrE* the whole quantity or number: *I can't believe you ate the whole lot!*
**9** ▶ **FILM** ◀ [C] a building and the land surrounding it where films are made; a film STUDIO (2): *the Universal Studios lot*
**10** ▶ **SB'S LOT** ◀ *sometimes humorous* the work, responsibilities, social position etc that you have, especially when they could be better: *She seems happy enough with her lot in life.*
**11** ▶ **PEOPLE** ◀ [singular] *BrE informal* a group of people, especially one you do not completely approve of: *Come on you lot, hurry up!*|**the lot of you/them etc** (=all of you, them etc) *Outside, the lot of you!*
**12** ▶ **GROUP OF THINGS** ◀ *BrE informal* a group of things: *Let's drop this lot off and go home.*
**13** ▶ **OF LAND** ◀ [C] *especially AmE* an area of land used for building on or for another particular purpose: *We could turn that vacant lot into a playground.*|*a used-car lot* —see also PARKING LOT
**14 have a lot on your plate** *informal especially BrE* to have a lot of difficult problems to deal with: *Leave Mum alone – she's got a lot on her plate at the moment.*
**15 draw lots** to decide on someone or something by choosing one piece of paper, object etc from among many: *They drew lots to see who would go first.*
**16 throw in/cast your lot with sb** to join or support someone, so that what happens to you depends on what happens to them: *They threw their lot in with the allies.*
**17 by lot** by drawing lots: *In Athens at that time, judges were chosen by lot.* —see also **bad egg/lot/sort/type** (BAD[1] (16)), **fall to sb's lot** (FALL[1]), **a fat lot of good/use** (FAT[1] (5))

**loth** /ləʊθ‖loʊθ/ *adj* [not before noun] another spelling of LOATH

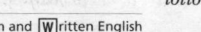

**lo·tion** /ˈləʊʃən‖ˈloʊ-/ *n* [C,U] a liquid mixture that you put on your skin or hair to clean or protect it: *suntan lotion*

**lot·sa** /ˈlɒtsə‖ˈlɑːt-/ *quantifier spoken* a short form of 'lots of'

S3 **lot·te·ry** /ˈlɒtəri‖ˈlɑː-/ *n* **1** [C] a system of raising money for the state or a CHARITY (2), in which people buy numbered tickets and some people win prizes: *a lottery ticket* —compare RAFFLE[1], DRAW[2] (2) **2** [singular] an uncertain or risky situation: *The legal system is nothing but a lottery these days.*

**lo·tus** /ˈləʊtəs‖ˈloʊ-/ *n* [C] **1** a white or pink flower that grows on the surface of lakes in Asia: *lotus blossom* **2** the shape of this flower used in decorative patterns, especially in ancient Egyptian art **3** a fruit that gives you a pleasant dreamy feeling after you eat it, according to Ancient Greek stories

**lotus-eat·er** /ˈ·· ˌ··/ *n* [C] someone who has a lazy, pleasant life and is not interested in other things

**loud**[1] /laʊd/ *adj* **1** making a lot of noise: *a loud bang*| *That music's too loud.* **2** someone who is loud talks too loudly and confidently: *The more Tom drank, the louder he became.* **3** loud clothes are unpleasantly bright: *Butch was wearing a loud checked suit.* **4 be loud in your praise/opposition etc** to express your approval or disapproval very strongly —**loudly** *adv* —**loudness** *n* [U]

**loud**[2] *adv* **1** loudly: *Could you speak a little louder?*| *You've got the telly on too loud.* **2 loud and clear** in a way that is very easily understood: *Sally got her message across loud and clear.* **3 out loud** in such a way that people can hear you; ALOUD: *Read it out loud, so we can all hear.*| *If you've got anything to say, say it out loud.*| **laugh out loud** *Leo laughed out loud at her suggestion.* —see also **actions speak louder than words** (ACTION (15), **for crying out loud** (CRY[1] (8))

**loud·hail·er** /ˌlaʊdˈheɪlə‖-ər/ *n* [C] *especially BrE* a thing shaped like a tube that is wide at one end, that you speak through to make your voice louder; MEGAPHONE

**loud·mouth** /ˈlaʊdmaʊθ/ *n* [C] someone who talks too much and says offensive or stupid things —**loud-mouthed** /ˈlaʊdmaʊðd/ *adj*

**loud·speak·er** /ˌlaʊdˈspiːkə, ˈlaʊdˌspiːkə‖-ər/ *n* [C] **1** a SPEAKER (3) **2** a piece of equipment used to make sounds louder: *Music blared from a loudspeaker.*

**lough** /lɒk, lɒx‖lɑːk, lɑːx/ *n* [C] *IrE* a lake or a part of the sea almost surrounded by land: *Lough Neagh*

**lounge**[1] /laʊndʒ/ *n* [C] **1** a small comfortable public room in a hotel or other building used by many people: *the television lounge* **2** a WAITING ROOM at an airport: *the departure lounge.* **3** *especially BrE* a comfortable room where you relax in your home **4** *BrE* a lounge bar —see also COCKTAIL LOUNGE, SUN LOUNGE

**lounge**[2] *v* [I] **1** [always + adv/prep] to stand or sit in a lazy way: [+ **in/on etc**] *young lads lounging in doorways* **2 lounge around/about** *BrE* to spend time doing nothing: *He was just lounging around all day.*

**lounge bar** /ˈ· ·/ *n* [C] *BrE* a room with comfortable furniture in a PUB; SALOON BAR

**loung·er** /ˈlaʊndʒə‖-ər/ *n* [C] **1** someone who is lazy and does no work **2** a piece of garden furniture like a light narrow bed, used for lying in the sun; SUN LOUNGER *AmE*

**lounge suit** /ˈ· ·/ *n* [C] *BrE old-fashioned* a suit that a man wears during the day, especially to work in an office; BUSINESS SUIT *AmE*

**lour** /ˈlaʊə‖-ər/ *v* [I] a British spelling of LOWER[3]

**louse**[1] /laʊs/ *n* [C] **1** *plural* **lice** a small wingless insect that lives on people's or animals' skin and hair **2** *plural* **louses** *informal* someone who is nasty and unpleasant: *"You louse!" she yelled.*

**louse**[2] *v*

**louse up** *phr v AmE informal* **1** [T **louse** sth **up**] to make something worse rather than better, or to spoil something: *I don't want to louse up your life.* **2** [I] to do something badly: [+ **on**] *Chris really loused up on his exams.*

**lou·sy** /ˈlaʊzi/ *adj* **lousier, lousiest** **1** *especially spoken* very bad, unpleasant etc: *What lousy weather!*| *I feel lousy.* **2** *spoken* small, useless, or unimportant: *Harry wouldn't lend me ten lousy quid!* **3 lousy with sth** *AmE spoken* **a)** a place that is lousy with people of a particular kind is too full of them: *The town was lousy with tourists.* **b)** someone who is lousy with money has a lot more of it than they need **4** covered with lice (LOUSE[1] (1))

**lout** /laʊt/ *n* [C] a rude, violent man: *Get up, you lazy lout!* —see also **lager lout** (LAGER (2)), —**loutish** *adj* —**loutishly** *adv* —**loutishness** *n* [U]

**lou·vre** *BrE*, **louver** *AmE* /ˈluːvə‖-ər/ *n* [C] **1** a narrow piece of wood, glass etc, in a door or window, sloping outwards to let some light in and keep rain or strong sun out **2 louvre window/door** a door or window made of these pieces of wood, glass etc —**louvred** *adj*: *louvred shutters*

**lov·a·ble, loveable** /ˈlʌvəbəl/ *adj* friendly and attractive: *a lovable kitten*| *not a very lovable child*

**love**[1] /lʌv/ *v* S1 W1

**1 ▶ ROMANTIC ATTRACTION ◀** [T not in progressive] to have a strong feeling of caring for and liking someone, combined with sexual attraction: *I love you, really. Do you love me?*| *He was the only man she had ever loved.*

**2 ▶ CARE ABOUT ◀** [T not in progressive] to care very much about someone, especially a member of your family or a close friend: *Children need to feel loved.*| **much-loved/greatly-loved/well-loved** *one of America's best-loved TV personalities*| **loved ones** (=people you love) *women caring for loved ones who had been injured in the war*

**3 ▶ LIKE/ENJOY ◀** [T not in passive] to like something very much or enjoy doing something very much: **love doing sth** *Max found that he really loved teaching.*| **love sth** *I love carrots.*| *She loves anything to do with figures.*| **love to do sth** *We all love to talk about ourselves.*| *I love the way she sings that.*| **I'd love to** *spoken* (=used to say you would really like to do something) *"Would you like to come swimming with us?" "I'd love to."*| *I'd have loved to have stayed till the end.*| *I'd love to know just why they did that.*

**4 I must love you and leave you** *spoken* used to tell someone that you have to go, especially when you wish you could stay longer

**5 ▶ LOYALTY ◀** [T not in progressive] to have a strong feeling of loyalty to your country, an institution etc: *He really loved the police force.*

**6 I love it!** *spoken* used when you are amused by something, especially by someone else's mistake or bad luck: *"Henry was telling the prof all about relativity." "I love it! I love it!"*

**7 she's going to love you/he's going to love this etc** *spoken* **a)** used to say that someone will enjoy something: *Listen guys, you're going to love this.* **b)** used jokingly to say that someone will not be pleased about something: *You did what? Oh, they're gonna love you, aren't they!?* —see also LOVER

**love**[2] *n* S1 W1

**1 ▶ FOR FAMILY/FRIENDS ◀** [U] a strong feeling of caring about someone, especially a member of your family or a close friend: *What these kids need is love and support.*| [+ **for**] *a mother's love for her child* —opposite HATE[2], HATRED

**2 ▶ ROMANTIC ◀** [U] a strong feeling of liking and caring about someone, especially combined with sexual attraction: *She's seen him every day this week – it must be love!*| *a love song*| **be/fall in love (with)** *I think I'm falling in love with your brother.*| **madly in love/very much in love/head over heels in love** *It was obvious that they were very much in love.*| **love at first sight** (=when you love someone the first time you see them)| **true love** (=strong romantic love that remains for ever)

**3 ▶ PERSON YOU LOVE ◀** [C] someone that you feel a strong romantic and sexual attraction to: *He was her first love.*| **the love of your life** (=the person that you have loved most of your life)

**4 ▶ PLEASURE/ENJOYMENT ◀** **a)** [singular, U] a strong feeling of pleasure and enjoyment that something gives you: **love of/for** *a love of nature* **b)** [C] something that gives you a lot of pleasure and enjoyment: *Sailing was her great love.*

**5 make love** **a)** to have sex with someone that you love: **make love to/with** *"I want to make love with*

*you," she breathed.* **b)** *old use* to say loving things to someone, to kiss them etc
**6 send your love (to)** to ask someone to give your loving greetings to someone else when they see them, write to them etc: *Aunt Mary sends her love to you.*
**7 give my love to** *spoken* used to ask someone to give your loving greetings to someone else: *"Bye! Give my love to Jackie."*
**8 love (from)/lots of love/all my love** expressions used at the end of a letter to a friend, a member of your family, or someone you love: *See you soon. Lots of love, Clare.*
**9 (my) love** *spoken* **a)** *especially BrE* a word used when you are talking to someone you love: *Hurry up, love!* **b)** *BrE* a friendly way of talking to someone who you do not know, especially to a woman: *Are you OK, love?*
**10 be a love and ... / ... there's a love** *spoken, especially BrE* expressions used when you are asking someone to do something, used especially to children and members of your family: *Say hello to your auntie, there's a love.*
**11 there is no love lost between** if there is no love lost between two people, they dislike each other: *There's never been any love lost between Paul and Geoff.*
**12 ▶ TENNIS ◀** [U] an expression meaning no points, used in the game of tennis
**13 not for love or/nor money** *informal* if you cannot get something or do something for love or money, it is impossible to obtain or to do: *I can't get hold of that book for love nor money.*
**14 for the love of God/Mike etc** *old-fashioned spoken* used to show that you are extremely angry, disappointed etc
**15 love nest** *humorous* a place where two people who are having a romantic relationship live or meet each other —see also **a labour of love** (LABOUR[1] (4))

**love af·fair** /ˈ· ·ˌ·/ *n* [C] **1** a romantic sexual relationship, usually between two people who are not married to each other: *a passionate love affair* —see also AFFAIR (3) **2** a strong enjoyment of something: *the great American love affair with the automobile*

**love·bird** /ˈlʌvbɜːd‖-bɜːrd/ *n* [C] **1** a small brightly coloured PARROT[1] (1) **2 lovebirds** *humorous* two people who show by their behaviour that they love each other very much

**love bite** /ˈ· ·/ *n* [C] *especially BrE* a red mark on someone's skin caused by someone else sucking it as a sexual act; HICKEY *AmE*

**love·child** /ˈlʌvtʃaɪld/ *n* [C] a word used especially in newspapers meaning a child whose parents are not married

**love·less** /ˈlʌvləs/ *adj* without love: *a loveless marriage*

**love let·ter** /ˈ· ˌ··/ *n* [C] a letter that someone writes to tell someone else how much they love them

**love life** /ˈ· ·/ *n* [C,U] the part of your life that involves your love relationships, especially sexual ones

**love·lorn** /ˈlʌvlɔːn‖-lɔːrn/ *adj literary* sad because the person you love does not love you

S2 W3 **love·ly¹** /ˈlʌvli/ *comparative* **lovelier** *superlative* **loveliest** *adj* **1** *especially BrE* beautiful or attractive: *What a lovely baby!|Her hair's a lovely shade of red.|***look lovely** *You look lovely in blue.* **2** *informal especially BrE* friendly and pleasant: *Richard's a lovely person.* **3** *BrE spoken* used to say that something is not at all enjoyable, or good: *"The cat threw up all over the carpet!" "Lovely!"|You've made a lovely mess in here.* **4** *spoken especially BrE* very pleasant, enjoyable, or good: *That was a lovely cup of tea.|Thank you for a lovely evening.* **5 lovely and warm/cold etc** *BrE spoken* used to emphasize how good something is: *This bread's lovely and fresh.* **6** *BrE spoken* used to show that you are pleased with something: *Push it right across. That's it, lovely.* —**loveliness** *n* [U]

**lovely²** *n* [C] *old-fashioned* an attractive woman: *Samantha, a nineteen year old Liverpool lovely*

**love·mak·ing** /ˈlʌvˌmeɪkɪŋ/ *n* [U] sexual activity, especially the act of having sex —see also **make love** (LOVE² (5))

W3 **lov·er** /ˈlʌvə‖-ər/ *n* [C] **1** a sexual partner: *a jealous lover* **2** someone who has a sexual relationship for a long time with someone they are not married to: *Arabella had had many lovers.* —compare MISTRESS (1) **3** someone who enjoys doing a particular thing very much or is very interested in it: *music lovers*

**love·seat** /ˈlʌvsiːt/ *n* [C] **1** a seat in the shape of an S for two people, designed so that they can face each other **2** *AmE* a small SOFA for two people

**love·sick** /ˈlʌvˌsɪk/ *adj* spending all your time thinking about someone you love, especially someone who does not love you: *You're acting like a lovesick teenager!*

**lov·ey** /ˈlʌvi/ *n* [C] *BrE spoken* a word used to address a woman or child, that many women think is offensive —see also LUVVIE

**lovey-dov·ey** /ˌlʌvi ˈdʌvi◂/ *adj informal* behaviour that is lovey-dovey is too romantic; SENTIMENTAL: *Josh went all lovey-dovey when I said I was pregnant.*

**lov·ing** /ˈlʌvɪŋ/ *adj* **1** [only before noun] behaving in a way that shows you love someone: *in memory of my loving wife|What that child needs is plenty of loving care and attention.* **2 peace-loving/home-loving etc** thinking that peace, your home etc is very important: *a peace-loving nation|Molly's a real home-loving type.* —**lovingly** *adv*: *Anna stroked the baby's cheek lovingly.*

**loving cup** /ˈ·· ·/ *n* [C] a very large cup with two handles that was passed around at formal meals in former times

**loving kind·ness** /ˌ·· ˈ··/ *n* [U] *especially literary* gentle and sincere friendship or love

a low wall

shallow water

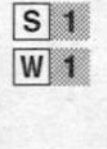
**low¹** /ləʊ‖loʊ/ *adj*
**1 ▶ NOT HIGH ◀ a)** having a top that is not far above the ground: *He jumped over the low wall.|a long low building* **b)** at a point that is not far above the ground: *low clouds|Put the books on the lowest shelf.* **c)** below the usual height: *a low bridge|The river is low for this time of year.*
**2 ▶ SMALL AMOUNT ◀ a)** small, or smaller than usual, in amount, value etc: *The price of oil is at its lowest for 10 years.|families existing on very low incomes|***low-cost/low-budget etc** *There's a desperate need for good low-cost housing.* **b) low in** having less than the usual amount of a substance or chemical: *food that is low in calories|***low-fat/low-salt etc** *I only smoke low-tar cigarettes.|low-alcohol beer* **c) in the low 20s/50s etc** a number, temperature etc in the low 20s etc is around 21, 22, or 23, but no higher: *Daytime temperature will be in the low 30s.*

**3 ► BELOW USUAL LEVEL ◄** small, or smaller than usual, in level or degree: *In this sort of investment, the risks are fairly low.* | *Morale has been low since the latest round of job-cuts.* | **low-risk/low-priority etc** *a low-security prison*
**4 ► STANDARDS/QUALITY ◄** below an acceptable or usual level or quality: *Their safety standards seem to be pretty low.* | *Cost-cutting has led to a lower quality of service.*
**5 ► SUPPLY ◄ a)** a supply of something that is low is nearly finished: **be/get/run low (on)** *We're running low on coffee.* | *Stocks are getting low.*
**6 ► SOUND ◄** a low voice, sound etc is quiet or deep: *I heard a low moaning noise.* | *The volume is too low – turn it up.* | *a low whisper*
**7 ► LIGHT ◄** a light that is low is not bright: *low romantic lighting in a restaurant*
**8 ► HEAT ◄** if you cook something on a low heat or in a low OVEN, you cook it using only a small amount of heat
**9 ► BATTERY ◄** a BATTERY that is low does not have much power left in it
**10 ► CLOTHES ◄** a low dress, BLOUSE etc does not cover your neck and the top of your chest
**11 ► UNHAPPY ◄** [not before noun] unhappy and without much hope for the future: *She's still feeling pretty low about failing that exam.* | **in low spirits** *Terry seems to be in rather low spirits today.*
**12 ► DISHONEST ◄** *old-fashioned or humorous* behaviour that is low is not fair or honest: *a low trick*
**13 of low birth/breeding** *old-fashioned* not from a high social class —see also **be at a low ebb** (EBB[1] (2)), **—lowness** *n* [U]

**low**[2] *adv* **1** in or to a low position or level: *He bent low over the engine.* | *Turn the heating down low.* **2** near the ground: *Watch out for low-flying aircraft.* **3** if you play or sing musical notes low, you play or sing them with quiet deep notes: *Sing those bars an octave lower.* **4 search/look high and low** *informal* to look everywhere in order to find something **5 lie low a)** to hide from people who are trying to catch you **b)** to wait and try not to be noticed by anyone: *Just lie low for a while.* **6 lay sb low** to knock someone down onto the ground or to make someone feel very weak: *laid low by flu* **7 be brought low** *old-fashioned* to become much less rich or important —see also LOWLY

**low**[3] *n* **1** [C] a low price or level: **fall to a new low/hit a new low** (=be worth less than ever before) *The pound has fallen to a new low against the dollar.* | **all-time low** (=much lower or worse than ever before) *Profits hit an all-time low this month.* **2** [C] a bad situation in someone's personal life: **all-time low** (=a worse situation than ever before) *1963 marked an all-time low in his family life.* | **highs and lows** (=good times and bad times) *the highs and lows in their marriage* **3** [C usually singular] **a)** an area of low pressure in the air: *a low moving in over the Pacific* **b)** a low temperature: *The overnight low will be 8°C.* **4 the lowest of the low a)** *informal* someone you think is completely unfair, cruel, immoral etc: *Property barons are among the lowest of the low.* **b)** *often humorous* someone from a low social class

**low**[4] *v* [I] *especially literary* if cattle low, they make a deep sound

**low beam** /ˌ· ˈ·/ *n* **be on low beam** if the lights at the front of a car are on low beam, they light only a short distance of the road ahead and are not very bright

**low·born** /ˌləʊˈbɔːn◂‖ˌloʊˈbɔːrn◂/ *adj old-fashioned* coming from a low social class

**low·brow** /ˈləʊbraʊ‖ˈloʊ-/ *adj* not interested in or connected with literature, art etc: *lowbrow television shows* —compare HIGHBROW

**low-cal, lo-cal** /ˌləʊ ˈkæl◂‖ˌloʊ-/ *adj informal* low-cal food or drink does not contain many CALORIES

**Low Church** /ˌ· ˈ·◂/ *n* [U] the part of the Church of England that believes in the importance of faith and studying the BIBLE rather than in religious ceremonies —compare HIGH CHURCH

**low-class** /ˌ· ˈ·◂/ *adj* **1** *old-fashioned* WORKING CLASS: *a low-class bar* **2** not good quality

**low-cut** /ˌ· ˈ·◂/ *adj* a low-cut dress is shaped so that it shows your neck and the top of your chest

**low·down** /ˈləʊdaʊn‖ˈloʊ-/ *n* **the lowdown (on)** *informal* the most important facts about something or someone: *Give me all the lowdown on what happened at the meeting.*

**low-down** /ˈ· ·/ *adj* [only before noun] *informal* dishonest and unkind: *What a low-down, dirty trick.*

**low·er**[1] /ˈləʊə‖ˈloʊər/ *adj* **1** [only before noun] below something else, especially beneath something of the same type: *Nina chewed her lower lip anxiously.* | *the lower limbs* (=legs) **2** [only before noun] at or near the bottom of something: *the lower slopes of the mountain* **3** smaller in number or amount: *Temperatures will be lower over the weekend.* **4** [only before noun] less important than something else of the same type: *the lower levels of management* S3

**lower**[2] *v*
**1 ► REDUCE ◄** [I,T] to reduce something in amount, degree, strength etc, or to become less: *After 20 minutes lower the temperature to 325°.* | *drugs to lower blood pressure* | **lower your voice** (=make it quieter) *Helen lowered her voice as they approached.*
**2 ► MOVE DOWN ◄** [T] to move something down from higher up: *The flags were lowered to half-mast.* | **lower sth down/into/between etc** *They lowered the coffin into the grave.*
**3 lower yourself** [usually in negatives] to behave in a way that makes people respect you less: *I wouldn't lower myself to speak to her after what she's done.*
**4 lower the tone** *often humorous* to make a conversation, a social situation etc less polite, for example by telling rude jokes: *They thought an influx of students would lower the tone of the neighborhood.*
**5 lower your eyes** to look down: *Katrina lowered her eyes demurely.* **—lowered** *adj*: *Zoe watched through lowered eyelashes.*

**low·er**[3] also **lour** *BrE* /ˈlaʊə‖-ər/ *v* [I] **1** when the sky or the weather lowers, it becomes dark because there is going to be a storm: *lowering clouds* **2** *literary* to look threatening or annoyed; FROWN[1]: *lowering at us across the table*

**lower case** /ˌ·· ˈ·◂/ *n* [U] letters in their small forms, such as a, b, c etc —compare CAPITAL[1] (3) —opposite UPPER CASE **—lower case** *adj*: *lower case letters*

**lower class** /ˌ·· ˈ·◂/ also **lower classes** *n* [C] *old-fashioned* the social class that has less money, power, or education than anyone else —see also WORKING CLASS **—lower-class** *adj*

**Lower House** /ˌ·· ˈ·/ also **Lower Cham·ber** /ˌ·· ˈ··/ *n* [singular] a group of elected representatives who make laws in a country, for example the HOUSE OF COMMONS in Britain or the HOUSE OF REPRESENTATIVES in the US

**lower or·ders** /ˌ·· ˈ··/ *n old-fashioned* **the lower orders** an expression meaning people of a low social class, used especially by people who consider themselves to be better and more important

**lowest com·mon de·nom·i·na·tor** /ˌ·· ˌ·· ·ˈ····/ *n* [U] **1** *technical* the smallest number that the bottom numbers of a group of fractions (FRACTION (2)) can be divided into exactly **2** the biggest possible number of people, including people who are very easily influenced or are willing to accept low standards: *Television quiz shows often seem to target the lowest common denominator.*

**lowest com·mon mul·ti·ple** /ˌ·· ˌ·· ˈ···/ *n* [C] *technical* the smallest number that two or more numbers divide into exactly: *12 is the lowest common multiple of 4 and 6.*

**low-fat** /ˌ· ˈ·◂/ *adj* containing or using only a small amount of fat: *a low-fat, high-fibre diet*

**low-fly·ing** /ˌ· ˈ··◂/ *adj* flying close to the ground

**low gear** /ˌ· ˈ·/ *n* [C,U] one of a vehicle's GEARS that you use when you are driving at a slow speed

**low-key** /ˌ· ˈ·◂/ *adj* not intended to attract a lot of attention to an event, subject, or thing: *The reception was a low-key affair.* | *a low-key approach to establishing women's rights*

**low·lands** /ˈləʊləndz‖ˈloʊ-/ *n* [plural] an area of land that is lower than the land around it: *the Scottish lowlands* —**lowland** *adj* [only before noun]: *lowland farming* —**lowlander** *n* [C] —compare HIGHLANDS

**low-lev·el** /ˌ· ˈ··/ *adj* a low-level computer language is used to give instructions to a computer and is similar to the language that the computer operates in —compare HIGH-LEVEL (4)

**low life** /ˈ· ·/ *n* **1** [U] the life and behaviour of people from a low social class, especially those who are involved in criminal activities: *a novel about low life in Chicago in the 1930s* **2** also **lowlife** [C] *AmE informal* someone who is involved in crime or who is bad: *Pete turned out to be a real lowlife.* —**low-life** *adj AmE informal*: *some low-life hooker Joe's taken up with*

**low·lights** /ˈləʊlaɪts‖ˈloʊ-/ *n* [plural] a dark colour that can be added to change the natural colour of some of your hair —compare **highlights** (HIGHLIGHT[2] (2))

**low·ly** /ˈləʊli‖ˈloʊ-/ *adj sometimes humorous* low in rank, importance, or social class; HUMBLE[1] (1): *He had left his lowly origins far behind.* | *Don't ask me, I'm just a lowly cleaner.* —**lowliness** *n* [U]

**low-ly·ing** /ˌ· ˈ··◂/ *adj* **1** low-lying land is not far above the level of the sea **2** below the usual level: *low-lying mist*

**low-paid** /ˌ· ˈ·◂/ *adj* providing or earning only a small amount of money: *low-paid jobs in catering*

**low-pitched** /ˌ· ˈ·◂/ *adj* **1** a low-pitched musical note or sound is deep: *the low-pitched hum of the generator* **2** a low-pitched roof is not steep

**low point** /ˈ· ·/ *n* [C usually singular] the worst moment of a situation or activity: *For him, the low point came with a phone call from the police.*

**low-pressure** /ˌ· ˈ··/ *n* [U] a condition of the air over a large area that affects the weather

**low pro·file** /ˌ· ˈ··/ *n* **keep a low profile** to be careful not to attract attention to yourself or your actions: *We'd better keep a low profile until the whole thing blows over.* —**low-profile** *adj*: *a low-profile campaign*

**low·rid·er** /ˈləʊraɪdə‖ˈloʊraɪdər/ *n* [C] *AmE* a big car that has its bottom very close to the ground, or a young man who drives this type of car

**low-rise** /ˈ· ·/ *adj* [only before noun] a low-rise building does not have many STOREYS —compare HIGH-RISE

**low-risk** /ˌ· ˈ·◂/ *adj* [only before noun] likely to be safe or without difficulties: *a low-risk investment*

**low sea·son** /ˈ· ˌ··/ *n BrE* the time of year when there is the least business for hotels, shops etc; OFF-SEASON —compare HIGH SEASON

**low-spir·it·ed** /ˌ· ˈ···◂/ *adj* unhappy; DEPRESSED (1): *He was a dull, low-spirited companion.*

**low-tech** /ˌ· ˈ·◂/ *adj* not using the most modern machines or methods in business or industry —opposite HIGH-TECH

**low tide** /ˌ· ˈ·/ *n* [C,U] the time when sea water is at its lowest level: *You can walk across to the island at low tide.* —opposite HIGH TIDE (1)

**low wa·ter** /ˌ· ˈ··/ *n* [U] the time when the water in a river or the sea is at its lowest level because of the TIDE[1] (1)

**low water mark** /ˌ· ˈ·· ˌ·/ *n* [C] **1** a mark showing the lowest level reached by a river or other area of water **2** the worst time in someone's life, job etc: *Our fortunes had reached their low water mark.*

**lox** /lɒks‖lɑːks/ *n* [U] *especially AmE* SALMON that has been treated with smoke in order to preserve it

**loy·al** /ˈlɔɪəl/ *adj* always supporting your friends, principles, country etc: [+ **to**] *Dennis will always be loyal to this government, whatever it does.* | *a loyal supporter of the team* —**loyally** *adv*

**loy·al·ist** /ˈlɔɪəlɪst/ *n* [C] someone who continues to support a government or country, when a lot of people want to change it —**loyalist** *adj*

**loy·al·ty** /ˈlɔɪəlti/ *n* **1** [U] the quality of remaining faithful to your friends, principles, country etc: [+ **to/towards**] *These people feel a lot of loyalty to the company.* **2** [C usually plural] a feeling of support for someone or something: *Don't let political loyalties affect your judgment.* | **divided loyalties** (=two strong feelings of loyalty that you must choose between) *the agony of divided loyalties for the children in a divorce*

**loz·enge** /ˈlɒzɪndʒ‖ˈlɑː-/ *n* [C] **1** a small flat sweet, especially one that contains medicine: *a cough lozenge* **2** a shape similar to a square, with two angles of less than 90° opposite each other and two angles of more than 90° opposite each other

**LP** /ˌel ˈpiː/ *n* [C] long playing record; a record that turns 33 times per minute, and usually plays for between 20 and 25 minutes on each side

**L-plate** /ˈel pleɪt/ *n* [C] a flat white square with a red letter L on it, that must be fixed to the back and front of a car being driven by a learner in Britain

**LRV** /ˌel ɑː ˈviː‖-ɑːr-/ *n* [C] Light Rail Vehicle; a type of train whose tracks run in or between streets, used especially in cities in the US

**LSD** /ˌel es ˈdiː/ *n* [U] an illegal drug that makes you see things as more beautiful, strange, frightening etc than usual, or see things that do not exist; ACID[1] (2)

**Lsd, £sd** /ˌel es ˈdiː/ *n* [U] *BrE old-fashioned* **1** the abbreviation of pounds, SHILLINGS, and pence, the system of money used in Britain before 1971 **2** money

**Lt.** the written abbreviation of LIEUTENANT

**Ltd** the written abbreviation of LIMITED (2), used in the names of companies or businesses: *M. Dixon & Son Ltd* —compare INC, PLC

**lu·bri·cant** /ˈluːbrɪkənt/ *n* [C,U] a substance such as oil that you put on surfaces that rub together, especially parts of a machine, in order to make them move smoothly and easily

**lu·bri·cate** /ˈluːbrɪkeɪt/ *v* [T] to put a lubricant on something in order to make it move more smoothly: *Lubricate all moving parts with grease.* —**lubrication** /ˌluːbrɪˈkeɪʃən/ *n* [U]

**lu·bri·cious** /luːˈbrɪʃəs/ *adj formal* too interested in sex, in a way that seems unpleasant or unacceptable —**lubriciously** *adv*

**lu·cid** /ˈluːsɪd/ *adj* **1** expressed in a way that is clear and easy to understand: *a lucid and accurate account of the day's events* **2** a word meaning able to understand and think clearly, used especially about someone who is not always able to do this: *In her more lucid moments the old lady would talk about her past.* —**lucidly** *adv* —**lucidity** /luːˈsɪdɪti/ *n* [U]

**Lu·ci·fer** /ˈluːsɪfə‖-ər/ *n* the devil

**luck[1]** /lʌk/ *n* [U] S2 W3

**1** ▶ **GOOD FORTUNE** ◀ something good that happens by chance: **have luck (with sth)** *Did you have any luck with the job application?* | *You're not having much luck today, are you?* | **Good luck!/Best of luck!** *Good luck tomorrow in the exam!* | **wish sb luck** *Tom wished me luck in the race and left.*

**2** ▶ **CHANCE** ◀ the way in which good or bad things happen to people by chance: *There's no skill in roulette, it's all a matter of luck.* | **good/bad luck** *We seem to have had a lot of bad luck lately.* | **sheer/pure luck** *It was sheer luck you were there to help.*

**3 any luck?** *spoken* used to ask someone if they have succeeded in doing something: *"I phoned them about the car." "Any luck?" "Yes, it'll be ready on Tuesday."*

**4 do sth for luck** to do something because you think it might bring you good luck: *John always carried a rabbit's foot for luck.*

**5 be in luck** to be able to do or get something, especially when you did not expect to: *We're in luck – the train hasn't gone yet.*

**6 be out of luck** to be prevented from getting or doing something by bad luck: *I'm sorry, you're out of luck! I sold the last one this morning.*

**7 just my luck!** *spoken* used to say that you are not surprised something bad has happened to you, because you are usually unlucky: *He's married, is he? Just my luck!*

**8 no such luck!** *spoken* used to say you are disappointed, because something good that could have happened did not happen: *"Did you get a rise then?" "No such luck!"*

**9 with (any) luck/with a bit of luck** *spoken* if things

L

happen in the way that you want; HOPEFULLY: *With any luck, there'll be some food left.*
**10 better luck next time!** used to say that you hope someone will be more successful the next time they try to do something
**11 good luck to sb** *spoken* used to say that you do not mind what someone does, because it does not affect you and may help them: *Well if she wants to go on her own, good luck to her, but I'm staying here.*
**12 luck is on sb's side** if luck is on someone's side, things go well for them: *Luck was on my side; all the traffic lights were green.*
**13 as luck would have it** used to say that something happened by chance: *As luck would have it, the bar was shut when we got there.*
**14 be down on your luck** to have no money because you have had a lot of bad luck over a period of time: *You really find out who your friends are when you're down on your luck!*
**15 the luck of the draw** the result of chance rather than something you can control: *You can't be sure of getting a ticket – it's all in the luck of the draw.*
**16 stroke of luck** something very fortunate, happening by chance: *What a stroke of luck, bumping into David in the street like that!*
**17 some people have all the luck!** *spoken* used when someone else has got something that you would like: *Rich parents as well? Some people have all the luck!*
**18 a run of bad luck** a period of time when a lot of bad things happen to you
**19 try/chance your luck** to do something because you hope you will be successful, even though you know you may not be: *The Hotel Europa was full, so we decided to try our luck elsewhere.*
**20 bad/hard/tough luck!** *spoken especially BrE* used to express sympathy when something unpleasant has happened to someone: *Oh bad luck! I'm sure you'll pass next time.* —compare **tough luck** (TOUGH[1] (7))
**21 worse luck!** *BrE spoken* unfortunately: *I've got to work this Saturday, worse luck!*
**22 (one) for luck** *spoken* used when you take or add something for no particular reason
**23 trust to luck** to hope that things will happen in the way that you want, even though you cannot control them: *I decided to just apply for the job and trust to luck for the rest.* —see also **hard-luck story** (HARD[1] (23)), **push your luck** (PUSH[1] (10))

**luck[2]** *v*
**luck out** *phr v* [I] *AmE informal* to be lucky: *Yeah, we really lucked out, got a parking space right in front.*

S3 **luck·i·ly** /ˈlʌkɪli/ *adv* as a result of good luck: *Luckily she can take a joke.* | **luckily for sb** *Luckily for us, the rain held off all day.*

**luck·less** /ˈlʌkləs/ *adj literary* having no luck in something you are trying to do: *He died in the desert like so many other luckless explorers.*

S2 W3 **luck·y** /ˈlʌki/ *adj* **1** having good luck; fortunate: **be lucky (enough) to do/be** *You were lucky to catch him in.* | *John was lucky enough to be selected for the team.* | **lucky (that)** *He's lucky he didn't break his neck.* | [+ **with**] *We've been very lucky with the weather.* | **think/count yourself lucky** *You can count yourself lucky he didn't hear you.* **2** resulting from good luck: *I didn't really know your name – it was just a lucky guess.* | *a lucky escape* **3** bringing good luck: *a lucky charm* **4 I/you should be so lucky!** *spoken* used to say that someone wants something that is unreasonable and not likely to happen: *You want a transfer to the London office? You should be so lucky!* **5 lucky you/me etc!** *spoken* used to say that someone is fortunate to be able to do something: *"I'm going out tonight." "Lucky you."* —see also **thank your lucky stars** (THANK (6)), **third time lucky** (THIRD[1] (2))

**lucky dip** /ˌ·· ˈ·/ *n BrE* **1** [C] a game in which you put your hand into a container filled with small objects, and choose one without looking; GRAB BAG (1) *AmE* **2** [singular] a situation in which what happens depends on chance

**lu·cra·tive** /ˈluːkrətɪv/ *adj* a job or activity that is lucrative lets you earn a lot of money; PROFITABLE: *Flynn had a lucrative contract at Warners.*

**lu·cre** /ˈluːkə‖-ər/ *n* **filthy lucre** money or wealth, used to show disapproval

**Lud·dite** /ˈlʌdaɪt/ *n* [C] someone who is strongly opposed to using modern machines and methods

**lu·di·crous** /ˈluːdʒkrəs/ *adj* completely unreasonable, stupid, or unsuitable; RIDICULOUS: *She turned up wearing a ludicrous flowery hat.* —**ludicrously** *adv*: *The test was ludicrously easy.* —**ludicrousness** *n* [U]

**lu·do** /ˈluːdəʊ‖-doʊ/ *n* [U] *BrE trademark* a game played with COUNTERS (=small flat round objects) on a board; PARCHEESI *AmE*

**lug[1]** /lʌg/ **lugged, lugging** *v* [T] to pull or carry something heavy with difficulty: **lug sth up/down/around etc** *I lugged my suitcase up the stairs and rang the bell.*

**lug[2]** *n* [C] **1** a part of something that sticks out and can be used as a handle or a support **2** *BrE humorous* an ear; LUGHOLE **3** a LUGWORM **4** *AmE old-fashioned* a rough, stupid, or awkward person: *You big lug!*

**luge** /luːʒ/ *n* [C] a vehicle with blades instead of wheels on which you slide down a track made of ice

**lug·gage** /ˈlʌgɪdʒ/ *n* [U] the cases, bags etc carried by someone who is travelling —see also HAND LUGGAGE

**luggage rack** /ˈ·· ·/ *n* [C] a shelf in a train, bus etc for putting luggage on —see picture at RACK[1]

**luggage van** /ˈ·· ·/ *n* [C] *BrE* the part of a train that boxes, cases etc are carried in

**lug·ger** /ˈlʌgə‖-ər/ *n* [C] a small boat with one or more lugsails

**lug·hole** /ˈlʌghəʊl, ˈlʌgəʊl‖-oʊl/ *n* [C] *BrE humorous* an ear

**lug·sail** /ˈlʌgseɪl, -səl/ *n* [C] a four-sided sail that hangs down from a pole attached to the MAST (1)

**lu·gu·bri·ous** /lʊˈguːbriəs/ *adj literary or humorous* very sad and serious: *a lugubrious voice* —**lugubriously** *adv* —**lugubriousness** *n* [U]

**lug·worm** /ˈlʌgwɜːm‖-wɜːrm/ *n* [C] a small WORM that lives in sand by the sea, often used to catch fish

**luke·warm** /ˌluːkˈwɔːm◂‖-ˈwɔːrm◂/ *adj* **1** food, liquid etc that is lukewarm is slightly warm and often not as hot or cold as it should be; TEPID: *Why do British people like lukewarm beer?* —see picture at HOT[1] **2** not showing much interest or excitement: *His plan got only a lukewarm response from the committee.*

**lull[1]** /lʌl/ *v* [T] **1** to make someone feel calm or sleepy: *The movement of the train gradually lulled me to sleep.* **2** to make someone feel safe and confident so that they are completely surprised when you attack or cheat them: **lull sb into (doing) sth** *Felix's charm lulled me into believing he loved me.* | **lull sb into a false sense of security** (=make someone think they are safe when they are not)

**lull[2]** *n* [C] **1** a short period of time when there is less activity or less noise than usual: [+ **in**] *a brief lull in the conversation* | *a lull in the fighting* **2 the lull before the storm** a short period of time when things are calm that is followed by a lot of activity, noise, or trouble

**lul·la·by** /ˈlʌləbaɪ/ *n* [C] a slow, quiet song sung to children to make them go to sleep

**lu·lu** /ˈluːluː/ *n* [C] *AmE informal* **1** something very good or exciting: *The roller coaster at Magic Mountain is a real lulu.* **2** something extremely silly, bad, embarrassing etc: *She's said some stupid things in her life, but that one was a real lulu!*

**lum·ba·go** /lʌmˈbeɪgəʊ‖-goʊ/ *n* [U] pain in the lower part of the back

**lum·bar** /ˈlʌmbə‖-bɑːr/ *adj technical* related to the lower part of the back: *pain in the lumbar region*

**lum·ber[1]** /ˈlʌmbə‖-ər/ *v* **1** [I always + adv/prep] to move in a slow, awkward way: [+ **after/into/along etc**] *Mrs Moffat lumbered over to us, complaining about her arthritis.* **2** [T] *informal* to give someone a job or responsibility that they do not want: **get/be lumbered with** *As usual, Joe got lumbered with the babysitting.* **3** [I] *AmE* to cut down trees to make TIMBER (1)

L

**lumber²** *n* [U] **1** *BrE informal* large objects that are no longer useful or wanted **2** trees that have been cut down to be used as wood; TIMBER (1)

**lum·ber·jack** /ˈlʌmbədʒæk‖-ər-/ *n* [C] someone whose job is cutting down trees for wood

**lumber jack·et** /ˈ·· ˌ··/ *n* [C] a thick wool jacket, often with a CHECK² (5) pattern

**lum·ber·man** /ˈlʌmbəmən‖-bər-/ *n* [C] someone whose job is cutting down trees or selling wood

**lum·ber·mill** /ˈlʌmbəmɪl‖-bər-/ *n* [C] *AmE* a building where trees are cut up to make wood; SAWMILL *BrE*

**lumber room** /ˈ·· ·/ *n* [C] *BrE* a room where old furniture, broken machines etc are kept

**lum·ber·yard** /ˈlʌmbəjɑːd‖-bərjɑːrd/ *n* [C] *AmE* a place where wood is kept before it is sold

**lu·mi·na·ry** /ˈluːmɪ̈nəri‖-neri/ *n* [C] someone who is very famous or highly respected for their skill at, or knowledge of, a particular subject: *luminaries of the women's movement*

**lu·mi·nous** /ˈluːmɪ̈nəs/ *adj* **1** made of a substance or material that shines in the dark: *luminous paint*| *luminous road signs* **2** very brightly coloured, especially in green, pink, or yellow: *luminous socks* —**luminously** *adv* —**luminosity** /ˌluːmɪ̈ˈnɒsɪ̈ti‖-ˈnɑː-/ *n* [U]

**lum·me** /ˈlʌmi/ *interjection BrE old-fashioned* used to express surprise

S2 **lump¹** /lʌmp/ *n* [C] **1** a small piece of something solid, without a particular shape: *There were lumps in the sauce.*|[+ **of**] *a lump of coal* —see picture on page 416 **2** something small that sticks out from someone's skin or grows in their body, usually because of an illness: *Check monthly for lumps on your breasts.* **3** a small square block of sugar: *One lump or two?* **4 bring a lump to sb's throat** to make someone feel as if they want to cry: *The scene where Laddie dies brought a lump to my throat.* **5 take your lumps** *AmE informal* to accept the bad things that happen to you and not let them affect you: *Forget about it, Rob, you have to take your lumps and go on.* **6** *BrE spoken* someone who is stupid, or CLUMSY (1): *You stupid great lump!*

**lump²** *v* **lump it** *informal* to accept a situation or decision you do not like because you cannot change it: **like it or lump it** *I'm going to that party! Like it or lump it!*

**lump** sth **together** *phr v* [T] to consider two or more different things as a single type or group, rather than individually or separately: *Pacifists, atheists and journalists were all lumped together as 'troublemakers'.*

**lump·ec·to·my** /lʌmpˈektəmi/ *n* [C] an operation in which a TUMOUR is removed from someone's body, especially from a woman's breast

**lump·ish** /ˈlʌmpɪʃ/ *adj* awkward or stupid

**lump sum** /ˌ· ˈ·/ *n* [C] an amount of money given in a single payment: *When you retire you'll get a lump sum of £80,000.*

**lump·y** /ˈlʌmpi/ *adj* covered with or containing small solid pieces: *a lumpy mattress*

**lu·na·cy** /ˈluːnəsi/ *n* [U] **1** a situation or behaviour that is completely crazy: **complete/sheer/pure lunacy** *It would be sheer lunacy to turn down an offer like that.* **2** *old-fashioned* mental illness: *the cause of Hamlet's lunacy* —see also LUNATIC

**lu·nar** /ˈluːnə‖-ər/ *adj* connected with the moon or with travel to the moon: *a lunar eclipse*

**lunar month** /ˌ·· ˈ·/ *n* [C] a period of 28 or 29 days between one NEW MOON and the next

**lu·na·tic** /ˈluːnətɪk/ *n* [C] **1** someone who behaves in a crazy or very stupid way: *You lunatic – you nearly drove straight into me!* **2** *old-fashioned* someone who is mentally ill: *a dangerous lunatic* **3 the lunatic fringe** *BrE* the people in a political group or organization who have the most extreme opinions or ideas —**lunatic** *adj*: *lunatic behaviour*

**lunatic a·sy·lum** /ˈ··· ·ˌ··/ *n* [C] *old-fashioned* a hospital where people who are mentally ill are cared for

**lunch¹** /lʌntʃ/ *n* [C,U] **1** a meal eaten in the middle of the day: **at lunch** *Anna said something at lunch about leaving.*|**have lunch** *When do you usually have lunch?*|**have some lunch** *I'm starved. Let's have some lunch.*|**have sth for lunch** *All I had for lunch was a salad sandwich.*|**take sb out to lunch** *He decided to take her out to lunch.*|**go to lunch** (=go somewhere to eat lunch) *Rory went to lunch in a small Italian restaurant.*|**a working lunch** (=when you discuss business and eat)|**packed lunch** *BrE*/**bag lunch** *AmE* (=food, usually SANDWICHes, that you take with you to work, school etc) **2 out to lunch** *informal* behaving in a strange and confused way S1 W2

**lunch²** *v formal* **1** [I] to eat lunch **2** [T] to buy someone lunch

**lunch·box** /ˈlʌntʃbɒks‖-bɑːks/ *n* [C] a box in which food is carried to school, work etc

**lunch break** /ˈ· ·/ *n* [C] LUNCH HOUR

**lunch·eon** /ˈlʌntʃən/ *n* [C,U] *formal* lunch

**luncheon meat** /ˈ·· ·/ *n* [U] meat that has been cooked, then pressed down, and is often sold in a can

**luncheon vou·cher** /ˈ·· ˌ··/ *n* [C] a special ticket sometimes given to people in Britain by their employers, that can be used to buy meals or food

**lunch hour** /ˈ· ·/ *n* [C] the period of time in the middle of the day when people stop working in order to eat

**lunch·room** /ˈlʌntʃruːm, -rʊm/ *n* [C] *AmE* a large room in a school or office where people can eat —compare CAFETERIA

**lunch·time** /ˈlʌntʃtaɪm/ *n* [C,U] the time in the middle of the day when people usually eat their LUNCH: *a lunchtime drink* S3

**lung** /lʌŋ/ *n* [C] one of the two organs in your body that you breathe with: *Smoking can cause lung cancer.* —see also IRON LUNG —see picture at RESPIRATORY

**lunge** /lʌndʒ/ *v* [I] to make a sudden strong movement towards someone or something, especially using your arm and to attack them: [+ **forwards/at/towards**] *They both lunged forwards to catch the ball.* —**lunge** *n* [C]: *Brad made a lunge towards his opponent, but missed.*

**lunk·head** /ˈlʌŋkhed/ *n* [C] *AmE informal* someone who is very stupid

**lu·pin** *BrE*, **lupine** *AmE* /ˈluːpɪ̈n/ *n* [C] a plant with a tall stem and many small flowers

**lurch¹** /lɜːtʃ‖lɜːrtʃ/ *v* [I] **1** to move suddenly forwards or sideways, usually because you cannot control your movements: [+ **across/into/along etc**] *Frank lurched back to his seat.*|*The car lurched forward across the grass.* **2 your heart/stomach lurches** used to say that your heart or stomach seems to move as you suddenly feel shocked, frightened etc **3 lurch from one crisis to the next/lurch from one extreme to the other etc** to seem to have no plan and no control over what you are doing

**lurch²** *n* [C] **1** a sudden movement forwards or sideways, usually made because you cannot control your body or a machine: *The train gave a violent lurch.* **2 leave sb in the lurch** to leave someone at a time when you should stay and help them; DESERT² (1)

**lure¹** /lʊə, ljʊə‖lʊr/ *v* [T] to persuade someone to do something, especially something wrong, by promising them something they want; TEMPT: **lure sb into/to/away etc** *I think he's trying to lure you away from Jerry.*|*prospectors lured to Alaska by the promise of gold*

**lure²** *n* **1** [C usually singular] something that you think is attractive, or the power that something has to attract you: [+ **of**] *Settlers were drawn to the West by the lure of free land.* **2** [C] a piece of equipment, such as a plastic bird or fish, used to attract animals or fish so that they can be caught; DECOY (2)

**Lu·rex** /ˈljʊəreks‖ˈlʊr-/ *n* [U] *trademark* a type of thread that looks like metal, usually gold or silver, used in material for making clothes: *a gold Lurex top*

**lur·gy** /ˈlɜːgi‖ˈlɜːr-/ *n* [singular] *BrE humorous* an illness, especially one that is infectious but not serious: *Anne's got the dreaded lurgy.*

**lu·rid** /ˈlʊərɪ̵d, ˈljʊərɪ̵d‖ˈlʊrɪ̵d/ *adj* **1** a description, story etc that is lurid is deliberately shocking and involves sex or violence: *lurid headlines|He told me in lurid detail what would happen to me.* **2** too brightly coloured; GAUDY: *a lurid orange dress* —**luridly** *adv* —**luridness** *n* [U]

**lurk** /lɜːk‖lɜːrk/ *v* [I always +adv/prep] **1** to wait somewhere quietly and secretly, usually because you are going to do something wrong: [+ **around/in/beneath etc**] *A man was lurking around outside the shop.* **2** to exist almost without being seen or known about: *childish fears that lurk in all our hearts*

**lus·cious** /ˈlʌʃəs/ *adj* **1** extremely good to eat: *a luscious peach* **2** *informal* a word meaning very sexually attractive, used especially by men: *a luscious young starlet*

**lush**[1] /lʌʃ/ *adj* **1** plants that are lush grow many leaves and look healthy and strong: *lush tropical vegetation* **2** very beautiful, comfortable, and expensive: *lush carpets*

**lush**[2] *n* [C] *AmE informal* an ALCOHOLIC

**lust**[1] /lʌst/ *n* **1** [C,U] very strong sexual desire, especially when it does not include liking or love: *What Len felt for her was pure lust.* **2** [U + **for**] a very strong desire to have something, usually power or money: *hard-faced men driven by a lust for gain*

**lust**[2] *v*

**lust after** sb/sth *phr v* [T] *often humorous* **1** to be strongly sexually attracted to someone, and think about having sex with them: *He thinks I'm only lusting after his body!* **2** to want something very much, especially something that you do not really need: *This is the shop for those of you lusting after designer clothes.*

**lus·ter** /ˈlʌstə‖-ər/ *n* [singular, U] the American spelling of LUSTRE

**lust·ful** /ˈlʌstfəl/ *adj* feeling or showing strong sexual desire: *a jealous, lustful man* —**lustfully** *adv*: *Max stared at her lustfully.*

**lus·tre** *BrE*, **luster** *AmE* /ˈlʌstə‖-ər/ *n* [singular,U] **1** an attractive shiny appearance: **add/give lustre to** *A little conditioner will give lustre to your hair.* **2** the quality that makes something interesting or exciting: **add/give luster to** *Arnold's singing will add lustre to the affair*

**lus·trous** /ˈlʌstrəs/ *adj* shining in a soft, gentle way: *lustrous black hair*

**lust·y** /ˈlʌsti/ *adj* strong and healthy; powerful: *The baby gave a lusty cry.|lusty young men* —**lustily** *adv*: *cheering lustily* —**lustiness** *n* [U]

**lute** /luːt/ *n* **1** [C] a musical instrument similar to a GUITAR with a round body, played especially in former times **2** [U] *technical* a type of clay or CEMENT used to fill holes or cracks

**Lu·ther·an** /ˈluːθərən/ *n* [C] a member of the church that follows the teachings and ideas of Martin Luther —**Lutheran** *adj*

**luv** /lʌv/ *n BrE informal* an informal way of spelling LOVE when it is used to address someone: *Come on, luv, don't cry.*

**luv·vie** /ˈlʌvi/ *n BrE* **1** another spelling of LOVEY **2** [C] *informal* an actor or actress who behaves to other people in a very friendly way that is not sincere

**lux·u·ri·ant** /lʌgˈzjʊəriənt, ləgˈʒʊəriənt‖ləgˈʒʊriənt/ *adj* **1** growing strongly and thickly: *a luxuriant black beard|luxuriant vegetation* **2** giving a rich effect: *luxuriant prose* —**luxuriantly** *adv* —**luxuriance** *n* [U]

**lux·u·ri·ate** /lʌgˈzjʊərieɪt, ləgˈʒʊəri-‖ləgˈʒʊri-/ *v*

**luxuriate in** sth *phr v* [T] to relax and consciously enjoy something: *Melanie was luxuriating in the sunshine when they arrived.*

**lux·u·ri·ous** /lʌgˈzjʊəriəs, ləgˈʒʊəriəs‖ləgˈʒʊriəs/ *adj* very expensive, beautiful, and comfortable: *The bathroom was luxurious, with gold taps and a thick carpet.* —**luxuriously** *adv* —**luxuriousness** *n* [C]

**lux·u·ry** /ˈlʌkʃəri/ *n* **1** [U] very great comfort and pleasure, such as you get from expensive food, beautiful houses, cars etc: *Caviar for breakfast! I was not used to such luxury.*|**a life of luxury** *They led a life of luxury, in a huge house in the countryside.*|**luxury apartment/flat/car etc** (=expensive and large) **2** [C] something expensive that you do not need, but you buy for pleasure and enjoyment: *We can't afford luxuries like piano lessons any more.* —see also **in the lap of luxury** (LAP[1] (4)) —compare NECESSITY (1)

**LW** the written abbreviation of LONG WAVE

**-ly** /li/ *suffix* **1** [in adverbs] in a particular way: *He did it very cleverly.* (=in a clever way)|*walking slowly* **2** [in adverbs] considered in a particular way: *Politically speaking it was a rather unwise remark.|a financially sound proposal* **3** [in adjectives and adverbs] happening at regular periods of time: *an hourly check* (=done every hour)|*They visit monthly.* (=once a month) **4** [in adjectives] like a particular thing in manner, nature, or appearance: *with queenly grace|a motherly woman* (=showing the love, kindness etc of a mother)

**ly·ce·um** /laɪˈsiːəm/ *n* [C] *AmE old-fashioned* a building used for public meetings, concerts, speeches etc

**ly·chee, litchi** /ˈlaɪtʃiː‖ˈliː-/ *n* [C] a small round fruit with a rough pink-brown shell outside and sweet white flesh inside —see picture on page 413

**lych·gate, lichgate** /ˈlɪtʃgeɪt/ *n* [C] a gate with a roof leading into the area surrounding a church

**Ly·cra** /ˈlaɪkrə/ *n* [U] *trademark* a material that stretches, used especially for making tight-fitting sports clothes

**ly·ing** /ˈlaɪ-ɪŋ/ the present participle of LIE[1]

**lying-in** /ˌ·· ˈ·/ *n* [singular] *old-fashioned* the period of time during which a woman stays in bed before and after the birth of a child; CONFINEMENT (2)

**lying in state** /ˌ·· · ˈ·/ *n* [singular] the period of time when people can come and see the body of someone such as a president or king who has died, to show their respect

**Lyme dis·ease** /ˈlaɪm dɪˌziːz/ *n* [U] a serious illness that is caused by a bite from a TICK[1] (2)

**lymph** /lɪmf/ *n* [U] a clear liquid that is formed in your body and passes into your blood system —**lymphatic** /lɪmˈfætɪk/ *adj*

**lymph gland** /ˈ· ·/ *n* [C] a lymph node

**lymph node** /ˈ· ·/ *n* [C] a small rounded SWELLING in your body through which lymph passes to be made pure before entering your blood system

**lynch** /lɪntʃ/ *v* [T] if a crowd of people lynches someone, they HANG[1] (3) them as a punishment, without using the usual legal process: *At that time you could be lynched for being black.* —**lynching** *n* [C]

**lynch mob** /ˈ· ·/ *n* [singular] a group of people that kills someone by hanging (HANG[1] (3)) them, without a legal TRIAL[1] (1)

**lynchpin** /ˈlɪnʃ pɪn/ *n* [C] another spelling of LINCHPIN

**lynx** /lɪŋks/ *n* [C] a large wild cat that has no tail and lives in forests; BOBCAT *AmE*

**lyre** /laɪə‖laɪr/ *n* [C] a musical instrument with strings across a U-shaped frame, used especially in ancient Greece

**lyre·bird** /ˈlaɪəbɜːd‖ˈlaɪrbɜːrd/ *n* [C] a bird with a long U-shaped tail, that lives in Australia

**lyr·ic**[1] /ˈlɪrɪk/ *adj* [only before noun] expressing strong personal emotions such as love, in a way that is similar to music in its sounds and RHYTHM (1): *Wordsworth was one of the greatest lyric poets of his time.*

**lyric**[2] *n* **1 lyrics** [plural] the words of a song, especially a modern popular song: *music and lyrics by the Gershwin brothers* **2** [C] *technical* a poem, usually a short one, written in a lyric style

**lyr·i·cal** /ˈlɪrɪkəl/ *adj* **1** beautifully expressed in words, poetry, or music: *Lawrence's lyrical descriptions of the natural world* **2 wax lyrical** to talk about and praise something in a very eager way: *Simon waxed lyrical on the joys of hill-walking.* —**lyrically** /-kli/ *adv*

**lyr·i·cis·m** /ˈlɪrɪ̵sɪzəm/ *n* [U] the romantic or song-like expression of something in writing or music

**lyr·i·cist** /ˈlɪrɪ̵sɪ̵st/ *n* [C] someone who writes the words for songs, especially modern popular songs

**M, m** /em/ *plural* **M's, m's** *n* [C] **1** the 13th letter of the English alphabet **2** the number 1000 in the system of ROMAN NUMERALS

**M** *BrE* the abbreviation of MOTORWAY: *M25|M1*

**m** the written abbreviation of **a)** metre **b)** mile **c)** million **d)** male **e)** married **f)** medium

**MA** /ˌem ˈeɪ/ *n* [C] Master of Arts; a university degree in an arts subject (ART[1] (5)) that you get after studying for a year or two longer after your first degree: *an MA in English literaure|Vanessa Clark, MA* —compare MSC

**Ma, ma** /mɑː/ *n* [C] *informal* **1** mother: *What's for dinner, Ma?* **2** a word meaning 'Mrs', used in some country areas of the US: *old Ma Harris*

**ma'am** /mæm, mɑːm, məm‖mæm/ *n* **1** *AmE spoken* a polite way of addressing a woman: *May I help you, ma'am?* **2** *BrE spoken* a way of addressing the Queen, some women in authority, and, especially in the past, women of high social class

**mac** /mæk/ *n* [C] *BrE* a coat worn to keep out the rain; MACKINTOSH

**Mac** *n AmE informal* used to address a man whose name you do not know

**ma·ca·bre** /məˈkɑːbrə, -bə ‖ -brə, -bər/ *adj* very strange and unpleasant and connected with death, serious accidents etc: *a macabre tale|a macabre sense of humour*

**ma·cad·am** /məˈkædəm/ *n* [U] a road surface made of a mixture of broken stones and TAR[1] (1) or ASPHALT; TARMAC[1] (1) *BrE*

**mac·a·ro·ni** /ˌmækəˈrəʊni◂‖-ˈroʊ-/ *n* [U] a type of PASTA in the shape of small tubes, which is cooked in boiling water: *a plate of macaroni*|**macaroni cheese** (=macaroni with a cheese sauce) —see picture at PASTA

**mac·a·roon** /ˌmækəˈruːn/ *n* [C] a small round cake made of sugar, eggs, and crushed ALMONDS or COCONUT

**ma·caw** /məˈkɔː‖-ˈkɒː/ *n* [C] a large brightly coloured bird like a PARROT[1] (1), with a long tail

**mace** /meɪs/ *n* **1** [U] powder made from the dried shell of a NUTMEG, used to give food a special taste **2** [C] a heavy ball with sharp points on a short metal stick, used in the past as a weapon **3** [C] a decorated stick that is carried by an official in some ceremonies as a sign of power **4 Mace** [U] *trademark* a chemical which makes your eyes and skin sting painfully, which some women carry to defend themselves

**ma·cer·ate** /ˈmæsəreɪt/ *v* [I,T] *technical* to make something soft by leaving it in water, or to become soft in this way —**maceration** /ˌmæsəˈreɪʃən/ *n* [U]

**ma·chet·e** /məˈʃeti, məˈtʃeɪti/ *n* [C] a large knife with a broad heavy blade, used as a weapon or a tool

**Mach·i·a·vel·li·an** /ˌmækiəˈveliən◂/ *adj* using clever but immoral methods to get what you want

**mach·i·na·tions** /ˌmækɪ̵ˈneɪʃənz, ˌmæʃɪ̵-/ *n* [plural] secret and clever plans

**ma·chine**[1] /məˈʃiːn/ *n* [C] **1** a piece of equipment that uses power such as electricity to do a particular job: *a machine that fills the bottles|Could you get me a Coke from the machine?*|**sewing/washing machine etc** (=a machine that can sew, wash clothes etc)|**by machine** *The letters are sorted by machine.* **2** a computer: *a powerful machine that is ideal for software development* **3** a group of people that controls an organization, especially a political party: *the party machine|the government's propaganda machine* **4 like a well-oiled machine** working very smoothly and effectively: *The office runs like a well-oiled machine.* **5** *informal* a vehicle: *That's an impressive-looking machine you've got there.* **6** someone who works without stopping, or who seems to have no feelings or independent thoughts: *He was a running machine, born to do nothing but win medals.* —see also cash machine, FRUIT MACHINE, TIME MACHINE

**USAGE NOTE: MACHINE**

WORD CHOICE: **machine, device, thing, appliance, gadget**

You do not usually work a **machine** directly by hand, and it may be large. Often the word is used with another word before it that describes its purpose: *The coffee machine has broken down.*

**Device** is more formal. A device may be worked by hand, or be electrical: *a device for opening bottles*. In spoken English people say **thing**: *a thing to open bottles with*. **Device** is used especially for something that is used to measure or protect something else: *a device to find faults in plastic|a contraceptive device*

An **appliance** is a machine used for a particular purpose in the home, and is called this especially by the people who produce and sell them: *a household appliance such as a dishwasher|domestic appliances*

A **gadget** is a cleverly designed small machine, often one that does a complicated action, and is usually modern: *My latest gadget is a breadmaker.*

SPOKEN-WRITTEN

When the word before it describes what the machine is for, people sometimes leave out the word **machine**: *Can I use your fax (machine)?*

When the word before **machine** ends in *-ing*, you can sometimes use the same word ending in *-er* on its own: *Lianne is in charge of the photocopier* (formal **photocopying machine**).

Often you do not use the word **machine** at all to talk about a particular machine. For example, you say **dishwasher**, not **dishwashing machine** and **tumble-drier** not **tumble-drying machine**.

**machine**[2] *v* [T] **1** to fasten pieces of cloth together using a SEWING MACHINE **2** to make or shape something using a machine

**machine code** /·ˈ· ˌ·/ *n* [C,U] *technical* instructions in the form of numbers which are understood by a computer

**machine gun** /·ˈ· ·/ *n* [C] a gun that fires a lot of bullets very quickly —**machinegun** *v* [T]

**machine lan·guage** /·ˈ· ˌ··/ *n* [C,U] instructions in a form such as numbers that can be used by a computer

**machine-made** /·ˈ· ·/ *adj* made using a machine —compare HANDMADE

**machine-read·a·ble** /·ˌ· ˈ···◂/ *adj* in a form that can be understood and used by a computer: *information stored in machine-readable form*

**ma·chin·e·ry** /məˈʃiːnəri/ *n* [U] **1** machines, especially large ones: *agricultural machinery|an expensive piece of machinery.* **2** the parts inside a machine that make it work: *Jack keeps tinkering with the machinery, but the car still won't go.* **3** system or set of processes for doing something: *the machinery of government* S3

**machine tool** /·ˈ· ˌ·/ *n* [C] a tool used for cutting and shaping metal, wood etc, usually run by electricity

**machine trans·la·tion** /·ˈ· ·ˌ··/ *n* [U] translation done by a computer

**ma·chin·ist** /məˈʃiːnɪ̵st/ *n* [C] someone who operates a machine, especially in a factory

**ma·chis·mo** /məˈtʃɪzməʊ, -ˈkɪz-‖mɑːˈtʃɪzmoʊ, mə-/ *n* [U] traditional male behaviour that emphasizes how brave, strong, and sexually attractive a man is

**mach·o** /ˈmætʃəʊ‖ˈmɑːtʃoʊ/ *adj informal* macho behaviour emphasizes a man's physical strength, lack of sensitive feelings, and other qualities considered to be typical

of men: *Jim likes to pretend he's macho but he's actually quite a vulnerable guy.* | *He's so concerned with his macho image.*

**macho man** /ˈ·· ·/ *n* [C] a man who is always trying to show that he is strong, brave etc

**mack** /mæk/ *n* [C] *BrE* another spelling of MAC

**mack·e·rel** /ˈmækərəl/ *n plural* **mackerel** [C] a sea fish that has oily flesh and a strong taste

**mack·in·tosh** /ˈmækɪ̵ntɒʃ‖-tɑːʃ/ *n* [C] *old fashioned especially BrE* a coat worn to keep out the rain; MAC

**ma·cra·mé** /məˈkrɑːmi‖ˌmækrəˈmeɪ/ *n* [U] the art of knotting string together in patterns for decoration

**mac·ro** /ˈmækrəʊ‖-roʊ/ *n plural* **macros** [C] a set of instructions for a computer, stored and used as a unit

**macro-** /ˈmækrəʊ‖-roʊ/ *prefix technical* large, especially concerning a whole system rather than particular parts of it: *macroeconomics* | *macromolecular structures* —compare MICRO-

**mac·ro·bi·ot·ic** /ˌmækrəʊbaɪˈɒtɪk‖-kroʊbaɪ‖-ˈɑːtɪk◂/ *adj* macrobiotic food consists mainly of grains and vegetables, with no added chemicals

**mac·ro·cos·m** /ˈmækrəʊkɒzəm‖-kroʊkɑː-/ *n* [C] a large, complicated system such as the whole universe or a society, considered as a single unit —compare MICROCOSM

**mac·ro·ec·o·nom·ics·** /ˌmækrəʊekəˈnɒmɪks,-iːkə-‖-kroʊekəˈnɑː-,-iːkə-/ *n* [U] the study of large economic systems such as those of a whole country or area of the world —**macroeconomic** *adj*

S2 W3 **mad** /mæd/ *adj* **madder, maddest**

**1 ►ANGRY◄** [not before noun] *informal especially AmE* angry: *You make me so mad!* | *Stay clear of Tucker – he's mad as hell and looking for a fight.* | **mad at sb** *AmE*: *Don't get mad at me, I'm just telling you what Ray said.* | **mad with sb** *BrE*: *Mum's really mad with Peter since he borrowed her car.* | **go mad** *BrE informal* (=become extremely angry) *Joe will go mad when he finds out how much I paid for that dress.* | **hopping mad** (=very angry) | **as mad as a wet hen** *AmE* (=very angry)

**2 ►CRAZY◄** *BrE* very silly or unwise; crazy: *Surely no one would be mad enough to fly in this weather?* | *You've agreed to marry him! Are you mad?* | **stark raving mad** (=completely crazy) *My friends all think I'm stark raving mad.* | **barking mad** (=completely crazy, with very strange ideas)

**3 ►MENTALLY ILL◄** *old-fashioned, not technical* mentally ill; INSANE (2): *Mr Rochester's mad wife* | *There was a mad gleam in his bloodshot eyes.*

**4 ►WILD/UNCONTROLLED◄** *especially BrE* behaving in a wild, uncontrolled way, without thinking about what you are doing: **a mad dash/rush etc** *We all made a mad dash for the door.* | **be mad with rage/grief etc** *She was mad with grief when she heard about her son's death.*

**5 go mad a)** *not technical* to become mentally ill **b)** *especially BrE* to start behaving in an excited or uncontrolled way: *When Italy scored, the crowd went mad.* | *We went a bit mad and ordered a bottle of champagne.* **c)** *BrE* to start feeling crazy because you are very bored, annoyed, or anxious: *Sometimes I thought I'd go mad with loneliness.* | *I'll go mad if I have to spend another day in that place.* **d)** *BrE informal* to become very angry: *Mum will go mad when she finds out what I paid for this dress.*

**6 don't go mad** *BrE spoken* used to tell someone not to work too hard or to get too excited: *I know you've got a lot to do before tomorrow morning but don't go mad.*

**7 you/she etc must be mad (to do sth)** *BrE spoken* used when you think someone is very silly or stupid to do something: *You've given up your job? You must be mad!*

**8 be mad about/on sb** *BrE informal* to love someone in a strong, uncontrolled way: *I was totally mad about him.*

**9 be mad about/on sth** *informal BrE* | to be very interested in an activity and spend a lot of time on it: *He's completely mad about computer games.*

**10 be mad keen on** *BrE informal* to be very interested in something or like it very much: *Giles was mad keen on planes from an early age.*

**11 run/work etc like mad** *BrE informal* to run, work etc as quickly as you can: *She ran like mad to catch the bus.* | *We've been working like mad to get the job finished.*

**12 drive sb mad** *BrE* to make someone so bored, annoyed, or anxious that they feel as if they are going crazy: *I wish you'd stop making that noise, it's driving me mad!*

**13 power-mad/money-mad/sex-mad etc** only interested in power, money etc: *a power-mad dictator*

**14 as mad as a hatter** *informal* behaving in a way that is very silly or strange, but unlikely to do any harm

**mad·am** /ˈmædəm/ *n* **1** a polite way of addressing a woman, especially a customer in a shop: *Are you being served, Madam?* **2 Dear Madam** used at the beginning of a business letter to a woman **3 Madam President/Ambassador etc** a way of addressing a woman who has an important official position **4** [C] a woman who is in charge of a BROTHEL (=place where women are paid to have sex with men) **5 a (proper) little madam** *BrE informal* a young girl who expects other people to do what she wants

**Mad·ame** /ˈmædəm, məˈdɑːm/ *n plural* **Mesdames** /meɪˈdæm‖meɪˈdɑːm/ a title used to address a French-speaking woman, especially a married one; MRS: *Madame Lefevre*

**mad·cap** /ˈmædkæp/ *adj* a madcap idea seems crazy and unlikely to succeed

**mad cow dis·ease** /ˌ· ˈ· ·ˌ·/ *n* [U] *not technical* BSE

**mad·den** /ˈmædn/ *v* [T usually passive] to make someone extremely angry or annoyed

**mad·den·ing** /ˈmædənɪŋ/ *adj* extremely annoying: *maddening delays* —**maddeningly** *adv*

**made** /meɪd/ **1** the past tense and past participle of MAKE[1] **2 be made for each other** *informal* to be completely suitable for each other, especially as husband and wife: *Jacinta and Dermot were made for each other.* **3 have (got) it made** *informal* to have everything that you need for a happy life: *Nice house, good job, lovely family – you've got it made!* **4 see what sb is (really) made of** *informal* to find out how strong, brave etc someone is **5 I'm not made of money** *spoken* used to say that you cannot afford something: *I can't buy you shoes as well – I'm not made of money!* **6 be made (for life)** *informal* to be so rich that you will never have to work again: *If the deal is successful I'll be made for life.* **7 I wasn't made for** *BrE spoken* used to say that you are not enjoying a job or activity: *I wasn't made for housework.*

**Ma·dei·ra** /məˈdɪərə‖-ˈdɪrə/ *n* [U] a strong sweet wine

**Madeira cake** /·ˈ·· ·/ *n* [U] a kind of plain yellow cake

**Mad·e·moi·selle** /ˌmædəmwəˈzel/ *n plural* **Mesdemoiselles** /ˌmeɪdəmwəˈzel/ a title used to address a young unmarried French-speaking woman; MISS[2](1): *Mademoiselle Dubois*

**made-to-mea·sure** /ˌ· · ˈ··◂/ *adj* made-to-measure clothes are specially made to fit you

**made-to-or·der** /ˌ· · ˈ··◂/ *adj AmE* made-to-order clothing, furniture etc is made for one particular customer

**made-up** /ˌ· ˈ·◂/ *adj* **1** a story that is made-up is not true: *This tale of hers is totally made-up.* —see also **make up** (MAKE[1]) **2** wearing MAKE-UP (1) on your face: *She was heavily made-up.*

**mad·house** /ˈmædhaʊs/ *n* [C] **1** a place with lot of people, noise, and activity: *This office is like a madhouse.* **2** *old use* a MENTAL HOSPITAL

**mad·ly** /ˈmædli/ *adv* **1** in a wild, uncontrolled way: *She was beating madly on the door with her fists.* **2 madly in love** very much in love

**mad·man** /ˈmædmən/ *n plural* **madmen** /-mən/ [C] **1 like a madman** in a wild, uncontrolled way: *He went racing off like a madman!* **2** *not technical* a man who is mentally ill

**mad·ness** /ˈmædnɪ̵s/ *n* [U] **1** *especially BrE* very stupid behaviour that could be dangerous: **it is/would be madness to do sth** *It would be sheer madness to try to cross the desert on your own.* **2** *not technical* serious mental illness —see also **there's method in sb's madness** (METHOD (3))

**Ma·don·na** /mə'dɒnə‖mə'dɑː-/ *n* **1 the Madonna** Mary, the mother of Jesus, in the Christian religion **2** [C] a picture or figure of Mary

**ma·dras** /mə'drɑːs,-dræs/ *n* **1** [C,U] a kind of CURRY (=hot-tasting Indian dish) usually made with meat **2** [U] a kind of cotton cloth with stripes

**mad·ri·gal** /'mædrɪgəl/ *n* [C] a song for several singers without musical instruments, popular in the 16th and 17th centuries

**mad·wom·an** /'mædwʊmən/ *n plural* **madwomen** /-wɪmɪn/ [C] *not technical* a woman who is mentally ill

**mael·strom** /'meɪlstrəm/ *n* [C] **1** a situation full of uncontrollable events or strong emotions that make people feel weak or frightened: *a maelstrom of conflicting emotions* **2** a violent storm

**maes·tro** /'maɪstrəʊ‖-roʊ/ *n* [C] someone who can do something very well, especially a musician

**maf·i·a** /'mɑːfiə‖'mɑː-, 'mæ-/ *n* [singular] **1 the Mafia** a large organised group of criminals who control many illegal activities especially in Italy and the US **2** a powerful group of people within an organization or profession who support and protect each other: *the medical mafia*

**maf·i·o·so** /ˌmɑːfi'əʊsəʊ, ˌmæ-‖-'oʊsoʊ/ *n plural* **mafiosi**/-si/ [C] a member of the Mafia

**mag** /mæg/ *n* [C] *informal* a magazine

S2 W2 **mag·a·zine** /ˌmægə'ziːn‖'mægəziːn/ *n* [C] **1** a large thin book with a paper cover that contains news stories, articles, photographs etc, and is sold weekly or monthly: *a glossy fashion magazine|a literary magazine* **2** the part of a gun that holds the bullets —see picture at GUN[1] **3** the container that holds the film in a camera or PROJECTOR **4** a room or building for storing weapons, explosives etc

**ma·gen·ta** /mə'dʒentə/ *n* [U] a bright pink colour —**magenta** *adj* —see picture on page 411

**mag·got** /'mægət/ *n* [C] a small creature like a WORM that is the young form of a FLY and lives in decaying food, flesh etc

**Ma·gi** /'meɪdʒaɪ/ *n* [plural] **the Magi** the three wise men who brought gifts to the baby Jesus, according to the Christian religion

**ma·gic[1]** /'mædʒɪk/ *n* [U] **1** a secret power used to control events or do impossible things, by saying special words or performing special actions: *Do you believe in magic?*|**work/do magic** *tales of wizards who could work magic* —see also BLACK MAGIC, WHITE MAGIC **2** a special, attractive or exciting quality: *These old stories still retain their magic.* **3** the skill of doing tricks that look like magic, used by a MAGICIAN, or the tricks a magician does **4 like magic/as if by magic** in a surprising way that seems impossible to explain: *The bottle had disappeared as if by magic.*|**work like magic** (=be very effective)

**magic[2]** *adj* **1** [only before noun] having special powers that are not normal or natural, so that you can do impossible things: *There is no magic formula for instant success.*|**magic spell/charm etc** *a magic hat that makes her invisible*|**magic trick** (=a trick in which something happens in a way that seems impossible to explain) *His best magic trick is sawing a lady in half.* **2 magic number/word** a number or word that is very important or that has a powerful effect on people **3 have a magic touch** to have a special ability to make things work well or to make people happy: *The baby's always quiet for Gary – he has a magic touch.* **4** [not before noun] *BrE spoken* very good or very enjoyable: *"Did you have a good time?" "Yeah, it was magic!"* **5 magic bullet** *informal* a quick, painless cure for illness, or something that solves a difficult problem in an easy way

**magic[3]** *v* **magicked, magicking** *BrE*

**magic** sth/sb **away** *phr v* [T] to make someone or something disappear by using magic: *I wish I could magic us away to a warm beach.*

**magic** sth ↔ **up** *phr v* [T] to make something appear suddenly and unexpectedly

**ma·gic·al** /'mædʒɪkəl/ *adj* **1** very enjoyable, exciting or romantic, in a strange or special way: *that magical evening we spent together* **2** containing magic, or done using magic: *magical powers* —**magically** /-kli/ *adv*

**magic car·pet** /ˌ·· '··/ *n* [C] a CARPET[1] (1) that people use to travel through the air in children's stories

**magic eye** /ˌ·· '·/ *n* [C] *informal* a PHOTOELECTRIC CELL

**ma·gi·cian** /mə'dʒɪʃən/ *n* [C] **1** someone in stories who can use magic; WIZARD (1) **2** an entertainer who performs magic tricks; CONJURER

**magic lan·tern** /ˌ·· '··/ *n* [C] a piece of equipment used in the past to make pictures shine onto a white wall or surface

**magic mush·room** /ˌ·· '··/ *n* [C] a type of MUSHROOM that has an effect like some drugs, and makes you see things that are not really there

**magic wand** /ˌ·· '·/ *n* [C] **1** a small stick used by a MAGICIAN **2 wave a magic wand** *humorous* to solve problems or difficulties immediately: *I can't just wave my magic wand and make your problems disappear!*

**ma·gis·te·ri·al** /ˌmædʒɪ'stɪəriəl◂‖-'stɪr-/ *adj* **1** a magisterial way of behaving or speaking shows that you think you have authority: *his magisterial voice* **2** a magisterial book is written by someone who has very great knowledge about a subject: *his magisterial study of the First World War* **3** connected with or done by a magistrate: *magisterial district* —**magisterially** *adv*

**ma·gis·tra·cy** /'mædʒɪstrəsi/ *n* [U] **1** the official position of a magistrate, or the time during which someone has this position **2 the magistracy** magistrates considered together as a group

**ma·gis·trate** /'mædʒɪstreɪt, -strɪt/ *n* [C] someone who judges less serious crimes in a court of law

**Magistrates' Court** /'··· ˌ·/ *n* [C] the lowest court of law in England and Wales, which deals with less serious crimes

**mag·ma** /'mægmə/ *n* [U] *technical* hot melted rock below the surface of the Earth

**magna cum lau·de** /ˌmægnə kʌm 'lɔːdi, -kʊm 'laʊdeɪ‖-kʊm 'laʊdi/ *adj, adv Latin* at the second of the three highest levels of achievement that American students can reach when they finish their college studies —compare CUM LAUDE, SUMMA CUM LAUDE

**mag·nan·i·mous** /mæg'nænɪməs/ *adj* kind and generous, especially to someone that you have defeated in some way: *a magnanimous gesture* —**magnanimously** *adv* —**magnanimity** /ˌmægnə'nɪmɪti/ *n* [U]

**mag·nate** /'mægneɪt, -nɪt/ *n* [C] **steel/oil/shipping magnate** a rich and powerful person in a particular industry

**mag·ne·sia** /mæg'niːʃə, -ʒə/ *n* [U] a light, white powder used in medicine and in industry —see also MILK OF MAGNESIA

**mag·ne·si·um** /mæg'niːziəm/ *n* [U] a common silver-white metal that burns with a bright yellow light

**mag·net** /'mægnɪt/ *n* [C] **1** a piece of iron or steel that can make other metal objects move towards it **2** a person or place that attracts many other people or things: *The region has become a magnet for small businesses.*

**mag·net·ic** /mæg'netɪk/ *adj* **1** connected with or produced by MAGNETISM: *magnetic forces|a magnetic disk* **2 magnetic personality/charm etc** a personality etc that makes other people feel strongly attracted towards you **3** having the power of a magnet: *a magnetic bulletin board* —**magnetically** /-kli/ *adv*

**magnetic field** /ˌ·‥ ˈ·/ *n* [U] an area around an object that has magnetic power

**magnetic head** /ˌ·‥ ˈ·/ *n* [C] **1** the part of a TAPE RECORDER that records sound **2** the part of a computer that reads and writes DATA

**magnetic me·di·a** /ˌ·‥ ˈ···/ *n* [plural, U] magnetic methods of storing information for computers, for example FLOPPY DISKS or MAGNETIC TAPE

**magnetic north** /ˌ·‥ ˈ·/ *n* [U] the northern direction shown by the needle on a COMPASS (1) —compare TRUE NORTH

**magnetic pole** /ˌ·‥ ˈ·/ *n* [C] **1** one of the two points that are not firmly fixed but are near the North and South Poles of the Earth, towards which the needle on a COMPASS (1) points **2** a POLE[1] (5a)

**magnetic tape** /ˌ·‥ ˈ·/ *n* [U] TAPE[1] (1a) on which sound, pictures, or computer information can be recorded using magnetism

**mag·net·is·m** /ˈmægnᵻtɪzəm/ *n* [U] **1** the physical force by which a MAGNET (1) attracts metal, or which is produced when an electric current is passed through iron or steel **2** a quality that makes other people feel attracted to you: *his extraordinary personal magnetism*

**mag·net·ize** also **-ise** *BrE* /ˈmægnᵻtaɪz/ *v* [T] **1** to make iron or steel able to attract other pieces of metal **2** to have a powerful effect on people so that they feel strongly attracted to you: *His dark flashing eyes magnetized those around him.*

**mag·ne·to** /mægˈniːtəʊ‖-toʊ/ *n* [C] a piece of equipment containing one or more magnets that is used for producing electricity, especially in the engine of a car

**magnet school** /ˈ·· ˌ·/ *n* [C] *AmE* a school that has more classes in a particular subject than usual, and so attracts students from a wide area

**mag·ni·fi·ca·tion** /ˌmægnᵻfᵻˈkeɪʃən/ *n* **1** [U] the act of magnifying: *The fingerprints showed up clearly under magnification.* **2** [C] the degree to which something is able to magnify things: *binoculars with a magnification of ×12*

**mag·nif·i·cent** /mægˈnɪfᵻsənt/ *adj* extremely impressive because of being very big, beautiful etc: *The view from the summit was magnificent.* | *a magnificent collection of Mexican art* | *her magnificent mane of red hair* —**magnificently** *adv* —**magnificence** *n* [U]

**magnify**

**mag·ni·fy** /ˈmægnᵻfaɪ/ *v* [T] **1** to make something look bigger than it is: *The photo shows a human embryo, magnified 150 times.* **2** to make something seem more important than it really is: *This report tends to magnify the risks involved.* **3** *formal* to make a problem much worst or more serious: *The results of economic mismanagement were magnified by a series of natural disasters.* **4** *biblical* to praise God —**magnifier** *n* [C]

**magnifying glass** /ˈ····ˌ·/ *n* [C] a round piece of glass with a handle, used to make objects or print look bigger —see picture at MAGNIFY

**mag·ni·tude** /ˈmægnᵻtjuːd‖-tuːd/ *n* **1** [U] greatness of size or importance: *They didn't seem to appreciate the magnitude of the problem.* **2** [C] *technical* the degree of brightness of a star —see also ORDER OF MAGNITUDE

**mag·no·li·a** /mægˈnəʊliə‖-ˈnoʊ-/ *n* **1** [C] a tree with large white, pink, yellow, or purple flowers that smell sweet **2** [U] a very pale pinkish-white colour

**mag·num** /ˈmægnəm/ *n* [C] **1** a large bottle containing about 1.5 litres of wine, CHAMPAGNE etc **2** a type of large PISTOL: *a 44 magnum*

**magnum o·pus** /ˌ·‥ ˈ··/ *n* [singular] *Latin* the most important piece of work by a writer or artist

**mag·pie** /ˈmægpaɪ/ *n* [C] **1** a bird with black and white feathers and a long tail **2** *informal* someone who likes collecting things

**mag tape** /ˌ· ˈ·/ *n* [U] *BrE informal* MAGNETIC TAPE

**ma·ha·ra·jah, maharaja** /ˌmɑːhəˈrɑːdʒə/ *n* [C] an Indian prince or king

**ma·ha·ra·ni, maharanee** /ˌmɑːhəˈrɑːniː/ *n* [C] an Indian PRINCESS or queen

**ma·ha·rish·i** /ˌmɑːhəˈriːʃi/ *n* [C] a HINDU holy teacher

**ma·hat·ma** /məˈhætmə‖məˈhɑːt-/ *n* a title used for a wise and holy man in India

**mahjong, mahjongg** /ˌmɑː ˈdʒɒŋ‖-ˈʒɑːŋ/ *n* [U] a Chinese game played with small pieces of wood or bone

**ma·hog·a·ny** /məˈhɒgəni‖məˈhɑː-/ *n* **1** [C, U] a type of hard reddish brown wood used for making furniture, or the tree that produces this wood **2** [U] a dark, reddish brown colour —**mahogany** *adj*

**ma·hout** /mɑːˈhuːt, məˈhaʊt‖məˈhaʊt/ *n* [C] *IndE* someone who rides and trains elephants

**maid** /meɪd/ *n* [C] **1** a female servant, especially in a large house: *a kitchen maid* **2** *old use* a woman or girl who is not married —see also OLD MAID

**maid·en[1]** /ˈmeɪdn/ *n* [C] *literary* a girl who is not married

**maiden[2]** *adj* **1 maiden flight/voyage** the first journey that a plane or ship makes **2 maiden speech** *BrE* the first speech that someone makes in parliament

**maiden aunt** /ˌ·· ˈ·/ *n* [C] an AUNT who has never married

**mai·den·hair** /ˈmeɪdnheə‖-her/ *n* [U] a kind of FERN

**maid·en·head** /ˈmeɪdnhed/ *n old use* **1** [U] the state of being a female VIRGIN **2** [C] a HYMEN

**maid·en·ly** /ˈmeɪdnli/ *adj old use* typical of a girl or young woman: *maidenly modesty*

**maiden name** /ˈ·· ·/ *n* [C] the family name that a woman had before she got married

**maid of hon·our** /ˌ· · ˈ··/ *n* [C] **1** the chief BRIDESMAID at a wedding **2** an unmarried lady who serves a queen or a PRINCESS **3** *BrE* a type of small cake

**maid·ser·vant** /ˈmeɪdˌsɜːvənt‖-ɜːr-/ *n* [C] *old use* a female servant —compare MANSERVANT

**mail[1]** /meɪl/ *n* **1 the mail** *especially AmE* the system of collecting and delivering letters, packages etc; POST[1] (1): *The mail here's really slow and unreliable.* | **in the mail** *Your photos are in the mail.* | *I'll put the check in the mail.* | **by mail** *Did you send it by mail?* —see also ELECTRONIC MAIL, SNAIL MAIL **2** [U] the letters, packages etc that are delivered to a particular person or at a particular time: *Did we get any mail this morning?* | **in the mail** *Anything interesting in the mail?* —see also JUNK MAIL **3** [U] armour made of metal worn in the Middle Ages S3 W3

**mail[2]** *v* [T] *especially AmE* to send a letter, package etc to someone; POST[2] (1) *BrE*: **mail sth to sb** *I'll mail it to you tomorrow.* S3

**mail·bag** /ˈmeɪlbæg/ *n* [C] **1** a large, strong bag used for carrying mail on trains etc **2** *AmE* a bag used to deliver letters to people's houses; POSTBAG *BrE*

**mail·box** /ˈmeɪlbɒks‖-bɑːks/ *n* [C] *AmE* **1** a box, usually outside a house, where someone's letters are delivered or collected —compare LETTERBOX **2** a container where you post letters; POSTBOX *BrE*

**mail car·ri·er** /ˈ· ˌ···/ *n* [C] *AmE old-fashioned* someone who delivers mail to people's houses

**mail drop** /ˈ· ·/ *n* [C] *AmE* **1** an address where someone's mail is delivered, which is not where they live **2** a box in a post office where your mail can be left

**mail·er** /ˈmeɪlə‖-ər/ *n* [C] *especially AmE* a container or envelope used for sending something small by mail

**mailing list** /ˈ·· ·/ *n* [C] a list of names and addresses kept by an organization, so that it can send information or advertising material by mail

**mail·man** /ˈmeɪlmæn/ *n plural* **mailmen** /-men/ [C] *AmE* a man who delivers mail to people's houses; POSTMAN *BrE*

**mail or·der** /ˌ· ˈ··◂/ *n* [U] a method of buying and selling in which the buyer chooses goods at home and orders them from a company which sends them by mail

**mail·shot** /ˈmeɪlʃɒt‖-ʃɑːt/ *n* [C] advertisements or information sent to many people at one time by mail

**mail train** /ˈ· ·/ *n* [C] a train that carries mail

**maim** /meɪm/ *v* [T] to wound or injure someone very seriously and often permanently: *landmines that kill or maim people in the rural areas* | **maimed for life** *Rod was maimed for life in a car smash.*

S1 W1 **main¹** /meɪn/ *adj* [only before noun] **1** bigger or more important than all other things, ideas, influences etc of the same kind: *I noted down the main points of her speech.* | *The main bedroom is at the back of the house.* | *Lack of confidence was the main reason behind the team's defeat.* | *Our main concern is that the children are safe.* | *The main female character in the movie.* **2 the main thing** *spoken* used to say what is the most important thing in a situation: *As long as you're not hurt, that's the main thing.* | *The main thing is not to panic.* —see also **with an eye to the main chance** (EYE¹ (36)), **the main drag** (DRAG² (7))

**main²** *n* **1** [C] a large pipe or wire carrying the public supply of water, electricity or gas: *a burst water main in the street* **2 the mains** *BrE* **a)** the place on a wall you can connect something to a supply of electricity: *You can run it off batteries or plug it into the mains.* | **at the mains**: *Make sure that the television is turned off at the mains.* **b) mains gas/electricity/water** The public supply of of gas etc through large pipes or wires: *The heater will run off mains gas or bottled gas.* **3 in the main** mostly: *Her fellow students were in the main from wealthy backgrounds.* —see also **with might and main** (MIGHT² (1))

**main clause** /ˌ· ˈ·/ *n* [C] *technical* a CLAUSE that can form a sentence on its own

**main course** /ˈ· ·/ *n* [C] the main part of a meal

**main drag** /ˌ· ˈ·/ *n* **the main drag** *AmE informal* the main street in a town or city where big shops and businesses are: *cruising along the main drag in Las Vegas*

**main·frame** /ˈmeɪnfreɪm/ *n* [C] a large computer that can work very fast and that a lot of people can use at the same time

**main·land** /ˈmeɪnlənd, -lænd/ *n* **the mainland** the main area of land that forms a country, as compared to islands near it that are also part of that country: *a ferry service between the islands and the mainland* —**mainland** *adj*: *mainland Britain*

**main line** /ˌ· ˈ·◂/ *n* [C] an important railway that connects two cities: *the main line to Moscow* —**mainline** *adj*: *a mainline station*

**main·line** /ˈmeɪnlaɪn/ *v* [I,T] *slang* to INJECT illegal drugs into your blood: *By that time he was mainlining heroin.*

S2 W2 **main·ly** /ˈmeɪnli/ *adv* as the largest or most important reason, thing, part of something etc: *Her illness was caused mainly by worry and stress.* | *The workforce is mainly made up of women.* | *the mainly Zulu Inkatha Freedom Party* | [sentence adverb]: *"What did you do all evening?" "Well, we just talked mainly."* | **mainly because**: *I don't go out much, mainly because I have to look after the kids.* | **mainly due to** (=caused to a great degree by) *Increased sales during the summer were mainly due to tourism.* | **mainly why/what/how** *spoken*: *Boredom was mainly why I decided to quit.*

**main·mast** /ˈmeɪnmɑːst, -məst‖-mæst, -məst/ *n* [C] the largest or most important of the MASTS that hold up the sails on a ship

**main road** /ˌ· ˈ·/ *n* [C] a large and important road

**main·sail** /ˈmeɪnsəl, *not tech* -seɪl/ *n* [C] the largest and most important sail on a ship —see picture at YACHT

**main·spring** /ˈmeɪnsprɪŋ/ *n* [C] **1 the mainspring of/for** the most important reason or influence that makes something happen: *Romantic love had been the mainspring of Augustini's poetry* **2** the most important spring in a watch or clock

**main·stay** /ˈmeɪnsteɪ/ *n* **the mainstay of a)** an important part of something that makes it possible for it to work properly or continue to exist: *Agriculture is still the mainstay of the country's economy.* **b)** someone who does most of the important work for a group or organization: *She was the mainstay of the team.*

**main·stream¹** /ˈmeɪnstriːm/ *n* **1 the mainstream of** the most usual way of thinking about something or doing something: *Environmental ideas have been absorbed into the mainstream of European politics.* **2 the mainstream** the people whose ideas about a subject are shared by most people and regarded as normal: *Genet started as a rebel, but soon became part of the literary mainstream.* —**mainstream** *adj*: *mainstream economic theory*

**mainstream²** *v* [T] *AmE* to include a child with physical or mental problems in an ordinary class

**Main Street** /ˈ· ·/ *n* **1** [C] the most important street, with many shops and businesses on it, in many small towns in the US —compare HIGH STREET **2** [U] *AmE* ordinary people who believe in traditional American values: *The President's new tax hikes won't go down too well on Main Street.*

**main·tain** /meɪnˈteɪn, mən-/ *v* [T] S3 W2

**1 ▶ MAKE STH CONTINUE ◀** to make something continue in the same way or at the same high standard as before: *Britain wants to maintain its position as a world power.* | *our commitment to maintaining a high-quality service*

**2 ▶ LEVEL/RATE ◀** to make a level or rate of activity, movement etc stay the same: *It is important to maintain a constant temperature inside the greenhouse.*

**3 ▶ MACHINE/BUILDING ◀** to keep a machine, building etc in good condition by looking after it: *The report found that safety equipment had been very poorly maintained.*

**4 maintain your silence/opposition/ etc** to continue to be silent, to oppose something etc: *Evans has always maintained his allegiance to the trade union movement.*

**5 ▶ SAY ◀** to strongly express your belief that something is true: **maintain (that)** *Critics maintain that these reforms will lead to a decline in educational standards.* | **maintain your innocence** (=continue to say that you are not guilty of something)

**6 ▶ MONEY/FOOD ◀** to provide someone with the things they need, such as money or food: *How can you maintain a family on $900 a month?*

**7 maintain life** to provide animals, plants etc with the things they need in order to exist

**main·te·nance** /ˈmeɪntənəns/ *n* [U] **1** the repairs, painting etc that are necessary to keep something in good condition: [**+ of**] *The caretaker is responsible for the maintenance of the school buildings.* | **car/building etc maintenance** *evening classes in car maintenance* | **maintenance man** (=a man who looks after buildings and equipment for a school or company) **2** *BrE* money paid by someone who is DIVORCED to their former wife or husband; CHILD SUPPORT *AmE* **3** the act of making a state or situation continue: *the maintenance of good relations between the two countries* S2 W3

**mai·son·ette** /ˌmeɪzəˈnet/ *n* [C] *BrE* an apartment, usually on two floors, that is part of a larger house

**mai·tre d'** /ˌmetrə ˈdiː‖ˌmeɪ-/ also **maître d'hôtel**

/ˌmetrə dəʊˈtel‖ˌmeɪtrə doʊ-/ *n* [C] *French* someone who is in charge of a restaurant, and who welcomes guests, gives orders to the waiters etc —see picture on page 838

**maize** /meɪz/ *n* [U] *BrE* a type of tall plant with large yellow seeds which are used for food; CORN (2a) *AmE*

**Maj.** the written abbreviation of MAJOR² (1)

**ma·jes·tic** /məˈdʒestɪk/ *adj* very big and impressive: *the majestic temples of Bangkok* —**majestically** /-kli/ *adv*

**ma·jes·ty** /ˈmædʒɪ̌sti/ *n* [U] **1 Your/Her/His Majesty** used when talking to or about a king or queen: *The Prime Minister is here to see you, Your Majesty.* | *His Majesty the King* **2** the quality of being impressive and powerful that something big has: *the awesome majesty of the snow-capped Rocky Mountains*

S3 W2 **ma·jor¹** /ˈmeɪdʒə‖-ər/ *adj* **1** [usually before noun] very large or important, when compared to other things or people of a similar kind: *There are two major political parties in the US.* | *Mahler's music was a major influence on the young composer.* | *one of the major causes of cancer* —opposite MINOR¹ (1) **2** [usually before noun] having very serious or worrying results: *The loss of Cantona through injury was a major setback for the team.* | **major problem** *This could create major traffic problems.* **3** [not before noun] *AmE spoken* very important: *This is major? You got me out of bed for this?* **4** a major key (KEY¹ (4)) is based on a musical SCALE in which there are SEMITONES between the third and fourth and the seventh and eighth notes: *a symphony in D major* —compare MINOR¹ (2)

**major²** *n* [C] **1** an officer of middle rank in the British or US army or MARINES, or in the US airforce —see table on page B3 —see also DRUM MAJOR **2** *especially AmE* the main subject that a student studies at college or university: *Her major is history.* —compare MINOR² (2) **3** *AmE* someone studying a particular subject as their main subject at college or university: *She's a history major.* **4 the majors** [plural] the MAJOR LEAGUES —compare MINOR LEAGUE

**major³** *v*

**major in** sth *phr v* [T] *especially AmE* to study something as your main subject at college or university: *He's majoring in Political Science.*

**ma·jor·do·mo** /ˌmeɪdʒəˈdəʊməʊ‖-dʒər ˈdoʊmoʊ/ *n* [C] *old-fashioned* someone in charge of the servants in a large house

**ma·jor·ette** /ˌmeɪdʒəˈret/ *n* [C] a girl who spins a BATON while marching with a band

**major gen·e·ral** /ˌ·· ˈ···◂/ *n* [C] an officer of high rank in the British or US army or the US airforce —see table on page B4

**ma·jor·i·ty** /məˈdʒɒrɪ̌ti‖məˈdʒɔː-, məˈdʒɑː-/ *n* **1** [singular] most of the people or things in a particular group: [+ **of**] *The majority of lone parents are divorced or separated women.* | [also + plural verb *BrE*] *Among trade union leaders, a majority still believe in public ownership.* | **the great/vast majority** (=almost all of a group) *In the vast majority of cases the disease proves fatal.* | **a majority decision** (=a decision made by more people voting for it than against it) **2 be in the majority** to form the largest part of a group: *Young people were in the majority at the meeting.* **3** [C] the difference between the number of votes gained by the winning party or person in an election and the number of votes gained by other parties or people: *Their majority in the House was reduced by 20.* | **overall majority** (=a situation in which one party wins more votes in an election than all the other parties) | **by/with a majority** *He won by a majority of 500.* **4** [U] *law* the age when someone legally becomes a responsible adult —opposite MINORITY S3 W2

**majority lead·er** /·ˈ···ˌ··/ *n* [C] the person who organizes the members of the political party that has the most people elected, in either the House of Representatives or the US Senate —compare MINORITY LEADER

**major-league** /ˌ··ˈ/ *adj* [usually before noun] **1** connected with the Major Leagues: *playing major-league baseball* **2** *especially AmE* important or influential: *a major-league player in California politics*

**Major Leagues** /ˌ·· ˈ·/ *n* [plural] the group of teams that make up American professional baseball

S1 W1

## make¹ /meɪk/ *v past tense and past participle* made /meɪd/

① PRODUCE STH
② DO STH
③ CAUSE A STATE/SITUATION
④ FORCE SB TO DO STH
⑤ MONEY
⑥ BE ADDED TOGETHER
⑦ BE SUITABLE
⑧ PRETEND
⑨ MAKE IT
⑩ CALCULATE
⑪ MANAGE
⑫ MAKE WAY
⑬ ARRIVE
⑭ BE GOOD/IMPORTANT
⑮ OTHER MEANINGS

### ① PRODUCE STH

**1** [T] to produce something by working: *I'm going to make a cake for Sam's birthday.* | *Did you make that dress yourself?* | *a car made in Japan* | *They're making a documentary about the Civil War.* | **make sth out of** *You could make some cushion covers out of those old curtains.* | **make sth from** *We made a shelter from leaves and branches.* | **make sb sth** *Shall I make you a cup of coffee?* | **made (out) of** *a blouse made of silk*
**2** to produce something by doing something, often by accident: | **make a hole/dent etc** *Make a hole in the paper.* | **make a mark/scratch etc** *Who made those marks on the wall?*

### ② DO STH

**3** [T] **a)** used with some nouns to mean that someone performs the action of the noun: **make a decision/mistake etc** *It's time to make a decision.* (=to decide) | *Come on, you guys – make an effort!* | *The company was about to make a major purchase.* **b)** used with some nouns of speaking, to mean that someone says something: **make a suggestion/comment/observation etc** *May I make a suggestion?* | *Jackson made a short statement to the press, denying all the charges.*
**4 make an appointment/arrangement/date etc** to arrange to do something, meet someone etc
**5 make a contribution/donation/charge etc** to give or ask for money for a particular purpose: *We have to make a small charge for use of the facilities.*
**6 make an appearance/entrance etc** to suddenly appear somewhere or enter a room
**7 make a start** to begin doing something: [+ **on/with**] *I'd better make a start on the ironing.*

### ③ CAUSE A STATE/SITUATION

**8** [T] to cause a particular state or situation, or make something happen: **make sb/sth do sth** *That tune makes me want to dance.* | *This lever here makes the heating come on.* | *I like him because he makes me laugh.* | **make sb/sth** *You could make this a really nice room if you got a new carpet.* | *the movie that made him a star* | **make sb ill/happy/popular etc** *The decision made her very unpopular with the staff.* | *It makes me so angry to see children being treated like that.* | **make sb feel good/guilty/sick etc** *Jo's reassuring comments made me feel better.* | **make sb look old/thin etc.** *This photo makes her look much older than she really is.* | *I like the dress Jan, it makes you look really slim.* | **make yourself heard/understood etc** *I had to shout to make myself heard above the music.* | **make it clear (that)** *I want to make it clear that I don't agree with this policy.* | **make it known (that)** *He made it known that he would not be running for re-election.*
**9 make trouble/a noise/a mess etc** to do something that causes trouble, noise etc: *The kids had made a terrible mess.* | *Do you have to make such a row?*
**10 make sb captain/leader etc** to give someone a new job or position in a group, organization etc: *She's now been made a full partner.*
**11 make sth the best/worst/most expensive etc** to result in something being the best, worst etc of a particular type: *These findings make Britain the country with the worst record on pollution.*

### ④ FORCE SB TO DO STH

**12** [T] to force someone to do something, or force something to happen: **make sb do sth** *They made us write it out again ten times.* | *Marcia made the poor girl cry.* | **be made to do sth** *I was made to wait two hours for an appointment.*

### ⑤ MONEY

**13** [T] to earn or get money: *She makes about £25,000 a year.* | *We made $10,000 out of selling the house.* | **make money** *Dunson's one aim in life was to make money.*
**14 make a living (doing sth)** to earn the money that you need: *He makes a living repairing secondhand cars.*
**15 make a profit/loss** to get or lose money in a trade or business: *The company has made a big loss this year.* —see GAIN[1] (USAGE)

### ⑥ BE ADDED TOGETHER

**16** [linking verb] to be a particular number or amount when added together: *Two and two make four.* | *So if Jan comes that makes four of us.*

### ⑦ BE SUITABLE

**17** [linking verb] to have the qualities, character etc necessary for a particular job, use, or purpose: *I'm sure Penny will make a very good teacher.* | *The hall would make an excellent theatre.* | *An old cardboard box makes a comfortable bed for a kitten.*

### ⑧ PRETEND

**18 make believe** to pretend that something is true, especially as a game: *We made believe we were on a secret island.* —see also MAKE-BELIEVE
**19 make like** *AmE spoken* to behave in a way that you hope will give people a particular opinion of you: *He makes like he's got it all figured out.*
**20 make as if to do sth** to move in a way that makes it seem that you are going to do something: *Fred, still grinning, made as if to hit me.*

### ⑨ MAKE IT

**21 make it** *informal* **a)** to arrive somewhere in time for something: *If we run, we should make it.* | [+ **to**] *I just made it to the bathroom before throwing up.* **b)** to be successful in a particular activity or profession: *I never thought Clare would make it as an actress.* | **make it big** *AmE* (=be very successful) *They've made it big in show business.* **c)** *spoken* to be able to go to an event, meeting etc that has been arranged: *I'm really sorry, but I won't be able to make it on Sunday after all.* | *We didn't make it to the party in the end.* **d)** to live through an illness or after an accident, or manage to deal with a very difficult experience: *Frank was very ill, and the doctors didn't think he'd make it.* | [+ **through**] *I don't know how I'm going to make it through the day.*
**22 make it up** *BrE* to become friendly with someone again after you have had an argument: *Have you made it up with your sister yet?*
**23 make it up to** to do something good for someone because you feel responsible for something bad that happened to them: *I'll make it up to you one day, I promise.*
**24 make it quick/snappy** *spoken* used to tell someone to do something as quickly as possible: *Two coffees please, and make it snappy.*
**25 make it 6 o'clock/4.30 etc** *BrE spoken* to think that it is a particular time, according to your watch: *"What time do you make it?" "I make it half past two."*
**26 make it with** *AmE* to have sex with someone

### ⑩ CALCULATE

**27** [T] to decide that something is a particular amount or total by calculating: *I make that $150 altogether.*

### ⑪ MANAGE

**28 make do (with/without)** to manage with or without something, even though this is not completely satisfactory: *New clothes are expensive, so you'll just have to make do with what you've got.*

### ⑫ MAKE WAY

**29 make way a)** to move to one side so that someone or something can pass: [+ **for**] *The crowd stepped aside, making way for the riders.* **b)** to be removed so that something newer or better can be used or made instead: [+ **for**] *Several houses were demolished to make way for an office development.*
**30 make your way a)** to move towards something, especially slowly or with difficulty: *We made our way down the hill towards the town.* **b)** to slowly become successful in a particular job, activity, or profession: *Gradually, Henderson began to make his way in politics.*

### ⑬ ARRIVE

**31** [T] *informal* to arrive at or get to a particular place: *I don't think we're going to make the town before nightfall.* | *We didn't make the 6:30 train.*
**32 make the meeting/the party/Tuesday etc** *spoken* to be able to go to something that has been arranged for a particular date or time: *I'm sorry, I can't make Friday after all.* | *Will you be able to make the next meeting?*
**33 make a deadline/target/rate** to succeed in doing something by a particular time, producing a particular amount etc

### ⑭ BE GOOD/IMPORTANT

**34 make the papers/headlines/front page etc** to be interesting or important enough to be printed in the papers etc: *News of their divorce made the headlines.*
**35 make the team/squad etc** to be good enough to be chosen to play in a sports team: *He'll never make the football team.*

### ⑮ OTHER MEANINGS

**36 make a difference** to cause a change, especially an improvement, in a situation: *Their help has made a big difference to the team's success.* | *I tried to reason with him, but it made no difference.* | **make all the difference** *That one extra day off made all the difference.*
**37 make a (phone) call** to speak to someone using a telephone: *I have to make a few calls.*
**38 make time** to find enough time to do something, even though you are busy: *Somehow, she always makes enough time to take the kids out.*
**39 make the bed** to pull the sheets and covers over a bed so that it is tidy after someone has slept in it

[continued on next page]

[continued from previous page]
**40 make or break** to cause either great success or complete failure: *Critics can make or break a young performer.*
**41 it makes a change** *spoken especially BrE* used to say that something is pleasantly different from normal: *It makes a change to get something other than bills in the post!*
**42 that makes two of us** *spoken* used to agree with someone's opinion or to say that something that happened to them has also happened to you: *"I think I've hade enough of this party." "That makes two of us."*
**43 make to do sth** *old use* to seem to be starting to do something: *Greg made to speak, but I stopped him.*
**44 ▶ MAKE STH PERFECT ◀** [T] *informal* to provide the qualities that make something complete or successful: *The hat really makes the outfit.* —see also MADE, **make sb's day** (DAY[1] (35)), **make friends** (FRIEND (2)), **make good** (GOOD[1] (43)), **make sense** (SENSE[1] (9))

**make away with** sb/sth *phr v* [T] **1** *informal* to steal something: *Thieves made away with thousands of dollars worth of jewelry.* **2** *old-fashioned* to kill someone

**make for** sth *phr v* [T] **1** to move towards something, or move in a particular direction: *We made for St. Louis as fast as possible.* **2** to be likely to have a particular result or make something possible: *The larger print makes for easier reading.* | *Such statements don't exactly make for racial harmony.* —see also **be made for each other** (MADE (2))

**make** sb/sth **into** sth *phr v* [T] **1** to change something so that it has a different form or purpose: *We can make your room into a study.* **2** [T] to change someone's character, job, or position in society: *a film which made her into a star overnight*

**make** sth **of** sb/sth *phr v* [T] **1** to understand something in a particular way, or have a particular opinion about something: *I don't know what to make of Kristin's recent behaviour at all.* | *What do you make of this latest idea?* **2** to use the chances, opportunities etc you have in a way that achieves a particular result: *Your college career is whatever you make of it.* | *I want to make something of my life.* | **make the most of** (=use an opportunity as successfully or usefully as possible) *We only have one day in Paris, so we'd better make the most of it.* **3 make a go of sth** *BrE informal* to make something as successful as possible by trying hard or working hard: *She's determined to make a go of the business this time.* **4 make too much of** to treat something as if it is more important than it really is: *The press made too much of what was only meant as a joke.*
**5 make a day/night/evening of it** *informal* to decide to spend a whole day, night etc doing something: *Why don't we go for a meal after the movie and really make an evening of it.* **6 do you want to make sth (out) of it?** *spoken* used to say that you are willing to have a fight or argument with someone —see also **see what sb is (really) made of** (MADE (4))

**make off** *phr v* [I] to leave quickly, especially in order to escape

**make off with** sth *phr v* [T] *informal* to take something that does not belong to you: *Two young men attacked him and made off with his wallet.*

**make out** *phr v* **1** [T **make** sth ↔ **out**] to be only just able to hear, see, or understand something: *I can scarcely make out his writing.* | **make out who/how/when etc** *We couldn't make out what they were talking about.* **2** [T **make** sb ↔ **out**] *informal* to understand someone's character, or what they think, feel, want etc: *Stuart's a strange guy – I can't make him out at all.*
**3 make out a cheque/bill etc** to write a cheque, bill etc: *Make the cheque out to 'Spencer Cross Ltd'.* **4** [T] *informal* to claim or pretend that something is true when it is not: **make out (that)** *She always makes out she's the only one who does any work.* | **make sb out to be sth** *Oh, Sean's not as bad as he's made out to be.*
**5 make out a case (for)** to find good enough reasons to prove something or explain why you need something: *I'm sure we can make out a case for hiring another assistant.* **6** [I] *especially AmE* to succeed or progress in a particular way: *How did you make out at the interview?* **7** [I] *informal, especially AmE* to kiss and touch someone in a sexual way: *making out in the back seats of cars* **8 make out like a bandit** *AmE informal* to get a lot of money or gifts, win a lot etc: *Those kids make out like bandits every Christmas.*

**make** sth ↔ **over** *phr v* [T] **1** to officially and legally give money or property to someone else: *He made over the whole estate to his son.* **2** *AmE* to change something so that it looks different or has a different use: *I've made that old blue dress over into a skirt.* —see also MAKEOVER

**make towards** sth *phr v* [T] to start moving towards something. *She made towards the door.*

**make up** *phr v*
**1 ▶ EXCUSE/EXPLANATION ◀** [T **make** sth ↔ **up**] to invent a story, explanation etc in order to deceive someone: *I think they're making the whole thing up.* —see also MADE-UP
**2 ▶ SONG/POEM ◀** [T **make** sth ↔ **up**] to invent the words or music for a new song, story, poem etc: *We even made up a rude song about it.*
**3 ▶ SB'S FACE ◀** [I,T **make** sb ↔ **up**] to put special paint, colour etc on someone's face in order to change the way they look: *They made him up as an old man for the last act of the play.* —see also MADE-UP, MAKE-UP
**4 ▶ PREPARE/ARRANGE ◀** [T **make** sth ↔ **up**] to prepare or arrange something by putting things together: *I could make up a bed for you on the couch.* | *Get the chemist to make up this prescription for you.*
**5 ▶ FORM/BE ◀** [T **make up** sth] to combine together to form a particular system, group, result etc; CONSTITUTE: *Women make up only 30% of the work force.* **be made up of** *The committee is made up of representatives from every state.* —see COMPRISE (USAGE)
**6 ▶ NUMBER/AMOUNT ◀** [T **make up** sth] *especially BrE* to complete an amount or number to the level that is needed: *I saved as much as I could, and my mum made up the rest of the money.* | *Do you want to make up a four for tennis?*
**7 ▶ TIME/WORK ◀** [T **make** sth ↔ **up**] to work at times when you do not usually work, so that you do all the work that you should have done: *I'm trying to make up the time I lost while I was sick.* | *Is it OK if I make the work up next week?*
**8 ▶ FROM CLOTH ◀** [T **make** sth ↔ **up**] to produce something from cloth by cutting and sewing: [**+ into**] *I plan on making that material up into a dress.*
**9 ▶ FRIENDS ◀** [I] *informal* to become friendly with someone again after you have had an argument: [**+ with**] *Have you made up with Patty yet?* | **kiss and make up**: *When are you two going to kiss and make up?* —see also **make up your mind** (MIND[1] (4))

**make up for** sth *phr v* [T] **1** to make a bad or unpleasant situation seem better, by providing something pleasant: *That one weekend made up for all the disappointments I'd had.* **2** to have so much of one quality that it does not matter that you do not have enough of something else: **make up for sth in/with** *What Jay lacked in experience, he made up for in enthusiasm.* **3 make up for lost time a)** to work more quickly, or at times when you do not usually work, because something has prevented you from working before: *We rehearsed all day Saturday, to make up for lost time.* **b)** to become involved in an activity very eagerly, because you wish you could have done it earlier in your life: *After all those years apart, we're making up for lost time getting to know each other!*

**make up to** sb *phr v* [T] to try to get someone's attention or approval by being friendly or praising them, especially in order to get an advantage for yourself —see also **make it up to** (MAKE[1] (24))

### USAGE NOTE: MAKE

COLLOCATION

There is no simple rule for when to use **make** or **do**. Generally you **make** something that did not exist before: you *make lunch/ trouble/ peace/ a noise/ a plan/ a joke/ a mistake/ a speech/ a promise.* But other verbs are used in phrases like these: *I asked a question.|He gave an answer.|We nearly had an accident.*

**Make** is also used when someone or something is changed in some way: *She made him comfortable.|He made a success of it.|They made friends.|How much money did Shane make?* But *They did a lot of harm/damage.*

When travel is involved, it is safer to use **go**: *They went shopping/for a picnic/on vacation/on a trip.* But you can also say: *They did the shopping* and *They made a trip to Boston.*

You **do** other actions: *They did some exercises/ some research/ a test/ the TOEFL exam.|Would you do me a favour?* But you *make fun of someone, make use of something,* and *make an effort/ attempt/ start.* Sometimes you would use **take** instead —you *take a class/take a look at something/take a ride on something*

**Do** is especially frequent with words that describe work and activities, often ending in *-ing*: *Her husband does all the shopping and cooking.*

GRAMMAR

Apart from in certain fixed phrases, you do not use an adjective immediately after **make**: *She always makes her classes interesting* (NOT *She always makes interesting her classes*).

You **make** someone do something: *The police officer made them empty their pockets.* (NOT *The police officer made them to empty their pockets.*)

However, you do use **to** for the second verb when you are writing or speaking in the passive tense: *They were made to empty their pockets.*

**make²** *n* **1** a particular type of product, made by one company: *What make is your car?*|[+ **of**] *a different make of computer* **2 be on the make** *informal* **a)** to be always trying to get an advantage for yourself **b)** to be trying to have a sexual relationship with someone

**make-be·lieve** /ˈ· ·ˌ·/ *n* [U] a state of imagining or pretending that something is real: *She told me her parents are millionaires, but it's all just make-believe.*

**make·o·ver** /ˈmeɪkəʊvə‖-oʊvər/ *n* [C] a process of improving your own or someone else's appearance with new clothes, a new haircut, MAKE-UP (1) etc

**mak·er** /ˈmeɪkə‖-ər/ *n* [C] **1 mapmaker/watchmaker etc** someone who makes or produces maps etc **2 decision maker/peacemaker etc** someone who is good at or responsible for making decisions, stopping arguments etc: *She was the peacemaker in a family that was always quarreling.* see also TROUBLEMAKER **3** also **makers** [plural] *especially BrE* —a firm that makes or produces something: *There's something wrong with my camera; I'm sending it back to the makers.* **4 meet your maker** *humorous* to die

**make·shift** /ˈmeɪkʃɪft/ *adj* made for temporary use when you need something and there is nothing better available: *a makeshift sofa of crates and cushions*

**make-up** /ˈ· ·/ *n* **1** [U] substances such as powder, creams, and LIPSTICK that some women and also actors put on their faces to improve or change their appearance: *eye make-up* —see also **make up** (MAKE¹) **2** [singular] a particular combination of people or things that form a group or whole: *The make-up of the team should include both young and experienced players.* **3 sb's make-up** the qualities, attitudes etc in someone's character: *It's in Bill's make-up to keep on fighting till the end.* **4** [C] *AmE* a test taken in school because you were not able to take a previous test

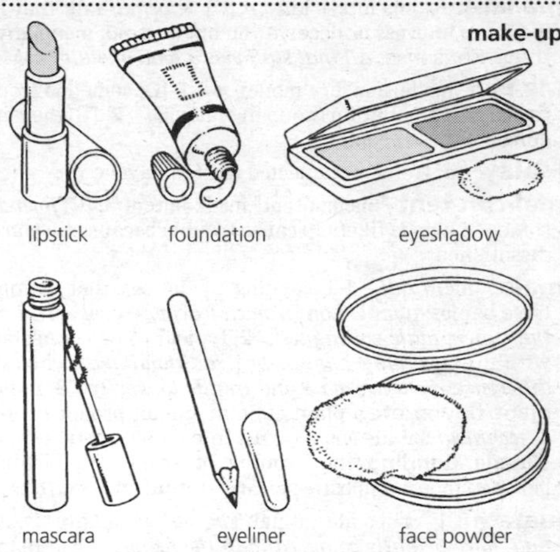


**make-weight** /ˈ· ·/ *n* [C] someone or something that is added only to make a necessary number or quantity

**make-work** /ˈ· ·/ *n* [U] *AmE* work that is not important but is given to people to keep them busy

**mak·ing** /ˈmeɪkɪŋ/ *n* **1** [U] the process or business of making or producing something: **the making of** *an interesting programme about the making of 'Jurassic Park'|involved in the making of policy*|**dress making/decision making etc** *a region famous for cheese making* **2 be the making of sb** to make someone a much better or more successful person: *It's a tough course, but I'm sure it will be the making of him.* **3 have the makings of** to have the qualities or skills needed to become a certain kind of person or thing: *Giggs has the makings of a world-class footballer.* **4 in the making** in the process of being made or produced: *His book was 20 years in the making.* **5 of your own making** problems or difficulties that are of your own making have been caused by you and no-one else

**mal-** /mæl/ *prefix* bad or badly: *a malformed limb* (=wrongly shaped)|*She maltreats her children.* (=treats them cruelly)

**mal·ad·just·ed** /ˌmæləˈdʒʌstɪ̣d◂/ *adj* unable to form good relationships with people because of problems in your character and attitudes —**maladjustment** *n* [U]

**mal·ad·min·i·stra·tion** /ˌmælədmɪnɪ̣ˈstreɪʃən/ *n* [U] *formal* careless or dishonest management

**mal·a·droit** /ˌmæləˈdrɔɪt◂/ *adj formal* not good at dealing with people or problems—**maladroitly** *adv*—**maladroitness** *n* [U]

**mal·a·dy** /ˈmælədi/ *n* [C] **1** *formal* something that is wrong with a system or organization: *Public education suffers from the same malady as many other government programs.* **2** *old use* an illness

**ma·laise** /məˈleɪz, mæ-/ *n* [singular, U] **1** a feeling of anxiety, dissatisfaction, and lack of confidence within a group of people that is not clearly expressed or understood: *We detected a certain malaise among the staff.* **2** a feeling of being slightly ill that usually does not last very long

**mal·a·prop·is·m** /ˈmæləprɒpɪzəm‖-prɑː-/ *n* [C] an amusing mistake made by using a word that sounds similar to the word you intended to say but means something completely different

**ma·lar·i·a** /məˈleəriə‖-ˈler-/ *n* [U] a disease common in hot countries that is caused when an infected MOSQUITO bites you —**malarial** *adj*: *malarial fever*

**ma·lar·key** /məˈlɑːki‖-ˈlɑːr-/ *n* [U] *informal* talk that is meant to impress or deceive you but does not mean anything; NONSENSE: *All that stuff was a load of malarky!*

**Ma·lay**[1] /məˈleɪ‖məˈleɪ, ˈmeɪleɪ/ *n* **1** [C] someone from the largest population group in Malaysia **2** [U] the language of these people

**Malay**[2] *adj* from or connected with Malaysia

**mal·con·tent** /ˈmælkəntent‖ˌmælkənˈtent/ *n* [C] *formal* someone who is likely to cause trouble because they are dissatisfied

S3 W2 **male**[1] /meɪl/ *adj* **1** belonging to the sex that cannot have babies: *a male lion|Women teachers often earn less than their male colleagues.* **2** typical of or connected with this sex: *male aggression|traditional male values|differences between male and female longevity* **3 male plant/flower etc** a plant etc that cannot produce fruit **4** *technical* a male PLUG[1] (1) fits into a hole or SOCKET (1) **5 male bonding** the forming of strong friendships between men —opposite FEMALE[2] —**maleness** *n* [U]

W3 **male**[2] *n* [C] **1** a male animal: *The male is usually bigger and more brightly coloured than the female.* **2** a man, especially a typical man: *She wouldn't appeal to your average male.|Police described her attacker as a white male aged about 25.*

**male chau·vin·ist** /ˌ· ˈ···◂/ *n* [C] a man who believes that men are better than women and who has fixed, traditional ideas about the way men and women should behave: *Bill was very much the male chauvinist, and wouldn't let his wife go out to work.*|**male chauvinist pig** (=an insulting name for a male chauvinist)

**mal·e·dic·tion** /ˌmæləˈdɪkʃən/ *n* [C] *formal* a wish or prayer that something bad should happen to someone; CURSE[2] (2)

**mal·e·fac·tor** /ˈmæləfæktə‖-ər/ *n* [C] *formal* someone who does evil things

**ma·lef·i·cent** /məˈlefəsənt/ *adj formal* doing or able to do evil things —**maleficence** *n* [U]

**male men·o·pause** /ˌ· ˈ···/ *n* [singular] *humorous* a period in the middle of a man's life when he feels anxious and unhappy

**male-voice choir** /ˌ· · ˈ·/ *n* [C] a large group of male singers

**ma·lev·o·lent** /məˈlevələnt/ *adj* showing a desire to harm other people —**malevolence** *n* [U] —**malevolently** *adv*

**mal·feas·ance** /mælˈfiːzəns/ *n* [U] *law* illegal activity, especially by a government official

**mal·for·ma·tion** /ˌmælfɔːˈmeɪʃən‖-fɔːr-/ *n* **1** [C] a part of the body that is badly formed: *congenital malformations in young children* **2** [U] the state of being badly formed: *bone malformation*

**mal·formed** /ˌmælˈfɔːmd◂‖-ˈfɔːrmd◂/ *adj* badly formed

**mal·func·tion** /mælˈfʌŋkʃən/ *n* [C] a fault in the way a machine or computer operates —**malfunction** *v* [I]

**mal·ice** /ˈmæləs/ *n* [U] **1** the desire or intention to deliberately harm someone: *There was no need for Jane to tell them – she did it out of sheer malice.*|**bear sb no malice** (=not want to harm someone although they have behaved badly to you) **2 with malice aforethought** *law* a criminal act that is done with malice aforethought is done in a carefully planned and deliberate way

**ma·li·cious** /məˈlɪʃəs/ *adj* showing a desire to harm or hurt someone: *malicious gossip* —**maliciously** *adv* —**maliciousness** *n* [U]

**ma·lign**[1] /məˈlaɪn/ *v* [T usually passive] to say or write unpleasant things about someone that are untrue: *She had seen herself repeatedly maligned in the newspapers.*|**much maligned** (=criticized by a lot of people, often unfairly) *a much-maligned and controversial film*

**malign**[2] *adj formal* harmful: *a malign influence* —**malignly** *adv* —**malignity** /məˈlɪgnəti/ *n* [U]

**ma·lig·nan·cy** /məˈlɪgnənsi/ *n* **1** [C] *technical* a TUMOUR **2** [U] *formal* feelings of great hatred

**ma·lig·nant** /məˈlɪgnənt/ *adj* **1** *technical* a malignant TUMOUR, disease etc is one that develops uncontrollably and is likely to cause death —compare BENIGN (2) **2** *formal* showing hatred and a strong desire to harm someone: *He advanced towards them with a malignant look.* —**malignantly** *adv*

**ma·lin·ger** /məˈlɪŋgə‖-ər/ *v* [I] to avoid work by pretending to be ill —**malingerer** *n* [C]

**mall** /mɔːl, mæl‖mɒːl/ *n* [C] *especially AmE* a large area where there are a lot of shops, usually a covered area where cars are not allowed

**mal·lard** /ˈmælɑːd‖-ərd/ *n* [C] a kind of wild duck

**mal·le·a·ble** /ˈmæliəbəl/ *adj* **1** something that is malleable is easy to press or pull into a new shape: *malleable steel* **2** someone who is malleable is easily influenced, changed, or trained —**malleability** /ˌmæliəˈbɪləti/ *n* [U]

**mal·let** /ˈmælət/ *n* [C] **1** a wooden hammer with a large end —see picture at TOOL[1] **2** a wooden hammer with a long handle used when playing CROQUET and POLO

**mal·low** /ˈmæləʊ‖-loʊ/ *n* [C,U] a plant with pink or purple flowers and long stems —see also MARSHMALLOW (2)

**mal·nour·ished** /ˌmælˈnʌrɪʃt◂‖-ˈnɜː-,-ˈnʌ-/ *adj* ill or weak because of not having enough food to eat, or because of not eating good food

**mal·nu·tri·tion** /ˌmælnjʊˈtrɪʃən‖-nʊ-/ *n* [U] illness or weakness caused by not having enough food to eat, or by not eating good food

**mal·o·dor·ous** /ˌmælˈəʊdərəs‖-ˈoʊ-/ *adj literary* smelling unpleasant

**mal·prac·tice** /ˌmælˈpræktəs/ *n* [C,U] the act of failing to do a professional duty properly, or of making a mistake while doing it: *She sued her doctor for malpractice.*

**malt**[1] /mɔːlt‖mɑːlt/ *n* **1** [U] grain, usually BARLEY, that has been kept in water for a time and then dried, used for making beer, WHISKY etc **2** [C] *AmE* a drink made from milk treated with malt, with ICE CREAM and something else such as chocolate added: *Two strawberry malts, please.* **3** [C,U] also **malt whisky** —a type of high quality WHISKY from Scotland

**malt**[2] *v* [T] to make grain into malt

**malt·ed** /ˈmɔːltəd‖ˈmɒːl-/ *n* [C] *AmE* a MALT[1] (2)

**Mal·tese** /ˌmɔːlˈtiːz◂‖ˌmɒːl-/ *adj* from or connected with Malta

**Mal·tese Cross** /ˌ·· ˈ·/ *n* [C] a cross with four pieces that become wider as they go out from the centre

**malt liq·uor** /ˌ· ˈ··/ *n* [U] *AmE* a type of beer

**mal·treat** /mælˈtriːt/ *v* [T] to treat a person or animal cruelly —**maltreatment** *n* [U]

**mam** /mæm/ *n* [C] *informal ScotE & NEngE* a mother

**ma·ma**[1], **mamma** /ˈmɑːmə/ also **momma** *n* [C] *AmE informal* a word meaning mother, used by or to children

**ma·ma**[2] /məˈmɑː/ *n* [C] *BrE old-fashioned* a mother

**mama's boy** /ˈmɑːməz ˌbɔɪ/ *n* [C] *AmE* a boy or man who lets his mother look after him and protect him too much, so that people think he is weak; MUMMY'S BOY *BrE*

**mam·ba** /ˈmæmbə‖ˈmɑːmbə, ˈmæmbə/ *n* [C] a poisonous African snake that is black or green

**mam·ma** /ˈmɑːmə/ *n* [C] another spelling of MAMA[1]

**mam·mal** /ˈmæməl/ *n* [C] one of the class of animals that drinks milk from its mother's body when it is young —**mammalian** /mæˈmeɪlien/ *adj*

**mam·ma·ry** /ˈmæməri/ *adj technical* [only before noun] connected with or relating to the breasts

**mammary gland** /'··· ˌ·/ *n* [C] *technical* the part of a woman's breast that produces milk, or a similar part of a female animal

**mam·mo·gra·phy** /mæ'mɒgrəfi‖-'mɑː-/ *n* [U] examination of the breasts using X-RAYS to check for signs of CANCER

**mam·mon** /'mæmən/ *n* [U] money, wealth, and profit, regarded as something that people want or think about too much

**mam·moth¹** /'mæməθ/ *adj* [only before noun] extremely large: *a mammoth task | a mammoth corporation*

**mammoth²** *n* [C] a large hairy ELEPHANT that lived on Earth thousands of years ago

**mam·my** /'mæmi/ *n* [C] *especially IrE* a mother

S1 W1 **man¹** /mæn/ *n plural* **men** /men/ [C]

**1 ▶ MALE PERSON ◀** [C] an adult male human: *There were two men and a woman in the car. | He's a very kind man. | a man's watch | Don't keep him waiting – he's a busy man.*

**2 ▶ STRONG/BRAVE MAN ◀** [C usually singular] a man who has the qualities that people think a man should have, such as being brave, strong etc: **be a man** *Go on, be a man. Tell him he has to pay you more.* | **be man enough to do sth** (=be strong or brave enough) | **make a man (out) of** (=make a boy or young man start behaving in a confident way) *running his own business has really made a man out of Terry.*

**3 ▶ HUMAN BEING ◀ a)** [C] *old-fashioned* a person, either male or female: *All men are equal in the eyes of the law.* **b)** [U] people as a group: *This is one of the worst diseases known to man. | the evolution of man |* **prehistoric/stone-age man** (=the types of people who lived in the early stages of human development)

**4 ▶ WORKER ◀** [C] **a)** [usually plural] a man who works for an employer: *Bad conditions and low wages were making the men restless.* **b)** a man who comes to your house to do a job for you, especially to repair something: *Has the man been to fix the TV?* | **the gas man/rent man etc** *I waited in all day for the man to come and connect the heater.*

**5 ▶ PARTICULAR KIND OF MAN ◀ a ... man a)** a man who belongs to a particular organization, comes from a particular place, does a particular type of work etc: *Bernard was a typical Foreign Office Man. | I got it from the vegetable man in the market. | I think she married a Belfast man.* | **an Oxford/Yale/Cambridge man** (=one who has been to a particular university) **b)** a man who likes, or likes doing, a particular thing: *I'm more of a jazz man myself. | Are you a betting man?*

**6 Man!** *spoken* **a)** used for addressing an adult male, especially when you are excited, angry etc: *Stop talking nonsense, man!* **b)** *especially AmE, CarE* used for addressing someone, especially an adult male: *This party's really great, man!*

**7 ▶ SOLDIER ◀** [C usually plural] a soldier or SAILOR who is under the authority of an officer: *The Captain ordered his men to fire.*

**8 ▶ HUSBAND ◀** [C] *informal* a woman's husband or sexual partner: *She spent five years waiting for her man to come out of prison.*

**9 the man** *spoken* **a)** used to talk about a man you dislike, a man who has done something stupid etc: *I don't know why she married him – I can't stand the man myself | Don't listen to him the man's a complete idiot.* **b)** *AmE* someone who has authority over you, especially a white man or police officer

**10 a man** *old fashioned spoken* used by a man to mean himself: *Can't a man read his paper in peace?*

**11 he's your/our man** *spoken* used to say that a man is the best person for a particular job, situation etc: *If you need repairs done in the house, Brian's your man.*

**12 a man of his word** a man you can trust, who will do what he has promised to do

**13 a man of few words** a man who does not talk very much

**14 be your own man** to behave and think independently without worrying about what other people think

**15 it's every man for himself** *spoken* used to say that people will not help each other: *In journalism it's every man for himself.*

**16 the man in the street** the average man or the average person: *This kind of music doesn't appeal to the man on the street.*

**17 a man of the people** a man who understands and expresses the views and opinions of ordinary people

**18 a man's man** a man who enjoys being with other men and doing male activities, and is popular with men rather than women

**19 ladies' man** a man who is popular with women and who likes to go out with a lot of different women

**20 man and boy** if a man has done something man and boy, he has done it all his life: *I've worked on that farm man and boy.*

**21 be man and wife** to be married

**22 live as man and wife** to behave as though you are married, although you may not be

**23 as one man** *especially literary* if a group of people do something as one man, they do it together: *The audience rose as one man to applaud the singers.*

**24 to a man/to the last man** *especially literary* used to say that all the men in a group do something or have a particular quality: *a disreputable crew, robbers and cutthroats to a man.*

**25 man-about-town** a rich man who spends a lot of time at parties, clubs, theatres etc:

**26 man of God** a religious man, especially a priest

**27 my (good) man** *BrE old-fashioned spoken* used when talking to someone of a lower social class

**28 my man** *spoken* used by some black British and American men to greet a friend

**29 your man** *IrE spoken* used to mean a particular man: *I think your man over there's organizing the music.*

**30 ▶ SERVANT ◀** [C] *old-fashioned* a male servant: *My man will drive you to the station.*

**31 ▶ GAME ◀** [C] one of the pieces you use in a game such as CHESS

**32 every man jack** *old-fashioned* each person in a group

**33 kick/hit a man when he's down** to treat someone badly when you know that they already have problems

**34 man's best friend** a dog

**35 the man on the Clapham omnibus** *BrE* someone who is supposed to represent the attitudes of ordinary people —see also BEST MAN, MAN-TO-MAN, NEW MAN, OLD MAN, **man/woman of the world** (WORLD¹ (26))

**USAGE NOTE: MAN**

POLITENESS

Many people no longer use **man** to mean 'men and women in general' because it gives the impression that women are not included. They prefer to use **humans** or **human beings**: *abilities found in humans* (rather than *in man*). Also you might see: *every disease known to human kind* rather than *every disease known to man/mankind*.

Generally you use the word **person** when it is not important to say whether you are talking about a man or a woman: *Sandy's a really nice person. | unemployed people*

It is also advisable not to use words that contain **man** in the names of jobs, because this seems to mean that only men do that job or that the person is a man. So say that someone is a **chairperson**, rather than a **chairman**, especially when it is a woman. Similarly it is better to say **spokesperson**, **businesspeople**, or **salesperson**.

Sometimes you do not need to use **-man**, **-woman**, or **-person** in the names of jobs at all. For example, people are more likely to say **firefighter** than **fireman**, **police officer** rather than **policeman**, and in British English, **headteacher** or **head** instead of **headmaster** or **headmistress**.

**man²** *v* **manned, manning** [T] to work at, use, or operate a system, piece of equipment etc: *The information desk is manned 24 hours a day.* | *the first manned spacecraft*

**man³** *interjection especially AmE* used to emphasize what you are saying: *Man, that was a lucky escape!*

**man·a·cle** /ˈmænəkəl/ *n* [C usually plural] an iron ring on a chain that is put around the hands or feet of prisoners —**manacled** *[adj]*

S1 W1 **man·age** /ˈmænɪdʒ/ *v*

**1** ▶ **DO STH DIFFICULT** ◀ [I,T] to succeed in doing something difficult, especially after trying very hard: **manage to do sth** *Jenny managed to pass her driving test on the fifth attempt.* | *How do you manage to stay so slim?* | *We eventually managed to track down the elusive Ms Lewis.* | **manage sth** *He tried to walk, but managed only a few shaky steps.* | **manage it** *I said we'd be there by seven, do you think we'll manage it?*

**2** ▶ **DEAL WITH PROBLEMS** ◀ [I] *especially spoken* to succeed in dealing with problems, living in a difficult situation etc: *Frankly, I don't know how single parents manage.* | [+ **without**] *How on earth do you manage without a washing machine?* | **manage with** (=use something even though it is not the best or most suitable thing) *I can't afford to get you a new coat – you'll have to manage with the one you've got.*

**3** ▶ **LIVE WITHOUT MUCH MONEY** ◀ [I] to succeed in buying the things you need to live even though you do not have very much money: *I honestly don't know how we'll manage now Keith's lost his job* | [+ **on**] *People like Jim have to manage on as little as $75 a week.*

**4** ▶ **NOT NEED HELP** ◀ [I,T] *especially spoken* to be able to do something or carry something without help: *"Do you want a hand with those bags?" "No, it's OK, I can manage."* | **manage sth** *You'll never manage that heavy suitcase; let me take it.*

**5** ▶ **CAUSE PROBLEMS** ◀ [T] *especially spoken* used jokingly to mean to do something that causes problems: **manage to do sth** *The kids had managed to spill paint all over the carpet.* | *I don't know how I managed to arrive so late.*

**6** ▶ **BUSINESS** ◀ [T] to direct or control a business and the people who work in it; to be the manager of: *Managing four restaurants is extremely hard work.* | *He used to manage a famous rock band.* | *The company had been very badly managed.*

**7** ▶ **TIME/MONEY** ◀ [T] to use your time or money effectively, without wasting them: *Helena's never been very good at managing her money.*

**8** ▶ **KEEP TIDY** ◀ [T] to succeed in keeping something neat and tidy: *He'll never manage such a big garden on his own.* | *Silkesse conditioner makes hair easier to manage.*

**9** ▶ **CONTROL** ◀ [T] to control the behaviour of a person or animal, so that they do what you want: *Audrey has the knack for managing difficult children.*

**10** ▶ **BE STRONG ENOUGH** ◀ [T] to be able to do something because you are strong enough or healthy enough: *Grandad can't manage the stairs any more.* | *I can only manage three sit-ups.*

**11** ▶ **EAT/DRINK** ◀ [T] to be able to eat or drink something: *I think I could manage another glass of wine.*

**12 manage a smile/a few words etc** to make yourself say or do something when you do not really want to: *Tina managed a reluctant smile for the camera.*

**13** ▶ **HAVE TIME FOR** ◀ **manage Wednesday/7:30/lunch etc** to agree to meet someone or do something with them, even though you are busy: *We should meet soon, can you manage Wednesday evening?*

**man·age·a·ble** /ˈmænɪdʒəbəl/ *adj* easy to control or deal with: *My hair's more manageable since I had it cut.* —opposite UNMANAGEABLE —**manageability** /ˌmænɪdʒəˈbɪləti/ *n* [U]

**man·age·ment** /ˈmænɪdʒmənt/ *n* **1** [U] the act or skill of directing and organizing the work of a company or organization: *He left the management of the firm to his son.* | *They sent me on one of those management training courses.* | **good/bad management** *The company's failure was mainly due to bad management.* **2** [singular, U] the people who are in charge of a company or organization: *Targets were agreed in consultation between management and staff.* | [also + plural verb *BrE*] *The management are blaming the workers for the dispute.* | *a management decision* | **senior/junior management** *talks with senior management* | **middle management** (=in charge of small groups within an organization) **3** [U] the act or skill of dealing with a situation that needs to be controlled in some way: *traffic management* | *better management of the Earth's natural resources* S1 W1

**management buy·out** /ˌ···ˈ··/ *n* [C] the buying of shares (SHARE² (5)) of a company by the management so that they control the company

**management con·sult·ant** /ˈ··· ·ˌ··/ *n* [C] someone who is paid to advise the management of a company how to improve their organization and working methods

**man·ag·er** /ˈmænɪdʒə‖-ər/ *n* [C] **1** someone whose job is to manage part or all of a company or other organization: *a bank manager* | *the General Manager of Chevrolet* | *one of our regional managers* | *Can I speak to the manager?* **2** someone who is in charge of the business affairs of a singer, an actor etc **3** someone who is in charge of training and organizing a sports team: *Jack Charlton, the Ireland manager* —see also LINE MANAGER S1 W1

**man·ag·er·ess** /ˌmænɪdʒəˈres‖ˈmænɪdʒərɪ̀s/ *n* [C] *old-fashioned* a woman who is in charge of a business, especially a shop or restaurant

**man·a·ge·ri·al** /ˌmænɪ̀ˈdʒɪəriəl‖-ˈdʒɪr-/ *adj* connected with the job of a manager: *a managerial post*

**managing di·rec·tor** /ˌ··· ·ˈ··/ *n* [C] *BrE* someone who is in charge of a large company or organization

**ma·ña·na** /mænˈjɑːnə‖mən-/ *adv, adj n Spanish* a word meaning tomorrow, used when talking about someone who seems too relaxed and always delays doing things: *a mañana attitude*

**man-at-arms** /ˌ· ·ˈ·/ *n* [C] *old use* a soldier

**Man·cu·ni·an** /mænˈkjuːniən/ *n* [C] someone who lives in or comes from Manchester —**Mancunian** *adj*

**man·da·la** /ˈmændələ, mænˈdɑːlə/ *n* [C] a picture of a circle around a square, that represents the universe in Hindu and Buddhist religions

**Man·da·rin** /ˈmændərɪn/ *n* [U] the official language of China, spoken by most educated Chinese people

**mandarin** *n* [C] **1** a kind of small orange with skin that is easy to remove **2** *BrE* an important official in the Civil Service, especially one who is regarded as having too much influence: *the mandarins of Whitehall* **3** an important government official in the former Chinese EMPIRE (1)

**mandarin or·ange** /ˌ··· ˈ··/ *n* [C] a MANDARIN (1)

**man·date¹** /ˈmændeɪt/ *n* **1** [C] the right and power to carry out certain policies, which is given to a government or elected official by the people who voted for them: **mandate to do sth** *The President was elected with a clear mandate to tackle violent crime.* | **seek a mandate** *They are seeking a mandate for tax reforms.* **2** [C] an official command given to a person or organization to do something: *an envoy carrying out the Archbishop's mandate* **3** [C,U] the power given to one country to govern another country

**man·date²** /mænˈdeɪt/ *v* [T] **1** *especially AmE* to give an official command that something must be done: *Austerity measures were mandated by the International Monetary Fund.* **2** [often passive] to give someone the right or power to do something

**man·dat·ed** /mænˈdeɪtɪ̣d/ *adj* a mandated country has been placed under the control of another country: *mandated territories*

**man·da·to·ry** /ˈmændət*ə*ri‖-tɔːri/ *adj* something that is mandatory must be done because the law says it must be done; COMPULSORY, OBLIGATORY: *Inspection of imported meat is mandatory.|Drug smuggling carried a mandatory death penalty.*

**man·di·ble** /ˈmændɪ̣b*ə*l/ *n* [C] *technical* **1** the jaw of an animal or fish, especially the lower jaw **2** the upper or lower part of a bird's beak **3** a part like a jaw at the front of an insect's mouth

**man·do·lin** /ˌmændəˈlɪn/ *n* [C] a musical instrument with eight metal strings and a round back

**man·drake** /ˈmændreɪk/ *n* [C] a plant from which drugs can be made which help people to sleep, and which was once thought to have magic powers

**man·drill** /ˈmændrɪl/ *n* [C] a large monkey like a BABOON with a brightly coloured face

**mane** /meɪn/ *n* [C] **1** the long hair on the back of a horse's neck, or around the face and neck of a lion —see picture at HORSE[1] **2** *informal* a person's long thick hair

**man-eat·er** /ˈ· ˌ··/ *n* [C] **1** an animal that eats human flesh **2** *humorous* a woman who has many sexual partners —**man-eating** *adj: a man-eating tiger*

**ma·neu·ver** /məˈnuːvə‖-ər/ *n, v* the American spelling of MANOEUVRE

**ma·neu·ve·ra·ble** /məˈnuːv*ə*rəb*ə*l/ *adj* the American spelling of MANOEUVRABLE

**ma·neu·ve·ring** /məˈnuːv*ə*rɪŋ/ *n* [C,U] the American spelling of MANOEUVRING

**man·ful·ly** /ˈmænf*ə*li/ *adv* in a brave, determined way: *They struggled manfully on through the wind and rain.* —**manful** *adj*

**man·ga·nese** /ˈmæŋgəniːz/ *n* [U] a greyish-white metal used for making glass, steel etc

**mange** /meɪndʒ/ *n* [U] a skin disease of animals that makes them lose small areas of fur

**man·ger** /ˈmeɪndʒə‖-ər/ *n* [C] a long open container that horses, cattle etc eat from —see also **dog in the manger** (DOG[1] (10))

**mange·tout** /ˌmɒnʒˈtuː‖ˌmɑːnʒ-/ *n* [C] *BrE* a kind of flat PEA whose outer part is eaten as well as the seeds; SNOW PEA *AmE*

**man·gle**[1] /ˈmæŋg*ə*l/ *v* [T] **1** [often passive] to damage or injure something badly by crushing or twisting it: *The trap closed round her leg, badly mangling her ankle.* **2** to put clothes through a mangle

**mangle**[2] *n* [C] a machine with two rollers (ROLLER (1)), used to remove water from washed clothes

**man·go** /ˈmæŋgəʊ‖-goʊ/ *n* [C] a tropical fruit with a thin skin and sweet yellow flesh —see picture on page 413

**man·grove** /ˈmæŋgrəʊv‖-groʊv/ *n* [C] a tropical tree that grows in or near water and grows new roots from its branches: *a mangrove swamp*

**mang·y** /ˈmeɪndʒi/ *adj* **1** suffering from MANGE: *emaciated mangy dogs* **2** *informal* dirty and in bad condition: *a mangy-looking rug*

**man·han·dle** /ˈmænhændl/ *v* [T] **1** to push or handle someone roughly: **manhandle sb into/through etc** *The police manhandled him into the car.* **2** to move a heavy object using force: **manhandle sth up/into etc** *We managed to manhandle the piano up the stairs.*

**man·hole** /ˈmænhəʊl‖-hoʊl/ *n* [C] a hole on the surface of a road covered by a lid, used to examine pipes, wires etc

**man·hood** /ˈmænhʊd/ *n* **1** [U] qualities such as strength, courage, and especially sexual power, that people think a man should have; VIRILITY: *He took this remark as an insult to his manhood.* **2** [U] the state of being a man and no longer a boy: *He had barely reached manhood when he married.* **3** [singular] *especially literary* a word meaning PENIS, used in order to avoid saying this directly **4** [U] *literary* all the men of a particular nation: *America's manhood* —compare WOMANHOOD

**man-hour** /ˌ· ˈ·/ *n* [C] the amount of work done by one person in one hour

**man·hunt** /ˈmænhʌnt/ *n* [C] an organized search, especially for a criminal or a prisoner who has escaped

**ma·ni·a** /ˈmeɪniə/ *n* [C,U] **1** a very strong desire for something or interest in something, especially one that affects a lot of people at the same time: [+ **for**] *A mania for a game called Nibs ran through the school.*|**religious/football/disco etc mania** *The whole country is in the grip of football mania.* **2** *technical* a serious mental illness

**ma·ni·ac** /ˈmeɪniæk/ *n* [C] **1** *informal* someone who behaves in a stupid or dangerous way: *Some maniac overtook us on a bend.* **2 a religious maniac/sex maniac etc** *informal* someone who thinks about religion, sex etc all the time: *The woman's a sex maniac if you ask me.* **3** *old-fashioned* someone who is mentally ill

**ma·ni·a·cal** /məˈnaɪək*ə*l/ *adj* behaving as if you are crazy: *maniacal laughter* —**maniacally** /-kli/ *adv*

**man·ic** /ˈmænɪk/ *adj* **1** *informal* behaving in a very anxious or excited way: *She seemed slightly manic.* **2** *technical* connected with a feeling of great happiness and excitement that is part of a mental illness

**manic de·pres·sion** /ˌ·· ·ˈ··/ *n* [U] a mental illness that makes people sometimes feel extremely happy and excited and sometimes extremely sad and hopeless

**manic de·pres·sive** /ˌ·· ·ˈ··/ *n* [C] someone who suffers from manic depression —**manic-depressive** *adj*

**man·i·cure** /ˈmænɪ̣kjʊə‖-kjʊr/ *n* [C,U] a treatment for the hands and nails that includes cutting and polishing the nails —**manicure** *v* [T]

**man·i·cured** /ˈmænɪ̣kjʊəd‖-kjʊrd/ *adj* **1** manicured hands have nails that are neatly cut and polished **2** manicured gardens or LAWNs are very neat and tidy —**manicurist** *n*

**man·i·fest**[1] /ˈmænɪ̣fest/ *v* [T] *formal* **1** to show a feeling, attitude etc: *They have so far manifested a total indifference to our concerns.* **2 manifest itself** to appear or to become easy to see: *Food allergies manifest themselves in a variety of ways.*

**manifest**[2] *adj formal* plain and easy to see; OBVIOUS: *a manifest error of judgment*|**be made manifest** (=be clearly shown) *Their devotion to God is made manifest in ritual prayer.* —**manifestly** *adv:manifestly untrue*

**man·i·fes·ta·tion** /ˌmænɪ̣feˈsteɪʃ*ə*n‖-fə-/ *n formal* **1** [C] a very clear sign that a particular situation or feeling exists: [+ **of**] *These latest riots are a clear manifestation of growing discontent.* **2** [U] the act of appearing or becoming clear: *Manifestation of the disease often doesn't occur until middle age.* **3** [C] the appearance of a GHOST or a sign of its presence

**man·i·fes·to** /ˌmænɪ̣ˈfestəʊ‖-toʊ/ *n* [C] a written statement by an organized group, especially a political party, saying what they believe in and what they intend to do

**man·i·fold**[1] /ˈmænɪ̣fəʊld‖-foʊld/ *adj formal* many and of different kinds: *manifold cultural differences*

**manifold**[2] *n* [C] *technical* an arrangement of pipes through which gases enter or leave a car engine: *an exhaust manifold* —see picture at ENGINE

**man·i·kin, mannikin** /ˈmænɪkɪ̣n/ *n* [C] **1** a model of the human body, used in art classes or for teaching medical students **2** *old use* a little man; DWARF[1]

**ma·nil·a, manilla** /məˈnɪlə/ *n* [U] *old use* strong brown paper used for making envelopes

**ma·nip·u·late** /məˈnɪpjɪ̣leɪt/ *v* [T] **1** to make someone think and behave exactly as you want them to, by skilfully deceiving them or influencing them : *I don't like the way she manipulates people.*|*It was a shameless attempt to manipulate public opinion* **2** to work skilfully with information, systems etc to achieve the result that you

want: *Researchers can manipulate the data in a variety of ways.* **3** *technical* to skilfully move and press a joint or bone into the correct position **4** to use skill in moving or handling something —**manipulation** /məˌnɪp-jᵊˈleɪʃən/ *n* [U]

**ma·nip·u·la·tive** /məˈnɪpjᵊlətɪv‖-leɪ-/ *adj* **1** clever at controlling or deceiving people to get what you want: *She has a very manipulative side to her character.* **2** *technical* connected with the skill of moving bones and joints into the correct position: *manipulative treatment* **3** *technical* connected with the ability to handle objects in a skilful way: *manipulative techniques*

**ma·nip·u·la·tor** /məˈnɪpjᵊleɪtə‖-ər/ *n* [C] someone who is good at getting what they want by cleverly controlling or deceiving other people

**man·kind** /ˌmænˈkaɪnd/ *n* [U] all humans considered as a group: *a great step forward for mankind.* —compare WOMANKIND —MAN[1] (USAGE)

**man·ky** /ˈmæŋki/ *adj BrE informal* looking dirty and unattractive: *a manky old sweater*

**man·ly** /ˈmænli/ *adj* having qualities that people expect and admire in a man, such as being brave and strong: *a deep manly voice* —**manliness** *n* [U]

**man-made** /ˌ· ˈ·◂/ *adj* produced by people; not natural: *a man-made lake | man-made fibres* —compare ARTIFICIAL, NATURAL[1]

**man·na** /ˈmænə/ *n* **1 manna from heaven** something that you need, which you suddenly or unexpectedly get or are given **2** [U] the food which, according to the Bible, was provided by God for the Israelites in the desert after their escape from Egypt

**man·ne·quin** /ˈmænɪkɪ̬n/ *n* [C] **1** a model of the human body used for showing clothes in shop windows **2** *old-fashioned* a woman whose job is to wear fashionable clothes and show them to people; MODEL[1] (2)

S3 W2 **man·ner** /ˈmænə‖-ər/ *n*

**1 ▶ WAY ◀** [singular] *formal* the way in which something is done or happens: **manner of doing sth** *This seems rather an odd manner of deciding things.* | **in a ... manner** *I felt stupid for reacting in such an impulsive manner.* | *The matter should be submitted to the accounts committee in the usual manner.*

**2 ▶ WAY OF SPEAKING/BEHAVING ◀** [singular] the way in which someone behaves towards or talks to other people: *She has a calm relaxed manner.* | *I thought I noticed a certain coldness in his manner.*

**3 manners** [plural] **a)** polite ways of behaving in social situations | **good/bad manners** *She has such good manners.* | **it's good/bad manners (to do sth)** *spoken* (=used to tell a child how to behave) *It's bad manners to point at people.* | **she/he has no manners** *spoken*: *"Vic and Lesley just got up and left." "Some people have no manners."* | **where are your manners?** *spoken* (=used to tell someone, especially a child, that they are behaving impolitely) | **table manners** (=the way that you behave at meals) **b)** *formal* the customs of a particular group of people: *a book on the life and manners of Victorian London*

**4 in a manner of speaking** in some ways though not exactly: *I suppose you could call us refugees in a manner of speaking.*

**5 in the manner of** in the style that is typical of a particular person or thing: *a painting in the manner of the early Impressionists*

**6 all manner of** *formal* many different kinds of things or people: *We would discuss all manner of subjects.*

**7 not by any manner of means** *BrE spoken* not at all: *It's not over yet, by any manner of means.*

**8 what manner of...?** *literary* what kind of: *What manner of son would treat his mother in such a way?*

**9 (as) to the manner born** in a natural confident way doing something, as if you have done it many times before —see also COMEDY OF MANNERS

**man·nered** /ˈmænəd‖-ərd/ *adj* **1 well-mannered/bad-mannered/mild-mannered etc** polite, impolite etc in the way you behave in social situations **2** behaving or speaking in an unnatural way, because you want to impress people: *He gave a very mannered performance in the lead rôle.*

**man·ner·is·m** /ˈmænərɪzəm/ *n* **1** [C,U] a way of speaking or moving that is typical of a particular person: *He has the same mannerisms as his father.* **2** [U] the use of a style in art that does not look natural

**man·ni·kin** /ˈmænɪkɪ̬n/ *n* [C] a MANIKIN

**man·nish** /ˈmænɪʃ/ *adj* a woman who is mannish looks or behaves like a man, especially in a way that is considered unattractive: *She had strong, almost mannish features.* —**mannishly** *adv*

**ma·noeu·vra·ble** *BrE*, **maneuverable** *AmE* /məˈnuː-vərəbəl/ *adj* easy to move or turn within small spaces: *an easily manoeuvrable car* —**manoeuvrability** /məˌnuːvərəˈbɪlᵊti/ *n* [U]

**ma·noeu·vre[1]** *BrE*, **maneuver** *AmE* /məˈnuːvə‖-ər/ *n* **1** [C] a skilful or careful movement that you make, for example in order to avoid something or go through a narrow space: *basic skiing manoeuvres* **2** [C,U] a skilful or carefully planned action intended to deceive someone or achieve something: *They tried by diplomatic maneuvers to obtain an agreement.* **3 manoeuvres** [singular] a military exercise like a battle done to train soldiers: **on manoeuvres** (=practising military exercises) *The regiment is abroad on manoeuvres.* **4 room for manoeuvre/freedom of manoeuvre** the possibility of changing your plans or decisions: *They haven't left us much freedom of manoeuvre.*

**manoeuvre[2]** *BrE*, **maneuver** *AmE* — *v* **1** [I always + adv/prep, T always + adv/prep] to move or turn skilfully or to move or turn something skilfully, especially something large and heavy: *She managed to manoeuvre expertly into the parking space.* | **manoeuvre sth along/into/out etc** *Josh manoeuvred himself out of bed and hobbled to the door.* **2** [I,T] to use cleverly planned and often dishonest methods to get the result that you want: **manoeuvre sb into/out of sth** *It was a well-organized plan to maneuvre the President out of office.*

**ma·noeu·vring** *BrE*, **maneuvering** *AmE* /məˈnuː-vərɪŋ/ *n* [C,U] the use of clever and sometimes dishonest methods to get what you want: *diplomatic manoeuvrings*

**man of let·ters** /ˌ· · ˈ··/ *n* [C] a male writer, especially one who writes NOVELS or writes about literature

**man-of-war** /ˌ· · ˈ·/ also **man-o'-war** —*n* [C] *old use* a fighting ship in the navy

**man·or** /ˈmænə‖-ər/ *n* [C] **1** a big old house with a large area of land around it **2** the land that belonged to an important man, under the FEUDAL system **3** *BrE slang* an area that a particular POLICE STATION is responsible for —**manorial** /məˈnɔːriəl/ *adj*

**manor house** /ˈ·· ·/ *n* [C] a big old house in the countryside with a large area of land around it

**man·pow·er** /ˈmænˌpaʊə‖-ər/ *n* [U] all the workers available for a particular kind of work: *a lack of trained manpower*

**man·qué** /ˈmɒŋkeɪ‖mɑːŋˈkeɪ/ *adj French* **artist/actor/teacher manqué** someone who could have been successful as an artist etc, but never became one

**man·sard** /ˈmænsɑːd‖-ɑːrd/ also **mansard roof** /ˈ·· ·/ *n* [C] a roof whose lower part slopes more steeply than its upper part

**manse** /mæns/ *n* [C] a house that is lived in by a priest, in certain Christian churches

**man·ser·vant** /ˈmænˌsɜːvənt‖-ɜːr-/ *n* [C] *old-fashioned* a male servant, especially a man's personal servant

**-manship** /mənʃɪp/ *suffix* [in U nouns] the art or skill of a particular type of person: *seamanship* (=sailing skill) | *statesmanship* | *horsemanship* (=skill at horse-riding)

**man·sion** /ˈmænʃən/ *n* [C] a large impressive-looking house

**man-sized** /ˈ· ·/ —also **man-size** *adj* [only before noun] large and considered suitable for a man: *That's a man-sized breakfast!* | *man-sized paper handkerchiefs*

**man·slaugh·ter** /ˈmænˌslɔːtə‖-ˌslɒːtər/ *n* [U] *law* the crime of killing someone illegally but not deliberately —compare MURDER¹ (1)

**man·tel** /ˈmæntl/ *n* [C] *especially AmE* a mantelpiece

**man·tel·piece** /ˈmæntlpiːs/ *n* [C] a frame surrounding a FIREPLACE, especially the top part that can be used as a shelf

**man·tel·shelf** /ˈmæntlʃelf/ *n* [C] *BrE* the top part of a mantelpiece that can be used as a shelf

**man·til·la** /mænˈtɪlə/ *n* [C] a decorative piece of thin material that covers the head and shoulders, traditionally worn by Spanish women

**man·tis** /ˈmæntɪ̈s/ *n* [C] a PRAYING MANTIS

**man·tle¹** /ˈmæntl/ *n* **1 take on/assume/wear the mantle of** *formal* to accept or have a particular duty or responsibility: *It is up to Europe to take on the mantle of leadership in environmental issues.* **2 a mantle of snow/darkness etc** *literary* something such as snow or darkness that covers a surface or area: *A mantle of snow lay on the trees.* **3** [C] a loose piece of outer clothing without SLEEVES, worn in former times **4** [C] a cover put over the flame of a gas or oil lamp to make it shine more brightly **5** [C] *technical* the part of the Earth around the central CORE¹ (6)

**mantle²** *v* [T] *literary* to cover the surface of something

**man-to-man** /ˌ· · ˈ·◂/ *adv informal* if two men talk about something man-to-man, they discuss it in an honest, direct way: *You two need to discuss this man-to-man.* —**man-to-man** *adj*: *a man-to-man discussion*

**man·tra** /ˈmæntrə/ *n* [C] **1** a piece of holy writing in the Hindu religion **2** a word or sound that is repeated as a prayer or to help people MEDITATE in the Hindu and Buddhist religions

**man·u·al¹** /ˈmænjuəl/ *adj* **1** involving the use of the hands: *manual work* | *manual skills* **2** operated or done by hand or without the help of electricity, computers etc: *a manual typewriter* | *It would take too long to do a manual search of all the data.* —**manually** *adv*

**manual²** *n* [C] **1** a book that gives instructions about how to use a machine: *an instruction manual* **2 on manual** if a machine is on manual it can only be operated by using your hands and not by AUTOMATIC means

**manual la·bour** *BrE*, **manual labor** *AmE* /ˌ··· ˈ··/ *n* [U] work done with your hands that does not need much thought or skill —**manual labourer** *n* [C]

**manual work·er** /ˈ··· ˌ··/ *n* [C] someone whose work involves using their hands rather than their mind —**manual work** *n* [U]

**man·u·fac·ture¹** /ˌmænjɪ̈ˈfæktʃə‖-ər/ *v* [T] **1** to make or produce large quantities of goods to be sold, using machinery: *the company that manufactured the drug* | *manufactured goods* **2** *technical* if your body manufactures a particular substance, it produces it: *Bile is manufactured by the liver.* **3** to invent an untrue story, excuse etc

**manufacture²** *n* **1** [U] *formal* the process of making or producing large quantities of goods to be sold: *Cost will determine the methods of manufacture.* **2 manufactures** [plural] *technical* goods that are produced in large quantities using machinery

S3 W2 **man·u·fac·tur·er** /ˌmænjɪ̈ˈfæktʃərə‖-ər/ *n* [C] also **manufacturers** [plural] —a company or industry that makes large quantities of goods: *Read the manufacturer's instructions before using your new dishwasher.* | *The fridge was sent back to the manufacturers.*

W3 **man·u·fac·tur·ing** /ˌmænjɪ̈ˈfæktʃərɪŋ/ *n* [U] the process or business of producing goods in factories: *Thousands of jobs had been lost in manufacturing.*

**ma·nure** /məˈnjʊə‖məˈnʊr/ *n* [U] waste matter from animals that is mixed with chemicals and put onto soil to produce better crops —**manure** *v* [T]

**man·u·script** /ˈmænjɪ̈skrɪpt/ *n* [C] **1** a book or piece of writing before it is printed: *I read his novel in manuscript.* **2** a book or document written by hand before printing was invented

**Manx** /mæŋks/ *adj* from or connected with the Isle of Man

**man·y** /ˈmeni/ *quantifier* **1** [used especially in formal English, or in ordinary written or spoken English when in questions and negative sentences] a large number of people or things: **many people/things/places etc** *Many people find this kind of movie unpleasant.* | *Rain has been forecast in many areas of the country.* | *Does she have many friends?* | **many of** *Many of our staff are actually part time workers.* | *Thousands of soldiers were sent into battle, many of them killed outright.* | **for many** *For many, the entrance exam proved too difficult.* | **how many...?** *How many brothers and sisters do you have?* | **not many** (=only a few) *There weren't many people at the party.* —see graph at FEW | **the many people/things/places etc** *The committee would like to thank the many visitors who gave money so generously.* | **many a person/thing/place etc** *Through many a crisis it was his family that helped him survive.* —compare LOT (1) **2 as many** the same number as another particular number: *Those cookies were great. I could eat as many again.* (=the same number again) | **as many as** *Grandfather claimed to have as many medals as the general himself.* | **in as many days/weeks etc** *A great trip! We visited five countries in as many days.* | **twice/three times etc as many** *The company now employs four times as many women as men.* | **one/two etc too many** (=one more than necessary) *You've bought one too many. There are only three of us who need tickets.* **3 a) many a time** *old-fashioned* often: *I've sat here many a time and wondered what became of her.* **b) many's the time/day (that/when)** used to say that a particular thing happens often: *Many's the time we've had to borrow money in order to get through the month.* **4 a good many** a fairly large number of people or things: *Stop complaining! A good many people would be happy to have work.* **5 a great many** a very large number of people or things: *Most of the young men went off to the war, and a great many never came back.* **6 have had one too many** *informal* to be drunk: *Don't pay any attention to him – he's had one too many.* **7 the many** *formal* a very large group of people, especially the public in general: *This war is another example of the few sacrificing so much for the many.* **8 be one too many for** *BrE old-fashioned* to be so clever that someone cannot gain advantage over you —opposite FEW —compare MORE, MOST —see also MUCH, **not in so many words** (WORD¹ (19))

**many-sid·ed** /ˌ·· ˈ··◂/ *adj* consisting of many different qualities or features: *a complex many-sided personality*

**Mao·is·m** /ˈmaʊɪzəm/ *n* [U] the system of political thinking invented by Mao Zedong —**Maoist** *n, adj*

**Mao·ri** /ˈmaʊri/ *n* **1** [C] someone who belongs to the race who first lived in New Zealand and who now form only a small part of the population **2** [U] the language of the Maori people —**Maori** *adj*: *a Maori tradition*

**map¹** /mæp/ *n* [C] **1** a drawing of an area of country showing rivers, roads, mountains, towns etc, or of a whole country or several countries: *According to the map we should turn left.* | [+ **of**] *a map of the world* | **a street/road map**: *a street map of Istanbul* | **read a map** (=understand the information it gives) **2 put sth on the map** to make a place famous, so that everyone knows it and talks about it: *It was the Olympic Games that really put Seoul on the map.* **3 off the map** *informal* a long way from towns or places where many people go —see also **wipe sth off the map** (WIPE¹ (8)) S2 W2

**map²** *v* **mapped, mapping** [T] **1** to make a map of a particular area: *Scientists have mapped the surface of the moon.* **2** to discover or show the shape and arrangement of something: *to map the part of the brain responsible for perception*

**map** sth ↔ **out** *phr v* [T] to plan something carefully: *They had mapped out a demanding schedule for us.*

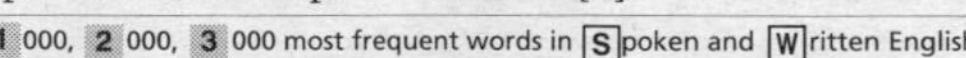

**ma·ple** /ˈmeɪpəl/ *n* **1** [C] a tree with pointed leaves that grows in northern countries such as Canada **2** [U] the wood from a maple

**maple syr·up** /ˌ·· ˈ··/ *n* [U] a sweet sticky liquid, obtained from some kinds of maple tree

**map·ping** /ˈmæpɪŋ/ *n* [C] *technical* a relationship between two mathematical sets in which a member of the first set is exactly matched by a member of the second

**map-read·ing** /ˈ· ˌ··/ *n* [U] the practice of using a map to find which way you should go —**map-reader** *n* [C]

**Mar** the written abbreviation of MARCH

**mar** /mɑː‖mɑːr/ *v* **marred, marring** [T often passive] to make something less attractive or enjoyable; spoil: *His appearance was marred by a scar on his left cheek.*

**mar·a·bou, marabout** /ˈmærəbuː/ *n* [C] a large African STORK (=a long-legged bird)

**ma·ra·cas** /məˈrækəz‖-ˈrɑː-, -ˈræ-/ *n* [plural] a pair of hollow balls, filled with small objects such as stones, that are shaken and used as a musical instrument

**mar·a·schi·no** /ˌmærəˈskiːnəʊ, -ˈʃiː-‖-noʊ/ *n* **1** [U] a sweet alcoholic drink made from a type of black CHERRY **2** [C] a CHERRY that has been kept in maraschino and is used for decorating cakes, drinks etc

**mar·a·thon**[1] /ˈmærəθən‖-θɑːn/ *n* [C] **1** a long race of about 26 miles or 42 kilometres: *the Boston Marathon* | **run a/the marathon** *Garcia ran the marathon in just under three hours.* **2** an activity that lasts a long time and needs a lot of energy, patience, or determination: *We finished the job but it was quite a marathon.*

**marathon**[2] *adj* [only before noun] a marathon event lasts a long time and needs a lot of energy, patience, or determination: *After a marathon round of negotiations, the two leaders reached an agreement.*

**ma·raud·ing** /məˈrɔːdɪŋ‖-ˈrɒː-/ *adj* [only before noun] a marauding person or animal moves around looking for something to destroy or kill: *Local residents live in fear of marauding street-gangs.* —**marauder** *n* [C]

**mar·ble** /ˈmɑːbəl‖ˈmɑːr-/ *n* **1** [U] a type of hard white rock that becomes smooth when polished, and is used for making buildings, STATUES etc: *The columns were of white marble.* | *A marble statue* **2** [C] a very small, coloured glass ball that children roll along the ground as part of a game **3 marbles** [U] a children's game played with marbles **4 lose your marbles** *informal* to start behaving in a crazy way **5** [C] *technical* a STATUE or SCULPTURE made of marble

**mar·bled** /ˈmɑːbəld‖ˈmɑːr-/ *adj* having an irregular pattern of lines and colours: *a marbled book cover*

**march**[1] /mɑːtʃ‖mɑːrtʃ/ *v* **1** [I] to walk quickly and with firm, regular steps like a soldier: *Wellington's army marched until nightfall.* | [+ **across/along/through**] *They had to march across the desert.* | **march 20km/40 miles etc** *We marched 50km across the foothills.* **2** [I always + adv/prep] to walk somewhere quickly and with determination, often because you are angry: [+ **down/off etc**] *Brett marched out of the office, slamming the door behind him.* **3** [I always + adv/prep] to walk somewhere slowly and in a large group to protest about something: *Hundreds of demonstrators are exptected to march on the Council offices.* **4** [T always + adv/prep] to force someone to walk somewhere with you, often pushing or pulling them roughly: **march sb to/along/into etc** *Mr Carter marched us to the principal's office.* **5 be given/get your marching orders** *BrE informal* to be ordered to leave a particular place —**marcher** *n* [C]

**march**[2] *n* [C] **1** the act of walking with firm regular steps like a soldier: *The soldiers did a march around the parade ground.* **2** an organized event in which many people walk together to protest about something: *a massive Civil Rights march in Washington* | **go on a march** *I went on a lot of peace marches when I was a student.* **3** a piece of music with a regular beat for soliders to march to **4 a day's march/two weeks' march etc** the amount of time it takes to march somewhere: *Lake Van was still three days' march away.* **5 marches** [plural] the area around the border of England and Wales or of England and Scotland **6 on the march a)** an army that is on the march is marching somewhere **b)** a belief, idea etc that is on the march is becoming stronger and more popular: *Fascism is on the march again in some parts of Europe.* **7 the march of time/history/events etc** *formal* the progress of time and of things happening that cannot be stopped —see also **steal a march on** (STEAL[1] (8))

**March** written abbreviation **Mar** *n* [C,U] the third month of the year, between February and April: **in March** *The theatre opened in March 1991.* | **last/next March** *She started work here last March.* | **on March 6th/on 6th March**: *The meeting will be on March 6th.* (spoken as: *on the sixth of March* or *on March the sixth* (*BrE*) or *on March sixth* (*AmE*))

**marching band** /ˈ·· ˌ·/ *n* [C] a group of people who play musical instruments while they march

**mar·chio·ness** /ˌmɑːʃəˈnes‖ˈmɑːrʃənɪ̣s/ *n* [C] **1** the wife of a MARQUIS **2** a woman who has the rank of MARQUIS

**march-past** /ˈ· ·/ *n* [C] the march of soldiers past an important person during a ceremony

**Mar·di Gras** /ˌmɑːdi ˈgrɑː‖ˈmɑːrdi grɑː/ *n* [singular] the day before Lent, or the music, dancing etc that celebrate this day in some countries

**mare** /meə‖mer/ *n* [C] **1** a female horse or DONKEY —compare STALLION **2 mare's nest a)** a discovery that seems important but is actually of no value **b)** a confused situation or a very untidy place

**mar·ga·rine** /ˌmɑːdʒəˈriːn, ˌmɑːgə-‖ˈmɑːrdʒərɪ̣n/ *n* [U] a yellow substance that is similar to butter but is not made from milk, which you eat with bread or use for cooking

**mar·ga·ri·ta** /ˌmɑːgəˈriːtə‖ˌmɑːr-/ *n* [C] an alcoholic drink made with TEQUILA and LEMON or LIME juice

**marge** /mɑːdʒ‖mɑːrdʒ/ *n* [U] *BrE spoken* margarine

**mar·gin** /ˈmɑːdʒɪ̣n‖ˈmɑːr-/ *n* [C] **1** the empty space that goes down the side of a page: **in the margin** *She scribbled some notes in the margin.* **2** the number of votes, or the amount of time or distance, by which an election or competition is won or lost: **by a (wide/narrow) margin** *The election was won by a margin of only 200 votes.* **3** the difference between what a business pays for something and what they sell it for —see also PROFIT MARGIN **4 on the margin(s)** not belonging to the main or central part of a society, group, or activity: *unemployed youths living on the margins of society* **5 margin of error** the degree to which a calculation can be wrong without affecting the final results **6** *literary* the edge of a forest, island, or other area S W

**mar·gin·al** /ˈmɑːdʒɪ̣nəl‖ˈmɑːr-/ *adj* **1** too small to make a difference: *a marginal increase in the unemployment figures* **2 marginal seat/constituency** *BrE* a SEAT[1] (5) in a parliament or similar institution, which can be won or lost by a small number of votes **3 marginal land** land that cannot produce good crops **4** written in a margin: *marginal notes* —see also MARGINALLY

**mar·gin·al·ize** also **-ise** *BrE* /ˈmɑːdʒɪ̣nəlaɪz‖ˈmɑːr-/ *v* [T] to make a group of people unimportant and powerless: *The decline of these industries marginalized the unions.*

**mar·gin·al·ly** /ˈmɑːdʒɪ̣nəl-i‖ˈmɑːr-/ *adv* not enough to make an important difference: *Gina's grades have improved marginally since last term.* | [+ adj/adv] *The new system is only marginally more efficient than the old one.*

**ma·ri·a·chi** /ˌmɑːriˈɑːtʃi/ *n* [U] a kind of Mexican dance music

**mar·i·gold** /ˈmærɪ̣gəʊld‖-goʊld/ *n* [C] a plant with golden-yellow flowers

**mar·i·jua·na, marihuana** /ˌmærɪ̣ˈwɑːnə, -ˈhwɑːnə/ *n* [U] an illegal drug smoked like a cigarette, made from the dried leaves of the HEMP plant

**ma·rim·ba** /məˈrɪmbə/ *n* [C] a musical instrument like a XYLOPHONE

**ma·ri·na** /məˈriːnə/ *n* [C] a small port or area of water where people keep boats that are used for pleasure

**mar·i·nade** /ˌmærəˈneɪd/ *n* [C,U] a mixture of oil, wine and SPICES in which meat or fish is put for a time before cooking

**mar·i·nate** /ˈmærəneɪt/ also **marinade** *v* [I,T] to put meat or fish in a marinade, or to be left in a marinade for some time

**Ma·rine** /məˈriːn/ *n* [C] **1** a soldier who serves on a ship, especially a member of the Royal Marines or the Marine Corps —see also MERCHANT NAVY —see table on page B4 **2 the Marines a)** the Marine Corps **b)** the Royal Marines **3 tell that to the Marines!** *spoken* used to say that you do not believe what someone has told you

**marine** *adj* [only before noun] **1** connected with the sea and the creatures that live there: *marine biology* **2** connected with ships or the navy

**Marine Corps** /ˈ· · ·/ *n* [singular] one of the main parts of the US armed forces, consisting of soldiers who serve on ships

**mar·i·ner** /ˈmærənə‖-ər/ *n* [C] *literary* a SAILOR

**mar·i·o·nette** /ˌmæriəˈnet/ *n* [C] a PUPPET whose arms and legs are moved by pulling strings

**mar·i·tal** /ˈmærətl/ *adj* connected with marriage: *marital difficulties* | **marital bliss** *humorous* (=the state of being very happily married) | **marital status** (=an expression used on official forms to ask if someone is married)

**mar·i·time** /ˈmærətaɪm/ *adj* **1** connected with the sea or ships **2** near the sea: *the Canadian maritime provinces*

**mar·jo·ram** /ˈmɑːdʒərəm‖ˈmɑːr-/ *n* [U] a HERB that smells sweet and is used in cooking

S3 W2 **mark¹** /mɑːk‖mɑːrk/ *v*

**1 ► MAKE A MARK ◄** [I,T] to make a mark on something in a way that spoils its appearance, or to become spoiled in this way: *We were careful not to mark the paintwork.* | *The disease had marked her face for life.* | *It's a beautiful table, but it marks very easily.*

**2 ► SHOW POSITION ◄** [T] to show where something is: *A simple wooden cross marked her grave.* | *He had marked the route in red.* | **mark your place** (=put something in a book to show the page you had reached)

**3 ► CELEBRATE ◄** [T] to celebrate an important event: *a festival to mark the town's 200th anniversary*

**4 ► SHOW A CHANGE ◄** [T] to be a sign of an important change or an important stage in the development of something: *His third film marks a major advance in cinematic techniques.*

**5 be marked by** to have a particular quality that is very typical of the way in which someone does something: *Her writing is marked by a subtle irony.*

**6 ► STUDENT'S WORK ◄** [T] *especially BrE* to read a piece of written work and put a number or letter on it to show what standard it is; GRADE¹ (5) *AmE*: *I've got a pile of exam papers to mark.*

**7 ► WRITE ON STH ◄** [T] to write or draw on something, so that someone will notice what you have written: *I've marked the pages you need to look at.* | *a document marked 'private and confidential'*

**8 ► SPORT ◄** [T] *BrE* to stay close to a player of the opposite team during a game

**9 (you) mark my words!** *old-fashioned spoken* used to tell someon that they should pay attention to what you are saying: *There'll be trouble, you mark my words.*

**10 mark you** *old-fashioned spoken* used to emphasize something you say: *Her uncle's just given her a car – given, mark you, not lent.*

**11 mark time a)** *informal* to spend time not doing very much except waiting for something else to happen: *I was just marking time until a better job came up.* **b)** if soldiers mark time, they move their legs as if they were marching, but remain in the same place

**12 mark sb present/absent** to write on an official list that someone is there or not there, especially in school —see also MARKED

**mark** sb/sth ↔ **down** *phr v* [T] **1** to write something down, especially in order to keep a record: *Mark down everything you eat on your daily chart.* | **mark sb down as absent/present** *The teacher marked him down as absent.* **2** to reduce the price of items that are being sold: *Winter coats have been marked down from $80 to $50.* **3** to form an opinion about someone when you first meet them: **mark sb down as sth** *When I first saw Gilbert play I marked him down as a future England player.* **4** to give someone a lower result in a test or exam because of something they have done wrong: *Write neatly as you can be marked down if your paper looks messy.*

**mark** sb/sth ↔ **off** *phr v* [T] **1** to make an area separate by drawing a line around it, putting a rope around it etc: *The competitors' arena had been marked off with cones.* **2** to make a person, period of time etc seem different from others: *Sara's natural flair for languages marked her off from the other students.* **3** to make a mark on a list to show that something has been done or completed: *I've marked off all the places we've already tried.*

**mark** sb/sth ↔ **out** *phr v* [T] **1** to show the shape or position of something by drawing lines around it: *A volleyball court had been marked out on the grass.* **2** to make someone or something seem very different from or much better than other people or things: **mark sb out as sth** *His efficient manner marked him out as a professional.* | **mark sb out for sth** *She seemed marked out for success.*

**mark** sb/sth ↔ **up** *phr v* [T] **1** to increase the price of something, so that you sell it for more than you paid for it: *Compact disks may be marked up as much as 80%.* —see also MARK-UP **2** to write notes or instructions on a piece of writing, music etc: *Someone had already marked up the alto part.*

**mark²** *n* S3 W2

**1 ► DIRT ◄** [C] a spot or small area on a surface, piece of clothing etc which is darker or dirtier than the rest and spoils its appearance: *I can't get these marks out of my T-shirt.* | *His feet left dirty marks all over the floor.* | **finger marks** *There were finger marks smeared on the window.*

**2 ► DAMAGE ◄** [C] a cut, hole, or other small sign of damage: *a burn mark on the kitchen table* | **bite mark/scratch mark etc** *Her teeth left bite marks in the apple.*

**3 ► COLOURED AREA ◄** [C] a small area of darker or lighter colour on a plain surface such as a person's skin or an animal's fur: *The kitten is mainly white with black marks on her back.* —see also BIRTH MARK

**4 ► SIGN ◄** [C] a shape or sign that is written or printed: *What do those strange marks at the top mean?* | **question mark/punctuation mark etc** *Her letter was full of exclamation marks.*

**5 ► STUDENT'S WORK ◄** [C] *especially BrE* a letter or number given by a teacher to show what standard a piece of work is; GRADE¹ (5) *AmE*: *The highest mark was a B+.* | *Her marks have been a lot lower this term.* | **pass mark** (=the mark you needed in order to pass an exam) *The pass mark was 50%.* | **full marks** (=the highest possible mark)

**6 full marks for effort/trying etc** *BrE* used to praise someone for trying hard to do something, even though they did not succeed

**7 mark 2/6 etc a)** a particular type of a car, machine etc: *The Mark 4 gun is much more powerful than the old Mark 3.* **b)** *BrE* a measurement of the temperature of a gas OVEN: *Cook for 40 minutes at gas mark 6.*

**8 ► MONEY ◄** [C] the standard unit of money in Germany

**9 a mark of** a sign that something is true or exists: *She was carrying bags full of toys and clothes – the mark of a mother on the run.* | **a mark of respect** *There was a 2-minute silence as a mark of respect for the dead.*

**10 hit/miss the mark a)** to hit or miss the thing that you were shooting at **b)** to succeed or fail to have the effect you wanted: *His jibe had evidently hit the mark, for she laughed a little awkwardly.*

**11 off the mark/wide of the mark** not correct; INACCURATE: *Our cost estimate was way off the mark.*

**12 make your mark** to become successful or famous: *Wilkins was quick to make his mark, scoring the touchdown.* | [+ on] *Margaret Thatcher made an unforgettable mark on British politics.*

**13 leave its/their mark on** to have an effect on someone or something that changes them in a permanent or very noticeable way: *The years of hardship and poverty had left their mark on her.*
**14 not up to the mark** *BrE* **a)** not good enough: *Her work just isn't up to the mark.* **b)** *old-fashioned* not well and healthy: *I'm not feeling quite up to the mark today.*
**15 be quick/slow off the mark** *informal* to be quick or slow to understand things or react to situations
**16 reach the 60 second/two-mile/£20 etc mark** to reach a particular time, distance, or amount: *Membership is approaching the two million mark.*
**17 the halfway mark** the point in a race, journey, or event that is half way between the start and the finish
**18 on your marks, get set, go!** *spoken* used to start a race
**19 ▶ SIGNATURE ◀** [C] *old use* a sign in the form of a cross, used by someone who is not able to write their name
**20 ▶ CRIME ◀** [C] *AmE* someone that a criminal has decided to steal from or trick —see also EXCLAMATION MARK, **overstep the mark** (OVERSTEP (2)), PUNCTUATION MARK, QUESTION MARK, QUOTATION MARK, SPEECH MARKS

**mark·down** /ˈmɑːkdaʊn‖ˈmɑːrk-/ *n* [C] a reduction in the price of something: *a markdown of $10*

W3 **marked** /mɑːkt‖mɑːrkt/ *adj* **1** very clear and easy to notice: *He showed a marked lack of interest.* | *a marked improvement in the patient's condition* | **in marked contrast** *Sara wore red, in marked contrast to her sister's sombre colours.* **2 a marked man** a man who is in danger because an enemy wants to harm him —**markedly** /ˈmɑːkɪ̣dli‖ˈmɑːr-/ *adv*: *They have a markedly different approach to the problem.*

**mark·er** /ˈmɑːkə‖ˈmɑːrkər/ *n* [C] **1** an object, sign etc that shows the position of something **2** a pen with a thick point made of FELT, used for marking or drawing things —see picture at PEN[1] **3 put down a marker** to say or do something that makes your future intentions clear

**marker pen** /ˈ··· ·/ *n* [C] *BrE* a pen with a thick point made of FELT

S1 W1 **mar·ket**[1] /ˈmɑːkɪ̣t‖ˈmɑːr-/ *n*
**1 ▶ PLACE TO BUY THINGS ◀** [C] **a)** a place where people buy and sell goods, especially in an open area or a large building: *There's a good antiques market here on Sundays.* | *I usually buy all my vegetables at the market.* | **street market** (=with a lot of different people selling things from tables, STALLS etc in the street) **b)** *AmE* a shop that sells food and things for the home
**2 the market a)** the STOCK MARKET: *Most analysts are forecasting a further downturn in the market.* | **play the market** (=risk money on the stock market) | **the markets** (=stock markets around the world) *The markets are nervous at the moment.* **b)** the total amount of trade in a particular kind of goods: *Honda is trying to increase its share of the market.* | **the art/diamond/bond etc market** *The art market is rather depressed.* | **the market in** *the world market in aluminum* **c)** the system in which all prices and wages depend on what goods people want to buy, how many they buy etc: *a naive belief in leaving everything to the market*
**3 on the market** available for people to buy: *There are thousands of different computer games on the market.* | **put a house/business etc on the market (=offer it for sale)** *We put our house on the market at the wrong time.* | **come onto the market** (=become available for people to buy) *a revolutionary new drug that has just come onto the market* | **on the open market** (=generally available for people to buy without any official restrictions) *In some areas, handguns were freely available on the open market.*
**4 ▶ COUNTRY/AREA ◀** [C] a particular country or area where a company sells its goods or where a particular type of goods is sold: *Our main overseas market is Japan.* | *cars intended for the domestic market* | [+ **for**] *The main market for computer software is still in the US.*
**5 ▶ PEOPLE WHO BUY ◀** [singular] the number of people who want to buy something, or the kind of people who want to buy it: [+ **for**] *The market for specialist academic books is pretty small.* | **there is a market for** (=people want to buy a product) *There isn't much of a market for second-hand mainframe computers.*
**6 be in the market for** to be interested in buying something: *Several terrorist groups were believed to be in the market for nuclear technology.*
**7 the job market/the labour market** the number of jobs that are available: *The job market has been badly hit by the recession.*
**8 a buyer's/seller's market** a time that is better for buyers because prices are low, or better for sellers because prices are high —see also BLACK MARKET, FLEA MARKET, **corner the market** (CORNER[2] (3)), **price yourself out of the market** (PRICE[2] (4))

**market**[2] *v* [T] **1** to try to persuade people to buy a product by advertising it in a particular way, using attractive packages etc: *The success of any beauty product depends on the way it is marketed.* **2** to make a product available in shops: *The turkeys are marketed ready-to-cook.*

**mar·ket·a·ble** /ˈmɑːkɪ̣təbəl‖ˈmɑːr-/ *adj* marketable goods, skills etc can be sold easily because people want them: *It's a very marketable qualification.* —**marketability** /ˌmɑːkɪ̣təˈbɪlɪ̣ti‖ˌmɑːr-/ *n* [U]

**market day** /ˈ·· ˌ·/ *n* [C] *especially BrE* the day in the week when there is a market in a particular town

**market-driv·en** /ˌ·· ˈ··◂/ *adj* MARKET-LED

**market e·con·o·my** /ˌ·· ·ˈ···/ *n* [C] a system of producing wealth based on the free operation of business and trade without government controls

**mar·ket·eer** /ˌmɑːkɪ̣ˈtɪə‖ˌmɑːrkɪ̣ˈtɪr/ *n* [C] **anti-Marketeer/pro-Marketeer** *old-fashioned* someone who is against/in favour of Britain being a member of the European Union —see also BLACK MARKETEER, FREE MARKETEER

**market forc·es** /ˌ·· ˈ··/ *n* [plural] the free operation of business and trade without any government controls, which decides the level of prices and wages at a particular time

**market gar·den** /ˌ·· ˈ··/ *n* [C] *BrE* an area of land where vegetables and fruit are grown so that they can be sold; TRUCK FARM *AmE* —**market gardener** *n* [C]

**mar·ket·ing** /ˈmɑːkɪ̣tɪŋ‖ˈmɑːr-/ *n* [U] **1** the activity of trying to sell a company's products by advertising, using attractive packages etc: *a marketing executive* | *a clever marketing ploy* **2 do the marketing/go marketing** *AmE old-fashioned* to go to the shops to buy things, especially food S W

**market lead·er** /ˌ·· ˈ··/ *n* [C] the company that sells the most of a particular kind of product, or the product that is the most successful one of its kind: *Kodak is still the market leader.*

**market-led** /ˌ·· ˈ·◂/ *adj* market-led products, developments etc are a result of public demand for a particular product, service, or skill

**market mak·er** /ˈ·· ˌ··/ *n* [C] *technical* someone who works on the STOCK MARKET buying and selling stocks (STOCK[1] (6)) and shares (SHARE[2] (6))

**mar·ket·place** /ˈmɑːkɪ̣tpleɪs‖ˈmɑːr-/ *n* [C] **1 the marketplace** the part of business activity which is concerned with selling goods: *his uncanny ability to see new opportunities in the marketplace* **2** an open area in a town where a market is held

**market price** /ˌ·· ˈ·/ *n* [singular] the price that people will actually pay for something at a particular time

**market re·search** /ˌ··ˈ··, ·· ˈ··/ *n* [U] a business activity which involves collecting information about what goods people buy and why

**market town** /ˈ·· ·/ *n* [C] *BrE* a town where there is an outdoor market, usually once or twice a week

**market val·ue** /ˌ·· ˈ··/ *n* [singular] the value of a product, building etc based on the price that people are willing to pay for it rather than the cost of producing it or building it

**mark·ing** /ˈmɑːkɪŋ‖ˈmɑːr-/ *n* **1** [C usually plural, U] the coloured patterns and shapes on an animal's fur, on leaves etc: *The leopard has beautiful markings.* **2** [C usually plural, U] colours and shapes painted on aircraft, army vehicles etc **3** [U] *especially BrE* the activity of checking students' written work: *I have to do a lot of marking tonight.*

**marks·man** /ˈmɑːksmən‖ˈmɑːrks-/ *plural* **marksmen** /-mən/ *n* [C] someone who can shoot very well

**marks·man·ship** /ˈmɑːksmənʃɪp‖ˈmɑːrks-/ *n* [U] the ability to shoot very well

**mark-up** /ˈ· ·/ *n* [C] an increase in the price of something, especially from the price a shop pays for something to the price it sells it for: *The retailer's mark-up is 50%.*

**mar·lin** /ˈmɑːlɨn‖ˈmɑːr-/ *n* [C] a large sea fish with a long sharp nose, which people hunt for sport

**mar·ma·lade** /ˈmɑːməleɪd‖ˈmɑːr-/ *n* [U] a JAM made from fruit such as oranges, LEMONS or GRAPEFRUIT, usually eaten at breakfast

**mar·mo·re·al** /mɑːˈmɔːriəl‖mɑːr-/ *adj literary* like MARBLE

**mar·mo·set** /ˈmɑːməzet‖ˈmɑːrməset, -zet/ *n* [C] a type of small monkey with long hair and large eyes that lives in Central and South America

**ma·roon¹** /məˈruːn/ *n* [U] a very dark red-brown colour —maroon *adj* —see picture on page 411

**maroon²** *v* **be marooned** to be left in a place where there are no other people and where you cannot escape: *The car broke down leaving us marooned in the middle of nowhere.*

**maroon³** *n* [C] a small ROCKET used as a signal by ships

**marque** /mɑːk‖mɑːrk/ *n* [C] the well-known name of a type of car or other product, especially an expensive one: *the prestigious Ferrari marque*

**mar·quee** /mɑːˈkiː‖mɑːr-/ *n* [C] **1** a large tent at an outdoor event or celebration, used especially for eating or drinking in **2** *AmE* a sign above the door of a theatre or cinema which gives the name of the play or film

**mar·quess** /ˈmɑːkwɨs‖ˈmɑːr-/ *n* [C] *BrE* a MARQUIS

**mar·quet·ry** /ˈmɑːkɨtri‖ˈmɑːr-/ *n* [U] a pattern made of coloured pieces of wood fastened together, or the art of making these patterns

**mar·quis** /ˈmɑːkwɨs‖ˈmɑːr-/ *n* [C] a man who, in the British system of NOBLE titles, has a rank between DUKE and EARL: *the Marquis of Bath*

S2 W2 **mar·riage** /ˈmærɪdʒ/ *n* **1** [C] the relationship between two people who are married: *They have a very happy marriage.* | *One in three marriages ends in divorce.* **2** [U] the state of being married: *My parents disapprove of sex before marriage.* **3** [C] the ceremony in which two people get married; WEDDING: *The marriage took place at St Bartholomew's church.* **4 by marriage** if you are related to someone by marriage, they are married to someone in your family

**mar·riage·a·ble** /ˈmærɪdʒəbəl/ *adj old-fashioned* suitable for marriage: *a young woman of marriageable age* —**marriageability** /ˌmærɪdʒəˈbɪlɨti/ *n* [U]

**marriage bu·reau** /ˈ·· ˌ··/ *n* [C] an organization that helps people find partners to marry

**marriage cer·tif·i·cate** /ˈ·· ·ˌ··/ *n* [C] an official document that proves that two people are married

**marriage guid·ance** /ˌ·· ˈ··/ *n* [U] advice given to people who are having difficulties in their marriage

**marriage li·cence** /ˈ·· ˌ··/ *n* [C] an official written document saying that two people are allowed to marry

**marriage lines** /ˈ·· ·/ *n* [plural] *old-fashioned BrE* a MARRIAGE CERTIFICATE

**marriage of con·ve·ni·ence** /ˌ·· · ·ˈ···/ *n* [C] a marriage for political or economic reasons, not for love

**marriage vows** /ˈ·· ·/ *n* [plural] the promises that you make during the marriage ceremony

S2 W2 **mar·ried** /ˈmærid/ *adj* **1** having a husband or a wife: *Are you married or single?* | *They've been married for 28 years.* | *More and more married women were returning to the workplace.* | [+ **to**] *She's married to my brother.* | **get married** *We're getting married next month.* | **married life** (=your life when you are married) *How are you enjoying married life?* **2 be married to sth** to give most of your time and attention to a job or activity —see also MARRY, YOUNG MARRIEDS

**mar·row** /ˈmærəʊ‖-roʊ/ *n* **1** [U] the soft fatty substance in the hollow centre of bones; BONE MARROW: *a bone marrow transplant* **2** [C,U] a large long dark green vegetable that grows along the ground —compare SQUASH² (3) —see picture on page 414 **3 chilled/frozen/shocked to the marrow** very cold or shocked: *She had walked all the way home, frozen to the marrow.*

**marrow bone** /ˈ·· ·/ *n* [C,U] a large bone that contains a lot of MARROW (1)

**mar·ry** /ˈmæri/ *v* **marries, married, marrying** S1 W2
**1** [I,T] to become someone's husband or wife: **get married (to)** *I got married when I was 18.* | *Billy got married to the first girl he went out with.* | **marry sb** *one of those romances about a rich tycoon who marries his secretary* | **marry money** (=marry someone who is rich) **2** [T] to perform the ceremony at which two people get married: *The priest who married us was really nice.* **3** [T] to find a husband or wife for one of your children: **marry sb to sb** *She's determined to marry all her daughters to rich men.* **4** [T] *formal* to combine two quite different ideas, designs, tastes etc together: **marry sth with sth** *The design marries traditional styles with modern materials.* **5 not the marrying kind** not the kind of person who wants to get married

**marry into** sth *phr v* [T] to join a family or social group by marrying someone who belongs to it: *She married into a very wealthy family.*

**marry** sb ↔ **off** *phr v* [T] to find a husband or wife for someone: [+ **to**] *They married her off to the first young man who came along.*

> **USAGE NOTE: MARRY**
>
> GRAMMAR
>
> You *marry someone* or *get/are married to someone*, not *with* them. But you can be *married with four children*.
>
> SPOKEN-WRITTEN
>
> **Get married** is more informal and more common in spoken English than **marry**: *Marti is getting married to Jeff next week* (compare *Marti is marrying Jeff next week*).
>
> In spoken English, speakers often avoid *to* with **married** by saying, for example: *Jeff and Marti got married/are married.*

**Mars** /mɑːz‖mɑːrz/ *n* [singular] the PLANET that is fourth in order from the sun, is nearest to the Earth, and is a red colour —see picture at SOLAR SYSTEM

**Mar·seil·laise** /ˌmɑːsəˈleɪz, -seɪˈez‖ˌmɑːr-/ *n* [singular] the national song of France

**marsh** /mɑːʃ‖mɑːrʃ/ *n* [C,U] an area of low flat land that is always wet and soft —compare SWAMP¹, BOG¹ (1) —**marshy** *adj*: *marshy ground*

**mar·shal¹** /ˈmɑːʃəl‖ˈmɑːr-/ *n* [C] **1** an officer of the highest rank in an army or airforce: *Marshal Zhukov* —see table on page B4 **2** *especially BrE* an official in charge of an important public event or ceremony **3** an official in charge of a race or sports event **4** *AmE* an official in a court of law; SHERIFF **5** *AmE* the officer in charge of a city's police force or fire-fighting department

**marshal²** *v* **marshalled, marshalling** *BrE*, **marshaled, marshaling** *AmE* [T] **1 marshal your arguments/ideas/facts etc** to organize your arguments, ideas etc so that they are effective or easy to understand: *Briggs paused for a moment as if to marshal his thoughts.* **2** to control or organize a large group: *Extra stewards had to be employed to marshal the huge crowds.* **3 marshal your forces** to organize all the people and things that you need in order to be ready for a battle, election etc

**marshalling yard** /ˈ··· ·/ *n* [C] *BrE* a place where railway WAGONS are brought together to form trains

**Marshal of the Roy·al Air·force** /ˌ···· ˌ·· ˈ··/ *n* [C] an officer of high rank in the British airforce

**marsh gas** /ˈ· ·/ *n* [U] gas formed from decaying plants under water in a MARSH; METHANE

**marsh·land** /ˈmɑːʃlænd‖ˈmɑːrʃ-/ *n* [U] an area of land where there is a lot of MARSH

**marsh·mal·low** /ˌmɑːʃˈmæləʊ‖ˈmɑːrʃmeloʊ/ *n* [C,U] **1** a very soft light sweet that is white or pink **2** a tall wild plant with pink flowers

**mar·su·pi·al** /mɑːˈsuːpiəl,-ˈsjuː-‖mɑːrˈsuː-/ *n* [C] an animal such as a KANGAROO which carries its babies in a pocket of skin on its body

**mart** /mɑːt‖mɑːrt/ *n* [C] a market: *the biggest cattle mart in the region*

**mar·ten** /ˈmɑːtɪn, -tn‖ˈmɑːrtn/ *n* [C] a small flesh-eating animal that lives mainly in trees

**mar·tial** /ˈmɑːʃəl‖ˈmɑːr-/ *adj* [only before noun] connected with war and fighting: *martial music*

**martial art** /ˌ·· ˈ·/ *n* [C usually plural] a sport such as JUDO or KARATE, in which you fight with your hands and feet, and which was developed in Eastern countries

**martial law** /ˌ·· ˈ·/ *n* [U] a situation in which the army controls an area instead of the police, especially because of fighting against the government: *Fighting in the capital led to the imposition of martial law.*

**Mar·tian** /ˈmɑːʃən‖ˈmɑːr-/ *n* [C] an imaginary creature from the PLANET Mars —**Martian** *adj*

**mar·tin** /ˈmɑːtɪn‖ˈmɑːrtn/ *n* [C] a small bird like a SWALLOW[2] (1)

**mar·ti·net** /ˌmɑːtɪˈnet‖ˌmɑːr-/ *n* [C] *formal* someone who is very strict and makes people obey rules exactly

**mar·ti·ni** /mɑːˈtiːni‖mɑːr-/ *n* [C,U] an alcoholic drink made by mixing GIN or VODKA with VERMOUTH

**mar·tyr¹** /ˈmɑːtə‖ˈmɑːrtər/ *n* [C] **1** someone who is killed or punished because of their religious or political beliefs **2** someone who tries to get other people's sympathy by complaining about how hard their life is: *She's such a martyr!* **3 be a martyr to** *old-fashioned* to suffer a lot because of an illness: *She's a martyr to her arthritis.*

**martyr²** *v* **be martyred** to be killed or punished because of your religious beliefs

**mar·tyr·dom** /ˈmɑːtədəm‖ˈmɑːrtər-/ *n* [U] the death or suffering of a martyr

**mar·tyred** /ˈmɑːtəd‖ˈmɑːrtərd/ *adj* [only before noun] a martyred look or expression is an unhappy one, as if you want to make other people feel sorry for you: *I wish you'd stop giving me those martyred looks.*

**mar·vel¹** /ˈmɑːvəl‖ˈmɑːr-/ *v* **marvelled, marvelling** *BrE*, **marveled, marveling** *AmE* [I, T] to feel great surprise or admiration for something, especially someone's behaviour: [+ **at**] *I marvelled at my mother's ability to remain calm in a crisis.* | **marvel that** *I marvelled that anyone could be so stupid.*

**marvel²** *n* [C] something or someone surprisingly useful or skilful, that you like and admire very much: *the marvels of modern science* | *an electronic marvel* | *I don't know how he did it – he's a bloody marvel!*

S2 **mar·vel·lous** *BrE*, **marvelous** *AmE* /ˈmɑːvələs‖ˈmɑːr-/ *adj* extremely good, enjoyable, or impressive etc: *"How was your holiday?" "Marvellous!"* | *It sounds like a marvellous idea.* | *It's marvelous what they can do with plastic surgery these days.* —**marvellously** *adv*

**Marx·is·m** /ˈmɑːksɪzəm‖ˈmɑːr-/ *n* [U] the system of political thinking invented by Karl Marx, which explains changes in history as the result of a struggle between social classes —**Marxist** *n* [C]

**mar·zi·pan** /ˈmɑːzɪpæn‖ˈmɑːrtsɪ-, ˈmɑːrzɪ-/ *n* [U] a sweet food made from ALMONDS, sugar, and eggs, used to make sweets and for covering cakes

**masc** the written abbreviation of MASCULINE

**mas·ca·ra** /mæˈskɑːrə‖mæˈskærə/ *n* [U] a dark substance used by women to colour their EYELASHES and make them look thicker —see picture at MAKE-UP

**mas·cot** /ˈmæskət‖ˈmæskɑːt/ *n* [C] an animal, toy etc that represents a team or organization, and is thought to bring them good luck: *The team mascot is a grizzly bear.*

**mas·cu·line** /ˈmæskjʊlɪn/ *adj* **1** belonging to men, done by men, or considered to be typical of men: *a masculine approach to the problem* | *traditionally masculine subjects such as physics* | *a dark, masculine face* **2** if a woman's appearance or voice is masculine, it is like a man's **3** belonging to the class of words for males: *'Drake' is the masculine word for 'duck'.* **4** a masculine noun, PRONOUN etc belongs to a class of words that have different INFLECTIONS from FEMININE or NEUTER words: *The word for 'book' is masculine in French.*

**mas·cu·lin·i·ty** /ˌmæskjʊˈlɪnɪti/ *n* [U] the characteristics and qualities considered to be typical of men: *Children's ideas of masculinity tend to come from their fathers.*

**ma·ser** /ˈmeɪzə‖-ər/ *n* [C] a piece of equipment that produces a very powerful electric force —compare LASER

**mash¹** /mæʃ/ also **mash up** *v* [T] to crush something, especially a food that has been cooked, until it is soft and smooth: *Mash the banana and add it to the batter.* —**masher** *n* [C] —see picture on page 834

**mash²** *n* [U] **1** *BrE informal* potatoes that have been boiled and then crushed until they are smooth; MASHED POTATO: *bangers and mash* **2** a mixture of grain cooked with water to make a food for animals **3** a mixture of MALT[1] (1) or crushed grain and hot water, used to make beer or WHISKY

**mashed po·ta·to** /ˌ· ·ˈ··/ also **mashed potatoes** —*n* [U] potatoes that have been boiled and then crushed until they are smooth

**masks**

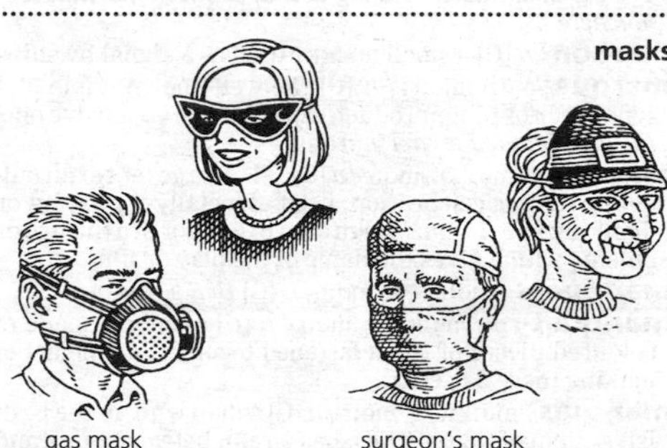


**mask¹** /mɑːsk‖mæsk/ *n* [C] **1** something that covers all or part of your face, to protect or to hide it: *a surgical face mask* **2** something that covers your face, and has another face painted on it: *special masks used in Kabuki theater* **3** [usually singular] an expression or way of behaving that hides your real emotions or character: *Her sarcasm is only a mask for her insecurity.* —see also DEATH MASK, GAS MASK

**mask²** *v* [T] **1** to cover something so that it cannot be properly seen: *an ugly concrete wall partially masked by straggling ivy* **2** a smell, taste, sound etc that is masked by a stronger one cannot be noticed because of it **3** to hide the truth about a situation, about how you feel etc: *His clownishness masks his loneliness.* | *so-called democratic institutions that mask the reality of power in Britain*

**masked** /mɑːskt‖mæskt/ *adj* wearing a mask

**masked ball** /ˌ· ˈ·/ *n* [C] a formal dance at which everyone wears masks

**masking tape** /ˈ·· ·/ *n* [U] long narrow paper that is sticky on one side, used especially to protect the edge of an area which you are painting

**mas·o·chis·m** /ˈmæsəkɪzəm/ *n* [U] **1** enjoyment of being hurt or punished **2** sexual behaviour in which you gain pleasure from being hurt —**masochist** *n* [C] —**masochistic** /ˌmæsəˈkɪstɪk◂/ *adj*: *masochistic behavior* —compare SADISM

**ma·son** /ˈmeɪsən/ *n* [C] **1** a STONEMASON **2** a FREEMASON

**Mason-Dix·on line** /ˌmeɪsən ˈdɪksən laɪn/ *n* [singular] the border between the American states of Pennsylvania and Maryland, considered as the dividing line between the northern and southern US

**Ma·son·ic** /məˈsɒnɪk‖-ˈsɑː-/ *adj* involved or connected with Freemasons: *a Masonic lodge*

**Mason jar** /ˈ·· ·/ *n* [C] *AmE* a glass pot with a tight lid used for preserving fruit and vegetables

**ma·son·ry** /ˈmeɪsənri/ *n* [U] **1** the stones and MORTAR (=material which holds stones together) from which a building, wall etc is made: *Several people had been buried under falling masonry.* **2** the skill of building with stone **3** FREEMASONRY

**masque** /mɑːsk‖mæsk/ *n* [C] a play written in the 16th and 17th centuries that was written in poetry and included music, dancing, and songs

**mas·que·rade¹** /ˌmæskəˈreɪd, ˈmɑːs-‖ˌmæs-/ *n* **1** [C] a formal dance where people wear MASKS and unusual clothes **2** [C,U] a way of behaving or speaking that hides your true thoughts or feelings: *She didn't really love him, but she kept up the masquerade for years.* **3** [C] *AmE old-fashioned* a party at which people wear unusual clothes

**masquerade²** *v* [I] to pretend to be something or someone different: **[+ as]** *secret police officers masquerading as demonstrators*

**Mass** /mæs/ *n* **1** [C,U] the main ceremony in some Christian churches, especially the Roman Catholic Church: **say/celebrate Mass** (=perform this ceremony as a priest) **2** [C] a piece of music written to be played at this ceremony: *Mozart's Mass in C Minor*

W2 **mass¹** *n*

**1 ▶LARGE AMOUNT◀ a)** [C] a large amount of a substance, liquid, or gas, that does not have a clear shape: *The food had all congealed into a sticky mass.* | **[+ of]** *A mass of almost pure white cloud lay below us.* **b) a mass of** a large amount or quantity of something: *a huge mass of data* | *The yard was just a mass of weeds.* **c) masses of** *BrE informal* a large amount of something, or a lot of people or things: *Masses of books covered every surface in the room.* | *We still had masses of time to spare.*

**2 ▶CROWD◀** [singular] a large crowd: **[+ of]** *There was a mass of people around the club entrance.* | **a solid mass** *The road was blocked by a solid mass of protesters.*

**3 the masses** all the ordinary people in society who do not have power or influence, and are thought of as not being very educated

**4 the mass of people/workers/the population etc** most of the people in a group or society; the MAJORITY: *The mass of black children there have fewer educational opportunities than their white counterparts.*

**5 ▶SCIENCE◀** [U] *technical* in science, mass is the amount of material in something: *the mass of a star*

W3 **mass²** *adj* [only before noun] **1** involving or intended for a very large number of people: *Radio can reach mass audiences.* | *a mass protest* **2 mass murderer** someone who has murdered a lot of people

**mass³** *v* [I, T] to come together, or make people or things come together, in a large group: *grey clouds massing behind the mountains* | *The country massed several divisions of troops along its border.*

**mas·sa·cre¹** /ˈmæsəkə‖-ər/ *v* [T] **1** to kill a lot of people, especially people who cannot defend themselves: *The army massacred 642 French civilians.* —see KILL¹ (USAGE) **2** *informal* to defeat someone very badly in a game or competition

**massacre²** *n* **1** [C,U] the killing of a lot of people, especially people who cannot defend themselves: *One man, the only survivor of the massacre, lived to tell the gruesome story.* **2** [C] *informal* a very bad defeat in a game or competition: *United lost in a 9-0 massacre.*

**mas·sage¹** /ˈmæsɑːʒ‖məˈsɑːʒ/ *n* [C,U] the action of pressing and rubbing someone's body with your hands, to help them relax or to reduce pain in their muscles: *Massage helps ease the pain.* | **give/have a massage** *She gave me a relaxing massage.*

**massage²** *v* [T] **1** to press and rub someone's body with your hands, to help them relax or to reduce pain in their muscles: *Alex massaged Helena's aching back.* —see picture on page 1259 **2** to change official numbers or information in order to make them seem better than they are: *massaging the unemployment statistics* **3 massage sb's ego** to try to make someone feel that they are important, attractive, intelligent etc: *secretaries who are expected to drop everything to get coffee or massage their boss's ego*

**massage par·lour** *BrE*, **massage parlor** *AmE* /ˈ·· ˌ··‖·ˈ· ˌ··/ *n* [C] **1** a word meaning a BROTHEL (=place where people pay to have sex), used to pretend that it is not a brothel **2** a place where you pay to have a MASSAGE

**masse** —see EN MASSE

**massed** /mæst/ *adj* **massed bands/choirs etc** a large number of musical groups playing together as one very large group

**mas·seur** /mæˈsɜː, mə-‖-ˈsɜːr/ *n* [C] someone who gives MASSAGES

**mas·seuse** /mæˈsɜːz, mæˈsuːz, mə-/ *n* [C] a woman who gives MASSAGES

**mas·sif** /ˈmæsiːf‖mæˈsiːf/ *n* [C] *technical* a group of mountains forming one large solid shape

**mas·sive** /ˈmæsɪv/ *adj* **1** very large, solid, and heavy: *The bell is massive, weighing over 40 tons.* | *the castle's massive walls* **2** unusually large, powerful, or damaging: *a massive tax bill* | *I had a massive argument with Vicky yesterday.* | **a massive stroke/heart attack etc** *He suffered a massive haemorrhage.* S2 W3

**mass me·di·a** /ˌ· ˈ···/ *n* **the mass media** all the people and organizations that provide information and news for the public, including television, radio, and newspapers

**mass-pro·duced** /ˌ· ·ˈ·◂/ *adj* produced in large numbers using machinery, so that each object is the same and can be sold cheaply: *mass-produced furniture* —**mass-produce** *v* [T] —**mass production** *n* [U]

**mast** /mɑːst‖mæst/ *n* [C] **1** a tall pole on which the sails or flags on a ship are hung: **two/three masted** (=having two or three masts) —see picture at YACHT **2** *BrE* a tall metal tower that sends out radio and television signals **3** a tall pole on which a flag is hung —see also HALF-MAST

**mas·tec·to·my** /mæˈstektəmi/ *n* [C] *technical* a medical operation to remove a breast

**Mas·ter** /ˈmɑːstə‖ˈmæstər-/ *n* [C] **1** *old-fashioned* a way of addressing or referring to young boys: *How's young Master Toby today?* **2** a religious leader in some religions: *a Sufi Master* **3** the person who is in charge of some British university colleges: *the Master of Trinity College, Cambridge*

**master¹** *n* [C]

**1 ▶OWNER/LEADER◀** *old-fashioned* a man who has control or authority over other people, for example servants or workers: *His staff were always very loyal to their master.* | **be your own master** (=control your own work or life) *I started this business because I wanted to be my own master.* —compare MISTRESS

**2 be master of** to be in complete control of a situation: *Without these changes, Africa cannot be master of its own economic destiny.*

**3 ▶SKILLED◀** someone who is very skilled at something: *Runyon was a master of the short story.* | *learning from an acknowledged master*

**4 be a past master** to be very good at doing something because you have done it a lot: **[+ at/in/of]** *He's a past master at getting free drinks out of people.*

**5 ▶ORIGINAL◀** a document, record etc from which copies are made: *I gave him the master to copy.*

**6 ▶TEACHER◀** *BrE old-fashioned* a male teacher: *the maths master* —see also HEADMASTER

**7 ▶DOG OWNER◀** the male owner of a dog: *a dog and its master*

**8 ▶SHIP◀** someone who commands a ship —see also GRAND MASTER, OLD MASTER, QUIZMASTER

**master²** *v* [T] **1** to learn a skill or a language so well that you understand it completely and have no difficulty with it: *that well-known difficulty of mastering the Chinese writing system* **2 master your fear/weakness etc** to manage to control a strong emotion

**master³** *adj* [only before noun] **1 master copy/list/tape etc** the original thing from which copies are made: *the master list of telephone numbers* **2** most important or main: *the master control center at NASA* **3 master craftsman/chef/plumber etc** someone who is very skilled at a particular job, especially a job that involves working with your hands

**master-at-arms** /ˌ·· · ˈ·/ *n* [C] an officer with police duties on a ship

**master bed·room** /ˈ·· ˌ··/ *n* [C] the largest bedroom in a house or apartment, often with its own bathroom

**master class** /ˈ·· ·/ *n* [C] a lesson, especially in music, given to very skilful students by someone famous

**mas·ter·ful** /ˈmɑːstəfəl‖ˈmæstər-/ *adj* **1** controlling people or situations in a skilful and confident way: *We allowed him to take charge in his masterful way.* **2** done with great skill and understanding: *a masterful analysis of the text* —**masterfully** *adv*

**master key** /ˈ·· ˌ·/ *n* [C] a key that will open all the door locks in a building

**mas·ter·ly** /ˈmɑːstəli‖ˈmæstərli/ *adj* done or made very skilfully: *a masterly analysis of the situation*

**mas·ter·mind¹** /ˈmɑːstəmaɪnd‖ˈmæstər-/ *n* [singular] someone who plans and organizes a complicated operation, especially a criminal operation: *the mastermind of an ingenious financial swindle*

**mastermind²** *v* [T] to think of, plan, and organize a large, important, and difficult operation: *The election campaign was masterminded by Peter Walters.*

**Master of Arts** /ˌ·· · ˈ·/ *n* [C] an MA

**master of ce·re·mo·nies** /ˌ·· · ˈ····/ *n* [C] someone who introduces speakers or performers at a social or public occasion; EMCEE *AmE*: *the master of ceremonies for the Miss World Pageant*

**Master of Sci·ence** /ˌ·· · ˈ··/ *n* [C] an MSc

**mas·ter·piece** /ˈmɑːstəpiːs‖ˈmæstər-/ *n* [C] a work of art, piece of writing or music etc that is of very high quality or that is the best that a particular artist, writer etc has produced: *Mary Shelley was just 18 when she wrote the horror masterpiece 'Frankenstein'.*|**a masterpiece of** (=a very good example of) *His speech was a masterpiece of ambiguity.*

**master plan** /ˈ·· ·/ *n* [C usually singular] a detailed plan for controlling everything that happens in a complicated situation: *an irrigation master plan*

**mas·ter's** /ˈmɑːstəz‖ˈmæstərz/ *n* [C] *informal* a MASTER'S DEGREE

**master's de·gree** /ˈ·· ·ˌ·/ *n* [C] a university degree such as an MA or an MSc, which you get by studying for one or two years after your first degree

**mas·ter·stroke** /ˈmɑːstəstrəʊk‖ˈmæstərstroʊk/ *n* [C] a very clever, skilful, and often unexpected action that is completely successful: *a masterstroke of diplomacy*

**master switch** /ˈ·· ˌ·/ *n* [C] the SWITCH that controls the supply of electricity to the whole of a building or area

**master·work** /ˈmɑːstəwɜːk‖ˈmæstərwɜːrk/ *n* [C] a painting, SCULPTURE, piece of music etc that is the best that someone has done; MASTERPIECE

**mas·ter·y** /ˈmɑːstəri‖ˈmæ-/ *n* [U] **1** complete control or power over someone or something: [+ **of/over**] *man's mastery over his environment* **2** thorough understanding or great skill: [+ **of/over**] *She combines technical mastery of her instrument with great flair and originality.*

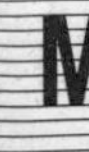

**mast·head** /ˈmɑːsthed‖ˈmæst-/ *n* [C] **1** the name of a newspaper, magazine etc printed in a special design at the top of the first page **2** the top of a MAST on a ship

**mas·tic** /ˈmæstɪk/ *n* [U] a type of glue that does not crack or break when it is bent

**mas·ti·cate** /ˈmæstɪkeɪt/ *v* [I, T] *technical* to CHEW (=crush food between the teeth) —**mastication** /ˌmæstɪˈkeɪʃən/ *n* [U]

**mas·tiff** /ˈmæstɪf/ *n* [C] a large, strong dog often used to guard houses

**mas·tur·bate** /ˈmæstəbeɪt‖-tər-/ *v* [I] to make yourself sexually excited by touching or rubbing your sexual organs —**masturbation** /ˌmæstəˈbeɪʃən‖-tər-/ *n* [U]

**mat¹** /mæt/ *n* [C] **1** a small piece of thick rough material which covers part of a floor: *Wipe your feet on the mat.* **2** a small flat piece of wood, cloth etc which protects a surface, especially on a table **3** a piece of thick soft material used in some sports for people to fall onto **4 a mat of hair/fur/grass etc** a thick mass of pieces of hair etc which are stuck together —see also MATTING

**mat²** *adj* another spelling of MATT

**mat·a·dor** /ˈmætədɔː‖-ɔːr/ *n* [C] a man who fights and kills BULLS during a BULLFIGHT

matador

**match¹** /mætʃ/ *n*

**1 ► FIRE ◄** [C] a small wooden or paper stick, used to light a fire, cigarette etc: *a box of matches*|**strike a match** (=rub a match against a surface to produce a flame)|**put a match to** (=make something burn by using a match) *I tore up the letter and put a match to it.* —see picture at LABORATORY

**2 ► GAME ◄** [C] *especially BrE* an organized sports event between two teams or people: *a violent incident during Chelsea's match against Liverpool*|*a cricket match*

**3 ► COLOURS/PATTERNS ◄** [singular] something that is the same colour or pattern as something else, or looks attractive with it: [+ **for**] *That shirt's a perfect match for your blue skirt.*

**4 be more than a match for** to be much stronger, cleverer etc than an opponent

**5 be no match for** to be much less strong, clever etc than an opponent: *Carlos was no match for the champion.*

**6 a slanging/shouting match** a loud angry argument in which two people insult each other

**7 be a perfect match** if two people who love each other are a perfect match, they are very suitable for each other

**8 make a good match** *old-fashioned* to marry a suitable person

**9 ► SUITABILITY ◄** [singular] a situation in which something is suitable for something else, so that the two things work together successfully: [+ **between**] *We need to establish a match between students' needs and teaching methods.* —see also **meet your match** (MEET¹ (16)), **mix and match** (MIX¹ (7))

**match²** *v*

**1 ► LOOK GOOD TOGETHER ◄** [I,T] if one thing matches another, or if two things match, they look attractive together because they have a similar colour, pattern etc: *The towels match the color of the bathroom tiles.*|**sth to match** (=something which matches) *a dining table with four chairs to match* —see also MATCHING —see FIT¹ (USAGE)

**2 ► LOOK THE SAME ◄** [I,T] if one thing matches another or if two things match, they look the same: *Your socks don't match.*

**3 ► SEEM THE SAME ◄** [I,T] if two reports or pieces of information match, or if one matches the other, there is no important difference between them: *The witnesses' stories just didn't match.*|*Traces of blood on the knife matched the suspect's blood-type.*

**4 ▶ PROVIDE WHAT IS NEEDED ◀** [T] to provide something that is suitable for a situation or enough for the people who need it: *creating sufficient employment to match the rising population|teaching materials that match the individual needs of students*
**5 ▶ FIND STH/SB SIMILAR ◀** [T] to find something that is similar to or suitable for something else: **match sth/sb to** *We get the children to match the animal pictures to the correct sounds.*
**6 ▶ BE AS GOOD AS ◀** [T] to be as skilful, intelligent etc as something or someone else: *No one can match Holden when it comes to winning an argument.|I've never seen a goal to match that one.*
**7 well-matched/ill-matched** very suitable/very unsuitable for each other: *a well-matched pair*
**8 evenly matched** if two competitors are evenly matched they are equal in strength, skill, speed etc
**9 ▶ GIVE MONEY ◀** [T] to give a sum of money equal to a sum given by someone else: *The government has promised to match any private donations to the earthquake fund.*
**10 ▶ MAKE EQUAL ◀** [T] to make something equal to or suitable for something else: **match sth to sth** *Match your spending to your income.*
**11 be matched with/against** to be competing against someone else in a game or competition: *Agassi will be matched against Sampras in the men's final.*

**match up** *phr v* **1** [I] if two reports or pieces of information match up, they seem the same **2** [**match** sth **up** to sth] to find something that is similar to or suitable for something else **3 match up to your hopes/expectations/ideals etc** to be as good as you expected, hoped etc

**match·book** /ˈmætʃbʊk/ *n* [C] a small folded piece of thick paper containing paper matches

**match·box** /ˈmætʃbɒks‖-bɑːks/ *n* [C] a small box containing matches

**match·ing** /ˈmætʃɪŋ/ *adj* having the same colour, style, or pattern as something else: *pink cushions and a matching bedspread*

**match·less** /ˈmætʃləs/ *adj literary* more intelligent, beautiful etc than anyone or anything else: *the matchless beauty of the Parthenon*

**match·mak·er** /ˈmætʃˌmeɪkə‖-ər/ *n* [C] someone who tries to find a suitable partner for someone else to marry —**matchmaking** *n* [U]

**match point** /ˌ· ˈ·‖ˈ· ·/ *n* **1** [U] a situation in tennis when the person who wins the next point will win the match **2** [C] the point that a player must win in order to win the match —compare GAME POINT

**match·stick** /ˈmætʃˌstɪk/ *n* [C] **1** a wooden MATCH¹ (1) **2 matchstick men/figures** people drawn with thin lines to represent their arms, legs, and bodies, as if by a child

**match·wood** /ˈmætʃwʊd/ *n* **break/splinter etc into matchwood** to be broken into very small pieces of wood: *Their boat hit the rocks and splintered into matchwood.*

S3 **mate¹** /meɪt/ *n*
**1 schoolmate/roommate/workmate etc** someone you study with, live with etc: *My flatmate and I aren't getting on very well!* —see also RUNNING MATE, SOUL MATE
**2 ▶ FRIEND ◀ a)** [C] *BrE informal* a friend: *I'm going out with my mates tonight.* **b)** *BrE and AustrE informal* used by men as a friendly way to address a man: *What's the time, mate?*
**3 ▶ ANIMAL ◀** [C] the sexual partner of an animal
**4 ▶ HUSBAND/WIFE ◀** *especially AmE* a word meaning your husband or wife, used especially in magazines: *Does your mate snore?*
**5 ▶ PAIR OF OBJECTS ◀** [C] *especially AmE* one of a pair of objects: *I can't find the mate to my glove.*
**6 ▶ SAILOR ◀** [C] a ship's officer who is one rank below the captain
**7 ▶ NAVY OFFICER ◀** [C] a US Navy PETTY OFFICER
**8 builder's mate/plumber's mate etc** *BrE* someone who works with and helps a skilled worker; ASSISTANT
**9 ▶ GAME ◀** [C, U] CHECKMATE in the game of CHESS

**mate²** *v* **1** [I + **with**] if animals mate, they have sex to produce babies **2** [T] to put animals together so that they will have sex and produce babies **3** [T] to achieve the CHECKMATE of your opponent in CHESS

**ma·ter** /ˈmeɪtə, ˈmɑː-‖ˈmeɪtər/ *n* [C] *BrE old-fashioned or humorous* mother —compare PATER

**ma·te·ri·al¹** /məˈtɪəriəl‖-ˈtɪr-/ *n* **1** [C,U] cloth used for making clothes, curtains etc; FABRIC (1): *curtain material* —see picture at CLOTHES **2** [C,U] a solid substance such as wood, plastic, or metal from which things can be made: *building materials* **3** [U] also **materials** [plural]—the things that are used for making or doing something: *Videos often make good teaching material.|artists' materials* **4** [U] information or ideas used in books, films etc: *His act contains a lot of new material.*|[+ **for**] *Anita is collecting material for her new novel.* **5 officer material/executive material etc** someone who is good enough for a particular job or position: *He's a good soldier, but not really officer material.* 

**material²** *adj* [usually before noun] **1** connected with people's money, possessions, living conditions etc, rather than the needs of their mind or soul: **material comforts/needs/well-being etc** *Improvements in health were linked to increasing material prosperity.* **2** connected with the real world and physical objects: *material existence* **3** *law* important and needing to be considered when making a decision: *material evidence*|[+ **to**] *facts material to the investigation* **4** important and having a noticeable effect: *material changes* —see also MATERIALLY, RAW MATERIALS W3

**ma·te·ri·al·is·m** /məˈtɪəriəlɪzəm‖-ˈtɪr-/ *n* [U] **1** the belief that money and possessions are more important than art, religion, moral goodness etc **2** *technical* the belief that only physical things really exist —**materialist** *adj, n* [C]

**ma·te·ri·a·lis·tic** /məˌtɪəriəˈlɪstɪk◂‖-ˌtɪr-/ *adj* caring only about money and possessions rather than things of the mind such as art or religion: *People nowadays are so materialistic.* —**materialistically** /-kli/ *adv*

**ma·te·ri·al·ize** also **-ise** *BrE* /məˈtɪəriəlaɪz‖-ˈtɪr-/ *v* [I] **1** to happen or appear in the way that you planned or expected: *The money we had been promised failed to materialize.* **2** to appear in an unexpected and strange way: *The figure of a man suddenly materialized in the shadows.* —**materialization** /məˌtɪəriəlaɪˈzeɪʃən‖-lə-/ *n* [U]

**ma·te·ri·al·ly** /məˈtɪəriəli‖-ˈtɪr-/ *adv* **1** in a big enough or strong enough way to change a situation: *This would materially affect US security.|This improvement is not materially significant.* **2** in a way that concerns possessions and money, rather than the needs of a person's mind or soul: *Materially we are better off than ever before.*

**ma·té·ri·el** /məˌtɪəriˈel‖-ˌtɪr-/ *n* [U] supplies of weapons used by an army

**ma·ter·nal** /məˈtɜːnl‖-ɜːr-/ *adj* **1** typical of the way a good mother behaves or feels: *I'm not maternal enough to have kids.|She kept a maternal eye on them all.*| **maternal instincts** (=the desire to have babies and take care of them) **2** [only before noun] of a mother or connected with being a mother: *the relationship between maternal age and infant mortality* **3 maternal grandfather/aunt etc** your mother's father, sister etc —compare PATERNAL —**maternally** *adv*

**ma·ter·ni·ty¹** /məˈtɜːnɪti‖-ɜːr-/ *adj* [only before noun] **1 maternity clothes/dress etc** clothes etc used by women who are PREGNANT (=going to have a baby) **2 maternity benefits/pay/allowance** the money that a woman is given by an employer or a government when she has a baby

**maternity²** *n* [U] the state of being a mother

**maternity leave** /·ˈ··· ˌ·/ *n* [U] time that a mother is allowed to spend away from work when she has a baby

**maternity ward** /·ˈ··· ˌ·/ *n* [C] a department in a hospital where women who are having babies are cared for

**mat·ey¹** /ˈmeɪti/ *adj BrE informal* behaving as if you were someone's friend: *She's been very matey with the boss recently.*

**matey²** *n BrE* used by men as a very informal or disrespectful way of addressing other men

S2 **math** /mæθ/ *n* [U] *AmE* mathematics

**math·e·mat·i·cal** /ˌmæθəˈmætɪkəl◂/ *adj* **1** connected with or using mathematics: *a mathematical equation* | *mathematical analysis* **2** calculating things in a careful, exact way: *The whole trip was planned with mathematical precision.* **3 a mathematical certainty** something that is completely certain to happen **4 a mathematical chance (of)** a very small chance that something will happen —**mathematically** /-kli/ *adv*

**math·e·ma·ti·cian** /ˌmæθəməˈtɪʃən/ *n* [C] someone who studies or teaches mathematics, or is a specialist in mathematics

**math·e·mat·ics** /ˌmæθəˈmætɪks/ *n* [U] the science of numbers and of shapes, including ALGEBRA, GEOMETRY, and ARITHMETIC

**mathematical notations**

- = is equal to
- ≠ is not equal to
- > is greater than
- < is less than
- ≥ is greater than or equal to
- ≤ is less than or equal to
- + add
- − subtract
- ÷ divide
- × multiply

S2 **maths** /mæθs/ *n* [U] *BrE informal* mathematics

**mat·i·née** /ˈmætəneɪ‖ˌmætənˈeɪ/ *n* [C] a performance of a play or film in the afternoon

**matinée i·dol** /ˈ··· ˌ··‖··ˈ· ˌ··/ *n* [C] *old-fashioned* an actor who is very popular with women

**matinée jack·et** /ˈ··· ˌ··‖··ˈ· ˌ··/ *n* [C] *old-fashioned BrE* a short coat for a baby

**mat·ing** /ˈmeɪtɪŋ/ *n* [U] sex between animals: *the mating season*

**mat·ins, mattins** /ˈmætənz‖ˈmætnz/ *n* [U] the first prayers of the day in the Christian religion; MORNING PRAYER

**matri-** /meɪtrɪ, mætrə/ *prefix* **1** concerning mothers: *matricide* (=killing one's own mother) **2** concerning women: *a matriarchal society* (=controlled by women) —compare PATRI-

**ma·tri·arch** /ˈmeɪtriɑːk‖-ɑːrk/ *n* [C] a woman, especially an older woman, who controls a family or a social group —compare PATRIARCH¹

**ma·tri·ar·chal** /ˌmeɪtriˈɑːkəl◂‖-ˈɑːr-/ *adj* **1** ruled or controlled by women: *a matriarchal society* **2** connected with or typical of a matriarch

**ma·tri·ar·chy** /ˈmeɪtriɑːki‖-ɑːr-/ *n* [C,U] **1** a social system in which the oldest woman controls a family and its possessions **2** a society in which women hold all the power —compare PATRIARCHY

**mat·ri·cide** /ˈmætrəsaɪd/ *n* [U] the crime of murdering your own mother —compare PARRICIDE (1), PATRICIDE

**ma·tric·u·late** /məˈtrɪkjəleɪt/ *v* [I] to officially start a course as a student at a university —**matriculation** /məˌtrɪkjəˈleɪʃən/ *n* [U]

**mat·ri·mo·ny** /ˈmætrəməni‖-moʊni/ *n* [U] *formal* the state of being married —**matrimonial** /ˌmætrəˈməʊniəl‖-ˈmoʊ-/ *adj*

**ma·trix** /ˈmeɪtrɪks/ *n plural* **matrices** /-trəsiːz/ *or* **matrixes** [C] *technical* **1** an arrangement of numbers, letters, or signs on a GRID (=a background of regular lines) used in mathematics, science etc **2** a situation from which a person or society can grow and develop: *the cultural matrix* **3** a living part in which something is formed or developed, such as the substance out of which the FINGERNAIL*s* grow **4** a MOULD (=a hollow container) into which melted metal, plastic, etc is poured to form a shape **5** the rock in which hard stones or jewels have formed —see also DOT-MATRIX PRINTER

**ma·tron** /ˈmeɪtrən/ *n* [C] **1** *BrE* a woman who works as a nurse in a school **2** *especially AmE* a woman who is in charge of women and children, for example in a prison **3** *BrE old-fashioned* a nurse who is in charge of the other nurses in a hospital **4** *especially literary* an older married woman

**ma·tron·ly** /ˈmeɪtrənli/ *adj* a word to describe a woman who is fairly fat and no longer young, used to avoid saying this directly

**matron of hon·our** *BrE*, **matron of honor** *AmE* /ˌ·· ·ˈ··/ *n* [C] a married woman who helps the bride on her wedding day —compare BRIDESMAID

**matt, mat, matte** /mæt/ *adj* matt paint, colour, or photographs have a dull surface; not shiny: *matt black* —compare GLOSS¹ (4)

**mat·ted** /ˈmætəd/ *adj* twisted or stuck together in a thick mass: *matted fur* | *His hair was dirty and matted.*

## mat·ter¹ /ˈmætə‖-ər/ *n*

① SUBJECT/SITUATION
② STH WRONG WITH
③ NO MATTER
④ AS A MATTER OF
⑤ IT'S A MATTER OF
⑥ SMALL AMOUNT
⑦ BOOKS/NEWSPAPERS
⑧ SUBSTANCE
⑨ OTHER MEANINGS

### ① SUBJECT/SITUATION

**1** [C] a subject or situation that you have to think about or deal with: *You do realize this is a serious matter, don't you?* | *He wasn't particularly interested in financial matters.* | **a matter of importance/concern/regret etc** (=a subject that is important, that people worry about etc) *Wilson always consulted Landers on matters of importance.* | *The King's mental state was becoming a matter of concern.* | **be a matter for** (=be something that a particular person or group should deal with) *If he was murdered, it's a matter for the police.* | **the heart/crux of the matter** (=the most important part of a situation) *The report didn't get to the heart of the matter.* | **raise the matter with** (=discuss a subject with someone) *Have you raised the matter with your union representative?* | **let the matter rest/drop** (=decide to stop worrying about something) *I'm prepared to let the whole matter drop if he apologizes.* | **the matter at/in hand** (=the thing that you should be dealing with now) *Could we please concentrate on the matter in hand?*

**2 subject matter** the subject that is discussed or shown in a book, film, article etc: *Because of its adult subject matter, the film is not suitable for under-16s.*

**3 it's no small/laughing matter** used to say that something must be treated seriously: *He ended up with a broken pelvis, which is no laughing matter, I can tell you.*

**4 that's the end of the matter/let that be an end to**

[continued on next page]

[continued from previous page]
**the matter** *spoken* used to tell someone that you do not want to talk about something any more: *We will not let you date until you're 16, and that's the end of the matter.*
**5 be a different matter** also **be quite another matter** *especially BrE* —used to say that one situation or problem is much more serious than another: *Having the occasional drink is one thing, but being drunk every night is quite another matter.*
**6 matters** *plural* a situation that you are in or have been describing: *Maybe some of these suggestions will help to improve matters.* | **not help matters** *spoken* (=make a situation worse) *I had a headache when I took the test, which didn't help matters.*
**7 to make matters worse** making a bad situation even worse: *The car had broken down, and to make matters worse, it was beginning to rain.*
**8 take matters into your own hands** to deal with a problem yourself because other people have failed to deal with it: *Local people took matters into their own hands and hired their own security guards.*

### ② STH WRONG WITH

**9 what's the matter?/is anything the matter?** *spoken* used when someone seems upset, unhappy, or ill and you are asking them why: *What's the matter, Mary? Have you been crying?*
**10 what's the matter with** *spoken* used to ask why something is not working normally, someone seems upset or ill, or something looks wrong: *What's the matter with Bill?* | *"The television had to go back to the store." "Why, what's the matter with it?"*
**11 there's something the matter with/something's the matter with** *spoken* used to say that something is not working normally, someone is upset or ill, or something looks wrong: *There's something the matter with the washing machine – it keeps leaking.*
**12 there's nothing the matter with** *spoken* used to say that someone is not ill or upset, or that something is working properly or looks good: *There was nothing the matter with it when I lent it to him.* | *There's nothing the matter with your haircut – I really like it!*

### ③ NO MATTER

**13 no matter how/where/what etc** used to say that something is always the same whatever happens, or in spite of someone's efforts to change it: *No matter how hard he tried, he couldn't get her to change her mind.* | *My parents always waited up for me, no matter what time I got home.*
**14 no matter what (happens)** *spoken* used to say that you will definitely do something: *I'll call you tonight no matter what.*
**15 no matter** *spoken* used to say that something you have asked about is not important: *"She's not in her office." "No matter, I'll try and call her at home."*

### ④ AS A MATTER OF

**16 as a matter of fact** *especially spoken* **a)** used when saying something, especially something surprising, that is connected with what you are talking about: *I knew him when we were in college – as a matter of fact we were on the same course.* **b)** used when you do not agree with what someone has just said: *No, I wasn't annoyed. As a matter of fact I was very glad to see them.*
**17 as a matter of interest** *BrE spoken* used when you want to ask or tell someone something that is not really necessary: *Just as a matter of interest, Tony, how much did you pay for your house?*
**18 as a matter of course/routine** as the correct and usual thing to do in a particular situation: *We will contact your former employer as a matter of course.*
**19 as a matter of principle/belief/policy etc** because of your personal beliefs about what you should do: *They're supporting him as a matter of principle.*
**20 as a matter of urgency/priority** *formal* done as quickly as possible because it is very important: *I want a full safety check as a matter of urgency.*

### ⑤ IT'S A MATTER OF

**21 it's/that's a matter of opinion** used to say that people have different opinions about a subject: *Personally I can't stand rock music, but I suppose it's all a matter of opinion.*
**22 it's only/just a matter of time** used to say that something will definitely happen eventully: *It's only a matter of time before somebody gets hurt.*
**23 it's a matter of life and death** used to say that a situation is extremely serious or dangerous and something must be done immediately: *We wouldn't usually operate on a pregnant woman, unless it's a matter of life and death.*
**24 it's (just) a matter of (doing) sth** *spoken* used to say that you only have to do a particular thing, or do something in a particular way, in order to be successful: *Anyone can take good photographs – it's just a matter of being in the right place at the right time.*
**25 it's a matter of taste/cost/luck etc** used to say that what happens or what you decide depends on your judgment, how much something costs, how lucky you are etc: *I can't say which wine is best – it's a matter of personal taste.*
**26 the fact/truth of the matter (is)** used to say what you think is really true: *The sad fact of the matter is that Alice is just not good enough for the job.* | *He doesn't love her any more – that's the truth of the matter.*

### ⑥ SMALL AMOUNT

**27 a matter of seconds/months/metres etc** only a few seconds, metres etc: *The ambulance was there in a matter of minutes.* | *In 1914 everyone expected the war to be over in a matter of months.*

### ⑦ BOOKS/NEWSPAPERS

**28 reading/printed etc matter** things that are written for people to read

### ⑧ SUBSTANCE

**29 waste/solid/organic/vegetable etc matter** a substance that consists of waste material, solid material etc
**30** [U] *technical* the material that everything in the universe is made of, including solids, liquids, and gases
**31** [U] a yellow or white substance that is found in wounds or next to your eye

### ⑨ OTHER MEANINGS

**32 or ... for that matter** *spoken* used to say that what you are saying about one thing is also true about something else: *Ben never touched beer, or any kind of alcohol for that matter.*
**33 there's the little matter of** *spoken* used jokingly to remind someone about something important that they may have forgotten: *OK, that's settled – but there's still the little matter of my fee to discuss.* —see also GREY MATTER, **not mince matters** (MINCE[1] (3)), **mind over matter** (MIND[1] (50))

S1 W3 **matter²** *v* [I] **1** to be important, especially to be important to you personally or to have a big effect on what happens: **it doesn't matter/it won't matter etc** *"We've missed the train!" "It doesn't matter, there's another one in 10 minutes."* | **matter if** *Will it matter if I'm a little late?* | **matter about** *It won't matter about the mess – I'll clear it up later.* | **matter who/why/what etc** *It doesn't matter what you wear, as long as you look neat and tidy.* | *Does it matter who goes first?* | **matter to sb** *It doesn't really matter to me if we don't see the film – I've seen it already anyway.* | **it matters a lot/a great deal** (=it is very important) *It mattered a great deal to her what*

other people thought of her. | **all that matters/the only thing that matters** (=the only thing that is important) *All that matters is that you're safe.* | *Money was the only thing that mattered to these people.* | **what matters is** *I don't care what it looks like – what matters is that it works.* | **nothing else matters** *He wanted to win the championship – nothing else really mattered to him.* **2 it doesn't matter** *spoken* **a)** used to tell someone that you are not angry or upset about something, especially something that they have done: *"I've spilled some coffee on the carpet." "It doesn't matter."* **b)** used to say that you do not mind which one of two things you have: *"Red or white wine?" "Oh, either. It doesn't matter."* **3 what does it matter (if)** *spoken* used to say that something is not very important: *What does it matter if he drinks a little, at least he's happy.*

Frequencies of the verb **matter** in spoken and written English.

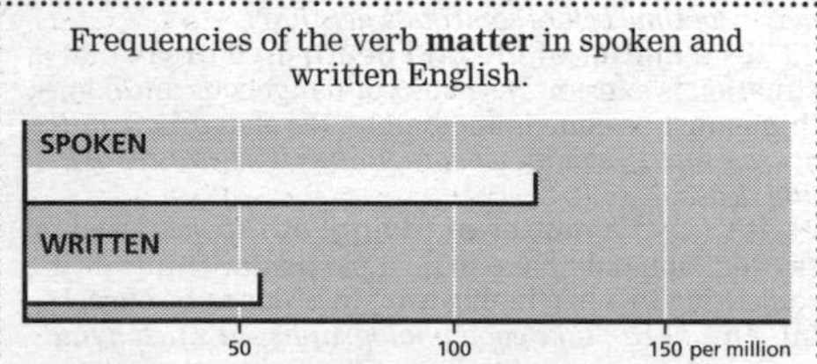


Based on the British National Corpus and the Longman Lancaster Corpus

This graph shows that the verb **matter** is much more common in spoken English than in written English. This is because it is used in a lot of common spoken phrases.

**matter-of-fact** /ˌ·· · ˈ·◂/ *adj* showing no emotion when you are talking about something exciting, frightening, upsetting etc: *Jan was surprisingly matter-of-fact about her divorce.* —**matter-of-factly** *adv* —**matter-of-factness** *n* [U]

**mat·ting** /ˈmætɪŋ/ *n* [U] strong rough material, used for making mats (MAT[1] (1)): *straw matting*

**mat·tins** /ˈmætɪ̣nz‖ˈmætnz/ *n* [U] another spelling of MATINS

**mat·tock** /ˈmætək/ *n* [C] a tool used for digging, with a long handle and a metal blade

**mat·tress** /ˈmætrɪ̣s/ *n* [C] the soft part of a bed that you lie on: *an old, lumpy mattress*

**ma·tu·ra·tion** /ˌmætʃʊ̈ˈreɪʃən/ *n* [U] *formal* the period during which something grows and develops

**ma·ture[1]** /məˈtʃʊə ‖ -ˈtʃʊr/ *adj*

**1 ▶ SENSIBLE ◀** a child or young person who is mature behaves in a sensible and reasonable way, as you would expect an older person to behave: *She's very mature for her age.* | *John has always shown a mature attitude to his work.* —opposite IMMATURE

**2 ▶ FULLY GROWN ◀** fully grown and developed: *The mature eagle has a wingspan of over six feet.*

**3 ▶ WINE/CHEESE ETC ◀** mature cheese, wine etc has a good strong flavour which has developed during a long period of time: *mature cheddar*

**4 ▶ OLDER ◀** a polite or humorous way of describing someone who is no longer young; MIDDLE-AGED: *We design clothes for the maturer woman.* | **of mature years** *a respectable gentleman of mature years*

**5 ▶ NOVEL/PAINTING ETC ◀** a mature piece of work by a writer or an artist shows a high level of understanding or skill

**6 on mature reflection/consideration** *formal* after thinking about something carefully: *On mature reflection we have decided to decline their offer.*

**7 ▶ FINANCIAL ◀** *technical* a mature BOND[1] (1) or POLICY (2) is ready to be paid —**maturely** *adv*

**mature[2]** *v* **matured, maturing 1** [I] to become fully grown or developed: *A kitten matures when it is about a year old.* **2** [I] to become sensible and start to behave like an adult: *He has matured a lot since he left home.* **3** [I,T] if a cheese, wine, WHISKY etc matures or is matured, it develops a good strong flavour over a period of time **4** [I] *technical* if a financial arrangement such as a BOND[1] (1) or POLICY (2) matures, it becomes ready to be paid

**mature stu·dent** /ˌ·ˌ· ˈ··/ *n* [C] *BrE* a student at a university or college who is over 25 years old

**ma·tu·ri·ty** /məˈtʃʊərɪ̣ti‖-ˈtʃʊr-/ *n* [U] **1** the quality of behaving in a sensible way like an adult: *Beth remained calm, showing a maturity way beyond her 16 years.* **2** the time when a person, animal, or plant is fully grown or developed: **reach maturity** *These insects reach maturity after a few weeks.* **3** *technical* the time when a financial arrangement such as a BOND[1] (1) or POLICY (2) becomes ready to be paid

**mat·zo** /ˈmɒtsə‖ˈmɑː-/ *n* [C] a type of flat bread eaten especially by Jewish people during PASSOVER

**maud·lin** /ˈmɔːdlɪn‖ˈmɒː-/ *adj* talking or behaving in a sad, silly way, because you are drunk

**maul** /mɔːl‖mɒːl/ *v* [T] **1** to injure someone badly by tearing their flesh: *The woman had been mauled by a panther.* **2** to write very unfavourable comments about a new book, play etc: *Her latest book was absolutely mauled by the critics.* **3** to touch someone in a rough sexual way which they think is unpleasant: *Some guy came over and started mauling Jane.*

**maun·der** /ˈmɔːndə‖ˈmɒːndər/ *v* [I + **on**] *especially BrE* to talk or complain about something for a long time in a boring way: *What are you maundering on about, Sid?*

**Maun·dy Thurs·day** /ˌmɔːndi ˈθɜːzdi‖ˌmɒːndi ˈθɜːr-/ *n* [U] the Thursday before Easter

**mau·so·le·um** /ˌmɔːsəˈliːəm‖ˌmɒː-/ *n* [C] a large stone building containing many graves or built over a grave

**mauve** /məʊv‖moʊv/ *n* [U] a pale purple colour —**mauve** *adj* —see picture on page 411

**ma·ven** /ˈmeɪvən/ *n* [C] *AmE* someone who knows a lot about a particular subject: *The café is a hangout for the cultural mavens.*

**mav·e·rick** /ˈmævərɪk/ *n* [C] an unusual person who has different ideas and ways of behaving from other people, and is often very successful: *Charles was always a bit of a maverick, even at school.* —**maverick** *adj*: *maverick tendencies*

**maw** /mɔː‖mɒː/ *n* [C] **1** *formal* something which seems to swallow things completely: *Millions of dollars were poured into the maw of defense spending.* **2** *literary* an animal's mouth or throat

**mawk·ish** /ˈmɔːkɪʃ‖ˈmɒː-/ *adj* showing too much emotion in a way that is embarrassing; SENTIMENTAL: *a mawkish love story* —**mawkishly** *adv* —**mawkishness** *n* [U]

**max[1]** /mæks/ *n* [U] **1** an abbreviation of MAXIMUM **2** *informal* at the most: *It'll cost about ten dollars max.* **3 to the max** *AmE slang* **a)** an expression meaning extremely, used to emphasize how good, bad etc something is: *"He's gorgeous, isn't he?" "To the max!"* **b)** if you push yourself to the max, you try as hard as you can to succeed

**max[2]** *v*

**max out** *phr v* [I] *AmE slang* **1** to do something with as much effort and determination as you can: *Hilary maxed out on the campaign.* **2** to do too much, eat too much etc: [+ **on**] *"Want a beer?" "Nah, I maxed out on booze this weekend."* —**maxed out** *adj*

**max·im** /ˈmæksɪ̣m/ *n* [C] a well-known phrase or saying, especially one that gives a rule for sensible behaviour

**max·i·mal** /ˈmæksɪ̣məl/ *adj technical* as much or as large as possible: *the right conditions for a maximal increase in employment* —**maximally** *adv*

**max·i·mize** also **-ise** *BrE* /ˈmæksɪ̣maɪz/ *v* [T] to increase something such as profit or income as much as possible: *The company's main function is to maximize profit.* —compare MINIMIZE —**maximization** /ˌmæksɪ̣maɪˈzeɪʃən‖-sɪ̣mə-/ *n* [U]

2 3 **max·i·mum¹** /ˈmæksɪ̣məm/ *adj* [only before noun] the maximum amount, quantity, speed etc is the largest that is possible or allowed: *The car has a maximum speed of 120 mph.* | *The maximum number of students in each class is thirty.* | *We must make maximum use of the resources available.* | **for maximum effect** (=to get the best possible results) *Display it under a strong light for maximum effect.* —compare MINIMUM¹

**maximum²** *n plural* **maxima** /-mə/ *or* **maximums** [C] the largest number or amount that is possible or is allowed: **[+ of]** *Temperatures will reach a maximum of 45° C.* | **the maximum** *40 students per class is the absolute maximum.*

**May** /meɪ/ *n* [C,U] the fifth month of the year, between April and June: **in May** *The theatre opened in May 1991.* | **last/next May** | *She started work here last May.* | **on 6th May/on May 6th** *The meeting will be on 6th May* (spoken as: *on the sixth of May* or *on May sixth (AmE)* or *on May the sixth (BrE)*)

S1 W1 **may¹** *modal verb negative short form* **mayn't** *old-fashioned BrE*

**1** ▶ **POSSIBILITY** ◀ if something may happen or may be true, there is a possibility that it will happen or be true but this is not certain: *I may be late so start without me.* | *Who knows what will happen. You may even have married by then.* | *It is feared that many workers may lose their jobs this winter.* | *£50 may not be enough.* | *Ian may be able to help.* —compare MIGHT¹

**2** ▶ **PERMISSION** ◀ **may I** **a)** *spoken* used to ask politely if you can do something: *May I speak to you for a moment in private, please?* | *I'd like to open a window, if I may.* **b)** *formal* used to say that someone is allowed to do something: *Thank you, you may go now.* | *You may start writing now – the examination will finish in three hours.* | *Firearms may be used in an emergency.* **c) may I say/ask/suggest etc** *formal* used to say, ask, or suggest something politely: *May I just add that Oliver was a pleasure to work with and will be missed by everyone in the team.* —compare CAN¹, MIGHT¹

**3 may you/he/they etc do sth** *formal* used to say that you hope that a particular thing will happen to someone: *May both the bride and groom have long and happy lives.*

**4 may ... but ...** used to say that although one thing is true, something else which seems very different is also true: *He may be lazy, but he can work very hard when he feels like it.* | *You may think you're smart but you don't understand this kind of work at all.* —compare MIGHT¹

**5 may well** if something may well happen or may well be true, it is fairly likely to happen or be true: *These are excellent photographs and we may well be able to use them in our magazine.* —compare **might well** (MIGHT¹ (7))

**6 may as well** *spoken* used to say that you will do something that you do not really want to do, because you cannot think of anything better: *I may as well go out tonight. There's nothing on television.* | *If you're not going to eat that pizza I may as well throw it out.*

**7** ▶ **PURPOSE** ◀ *formal* used like 'can' after 'so that', to say that someone does something in order to make something else possible: *He gave up his life so that we may all live in a free and fair world.* —compare MIGHT¹

**8** ▶ **POSSIBLE TO DO STH** ◀ if something may be done, completed etc in a particular way, that is how it is possible to do it: *The problem may be solved in a number of ways, but there is only one correct answer.* —see (USAGE) CAN

**may²** *n* [U] HAWTHORN flowers

S1 W2 **may·be** /ˈmeɪbi/ *adv* [sentence adverb] **1** used like 'perhaps' to say that something may happen or may be true but you are not certain: *"Do you think he'll come back?" "Maybe."* | *Maybe I was wrong about Karen; I don't know.* | *He said he'd finish the work soon – maybe tomorrow.* —see graph at PERHAPS **2** used to show that you are not sure of an amount or number: *There were three, maybe four hundred people at the concert.* **3** used to make a suggestion you are not quite sure about: *We thought maybe we should lower the price we were asking for our house.* **4** used when politely asking someone to do something or offering to help them: *Maybe you could help me tidy the livingroom.* **5** *spoken* used to reply to a suggestion or idea when either you are not sure if you agree with it, or you do not want to say 'yes' or 'no': *"I think Sheila would be an excellent managing director." "Maybe."* | *"Well, are you going to take the job or not?" "Maybe ..."* **6 maybe ... but** *spoken* used to agree with someone but say that there are also other facts to be considered: *"Mike should rent his own apartment and get away from home." "Maybe, but where would he get the money from?"*

> **USAGE NOTE: MAYBE**
> FORMALITY
> **Maybe** and **perhaps** mean the same thing, but **maybe** is more informal. To a friend you might say or write: *I'll maybe see you in August.* To someone you do not know well you might say: *Perhaps we could meet next week.* When you write a report or story you might put: *New York is perhaps the most interesting city in the US.* In a speech you might say: *Perhaps in closing I could just thank everyone for coming*, but it would be less formal to say *Maybe...*
> SPELLING
> **Maybe** is always spelt as one word when it means 'perhaps': *Maybe it'll be fun.* Compare *It may be fun.*

**may·bug** /ˈmeɪbʌg/ *n* [C] a COCKCHAFER

**May Day** /ˈ· ·/ *n* [C,U] the first day of May, when LEFT-WING political parties have celebrations, and when people traditionally used to celebrate the arrival of spring

**may·day** /ˈmeɪdeɪ/ *n* [singular] a radio signal used to ask for help when a ship or plane is in serious danger —compare SOS

**may·est** /ˈmeɪəst/ *v* **thou mayest** *old use* you may

**may·fly** /ˈmeɪflaɪ/ *n plural* **mayflies** [C] a small insect that lives near water, and only lives for a short time

**may·hem** /ˈmeɪhem/ *n* [U] an extremely confused situation in which people are very frightened or excited; CHAOS: *There was complete mayhem after the explosion.*

**may·n't** /ˈmeɪənt/ *old-fashioned BrE* the short form of 'may not'

**may·o** /ˈmeɪəʊ‖-oʊ/ *n* [U] *AmE informal* mayonnaise

**may·on·naise** /ˌmeɪəˈneɪz‖ˈmeɪəneɪz/ *n* [U] a thick white SAUCE eaten with cold SALADS, on CHIPS etc

**mayor** /meə‖ˈmeɪər/ *n* [C] **1** someone who is chosen or elected each year in Britain to represent a town or city at official public ceremonies **2** the person who has been elected to lead the government of a town or city in the US —**mayoral** *adj*: *mayoral duties*

**mayor·al·ty** /ˈmeərəlti‖ˈmeɪərəlti/ *n* [U] *formal* the position of mayor, or the period when someone is mayor

**mayor·ess** /ˈmeərɪ̣s‖ˈmeɪərɪ̣s/ *n* [C] *BrE* the wife of a mayor, or a woman who shares the work of a mayor

**may·pole** /ˈmeɪpəʊl‖-poʊl/ *n* [C] a tall pole around which people danced on May Day in England in the past

**mayst** /meɪst/ *v old use* **thou mayst** you may

**may've** /ˈmeɪəv/ the short form of 'may have': *You may've heard this story before.*

**maze** /meɪz/ *n* [C] **1 a maze of streets/paths/wires etc** a complicated and confusing arrangement of streets etc: *the maze of tiny streets in the old part of the city* **2 a maze of rules/regulations/details etc** a large number of rules etc which are complicated and difficult to understand **3** a specially designed system of paths, often in a park or public garden, which is difficult to find your way through: *We got completely lost in the maze.* **4** a children's game in which you draw a line through a complicated group of lines without crossing any of them

**MB** /ˌem ˈbiː/ the abbreviation of Bachelor of Medicine

**MBA** /ˌem biː ˈeɪ/ *n* [C] Master of Business Administration; a university degree in the skills needed to be in charge of a business

**MBE** /ˌem biː ˈiː/ *n* [C] Member of the Order of the British Empire; a special honour given to some British people for things they have done for their country

**MBSc** /ˌem biː es ˈsiː/ the abbreviation of Master of Business Science

**MC** /ˌem ˈsiː/ *n* [C] **1** the abbreviation of Master of Ceremonies —see also EMCEE **2** Military Cross; a MEDAL given to British army officers for bravery **3** *AmE* the written abbreviation of Member of Congress

**McCoy** /məˈkɔɪ/ **the real McCoy** *informal* something that is real and is not a copy, especially something valuable: *"Is it a Rolex?" "Yes, it's the real McCoy."*

**MD** /ˌem ˈdiː/ *n* [C] **1** the written abbreviation of Doctor of Medicine **2** *especially spoken* the MANAGING DIRECTOR of a company

**ME** /ˌem ˈiː/ *n* [U] *BrE* myalgic encephalomyelitis; an illness that makes you feel very tired and weak and can last for a long time; EPSTEIN-BARR VIRUS *AmE*

S1 W1 **me** /mi; *strong* miː/ *pron* the object form of I: *It fell off and hit me on the head.* | *He bought me a drink.* | *Give that book to me.* | *She's two years older than me.* | *That's me, standing on the left of the bride.*

**USAGE NOTE: ME**

FORMALITY: **me, her, him, us, we, they, them**

When you are speaking you usually use **me, her, him, us,** and **them** after **as, than,** and the verb **to be**, and with **and** and **or** in a phrase that is the subject of a clause: *I'm not as pretty as her.* | *She's older than him.* | *It's them.* | *Tanya and me are off to Acapulco*, or even *Me and Tanya are off to Acapulco.*

In very formal or old-fashioned writing you may see **I, she, he, we** and **they** used instead: *None was as rich as he.* You may also hear this in spoken English, but it often sounds much too formal or pompous: *It was they.* | *My husband and I are going to the opera.*

You can avoid using either by rephrasing your sentence: *No one was as rich as he was.* | *They were the ones.* | *I am going to the opera with my husband.*

**me·a cul·pa** /ˌmeɪə ˈkʊlpə/ *interjection Latin humorous* used to admit that something is your fault

**mead** /miːd/ *n* **1** [U] an alcoholic drink made from HONEY **2** [C] *poetical* a meadow

**mead·ow** /ˈmedəʊ‖-doʊ/ *n* [C] a field with wild grass and flowers —see also WATER MEADOW

**mead·ow·lark** /ˈmedəʊlɑːk‖-doʊlɑːrk/ *n* [C] a brown North American bird with a yellow front

**mea·gre** *BrE*, **meager** *AmE* /ˈmiːgə‖-ər/ *adj* a meagre amount of food, money etc is too small and is much less than you need: *meagre wages* | *a meager diet* —**meagrely** *adv* —**meagreness** *n* [U]

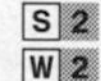

S2 W2 **meal** /miːl/ *n* **1** [C] an occasion when you eat food, for example breakfast or lunch: *Dinner is the main meal of the day for most people.* | *What time are you having your meal?* | **go (out) for a meal** *After the movie we went for a meal in a Chinese restaurant.* | **take/ask sb out for a meal** *Why don't you ask her out for a meal?* **2** [C] the food that you eat on a particular occasion: *Michel cooked us a lovely French meal.* | *a five-course meal* —see also **square meal** (SQUARE² (7)) **3** [U] grain that has been crushed into a powder, for making flour or animal food —see also BONE MEAL **4 make a meal of** *informal* to spend too much time or effort doing something: *He made a real meal out of parking the car.*

**mea·lie** /ˈmiːli/ *n* [C, U] *SAfrE* MAIZE, or a piece of maize

**meal tick·et** /ˈ· ˌ··/ *n* [C] **1** *informal* something or someone that you depend on to give you money or food **2** a card that gives you the right to have free or cheaper meals at school or work in the US

**meal·time** /ˈmiːltaɪm/ *n* [C] a time during the day when you have a meal: *The only time I see them is at mealtimes.*

**meal·y** /ˈmiːli/ *adj* **1** fruit or vegetables that are mealy are dry and do not taste good: *mealy potatoes* **2** containing MEAL (3)

**mealy-mouthed** /ˌ·· ˈ·◂/ *adj* not brave enough or honest enough to say clearly and directly what you really think

**mean¹** /miːn/ *v* [T] *past tense and past participle* **meant** /ment/ S W

**1 ▶ HAVE A PARTICULAR MEANING ◀** [not in progressive] to have or represent a particular meaning: *"What does 'Konbanwa' mean in English?" "It means 'Good Evening'."* | *The red light means 'Stop.'* | **what is meant by** (=what something means) *What is meant by the term 'random access'?* | **mean (that)** *This signal means your message has been received.*

**2 ▶ INTEND TO SAY STH ◀** [not in progressive] to intend a particular meaning when you say something: **mean (that)** *I meant we'd have to leave early – that's all.* | **what you mean/what she means etc** *So what he means is that we'll have to start the whole thing again.*

**3 I mean** *spoken* **a)** used when explaining or giving an example of something, or when pausing to think about what you are going to say next: *He's really very rude – I mean he never even says 'Good Morning'.* | *It's just not right. I mean it's unfair isn't it?* **b)** used to quickly correct something you have just said: *She plays the violin, I mean the viola, really well.*

**4 do you know what I mean?/if you know what I mean** *spoken* used when checking that someone has understood what you are saying: *This year I want to buy her something really special. Do you know what I mean?*

**5 (do) you mean ...?** *spoken* used when checking that you have understood what someone has said: *You mean we're supposed to tell you if we want to leave early?*

**6 I know what you mean** *spoken* used to tell someone that you understand what they are talking about, because you have had the same experience yourself: *Oh, I know exactly what you mean. Things like that drive me crazy too.*

**7 I see what you mean** *spoken* used to tell someone that you now understand what they have been saying: *Yes, I see what you mean. That would be the best way to do it.*

**8 see what I mean?** *spoken* used when checking that someone has understood something you have said, often by showing them an example of it: *See what I mean? Every time she calls me up she wants me to do something for her.*

**9 that's what I mean** *spoken* used when someone is saying the same thing that you were trying to say earlier: *"We might not have enough money." "That's what I mean, so we'd better find out the price first."*

**10 how do you mean?** *spoken* used to ask someone to explain what they have just said or tell you more about it: *"He says he finds it difficult at times." "How do you mean?"*

**11 what do you mean ...?** *spoken* **a)** used when you do not understand what someone is trying to say **b)** used when you are very surprised or annoyed by what someone has just said: *What do you mean, you've cancelled the holiday?* | *What do you mean by that?*

**12 I mean to say** *spoken* used when adding a reason or explanation for something you have just said, especially something you feel strongly about: *Of course she wants to see the children, I mean to say, it's only natural isn't it?*

**13 ▶ SAY WHICH PERSON/THING ◀ I mean sb/sth** *usually spoken* used to say that a particular person or thing is the one that you are talking about, pointing to etc: *"Hey you!" "Do you mean me?"* | *I didn't mean that one, I meant this one.*

**14 ▶ INTEND (SB) TO DO (STH) ◀** *especially spoken* to intend to do something or intend that someone else should do something: **mean to do sth** *I've been meaning to phone you all week.* | *I didn't mean to interrupt your meal.* | **mean sb to do sth** *Oh no! I never meant her to read those comments.* | **mean for sb to do sth** *especially AmE*: *I didn't mean for her to get hurt.* —see also **mean no harm** (HARM¹ (3))

**15 mean business** to be determined to do something even if it involves hurting someone, or be very serious about something: *We've got to show these gangsters we mean business.* | *Get upstairs now! I mean business!*

**16 he/she means well** *spoken* used to say that someone intends to be helpful or kind, but often makes a situation worse: *He may sound a bit rude at times, but he means well.* —see also WELL-MEANING, WELL-MEANT
**17 I/he etc meant it for the best** *especially spoken* used to say that someone wanted to do something helpful, but their actions had the wrong effect: *I wasn't criticizing you, I really meant it for the best.*
**18 mean mischief/trouble** to intend to cause trouble: *I could tell from the look on his face that he meant mischief.*
**19 what do you mean by doing sth?** *spoken* used to tell someone that you are very annoyed because of what they have done: *What do you mean by calling me at this time of night?*
**20 ▶ SAY STH SERIOUSLY ◀** [not in progressive] to have a serious purpose in something you say or write: **mean it** *We've heard these threats before, but I think he means it this time.* | **mean what you say** *She meant what she said – you'll have to watch out.* | **really mean** *You don't really mean that, do you?*
**21 I didn't mean it** *spoken* used to say that you did not intend to upset or hurt someone: *I'm sorry, I didn't mean it – it was just a stupid thing to say.* | *I'm sure she didn't mean it, really.*
**22 ▶ RESULT IN STH ◀** [not in progressive] to have a particular result: *The pit closures will mean a large rise in unemployment.* | **mean (that)** *His injury meant that he could no longer continue work.*
**23 that doesn't mean** used to say that something is not definitely true, or is not definitely going to happen, even though it may seem to be true because of something else you have mentioned: *Just because he's been in prison that doesn't mean he's some kind of violent criminal.*
**24 ▶ INVOLVE DOING STH ◀** [not in progressive] to involve having to do a particular thing: **mean doing sth** *I'm determined to solve this mystery even if it means traveling to New York myself.*
**25 ▶ SHOW STH IS TRUE/WILL HAPPEN ◀** [not in progressive] to be a sign that something is true or will happen: *When the boss sends for me it usually means trouble.* | **mean (that)** *If the sky is red in the evening, it usually means it'll be fine the next day.*
**26 sth means a lot to sb** used to say something is very important to someone: *Her job means a lot to her.* | **sth means everything/the world to sb** *Their grandchildren mean everything to them.*
**27 mean nothing to sb a)** to be unfamiliar to someone or impossible for them to understand: *"Who's that message for?" "No idea. It means nothing to me."* **b)** to not be important to someone: *Public honours mean nothing to her.*
**28 mean something/anything to sb a)** to be familiar to someone: *Does the name 'Kanafani' mean anything to you?* **b)** to be important to someone: *I spent years believing that I actually meant something to him.*
**29 be meant to do sth a)** if you are meant to do something, you should do it, especially because someone has told you to or because it is your responsibility: *We're meant to write our names at the top of the paper.* | *I thought the police were meant to protect people.* **b)** to be intended to do something: *The diagram is meant to show the different stages of the process.*
**30 be meant for** to be intended for a particular person or purpose: *These chairs are meant for guests.*
**31 sb was never meant for sth/to be sth** used to say that someone is not at all suitable for a particular job or activity: *I was never meant for the army.*
**32 be meant for each other** if two people are meant for each other, they are very suitable as partners for each other: *Monique and Didier were meant for each other.*
**33 sth was meant to be** used to say that you think a situation was certain to happen and that no one had any power to prevent it: *They met in August, and were married within a month, so I guess it was just meant to be.*
**34 know/understand what it means to be sth** to have experienced a particular situation, so that you know what it is like: *I understand your problems because I know what it means to be poor.*

Frequencies of the verb **mean** in spoken and written English.

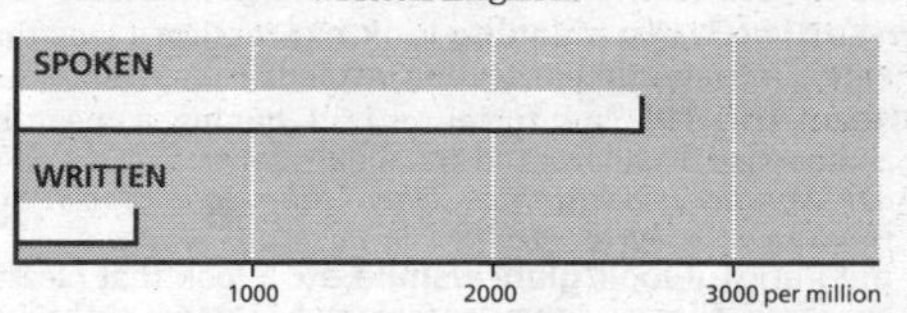


Based on the British National Corpus and the Longman Lancaster Corpus

This graph shows that the verb **mean** is much more common in spoken English than in written English. This is because it is used in a lot of common spoken phrases.

**mean²** *adj* **1** unkind or nasty: *That was a mean thing to do.* | [+ **to**] *Don't be so mean to her!* **2** *BrE* unwilling to spend any money or share what you have with other people; CHEAP¹ (6), STINGY: [+ **with**] *He's always been mean with his money.* **3** *especially AmE* cruel and bad-tempered: *That's a mean dog. Be careful it doesn't bite you.* **4 no mean achievement/feat/task etc** something that is very difficult to do, so that someone who does it deserves to be admired: *Winning that competition was no mean feat.* **5 be no mean performer/player etc** to be very good at doing something: *He was no mean batsman in those days.* **6** *AmE informal* very good and skilful: *She's one mean tennis-player.* | *Brock plays a mean game of poker.* **7** [only before noun] *technical* average: *the mean rate of consumption* **8** [only before noun] *literary* poor or looking poor: *these mean streets* **9** [only before noun] *old use* belonging to a low social class: *a man of mean birth* —**meanly** *adv* —**meanness** *n* [U]

**mean³** *n* **1 the mean** *technical* the average amount, figure, or value: *The mean of 7, 9 and 14 is 10.* **2 the/a mean between sth and sth** a method or way of doing something which is between two very different methods, and better than either of them: *It's a case of finding the mean between firmness and compassion.* —see also MEANS

**me·an·der** /miˈændə‖-ər/ *v* [I] **1** if a river or stream meanders, it turns a lot as it flows: *a flat plain of meandering rivers* **2** [always + adv/prep] to walk in a slow, relaxed way, not in any particular direction: [+**along/through etc**] *We meandered aimlessly along the lanes.* **3** also **meander on**— to talk for a long time in a way that is unclear or boring: *Will meandered on for hours.* —**meanderings** *n* [plural] —**meander** *n* [C]

**mean·ie, meany** /ˈmiːni/ *n* [C] *spoken* a word meaning an unkind person, used especially by children: *Don't be such a meanie!*

**mean·ing¹** /ˈmiːnɪŋ/ *n* S2 W1
**1 ▶ OF A WORD/SIGN ETC ◀** [C,U] the thing or idea that a word, expression, or sign represents: [+ **of**] *Can you explain the meaning of this word?* | *The expression has two very different meanings in English.*
**2 ▶ OF WHAT SB SAYS ◀** [U] the things or ideas that someone wants you to understand from what they say: [+ **of**] *We couldn't work out the meaning of this last remark.* | **get/catch/understand sb's meaning** (=understand what they are trying to tell you) *Barry could make things pretty unpleasant for us, if you get my meaning.*
**3 what's the meaning of this?** *spoken* used to demand an explanation: *What's the meaning of this? I asked you to be here an hour ago!*
**4 ▶ OF A BOOK/FILM ETC ◀** [U] the ideas that a writer, artist etc wants to show in a book, picture, film etc
**5 ▶ PURPOSE/SPECIAL QUALITY ◀** [U] the quality that makes something seem important and makes people feel that their life, work etc has a purpose and value: **lose its meaning** *Life seemed to have lost its meaning since Janet's death.* | **have meaning** *Her studies no longer seemed to have any meaning.*
**6 ▶ TRUE NATURE ◀** [U] the true nature and importance of something: [+ **of**] *I was starting to realize the full meaning of the night's events.*
**7 (not) know the meaning of** to (not) have experience

and understanding of a particular situation or feeling: *Living in that area, they knew the meaning of fear.*| *"Guilty, she doesn't know the meaning of the word!"*

**meaning²** *adj* **a meaning look/expression** a look that expresses a particular feeling strongly

**mean·ing·ful** /ˈmiːnɪŋfəl/ *adj* **1** having a meaning that is easy to understand and makes sense: *The statistics are not very meaningful when taken out of context*| *Standards must be specified in meaningful terms.* **2 a meaningful look/glance/smile etc** a look that clearly expresses the way someone feels, even though nothing is said: *John gave us a meaningful look as if to say 'I told you so'.* **3 a meaningful relationship/experience/argument etc** a relationship etc that is serious, important, or useful —**meaningfully** *adv*

**mean·ing·less** /ˈmiːnɪŋləs/ *adj* **1** something that is meaningless has no purpose or importance and does not seem worth doing or having; FUTILE: *a meaningless existence* **2** not having a meaning that you can understand or explain: *To me the marks on the page were just meaningless symbols.* —**meaninglessness** *n* [U]

S2 W2 **means** /miːnz/ *n plural* **means**
**1 ► METHOD ◄** [C] a method, system, object etc that you use as a way of achieving a result: **[+ of]** *What would be the most effective means of advertising our product?*| **means of transport** *BrE*/**transportation** *AmE*: *We had no means of transport except for two bicycles.*| **by honest/fair etc means** *The money was acquired by dishonest means.*| **means of identification** (=something that shows your name and address)
**2 by means of** using a particular method or system: *The blocks are raised by means of pulleys.*
**3 by all means** *spoken* used to mean 'of course' when politely allowing someone to do something or agreeing with a suggestion: *"Can I bring Alan to the party?" "By all means!"*| *By all means try the jacket on, but I think it will be too big for you.*
**4 by no means/not by any means** not at all: *It is by no means certain that the game will take place.*| *She's not a bad kid, by any means.*
**5 a means to an end** something that you do only to achieve a result, not because you want to do it: *For Geoff, the job was simply a means to an end.*
**6 ► MONEY ◄** [plural] the money or income that you have: **have the means to do sth** *I don't have the means to support a family.*| **according to your means** *Each member contributes according to his or her means.*| **beyond your means** (=costing more than you can afford) *These medical costs are beyond the means of most working people.*| **within your means** (=not costing more than you can afford) *The cost should be well within the means of the average family.*
**7 man/woman of means** *literary* someone who is rich
**8 the means of production** *technical* the material, tools, and equipment that are used in the production of goods: *public ownership of the means of production* —see also **by fair means or foul** (FAIR¹ (13)), **ways and means** (WAY¹ (3))

**mean-spir·it·ed** /ˌ· ˈ···◂/ *adj* not generous or sympathetic: *a mean-spirited, jealous man*

**means test** /ˈ· ·/ *n* [C] an official check in order to find out whether someone is poor enough to need money from the state —**means tested** *adj*: *means-tested benefits*

**meant** /ment/ *v* the past tense and past participle of MEAN¹

**mean·time** /ˈmiːntaɪm/ *adv* **1 in the meantime** in the period of time between now and a future event, or between two events in the past: *The doctor will be here soon. In the meantime, try and relax.*| *I didn't see her for another five years, and in the meantime she had got married and had a couple of kids.* **2 for the meantime** for the present time, until something happens: *The power supply should be back soon – for the meantime we'll have to use candles.* **3** [sentence adverb] *spoken* in the present period, before something else happens: *Dinner will be at 7. Meantime, just make yourselves at home.*

W **mean·while** /ˈmiːnwaɪl/ *adv* [sentence adverb] **1** in the period of time between two events: *The flight will be announced soon. Meanwhile, please remain seated.*| **in the meanwhile** *I knew I wouldn't get my exam results for several weeks, and I wasn't sure what to do in the meanwhile.* **2** while something else is happening: *Jim went to answer the phone. Meanwhile Pete started to prepare lunch.* **3** used to compare two things that are happening at the same time: *The incomes of male professionals went up by almost 80%. Meanwhile, part-time women workers saw their earnings fall.*

**mean·y** /ˈmiːni/ *n* [C] another way of spelling MEANIE

**mea·sles** /ˈmiːzəlz/ *n* [U] also **the measles**— an infectious illness in which you have a fever and small red spots on your face and body —see also GERMAN MEASLES

**meas·ly** /ˈmiːzli/ *adj informal* very small and disappointing in size, quantity, or value: *All I got was a measly £5.*

**mea·su·ra·ble** /ˈmeʒərəbəl/ *adj* **1** large or important enough to have a definite effect: *The tax will not have any measurable impact on the lives of most people.* **2** able to be measured: *measurable results* —**measurably** *adv*: *His mood had improved measurably.*

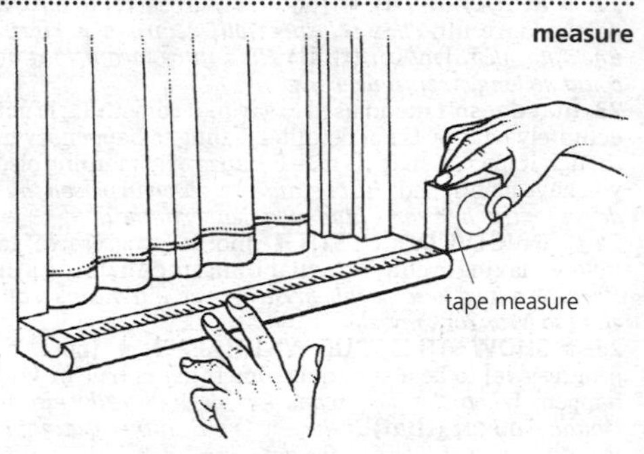


W **mea·sure¹** /ˈmeʒə‖-ər/ *n*
**1 ► OFFICIAL ACTION ◄** [C] an official action that is intended to deal with a particular problem: *Stronger measures are needed to combat crime.*
**2 half measures** things done to deal with a difficult situation that are not effective or firm enough: *This was no time for half measures and compromises.*
**3 ► A CERTAIN AMOUNT ◄ a measure of success/agreement/freedom etc** a certain amount of a good or useful quality: *new legislation giving women a measure of economic independence*
**4 ► UNIT OF MEASUREMENT ◄** [C] an amount or unit in a measuring system: *A centimetre is a measure of length.*| *a table of weights and measures*
**5 a measure of alcohol/whisky/etc** a standard amount of an alcoholic drink
**6 ► SIGN/PROOF ◄ be a measure of sth** *formal* to be a sign of the importance, strength etc of something: *It is a meansure of his popularity that he was able to travel around without a bodyguard.*
**7 ► WAY OF JUDGING STH ◄ a measure of** a way of testing or judging something: *Exams are not necessarily the best measure of students' abilities.*
**8 beyond measure** *formal* very great or very much: *The pride he felt was beyond measure.*| *Her work has improved beyond measure.*
**9 for good measure** in addition to what you have already done or given: *She tasted the mixture and added another glass of brandy for good measure.*
**10 in large measure/in some measure** to a great degree or to some degree: *The improvements are due in large measure to his leadership.*
**11 in full measure** if someone gives something back in full measure, they give back as much as they received: *They returned our hospitality in full measure.*

**12 the full measure of** *formal* the whole of something: *Ralph received the full measure of his mother's devotion.* **13 get the measure of sb/take sb's measure** to form a judgment of someone's abilities or character, so that you are able to deal with them or defeat them: *She soon got the measure of her opponent.*
**14 ▶THING USED FOR MEASURING◀** [C] something such as a piece of wood or a container used for measuring —see also TAPE MEASURE
**15 ▶SYSTEM FOR MEASURING◀** [U] a system for measuring amount, size, or weight: *liquid measure.*
**16 ▶MUSIC◀** [C] *AmE* one of a group of notes and rests (REST[1] (12)), separated by VERTICAL lines, into which a line of written music is divided —see also MADE-TO-MEASURE, **give sb short measure** (SHORT[1] (14))

S2 W2 **measure²** *v* **1** [T] to find the size, length, or amount of something using standard units: *Could you measure the height of the wall for me?| The rainfall was measured over a three-month period.* | **measure sb for sth** (=measure someone in order to make clothes for them) *She was being measured for her wedding dress.* **2** [T] to judge the importance, value, or true nature of something: *What criteria can we use to measure women's progress in the workforce?*| **measure sth by sth** *Education shouldn't be measured purely by examination results.* **3** [linking verb] to be a particular size, length, or amount: *That old tree must measure at least 30 metres from top to bottom.* | *an earthquake measuring 6.5 on the Richter scale* **4** [T] to show or record a particular kind of measurement: *an instrument for measuring tiny amounts of electrical current* **5 measure your length** *old use* to fall down flat on the ground

**measure** sb/sth **against** *phr v* [T] to judge someone or something by comparing them with another person or thing: *When measured against the work of a professional, her efforts look unimpressive.*

**measure** sth ↔ **off** *phr v* [T] to measure a length of material and cut it from a larger piece: *The assistant measured off enough fabric for three dresses.*

**measure** sth ↔ **out** *phr v* [T] to take a certain amount of liquid, powder etc from a larger amount: *Measure out 100 grams of flour.*

**measure up** *phr v* **1** [I] to be good enough to do a particular job or to reach a particular standard: **[+ to]** *How will the Secretary General measure up to his new responsibilities?| We'll give you a week's trial in the job to see how you measure up.* **2** [I,T] to measure something: *I'd better measure up before I start laying the carpet.*

**mea·sured** /ˈmeʒəd‖-ərd/ *adj* careful and slow or steady: *a calm measured voice | a measured response*

**mea·sure·less** /ˈmeʒələs‖-ʒər-/ *adj literary* too big to be measured: *falling through the measureless ocean*

W3 **mea·sure·ment** /ˈmeʒəmənt‖-ʒər-/ *n* **1** [C usually plural] the length, height etc of something: **waist/chest etc measurement** *What's your waist measurement?*| **make/take measurements** (=measure something) *The builders made careful measurements.* | **take sb's measurements** (=measure someone in order to make or find clothes for them) **2** [U] the act of measuring something: *the measurement of performance*

**measuring cup** /ˈ··· ˌ·/ *n* [C] *especially AmE* a cup used for measuring food or liquid when cooking

**measuring jug** /ˈ··· ˌ·/ *n* [C] *especially BrE* a glass or plastic container used for measuring liquid when cooking —see picture at JUG[1]

**measuring tape** /ˈ··· ˌ·/ *n* [C] a long piece of cloth or steel used for measuring; TAPE MEASURE

S2 W3 **meat** /miːt/ *n* **1** [U] the flesh of animals and birds eaten as food: *I gave up eating meat a few months ago.* | *meat pie* **2** [C] a type of meat: *a selection of cold meats* **3** [U] something that is interesting or important in a talk, book etc: *The lecture was well-delivered but there wasn't much meat in it.* | **the meat of** (=the main and most interesting part) *We then got down to the real meat of the debate.* **4 sb doesn't have much meat on him/her** *informal* used to say that someone looks very thin: *George doesn't have much meat on him, does he?* **5 easy meat** *informal* someone who it is easy to deceive or hurt **6 meat and drink to sb** something that someone enjoys doing or finds very easy to do: *The first five questions were on basketball, which was meat and drink to Larry.| Repairing cars is meat and drink to him.* **7 be the meat in the sandwich** *BrE informal* to be friendly with two people or groups who are quarrelling **8 one man's meat is another man's poison** used to say that something that one person likes may not be liked by someone else **9 the meat and potatoes** *AmE informal* the most important part of a discussion: *Let's get down to the meat and potatoes; how much are you going to pay me for this?*

**meat·ball** /ˈmiːtbɔːl‖-bɒːl/ *n* [C] a small round ball made from thin pieces of meat pressed together

**meat grind·er** /ˈ· ˌ··/ *n* [C] *AmE* a machine that cuts meat into very small pieces by forcing it through small holes; MINCER *BrE*

**meat·loaf** /ˈmiːtləʊf‖-loʊf/ *n* [C,U] a type of food made from meat and other foods which are mixed together in the shape of a LOAF and baked

**meat-pack·ing** /ˈ· ˌ··/ *n* [U] *AmE* the preparation of dead animals so that they can be sold as meat: *the meat-packing industry* —**meat-packer** *n* [C]

**meat·y** /ˈmiːti/ *adj* **1** containing a lot of meat or tasting strongly of meat: *a delicious meaty gravy* **2** *informal* big and fat, with a lot of flesh: *a tall guy with meaty shoulders* **3** *informal* containing a lot of interesting ideas or information: *The lecture wasn't very meaty.*

**mec·ca** /ˈmekə/ *n* [singular] **1** a place that many people want to visit for a particular reason: **[+ for]** *Florence is a mecca for students of Art History.* **2 Mecca** a city in Saudi Arabia which is the holiest city of Islam

**me·chan·ic** /mɪˈkænɪk/ *n* **1** [C] someone who is skilled at repairing motor vehicles and machinery **2 mechanics** [U] the science that deals with the effects of forces on objects —see also QUANTUM MECHANICS **3 the mechanics of (doing) sth** the way in which something works or is done: *I still don't understand the mechanics of transferring computer files onto a different machine.*

**me·chan·i·cal** /mɪˈkænɪkəl/ *adj* **1** using power from an engine to do a particular kind of work: *a mechanical digger* **2** affecting or involving a machine: *The pump shut off as a result of a mechanical failure.* **3** a mechanical action, reply etc is done without thinking, and has been done many times before: *He was asked the same question so many times that the answer became mechanical.* **4** *informal* someone who is mechanical understands how machines work **5** *technical* connected with or produced by physical forces: *the mechanical properties of solids* —**mechanically** /-kli/ *adv*

**mechanical en·gi·neer·ing** /·ˌ··· ··ˈ··/ *n* [U] the study of the design and production of machines and tools —**mechanical engineer** *n* [C]

**mechanically mind·ed** /·ˌ··· ˈ··◂/ *adj* good at understanding how machines work and repairing them

**mechanical pen·cil** /·ˌ··· ˈ··/ *n* [C] *AmE* a pencil made of metal or plastic, with a thin piece of LEAD (=the part that you write with) inside; PROPELLING PENCIL *BrE*

**mech·a·nis·m** /ˈmekənɪzəm/ *n* [C] **1** part of a machine that does a particular job: *the brake mechanism* **2** a system that is intended to achieve something or deal with a problem: *mechanisms to stop the spread of nuclear weapons| The market system is an imperfect mechanism for achieving full employment.* **3** the way that something works: *the mechanism of the brain* **4 defence/survival/escape mechanism** a way of behaving that helps you to avoid or deal with something that is difficult or dangerous: *His aggression is actually a defence mechanism against rejection.*

**mech·a·nis·tic** /ˌmekəˈnɪstɪk◂/ *adj* tending to explain the actions and behaviour of living things as if they were machines: *a mechanistic view of the universe* —**mechanistically** /-kli/ *adj*

**mech·a·nize** also **-ise** *BrE* /ˈmekənaɪz/ *v* [I,T] to change

M

the way that something is made or done, so that the work is done by machines instead of people or animals: *Almost the entire process of car manufacturing has been mechanized.* —**mechanized** *adj*: mechanized farming —**mechanization** /ˌmekənaɪˈzeɪʃən‖-nə-/ *n* [U]

**M Econ** *n BrE* Master of Economics; a university higher degree in ECONOMICS that you get after your first degree

**M Ed** /ˌem ˈed/ *n* Master of Education; a university higher degree in teaching that you get after your first degree

**Med** /med/ *n* **the Med** *BrE informal* the area surrounding the Mediterranean Sea

**med·al** /ˈmedl/ *n* [C] a round flat piece of metal given to someone who has won a competition or who has done something brave: *an Olympic gold medal* —see also **deserve a medal** (DESERVE (3))

**med·al·ist** /ˈmedl-ɪ̈st/ *n* [C] the American spelling of medallist

**me·dal·li·on** /mɪ̈ˈdæliən/ *n* [C] a piece of metal shaped like a large coin, worn as jewellery on a chain around the neck

**med·al·list** /ˈmedl-ɪ̈st/ *n* [C] *BrE* someone who has won a medal in a competition: *the Olympic silver medallist*

**Medal of Hon·our** /ˌ‧‧ ‧ ˈ‧‧/ *n* [C] the highest award given by Congress to a soldier, sailor etc who has done something extremely brave

**med·dle** /ˈmedl/ *v* [I] **1** to deliberately become involved in a situation that does not concern you, or that you do not understand: [+ **in/with**] *I wish you wouldn't meddle in my affairs.* **2** to touch something carelessly in a way that might break it: [+ **with**] *The kids are always meddling with the ornaments.* —**meddler** *n* [C]

**med·dle·some** /ˈmedlsəm/ *adj* tending to become involved in situations that do not concern you, in a way that annoys people: *that meddlesome old woman*

S2 W2 **me·di·a** /ˈmiːdiə/ *n* **1 the media** all the organizations, such as television, radio, and the newspapers, that provide information for the public: *The letter was leaked to the media by a White House official.* | [also + plural verb *BrE*] *The media have launched a bitter attack on the Health Minister.* | **media coverage** (=the amount of time or space given to an event by the media) *The war got massive media coverage.* | **media event** (=an event that the media give a lot of attention to) | **media hype** (=a lot of attention given to an event by the media, making it seem much more important than it really is) **2** the plural of MEDIUM —see also MASS MEDIA

**med·i·ae·val** /ˌmediˈiːvəl◂‖ˌmiː-/ *adj* another spelling of MEDIEVAL

**me·di·an**[1] /ˈmiːdiən/ *n* **1** [C] *AmE* a thin area of land running down the middle of a road to keep traffic travelling in different directions apart; CENTRAL RESERVATION *BrE* **2** [C] the middle measurement in a set of measurements that are arranged in order **3** [C] *technical* a line passing from one of the points of a TRIANGLE to the opposite side

**median**[2] *adj* [only before noun] *technical* **1** in or passing through the middle **2** *technical* related to a line passing from one of the points of a TRIANGLE to the opposite side

**median strip** /ˈ‧‧‧ ˌ‧/ *n* [C] *AmE* MEDIAN[1] (1) —see picture on page 415

**media stud·ies** /ˈ‧‧‧ ˌ‧‧/ *n* [U] *BrE* the study of newspapers, radio and television

**me·di·ate** /ˈmiːdieɪt/ *v* **1** [I,T] to try to end a quarrel between two people or groups: [+ **between**] *The U.N. attempted to mediate between the warring factions.* | **mediate sth** *The court was set up to mediate civil disputes.* **2** [T] to find an agreement or solution by talking to two people or groups who are quarrelling: *They've succeeded in mediating a ceasefire.* **3** [T] usually passive] *formal or technical* if the effect of something is mediated by another thing, it changes because of that other thing: *child mortality is mediated by economic factors* —**mediator** *n* [C] —**mediation** /ˌmiːdiˈeɪʃən/ *n* [U]

**med·ic** /ˈmedɪk/ *n* [C] **1** *informal* a medical doctor **2** *BrE* a medical student **3** *AmE* someone in the army who gives medical treatment

**Med·i·caid** /ˈmedɪkeɪd/ *n* [U] a system in the US by which the government helps to pay the cost of medical treatment for poor people —compare MEDICARE

**med·i·cal**[1] /ˈmedɪkəl/ *adj* connected with medicine and the treatment of disease or injury: *The injury required urgent medical attention.* | *medical college* | *Poor people can only afford the most basic medical treatment.* | **the medical profession** (=doctors, nurses, and other people who treat people who are ill) —**medically** /-kli/ *adv* S2 W2

**medical**[2] *n* [C] *BrE* an examination of your body by a doctor to see if you are healthy; PHYSICAL[2] *AmE*: *You'll need to have a medical before starting the new job.*

**medical cer·tif·i·cate** /ˈ‧‧‧ ‧ˌ‧‧‧/ *n* [C] an official piece of paper signed by a doctor saying that you are too ill to work or that you are completely healthy

**medical prac·ti·tion·er** /ˌ‧‧‧ ‧ˈ‧‧‧/ *n* [C] *BrE formal* a doctor

**medical school** /ˈ‧‧‧ ‧/ *n* [C,U] a college or university where people study to become doctors

**me·dic·a·ment** /mɪˈdɪkəmənt, ˈmedɪ-/ *n* [C] *formal* a substance used on or in the body to treat a disease

**Med·i·care** /ˈmedɪkeə‖-ker/ *n* [U] a system by which the US government helps to pay for the medical treatment of old people —compare MEDICAID

**med·i·cated** /ˈmedɪ̈keɪtɪ̈d/ *adj* medicated soap or SHAMPOO contains a substance to help small medical problems of your skin or hair

**med·i·ca·tion** /ˌmedɪ̈ˈkeɪʃən/ *n* [C,U] medicine or drugs given to people who are ill: **be on medication** *She's on medication for her heart.*

**me·di·ci·nal** /mɪ̈ˈdɪsənəl/ *adj* **1** a medicinal substance can cure illness or disease: **medicinal properties** *Evening primrose oil is thought to have medicinal properties.* **2 for medicinal purposes** *humorous* used to say jokingly that you drink alcohol because it is good for your health: *I keep a bottle of brandy handy – purely for medicinal purposes.* —compare MEDICAL[1] —**medicinally** *adv*

**medi·cine** /ˈmedsən‖ˈmedɪ̈sən/ *n* **1** [C,U] a substance used for treating illness, especially a liquid you drink: **take medicine** *Have you taken your medicine?* **2** [U] the treatment and study of illnesses and injuries: *He studied medicine at Yale.* | *homeopathic medicine* **3 the best medicine** the best way of making you feel better when you are sad: *Laughter is the best medicine.* **4 give someone a dose/taste of their own medicine** to treat someone as badly as they have treated you: *I love 'em and leave 'em, she said. I do it to give men a taste of their own medicine.* **5 take your medicine (like a man)** to accept an unpleasant situation that you have caused, or a punishment, without complaining —see also ALTERNATIVE MEDICINE 

**medicine chest** /ˈ‧‧ ‧‖ˈ‧‧‧ ‧/ *n* [C] a small cupboard used to store medicines

**medicine man** /ˈ‧‧ ‧‖ˈ‧‧‧ ‧/ or **medicine wom·an** /ˈ‧‧ ˌ‧‧‖ˈ‧‧‧ ˌ‧‧/ *n* [C] a person in a Native American tribe who is considered to have the ability to cure illness and disease

**med·i·co** /ˈmedɪkəʊ‖-koʊ/ *n* [C] *informal* a MEDIC

**med·i·e·val, mediaeval** /ˌmediˈiːvəl◂‖ˌmiː-/ *adj* **1** connected with the Middle Ages (=the period between about AD 1100 and 1500): *medieval literature* | *medieval Europe* **2** *humorous* very old or old-fashioned: *The plumbing in this house is positively medieval!* W3

**me·di·o·cre** /ˌmiːdiˈəʊkə◂‖-ˈoʊkər◂/ *adj* not very good: *I thought the film was pretty mediocre.* | *a mediocre student* —**mediocrity** /ˌmiːdiˈɒkrɪ̈ti‖-ˈɑːk-/ *n* [U]

**med·i·tate** /ˈmedɪ̈teɪt/ *v* **1** [I] to empty your mind of thoughts and feelings, in order to relax completely or for religious purposes: *I try to meditate for half an hour every evening.* **2** [I] to think seriously and deeply about something: [+ **on/upon**] *She sat quietly, meditating on the* *day's events.* **3** [T] to plan to do something, usually something unpleasant: *Silently she meditated revenge.*

**med·i·ta·tion** /ˌmedʒˈteɪʃən/ *n* **1** [U] the practice of emptying your mind of thoughts and feelings, in order to relax completely or for religious reasons: *Try to set aside an hour each day for meditation.* **2** [C usually plural, U] the act of thinking deeply and seriously about something: *He stood gazing into the water, lost in meditation.* | *Rob interrupted his father's meditations.* **3** [C usually plural] serious thoughts about a particular subject: [+ **on**] *meditations on death and loss*

**med·i·ta·tive** /ˈmedʒtətɪv‖-teɪtɪv/ *adj* thinking deeply and seriously about something: *Dr Wijk contemplated the picture in meditative silence.* —**meditatively** *adv*

**Med·i·ter·ra·ne·an**[1] /ˌmedʒtəˈreɪniən◂/ *n* **the Mediterranean** the sea that is surrounded by the countries of southern Europe, North Africa, and the Middle East

**Mediterranean**[2] *adj* from or connected with the Mediterranean Sea, or typical of the area of Southern Europe around it: *the Mediterranean way of life*

S3 **me·di·um**[1] /ˈmiːdiəm/ *adj* **1** of middle size between large and small, of middle height between tall and short etc: *What size do you want – large, medium, or small?* | **medium sized/medium size** *a medium-sized onion* | **of medium height/length/build etc** *She's of medium height.* | *The man is of medium build and is in his late 20s.* | *hair of medium length* | **medium to large** *medium to large companies* | **medium heat/oven** (=at a temperature that is warm but not too high or low) *Bake in a medium oven for 25 minutes.* **2 medium brown/blue etc** a colour which is neither light nor dark: *His jacket's a medium brown colour.*

**medium**[2] *n plural* **media** /-diə/ or **mediums** [C] **1** a way of communicating information and news to people, such as newspapers, television etc: *Politicians prefer to use the medium of television.* —see also MEDIA **2** a way of expressing your ideas, especially as a writer or an artist: [+ **for**] *the novel as a medium for satire* | *the visual media* **3 medium of instruction** a language that is used for teaching: *English is still the main medium of instruction in Nigeria.* **4 medium of exchange** money or other ways of paying for things **5** *technical* a substance or material in which things grow or exist **6** *technical* a substance through which a force travels —see also MAGNETIC MEDIA, **happy medium** (HAPPY (7))

**medium**[3] *n plural* **mediums** [C] someone who claims to have the power to receive messages from the spirits of the dead

**medium term** /ˈ··· ˌ·/ *n* [singular] the period of time a few weeks or months ahead of the present: **in the medium term** *The company's prospects look good in the medium term.* | *medium term investments* —compare SHORT-TERM, LONG-TERM

**medium wave** /ˈ··· ·/ *written abbreviation* **MW** *n* [U] a system of radio broadcasting using radio waves (WAVE[2] (3)) that are between 100 and 1000 metres in length

**med·ley** /ˈmedli/ *n* [C] **1** a group of songs or tunes sung or played one after the other as a single piece of music: *a medley of Eighties hits* **2** a swimming race in which the competitors swim using four different strokes (STROKE[1] (2b)) **3** [usually singular] a mixture of different kinds of the same thing which produces an interesting or unusual effect: *a medley of architectural styles*

**meek** /miːk/ *adj* very quiet and gentle and unwilling to argue or express an opinion: *a meek and obedient child* | **meek and mild** (=extremely quiet and gentle) *She'd never stand up for herself, she's too meek and mild.* —**meekly** *adv. She smiled meekly.* —**meekness** *n* [U]

S1 W1 **meet**[1] /miːt/ *v past tense and past participle* **met** /met/

**1 ▸ BE IN THE SAME PLACE ◂** [I,T not in passive] **a)** to be in the same place as someone else because you have arranged to do this: *Meet me at 8.00.* | *We agreed to meet in front of the theatre.* | *Why don't we meet for lunch on Friday?* **b)** to see someone by chance and talk to them: *James and Tim met in the park.* | *You'll never guess who I met yesterday – my old teacher!*

**2 ▸ SEE SB FOR THE FIRST TIME ◂** [I,T not in passive] to see and talk to someone for the first time, or be introduced to them: *Diego and Susan met on vacation and were married six months later.* | *Jane, come and meet Alan and Dave.* | *I met my husband at University.*

**3 nice/pleased/glad to meet you** *spoken especially BrE* also **nice meeting you** *AmE spoken* used when meeting someone for the first time, especially when another person has introduced you to each other: *"Farrah, this is Jean-Paul." "Nice to meet you."*

**4 ▸ AT AN AIRPORT/STATION ETC ◂** [T] to meet someone who has arrived at an airport, station etc: *Rob came to meet us at the airport.*

**5 ▸ COMMITTEE, GROUP ETC ◂** [I] to be together in the same place, usually in order to discuss something: *The committee meets once a month.*

**6 ▸ OPPONENT ◂** [I,T not in passive] to play against another person or team in a competition, or to fight another army in a war: *Manchester United will meet Blackburn Rovers in the sixth round of the Cup.*

**7 ▸ RIVERS/ROADS/LINES ETC ◂** [I,T not in passive] to join together at a particular place: *The two roads meet just north of Flagstaff.* | **meet sth** *You can see on the map where the land meets the sea.*

**8 ▸ PROBLEM/ATTITUDE/SITUATION ◂** [T] to experience a particular kind of problem, attitude, or situation; ENCOUNTER[1]: *I've never met this kind of problem before.*

**9 meet a demand/need/requirement** to satisfy a demand etc: *The company is unable to meet these wage claims.*

**10 meet an aim/goal/target etc** to achieve an aim etc: *It's virtually impossible to meet the weekly sales targets.*

**11 meet debts/costs/expenses etc** to pay debts etc: *The firm has found itself unable to meet its debts.*

**12 there's more to sb/sth than meets the eye** used to say that someone or something is more interesting, intelligent etc than they seem to be

**13 our/their eyes meet** if two people's eyes meet they look at each other, because they are attracted to each other or because they are thinking the same thing: *Their eyes met across the crowded room.*

**14 meet sb's eye/gaze/glance etc** to look directly at someone who is looking at you: *Martin met his father's accusing glance defiantly.*

**15 meet your eye/ear** to be heard or seen: *At the top of the mountain a scene of extraordinary beauty met our eyes.*

**16 meet your match** to have an opponent who is stronger or more skilful than you are: *I think he's finally met his match.*

**17 meet sb halfway** to do some of the things that someone wants, in order to reach an agreement with them: *They won't pay all our expenses but they might be prepared to meet us halfway.*

**18 ▸ TOUCH/HIT ◂** [I,T] to touch or hit another object: *Their hands met under the table.*

**19 meet (sth) head-on a)** if two vehicles or people that are moving quickly towards each other meet head-on, they hit each other suddenly and violently **b)** if you meet a problem head-on, you deal with it directly without trying to avoid it

**20 meet your death/end** to die in a particular way: *The general met a violent end at the hands of a paid assassin.*

**21 meet your maker** *informal humorous* to die

**22 sb has met their Waterloo** used to say that someone will be defeated —see also **make ends meet** (END[1] (17))

**meet up** *phr v* [I] **1** to meet someone in order to do something together: *We often meet up after work and go for a drink.* | [+ **with**] *Pete met up with us after the game.* **2** if roads, paths etc meet up they join together at a particular place: [+ **with**] *The path eventually meets up with the main road.*

**meet with** sb/sth *phr v* [T] **1** to have a meeting with someone: *Representatives of EC countries will meet with senior American politicians.* **2** to get a particular reaction or result: **meet with approval/disapproval/opposition** *The senator's suggestions met with widespread disapproval.* | **meet with success/failure** (=succeed or fail) *Our attempts at negotiation finally met with some success.* **3 meet with an accident/danger/death** *formal* to experience something by chance, often something unpleasant: *Rizzio met with a fatal accident at Hollyrood Palace.*

**meet²** *n* [C] **1 track/sports meet** *especially AmE* a sports competition, especially a competition between people running races **2** *BrE* an occasion when a group of people riding horses go out to hunt foxes (FOX¹ (1))

**meet³** *adj old use* right or suitable

S1 W1 **meet·ing** /ˈmiːtɪŋ/ *n* **1** [C] an event at which people meet to talk and decide things: **attend a meeting** *Over a hundred people attended the meeting.* | **be in/at a meeting** *Mrs Lavelle is in a meeting at the moment.* | **hold a meeting** *A meeting will be held in the City Hall on Thursday at 2pm.* **2 the meeting** *formal* all the people who attend a meeting: *I'd like to put a few ideas before the meeting.* **3** [usually singular] a situation of two or more people meeting each other by chance or because they have arranged to do this: *I had felt drawn to Alice ever since our first meeting.* **4** [C] a sports competition or a set of races for horses **5 meeting of minds** a situation in which two people have very similar ideas and understand each other very well: *There was a real meeting of minds between the composer and his young pupil.* **6** an event at which a group of Quakers (=a Christian religious group) worship together

**meeting-house** /ˈ·· ·/ *n* [C] a building where Quakers worship

**meg·a** /ˈmegə/ *adj slang* very big and impressive or enjoyable: *a really mega party* —**mega** *adv*: *a mega big rock star*

**mega-** /megə/ *prefix* **1** a million times a particular unit of something: *a 100-megaton bomb* —see table on page B2 **2** *informal* much larger than usual in amount, importance, or size: *Hollywood megastars* | *Frank told me her new boyfriend is megarich.*

**meg·a·bit** /ˈmegəbɪt/ *n* [C] *technical* a million bits (BIT¹ (12))

**meg·a·bucks** /ˈmegəbʌks/ *n* [plural] *informal* a large amount of money: *She's earning megabucks now.*

**meg·a·byte** /ˈmegəbaɪt/ *n* [C] a million BYTES

**meg·a·death** /ˈmegədeθ/ *n* [U] a word meaning one million deaths, used when talking about a NUCLEAR WAR

**meg·a·hertz** /ˈmegəhɜːts‖-ɜːr-/ written abbreviation **MHz** *n* a million HERTZ

**meg·a·lith** /ˈmegəlɪθ/ *n* [C] a large tall stone put in an open place by people in ancient times, possibly as a religious sign —**megalithic** /ˌmegəˈlɪθɪk◂/ *adj*: *a megalithic monument*

**meg·a·lo·ma·ni·a** /ˌmegələʊˈmeɪniə‖-loʊ-/ *n* [U] the belief that you are extremely important and powerful, which makes you want to control other people's lives, and is often a kind of mental illness

**meg·a·lo·ma·ni·ac** /ˌmegələʊˈmeɪniæk‖-loʊ-/ *n* [C] someone who believes they are extremely important or powerful and tries to control other people's lives —**megalomaniac** *adj*

**meg·a·phone** /ˈmegəfəʊn‖-foʊn/ *n* [C] a piece of equipment like a large horn which you talk through to make your voice sound louder, when speaking to a crowd

**meg·a·star** /ˈmegəstɑː‖-stɑːr/ *n* [C] *informal* a very famous singer or actor: *rock megastar David Bowie*

**meg·a·ton** /ˈmegətʌn/ *n* [C] a measure of the power of an explosive that is equal to that of a million TONS of TNT (=a powerful explosive): *a five megaton atomic bomb*

**mel·a·mine** /ˈmeləmiːn/ *n* [U] a material like plastic used to make hard smooth surfaces on tables and shelves

**mel·an·cho·li·a** /ˌmelənˈkəʊliə‖-ˈkoʊ-/ *n* [U] *technical* a feeling of great sadness and lack of energy, often caused by mental illness; DEPRESSION (1)

**mel·an·chol·ic** /ˌmelənˈkɒlɪk◂‖-ˈkɑː-/ *adj formal* feeling or tending to be very sad, often because you are mentally ill: *the cause of Emilia's melancholic condition*

**mel·an·chol·y¹** /ˈmelənkəli‖-kɑːli/ *adj* sad or making you feel sad: *a melancholy expression* | *the seagulls' melancholy cry*

**melancholy²** *n* [U] *formal* a feeling of sadness for no particular reason: *They sank into a mood of deep melancholy.* | *the lingering melancholy of "Gloomy Sunday"*

**me·lange** /meɪˈlɑːnʒ/ *n* [singular] *French* a mixture of different things: *a melange of sounds and smells*

**mel·a·nin** /ˈmelənɪn/ *n* [U] a natural dark brown colour in human skin, hair, and eyes

**mel·a·no·ma** /ˌmeləˈnəʊmə‖-ˈnoʊ-/ *n* [C] *technical* a TUMOUR on the skin which causes CANCER

**Mel·ba toast** /ˌmelbə ˈtəʊst‖-ˈtoʊst/ *n* [U] a kind of thin toast which breaks easily into small bits

**mel·ée** /ˈmeleɪ‖ˈmeɪleɪ, meɪˈleɪ/ *n* [usually singular] a situation in which people rush around in a confused way: *Richard was thrown from his horse in the melée.*

**mel·li·flu·ous** /mɪˈlɪfluəs/ *adj formal* having a pleasant musical sound: *a mellifluous voice* —**mellifluously** *adv*

**mel·low¹** /ˈmeləʊ‖-loʊ/ *adj* **1** a mellow colour or light looks soft, warm, and not too bright: *the mellow, golden light of early evening* | *mellow shades of brown and orange* **2** a mellow sound is pleasant and smooth: *the mellow sound of a trombone* | *a friendly, mellow voice* **3** mellow wine or fruit has a smooth, ripe taste: *a mellow red wine* **4** gentle, calm, and sympathetic because of age or experience: *Tina's become more mellow since having children of her own.* **5** feeling calm and relaxed, especially after drinking alcohol: *They were feeling pleasantly mellow.* —**mellowness** *n* [U]

**mellow²** *v* [I,T] **1** if colours mellow or are mellowed, they begin to look warm and soft **2** if someone mellows or is mellowed, they become gentler and more sympathetic: *Paul's certainly mellowed over the years.* **3** if wine mellows or is mellowed it gets a smooth taste

**mellow out** *phr v* [I,T] *AmE informal* to become relaxed and calm, or make someone relaxed and calm: *Mellow out, OK? It's no big deal!*

**me·lod·ic** /mɪˈlɒdɪk‖mɪˈlɑː-/ *adj* **1** *technical* concerned with the main tune in a piece of music: *the melodic structure of Beethoven's symphonies* **2** having a pleasant tune or a pleasant sound like music: *a sweet melodic voice*

**me·lo·di·ous** /mɪˈləʊdiəs‖-ˈloʊ-/ *adj formal* having a pleasant tune or a pleasant sound like music: *The piece was melodious and simple.* —**melodiously** *adv* —**melodiousness** *n* [U]

**mel·o·dra·ma** /ˈmelədrɑːmə‖-drɑːmə,-dræmə/ *n* [C,U] **1** a story or play with many sudden exciting events, and very good or bad characters, who show feelings that are too strong or simple to seem real **2** a situation in which people behave with too much emotion and excitement: *Let's not make a melodrama out of this little problem.*

**mel·o·dra·mat·ic** /ˌmelədrəˈmætɪk◂/ *adj* behaving or talking in an excited way with strong emotion: *Stop being so melodramatic!* —**melodramatically** /-kli/ *adv*

**mel·o·dy** /ˈmelədi/ *n* **1** [C,U] a song or tune: *a haunting melody* **2** [C] the main tune in a complicated piece of music: *variations on the original melody* **3** [U] the arrangement of musical notes in a way that is pleasant to listen to

**mel·on** /ˈmelən/ *n* [C,U] a large round fruit with yellow, green, or red sweet juicy flesh —see picture on page 413

**melt** /melt/ *v* **1** [I,T] if something solid melts or if heat melts it, it becomes liquid: *The snow was melting in the early morning sun.* | **melt sth** *Melt the butter and mix it with the eggs.* —compare FREEZE[1] (1), THAW[1] (1) **2** also **melt away** [I] to gradually disappear: *Julie's anger slowly melted away.* | **melt into a crowd** *The man melted into the crowd and I lost sight of him.* **3** [I,T] to become or make someone become more gentle and sympathetic than before: **your heart melts** (=you suddenly feel very sympathetic) *He shouted at the little girl, but his heart melted when he saw her crying.* **4 melt into** if one sound, colour, or feeling melts into another one, it gradually becomes part of it until there is no difference between them: *The sound of the trumpet melted into the strains of the orchestra.* **5 melt in your mouth** if food melts in your mouth, it is soft and delicious —see also **butter wouldn't melt in sbs mouth** (BUTTER[1] (2))

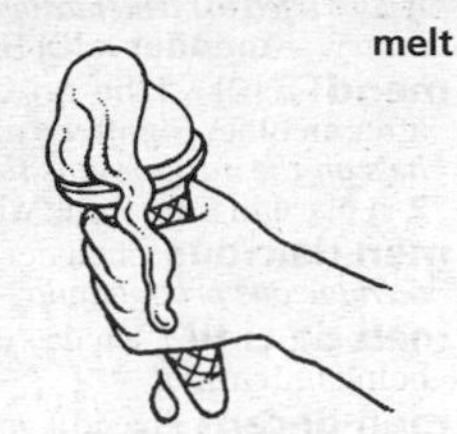
melt

**melt** sth ↔ **down** *phr v* [T] to heat a metal object until it becomes a liquid, especially so that you can use the metal again: *People were melting down coins to make earrings and ornaments.*

**melt·down** /ˈmeltdaʊn/ *n* [C,U] a very dangerous situation in which the material in a NUCLEAR REACTOR melts and burns through its container, allowing RADIOACTIVITY to escape

**melt·ing** /ˈmeltɪŋ/ *adj* [usually before noun] a melting look, voice, or expression makes you feel strong feelings of pity, love, or sympathy —**meltingly** *adv*

**melting point** /ˈ·· ·/ *n* [singular] the temperature at which a solid substance becomes a liquid

**melting pot** /ˈ·· ·/ *n* [C usually singular] **1** a place where people from different races, countries, or social classes come to live together: *America has been a melting pot since the beginning of European immigration.* **2** a situation or place in which many different ideas are discussed **3 in the melting pot** *BrE* still changing and not yet in a final state

S1  W1 **mem·ber** /ˈmembə‖-ər/ *n* [C] **1** someone who has joined a particular club, group, or organization: *I'm a member of the local tennis club.* | **club/union/party etc members** *The strike was approved by a majority of union members.* | **member states/countries/organizations etc** (=the states etc that have joined a particular group) *UN member states* | **full member** (=a member in the most complete way) *Turkey wants to become a full member of the EC.* **2** one of a particular group of people or things: *Dogs and wolves are both members of the same species.* | **member of a family** *The other members of his family were against the marriage.* | **member of staff** (=a worker at a particular company) *All members of staff must wear uniform* **3** *BrE* a Member of Parliament: *the member for Truro* **4** *technical or humorous* the male sex organ; PENIS **5** *old use* a part of the body, especially an arm or leg

**Member of Par·lia·ment** /ˌ·· · ˈ···/ *n* [C] an MP (1)

S2 W2 **mem·ber·ship** /ˈmembəʃɪp‖-ər-/ *n* **1** [U] the state of being a member of a club, group, organization, or system, and receiving the advantages of belonging to that group: [+ **of**] *Only full-time employees can apply for membership of the company pension plan.* | [also + **in** *AmE*] *I forgot to renew my membership in the sailing club.* | **membership card** (=a card that shows you are a member) **2** [singular] all the members of a club, group, or organization: *The membership voted to change the rules.* **3** [U] the number of people who belong to a club, group, or organization: *We're trying to increase our membership.*

**mem·brane** /ˈmembreɪn/ *n* [C,U] **1** a very thin piece of skin that covers or connects parts of the body: *a vibrating membrane in the ear which conveys sound* **2** a very thin piece of material that covers or connects something —**membranous** /ˈmembrənəs/ *adj*

**me·men·to** /mɪ̵ˈmentəʊ‖-toʊ/ *n plural* **mementos** [C] a small thing that you keep to remind you of someone or something: [+ **of**] *a memento of her time in Spain*

**mem·o** /ˈmeməʊ‖-moʊ/ *n plural* **memos** [C] a short official note to another person in the same company or organization: *She dictated an urgent internal memo.* S3

**mem·oir** /ˈmemwɑː‖-wɑːr/ *n* **1 memoirs** [plural] an account written by someone, especially a famous person, about their life and experiences: *Lady Thatcher had just published her memoirs.* **2** [C] *formal* a short piece of writing about someone or something that you know well

**mem·o·ra·bil·i·a** /ˌmemərəˈbɪliə/ *n* [plural] things that you keep or collect because they are connected with a famous person, event, or time: *Elvis Presley memorabilia*

**mem·o·ra·ble** /ˈmemərəbəl/ *adj* very good, enjoyable, or unusual, and worth remembering: *a truly memorable performance* | [+ **for**] *The play was memorable for its beautiful costumes.* —**memorably** *adv*

**mem·o·ran·dum** /ˌmeməˈrændəm/ *n plural* **memoranda** *or* **memorandums** [C] **1** *formal* a MEMO **2** *law* a short legal document recording the conditions of an agreement

**me·mo·ri·al**[1] /mɪ̵ˈmɔːriəl/ *adj* [only before noun] made, held, or done in order to remind people of someone who has died | **memorial service/ceremony** *A memorial service will be held at 7 pm on Saturday.* | **memorial prize/scholarship/fund etc** *the John Kobal memorial prize for best young photographer*

**memorial**[2] *n* **1** [C] something, especially a stone with writing on it, to remind people of someone who has died: *the Albert memorial* | [+ **to**] *a memorial to the men who died in the war* **2** [singular] an achievement that reminds people of someone who has died: *The college is his true memorial.* —see also WAR MEMORIAL

**mem·o·rize** also **-ise** *BrE* /ˈmeməraɪz/ *v* [T] to learn words, music etc

**mem·o·ry** /ˈeməri/ *n* S1 W1

**1 ▶ ABILITY TO REMEMBER ◀** [C,U] the ability to remember things, places, experiences etc: *Grandpa was getting old and his memory wasn't so good.* | **have a good/bad memory for sth** (=be good or bad at remembering things of a particular kind) *I have a terrible memory for names.* | **have a short/long memory** (=remember something for a short time or for a long time) | **do sth from memory** (=do something such as say a poem or play a piece of music by remembering it) *The cellist played the whole piece through from memory.*

**2 ▶ STH YOU REMEMBER ◀** [C usually plural] something that you remember from the past about a person, place, or experience: [+ **of**] *memories of the war* | **happy/good/bad etc memories** *He has lots of happy memories of his stay in Japan.* | **childhood memories** (=memories of the time when you were a child) *One of my earliest childhood memories is of my mother reading stories to me by the fire.* | **bring back memories** (=to remind you of pleasant events) *Those old songs bring back memories.*

**3 a)** [C] the part of a computer in which information can be stored **b)** [U] the amount of space that can be used for storing information on a computer: *30 megabytes of memory*

**4 if my memory serves me (well/correctly)** used when you are almost sure that you have remembered something correctly: *We first moved here in 1962, if my memory serves me correctly.*

**5 speaking from memory** *spoken* used to say that you are telling someone what you remember about something

**6 have a memory like a sieve** *spoken* to be very bad at remembering things

**7 sb's memory is playing tricks on them** *spoken* used to say that someone is remembering things incorrectly: *My*

*memory must be playing tricks on me; I'm sure I put that book on the desk.*
**8 take a walk/trip down memory lane** spend some time remembering the past
**9 in living memory** since the earliest time that people now alive can remember: *the hottest summer in living memory*
**10 within sb's memory** during the time that someone can remember: *There have been two world wars within the memory of my grandfather.*
**11 in memory of** also **to the memory of** for the purpose of remembering someone and reminding other people of them after they have died: *She set up a charitable fund in memory of her father.*
**12 sb's memory lives on** used to say that people still remember someone after they have died or gone away
**13 sb's memory** the way you think about someone who has died who you knew very well: *a rose garden dedicated to his memory* —see also **commit to memory** (COMMIT (6)), **jog sb's memory** (JOG[1] (3)), **lose your memory** (LOSE (4)), **photographic memory** (PHOTOGRAPHIC (2)), **refresh sb's memory** (REFRESH (2))

This graph shows some of the words most commonly used with the noun **memory**.

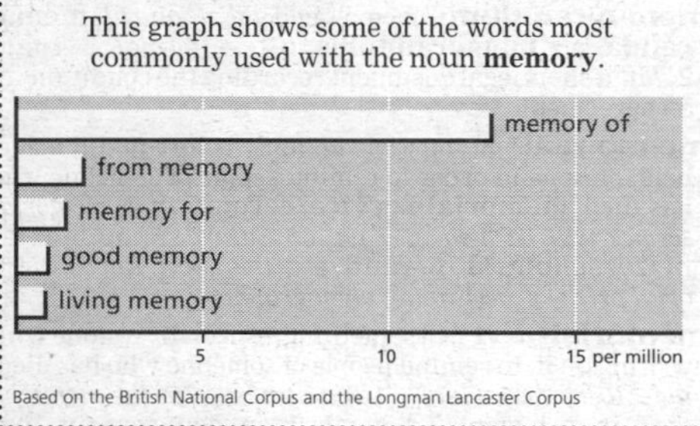


**memory bank** /'··· ,·/ *n* [C] the part of a big computer system that stores information
**mem·sahib** /'mem,sɑːb‖-,sɑːhɪb, -,sɑːb/ *n* [C] *IndE, PakE old-fashioned* a European woman
**men** /men/ *n* the plural of MAN
**men·ace[1]** /'menɨs/ *n* **1** [C] something or someone that is dangerous: [+ **to**] *hazardous chemicals that are a menace to public safety | That man's a menace to society!* **2** [U] a threatening quality or manner: *There was menace in her eyes as she spoke.* **3** [C] a person, especially a child that is annoying or causes trouble; NUISANCE
**menace[2]** *v* [T] *formal* to threaten
**men·ac·ing** /'menɨsɪŋ/ *adj* making you expect something unpleasant; THREATENING: *dark, menacing clouds | a low, menacing laugh* —**menacingly** *adv*
**mé·nage** /'meɪnɑːʒ‖mə'nɑːʒ/ *n* [C] *formal or humorous* all the people who live in a particular house; HOUSEHOLD (2)
**ménage à trois** /,meɪnɑːʒ ɑː 'trwɑː‖mə,nɑːʒ-/ *n* [singular] *French* a sexual relationship involving three people who live together
**me·na·ge·rie** /mɨ'nædʒəri/ *n* [C] a collection of wild animals kept privately or for the public to see
**mend[1]** /mend/ *v*
**1 ▶ REPAIR ◀** [T] **a)** to repair a tear or hole in a piece of clothing: *My father used to mend our shoes.* **b)** *BrE* to repair something that is broken or not working; FIX[1] (1): *When are you going to mend that light in the hall?* —see graph at REPAIR[1]
**2 ▶ BECOME HEALTHY ◀** [I] **a)** *informal* if a broken bone mends, it becomes whole again **b)** [I] *old-fashioned* to become healthy again after being ill
**3 mend your ways** to improve the way you behave after behaving badly for a long time
**4 mend (your) fences** to talk to someone you have offended or argued with, and try to persuade them to be friendly with you again
**5 ▶ END A QUARREL ◀** [T] to end a quarrel or difficult situation by dealing with the problem that is causing it: *I've tried to mend matters between us, but she's still very angry.* —**mender** *n* [C] *BrE*
**mend[2]** *n* [C] **1 be on the mend** to be getting better after an illness or after a difficult period: *He's had flu, but he's on the mend. | signs that the economy is on the mend* **2** a place in something where it has been repaired
**men·da·cious** /men'deɪʃəs/ *adj formal* not truthful: *mendacious propaganda* —**mendaciously** *adv*
**men·da·ci·ty** /men'dæsɨti/ *n* [U] *formal* the quality of being untruthful
**men·di·cant** /'mendɨkənt/ *n* [C] *formal* someone who begs for money in order to live, usually for religious reasons —**mendicant** *adj*: *a mendicant monks' order such as the Franciscans*
**mend·ing** /'mendɪŋ/ *n* [U] clothes that need to be mended
**men·folk** /'menfəʊk‖-foʊk/ *n* [plural] *old-fashioned* a word used by women meaning men, especially their male relatives: *Round up the menfolk for dinner, please.*
**me·ni·al[1]** /'miːniəl/ *adj* menial work is boring, needs no skill, and is not important —**menially** *adv*
**menial[2]** *n* [C] someone who does menial work, especially a servant in a house
**men·in·gi·tis** /,menɨn'dʒaɪtɨs/ *n* [U] a serious illness in which the outer part of the brain becomes swollen
**men·o·pause** /'menəpɔːz‖-pɒːz/ *n* [U] the time when a woman stops menstruating (MENSTRUATE), which usually occurs around age 50 —**menopausal** /,menəʊ'pɔːzəl◂‖-nə'pɒː-/ *adj*
**me·no·rah** /mə'nɔːrə/ *n* [C] a Jewish CANDLESTICK that holds seven CANDLES
**mensch** /menʃ/ *n* [C] *AmE spoken* someone that you like and admire, especially because they have done something good for you: *You've been a real mensch.*
**men·ses** /'mensiːz/ *n* [plural] *technical* the blood that flows out of a woman's body each month
**men's room** /'· ·/ *n* [C] *especially AmE* the men's toilet; gents GENT (2) *BrE*
**men·stru·al** /'menstruəl/ *adj* connected with the time each month when a woman menstruates
**menstrual pe·ri·od** /'··· ,···/ *n* [C] *formal* the time each month when a woman menstruates; PERIOD[1] (4)
**men·stru·ate** /'menstrueɪt/ *v* [I] *technical* when a woman menstruates, blood flows from her body every month —**menstruation** /,menstru'eɪʃən/ *n* [C,U]
**mens·wear** /'menzweə‖-wer/ *n* [U] clothing for men: *a menswear shop*
**-ment** /mənt/ *suffix* [in nouns] **1** the act, cause, means, or result of doing something: *the need for strong government* (=strong governing) | *the replacement* (=replacing) *of obsolete machinery | some interesting new developments* **2** the condition of being treated in a particular way: *his confinement* (=being shut up) *in prison* —**mental** *suffix* [in adjectives]: *governmental*
**men·tal** /'mentl/ *adj* S2 W2
**1 ▶ MIND ◀** affecting the mind or happening in the mind: *mental health | a child's mental development |* **mental picture/image** (=a picture that you form in your mind) *I tried to get a mental picture of him from her description.*
**2 ▶ MENTAL ILLNESS ◀** [only before noun] concerned with illnesses of the mind, or with treating illnesses of the mind: *Mental patients have to be kept under strict supervision. | a mental institution* —see also MENTAL HOME, MENTAL HOSPITAL
**3 mental block** a difficulty in remembering something or in understanding something: *I got a complete mental block as soon as the interviewer asked me a question. | Julie has a mental block when it comes to math.*
**4 make a mental note** to make a special effort to remember something
**5 ▶ CRAZY ◀** [not before noun] *BrE slang* thinking or behaving in a way that seems crazy or strange: *He must be mental!*
**6 go mental** *BrE slang spoken* **a)** to get very angry:

*She'll go mental if she finds out.* **b)** to start behaving in a crazy way: *I can't understand why she's doing this – has she gone mental or something?* —**mentally** *adv*: *mentally ill*

S3 **mental age** /ˌ·· ˈ·‖ˈ·· ·/ *n* [C] a measure of someone's ability to think, obtained by comparing their ability with the average ability of children at various ages: *a 25-year-old man with a mental age of seven*

**mental a·rith·me·tic** /ˌ·· ·ˈ···/ *n* [U] the act of adding numbers together, multiplying them etc in your mind, without writing them down

**mental home** /ˈ·· ·/ *n* [C] *BrE old-fashioned* a mental hospital

**mental hos·pi·tal** /ˈ·· ˌ···/ *n* [C] a hospital where people with mental illnesses are treated; PSYCHIATRIC HOSPITAL

**men·tal·i·ty** /menˈtælɪ̈ti/ *n* [C] a particular kind of attitude or way of thinking, especially one that you think is wrong or stupid: *a get-rich-quick mentality*

**mentally han·di·capped** /ˌ··· ˈ···/ *adj* **1** a mentally handicapped person has a problem with their brain that affects their ability to think or control their body movements, usually from birth **2** [plural] **the mentally handicapped** people who are mentally handicapped

**men·thol** /ˈmenθɒl‖-θɒːl, -θɑːl/ *n* [U] a substance that smells and tastes of MINT to give cigarettes and sweets a special taste

**men·tho·la·ted** /ˈmenθəleɪtɪ̈d/ *adj* containing menthol

S1 **men·tion**[1] /ˈmenʃən/ *v* [T] **1** to talk about something
W1 or someone in a conversation, piece of writing etc, especially without saying very much or giving details: *As I mentioned earlier, this has been a very successful year for our company.* | *Jill mentioned something about a party on Saturday.* | *Was my name mentioned at all?* | **mention sth to sb** *I mentioned the idea to Joan, and she seemed to like it.* | **mention (that)** *He mentioned that he was having problems, but he didn't explain.* | **it is worth mentioning that** (=this is a useful or important piece of information) *It's worth mentioning that the new regulations don't actually come into force until next year.* **2 don't mention it** *spoken* used to say politely that there is no need for someone to thank you for helping them: *"Thanks for the ride home!" "Don't mention it."* **3 not to mention** used to introduce an additional thing that makes a situation even more difficult, surprising, interesting etc: *They already take pension and social security payments off my pay, not to mention state taxes.* **4 mention sth in passing** to mention something quickly without paying much attention to it: *Sue mentioned the party in passing, but I couldn't go.* **5 above mentioned/mentioned above** mentioned earlier in a piece of writing **6 mentioned in dispatches** *BrE* honoured for being brave in a battle by being mentioned on an official list

**mention**[2] *n* [C usually singular, U] the act of mentioning something or someone in a conversation, piece of writing etc: *Just the mention of her name still upsets him.* | **there's no mention** (=something is not mentioned) *There was no mention of any trip to Holland in his diaries.* | **get a mention** (=be mentioned when someone is talking or writing about something) *I didn't even get a mention in the list of contributors.* | **make no mention** (=not say anything about) *He made no mention of his wife's illness to me.* —see also HONOURABLE MENTION

**men·tor** /ˈmentɔː‖-tɔːr/ *n* [C] an experienced person who advises and helps a less experienced person

**men·tor·ing** /ˈmentɔːrɪŋ/ *n* [U] a system of using people with a lot of experience, knowledge etc to advise other people at work, or in their professional life: *Support for you in your new job will be provided by a system of mentoring*

**men·u** /ˈmenjuː/ *n* [C] **1** a list of all the kinds of food that are available for a meal, especially in a restaurant: *Is there any fish on the menu?* | *Could we have the menu, please?* —see picture on page 838 **2** a list of things that you can choose from or ask a computer to do, that is shown on the SCREEN of the computer: **menu-driven** (=operated by using a menu)

**me·ow** /miˈaʊ/ *v* [I] the usual American spelling of MIAOW —**meow** *n* [C]

**MEP** /ˌem iː ˈpiː/ *n* [C] Member of the European Parliament; someone who has been elected as a member of the Parliament of the European Union

**Meph·i·stoph·e·les** /ˌmefɪ̈ˈstɒfɪ̈liːz‖-ˈstɑː-/ *n* the Devil, especially in the story of Faust —**Mephistophelean** /ˌmefɪstəˈfiːliən◂/ *adj*

**mer·can·tile** /ˈmɜːkəntaɪl‖ˈmɜːrkəntiːl,-taɪl/ *adj* [only before noun] *formal* concerned with trade; COMMERCIAL[1] (1): *mercantile law*

**mercantile ma·rine** /ˌ···· ·ˈ·/ *n* [singular] *BrE* the MERCHANT NAVY

**Mer·ca·tor pro·jec·tion** /məˌkeɪtə prəˈdʒekʃən‖mərˌkeɪtər-/ also **Mercator's projection** —*n* [U] a way of drawing a map of the world so that it can be divided into regular squares, instead of getting thinner at the northern or southern edges

**mer·ce·na·ry**[1] /ˈmɜːsənəri‖ˈmɜːrsəneri/ *n* [C] a soldier who fights for any country or group that is willing to pay him: *The Emperor hired an army of Saxon mercenaries.*

**mercenary**[2] *adj* only interested in money, and not caring about whether your actions are right or wrong or about the effect of your actions on other people: *It's a purely mercenary relationship, not a friendship.*

**mer·cer·ized cot·ton** /ˌmɜːsəraɪzd ˈkɒtn‖ˌmɜːrsəraɪzd ˈkɑːtn/ *n* [U] cotton that has been treated with chemicals to make it shiny and strong

**mer·chan·dise**[1] /ˈmɜːtʃəndaɪz, -daɪs‖ˈmɜːr-/ *n* [U] goods that are produced in order to be sold, especially goods that are shown in a shop for people to buy W3

**merchandise**[2] *v* [T] to try to sell goods or services using methods such as advertising: *If the product is properly merchandised, it should sell very well.*

**mer·chan·dis·ing** /ˈmɜːtʃəndaɪzɪŋ‖ˈmɜːr-/ *n* [U] toys, clothes, and other products based on a popular film, TV show etc and sold to make additional profits

**mer·chant** /ˈmɜːtʃənt‖ˈmɜːr-/ *n* [C] **1** someone who buys and sells goods in large quantities: *He's a wine merchant.* **2 con merchant/speed merchant etc** *BrE informal* someone who is involved in a particular activity, such as tricking people or driving very fast

**merchant bank** /ˌ·· ˈ·/ *n* [C] a bank that provides banking services for business

**mer·chant·man** /ˈmɜːtʃəntmən‖ˈmɜːr-/ *n* [C] *old-fashioned* a ship used for carrying goods

**merchant na·vy** /ˌ·· ˈ··/ *BrE*, **merchant ma·rine** *AmE* /ˌ·· ·ˈ·/ *n* [singular] all of a country's ships that are used for trade, not war, and the people who work on these ships: *John worked as a chef in the merchant navy.*

**merchant sea·man** /ˌ·· ˈ··/ *n* [C] a sailor in the merchant navy

**mer·ci·ful** /ˈmɜːsɪfəl‖ˈmɜːr-/ *adj* **1 merciful death/end/release** a death that seems fortunate because it ends someone's suffering or difficulty: *The final whistle came as a mericful relief.* **2** being kind to people and forgiving them rather than punishing them or being cruel: *Merciful God, save us.*

**mer·ci·ful·ly** /ˈmɜːsɪfəli‖ˈmɜːr-/ *adv* fortunately or luckily, because a situation could have been much worse: *Mercifully, I managed to stop the car just in time.*

**mer·ci·less** /ˈmɜːsɪləs‖ˈmɜːr-/ *adj* cruel and showing no kindness or forgiveness: *a merciless attack on a defenceless village* —**mercilessly** *adv* —**mercilessness** *n* [U]

**mer·cu·ri·al** /mɜːˈkjʊəriəl‖mɜːrˈkjʊr-/ *adj* **1** *literary* changing mood suddenly and unexpectedly: *an actor noted for his mercurial temperament* **2** *literary* quick and lively: *her mercurial wit* **3** *technical* containing mercury

**Mer·cu·ry** /ˈmɜːkjɪ̈ri‖ˈmɜːr-/ *n* [singular] the PLANET that is nearest the sun —see picture at SOLAR SYSTEM

**mercury** *n* [U] a heavy silver-white metal that is liquid at ordinary temperatures, and is used in THERMOMETERS

**mer·cy** /ˈmɜːsi‖ˈmɜːrsi/ *n* **1** [U] kindness, pity, and a willingness to forgive, which you show towards someone that you have power over: **show no mercy** *The terrorists showed no mercy to the hostages.* | **have mercy (on)** *Oh Lord, have mercy on us sinners.* **2 it's a mercy** *spoken* used to say that it is lucky that a worse situation was avoided: *It's a mercy the accident happened so near the hospital.* **3 at the mercy of** unable to do anything to protect yourself from someone or something: *They were lost at sea, at the mercy of wind and weather.* | *a housing policy that leaves people at the mercy of unscrupulous landlords* **4 leave sb to sb's (tender) mercies** *often humorous* to let someone be dealt with by another person, who may treat them very badly or strictly **5 be thankful/grateful for small mercies** to be pleased that a bad situation is not even worse **6 mercy flight/mission etc** a journey taken to bring help to people: *a mercy dash to rescue stranded tourists* **7 throw yourself on sb's mercy** to BEG someone to help you or not to punish you

**mercy kill·ing** /ˈ·· ˌ··/ *n* [C,U] the act of killing someone who is very ill or old so that they do not have to suffer any more; EUTHANASIA

W3 **mere¹** /mɪə‖mɪr/ *adj* [only before noun, no comparative] **1** used to emphasize how small or unimportant something or someone is: *She lost the election by a mere 20 votes.* | *He's a mere child.* **2** also **the merest** used when something small or unimportant has a big effect: *The merest little noise makes him nervous.* | *The mere presence of a police officer made him feel guilty.*

**mere²** *n* [C] *literary* a lake

S2 **mere·ly** /ˈmɪəli‖ˈmɪrli/ *adv* **1** used to emphasize that
W2 something or someone is very small or unimportant, especially when compared with something else; ONLY: *It is an issue of merely local importance.* | *This is merely the latest example of government interference.* **2** *spoken* used to emphasize that you are doing something only for the reason you say: *I'm not trying to criticize you, I'm merely trying to find out how the accident happened.*

**mer·e·tri·cious** /ˌmerɪ̈ˈtrɪʃəs◂/ *adj formal* seeming attractive but having no real value or not based on the truth: *a meretricious argument* —**meretriciously** *adv* —**meretriciousness** *n* [U]

**merge** /mɜːdʒ‖mɜːrdʒ/ *v* **1** [I,T] to combine or join together to form one thing: [**+ with**] *Rover is to merge with BMW, the German car manufacturer.* | **merge sth** *The company plans to merge its subsidiaries in the US.* | [**+ together**] *The sounds of the wind and the water merged together.* **2 merge into sth** to seem to disappear into something and become part of it: *As night fell, their outlines merged into the landscape.* **3 merge into the background** *BrE informal* to behave very quietly in social situations, so that people do not notice you

**merg·er** /ˈmɜːdʒə‖ˈmɜːrdʒər/ *n* [C] the act of joining together two or more companies or organizations to form one larger one: *job losses as a result of the merger*

**me·rid·i·an** /məˈrɪdiən/ *n* **1** [C] an imaginary line drawn from the NORTH POLE to the SOUTH POLE over the surface of the Earth, used to show the position of places on a map **2 the meridian** *technical* the highest point reached by the sun or another star, when seen from a point on the Earth's surface

**me·ringue** /məˈræŋ/ *n* [C,U] a light sweet food made by baking a mixture of sugar and the white part of eggs

**me·ri·no** /məˈriːnəʊ‖-noʊ/ *n* [U] a kind of sheep with long wool, or cloth made from this wool

**mer·it¹** /ˈmerɪ̈t/ *n* **1** [C usually plural] one of the good features of something such as a plan or system: *The committee will look at the relative merits of the two proposals.* —opposite DEMERIT (1) **2** [U] *formal* a good quality that makes something deserve praise or admiration: **have merit/be of merit** (=be good) *The arguments for legalizing marijuana have considerable merit.* | **artistic/literary merit** *a film lacking any kind of artistic merit* **3 judge sth on its (own) merits** to judge something only by how good it is, without considering anything else

**merit²** *v* [T not in progressive forms] *formal* to deserve something: *Your suggestion merits serious consideration.*

**mer·i·toc·ra·cy** /ˌmerɪ̈ˈtɒkrəsi‖-ˈtɑː-/ *n especially BrE* **1** [C] a social system that gives the greatest power and highest social positions to people with the most ability **2** [singular] the people who have power in this kind of system

**mer·i·to·ri·ous** /ˌmerɪ̈ˈtɔːriəs◂/ *adj formal* very good and deserving praise —**meritoriously** *adv*

**mer·maid** /ˈmɜːmeɪd‖ˈmɜːr-/ *n* [C] a woman in stories who has a fish's tail instead of legs

mermaid

**mer·ri·ment** /ˈmerɪmənt/ *n* [U] *formal* laughter, fun, and enjoyment: *His new hairstyle was the cause of much merriment.*

**mer·ry** /ˈmeri/ *adj* **1 Merry Christmas!** used to say that you hope someone will have a happy time at Christmas **2** cheerful and happy: *He marched off, whistling a merry tune.* **3 the more the merrier** *spoken* used to tell someone that you will be happy if they join you in something you are doing: *"Do you guys mind if I come with you?" "Sure – the more the merrier".* **4** [not before noun] *BrE informal* slightly drunk: *We were all quite merry at the party last night.* **5 make merry** *literary* to enjoy yourself by drinking, singing etc **6** *old use* pleasant: *the merry month of June* —**merrily** *adv* —**merriness** *n* [U]

**merry-go-round** /ˈ··· ˌ·/ *n* **1** [C] a machine that turns around and around, and has model animals or cars for children to sit on, CAROUSEL *AmE* **2** [singular] a series of similar events that happen very quickly one after another: *the endless Washington merry-go-round of parties and socializing*

**merry-mak·ing** /ˈ·· ˌ··/ *n* [U] *literary* fun and enjoyment, especially drinking, dancing, and singing —**merry-makers** *n* [C]

**me·sa** /ˈmeɪsə/ *n* [C] a hill with a flat top and steep sides, in the southwestern USA

**mes·ca·lin, mescaline** /ˈmeskəliːn, -lɪ̈n/ *n* [U] a drug made from a CACTUS plant that makes people imagine that they can see things that do not really exist

**mesh¹** /meʃ/ *n* [C,U] **1** a piece of material made of threads or wires that have been woven together like a net: *Wire mesh covered all the windows to keep out flies.* **2** a complicated situation that makes you feel confused and trapped: [**+ of**] *He was caught in the mesh of emotions between the mother and her daughter.*

**mesh²** *v* [I] **1** if two ideas or qualities mesh, they go well together and are suitable for each other: *music in which classical harmonics mesh with the hypnotic rhythms of jazz* **2** *technical* if two parts of an engine or machine mesh, they fit closely together and connect with each other

**mes·mer·ize** also **-ise** *BrE* /ˈmezməraɪz/ *v* [T often passive] to make someone feel that they must watch or listen to something or someone, because they are so interested in it or attracted by it: *He was mesmerized by her charm and beauty.* —**mesmerizing** *adj*

**mess¹** /mes/ *n* S2

**1** ▶ **DIRTY/UNTIDY** ◀ [singular, U] a situation in which a place looks very untidy or dirty, with things spread all around: *Clean up this mess!* | *The house was an awful mess after the party.* | **make a mess** *You can make cookies if you promise not to make a mess in the kitchen.*

**2** ▶ **PROBLEMS/DIFFICULTIES** ◀ [singular] *informal*

a situation in which there are a lot of problems and difficulties, especially as a result of mistakes or carelessness: *We have to sort this problem out – the whole thing's a mess.* | *You got us into this mess, Terry. You can get us out of it.*

**3 be in a mess** to be very untidy or dirty, very disorganized or full of problems: *The previous chairman had left the company in a terrible mess.* | *My life was in a real mess and I didn't know what to do.*

**4 make a mess of** *informal* to do something badly and make a lot of mistakes: *I made a complete mess of that test.* | *They've made such a mess of the economy.*

**5 a mess of** *AmE informal* a lot of: *The dress had a high neck with a mess of buttons coming down the back.*

**6 ▶ARMY/NAVY◀** [C] a room in which members of the army, navy etc eat and drink together

**7 ▶WASTE MATTER◀** [C,U] *informal especially BrE* solid waste material from a baby or animal: *The dog's made a mess on the carpet!*

S3 **mess²** *v* [I] to have meals in a room where members of the army, navy etc eat together

**mess around** also **mess about** *BrE phr v informal* **1** [I] to spend time lazily, doing things slowly and in a way that is not planned: *He spent his vacation messing around on the farm.* **2** [I] to behave in a silly way when you should be working or paying attention: *Stop messing around and help me move this furniture.* **3** [T **mess** sb **around/about**] to cause a lot of problems for someone, especially by changing your mind often or preventing them from getting what they want: *Don't mess me about – I want the money you promised me.*

**mess around with** also **mess about with** *BrE phr v* [T] *informal* **1** to have a sexual relationship with someone that you should not have a sexual relationship with: *She'd been messing around with another man.* **2** to spend time playing with something, repairing it etc: *Dave likes messing around with old cars.*

**mess up** *phr v informal* **1** [T **mess** sth ↔ **up**] to spoil or ruin something, especially something important or something that has been carefully planned: *It took me ages to get this right – I don't want some idiot to mess it up.* | *She felt she'd messed up her whole life.* **2** [T **mess** sth ↔ **up**] to make something dirty or untidy: *Who messed up the kitchen?* **3** [I,T **mess sth ↔ up**] to make a mistake and do something badly: *It doesn't matter if you mess it up, you can always try again.* | [+ **on**] *I think I messed up on the last question.* —see also MESSED UP, MESS-UP

**mess with** *phr v* [I,T] **don't mess with** *spoken* **a)** used to warn someone not to annoy or argue with someone: *Don't mess with me, buddy.* **b)** used to warn someone not to get involved with something that is dangerous or harmful: *Don't mess with illegal drugs. Just say no!*

S1 W2 **mes·sage** /ˈmesɪdʒ/ *n* [C] **1** a spoken or written piece of information that you send to another person: *Did you get my message?* | **leave a message** *He left a message saying he would probably be a little late.* | **can I take a message?** *spoken* (=used on the telephone when offering to give a message to someone) *I'm sorry, she's out right now, can I take a message?* **2** [singular] the main or most important idea that someone is trying to tell people about in a film, book, speech etc: *The message of the film is that good always triumphs over evil.* **3 get the message** *informal* to understand what someone means or what they want you to do: *OK, I get the message – I'm going!*

**messed up** /ˌ· ˈ·/ *adj informal* someone who is messed up is very unhappy and has mental problems because of something that has happened to them: *He's been really messed up since his wife left him.*

**mes·sen·ger** /ˈmesɪndʒə, -sən-‖ -ər/ *n* [C] **1** someone who takes messages to people **2 blame/shoot the messenger** to be angry with someone for telling you about something bad that has happened

**mess hall** /ˈ· ·/ *n* [C] a large room where soldiers eat

**mes·si·ah** /mɪ̯ˈsaɪə/ *n* [singular] **1 the Messiah a)** Jesus Christ, who is believed by Christians to be sent by God to save the world **b)** a great religious leader who, according to Jewish belief, will be sent by God to save the world **2** someone who people believe will save them from great social or economic problems: *He was seen as an economic messiah.*

**mes·si·an·ic** /ˌmesiˈænɪk◂/ *adj formal* **1** someone who has messianic beliefs or feelings wants to make very big social or political changes connected with the belief that the world should be completely changed: *messianic zeal* **2** connected with the Messiah

**Mes·srs** *BrE*, **Messrs.** *AmE* /ˈmesəz‖-ərz/ the plural of MR, used especially in the names of companies: *Messrs Ford and Dobson*

**mess-up** /ˈ· ·/ *n* [C] *informal* a situation in which someone has done something badly or made a lot of mistakes: *The whole thing had been a mess-up from start to finish.*

**mess·y** /ˈmesi/ *adj* **1** dirty or untidy: *messy saucepans* | *Sorry the place is so messy, I haven't had time to clear up.* S3 **2** *informal* a messy situation is complicated and unpleasant to deal with: *He's just been through a particularly messy divorce.* —**messily** *adv* —**messiness** *n* [U]

**mes·ti·zo** /meˈstiːzəʊ‖-zoʊ/ *n plural* **mestizos** [C] someone who has one Spanish parent and one Native American parent

**Met** /met/ *n* **the Met** *informal* **a)** the Metropolitan Opera Company; the main OPERA company in New York **b)** the Metropolitan Police; the police force in London

**met** the past tense and past participle of MEET¹

**meta-** /metə/ *prefix technical* beyond the ordinary or usual: *metaphysical* (=beyond ordinary physical things)

**me·tab·o·lis·m** /mɪ̯ˈtæbəlɪzəm/ *n* [C,U] the chemical activity in your body that uses food to produce the energy you need to work and grow —**metabolic** /ˌmetəˈbɒlɪk◂‖-ˈbɑː-/ *adj*: *An animal's lifespan is linked to its metabolic rate.*

**me·ta·bol·ize** *also* **-ise** *BrE* /mɪ̯ˈtæbəlaɪz/ *v* [T] to break down food in the body by chemical activity and use it to produce energy

**met·al** /ˈmetl/ *n* [C, U] a hard, usually shiny substance such as iron, gold, or steel: *The frame is made of metal.* | *a metal box* | **precious metal** (=expensive metal used for making jewellery) —see also HEAVY METAL, METALLIC S2 W2

**met·a·lan·guage** /ˈmetəˌlæŋgwɪdʒ/ *n* [C,U] words used for talking about or describing language

**metal de·tect·or** /ˈ·· ·ˌ··/ *n* [C] **1** a machine used to find pieces of metal that are buried under the ground **2** a special frame that you walk through at an airport, used to check for weapons made of metal

**metal fa·tigue** /ˈ·· ·ˌ·/ *n* [U] a weakness in metal that makes it likely to break, caused for example by frequent shaking over a long period

**me·tal·lic** /mɪ̯ˈtælɪk/ *adj* **1** like metal in colour, appearance, or taste: *The sea was a dull metallic grey.* **2** a metallic noise sounds like pieces of metal hitting each other: *The pans made a metallic clatter as they crashed to the floor.* **3** made of or containing metal: *metallic elements*

**met·al·lur·gy** /mɪ̯ˈtælədʒi‖ˈmetəlɜːrdʒi/ *n* [U] the scientific study of metals and their uses —**metallurgist** *n* [C] —**metallurgical** /ˌmetəˈlɜːdʒɪkəl◂‖-ɜːr-/ *adj*

**met·al·work** /ˈmetlwɜːk‖-wɜːrk/ *n* [U] **1** the activity or skill of making metal objects: *metalwork classes* **2** objects made by shaping metal —**metalworker** *n* [C]

**met·a·mor·pho·sis** /ˌmetəˈmɔːfəsɪ̯s‖-ˈmɔːr-/ *n plural* **metamorphoses** [C,U] **1** *formal* a process in which something changes completely into something very different: *the metamorphosis of China under Deng's economic reforms* **2** a process in which a young insect, frog etc changes into another stage in its development —**metamorphose** /ˌmetəˈmɔːfəʊz‖-ˈmɔːrfoʊz/ *v* [I,T]

**met·a·phor** /ˈmetəfə, -fɔː‖-fɔːr/ *n* [C,U] **1** a way of describing something by comparing it to something else that has similar qualities, without using the words 'like' or 'as': *'The sunshine of her smile' is a metaphor.|His poetry is brought alive by his masterful use of metaphor.* —compare SIMILE **2 mixed metaphor** the use of two different metaphors at the same time to describe something, especially in a way that seems silly or funny **3** [C,U] something in a book, painting, film etc that is intended to represent a more general idea or quality; SYMBOL: [+ **for**] *Their relationship is a metaphor for the failure of communication in the modern world.*

**met·a·phor·i·cal** /ˌmetəˈfɒrɪkəl◂‖-ˈfɔː-, -ˈfɑː-/ *adj* using words to mean something different from their ordinary meaning when describing something in order to achieve an effect —**metaphorically** /kli/ *adv*: *He's got a big head – metaphorically speaking of course!*

**met·a·phys·i·cal** /ˌmetəˈfɪzɪkəl◂/ *adj* **1** concerned with the study of metaphysics **2** *spoken* used to describe a complicated arrangement of words and ideas —**metaphysically** /-kli/ *adv*

**met·a·phys·ics** /ˌmetəˈfɪzɪks/ *n* [U] the part of the study of PHILOSOPHY that is concerned with trying to understand and describe the nature of reality

**mete** /miːt/ *v*

**mete** sth ↔ **out** *phr v* [T] *formal* to give someone a punishment: *Judges are meting out increasingly harsh sentences for car theft.*

**me·te·or** /ˈmiːtiə‖-ər/ *n* [C] a piece of rock or metal that floats in space, and makes a bright line in the night sky when it falls through the Earth's ATMOSPHERE (1)

**me·te·or·ic** /ˌmiːtiˈɒrɪk◂‖-ˈɔːrɪk◂, -ˈɑːrɪk◂/ *adj* **1** happening very suddenly and quickly: **meteoric rise/career** *her meteoric rise to fame* **2** from a METEOR: *meteoric stones* —**meteorically** /-kli/ *adv*

**me·te·o·rite** /ˈmiːtiəraɪt/ *n* [C] a piece of rock or metal that has come from space and has landed on Earth

**me·te·o·rol·o·gy** /ˌmiːtiəˈrɒlədʒi‖-ˈrɑː-/ *n* [U] the scientific study of weather conditions —**meteorologist** *n* [C] —**meteorological** /ˌmiːtiərəˈlɒdʒɪkəl◂‖-ˈlɑː-/ *adj*

**-meter[1]** /miːtə, mɪtə‖-tər/ *suffix* [in nouns] an instrument for measuring: *an altimeter* (=for measuring the height at which an aircraft is flying)

**-meter[2]** *suffix* the American spelling of -METRE

**me·ter[1]** /ˈmiːtə‖-ər/ *n* **1** [C] a machine that measures and shows the amount of something you have used or the amount of money that you must pay: *The taxi driver turned off his meter.* **2** [C,U] the American spelling of METRE —see also PARKING METER

**meter[2]** *v* [T] to measure something with a meter, or supply gas, electricity etc through a meter

**meter maid** /ˈ·· ·/ *n* [C] *AmE* a woman whose job is to make sure that cars are not parked in the wrong place or for longer than is allowed; TRAFFIC WARDEN *BrE*

**meth·a·done** /ˈmeθədəʊn‖-doʊn/ *n* [U] a drug that is often given to people who are trying to stop taking HEROIN

**me·thane** /ˈmiːθeɪn‖ˈme-/ *n* [U] a colourless gas with no smell that can be burned to give heat

**meth·a·nol** /ˈmeθənɒl‖-nɔːl,-nɑːl/ *n* [U] a poisonous alcohol that can be made from wood

**me·thinks** /mɪˈθɪŋks/ *v past tense* **methought** /-ˈθɔːt‖-ˈθɒːt/ *old use or humorous* I think: *a holiday somewhere nice, Florida methinks*

S1 W1 **meth·od** /ˈmeθəd/ *n* **1** [C] a planned way of doing something, especially one that a lot of people know about and use: *traditional teaching methods|I think we should try again using a different method.|*[+ **of**] *There are several possible methods of payment.|*[+ **for**] *a new method for the early detection of cancer* **2** [U] *formal* proper planning of the way that something is done: *There's no method in the way they do their accounts.* **3 there's method in sb's madness** used to say that even though someone seems to be behaving strangely, there is a sensible reason for what they are doing

**me·thod·i·cal** /mɪ̈ˈθɒdɪkəl‖mɪ̈ˈθɑː-/ *adj* **1** done in a careful and well organized way: *a methodical piece of work* **2** always doing things carefully, using an ordered system: *She's a very methodical person.* —**methodically** /-kli/ *adv*: *The detective went through the papers methodically, one by one.*

**Meth·o·dist** /ˈmeθədɪ̈st/ *n* [C] someone who belongs to a Christian religious group that follows the teachings of John Wesley —**Methodist** *adj* —**Methodism** *n* [U]

**meth·o·dol·o·gy** /ˌmeθəˈdɒlədʒi‖-ˈdɑː-/ *n* [C,U] the set of methods and principles that are used when studying a particular subject or doing a particular kind of work: *teaching methodology* —**methodological** /ˌmeθədəˈlɒdʒɪkəl◂‖-ˈlɑː-/ *adj* —**methodologically** /kli/ *adv*

**me·thought** /mɪˈθɔːt‖-ˈθɒːt/ the past tense of METHINKS

**meths** /meθs/ *n* [U] *BrE informal* METHYLATED SPIRITS

**Me·thus·e·lah** /ˌməˈθjuːzɪ̈lə‖-ˈθuː-/ *n* **as old as Methuselah** very old

**meth·yl al·co·hol** /ˌmeθɪ̈l ˈælkəhɒl, *tech* ˌmiːθaɪl-‖-hɒːl/ *n* [U] a poisonous alcohol that can be made from wood; METHANOL —compare ETHYL ALCOHOL

**meth·yl·at·ed spir·its** /ˌmeθɪ̈leɪtɪ̈d ˈspɪrɪ̈ts/ *n* [U] a kind of alcohol that is burned in lamps, heaters etc

**me·tic·u·lous** /mɪ̈ˈtɪkjʊ̈ləs/ *adj* **1** very careful about small details, and always making sure that everything is done correctly: *He kept meticulous accounts.|She pasted the cuttings into the scrapbook with meticulous care.* **2** if you are meticulous about doing something, you are very careful to always do it: [+ **in/about**] *He's meticulous about replying to correspondence.* —**meticulously** *adv* —**meticulousness** *n* [U]

**met·i·er** /ˈmetieɪ,ˈmeɪ-‖meˈtjeɪ,ˈmetjeɪ/ *n* [C usually singular] *formal* a kind of work or activity that you enjoy doing because you have a natural ability to do it well: **not be sb's metier** *Modern music is not his metier.*

**-metre** /ˈmiːtə, mɪtə‖-tər/ *BrE*, **-meter** *AmE suffix* [in nouns] part of a metre, or a number of metres: *a millimetre|a kilometre*

**me·tre** *BrE*, **meter** *AmE* /ˈmiːtə‖-ər/ *n* **1** [C] the basic unit for measuring length in the METRIC SYSTEM —see table on page B2 **2** [C,U] the arrangement of sounds in poetry into patterns of strong and weak beats —compare RHYTHM (1) S2 W3

**met·ric** /ˈmetrɪk/ *adj* **1** using or connected with the metric system of weights and measures: *the metric tonne|metric sizes* **2** metrical —compare IMPERIAL (2)

**met·ri·cal** /ˈmetrɪkəl/ *adj technical* written in the form of poetry, with regular beats —**metrically** /-kli/ *adv*

**met·ri·ca·tion** /ˌmetrɪˈkeɪʃən/ *n* [U] the change to using the metric system of weights and measures

**metric sys·tem** /ˈ·· ˌ··/ *n* [singular] the system of weights and measures that is based on the metre and the kilogram

**metric ton** /ˌ·· ˈ·/ *n* [C] a unit for measuring weight equal to 1000 kilograms

**met·ro** /ˈmetrəʊ‖-troʊ/ *n* [C] a railway system that runs under the ground below a city: *the Paris Metro*

**met·ro·nome** /ˈmetrənəʊm‖-noʊm/ *n* [C] a piece of equipment that shows the speed at which music should be played, by making a regular noise

**me·trop·o·lis** /mɪ̈ˈtrɒpəlɪ̈s‖mɪ̈ˈtrɑː-/ *n* [C] a very large city that is the most important city in a country or area

**met·ro·pol·i·tan** /ˌmetrəˈpɒlɪ̈tən◂‖-ˈpɑː-/ *adj* **1** connected with or belonging to a very large city: *the Los Angeles metropolitan area* **2** *technical* connected with France, rather than its colonies (COLONY (1)): *metropolitan France*

**Metropolitan Po·lice** /ˌ····· ·ˈ·/ *n* [singular] the police force that is responsible for London

**met·tle** /ˈmetl/ *n* [U] **1** courage and determination to do something even when it is very difficult: *a man of mettle|***show/prove your mettle** (=show that you can do something well, in spite of difficulties) *It'll be a hard game, but it should give the team a chance to show their mettle.* **2 be on your mettle** to be ready to try as hard as possible because your abilities are being tested: *You'll have to be on your mettle in the oral exam.*

**met·tle·some** /ˈmetlsəm/ *adj literary* full of energy and determination

**mew** /mjuː/ *v* [I] to make the soft high crying sound that a cat makes —**mew** *n*

**mews** /mjuːz/ *n plural BrE* a small street or yard surrounded by houses in a city, where horses used to be kept

**Mex·i·can¹** /ˈmeksɪkən/ *adj* from or connected with Mexico

**Mexican²** *n* [C] someone from Mexico

**Mexican wave** /ˌ··· ˈ·/ *n* [singular] *BrE* the effect that is made when all the people watching a game of football, BASEBALL etc stand up, move their arms up and down, and sit down again one after the other in a continuous movement

**mez·za·nine** /ˈmezəniːn, ˈmetsə-‖ˈmezə-/ *n* [C] **1** a small floor that is built between two other floors in a building **2** *AmE* the lowest BALCONY in a theatre, or the first few rows of seats in that balcony

**mez·zo¹** /ˈmetsəʊ‖-soʊ/ *adv* **mezzo forte/piano etc** *technical* a word meaning quite or not very loud, softly etc, used in instructions for performing music

**mezzo²** *n* [C] a mezzo-soprano voice

**mezzo-so·pra·no** /ˌ·· ·ˈ··/ *n* [C] **1** a voice that is lower than a SOPRANO*'s* but higher than an ALTO*'s* **2** a woman who sings with this kind of voice

**mez·zo·tint** /ˈmetsəʊˌtɪnt‖-soʊ-/ *n* [C,U] a picture printed from a metal plate that is polished in places to produce areas of light and shade

**MFA** /ˌem ef ˈeɪ/ *n* [C] *AmE* Master of Fine Arts; a university degree in a subject such as painting or SCULPTURE

**mg** the written abbreviation of MILLIGRAM

**MHz** the written abbreviation of MEGAHERTZ

**mi** /miː/ *n* [singular] the third note in a musical SCALE¹ (8) according to the SOL-FA system

**MI5** /ˌem aɪ ˈfaɪv/ *n* [not with *the*] a secret British government organization whose job it is to keep Britain safe from attack by enemies inside the country, such as foreign spies (SPY¹) or TERRORISTS

**MI6** /ˌem aɪ ˈsɪks/ *n* [not with *the*] a secret British government organization that sends people to foreign countries to try and find out secret political and military information

**MIA** /ˌem aɪ ˈeɪ/ *n* [C] *AmE* missing in action; a soldier who has disappeared in a battle and who may still be alive

**mi·aow, meow** /miˈaʊ/ *v* [I] to make the crying sound that a cat makes —**miaow** *n* [C]

**mi·as·ma** /miˈæzmə, maɪ-/ *n* [singular, U] *literary* **1** a thick, unhealthy, unpleasant mist: *A foul miasma lay over the town.* **2** an evil influence or feeling: *The miasma of defeat hung over them.*

**mi·ca** /ˈmaɪkə/ *n* [U] a mineral that consists of small flat transparent pieces of rock, which is used to make electrical instruments

**mice** /maɪs/ the plural of mouse

**Mich·ael·mas** /ˈmɪkəlməs/ *n* [C,U] 29th September, a Christian holy day in honour of Saint Michael

**mick** /mɪk/ *n* [C] *BrE* an insulting word for someone from Ireland

**mick·ey** /ˈmɪki/ *n* **1 take the mickey (out of sb)** *informal especially BrE* to make someone look silly often in a friendly way, for example by copying them or by pretending something is true when it is not: *Why are people always taking the mickey out of Nigel?* **2** also **Mickey Finn** [C] a type of drug that you give to someone to make them unconscious

**Mickey Mouse** /ˌ·· ˈ··◂/ *adj* **a Mickey Mouse operation/organization/outfit** a company or organization that is very small and unimportant, and not very good

**mi·cro** /əmaɪkrəʊ‖-kroʊ/ *n* [C] *old-fashioned* a small computer; a PC (1)

**micro-** /ˈmaɪkrəʊ, -krə‖-kroʊ, -krə/ *prefix technical* extremely small: *a microcomputer | microelectronics* —see table on page B2 —compare MACRO-, MINI-

**mi·crobe** /ˈmaɪkrəʊb‖-kroʊb/ *n* [C] a living thing which is so small that it cannot be seen without a microscope, and which can sometimes cause disease

**mi·cro·bi·ol·o·gy** /ˌmaɪkrəʊbaɪˈɒlədʒi‖-kroʊbaɪˈɑːl-/ *n* [U] the scientific study of very small living things such as BACTERIA —**microbiologist** *n* [C] —**microbiological** /ˌmaɪkrəʊbaɪəˈlɒdʒɪkəl‖-kroʊbaɪəˈlɑː-/ *adj*

**mi·cro·chip** /ˈmaɪkrəʊˌtʃɪp‖-kroʊ-/ *n* [C] a very small piece of SILICON containing a set of electronic parts which is used in computers and other machines; a CHIP¹ (4a)

**mi·cro·com·put·er** /ˈmaɪkrəʊkəmˌpjuːtə‖-kroʊkəmˌpjuːtər/ *n* [C] *old-fashioned* a small computer; a PC (1)

**mi·cro·cos·m** /ˈmaɪkrəʊkɒzəm‖-kroʊkɑː-/ *n*[C] a small group, society, or place that has the same qualities as a much larger one —compare MACROCOSM —**microcosmic** /ˌmaɪkrəʊˈkɒzmɪk◂‖-kroʊˈkɑːz-/ *adj*

**mi·cro·dot** /ˈmaɪkrəʊdɒt‖-kroʊdɑːt/ *n* [C] a secret photograph of something such as a document, that is reduced to the size of a DOT so that it can easily be hidden

**mi·cro·e·lec·tron·ics** /ˌmaɪkrəʊɪlekˈtrɒnɪks‖-kroʊɪlekˈtrɑː-/ *n* [U] the practice or study of designing very small PRINTED CIRCUITS that are used in computers —**microelectronic** *adj*

**mi·cro·fiche** /ˈmaɪkrəʊfiːʃ‖-kroʊ-/ *n* [C,U] a sheet of film on which written information is stored in a very small form, and which can only be read using a special machine

**mi·cro·film** /ˈmaɪkrəʊfɪlm‖-kroʊ-/ *n* [C,U] very small film for photographing maps, documents etc so that they can be easily stored —**microfilm** *v* [T]

**mi·cro·light** /ˈmaɪkrəʊlaɪt‖-kroʊ-/ *n* [C] a very light small aircraft for one or two people

**mi·crom·e·ter** /maɪˈkrɒmɪtə‖-ˈkrɑːmɪtər/ *n* [C] an instrument for measuring very small distances

**mi·cron** /ˈmaɪkrɒn‖-krɑːn/ *n* [C] one millionth of a metre

**mi·cro·or·gan·is·m** /ˌmaɪkrəʊˈɔːgənɪzəm‖-kroʊˈɔːr-/ *n* [C] a living thing which is so small that it cannot be seen without a microscope

**mi·cro·phone** /ˈmaɪkrəfəʊn‖-foʊn/ *n* [C] a piece of equipment that you speak into to record your voice or make it louder when you are speaking or performing in public

**mi·cro·pro·ces·sor** /ˈmaɪkrəʊˌprəʊsesə‖-kroʊˌprɑːsesər/ *n* [C] the central CHIP¹ (4a) in a computer, which controls most of its operations

**mi·cro·scope** /ˈmaɪkrəskəʊp‖-skoʊp/ *n* [C] **1** a scientific instrument that makes extremely small things look larger —see picture at LABORATORY **2 put sth under the microscope** to examine a situation very closely and carefully

**mi·cro·scop·ic** /ˌmaɪkrəˈskɒpɪk◂‖-ˈskɑː-/ *adj* **1** extremely small and therefore very difficult to see: *His handwriting is microscopic! | The insect's legs are covered with microscopic hairs.* **2** [only before noun] using a microscope: *The cells were identified through microscopic analysis.* —**microscopically** /-kli/ *adv*

**mi·cro·sec·ond** /ˈmaɪkrəʊˌsekənd‖-kroʊ-/ *n* [C] one millionth of a second

**mi·cro·wave¹** /ˈmaɪkrəweɪv/ *n* [C] **1** also **microwave ov·en** /ˌ··· ˈ··/ a type of OVEN that cooks food very quickly using very short electric waves instead of heat —see picture on page 833 **2** a very short electric wave that is used in cooking food, sending messages by radio, and in RADAR

**microwave²** *v* [T] to cook something in a microwave oven —**microwaveable, microwavable** *adj*

**mid** /mɪd/ *prep poetic* among or in the middle of

**mid-** /mɪd/ *prefix* middle: *She's in her mid-20s.* (=is about 25 years old) | *in mid-July* | *a cold midwinter night*

**mid·air** /ˌmɪdˈeə◂‖-ˈer◂/ *n* **in midair** in the air or the sky, away from the ground: *The planes collided in midair.* —**midair** *adj*: *a midair collision*

**mid At·lan·tic** /ˌ· ·ˈ··◂/ *adj* **mid Atlantic accent** a way of

speaking that uses a mixture of American and British English sounds and words

**mid·day** /ˌmɪdˈdeɪ◂‖ˈmɪd-deɪ/ *n* [U] the middle of the day; twelve o'clock: **at midday** *I'm meeting him at midday.* | **midday meal/sun etc** *the full heat of the midday sun* —compare MIDNIGHT (1)

**mid·den** /ˈmɪdn/ *n* [C] *old use* a pile of something such as animal waste or rubbish

S1 W2 **mid·dle¹** /ˈmɪdl/ *n* **1 the middle a)** the part that is furthest from the sides, edges, or ends: *a seat in the middle of the front row* | *Here's a photo of us on holiday – that's me in the middle.* | **right in the middle/right down the middle etc** *The other car was driving right in the middle of the road.* | *Going through the middle of Tokyo in the rushhour can be a nightmare.* **b)** the part that is between the beginning and the end of an event, story, period etc: *Why don't we meet sometime in the middle of the week?* | *She started to feel sick in the middle of the exam.* | *I arrived in Athens in the middle of a heatwave.* **c)** the position or rank that is between the highest and the lowest position in a list of people or things: *Janine graduated top of the class and I finished somewhere around the middle.* **d)** the inside part of an object such as a ball, or piece of fruit: *Urgh! There's a maggot in the middle of this apple!* **2 be in the middle of (doing sth)** to be busy doing something: *Can I call you back – I'm in the middle of a meeting.* | *She was just in the middle of getting the dinner ready.* **3** [C usually singular] *informal* the waist and the part of the body around the stomach: *Nick seems to be getting a bit fat round his middle.* **4 in the middle of nowhere** a long way from the nearest town or from any interesting places: *So there we were, in the middle of nowhere, and out of gas.* **5 divide/split sth down the middle** to divide something into equal halves or groups: *The votes are divided right down the middle on this issue.* —see also **piggy in the middle** (PIGGY¹ (2))

S1 W2 **middle²** *adj* [only before noun] **1** nearest the centre, especially of a row, list, or group of things or people: *the middle house in a row of five* | *Two of his middle front teeth were missing.* | *the middle drawer of the filing cabinet* **2** halfway through an event or period of time: *They spent the middle part of their vacation in Florida.* **3 in your middle twenties/thirties etc** about 25, 35 etc years old **4 middle brother/child/daughter etc** the brother etc who is between the oldest and the youngest **5 middle course/way etc** a way of dealing with something that is between two opposite and often extreme ways: *The administration is trying to follow a middle course on health care reform.* **6 Middle English/French etc** an old form of English, French etc, used in the Middle Ages (=between 1100 and 1500 AD) —see also MIDDLE FINGER, MIDDLE NAME

**middle age** /ˌ·· ˈ··◂/ *n* [U] the period of your life when you are no longer young but are not yet old: *The new technique allows women to have children well into middle age.*

**middle-aged** /ˌ·· ˈ·◂/ *adj* **1** no longer young but not yet old: *a middle-aged businessman* **2** middle-aged attitudes or ways of behaving are rather boring or old-fashioned: *a middle-aged outlook on life* **3 middle aged spread** an area of fat that many people develop around their waist as they grow older

**Middle Ag·es** /ˌ·· ˈ···/ *n* **the Middle Ages** the period in European history between about 1100 and 1500 AD

**Middle A·mer·i·ca** /ˌ·· ·ˈ···/ *n* [U] **1** the mid-western part of the United States **2** Americans who are neither very rich nor very poor and who usually have traditional ideas about morality, education etc

**mid·dle·brow** /ˈmɪdlbraʊ/ *adj* middlebrow books, television programmes etc are not very difficult to understand —compare HIGHBROW, LOWBROW

**middle C** /ˌmɪdl ˈsiː/ *n* [singular] the musical note C which is at the middle point of a piano KEYBOARD

**middle class** /ˌ·· ˈ·◂/ *n* **the middle class** also **the middle classes** the social class that includes professional people such as teachers or managers, but does not include people who are very rich or people who work mainly with their hands —compare LOWER CLASS, UPPER CLASS, WORKING CLASS

**middle-class** *adj* **1** belonging to or typical of the middle class: *a middle-class suburb* | *She comes from a middle-class background.* **2** middle-class attitudes, values etc are typical of middle-class people and are often concerned with work, education, and possessions

**middle dis·tance** /ˌ·· ˈ···/ *n* **the middle distance** the part of a picture or a view that is between the nearest part and the part that is farthest away

**middle-dis·tance** /ˈ·· ··/ *adj* [only before noun] a middle-distance race is neither very short nor very long, for example 800 or 1500 metres

**middle ear** /ˌ·· ˈ·/ *n* [singular] the central part of the ear, between the outside part and the EARDRUM

**Middle East** /ˌ·· ˈ·◂/ *n* **the Middle East** the area including Iran and Egypt and the countries which are between them —compare FAR EAST —**Middle Eastern** *adj*

**middle fin·ger** /ˌ·· ˈ··/ *n* [C] the longest finger, which is the middle one of the five fingers on your hand

**middle ground** /ˌ·· ˈ·/ *n* [U] something that two opposing groups can both agree about: *The negotiators could find no middle ground.*

**mid·dle·man** /ˈmɪdlmæn/ *plural* **middlemen** /-men/ *n* [C] someone who buys things in order to sell them to someone else, or who helps to arrange business deals for other people: *He acts as a middleman for British companies seeking contracts in the Gulf.* | **cut out the middleman** (=avoid having to use a middleman): *Buy direct from the manufacturer and cut out the middleman.*

**middle man·age·ment** /ˌ·· ˈ···/ *n* [U] managers who are in charge of small groups of people but do not take the most important decisions —**middle manager** *n* [C]

**middle name** /ˌ·· ˈ·/ *n* [C] **1** the name that is between your first name and your family name **2 sth is sb's middle name** *informal* used to say that someone has a lot of a particular personal quality: *Generosity's her middle name.*

**middle-of-the-road** /ˌ·· · · ˈ·◂/ *adj* middle-of-the-road ideas, opinions etc are not extreme, and are similar to the ideas that most people have: *Her political views are fairly middle-of-the-road.*

**middle school** /ˈ·· ·/ *n* **1** [C,U] a school in Britain for children between the ages of 8 and 12 **2** [C,U] a school in the US for children between the ages of 11 and 14

**middle-sized** /ˌ·· ˈ·◂/ *adj* neither very large nor very small: *a middle-sized house*

**mid·dle·weight** /ˈmɪdlweɪt/ *n* [C] a BOXER who is lighter than a LIGHT HEAVYWEIGHT and heavier than a WELTERWEIGHT

**Middle West** /ˌ·· ˈ·/ *n* **the Middle West** another form of the MIDWEST

**mid·dling** /ˈmɪdəlɪŋ/ *adj informal* not very good or bad, not very big or small etc; average: **fair to middling** (=about average) *"How are you?" "Oh, fair to middling."*

**mid·field** /ˈmɪdfiːld/ *n* [U] **1** the middle part of the area where a game such as football or BASEBALL is played: *a midfield player* **2** the members of a football team who play in this area

**mid·field·er** /ˈmɪdfiːldə‖-ər/ *n* [C] a player who usually plays in the midfield

**midge** /mɪdʒ/ *n* [C] a small flying insect that bites people

**midg·et¹** /ˈmɪdʒɪ̈t/ *n* [C] **1** a very small person who will never grow tall because there is something wrong with their body **2** *BrE informal* someone who is not very tall

**midget²** *adj* **midget car/camera etc** a very small CAR etc

**Mid·lands** /ˈmɪdləndz/ *n* **the Midlands** *plural* the central part of England —**Midland** *adj* —**Midlander** *n* [C]

**mid·life cri·sis** /ˌmɪdlaɪf ˈkraɪsɪ̈s/ *n* [C] feelings of worry and lack of confidence, when you are between 40 and 50 years old

**mid·night** /ˈmɪdnaɪt/ *n* [U] **1** 12 o'clock at night: *We* *close at midnight.* | *the midnight train to Glasgow* —compare MIDDAY **2 midnight feast** a secret meal eaten late at night, especially by children —see also **burn the midnight oil** (BURN[1] (24))

**midnight sun** /ˌ·· ˈ·/ *n* **the midnight sun** the sun seen in the middle of the night in summer in the far north or south of the world

**mid·point** /ˈmɪdpɔɪnt/ *n* [C usually singular] a point that is halfway through or along something: [+ **of**] *We are now at the midpoint of this government's term of office.*

**mid·riff** /ˈmɪdrɪf/ *n* [C] the part of the body between your chest and your waist

**mid·ship·man** /ˈmɪdʃɪpmən/ *n* [C] the rank of someone who is training to become an officer in the British Navy —see table on page B4

**midst[1]** /mɪdst/ *n* **1 in the midst of a)** in the middle of a period, situation, or event: *in the midst of the Cold War* **b)** in the middle of a place or a group of things **2 in our/their midst** *formal* in a particular group: *We have a traitor in our midst.*

**midst[2]** *prep old use* in the middle of or among

**mid·sum·mer** /ˌmɪdˈsʌmə◂‖-ər◂/ *n* [U] the middle of summer: *one bright midsummer afternoon*

**Midsummer Day** /ˌ··· ˈ·/ also **Midsummer's Day** *n* [singular] *BrE* the 24th of June

**mid·term[1]** /ˌmɪdˈtɜːm◂‖-ˈtɜːrm◂/ *n* **1** [U] the middle period of an elected government's time in power: *Nixon was the first president to resign in midterm.* **2** [C] *AmE* an examination in the middle of one of the main periods in the year at university

**mid·term[2]** /ˈmɪdtɜːm‖-tɜːrm/ *adj* [only before noun] during or in the middle of one of the main periods in the school year, or in the middle of an elected government's time in power: *midterm tests* —compare HALF-TERM

**mid·town** /ˌmɪdˈtaʊn◂/ *adj, adv AmE* in the area of a city that is near the centre but is not the main business area —compare DOWNTOWN, UPTOWN —**midtown** *n* [U]

**mid·way** /ˌmɪdˈweɪ◂‖ˈmɪdweɪ/ *adj, adv* **1** halfway between two places or along a line: [+ **between/along**] *midway between Madagascar and the coast of Tanzania* **2** halfway through a period of time: *Tyson knocked out his opponent midway through the third round.*

**mid·week** /ˌmɪdˈwiːk◂‖ˈmɪdwiːk/ *adj, adv* on one of the middle days of the week: *a midweek match against Liverpool* | *I don't go out much midweek anymore.*

**Mid·west** /ˌmɪdˈwest/ *n* **the Midwest** the central area of the United States —**Midwestern** *adj*

**mid·wife** /ˈmɪdwaɪf/ *n plural* **midwives** /-waɪvz/ [C] a specially trained nurse, usually a woman, whose job is to help women when they are having a baby

**mid·wif·e·ry** /ˈmɪdˌwɪfəri‖-ˌwaɪfəri/ *n* [U] the skill or work of a midwife

**mid·win·ter** /ˌmɪdˈwɪntə◂‖-ər◂/ *n* [U] the middle of winter: *They crossed the Great Smoky Mountains in midwinter.*

**mien** /miːn/ *n* [singular] *literary* someone's typical expression or way of behaving: *a thoughtful and solemn mien*

**miffed** /mɪft/ *adj spoken* slightly annoyed or upset: *I was a bit miffed that you'd left without me.*

S1 W1 **might[1]** /maɪt/ *modal verb negative short form* mightn't **1** if something might happen or might be true, there is a possibility that it may happen or be true but you are not certain: *Who knows – England might win the next World Cup!* | *"Are you going to write her a letter?" "I might, I might not."* | *You might not have noticed but I've put up a 'no smoking' sign in here.* | *Did you see the way he was driving? I might have been killed.* **2** the past tense of may: *Thinking it might rain, I decided to go in the car.* | *She asked if she might open a window.* **3** used to give advice or make a suggestion: *If the police can't help, you might try the Citizens Advice Bureau.* | *I thought we might spend the lesson studying irregular verbs.* **4 a)** *spoken old-fashioned* used to ask politely if you can do something: *Might I come in?* **b) might I say/ask/add etc** *spoken* used to politely give more information, ask a question, interrupt etc: *Might I just add that Miriam has been a pleasure to work with and we wish her every success in the future.* **5** used when you are angry or surprised when someone has not done something that you think they should do: *You might have cleaned up before you left!* | *Don't you think he might at least say thank you?* **6 I might have known/guessed etc** *spoken* used to say that you are not surprised at a situation: *Jake Thompson! I might have known you'd be behind all this!* **7 might well** if something might well happen or might well be true you think it is fairly likely to happen or be true: *You might well find that you'll need more by the weekend.* **8 might (just) as well** *usually spoken* used to suggest doing something that you do not really want to do, because you have no better ideas: *It's no good waiting for the bus. We might as well walk.* **9 might...but...** used to tell someone that although what they said is true, something else which seemed very different is also a fact: *You might be a strong swimmer but that doesn't mean you can win a triathlon.* **10** *formal* used to say why something happens or the reason why someone does something: *Samuel left his children a letter, so that his family might understand why he had to go away.* **11** *old-fashioned humorous* used to politely ask for information: *And who might you be, young man?* —compare MAY[1]

**might[2]** *n* [U] **1** great strength and power: *the full might of the Russian army* | **with all your might** (=using all your strength and a lot of effort) *He swung the ax with all his might.* | **with might and main** *literary* (=with a lot of strength) **2 might is right** *BrE* **might makes right** *AmE* used to say that powerful people and countries can do whatever they want

**might-have-beens** /ˈ· · ˌ·/ *n* [plural] things that you wish had happened in the past but which never did

**might·i·ly** /ˈmaɪtəli/ *adv especially literary* **1** very: *She seemed mightily impressed by his story.* **2** using great strength: *Fred swung mightily at the ball.*

**might·n't** /ˈmaɪtənt/ *informal, especially BrE* the short form of 'might not'

**might·y[1]** /ˈmaɪti/ *adj especially literary* very strong and powerful, or very big and impressive: *the mighty Mississippi river* | *a mighty king* —see also **high and mighty** (HIGH[1] (19))

**mighty[2]** *adv* [+ adj/adv] *AmE informal* very: *It's mighty good to see you.*

**mi·graine** /ˈmiːgreɪn, ˈmaɪ-‖ˈmaɪ-/ *n* [C] an extremely bad headache, during which you feel sick and have pain behind your eyes

**mi·grant** /ˈmaɪgrənt/ *n* [C] **1** someone who goes to another area or country, especially in order to find work: **migrant worker/labour/groups** *migrant workers in the depression of the 1930s* | **economic migrant** (=someone who goes to another country because living conditions are better there) **2** a bird or animal that travels from one part of the world to another, especially in the autumn and spring —compare EMIGRANT, IMMIGRANT

**mi·grate** /maɪˈgreɪt‖ˈmaɪgreɪt/ *v* [I + **from/to**] **1** if birds or animals migrate, they travel from one part of the world to another, especially in the autumn and spring **2** to go to another area or country, especially in order to find work —compare EMIGRATE, IMMIGRATE

**mi·gra·tion** /maɪˈgreɪʃən/ *n* [C] the movement from one place to another of a large group of people, birds, animals etc: *the great migrations to America of the 19th century* 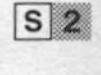

**mike[1]** /maɪk/ *n* [C] *informal* a MICROPHONE —see also OPEN MIKE, **for the love of Mike** (LOVE[2] (14))

**mike[2]** *v*

**mike** sb **up** *phr v* [T] *informal* to put a MICROPHONE on someone so that their voice can be recorded or made louder

**mi·la·dy** /mɪˈleɪdi/ *n* [singular] another spelling of M'LADY

**milch cow** /ˈmɪltʃ kaʊ/ *n* [C] another spelling of MILK COW

**mild¹** /maɪld/ *adj*
**1** ▶ **WEATHER** ◀ not too cold or wet, and sometimes pleasantly warm: *We had an exceptionally mild winter last year.*
**2** ▶ **ILLNESS** ◀ a mild illness or health problem is not serious: *It's nothing – just a mild throat infection.*
**3** ▶ **FOOD/TASTE** ◀ not very strong or hot-tasting: *a mild curry*
**4** ▶ **PUNISHMENT/CRITICISM** ◀ not severe or strict: *a mild rebuke*
**5** ▶ **SMALL EFFECT** ◀ not serious enough to cause much suffering: *The recession in Germany has been comparatively mild.* | *a mild earthquake*
**6** ▶ **CHARACTER/MANNER** ◀ having a gentle character and not easily getting angry: *Joe was a mild man who rarely raised his voice.*
**7** ▶ **SOAP ETC** ◀ soft and gentle to your skin: *a mild washing-up liquid* —see also MILDLY

**mild²** *n* [U] *BrE* dark beer with a mild taste —compare BITTER² (1)

**mil·dew** /ˈmɪldjuː‖-duː/ *n* [U] a white or grey substance that grows on leaves, walls, or other surfaces in wet, slightly warm conditions —**mildewed** *adj*

**mild·ly** /ˈmaɪldli/ *adv* **1** [+ adj] slightly: *The drug is only mildly addictive.* **2** **to put it mildly** *spoken* used when saying that you could use much stronger words to describe something: *The manager wasn't very happy, to put it mildly, when you came in two hours late for the meeting.* **3** in a gentle way without being angry: *"Of course I don't mind," she answered mildly.*

**mild-man·nered** /ˌ· ˈ··◂/ *adj* gentle and polite: *She had always struck me as being mild-mannered and quiet.*

**mile** /maɪl/ *n* [C] **1** a unit for measuring distance or length, equal to 1609 metres —see table on page B4 **2** **the mile** a race that is a mile in length: *the world record holder in the mile* **3** **miles** *informal* a very long distance: *We were miles from home, and very tired.* | **for miles** (=for a very long distance) *You can see for miles from the top of the hill.* | **miles from anywhere/nowhere** (=a long way from the nearest town or city) *They lived in a little cottage miles from nowhere.* **4** **go the extra mile** to try a little harder in order to achieve something, after you have already used a lot of effort: *Neither of the negotiating teams seems willing to go the extra mile.* **5** **sth sticks out/stands out a mile** also **you can tell sth a mile away/off** *informal* used to say that something is very clear from someone's appearance or behaviour: *It's obvious she's English – you can tell it a mile away.* **6** **talk a mile a minute** to speak very quickly without stopping **7** **be miles away** *spoken* to not be paying attention to anything that is happening around you: *"Kate!" "Sorry, I was miles away!"* **8** **miles older/better/too difficult etc** *BrE informal* very much older, better, too difficult etc: *You're going out with John? But he's miles older than you!* **9** **miles out** *BrE informal* a measurement, guess, or calculation that is miles out is completely wrong—see also NAUTICAL MILE, **run a mile** (RUN¹ (47)), **a miss is as good as a mile** (MISS² (8))

**mile·age** /ˈmaɪlɪdʒ/ *n* **1** [C usually singular, U] the number of miles a vehicle has travelled since it was made: *For sale Red Ford Escort. Low Mileage.* **2** [C usually singular, U] the number of miles a vehicle can travel using one GALLON or litre of fuel **3** [U] the amount of use or advantage you get from something: *The newspapers have had a lot of mileage out of the Royal divorce story.* **4** [C usually singular, U] also **mileage allowance** an amount of money paid for each mile that is travelled by someone using a car for work **5** [U] a distance in miles that is covered by a country's roads or railways

**mile·om·e·ter, milometer** /maɪˈlɒmɪ̣tə‖-ˈlɑːmɪ̣tər/ *n* [C] *BrE* an instrument in a car that shows how many miles it has travelled; ODOMETER *AmE* —see picture on page 409

**mile·post** /ˈmaɪlpəʊst‖-poʊst/ *n* [C] *especially AmE* a post next to a road or railway that shows the distance in miles to the next town

**mil·er** /ˈmaɪlə‖-ər/ *n* [C] a person or horse that competes in one-mile races

**mile·stone** /ˈmaɪlstəʊn‖-stoʊn/ *n* [C] **1** [usually singular] a very important event in the development of something: [+ **in**] *The agreement was a milestone in the history of US-Soviet relations.* **2** a stone next to a road that shows the distance in miles to the next town

**mi·lieu** /ˈmiːljɜː‖miːˈljɜː, -ˈljuː/ *n plural* **milieux** /-ljɜːz, -ljɜː‖-ˈljɜːz, -ˈljuːz, -ˈljɜː, -ˈljuː/ *or* **milieus** [C,U] *French formal* the things and people that surround you and influence the way you live and think: *Proust wrote exclusively about his own social and cultural milieu.*

**mil·i·tant** /ˈmɪlɪ̣tənt/ *adj* a militant organization or person is willing to use strong or violent action in order to achieve political or social change: *militant trade unionists* | *After the assassination of Martin Luther King, black leaders became more militant.* —**militant** *n* [C] —**militancy** *n* [U] —**militantly** *adv*

**mil·i·ta·ris·m** /ˈmɪlɪ̣tərɪzəm/ *n* [U] the belief that a country should build up its military forces and use them to get what it wants —**militarist** *n* [C] —**militaristic** /ˌmɪlɪ̣təˈrɪstɪk◂/ *adj*

**mil·i·ta·rized** also **-ised** *BrE* /ˈmɪlɪ̣təraɪzd/ *adj* a militarized area is one that has a lot of soldiers and weapons in it

**mil·i·ta·ry¹** /ˈmɪlɪ̣təri‖-teri/ *adj* used by or connected with war or the army, navy, or airforce: *a military helicopter* | *the use of military power* | *the supreme US military commander in Europe* —**militarily** *adv* S2 W1

**military²** *n* **the military** the military forces of a country [also + plural verb *BrE*]: *The military have taken control of the government.* | **in the military** *AmE* (=in the army, navy etc) *My brother is in the military.*

**Military A·cad·e·my** /ˌ····· ·ˈ···/ *n* [C] **1** a national college where people are trained to be officers in the military forces **2** a private school in the US that gives students military training

**Military Cross** /ˌ···· ˈ·/ *n* [C] a MEDAL given to British army officers for being brave in battle

**military po·lice** /ˌ···· ·ˈ·/ *n* [singular] a special police force whose job is to deal with members of the army etc who break the rules —see also MP (2)

**military ser·vice** /ˌ···· ˈ··/ *n* [U] the system in which every adult man in a country has to be in the army, navy, or airforce, for a period of time —compare DRAFT¹ (2)

**mil·i·tate** /ˈmɪlɪ̣teɪt/ *v*
**militate against** *phr v* [T] *formal* to prevent something or make it less likely to happen: *Environmental factors militate against building the power station in this area.*

**mi·li·tia** /mɪ̣ˈlɪʃə/ *n* [C] a group of people trained as soldiers, who are not part of the permanent army

**mi·li·tia·man** /mɪ̣ˈlɪʃəmən/ *n* [C] a member of a militia

**milk¹** /mɪlk/ *n* [U] **1** a white liquid produced by cows or goats that is drunk by people: *a bottle of milk* | *Would you like some milk in your tea?* **2** a white liquid produced by female animals and women for feeding their babies **3** a liquid or juice produced by certain plants, especially the COCONUT (1) **4** **the milk of human kindness** *literary* ordinary kindness and sympathy for other people —see also EVAPORATED MILK, SKIMMED MILK, **cry over spilt milk** (CRY¹ (5)), **land of milk and honey** (LAND¹ (8)) S2 W3

**milk²** *v* [T] **1** to take milk from a cow or goat **2** *informal* to get as much money or as many advantages as you can from a situation, in a very determined and sometimes dishonest way: **milk sb for sth** *Their landlord regularly milks them for extra money by claiming for damage to his property.* | **milk sth for all it is worth** *Reporters were milking Nixon's resignation for all it was worth.* **3** to take the poison from a snake

**milk choco·late** /ˌ· ˈ···◂‖ˌ· ˈ····◂/ *n* [U] chocolate made with milk and sugar —see also DARK CHOCOLATE, PLAIN CHOCOLATE

**milk churn** /ˈ· ·/ *n* [C] *BrE* a large metal container with a lid used to carry milk from farms

**milk cow** /ˈ· ·/ also **milking cow** /ˈ· · ·/ *n* [C] a cow kept to give milk rather than for meat

**milk float** /ˈ· ·/ *n* [C] *BrE* a vehicle used for delivering milk to people's houses, which is usually powered by electricity

**milking ma·chine** /ˈ· · ˌ·/ *n* [C] a machine used for taking milk from cows

**milking par·lour** *BrE*, **milking parlor** *AmE* /ˈ· · ˌ· ·/ *n* [C] a building on a farm where milk is taken from the cows

**milk loaf** /ˈ· ·/ *n plural* **milk loaves** [C] *BrE* a LOAF of white bread made with milk

**milk·maid** /ˈmɪlkmeɪd/ *n* [C] *old use* a woman who gets milk from cows on a farm

**milk·man** /ˈmɪlkmən/ *n plural* **milkmen** /-mən/ [C] someone who delivers milk to houses each morning

**milk of mag·ne·sia** /ˌ· · · ˈ· ·/ *n* [U] a thick white liquid medicine used for stomach problems and CONSTIPATION

**milk pud·ding** /ˌ· ˈ· ·/ *n* [C] *BrE* a sweet food made of rice, TAPIOCA, or SAGO, baked in milk

**milk round** /ˈ· ·/ *n BrE* **1** [C] the regular journey a milkman makes every day to deliver milk **2 the milk round** *BrE* a series of visits to universities made each year by large companies to find people they may want to employ

**milk run** /ˈ· ·/ *n* [C] **1** *BrE informal* a familiar, easy journey that you do regularly **2** *AmE informal* a train journey or regular plane flight that stops in many places

**milk shake** /ˌ· ˈ·‖ˈ· ·/ *n* [C] **1** *BrE* a drink made of milk mixed with fruit or chocolate **2** *AmE* a drink made of milk, ICE CREAM, and fruit or chocolate

**milk·sop** /ˈmɪlksɒp‖-sɑːp/ *n* [C] *old-fashioned* a boy or man who is too gentle and weak, and who is afraid to do anything dangerous

**milk·toast** /ˈmɪlktəʊst‖-toʊst/ *n* [C] another spelling of MILQUETOAST

**milk tooth** /ˈ· ·/ *n plural* **milk teeth** [C] *BrE* one of the first set of teeth developed by young children; BABY TOOTH

**milk·weed** /ˈmɪlkwiːd/ *n* [U] a common North American plant that produces a bitter white substance when its stem is broken

**milk·y** /ˈmɪlki/ *adj* **1** a drink that is milky contains a lot of milk: *milky coffee* **2** water or other liquids that are milky are not clear and look like milk **3** milky skin is white and smooth —**milkiness** *n* [U]

**Milky Way** /ˌ· · ˈ·/ *n* **the Milky Way** the pale white band of stars that can be seen across the sky at night

W3 **mill**[1] /mɪl/ *n* [C] **1** a building containing a large machine for crushing grain into flour, or the machine itself: *an old mill with a ruined water-wheel* **2** a factory that produces materials such as cotton, cloth, steel: *a woollen mill* **3 coffee/pepper mill** a small machine for crushing coffee or pepper **4 go through the mill** to go through a time when you experience a lot of difficulties and problems: *Go easy on him – he's been through the mill lately.* **5 put sb through the mill** to make someone answer a lot of difficult questions or do a lot of difficult things in order to test them **6** *AmE* a unit of money equal to 1/10 of a cent, used in setting taxes and for other financial purposes —see also RUN-OF-THE-MILL, **(all) grist to the mill** (GRIST)

**mill**[2] *v* [T] **1** to produce flour by crushing grain in a mill **2** to press, roll, or shape metal in a machine **3** to mark the edge of a coin with regular lines

**mill around/about** *phr v* [I] *informal* if a lot of people mill around, they move around a place in different directions without any particular purpose: *Crowds of students were milling around in the street.*

**mil·len·ni·um** /mɪˈleniəm/ *n plural* **millennia** /-nɪə/ **1** [C] a period of 1000 years **2** [C] the time when a new 1000-year period begins: *plans for celebrating the millennium, in the year 2000* **3 the millennium** the time in the future when Jesus Christ will return and rule on Earth for 1000 years —**millennial** *adj*

**mil·le·pede** /ˈmɪlɪ̈piːd/ another spelling of MILLIPEDE

**mill·er** /ˈmɪlə‖-ər/ *n* [C] someone who owns or operates a mill which makes flour

**mil·let** /ˈmɪlɪ̈t/ *n* [U] the small seeds of a plant similar to grass, used as food

**milli-** /mɪlɪ̈/ *prefix* a 1000th part of a particular unit of something: *a millilitre* (=0.001 litres) —see table on page B1

**mil·li·bar** /ˈmɪlɪ̈bɑː‖-bɑːr/ *n* [C] *technical* a unit for measuring the pressure of air

**mil·li·gram** /ˈmɪlɪ̈græm/ written abbreviation **mg** *n* [C] a unit for measuring weight. There are 1000 milligrams in one gram. —see table on page B2

**mil·li·li·tre** *BrE*, **milliliter** *AmE* /ˈmɪlɪ̈ˌliːtə‖-ər/ written abbreviation **ml** *n* [C] a unit for measuring the amount of a liquid. There are 1000 millilitres in one litre. —see table on page B2

**mil·li·me·tre** *BrE*, **millimeter** *AmE* /ˈmɪlɪ̈ˌmiːtə‖-ər/ S3 written abbreviation **mm** *n* [C] a unit for measuring length. There are 1000 millimetres in one metre. —see table on page B2

**mil·li·ner** /ˈmɪlɪ̈nə‖-ər/ *n* [C] *old-fashioned* someone who makes and sells women's hats

**mil·li·ne·ry** /ˈmɪlɪ̈nəri‖-neri/ *n* [U] **1** a word meaning hats, used in shops and in the fashion industry **2** the activity of making women's hats

**mil·lion** /ˈmɪljən/ *plural* **million** or **millions** *number, quantifier* **1** 1,000,000: *three million dollars|a population of 12 million people* **2** also **millions** an extremely large number of people or things: *Millions of people will see that film.|He made millions* (=a lot of money) *on that deal.|I've heard that excuse a million times.* **3 not/never in a million years** *spoken* used to emphasize that something is impossible or very unlikely to happen: *I'd never marry him – not in a million years.* **4 feel/look like a million dollars/bucks** *informal especially AmE* to feel or look very well or very attractive: *Wow! You look like a million dollars tonight!* **5 one in a million** also **a wife/teacher/writer etc in a million** *informal* one of the best possible wives, teachers etc —**millionth** *determiner, n, pron, adj*

**mil·lion·aire** /ˌmɪljəˈneə‖-ˈner/ *n* [C] someone who is very rich and has at least a million pounds or dollars

**mil·lion·air·ess** /ˌmɪljəˈneərɪ̈s‖-ˈner-/ *n* [C] *old-fashioned* a woman who is very rich and has at least a million pounds or dollars

**mil·li·pede** /ˈmɪlɪ̈piːd/ *n* [C] a long thin insect with a lot of legs

**mill·pond** /ˈmɪlpɒnd‖-pɑːnd/ *n* [C] a very small lake that supplies water to turn the wheel of a WATERMILL

**mill·stone** /ˈmɪlstəʊn‖-stoʊn/ *n* [C] **1** one of the two large circular stones that crush grain into flour in a MILL[1] (1) **2 a millstone around your neck** something that causes you a lot of problems and prevents you from doing what you would like to do: *His fame, so pleasant at first, became a millstone around his neck.*

**mill·wheel** /ˈmɪlwiːl/ *n* [C] *especially BrE* a large wheel that is turned by water flowing past it to provide power to the machinery in a MILL[1] (1)

**mil·om·e·ter** /maɪˈlɒmɪ̈tə‖-ˈlɑːmɪ̈tər/ *n* [C] another spelling of MILEOMETER

**milque·toast, milktoast** /ˈmɪlktəʊst‖-toʊst/ *n* [C] *AmE old-fashioned* a weak, quiet man with no courage; WIMP[1] (1)

**mime**[1] /maɪm/ *n* **1** [C,U] the use of actions or movements to express what you want to say without using words **2** [C] a simple play performed without using words: *a mime artist* **3** [C] an actor who performs without using words

**mime²** *v* [I,T] to act something using actions and movements without any words: *The children mimed the whole story for the rest of the class.*

**mi·met·ic** /mɪ̇ˈmetɪk/ *adj technical* copying the movements or appearance of someone or something else

**mim·ic¹** /ˈmɪmɪk/ *v past tense and past participle* **mimicked** [T] **1** to copy the way someone speaks or behaves, especially in order to make people laugh: *Sally used to keep us entertained by mimicking the teacher.* **2** to behave or operate in exactly the same way as something or someone else: *Will computers ever be able to mimic the way humans think?* **3** if an animal mimics something it tries to look or sound like something in order to protect itself: *an insect that mimics the appearance of a wasp* —**mimicry** *n* [U]

**mimic²** *n* [C] **1** an entertainer who copies the way famous people speak or behave **2** a person or animal that is good at copying the movements, sound, or appearance of someone or something else

**mimic³** *adj* [only before noun] **1** *technical* providing protection by looking exactly like something else **2** imitating behaviour or movements: *the mimic marching of the children playing soldiers*

**mi·mo·sa** /mɪˈməʊzə‖-ˈmoʊsə/ *n* [C,U] a small tree that grows in hot countries and has small yellow flowers

**min** **1** the written abbreviation of MINIMUM **2** the written abbreviation of minute or minutes

**min·a·ret** /ˌmɪnəˈret, ˈmɪnəret/ *n* [C] a tall thin tower on a MOSQUE from which Muslims are called to prayer

**min·a·to·ry** /ˈmɪnətəri‖-tɔːri/ *adj formal* threatening

**mince¹** /mɪns/ *v* **1** [T] to cut food, especially meat, into very small pieces, usually in a machine: *minced lamb* **2** [I always + adv/prep] to walk in an unnatural way, taking short steps and moving your hips: [+ **across/down/along etc**] *She minced across the hall to her desk.* **3 not mince matters/your words** to say exactly what you think even if this may offend people: *He's a brash New Yorker who doesn't mince his words.*

**mince²** *n* [U] *BrE* meat, especially BEEF, that has been cut into very small pieces using a special machine; GROUND BEEF *AmE*

**mince·meat** /ˈmɪns-miːt/ *n* [U] **1** a mixture of apples, RAISINS, SUET, and SPICES, but no meat, put inside PASTRY (1) and baked **2 make mincemeat of** *informal* to completely defeat someone in an argument, fight, or game: *They made mincemeat of the opposition's arguments.*

**mince pie** /ˌ· ˈ·/ *n* [C] **1** a small PIE filled with mincemeat that is eaten especially at Christmas **2** *AmE* a large PIE filled with mincemeat

**minc·er** /ˈmɪnsə‖-ər/ *n* [C] *BrE* a machine that cuts meat into very small pieces by forcing it through small holes; MEAT GRINDER *AmE*

**minc·ing·ly** /ˈmɪnsɪŋli/ *adv* with little short steps

**mind¹** *n* see below

**mind²** *v* S1 W2

**1 ▶ FEEL ANNOYED ◀** [I,T not in progressive or passive, usually in questions and negatives] to feel annoyed or upset about something: *We'll have to leave early. Do you mind?* | *I wouldn't have minded so much if he'd apologized.* | **mind sth** *He didn't mind the lie she'd told him, it was the fact that she'd made him look stupid.* | **mind sb doing sth** *I hope you don't mind me bringing the dog with me.* | **mind that** *She didn't mind that he was late as long as he got there.*

**2 not mind doing sth** to be willing to do something: *I don't mind driving if you're tired.*

**3 ▶ NOT CARE WHICH ONE ◀ not mind** [I,T not in progressive or passive] *especially BrE* to not care what is decided because you are equally happy with whatever is decided: *I don't mind whether we see the film or not.*

**4 ▶ TAKE CARE OF ◀** [T] *BrE* **a)** to be responsible for something for a short time; WATCH¹ (3): *Will you mind my bag while I buy my ticket?* **b)** to take care of a child while their parents are not there; WATCH¹ (3): *My sister minds the baby so I can go to my yoga class.*

**5 mind your own business** to not get involved in or ask questions about other people's lives or personal details: *Why don't you just mind your own business and leave me in peace?*

**6 mind the store** *AmE informal* to be in charge of something, especially while the person who is usually in charge is not there: *If the president didn't know about the arms sales to Iran, who is really minding the store?*

**7 mind your manners/language/p's and q's** to be careful about what you say or how you behave so that you do not offend anyone

**8 ▶ OBEY ◀** [T not in progressive] *AmE* to obey someone's instructions or advice: *Mind what your mother says, Anthony.*

[continued on page 906]

S1 W1

## mind¹ /maɪnd/ *n*

| | |
|---|---|
| ① BRAIN/THINKING PROCESS | ⑧ OPINION |
| ② DECIDE | ⑨ STRONG/DETERMINED |
| ③ THINKING ABOUT STH | ⑩ ATTENTION |
| ④ WORRY/STOP WORRYING | ⑪ IMAGINE |
| ⑤ CRAZY/MENTALLY ILL | ⑫ INTEND/WANT |
| ⑥ FORGET | ⑬ INTELLIGENCE |
| ⑦ REMEMBER | ⑭ OTHER MEANINGS |

### ① BRAIN/THINKING PROCESS

**1** [C,U] the part of a person, usually considered to be their brain, that they use to think and imagine things: *I have a picture of him in my mind – tall, blond and handsome.* | *I don't know what's going on in her mind.*

**2 get sb/sth out of your mind** to stop yourself thinking about someone or something: *I just can't seem to get her out of my mind.*

**3 go over sth/turn sth over in your mind** to keep thinking about something because you are trying to understand it or solve a problem: *I kept turning the conversation over in my mind.*

### ② DECIDE

**4 make up your mind a)** to decide which of two or more choices you want, especially after thinking for a long time: *I just couldn't make up my mind, so in the end I bought both.* | *I wish you'd make your mind up whether you're coming or not.* **b)** to become very determined to do something, so that you will not change your decision: *I'm sorry but my mind's made up – I'm leaving.* | **make up your mind to do sth** *He's made his mind up to resign, and that's final.* | **make up your mind that** *They made up their mind that they would buy a new house once Larry changed jobs.*

**5 change your mind** to change your opinion or decision about something: *I've changed my mind – I'll have a beer instead.* | [+ **about**] *Try and get her to change her mind about coming with us.*
**6 be in two minds about** *informal* to be unable to make a decision about something: *We're in two minds about whether to sell the house or not.*
**7 set your mind on (doing) sth** to decide that you want to do something very much: *Tom had set his mind on a trip to the Seychelles.*

### ③ THINKING ABOUT STH
**8 be the last thing on sb's mind** to be the thing that someone is least likely to be thinking about: *One thing was for sure, marriage was the last thing on Nick's mind.*
**9 come/spring to mind** [not in progressive] if something comes to mind or springs to mind you suddenly think of it: *We needed someone to look after the kids, and your name sprang to mind.*
**10 cross/enter your mind (that)** [not in progressive] if something crosses or enters your mind, you have a particular thought or idea, especially for a short time: *It never crossed my mind that Lisa might be lying.*
**11 turn your mind to** to begin to think about a subject after you have been thinking about something else: *Let's now turn our minds to tomorrow's meeting.*

### ④ WORRY/STOP WORRYING
**12 take your mind off sth** to make yourself stop thinking about something that is worrying you: *I decided to clean the car to take my mind off the events of the day.*
**13 set/put sb's mind at rest** to make someone feel less worried or anxious: *Call your mom and tell her you've arrived safely, just to set her mind at rest.*
**14 be out of your mind with grief/worry etc** to be extremely worried, sad etc: *Since her son was reported missing she's been out of her mind with worry.*
**15 be a load/weight off your mind** *informal* to be something that you no longer need to worry about: *The police said the accident wasn't my fault. Boy, was that a load off my mind.*
**16 on your mind** if something is on your mind, you keep thinking about it and worrying about it: *You look worried, Sarah. Is there something on your mind?* | **have a lot on your mind** (=have a lot of problems to worry about) *With Jim losing his job and her mother being sick, Michelle has had a lot on her mind lately.*

### ⑤ CRAZY/MENTALLY ILL
**17 be out of your mind/not be in your right mind** *informal* to behave in a way that is crazy or stupid: *Nobody in their right mind would go out on a night like this.* | *She must be out of her mind to marry him.*
**18 go out of your mind/lose your mind** *informal* to start to become mentally ill or behave in a strange way: *I have so much to do – I feel like I'm going out of my mind.*
**19 be of sound mind** *law* to have the ability to think clearly and be responsible for your actions

### ⑥ FORGET
**20 your mind goes blank** *informal* if your mind goes blank, you suddenly cannot remember something: *My mind went blank as soon as I went into the exam room.*
**21 out of sight, out of mind** used to say that if you cannot see someone or something, you stop thinking about them and forget about them
**22 put sth out of your mind** to deliberately try to forget about something unpleasant: *Put the whole experience out of your mind and try to sleep.*
**23 go (right) out of your mind/slip your mind** if something goes out of your mind, you forget it, especially because you are too busy doing other things: *Her birthday had gone right out of Jerry's mind.* | **slip sb's mind that** *It slipped my mind that I'd agreed to meet him.*

### ⑦ REMEMBER
**24 bring/call sth to mind a)** to make yourself remember a name, fact etc: *I couldn't quite call his name to mind.* **b)** to remind you of something: *These violent scenes bring to mind the riots of last year.*
**25 keep sth in mind** to remember a fact or piece of information because it will be useful to you in the future: *It's a good idea – I'll keep it in mind.*
**26 bear sth in mind** to remember a useful or important piece of information: *You should bear in mind that these exams affect your final result.*
**27 stick in your mind** if a name, fact etc sticks in your mind, you remember it for a long time: *For some reason the name really stuck in Joe's mind.*
**28 at/in the back of your mind** if something is at the back of your mind, you keep remembering it or feeling it, but you do not think about it directly: *At the back of his mind, Matt had been hoping that Beth would stay.*
**29 put you in mind of** [not in progressive] *old-fashioned* to remind you of a person or thing from your past: *Seeing the movie put me in mind of my army days.*

### ⑧ OPINION
**30 to my mind** *BrE spoken* used when you are giving your opinion about something: *To my mind this is the finest building in Paris.*
**31 speak your mind** to say exactly what you think about something, even when this might offend people
**32 keep/have an open mind (about)** to be willing to think about and accept new ideas or ways of doing things: *My parents have a very open mind about sex before marriage.*
**33 have a closed mind (about)** to refuse to think about or accept new ideas or ways of doing things
**34 be of one mind/of the same mind/of like mind** to agree with someone about something: *It's not often that I meet people who are of like mind in politics.* | [+ **on/about**] – *We're all of the same mind on this issue.*

### ⑨ STRONG/DETERMINED
**35 have a mind of your own** to decide on your opinions and make your own decisions: *Even at the age of two, Joey had a mind of his own.*
**36 know your own mind** to be very clear about what your opinions or beliefs are and not be influenced by what other people think
**37 put your mind to** to decide to do something or achieve something by thinking and working very hard at it: *It won't take long to sort it out once you put your mind to it.*

### ⑩ ATTENTION
**38 sb's mind is not on sth** to not be thinking about what you are doing, because you are thinking or worrying about something else: *Steve's mind just doesn't seem to be on the job these days. Is something wrong at home?*
**39 keep your mind on** to keep paying attention to something even if it is boring or if you want to think about something else: *It was difficult to keep our minds on the job with all the talk of war.*
**40 pay sb/sth no mind** *AmE* to not pay any attention to someone or something or not care about what they are saying or doing
**41 your mind wanders** if your mind WANDERS, you no longer pay attention to something, especially because you are bored

### ⑪ IMAGINE
**42 it's all in your mind** used to tell someone that they have imagined something and it does not really exist: *one of those doctors who say you're not really sick and it's all in your mind*
**43 in your mind's eye** if you see something in your mind's eye, you can imagine what it looks like because you remember it: *She could see in her mind's eye the whitewashed cottage of her childhood.*

[continued on next page]

[continued from previous page]

### ⑫ INTENDI/WANT

**44 have sth/sb in mind** to be thinking about or considering a particular person, plan etc for a particular purpose: *It's a nice house, but it wasn't quite what we had in mind.*
**45 have it in mind to do sth** to intend to do something: *Once she had it in mind to win that trophy, nothing would have stopped her.*
**46 have a good mind/half a mind to do sth** **a)** used as a not very serious threat when you want to show your disapproval of what someone has done: *I've a good mind to phone him up and tell him exactly what I think.* **b)** used when you are considering doing something but are not sure you will: *I have half a mind just to take a cab home.*

### ⑬ INTELLIGENCE

**47** [C usually singular] intelligence and ability to think rather than emotions; INTELLECT: *Paul says he's doing the course to improve his mind.*|*a bright child with an enquiring mind*
**48** [C] someone who is very intelligent, especially in a particular area of study or activity: *She is one of the finest political minds in the country.*
**49 great minds think alike** *spoken* used to say jokingly that you and someone else must be very intelligent because you both agree about something
**50 mind over matter** an expression used when someone uses their intelligence to control a difficult situation

### ⑭ OTHER MEANINGS

**51 frame/state of mind** the way someone is thinking and feeling at a particular time: *I'm not going to argue with you while you're in this frame of mind.*
**52 give sb a piece of your mind** *informal* to tell someone how angry you are with them
**53 bored out of your mind** *informal* extremely bored
**54 stoned/drunk etc out of your mind** affected by drugs or alcohol so that you do not really know what you are doing
**55 time out of mind** more often than you can remember: *I've told you time out of mind to close that door when you leave the room.*
**56 ▶CHARACTER◀** [C] a particular way of thinking that is part of someone's character: *If you ask me O'Rourke has a very devious mind.* —see also ONE-TRACK MIND, **blow your mind** (BLOW[1] (17)), **the mind boggles** (BOGGLE (1)), **meeting of minds** (MEETING (5)), **peace of mind** (PEACE (4)), PRESENCE OF MIND, **read sb's mind** (READ[1] (12))

Frequencies of the verb **mind** in spoken and written English.

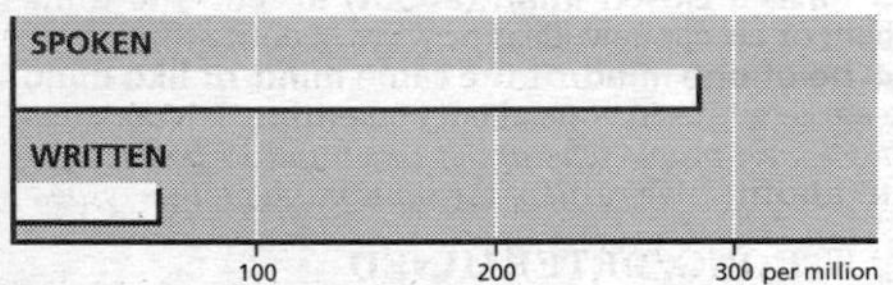


Based on the British National Corpus and the Longman Lancaster Corpus

This graph shows that the verb **mind** is much more common in spoken English than in written English. This is because it is used in a lot of common spoken phrases.

**mind (v) SPOKEN PHRASES**

**9 never mind** **a)** used to say that something is not important or serious, especially when someone seems worried or is saying sorry to you: *"I'm afraid I've broken the chair." "Never mind, I can easily get it fixed."* **b)** used to emphasize that something is impossible, because even something that should be easier is also impossible: *I can't even explain the problem to my colleagues, never mind anyone else.* **c)** used to emphasize that something else is also true, apart from the thing you have just mentioned: *Cars kill thousands of people each year, never mind the damage they do to the environment.* **d)** used to tell someone not to do something now, because it is less important than something else, or because you will do it later yourself: **never mind sth** *Never mind the dishes – I'll do them later.*| **never mind doing something** *Never mind looking at the boys, we're supposed to be playing tennis.* **e)** used to say that you do not really care about something because it is much less important than something else: *I want the best , never mind the cost!*|[+ **about**]|*Let's get the economy right, never mind about the unemployed.*
**10 never you mind** *especially BrE* used to tell someone that you are not going to tell them something because it is private or secret: *"What's that you were saying to dad?" "Never you mind."*
**11 mind you** *BrE* used to say something that is the opposite of what you have just said, or that emphasizes it: *The photos look very old. Mind you, she did take them over 20 years ago.*
**12 would/do you mind** used to ask someone something politely: **would/do you mind doing sth** *Would you mind opening the window please?*|**would/do you mind if** *Do you mind if I smoke?*
**13 I wouldn't mind** used to politely ask for something: *I wouldn't mind a drink if you have one.*
**14 do you mind!** used when you are annoyed at something that someone has done: *Do you mind! I just washed that floor!*
**15 if you don't mind** **a)** used when checking that someone is willing to do something or let you do something: *I'll come along if you don't mind.* **b)** used, sometimes rudely, when you do not want to do something that someone has suggested: *I can handle this myself, if you don't mind!*
**16 if you don't mind my saying so** used when you want to give advice or an opinion that you think might offend somene: *I don't think you should ever hit a child, if you don't mind my saying so.*
**17 mind!** *BrE* used to warn someone to be careful because something bad or dangerous might happen: *Mind! That's my foot you're standing on.*|**mind sth** *Mind the window! It's only just been repaired.*|**mind sb/sth doesn't do sth** *Mind you don't fall off the chair.*|**mind how/where/who etc** *Mind where you're walking. The floor's a bit slippery.*|**mind your head/back/fingers etc** *Mind your head. The ceiling's very low in here.*
**18 mind out!** *BrE* **a)** used to warn someone that they are in danger: *Mind out! There's a car coming!* **b)** used to ask someone to move so that you can pass them: *Mind out! You're sitting right in front of the door.*
**19 don't mind me** used to tell someone not to pay any attention to you: *Just get on with your work, don't mind us!*
**20 I don't mind if I do** *humorous* used when politely accepting something such as food or drink that has been offered to you: *"Would you like a cigar?" "I don't mind if I do, thank you."*

**mind-bend·ing** /ˈ· ˌ··/ *adj informal* difficult to understand: *Filing letters is not exactly a mind-bending task.*

**mind-blow·ing** /ˈ· ˌ··/ *adj informal* very exciting, shocking, or strange: *The astronauts had mind-blowing views of planet Earth.*|*a mind-blowing experience* —see also **it blows your mind** (BLOW[1] (17))

**mind-bog·gling** /ˈ· ˌ··/ *adj informal* difficult to imagine and very big, strange, or complicated: *He's made a mind-boggling profit with his investments.*

**mind·ed** /ˈmaɪndᵻd/ *adj* **1 serious-minded/evil-minded etc** having a particular attitude or way of thinking: *a very serious-minded girl who studies hard* **2 safety-minded/efficiency-minded etc** believing in the importance of safety etc: *People need to be more safety-minded in the home.* **3 be minded to do sth** *formal* to want or intend to do something: *He has enough money to travel, if he were minded to do so.*

**mind·er** /ˈmaɪndə‖-ər/ *n* [C] *BrE* **1** someone who is employed to protect another person **2 machine minder, child minder etc** a person whose job it is to look after a machine, a child etc

**mind·ful** /ˈmaɪndfəl/ *adj* **mindful of** behaving in a way that shows you remember a particular rule or fact: *Mindful of the guide's warning they returned before dark.*

**mind·less** /ˈmaɪndləs/ *adj* **1** completely stupid and without any purpose: *mindless vandals* **2** mindless work or a mindless activity can be done without intelligence or thought: *a completely mindless task* | *mindless game shows on TV* **3 mindless of** not paying attention to or thinking about danger or warnings; HEEDLESS —**mindlessly** *adv* —**mindlessness** *n* [U]

**mind read·er** /ˈ·,··/ *n* [C] *often humorous* someone who knows what someone else is thinking without being told

**mind·set** /ˈmaɪndset/ *n* [C] someone's way of thinking about things, which is often difficult to change: *You need a logical mindset to develop computer programs.*

S1 **mine¹** /maɪn/ *pron* [possessive form of 'I'] the one or the ones that belong to me: *"Whose is this coat?" "It must be mine."* | *Can I borrow your CD player? Mine's broken.* | **a friend/cousin etc of mine** *an old teacher of mine*

S2 W3 **mine²** *n* [C] **1** a deep hole or series of holes under the ground that are dug in order to find coal, gold, tin etc: **coal/gold/copper mine etc**: *He works in the coal mines.* —compare QUARRY¹ (1) **2** a type of bomb that is hidden just below the ground or under water and that explodes when it is touched **3 a mine of information/gossip etc** someone who knows a lot about something or a book that tells you a lot about a subject **4** a passage dug beneath the place where an enemy army is

**mine³** *v* **mined, mining 1** [I,T] to make holes or passages under the ground in order to take out coal, gold etc, or to take coal, gold etc from these holes: [+ **for**] *mining for coal* **2** [T often passive] to hide bombs in the sea or under the ground: *All the roads leading to the city had been mined.* **3** [T] to dig a passage under the ground beneath the place where an enemy army is

**mine⁴** *determiner old use* a way of saying 'my', before a vowel sound or 'h', or after a noun: *mine host*

**mine·field** /ˈmaɪnfiːld/ *n* **1** [C] an area where a lot of bombs have been placed just below the ground or under water **2** [singular] something that has hidden dangers or difficulties: *The legal system is a minefield for the ordinary person.*

**min·er** /ˈmaɪnə‖-ər/ *n* [C] someone who works under the ground in a MINE² (1) taking out coal, gold etc: *a coal miner*

**min·e·ral** /ˈmɪnərəl/ *n* [C] **1** a substance that is formed naturally in the earth, especially a solid substance such as coal, salt, stone, or gold: *an area rich in minerals* **2** a natural substance such as CALCIUM or iron that is present in some foods and that is important for good health **3** *BrE formal* a SOFT DRINK

**min·e·ral·o·gy** /ˌmɪnəˈrælədʒi‖-ˈrɑː-, -ˈræ-/ *n* [U] the scientific study of minerals —**mineralogist** *n* [C]

**mineral wa·ter** /ˈ··· ˌ··/ *n* [C,U] water that comes from under the ground and contains minerals

**min·e·stro·ne** /ˌmɪnᵻˈstrəʊni‖-ˈstroʊ-/ *n* [U] an Italian soup containing vegetables and small pieces of PASTA

**mine·sweep·er** /ˈmaɪnˌswiːpə‖-ər/ *n* [C] a ship that has equipment for removing bombs from under water —**minesweeping** *n* [U]

**min·gle** /ˈmɪŋgəl/ *v* **mingled, mingling 1** [I,T] if two feelings, sounds, smells etc mingle or are mingled, they combine with each other but can still be recognized separately: [+ **with**] *excitement mingled with nervousness.* | [+ **together**] *The smell of sweat and stale cigar smoke mingled together.* **2** [I] to mix with different groups of people at a social occasion and talk to people that you do not already know; CIRCULATE (4): *The cast and crew mingled as everyone started to relax.* —**mingled** *adj*

**min·gy** /ˈmɪndʒi/ *adj BrE informal* not at all generous; STINGY: *Don't be so mingy.* | *mingy portions*

**min·i** /ˈmɪni/ *n* [C] **1** a very short skirt or dress; MINISKIRT **2** a type of very small British car

**min·i-** /mɪni/ *prefix* very small compared with others of its kind: *a minibreak* (=a short holiday) | *a miniskirt* (=very short) —compare MICRO-

**min·ia·ture¹** /ˈmɪnᵻtʃə‖ˈmɪniətʃər/ *adj* **miniature camera/railway/garden etc** a camera etc that is much smaller than a normal one

**miniature²** *n* **1 in miniature** exactly like something or someone but much smaller: *She's her mother in miniature.* **2** [C] a very small painting, usually of a person: *a collection of Victorian miniatures*

**miniature golf** /ˌ··· ˈ·‖ˌ···· ˈ·/ *n* [U] *AmE* a GOLF game, played for fun, in which you hit a small ball through passages, over bridges and small hills etc; CRAZY GOLF *BrE*

**min·ia·tur·ist** /ˈmɪnᵻtʃərᵻst‖ˈmɪniətʃʊ-/ *n* [C] someone who paints very small pictures

**min·ia·tur·ize** also **-ise** *BrE* /ˈmɪnᵻtʃəraɪz‖ˈmɪniə-/ *v* [T] to make something in a very small size —**miniaturized** *adj* —**miniaturization** /ˌmɪnᵻtʃəraɪˈzeɪʃən‖ˌmɪniətʃərə-/ *n* [U]

**min·i·bus** /ˈmɪnibʌs/ *n* [C] *especially BrE* a small bus with seats for six to twelve people

**min·i·cab** /ˈmɪnikæb/ *n* [C] *BrE* a taxi that you can call for on the telephone but cannot stop in the street

**min·i·com·put·er** /ˈmɪnikəmˌpjuːtə‖-ər/ *n* [C] a computer that is larger than a PERSONAL COMPUTER and smaller than a MAINFRAME, used by businesses and other large organizations

**min·im** /ˈmɪnᵻm/ *n* [C] *BrE* a musical note that continues for half the length of a SEMIBREVE; HALF NOTE *AmE* —see picture at MUSIC

**min·i·mal** /ˈmɪnᵻməl/ *adj* very small in degree or amount, especially the smallest degree or amount possible: *The storm caused only minimal damage.* —**minimally** *adv*

**min·i·mal·is·m** /ˈmɪnᵻməlɪzəm/ *n* [U] art, music etc that uses very simple ideas or patterns that are repeated often —**minimalist** *n* [C]

**min·i·mart** /ˈmɪnimɑːt‖-mɑːrt/ *n* [C] *especially AmE* a small shop that stays open very late and that sells food, cigarettes etc

**min·i·mize** **-ise** *BrE* /ˈmɪnᵻmaɪz/ *v* [T] **1** to reduce something to the smallest possible amount or degree: *We need to minimize disruptions to the schedule.* **2** to make something seem less serious or important than it really is: *a tendency to minimize the problem of sexual harassment in the workplace* —compare MAXIMIZE

**min·i·mum¹** /ˈmɪnᵻməm/ *adj* [only before noun] the minimum number, degree, or amount of something is the smallest or least that is possible, allowed, or needed: *The minimum requirements for the job are a degree and two years' experience.* | *a minimum price* —compare MAXIMUM¹ S2 W3

**minimum²** *n* [singular] **1** the smallest amount, number, or degree of something that is possible, allowed, or needed: [+ **of**] *Looking after a horse costs a minimum of £2000 a year.* | **absolute/bare minimum** (=the very least amount or number): *Staffing levels at the hospital have been slashed to an absolute minimum.* **2 keep/reduce sth to a minimum** to limit something, especially something bad, to the smallest amount or degree possible: *The school manages to keep bullying to a minimum.*

**minimum se·cu·ri·ty pris·on** /ˌ··· ·ˈ··· ˌ··/ *n* [C] *AmE* a prison that does not restrict prisoners' freedom as much as ordinary prisons; OPEN PRISON *BrE*

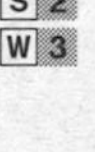


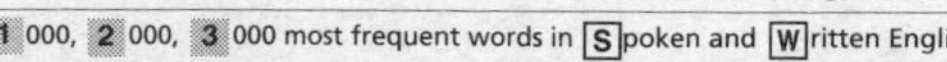

**minimum wage** /ˌ··· ˈ·/ *n* [C singular] the lowest amount of money that can legally be paid per hour to a worker

**min·ing** /ˈmaɪnɪŋ/ *n* [U] the action or industry of getting minerals out of the earth —see also STRIP MINING

**min·ion** /ˈmɪnjən/ *n* [C] a very unimportant person in an organization, who just obeys other people's orders

**mini-round·a·bout** /ˌ·· ˈ···/ *n* [C] *BrE* a white circle painted on the road that vehicles must drive around at a place where several roads meet

**min·is·cule** /ˈmɪnɪskjuːl/ *adj* another spelling of MINUSCULE

**min·i·se·ries** /ˈmɪniˌsɪəriz‖-ˌsɪr-/ *n* [C] a television film that is divided into several parts, which are usually shown once a night for several days

**min·i·skirt** /ˈmɪniskɜːt‖-skɜːrt/ *n* [C] a very short skirt; MINI

S1 W1 **min·is·ter¹** /ˈmɪnɪstə‖-ər/ *n* [C] **1** a politician who is a member of the government and is in charge of a government department, in Britain and some other countries: [+ **of/for**] *the Minister of Education* —see also PRIME MINISTER **2** a priest in some Christian churches —see PRIEST (USAGE) **3** someone whose job is to represent their country in another country, but who is lower in rank than an AMBASSADOR **4** a MINISTER OF STATE

**minister²** *v*

**minister to** sb/sth *phr v* [T] *formal* to give help to someone who needs it: *ministering to the sick*

**min·is·ter·i·al** /ˌmɪnɪˈstɪəriəl◂‖-stɪr-/ *adj* connected with or relating to a government minister or a minister in the Christian church: *ministerial duties*

**minister of state** /ˌ···· ˈ·/ *n* [C] a member of the government in Britain who has an important job in a government department but is not the chief minister

**min·i·stra·tions** /ˌmɪnɪˈstreɪʃənz/ *n* [plural] *formal* the giving of help and service, especially to people who are ill or who need the help of a priest

W2 **min·is·try** /ˈmɪnɪstri/ *n* **1** [C] a government department that is responsible for one of the areas of government work, such as education, health, or defence: [+ **of**] *the Ministry of Agriculture* **2 the ministry** the profession of being a church leader, especially in the Protestant church: *James wants to join the ministry.* **3** [U] the work done by a priest or other religious person: *the ministry of Jesus*

**min·i·van** /ˈmɪnivæn/ *n* [C] *AmE* a large car for up to eight people

**mink** /mɪŋk/ *n plural* **mink** [C,U] a very valuable brown fur used to make coats, hats etc, or the animal from which this fur is obtained

**min·now** /ˈmɪnəʊ‖-noʊ/ *n* [C] **1** a very small fish that lives in rivers and lakes **2** an organization, company etc that is small and unimportant: *one of the minnows of the computer industry*

S2 W2 **mi·nor¹** /ˈmaɪnə‖-ər/ *adj* **1** small and not very important or serious, especially when compared with other things: *We have made some minor changes to the program.* | *an issue of minor importance* | **minor illness/operation/injury** (=one that is not very serious or dangerous) *minor head injuries* —opposite MAJOR¹ (1) **2** based on a musical SCALE¹ (8) in which the third note of the related MAJOR¹ (4) scale has been lowered by a SEMITONE: *a minor key* | *a symphony in D minor*

**minor²** *n* [C] **1** *law* someone who is below the age at which they are considered by law to be an adult and completely responsible for their actions **2** *especially AmE* a subject studied at university that has less importance and needs less work than your MAJOR (=main subject) **3 the minors** the MINOR LEAGUES

**minor³** *v*

**minor in** sth *phr v* [T] *especially AmE* to study an additional subject at university that is less important than your main subject —opposite MAJOR³

S3 W2 **mi·nor·i·ty¹** /maɪˈnɒrɪti‖məˈnɔː-, mɪˈnɑː-/ *n* **1** [singular] a small group of people or things within a much larger group: *Gaelic is still spoken in Ireland by a tiny minority.* | [+ **of**] *It's only in a minority of cases that the illness is fatal.* | [also + plural verb *BrE*] *Only a minority support these new laws.* **2** [C usually plural] **a)** a group of people in a country who are different from the rest in race or religion: *People from ethnic minorities often face prejudice and discrimination.* **b)** *AmE* someone who belongs to a group like this: *hiring minorities and women* **3 be in the/a minority** to form less than half of a larger group: *Boys are very much in the minority at the dance class.* **4 be in a minority of one** to be the only person in a group who has a particular opinion **5** [U] *law* the period of time when someone is below the age at which they become legally responsible for their actions —opposite MAJORITY

**minority²** *adj* [only before noun] relating to people who form less than half of a larger group of people: *a series of television programmes designed to appeal to minority interests* | *a minority language*

**minority gov·ern·ment** /·ˌ··· ˈ···/ *n* [C] a government that does not have enough politicians in parliament to control it without the support of other parties

**minority lead·er** /·ˈ··· ˌ··/ *n* [C] *AmE* a leader of the political party that has fewer politicians in the law-making institutions than the leading party —compare MAJORITY LEADER

**minor league** /ˈ·· ·/ *n* [C] **1** a group of professional BASEBALL teams in the US that are not as good as the teams in the MAJOR LEAGUES **2** *informal* small businesses and organizations, rather than large powerful ones —**minor-league** *adj*

**min·ster** /ˈmɪnstə‖-ər/ *n* [C] *BrE* a large or important church: *York Minster*

**min·strel** /ˈmɪnstrəl/ *n* [C] **1** a singer or musician in the Middle Ages **2** one of a group of singers and dancers who performed in popular shows in the 1920s

**mint¹** /mɪnt/ *n* **1** [C,U] a sweet that tastes of PEPPERMINT (=a strong tasting substance obtained from a plant) **2** [U] a small plant with leaves that have a fresh smell and taste and are used in cooking **3 in mint condition** looking new and in perfect condition: *A copy in mint condition would fetch about £2,000.* **4 a mint** *informal* a large amount of money: *Lynn won a mint in that competition!* **5** [C] a place where coins are officially made

**mint²** *v* [T] **1** to make a coin **2** to invent new words, phrases, or ideas: *a recently minted phrase*

**mint ju·lep** /ˌ· ˈ··/ *n* [C] *AmE* a drink in which alcohol and sugar are mixed with ice and mint leaves are added

**mint·y** /ˈmɪnti/ *adj* tasting or smelling of mint

**min·u·et** /ˌmɪnjuˈet/ *n* [C] a slow graceful dance of the 17th and 18th century, or a piece of music for this dance

**mi·nus¹** /ˈmaɪnəs/ *prep* **1** used in mathematics when you SUBTRACT one number from another: *17 minus 5 is 12 (17–5 = 12)* **2** minus 5, 20 etc less than zero, especially less than zero degrees in temperature: *At night the temperature can go as low as minus 30.* **3** *informal* without something that would normally be there: *He came back minus a couple of front teeth.* —opposite PLUS³

**minus²** *n* [C] **1** also **minus sign** a sign (–) showing that a number is less than zero, or that the second of two numbers is to be subtracted (SUBTRACT) from the first **2** something that is a disadvantage because it makes a situation unpleasant: *There are both pluses and minuses to living in a big city.* —opposite PLUS¹

**minus³** *adj* **1 minus point/factor** *BrE* a quality that makes something or someone seem less good: *Kirsten's very keen, but her inexperience is a definite minus factor.* **2 A minus, B minus etc** a mark used in a system of marking students' work, A minus is lower than A, but higher than B plus —opposite PLUS²

**min·us·cule, miniscule** /ˈmɪnɪskjuːl/ *adj* extremely small: *a minuscule amount* | *Her office is miniscule.*

S1 W1 **min·ute¹** /ˈmɪnɪ̟t/ *n* [C]
**1 ▶ TIME ◀** one of the 60 parts into which an hour is divided: *It takes me ten minutes to walk to work.* | *The train arrived at four minutes past eight.*
**2 at the last minute** at the last possible time, just before it is too late: *Clare changed her mind at the last minute and came with us.* —see also LAST-MINUTE
**3 by the minute** also **every minute, minute by minute** *spoken* increasingly as time passes: *"Do you still feel sick?" "No, I'm feeling better by the minute."*
**4 love/enjoy/hate etc every minute of** *informal* to love, enjoy etc all of something: *I went camping for a week and enjoyed every minute of it.*
**5 within minutes** very soon after something has happened: *The ambulance was there within minutes.*
**6 ▶ MEETING ◀ minutes** [plural] an official written record of what is said and decided at a meeting
**7 ▶ NOTE ON A REPORT ◀** a short official note on or about a document
**8 ▶ MATHEMATICS ◀** *technical* one of the 60 parts into which a degree of angle is divided —see also UP-TO-THE-MINUTE

Frequencies of the noun **minute** in spoken and written English.

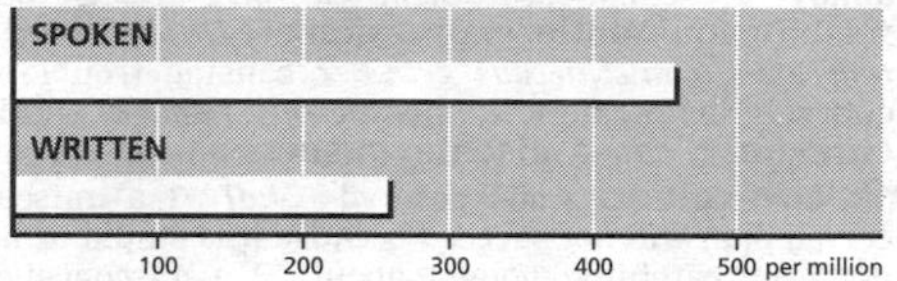


Based on the British National Corpus and the Longman Lancaster Corpus

This graph shows that the noun **minute** is much more common in spoken English than in written English. This is because it is used in a lot of common spoken phrases.

**minute (n)) SPOKEN PHRASES**

**9 a minute** a very short period of time; MOMENT (2): *He was there a minute ago.* | *Stay there a minute.*
**10 in a minute** very soon: *All right, I'll do it in a minute.* | *Mr Gregson will be with you in a minute.*
**11 wait a minute/just a minute/hold on a minute/hang on a minute a)** used to tell someone you want them to wait for a short time while you do or say something else: *Wait a minute, I have to turn off the cooker.* | *Just a minute, I'll see if she's in.* **b)** used to tell someone to stop speaking or doing something for a short time because they have said or done something wrong: *Hold on a minute! That can't be right.*
**12 any minute now** used to say that something will happen extremely soon: *We're expecting them any minute now.*
**13 have you got a minute?** *BrE* **do you have a minute?** *AmE* used to ask someone if it is convenient for you to talk to them for a short time: *Have you got a minute? I've got a problem.*
**14 one minute a)** used to say that a situation suddenly changes: *One minute they're madly in love and the next they've split up again.* **b)** used to ask someone to wait for a short time while you do something else: *One minute Stephen, let me finish this.*
**15 the minute sb does sth** as soon as someone does something: *Tell him I need to see him the minute he arrives.*
**16 the next minute** immediately afterwards: *I put down the phone and the next minute it rang again.*
**17 not think/believe/etc for one minute** used to say that you certainly do not think something, believe something etc: *I don't think for one minute that he'll do it but I have to ask.*
**18 this minute** used to tell someone, often angrily, to do something immediately: *Johnny! Get inside, this minute!*

**mi·nute²** /maɪˈnjuːt‖-ˈnuːt/ *adj* **1** extremely small: *There's been a minute improvement in sales figures.* | *Her handwriting is minute.* **2** paying careful attention to the smallest details: *a minute examination of the rock* | **in minute detail** *He explained the plan in minute detail.* —**minutely** *adv* —**minuteness** *n* [U]

**min·ute³** /ˈmɪnɪ̟t/ *v* [T] *especially BrE* to make an official note of something in the record of a meeting

**minute hand** /ˈmɪnɪ̟t hænd/ *n* [C] the long thin piece of metal that points to the minutes on a clock or watch

**min·ute·man** /ˈmɪnɪ̟tmæn/ *n* [C] *AmE* one of a group of men in the past who were not official soldiers but who were ready to fight at any time

**mi·nu·ti·ae** /maɪˈnjuːʃiaɪ, mɪ̟-‖mɪ̟ˈnuː-/ *n* [plural] very small and exact but unimportant details

**minx** /mɪŋks/ *n* [C] *old-fashioned* a girl who is not RESPECTFUL and is very good at getting what she wants

**mips** /mɪps/ *n* [plural] *technical* millions of instructions per second; a way of measuring how fast a computer works

**mir·a·cle** /ˈmɪrəkəl/ *n* [C] **1** something lucky that you did not expect to happen or did not think was possible: *By some miracle, we managed to catch the plane.* | **it is a miracle (that)** *It's a miracle you weren't killed!* **2** an action or event that is impossible according to the ordinary laws of nature, believed to be done by God: *the miracles of Jesus* **3 miracle cure/drug** a very effective medical treatment that cures even serious diseases **4 work/perform miracles** to have a very good effect or result: *Maybe you should try yoga – it worked miracles for me.* **5 a miracle of engineering/design etc** something that is produced or invented that is a very impressive example of a particular quality or skill: *This new electronic notebook is a miracle of miniaturization.*

**mi·rac·u·lous** /mɪˈrækjɪ̟ləs/ *adj* completely unexpected and usually resulting from extreme good luck: **miraculous recovery/escape/improvement** *It was thought she only had a month to live but she made a miraculous recovery.* —**miraculously** *adv*

**mi·rage** /ˈmɪrɑːʒ‖mɪ̟ˈrɑːʒ/ *n* [C] **1** a strange effect caused by hot air in a desert, in which you think you can see objects when they are not actually there **2** a dream, hope, or wish that cannot come true

**mire¹** /maɪə‖maɪr/ *n* [U] *literary* **1 drag sb's name through the mire** to talk about someone publicly in a way that brings shame on them **2 in/into the mire** more and more deeply involved in problems: *The Party sank deeper into the mire of conflict.* **3** deep mud

**mire²** *v* **be mired (down) in** *especially literary* **a)** to be stuck in deep mud: *The plane's wheels were deeply mired in waterlogged ground.* **b)** to be in a very difficult situation

**mir·ror¹** /ˈmɪrə‖-ər/ *n* [C] **1** a piece of special flat glass that you can look at and see yourself in: *Check your rear-view and side mirrors before you drive away* —see picture on page 409. **2 a mirror of** something that gives a clear idea of what something else is like: *We believe the polls are an accurate mirror of public opinion.* S3 W3

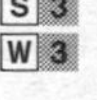

**mirror²** *v* [T] **1** if something mirrors a situation, fact, belief etc, it is very similar to it and gives a clear idea of what it is like: *The discussion mirrored the general attitudes prevalent in the local area.* **2** to be very similar to something or a copy of it: *Victor's expression mirrored her own, both of them staring in amazement.*

**mirror im·age** /ˈ·· ˌ··/ *n* [C + **of**] **1** an image of something in which the right side appears on the left, and the left side appears on the right **2** something that is either very similar to something else or is the complete opposite of it: *Davy's messiness is the mirror image of his sister Dora's neatness.*

**mirth** /mɜːθ‖mɜːrθ/ *n* [U] *literary* happiness and laughter: *Stifled laughter and cries of suppressed mirth issued from the next room.* —**mirthful** *adj* —**mirthfully** *adv*

**mirth·less** /ˈmɜːθləs‖ˈmɜːrθ-/ *adj literary* mirthless laughter or a mirthless smile does not seem to be caused by real amusement or happiness: *Now it's your turn, he said with a mirthless grin.* —**mirthlessly** *adv*

M

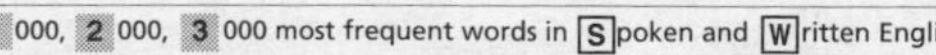

**mis-** /mɪs/ *prefix* **1** bad or badly: *misfortune* (=bad luck)|*He's been misbehaving.* **2** wrong or wrongly: *a miscalculation*|*I misunderstood what you said.* **3** shows an opposite or the lack of something: *mistrust*

**mis·ad·ven·ture** /ˌmɪsədˈventʃə‖-ər/ *n* [C,U] **1 death by misadventure** *BrE law* the official name for an accidental death **2** *literary* bad luck or an accident

**mis·al·li·ance** /ˌmɪsəˈlaɪəns/ *n* [C] *formal* a situation in which two people or organizations have mistakenly agreed to work together, marry each other etc, but are not suitable for each other

**mis·an·thro·pist** /mɪsˈænθrəpɪst/ also **misanthrope** /ˈmɪsənθrəʊp‖-θroʊp/ *n* [C] *formal* someone who dislikes other people and prefers to be alone —**misanthropic** /ˌmɪsənˈθrɒpɪk◂‖-ˈθrɑː-/ *adj* —**misanthropy** *n* [U]

**mis·ap·ply** /ˌmɪsəˈplaɪ/ *v* [T] to use a principle, rule etc incorrectly or for a wrong purpose —**misapplication** /ˌmɪsæplɪˈkeɪʃən/ *n* [U + **of**]: *a misapplication of the law*

**mis·ap·pre·hend** /ˌmɪsæprɪˈhend/ *v* [T] *formal* to understand something wrongly

**mis·ap·pre·hen·sion** /ˌmɪsæprɪˈhenʃən/ *n* [C] *formal* a mistaken belief or a wrong understanding of something: **(labour) under a misapprehension** (=believe something is true when in fact it is not) *I wonder if others are under the misapprehension that screwdrivers used to test electricity are infallible.*

**mis·ap·pro·pri·ate** /ˌmɪsəˈprəʊprieɪt‖-ˈproʊ-/ *v* [T] *formal* to dishonestly take something that you have been trusted to keep safe, for example to take money that belongs to your employer; EMBEZZLE —**misappropriation** /ˌmɪsəprəʊpriˈeɪʃən‖-proʊ-/ *n* [U + **of**]: *the misappropriation of treasury funds*

**mis·be·got·ten** /ˌmɪsbɪˈgɒtn◂‖-ˈgɑː-/ *adj* [only before noun] **1** a misbegotten plan, idea, etc is not likely to succeed because it is badly planned or not sensible **2** *formal or humorous* a misbegotten person is completely stupid or useless: *You misbegotten fool!*

**mis·be·have** /ˌmɪsbɪˈheɪv/ *v* [I] also **misbehave yourself** to behave badly, and cause trouble or annoy people: *William has been misbehaving himself at school.*

**mis·be·ha·viour** *BrE* **misbehavior** *AmE* /ˌmɪsbɪˈheɪvjə‖-ər/ *n* [U] behaviour that is not acceptable to other people: *Even the most minor forms of misbehaviour were punished.*

**mis·cal·cu·late** /ˌmɪsˈkælkjʊleɪt/ *v* [I,T] **1** to make a mistake when deciding how long something will take to do, how much money you will need etc: *The contractor miscalculated the costs of rebuilding.* **2** to make a wrong judgment about a situation

**mis·cal·cu·la·tion** /mɪsˌkælkjʊˈleɪʃən/ *n* [C] **1** a mistake made in deciding how long something will take to do, how much money you will need etc **2** a wrong judgment about a situation

**mis·car·riage** /ˌmɪsˈkærɪdʒ, ˈmɪskærɪdʒ/ *n* [C,U] the act of accidentally giving birth too early for the baby to live: **have a miscarriage** *Unfortunately, she had a miscarriage at four months.* —compare ABORTION, STILLBIRTH

**miscarriage of jus·tice** /ˌ·· ˈ··, ˌ··· ˈ··/ *n* [C,U] a situation in which someone is wrongly punished by a court of law for something they did not do

**mis·car·ry** /mɪsˈkæri/ *v* [I] **1** to give birth to a baby too early for it to live —compare ABORT (3) **2** *formal* if a plan miscarries, it is not successful

**mis·cast** /ˌmɪsˈkɑːst‖-ˈkæst/ *v past tense and past participle* **miscast** [T usually passive] to choose an unsuitable actor to play a particular character in a play or film

**mis·ce·ge·na·tion** /ˌmɪsɪdʒɪˈneɪʃən‖-sedʒ-/ *n* [U] *formal* the act of having children by parents of different races, especially when one of the parents is white

**mis·cel·la·ne·ous** /ˌmɪsəˈleɪniəs◂/ *adj* [only before noun] made up of many different things or people who do not seem to be connected with each other: *a miscellaneous assortment of books*|*miscellaneous expenses*

**mis·cel·la·ny** /mɪˈseləni‖ˈmɪsɪleɪni/ *n* [C] a collection of different things: *a miscellany of American short stories*

**mis·chance** /ˌmɪsˈtʃɑːns‖-ˈtʃæns/ *n* [C,U] bad luck, or a situation that results from bad luck: *As mischance would have it we ran into Sue – just the person we wanted to avoid.*

**mis·chief** /ˈmɪstʃɪf/ *n* **1** [U] bad behaviour, especially by children, that causes trouble or damage, but no serious harm: **get into mischief** (=behave in a way that causes trouble) *Now run along, and don't get into mischief.*|**be up to mischief** (=plan or do something you know you should not do) *If you can't see Nick, you can be sure he's up to some mischief.*|**keep (sb) out of mischief** *They've got enough toys to keep them out of mischief for a while.* **2** [U] enjoyment of playing tricks on people or embarrassing them: *Helena's eyes flashed with amusement and mischief.* **3 make mischief (between)** *informal* to deliberately cause quarrels or unfriendly feelings between people **4 do yourself a mischief** *BrE humorous* to injure yourself slightly: *If you try to lift that box, you'll do yourself a mischief.* **5** [U] *formal* damage or harm that may or may not have been intended

**mischief-mak·er** /ˈ·· ˌ··/ *n* [C] someone who deliberately causes trouble or quarrels

**mis·chie·vous** /ˈmɪstʃɪvəs/ *adj* **1** liking to have fun, especially by playing tricks on people or doing things to annoy or embarrass them: *a mischievous boy*|**mischievous smile/expression etc** *Gabby looked at him with a mischievous grin.* **2** causing trouble or quarrels deliberately: *a mischievous remark* —**mischievously** *adv* —**mischievousness** *n* [U]

**mis·con·ceived** /ˌmɪskənˈsiːvd◂/ *adj* **1** a misconceived plan will not succeed because it is stupid or has not been carefully thought about **2** a misconceived idea is based on a wrong understanding of something: *a misconceived notion of what acting really involves*

**mis·con·cep·tion** /ˌmɪskənˈsepʃən/ *n* [C,U] an idea which is wrong or untrue, but which people believe because they do not understand it properly: [+ **that**] *the misconception that unemployment can be cured by government intervention*|**a popular/common misconception** (=a wrong idea that a lot of people believe) *It is a popular misconception that eye problems result in headaches.*

**mis·con·duct** /ˌmɪsˈkɒndʌkt‖-ˈkɑːn-/ *n* [U] *formal* bad or dishonest behaviour by someone in a position of authority or trust: *allegations of misconduct by council officials*|**gross misconduct** (=very serious misconduct) *One of the doctors had been dismissed for gross professional misconduct.*

**mis·con·struc·tion** /ˌmɪskənˈstrʌkʃən/ *n* [C,U] *formal* an incorrect or mistaken understanding of something: **open to misconstruction** (=easy to misunderstand) *A law must be worded so carefully that it is not open to misconstruction.*

**mis·con·strue** /ˌmɪskənˈstruː/ *v* [T] *formal* to misunderstand something that someone has said or done

**mis·count** /ˌmɪsˈkaʊnt/ *v* [I,T] to count wrongly: *Oops! Sorry, I miscounted – we need ten copies, not nine.*

**mis·cre·ant** /ˈmɪskriənt/ *n* [C] *old use* a bad person who causes trouble, hurts people etc

**mis·deed** /ˌmɪsˈdiːd/ *n* [C] *formal* a wrong or illegal action: *No one ever suspected the seriousness of his misdeeds.*

**mis·de·mea·nour** *BrE*, **misdemeanor** *AmE* /ˌmɪsdɪˈmiːnə‖-ər/ *n* [C] **1** *formal* a bad or unacceptable action that is not very serious: *Alfred beat his children for even the smallest misdemeanour.* **2** *law* a crime that is not very serious —compare FELONY

**mis·di·ag·nose** /ˌmɪsdaɪəgˈnəʊz‖-ˈnoʊs/ *v* [T usually passive] to give an incorrect explanation of an illness, a problem in a machine etc

**mis·di·rect** /ˌmɪsdɪˈrekt/ *v* [T usually passive] **1** *formal* to use your efforts, energy or abilities in a wrong or unsuitable way: *We believe their efforts to prevent animal testing are misdirected.* **2** if a judge misdirects a JURY (=the group of people who decide a legal case), he or she gives them incorrect information about the law **3** *formal* to send someone or something to the wrong place —**misdirection** /-'rekʃən/ *n* [U]

**mise-en-scène** /ˌmiːz ɒn 'sen,-'seɪn‖-ɑːn-/ *n* [C] *French* **1** *technical* the arrangement of furniture and other objects used on the stage in a theatre play **2** *formal* the environment in which an event takes place

**mi·ser** /'maɪzə‖-ər/ *n* [C] someone who hates spending money and likes saving it: *A typical miser, he hid his money in the house in various places.*

**mis·e·ra·ble** /'mɪzərəbəl/ *adj* **1** extremely unhappy, for example because you feel lonely, cold, or badly treated: *You're making my life miserable!* | *There's nothing like a bad cold to make you feel miserable.* | *You look miserable. What's up?* **2** always unhappy, dissatisfied, or complaining: *He's a miserable old devil.* **3** [usually before noun] making you feel very unhappy, uncomfortable etc: *They endured hours of backbreaking work in miserable conditions.* **4** [only before noun] very bad in quality, or very small in amount: *I can hardly afford the rent on my miserable income.* —**miserably** *adv*: *miserably cold and wet*

**mi·ser·ly** /'maɪzəli‖-zər-/ *adj* **1** a miserly amount, salary etc is one that is much too small: *a miserly 4% pay rise* **2** a miserly person is one who hates spending money —**miserliness** *n* [U]

S3 **mis·e·ry** /'mɪzəri/ *n* **1** [C,U] great suffering or discomfort, caused for example by being very poor or very sick: *the awful shanty-towns, so full of human misery* | [+ **of**] *The cold increased the misery of the retreating army.* **2** [C,U] great unhappiness: *Her face was a picture of misery.* **3 make sb's life a misery** to cause so much trouble for someone that they cannot enjoy their life: *Competitive mothers can make their daughters' lives a misery.* **4 put sth/sb out of their misery a)** *informal* to make someone stop feeling worried, especially by telling them something they are waiting to hear: *Go on, put them out of their misery and announce the winner.* **b)** to kill an animal in order to end its suffering **5** [C] *BrE spoken* someone who is always complaining and never enjoys anything: *Don't be such a misery.* | **misery guts** (=a name for someone who is like this) *You don't want to be like old misery guts over there.*

**mis·field** /ˌmɪs'fiːld/ *v* [I,T] to make a mistake in catching or throwing the ball in some ball games, such as cricket —**misfield** /'mɪsfiːld/ *n* [C]

**mis·fire** /ˌmɪs'faɪə‖-'faɪr/ *v* [I] **1** if a plan or joke misfires, it does not have the result that you intended **2** if an engine misfires, the petrol mixture does not burn at the right time **3** if a gun misfires, the bullet does not come out —**misfire** /'mɪsfaɪə‖-faɪr/ *n* [C]

**mis·fit** /'mɪs,fɪt/ *n* [C] someone who does not seem to belong in a place because they are very different from the other people there: *a social misfit*

**mis·for·tune** /mɪs'fɔːtʃən‖-ɔːr-/ *n* [C,U] very bad luck, or something that happens to you as a result of bad luck: *It seems the banks always profit from farmers' misfortunes.* | **have the misfortune to do sth** *The French soldiers had the misfortune to be caught in the crossfire.*

**mis·giv·ing** /ˌmɪs'gɪvɪŋ/ *n* [C,U] a feeling of doubt, distrust, or fear about what might happen or about whether something is right: *She eyed Bert's pistol with misgiving.* | **have deep/serious misgivings** *Opponents of nuclear energy have deep misgivings about its safety.*

**mis·guid·ed** /mɪs'gaɪdɪd/ *adj* **1** intended to be helpful but in fact making a situation worse: *a well-meaning but misguided attempt to bring her parents back together* **2** a misguided idea or opinion is wrong because it is based on a wrong understanding of a situation: *They cling to the misguided belief that only big name managers can bring big time success.* —**misguidedly** *adv*

**mis·han·dle** /ˌmɪs'hændl/ *v* [T] **1** to deal with a situation badly, because of a lack of skill or care: *The Prime Minister admitted that the water privatisation had been mishandled.* **2** to treat something roughly, often causing damage

**mis·hap** /'mɪshæp/ *n* [C,U] a small accident or mistake that does not have very serious results: *a slight mishap with the glasses* | **without mishap** *Only one horse finished the course without mishap.*

**mis·hear** /ˌmɪs'hɪə‖-'hɪr/ *v past tense and past participle* **misheard** /'hɜːd‖-'hɜːrd/ [I,T] to not properly hear what someone says, so that you think they said something different: *It seemed a strange question; I wondered if I had misheard.*

**mis·hit** /ˌmɪs'hɪt/ *v* [T] to hit a ball badly, especially in GOLF —**mishit** /'mɪshɪt/ *n* [C]

**mish·mash** /'mɪʃmæʃ/ *n* [singular] *informal* a mixture with no particular order in its design or in the choice of what is included; HOTCHPOTCH *BrE*: [+ **of**] *The magazine is a jumbled mishmash of jokes, stories, and serious news.*

**mis·in·form** /ˌmɪsɪn'fɔːm‖-ɔːrm/ *v* [T usually passive] to give someone information that is incorrect or untrue

**mis·in·for·ma·tion** /ˌmɪsɪnfə'meɪʃən‖-fər-/ *n* [U] incorrect information, especially when deliberately intended to deceive people —compare DISINFORMATION

**mis·in·ter·pret** /ˌmɪsɪn'tɜːprɪt‖-ɜːr-/ *v* [T] to not understand the correct meaning of something that someone says or does, or to explain something wrongly to other people: *Liam misinterpreted her friendly offer of a lift home.* —**misinterpretation** /ˌmɪsɪntɜːprɪ'teɪʃən‖-tɜːr-/ *n* [C,U]: *a misinterpretation of the test results*

**mis·judge** /ˌmɪs'dʒʌdʒ/ *v* [T] **1** to form a wrong or unfair opinion about a person or situation: *The defeat showed how badly he'd misjudged the mood of the electorate.* **2** to guess an amount, distance etc wrongly: *I misjudged the turn and hit the sidewalk.* —**misjudgment** or **misjudgement** *n* [C,U]

**mis·lay** /mɪs'leɪ/ *v past tense and past participle* **mislaid** /-'leɪd/ [T] to put something somewhere, then forget where you put it; MISPLACE: *I've mislaid my glasses again.*

**mis·lead** /mɪs'liːd/ *v past tense and past participle* **misled** /-'led/ [T] to make someone believe something that is not true by giving them false or incomplete information: *McFarlane admitted that he had misled Congress about aid to the Contras.* | **don't be misled by** *Don't be misled by appearances, he's a very competent worker.*

**mis·lead·ing** /mɪs'liːdɪŋ/ *adj* likely to make someone believe something that is not true: *The article was misleading, and the newspaper has apologized.* —**misleadingly** *adv*: *"You imply, misleadingly, that you knew nothing about it", accused the prosecutor.*

**mis·man·age** /ˌmɪs'mænɪdʒ/ *v* [T] if someone mismanages something they are in charge of, they deal with it badly: *The nation's finances had been badly mismanaged.* —**mismanagement** *n* [U]

**mis·match** /'mɪsmætʃ/ *n* [C] a combination of things or people that do not work well together or are not suitable for each other: *the mismatch between the demand for health care and the supply* —**mismatched** /ˌmɪs'mætʃt◂/ *adj*: *a brilliant woman tragically mismatched with an incompetent, dull man*

**mis·no·mer** /mɪs'nəʊmə‖-'noʊmər/ *n* [C] a wrong or unsuitable name: *The word 'new' in their New Development was now something of a misnomer given that building had not even started.*

**mi·so·gy·nist** /mɪ'sɒdʒɪnɪst‖mɪ'sɑː-/ *n* [C] a man who hates women —**misogyny** *n* [U] *formal*

**mis·place** /ˌmɪs'pleɪs/ *v* [T] to lose something for a short time by putting it in the wrong place; MISLAY: *Oh dear, I seem to have misplaced the letter.*

**mis·placed** /ˌmɪs'pleɪst◂/ *adj* misplaced feelings of trust, love etc are wrong and unsuitable, because the person that you have these feelings for does not deserve them: *her misplaced sense of loyalty*

**mis·print** /'mɪs-prɪnt/ *n* [C] a mistake, especially a spelling mistake, in a book, magazine etc

**mis·pro·nounce** /ˌmɪsprə'naʊns/ *v* [T] to pronounce a

word or name wrongly —**mispronunciation** /ˌmɪsprəˌnʌnsiˈeɪʃən/ *n* [C,U]

**mis·quote** /ˌmɪsˈkwəʊt‖-ˈkwoʊt/ *v* [T] to make a mistake in reporting what someone else has said: *Dr Hall said he had been misquoted in the press.* —**misquotation** /ˌmɪskwəʊˈteɪʃən‖-kwoʊ-/ *n* [C,U]

**mis·read** /ˌmɪsˈriːd/ *v past tense and past participle* **mis·read** /-ˈred/ [T] **1** to make a wrong judgment about a person or situation: *Negotiators misread the clues as to the enemy's true intentions.* **2** to read something incorrectly —**misreading** *n* [C,U] *a misreading of the situation*

**mis·re·port** /ˌmɪsrɪˈpɔːt‖-ˈpɔːrt/ *v* [T usually passive] to give an incorrect or untrue account of an event or situation: *The facts of the story have been misreported.*

**mis·rep·re·sent** /ˌmɪsreprɪˈzent/ *v* [T] to deliberately give a wrong description of someone's opinions or of a situation: *These statistics grossly misrepresent the reality.* —**misrepresentation** /ˌmɪsreprɪzenˈteɪʃən/ *n* [C,U]

**mis·rule** /ˌmɪsˈruːl/ *n* [U] *formal* bad government: *15 years of misrule by a weak and corrupt government*

**miss¹** *v* see below

S 2 **miss²** *n*

**1 Miss Smith/Cleveland etc** used in front of the family name of a woman who is not married to address her politely, to write to her, or to talk about her —compare MRS, MS —see MR (USAGE)

**2 ▶ TEACHER ◀** *BrE* used by children when addressing a female teacher, whether she is married or not: *I know the answer, Miss.* —compare SIR (5)

**3 Miss Italy/Ohio/World etc** used before the name of a country, city etc which a woman represents in a beauty competition

**4 ▶ YOUNG WOMAN ◀** *old-fashioned* used as a polite way of addressing a young woman when you do not know her name: *Excuse me, miss, you've dropped your umbrella.* —compare MADAM (1), SIR (2)

**5 ▶ YOUNG GIRL ◀** [C] *BrE* a young girl, especially one who has been naughty or rude: *a cheeky little miss*

**6 give sth a miss** *informal especially BrE* to decide not to do something: *I think I'll give aerobics a miss this week.*

**7 ▶ NOT HIT/CATCH ◀** [C] a failed attempt to hit, catch, or hold something: *an exciting game with three shots at goal and only two misses*

**8 a miss is as good as a mile** used to say that although someone failed by only a small amount to do something, they were still unsuccessful —see also HIT-AND-MISS

**mis·sal** /ˈmɪsəl/ *n* [C] a book containing all the prayers said during each Mass for a whole year in the Roman Catholic church

**mis·shap·en** /ˌmɪsˈʃeɪpən, mɪˈʃeɪ-/ *adj* not the normal or natural shape: *Ballerinas often have blunted, misshapen toes.*

**mis·sile** /ˈmɪsaɪl‖ˈmɪsəl/ *n* [C] **1** a weapon that can fly over long distances and that explodes when it hits the thing it has been aimed at: *a nuclear missile* **2** an object that is thrown at someone in order to hurt them: *Many of the hooligans were throwing missiles at the police.*

**miss·ing** /ˈmɪsɪŋ/ *adj* **1** something that is missing is not in its usual place and you cannot find it: *We found the missing piece of the jigsaw under the chair.* | [+ **from**] *Fifty dollars were missing from my wallet.* **2** if part of something is missing, it has been removed, destroyed etc and no longer exists: *Two of her front teeth were missing.* **3** someone who is missing has disappeared, and no one knows where they are: *The soldiers were reported missing, presumed dead.* **4** not included, although it ought to have been: [+ **from**] *Why is my name missing from the list?* **5 go missing** *BrE* to disappear or become lost: *My cat's gone missing again.* S 3

**missing link** /ˌ·· ˈ·/ *n* [C] **1** a piece of information that you need in order to solve a problem: *a discovery which could provide a new direction towards finding the missing link in the search for a cure for cancer* **2 the missing link** an animal similar to humans that may have existed at the time when apes (APE¹ (1)) developed into humans: *The race is on to find the missing link in our evolution.*

**missing per·son** /ˌ·· ˈ··/ *n plural* **missing persons** [C] **1** someone who has disappeared and whose family has asked the police to try to find them **2 Missing Persons** the police department responsible for trying to find people who have disappeared

**mis·sion** /ˈmɪʃən/ *n* [C] W 3

**1 ▶ AIRFORCE/ARMY ETC ◀** an important job done by a member of the airforce, army etc, especially an attack on the enemy: *He was sent on over 200 missions before being killed in action.* | *a space misssion*

## miss¹ /mɪs/ *v*

① NOT DO STH/FAIL TO DO STH
② BE TOO LATE
③ FEEL SAD WITHOUT
④ NOT NOTICE
⑤ AVOID STH
⑥ NOTICE STH ISN'T THERE
⑦ OTHER MEANINGS

### ① NOT DO STH/FAIL TO DO STH

**1** [T] to not go somewhere or do something, especially when you want to but cannot: *I'm really hungry. I missed breakfast.* | *Donna had to miss a week of school because of chickenpox.*

**2 ▶ NOT HIT/GET HOLD OF ◀** [I,T] to not hit something or catch something: *She fired at the target but missed.* | **miss sth** *He ran to catch the ball but missed it.* | **miss doing sth** *The car came screeching round the corner and just missed hitting a little boy who was crossing the road.* —see picture on page 1264

**3 miss a chance/opportunity** to fail to use an opportunity to do something: *A free trip to Jamaica was an opportunity he couldn't miss.*

**4 I wouldn't miss it for the world** *spoken* used to say that you really want to go to an event, see something etc

**5 miss the boat/bus** *informal* to fail to take an opportunity: *You'll miss the boat if you don't buy these shares now.*

### ② BE TOO LATE

**6** [T] to be too late for something: *By the time we got there we'd missed the beginning of the movie.* | **miss the train/bus etc**: *I overslept and missed the train.* —opposite CATCH¹ (8)

### ③ FEEL SAD WITHOUT

**7 ▶ MISS SB ◀** [T] to feel sad because someone you love is not with you: *When George went away I really missed him.* | *Will you miss me?*

**8 ▶ MISS STH ◀** to feel sad because you do not have something or cannot do something you had or did before: *I miss the car, but the bus system is good.* | *We really missed being able to go to the beach whenever we wanted.*

④ **NOT NOTICE**
**9** [T] to not see, hear, or notice something, especially when it is difficult to notice: *Grandpa Joe spoke very slowly so that Charlie wouldn't miss a word.* | *J.D. noticed a design fault in the engine that everyone else had missed.*
**10 you can't miss it/him etc** *spoken* used to say that it is very easy to notice or recognize someone or something: *He's the one in the red hat. You can't miss him.*
**11 sb doesn't miss much** *spoken* used to say that someone is good at noticing things, even small details: *Old Mr Staines doesn't miss much, does he?*
**12 sb doesn't miss a trick** *spoken* used to say that someone notices every opportunity to get an advantage: *The cunning old devil – he never misses a trick.*
⑤ **AVOID STH**
**13 ▶AVOID STH◀** [T] to avoid doing something or going somewhere, especially deliberately: *If we leave now we should miss the traffic.* | *They narrowly missed being killed in the fire.*
⑥ **NOTICE STH ISN'T THERE**
**14** [T] to notice that something or someone is not in the place you expect them to be: *I didn't miss my wallet till it came to paying the bill.*
⑦ **OTHER MEANINGS**
**15 miss the point** to not understand the main point of what someone is saying
**16 sb's heart misses a beat** used to say that someone is very excited, surprised, or frightened: *When I spotted Christophe my heart missed a beat.*
**17 without missing a beat** if you do something without missing a beat, you do it without showing that you are very surprised or shocked: *"I hear you're a private detective," he said, without missing a beat.*
**18 ▶ENGINE◀** [I] if an engine misses, it stops working for a very short time and then starts again
**miss out** *phr v* **1** [I] to not have the chance to do something that you enjoy: *Some children miss out because their parents can't afford to pay for school trips.* | [+ **on**] *She married young and felt she was missing out on life.* **2** [T **miss** sb/sth ↔ **out**] *BrE* to not include someone or something: *Make sure you don't miss any details out.*

**2 ▶GOVERNMENT/GROUP◀** a group of important people who are sent by their government to another country to discuss something or collect information: *a British trade mission to Moscow*
**3 ▶JOB◀** an important job that someone has been given to do especially when they are sent to another place: *His mission was to improve staff morale and output.*
**4 ▶DUTY◀** something that you feel you must do because it is your duty: **mission in life** *He always felt that his mission in life was to help old people.*
**5 ▶RELIGION◀ a)** the work of a religious leader or organization, that has gone to a foreign country, in order to teach people about Christianity or help poor people: *After he trained as a priest he went to work for the missions in Africa.* **b)** a building where this kind of work is done
**6 mission accomplished** used when you have finished a job that someone has asked or told you to do
**mis·sion·a·ry** /ˈmɪʃənəri‖-neri/ *n* [C] someone who has been sent to a foreign country to teach people about Christianity and persuade them to become Christians: *She spent 20 years in Africa as a missionary.*
**missionary po·si·tion** /ˈ···· ·ˌ··/ *n* [singular] the sexual position in which the woman lies on her back with the man on top of her and facing her
**mission con·trol** /ˌ·· ·ˈ·/ *n* [singular] the people on earth who control, communicate with and guide a group of people on a space flight
**mission state·ment** /ˈ·· ˌ··/ *n* [C] a clear statement about the aims of a company or organization
**mis·sis** /ˈmɪsɪz/ *n* another spelling of MISSUS
**mis·sive** /ˈmɪsɪv/ *n* [C] *humorous* a letter: *An anonymous missive had been pushed under her door.*
**mis·spell** /ˌmɪsˈspel/ *v past tense and past participle* **misspelt** /-ˈspelt/ or **misspelled** [T] to spell a word wrongly —**misspelling** *n* [C, U]
**mis·spend** /ˌmɪsˈspend/ *v past tense and past participle* **misspent** /-ˈspent◂/ [T] **1 misspent youth** *often humorous* someone who had a misspent youth wasted their time or behaved badly when they were young **2** to use time, money, etc badly, and not carefully or effectively
**mis·step** /ˈmɪs-step/ *n* [C] *AmE* a mistake, especially one that is caused by not understanding a situation correctly: *He has made a number of missteps over health care.*
**mis·sus, missis** /ˈmɪsɪz/ *n* [singular] **1** *informal* a man's wife: *How's the missus?* **2** *spoken, especially BrE* used when addressing a woman whose name you do not know: *Hey, missus, are these your kids?*
**mist¹** /mɪst/ *n* **1** [C,U] a light cloud low over the ground that makes it difficult for you to see very far: *We could just see the outline of the house through the mist.* —compare FOG¹ (1) —see picture on page 836 **2** [singular] air that is filled with very small drops of a particular liquid: *a treatment for asthma in the form of an aerosol mist*
**3 lost in the mists of time** if something such as a fact or secret is lost in the mists of time, no one remembers it because it happened so long ago: *The real reasons for the war are now lost in the mists of time.*
**mist²** *v* **1** [T] to cover something with very small drops of liquid in order to keep it wet: *The plant has to be misted every day.*
**mist over** *phr v* [I] **1** if someone's eyes mist over, they become filled with tears: *His eyes misted over at the memory of his wife.* **2** to mist up
**mist up** *phr v* [I, T] if a piece of glass mists up or if something mists it up, it becomes covered with very small drops of water so that you cannot see through it: *I can't see where I'm going, the windows have misted up.*
**mis·take¹** /mɪˈsteɪk/ *n* [C] S2 W2
**1 ▶INCORRECT ACTION/OPINION ETC◀** something that has been done incorrectly, or an opinion or statement that is incorrect: *Hitting the ball too hard in golf is a typical beginner's mistake.* | **make a mistake** *I think you've made a mistake – this isn't my coat.* | **there must be some mistake** (=used when you think someone has made a mistake) *There must be some mistake – I already paid my hotel bill.* | **learn from your mistakes** (=learn how to do something correctly by doing it the wrong way first) —see graph at ERROR
**2 by mistake** if you do something by mistake, you do it without intending to: *Someone must have left the door open by mistake.*
**3 ▶STUPID ACTION◀** something unwise or stupid that someone does, which they regret doing afterwards: *Buying the house seemed a great idea at the time, but now I can see it was a mistake.* | **make a mistake** *It's your decision, but I warn you – you're making a mistake.* | **big mistake** *Marrying him was the biggest mistake she ever made.* | **make the mistake of doing sth** *I stupidly made the mistake of giving them my phone number.* | **it is a mistake to do sth** *It would be a mistake to underestimate the amount of support for his victims.*
**4 ▶IN SPEECH OR WRITING◀** something that is said or written incorrectly, for example in a piece of school work: *Ivan's work is always full of mistakes.* | **make a mistake** *At this level, students tend to make a lot of basic mistakes.* | **spelling mistake** *There are a lot of spelling mistakes in this letter.*
**5 we all make mistakes** *spoken* used when telling someone not to be worried because they have made a mistake
**6 make no mistake (about it)** *spoken* used to emphasize what you are saying, especially when you are warning someone: *He'll get his revenge, make no mistake about it!*

**7 and no mistake** *spoken* used to show that you are very certain about something that you have just said: *Miles was a heartbreaker, and no mistake!* —compare ERROR

**mistake²** *past tense* **mistook** /mɨˈstʊk/ *past participle* **mistaken**/mɨˈsteɪkən/ *v* [T] **1** to understand something wrongly: *Ken mistook her concern, thinking she was interested in him for another reason.* | *She mistook my meaning entirely.* **2 you can't mistake sb/sth** used to say that someone or something is very easy to recognize: *You can't mistake her. She's the one with the long red hair.* **3 there is no mistaking sb/sth** used to say that you are certain about something: *There's no mistaking whose children they are – they all look just like Joe.*

**mistake** sb/sth **for** sb/sth *phr v* [T] to think that one person or thing is someone or something else: *I mistook the poor woman for my sister.* | *The doctor mistook the symptoms for blood poisoning.* (=and it was something else)

**mis·tak·en** /mɨˈsteɪkən/ *adj* **1** [not before noun] someone who is mistaken is wrong about something: **be mistaken** *I thought I saw her at the movies but I guess I was mistaken.* **2 mistaken idea/belief/impression etc** a mistaken belief etc is not correct or is based on bad judgment: *Marijuana has few withdrawal effects, and this has given rise to the mistaken belief that it is not addictive.* **3 a case of mistaken identity** a situation in which someone believes that they have seen a particular person taking part in a crime, when in fact it was someone else: *The police arrested her but it turned out to be a case of mistaken identity.* —**mistakenly** *adv*

**mis·ter** /ˈmɪstə‖-ər/ *n* **1 Mister** the full form of MR **2** *spoken especially AmE* used to address a man whose name you do not know: *Hey, mister, you dropped your paper.*

**mis·time** /ˌmɪsˈtaɪm/ *v* [T] to do something at the wrong time or at an unsuitable time. *We mistimed a scene where a door slams in my face and I ended up with a broken nose.*

**mis·tle·toe** /ˈmɪsəltəʊ‖-toʊ/ *n* [U] a plant with small white berries, which grows over other trees, and is often used as a decoration at Christmas

**mis·took** /mɨˈstʊk/ the past tense of MISTAKE (2)

**mis·tral** /ˈmiːstrɑːl/ *n* [singular] a strong cold dry wind that blows from the north into the south of France

**mis·tress** /ˈmɪstrɨs/ *n* [C] **1** a woman that a man has a sexual relationship with even though he is married to someone else: *The Prince had shocked society by living openly with his mistress.* **2** *BrE old-fashioned* a female teacher: *the new English mistress* **3** the female owner of a dog, horse etc **4** *old-fashioned* the female employer of a servant: *You'll have to deal with the mistress of the house.* **5 be mistress of** if a woman is a mistress of something she is in control of it, highly skilled at it etc: *She appeared to be very much the mistress of the situation.* **6 Mistress** *old use* used with a woman's family name as a polite way of addressing her —compare MASTER¹ (1)

**mis·tri·al** /ˌmɪsˈtraɪəl/ *n* [C] a trial during which a mistake in the law is made, so that a new trial has to be held

**mis·trust¹** /mɪsˈtrʌst/ *n* [U] the feeling that you cannot trust someone, especially because you think they may treat you unfairly or dishonestly: **[+ of]** *He had a deep mistrust of the legal profession.* —compare DISTRUST¹

**mistrust²** *v* [T] to not trust someone, especially because you think they may treat you unfairly or dishonestly: *As a very small child she had learned to mistrust adults.* —compare DISTRUST² —**mistrustful** *adj: Some people are very mistrustful of computerised banking.* —**mistrustfully** *adv*

**mist·y** /ˈmɪsti/ *adj* **mistier, mistiest** **1** misty weather is weather with a lot of mist: *The forecast says it will be wet and misty tomorrow.* **2** *literary* full of tears: *Her eyes became misty.* **3** not clear or bright: *Without my glasses everything is just a misty blur.*

**mis·un·der·stand** /ˌmɪsʌndəˈstænd‖-ər-/ *v past tense and past participle* **misunderstood** [I, T] to think that something means one thing when in fact it means something different: *I don't think we should be seen travelling together – people might misunderstand.*

**mis·un·der·stand·ing** /ˌmɪsʌndəˈstændɪŋ‖-ər-/ *n* **1** [C,U] a problem caused by someone not understanding a question, situation, or instruction correctly: *I think there must have been some misunderstanding. I didn't order all these books.* **2** [C] an argument or disagreement that is not very serious: *We had a little misunderstanding with our neighbors last night.*

**mis·use¹** /ˌmɪsˈjuːz/ *v* [T] **1** to use something in the wrong way or for the wrong purpose: *The term schizophrenia is often misused.* **2** to treat someone badly or unfairly

**mis·use²** /mɪsˈjuːs/ *n* [C,U] the use of something in the wrong way or for the wrong purpose: *A system designed to prevent credit card misuse.* | *the misuse of power*

**mite** /maɪt/ *n* [C] **1** a very small insect that lives in plants, carpets etc **2** a small child, especially one that you feel sorry for: *Poor mite! You must be starving!* **3 a mite shy/boring/nervous etc** slightly shy, boring, nervous etc **4 a mite of** *old-fashioned* a small amount

**mit·i·gate** /ˈmɪtɨgeɪt/ *v* [T] *formal* to make a situation or the effects of something less unpleasant, harmful, or serious: *Measures need to be taken to mitigate the environmental effects off burrning more coal.*

**mit·i·gat·ing** /ˈmɪtɨgeɪtɪŋ/ *adj* **mitigating circumstances/factors etc** facts about a situation that make a crime or bad mistake seem less serious: *a reduced prison sentence due to mitigating circumstances*

**mit·i·ga·tion** /ˌmɪtɨˈgeɪʃən/ *n* [U] **1 in mitigation** *law* if you say something in mitigation, you try to make someone's crime or mistake seem less serious or show that they were not completely responsible: *The captain added, in mitigation, that the engines may have been faulty.* **2** *formal* a reduction in how unpleasant, harmful, or serious a situation is: *His marriage had brought slight mitigation of the monotony of his existence.*

**mi·tre** *BrE*, **miter** *AmE* /ˈmaɪtə‖-ər/ *n* [C] **1** a tall pointed hat worn by BISHOPS and ARCHBISHOPS **2** also **mitre joint** a joint between two pieces of wood, in which each piece is cut at an angle

**mitt** /mɪt/ *n* [C] **1** a type of GLOVE that does not have separate parts for each finger; MITTEN **2** a GLOVE made of thick material, worn to protect your hand: *an oven mitt* | *ski mitts* **3** a type of leather GLOVE used to catch a ball in BASEBALL —see picture on page 1263 **4** *informal, especially BrE* someone's hand: *Robert's put his sticky mitts all over it.*

**mit·ten** /ˈmɪtn/ *n* [C] a type of GLOVE that does not have separate parts for each finger —see picture at GLOVE

**mix¹** /mɪks/ *v* **1** [I,T] if you mix two or more substances or if they mix, they combine to become a single substance, and they cannot be easily separated: *Mix the blue and yellow paint to make green.* | *Oil and water don't mix.* | **mix sth together/in etc** *First mix the butter and sugar together, then add the milk.* | **mix sth with sth** *Shake the bottle well so that the oil mixes with the vinegar.* —see picture on page 834 **2** [I,T] to combine two or more different activities, ideas, groups of things etc: **mix sth with sth** *His books mix historical fact with fantasy.* | **mix business with pleasure** (=combine business and social activities at the same time) **3 not mix** if two different ideas, activities etc do not mix, they are not suitable for each other and cause problems when they are combined: *We all know that drink, drugs and knives do not mix.* **4** [T] to prepare something, especially food or drink, by mixing things together: *Will you mix us some martinis, Bill?* **5** [I] to enjoy meeting, talking, and spending time with other people, especially people you do not know very well: **[+ with]** *Charlie doesn't mix well with the other children.* **6** [T] *technical* to control the balance of sounds in a record or film **7 mix and match** to try wearing different pieces of clothing together to see whether they look good **8 mix it (up) with** to argue or

S2 W3

threaten to fight with someone: *You don't want to mix it with him. He's been drinking since noon.*

**mix** sb/sth ↔ **up** *phr v* [T] **1** [**mix** sb/sth ↔ **up**] to make the mistake of thinking that someone or something is another person or thing: [+ **with**] *I always mix him up with his brother. They look so much alike.* **2** [**mix** sth ↔ **up**] to change the way things have been arranged, often by mistake, so that they are no longer in the same order: *Don't mix up those papers, or we'll never find the ones we need.* **3** [**mix** sb **up**] to make someone feel confused: *They kept trying to mix me up.* —see also MIXED UP, MIX-UP

**mix²** *n* **1** [singular] the particular combination of things or people that form a group: [+ **of**] *There's a real mix of ethnic groups in that area of the city.* | *We have to come up with a mix of policies to please the voters.* **2** [C,U] a combination of substances that you mix together to make something such as a cake: **cake/soup etc mix** *Add water to the cake mix and cook at 375°.*

S2 **mixed** /mɪkst/ *adj* **1** [only before noun] consisting of many different types of things or people: *The doctor suggested a mixed diet of fruits and vegetables.* | *a mixed race community* **2 mixed reaction/response/reviews etc** if something gets a mixed reaction etc, some people say they like it or agree with it, but others dislike it or disagree with it: *The film has had mixed reviews from the critics.* **3 have mixed emotions/feelings about** to be unsure about whether you like or agree with something or someone: *I must admit I have rather mixed feelings about my brother's new wife.* **4** *especially BrE* for both males and females: *a mixed school* **5 a mixed blessing** something that is good in some ways but bad in others: *Having your parents living nearby is a mixed blessing.* **6 a mixed bag** a group of things or people that are all very different from each other: [+ **of**] *The concert was a mixed bag of classical and modern music.* **7 in mixed company** when you are with people of both sexes: *It's not the sort of joke you tell in mixed company.*

**mixed a·bil·i·ty** /ˌ· ·ˈ···◂/ *adj* [only before noun] a mixed ability school or class teaches all children of the same age together, even if they have different levels of ability

**mixed doub·les** /ˌ· ˈ··/ *n* [U] a game in a sport such as tennis in which a man and a woman play against another man and woman

**mixed e·con·o·my** /ˌ· ·ˈ···/ *n* [C] *technical* an economic system in which some industries are owned by the government and some are owned by private companies

**mixed farm·ing** /ˌ· ˈ··/ *n* [U] a system of farming in which you grow crops and keep animals

**mixed grill** /ˌ· ˈ·/ *n* [C] *BrE* a dish consisting of meats such as SAUSAGE, BACON, LIVER etc which have all been grilled (GRILL¹ (1))

**mixed mar·riage** /ˌ· ˈ··/ *n* [C,U] a marriage between two people from different races or religions

**mixed up** /ˌ· ˈ·◂/ *adj* **1 be mixed up in** to be involved in an illegal or dishonest activity: *He's the last person I'd expect to be mixed up in something like this.* **2 be mixed up with** to be involved with someone who has a bad influence on you: *When he left college he got mixed up with the wrong people.* **3** [not before noun] confused, for example because you have too many different details to remember or think about: *I get all mixed up over the money whenever I travel abroad.* **4** *informal* confused and suffering from emotional problems: *She's just a crazy mixed up kid.* —see also **mix up** (MIX¹), MIX-UP

**mix·er** /ˈmɪksə‖-ər/ *n* [C] **1** a piece of kitchen equipment used to mix flour, sugar, butter etc together: *an electric food mixer* **2** a drink that can be mixed with alcohol, especially to make a COCKTAIL: *We can use tonic water or orange juice as mixers.* **3 a good/bad mixer** someone who finds it easy or difficult to make friends with people and talk to strangers **4** someone whose job is to control the sound when making a record or tape of a piece of music, or to control the quality of the picture when making a film **5** *AmE old-fashioned* a party held so that people who have just met can get to know each other better: *Are you going to the freshman mixer?*

**mix·ing bowl** /ˈ·· ·/ *n* [C] a large bowl used for mixing things such as flour and sugar for making cakes

**mix·ture** /ˈmɪkstʃə‖-ər/ *n* **1** [C] a combination of two or more people, things, feelings, or ideas that are different: *People are a mixture of good and evil.* | *the mixture of different people living in a city* | *He looked at her with a mixture of amusement and despair.* **2** [C, U] a liquid or other substance made by mixing several substances together: *Pour the cake mixture into the pan slowly and then bake on a low heat.* **3** [C] *technical* a combination of substances that are put together but do not mix with each other —compare COMPOUND¹ **4** [U] *formal* the action of mixing things or the state of being mixed S3 W3

**mix-up** /ˈ· ·/ *n* [C] *informal* a mistake that causes confusion about details or arrangements: *There was a mix-up over the reservations and we had to share a room.*

**miz·zen** /ˈmɪzən/ *n* [C] **1** also **mizzen mast** the MAST behind the main mast on a sailing ship **2** also **mizzen sail** the main sail set lengthways on a mizzen on a sailing ship

**Mk** the written abbreviation of MARK² (7)

**ml** the written abbreviation of MILLILITRE(s)

**m'lady, milady** /mɪˈleɪdi/ *n old use* a word used by a servant to address a woman who belongs to a NOBLE family: *Will that be all, m'lady?*

**MLitt** /ˌem ˈlɪt/ Master of Letters; a university degree that you can get at some British universities by studying for two years after your first degree

**M'lord** /mḷˈlɔːd‖-ˈlɔːrd/ *n* **1** a word used to address a judge **2** *old use* a word used by a servant to address a man who belongs to a NOBLE family

**M'lud** /mḷˈlʌd/ *n* used to address a judge in a British court of law (=short for 'my lord')

**mm¹** /m/ *interjection spoken* used when someone else is speaking and you want to show that you are listening or that you agree with them

**mm²** the written abbreviation of MILLIMETRE(*s*)

**mne·mon·ic** /nɪˈmɒnɪk‖nɪˈmɑː-/ *n* something, such as a poem, or a sentence that you use to help you remember a rule, a name etc —**mnemonic** *adj* —**mnemonically** /-kli/ *adv*

**MO** /ˌem ˈəʊ‖-ˈoʊ/ *n informal* **1** [C] *especially BrE* medical officer; an army doctor **2** [singular] modus operandi; a way of doing something that is typical of one person or a group

**mo** /məʊ‖moʊ/ *n* [singular] *BrE spoken* a very short period of time; MOMENT (2): *Wait a mo!*

**mo.** *AmE* the written abbreviation for MONTH

**moan¹** /məʊn‖moʊn/ *v* **1** [I] to make a long low sound expressing pain, unhappiness, or sexual pleasure: *The sick child moaned a little and then fell asleep.* **2** [I, T] *BrE informal* to complain in an annoying way, especially in an unhappy voice and without good reason: *You've done nothing but moan all day.* | [+ **at**] *My mum never stops moaning at me.* | [+ **that**] *He's always moaning that we use too much electricity.* **3** [I] *literary* if the wind moans it makes a long low sound: *She was awakened by the low moaning of the wind in the trees.* —**moaner** *n* [C]

**moan²** *n* [C] **1** a long low sound expressing pain, unhappiness, or sexual pleasure: *There was a moan of pain from the injured man.* | **give a moan** *She gave a little moan of pleasure.* **2 have a moan** *BrE informal* to complain about something: *We were just having a moan about work.* **3** *literary* a low sound made by the wind

**moat** /məʊt‖moʊt/ *n* [C] **1** a deep wide hole, usually filled with water, around a castle or fort as a defence **2** a deep wide hole dug around an area used for animals in a zoo to stop them from escaping —**moated** *adj*

**mob¹** /mɒb‖mɑːb/ *n* [C] **1** a large, noisy crowd, especially one that is angry and violent: *a mob of demonstrators* | **mob rule** (=when a mob controls the situation rather than the government or the law) **2** *informal* a group of people of the same type: *The usual* *mob of teenagers were standing on the corner.* **3 the Mob** the MAFIA (=a powerful organization of criminals) **4 the mob** *old use* an insulting expression meaning all the poorest and least educated people in society **5 a mob of sheep/cattle** *AustrE, NZE* a large group of sheep or cattle

**mob²** *v* **mobbed, mobbing** [T] to form a crowd around someone in order to express admiration or to attack them: *The actress was mobbed by doting fans.*

**mob cap** /ˈ· ·/ *n* [C] a light cotton hat with a decorative edge, worn by women in the 18th and 19th centuries

**mo·bile¹** /ˈməʊbaɪl‖ˈmoʊbəl, -baɪl/ *adj* **1** able to move or travel easily: *She's more mobile now that she has her own car.* **2** not fixed in one position, and easy to move and use in different places: *mobile air-conditioners* **3 mobile library/shop/clinic etc** *BrE* a shop etc that is kept in a vehicle and driven from place to place **4** tending to move or able to move from one social class, job, or place to another: *People these days are much more socially mobile.* **5 mobile face/features** a face that can change its expression quickly —see also IMMOBILE, UPWARDLY MOBILE

**mo·bile²** /ˈməʊbaɪl‖ˈmoʊbiːl/ *n* [C] **1** a decoration made of small objects tied to wires or string and hung up so that the objects move when air blows around them **2** a MOBILE PHONE

**mobile home** /ˌ·· ˈ·/ *n* [C] **1** *AmE* a type of house that looks like an ordinary house but can be moved to another place **2** *BrE* a large CARAVAN which stays permanently in one place and is used as a house; TRAILER (1) *AmE*

**mobile phone** /ˌ·· ˈ·/ *n* [C] a telephone that you can carry with you and use in any place

**mobile phone**

**mo·bil·i·ty** /məʊˈbɪlɪ̥ti‖moʊ-/ *n* [U] **1** the ability to move easily from one job, place to live, or social class to another: **social/job mobility** *In America, social mobility is an everyday reality.* **2** the ability to move easily from place to place: *Arthritis restricted his mobility.*|*The key to the Army's effectiveness is its increased mobility.*

**mo·bil·ize** also **-ise** *BrE* /ˈməʊbɪ̥laɪz‖ˈmoʊ-/ *v* **1** [T] to bring people together so that they can all work to achieve something important: *to mobilize the rural population in a drive for self-sufficiency* **2 mobilize support/resources etc** to bring together the supporters, resources etc that you need and prepare them for action: *Owen was trying to mobilize support for a new political party.* **3** [I,T] if a country mobilizes or mobilizes its army, it prepares to fight a war —see also DEMOBILIZE —**mobilization** /ˌməʊbɪ̥laɪˈzeɪʃən‖ˌmoʊbɪ̥lə-/ *n* [C,U]

**mob·ster** /ˈmɒbstə‖ˈmɑːbstər/ *n* [C] *especially AmE* a member of an organized criminal group; GANGSTER

**moc·ca·sin** /ˈmɒkəsɪn‖ˈmɑː-/ *n* [C] a flat comfortable shoe made of soft leather —see picture at SHOE¹

**moch·a** /ˈmɒkə‖ˈmoʊkə/ *n* [U] **1** a type of coffee **2** *AmE* a combination of coffee and chocolate

**mock-** /mɒk‖mɑːk/ *prefix* **1** only pretendingly: *a mock-serious expression* **2** not real: *a mock-Tudor fireplace*

**mock¹** /mɒk‖mɑːk/ *v* **1** [I,T] *formal* to laugh at someone or something and try to make them look stupid by making unkind remarks about them or by copying them; make fun of: **mock sth/sb** *They have insulted us and mocked our religion.*|*It's easy for you to mock, but we put a lot of work into this play.*|*mocking laughter* **2** [T] *formal* to make something seem completely useless: *His silence mocked her efforts to start a conversation.* —**mocker** *n* [C] —**mockingly** *adv His lips twisted mockingly.*

**mock** sth ↔ **up** *phr v* [T] to make a full-size model of something so that it looks real —see also MOCK-UP

**mock²** *adj* [only before noun] **1** not real, but intended to be very similar to a real situation, substance etc: *war games with mock battles*|*a mock interview* **2 mock surprise/horror/indignation etc** surprise etc that you pretend to feel, especially as a joke: *He pulled at his hair in mock distress.* **3 mock Tudor/Georgian** copying the style of Tudor or Georgian buildings

**mock³** *n* **1 mocks** [plural] *BrE* school examinations taken as practice before official examinations **2 make mock of** *literary* to mock someone *He makes mock of my dreams.*

**mock·ers** /ˈmɒkəz‖ˈmɑːkərz/ *n* [plural] **put the mockers on** *BrE informal* to spoil an event or someone's plans: *Oh well, if you've got the car that puts the mockers on my plans to go out!*

**mock·e·ry** /ˈmɒkəri‖ˈmɑː-/ *n* **1 make a mockery of** to make something such as a plan, system, or organization seem completely useless or ineffective: *The continued flouting of Security Council resolutions is making a mockery of the UN.* **2** [U] a feeling or attitude of laughing at someone or something or of trying to make them seem completely stupid: *There was an element of mockery in the politeness he showed the inspector.* **3** [singular] something that is completely useless or ineffective: *The driving test was a mockery as a test of real driving skill.*

**mock·ing·bird** /ˈmɒkɪŋbɜːd‖ˈmɑːkɪŋbɜːrd/ *n* [C] an American bird that copies the songs of other birds

**mock tur·tle** /ˌ· ˈ··/ *n* [C] *AmE* a shirt or SWEATER with a high, close-fitting band around the neck; TURTLENECK *BrE* —see picture on page 840

**mock-up** /ˈ· ·/ *n* [C] a full-size model of something that is going to be made or built, which shows how it will look: *a mock-up of the space shuttle* —see also **mock up** (MOCK¹)

**mod** /mɒd‖mɑːd/ *n* [C] *BrE* a member of a group of young people in Britain in the 1960s who wore a particular type of neat clothes, listened to SOUL MUSIC, and drove MOTOR SCOOTERS —compare ROCKER (3)

**mo·dal¹** /ˈməʊdl‖ˈmoʊ-/ *n* [C] a modal verb

**modal²** *adj technical* **1** [only before noun] related to the MOOD (6) of a verb **2** related to or written in a musical MODE (5) —**modally** *adv*

**modal aux·il·ia·ry** /ˌ·· ·ˈ···/ *n* [C] a modal verb

**modal verb** /ˌ··ˈ·/ *n* [C] *technical* one of these verb forms: can, could, may, might, shall, should, will, would, must, ought to, used to, need, had better, and DARE. They are all used with other verbs to change their meaning by expressing ideas such as possibility, permission, or intention —see also AUXILIARY VERB

**mod cons** /ˌmɒd ˈkɒnz‖ˌmɑːð ˈkɑːnz/ *n* **all mod cons** *BrE informal* all the things that are fitted in modern houses to make life easy and comfortable: *a property with many interesting features and all mod cons*

**mode** /məʊd‖moʊd/ *n* [C] **1** *formal* a particular way or style of behaving, living or doing something: *They have a relaxed mode of life that suits them well.*|*a highly efficient mode of transport* **2** *technical* a particular way in which a machine operates when it is doing a particular job: *a spacecraft in re-entry mode*|*To get out of the 'auto' mode on the camera, turn the knob to 'M'.* **3 be in work mode/holiday mode etc** *informal,* to be in a particular state of mind: *With only 10 minutes to go, we were now in panic mode.* **4 be the mode** *formal* to be fashionable at a particular time: *Long skirts were then the latest mode.* **5** *technical* one of various systems of arranging notes in music, such as MAJOR and MINOR in Western music —see also À LA MODE, MODISH W3

**mod·el¹** /ˈmɒdl‖ˈmɑːdl/ *n* [C] S2
**1** ► **SMALL COPY** ◄ a small copy of a building, vehicle, machine etc, especially one that can be put together from separate parts: *He enjoys making airplane models.*|[+ **of**] *They brought us a little model of the Taj* W1

*Mahal.* | **working model** (=one in which the parts move) *a working model of a steam engine*
**2 ▶ FASHION ◀** someone whose job is to show clothes, hair styles etc by wearing them and being photographed: *a top fashion model* | *a male model*
**3 ▶ ART ◀** someone who is employed by an artist or photographer to be painted or photographed
**4 ▶ GOOD/SPECIAL PERSON ◀** someone you should imitate because of their good qualities or behaviour: [+ **of**] *As a politician, she was a model of integrity and decency.* | **role model** (=someone that you try to copy because they have qualities you would like to have) *A woman teacher can become a role model for female students.*
**5 ▶ GOOD /SUCCESSFUL THING ◀** a way of doing something that is successful or useful and therefore worth copying: [+ **of**] *Scarman's report is a model of fairness and clarity.* | *The science of astronomy was developed first and became a model for the other sciences.*
**6 ▶ DESCRIPTION ◀** a simple description of a system or structure that is used to help people understand similar systems or structures: *a computer model of the main factors determining a company's market share*
**7 ▶ TYPE OF CAR ETC ◀** a particular type or design of a vehicle or machine: *the cheapest model in the Volkswagen range.* | **latest model** (=the newest design produced by a company) *Our dishwasher is the latest model.*

**model²** *adj* **1 model airplane/train/car etc** a small copy of an airplane etc, especially one that a child can play with or put together from separate parts **2 model wife/employee/student etc** someone who behaves like a perfect wife, employee etc: *His lawyers tried to show him as a model husband and father.* **3 model prison/farm/school etc** a prison etc that has been specially designed or organized to be as good as possible

**model³** *v* **modelled, modelling** *BrE*, **modeled, modeling** *AmE* **1** [I, T] to wear clothes in order to show them to possible buyers: *She's modeling Donna Karan's fall collection of skirts.* **2 model yourself on** to try to be like someone else because you admire them: *Jim had always modelled himself on his great hero, Martin Luther King.* **3 be modelled on** to be designed in a way that copies another system or way of doing something: *Their education system is modelled on the French one.* **4** [T] to make small objects from materials such as wood or clay: *She was modeling the plasticine into little animal figures.*

**mod·el·ling** *BrE*, **modeling** *AmE* /ˈmɒdl-ɪŋ‖ˈmɑː-/ *n* [U] **1** the work of a MODEL¹ (2): *a career in modelling* **2** the activity of making model ships, planes, figures etc

**mo·dem** /ˈməʊdəm, -dem‖ˈmoʊ-/ *n* [C] a piece of electronic equipment that allows information from one computer to be sent along telephone wires to another computer —see picture on page 837

**mod·e·rate¹** /ˈmɒdərɪ̣t‖ˈmɑː-/ *adj* **1** neither very big nor very small, very hot nor very cold, very fast nor very slow etc: *Bake the pie for 30 minutes in a moderate oven.* | *We're looking for a house with a moderate-sized garden.* | *a moderate degree of success* | *a student of only moderate ability.* **2** having opinions, or beliefs especially about politics, that are not extreme and that most people consider reasonable or sensible: *Her views represent the moderate wing of the party.* | *a moderate politician* **3** staying within reasonable or sensible limits: *a moderate smoker* | *moderate wage demands* —see also MODERATELY

**mod·e·rate²** /ˈmɒdəreɪt‖ˈmɑː-/ *v* [I,T] **1** *formal* to make something less extreme or violent, or to become less extreme or violent: *The students moderated their demands.* | *We couldn't leave the harbour until the storm moderated.* **2** *BrE* to do the work of a MODERATOR

**mod·e·rate³** /ˈmɒdərɪ̣t‖ˈmɑː-/ *n* [C] someone whose opinions or beliefs, especially about politics, are not extreme and are considered reasonable by most people: *Carter appointed moderates to the Supreme Court.*

**mod·e·rate·ly** /ˈmɒdərɪ̣tli‖ˈmɑː-/ *adv* fairly but not very: *a moderately successful film*

**mod·e·ra·tion** /ˌmɒdəˈreɪʃən‖ˌmɑː-/ *n* [U] **1 in moderation** if you do something in moderation, such as drinking alcohol or smoking, you do not do it too much: *Some people think drinking in moderation is healthy.* **2** *formal* control of your behaviour, so that you keep your actions, feelings, habits etc within reasonable or sensible limits: [+ **in**] *Moderation in diet is the way to good health.* **3** *formal* reduction in force, degree, speed etc: *Even after sunset there was little moderation in the temperature.*

**mod·e·ra·to** /ˌmɒdəˈrɑːtəʊ‖ˌmɑːdəˈrɑːtoʊ/ *adj, adv* a word meaning at an average speed, used as an instruction on how fast to play a piece of music

**mod·e·ra·tor** /ˈmɒdəreɪtə‖ˈmɑːdəreɪtər/ *n* [C] **1** someone whose job is to control a discussion or argument and to help people reach an agreement **2** *BrE* someone who makes sure that an examination is fair, and that the marks given are fair and correct **3** someone who asks questions and keeps the marks of competing teams in a spoken game or competition **4** a religious leader who is in charge of the council of the Presbyterian and United Reformed Churches

**mod·ern** /ˈmɒdn‖ˈmɑːdərn/ *adj* **1** [only before noun] time belonging to the present time or most recent time: *a book about modern history* | *Traditional treatments, once shunned by modern medicine, are now being examined scientifically.* | *The original supermarkets were small by modern standards.* **2** made or done using the most recent methods; UP-TO-DATE: *Their offices are in a modern 25-storey skyscraper.* | *modern surgical techniques* **3** using or willing to use very recent ideas, fashions, or ways of thinking: *The school is very modern in its approach to sex education.* **4** [only before noun] modern art, music, literature etc uses styles that have been recently developed and are very different from traditional styles: *Modern dance looks more spontaneous than traditional ballet.* **5 Modern Greek/Hebrew/English** the form of the Greek etc language that is used today —see also SECONDARY MODERN S1 W1

**modern-day** /ˈ·· ·/ *adj* [only before noun] existing in the present time, but considered in relation to someone or something else in the past: *She's a modern-day Joan of Arc.* | *The modern-day diet has too little fiber in it.*

**mod·ern·is·m** /ˈmɒdənɪzəm‖ˈmɑːdər-/ *n* [U] a style of art, building etc that was popular especially from the 1940s to the 1960s, in which artists used simple shapes and modern artificial materials —compare POST-MODERNISM —**modernist** *adj, n* [C]: *the modernist school*

**mod·ern·ist·ic** /ˌmɒdəˈnɪstɪk◂‖ˌmɑːdər-/ *adj* designed in a way that looks very modern and very different from previous styles: *a modernistic office building*

**mo·der·ni·ty** /mɒˈdɜːnɪ̣ti‖məˈdɜːr-/ *n* [U] *formal* the quality of being modern: *a conflict between tradition and modernity*

**mod·ern·ize** also **-ise** *BrE* /ˈmɒdənaɪz‖ˈmɑːdər-/ *v* **1** [T] to change something so that it is more suitable for the present time by using new equipment or methods: *NATO is determined to modernize its ground forces.* | *a tastefully modernized old farmhouse* **2** [I] to start using more modern methods and equipment: *The business will lose money if it doesn't modernize.* —**modernization** /ˌmɒdənaɪˈzeɪʃən‖ˌmɑːdərnə-/ *n* [C,U]

**modern lan·gua·ges** /ˌ·· ˈ···/ *n* [plural] *BrE* modern European languages, such as French or Italian, studied as a subject at school or university

**mod·est** /ˈmɒdɪ̣st‖ˈmɑː-/ *adj* **1** unwilling to talk proudly about your abilities and achievements: [+ **about**] *He was always surprisingly modest about his role in the Everest expedition.* **2** not very big, expensive etc, especially less big, expensive etc than you would expect: *quite a modest salary for such an important job* | *his modest ambitions* | **a modest amount/improvement etc** *House prices rose by a modest amount in the last quarter.* **3** shy about showing your body or attracting sexual interest, because you are easily embarrassed:

*Children often become very modest at around age 11.* **4** *old-fashioned* modest clothing covers the body in a way that does not attract sexual interest: *a modest knee-length dress* —**modestly** *adv*

**mod·es·ty** /ˈmɒdɪ̈sti‖ˈmɑː-/ *n* [U] **1** a modest way of behaving or talking: *the great player's modesty* **2 in all modesty** *spoken* used to say that you do not want to seem too proud of something you have done, when in fact you are: *I think in all modesty that I can take some small credit for the team's success.* **3** unwillingness to show your body or do anything that may attract sexual interest **4 modesty forbids** *spoken* used when saying jokingly that you do not want to talk about your achievements —see also **false modesty** (FALSE (4))

**mod·i·cum** /ˈmɒdɪkəm‖ˈmɑː-/ *n* **a modicum of** *formal* a small amount of something, especially a good quality: *a modicum of common sense*

**mod·i·fi·ca·tion** /ˌmɒdɪ̈fɪ̈ˈkeɪʃən‖ˌmɑː-/ *n* **1** [C] a small change made in something such as a design, plan, or system: *We've made one or two minor modifications to the original design.* **2** [U] the act of modifying something, or the process of being modified: *The fuel can be used in diesel engines without modification.*

**mod·i·fi·er** /ˈmɒdɪ̈faɪə‖ˈmɑːdɪ̈faɪər/ *n* [C] *technical* a word or group of words that give additional information about another word. Modifiers can be adjectives (such as 'fierce' in 'the fierce dog'), adverbs (such as 'loudly' in 'the dog barked loudly'), or phrases (such as 'with a short tail' in 'the dog with a short tail').

**mod·i·fy** /ˈmɒdɪ̈faɪ‖ˈmɑː-/ *v* [T] **1** to make small changes to something in order to improve it and make it more suitable or effective: *The present law needs to be modified.* **2** *technical* if an adjective, adverb etc modifies another word it describes it or limits its meaning: *In the phrase 'walk slowly', the adverb 'slowly' modifies the verb 'walk'.*

**mod·ish** /ˈməʊdɪʃ‖ˈmoʊ-/ *adj* modish ideas, designs etc are modern and fashionable —**modishly** *adv*

**mod·u·lar** /ˈmɒdjʊ̈lə‖ˈmɑːdʒələr/ *adj* based on modules or made using modules: *a modular course in business studies|modular furniture*

**mod·u·late** /ˈmɒdjʊ̈leɪt‖ˈmɑːdʒə-/ *v* **1** [T] *formal* to change the sound of your voice or the strength of something **2** [I + **from/to**] *technical* to move from one KEY to another in a piece of music using a series of related chords (CHORD (1)) **3** [T] *technical* to change the form of a radio signal so that it can be broadcast more effectively —**modulation** /ˌmɒdjʊ̈ˈleɪʃən‖ˌmɑːdʒə-/ *n* [C]

W2 **mod·ule** /ˈmɒdjuːl‖ˈmɑːdʒuːl/ *n* [C] **1** *especially BrE* one of the units that a course of study has been divided into, each of which can be studied separately: *a module in mathematics* **2** a part of a SPACECRAFT that can be separated from the main part and used for a particular purpose **3** one of several separate parts that can be combined to form a larger object, such as a machine or building

**mo·dus op·e·ran·di** /ˌməʊdəs ɒpəˈrændi‖ˌmoʊdəs ˌɑːpə-/ *n* [singular] *Latin formal* a way of doing something that is typical of one person or group

**modus vi·ven·di** /ˌməʊdəs vɪˈvendi‖ˌmoʊ-/ *n* [singular] *Latin formal* an arrangement between people with very different opinions or habits that allows them to live or work together without quarrelling

**mog·gy, moggie** /ˈmɒgi‖ˈmɑːgi, ˈmɒːgi/ *n* [C] *BrE informal* a cat

**mo·gul** /ˈməʊgəl‖ˈmoʊ-/ *n* [C] **movie/record/tennis mogul etc** someone who has great power and influence in a particular industry or activity

**mo·hair** /ˈməʊheə‖ˈmoʊher/ *n* [U] expensive wool made from the hair of the ANGORA goat: *a mohair sweater* —see picture on page 839

**Mo·ham·me·dan** /məʊˈhæmɪ̈dən, mə-‖moʊ-, mə-/ *n* [C] a word meaning Muslim, now considered offensive by most Muslims —**Mohammedan** *adj*

**Mo·ham·me·dan·is·m** /məʊˈhæmɪ̈dənɪzəm, mə-‖moʊ-, mə-/ *n* [U] a word meaning the Muslim religion, now considered offensive by most Muslims; ISLAM

**moi** /mwɑː/ *pron spoken humorous* me: *Difficult, moi?*

**moi·e·ty** /ˈmɔɪɪ̈ti/ *n* [C + **of**] *law or literary* a half share

**moist** /mɔɪst/ *adj* slightly wet but not too wet, especially in a way that seems pleasant or suitable: *Make sure the soil is moist before planting the seeds.|a moist chocolate cake* —compare DAMP[1] (1) —**moistness** *n* [U]

**moist·en** /ˈmɔɪsən/ *v* [I,T] to become slightly wet, or to make something slightly wet: *Moisten the clay if it seems too dry.*

**mois·ture** /ˈmɔɪstʃə‖-ər/ *n* [U] small amounts of water that are present in the air, in a substance, or on a surface: *Plants use their roots to absorb moisture from the soil.*

**mois·tur·ize** also **-ise** *BrE* /ˈmɔɪstʃəraɪz/ *v* [T] **1** to make your skin less dry by using special cream **2 moisturizing cream/lotion/oil** cream, oil etc which you put on your skin to make it less dry

**mois·tur·iz·er** also **-iser** *BrE* /ˈmɔɪstʃəraɪzə‖-ər/ *n* [C,U] cream that you put on your skin to make it less dry

**mo·lar** /ˈməʊlə‖ˈmoʊlər/ *n* [C] one of the large teeth at the back of the mouth used for breaking up food —compare INCISOR —**molar** *adj* —see picture at TEETH

**mo·las·ses** /məˈlæsɪ̈z/ *n* [U] *AmE* a thick dark sweet liquid that is obtained from raw sugar plants when they are being made into sugar; TREACLE *BrE*

**mold** /məʊld‖moʊld/ *n* [U] the American spelling of MOULD —**molding** *n* [C,U]

**mol·der** /ˈməʊldə‖ˈmoʊldər/ *v* [I] the American spelling of MOULDER

**mold·y** /ˈməʊldi‖ˈmoʊl-/ *adj* the American spelling of MOULDY —**moldiness** *n* [U]

**mole** /məʊl‖moʊl/ *n* [C] **1** a small furry almost blind animal that usually lives under the ground **2** a small dark brown mark on the skin that is slightly higher than the skin around it **3** someone who works for an organization while secretly giving information to its enemies **4** *technical* a scientific unit for measuring the quantity of a substance

**mol·e·cule** /ˈmɒlɪkjuːl‖ˈmɑː-/ *n* [C] the smallest unit into which any substance can be divided without losing its own chemical nature, usually consisting of two or more atoms —**molecular** /məˈlekjʊ̈lə‖-ər/ *adj*: *molecular structure*

**mole·hill** /ˈməʊlˌhɪl‖ˈmoʊl-/ *n* [C] a small pile of earth made by a MOLE —see also **make a mountain out of a molehill** (MOUNTAIN (4)) —see picture at MOLE

**mole·skin** /ˈməʊlˌskɪn‖ˈmoʊl-/ *n* [U] **1** thick dark cloth **2** the skin of a MOLE

**mo·lest** /məˈlest/ *v* [T] **1** to attack or harm someone, especially a child, by touching them in a sexual way or trying to have sex with them: *men who molest young boys* —compare ABUSE[2] (2) **2** *old-fashioned* to attack and physically harm someone: *a dog that was molesting sheep* —**molester** *n* [C]|*a convicted child molester* —**molestation** /ˌməʊleˈsteɪʃən‖ˌmoʊ-/ *n* [U]

**moll** /mɒl‖mɑːl/ *n* [C] *old-fashioned, slang especially AmE* a criminal's girlfriend: *a gangster's moll*

**mol·li·fy** /ˈmɒlɪ̈faɪ‖ˈmɑː-/ *v* [T] to make someone feel less angry and upset about something: *The old man seemed mollified by the flattery.* —**mollification** /ˌmɒlɪ̈fɪ̈ˈkeɪʃən‖ˌmɑː-/ *n* [U]

**mol·lusc** *BrE*, **mollusk** *AmE* /ˈmɒləsk‖ˈmɑː-/ *n* [C] a type of sea or land animal that has a soft body covered by a hard shell: *snails and other molluscs*

**mol·ly·cod·dle** /ˈmɒliˌkɒdl‖ˈmɑːliˌkɑːdl/ *v* [T] to treat someone too kindly: *rather a weak young man who had always been mollycoddled as a boy*

M

**Mol·o·tov cock·tail** /ˌmɒlətɒf ˈkɒkteɪl‖ˌmɑːlətɔːf ˈkɑːk-, ˌmɔːl-/ *n* [C] a simple bomb consisting of a bottle filled with petrol with a piece of cloth at the end

**molt** /məʊlt‖moʊlt/ *v* [I] the American spelling of MOULT

**mol·ten** /ˈməʊltən‖ˈmoʊl-/ *adj* [usually before noun] molten metal or rock has been made into a liquid by being heated to a very high temperature: *molten lava*

**mol·to** /ˈmɒltəʊ‖ˈməʊltoʊ ˈmɔːl-/ *adv* a word used in music meaning 'very': *molto allegro* (=very fast)

**mo·lyb·de·num** /məˈlɪbdənəm/ *n* [U] a pale-coloured metal used especially to strengthen steel

S1 W2 **mom** /mɒm‖mɑːm/ *n* [C] *AmE informal* mother; MUM[1] (1) *BrE*: *fourteen-year-old girls and their moms and dads arguing about a moral issue*|*"My mom got this for me." "Oh, isn't that pretty?"*

**mom-and-pop** /ˌ· · ˈ·◂/ *adj* [only before noun] *AmE* a mom-and-pop business is owned and operated by a family or a husband and wife: *a real mom-and-pop operation*

S1 W1 **mo·ment** /ˈməʊmənt‖ˈmoʊ-/ *n*

**1 ▶ POINT IN TIME ◀** [C] a particular point in time: *They've been arguing from the moment they walked in the door.*|*There were a few worrying moments, but on the whole the play went well.*|**at the moment** *especially spoken BrE, formal AmE* (=used to say that something is happening or true now) *Julia's on holiday in Spain at the moment.*|*At the moment, the situation in Haiti is very tense.*|**for the moment** (=used to say that something is happening or true now but will probably change in the future) *Well, for the moment we're just friends.*|*For the moment the troops had stopped firing and there was an eerie hush.*|**at this/that moment** (=used to emphasize that something is happening now or at a particular time in the past) *Just at that moment there was a knock on the door.*|*John's listening to the programme at this moment, in fact.*|**at this moment in time** (=used especially by politicians, newspapers etc to mean now): *At this moment in time it would be inappropriate to speculate on Castro's intentions.*|**just this moment** (=used to emphasize that something has only just happened) *I just this moment arrived, and already Dan wants to know when I'm leaving.*

**2 ▶ SHORT TIME ◀** [C] a very short period of time: *But you said a moment ago you weren't going to see him again!*|*Can you spare a few moments to answer some questions?*|**in a moment** (=very soon) *I'll come back to that point in a moment.*|**for a moment** *It was quiet for a moment, then Rae asked what time he'd be back.*|**wait/just a moment** (=used when you want someone to wait a short time while you do or say something) *Just a moment, let me put these away first.*

**3 the moment (that) sb does/says sth** as soon as someone does something or says something: *He said he'd phone you the moment he got home.*

**4 the last moment** if you do something at the last moment or wait until the last moment to do it, you do it at the last possible time: *How could you leave buying your wedding dress to the last moment?!*

**5 not believe/think/do sth for a moment** *especially spoken* used to say that you did not believe etc something at all: *He didn't fool me for a moment.*

**6 any moment** extremely soon: *The plumber should be here any moment now.*|**at any moment** *The roof could collapse at any moment.*

**7 of the moment** the job, person, event etc of the moment is the one that is most important or famous at the present time: *her boyfriend of the moment*

**8 ▶ OPPORTUNITY ◀** [C usually singular] a particular period of time when you have a chance to do something: **big moment** (=a time when you have a chance to show other people how skilled, intelligent etc you are) *It was André's big moment; he breathed deeply and began to play.*|**choose/pick your moment** (=an expression meaning to choose a good time to do something, often used if you choose a very bad time to do it)

**9 have its/your moments** to have periods of being good or interesting: *a movie that had its moments*

**10 not a moment too soon** almost too late: *The ambulance finally arrived, and not a moment too soon.*

**11 the moment of truth** the time when you will find out if something will work properly, be successful etc

**12 of great moment** *old-fashioned* important

**mo·men·tar·i·ly** /ˈməʊməntərəli‖ˌmoʊmənˈterəli/ *adv* **1** for a very short time: *She paused momentarily and glanced over her shoulder.* **2** *AmE* very soon: *Mr Johnson will be with you momentarily.*

**mo·men·ta·ry** /ˈməʊməntəri‖ˈmoʊmənteri/ *adj* lasting for a very short time: *There was a momentary pause.*

**mo·men·tous** /məʊˈmentəs, mə-‖moʊ-,mə-/ *adj* a momentous event, occasion, decision etc is very important or serious, especially because it will have a great influence on the future: *a momentous decision*|*1789 was a momentous year in European history.*

**mo·men·tum** /məʊˈmentəm, mə-‖moʊ-,mə-/ *n* [U] **1** the ability to keep increasing, developing, or being more successful: **lose momentum** (=stop increasing or developing) *The business did well at first but it seems to be losing momentum.*|**gain/gather momentum** (=begin to increase or develop more quickly) *The trend towards political change in South Africa was gathering momentum.* **2** the force that makes a moving object keep moving: **gain/gather momentum** (=move faster) *The hill got steeper and the sled gained momentum.*|**lose momentum** (=move more slowly) **3** *technical* the force or power contained in a moving object calculated by multiplying its weight by its speed

**mom·ma** /ˈmɒmə‖ˈmɑːmə/ *n* [C] *AmE* another spelling of MAMA[1]

**mom·my** /ˈmɒmi‖ˈmɑːmi/ *n* [C] *AmE* a word meaning mother, used by or to young children; MUMMY (1) *BrE* S3

**Mon** the written abbreviation of MONDAY

**mon·arch** /ˈmɒnək‖ˈmɑːnərk, -ɑːrk/ *n* [C] a king or queen —**monarchic** /məˈnɑːkɪk‖-ˈnɑːr-/ also **monarchical** *adj*: *monarchic rule*

**mon·arch·ist** /ˈmɒnəkɪst‖ˈmɑːnər-/ *n* [C] someone who supports the idea that their country should be ruled by a king or queen —**monarchism** *n* [U]

**mon·ar·chy** /ˈmɒnəki‖ˈmɑːnərki/ *n* **1** [U] the system in which a country is ruled by a king or queen: *the abolition of the monarchy* **2** [C] a country that is ruled by a king or queen: *Britain is a constitutional monarchy.* —compare REPUBLIC

**mon·as·tery** /ˈmɒnəstri‖ˈmɑːnəsteri/ *n* [C] a building or group of buildings in which MONKS live —compare CONVENT, NUNNERY

**mo·nas·tic** /məˈnæstɪk/ *adj* **1** concerned with or relating to MONKS or monasteries: *monastic lands* **2** someone who has a monastic way of life lives alone and very simply —**monastically** /-kli/ *adv* —**monasticism** *n* [U]

**Mon·day** /ˈmʌndi/ *n* [C,U] the day between Sunday and Tuesday. In Britain, Monday is considered the first day of the week, and in the US, it is considered the second day of the week: *It was raining on Monday.*|*I found it hard to get out of bed for work on Monday morning.*|*Sasha will arrive Monday.*|**on Mondays** (=each Monday) *We play football on Mondays.*|**a Monday** (=one of the Mondays in a year) *Does Christmas fall on a Monday this year?*

**mon·e·ta·ris·m** /ˈmʌnɪtərɪzəm‖ˈmɑː-/ *n* [U] the belief that the best way to manage and control a country's economic system is to limit the amount of money that is available and being used —**monetarist** *adj, n* [C]

**mon·e·ta·ry** /ˈmʌnɪtəri‖ˈmɑːnɪteri/ *adj* concerned with or relating to money, especially all the money in a particular country: *monetary growth*|*a monetary unit* W3

**mon·ey** /ˈmʌni/ *n* [U] **1** what you earn by working and what you spend in order to buy things: *The repairs will cost a lot of money.*|**earn money** *She barely earns enough money to live on.*|**save money** *We're not going on holiday this year – we're trying to save money.*|**get/be given your money back** *If it doesn't fit, just take it back* S1 

to the shop and they'll give you your money back. | **spend money** *I spent so much money at the weekend I can't afford to come.* | **borrow money** *Maybe you could borrow some money from the bank to pay for your course.* | **make money** (=earn money or make a profit) *John's making a lot of money from his computer games.* | *His business has finally started making money.* | **charge money** *I said I didn't want it if they were gong to charge me a lot of money for it.* | **good money** (=good wages for your work) *She's making about $40,000 a year, which is pretty good money.* | **raise money** (=collect money for a purpose) *We're trying to raise money for the victims of the earthquake.* | **birthday money/redundancy money etc** (=money you receive on a particular occasion or in a particular situation) *They're using part of his redundancy money to go on a cruise.* | **put money into** (=lend money or allow a business to use your money, especially in order to make a profit) *George has decided to put some of his money into the business.* | **put money on a race/horse etc** (=risk money on the result of a race etc) **2** money in the form of coins or notes; CASH[1] (1): *My bag came open, and all my money fell on the floor.* | **have money on you** (=carry money with you) *Do you have enough money on you to pay for the meal?* **3 French/Japanese/Turkish money** the money that is used in a particular country; CURRENCY: *Don't forget to get some French money before you leave.* **4** all the money that a person, organization, or country owns: *The business collapsed and we lost all our money.* | *She's only marrying him for his money.* | **make your money** (=earn all your money) *I think he made his money in property speculation.* **5 pay good money for** *spoken* to spend a lot of money on something: *I paid good money for that sofa, so it should last.* **6 there's money (to be made) in** *spoken* used to say that you can get a lot of money from a particular activity or from buying and selling something: *Apparently there's a lot of money in ostrich farming.* **7 be rolling in money/be rolling in it** *informal* to be very rich: *They're always going on vacation – they must be rolling in money!* **8 I'm not made of money** *spoken* used to say that you do not have a lot of money when someone asks you for some **9 he/she must have money to burn** used when you think someone is wasting their money on unnecessary things **10 get your money's worth** to get something worth the price that you paid: *At that price you want to make sure you get your money's worth.* **11 be in the money** *informal* to have a lot of money, especially suddenly or when you did not expect to **12 money is no object** *informal* used to say that you can spend as much money as you want to on something: *Choose whatever you like, money is no object.* **13 for my money** *spoken* used when giving your opinion about something to emphasize that you believe it strongly: *For my money, Torville and Dean were by far the best skaters.* **14 I'd put money on it** *spoken* used to emphasize that you are completely sure about something: *"Do you really think that she'll get the gold medal?" "I'd put money on it."* **15 my money's on** *spoken* used to say that you think someone will probably win, or a situation will probably have a particular result: *My money's on a draw – I don't think either team can win now.* **16 money for old rope/money for jam** *BrE spoken* money that you earn very easily **17 put your money where your mouth is** *informal, often humorous* to show by your actions that you really believe what you say **18 money doesn't grow on trees** *spoken* used to tell someone that they should not waste money **19 money talks** *spoken* used to say that money is powerful, and people who have money can get what they want **20 be (right) on the money** *AmE spoken* used when something is perfect or exactly right for the situation: *Her solution was right on the money – the clients loved it.* **21 marry (into) money** to marry someone whose family is rich —see also BLOOD MONEY, HUSH MONEY, POCKET MONEY, **have a (good) run for your money** (RUN[2] (11)), **throw money at** (THROW[1] (20))

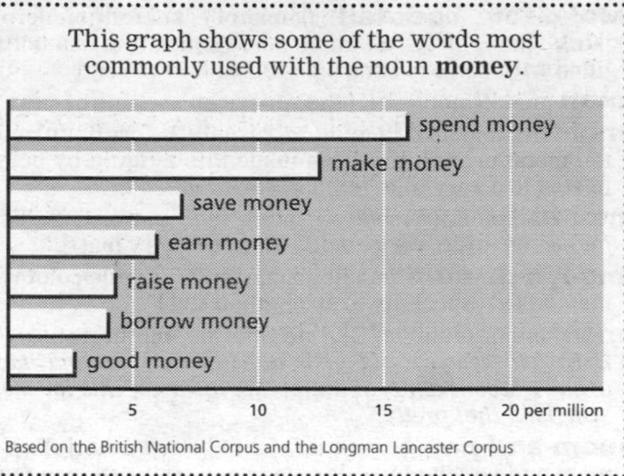


This graph shows some of the words most commonly used with the noun **money**.

Based on the British National Corpus and the Longman Lancaster Corpus

**USAGE NOTE: MONEY**

WORD CHOICE: **money, cash, change, funds**

**Money** is the most general word: *Where can I change money?* | *How much money do you have?* | *taxpayers' money*

**Cash** usually means money in coins or notes rather than cheques or credit cards: *"May I pay by Visa?" "I'm sorry, we only take cash."* But it can also mean money in any form that is available to be spent: *We're going to Australia next year if we have the cash.*

**Change** is used for the amount of money that is given back to you when you have given more for something than the amount it costs: *three dollars fifty change.* **Change** can also mean money in low-value coins or notes: *Can you give me change for a ten pound note?* | *I keep all my small change for the coffee machine.*

Money collected for a particular purpose may be called **funds**: *I need more funds if I'm to study abroad.* | *We're short of funds at the moment.*

**mon·ey·bags** /ˈmʌnibæɡz/ *n* [singular] *informal humorous* someone who has a lot of money

**mon·ey·box** /ˈmʌnibɒks‖-bɑːks/ *n* [C] *especially BrE* a box for saving money in

**mon·ey·chang·er** /ˈmʌniˌtʃeɪndʒə‖-ər/ *n* [C] someone whose business is to exchange one country's money for money from another country, sometimes unofficially

**mon·eyed, monied** /ˈmʌnid/ *adj* [only before noun] *formal* rich: *the new moneyed classes*

**mon·ey·grab·bing** /ˈmʌniɡræbɪŋ/ also **moneygrubbing** /ˈmʌniɡrʌbɪŋ/ *adj* [only before noun] *informal* determined to get money, even by unfair or dishonest methods: —**moneygrabber, moneygrubber** *n* [C]

**mon·ey·lend·er** /ˈmʌniˌlendə‖-ər/ *n* [C] someone whose business is to lend money to people, especially at very high rates of INTEREST[1] (4)

**mon·ey·mak·er** /ˈmʌniˌmeɪkə‖-ər/ *n* [C] a product or business that earns a lot of money; MONEY-SPINNER *BrE*: *The movie has turned into a real moneymaker.*

**money mar·ket** /ˈ·· ˌ··/ *n* [C] the banks and other institutions who buy, sell, lend, or borrow money, especially foreign money, for profit

**money or·der** /ˈ·· ˌ··/ *n* [C] an official document that you buy in a post office or a bank and send to someone so that they can exchange it for money in a bank —compare POSTAL ORDER

**money-spin·ner** /ˈ·· ˌ··/ *n* [C] *BrE* MONEYMAKER: *The hotel's a real moneyspinner in the summer months.*

**money sup·ply** /ˈ·· ·ˌ·/ *n* [singular] *technical* all the money that exists in a country's economic system at a particular time

**-mon·ger** /mʌŋɡə‖mɑːŋɡər, mʌŋ-/ *suffix* [in nouns] **1** someone who sells a particular thing: *a fishmonger* **2** someone who likes to say or encourage something unpleasant: *the rumour-mongers* (=people who say untrue things about other people) | *capitalist warmongers*

**mon·gol** /ˈmɒŋɡəl‖ˈmɑːŋ-/ *n* [C] *old-fashioned* someone with DOWN'S SYNDROME —**mongolism** *n* [U]

**mon·goose** /ˈmɒŋɡuːs‖ˈmɑːŋ-/ *n plural* **mongooses** [C] a small furry tropical animal that kills snakes and rats

**mon·grel** /ˈmʌŋɡrəl‖ˈmɑːŋ-, ˈmʌŋ-/ *n* [C] a dog that is a mix of several breeds of dog

**mon·ied** /ˈmʌnid/ *adj* another spelling of MONEYED

**mon·ies** /ˈmʌniz/ *n* [plural] *law* money

**mon·i·ker** /ˈmɒnɪkə‖ˈmɑːnɪkər/ *n* [C] *humorous* someone's name, signature, or NICKNAME

S3 W3 **mon·i·tor**[1] /ˈmɒnɪ̣tə‖ˈmɑːnɪ̣tər/ *v* [T] **1** to carefully watch and check a situation in order to see how it changes or progresses over a period of time: *British Aerospace has built a scanner that monitors damage to the ozone layer.* | *Their job is to monitor healthcare costs.* **2** to secretly listen to other people's phone calls, foreign radio broadcasts etc *The Security Police had monitored all of his phone calls.*

**monitor**[2] *n* [C] **1** a television that shows a picture of what is happening in a particular place: *a row of monitors covering key areas of the building* **2** the part of a computer that looks like a television and that shows information; VDU —see picture on page 837 **3** a piece of equipment that receives and shows information about what is happening inside someone's body: *a monitor that shows the baby's heartbeat* **4** a child who has been chosen to help the teacher in some way: *the milk monitors* **5** someone whose job is to listen to news, messages etc from foreign radio stations and report on them

**monk** /mʌŋk/ *n* [C] a member of an all-male religious group that lives apart from other people in a MONASTERY —compare NUN —**monkish** *adj*: *a monkish silence*

**mon·key**[1] /ˈmʌŋki/ *n* [C]

**1** ► **ANIMAL** ◄ a small brown animal with a long tail, which uses its hands to climb trees and lives in hot countries

**2** ► **CHILD** ◄ *informal* a small child who is very active and likes to play tricks: *Stop that, you little monkey!*

**3 monkey business** *informal* behaviour that may cause trouble or may be dishonest: *The boys are awfully quiet – I think they're up to some monkey business.*

**4 make a monkey (out) of sb** to make someone seem stupid: *They got into the palace in broad daylight, and made monkeys out of the security men.*

**5 I don't give a monkey's** *BrE spoken* used to say that you do not care at all about something: *To be honest I don't give a monkey's what they do.*

**6 a monkey on your back** *AmE informal* a serious problem that makes your life very difficult, especially being dependent on drugs

**monkey**[2] *v*

**monkey around** also **monkey about** *phr v* [I] *BrE informal* to behave in a stupid or careless way: *They were monkeying around in the playground and one of them got hurt.* | [+ **with**] *I wish those kids would stop monkeying around with the remote control!*

**monkey bars** /ˈ·· ·/ *n* [plural] **1** *AmE* a structure for children to climb and play on; CLIMBING FRAME *BrE* **2** *BrE* bars fixed to the wall in a GYM (1)

**monkey nut** /ˈ·· ·/ *n* [C] *BrE informal* a PEANUT in its shell

**mon·key·shines** /ˈmʌŋkiʃaɪnz/ *n* [plural] *AmE informal* tricks or jokes: *Jo's monkeyshines finally cost him his job.*

**monkey suit** /ˈ·· ·/ *n* [C] *old-fashioned* a formal suit, especially with black trousers and jacket and a BOW TIE

**monkey wrench** /ˈ·· ·/ *n* [C] *AmE* **1** a tool that is used to hold or turn things, especially nuts (NUT[1] (2)); ADJUSTABLE SPANNER *BrE* —see picture at TOOL[1] **2 throw a monkey wrench in the works** *AmE informal* to do something that will cause problems or spoil what someone else is planning

**mono-** /mɒnəʊ, -nə‖-noʊ, -nə/ *prefix* one; single: *a monoplane* (=plane with only one wing on each side) | *a monolingual dictionary* (=dealing with only one language)

**mon·o**[1] /ˈmɒnəʊ‖ˈmɑːnoʊ/ *n* [U] *informal* **1** *AmE* an infectious illness that makes your LYMPH GLANDS swell and makes you feel weak and tired for a long time afterwards; GLANDULAR FEVER *BrE* **2** a system of recording or broadcasting sound, in which the sound comes from only one direction —compare STEREO[1]

**mono**[2] *adj* using a system of recording or broadcasting sound in which all the sound comes from only one direction: *a mono recording* —compare STEREO[2]

**mon·o·chrome** /ˈmɒnəkrəʊm‖ˈmɑːnəkroʊm/ *adj* **1** in shades of only one colour, especially shades of grey: *The landscape was dull, misty, and monochrome.* **2** using or appearing in only black, white, and grey: *a monochrome television* **3** a monochrome computer MONITOR uses one colour as a background and only one other colour for the letters on the SCREEN —opposite COLOUR[3]

**mon·o·cle** /ˈmɒnəkəl‖ˈmɑː-/ *n* [C] a single LENS (=ROUND PIECE OF GLASS) that you hold in front of one eye to help you to see better

**mo·nog·a·my** /məˈnɒɡəmi‖məˈnɑː-/ *n* [U] the custom or practice of being married to only one husband or wife —compare BIGAMY, POLYGAMY —**monogamous** *adj* —**monogamously** *adv*

**mon·o·gram** /ˈmɒnəɡræm‖ˈmɑː-/ *n* [C] two or more letters, usually the first letters of someone's names, that are put together to form a design —**monogrammed** *adj*

**mon·o·graph** /ˈmɒnəɡrɑːf‖ˈmɑːnəɡræf/ *n* [C + **on**] a serious article or short book about a subject

**mon·o·ling·ual** /ˌmɒnəʊˈlɪŋɡwəl◄‖ˌmɑːnə-/ *adj* speaking or using only one language: *a monolingual dictionary* —compare BILINGUAL, MULTILINGUAL

**mon·o·lith** /ˈmɒnəlɪθ‖ˈmɑː-/ *n* [C] **1** an organization, government etc that is very large and powerful and difficult to change: *the break-up of the Soviet monolith* **2** a large tall block of stone, especially one that was put in place in ancient times, possibly for religious reasons

**mon·o·lith·ic** /ˌmɒnəˈlɪθɪk◄‖ˌmɑː-/ *adj* **1** very large, solid, and impressive: *huge monolithic office buildings* **2** a monolithic organization, political system etc is very large and powerful and difficult to change

**mon·o·logue** also **monolog** *AmE* /ˈmɒnəlɒɡ‖ˈmɑːnl-ɒːɡ, -ɑːɡ/ *n* [C] **1** *informal* a long period of talking by one person that prevents other people from taking part in a conversation: *Charles listened patiently to a fifteen-minute monologue before finally interrupting.* **2** a long speech by one character in a play or film: *Hamlet's famous monologue* —compare DIALOGUE, SOLILOQUY

**mon·o·ma·ni·a** /ˌmɒnəʊˈmeɪniə‖ˌmɑːnoʊ-/ *n* [U] an unusually strong interest in a particular idea or subject; OBSESSION: *the victims of a computing monomania* —**monomaniac** /-niæk/ *n adj*

**mon·o·nu·cle·o·sis** /ˌmɒnəʊnjuːkliˈəʊsɪ̣s‖ˌmɑːnoʊnuːkliˈoʊ-/ *n* [U] *AmE technical* MONO[1] (1)

**mon·o·plane** /ˈmɒnəʊpleɪn‖ˈmɑːnoʊ-/ *n* [C] a plane with only one wing on each side, like most modern planes —compare BIPLANE

**mo·nop·ol·is·tic** /məˌnɒpəˈlɪstɪk◄‖-ˌnɑː-/ *adj* controlling or trying to control something completely, especially an industry or business activity: *monopolistic corporations*

**mo·nop·o·lize** also **-ise** *BrE* /məˈnɒpəlaɪz‖məˈnɑː-/ *v* [T] **1** to have complete control over something so that other people cannot share it: *This small group monopolized the key positions in government for many years.* | *to monopolize a conversation* **2** to demand or need a lot of someone's time and attention: *Virtually all her time and energy is now monopolized by the children.* —**monopolization** /məˌnɒpəlaɪˈzeɪʃən‖-ˌnɑːpələ-/ *n* [U]

**mo·nop·o·ly** /məˈnɒpəli‖məˈnɑː-/ *n* **1** [C] the control of

all or most of a business activity by a single company or by a government, so that other organizations cannot easily compete with them: *Cigarette production is a state monopoly in China.* | [+ **on/of**] *For years Bell Telephone had a monopoly on phone services in the US.* **2** [singular] something that belongs to only one person, group, or organization, so that other people cannot share it: *Good healthcare shouldn't be the monopoly of the rich.* | **have/hold a monopoly on** *Universities do not hold a monopoly on intellectual life.*

**mon·o·rail** /ˈmɒnəʊreɪl‖ˈmɑːnə-/ *n* **1** [U] a railway system that uses a single RAIL[1] (3) , usually high above the ground **2** [C] a train on this system

**mon·o·sod·i·um glu·tam·ate** /ˌmɒnəʊˌsəʊdiəm ˈgluːtəmeɪt‖ˌmɑːnəsoʊ-/ *n* [U] *technical* MSG

**mon·o·syl·lab·ic** /ˌmɒnəsɪˈlæbɪk◂‖ˌmɑː-/ *adj* **1** someone who is monosyllabic or makes monosyllabic remarks seems rude because they do not say much: *Jim became more and more monosyllabic.* **2** *technical* a monosyllabic word has only one SYLLABLE

**mon·o·syl·la·ble** /ˈmɒnəˌsɪləbəl‖ˈmɑː-/ *n* [C] *technical* a word with one SYLLABLE

**mon·o·the·is·m** /ˈmɒnəʊθiːɪzəm‖ˈmɑːnə-/ *n* [U] *technical* the belief that there is only one God —compare POLYTHEISM —**monotheist** *n* [C] —**monotheistic** /ˌmɒnəʊθiˈɪstɪk◂‖ˌmɑːnə-/ *adj*: *Christianity is a monotheistic religion.*

**mon·o·tone** /ˈmɒnətəʊn‖ˈmɑːnətoʊn/ *n* [singular] a sound or way of speaking or singing that continues on the same note without getting any louder or softer, and therefore sounds very boring: *Mr Major was talking in a flat, slow monotone.*

**mo·not·o·nous** /məˈnɒtənəs‖məˈnɑː-/ *adj* boring because there is no variety: *He was speaking in a low monotonous voice.* | *a monotonous factory job* —**monotonously** *adv*: *The rain poured monotonously out of the grey sky*

**mo·not·o·ny** /məˈnɒtəni‖məˈnɑː-/ *n* [U] a lack of variety that makes you feel bored: *A small group of houses relieved the monotony of the landscape.*

**mo·nox·ide** /məˈnɒksaɪd‖məˈnɑːk-/ *n* [C,U] *technical* a chemical compound containing one atom of oxygen to every atom of another substance: *carbon monoxide*

**Mon·sieur** /məˈsjɜː‖-ˈsjɜːr/ *n plural* **Messieurs** /meɪˈsjɜːz‖-ˈsjɜːrz/ [C] *French* a way of addressing or referring to a French-speaking man: *Monsieur Bonnet*

**Mon·si·gnor** /mɒnˈsiːnjə‖mɑːnˈsiːnjər/ *n* [C] a way of addressing or referring to a priest of high rank in the Roman Catholic Church

**mon·soon** /mɒnˈsuːn‖mɑːn-/ *n* [C] **1** [usually singular] the season, from about April to October, when it rains a lot in India and other southern Asian countries **2** the rain that falls during this season or the wind that brings the rain

**mon·ster**[1] /ˈmɒnstə‖ˈmɑːnstər/ *n* [C]
**1** ▶ **IN STORIES** ◀ a large ugly frightening creature, especially an imaginary one: *the Kraken and other legendary sea monsters* | *a prehistoric monster*
**2** ▶ **CRUEL PERSON** ◀ someone who is very cruel and evil: *Only a monster could kill all those women and feel no remorse.*
**3** ▶ **CHILD** ◀ *often humorous* a small child, especially one who is behaving badly: *I've got to get home and feed this little monster.*
**4** ▶ **STH LARGE** ◀ *informal* an object, animal etc that is unusually large: *That car of his is an absolute monster!*
**5** a dangerous or threatening problem, especially one that develops gradually: *It was years before people realized what a monster industrialization had created.*

**monster**[2] *adj* [only before noun] *informal* unusually large: *the monster fortunes of the Mellons and DuPonts*

**mon·stros·i·ty** /mɒnˈstrɒsɪ̀ti‖mɑːnˈstrɑː-/ *n* [C] something large and ugly, especially a building: *The office complex is yet another monstrosity in the very center of the city.*

**mon·strous** /ˈmɒnstrəs‖ˈmɑːn-/ *adj* **1** very wrong, immoral, or unfair: *It's monstrous to charge that much for a hotel room.* | *a monstrous injustice* **2** unusually large and ugly: *a monstrous castle* —**monstrously** *adv*

**mon·tage** /ˈmɒntɑːʒ‖mɑːnˈtɑːʒ/ *n* **1** [U] an art form in which a picture, film, piece of writing etc is made from parts of different pictures etc, that are combined to form a whole **2** [C] something made using this process

**month** /mʌnθ/ *n* [C] **1** one of the twelve named periods of time that a year is divided into: *It snowed heavily during the month of January.* | *Phil is coming home for a visit next month.* | *She'll be thirteen this month.* | *a tremendous article in this month's American Indian Review* **2** a period of about four weeks: *She has an eight-month old daughter.* | *He'll be away for two months.* **3 once/twice etc a month** *We update the schedule at least once a month.* **4 months** a long time, especially several months: *Redecorating the kitchen took months.* | **for/in months** (=for a long time) *I haven't seen him for months.* **5 month after month** used to emphasize that something happens regularly or continuously for several months: *I felt I was doing the same old thing week after week, month after month.* **6 month by month** used when you are talking about a situation that develops over several months: *Unemployment figures are rising month by month.* **7 never in a month of Sundays** *spoken* used to emphasize that something will definitely never happen: *You'll never guess it in a month of Sundays.* S1 W1

**month·ly**[1] /ˈmʌnθli/ *adj* [only before noun] **1** happening once a month: *The mortgage is payable in monthly instalments.* | *a monthly publication* **2** a monthly income, figure etc is the total amount that is received, paid, measured etc in a month: *a monthly salary of $850* | *Monthly rainfall in the area goes down from four inches in January to nothing at all in July.* **3** a monthly ticket, PASS[2] (1) etc can be used for a period of one month —**monthly** *adv*: *They meet monthly to discuss progress.* S3

**monthly**[2] *n* [C] **1** a magazine that appears once a month **2 monthlies** *BrE old-fashioned* a woman's PERIOD (=flow of blood from the body each month)

**mon·u·ment** /ˈmɒnjʊ̀mənt‖ˈmɑː-/ *n* [C] **1** a building or other large structure that is built to remind people of an important event or famous person: [+ **of/to**] *a monument to soldiers killed in battle* | *The Victor Emmanuel monument was built to commemorate the unity of Italy.* **2** a very old building or place that is important historically: *The Alhambra is the last and most exquisite monument of Arab civilization in Europe.* **3 be a monument to** to be a very clear example of what can happen as a result of a particular quality: *The house, built just before the stock market crash, was a monument to miscalculation.*

**mon·u·ment·al** /ˌmɒnjʊ̀ˈmentl◂‖ˌmɑː-/ *adj* **1** [usually before noun] a monumental achievement, piece of work, etc is very important and influential, and is usually based on many years of work: *a monumental contribution to the field of medicine* | *Charles Darwin's monumental study, 'The Origin of Species'.* **2** [only before noun] extremely large, bad, good, impressive etc: *There was a monumental traffic jam on the freeway.* | *This is yet more evidence of his monumental incompetence.* **3** [only before noun] appearing on a monument or built as a monument: *a monumental temple*

**mon·u·ment·al·ly** /ˌmɒnjʊ̀ˈmentəli‖ˌmɑː-/ *adv* extremely: [+ adj/adv] *It was a monumentally stupid thing to do.*

**moo**[1] /muː/ *v* [I] to make the sound a cow makes

**moo**[2] *n* [C] **1** the sound that a cow makes **2** *BrE old-fashioned* a stupid woman: *You silly old moo!*

**mooch** /muːtʃ/ *v* [T] *AmE informal* to get something by asking someone to give you it, instead of paying for it; CADGE: *He tried to mooch a drink from me.*

**mooch around** also **mooch about** *BrE phr v* [I] *informal* to walk around without any purpose: *"Where've you been?" "Oh, just mooching around."*

**mood** /muːd/ *n* S3
**1** ▶ **WAY YOU FEEL** ◀ [C] the way you feel at a W3

particular time: *His moods change very quickly – one moment he's cheerful and the next he's sunk in despair.* | *It takes a couple of days to get into the holiday mood.* | **be in a good mood/bad mood etc** (=be happy, annoyed, angry etc) *You're in a good mood this morning!* | *The kids were in a really silly mood after the party.* | **be in a foul/filthy mood** (=be very angry or upset) *Don't talk to Jean; she's in a filthy mood!* | **put sb in a good/bad mood** (=make them feel happy or annoyed) *I'd been stuck in the traffic for hours, which put me in a really bad mood.*
**2 be in a mood** to feel unhappy or angry: *She's been in a real mood all day.* | **be in one of your/his moods** (=used when someone often gets in a bad mood)
**3 be in no mood for sth/to do sth** to not want to do something, or be determined not to do something: *The boss is in no mood for compromise on this point.* | *I was in no mood to argue any more.*
**4 be/feel in the mood (for sth/to do sth)** to want to do something or feel that you would enjoy doing something: *She was in the mood for a romantic walk in the woods.* | *I don't want to talk about it now. I'm not in the mood.*
**5 ▶ WAY PEOPLE FEEL ◀** [singular] the way a group of people feels about something or about life in general: **[+ of]** *The president had misjudged the mood of the people on this issue.* | *The novel captures the mood of postwar France.*
**6 ▶ GRAMMAR ◀** [C] *technical* one of the sets of verb forms in grammar such as the INDICATIVE (=expressing a fact or action), the IMPERATIVE (=expressing a command) or the SUBJUNCTIVE (=expressing a doubt or wish)

**mood mu·sic** /ˈ· ,··/ *n* [U] music that is supposed to make you feel particular emotions, especially romantic feelings

**mood·y** /ˈmuːdi/ *adj* **moodier, moodiest 1** easily becoming annoyed or unhappy when there is no good reason to feel that way: *She had been moody and difficult all day.* | *They kept apart in moody silence.* **2** having moods that change often and quickly: *a moody child* —**moodily** *adv: She was staring moodily into the fire.* —**moodiness** *n* [U]

**moo·la, moolah** /ˈmuːlə/ *n* [U] *AmE slang* money

W3 **moon¹** /muːn/ *n* **1 the moon** the round object that you can see shining in the sky at night, and that moves around the Earth every 28 days: *the first man on the moon* **2** [singular] the shape of this object as it appears at a particular time: *a crescent moon* | *There's no moon tonight.* (=it cannot be seen) **3** [C] a round object that moves around a PLANET other than Earth: *the moons of Saturn* **4 ask for the moon** also **cry for the moon** *BrE informal* to ask for something that is difficult or impossible to obtain **5 over the moon** *BrE informal* very happy: *She's over the moon about her new job.* **6 throw a moon** *BrE* **shoot the moon** *AmE informal* to show your bare BUTTOCKS to someone as a joke or a way of insulting someone **7 many moons ago** *poetic* a long time ago: *It all happened many moons ago.* —see also FULL MOON, HALF MOON, NEW MOON, **once in a blue moon** (BLUE¹ (4)), **promise sb the moon** (PROMISE¹ (3))

**moon²** *v* [I, T] *informal* to bend over and show your bare BUTTOCKS as a joke or a way of insulting someone

**moon about/around** *phr v* [I] *BrE informal* to spend your time lazily, moving around with no real purpose: *I wish you'd stop mooning about and do something useful!*

**moon over sb/sth** *phr v* [T] *informal* to spend your time thinking and dreaming about someone or something that you love: *She sits mooning over his photograph for hours.*

**moon·beam** /ˈmuːnbiːm/ *n* [C] a beam of light from the moon

**moon boot** /ˈ· ·/ *n* [C] a thick warm cloth or plastic boot worn in snow and cold weather

**Moon·ie** /ˈmuːni/ *n* [C] a member of a religious group started by the Korean businessman Sun Myung Moon

**moon·less** /ˈmuːnləs/ *adj* a moonless sky or night is dark because the moon cannot be seen: *a cloudy, moonless night*

**moon·light¹** /ˈmuːnlaɪt/ *n* [U] **1** the light of the moon: *The hills were bathed in pale moonlight.* **2 do a moonlight** also **do a moonlight flit** *BrE* leave a place secretly in the middle of the night in order to avoid paying money that you owe: *Two of the hotel guests had done a moonlight without paying their bills.*

**moonlight²** *v past tense and past participle* **moonlighted** [I] *informal* **1** to have a second job in addition to your main job, especially without the knowledge of the government tax department: *She's been moonlighting as a waitress in the evenings.* **2** *BrE* to do paid work although you are getting money from the government because you do not officially have a job; DOUBLE-DIP² *AmE* —**moonlighter** *n* [C] —**moonlighting** *n* [U] *He's been doing some moonlighting for another company.*

**moon·lit** /ˈmuːn,lɪt/ *adj* [only before noun] made brighter by the light of the moon: *a moonlit garden*

**moon·scape** /ˈmuːnskeɪp/ *n* [C] a bare empty area of land that looks like the surface of the moon

**moon·shine** /ˈmuːnʃaɪn/ *n* [U] *informal* **1** a stupid or impractical remark, idea, or plan: *He regarded her plans as romantic moonshine.* **2** *especially AmE* strong alcoholic drink that is produced illegally

**moon·shot** /ˈmuːnʃɒt‖-ʃɑːt/ *n* [C] a SPACESHIP flight through space to the moon

**moon·stone** /ˈmuːnstəʊn‖-stoʊn/ *n* [C,U] a milky-white stone used in making jewellery: *a moonstone necklace*

**moon·struck** /ˈmuːnstrʌk/ *adj informal* slightly mad

**moor¹** /mʊə‖mʊr/ *n* [C] **1** usually **moors** [plural] *especially BrE* a wild open area of high land, covered with rough grass or low bushes and HEATHER, that is not farmed because the soil is not good enough: *They went grouse shooting up on the moors.* | *the Yorkshire moors* **2 Moor** one of the Muslim people of the Arab race who were in power in Spain from 711 to 1492

**moor²** *v* [I,T] to fasten a ship or boat to the land or to the bottom of the sea using ropes or an ANCHOR: *We moored in the estuary, waiting for high tide.*

**moor·hen** /ˈmʊəhen‖ˈmʊr-/ *n* [C] a black bird that lives beside streams and lakes

**moor·ing** /ˈmʊərɪŋ‖ˈmʊr-/ *n* [C] **1 moorings** [plural] the ropes, chains, ANCHORS etc used to moor a ship or boat: *Several ships had broken their moorings during the storm.* **2** the place where a ship or boat is moored: *a temporary mooring*

**Moor·ish** /ˈmʊərɪʃ‖ˈmʊr-/ *adj* connected with the MOORS: *Moorish architecture in Spain*

**moor·land** /ˈmʊələnd‖ˈmʊr-/ also **moorlands** *n* [U] *especially BrE* wild open countryside covered with rough grass and low bushes —**moorland** *adj: a moorland cottage*

**moose** /muːs/ *n plural* **moose** [C] a large brown animal like a DEER that has very large flat ANTLERS (=horns that grow like branches), and lives in North America and northern Europe

**moot¹** /muːt/ *adj* **1 a moot point/question** something that has not yet been decided, and about which people have different opinions: *Whether these controls will really reduce violent crime is a moot point.* **2** *AmE* a situation or possible action that is moot, is no longer likely to happen or exist: *The fear that airstrikes could endanger troops is moot now that the army is withdrawing.*

**moot²** *v* [T] **be mooted** to be suggested for people to consider: *The question of changing the membership rules was mooted at the last meeting.*

**moot court** /ˈ· ·/ *n* [C] *AmE* a court in which law students practise holding trials

**mop¹** /mɒp‖mɑːp/ *n* [C] **1** a thing for washing floors with, consisting of a long stick with threads of thick string or a piece of SPONGE¹ (1) fastened to one end **2** a thing for cleaning dishes with, consisting of a short stick with a piece of SPONGE¹ (1) fastened to one end **3** [usually singular] *informal* a large amount of thick, often untidy hair: **[+ of]** *a baby with a mop of golden curls*

**mop²** **mopping, mopped** *v* [T] **1** [I,T] to wash a floor with a wet mop —see picture at CLEAN² **2** [T] to dry your face by rubbing it with a cloth or something soft: *It was so hot he had to keep stopping to mop his face.* | **mop your brow** (=remove SWEAT² (1) from your forehead) **3** [I,T] to remove liquid from a surface by rubbing it with a cloth or something soft: **mop sth from sth** *The nurse gently mopped the blood from the wound.* | **mop sth away** *She mopped the tears away with a lacy handkerchief.* **4 mop the floor with** *AmE* **wipe the floor with** *BrE* to completely defeat someone, for example in a game or argument: *We mopped the floor with the team from Pomona High.*

**mop** sth ↔ **up** *phr v* [T] **1** to remove liquid with a mop, cloth, or something soft, especially in order to clean a surface: *Can you mop up the milk you've spilled?* | *Mop up the sauce with your bread.* **2** to deal with the remaining members of a defeated army by killing them or making them prisoners: *mopping up isolated pockets of resistance* | **mopping-up operations** *The rebellion has been crushed, but mopping-up operations may take several weeks.* **3** *BrE* to complete a piece of work or finish dealing with something or someone: *I've just got a couple of jobs to mop up before I go on holiday.*

**mope** /məʊp‖moʊp/ *v* [I] to feel sorry for yourself, without making any effort to be more cheerful: *Don't lie there moping on a lovely morning like this!*

**mope around** also **mope about** *phr v* [I,T] *BrE* to move around a place in a sad, slow way: *She spends her days moping around the house.*

**mo·ped** /ˈməʊped‖ˈmoʊ-/ *n* [C] a small two-wheeled vehicle with an engine —compare MOTORCYCLE

**mo·quette** /mɒˈket‖moʊ-/ *n* [U] a thick soft material used for covering furniture: *a moquette armchair*

**mo·raine** /məˈreɪn/ *n* [C] *technical* a mass of earth or pieces of rock left in a line at the bottom or edge of a GLACIER —see picture on page 835

S3 W2 **mor·al¹** /ˈmɒrəl‖ˈmɔː-/ *adj*

**1 ▶ ABOUT RIGHT AND WRONG ◀** [only before noun] connected with the principles of what is right and wrong behaviour, and with the difference between good and evil: *a man of high moral standards* | *You don't know the circumstances of the divorce, so don't make moral judgments about it.* | **moral dilemma/issue** (=a subject that involves morals) *the abortion issue, one of the great moral dilemmas* | **moral sense** (=ability to understand the difference between right and wrong) *Babies are born without a moral sense.*

**2 ▶ BASED ON WHAT IS RIGHT ◀** [only before noun] based on your ideas about what is right, rather than on what is legal or practical: **moral responsibility/duty** *You have a moral responsibility to help people in need.* | **moral courage** (=the courage to do what you believe is right) *Does he have the moral courage necessary to lead the country?* | **moral authority** (=influence that you have because people accept that your beliefs are right) *The UN feels that it has the moral authority to send troops to the area.* | **moral fibre** *BrE*/**fiber** *AmE* (=the emotional strength to do what you believe is right)

**3 moral support** encouragement that you give by expressing approval or interest, rather than by giving practical help: *He went along to give moral support.*

**4 moral victory** a situation in which you show that your beliefs are right and fair, even if you do not win the argument: *We felt we had won a moral victory in the debate.*

**5 ▶ STORY ◀** a moral story, play etc is one that teaches or shows good behaviour

**6 ▶ PERSON ◀** always behaving in a way that is based on strong principles about what is right and wrong —compare AMORAL, IMMORAL —see also MORALLY

**moral²** *n* [C] **1 morals** [plural] principles or standards of good behaviour, especially in matters of sex: *The novel reflects the morals and customs of the time.* | **public morals** (=the standards of behaviour, especially sexual behaviour, expected by society) *The sex shop was deemed a danger to public morals.* | **loose morals** *old-fashioned or humorous* (=low standards of sexual behaviour resulting in someone having many sexual partners) **2** a practical lesson about what to do or how to behave, which you learn from a story or from something that happens to you: **the moral of sth is** *The moral of the film was that crime does not pay.* | **draw a moral** (=understand what a story or event is teaching you)

**mo·rale** /məˈrɑːl‖məˈræl/ *n* [U] the level of confidence and positive feelings, especially among a group of people who work together, belong to the same team etc: *The team's morale was low after losing.* | *A few words of praise are always good for morale.* | **keep up/maintain morale** *the benefits of regular exercise in keeping up students' morale* | **boost/raise/improve morale** *Churchill's visit did a great deal to boost morale among the troops.*

**mor·al·ist** /ˈmɒrəlɪst‖ˈmɔː-/ *n* [C] **1** someone who has very strong beliefs about what is right and wrong, and who tries to control other people's morals **2** a teacher of moral principles

**mor·al·ist·ic** /ˌmɒrəˈlɪstɪk◂‖ˌmɔː-/ *adj* having very strong unchanging beliefs about what is right and wrong, especially when this makes you judge other people's behaviour: *It's difficult to talk to teenagers about drugs without sounding too moralistic.* —**moralistically** /-kli/ *adv*

**mo·ral·i·ty** /məˈrælɪti/ *n* **1** [U] beliefs or ideas about what is right and wrong and about how people should behave: *traditional morality* | *declining standards of morality* **2** [U] the degree to which something is right or acceptable: [+ **of**] *a discussion on the morality of abortion* **3** [C,U] a system of beliefs and values concerning how people should behave, which is accepted by a particular person or group: *Christian morality* | *a direct clash in moralities* —opposite IMMORALITY

**mor·al·ize** also **-ise** *BrE* /ˈmɒrəlaɪz‖ˈmɔː-/ *v* [I] to tell other people your ideas about right and wrong behaviour, especially when they have not asked for your opinion: [+ **about/on**] *politicians moralizing about people's sexual behaviour* —**moralizer** *n* [C]

**mor·al·ly** /ˈmɒrəli‖ˈmɔː-/ *adv* **1** according to moral principles about what is right and wrong: *What you did wasn't illegal, but it was morally wrong.* | *The president is morally opposed to capital punishment.* | **morally responsible** *He held himself morally responsible for the accident.* **2** in a way which is good or right: *one of the few politicians who always behaves completely morally* **3 morally certain** *old-fashioned* very probable: *It's morally certain that he'll be the next President.*

**moral ma·jor·i·ty** /ˌ·· ·ˈ···/ *n* [singular] a group of people in the US with strong Christian principles, who have very traditional beliefs about the family, crime and punishment, people's sexual behaviour etc

**mo·rass** /məˈræs/ *n* **1** [singular] a complicated and confusing situation that is very difficult to get out of: [+ **of**] *We were bogged down in a morass of detail.* **2** [C] *especially literary* a dangerous area of soft wet ground; MARSH

**mor·a·to·ri·um** /ˌmɒrəˈtɔːriəm‖ˌmɔː-/ *n* [C usually singular] **1** an official stopping of an activity for a period of time: [+ **on**] *the proposed moratorium on nuclear testing* **2** a law or an agreement that gives people more time to pay their debts

**mor·bid** /ˈmɔːbɪd‖ˈmɔːr-/ *adj* **1** having a strong and unhealthy interest in unpleasant subjects, especially death: *He wanted to know all the morbid details about the accident.* | *a morbid fascination with instruments of torture* **2** *technical* connected with or caused by a disease: *a morbid gene* —**morbidly** *adv* —**morbidity** *n* [U]

**mor·dant** /ˈmɔːdənt‖ˈmɔːr-/ *adj*: **mordant criticism/wit/humour** *formal* cruel and insulting criticism, wit etc

**more¹** /mɔː‖mɔːr/ *adv* **1** [+ adj/adv] having a particular quality or characteristic to a greater degree than someone or something else: **more interesting/expensive etc** *We can make the test more difficult by*

*adding a time limit.* | *It could have been an infection but it's more likely to have been something you ate.* | **more interesting/expensive etc than** *Who knows if there are beings more advanced than ourselves out there on other planets?* | **much/a lot/far more** *Many of the children feel much more confident if they work in groups.* —opposite LESS² (1) **2** used to say that something happens more often or for a longer time than before or than something else: *He's managed to master the basics of tennis but needs to practice a bit more.* | **more than** *Businesses use computers more than they used to.* | **far/much/a lot more** *He goes out a lot more now he has the car.* —opposite LESS² (1) **3** used to say that something such as a feeling or opinion is felt or believed to a greater degree: *I couldn't agree more.* | **more than** *It's her manner I dislike, more than what she actually says.* | **much/far/a lot more** *She cares far more for her dogs than she does for me.* —opposite LESS² (1) **4 more and more** if something happens or is done more and more it happens or is done more than before and is becoming common: *More and more I see young boys with no prospects turning to crime or drugs.* **5 more and more tired/angry etc** increasingly tired, angry etc as time passes: *As the disease worsened he found walking more and more difficult.* **6 once more a)** if you do something once more you do it again and usually for the last time: *Can we rehearse the scene once more before the show starts?* **b)** *especially literary* again: *Once more the soldiers attacked and once more they were defeated.* **7 not any more** also **no more** *literary* no longer: *Didn't you know? Paul and Ann aren't going out together any more.* | *No more is it possible to stand on the football terraces and cheer on your local team.* **8 more often than not** used to say that something usually happens: *More often than not people don't realise what their rights are.* **9 be more than pleased/sorry etc** used to emphasize that you are very pleased, very sorry etc: *The store is more than happy to deliver goods to your home.* | *"I suppose you will be working late again tonight?" "More than likely, yes."* **10 be more than a little angry/sad etc** used to emphasize how angry or sad you are: *We're more than a little concerned about the state of his financial affairs.* **11 more...than...** used to emphasize that one thing is truer, more important etc than something: *Don't be too hard on him. He's more misled than stupid.* | *She's known more for her wild private life than her acting ability.* **12 a) no more than** used to say that something is needed or suitable: *It's no more than you deserve.* **b)** also **little more than** used to say that someone or something is less important than they seem: *He's no more than a glorified accountant.* | *It was little more than a scratch.* **13 (and) what's more** used to add more information that emphasizes what you are saying: *He enjoyed the meal and what's more he ate the lot!* **14 no more...than...** used to emphasize that something is not true, not suitable etc: *He's no more fit to be a priest than I am!* **15 no more can she/no more do I etc** neither can she, neither do I etc: *I don't have time to do the filing and no more do you!* **16 (then) more fool you** *BrE* used to say that you think someone is being stupid: *If you want to get up so early in the morning then more fool you!*

**USAGE NOTE: MORE**

GRAMMAR

**More** is used with an adjective instead of the *-er* form, not as well as it: *This year's exam was harder for me* (NOT *more harder*).

It is also used when an adjective does not have an *-er* form: *This year's exam was more difficult than last year's.*

S1 W1 **more²** *quantifier comparative of many, much* **1** used to say that a particular number or amount is larger than another: **more people/things etc than...** *More cars are failing the emissions test than was anticipated.* | *She makes more phone calls in one day than anyone else I know.* | **more than 10/100 etc** *More than 500 people had to be helped to safety when the stadium collapsed.* | **more than sth** *In some places bottled water costs more than a glass of beer.* | *It is possible to earn $100 a day, some days more.* | *I'd ask Veronica – she knows far more about it.* | [+ **of**] *We sell more of these maps because they're so colourful.* | **much/far/a lot more** *Recent anti-smoking campaigns have driven a lot more smokers to give up.* —opposite LESS¹ or FEWER **2** used when you mean another number or amount in addition to what you have, expect, or have mentioned: *You'll have to pay more for a double room.* | *A free trip to Jamaica? Tell me more!* | **2/10 etc more** *That was Jim on the phone. He needs two more tickets for the play.* | **some/any/a few etc more** *We have some wonderful people volunteering to help out but many more are needed.* | **more people/things etc** *I think I'd need to know some more facts before I could agree to the trip.* | *I'm sorry sir, your meal will be five minutes more, I'm afraid.* [+ **of**] | *Can I have some more of that apple pie please?* | *You've had a week to do it. How much more time do you need?* —opposite LESS¹ **3 more and more** an increasing number of something: *More and more people are taking early retirement these days.* —opposite **less and less** (LESS² (2)) **4 more or less a)** almost: *By the time of the dress rehearsal she knew her lines more or less by heart.* **b)** APPROXIMATELY: *We're expecting 150 delegates at the conference, more or less.* **5 not/no more than** used to say that a price, distance etc is only a particular number or amount: *It's a beautiful cottage not more than five minutes from the nearest beach.* **6 the more..., / the more..., the less** used to say that when you do something or something happens, a particular situation will be the result of it: *It's simple. The more preparation you do now, the less nervous you'll be before the exam.* —see also **more's the pity** (PITY¹ (5))

**more·ish** /ˈmɔːrɪʃ/ *adj BrE spoken* food that is moreish tastes very good, and makes you want to eat more of it

**more·o·ver** /mɔːrˈəʊvə‖-ˈoʊvər/ *adv* [sentence adverb] W2 *formal* a word meaning 'in addition', used to introduce information that adds to or supports what has previously been said: *The rent is reasonable and, moreover, the location is perfect.*

**USAGE NOTE: MOREOVER**

FORMALITY

**Moreover** is very formal and not common in spoken English. But you may see it used in a report: *Local people would like a new road. Moreover, there are good economic reasons for building one.*

**Also** is a less formal way of adding a reason or idea. It can be used at the beginning of a sentence to link it to the previous one: *You can stay at our house. Also, I can check the plane times for you.* Or it can be used within a sentence: *I can also check the plane times for you.*

**Besides (that)** is more informal and used especially to add a reason. *June isn't a good month to go there. Besides, I want to finish my exams first.*

People also often add reasons and ideas within one sentence using **and** made stronger with **moreover/also/besides**: *You should switch to a healthier diet and moreover/also/besides that stop smoking.*

**mo·res** /ˈmɔːreɪz/ *n* [plural] *formal* the customs, social behaviour, and moral values of a particular group: *American social and sexual mores*

**morgue** /mɔːg‖mɔːrg/ *n* [C] **1** a building or room, for example in a hospital, where dead bodies are kept until they are buried or cremated (CREMATE); MORTUARY¹ (1) *BrE* **2** *often humorous* a quiet place where not much happens, so that you feel sad or bored

**mor·i·bund** /ˈmɒrɪ̇bʌnd‖ˈmɔː-, ˈmɑː-/ *adj* **1** a moribund industry, institution, custom etc is no longer active or effective and therefore coming to an end: *The eastern*

*region's heavy industry is inefficient and moribund.* **2** *literary* slowly dying

**Mor·mon** /ˈmɔːmən‖ˈmɔːr-/ *n* [C] a member of a religious organization formed in 1830 in the US, officially called The Church of Jesus Christ of Latter-day Saints —**Mormon** *adj* —**Mormonism** *n* [U]

**morn** /mɔːn‖mɔːrn/ *n* [C usually singular] *poetic* morning

S1 W1 **morn·ing¹** /ˈmɔːnɪŋ‖ˈmɔːr-/ *n* [C,U] **1** the early part of the day, from when the sun rises until the middle of the day: *a sunny morning | six o'clock in the morning | I had a letter from George this morning. | We're leaving on Tuesday morning.* **2** the part of the day from midnight until the middle of the day: *The phone rang at three in the morning.* **3 in the morning** tomorrow morning: *I'll deal with that in the morning.* **4 mornings** during the morning each day: *She works mornings at the local school.* **5 morning, noon, and night** used to emphasize that something happens a lot or continuously: *That girl is on the phone morning, noon, and night!* —see also COFFEE MORNING

**morning²** *interjection* used to greet someone in the morning: *Morning, Dave. How are you?*

**morning-af·ter pill** /ˌ·· ˈ·· ˌ·/ *n* [C] a drug that a woman can take after having sex to prevent her from having a baby

**morning coat** /ˈ·· ·/ *n* [C] a formal black coat with a long back that is worn as part of morning dress

**morning dress** /ˈ·· ·/ *n* [U] *especially BrE* men's formal clothes that include a morning coat, trousers, and a TOP HAT, worn at daytime ceremonies such as weddings

**morning glo·ry** /ˌ·· ˈ··‖ˈ·· ˌ··/ *n* [C,U] a plant that has white, blue, or pink flowers that open in the morning and close in late afternoon

**Morning Prayer** /ˌ·· ˈ··/ *n* [U] a morning church service in the Church of England and the Episcopal Church in the US; MATINS

**morning room** /ˈ·· ·/ *n* [C] *old-fashioned* a comfortable room that is used in the morning, usually in a large house

**morning sick·ness** /ˈ·· ˌ··/ *n* [U] a feeling of sickness that some women have before they have a baby

**morning star** /ˌ·· ˈ·/ *n* [singular] a bright PLANET, usually Venus, you can see in the eastern sky when the sun rises —compare EVENING STAR

**morning suit** /ˈ·· ·/ *n* [C] a man's suit that is worn at formal ceremonies during the day, especially weddings

**mo·roc·co** /məˈrɒkəʊ‖məˈrɑːkoʊ-/ *n* [U] fine soft leather used especially for covering books

**mo·ron** /ˈmɔːrɒn‖-rɑːn/ *n* [C] **1** *informal* someone who is very stupid: *Don't leave it there, you moron!* **2** *technical old use* someone whose intelligence has not developed to the normal level —**moronic** /məˈrɒnɪk/ *adj*: *a moronic grin* —**moronically** /-kli/ *adv*

**mo·rose** /məˈrəʊs‖-ˈroʊs/ *adj* bad-tempered, unhappy, and silent: *Daniel seems very morose and gloomy.* —**morosely** *adv* —**moroseness** *n* [U]

**mor·pheme** /ˈmɔːfiːm‖ˈmɔːr-/ *n* [C] *technical* the smallest meaningful unit of language, consisting of a word or part of a word that cannot be divided without losing its meaning: *'Gun' contains one morpheme but 'gun-fight-er' contains three.*

**Mor·phe·us** /ˈmɔːfiəs, -fjuːs‖ˈmɔːr-/ *n* **in the arms of Morpheus** *literary* asleep

**mor·phi·a** /ˈmɔːfiə‖ˈmɔːr-/ *n* [U] *old-fashioned* morphine

**mor·phine** /ˈmɔːfiːn‖ˈmɔːr-/ *n* [U] a powerful and ADDICTIVE drug used for stopping pain and making people calmer

**morph·ing** /ˈmɔːfɪŋ‖ˈmɔːr-/ *n* [U] a computer method that is used to make one image gradually change into a different one

**mor·phol·o·gy** /mɔːˈfɒlədʒi‖mɔːrˈfɑː-/ *n technical* **1** [U] the study of the MORPHEMES of a language and of the way in which they are joined together to make words —compare SYNTAX **2** [U] the scientific study of how animals, plants, and their parts are formed **3** [C,U] the structure of an object or system or the way it was formed —**morphological** /ˌmɔːfəˈlɒdʒɪkəl◂‖ˌmɔːrfəˈlɑː-/ *adj*

**mor·ris danc·ing** /ˈmɒrɪ̈s ˌdɑːnsɪŋ‖ˈmɔːrɪ̈s ˌdænsɪŋ, ˈmɑː-/ *n* [U] traditional English country dancing performed by men wearing white clothes —**morris dancer** *n* [C]

**mor·row** /ˈmɒrəʊ‖ˈmɔːroʊ, ˈmɑː-/ *n* **1 the morrow a)** the next day: *They were to arrive on the morrow.* **b)** the future: *We wondered what the morrow would bring.* **2 the morrow of** *literary* the time immediately after a particular event: *the morrow of victory* **3 good morrow** *old use* good morning

**Morse code** /ˌmɔːs ˈkəʊd‖ˌmɔːrs ˈkoʊd-/ *n* [U] a system of sending messages in which the alphabet is represented by signals made of DOTS (=short signals) and DASHes (=long signals) in sound or light

**mor·sel** /ˈmɔːsəl‖ˈmɔːr/ *n* [C] **1** a small piece of food: [+ **of**] *a morsel of bread | tasty morsels* **2 morsel of hope/wisdom/gossip etc** a small amount of hope etc: *That's the best morsel of scandal we've had for ages.*

**mor·tal¹** /ˈmɔːtl‖ˈmɔːrtl/ *adj* **1** not living for ever: *Her father's death reminded her that she was mortal. | mortal creatures* —opposite IMMORTAL (1) **2 mortal blow/injuries/danger etc** causing death or likely to cause death: *He was dealt a mortal blow in the battle.* | **mortal combat** (=fighting until one person kills the other) *two gladiators locked in mortal combat* —compare LETHAL (1) **3 mortal enemy/foe** an enemy that you hate very much and always will hate **4 mortal fear/terror/dread** extreme fear: *She lives in mortal fear of her husband's anger.* **5** [only before noun] *old-fashioned* used to emphasize the word that follows it, especially to show that you are annoyed: *Now I've lost every mortal thing I owned.* **6** *poetic* belonging to a human: *a sight as yet unseen by mortal eyes* —see also MORTALLY

**mortal²** *n* [C] **1 lesser/ordinary/mere mortals** *humorous* ordinary people, as compared with people who are more important or more powerful: *Of course, she dines in the executive suite, while we lesser mortals use the staff cafeteria.* **2** *especially literary* a word meaning a human, used especially when comparing humans with gods, spirits etc

**mor·tal·i·ty** /mɔːˈtælɪ̈ti‖mɔːr-/ *n* [U] **1** also **mortality rate** /ˈ·ˈ··· ·/ the number of deaths during a certain period of time among a particular type or group of people: *Mortality from heart disease varies widely across the world.* | **infant mortality** (=the rate at which babies die) **2** the condition of being human and having to die —opposite IMMORTALITY

**mor·tal·ly** /ˈmɔːtəl-i‖ˈmɔːr-/ *adv* **1** in a way that will cause death: *Arthur, mortally wounded, was attended by Sir Bedivere.* **2** extremely or greatly: *We hid, mortally afraid, in the cellar.*

**mortal sin** /ˌ·· ˈ·/ *n* [C] something that you do that is so bad, according to the Roman Catholic Church, that it will bring unending punishment to your soul after death unless it is forgiven

**mor·tar** /ˈmɔːtə‖ˈmɔːr-/ *n* **1** [U] a mixture of LIME¹ (3), sand, and water, used in building for joining bricks or stones together **2** [C] a heavy gun that fires bombs or shells (SHELL¹ (2)) in a high curve **3** [C] a hard bowl in which substances are crushed into powder with a PESTLE (=tool with a heavy round end) into very small pieces or powder: *Pound the garlic with a mortar and pestle.* —see picture at LABORATORY

**mor·tar·board** /ˈmɔːtəbɔːd‖ˈmɔːrtərbɔːrd/ *n* [C] a black cap with a flat square top worn by members of some universities on formal occasions —see picture at CAP¹

**mort·gage¹** /ˈmɔːgɪdʒ‖ˈmɔːr-/ *n* [C] **1** a legal arrangement by which you borrow money from a bank or similar organization in order to buy a house, and pay back the money over a period of years: *Your building society or bank will help arrange a mortgage.* | **take out a mortgage** (=borrow money for a mortgage) *They've taken out* W3 *a 30 year mortgage.* | **pay off a mortgage** (=pay back all the money you borrowed for a mortgage) | **mortgage rate/payment etc** *Mortgage interest rates are set to rise again in the spring.* **2** the amount of money you owe on a mortgage: *a mortgage of $90,000*

**mortgage²** *v* [T] **1** to give someone, usually a bank, the right to own your house, land, or property if you do not pay back the money they lent you within a certain period of time: *He's mortgaged all his assets to try and save the business.* **2 be mortgaged to the hilt** to have everything that you own mortgaged

**mor·ti·cian** /mɔːˈtɪʃən‖mɔːr-/ *n* [C] *AmE* someone whose job is to arrange funerals and prepare bodies for burial; UNDERTAKER *BrE*

**mor·ti·fy** /ˈmɔːtʒfaɪ‖ˈmɔːr-/ *v* [T] **1 be mortified** to feel extremely embarrassed or ashamed: *She was mortified to think that he had read her diary.* **2 mortify the flesh/yourself** *formal* to try to control your natural physical desires and needs by making your body suffer pain —**mortification** /ˌmɔːtʒfʒˈkeɪʃən‖ˌmɔːr-/ *n* [U]: *To my utter mortification I could not remember his name.*

**mor·ti·fy·ing** /ˈmɔːtʒfaɪ-ɪŋ‖ˈmɔːr-/ *adj* extremely embarrassing: *The princess now faced further mortifying revelations in the tabloid press.*

**mor·tise** /ˈmɔːtʒs‖ˈmɔːr-/ *n* [C] *technical* a hole cut in a piece of wood or stone to receive the TENON (=the shaped end) of another piece and form a joint

**mortise lock** /ˈ·· ·/ *n* [C] *BrE* a lock that fits into a hole cut in the edge of a door; DEAD BOLT *AmE*

**mor·tu·a·ry¹** /ˈmɔːtʃuəri‖ˈmɔːrtʃueri/ *n* [C] **1** *BrE* a building or room, for example in a hospital, where dead bodies are kept before they are buried or cremated (CREMATE); MORGUE (1) **2** *AmE* the place where a body is kept before a funeral and where the funeral is sometimes held

**mortuary²** *adj* [only before noun] *formal* connected with death or funerals: *a mortuary urn*

**Mo·sa·ic** /məʊˈzeɪ-ɪk‖moʊ-/ *adj* connected with or relating to Moses, the great leader of the Jewish people in ancient times: *Mosaic law*

**mosaic** *n* **1** [C,U] a pattern or picture made by fitting together small pieces of coloured stone, glass etc: *a Roman stone mosaic* | *mosaic tiles* **2** [C usually singular] a group of various things that are seen or considered together as a pattern: *The forest floor was a mosaic of autumn colours.*

**Mo·ses bas·ket** /ˈməʊzʒz ˌbɑːskʒt‖ˈmoʊzʒz ˌbæ-/ *n* [C] *BrE* a large basket with handles, in which a baby can sleep and be carried

**mo·sey** /ˈməʊzi‖ˈmoʊ/ *v* [I always + adv/prep] *AmE informal, often humorous* **1** to walk somewhere in a slow relaxed way: [**+around/down etc**] *I guess I'll mosey on down to the store now.* **2 mosey along** to leave: *I'd better mosey along – it's getting late.* —**mosey** *n* [singular]

**Mos·lem** /ˈmɒzlʒm‖ˈmɑːz-/ *n* [C] another spelling of MUSLIM, which is unacceptable to some Muslims

**mosque** /mɒsk‖mɑːsk/ *n* [C] a building in which Muslims worship: *the famous mosque in Regents Park*

**mos·qui·to** /məˈskiːtəʊ‖-toʊ/ *n plural* **mosquitoes** or **mosquitos** [C] a small flying insect that sucks the blood of people and animals.

**mosquito net** /-ˈ·· ·/ *n* [C] a net placed over a bed as a protection against mosquitoes

**moss** /mɒs‖mɒːs/ *n* [C,U] a small flat green or yellow plant that grows in a thick furry mass on wet soil or rock: *rocks covered in moss* —compare LICHEN —**mossy** *adj*

**-most** /məʊst‖moʊst/ *suffix* [in adjectives] nearest to something: *the northernmost town in Sweden* (=the town that is furthest to the north) | *the topmost branches of the tree*

S1 W1 **most¹** /məʊst‖moʊst/ *adv* [+ adj/adv] **1** used for forming the SUPERLATIVE of most adjectives and adverbs with more than two SYLLABLES, and many that only have two: *the most boring book I've ever read* | *She's one of the most experienced teachers in the district.* | *The excuse I get told most often is that the train was late.* | *In high school Kelly had been voted 'girl most likely to succeed'.* **2** more than anything else: *The food I eat most is pasta.* | *What annoyed him most was the way she wouldn't even listen to his reasons.* | **most of all** *Unfortunately they'd run out of the paint colour I liked most of all.* **3** *formal* very: *I was most surprised to hear of your engagement.* | *Do you realise we'll most probably end up bankrupt.* | **a most interesting/expensive etc sth** *That really was a most illuminating lecture, Professer Jordan.* **4** *AmE informal* almost: *He plays poker most every evening.*

> **USAGE NOTE: MOST**
>
> GRAMMAR
>
> **Most** meaning 'nearly all' is followed directly by a noun when you are speaking generally: *Most cheese contains a lot of fat* (NOT *most of cheese*). | *Most Americans own cars.*
>
> You use **most of the** when you are talking about part of a particular thing, group, etc: *Greg has eaten most of the cheese that was in the fridge.* | *Most of the Americans we asked owned cars.*
>
> You can also say: *Most Americans we asked own cars* without using **of the** to talk about that particular group.
>
> **The most** can be followed directly by a plural or uncountable noun, when it means 'more than any other(s)': *The most damage was done to the houses nearest the cliff* means more damage was done to those houses than any others.
>
> You use **most** meaning 'more than anything else' in these ways: *My swimming is the thing I most want to improve.* | *I want to improve my swimming most.* | *I most want to improve my swimming* (NOT *The most thing I want to improve is my swimming*).
>
> Remember that most short adjectives have a form ending in *-est* that you usually use when you want to say 'more than any other', and you should not use **most** with them: *Manhattan is the richest area in New York* (NOT *the most rich* or *the most richest*). | *The dullest people I've ever met* (NOT *most dull*).
>
> Note that you use the phrase **most of the time**, not *the most time* or *most of times*.

**most²** *quantifier* [superlative of **many**, **much**] S1 W1 **1** almost all of a particular group of people or things **most things/food etc** *These days most crime is against property, not people.* | *Like most people, I try to take a vacation every year.* | **most of** *It was afternoon and most of the shops were shut.* | *Tim spent most of his salary on alcohol and cigarettes.* | **most** *Of all the money donated, most is spent on food and clothing for the refugees.* **2** more people or things than anyone else: **the most people/food etc** *It's the best hotel in town and it also has the most rooms.* | *This is the most votes any candidate has ever received.* | **the most** *It's unfair that you should have to pay the most when you earn so little.* | **most** *Whoever scores most in the penalty competition will be awarded the trophy.* **3** the largest number or amount possible. **most people/food etc** *How can we plan the campaign to reach most people?* | **the most people/food etc** *To get the most use out of the machine, recharge the batteries overnight.* | **the most** *The most you can hope to achieve is to just get him to listen to your ideas.* **4 at (the) most** used to say that a number or amount could not be larger: *You could buy a good washing machine for about £350, £400 at most.* | **at (the) very most** *At the very most the temperature in summer goes up to about 38°C.* —compare **at (the) very least** (LEAST¹ (1)) **5 for the most part** used when a statement or fact is generally true but not completely true: *For the most part the relationship between private investment and government interests has not been a successful one.* **6 make the most of sth** to get the most advantage from a good situation because it

will not last a long time: *You should be outside making the most of the sunshine.*

S2 W3 **most·ly** /ˈməustli‖ˈmoust-/ *adv* in most cases or most of the time: *I mostly worked as a researcher, writer, or teacher.* | *More immigrants arrived, mostly Europeans.*

**MOT** /ˌem əu ˈtiː‖-ou-/ *n* [C] a regular official examination in Britain of the condition and safety of cars that are more than three years old: *Will the car pass its MOT?*

**mote** /məut‖mout/ *n* [C] *old-fashioned* a very small piece of dust

**mo·tel** /məuˈtel‖mou-/ *n* [C] a hotel for people travelling, where you can park your car outside your room

**moth** /mɒθ‖mɔːθ/ *n* [C] **1** an insect related to the BUTTERFLY that flies mainly at night and is attracted to lights **2** also **clothes moth** a moth whose young eat holes in cloth

**moth·ball¹** /ˈmɒθbɔːl‖ˈmɔːθbɒːl-/ *n* [C usually plural] **1** a small ball made of a strong-smelling chemical, used for keeping moths away from clothes **2 in mothballs** stored and not used for a long time: *With the end of the Cold War several warships were put into mothballs.*

**mothball²** *v* [T] to close a factory or to decide not to use plans or machinery for a long time: *The company announced that plans to create new offices have been mothballed.*

**moth-eat·en** /ˈ· ˌ··/ *adj* **1** cloth that is moth-eaten has holes eaten in it by moths: *a moth-eaten sweater* **2** old and in bad condition: *a moth-eaten old sofa*

S1 W1 **moth·er¹** /ˈmʌðə‖-ər/ *n* [C]
**1** ▶ **PARENT** ◀ a female parent of a child or animal: *His mother and father are both doctors.* | *Can I borrow your car please, Mother?* | **mother hen/cat/dog etc** (=an animal that is a mother) —see picture at FAMILY
**2 be (like) a mother to** to care for someone as if you were their mother
**3 mother's boy** *BrE*, **mama's boy** *AmE* a man or boy who allows his mother to protect him too much and is considered weak
**4 mother hen** someone who tries to protect her children too much and worries about them all the time
**5 learn/be taught sth at your mother's knee** to learn something as a very young child: *She had learned to flirt at her mother's knee.*
**6** ▶ **BIG** ◀ *spoken especially AmE* something very large and usually very good: *a real mother of a car*
**7** ▶ **SLANG** ◀ *AmE taboo spoken* MOTHERFUCKER
**8 every mother's son** *old-fashioned* an expression meaning every man, used for emphasis: *I'd jail every mother's son of them.*
**9 Mother a)** used to address the woman who is head of a CONVENT **b)** *old use* used by a man to address an old woman
**10 the mother of a)** the origin or cause of something: *Westminster is known as 'the mother of parliaments'.* **b)** *informal* a very bad or severe type of something: *I woke up with the mother of all hangovers.*

**mother²** *v* [T] to look after and protect someone as if you were their mother, especially by being too kind and doing everything for them: *Tom was constantly mothered by his wife, and resented it.*

**moth·er·board** /ˈmʌðəbɔːd‖-ərbɔːrd/ *n* [C] *technical* a board where all the circuits (CIRCUIT (4)) of a computer are placed

**mother coun·try** /ˈ·· ˌ··/ *n* [C usually singular] the country where you were born

**Mother Earth** /ˌ·· ˈ·/ *n* [U] the world considered as the place or thing from which everything comes

**moth·er·fuck·er** /ˈmʌðəˌfʌkə‖-ðərˌfʌkər/ *n* [C] *AmE taboo spoken* someone that you dislike very much or that you are very angry with —**motherfucking** *adj*

**moth·er·hood** /ˈmʌðəhud‖-ðər-/ *n* [U] the state of being a mother: *teenage motherhood* | *She's enjoying motherhood.*

**Mothering Sun·day** /ˈ··· ˌ··/ *n* [C,U] *BrE old-fashioned* MOTHER'S DAY

**mother-in-law** /ˈ··· ˌ·/ *n plural* **mothers-in-law** *or* **mother-in-laws** [C] the mother of your wife or husband —see picture at FAMILY

**moth·er·land** /ˈmʌðəlænd‖-ðər-/ *n* [C usually singular] the country where you were born or that you feel you belong to —see also FATHERLAND, MOTHER COUNTRY

**moth·er·less** /ˈmʌðələs‖-ðər-/ *adj* a motherless child is one whose mother has died: *Alone and motherless, David set out to find fame and fortune.*

**mother lode** /ˈ·· ·/ *n* [C usually singular] *AmE* **1** a mine that is full of gold, silver etc **2** a place where you can find a lot of a particular type of object: *The Sharper Image catalog has a mother lode of men's gadgets and toys.*

**moth·er·ly** /ˈmʌðəli‖-ðər-/ *adj* similar to or typical of a good mother: *a kind, motherly woman* —see also MATERNAL (1) —**motherliness** *n* [U]

**Mother Na·ture** /ˌ·· ˈ··/ *n* [U] an expression used to talk about the world and living creatures as a person: *We can hardly expect Mother Nature not to protest at the pollution we've been creating for the last half century.*

**Mother of God** /ˌ·· · ˈ·/ *n* [singular] a title for Mary, the mother of Jesus Christ, used in the Roman Catholic Church

**mother-of-pearl** /ˌ·· · ˈ·/ *n* [U] a pale-coloured hard smooth shiny substance that forms the inside of some SHELLFISH, and is used for making buttons, jewellery etc

**Mother's Day** /ˈ·· ·/ *n* [C,U] a day on which people give cards and presents to their mother

**mother ship** /ˈ·· ·/ *n* [C] a large ship or SPACECRAFT from which smaller boats or spacecraft are sent out

**mother's ru·in** /ˌ·· ˈ··/ *n* [U] *BrE old-fashioned humorous* GIN (=a strong alcoholic drink)

**Mother Su·pe·ri·or** /ˌ·· ·ˈ···/ *n* [C usually singular] the woman who is the leader of a CONVENT

**mother-to-be** /ˌ·· · ˈ·/ *n plural* **mothers-to-be** [C] a woman who is going to have a baby

**mother tongue** /ˌ·· ˈ·/ *n* [C] the first and main language that you learn as a child: *Her mother tongue is French.*

**mo·tif** /məuˈtiːf‖mou-/ *n* [C] **1** an idea, subject, or pattern that is regularly repeated and developed in a book, film, work of art etc: *The theme of creation is a recurrent motif in Celtic mythology.* **2** a small picture or pattern used to decorate something plain: *a cat motif on a child's pyjamas* **3** an arrangement of notes that is often repeated in a musical work

**mo·tion¹** /ˈməuʃən‖ˈmou-/ *n* W3
**1** ▶ **MOVEMENT** ◀ [U] the process of moving or the way that someone or something moves: *The rocking motion of the boat made Sylvia feel sick.*
**2** ▶ **MOVING YOUR HEAD OR HAND** ◀ [C] a single movement of your hand or head, especially done in order to communicate something: *He summoned the waiter with a motion of his hand.*
**3** ▶ **SUGGESTION AT A MEETING** ◀ [C] a proposal that is made formally at a meeting and then decided on by voting: **motion to do sth/motion that** *We will now vote on the motion that membership charges should rise by 15%.* | **pass/carry a motion** (=accept it by voting) *The motion was carried by 15 votes to 10.* | **propose/put forward a motion** (=make a proposal) *I'd like to propose a motion to move the weekly meetings to Thursdays.* | **reject a motion** (=not accept it) | **motion denied** (=used by a judge in a law court to refuse a suggestion by one of the lawyers)
**4 in motion** *formal or technical* moving from one place or position to another: *a photograph of a frog in motion*
**5 go through the motions** to do something because you have to, even though you do not want to do it: *The mayor said he enjoyed the party, but you could see he was only going through the motions.*
**6 set/put sth in motion** to start a process or series of events that will continue for some time: *The Church voted to set in motion the process allowing women to be priests.*

**7 in slow motion** if a film is shown in slow motion, it is shown more slowly than usual so that all the actions can be clearly seen: *Let's look at that goal in slow motion.* **8 ▶ BOWELS ◀** [C] *especially BrE* a word meaning an act of emptying your BOWELS, used especially by doctors and nurses —see also TIME AND MOTION STUDY

**motion²** *v* [I,T] to give someone directions or instructions by moving your hands: **motion (for) sb to do sth** *The police officer motioned for me to pull over.* | **motion to sb to do sth** *He motioned to her to be quiet.* | **motion sb in/out etc** *I saw her motioning me into the room.*

**mo·tion·less** /ˈməʊʃənləs‖ˈmoʊ-/ *adj* not moving at all: *Helen sat motionless and silent.* —**motionlessly** *adv*

**motion pic·ture** /ˌ·· ˈ··◂/ *n* [C] *AmE* a film made for the cinema: *the motion picture industry*

**motion sick·ness** /ˈ·· ˌ··/ *n* [U] *AmE* travel sickness (TRAVEL SICK): *I always get motion sickness when I sit in the back of a car.*

**mo·ti·vate** /ˈməʊtɪ̣veɪt‖ˈmoʊ-/ *v* [T] **1** to make someone want to achieve something and make them willing to work hard in order to do it: *A good teacher has to be able to motivate her students.* | **motivate sb to do sth** *The profit-sharing plan is designed to motivate the staff to work hard.* **2** [often passive] to provide the reason why someone does something: *Would you say that he was motivated solely by a desire for power?*

**mo·ti·va·ted** /ˈməʊtɪ̣veɪtɪ̣d‖ˈmoʊ-/ *adj* **1** very keen to do something or achieve something, especially because you find it interesting or exciting: *They're a really good bunch of students – highly motivated and very intelligent.* **2 politically/financially/commercially motivated etc** done for political, financial etc reasons: *a politically-motivated decision* | *Police believe the attack was racially motivated.*

**mo·ti·va·tion** /ˌməʊtɪ̣ˈveɪʃən‖ˌmoʊ-/ *n* **1** [U] eagerness and willingness to do something without needing to be told or forced to do it: *Jack is an intelligent pupil, but he lacks motivation.* **2** [C] the reason why you want to do something: [+ **for**] *What was your motivation for becoming a teacher?*

**mo·tive¹** /ˈməʊtɪv‖ˈmoʊ-/ *n* [C] **1** the reason that makes someone do something, especially when this reason is kept hidden: *The police believe the motive for this murder was jealousy.* **2** a MOTIF —**motiveless** *adj: an apparently motiveless killing*

**motive²** *adj* [only before noun] *technical* a motive power or force is one that causes movement

**mot juste** /ˌməʊ ˈʒuːst‖ˌmoʊ-/ *plural* **mots justes** (*same pronunciation*) *n* [C] *French* exactly the right word or phrase: *How can I describe her? I'm searching for the mot juste ... Yes, that's it – slender.*

**mot·ley¹** /ˈmɒtli‖ˈmɑːtli/ *adj* [only before noun] **1 a motley crew/bunch/assortment etc** a group of people of very different kinds especially people that you do not approve of: *I looked at the motley bunch we were sailing with and began to feel uneasy about the trip.* **2** a motley group of things contains objects that are all different in shape, size etc and that do not seem to belong together: *His pockets contained a motley collection of coins, movie ticket stubs, and old peppermint candies.* **3** *literary* having a strange mixture of of many different colours: *a court jester in motley garb*

**motley²** *n* [U] *technical* the clothes worn by a JESTER

**mo·to·cross** /ˈməʊtəʊkrɒs‖ˈmoʊtoʊkrɔːs/ *n* [U] the sport of racing MOTORCYCLES over rough land, up hills, through streams etc

**mo·tor¹** /ˈməʊtə‖ˈmoʊtər/ *n* [C] **1** the part of a machine that makes it work or move, by changing power, especially electrical power, into movement: *The lawnmower is powered by a small motor.* | *We had to replace the starter motor in the car's engine.* **2** *BrE informal* a car: *That's a nice motor you've got, Dave.*

**motor²** *adj* [only before noun] **1** *especially BrE* connected with cars or other vehicles with engines: *a motor accident* | *the motor industry* | *motor insurance* **2** using power provided by an engine: *a motor scooter* **3** *technical* related to a nerve that makes a muscle move: *impaired motor function*

**motor³** *v* [I] *BrE old-fashioned* to travel by car: *Bertie is motoring down from London this weekend.*

**motorbike**

motorbike / motorcycle *AmE* scooter

**mo·tor·bike** /ˈməʊtəbaɪk‖ˈmoʊtər-/ *n* [C] *especially BrE* a fast two-wheeled vehicle with an engine

**mo·tor·boat** /ˈməʊtəbəʊt‖ˈmoʊtərboʊt/ *n* [C] a small fast boat with an engine

**mo·tor·cade** /ˈməʊtəkeɪd‖ˈmoʊtər-/ *n* [C] a group of cars and other vehicles that travel together and surround a very important person's car: *the President's motorcade*

**motor car** /ˈ··· ·/ *n* [C] *BrE formal or old-fashioned* a car

**mo·tor·cy·cle** /ˈməʊtəˌsaɪkəl‖ˈmoʊtər-/ *n* [C] a fast, usually large, two-wheeled vehicle with an engine —see picture at MOTORBIKE

**mo·tor·drome** /ˈməʊtədrəʊm‖ˈmoʊtərdroʊm/ *n* [C] *AmE* a track where people can watch car or motorcycle races

**motor home** /ˈ·· ·/ *n* [C] a large vehicle with beds, a kitchen, toilet etc built into it, used for travelling and holidays —see also RV

**mo·tor·ing** /ˈməʊtərɪŋ‖ˈmoʊ-/ *n* [U] *BrE old-fashioned* the activity of driving a car: *a motoring enthusiast*

**motor inn** /ˈ·· ·/ *n* [C] *AmE* a MOTEL

**mo·tor·ist** /ˈməʊtərɪ̣st‖ˈmoʊ-/ *n* [C] *especially BrE* someone who drives a car *12,000 motorists were stopped for speeding in the police crackdown.*

**mo·tor·ized** also **-ised** *BrE* /ˈməʊtəraɪzd‖ˈmoʊ-/ *adj* [only before noun] **1** fitted with an engine, especially when something does not usually have an engine: *a motorized bicycle* **2** a motorized army or group of soldiers is one that uses motor vehicles —**motorize** *v* [T]

**motor lodge** /ˈ··· ·/ *n* [C] *AmE* a MOTEL

**mo·tor·mouth** /ˈməʊtəmaʊθ‖ˈmoʊtər-/ *n* [C] *informal* someone who talks too much and too loudly

**motor neu·rone dis·ease** /ˌməʊtə ˈnjʊərəʊn dɪˌziːz‖ˌmoʊtər ˈnʊroʊn-/ *n* [U] a disease that causes a gradual loss of control over the muscles and nerves of the body, resulting in death

**motor pool** /ˈ··· ·/ *n* [C] *AmE* CAR POOL¹ (2)

**motor rac·ing** /ˈ·· ˌ··/ *n* [U] the sport of racing fast cars on a special track

**motor scoot·er** /ˈ·· ˌ··/ *n* [C] a SCOOTER (1)

**motor ve·hi·cle** /ˈ·· ˌ···/ *n* [C] the official word for any vehicle which is powered by an engine, such as a car, bus, or TRUCK: *This road is closed to motor vehicles.*

**mo·tor·way** /ˈməʊtəweɪ‖ˈmoʊtər-/ *n* [C] *BrE* a very wide road for travelling fast over long distances, especially between cities —compare EXPRESSWAY, FREEWAY, HIGHWAY (1) S2

**mot·tled** /ˈmɒtld‖ˈmɑː-/ *adj* covered with patterns of light and dark colours of different shapes: *mottled like an* *owl's feathers | His red, mottled face showed the effect of too much whiskey.*

**mot·to** /ˈmɒtəʊ‖ˈmɑːtoʊ/ *n plural* **mottos** also **mottoes** [C] **1** a short statement giving a rule on how to behave, which expresses the aims or beliefs of a person, school, or institution: *'Be prepared' is the motto of the boy scouts.* **2** *BrE* an amusing remark or joke printed on a piece of paper in a CHRISTMAS CRACKER

**mould¹** *BrE*, **mold** *AmE* /məʊld‖moʊld/ *n* **1** [U] a soft green or black substance that grows on food which has been kept too long, and on objects that are in warm, wet air: *Throw that bread away, there's mold on it. | There was mould on the bathroom ceiling.* —see also LEAF MOULD **2** [C] a hollow container that you pour liquid into, so that when the liquid becomes solid, it takes the shape of the container: *a jelly mould | a candle mold* **3** [singular] if someone is in, or fits into, a particular mould, they have all the attitudes, and qualities, typical of a certain type of person: *a sex symbol in the traditional Hollywood mold | She didn't quite fit into the standard 'high-flying businesswoman' mould.* **4 break the mould** to change a situation completely, by doing something that has not been done before: *an attempt to break the mould of British politics*

**mould²** *BrE*, **mold** *AmE v* **1** [T] to shape a soft substance by pressing or rolling it or by putting it into a mould: **mould sth into sth** *Mould the sausage meat into little balls.* | **mold sth** *moulded plastic piping* **2** [T] to influence the way someone's character or attitudes develop: *I enjoy working with children, helping to mold their young minds. | an attempt to mold public opinion* **3** [I,T] to fit closely to the shape of something: *Her wet dress was moulded to her body.*

**moul·der** *BrE*, **molder** *AmE* /ˈməʊldə‖ˈmoʊldər/ also **moulder away** *v* [I] to decay slowly and gradually: *old papers mouldering away in the attic | the discovery of a dead body, mouldering in the woods*

**mould·ing** *BrE*, **molding** *AmE* /ˈməʊldɪŋ‖ˈmoʊl-/ *n* **1** [C,U] a thin decorative line of stone or wood around the edge of a wall, a piece of furniture, a picture frame etc **2** [C] an object produced from a mould

**mould·y** *BrE*, **moldy** *AmE* /ˈməʊldi‖ˈmoʊl-/ *adj* **mouldier, mouldiest** covered with MOULD¹ (1): *mouldy cheese* | **go mouldy** *BrE* (=become mouldy) *The bread's gone mouldy.*

**moult** *BrE*, **molt** *AmE* /məʊlt‖moʊlt/ *v* [I] when a bird or animal moults, it loses hair or feathers so that new ones can grow —**moult** *n* [C,U]

**mound** /maʊnd/ *n* [C] **1** a pile of earth or stones that looks like a small hill **2** a large pile of something: [+ **of**] *There's a mound of papers on my desk. | The waiter appeared with a huge mound of spaghetti.* **3** the small hill that the PITCHER stands on in the game of BASEBALL —see picture on page 1263

**mount¹** /maʊnt/ *v*

**1** ▶ **INCREASE** ◀ [I] to increase gradually, especially in a way that makes a situation worse: *The tension here is mounting, as we await the final result. | For days after the accident, the death toll continued to mount.* —see also MOUNTING¹

**2 mount a campaign/attack/exhibition etc** to plan, organize, and begin an event or a course of action: *Scott mounted an expedition to the South Pole.*

**3** ▶ **HORSE/BICYCLE** ◀ [I,T] to get on a horse, bicycle etc: *She mounted and rode off.* —opposite DISMOUNT (1)

**4** ▶ **CLIMB STAIRS** ◀ [T] *formal* to go up something such as a set of stairs: *We mounted some stone steps to a gallery.*

**5 be mounted to/on** to be fixed to something and supported by it: *The statue was mounted on a marble plinth.*

**6** ▶ **PICTURE** ◀ [T] to fix a picture or photograph to a larger piece of stiff paper so that it looks more attractive

**7** ▶ **SEX** ◀ [T] *technical* if a male animal mounts a female animal, he gets up onto her back to have sex

**8 mount guard (over)** *formal* to guard a place, especially as a military duty

**mount up** *phr v* [I] to gradually increase in size or amount: *Our debts are beginning to mount up again.*

**mount²** *n* [C] **1 Mount** part of the name of a mountain: *Mount Everest* **2** a horse that you ride on **3** *old use* a mountain

**moun·tain** /ˈmaʊntɪ̣n‖ˈmaʊntn/ *n* [C] S3 W2 **1** a very high hill: *the Rocky Mountains | a mountain rescue team* —see picture on page 835 **2** also **mountains** *plural* a very large pile or amount of something: *My mother-in-law always gives me a mountain of potatoes from her garden. | I've got mountains of washing to do.* **3 butter/grain etc mountain** a very large amount of food that is stored in order to prevent prices from becoming lower, especially by the European Union —compare LAKE (2) **4 make a mountain out of a molehill** to treat a problem as if it was very serious when in fact it is not

**mountain ash** /ˌ·· ˈ·/ *n* [C] a type of tree with red or orange-red berries; ROWAN

**mountain bike** /ˈ·· ˌ·/ *n* [C] a strong bicycle with a lot of GEARS and wide tyres, specially designed for riding up hills and on rough ground

**moun·tain·eer** /ˌmaʊntɪ̣ˈnɪə‖ˌmaʊntnˈɪr/ *n* [C] someone who climbs mountains as a sport

**moun·tain·eer·ing** /ˌmaʊntɪ̣ˈnɪərɪŋ‖ˌmaʊntnˈɪrɪŋ/ *n* [U] the sport of climbing mountains

**mountain goat** /ˈ·· ˌ·/ *n* [C] an animal with thick white fur which looks like a goat and lives in the western mountains of North America

**mountain laur·el** /ˌ·· ˈ··/ *n* [C] a bush with glossy leaves and pink or white flowers that grows in North America

**mountain li·on** /ˈ·· ˌ··/ *n* [C] a COUGAR

**moun·tain·ous** /ˈmaʊntɪ̣nəs‖ˈmaʊntnəs/ *adj* **1** having a lot of mountains: *the mountainous coast of Wales | a mountainous region* **2** very large in amount or size: *a mountainous woman in a floral swimsuit*

**mountain range** /ˌ·· ˈ·/ *n* [C] a long row of mountains that covers a large area

**moun·tain·side** /ˈmaʊntɪ̣nsaɪd‖ˈmaʊntn-/ *n* [C] the side of a mountain: *Great rocks rolled down the mountainside.*

**moun·tain·top** /ˈmaʊntɪ̣ntɒp‖ˈmaʊntntɑːp/ *n* [C] the top part of a mountain

**moun·te·bank** /ˈmaʊntɪbæŋk/ *n* [C] *literary* a dishonest person who tricks and deceives people

**moun·ted** /ˈmaʊntɪ̣d/ *adj* mounted soldiers or police officers ride on horses: *the mounted police*

**Mount·ie** /ˈmaʊnti/ *n* [C] *informal* a member of the Royal Canadian Mounted Police

**mount·ing¹** /ˈmaʊntɪŋ/ *adj* [only before noun] **1 mounting excitement/anger/violence** gradually increasing or becoming worse: *mounting violence in urban areas | With mounting excitement the children waited for Christmas morning.* **2 mounting inflation/debts/losses** gradually increasing and causing serious problems: *the mounting costs of the project*

**mounting²** *n* [C] an object to which other things, especially parts of a machine, are fastened to keep them in place: *The engine is supported by four rubberized mountings.*

**mourn** /mɔːn‖mɔːrn/ *v* [I, T] **1** to feel very sad because someone that you love has died, and show this in the way you behave: **mourn sb's death/loss** *She still mourns her son's death.* | [+ **for**] *They mourned for their children, killed in the war.* **2** to feel very sad because something no longer exists or is no longer as good as it used to be: *The old steam trains were much-loved, and we all mourn their passing.*

**mourn·er** /ˈmɔːnə‖ˈmɔːrnər/ *n* [C] someone who attends a funeral, especially a relative of the dead person

**mourn·ful** /ˈmɔːnfəl‖ˈmɔːrn-/ *adj* very sad: *Durant was thin, mournful and silent. | the slow, mournful music of the bagpipes* —**mournfully** *adj* —**mournfulness** *n* [U]

**mourn·ing** /ˈmɔːnɪŋ‖ˈmɔːr-/ *n* [U] **1** great sadness because someone has died: *The drawn curtains and* *solemn hush told me that this was a house of mourning.* **2** black clothes worn to show that you are very sad that someone has died: *She was recently widowed and wearing mourning.* **3 be in mourning a)** to be very sad because of someone's death: *It was the custom to visit those in mourning and sit quietly with them.* **b)** to be dressed in black clothes to show that you are mourning

S2 W3 **mouse** /maʊs/ *n* [C] **1** *plural* **mice** /maɪs/ a small furry animal with a long tail that lives in people's houses or in fields, and that looks like a small rat: *I think we have mice in the kitchen.* | *a field mouse* **2** *technical* a small object connected to a computer by a wire, which you move with your hand to give commands to the computer —see picture on page 837 **3** [usually singular] *informal* a quiet, nervous person —see also **play cat and mouse with** (CAT (4))

mouse

**mous·er** /ˈmaʊsə‖-ər/ *n* [C] a cat that catches mice

**mouse·trap** /ˈmaʊs-træp/ *n* [C] a trap for catching mice

**mous·sa·ka** /muːˈsɑːkə/ *n* [U] a Greek dish made from meat, cheese, and AUBERGINES

**mousse** /muːs/ *n* [C,U] **1** a sweet food made from a mixture of cream, eggs, and fruit or chocolate which is eaten when it is cold: *chocolate mousse* **2** a white slightly sticky substance that you put in your hair to make it look thicker or to hold it in place

**mous·tache** also **mustache** *AmE* /məˈstɑːʃ‖ˈmʌstæʃ/ *n* [C] hair that grows on a man's upper lip: *He's shaved off his moustache.* —compare BEARD (1)

**mous·tach·i·oed** /məˈstæʃiəʊd, -ˈstɑː-‖-ʃioʊd/ *adj* an American spelling of MUSTACHIOED

**mous·y, mousey** /ˈmaʊsi/ *adj* **1** mousy hair is a dull brown colour **2** a mousy woman is quiet and unattractive —**mousiness** *n* [U]

S2 W1 **mouth¹** /maʊθ/ *n plural* **mouths** /maʊðz/

**1** ▶ **FACE** ◀ [C] the part of your face which you put food into, or which you use for speaking: *Don't talk with your mouth full of food!* —see picture at HEAD¹

**2 keep your mouth shut** *informal* **a)** to not tell other people about a secret: *I don't want my parents finding out about this, so you'd better keep your mouth shut.* **b)** to not say anything because you might make a mistake, or annoy someone or upset them: *She started to cry, and I wished I'd kept my mouth shut.*

**3 open your mouth** to start to speak, especially in a situation where you feel you should not say anything: *I didn't dare open my mouth in case I offended her.*

**4** ▶ **OPENING** ◀ [C] **a)** the entrance to a large hole or CAVE **b)** the open part at the top of a bottle or container

**5** ▶ **RIVER** ◀ [C] the part of a river where it joins the sea —see picture on page 835

**6 big mouth** *informal* someone who is a big mouth or has a big mouth is annoying because they cannot keep secrets or they often say things they should not say

**7 me and my big mouth/you and your big mouth etc** *spoken* used when you are annoyed with yourself or with someone else for telling other people a secret or saying something that should not be said

**8 he/she is all mouth** *spoken* used when you think that someone is not really brave enough, strong enough etc to do what they say they can do

**9 mouth to feed** someone who you must provide food for, especially one of your children: *To these parents, a new baby is just another hungry mouth to feed.*

**10 make your mouth water** if food makes your mouth water, it looks so good you want to eat it immediately —see also MOUTH-WATERING

**11 down in the mouth** *informal* looking very unhappy: *Why's Tim so down in the mouth?*

**12 open-mouthed/wide-mouthed etc** with an open, wide etc mouth

**13 out of the mouths of babes (and sucklings)** *humorous* used when a small child has just said something clever or interesting —see also **by word of mouth** (WORD¹ (29)), **foam at the mouth** (FOAM² (2)), FROM HAND TO MOUTH, **put your foot in your mouth** (FOOT¹ (12)), **shut your mouth** (SHUT¹ (3)), **shoot your mouth off** (SHOOT¹ (7))

**mouth²** /maʊð/ *v* [T] **1** to move your lips as if you are saying words, but without making any sound: *Brook was waving and mouthing over the noise at the others to stand aside.* **2** to say things that you do not really believe or that you do not understand: *a third-rate politician, capable only of mouthing the current party line* | **mouth platitudes** (=give opinions that are not original) *people at cocktail parties mouthing platitudes about the starving millions*

**mouth off** *phr v* [I + **at/about**] *informal* to complain angrily and noisily about something, or talk as if you know more than anyone else

**mouth·ful** /ˈmaʊθfʊl/ *n* [C] **1** an amount of food or drink that you put into your mouth at one time: *That was a great steak! I enjoyed every mouthful.* **2 a mouthful** *informal* a long word or phrase that is difficult to say: *Her real name is a bit of a mouthful, so we just call her Dee.* **3 give sb a mouthful** *informal especially BrE* to speak angrily to someone, often swearing at them **4 say a mouthful** *AmE informal* to say a lot of true and important things about something in a few words

**mouth or·gan** /ˈ· ,··/ *n* [C] a small musical instrument which you hold close to your lips and blow or suck; HARMONICA

**mouth·piece** /ˈmaʊθpiːs/ *n* [C] **1** [usually singular] a person, newspaper etc that expresses the opinions of a government or a political organization: *Pravda was the official mouthpiece of the Communist Party.* **2** the part of a musical instrument, telephone etc that you put in your mouth or next to your mouth

**mouth-to-mouth re·sus·ci·ta·tion** /,· · ,· ·,·· ˈ··/ *n* [U] a method used to make someone start breathing again by blowing air into their mouth

**mouth·wash** /ˈmaʊθwɒʃ‖-wɒːʃ, -wɑːʃ/ *n* [C,U] a liquid used to make your mouth smell fresh or to get rid of infection in your mouth

**mouth-wa·ter·ing** /ˈ· ,···/ *adj* food that is mouth-watering looks or smells extremely good: *a mouth-watering aroma coming from the kitchen*

**mov·a·ble¹, moveable** /ˈmuːvəbəl/ *adj* able to be moved and not fixed in one place or position: *a teddy bear with movable arms and legs*

**movable²** also **moveable** *n* [C usually plural] *law* a personal possession such as a piece of furniture

**movable feast** /,··· ˈ·/ *n* [C] **1** *BrE informal* something that happens at different times, so that you are not sure exactly when it will happen **2** a special religious day, such as Easter, the date of which changes

**move¹** /muːv/ *v* S1 W1

**1** ▶ **CHANGE PLACE** ◀ [I,T] to change your place or position, or to make something do this: *Don't move or I'll shoot.* | *You mustn't get off the train while it's still moving.* | **move sth** *Can you move your car – it's blocking the road.* | *We'll have to move the bed closer to the wall.* | **move about** *BrE*/**around** *I could hear someone moving around upstairs.* | **can't move** (=be stuck or trapped) *Get me out of here – I can't move.*

**2** ▶ **NEW HOUSE/OFFICE** ◀ [I, T] to go to live or work in a different place: [+ **to**] *When are you moving to Memphis?* | [+ **into**] *They've moved into a bigger office.* | **move house/home** *BrE* (=go to live in a different house) *My parents kept moving house because of my dad's job.*

**3** ▶ **CHANGE JOB/CLASS ETC** ◀ [I,T] to change to a different job, class etc, or to make someone change to a different job, class etc: **move sb to/into** *His teacher*

M

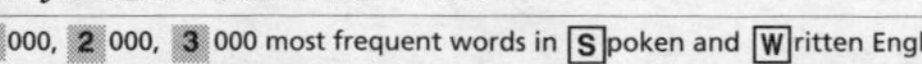

*wants him moved to a higher class.* | **move to/from** *She's just moved from the sales department.*

**4 ▶ CHANGE YOUR OPINION ◀ a)** [I] to change from one opinion or way of thinking to another: *Neither side is willing to move on the issue of territory.* | [+ **towards/away from**] *The two political parties have moved closer towards each other in recent months.* **b)** [T] to persuade someone to change their opinion: *She won't be moved – it doesn't matter what you say to her.*

**5 ▶ MAKE SB SAD ◀** [T] to make someone feel strong feelings, especially of sadness or sympathy: **be deeply/greatly moved** *I was deeply moved by their story.* | **move sb to tears** *The child's suffering moved us to tears.* —see also MOVING

**6 ▶ PROGRESS ◀** [I] to progress in a particular way or at a particular rate: *Things moved quickly once the contract was signed.* | *The negotiations seem to be moving in the right direction.*

**7 be/feel moved to do sth** to want to do something because you feel angry, sad etc: *Hearing so much nonsense talked, I felt moved to speak on the subject.*

**8 get moving** *informal* **a)** used when telling someone to hurry or when saying that you must hurry: *We'd better get moving if we're going to catch that plane.* **b)** *spoken* used to tell someone that you need to leave a place: *It's time we got moving – I have to be up early tomorrow.*

**9 get things moving** *informal* to make a process or event start happening

**10 ▶ CHANGE ARRANGEMENTS ◀** [T] to change the time or order of something: **move sth to/from** *Could we move the meeting to Thursday?*

**11 ▶ CHANGE SUBJECT/ACTIVITY ◀** [I] to change from one subject or activity to another: [+ **away from/off**] *We seem to be moving away from the main point of the discussion.* —see also **move on**

**12 ▶ START DEALING WITH ◀** [I] to start doing something, especially in order to achieve something or deal with a problem: [+ **on/against etc**] *The governor has yet to move on any of the recommendations in the report.* | **move fast/quickly** *You'll have to move fast if you want to get a place on the course.*

**13 ▶ LEAVE ◀** [I] *BrE especially spoken* to go somewhere or leave a place: *It's time we were moving.*

**14 ▶ GAMES ◀** [I,T] to change the position of one of the pieces used to play a game such as CHESS

**15 ▶ AT A MEETING ◀** [I,T] *formal* to officially make a proposal at a meeting: **move that** *The chairman moved that the meeting be adjourned.* | **move an amendment** *BrE* (=propose a change) *They want to move an amendment to the bill.*

**16 ▶ GO FAST ◀** [I] *informal* to travel very fast: *This car can really move!*

**17 ▶ SELL STH ◀** [I] *informal* to sell something quickly: *You should watch these juggling kits move. The kids love 'em.*

**18 not move a muscle** to stay completely still

**19 move with the times** to change the way you think and behave, as the world changes around you

**20 you can't move/you can hardly move** *spoken* used to say that a place is very full and there is not much space: *The bar was so crowded you could hardly move.*

**21 you can't move for** *spoken* used to say that a place is full of a particular kind of people or things: *You couldn't move for police in town this morning.*

**22 move in a society/world/circle** to spend a lot of time with a particular kind of people and know them well: *Lady Olga moved in a different social world from me.* —see also **move the goalposts** (GOALPOST (2)), **move in for the kill** (KILL² (2)), **move heaven and earth** (HEAVEN (10)), **when the spirit moves you** (SPIRIT¹ (13))

**move along** *phr v* **1** [I] *BrE* to move further towards the back or front of something: *The bus-driver asked us all to move along.* **2** [T **move** sb **along**] *especially BrE* to officially order someone to leave a public place: *The police moved us along almost as soon as we started playing.*

**move away** *phr v* [I] to go to live in a different area: *Her children had moved away and she was left on her own.*

**move in** *phr v* [I] **1** to start living in a new house: *We decided not to move in until we'd finished decorating.* **2** to start living with someone in the same house: [+ **with**] *She wants her boyfriend to move in with her.* **3** to take control of a situation, often using your power and influence unfairly: *The big multinationals moved in and started pushing up prices.* **4** to go towards a place or group of people in order to attack them or take control of them: [+ **on**] *Already a special police task force was preparing to move in on the gang.*

**move off** *phr v* [I] if a vehicle or group of people moves off, they start to leave the place where they are: *The conductor blew his whistle and the train slowly moved off.*

**move on** *phr v*

**1 ▶ CONTINUE JOURNEY ◀** [I] to leave the place where you have been staying and continue your journey: *That's enough rest – it's time to move on.*

**2 ▶ CHANGE SUBJECT ◀** [I] to start talking about a new subject in a discussion, book etc: *I think we've covered this topic – is it all right if we move on?*

**3 ▶ CHANGE JOB/CLASS ◀** [I] to leave your present job, class, or activity and start doing another one: [+ **to**] *Children usually move on to secondary school at 11.*

**4 ▶ PROGRESS/DEVELOP ◀** [I] **a)** to develop in your life, and become older and more experienced: [+ **from**] *I felt that I'd moved on from my college days, and didn't want to go back.* **b)** to become more modern, advanced, or complicated than before: *In my day you could only get them in black-and-white, but things have moved on since then.*

**5 move on to higher/better things** *humorous* to get a better job or social position: *I expect you'll be moving on to higher things now that you have your degree.*

**6 ▶ TIME ◀** [I] if time moves on, the year moves on etc, the time passes

**7 time is moving on** *BrE spoken* used to say that you must leave soon or do something soon, because it is getting late: *Time's moving on – we'd better get back to the car.*

**8 ▶ MAKE SB LEAVE ◀** [T **move** sb **on**] *BrE* to officially order someone to leave a public place: *We got moved on by the police for making too much noise.*

**move out** *phr v* [I] **1** to leave the house where you are living now in order to go and live somewhere else: [+ **of**] *They want to find a house somewhere and move out of their apartment.* **2** if a group of soldiers moves out, they leave a place **3** *AmE informal* to leave: *Is everything packed? Then let's move out.*

**move over** *phr v* [I] **1** to change position so that there is more space for someone else: *Move over so that we can all sit down.* **2** to change to a different system, opinion, group of people etc: [+ **to**] *Most companies have moved over to computer-aided design systems.*

**move up** *phr v* [I] **1** *BrE* to change position in order to make more space for other people or things, or to be near someone else: *There's room for one more if everyone moves up a bit.* **2** to get a better job in a company, or move to a higher class in a school: *Everyone here's very ambitious – they all want to move up as quickly as possible.* **3 move up in the world** *often humorous* to get a better job or social position: *John's moved up in the world since you knew him – he's a director now.*

**move²** *n* S2 W1

**1 ▶ ACTION ◀** [singular] something that you decide to do: *She's still thinking about her next move.* | **a good/wise/smart etc move** *He said he was starting his own company, which sounded like a smart move.*

**2 make a move a)** to move in a particular direction, especially in order to attack someone or to escape: *If anyone makes a move, I'll shoot.* | [+ **towards/for**] *He suddenly made a move towards the door.* **b)** to do something to achieve a particular result: *Neither side had made a move to resolve the dispute.* **c)** *BrE informal* to leave a place: *It's getting late – we ought to make a move.*

**3 be on the move a)** to be travelling from one place to the next: *We have received reports that the rebel army is on the move.* **b)** to be busy and active: *She's always on the*

*move, isn't she?* **c)** to be changing and developing a lot: *Georgian England was a society on the move.*
**4 get a move on** *spoken* used to tell someone to hurry: *Get a move on or we'll be late!*
**5 make the first move** to do something first, especially in order to end a quarrel or start a relationship: *Neither was willing to make the first move towards reconciliation.*
**6 watch/follow sb's every move** to carefully watch everything that someone does, especially because you think they are doing something illegal: *I have three officers watching his every move.*
**7 make no move to do sth** to make no attempt to prevent someone from doing something: *They were staring, but made no move to stop us.*
**8 ▶ GOING TO A NEW PLACE ◀** [singular] the process of leaving one house, office etc, and going to live or work in a different one: *"How was the move?" "Exhausting!"*
**9 ▶ PROGRESS ◀** [C] something that is done to improve a situation: *It's a move in the right direction.*
**10 ▶ GAMES ◀** [C] **a)** an act of changing the position of one of the objects in a game such as CHESS **b)** a way in which this may be done, according to the rules: *I'm learning all the different moves.* **c)** the time when a player can move one of these objects: *It's your move.*

**move·a·ble** /ˈmuːvəbəl/ *adj* another spelling of MOVABLE

S1 W1 **move·ment** /ˈmuːvmənt/ *n*
**1 ▶ GROUP ◀** [C] a group of people who share the same ideas or beliefs and work together to achieve a particular aim: *the civil rights movement* | *The nationalist movement did not have widespread support.*
**2 ▶ MOVING ◀ a)** [C,U] a change in the place or position of something or someone: *reports of troop movement in the area* **b)** [C] an act of moving your body, or the way someone moves their body: *the dancer's graceful movements*
**3 ▶ CHANGE DEVELOPMENT ◀ a)** [U] a change that brings progress or improvement in a situation: *There's been no movement in the dispute since Thursday.* **b)** [C] a gradual change or development in people's attitudes or behaviour: *a growing movement among consumers away from buying processed foods*
**4 sb's movements** all of a person's activities over a certain period: *Police are trying to trace Carter's movements over the last 48 hours.*
**5 ▶ MUSIC ◀** [C] one of the main parts into which a piece of music is divided, especially in a SYMPHONY
**6 ▶ CLOCK/WATCH ◀** the moving parts of a piece of machinery, especially a clock or watch
**7 ▶ BODY WASTE ◀** [C] *formal* an act of getting rid of waste matter from the bowels (BOWEL (1))

**mov·er** /ˈmuːvə‖-ər/ *n* [C] **1** someone who makes a formal proposal at a meeting: *The mover of the motion has a right of reply to the discussion.* **2** someone or something that moves in a particular way: *Saturn is the slowest mover of all the planets.* **3** *especially AmE* someone whose job is to help people move from one house to another **4 movers and shakers** powerful and influential people: *The movers and shakers in the stock market predicted a rise in share-dealing.* —see also PRIME MOVER, KEY MOVER/PLAYER (KEY[2])

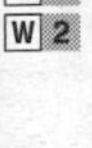
**mov·ie** /ˈmuːvi/ *n* [C] *especially AmE* **1** a film made to be shown at the cinema: *a Hollywood movie* **2 the movies** the cinema: **go to the movies** (=go to watch a movie at the cinema)

**mov·ie·go·er** /ˈmuːviˌgəʊə‖-ˌgoʊər/ *n* [C] *especially AmE* someone who goes to see films, especially regularly

**movie star** /ˈ... ./ *n* [C] *especially AmE* a famous film actor or actress

**movie thea·ter** /ˈ.. ˌ../ *n* [C] *AmE* CINEMA (1) *BrE*

**mov·ing** /ˈmuːvɪŋ/ *adj* **1** making you feel strong emotions, especially sadness or sympathy: *Jackson's speech was so moving, it made me cry.* | **moving account/experience/story etc** *a moving account of life in the refugee camps* **2** [only before noun] changing from one position to another: *a moving stage* | **fast/slow moving etc** *Be very careful when changing lanes in fast moving traffic.* **3 the moving spirit** someone who makes something start to happen: *Mr Arkwright was the moving spirit behind the founding of the union.* —**movingly** *adv*: *the sufferings of the famine victims, so movingly described in Buerk's TV reports*

**moving part** /ˌ.. ˈ./ *n* [C] a part of a machine that moves when it is operating: *Keep the moving parts well oiled.*

**moving pic·ture** /ˌ.. ˈ..◂/ *n* [C] *old-fashioned, especially AmE* a film made to be shown at the cinema

**moving stair·case** /ˌ.. ˈ../ *n* [C] *old-fashioned* an ESCALATOR

**moving van** /ˈ.. ˌ./ *n* [C] *AmE* REMOVAL VAN *BrE*

**mow** /məʊ‖moʊ/ *v past participle* **mowed** *or* **mown** /məʊn‖moʊn/ [I,T] **1** to cut grass or wheat using a machine or tool with special blades: *It's time to mow the lawn again.* **2 new-mown hay/grass etc** recently cut grass etc

**mow** sb ↔ **down** *phr v* [T] to kill large numbers of people at the same time, especially by shooting them: *The battalion was mown down by enemy tanks.*

**mow·er** /ˈməʊə‖ˈmoʊər/ *n* [C] **1** a machine used for cutting grass; LAWNMOWER **2** *old use* someone who mows

**mox·ie** /ˈmɒksi‖ˈmɑː-/ *n* [U] *AmE informal* courage and determination: *He's always had plenty of moxie.*

**MP** /ˌem ˈpiː/ *n* [C] **1** MEMBER OF PARLIAMENT; someone who has been elected to represent the people in a parliament: *She's the MP for Liverpool North.* | *Ken Newton, MP* **2** *informal* a member of the MILITARY POLICE

**mpg** /ˌem piː ˈdʒiː/ the abbreviation of miles per GALLON, used to describe the amount of petrol used by a car: *a car that does 35 mpg*

**mph** /ˌem piː ˈeɪtʃ/ the abbreviation of miles per hour, used to describe the speed of a vehicle: *speeding along at 100 mph*

**MPhil** /ˌem ˈfɪl/ *n* [C] *BrE* Master of PHILOSOPHY; a university degree that you get after your first degree

**Mr** *BrE*, **Mr.** *AmE* /ˈmɪstə‖-ər/ **1** a title used before a man's family name when you are speaking to him or writing to him and want to be polite: *Mr Smith* | *Mr. John Smith* | *Mr and Mrs Smith* **2** a title used when addressing a man in an official position: *Mr Chairman* | *Mr. President* —compare MADAM (3) **3 Mr Right** a man who would be the perfect husband for a particular woman: *She's spent years waiting for Mr Right to come along.* **4 Mr Big** *informal* the leader or most important person in a group, especially a criminal group **5 Mr Clean** *informal* someone who is honest and always obeys the law **6** *spoken* used before the name of a personal quality or kind of behaviour as a humorous name for a man who has that quality: *I don't think we need any comments from Mr Sarcasm here.* —see also **no more Mr nice Guy!** (GUY[1] (5))

**USAGE NOTE: MR**

COLLOCATION

**Mr, Mrs, Miss,** and **Ms** are only used with full names or last names (surnames): *Hello Mr Gray* | *The next candidate for the job is Mrs Betty Schwarz* (NOT *Please Miss teacher* or *Good morning Mr Jerry*).

When you are talking or writing to someone directly, you do not usually use their full name: *Hello, Mr Smith* (NOT *Hello, Mr Alan Smith*).

Usually **Mr, Ms** etc is not used with names of people you know well or who are famous: *This is my friend Annie Walker.* | *the defeat of Adolf Hitler* | *Clinton's health care policy* | *'The Wave' by Hokusai*

POLITENESS

Many women prefer to be addressed as **Ms** rather than **Miss** or **Mrs**, as **Ms** does not unnecessarily draw attention to whether or not the woman is married.

**Mrs** *BrE*, **Mrs.** *AmE* /ˈmɪsɪz/ **1** a title used before a married woman's family name when you are speaking or

writing to her and want to be polite: *Mrs. Smith* | *Mr and Mrs David Smith* —compare MISS[2] MS —see MR (USAGE) **2** *spoken* used before the name of a personal quality or type of behaviour as a humorous name for a married woman who has that quality: *Mrs Superefficiency*

**MS** /ˌem ˈes/ *n* **1** [C] *AmE* Master of Science; a university degree in science that you get after your first degree **2** [U] multiple sclerosis; a serious illness that gradually destroys your nerves, making you weak and unable to move

**Ms** *BrE*, **Ms.** *AmE* /mɪz, məz/ a title used before a woman's family name because it is not important to say whether she is married or not, or when you do not know whether she is married or not —compare MISS[2], MRS —see MR (USAGE)

**ms** *n plural* **mss** the written abbreviation of MANUSCRIPT

**MSc** /ˌem es ˈsiː/ *n* [C] Master of Science; a university degree in science that you get after your first degree; MS (1) *AmE* —compare MA

**MS-DOS** /ˌem es ˈdɒs‖-ˈdɑːs/ *n* [U] *trademark* one of the most common OPERATING SYSTEMS for a computer

**MSG** /ˌem es ˈdʒiː/ *n* [U] MONOSODIUM GLUTAMATE; a chemical compound added to food

**Mt** the written abbreviation of MOUNT[2] (1): *Mt Everest*

**much[1]** /mʌtʃ/ *adv* **1 much taller/much more difficult etc** used especially before comparatives and superlatives to mean a lot taller, a lot more difficult: *You get a much better view if you stand on a chair.* | *She looks much fatter in real life than she does on TV.* | **much too old/much too tall etc** *You can't marry him. He's much too old.* | **much the bigger/much the more interesting** *Her second novel was much the more exciting.* | **much the biggest/much the most interesting etc** *He is much the most handsome man I've ever met.* | **much loved/much admired** *Maturity and wider experience are much sought after commodities in teaching these days.* **2 too much/so much/very much/how much etc** used to show the degree which someone does something or something happens: *If he didn't talk so much he'd do a lot better.* | *The divorce was messy and at the time upset her very much.* | *I've so much looked forward to your visit.* | *However much you hate walking you still have to go to the top.* **3 not much a)** only a little, only to a small degree etc: *"Did you enjoy the performance?" "Not much!"* | *I haven't seen Tony for over 20 years. He hasn't changed much.* | *It was only a young dog – not much higher than my knee.* **b)** used to say that something does not happen often: *We don't go to the theatre much these days.* | *The new compact discs mean you don't see LPs in the shops as much.* —see graph at LITTLE **4 much like/much as/much the same** used to say that something is very similar to something else: *The house was very much as I'd remembered it.* | *It's easy to confuse us, we're much the same build and have the same coloured hair.* **5 not be much good at something** to not be able to do something such as play a sport, speak a foreign language etc very well: *Brian's never been much good at understanding other people's feelings.* **6 much less** used to say that one thing is even less true, possible etc, than another: *He can hardly afford beer, much less champagne.* **7 be too much/a bit much** *spoken* used to say that someone's behaviour is rude or impolite: *I thought breaking your window and expecting you to pay for it was a bit much!* **8 not so much...as...** used to show that something is bigger, more difficult etc than people may think: *In many cases nursing is not so much a job as a way of life.* **9 much as sb does sth** used to mean that although one thing is true, something else is also true: *Much as I enjoy Shakespeare, I was glad when the play was over.* **10 much to sb's surprise/disgust etc** *formal* used to say that someone was very surprised, very disgusted etc: *Much to my displeasure some of the pupils in the school have been smoking outside the gates.* **11 so much the better (for sb)** *especially spoken* used to say that you think a situation, idea etc is very good: *If he wants to not drink and drive everyone home, so much the better for us!* **12 Not much!** used to emphasize that you really do want to do something, that you really are excited about something etc: *"You don't want any cake, do you Tom?" "Not much!"*

**USAGE NOTE: MUCH**

GRAMMAR POINTS

**Much**, with or without *very*, is only used with nouns if they are uncountable, and then only with negative clauses or in questions: *Did you get very much work done?* | *How much money do you have?*

For positive statements and with countable nouns, you use **a lot** or **many**: *She's done a lot of work.* | *They visited many/a lot of countries.* | *Were there many people there?*

You often use **(very) much** with verbs in negative or question contexts. In questions, it usually comes at the end of a clause: *Do you go to London much?* In negative contexts, it may come before the verb, or, more often, at the end. So you would say: *I don't much like living in London.* | *I don't like living in London much* (NOT *I don't like living much in London*).

**So much, as much, much more** and **too much** are often used in positive contexts with verbs and uncountable nouns: *I go to restaurants so much I'm tired of them.* | *She smokes too much.* | *Try to relax as much as possible.* | *We'll need much more money than that.*

With some verbs, especially with the general meaning 'like', **very much** can be used in positive contexts as well. Using **very much** before a verb is particularly common in British English: *Rhoda very much enjoys skiing* (NOT *Rhoda enjoys very much skiing*). | *I love her very much.* You also say: *Thank you very much.*

**(Very) much** is used with most adjectives only before **more** and **too**, or when they are in the **-er** form. You cannot use it simply instead of **very**: *This is much more/too difficult.* But note that you say: *I am very sorry* (NEVER *I am much sorry*, or *I am sorry very much*).

Some adjectives end in **-ed** or **-ing** and look like forms of verbs, but they take **very** rather than **much** (unless **more** or **too** is there as well). So you would use much in this sentence: *She was a much-loved colleague* because **loved** is a passive verb, but you would use **very** in this one: *The kids are getting very tired*, because **tired** is an adjective.

**much[2]** *quantifier* **1** used to mean a lot of something especially in spoken English in questions and negatives or in formal written English: *There isn't much time. Pack the bag quickly.* | *He didn't say much about it but I think his wife left him.* | *Do you get much chance to travel in your job?* | *After much deliberation the judges awarded the prize to Miss Venezuela.* | **how much?** | *How much is the dress with the white collar?* | **much of** *Much of the city was destroyed in the attack.* **2 so much/too much** used to talk about a particularly large amount of something, especially more than necessary: *I think it would taste nicer if you didn't use so much salt.* | *There was too much work for one person.* | **far/much etc too much**: *Easy on the gin! You've put in much too much!* **3 not much** used to mean that something is not important, interesting, worthy etc: *The car may not be much to look at but it's very reliable.* | *Spend the vacation decorating? I don't think much of that idea.* | *I think we should leave. There's nothing much we can do to help.* | *The sequel was slightly better than the first movie but that's not saying much.* **4 not be up to much** *spoken especially BrE* to be fairly bad: *The restaurant's very grand but the food isn't up to much.* **5 not be much of a dancer/swimmer etc** to not be a good dancer, swimmer etc: *Greg's not much of a footballer but you can't fault his motivation.* **6 it was as much as I/she etc could do** used to say that someone could only just manage to do something: *He looked so absurd, it was as much as I could do to keep a straight face.* **7 be too much for sb** to be too difficult for someone to do: *Climbing the stairs is too much for her now that she's in her 90s.* **8 think/say etc as much** to think or say what you have just mentioned: *She believed that the company should abandon such a risky proposal and said as much at the meeting.* **9 make much of sb/sth a)** to treat information, a situation etc as though you think it is very important or serious: *The press didn't make as much of the discovery as they might have done.* **b)** to think that something is very good or very impressive: *I didn't make much of her latest novel.* **c)** to treat someone very kindly because you like them a lot: *A childless couple, they always made much of thier nephews and nieces.* —compare **make little of** (LITTLE[2] (8)) **10 not/without so much as** used when you are surprised or annoyed that someone did not do something: *He left without so much as saying goodbye.* | *Sonia didn't so much as thank her for her help.* **11 I'll say this/that much for** used to praise someone or something when they are being criticized a lot: *I'll say this much for Fiona – she has plenty of spirit!* **12 so much for** used to say that it was not worth using something because it had little effect, it was useless etc: *So much for worrying she'd be lonely – she's having a party tonight!* **13 as much again** the same amount or number as the one mentioned before: *The car only cost me £500 but it cost as much again to get it insured.*

**much-her·ald·ed** /ˌ· ˈ···◂/ *adj* [only before noun] talked about a lot before it actually appears: *Ford's much-heralded new family saloon*

**much·ness** /ˈmʌtʃnɪ̆s/ *n* **be much of a muchness** *BrE informal* to be very similar: *It was hard to choose between the candidates – they were all much of a muchness.*

**mu·ci·lage** /ˈmjuːsɪ̆lɪdʒ/ *n* [U] a sticky liquid obtained from plants and used as a glue —**mucilaginous** /ˌmjuːsɪ̆ˈlædʒɪ̆nəs/ *adj*: *the mucilaginous fruit of the okra plant*

**muck¹** /mʌk/ *n* [U] *informal* **1** *especially BrE* something such as dirt, mud, or another sticky substance that makes something dirty: *Come on, let's wipe that muck off your face.* **2** *BrE* waste matter from animals, especially waste matter that is put on land to make plants grow better: *dog muck* | *They were shovelling muck onto the fields.* **3** something that is unpleasant or of very bad quality: *How can you eat that muck? It looks disgusting.* | *All that paper ever prints is muck about people's sex lives.* **4 as common as muck** *BrE old-fashioned* an insulting way of describing someone of a low social class

**muck²** *v*

**muck about/around** *phr v BrE informal* **1** [I] to behave in a silly way, especially when you should be working or paying attention to something; mess around (MESS²): *Stop mucking about and listen!* | *We spent the days mucking around on the beach.* **2** [T **muck** sb/sth **about/around**] to cause trouble and inconvenience for someone, especially by changing your mind a lot; mess around (MESS²): *The travel agent has really been mucking me around over this holiday.*

**muck in** *phr v* [I] *BrE informal* **1** to work together with other people in order to get a job done; pitch in (PITCH¹): *Oh, stop moaning – we've all got to muck in!* **2** to share things with other people: *We're a bit short of space. Do you mind mucking in with the other boys?*

**muck** sth ↔ **out** *phr v* [I,T] to clean the place where an animal lives: *to muck out the stables*

**muck** sth ↔ **up** *phr v* [T] *BrE informal* **1** to do something wrong or badly, so that you fail to achieve something: *I really mucked up those last two exams.* **2** to spoil something, especially an arrangement or plan: *The bad weather mucked up our plans for a picnic.* **3** to make something dirty: *Don't muck up your shirt.*

**muck·heap** /ˈmʌkhiːp/ *n* [C] *BrE* a pile of MANURE (=animal waste matter) in a farmyard

**muck·rak·ing** /ˈmʌk-reɪkɪŋ/ *n* [U] the practice of telling or writing unpleasant and perhaps untrue stories about people's private lives, especially famous people: *low quality magazines specializing in muckraking* —**muckraking** *adj* —**muckraker** *n* [C]

**muck·spread·er** /ˈmʌkspredə‖-ər/ *n* [C] *BrE* a machine used on a farm to spread MANURE (=animal waste matter) onto farm land —**muckspreading** *n* [U]

**muck·y** /ˈmʌki/ *adj BrE informal* **1** dirty, for example with mud or oil: *Your hands are all mucky.* **2** a mucky joke or story etc is slightly rude and about sex **3** mucky weather is cold and wet

**mu·cous mem·brane** /ˌmjuːkəs ˈmembreɪn/ *n* [C] the thin surface that covers certain inner parts of the body, such as the inside of the nose, and produces mucus

**mu·cus** /ˈmjuːkəs/ *n* [U] a liquid produced in parts of your body such as your nose —**mucous** *adj*

**mud** /mʌd/ *n* [U] **1** wet earth that has become soft and sticky: *His shoes were covered with mud.* **2 your name is mud** *spoken* if your name is mud, people are annoyed with you because you have caused trouble: *His name is mud in the office after what happened.* **3** earth used for building: *a mud hut* **4 here's mud in your eye** *spoken old-fashioned* used for expressing good wishes when having a drink with someone; CHEERS (1) —see also **as clear as mud** (CLEAR¹ (19))

**mud·bath** /ˈmʌdbɑːθ‖-bæθ/ *n* **1** [C] a health treatment in which heated mud is put onto your body, used especially to reduce pain **2** [singular] a large area of mud: *Heavy rain had turned the playing field into a mudbath.*

**mud·dle¹** /ˈmʌdl/ *n* [C usually singular] **1** a state of confusion or untidiness, that results in things being done wrong: *There was a bit of a muddle over our reservations.* | *We had to get an accountant in to sort out the muddle.* **2 be in a muddle a)** to be in an untidy and confused state: *The papers were all in a muddle.* **b)** to be confused because you have too much to do: *I'm in such a muddle, I'd completely forgotten you were coming today.*

**muddle²** *v* also **muddle up** [T] *especially BrE* **1** to put something in the wrong order or mix something up: *Someone's muddled up all the papers on my desk.* | *Your invoice got muddled up with Mr Clark's.* **2 get muddled (up)** to get confused between one thing or person and another, and make a mistake: *Sorry, I got a bit muddled up over the dates.* | **get sb/sth muddled (up)** *I'm not quite sure of their ages, I get them muddled up.* —**muddled** *adj*: *muddled thinking* —**muddling** *adj*

**muddle along/on** *phr v* [I] *BrE* to continue doing something without having any clear plan: *We just seem to muddle along but never make any real progress.*

**muddle through** *phr v* [I] *especially BrE* to achieve something even though you do not have a clear plan or use the best methods or equipment: *Jack got some difficult questions but he managed to muddle through.*

**muddle-head·ed** /ˌ·· ˈ··◂/ *adj BrE* confused or not able to think clearly —**muddle-headedness** *n* [U]

**mud·dy¹** /ˈmʌdi/ *adj* **muddier, muddiest** **1** covered with mud or containing mud: *the muddy banks of the river* | *Take your boots off outside if they're muddy.* **2** colours that are muddy are dull **3** confused and not clear: *muddy thinking* —**muddiness** *n* [U]

**muddy²** *v* **muddied, muddying** [T] **1** to make something dirty with mud: *She was taking care not to muddy her new shoes.* **2 muddy the waters/the issue** to make things more complicated or confusing in a situation that was simple before

**mud·flap** /ˈmʌdflæp/ *n* [C] *BrE* a piece of rubber that hangs behind the wheel of a vehicle to prevent mud from flying up; SPLASH GUARD *AmE* —see picture on page 409

**mud·flat** /ˈmʌdflæt/ *n* [C often plural] **1** an area of muddy land, covered by the sea when it comes up at HIGH TIDE and uncovered when it goes down at LOW TIDE **2** *AmE* the muddy bottom of a dry lake

**mud·guard** /ˈmʌdgɑːd‖-gɑːrd/ *n* [C] *BrE* a curved piece of metal or plastic over the wheel of a bicycle that

prevents the mud from flying up; FENDER (4) *AmE* —see picture at BICYCLE[1]

**mud·pack** /ˈmʌdpæk/ *n* [C] a soft mixture containing clay that you spread over your face and leave there for a short time to improve your skin

**mud pie** /ˌ· ˈ·/ *n* [C] a little ball of wet mud made by children as a game

**mud·sling·ing** /ˈmʌdslɪŋɪŋ/ *n* [U] the practice of saying bad and often untrue things about someone in order to make other people have a low opinion of them: *There has been a lot of political mudslinging in the battle for votes.* —**mudslinger** *n* [C]

**mues·li** /ˈmjuːzli/ *n* [U] grains, nuts, and dried fruits, mixed together and eaten with milk as a breakfast food; GRANOLA *AmE*

**mu·ez·zin** /muːˈezǝn, ˈmwezǝn/ *n* [C] a man who calls Muslims to prayer from a MOSQUE

**muff**[1] /mʌf/ *n* [C] a short tube of thick cloth or fur that you can put your hands into to keep them warm in cold weather —see also EARMUFFS

**muff**[2] *v* [T] **1** also **muff up** *informal* to spoil a chance to do something well: *I wanted to impress her with my efficiency but I muffed it up.* **2 muff a catch/muff it** to fail to catch or hold a ball in a game or sport

**muf·fin** /ˈmʌfǝn/ *n* [C] **1** *BrE* a small thick round kind of bread, usually eaten hot with butter; ENGLISH MUFFIN *AmE* **2** *AmE* a small usually sweet cake that sometimes has bits of fruit in it: *blueberry muffins*

**muf·fle** /ˈmʌfəl/ *v* [T usually passive] **1** to make a sound less loud and clear: *The falling snow muffled the noise of the traffic.* **2** also **muffle up** to cover yourself with something thick and warm: *He went out into the snow muffled up in his scarf and thick overcoat.*

**muf·fled** /ˈmʌfəld/ *adj* muffled sounds or voices cannot be heard clearly, for example because they come from behind a door or wall: *I heard the muffled thump of a car door slamming.* | *Muffled voices could be heard in the next room.*

**muf·fler** /ˈmʌflə‖-ər/ *n* [C] **1** a thick long piece of cloth worn to keep your neck warm **2** *AmE* SILENCER (2)

**muf·ti** /ˈmʌfti/ *n* **1 in mufti** *old-fashioned* wearing ordinary clothes instead of a uniform: *soldiers in mufti* **2** [C] someone who officially explains Muslim law

S 3 **mug**[1] /mʌg/ *n* [C] **1** a large cup with straight sides used for drinking tea, coffee etc —see picture at CUP[1] **2** a large glass with straight sides and a handle, used especially for drinking beer: *rugby players swilling mugs of beer at the bar* **3** also **mugful** a mug and the liquid inside it: *Two mugs of tea, please.* **4** *BrE spoken* someone who is stupid and easy to deceive: *I expect they'll find some poor mug to buy their car.* **5** *spoken* a face: *What an ugly mug!* **6 a mug's game** *BrE spoken* something that is not likely to be successful or profitable: *Gambling is a mug's game, Jonah.*

**mug**[2] *v* **mugged, mugging** **1** [T] to attack someone and rob them in a public place: *A lot of people won't go out alone at night for fear of being mugged.* **2** [I] *AmE informal* to make silly expressions with your face or behave in a silly way, especially in a photograph or a play: *Scotty's always mugging for the camera.*

**mug up** *phr v* [I,T] *BrE informal* to study something very hard, especially when preparing for an exam: **mug sth↔ up** *He's got to mug up some facts about pollution.* | [+ **on**] *She's mugging up on Racine for her French paper.*

**mug·ger** /ˈmʌgə‖-ər/ *n* [C] someone who attacks people and robs them in a public place

**mug·ging** /ˈmʌgɪŋ/ *n* [C,U] an attack on someone in which they are robbed in a public place: *There has been an increase in muggings in the park.*

**mug·gins** /ˈmʌgɪnz/ *n* [singular] *spoken BrE* used jokingly to mean yourself, when you know you have been stupid and let other people treat you unfairly: *Everyone disappeared after supper, leaving muggins here to do the washing-up.*

**mug·gy** /ˈmʌgi/ *adj* **muggier, muggiest** *informal* muggy weather is unpleasantly warm and the air seems wet: *The air was muggy and damp, threatening a storm later.* —**mugginess** *n* [U]

**mug·shot** /ˈmʌgʃɒt‖-ʃɑːt/ *n* [C] *informal* a photograph of a criminal's face, taken by the police: *Can you look through some mugshots to identify the man who attacked you?*

**Mu·ham·ma·dan** /mʊˈhæmǝdən, mə-/ *n, adj old-fashioned* a word meaning Muslim, now considered offensive by most Muslims —**Muhammadanism** *n* [U]

**mu·ja·hed·din** /ˌmuːdʒəheˈdiːn/ *n* [plural] Muslim soldiers with strong religious beliefs

**muk·luks** /ˈmʌklʌks/ *n* [plural] *AmE* boots made of animal skin with a thick bottom, used for walking in snow

**mu·lat·to** /mjuːˈlætəʊ‖mʊˈlætoʊ/ *n* [C] an insulting word for someone with one black parent and one white parent

**mul·ber·ry** /ˈmʌlbəri‖-beri/ *n* **1** [C] a dark purple fruit that can be eaten, or the tree on which this fruit grows **2** [U] the dark purple colour of these fruit

**mulch**[1] /mʌltʃ/ *n* [singular] decaying leaves that are put on the soil to improve its quality, to protect the roots of plants, and to stop WEEDS (=unwanted plants) growing

**mulch**[2] *v* [T] to cover the ground with a mulch

**mule** /mjuːl/ *n* [C] **1** an animal that has a DONKEY and a horse as parents **2** [usually plural] a shoe or SLIPPER without a back, that has a piece of material across the toes to hold it on your foot **3** *slang* someone who brings illegal drugs into a country by hiding them on or in their body —see also **stubborn as a mule** (STUBBORN (1))

**mu·le·teer** /ˌmjuːlǝˈtɪə‖-ˈtɪr/ also **mule·skin·ner** *AmE* /ˈmjuːlskɪnə‖-ər/ —*n* [C] someone who leads mules

**mul·ish** /ˈmjuːlɪʃ/ *adj* refusing to do something or agree to something in an unreasonable way; STUBBORN: *mulish obstinacy* —**mulishly** *adv* —**mulishness** *n* [U]

**mull**[1] /mʌl/ *v* [T] to heat wine or beer with sugar and SPICES

**mull** sth↔ **over** *phr v* [T] to think about a problem, plan etc and consider it for a long time: *Victor mulled over the idea and finally decided that it made sense.*

**mull**[2] *n* [C] *ScotE* an area of land that sticks out into the sea; PROMONTORY: *Mull of Kintyre*

**mul·lah** /ˈmʌlə, ˈmʊlə/ *n* [C] a Muslim teacher of law and religion

**mulled wine** /ˌ· ˈ·/ *n* [U] wine that has been heated with sugar and SPICES: *mulled wine with lots of cloves and cinnamon*

**mul·let** /ˈmʌlǝt/ *n* [C] a fairly small sea fish that can be eaten

**mul·li·ga·taw·ny** /ˌmʌlɪgəˈtɔːni‖-ˈtɒːni, -ˈtɑːni/ *n* [U] a soup that tastes hot because it contains hot SPICES

**mul·lion** /ˈmʌljən/ *n* [C] a piece of stone, metal, or wood that divides a window between the glass parts —**mullioned** *adj*: *mullioned windows*

**multi-** /mʌltǝ/ *prefix* more than one; many: *multicoloured* (=with many colours) | *a multistorey office block*

**mul·ti·choice** /ˈmʌltitʃɔɪs/ *adj* MULTIPLE CHOICE

**mul·ti·col·oured** *BrE*, **multicolored** *AmE* /ˈmʌltiˌkʌləd‖-ərd/ *adj* having many different colours: *a multicoloured sweatshirt*

**mul·ti·cul·tur·al** /ˌmʌltiˈkʌltʃərəl◂/ *adj* involving or including people or ideas from several different countries, races, or religions: *a multicultural society*

**mul·ti·cul·tu·ral·is·m** /ˌmʌltiˈkʌltʃərəlɪzəm/ *n* [U] the belief that it is important and good to include people or ideas from many different countries, races, or religions —**multiculturalist** *n* [C]

**multi-faith** /ˌ·· ˈ·◂/ *adj* [only before noun] including or involving people from several different religious groups: *a multi-faith service of thanksgiving*

**mul·ti·far·i·ous** /ˌmʌltǝˈfeəriəs◂‖-ˈfer-/ *adj* of very many different kinds: *her multifarious business activities* —**multifariously** *adv* —**multifariousness** *n* [U]

**multi-func·tion** /ˌ·· ˈ··◂/ **multi-func·tion·al** /ˌ·· ˈ···◂/ *adj* [only before noun] a multi-function machine, piece of equipment, building etc is designed to have several different uses

**mul·ti·lat·e·ral** /ˌmʌltɪˈlætərəl◂/ *adj* **multilateral agreements/trade etc** agreements, trade etc that involve the governments of several different countries —compare BILATERAL, UNILATERAL —**multilaterally** *adv*

**mul·ti·lin·gual** /ˌmʌltɪˈlɪŋgwəl◂/ *adj* **1** able to speak several different languages: *a multilingual secretary* **2** written in several different languages: *a multilingual phrasebook covering English, French, German, and Italian* —compare BILINGUAL, MONOLINGUAL —**multilingualism** *n* [U]

**mul·ti·me·di·a** /ˌmʌltiˈmiːdiə◂/ *adj* [only before noun] using a mixture of sound, pictures, film, and writing to give information, especially with computers: *Encarta, the latest multimedia encyclopedia* —**multimedia** *n* [U]

**mul·ti·mil·lion** /ˌmʌltiˈmɪljən◂/ *adj* | **multimillion-pound, multimillion-dollar etc** worth or costing many millions of pounds, dollars etc: *Gascoigne's multimillion-pound move to Lazio*

**mul·ti·mil·lio·naire** /ˌmʌltɪˌmɪljəˈneə‖-ˈner/ *n* [C] an extremely rich person, who has many millions of pounds or dollars

**mul·ti·na·tion·al**[1] /ˌmʌltɪˈnæʃənəl◂/ *adj* **1** a multinational company has factories, offices, and business activities in many different countries: *a multinational motor-manufacturing corporation* **2** involving people from several countries: *a multinational force sponsored by the UN* —**multinationally** *adv*

**multinational**[2] *n* [C] a large company that has offices, factories etc in many different countries: *a giant food multinational* | *the growth of the multinationals*

**mul·ti·ple**[1] /ˈmʌltəpəl/ *adj* including or involving many things, people, events etc: | **multiple injuries/burns** *Baxter was rushed to the hospital with multiple stab wounds.* | **multiple collision/crash/accident** (=an accident involving many cars) | **multiple birth** (=an occasion when several babies are born to the same mother at the same time)

**multiple**[2] *n* [C] **1** a number that contains a smaller number an exact number of times: *20 is a multiple of 5.* —see also LOWEST COMMON MULTIPLE **2** a multiple store

**multiple choice** /ˌ··· ˈ·◂/ *adj* a multiple choice examination or question shows several possible answers and you have to choose the correct one

**multiple scle·ro·sis** /ˌ···· ·ˈ··/ also **MS** —*n* [U] a serious illness that gradually destroys your nerves making you weak and unable to walk, often involving weakening eyesight and slow speech

**multiple store** /ˌ··· ˈ·/ *n* [C] *BrE* a word used especially in business meaning a CHAIN STORE

**mul·ti·plex** /ˈmʌltəpleks/ *adj* **1** a multiplex cinema shows several different films at the same time **2** *technical* having several different parts

**mul·ti·pli·ca·tion** /ˌmʌltəpləˈkeɪʃən/ *n* [U] **1** a method of calculating in which you add the same number to itself a particular number of times **2** *formal* a large increase in the size or number of something: *the multiplication in the number of claim forms that have to be filled out*

**multiplication sign** /ˌ···ˈ·· ·/ *n* [C] a sign (×) showing that one number is multiplied by another —see picture at MATHEMATICS

**multiplication ta·ble** /ˌ···ˈ·· ˌ··/ *n* [C] a list showing the result of numbers between one and twelve that have been multiplied together, used by children in schools

**mul·ti·pli·ci·ty** /ˌmʌltəˈplɪsəti/ *n* [C,U] a large number or great variety of things: [+ **of**] *the baffling multiplicity of courses available to language students*

**mul·ti·ply** /ˈmʌltəplaɪ/ *v* **1** [I,T] to increase greatly or make something increase greatly: *Our chances of success had multiplied several times over.* | *This vast stock of computerized images has multiplied the possibilities open to the artist.* **2** [I,T] to do a calculation in which you add a number to itself a particular number of times: **multiply sth by sth** *3 multiplied by 4 is 12.* —compare DIVIDE[1] (4) **3** [I] to breed: *The bugs can easily multiply to give a nasty bout of food poisoning.*

**mul·ti·pur·pose** /ˌmʌltiˈpɜːpəs◂‖-ˈpɜːr-/ *adj* a multipurpose tool, building etc is designed to be used for many different purposes

**mul·ti·ra·cial** /ˌmʌltɪˈreɪʃəl◂/ *adj* including or involving several different races of people: *a multiracial society*

**multi-sto·rey**[1] /ˌ·· ˈ··◂/ *adj* [only before noun] *BrE* a multi-storey building has many levels or floors

**multi-storey**[2] *n* [C] *BrE spoken* a multi-storey CAR PARK

**mul·ti·tude** /ˈmʌltətjuːd‖-tuːd/ *n* [C] **1 a multitude of** *formal or literary* a very large number of people or things: *The captain sat before a multitude of dials and levers.* | *a multitude of possible interpretations* **2 the multitude a)** ordinary people, especially when they are thought of as not being very well educated: *Political power has been placed in the hands of the multitude.* **b)** *literary or biblical* a large crowd of people **3 cover/hide a multitude of sins** *especially humorous* to make faults or problems seem less clear or noticeable

**mul·ti·tu·di·nous** /ˌmʌltəˈtjuːdənəs◂‖-ˈtuː-/ *adj formal* very many: *language in all its multitudinous forms*

**mum**[1] /mʌm/ *n* [C] **1** *BrE* mother; MOM *AmE* **2 mum's the word** used to tell someone that they must not tell other people about a secret: *Remember, mum's the word! I don't want anyone else finding out about this!* S1 W2

**mum**[2] *adj* **keep mum** *informal* to not tell anyone about a secret

**mum·ble** /ˈmʌmbəl/ *v* **mumbled, mumbling** [I,T] to say something too quietly and not clearly enough, so that it is difficult or impossible to hear: *The little boy mumbled something about wanting to go to the toilet.* | *Stop mumbling and speak up!* —**mumbler** *n* [C] —**mumble** *n* [C]

**mum·bo-jum·bo** /ˌmʌmbəʊ ˈdʒʌmbəʊ‖-boʊ/ *n* [U] **1** talk or writing on a technical subject that is difficult to understand and seems to have no sense: *Psychology books are often full of meaningless mumbo-jumbo.* **2** religious beliefs or activities that seem without sense or meaning

**mum·mer** /ˈmʌmə‖-ər/ *n* [C] an actor in a simple traditional play without words —**mumming** *n* [U]

**mum·mi·fy** /ˈmʌmɪfaɪ/ *v* [T] to preserve a dead body by putting special oils on it and wrapping it with cloth —**mummification** /ˌmʌmɪfəˈkeɪʃən/ *n* [U]

**mum·my** /ˈmʌmi/ *n* [C] **1** *BrE* a word meaning mother, used by or to young children; MOMMY *AmE* **2** a dead body that has been preserved by wrapping it in cloth, expecially in ancient Egypt S2

**mummy's boy** /ˈ·· ·/ *n* [singular] *informal* a mother's boy (MOTHER[1] (3))

**mumps** /mʌmps/ also **the mumps** *n* [U] an infectious illness which makes your neck swell and become painful, and is common among children

**mum-to-be** /ˌ· ·ˈ·/ *n* [C] *BrE informal* a MOTHER-TO-BE,

**munch** /mʌntʃ/ *v* [I,T] to eat something noisily: *My father went on munching his toast.* | [+ **on/at**] | *She was busily munching on an apple.*

**munch·ies** /ˈmʌntʃiz/ *n* [plural] *informal* **1 have the munchies** to feel hungry **2** small pieces of food, that you can eat with drinks at a party

**mun·dane** /mʌnˈdeɪn/ *adj* **1** ordinary and uninteresting: *Initially, the work was pretty mundane.* | *She led a mundane existence in the drab suburbs of Paris.* **2** *formal* concerned with ordinary daily life rather than religious matters; WORLDLY (2) —**mundaneness** *n* [U] —**mundanely** *adv*

**mung bean** /ˌmʌŋ ˈbiːn/ *n* [C] a small green bean, usually eaten as a BEANSPROUT

**mu·ni·ci·pal** /mjuːˈnɪsəpəl‖mjʊ-/ *adj* belonging to or

concerned with the government of a town or city: *the municipal waste dump|municipal elections* —**municipally** *adv*

**mu·ni·ci·pal·i·ty** /mjuːˌnɪsɪ̯ˈpælɪ̯ti‖mjʊ-/ *n* [C] **1** a town, city, or other small area, which has its own government that makes decisions about local affairs **2** the government of a town, city etc, which makes decisions about local affairs

**mu·nif·i·cent** /mjuːˈnɪfɪ̯sənt‖mjʊ-/ *adj formal* very generous: *a munificent gift* —**munificence** *n* [U] *She thanked the committee for their munificence.* —**munificently** *adv*

**mu·ni·tions** /mjuːˈnɪʃənz‖mjʊ-/ *n* [plural] military supplies such as bombs and large guns: *a munitions factory* —**munition** *adj* [only before noun]: *munition workers*

**mu·ral** /ˈmjʊərəl‖ˈmjʊrəl/ *n* [C] a painting that is painted on a wall, either inside or outside a building —compare FRESCO —**mural** *adj* [only before noun]

S3 W2 **mur·der¹** /ˈmɜːdə‖ˈmɜːrdər/ *n* **1** [C,U] the crime of deliberately killing someone: *He is charged with the horrific murder of two young boys.*| **commit (a) murder** *4600 murders were committed in the US in 1975.*|*the murder weapon* —compare MANSLAUGHTER **2** [U] unnecessary loss of human life caused by stupidity, especially in war: *Sending untrained men into the battle was sheer murder.* **3 get away with murder** *informal* if someone gets away with murder they are not punished for their actions and are allowed to do anything they want: *She lets those kids get away with murder.* **4 it's murder** *spoken* used to say that something is very difficult or unpleasant: *It's murder trying to find somewhere to park in Cambridge these days.* **5 it's murder on your feet/back etc** *spoken* used to say that something makes a part of your body feel very uncomfortable: *It's murder on your feet wearing high-heels all day.* —see also **scream/shout blue murder** (BLUE¹ (5))

**murder²** *v* [T] **1** to kill someone deliberately and illegally: *She murdered him for his money.*|*Thousands of civilians have been brutally murdered by right-wing death squads.*|*the murdered man* —see KILL¹ (USAGE) **2** *informal* to spoil a song, play etc completely by performing it very badly: *It's a beautiful song, but they murdered it.* **3** *informal* to defeat someone completely: *They murdered us in the final.* **4 I could murder a beer/pizza etc** *BrE spoken* used to say that you very much want to eat or drink something **5 sb will murder you** *spoken* used to tell someone that another person will be very angry with them: *Your dad'll murder you when he hears about it.*

**mur·der·er** /ˈmɜːdərə‖ˈmɜːrdərər/ *n* [C] someone who murders another person: *a convicted murderer*

**mur·der·ess** /ˈmɜːdərɪ̯s‖ˈmɜːr-/ *n* [C] *old-fashioned* a woman who murders another person

**mur·der·ous** /ˈmɜːdərəs‖ˈmɜːr-/ *adj* **1** very dangerous and likely to kill people: *Captain Bligh's murderous crew|murderous weapons of war* **2 murderous look/expression** an expression or look which shows that someone is very angry: *She kept giving me murderous looks every time I mentioned her husband.* —**murderously** *adv* —**murderousness** *n* [U]

**murk** /mɜːk‖mɜːrk/ *n* [U] *literary* darkness caused by smoke, dirt, or cloud; GLOOM (1): *the misty murk of the lagoon*

**murk·y** /ˈmɜːki‖ˈmɜːr-/ *adj* **1** dark and difficult to see through: *the murky grey light of dawn|He plunged into the murky waters of Honolulu harbour.* **2** involving dishonest or illegal activities that are kept hidden or secret: *It's a murky business.*| **a murky past** *a politician with a murky past* —**murkily** *adv* —**murkiness** *n* [U]

**mur·mur¹** /ˈmɜːmə‖ˈmɜːrmər/ *v* **1** [I,T] to say something in a soft low voice which is difficult to hear clearly: *He began stroking her hair and gently murmuring her name.* **2** [I] to complain to friends and people you work with, but not officially: [+ **about/against**] *Within the city there was much murmuring against the new ruler.* **3** [I] to make a soft, low sound: *The wind murmured through the trees.* —**murmuring** *n* [C,U] *vague murmurings of discontent*

**murmur²** *n* [C] **1** a soft low sound made by people speaking quietly or from a long way away: *the murmur of voices from down the corridor|She replied in a low murmur.* **2** a complaint, especially one made to friends and people you work with, but not officially: *There have been some murmurs of discontent over new city taxes.*| **without a murmur** (=without complaining or opposing) *Congress had accepted the treaty almost without a murmur.* **3** the soft low sound made by a stream, the wind etc: *the murmur of the little brook* **4** [usually singular] an unusual sound made by the heart which shows that there may be something wrong with it: *a heart murmur*

**Mur·phy's law** /ˌmɜːfiz ˈlɔː‖ˌmɜːrfiz ˈlɒː/ *n* [singular] *especially AmE* a tendency for bad things to happen whenever it is possible for them to do so; SOD'S LAW

**mus·ca·tel** /ˌmʌskəˈtel/ *n* [C,U] a sweet light-coloured wine, or the type of GRAPE that is used to make it

**mus·cle¹** /ˈmʌsəl/ *n* **1** [C,U] one of the pieces of flesh inside your body that connects your bones together and that you use when you move: *The next day the muscles in my arm felt sore.*| **arm/chest/stomach muscles** *bulging chest muscles*| **pull a muscle** (=injure a muscle so that it becomes painful) *My leg hurts – I think I've pulled a muscle.* **2** [U] physical strength and power: *It must have taken a lot of muscle to get that piano up those stairs.*| **put some muscle into it** *spoken* (=used to tell someone to try harder and use more effort) **3 military/political/financial etc muscle** military, political, or financial power or influence **4 not move a muscle** to remain completely still: *I shouted at him, but he didn't move a muscle.* **5** [U] *slang* strong men who are paid to protect or attack someone, especially by criminals —see also **flex your muscles** (FLEX¹ (2)) S2 W3

**muscle²** *v* **muscled**, **muscling**

**muscle in** *phr v* [I] to use your strength, power, or influence to get control of someone else's business or to interfere in their affairs: [+ **on**] *Another gang was trying to muscle in on their territory.*

**mus·cle·bound** /ˈmʌsəlbaʊnd/ *adj* having large stiff muscles because of too much physical exercise: *musclebound he-men with no imagination*

**mus·cle·man** /ˈmʌsəlmæn/ *plural* **musclemen** /-men/ *n* [C] **1** a man who has developed big strong muscles by doing exercises **2** a strong man who is employed to protect someone, usually a criminal

**Mus·co·vite** /ˈmʌskəvaɪt/ *n* [C] someone from Moscow

**mus·cu·lar** /ˈmʌskjɪ̯lə‖-ər/ *adj* **1** having a lot of big muscles; strong-looking: *strong muscular arms|She liked men who were tall and muscular.* **2** concerning or affecting the muscles: *muscular injuries* —**muscularly** *adv* —**muscularity** /ˌmʌskjɪ̯ˈlærɪ̯ti/ *n* [U]

**muscular dys·tro·phy** /ˌmʌskjɪ̯lə ˈdɪstrəfi‖-lər-/ *n* [U] a serious illness in which the muscles become weaker over a period of time

**muse¹** /mjuːz/ *v* **1** [I] to think carefully about something for a long time: [+ **on/over**] *He lit a cigarette and sat musing over the problems of the world.* **2** [T] to say something in a thoughtful way, especially a question that you are trying to find the answer to: *"I wonder why she was killed," mused Poirot.* —**musingly** *adv*

**muse²** *n* [C] **1** someone's muse is the force or person that makes them want to write, paint, or make music, and helps them to have good ideas; INSPIRATION (3): *She was the artist's lover and his creative muse.* **2 the Muses** a group of ancient Greek goddesses, each of whom represented a particular art or a science

**mu·se·um** /mjuːˈziːəm‖mjʊ-/ *n* [C] a building where important cultural, historical, or scientific objects are kept and shown to the public: *the Museum of Modern Art* S3 W2

**museum piece** /ˈ·ˌ·· ·/ *n* [C] **1** *often humorous* a very old-fashioned piece of equipment: *Some of the weapons* *used by the rebels are museum pieces.* **2** an object that is so valuable or interesting that it should be in a museum

**mush¹** /mʌʃ/ *n* **1** [singular, U] an unpleasant soft mass of a substance, especially food, which is partly liquid and partly solid: *The cabbage had been boiled down into a flavourless mush.* **2** [U] *AmE* a thick PORRIDGE made from CORN MEAL **3** [U] a book or film that is mush is about love and is SENTIMENTAL —**mushy** *adj*

**mush²** /mʊʃ/ *n* [singular] *BrE spoken* an angry and insulting way of addressing someone: *Oi, mush! Get your hands off my car!*

**mush·room¹** /ˈmʌʃruːm, -rʊm/ *n* [C] one of several kinds of FUNGUS with a flat top, some of which can be eaten: *mushroom soup* —see also MAGIC MUSHROOM —see picture on page 414

**mushroom²** *v* [I] **1** to grow and develop very quickly: *New housing developments mushroomed on the edge of town.* **2** [+ adv/prep] to spread up into the air in the shape of a mushroom

**mushroom cloud** /ˈ·· ˌ·/ *n* [C usually singular] a big cloud shaped like a mushroom, which is caused by a NUCLEAR explosion

**mushy peas** /ˌ·· ˈ·/ *n* [plural] *BrE* soft cooked PEAS, eaten especially in the north of England

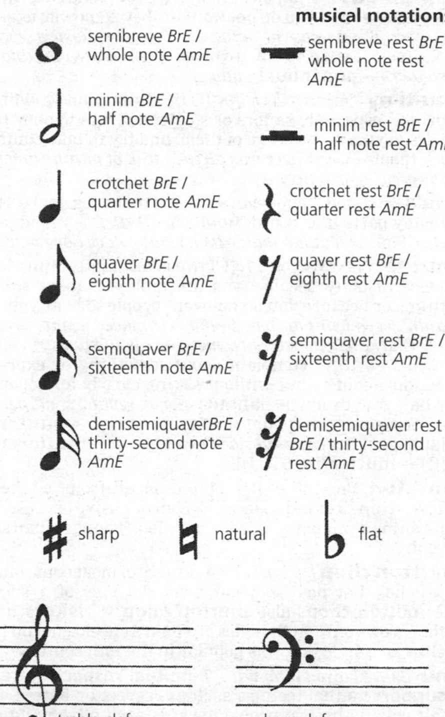


S1 W1 **mu·sic** /ˈmjuːzɪk/ *n* [U] **1** the arrangement of sounds made by instruments or voices in a way that is pleasant or exciting: *loud pop music | I like all kinds of music.* | **a piece of music** *The Moonlight Sonata is one of my favourite pieces of music.* | **write/compose music** *Nyman writes the music for most of Peter Greenaway's films.* **2** the art of writing or playing music: *studying music at college | music lessons* **3** a set of written marks representing music, or paper with the written marks on it: **read music** (=understand the sounds that written music represents) *Can you read music? | organ/piano/pop music* **4 be music to your ears** if someone's words are music to your ears, they make you very happy or pleased **5 set/put sth to music** to write music so that the words of a poem, play etc can be sung —see also **face the music** (FACE² (8))

**mu·sic·al¹** /ˈmjuːzɪkəl/ *adj* **1** [only before noun] connected with music or consisting of music: *a musical entertainment | We share the same musical tastes.* **2** good at or interested in playing or singing music: *I wasn't very musical when I was at school.* **3** having a pleasant sound like music: *She had a sweet musical voice.* —see also MUSICALLY 

**musical²** also **musical com·e·dy** /ˌ··· ˈ···/ *n* [C] a play or film that uses singing and dancing to tell a story: *'West Side Story', a musical with music by Leonard Bernstein*

**musical box** /ˈ··· ·/ *n* [C] *especially BrE* a box that plays a musical tune when you open it

**musical chairs** /ˌ··· ˈ·/ *n* [U] a children's game in which all the players must sit down when the music stops, but there are never enough chairs

**musical in·stru·ment** /ˌ··· ˈ···/ *n* [C] something that you use for playing music, such as a piano or GUITAR

**mu·sic·ally** /ˈmjuːzɪkli/ *adv* **1** with regard to music: *The band aren't much good musically, but they're very good-looking. | Musically speaking, the concert was only average.* **2** in a way that sounds like music: *Welsh people are supposed to pronounce English words musically.*

**music box** /ˈ·· ˌ·/ *n* [C] *especially AmE* a musical box

**music hall** /ˈ·· ·/ *n* **1** [U] a type of entertainment in the theatre, especially in the 19th and early 20th century consisting of singers, dancers, and people telling jokes; VAUDEVILLE *AmE* **2** [C] *BrE* a theatre used for this kind of entertainment

**mu·si·cian** /mjuːˈzɪʃən‖mjʊ-/ *n* [C] a person who plays a musical instrument, especially very well or as a job: *a talented young musician*

**mu·si·cian·ship** /mjuːˈzɪʃənʃɪp‖mjʊ-/ *n* [U] skill in playing music: *His musicianship was superb, really beyond compare.*

**mu·si·col·o·gy** /ˌmjuːzɪˈkɒlədʒi‖-ˈkɑː-/ *n* [U] the study of music, especially the history of different types of music —**musicologist** *n* [C] —**musicological** /ˌmjuːzɪkəˈlɒdʒɪkəl‖-ˈlɑː-/ *adj*

**music stand** /ˈ·· ·/ *n* [C] a metal frame for holding written music, so that you can read it while playing an instrument or singing

**musk** /mʌsk/ *n* [U] a strong smelling substance used to make PERFUME

**mus·ket** /ˈmʌskɪ̣t/ *n* [C] a type of gun used in former times

**mus·ket·eer** /ˌmʌskɪ̣ˈtɪə‖-ˈtɪr/ *n* [C] a soldier who uses a musket

**musk mel·on** /ˈ· ˌ··/ *n* [C] a type of sweet MELON

**musk·rat** /ˈmʌskræt/ *n* [C] an animal which lives in water in North America and is hunted for its fur

**musk·y** /ˈmʌski/ *adj* like MUSK: *a musky smell* —**muskiness** *n* [U]

**Mus·lim** /ˈmʊzlɪ̣m, ˈmʌz-, ˈmʊs-/ *n* [C] someone whose religion is Islam —**Muslim** *adj*

**mus·lin** /ˈmʌzlɪ̣n/ *n* [U] a very fine thin cotton cloth used for making dresses and curtains, especially in past times

**muss** /mʌs/ *v* [T + **up**] *informal especially AmE* to make something untidy, especially someone's hair

**mus·sel** /ˈmʌsəl/ *n* [C] a small sea animal, with a soft body that can be eaten and a black shell that is divided into two parts —see picture at SHELL¹

**must¹** /məst; *strong* mʌst/ *modal verb* [negative short form **mustn't**] **1** [past usually **had to**] to have to do something because the situation forces you, because of a rule or law, or because you feel that you should: *All passengers must wear seat belts. | You mustn't tell anyone about this – it's a secret. | I don't really want to make the* 

*appointment, but I suppose I must.* | *Under no circumstances must any member of staff socialize with the patients.* | *Apologize? Must I? It was all her own fault.* | **I must admit/say etc** *I must admit, I was surprised when he passed his driving test first time.* —compare HAVE³ —see graph at OBLIGE **2** [past usually **must have**] used when you are guessing that something is true or that something has happened because there seems to be no other possibility: *Sam must be nearly 90 years old now.* | *Buying roses? It must be love.* | *He must have been drunk to say that.* | *There must have been ten of them, all hiding in my attic.* **3 a)** used to suggest that someone does something, especially because you think they will enjoy it very much or you think it is a very good idea: *You must go and see the new Spielberg movie, the special effects are amazing.* **b)** used when you want to do something and hope to do it soon: *We must come over and try out that new barbecue of yours.* **4 if you must** used to tell someone that they are allowed to do something but that you do not approve or agree with it: *"Can I borrow your car, Mum?" "If you must."* | **if you must do sth** *If you must smoke, do it outside please.* **5 you must be joking** used when you think someone's suggestion is silly or stupid: *£2000 for that old car? You must be joking!*

**must²** /mʌst/ *n* **1 a must** something that you must do or must have: *Warm clothes are a must in the mountains.* **2** [U] the liquid from which wine is made; GRAPE juice

**mus·tache** /məˈstɑːʃ‖ˈmʌstæʃ/ *n* [C] the usual American spelling of MOUSTACHE

**mustachioed**, **moustachioed** /məˈstæʃiəʊd, -ˈstɑː-‖-ʃiəʊd/ *adj* having a large curly MOUSTACHE

**mus·tang** /ˈmʌstæŋ/ *n* [C] a small American wild horse

**mus·tard** /ˈmʌstəd‖-ərd/ *n* [U] **1** a yellow sauce that tastes hot, eaten especially with meat **2** a plant with yellow flowers whose seeds can be used to make the powder used to make this **3 not cut the mustard** to not be good enough for a particular job: *He'll never cut the mustard as a manager.* **4** a yellow-brown colour —see also **keen as mustard** (KEEN¹ (8)) —see picture on page 411

**mustard gas** /ˈ·· ·/ *n* [U] a poisonous gas that burns the skin, which was used during the First World War

**mus·ter¹** /ˈmʌstə‖-ər/ *v* **1 muster (up) courage/support/energy etc** to try to find as much courage, support etc as you can in order to do something difficult: *Finally I mustered up the courage to ask her out.* | *Senator Newbolt has been trying to muster support for his proposals.* **2** [I,T] to gather a group of people, especially soldiers, together in one place, or to come together as a group: *In April 1185 he began to muster an army.*

**muster²** *n* **1 pass muster** to be accepted as good enough: *Jackson wasn't a great player, but he just about passed muster.* **2** [C] *especially literary* a group of people, especially soldiers, that have been gathered together

**must·n't** /ˈmʌsənt/ the short form of 'must not': *You mustn't tell Jerry what I've bought.*

**must·y** /ˈmʌsti/ *adj* a musty room, house, or object has a damp and unpleasant smell, because it is old and has not had any fresh air for a long time: *musty old books* | *the stale musty smell of the attic* —**mustiness** *n* [U]

**mu·ta·ble** /ˈmjuːtəbəl/ *adj formal* able or likely to change —**mutability** /ˌmjuːtəˈbɪlɪti/ *n* [U] —opposite IMMUTABLE

**mu·ta·gen** /ˈmjuːtədʒən, -dʒen/ *n* [C] *technical* a substance that causes a living thing to mutate

**mu·tant** /ˈmjuːtənt/ *n* [C] an animal or plant that is different in some way from others of the same kind, because of a change in its GENETIC structure —**mutant** *adj*

**mu·tate** /mjuːˈteɪt‖ˈmjuːteɪt/ *v* [I] if a plant or animal mutates, it develops a feature that makes it different from other plants or animals of the same kind, because of a change in its GENETIC structure

**mu·ta·tion** /mjuːˈteɪʃən/ *n* [C,U] **1** a change in the GENETIC structure of an animal or plant, that makes it different from others of the same type: *random mutation* **2** *technical* a change in a speech sound, especially a vowel, because of the sound of the one next to it

**mute¹** /mjuːt/ *adj* **1** not speaking or refusing to speak: *Helena glared at me in mute anger.* **2** *old-fashioned* unable to speak; DUMB **3** *technical* not pronounced: *a mute 'e'* —**mutely** *adv* —**muteness** *n* [U]

**mute²** *v* [T] **1** to make a sound quieter: *He placed a hand across her mouth to mute her screams.* **2** to make a musical instrument sound softer

**mute³** *n* [C] **1** something that is placed over or into a musical instrument to make it sound softer **2** someone who cannot speak —see also DEAF-MUTE

**mut·ed** /ˈmjuːtɪd/ *adj* **1 muted criticism/support/response etc** criticism etc that is not expressed strongly: *At first, criticism of the war was fairly muted.* **2** quieter than usual: *We could hear the muted cries of newpaper-sellers in the street outside.* **3** a muted colour is not bright but soft and gentle: *muted pinks and blues*

**mu·ti·late** /ˈmjuːtɪleɪt/ *v* [T often passive] **1** to severely and violently damage someone's body, especially by removing part of it: *Many people were mutilated and maimed in the blast.* **2** to damage or change something so much that it is completely spoiled or ruined —**mutilation** /ˌmjuːtɪˈleɪʃən/ *n* [C,U]

**mu·ti·neer** /ˌmjuːtɪˈnɪə‖ˌmjuːtnˈɪr/ *n* [C] someone who is involved in a mutiny

**mu·ti·nous** /ˈmjuːtɪnəs‖-tn-əs/ *adj* **1** behaving in a way that shows you do not want to obey someone; REBELLIOUS: *There was a mutinous look in Rosie's eyes.* | *mutinous teenagers* **2** involved in a mutiny: *mutinous soldiers* —**mutinously** *adv*

**mu·ti·ny** /ˈmjuːtɪni‖-tn-i/ *n* [C,U] a situation in which people, especially sailors or soldiers, refuse to obey the person who is in charge of them, and try to take control for themselves: *There was already talk of mutiny among the crew.* —**mutiny** *v* [I]

**mutt** /mʌt/ *n* [C] *informal* **1** a dog that does not belong to any particular breed; MONGREL **2** *BrE* a stupid person; fool: *You dumb mutt – look what you've done now!*

**mut·ter** /ˈmʌtə‖-ər/ *v* **1** [I,T] to speak quietly or in a low voice, usually because you are annoyed about something, or because you do not want people to hear you: *"I didn't even want to come in the first place" he muttered.* | *Mr Clarke left, muttering something about having to see a client.* **2** [I] to complain about something or express doubts about it, but without saying clearly and openly what you think: [+ **about**] *Some senators muttered darkly about the threat to national security.* —**mutter** *n* [singular] *His voice subsided to a mutter.* —**mutterer** *n* [C] —**muttering** *n* [C,U]

**mut·ton** /ˈmʌtn/ *n* [U] **1** the meat from a sheep **2 mutton dressed as lamb** *BrE* an offensive expression meaning a woman who is trying to look younger than she really is

**mutton chop** /ˌ·· ˈ·/ *n* [C] **1** a piece of meat containing a bone, that has been cut from the RIBS of a sheep **2 mutton chops** also **mutton chop whiskers** hair that grows only on the sides of a man's cheeks, not on his chin, in a style that was popular in the 19th century

**mu·tu·al** /ˈmjuːtʃuəl/ *adj* **1 mutual respect/hatred/support** mutual feelings such as respect or hatred are felt equally by two people towards each other: *Mutual respect is necessary for the partnership to work.* | **the feeling is mutual** (=used to say that you have the same feeling about someone else as they have about you, especially when you dislike each other) *I didn't like Dev, and the feeling seemed to be mutual.* —compare RECIPROCAL **2 mutual friend/interest** a friend or interest that two people both have: *We discovered a mutual interest in gardening.* **3 mutual admiration society** *humorous* a situation in which two people praise each other a lot —**mutuality** /ˌmuːtʃuˈælɪti/ *n* [U]

**mutual fund** /ˈ··· ·/ *n* [C] *AmE* a UNIT TRUST *BrE*

**mu·tu·al·ly** /ˈmjuːtʃuəli/ *adv* **1** done or experienced equally by two people: *a mutually beneficial arrangement* **2 mutually exclusive/contradictory** two ideas or beliefs that are mutually exclusive cannot both exist or be true at the same time

**muu-muu** /ˈmuː muː/ *n* [C] *AmE* a long loose dress

**mu·zak** /ˈmjuːzæk/ *n* [U] *trademark* recorded music that is played continuously in airports, shops, hotels etc

**muz·zle¹** /ˈmʌzəl/ *n* [C] **1** the nose and mouth of an animal such as a dog or horse: *a grey dog with a black muzzle* —see picture at HORSE¹ **2** something that you put over a dog's mouth to stop it from biting people **3** the end of the BARREL of a gun —see picture at GUN¹

**muzzle²** *v* [T] **1** to prevent someone from speaking freely or expressing their opinions: *an attempt to muzzle the press and ban opposition newspapers* **2** to put a muzzle over a dog's mouth so that it cannot bite people

**muz·zy** /ˈmʌzi/ *adj BrE* **1** unable to think clearly, especially because you are ill or drunk; CONFUSED: *I was feeling a bit muzzy by that time, and decided to go home.* **2** not clear; BLURRED: *a muzzy TV picture* —**muzzily** *adv* —**muzziness** *n* [U]

**MW** a written abbreviation for MEDIUM WAVE

S1 W1 **my** /maɪ/ *determiner* [possessive form of 'I'] **1** of or belonging to me: *Have you seen my car keys?|My mother phoned last night.|You should take my advice.|I'm sure you don't want to listen to all my problems.* **2** used when you are surprised about something: *My! What a clever boy you are.* **3** used when you are shocked or angry about something: *Oh my God! The house is on fire!* **4** used when addressing people who you love or like a lot: *Goodnight, my dear. Sleep well.*

**my·col·o·gy** /maɪˈkɒlədʒi‖-ˈkɑː-/ *n* [U] the study of fungi (FUNGUS)

**my·nah bird** /ˈmaɪnə bɜːd‖-bɜːrd/ also **mynah** —*n* [C] a large dark Asian bird that can copy human speech

**my·o·pi·a** /maɪˈəʊpiə‖-ˈoʊ-/ *n* [U] **1** inability to imagine what the results of your actions will be or how they will affect other people **2** *formal* inability to see things clearly that are far away

**my·o·pic** /maɪˈɒpɪk‖-ˈɑːpɪk/ *adj* **1** unwilling or unable to think about the future results of your actions: *the government's myopic refusal to take environmental issues seriously* **2** *technical* unable to see things clearly that are faraway; SHORTSIGHTED (1) —**myopically** /-kli/ *adv*

**myr·i·ad¹** /ˈmɪriəd/ *adj* [only before noun] *literary* too many to count: *Myriad bright stars shone in the sky above.*

**myriad²** *n* [C] *especially literary* a very large number of something: [+ **of**] *myriads of small islands*

**myrrh** /mɜː‖mɜːr/ *n* [U] a sticky brown substance that is used for making PERFUME and INCENSE

**myr·tle** /ˈmɜːtl‖ˈmɜːr-/ *n* [C] a small tree with shiny green leaves and sweet-smelling white flowers

S1 W1 **my·self** /maɪˈself/ *pron* **1** [reflexive form of 'I']: *I hurt myself|I passed the exam so I'm feeling pretty pleased with myself.|Those dishwashers are great. I think I'll get one for myself.* **2** used to emphasize the pronoun I: *Why do I always have to do everything myself?|I'm sorry, I'm a stranger here myself.|I myself might have done things differently.* **3 not be/feel etc myself** to not feel or behave in the way you usually do because you are nervous or upset: *I do apologise — I haven't been feeling myself lately* **4 (all) by myself a)** alone: *If you don't mind, I'd like to be by myself for a while.* **b)** without help: *It's hard to believe but I painted the house all by myself.* **5 (all) to myself** if you have something to yourself, you do not have to share it with anyone: *I always dreamt of having a room all to myself.* —see also YOURSELF

**mys·te·ri·ous** /mɪˈstɪəriəs‖-ˈstɪr-/ *adj* **1** mysterious events, behaviour, or situations are difficult to explain or understand: *His father died of a mysterious disease.|a mysterious smile|* **in mysterious circumstances** *Benson later disappeared in mysterious circumstances.* **2** a mysterious person is someone who you know very little about and who seems strange or interesting: *Who was this mysterious stranger?* **3** saying very little about what you are doing; SECRETIVE: [+ **about**] *Helen's being very mysterious about her plans.* —**mysteriously** *adv* —**mysteriousness** *n* [U]

**mys·te·ry** /ˈmɪstəri/ *n* **1** [C] something that is impossible to understand or explain or about which little is known: **remain a mystery** *Twenty years after the event, his death remains a mystery.|* **solve/unravel a mystery** (=find an explanation for it) *They never solved the mystery of Gray's disappearance.|* **a mystery phone call/lover/package etc** (=one that you know very little about, which therefore seems strange and interesting) *If I tell you the mystery ingredient, my recipe won't be a secret.|* **be a mystery to** (=used to say that you do not know or understand much about something) *Jean's business affairs were always a mystery to him.* **2 It's a mystery to me** *spoken* used to say that you cannot understand something at all: *It's a mystery to me how she manages to work so fast.* **3** [U] a quality that makes someone or something seem strange, secret, or difficult to explain| **an air of mystery** *There was an air of mystery about him.|* **be shrouded/veiled in mystery** *The circumstances of his death were veiled in mystery.* **4** [C] *formal* a quality that something has that cannot be explained in any practical or scientific way, especially because it is connected with God and religion: [+ **of**] *the mystery of creation* **5** [C] a story about a murder, in which you are not told who the murderer is until the end: *a murder mystery* W3

**mystery play** /ˈ··· ·/ *n* [C] a religious play from the Middle Ages based on a story from the Bible

**mystery tour** /ˈ··· ·/ *n* [C] *BrE* a trip, usually by bus, in which people do not know where they will be taken

**mys·tic¹** /ˈmɪstɪk/ *n* [C] someone who practises MYSTICISM

**mystic²** *adj* another word for MYSTICAL

**mys·tic·al** /ˈmɪstɪkəl/ *adj* **1** involving religious, spiritual, or magical powers that people cannot understand: *a mystical union with nature|the mystical significance of names and numbers* **2** connected with mysticism —**mystically** /-kli/ *adv*

**mys·ti·cis·m** /ˈmɪstɪsɪzəm/ *n* [U] a religious practice in which people try to get knowledge of truth and to become united with God through prayer and MEDITATION

**mys·ti·fy** /ˈmɪstɪfaɪ/ *v* [T] to be impossible for someone to understand or explain; BAFFLE¹: *a case that mystified the police* —**mystifying** *adj* —**mystification** /ˌmɪstɪfɪˈkeɪʃən/ *n* [U]

**mys·tique** /mɪˈstiːk/ *n* [U] a quality that makes someone or something seem different, mysterious, or special: *Hollywood has lost none of its mystique.*

**myth** /mɪθ/ *n* **1** [C,U] an idea or story that many people believe, but which is not true: *the myth of male superiority|Most people think that bats are blind, but in fact this is a myth.|* **popular myth** (=one that a lot of people believe) *Contrary to popular myth, there is no evidence that long jail sentences really deter young offenders.|* **explode/dispel a myth** (=prove that it is not true) **2** [C] an ancient story, especially one invented in order to explain natural or historical events: *the myth of Orpheus* **3** [U] this kind of ancient story in general: *the giants of myth and fairy-tale*

**myth·ic** /ˈmɪθɪk/ *adj* like something or someone in a myth: *mythic powers|mythic beauty*

**myth·i·cal** /ˈmɪθɪkəl/ *adj* **1** connected with or only existing in an ancient story: *a mythical creature like the Minotaur* **2** imagined or invented; FICTITIOUS: *all these mythical 'job prospects' he keeps talking about*

**my·thol·o·gy** /mɪˈθɒlədʒi‖-ˈθɑː-/ *n* [C,U] **1** ancient myths in general, and the beliefs they represent: *scenes from classical mythology* **2** ideas or opinions that many people believe, but that are wrong or not true: *popular mythology about the lives of the royal family* —**mythologist** *n* [C] —**mythological** /ˌmɪθəˈlɒdʒɪkəl◂‖-ˈlɑː-/ *adj|a mythological hero*

**myx·o·ma·to·sis** /ˌmɪksəməˈtəʊsɪs‖-ˈtoʊ-/ *n* [U] a disease that kills rabbits

**N,n** /en/ *plural* **N's, n's** *n* [C] the 14th letter of the English alphabet

**n** the written abbreviation of NOUN

**N** the written abbreviation of north or northern

**n** /ən/ a short form of 'and': *rock 'n' roll*

**N/A** not applicable; written on a form to show that you do not need to answer a question

**NAACP** /ˌen eɪ eɪ siː ˈpiː/ *n* [singular] the National Association for the Advancement of Colored People; an American organization that works for the rights of African-American people

**Naaf·i** /ˈnæfi/ *n* [C] a shop or eating place in a British military establishment

**naan** /nɑːn/ *n* [U] another spelling of NAN[2]

**nab** /næb/ *v* **nabbed, nabbing** [T] *informal* **1** to catch someone doing something illegal; ARREST[1] (1) **2** to get something quickly: *See if you can nab a seat.*

**na·bob** /ˈneɪbɒb‖-bɑːb/ *n* [C] an Englishman in the 18th or 19th century who became rich in India and returned to Europe

**nach·os** /ˈnætʃəʊz‖-oʊz/ *n* [plural] hot-tasting Mexican food consisting of small pieces of TORTILLAS covered with cheese, beans etc

**na·cre** /ˈneɪkə‖-ər/ *n* [U] MOTHER-OF-PEARL: *Buzz's gift, a nacre box, lay on the table.* —**nacreous** *adj*

**na·dir** /ˈneɪdɪə‖-dər/ *n* [singular] *literary* the time when a situation is at its worst: *By 1932, the depression had reached its nadir.*

**naff**[1] /næf/ *adj BrE slang* silly, especially in a way that shows a lack of good judgement about style, fashion etc: *a really naff film*

**naff**[2] *v* **naff off** *BrE spoken* used to tell someone rudely to go away.

**nag**[1] /næg/ *v* **nagged, nagging** [I,T] **1** to keep complaining to someone about their behaviour or asking them to do something, in a way that is very annoying: *I wish you'd stop nagging!* | **nag sb to do sth** *Nadia's been nagging me to fix the lamp.* | **nag sb for** *The kids are always nagging me for new toys.* **2** to make someone feel continuously worried or uncomfortable: [**+ at**] *a problem that had been nagging at him for days.* | **nagged by doubts/worries/fears** *Karen lay awake all night, nagged by doubts.*

**nag**[2] *n* [C] *informal* **1** a person who nags continuously **2** a horse, especially one that is old or in bad condition

**nag·ging** /ˈnægɪŋ/ *adj* [only before noun] making you worry or feel pain all the time: **nagging doubt/fear/feeling etc** *It was a week before the wedding, and there was still the nagging doubt in the back of her mind.* | **nagging toothache/headache/pain etc** *Lee had a nagging pain in her back.*

**nai·ad** /ˈnaɪæd‖ˈneɪæd, ˈnaɪ-, -əd/ *n* [C] a female spirit who, according to ancient Greek stories, lived in a lake, stream, or river

S3 **nail**[1] /neɪl/ *n* [C] **1** a thin pointed piece of metal which you force into a piece of wood with a hammer to fasten the wood to something else **2** the hard smooth layer on the ends of your fingers and toes *Damn! I've just broken a nail.* **3 a nail in sb's/sth's coffin** something bad which will help to destroy someone's success or hopes: *This latest scandal was one more nail in the coffin of Manley's ambitions.* **4 on the nail a)** *BrE* if you pay money on the nail, you pay it immediately **b)** *AmE* completely correct in what you say or when you guess something: *Ed was right on the nail when he guessed Sue's age.* —see also **as hard as nails** (HARD[1] (27)), **hit the nail on the head** (HIT[1] (24))

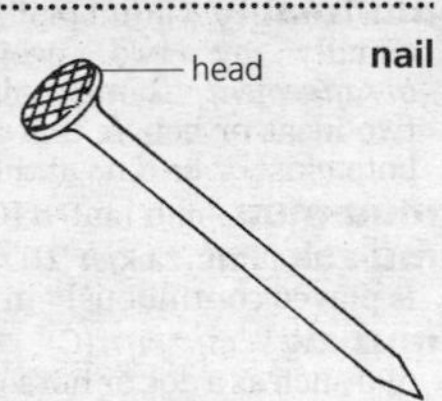

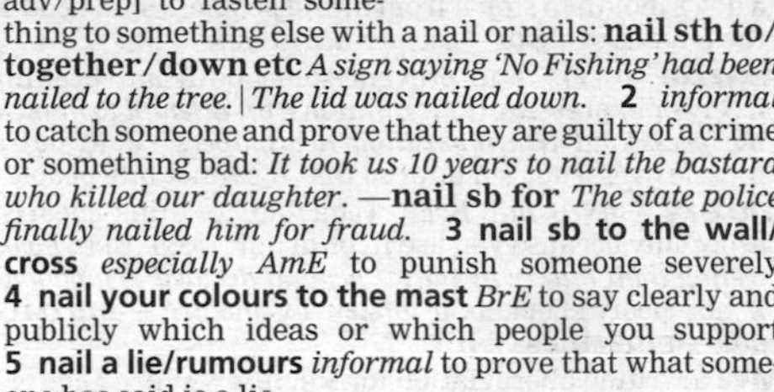


**nail**[2] *v* [T] **1** [always + adv/prep] to fasten something to something else with a nail or nails: **nail sth to/together/down etc** *A sign saying 'No Fishing' had been nailed to the tree.* | *The lid was nailed down.* **2** *informal* to catch someone and prove that they are guilty of a crime or something bad: *It took us 10 years to nail the bastard who killed our daughter.* —**nail sb for** *The state police finally nailed him for fraud.* **3 nail sb to the wall/cross** *especially AmE* to punish someone severely **4 nail your colours to the mast** *BrE* to say clearly and publicly which ideas or which people you support **5 nail a lie/rumours** *informal* to prove that what someone has said is a lie

**nail sb/sth ↔ down** *phr v* [T] *informal* **1** to force someone to say clearly what they want or what they intend to do **nail sb down to sth** *Before they repair the car, nail them down to a price.* **2** *AmE* to reach a final and definite decision about something: *Two days isn't enough time to nail down the details of an agreement.*

**nail-bit·er** /ˈ· ˌ··/ *n* [C] *informal* a very exciting story, film etc

**nail-bit·ing** /ˈ· ˌ··/ *adj* [only before noun] extremely exciting because you do not know what is going to happen next: *a nail-biting finish to the tennis final*

**nail·brush** /ˈ· ·/ *n* [C] a small, stiff brush for cleaning your fingernails —see picture at BRUSH

**nail file** /ˈ· ·/ *n* [C] a thin piece of metal with a rough surface used for making your fingernails a nice shape

**nail pol·ish** /ˈ· ˌ··/ also **nail e·nam·el** /ˈ· ·ˌ··/, **nail var·nish** /ˈ· ˌ··/ *BrE n* [U] coloured or transparent liquid which is painted on women's fingernails or toenails to make them look attractive: *pink nail polish*

**nail scis·sors** /ˈ· ˌ··/ *n* [plural] a small pair of scissors for cutting fingernails or toenails —see picture at SCISSORS

**na·ive** /naɪˈiːv/ *adj* not having much experience of how complicated life is so that you trust people too much and believe that good things will always happen: *a group of young, naive revolutionaries* | *You really believe him? How can you be so naive?* —**naively** *adv*: *I had naively imagined that he was in love with me.* —**naivety** /naɪˈiːvəti/ also **naiveté** /naɪˈiːvəteɪ/ *n* [U] *dangerous political naivety*

**na·ked** /ˈneɪkɪd/ *adj* **1** not wearing clothes or not covered by clothes; NUDE[1]: *The children swam naked in the lake.* | **stark naked** also **buck naked/naked as a jaybird** *AmE* (=completely naked) **2 with the naked eye** without the help of any instrument: *Bacteria can't be seen with the naked eye.* **3 naked sword/light/flame etc** a sword etc that is not enclosed by a cover: *The naked light bulb glared in her eyes.* **4 naked truth/self-interest/aggression etc** truth etc that is not hidden and is shocking: *Their claim was based on naked self-interest.* —**nakedly** *adv* —**nakedness** *n* [U] S3

**nam·by-pam·by** /ˌnæmbi ˈpæmbi◂/ *adj informal* too weak and gentle and lacking determination: *To these soldiers writing poetry must have seemed a namby-pamby sort of occupation.* —**namby-pamby** *n* [C]

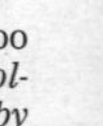

**name**[1] /neɪm/ *n* **1** [C] the word that someone or something is called or known by: *What's the name of that river?* | *Her name is Mandy Wilson.* | **first name/Christian name** *Her first name is Mandy.* | **last name/surname/family name** *Her surname is Wilson.* | **middle name** *Lots of girls have Elizabeth as their middle name.* | **full name** (=complete name) *Please leave your*

*full name and address with reception.* | **know sb by name** (=know what someone is called) *It's a big school but the principal knows everyone by name.* | **by the name of** (=whose name is...) *Is there anyone here by the name of Sommerville?* | **go by the name of** (=call yourself a particular name which may not be your real name) *a wrestler who went by the name of Mazambula* | **under the name (of)** (=using a name that is different from your own) *H. H. Munro wrote under the name Saki.* **2 call sb names** to say something nasty or insulting about someone | **call sb all the names under the sun** (=say rude and insulting things about someone) **3** [singular] the opinion that people have about a person or organization; REPUTATION: **have a name for** (=be known by people to have a particular quality) *The company has a name for reliability.* | **get a good/bad name** *The restaurant got a bad name for slow service.* | **make a name for yourself** (=become known and admired by many people) *Manyac made a name for himself in the Parisian art world.* **4 big/famous/household name** *informal* someone who is famous: *some of the biggest names in show business* **5 not have a penny to your name** *informal* to be very poor **6 in sb's name** if an official document, a hotel room etc is in someone's name it officially belongs to them or is for them: *The mortgage is in my husband's name.* **7 do sth in the name of science/religion etc** to do something that is wrong and believe that you are doing it to support the work of science etc: *cruel experiments on animals carried out in the name of science* **8 in the name of sb** doing something as someone else's representative: *I claim this land in the name of the King!* **9 in name only** if something exists in name only it does not really exist although it is officially said to: *a democracy in name only* **10 in all but name** if a situation exists in all but name, it is the real situation but people do not admit that it is: *She was his wife in all but name.* **11 I can't put a name to it** *spoken* used when you cannot remember what something is called: *I know the tune but I can't put a name to it.* **12 take sb's name in vain** *often humorous* to talk about someone without showing respect **13 the name of the game** *informal* the most important thing or quality needed for a particular activity: *In fishing, patience is the name of the game.* **14 sb's name is mud** *informal* used to say that people are angry with someone because of something he or she has done —see also PEN NAME, **clear sb's name** (CLEAR² (3))

S 2 W 2 **name²** *v* [T]

**1 ► GIVE SB A NAME ◄** to give someone or something a particular name: **name sb John/Ann etc** *We named our daughter Sarah.* | *I name this ship 'Arcadia'.* | **name sb after** *BrE* **/name sb/sth for** *AmE* (=give someone the same name as) *Bill is named after his father.* | *The college is named for George Washington.*

**2 ► SAY SB'S OR STH'S NAME ◄** to say what the name of someone or something is: *Can you name this tune?* | *The two murder victims have yet to be named.* | **name names** (=name the people who were involved in something, especially something bad or illegal) *She has secret information and is threatening to name names.*

**3 ► CHOOSE SB ◄** to officially choose someone or something: **name sb as** *Gerry's been named as successor to the present manager.* | **name sb to sth** *AmE*: *Fitzgerald was named to the committee by the chairman.*

**4 to name but a few** used after a short list of things or people to say that there are many more you could mention: *Gina Fratini, David Neil and Benny Ong, to name but a few, became famous when the Princess wore their designs.*

**5 you name it** *spoken* used after a list of things to mean that there are many more you could mention: *Clothes, furniture, books – you name it, they sell it!*

**6 name the day** to decide on a date for your wedding

**7 name your price** used to mean that you can decide how much money you want to buy or sell something for

**name-cal·ling** /ˈ· ˌ··/ *n* [U] the act of saying nasty things about someone: *children subjected to jibes and name-calling*

**name day** /ˈ· ·/ *n* [C] the day each year when the Christian church gives honour to the particular SAINT (=holy person) whose name you have been given

**name·drop** /ˈneɪmdrɒp‖-drɑːp/ *v* [I] *informal* to mention famous or important people's names to make it seem that you know them personally —**namedropping** *n* [U]

**name·less** /ˈneɪmləs/ *adj* **1** not known by name; ANONYMOUS: *the work of a nameless 13th century writer* **2 a)** [only before noun] *literary* difficult to describe: *Nameless fears made her tremble.* **b)** too terrible to name or describe: *nameless crimes* **3** having no name: *hundreds of nameless canyons* **4 who shall remain nameless** *spoken* used when you want to say that someone has done something wrong but without mentioning their name: *A certain person, who shall remain nameless, forgot to lock the front door.*

**name·ly** /ˈneɪmli/ *adv* used to introduce additional information which makes it clear exactly who or what you are talking about: *Three students were mentioned, namely John, Sarah and Sylvia.*

**name·plate** /ˈneɪmpleɪt/ *n* [C] a piece of metal or plastic fastened to something, showing the name of the owner or maker, or the person who lives or works in a place

**name·sake** /ˈneɪmseɪk/ *n* [C] **sb's namesake** another person, especially a more famous person, who has the same name as someone: *Like his famous namesake, young Nelson had a brave, adventurous spirit.*

**name tag** /ˈ· ·/ *n* [C] a small sign with your name on it that you wear

**name-tape** /ˈ· ·/ *n* [C] *BrE* a small piece of cloth with your name on it that is sewn onto clothes; LABEL¹ (1) *AmE*

**nan¹** /næn/ *n* [C] *BrE informal* a word meaning grandmother, used by children

**nan², naan** /nɑːn/ *n* [U] a type of bread made without YEAST and eaten with Indian food

**nan·ny** /ˈnæni/ *n* [C] **1** a woman whose job is to take care of the children in a family, usually in the children's own home **2** *BrE informal* a word meaning grandmother, used by children: *It's my Nanny's birthday* **3 the nanny state** *especially BrE* a government which tries to control the lives of citizens too much

**nanny goat** /ˈ·· ·/ *n* [C] a female goat

**nano-** /nænəʊ/ *prefix* one thousand millionth of a particular unit: *nanometre* (=one thousand millionth of a metre) —see table on page B2.

**nan·o·sec·ond** /ˈnænəʊˌsekənd‖-noʊ-/ *n* [C] a unit for measuring time. There are one thousand million nanoseconds in a second.

**nap¹** /næp/ *n* **1** [C] a short sleep, especially during the day: **have/take a short nap** *I usually take a nap after lunch.* **2** [singular] the soft surface on some cloth and leather, made by brushing the short, fine threads or hairs in one direction —compare PILE¹ (4) **3** [C] information about the horse likely to win a race

**nap²** *v* **napped, napping** **1** [I] to sleep for a short time during the day **2 be caught napping** *informal* to not be ready to deal with something when it happens, although you should be ready for it **3** [T] to give advice about which horse is likely to win a race

**na·palm** /ˈneɪpɑːm‖-pɑːm, -pɑːlm/ *n* [U] a thick liquid made from petrol, which is used in bombs

**nape** /neɪp/ *n* [singular] the back of your neck: *He nuzzled the soft, warm nape of her neck.*

**naph·tha** /ˈnæfθə/ *n* [U] a chemical compound like petrol

**nap·kin** /ˈnæpkɪn/ *n* [C] **1** a square piece of cloth or paper used for protecting your clothes and for cleaning your hands and lips during a meal —see picture on page 833 **2** SANITARY PAD *AmE*

**napkin ring** /ˈ·· ˌ·/ *n* [C] a small ring in which a napkin is put and kept for someone to use at the next meal

**nap·py** /ˈnæpi/ *n* [C] *BrE* a piece of soft cloth or paper worn by a baby between its legs and fastened around its waist to hold its liquid and solid waste; DIAPER *AmE* S 3

**nappy rash** /ˈ·· ·/ *n* [U] *BrE* sore skin between a baby's legs and on its BUTTOCKS caused by a wet or dirty nappy; DIAPER RASH *AmE*

**narc[1]** /nɑːk‖nɑːrk/ *n* [C] *AmE informal* a police officer who deals with the problem of illegal drugs

**narc[2]** *v* [I + on] *AmE slang* to secretly tell the police about someone else's criminal activities, especially activities involving illegal drugs

**nar·cis·sis·m** /ˈnɑːsɪ̇sɪzəm‖ˈnɑːr-/ *n* [U] a tendency to admire your own physical appearance or abilities: *He went to the gym to train every day, driven purely by narcissism.* —**narcissist** *n* [C] —**narcissistic** /ˌnɑːsɪ̇ˈsɪstɪk◂‖ˌnɑːr-/ *adj*

**nar·cis·sus** /nɑːˈsɪsəs‖nɑːr-/ *n* [C] a white or yellow spring flower, such as the DAFFODIL

**nar·cot·ic[1]** /nɑːˈkɒtɪk‖nɑːrˈkɑː-/ *n* **1 narcotics** [plural] *especially AmE* illegal drugs that affect the mind in a harmful way | **narcotics agent** (=a police officer who deals with the problems of narcotics) **2** [C] a type of drug which makes you sleep and reduces pain

**narcotic[2]** *adj* **1** [only before noun] *especially AmE* connected with illegal drugs: *narcotic addiction* **2** a narcotic drug takes away pain or makes you sleep

**nark[1]** /nɑːk‖nɑːrk/ *n* [C] *BrE slang* someone who is friendly with criminals and who secretly tells the police about their activities; STOOLPIGEON *AmE*

**nark[2]** *v BrE slang* **1 be/get narked** to be angry or get angry about something someone has done: *I was really narked when she wouldn't listen to me.* **2** [I + on] to secretly tell the police about someone else's criminal activities

**nark·y** /ˈnɑːki‖ˈnɑːr-/ *adj BrE slang* bad-tempered

**nar·rate** /nəˈreɪt‖ˈnæreɪt, næˈreɪt, nə-/ *v* [T] *formal* to tell a story by describing all the events in order: *a wild life film narrated by David Attenborough*

**nar·ra·tion** /nəˈreɪʃən‖næ-, nə-/ *n* [C,U] *formal* **1** the act of telling a story **2** a spoken description or explanation which is given during a film, play etc

**nar·ra·tive** /ˈnærətɪv/ *n* **1** [C,U] *formal* something that is told as a story: *The last chapter of the book brings the narrative of his journey to an end.* **2** [U] the art of telling a story —**narrative** *adj*: *a narrative poem*

**nar·ra·tor** /nəˈreɪtə‖ˈnæreɪtər, næˈreɪtər, nə-/ *n* [C] a person in some books, plays etc who tells the story

S3 W2 **nar·row[1]** /ˈnærəʊ‖-roʊ/ *adj*

**1 ▶ NOT WIDE ◀** not wide, especially in comparison with length or with what is usual: *a narrow winding valley* | *a long narrow room* | *There are plans to widen the narrowest sections of the road.* —compare BROAD[1] (1) —opposite WIDE[1] (1) —see picture at THIN[1]

**2 narrow escape** a situation in which you only just avoid danger, difficulties, or trouble: *Peter had a narrow escape from drowning when he fell overboard.*

**3 narrow majority/victory/defeat etc** one that is only just achieved or happens by only a small amount

**4 by a narrow margin** if you win or lose by a narrow margin, you do it by only a small amount

**5 ▶ IDEAS/ATTITUDES ◀** a narrow attitude or way of looking at a situation is too limited and does not consider enough possibilities: *The company takes too narrow a view of possible export markets.* | *Each group has their own narrow economic interest.* —see also NARROW-MINDED

**6 narrow squeak** *informal* a situation in which you only just escape from danger or avoid an accident

**7** *formal* careful and thorough: *a narrow examination of events* —see also NARROWLY, NARROWS **keep to/stray from the straight and narrow** (STRAIGHT[3] (4)), —**narrowness** *n* [U]

**narrow[2]** *v* [I,T] **1** to become narrower or make something narrower: *The river narrows at this point.* | *He narrowed his eyes against the sun.* **2** also **narrow down** to become less or make something less in range, difference etc: *The police have narrowed down their list of suspects.* | *New tax laws will narrow the gap between rich and poor.* | *The choice of goods available is narrowing.*

**narrow boat** /ˈ·· ˌ·/ *n* [C] *BrE* a long, narrow boat for use on CANALS

**narrow gauge** /ˈ·· ˌ·/ *n* [C] a size of railway track of less than standard width —see also GAUGE[1] (3)

**nar·row·ly** /ˈnærəʊli‖-roʊ-/ *adv* **1** only by a small amount: *We narrowly missed hitting the other car.* | *The amendment was narrowly defeated.* **2** looking at or considering only a small part of something: *The law is being interpreted too narrowly.* **3** *formal* in a thorough way, looking for detail: *The teacher questioned the boy narrowly about why he was late.*

**narrow-mind·ed** /ˌ·· ˈ··◂/ *adj* unwilling to accept or understand new or different ideas or customs; PREJUDICED —opposite BROADMINDED —**narrow-mindedness** *n* [U] —**narrow-mindedly** *adv*

**nar·rows** /ˈnærəʊz‖-roʊz/ *n* [plural] **1** also **Narrows** [plural] a narrow passage of water between two pieces of land which connects two larger areas of water **2** *AmE* a narrow part of a river, lake etc

**na·ry** /ˈneəri‖ˈneri/ *adv old use* not one: *They said nary a word.*

**NASA** /ˈnæsə/ *n* [singular] National Aeronautics and Space Administration; a US government organization that controls space travel and the scientific study of space

**na·sal[1]** /ˈneɪzəl/ *adj* **1** related to the nose: *the nasal passage* —see picture at RESPIRATORY **2** a sound or voice that is nasal comes mainly through your nose: *He spoke in a high nasal voice.* **3** *technical* a nasal CONSONANT or vowel such as /n/ or /m/ is one that is produced wholly or partly through your nose —**nasally** *adv*

**nasal[2]** *n* [C] *technical* a particular speech sound, such as /m/, /n/, or /ŋ/ that is made through your nose

**na·sal·ize** also **-ise** *BrE* /ˈneɪzəl-aɪz/ *v* [T] to make a sound partly through your nose: *nasalized vowels*

**nas·cent** /ˈnæsənt/ *adj formal* coming into existence or starting to develop: *South Africa's nascent democracy*

**nas·tur·tium** /nəˈstɜːʃəm‖-ɜːr-/ *n* [C] a garden plant with orange, yellow, or red flowers and circular leaves

**nas·ty** /ˈnɑːsti‖ˈnæsti/ *adj* S

**1 ▶ BEHAVIOUR ◀** nasty behaviour or remarks are extremely unkind and unpleasant; MALICIOUS: *a nasty temper* | *That's a nasty thing to say!* | *There's a nasty streak in her character.* | **be nasty to** (=treat someone in an unkind way) *Don't be so nasty to your mum.* | **get/turn nasty** *especially BrE* (=suddenly start behaving in a threatening way) *Don't tease the dog. He might turn nasty.*

**2 ▶ SIGHT/SMELL ETC ◀** having a bad appearance, smell, taste etc: *The medicine tastes nasty, but it works.* | **cheap and nasty** *cheap and nasty furniture*

**3 nasty illness/cut/wound etc** an illness etc that is severe or very painful: *a nasty cut on the head*

**4 ▶ EXPERIENCE/SITUATION ◀** a nasty experience, feeling or situation is unpleasant: *nasty weather* | *It gave me a nasty shock.* | *I have a nasty suspicion that he's going to make us pay for everything.* | **leave a nasty taste in the mouth** (=make you feel upset or angry afterwards) *When you feel you've been cheated, it always leaves a nasty taste in the mouth.*

**5 ▶ OFFENSIVE ◀** morally bad or offensive; OBSCENE (1): *nasty language* | *You've got a nasty mind.*

**6 a nasty piece of work** *BrE* someone who is dishonest, violent, or likely to cause trouble —see also VIDEO NASTY —**nastily** *adv* —**nastiness** *n* [U]

**na·tal** /ˈneɪtl/ *adj technical* connected with birth: *the salmon's natal stream*

**natch** /nætʃ/ *adv* [sentence adverb] *slang* used to say that something is exactly as you would expect: *"What does he drive?" "A BMW, natch."*

**na·tion** /ˈneɪʃən/ *n* [C] **1** a country, considered especially in relation to its people and its social or economic structure: *the President's radio broadcast to the nation* | *the world's leading industrial nations* **2** a large group of people of the same race and language: *the Cherokee nation* —see RACE[1] (USAGE)

**na·tion·al[1]** /ˈnæʃənəl/ *adj* **1** related to a whole nation as opposed to any of its parts: *national and local news*

2 related to a nation as opposed to other nations: *We refuse to sign any treaty that is against our national interests.*|*selling to national and international markets* **3** [only before noun] owned or controlled by the central government of a country: *a national bank*|*the National Health Service* —see also NATIONALLY

**national²** *n* [C] someone who is a citizen of a particular country but is living in another country: *Foreign nationals were advised to leave the country.* —compare ALIEN ² (1) CITIZEN (2), SUBJECT ¹ (6)

**national an·them** /ˌ··· ˈ··/ *n* [C] the official song of a nation that is sung or played on certain formal occasions

**national cos·tume** /ˌ··· ˈ··/ *n* [C,U] special clothing traditionally worn by the people of a particular country; NATIONAL DRESS: *folk dancers in national costume*

**national debt** /ˌ··· ˈ·/ *n* [C] the total amount of money owed by the government of a country

**national dress** /ˌ··· ˈ·/ *n* [U] national costume

**national grid** /ˌ··· ˈ·/ *n* [C] the system of numbered squares printed on a map to show the exact position of a place

**National Guard** /ˌ··· ˈ·/ *n* [singular] a military force in each state of the US which can be used when it is needed by the state or the US government

**National Health Ser·vice** /ˌ··· ˈ· ˌ··/ *n* [singular] the NHS

**National In·sur·ance** /ˌ··· ·ˈ··/ *n* [U] a system of insurance organized by the British Government into which workers and employers make regular payments, and which provides money for people who are unemployed, old, or ill

**na·tion·al·ise** /ˈnæʃənəlaɪz/ *v* [T] *BrE* another spelling of NATIONALIZE

**na·tion·al·is·m** /ˈnæʃənəlɪzəm/ *n* [U] **1** desire by a group of people of the same race, origin, language, etc to form an independent country: *Scottish nationalism* **2** the belief that your own country is better than any other country: *the rise of nationalism in Eastern Europe*

**na·tion·al·ist¹** /ˈnæʃənəlɪst/ *adj* [only before noun] a nationalist organization, party etc wants to get or keep political independence for their country and people

**nationalist²** *n* [C] someone who is involved in trying to gain or keep political independence for their country: *Welsh nationalists*

**na·tion·al·is·tic** /ˌnæʃənəˈlɪstɪk◂/ *adj* someone who is nationalistic believes that their country is better than other countries, and often has no respect for people from other countries —**nationalistically** /-kli/ *adv*

**na·tion·al·i·ty** /ˌnæʃəˈnæləti/ *n* **1** [C,U] the legal right of belonging to a particular country: *people of the same nationality*|**French/Brazilian etc nationality** *He has British nationality.*|**dual nationality** (=the legal right of being a citizen of two countries) **2** [C] a large group of people with the same race, origin, language etc: *the different nationalities within the former USSR*

**na·tion·al·ize** also **-ise** *BrE* /ˈnæʃənəlaɪz/ *v* [T] if a government nationalizes a very large industry or service such as water, gas or electricity, it buys or takes control of it: *The British government nationalized the railways in 1948.*|*a nationalised industry* —compare PRIVATIZE —**nationalization** /ˌnæʃənəlaɪˈzeɪʃən‖-nələ-/ *n* [C,U]

**National League** /ˌ··· ˈ·/ *n* [singular] one of the two organizations that arranges professional BASEBALL games in the US

**na·tion·al·ly** /ˈnæʃənəli/ *adv* by or to everyone in the nation: *The programme will be broadcast nationally.*

**national mon·u·ment** /ˌ··· ˈ···/ *n* [C] a building, special feature of the land etc that is kept and protected by a government for people to visit: *the Death Valley National Monument in California*

**national park** /ˌ··· ˈ·/ *n* [C] an area of natural, historical, or scientific interest which is kept and protected by a government for people to visit: *Yosemite National Park*

**national se·cu·ri·ty** /ˌ··· ·ˈ···/ *n* [U] the idea that a country must keep its secrets safe and its army strong in order to protect its citizens: *a matter of national security*

**national ser·vice** /ˌ··· ˈ··/ *n* [U] *BrE* the system of making all men serve in the army for a limited time, whether the country is involved in a war or not

**National Trust** /ˌ··· ˈ·/ *n* [singular] a British organization which owns and takes care of many beautiful places and historic buildings in England and Wales

**nation state** /ˌ·· ˈ·/ *n* [C] a nation that is a politically independent country: *European union is seen as a threat to the sovereignty of the nation state.*

**na·tion·wide** /ˌneɪʃənˈwaɪd◂, ˈneɪʃənwaɪd/ *adj* happening or existing in every part of the country: *a nationwide radio broadcast*|*a nationwide search for the criminals* —**nationwide** *adv*: *We have 350 sales outlets nationwide.*

**na·tive¹** /ˈneɪtɪv/ *adj* [only before noun] W3
**1** ▸ **COUNTRY** ◂ your native country, town etc is the place where you were born: *a visit by the Pope to his native Poland*|*They never saw their native land again.*
**2 native New Yorker/Londoner/Californian etc** a person who has always lived in New York, London etc
**3 native language/tongue** the language you spoke when you first learned to speak: *Lara's native language is Swedish.*
**4** ▸ **PLANT/ANIMAL** ◂ growing, living, produced etc in one particular place; INDIGENOUS: [+ **to**] *The oregano plant is native to Italy.*|*the region's native birds*
**5** ▸ **ART/CUSTOM** ◂ related to the people of a country who were the earliest people to live there: *the native art of Peru*
**6 native intelligence/wit etc** a quality that you have naturally from birth: *native genius*
**7 go native** *humorous* to behave, dress, or speak like the people who live in the country where you have come to stay or work: *I once knew an anthropologist who went native and married a Masai warrior.*

**native²** *n* [C] **1** a person who was born in a particular place: [+ **of**] *a native of Texas* **2** someone who lives in a place all the time or has lived there a long time: [+ **of**] *Are you a native of these parts?* **3** [often plural] a word that is now considered offensive, in former times used by Europeans to mean one of the people who lived in Africa, S. Asia etc before Europeans arrived **4** a plant or animal that grows or lives naturally in a place: [+ **of**] *The bear was once a native of Britain.*

**Native A·mer·i·can** /ˌ·· ·ˈ···/ *n* [C] one of the people who were living in N. America before white people arrived there

**native speak·er** /ˌ·· ˈ··/ *n* [C] someone who has learned a particular language as their first language, rather than as a foreign language: *a native speaker of English*

**Na·tiv·i·ty** /nəˈtɪvəti/ *n* **1** [singular] the birth of Jesus Christ **2** [C] a picture or model of the baby Jesus Christ and his parents in the place where he was born

**Nativity play** /·ˈ···· ˌ·/ *n* [C] a play telling the story of the birth of Jesus Christ performed by children at Christmas

**NATO** /ˈneɪtəʊ‖-toʊ/ *n* [singular] the North Atlantic Treaty Organization; a group of countries including the US and several European countries, which give military help to each other: *our allies in NATO*|*a NATO country*

**nat·ter¹** /ˈnætə‖-ər/ *v* [I] *BrE informal* to talk continuously about unimportant things: *Lynne's been nattering on about the wedding for weeks.*

**natter²** *n* [singular] *BrE informal* the act of talking about unimportant things for fun: **have a natter** *Come round after work and we'll have a natter.*

**nat·ty** /ˈnæti/ *adj informal* very neat and fashionable in appearance: *a natty suit* —**nattily** *adv*

**nat·u·ral¹** /ˈnætʃərəl/ *adj*

**1** ▸ **NORMAL** ◂ normal and what you would expect in a particular situation or at a particular time: *Don't worry – it's a perfectly natural reaction.*|**it's only natural**

*spoken: It's only natural to be afraid sometimes.* | **it is natural for sb to do sth** *It's not natural for a child of his age to be so quiet.* —opposite UNNATURAL (1), ABNORMAL
**2 ▶ NOT ARTIFICIAL ◀** not caused, made, or controlled by human beings: *an area of spectacular natural beauty* | *natural disasters* | *death from natural causes* —compare ARTIFICIAL, MAN-MADE
**3 ▶ TENDENCY/ABILITY ◀ a)** a natural tendency or type of behaviour is part of your character when you are born, rather than one that you learn later; INNATE: *Cats have a natural aversion to water.* **b)** [only before noun] having a particular quality or skill without needing to be taught and without needing to try hard: *a natural musician* | *Cheryl has a natural elegance about her.*
**4 ▶ NOT PRETENDING ◀** behaving in a way that is normal and shows you are relaxed and not trying to pretend: *Try to look natural for your photograph.*
**5 natural parent/mother etc** the parent from whom a child is born: *John was adopted; he never knew his natural parents.*
**6 ▶ NOT MAGIC ◀** not connected with gods, fairies, or spirits: *I'm sure there's a perfectly natural explanation.* —opposite SUPERNATURAL [1]
**7 ▶ FOOD ◀** with nothing added to change the taste: *natural yoghurt*
**8** a musical note that is natural has been raised from a FLAT [2] (3) by one SEMITONE or lowered from a SHARP [3] (1) by one semitone
**9 natural child/son/daughter** *old use* a child whose parents are not married —**naturalness** *n* [U]

**natural**[2] *n* [C] **1 be a natural** to be good at doing something without having to try hard or practise: *Look how he swings that bat – he's a natural.* **2 a)** a musical note that has been changed from a FLAT [2] (3) to be a SEMITONE higher, or from a SHARP [3] (1) to be a semitone lower **b)** the sign (♮) in written music that shows this —see picture at MUSIC

**natural-born** /ˈ··· ·/ *adj* **natural-born fool/singer etc** *AmE informal* someone who has always had a particular quality or skill without having to try hard

**natural child·birth** /ˌ··· ˈ··/ *n* [U] a method of giving birth to a baby in which a woman chooses not to use drugs

**natural gas** /ˌ··· ˈ·/ *n* [U] gas used for heating and lighting, taken from under the earth or under the sea

**natural his·to·ry** /ˌ··· ˈ···/ *n* [U] the study of plants, animals, and minerals: *the Natural History Museum*

**nat·u·ral·is·m** /ˈnætʃərəlɪzəm/ *n* [U] a style of art or literature which tries to show the world and people exactly as they are

**nat·u·ral·ist** /ˈnætʃərəlɪst/ *n* [C] **1** someone who studies plants or animals, especially outdoors **2** someone who believes in naturalism in art or literature

**nat·u·ral·is·tic** /ˌnætʃərəˈlɪstɪk◂/ also **naturalist** *adj* painted, written, etc according to the ideas of naturalism —**naturalistically** /-kli/ *adv*

**nat·u·ral·ize** also **-ise** *BrE* /ˈnætʃərəlaɪz/ *v* **be naturalized a)** if someone who was born outside a particular country is naturalized, they become a citizen of that country **b)** if a foreign word or phrase is naturalized in another language, it has become part of it —**naturalization** /ˌnætʃərəlaɪˈzeɪʃən‖-lə-/ *n* [U]

S2 W3 **nat·u·ral·ly** /ˈnætʃərəli‖-tʃərəli, -tʃərli/ *adv* **1** [sentence adverb] used to mean that the fact you are mentioning is just what you would have expected: *Naturally, you'll want to discuss this with your wife.* | *"How do you feel about it?" " Well, naturally, we're very disappointed, but ..."* —see SURELY (USAGE) **2** *spoken* used to say 'yes' when you think the person who asked the question should know that your reply will be yes: *"You'll write to me, won't you?" "Naturally."* —see OF COURSE (USAGE) **3** as a natural feature or quality: *My hair is naturally curly.* | **come naturally (to)** (=be easy for you to do because you have a natural ability) *Speaking in public seems to come quite naturally to her.* **4** in a relaxed manner without trying to look or sound different from usual: *Just speak naturally and pretend the microphone isn't there.*

**natural phi·los·o·phy** /ˌ··· ·ˈ···/ *n* [U] *old use* science

**natural re·sourc·es** /ˌ··· ·ˈ··, ˌ··· ˈ···/ *n* [plural] all of the land, minerals, natural energy etc that exist in a country: *a country rich in natural resources*

**natural sci·ence** /ˌ··· ˈ··/ *n* [C,U] chemistry, BIOLOGY, and PHYSICS considered together as subjects for study, or one of these subjects

**natural se·lec·tion** /ˌ··· ·ˈ··/ *n* [U] *technical* the process by which only plants and animals that are naturally suitable for life in their environment will continue to live, while all others will die —see also **survival of the fittest** (SURVIVAL (2))

**natural wast·age** /ˌ··· ˈ··/ *n* [U] a reduction in the number of people employed by an organization, which happens when people leave their jobs and the jobs are not given to anyone else

**na·ture** /ˈneɪtʃə‖-ər/ *n* S W
**1 ▶ PLANTS/ANIMALS ETC ◀** also **Nature** [U] everything in the physical world that is not controlled by humans, such as wild plants and animals, earth and rocks, and the weather: *We grew up in the countryside, surrounded by the beauties of nature.* | *the fundamental forces of nature*
**2 ▶ SB'S CHARACTER ◀** [C,U] someone's character: *Eric's got a lovely easy-going nature.* | **be in sb's nature** *Jana wouldn't lie, it's not in her nature.* | **by nature** *He was, by nature, a man of few words.* | **sb's better nature** (=your feelings of kindness) *I've tried appealing to her better nature, but she still refuses to help.* | **human nature** (=the feelings and natural qualities that everyone has) *Of course she's jealous – it's only human nature.*
**3 ▶ CHARACTER OF STH ◀** [C,U] a particular combination of qualities that makes something what it is and makes it different from other things: *the true nature of their difficulties* | **by its very nature** *Companies are, by their very nature, conservative.*
**4 ▶ TYPE ◀** [singular] a particular kind of thing: **of a personal/political/difficult nature** *books of an erotic nature* | *The support being given is primarily of a practical nature.* | **of that nature** (=of that kind) *I never trouble myself with affairs of that nature.* | **be in the nature of sth** (=to be like something) *The cruise was to be in the nature of a 'rest cure'.*
**5 in the nature of things** according to the natural way things happen: *In the nature of things, there is bound to be the occasional accident.*
**6 let nature take its course** to allow events to happen without doing anything to change the results: *Sometimes the best cure is just to let nature take its course.*
**7 in a state of nature a)** in a natural state, not having been affected by the modern world **b)** *humorous* not wearing any clothes
**8 back to nature** a style of living in which people try to live more simply —see also SECOND NATURE, **the call of nature** (CALL [2] (12))

**nature re·serve** /ˈ·· ·ˌ·/ *n* [C] an area of land in which animals and plants, especially rare ones, are protected

**nature stud·y** /ˈ·· ˌ··/ *n* [U] the study of plants, animals etc as a school subject

**na·tur·ist** /ˈneɪtʃərɪst/ *n* [C] someone who enjoys not wearing any clothes because they believe it is natural and healthy; NUDIST —**naturism** *n* [U]

**na·tu·ro·path** /ˈneɪtʃərəpæθ/ *n* [C] someone who tries to cure illness using natural things such as plants, rather than drugs —**naturopathy** /ˌneɪtʃəˈrɒpəθi‖-ˈrɑː-/ *n* [U] —**naturopathic** /ˌneɪtʃərəˈpæθɪk◂/ *adj*

**naught** /nɔːt‖nɒːt, nɑːt/ *n* [U] *old use* nothing: *He cared naught for public opinion.* | **come to naught** (=fail) *All their plans came to naught.*

**naugh·ty** /ˈnɒːti‖ˈnɔːti, ˈnɑːti/ *adj* **1** a naughty child behaves badly and is rude and disobedient: *You're a very*

*naughty boy! Look what you've done!* **2** *especially BrE* used jokingly about an adult when you are pretending to disapprove of their behaviour: **it's naughty of sb to do sth** *spoken*: *It was a bit naughty of me to stay out so late last night.* **3 naughty jokes/magazines/pictures etc** *BrE* naughty jokes etc deal with sex in a rude but not very serious way —**naughtily** *adv* —**naughtiness** *n* [U]

**nau·se·a** /ˈnɔːziə, -siə‖ˈnɒːziə, -ʃə/ *n* [U] *formal* the feeling that you have when you think you are going to VOMIT (=bring food up from your stomach through your mouth): *Early pregnancy is often accompanied by nausea.* —see also AD NAUSEAM

**nau·se·ate** /ˈnɔːzieɪt, -si-‖ˈnɒːzi-, -ʃi-/ *v* [T] to make someone feel NAUSEA: *Even clear fluids were making him feel nauseated.* | *It nauseates me the way Keith bullies you.*

**nau·se·a·ting** /ˈnɔːzieɪtɪŋ, -si-‖ˈnɒːzi-, -ʃi-/ *adj* **1** making you feel NAUSEA: *In summer the smell of the farmyard was nauseating.* **2** making you feel angry: *It's nauseating how the coach always picks his favorites.* —compare DISGUSTING —**nauseatingly** *adv*

**nau·se·ous** /ˈnɔːziəs, -siəs‖ˈnɒːziəs, -ʃəs/ *adj* **1** *especially AmE* feeling nausea: *I awoke from my drunken stupor feeling nauseous.* **2** *formal* making you feel NAUSEA: *the nauseous stench of the durian fruit* —**nauseously** *adv* —**nauseousness** *n* [U]

**nau·ti·cal** /ˈnɔːtɪkəl‖ˈnɒː-/ *adj* connected with ships or sailing —**nautically** /-kli/ *adv*

**nautical mile** /ˌ··· ˈ·/ *n* [C] a measure of distance used at sea, equal to 1853 metres; SEA MILE —see table on page B2

**na·val** /ˈneɪvəl/ *adj* [only before noun] connected with or used by the navy: *a naval officer* | *naval battles*

**nave** /neɪv/ *n* [C] the long central part of a church

**na·vel** /ˈneɪvəl/ *n* [C] **1** the small hollow or raised place in the middle of your stomach —see picture at BODY **2 gaze at/contemplate your navel** *humorous* to spend too much time thinking about your own problems

**nav·i·ga·ble** /ˈnævɪ̈gəbəl/ *adj* a river, lake etc that is navigable is deep and wide enough for ships to travel on: *The St Lawrence River is navigable from the Great Lakes to the Atlantic.* —**navigability** /ˌnævɪ̈gəˈbɪlɪ̈ti/ *n* [U]

**nav·i·gate** /ˈnævɪ̈geɪt/ *v* **1** [I,T] to find the way to a place, especially by using maps: *I'll drive, you take the map and navigate.* | **navigate by the stars/sun** *Early explorers used to navigate by the stars.* **2** [T] to sail all the way across or along an area of water

**nav·i·ga·tion** /ˌnævɪ̈ˈgeɪʃən/ *n* [U] **1** the science of planning the way along which you travel from one place to another: *compasses and other instruments of navigation* **2** the act of sailing a ship or flying a plane along a particular line of travel: *Navigation becomes more difficult further up the river.* **3** the movement of ships or aircraft: *open to navigation* —**navigational** *adj*

**nav·i·ga·tor** /ˈnævɪ̈geɪtə‖-ər/ *n* [C] an officer on a ship or aircraft who plans the way along which it is travelling

**nav·vy** /ˈnævi/ *n* [C] *BrE* an unskilled worker who does tiring physical work, such as building roads

3 **na·vy** /ˈneɪvi/ *n* [C] **1** the part of a country's military forces that is organized for fighting a war at sea: *My father joined the Navy during the war* **2** the war ships belonging to a country: *demands for a larger navy*

**navy blue** /ˌ·· ˈ··◂/ also **navy** *adj* very dark blue —**navy blue** *n* [U] —see picture on page 411

**nay¹** /neɪ/ *adv* **1** [sentence adverb] *literary* used when you are adding something to emphasize what you have just said: *a bright – nay, a blinding light* **2** *old use or dialect* used to say no: *Nay, lad. It's not that bad.*

**nay²** *n* [C] a vote against or someone who votes against an idea, plan, etc —opposite AYE¹ (1), YEA²

**Na·zi** /ˈnɑːtsi/ *n plural* **Nazis** [C] **1** a member of the National Socialist Party of Adolf Hitler which controlled Germany from 1933 to 1945 **2** someone who likes to use their authority in an unreasonably strict way: *Some of the traffic wardens are real Nazis.* —**Nazi** *adj* —**Nazism** *n* [U]

**NB, nb** *Latin* nota bene; used to make a reader pay attention to an important piece of information

**NBA** /ˌen biː ˈeɪ/ *n* [singular] National Basketball Association; the American organization which arranges BASKETBALL games

**NBC** /ˌen biː ˈsiː/ *n* [U] National Broadcasting Company; one of three main American television companies

**NCO** /ˌen siː ˈəʊ‖-ˈoʊ/ *n* [C] noncommissioned officer; a soldier such as a CORPORAL or SERGEANT

**-nd** /nd/ *suffix* forms written ORDINAL numbers with 2: *the 2nd (=second) of March* | *her 22nd birthday*

**NE** the written abbreviation of northeast or northeastern: *NE Scotland*

**ne·an·der·thal** /niˈændəˌtɑːl‖-dərˌθɒːl, -ˌtɑːl/ *n* [C] **1** *humorous* a big, ugly, stupid man **2** someone who opposes all change without even thinking about it **3** a Neanderthal man —**Neanderthal** *adj*

**Neanderthal man** /·ˈ··· ·/ *n* an early type of human being who lived in Europe during the STONE AGE

**nea·pol·i·tan** /nɪəˈpɒlɪ̈tən‖-ˈpɑː-/ *adj* neapolitan ICE CREAM has layers of different colours and tastes

**neap tide** /ˈniːp taɪd/ *n* [C] a very small rise and fall of the level of the sea at the times of the first and third quarters of the moon

**near¹** /nɪə‖nɪr/ *adv, prep* **1** only a short distance from a person or thing: *Bob was standing near enough to hear what they said.* | *Why don't you move your chair nearer mine?* | **near to** *Don't sit too near to the screen.* | **go/come/get etc near** (=to move near someone or something) *Don't come any nearer – I have a gun.* | *As the car drew nearer I realised the man was a stranger.* **2 come/be near (to) sth** to almost do something or almost be in a particular state | *She had what came near to a perfect singing voice.* | **come/be near (to) tears/death etc** *Sarah was trembling, and near to tears.* | **come/be near to doing sth** *especially BrE Samuel came very near to rejecting the award before accepting graciously.* **3** soon before a particular time or event: *Near the day of the wedding she started to have second thoughts.* | [+to] *Remind me nearer the time of the meeting.* | **draw near** *As my birthday drew near, I began to dread being fifty.* **4 near perfect/impossible etc** almost perfect etc: *The dye left a near transparent liquid on the surface of her skin.* **5 (as) near as dammit** *BrE spoken* used to say that something is very nearly true or correct: *The repairs will cost us £1000, as near as dammit.* S1 W1

**near²** *adj* **1** only a short distance away from someone or something: *It's a beautiful house but it's 20 miles away from the nearest town.* | *We can meet at the pub or in the restaurant, whichever's nearer for you.* | [+to] *Of course I've heard of the Littleton sports centre – it's near to my college.* **2** if something is near something else, it is similar to it: [+to] *It seems that his diaries are as near to the truth as we'll ever get.* | *Hyde Park is the nearest thing we have to the countryside round here.* | *It may not be an exact replica but it's pretty damn near.* **3 a near disaster/collapse etc** almost a disaster, a collapse etc: *The factory has seen a near doubling of it's output this year alone.* **4 be a near thing a)** if something you succeed in doing is a near thing, you manage to succeed but you nearly failed: *They won the championship, but it was a near thing.* **b)** used to say that you just managed to avoid a dangerous or unpleasant situation: *That was a near thing – that truck was heading straight for us.* **5 be a near miss** if a bomb, shot etc is a near miss it seemed as if it would hit something but did not **6 in the near future** soon: *They promised to contact us again some time in the near future.* **7 to the nearest £10/hundred etc** an amount to the nearest £10, hundred etc is the number nearest to it that can be divided by £10, a hundred etc: *Give me the car mileage to the nearest thousand.* **8 a) near relative/relation** a relative who is very closely related to you such as a parent: *You are only allowed time off if the funeral is for a near relative.*

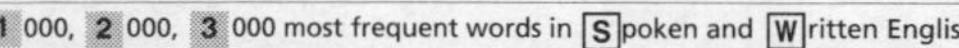

**b) sb's nearest and dearest** *humorous* someone's family **9** [only before a noun, no comparative] **a)** used to describe the side of something that is closest to where you are: *the near bank of the river* **b)** used when talking about the wheels on a vehicle to mean the one on the left side: *the near wheel of a car* —opposite OFF[3] (3) —see also NEARLY, **nowhere near** (NOWHERE (4)) —**nearness** *n* [U]

**near[3]** *v* **1** [T] to come closer to a particular place, time, or state; APPROACH[1]: *Work is nearing completion.*|*The ship was nearing harbour.* **2** [I] if a time nears, it gets closer and will come soon: *He got more and more nervous as the day of his departure neared.*

**near·by** /ˈnɪəbaɪ‖ˈnɪr-/ *adj* [only before noun] not far away: *Lucy was staying in the nearby town of Hamilton.* —**nearby** /nɪəˈbaɪ‖nɪr-/ *adv*: *Dan found work on one of the farms nearby.*

**Near East** /ˌ· ˈ·/ *n* **the Near East** the Middle East —**Near Eastern** *adj*: *Ancient Near Eastern literature*

S1 W1 **near·ly** /ˈnɪəli‖ˈnɪrli/ *adv* **1** *especially BrE* almost, but not quite or not completely: *It took nearly two hours to get here.*|*Michelle's nearly twenty.*|*Is the job nearly finished?*|*He's nearly always right.*|*Louise is nearly as tall as her mother.*|**very nearly** *He very nearly died.*|**not nearly enough** (=much less than enough) *I can earn some money, but not nearly enough to live on.* —see ALMOST (USAGE) **2** *old use* closely: *a problem which concerns me nearly*

**near·side** /ˈnɪəsaɪd‖ˈnɪr-/ *adj* [only before noun] *BrE* on the side of a vehicle that is nearest the edge of the road: *a scratch on the nearside front wing of the car* —**nearside** *n* [singular] —opposite OFFSIDE[2]

**near·sight·ed** /ˌnɪəˈsaɪtɪ̈d◂‖ˈnɪrsaɪtɪ̈d/ *adj* unable to see things clearly unless they are close to you; SHORTSIGHTED *BrE* —**nearsightedly** *adv* —**nearsightedness** *n* [U]

S2 **neat** /niːt/ *adj* **1** tidy and carefully arranged: *neat handwriting*|*She wears her hair short and neat.*|*He folded his clothes in a neat pile on the chair.*|**neat and tidy** *Can't you keep your bedroom neat and tidy?* **2** *AmE spoken* very nice or pleasant: *The party was really neat – we had a good time.*|*I liked working for him – he was a neat guy.* **3** simple and effective: *a neat turn of phrase*|*There are no neat solutions to this problem.* **4** neat alcoholic drinks have no ice or water or any other liquid added; STRAIGHT[1] (12): *She likes her whisky neat.* **5** someone who is neat likes to keep things tidy: *The new lodger was fortunately a neat person.* —**neatly** *adv*: *He arranged the books neatly on the shelf.* —**neatness** *n* [U]

**neath** /niːθ/ *prep poetic* below: *neath the stars*

**neb·u·la** /ˈnebjʊ̈lə/ *n* [C] **1** a mass of gas and dust among the stars, often appearing as a bright cloud in the sky at night **2** a GALAXY (=mass of stars) which has this appearance —**nebular** *adj*

**neb·u·lous** /ˈnebjʊ̈ləs/ *adj formal* **1** an idea that is nebulous is not at all clear or exact; VAGUE: *The reasons he gave were rather nebulous.* **2** a shape that is nebulous is misty and has no definite edges: *a nebulous ghostly figure* —**nebulously** *adv* —**nebulousness** *n* [U]

S1 W2 **ne·ces·sar·i·ly** /ˈnesɪ̈sərɪ̈li, ˌnesɪ̈ˈserɪ̈li‖ˌnesɪ̈ˈserɪ̈li/ *adv* **1 not necessarily** possibly but not certainly: *Expensive restaurants are not necessarily the best.*|*"We'll need to employ another engineer, then." "Not necessarily."*|*It does not necessarily follow that a larger workforce will be more productive.* **2** in a way that cannot be different or be avoided; INEVITABLY: *Testing criteria are necessarily subjective.*

S1 W1 **ne·ces·sa·ry[1]** /ˈnesɪ̈səri‖-seri/ *adj* **1** something that is necessary is what you need to have or need to do; ESSENTIAL: *I'll leave it to you to make all the necessary arrangements.*|[+ **for**] *Food is necessary for life.*|**it is necessary (for sb) to do sth** *It's not necessary to wear a tie.*|*The doctor says it may be necessary for me to have an operation.*| **make it necessary (for sb) to do sth** *The heavy rain made it necessary to close several roads.*|**is it really necessary to do sth?** *spoken* (=used to complain about something that someone is doing) *Is it really necessary to make all that noise!*|**if necessary** (=if it is necessary): *I'll stay up all night, if necessary, to get it finished.*|**hardly necessary** (=almost not necessary) *Taking notes was hardly necessary – she had a brilliant memory.* **2 necessary connection/consequence etc** a connection, result etc that must exist: *the necessary connection between wage rates and the price of food* **3 a necessary evil** something bad or unpleasant that you have to accept in order to achieve what you want: *Mr Hurst regarded work as a necessary evil.*

**necessary[2]** *n* **1 the necessaries** things that you need, such as food or money, especially for a journey **2 do the necessary** *spoken* to do what is necessary: *Leave it to me – I'll do the necessary.*

**ne·ces·si·tate** /nɪ̈ˈsesɪ̈teɪt/ *v* [T] *formal* to make it necessary for you to do something: *Lack of money necessitated a change of plan.*|**necessitate doing sth** *This change would necessitate starting all over again.*

**ne·ces·si·tous** /nəˈsesɪ̈təs/ *adj* a word meaning 'poor' used when people are trying to sound important or want to avoid saying 'poor' directly —**necessitously** *adv*

**ne·ces·si·ty** /nɪ̈ˈsesɪ̈ti/ *n* **1** [C] something that you need to have: *A telephone is an absolute necessity for this job.*|*We went to buy the basic necessities for our stay.*|**bare necessities** (=basic things that you must have) *Food and clothing are the bare necessities of life.* —compare LUXURY (2) **2** [U] the fact of something being necessary: [+ **for**] *the necessity for decent, affordable housing*|**necessity of doing sth** *Martell Bakeries was faced with the necessity of firing many of its employees.*|**necessity to do sth** *There's no necessity to buy tickets in advance.* **3** [C] something that must happen, even if it is unpleasant or undesirable: *Taxes are a regrettable necessity.*|*The treaty is considered a diplomatic necessity.* **4** [U] the condition of urgently needing money or food: *He was forced by necessity to steal a loaf of bread.*|**dire necessity** (=great need) **5 of necessity** used when something happens in a particular way because that is the only possible way it can happen: *The summary of his findings is, of necessity, very brief.* **6 necessity is the mother of invention** used to say that if someone really needs to do something they will find a way of doing it

S2 W2 **neck[1]** /nek/ *n*

**1 ▶ PART OF THE BODY ◀** [C] the part of your body that joins your head to your shoulders: *She wore a string of pearls around her neck.* —see picture at HEAD [1]

**2 ▶ CLOTHING ◀** [C] the part of a piece of clothing that goes around your neck: *the neck of the shirt*|*The colour's all right, but the neck's a bit low.* —see also **crew neck, polo neck, scoop neck, turtleneck, V-neck** —see picture on page 840

**3 ▶ BOTTLE ◀** [C] the narrow part of a bottle

**4 be up to your neck in** to be in a difficult situation, or to be very busy doing something: *Jim's always up to his neck in debt.*|*I've been up to my neck in paperwork all week.*

**5 breathe down sb's neck** to watch what someone is doing very carefully, in a way that makes them nervous or annoyed: *How can I, with accountants breathing down my neck the whole time!*

**6 V-necked/open-necked etc** also **V-neck/open-neck etc** if a piece of clothing is V-necked etc, it has that type of neck: *a navy V-necked sweater*

**7 I'll break/wring your neck** *spoken* used to tell someone that you are so angry with them you feel like hurting them

**8 (hanging) around your neck** if a problem or difficult situation is hanging around your neck, you are responsible for it, and this makes you worry

**9 get it in the neck** *BrE spoken* to be severely punished: *You'll really get it in the neck if you lose that watch!*

**10 ▶ MEAT ◀** [U] the neck of an animal, used as food: *neck of lamb*

**11 neck and neck** *informal* if two things are neck and neck in a competition or race, they both have an equal chance of winning
**12 in this neck of the woods** *informal* in this area or part of the country: *What are you doing in this neck of the woods?*
**13 by a neck** *informal* if a race is won by a neck, the winner is only a very short distance in front: *Our horse won by a neck.* —see also **pain in the neck** (PAIN[1] (4)), **risk your neck** (RISK[2] (1)), **save your own skin/neck** (SAVE[1] (10)), **stick your neck out** (STICK [1])
**14 ▶ LAND ◀** a narrow piece of land that comes out of a wider part

neck and neck

**neck²** *v* [I] *informal* if two people neck, they kiss for a long time in a sexual way —**necking** *n* [U]

**neck·band** /ˈnekbænd/ *n* [C] a narrow piece of material around the neck of a piece of clothing: *a velvet neckband*

**neck·er·chief** /ˈnekətʃiːf‖-ər-/ *n* [C] a square piece of cloth that is folded and worn tied around the neck

**neck·lace** /ˈnek-lɪ̵s/ *n* [C] a string of jewels, BEADS etc or a thin gold or silver chain: *a diamond necklace* | *a pearl necklace* —see picture at JEWELLERY

**neck·let** /ˈnek-lɪ̵t/ *n* [C] a short necklace

**neck·line** /ˈnek-laɪn/ *n* [C usually singular] the shape made by the upper edge of a piece of woman's clothing around or below the neck: *a flattering scoop neckline* | **low/plunging neckline** (=leaving part of the chest uncovered) *Her evening gown had a plunging neckline.*

**neck·tie** /ˈnektaɪ/ *n* [C] *AmE formal* a man's TIE

**nec·ro·man·cy** /ˈnekrəmænsi/ *n* [U] **1** magic, especially evil magic **2** *literary* the practice of claiming to talk with the dead —**necromancer** *n* [C]

**nec·ro·phil·i·a** /ˌnekrəʊˈfɪliə, -krə-‖-kroʊ-, -krə-/ *n* [U] sexual interest in dead bodies

**nec·tar** /ˈnektə‖-ər/ *n* [U] **1** the sweet liquid that BEES collect from flowers: *The sunbird feeds on nectar.* **2** the drink of the gods, in the stories of ancient Greece **3** thick juice made from certain fruits: *mango nectar*

**nec·ta·rine** /ˈnektəriːn/ *n* [C] a type of fruit like a PEACH that has a smooth skin, or the tree that produces this fruit —see picture on page 413

**née** /neɪ/ *adj* a word used after a woman's married name and before the family name that she had when she was born: *Mrs Carol Cook née Williams*

S1 **need¹** /niːd/ *v* [T not in progressive]
W1 **1 ▶ MUST ◀** to feel that you must have something or must do something; REQUIRE: **need sth** *That was what I needed – strong, hot coffee.* | *I don't need your approval, thank you very much.* | **need to do sth** *I need to think about this before I make a decision.* | **need sth for** *He said he needed the information for an article he was writing.* | **need sb to do sth** *We need volunteers to clean up after the performance.* | **need sth badly** *Money was tight and he needed a job badly.* —see graph at REQUIRE
**2** to have to do something because you feel you should do it or because you think it is necessary: **need (to) do sth** *Do you think I need to go to the meeting?* | *You need to work harder if you're going to pass those exams.* | *Nobody need feel jealous.* | **need not do sth** *BrE You needn't worry. I've taken care of it.* | **do not need to do sth** *Honestly, you don't need to get changed. You look fine as you are.* | **need not have done sth** *BrE* (=used when someone does something that was not necessary) *Terence has done so little work, he needn't have bothered to come to school today.* | **did not need to do sth** *What a beautiful day! I didn't need to bring my umbrella after all.* | **need sb do sth?** *BrE old-fashioned: Need we leave so soon? I'm having a wonderful time.*
**3 need cleaning/mending/fixing etc** if something needs cleaning or needs to be cleaned, someone should clean it because it is dirty: *That fence needs fixing.* | **need washing/mending etc** *The children need collecting at 4 o'clock.* | **need to be washed/to be mended etc** *I think these potatoes need to be cooked a little longer.* | **need a wash/a mend etc** *He looked tired and looked like he needed a shave.*
**4** if a job or activity needs a particular quality, you need to have that quality in order to do it well: *A job like nursing needs patience and understanding.*
**5 I need hardly say/tell/remind etc** used when you think that people should already know what you are going to say: *I need hardly remind you that people will judge the school by the way you behave.*
**6 need you ask/need I ask** *spoken* used to say that someone already knows what they are asking about: *"Who did it?" "Need you ask? It was Joe, of course."*
**7 who needs it?** *spoken* used to say you are not interested in something: *To hell with enlightenment, who needs it?*

This graph shows how common different grammar patterns of the verb **need** are.

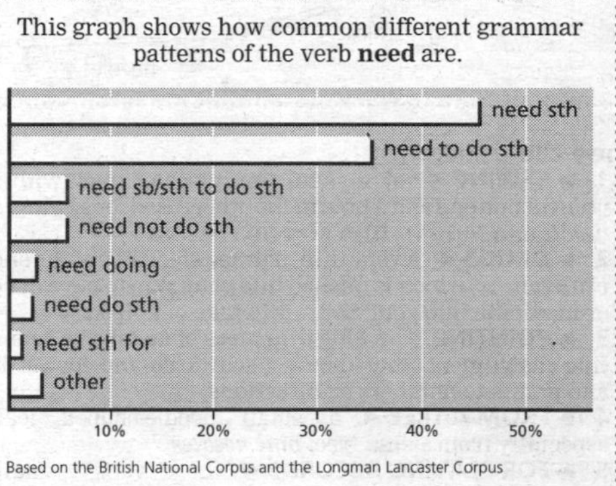


**need²** *n* S1 W1
**1 ▶ WHEN STH IS NECESSARY ◀** [singular] a situation in which something is necessary, especially something that is not happening yet or is not yet available: [+ **for**] *the need for stricter safety regulations* | *There's a growing need for new housing in many rural areas.* | **the need to do sth** *We fully recognize the need to improve communications.* | *Don't you ever feel the need to take a vacation?* | **as the need arises** (=whenever it is necessary) *We draw money from the account as the need arises.* | **if need be** (=if it is necessary) *I'll work all night if need be.*
**2 there's no need (for sb) to do sth a)** used to say that someone does not have to do something: *There's no need for you to come if you don't want to.* **b)** *spoken* used to tell someone to stop doing something: *There's no need to shout; I'm not deaf!*
**3 be in need of a)** to need to be cleaned, repaired, or given attention in some way: *The whole house is in need of decorating.* **b)** to need help, advice, money etc, because you are in a difficult situation: *I felt lonely and in need of some companionship.* | **be in dire need of** (=need something urgently) *Many of the refugees are in dire need of medical treatment.*
**4 have no need of** to not need something: *Japan has its own space technology and has no need of American help.*

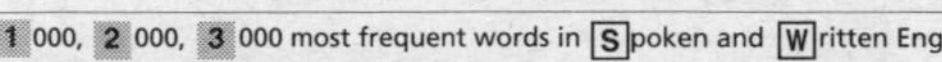

5 ▶ **WHAT YOU NEED** ◀ [C usually plural] what someone needs to have in order to live a normal healthy comfortable life: **sb's needs** *We must look after the needs of the elderly.* | **meet/answer/fill a need** (=provide something that people want or need) *meeting the educational needs of every child* | **your every need** *a service that caters for your every need*
6 ▶ **LACK OF MONEY** ◀ [U] the state of not having enough food or money: *cases of severe need in the inner cities* | **in need** (=not having enough food or money) *Our aim is to provide adequate food for those families in need.*
7 **in your hour of need** when you are in trouble: *a friend you can turn to in your hour of need*

**need·ful** /ˈniːdfəl/ *adj formal* necessary: *needful expenditure* —**needfully** *adv*

**needles**

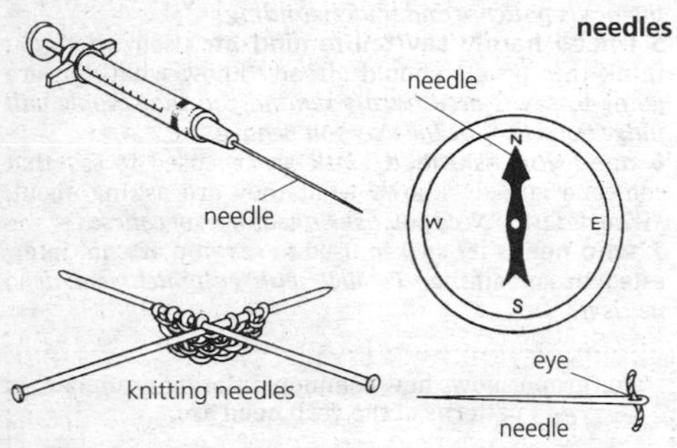


**nee·dle**[1] /ˈniːdl/ *n* [C]
1 ▶ **SEWING** ◀ **a)** a small thin piece of steel, with a point at one end and a hole in the other, used for sewing: *a needle and thread* **b)** a KNITTING NEEDLE
2 ▶ **DRUGS** ◀ a very thin, pointed steel tube at the end of a SYRINGE, which is pushed into your skin to put a drug or medicine into your body or to take out blood
3 ▶ **POINTING** ◀ a long thin piece of metal on a scientific instrument, that moves backwards and forwards and points to numbers or directions
4 ▶ **FROM A TREE** ◀ a small needle-shaped leaf, especially from a PINE tree: *pine needles*
5 ▶ **FOR PLAYING RECORDS** ◀ the very small, pointed part in a RECORD PLAYER that picks up sound from the records; STYLUS (1)
6 **like looking for a needle in a haystack** *informal* used to say that something is almost impossible to find
7 **a needle match** *BrE* a game in which both teams are determined to win because they do not like each other

**needle**[2] *v* [T] *informal* to deliberately annoy someone by continuously making unkind remarks or stupid jokes: *She's always needling me about my accent.*

**nee·dle·point** /ˈniːdlpɔɪnt/ *n* [U] pictures made by covering a piece of material with small stitches

**need·less** /ˈniːdləs/ *adj* 1 needless troubles, suffering, loss etc are unnecessary because they could easily have been avoided: *the needless loss of life* | *needless expense* | *a lot of needless worry* 2 **needless to say** used when you are telling someone something that they probably know or expect: *Needless to say, we'll pay your expenses.* —**needlessly** *adv*: *Thousands of women die needlessly every year because of poor medical care.*

**nee·dle·wom·an** /ˈniːdl,wʊmən/ *n* [C] a woman who is good at sewing

**nee·dle·work** /ˈniːdlwɜːk‖-wɜːrk/ *n* [U] the activity or art of sewing, or things made by sewing

**need·n't** /ˈniːdnt/ *especially BrE* the short form of 'need not': *I needn't have put on this thick coat.*

**need·y** /ˈniːdi/ *adj* 1 having very little food or money: *a needy family* 2 **the needy** needy people: *money to help the needy* —**neediness** *n* [U]

**ne'er** /neə‖ner/ *adv poetic* never

**ne'er-do-well** /ˈneə duː ˌwel‖ˈner-/ *n* [C] *old use* a lazy useless person

**ne·far·i·ous** /nɪˈfeəriəs‖-ˈfer-/ *adj formal* evil or criminal: *nefarious activities such as drug trafficking and fraud* —**nefariously** *adv* —**nefariousness** *n* [U]

**neg** the written abbreviation of NEGATIVE

**ne·gate** /nɪˈgeɪt/ *v* [T] *formal* 1 to prevent something from having any effect: *Efforts to expand the tourist industry could be negated by reports that the sea is highly polluted.* 2 to state that something does not exist or is untrue; DENY (1) —**negation** /nɪˈgeɪʃən/ *n* [U]

**neg·a·tive**[1] /ˈnegətɪv/ *adj* S W
1 ▶ **EFFECT** ◀ bad or harmful: *socialist policies that have had a negative effect on the country's economy* | *I think our relationship was very negative and destructive.* —opposite POSITIVE (7)
2 ▶ **ATTITUDE** ◀ considering only the bad qualities of a situation, person etc and not the good ones: *Her negative attitude really annoys me.* | *The play was criticized for its violence, and its bleak, negative message.* | **be negative (about)** *Don't be so negative – of course you can win!* —opposite POSITIVE (2)
3 ▶ **NO/NOT** ◀ **a)** saying or meaning no: *a negative response to our request* **b)** containing one of the words 'no', 'not', 'nothing', 'never' etc; for example 'cannot' and 'can't' are the negative forms of 'can' —opposite AFFIRMATIVE (1)
4 ▶ **SCIENTIFIC TEST** ◀ not showing any sign of the chemical or medical condition that was being looked for: *The pregnancy test was negative.* —opposite POSITIVE (6)
5 ▶ **ELECTRICITY** ◀ *technical* of the type that is carried by ELECTRONS —opposite POSITIVE (11)
6 ▶ **NUMBER/QUANTITY** ◀ less than zero: *a negative return to our investment* (=a loss)
7 ▶ **BLOOD** ◀ *technical* not having RHESUS FACTOR in your blood —opposite POSITIVE (13) —**negatively** *adv*

**negative**[2] *n* 1 [C] a statement or expression that means 'no': **in the negative** *formal* (=saying 'no') *He answered in the negative.* —opposite AFFIRMATIVE [2] 2 a photographic image that shows dark areas as light and light areas as dark, from which the final picture is printed

**negative**

**negative**[3] *v* [T] *formal* 1 to refuse to accept a proposal or request 2 to prove something to be untrue

**negative pole** /ˌ··· ˈ·/ *n* [C] *technical* 1 the end of a MAGNET which turns naturally to the south 2 a CATHODE

**ne·glect**[1] /nɪˈglekt/ *v* [T] 1 to not look after someone or something properly: *They were accused of neglecting the children.* | *a neglected garden* | *I suppose I had neglected myself – put on a bit of weight and so on.* 2 to pay too little attention to something that you should do: *Many of these ideas have been neglected by modern historians.* 3 **neglect to do sth** *formal* to not do something: *The agent had neglected to warn us about delays.*

**neglect**[2] *n* [U] 1 failure to look after something or someone properly because you do not care enough about them: [+ **of**] *Tenants are complaining about the landlord's neglect of the property.* 2 the condition of not being properly looked after: *Grass grew on the sidewalk. The whole district had an air of abandonment and neglect.*

**ne·glect·ful** /nɪˈglektfəl/ *adj formal* not looking after something properly, or not giving it enough attention:

[+of] *She became more and more neglectful of her responsibilities.* —**neglectfully** *adv* —**neglectfulness** *n* [U]

**neg·li·gee** /ˈneglɪ̈ʒeɪ‖ˌneglɪ̈ˈʒeɪ/ *n* [C] a very thin, pretty coat, worn over a NIGHTDRESS

**neg·li·gence** /ˈneglɪdʒəns/ *n* [U] failure to take enough care over something that you are responsible for: *negligence in carrying out safety procedures*| *The bridge's architect was sued for criminal negligence.*

**neg·li·gent** /ˈneglɪdʒənt/ *adj* **1** not taking enough care over something that you are responsible for, with the result that serious mistakes are made: *The report stated that Dr Brady had been negligent in not giving the patient a full examination.* **2** a negligent manner or way of dressing is careless, but in a pleasantly relaxed way: *He dresses with negligent grace.* —**negligently** *adv*

**neg·li·gi·ble** /ˈneglɪdʒɪ̈bəl/ *adj* too slight or unimportant to have any effect: *The damage done to his property was negligible.* —**negligibly** *adv*

**ne·go·ti·a·ble** /nɪˈgəʊʃiəbəl, -ʃə-‖-ˈgoʊ-/ *adj* **1** an offer, price, contract etc that is negotiable can be discussed and changed before being agreed on: *Part-time barman required. Hours and salary negotiable.* **2** a road, path etc that is negotiable can be travelled along: *The road is only negotiable in the dry season.* **3** *technical* a cheque that is negotiable can be exchanged for money

3 3 **ne·go·ti·ate** /nɪˈgəʊʃieɪt‖-ˈgoʊ-/ *v* **1** [I,T] to discuss something in order to reach an agreement, especially in business or politics: [**+ with**] *The government refuses to negotiate with terrorists.*| **negotiate an agreement/contract etc** *Union leaders have negotiated an agreement for a shorter working week.*| **come to the negotiating table** (=start official discussions) *The French have brought new proposals to the negotiating table.* **2** [T] to succeed in getting past or over a difficult place on a path, road etc: *Eliot negotiated the steep stairs and walked across the courtyard.* —**negotiator** *n* [C]

2 2 **ne·go·ti·a·tion** /nɪˌgəʊʃiˈeɪʃən‖-ˌgoʊ-/ *n* [C usually plural, U] official discussions between the representatives of opposing groups, who are trying to reach an agreement, especially in business or politics: *The treaty was a result of long and complex negotiations.*| *Through negotiation we were able to reach a compromise.*| **be open to negotiation** (=can be negotiated and changed) *The terms of the contract are still open to negotiation.*| **enter into negotiation** (=start negotiation)

**Ne·gress** /ˈniːgrɪ̈s/ *n* [C] *old-fashioned* a word meaning a black woman, which is now usually considered offensive

**Ne·gro** /ˈniːgrəʊ‖-groʊ/ *plural* **Negroes** *n* [C] *old-fashioned* a word meaning a black person, which is now usually considered offensive —**negro** *adj*

> USAGE NOTE: NEGRO
>
> POLITENESS
>
> People of African origin (recent or long ago) usually prefer to be called **black**, or in the US, often **African-American**. In the UK the term **Afro-Caribbean** is often used.
>
> Some people think that it is polite to use the word **coloured** but this is now considered to be offensive and unacceptable.

**ne·groid** /ˈniːgrɔɪd/ *adj technical* having the physical features of a black person from Africa

**Negro spir·i·tu·al** /ˌ·· ˈ····/ *n* [C] a religious song of the type sung by the black people of the US

**neigh** /neɪ/ *v* [I] if a horse neighs, it makes a long loud noise —**neigh** *n* [C]

2 2 **neigh·bour** *BrE*, **neighbor** *AmE* /ˈneɪbə‖-ər/ *n* [C] **1** someone who lives next to you or near you: **next-door neighbour** (=in the house next to you): *Our next-door neighbours are so noisy we can hardly sleep some nights.* **2** someone who is sitting or standing next to you: *The teacher saw Bobby passing a note to his neighbour* **3** a country's neighbour is the country next to it *The USA is Canada's only neighbor.*

**neigh·bour·hood** *BrE*, **neighborhood** *AmE* /ˈneɪbəhʊd‖-ər-/ *n* [C] **1** a small area of a town, or the people who live there: *You're going to wake up the whole neighbourhood with that noise.*| *I grew up in a quiet neighborhood of Boston.*| *a neighbourhood school* **2 in the neighbourhood** in the area around you or around a particular place: *Are there any hotels in the neighbourhood?*| [**+ of**] *somewhere in the neighbourhood of Chester* **3 in the neighbourhood of** either a little more or a little less than a particular number or amount; APPROXIMATELY: *I'm hoping to buy one for something in the neighbourhood of £500.*

**neighbourhood watch** /ˌ··· ˈ·/ *n* [U] a system for preventing crime by which people living in an area watch each other's houses

**neigh·bour·ing** *BrE*, neighboring *AmE* /ˈneɪbərɪŋ/ *adj* [only before noun] near the place where you are or the place you are talking about; NEARBY: **neighbouring country/town/house etc** *The fair attracted hundreds of people from the neighbouring towns and villages.*

**neigh·bour·ly** *BrE*, **neighborly** *AmE* /ˈneɪbəli‖-ər-/ *adj* friendly and helpful towards your neighbours: *Since we've moved in people have been very neighbourly.* —**neighbourliness** *n* [U]

**nei·ther¹** /ˈnaɪðə‖ˈniːðər/ *determiner, pron* not one or the other of two people or things: **neither person/thing etc** *Neither parent cares what happens to the child.*| **neither of them/the people etc** *Both players have been warned, but neither of them seem to take it seriously.*| **neither** *"Would you like tea or coffee?" "Neither, thanks."*| *We went to see a couple of houses, but neither was suitable.* —compare EITHER, NONE¹ —see EACH (USAGE) W3

**neither²** *adv* **1** used to add a negative statement to one that has just been mentioned: **neither can I/neither does John etc** *"I have never been to Paris before." "No, neither have we."*| *Tom didn't believe a word she said and neither did the police.*| **me neither/John neither etc** *"I don't like horror movies." "Me neither."* —see ALSO (USAGE) **2** *formal* used to emphasize or add information to a negative statement: *The authorities were not sympathetic to the students' demands, neither would they tolerate any disruption.* —compare ANY, EITHER⁴ S2 W3

**neither³** *conjunction* **1 neither... nor...** used when two states, facts, actions etc are mentioned and both are not true or not possible: *The equipment is neither accurate nor safe.*| *She was expressionless, neither laughing nor crying.* **2 be neither here nor there** *especially spoken* used to say that something is not important because it does not affect or change another fact or situation: *The fact that she needed the money for her children is neither here nor there, it's still stealing.*

**nel·ly, nellie** /ˈneli/ *n* **not on your nelly** *BrE spoken* used to tell someone humorously or rudely that you are definitely not going to do something

**nem con** /ˌnem ˈkɒn‖-ˈkɑːn/ *adv Latin law* without any opposition: *The motion was passed nem con.*

**nem·e·sis** /ˈnemɪ̈sɪ̈s/ *n* [singular] *literary* a punishment that is deserved and cannot be avoided

**neo-** /niːəʊ, niːə‖niːoʊ, niːə/ *prefix* [in nouns and adjectives] a recent or later kind of a former system, style etc; new: *neoclassical architecture* (=copying that of ancient Greece and Rome)| *neocolonialism* (=the control of other countries by large modern states)

**ne·o·clas·si·cal** /ˌniːəʊˈklæsɪkəl◂‖ˌniːoʊ-/ *adj* neoclassical art copies the style of ancient Greece or Rome

**ne·o·co·lo·ni·al·is·m** /ˌniːəʊkəˈləʊniəlɪzəm‖ˌniːoʊkəˈloʊ-/ *n* [U] the economic and political influence which a powerful country uses to control another country

**ne·o·lith·ic** /ˌniːəˈlɪθɪk◂/ *adj* connected with the latest period of the STONE AGE about 10,000 years ago, when people began to settle in villages and make stone tools and weapons: *the discovery of a Neolithic burial mound*

**ne·ol·o·gis·m** /niːˈɒlədʒɪzəm‖-ˈɑːl-/ *n* [C] a new word or expression, or a word used with a new meaning

N

**ne·on** /ˈniːɒn‖-ɑːn/ *n* [U] gas that produces a bright light when electricity is passed through it

**neon light** /ˌ·· ˈ·/ *n* [C] a glass tube filled with neon that produces a bright light when electricity is passed through it: *the neon lights of Las Vegas*

**neon sign** /ˌ·· ˈ·/ *n* [C] an electric advertising sign consisting of neon lights in the form of shapes and words

**ne·o·phyte** /ˈniːəfaɪt/ *n* [C] *formal* **1** someone who has just started to learn a particular skill, art, trade etc **2** a new member of a religious group

**neph·ew** /ˈnefjuː, ˈnev-‖ˈnef-/ *n* [C] the son of your brother or sister, or the son of your husband's or wife's brother or sister: *I've got one nephew. He's two.* —see picture at FAMILY —compare NIECE

**nep·o·tis·m** /ˈnepətɪzəm/ *n* [U] the practice of giving the best jobs to members of your family when you are in a position of power —**nepotistic** *adj*

**Nep·tune** /ˈneptjuːn‖-tuːn/ *n* [singular] the PLANET eighth in order from the sun —see picture at SOLAR SYSTEM

**nerd** /nɜːd‖nɜːrd/ *n* [C] *informal* **1** someone who is boring and unfashionable **2** someone who is extremely interested in computers —**nerdy** *adj*: *nerdy glasses*

**ner·e·id** /ˈnɪəri-ɪd‖ˈnɪr-/ *n* [C] a female spirit who lives in the sea according to ancient Greek stories

S3 W3 **nerve¹** /nɜːv‖nɜːrv/ *n*

**1 ▶FEELINGS◀ nerves** [plural] the feeling of being nervous because you are worried or a little frightened: *"What's wrong?" "It's just nerves. He's got his exams tomorrow."* | **be a bundle/bag of nerves** *informal* (=be extremely worried or frightened) *I remember you were a bundle of nerves on your wedding day.* | **calm/steady your nerves** (=stop yourself feeling worried or frightened) *Sean drank a large glass of brandy to calm his nerves.* | **live on your nerves** (=be always worried) *He's the type of person who lives on his nerves.*

**2 get on sb's nerves** *informal* to annoy someone, especially by repeatedly doing something: *She's always moaning. It really gets on my nerves.*

**3 ▶COURAGE◀** [U] the ability to stay calm and confident in a dangerous, difficult or frightening situation: **have the nerve to do sth** *Not many people have the nerve to stand up and speak in front of a large audience.* | **it takes a lot of nerve to do sth** *spoken*: *It takes a lot of nerve to report a colleague for sexual harassment.* | **lose your nerve** *He'd have won if he hadn't lost his nerve.*

**4 have a nerve** *spoken* to be surprisingly rude without seeming ashamed or embarrassed: *He's got a nerve asking for more money.* | **have the nerve to do sth** *She lets me do all the work, and then she has the nerve to criticise my cooking.* | **what a nerve!** *What a bloody nerve! Telling me how to do something I've been doing for years!*

**5 ▶BODY PART◀** [C] one of the thin parts like threads inside your body, along which feelings and messages are sent to the brain: *The dentist was drilling and he hit a nerve. The pain was incredible!* —see picture at TEETH

**6 hit/touch a raw nerve** to say something that someone else is very sensitive about especially accidentally —see also **touch a raw nerve** (RAW¹ (6)), **strain every nerve** (STRAIN¹ (7))

**nerve²** *v* **nerve yourself** to force yourself to be brave enough to do something difficult or dangerous: [+ **for**] *The parachutist nerved himself for the jump.*

**nerve cen·tre** *BrE*, **nerve center** *AmE* /ˈ· ˌ··/ *n* [C] the place from which a system, activity, organization etc is controlled: *The bridge is the ship's nerve center.*

**nerve gas** /ˈ· ·/ *n* [U] a poisonous gas that is used in war and that damages your CENTRAL NERVOUS SYSTEM

**nerve·less** /ˈnɜːvləs‖ˈnɜːrv-/ *adj* nerveless fingers, feet, hands etc have no strength or feeling in them

**nerve-wrack·ing, nerve-racking** /ˈ· ··/ *adj* a nerve-wracking situation makes you feel very nervous because it is difficult or frightening: *Your first appearance on stage is always a nerve-wracking experience.*

**ner·vous** /ˈnɜːvəs‖ˈnɜːr-/ *adj* **1** worried or frightened about something that may happen so that you cannot relax: [+ **about**] *I was so nervous about my exams that I couldn't sleep* | [+ **of**] *Jill's always been a little nervous of dogs.* **2** often becoming worried or frightened and easily upset: *She's a nervous, sensitive child.* | **nervous wreck** (=someone whose health and confidence have been destroyed by worry, fear etc) *This job is turning me into a nervous wreck.* | **of a nervous disposition** *This film is unsuitable for people of a nervous disposition.* **3 nervous exhaustion/strain etc** a mental condition in which you feel very tired, usually caused by working too hard or by difficult emotional problems **4** related to the nerves in your body: *a nervous disorder* —**nervously** *adv*: *She smiled nervously.* —**nervousness** *n* [U] | *Minelli's nervousness showed in his voice.*

**USAGE NOTE: NERVOUS**

WORD CHOICE: **nervous, uneasy, concerned, anxious, worried**

You are **nervous** about something difficult or strange that you are doing, or when you are worried and a little frightened about something that might happen or is going to happen, so that you cannot relax: *Don't drive so fast —you're making me nervous!* | *She gets nervous about walking home alone late at night.* You are **uneasy** when you are unable to relax because you think but do not know for certain that something bad is happening or is going to happen: *When Jody didn't call for the next three days I started to get uneasy.*

You are **concerned** when there is a problem or when someone has a problem that you wish you could do something about: *I'm rather concerned about Harvey's health.* **Worried** is stronger. If you are **worried** you are unhappy and cannot stop thinking about a problem or about something bad that might happen: *Martha's very worried about her son's disappearance.* **Anxious** is stronger still. You are **anxious** when you are very worried and frightened about something that is happening or might happen: *the little girl's anxious face as she searched the crowds for her mother*

**nervous break·down** /ˌ·· ˈ··/ *n* [C] *not technical* a mental illness in which someone becomes extremely anxious and tired and cannot deal with the things they usually do

**nervous sys·tem** /ˈ·· ˌ··/ *n* [C] the parts of your body, including your nerves, brain, and SPINAL CORD, by means of which you feel pain, heat etc and control your movements

**nerv·y** /ˈnɜːvi‖ˈnɜːr-/ *adj* **1** *informal* nervous and easily frightened **2** *AmE informal* brave and confident

**-ness** /nɪ̈s/ *suffix* [in nouns] the condition, quality, or degree of being something: *loudness* | *sadness* | *warm-heartedness* | *the many kindnesses you've done me*

**nest¹** /nest/ *n* [C] **1** a hollow place made or chosen by a bird to lay its eggs in and to make its home in **2** a place where insects or small animals live: *a field mouse's nest* **3 a nest of spies/criminals/vice etc** a place where there are many bad people or evil activities **4 leave the nest** to leave your parents' home **5 nest of tables/boxes** a set of tables etc that fit inside of one another —see also **feather your nest** (FEATHER² (1)), **stir up a hornets' nest** (HORNET (2)), **mare's nest** (MARE (2)), **love nest** (LOVE)

**nest²** *v* [I] to build or use a nest: *gulls nesting on the cliffs*

**nest egg** /ˈ· ·/ *n* [C] an amount of money that you have saved

**nes·tle** /ˈnesəl/ *v* **1** [I always + adv/prep, T always + adv/prep] To move into a comfortable position, pressing your head or body against someone or against something soft: **nestle against/beside/by etc** *Sarah lay there peacefully, the child nestling by her side.* | **nestle sth against/beside etc** *He nestled his head against her shoulder.* **2** [I always + adv/prep] to be in a position that seems to be protected by the hills etc around:

[+ **among/between etc**] *several small villages nestling among the mountains*

**nest·ling** /ˈnestlɪŋ, ˈneslɪŋ/ *n* [C] a very young bird

W3 **net**[1] /net/ *n* **1** [C,U] a piece of material consisting of strings, threads, or wires woven across each other with regular spaces in between, used, for example, for catching fish, protecting vegetables etc: *a fishing net* **2 the net a)** a long net used in games such as tennis that the players must hit the ball over —see picture at TENNIS **b)** a net forming an enclosure at the back of the GOAL in football, HOCKEY etc: *Cole slammed the ball into the back of the net.* **3** [U] very thin material made from fine threads woven together with very small spaces between: *net curtains* **4** [C] a bag made of net on the end of a stick used for catching butterflies (BUTTERFLY (1)) etc **5** [C] a communications or computer network **6 the Net** *technical* the Internet; a system that allows millions of computer users around the world to exchange information —see also **cast your net wide** (CAST[1] (18)), HAIRNET, SAFETY NET

W2 **net**[2] *v* **netted, netting** [T] **1** to catch a fish in a net: *We netted three fish in under an hour.* **2** *especially AmE* to earn a particular amount of money as a profit after tax has been paid: *I was netting around $64,000 a year.* **3** *informal* to hit or kick the ball into the net in sport **4** to succeed in getting something by using your skill: *a company that has netted several large contracts*

**net**[3] also **nett** *BrE* —*adj* [only before noun] **1** a net amount of money is the amount that remains after everything has been taken away from it: **net profit** (=profit after tax, rent etc are paid) *He took 50% of the net revenue.* —compare GROSS[1] (1) **2 net weight** the weight of something without its container | **2lb/500g etc net** *jars of coffee weighing 450 grams net* **3 net result (of)** the final result of something: *The net result of this policy was even worse inflation.*

**net·ball** /ˈnetbɔːl‖-bɒːl/ *n* [U] a game similar to BASKETBALL played in Britain especially by girls

**neth·er** /ˈneðə‖-ðər/ *adj* [only before noun] *literary or humorous* lower down: *the nether regions*

**neth·er·most** /ˈneðəməʊst‖-ðərmoʊst/ *adj literary* lowest *the nethermost fiery pit of hell*

**nett** /net/ *adj* a British spelling of NET[3]

**net·ting** /ˈnetɪŋ/ *n* [U] material consisting of string, wire etc that has been woven into a net: *a fence of wire netting*

**net·tle**[1] /ˈnetl/ *n* [C] a wild plant with rough leaves that sting you —see also **grasp the nettle** (GRASP[1] (4))

**nettle**[2] *v* [T] **be nettled** *informal* to be annoyed by someone's behaviour: *She was nettled by Holman's remark.*

**nettle rash** /ˈ·· ·/ *n* [C,U] *BrE* a condition that causes areas of red spots on your skin

**network**

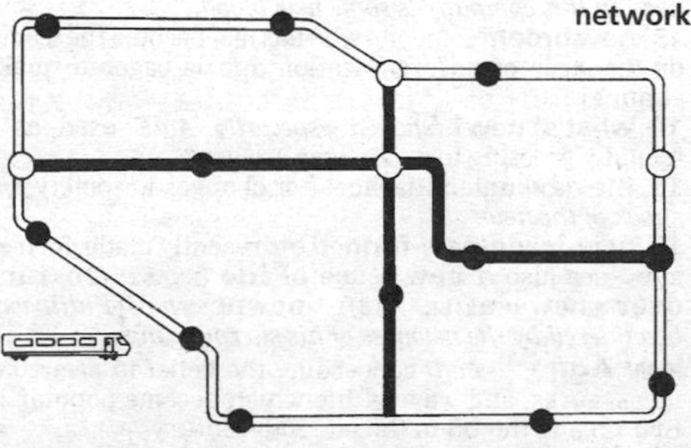

W3 **net·work**[1] /ˈnetwɜːk‖-wɜːrk/ *n* [C] **1** a group of radio or television stations, which broadcast many of the same programmes, but in different places **2** a system of lines, tubes, wires, roads etc that cross each other and are connected to each other: [+ **of**] *an elaborate network of canals | the network of blood vessels in the body.* **3** a group of people, organizations etc that are connected or that work together: [+ **of**] *It's important to build up a network of professional contacts.* **4** a set of computers that are connected to each other and can be used to send information or messages

**net·work**[2] *v* [I,T] **1** to broadcast a radio or television programme on several different channels (CHANNEL[1] (1,2)) at the same time **2** to connect several computers together so that you can send information between them

**net·work·ing** /ˈnetwɜːkɪŋ‖-wɜːr-/ *n* [U] the practice of meeting other people involved in the same kind of work, to share information, support each other etc

**neur-** /njʊər‖nʊr/ *prefix* another form of the prefix NEURO-

**neu·ral** /ˈnjʊərəl‖ˈnʊr-/ *adj technical* related to a nerve or the NERVOUS SYSTEM: *neural networks*

**neu·ral·gia** /njʊˈrældʒə‖nʊ-/ *n* [U] a sharp pain along the length of a nerve —**neuralgic** *adj*

**neuro-** /njʊərəʊ, -rə‖nʊroʊ, -rə/ *prefix* also **neur-** *technical* concerning the nerves: *neuropathology | a neurosurgeon* (=who specializes in the body's nervous system)

**neu·rol·o·gy** /njʊˈrɒlədʒi‖nʊˈrɑː-/ *n* [U] the scientific study of the NERVOUS SYSTEM and its diseases —**neurologist** *n* [C] *consultant neurologist David Hart* —**neurological** /ˌnjʊərəˈlɒdʒɪkəl◂‖ˌnʊrəˈlɑː-/ *adj*

**neu·ro·sis** /njʊˈrəʊsɪ̇s‖nʊˈroʊ-/ *n plural* **neuroses** /siːz/ [C,U] a mental illness that makes someone unreasonably worried or frightened

**neu·rot·ic** /njʊˈrɒtɪk‖nʊˈrɑː-/ *adj* **1** unreasonably anxious or afraid: *He seemed a neurotic, self-obsessed character.* **2** connected with or affected by neurosis: *neurotic disorders* —**neurotically** /-kli/ *adv* —**neurotic** *n* [C]

**neu·ter**[1] /ˈnjuːtə‖ˈnuːtər/ *adj* **1** plants or animals that are neuter have undeveloped sex organs or no sex organs **2** *technical* a neuter noun, PRONOUN etc belongs to a class of words that have different inflections (INFLECTION (1)) from MASCULINE (4) or FEMININE (2) words

**neuter**[2] *v* [T] to remove part of the sex organs of an animal so that it cannot produce babies: *a neutered tomcat*

**neu·tral**[1] /ˈnjuːtrəl‖ˈnuː-/ *adj*

**1 ▸ IN AN ARGUMENT ETC ◂** not supporting either of the people or groups involved in an argument or disagreement: *I always tried to remain neutral when they started arguing.*

**2 ▸ IN A WAR ◂** a country that is neutral does not support any of the countries involved in a war: *During the Second World War, Sweden was neutral.* | **neutral territory/waters** (=land or sea that is not controlled by any of the countries involved in a war)

**3 be on neutral ground** if two opposing teams or representatives are on neutral ground they are in a place that is not favourable to either of them

**4 ▸ LANGUAGE ◂** language, words etc that are neutral are deliberately chosen to avoid expressing any strong opinion or feeling: *the neutral language of an offical news report*

**5 ▸ COLOUR ◂** a neutral colour is not very strong or bright, for example grey or light brown

**6 ▸ WIRE ◂** *technical* a neutral wire has no electrical CHARGE[1] (7)

**7 ▸ CHEMICAL ◂** *technical* a neutral substance is neither acid nor ALKALI —**neutrally** *adv*

**neutral**[2] *n* **1** [U] the position of the gears (GEAR[1] (2)) of a car or machine in which the engine does not turn the wheels: **in/into neutral** *When you start the engine, be sure the car's in neutral.* **2** [C] a country or person that is not fighting for or helping any of the countries involved in a war

**neu·tra·list** /ˈnjuːtrəlɪ̇st‖ˈnuː-/ *adj AmE* tending not to support either side in a war, quarrel etc —**neutralist** *n* [C]

**neu·tral·i·ty** /njuːˈtrælɪ̇ti‖nuː-/ *n* [U] the state of not supporting either side in an argument or war

**neu·tral·ize** also **-ise** *BrE* /ˈnjuːtrəlaɪz‖ˈnuː-/ *v* [T] **1** to prevent something from having any effect: *Rising prices tend to neutralize increased wages.* **2** *technical* to make a substance chemically NEUTRAL: *a medicine that neutralizes the acid in the stomach* **3** to make a country or population NEUTRAL in war **—neutralization** /ˌnjuːtrəlaɪˈzeɪʃən‖ˌnuːtrələ-/ *n* [U]

**neu·tron** /ˈnjuːtrɒn‖ˈnuːtrɑːn/ *n* [C] a part of an atom that has no electrical charge (CHARGE [1] (7))

**neutron bomb** /ˈ·· ˌ·/ *n* [C] a kind of NUCLEAR bomb which kills people but which does not cause much damage to property

S1 W1 **nev·er** /ˈnevə‖-ər/ *adv*

**1 ▶ NOT AT ANY TIME ◀** not once or not at any time: *We've never been to Paris.* | *I'll never forget what my mother said.* | **never...again** *Never let me hear you use that word again!* | **never in all my life** *spoken* (=used to emphasize how bad something was) *Never in all my life have I felt so humiliated.* | **never ever** *spoken* (=used to emphasize 'never') *I'll never ever forgive him for leaving me* | **never once** *spoken* (=used when you are annoyed because someone never did something although they had many opportunities) *Never once did she offer to look after the children.* | **never for one moment** *especially spoken* (=used to emphasize that you never thought, imagined, or doubted something) *Never for one moment did I think that we were going to encounter so many problems.* | **sb/sth has never been known to do something** (=used to mean that something is strange because it has never happened before) *Max had never been known to leave home without telling someone.* —see picture at FREQUENCY

**2 never mind** *spoken* used to tell someone that something is not important or serious, so that there is no need to worry or feel sorry: *"We've missed the train." "Never mind, there's another one in ten minutes."*

**3 never you mind** *spoken* used to tell someone not to ask questions about something because you do not want to tell them about it: *"What were you talking about just now?" "Never you mind."*

**4 you never know** *spoken* used to say that something which seems unlikely may happen: *Try it! You never know, you might be lucky.*

**5 that would never do** *spoken* used to say that you would not want something to happen: *Someone might discover our secret and that would never do.*

**6 I never knew (that)** *spoken* used to mean that you did not know something until now: *I never knew Texas was so big.* | *I've just learned something I never knew before.*

**7 well, I never (did)!** *spoken* used to say that you are very surprised: *Well, I never! I wouldn't have thought she was that old.*

**8 never!** *BrE spoken* used when you are surprised by something, because you think it is not possible: *He's never going to cycle all the way to Manchester!* | *Never! I don't believe it!*

**9 never so much as** not even: *The thought that Laura might be having an affair had never so much as crossed his mind.*

**10 no I never!** *BrE spoken* used by a child to say that they did not do something bad when someone else is saying that they did: *"You cheated, didn't you?" "No, I never."*

**11 never fear** *old-fashioned* used to tell someone not to worry: *She'll be back, never fear.*

**12 never say die** used to encourage someone when they are losing hope

**never-end·ing** /ˌ·· ˈ··◂/ *adj* seeming to continue for a very long time: *The work is never-ending.*

**nev·er·more** /ˌnevəˈmɔː‖-vərˈmɔːr/ *adv poetic* never again

**never-never** /ˌ·· ˈ··/ *n* **on the never-never** *BrE humorous* if you buy something on the never-never, you buy it on HIRE PURCHASE (=by making small regular payments)

**never-never land** /ˌ·· ˈ·· ·/ *n* [U] an imaginary place where everything is perfect

**nev·er·the·less** /ˌnevəðəˈles‖-vər-/ *adv* [sentence adverb] *formal* in spite of a fact that you have just mentioned: *What you said was true. It was, nevertheless, a little unkind.* | *He insisted that everything would be alright. Nevertheless, I could not help feeling anxious.*

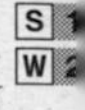

**new** /njuː‖nuː/ *adj*

**1 ▶ RECENTLY MADE ◀** recently made, built, or invented: *the city's new hospital* | *Renault's new GTI hatchback* | *the new issue of 'Time' magazine* | *the new fashions* | *a new way of organizing data*

**2 ▶ RECENTLY BOUGHT ◀** recently bought: *Do you like my new dress?* | *That's a nice bag – is it new?*

**3 ▶ NOT THERE BEFORE ◀** having just developed: *new buds on the trees* | *a young woman with new ideas* | *the new nations of Africa* | **new hope/confidence/optimism etc** (=hope etc that you have only just started to feel) *a medical breakthrough that offers new hope to cancer patients*

**4 ▶ NOT USED BEFORE ◀** [no comparative] not used or owned by anyone before: *New and second hand books for sale.* | **buy sth new** *I got a used video camera for £300 – it would have cost £1000 if I'd bought it new.* | **brand new** (=completely new) *When did you buy this sofa? It looks brand new.*

**5 like new/as good as new** in excellent condition: *Your watch just needs cleaning and it'll be as good as new.* | *We polished the car till it looked like new.*

**6 ▶ UNFAMILIAR ◀** not recognised or not experienced before: *learning a new language* | *Living in the city was a new experience for Philip.* | **be new to sb** *The fruit had a delicate taste that was completely new to me.* | **that's a new one on me** *spoken* (=used to say that you have never heard a particular word, name etc before)

**7 ▶ RECENTLY ARRIVED ◀** having recently arrived in a place, joined an organisation, or started a new job: *You're new here aren't you?* | **be new to sth/be new at sth** *Don't worry if you make mistakes you're still new to the job* | **new member/employee/student etc** (=people who are not already members) *training for new employees* | *The party is anxious to recruit new members.* | **new arrival** (=someone who has recently arrived in a place) *As a new arrival, Maria was obviously going to have problems with the language.* | **be the new kid on the block** *AmE informal* (=be the newest person in a job, school etc) *It's not always easy being the new kid on the block.* | **be the new boy/girl** *BrE humorous* (=be the newest person in a job, organization etc)

**8 new owner/address/job etc** the owner etc that has recently replaced the previous one: *Have you met Keith's new girlfriend?* | *I'll let you have my new phone number.*

**9 ▶ RECENTLY DISCOVERED ◀** recently discovered: *the discovery of a new planet* | *new oilfields in Alaska* | *important new evidence that may prove her innocence*

**10 new life/day/era** a period that is just beginning and seems to offer better opportunities: *They went to Australia to start a new life there.*

**11 feel (like) a new man/woman** to feel much healthier and have a lot more energy than before

**12 new blood** new members of a group or organization who will bring new ideas and be full of energy: *What we need in this company is some new blood.*

**13 new broom** someone who has just become the leader or manager of an organization and is eager to make changes

**14 what's new?** *spoken especially AmE* used as a friendly greeting to mean 'how are you?'

**15 the new** unfamiliar ideas or changes in society: *the shock of the new*

**16 new-made/new-formed etc** recently made, formed etc —see also **a new lease of life** (LEASE[1] (2)), **turn over a new leaf** (LEAF[1] (3)) **—newness** *n* [U] *Philip was bewildered by the newness of his surroundings.*

**New Age** /ˌ· ˈ·◂/ *adj* concerning the belief in SPIRITUAL ideas, cures, and ways of life which became popular in Britain and the US in the late 20th century

**New Age trav·el·lers** /ˌ· · ˈ···/ *n* [plural] people in Britain who refuse to live the way other people live in ordinary society, and go from place to place living in vehicles

**new·born** /ˈnjuːbɔːn‖ˈnuːbɔːrn/ *adj* **newborn child/baby/son etc** a child that has just been born: *He took his newborn baby in his arms.* **—newborn** *n* [C]

**new·com·er** /ˈnjuːkʌmə‖ˈnuːkʌmər/ *n* [C] someone who has only recently arrived somewhere or only recently started a particular activity: **[+ to]** *I'm a relative newcomer to the retail business.*|*Promising newcomer Gillespie won outright.*

**new·fan·gled** /ˌnjuːˈfæŋgəld◂‖ˌnuː-/ *adj* newfangled ideas, machines etc have been recently invented but you think they are too complicated or unnecessary: *newfangled ideas about education*

**new-found** /ˌ· ˈ·◂/ *adj* **newfound confidence/freedom/happiness etc** confidence, freedom etc that someone has only recently gained: *At first Mozart enjoyed his new-found freedom, earning enough to rent a big apartment.*

**new-laid** /ˌ· ˈ·◂/ *adj* a new-laid egg is fresh

**new-look** /ˈ· ·/ *adj* recently made more modern or more attractive: *the new-look Labour party*

W3 **new·ly** /ˈnjuːli‖ˈnuːli/ *adv* **newly formed/created/appointed/married etc** formed etc very recently: *the newly appointed director*|*newly fallen snow*

**new·ly·weds** /ˈnjuːliwedz‖ˈnuː-/ *n* [plural] a man and a woman who have recently got married —**newlywed** *adj*

**New Man** /ˌ· ˈ·/ *n* [C] a man who is considered to be very modern because he enjoys looking after his children and helping his partner with the care of the home: *He is a New Man, freely admitting to doing cleaning in place of his career-woman wife.*

**new maths** /ˌ· ˈ·/ *BrE*, **new math** *AmE n* [U] a way of teaching and understanding mathematics, first used in schools in the early 1970s

**new mon·ey** /ˌ· ˈ··/ *n* [U] people who have recently or suddenly become very rich, as opposed to people whose families have always been rich

**new moon** /ˌ· ˈ·/ *n* **1** [C] the moon when it first appears in the sky as a thin CRESCENT **2** [C,U] the time of the month at which this is first seen **3** [C] *technical* the time when the moon is between the Earth and the sun, and cannot be seen —compare FULL MOON, HALF MOON

**new-mown** /ˌ· ˈ·◂/ *adj* **new-mown hay/grass** grass that has recently been cut: *the sweet smell of new-mown grass*

**new po·ta·to** /ˌ· ·ˈ··/ *n* [C] a potato from one of the first crops of a year

**new rich** /ˌ· ˈ·◂/ *n* **the new rich** *AmE* people who have recently or suddenly become very rich, as opposed to people whose families have always been rich —**new rich** *adj*

S1 W1 **news** /njuːz‖nuːz/ *n* [U] **1** information about something that has happened recently: *That's great news!*|*Sit down and tell me all your news.*|**[+ about/of]** *There hasn't been any news of him since he left home.*|**[+ that]** *Our delegates returned with the news that negotiations had broken down.*|**good/bad news** *You're looking upset – not bad news, I hope?*|**hear news** (=receive news) *Have you heard any news from Emily yet?*|**piece of news** *Your brother's just told me an interesting piece of news.*|**have news for** *I've some good news for you – they've signed the contract.*|**I've got news for you** (=some bad news) *You may think you've fooled him, but I've got news for you —he's wise to your little trick.*|**break the news to** (=tell someone some bad news) *I don't know how to break the news to her.* **2** reports of recent events in the newspapers or on the radio or television: **[+ of/about]** *News is coming in of a major explosion at the World Trade Centre.*|*We'll bring you more news about the election at 11 o'clock.*|**news that** *Several evening papers carried the news that a cabinet minister was about to resign.*|**latest news** *the latest news from the Olympic stadium*|**local/national etc news** *a programme bringing you national and international news*|**make the news** (=be considered important enough to be in the news) *Twenty years ago environmental issues rarely made the news.*|**be in the news** *I see Michael Jackson's in the news again.*|**be front page news** (=be interesting enough to be on the front page of a newspaper) *Wallace's resignation was front page news.*|**news story/report** *Wilks had been paid by journalists to simply invent bogus news stories.* **3 the news** a regular television or radio programme that gives you reports of recent events: **on the news** *It must be true – I heard it on the news last night.* **4 be good/bad news for** if the facts about something are good or bad news for someone, they are likely to make life better or worse for them: *House prices are very low at the moment, which is good news for first-time buyers.* **5 he's/she's bad news** *informal* used to say that someone is likely to cause trouble: *Stay away from that guy, he's bad news.* **6 that's news to me!** *spoken* used when you are surprised or annoyed because you have not been told something earlier: *So, the meeting's been cancelled? Well that's news to me!* **7 no news is good news** *spoken* used when you have not received any news about someone and you hope this means that nothing bad has happened

This graph shows some of the words most commonly used with the noun **news**.

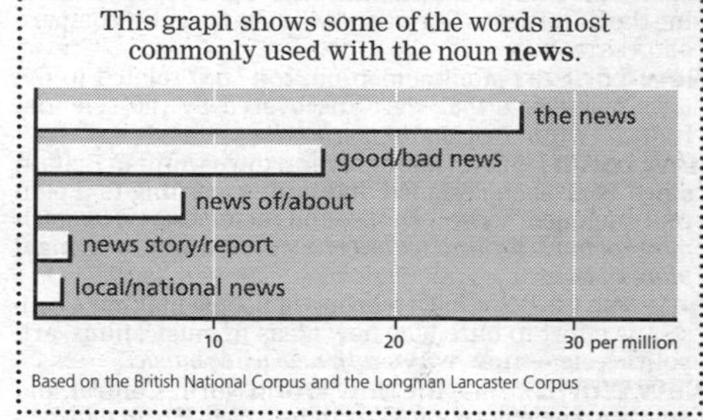


Based on the British National Corpus and the Longman Lancaster Corpus

**news a·gen·cy** /ˈ· ˌ···/ *n* [C] a company that supplies information to newspapers, radio and television

**news·a·gent** /ˈnjuːzˌeɪdʒənt‖ˈnuːz-/ *n* [C] *BrE* someone who owns or works in a shop that sells newspapers and magazines: **newsagent's** (=a newsagent's shop)

**news bul·le·tin** /ˈ· ˌ···/ *n* [C] **1** *BrE* a short news programme on radio or television, reporting only the most important information **2** *AmE* a very short news programme on radio or television, broadcast suddenly in the middle of another programme when something very important has happened; NEWSFLASH *BrE*

**news·cast** /ˈnjuːzkɑːst‖ˈnuːzkæst/ *n* [C] *AmE* a news programme on radio or television

**news·cast·er** /ˈnjuːzˌkɑːstə‖ˈnuːzˌkæstər/ *n* [C] someone who reads the news on radio or television; NEWSREADER *BrE*

**news con·fer·ence** /ˈ· ˌ···/ *n* [C] a PRESS CONFERENCE

**news·flash** /ˈnjuːzflæʃ‖ˈnuːz-/ *n* [C] *especially BrE* a very short news programme on radio or television, broadcast suddenly in the middle of another programme when something very important has happened; NEWS BULLETIN *AmE*: *We interrupt this programme to bring you a newsflash from the Malabar front.*

**news·hound** /ˈnjuːzhaʊnd‖ˈnuːz-/ *n* [C] *informal* someone who writes for a newspaper and is always looking for exciting new stories but sometimes upsets people by being too eager

**news·let·ter** /ˈnjuːzˌletə‖ˈnuːzˌletər/ *n* [C] one or several sheets of printed news sent regularly to a particular group of people: *Have you seen the church newsletter?*

**news·pa·per** /ˈnjuːsˌpeɪpə‖ˈnuːzˌpeɪpər-/ *n* **1** [C] a set of large folded sheets of paper containing news, articles, pictures, advertisements etc printed and sold daily or weekly: *a national newspaper* **2** [U] sheets of paper from old newspapers: *Wrap the plates in newspaper to stop them from breaking.* **3** [C] a company that produces a newspaper: *I think he works for a local newspaper.* 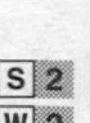 S2 W2

**newspaper stand** /ˈ··· ˌ·/ *n* [C] a NEWSSTAND

**news·print** /ˈnjuːzˌprɪnt‖ˈnuːz-/ *n* [U] *technical* cheap paper used mostly for printing newspapers on

**news·read·er** /ˈnjuːzˌriːdə‖ˈnuːzˌriːdər/ *n* [C] *especially BrE* someone who reads the news on television or radio

**news·reel** /ˈnjuːzriːl‖ˈnuːz-/ *n* [C] a cinema film of news

**news re·lease** /ˈ· ·ˌ·/ *n* [C] a PRESS RELEASE

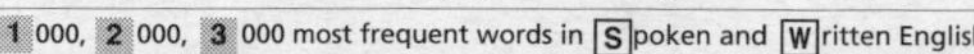

N

**news·room** /'nju:zrum, -ru:m‖'nu:z-/ *n* [C] the office in a newspaper or broadcasting company where news is received and news reports are written

**news·stand** /'nju:zstænd‖'nu:z-/ *n* [C] *n* a place on a street where newspapers and magazines are sold

**news ven·dor** /'· ,··/ *n* [C] *especially BrE* someone who sells newspapers

**news·wor·thy** /'nju:z,wɜ:ði‖'nu:z,wɜ:rði/ *adj* important or interesting enough to be reported as news: *The reporter's task is to report what is newsworthy about an event.*

**news·y** /'nju:zi‖'nu:zi/ *adj* a newsy letter is from a friend or relative and contains a lot of news about them

**newt** /nju:t‖nu:t/ *n* [C] a small animal with a long body, four legs and a tail, that lives in water

**New Tes·ta·ment** /,· '···/ *n* **the New Testament** the part of the Bible which includes the four Gospels describing the life of Jesus Christ and what he taught —compare OLD TESTAMENT

**New·toni·an** /nju:'təuniən‖nu:'tou-/ *adj* related to the laws of PHYSICS that were discovered by the scientist Isaac Newton: *Newtonian mechanics*

**new town** /'· ·/ *n* [C] one of several towns built in Britain since 1946, each designed and built according to a plan that included houses, shops, and factories: *A new town may not be very attractive but is certainly a very convenient place to live.*

**new wave** /,· '·◂/ *n* [C] a group of people making a conscious effort to introduce new ideas in music, films, art, politics etc —**new wave** *adj*: *new wave music*

**New World** /,· '·◂/ *n* **the New World** North, Central, and South America —**New World** *adj*: *New World wines*

**New Year, new year** /,· '·◂/ *n* [U] **1** the time at the beginning of the year when you celebrate: *We're going to spend Christmas and New Year with my parents.* | **Happy New Year** (=used as a greeting) | **see in the new year** (=celebrate the beginning of the year) *Our neighbours invited us round to see in the new year.* **2 the new year** the first few weeks of the year: *Let's hope things will begin to improve in the new year.* | **new year resolution** (=a decision to improve yourself in the new year) *I haven't made any new year resolutions – I never stick to them anyway.*

**New Year's Day** /,· · '·/ *n* [singular, U] 1st January, the first day of the year

**New Year's Eve** /,· · '·/ *n* [singular, U] 31st December, the last day of the year

S1 W1 **next¹** /nekst/ *determiner* **1** the next house, room etc is the one that is closest to you: *I asked the woman at the next table what time it was.* | *They could be heard arguing from the next room.* **2** the next event, day, time etc is the one that happens after the present one: **the next train/meeting/class etc** *The next episode was watched by over 10 million anxious viewers.* | *If they win the next election they have promised to reform the health service.* | *I've just missed the flight to Chicago, what time's the next one?* | **the next few weeks/three years etc** *Over the next couple of months, try to relax more and take more exercise.* | **next Monday/July/year etc** *We're hoping to reopen the factory some time next year.* | **(the) next day** *She called me and we arranged to meet the next day.* | **(the) next time** *Next time I take a cab, I'll be more careful.* —compare LAST¹ (1) **3** the next person or thing in a list, a series, a line of people etc is the one that you come to after the one that you are dealing with at the present time: *The letter continues on the next page.* | *The next interviewee has a degree in geography and plenty of work experience.* | *The cottage is just around the next bend in the road.* **4 a) the next biggest/smallest etc** the one that is a bit bigger, smaller etc than the one you are talking about: *The hotel was full and the next nearest was over 20 miles away.* **b) the next best thing** the thing that is almost as good as something else: *If butter is too expensive use the next best thing – margarine.* —see also **next of kin** (KIN (2))

S1 W1 **next²** *adv* **1** immediately afterwards: *Being a doctor is a great life, you never know what will happen next.* | *The mixture is heated to a temperature of 40°C. Next, it is poured into a mould and left to cool.* | *Where do you think you'll travel next?* **2 next to a)** situated very close to someone or something with nothing in between: *There was a little girl sitting next to him.* | *The church is on the left, next to the school.* —see picture on page 1257 **b)** used when giving a list of things you like or prefer etc in order to say what is first in the list: *Next to soccer, squash is the sport I'm best at.* **3 next to nothing** very little: *He knows next to nothing about antiques.* **4** the next time: *When I next saw her she completely ignored me.*

**next³** *pron* **1** the person or thing in a list, a series, a line of people etc that you come to after the one that you are dealing with at the present time: *Un, deux, trois...what comes next?* | *You're next Mrs Williams. The doctor will be ready in a moment.* **2 the day/week etc after next** the day, week etc that follows the next one: *Have you remembered it's Susie's birthday the week after next?* **3 the next to last** the one before the last one: *We'll need to buy some more ink. I'm on the next to last bottle at the moment.* **4 next (please)** used to tell someone that it is now their turn to speak or their turn to do something **5 be next in line** to be the next person to become king, a leader etc

**next door¹** /,· '·/ *adv* **1** in the house, room etc next to yours or someone else's: *the boy next door* | *the people who've just moved in next door* | *Her office is just next door.* **2 next door to a)** next to another building, room etc: *He runs that small restaurant next door to the theatre.* **b)** almost the same as: *Leaving a man to die is next door to murder.*

**next door²** *n* [U] *BrE informal* the people living in the house or apartment next to yours: *Have you seen next door's new car?*

**next-door³** /,· '·◂/ *adj* **1 next-door neighbour** the person who lives in the house or apartment next to yours *I met my new next-door neighbour for the first time last night.* **2 next door apartment/office etc** the apartment etc that is next to yours

**nex·us** /'neksəs/ *n plural* **nexus** [C + **of**] *formal* a connection or network of connections between a number of people, things or ideas: *Beneath the apparent certainty was a nexus of contradictions.*

**NHS** /,en eɪtʃ 'es/ *n* **the NHS** the National Health Service; the British system that provides free medical treatment for everyone, paid for by taxes: *NHS hospitals* | **on the NHS** (=paid for by the NHS) *Can I get my glasses on the NHS?*

**nib** /nɪb/ *n* [C] **1** the pointed metal part at the end of a pen **2 his/her nibs** *old-fashioned* someone of a higher social rank than you or someone who thinks they are important: *His nibs has wine with his meal – we get water.*

**nib·ble¹** /'nɪbəl/ *v* **1** [I,T] to eat small amounts of food by taking very small bites: *He nibbled the biscuit cautiously.* | [+ **at**] *She nibbled at her sandwich.* **2** [I + **at**] to show slight interest in an offer or suggestion

**nibble away at** sth *phr v* [T] to keep reducing a large amount by taking smaller amounts from it: *All these expenses are nibbling away at our savings.*

**nibble²** *n* [C] **1** a small bite of something: *taking tiny nibbles of a biscuit* **2 nibbles** [plural] *informal* small things to eat, especially at a party **3** an expression of slight interest in an offer or suggestion: *We've had the house on the market for a month and not even a nibble yet.*

**nice** /naɪs/ *adj* S1 W2

**1** ▸ **ENJOYABLE/ATTRACTIVE** ◂ pleasant, attractive or enjoyable: *That's a nice dress.* | *We had a really nice day at the beach.* | *not too hot, just a nice temperature* | *"We could take a picnic." "Yes, that'd be nice."* | **it is nice to do something** *It's nice to have a sit down.* | *It's really nice to see you again.* | **look/taste/smell nice** *You look nice in that suit.* | *If it doesn't taste nice, don't eat it.* | **nice big/new/long etc** *spoken*: *I had a nice long letter from your mother.* | **nice and warm/nice and sweet etc** *Have one of these oranges – they're nice and juicy.* | **one of the nice things about...** *One of the nice things about Christmas is having all the family together.*

**2 ▶ FRIENDLY ◀** friendly or kind: *Dave's a really nice guy.* | *He told me, in the nicest possible way, that I was interfering too much.* | *Did she really say all those nice things about me?* | **be nice to** *Be nice to Grandad. He's not feeling very well today.* | **it is nice of sb (to do sth)** *It was nice of you to help.*
**3 it's nice to know (that)** *spoken* used to mean that you feel happier when you know something: *I still haven't heard any news – it would be nice to know what's happening*
**4 ▶ NOT NICE AT ALL ◀** *spoken* used when you think that something or someone is not nice at all: *That's a nice way to treat a friend, I must say!* | *You've got us into a nice old mess, haven't you?*
**5 be as nice as pie** *spoken* if someone is as nice as pie, they are very nice to you when you were expecting them to be angry: *I told her about the broken window and she was as nice as pie about it.*
**6 have a nice day!** *spoken especially AmE* used to say goodbye to someone, especially to customers in shops and restaurants when they are leaving
**7 nice to meet you** *spoken* used as a friendly greeting when you meet someone for the first time: *Hello. It's nice to meet you at last.*
**8 it's been nice meeting you** *spoken* used when you say goodbye to someone you have just met
**9 nice one!** *BrE spoken* used to say that you think someone has just said or done something clever, amusing, helpful etc: *"Dad said he'd give us some money to help pay for it." "Nice one!"*
**10 nice work!** *BrE spoken* used to praise someone when they have succeeded in doing something: *"I've traced those missing files, sir." "Nice work, Cardew!"*
**11 ▶ DETAIL ◀** *formal* involving a very small difference or detail: *a nice point of law*
**12 ▶ RESPECTABLE ◀** *old-fashioned* having high standards of moral and social behaviour: *the kind of nightclubs nice people don't go to* —**niceness** *n* [U] —see also **no more Mr Nice Guy!** (GUY [1] (5))

**USAGE NOTE: NICE**
GRAMMAR
**Nice** is often joined to another adjective by *and* when it follows **is, seems** etc without a noun. (But you do not use 'nice and' before a noun): *Your new house looks nice and big*. Compare: *This is a nice big house!*

SPOKEN-WRITTEN
**Nice** is very frequent in spoken English, but many people feel you should not use it too much in writing. Often it is better to think of a word that describes what you mean more exactly. For example, look at this sentence: *That area of France is really nice.* Here you could make your meaning clearer by using more specific adjectives such as **interesting** or **beautiful**.

**nice-look·ing** /ˌ· ˈ··/ *adj* attractive: *Do you really think he's nice-looking?*

S3 **nice·ly** /ˈnaɪsli/ *adv*
**1 ▶ WELL ◀** in a satisfactory or pleasing way: *The car seems to be running nicely now it's been fixed.* | *We were managing quite nicely till you started interfering.* | *My legs are getting nicely tanned.*
**2 ▶ IN A FRIENDLY/PLEASANT WAY ◀** in a pleasant, polite, or friendly way: *I hope you thanked Mrs Deville nicely.*
**3 be doing nicely (for yourself)** to be successful and be earning a lot of money: *I've heard Malcom's doing very nicely for himself out in Japan.*
**4 will do nicely** *spoken* if something will do nicely, it is suitable for a particular purpose: *"Is this knife big enough?" "Yes, it'll do nicely."*
**5 ▶ EXACTLY ◀** *formal* exactly or carefully: *a nicely calculated distance*

**ni·ce·ty** /ˈnaɪsəti/ *n* **1** [C usually plural] a small and exact point of difference or detail: *legal niceties* | **[+ of]** *the niceties of etiquette* **2 to a nicety** *formal* exactly

**niche** /niːʃ, nɪtʃ‖nɪtʃ/ *n* **1** [C] a job or activity that is perfect for someone: *She's found a niche for herself in the book trade.* **2** [C] a hollow place in a wall, often made to hold a STATUE **3** [singular] *technical* all the people who buy a particular product or use a particular service

**niche mar·ket·ing** /ˈ· ˌ···/ *n* [U] the practice of trying to sell a product to a particular group of people

**nick**[1] /nɪk/ *n* **1 in the nick of time** just before it is too late or just before something bad happens: *Luckily, help arrived in the nick of time.* **2** [C] a very small cut made on the edge or surface of something **3 in good nick/in bad nick etc** *BrE informal* in good condition or in bad condition: *It's an old car but it's in good nick.* **4 the nick** *BrE informal* prison or a POLICE STATION

**nick**[2] *v* [T] **1** to make a small cut in the surface or edge of something, usually by accident: *A bullet nicked his leg.* **2** *BrE informal* to steal something: *Someone's nicked my bike.* **3** *BrE informal* if the police nick you, they catch you and charge you with a crime; ARREST [1] (1)

**nick·el** /ˈnɪkəl/ *n* **1** [U] a hard silver-white metal that is an ELEMENT (=a simple substance) and is used in the production of other metals **2** [C] a coin in the US or Canada that is worth five cents

**nickel-and-dime** /ˌ·· · ˈ·◂/ *adj AmE* unimportant and not costing a lot of money

**nick-nack** /ˈnɪk næk/ *n* [C] another spelling of KNICK-KNACK

**nick·name** /ˈnɪkneɪm/ *n* [C] a name given to someone, especially by their friends or family, that is not their real name and is often connected with what they look like or something they have done —**nickname** *v* [T] *Frank Sinatra, nicknamed 'Old Blue Eyes'*

**nic·o·tine** /ˈnɪkətiːn/ *n* [U] a substance in tobacco which makes it difficult for people to stop smoking

**nicotine patch** /ˈ··· ˌ·/ *n* [C] a small piece of material containing nicotine which you stick on your skin to help you stop smoking

**niece** /niːs/ *n* [C] the daughter of your brother or sister, or the daughter of your wife's or husband's brother or sister —compare NEPHEW —see picture at FAMILY

**niff** /nɪf/ *n* [singular] *BrE informal* a bad smell —**niffy** *adj*

**nif·ty** /ˈnɪfti/ *adj informal* very good, fast, or effective: *a nifty little gadget for squeezing oranges* | *a nifty little car*

**nig·gard·ly** /ˈnɪɡədli‖-ər-/ *adj* **1** unwilling to spend money or be generous; STINGY: *The landlord was niggardly about repairs.* **2** a niggardly gift, amount, salary etc is not worth very much and is given unwillingly: *niggardly wages* —**niggard** *n* [C] —**niggardliness** *n* [U]

**nig·ger** /ˈnɪɡə‖-ər/ *n* [C] *taboo* an extremely offensive word for a black person —see NEGRO (USAGE)

**nig·gle**[1] /ˈnɪɡəl/ *v* **1** [T] if something niggles you, it worries or annoys you slightly and you cannot forget about it: *Something's been niggling her all day.* **2** [I] to argue or make criticisms about small unimportant details: **[+ about/over]** *She niggled over every detail of the bill.* —**niggle** *n* [C] —**niggler** *n* [C]

**nig·gling** /ˈnɪɡəlɪŋ/ *adj* **niggling doubt/worry/suspicion etc** a doubt etc that keeps worrying you slightly and that you cannot stop thinking about: *A niggling doubt about Marlow's motives suddenly entered his mind.*

**nigh** /naɪ/ *adv* **1 nigh on** *old-fashioned* almost: *There were nigh on 40 people there.* **2** *literary* near: **draw nigh** (=come near or be about to happen soon) *Winter draws nigh.* —see also **well-nigh**

**night** /naɪt/ *n* S1 W1
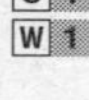
**1 ▶ WHEN IT IS DARK ◀** [C,U] the dark part of each 24-hour period when the sun cannot be seen: *a starry night* | **at night/by night** (=when it is dark) *At night the temperature drops below zero.* | *They travelled by night and slept during the day.* | **all night (long)** (=through the

whole night) *In New York, some stores stay open all night long.* | *The party went on all night.* | **night train/flight/bus** (=a train, plane, bus etc that travels at night) *We took the night train to Glasgow.* | **the night sky/air** *the cold night air* | **at dead of night** (=in the middle of the night when it is quiet) *Their meetings were held in secret at dead of night.* | **night falls** (=it becomes dark) *Night was beginning to fall as we sailed into Vera Cruz.*

**2 ▶ WHEN YOU SLEEP ◀** the time when most people are in bed: *I didn't sleep too well last night.* | *We had to get up in the middle of the night.* | *14 nights in a 5 star hotel* | **at night** (=when it is night) *She's so worried she can't sleep at night.* | **in the night** (=during the night) *The baby woke up twice in the night.* | **spend the night** *We spent the first two nights of our vacation in a cheap motel.* | **spend the night with sb** (=and have sex with someone) | **stay the night** (=sleep at someone's house) *If you miss the last bus home, you can always stay the night.* | **a good night's sleep** (=when you sleep well all night) *You look exhausted! What you need is a good night's sleep.* | **have a bad night** *BrE* (=not sleep much)

**3 ▶ EVENING ◀** [C,U] the time during the evening until you go to bed: *Most nights we just stay at home and watch television.* | **last night** *Where did you go last night?* | **at night** *Do you mean 9:30 in the morning or 9:30 at night?* | **tomorrow night** *My parents are coming for dinner tomorrow night.* | **the other night** *spoken* (=a few nights ago) *Did I tell you I saw Nicky Ansell the other night?* | **Friday night/Saturday night etc** *There's a party at Ben's place on Saturday night.* | **a night out** (=a night when you go to a party, restaurant, theatre etc) *Let's go see a band – I could do with a night out.* | **late at night** *Anna doesn't like him walking home late at night.*

**4 nights** *especially AmE* if you do something nights, you do it regularly or often at night: *I lie awake nights.* | **work nights** *I'd hate to work nights – it's so antisocial.*

**5 night!** *spoken* used to say goodbye to someone when it is late in the evening or when they are going to bed: *Night! See you tomorrow!*

**6 night night!** *spoken* used to say goodbye to someone, especially a child, when they are going to bed

**7 night after night** every night for a long period: *He's out drinking night after night.*

**8 night and day/day and night** all the time: *The store is guarded day and night.*

**9 late night** a night when you go to bed later than usual: *You're looking sleepy this morning. Too many late nights!* —see also LATE-NIGHT

**10 have an early night** to go to bed earlier than usual: *I'm exhausted – I think I'll have an early night.*

**11 last thing at night** just before you go to bed: *You should never eat cheese last thing at night.*

**12 at this time of night!** *spoken* used when you are surprised because something happens late at night: *Who on earth could be calling at this time of night?*

**13 first night/opening night** the first performance of a play or show: *We saw 'Miss Saigon' on its opening night.*

**14 make a night of it** to stay out late drinking, dancing etc —see also NIGHTLY

**night·cap** /ˈnaɪtkæp/ *n* [C] **1** an alcoholic drink that you have just before you go to bed **2** a soft cap that people in the past used to wear in bed

**night·clothes** /ˈnaɪtkləʊðz, -kləʊz‖-kloʊ-/ *n* [plural] clothes that you wear in bed

**night·club** /ˈnaɪtklʌb/ *n* [C] a place of entertainment open late at night where people can dance and drink

**night·club·bing** /ˈnaɪtˌklʌbɪŋ/ *n* [U] **go nightclubbing** *BrE* to spend an evening at a nightclub

**night de·pos·it·o·ry** /ˈ· ·ˌ····/ *n* [C] *AmE* NIGHT SAFE

**night·dress** /ˈnaɪtdres/ *n* [C] a piece of clothing, like a thin dress, that women wear in bed

**night·fall** /ˈnaɪtfɔːl‖-fɒːl/ *n* [U] the time when it begins to get dark in the evening; DUSK: *We rushed to reach home before nightfall.*

**night·gown** /ˈnaɪtgaʊn/ *n* [C] a nightdress

**night·hawk** /ˈnaɪthɔːk‖-hɒːk/ *n* [C] *especially AmE informal* someone who enjoys staying awake all night

**night·ie** /ˈnaɪti/ *n* [C] *informal* a NIGHTDRESS

**nigh·tin·gale** /ˈnaɪtɪŋgeɪl/ *n* [C] a small bird that sings very beautifully, especially at night

**night·life** /ˈnaɪtlaɪf/ *n* [U] entertainment in the evening: *It's a beautiful place but there's not much nightlife.*

**night·light** /ˈnaɪtlaɪt/ *n* [C] a small electric light that you put in a child's room at night

**night·long** /ˈnaɪtlɒŋ‖-lɒːŋ/ *adj* [only before noun] *literary* lasting all night: *a nightlong vigil*

**night·ly** /ˈnaɪtli/ *adv* every night: *The band performed nightly.* —**nightly** *adj*: *nightly news broadcasts*

**night·mare** /ˈnaɪtmeə‖-mer/ *n* [C] **1** a very frightening dream: *Years after the accident I still have nightmares about it.* **2** a very unpleasant or frightening experience: *He kept trying to hold my hand all the time – it was a real nightmare!* | **nightmare journey/situation etc** (=the worst journey etc you can imagine) *a nightmare sea voyage in a raging storm* **3** something terrible that you fear may happen in the future: [+ **of**] *the nightmare of a nuclear war* | **nightmare scenario** (=the worst or most frightening situation that you can imagine) —**nightmarish** *adj*

**night owl** /ˈ· ·/ *n* [C] *informal* someone who enjoys staying awake all night

**night por·ter** /ˌ· ˈ··/ *n* [C] someone who works at the main entrance of a hotel during the night

**night safe** /ˈ· ·/ *n* [C] *BrE* a special hole in the outside wall of a bank into which a customer can put money or documents when the bank is closed; NIGHT DEPOSITORY *AmE*

**night school** /ˈ· ·/ *n* [U] classes that take place in the evening for people who work during the day

**night shift** /ˈ· ·/ *n* [C] **1** a period of time at night during which people regularly work, especially in a factory: *She's on the night shift this week.* **2** the group of people who work at this time: *the night shift was just arriving*

**night·shirt** /ˈnaɪt-ʃɜːt‖-ʃɜːrt/ *n* [C] a long loose shirt that people, especially men, wear in bed

**night soil** /ˈ· ·/ *n* [U] *technical* human waste used in growing crops

**night spot** /ˈ· ·/ *n* [C] a place people go to at night for entertainment: *my favourite New York night spot*

**night·stand** /ˈnaɪtstænd/ *n* [C] *AmE* a small table beside a bed

**night·stick** /ˈnaɪtˌstɪk/ *n* [C] *AmE* a short thick stick carried as a weapon by police officers; TRUNCHEON *BrE*

**night·time** /ˈnaɪtˌtaɪm/ *n* [U] the time during the night: **at nighttime** *animals that hunt at nighttime* —opposite DAYTIME

**night watch** /ˈ· ·/ *n* **the night watch** a kind of police force in the past, who looked after a town at night

**night watch·man** /ˌ· ˈ··/ *n* [C] someone whose job is to guard a building at night

**night·wear** /ˈnaɪtweə‖-wer/ *n* [U] clothes that you wear in bed at night

**nig·nog** /ˈnɪg nɒg‖-nɑːg/ *n* [C] *BrE old-fashioned taboo* an extremely offensive word for a black person

**ni·hil·is·m** /ˈnaɪɪlɪzəm/ *n* [U] **1** the belief that nothing has any meaning or value **2** the idea that all social and political institutions should be destroyed —**nihilist** *n* [C] —**nihilistic** /ˌnaɪɪˈlɪstɪk◂/ *adj*

**-nik** /nɪk/ *suffix informal (in nouns)* someone who is connected with something or enjoys something: *a computernik* (=someone who works with or is very keen on computers) *a peacenik* (=someone who supports peace)

**nil** /nɪl/ *n* [U] **1** nothing: *The new machine reduced labour costs to almost nil.* **2** *BrE* the number zero, used in sports results: *Our team won by two goals to nil.* S3

**nim·ble** /ˈnɪmbəl/ *adj* **1** able to move quickly and easily with light neat movements: *a nimble climber* | *nimble fingers* **2 a nimble mind/brain/wit** an ability to think quickly or understand things easily: *They liked his nimble mind – his ability to come up with original ideas.* —**nimbly** *adv* —**nimbleness** *n* [U]

**nim·bus** /ˈnɪmbəs/ *n* **1** [C,U] a dark cloud that may bring rain or snow **2** [C] a HALO

**nim·by** /ˈnɪmbi/ *n* [C] not in my backyard; someone who does not want a particular activity or building near their home —**nimby** *adj*: *nimby attitudes*

**nin·com·poop** /ˈnɪŋkəmpuːp/ *n* [C] *old-fashioned* a stupid person

**nine** /naɪn/ *number* **1** 9 —see table on page B1 **2 nine times out of ten** almost always: *Nine times out of ten it's careless driving that causes an accident.* **3 nine days' wonder** a thing or event that makes people very excited for a short time —see also **dressed up to the nines** (DRESSED (5)), **be on cloud nine** (CLOUD[1] (4))

**nine·pins** /ˈnaɪnˌpɪnz/ *n* [U] a game in which you roll a ball at nine bottle-shaped objects to try to knock them down

**nine·teen** /ˌnaɪnˈtiːn◂/ *number* **1** 19 —see table on page B1 **2 nineteen to the dozen** if you talk nineteen to the dozen, you talk very quickly and without stopping: —**nineteenth** *adj*

**nine·teenth** /ˌnaɪnˈtiːnθ◂/ *number* [singular] *humorous* an expression used by GOLF players meaning the bar where they drink after playing

**nine-to-five** /ˌ· · ˈ·◂/ *adv* **work nine-to-five** to work from 9 o'clock until 5 o'clock; the normal working hours of an office worker —**nine-to-five** *adj*: *a nine-to-five job*

**nine·ty** /ˈnaɪnti/ *number* **1** 90 —see table on page B1 **2 the nineties** also **the '90's, the 1990's;** the years from 1990 to 1999 **3 be in your nineties** to be aged from ninety to ninety-nine: *My grandparents are both in their nineties.* —**ninetieth** *number*

**nin·ja** /ˈnɪndʒə/ *n* [C] a member of a Japanese class of professional killers in former times: *a ninja warrior*

**nin·ny** /ˈnɪni/ *n* [C] *old-fashioned* a silly person

**ninth[1]** /naɪnθ/ *number* 9th —see table on page B1

**ninth[2]** *number* [C] one of nine equal parts of something

**nip[1]** /nɪp/ **nipped, nipping** *v* **1** [T] to bite someone or something lightly: *The dog nipped my ankles.* **2** [I always + adv/prep] *BrE informal* to go somewhere quickly or for a short time: [+ **in/down/out etc**] *I'm just nipping out to the shops – I'll be back in five minutes.* | *Another car nipped in* (=nipped into a space) *in front of me.* **3 nip sth in the bud** to prevent something from becoming a problem by stopping it as soon as it starts: *If you feel a cold coming on try to nip it in the bud by keeping warm and getting a lot of sleep.* **4** [T] *BrE* to suddenly and accidentally press something tightly between two edges or surfaces: *He nipped his finger in the door.*

**nip** sth ↔ **off** *phr v* [T] to remove a small part of something, especially a plant, by pressing it tightly between your finger and thumb: *She nipped off a dead flower.*

**nip[2]** *n* [C] **1** the act or result of pressing something between two edges or biting it lightly **2** a small amount of strong alcoholic drink: [+ **of**] *a nip of brandy* **3 a nip in the air** coldness in the air **4 nip and tuck** *AmE informal* **a)** if two competitors are nip and tuck in a race or competition, they are doing equally well; **neck and neck** (NECK [1] (11): *They were nip and tuck in the last lap of the race.* **b)** equally likely to happen or not happen: *I might just make it to the airport, but it'll be nip and tuck.*

**nipp·er** /ˈnɪpə‖-pər/ *n* [C] *BrE informal* a child, especially a small boy

**nip·ple** /ˈnɪpəl/ *n* [C] **1** the small dark circular part of a woman's breast, through which a baby sucks milk —see picture at BODY **2** one of the two small dark circular parts on a man's chest —see picture at BODY **3** *AmE* the rubber part on a baby's bottle that a baby sucks milk through; TEAT (1) *BrE* **4** a small thing shaped like a nipple on a machine, with a hole in it which you pour oil through

**nip·py** /ˈnɪpi/ *adj informal* **1** weather that is nippy is slightly cold: *It's rather nippy out there.* **2** *BrE* moving quickly or able to move quickly: *a nippy little car* —**nippiness** *n* [U] —**nippily** *adv*

**nir·va·na** /nɪəˈvɑːnə, nɜː-‖nɪr-, nɜːr-/ *n* [U] **1** *technical* a state of knowledge or understanding that is beyond life and death, suffering, and change, and is the aim of believers in Buddhism **2** *informal* a condition of great happiness and a feeling of peace

**ni·si** /ˈnaɪsaɪ/ *n* —see **decree nisi**

**nit** /nɪt/ *n* [C] **1** an egg of a LOUSE (=a small insect that sucks blood), that is sometimes found in people's hair **2** *BrE informal* a silly person

**nit·pick·ing** /ˈnɪtˌpɪkɪŋ/ *n* [U] *informal* the annoying habit of arguing about unimportant details, especially in someone's work —**nitpicking** *adj* —**nitpicker** *n* [C]

**ni·trate** /ˈnaɪtreɪt, -trɪ̇t/ *n* [C,U] a chemical compound that is mainly used to improve the soil for growing crops

**ni·tre** *BrE*, **niter** *AmE* /ˈnaɪtə‖-ər/ *n* [U] one of several natural nitrates, including SALTPETRE

**nitric ac·id** /ˌnaɪtrɪk ˈæsɪ̇d/ *n* [U] a powerful acid that is used in explosives and other chemical products

**ni·tro·gen** /ˈnaɪtrədʒən/ *n* [U] a gas that is an ELEMENT (=a simple substance) without colour or smell, that forms most of the Earth's air

**ni·tro·gly·ce·rine, nitroglycerin** /ˌnaɪtrəʊˈglɪsərɪ̇n, -riːn‖-troʊˈglɪsərɪ̇n/ *n* [U] a powerful liquid explosive

**nit·ty-grit·ty** /ˌnɪti ˈgrɪti/ *n informal* **the nitty-gritty** the basic and practical facts of a subject or activity: **get down to the nitty-gritty** *Let's get down to the nitty-gritty and work out the costs, shall we?*

**nit·wit** /ˈnɪt-wɪt/ *n* [C] *informal* a silly person

**nix[1]** /nɪks/ *adv AmE old-fashioned* no

**nix[2]** *v* [T] *AmE old-fashioned* to answer no to something or FORBID something: *They nixed the idea of filming in Ireland.*

**no** *plural* **nos.** the written abbreviation of NUMBER

**no[1]** /nəʊ‖noʊ/ *adv* **1** *spoken* used to give a negative reply to a question, offer, or request: *"Are you Italian?" "No, I'm Spanish."* | *"Do you want any more?" "No thanks."* | *"Could you help me write this?" "No, sorry, I haven't got time at the moment."* | **say no** *Would you be terribly offended if I said no?* | **the answer's no** *If she asks to borrow any money, the answer's no!* —opposite YES [1] (1) **2** *spoken* used to say that you disagree with a statement: *"You're always complaining about things." "No, I'm not!"* **3** *spoken* used to say that you agree with a negative statement: *"They shouldn't be charging such high prices." "No, it's ridiculous!"* **4 won't take no for an answer** if someone won't take no for an answer, they say firmly that you must do something: *You simply must come to dinner, and I won't take no for an answer.* **5** *spoken* used to show that you are shocked, surprised, annoyed, or disappointed by what someone has just told you, or by what has just happened: *"This skirt cost me £7." "No!"* | **Oh no** *Oh no, not another false alarm?* **6 no good/no use etc** not at all good, not at all useful etc: *This map's no use – it's out of date.* | *I'm no good at physics.* **7 no better/no more/no less etc** not better, not more etc: *They've written no fewer than ten letters of complaint and still nothing's been done.* **8 no small part/no great matter etc** *formal* a large part, a small matter etc: *a question of no great importance* (=of little importance) | *She had no small part* (=had a large part) *in its success.* S1 W1

**no[2]** *determiner* **1** not one or not any: *Do you mind having black coffee. There's no milk.* | *There're no buses in this part of town.* | *a house with no central heating* | **be no reason why** *There's no reason at all why Jenny shouldn't come along too.* **2** used on a notice to say that something is forbidden: *No parking* | *No smoking* **3 in no time** *informal* very little or hardly any: *We're almost home now – we'll be there in no time.* **4 there's no knowing/telling/saying etc** *spoken* used to say that it is impossible to guess what will happen or what is true: *He's such a strange person – there's no knowing what he'll do next.* **5 be no fool/expert/friend etc** to be not at all stupid etc: | *Larry's no friend of mine.*

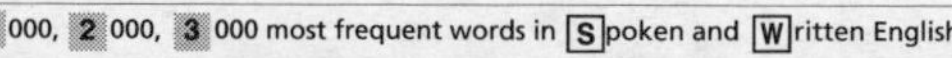

**USAGE NOTE: NO**

GRAMMAR

**No** is used before nouns and adjectives when it means 'not any': *No problem.* | *That's no good – it's broken.* | *He's no slimmer than he was before.*

Otherwise **not** is used, especially before *a, all, many, much,* and *enough*: *Not many tourists come here.* | *not enough food for all of us* | *She's not stupid.* | *The news was not good.*

SPELLING

**Nobody** meaning 'no one' is always spelt as one word: *There was nobody there* (=no person). Compare: *There was no body there* (=there was not a dead body there).

**no³** *n plural* **noes** **1** [singular] a negative answer or decision: *The answer was a definite no.* **2 noes** [plural] votes against a proposal in parliament

**No. 10** /ˌnʌmbə 'ten‖-bər-/ *n* [singular] No. 10 Downing Street; the address of the official home of the British Prime Minister

**no-ac·count** /'· ·ˌ·/ *adj AmE* another form of the word NO-COUNT: *a series of no-account boyfriends who drank too much*

**No·ah's ark** /ˌnəʊəz 'ɑːk‖ˌnoʊəz 'ɑːrk/ *n* [singular] the large boat which Noah built, according to the Bible, to save his family and two of every type of animal from a flood sent by God

**nob** /nɒb‖nɑːb/ *n* [C] *BrE old-fashioned* a rich person with a high social position: *They watched the nobs in their satin and feathers.*

**no ball** /'· ·/ *n* [C] an act of bowling (BOWL² (1,2)) the ball, in games such as CRICKET, in a way not allowed by the rules

**nob·ble** /'nɒbəl‖'nɑː-/ *v* [T] *BrE informal* **1** to get someone's attention, especially in order to persuade them to do something: *I'll try to nobble Jim and ask him if he'll help us.* **2** to make someone do what you want by offering them money or threatening them **3** to prevent a horse from winning a race, especially by giving it drugs

**No·bel Prize** /nəʊˌbel 'praɪz, ˌnəʊbel-‖noʊ-/ *n* [C] a prize given in Sweden each year to people from any country for important work in science, medicine, literature, economics, or work towards world peace

**no·bil·i·ty** /nəʊ'bɪləti, nə-‖noʊ-, nə-/ *n* **1 the nobility** the group of people in some countries who belong to the highest social class and have titles such as Duke or Countess; the ARISTOCRACY **2** [U] the quality of being noble in character or appearance: *For him, true nobility is found in hard work.*

**no·ble¹** /'nəʊbəl‖'noʊ-/ *adj* **1** someone who is noble behaves in a morally good or generous way that should be admired: *It's very noble of you to spend all your weekends helping the old folk.* | *noble ideals* **2** something that is noble is very impressive and beautiful: *this noble monument to our war heroes* **3** belonging to the nobility: *a man of noble birth* **4** a noble metal, such as gold or silver, is not affected chemically by the air —compare BASE METAL

**noble²** *n* [C] a member of the highest social class with a title such as Duke or Countess, especially in the past: *a vast gathering of kings and nobles* —compare COMMONER

**no·ble·man** /'nəʊbəlmən‖'noʊ-/ *n plural* **noblemen** /-mən/ [C] a man who is a member of the highest social class and has a title such as Duke

**no·blesse o·blige** /nəʊˌbles ə'bliːʒ‖noʊ-/ *n French* used to mean that people who belong to a high social class should be generous and behave with honour

**no·ble·wom·an** /'nəʊbəlˌwʊmən‖'noʊ-/ *n plural* **noblewomen** /-ˌwɪmən/ [C] a woman who is a member of the highest social class with a title such as Duchess

**no·bly** /'nəʊbli‖'noʊ-/ *adv* **1** in a morally good or generous way that should be admired: *great pain nobly borne* **2 nobly born** *literary* having parents who are members of the NOBILITY (1)

S1 W2 **no·bod·y¹** /'nəʊbədi‖'noʊbɑːdi, -bədi/ *pron* no one: *I knocked on the door but nobody answered.* —see also **like nobody's business** (BUSINESS (27)), **sb is nobody's fool** (FOOL ¹ (3)) —see NO² (USAGE)

**nobody²** *n* [C] someone who is not important and has no influence: *I'm tired of being a nobody!*

**no-claims bo·nus** /·'· ˌ··/ *n* [C] *BrE* a reduction in the amount that you have to pay for car insurance, because you have not made any claims

**no-count** /'· ·/ *adj* [only before noun] *AmE* a no-count person never achieves very much because they are very lazy: *my no-count good-for-nothing nephew*

**noc·tur·nal** /nɒk'tɜːnl‖nɑːk'tɜːr-/ *adj* **1** *technical* an animal that is nocturnal is active at night: *Hamsters are nocturnal creatures.* **2** *formal* happening at night: *nocturnal visits* —**nocturnally** *adv*

**noc·turne** /'nɒktɜːn‖'nɑːktɜːrn/ *n* [C] a piece of music, especially a soft beautiful piece of piano music

nod

The lady nodded her head. Sam shook his head.

**nod¹** /nɒd‖nɑːd/ *v* **nodded, nodding** [I,T] **1** to move your head up and down, especially in order to show agreement or understanding: *I asked her if she was ready to go, and she nodded.* | **nod your head** *Jane nodded her head sympathetically.* | **nod your approval/agreement etc** (=show your approval etc by nodding) **2** to move your head down and up again once in order to greet someone or give someone a sign to do something: [+ **at/to**] *The judge nodded at the foreman to proceed.* | *She nodded to us as she walked by.* **3 be on nodding terms(with)/have a nodding acquaintance(with)** to know someone slightly or know a little about a subject: *Burke was already on nodding terms with a number of senators.* | *a nodding acquaintance with local history* W2

**nod off** *phr v* [I] to begin to sleep, when you do not intend to: *I missed the movie because I'd nodded off.*

**nod²** *n* **1** [C] an act of nodding: *The woman greeted us with a nod of the head.* | **give a nod** *I showed the doorman my card and he gave a friendly nod.* **2 give sb the nod** *BrE informal* to give someone permission to do something: *We're waiting for the boss to give us the nod on this one.* **3 a nod's as good as a wink** *humorous* used to tell someone that you have understood something, although it was said in an indirect way **4 on the nod** *BrE informal* by general agreement and without discussion: *The chairman's proposals are usually passed on the nod.* —see also **the land of nod** (LAND ¹ (9))

**no·dal** /'nəʊdl‖'noʊ-/ *adj technical* connected with nodes: *nodal root systems*

**nod·dle** /'nɒdl‖'nɑːdl/ *n* [C] *BrE old-fashioned* your head or brain; NOODLE *AmE*: *It's easy enough to do if you just use your noddle.*

**node** /nəʊd‖noʊd/ *n* [C] **1** the place on the stem of a plant from which a leaf or branch grows **2** a place where lines in a network, GRAPH etc meet or join **3** a LYMPH NODE

**nod·ule** /'nɒdjuːl‖'nɑːdʒuːl/ *n* [C] a small round raised part, especially a small swelling on a plant or someone's body —**nodular** *adj*

**No·el** /nəʊ'el‖noʊ-/ *n* [U] a word used in songs, on cards etc meaning CHRISTMAS

**noes** /nəʊz‖noʊz/ the plural of NO³

**no-fly zone** /ˌ· ˈ· ˌ·/ *n* [C] an area that no airplane is allowed to enter, and in which it would be attacked

**nog·gin** /ˈnɒgɪ̈n‖ˈnɑː-/ *n* [C] *old-fashioned* **1** a small amount of an alcoholic drink **2** *informal* your head or brain: *Use your noggin. Don't light a match in here.*

**no-go ar·e·a** /ˌ· ˈ· ˌ···/ *n* [C] **1** an area in a city that is controlled by a violent group and is dangerous for anyone else to enter: *They had taken a wrong turning and now found themselves in one of the most dangerous no-go areas in the city.* **2** a subject that cannot be discussed because it may offend people

**no·how** /ˈnəʊhaʊ‖ˈnoʊ-/ *adv usually humorous* not in any way or in any situation: *I never liked her nohow.*

S2 W2 **noise¹** /nɔɪz/ *n*
**1** ▶**SOUND**◀ [C,U] sound, especially a loud or unpleasant sound: *the noise of the traffic | a loud cracking noise* | **make (a) noise** *Try not to make a noise when you go upstairs. | Stop making so much noise.*
**2 make polite/encouraging etc noises** to talk in a way that sounds polite, encouraging etc: *My teacher made encouraging noises when I told her I wanted to go to university.* | **make the right noises** (=pretend to be concerned about or interested in what someone is saying)
**3 make a noise about** to complain a lot about something so that other people will notice
**4** ▶**ELECTRICAL**◀ [U] *technical* unwanted signals produced by an electrical CIRCUIT
**5** ▶**COMPUTERS**◀ [U] *technical* pieces of unwanted information that can prevent a computer from working effectively —see also BIG NOISE

> **USAGE NOTE: NOISE**
> WORD CHOICE: **noise, sound, racket, voice**
> A **sound** is anything that you hear: *I love the sound of the sea. | the sound of voices/a guitar/breaking glass*
> A **noise** is usually an unpleasant sound, often not made by a person: *'What's that noise?' she asked nervously. | They had to shout to make themselves heard above the noise of the machines.*
> A **voice** is the sound of a person speaking or singing: *We heard voices outside. | She has rather a high-pitched voice.*
> **Racket** is an informal word for a loud unpleasant noise: *They're making a hell of a racket next door.*

**noise²** *v* **be noised abroad/about/around** *old-fashioned, especially BrE* if news or information is noised abroad people are talking about it: *Rumours of an election are being noised abroad.*

**noise·less·ly** /ˈnɔɪzləsli/ *adv* without making any sound: *We crept noiselessly down the hall.* —**noiseless** *adj*: *noiseless tears* **noiselessness** *n* [U]

**noise pol·lu·tion** /ˈ· ·ˌ··/ *n* [U] very loud or continuous loud noise which is considered to be harmful to people

**noi·some** /ˈnɔɪsəm/ *adj literary* extremely unpleasant: *The workers lived in noisome slums.*

S3 **nois·y** /ˈnɔɪzi/ *adj* making a lot of noise, or full of noise: *The kids have been really noisy today. | The bar was too noisy and crowded. | a noisy engine* —**noisily** *adv*: *The children chattered noisily.* —**noisiness** *n* [U]

**no·mad** /ˈnəʊmæd‖ˈnoʊ-/ *n* [C] a member of a tribe that travels from place to place, especially to find grass for their animals —**nomadic** /nəʊˈmædɪk‖noʊ-/ *adj*: *a nomadic people*

**no-man's-land** /ˈ· · ˌ·/ *n* [singular, U] an area of land that no one owns or controls, especially an area between two borders or opposing armies

**nom de plume** /ˌnɒm də ˈpluːm‖ˌnɑːm-/ *n* [C] a name used by a writer instead of their real name

**no·men·cla·ture** /nəʊˈmeŋklətʃə‖ˈnoʊmənkleɪtʃər/ *n* [C,U] *formal* a system of naming things, especially in science: *medical nomenclature*

**nom·i·nal** /ˈnɒmɪ̈nəl‖ˈnɑː-/ *adj* **1 nominal head/leader etc** someone who has the title of leader etc but is not really doing that job: *Longo was the real power in the Communist Party while Togliatti was merely the nominal head.* **2** a nominal sum of money is very small, especially when compared with the usual amount that would be paid for something: *Golfers may play this course for a nominal fee in the off-peak season.* **3** *technical* connected with or used as a noun: *nominal endings such as 'ness' and 'ation'.*

**nom·i·nal·ly** /ˈnɒmɪnəli‖ˈnɑː-/ *adv* officially described as something when this is not really true: *Although Banda is nominally a Christian island, few of its inhabitants actually attend church.*

**nom·i·nate** /ˈnɒmɪ̈neɪt‖ˈnɑː-/ *v* [T] **1** to officially suggest someone for an important position, duty, or prize: **nominate sb for sth** *He was nominated for the Nobel Prize.* | **nominate sb as** *BrE I wish to nominate Jane Morrison as president of the club.* | **nominate sb to do sth** *I nominate John to represent us at the meeting.* **2** to choose someone for a particular job: **nominate sb as** *The director nominated me as her official representative at the conference.* | **nominate sb to sth** *She was nominated to the legislative council.*

**nom·i·na·tion** /ˌnɒmɪ̈ˈneɪʃən‖ˌnɑː-/ *n* **1** [C,U] the act of officially suggesting someone for a position, honour or prize, or the fact of being suggested for it: [**+ for**] *Who will get the Republican nomination for president? | All the committee's nominations were approved.* **2** [C] the name of a book, film, actor etc that has been suggested to receive an honour or prize: *'Schindler's List' was an obvious nomination for an Oscar.* **3** [C,U] the act of choosing someone for a particular job, or the fact of being chosen: [**+ as**] *O'Neil's nomination as chief executive*

**nom·i·na·tive** /ˈnɒmɪ̈nətɪv, ˈnɒmnə-‖ˈnɑː-/ *n* [C] *technical* a particular form of a noun in some languages, such as Latin and German, which shows that the noun is the SUBJECT¹ (5) of a verb —**nominative** *adj*

**nom·i·nee** /ˌnɒmɪ̈ˈniː‖ˌnɑː-/ *n* [C] someone who has been suggested for a prize, duty, or honour: *Oscar nominee Whoopi Goldberg*

**non-** /nɒn‖nɑːn/ *prefix* **1** in some adjectives and nouns, shows a negative; not: *a nonalcoholic drink | a nonsmoker* (=someone who does not smoke) | a nonstick frying pan (=which food does not stick to) **2** *informal* in some nouns, means something not deserving a particular name: *a non-event* (=something boring)

**no·na·ge·nar·i·an** /ˌnəʊnədʒɪ̈ˈneəriən, ˌnɒn-‖ˌnoʊnədʒɪ̈-ˈner-,ˌnɑːn-/ *n* [C] someone between 90 and 99 years old

**non-ag·gres·sion** /ˌ· ·ˈ··/ *n* [U] the idea that countries should not attack each other: *a policy of non-aggression* | **non-aggression pact/treaty** *In 1939 Stalin and Hitler signed a non-aggression pact.*

**non-al·co·hol·ic** /ˌ· ··ˈ··◀/ *adj* a drink that is non-alcoholic does not contain alcohol

**non-a·ligned** /ˌ· ·ˈ·◀/ *adj* a non-aligned country does not support, or is not dependent on, any of the powerful countries in the world —**non-alignment** *n* [U]

**nonce¹** /nɒns‖nɑːns/ *adj technical* a nonce word or phrase is only invented once for a particular occasion

**nonce²** *n* **for the nonce** *literary or humorous* for the present time or for this particular occasion

**non·cha·lant** /ˈnɒnʃələnt‖ˌnɑːnʃəˈlɑːnt/ *adj* behaving calmly and seeming not to worry or care about anything: *He was leaning on the bar, trying to look nonchalant.* —**nonchalance** *n* [U] —**nonchalantly** *adv*

**non·com·ba·tant** /ˌ· ˈ···‖ˌ· ·ˈ··/ *n* [C] someone who is in the army, navy etc during a war but who does not actually fight, for example an army doctor

**non-commis·sioned of·fi·cer** /ˌ· ··· ˈ···/ *n* [C] an NCO

**non·com·mit·tal** /ˌnɒnkəˈmɪtl◀‖ˌnɑːn-/ *adj* not expressing a definite opinion or intention: [**+ about**] *The doctor was noncommittal about his chances of making a full recovery. | a noncommital answer* —**noncommitally** *adv*

**non com·pos men·tis** /ˌnɒn ˌkɒmpəs ˈmentɪ̈s‖ˌnɑːn-ˌkɑːm-/ *adj* [not before noun] *Latin* unable to think clearly or be responsible for your actions

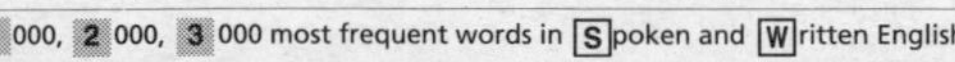

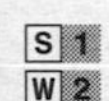

**Non·con·form·ist** /ˌnɒnkənˈfɔːmɪst◂‖ˌnɑːnkənˈfɔːr-/ *adj* belonging to one of the Protestant Christian churches that have separated from the Church of England —**Nonconformist** *n* [C] —**Nonconformism** *n* [U]

**nonconformist** *n* [C] someone who does not follow ways of living, thinking, or behaving accepted by most people: *a political nonconformist* —**nonconformist** *adj*: *nonconformist attitudes* —**nonconformity** *n* [U]

**non·con·trib·u·to·ry** /ˌnɒnkənˈtrɪbjʊtəri◂‖ˌnɑːnkənˈtrɪbjʊtɔːri◂/ *adj* a noncontributory PENSION or insurance plan is paid for by the employer only, and not by the worker

**non-co·op·e·ra·tion** /ˌ· ····ˈ··/ *n* [U] the refusal to do any more than you officially have to, as a protest

**non·cus·to·di·al** /ˌnɒnkʌˈstəʊdiəl◂‖ˌnɑːnkʌˈstoʊ-/ *adj* **noncustodial sentence** a form of punishment which does not involve being kept in prison

**non·de·script** /ˈnɒndɪˌskrɪpt‖ˌnɑːndɪˈskrɪpt/ *adj* very ordinary looking and without any interesting or unusual qualities or features: *a nondescript suburban house*

S1 W2 **none**[1] /nʌn/ *pron* **1** not any of something: *I was going to offer you some cake but there's none left.* | **none of** *Everyone was talking about it – it did not matter to them that none of it was true.* | *She had inherited none of her mother's beauty.* | **none at all/none whatsoever** *"Any mail arrive today?" "None whatsoever."* **2** not any of a number of people or things: **none of** *None of my friends phone me anymore.* | *None of you need worry.* | *None of their promises were kept.* | **none** *Of all the movies Hepburn made none is more memorable than 'Breakfast at Tiffany's'.* | *Perhaps none felt the effects more than Peter.* **3** not one thing or person: *Even an old car is better than none.* | **none at all** *It'd be better to make some sort of decision than none at all.* **4 have none of sth** to not allow someone to do something or to not allow someone to behave in a particular way: *This time I'll have none of her tears and tantrums.* | *We offered to pay our half of the cost but Charles would have none of it.* **5 none but** *literary* only: *None but she would have been capable of such strength and courage.* **6 none other (than)** used when you are surprised that a particular person, especially someone famous, has done something: *The mystery guest turned out to be none other than Cher herself.* —see also NONETHELESS, **second to none** (SECOND[1] (6)), **bar none** (BAR[3] (2))

> **USAGE NOTE: NONE**
> FORMALITY
> When **none of** is followed by a plural noun, it usually takes a plural verb in ordinary spoken English: *None of us are ready yet.*
> In formal writing a singular verb is used: *None of our factories is in operation yet.* Some people believe the singular is the only correct form.

**none**[2] *adv* **1 none the worse/better etc** not at all worse, better etc than before: *She seems none the worse for her experience.* | **none the wiser** (=not knowing any more about something than you did at the beginning) *I've read the instruction book from cover to cover, but I'm still none the wiser.* **2 none too** *informal* not at all: *I was none too pleased to have to take the exam again.*

**non·en·ti·ty** /nɒˈnentɪti‖nɑː-/ *n* [C] someone who has no importance, power, or ability, and who you have no respect for: *Chomsky was the only speaker of any importance – the rest were nonentities.*

**non·es·sen·tial** /ˌ· ·ˈ··◂/ *adj* not completely necessary: *The US has imposed a ban on non-essential aerosols.*

**none·such, nonsuch** /ˈnʌnsʌtʃ/ *n* [singular] *old use* a person or thing that is better than all the others of the same kind

**none·the·less** /ˌnʌnðəˈles◂/ *adv* [sentence adverb] *formal* in spite of the fact that has just been mentioned; NEVERTHELESS: *These islands are not a popular holiday destination, but are worth considering nonetheless.* | *The region was extremely beautiful. Nonetheless Gerard could not imagine spending the rest of his life there.*

**non·e·vent** /ˌ· ·ˈ·/ *n* [C usually singular] an event that is disappointing because it is much less interesting and exciting than you expected: *The conference was a bit of a non-event – hardly anyone turned up for it.*

**non·ex·ec·u·tive di·rec·tor** /ˌ· ····· ·ˈ··/ *n* [C] one of the directors (DIRECTOR (1)) of a company who gives advice, but does not have any responsibility for how the company is managed

**non·ex·ist·ent** /ˌnɒnɪɡˈzɪstənt◂‖ˌnɑːn-/ *adj* not existing at all, or not present in a particular place: *We were expected to sit on non-existent chairs.* | *Their sex life was practically nonexistent.* —**non-existence** *n* [U]

**non·fic·tion** /ˌ· ˈ··◂/ *n* [U] books, articles etc about real facts or events, not imagined ones —**non-fiction** *adj*

**non·fi·nite** /ˌ· ˈ··/ *adj* **1** a non-finite verb is not marked to show a particular sense or subject, and is either the INFINITIVE or the PARTICIPLE form of the verb, for example 'go' in the sentence 'Do you want to go home?' **2** not having an end or limit; INFINITE —opposite FINITE

**non·flam·ma·ble** /ˌnɒnˈflæməbəl‖ˌnɑːn-/ *adj* nonflammable materials or substances do not burn easily or do not burn at all —opposite FLAMMABLE, INFLAMMABLE

**non·in·ter·ven·tion** /ˌ· ··ˈ··/ *n* [U] the practice by a government of not trying to influence or become involved in the affairs of other countries or organizations: *a policy of non-intervention in internal affairs*

**non·i·ron** /ˌ· ˈ··◂/ *adj* non-iron materials do not need to be ironed (IRON[2]) after washing

**non·ne·go·ti·a·ble** /ˌ· ·ˈ····/ *adj* **1** rights and conditions that are non-negotiable are parts of a law or contract that cannot be discussed or changed **2** a cheque that is non-negotiable can only be exchanged for money by the person whose name is on it

**no-no** /ˈ· ·/ *n* [C] *informal* something that you must not do because it is considered to be unacceptable behaviour: *Colouring your hair was a distinct no-no at that time.*

**no-non·sense** /ˌ· ˈ··◂/ *adj* [only before noun] very practical and direct, without wasting time on unnecessary and unimportant things: *His clients admired his straightforward no-nonsense attitude to business.*

**non·pa·reil** /ˈnɒnpərəl, -pəreɪl‖ˌnɑːnpəˈrel/ *n* **1 nonpareils** [plural] *AmE* very small pieces of coloured sugar used to decorate cakes **2** [C] *AmE* a piece of chocolate covered with nonpareils **3** [singular] *literary* someone or something that is much better than all the others: *reviews by film critic nonpareil Pauline Kael* —**nonpareil** *adj*

**non·par·ti·san** /ˌ· ··ˈ··◂‖ˌ· ˈ···/ *adj* not supporting the ideas of any political party or group: *a non-partisan approach to the housing problem*

**non·pay·ment** /ˌ· ˈ··/ *n* [U] failure to pay money that you owe in tax, rent etc: [+ **of**] *non-payment of rent.*

**non·plussed** also **nonplused** *AmE* /nɒnˈplʌst‖nɑːn-/ *adj* so surprised by something that you do not know what to say or do: *He stood, nonplussed, the letter still in his hand.*

**non·prof·it·mak·ing** /ˌnɒnˈprɒfɪtmeɪkɪŋ‖ˌnɑːnˈprɑː-/ *BrE*, **non·prof·it** /ˌ· ˈ··/ *AmE adj* a non-profitmaking organization uses the money it earns to help people

**non·pro·lif·e·ra·tion** /ˌ· ···ˈ··/ *n* [U] the aim of limiting the number of NUCLEAR or CHEMICAL WEAPONS in the world, especially by stopping countries that do not yet have them from developing them: *the nuclear non-proliferation treaty*

**non·re·new·a·ble** /ˌ· ·ˈ···◂/ *adj* non-renewable types of energy such as coal or gas cannot be replaced after they have been used: *the diminishing non-renewable resource of coal*

**non·res·i·dent** /· ˈ···/ *n* [C] **1** someone who is not staying in a particular hotel: *The hotel restaurant is open to non-residents.* **2** someone who is not living in a particular place or country —**non-resident** *adj*

**non·res·i·den·tial** /ˌnɒnrezɪˈdenʃəl◂‖ˌnɑːn-/ *adj* not providing somewhere for people to live or stay at night: *The course is nonresidential.* | *nonresidential care for the elderly*

**non-re·strict·ive** /ˌ· ˈ··◂/ *adj technical* a non-restrictive RELATIVE CLAUSE gives additional information about a particular person or thing rather than saying which person or thing is being mentioned, for example in the sentence 'Perry, who is 22, was arrested yesterday.', the phrase 'who is 22' is a non-restrictive clause

S3 **non·sense** /ˈnɒnsəns‖ˈnɑːnsens/ *n* [U]
**1 ▶ STUPID/UNTRUE ◀** [U] ideas, opinions, statements etc that are untrue or stupid: *all this nonsense about health foods | "She says she's 39." "Nonsense!"* | **a load of nonsense** (=a lot of nonsense) *If you ask me, these modern teaching methods are a load of nonsense.* | **talk nonsense**: *He was talking utter nonsense as usual.* | **be a nonsense**: *The whole idea's a complete nonsense.*
**2 ▶ WITHOUT MEANING ◀** speech or writing that has no meaning or cannot be understood: *Computer programs look like complete nonsense to me.*
**3 nonsense poems/verse** poetry that is humorous because it does not have a normal sensible meaning
**4 ▶ ANNOYING BEHAVIOUR ◀** behaviour that is stupid and annoying: *I wish they'd stop all this nonsense and be nice to each other for a change.* | **not stand any nonsense** (=be very strict) *She won't stand any nonsense from the kids in her class.*
**5 make (a) nonsense of** *BrE* to show that a previous action or idea was useless and had no meaning: *Having the army still in power makes a nonsense of last year's democratic elections.*

**non·sen·si·cal** /nɒnˈsensɪkəl‖nɑːn-/ *adj* not reasonable or sensible: *nonsensical ideas* —**nonsensically** /-kli/ *adv*

**non seq·ui·tur** /ˌnɒn ˈsekwɪtə‖ˌnɑːnˈsekwɪtər/ *n* [C] a statement which does not seem to be connected in a reasonable or sensible way with what was said before

**non-shrink** /ˌ· ˈ·◂/ *adj* non-shrink materials do not become smaller when they are washed

**non-smok·er** /ˌ· ˈ··/ *n* [C] someone who does not smoke

**non-smok·ing** /ˌ· ˈ··◂/ *adj* a non-smoking area is one where you are not allowed to smoke

**non-stan·dard** /ˌ· ˈ··◂/ *adj* **1** not the usual size or type: *a non-standard disk size* **2** non-standard words, expressions, or pronunciations are not usually considered to be correct by educated speakers of a language, for example 'gotta' in the sentence 'I gotta go.'

**non·start·er** /ˌnɒnˈstɑːtə‖ˌnɑːnˈstɑːrtər/ *n* [C] **1** [usually singular] *informal* a person, idea, or plan that has no chance of success: *The whole thing sounds like a nonstarter to me.* **2** a horse that is supposed to take part in a race but does not run

**non-stick** /ˌ· ˈ·◂/ *adj* a non-stick cooking pan has a special inside surface which prevents food from sticking to it

**non·stop** /ˌnɒnˈstɒp◂‖ˌnɑːnˈstɑːp◂/ *adj, adv* without stopping: *She talked nonstop for over an hour.* | *a non-stop flight to Los Angeles*

**non·such** /ˈnʌnsʌtʃ/ *n* [singular] another spelling of NONESUCH

**non-u·nion** /ˌ· ˈ··◂/ *adj* [usually before noun] **1** not belonging to a TRADE UNION (=official organization for workers) *non-union members* **2** not officially accepting TRADE UNIONS, or not employing their members: *non-union factories* —**non-unionized** *adj*

**non·ver·bal** /ˌnɒnˈvɜːbəl◂‖ˌnɑːnˈvɜːr-/ *adj* not using words: *non-verbal communication* —**nonverbally** *adv*

**non-vi·o·lence** /ˌ· ˈ···/ *n* [U] political opposition without fighting, shown especially by not obeying laws or orders: *Gandhi's policy of non-violence and negotiation* —**non-violent** *adj*: *non-violent protests* —**non-violently** *adv*

**non-white** /ˌ· ˈ·/ *n* [C] *especially SAfrE* someone who does not belong to a white race —**non-white** /ˌ· ˈ·◂/ *adj*

**noo·dle** /ˈnuːdl/ *n* **1 noodles** [plural] long thin pieces of food made from a mixture of flour, water, and eggs, usually cooked in soup or boiling water: *egg noodles* **2** [C] *old-fashioned* a silly person **3** [C] *AmE old-fashioned* your head or brain: *Use your noodle!*

**nook** /nʊk/ *n* [C] **1** a small quiet place which is sheltered by a rock, a big tree etc: *a shady nook* **2** a small space in a corner of a room: *a cozy little nook next to the fireplace* **3 nook and cranny** every part of a place: *We searched every nook and cranny.*

**nook·ie** /ˈnʊki/ *n* [U] *humorous* the activity of having sex

**noon** /nuːn/ *n* [U] 12 o'clock in the daytime; MIDDAY: *We left home at noon.* | *He rarely gets up before noon.* —see also **morning, noon and night** (MORNING [1] (5))

**noon·day** /ˈnuːndeɪ/ *adj literary* happening or appearing at noon: *in the heat of the noonday sun*

**no one** /ˈ· ·/ *pron* not anyone; NOBODY: *No one likes being criticized.* | *There's no-one else I really want to invite apart from you.* | *I see no one new has joined the department in my absence.* | *No one can say I didn't warn you.* —see EACH[1] (USAGE) S1 W2

**noose** /nuːs/ *n* **1** [C] a ring formed by the end of a piece of rope or string, which closes more tightly as it is pulled **2 the noose** punishment by hanging: *The outlaws managed to escape the hangman's noose.*

**nope** /nəʊp‖noʊp/ *adv spoken* used to say 'no' when you answer someone: *"Hungry?" "Nope, I just ate."* S3

**no place** /ˈ· ·/ *adv informal, especially AmE* nowhere: *There's no place left to hide.*

**nor'-** /nɔː‖nɔːr/ *prefix* a prefix meaning 'north', used especially by sailors: *nor'east* | *nor'west*

**nor[1]** /nɔː‖nɔːr/ *conjunction* **1 neither... nor...** used when two states, facts, actions etc are mentioned and both are not true or not possible: *He can neither read nor write.* | *Hilary was neither shocked nor surprised by the news.* **2** *formal* used after a negative statement to mean 'and not something else too': *I wasn't very impressed by his replies, nor his reasons.* S2 W1

**nor[2]** *adv* **1 nor can I/nor does John etc** *especially BrE* used to add a negative statement to one that has just been mentioned: *She couldn't work out the answer, and nor could I.* **2** *formal* used to emphasize or add information to a negative statement: *I don't expect children to be rude, nor do I expect to be disobeyed.* | *I am not, nor have I ever been a wealthy man.* —see also NEITHER

**Nor·dic** /ˈnɔːdɪk‖ˈnɔːr-/ *adj* from or connected with the Northern European countries of Denmark, Norway, Sweden, Iceland, and Finland: *Nordic beauty*

**norm** /nɔːm‖nɔːrm/ *n* **1** [C] the usual or normal situation, way of doing something etc: *Joyce's style of writing was a striking departure from the literary norm.* | **be the norm** *Short term contracts are now the norm with some big companies.* **2 norms** [plural] generally accepted standards of social behaviour: *terrorists who violate the norms of civilized society*

**nor·mal** /ˈnɔːməl‖ˈnɔːr-/ *adj* **1** not unusual in any way, but happening just as you would expect: *normal working hours* | **it is normal for sb to do sth** *In the West it's becoming quite normal for couples to live together before they are married.* | **back to normal** *Train services are back to normal again after the strike.* | **above/below normal** *The rainfall has been below normal for this time of year.* **2** a normal person, especially a child, is physically and mentally healthy and does not behave strangely: *a normal healthy baby* | **perfectly normal** *He seems a perfectly normal little boy.* —compare ABNORMAL S1 W1

**nor·mal·i·ty** /nɔːˈmælɪti‖nɔːr-/ also **nor·mal·cy** /ˈnɔːməlsi‖ˈnɔːr-/ *AmE* —*n* [U] a situation in which things happen in the usual or expected way: *a return to normality* | *a comforting sense of normality*

**nor·mal·ize** also **-ise** *BrE* /ˈnɔːməlaɪz‖ˈnɔːr-/ *v* [I,T] if you normalize a situation, or if it normalizes, it becomes normal again: **normalize relations** (=start having a normal friendly relationship with a country again after a period of war or disagreement) —**normalization** /ˌnɔːməlaɪˈzeɪʃən‖ˌnɔːrmələ-/ *n* [U]

**nor·mal·ly** /ˈnɔːməli‖ˈnɔːr-/ *adv* **1** *especially BrE* usually, or under normal conditions: [sentence adverb] *Normally, I get home about 6 o'clock.* | *The illness normally lasts about a week or ten days.* **2** in a normal ordinary way: *The patient started breathing normally again.* S1 W2

**Nor·man** /ˈnɔːmən‖ˈnɔːr-/ *adj* **1** built in the style that was popular during the 11th and 12th centuries in Europe: *a Norman church* **2** connected with the Normans, the northern French people who took control of England in the 11th century

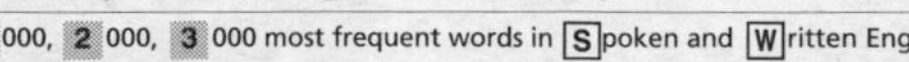

**nor·ma·tive** /ˈnɔːmətɪv‖ˈnɔːr-/ *adj formal* describing or establishing a set of rules or standards of behaviour: *a normative social structure*

**Norse** /nɔːs‖nɔːrs/ *adj* connected with the people of ancient Scandinavia or their language: *Norse legends*

**Norse·man** /ˈnɔːsmən‖ˈnɔːrs-/ *n* [C] *literary* a VIKING

S1 W2 **north¹, North** /nɔːθ‖nɔːrθ/ written abbreviation **N** *n* [singular, U] **1** the direction that is at the top of a map of the world, above the EQUATOR, and is on the left of a person facing the rising sun: *Which way is north?* | **from/towards the north** *a strong wind was blowing from the north* | **to the north (of)** *Cheshunt is a few miles to the north of London.* | **in the north** *A strange light appeared in the north.* | *The wind is in the north.* (=is coming from the north) **2 the North a)** the northern part of a country: *The North will be dry and bright.* | *in the north of England* **b)** the northeastern states of the US, which fought against the South in the American Civil War **c)** the richer countries of the world, especially Europe and N America

**north²** written abbreviation **N** *adj* **1** in the north or facing the north: *The north side of the building doesn't get much sun.* | *He lives in North Wales.* **2** a north wind comes from the north

**north³** written abbreviation **N** *adv* **1** towards the north: *The birds fly north in summer.* | *Chicago is four hours north of Indianapolis.* | *a north-facing window* **2 up north** *informal* to or in the north of the country: *They've moved up north.*

**north·bound** /ˈnɔːθbaʊnd‖ˈnɔːrθ-/ *adj* travelling or leading towards the north: *a northbound bus* | *the northbound lane of the A1*

**north·east¹** /ˌnɔːθˈiːst◂‖ˌnɔːrθ-/ written abbreviation **NE** *n* [U] **1** the direction that is exactly between north and east **2 the northeast** the northeastern part of a country —**northeast** *adv*: *This road goes northeast.*

**northeast²** written abbreviation **NE** *adj* **1** a northeast wind comes from the northeast **2** in the northeast of a place: *the northeast outskirts of Las Vegas*

**north·east·er** /ˌnɔːθˈiːstə‖ˌnɔːrθˈiːstər/ *n* [C] a strong wind or storm coming from the northeast

**north·east·er·ly** /ˌnɔːθˈiːstəli‖ˌnɔːrθˈiːstərli/ *adj* **1** towards or in the northeast: *They set off in a northeasterly direction.* **2** a northeasterly wind comes from the northeast

**north·east·ern** /ˌnɔːθˈiːstən‖ˌnɔːrθˈiːstərn/ *adj* in or from the northeast part of a country or area: *the northeastern states of the US*

**north·east·wards** /ˌnɔːθˈiːstwədz‖ˌnɔːrθˈiːstwərdz/ also **northeastward** —*adv* towards the northeast —**northeastward** *adj*

**nor·ther·ly** /ˈnɔːðəli‖ˈnɔːrðərli/ *adj* **1** towards or in the north: *a northerly direction* **2** a northerly wind comes from the north

S2 W2 **nor·thern** /ˈnɔːðən‖ˈnɔːrðərn/ *adj* in or from the north of a country or area: *a man with a northern accent* | *Northern Europe*

**nor·thern·er** /ˈnɔːðənə‖ˈnɔːrðərnər/ *n* [C] someone who comes from the northern part of a country

**northern hem·is·phere** /ˌ·· ˈ···/ *n* [singular] the half of the world that is north of the EQUATOR —see picture at EARTH

**Northern Lights** /ˌ·· ˈ·/ *n* [plural] bands of coloured light that are seen in the night sky in the most northern parts of the world; AURORA BOREALIS

**nor·thern·most** /ˈnɔːðənməʊst‖ˈnɔːrðərnmoʊst/ *adj* furthest north: *the northernmost tip of the island*

**North Pole** /ˌ· ˈ·/ *n* [singular] the most northern point on the surface of the earth, or the area around it —see also SOUTH POLE —see picture at EARTH

**north·wards** /ˈnɔːθwədz‖ˈnɔːrθwərdz/ also **northward** —*adv* towards the north: *We sailed northward.* —**northward** *adj*

**northwest¹** /ˌnɔːθˈwest◂‖ˌnɔːrθ-/ written abbreviation **NW** *n* [U] **1** the direction that is exactly between north and west **2 the northwest** the northwestern part of a country —**northwest** *adv*: *The house faces northwest.*

**northwest²** written abbreviation **NW** *adj* **1** a northwest wind comes from the northwest **2** in the northwest of a place: *the northwest suburbs of the city*

**north·west·er** /ˌnɔːθˈwestə‖ˌnɔːrθˈwestər/ *n* [C] a strong wind or storm coming from the northwest

**north·west·er·ly** /ˌnɔːθˈwestəli‖ˌnɔːrθˈwestərli/ *adj* **1** towards or in the northwest **2** a northwesterly wind comes from the northwest

**north·west·ern** /ˌnɔːθˈwestən‖ˌnɔːrθˈwestərn/ *adj* in or from the northwest part of a country or area: *northwestern Canada*

**north·west·wards** /ˌnɔːθˈwestwədz‖ˌnɔːrθˈwestwərdz/ also **northwestward** —*adv* towards the northwest

**nos.** the written abbreviation of numbers: *nos. 17-33*

**nose¹** /nəʊz‖noʊz/ *n* 

**1 ▶ ON YOUR FACE ◀** [C] the part of your face that you smell with and breathe through: *a broken nose* | *Marty punched him on the nose.* | **blow your nose** (=clear it by blowing strongly into a piece of cloth or soft paper) *Here, take this hanky and blow your nose.* —see picture at HEAD ¹

**2 red-nosed/long-nosed etc** having a nose that is red, long etc

**3 (right) under sb's nose** so close to someone that they ought to notice, but they do not: *The drugs were smuggled in right under the noses of security guards.*

**4 stick/poke your nose into** to show too much interest in private matters that do not concern you: *She always has to stick her nose into everything, doesn't she?* —see also NOSY

**5 keep your nose out (of)** *spoken* to stop showing too much interest in private matters that do not concern you: *I'd prefer you to keep your nose right out of my business!*

**6 turn your nose up (at)** *informal* to refuse to accept something because you do not think it is good enough for you: *My children turn their noses up at home cooking.*

**7 look down your nose at** *informal* to behave as if you think someone or something is not good enough for you: *The Taggarts have always looked down their noses at their neighbours.*

**8 with your nose in the air** behaving as if you are more important than other people and not talking to them: *Maria flounced past with her nose in the air.*

**9 have a nose round** *BrE spoken* to look around a place or to look for something: *Let's have a nose round while there's no one here.*

**10 have a (good) nose (for) a)** to be naturally good at finding and recognizing something: [+ **for**] *a reporter with a nose for a story* **b)** to be good at recognizing smells: *a dog with a good nose*

**11 get up sb's nose** *BrE spoken* to annoy someone very much: *His manner really gets up my nose.*

**12 follow your nose** to keep going straight ahead: *Turn left at the post office and then just follow your nose.*

**13 keep your nose clean** *spoken* to make sure you do not get into trouble, or do anything wrong or illegal

**14 on the nose** *AmE spoken* exactly: *Guess how much I paid. That's right; $50 on the nose!*

**15 keep your nose to the grindstone** *informal* to work very hard, without stopping to rest

**16 have your nose in a book** to be giving all your attention to what you are reading

**17 by a nose** if a horse wins a race by a nose, it only just wins

**18 put sb's nose out of joint** *informal* to annoy someone, especially by attracting everyone's attention away from them

**19 nose to tail** *especially BrE* cars, buses etc that are nose to tail are moving very slowly without much space between them: *Traffic was nose to tail for three miles.*

**20 ▶ PLANE ◀** [C] the pointed front end of a plane, ROCKET etc —see picture at AIRCRAFT —see also HARD-NOSED, BROWN-NOSE, **cut off your nose to spite your face** (CUT¹ (8)), NOSE JOB¹, **pay through the nose** (PAY¹ (13)), **powder your nose** (POWDER² (3)), **thumb your nose at** (THUMB² (2))

**nose**[2] *v* **1** [I always + adv/prep] *informal* to try to find out things about other people in a way that is annoying: **nose about** *BrE*/**around/into** *The landlady was nosing around the house while we were out.* | *Stop nosing into my affairs!* **2** [I always + adv/prep, T always + adv/prep] if a vehicle, boat etc noses forward, or if you nose it forward, it moves forward slowly: [**+ out/through etc**] *The boat nosed out into Nantucket Sound.* | **nose sth out/through etc** *She carefully nosed the car forward through the traffic.*

**nose** sth ↔ **out** *phr v* [T] *informal* to discover information by searching carefully for a long time: *The reporters have nosed out some interesting facts about the politician's past life.*

**nose·bag** /ˈnəʊzbæg‖ˈnoʊz-/ *n* [C] a bag that holds food and can be hung around a horse's head; FEEDBAG *AmE*

**nose·bleed** /ˈnəʊzbliːd‖ˈnoʊz-/ *n* [C] **have a nosebleed** to have blood coming out of your nose

**nose·cone** /ˈnəʊzkəʊn‖ˈnoʊzkoʊn/ *n* [C] the pointed front part of a MISSILE

**nose·dive**[1] /ˈnəʊzdaɪv‖ˈnoʊz-/ *n* [C] **1** a sudden drop in amount, price, rate etc: *The pound took a nosedive on the foreign exchange market today.* **2** a sudden steep drop made by a plane with its front end pointing towards the ground: *Everyone screamed as the plane suddenly went into a nosedive.*

**nosedive**[2] *v* [I] **1** if a price, rate, amount etc nosedives, it becomes smaller or reduces in value suddenly **2** if a plane nosedives, it drops suddenly and steeply with its front end pointing towards the ground

**nose·gay** /ˈnəʊzgeɪ‖ˈnoʊz-/ *n* [C] *old-fashioned* a small arrangement of flowers

**nose job** /ˈ· ·/ *n* [C] *informal* a medical operation on someone's nose to improve its appearance

**nos·ey** /ˈnəʊzi‖ˈnoʊ-/ *adj* another spelling of NOSY

**nosh**[1] /nɒʃ‖nɑːʃ/ *n informal* **1** [U] *BrE* food: *They serve good nosh there.* **2** [singular] *BrE* a meal **3** [singular] *AmE* a small amount of food eaten between meals; SNACK

**nosh**[2] *v* [I] *informal* to eat

**no-show** /ˌ· ˈ·/ *n* [C] someone who is expected to arrive somewhere, for example at a restaurant or plane, but does not arrive: *How many no-shows were there?* —**no-show** *v* [I,T] *AmE.*

**nosh-up** /ˈ· ·/ *n* [singular] *BrE informal* a big satisfying meal

**nos·tal·gia** /nɒˈstældʒə‖nɑː-/ *n* [U] the slightly sad feeling of remembering happy events or experiences from the past: *He thought with nostalgia of his carefree childhood.* | [**+ for**] *nostalgia for the good old days*

**nos·tal·gic** /nɒˈstældʒɪk‖nɑː-/ *adj* feeling or expressing a slight sadness when remembering happy events or experiences from the past: *Seeing those old school photographs has made me quite nostalgic.* | *a nostalgic look back at the 1950s* —**nostalgically** /-kli/ *adv*

**nos·tril** /ˈnɒstrəl‖ˈnɑː-/ *n* [C] one of the two openings at the end of your nose, through which you breathe and smell things —see picture at HEAD[1]

**nos·trum** /ˈnɒstrəm‖ˈnɑː-/ *n* [C] **1** *formal* an idea that someone thinks will solve a problem easily, but probably will not help at all: *an economic nostrum* **2** *old-fashioned* a medicine that is probably not effective and is not given by a doctor

**nos·y, nosey** /ˈnəʊzi‖ˈnoʊ-/ *adj* always wanting to find out things that do not concern you, especially other people's private affairs: *Don't be so nosy! It's none of your business.* —**nosiness** *n* [U]

**nosy park·er** /ˌ·· ˈ··/ *n* [C] *BrE informal* a nosy person

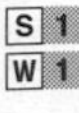

**not** /nɒt‖nɑːt/ *adv* **1** used to make a word or expression negative: *"Can we go to the park?" "No, not today, dear."* | *Lorna was not a tidy child and left toys everywhere.* | *The store is open all week but not on Sundays.* | *Sally will not eat meat.* | *You were wrong not to inform the police.* | **not at all easy/difficult etc** *I was not at all surprised to see her at the meeting.* | **not at all** *I don't like his attitude at all.* —compare NO[1] —see also -N'T —see NO[2] (USAGE) **2** used instead of a word or expression to mean the opposite of something that has been mentioned before it: *Are you ready to eat or not?* | *I hope to see you tomorrow, but if not, leave me a message.* | **hope/think/be afraid etc not** *"Is Fiona coming?" "I hope not, she's so boring."* | *I asked if she would be able to help out but she said not.* —compare SO[1] (4) **3** used to give a word or expression the opposite meaning: *"Will the journey take much longer?" "Oh, it's not far now."* | *Madeline is such a caring person, not without problems of her own.* | *In the war years diptheria was not an uncommon disease.* | *They want a cheap service but they're not slow to complain if the trains break down.* | **not very tall/expensive etc** (=fairly short, cheap etc) *These teabags aren't very good, are they?* | **not a little/a few etc** (=quite a lot) *He drank not a little of the wine.* | **not a lot/much/many etc** (=only a few/a little etc) *It's a new remedy for hay fever which not many people have heard of.* **4 not a/not one** not any person or thing: *Since she went abroad she hasn't even written a letter, not one word!* | **not even a** *Her face was stony, not even a smile.* | **not a single** *He has none of his savings left, not a single penny!* **5 not at all** *especially BrE* used to be polite when someone has thanked you or asked you to do something: *"Would you mind helping me with my suitcase?" "Not at all."* **6 not only** used to say that besides someone doing one thing they have also done something else: **not only...but (also)...** *Shakespeare was not only a writer but also an actor.* | **not only do/will/can etc** *Not only do the nurses want a pay increase, they want reduced hours as well.* **7 not that I care/not that it is important etc** used to mean that you do not care, that it is not important etc: *Sarah's found herself a new boyfriend – not that I care about it.* **8 – not!** *spoken* used, especially by young people, to say that you really mean the opposite of what you have just said: *I really like spending my Saturday afternoons tidying the house – not!* —see also **not half** (HALF[3] (5)), **not to say** (SAY[1] (43))

**USAGE NOTE: NOT**

FORMALITY

In spoken English and informal writing **not** is usually shortened to **n't** with *is, are, was, were, has, have, had, do, does etc. Shall not* becomes *shan't,* and *will not* becomes *won't.* (Note however that **shan't** is only used in British English).

SPELLING

The short form of **not** is **n't** not *'nt.*

**Can** with the full form **not** is written as one word: *The two sides in the dispute still cannot reach an agreement.* | *I simply cannot understand what he's talking about.*

**no·ta·bil·i·ty** /ˌnəʊtəˈbɪləti‖ˌnoʊ-/ *n* [C usually plural] *formal* an important person

**no·ta·ble** /ˈnəʊtəbəl‖ˈnoʊ-/ *adj* important, interesting, excellent, or unusual and therefore deserving to be noticed or mentioned: *a notable achievement* | *a notable lack of enthusiasm* | [**+ for**] *The book is notable for its striking illustrations.* | **a notable example/exception etc** *Most birds sing only in daylight, one notable exception being the nightingale.*

**no·ta·bles** /ˈnəʊtəbəlz‖ˈnoʊ-/ *n* [plural] important or famous people

**no·ta·bly** /ˈnəʊtəbli/ *adv* **1** particularly; especially: *Some early doctors, notably Hippocrates, thought that diet and hygiene were important.* **2** in a way that is noticeably different, important, or unusual: *Emigration has notably increased.* W3

**no·ta·rize** also **-ise** *BrE* /ˈnəʊtəraɪz‖ˈnoʊ-/ *v* [T often passive] if a notary notarizes a document or written statement they make it official

**no·ta·ry** /ˈnəʊtəri‖ˈnoʊ-/ also **notary pub·lic** /ˌ·· ˈ··/ *n* [C] someone, especially a lawyer, who has the legal power to make a signed statement or document official

**no·ta·tion** /nəʊˈteɪʃən‖noʊ-/ *n* [C,U] a system of written marks or signs used to represent something such as music, mathematics, or scientific ideas

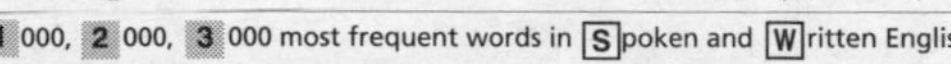

**notch¹** /nɒtʃ‖nɑːtʃ/ *n* [C] **1** a V-shaped cut in a surface or edge: *He made three notches in the stick.* **2** a degree or level on a scale of achievement, social position etc: *Her new book is several notches above anything else she has written.* **3** *AmE* a passage between two mountains or hills —see also TOP-NOTCH

**notch²** *v* [T] to cut a usually V-shaped mark into something, especially as a way of showing the number of times something has been done

**notch** sth ↔ **up** *phr v* [T] to achieve something, especially a victory or a particular total or SCORE: *The Houston Astros have notched up another win.*

S1 W1 **note¹** /nəʊt‖noʊt/ *n*

**1 ▶TO REMIND YOU◀** [C] something that is written down to remind you of something you need to do, say, or remember: *I'll write myself a note so I don't forget to ring the bank.*|*She gave a brilliant speech – and without any notes.*|**make a note of sth** (=write something down so that you can look at it later) *I made a note of her address and phone number.*

**2 ▶SHORT LETTER◀** [C] a short, usually informal letter: *There was a note on the table – 'Gone to movies – Back about 11:30'*|**thank-you note** (=a note to thank someone for a present etc)

**3 ▶FOR STUDYING◀ notes** [plural] pages written by a student containing information from a book, lesson etc: *There is no textbook, so you must rely on your lecture notes.*|**take/make notes** (=write notes) *She sat quietly in the corner making careful notes.*

**4 ▶MUSIC◀** [C] **a)** a particular musical sound or PITCH² (3a): *She has a good voice but has trouble hitting the high notes.* **b)** a sign in a piece of music that represents a particular musical sound or pitch and that is of a particular length —see picture at MUSIC **c) the black/white notes** the black or white KEYS of a piano

**5 ▶MONEY◀** [C] *BrE* a piece of paper that is used as money: BILL¹ (3) *AmE*: *Alice took out a ten-pound note.*

**6 ▶VOICE◀** [singular] if there is a particular note in someone's voice, they show what they are thinking or feeling by the way their voice sounds: *There was a strained note in Fischer's normally relaxed voice.*|**a note of anger/jealousy/anxiety etc** *I detected a note of jealousy in his voice.*

**7 ▶PARTICULAR QUALITY◀** [singular] something that adds a particular quality to a situation, statement, or event: *Her story brought a personal note to the debate on child care.*|**a note of humour/sadness/dissent etc** *We need to add a note of caution to such optimism.*

**8 ▶ADDITIONAL INFORMATION◀** [C] a short piece of writing at the bottom of a page or at the end of a book, that gives more information about something written in the main part: *the notes at the back of the book*

**9 ▶LETTER◀** [C] a formal letter between governments: *a diplomatic note*

**10 of note:** important or famous: *The school has produced several architects of note.*

**11 worthy/deserving of note** important or interesting and deserving to be noticed: *History has been called 'the record of what one age finds worthy of note in another'.*

**12 take note** to pay careful attention to something: [+ **of**] *People were beginning to take note of her talents.*

**13 hit/strike the right/wrong note** to succeed or not succeed in being right and suitable for a particular occasion —see also **compare notes** (COMPARE¹ (6))

**note²** *v* [T] *formal* **1** to notice or pay careful attention to something: **note that** *Please note that the bill must be paid within ten days.*|**note sth** *The children should be encouraged to note the colours and textures of the fabrics.*|**note who/what/how etc** *I noted how her face reddened every time Ben's name was mentioned.* **2** to mention something because it is important or interesting: *The report noted a complete disregard for the safety regulations.*|**note that** *We have already noted that soybeans are a good source of protein.* **3** also **note down** to write something down so that it will be remembered: *Note any adverse reaction to the medication on the chart.*

**note·book** /ˈnəʊtbʊk‖ˈnoʊt-/ *n* [C] **1** a book made of plain paper on which you can write notes **2** a very small PERSONAL COMPUTER that is the size of a book —see picture on page 837

**note card** /ˈ· ·/ *n* [C] *AmE* a NOTELET

**not·ed** /ˈnəʊtɪ̣d‖ˈnoʊ-/ *adj* well known, especially because of some special quality or ability: *restaurants noted for the excellence of their cuisine*

**note·let** /ˈnəʊtlɪ̣t‖ˈnoʊt-/ *n* [C] *BrE* a small folded piece of paper with a picture on it, for writing a short letter; NOTECARD *AmE*

**note·pad** /ˈnəʊtpæd‖ˈnoʊt-/ *n* [C] a number of sheets of paper fastened together at the top, used for writing notes

**note·pa·per** /ˈnəʊtˌpeɪpə‖ˈnoʊtˌpeɪpər/ *n* [U] paper used for writing letters etc: **headed notepaper** (=with someone's address printed on it)

**note·wor·thy** /ˈnəʊtˌwɜːði‖ˈnoʊtˌwɜːr-/ *adj* something such as an event that is noteworthy deserves attention because it is important, interesting, or unusual: *a noteworthy achievement*|*a noteworthy piece of architecture*

**not-for-prof·it** /ˌ· ·ˈ··/ *adj AmE* NON-PROFITMAKING

**noth·ing¹** /ˈnʌθɪŋ/ *pron* **1** not anything; no thing: S1 W1 *Nothing ever happens in this town.*|*There's nothing in this box. Throw it away.*|*He said nothing about it to me.*|**nothing new/bad etc** *Why are you still in bed when there's nothing wrong with you?*|**nothing to do/to eat etc** *If you have nothing to do how about helping me in the garden?*|**nothing else** (=nothing more) *I had nothing else to say so I signed the letter.*|**nothing at all** (=absolutely nothing) *You must eat nothing at all before the operation.* **2** something which is considered unimportant, not interesting or not worth worrying about: *A harmless kiss. It meant nothing.*|*It's nothing, just a scratch.*|*There's nothing on television tonight.*|*It was nothing for a family to have ten children in those days.* **3** *especially AmE* zero: *We beat them ten to nothing.* **4 for nothing a)** without paying for something or being paid for something: *Why pay a plumber when my brother will do it for nothing*|*She knows the club manager so we always get in for nothing.* **b)** without having a good reason or purpose: *We went all that way for nothing.*|*They don't call him Babyface Dickson for nothing!* **5 have/be nothing to do with sb/sth** [not in progressive] **a)** if something has nothing to do with a particular fact or situation it is not connected with that fact or situation: *Our decision has nothing to do with the fact that her father is on the committee.* **b)** if a situation has nothing to do with someone, it is personal and private: *It's nothing to do with you. Mind your own business.* **6 have/want nothing to do with** to not be involved in something, especially because you disapprove: *He told the police that he had wanted nothing to do with the whole thing.* **7 nothing special** not very bad and not very good; average: *The meal was nothing special, just a little fish with a cheese sauce.* **8 nothing but** *formal* only: *He's nothing but a common criminal.* **9 nothing much** very little: *"What did you do last weekend?" "Oh, nothing much."* **10 there's nothing like** used to say that something is very good: *There's nothing like a long hot bath after a day's climbing.* **11 there's nothing in/to sth** used to say that what people are saying about someone else's personal life is not true: *It seems there's nothing in the rumours that she's pregnant.* **12 there's nothing for it but to do sth** used when there is only one thing you can do in a particular situation: *With the bridge destroyed there was nothing for it but to swim.* **13 nothing doing** *spoken* used to refuse to do something: *Lend you £500? Nothing doing!* **14 be nothing if not** used to emphasize a particular quality that someone or something has: *You've got to admit – he's nothing if not persistent.* **15 nothing to it** *spoken* used when something is easy to do: *Anyone can use a computer. There's nothing to it!* **16 it was nothing/think nothing of it** *spoken* used when someone has thanked you a

lot for something you have done for them: *"You really shouldn't have gone to so much trouble" "Oh, think nothing of it."* **17 nothing of the sort** *spoken* used to strongly refuse to do something or when you feel strongly that something is not true: *What do you mean you're going to borrow my car? You'll do nothing of the sort!* —see also **sweet nothings** (SWEET[1] (12)), **to say nothing of** (SAY[1] (47)) **nothing on earth** (EARTH[1] (11))

**nothing**[2] *adv* **1 be nothing like sb/sth** to have no qualities or features that are similar to someone or something else: *She's nothing like her brother. He's dark and she's fair.* **2 be nothing short of sth** if someone's behaviour is nothing short of something such as laziness, corruption etc, they are extremely lazy or corrupt: *His behaviour was nothing short of rudeness.*

**noth·ing·ness** /ˈnʌθɪŋnɪ̟s/ *n* [U] **1** empty space or the complete absence of everything: *Natalie found him standing very still, looking into nothingness.* **2** the state of not existing: *Is there only nothingness after death?*

S1 W2 **no·tice**[1] /ˈnəʊtɪ̟s‖ˈnoʊ-/ *v* [I, T not in progressive] **1** to see, hear, or feel something: *He spilled the tea, but Miss Whitley did not notice.* | **notice sth/sb** *You may notice a numb feeling in your fingers.* | **notice that** *Catherine noticed that Isabella was restless.* | **notice who/what/how etc** *He was too tired even to notice how hungry and thirsty he was.* | **notice sb/sth doing sth** *Did you notice him leaving the party early?* **2 be/get noticed** to get attention from someone: *a young actress trying to get herself noticed*

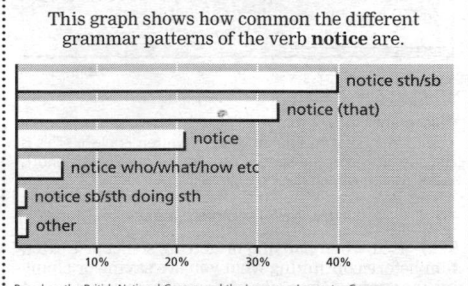

This graph shows how common the different grammar patterns of the verb **notice** are.

| Pattern | Approx. frequency |
|---|---|
| notice sth/sb | ~40% |
| notice (that) | ~30% |
| notice | ~20% |
| notice who/what/how etc | ~6% |
| notice sb/sth doing sth | ~1% |
| other | ~1% |

10% 20% 30% 40%

Based on the British National Corpus and the Longman Lancaster Corpus

S2 W2 **notice**[2] *n*
**1 take notice (of)** to pay attention to something or someone and let them affect or influence you: **not take any notice/take no notice** *I keep complaining but nobody takes any notice.* | *Take no notice of Henry – he's just being silly.* | *I hope you'll take notice of what I'm going to tell you.*
**2 ▶ ON PAPER ◀** [C] a written or printed statement that gives information or a warning to people: *That notice on the wall says 'No smoking'.* | *I'll put up a notice about the meeting.*
**3 ▶ WARNING/TIME TO PREPARE ◀** [U] information or a warning about something that is going to happen: *These rules are subject to change without notice.* | **ten days' notice/three months' notice etc** (=a warning ten days etc before) *Either party may terminate the contract upon three month's notice.* | **at short notice/at a moment's notice** (=allowing only a short time to prepare for something): *You can't expect me to produce a meal at a moment's notice.* | **give sb some notice** *If they'd given me more notice, I'd have had everything ready.* | **serve notice** *formal* (=officially warn someone that something is going to happen)
**4 give sb notice a)** to tell someone that they must leave their job in a week, a month etc: *They closed the factory, giving the workers only a week's notice.* **b)** to tell someone officially that they must leave the place they are renting by a particular date | **give sb notice to quit/leave** *BrE*: *I've been given notice to leave my flat.*
**5 hand in/give in your notice** to inform your employer that you will be leaving your job soon, especially by writing a formal letter
**6 come to sb's notice** *formal* [U] if a fact, problem etc comes to your notice, you notice it or find out about it: *It has come to my notice that your account is overdrawn by £200.* | **bring sth to sb's notice** (=tell someone about something) *There are several important matters I'd like to bring to your notice.* | **escape sb's notice** (=not be noticed by someone) *It may have escaped your notice but your father is much too ill to travel.*
**7 until further notice** from now until another change is announced: *The office is closed until further notice.*
**8 ▶ BOOK/PLAY ETC ◀** [C usually plural] a statement of opinion, especially one written for a newspaper or magazine, about a new play, book, film etc; REVIEW[1] (2): *The new play got mixed notices* (=some good, some bad) *in the newspapers* | **sit up and take notice** (SIT)

**no·tice·a·ble** /ˈnəʊtɪ̟səbəl‖ˈnoʊ-/ *adj* easy to notice: *However much he drank it had no noticeable effect on him.* | *There was a noticeable lack of interest in the idea.* | **it is noticeable that** *It was noticeable that she invited everybody except Gail.* —**noticeably** *adv*: *The atmosphere at the dinner table was noticeably less relaxed.*

**no·tice·board** /ˈnəʊtɪ̟sˌbɔːd‖ˈnoʊtɪ̟sˌbɔːrd/ *n* [C] *BrE* a special board on a wall which notices can be fixed to; BULLETIN BOARD *AmE* —see picture at BOARD[1]

**no·ti·fi·a·ble** /ˈnəʊtɪ̟faɪəbəl‖ˈnoʊ-/ *adj BrE technical* a notifiable disease is one that by law must be reported to an office of public health

**no·ti·fi·ca·tion** /ˌnəʊtɪ̟fɪ̟ˈkeɪʃən‖ˌnoʊ-/ *n* [C,U] *formal* an act of officially informing someone about something: **[+ of]** *Notification of any changes should be in writing.*

**no·ti·fy** /ˈnəʊtɪ̟faɪ‖ˈnoʊ-/ *v* [T] to formally or officially tell someone about something; inform: **notify sb of** *You will be notified of any changes in the system.*

**no·tion** /ˈnəʊʃən‖ˈnoʊ-/ *n* [C] **1** an idea, belief or opinion, especially one that is false or not very clear: **[+ of]** *misguided notions of male superiority* | *We haven't the faintest notion of her whereabouts.* | **notion that** *the notion that human beings are basically good* **2** a sudden desire to do something; WHIM: **notion to do sth** *At midnight she had a sudden notion to go to the beach.* **3 notions** [plural] *AmE* small things used for sewing W3

**no·tion·al** /ˈnəʊʃənəl‖ˈnoʊ-/ *adj* existing only in the mind as an idea or plan, and not existing in reality: *Their calculations were based on a notional minimum wage.*

**no·to·ri·e·ty** /ˌnəʊtəˈraɪəti‖ˌnoʊ-/ *n* [U] the state of being famous or well-known because of something bad: *His affairs with young actresses earned him great notoriety.*

**no·to·ri·ous** /nəʊˈtɔːriəs, nə-‖noʊ-, nə-/ *adj* famous or well-known for something bad: *a notorious bandit* | **[+ for]** *The region is notorious for its terrible snowstorms.* —**notoriously** *adv*: *a notoriously inefficient company* — see FAMOUS (USAGE)

**not·with·stand·ing** /ˌnɒtwɪθˈstændɪŋ, -wɪð-‖ˌnɑːt-/ *prep formal* in spite of something: *The government is determined to proceed with the housing policies, notwithstanding public opposition.* | *The EC nations embarked upon the trade agreement, a few exceptions notwithstanding.* —**notwithstanding** *adv*

**nou·gat** /ˈnuːgɑː‖-gət/ *n* [U] a sticky pink or white sweet made of sugar, nuts, and small pieces of fruit

**nought** /nɔːt‖nɒːt/ *n* **1** [C] *BrE* the number 0; zero: *A billion is 1 with 9 noughts after it.* **2** [U] *old use* nothing

**noughts and cross·es** /ˌ· · ˈ··/ *BrE n* [U] a game in which two players write 0 or X in a pattern of nine squares, trying to win with a row of three 0s or three Xs; TICK-TACK-TOE *AmE*

**noun** /naʊn/ *n* [C] a word or group of words that represent a person (such as 'Michael' or 'teacher' or 'police officer'), a place (such as 'France' or 'school'), a thing or activity (such as 'coffee' or 'football'), or a quality or idea (such as 'danger' or 'happiness'). Nouns can be used as the subject or object of a verb (as in 'The teacher arrived' or 'We like the teacher') or as the object of a PREPOSITION (as in 'good at football'). —see also COMMON NOUN, COUNT NOUN, PROPER NOUN, VERBAL NOUN

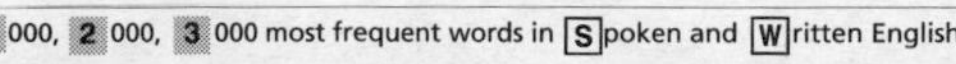

**nour·ish** /ˈnʌrɪʃ‖ˈnɜːrɪʃ, ˈnʌ-/ *v* [T] **1** to give a person or other living thing the food they need in order to live, grow, and stay healthy: *a well nourished baby* **2** *formal* to keep a feeling, idea, or belief strong or help it to grow stronger: *The beauty of the region has nourished the imagination of countless artists.*

**nour·ish·ing** /ˈnʌrɪʃɪŋ‖ˈnɜː-, ˈnʌ-/ *adj* food that is nourishing makes you strong and healthy

**nour·ish·ment** /ˈnʌrɪʃmənt‖ˈnɜːrɪʃ-, ˈnʌ-/ *n* [U] *formal* food that is needed to live, grow, and stay healthy: *The child has taken no nourishment all day.*

**nous** /naʊs‖nuːs/ *n* [U] *BrE informal* intelligence and the ability to make good practical decisions; COMMON SENSE: *She did have the nous to ring and tell us she'd be late.*

**nou·veau riche** /ˌnuːvəʊ ˈriːʃ‖-voʊ-/ *plural* **nouveaux riches** (*same pronunciation*) *n* [C] someone who has only recently become rich and spends a lot of money —**nouveau riche** *adj*

**nou·velle cui·sine** /ˌnuːvel kwɪˈziːn/ *n* [U] a style of cooking from France that uses fresh fruit and vegetables cooked in a simple way and attractively served

**Nov.** the written abbreviation of NOVEMBER

**no·va** /ˈnəʊvə‖ˈnoʊ-/ *plural* **novas** *or* **novae** /-viː/ *n* [C] a star which explodes and suddenly becomes much brighter for a short time

W3 **nov·el**[1] /ˈnɒvəl‖ˈnɑː-/ *n* [C] a long written story in which the characters and events are usually imaginary: *an Agatha Christie novel*

**novel**[2] *adj* not like anything known before and often thought of as new, unusual, and interesting: *That's a novel idea – opening an English restaurant in France.*

**nov·el·ist** /ˈnɒvələ̇st‖ˈnɑː-/ *n* [C] someone who writes novels

**no·vel·la** /nəʊˈvelə‖noʊ-/ *n* [C] a story that is shorter than a novel, but longer than a SHORT STORY

**nov·el·ty** /ˈnɒvəlti‖ˈnɑː-/ *n* **1** [C] something new and unusual which attracts people's attention and interest: *Cars were still something of a novelty at the beginning of the century.* **2** [U] the quality of being new, unusual, and interesting: *I was intrigued by the novelty of her ideas.* | **the novelty wears off** (=used to say that something gradually loses its novelty) *I enjoyed living in Paris at first but the novelty soon wore off.* **3** [C often plural] an unusual, small, cheap object, suitable to be given as a present: *Christmas novelties* | *a novelty key-ring*

**No·vem·ber** /nəʊˈvembə, nə-‖noʊˈvembər, nə-/ written abbreviation **Nov.** *n* [C,U] the 11th month of the year, between October and December: **in November** *This office opened in November 1991.* | **last/next November** *He started work here last November.* | **on November 6th** (also **on 6th November** *BrE*) *It happened on November 6th* (spoken as *on the sixth of November* or *AmE*: *on November the sixth* or *on November sixth*)

**nov·ice** /ˈnɒvə̇s‖ˈnɑː-/ *n* [C] **1** someone who has no experience in a skill, subject, or activity; beginner: *You'll have to show me what to do – I'm a complete novice.* | **a novice skier/driver etc** *The novice pilot had to take the controls.* **2** someone who has recently joined a religious group to become a MONK or NUN

**no·vi·ti·ate, noviciate** /nəʊˈvɪʃiə̇t, nə-, -ʃieɪt‖noʊˈvɪʃə̇t/ *n* [C] *technical* the period of being a novice

**No·vo·cain** /ˈnəʊvəkeɪn‖ˈnoʊ-/ *n* [U] *AmE trademark* a drug used for stopping pain during a small operation, especially on your teeth

S1 W1 **now**[1] /naʊ/ *adv* **1** at the present time: *If we leave now we'll be there before dark.* | *They now live in the city centre.* | **right now** (=exactly now): *Right now I couldn't give a damn about your broken window.* | **just now** *especially BrE* (=at the present time) *There are a lot of bargains in the shops just now.* | **up to now/until now** *It's been a good game up to now but it would be nice to see a few more goals.* | **by/before now** (=before the present time) *Sonia should be home by now. Do you think she's had an accident?* | **from now on/as of now** (=starting from now) *From now on Bill wishes to be addressed as Mr Wilson by all the staff.* | **for now** (=used when something is happening at the present time but may change in the future) *That's enough talk for now. Take a break and we'll try again after lunch.* **2** immediately: *I've already told you to clean up. I said now and I mean now.* | *The bell has rung – stop writing now.* **3** used when you know or understand something because of something you have just seen, just been told etc: *Having met the rest of the family, she now saw where he got his temper from.* **4** **3 weeks/2 years etc now** starting 3 weeks, 2 years etc ago and continuing into the future: *They've been going out together for a long time now.* | *It's been over five years now since I started working here.* | **it is now 3 weeks/2 years etc** *It's now a month since we bought the car and it's broken down three times already.* **5** **any day/minute etc now** very soon: *The guests will arrive any minute now.* **6** **(every) now and then/now and again** sometimes: *I try to buy myself something every now and then.* **7** used in stories when you mean at the time that the event or story is happening: *She blew out the candle. Now she could hear the sound of the wind howling in the trees outside.* **8** **now...now...** *literary* used to say that at one moment someone does one thing and immediately after they do something else: *The eagle glided through the sky, now rising, now swooping.*

Frequencies of the adverb **now** in spoken and written English.

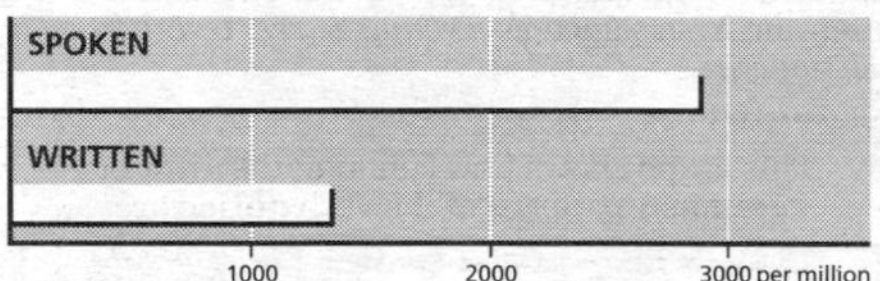


Based on the British National Corpus and the Longman Lancaster Corpus

This graph shows that the adverb **now** is much more common in spoken English than in written English. This is because it has some special uses in spoken English and is used in a lot of common spoken phrases.

**now** (*adv*) **SPOKEN PHRASES**

**9 a)** used when pausing or getting someone's attention before continuing what you are saying or changing the subject: *Now, what did you say your name was?* | *Now, let's move on to the question of payment.* **b)** used when pausing when you are thinking what to say next: *Now, let's see, oh yes – they wanted to know what time you'll be back on Friday.* **c)** used to say that if the situation was different, something different would happen: *Now, if I'd been in charge there's no way I'd have let them use the van.* **d)** used to make someone calm or comfort them when they are angry, upset etc: *Come on now, don't cry.* **e)** used when telling or reminding someone to do something: *Don't forget now – put the keys in the right hand drawer.* | *Now hurry up! I haven't got all day.* **10** **right now** at the moment: *I'm really busy right now, can I call you back?* **11** **just now** *especially BrE* **a)** at the moment: *I can't do it just now, I'm busy.* **b)** a moment ago: *Where have I put that pen? I was using it just now.* **12** **now then** used to get someone's attention before telling them to do something or asking them a question: *Now then, what's the matter?* **13** **well now** used when giving an opinion or asking someone to tell you something: *Well now, what's all this I hear about you getting married?* **14** **now for** used when saying what you are going to do next: *That's done. Now for a nice cup of coffee.* **15** **and now a)** used when introducing the next activity, performer etc: *And now, live from New York, Diana Ross.* **b)** to ask someone what the situation is like at the moment when they have been telling you what it was like in the past: *"It was terrible, she nearly died." "And now?" "Oh, she's back to normal now."* **16** **now now a)** used to make someone calm or comfort them when they are angry, upset etc: *Now now, don't worry, everything will be okay.*

**b)** *especially BrE* used when telling someone not to behave badly: *Now now, leave her alone, it's not fair to blame her.* **17 not now** used to tell someone that you do not want to talk to them or do something now, because you are busy, tired etc: *"Tell me a story." "Not now, Daddy's working."* **18 it's now or never** used to say that if someone does not do something now, they will not get another chance to do it **19 now's the time** used to say that someone should do something now, because it is the right time to do it: *Now's the time to buy a suit, while there are still sales on.* **20 now I know** used when you have just found out something you didn't know before: *Okay, now I know. I won't do it again, I'm sorry.* **21 what is it now?** used when you are annoyed because someone keeps interrupting you or asking you things: *What is it now? I wish you'd leave me alone!* **22 now you tell me!** used when you are annoyed or amused because someone has just told you something they should have told you before: *Now she tells me! After I spent hours waiting for you all to arrive!*

S1 W3 **now²** *conjunction* also **now that** because of something or as a result of something: *Now that they've got to know each other a little better, they get along just fine.* | *Now you're here, why not have a drink.*

S2 **now·a·days** /ˈnaʊədeɪz/ *adv* now, compared with what happened in the past: *Nowadays young people are much more aware of ecological issues than they used to be.*

S2 **no way** /ˌ· ˈ·/ *adv spoken* certainly not: *"Are you going to offer to work over the weekend?" "No way!"* | *No way will we be finished by five o' clock.* | **there's no way...** *There's no way I'm going to pay £300 just for a weekend in Paris.*

S2 **no·where** /ˈnəʊweə‖ˈnoʊwer/ *adv* **1** also **no place** *AmE informal* not in any place or to any place: *I have no job and nowhere to live.* | **nowhere else** (=no other place) *You've got to help me. I've nowhere else to go.* **2 get nowhere** to have no success or make no progress: *It's a good idea but it will get nowhere without more financial support.* | **get sb nowhere** *Taking that kind of attitude will get us nowhere.* | **get nowhere with** *Flaherty was getting nowhere with the Americans, and decided on a different approach.* | **get nowhere fast** *I soon realised that being tough was getting me nowhere fast.* **3 be nowhere to be seen/found/heard** not to be seen, found, or heard anywhere: *Typical – another street crime and the police are nowhere to be seen.* **4 nowhere near a)** far from a particular place: *He swore he was nowhere near her house on the night she died.* **b)** not at all: **nowhere near ready/full/finished etc** *The building's nowhere near finished.* | **nowhere near as good as etc** *Sarah's nowhere near as fit as I am.* **5 out of/from nowhere** happening or appearing suddenly and without warning: *In the last few seconds Gunnell came from nowhere to win another gold medal.* | *From out of nowhere he asks me to marry him!*

**no-win sit·u·a·tion** /ˌ·ˈ· ··ˈ··/ *n* [C] a situation which will end badly whatever you decide to do

**no·wise** /ˈnəʊwaɪz‖ˈnoʊ-/ *adv old use* not at all

**nox·ious** /ˈnɒkʃəs‖ˈnɑːk-/ *adj formal* harmful or poisonous: *noxious gases*

**noz·zle** /ˈnɒzəl‖ˈnɑː-/ *n* [C] a short tube fitted to the end of a HOSE, pipe etc to direct and control the stream of liquid or gas pouring out

**nozzle**

**nr** *BrE* the written abbreviation of 'near', used in addresses

**NSPCC** /ˌen es ˌpiː siː ˈsiː/ *n* the National Society for the Prevention of Cruelty to Children; a British organization that protects children who are being badly treated

**NSU** /ˌen es ˈjuː/ *n* [U] non-specific urethritis; an infection of the URETHRA

**n't** /ənt/ the short form of 'not': *hadn't* | *didn't* | *wouldn't* | *isn't* —see NOT (USAGE)

**nth** /enθ/ *adj* **1** [only before noun] *informal* the most recent of a long series of similar things that have happened: *Even after I'd reminded him for the nth time, he forgot.* **2 to the nth degree** *informal* extremely, or as much as possible: *It was boring to the nth degree.*

**nu·ance** /ˈnjuːɑːns‖ˈnuː-/ *n* [C,U] a very slight, hardly noticeable difference in manner, colour, meaning etc: *He was aware of every nuance in her voice.*

**nub** /nʌb/ *n* **the nub of the problem/matter/argument etc** the main point of a problem etc: *Differing social attitudes lie at the nub of the dispute.*

**nu·bile** /ˈnjuːbaɪl‖ˈnuːbəl/ *adj formal or humorous* a woman who is nubile is young and sexually attractive

**nu·cle·ar** /ˈnjuːkliə‖ˈnuːkliər/ *adj* **1** using or connected with nuclear energy: *a nuclear power station* | *a nuclear-powered submarine* **2** concerning the NUCLEUS (1) of an atom: *nuclear fission* **3** connected with or involving the use of NUCLEAR WEAPONS: **nuclear bomb/war** *the threat of nuclear war* | **nuclear tests** (=for testing nuclear bombs) | **nuclear disarmament** (=getting rid of nuclear weapons) | **the nuclear deterrent** (=nuclear weapons used as a threat to stop an enemy attacking) W3

**nuclear en·er·gy** /ˌ··· ˈ···/ *n* [U] the powerful force that is produced when the NUCLEUS (=central part) of an atom is either split or joined to another atom

**nuclear fam·i·ly** /ˌ··· ˈ···/ *n* [C] a family unit that consists only of husband, wife and children

**nuclear fis·sion** /ˌ··· ˈ··/ *n* [U] the splitting of the NUCLEUS (=central part) of an atom which results in a lot of power being produced

**nuclear-free** /ˌ··· ˈ·◂/ *adj* places that are nuclear-free do not allow NUCLEAR materials to be carried, stored or used in that area: *a nuclear-free zone*

**nuclear fu·sion** /ˌ··· ˈ··/ *n* [U] a NUCLEAR (2) reaction in which the nuclei (NUCLEUS (1)) of light atoms join with the nuclei of heavier atoms, which produces power without producing any waste

**nuclear phys·ics** /ˌ··· ˈ··/ *n* [U] the area of PHYSICS which is concerned with the structure and features of the NUCLEUS (=central part) of atoms

**nuclear pow·er** /ˌ··· ˈ··/ *n* [U] power, usually in the form of electricity, from NUCLEAR ENERGY

**nuclear re·ac·tion** /ˌ··· ·ˈ··/ *n* [C] a process in which the parts of the NUCLEUS (=central part) of an atom are rearranged to form new substances

**nuclear re·ac·tor** /ˌ··· ·ˈ··/ *n* [C] a large machine that produces NUCLEAR ENERGY, especially as a means of producing electricity

**nuclear waste** /ˌ··· ˈ·/ *n* [U] waste material from NUCLEAR REACTORS, which is RADIOACTIVE: *There are no easy solutions to the problems of nuclear waste disposal.*

**nuclear weap·on** /ˌ··· ˈ··/ *n* [C] a very powerful weapon which uses atomic power to cause death and destruction over a large area: *The controversy over nuclear weapons testing*

**nu·cle·ic ac·id** /njuːˌkliːɪk ˈæsɪ̣d, -ˌkleɪ-‖nuː-/ *n* [C,U] one of the two acids, DNA and RNA, that exist in the cells of all living things

**nucleus**

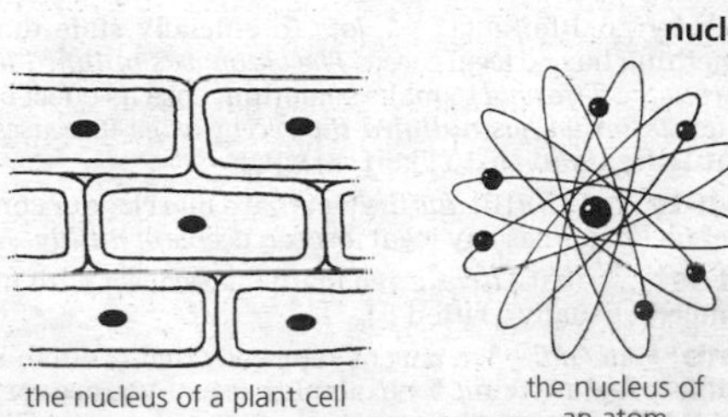

the nucleus of a plant cell

the nucleus of an atom

**nu·cle·us** /ˈnjuːkliəs‖ˈnuː-/ *n plural* **nuclei** /-kliaɪ/ [C] **1** the central part of an atom, made up of NEUTRONS, PROTONS, and other ELEMENTARY PARTICLES **2** the central part of almost all the cells of living things **3** a small, important group at the centre of a larger group or organization: *the nucleus of an effective team*

**nude¹** /njuːd‖nuːd/ *adj* **1** not wearing any clothes; NAKED **2** done by or involving people who are not wearing any clothes: *There are several nude scenes in the film.*

**nude²** *n* **1** [C] a painting, STATUE etc of someone not wearing clothes **2 in the nude** not wearing any clothes: *He was standing there in the nude.*

**nudge** /nʌdʒ/ *v* **1** [T] to push someone gently, usually with your elbow, in order to get their attention: *"Look!" Benjamin nudged his mother. "There's my teacher, Miss Watts."* —see picture on page 1260 **2** [T always + adv/prep] to move something or someone a short distance by gently pushing: **nudge sth/sb towards/away etc** *She nudged the glass towards me.* | *David nudged me out of the way.* **3** also **nudge your way** [I always + adv/prep] to move forward slowly by pushing gently: [+ **to/through/forward etc**] *I started to nudge my way to the front of the crowd.* **4** [T always + adv/prep] to gently persuade or encourage someone to take a particular decision or action: [+ **into/towards**] *We're trying to nudge them towards a practical solution.* **5** [T usually in progressive] to almost reach a particular level or amount: *For the first time in my life I was nudging 80kg.* —**nudge** *n* [C] *Hannah gave me a sharp nudge.*

**nud·ist** /ˈnjuːdɪst‖ˈnuː-/ *n* [C] someone who enjoys not wearing any clothes because they believe it is natural and healthy; NATURIST —**nudist** *adj*: *a nudist camp* —**nudism** *n* [U]

**nu·di·ty** /ˈnjuːdɪti‖ˈnuː-/ *n* [U] the state of not wearing any clothes

**nug·get** /ˈnʌgɪt/ *n* [C] **1** a small rough piece of a valuable metal found in the earth: *gold nuggets* **2** a small, round piece of food: *chicken nuggets* **3 nugget of information/wisdom etc** a piece of valuable information, advice etc: *It took ages to extract that nugget of information from him.*

S3 **nui·sance** /ˈnjuːsəns‖ˈnuː-/ *n* **1** [C usually singular] a person, thing, or situation that annoys you or causes problems: *Those dogs next door are a thorough nuisance.* | **What a nuisance!** *spoken*: *What a nuisance! I've forgotten my ticket.* | **make a nuisance of yourself** (=behave in a way that annoys other people) *Stop making a nuisance of yourself.* **2** [C,U] *law* the use of a place or property in a way that causes public annoyance: *She was charged with causing a nuisance in a public place.* **3 nuisance value** *BrE* something that has nuisance value is useful because it causes problems for your opponents

**nuke¹** /njuːk‖nuːk/ *v* [T] *informal* to attack a place using NUCLEAR WEAPONS

**nuke²** *n* [C] *informal* a NUCLEAR WEAPON

**null** /nʌl/ *adj* **null result/effect etc** *technical* a result etc that is zero or nothing

**null and void** /ˌ· · ˈ·/ *adj law* having no legal effect; INVALID¹ (1): *The contract was declared null and void.*

**nul·li·fy** /ˈnʌlɪfaɪ/ *v* [T] **1** *law* to officially state that something has no legal force: *The claim was nullified by the court.* **2** *formal* to make something lose its effect or value: *Inflation has nullified the recent wage increases.* —**nullification** /ˌnʌlɪfɪˈkeɪʃən/ *n* [U]

**nul·li·ty** /ˈnʌlɪti/ *n* [U] *law* the fact that a marriage or contract no longer has any legal force: *a decree of nullity*

**null set** /ˌ· ˈ·/ *n* [C] *technical* a mathematical set with no members, usually written { }

**numb¹** /nʌm/ *adj* **1** a part of your body that is numb is unable to feel anything, for example because you are very cold: *My fingers were so numb I could hardly write.* | *The anaesthetic had made his whole face go numb.* **2** unable to think, feel, or react in a normal way: **numb with shock/fear/terror etc**: *I just sat there, numb with terror.* —**numbly** *adv* —**numbness** *n* [U]

**numb²** *v* [T] **1** to make someone unable to feel pain or other sensations: *fingers numbed with cold* | *the numbing effect of the drug* **2** to make someone unable to think, feel, or react in a normal way: *He was numbed by the shock of his wife's death.*

**number¹** /ˈnʌmbə‖-ər/ *n* S1 W1

**1** ▶ **NUMBER** ◀ [C] a word or sign which represents an amount or a quantity: *Add together the following numbers: 1027, 643, and 378.* | **high/low number** *Choose a fairly low number – under 100, say.* | **even number** (=2, 4, 6, 8, 10 etc) | **odd number** (=1, 3, 5, 7, 9 etc) | **round number** (=a number ending in 0) *I'll give her £17 - no, make it £20. That's a good round number.* | **be good/no good etc with numbers** *informal* (=to be good, bad etc at calculating things using numbers) —see also CARDINAL NUMBER, ORDINAL NUMBER, PRIME NUMBER, WHOLE NUMBER

**2** ▶ **IN A SET/LIST** ◀ [C] a number used to show the position of something in an ordered set or list: *We live at number 107 Castle Street.* | *Answer question number 4.* | *a number 17 bus* —see also E NUMBER, NO. 10, NUMBER ONE

**3 model/account/fax etc number** a number used to communicate with someone, to find information about someone or something etc: *What is your account number, please?* —see also BOX NUMBER, PIN, SERIAL NUMBER

**4** ▶ **TELEPHONE** ◀ [C] a telephone number: *My new number is 502655.* | **sb's home/office/work number** *I gave him my home number.* | **wrong number** *"Is that 70348?" – "No, I'm afraid you have the wrong number."*

**5** ▶ **CAR** ◀ [C] *BrE* the official series of numbers and letters shown on a motor vehicle; REGISTRATION NUMBER: *Did you get the number of the car?*

**6** ▶ **AMOUNT** ◀ [singular] also **numbers** *plural* an amount of something that can be counted; a QUANTITY: *The number of cars on our roads rose dramatically last year.* | *Estimates put the number of deaths at between three and five thousand.* | **a large/great/small etc number of** also **large/great/small etc numbers of** *Doctors believe only a tiny number of people are at risk.* | **in large/great/small etc numbers** *They were printed in limited numbers.* | **bring the number of sth to five/ten etc** *This latest bomb brings the number of terrorist attacks this year to seven.* | **ten/twelve etc in number** *formal*: *A small number of protesters, about 20 in number, gathered outside.* —see AMOUNT¹ (USAGE)

**7 numbers** [plural] how many people there are, especially people attending an event or doing an activity together: *Can you give me some idea of numbers?* | **student/client etc numbers** *Visitor numbers increase in the summer.*

**8 by (sheer) force/weight of numbers** if a group of people is defeated by force of numbers, it is defeated because many more people are attacking or opposing it

**9 a number of** *formal* several: *She has written a number of articles for the local paper.* | **a good number of/quite a number of** (=a lot of) *Darke knew a good number of people with government connections.* | **a number of ways/reasons/factors etc** (=various different ways etc) *These paintings differ from his earlier ones in a number of ways.* | **any number of** *There could be any number of reasons why she's late.*

**10 some/none/20 etc of sb's number** *formal* some etc of a group of people: *Only three of our number could speak Italian.*

**11** ▶ **MUSIC** ◀ [C] a piece of popular music that forms part of a longer performance: *Madonna sang several numbers from her latest album.* —see also PRODUCTION NUMBER

**12 a recent/an old/last month's number** *BrE* a copy of a magazine printed recently, a long time ago etc; ISSUE¹ (2) *AmE*: **back number** (=an old copy of a magazine)

**13 have sb's number** *informal* to understand something about someone that helps you deal with them: *You'll never fool her, Mike – she's got your number!*

**14 sb's number is up/has come up** *informal* someone will suffer or be punished: *Your number's up Hanks!*

**15 black/elegant etc (little) number** *informal* a black etc dress: *Sue turned up in a very elegant number.*
**16 sb's number comes up** someone has the winning number in a competition
**17 the number of times I've**...*spoken* used to say that you have done something many times, without any result: *Honestly, the number of times I've told that girl not to walk home alone.*
**18 the numbers** an illegal game in the US in which people risk money on the appearance of a combination of numbers in a newspaper: *playing the numbers*
**19 beyond/without number** *literary* if things are beyond number, there are so many of them that no one could count them all
**20 ▶ GRAMMAR ◀** [U] *technical* the form of a word, depending on whether one thing or more than one thing is being talked about: *'Horses' is plural in number, 'horse' is singular.*

**number²** *v* **1** [T] to give a number to something that is part of an ordered set or list: *They haven't numbered the pages of the report.*|*All the seats in the theatre are numbered.*|**number sth (from) 1 to 10/100 etc** *Number the questions 1 to 25.*|*a numbering system* **2 his/their/its days are numbered** someone or something cannot live or continue much longer **3 number several thousands/almost a million etc** to be several thousands etc: *The crowd numbered at least 7000*|*The men on strike now number 5% of the workforce.* **4 number among/ be numbered among** *formal* to be included as one of a particular group: *Amis numbers among the best of our younger writers.* **5** [T] *literary* to count: *Who can number the stars?*

**number off** *phr v* [I] *BrE technical* if soldiers number off, they call out their number when their turn comes; COUNT off *AmE*

**number crunch·er** /ˈ·· ˌ··/ *n* [C] *informal humorous* **1** someone who works with numbers, such as an ACCOUNTANT **2** a computer designed to work with numbers and calculate results

**number crunch·ing** /ˈ·· ˌ··/ *n* [U] *informal humorous* the process of working with numbers and calculating results —**number-crunching** *adj*

**num·ber·less** /ˈnʌmbələs‖-bər-/ *adj* too many to be counted; INNUMERABLE: *numberless possibilities*

**number one¹** /ˌ·· ˈ·◂/ *n* [singular] **1** the most important or successful person or thing: *George is number one in this organization.*|*Kline had so many great plans – number one being to star in a movie.* **2** the musical record that is the most popular at a particular time: *number one in the charts* **3 look out for number one/look after number one** *spoken* to look after yourself and not worry about other people: *Suzanne's only bothered about looking after number one.*

**number one²** /ˌ·· ˈ·◂/ *adj* **1** most important or successful in a particular situation: *Obedience was the organization's number one priority.*|*Sweden's number one model* **2** first on a list of several things to be considered, done etc: *item number one on the agenda*

**num·ber·plate** /ˈnʌmbəpleɪt‖-ər-/ *n* [C] *BrE* one of the signs at the front and back of a car showing its REGISTRATION NUMBER; LICENSE PLATE *AmE* —see picture on page 409

**Number Ten** /ˌ·· ˈ·/ *n* [singular] —see NO. 10

**numb·skull** /ˈnʌmskʌl/ *n* [C] another spelling of NUMSKULL

**nu·me·ral** /ˈnjuːmərəl‖ˈnuː-/ *n* [C] a written sign that represents a number —**numeral** *adj*

**nu·me·rate** /ˈnjuːmərɪ̣t‖ˈnuː-/ *adj* able to do calculations and understand simple mathematics: *We need someone who's numerate.* —opposite INNUMERATE —compare LITERATE (1) —**numeracy** *n* [U]

**nu·me·ra·tion** /ˌnjuːməˈreɪʃən‖ˌnuː-/ *n* [C,U] *technical* a system of counting or the process of counting

**nu·me·ra·tor** /ˈnjuːməreɪtə‖ˈnuːməreɪtər/ *n* [C] *technical* the number above the line in a FRACTION (2), for example 5 is the numerator in $\frac{5}{6}$—compare DENOMINATOR

**nu·mer·i·cal** /njuːˈmerɪkəl‖nuː-/ *adj* expressed or considered in numbers: *a numerical code*|*the numerical superiority of the government forces* (=the fact that they were greater in number) —**numerically** /-kli/ *adv: numerically equal*

**nu·me·rous** /ˈnjuːmərəs‖ˈnuː-/ *adj formal* many: *Numerous attempts have been made to hide the truth.*|*on numerous occasions* W3

**nu·mi·nous** /ˈnjuːmɪ̣nəs‖ˈnuː-/ *adj literary* having a mysterious and holy quality, which makes you feel that God is present

**nu·mis·mat·ics** /ˌnjuːmɪ̣zˈmætɪks‖ˌnuː-/ *n* [U] *technical* the activity of collecting and studying coins and MEDALS —**numismatic** *adj* —**numismatist** /njuːˈmɪzmətɪ̣st‖nuː-/ *n* [C]

**num·skull, numbskull** /ˈnʌmskʌl/ *n* [C] *informal* a very stupid person; IDIOT: *Look what you've done now, you numskull!*

**nun** /nʌn/ *n* [C] a member of an all female religious group who live together in a CONVENT —compare MONK

**nun·ci·o** /ˈnʌnsiəʊ‖-sioʊ/ *n* [C] *plural* **nuncios** a representative of the Pope in a foreign country

**nun·ne·ry** /ˈnʌnəri/ *n* [C] *literary* a CONVENT

**nup·tial** /ˈnʌpʃəl/ *adj formal or humorous* connected with marriage or the marriage ceremony: *the nuptial day*|*nuptial bliss*

**nup·tials** /ˈnʌpʃəlz/ *n* [plural] *formal or humorous* a wedding

**nurse¹** /nɜːs‖nɜːrs/ *n* [C] **1** someone who is trained to look after people who are ill or injured, usually in a hospital: *The nurse is coming to give you an injection.*|*a student nurse* (=someone learning to be a nurse)|*Nurse Jones*|*a male nurse* **2** *old-fashioned* a woman employed to look after a young child; NANNY (1) —see also WET NURSE S3 W3

**nurse²** *v*
**1 ▶ SICK PEOPLE ◀ a)** [T] to look after someone who is ill or injured: *nursing an elderly relative*|**nurse sb back to health** (=nurse someone until they are well again) **b)** [I usually in progressive] to work as a nurse: *She spent several years nursing in a military hospital.*
**2 ▶ YOUR FEELINGS ◀** [T not in passive] to secretly have a feeling or idea in your mind for a long time, especially an angry feeling: **nurse a grudge/grievance/ambition etc** *For years he had nursed a grievance against his former employer.*
**3 ▶ YOUR ILLNESS/INJURY ◀** [T not in passive] to rest when you have an illness or injury so that it will get better: *Andrea was at home, nursing a cold.*
**4 ▶ TAKE CARE OF STH ◀** [T] to take special care of something especially during a difficult situation: **nurse sth through/along etc** *Royton succeeded in nursing the company through a financially difficult period.*
**5 ▶ HOLD ◀** [T] to hold something carefully in your hands or arms close to your body: *a child nursing a kitten*|*Frank sat there nursing his glass of beer.*
**6 ▶ FEED A BABY ◀ a)** [I,T] if a woman nurses a baby, she feeds it with milk from her breasts; BREASTFEED **b)** [I] if a baby nurses, it sucks milk from its mother's breast

**nurse·ling** /ˈnɜːslɪŋ‖ˈnɜːr-/ *n* [C] another spelling of NURSLING

**nurse·maid** /ˈnɜːsmeɪd‖ˈnɜːrs-/ *n* [C] *old-fashioned* a woman employed to look after young children

**nur·se·ry** /ˈnɜːsəri‖ˈnɜːr-/ *n* [C] **1** a place where young children are taken care of during the day while their parents are at work, shopping etc —see also DAY CARE (1) **2 nursery education/school/unit/teacher etc** education etc for young children from three to five years old —see also KINDERGARTEN **3** *old-fashioned* a baby's bedroom or a room where young children play, in a private house **4** a place where plants and trees are grown and sold; GARDEN CENTRE *BrE*

N

**nur·se·ry·man** /ˈnɜːsərimən‖ˈnɜːr-/ *n* [C] *plural* **nurserymen** /-mən/ someone who grows plants and trees in a nursery

**nursery nurse** /ˈ··· ˌ·/ *n* [C] *BrE* someone who has been trained to work with and look after young children

**nursery rhyme** /ˈ··· ·/ *n* [C] a short traditional song or poem for children

**nursery slope** /ˈ··· ˌ·/ *n* [C] *BrE* a slope that is not very steep, where people are taught to SKI ; BUNNY SLOPE *AmE*

**nurs·ing** /ˈnɜːsɪŋ‖ˈnɜːr-/ *n* [U] the job or skill of looking after people who are ill, injured, or old: *I'd love to go into nursing.*

**nursing home** /ˈ·· ·/ *n* [C] a type of small private hospital for old people who cannot look after themselves

**nursing moth·er** /ˌ·· ˈ··/ *n* [C] a mother who is feeding her baby from her breast

**nurs·ling, nurseling** /ˈnɜːslɪŋ‖ˈnɜːr-/ *n* [C] *old use* a baby who is being fed from the breast, or who is being looked after by a nurse

**nur·tur·ance** /ˈnɜːtʃərəns‖ˈnɜːr-/ *n* [U] *AmE* loving care and attention that you give to someone: *the feminine virtue of nurturance* —**nurturant** *adj*

**nur·ture**[1] /ˈnɜːtʃə‖ˈnɜːrtʃər/ *v* [T often passive] *formal* **1** to feed and take care of a child or a plant while it is growing: *children nurtured in an overprotective environment | plants nurtured in the greenhouse* **2** to help a plan, idea, feeling etc to develop: *European union is an ideal that has been nurtured since the post-war years.*

**nurture**[2] *n* [U] *formal* the education and care that you are given as a child, and the way it affects your later development and attitudes

S3 **nut**[1] /nʌt/ *n* [C]

**1 ▶ FOOD ◀** a dry brown fruit inside a hard shell, that grows on a tree: *crack a nut | a cashew nut*

**2 ▶ TOOL ◀** a small piece of metal with a hole through the middle which is screwed onto a BOLT[1] (2) to fasten things together

**3 ▶ CRAZY PERSON ◀** *informal especially AmE* someone who is crazy or behaves strangely: *He's kind of a nut, but I like him.*

**4 a golf/opera etc nut** *informal* someone who is very interested in golf etc: *She's a Clark Gable nut.*

**5 ▶ SEXUAL ORGAN ◀** *slang* a man's testicles: *He got kicked in the nuts.*

**6 the nuts and bolts of** *informal* the practical details of a subject or job: *the nuts and bolts of the project*

**7 a tough/hard nut** *informal* someone who is difficult to deal with: *Johnny Stone was a tough nut.*

**8 a hard/tough nut to crack** a difficult problem or situation: *Saturday's match will be a tough nut to crack.*

**9 ▶ HEAD ◀** *BrE spoken* your head or brain: *Oh come on, use your nut!*

**10 be off your nut** *BrE spoken* to be crazy: *You must be off your nut!*

**11 do your nut** *BrE spoken* to become very angry or worried: *I didn't get home till three – my Mum did her nut!*

**12 sb can't ... for nuts** *spoken* used to say that someone is completely unable to do something: *She can't sing for nuts.* —see also NUTS[1]

**nut**[2] *v* [T] *BrE informal* to hit someone with your head; HEADBUTT: *He just turned round and nutted me!*

**nut·case** /ˈnʌtkeɪs/ *n* [C] *informal humorous* someone who is crazy or mentally ill: *That man's a complete nutcase.*

**nut·crack·er** /ˈnʌtˌkrækə‖-ər/ *n* [C] also **nutcrackers** [plural] *BrE* a tool for cracking the shells of nuts

**nut·house** /ˈnʌthaʊs/ *n* [C] *slang* an offensive word for a PSYCHIATRIC HOSPITAL

**nut·meg** /ˈnʌtmeg/ *n* **1** [U] a brown powder used as a SPICE[1] (1) to give a particular taste to food **2** [C] the seed of a tropical tree from which this powder is made

**nu·tri·ent** /ˈnjuːtriənt‖ˈnuː-/ *n* [C] a chemical or food that provides what is needed for plants or animals to live and grow: *The plant absorbs nutrients from the soil.* —**nutrient** *adj*

**nu·tri·ment** /ˈnjuːtrɪ̈mənt‖ˈnuː-/ *n* [U] *formal* substances that plants and animals need in order to live and grow; NOURISHMENT

**nu·tri·tion** /njuːˈtrɪʃən‖nuː-/ *n* [U] the process of giving or getting the right kind of food for good health and growth: *Nutrition and exercise are essential to fitness and health.* —**nutritional** *adj*: *the nutritional value of fresh vegetables* —**nutritionally** *adv*

**nu·tri·tious** /njuːˈtrɪʃəs‖nuː-/ *adj* food that is nutritious is full of the natural substances that your body needs to stay healthy or to grow properly; NOURISHING: *Wholemeal bread is more nutritious than white bread.*

**nu·tri·tive** /ˈnjuːtrɪ̈tɪv‖ˈnuː-/ *adj* **1** [no comparative] *technical* relating to nutrition **2** *formal* nutritious

**nuts**[1] /nʌts/ *adj* [not before noun] *informal* **1** crazy: **go nuts** (=become crazy) *I'll go nuts if I have to wait any longer.* | **drive sb nuts** (=annoy someone very much) *Turn that radio off. It's driving me nuts.* **2 be nuts about/on/over** to like someone or something very much: *She's nuts about the boy next door.*

**nuts**[2] *interjection AmE old-fashioned* used when you are angrily refusing to listen to someone: *"Nuts to you, wise guy," he sneered.*

**nut·shell** /ˈnʌt-ʃel/ *n* [C] **1 (to put it) in a nutshell** *spoken* used when you are stating the main facts about something in a short, clear way: *To put it in a nutshell, the show was a total disaster.* **2** the hard outer part of a nut

**nut·ter** /ˈnʌtə‖-ər/ *n* [C] *BrE informal* a crazy person: *an absolute nutter*

**nut·ty** /ˈnʌti/ *adj* **1** tasting like nuts: *This coffee has a rich nutty flavour.* **2** containing or filled with nuts: *a nutty cake* **3** *informal* crazy: *another of his nutty ideas* | **nutty as a fruitcake** (=completely crazy) —**nuttiness** *n* [C]

**nuz·zle** /ˈnʌzəl/ also **nuzzle up** *v* [I always + adv/prep, T] to gently rub or press your nose or head against someone to show you like them: *The horses were nuzzling up against each other.* | *Tim nuzzled Clare's neck.*

**NW** the written abbreviation of NORTHWEST or NORTHWESTERN

**ny·lon** /ˈnaɪlɒn‖-lɑːn/ *n* [U] **1** a strong artificial material that is used to make plastics, clothes, rope etc: *shirts made of nylon | nylon thread* **2 nylons** *old-fashioned* women's STOCKINGS or TIGHTS made of nylon

**nymph** /nɪmf/ *n* [C] **1** one of the spirits of nature, who, according to ancient Greek and Roman stories, appeared as young girls living in trees, mountains, streams etc **2** *poetic* a girl or young woman

**nym·phet** /nɪmˈfet, ˈnɪmfɪ̈t‖nɪmˈfet/ *n* [C] *humorous* a young girl who is very sexually attractive

**nym·pho·ma·ni·ac** /ˌnɪmfəˈmeɪniæk/ also **nympho** *informal n* [C] a woman who always wants to have sex, with a lot of different men —**nymphomaniac** *adj*: *nymphomaniac tendencies* —**nymphomania** /-niə/ *n* [U]

**NZ** the written abbreviation of New Zealand

# O,o

**O, o** /əʊ‖oʊ/ *plural* **O's, o's** 1 the 15th letter of the English alphabet 2 *spoken* a zero

**O** /əʊ‖oʊ/ *interjection* 1 *poetic* used when addressing someone or something: *O Death, where is thy sting?* 2 another form of OH

**o'** /ə/ *prep* 1 a way of writing 'of' as it is usually said in speech: *a pint o' beer* 2 *literary* on

**oaf** /əʊf‖oʊf/ *n* [C] a stupid awkward man or boy: *You clumsy oaf!* —**oafish** *adj* —**oafishly** *adv* —**oafishness** *n* [U]

S3 **oak** /əʊk‖oʊk/ *n* [C,U] a large tree that is common in northern countries, or the hard wood of this tree: *ancient oaks | an oak door | polished oak*

**oak ap·ple** /'· ,··/ *n* [C] a raised part on the leaf or stem of an oak tree, caused by an insect

**oak·en** /'əʊkən‖'oʊ-/ *adj especially literary* made of oak

**oa·kum** /'əʊkəm‖'oʊ-/ *n* [U] small pieces of old rope used for filling up small holes in the sides of wooden ships

**OAP** /,əʊ eɪ 'piː‖,oʊ-/ *n* [C] *BrE* Old Age Pensioner; a person who is old enough to receive a PENSION from the state

**oar** /ɔː‖ɔːr/ *n* [C] 1 a long pole with a wide flat blade at one end, used for rowing a boat —compare PADDLE[1] (1) 2 **put/shove/stick your oar in** *BrE informal* to join in a discussion without being asked to

**oar·lock** /'ɔːlɒk‖'ɔːrlɑːk/ *n* [C] *AmE* a ROWLOCK

**oars·man** /'ɔːzmən‖'ɔːrz-/ *n plural* **oarsmen** /-mən/ [C] someone who rows a boat, especially in races

**oars·wom·an** /'ɔːz,wʊmən‖'ɔːrz-/ *n plural* **oarswomen** /-,wɪmɪn/ [C] a woman who rows a boat, especially in races

**o·a·sis** /əʊ'eɪsɪs‖oʊ-/ *n plural* **oases** /-siːz/ [C] 1 a place with water and trees in a desert 2 a peaceful or pleasant place that is very different from everything around it: *the one oasis of calm in the war-torn city*

**oast house** /'əʊst haʊs‖'oʊst-/ *n* [C] *BrE* a round building with a pointed top, built for drying HOPS[2] (4)

**oat cake** /'əʊt keɪk‖'oʊt-/ *n* [C] a flat cake made of oatmeal

**oath** /əʊθ‖oʊθ/ *n* [C] *plural* **oaths** /əʊðz‖oʊðz/ 1 a formal and very serious promise: **swear/take an oath** *The knights swore an oath of loyalty to their king.* 2 **be on/under oath** *law* to have made a formal promise to tell the truth in a court of law: *evidence given under oath* 3 **take the oath** to make an official promise to tell the truth in a court of law 4 an expression of strong feeling that uses religious or sexual words in an offensive way: *He shouted oaths and curses as they took him away.*

**oat·meal** /'əʊtmiːl‖'oʊt-/ *n* [U] 1 crushed OATS used for making cakes and PORRIDGE (1) 2 *AmE* a soft breakfast food made by boiling crushed oats; PORRIDGE (1) *BrE*

**oats** /əʊts‖oʊts/ *n* [plural] 1 a grain that is eaten by people and animals 2 oatmeal 3 **feel your oats** *informal* to feel full of energy 4 **get your oats** *BrE informal* to have sex regularly 5 **be off your oats** *BrE informal* to have lost the desire to eat

**ob·du·ra·cy** /'ɒbdjərəsi‖'ɑːbdə-/ *n* [U] *formal* an unreasonable refusal to change your beliefs or feelings

**ob·du·rate** /'ɒbdjərɪt‖'ɑːbdə-/ *adj formal* unreasonably determined not to change your beliefs or feelings; STUBBORN: *She remained obdurate despite their pleas.* —**obdurately** *adv*

**o·be·di·ence** /ə'biːdiəns/ *n* [U] obedient behaviour; doing what you are told to do by your parents etc: [+ **to**] *obedience to her father's wishes* | **demand obedience** *a master who demanded absolute obedience from his servants*

**o·be·di·ent** /ə'biːdiənt/ *adj* 1 always doing what you are told to do by your parents, by someone in authority etc: *an obedient and dutiful child* 2 **your obedient servant** *old use* used to end a very formal letter —opposite DISOBEDIENT —**obediently** *adv*: *She obediently did as she was told.*

**o·bei·sance** /əʊ'beɪsəns‖oʊ-/ *n* [C,U] *formal* an act of showing respect and obedience, by bending your head or the upper part of your body

**ob·e·lisk** /'ɒbəlɪsk‖'ɑː-, 'oʊ-/ *n* [C] 1 a tall pointed stone PILLAR (1) 2 a DAGGER (1) sign used in printing

**o·bese** /əʊ'biːs‖oʊ-/ *adj technical* very fat in a way that is unhealthy —see FAT[1] (USAGE)

**o·be·si·ty** /əʊ'biːsəti‖oʊ-/ *n* [U] *technical* the condition of being too fat in a way that is dangerous to your health

**o·bey** /əʊ'beɪ, ə-‖oʊ-, ə-/ *v* [I,T] to do what someone in a position of authority tells you to do, or to do what a law or rule says you must do: *The men always obey him.* | *"Stand still!" he bellowed. Only a few obeyed.* | **obey an order/command** *Soldiers are expected to obey orders.* | **obey the law/laws/rules** *You'll have to obey the rules if you want to live here.* —opposite DISOBEY

**ob·fus·cate** /'ɒbfəskeɪt‖'ɑːb-/ *v* [T] *formal* to deliberately make something unclear or difficult to understand —**obfuscation** /,ɒbfə'skeɪʃən‖,ɑːb-/ *n* [U]

**ob/gyn** /,əʊ biː ,dʒiː waɪ 'en ‖,oʊ-/ *n* [U] *informal, especially AmE* OBSTETRICS and GYNAECOLOGY

**o·bit·u·a·ry** /ə'bɪtʃuəri‖-tʃueri/ *n* [C] a report in a newspaper about the life of someone who has just died

**ob·ject**[1] /'ɒbdʒɪkt‖'ɑːb-/ *n* S3 W2

1 ▶ **THING** ◀ [C] a solid thing, especially something that you can hold or touch: *some kind of heavy blunt object*

2 **an object of pity/desire/contempt etc** someone or something that is pitied, desired etc: *Once famous, he was now a mere object of pity.* —see also SEX OBJECT

3 ▶ **AIM** ◀ [singular] the intended result of a plan, action, or activity: [+ **of**] *The object of the game is to score 100 points.* | *His primary object was to gain publicity.* | **the object of the exercise** (=the object of whatever you are doing) *The customer will benefit most, and that after all is the object of the exercise.*

4 **money/expense is no object** used to say that you are willing to spend a lot of money

5 **object lesson** an event or story that shows you the right or wrong way of doing something: *The whole weekend was an object lesson in how not to attract a woman.*

6 ▶ **IN GRAMMAR** ◀ [C] a noun, noun phrase, or PRONOUN representing **a)** the person or thing that something is done to, for example 'the house' in 'We built the house.'; DIRECT OBJECT **b)** the person who is concerned in the result of an action, for example 'her' in 'I gave her the book.'; INDIRECT OBJECT **c)** the person or thing that is joined by a PREPOSITION to another word or phrase, for example 'table' in 'He sat on the table.'

**ob·ject**[2] /əb'dʒekt/ *v* 1 [I] to complain or protest about something, or to feel or say that you oppose it or disapprove of it: *Do you think anyone would object if I park my car here?* | [+ **to**] *My mother objected to every boy I brought home.* | **object to being called/being told etc** *I object to being spoken to like that.* | **I object** (=used in formal arguments) *Mr. Chairman, I object. That is an unfair allegation.* 2 [T + **that**] to state a fact or opinion as a way of opposing something or complaining: *Mom objected that we were too young to go on vacation alone.* | *"My name's not Sonny," the child objected.* —see also OBJECTOR S2

**object code** /'·· ,·/ *n* [U] MACHINE CODE

**ob·jec·tion** /əb'dʒekʃən/ *n* [C] 1 something that you say to show that you oppose or disapprove of an action, idea etc: [+ **to**] *objections to the Governor's plan* | **have an objection** *If no one has any objection, I'll declare the meeting closed.* | **raise/voice an objection** (=state an objection) 2 a reason against doing something: [+ **to/against**] *The only objection to hiring him is that he can't drive.* S3

**ob·jec·tio·na·ble** /əb'dʒekʃənəbəl/ *adj* unpleasant and likely to offend people; offensive: *a most objectionable remark* | *What an objectionable man he is!* —**objectionably** *adv*

**ob·jec·tive**[1] /əb'dʒektɪv/ *n* [C] 1 an aim that you are trying to achieve, especially in business or politics: *The main objective of this policy is to reduce unemployment.* W3

2 a place that you are trying to reach, especially in a military attack: *The valley was our primary objective.*

S3 **objective**[2] *adj* **1** not influenced by your own feelings or opinions, when you have to make a judgment or decision: *I need an objective opinion from someone who's not involved.* —opposite SUBJECTIVE (1) **2** *formal* existing outside the mind; real: *objective facts* **3** *technical* connected with the object —**objectivity** /ˌɒbdʒekˈtɪvɪ̈ti‖ˌɑːb-/ *n* [U]

O

**ob·jec·tive·ly** /əbˈdʒektɪvli/ *adv* if you consider something objectively, you try to think about it without being influenced by your own feelings or opinions

**ob·jec·tor** /əbˈdʒektə‖-tər/ *n* [C] someone who states or shows that they oppose something: *objectors to the new motorway*

**ob·jet d'art** /ˌɒbʒeɪ ˈdɑː‖ˌɑːbʒeɪ ˈdɑːr/ *plural* **objets d'art** (*same pronunciation*) *n* [C] a small object, used for decoration, that has some value as art

**ob·la·tion** /əˈbleɪʃən/ *n* [C,U] *formal* a gift that is offered to God or a god, or the act of offering the gift

**ob·li·gat·ed** /ˈɒblɪ̈geɪtɪ̈d‖ˈɑːb-/ *adj especially AmE* **1 be obligated (to do something)** to have to do something or have a duty to do it: *IBM's European customers will be obligated to make more drastic cutbacks in mainframe expenditure.* **2 be/feel obligated to someone** to owe someone loyalty, thanks, or money, because they have done something for you

W3 **ob·li·ga·tion** /ˌɒblɪ̈ˈgeɪʃən‖ˌɑːb-/ *n* [C,U] **1** a moral or legal duty to do something: **obligation to do sth** *You can look at the books without any obligation to buy.* | [+ **to**] *I have certain obligations to my family.* | **meet/fulfil an obligation** (=do something that is your duty) | *Have the employers met their contractual obligations?* | **a sense of obligation** (=feeling that you ought to do something) *I helped you because I wanted to, not out of any sense of obligation.* **2 be under an obligation a)** to have to do something because it is a legal or moral duty: **be under no obligation to do sth** *We are invited but we are under no obligation to go.* | **place sb under an obligation** *Signing a contract places you under a long-term obligation.* **b)** to owe someone loyalty, thanks, or money because they have done something for you: [+ **to**] *I don't want to be under an obligation to anyone.*

**ob·lig·a·to·ry** /əˈblɪgətəri‖-tɔːri/ *adj* **1** *formal* something that is obligatory must be done because of a law, a rule etc; COMPULSORY, MANDATORY: *Attendance is obligatory.* **2** *often humorous* used to describe something that is usually done, worn, or included because many people also do it, or you have always done it in the past: *Paula was smartly dressed in a new tweed suit with the obligatory matching bag and shoes.*

Frequencies of **be obliged to**, **must**, and **have/got to** in spoken and written English.

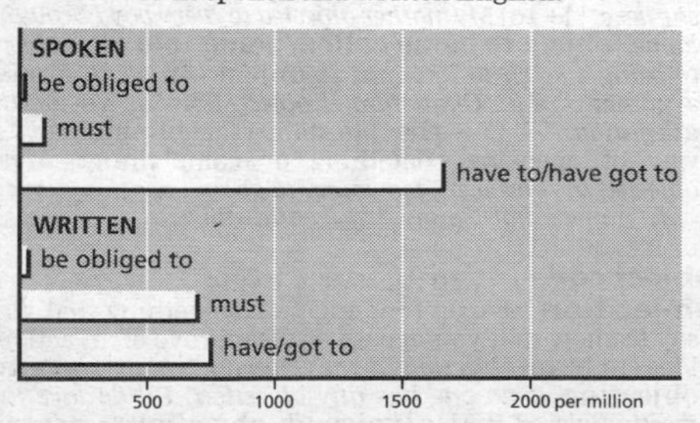


Based on the British National Corpus and the Longman Lancaster Corpus

This graph shows that the expressions **have to** and **have got to** are much more common in spoken English than **must** or **be obliged to**. **Have got to** is only used in British English. **Must** is more common in written English. **Be obliged to** is much less common than the others and is only used to say that someone must do something because of a rule or law, or because the situation forces them to do it.

**o·blige** /əˈblaɪdʒ/ *v formal* **1** [T usually passive] to make it necessary for someone to do something: **be obliged to do sth** *As a result of falling profits we were obliged to close the factory.* | **feel obliged to do sth** (=feel that you have a duty to do something) *Don't feel obliged to play if you don't want to.* **2** [I,T] to do something that someone has asked you to do: *Would you oblige me by taking this letter to the Director?* | **happy/glad/ready to oblige** *If you need a ride home, I'd be happy to oblige.* **3 I'd be obliged if** *spoken* used to make a polite request: *I'd be obliged if you'd treat this matter as strictly confidential.* **4 (I'm) much obliged (to you)** *spoken* used to thank someone very politely S3

**o·blig·ing** /əˈblaɪdʒɪŋ/ *adj* willing and eager to help: *What an obliging child!* —**obligingly** *adv*: *"Of course I'll do it", she said obligingly.*

**o·blique**[1] /əˈbliːk/ *adj* **1** not expressed in a direct way: *oblique references to his drinking problems* **2** not looking or pointing directly at something: *an oblique glance* **3 oblique line/stroke etc** a sloping line etc **4 oblique angle** *technical* an angle that is not 90°, 180°, or 270° —**obliquely** *adv* —**obliqueness** *n* [U]

**oblique**[2] *n* [C] a mark (/) used for writing FRACTIONS (2) or for separating numbers, letters, words etc; SLASH[2] (2)

**o·blit·er·ate** /əˈblɪtəreɪt/ *v* [T] **1** to destroy something so completely that no sign of it remains: *The entire village was obliterated by incendiary bombs.* **2** to cover something completely so that it cannot be seen **3** to remove a thought, feeling, or memory from someone's mind: *Nothing could obliterate the memory of those tragic events.* —**obliteration** /əˌblɪtəˈreɪʃən/ *n* [U]

**o·bliv·i·on** /əˈblɪviən/ *n* [U] **1** the state of being completely forgotten: *The loser's name is consigned to oblivion.* **2** the state of being unconscious or of not noticing what is happening: *the oblivion of sleep*

**o·bliv·i·ous** /əˈblɪviəs/ *adj* [not before noun] not knowing about, or not noticing, something that is happening around you; UNAWARE: [+ **of/to**] *Mallory set off, utterly oblivious of the danger.* —**obliviousness** *n* [U]

**ob·long** /ˈɒblɒŋ‖ˈɑːblɔːŋ/ *adj* **1** *AmE* an oblong shape is much longer than it is wide: *an oblong leaf* **2** *BrE* an oblong shape has four straight sides at 90° to each other, two of which are much longer than the other two: *an oblong frame* —compare RECTANGLE —**oblong** *n* [C]

**ob·lo·quy** /ˈɒbləkwi‖ˈɑːb-/ *n* [U] *formal* **1** very strong, offensive criticism **2** loss of respect and honour

**ob·nox·ious** /əbˈnɒkʃəs‖-ˈnɑːk-/ *adj* extremely unpleasant or rude: *You obnoxious little creep!* | *an obnoxious smell* —**obnoxiously** *adv* —**obnoxiousness** *n* [U]

**o·boe** /ˈəʊbəʊ‖ˈoʊboʊ/ *n* [C] a wooden musical instrument, shaped like a narrow tube, which you play by blowing air through a REED (2)

**o·bo·ist** /ˈəʊbəʊɪ̈st‖ˈoʊboʊ-/ *n* [C] someone who plays the oboe

**ob·scene** /əbˈsiːn/ *adj* **1** dealing with sex in a socially unacceptable and offensive way; INDECENT (1): *The condemned man made an obscene gesture at the jury.* | *obscene publications* | **obscene phone calls** (=from an unknown person saying obscene things) **2** extremely immoral and unfair in a way that makes you angry: *an obscene indifference to the needs of the poor* —**obscenely** *adv*

**ob·scen·i·ty** /əbˈsenɪ̈ti/ *n* **1** [U] sexually offensive language or behaviour, especially in a book, play, film etc **2** [C usually plural] a sexually offensive word or action: *He ran off, shouting obscenities at them.*

**ob·scu·ran·tis·m** /ˌɒbskjʊ̈ˈræntɪzəm‖ˌɑːb-/ *n* [U] *formal* the practice of deliberately stopping ideas and facts from being known —**obscurantist** *adj*

**ob·scure**[1] /əbˈskjʊə‖-ˈskjʊr/ *adj* **1** not at all well known and usually not very important: *an obscure poet* | *The exact origin of the paisley design is obscure.* **2** difficult to understand: *obscure legal phrases* —**obscurely** *adv*

**obscure**[2] *v* [T] **1** to make something difficult to know or understand: **obscure the fact/issue etc** *Recent successes obscure the fact that the company is still in trouble.* **2** to prevent something from being seen or heard clearly: *Thick cloud obscured the stars from view.*

**ob·scu·ri·ty** /əbˈskjʊərɪ̣ti‖-ˈskjʊr-/ *n* **1** [U] the state of not being known or remembered: [+ **in**] *O'Brien retired from politics and died in obscurity.* **2** [C,U] something that is difficult to understand, or the quality of being difficult to understand: *After years of analysis, a great many obscurities remain in the text.* **3** [U] *literary* darkness

**ob·se·quies** /ˈɒbsɪ̣kwiz‖ˈɑːb-/ *n* [plural] *formal* a funeral ceremony

**ob·se·qui·ous** /əbˈsiːkwiəs/ *adj* too eager to serve people and agree with them; SERVILE (1): *The salesman's obsequious manner was beginning to irritate me.* —**obsequiously** *adv* —**obsequiousness** *n* [U]

**ob·ser·va·ble** /əbˈzɜːvəbəl‖-ɜːr-/ *adj* something that is observable can be seen or noticed: *unemployment and other observable effects of the recession* —**observably** *adv*

**ob·ser·vance** /əbˈzɜːvəns‖-ɜːr-/ *n* **1** [U] the practice of obeying a law or doing what is expected according to a custom or ceremony: [+ **of**] *strict observance of the rules* | *the observance of Chinese New Year* **2** [C] a part of a religious ceremony: *ritual observances*

**ob·ser·vant** /əbˈzɜːvənt‖-ɜːr-/ *adj* **1** good or quick at noticing things: *Luckily, an observant passerby spotted the broken cable.* | [+ **of**] *Artists tend to be more observant of their surroundings.* **2** [+ **of**] obeying laws, religious rules etc

W3 **ob·ser·va·tion** /ˌɒbzəˈveɪʃən‖ˌɑːbzər-/ *n* **1** [C,U] the process of watching something or someone carefully for a period of time: *a study based on detailed observation of a group of 20 patients* | *a result of scientific observation* | **under observation** (=being watched continuously by police, doctors etc) *She's in hospital under observation.* | *Detectives are keeping the place under observation.* **2** [C] a spoken or written remark about something you have noticed: [+ **on**] *Darwin's observations on the habits of certain birds* | **make an observation** *I'd like to make a few observations about the current style of management.* **3 powers of observation** a natural ability to notice what is happening around you **4 escape observation** to avoid being noticed **5** [U] the act of obeying a law etc; OBSERVANCE (1) —**observational** *adj*

**observation post** /ˌ··ˈ·· ·/ *n* [C] a position from which an enemy can be watched

**ob·ser·va·to·ry** /əbˈzɜːvətəri‖əbˈzɜːrvətɔːri/ *n* [C] a special building from which scientists watch the moon, stars, weather etc: *the Greenwich Observatory*

W2 **ob·serve** /əbˈzɜːv‖-ɜːrv/ *v* [T] **1** [not in progressive] *formal* to see and notice something: **observe sb doing sth** *Ben knew that someone had observed him meeting Ryan.* | [+ **that**] *She observed that the pond was drying up.* | **observe sth** *The car I had observed earlier was no longer there.* **2** to watch something or someone carefully: *The police have been observing his movements.* | **observe what/how/where** *I sat in a corner and observed what was going on.* **3** to do what you are supposed to do according to a law, agreement, or custom: *So far the ceasefire has been observed by both sides.* | **observe Christmas/May Day etc** (=celebrate a traditional holiday) **4** *formal* to say what you have noticed about a situation: *"Michael's looking very anxious," I observed.* | **observe that** *Keynes observed that humans fall into two classes.* **5 closely observed** a play, character etc that is closely observed is very like a situation, character etc in real life

**ob·serv·er** /əbˈzɜːvə‖-ɜːrvər/ *n* [C] **1** someone who sees or notices something: *Shocked observers told police about the robbery.* | **casual observer** (=one who is not specially interested) *To a casual observer she may have seemed fine, but I knew better.* **2** someone who regularly watches or pays attention to particular things: [+ **of**] *an impartial observer of the current political scene* | *an observer of nature* **3** someone who attends meetings, classes etc to check what is happening: *The UN sent a team of observers to the peace talks.*

**ob·sess** /əbˈses/ *v* **1** [T usually passive] if something or someone obsesses you, you think about them all the time and you cannot think of anything else: **be obsessed with** *You've always been obsessed with making money.* | *He had become obsessed with another man's wife.* | **obsess sb** *Minute details seem to obsess lawyers.* **2** [I] *AmE* to think about something or someone much more than is necessary or sensible: [+ **over/about**] *Stop obsessing about your weight. You look fine.*

**ob·ses·sion** /əbˈseʃən/ *n* [C] an unreasonably strong and continuous interest in something, or worry about something, which stops you from thinking about anything else: *He's convinced he was unfairly treated and it's become an obsession.* | [+ **with/about**] *an unhealthy obsession with death* —**obsessional** *adj*: *She had an almost obsessional desire to win.*

**ob·ses·sive**[1] /əbˈsesɪv/ *adj* an obsessive feeling, interest or attitude makes you think all the time about a particular thing or person: *an obsessive need for excitement* | *She's becoming obsessive about hygiene.* —**obsessively** *adv*

**obsessive**[2] *n* [C] *technical* someone whose behaviour is obsessive

**ob·sid·i·an** /əbˈsɪdiən/ *n* [U] a type of dark rock which looks like glass

**ob·so·les·cence** /ˌɒbsəˈlesəns‖ˌɑːb-/ *n* [U] **1** the state of becoming old-fashioned and no longer useful, because something else that is newer and better has been invented **2 planned/built-in obsolescence** the practice of making a product in such a way that it will soon become unfashionable or impossible to use

**ob·so·les·cent** /ˌɒbsəˈlesənt◂‖ˌɑːb-/ *adj* becoming obsolete

**ob·so·lete** /ˈɒbsəliːt‖ˌɑːbsəˈliːt◂/ *adj* no longer useful because something newer and better has been invented: *obsolete weapons* | **render sth obsolete** (=make it obsolete) *Current production methods will soon be rendered obsolete.*

**ob·sta·cle** /ˈɒbstəkəl‖ˈɑːb-/ *n* [C] **1** something that makes it difficult for you to achieve your aim: [+ **to**] *Fear of change is the greatest single obstacle to progress.* | **put obstacles in the way (of)** (=try to prevent something by causing difficulties) *They tried to put obstacles in the way of our marriage.* **2** an object which blocks your way, so that you must try to go around it

**obstacle course** /ˈ··· ˌ·/ *n* [C] **1** a line of objects which runners in an OBSTACLE RACE have to jump over, climb through etc **2** a series of difficulties which must be dealt with to achieve a particular aim **3** *AmE* an ASSAULT COURSE

**obstacle race** /ˈ··· ˌ·/ *n* [C] a type of race in which runners have to jump over or climb through various objects

**ob·ste·tri·cian** /ˌɒbstɪ̣ˈtrɪʃən‖ˌɑːb-/ *n* [C] a doctor who has special training in obstetrics

**ob·stet·rics** /əbˈstetrɪks/ *n* [U] the part of medical science concerned with the birth of children —**obstetric** *adj*

**ob·sti·na·cy** /ˈɒbstɪ̣nəsi‖ˈɑːb-/ *n* [U] an unreasonable determination not to change your mind

**ob·sti·nate** /ˈɒbstɪ̣nɪ̣t‖ˈɑːb-/ *adj* **1** unreasonably refusing to change your ideas of behaviour, even though people try to persuade you: *Harry was obstinate and wouldn't admit he was wrong.* | *a sulky, obstinate child* | *an obstinate refusal to face facts* **2** [only before noun] difficult to deal with or get rid of: *strong enough to remove the most obstinate stains* | *an obstinate cough* —**obstinately** *adv*

**ob·strep·e·rous** /əbˈstrepərəs/ *adj* obstreperous behaviour is noisy and cheerful or angry —**obstreperously** *adv* —**obstreperousness** *n* [U]

**ob·struct** /əbˈstrʌkt/ *v* [T] **1** to block a road, passage etc: *A small aircraft now obstructed the runway.* | *an* *accident obstructing northbound traffic | Our view was obstructed by a high wall.* **2** to try to prevent someone from doing something by making it difficult for them: *A small minority obstructed policies that would help the majority of people. | obstructing a police officer in the course of his duty*

**ob·struc·tion** /əb'strʌkʃən/ *n* **1** [U] the act of trying to prevent or delay a legal or political process: [+ **of**] *obstruction of vital legislation* **2** [U] the act of blocking a road, passage, tube etc: [+ **of**] *obstruction of the public highway* **3** [C] something that blocks a road, passage, tube etc: *There's an obstruction in the fuel pipe.* **4** *v* an offence in football, HOCKEY etc in which a player gets between an opponent and the ball —see picture on page 1264

**ob·struc·tion·is·m** /əb'strʌkʃənɪzəm/ *n* [U] the practice of trying to prevent or delay a legal or political process —**obstructionist** *n* [C]

**ob·struc·tive** /əb'strʌktɪv/ *adj* trying to prevent someone from doing something by deliberately making it difficult for them: *an obstructive official | obstructive tactics* —**obstructively** *adv* —**obstructiveness** *n* [U]

S2 W2 **ob·tain** /əb'teɪn/ *v formal* **1** [T] to get something that you want, especially through your own effort, skill, or work: *Further information can be obtained from head office. | They've extended the growing season to obtain a larger crop. | the difficulty of obtaining credit* **2** [I not in progressive] if a situation, system, or rule obtains, it continues to exist: *These conditions no longer obtain.*

**USAGE NOTE: OBTAIN**

WORD CHOICE: **obtain, get, get hold of, find out, achieve, receive**

**Obtain** is formal and often sounds unnatural in spoken English or in a personal letter: *Where can I obtain a list of restaurants? | Fresh fruit and vegetables were especially difficult to obtain.*

**Get** is the most common word in spoken English and informal writing meaning to come to have something. However, some people feel that **get** should not be used too often in writing: *Where did you get that painting? | He gets about $200 a week at the textile mill.*

You can also **get hold of** things, or information, especially after some difficulty (informal): *I need to get hold of a powerful computer. | At last I managed to get hold of her address.*

You **find out** information: *I need to find out where my classes are.*

If you get yourself into a better situation through you own efforts, you **achieve** something: *We are working to achieve better results/equality/independence. | Regular exercise helps people achieve better health.*

If what you get comes naturally or is given to you, you can use the word **receive** (slightly formal): *The charity receives most of its money through private donations.*

**ob·tai·na·ble** /əb'teɪnəbəl/ *adj* something that is obtainable can be obtained: *Most of the ingredients for Chinese cooking are obtainable at the supermarket.*

**ob·trude** /əb'truːd/ *v* [I,T] *formal* **1** if something obtrudes, or you obtrude something, it becomes noticed where it is not wanted: [+ **into/upon**] *Personal taste is bound to obtrude into a book about wine.* —compare INTRUDE (1), PROTRUDE **2** to stick out or make something stick out

**ob·tru·sive** /əb'truːsɪv/ *adj* noticeable in a way that is unpleasant: *large obtrusive TV antennas | He was here just now, being kind of obtrusive and polite at the same time.* —opposite UNOBTRUSIVE —**obtrusively** *adv* —**obtrusiveness** *n* [U]

**ob·tuse** /əb'tjuːs‖-'tuːs/ *adj* **1** slow to understand things, in a way that is annoying: *an obtuse lout of a man | be obtuse* (=pretend to not understand something) *Is he being deliberately obtuse?* **2 obtuse angle** *technical* an angle between 90 and 180 degrees —**obtusely** *adv* —**obtuseness** *n* [U] —see picture at ANGLE[1]

**ob·verse** /'ɒbvɜːs‖'ɑːbvɜːrs/ *n* **1** *formal* the opposite of a particular situation or feeling: [+ **of**] *Defeat is the obverse of victory.* **2 the obverse** *technical* the front side of a coin or MEDAL —opposite REVERSE[2] (6)

**ob·vi·ate** /'ɒbvieɪt‖'ɑːb-/ *v* [T] **1 obviate the need** *formal* to make something unnecessary: *The use of a credit card obviates the need to carry a lot of money.* **2** to remove a difficulty

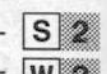 **ob·vi·ous** /'ɒbviəs‖'ɑːb-/ *adj* **1** easy to notice or understand: *the obvious advantages of co-operation | For obvious reasons we have had to cancel tonight's performance. | "Why is she leaving?" "Well, it's pretty obvious isn't it?"* | **it is obvious (to sb) that** *It was obvious to everyone that Gina was lying.* **2 obvious statement/remark etc** a statement that is unnecessary because it states what is obvious to everyone **3 the obvious choice** the person or thing that you would expect everyone to choose: *Nicholson was the obvious choice for team leader.* **4 the obvious thing (to do)** what clearly seems the best thing to do: *The obvious thing would have been to travel with her husband, but she couldn't.* **5 state the obvious** to say something that is already obvious and is therefore unnecessary —**obviousness** *n* [U]

 **ob·vi·ous·ly** /'ɒbviəsli‖'ɑːb-/ *adv* used to mean that a fact can easily be noticed or understood: [sentence adverb] *We're obviously going to need more help. | "Is she sorry?" "Obviously not! Look at her."* | [+ adj/adv] *The woman was lying across the chairs, obviously unwell.* —see OF COURSE (USAGE) —compare APPARENTLY, EVIDENTLY

 **oc·ca·sion**[1] /ə'keɪʒən/ *n*

**1 ▶ TIME ◀ a)** [C] a time when something happens: **on an occasion** *She had met Zahid on an earlier occasion. | I've seen Jana with them on several occasions.* **b)** [singular] a suitable or favourable time: [+ **for**] *We used the meeting as an occasion for announcing the restructuring.*

**2 ▶ SPECIAL EVENT ◀** [C] an important social event or ceremony: *I'm saving this bottle of champagne for a special occasion.* | **quite an occasion** (=a very exciting or impressive occasion) *The opening of the new library turned out to be quite an occasion.*

**3 ▶ CAUSE/REASON ◀** [singular] *formal* a direct cause or reason: **be the occasion of** *His remark was the occasion of a bitter quarrel.* | **have occasion to do sth** (=need to do something) *More than once Dr Standish had occasion to warn his son about his irresponsible behaviour.*

**4 if (the) occasion arises** *formal* if a particular action ever becomes necessary: *I am ready to defend our policies if the occasion arises.*

**5 on occasion** sometimes but not often: *I have on occasion visited her at home.*

**6 on the occasion of** *formal* at the time of an important event: *on the occasion of her 50th birthday*

**7 rise to the occasion** to deal well with an unexpected and difficult situation —see also **sense of occasion** (SENSE[1] (20))

**occasion**[2] *v* [T] *formal* to cause something: *disputes occasioned by greed and intolerance* | **occasion sb sth** *Your behaviour has occasioned us a great deal of anxiety.*

 **oc·ca·sion·al** /ə'keɪʒənəl/ *adj* **1** happening sometimes but not often: *Expect occasional showers today. | He smokes an occasional cigar.* **2** *formal* written or intended for a special occasion: *occasional poems*

  **oc·ca·sion·al·ly** /ə'keɪʒənəli/ *adv* sometimes, but not regularly and not often: *Occasionally Alice would look up from her books.* | **very occasionally** (=rarely) *We only see each other very occasionally.* —see picture at FREQUENCY

**occasional ta·ble** /·'··· ,··/ *n* [C] *BrE* a small light table that can be easily moved

**Oc·ci·dent** /ˈɒksɪ̈dənt‖ˈɑːksɪ̈dənt, -dent/ *n* **the Occident** *literary* the western part of the world, especially Europe and the Americas —compare ORIENT²

**oc·ci·den·tal** /ˌɒksɪ̈ˈdentəl◂‖ˌɑːk-/ *n* [C] *formal* someone from the western part of the world —compare ORIENTAL² —**occidental** *adj*

**oc·cult¹** /ˈɒkʌlt, əˈkʌlt‖əˈkʌlt, ˈɑːkʌlt/ *n* **the occult** mysterious practices and powers involving magic and spirits: *He was a strange man who dabbled in the occult.*

**occult²** *adj* magical and mysterious: *the occult powers*

**oc·cu·pan·cy** /ˈɒkjɪ̈pənsi‖ˈɑːk-/ *n* [U] *formal* someone's use of a building, piece of land, or other space, for living or working in: *their occupancy of the apartment*

**oc·cu·pant** /ˈɒkjɪ̈pənt‖ˈɑːk-/ *n* [C] *formal* **1** someone who lives in a house, room etc, though without necessarily owning it: *Furniture left by the previous occupants.* **2** someone who is in a room, vehicle etc at a particular time: *Neither of the car's two occupants was injured.*

S3 W3 **oc·cu·pa·tion** /ˌɒkjɪ̈ˈpeɪʃən‖ˌɑːk-/ *n* **1** [C] a job or profession: *Please state your name, address and occupation.* —see JOB (USAGE) **2** [C] a way of spending your time; PASTIME: *Marcus regarded stamp-collecting as a childish occupation.* **3** [U] the act of living or staying in a building or place: *In many of the caves there is evidence of human occupation.* **4** [U] the act of entering a place in a large group and keeping control of it, especially by military force: [+ **of**] *the German occupation of France* | *Demonstrators are continuing their occupation of the building.*

**oc·cu·pa·tion·al** /ˌɒkjɪ̈ˈpeɪʃənəl◂‖ˌɑːk-/ *adj* [only before noun] related to, or caused by your job: *an occupational disease* | **occupational hazard** (=a risk that always exists in a particular job) —**occupationally** *adv*

**occupational ther·a·py** /ˌ····· ˈ···/ *n* [U] a form of treatment for helping people to get back their health after illness by giving them special work —**occupational therapist** *n* [U]

**oc·cu·pi·er** /ˈɒkjɪ̈paɪə‖ˈɑːkjɪ̈paɪr/ *n* [C] *especially BrE* someone who lives in or uses a particular house, piece of land etc, especially temporarily —see also OWNER-OCCUPIER

S3 W2 **oc·cu·py** /ˈɒkjɪ̈paɪ‖ˈɑːk-/ *v* [T]
**1** ► **STAY IN A PLACE** ◄ *formal* to live or stay in a place: *The Jackson family have occupied this apartment for the past six months.*
**2 be occupied** if a room, seat, or bed is occupied, someone is in it or using it
**3** ► **SEIZE AND CONTROL** ◄ to enter a place in a large group and keep control of it, for example by military force: *Bosnian Serb forces have occupied the city for 8 months.* | *an occupying army*
**4** ► **FILL TIME/SPACE** ◄ to fill a space or period of time: *Soccer occupies most of my leisure time.* | *Traditional paintings occupy most of the wall-space in the gallery.*
**5 occupy sb's mind/thoughts/attention** if something occupies your mind etc, you think about that thing more than anything else
**6** ► **BUSY** ◄ **a) occupy sb/keep sb occupied** to keep someone busy: *I've invented a game that will keep the kids occupied for hours.* | *Hannah gets so bored – she needs something to occupy her.* **b) be occupied with** to be busy doing something: *Helen was fully occupied with business matters, so we didn't want to bother her.*
**7** ► **OFFICIAL POSITION** ◄ to have an official position or job: *Before becoming prime minister, Mrs Thatcher had already occupied several cabinet posts.*

S1 W1 **oc·cur** /əˈkɜː‖əˈkɜːr/ *v* **occurred, occurring** [I] *formal* **1** to happen: *Many accidents occur in the home.* | *Climatic changes have occurred at intervals throughout the millenium.* **2** [always + adv/prep] to happen or exist in a particular place or situation: [+ **in/among etc**] *Whooping cough occurs mainly in young children.*

**occur to** sb *phr v* [T not in passive] if an idea or thought occurs to you, it suddenly comes into your mind: **it occurs to sb that** *Didn't it occur to you that your husband might be late?* | *The possibility that she might be wrong never occurred to her.* | **it occurs to sb to do sth** *I suppose it never occurred to you to phone the police?*

**USAGE NOTE: OCCUR**

WORD CHOICE: **occur to, strike, occur, there is, happen, take place, arise, crop up**

If a thought comes into your mind it **occurs to** you or **strikes** you: *It suddenly occurred to/struck me I hadn't seen Peter all day.*

**Occur** meaning 'happen' is rather formal and not common in spoken English: *The court will decide what really occurred.* **Occur to** is not used in this sense: *A problem occurred to me* means 'I thought of a problem' NOT 'I had a problem'.

Usually people use **there is...**: *There was a loud bang from outside.* | *There's been an accident.* | *There's going to be a meeting next Tuesday.* When the person who something happens to is mentioned, you use **have**: *He had an interview last week.* | *She's bound to have trouble with the customs officials.*

Events and processes **happen** or **happen to** you, especially if they are not planned: *All sorts of unexpected things might happen.* | *The Industrial Revolution happened in the eighteenth century.* | *What's happening to us?*

If you are talking about something that is planned or arranged, you often use **take place**: *The wedding will take place in St Peter's Church.*

Problems or difficulties **arise** (formal) and something that happens suddenly and unexpectedly **crops up** (informal): *Let's consider what kind of difficulties might arise from the situation.* | *I have to go home early – something's cropped up.*

SPELLING POINT

Remember that there are two 'r's in *occurred* and *occurring.*

**oc·cur·rence** /əˈkʌrəns‖əˈkɜː-/ *n* **1** [C] something that happens: **a common/rare/regular occurrence:** *Flooding under this bridge is a common occurrence.* | *Laughter was a rare occurrence in his classroom.* **2** [U] the fact of something happening: *the frequent occurrence of violent storms in the area*

**o·cean** /ˈəʊʃən‖ˈoʊ-/ *n* **1 the ocean** *especially AmE* the great mass of salt water that covers most of the Earth's surface: *She stood on the beach, gazing at the ocean.* **2** [C] one of the very large areas of sea on the Earth's surface: *the Pacific Ocean* **3 oceans of** *informal* a great mass or amount of something —see also **a drop in the ocean** (DROP² (8)) —**oceanic** /ˌəʊʃiˈænɪk◂‖ˌoʊ-/ *adj* S3 W2

**o·cean·go·ing** /ˈəʊʃənˌɡəʊɪŋ‖ˈoʊʃənˌɡoʊ-/ *adj* an ocean-going ship is designed to sail across the sea: *an ocean-going tanker*

**o·cean·og·ra·phy** /ˌəʊʃənˈɒɡrəfi‖ˌoʊʃənˈɑːɡ-/ *n* [U] the scientific study of the ocean —**oceanographer** *n* [C]

**oc·e·lot** /ˈɒsɪ̈lɒt‖ˈɑːsɪ̈lɑːt, ˈoʊ-/ *n* [C] a large American wild cat that has a pattern of spots on its back

**och** /ɒx‖ɒːx/ *interjection ScotE* used to express surprise or to emphasize a remark; OH (3)

**o·chre** usually **ocher** *AmE* /ˈəʊkə‖ˈoʊkər/ n [U] **1** a reddish-yellow earth used in paints **2** the colour of ochre —**ochre** *adj*

**ock·er** /ˈɒkə‖ˈɑːkər/ *n* [C] *AustrE, NZE* a word for an Australian man, also used in Australia by men speaking to or about each other: *G'day Ocker – how's it going?*

**o'clock** /əˈklɒk‖əˈklɑːk/ *adv* **one o'clock/two o'clock etc** one of the times when the clock shows the exact hour as a number from 1 to 12: *"What time is it?" "It's 9 o'clock."* S1 W3

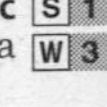

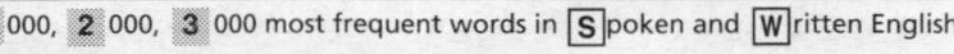

**USAGE NOTE: O'CLOCK**

UK-US DIFFERENCE

**O'clock** is used only when you are talking about the exact hour: *nine o'clock*. Compare: *ten to nine*

Minutes after the hour are expressed with **past** (usually **after** in American English): *five/a quarter/ten past nine* Compare: *five/ten/a quarter after nine* (American English only). In British English you can say 'half past' the hour, but it is not possible in American English to say 'half after' the hour.

You talk about minutes before the hour using **to** (and also **of** in American English): e.g. *twenty/a quarter to eight*. Compare: *It's five minutes of two/a quarter of eight* (American English only).

Time can also be expressed by using the numbers alone: *The meeting is at 10.15.* | *I'll pick you up about 3.20.* (=said three-twenty).

**-oc·ra·cy** /ɒkrəsi‖ɑːk-/ also **-cracy** *suffix (in nouns)* **1** government by a particular sort of people or according to a particular principle: *democracy* (=government by the people) | *mobocracy* **2** a society or country governed in this way: *the Western democracies* (=countries governed by their people) | *a meritocracy* **3** the powerful social class made up of a particular sort of people: *the aristocracy* (=people with noble titles)

**-o·crat** /əkræt/ also **-crat** *suffix* (in nouns) **1** a believer in a particular principle of government: *a democrat* (=someone who believes in government by the people) **2** a member of a powerful or governing social class or group: *a technocrat* (=scientist who controls organizations etc) —**-ocratic** /əkrætɪk/ *suffix* —**-ocratically** /əkrætɪkli/ *suffix*

**Oct** the written abbreviation of October

**oc·ta·gon** /ˈɒktəgən‖ˈɑːktəgɑːn/ *n* [C] a flat shape with eight sides and eight angles —**octagonal** /ɒkˈtægənəl‖ɑːk-/ *adj*: *an octagonal room*

**oc·tane** /ˈɒkteɪn‖ˈɑːk-/ *n* [U] **high octane petrol/fuel etc** petrol etc of the highest quality

**oc·tave** /ˈɒktɪ̵v, -teɪv‖ˈɑːk-/ *n* [C] **a)** the range of musical notes between the first note of a SCALE[1] (8) and the last one **b)** the first and last notes of a musical SCALE[1] (8) played together

**oc·tet** /ɒkˈtet‖ɑːk-/ *n* [C] **1** eight singers or musicians performing together **2** a piece of music for an octet

**Oc·to·ber** /ɒkˈtəʊbə‖ɑːkˈtoʊbər/ written abbreviation **Oct** *n* [C,U] the tenth month of the year, between September and November: *It happened on October the third.* | *on the third of October* | *on October third* | *in October 1991*

**oc·to·ge·nar·i·an** /ˌɒktəʊdʒɪ̵ˈneəriən, -tə-‖ˌɑːktoʊdʒɪ̵ˈner-/ *n* [C] a person who is between 80 and 89 years old

**oc·to·pus** /ˈɒktəpəs‖ˈɑːk-/ *n plural* **octopuses** [C] a sea creature with eight TENTACLES (=arms)

octopus

tentacle

**oc·u·lar** /ˈɒkjɪ̵lə‖ˈɑːkjɪ̵lər/ *adj technical* related to the eyes: *ocular muscles*

**oc·u·list** /ˈɒkjɪ̵lɪ̵st‖ˈɑːk-/ *n* [C] *old-fashioned* a doctor who examines and treats people's eyes

**OD** /ˌəʊ ˈdiː‖ˌoʊ-/ *v* [I + **on**] *slang* **1** to take too much of a dangerous drug; OVERDOSE **2** to see, hear too much of something —**OD** *n* [C]

**o·da·lisque** /ˈəʊdəlɪsk‖ˈoʊ-/ *n* [C] *literary* a beautiful female slave in former times

**odd** /ɒd‖ɑːd/ *adj* S1 W3

**1** ▶ **STRANGE** ◀ different from what is normal or expected: *an odd character* | *Isn't that odd? She's never done that before.* | *An odd thing happened last night!* | **it is odd (that)** *It's odd that Diana never answered your letter.* | **the odd thing is...** *The odd thing is no one seems to know who actually bought the picture.*

**2 odd-looking/sounding** looking or sounding strange or unusual: *He was an odd-looking bloke.*

**3 the odd drink/word/moment etc** *especially BrE* a few drinks etc at various times but not often and not regularly; OCCASIONAL (1): *We get the odd complaint from customers.* | *We have the odd drink together now and again.*

**4** ▶ **VARIOUS** ◀ [only before noun] not specially chosen or collected: *He'd written the addresses on odd scraps of paper.* | **odd jobs** (=many different small pieces of work) *He sometimes does odd jobs around the estate.*

**5** ▶ **NOT IN A PAIR/SET** ◀ [only before noun] separated from its pair or set: *an odd shoe* | **odd socks/gloves etc** (=not a matching pair of socks etc)

**6 odd number** a number that cannot be divided exactly by two, for example 1, 3, 5, 7 etc —opposite EVEN[2] (4)

**7 20-odd/30-odd etc** *spoken* a little more than 20 etc: *I have 20-odd years to work before I retire.*

**8 odd man out/odd one out a)** *especially BrE* someone or something that is different from the rest of the group: *Which of these three shapes is the odd one out?* **b)** *BrE informal* someone who is not usually included in groups of people or friends: *I was always the odd one out in my class at school.* —see also ODDLY —**oddness** *n* [U]

**odd·ball** /ˈɒdbɔːl‖ˈɑːdbɒːl/ *n* [C] *especially AmE informal* someone who behaves in a strange or unusual way —**oddball** *adj*: *Ernest, the odd-ball comedian in 'Ernest goes to Jail'*

**odd·i·ty** /ˈɒdɪ̵ti‖ˈɑː-/ *n* **1** [C] a strange or unusual person or thing: *He was something of an oddity in the neighborhood with his neat suits.* **2** [C,U] a strange quality in someone or something: *fashions that are remembered for their oddity*

**odd-job man** /· ˈ· ·/ *n* [C] a man who does various jobs in or around people's houses

**odd·ly** /ˈɒdli‖ˈɑːdli/ *adv* **1** in a strange or unusual way: *Brenda's been acting oddly this week.* **2** also **oddly enough** [sentence adverb] used to say that something seems strange or surprising: *Oddly enough, her anger made her seem more attractive.* **3 oddly matched/assorted** very different and looking strange together

**odd·ments** /ˈɒdmənts‖ˈɑːd-/ *n* [plural] small things of no value, or pieces of stuff that were not used when something was made

**odds** /ɒdz‖ɑːdz/ *n* [plural] S3

**1** ▶ **PROBABILITY** ◀ how likely it is that something will or will not happen, especially when this can be stated in numbers: *If you are male, the odds are about 1 in 12 of being colour-blind.* | **the odds are (that)** (=it is likely) *Invest now – the odds are that the share prices will rise after the budget.* | **odds in favour of** *The odds are in favour of a Russian victory.* | **odds against** *The odds against you getting killed in a plane crash are around a million to one.*

**2** ▶ **DIFFICULTIES** ◀ **a) enormous/heavy odds** difficulties which make a good result seem very unlikely: *Theresa has overcome enormous odds to get where she is today.* **b) against all (the) odds** in spite of great difficulties: *Against all the odds, racing driver Lauda recovered from his terrible injuries.*

**3 be at odds (with) a)** to disagree: *Briggs found himself at odds with his colleagues at NASA.* **b)** if two statements, descriptions, actions etc are at odds with each other, they are different although they should be the same: *Burt's latest evidence is at odds with his earlier statements.*

**4** ▶ **HORSE RACING ETC** ◀ numbers based on the probability of a horse winning a race, or a particular result in any competition, which show by how much you can increase your money if you BET[1] (1) on the one that

wins: *I bet £10 on Broadway Flyer with the odds at 6–1.* | **lay/offer (sb) odds** *I laid him odds of 7–2.* | **long/short odds** (=odds based on a high or low risk of losing)
**5 it makes no odds/what's the odds?** *BrE spoken* it makes no difference: *You can pay me now or later – it makes no odds.*
**6 pay/charge over the odds** *BrE informal* to pay or charge a higher price than is usual or reasonable: *There's always somebody ready to pay over the odds for a designer jacket.* —see also **have the odds stacked against you** (STACK² (3))

**odds and ends** /ˌ· · ˈ·/ *n* [plural] small things of various kinds without much value: *He didn't keep much in his desk – just odds and ends.*

**odds and sods** /ˌ· · ˈ·/ *n* [plural] *BrE informal* odds and ends

**odds-on** /ˌ· ˈ·◂/ *adj* **1 the odds-on favourite** a competitor that is very likely to win, especially a horse in a race **2** *informal* **it's odds on (that)** used to say that something is very likely to happen: *It's odds-on that she won't come.*

**ode** /əʊd‖oʊd/ *n* [C] a long poem addressed to a person or thing: *Keats' 'Ode to A Grecian Urn'*

**o·di·ous** /ˈəʊdiəs‖ˈoʊ-/ *adj formal* extremely unpleasant: *an odious and conceited little man* —**odiously** *adv*

**o·di·um** /ˈəʊdiəm‖ˈoʊ-/ *n* [U] *formal* hatred that a lot of people feel for someone

**o·dom·e·ter** /əʊˈdɒmɪ̣tə‖oʊˈdɑːmɪ̣tər/ *n* [C] *AmE* MILEOMETER *BrE*

**o·do·rif·er·ous** /ˌəʊdəˈrɪfərəs◂‖ˌoʊ-/ *adj old use* odorous

**o·do·rous** /ˈəʊdərəs‖ˈoʊ-/ *adj literary* having a smell, especially a pleasant one

**o·dour** *BrE*, **odor** *AmE* /ˈəʊdə‖ˈoʊˌdər/ *n* [C] **1** a smell, especially an unpleasant one: *Get rid of unpleasant household odours with new Fleur!* **2 be in bad odour (with)** if you are in bad odour with someone, they are not pleased with something you have done —see also BODY ODOUR

**o·dour·less** *BrE*, **odorless** *AmE* /ˈəʊdələs‖ˈoʊdər-/ *adj* not having a smell: *Water is a colorless, odorless liquid.*

**od·ys·sey** /ˈɒdɪ̣si‖ˈɑː-/ *n literary* [C] a long journey with lots of adventures

**OECD** /ˌəʊ iː siː ˈdiː‖ˌoʊ-/ *n* **the OECD** the Organization for Economic Cooperation and Development; a group of rich countries who work together to develop trade and economic growth

**oe·di·pal** /ˈiːdɪ̣pəl‖ˈe-/ *adj* related to an Oedipus complex: *oedipal fantasies*

**Oe·di·pus com·plex** /ˈiːdɪ̣pəs ˌkɒmpleks‖ˈedɪ̣pəs ˌkɑːm-/ *n* an unconscious sexual desire that a son feels for his mother, combined with a hatred for his father, according to Freudian PSYCHOLOGY

**o'er** /əʊə‖ɔːr/ *adv, prep poetic* over: *o'er vales and hills*

**oe·soph·a·gus** *especially BrE usually* **esophagus** *AmE* /ɪˈsɒfəgəs‖ɪˈsɑː-/ *n* [C] the tube from your mouth to your stomach, down which food passes —see picture at DIGESTIVE SYSTEM

**oes·tro·gen** *BrE*, **estrogen** *AmE* /ˈiːstrədʒən‖ˈes-/ *n* [U] a substance that is produced in a woman's ovaries (OVARY), and causes changes in her body that prepare it for having babies

**oeu·vre** /ˈɜːvrə/ *n* [C] *French* all the works of an artist, such as a painter or writer

S1 W1 **of** /əv, ə; *strong* ɒv‖əv, ə; *strong* ɑːv/ *prep* **1 a)** used to show a feature or quality that something has: *the colour of her dress* | *the width of the road* | *the size of John's overdraft* **b)** used to say that something is part of something else: *the leg of the table* | *the roots of her hair* | *the last scene of the movie* **2** used to show that something belongs to someone: *a friend of my parents* | *a computer of her own* | *a habit of his* **3** used to talk about a group or collection of particular people or things: *a herd of elephants* **4** used to talk about a particular amount or measurement of something: *two kilos of sugar* | *lots of money* | *a drop of water* | *a cup of coffee* **5** used to talk about a particular person or thing from a larger group of the same people or things: *a member of the soccer team* | *both of us* | *The Mona Lisa is one of his finest works.* | *the leading brand of shampoo.* **6 a)** used in dates: *the 27th of July* **b)** *AmE* used in giving the time to mean before: *a quarter of seven* (=6.45) **7** used when giving the name of something or being more specific about something that is very general: *the city of New York* | *the art of painting* | *the age of eight* | *the problem of unemployment* **8 a)** used after nouns describing actions, to show who the action is done to: *the killing of innocent children* (=the children are killed) **b)** used after nouns describing actions, to show who does the action: *the barking of the dogs* (=the dogs bark) **9** used to say what subject, person, thing etc another subject, person or thing is connected with: *the Queen of England* | *disease of the liver* | *the results of the meeting* | *the advantages of using a computer* **10** used to say what something is made from: *a dress of pure silk* | *These bowls are made of plastic.* **11 a) the day/year etc of** the day, year etc that something happened: *the day of the accident* | *the week of the festival* **b) of the day/year etc** the best or most important person or thing or a particular day or year: *She has been voted 'Woman of the Year'.* **c) of an evening/of a weekend** used to say that you often do something in the evenings, at weekends etc: *We always like to walk by the river of an evening.* **12** used to show that something is the result of something else: *She left of her own free will.* | *He died of cancer.* | *the effects of radiation* **13 a)** used to say who writes a play, who paints a painting etc: *the plays of Shakespeare* | *The building is the work of a great artist.* **b)** used to show what a picture, story etc is about or who is in it: *a photo of Elizabeth* | *a map of Indonesia* | *a story of love and loss* **14** about: *He's never heard of John Lennon.* | *Rumours of his infidelity filled the newspapers.* **15** used to show where something is or how far something is from something else: *east of Suez* | *I live within a mile of here.* **16** used to describe a particular person or thing: *a woman of tremendous spirit* | *a matter of no importance* **17** *especially literary* used to say where someone comes from: *Jesus of Nazareth* | *the people of China* **18 it is kind of/it was wrong of etc** used to say that something that someone has done shows that they are kind, wrong etc: *It was silly of him to think he could cheat.*

**USAGE NOTE: OF**

GRAMMAR

You use **'s** or plural **s'** rather than **of** to mean 'belonging to someone': *the students' grades* | *my friend's car* | *Clive's new hairstyle*

When you talk about something that belongs to or is part of something, you can use **of**: *the corner of the street* | *the top of the mountain* | *the street corner* | *the mountain top*

*You also use* **'s** and **s'** to talk about periods of time, for example: *a day's work* | *three weeks' vacation*

**'s** is increasingly used with the names of places, especially in newspapers and American English: *Chicago's favorite son* | *China's recent history*

When you use words like **a, some, the, this** etc with the word for something that belongs to someone, or the person you are talking about in connection with them, you can use both **of** and **'s** together: *that old bike of Cathy's* | *a friend of Terry's*

**of course** /· ˈ·/ *adv* **1** certainly: *Of course I'll give you your money back.* | *"Were you glad to leave?" "Of course not!"* | *Of course you must make a profit, but not if it involves exploiting people.* **2** used when you think that someone should know something, or should not be surprised by something: *You should of course keep copies of all correspondence.* | *Well, she won, of course.* S1 W1

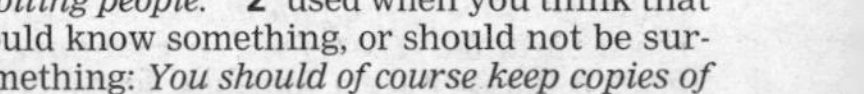

**USAGE NOTE: OF COURSE**

POLITENESS

You use **of course** as a polite and friendly way of agreeing to something or agreeing to do something someone has asked you: *"May I borrow this book?" "Of course you can."* | *"Do you think I was wrong?" "Of course not."*

It is not usually polite to use **of course** or **of course not** as a reply to a request for information. If for example someone asked you: *"Is this the way to the station?"* and you replied *"Of course (it is)"*, this would sound as if you think the answer to the question is very clear and you think the person is stupid to need to ask you.

STYLE

Except when you are answering questions, **of course** is not usually used at the beginning of a sentence. Instead of saying: *We play a lot of tennis and polo. Of course we have our own swimming pool,* you would say: *We also have our own swimming pool, of course* or *...and of course we have our own swimming pool.*

S1 W1 **off**[1] /ɒf‖ɒːf/ *adv, adj* [not before noun] **1** away or from where something is: *Travis got into his car and drove off.* | *Suddenly they turned off and parked in a side road.* | **be off** (=to leave) *We're off now. Thanks for the meal!* | **be off to** (=to go to a particular place) *They're off to Jamaica for a hard-earned vacation.* **2** out of a bus, train, car etc: *I'll get off at the next stop.* **3** removed; no longer connected or fastened to something: *Can anyone get the lid off?* | *Take off your shoes.* | *Waxing the table is a really good way of keeping the dust off.* **4** a machine, piece of equipment etc that is off is not working or operating: *Will someone switch the radio off?* —opposite ON[2] (6) **5** not at work, school etc because you are ill or on holiday: *You look tired. Why don't you take tomorrow off?* | **day/afternoon etc off** *I'm entitled to 25 days off a year.* | **be off** (=to be absent) *Mary is off with the flu today.* **6 a) be/go off** *especially BrE* food that is off is beginning to decay: *Ugh! This milk is off.* **b) be off** not be available to be eaten in a restaurant: *The fish is off today, sir.* **7 a) 4 kilometres/3 days' walk etc off** a particular distance away: *The hostel is at least two more miles off.* **b) 4 hours/10 years etc off** a particular amount of time away in the future: *The game is only two days off and our top player has been injured.* **8** a particular amount of money off is how much the price has been reduced by: *If you buy more than ten, they knock 10% off.* **9** *BrE* behaviour that is off is rude or not what is expected: *I thought it was a little off when he said he wished he'd never been invited.* | *Look, I know when someone's being off with me. OK?* **10** an arranged event that is off will no longer happen: *The wedding's off!* —compare ON[2] (8) **11 a) be badly/well off** to be poor or rich: *They have to be fairly well off to have that big a house.* **b) be badly/well off for sth** *informal* to have a small amount or large amount of something: *The school's fairly well off for books these days.* | **how are you off for sth?** *How are you off for jeans?* (=do you have enough pairs of jeans?) **12 be better off** *especially spoken* to be in a situation where you would gain more advantage: **be better off with** *I always said she was better off with a boyfriend of her own age.* | **be better off doing sth** *You'd be better off resigning and working part time.* **13 off and on** also **on and off** for short periods but not regularly, over a long period of time: *We've been going out together for five years, off and on.* **14 right off/straight off** *especially BrE informal* immediately **15** not on the stage but still able to be heard in the theatre; OFFSTAGE (1): *noises off*

S1 W1 **off**[2] *prep* **1** not on something or not touching something: *Keep off the grass.* | *Get off your backside and start digging.* | *I hope your dirty feet are off my clean floor.* —opposite ON[1] (1) **2** away from a particular person or thing: *Once we were off the main freeway the trip felt more like a vacation.* | *The referee ordered three players off the field.* **3** taken from someone or something: *Tom borrowed £500 off his sister.* | *I got this necklace off a woman outside the market.* | *What do you plan to live off while you're studying?* **4** out of a bus, train, car etc: *Both robbers jumped off the train while it was still moving.* **5** no longer held or supported by a particular thing: *Take your coat off the hook.* | *Suddenly the trophy fell off the platform.* **6** no longer connected or fastened to something; REMOVED: *A button has come off my shirt.* | *Cut about an inch off my bangs please.* **7 a)** at a particular distance from something; REMOVED: *My house is about 50 yards off Main Street.* **b)** in the sea but near the land: *an island off the coast of France* | *The ship began to sink 30 miles off Portsmouth.* **8** if one room is off another, you get to the second room by passing through the first: *Off the main bedroom was a beautiful en suite bathroom.* **9** *informal* not in a particular building, area etc: *Smoking is only allowed off the hospital premises.* **10 a)** no longer interested in something: *Toby's been off his food for a few days.* | **go right off** *BrE*: *I've gone right off her books.* **b)** no longer taking something such as medicine: *The operation was a success, and she's off the morphine.* **11 off the top of your head** if you say something off the top of your head, you are guessing

**off**[3] *adj* [only before noun, no comparative] **1 off day/week etc** a day, week etc when you are not doing something as well as you usually do: *Brian never forgets the words – he must be having one of his off days.* **2 off period/season etc** a period or season which is not as busy as other times of the year: *In the off season there's hardly anyone in the hotel at all.* **3** used when talking about a pair of things such as wheels on a car, to mean the one on the right —opposite NEAR[1] (96)

**off**[4] *n* **the off** the start, especially of a race or a journey: *The horses were in line, ready for the off.*

**off**[5] *v* [T] *AmE slang* to kill someone

**of·fal** /ˈɒfəl‖ˈɒː-, ˈɑː-/ *n* [U] the inside organs of an animal, for example the heart, LIVER, and KIDNEYS used as food

**off-bal·ance** /ˌ· ˈ··/ *adj* [not before noun] **1** in an unsteady position so that you are likely to fall: **throw/knock/push sb off-balance** *Lee caught hold of my wrist and pulled me off-balance.* **2** unprepared for something, so that it surprises or shocks you: **catch sb off-balance** *This time poor old Simpson had been caught off-balance by events.*

**off·beat** /ˌɒfˈbiːt◂‖ˌɒːf-/ *adj informal* unusual and not what people normally expect: *a slightly offbeat lifestyle*

**off-cen·tre** *BrE*, **off-center** *AmE* /ˌ· ˈ··◂/ *adj* not exactly in the centre of something: *Here, the photo is slightly off-centre.*

**off-chance** /ˈ· ·/ *n* **on the off-chance** hoping that something will happen, although it is unlikely: *I just stopped by on the off-chance that Pippa might be here.*

**off-col·our** *BrE*, **off-color** *AmE* /ˌ· ˈ··◂/ *adj* **1** sexually offensive: *Lou followed that up with some fairly off-color jokes.* **2** [not before noun] *especially BrE* slightly ill: *She's been feeling a bit off-colour lately.*

**off-cut** /ˈ· ·/ *n* [C] a piece of wood, paper etc that is left after the main piece has been cut and removed

**off day** /ˈ· ·/ *n* [C] **have an off day** to not do things as well as you usually do on a particular day

**off-du·ty** /ˌ· ˈ··◂/ *adj* someone such as a policeman, nurse, or soldier is off-duty during the hours when they are not working: *an off-duty guard* | *Sorry, I'm off-duty now.*

**of·fence** *BrE, usually* **offense** *AmE* /əˈfens/ n **1** [C] an illegal action or a crime: *Driving while drunk is a serious offence.* | *a parking offense* | [+ **against**] *sexual offences against children* | **commit an offence** (=do something that is an offence) | **first offence** (=the first illegal thing that someone has done) | **criminal offence** *Possession of stolen property is a criminal offence.* | **serious offence** *serious offences under the Prevention of Terrorism Act* | **capital offence** (=a crime for which death is the punishment) | **minor offence** (=one that is not very serious) **2** [U] behaviour which offends someone: **cause/give offence** (=offend someone) *The problem was how to get rid of her without causing offence.* | **mean no offence** (=have no intention of offending someone) *Don't be upset by what he said; he meant no offence.* **3 no** W3

**offence** *spoken* used to tell someone that you do not want to offend them by what you are saying: *No offense, but this cheese tastes like rubber.* **4 take offence** to feel offended because of something someone has said or done: *She's always quick to take offence.* **5** [U] *formal* the act of attacking: *It depends on whether it was used as a weapon of offence or defence.* **6** [U] *BrE* the part of a game such as football concerned with getting points and winning —see also OFFENSE

**of·fend** /ə'fend/ *v* **1** [T usually passive] to make someone angry or upset: **be offended** *Richard was deeply offended that people thought he'd faked the story.* | *I hope you won't be offended if I leave early.* | **offend sb** *I'm sorry; have I done something to offend you?* **2** [T] to seem bad or unpleasant to someone: *Cruelty to animals offends many people.* | **offend the eye/ear** (=look very ugly or sound very bad) **3** [I] to do something that is a crime: *Many criminals offend again within a year of their release from prison.* **4** [I,T] *formal* to go against people's feelings of what is morally right: [+ **against**] *behaviour that offends against common decency*

**of·fend·er** /ə'fendə‖-ər/ *n* [C] **1** someone who is guilty of a crime: *an institute for young offenders* | **first offender** (=one who has done a criminal action for the first time) **2** someone or something that is the cause of something that is bad: *Among causes of air pollution, car exhaust fumes may be the worst offender.*

**of·fend·ing** /ə'fendɪŋ/ *adj* **the offending ...** *often humorous* the thing that is causing a problem: *I decided to have the offending tooth removed.*

**of·fense¹** /ə'fens/ *n* [C,U] the usual American spelling of OFFENCE

**of·fense²** /'ɒːfens, 'ɑː-/ *n* [U] *AmE* the part of a game such as football concerned with getting points and winning: *The Bears are going to have to work on their offense this season.* —opposite DEFENSE²

**of·fen·sive¹** /ə'fensɪv/ *adj* **1** very rude or insulting and likely to upset people: *I found her remarks deeply offensive.* | [+ **to**] *crude jokes that are offensive to women* —opposite INOFFENSIVE¹ (1) **2** *formal* unpleasant: *an offensive smell* **3** [only before noun] for attacking: *offensive weapons* | *The troops took up offensive positions.* —opposite DEFENSIVE **4** *AmE* concerned with getting points and getting a game, as opposed to stopping the other team from getting points: *offensive play* | *an offensive coach* —opposite DEFENSIVE —**offensively** *adv*: *His clothes smelled slightly, but not offensively.* | *The planes were too few to be used offensively.* —**offensiveness** *n* [U]

**offensive²** *n* [C] **1** a planned military attack involving large forces over a long period: *On March 6th they launched a full-scale offensive.* **2 be on the offensive** to be ready to attack or criticize people **3 take the offensive/go on the offensive** to be the first to make an attack or strong criticism **4 sales/charm/PR offensive** a planned set of actions intended to influence a lot of people

S1 W1 **of·fer¹** /'ɒfə‖'ɒːfər, 'ɑː-/ *v* **1** [T] to say that you are willing to give someone something, or to hold something out to them so that they can take it: **offer sb sth** *You haven't offered Grandma any ice cream.* | *They offered him a very good job but he turned it down.* | **offer sth to sb** *Offer some coffee to the guests.* **2** [T] to say that you are willing to pay a particular amount of money: **offer (sb) sth for** *They've offered us £75,000 for the house.* | *The police are offering a reward for any information.* **3** [I,T] to say that you are willing to do something: *I don't need any help, but it was nice of you to offer.* | **offer to do sth** *My dad has offered to pick us up.* | *Shelly didn't even offer to help.* **4** [T] to provide something that people need or want: *He offered no explanation for his actions.* | **offer sth to sb** *Senator Joseph's speech will have offered little comfort to bankrupt businessmen.* | **have sth to offer (to sb)** *Edinburgh has a great deal to offer to visitors in the way of entertainment.* **5 offer (up) a prayer/sacrifice etc** to pray to God or give something to God **6 offer itself** *formal* if an opportunity offers itself, it happens for you: *I shall be ready to raise the matter with him when a suitable occasion offers itself.* **7 offer your hand to sb** to hold out your hand in order to shake hands with someone

**offer²** *n* [C] **1** a statement that you are willing to give someone something or do something for them: [+ **of**] *an offer of assistance* | **offer to do sth** *an offer to help* | **turn down/refuse/decline an offer** (=say no to an offer) *He turned down the offer of a free trip to Milan.* **2** an amount of money that you are willing to pay for something: **make (sb) an offer (for)** *I'm prepared to make you a generous offer for the house.* | **accept an offer** *They've accepted our offer of £50,000.* | **be open to offers** (=be ready to consider people's offers) *We're asking £2500, but we're open to offers.* **3** a reduction of the price of something in a shop for a short time: **special offer** *They have a special offer on this week – buy two, get one free.* **4 on offer a)** available to be bought or used: *a whole range of services on offer* **b)** *BrE* for sale at a very cheap price for a short time: *Olive oil is on offer this week.* **5 be under offer** *BrE* if a house that is for sale is under offer, someone has offered money for it S2 W1

**of·fer·ing** /'ɒfərɪŋ‖'ɒː-, 'ɑː-/ *n* **1** [C] a book, play, piece of music etc that someone has written recently: *the latest offering from Nancy Griffith* **2** something that is given to God or given as a present to please someone —see also **burnt offering** (BURNT² (2)), PEACE OFFERING

**of·fer·to·ry** /'ɒfətəri‖'ɒːfətɔːri, 'ɑː-/ *n plural* **offertories** [C] **1** the money people give during a religious ceremony in church —see also COLLECTION (2a) **2** the offering of the bread and wine to God at COMMUNION (2)

**off-guard** /ˌ· '·◂/ *adj* [not before noun] not expecting something surprising or dangerous to happen, and not prepared to deal with it: **catch/take sb off-guard** *Caught off-guard, Paul blushed and looked away in embarrassment.*

**off·hand¹** /ˌɒf'hænd◂‖ˌɒːf-/ *adj* not giving people much time or attention, when you are talking to them: *She said you were a bit offhand with her this afternoon.* —**offhandedly** *adv* —**offhandedness** *n* [U]

**offhand²** *adv* immediately, without time to think about it or find out about something: *I can't remember offhand what shifts I'm working next week.*

**of·fice** /'ɒfɪ̈s‖'ɒː-, 'ɑː-/ *n* S1 W1

**1 ▶ BUILDING ◀** [C] the building that belongs to a company or organization, with a lot of rooms where people work: *The company is moving to new offices in central London.* | **head office** (=main office) | **the office** *Did you go to the office today?* | **at the office** *I must have left my keys at the office.* | **work in an office** *I'd hate to work in an office, but I could use a regular income.*

**2 ▶ ROOM ◀** [C] a room where you do work that involves writing, calculating, or talking to people: *the manager's office* | *My office gets really hot and sticky in the summer.* —see picture on page 837

**3 office hours** the time between about nine in the morning and five in the afternoon, when the people in offices are working: *You can contact us during office hours.*

**4 information/ticket etc office** a room or building where people go to ask for information —see also BOX OFFICE, POST OFFICE

**5 ▶ IMPORTANT JOB ◀** [C,U] an important job or position with power, especially in government: *the office of President* | **in office** (=in an important position) *His decision to resign after 30 years in office came as a great shock.* | **hold office** *She had previously held office as Minister of Education.* | **take office** (=start an important job)

**6 Office** used in the names of British government departments: *the Foreign Office*

**7 sb's good offices** *formal* help given by someone who has authority or can influence people: *I managed to get a visa through the good offices of a friend in the Service.*

**office block** /'· · ·/ *n* [C] *BrE* a large building with many offices in it; OFFICE BUILDING *AmE*

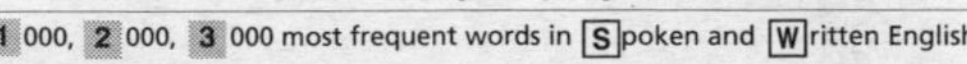

**office build·ing** /ˈ·· ˌ··/ *n* [C] *AmE* a large building with many offices in it; OFFICE BLOCK *BrE*

**office girl** /ˈ·· ·/ *n* [C] a young woman who does unimportant work in an office

**office hold·er** /ˈ·· ˌ··/ *n* [C] someone who has an official position, especially in the government

**office par·ty** /ˈ·· ˌ··/ *n* [C] a party just before Christmas in the office of a company, government department etc for the people who work there

S1 W1 **of·fi·cer** /ˈɒfɪ̈sə‖ˈɔːfɪ̈sər, ˈɑː-/ *n* [C] **1** someone who is in a position of authority in the army, navy etc: *a naval officer|Report to your commanding officer.* **2** someone who has an important position in an organization, such as a government, company etc: *a local government officer|a personnel officer* **3** a policeman or policewoman: *What's the problem, officer?|the officer in charge of the murder inquiry* **4 Officer** *AmE* a title for a policeman or policewoman: *Officer Maloney will help you.*

W3 **of·fi·cial¹** /əˈfɪʃəl/ *n* [C] someone who has a responsible position in an organization: *trade union members and officials|a government official*

S3 W2 **official²** *adj* **1** approved of or done by someone in authority, especially the government: *You have to get official permission to build a new house.|an official inquiry |The official languages of Canada are English and French.* **2** done as part of your job and not for your own private purposes: *Are you here in your official capacity?|the Queen's official visit to the Bahamas* **3** official information, reasons etc are given formally and publicly, but may not always be true: *The official motive for his resignation was that he wanted to spend more time with his children.|The news is not yet official.* (=has not been publicly announced) **4** chosen to represent someone or an organization, or do something for them: *official photographer to the Royal Family their official logo* **5** an official event is a formal, public event: *the official opening of the new store*

**of·fi·cial·dom** /əˈfɪʃəldəm/ *n* [U] a word meaning government departments or the people who work in them, used when you think they are unhelpful

**of·fi·cial·ese** /əˌfɪʃəlˈiːz/ *n* [U] *informal* a way of talking or writing used by government officials, that is unnecessarily difficult to understand

**of·fi·cial·ly** /əˈfɪʃəli/ *adv* **1** publicly and formally: *They have officially announced their engagement.|The new clinic was officially opened this morning.|The two countries are still not officially at war.* **2** [sentence adverb] according to what you say publicly, even though this may not be true: *Officially, he's on vacation, but there's a rumor that he's very ill.*

**official re·ceiv·er** /ˌ·· ·ˈ··/ *n* [C] someone whose job is to take care of the financial affairs of a company or a person that is BANKRUPT

**of·fi·ci·ate** /əˈfɪʃieɪt/ *v* [I + **at**] to do official duties, especially at a religious ceremony

**of·fi·cious** /əˈfɪʃəs/ *adj* too eager to tell people what to do: *An officious little guard came and told me not to whistle in the museum.* —**officiously** *adv* —**officiousness** *n* [U]

**off·ing** /ˈɒfɪŋ‖ˈɔː-, ˈɑː-/ *n* **be in the offing** to be about to happen or to be possible: *Everything's topsy-turvy at the moment with this big trip in the offing.*

**off·ish** /ˈɒfɪʃ‖ˈɔːf-/ *adj informal* behaving in a slightly unfriendly or impolite way: *I don't know why but she seemed a bit offish to me.*

**off-key** /ˌ· ˈ·◂/ *adj* music that is off-key sounds unpleasant because it is played slightly above or below the correct PITCH² (3): *The band sounds slightly off-key.* —**off-key** *adv*: *Someone upstairs was singing off-key.*

**off-li·cence** /ˈ· ··/ *n* [C] *BrE* a shop that sells wine, beer, and other alcoholic drinks, in bottles or cans; LIQUOR STORE *AmE*

**off lim·its** /ˌ· ˈ··/ *adj* **be off limits** if a place is off limits, you are not allowed to go there: [+ **to**] *Under the proposal, the Antarctic would be declared off-limits to whalers.*

**off·line** /ˈɒflaɪn‖ˈɔːf-/ *adj* not directly connected to a computer or directly controlled by it: *an offline terminal|offline storage of data* —opposite ONLINE —**offline** *adv*

**off-load** /ˌ· ˈ·/ *v* **1** [T] to get rid of something that you do not need by giving it to someone else: **off-load sth onto sb** *We managed to off-load all those old typewriters onto a friend of mine.* **2 off-load your problems/guilt/troubles etc** to tell someone about your problems etc in order to make yourself feel better

**off-peak** /ˌ· ˈ·◂/ *adj* **1** off-peak hours or periods are times when fewer people want to do or use something: *Telephone charges are lower during off-peak periods.* **2** off-peak travel, electricity etc is cheaper because it is done or used at these times

**off·print** /ˈɒfprɪnt‖ˈɔːf-/ *n* [C] an article from a magazine that is printed and sold separately

**off-put·ting** /ˈ· ˌ··/ *adj* if someone's behaviour or the appearance of something is off-putting, it is strange or unpleasant and stops you from liking or being interested in them: *Jack's aggressiveness is really off-putting.* —see also **put sb/sth off** (PUT) —**off-puttingly** *adv*

**off-ramp** /ˈ· ·/ *n* [C] *AmE* a road for driving off a HIGHWAY (1)

**off-road ve·hi·cle** /ˌ· · ˈ···/ *n* [C] a vehicle that is built very strongly so that it can be used on rough ground

**off-screen** /ˌ· ˈ·◂/ *adv* when a film actor is not acting: *What's he like off-screen?* —**off-screen** *adj*: *The fan magazines are full of her off-screen romances.*

**off-sea·son** /ˌ· ˈ··◂/ *n* **the off-season** the time of the year when there is not much work or activity, especially in farming or the tourist industry: *Most hotels are closed in the off-season.* —**off-season** *adj, adv*: *Take advantage of our special off-season fares.*

**off·set¹** /ˈɒfset, ˌɒfˈset‖ˈɔːfset, ˌɔːfˈset/ *v past tense and past participle* **offset** *present participle* **offsetting** [T] **1** if something such as a cost or sum of money offsets another cost, sum etc or is offset against it, it has an opposite effect so that the situation remains the same: **be offset by** *In 1992 the cost of the layoffs was offset by the savings on the payroll.|* **offset sth against sth** *He was able to offset his travel expenses against tax.* **2** to make something look better by being close to it and different: *Streaks of blond in his hair offset his deep tan.*

**off·set²** /ˈɒfset‖ˈɔːf-/ *n* [C,U] a method of printing in which ink is put onto rollers (ROLLER (1)) and the paper then passes between the rollers —**offset** *adj*

**off·shoot** /ˈɒfʃuːt‖ˈɔːf-/ *n* [C] **1** an organization, system of beliefs etc which has developed from a larger or earlier one: *Marxism-Leninism and its various offshoots|* [+ **of**] *The company was originally an offshoot of Bell Telephones.* **2** a new stem or branch on a plant

**off·shore** /ˌɒfˈʃɔː◂‖ˌɔːfˈʃɔːr◂/ *adj* **1** connected with work that is done on or under the sea: **offshore fishing/oil rig/exploration etc** *more than 10,000 offshore workers based in Orkney* **2 offshore bank/company/investment etc** a bank etc that is based abroad in a country where you pay less tax than in your home country **3 offshore wind/current etc** a wind etc that is blowing or moving away from the land —compare INSHORE, ONSHORE —**offshore** *adv*: *a boat anchored offshore*

**off·side¹** /ˌɒfˈsaɪd◂‖ˌɔːf-/ *adj, adv* in a position where you are not allowed to play the ball in sports such as football —opposite ONSIDE

**offside²** /ˈɒfsaɪd‖ˈɔːf-/ *n* **the offside** *BrE* the side of a car that is nearest to the middle of the road when you are driving it —opposite NEARSIDE —**offside** *adj*: *the offside headlight*

**off·spring** /ˈɒfˌsprɪŋ‖ˈɔːf-/ *n plural* **offspring** [C] **1** someone's child or children: *one of her numerous offspring* **2** an animal's baby or babies

**off·stage** /ˌɒfˈsteɪdʒ◂‖ˌɔːf-/ *adv* **1** just behind or to the side of a stage in a theatre, where the people watching a play cannot see: *There was a loud crash offstage.* **2** when an actor is not acting: *Offstage Peter always seemed a quiet, shy sort of person.* —**offstage** *adj*

**off-street** /ˌ· ˈ·/ *adj* **off-street parking** places for parking that are not on main streets

**off-the-cuff** /ˌ· · ˈ·◂/ *adj* [usually before noun] an off-the-cuff remark, reply etc is one that you make without thinking about it first —**off-the-cuff** *adv*

**off-the-peg** /ˌ· · ˈ·◂/ *adj BrE* off-the-peg clothes are not made to fit one particular person but are made in standard sizes; OFF-THE-RACK *AmE* —compare MADE-TO-MEASURE —**off-the-peg** *adv*: *It was only a cheap suit, bought off-the-peg.*

**off-the-rack** /ˌ· · ˈ·◂/ *adj AmE* OFF-THE-PEG

**off-the-rec·ord** /ˌ· · ˈ··◂/ *adj* an off-the-record remark is unofficial and is not supposed to be made public: *The Prime Minister's remarks were strictly off-the-record.* —**off-the-record** *adv*

**off-the-shelf** /ˌ· · ˈ·◂/ *adj, adv* already made and available in shops: *off-the-shelf database software*

**off-the-wall** /ˌ· · ˈ·◂/ *adj informal* a little strange or unusual: *an off-the-wall idea*

**off·track** /ˈɒftræk‖ˈɒːf-/ *adj* AmE away from a place where horses race: *Few states allow offtrack betting.*

**off-white** /ˌ· ˈ·◂/ *n* [U] a white that has some yellow or grey in it —**off-white** *adj*: *an off-white blouse*

**off-year** /ˈ· ·/ *n* [C usually singular] **1** a year when something is not as successful as usual: [+ **for**] *an off-year for car sales* **2** *AmE* a year in which no elections happen

**oft** /ɒft‖ɒːft/ *adv poetical or formal* often: **oft-repeated/quoted etc** *oft-repeated advice*

S1 W1 **of·ten** /ˈɒfən, ˈɒftən‖ˈɒː-/ *adv* **1** if something happens often, or you do something often, it happens regularly or many times: *Rosi often works till 7 or 8 o'clock in the evening.* | *If you wash your hair too often, it tends to make it greasy.* | **how often?** *How often do you go to the movies?* | **very/quite often** *Tom quite often goes to his Mum's on Saturday for tea.* | **not often** *It's not often that you meet people who are so willing to help.* —see picture at FREQUENCY **2** [sentence adverb] if something happens often, it happens in many situations or cases: *It's often difficult to translate poetry.* | **very/quite often** *Very often you find that children with behavioral problems come from broken homes.* **3 all too often** *also* **only too often** used to say that something sad, disappointing, or annoying happens too much: *All too often victims of bullying are too frightened to ask for help.* | *These loopholes in the tax laws are exploited only too often.* **4 every so often** sometimes: *An inspector would come round every so often to check the premises.* **5 as often as not** *also* **more often than not** *spoken* usually: *More often than not he'll come and apologize within minutes of shouting at us.*

**of·ten·times** /ˈɒfəntaɪmz‖ˈɒːf-/ *adv old use* often

**o·gle** /ˈəʊgəl‖ˈoʊ-/ *v* [I,T] to look at someone in an offensive way that shows you think they are sexually attractive: *A small fat man sat there most days, ogling girls' legs.*

**O grade** /ˈəʊ greɪd‖ˈoʊ-/ *n* [C] an examination in a particular subject, taken in Scotland, usually at the age of 16 —see also O LEVEL

**o·gre** /ˈəʊgə‖ˈoʊgər/ *n* [C] **1** a large character in children's stories who eats people **2** someone who seems fierce, cruel, and frightening: *My boss is a real ogre.*

**oh** /əʊ‖oʊ/ *interjection* **1** used to make a slight pause, especially before replying to a question or giving your opinion on something: *"What time are you going into town?" "Oh, I haven't decided yet."* | *"I don't like the new boss." "Oh, I think she's quite nice."* **2** used to get or keep someone's attention so that you can ask them a question or continue what you are saying: *Oh, Janet, could you get me a paper while you're out?* | *Milk, cereal, juice – oh, and put lettuce on the list too.* **3** used to express a strong emotion or to emphasize what you think about something: *Oh, aren't those flowers gorgeous!* | *Oh, how awful!* | *She got the job? Oh great!* **4 oh, did he?/oh, are you?/oh, was she? etc** used to show that you did not previously know what someone has just told you: *"Frances has left her husband, you know." "Oh, has she?"*

**ohm** /əʊm‖oʊm/ *n* [C] *technical* the standard unit of electrical RESISTANCE (5) which allows one AMP (1) to flow under a pressure of one VOLT

**o·ho** /əʊˈhəʊ‖oʊˈhoʊ/ *interjection old-fashioned* used to show surprise or satisfaction

**-oid** /ɔɪd/ *suffix technical (in adjectives)* like or in the form of something: *humanoid creatures* (=similar to humans) | *ovoid* (=egg shaped)

**oik** /ɔɪk/ *n* [C] *BrE slang* a rude unintelligent man who is likely to cause trouble —**oikish** *adj*

**oil¹** /ɔɪl/ *n* **1** [U] a smooth thick mineral liquid that is burned to produce heat, or used to make machines run easily: *Check the oil level in your car every week.* | **oil-burning/oil-fired** *oil-fired central heating* **2** [U] the thick, dark liquid from under the ground from which oil and petrol are produced; PETROLEUM: *the oil industry* **3** [C,U] a smooth, thick liquid made from plants or animals, used in cooking or for making beauty products: *olive oil* | *coconut oil shampoo* **4 oils** [plural] paints that contain oil; OIL PAINTS: **in oils** *Mostly I paint in oils.* —see also **burn the midnight oil** (BURN¹ (24)), **pour oil on troubled waters** (POUR (8)) S3 W2

**oil²** *v* [T] **1** to put oil into or onto something, such as a machine, in order to make it work more smoothly: *Isabel went upstairs to oil the attic lock and door hinges.* **2 oil the wheels** to help something to be done in business, politics etc successfully and easily

**oil-bear·ing** /ˈ· ˌ··/ *adj* oil-bearing rock contains oil

**oil·cake** /ˈɔɪlkeɪk/ *n* [C] a type of food for cattle

**oil·can** /ˈ· ·/ *n* [U] a metal container for oil with a long thin tube for pouring

**oil·cloth** /ˈɔɪlklɒθ‖-klɒːθ/ *n* [U] cloth treated with oil to give it a smooth surface

**oiled** /ɔɪld/ *adj* **well oiled** *BrE informal* very drunk

**oil·field** /ˈɔɪlfiːld/ *n* [C] an area of land or sea under which there is oil

**oil-fired** /ˈ· ·/ *adj* an oil-fired heating system burns oil to produce heat

**oil·man** /ˈɔɪlmæn/ *n plural* **oilmen** /-mən/ [C] someone who owns an oil company or works in the oil industry

**oil paint** /ˈ· ·/ *n* [C,U] paint that contains oil

**oil paint·ing** /ˈ· ˌ··/ *n* **1** [C] a picture painted with oil paint **2** [U] the art of painting with oil paint **3 he's/she's no oil painting** *BrE humorous* used to say that someone is unattractive or ugly

**oil pan** /ˈ· ·/ *n* [C] *AmE* a part of an engine that holds the supply of oil; SUMP (2) *BrE*

**oil plat·form** /ˈ· ˌ··/ *n* [C] an oil rig

**oil rig** /ˈ· ·/ *n* [C] a large structure with equipment for getting oil from under the ground, especially from under the sea bottom

**oil·seed rape** /ˌɔɪlsiːd ˈreɪp/ *n* [U] RAPE² (3)

**oil·skin** /ˈɔɪl-skɪn/ *n* **1** [U] cloth treated with oil so that water will not pass through it **2 oilskins** [plural] a coat and trousers made of oilskin

**oil slick** /ˈ· ·/ *n* [C] a layer of oil floating on water

**oil tank·er** /ˈ· ˌ··/ *n* [C] a ship that has large containers for carrying oil

**oil well** /ˈ· ·/ *n* [C] a hole that is dug in the ground to obtain oil

**oil·y** /ˈɔɪli/ *adj* **1** covered with oil or containing a lot of oil: *oily skin* | *oily rags* **2** looking or feeling like oil: *an oily liquid* **3** unpleasantly polite —**oiliness** *n* [U]

**oink** /ɔɪŋk/ *interjection* used to represent the sound that a pig makes —**oink** *n* [C]

**oint·ment** /ˈɔɪntmənt/ *n* [C,U] a soft substance made of solid oil that you rub into your skin, especially as a medical treatment —see also **fly in the ointment** (FLY³ (5))

**OJ** /ˈəʊ dʒeɪ‖ˈoʊ-/ *n* [U] *AmE informal* orange juice

**o·ka·pi** /əʊˈkɑːpi‖oʊ-/ *n* [C] an African animal like a GIRAFFE, but with a shorter neck

S1 **o·kay¹, OK** /əʊˈkeɪ‖oʊ-/ *adj spoken* **1** [not before noun] not ill, injured, unhappy etc: *Do you feel OK now?* **2** used to say that something is acceptable: *"Sorry I'm late." "That's okay."|Does my hair look OK?* **3** [not before noun] satisfactory but not extremely good: *Well, it was OK, but I liked the other one better.* **4 is it OK...?/...OK?** used to ask if you can do something or to tell someone they can do it: *Is it OK if I take Monday off?|I'll go first, OK?|* **it is okay for sb to do sth** *It's okay for you to go home now.|* **it is okay with/by sb** *If it's OK with your mom, it's OK by me.* **5** *especially AmE* nice, helpful, honest etc: *Dwight's OK – you can trust him.|an OK kind of guy* —**okay**, **OK** *adv*: *Mum's doing OK now.|Yeah, the TV's working okay.*



S1 **okay², OK** *interjection* **1** used when you start talking about something else, or when you pause before continuing: *OK, let's go on to item B.|OK, any questions so far?* **2** used to express agreement or give permission: *"Can I take the car today?" "Okay."* **3** used to stop people arguing with you: *OK, OK, so I made a mistake, I've told you I'm sorry.* **4** used when you think people are being unreasonable: *Look, I'm doing my best, OK?*

**okay³, OK** *v* **okayed, okaying** [T] *informal* to say officially that you will agree to something or allow it to happen: *Has the bank okayed your request for a loan?*

**okay⁴, OK** *n informal* **give (sb) the okay/get the okay** to give or get permission to do something: *I got the OK to leave early today.*

Frequencies of the word **okay** in spoken and written English.

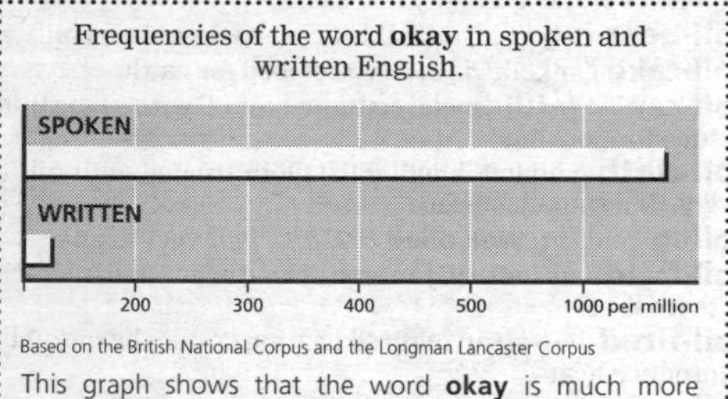


Based on the British National Corpus and the Longman Lancaster Corpus

This graph shows that the word **okay** is much more common in spoken English than in written English.

**o·key-doke** /ˌəʊki ˈdəʊk‖ˌoʊki ˈdoʊk/ also **okey-do·key** /-ˈdəʊki‖-ˈdoʊ-/ *adj, adv spoken* used like 'okay' to express agreement

**o·kra** /ˈɒkrə, ˈəʊ-‖ˈoʊ-/ *n* [U] a green vegetable used in cooking in Asia and the southern US —see picture on page 414

S1 W1 **old** /əʊld‖oʊld/ *adj*

**1** ▶ **USED OR NOT NEW** ◀ having existed for a long time, or having been used a lot before: *an old winter coat|a big old house|an old saying|My car's older than yours.*| **be (as) old as the hills** (=be extremely old)

**2** ▶ **NOT YOUNG** ◀ having lived for a long time: *an old man|* **get/grow old** (=become old) *The next time Robbie saw Mrs Dawes he thought she had grown very old.*

**3 the old** old people: *taking care of the old and the sick*

**4** ▶ **AGE** ◀ **be ... old** to be a particular age: *How old are you?|* **be 5/10/50 etc years old** *Our house is 60 years old.|* **5-year-old/10-year-old etc**: *our 12-year-old son|a six-week-old baby|* **old enough/too old** *I think you're old enough to make your own decisions.*

**5 old house/job/teacher etc** a house, job etc that you had before but do not have now: *I saw Phil with one of my old girlfriends.|My old car didn't have air conditioning.*

**6 he's old enough to be your father/she's old enough to be your mother** *informal* used to say that someone is too old for someone to have a sexual relationship with

**7 be old beyond your years** to be wiser or more sensible than most people your age

**8 be old before your time** to behave like someone much older than you, because bad things have happened to you

**9 sb is old enough to know better** used to say that you think someone should have behaved more sensibly

**10 an old friend/enemy etc** someone you have known for a long time: *Bob's an old friend of mine.*

**11 an old head on young shoulders** a young person who seems to think and behave like an older person

**12** ▶ **FAMILIAR** ◀ [only before noun] experienced, heard, or seen many times before; familiar: *It's good to get back into the old routine.|the old familiar faces|* **the same old** (=often used to say that you are bored with something) *We get tired of hearing the same old stuff.* —see also **it's the same old story** (STORY (10))

**13 old flame** someone with whom you used to have a romantic relationship

**14 the old country** *especially AmE* the country that you were born in, but that you no longer live in, used especially to mean Europe

**15 the old days** times in the past: *In the old days people used to fetch water from the pump.*

**16 the good old days/the bad old days** an earlier time in your life, or in history, when things seemed better or worse than now: *We like to chat about the good old days.*

**17 of old a)** *literary* long ago in the past: *in days of old* **b)** if you know someone of old you know them from a long time ago

**18 for old times' sake** if you do something for old times' sake, you do it to remind yourself of a happy time in the past

**19 be/feel/look like your old self** to feel or look better again after you have been ill or very unhappy: *Glad to see you looking more like your old self again.*

**20 Old English/Old Icelandic etc** an early form of English, Icelandic etc

**21 good old/poor old/silly old etc** *spoken* used to talk to or about someone you are fond of: *Good old Keith!|You poor old thing!*

**22 the old ...** used to talk about something that you often use or are very familiar with: *So I got the old paint brushes out and set to work.*

**23 you old .../the old ...** used to show that you are surprised or amused by what someone has said or done: *You told her that? You old liar!|Don't ask him, the old miser.*

**24 old fool/old cow etc** *spoken* used to talk about someone you do not like: *the old bastard|silly old fool*

**25 a good old** also **a right old** *BrE spoken* used to talk about something you enjoy: *We had a good old talk.*

**26 any old thing/hat/place etc** *informal* used to say that it does not matter which thing, place etc you choose: *Oh, just wear any old thing.|You can't just turn up at any old time, you know.*

**27 any old how/way** *informal* untidily or carelessly: *Put these away properly, don't shove them in any old how.*

**28 pay/settle an old score** to punish someone for something wrong that they did to you in the past

**29 of the old school** old-fashioned and believing in old ideas and customs: *a real English lady of the old school*

**30 old wives' tale** a belief based on old ideas that are now considered to be untrue

**31 be an old hand at** to have a lot of experience of something: *I'm an old hand at this game.*

**32 the old guard** a group of people within an organization or club who do not like changes or new ideas: *The old guard will vote against letting women into the club.*

**33 the Old Bill** *BrE informal* the police —see also **the old school tie** (TIE¹ (8))

**USAGE NOTE: OLD**

WORD CHOICE: **older, elder, elderly, senior citizen, OAP**

You can use **older** to describe either people or things. **Elder** means the same thing but you only use it to talk about people and usually only your close family: *My elder/older daughter is at university.* | *Shane is the elder brother of the two.* But you can also say: *elder members of the community*

**Older** but not **elder** can be used with **than**: *Shane is older than Mark* (NOT *elder than*).

When you are talking about people, **elderly** (NOT *elder*) is a polite way of saying **old.** Compare *an old church* and *an old/elderly lady*. Most people however now prefer to be called **senior citizens**, and this is the most common, polite, and acceptable expression to use.

In British English, especially in official notices, you might see OAP, which is short for 'old age pensioner'.

**old age** /ˌ· '·◂/ *n* [U] the part of your life when you are old: *the effects of old age* | **in your old age** *My aunt needed to be cared for in her old age.*

**old age pen·sion** /ˌ· · '··/ *n* [U] *BrE* money paid regularly by the state to old people; SOCIAL SECURITY (2) *AmE*

**old age pen·sion·er** /ˌ· · '···/ *n* [C] *BrE* someone who does not work any more and who receives an old age pension —see also OAP

**old boy** /'. .(for 1, 2), ˌ. '. (for 3, 4)/ *n* [C] **1** *BrE* a man who used to be a student at a particular school: *an old boys' reunion* **2 the old-boy network** the system by which men from rich families, men who went to the same school, belong to the same club etc, use their influence to help each other **3** *BrE spoken* an old man: *the old boy from down the road* **4** *BrE old-fashioned* a way of addressing a male friend: *How are you, old boy?* —compare OLD GIRL

**old·e** /'əʊldi‖'oʊldi/ *adj* another spelling of old, used in the names of shops, products etc to make them seem traditional: *ye olde tea shoppe*

**old·en** /'əʊldən‖'oʊl-/ *adj* **in olden days/times** a long time ago: *In olden times life was simpler.*

**Old En·glish Sheep·dog** /ˌ· ·· '··/ *n* [C] a large dog with long thick grey and white hair

**olde-world·e** /ˌəʊldi 'wɜːldi◂‖ˌoʊldi 'wɜːr-/ *adj BrE informal* a place that is olde-worlde has been decorated so that it looks old-fashioned: *an olde-worlde country pub*

**old-fash·ioned**[1] /ˌ· '··◂/ *adj* **1** not modern and considered not to be fashionable any more: *Gwen's clothes are so old-fashioned!* | *'Wireless' is an old-fashioned word for 'radio'.* **2** someone who is old-fashioned believes in ways of doing things that are not usual any more: *Dad's kind of old-fashioned in his views on sex before marriage.* **3 an old-fashioned look/expression** *BrE old use* a disapproving look or expression

**old-fashioned**[2] *n* [C] *AmE* an alcoholic drink made with WHISKEY

**old fo·gey** /ˌəʊld 'fəʊgi‖ˌoʊld 'foʊ-/ *n* [C] *informal* someone who is old, or has old-fashioned ideas about things: *Oh come on, it's only 10 o'clock, don't be such an old fogey!*

**old folk** /'· ˌ·/ *BrE* also **old folks** *especially AmE n* [plural] an expression meaning old people, used especially when speaking of them in a kind way: *We always try to do something for the old folk at Christmas.*

**old folks' home** /ˌ· '· ˌ·/ *n* [C] *informal* an OLD PEOPLE'S HOME

**old girl** /'. . (for 1), ˌ. '. (for 2)/ *n* [C] *BrE* **1** a woman who is a former student of a particular school **2** *spoken* an old woman: *Don't tell me the old girl still drives!* —compare OLD BOY

**Old Glo·ry** /ˌ· '··/ *n* [U] *AmE* the flag of the US

**Old Har·ry** /ˌ· '··/ *n BrE old-fashioned* the devil

**old hat** /ˌ· '·/ *adj* [not before noun] familiar or old-fashioned, and therefore boring: *Most of this is probably old hat to you, isn't it?*

**old·ie** /'əʊldi‖'oʊldi/ *n* [C] *informal* someone or something that is old: **oldie but goodie** *It's all nostalgia – they play the oldie-but-goodie records.* —see also **golden oldie** (GOLDEN (7))

**old·ish** /'əʊldɪʃ‖'oʊld-/ *adj* not very old, but not young or new either

**old la·dy** /ˌ· '··/ *n slang* **1** an expression meaning someone's wife: *Gotta go home to my old lady, I guess.* **2** an expression meaning your mother

**old lag** /ˌ· '·/ *n BrE old-fashioned* someone who has been in prison many times

**old maid** /ˌ· '·/ *n* [C] **1** an offensive expression meaning a woman who has never married and is not young any more **2** *informal* someone who pays too much attention to unimportant matters and has old-fashioned ideas —**old-maidish** *adj*

**old man** /ˌ· '·/ *n* [C] **1** *slang* an expression meaning someone's husband: *I heard her old man beats her.* **2** *slang* an expression meaning your father **3** *BrE old-fashioned* used to address a male friend: *Could I have a word with you, old man?*

**old mas·ter** /ˌ· '··/ *n* [C] a famous painter, especially from the 15th to 18th century, or a painting by one of these painters: *a priceless collection of old masters*

**Old Nick** /ˌ· '·/ *n BrE old-fashioned* the devil

**old peo·ple's home** /ˌ· '·· ˌ·/ *n* [C] a place where old people live together and are cared for

**old salt** /ˌ· '·/ *n* [C] *old-fashioned* a SAILOR who has had a lot of experience of sailing

**old·ster** /'əʊldstə‖'oʊldstər/ *n* [C] *informal* an old person

**Old Tes·ta·ment** /ˌ· '···◂/ *n* **the Old Testament** the first part of the Christian Bible containing ancient Hebrew writings about the time before the birth of Christ —compare NEW TESTAMENT

**old tim·er** /ˌ· '··/ *n* [C] **1** someone who has been in a particular job, place etc for a long time and knows a lot about it **2** *especially AmE* an old man

**old wom·an** /ˌ· '··/ *n BrE slang* **1 the old woman** an offensive expression meaning someone's wife or mother **2** [C] a man who pays too much attention to unimportant details —**old womanish** *adj*

**Old World** /ˌ· '·◂/ *n* **the Old World** *old use* the Eastern Hemisphere, especially Europe, Asia and Africa —compare NEW WORLD

**old-world** /'· · / *adj* [only before noun] an old-world place or quality is attractive because it is old or reminds you of the past: *the old-world charm of the village*

**ole** /əʊl‖oʊl/ *adj* used in written English to represent the way some people say 'old': *The poor ole guy!*

**o·le·ag·i·nous** /ˌəʊli'ædʒɪnəs‖ˌoʊ-/ *adj technical* containing, producing, or like oil

**o·le·an·der** /ˌəʊli'ændə‖ˌoʊli'ændər/ *n* [C,U] a green bush with white, red, or pink flowers

**O lev·el** /'əʊ ˌlevəl‖'oʊ-/ *n* **1** [U] Ordinary level; an examination taken in schools in England and Wales before 1988, usually at the age of 16 **2** [C] one of these examinations in a particular subject: *He left school with five O levels.* | *O level German* —compare A LEVEL, GCSE

**ol·fac·to·ry** /ɒl'fæktəri‖ɑːl-, oʊl-/ *adj technical* connected with the sense of smell: *the olfactory ducts*

**ol·i·gar·chy** /'ɒlɪgɑːki‖'ɑːlɪgɑrːki, 'oʊ-/ *n* **1** [U] government or control by a small group of people **2** [C usually singular] a state governed by a small group of people, or the group who govern such a state —**oligarch** *n* [C]

**ol·ive** /'ɒlɪv‖'ɑː-/ *n* **1** [C] a tree grown in Mediterranean countries that has small bitter egg-shaped fruits, usually black or green: *an olive grove* **2** [C] the fruit of this tree, used for food and also for its oil **3** a deep yellowish green colour —see picture on page 411 **4 olive skin/complexion** skin colour that is yellowish brown **5 offer/hold out/extend the olive branch** to do something to show that you want to end an argument —**olive** *adj*: *an olive sweatshirt*

**olive drab** /ˌ·· '·/ *n* [U] *especially AmE* a greyish green colour, used especially in military uniforms —**olive drab** *adj*

**olive oil** /ˌ·· ˈ·/ *n* [U] a pale yellow or green oil obtained from olives and used in cooking

**-ol·o·gist** /ɒlədʒ̍st‖ɑːl-/ also **-logist** *suffix (in nouns)* a person who studies or specializes in a particular kind of science: *a biologist*

O

**-ology** /ɒlədʒi‖ɑːl-/ also **-logy**—*suffix (in nouns)* **1** the scientific study of something: *geology* (=the study of rocks and the Earth)|*climatology* (=the study of CLIMATE)|*Egyptology* (=the study of ancient Egypt) **2** *informal* something that is done or talked about as though it was a scientific study: *futurology* (=the practice of trying to say how the future will develop) **3** the things studied by a particular science: *The geology of north Devon is particularly interesting* (=it has interesting rocks, etc). —**-ological** /əlɒdʒɪkəl‖-lɑː-/ *suffix (in adjectives)* —**-ologically** /əlɒdʒɪkli‖-lɑː-/ *suffix (in adverbs)*: *geologically interesting*

**O·lym·pi·ad** /əˈlɪmpi-æd/ *n* [C] *formal* a particular occasion of the modern Olympic Games: *Welcome to the games of the 23rd Olympiad.*

**O·lym·pi·an¹** /əˈlɪmpiən/ *n* one of the ancient Greek Gods

**Olympian²** *adj* **1** like a god, especially by being calm and not concerned about ordinary things: *to view the world with an Olympian detachment* **2** connected with the ancient Greek gods

**O·lym·pic** /əˈlɪmpɪk/ *adj* [only before noun] connected with the Olympic Games: *an Olympic runner*

**Olympic Games** /·ˌ·· ˈ·/ *n* [plural] **1** an international sports event held every four years in different countries **2** a sports event held at Olympia in Greece every four years in ancient times

**O·lym·pics**/əˈlɪmpɪks/ *n* [plural] the Olympic Games

**OM** /ˌəʊ ˈem‖ˌoʊ-/ *n* [C] the Order of Merit; a special HONOUR¹ (4) given to someone by the Queen of England

**om·buds·man** /ˈɒmbʊdzmən‖ˈɑːm-/ *n* [C] someone who deals with complaints made by ordinary people against the government, banks, insurance companies etc

**o·me·ga** /ˈəʊm̍gə‖oʊˈmegə, -ˈmiː-, -ˈmeɪ-/ *n* [C] the last letter of the Greek alphabet

**ome·lette** also **omelet** *AmE* /ˈɒml̍t‖ˈɑːm-/ *n* [C] **1** eggs mixed together and cooked in hot fat, sometimes with other foods added: *a cheese omelette* **2 you can't make an omelette without breaking eggs** used to say that it is impossible to do something important without causing problems

**o·men** /ˈəʊmən‖ˈoʊ-/ *n* [C] a sign of what will happen in the future: **a good/bad/ill omen** *The sudden change in weather seemed to Frank to be a good omen.* —see also ILL-OMENED

**om·i·nous** /ˈɒm̍nəs‖ˈɑː-/ *adj* making you feel that something bad is going to happen: *The car is making an ominous rattling sound.* —**ominously** *adv*: *The sky looked ominously dark.*

**o·mis·sion** /əʊˈmɪʃən, ə-‖oʊ-, ə-/ *n* **1** [U] the act of not including or not doing something: *The omission of her name was not a deliberate act.* **2** [C] something that has been omitted: *It was one of many errors and omissions pushing up the cost of the road works.*|**a glaring omission** (=one that is very bad and easily noticed)

**o·mit** /əʊˈmɪt, ə-‖oʊ-, ə-/ **omitted, omitting** *v* [T] **1** to not include someone or something, either deliberately or because you forget to do it; **leave out** (LEAVE¹): *Please don't omit any details, however trivial they may seem.* **2 omit to do sth** *formal* to not do something, either because you forgot or deliberately: *Oliver omitted to mention that he was married.*

**om·ni-** /ɒmnɪ‖ɑːm-/ *prefix* everything or everywhere; all: *an omnivore* (=animal that eats all sorts of food)

**om·ni·bus** /ˈɒmnɪbəs, -ˌbʌs‖ˈɑːm-/ *n* [C] *especially BrE* **1** a book containing several stories, especially by one writer, that have already been printed separately **2** a radio or television programme made of several programmes that have previously been broadcast separately: *the Brookside omnibus* **3** *old use* a bus

**om·nip·o·tent** /ɒmˈnɪpətənt‖ɑːm-/ *adj formal* able to do everything —**omnipotence** *n* [U] *God's omnipotence*

**om·ni·pres·ent** /ˌɒmnɪˈprezənt◂‖ˌɑːm-/ *adj formal* present everywhere at all times —**omnipresence** *n* [U]

**om·nis·ci·ent** /ɒmˈnɪʃənt, -ˈnɪsiənt‖ɑːmˈnɪʃənt/ *adj formal* knowing everything: *Only God is omniscient.* —**omniscience** *n* [U]

**om·ni·vore** /ˈɒmn̍vɔː‖ˈɑːmn̍vɔːr/ *n* [C] *technical* an animal that eats both meat and plants

**om·niv·o·rous** /ɒmˈnɪvərəs‖ɑːm-/ *adj technical* **1** an animal that is omnivorous eats both meat and plants **2** interested in everything, especially in all books: *an omnivorous reader*

**on¹** /ɒn‖ɑːn, ɔːn/ *prep* **1** touching or being supported by a particular surface: *The plate's on the table.*|*You have mud on your shoes.*|*The answer is written on page 25.* —see picture on page 1257 **2** hanging from, supported by or connected to a particular thing: *Stand on one foot.*|*pictures stuck on the wall*|*a ball on a string* **3 a)** in a particular place, building or area of land: *Several bombs landed on the runway.*|*He grew up on a ranch in California.* **b)** *AmE* in a particular road: *We live on Mulberry Drive.*|*I met Amy on the street the other day.* **4** in a particular direction: *On my right sat the Chancellor.*|*As the troops marched on the city, the leaders planned their escape.* **5** used to show the person or thing affected by an action or someone's behaviour: *a tax on cigarettes*|*The divorce has had a particularly bad effect on the children.* **6** on one of the sides of something such as a river or road: *a cafe on the river*|*a beautiful village on the Austrian border*|*trees on both sides of the street* **7 on Friday/August 2nd/my birthday** at some time during a particular day: *They arrive on Tuesday.*|*I was born on July 1st.* **8** about a particular subject: *a book on India*|*advice on what to wear* **9** in a bus, train, aircraft etc: *Everyone on the plane was frightened.*|*He managed to be on the first train back to London.* —see also **on foot** (FOOT¹ (2)), **on horseback** (HORSEBACK) **10** used to say what food someone needs to survive, what FUEL¹ (1) something needs to operate etc: *We can't live on rice and water forever.*|*Many cars nowadays run on lead free petrol.* **11** used to say what money people use to live, the amounts of money someone earns etc: *Some families in the ghettos have been on welfare all their lives.*|*People on high salaries should pay more tax.* **12** *informal* used to say that someone takes a particular drug or medicine: *Since she's been on Prozac she's been a different person.* **13 on the radio/telephone** using a radio or telephone: *Shut up! I'm on the phone.* **14 on a trip/journey etc** during a trip, journey etc: *I met several people on the voyage.*|*On my way to work the car broke down.* **15** used to say what has been used to do something: *Phil had torn his shirt on a nail.*|*It's amazing what you can do on these new word processors.* **16** *formal* immediately after something has happened or after someone has done something: **on doing sth** *On hearing the news of the air attack most foreigners headed for the border.*|**on arrival/sb's return etc** *On arrival at reception, guests should sign the visitors' book.*| **on sth** *On the general's command, all soldiers must salute.* **17** used to say that someone is a member of a team, organization etc: *What team did you say your boyfriend was on?* **18** compared with another person or thing: *This essay is a definite improvement on your last one.*|*Sales are 10% up on last year.* **19 have/carry etc sth on you** *informal* to have a particular thing in your pocket, your bag etc: *How much cash do you have on you?* **20** *spoken* used to say that someone will pay for something such as a drink, a meal etc: *Drinks are on Harold!* **21** *informal* if a machine stops, breaks etc on you, it stops or breaks while you are using it: *Suddenly the telephone went dead on me.*

**on²** *adj, adv* [not before noun] **1** used to say that someone continues to do something or something continues to happen, without stopping: **play/read/talk etc on** (=to

continue playing, reading etc) *Both teams managed to play on into overtime, despite the blistering heat.* | **carry/keep/go on etc doing sth** *If you keep on eating like that you'll need to diet.* | **carry/keep/go on etc** *Carry on. You're doing very well.* **2** if you move, walk etc on, you move forward to a particular place: *If you walk on a little, you can see the coast.* | *You can have your letters sent on to you at your new address.* | **straight on** *Keep straight on and turn left at the bank.* **3** used to say that something happens at a time that is before or after another time: **earlier/later on** *Later on we learned that he got back to France safely.* | **from then on/from that day on etc** *From that moment on I never believed a word she told me.* **4** if you have something on, you are wearing it: *Put your coat on. It's freezing outside.* | *The poor child had absolutely nothing on.* **5** in a bus, train, aircraft etc: *The bus stopped and everyone rushed to get on.* **6** if a machine, light etc is on, it is operating: *Who left the hot water faucet on?* | *The TV's on but nobody seems to be watching it.* —opposite OFF[1] (4) **7** if a film, TV programme etc is on, it is being broadcast or shown at a theatre: *That new sitcom is on tonight.* **8** if an event is on, it is happening or will still happen: *There's a jazz festival on in Vancouver this week.* | *Are you sure the party's on for tonight?* **9 have a lot on** *informal* to be very busy: *We don't have much on at the moment. I could see you tomorrow.* **10 be on at sb** *informal* to keep asking someone to do something, so that they become annoyed: *Mildred's been on at him to fix that cupboard for weeks now.* **11 be/go on about sth** *informal BrE* to keep talking about something, in a way that is boring: *Will you stop going on about that goal! It was definitely a penalty.*
**12 on and off** also **off and on** if you do something during a period of time on and off, you do it for several short periods in that time but not continually: *He's been smoking for 10 years now, on and off.* **13 it's not on** *spoken BrE* used to say that you do not think something is socially acceptable or reasonable: *It's not on, is it? Leaving your children alone like that.* **14 head on/full on** if two things hit each other head on, they hit the front part of each other, usually very hard: *Both cars skidded, crashing head on at 80 miles an hour.* **15** if an actor is on, they are performing: *You're on in two minutes.*

**on-air** /ˈ· ·/ *adj* [only before noun] broadcast while actually happening: *an on-air interview*

S1 W1 **once¹** /wʌns/ *adv*
**1 ▶ ONE TIME ◀** on one occasion: *I've only met her once.* | **once before** *Paul's been to Wexford once before.*
**2 once a week/year etc** one time every week etc as a regular activity: *We do aerobics once a week.*
**3 at once a)** immediately or without delay: *Young lady, get upstairs and clean your room at once!* **b)** at the same time, together: *Don't all talk at once.*
**4 all at once** if something happens all at once, it happens suddenly when you do not expect it: *All at once there was a loud banging on the door.*
**5 once more** one more time or again: *Can we go please Daddy, just once more!*
**6 once again/once more** again, after happening several times before: *Once again she's refusing to help.*
**7 once or twice** a few times: *I've driven down here once or twice before.*
**8 once in a while** sometimes, although not often: *It'd be nice if you'd write to me once in a while.*
**9 ▶ IN THE PAST ◀** at some time in the past, but not now: *Franklyn had obviously been handsome once.* | **once-great/beautiful etc** *It was sad to see the once-great man looking so frail.*
**10 once in a blue moon** *informal* very rarely
**11 (just) for once** *spoken* used to say that something hardly ever happens, although it should happen often: *Just for once I'd like to see him cook dinner.* | *Well, for once he's being nice to me.*
**12 (just) this/the once** *spoken* used to emphasize that this is the only time that you will let someone do something, or ask someone to do something: *Go on, lend me the car, just this once.*
**13 once and for all a)** if you deal with something once and for all, you deal with it definitely and finally: *Let's settle this matter once and for all.* **b)** *spoken* used to say that you are asking someone to do something for the last time, and they must do it: *Once and for all, will you switch off that television!*
**14 once upon a time a)** used at the beginning of children's stories **b)** *spoken* at a time in the past that you think was much better than now: *Once upon a time you used to be able to leave your front door unlocked.*
**15 do sth once too often** to be hurt because of something dangerous or stupid that you have done
**16 the once** *spoken* on one particular occasion: *I've only met her the once.*
**17 once bitten, twice shy** used to say that people will not do something again if it has been a bad experience

**once²** *conjunction* from the moment that something happens: *Once she arrives, we can start.* | *Once in bed, the children usually stay there.* S1 W1

**once-o·ver** /ˈ· ˌ··/ *n* **give sb/sth the once-over** to look at someone or something quickly to check who they are or what they are like: *A guard gave us the once-over before letting us in the door.*

**on·com·ing** /ˈɒnˌkʌmɪŋ‖ˈɑːn-, ˈɔːn-/ *adj* **oncoming car/traffic etc** a car etc that is coming towards you

**one¹** /wʌn/ *number* **1** the number one: *one hundred and twenty one pounds (£121)* | *The answer is on page forty-one.* | *Can I have one coffee and two milkshakes please?* **2 one or two** a small number of people or things: *There are one or two things to sort out before I leave.* **3 in ones and twos** if people do something in ones and twos they do it on their own or in small groups: *Guests arrived in ones and twos.* **4 a)** *AmE* a one dollar bill **b)** *BrE* a one pound coin **5 for one thing** *spoken* used to introduce the first of several reasons: *You can't see in that fridge, for one thing the light's gone and for another the button's broken.* **6 one-armed/one-eyed/one-legged etc** having only one arm, eye, leg etc S1 W1

**one²** *determiner* **1** a person or thing, especially when there are other people or things of the same type or kind: *Sam's just heard that one of his houses has caught fire.* | *If there's one thing I can't stand it's people who bite their nails.* | *There's one person I really must thank.* **2 one day/afternoon/year etc a)** a particular day, afternoon etc in the past: *We first met one cloudy day last July.* | *One morning I was sitting at my desk when a policeman knocked at my door.* **b)** any day, afternoon etc at any time in the future: *One evening you and I should go out for a drink.* **3 sb's one fear/worry/concern etc** someone's main fear, worry etc: *My one fear is that her nerves will get the better of her.* **4 the one man/place etc** the only man, place etc: *Claire is the one person I can trust.* | *I'm sorry madam, we've only the one ticket left.* **5** used to talk about one person or thing in comparison with other similar or connected people or things: *It's impossible to tell one child from another in that family.* | *One of the gang broke into the safe while the other was keeping watch.* | **It's one thing ... but ...** *It's one thing passing your driving test but being a good driver is another.* **6** *formal* used before the name of someone who you do not know well: *It seems the inheritance went to an old family friend, one Joseph Nelson.* **7 one wonderful woman/one interesting job etc** *spoken especially AmE* a very wonderful woman, a very interesting job etc: *Hey, your brother is one amazing guy!* **8 one by one/one after another** if people do something one by one, first one person does it, then the next, then the next etc: *One by one each soldier approached the coffin and gave a final salute.* **9 I/John etc for one** used to emphasize that you are doing something, believe something etc and hope others will do the same: *If they continue to abuse civil rights, I for one will be boycotting any food they produce.* **10 (all) in one** if someone or something is many different things all in one, they are all of those things: *She's president, secretary and treasurer all in one.* **11 be one up (on sb)** to have an S1 W1

O

advantage over someone —see also ONE-UPMANSHIP **12 put one over on sb** *informal* to trick someone: *No one's going to put one over on me!* **13 get one over on sb** *informal* to get an advantage over someone: *The easiest way to get one over on bullies is to answer them back.* **14 the one and only** *informal* used to emphasize that someone is very famous: *"That wasn't George Best I saw you talking to, was it?" "The one and only!"* **15 be at one with sb/sth a)** to feel very calm or relaxed because of the calm situation or environment you are in: *a weekend in the country, when you can feel at one with nature* **b)** *formal* to agree with someone about something: **16 a) be as one** *formal* to agree about something: *The whole committee is as one on this – no women are allowed on the golf course.* **b) as one** if many people do something as one they all do it at the same time: *The whole team stood up as one and marched out of the room.* **17 got it in one!** *spoken* used to say that someone has guessed correctly: *"You're not painting the house again are you?" "Got it in one!"* **18 have one for the road** *informal* to have an alcoholic drink, especially the last one before you leave a place **19 you are/he is a one** *old-fashioned especially BrE* used to tell someone that they are being rude, foolish etc: *The patient in the end bed is a real one, I can tell you.* —see also ONE-TO-ONE

S1 W1 **one³** *pron plural* **ones** **1** used instead of a noun that has already been mentioned or which the person you are talking to already knows about: *I've always wanted a CD player and I've just saved enough money to buy one.* | *The train was crowded so we decided to catch a later one.* | **the one that/who/which etc** *Soufflés are so hard to cook. Why is it that the ones I make always sink?* | **this one/that one/these ones/those ones** *I'll take that one, the one with all the chocolate on top.* **2** *formal* used when you mean YOU¹ (2), especially when you do not mean any one person in particular: *One asks oneself where children learn to behave so badly.* **3 the one about ...** *especially spoken* a joke or humorous story: *Have you heard the one about the dog that thought it was a cat?* **4 a ... one** a particular kind of problem, question, story etc: *"Excuse me, can you tell me the way to the bank?" "Oh, that's a hard one, it's either the second or the third road on the left."* **5 not be one to do sth/not be one who does sth** *informal* to never do a particular thing, especially something that annoys people: *I'm never one to complain, as you know, but I do think you could come and visit me more often.* **6 be one for** *informal* to enjoy doing a particular sport, subject etc: *I've never been (a great) one for watersports.* **7 one and the same** the same person or thing: *Muhammad Ali and Cassius Clay are one and the same.* **8 one and all** *old-fashioned* everyone: *The bride was welcomed by the family, one and all.* **9 be one of the family/the boys** to be accepted as a member of a particular group of people: *It took me a while to settle in but I just feel like one of the family now.* **10 one of us** *especially spoken* used to say that someone is a member of the same group that you are in and has the same ideas, beliefs etc: *You can talk in front of Terry – he's one of us.* **11 the little/young ones** *humorous or old-fashioned* children, especially young children

> **USAGE NOTE: ONE**
>
> FORMALITY
>
> **One** meaning 'people in general' is very formal. Most people usually use **you** with the same meaning. Compare: *One can do what one likes here.* | *You can do what you like here.*
>
> You use **one** instead of repeating a noun phrase in both spoken and written English: *The reason is basically an economic one.*
>
> You can use **ones** when two adjectives are used to compare things, but it is best to avoid this in formal written English: *He buys German rather than British cars* (formal). | *He buys German cars rather than British ones* (informal).

**one an·oth·er** /ˌ· ·ˈ··/ *pron* each other: *Liz and I have known one another for years.* | *They often stay at one another's houses.* —compare EACH OTHER S3 W3

**one-armed ban·dit** /ˌ· · ˈ··/ *n* [C] a machine with a long handle, into which you put money in order to try to win more money; FRUIT MACHINE *BrE*; SLOT MACHINE *AmE*

**one-horse** /ˈ· ·/ *adj* **1 one horse town** *informal* a small and boring town: *I can't wait to get out of this one-horse town!* **2** pulled by one horse: *a one-horse plough*

**one-lin·er** /ˌ· ˈ··/ *n* [C] a very short joke or humorous remark

**one-man** /ˈ· ·/ *adj* [only before noun] performed, operated, controlled etc by one person: *He does a one-man show in Las Vegas.* | *a one-man business*

**one-man band** /ˌ· · ˈ·/ *n* [C] **1** *informal* an organization or activity in which one person does everything: *The company is really a one-man band.* **2** a street musician who plays several instruments at the same time

**one-night stand** /ˌ· · ˈ·/ *n* [C] **1** *informal* **a)** an occasion when two people have sex, but do not intend to meet each other again: *I'm not into one-night stands.* **b)** a person that you have sex with once and do not see again **2** a performance of music or a play that is given only once in a particular place: *The band had a series of one-night stands around the country.*

**one-off¹** /ˌ· ˈ·◂/ *adj* [only before a noun] *BrE* happening or done only once, not as part of a regular series; ONE-SHOT *AmE*: *Yours for a one-off payment of only £200.*

**one-off²** *n* [C] *BrE* **1** something that is done or made only once: *I missed my chance. The deal was a one-off.* **2** *informal* someone who is completely different from anyone else

**one-pa·rent fam·i·ly** /ˌ· ·· ˈ···/ *n* [C] a family in which there is only one parent who looks after the children

**one-piece** /ˈ· ·/ *adj* [only before noun] consisting of only one piece, not separate parts: *a one-piece bathing suit*

**o·ner·ous** /ˈɒnərəs, ˈəʊ-‖ˈɑː-, ˈoʊ-/ *adj formal* work or RESPONSIBILITY that is onerous is difficult and worrying or makes you tired: *an onerous task* | *onerous duties* —**onerously** *adv* —**onerousness** *n* [U]

**one·self** /wʌnˈself/ *pron formal* the reflexive form of ONE³ (2): *It is only through study that one really begins to know oneself.* —see ONE (USAGE), YOURSELF (USAGE)

**one-shot** /ˈ· ·/ *adj AmE* happening or done only once; ONE-OFF *BrE*: *It's a one-shot deal. You don't get any second chances.*

**one-sid·ed** /ˌ· ˈ··◂/ *adj* **1** considering or showing only one side of a question, subject etc in a way that is unfair: *The newspapers give a very one-sided account of the war.* **2** an activity or competition that is one-sided is one in which one person or side does what they want and the other can do nothing: *a very boring, one-sided game* | *I'd say the conversation was pretty one-sided.* —**one-sidedly** *adv* —**one-sidedness** *n* [U]

**one-star** /ˈ· ·/ *adj* **one-star hotel/restaurant etc** a hotel etc that is not of a very high standard

**one-stop** /ˈ· ·/ *adj AmE* **one-stop shop/store etc** a shop where you can buy many different things

**one-time** /ˈ· ·/ *adj* [only before noun] former: *Neil McMurtry, a one-time busdriver, is the lead singer.*

**one-to-one** /ˌ· · ˈ·◂/ *adj* **1** between only two people: *tuition on a one-to-one basis* **2** matching each other exactly: *a one-to-one correlation* —**one-to-one** *adv*: *I need to discuss it with him one-to-one.*

**one-track mind** /ˌ· · ˈ·/ *n* **have a one-track mind** to be continuously thinking about one particular thing: *All you ever talk about is sex! You've got a one-track mind.*

**one-two** /ˌ· ˈ·/ *n* [C] a movement in which a BOXER hits his opponent with one hand and then quickly with the other: *Ali gives his opponent the old one-two, and it's all over.*

**one-up·man·ship** /wʌn'ʌpmənʃɪp/ *n* [U] the skill of making yourself seem better than other people

**one-way** /ˌ· '·◂/ *adj* [usually before noun] **1** moving or allowing movement in only one direction: *one-way traffic | a one-way street* **2** *especially AmE* a one-way ticket is for travelling from one place to another but not back again; SINGLE² (4) *BrE* —opposite RETURN³ (9), ROUND-TRIP **3** a one-way process, relationship etc is one in which only one person makes any effort

**one-way mir·ror** /ˌ· · '··/ *n* [C] a mirror which can be used as a window by people secretly watching from the other side of it

**one-wom·an** /'· ··/ *adj* [only before a noun] performed, operated, controlled etc by only one woman: *a one-woman show*

**on·go·ing** /'ɒnˌgəʊɪŋ‖'ɑːnˌgoʊ-, 'ɔːn-/ *adj* [usually before noun] continuing, or continuing to develop: *an ongoing search for a new director | ongoing negotiations* —see also **go on** (GO¹)

**on·ion** /'ʌnjən/ *n* [C,U] **1** a round white vegetable with a brown skin and many layers, that has a strong taste and smell—see picture on page 414 **2 know your onions** *BrE informal* to know a lot about something

**on·ion·skin** /'ʌnjənskɪn/ *n* [U] *AmE* very thin light paper, used especially for writing letters on

**on·line** /'ɒnlaɪn‖'ɑːn-, 'ɔːn-/ *adj* directly connected to or controlled by a computer: *an online printer* —**online** *adv*

**on·look·er** /'ɒnˌlʊkə‖'ɑːnˌlʊkər, 'ɔːn-/ *n* [C] someone who watches something happening without being involved in it: *A crowd of onlookers had gathered at the scene of the accident.* —see also **look on** (LOOK¹)

S1 W1 **on·ly¹** /'əʊnli‖'oʊnli/ *adv* **1** not more than a particular amount, number, age etc: *Naomi was only 17 when she got married. | Only five minutes more, and then we can go home.* **2** nothing or no one except: *Only the president can authorize a nuclear attack. | Get me some peaches, but only pick the ones that are ripe.* | **staff/women/men etc only** *The car park is for staff only.* **3** not better, worse, or more important than: *I didn't mean what I said. It was only a joke. | It's no good asking me. I'm only the cleaner.* **4** in one place, situation, or way and no other, or for one reason and no other: *a plant that is only found in Madagascar | I only did it for the money. | I'll tell you, but only if you promise not to tell anyone else.* —see UNIQUE (USAGE) **5** no earlier than a particular time: *I only got here last night.* | **only yesterday/last week/recently** *They got married five weeks ago but I only heard about it yesterday.* | **only then** (=at that moment and not before) *Trevor sat in the dark, and it was only then that he realised how unhappy he was.* **6 only just** *especially BrE* **a)** a moment ago: *No wonder she looks sleepy – she's only just got up.* **b)** almost not; hardly: *There's only just room for the two of us on the back seat. | The dress fits her, but only just.* **7 I only wish/hope** *spoken* used to express a strong wish or hope: *"What's going to happen after the divorce?" "I only wish I knew."* **8 if only** used to express a strong wish: *If only I had a car, I could get out of this place.* **9 you'll only ...** used to tell someone that what they want to do will have a bad effect: *Don't interfere, you'll only make things worse.* **10 you only have to read/look at/listen to etc** *spoken* used to mean that it is easy to realise that something is true because you can see or hear things that prove it: *The situation's getting worse – you only have to look at the crime statistics.* **11 I can only assume/suppose etc** used to say that you can only think of one explanation for something surprising or disappointing: *I can only assume that there has been some kind of mistake.* **12 only to ...** used to say that someone did something, with a disappointing or surprising result: *Scott arrived at the South Pole on January 18th, only to find that Amundsen had got there before him.* **13 only too** very or completely: *Mark was only too ready to agree with her.* | **only too true/likely etc** (=used when something unpleasant is true etc) *"Is it true that there's going to be a war?" "Only too true, I'm afraid."* — see also **not only...but (also)** (NOT (6)), **only have eyes for sb** (EYE¹ (25))

**only²** *adj* [only before a noun] **1 the only thing/person/way etc** **a)** the one single thing, person etc that there is when there are no others: *Dan's the only guy in this office who smokes. | The only reason I came here was to see you.* **b)** the best: *She's the only person for this job. | I'd recommend Kensington. Honestly – it's the only place to live.* **2 the only thing is ...** *spoken* used when you are going to mention a problem or disadvantage about something: *I'd be happy to take you to the airport. The only thing is I think my mother needs the car.* **3 an only child** a child who has no brothers or sisters — see also **the one and only** (ONE² (13)), **(only) time will tell** (TIME¹ (77)) S1 W1

**only³** *conjunction informal* used like 'but' to introduce the reason why something is not possible: *I'd offer to help you, only I'm really busy just now.*

**o.n.o** *BrE* the written abbreviation of 'or nearest offer', used in advertisements to show that you may be willing to sell something for slightly less money than you have asked for: *Bicycle for sale; £60 ono*

**on·o·mat·o·poe·ia** /ˌɒnəmætə'piːə‖ˌɑː-/ *n* [U] *technical* the use of words that sound like the thing that they are describing, like 'hiss' or 'boom' —**onomatopoeic** *adj*

**on-ramp** /'· ·/ *n* [C] *AmE* a road for driving onto a HIGHWAY (1)—see picture on page 415

**on·rush** /'ɒnrʌʃ‖'ɑːn-, 'ɔːn-/ *n* [singular] a strong fast movement forward: **[+ of]** *the second onrush of demonstrators* —**onrushing** *adj*: *the onrushing tide*

**on-screen** /ˌ· '·◂/ *adv* if information appears or is written on-screen, it appears on the SCREEN of a computer: *I prefer to edit on-screen rather than on paper.* —**on-screen** *adj*

**on·set** /'ɒnset‖'ɑːn-, 'ɔːn-/ *n* **the onset of** the beginning of something, especially something unpleasant: *The enemy had to withdraw before the onset of winter.*

**on·shore** /ˌɒn'ʃɔː◂‖ˌɑːn'ʃɔːr◂, ˌɔːn-/ *adj* **1** on or near the land rather than in the sea: *onshore oil production* **2** moving towards the land: *strong onshore winds* —**onshore** *adv*

**on·side** /ˌɒn'saɪd◂‖ˌɑːn-, ˌɔːn-/ *adj, adv* in a position where you are allowed to play the ball in sports such as football —opposite OFFSIDE¹

**on·slaught** /'ɒnslɔːt‖'ɑːn-, 'ɔːn-/ *n* [C] a very strong attack against someone or something: *He was confident his armies could withstand the Allied onslaught.* | **[+ on]** *an onslaught on their whole culture and way of life*

**on-stream** /ˌ· '·◂/ *adv* in operation or ready to begin operation: *More hotel developments are due to come on-stream for the 1998–99 season.* —**on-stream** *adj*

**on·to** /'ɒntʊ; *before consonants* 'ɒntə‖'ɑn-, 'ɔːn-/ *prep* **1** used with verbs expressing movement meaning in or on a particular place: *The men managed to jump onto the train while it was moving. | Some paint was dripping off the ceiling onto the floor.* **2 a) be onto sb** *informal* to know who did something wrong, committed a crime etc: *The police are onto him.* **b) be/get onto sb** *especially BrE* to get in contact with someone: *Get onto the hospital and see if they can spare extra nurses.* **3 be onto a good thing/a winner** *informal* to be in a very good situation that gives you many advantages: *She's onto a real winner with that job.* **4** if something such as a room looks or gives onto another room, a view etc, that is what you can see from that room or where that room leads: *The main sitting area looked out onto a beautiful view of the hills.*

**on·tol·o·gy** /ɒn'tɒlədʒi‖ɑːn'tɑː-/ *n* [U] a subject of study in PHILOSOPHY that is concerned with the nature of existence —**ontological** /ˌɒntə'lɒdʒɪkəl◂‖ˌɑːntə'lɑː-/ *adj*

**o·nus** /'əʊnəs‖'oʊ-/ *n* **the onus** the responsibility for something: **the onus is on sb (to do sth)** *The onus is on the prosecution to provide proof of guilt.*

**on·ward** /'ɒnwəd‖'ɑːnwərd, 'ɔːn-/ *adj* [only before noun] **1** moving forward or continuing: *the onward journey* **2** developing over a period of time: *the onward march of scientific progress*

**on·wards** /'ɒnwədz‖'ɑːnwərdz, 'ɔːn-/ usually **onward** *AmE adv* **1** forwards: *The ship sailed majestically*

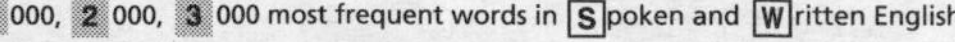

*onwards.* **2 from...onwards** beginning at a particular time and continuing after that time: *I'm on call at the hospital from midnight onwards.*

**on·yx** /ˈɒnɪks‖ˈɑː-/ *n* [U] a stone with lines of different colours in it, often used in jewellery

**oo·dles** /ˈuːdlz/ *n* [plural] *informal* a large amount of something: [+ **of**] *Give me oodles of cream. I love it.*

**O**

**oof** /uːf/ *interjection* the sound that you make when you have been hit, especially in the stomach

**ooh** /uː/ *interjection* used when you think something is very beautiful, unpleasant, surprising etc: *"Look what I've bought." "Ooh!"*

**ooh la la** /ˌuː lɑː ˈlɑː/ *interjection French humorous* used when you think that something or someone is surprising, unusual, or sexually attractive

**oomph** /ʊmf/ *n* [U] *informal* **1** energy: *It's not a bad song, but it needs more oomph.* **2** sexual attractiveness

**oops** /ʊps/ *interjection* used when someone has fallen, dropped something, or made a small mistake: *Oops! Sorry, Calvin, I didn't mean to bump into you like that.*

**oops-a-dai·sy** /ˈ· · ˌ··/ *interjection* used when someone has fallen, especially a child

**ooze¹** /uːz/ *v* **1** [I always + adv/prep, T] if a liquid oozes from something or if something oozes a liquid, liquid flows from it very slowly: [+ **from/out**] *Great tears oozed out from between her tight-shut eyelids.* | **ooze sth** *The stone walls of the cottage oozed moisture.* **2** [I,T] to show a lot of a particular quality or feeling: *oozing charm from every pore* | [+ **with**] *oozing with sexuality*

**ooze²** *n* **1** [U] very soft mud, especially at the bottom of a lake or the sea **2** [singular] a very slow flow of liquid

**ooz·y** /ˈuːzi/ *adj* soft and wet like mud

**Op** the written abbreviation of OPUS

**op** /ɒp‖ɑːp/ *n* [C] *BrE informal* a medical operation

**o·pac·i·ty** /əʊˈpæsɪ̥ti‖oʊ-/ *n* [U] **1** the quality of being difficult to understand **2** the quality of being difficult to see through: *different degrees of opacity and translucence*

**o·pal** /ˈəʊpəl‖ˈoʊ-/ *n* [C,U] a type of white stone with changing colours in it, or a piece of this stone used in jewellery

**o·pa·les·cent** /ˌəʊpəˈlesənt◂‖ˌoʊ-/ *adj* having colours that shine and seem to change: *The sky shone a pale, opalescent blue.* —**opalescence** *n* [U]

**o·paque** /əʊˈpeɪk‖oʊ-/ *adj* **1** glass, liquid etc that is opaque is too thick or too dark to see through: *There was a shower with an opaque glass door.* **2** speech or writing that is opaque is difficult to understand: *very opaque style of writing* —**opaquely** *adv* —**opaqueness** *n* [U] —compare TRANSPARENT —see also OPACITY

**op art** /ˈ· ·/ *n* [U] a form of art using patterns that seem to move or to produce other shapes as you look at them

**op cit** an abbreviation used in formal writing to refer to a book that has been mentioned before

**ope** /əʊp‖oʊp/ *v* [I, T] *poetic* to open

**OPEC** /ˈəʊpek‖ˈoʊ-/ *n* [U] Organization of Petroleum Exporting Countries; an organization of nations that produce and sell oil and which fixes the price of the oil

**op-ed** /ˌ· ˈ·/ *adj AmE informal* **op-ed page** the page in a newspaper that has articles containing opinions on various interesting subjects

S1 W1

**o·pen¹** /ˈəʊpən‖ˈoʊ-/ *adj*

① NOT CLOSED
② NOT ENCLOSED
③ NOT UNDER A ROOF/COVER
④ READY FOR SERVICE
⑤ AVAILABLE
⑥ NOT RESTRICTED
⑦ NOT DECIDED
⑧ NOT HIDING ANYTHING
⑨ OTHER MEANINGS

**open**

wide open

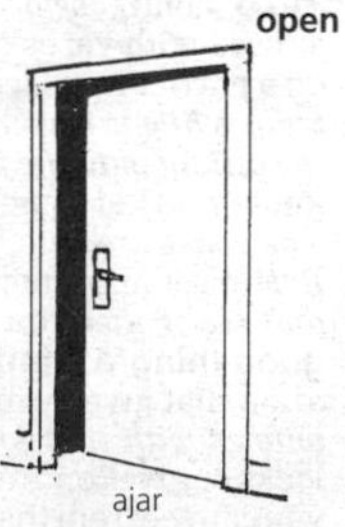

ajar

### ① NOT CLOSED

**1 ▶ DOOR/CONTAINER ◀** not closed, so that you can go through, take things out, or put things in: *an open window* | *I guess I did leave the door open.* | *I can't get this milk open.* | **wide open** (=completely open) *The door was wide open and we could hear everything she said.* | **fly/blow/burst open** *A suitcase fell off the cart and burst open.* | **push/slide/throw sth open** *Fran flung the window open and screamed.* | **tear/rip sth open** *He snatched the envelope from me and ripped it open.*

**2 ▶ EYES/MOUTH ◀** not closed: *I was so sleepy, I couldn't keep my eyes open.* | **wide open** (=completely open) *Ben gaped at me, his mouth wide open.*

**3 ▶ BOOK ◀** a book that is open has its pages moved apart so that you can read it: *A book lay open on the table.*

**4 ▶ NOT BLOCKED ◀** if a road or line of communication is open, it is not blocked and can be used: *We try to keep the mountain roads open all through the winter.*

**5 ▶ CLOTHES ◀** not fastened: *His shirt was open at the neck.*

### ② NOT ENCLOSED

**6** [only before noun] not behind a cover or surrounded by a structure: *goods displayed on the open shelves* | *An open fire is cosier than central heating.*

**7 open country/fields/space** countryside where there are no buildings, walls etc: *To the east, through miles of suburban streets, lay the open country.*

**8 the open sea** sea that is far from any land: *The battered boat slowly drifted out towards the open sea.*

**9 the open road** roads that you can travel on freely or quickly: *The thought of the open road is already making my feet itch.*

### ③ NOT UNDER A ROOF/COVER

**10 in the open air/(out) in the open** outdoors: *In the summer we have our meals in the open air.* | *It was too cold to spend the night out in the open.* —see also OPEN-AIR

**11 ▶ NOT COVERED ◀** without a roof or cover: *an*

*open limousine*|*an open sewer*|**open to the sky/elements** (=without a roof)

### ④ READY FOR SERVICE

**12 ▶SHOP/BANK ETC◀** [not before noun] allowing customers to enter and ready to serve them: *The bank is open until 12.00 on Saturdays.*

**13 ▶DECLARE STH OPEN◀** to officially state that a building is ready to be used, or that an organized event is ready to start: *I now declare the exhibition open.*

### ⑤ AVAILABLE

**14 ▶OPPORTUNITY◀ be open to sb** if an opportunity or possible action is open to you, you have the chance to do it: *training opportunities open to science graduates*|*There is only one course of action open to me.*

**15 ▶JOB◀** [not before noun] a job that is open is available: *Is the vacancy still open?*

### ⑥ NOT RESTRICTED

**16** an open competition, discussion etc is one that anyone can join in: *the British Open Squash Championships*|[+ **to**] *The competition is open to men and women of all ages.*|**throw sth open to sb** *The discussion was thrown open to the studio audience.*

**17 be open to the public/be open to visitors etc** if a place is open to the public etc, anyone can enter or visit it: *The bar is open to non-residents.*

**18 on the open market** if something is sold on the open market, it is made available for anyone to buy: *This house would sell for £300,000 on the open market.*

**19 an open invitation a)** an invitation to visit someone whenever you like **b)** something that makes it easier for criminals to steal, cheat etc: *An unlocked car is an open invitation to thieves.*

### ⑦ NOT DECIDED

**20** a choice or question that is open has been considered but not finally decided: *Who will lead the new party is still an open question.*|**leave it open** (=not decide yet)

**21 keep/leave your options open** to delay any decision so that you can choose later: *a flexible fare package for executives who need to keep their options open*

**22 be open to discussion/negotiation** if something is open to discussion etc, you can discuss it and suggest changes: *The terms are open to negotiation.*

**23 keep/have an open mind** to deliberately not make a decision or form a definite opinion about something: *Try to keep an open mind on the subject until you've heard all the evidence.*

**24 be open to suggestions/offers** to be ready to consider people's suggestions, or prices that people offer to pay: *We're always open to suggestions about how we can improve our service.*

### ⑧ NOT HIDING ANYTHING

**25** [only before noun] actions, feelings, or intentions that are open are not hidden or secret: *open threats against the president*|*Ralph was looking at her in open admiration.*|**open hostility/rivalry/rebellion** *open rivalry between two of the big TV channels*|**open government** (=a system of government where information is freely available)|**in open court** (=in a court of law where everything is public) *allegations made in open court*|**(out) in/into the open** (=no longer secret) *The public has a right to know what has been happening. Let's get it out in the open.*|**an open secret** (=something that is supposed to be secret but that most people know about) *It was an open secret that he had links with far-right extremists.*

**26 ▶HONEST◀** honest and not wanting to hide any facts from other people: [+ **with**] *Let's be completely open with each other.*|*frank and open discussions*|*a friendly open smile*|**open and above board** (=done in a completely honest and legal way) *We don't have to bribe anyone. It's all open and above board.*

### ⑨ OTHER MEANINGS

**27 be open to criticism/blame/suspicion** to be likely to be criticized, blamed etc: *Such a remark is open to misinterpretation.*|**lay yourself (wide) open to criticism etc** (=do or say something that will make it much easier for people to criticize you etc)

**28 be open to question** if someone's honesty, judgment etc is open to question there are doubts about it: *Their motives are open to question.*

**29 keep your eyes/ears open** to keep looking or listening so that you will notice anything that is important, dangerous etc

**30 greet/welcome sb with open arms** to be very pleased to see someone: *Wealthy investors are usually welcomed with open arms.*

**31 be an open book** to be something that you know and understand very well: *The natural world was an open book to him.*

**32 open weave/texture** cloth with an open weave or texture has wide spaces between the threads — see also **keep an eye open for sth** (EYE[1] (14)), **keep your eyes open** (EYE[1] (15)), **with your eyes open** (EYE[1] (38)), OPEN-EYED

## open[2] *v*

S1 W1

① OPEN
② START
③ SPREAD/UNFOLD
④ OTHER MEANINGS

### ① OPEN

**1 ▶DOOR/WINDOW ETC◀ a)** [T] to move a door, window etc so that people, things, air etc can pass through: *Open all the windows and let some fresh air in.* **b)** [I] to be moved in this way: *The bus doors open and close automatically.*

**2 ▶CONTAINER/PACKAGE◀** [T] to unfasten or remove the lid, top, or cover of a container, package etc: *I've asked the waiter to open a bottle of champagne.*|*She opened the letters one by one and read them in silence.*

**3 ▶EYES◀ a) open your eyes** to raise your EYELIDS so that you can see **b) open sb's eyes (to)** to make someone realize something that they had not realized before: *Dan's remarks opened my eyes to the fact that he was only interested in my money.*

**4 ▶MOUTH◀ open your mouth** to move your lips apart

**5 ▶BOOK◀** [T] to turn the covers and pages of a book so that you can read it: *Open your books to page 29.*

**6 ▶OPEN A WAY THROUGH◀** [T] to make it possible for cars, goods etc to pass through a place: *They were clearing away snow to open the tunnel.*|**open a border/frontier (to)** *The new republic has opened its borders to foreign trade.*

### ② START

**7 ▶SHOP/RESTAURANT ETC◀ a)** [I] if a shop or office opens at a particular time, it starts business at

[continued on next page]

[continued from previous page]
that time: *What time do the banks open?* **b)** [I,T] if a new business such as a shop or restaurant opens or is opened, someone starts it: *A new supermarket has opened.* | *plans to open a chain of restaurants*

**8 ▶START AN ACTIVITY◀ open an inquiry/investigation** to start gathering information or opinions from a lot of people: *Police have opened an investigation into the girl's disappearance.*

**9 ▶MEETING/EVENT◀** [I,T] if a meeting etc opens or is opened in a particular way, it starts in that way: *Our chairman opened the conference by welcoming new delegates.* | [+ **with**] *The concert opens with Beethoven's Egmont Overture.*

**10 ▶FILM/PLAY ETC◀** [I] to start being shown to the public: *Bertolucci's new film opens in London on March 15th.*

**11 ▶OFFICIAL CEREMONY◀** [T] to perform a ceremony in which you officially state that a building is ready to be used

**12 open an account** to start an account at a bank or other financial organization by putting money into it

**③ SPREAD/UNFOLD**

**13** [I,T] if something that is folded opens or you open it, you make it spread out into a wide shape: *His parachute failed to open.* | *I opened my umbrella.*

**14 ▶FLOWER/LEAF◀** [I] if a flower or BUD opens, it spreads out wide: *The buds are starting to open.*

**15 open your arms** to stretch your arms wide apart: *Marcus opened his arms in a welcoming gesture.*

**④ OTHER MEANINGS**

**16 open sth to the public** to let people come and visit a house, garden etc: *For the first time, Buckingham Palace has been made open to the public.*

**17 open the door/way to** to make an opportunity for something to happen: *a joint venture that opens the way to wider international co-operation* | **open doors** *A degree no longer opens doors in the way it used to.*

**18 open fire (on)** to start shooting at someone or something: *Troops opened fire on the rioters.*

**19 open your mind to** to be ready to consider or accept new ideas

**20 the heavens opened** it started to rain heavily

**21 open your heart (to)** to tell someone your real thoughts and feelings because you trust them —see also **open the floodgates** (FLOODGATES (1))

**open onto/into sth** *phr v* [T] if a room, door etc opens onto or into another place, you can enter that other place directly through it: *The living room opens into the dining room.* | *patio doors opening onto the garden*

**open out** *phr v* [I] **1** if a road, path, or passage opens out, it becomes wider: [+ **into**] *Beyond the forest the path opened out into a track.* **2** *BrE* if someone opens out, they become less shy: *As she got to know us better, Lizzie gradually started to open out.*

**open up** *phr v*

**1 ▶LAND◀** [I,T] if someone opens up an area of land, they make it easier to reach and ready for development: **open sth ↔ up** *They saw the new railroad as a means of opening up the far west of the country.*

**2 ▶SHOP/RESTAURANT ETC◀ a)** [I,T] if a shop, restaurant etc opens up or is opened up, someone starts it **b)** [I] if a shop, office etc opens up at a particular time, it starts business at that time

**3 ▶DOOR/BOX◀** [I,T] an expression meaning to open a door or something such as a box or case, often used to order someone to do this: *Open up, this is the police.* | **open sth ↔ up** *Is this your suitcase? Right, open it up.*

**4 ▶OPPORTUNITY◀** [I,T] if an opportunity opens up or is opened up, it develops: *A new life was opening up before her.* | **open sth ↔ up** *A move to New York would open up all kinds of exciting new possibilities.*

**5 ▶WITH A GUN◀** [I] to start shooting: *The enemy opened up with machine guns.*

**6 ▶DISAGREEMENT◀** [I,T] if a disagreement opens up or is opened up between people, it starts to divide them: *A rift has opened up, splitting the committee down the middle.* | **open sth ↔ up** *The abortion issue may open up a split in the Democratic party.*

**7 ▶TALK◀** [I] to stop being shy and say what you really think: *Once she knew she could trust me, Melissa started to open up.*

**8 ▶HOLE/CRACK ETC◀** [I,T] if a hole, crack etc opens up or is opened up, it appears and becomes wider

**USAGE NOTE: OPEN**

WORD CHOICE: **open, shut, close, undo, do up, turn on/off, switch on/off, open up**

You **open**, **shut** or **close** your mouth, eyes, doors, windows, boxes, bottles, and shops.

You **open** meetings and debates, but you can only **close** (NOT **shut**) them: *Madam Chair, I think we should close the meeting at eight.*

You **undo** or **do up** clothes: *She did up her boots/shirt.*

You **turn** water or gas **on** or **off**.

You **turn** or **switch** electrical things **on** or **off**: *Turn that radio off.* | *She opened her laptop and switched it on.*

You **open up** new opportunities or possibilities: *Plans to open up the world of higher education to people from poor backgrounds.*

**open**[3] *n* **the open** **1** outdoors: **in the open** *It must be wonderful to be able to take your meals in the open every day.* **2 in the open** not hidden or secret: *It was a great relief to know that it was all in the open at last.* | **bring sth (out) into the open** *an opportunity to bring all your gripes out into the open* **3 the Open** a national GOLF competition: *the US Open*

**open-air** /ˌ·· ˈ·◂/ *adj* [usually before noun] happening or existing outdoors, not in a building: *open-air concerts* | *an open-air swimming pool*

**open-and-shut case** /ˌ·· · · ˈ·/ *n* [C] a law case that is easy to prove and will not take a long time in court

**open bar** /ˌ·· ˈ·/ *n* [C] *AmE* a bar at an occasion such as a wedding, where drinks are served free

**o·pen·cast** /ˈəʊpənkɑːst‖ˈoʊpənkæst/ *adj BrE* **opencast mine/mining** mines where minerals, especially coal, are dug from large open holes in the ground

**open-cut** /ˈ·· ·/ *adj AmE* opencast

**open day** /ˈ·· ·/ *n* [C] *BrE* a day or time when a school, organization etc allows anyone to come in and see the work that is done there; OPEN HOUSE (2) *AmE*

**open door pol·i·cy** /ˌ·· ˈ· ˌ···/ *n* [C] **1** the principle of allowing people and goods to move into your country **2** the principle of allowing anyone to come and talk to you while you are working

**open-end·ed** /ˌ·· ˈ··◂/ *adj* **1** without a fixed ending time: *hiring workers on open-ended contracts* **2** not having rules that limit or restrict anything: *These interviews are fairly open-ended in format.*

**o·pen·er** /ˈəʊpənə‖ˈoʊpənər/ *n* [C] **1** a tool or machine used to open letters, bottles, or cans: *an electric can opener* **2** the first of a series of things such as sports competitions: *the opener against the 49ers* **3 for openers** as a beginning or first stage: *Well, for openers, it would be nice to know your name.*

**open-eyed** /ˌ·· ˈ·◂/ *adj, adv* **1** awake, or with your eyes open **2** accepting or taking notice of all the facts of a situation: *clear, open-eyed reasoning*

**open-faced sand·wich** /ˌ·· · ˈ··/ *n* [C] *AmE* an OPEN SANDWICH *BrE*

**open-hand·ed** /ˌ·· ˈ··◂/ *adj* generous and friendly: *an open-handed offer of help* —**openhandedness** *n* [U]

**open-heart·ed** /ˌ·· ˈ··◂/ *adj* kind and sympathetic

**open-heart sur·ge·ry** /ˌ·· ˌ· ˈ···/ *n* [U] a medical operation in which doctors operate on someone's heart

**open house** /ˌ·· ˈ·/ *n* **1** [U] a situation in which visitors are welcome at any time: *It's always open house at Beryl's.* **2** *AmE* [C] an occasion when a college, factory, or organization allows the public to come in and see the work that is done there; OPEN DAY *BrE* **3** [C] *AmE* an occasion on which someone who is selling their house lets everyone who is interested in buying it come to see it

**o·pen·ing¹** /ˈəupənɪŋ‖ˈou-/ *n* **1** [C] a hole or space in something through which air, light, objects etc can pass: *There was another opening to the cave.* **2** [C] an occasion when a new business, building, road etc starts working or being used: [+ **of**] *the opening of the new theatre* **3** [C usually singular] the beginning or first part of something: [+ **of**] *The opening of the novel is dull.*| *at the opening of each school day* **4** [C] a good chance for someone to do or say something: [+ **for**] *His question left an opening for me to say exactly what I thought.* **5** [C] a job or position that is available: *Are there any openings for computer programmers?* **6** [U] the act of opening something: [+ **of**] *the opening of markets in Eastern Europe*

**opening²** *adj* [only before noun] first or beginning: *the opening speech of the debate*

**opening hours** /ˈ··· ˌ·/ *n* [plural] the hours during which a shop, building etc is open to the public

**opening night** /ˌ··· ˈ·/ *n* [C] the first night that a new play, film etc is shown to the public

**opening time** /ˈ··· ˌ·/ *n* [C] the time that a business opens to the public, especially the time a PUB begins serving drinks: *It was nearly an hour till opening time.*

**opening up** /ˌ··· ˈ·/ *n* [singular] **1** the process of making something, especially land, available for use or development: *The opening up of new land brought a rush of immigrants.* **2** the process of becoming less restricted or limited: *the opening up of jobs for women*

**open let·ter** /ˌ·· ˈ··/ *n* [C] a letter to an important person, which is printed in a newspaper or magazine in order to protest or complain about something

**o·pen·ly** /ˈəupənli‖ˈou-/ *adv* in a way that does not hide your feelings or opinions: *Sarah talked openly about her abusive parents.*|*He was openly contemptuous of his colleagues.*

**open mike** /ˌ·· ˈ·/ *n* [U] *AmE* a time when anyone is allowed to tell jokes, sing etc in a bar or NIGHTCLUB

**open-mind·ed** /ˌ·· ˈ··◂/ *adj* willing to consider and accept other people's ideas, opinions etc: *I'm quite open-minded about this subject.* —**openmindedly** *adv* —**openmindedness** *n* [U]

**open-mouthed** /ˌ·· ˈ·◂/ *adj, adv* with your mouth wide open, because you are very surprised or shocked: *They stared open-mouthed at the extraordinary spectacle.*

**open-necked** /ˌ·· ˈ·◂/ *adj* an open-necked shirt is one on which the top button has not been fastened —see picture on page 840

**o·pen·ness** /ˌəupən-nəs‖ˈou-/*n* [U] **1** the quality of being honest and not keeping things secret: *dealing based on honesty and openness* **2** the quality of being willing to accept new ideas or people: *his openness to new experience* **3** the quality of being open and not enclosed: *the openness of the landscape*

**open-plan** /ˌ·· ˈ·◂/ *adj* an open-plan office, school etc does not have walls dividing it into separate rooms

**open pri·ma·ry** /ˌ·· ˈ···/ *n*[C] a PRIMARY ELECTION in the US in which any voter may vote for someone from any party

**open pris·on** /ˌ·· ˈ··/ *n* [C] *BrE* a prison that does not restrict the actions or freedom of prisoners as much as ordinary prisons; MINIMUM SECURITY PRISON *AmE*

**open sand·wich** /ˌ·· ˈ··/ *n* [C] *BrE* a single piece of bread with meat, cheese, etc on top; OPEN-FACED SANDWICH *AmE*

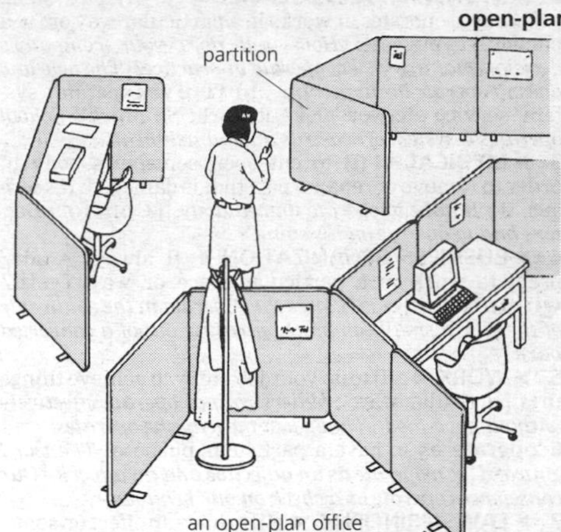

an open-plan office

**open sea·son** /ˈ·· ˌ··/ *n* [singular] **1** the period of time each year when it is legal to kill certain animals or fish as a sport: [+ **for/on**] *open season for deer* **2 open season (on sb)** a time when a lot of people take the opportunity to criticize someone: *The CNN broadcast, in effect, declared open season on Lester Coleman.* —opposite CLOSE SEASON (1)

**open ses·a·me** /ˌ·· ˈ···/ *n* [singular] a way to achieve something that is nearly impossible: *A degree isn't an open sesame to a good job.*

**open sys·tem** /ˈ·· ˌ··/ *n* [C] *technical* a computer system that is made so that it can be connected with similar computer systems made by other companies

**Open U·ni·ver·si·ty** /ˌ·· ··ˈ···/ *n* [singular] a British university that teaches adult students mainly in their own homes by means of radio and television programmes and courses of study sent by mail

**open ver·dict** /ˌ·· ˈ··/ *n* [C] a decision of a JURY (1) in a British court that the cause of someone's death is not known: *Johnson returned an open verdict.*

**open vow·el** /ˌ·· ˈ··/ *n* [C] *technical* a vowel that is pronounced with your tongue flat on the bottom of your mouth

**o·pen·work** /ˈəupənˌwɜːk‖ˈoupənˌwɜːrk/ *adj* [only before noun] using or containing a pattern that has spaces in between metal bars, pieces of thread etc: *a beautiful openwork screen* —**openwork** *n* [U]

**op·e·ra** /ˈɒpərə‖ˈɑː-/ *n* **1** [C] a musical play in which all of the words are sung: **go to the opera** (=go to a performance of an opera) *Helena had never been to the opera until that night.* **2** [U] these plays considered as a form of art: *Do you enjoy opera?*|*an opera lover* —see also COMIC OPERA, GRAND OPERA, SOAP OPERA —compare OPERETTA —**operatic** *adj* —**operatically** *adv*

**op·e·ra·ble** /ˈɒpərəbəl‖ˈɑː-/ *adj* a medical condition that is operable can be treated by an operation

**opera glass·es** /ˈ··· ˌ··/ *n* [plural] a small pair of special glasses used at the theatre for making things seem closer

**opera house** /ˈ··· ·/ *n* [C] a theatre where operas are performed: *the Sydney Opera House*

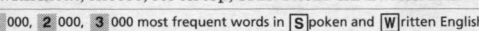

**op·e·rate** /ˈɒpəreɪt‖ˈɑː-/ *v*

**1** ▶ **MACHINE** ◀ **a)** [T] to use and control a machine or equipment: *If affected by drowsiness, do not drive or operate heavy machinery.*|*instructions for operating the central heating* **b)** [I always + adv/prep] if a machine operates in a particular way, it works in that way; FUNCTION²: [+ **in/at**] *a motor operating at high speeds*

2 ▶ **SYSTEM/PROCESS/SERVICE** ◀ **a)** [I] if a system, process etc operates, it works in a particular way or for a particular purpose: *How well does your company's decision-making system operate in practice?* | *The new law doesn't operate in our favour.* **b)** [T] if you operate a system, service etc, you make it work: *St. Mark's School operates a system of rewards and punishments.*
3 ▶ **MEDICAL** ◀ [I] to cut open someone's body in order to remove or repair a part that is damaged: *It's serious. We'll have to operate immediately.* | [+ **on/for**] *Doctors had to operate on his spine.*
4 ▶ **BUSINESS/ORGANIZATION** ◀ [I always + adv/prep] to work in a particular place or way: [+ **in/within/from**] *rival gangs that operate in the south side of the city* | *a small company operating out of a converted barn*
5 ▶ **WORK** ◀ [I] to do your job or try to achieve things in a particular way: *Soldiers cannot operate effectively without good food.* | *That's just the way she operates.*
6 **operate as** to have a particular purpose: *The word 'onward' can operate as an adjective and an adverb.* | *Our consciences operate as a check on our behaviour.*
7 ▶ **LAWS/PRINCIPLES** ◀ [I] to have an effect on something: *evolutionary principles operating in the physical world*

**op·e·rat·ing room** /'···· ,·/ *n* [C] *AmE* an OPERATING THEATRE

**operating sys·tem** /'···· ,··/ *n* [C] a system in a computer that helps all the programs (PROGRAM[1] (1)) in it to work together

**operating ta·ble** /'···· ,··/ *n* [C] a special table that you lie on to have a medical operation

**operating thea·tre** /'···· ,··/ *n* [C] *BrE* a room in a hospital where operations are done; OPERATING ROOM *AmE*

S1 W1 **op·e·ra·tion** /,ɒpə'reɪʃən‖,ɑː-/ *n*
1 ▶ **MEDICAL** ◀ [C] the process of cutting into someone's body to repair or remove a part that is damaged: *a heart bypass operation* | *She had a bad operation, she had a hysterectomy.* | [+ **on/for**] *She's going to have an operation on her knee.* | **perform an operation** *an operation only the most skilled surgeon could perform*
2 ▶ **SET OF ACTIONS** ◀ [C] a set of planned actions or activities for a particular purpose: *The whole operation should only take about ten minutes to perform.* | *a search and rescue operation, expertly performed*
3 ▶ **MACHINE/SYSTEM** ◀ [U] **a)** the way the parts of a machine or system work together: *to maintain proper engine operation* (=working) | **in operation** (=working) *Protective clothing must be worn when the machine is in operation.* **b)** the process of making a machine or system work: *Operation of the system is automatic.*
4 ▶ **BUSINESS** ◀ **a)** [C] a business, company, or organization, especially one with many parts: *Their huge interstate operation reportedly brings in $20 million a year.* **b)** [C,U] the work or activities done by a business, organization etc, or the process of doing this work: *Many small businesses fail in the first year of operation.* | **be in operation** *Chris's courier service has only been in operation for two months.*
5 ▶ **PRINCIPLE/LAW/PLAN ETC** ◀ [U] the way something such as a principle, law etc works or has an effect: *the operation of the laws of gravity* | **in operation** *a clear example of Murphy's law in operation* | **come/go into operation** (=begin to have an effect) *The Act will come into operation later this year.* | **put/bring sth into operation** (=make something start to work)
6 ▶ **MILITARY/POLICE ACTION** ◀ [C] a planned military or police action, especially one that involves a lot of people: *an espionage operation*
7 ▶ **COMPUTERS** ◀ [C] *technical* an action done by a computer: *a multitasking machine performing millions of operations per second*

**op·e·ra·tion·al** /,ɒpə'reɪʃənəl◂‖,ɑː-/ *adj* **1** working and ready to be used: *The new vehicle could be operational as early as 1994.* | **fully operational** *The new laboratory is fully operational and open for business.* —compare OPERATIVE[1] (1) **2** [only before noun] related to the operation of a business, government etc: *operational and budgetary planning officer* —**operationally** *adv*

**operational re·search** /,····· ·'·, ,····· '··/ *n* [U] *technical* the study of how best to build and use machines or plan organizations

**op·e·ra·tive[1]** /'ɒpərətɪv‖'ɑːpərə-, 'ɑːpəreɪ-/ *adj* **1** working and able to be used: *We had only one radar station operative.* | *operative missiles* —compare OPERATIONAL (1) **2 the operative word** used when you repeat a word from a previous sentence to draw attention to its importance: *He is supposed to supervise their work. 'Supposed', unfortunately, is the operative word.*

**operative[2]** *n* [C] **1** a word meaning a worker, especially a factory worker, used in business: *increased productivity from the operatives* **2** *AmE* someone who does work that is secret in some way, especially for a government organization: *Hunt was no ordinary consultant, but a political operative.*

**op·e·ra·tor** /'ɒpəreɪtə‖'ɑːpəreɪtər/ *n* [C] **1** someone who works on a telephone SWITCHBOARD, who you can call for help when you have problems: *Ask the operator to put you through.* —see TELEPHONE (USAGE) **2** someone who operates a machine or piece of equipment: *a tow truck operator* | *a computer operator* **3** a person or company that operates a particular business: *a tour operator* | *the largest road haulage operator in Alaska* **4** a disapproving word for someone who is able to get what they want by persuading people: *a supreme operator in congressional politics* | **a smooth/sharp operator** *He's a smooth operator with the women.*

**op·e·ret·ta** /,ɒpə'retə‖,ɑː-/ *n* [C] a short or romantic musical play in which some of the words are spoken and some are sung: *Strauss's operetta Die Fledermaus* —compare OPERA (1)

**oph·thal·mi·a** /ɒf'θælmiə‖ɑːf-/ *n* [U] *technical* an illness of the eyes that makes them red and swollen

**oph·thal·mic** /ɒf'θælmɪk‖ɑːf-/ *adj* related to the eyes and the illnesses that affect them: *an ophthalmic surgeon*

**oph·thal·mol·o·gist** /,ɒfθæl'mɒlədʒɪst‖,ɑːfθæl'mɑː-/ *n* [C] a doctor who treats people's eyes and does operations on them —compare OPTICIAN (1), OPTOMETRIST

**oph·thal·mol·o·gy** /,ɒfθæl'mɒlədʒi‖,ɑːfθæl'mɑː-/ *n* [U] *technical* the study of the eyes and diseases that affect them

**o·pi·ate** /'əupiɪt, -eɪt‖'ou-/ *n* [C] a type of drug that contains OPIUM and makes you want to sleep

**o·pine** /əu'paɪn‖ou-/ *v* [T + **that**] *formal* to say that you think something is true: *"She did right, if you ask me," opined Moreau.*

**o·pin·ion** /ə'pɪnjən/ *n* **1** [C] your ideas or beliefs about a particular subject: [+ **about**] *Sarah's parents have strong opinions about divorce.* | [+ **on**] *I went to my boss to ask him for his opinion on the matter.* | [+ **of**] *What's your opinion of her as a teacher?* | **the general opinion** (=what most people believe) *The general opinion is that the new working hours are a good thing.* —compare VIEW[1] (1) **2** [C] judgement or advice from a professional person about something: *When choosing an insurance policy it's usually best to get an independent opinion.* | **a second opinion** (=advice from a second person to make sure that the first advice is right) *My doctor says I need an operation, but I've asked for a second opinion.* **3 have a high/low/good/bad etc opinion of** to think that someone or something is very good or very bad: *They seem to have a very high opinion of Paula's work.* **4 in my opinion/if you want my opinion** used to tell someone what you think about a particular subject: *If you want my opinion, Phil's gone crazy.* **5 be of the opinion (that)** to think that something is true: *Aristotle was of the opinion that there would always be rich and poor in society.* —see also **a difference of opinion** (DIFFERENCE (4)), **it's/that's a matter of opinion** (MATTER[1] (21)), PUBLIC OPINION S1 W2

**o·pin·ion·at·ed** /ə'pɪnjəneɪtɪd/ *adj* expressing very strong opinions about things: *an opinionated old fool*

**opinion-mak·ers** /ˈ·· ˌ··/ *n* [plural] people who have great influence over the way other people think

**opinion poll** /ˈ··· ·/ *n* [C] an attempt to find out what the public thinks about something, especially politics, by asking many people the same questions: *The latest opinion polls show the Social Democrats leading by 10%.*

**o·pi·um** /ˈəʊpiəm‖ˈoʊ-/ *n* [U] a powerful illegal drug made from POPPY seeds, that used to be used legally as a PAINKILLER —see also HEROIN

**o·pos·sum** /əˈpɒsəm‖-ˈpɑː-, ˈpɑːsəm/ also **possum** *n* [C] one of various small animals from America and Australia that has fur and climbs trees

**opp.** the written abbreviation of OPPOSITE

W3 **op·po·nent** /əˈpəʊnənt‖əˈpoʊ-/ *n* [C] **1** someone who tries to defeat another person in a competition, game, fight, or argument: *Tyson knocked his opponent out in the first round.*|*Rumpole was a formidable opponent in court.* **2** someone who disagrees with a plan, idea etc, and wants to try and stop it: [+ **of**] *opponents of the Administration's plans to cut the Federal budget*

**op·por·tune** /ˈɒpətjuːn‖ˌɑːpərˈtuːn/ *adj formal* **1 an opportune moment/time** a time that is suitable for doing something: *Deborah was waiting for an opportune moment to ask for a raise.* **2** done at a very suitable time: *an opportune remark* —opposite INOPPORTUNE —**opportunely** *adv*

**op·por·tun·is·m** /ˌɒpəˈtjuːnɪzəm‖ˌɑːpərˈtuː-/ *n* [U] trying whenever possible to gain power or unfair advantages over other people: *a blatant piece of political opportunism*

**op·por·tun·ist** /ɒpəˈtjuːnɪst‖ˌɑːpərˈtuː-/ *n* [C] someone who uses every chance to gain power or unfair advantage over others —**opportunist** *adj*: *the opportunist policies of war-time leaders.* —**opportunistic** /ˌɒpətjuːˈnɪstɪk‖ˌɑːpərtuː-/ *adj*: *A recent police video reflects the increasing number of opportunistic thefts from drivers in heavy urban traffic.*

S1 W1 **op·por·tu·ni·ty** /ˌɒpəˈtjuːnɪti‖ˌɑːpərˈtuː-/ *n* **1** [C,U] a chance to do something or an occasion when it is easy for you to do something: *I just thought it was too good an opportunity to miss.*| **opportunity to do sth** *You have had plenty of opportunity to observe our way of doing things.*| [+ **for**] *When you're in school there are lots of opportunities for meeting people of the opposite sex.*| **take the opportunity to do sth** (=use a chance to say something you want to) *I'd like to take this opportunity to wish you a good trip.*| **at the earliest/first opportunity** (=as soon as possible) *He must have got rid of the body at the first opportunity.*| **at every opportunity** (=whenever possible) *I try to speak French at every available opportunity.* —CHANCE¹ (USAGE) **2** [C] a chance to get a job: *There are fewer opportunities for new graduates this year.* —see also **equal opportunities** (EQUAL¹ (2))

**opposable thumb** /ˌ·ˌ··· ˈ·/ *n* [C] a thumb that human beings, MONKEYS etc have that can be used for holding things

W3 **op·pose** /əˈpəʊz‖əˈpoʊz/ *v* [T] **1** to disagree with something such as a plan or idea and try to prevent it from happening or succeeding: *Congress is continuing to oppose the President's healthcare budget.*| **be opposed to sth** *Most of us are opposed to the death penalty.* **2** to fight or compete against another person or group in a battle, competition, or election: *He is opposed by two other candidates.*

**op·posed** /əˈpəʊzd‖əˈpoʊzd/ *adj* [not before noun] **1** two ideas that are opposed to each other are completely different from each other: [+ **to**] *The principles of capitalism and socialism are diametrically opposed to each other.* **2 as opposed to** used to compare two things and show that they are different from each other: *Students discuss ideas, as opposed to just copying from books.*|*his private as opposed to his public life*

Frequencies of **oppose**, **be opposed to** and **be against** in spoken and written English.

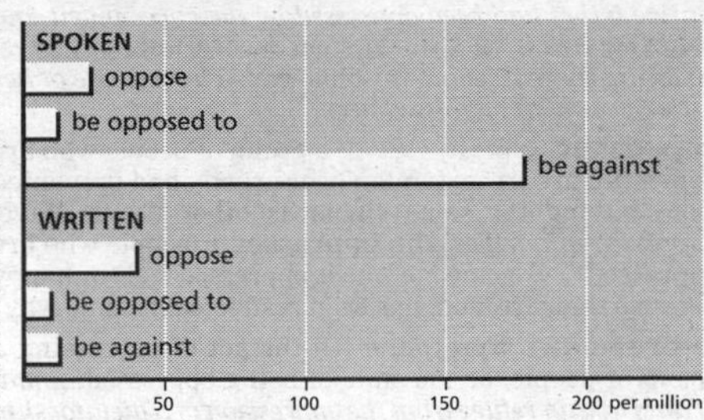


Based on the British National Corpus and the Longman Lancaster Corpus

This graph shows that it is much more usual in spoken English to say that you **are against** something, rather than to say that you **oppose** it or **are opposed to** it. This is because **be against** is more informal and more general than **oppose** and **be opposed to**, which often suggest not only disagreeing with and disapproving of something, but also taking action to prevent it.

**op·pos·ing** /əˈpəʊzɪŋ‖əˈpoʊ-/ *adj* **1** opposing teams, groups, forces etc are competing, arguing, or fighting against each other: *The opposing armies were already preparing for war.*|*The Socialist Party has split into two opposing camps.* **2** opposing ideas, opinions etc are completely different from each other: *Bobbie and Jo have opposing views on abortion.*

**op·po·site¹** /ˈɒpəzɪt‖ˈɑː-/ *prep* if one thing or person is opposite another, they are facing each other: *The people sitting opposite us looked very familiar.*|*It's easy to find – there's a church just opposite my house.* S2 W2

**opposite²** *adj* **1** as different as possible from something else: *I thought the medicine would make him sleep, but it had the opposite effect.*|*two parties at opposite ends of the political spectrum* **2** the opposite direction, way etc is directly away from someone or something: *The woman turned and walked off in the opposite direction.* **3** one thing that is opposite another is on the other side of the same area, often directly across from it: *The grocery store was on the opposite side of the street.*|*the houses opposite* —see FRONT¹ (USAGE) **4 at opposite ends of the city/country etc** on different sides of a city etc, and a long way apart: *We live at opposite ends of the city, so it's not always easy to meet.* **5 the opposite sex** the other sex: *He doesn't feel comfortable with the opposite sex.* **6 opposite number** someone who has the same job in another similar organization: *his opposite number in the KGB*

**opposite³** *n* [C] **1** a person or thing that is as different as possible from someone or something else: *The colors 'black' and 'white' are opposites.*| **be the opposite (of)** *She's tall and slim, and he's the complete opposite.* **2 not ... just/quite the opposite** used to say that something is completely different from what has just been said: *Martha's not shy at all – just the opposite in fact.*

**opposite⁴** *adv* in a position on the other side of the same area: *The Browns live just opposite*

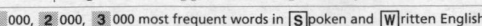

**op·po·si·tion** /ˌɒpəˈzɪʃən‖ˌɑː-/ *n* [U] **1** strong disagreement with, or protest against, something such as a plan, law, or system etc: **opposition to sth** *There was a great deal of opposition to the war.*| **strong/fierce opposition** *Plans to build a new airport met with fierce opposition from local farmers.*| **in opposition to (sth)** *The party was founded in opposition to the more moderate policies of the government.* **2** [also + plural verb *BrE*] the people who you are competing against: *He passed the ball to the opposition by mistake.* —see also RIVAL¹ (1) **3 the opposition** the main political party in a country's parliament that is not part of the government: *the leader of the Opposition*|*protests from the opposition* **4 in opposition** a political party that is in opposition is in parliament, but is not part of the government: *The Socialists were elected to power after 10 years in opposition.* S2 W1

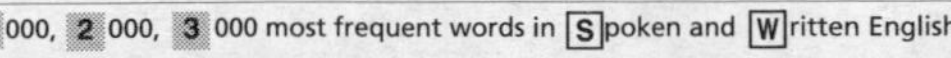

**op·press** /ə'pres/ *v* [T often passive] **1** to treat a group of people unfairly or cruelly, and prevent them from having the same rights that other people in society have: *Native tribes had been oppressed by the government and police for years.* **2** to make someone feel unhappy by restricting their freedom in some way: *The solitude of her little apartment oppressed her.*

**op·pressed** /ə'prest/ *adj* **1** a group of people who are oppressed are treated unfairly or cruelly and prevented from having the same rights as other people have: *oppressed minorities* | **the oppressed** (=people who are oppressed) **2** someone who is oppressed feels unhappy because their freedom has been restricted in some way

**op·pres·sion** /ə'preʃən/ *n* [U] the act of oppressing a group of people, or the state of being oppressed: *immigrants taking refuge from the oppression of a dictatorship*

**op·pres·sive** /ə'presɪv/ *adj* **1** powerful, cruel, and unfair: *an oppressive military regime* **2** weather that is oppressive is unpleasantly hot with no movement of air: *The evening gradually grew more and more oppressive.* **3** a situation that is oppressive makes you feel too uncomfortable to do or say anything: *The silence in the meeting was becoming oppressive.* **—oppressively** *adv* **—oppressiveness** *n* [U]

**op·pres·sor** /ə'presə‖-ər/ *n* [C] a person or group that oppresses people: *They rose up against their colonial oppressors.*

**op·pro·bri·ous** /ə'prəʊbriəs‖ə'proʊ-/ *adj formal* showing great disrespect **—opprobriously** *adv*

**op·pro·bri·um** /ə'prəʊbriəm‖ə'proʊ-/ *n* [U] *formal* strong public criticism, hatred, or shame: *in the face of public opprobrium*

**opt** /ɒpt‖ɑːpt/ *v* [I] to choose one thing or one course of action instead of another: [+ **for**] *GM workers opted for job security over pay increases.* | **opt to do sth** *Many young people are opting to go on to further education.*

**opt out** *phr v* [I] **1** to avoid doing a duty: [+ **of**] *You can't just opt out of all responsibility for the child!* **2** to decide not to join in a group or system: *Britain wants to opt out of the European Social Chapter.* **3** if a school or hospital in Britain opts out, it decides to control its own money, that it is given by the government, instead of being controlled by local government

**op·tic¹** /'ɒptɪk‖'ɑːp-/ *adj* [only before noun] concerning the eyes: *the optic nerve* —see picture at EYE¹

**optic²** *n* **1 optics** [U] the scientific study of light **2** [C] *BrE* a small plastic object on a bottle of alcohol that measures the amount to be poured into a glass

**op·ti·cal** /'ɒptɪkəl‖'ɑːp-/ *adj* **1** used for seeing images and light: *microscopes and other optical instruments* **2** concerned with the way light is seen: *an optical diagram* **3** using light, especially for the purpose of sending or storing information for use in a computer system: *optical character recognition* **—optically** /-kli/ *adv*

**optical fi·bre** /ˌ··· '··/ *n* [U] a thread-like piece of glass or plastic which is used for sending information, for example in a telephone or computer system

**optical il·lusion** /ˌ··· ·'··/ *n* [C] a picture or image that tricks your eyes and makes you see something that is not actually there

**op·ti·cian** /ɒp'tɪʃən‖ɑːp-/ *n* [C] **1** *BrE* someone who tests people's eyes and sells SPECTACLES in a shop **2** *AmE* someone who makes lenses (LENS (1)) for SPECTACLES

**op·ti·mal** /'ɒptɪ̈məl‖'ɑːp-/ *adj* the best or most suitable; OPTIMUM (1)

**op·ti·mis·m** /'ɒptɪ̈mɪzəm‖'ɑːp-/ *n* [U] a tendency to believe that good things will always happen: *the optimism of the postwar years* —opposite PESSIMISM

**op·ti·mist** /'ɒptɪ̈mɪst‖'ɑːp-/ *n* [C] someone who always believes that good things will happen: *I'm a born optimist.* —opposite PESSIMIST

**op·ti·mis·tic** /ˌɒptɪ̈'mɪstɪk◂‖ˌɑːp-/ *adj* **1** believing that good things will happen in the future: [+ **about**] *Foreign bankers are cautiously optimistic about the country's economic future.* **2** thinking that things will be better, easier or more successful than is actually possible: **over-optimistic** *They're being over-optimistic if they think that car can make an 800 mile trip.* **—optimistically** /-kli/ *adv* —opposite PESSIMISTIC

**op·ti·mize** also **-ise** *BrE* /'ɒptɪ̈maɪz‖'ɑːp-/ *v* [T] to make the way that something is done or used as effective as possible: *The company is seeking to optimize its use of financial resources by introducing performance-related pay.*

**op·ti·mum** /'ɒptɪ̈məm‖'ɑːp-/ *adj* [only before noun] **1** the best or most suitable for a particular purpose: *the optimum temperature for keeping wine* **2 the optimum** the best possible situation, conditions, amount of time etc for something to happen: *Make sure the fridge is kept at the optimum temperature.*

**op·tion** /'ɒpʃən‖'ɑːp-/ *n* S1 W2

**1** ▶ **A CHOICE** ◀ [C] a choice you can make in a particular situation: *As I see it, we have two options – either we sell the house or we rent it out.* | *I usually choose the vegetarian option in restaurants.* | **the option of doing sth** *I always had the option of going back to Canada.* | **have no option but to do sth** (=be forced to do something because there are no other choices) *Teenage mothers often have no option but to live with their parents.*

**2 keep/leave your options open** to wait before making a decision: *We should keep our options open until Jim can study the results of the survey.*

**3** ▶ **RIGHT TO BUY/SELL** ◀ [C] the right to buy or sell something in the future: [+ **on**] *The Saudi government has agreed to buy 20 planes, with an option on a further 10.*

**4** ▶ **COMPUTERS** ◀ [C] one of the possible choices you can make when using a computer PROGRAM¹ (1): *Press 'P' to select the print option.*

**5** ▶ **STH THAT IS ADDITIONAL** ◀ [C] something that is offered in addition to the standard equipment when you buy something new, especially a car

**6** ▶ **AT COLLEGE/UNIVERSITY** ◀ *BrE* [C] a subject that you can choose to study as part of a course: *I did an option in Korean Studies.*

**7 first option** the chance to buy or get something before anyone else: *They've agreed to give us the first option on their apartment.*

**8 the soft/easy option** the course of action that needs the least effort, chosen because you are being lazy: *Some people consider studying Expressive Arts to be a soft option.*

**op·tion·al** /'ɒpʃənəl‖'ɑːp-/ *adj* if something is optional, you do not have to do it or use it, but you can choose to if you want to: *Woodwork was an optional subject at our school.* | **an optional extra** (=something that you can choose to have in addition to what you would normally get) *Leather seats are an optional extra in the hatchback.*

**op·tom·e·trist** /ɒp'tɒmɪ̈trɪ̈st‖ɑːp'tɑː-/ *n* [C] someone who tests people's eyes and orders SPECTACLES for them

**op·u·lence** /'ɒpjɪ̈ləns‖'ɑːp-/ *n* [U] great wealth: *the opulence of ancient Rome*

**op·u·lent** /'ɒpjɪ̈lənt‖'ɑːp-/ *adj* **1 a)** very beautiful, highly decorated, and made from expensive materials; LUXURIOUS: *the opulent splendour of the Sultan's palace* **b)** very rich: *opulent officials in large limousines* **2** growing healthily and in large amounts; LUXURIANT

**o·pus** /'əʊpəs‖'oʊ-/ *n* [usually singular] **1** a piece of music by a great musician, numbered according to when it was written: *Beethoven's Opus 95 quartets* **2** an important work of art by a famous writer, painter etc: *Verdi's Requiem, his greatest opus* —see also MAGNUM OPUS

**-or** /ə‖ər/ *suffix (in nouns)* the form used for -ER in certain words: *an actor* (=someone who acts) | *an inventor*

1 1 **or** /ə; *strong* ɔː‖ər; *strong* ɔːr/ *conjunction* **1** used between two things or before the last in a list of possibilities, things that people can choose from etc: *Do you want to leave now or would you rather set off later?*| *Was it London, Paris or Rome where you first met Maxim?*| **or anything/something** *spoken* (=or something of the same kind) *Would you like a coffee or something?*| *I wasn't trying to push in or anything.*| **either... or...** *If either Lennie or Miranda calls, I'm not at home.* —compare EITHER[3] **2** used after a negative verb when you mean not one thing and also not another thing: *He doesn't have a television or a video.*| *Sonia never cleans or even offers to wash the dishes.* **3** used to warn or advise someone that if they do not do something, something they do not want will happen: *Wear your coat or you'll catch cold.*| **or else**: *You have to roll the clothes very tightly or else they won't all fit in the rucksack.*| *You'd better be there, or else.* (=used to threaten someone) **4** used to correct something that you have said or to give more specific information: *It's going to snow tomorrow, or that's what the forecast says.*| *She was born in Saigon, or Ho Chi Minh City as it is now called.*| **or rather** *The computer software is old, or rather very out of date.* **5** used to explain why something happens or to show that something must be true: *He must be very drunk or he wouldn't keep falling down.*| **or else** *It's either a coincidence they're so alike, or else they are related in some way.* **6 a minute/a mile/twenty etc or so** a particular amount or a little more: *They had to wait an hour or so for the police to arrive.* **7 a minute/a dollar etc or two** a small amount or number of something: *I saw Nigel leaving a second or two ago.*

**or·a·cle** /ˈɒrəkəl‖ˈɔː-, ˈɑː-/ *n* [C] **1** someone the ancient Greeks believed could communicate with the gods, who gave advice to people or told them what would happen: *Spartans would consult the oracle before going into battle.* **2** a message given by an oracle **3** *humorous* a person or book that gives advice and information

**o·rac·u·lar** /ɒˈrækjʊlə, ə-‖ɔːˈrækjʊlər, ə-/ *adj* **1** said by an oracle **2** difficult to understand

**o·ral**[1] /ˈɔːrəl/ *n* [C] **1** *BrE* a spoken test, especially in a foreign language: *I've got my French oral tomorrow* **2** *AmE* a spoken test for a MASTER'S DEGREE

**oral**[2] *adj* **1** spoken, not written: *oral history*|*a brief oral report* **2** concerned with or involving the mouth: *oral hygiene* —**orally** *adv*

**oral con·tra·cep·tive** /ˌ·· ··ˈ··/ *n* [C] a drug that a woman takes by mouth, so that she can have sex without having a baby; the **pill** (PILL (2))

**oral ex·am** /ˈ·· ·ˌ·/ *n* [C] an ORAL

**oral sex** /ˌ·· ˈ·/ *n* [U] touching someone's sex organs with the lips and tongue, to give sexual pleasure

**oral sur·geon** /ˈ·· ˌ··/ *n* [C] **1** a DENTIST who performs operations in the mouth **2** *AmE* a DENTIST

3 **or·ange** /ˈɒrɪndʒ‖ˈɔː-, ˈɑː-/ *n* [C] **1** a round fruit that has a thick orange skin and is divided into parts inside —see picture on page 413 **2** a colour that is between red and yellow: *The sky turned a brilliant orange.* —**orange** *adj*: *Carrots are orange.* —see picture on page 411

**or·ange·ade** /ˌɒrɪndʒˈeɪd‖ˌɔː-, ˌɑː-/ *n* [U] a drink that tastes like oranges

**or·an·ge·ry** /ˈɒrɪndʒəri‖ˈɔː-, ˈɑː-/ *n* [C] a place where orange trees are grown

**orange squash** /ˌ·· ˈ·/ *n* [U] *BrE* a drink that tastes like oranges, made by adding water to a strong tasting liquid

**o·rang·u·tang** /ɔːˌræŋuːˈtæŋ‖əˈræŋətæŋ/ also **o·rang·u·tan** /-tæn/ *n* [C] a large APE[1] (1) with long arms and long orange hair

**o·ra·tion** /əˈreɪʃən, ɔː-/ *n* [C] a formal public speech

**or·a·tor** /ˈɒrətə‖ˈɔːrətər, ˈɑː-/ *n* [C] someone who makes speeches and is good at persuading people

**or·a·to·ri·o** /ˌɒrəˈtɔːriəʊ‖ˌɔːrəˈtɔːrioʊ, ˌɑː-/ *n* [C] a long piece of music in which a large group of people sing

**or·a·tory** /ˈɒrətri‖ˈɔːrətɔːri, ˈɑː-/ *n* **1** [U] the skill of making powerful and persuasive speeches: *a dazzling display of oratory* **2** [U] language that includes long and formal words **3** [C] a small building or part of a church where people can go to pray —**oratorical** /ˌɒrəˈtɒrɪkəl◂‖ˌɔːrəˈtɔːr-, ˌɑːrəˈtɑː-/ *adj*: *Churchill's formidable oratorical skills* —**oratorically** /-kli/ *adv*

**orb** /ɔːb‖ɔːrb/ *n* [C] **1** *literary* a bright ball-shaped object, especially the sun or the moon: *the red orb of the sun* **2** a ball decorated with gold, carried by a king or queen on formal occasions as a sign of power

**or·bit**[1] /ˈɔːbɪt‖ˈɔːr-/ *v* [I,T] to travel in a circle around a much larger object such as the Earth, the sun etc: *The satellite orbits the Earth every 48 hours.*

**orbit**[2] *n* [C] **1** the path travelled by an object which is moving around another much larger object such as the Earth, the sun etc: *the Moon's orbit around the Earth*| **in orbit** (=travelling in this kind of path) *The Space Shuttle is now in orbit.* **2** an area of power and influence: *brought within orbit of the Central Office*

**or·bit·al** /ˈɔːbɪtl‖ˈɔːr-/ *adj* **1** concerned with the orbit of one object around another: *the Earth's orbital path* **2** *BrE* an orbital road goes around a large city: *the London orbital* —**orbital** *n* [C]

**or·chard** /ˈɔːtʃəd‖ˈɔːrtʃərd/ *n* [C] a place where fruit trees are grown: *a cherry orchard*

**or·ches·tra** /ˈɔːkɪstrə‖ˈɔːr-/ *n* [C also + plural verb *BrE*] a large group of musicians playing many different kinds of instruments and led by a CONDUCTOR (1)

**or·ches·tral** /ɔːˈkestrəl‖ɔːr-/ *adj* concerned with or written for an orchestra: *orchestral music*

**orchestra pit** /ˈ··· ·/ *n* [C] the space below the stage in a theatre where the musicians sit —see picture at THEATRE

**or·ches·trate** /ˈɔːkɪstreɪt‖ˈɔːr-/ *v* [T] **1** to organize an important event or a complicated plan, especially secretly: *The coup was orchestrated by the CIA.* **2** to arrange a piece of music so that it can be played by an orchestra —**orchestrated** *adj* —**orchestration** /ˌɔːkɪˈstreɪʃən‖ˌɔːr-/ *n* [C,U]

**or·chid** /ˈɔːkɪd‖ˈɔːr-/ *n* [C] a plant that has flowers with three parts, the middle one being shaped like a lip

**or·dain** /ɔːˈdeɪn‖ɔːr-/ *v* [T] **1** to officially make someone a priest or religious leader: *Desmond Tutu was ordained in 1960.*| **ordain sb (as) sth** *Paulson was ordained deacon.* —see also ORDINATION **2** *formal* to order that something should happen: *a duty ordained by God*|[+ **that**] *The King ordained that a feast should be prepared.*

**or·deal** /ɔːˈdiːl, ˈɔːdiːl‖ɔːrˈdiːl, ˈɔːrdiːl/ *n* [C] a terrible or painful experience: [+ **of**] *the ordeal of having your child kidnapped*| **it is an ordeal to do sth** *Some people find it an ordeal to appear before the TV camera.*

**or·der**[1] /ˈɔːdə‖ˈɔːrdər/ *n*

**1 ▶ FOR A PURPOSE ◀ a) in order to do sth** for the purpose of doing something: *politicians who make promises simply in order to win more votes*|*In order to understand how the human body works, you need to have some knowledge of chemistry.* **b) in order for/that** *formal* so that something can happen or so that someone can do something: **in order for sb/sth to do sth** *Sunlight is needed in order for photosynthesis to take place.*| **in order that** *I locked the door in order that we might continue our discussions undisturbed.* S1 W1

**2 ▶ ARRANGEMENT ◀** [C,U] the way that several things, events etc are arranged or put on a list, showing whether something is first, second, third etc; SEQUENCE: *The programme shows the order of events for the day.*| **In order** (=arranged in a particular way) *You should keep the files in order.*| *What order are these videos supposed to be in?*| **do sth in order** (=do things one after another, according to a plan) *Then they call out our names in order and we answer yes or no.*| **out of order** (=in the wrong order)| **in chronological/alphabetical/numerical order** *Let us examine these*

order

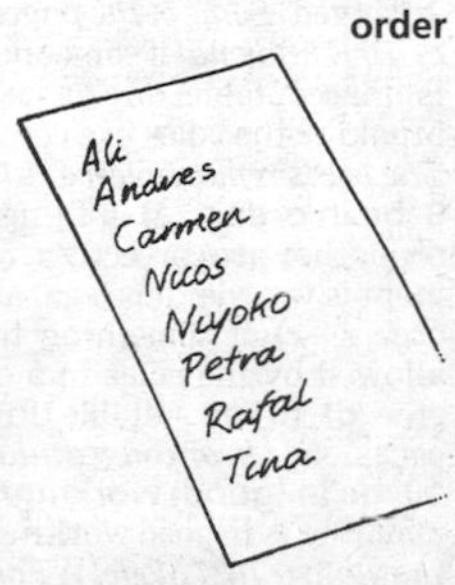


names in alphabetical order

*events in chronological order.* | **in the right/wrong order**: *Wait a minute, we've got these photos in the wrong order.* | **in order of importance/preference/appearance etc**: *characters are listed in order of appearance.* | **in reverse order** (=in the opposite order to what is usual) | **in ascending/descending order** (=starting with the lowest or highest number)

**3 ▶ REQUEST FOR GOODS ◀** [C] a request by a customer for a company to supply goods or for a meal in a restaurant: | **place an order** (=make an order) *The Canadian Air Force has placed a large order for electronic equipment.* | **order form** (=special piece of paper for writing orders on) *Have you filled out the order form?* | **on order** (=ordered but not yet received) *It's on order – it should be in next week.* | **have sth on order** (=be waiting for something you have ordered) | **take sb's order** (=write down what a customer in a restaurant wants) *The waiter came over to take my order.* | **make/supply sth to order** (=produce something especially for a particular customer) *We supply hand-made shoes to order.*

**4 ▶ GOODS/MEAL ◀** [C] goods or a meal that a customer has asked for: *Your order has arrived – you can collect it from the store any time.* | **side order** (=a small plate of food in addition to your main meal)

**5 ▶ NO TROUBLE OR CRIME ◀** [U] a situation in which rules are obeyed and authority is respected: **law and order** *the work of the police in maintaining law and order* | **public order** *Their speeches were clearly a threat to public order.* | **keep order/keep sb in order** (=stop people from behaving badly) *Some of the new teachers can't keep order.* | *Don't worry, I'll keep them in order.* | **restore order** *The army was called in to restore order.* | **call sb to order** (=order someone in a formal meeting or court of law to obey the rules) | **Order! Order!** (=used in parliament or in court to tell people to be quiet and obey the rules)

**6 ▶ COMMAND ◀** also **orders** [C] a command given by someone in authority: *I expect my orders to be obeyed.* | *You will report to me at eight o'clock tomorrow – and that's an order* | **give orders** *I'm the one who gives the orders around here – just remember that.* | **take orders from** (=obey someone) *I'm not taking orders from you!* | **order to do sth** *General Bradley gave the order to advance.* | **have orders to do sth** (=have been commanded to do something) *I have orders to search your house.* | **by order of/on the orders of** (=because of someone's order) *On Stalin's orders the target for the five year plan was raised once again.* | **under orders to do sth** (=having been commanded to do something) *A warship was dispatched, under orders to sail directly to Georgetown.*

**7 ▶ LEGAL DOCUMENT ◀** [C] an official statement from a court of law that something must be done; COURT ORDER

**8 be out of order a)** if a machine or piece of equipment is out of order, it is not working: *The phone at the street corner is out of order again.* **b)** if things on a list or in a series are out of order, they are not correctly arranged: *Some of the pages in this book are out of order.* **c)** *BrE informal* if someone's behaviour is out of order it is unacceptable; OUT OF LINE (LINE[1] (32)) *AmE* **d)** to be breaking the rules in a committee, court, parliament etc: *The MP's remarks were ruled out of order.*

**9 be in order a)** if things on a list or in a series are in order they are correctly arranged **b)** if an official document is in order it is legal and correct: *Is your passport in order?* **c)** if something that you do is in order, it is allowed by the rules in a committee, court, parliament etc **d)** to be a suitable thing to do or say on a particular occasion: *I hear congratulations are in order.*

**10 be in (good) working/running order** if a vehicle or machine is in good working or running order, it is working well: *a 1927 Model A Ford, still in good running order*

**11 ▶ WELL-ORGANIZED STATE ◀** [U] a situation in which everything is controlled, well organized, and correctly arranged: *Let's have some order in here. Someone put those desks straight.* | **put sth in order** (=organize or arrange something properly) *Uncle Bob put his business affairs in order before he died.* | **in apple-pie order** *AmE informal* (=very tidy and correctly arranged) *Tim's room was in apple-pie order.*

**12 leave/retreat/retire in good order** to leave in a controlled way, when people are angry or attacking you

**13 ▶ POLITICAL/SOCIAL SITUATION ◀** [singular] the political, social, or economic situation at a particular time: *the present economic order* | **the established order** (=the traditional rules and customs of society) *The gay rights movement emerged to challenge the established order.* | **the new order** (=the new situation after an important change in politics or society) *the new world order since the end of the Cold War*

**14 the (natural) order of things** the way that life and the world are organized and intended to be: *People accepted the class system as part of the natural order of things.*

**15 of a high/the highest/the first order** of a very good or of the best kind: *an achievement of the highest order*

**16 be the order of the day a)** to be suitable for a particular occasion or situation: *Casual clothes are the order of the day.* **b)** to be very common at a particular time: *Sexual explicitness seems to be the order of the day.*

**17 in the order of/of the order of** also **on the order of** *AmE* a little more or a little less than a particular amount; APPROXIMATELY: *a figure in the order of $7 million*

**18 in short order** *especially AmE* immediately: *The crisis was resolved in relatively short order.*

**19 ▶ RELIGIOUS GROUP ◀** [C] a society of MONKS or NUNS (=people who live a holy life according to religious rules): *the Benedictine Order* | [+ **of**] *the order of Jesuits*

**20 take (holy) orders** to become a priest

**21 ▶ SECRET SOCIETY ◀** [C] an organization or society whose members meet for secret ceremonies: *a Masonic order* | *the Royal Ancient Order of Boars*

**22 ▶ OFFICIAL HONOUR ◀** [C] **a)** a group of people who have received a special official reward from a king, president etc for their services or achievements: *the Order of the Garter* **b)** a special piece of metal, silk etc that members of the order wear at ceremonies

**23 ▶ MONEY ◀** [C] an official piece of paper that can be exchanged for money —see also POSTAL ORDER, BANKER'S ORDER, MONEY ORDER

**24 the lower orders** *BrE old-fashioned* people who belong to the lowest social class

**25 ▶ OF ANIMALS/PLANTS ◀** [C] *technical* a group of animals or plants that are considered together because they are descended from the same plant or animal in EVOLUTION (1) —compare CLASS[1] (6), KINGDOM (3), SPECIES

**26 ▶ COMPUTER ◀** [C] *AmE technical* a list of jobs that a computer has to do in a particular order; QUEUE *BrE* —see also POINT OF ORDER, **tall order** (TALL (3)), STANDING ORDER, PECKING ORDER, **be given/get your marching orders** (MARCH[1] (5)), **under starter's orders** (STARTER (3)), **set/put your own house in order** (HOUSE[1] (7))

This graph shows some of the words most commonly used with the noun **order**.

in order
first/highest/high order
out of order
give orders
good/working order
take orders
chronological/alphabetical order
right/wrong order

10 20 30 40 50 60 70 80 90 100 per million

Based on the British National Corpus and the Longman Lancaster Corpus

**order**[2] *v* **1** [I,T] to ask for goods or services: *Have you ordered yet, madam?* | **order sth** *She ordered a double brandy.* | **order sb sth** *We'll order you a taxi from the*

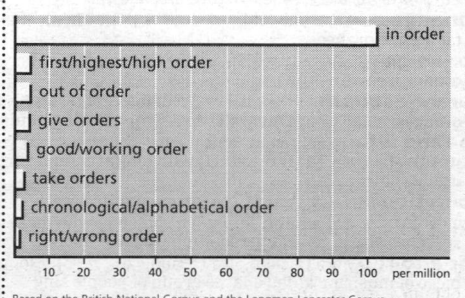

*station.* | **order sth for sb/sth** *I've ordered new curtains for the living room.* **2** [T] to tell someone to do something, using your authority or power: *"Stay right there," she ordered.* **order sb in/out etc** *If you make any more noise I'll order you out of the room.* | **order sb to do sth** *The commandant ordered them to line up against the wall.* | **order sth** *Only the king has the power to order the release of the prisoners.* | [+ **that**] *A grand jury has ordered that Schultz be sent for trial.* **3** [T] to arrange something in an order: *The diamonds are ordered according to size.* **4** [T] *old use* to arrange things neatly or effectively

**order** sb **about/around** *phr v* [T] *BrE* to continuously give someone orders in an annoying or threatening way: *Keith's older brother is always ordering him around.*

**order** sb ↔ **out** *phr v* [T] to order soldiers or police to go somewhere to stop violent behaviour by a crowd: *The Governor decided to order out the National Guard.*

**or·dered** /ˈɔːdəd‖ˈɔːrdərd/ also **well-ordered** *adj* well arranged or controlled: *a well-ordered household* | *an ordered existence* —compare DISORDERED (1)

**or·der·ly¹** /ˈɔːdəli‖ˈɔːrdərli/ *adj* **1** arranged or organized in a sensible or neat way: *an orderly household.* | *an orderly mind.* **2** peaceful or well-behaved: *An orderly crowd assembled at the gate.* —**orderliness** *n* [U]

**orderly²** *n* [C] **1** someone who does unskilled jobs in a hospital **2** a soldier who does unskilled jobs

**order pa·per** /ˈ·· ˌ··/ *n* [C] a list of subjects to be discussed in the British Parliament

**or·di·nal¹** /ˈɔːdɪ̣nəl‖ˈɔːr-/ *adj* showing a position in a set of numbers

**ordinal²** *n* [C] an ordinal number

**ordinal num·ber** /ˌ··· ˈ··/ *n* [C] one of the numbers such as first, second, third etc which show the order of things —compare CARDINAL NUMBER

**or·di·nance** /ˈɔːdɪ̣nəns‖ˈɔːrdənəns/ *n* [C] **1** an order given by a ruler or governing organization: *a Royal ordinance* **2** *AmE* a law, usually of a city or town, that forbids or restricts an activity: *contravening city ordinances*

**or·di·na·ri·ly** /ˈɔːdənərɪ̣li, ˌɔːdənˈeərɪ̣li‖ˌɔːrdənˈerɪ̣li/ *adv* **1** [sentence adverb] usually: *Ordinarily, the process of buying clothes irritates me.* | *It is ordinarily possible to predict the results with some accuracy.* **2** in an ordinary or normal way: *He was walking along quite ordinarily.*

S1 W2 **or·di·na·ry** /ˈɔːdənəri‖ˈɔːrdneri/ *adj* **1** average, common, or usual, not different or special: *part of a politician's ordinary routine* | *The new taxes came as a shock to ordinary Americans.* | **out of the ordinary** (=unusual or unexpected) *Nothing out of the ordinary had happened.* | **in the ordinary way** *BrE* (=normally) *Jim was not in the ordinary way a romantic, but he decided to bring Joanna some roses.* **2** not particularly good or impressive: *I thought the paintings were pretty ordinary.* —see also EXTRAORDINARY (1,2) —**ordinariness** *n* [U]

**ordinary sea·man** /ˌ···· ˈ··/ *n* —see table on page B4

**ordinary shares** /ˌ···· ˈ·/ *n* [plural] *technical* the largest part of a company's CAPITAL¹ (2), which is owned by people who have the right to vote at meetings and to receive part of the company's profits

**or·di·na·tion** /ˌɔːdɪ̣ˈneɪʃən‖ˌɔːr-/ *n* [C,U] the act or ceremony making someone a priest: *the ordination of women*

**ord·nance** /ˈɔːdnəns‖ˈɔːr-/ *n* [U] **1** large guns with wheels; ARTILLERY (1) **2** weapons, explosives, and vehicles used in fighting

**ordnance sur·vey map** /ˌ·· ˈ·· ·/ *n* [C] *BrE* a map which shows all the roads, paths, hills etc of an area in detail

**or·dure** /ˈɔːdjʊə‖ˈɔːrdʒər/ *n* [U] *formal* dirt, especially waste matter from the body

**ore** /ɔː‖ɔːr/ *n* [C,U] rock or earth from which metal can be obtained: *iron ore* | *veins of rich ore*

**o·reg·a·no** /ˌɒrɪˈɡɑːnəʊ‖əˈreɡənoʊ/ *n* [U] a plant used in cooking, especially in Italian cooking

W3 **or·gan** /ˈɔːɡən‖ˈɔːr-/ *n* [C]

**1** ▶ **BODY PART** ◀ **a)** a part of the body, such as the heart or lungs, that has a particular purpose: *inflammation affecting the internal organs* | *an organ transplant* **b)** a word meaning PENIS, used because you want to avoid saying this directly

**2** ▶ **MUSICAL INSTRUMENT** ◀ a large musical instrument used especially in churches, with one or more keyboards (KEYBOARD¹ (1)) and large pipes out of which the sound comes: *an organ recital in Westminster Cathedral*

**3** ▶ **ORGANIZATION** ◀ an organization that is part of, or works for, a larger organization or group: [+ **of**] *Giving too much power to any organ of government should be avoided.*

**4** ▶ **NEWSPAPER/MAGAZINE** ◀ *formal* a newspaper or magazine which gives information, news etc for an organization: [+ **of**] *This publication is the organ of the Conservative Party.*

**5** ▶ **PLANT** ◀ a part of a plant, such as a leaf or stem, that has a special purpose

**or·gan·die** also **organdy** *AmE* /ˈɔːɡəndi‖ˈɔːr-/ *n* [U] very thin, stiff cotton, used as dress material

**organ grind·er** /ˈ·· ˌ··/ *n* [C] a musician who plays a BARREL ORGAN in the street

**or·gan·ic** /ɔːˈɡænɪk‖ɔːr-/ *adj*

**1** ▶ **LIVING THINGS** ◀ living, or produced by or from living things: *Peat is decomposed organic matter.* —opposite INORGANIC (1)

**2** ▶ **BODY ORGANS** ◀ concerning the organs of the body: *organic diseases*

**3** ▶ **PART OF STH** ◀ **a)** made up of many parts that all depend on each other: *an organic system* | *an organic link between the music and the meaning* **b)** connected with the relationship between these parts

**4** ▶ **FARMING** ◀ using farming or gardening methods without artificial chemicals, or produced or grown by these methods: *organic vegetables* | *an organic farmer*

**5** ▶ **DEVELOPMENT** ◀ change or development which is organic happens in a natural way, without anyone planning it or forcing it to happen —**organically** /-kli/ *adv*

**organic chem·is·try** /·ˌ·· ˈ···/ *n* [U] the study of CARBON (1) compounds —compare INORGANIC CHEMISTRY

**or·gan·is·m** /ˈɔːɡənɪzəm‖ˈɔːr-/ *n* [C] **1** an animal, plant, human, or any other living thing: *the human organism* | *a microscopic organism living in the cow's stomach* **2** a system made up of parts that are dependent on each other: *A society is essentially an organism.* S3

**or·gan·ist** /ˈɔːɡənɪ̣st‖ˈɔːr-/ *n* [C] someone who plays the ORGAN (2): *a church organist*

**or·gan·i·za·tion** also **organisation** *BrE* /ˌɔːɡənaɪˈzeɪʃən‖ˌɔːrɡənə-/ *n* **1** [C] a group such as a club or business that has formed for a particular purpose: *a charitable organization* **2** [U] the act of planning and arranging things effectively: *Organisation's never been my strong point.* | [+ **of**] *The organization of the fund raisers has been left to Ellen.* **3** [U] the way in which the different parts of a system are arranged and work together: [+ **of**] *the social organization of primitive cultures* —**organizational** *adj*: *organizational ability* —**organizationally** *adv* S2 W1

**or·gan·ize** also **—ise** *BrE* /ˈɔːɡənaɪz‖ˈɔːr-/ *v* **1** [T] to make the necessary arrangements so that an activity can happen: *They organized a protest march.* | *Who's going to organise the party this year?* **2** [T] to arrange information, work, a group etc so that it works correctly: *Organize your thoughts before you begin to speak.* | *A team of professionals will organize the volunteers.* | **be organized in/along/around** *The political system is organized along party lines.* | *industrial towns organized around places of work* **3** [I,T] *especially AmE* to form a TRADE UNION (=an organization that protects workers' rights) or persuade people to join one; UNIONIZE

**or·gan·ized** also **organised** *BrE* /ˈɔːɡənaɪzd‖ˈɔːr-/ *adj* **1** achieving aims in an effective, ordered, and sensible way: *I'm sorry I forgot – I'm not very organized these days.* | *You can be sure the conference will be well organised*

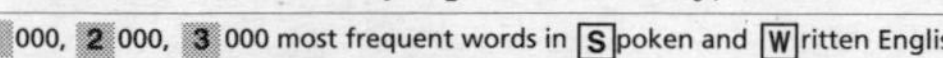
1 000, 2 000, 3 000 most frequent words in Spoken and Written English

*if Barb is in charge.* | **get organized** *spoken*: *I have to get organized and get some things done.* | **highly organized** (=very well organized) *a highly organized social system* —opposite DISORGANIZED **2** an organized activity is arranged for and done by many people: *organized religion* | *organized sports*

O

**organized crime** /ˌ··· ˈ·/ *n* [U] a large and powerful organization of criminals: *moves to combat terrorism, drug trafficking and organized crime*

**organizer** also **organiser** *BrE* /ˈɔːɡənaɪzə‖ɔːrɡənaɪzər/ *n* [C] someone who makes the arrangements for something that is planned to happen: *The organizers had expected about 50,000 people to attend the concert.*

**or·gas·m** /ˈɔːɡæzəm‖ˈɔːr-/ *n* [C, U] the greatest point of sexual pleasure

**or·gas·mic** /ɔːˈɡæzmɪk‖ɔːr-/ *adj* **1** *technical* related to orgasm **2** *slang* extremely exciting or enjoyable

**or·gy** /ˈɔːdʒi‖ˈɔːr-/ *n* [C] **1** a wild party with a lot of eating, drinking, and sexual activity **2** sexual activity in a group **3 an orgy of** a short time spent doing too much of an activity in a way that is not sensible or controlled: *an orgy of shopping* —**orgiastic** *adj*

**o·ri·el win·dow** /ˈɔːriəl ˌwɪndəʊ‖-doʊ/ *n* [C] *technical* an upper window that is built out from a wall

**o·ri·ent[1]** /ˈɔːriənt, ˈɒri-‖ˈɔː-/ also **orientate** *BrE* —*v* **1 be oriented to/towards** to be developed, trained, made etc for a particular purpose: *an English language course oriented towards the needs of businessmen* **2 be oriented around** if something is oriented around a particular idea, that idea is very important to it: *Wanda's whole life has been oriented around the children.* **3 orient yourself a)** to find your position with a map or a COMPASS (1): *The climbers stopped to orientate themselves.* **b)** to become familiar with a new situation: *I'll need a few days to orient myself.*

**o·ri·ent[2]** *n* **the Orient** *old-fashioned* the eastern part of the world, especially China and Japan and the countries near them —compare **the East** (EAST (1a)), OCCIDENT

**orient[3]** *adj poetic* **1** eastern **2 orient star/sun** a rising star or sun

**o·ri·en·tal[1]** /ˌɔːriˈentl◂, ˌɒ-‖ˌɔː-/ *adj* concerning or from the East or South-East Asia: *oriental countries* | *oriental culture*

**oriental[2]** *n* [C] *old-fashioned* a word meaning someone from an oriental country, which is now usually considered offensive —compare OCCIDENTAL

**o·ri·en·tal·ist** /ˌɔːriˈentəlɪst, ˌɒ-‖ˌɔː-/ *n* [C] someone who studies the languages and culture of oriental countries

**o·ri·en·tate** /ˈɔːriənteɪt, ˈɒ-‖ˈɔː-/ *v BrE* another form of the word ORIENT[1]: *an English language course orientated towards the needs of businessmen* | *The climbers stopped half way up the mountain to orientate themselves.* | *I'll need a few days to orientate myself.*

**o·ri·en·ta·tion** /ˌɔːriənˈteɪʃən,ˌɒ-‖ˌɔː-/ *n* [C, U] **1** the aims or interests of a particular activity or organization: [+ **towards/to**] *an orientation to world affairs* | [+ **of**] *the orientation of post-war policy* **2 political/religious orientation** the political views or religious beliefs that you have **3 sexual orientation** the fact that someone is HETEROSEXUAL or HOMOSEXUAL: *questions about race and sexual orientation* **4** [U] *especially AmE* training and preparation for a new job or activity: *This is orientation week for all the new students.* **5** [C] the angle or position of an object in relation to another object or a direction

**o·ri·ent·ed** /ˈɔːrientɪd, ˈɒ-‖ˈɔː-/ also **o·ri·en·ta·ted** /ˈɔːriənteɪtɪd, ˈɒ-‖ˈɔː-/ *BrE* —*adj* **politically oriented/family oriented etc** giving a lot of time, effort, or attention to politics, family etc: *The new generation doesn't seem to be politically oriented at all.*

**o·ri·en·teer·ing** /ˌɔːriənˈtɪərɪŋ, ˌɒ-‖ˌɔːriənˈtɪr-/ *n* [U] a sport in which people have to find their way quickly across unknown country using a map and a COMPASS (1)

**or·i·fice** /ˈɒrɪfɪs‖ˈɔː-, ˈɑː-/ *n* [C] **1** *technical or humorous* one of the holes in your body, such as your mouth, nose etc: *the dental orifice* **2** *formal* a hole or entrance

**o·ri·ga·mi** /ˌɒrɪˈɡɑːmi‖ˌɔː-/ *n* [U] the Japanese art of folding paper to make attractive objects

**or·i·gin** /ˈɒrɪdʒɪn‖ˈɔː-, ˈɑː-/ *n* **1** also **origins** [plural] the situation, place, or physical matter from which something begins: [+ **of**] *the origins of language* | **have your/its origin in sth** (=begin in a particular place, situation etc) *Many of the problems had their origin in post-war Europe.* **2** also **origins** [plural] the country, race or class from which someone or their family comes: *They are proud of their aristocratic origins.* **3** [C] *technical* the point where two axes (AXIS (3)) cross on a GRAPH W

**o·rig·i·nal[1]** /əˈrɪdʒɪnəl, -dʒənəl/ *adj* **1** [only before noun] existing or happening first, before being changed or replaced by something or someone else: *The land was returned to its original owner.* | *We still have the original stone floor.* **2** completely new and different from anything that anyone has thought of before: *a highly original style* | *an original thinker* | *What an original idea!* **3** [only before noun] not copied: *an original Holbein drawing* S W

**original[2]** *n* [C] **1** a painting, document, etc that is not a copy, but is the one produced by the writer or artist: *The colour was paler in the original.* | *I'll keep a copy, and give you the original.* **2 in the original** in the language that a book, play etc was first written in, before it was translated: *I read it in the original.* **3** *informal* someone whose behaviour, clothing etc is unusual and amusing

**o·rig·i·nal·i·ty** /əˌrɪdʒɪˈnælɪti/ *n* [U] the quality of being completely new and different from anything that anyone has thought of before: *poems of great originality*

**o·rig·i·nal·ly** /əˈrɪdʒɪnəli, -dʒənəli/ *adv* in the beginning: *The family originally came from France.* | *The book was originally conceived as an autobiography, but it became a novel.* | [sentence adverb] *Originally, we had planned a tour of Scotland but we never got further than Edinburgh.* S W

**original sin** /·ˌ··· ˈ·/ *n* [U] the state of disobedience to God which everyone is in from birth, according to some Christian teaching

**o·rig·i·nate** /əˈrɪdʒɪneɪt/ *v* **1** [I always + adv/prep, not in progressive] *formal* to start to develop in a particular place or from a particular situation: [+ **in/from/with**] *a custom originating in Chinese culture* | *How did the idea originate?* **2** [T] to have the idea for something and start it: *Who originated the present complaints procedures?*

**o·rig·i·nat·or** /əˈrɪdʒɪneɪtə‖-ər/ *n* [C] the person who first has the idea for something and starts it: [+ **of**] *the originator of a whole genre of detective fiction, Edgar Allan Poe*

**or·i·ole** /ˈɔːriəʊl‖-oʊl/ *n* [C] **1** a N. American bird that is black with a red and yellow stripe on its wing **2** a European bird with black wings and a yellow body

**or·i·son** /ˈɒrɪzən‖ˈɔːrɪsən-, ˈɑː-/ *n* [C] *old use* a prayer

**or·mo·lu** /ˈɔːməluː‖ˈɔːr-/ *n* [U] a gold-coloured mixture of metals, not containing real gold: *an ormolu clock*

**or·na·ment[1]** /ˈɔːnəmənt‖ˈɔːr-/ *n* **1** [C] an object that you keep in your house because it is beautiful rather than useful: *china ornaments* **2** [U] decoration that is added to something: *plain architecture with very little ornament* **3 be an ornament to** *old-fashioned* to add honour, importance, or beauty to something: [+ **to**] *She is an ornament to her profession.*

**ornament[2]** *v* **be ornamented with** to be decorated with something: *a silver goblet ornamented with pearls*

**or·na·men·tal** /ˌɔːnəˈmentl◂‖ˌɔːr-/ *adj* designed to decorate something: *ornamental gardens* | *These buttons are only ornamental.* —**ornamentally** *adv*

**or·na·men·ta·tion** /ˌɔːnəmenˈteɪʃən‖ˌɔːr-/ *n* [U] decoration: *the Victorian love of ornamentation*

**or·nate** /ɔːˈneɪt‖ɔːr-/ *adj* a lot of decoration, or too much decoration, especially with many complicated details: *a heavy ornate gold cigarette case* —**ornately** *adv* —**ornateness** *n* [U]

**or·ne·ry** /ˈɔːnəri‖ˈɔːr-/ *adj humorous AmE* behaving in an unreasonable and angry way

**or·ni·thol·o·gist** /ˌɔːnɪ̵ˈθɒlədʒɪ̵st‖ˌɔːrnɪ̵ˈθɑː-/ *n* [C] someone who studies birds

**or·ni·thol·o·gy** /ˌɔːnɪ̵ˈθɒlədʒi‖ˌɔːrnɪ̵ˈθɑː-/ *n* [U] the scientific study of birds —**ornithological** /ˌɔːnɪ̵θəˈlɒdʒɪkəl◂‖ˌɔːrnɪ̵θəˈlɑː-/ *adj*

**o·ro·tund** /ˈɒrəʊtʌnd‖ˈɔːrə-/ *adj formal* **1** an orotund sound or voice is strong and clear **2** orotund speech or writing is trying to sound important and impressive

**or·phan¹** /ˈɔːfən‖ˈɔːr-/ *n* [C] a child whose parents are both dead: *the plight of thousands of war orphans*

**orphan²** *v* **be orphaned** to become an orphan: *She was orphaned when her parents died in a plane crash.*

**or·phan·age** /ˈɔːfənɪdʒ‖ˈɔːr-/ *n* [C] a place where orphan children live: *He was raised in a Catholic orphanage.*

**or·tho·don·tics** /ˌɔːθəˈdɒntɪks‖ˌɔːrθəˈdɑːn-/ *n* [U] the practice or skill of making teeth grow straight when they have not been growing correctly —**orthodontic** *adj*: *orthodontic treatment*

**or·tho·don·tist** /ˌɔːθəˈdɒntɪ̵st‖ˌɔːrθəˈdɑːn-/ *n* [C] a DENTIST who is a specialist in making teeth grow straight when they have not been growing correctly

**or·tho·dox** /ˈɔːθədɒks‖ˈɔːrθədɑːks/ *adj* **1** ideas or behaviour that are orthodox are considered by most people to be normal, correct and acceptable: *orthodox theories of medicine* —see also UNORTHODOX **2** believing in and following all the traditional beliefs, laws, and practices of a religion: *an orthodox Jew* **3** believing in or following the usual form of a particular set of ideas: *orthodox monetarism*

**Orthodox Church** /ˌ··· ˈ·/ *n* [U] one of the Christian churches in eastern Europe and parts of Asia

**or·tho·dox·y** /ˈɔːθədɒksi‖ˈɔːrθədɑː-/ *n* **1** [C,U] an idea or set of ideas considered by most people to be normal, correct and acceptable: *The early feminists challenged the social and political orthodoxy of their time.* **2** the traditional ideas and beliefs of a group or religion, or the practice of following these strictly

**or·thog·ra·phy** /ɔːˈθɒgrəfi‖ɔːrˈθɑː-/ *n* [U] *technical* **1** the spelling of words **2** correct spelling —**orthographic** /ˌɔːθəˈgræfɪk◂‖ˌɔːr-/ *adj* —**orthographically** /-kli/ *adv*

**or·tho·pe·dic, orthopaedic** /ˌɔːθəˈpiːdɪk◂‖ˌɔːr-/ *adj* **1** connected with or providing medical treatment for problems affecting bones, muscles etc: *an orthopaedic surgeon* **2 orthopedic bed/chair/shoe etc** one that is designed to cure or prevent medical problems affecting your bones, muscles etc —**orthopedically** /-kli/ *adv*: *orthopedically designed seats*

**or·tho·pe·dics, orthopaedics** /ˌɔːθəˈpiːdɪks‖ˌɔːr-/ *n* [U] the area of medical science or treatment that deals with problems, diseases, or injuries of bones, muscles etc

**or·tho·pe·dist, orthopaedist** /ˌɔːθəˈpiːdɪ̵st‖ˌɔːr-/ *n* [C] a doctor with special training in orthopedics

**-ory¹** /əri‖ɔːri, əri/ *suffix (in nouns)* a place or thing used for doing something: *an observatory* (=where people look at things, especially the stars) | *a directory*

**-ory²** *suffix (in adjectives)* describes something that does a particular thing: *an explanatory note* (=that gives an explanation) | *a congratulatory telegram* (=that CONGRATULATES)

**Os·car** /ˈɒskə‖ˈɑːskər/ *n* [C] an American prize given each year for the best film, actor etc in the film industry: *the Oscar for best actress*

**os·cil·late** /ˈɒsɪ̵leɪt‖ˈɑː-/ *v* [I] **1** *technical* to keep moving regularly from side to side, between two limits **2** *formal* to keep changing between one feeling or attitude and another; VACILLATE: [+ **between**] *Her attitude towards her husband oscillated between tender affection and deep mistrust.* **3** if an electric current oscillates, it changes direction very regularly and very frequently —**oscillatory** /ˈɒsɪ̵lətəri‖ˈɑːsələˌtɔːri/ *adj*

**os·cil·la·tion** /ˌɒsɪ̵ˈleɪʃən‖ˌɑː-/ *n technical* **1** [U] the regular movement of something from side to side between two limits **2** [C] a single movement from side to side of something that is oscillating

**os·cil·la·tor** /ˈɒsɪ̵leɪtə‖ˈɑːsɪ̵leɪtər/ *n* [C] a machine that produces electrical oscillations

**-oses** /əʊsiːz‖oʊ-/ *suffix* the plural form of the suffix -OSIS

**o·si·er** /ˈəʊziə‖ˈoʊʒər/ *n* [C] a type of WILLOW tree whose branches are used for making baskets

**-osis** /əʊsɪ̵s‖oʊ-/ *suffix plural* **-oses** /əʊsiːz‖oʊ-/ *(in nouns)* **1** *technical* a diseased condition: *silicosis* (=a lung disease) | *neuroses* (=disorders of the mind) **2** a condition or process: *a metamorphosis* (=change from one state to another) —**-otic** /ɒtɪk‖ɑːtɪk/ *(in adjectives)*: *neurotic* | *hypnotic* —**-otically** /ɒtɪkli‖ɑːt-/ *(in adverbs)*

**os·mo·sis** /ɒzˈməʊsɪ̵s‖ɑːzˈmoʊ-/ *n* [U] **1 by osmosis** if you learn facts or receive ideas by osmosis, you gradually learn them by hearing them often: *I must have learnt it by osmosis.* **2** *technical* the gradual process of liquid passing through a MEMBRANE (2) —**osmotic** /ɒzˈmɒtɪk‖ɑːzˈmɑː-/ *adj* —**osmotically** /-kli/ *adv*

**os·prey** /ˈɒspri, -preɪ‖ˈɑː-/ *n* [C] a type of large bird that eats fish

**os·si·fy** /ˈɒsɪ̵faɪ‖ˈɑː-/ *v* **1** [I] to become unwilling to consider new ideas or change your behaviour **2** [I,T] *technical* to change into bone or to make something change into bone —**ossification** /ˌɒsɪ̵fɪ̵ˈkeɪʃən‖ˌɑːs-/ *n* [U] *the rapid ossification of the Soviet hardline position*

**os·ten·si·ble** /ɒˈstensɪ̵bəl‖ɑː-/ *adj* seeming to be the reason for or the purpose of something but usually hiding the real reason or purpose: *The ostensible purpose of the war was to liberate a small nation from tyranny.*

**os·ten·si·bly** /ɒˈstensɪ̵bli‖ɑː-/ *adv* if something is done ostensibly for a particular reason, it is not really done for this reason but people pretend that it is: *The big bosses went to Hawaii, ostensibly to launch the new project.*

**os·ten·ta·tion** /ˌɒstənˈteɪʃən, -ten-‖ˌɑː-/ *n* [U] an unnecessary show of wealth or knowledge intended to make people admire you: *Their simple style of dress and complete lack of ostentation made me like them even more.*

**os·ten·ta·tious** /ˌɒstənˈteɪʃəs◂, -ten-‖ˌɑː-/ *adj* **1** something that is ostentatious is large, looks expensive and is designed to make people think that its owner must be very rich: *The hotel loomed huge and ostentatious above the street.* **2** someone who is ostentatious likes to show everyone how rich they are: *I was vaguely annoyed by his generosity which seemed almost ostentatious.* —**ostentatiously** *adv*

**osteo-** /ɒstiəʊ, -tiə‖ɑːstioʊ, -tiə/ *prefix technical* concerning bones

**os·te·o·ar·thri·tis** /ˌɒstiəʊɑːˈθraɪtɪ̵s‖ˌɑːstioʊɑːr-/ *n* [U] *technical* a condition which makes your knees and other joints stiff and painful

**os·te·o·path** /ˈɒstiəpæθ‖ˈɑː-/ *n* [C] someone trained in osteopathy

**os·te·op·a·thy** /ˌɒstiˈɒpəθi‖ˌɑːstiˈɑː-/ *n* [U] the practice or skill of treating physical problems such as back pain by moving and pressing muscles and bones

**os·tler** /ˈɒslə‖ˈɑːslər/ also **hostler** *AmE* —*n* [C] a man who, in former times, took care of guests' horses at a hotel

**os·tra·cize** also **-cise** *BrE* /ˈɒstrəsaɪz‖ˈɑː-/ *v* [T] if a group of people ostracize someone, they stop accepting them as a member of the group: *Reg was ostracized by the whole squadron, who cursed his actions.* —**ostracism** /-sɪzəm/ *n* [U]

**os·trich** /ˈɒstrɪtʃ‖ˈɔː-, ˈɑː-/ *n* [C] **1** a large African bird with long legs, that runs very quickly but cannot fly **2** *informal* someone who refuses to accept that unpleasant problems exist instead of dealing with them

**OT** the written abbreviation of OLD TESTAMENT

**OTC** /ˌəʊ tiː ˈsiː◂‖ˌoʊ-/ the abbreviation of OVER-THE-COUNTER (2)

**oth·er** /ˈʌðə‖ˈʌðər/ *determiner, adj, pron* **1** used when there are two people, things etc to mean the one that is not being used, the one that you do not already have etc: **the** S1 W1

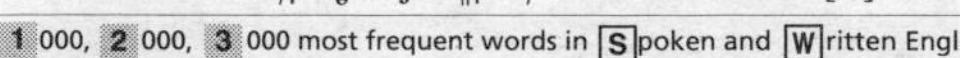

other *She was driving the car with one hand and wiping the window with the other.* | *I've got mud all over my trousers – are my others clean?* | **the other person, thing etc** *On weekends I do all my housework on one day so the other day I'm free to relax.* | **the other one** *I recognize one of the guitarists but who's the other one?* **2** used to mean all the people, things etc that are not the particular one you are talking about: **the other people/things etc** *Olivia is cleverer than all the other children in the class.* | *The museum may be closed but the other tourist places are open.* | **the others** *The wine glasses got broken but some of the others are alright.* | **other ones** *I bought this dress on sale. There were other ones that were nicer but I could only afford this one.* **3** used to mean more people or things in addition to the ones you already have or are talking about: **other people/things etc** *I know you've met Peter but I have two other brothers as well.* | *I'm sure if you asked other people they would say the same.* **4** used to mean the people or things which are different from the ones you already have or are talking about: *Making omelettes is one way to cook eggs but there are others you know.* | **some/any/no etc other thing** *I'm busy — we'll have to meet some other time.* | *Do you know of any other job where you get as many benefits as this one?* **5 others** [plural] other people or things: *some of these lapel microphones are better than others.* **6 other than** apart from a particular person or thing; except: *You should get a little stiffness but other than that there should be no side effects.* | *How can you say that religion is anything other than a way of controlling people?* **7 none other than** used when saying who someone is when you are surprised or shocked to find out exactly who they are: *The winner of 'journalist of the year' was none other than the editor's daughter.* **8 a) on the other side/bank etc** on the opposite side of the road, river etc, facing you: *There is a book store on the other side of the road.* **b) the other way/direction etc** in the opposite direction to the one you are moving in already: *She thought it unusual that all the traffic was going the other way.* **9 the other end/side etc** the end, side etc of something that is furthest away from where you are now: *My car broke down on the other side of town.* | *The woman on the other end of the phone didn't really understand what I'd asked for.* **10 the other way around/round** *BrE* if the situation is the other way around, it is actually the opposite of how you thought it was: *If you look at it the other way around, the soldiers were only trying to protect themselves.* **11 the other day/morning etc** *especially spoken* on a recent day, morning etc: *I saw Rufus the other day.* **12 something/someone etc or other** used to mean a particular thing, person etc or any thing or person that is similar: *Don't worry, we'll get the money somehow or other.* **13 in other words** used to express an idea or opinion in a way that is easier to understand: *The company claims it's got to rationalize its workforce, in other words many of the staff will lose their jobs.* —compare ANOTHER —see also EACH OTHER, **every other** (EVERY (7)), **on the one hand ... on the other hand** (HAND[1] (36))

**oth·er·ness** /ˈʌðənɪ̵s‖ˈʌðər-/ *n* [U] the quality of being strange or different

S1 W2 **oth·er·wise** /ˈʌðəwaɪz‖ˈʌðər-/ *adv* **1** [sentence adverb] a word meaning 'if not', often used when there will be a bad result if something does not happen: *You'll have to go now, otherwise you'll miss your bus.* | *They got two free tickets to Canada, otherwise they'd never have been able to afford to go.* | *A surveyor's inspection of the building revealed faults that might otherwise have been overlooked.* (=if there had not been an inspection) **2 say/think/decide etc otherwise** to say, think etc something different from what has been mentioned: *The government claims that the economy is improving, but this survey suggests otherwise.* **3** [sentence adverb] except for what has just been mentioned: *I could hear the distant rumbling of traffic. Otherwise all was still.* | *He was tired but otherwise in good health.* | [+ adj/adv] *a few mistakes in an otherwise excellent piece of work* **4 or otherwise** *especially BrE* or not: *We welcome any comments from viewers, favourable or otherwise.* **5 otherwise engaged** *formal* busy doing something else: *I was unable to attend the conference because I was otherwise engaged.* **6 otherwise known as** also called: *Albert DeSalvo, otherwise known as the Boston strangler* **7 it cannot be otherwise/how can it be otherwise?** used to mean that it is impossible for something to be different from the way it is: *Life in the military is hard – how can it be otherwise?*

**oth·er·world·ly** /ˌʌðəˈwɜːldli◂‖ˌʌðərˈwɜːr-/ *adj* more concerned with religious or SPIRITUAL[1] (1) thoughts than with normal daily life

**o·ti·ose** /ˈəʊʃiəʊs, ˈəʊti-‖ˈoʊʃioʊs, ˈoʊti-/ *adj formal* ideas or words that are otiose are unnecessary; REDUNDANT (2)

**OTT** /ˌəʊ tiː ˈtiː‖ˌoʊ-/ *adj BrE informal* OVER-THE-TOP

**ot·ter** /ˈɒtə‖ˈɑːtər/ *n* [C] a swimming animal that has smooth brown fur and eats fish

**ot·to·man** /ˈɒtəmən‖ˈɑː-/ *n* [C] **1** a piece of furniture like a big box with a soft top, used as a seat and for storing things **2** *AmE* a soft piece of furniture shaped like a box, used to rest your feet on when you are sitting down

**OU** /ˌəʊ ˈjuː‖ˌoʊ-/ the abbreviation of OPEN UNIVERSITY

**ou·bli·ette** /ˌuːbliˈet/ *n* [C] a small room or prison in an old castle where prisoners were kept

**ouch** /aʊtʃ/ *interjection* a sound that you make when you feel sudden pain: *Ouch! That hurt!*

**ought** /ɔːt‖ɒːt/ *modal verb* **1** used to say that someone should do something because it is the best or most sensible thing to do: **ought to do sth** *I think you ought to make more time for yourself to relax.* | *What you ought to have done is called the police.* | *If Veronica's trying to get to college she ought to study more.* **2** used to say that someone should do something because it is right: **ought to do sth** *You ought to be ashamed of yourself.* | *I don't care what you say – I still think he ought to have apologised.* | **ought (to)** *"I can't decide whether to tell him the truth." "Well you ought to."* **3** used to say that you think something will probably happen, probably be true etc: **ought to do sth** *He left 2 hours ago so he ought to be there by now.* | *They ought to win, they've trained hard enough.* | *This ought to be good.* —see also SHOULD S1 W2

**oughtn't** /ˈɔːtnt‖ˈɒː-/ the short form of 'ought not': *You oughtn't to drive if you are feeling so drowsy.*

**Oui·ja board** /ˈwiːdʒə bɔːd‖ˈwiːdʒiː bɔːrd/ *trademark n* [C] a board with letters and signs on it, used to try to receive messages from the spirits of dead people

**ounce** /aʊns/ *n* **1** [C] written abbreviation **oz** a unit for measuring weight equal to 28.35 grams —see table on page B2 —see also FLUID OUNCE **2 not an ounce of sense/truth/decency** no sense etc at all: *If you had an ounce of sense you wouldn't believe these stupid rumors!* **3 every (last) ounce of courage/ energy/ strength** all the courage etc that you have: *He clung to the rock with every last ounce of strength in his body.* S3

**our** /aʊə‖aʊr/ *determiner* [possessive form of **we**] **1** of or belonging to us: *Our daughter is in France at the moment.* | *Winning the Grand Prix was one of our finest sporting achievements.* | *It is important that we preserve our natural resources.* **2** *N Eng spoken* used to show that the person mentioned is your child, brother, or sister: *Our Sharon did really well in her exams.* S1 W1

**Our Fa·ther** /ˌ· ˈ··/ *n* [singular] the LORD'S PRAYER

**Our La·dy** /ˌ· ˈ··/ *n* [singular] Mary, the mother of Christ

**Our Lord** /ˌ· ˈ·/ *n* [singular] Jesus Christ

**ours** /aʊəz‖aʊrz/ *pron* [possessive form of **we**] the one or the ones that belong to us or that are of us: *I'll show you to your room. Ours is the one next door.* | *We wouldn't dream of wasting your time, so don't waste ours.* S1

**our·selves** /aʊəˈselvz‖aʊr-/ *pron* **1** the reflexive form of 'we': *It was strange seeing ourselves on television.* | *We all introduced ourselves before the meeting started.* **2** used to emphasize the pronoun we, a plural noun etc: *Not many people realise we built the house ourselves.* | *As* S1 W3 *we are parents ourselves we can understand what you've gone through.* **3 (all) by ourselves a)** alone: *Our teacher left us by ourselves for over an hour.* **b)** without help: *My sister and I learnt to use the computer all by ourselves.* **4 to ourselves** if we have something to ourselves, we do not have to share it with any other people: *Once Sam left town we had the house to ourselves.* —see also YOURSELF

**-ous** /əs/ *suffix (in adjectives)* describes something that causes or has a particular quality: *dangerous* (=full of danger) | *spacious* (=with much space)

**oust** /aʊst/ *v* [T] to force someone out of a position of power, especially so that you can take their place: **oust sb from** *an attempt to oust the Communists from power*

**ous·ter** /ˈaʊstə‖-ər/ *n* [C] *AmE* an act of moving someone from a position of power in order to take their place

S1 W1 **out¹** /aʊt/ *adv, adj* [adv only after verb, adj not before noun]

**1 ▶NOT INSIDE STH◀** from the inside of something: *She opened the envelope and took the letter out.* | [+ **of**] *The diary must have fallen out of her pocket.* | *Someone has torn the last page out of the book I'm reading.*

**2 ▶LEAVE A PLACE◀** from the inside part of something such as a building to the outside part: *Lock the door on your way out.* | [+ **of**] *I don't think I'd have the courage to jump out of a plane.* | **out jumped/walked etc** *The plane door slid open, and out walked the princess.* —see picture on page 1257

**3 ▶NOT HOME◀** away from your home, especially because you are in a restaurant, party etc: *Let's go out to eat tonight.* | *That guy she likes has finally asked her out.*

**4 ▶ABSENT◀** not in the place where you usually are, especially for a short time: *I'm sorry, my mother is out at the moment.* | *He went out at 11 o'clock.*

**5 ▶OUTSIDE◀** outside: *Many of the homeless have been sleeping out for years.* | *Billy was out playing in the street.* —see OUTSIDE (USAGE)

**6 ▶GIVEN TO MANY PEOPLE◀** used to say that something is given to many people, a situation affects many people etc: *The examination will start when all the question papers have been handed out.*

**7 ▶GET RID OF STH◀** used to say that something no longer exists or that someone has got rid of something: *These eggs are old, throw them out.* | [+ **of**] *There's this stuff you can buy to get the stains out of delicate fabrics.*

**8 ▶NOT INCLUDED◀** used to say that someone or something has not been included, not allowed to enter somewhere etc: *The house had a 'Keep Out' sign in front.* | [+ **of**] *Daniels has been left out of the team due to injury.*

**9 ▶FIND STH◀** used to say that someone finds or discovers something: [+ **of**] *If she knows what the plan is I'll soon get it out of her.*

**10 ▶PRODUCE STH◀** used to say that someone or something produces something: *factories throwing out pollution into the atmosphere* | [+ **of**] *A lot of good music came out of the hippy culture in the 1960s.*

**11 ▶STICK OUT◀** used to say that something is very easy to see, feel etc because it is not part of the main part of something: [+ **of**] *the nail sticking out of the chair* | *a small peninsula jutting out into the sea*

**12 ▶CHOOSE STH◀** used to say that one person or thing is chosen or taken from a larger group: *Pick out something to wear.* | *singled out for punishment*

**13 ▶DO STH COMPLETELY◀** used to say that something is done carefully and completely: *When the cupboard was cleared out I found some of my old books.* | *The work rota is a little confused but we'll sort it out.*

**14 ▶PRODUCT◀** used to say that a product is available to be bought: *When's Archer's new book out?* | *Sony have brought out a new portable music system.*

**15 ▶FREE◀** used to say that someone is no longer in prison or locked in a place against their will: *Once he was out it was only a matter of time till he reoffended.* | [+ **of**] *I like to let my parrots out of their cage once in a while.*

**16 ▶NOT FASHIONABLE◀** used to say that something is no longer fashionable: *You can't wear that, maxi skirts have been out for years.*

**17 ▶SECRET◀** used to say that some information is no longer a secret: *Her secret was out.* | *The word's out that Mel Gibson is in town.*

**18 ▶APPEAR◀** used to say that someone or something has suddenly appeared: *You don't often see daffodils out at this time of year.* | *The house looks so much better when the sun comes out.*

**19 read/shout etc sth out (loud)** to say something in a voice that is loud enough for others to hear: *The teacher made Ben read the note out to the whole class.* | *As I call out the winners' names, will you please approach the stage?*

**20 watch/listen/mind etc out** *especially spoken* used to tell someone to be careful: *Look out! There's a van coming.*

**21** a fire or light that is out is no longer burning or shining: *Blow the candles out.* | *Suddenly the lights went out.*

**22 ▶NOT AWAKE◀ a)** used to say that someone is asleep: **be/go out like a light** *The poor kid's exhausted. He went out like a light.* **flat out** *Ray spent the whole afternoon flat out on the sofa.* **b)** used to say that someone is no longer conscious: *He was out for about 10 minutes.* | **be out cold** *How hard did you hit him? He's out cold.*

**23 ▶DISTANT PLACE◀** used to say that someone goes to a place that is a long way away, very difficult to get to etc: *They've just moved out to a farm in Massachusetts.* | *He went out to Africa.*

**24 wear/tire etc out** to make someone feel extremely tired: *By the time she'd tidied up she was worn out.*

**25 be/run/sell etc out** to not have something because you have used it all, sold it all etc: *The album was sold out within minutes.* | [+ **of**] *We've run out of coffee.*

**26 think/plan etc it out** to think, plan etc something very carefully before you do it: *It would be wiser to work it out with your financial advisors.*

**27 ▶NOT WORKING◀** *especially AmE* if a machine, piece of equipment etc is out it is not working: *I don't believe it – the elevator's out again!* —see also **out of order** (ORDER (8))

**28 before the day/year etc is out** before the day, year etc has ended: *Don't cry, I'll be back before the week's out.*

**29 ▶MEASUREMENT◀** if a measurement, result etc is out, it is wrong because the numbers have not been calculated correctly: *He was out in his calculations, so there was a lot of carpet left over.* | **be out by £4/$5 etc** *The bill was out by over £10.* | **be way out** *These accounts are way out – the tax people will never accept them.*

**30 be out for sth/be out to do sth** *informal* to have a particular intention: *Mark my words – he's only out for one thing and that's her money.* | *These salesmen are out to trick you into buying something you just don't need.*

**31 ▶NOT IN POWER◀** used to say that someone, especially a political party, no longer has power or authority: *It's time we voted the Republicans out.*

**32 be the stupidest/silliest etc person out** *BrE* to be extremely stupid, silly etc: *You've got to be the luckiest man out!*

**33 ▶OFFICIAL PROTEST◀** *BrE* used to say that someone has stopped working as a way of protesting about something: *The doctors have come out in sympathy with the miners.*

**34 ▶HOMOSEXUAL◀** if a homosexual is or comes out, they tell people that they are homosexual

**35 sth's out** used to say that a suggestion is not possible: *"What are we going to do?" "Well bowling's out because my wrist is killing me."*

**36 ▶SEA◀** if the sea, the TIDE¹ (1) etc is out, it is at its lowest level

**37 ▶SPORT◀ a)** a player or team that is out in a game such as cricket or baseball is no longer allowed to play in the game: *Sussex were all out for 365.* **b)** a ball that is out in a game such as tennis or basketball is outside the line

**38 out with it!** used to tell someone to say something that they are having difficulty saying: *OK, out with it! What really happened?*

**39 out you go!** used to order someone to leave a room
**40 be out of luck/condition etc** used to say that someone or something is no longer in a particular state or situation: *She's not completely cured but at least she's out of danger.* | *This whole situation is getting out of control.*
**41 be out of earshot/sight** to be so far away from someone that they cannot hear you, see you etc: *I thought she was out of earshot or I wouldn't have said that.*
**42 out of curiosity/interest etc** because you are curious, interested etc: *Just out of curiosity, why did you take that job?*
**43 out of wood, metal etc** used to say what substance a particular thing is made of: *a little box made out of wood and decorated with flowers*
**44 9 out of 10, 4 out of a hundred etc** used to say that there are ten people or things and you are talking about nine of them: *Apparently they've lost three games out of seven already.*
**45 be out of work/a job etc** to not have a job: *those who have been out of work for over 6 months*
**46 ▶ MONEY ◀** used to say where the money has come from to pay for something or buy something: *Can you believe he used money out of our bank account to pay for his trips with another woman?*
**47 out of the way a)** a place that is out of the way is fairly far from any town: *The camp site is a little out of the way but the views are magnificent.* **b)** if you get a problem out of the way you solve it so that you can do something else: *So, that's got the salary thing out of the way, let's move on to productivity.*
**48 be out of your head/mind** *informal* **a)** to be very worried: *His parents were out of their minds with worry when he didn't come home.* **b)** to be very drunk: *By the time I got to the party most people were out of their heads.*
**49 be/feel out of it (all) a)** *informal* to feel different from the rest of a group of people: *It was nice but I felt really out of it because I was the only one who couldn't speak French.* **b)** *informal* to be drunk: *You were really out of it last night. What were you drinking?*
**50 ▶ HORSE ◀** *technical* having a particular horse as a mother [+**of**] *Golden Trumpet, by Golden Rain out of Silver Trumpet* —compare BY[2] —see also **out of the blue** (BLUE[2] (4)), **out of the question** (QUESTION[1] (8)), **out of sorts** (SORT[1] (5)), **out of this world** (WORLD[1] (13))

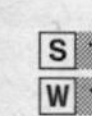
**out²** *prep informal* **a)** *AmE* used to say that someone or something is removed from inside something, leaves somewhere etc: **+of** *When I first came out of the army I worked in a drug store.* **b)** *BrE* used in a way which some people think is incorrect, to say that someone or something is removed from inside something, leaves somewhere etc: *Get out the car and push with the rest of us!*

**out³** *v* **1** [T usually passive] to publicly say that someone is homosexual when that person would prefer to keep it private: *Several gay politicians have been outed in recent months.* **2 truth/murder etc will out!** used to say that it is difficult to hide the truth, a murder etc

**out⁴** *n* **1** [singular] an excuse for not doing an activity or to avoid being blamed for something: *I have tons of work to do. At least that gives me an out.* **2** [C] the state of no longer being allowed to take part in a particular game in a sport such as baseball —see also INS AND OUTS

**out-** /aʊt/ *prefix* **1** used to form nouns and adjectives from verbs followed by 'out': *an outbreak of flu* (=from 'break out') | *outspoken comments* (=from 'speak out') **2** in some nouns and adjectives, means outside; beyond: *an outhouse* (=small additional building) | *outlying areas* (=far from the centre) **3 a)** beyond; further: *She outlived her brother.* (=he died before her) | *He's outgrown his clothes.* (=become too big for them) **b)** better than someone, so that you defeat them: *I can out-argue you any day.*

**out·age** /ˈaʊtɪdʒ/ *n* [C] *AmE* a period when a service such as the electricity supply is not provided: *a power outage*

**out-and-out** /ˌ· · ˈ·◂/ *adj* [only before noun] having all the qualities of a particular kind of person or thing; complete: *an out-and-out villain*

**out·back** /ˈaʊtbæk/ *n* **the outback** the Australian countryside far away from cities, where few people live

**out·bid** /aʊtˈbɪd/ *v past tense* **outbid** *present participle* **outbidding** [T] to offer a higher price than someone else, especially at an AUCTION[1]

**out·board mo·tor** /ˌaʊtbɔːd ˈməʊtə‖-bɔːrd ˈmoʊtər/ *n* [C] a motor fixed to the back end of a small boat

**out·bound** /ˈaʊtbaʊnd/ *adj* moving away from you or away from a town, country etc: *outbound traffic*

**out·break** /ˈaʊtbreɪk/ *n* [C] a sudden appearance or start of war, fighting, or serious disease: *a cholera outbreak* | [+ **of**] *renewed outbreaks of fighting* | *the outbreak of World War II* —see also **break out** (BREAK[1])

**out·build·ing** /ˈaʊtˌbɪldɪŋ/ *n* [C] a building such as a BARN (1) or SHED[1] (1) near a main building: *the farm and its outbuildings*

**out·burst** /ˈaʊtbɜːst‖-bɜːrst/ *n* [C] **1** a sudden powerful expression of strong emotion: *He later came to apologize to me for his outburst.* | [+ **of**] *I was surprised by this outburst of resentment.* **2** a sudden temporary increase in activity: *an outburst of creative energy*

**out·cast** /ˈaʊtkɑːst‖-kæst/ *n* [C] someone who is not accepted by the people they live among, or has been forced out of their home: *In these health-conscious times smokers are often treated as social outcasts.* —**outcast** *adj*

**out·caste** /ˈaʊtkɑːst‖-kæst/ *n* [C] someone who does not belong to or who has been forced out of a CASTE (=a traditional social class) in India

**out·class** /aʊtˈklɑːs‖-ˈklæs/ *v* [T often passive] to be much better than someone at doing something, or to be much better than something else: *The Pittsburgh Steelers were completely outclassed by their rivals.* | *There's never been a jet engine to outclass the Rolls Royce Avon.*

**out·come** /ˈaʊtkʌm/ *n* [singular] the final result of a meeting, discussion, war etc, especially when no-one knows what it will be until it actually happens: [+ **of**] *We are anxiously awaiting the outcome of the negotiations.* W3

**out·crop** /ˈaʊtkrɒp‖-krɑːp/ *n* [C] a rock or group of rocks above the surface of the ground

**out·cry** /ˈaʊtkraɪ/ *n* [singular] an angry protest by a lot of ordinary people: *The closure of our local hospital has caused a huge public outcry.* | [+ **against**] *an outcry against this waste of public money*

**out·dat·ed** /ˌaʊtˈdeɪtɪ̇d◂/ *adj* **1** unsuitable for the modern world and no longer used much; old-fashioned: *outdated teaching methods* | *We reject outdated notions of national sovereignty.* **2** a document that is outdated cannot be used because it is no longer effective: *an outdated passport*

**out·did** /aʊtˈdɪd/ the past tense of OUTDO

**out·dis·tance** /aʊtˈdɪstəns/ *v* [T] to run, ride etc faster than other people, especially in a race, so that you are far ahead: *Laura quickly outdistanced her pursuers.*

**out·do** /aʊtˈduː/ *v past tense* **outdid** /-ˈdɪd/, *past participle* **outdone** /-ˈdʌn/, *3rd person singular present tense* **outdoes** [T] **1** to be better or more successful than someone else at doing something: *The economies of South East Asia are already outdoing Western competitors.* | **outdo sb in** *skaters trying to outdo the others in grace and speed* **2 not to be outdone** in order not to let someone else do better than you: *Not to be outdone by the rival country-clubs, the Glen Hills golf club put in a new swimming pool.*

**out·door** /ˈaʊtdɔː‖-dɔːr/ *adj* **1** [only before noun] existing, happening, or used outside, not inside a building: *outdoor activities* | *outdoor clothing* | *a healthy outdoor life* —opposite INDOOR **2 outdoor type** a person who enjoys camping, walking in the countryside etc

**out·doors¹** /ˌaʊtˈdɔːz‖-ɔːrz/ *adv* outside, not inside a building; OUT OF DOORS: *I reckon it's warm enough to eat outdoors this evening.* —opposite INDOORS

**outdoors²** *n* **the (great) outdoors** the countryside far away from buildings and cities: *a love of the great outdoors*

**out·door·sy** /aʊtˈdɔːzi‖-ˈdɔːr-/ *adj informal* enjoying outdoor activities: *She's a real outdoorsy type.*

**out·draw** /aʊtˈdrɔː‖-ˈdrɒː/ *v* [T] to pull a gun out faster than someone else: *The Kid could outdraw any man in Texas.*

**out·er** /ˈaʊtə‖-ər/ *adj* [only before noun] **1** on the outside of something: *Remove the tough outer leaves before cooking.* **2** further from the centre of something: *the outer suburbs* —opposite INNER (1)

**out·er·most** /ˈaʊtəməʊst‖-tərmoʊst/ *adj* [only before noun] furthest outside or furthest from the middle: *the outermost stars* —opposite INMOST (2), INNERMOST (2)

**outer space** /ˌ·· ˈ·/ *n* [U] the space outside the Earth's air, where the PLANETS and stars are

**out·er·wear** /ˈaʊtəweə‖-tərwer/ *n* [U] clothes, such as coats, that are worn over ordinary clothes

**out·face** /aʊtˈfeɪs/ *v* [T] to deal bravely with a difficult situation or opponent

**out·fall** /ˈaʊtfɔːl‖-fɒːl/ *n* [C] a place where water flows out, especially from a DRAIN² (1) or river: *a sewage outfall*

**out·field** /ˈaʊtfiːld/ *n* **the outfield a)** the part of a cricket or BASEBALL field furthest from the player who is batting (BAT² (1)) **b)** the players in this part of the field —compare INFIELD —**outfielder** *n* [C]

S3 **out·fit¹** /ˈaʊtfɪt/ *n* [C] **1** a set of clothes worn together, especially for a special occasion: *She bought a new, elegant two-piece outfit in shades of apricot for the wedding.* **2** *informal* a group of people who work together as a team or organization: *a small advertising outfit* **3** a set of equipment that you need for a particular purpose or job: *a tyre repair outfit*

**outfit²** *v* **outfitted, outfitting** [T] to provide someone with a set of clothes or equipment for a special purpose

**out·fit·ter** /ˈaʊtfɪtə‖-ər/ *n* [C] **1** *BrE old-fashioned* a shop that sells men's clothes: *a firm of gentlemen's outfitters* **2** *AmE* a shop that sells equipment for outdoor activities such as camping

**out·flank** /aʊtˈflæŋk/ *v* [T] **1** to go around the side of an enemy during a battle and attack them from behind **2** to gain an advantage over an opponent, especially in politics: *The Tories found themselves outflanked by Labour on the issue of law and order.*

**out·flow** /ˈaʊtfləʊ‖-floʊ/ *n* [C,U] **1** the process in which money, goods etc leave a bank, country etc: *the outflow of gold from the US Federal Reserve* **2** the flow of water or air from something: *an outflow of gas escaping from the main duct | the outflow valve*

**out·fox** /aʊtˈfɒks‖-ˈfɑːks/ *v* [T] to gain an advantage over someone by being cleverer than they are; OUTWIT

**out front** /ˌ· ˈ·/ *adv AmE informal* **1** honest, in a way that other people can clearly see: *I just want you to know, out front, that I can't stand the guy, and I don't like spending time with him.* **2** taking a leading position: *The President has to be out front, not ducking responsibility for important issues.* —**out front** *adj*

**out·go·ing** /ˌaʊtˈgəʊɪŋ◂‖-ˈgoʊ-/ *adj* **1** liking to meet and talk to new people: *She's got a warm, outgoing personality.* **2 the outgoing president/chancellor etc** someone who is finishing their time as a president etc **3** [only before noun] going out or leaving a place: *the tray for outgoing mail | outgoing phone calls*

**out·go·ings** /ˈaʊtˌgəʊɪŋz‖-ˌgoʊ-/ *n* [plural] *especially BrE* amounts of money that you spend, especially money that you have to spend regularly: *My monthly outgoings come to about £500.*

**out·grow** /aʊtˈgrəʊ‖-ˈgroʊ/ *v past tense* **outgrew** /-ˈgruː/, *past participle* **outgrown** /-ˈgrəʊn‖-ˈgroʊn/ [T] **1** to grow too big for something; GROW OUT OF: *You've outgrown that coat; I'll have to buy you another one.* **2** to change as you become older, and no longer enjoy the things that you used to do: *Callahan had outgrown the radical idealism of his younger days.* **3** to grow faster than someone or something else: *a population outgrowing its resources* **4 outgrow your strength** *BrE* to grow too quickly when you are a child, so that you become weak or unhealthy

**out·growth** /ˈaʊtgrəʊθ‖-groʊθ/ *n* [C] **1** a natural result of something, especially an unpleasant one: *Crime is often an outgrowth of poverty.* **2** *technical* something that grows out of something else

**out·house** /ˈaʊthaʊs/ *n* [C] **1** *BrE* a small building which is near to and belongs to a larger main building **2** *AmE* an outside toilet

**out·ing** /ˈaʊtɪŋ/ *n* **1** [C] a short pleasure trip for a group of people: **a school/church/class etc outing** *a class outing to the ballet* **2** [C,U] the practice of publicly naming people as HOMOSEXUALS, when they do not want anyone to know this

**out·land·ish** /aʊtˈlændɪʃ/ *adj* strange and unusual: *He used to play guitar and wear outlandish costumes in a punk band.* —**outlandishly** *adv* —**outlandishness** *n* [U]

**out·last** /aʊtˈlɑːst‖-ˈlæst/ *v* [T] to continue to exist for a longer time than something else —compare OUTLIVE

**out·law¹** /ˈaʊtlɔː‖-lɒː/ *n* [C] someone who has done something illegal, and who is not protected by the law

**outlaw²** *v* [T] **1** to completely stop something by making it illegal or socially unacceptable: *Certain counties have outlawed the sale of alcohol.* **2** to officially state that someone is an outlaw

**out·lay** /ˈaʊtleɪ/ *n* [C,U] the amount of money that you have to spend in order to start a new business, activity etc: *For a relatively small outlay you can start manufacturing T-shirts.* | [+ **on/for**] *House buyers usually have a large initial outlay on carpets and furniture.*

**out·let** /ˈaʊtlet, -lət/ *n* [C] **1** a way of expressing or getting rid of strong feelings: [+ **for**] *I play racquet ball as an outlet for stress.* **2** a shop, company, or organization through which products are sold: **retail outlet** *Benetton has retail outlets in every major European city.* **3** a way through which something such as a liquid or gas can flow out **4** *AmE* a POWER POINT *BrE*

**out·line¹** /ˈaʊtlaɪn/ *n* [singular] **1** the main ideas or facts about something, without the details: *I'd like to see the proposal outline.* | *an outline of world history* | **broad/rough outline** (=a very general outline) | **in outline** (=giving an outline) *Chapter I describes in outline the way money circulates through the economy.* **2** a line around the edge of something which shows its shape: *the outline of a footprint in the snow* | **outline map/sketch etc** *an outline map of Europe* **3** *especially AmE* a plan for a report, story etc in which each new idea is separately recorded

**outline**

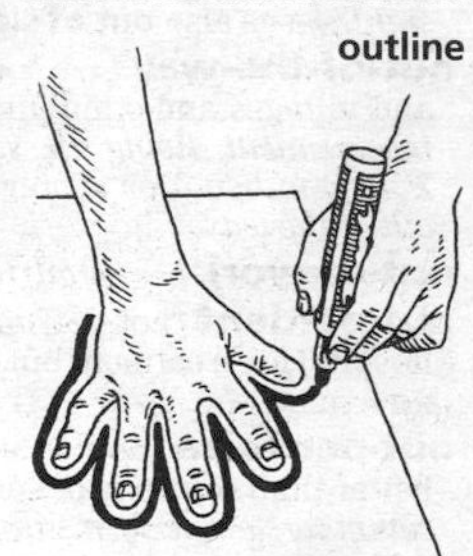

She is drawing an outline of her hand.

**outline²** *v* [T] **1** to describe something in a general way, giving the main points but not the details: *The President outlined his peace plan for the Middle East.* **2** [often passive] to make the outline of a shape very clear: *a map of the area with our property outlined in red*

**out·live** /aʊtˈlɪv/ *v* [T] **1** to live longer than someone else: *She outlived her husband by twenty years.* **2** to continue to exist after something else has ended or disappeared: *The military regime has outlived its statutory term by three years.* | **outlive its usefulness** (=become no longer useful) *As a commuter service the Seacombe Ferry had outlived its usefulness.*

**out·look** /ˈaʊtlʊk/ *n* [C] **1** your general attitude to life and the world: [+ **on**] *He's got a very positive outlook on life.|The farmers were narrowly provincial in their outlook.* **2** what is expected to happen in the future: [+ **for**] *The weather outlook for the weekend is bad.|The outlook for sufferers from this disease is not good.* **3** a view from a particular place: *a very pleasing outlook from the bedroom window*

**out·ly·ing** /ˈaʊtˌlaɪ-ɪŋ/ *adj* [only before noun] far from the centre of a city, town etc or from a main building: *one of the outlying suburbs|the outlying barns*

**out·ma·noeu·vre** *BrE*, **outmaneuver** *AmE* /ˌaʊtməˈnuːvə‖-ər/*v* [T] to gain an advantage over someone by using cleverer plans or methods than they do: *a woman who could outmanoeuvre even the Prime Minister*

**out·mod·ed** /aʊtˈməʊdɪ̇d‖-ˈmoʊ-/ *adj* no longer fashionable or useful: *an outmoded set of values*

**out·most** /ˈaʊtməʊst‖-moʊst/ *adj* furthest outside or furthest from the middle; OUTERMOST

**out·num·ber** /aʊtˈnʌmbə‖-ər/ *v* [T usually passive] to be more in number than another group: *We were completely outnumbered by the enemy.|In the nursing profession women still outnumber men by four to one.*

**out-of-bod·y** /ˌ· · ˈ··◂/ *adj* **out-of-body experience** the feeling that sometimes happens when someone is close to death that they are outside of their body and can look down on it from above

**out-of-court** /ˌ· · ˈ·◂/ *adj* **out-of-court settlement** an agreement to settle a legal argument, in which one side agrees to pay money to the other so that the problem is not brought to court —see also **settle sth out of court** (COURT[1] (1))

**out of date** /ˌ· · ˈ·◂/ *adj* no longer useful, correct or fashionable: *out of date theories on education|The information in last year's tourist guide is already out of date.*

**out of doors** /ˌ· · ˈ·/ *adv* outside, not in a building; OUTDOORS —see OUTSIDE (USAGE)

**out-of-pock·et ex·pens·es** /ˌ· · · · ˈ··/ *n* [plural] small amounts of money that you have to spend as part of your job, and get back from your employer

**out-of-sight** /ˌ· · ˈ·/ *adj AmE* an amount of money that is out-of-sight is extremely large: *The hotel bill was out-of-sight.* —see also **out of sight, out of mind** (SIGHT[1] (18))

**out-of-the-way** /ˌ· · · ˈ·◂/ *adj* **1** far from other towns and villages and often difficult to find: *Don't you find it inconvenient living in such an out-of-the-way place?* **2** *BrE* unusual or strange: *Her taste in music is a bit out-of-the-way.*

**out-of-work** /ˌ· · ˈ·◂/ *adj* unemployed: *out-of-work actors*

**out·pa·tient** /ˈaʊtˌpeɪʃənt/ *n* [C] someone who goes to a hospital for treatment but does not stay there —compare INPATIENT

**out·per·form** /ˌaʊtpəˈfɔːm‖-pərˈfɔːrm/ *v* [T] to perform better than someone or something else *The new Pentium computers outperform our 486s.*

**out·place·ment** /ˈaʊtˌpleɪsmənt/ *n* [C,U] the process of a company helping people to find new jobs after asking them to leave their employment

**out·play** /aʊtˈpleɪ/ *v* [T] to beat an opponent in a game by playing with more skill than they do

**out·point** /aʊtˈpɔɪnt/ *v* [T] to defeat an opponent in BOXING by gaining more points

**out·post** /ˈaʊtpəʊst‖-poʊst/ *n* [C] a small town or group of buildings in a distant lonely place, usually established as a military camp or a place for trade

**out·pour·ing** /ˈaʊtpɔːrɪŋ/ *n* **1 outpourings** [plural] continuous expressions of strong feeling: [+ **of**] *outpourings of grief* **2** [C,U] a lot of something that is produced suddenly: *an outpouring of creative energy*

W2 **out·put¹** /ˈaʊtpʊt/ *n* [C,U] **1** the amount of goods or work produced by a person, machine, factory etc: *Output is up 30% on last year.* **2** *technical* the information produced by a computer **3** *technical* the amount of electricity produced by a GENERATOR —compare INPUT[1]

**output²** *v past tense and past participle* **output** [T] if a computer outputs information, it produces it

**out·rage¹** /ˈaʊtreɪdʒ/ *n* **1** [U] a feeling of great anger and shock: *The injustice of the situation filled him with a sense of outrage.* **2** [C] a very cruel, violent, and shocking action or event: [+ **against**] *These terrorist attacks are an outrage against society.*

**outrage²** *v* [T usually passive] to make someone feel very angry and shocked: *People were outraged at the idea of the murderer Hindley being released.*

**out·ra·geous** /aʊtˈreɪdʒəs/ *adj* **1** very shocking and extremely unfair or offensive: *outrageous prices|I can't believe he's been allowed to spread such outrageous lies!*|**it is outrageous that** *It's outrageous that the poor should have to pay such high taxes.* **2** extremely unusual and slightly amusing or shocking: *an outrageous hairstyle|Mark will say the most outrageous things, especially when he's supposed to be polite.*

**out·ran** /aʊtˈræn/ the past tense of OUTRUN

**out·rank** /aʊtˈræŋk/ *v* [T] **1** to have a higher rank than someone else in the same group **2** to be more important than something else

**ou·tré** /ˈuːtreɪ‖uːˈtreɪ/ *adj French* strange, unusual, and slightly shocking: *the genius of artists as outré as Beardsley or Toulouse-Lautree*

**out·reach** /ˈaʊtriːtʃ/ *n* [U] *especially AmE* **1** services based close to people's homes to help those who cannot easily come to an office, hospital etc: **outreach service/center etc** *outreach centers for drug addicts* **2** the work a church does to teach or serve people who are not its members

**out·ride** /aʊtˈraɪd/ *v past tense* **outrode** /-ˈrəʊd‖-ˈroʊd/ *past participle* **outridden** /-ˈrɪdn/ [T] to ride faster or further than someone or something else

**out·rid·er** /ˈaʊtˌraɪdə‖-ər/ *n* [C] a guard or police officer who rides on a MOTORCYCLE or horse beside or in front of a vehicle in which an important person is travelling

**out·rig·ger** /ˈaʊtˌrɪgə‖-ər/ *n* [C] **1** a piece of wood shaped like a small narrow boat which is fixed to the side of a boat, especially a CANOE[1], to prevent it from turning over in the water **2** a boat fitted with one of these

**out·right¹** /aʊtˈraɪt/ *adv* **1** without trying to hide your feelings or intentions: *They laughed outright at my suggestion.|Tell him outright exactly what you think.* **2** completely: *The town was destroyed outright.|She won outright.* **3 buy/own sth outright** to own something such as a house completely because you have paid the full price with your own money **4 be killed outright** to be killed immediately

**out·right²** /ˈaʊtraɪt/ *adj* [only before noun] **1** clear and direct: *an outright refusal* **2** complete: *outright ban on the sale of pornographic films* **3 outright winner/victor** someone who has definitely and easily won

**out·ri·val** /aʊtˈraɪvəl/ *v* [T] to defeat someone in a competition

**out·rode** /aʊtˈrəʊd‖-ˈroʊd/ the past tense of OUTRIDE

**out·run** /aʊtˈrʌn/ *v past tense* **outran** /-ˈræn/ *past participle* **outrun** *present participle* **outrunning** [T] **1** to run faster or further than someone **2** to develop more quickly than something else: *The Reverend believes that technological progress has outrun our moral development.*

**out·sell** /aʊtˈsel/ *v past tense and past participle* **outsold** /-ˈsəʊld‖-ˈsoʊld/ [T] **1** to be sold in larger quantities than something else: *a detergent that outsells every other brand* **2** to sell more goods or products than a competitor

**out·set** /ˈaʊtset/ *n* **at/from the outset** at or from the beginning of an event or process: *It was clear right from the outset that there were going to be problems.*

**out·shine** /aʊtˈʃaɪn/ *v past tense and past participle* **outshone** /aʊtˈʃɒn‖-ˈʃoʊn/, *present participle* **outshining**

[T] **1** to be better at something than someone else: *Vera's flowers outshone all the others in the competition.* **2** to shine more brightly than something else

S1 W1 **out·side¹** /aʊt'saɪd, 'aʊtsaɪd/ *prep* **1** out of a particular building or room: *As soon as we were outside the door we burst out laughing.* —opposite INSIDE³ (2) **2** out of a building but still close to it: *I'll meet you outside the hardware store at 2 o'clock.* **3** beyond the limits of a city, country etc: *Add the area code 212 if you are calling from outside the New York area.* | **just outside** *Bolton is a beautiful mill town just outside Manchester.* **4** beyond the limits or range of a situation, activity etc: *It's outside my experience I'm afraid.* | *I don't care who you see outside working hours.* —opposite WITHIN —compare BEYOND¹ **5** if someone is outside a group of people, an organization etc they do not have the same ideas and beliefs: *Outside the party the official story was that he needed to spend more time with his family.*

S1 W3 **out·side²** /aʊt'saɪd/ *adv* **1** not inside a building: *Can't you kids go and play outside?* | *What do you want to go out for? It's still dark outside.* **2** not in a room or building but close to it: *I don't have time to chat, my husband's waiting outside.* | *What's happening at the stadium? There are lots of people standing outside.* **3 outside of** *informal especially AmE* **a)** apart from a particular person or thing; except: *What else can we do, outside of tearing the work up and starting from the beginning?* **b)** outside a particular place, building etc: *It was decided to run a campaign outside of Washington.*

**USAGE NOTE: OUT**

WORD CHOICE: **out, outside, outdoors/out of doors**

If you are **outside** a room or building, you are not in it but are close to it: *You have to go outside if you want to smoke.* | *It's cold outside.*

If you are **out**, you are away from a building, especially somewhere you live or spend a lot of time: *Let's go out for a meal/drive.* | *I'm sorry, Mr. Davies is out at the moment.*

You use **outdoors** (or **out of doors**) more informally to mean being out of any building: *I'd like a job where I can work outdoors.*

GRAMMAR

People or things go or come **out of** somewhere: *He comes out of prison next week* (NOT *out from prison*). | *Water poured out of the pipe.* (Also *out the pipe* in American English and informal spoken British English).

You go/are **out of** *the house*, but **away from** *home*.

**Outside** may be used alone or with **of** (especially in spoken and American English): *He lives outside (of) Miami* (NOT *outside from...*).

S2 W2 **out·side³** /'aʊtsaɪd/ *adj* [only before a noun] **1 outside wall/toilet etc** a wall, toilet etc that is not inside a building: *Most apartments have outside staircases in case of emergency.* | *The house will need a lot of outside repairs before we can sell it.* —opposite INSIDE⁴ (1) —see also OUTDOORS¹, OUTER **2 outside help/interest etc** help etc from people who do not belong to the same group or organization as you: *My family solved its problems without any outside interference.* **3 outside expert/consultant etc** an expert, consultant etc who does not work for your company or organization but who you pay to do some work for you: *A firm of outside caterers were brought in especially for the function.* **4 outside interests/experiences etc** interests, experiences etc that are different from those that you have in your job: *Ex-scientists can bring their outside knowledge into the teaching profession.* **5 the outside world** the rest of the world which is unknown to you because you have no communication with it, you are not involved in it etc: *Since the attack the city has been cut off from the outside world.* **6 an outside chance** a very small possibility that something will happen: *There's an outside chance that Regis might be sent to Uganda on business.* **7 an outside figure/estimate etc** a number or amount that is the largest something could possibly be **8 outside line/call etc** a telephone line or telephone call which is to or from someone not inside a building **9 the outside lane** the LANE (2) that is nearest the middle of the road —see picture on page 415

**out·side⁴** /aʊt'saɪd, 'aʊtsaɪd/ *n* **the outside 1** the outer walls, windows etc of something such as a building or vehicle: [+**of**] *We've decided to paint the outside of the house brown.* **2** the area of land around something such as a building, vehicle etc: *From the outside the hotel looked fairly rundown.* **3** the outer part or surface of something: [+**of**] *The outside of the cheese is red but this is just a protective wax.* —opposite INSIDE¹ (1) **4** someone who is on or from the outside is not involved in an activity or does not belong to a particular group, organization etc: *To anyone on the outside our discipline methods may seem a little severe.* **5 on the outside a)** used to describe the way someone appears to be or to behave: *On the outside she appeared gentle and kind but really she was the meanest person I ever met.* **b)** not in prison: *Life on the outside was not as easy as he'd first thought.* **6 at the (very) outside** used to say that a particular number or amount could be the largest something, and it might be less: *It's only a 20 minute walk, half an hour at the outside.* **7** the LANE (2) on a road that is nearest to the middle of the road: *In some countries it is only permissible to overtake on the outside.* —opposite INSIDE¹ (2)

**out·sid·er** /aʊt'saɪdə‖-ər/ *n* [C] **1** someone who is not accepted as a member of a particular social group: *We felt like complete outsiders when we first moved here.* **2** someone who does not seem to have much chance of winning a race or competition: *The champion was knocked out by an outsider.* **3** someone who does not belong to a particular company or organization: *The firm was obliged to seek the help of outsiders.*

**out·size** /'aʊtsaɪz/ *adj* also **out·sized** /-saɪzd/ **1** larger than normal: *peering through outsize spectacles* **2** made for people who are very large: *outsize clothes*

**out·skirts** /'aʊtskɜːts‖-skɜːrts/ *n* [plural] the parts of a town or city that are furthest from the centre: **on the outskirts** *They live on the outskirts of Paris.*

**out·smart** /aʊt'smɑːt‖-'smɑːrt/ *v* [T] to gain an advantage over someone using tricks or clever plans; OUTWIT: *The lizard can outsmart any predators by leaving its tail behind to confuse them.*

**out·sour·cing** /'aʊtˌsɔːsɪŋ/-sɔːr-/ *n* [U] the practice of using workers from outside a company

**out·spo·ken** /aʊt'spəʊkən‖-'spoʊ-/ *adj* expressing your opinions honestly, even when it is not popular to do so: *an outspoken critic of the country's human rights policies* —**outspokenly** *adv* —**outspokenness** *n* [U]

**out·spread** /ˌaʊt'spred◂/ *adj* spread out flat or completely: *He was lying on the beach with arms outspread.*

**out·stand·ing** /aʊt'stændɪŋ/ *adj* **1** extremely good: *an area of outstanding natural beauty* | *an outstanding performance* **2** not yet done, solved, or paid: *We've got quite a few debts still outstanding.* | *an outstanding problem* W3

**out·stand·ing·ly** /aʊt'stændɪŋli/ *adv* extremely well: *Varese played outstandingly.* | [+ adj/adv] *an outstandingly talented musician*

**out·stare** /aʊt'steə‖-'ster/ *v* [T] to look at someone for so long that they feel too uncomfortable to look at you

**out·stay** /aʊt'steɪ/ *v* [T] to stay somewhere longer than someone else: *As usual she outstayed all the other guests at the party.* —see also **outstay your welcome** WELCOME⁴ (3)

**out·stretched** /ˌaʊt'stretʃt◂/ *adj* stretched out to full length: *She ran to meet them with outstretched arms.*

**out·strip** /aʊt'strɪp/ *v* **outstripped, outstripping** [T] **1** to do something better than someone else: *We*

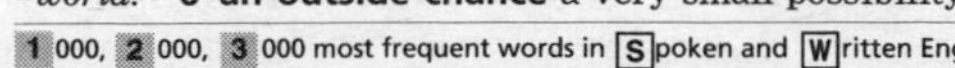

*outstripped all our competitors in sales last year.* **2** to be greater in quantity than something else: *Demand for energy is outstripping the supply.* **3** to run or move faster than someone or something else: *Dawson outstripped the other runners on the last lap.*

**out-take** /ˈ· ·/ *n* [C] a piece of a film or television show that is removed before it is broadcast, especially because it contains a mistake

**O**

**out tray** /ˈ· ·/ *n* [C] a box on an office desk to hold work and letters which are ready to be sent out or put away —compare IN TRAY

**out·vote** /aʊtˈvəʊt‖-ˈvoʊt/ *v* [T] to defeat a person or an idea by voting against them

**out·ward** /ˈaʊtwəd‖-wərd/ *adj* **1** [only before noun] concerning how someone seems to other people, rather than what they are actually like: *She managed to maintain her outward composure.* | *His house shows few outward signs of worldly success.* | **to all outward appearances** (=as much as you can judge by the way things seem) *To all outward appearances, Jayne seems to be dealing with the tragedy well.* **2 outward journey/voyage etc** a journey in which you are travelling away from home **3** [only before noun] directed towards the outside or away from something: *an outward movement of the arm* **4 outward bound** a train, ship, etc that is outward bound is leaving a place that it will return to later

**out·ward·ly** /ˈaʊtwədli‖-wərd-/ *adv* according to the way things seem: *Calvin remained outwardly calm but inside he was seething.* | [sentence adverb] *Outwardly, nothing seemed to have changed.*

**out·wards** /ˈaʊtwədz‖-wərdz/ also **outward** *AmE* —*adv* towards the outside or away from the centre of something: *The door opens outwards.*

**out·weigh** /aʊtˈweɪ/ *v* [T] to be more important or valuable than something else: *The advantages of this plan far outweigh the disadvantages.*

**out·wit** /aʊtˈwɪt/ *v* **outwitted, outwitting** [T] to gain an advantage over someone using tricks or clever plans: *My father spent years trying to build a bird feeder that would outwit the squirrels.*

**out·work** /ˈaʊtwɜːk‖-wɜːrk/ *n* [U] work for a business that is done by people at home —**outworker** *n* [C]

**out·worn** /ˌaʊtˈwɔːn◂‖-ˈwɔːrn◂/ *adj* [only before noun] old-fashioned, and no longer useful or important: *A lot of schools have abolished these outworn traditions.*

**ou·zo** /ˈuːzəʊ‖-zoʊ/ *n* [U] a Greek alcoholic drink that is drunk with water

**o·va** /ˈəʊvə‖ˈoʊ-/ *n* the plural form of OVUM

**o·val** /ˈəʊvəl‖ˈoʊ-/ *n* [C] a shape like a circle, but longer than it is wide —**oval** *adj*: *an oval mirror* —see picture at SHAPE¹

**Oval Of·fice** /ˌ·· ˈ··/ *n* the office of the US president, in the White House, Washington DC: *We're waiting for a reaction from the Oval Office.*

**o·var·i·an** /əʊˈveəriən‖oʊˈver-/ *adj* related to the ovary: *ovarian cancer*

**o·va·ry** /ˈəʊvəri‖ˈoʊ-/ *n plural* **ovaries** [C] **1** the part of a female that produces eggs **2** the part of a female plant that produces seeds

**o·va·tion** /əʊˈveɪʃən‖oʊ-/ *n* [C] *formal* if a group of people give someone an ovation they CLAP¹ (1) to show approval: *60,000 fans gave the rock group a thunderous ovation.* | **standing ovation** (=one in which people stand)

S3 **ov·en** /ˈʌvən/ *n* [C] **1** a thing inside which food is cooked, shaped like a box with a door on the front: **a medium/moderate oven** (=an oven that has not been made very hot) *Bake in a medium oven for 40 minutes.* **2 like an oven** *informal* uncomfortably hot: *It's like an oven in here! Open the window.* —see also **have a bun in the oven** (BUN (4))

**ov·en·proof** /ˈʌvənpruːf/ *adj* a dish, plate etc that is ovenproof will not be harmed by the high temperatures in an oven

**oven-read·y** /ˌ·· ˈ··◂/ *adj* oven-ready food is already prepared when you buy it, so you only have to cook it

**ov·en·ware** /ˈʌvənweə‖-wer/ *n* [U] cooking pots that can be put in a hot oven without cracking

**over¹** /ˈəʊvə‖ˈoʊvər/ *prep* **1** above or higher than something, without touching it: *A lamp hung over the table.* | *She leaned over the desk to answer the phone.* | *The sign over the door said 'Mind your head'.* —opposite UNDER¹ (1) —see also ABOVE¹, ACROSS¹ —see picture at ABOVE¹ **2** on something, so that it is covered: *Over the body lay a thin white sheet.* | *She wore a large jacket over her sweater.* —opposite UNDER¹ (1) **3** from one side of something to the other side of it: *Somehow the sheep had jumped over the fence.* | *The road over the mountains is steep and dangerous.* **4 over on** also **over** *BrE* on the opposite side of something from where you already are: *We live over on the other side of town.* **5** down from the edge of something: *Apparently the car fell over a cliff.* | *The shirt was hanging over the back of the chair.* **6** in many parts of a particular place, organization etc: *I've travelled over most of Europe but my favourite place was Austria.* | **all over** (=in every part) *They said they had cleaned up but there were bottles all over the place.* **7 be over sth** to feel better after an illness or bad situation: *I think I'm over the worst of it now.* **8** in control of someone or having authority to give orders to someone: *He rules over a large kingdom.* | *In this office there is one manager over a staff of 15 workers.* —opposite UNDER¹ (9) **9** more than a particular number, amount or level: *I've lost over 3 kilos in weight.* | *Children over 12 are not allowed in the swimming area.* | *The driver was found to have over the legal alcohol limit in his blood.* | **the over-30s/the over-50s etc** (=people who are more than a particular age) *a social club for the over-60s* **10** during: *Will you be home over the Christmas vacation?* | *Over a period of ten years he stole a million pounds from the company.* | *Can we talk about this over dinner?* **11** using something such as a telephone or radio: *I don't want to talk about this over the telephone.* **12** about a particular subject, person or thing: *He's having problems over his income tax.* | *a row over public expenditure* **13 over and above** an amount that is over and above another is an extra amount: *He gets a travel allowance over and above his existing salary.* —see also **all over** (ALL² (7))

**over²** *adv* **1 fall over/knock sth over etc** to fall etc so that you are lying down or knock something etc so that it is flat on a surface after being upright: *He was so drunk he fell over in the road.* | **knock sth etc so that it is** *A lot of work is being done to prevent the tower from toppling over.* **2 bend over/fold sth over etc** to bend etc so that you are no longer upright or fold something etc so that it is no longer straight or flat and is folded in the middle: *As Sheila bent over, a sudden pain shot up her back.* | *He silently folded the paper over and put it in his pocket.* **3** [only after verb] from one side of something to the other side: *There are only 3 canoes so some people will have to swim over.* | *I went over to say hello but Vincent didn't recognize me.* | **over to/from** *We flew over to the US to visit my Aunt Polly.* | *I took her over to Saginaw because she had a doctor's appointment.* **4** [only after verb] to or in a particular house, city etc. | *You really should come over and see our new house.* **5 hand over/sign over etc** to give something to another person: *The attacker was ordered to hand over his weapon and lie on the ground.* | *Most of the money has been signed over to his children.* **6 change over/swap over** if you change two things over you put one of the things in the place of the other: *The vases had been swapped over and nobody had spotted the fake.* | *The guards change over at midnight.* **7 turn over/roll over** if you turn something over you move it so that the side of it which could not be seen can now be seen: *Turn the page over.* | *The children spent hours rolling over and over in the sand.* **8 twelve years/90% etc and over** more than 12 years, 90% etc: *The film is suitable for people of 18 and over.* | *Sorry, this agency only deals with properties worth $200,000 and over.* —opposite S1 W1

UNDER **9** a particular amount of something that is over is what remains after some of it has been used: *We were over by about $300!* | **left over** *We had so much food left over we donated it to charity.* **10 covered over/ painted over etc** covered with a particular substance or material: *Most of the windows have been boarded over.* | [+ **with**] *The door had been painted over with a bright red varnish.* **11 read/think/talk etc sth over** to read something, think about something etc very carefully before deciding what to do: *After talking it over with my wife, I've decided to retire.* **12 over and over (again)** repeatedly: *The only way to learn the script is to say it to yourself over and over again.* **13 over to sb** used to say that it is now someone else's turn to do something, to speak etc: *I've done my best. Now it's over to the professionals.* | *We're going over live to our correspondent at the scene of the explosion.* **14 over!** *spoken* used when using a radio to show that you have finished speaking **15 over against** compared to someone or something else —see also **all over** (ALL[2] (7))

**over[3]** *adj* [not before noun] **1** if an event or period of time is over, it has finished: *When the game was over all the players shook hands.* **2 be over (and done) with** if an unpleasant situation or experience is over with, it has finished: *We don't have to mention the court case again! It's all over and done with now.* | **get sth over (and done) with** (=to do something so that the situation no longer exists) *The sooner you get it over with the better so phone up and make the appointment.*

**over[4]** *n* [C] the period of time in the game of CRICKET (2) during which six or eight balls are thrown by the same BOWLER (1) in one direction

**over-** /əʊvə‖oʊvər/ *prefix* **1** too much: *overpopulation* | *overcooked cabbage* **2** above; beyond; across: *overhanging branches* | *the overland route* (=not by sea or air) **3** outer; covering: *an overcoat* **4** additional: *working overtime* (=beyond the usual time)

**over-a·chiev·er** /ˌ·· ˈ··/ *n* [C] someone who works very hard to be successful and is very unhappy if they do not achieve everything they want to —**over-achieve** *v* [I]

**o·ver·act** /ˌəʊvərˈækt‖ˌoʊ-/ *v* [I,T] to act a part in a play with too much emotion or movement

**o·ver·ac·tive** /ˌəʊvərˈæktɪv◂‖ˌoʊ-/ *adj* too active, in a way that produces a bad result: *Paul's illness was due to an overactive thyroid.* | **have an overactive imagination** (=tend to imagine things that are untrue) *The rumor is probably just the result of someone's overactive imagination.*

**over-age** /ˌ·· ˈ·◂/ *adj* too old for a particular purpose or activity: *He looked like an over-age drummer from some sixties band.* —compare UNDERAGE

S3 W2 **o·ver·all[1]** /ˌəʊvərˈɔːl◂‖ˌoʊvərˈɒːl◂/ *adj* including everything: *My overall impression of his work is good.* | *What's the overall cost of repairs?*

**overall[2]** *adv* **1** including everything: *The fish measures 1.7 metres overall.* | *What will it cost, overall?* **2** [sentence adverb] generally: *Overall, prices are still rising.*

**o·ver·all[3]** /ˈəʊvərɔːl‖ˈoʊvərɒːl/ *n* **1** [C] *BrE* a loose-fitting piece of clothing like a coat, that is worn over clothes to protect them **2 overalls** [plural] *especially AmE* heavy cotton trousers with a piece covering your chest and held up by pieces of cloth that go over your shoulders; DUNGAREES (1) *BrE* **3 overalls** [plural] *BrE* also **overall** [C] *AmE* a piece of clothing like a shirt and trousers in one piece worn over other clothes to protect them

**overall ma·jor·i·ty** /ˌ···· ˈ····/ *n* [C] **1** more votes than all the other political parties together **2** *BrE* the difference between this number of votes and the total votes gained by all the other parties

**o·ver·arch·ing** /ˌəʊvərˈɑːtʃɪŋ◂‖ˌoʊvərˈɑːr-/ *adj* **1** including or influencing every part of something: *The project's overarching aim is the improvement of education.* **2** forming a curved shape over something: *the overarching sky*

**o·ver·arm** /ˈəʊvərɑːm‖ˈoʊvərɑːrm/ *adj, adv especially BrE* an overarm throw in a sport is when you throw the ball with your arm high above your shoulder; OVERHAND *AmE* —see picture on page 1264

**o·ver·awe** /ˌəʊvərˈɔː‖ˌoʊvərˈɒː/ *v* [T] to make someone feel respect or fear so that they become very quiet: *overawed by the great man's booming voice*

**o·ver·bal·ance** /ˌəʊvəˈbæləns‖ˌoʊvər-/ *v* [I,T] **1** *especially BrE* to shake and start to fall because you lose balance, or to make someone or something do this: *The horse reared, overbalanced, and fell.* **2** *AmE* OUTWEIGH *The lack of social life is overbalanced by the amount of money I'll save living here.*

**o·ver·bear** /ˌəʊvəˈbeə‖ˌoʊvərˈber/ *v* [T usually passive] *past tense* **overbore**, *past participle* **overborne** to defeat someone or something

**o·ver·bear·ing** /ˌəʊvəˈbeərɪŋ◂‖ˌoʊvərˈber-/ *adj* always trying to control other people without considering their wishes or feelings; DOMINEERING: *self-important overbearing attitudes of these high-up doctors.* —**overbearingly** *adv*

**o·ver·bid** /ˌəʊvəˈbɪd‖ˌoʊvər-/ *v* **1** [I + **for**] to offer too high a price for something, especially at an AUCTION[1] **2** [I,T] to offer more than the value of your cards in a card game such as BRIDGE[1] (4)

**o·ver·bite** /ˈəʊvəbaɪt‖ˈoʊvər-/ *n* [C] a condition in which someone's upper jaw is too far forwards beyond their lower jaw

**o·ver·blown** /ˌəʊvəˈbləʊn◂‖ˌoʊvərˈbloʊn◂/ *adj* **1** *formal* made to seem greater or more impressive; EXAGGERATED (1): *overblown news stories* **2** overblown flowers have opened too wide and become less beautiful

**o·ver·board** /ˈəʊvəbɔːd‖ˈoʊvərbɔːrd/ *adv* **1** over the side of a ship or boat into the water: *One of the crew fell overboard and drowned.* | *Man overboard!* **2 go overboard** *informal* to do or say too much because you are too eager or excited: *Dean knew he had gone overboard by sending six dozen roses.* **3 throw sth overboard** to get rid of an idea etc that is useless or unnecessary

**o·ver·book** /ˌəʊvəˈbʊk‖ˌoʊvər-/ *v* [I,T] to sell more tickets for a theatre, plane etc than there are seats available

**o·ver·bur·den** /ˌəʊvəˈbɜːdn‖ˌoʊvərˈbɜːrdn/ *v* [T usually passive] to give someone or a system too much work or too many problems to deal with: *an overburdened donkey* | [+ **with**] *a student overburdened with essays*

**o·ver·came** /ˌəʊvəˈkeɪm‖ˌoʊvər-/ *v* the past tense of OVERCOME

**o·ver·cap·i·tal·ize** also **-ise** *BrE* /ˌəʊvəˈkæpɪtl-aɪz‖ˌoʊvər-/ *v* [I,T] **1** to supply too much money for a business **2** to put too high a value on a business —**overcapitalization** /ˌəʊvəkæpɪtl-aɪˈzeɪʃən‖ˌoʊvər-kæpɪtlə-/ *n* [U]

**o·ver·cast** /ˌəʊvəˈkɑːst◂‖ˌoʊvərˈkæst◂/ *adj* dark with clouds: *an overcast day* | *an overcast sky* —see picture on page 836

**o·ver·charge** /ˌəʊvəˈtʃɑːdʒ‖ˌoʊvərˈtʃɑːrdʒ/ *v* **1** [I,T] to charge someone too much money for something: **overcharge sb** *The cashier overcharged me by at least $2.00.* **2** [T] too full of emotion or excitement: *The atmosphere in the stadium was overcharged with excitement.* **3** [T] to put too much power into a BATTERY (1) or electrical system

**o·ver·cloud** /ˌəʊvəˈklaʊd‖ˌoʊvər-/ *v* [T usually passive] **1** to cover the sky, sun etc with clouds **2** to fill someone or a situation with unhappy or worried feelings: *a look of fear suddenly overclouding his face*

**o·ver·coat** /ˈəʊvəkəʊt‖ˈoʊvərkoʊt/ *n* [C] a long, thick, warm coat worn over other clothes in cold weather

**o·ver·come** /ˌəʊvəˈkʌm‖ˌoʊvər-/ *v past tense* **overcame** /-ˈkeɪm/ *past participle* **overcome** **1** [T] to control a feeling or problem that prevents you from achieving something: *He struggled to overcome his shyness.* 

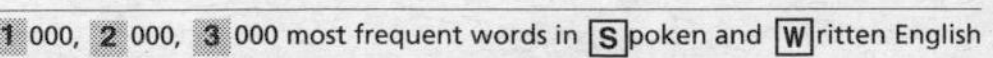

2 [I,T] to fight and win against someone or something: *They overcame the enemy after a long battle.* | *We shall overcome!* **3** [T usually passive] to have such a strong effect on someone that they become weak, unconscious, or unable to control their feelings: *She was overcome by emotion.* | *Those who died in the fire were overcome by the gas fumes.*

**o·ver·com·pen·sate** /ˌəʊvəˈkɒmpənseɪt, -pen-‖ˌoʊvər-kɑːm-/ *v* [I] to try to correct a weakness or mistake by doing too much of the opposite thing: *Zoe overcompensates for her shyness by talking a lot.* —**overcompensation** /ˌəʊvəkɒmpənˈseɪʃən, -pen-‖ˌoʊvərkɑːm-/ *n* [U]

**o·ver·crowd** /ˌəʊvəˈkraʊd‖ˌoʊvər-/ *v* [T] to fill a space or period of time with too many things or people: [+ **with**] *The courts overcrowd their calendars with too many trials.*

**o·ver·crowd·ed** /ˌəʊvəˈkraʊdɪd◂‖ˌoʊvər-/ *adj* filled with too many people or things: *an overcrowded room*

**o·ver·crowd·ing** /ˌəʊvəˈkraʊdɪŋ‖ˌoʊvər-/ *n* [U] the condition of living or working too close together, with too many people in a small space

**o·ver·de·vel·oped** /ˌəʊvədɪˈveləpt◂‖ˌoʊvər-/ *adj* too great or large: *Ryan has an overdeveloped sense of his own importance.*

**o·ver·do** /ˌəʊvəˈduː‖ˌoʊvər-/ *v past tense* **overdid** /-ˈdɪd/ *past participle* **overdone** /-ˈdʌn/ [T] **1** to do something more than is suitable or natural: *Don't overdo the praise. She wasn't that good.* | **overdo it** *I think Trudy's overdone it with the all the lace and frills in the bedroom.* **2** to use too much of something: *I think I overdid the salt.* **3** **overdo it** to work too hard or be too active so that you become tired: *She's been overdoing it lately.*

**o·ver·done** /ˌəʊvəˈdʌn◂‖ˌoʊvər-/ *adj* cooked too much: *The beef was overdone.* —compare UNDERDONE

**o·ver·dose** /ˈəʊvədəʊs‖ˈoʊvərdoʊs/ *n* [C] too much of a drug taken at one time: *a massive overdose of heroin* —**overdose** /ˌəʊvəˈdəʊs‖ˌoʊvərˈdoʊs/ *v* [I + **on**] *He overdosed on heroin.*

**o·ver·draft** /ˈəʊvədrɑːft‖ˈoʊvərdræft/ *n* [C] the amount of money you owe to a bank when you have taken out more money than you had in your bank account: *I have to find the money to pay off this overdraft.*

**overdraft fa·cil·i·ty** /ˈ··· ·ˌ···/ *n* [C] *BrE* an agreement with the bank that a customer may take more money from the bank than they have in their account, up to a certain amount

**o·ver·drawn** /ˌəʊvəˈdrɔːn‖ˌoʊvərˈdrɒːn/ *adj* **be overdrawn** if your bank account is overdrawn you have spent more than is in it and you owe the bank money: *I'm overdrawn at the moment.* | **be overdrawn by £50/$600 etc** *My account is overdrawn by £300.* —**overdraw** *v* [I]

**o·ver·dressed** /ˌəʊvəˈdrest◂‖ˌoʊvər-/ *adj* dressed in clothes that are too formal for the occasion: *I felt distinctly overdressed beside all those young people in jeans.* —**overdress** *v* [I]

**o·ver·drive** /ˈəʊvədraɪv‖ˈoʊvər-/ *n* [U] **1** an additional GEAR[1] (2) which allows a car to go fast while its engine produces the least power necessary: *Put the car in overdrive when you hit 50 mph.* **2** **go into overdrive** to become very excited or active: *You could see his imagination go into overdrive at the thought.*

**o·ver·due** /ˌəʊvəˈdjuː◂‖ˌoʊvərˈduː◂/ *adj* **1** a payment that is overdue should have been paid earlier: *an overdue gas bill* **2** **be overdue for** to have needed something done for a long time: *The car is overdue for a tune-up.* **3** something that is overdue should have happened or been done a long time ago: **long overdue** *This is a major, but long overdue reform which will benefit around 4 million low-paid people.* **4** [not before noun] a baby that is overdue was not born at the time that it was expected: *Collette's baby is a week overdue.* **5** a library book that is overdue was not returned to the library when it should have been

**o·ver·eat** /ˌəʊvərˈiːt‖ˌoʊ-/ *v past tense* **overate** /-ˈet, -ˈeɪt‖-ˈeɪt/ *past participle* **overeaten** /-ˈiːtn/ [I] to eat too much, or eat more than is healthy: *Pete's gained so much weight because he can't stop overeating.*

**o·ver·egg** /ˌəʊvərˈeg‖ˌoʊ-/ *v* **overegg the pudding** *BrE informal* to do more than is necessary, or add something that is not needed

**o·ver·es·ti·mate[1]** /ˌəʊvərˈestɪmeɪt‖ˌoʊ-/ *v* **1** [T] to judge something to be better than it really is: *I'm afraid we overestimated his abilities.* **2** [I,T] to guess an amount or value that is too high: *We overestimated the number of people who would come.* | [+ **by**] *I think Jo's overestimated by about 300.* —compare UNDERESTIMATE[1]

**o·ver·es·ti·mate[2]** /ˌəʊvərˈestɪmɪt‖ˌoʊ-/ *n* [C] a calculation, judgment, or guess that is too large

**o·ver·ex·cit·ed** /əʊvərikˈsaɪtɪd/ *adj* children who are overexcited are too excited to behave sensibly

**o·ver·ex·pose** /ˌəʊvərɪkˈspəʊz‖ˌoʊvərɪkˈspoʊz/ *v* [T] **1** to allow too much light to reach the film when taking or developing a photograph **2** **be overexposed** become less popular because of appearing too many times on television, in the newspapers etc —opposite UNDEREXPOSE

**over·ex·po·sure** /ˌ·· ·ˈ··/ *n* [U] the state of having received too much light, sun light, RADIATION etc, that is harmful to someone's skin, a photographic film etc

**o·ver·ex·tend** /ˌəʊvərɪkˈstend‖ˌoʊ-/ [T] to try to do or use too much of something, causing problems, illness, or damage: *The accountants have advised us not to overextend our resources.* | **overextend yourself** *Be careful not to overextend yourself. You've been very ill!*

**o·ver·flow[1]** /ˌəʊvəˈfləʊ‖ˌoʊvərˈfloʊ/ *v* **1** [I,T] if a river, lake, or container overflows, it is so full that the water, material etc inside flows over its edges: *The toilet's just overflowed again.* | [+ **with**] *a trash can overflowing with papers* | **overflow sth** *The river had overflowed its banks.* **2** **overflow with love/gratitude etc** to have a very strong feeling of love etc: *My heart was overflowing with gratitude for the old man.* **3** [I,T] if people overflow a place, there are too many of them to fit into it: [+ **into/onto**] *The crowd overflowed into the street.*

**o·ver·flow[2]** /ˈəʊvəfləʊ‖ˈoʊvərfloʊ/ *n* [C] **1** [singular] the amount of something or the number of people that cannot be contained in a place because it is already full: *The overflow will be accommodated in another hotel.* | [+ **of**] *the overflow of water from the lake* **2** [U] an act of overflowing something **3** [C] a pipe through which water flows out of a container when it becomes too full

**o·ver·fly** /ˌəʊvəˈflaɪ‖ˌoʊvər-/ *v* [T] to fly over an area or country in an aircraft

**o·ver·grown** /ˌəʊvəˈgrəʊn◂‖ˌoʊvərˈgroʊn◂/ *adj* **1** covered with plants that have grown in an uncontrolled way: [+ **with**] *The garden will be overgrown with weeds by the time we get back.* **2** **overgrown child/schoolboy/baby** used to describe an adult who behaves like a child: *Stop acting like an overgrown schoolboy.*

**o·ver·growth** /ˈəʊvəgrəʊθ‖ˈoʊvərgroʊθ/ *n* [U] plants and branches of trees growing above your head, usually in a forest

**o·ver·hand** /ˈəʊvəhænd‖ˈoʊvər-/ *adj, adv AmE* an overhand throw in a sport is when you throw the ball with your arm above the level of your shoulder; OVERARM *especially BrE* —opposite UNDERHAND[2]

**o·ver·hang[1]** /ˌəʊvəˈhæŋ‖ˌoʊvər-/ *v past tense and past participle* **overhung** /-ˈhʌŋ/ [I,T] to hang over something: *Our apple trees overhang the neighbors' yard.*

**o·ver·hang[2]** /ˈəʊvəhæŋ‖ˈoʊvər-/ *n* [usually singular] **1** a rock, roof etc that hangs over something else: *We* *stood under the overhang while it rained.* **2** the amount by which something hangs over something else

**o·ver·haul¹** /ˌəʊvəˈhɔːl‖ˌoʊvərˈhɒːl/ *v* [T] **1** to repair or change all the parts that need it, in a machine, system etc that is not working correctly: *overhaul an engine | an overhaul of civil court procedures to speed up and simplify cases* **2** to move up to a vehicle, ship, or person from behind and pass them; OVERTAKE (1)

**o·ver·haul²** /ˈəʊvəhɔːl‖ˈoʊvərhɒːl/ *n* [C] necessary changes or repairs made to a machine or system: *The Chevy needs a complete overhaul.*

**o·ver·head¹** /ˌəʊvəˈhed◂‖ˌoʊvər-/ *adv* above your head: *A plane flew overhead | Bullets whizzed overhead.* —**overhead** *adj*: *overhead wires* —see picture on page 1257

**o·ver·head²** /ˈəʊvəhed‖ˈoʊvər-/ *n* **1** [singular] *especially AmE* also **overheads** [plural] *especially BrE* money spent regularly on rent, insurance, electricity, and other things that are needed to keep a business operating: *Their offices are in London so the overheads are very high.* **2** [C] a piece of transparent material used with an overhead projector to show words, pictures etc

**overhead pro·jec·tor** /ˌ··· ·ˈ··/ *n* [C] a piece of electrical equipment used for making words, pictures etc look larger by showing them on a wall or large SCREEN¹ (1) so that many people can see —see picture on page 837

**o·ver·hear** /ˌəʊvəˈhɪə‖ˌoʊvərˈhɪr/ *v past tense and past participle* **overheard** /-ˈhɜːd‖-ˈhɜːrd/ [T] to accidentally hear what other people are saying, when they do not know that you have heard: *I overheard part of their conversation.* | **overhear sb saying sth** *Christie overheard the men saying they were going to rob the bank!* | **overhear sb say (that)** *We overheard the teacher say there would be a pop quiz today.* —compare EAVESDROP

**o·ver·heat** /ˌəʊvəˈhiːt‖ˌoʊvər-/ *v* [I,T] to become too hot, or to make something too hot: *I think the engine's overheating again.* | **overheat sth** *Try not to overheat the sauce.*

**o·ver·heat·ed** /ˌəʊvəˈhiːtɪ̬d◂‖ˌoʊvər-/ *adj* **1** too hot: *the overheated waiting room* **2** full of angry feelings: *an overheated quarrel that turned into a fight* **3** an ECONOMY¹ (1) that is overheated is too active to work properly

**o·ver·hung** /ˌəʊvəˈhʌŋ‖ˌoʊvər-/ *v* the past tense and past participle of OVERHANG¹

**o·ver·in·dulge** /ˌəʊvərɪnˈdʌldʒ‖ˌoʊ-/ *v* **1** [I] to eat or drink too much: *I'm getting too fat, so I mustn't overindulge.* **2** [T] to let someone have everything they want, or always let them do what they want: *Penny was overindulged by her parents.* —**overindulgence** *n* [U]

**o·ver·joyed** /ˌəʊvəˈdʒɔɪd‖ˌoʊvər-/ *adj* [not before noun] extremely pleased or happy: **overjoyed to hear/find/see sth** *We were overjoyed to hear that they were safe.* | [+ **at**] *Richard was overjoyed at the prospect of becoming a father.*

**o·ver·kill** /ˈəʊvəkɪl‖ˈoʊvər-/ *n* [U] **1** more of something than is necessary or desirable: *I thought 24 hours of television coverage of the election verged on overkill.* **2** more than enough weapons, especially NUCLEAR (3) weapons, to kill everyone in a country

**o·ver·la·den** /ˌəʊvəˈleɪdn‖ˌoʊvər-/ *v* a past tense and past participle of OVERLOAD

**o·ver·laid** /ˌəʊvəˈleɪd‖ˌoʊvər-/ *v* the past tense and past participle of OVERLAY¹

**o·ver·land** /ˌəʊvəˈlænd◂‖ˌoʊvər-/ *adv* across land, not by sea or air: *travelling overland to China* —**overland** *adj*

**o·ver·lap¹** /ˌəʊvəˈlæp‖ˌoʊvər-/ *v* **overlapped, overlapping** [I,T] **1** if two or more things overlap, part of one thing covers part of another thing: *One of Jilly's front teeth overlaps the other.* | *The tiles on the roof overlap.* **2** if two sets, subjects, ideas etc overlap, they include some but not all of the same things: [+ **with**] *This is where sociology overlaps with economics.* | **overlap sth** *Maxwell's responsibilities overlap yours, so you will be sharing some of the work.* **3** if two events or activities overlap, the first one finishes a short time after the second one starts: [+ **with**] *My vacation overlaps with yours, so we won't see each other for a month or so.* | **overlap sth** *The first shift overlaps the second.*

**overlap**

overlapping roof tiles

**o·ver·lap²** /ˈəʊvəlæp‖ˈoʊvər-/ *n* [C,U] the amount by which two things, activities etc overlap: [+ **between**] *The overlap between the two subjects is considerable.*

**o·ver·lay¹** /ˌəʊvəˈleɪ‖ˌoʊvər-/ *v past tense and past participle* **overlaid** /-ˈleɪd/ [T] *technical* **1 be overlaid with** to be thinly covered with something: *wood overlaid with silver* **2** [usually passive] to add an outer appearance to something that hides its real character: [+ **with**] *His ordinarily cheerful face was overlaid with gloom.*

**o·ver·lay²** /ˈəʊvəleɪ‖ˈoʊvər-/ *n* [C] **1** something laid over something else **2** a transparent sheet with a picture or drawing on it which is put on top of another picture to change it **3** an additional quality or feeling: *sad stories with an overlay of humour*

**o·ver·leaf** /ˌəʊvəˈliːf‖ˈoʊvərliːf/ *adv* on the other side of the page: *See the diagram overleaf.*

**o·ver·lie** /ˌəʊvəˈlaɪ‖ˌoʊvər-/ *v* [T] *technical* **1** to lie over something: *A thick layer of soil overlies the rocks.* **2** if a parent animal overlies its young it kills them by lying on them

**o·ver·load** /ˌəʊvəˈləʊd‖ˌoʊvərˈloʊd/ *v past participle* **overloaded** *or* **overladen** /-ˈleɪdn/ [T] **1** to load something with too many things: [+ **with**] *The bus was overloaded with tourists and their luggage.* **2** to put too much electricity through an electrical system or piece of equipment: *Don't overload the outlet by plugging in too many appliances.* **3** to give someone too much work: [+ **with**] *All the staff are overloaded with work.* —**overload** /ˈəʊvələʊd‖ˈoʊvərloʊd/ *n* [C,U]

**o·ver·long** /ˌəʊvəˈlɒŋ◂‖ˌoʊvərˈlɒːŋ◂/ *adj* continuing for too long: *an overlong performance*

**o·ver·look** /ˌəʊvəˈlʊk‖ˌoʊvər-/ *v* [T] **1** to not notice something: *It is easy to overlook a small detail like that.* **2** to ignore and forgive someone's mistake, bad behaviour etc: *I'll overlook your mistake this time.* **3** if a building, room, or window overlooks a place, you can look down on that place from it: *Our room overlooks the ocean.* | *My garden is overlooked by the neighbours.*

**o·ver·lord** /ˈəʊvəlɔːd‖ˈoʊvərlɔːrd/ *n* [C] a lord who ruled over other lords in the past

**o·ver·ly** /ˈəʊvəli‖ˈoʊvər-/ *adv* [often in negatives] too or very: *I wasn't overly impressed with her performance.* | *You're being overly critical.*

**o·ver·manned** /ˌəʊvəˈmænd◂‖ˌoʊvər-/ *adj* having more workers than are needed for a job; OVERSTAFFED —**overmanning** *n* [U]

**o·ver·mas·ter** /ˌəʊvəˈmɑːstə‖ˌoʊvərˈmæstər/ *v* [T] *literary* to gain control or power over someone

**o·ver·much** /ˌəʊvəˈmʌtʃ◂‖ˌoʊvər-/ *literary or humorous* too much: *It is unwise to indulge overmuch in strong drink.* | **not overmuch** *We didn't like each other overmuch.*

**o·ver·night¹** /ˌəʊvəˈnaɪt‖ˌoʊvər-/ *adv* **1** for or during the night: **stay overnight** *Pam's staying overnight at my house.* **2** *informal* suddenly: *Logan became famous overnight.*

**o·ver·night²** /ˈəʊvənaɪt‖ˈoʊvər-/ *adj* **1** continuing all night: *an overnight flight from Boston to London* **2** done in one night: *an overnight delivery service* **3 an overnight success** something that suddenly becomes very popular or successful: *The show was an overnight success on Broadway.*

**o·ver·night·er** /ˈ··· ,·/ *n* [C] a bag or small case which holds a few clothes and other things you need for a short trip

**over-op·ti·mis·tic** /,·· ··ˈ··◂/ *adj* expecting that things will be better than is possible or likely: *over-optimistic forecasts of economic growth*

**o·ver·pass** /ˈəʊvəpɑːs‖ˈoʊvərpæs/ *n* [C] *AmE* FLYOVER (1) —see picture on page 415

**o·ver·pay** /,əʊvəˈpeɪ‖,oʊvər-/ *v past tense and past participle* **overpaid** /-ˈpeɪd/ [T] to pay someone too much: *I think lawyers are overpaid for what they do.*

**o·ver·play** /,əʊvəˈpleɪ‖,oʊvər-/ *v* [T] **1** to make something seem more important than it is: *The poet's importance is overplayed by his biographer.* —opposite UNDERPLAY (1) **2 overplay your hand** to try to gain more advantage than you know you can reasonably expect: *If you're asking for more vacation time, don't overplay your hand by bringing salary into it too.*

**o·ver·pop·u·lat·ed** /,əʊvəˈpɒpjɡleɪtɡd◂‖,oʊvərˈpɑːp-/ *adj* a city or country that is overpopulated has too many people: *a programme of resettlement from the most overpopulated areas* —**overpopulation** /,əʊvəpɒpjɡˈleɪʃən‖,oʊvərpɑːp-/ *n* [U]

**o·ver·pow·er** /,əʊvəˈpaʊə‖,oʊvərˈpaʊər/ *v* [T] **1** to defeat someone because you are stronger: *The policeman and a dog handler struggled to overpower the man.* **2** if a smell, task, emotion etc overpowers someone or something it is too strong: *a full flavour slightly overpowered by saltiness;* OVERCOME (3)

**o·ver·pow·er·ing** /,əʊvəˈpaʊərɪŋ◂‖,oʊvər-/ *adj* **1** very strong; INTENSE (1): *an overpowering smell | an overpowering desire to slap her* **2** someone who is overpowering has such a strong character that they make other people feel uncomfortable or afraid; OVERBEARING —**overpoweringly** *adv*

**o·ver·priced** /,əʊvəˈpraɪst◂‖,oʊvər-/ *adj* too expensive: *The patisserie has good food, but it's overpriced.*

**o·ver·print** /,əʊvəˈprɪnt‖,oʊvər-/ *v* [T + **with/on**] to print additional words over a document, stamp etc that already has printing on it

**o·ver·proof** /,əʊvəˈpruːf‖,oʊvər-/ *adj* **10%/15% overproof** containing 10% etc more alcohol than PROOF SPIRIT does

**o·ver·pro·tec·tive** /,əʊvəprəˈtektɪv◂‖,oʊvər-/ *adj* so anxious to protect someone from harm, danger etc that you restrict their freedom: *I suppose I've been overprotective, but Mike's my only son.*

**o·ver·qual·i·fied** /,əʊvəˈkwɒlɡfaɪd◂‖,oʊvərˈkwɑː-/ *adj* having so much experience or training that people do not want to employ you for particular jobs: *The firm told me not to bother applying because I was overqualified.*

**o·ver·ran** /,əʊvəˈræn‖,oʊ-/ *v* the past tense of OVERRUN

**o·ver·rate** /,əʊvəˈreɪt‖,oʊ-/ *v* [T] to think that something is better or more important than it is: *'Titus Andronicus' is an overrated play in my opinion.* —opposite UNDERRATE

**o·ver·reach** /,əʊvəˈriːtʃ‖,oʊ-/ *v* [T] **overreach yourself** to try to do more than you have the ability or money to do: *The company overreached itself financially.*

**o·ver·re·act** /,əʊvəriˈækt‖,oʊ-/ *v* [I] to react to something with too much emotion, especially anger: [+ **to**] *You always overreact to criticism.* —**overreaction** /-riˈækʃən/ *n* [C,U]

**o·ver·ride** /,əʊvəˈraɪd‖,oʊ-/ *v past tense* **overrode** /-ˈrəʊd‖-ˈroʊd/ *past participle* **overridden** /-ˈrɪdn/ [T] **1** to ignore a decision or order made by someone with less authority than you: *The principal overrode the teacher's rule and let the children stay outside.* **2** to be regarded as more important than something else: *The needs of the mother should not override the needs of the child.*

**o·ver·rid·ing** /,əʊvəˈraɪdɪŋ◂‖,oʊ-/ *adj* [only before noun] more important than anything else: *a question of overriding importance | Our overriding obligation is to prepare our graduates for their future.*

**o·ver·rule** /,əʊvəˈruːl‖,oʊ-/ *v* [T] to change someone's order, or decision that you think is wrong, using your official power: *Parliament overruled the local authorities.*

**o·ver·run** /,əʊvəˈrʌn/ *v past tense* **overran** /-ˈræn/ *past participle* **overrun** **1** [T] if something unwanted overruns a place or area, it spreads over it in great numbers: *Rats had overrun the barn in the few years since we'd been there.* | **overrun by/with** *a tiny island overrun with tourists* **2** [I,T] to continue longer than intended: *The final speaker overran by at least half an hour.*

**o·ver·seas¹** /,əʊvəˈsiːz◂‖,oʊvər-/ *adv* to or in a foreign country somewhere across the sea: *Carmen is going to work overseas.* | *Most applications came from overseas.* W3

**o·ver·seas²** /ˈəʊvəsiːz‖ˈoʊvər-/ *adj* [only before noun] coming from or happening abroad: *overseas students | overseas trade*

**o·ver·see** /,əʊvəˈsiː‖,oʊvər-/ *past tense* **oversaw** /-ˈsɔː‖-ˈsɒː/ *past participle* **overseen** /-ˈsiːn/ *v* [T] to be in charge of a group of workers and check that a piece of work is done satisfactorily: *A team leader was appointed to oversee the project.* | *overseeing the workers*

**o·ver·seer** /ˈəʊvəsɪə‖ˈoʊvərsiːər/ *n* [C] someone in charge of a group of workers, who checks that their work is done properly

**o·ver·sell** /,əʊvəˈsel‖,oʊvər-/ *past tense and past participle* **oversold** /-ˈsəʊld‖-ˈsoʊld/ *v* [T] to praise someone or something too much

**o·ver·sen·si·tive** /,əʊvəˈsensɡtɪv◂‖,oʊvər-/ *adj* easily upset or offended: *I didn't mean that. Rod's just being oversensitive.*

**o·ver·sexed** /,əʊvəˈsekst◂‖,oʊvər-/ *adj* having too much interest in or desire for sex

**o·ver·shad·ow** /,əʊvəˈʃædəʊ‖,oʊvərˈʃædoʊ/ *v* [T] **1** to make someone or something else seem less important: *Her success has been overshadowed by her fears for her daughter, Maggie.* **2** if a tall building, mountain etc overshadows a place, it is very close to it: *a dark valley overshadowed by towering peaks* **3** to make an occasion or period of time less enjoyable by making people feel sad or worried: *The threat of war overshadowed the summer of 1939.*

**o·ver·shoe** /ˈəʊvəʃuː‖ˈoʊvər-/ *n* [C] a rubber shoe that you wear over an ordinary shoe to keep your feet dry

**o·ver·shoot** /,əʊvəˈʃuːt‖,oʊvər-/ *v past tense and past participle* **overshot** /-ˈʃɒt‖-ˈʃɑːt/ [I,T] **1** to drive past the place where you intended to stop or turn: *I didn't see the sign and overshot the turning.* **2 overshoot the mark** to make the mistake of going higher or further than the amount or distance you had aimed for | *We realized after a half hour that we'd overshot the mark, and had to turn back.*

**o·ver·sight** /ˈəʊvəsaɪt‖ˈoʊvər-/ *n* [C,U] **1** a mistake that you make by not noticing something or by forgetting to do something: *I assure you that this was purely an oversight on my part.* **2 have oversight of** to be in charge of a piece of work and check that it is satisfactory: *The works manager will have general oversight of the project.*

**o·ver·sim·pli·fy** /,əʊvəˈsɪmplɡfaɪ‖,oʊvər-/ *v* [I,T] to make a situation or problem seem less complicated than it really is, by ignoring important facts: *My research has been grossly oversimplified in your account.* —**oversimplification** /,əʊvəsɪmplɡfɡˈkeɪʃən‖,oʊvər-/ *n* [C,U]

**over-six·ties** /,·· ˈ··/ *n* [plural] people who are over sixty years old: *holidays for the over-sixties*

**o·ver·size** /,əʊvəˈsaɪz◂‖,oʊvər-/ also **o·ver·sized** /-ˈsaɪzd◂/ *adj* bigger than usual or too big: *His features were dwarfed by a pair of oversize spectacles.*

**o·ver·sleep** /,əʊvəˈsliːp‖,oʊvər-/ *v past tense and past participle* **overslept** /-ˈslept/ [I] to sleep for longer than you intended: *I had overslept that morning, and was late for work.* —compare **sleep in** (SLEEP²)

**o·ver·spend** /,əʊvəˈspend‖,oʊvər-/ *v past tense and past participle* **overspent** /-ˈspent/ [I] to spend more money than you can afford: *Credit cards have encouraged people* *to overspend.* —**overspend** /ˈəʊvəspend‖ˈoʊvər-/ *n* [C]: *an overspend of £200,000*

**o·ver·spill** /ˈəʊvəˌspɪl‖ˈoʊvər-/ *n* [U] *BrE* people who move out of a big city because there are too many people living there, and go to live in new houses outside the city: *a new town built to accommodate London's overspill*

**o·ver·staffed** /ˌəʊvəˈstɑːft◂‖ˌoʊvərˈstæft◂/ *adj* a company, organization etc that is overstaffed has more workers than it needs —opposite UNDERSTAFFED

**o·ver·state** /ˌəʊvəˈsteɪt‖ˌoʊvər-/ *v* [T] to talk about something in a way that makes it seem more important, serious etc than it really is; EXAGGERATE: *We must not frighten people by overstating the dangers.* —opposite UNDERSTATE

**o·ver·state·ment** /ˌəʊvəˈsteɪtmənt‖ˌoʊvər-/ *n* [C,U] the act of talking about something in a way that makes it seem more important, serious etc than it really is, or an example of this; EXAGGERATION: *It's a bit of an overstatement to say that the man's a fool, but he's not brilliant.*

**o·ver·stay** /ˌəʊvəˈsteɪ‖ˌoʊvər-/ *v* [T] to stay somewhere longer than you intended or longer than you should —see also **overstay your welcome** (WELCOME[4] (3))

**o·ver·step** /ˌəʊvəˈstep‖ˌoʊvər-/ *v* **overstepped, overstepping** [T] **1 overstep the rules/limits etc** to behave in a way that is not polite or not allowed by the rules **2 overstep the mark** to do or say more than you should, and offend people or make them angry: *I've been very patient with him so far, but he's really overstepped the mark this time!*

**o·ver·stock** /ˌəʊvəˈstɒk‖ˌoʊvərˈstɑːk/ *v* [I,T] to obtain more of something than is needed for a shop, hotel etc

**o·ver·sub·scribe** /ˌəʊvəsəbˈskraɪb‖ˌoʊvər-/ *v* [T] **be oversubscribed** if an activity, sale, service etc is oversubscribed, people are asking for more places, tickets etc than there are available: *Hostels for single people are normally oversubscribed.*

**o·vert** /ˈəʊvɜːt, əʊˈvɜːt‖ˈoʊvɜːrt, oʊˈvɜːrt/ *adj formal* actions that are overt are done publicly, without trying to hide anything: *an overt attempt to silence their political opponents|overt discrimination* —opposite COVERT —**overtly** *adv*

**o·ver·take** /ˌəʊvəˈteɪk‖-ˌoʊvər-/ *v past tense* **overtook** /-ˈtʊk/ *past participle* **overtaken** /-ˈteɪkən/ **1** [I,T] to go past a moving vehicle or person because you are going faster than them and want to get in front of them: *He pulled out to overtake the red van.* —see picture on page 415 **2** [T] if something bad overtakes you, it happens to you suddenly and prevents you from doing what you had planned to do: [+ **by**] *We'd both been overtaken by sheer fatigue* **3** [T] to develop or increase more quickly than someone or something else and become bigger, better, or more advanced than them: *By 1970 the Americans had overtaken the Russians in space technology.* **4 be overtaken by events** if you are overtaken by events, the situation changes, so that your plans or ideas are not useful any more *His last years were spent working from a theory that was rapidly being overtaken by events.*

**o·ver·tax** /ˌəʊvəˈtæks‖ˌoʊvər-/ *v* [T] **1** to make someone do more than they are really able to do, so that they become very tired: **overtax yourself** *Don't overtax yourself!* **2** to make people pay too much tax

**over-the-coun·ter** /ˌ·· · ˈ··◂/ *adj* [only before noun] **1** over-the-counter drugs can be obtained without a PRESCRIPTION (=a written order) from a doctor **2** *AmE* abbreviation **OTC** over-the-counter business shares are ones that do not appear on an official STOCK EXCHANGE (2) list

**over-the-top** /ˌ··· ˈ·◂/ abbreviation **OTT** *adj BrE informal* remarks, behaviour etc that are over-the-top are so exaggerated (EXAGGERATE) or unreasonable that they seem stupid or offensive: *It's a bit over-the-top to call him a fascist.*

**o·ver·throw**[1] /ˌəʊvəˈθrəʊ‖ˌoʊvərˈθroʊ/ *v past tense* **overthrew** /-ˈθruː/ *past participle* **overthrown** /-ˈθrəʊn‖-ˈθroʊn/ [T] **1** to remove a leader or government from a position of power: *Rebels were already plotting to overthrow the government.* **2** to get rid of the rules of a society: *a social revolution that has overthrown basic standards of morality*

**o·ver·throw**[2] /ˈəʊvəθrəʊ‖ˈoʊvərθroʊ/ *n* [U] the defeat and removal from power of a leader or government, especially by force: [+ **of**] *The organization was dedicated to the overthrow of capitalism.|the overthrow of Mussolini*

**o·ver·time** /ˈəʊvətaɪm‖ˈoʊvər-/ *n* [U] **1** time that you spend working in your job in addition to your normal working hours: *six hours' overtime|overtime pay|* **work overtime** *They're working overtime to get the job finished.* **2** the money that you are paid for working more hours than usual: *A miner could earn £250 a week, including overtime.* **3 be working overtime** *informal* to be very active: *After nine months of pregnancy your hormones are working overtime.* **4** *AmE* EXTRA TIME *BrE*

**o·ver·tone** /ˈəʊvətəʊn‖ˈoʊvərtoʊn/ *n* **1 overtones** [plural] signs of an emotion or attitude that is not expressed directly: *His words were polite, but there were overtones of anger in his voice.|heavy moral overtones* **2** [C] *technical* a higher musical note that sounds together with the main note: HARMONIC —see also UNDERTONE

**o·ver·took** /ˌəʊvəˈtʊk‖ˌoʊvər-/ the past tense of OVERTAKE

**o·ver·top** /ˌəʊvəˈtɒp‖ˌoʊvərˈtɑːp/ *v* **overtopped, overtopping** [T] *formal* to be higher or more important than something

**o·ver·ture** /ˈəʊvətjʊə, -tʃʊə, -tʃə‖ˈoʊvərtjʊr, -tʃʊr, -tʃər/ *n* **1** [C] a short piece of music written as an introduction to a long piece of music, especially an OPERA **2 overtures** an attempt to begin a friendly relationship with a person, country etc: [+ **of**] *overtures of friendship|* **make overtures to** *They began making overtures to the Irish government in the hope of gaining their support.* **3 be an overture** if an event is an overture to a more important event, it happens just before it and makes you expect it: *This encounter was a sort of overture to their first real meeting.*

**o·ver·turn** /ˌəʊvəˈtɜːn‖ˌoʊvərˈtɜːrn/ *v* **1** [I,T] if you overturn something or if it overturns, it turns upside down or falls over on its side: *Leslie leapt to her feet, overturning her chair.|One of the boats had overturned.* **2** [T] **overturn a decision/verdict etc** to change a decision or result so that it becomes the opposite of what it was before: *The decision was finally overturned by the Supreme Court last year.* **3** [T] to suddenly remove a government from power, especially by using violence; OVERTHROW[1] (1)

**o·ver·val·ue** /ˌəʊvəˈvæljuː‖ˌoʊvər-/ *v* [T] to believe or say that something is more valuable or more important than it really is —**overvaluation** *n* [U]

**o·ver·view** /ˈəʊvəvjuː‖ˈoʊvər-/ *n* [C] a short description of a subject or situation that gives the main ideas without explaining all the details: [+ **of**] *an overview of the issues involved|* **give an overview** *Professors often give an overview of the subject at the start of the lecture.*

**o·ver·ween·ing** /ˌəʊvəˈwiːnɪŋ◂‖ˌoʊvər-/ *adj formal* too proud and confident; ARROGANT: *overweening vanity* —**overweeningly** *adv*

**o·ver·weight** /ˌəʊvəˈweɪt◂‖ˌoʊvər-/ *adj* **1** someone who is overweight is too heavy and fat: **10 kilos/20 lbs etc overweight** *Sally was three stone overweight.* **2** something such as a package that is overweight weighs more than it is supposed to weigh: *My luggage was overweight by five kilos.* —compare UNDERWEIGHT —see FAT[1] (USAGE)

**o·ver·whelm** /ˌəʊvəˈwelm‖ˌoʊvər-/ *v* [T]
**1 ► EMOTION ◄** if someone is overwhelmed by an emotion, they feel it so strongly that they cannot think clearly: *He was suddenly overwhelmed by a strong feeling of his insignificance.|Grief overwhelmed me.*
**2 ► SURPRISE SB ◄** to surprise someone very much,

so that they do not know how to react: *I was completely overwhelmed by his generosity.*
**3 ▶ DEFEAT SB ◀** to defeat an army completely: *In 1532 the Spaniards finally overwhelmed the armies of Peru.*
**4 ▶ PROBLEM ◀** if a problem overwhelms someone or something, it has such a great effect that nothing can be done to deal with it: *Decades of war and natural catastrophes had overwhelmed the city's finances.*
**5 ▶ WATER ◀** *literary* if water overwhelms an area of land, it covers it completely and suddenly

**o·ver·whelm·ing** /ˌəʊvəˈwelmɪŋ‖ˌoʊvər-/ *adj* **1** having such a great effect on you that you feel confused and do not know how to react: *The sheer size of the place will seem overwhelming and confusing at first.* | *overwhelming generosity* **2 overwhelming numbers/majority/odds etc** very large numbers etc: *An overwhelming majority of the members were against the idea.* —**overwhelmingly** *adv*: *Congress voted overwhelmingly in favor of the bill.*

**o·ver·win·ter** /ˌəʊvəˈwɪntə‖ˌoʊvərˈwɪntər/ *v* [I,T] to live through the winter, or to make it possible for something to live through the winter: *These birds generally overwinter in tropical regions.*

**o·ver·work¹** /ˌəʊvəˈwɜːk‖ˌoʊvərˈwɜːrk/ *v* [I,T] to work too much, or to make someone work too much: *Batson overworked his staff mercilessly.* | *You've been overworking – why don't you take a week off?*

**overwork²** *n* [U] too much hard work: *a heart attack brought on by overwork*

**o·ver·worked** /ˌəʊvəˈwɜːkt◂‖ˌoʊvərˈwɜːrkt◂/ *adj* **1** made to work too hard: *an overworked doctor* **2** a word or phrase that is overworked is used too much and has become less effective: *overworked metaphors*

**o·ver·wrought** /ˌəʊvəˈrɔːt◂‖ˌoʊvəˈrɒːt◂/ *adj* very upset, nervous, and worried: *Clara was tired and overwrought after the upheavals of the last few days.*

**o·vi·duct** /ˈəʊvɪdʌkt‖ˈoʊvə-/ *n* [C] *technical* one of the two tubes in a female through which eggs pass to the WOMB

**o·vip·a·rous** /əʊˈvɪpərəs‖oʊ-/ *adj technical* an animal, fish, bird etc that is oviparous produces eggs that develop outside its body

**o·void** /ˈəʊvɔɪd‖ˈoʊ-/ *adj* shaped like an egg —**ovoid** *n* [C]

**ov·u·late** /ˈɒvjɡleɪt‖ˈɑːv-/ *v* [I] when a woman or female animal ovulates, she produces eggs inside her body —**ovulation** /ˌɒvjɡˈleɪʃən‖ˌɑːv-/ *n* [U]

**o·vum** /ˈəʊvəm‖ˈoʊ-/ *n plural* **ova** /ˈəʊvə‖ˈoʊ-/ [C] *technical* an egg, especially one that develops inside the mother's body

**ow** /aʊ/ *interjection* used to express sudden pain: *"Ow, that hurts!"*

S2 W3 **owe** /əʊ‖oʊ/ *v* [T]
**1 ▶ MONEY ◀** to have to pay someone for something that they have done for you or sold to you, or to have to give someone back money that they have lent you: **owe sb sth** *I owe my brother $50.* | **owe sb for sth** *We still owe the garage for those repairs.* | **owe sth** *How much do you owe?*
**2 ▶ STH DONE/GIVEN ◀** to feel that you should do something for someone, give someone something etc because they have done something for you or given something to you: **owe sb a drink/letter etc** *I'll write and tell Marie; I owe her a letter anyway.* | **owe sb a favour**: *One of the neighbours owes me a favor, I'm sure they'll take care of the cat.* | **I owe you one** (=used when saying thank you, when they have helped you and you are willing to help them) *Thanks a lot for being so understanding about all this – I owe you one!* | **owe sb** *informal* be in a position in which someone has helped you, so that you should help them: *Let's go and see Joe – he owes me!*
**3 owe sb an explanation/apology** to feel that you should give someone an explanation of why you did something, or say you are sorry: *"I owe you an apology, Margaret," he said sheepishly.*
**4 ▶ STH YOU HAVE/ACHIEVE ◀ a)** to have something or achieve something because of what someone else has done: **owe sth to sb** *Helena probably owed her rapid recovery to her husband's devoted care.* | **owe sb sth** *I knew that I owed Shanklin my life.* **b)** to know that someone's help has been important to you in achieving something: **owe sb a lot/owe sb a great deal** *"I owe my parents a lot," he admitted.* | *He owes a great deal to his publishers.* | **owe it all to/owe everything to** *I owe it all to you.* | **owe sb a debt (of gratitude)** *the debt that we owe to our teachers*
**5 owe it to sb to do sth** to feel you should do something for someone because they have helped you or given you support: *You owe it to your supporters not to give up now.*
**6 owe it to yourself to do sth** to feel you should try to achieve something because it is what you deserve: *You owe it to yourself to take some time off.*
**7 ▶ GOOD EFFECT ◀** to be successful because of the good effect of something: *Their success owes more to good luck than to careful management.*
**8 owe loyalty/allegiance etc** to have a duty to obey someone: *From then on English and Scottish citizens owed allegiance to the same king.*
**9 think that the world owes you a living** to be unwilling to work in order to get things, and expect them to be provided for you

**ow·ing** /ˈəʊɪŋ‖ˈoʊ-/ *adj* **1** [not before noun] *especially BrE* if money is owing, it has not yet been paid to the person who should receive it: *There's still over £100 owing to the bank.* **2 owing to** because of: *Owing to a lack of funds, the project will not continue next year.*

**USAGE NOTE: OWING**

WORD CHOICE: **owing to, due to, because of, thanks to**

**Owing to** is less common in spoken English than **due to**, but both are slightly formal and are often used in official notices or public statements: *All flights into London Heathrow have been delayed due to/owing to thick fog.*

You would usually use **because of** in spoken English: *All the flights have been delayed because of fog.*

**Thanks to** is not formal and is used especially to explain why or how something good has happened: *Thanks to the public's generosity, we've been able to build two new schools in the area.*

GRAMMAR

You do not use **owing to** directly after the verb **to be**, but with other verbs.

Some people think **due to** should only be used after the verb **to be**, but many people use it with other verbs as well: *The accident was largely due to human error.* | *Prices have risen due to an increase in demand.*

**owl** /aʊl/ *n* [C] a bird with large eyes that hunts at night

**owl·et** /ˈaʊlɡt/ *n* [C] a young owl

**owl·ish** /ˈaʊlɪʃ/ *adj* looking like an owl and seeming serious and clever: *Professor Jay looked owlish in his horn-rimmed spectacles.* —**owlishly** *adv*

**own¹** /əʊn‖oʊn/ *determiner, pron* **1** belonging to you and no one else: **your own house/car etc** *He was so drunk he even forgot his own name.* | *He tells people how to bring up their children but is so lenient with his own.* | **a house/car etc of your own** *He left the company to start a business of his own.* | **your very own** (=used to add emphasis) *When you grow up you can have your very own room.* **2** done or caused without the help or influence of someone else: *Why buy clothes when you can make your own more cheaply?* | *You've got to learn to make your own decisions.* | *It's your own fault for leaving the window open.* **3 get your own back (on sb)** *informal* to get REVENGE¹ (1) for something someone has done to you: *All I wanted was to get my own back on my stepfather for* S1 W1 *punishing me.* **4 (all) on your own** **a)** alone: *I've been living on my own for four years now.* **b)** without anyone's help: *I made this wardrobe all on my own.* —see graph at ALONE[1] **5 be your own man/woman** to have your opinions and not be influenced by others —see also **come into your own** (COME[1]), **hold your own** (HOLD[1] (39))

> **USAGE NOTE: OWN**
> GRAMMAR
> You use **own** only after possessive words like *my, John's, the company's*, etc: *He has his own room/a room of his own.*
> **Own** can be made stronger by adding **very**: *He has his very own room/a room of his very own.*

S2 W2 **own**[2] *v* [T not in progressive] **1** to have something when it is legally yours, especially because you have bought it, been given it etc: *Who owns that beautiful house?|Mr Silver owned a large printing firm.* **2 behave as if you own the place** also **act like you own the place** *informal* to behave in a way that is too confident and upsets other people: *She's only been here five minutes and she's already acting like she owns the place!* **3** *old-fashioned* to admit that something is true: **own (that)** *I own that I judged her harshly at first.*|[+ **to**] *I must own to a feeling of anxiety.*

**own up** *phr v* [I] to admit that you have done something wrong, especially something that is not serious: *Unless the guilty person owns up, the whole class will be punished.*| **own up to sth/to doing sth** *No one owned up to breaking the window.*

**own brand** /ˌ· ˈ·◂/ *adj BrE* own brand goods are specially produced and sold by particular shops and have the name of the shop on them; STORE BRAND *AmE*: *Sainsbury's own brand tomato sauce*

S2 W2 **own·er** /ˈəʊnə‖ˈoʊnər/ *n* [C] someone who owns something: [+ **of**] *I met the owner of the local hotel.*|**the proud owner of** *the proud owner of a bright red sports car*|**car-owner/dog-owner etc** *Dog-owners have been warned to keep their animals under control.*|**home-owner** (=someone who owns their house)

**owner-oc·cu·pied** /ˌ·· ˈ···◂/ *adj* houses, apartments etc that are owner-occupied are lived in by the people who own them: *Most of these properties are owner-occupied.*

**owner-oc·cu·pi·er** /ˌ·· ˈ····/ *n* [C] someone who owns the house or apartment etc that they live in

S3 W3 **own·er·ship** /ˈəʊnəʃɪp‖ˈoʊnər-/ *n* [U] the fact of owning something: *a dispute over the ownership of the land*

**own goal** /ˌ· ˈ·/ *n* [C] *BrE* **1** a GOAL that you accidentally SCORE[2] (1) against your own team without intending to in a game of football, HOCKEY etc **2** *informal* an action or remark that has the opposite effect from what you intended: *the minister's spectacular own goal when he admitted that his own department had leaked the document*

**own la·bel** /ˌ· ˈ··◂/ *adj* [U] *BrE* OWN BRAND

**ox** /ɒks‖ɑːks/ *n plural* **oxen** /ˈɒksən‖ˈɑːk-/ [C] **1** a BULL whose sex organs have been removed, often used for working on farms etc **2** a large cow or BULL

**Ox·bridge** /ˈɒksˌbrɪdʒ‖ˈɑːks-/ *n* [U] the universities of Oxford and Cambridge —compare REDBRICK

**ox·cart** /ˈɒkskɑːt‖ˈɑːkskɑːrt/ *n* [C] a vehicle pulled by oxen

**ox-eye** /ˈ· ·/ *n* [C] a yellow flower like a DAISY

**Ox·fam** /ˈɒksfæm‖ˈɑːks-/ *n* [singular] the Oxford Committee for Famine Relief; a British CHARITY organization that aims to help people in poor countries

**ox·ford** /ˈɒksfəd‖ˈɑːksfərd/ *n AmE* **1** [C] a type of shirt made of thick cotton **2 oxfords** [plural] a type of leather shoes that fasten with SHOELACES

**ox·ide** /ˈɒksaɪd‖ˈɑːk-/ *n* [C,U] *technical* a chemical compound in which another substance is combined with oxygen: *iron oxide*

**ox·i·dize** also **-ise** *BrE* /ˈɒksɪ̣daɪz‖ˈɑːk-/ *v* [I,T] *technical* to combine with oxygen, or make something combine with oxygen, especially in a way that causes RUST —**oxidation** /ˌɒksɪ̣ˈdeɪʃən‖ˌɑːk-/ also **oxidization** /ˌɒksɪ̣daɪˈzeɪʃən‖ˌɑːksədə-/ *n* [U]

**Ox·on** /ˈɒksɒn‖ˈɑːksɑːn/ used after the title of a degree from Oxford University: *David Jones, BA (Oxon)*

**ox·tail** /ˈɒksteɪl‖ˈɑːks-/ *n* [U] the meat from the tails of cattle, used especially in soup: *oxtail soup*

**ox·y·a·cet·y·lene** /ˌɒksiəˈsetəliːn◂‖ˌɑːksiəˈsetl-iːn◂, -ən◂/ *n* [U] *technical* a mixture of oxygen and ACETYLENE that produces a hot white flame that can cut steel

**ox·y·gen** /ˈɒksɪdʒən‖ˈɑːk-/ *n* [U] a gas with no colour, smell, or taste, that is present in air and is necessary for most animals and plants to live

**ox·y·gen·ate** /ˈɒksɪdʒəneɪt‖ˈɑːk-/ *v* [T] *technical* to add oxygen to something —**oxygenation** /ˌɒksɪdʒɪ̣ˈneɪʃən‖ˌɑːk-/ *n* [U]

**oxygen mask** /ˈ··· ·/ *n* [C] a piece of equipment that fits over someone's mouth and nose to provide them with oxygen

**oxygen tent** /ˈ··· ·/ *n* [C] a piece of equipment shaped like a tent that is put around people who are very ill in hospital, to provide them with oxygen

**ox·y·mo·ron** /ˌɒksiˈmɔːrɒn‖ˌɑːksiˈmɔːrɑːn/ *n* [C] *technical* a deliberate combination of two words that seem to mean the opposite of each other, such as 'cruel kindness'

**o·yez** /əʊˈjez‖oʊ-/ *interjection* a word used by law officials or by TOWN CRIERS in the past to get people's attention

**oy·ster** /ˈɔɪstə‖-ər/ *n* [C] **1** a type of SHELLFISH that can be eaten cooked or uncooked, and that produces a jewel called a PEARL (1) —see picture at SHELL[1] **2 the world is your oyster** used to tell someone that they can achieve whatever they want

**oyster bed** /ˈ·· ·/ *n* [C] an area at the bottom of the sea where oysters live

**oyster-catch·er** /ˈ·· ˌ··/ *n* [C] a black and white bird that eats SHELLFISH

**Oz** /ɒz‖ɑːz/ *n BrE, AustrE informal* Australia

**oz** the written abbreviation of OUNCE or ounces

**o·zone** /ˈəʊzəʊn‖ˈoʊzoʊn/ *n* [U] **1** *technical* a poisonous blue gas that is a type of oxygen **2** *informal* air near the sea, thought to be fresher and healthier

**ozone-friend·ly** /ˌ·· ˈ··◂/ *adj* not containing chemicals that damage the ozone layer: *an ozone-friendly aerosol*

**ozone lay·er** /ˈ·· ˌ··/ *n* [singular] a layer of gases that prevents harmful RADIATION (2) from the sun from reaching the Earth: *CFCs, the chemicals responsible for the hole in the ozone layer.*

**P,p** /piː/ *plural* **P's, p's** *n*[C] the 16th letter of the English alphabet —see also **mind your p's and q's** (MIND[2] (7))

**p** **1** the written abbreviation of page **2** *BrE* pence or PENNY: *'The Times' now costs only 30p.* **3** the written abbreviation of PARTICIPLE **4** the written abbreviation of population **5** used in written music to show that a part should be played or sung quietly

**p & p** the written abbreviation of **postage and packing:** *Please send 20p to cover p & p.*

**PA** /ˌpiː ˈeɪ/ *n* **1** [C, usually singular] public address system; a set of electronically controlled pieces of equipment that makes someone's voice loud enough to be heard by large groups of people **2** [C] *BrE* personal assistant; a special secretary who looks after the affairs of just one person

**p.a.** the written abbreviation of PER ANNUM

**pa** /pɑː/ *n* [C] *old-fashioned* a word meaning 'father' used by or to children

W3 **pace[1]** /peɪs/ *n*

**1 ▶ WALK/RUN ◀** [singular] the speed at which you walk or run: *They've run the first mile in under six minutes – can they keep up this pace?* | **at a steady/gentle/brisk pace** *The troops marched at a steady pace.*

**2 ▶ SPEED STH HAPPENS ◀** [singular] the rate or speed at which something happens or at which someone does something: **[+ of]** *The pace of change in Eastern Europe has been breathtaking.* | **at your own pace** (=at the pace that suits you) *He liked to work at his own pace.*

**3 ▶ A STEP ◀** [C] a single step when you are running or walking, or the distance moved in one step: *I moved forward a couple of paces.*

**4 force the pace** to make something happen or develop more quickly than it would do normally: *Gorbachev favoured gradual reform and felt it was dangerous to force the pace.*

**5 keep pace (with)** to move or change as fast as someone or something else: *She followed Bobby, barely keeping pace with him.* | *Pensions and benefits have failed to keep pace with the rate of inflation.*

**6 put sb/sth through their paces** to make a person or a machine show how well they can do something: *a series of tests to put candidates through their paces*

**7 set the pace a)** to establish a speed at which others try to do something, or a quality they to try to achieve: *Japanese firms have been setting the pace in electronic engineering.* **b)** to run at a speed that other runners try to keep to, at the beginning of a race

**8 stand the pace** to be able to deal with situations where you are very busy and have to think and act very quickly: *If you can stand the pace, working in advertising pays well.*

**9 show your paces** to show your skill or speed in an activity

**10 the pace of life** the amount of activity in people's lives and how busy they are: *The pace of life in the village was slow and restful.*

**11 ▶ HORSE ◀** [C] one of the ways that a horse walks or runs

**pace[2]** *v* **1** [I always + adv/prep, T] to walk with slow, regular, steady steps, usually backwards and forwards: **pace up and down** *He paced nervously up and down the hospital room, waiting for news.* | **pace the floor/room etc** *Ben stood up and paced the floor, deep in thought.* —see picture on page 1262 **2 pace yourself a)** to set a controlled regular speed for yourself, especially in a race: *I paced myself so that I was not too far ahead of the others.* **b)** to do something at a steady speed without rushing **3 pace someone** to set a speed for someone running or riding, especially in a race **4** also **pace off, pace out** [T] to measure a distance by taking steps of an equal length: *The director paced out the length of the stage.*

**pace·mak·er** /ˈpeɪsˌmeɪkə‖-ər/ *n* [C] a small machine that is fixed inside someone's chest in order to make weak or irregular beats of the heart regular

**pace·set·ter** /ˈpeɪs-setə‖-ər/ *n* [C] **1** a team that is ahead of others in a competition **2** someone or something that sets an example for others: *Industry is the pacesetter of modern life.* **3** someone who runs at the front at the beginning of a race and sets the speed at which others must run

**pach·y·derm** /ˈpækɪdɜːm‖-dɜːrm/ *n* [C] *technical* a thick-skinned animal such as an elephant or a RHINOCEROS

**pa·cif·ic** /pəˈsɪfɪk/ *adj literary* **1** peaceful or loving peace: *a normally pacific community* **2** helping to cause peace —**pacifically** /-kli/ *adv*

**Pacific Rim** /ˌ·ˌ·· ˈ·/ *n* **the Pacific Rim (countries)** the countries or parts of countries that border the Pacific Ocean, such as Japan, Australia, and the west coast of the US, considered as an economic group

**pac·i·fi·er** /ˈpæsɪ̇faɪə‖-faɪr/ *n* [C] **1** *AmE* a specially shaped rubber object that you give a baby to suck so that it does not cry; DUMMY[1] (3) *BrE* **2** something that makes people calm

**pac·i·fis·m** /ˈpæsɪ̇fɪzəm/ *n* [U] the belief that all wars and all forms of violence are wrong

**pac·i·fist** /ˈpæsɪ̇fɪ̇st/ *n* [C] someone who believes that all wars are wrong and who refuses to use violence

**pac·i·fy** /ˈpæsɪ̇faɪ/ *v* [T] **1** to make someone calm, quiet, and satisfied after they have been angry or upset: *Gregory knew his wife would be furious and he was trying to think how to pacify her.* **2** to bring peace to an area or to end war in a place: *It was hoped the new ruler could pacify the region.* —**pacification** /ˌpæsɪ̇fɪ̇ˈkeɪʃən/ *n* [U]

pack

S W **pack[1]** /pæk/ *v*

**1 ▶ IN BOXES, CASES ETC ◀** also **pack up** [I,T] to put things into cases, boxes etc for taking somewhere or storing: *I forgot to pack my razor.* | *They packed up the contents of their house.* | *We're off to Greece tomorrow and I haven't even started packing yet.* | **pack sb sth** *Have you packed the kids a lunch?*

**2 pack a bag/case etc** to put things into a bag, case etc: *She packed her suitcase and headed for the airport.* —opposite UNPACK (1)

**3 ▶ CROWD OF PEOPLE ◀** [I always + adv/prep, T always + adv/prep] to go in large numbers into a space that is not big enough, or to make a lot of people or things do this: **[+ into/in/onto]** *When the door was opened people began to pack into the hall.* | *They packed as many people as possible onto the bus.*

**4 ▶ PROTECT STH ◀** [T] to cover, fill, or surround an object closely with a protective material: *Pack the newspaper around the china so that it doesn't break.* | **[+ in/with]** *china cups packed with paper*

**5 pack your bags** *informal* to leave a place and not return, especially because of a disagreement: *Why don't you pack your bags and find another job?*

**6 ▶ SNOW/SOIL ETC ◀** [T] to press soil, sand etc into a firm mass: *pack soil firmly around the stem*
**7 ▶ MEAT ETC ◀** [T] to prepare food and put it into containers for preserving or selling
**8 pack a committee/jury/meeting etc** [T] to secretly and dishonestly arrange for a committee etc to be filled with people who support you
**9 pack a gun** *AmE* to regularly carry a gun
**10 pack a (hard) punch** *informal* **a)** to be able to hit another person hard in a fight **b)** to be able to speak very effectively in an argument or discussion —see also **send sb packing** (SEND (9))

**pack** sth ↔ **away** *phr v* [T] to put something back in a box, case etc where it is usually kept: *We packed away the picnic things.*

**pack** sb/sth ↔ **in** *phr v* [T] **1** *informal* to attract people in large numbers: *"Pulp Fiction" is really packing them in.* **2** also **pack** sth **into** sth to fit a lot of something into a space, place, or period of time: *They packed so much into their holiday, they returned exhausted.* **3** *informal especially BrE* to stop doing something, especially a job that you find unpleasant or annoying: *At times like this I feel like packing it all in and going off travelling.* **4 pack it in** *spoken* used to tell someone to stop doing something that is annoying you: *Pack it in you two. I'm tired of hearing you arguing.* **5** *BrE informal* to end a romantic relationship with someone

**pack** sb/sth **off** *phr v* [T] *informal* to send someone away quickly, to avoid trouble or because you want to get rid of them: *My parents packed us off to camp every summer.*

**pack up** *phr v* **1** [I] *informal* to finish work: *Business was slack and she packed up early.* **2** [I] *informal especially BrE* if a machine packs up it stops working: *The engine's packed up!* **3** [T] *informal BrE* to stop doing something such as a job: *He's packed up his job after only three months.*

S2 W3 **pack²** *n* [C]
**1 ▶ THINGS WRAPPED TOGETHER ◀** several things wrapped or tied together or put in a case, to make them easy to carry, sell, or give to someone: *Send away for your free information pack today.* —see also SIX-PACK
**2 ▶ SMALL CONTAINER ◀** *especially AmE* a small container, usually made of paper, with a set of things in it; PACKET¹ (1,2) [+ **of**] *a pack of cigarettes* | *a pack of gum* *BrE* —see picture at CONTAINER
**3 ▶ BAG ◀** [C] *BrE* a bag carried by a climber, walker, or soldier, that is fastened to their shoulders and is used to carry equipment, clothes etc
**4 ▶ ANIMALS ◀** a group of wild animals that hunt together, or a group of dogs trained together for hunting: *a wolf pack* | *a pack of hounds*
**5 ▶ GROUP OF PEOPLE ◀** a group of people who do something together, especially a group who you do not approve of: *a pack of thieves* | *the Hollywood brat pack*
**6 ▶ MILITARY ◀** a group of aircraft, SUBMARINES, etc that fight the enemy together
**7 be a pack of lies** *informal* to be completely untrue: *Don't you believe what it says in the paper – it's a pack of lies.*
**8 ▶ CARDS ◀** a complete set of PLAYING CARDS: *Please shuffle the pack and deal.*
**9 Cub/Brownie pack** a group of children belonging to a children's organization —see CUB SCOUT, BROWNIE
**10 ▶ ON A WOUND ◀** a thick mass of soft cloth that you press on a wound to stop the flow of blood; COMPRESS² —see also ICE PACK
**11 ▶ BEAUTY TREATMENT ◀** a substance, often a special mud or clay, that you put on your skin to make you feel better —see also FACE PACK, MUDPACK

S2 W2 **pack·age¹** /ˈpækɪdʒ/ *n* [C] **1** an amount of something, or several things, packed together firmly and wrapped in paper etc; PARCEL¹ (1): [+ **of**] *Can you deliver a large package of books?* **2** *AmE* the box, bag etc that foods are put in for selling **3** a set of related things or services sold or offered together: *a new software package* | *The bank is offering a special financial package for students.*

**package²** also **package up** *v* [T] **1** to make something into a package or tie it up as a package: *She packaged up the clothes to send to her daughter.* **2** to put something in a special package ready to be sold

**pack·aged** /ˈpækɪdʒd/ *adj* specially wrapped and put in a container for selling: *The soap was beautifully packaged in a special gift box.*

**package deal** /ˈ·· ·/ *n* [C] an offer or agreement that includes several things that must all be accepted together

**package hol·i·day** /ˈ·· ˌ···/ *n* [C] *BrE* a package tour

**package store** /ˈ·· ·/ *n* [C] *AmE old-fashioned* a store where alcohol is sold; OFF LICENCE *BrE*

**package tour** /ˈ·· ·/ *n* [C] a completely planned holiday arranged by a company at a fixed price, which includes travel, hotels, meals etc

**pack·ag·ing** /ˈpækɪdʒɪŋ/ *n* [U] **1** material used to cover a product that is sold in a shop: *Packaging adds to the cost of food.* **2** [U] the process of wrapping food for sale: *Prepacked bacon carries the date of packaging.* **3** a way of making a plan or a politician seem better than they are: *the imaginative packaging of an unacceptable tax*

**pack an·i·mal** /ˈ· ˌ···/ *n* [C] an animal, such as a horse, used for carrying heavy loads

**packed** /pækt/ *adj* **1** extremely full of people: *a packed dance floor* **2 packed with/packed full of** containing a lot of a particular kind of thing*a new magazine packed with exciting recipes* **3** [not before noun] if you are packed, you have put everything you need into boxes or cases before going somewhere **4 loosely packed** packed without being pressed closely together: *loosely packed cigarettes* **5 tightly packed** pressed into a small space: *tightly packed fibres*

**packed lunch** /ˌ· ˈ·/ *n* [C] *BrE* a cold meal of SANDWICHES, fruit etc packed into a box

**packed out** /ˌ· ˈ·/ *adj* [not before noun] *informal* a cinema, restaurant etc that is packed out is completely full

**pack·er** /ˈpækə‖-ər/ *n* [C] someone who works in a factory, preparing food and putting it into containers

**pack·et** /ˈpækɪt/ *n* [C] **1** *BrE* a small container, usually made of paper, with several things of the same kind in it; PACK *AmE*: [+ **of**] *a packet of envelopes* | *a packet of cigarettes* **2** a very small packet like an envelope: *a packet of seeds* —see picture at CONTAINER **3 cost a packet** *BrE informal* to cost a lot of money: *That car cost me a packet.* **4** a packet boat **5 catch/cop/get/stop a packet** *BrE old-fashioned* to get into serious trouble or receive a severe punishment S2

**packet boat** /ˈ··· ·/ *n* [C] *old-fashioned* a boat that carries mail and usually passengers at regular times

**packet-switch·ing** /ˈ·· ˌ··/ *n* [C] a method of sending DATA (=information stored on a computer) on telephone lines, that breaks long messages into pieces and puts them together again when they are received

**pack horse** /ˈ· ·/ *n* [C] a horse used for carrying heavy loads

**pack ice** /ˈ· ·/ *n* [U] sea ice in a large floating mass

**pack·ing** /ˈpækɪŋ/ *n* [U] **1** the act of putting things into cases or boxes so that you can send or take them somewhere: **do the packing** *I'll do my packing the night before we leave.* **2** paper, plastic, cloth etc used for packing things

**packing case** /ˈ·· ·/ *n* [C] a large strong wooden box in which things are packed to be sent somewhere or stored

**pack rat** /ˈ· ·/ *n* [C] *AmE* someone who collects and stores things that they do not really need

**pack sad·dle** /ˈ· ˌ··/ *n* [C] a SADDLE¹ (1) that you fasten bags to so that a horse or other animal can carry them

**pack trip** /ˈ· ·/ *n* [C] *AmE* a trip through the countryside on horses, for fun or as a sport; PONY-TREKKING *BrE*

**pact** /pækt/ *n* [C] a formal agreement between two groups, nations, or people, especially to help each other or fight together against an enemy: **make/sign a pact** *The two countries signed a non-aggression pact.* | **a pact to do sth**

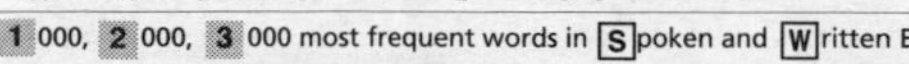

*an electoral pact to keep out the Fascists* —see also SUICIDE PACT

S3 **pad¹** /pæd/ *n* [C]
**1 ▶ SOFT MATERIAL ◀** something made of or filled with soft material, that is used to protect something or make it more comfortable: *She put a sterile pad of cotton over the wound.* | *a foam rubber pad* | **knee/elbow/shoulder pad** (=a pad sewn into someone's clothes to protect their knee etc or make them look bigger)
**2 ▶ PAPER ◀** several sheets of paper fastened together, used for writing letters, drawing pictures etc: *a writing pad*
**3 ▶ ANIMAL'S FOOT ◀** the flesh on the bottom of the foot of a cat, dog, etc

**4 ▶ APARTMENT ◀** *informal* a room or apartment where someone lives: *a bachelor pad in Mayfair*
**5 ▶ QUIET SOUND ◀** [singular] a soft sound made by someone walking quietly: *I heard the pad and squeak of footsteps in the snow.*
**6 ▶ WATER PLANT ◀** *technical* the large floating leaf of some water plants such as the WATER LILY
**7 ▶ FOR WOMEN ◀** a soft material like paper, worn by a woman during her PERIOD¹ (4) to take up the blood
**8 ▶ FOR INK ◀** a piece of material that has been made wet with ink and is used for covering a STAMP² (1) with ink; INK PAD —see also LAUNCH PAD, HELICOPTER PAD

**pad²** *v* **padded, padding** **1** [I always + adv/prep] to walk softly and quietly: *The boy's dog padded after him.* **2** [T] to protect something, shape it, or make it more comfortable by covering or filling it with soft material. **3** [T] *AmE* to dishonestly make bills more expensive than they really are: *padding the bills of medicare patients*
**pad** sth ↔ **out** *phr v* [T] to make a sentence, speech etc longer by adding unnecessary words: *The last two chapters are padded out with boring stories.*

**pad·ded** /ˈpædɪ̈d/ *adj* something that is padded is filled or covered with a soft material to make it thicker or more comfortable: *a jacket with padded shoulders*

**padded cell** /ˌ·· ˈ·/ *n* [C] a special room with thick, soft walls in a MENTAL HOSPITAL, used to stop people who are being violent from hurting themselves

**pad·ding** /ˈpædɪŋ/ *n* [U] **1** soft material used to fill or cover something to make it softer or more comfortable **2** unnecessary words that are added to make a sentence, speech etc longer

**pad·dle¹** /ˈpædl/ *n* [C] **1** a short pole that is wide and flat at one end or both ends, used for moving a small boat along —compare OAR —see picture at CANOE **2** [singular] *BrE* the action of walking about in water which is not very deep: **have a paddle/go for a paddle** *I'm just going for a quick paddle to cool my feet down.* **3** *AmE* a small round BAT¹ (2b) with a short handle, used for hitting the ball in TABLE TENNIS **4** one of the wide blades on the wheel of a PADDLE STEAMER **5** a tool like a flat spoon, used for mixing food: *a paddle for making the butter* **6** *AmE* a piece of wood with a handle, used for hitting a child to punish them —see also DOG PADDLE

**paddle²** *v* **paddled, paddling** **1** [I,T] to move a small light boat through water, using one or more paddles: [+ **along/upstream/towards**] *We got out the canoe and paddled upstream.* | **paddle sth** *They paddled the canoe across the lake.* —compare ROW³ —see picture on page 1262 **2** [I] *BrE* to walk about in water that is not very deep: *The children paddled in the sea.* **3** [I] to swim by moving your hands and feet up and down **4** [T] *AmE informal* to hit a child with a piece of wood as a punishment **5 paddle your own canoe** *informal* to depend on yourself and no one else

**paddle boat** /ˈ·· ·/ *n* [C] a paddle steamer

**paddle steam·er** /ˈ·· ˌ··/ *n* [C] *BrE* a STEAMBOAT (=a large boat driven by steam) which is pushed forward by two large wheels at the sides; SIDE-WHEEL *AmE*

**paddle ten·nis** /ˈ·· ˌ··/ *n* [U] *AmE* TABLE TENNIS

**paddling pool** /ˈ·· ·/ *n* [C] *BrE* **1** a small pool, which is not very deep, for children to play in **2** a plastic container that is filled with water, for small children to play in; WADING POOL *AmE*

**pad·dock** /ˈpædək/ *n* [C] **1** a small field near a house or STABLE in which horses are kept or exercised **2** a place where horses are brought together before a race so that people can look at them **3** *AustrE, NZE* a field, especially one with grass

**Pad·dy** /ˈpædi/ *n* [C] *informal* a joking word for an Irishman, that is often considered offensive

**pad·dy** /ˈpædi/ *n* [C] **1 be in a paddy** *BrE* to be in a bad temper **2** a paddy field

**paddy field** /ˈ·· ·/ *n* [C] a field in which rice is grown in water; RICE PADDY

**paddy wag·on** /ˈ·· ˌ··/ *n* [C] *AmE informal* a police vehicle

**pad·lock** /ˈpædlɒk‖-lɑːk/ *n* [C] a small lock that you can put on a door, cupboard, bicycle etc —**padlock** *v* [T]

**pa·dre** /ˈpɑːdri, -reɪ/ *n* [C] *informal* a priest, especially one in the army —see PRIEST (USAGE)

**pae·an** /ˈpiːən/ *n* [C] *literary* a happy song of praise, thanks, or victory

**paed·e·rast** *BrE,* **pederast** *AmE* /ˈpedəræst/ *n* [C] *technical* a man who has sex with a boy —**paederasty** *n* [U]

**pae·di·a·tri·cian** *BrE,* **pediatrician** *AmE* /ˌpiːdiəˈtrɪʃən/ *n* [C] a doctor who looks after children and treats their illnesses

**pae·di·at·rics** *BrE,* **pediatrics** *AmE* /ˌpiːdiˈætrɪks/ *n* [U] the branch of medicine connected with children and their illnesses —**paediatric** *adj: a pediatric hospital*

**pae·do·phile** *BrE,* **pedophile** *AmE* /ˈpiːdəfaɪl/ *n* [C] someone who is sexually attracted to young children

**pa·el·la** /paɪˈelə‖pɑː-/ *n* [U] a Spanish dish of rice cooked with pieces of meat, fish, and vegetables

**pa·gan¹** /ˈpeɪgən/ *adj* pagan religious beliefs and customs do not belong to any of the main religions of the world, and may come from a time before these religions: *Christmas is held around the time of an old pagan festival.*

**pagan²** *n* [C] **1** someone who believes in a pagan religion **2** *humorous* someone who has few or no religious beliefs —**paganism** *n* [U]

**page¹** /peɪdʒ/ *n* [C] S W
**1 ▶ PAPER ◀** one side of a sheet of paper in a book, newspaper etc, or the sheet of paper itself: *There's a picture on the next page.* | *I've made several pages of notes.* | *an eight-page booklet* | **front/back page** (=of a newspaper) *The story was all over the front page.* | **see/turn to page 5/20 etc** *See page 5 for further details.* | **turn a page** *idly turning the pages* | **the opposite/facing page** *the diagram on the facing page* | **over the page** (=on the next page) | **the sports pages/the fashion page etc** (=part of a newspaper) | **a blank page** (=a page that is empty)
**2 ▶ COMPUTER ◀ a)** a piece of TEXT (=writing) or a picture on a computer screen that will fill one side of a piece of paper when it is printed **b)** all the text that can be seen at one time on a computer screen
**3 ▶ BOY ◀** a PAGEBOY (1,2)
**4 ▶ MIDDLE AGES ◀** a boy who served a KNIGHT during the Middle Ages as part of his training to become a knight himself
**5 ▶ STUDENT ◀** *AmE* a student who works as a helper to a member of the US Congress
**6 page in history** an important event or period of time: *a significant page in our country's history*
**7 ▶ SERVANT ◀** *old use* a boy who is a servant to a person of high rank

**page²** *v* [T] **1** to call someone's name out in a public place, especially using a LOUDSPEAKER, in order to find them: *I couldn't find Jenny at the airport, so I had her paged.* **2** to call someone by sending a message to their PAGER (=a small machine they carry that receives signals) *If you need me for anything, just page me.*
**page through** sth *phr v* [T] *AmE* to look at a book, magazine etc: *paging through old newspapers*

**pag·eant** /ˈpædʒənt/ *n* **1** [C] a public show or ceremony, often performed outdoors, with people dressed in beautifully decorated clothes or actors acting historical scenes **2** [singular] *literary* history or a continuous series of events that are interesting and impressive: *the dramatic pageant of life in the upland valleys* **3** [C] *AmE* a public competition for young women in which their appearance, and sometimes other qualities, are compared and judged; BEAUTY CONTEST **4** [U] behaviour or ceremonies which look impressive or grand, but have no real meaning

**pag·eant·ry** /ˈpædʒəntri/ *n* [U] impressive ceremonies or events, involving many people wearing special clothes: *the pageantry of a military ceremony*

**page·boy** /ˈpeɪdʒbɔɪ/ *n* [C] **1** *BrE* a boy chosen to help a BRIDE as part of a wedding ceremony **2** *old-fashioned* a boy or young man employed in a hotel, club, theatre etc to deliver messages, carry bags etc **3** a style of cutting women's hair in which the hair is cut fairly short and has its ends turned under

**pag·er** /ˈpeɪdʒə‖-ər/ *n* [C] a small machine that you carry in a pocket, that makes short high noises to tell the person who is wearing it that they must telephone someone

**pa·gi·na·tion** /ˌpædʒəˈneɪʃən/ *n* [U] *technical* the process of giving a number to each page of a book, magazine etc —**paginate** /ˈpædʒəneɪt/ *v* [T]

**pa·go·da** /pəˈgəʊdə‖-ˈgoʊ-/ *n* [C] a Buddhist TEMPLE that has several levels with a decorated roof at each level

**pah** /pɑː/ *interjection* used to show that you disapprove strongly of something

S2 **paid** /peɪd/ the past tense and past participle of PAY —see also **put paid to sth** (PUT (19))

**paid-up** /ˌ· ˈ·◂/ *adj* **1 paid-up member** someone who has paid the money necessary to be a member of a club, political party etc **2 a fully paid-up** used when saying that someone who is definitely a particular kind of person or a member of a particular group: *a fully paid-up heavy metal fan*

**pail** /peɪl/ *n* [C] *especially AmE* **1** a container with a handle for carrying liquids or used by children when playing on the beach: *a milk pail* | *The kids bought shovels and pails to the beach.* **2** also **pail·ful** /-fʊl/ the amount a pail will hold: *It takes about ten pails of water to fill the trough.*

**pail·lasse** /ˈpæliæs‖ˌpæliˈæs/ *n* [C] another spelling of PALLIASSE

S2 **pain¹** /peɪn/ *n*

W2 **1** ▶ **PHYSICAL** ◀ [C,U] the feeling you have when part of your body hurts: **be in pain** (=having a pain in part of your body) *Take these tablets if you're in pain.* | **feel pain** *We've given him an anaesthetic so he shouldn't feel any pain.* | **be in great pain** *Her face was contorted and she was clearly in great pain.* | **severe pain** *She started getting severe back pains and had to stay off work.* | **relieve pain** (=stop pain) *drugs to relieve the pain.* | **ease the pain** (=reduce the pain). | **a sharp pain** (=one that you feel very severely, usually for a short time). | **a dull pain** (=one that is not very strong but which continues for a long time). **have a pain in your chest/leg/back etc** *I've got a terrible pain in my left side.* | **labour pains** (=pain felt by women beginning to have a baby) —see also GROWING PAINS (1).

**2** ▶ **MENTAL** ◀ [C,U] emotional or mental suffering, or a particular experience of this suffering: *life with its pleasures and pains* | **cause (sb) pain/inflict pain on sb** *She hated to say the words, for fear of causing pain.*

**3 a pain in the ass/butt** *AmE* also **pain in the arse/backside** *BrE spoken* an impolite expression meaning someone or something extremely annoying: *What's wrong with Dave? He's becoming a total pain in the ass.*

**4 a pain** also **a pain in the neck** *spoken* someone or something that you have to do that is very annoying: *My commute to work is a real pain.* | *He's such a pain in the neck.*

**5 aches and pains** many small pains in various parts of your body: *everyday aches and pains increase*

**6 take pains to do sth** also **take pains with/over sth** to make a special effort to do something, or to be very careful in doing something: *Take pains to present a smart, efficient appearance.*

**7 be at pains to do sth** to be especially careful to do something, or try very hard to do something: *Major and Clinton were clearly at pains to avoid a row.*

**8 for your pains** used when saying that you got something, especially an unfairly small payment, as a reward for your efforts: *I drive them sixty miles, and I only get a fifty-cent tip for my pains!*

**9 on/under pain of death** at the risk of being killed as punishment: *You are sworn to keep the secret, on pain of death.*

This graph shows some of the words most commonly used with the noun **pain**.

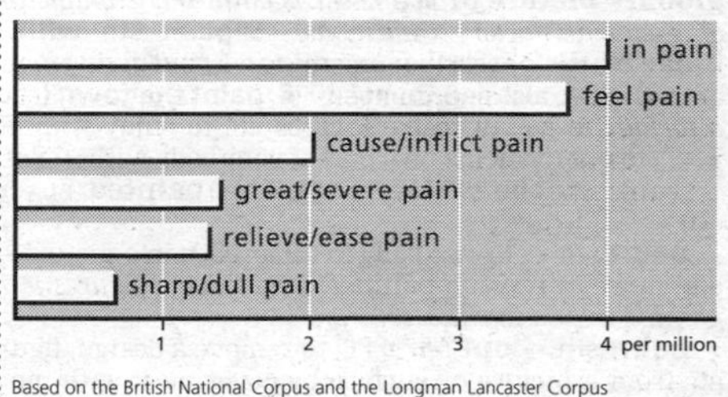


Based on the British National Corpus and the Longman Lancaster Corpus

**pain²** *v* [T] **1 it pains sb to do sth** *formal* it is very difficult and upsetting for someone to have to do something: *It pains me to leave you.* **2** *old use* if a part of your body pains you, it hurts

**pained** /peɪnd/ *adj* worried and upset: *Every time she saw us smoking, my mother got a pained look on her face.*

**pain·ful** /ˈpeɪnfəl/ *adj* **1** making you feel very upset, or very difficult and unpleasant for you: **be painful for sb (to do sth)** *It's still painful for her to talk about the divorce.* | **painful memories/experience** *Hearing about the war again brings back painful memories for many people.* | **painful decision/choice/task etc** *Wendy took the painful decision to switch off their son's life support system.* | **painful to watch/hear etc** *It was painful to hear those words.* **2** if part of your body is painful, you feel pain in it: *My leg's still really painful.* **3** causing physical pain: *painful cosmetic surgery* | *Brynner's excruciatingly painful death from cancer.* **4** very bad and embarrassing for other people to watch, hear etc: *The poor script and bad acting make the film painful to watch.* | *the boy's painful shyness* —**painfulness** *n* [U]

**pain·ful·ly** /ˈpeɪnfəli/ *adv* **1** with pain or causing pain: *The prince walked slowly and painfully.* | *The ball hit him painfully on the shin.* **2 painfully obvious/clear/evident** easy to see and disappointing or embarrassing: *It was becoming painfully obvious that I would never be a singer.* **3** with a lot of effort and trouble: *all the knowledge that he had so painfully acquired* | **painfully slow** *Progress in the negotiations has been painfully slow.* **4** in a way that makes you sad or upset: *the painfully early death of someone who was very close to her*

**pain·kill·er** /ˈpeɪnˌkɪlə‖-ər/ *n* [C] a medicine which reduces or removes pain

**pain·less** /ˈpeɪnləs/ *adj* **1** causing no pain: *A visit to the dentist should be quite painless.* **2** *informal* needing no effort or hard work: *a painless way to learn a foreign language* —**painlessly** *adv*

**pains·tak·ing** /ˈpeɪnzˌteɪkɪŋ/ *adj* very careful and thorough: *fourteen months of painstaking investigation* —**painstakingly** *adj*

**paint¹** /peɪnt/ *n* **1** [U] a liquid that you put on a surface to make it a particular colour: *a can of blue paint* | **a coat of paint** (=a layer of paint) *The whole house could do with* 

*a fresh coat of paint.* | **wet paint** (=used as a warning on a sign) **2 paints** [plural] a set of small tubes or dry blocks of coloured substance, used for painting pictures: *oil paints* **3** [U] *old-fashioned* MAKE-UP

S2 W3 **paint²** *v* **1** [I,T] to put paint on a surface: *I wear old clothes when I'm painting.* | *The ceiling needs painting.* | **paint sth blue/red/green etc** *We painted the door blue.* **2 a)** [T] to make a picture, design etc using paint: **paint a picture/portrait etc** *Turner is famous for painting landscapes.* **b)** [I] to use paint to make pictures or designs: **paint in oils/watercolours etc** (=using a particular kind of paint) *Jana likes to paint in watercolours.* **c)** [T] to make a picture of someone or something using paint: *I'll paint the view from the window.* **3** [T] to put a coloured substance on part of your face or body to make it more attractive: **paint your lips/fingernails etc** *Her lips and fingernails were painted bright red.* **4 paint a picture of sth** to describe something in a particular way: **paint a grim/rosy/gloomy picture of sth** *Dickens painted a grim picture of Victorian factory conditions.* **5 paint sth with a broad brush** to describe something without giving many details —see also BROADBRUSH **6 paint the town (red)** *informal* to go out to bars, clubs etc to enjoy yourself **7** [T] to put medicine on a part of your body with a brush —see also **not be as black as you are painted** (BLACK[1] (7))

**paint** sth ↔ **in** *phr v* [T] to fill a space in a picture or add more to it using paint: *The additional figures were painted in at a later date.*

**paint** sth ↔ **out** *phr v* [T] to remove a design, figure etc from a picture or surface by covering it with more paint: *On the side of the van the company name had been painted out.*

**paint** sth ↔ **over** *phr v* [T] to cover a picture or surface with new paint

**paint·box** /ˈpeɪntbɒks‖-bɑːks/ *n* [C] a small box containing dry blocks of paint that can be mixed with water

**paint·brush** /ˈpeɪntbrʌʃ/ *n* [C] a brush for spreading paint on a surface —see picture at BRUSH[1]

**paint·er** /ˈpeɪntə‖-ər/ *n* [C] **1** someone who paints pictures; ARTIST: *a landscape painter* | *a portrait painter* **2** someone whose job is painting houses, rooms etc **3** a rope for tying a small boat to a ship or to a post on land

**paint·er·ly** /ˈpeɪntəli‖-tər-/ *adj* typical of painters or painting: *painterly images*

S3 W2 **paint·ing** /ˈpeɪntɪŋ/ *n* **1** [C] a painted picture: *A large painting hung in the hallway.* **2** [U] the act of making a picture using paint: *I've always admired O'Keefe's style of painting.* **3** [U] the act of covering a wall, house etc with paint: *painting and decorating*

**paint strip·per** /ˈ· ˌ··/ *n* [U] a substance used to remove paint from walls, doors etc

**paint·work** /ˈpeɪntwɜːk‖-wɜːrk/ *n* [U] paint on a car, house etc: *the drab office with its faded paintwork and nicotine-stained ceiling*

S2 W2 **pair¹** /peə‖per/ *n plural* **pairs** or **pair** [C]

**1 ▶ TROUSERS ETC ◀** a single thing made of two similar parts that are joined together: **a pair of jeans/trousers/scissors/glasses etc** *Go put on a clean pair of jeans.* | *a new pair of sunglasses*

**2 ▶ SHOES ETC ◀** two things of the same kind that are used together: **a pair of shoes/socks/gloves etc** *three pairs of socks* | *a pair of candlesticks* | **a matching pair** (=two things that are exactly alike)

**3 in pairs** in groups of two: *OK class, get in pairs for the next activity.* | *earrings sold in pairs*

**4 ▶ TWO PEOPLE ◀** [singular] two people who are standing or doing something together, or are connected with each other in some way: [+ **of**] *a pair of dancers* | *a pair of scruffy kids*

**5 the pair of you/them** *BrE spoken* used when you are angry or annoyed: *Oh get out, the pair of you.* | *They're crooks, the pair of them.*

**6 ▶ TWO ANIMALS ◀** [singular] **a)** two animals, one male and one female, that come together to have sex: [+ **of**] *a pair of doves* | *the mating pair* **b)** *old use* two horses that work together: *a carriage and pair*

**7 I've only got one pair of hands** *spoken* used to say that you are busy and cannot do any more than you are doing

**8 ▶ CARDS ◀** two PLAYING CARDS which have the same value: [+ **of**] *a pair of jacks*

**9 the happy pair** two people who have just become married

**USAGE NOTE: PAIR**

WORD CHOICE: **pair, couple**

A **pair** is a set of two things which are joined or normally used together, or two people who work or do something together: *a pair of jeans/slippers* | *drug dealers often work in pairs*

A **couple** is two or a few things of the same kind: *I've found two/a couple of socks but they aren't a pair.* | *Can you lend me a couple of dollars (= a few dollars)?*

*Note that two married people or two people in a lasting relationship are a* **couple** *not a* **pair**: *a childless couple*

GRAMMAR

Things that come in pairs and are joined can only be counted using the word **pair**, even though they are plural: *two pairs of jeans* | *a pair of glasses* (NOT *a glasses*) | *both pairs of scissors*

Things that come in pairs but are not joined can be counted either in pairs or separately: *one shoe* | *two/both shoes* | *a pair of shoes*

**pair²** also **pair up** *v* [I, T usually passive] to form groups of two or be put into groups of two: **be paired with sb** *We were each paired with a newcomer to help with training.*

**pair off** *phr v* [I,T] to come together or bring two people together to have a romantic relationship: *All the others were pairing off and I was left on my own.* | **pair sb off with sb** *They want to pair their daughters off with rich men.*

**pair up** *phr v* [I] **1** to become friends and start to have a relationship **2** to agree to start to work together with someone

**pais·ley** /ˈpeɪzli/ *adj* made from cloth that is covered with a pattern of shapes that look like curved drops of rain: *a paisley shawl* —see picture on page 839

**pa·ja·mas** /pəˈdʒɑːməz‖-ˈdʒɑː-, -ˈdʒæ-/ *n* [plural] the usual American spelling of PYJAMAS —**pajama** *adj*

**Pa·ki** /ˈpæki/ *n* [C] *BrE taboo* a very offensive word for a person from Pakistan, or a person born in Britain whose parents were from Pakistan

**Pak·i·sta·ni** /ˌpækɪˈstɑːni◂‖-ˈstæni/ *n* [C] **1** someone from Pakistan **2** from or connected with Pakistan

**pal¹** /pæl/ *n* [C] **1** *informal* a close friend: *an old pal of mine* | *We just weren't pals any more.* **2** *spoken* used to address a man in an unfriendly way: *Listen, pal, I don't want you hanging around my sister any more.*

**pal²** *v*

**pal around** *phr v* [I + **with**] *AmE* to go places and do things with someone as a friend: *It was nice having someone to pal around with.*

**pal up** *phr v* [I + **with**] *BrE* to become someone's friend: *They palled up while travelling round Europe.*

**pal·ace** /ˈpælɪ̣s/ *n* [C] **1** often **Palace** a large grand house where a ruling king or queen, or a British BISHOP or ARCHBISHOP, officially lives: *Buckingham Palace* **2** a large, grand, beautifully decorated house: *The nobles of Florence built splendid palaces.* W

**palace rev·o·lu·tion** /ˌ·· ··ˈ··/ *n* [C] a situation in which a ruler or an important person in a large organization, has their power taken away by the less important people who work with them

**pal·a·din** /ˈpælədɪn/ *n* [C] **1** *literary* a respected person who strongly supports a particular action or opinion;

CHAMPION[1] (2) **2** a KNIGHT (=a soldier of high rank) in the Middle Ages who fought loyally for his prince

**palaeo-** /pæliəʊ‖peɪlioʊ/ *prefix* another spelling of PALEO-

**pal·ae·o·lith·ic** /ˌpæliəʊˈlɪθɪk◂‖ˌpeɪliə-/ *adj* the British spelling of PALEOLITHIC

**pal·ae·on·tol·o·gy** /ˌpæliɒnˈtɒlədʒi‖ˌpeɪliɑːnˈtɑː-/ *n* [U] the British spelling of PALEONTOLOGY

**pal·ais** /ˈpæleɪˈpæli‖pæˈleɪ/ also **palais de danse** /ˌpæleɪ dʼ ˈdɑːns‖pæˌleɪ də ˈdæns/ *n* [C] *BrE* a large public building used for dancing in the past

**pal·an·quin, palankeen** /ˌpælənˈkiːn/ *n* [C] a box-shaped container with a seat or bed inside it for one person, carried on poles by other people

**pal·a·ta·ble** /ˈpælətəbəl/ *adj* **1** having a pleasant or acceptable taste: *a palatable wine* **2** something such as an idea, suggestion etc that is palatable is acceptable or pleasant: [+ **to**] *We need to find a compromise that's more palatable to the voters.* —opposite UNPALATABLE —**palatably** *adv*

**pal·a·tal** /ˈpælətl/ *n* [C] *technical* a CONSONANT[1] (1) sound made by putting your tongue against or near your HARD PALATE —**palatal** *adj*

**pal·ate** /ˈpælɪ̈t/ *n* **1** [C] the ROOF (=top inside part) of the mouth —see also CLEFT PALATE, HARD PALATE, SOFT PALATE **2** [C,U] the sense of taste: *a crisp salad to refresh the palate | too spicy for my palate*

**pa·la·tial** /pəˈleɪʃəl/ *adj* very large and beautifully decorated, like a palace: *a palatial home* —**palatially** *adv*

**pa·lat·i·nate** /pəˈlætɪ̈nɪ̈t/ *n* [C] an area which in past times was ruled over by a man of high rank who was the representative of a higher ruler

**pa·la·ver** /pəˈlɑːvə‖-ˈlævər/ *n* **1** [U, singular] *informal* unnecessary trouble and anxiety over small matters; BOTHER[2] (1) ; FUSS[1] (1): *all the palaver of booking a flight and getting a passport | What a palaver!* **2** [U] *informal* a lot of silly and meaningless talk: *What's all the palaver about?* **3** [C] *old use* a long talk about something important

W3 **pale[1]** /peɪl/ *adj* **1** having a much whiter skin colour than usual, especially because you are ill, worried etc: *She suddenly noticed how pale and drawn he looked. | a pale complexion* —see picture on page 412 **2** a pale colour is much lighter than the standard colour: **pale blue/pink/green etc** *pale blue curtains* —compare DEEP[1] (7), LIGHT[3] (1) **3** pale light is not bright: *the pale light of early morning* —**palely** *adv* —**paleness** *n* [U]

**pale[2]** *v* [I] **1** if your face pales, it becomes much whiter than usual because you have had a shock: *Kent's face paled when he saw Rob had a knife.* **2 pale into insignificance** to seem much less important when compared to something else, especially something much worse that has happened: *All her anger, her jealousy, paled into insignificance beside this momentous news.* **3 pale in/by comparison** to seem small or unimportant compared to something else: *This year's profits pale in comparison to last year's.*

**pale[3]** *n* **1 beyond the pale** behaviour that is beyond the pale is offensive or unacceptable **2** [C] a PALING

**pale ale** /ˌ· ˈ·/ *n* [C,U] a type of beer that does not contain much ALCOHOL and is sold in bottles

**pale·face** /ˈpeɪlfeɪs/ *n* [C] an insulting word for a white person used by Native Americans in films

**paleo-**, **palaeo-** /pæliəʊ‖peɪlioʊ/ *prefix technical* extremely ancient, before historical times: *paleobotany*

**pal·e·o·lith·ic, palaeolithic,** often **Paleolithic** /ˌpæliəʊˈlɪθɪk◂, ˌpeɪ-‖ˌpeɪlioʊ-/ *adj* connected with the earliest period of the STONE AGE (=the period thousands of years ago when people made stone tools and weapons) *a paleolithic axe* —compare NEOLITHIC

**pal·e·on·tol·o·gy, palaeontology** /ˌpæliɒnˈtɒlədʒi, ˌpeɪ-‖ˌpeɪliɑːnˈtɑː/ *n* [U] the study of FOSSILS (=ancient animals and plants that have been preserved in rock) —**paleontologist** *n* [C]

**pal·ette** /ˈpælɪ̈t/ *n* [C] **1** a board with a curved edge and a hole for your thumb, on which a painter mixes colours **2** [usually singular] *technical* the particular colours used by a painter or for a picture

**palette knife** /ˈ·· ·/ *n* [C] a thin knife that bends easily and has a rounded end, used in cooking and by painters

**pal·frey** /ˈpɔːlfri‖ˈpɒːl-/ *n* [C] *old use* a horse trained to be ridden, especially by a woman

**pa·li·mo·ny** /ˈpælɪ̈məni‖-moʊni/ *n* [U] *AmE* money that someone is ordered to pay regularly to a former partner, when they have lived together without being married

**pal·imp·sest** /ˈpælɪ̈mpsest/ *n* [C] an ancient written document which had its original writing rubbed out, not always completely, so that it could be used again

**pal·in·drome** /ˈpælɪ̈ndrəʊm‖-droʊm/ *n* [C] a word or phrase such as 'deed' or 'level', which is the same when you read it backwards

**pal·ing** /ˈpeɪlɪŋ/ *n* **1** [C usually plural] a pointed piece of wood used with other pointed pieces in making a fence **2 palings** [plural] a fence made out of palings

**pal·i·sade** /ˌpælɪ̈ˈseɪd/ *n* [C] **1** a fence made of strong pointed poles, used for defence in past times **2** [plural] also **palisades** *especially AmE* a line of high straight cliffs, especially along a river or beside the sea

**pal·ish** /ˈpeɪlɪʃ/ *adj* slightly pale

**pall[1]** /pɔːl‖pɒːl/ *v* [T + **on/upon**] if something palls on you, it becomes uninteresting or unpleasant, because you have done, used, heard, or seen it too often or for too long: *Gradually the novelty of city life began to pall.*

**pall[2]** *n* **1 a pall of smoke/dust etc** something heavy or dark, which covers something else, like a cloud: *A pall of grey smoke hung over the buildings.* **2 cast a pall on/over** to spoil an event or occasion that should have been happy and enjoyable: *The drugs scandal cast a pall over the athletics championships.* **3** [C] a large piece of cloth spread over a COFFIN (=box in which a dead body is carried) **4** [C] a COFFIN with a body inside

**pall·bear·er** /ˈpɔːlˌbeərə‖ˈpɒːlˌberər/ *n* [C] someone who walks beside a COFFIN (=a box with a dead body inside) or helps to carry it at a funeral

**pal·let** /ˈpælɪ̈t/ *n* [C] **1** a large metal plate or flat wooden frame on which heavy goods can be lifted, stored, or moved **2** *old-fashioned* a temporary bed, or a cloth bag filled with STRAW (1a) for sleeping on

**pal·li·asse, paillasse** /ˈpæliæs‖ˌpæliˈæs/ *n* [C] *old use* a cloth bag filled with STRAW (1a) for sleeping on

**pal·li·ate** /ˈpælieɪt/ *v* [T] *formal* **1** to reduce the unpleasant effects of illness, pain etc without curing them **2** to make a bad situation seem better than it really is by giving excuses —**palliation** /ˌpæliˈeɪʃən/ *n* [U]

**pal·li·a·tive** /ˈpæliətɪv‖-ətɪv, -eɪtɪv/ *n* [C] *formal* **1** an action taken to make a bad situation seem better, but which does not solve the problem: *Promises of reform are mere palliatives.* **2** a medical treatment that will not cure a problem but will reduce the pain —**palliative** *adj*: *palliative surgery*

**pal·lid** /ˈpælɪ̈d/ *adj* **1** unusually or unhealthily pale: *Paul was still pallid and sick.* **2** boring, without any excitement —**pallidly** *adv* —**pallidness** *n* [U]

**pal·lor** /ˈpælə‖-ər/ *n* [singular] unhealthy paleness of the skin or face: *Her skin had a deathly pallor.*

**pal·ly** /ˈpæli/ *adj* [not before noun] *informal* very friendly with someone: *She's getting very pally with the boss these days.* | **be pally with sb** *I didn't know you were pally with her.*

**palm[1]** /pɑːm‖pɑːm, pɑːlm/ *n* [C] **1** the inside surface of your hand between the base of your fingers and your wrist: *He held the pebble in the palm of his hand.* **2** a palm tree **3 hold/have sb in the palm of your hand** to have a strong influence on someone, so that they do what you want them to do: *She's got the whole committee in the palm of her hand.* **4 read sb's palm** to tell someone what is going to happen to them by looking at their hand —see also **itchy palm** (ITCHY (6)), **cross sb's palm (with silver)** (CROSS[1] (16)), **grease sb's palm** (GREASE[2] (2))

**palm[2]** *v* [T] to hide something in the palm of your hand, especially when performing a magic trick or stealing something

**palm off** *phr v* [T **palm** sth/sb ↔ **off**] to persuade someone to accept or buy something, especially by deceiving them: **palm sth off on/onto sb** *The fruit seller palmed some damaged apples off onto an old lady.*| **palm sth off as** *He tried to palm it off as a real Renoir.*| **palm sb off with sth** *They palmed her off with an obsolete computer.*

P

**pal·met·to** /pælˈmetəʊ‖-toʊ/ *n* [C] a small PALM TREE that grows in the south-eastern US

**palm·ist** /ˈpɑːmɪ̣st‖ˈpɑːm-, ˈpɑːlm-/ *n* [C] *BrE* someone who claims they can tell what a person is like or what will happen to them, by looking at the palm of their hand; —compare FORTUNE-TELLER

**palm·ist·ry** /ˈpɑːmɪ̣stri‖ˈpɑːm-, ˈpɑːlm-/ *n* [U] the art of looking at the palm of a person's hand to tell what they are like or what will happen to them

**palm oil** /ˈ· ·/ *n* [U] the oil obtained from the nut of an African PALM TREE

**palm read·ing** /ˈ· ˌ··/ *n* [U] palmistry —**palm reader** *n* [C]

**Palm Sun·day** /ˌ· ˈ··/ *n* the Sunday before Easter in the Christian Church

**palm·top** /ˈpɑːmtɒp‖ˈpɑːmtɑːp, ˈpɑːlm-/ *n* [C] a very small computer that you can hold in your hand

**palm tree** /ˈ· ·/ *n* [C] a tropical tree which typically grows near beaches or in deserts, with a long straight trunk and large pointed leaves at the top

**palm·y** /ˈpɑːmi‖ˈpɑːmi, ˈpɑːlmi/ *adj* used to describe a period of time when people have money and life is good: *in the palmy days of Elizabeth I*

**pal·o·mi·no** /ˌpæləˈmiːnəʊ◂‖-noʊ/ *n* [C] a horse of a golden or cream colour, with a white MANE and tail

**pal·pa·ble** /ˈpælpəbəl/ *adj formal* **1** easily and clearly noticed; OBVIOUS (1): *a palpable lie* **2** able to be touched or physically felt; TANGIBLE (2): *an almost palpable atmosphere of mistrust* —opposite IMPALPABLE —**palpably** *adv: What he said was palpably false.*

**pal·pate** /pælˈpeɪt‖ˈpælpeɪt/ *v* [T] *technical* to give someone a medical examination by touching their body: *The doctor palpated his abdomen.* —**palpation** /pælˈpeɪʃən/ *n* [C,U]

**pal·pi·tate** /ˈpælpɪ̣teɪt/ *v* [I] **1** if your heart palpitates, it beats quickly and irregularly **2** to tremble: [+ **with**] *He was positively palpitating with excitement.*

**pal·pi·ta·tions** /ˌpælpɪ̣ˈteɪʃənz/ *n* [plural] irregular or extremely fast beating of your heart, caused by illness or too much effort

**pal·sied** /ˈpɔːlzid‖ˈpɒːl-/ *adj not technical* suffering from an illness that makes your arms and legs shake because you cannot control your muscles

**pal·sy** /ˈpɔːlzi‖ˈpɒːl-/ *n* [U] **1** *old use* PARALYSIS (1) **2** an illness that makes your arms and legs shake because you cannot control your muscles —see also CEREBRAL PALSY

**pal·sy-wal·sy** /ˌpælzi ˈwælzi/ *adj BrE spoken* very friendly, especially in a way that seems insincere

**pal·try** /ˈpɔːltri‖ˈpɒːl-/ *adj* **1** a paltry amount of something such as money is too small to be useful or important: *The management offered us a paltry 3% pay increase.* **2** worthless and silly: *paltry excuses*|*her paltry little observations on Russia*

**pam·pas** /ˈpæmpəz, -pəs/ *n* **the pampas** the large wide flat areas of land covered with grass in some parts of South America

**pampas grass** /ˈ·· ·/ *n* [U] a kind of tall grass with silver-white feathery flowers

**pam·per** /ˈpæmpə‖-ər/ *v* [T] to look after someone too kindly or very kindly: *a pampered cat*|*Pamper yourself with a long, luxurious bath.*

**pam·phlet** /ˈpæmflɪ̣t/ *n* [C] a very thin book with paper covers, giving information about something

**pam·phle·teer** /ˌpæmflɪ̣ˈtɪə‖-ˈtɪr/ *n* [C] someone who writes pamphlets giving political opinions

**pan-, Pan-** /pæn/ *prefix* including all: *pan-African unity*| *Pan-Arabism* (=political union of all Arabs)

**pans**

**pan[1]** /pæn/ *n* [C]
**1** ▶ **FOR COOKING** ◀ a round metal container used for cooking usually, with one long handle and a lid; SAUCEPAN: *Cook the pasta in a large pan of boiling salted water.*
**2** ▶ **FOR BAKING CAKES ETC** ◀ *AmE* a metal container for baking things in; TIN *BrE*: *a 9" cake pan*
**3** ▶ **FOR WEIGHING** ◀ one of the two dishes on a pair of SCALES (=a small weighing machine)
**4** ▶ **TOILET** ◀ *especially BrE* the bowl of a toilet
**5** ▶ **DRUM** ◀ a metal drum that is played in a STEEL BAND
**6** ▶ **FOR FINDING GOLD** ◀ *AmE* a container used to separate gold from other substances, by washing them in water
**7** **go down the pan** *BrE slang* to be wasted or become useless or ruined —see also FRYING PAN, SKIDPAN, WARMING PAN, **a flash in the pan** (FLASH[2] (8))

**pan[2]** *v* **panned, panning**
**1** ▶ **CRITICIZE** ◀ [T] *informal* to strongly criticize a film, play etc in a newspaper or on television or radio: *a production that was panned by the critics*
**2** ▶ **CAMERA** ◀ **a)** [I always + adv/prep] if a film or television camera pans in a particular direction, it moves and follows the thing that is being filmed: *The camera panned slowly across the crowd.* **b)** [I,T] to move a camera in this way
**3** ▶ **GOLD** ◀ **a)** [I,T] to wash soil in a pan to separate gold from it: [+ **for**] *panning for gold* **b)** also **pan out, pan off** to get or separate gold in this way

**pan out** *phr v* [I] to happen or develop in a particular way: *I wonder how it will all pan out.*

**pan·a·cea** /ˌpænəˈsɪə/ *n* [C] **1** something that people think will make everything better and solve all their problems: *Battery-powered cars are not a panacea for the pollution problem.* **2** a medicine or form of treatment that is supposed to cure any illness

**pa·nache** /pəˈnæʃ, pæ-/ *n* [U] a way of doing things that is exciting and makes them seem easy, and makes other people admire you: *a designer with flair and panache | They sang their songs with great panache.*

**pan·a·ma** /ˌpænəˈmɑː◂, ˈpænəmɑː/ also **panama hat** /ˌ··· ˈ·/ *n* [C] a light hat for men, made from STRAW —see picture at HAT

**pan·a·tel·la** /ˌpænəˈtelə/ *n* [C] a long thin CIGAR

**pan·cake** /ˈpænkeɪk/ *n* **1** [C] *BrE* a very thin, flat round cake made from flour, milk, and eggs, that has been cooked in a flat pan, and is eaten hot; CREPE *AmE* **2** [C] *AmE* a thick round cake made from flour, milk, and eggs that has been cooked in a flat pan and is eaten for breakfast, often with MAPLE SYRUP; FLAPJACK (2); HOT CAKE *AmE* **3** [U] very thick MAKE-UP for the face

**Pancake Day** /ˈ·· ·/ *n* [C,U] *BrE informal* SHROVE TUESDAY, when people in Britain traditionally eat pancakes

**pancake land·ing** /ˌ·· ˈ··/ *n* [C] an act of bringing an aircraft down to the ground in such a way that it drops flat from a low height

**pancake roll** /ˌ·· ˈ·/ *n* [C] *BrE* a SPRING ROLL

**Pancake Tues·day** /ˌ·· ˈ··/ *n* [C,U] Pancake Day

**pan·cre·as** /ˈpæŋkriəs/ *n* [C] a GLAND inside your body, near your stomach, that produces INSULIN and a liquid that helps your body to use the food that you eat —**pancreatic** /ˌpæŋkriˈæt◂/ *adj* —see picture at DIGESTIVE SYSTEM

**pan·da** /ˈpændə/ *n* [C] **1** a large black and white animal that looks like a bear and lives in the mountains of China; GIANT PANDA **2** a small animal with red-brown fur and a long tail, living in the south-eastern Himalayas

**Panda car** /ˈ·· ·/ *n* [C] *BrE* a small police car used by local police; PATROL CAR

**pan·dem·ic** /pænˈdemɪk/ *n* [C] *technical* an illness or disease that affects the population of a large area —**pandemic** *adj* —compare ENDEMIC

**pan·de·mo·ni·um** /ˌpændɪ̵ˈməʊniəm‖-ˈmoʊ-/ *n* [U] a situation in which there is a lot of noise because people are angry, confused or frightened: *Pandemonium broke out when the results were announced.*

**pan·der** /ˈpændə‖-ər/ *v*

**pander to** sth/sb *phr v* [T] to give someone what they want, when you know it is not good for them: *newspapers that pander to people's interest in sex*

**pan·dit** /ˈpʌndɪ̵t, ˈpæn-/ *n* [C] a title of respect for a wise man, used in India: *Pandit Nehru*

**Pan·do·ra's box** /pænˌdɔːrəz ˈbɒks‖-ˈbɑːks/ *n* **open Pandora's box** to cause a lot of problems that did not exist before

**pane** /peɪn/ *n* [C] a sheet of glass used in a window or door —see also WINDOWPANE —see picture on page 416

**pan·e·gyr·ic** /ˌpænɪ̵ˈdʒɪrɪk/ *n* [C + **on/upon**] *formal* a speech or piece of writing that praises someone or something very highly

S1 W2 **pan·el¹** /ˈpænl/ *n* [C]

**1** ▶**PART**◀ **a)** a flat piece of wood, glass etc with straight sides, which forms part of a door, wall, fence etc: *a stained glass panel* **b)** a piece of metal that forms part of the outer structure of a vehicle **c)** a piece of material that forms part of a piece of clothing

**2** ▶**GROUP OF PEOPLE**◀ **a)** a group of people with skills or specialist knowledge who have been chosen to give advice or opinions on a particular subject: *A panel of experts was consulted. | a crime prevention panel* **b)** a group of well-known people who answer questions on a radio or television programme: *Let me introduce tonight's panel.* —see also PANELLIST **c)** a group of people who are chosen to listen to a case in a court of law and to decide the result; JURY

**3 instrument/control panel** a board in a car, plane, boat etc on which the controls are fixed

**4** ▶**PICTURE**◀ a thin board with a picture painted on it —see also SOLAR PANEL

**panel²** *v* **panelled, panelling** *BrE*, **paneled, paneling** *AmE* [T usually passive] to cover or decorate something with flat pieces of wood, glass etc: **be panelled with** *The walls were panelled with oak.* | **oak-panelled/glass-panelled etc** *an oak-panelled library*

**panel-beat·er** /ˈ·· ˌ··/ *n* [C] *BrE* someone whose job is to repair the outer structure of cars, for example after an accident, by beating the metal with a hammer

**pan·el·ling** *BrE*, **paneling** *AmE* /ˈpænəl-ɪŋ/ *n* [U] wood, especially in long or square pieces, used to decorate walls etc: *oak panelling*

**pan·el·list** *BrE*, **panelist** *AmE* /ˈpænəl-ɪ̵st/ *n* [C] one of a group of well-known people who answer questions on a radio or television programme

**panel pin** /ˈ·· ·/ *n* [C] a short, thin nail used for fastening thin pieces of wood together

**panel truck** /ˈ·· ·/ *n* [C] *AmE* a small motor vehicle used for delivering goods

**pang** /pæŋ/ *n* [C] a sudden feeling of pain, sadness etc: [+ **of**] *pangs of jealousy | hunger pangs*

**pan·han·dle¹** /ˈpænˌhændl/ *n* [C] *AmE* a thin piece of land that is joined to a larger area like the handle of a pan: *the Alaskan panhandle*

**panhandle²** *v* [I] *especially AmE* to ask for money in the streets: *a ban on panhandling in New York's subway* —**panhandler** *n* [C]

**pan·ic¹** /ˈpænɪk/ *n* **1** [C usually singular, U] a sudden strong feeling of fear or nervousness that makes you unable to think clearly or behave sensibly: **get into a panic/be thrown into (a) panic** *She got into a real panic when she thought she'd lost the tickets.* | **in (a) panic** *Shoppers fled the street in panic after two bombs exploded in central London.* | **panic attack** *Philip sometimes gets panic attacks and can't breathe properly.* **2** [C usually singular, U] a situation in which people are suddenly made very anxious, and make quick decisions without thinking carefully: *the recent panic over the contamination of food by listeria and salmonella* | **panic buying/selling** *a wave of panic selling in Hong Kong shook the city yesterday* **3** [singular] *especially BrE* a situation in which there is a lot to do and not much time to do it in: *There was the usual last minute panic just before the deadline.* **4 press/push the panic button** *BrE* to do something quickly without thinking enough about it, because something unexpected or dangerous has suddenly happened **5 panic stations** *BrE* a state of confused anxiety because something needs to be done urgently: *It was panic stations here on Friday.* S3

**panic²** *v* **panicked, panicking** [I, T] to suddenly become so frightened that you cannot think clearly or behave sensibly, or to make someone do this: *The crowd panicked at the sound of the gunfire. | He panicked thinking it was a shark.* | **Don't panic!** (=used to tell people to stay calm) | **panic sb into doing sth** *The protests became more violent and many landowners were panicked into leaving the country.*

**pan·ic·ky** /ˈpænɪki/ *adj informal* very nervous or anxious: *Emily always gets panicky about exams.*

**panic-strick·en** /ˈ·· ˌ··/ *adj* so frightened that you cannot think clearly or behave sensibly: *the panic-stricken faces of the hostages*

**pan·ni·er** /ˈpæniə‖-ər/ *n* [C] **1** one of a pair of baskets or bags carried one on each side of an animal or a bicycle **2** a basket used to carry a load on someone's back

**pan·ni·kin** /ˈpænɪkɪ̵n/ *n* [C] *BrE old use* a small metal drinking cup

**pan·o·ply** /ˈpænəpli/ *n* [U + **of**] **1** an impressive show of special clothes, decorations etc, especially at an important ceremony: *the whole panoply of a royal wedding* **2** a large amount of equipment, weapons etc —**panoplied** *adj*

**pan·o·ra·ma** /ˌpænəˈrɑːmə‖-ˈræmə/ *n* [C usually singular] **1** an impressive view of a wide area of land: *A breathtaking panorama of mountains and lakes spread out in front of them.* | [+ **of**] *a vast panorama of roof tops* **2** a description or series of pictures that shows all the features of a subject, historical period etc: [+ **of**] *a panorama of life in England 400 years ago* —**panoramic** /ˌpænəˈræmɪk◂/ *adj*: *a panoramic view of the valley* —**panoramically** /-kli/ *adv*

**pan·pipes** /ˈpænpaɪps/ *n* [plural] a simple musical instrument made of several short wooden pipes of different lengths, that are played by blowing across their open ends

**pan·sy** /ˈpænzi/ *n* [C] **1** a small garden plant with flat brightly coloured flowers **2** *informal* an insulting word for a man who seems weak and too much like a woman

**pant** /pænt/ *v* **1** [I] to breathe quickly with short noisy breaths because you have been running, climbing etc or because it is very hot: *He was panting after his exertions.* | *The dog lay panting on the doorstep.* **2** [T] to say something while panting: *"I can't run any farther," she panted.*

**pant for** sth *phr v* [T] to want something very much: *He was panting for a chance to speak.* —**pant** *n* [C]

**pan·ta·loons** /ˌpæntəˈluːnz/ *n* [plural] long trousers with wide legs, which are gathered in again at the ankles

**pan·tech·ni·con** /pænˈteknɪkən‖-kɑːn/ *n* [C] *BrE old-fashioned* a REMOVAL VAN

**pan·the·is·m** /ˈpænθi-ɪzəm/ *n* [U] the religious idea that God and the universe are the same thing and that God is present in all natural things —**pantheist** *n* [C] —**pantheistic** /ˌpænθiˈɪstɪk◂/ *adj*

**pan·the·on** /ˈpænθiən‖-θiɑːn/ *n* [C] **1** all the gods of a particular people or nation: *the Roman pantheon* **2** *literary* a group of famous and important people: *a leading figure in the pantheon of 20th century designers* **3** a TEMPLE built in honour of all gods

**pan·ther** /ˈpænθə‖-ər/ *n plural* **panthers** or **panther** [C] **1** a black LEOPARD **2** *AmE* a COUGAR or JAGUAR

**pan·ties** /ˈpæntiz/ *n* [plural] a piece of women's underwear that covers the area between their waist and the top of their legs; KNICKERS *BrE*: *a pair of lacy panties* —see picture at UNDERWEAR

**pan·ti·hose** /ˈpæntihəʊz‖-hoʊz/ *n* [plural] *AmE* another spelling of PANTYHOSE

**pan·tile** /ˈpæntaɪl/ *n* [C usually plural] a curved roof TILE

**pan·to** /ˈpæntəʊ‖-toʊ/ *n* [C] *BrE informal* pantomime

**pan·to·graph** /ˈpæntəgrɑːf‖-græf/ *n* [C] **1** an instrument used to make a smaller or larger exact copy of a drawing, plan etc **2** the metal structure on top of an electric train that takes power from the wires above the track

**pan·to·mime** /ˈpæntəmaɪm/ *n* **1** [C,U] a type of play for children that is performed in Britain around Christmas, in which traditional stories are performed with jokes, music, and songs **2** [C,U] a method of performing using only actions and not words, or a play performed using this method; MIME[1] (1)

**pan·try** /ˈpæntri/ *n plural* **pantries** [C] **1** a very small room in a house where food is kept; LARDER **2** a room in a big house, hotel etc where glasses, dishes etc are kept

S3 **pants** /pænts/ *n* [plural] **1** *AmE* a piece of clothing that covers you from your waist to your feet and has a separate part for each leg; TROUSERS *especially BrE* —see graph at TROUSERS —see picture on page 840 **2** *BrE* a piece of underwear that covers the area between your waist and the top of your legs **3 bore/charm/beat etc the pants off** *spoken* to make you feel very bored, very frightened etc: *She always bores the pants off me.* **4 he/she puts his/her pants on one leg at a time** *AmE spoken* used to say that someone is just like everyone else: *Go on, ask him for his autograph – he puts his pants on one leg at a time just like you do.* **5 be in short pants** *informal* to still be a very young boy: *I've known Eric since he was in short pants.* —see also **by the seat of your pants** (SEAT[1] (9)), **catch sb with their pants down** (CATCH[1] (3)), **wear the pants/trousers** (WEAR[1] (8))

**pant·suit** /ˈpæntsuːt, -sjuːt‖-suːt/ *n* [C] *AmE* a TROUSER SUIT *BrE*

**pan·ty·hose, pantihose** /ˈpæntihəʊz‖-hoʊz/ *n* [plural] *AmE* a very thin piece of women's clothing that covers their legs from the toes to the waist and is usually worn with dresses or skirts; TIGHTS *BrE*

**pan·ty·lin·er** /ˈpæntilaɪnə‖-ər/ *n* [C] a very thin SANITARY PAD

**pap** /pæp/ *n* [U] **1** books, television programmes etc that people read or watch for entertainment but which have no serious value: *Telly snobs dismiss the show as lightweight pap.* **2** very soft food eaten by babies or sick people —see also PAP SMEAR

**pap·a** /pəˈpɑː‖ˈpɑːpə/ *n* [C] *AmE or old-fashioned BrE* a way of talking about your father: *Good morning, Papa!*

**pa·pa·cy** /ˈpeɪpəsi/ *n* **1 the papacy** the position and authority of the POPE **2** [U] the time during which a particular POPE is in power

**pap·a·dum** /ˈpæpədəm‖ˈpɑː-/ *n* [C] another spelling of POPADUM

**pa·pal** /ˈpeɪpəl/ *adj* [only before noun] connected with or belonging to the POPE: *papal authority*

**pap·a·raz·zi** /ˌpæpəˈrætsi‖ˌpɑːpəˈrɑː-/ *n* [plural] newspaper writers or photographers who follow famous people

**pa·pa·ya** /pəˈpaɪə/ *n* [C] the large yellow-green fruit of a tropical tree —see picture on page 413

**pa·per**[1] /ˈpeɪpə‖-ər/ *n* S1 W1

**1 ▶ FOR WRITING ON ◀** [U] material in the form of thin sheets that is used for writing on, wrapping things etc: *a piece of paper* | *wrapped in brown paper* | **writing/wrapping/drawing paper** *sheets of writing paper*

**2 ▶ NEWSPAPER ◀** [C] a newspaper: *Have you seen today's paper?* | *Why don't you put an ad in the local paper?* | **daily/evening/Sunday paper** *The story was all over the Sunday papers.*

**3 ▶ DOCUMENTS/LETTERS ◀ a) papers** [plural] pieces of paper with writing on them that you use in your work, at meetings etc: *I left some important papers in my briefcase.* **b)** documents and letters concerning someone's private or public life: *I found this photograph among his private papers.* **c)** official documents such as your PASSPORT, IDENTITY CARD etc: *After checking our papers, the border guards let us through.* —see also WHITE PAPER, GREEN PAPER, ORDER PAPER

**4 on paper a)** if you put ideas or information on paper, you write them down: *As soon as you have an idea, get it down on paper so you don't forget it.* **b)** if something seems true on paper, it seems to be true as an idea, but may not be true in a real situation: *It's a nice idea on paper, but you'll never get it to work.*

**5 ▶ EXAMINATION ◀ a)** [C] *BrE* a set of printed questions used as an examination in a particular subject: *an exam paper* | **history/French etc paper** *The history paper was really easy.* **b)** the answers that have been written to these questions: *I have a stack of papers to mark.*

**6 ▶ ABOUT A SUBJECT ◀** [C] **a)** a piece of writing or a talk by someone who has made a study of a particular subject: *a scientific paper* | **give a paper on** (=give a talk about) *Professor Usborne gave a paper on recent developments in the field of cognitive psychology.* | **working paper** (=an official document that makes suggestions about a subject or problem) **b)** *especially AmE* a piece of writing that is done as part of a course at school or university: [+ **on**] *I have a paper to write on the Civil War.*

**7 ▶ FOR WALLS ◀** [C,U] paper for covering and decorating the walls of a room; WALLPAPER: *We've chosen a floral paper for Pauline's bedroom.*

**8 not worth the paper it is written on/printed on** if something such as a contract is not worth the paper it is written on, it has no value because whatever is promised in it will not happen —see also **put/set pen to paper** (PEN[1] (3)), TOILET PAPER, WASTE PAPER

**paper**[2] *adj* [only before noun] **1** made of paper: *a paper cup* **2 paper qualifications** an expression meaning documents showing that you have passed certain examinations used specially when you think that someone's experience and knowledge of a subject are more important **3** existing only as an idea but not having any real value: *paper profits|paper promises* **4 paper tiger** an enemy or opponent who seems powerful but actually is not

**paper³** *v* [T] **1** to decorate the walls of a room by covering them with special paper **2 paper over the cracks/a problem etc** to try to hide disagreements or difficulties

**pa·per·back** /ˈpeɪpəbæk‖-ər-/ *n* [C] a book with a stiff paper cover: *a shelf full of paperbacks*|**in paperback** *His first novel sold over 20,000 copies in paperback.* —compare HARDBACK

**pa·per·boy** /ˈpeɪpəbɔɪ‖-ər-/ *n* [C] a boy who delivers newspapers to people's houses

**paper chase** /ˈ·· ·/ *n* [C] **1** *especially BrE* a game in which someone runs ahead of a group of people dropping pieces of paper which they have to follow **2** *AmE* an attempt to gain a university degree

**pa·per·clip** /ˈpeɪpəklɪp‖-ər-/ *n* [C] a small piece of curved wire used for holding sheets of paper together

**paper doll** /ˌ·· ˈ·/ *n* [C] a piece of stiff paper cut in the shape of a person

**paper fas·ten·er** /ˈ·· ˌ···/ *n* [C] *BrE* a small metal object like a button used to hold several pieces of paper together; BRAD *AmE*

**paper girl** /ˈ·· ·/ *n* [C] a girl who delivers newspapers to people's houses

**pa·per·hang·er** /ˈpeɪpəˌhæŋə‖-pərˌhæŋər/ *n* [C] someone whose job is to decorate rooms with WALLPAPER

**paper knife** /ˈ·· ·/ *n* [C] *BrE* a knife for opening envelopes

**paper mon·ey** /ˈ·· ˌ··/ *n* [U] money consisting of small sheets of paper, not coins

**paper-push·er** /ˈ·· ˌ··/ *n* [C] someone whose job is doing unimportant office work

**paper round** /ˈ·· ·/ *n* [C] *BrE* the job of delivering newspapers to a group of houses: *Harry used to do a paper round before breakfast.*

**paper route** /ˈ·· ·/ *n* [C] *AmE* a paper round

**paper shop** /ˈ·· ·/ *n* [C] *BrE* a shop that sells newspapers and magazines; NEWSAGENT *BrE*

**paper-thin** /ˌ·· ˈ·◂/ *adj* very thin

**paper tow·el** /ˌ·· ˈ··/ *n* [C] a sheet of soft thick paper that you use to dry your hands

**pa·per·weight** /ˈpeɪpəweɪt‖-ər-/ *n* [C] a small heavy object used to hold pieces of paper in place

**pa·per·work** /ˈpeɪpəwɜːk‖-pərwɜːrk/ *n* [U] **1** work such as writing letters or reports, which must be done but is not very interesting: *The job involves a lot of paperwork.* **2** the documents that you need for a business deal, a journey etc: *I'm leaving the solicitors to sort out the paperwork.*

**pa·per·y** /ˈpeɪpəri/ *adj* something such as skin or leaves that is papery is very dry and thin and a little stiff: *the papery skin of her hands*

**pap·ier-mâ·ché** /ˌpæpieɪ ˈmæʃeɪ, ˌpeɪpə-‖ˌpeɪpər məˈʃeɪ/ also **paper-mâché** *AmE n* [U] a soft substance made from a mixture of paper, water, and glue, which becomes hard when it dries and is used for making boxes, pots etc

**pa·pist** /ˈpeɪpɪst/ *n* [C] an insulting word for a member of the Roman Catholic Church

**pa·poose** /pəˈpuːs‖pæ-/ *n* [C] **1** a type of bag fixed to a frame, used to carry a baby on your back **2** *old use* a Native American baby or young child

**pap·py** /ˈpæpi/ *n* [C] *AmE old-fashioned* a father

**pap·ri·ka** /ˈpæprɪkə‖pəˈpriːkə/ *n* [U] a red powder made from a type of SWEET PEPPER, used to give a strong taste to food

**Pap smear** /ˈ· ·/ *n* [C] *AmE* a medical test that takes cells from a woman's CERVIX and examines them for signs of CANCER; SMEAR TEST *BrE*

**pa·py·rus** /pəˈpaɪərəs‖-ˈpaɪrəs/ *n plural* **papyruses** or **papyri** /-raɪ/ **1** [U] a plant like grass that grows in water **2** [C,U] a type of paper made from this plant and used in ancient Egypt, or a piece of this paper

**par** /pɑː‖pɑːr/ *n* [U] **1 be on a par (with)** to be at the same level or standard: *The wages of clerks were on a par with those of manual workers.* **2 be below/under par a)** to feel a little ill or lacking in energy: *I've been feeling a little under par the last couple of weeks.* **b)** also **not be up to par** to be less good than usual or below the proper standard: *None of the people who'd auditioned were really up to par.* **3 be par for the course** to be what you would normally expect to happen: *The train's late again – I guess that's about par for the course.* **4** the number of STROKES a player should take to hit the ball into a hole in the game of GOLF **5** also **par value** the value of a STOCK or BOND that is printed on it when it is first sold: *a par value of $40 million* —see also PAR EXCELLENCE

**para-** /pærə/ *prefix* **1** beyond: *the paranormal* (=strange unnatural events) **2** very similar to something: *terrorists wearing paramilitary uniforms|paratyphoid* **3** connected with a profession and helping more highly trained people: *paramedical workers such as ambulance drivers*

**par·a¹** /ˈpærə/ *n BrE informal* a PARATROOPER

**para²** also **par** the written abbreviation of PARAGRAPH

**par·a·ble** /ˈpærəbəl/ *n* [C] a short simple story that teaches a moral or religious lesson, especially one of the stories told by Jesus in the Bible

**pa·rab·o·la** /pəˈræbələ/ *n* [C] *technical* a curve in the shape of the imaginary line a ball makes when it is thrown high in the air and comes down a little distance away —**parabolic** /ˌpærəˈbɒlɪk◂‖ˈbɑ/ *adj*

**par·a·ce·ta·mol** /ˌpærəˈsiːtəmɒl,-ˈset-‖-mɑːl, -mɒːl/ *n* [C, U] *BrE* a common drug used to reduce pain, which does not contain ASPIRIN

**par·a·chute¹** /ˈpærəʃuːt/ *n* [C] the thing that you wear fastened to your back to make you fall through the air slowly when you jump out of a plane: *a parachute jump*

**parachute²** *v* **1** [I always + adv/prep] to jump from a plane using a parachute: [+ **into/on**] *We parachuted into Vietnam in September 1968.* **2** [T always + adv/prep] to drop something from a plane with a parachute: **parachute sth to/into** *It may be possible to parachute supplies to the garrison.*

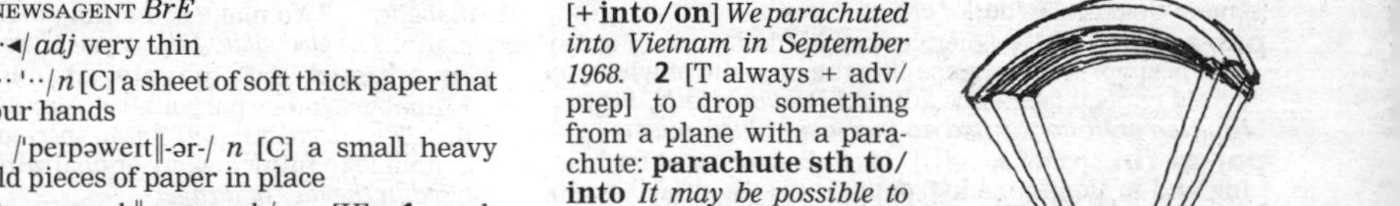
parachute

**par·a·chut·ist** /ˈpærəʃuːtɪst/ *n* [C] someone who jumps from a plane with a parachute

**pa·rade¹** /pəˈreɪd/ *n* [C] **1** a public celebration when musical bands, brightly decorated vehicles etc move down the street: *a victory parade* **2** a military ceremony in which soldiers stand or march together so that important people can examine them: *a passing-out parade*|**be on parade** (=be standing or marching in a parade) **3** a line of people moving along so that other people can watch them: **fashion parade** (=a show of different styles of clothes) **4** *especially BrE* a street with a row of small shops —see also IDENTIFICATION PARADE, HIT PARADE

**parade²** *v*
**1** ▶ **CELEBRATE/PROTEST** ◀ [I always + adv/prep] to walk or march together to celebrate or protest about something: [+ **around/past etc**] *The marchers paraded peacefully through the center of the capital.*
**2** ▶ **SHOW STH** ◀ [T] to show your possessions, knowledge etc in order to make people admire you: *He loves to parade his knowledge in front of his students.*
**3** ▶ **WALK AROUND** ◀ [I always + adv/prep] to walk

around, especially in a way that shows that you want people to notice and admire you: [+ **around/past etc**] *A trio of girls in extremely brief bikinis paraded up and down.*
**4** ▶ **SHOW SB** ◀ [T always + adv/prep] to proudly show someone to other people, often to prove that you have control over them: *The prisoners were paraded in front of the TV cameras.*
**5** ▶ **SOLDIERS** ◀ [I,T] if soldiers parade or if an officer parades them, they march together so that an important person can watch them: *Two thousand of his warriors paraded before him.*
**6 parade as/be paraded as** if something parades as something else that is better, someone is pretending that it is the other better thing: *It's just self-interest parading as concern for your welfare.*

**parade ground** /·'· ˌ·/ *n* [C] a large flat area where soldiers practise marching or standing together in rows

**par·a·digm** /'pærədaɪm/ *n* [C] **1** *formal* a very clear or typical example of something: [+ **of**] *The Holocaust, to me, is a paradigm of evil.* **2** *technical* a model or example that shows how something works or is produced **3** *technical* an example or pattern of a word, showing all its forms in grammar, like child's, children, children's —**paradigmatic** /ˌpærədɪg'mætɪk◂/ *adj* —**paradigmatically** /-kli/ *adv*

**par·a·dise** /'pærədaɪs/ *n* **1** [U] a place or situation that is extremely pleasant, beautiful, or enjoyable: *the beautiful Thai holiday paradise of Phuket* | *The hotel felt like paradise after two weeks of camping.* **2** [singular] a place that has everything you need for doing a particular activity: *The market is a shopper's paradise.* | [+ **for**] *Hawaii is a paradise for surfers.* **3 Paradise** [singular] **a)** Heaven, thought of as the place where God lives and where there is no illness, death, or evil **b)** the garden where Adam and Eve lived (=the first humans, according to the Bible) —see also BIRD OF PARADISE, **be living in a fool's paradise** (FOOL[1] (8))

**par·a·dox** /'pærədɒks‖-dɑːks/ *n* **1** [C] a situation that seems strange because it involves two ideas or qualities that are very different: *It's a paradox that in such a rich country there can be so much poverty.* **2** [C] a statement that seems impossible because it contains two opposing ideas that are both true **3** [U] the use of such statements in writing or speech —**paradoxical** /ˌpærə'dɒksɪkəl◂‖-'dɑːk-/ *adj*

**par·a·dox·i·cally** /ˌpærə'dɒksɪkli‖-'dɑːk-/ *adv* in a way that is surprising because it is the opposite of what you would expect: [sentence adverb] *Paradoxically, the prohibition of liquor caused an increase in alcoholism.*

**par·af·fin** /'pærəfɪn/ *n* [U] **1** *BrE* an oil used for heating and in lamps, made from PETROLEUM or coal; KEROSENE *AmE* **2** paraffin wax

**paraffin wax** /'··· ˌ·/ *n* [U] a soft white substance used for making CANDLES, made from PETROLEUM or coal

**par·a·glid·ing** /'pærəˌglaɪdɪŋ/ *n* [U] a sport in which you jump off a hill and use a PARACHUTE to float back down to the ground

**par·a·gon** /'pærəgən‖-gɑːn/ *n* [C] someone who is perfect or is extremely brave, good etc: [+ **of**] *a paragon of virtue*

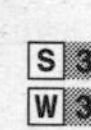
**par·a·graph** /'pærəgrɑːf‖-græf/ *n* [C] a group of several sentences in a piece of writing, the first sentence of which starts on a new line —**paragraph** *v* [T]

**par·a·keet** /'pærəkiːt/ *n* [C] a small brightly coloured bird with a long tail

**par·a·le·gal** /ˌpærə'liːgəl/ *n* [C] *AmE* LEGAL EXECUTIVE

**par·al·lel[1]** /'pærəlel/ *n* [C] **1** a connection between two things, especially things that exist or happen in different places or at different times: [+ **between**] *There are certain parallels between Europe today and 100 years ago.* | [+ **with**] *The study of philosophy has close parallels with the study of linguistics.* | **draw a parallel between** (=show that two things are similar) *The book draws a parallel between ancient and modern theories of education.* **2** something that is very similar to something else: *Modern styles of painting have their parallels in music and literature.* | **have no parallel/be without parallel** (=be greater, better, worse etc than anything else) *a social revolution without parallel in history* **3 in parallel with** together with and at the same time as something else: *private organizations working in parallel with the state education system* **4** an imaginary line drawn on a map of the Earth, that is parallel to the EQUATOR: *the 38th parallel* **5 be in parallel** *technical* if two electrical CIRCUITS (=complete circular paths) are in parallel, they are connected so that any electric current is divided equally between them

**parallel[2]** *adj* **1** two lines that are parallel to each other are the same distance apart along their whole length: *Lines AB and CD are parallel.* | [+ **to/with**] *Parallel with the old fence was a new one of barbed wire.* | *The road runs parallel to the railway.* **2** *formal* similar and happening at the same time: *Social changes in Britain are matched by parallel trends in other countries.*

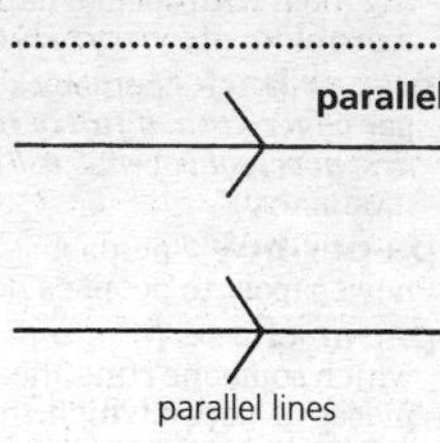


**parallel[3]** *v* [T] *formal* **1** to be as good as something else: *a level of economic prosperity paralleled by few other countries* **2** to be similar to something else: *Does the geology of Mars parallel in any way that of Earth?*

**parallel bars** /ˌ··· '·/ *n* [plural] two wooden bars that are held parallel to each other on four posts, used in GYMNASTICS (1)

**par·al·lel·is·m** /'pærəlelɪzəm/ *n* **1** [U] the state of being PARALLEL with something **2** [C] a similarity

**par·al·lel·o·gram** /ˌpærə'leləgræm/ *n* [C] a flat shape with four sides in which each side is the same length as the side opposite it and parallel to it —see picture at SHAPE[1]

**parallel pro·cess·ing** /ˌ··· '···/ *n* [U] *technical* the method of using several computers to work on a single problem at one time

**par·a·lyse** *BrE*, **paralyze** *AmE* /'pærəlaɪz/ *v* [T] **1** to make someone lose the ability to move part or all of their body, or to feel anything in it: *Mrs Burrows had been paralysed by a stroke.* **2 be paralysed** to be unable to move, or to deal with a situation, because you are frightened or surprised: *She was paralysed by shock and disbelief.* **3** to make something unable to operate normally: *The electricity failure paralysed the city.*

**par·a·lysed** *BrE*, **paralyzed** *AmE* /'pærəlaɪzd/ *adj* **1** unable to move part or all of your body or feel things in it: *The accident left him permanently paralysed.* **2** unable to think clearly or deal with a situation: *paralysed in the face of danger*

**pa·ral·y·sis** /pə'rælɪsɪs/ *n* [U] **1** the loss of the ability to move all or part of your body or feel things in it: *He suffered a stroke and partial paralysis.* **2** a state of being unable to take action, make decisions, or operate normally —see also INFANTILE PARALYSIS

**par·a·lyt·ic[1]** /ˌpærə'lɪtɪk◂/ *adj* **1** [not before noun] *BrE informal* very drunk **2** [only before noun] suffering from PARALYSIS —**paralytically** /-kli/ *adv*

**paralytic[2]** *n* [C] someone who is PARALYSED

**par·a·lyze** /'pærəlaɪz/ the American spelling of PARALYSE

**par·a·med·ic** /ˌpærə'medɪk/ *n* [C] someone who has been trained to help people who are hurt or to do medical work, but who is not a doctor or nurse

**par·a·med·i·cal** /ˌpærə'medɪkəl◂/ *adj* helping or supporting doctors, nurses, or hospitals: *paramedical staff*

**pa·ram·e·ter** /pə'ræmɪtə‖-ər/ *n* [C usually plural] a set of fixed limits that control the way that something should be done: **establish/set/lay down parameters** *The inquiry has to stay within the parameters laid down by Congress.*

**par·a·mil·i·ta·ry** /ˌpærə'mɪlɪtəri◂‖-teri◂/ *adj* [usually before noun] **1** a paramilitary organization fights and kills people illegally in order to achieve political aims: *extremist paramilitary groups* **2** connected with or helping a military organization: *Their police have paramilitary duties.* —**paramilitary** *n* [C]

**par·a·mount** /ˈpærəmaʊnt/ *adj* more important than anything else: *The interests of the consumer should be paramount.* | **of paramount importance** *A balanced budget is of paramount importance.* —**paramountcy** *n* [U]

**par·a·mour** /ˈpærəmʊə‖-mʊr/ *n* [C] *literary* someone who you have a romantic or sexual relationship with, but who you are not married to; LOVER (2)

**par·a·noi·a** /ˌpærəˈnɔɪə/ *n* [U] **1** an unreasonable belief that you cannot trust other people, or that they are trying to harm you or saying bad things about you: *No one's blaming her – it's pure paranoia!* **2** *technical* a serious mental illness that makes someone believe that people hate them and treat them badly

**par·a·noi·ac** /ˌpærəˈnɔɪæk◂/ *adj* paranoid —**paranoiac** *n* [C]

**par·a·noid** /ˈpærənɔɪd/ *adj* **1** believing unreasonably that you cannot trust other people, or that they are trying to harm you or are saying bad things about you: *You think I'm just being paranoid, but something's going on!* | *She's getting paranoid about being burgled.* **2** *technical* suffering from a mental illness that makes you believe that other people are trying to harm you

**par·a·nor·mal** /ˌpærəˈnɔːməl◂‖-ˈnɔːr-/ *adj* **1** paranormal events cannot be explained by science and seem strange and mysterious: *ESP and other paranormal phenomena* **2 the paranormal** these events in general —compare SUPERNATURAL[1]

**par·a·pet** /ˈpærəpɪ̣t, -pet/ *n* [C] **1** a low wall at the edge of a high roof, bridge etc **2** a protective wall of earth or stone built in front of a TRENCH[2] in a war

**par·a·pher·na·li·a** /ˌpærəfəˈneɪliə‖-fər-/ *n* [U] **1** a lot of small things that belong to someone, or are needed for a particular activity: *camping paraphernalia* **2** the things and events that are connected with a particular activity: *all the usual paraphernalia of bureaucracy*

**par·a·phrase**[1] /ˈpærəfreɪz/ *v* [T] to express in a shorter or clearer way what someone has written or said: *To paraphrase Finkelstein: mathematics is a language, like English.*

**paraphrase**[2] *n* [C] a statement that expresses in a shorter or clearer way what someone has said or written

**par·a·ple·gi·a** /ˌpærəˈpliːdʒiə, -dʒə/ *n* [U] inability to move your legs and the lower part of your body

**par·a·ple·gic** /ˌpærəˈpliːdʒɪk◂/ *n* [C] someone who is unable to move the lower part of their body including their legs —**paraplegic** *adj*

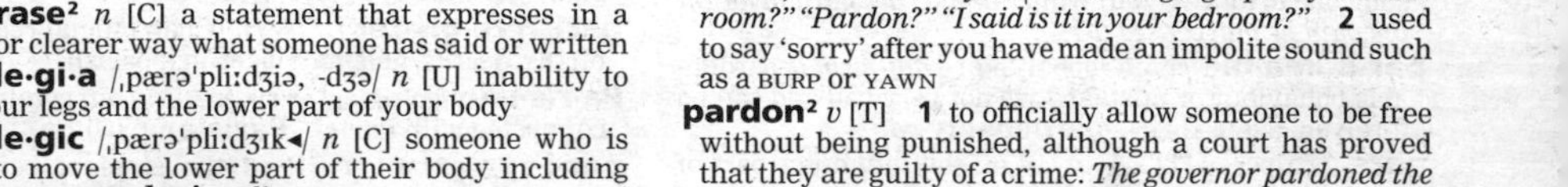

**par·a·psy·chol·o·gy** /ˌpærəsaɪˈkɒlədʒi‖-ˈkɑː-/ *n* [U] the scientific study of mysterious abilities that some people claim to have, such as knowing what will happen

**par·a·quat** /ˈpærəkwɒt‖-kwɑːt/ *n* [U] a strong poison used to kill WEEDS

**par·a·sail·ing** /ˈpærəˌseɪlɪŋ/ *n* [U] a sport in which you wear a PARACHUTE and are pulled behind a motor boat so that you sail through the air

**par·as·cend·ing** /ˈpærəˌsendɪŋ/ *n* [U] a sport in which you wear a PARACHUTE, go up into the sky by being pulled along behind a car, and float back down to the ground

**par·a·site** /ˈpærəsaɪt/ *n* [C] **1** a plant or animal that lives on or in another plant or animal and gets food from it **2** a lazy person who does not work but depends on other people: *He thinks students are just parasites.*

**par·a·sit·ic** /ˌpærəˈsɪtɪk◂/ also **parasitical** /-ˈsɪtɪkəl/ *adj* **1** living in or on another plant or animal and getting food from them: *parasitic fungi* **2** a parasitic person is lazy, does no work, and depends on other people **3** a parasitic disease is caused by parasites —**parasitically** /-kli/ *adv*

**par·a·sol** /ˈpærəsɒl‖-sɔːl, -sɑːl/ *n* [U] a type of UMBRELLA used to provide shade from the sun

**par·a·troop·er** /ˈpærəˌtruːpə‖-ər/ *n* [C] a soldier who is trained to jump out of a plane using a PARACHUTE

**par·a·troops** /ˈpærətruːps/ *n* [plural] a group of paratroopers that fights together as a military unit

**par·a·ty·phoid** /ˌpærəˈtaɪfɔɪd/ *n* [U] a disease that causes fever and severe pain in your INTESTINE

**par·boil** /ˈpɑːbɔɪl‖ˈpɑːr-/ *v* [T] to boil something until it is partly cooked

**par·cel**[1] /ˈpɑːsəl‖ˈpɑːr-/ *n* [C] **1** *especially BrE* an object that has been wrapped in paper or put in a special envelope, especially so that it can be sent by mail; PACKAGE[1] (1) *AmE*: *She tied up the parcel with string.* **2** an area of land that is part of a larger area which has been divided up: *a parcel of farmland* **3** *BrE* a small quantity of food that has been wrapped up, usually in PASTRY (1): *parcels of cod* —see also **part and parcel** (PART[1] (25)) S3

**parcel**[2] *v* **parcelled, parcelling** *BrE*, **parceled, parceling** *AmE*

**parcel** sth ↔ **out** *phr v* [T] to divide or share something among several people: *Government posts have already been parcelled out among the President's friends.*

**parcel** sth ↔ **off** *phr v* [T] to divide something into small parts so that it can be sold

**parcel** sth ↔ **up** *phr v* [T] *BrE* to make something into a parcel by wrapping it up

**parcel post** /ˈ·· ·/ *n* [U] the system of sending parcels by mail in the US

**parch** /pɑːtʃ‖pɑːrtʃ/ *v* [T] if sun or wind parches land, plants etc, it makes them very dry

**parched** /pɑːtʃt‖pɑːrtʃt/ *adj* **1** very dry, especially because of hot weather: *the parched African landscape* | *He raised the water bottle to his parched lips.* —see picture on page 836 **2 be parched** *informal* to be very thirsty

**Par·chee·si** /pɑːˈtʃiːzi‖pɑːr-/ *n* [U] *AmE trademark* a children's game in which you move a small piece of plastic around a board after throwing DICE; LUDO *BrE*

**parch·ment** /ˈpɑːtʃmənt‖ˈpɑːr-/ *n* **1** [U] a material used in the past for writing on, made from the skin of a sheep or a goat **2** [U] thick yellow-white writing paper, sometimes used for official documents **3** [C] a document written on this paper or material

**pard·ner** /ˈpɑːdnə‖ˈpɑːrdnər/ *n AmE humorous spoken* a way of addressing someone you know well: *Howdy, pardner!*

**par·don**[1] /ˈpɑːdn‖ˈpɑːrdn/ *interjection especially BrE* **1** used when you want someone to repeat something because you did not hear it: *Pardon, you'll have to talk louder, I can't hear you.* | *"Is it hanging up in your bedroom?" "Pardon?" "I said is it in your bedroom?"* **2** used to say 'sorry' after you have made an impolite sound such as a BURP or YAWN S2

**pardon**[2] *v* [T] **1** to officially allow someone to be free without being punished, although a court has proved that they are guilty of a crime: *The governor pardoned the two offenders.* **2** [not in progressive] *old-fashioned* to forgive someone for behaving badly: *I hope you will pardon my son's little outburst at dinner.* **3 sb may be pardoned for doing sth** used to say that it is easy to understand why someone has done something or why they think something: *Anyone reading the advertisement might be pardoned for thinking that the offer was genuine.*

Frequencies of the verb **pardon** in spoken and written English.

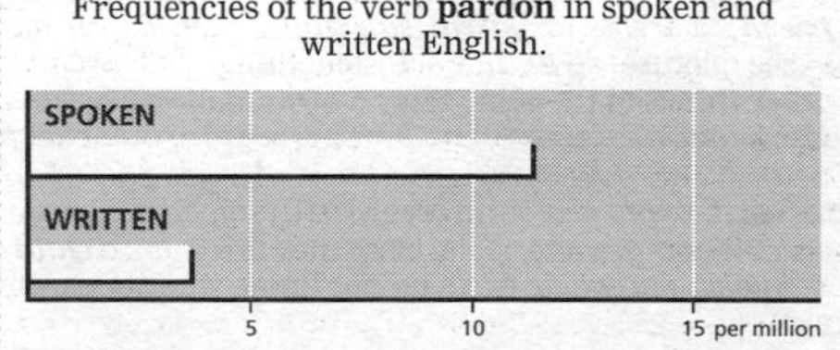


Based on the British National Corpus and the Longman Lancaster Corpus

This graph shows that the verb **pardon** is much more common in spoken English than in written English. This is because it is used in a lot of common spoken phrases.

**pardon** (*v*) **SPOKEN PHRASES**

**4 a) pardon me** used to say 'sorry' politely when you have accidentally pushed someone, interrupted them etc: *Oh, pardon me, I didn't mean to disturb you.* **b)** used to say 'sorry' politely after you have made an impolite sound such as a BURP (1) or a YAWN[2] (1) **c)** used before you politely correct someone or disagree with them: *Pardon me, but I think you've got your* *facts wrong.* **d)** *old-fashioned, especially AmE* used to politely get someone's attention in order to ask them a question: *Pardon me, can you direct me to City Hall?* **5 pardon me for interrupting/asking/saying** *especially BrE* used to politely ask if you can interrupt someone, ask something etc: *Pardon me for saying so, but you're doing that all wrong.* **6 pardon my ignorance/rudeness etc** used when you think that you may seem not to know enough, not to be polite enough etc: *Pardon my ignorance, but what does OPEC stand for?* **7 if you'll pardon the expression** used when you are saying sorry for using a slightly impolite phrase: *It was a bit of a cock-up, if you'll pardon the expression.* **8 pardon my French** *humorous* used to say sorry after you have said an impolite word **9 pardon me for breathing/living** used when you are annoyed because you think someone has answered you angrily for no good reason

**pardon³** *n* **1 (I) beg your pardon a)** *spoken* used when politely saying sorry because you have just made a mistake: *I beg your pardon, I meant the green one.* | *I do beg your pardon, I thought you were someone else.* **b)** used to politely ask someone to repeat something because you did not hear it: *"I think the radiator's leaking." "Beg your pardon?" "The radiator, I think it's leaking."* **c)** used to politely say sorry because you have accidentally touched someone, stepped on their foot, burped (BURP (1)) etc **d)** used when you are strongly or angrily disagreeing with what someone has just said: *I beg your pardon, I never said that at all.* **e)** used when you are surprised or shocked by what someone has just said: *"I'm ready to pay £20,000." "I beg your pardon, are you serious?"* —see EXCUSE¹ (USAGE) **2** [C] an official order allowing someone to be free and stopping their punishment, although a court has proved them guilty of a crime: **grant/give sb a pardon** *Tyler was convicted but was granted a royal pardon.* **3** [U] *old-fashioned* the act of forgiving someone: **ask/beg sb's pardon (for)** (=ask someone to forgive you) *Walter begged her pardon for all the pain he had caused her.*

**par·don·a·ble** /ˈpɑːdənəbəl‖ˈpɑːr-/ *adj formal* pardonable behaviour or mistakes are not very bad and can be forgiven; EXCUSABLE —**pardonably** *adv*

**pare** /peə‖per/ *v* [T] **1** to cut off the thin outer part of something using a sharp knife: *Pare the onions then cut them.* **2** to cut your nails so that they look neat

**pare** sth **down** *phr v* [T] to gradually reduce an amount or number: *The workforce has been pared down from 1400 to 700.* | **pare sth down to the bone** (=reduce an amount or number as much as possible) —**pared-down** *adj*

S1 W1 **par·ent** /ˈpeərənt‖ˈper-/ *n* [C] **1** the father or mother of a person or animal: *I don't really get on with my boyfriend's parents.* | *a parent substitute, such as an aunt* —see picture at FAMILY **2** something that produces other things of the same type: *Shares in Mercury parent Cable and Wireless went up by 3p.* —see also ONE-PARENT FAMILY, SINGLE PARENT

**par·ent·age** /ˈpeərəntɪdʒ‖ˈper-/ *n* [U] someone's parents and the country and social class they are from: *a child of unknown parentage* (=we do not know who its parents are)

**pa·rent·al** /pəˈrentl/ *adj* connected with one parent or both parents: *parental responsibilities*

**parent com·pa·ny** /ˈ·· ˌ···/ *n* [C] a company that controls a smaller company or organization

**pa·ren·the·sis** /pəˈrenθɪ̇sɪ̇s/ *n plural* **parentheses** /-siːz/ [usually plural] *especially AmE* a round BRACKET: **in parentheses** *The figures in parentheses refer to page numbers.* —see picture at PUNCTUATION MARK

**par·en·the·t·ical** /ˌpærənˈθetɪkəl◂/ **parenthetic** *adj* said or written as an extra remark about something you are talking about —**parenthetically** /-kli/ *adv*

**par·ent·hood** /ˈperənthʊd‖ˈper-/ *n* [U] the state of being a parent

**par·ent·ing** /ˈpeərəntɪŋ‖ˈper-/ *n* [U] the skill or activity of looking after children as a parent

**par ex·cel·lence** /ˌpɑːr ˈeksələːns‖-eksəˈlɑːns/ *adj* [only after noun] *French* the very best: *Auguste Escoffier, master-chef par excellence*

**par·fait** /pɑːˈfeɪ‖pɑːr-/ *n* [U] *AmE* a sweet food made of layers of ICE CREAM and fruit

**pa·ri·ah** /pəˈraɪə, ˈpæriə/ *n* [C] **1** someone who is hated and avoided by other people: *a social pariah* **2** *old use* a member of a very low social class in India

**par·i·mu·tu·el** /ˌpæriˈmjuːtʃuəl/ *n French* **1** [U] a system in which the money that people have risked on a horse race is shared between the people who have won **2** [C] *AmE* a machine used to calculate the amount of money people can win by risking it on horse races; TOTE² *BrE*

**par·ings** /ˈpeərɪŋz‖ˈper-/ *n* [plural] thin pieces of something that have been cut off: *nail parings* | *cheese parings*

**par·ish** /ˈpærɪʃ/ *n* [C] **1** the area that a priest is responsible for: *a parish priest* **2** *BrE* a small area, especially a village, that has its own local government: *a parish boundary* **3 the parish** the people who live in a particular area, especially those who go to church **4 sb's parish** *BrE old-fashioned* something which someone knows a lot about or which they are responsible for

**parish church** /ˌ·· ˈ·/ *n* [C] the main church in a particular area

**parish clerk** /ˌ·· ˈ·/ *n* [C] an official who works for a church in a particular town or area

**parish coun·cil** /ˌ·· ˈ··/ *n* [C] a group of people who are responsible for taking decisions about a small area, especially a village

**pa·rish·io·ner** /pəˈrɪʃənə‖-ər/ *n* [C] someone who lives in a parish, especially someone who regularly goes to the church there

**parish pump** /ˌ·· ˈ·/ *adj* [only before noun] *BrE old-fashioned* concerned only with a small local area: *parish-pump politics*

**parish re·gis·ter** /ˌ·· ˈ···/ *n* [C] an official record of the births, deaths, and marriages in a parish

**Pa·ris·i·an** /pəˈrɪziən‖pəˈrɪʒən, -ˈriː-/ *adj* coming from or connected with Paris —**Parisian** *n* [C]

**par·i·ty** /ˈpærɪ̇ti/ *n* [U] **1** the state of being equal, especially having equal pay, rights, or power: **[+ with]** *Women workers are demanding parity with their male colleagues.* **2** *technical* equality between the units of money from two different countries: *until the time the pound has parity with the dollar* **3** *technical* a system for finding mistakes in the sending of information from one computer to another: *parity checking*

**park¹** /pɑːk‖pɑːrk/ *n* [C] **1** a large open area with grass and trees, especially in a town, where people can walk, play games etc: *Let's go for a walk in the park.* | *a park bench* **2** a large enclosed area of land, with grass and trees, around a big house in the countryside **3 the park** *BrE informal* the field where a game of football or RUGBY is played **4** *AmE informal* the field where a game of BASEBALL is played —see also AMUSEMENT PARK, BALL PARK, CAR PARK, NATIONAL PARK, SAFARI PARK, SCIENCE PARK, THEME PARK, TRAILER PARK S1 W2

**park²** *v* **1** [I,T] to put a car or other vehicle in a particular place for a period of time: *You can't park here – it's private property.* | **park sth** *We couldn't find anywhere to park the van.* | *There's a police car parked outside our house.* | *parked cars* | *I'm parked over there.* (=I've parked my car over there) **2** [T] *spoken* to put something in a particular place for a period of time, in a way that is inconvenient or annoying: **park sth in/on/here etc** *He parked a load of papers on my desk.* **3 park yourself** *spoken* to sit or stand in a particular place, that is inconvenient for other people: *Alma parked herself in the hotel lobby and refused to budge.* S2

**par·ka** /ˈpɑːkə‖ˈpɑːrkə/ *n* [C] a thick warm JACKET with a HOOD —see picture at COAT¹

**park and ride** /ˌ· · ˈ·/ *n* [U] a system in which you leave your car just outside a town or city and then take a special bus to the centre of the town

**par·kin** /ˈpɑːkɪn‖ˈpɑːr-/ *n* [U] *BrE* a type of cake made with OATMEAL and GINGER

S3 **park·ing** /ˈpɑːkɪŋ‖ˈpɑːr-/ *n* [U] **1** the act of parking a car or other vehicle: *No Parking.* | *a parking fine* | *a parking space* **2** spaces in which you can leave a car or other vehicle: *There's plenty of parking at the shopping mall.*

**parking ga·rage** /ˈ·· ˌ·‖ˈ·· ·ˌ·/ *n* [C] *AmE* MULTISTOREY CAR PARK

**parking light** /ˈ·· ˌ·/ *n* [C] *AmE* SIDELIGHT —see picture on page 409

**parking lot** /ˈ·· ·/ *n* [C] *AmE* an open area for cars to park in; CAR PARK *BrE*

**parking me·ter** /ˈ·· ˌ··/ *n* [C] a machine which you put money into when you park your car next to it —see picture on page 415

**parking tick·et** /ˈ·· ˌ··/ *n* [C] an official notice fixed to a vehicle, saying that you have to pay money because you have parked your car in the wrong place or for too long

**Par·kin·son's dis·ease** /ˈpɑːkənsənz dɪˌziːz‖ˈpɑːr-/ also **Parkinson's** *n* [U] a serious illness in which your muscles become very weak and your arms and legs shake

**Parkinson's law** /ˈ··· ˌ·/ *n* [singular] the idea that the amount of work you have to do increases to fill the amount of time you have to do it in

**park keep·er** /ˈ· ˌ··/ *n* [C] *BrE* someone whose job is to look after a park

**park·land** /ˈpɑːk-lænd‖ˈpɑːrk-/ *n* [U] **1** *BrE* an area of land with grass and trees, surrounding a big house in the countryside **2** land with grass and trees which is used as a park

**park ran·ger** /ˈ· ˌ··/ *n* [C] *AmE* a RANGER (1)

**park·way** /ˈpɑːkweɪ‖ˈpɑːrk-/ *n* [C] *AmE* a wide road with an area of grass and trees in the middle or along the sides

**par·ky** /ˈpɑːki‖ˈpɑːrki/ *adj BrE informal* cold: *It's a bit parky outside today.*

**par·lance** /ˈpɑːləns‖ˈpɑːr-/ *n* **in common/medical/advertising etc parlance** expressed in words that most people, or a particular group of people, would use: *This is called a unique selling proposition in advertising parlance.*

**par·lay** /ˈpɑːli‖ˈpɑːrleɪ/ *v* [T] *AmE* to increase the value of something that you have, especially your abilities, previous success, or money, by using all your opportunities well: **parlay sth into** *He parlayed his athletic achievements into a successful sports broadcasting career.*

**par·ley** /ˈpɑːli‖ˈpɑːrli/ *n* [C] *old-fashioned* a discussion in which enemies try to achieve peace —**parley** *v* [I]

W2 **par·lia·ment** /ˈpɑːləmənt‖ˈpɑːr-/ *n* [C] **1** the group of people who are elected to make a country's laws and discuss important national affairs **2 Parliament** the main law-making institution in the United Kingdom, which consists of the HOUSE OF COMMONS and the HOUSE OF LORDS: **enter Parliament/get into Parliament** (=be elected as a member of Parliament) **3** the period during which this institution meets: *We expect to get these laws passed during the present parliament.*

**par·lia·men·tar·i·an** /ˌpɑːləmənˈteəriən‖ˌpɑːrləmən-ˈter-/ *n* [C] a skilled and experienced member of a parliament

W3 **par·lia·men·ta·ry** /ˌpɑːləˈmentəri◂‖ˌpɑːr-/ *adj* connected with or governed by a parliament: *the world's oldest parliamentary democracy*

**par·lor** /ˈpɑːlə‖ˈpɑːrlər/ *n* [C] the American spelling of PARLOUR

**parlor car** /ˈ·· ·/ *n* [C] *AmE* a special railway carriage which has comfortable seats —compare PULLMAN

**par·lour** *BrE*, **parlor** *AmE* /ˈpɑːlə‖ˈpɑːrlər/ *n* [C] **1 ice cream/massage/funeral etc parlour** a shop or type of business that provides a particular service **2** *old-fashioned* a room in a house which has comfortable chairs and is used for meeting guests —see also MILKING PARLOUR

**parlour game** *BrE*, **parlor game** *AmE* /ˈ·· ·/ *n* [C] *old-fashioned* a game that can be played indoors, such as a guessing game or a word game

**parlour maid** *BrE*, **parlor maid** *AmE* /ˈ·· ·/ *n* [C] a female servant who was employed in former times in a large house to clean the rooms, serve guests etc

**par·lous** /ˈpɑːləs‖ˈpɑːr-/ *adj formal* in a very bad or dangerous condition: *the parlous state of the country*

**Par·me·san** /ˌpɑːməˈzæn◂‖ˈpɑːrməzɑːn, -zæn/ also **Parmesan cheese** /ˌ··· ˈ·/ *n* [U] a hard strong-tasting Italian cheese

**pa·ro·chi·al** /pəˈrəʊkiəl‖-ˈroʊ-/ *adj* **1** only interested in the things that affect you and your local area, and not interested in more important matters: *Local newspapers tend to be very parochial.* **2** [only before noun] concerned with a PARISH —**parochialism** *n* [U] —**parochially** *adv*

**parochial school** /·ˈ··· ˈ·/ *n* [C] *especially AmE* a private school which is run by or connected with a church

**par·o·dy**[1] /ˈpærədi/ *n* **1** [C,U] a piece of writing or music that copies a particular well-known style in an amusing way: [+ **on/of**] *The play is a parody of James Joyce's book 'Ulysses'.* **2** [C] something that is so bad that it seems like a very bad copy of another thing: *a grotesque parody of her former self* **3 a parody of justice** something that is extremely unfair

**parody**[2] *v* [T] to copy someone's style or attitude: *East end working class attitudes have been parodied by the TV character Alf Garnett.* —**parodist** *n* [C]

**pa·role**[1] /pəˈrəʊl‖-ˈroʊl/ *n* [U] permission for someone to leave prison, on the condition that they promise to behave well: **on parole** *He was released on parole after serving 2 years.* | **break parole** (=not behave as you are supposed to when you are on parole)

**parole**[2] *v* [T] to allow someone to leave prison on the condition that they promise to behave well

**par·ox·ys·m** /ˈpærəksɪzəm/ *n* [C] **1 a paroxysm of rage/jealousy/laughter etc** a sudden uncontrollable expression of strong feeling: *Joshua suddenly broke out into a paroxysm of sobbing.* **2** a sudden, short attack of pain, coughing, shaking etc: [+ **of**] *paroxysms of coughing* —**paroxysmal** /ˌpærəkˈsɪzməl◂/ *adj*

**par·quet** /ˈpɑːkeɪ, ˈpɑːki‖pɑːrˈkeɪ/ *n* [U] small flat blocks of wood fitted together in a pattern that cover the floor of a room: *a parquet floor*

**par·ri·cide** /ˈpærəsaɪd/ *n* **1** [U] *formal* the crime of killing your father, mother, or any other close relative **2** [C] *technical* someone who is guilty of this crime —compare MATRICIDE, PATRICIDE

**par·rot**[1] /ˈpærət/ *n* [C] **1** a tropical bird with a curved beak and brightly coloured feathers that can be taught to copy human speech **2 parrot fashion** *BrE* repeating what someone has just said without understanding it: *reciting poems parrot-fashion* —see also **sick as a parrot** (SICK[1] (8))

**parrot**[2] *v* [T] to repeat someone else's words or ideas without really understanding what you are saying

**par·ry** /ˈpæri/ *v* [T] **1** to avoid answering a difficult question: *White House spokesmen tired of parrying journalists' questions* **2** to defend yourself against someone who is attacking you by pushing their weapon or hand to one side; DEFLECT —**parry** *n* [C]

**parse** /pɑːz‖pɑːrs/ *v* [T] *technical* to describe the grammar of a word when it is in a particular sentence, or the grammar of the whole sentence —**parser** *n* [C] *a powerful parser that analysed errors in word processed letters*

**Par·see**, **Parsi** /pɑːˈsiː‖ˈpɑːrsiː/ *n* [C] a member of an ancient Persian religious group in India —**Parsee** *adj*

**par·si·mo·ni·ous** /ˌpɑːsəˈməʊniəs◂‖ˌpɑːrsəˈmoʊ-/ *adj formal* extremely unwilling to spend money; MEAN[2] (2) —**parsimoniously** *adv* —**parsimony** /ˈpɑːsəməni‖ˈpɑːrsəmoʊni/ *n* [U]

**pars·ley** /ˈpɑːsli‖ˈpɑːr-/ *n* [U] a small plant with curly leaves that have a strong taste, used in cooking or as decoration on food

**pars·nip** /ˈpɑːsnɪp‖ˈpɑːr-/ *n* [C,U] a plant with a thick white or yellowish root that is eaten as a vegetable —see picture on page 414

**par·son** /ˈpɑːsən‖ˈpɑːr-/ *n* [C] *old-fashioned* a Christian priest or minister responsible for a small area, especially in the Church of England

**par·son·age** /ˈpɑːsənɪdʒ‖ˈpɑːr-/ *n* [C] the house where a parson lives

**parson's nose** /ˌ·· ˈ·/ *n* [C] *BrE informal* the piece of flesh at the tail end of a bird, usually a chicken, that has been cooked; POPE'S NOSE *AmE*

S1 W1 **part**[1] /pɑːt‖pɑːrt/ *n*

**1 ▶ PIECE OF ◀** [C,U] a piece of something such as an object, area, event, or period of time: [+ **of**] *The front part of the car was badly damaged.* | *In parts of Canada, French is the first language.* | *What part of America do you come from?* | *I only saw the first part of the programme.* | **be (a) part of** *Falling over is part of learning how to ski.* | **late/early part** *She spent the early part of her life in Belfast.* | **best/worst part** *The best part of the holiday was the trip to the Islands.* | **hard/easy part** *Getting dad to agree will be the hard part.*

**2 ▶ MACHINE/OBJECT ◀** [C] one of the separate pieces that something such as a machine, object etc is made of: *I've glued it back together, but this part won't fit properly.* | *They send you the parts and you build it yourself.* | **spare part** (=kept for when a part breaks, needs replacing etc)

**3 ▶ NOT ALL ◀** [C,U] some but not all of a particular thing or group of things: [+ **of**] *Part of the castle was destroyed in the fire.* | **in parts** *The film is very violent in parts.* | **(only) part of the story/problem/explanation etc** *Poor working conditions are only part of the problem.*

**4 play a part a)** if something plays a part in something, it is one of the several causes that make it happen or be successful: [+ **in**] *This innovation has played a part in the company's success.* | **play a big/important part in** *Besides dieting, exercising plays an important part in losing weight.* **b)** to perform the actions, words etc of a particular character in a play, film etc: **play the part of** *Kenneth Brannagh played the part of Henry V.* **c)** to be involved in something: *Britain should play its full part in these negotiations.*

**5 take part** to be involved in an activity, sport, event etc together with other people: [+ **in**] *About 400 students took part in the protest.* | *She wanted to take part but she was too ill.* | **take an active/leading part** *At college I took an active part in student politics.*

**6 the best/better part of** nearly all of something: *We waited for the best part of an hour.*

**7 a good/large part of** a lot or more than half of something: *A large part of the budget will be spent on advertising.*

**8 in large part/for the most part** mostly, to a great extent, or in most places: *The team, for the most part, was confident of success.* | *The money was in large part raised by sponsorship.*

**9 form part of/form a part of** to be one of the things that together make up something larger or more important: *Practical work forms an integral part of the course.*

**10 ▶ HAIR ◀** *AmE* a PARTING

**11 ▶ ACTING ◀** [C] the words and actions of a particular character in a play, film etc, performed by an actor: *I have to learn the part of Romeo by Tuesday.*

**12 part of the body** a particular piece or area of a body: *More heat is lost through the head than through any other part of the body.* —see also PRIVATE PARTS

**13 ▶ BOOK ◀** [C] the different parts of something written such as a book, sometimes used as a title: **first/last part** *Please turn to the first part of the report.* | **Part One/Three/Six etc** *The first chapter of Part Two begins at the funeral.*

**14 ▶ MUSIC ◀** [C] a tune that a particular type of instrument or voice within a group plays or sings: *The tenor part carried the melody.*

**15 take/have/play/want no part in** not be involved in something, because you do not agree with or approve of it: *I played no part in leaking the information to the press.*

**16 ▶ YOUR PART IN ◀** what you yourself did, in an activity that was shared by several people, especially something bad: *They were sentenced for their part in a £14 million fraud.*

**17 in/round these parts** in the particular area, part of a country etc that you are in: *We don't get many tourists in these parts.*

**18 part of me/him etc** used when you have many different feelings or thoughts about something, so it is difficult to decide what you feel or what you should do: *Part of me just wants to leave, but I know I will be unhappy if I do.*

**19 take sb's part** to support someone when they are being criticized or attacked: *The school took the teacher's part and told Jamie to leave.*

**20 ▶ QUANTITY ◀** [C] a particular quantity of a substance used when measuring different substances together into a mixture: *Prepare the glue with one part powder to three parts water.*

**21 for the part of/for his part etc** used to say what someone's opinions are, when compared to someone else's opinions: *For my part I prefer living in the country.*

**22 on sb's part/on the part of sb** used to say that someone has done something or feels something: *It was probably just a mistake on her part.* | *There has never been any jealousy on my part.*

**23 in part** to some degree, but not completely: *The accident was due in part to my own carelessness.*

**24 take sth in good part** *old-fashioned* to be able to laugh at a joke, which is about you or affects you

**25 be part and parcel of** included in something else or connected with it: *Working irregular hours is all part and parcel of being a journalist.*

**part**[2] *v* **1** [T] to pull the two sides of something apart, making a space in the middle: *The sunlight flooded the room when he parted the curtains.* | **parted lips** (=your mouth open) *Ralph's lips parted into a delighted smile.* **2** [I] to separate from someone, or end a relationship with them: *They parted on amicable terms.* | *I hope we will never part.* | **be parted** *They were hardly ever parted in thirty years of marriage.* **3 part company a)** to separate from someone, or end a relationship with them: *The two women parted company outside their rooms.* **b)** to no longer agree with or think the same as someone else: *He parted company with Lloyd George over post-war diplomacy.* **4** [T] if you part your hair you separate it into two parts with a comb so that it looks tidy

**part with** sth *phr v* [T] to unwillingly give something to someone else or stop having it yourself: *I'm reluctant to part with any of the kittens, but we need the money.*

**part**[3] *adv* **part sth, part sth** if something is part one thing, part another, it consists of both of those things: *The medical exams are part written, part practical.* | *The room is really part sitting room, part bedroom.*

**part**[4] *adj* **part owner/payment etc** only owning, paying etc a bit of something, not all of it: *I gave them £10 in part payment.*

**par·take** /pɑːˈteɪk‖pɑːr-/ *v past tense* **partook** /-ˈtʊk/ *past participle* **partaken** /-ˈteɪkən/ [I] *formal* **1** to eat or drink something that is offered to you: [+ **of**] *Will you partake of a glass of wine?* **2** to take part in an activity or event; PARTICIPATE [+ **in**] *I like to partake in the festivities.*

**partake of** sth *phr v* [T] *formal* to have a certain amount of a particular quality: *a self-confident manner that partakes of arrogance*

**par·terre** /pɑːˈteə‖pɑːrˈter/ *n* [C] a part of a garden with flat areas of grass and flowers that make a formal pattern

**part-ex·change** /ˌ· ·ˈ·/ *n* [C,U] *BrE* a way of buying a new car, television etc in which you give your old car, television etc as part of the payment; TRADE-IN *AmE*

**par·the·no·gen·e·sis** /ˌpɑːθɪ̈nəʊˈdʒenɪ̈sɪ̈s‖ˌpɑːrθɪ̈noʊ-/

*n* [U] *technical* the production of a new plant or animal from a female without the sexual involvement of the male

**par·tial** /ˈpɑːʃəl‖ˈpɑːr-/ *adj* **1** not complete: *a partial success*| *The patient may only make a partial recovery.* **2 be partial to sth** *formal* to like something very much: *I'm very partial to cream cakes.* **3** unfairly supporting one person or one side against another —opposite IMPARTIAL

**par·ti·al·i·ty** /ˌpɑːʃiˈæləti‖ˌpɑːr-/ *n* [U] **1** unfair support of one person or one side against another; BIAS[1] (1): *Councillors were accused of partiality on land issues.* **2 partiality for** *formal* a special liking for something: *a partiality for Moorish architecture*

**par·tial·ly** /ˈpɑːʃəli‖ˈpɑːr-/ *adv formal* **1** not completely; partly: *He was only partially to blame for the accident.* **2** in a way that shows you unfairly support one person, side etc against another

W3 **par·tic·i·pant** /pɑːˈtɪsəpənt‖pɑːr-/ *n* [C] someone who is taking part in an activity or event: [+ **in**] *Would participants in the next race come forward?*

W3 **par·tic·i·pate** /pɑːˈtɪsəpeɪt‖pɑːr-/ *v* [I] *formal* to take part in an activity or event: [+ **in**] *Everyone in the class is expected to participate in these discussions.* —see JOIN[1] ((USAGE))

W3 **par·ti·ci·pa·tion** /pɑːˌtɪsəˈpeɪʃən‖pɑːr-/ *n* [U] the act of taking part in an activity or event: [+ **in**] *We want more participation in the decision-making.*| *entertainment with plenty of audience participation*

**par·ti·ci·pa·tory** /pɑːˌtɪsəˈpeɪtəri◂‖pɑːrˈtɪsəpətɔːri/ *adj formal* a way of making decisions that is participatory involves everyone who is affected by the decisions: *a participatory democracy*

**par·ti·cip·i·al** /ˌpɑːtəˈsɪpiəl‖ˌpɑːr-/ *adj technical* using a participle, or having the form of a participle —**participially** *adv*

**par·ti·ci·ple** /ˈpɑːtəsɪpəl◂‖ˈpɑːr-/ *n* [C] *technical* the form of a verb, usually ending in -ing or -ed, which is used to make compound forms of the verb or as an adjective —see also PAST PARTICIPLE, PRESENT PARTICIPLE

**par·ti·cle** /ˈpɑːtɪkəl‖ˈpɑːr-/ *n* [C] **1** a very small piece of something: *dust particles* —see also ELEMENTARY PARTICLE **2 not a particle of truth/evidence etc** no truth etc at all: *There's not a particle of truth in what he says.* **3** *technical* a type of word in grammar, such as a CONJUNCTION (3) or PREPOSITION, that is usually short and is not as important in a sentence as the subject or verb

**particle ac·cel·e·ra·tor** /ˈ··· ·ˌ····/ *n* [C] *technical* an ACCELERATOR (2)

**particle phys·ics** /ˈ··· ˌ··/ *n* [U] the study of the way ELEMENTARY PARTICLES (=very small bits of substance inside atoms) develop and behave

**par·ti-col·oured** /ˌpɑːtiˈkʌləd◂‖ˌpɑːrtiˈkʌlərd◂/ *adj* having different colours in different parts

S1 W1 **par·tic·u·lar[1]** /pəˈtɪkjələ‖pərˈtɪkjələr-/ *adj* **1** [only before noun] a particular thing or person is the one that you are talking about, and not any other: *Fred hasn't seen that particular film.*| *We expect budget pressures in this particular area.* **2** special or important enough to mention separately: *You should pay particular attention to spelling.*| *There was nothing of particular interest in the letter.*| *Is there any particular thing that's worrying you?* **3** very careful about choosing exactly what you like and not easily satisfied: [+ **about**] *Marty's very particular about his food.* **4 I'm not particular** *spoken* used to say that you do not care what is decided: [+ **what/how/where etc**] *I'm not particular how you do it, as long as it gets done.* **5** *formal* giving exact details: *She gave us a full and particular account of what had happened.*

**particular[2]** *n* **1 in particular** especially: *It was a good concert – I enjoyed the last song in particular.*| **anything/anyone in particular** *Was there anything in particular that you wanted to talk about?*| **nothing/no one in particular** *"What did you want?" "Oh, nothing in particular."* **2 particulars** [plural] the facts and details: [+ **of**] *I am not familiar with the particulars of the case.*| **sb's particulars** (=details such as their name, address, profession etc) **3 in every particular/in all particulars** *formal* in every detail: *The documents were identical in almost every particular.*

**par·tic·u·lar·i·ty** /pəˌtɪkjəˈlærəti‖pər-/ *n formal* **1** [U] the quality of being exact and paying attention to details **2** [C] a detail

**par·tic·u·lar·ize** *also* **-ise** *BrE* /pəˈtɪkjələraɪz‖pər-/ *v* [I,T] *formal* to give the details of something; ITEMIZE —**particularization** /pəˌtɪkjələraɪˈzeɪʃən‖pərˌtɪkjələrə-/ *n* [U]

**par·tic·u·lar·ly** /pəˈtɪkjələli‖pərˈtɪkjələrli/ *adv* S1 W1 **1** more than usual or more than others; ESPECIALLY: *Steve was in a particularly bad mood when he got back.*| *The restaurant is particularly popular with young people.*| *We are hoping to expand our business, particularly in Europe.* **2 not particularly a)** not very: *I'm not particularly impressed with their performance.* **b)** *spoken* not very much: *"Do you want to come to the party?" "Not particularly."*

**par·tic·u·lates** /pəˈtɪkjələts, -leɪts‖pər-/ *n* [plural] substances that consist of very small separate parts, especially substances in the air that come from car engines and seriously damage your health

**part·ing[1]** /ˈpɑːtɪŋ‖ˈpɑːr-/ *n* **1** [C,U] an occasion when two people leave each other: *It had been a melancholy parting in the rain.* **2** [C] *BrE* the line on your head made by dividing your hair with a comb; PART *AmE*: *a centre parting* —see picture on page 412 **3 the parting of the ways** the point at which two people or organizations decide to separate

**parting[2]** *adj* **1 a parting kiss/gift/glance etc** a kiss etc that you give someone as you leave **2 parting shot** an unpleasant remark that you make just as you are leaving, especially at the end of an argument: *As her parting shot, she told me never to phone her again.*

**par·ti·san[1]** /ˌpɑːtəˈzæn‖ˈpɑːrtəzən, -sən/ *adj* **1** supporting a particular party, plan or leader and disliking all others: *a partisan report* **2 partisan struggle/conflict** the continuing fight of an armed group against an enemy that has defeated its country

**partisan[2]** *n* [C] **1** someone who supports a party, plan, or leader **2** a member of an armed group that continues to fight against an enemy that has defeated its country

**par·ti·tion[1]** /pɑːˈtɪʃən‖pər-, pɑːr-/ *n* **1** [C] a thin wall that separates one part of a room from another —see picture at OPEN-PLAN **2** [U] the division of a country into two or more independent countries: *the partition of India*

**partition[2]** *v* [T + **into**] to divide a country, building, or room into two or more parts

**partition** sth ↔ **off** *phr v* [T] to divide part of a room from the rest by using a partition: *They partitioned off part of the living room to make a study.*

**par·ti·tive** /ˈpɑːtətɪv‖ˈpɑːr-/ *n technical* a word which comes before a noun and shows that part of something is being described, not the whole of it, for example the word 'some' in the phrase 'some of the cake' —**partitive** *adj*

**part·ly** /ˈpɑːtli‖ˈpɑːr-/ *adv* to some degree, but not completely: *It was partly my fault.*| *The company's problems are partly due to bad management.*| *The track was partly covered by long grass.* S2 W2

**part·ner[1]** /ˈpɑːtnə‖ˈpɑːrtnər/ *n* [C] S3 W2
**1** ▶ **MARRIAGE ETC** ◀ one of two people who are married, or who live together and have a sexual relationship
**2** ▶ **BUSINESS** ◀ one of the owners of a business, who share the profits and losses: *She's a partner in a law firm.* —see also SLEEPING PARTNER
**3** ▶ **DANCING/GAMES ETC** ◀ someone you do a particular activity with, for example dancing or playing a game against two other people: *Clare's my tennis partner.*
**4** ▶ **COUNTRY** ◀ a country that your country has an agreement with: *Britain's new trading partners in Eastern Europe.*

**5 partners in crime** *humorous* two people who have

planned and done something together, especially something that slightly annoys other people

**partner²** *v* [T] to be someone's partner in a dance, game etc: *I used to partner him in tennis matches.*

**partner up** also **partner off** *phr v* [I,T] to become or make people become partners: **partner sb ↔ up with sb** *The host tried to partner me up with Janice.*

W3 **part·ner·ship** /ˈpɑːtnəʃɪp‖ˈpɑːrtnər-/ *n* **1** [U] the state of being a partner in business: **be in partnership** *We've been in partnership for five years.* | **go into partnership** *She's gone into partnership with two local doctors.* **2** [C] a business owned by two or more partners who share the profits and losses: *It's one of the most profitable partnerships in the country.* **3** [C] a relationship between two people, organizations, or countries that work together regularly: *Laurel and Hardy – a comedy partnership that lasted all through the 1930s*

**part of speech** /ˌ· · ˈ·/ *n* [C] *technical* one of the types into which words are divided in grammar according to their use, such as noun, verb, or adjective

**par·took** /pɑːˈtʊk‖pɑːr-/ the past tense of PARTAKE

**par·tridge** /ˈpɑːtrɪdʒ‖ˈpɑːr-/ *n* [C] a fat bird with a short tail which is shot for sport and food

**part-sing·ing** /ˈ· ˌ··/ *n* [U] the singing of part-songs

**part-song** /ˈpɑːtsɒŋ‖ˈpɑːrtsɔːŋ/ *n* [C] a song that consists of three or more musical lines that are sung together

S3 **part-time** /ˌ· ˈ·◂/ *adj* [only before noun] a part-time worker works regularly for a part of the usual working time: *Mattie had a part-time job in the evenings.* —compare FULL-TIME —**part-time** *adv*: *She'll work part-time after she's had the baby.* —**part-timer** *n* [C] *informal*: *A part-timer helps us out in the mornings.*

**part·way** /ˈpɑːtweɪ‖ˈpɑːrt-/ *adv informal* some of the way into a space, or after some of a period of time has passed: *She slid partway into the room.* | *He came in partway through the presentation.*

S1 W1 **par·ty¹** /ˈpɑːti‖ˈpɑːrti/ *n plural* **parties** [C]

**1 ▶ FOR FUN ◀** an occasion when people meet together, to enjoy themselves by eating, drinking, dancing etc: *a birthday party* | *a garden party* | *Want to come to a party on Saturday?* | *Let's have a party here before we move out.* | **give/throw a party** *Robin threw a party while his parents were away.* | **party dress/clothes/hat** (=worn at a party) | **party game/trick** (=played or done at a party) | **party animal** *informal* (=someone who enjoys parties) | **party house/school** *AmE informal* (=a place that often has noisy parties) —see also HEN PARTY, HOUSE PARTY, STAG PARTY

**2 ▶ IN POLITICS ◀** an organization of people with the same political beliefs and aims, that you can vote for in elections: *The Democratic Party increased its majority.* | [also + plural verb] *BrE*: *The Labour party have launched their manifesto.* | *an all-party committee* | **party leader/member** *Party leaders met to discuss their housing policy.* | **the party faithful** (=its most loyal members) —see also PARTY LINE (1)

**3 ▶ GROUP OF PEOPLE ◀** a group of people that someone has formed in order to go somewhere or do something in an organized way: *a search party* | *a rescue party* | *The bus was rented by a party of tourists.* —see also WORKING PARTY

**4 ▶ IN AN ARGUMENT/LAW ◀** one of the people or groups involved in an argument, agreement etc, especially a legal one: *The two parties are having difficulty agreeing.* —see also THIRD PARTY

**5 the guilty party** the person who has done something illegal or wrong

**6 be (a) party to sth** *formal* to be involved in or have your name connected with an activity: *I insist on being a party to this discussion.*

**party²** also **party down** *v* [I] *informal especially AmE* to enjoy yourself, especially by drinking alcohol, eating, dancing etc: *All right! Let's party!*

**party fa·vors** /ˌ·· ˈ··/ *n* [plural] *especially AmE* small gifts such as paper hats or toys given to children at a party

**party line** /ˈ·· ·/ *n* [C] **1** the official opinion of a political party, which its members are expected to agree with and support: *He follows the party line fairly closely.* —see also **toe the line** (TOE²) **2** a telephone line connected to two or more telephones belonging to different people

**party piece** /ˈ·· ˌ·/ *n* [C] something that you usually do to entertain people at a party, for example a song that you sing

**party po·lit·i·cal** /ˌ·· ·ˈ···◂/ *adj* [only before noun] *especially BrE* related to party politics: *party-political conflict* | *a party political broadcast*

**party pol·i·tics** /ˌ·· ˈ···/ *n* [U] activities that are concerned with getting support for a political party rather than with doing things to improve the situation in a country

**party poop·er** /ˈpɑːti ˌpuːpə‖ˈpɑːrti ˌpuːpər/ *n* [C] *informal* someone who spoils other people's fun

**party wall** /ˌ·· ˈ·/ *n* [C] a dividing wall between two houses, apartments etc which belong to both owners

**par·ve·nu** /ˈpɑːvənjuː‖ˈpɑːrvənuː/ *n* [C] *formal* someone from a low social position who suddenly becomes rich or powerful: *Aristocratic families found themselves associating with parvenus.* —**parvenu** *adj*

**PASCAL** /ˈpæskæl‖pæˈskæl/ *n* [U] a computer language that works well on small computer systems and is used in teaching

**pas·chal** /ˈpæskəl/ *adj* **1** related to the Jewish holiday of Passover **2** related to the Christian holiday of Easter

**pas de deux** /ˌpɑː də ˈdɜː‖-ˈduː/ *n* [C] a dance in BALLET performed by a man and a woman

**pass¹** /pɑːs‖pæs/ *v* S1 W1

**1 ▶ GO PAST ◀** [I,T] to come up to a particular point or object and go past it: *The crowd parted to let the truck pass.* | *They kept quiet until the soldiers had passed.* | **pass sb/sth** *We passed each other on the staircase.* | *I pass the sports centre on the way to work.*

**2 ▶ MOVE/GO ◀ a)** [I always + adv/prep] to move, go, or travel from one place to another, following a particular direction: [+ **through/into/from etc**] *We saw her arrive, passing through the little gate into the garden.* | *A few seconds later, I heard his footsteps pass along the deck above my head.* | *Light bends as it passes from air to water.* | **be (just) passing through** *spoken* (=be travelling through a place) *We were just passing through and thought we'd call in and see you.* **b)** [T always + adv/prep] to move something or place something across, through, around etc something else: **pass sth around/along/across etc** *Pass the rope around the tree.*

**3 ▶ ROAD/RIVER ETC ◀** [I always + adv/prep] if a road, river, railway line etc passes through a place, it goes through that place: *The new road passes immediately behind the theatre.*

**4 ▶ TIME ◀ a)** [I] if time passes, it goes by: *The days passed slowly.* | *Several years passed before she realized the truth.* | **with each day that passes/with every passing day** *The situation seems to get worse with each day that passes.* | **not a day/hardly a day passes without** *Hardly a day passes without me thinking about Ian.* **b)** [T] if you pass time or pass your life in a particular way, you spend it in that way: *We passed the winter pleasantly enough.* | **pass the time** (=when you are bored or waiting for something) *We played cards to pass the time until morning.*

**5 ▶ EXAM/TEST ◀** [I,T] **a)** to succeed in an examination or test: *Do you think you'll pass?* | *I passed my driving test first time.* | **pass (sth) with flying colours** (=get very high marks) **b)** [T] to officially decide that someone has passed an examination or test: *The examiners finally passed her.*

**6 ▶ LAW/PROPOSAL ◀ a)** [T] to officially accept a law or proposal, especially by voting: **pass a law/motion/resolution etc** *Parliament passed a series of important measures in 1994.* | *The motion was passed unanimously.* **b)** [I,T] if a law or proposal passes an

official group, it is officially accepted by that group: *The bill failed by 17 votes to pass the House of Representatives.*
**7 ▶ GIVE ◀** [T] to take something and put it in someone's hand, especially because they cannot reach it: *Pass the salt, please.* | **pass sb sth** *Can you pass me that bag that's on the floor by your feet?* | **pass sth to sb** *I passed the note back to her.* —see also **pass around**
**8 ▶ SAY/COMMUNICATE ◀ a)** [I always + adv/prep] if words, looks, or signs pass between two or more people, they exchange them with one another: [+ **between/through etc**] *A glance of understanding passed between them.* | *The news passed quickly through the crowd outside the palace.* **b) pass a remark/comment/opinion etc** to say something or give your opinion: *She sat and watched the game, passing the occasional witty comment.*
**9 let sth pass** to deliberately not say anything or not react when someone says or does something that you do not like: *Carla made some comment about my work but I decided to let it pass.*
**10 ▶ END ◀** [I] to gradually come to an end: *The storm soon passed.* | *You may feel a little stiff, but it'll pass.*
**11 ▶ SPORT ◀** [I,T] to kick, throw, or hit a ball etc to a member of your own team: *Maradona quickly passed to Jaires.* | **pass sth** *Pass the baton, you idiot!* —see picture on page 1263
**12 pass 600/pass the $5000 mark etc** to go past a particular number or amount, as a total gradually increases or is added to: *Contributions to the disaster fund have already passed the $2 million mark.*
**13 pass unnoticed** to happen without anyone noticing or saying anything
**14 pass the time of day (with sb)** to talk to someone for a short time in order to be friendly
**15 ▶ CHANGE CONTROL ◀** [I] *formal* to go from one person's control or ownership to someone else's: [+ **to/into**] *On his death his lands passed to his son.*
**16 ▶ CHANGE ◀** [I] *formal* if a substance passes from one condition into another, it changes into another condition: [+ **from/to**] *Ice passes from a solid to a liquid state.*
**17 ▶ FALSE MONEY ◀** [T] to use false money to pay for something: *She tried to pass a counterfeit $100 bill.*
**18 ▶ PROBLEM ◀** [T always + adv/prep] to send a problem or question to another person or group so that they can deal with it: **pass sth (across/back/on) to sb** *They passed your enquiry over to us.*
**19 pass (a) sentence (on sb)** to officially decide how a criminal will be punished, and to announce what the punishment will be
**20 pass judgment (on sb)** to give your opinion about someone's behaviour
**21 ▶ GIVE NO ANSWER ◀** [I] to give no answer to a question because you do not know the answer: *"Who won the Cup in 1966?" "Pass."*
**22 pass urine/stools/blood etc** *formal or technical* to send out something as waste material or in waste material from your BLADDER OR BOWELS
**23 pass water** *technical* to send out URINE (=liquid waste) from your body
**24 pass understanding/comprehension/belief** *formal* to be impossible to understand or believe
**25 come to pass** *literary or biblical* to happen —see also PASSING, **pass the buck** (BUCK[1] (2)), **pass muster** (MUSTER[2] (1))

**pass as** sb/sth *phr v* [T] **pass for** (PASS[1])

**pass** sth ↔ **around** *phr v* [T] **1** to offer something to each person in a group: *Pass the cookies around, would you?* **2** to give something to one person in a group for them to give to the person next to them: *He took a cigar and passed the box around.* —see also **pass the hat round** (HAT (5))

**pass away** *phr v* [I] an expression meaning to die, used because you want to avoid upsetting someone by saying this directly

**pass by** *phr v* **1** [I, T] to move past or go past a person, place, vehicle etc: *I'd lie on my back and look at the clouds passing by.* | **pass by sb/sth** *Call in and see us if you're ever passing by the house.* —see also PASSERBY **2** [T **pass** sb ↔ **by**] if something passes you by, it is there but you do not get any profit or advantage from it: *She felt that life was passing her by.*

**pass** sth ↔ **down** *phr v* [T often passive] to give or teach something, such as knowledge or traditions, to people who are younger than you or live after you: **pass sth down (from sb) to sb** *They pass their knowledge down from one generation to the next in stories and rhymes.*

**pass for** sb/sth *phr v* [T] if someone or something passes for something, people think that they are that thing, although they are not really: *With my hair cut short I could have passed for a boy.* | **what passes for** *Davis then encountered the police, or what passed for the police in those peculiar conditions.*

**pass off** *phr v* **1** [T **pass** sb/sth **off as** sth] to try to make people think that something or someone is something that it is not, especially something valuable: *There is rarely any attempt to pass these copies off as originals.* **2 pass off well/badly etc** if an event passes off well, badly etc, it happens and is completed in that way: *The presidential tour passed off without a hitch.*

**pass on** *phr v* **1** [T **pass** sth ↔ **on**] to tell someone a piece of information that someone else has told you: **pass sth on to sb** *She said she'd pass the message on to the other students.* **2** [T **pass** sth ↔ **on**] **a)** to give something, especially a disease, to your children through your GENES **b)** to give a slight illness to someone else: *I stayed off work, as I didn't want to pass my cold on to anyone.* **3** [T **pass** sth ↔ **on**] to make someone else pay the cost of something: *Any increase in wage costs is bound to be passed on to the consumer.* **4** [I] **pass away** (PASS[1])

**pass out** *phr v* **1** [I] to faint: *He always passes out at the sight of blood.* **2** [T **pass** sth ↔ **out**] to give something to each one of a group of people: *Their teacher passed out the dictionaries.* **3** [I] *especially BrE* to finish a course of study at a military school or police college

**pass over** *phr v* [T] **1** [**pass** sb ↔ **over** usually passive] if you pass someone over for a job, you choose someone else who is younger or lower in the organization than them: **be passed over for promotion** (=someone else got the promotion) **2** [**pass over** sth] if you pass over a remark or a subject in a conversation, you do not spend any time discussing it: *I think we'd better pass over that last remark.*

**pass** sth ↔ **round** *phr v* [T] *BrE* to pass something around

**pass up** *phr v* **pass up a chance/opportunity/offer** to not make use of a chance to do something: *Why did you pass up the opportunity to go to university?*

**pass**[2] *n* [C] **1** an official piece of paper which shows that you are allowed to enter a building, travel on something without paying, etc: *The guard checked our passes.* | **bus pass/train pass etc** *She issued us with a one-day bus pass.* **2** a successful result in an examination: **a pass in** *delighted with her pass in geography* | **pass mark** (=the mark you need to succeed in an examination) **3** a single act of kicking, throwing, or hitting a ball etc to another member of your team: *Holden intercepted a short pass by Maradona.* **4 make a pass at** *informal* to try to kiss or touch another person with the intention of starting a sexual relationship with them **5** a road or path which goes through a place that is difficult to cross: *The road wound over a narrow mountain pass.* | *at the top of the pass into Italy* —see picture on page 835 **6 this pass/the first etc pass** this, the first etc stage in a process, especially one which involves separating unwanted things out from a group: *On the second pass we eliminated all the candidates with less than a year's experience.* **7 a pretty/sorry/fine etc pass** *old-fashioned informal* an unpleasant situation: **come to a pretty pass** *Things have come to a pretty pass if we can't even afford to get a newspaper!* **8 a)** a single movement of your hands or of a WAND over something **b)** a single movement of an aircraft over a place which it is attacking  S2 W3

**pass·a·ble** /ˈpɑːsəbəl‖ˈpæ-/ *adj* **1** just good enough to be acceptable, but not very good: *a passable piece of work* **2** a road or river that is passable is not blocked, so you can travel along or across it: *The mountain path is not passable in winter.* —**passably** *adv*: *passably well*

S3 W2 **pas·sage** /ˈpæsɪdʒ/ *n*
**1** ▶ **IN A BUILDING** ◀ [C] a long narrow way with walls on either side which connects one room or place to another; CORRIDOR (1): *Vaughan's room is just along the passage.* | *an underground passage*
**2** ▶ **A WAY THROUGH** ◀ [singular] a way through something: [+ **through**] *We forced a passage through the crowd.*
**3** ▶ **FROM A BOOK ETC** ◀ [C] a short part of a book, poem, speech, piece of music etc
**4** ▶ **OF A LAW** ◀ [U] the process of getting a BILL through a parliament or Congress so that it can become law: [+ **through**] *The bill was amended several times during its passage through Congress.*
**5** ▶ **MOVEMENT** ◀ [U] *formal* the action of going across, over, along etc something: *The bridge isn't strong enough to allow the passage of heavy vehicles.*
**6 the passage of time** the passing of time: *With the passage of time, things began to look more hopeful.*
**7** ▶ **INSIDE A BODY** ◀ a tube in your body that air or liquid can pass through: *nasal passages*
**8** ▶ **JOURNEY** ◀ [singular] the cost of a journey on a ship: [+ **to**] *My parents couldn't afford the passage to America.* | **work your passage** (=pay for a journey by working on the ship) —see also **rite of passage** (RITE (2))

**pas·sage·way** /ˈpæsɪdʒweɪ/ *n* [C] a PASSAGE (1)

**pas·sant** /ˈpæsɒŋ‖pɑːˈsɑːn/ *adv* —see EN PASSANT

**pass·book** /ˈpɑːsbʊk‖ˈpæs-/ *n* [C] **1** a book in which a record is kept of the money you put into and take out of a BUILDING SOCIETY or SAVINGS AND LOAN ASSOCIATION **2** *AmE* a BANK BOOK

**pas·sé** /ˈpæseɪ, ˈpɑː-‖pæˈseɪ/ *adj* no longer modern or fashionable: *passé colours typical of the 80s*

**pas·sel** /ˈpæsəl/ *n* [C + **of**] *AmE old-fashioned* a group of people or things: *a whole passel of kids*

**pas·sen·ger** /ˈpæsɪndʒə, -sən-‖-ər/ *n* [C] **1** someone who is travelling in a vehicle, plane, boat etc, but is not driving it or working on it: *Neither the driver nor the passengers were hurt.* | **passenger train/carriage/car** (=for people, not for goods) **2** *BrE* someone in a team who does not do their share of the group's work

**passenger seat** /ˈ··· ˌ·/ *n* [C] the seat in the front of a vehicle next to the driver

**pass·er·by** /ˌpɑːsəˈbaɪ‖ˌpæsər-/ *n plural* **passersby** [C] someone who is walking past a place by chance: *A few passersby witnessed the accident.*

**pas·sim** /ˈpæsɪm/ *adv technical* used in the notes to a book or article to show that a particular word or name appears many times

**pass·ing¹** /ˈpɑːsɪŋ‖ˈpæ-/ *n* [U] **1 the passing of time/the years** the process of time going by: *With the passing of years, he grew more bad-tempered.* **2 mention/note in passing** if you say something in passing, you mention it while you are mainly talking about something else: *He did mention his brother's wife, but only in passing.* **3** the fact of something ending or disappearing: *The old regime was defeated, and few people mourned its passing.* **4** a word meaning death, used when you want to avoid saying this directly

**passing²** *adj* [only before noun] **1** going past: *Michael watched the passing cars.* **2 with each passing day/week/year** *literary* continuously as time passes: *With each passing day she grew stronger.* **3** short, or disappearing after only a short time; BRIEF¹ (1): *He didn't even give the matter a passing thought.* | *a passing reference*

**passing³** *adv old use* very: *passing strange*

W3 **pas·sion** /ˈpæʃən/ *n* **1** [C,U] a very strong, deeply felt emotion, especially of sexual love, of anger, or of belief in an idea or principle: *a sermon full of passion and inspiration* | [+ **for**] *Paolo's burning passion for an older woman.* | **fly into a passion** (=suddenly become very angry) **2** [C] a strong liking for something: [+ **for**] *the Cubans' passion for baseball* **3 the Passion** *technical* the suffering and death of Christ —see also **crime of passion** (CRIME (5)) —**passionless** *adj*

**pas·sion·ate** /ˈpæʃənɪ̣t/ *adj* **1** having or involving very strong feelings of sexual love: *a passionate kiss* **2** having or expressing a very strong feeling, especially belief in an idea or principle: *Lewis is a passionate supporter of women's rights.* **3** very eager; INTENSE: *Brian is passionate about football.* —**passionately** *adv*: *Peter is passionately involved in environmental issues.*

**pas·sion·flow·er** /ˈpæʃənˌflaʊə‖-ˌflaʊr/ *n* [C] a climbing plant with large flowers

**passion fruit** /ˈ·· ·/ *n* [C,U] a small fruit that grows on some types of passionflower —see picture on page 413

**passion play** /ˈ·· ·/ *n* [C] a play telling the story of the suffering and death of Christ

**pas·sive¹** /ˈpæsɪv/ *adj* **1** tending to accept situations or things that other people do, without attempting to change or fight against them; SUBMISSIVE: *They accepted their defeat with passive resignation.* | *Kathy seems to take the passive role in the relationship.* **2** *technical* a verb or a sentence that is passive has as its subject the person or thing to which an action is done, as in 'The boy was thrown from his horse.' —compare ACTIVE¹ (7) —see also —**passively** *adv* —**passiveness, passivitiy** *n* [U]

**passive²** *n* **the passive** *technical* the passive form of a verb, for example 'was kicked' in the sentence 'The ball was kicked by the boy.' —compare ACTIVE²

**passive re·sis·tance** /ˌ·· ·ˈ··/ *n* [U] a way of opposing or protesting against something without using violence: *Gandhi's campaign of passive resistance*

**passive smok·ing** /ˌ·· ˈ··/ *n* [U] the act of breathing in smoke from someone else's cigarette, PIPE etc

**passive voice** /ˈ·· ˌ·/ *n* [singular] the PASSIVE²

**pas·siv·ize** also **-ise** *BrE* /ˈpæsɪvaɪz/ *v* [I,T] *technical* to make a verb PASSIVE, or to become passive —**passivization** /ˌpæsɪvaɪˈzeɪʃən‖-və-/ *n* [U]

**pass·key** /ˈpɑːs-kiː‖ˈpæs-/ *n* [C] **1** a key given to a few people for a door that only they are allowed to use **2** a key that will open a number of different locks

**Pass·o·ver** /ˈpɑːsəʊvə‖ˈpæsoʊvər/ *n* [singular] an important Jewish religious holiday when the escape of the Jews from Egypt is remembered

**pass·port** /ˈpɑːspɔːt‖ˈpæspɔːrt/ *n* [C] **1** a small official book given by a government to a citizen that proves who that person is and allows them to leave the country and enter other countries **2 a passport to success/romance/a good job etc** something that makes success, romance etc possible and likely: *Erin saw marriage as a passport to happiness.* 

**passport con·trol** /ˈ·· ·ˌ·/ *n* [U] the place where your passport is checked when you leave or enter a country

**pass·word** /ˈpɑːswɜːd‖ˈpæswɜːrd/ *n* [C] **1** a secret word or phrase that someone has to speak before they are allowed to enter a place such as a military camp **2** a secret group of letters or numbers that must be put into a computer before you can use a system or PROGRAM

**past¹** /pɑːst‖pæst/ *adj* 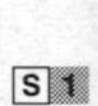
**1** ▶ **PREVIOUS** ◀ [only before noun] done, used, or experienced before now: *Judging by her past performance, I'd say Rowena should do very well.* | *From past experience she knew not to ask him where he'd been.* | *Study some past exam papers to get an idea of the questions.*
**2** ▶ **RECENTLY** ◀ a little earlier than the present or up until now: **in the past 24 hours/year/few weeks etc** *In the past year Shane's changed jobs 3 times.* | **for the past 24 hours/year/few weeks etc** *Ben hasn't been feeling too good for the past week.*
**3** ▶ **FINISHED** ◀ finished or having come to an end: *Winter is past and spring has come at last.* | *Sarah's eyes shone with memories of past happiness.* | **past life** (=part of your life that you have no connection with any more) *a sleep filled with dreams of my past life in the East*

**4 ▶ FORMER ◀** [only before noun] achieving something in the past, or holding a particular important position in the past: **past president/champion/heroes etc** *celebrating in honour of all our nation's past heroes* **5 be past it** *spoken* to be too old to do something: *Talbot's past it – they should have dropped him.* **6 ▶ GRAMMAR ◀** [only before noun] *technical* being the form of a verb that is used to show a past action or state: *the past tense*

S1 W2 **past²** *prep* **1** further than: *The hospital's just up this road about a mile past the school on your left.* | **just past** (=a little further than) *There are parking spaces over there, just past the garage.* —see picture on page 1257 **2** up to and beyond: *Will you be going past my house on your way home?* | **straight past** (=directly past without stopping) *Eva had changed so much I walked straight past her and didn't recognize her.* **3 I wouldn't put it past sb (to do sth)** *spoken* used to say that you would not be surprised if someone did something bad or unusual because it is typical of them to do that type of thing: *I'm not sure if he actually did cheat in the exams, but I wouldn't put it past him!* **4 be past caring/being interested/hope etc** to not care any more, be interested in something any more etc: *I used to get really upset when he wouldn't see me, but I'm past caring now.*

S1 W2 **past³** *n* **1 the past a)** the time that existed before the present: *James has done many things in the past, but he's happiest now in his job as a teacher.* | **a thing of the past** (=something that does not exist any more) *Good manners seem to have become a thing of the past.* **b)** the form of a verb that shows that the action or state described by the verb happened or existed some time before the present time: *Change the following verbs into the past.* **2 it's all in the past** *spoken* used to say that an unpleasant experience has ended and can be forgotten: *You mustn't think about it. It's all in the past now.* **3 sb's/sth's past** all the things that have happened to someone or something in the past: *There were certain things in his past which were very painful for Neil to remember.* **4** [singular] part of someone's life that they try to keep secret because they did things that are considered to be wrong: **a shady past** *There was something odd about him which suggested he had a shady past.*

S2 **past⁴** *adv* **1** up to and beyond a particular place: *Hal and his friends came running past at top speed.* **2 go past** if a period of time goes past, it passes: *Weeks went past without any news of them.*

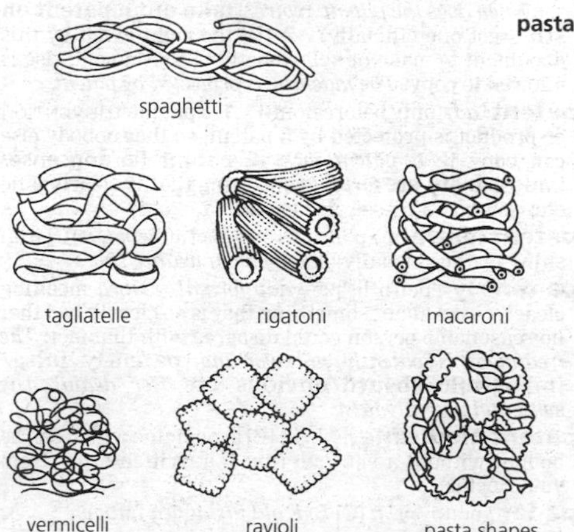


**pas·ta** /ˈpæstə‖ˈpɑː-/ *n* [U] an Italian food made from flour, eggs, and water and cut into various shapes, usually eaten with a sauce

**paste¹** /peɪst/ *n* **1 meat/fish/tomato etc paste** a soft mixture made from crushed solid food that is used in cooking or is spread on bread **2** [C,U] a soft thick mixture that can easily be shaped or spread: *Mix the powder with enough water to make a smooth paste.* **3** [C,U] a kind of glue that is used for sticking paper onto things: *wallpaper paste* **4** [U] artificial diamonds

**paste²** *v* **1** [T always + adv/prep] to stick paper to a surface using paste: [+ **on/over/down etc**] *A notice had been pasted to the door.* | *Paste down the edges of the label.* **2** [I,T] to make words appear in a new place on a computer SCREEN —see also PASTE-UP, PASTING

**paste·board** /ˈpeɪstbɔːd‖-bɔːrd/ *n* [U] flat stiff CARDBOARD made by sticking sheets of paper together

**pas·tel¹** /ˈpæstl‖pæˈstel/ *n* **1 a)** [C,U] a small coloured stick for drawing pictures with, made of a substance like CHALK **b)** [C] a picture drawn with pastels **2** [C usually plural] a soft pale colour, such as pale blue or pink

**pastel²** *adj* [only before noun] **1** a pastel colour is pale and light: *pastel blue* **2** drawn using pastels

**pas·tern** /ˈpæstɜːn‖-ɜːrn/ *n* [C] *technical* the narrow upper part of a horse's foot, just above the HOOF —see picture at HORSE¹

**paste-up** /ˈ· ·/ *n* [C] a piece of paper with writing and pictures stuck on it that show what a page will look like when a book or magazine is produced

**pas·teur·ize** also **-ise** *BrE* /ˈpɑːstʃəraɪz, -stə-‖ˈpæs-/ *v* [T] to heat a liquid in a special way that kills any BACTERIA in it: *pasteurized milk* —**pasteurization** /ˌpɑːstʃəraɪˈzeɪʃən -stə-‖ˌpæstʃərə-/ *n* [U]

**pas·tiche** /pæˈstiːʃ/ *n* **1** [C] a piece of writing, music etc that is deliberately made in the style of another artist: *The concert was a weird mixture of traditional classics and slightly embarrassing Beatles pastiches.* **2** [C] a work of art that consists of a variety of different styles put together **3** [U] the style or practice of making works of art in either of these ways

**pas·tille** /pæˈstiːl/ *n* [C] *especially BrE* a small round sweet, sometimes containing medicine for a sore throat; LOZENGE (1): *fruit pastilles*

**pas·time** /ˈpɑːstaɪm‖ˈpæs-/ *n* [C] something that you do because you find it enjoyable or interesting: *Reading was her favourite pastime.*

**past·ing** /ˈpeɪstɪŋ/ *n* **1 give sb a pasting** *informal especially BrE* **a)** to punish someone by hitting them hard: *You'll get a pasting if your dad finds out.* **b)** to defeat someone easily in a game or other competition **2** [U] the activity of moving words from one place to another on a computer screen: *cutting and pasting*

**pas·tor** /ˈpɑːstə‖ˈpæstər-/ *n* [C] a Christian priest in some protestant churches

**pas·tor·al** /ˈpɑːstərəl‖ˈpæ-/ *adj* **1** connected with the duties of a priest, minister etc towards the members of their religious group: *The Rabbi makes pastoral visits on Tuesdays.* **2** *literary* typical of the simple peaceful life in the country: *a charming pastoral scene* **3** connected with the duties of a teacher in advising students about their personal needs outside of lessons

**past par·ti·ci·ple** /ˌ· ˈ····/ *n* [C] *technical* a participle that can be used in compound forms of a verb to show the PASSIVE or the PERFECT tenses (for example 'broken' in 'I have broken my leg'), or sometimes as an adjective (for example 'broken' in 'a broken leg')

**past per·fect** /ˌ· ˈ··/ *n* [singular] *technical* the form of a verb that shows that the action described by the verb was completed before a particular time in the past, formed in English with 'had' and a past participle —**past perfect** *adj*

**pas·tra·mi** /pəˈstrɑːmi/ *n* [U] smoked BEEF that contains a lot of SPICES

**pas·try** /ˈpeɪstri/ *n* **1** [U] a mixture of flour, fat, and milk or water, used to make the outer part of baked foods such as PIES **2** [C] a small sweet cake, made using this substance: *a Danish pastry* S3

**pas·tur·age** /ˈpɑːstʃərɪdʒ‖ˈpæs-/ *n* [U] **1** *technical* the right to use an area of land for feeding your sheep, cattle, horses etc **2** pasture

**pas·ture**[1] /ˈpɑːstʃə‖ˈpæstʃər-/ *n* [C,U] **1** land or a field that is covered with grass and is used for cattle, sheep etc to feed on: *Stone walls divided pasture from arable land.*| *the rolling pastures of southern England* **2 put sth/sb out to pasture a)** to move cattle, horses etc into a field to feed on the grass **b)** *informal* to make someone leave their job because you think they are too old to do it properly **3 pastures new/greener** *humorous* a new and exciting or better job, place or activity: *"I'd like to say goodbye to Paul who leaves us for pastures new."*

**pasture**[2] *v* **1** [T] to put animals outside in a field to feed on the grass **2** [I + **on**] if animals pasture on a particular area of land, they eat the grass that is growing there

**pas·ture·land** /ˈpɑːstʃəlænd‖ˈpæstʃər-/ *n* [U] pasture

**past·y**[1] /ˈpeɪsti/ *adj* a pasty face looks very pale and unhealthy

**past·y**[2] /ˈpæsti/ *n* [C] *BrE* a small case of PASTRY (1) filled with meat, vegetables etc and baked: *a Cornish pasty*

**pasty-faced** /ˈpeɪsti feɪst/ *adj* having a very pale face that looks unhealthy

**pat**[1] /pæt/ *v* **patted, patting** [T] **1** to repeatedly touch someone or something lightly with your hand flat, especially to give comfort: *He patted the dog affectionately as he spoke.* **2 pat sb/yourself on the back** to praise someone or yourself for doing something well: *You can pat yourselves on the back for a job well done.* —see picture on page 1260

**pat**[2] *n* [C] **1** a friendly act of touching someone with your hand flat: *Mrs Dodd gave the child a pat on the head.* **2** the sound made by hitting something lightly with a flat object **3 a pat of butter** a small flat lump of butter **4 a pat on the back** *informal* praise for something that you have done well: *Alex deserves a pat on the back for all his hard work.* —see also COWPAT

**pat**[3] *adj* [usually before noun] a pat answer or explanation is made quickly and sounds as if it has been used before: *Don't give me any of your pat answers.*

**pat**[4] *adv* **1 have sth off pat** *BrE*, **have sth down pat** *AmE* to know something thoroughly so that you can say it, perform it etc immediately without thinking about it **2 stand pat** *especially AmE* to refuse to change your opinion or decision

**patch**[1] /pætʃ/ *n* [C]

**1 ▶ PART OF AN AREA ◀** a part of an area that is different or looks different from the parts that surround it: *Lost: a small dog, white with brown patches.*| **patch of dirt/grease/damp etc** *Watch out for icy patches on the roads.*| **patch of light/sky etc** *Patches of blue sky peeked through the clouds.*

**2 ▶ OVER A HOLE ◀** a small piece of material used to cover a hole in something: *a jacket with leather patches at the elbows*

**3 ▶ FOR GROWING STH ◀** a small area of ground for growing fruit or vegetables: *a strawberry patch*

**4 ▶ ON YOUR EYE ◀** a piece of material that you wear over your eye to protect it when it has been hurt

**5 ▶ DECORATION ◀** a small piece of cloth with words or pictures on it that you can stitch onto clothes

**6 a bad/difficult/sticky patch** *informal especially BrE* a period of time when you are having a lot of difficulty: *Gemma's going through a bad patch right now.*

**7 sb's patch** *BrE informal* an area that someone knows very well because they work or live there; TURF[1] (4) *AmE*: *The boss knows everything that's going on in our patch.*

**8 not be a patch on** *BrE informal* to be much less attractive, good etc than something or someone else: *She's no great beauty – not a patch on Maria.*

**9 good/interesting/boring etc in patches** *especially BrE* good etc in some parts, but not all the time

**patch**[2] *v* [T] to put a piece of cloth over a hole, especially in a piece of clothing

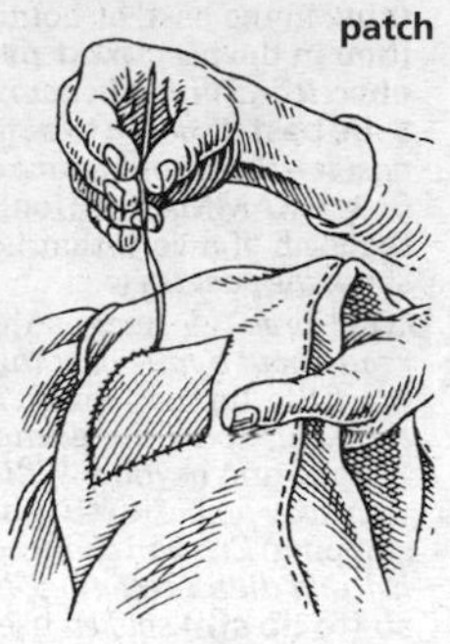


**patch** sth ↔ **together** *phr v* [T] to make something quickly or carelessly from a number of different pieces or ideas: *A new plan was quickly patched together.*

**patch** sth/sb ↔ **up** *phr v* [T] **1** to end an argument because you want to stay friendly with someone: *Try to patch up your differences before he leaves.*| **patch it up (with)** *I've patched it up with the landlord.* **2** to repair something by adding a new piece of material to it: *We'd better patch up the roof – we can't afford a new one.* **3** to give quick and basic medical treatment to someone who is hurt: *We just patch up the wounded as best we can.*

**patch pock·et** /ˌ· ˈ··/ *n* [C] a pocket made by SEWING a square piece of cloth onto a piece of clothing

**patch·work** /ˈpætʃwɜːk‖-wɜːrk/ *n* [U] **1** a type of needlework in which many coloured squares of cloth are stitched together to make one large piece: *a patchwork quilt* —see picture on page 839 **2 a patchwork of fields/villages etc** a pattern that fields and villages seem to make when you see them from far above **3 a patchwork of ideas/techniques etc** a combination of many different ideas etc: *a patchwork of architectural styles*

**patch·y** /ˈpætʃi/ *adj* **1** happening or existing irregularly in a number of small separate areas: *patchy fog* **2** not complete enough to be useful: *His knowledge of French remained pretty patchy.*| *patchy evidence* **3** *especially BrE* good in some parts but bad in others: *I thought the performance was patchy.* —**patchiness** *n* [U]

**pate** /peɪt/ *n* [C] *old use* the top of your head: *his bald pate*

**pâ·té** /ˈpæteɪ‖pɑːˈteɪ, pæ-/ *n* [C,U] a smooth, soft substance made from meat or fish that can be spread on bread

**pa·tel·la** /pəˈtelə/ *n* [C] *technical* your KNEECAP[1] —see picture at SKELETON

**pa·tent**[1] /ˈpeɪtnt, ˈpæ-‖ˈpæ-/ *n* **1** [C] a special document that says that you have the right to make or sell a new INVENTION or product and that no one else is allowed to do so: *When does the patent expire?*| **take out a patent on sth** (=get one officially) **2** [U] the right given by this document to make or sell something that no one else is allowed to copy: *The machine is protected by patent.*

**patent**[2] *adj* [only before noun] **1** a patented INVENTION or product is protected by a patent, so that nobody else can copy it: *a patent lock* **2 patent lie/nonsense/impossibility etc** *formal* something that is clearly a lie etc; OBVIOUS (1) —see also PATENTLY

**patent leath·er** /ˌpeɪtnt ˈleðə◂‖ˌpætnt ˈleθər/ *n* [U] thin shiny leather, usually black: *patent leather shoes*

**pa·tent·ly** /ˈpeɪtntli‖ˈpæ-/ *adv formal* a word meaning clearly, used about something that is so clearly bad that no reasonable person could disagree with that fact: *The treatment is patently not working.*| **patently false/impossible/absurd/obvious etc** *Her denial was swift and patently false.*

**patent medi·cine** /ˌ·· ˈ···/ *n* [C] a medicine which can be bought without a PRESCRIPTION (=a written order from your doctor)

**pa·ter** /ˈpeɪtə‖-ər/ *n* [C] *BrE old-fashioned* father

**pa·ter·fa·mil·ias** /ˌpeɪtəfəˈmiːliæs‖ˌpɑːtərfəˈmiːliəs/ *n* [C] *formal* a father or a man who is the head of a family

**pa·ter·nal** /pəˈtɜːnl‖-ɜːr-/ *adj* **1** paternal feelings or behaviour are like those of a father for his children: *Dan took a paternal interest in my work.* **2 paternal grandmother/uncle etc** your father's mother, brother etc —compare MATERNAL —**paternally** *adv*

**pa·ter·nal·is·m** /pəˈtɜːnəl-ɪzəm‖-ɜːr-/ *n* [U] a system of controlling people or organizations in which people are protected, and their needs are satisfied, but they do not have any freedom or responsibility —**paternalist, paternalistic** /pəˌtɜːnəlˈɪstɪk◂‖-ɜːr-/ *adj*

**pa·ter·ni·ty** /pəˈtɜːnɪ̣ti‖-ɜːr-/ *n* [U] *law* the fact of being the father of a particular child, or the question of who the child's father is: *The paternity of the child is in dispute.*

**paternity leave** /-ˈ··· ˌ·/ *n* [U] a period of time away from work that a father of a new baby is allowed

**paternity suit** /-ˈ··· ˌ·/ *n* [C] a legal action in which a mother asks a court of law to say that a particular man is the father of her child

**pa·ter·nos·ter** /ˌpætəˈnɒstə‖-tərˈnɑːstər/ *n* [C] the LORD'S PRAYER

S2 W2 **path** /pɑːθ‖pæθ/ *n plural* **paths** /pɑːðz‖pæðz/ [C]
**1** ▶ **TRACK** ◀ a track that people walk along over an area of ground: *I walked nervously up the path towards the front door.* | *A path had been worn across the grass.*
**2** ▶ **WAY THROUGH STH** ◀ a way through something, that is made by opening a space to allow you to move forward: *The crowd moved aside to make a path for them.* | [+ **through**] *They used axes to clear a path through the jungle.*
**3** ▶ **DIRECTION** ◀ the direction or line along which someone or something moves: *Sherman's army burned and looted everything that lay in its path.* | *the orbital path of the moon around the earth*
**4** ▶ **PLAN** ◀ what you intend to do over a long period of time: *a career path* | [+ **to**] *Shamira saw a college degree as her path to independence.*
**5 sb's paths cross** if two people's paths cross, they meet by chance: *Our paths did not cross again until 1941.* —see also **beat a path (to sb's door)** (BEAT[1] (23)), **lead sb up the garden path** (LEAD[1] (18)), **stand in sb's way/path** (STAND[1] (48))

S3 **pa·thet·ic** /pəˈθetɪk/ *adj* **1** something or someone that is pathetic is so useless, unsuccessful, or badly done that they annoy you: *You're pathetic! Here, let me do it.* | *It's a pretty pathetic computer, basically.* | *Vic made a pathetic attempt to apologise.* **2** making you feel pity or sympathy: *a pathetic sight* —**pathetically** /-kli/ *adv*

**pathetic fal·la·cy** /-ˌ·· ˈ···/ *n* [U] *technical* the idea of describing the sea, rocks, weather etc in literature as if they were human

**path·find·er** /ˈpɑːθˌfaɪndə‖ˈpæθˌfaɪndər/ *n especially AmE* **1** [C] a person who goes ahead of a group and finds the best way through unknown land **2** a person who discovers new ways of doing things; TRAILBLAZER

**path·o·gen** /ˈpæθədʒən, -dʒen/ *n* [C] *technical* something that causes disease in your body —**pathogenic** /ˌpæθəˈdzenɪk◂/ *adj*

**path·o·log·i·cal** /ˌpæθəˈlɒdʒɪkəl◂‖-ˈlɑː-/ *adj* **1** pathological behaviour or feelings happen regularly, are unreasonable, and impossible to control: *a pathological liar* | *a pathological hatred of women* **2** a mental or physical condition that is pathological is caused by disease **3** *technical* connected with pathology —**pathologically** /-kli/ *adv*: *pathologically jealous*

**pa·thol·o·gy** /pəˈθɒlədʒi‖-ˈθɑː-/ *n* [U] the study of the causes and effects of illnesses —**pathologist** *n* [C]

**pa·thos** /ˈpeɪθɒs‖-θɑːs/ *n* [U] the quality that a person or a situation has that makes you feel pity and sadness: *a scene full of pathos*

**path·way** /ˈpɑːθweɪ‖ˈpæθ-/ *n* [C] a path

S3 **pa·tience** /ˈpeɪʃəns/ *n* [U] **1** the ability to wait calmly for a long time and accept delays without becoming angry or anxious: *You'll need patience if you want to be served in this shop.* | *Marianna listened to his story with patience.* **2** the ability to accept trouble and other people's annoying behaviour without complaining or becoming angry: **have no patience with** *She has no patience with time-wasters.* | **lose patience (with)** (=stop being patient and get angry) *I'm beginning to lose patience with you people.* | **the patience of Job/the patience of a saint** (=very great patience when someone is annoying you) | **try sb's patience** (=make someone lose their patience) *Henry began to try Isabel's patience with his negative attitude.* **3** the ability to continue to give your attention to work that is difficult or tiring: **have the patience to do sth** *I wouldn't have the patience to sit sewing all day.* **4** *BrE* a card game for one player; SOLITAIRE (3) *AmE*

S2 W1 **pa·tient¹** /ˈpeɪʃənt/ *n* [C] someone receiving medical treatment from a doctor

W3 **patient²** *adj* able to wait calmly for a long time or to accept difficulties, people's annoying behaviour etc without becoming angry: [+ **with**] *Louise was very patient with me when I was ill and crabby.* —**patiently** *adv*

**pat·i·na** /ˈpætɪ̣nə‖pəˈtiːnə/ *n* [singular, U] **1** a greenish layer that forms naturally on the surface of copper or BRONZE **2** a smooth, shiny surface that gradually develops on wood, leather etc **3 the patina of wealth/success etc** the attractive or impressive appearance of wealth etc

**pat·i·o** /ˈpætiəʊ‖-oʊ/ *n plural* **patios** [C] a flat area with a stone floor next to a house, used for sitting outside

**patio doors** /ˈ··· ˌ·/ *n* [plural] *especially BrE* glass doors that open from a living room onto a patio

**pa·tis·se·rie** /pəˈtiːsəri, ˈtɪs/ *n* [C] *French* a shop that sells French cakes and pies, or the cakes it sells

**pa·tois** /ˈpætwɑː/ *n plural* **patois** /-twɑːz/ [C,U] a spoken form of a language used by the people of a small area and different from the national or standard language

**patri-** /peɪtrɪ̣, pætrɪ̣/ *prefix* **1** concerning fathers: *patricide* (=killing one's father) **2** concerning men: *a patriarchal society* (=controlled by men) —compare MATRI-

**pa·tri·al** /ˈpeɪtriəl, ˈpæ-/ *n* [C] *BrE technical* someone who has a legal right to come to live in the United Kingdom because their parents, grandfather, or grandmother were born there

**pa·tri·arch** /ˈpeɪtriɑːk‖-ɑːrk/ *n* [C] **1** an old man who is respected as the head of a family or tribe —compare MATRIARCH **2** a BISHOP (1) in the early Christian church **3** a chief BISHOP (1) of the Orthodox Christian churches

**pa·tri·arch·al** /ˌpeɪtriˈɑːkəl◂‖-ˈɑːr-/ *adj* **1** ruled or controlled only by men: *a patriarchal system* **2** connected with being a patriarch, or typical of a patriarch: *patriarchal attitudes*

**pa·tri·arch·y** /ˈpeɪtriɑːki‖-ɑːr-/ *n* [C,U] **1** a social system in which the oldest man rules his family and passes power and possessions on to his sons **2** a social system in which men have all the power —compare MATRIARCHY

**pa·tri·cian** /pəˈtrɪʃən/ *adj* **1** typical of a member of the highest class in society; ARISTOCRATIC: *a patrician face* **2** belonging to the governing classes in ancient Rome —compare PLEBEIAN —**patrician** *n* [C]

**pat·ri·cide** /ˈpætrɪ̣saɪd/ *n* [U] the crime of murdering your father —compare MATRICIDE, PARRICIDE (1)

**pat·ri·mo·ny** /ˈpætrɪ̣məni‖-moʊni/ *n* [U, singular] *formal* property given to you after the death of your father, which was given to him by your grandfather etc; INHERITANCE (1) —**patrimonial** /ˌpætrɪ̣ˈməʊniəl◂‖-ˈmoʊ-/ *adj*

**pat·ri·ot** /ˈpætriət, -triɒt, ˈpeɪ-‖ˈpeɪtriət, -triɑːt/ *n* [C] someone who loves their country and is willing to defend it: *Mr Bush praised Weinburger as 'a true American patriot'.*

**pat·ri·ot·ic** /ˌpætriˈɒtɪk◂, ˌpeɪ-‖ˌpeɪtriˈɑːtɪk◂/ *adj* having or expressing a great love of your country: *good patriotic Americans* | *patriotic songs* —**patriotism** /ˈpætriətɪzəm, ˈpeɪ‖ˈpeɪ/ *n* [U]

**pa·trol¹** /pəˈtrəʊl‖ˈtroʊl/ *v* **patrolled, patrolling** [I always+adv/prep, T] **1** to go around the different parts of an area or building at regular times to check that there is no trouble or danger: *waters patrolled by enemy submarines* | *Armed guards with dogs patrolled the exhibition.* **2** to drive or walk repeatedly around an area in a threatening way: *Gangs of youths patrolled the streets at night.*

**patrol²** *n* **1** [C,U] the act of going around different parts of an area at regular times to check that there is no trouble or danger: *Security guards carry out regular patrols of the factory premises.*|*patrol duty*|**on patrol** *submarines on patrol in the North Atlantic*|**patrol boat/car** (=used by the army or police) **2** [C] a group of police, soldiers, vehicles, planes etc sent out to search a particular area: *the US border patrol* **3** [C] a small group of BOY SCOUTS or GIRL GUIDES —see also HIGHWAY PATROL

**patrol car** /·ˈ·· ·/ *n* [C] a police car that drives around the streets of a city

**pa·trol·man** /pəˈtrəʊlmən‖-ˈtroʊl-/ *n* [C] **1** *AmE* a police officer who regularly walks or drives around a particular area to prevent crime from happening **2** someone employed by a car owners' association in Britain who drives along roads to give help to drivers

**patrol wag·on** /·ˈ· ˌ··/ *n* [C] *AmE* a police vehicle used to move prisoners; BLACK MARIA *BrE*

**pa·tron** /ˈpeɪtrən/ *n* [C] **1** someone who supports the activities of an organization, for example by giving money; BENEFACTOR: *a patron of the arts*|*patron companies* **2** *formal* someone who uses a particular shop, restaurant or hotel —compare CUSTOMER (1)

**pat·ron·age** /ˈpætrənɪdʒ/ *n* [U] **1** the support, especially financial support, that is given to an organization or activity by a patron **2** *AmE* the support that you give a particular shop, restaurant etc by buying their goods or using their services; CUSTOM (3) *BrE*: *Thank you for your patronage.* **3** a system by which someone in a powerful position gives people generous help or important jobs in return for their support

**pat·ron·ize** /ˈpætrənaɪz‖ˈpeɪ-, ˈpæ-/ *v* [T] **1** to talk to someone as if they are stupid when in fact they are not: *Don't patronize me – I'm not a fool.* **2** *formal* to use or visit a shop, restaurant etc: *tourists who patronize the shopping and recreational facilities* **3** to support or give money to an organization or activity

**pat·ro·niz·ing** /ˈpætrənaɪzɪŋ‖ˈpeɪ-, ˈpæ-/ *adj* someone who is patronizing talks to you as if they think you are less intelligent or important than them: *Try not to sound so patronizing when you talk to the students.*|*a patronizing attitude* —**patronizingly** *adv*

**patron saint** /ˌ·· ˈ·/ *n* [C + **of**] a Christian SAINT (=very holy person) who is believed to give special protection to a particular place, activity, or person: *St. Christopher, patron saint of travellers*

**pat·ro·nym·ic** /ˌpætrəˈnɪmɪk/ *n* [C] *technical* a name formed from the name of your father, grandfather etc —**patronymic** *adj*

**pat·sy** /ˈpætsi/ *n* [C] *AmE informal* someone who is easily tricked or deceived, especially into taking the blame for someone else's crime

**pat·ten** /ˈpætn/ *n* [C] a wooden shoe with pieces of iron on the bottom

**pat·ter¹** /ˈpætə‖-ər/ *v* [I] **1** to make the quiet sound of something hitting a surface lightly, quickly, and repeatedly: *rain pattering on the window panes* **2** [always + adv/prep] to walk or run with light steps making this sound: [+ **around/along etc**] *I can hear the dog pattering around downstairs.*

**patter²** *n* **1** [singular] the repeated sound of something hitting a surface lightly and quickly: [+ **of**] *the patter of hooves on the street* **2** [U, singular] very fast, continuous, and usually amusing talk, used by someone telling jokes or trying to sell something: *It's difficult to look at the cars without getting the sales patter.* **3 the patter of tiny feet** *humorous* used to mean that someone is going to have a baby: *Are we going to hear the patter of tiny feet?*

S3 W1 **pat·tern¹** /ˈpætən‖ˈpætərn/ *n* [C]
**1 ▶ OF EVENTS ◀** the regular way in which something happens, develops, or is done: *Watch for changes in her breathing pattern.*|*a strange pattern of events*|**follow a set pattern** (=always happen or develop in the same fixed way) *Romantic novels tend to follow a set pattern.*
**2 ▶ DESIGN ◀ a)** a regularly repeated arrangement of shapes, colours, or lines on a surface usually intended as decoration: *a cotton dress with a flowery pattern*|*tracing an intricate pattern in the sand* **b)** a regularly repeated arrangement of sounds or words: *A sonnet has a fixed rhyming pattern.*
**3 ▶ EXAMPLE ◀** [usually singular] a thing, form, or person that is an example to copy: **set a pattern (for)** (=become a pattern) *a successful course that set a pattern for the training of all new employees*
**4 ▶ MAKING THINGS ◀** a shape used as a guide for making something, especially a thin piece of paper used when cutting material to make clothing: *a dress pattern*
**5 ▶ CHOOSING ◀** a small piece of cloth, paper etc that shows what a larger piece will look like; SAMPLE¹

**pattern²** *v* **be patterned on** to be designed or made in a way that is copied from something else: *a planned economy patterned on the Stalinist model*

**pat·terned** /ˈpætənd‖-tərnd/ *adj* decorated with a pattern: *a patterned carpet*|*wallpaper patterned with roses*

**pat·tern·ing** /ˈpætənɪŋ‖-tər-/ *n* [U] **1** *technical* the development of fixed ways of behaving, thinking, doing things etc as a result of copying and repeating actions, language etc: *cultural patterning* **2** patterns of a particular kind, especially on an animal's skin

**pat·ty** /ˈpæti/ *n plural* **patties** [C] **1** *especially AmE* small, flat pieces of cooked meat or other food: *a hamburger patty* **2** *BrE dialect* a PASTY

**patty melt** /ˈ·· ·/ *n* [C] a flat round piece of BEEF that is cooked with cheese on top and served on bread in the US

**pau·ci·ty** /ˈpɔːsəti‖ˈpɒː-/ *n* **a paucity of** *formal* less than is needed of something: *a paucity of information*

**paunch** /pɔːntʃ‖pɒːntʃ/ *n* [C] *often humorous* a man's fat stomach —**paunchy** *adj*

**pau·per** /ˈpɔːpə‖ˈpɒːpər/ *n* [C] *old-fashioned* someone who is very poor

**pau·per·ize** also **-ise** *BrE* /ˈpɔːpəraɪz‖ˈpɒː-/ *v* [T] *technical* to make people poor —**pauperization** /ˌpɔːpəraɪˈzeɪʃən‖ˌpɒːpərə-/ *n* [U]

**pause¹** /pɔːz‖pɒːz/ *v* [I] to stop speaking or doing something for a short time before starting again: *I paused for breath, almost choking with rage.*|*Please pause to consider the matter.* 

**pause²** *n* [C] **1** a short time during which someone stops speaking or doing something before starting again: *"Yes," said Philip after a moment's pause.*|[+ **in**] *an awkward pause in the conversation* **2** a mark (⌒) over a musical note, showing that the note is to be played or sung longer than usual **3 give sb pause (for thought)** to make someone stop and consider carefully what they are doing: *an avoidable accident that should give us all pause for thought*

**pa·vane** /pəˈvæn, ˈpævən‖pəˈvɑːn, pəˈvæn/ *n* [C,U] a formal dance of the 16th and 17th centuries, or the music for this dance

**pave** /peɪv/ *v* [T usually passive] **1** to cover a path, road, area etc with a hard level surface such as blocks of stone or CONCRETE: *The road was only paved last year.*|*a paved courtyard* **2 pave the way for** to make a later event or development possible by producing the right conditions: *The Supreme Court decision paved the way for further legislation on civil rights.* **3 the streets are paved with gold** used to say that it is easy to become rich quickly in a particular place

**pave·ment** /ˈpeɪvmənt/ *n* **1** [C] *BrE* a hard level surface or path at the side of a road for people to walk on; SIDEWALK *AmE* —see picture on page 410 **2** [U] *AmE* the hard surface of a road **3** [C,U] paved surface or area of any kind; PAVING (2)

This graph shows how common the nouns **pavement** and **sidewalk** are in British and American English.

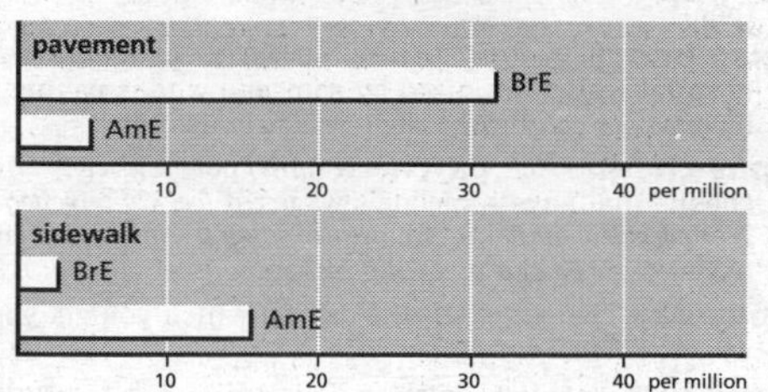


Based on the British National Corpus and the Longman Lancaster Corpus

In British English the word **pavement** means the path for people to walk on at the side of a road. Americans use the word **sidewalk** for this meaning. In American English, **pavement** is used to mean the hard surface of a road, or a paved surface.

**pavement art·ist** /ˈ·· ˌ··/ *n* [C] *BrE* someone who draws coloured pictures on a pavement, hoping that people passing will give them money; SIDEWALK ARTIST *AmE*

**pa·vil·ion** /pəˈvɪljən/ *n* [C] **1** a large, light structure that is built to be used for only a short time especially for public entertainments or EXHIBITIONS: *the German pavilion at the World Trade Fair* **2** *especially BrE* a building beside a sports field, especially a CRICKET field, used by the players and people watching the game

**pav·ing** /ˈpeɪvɪŋ/ *n* **1** [U] material used to form a hard, level surface on a path, road, area etc **2** [U] any kind of paved (PAVE) surface **3** [C] a paving stone

**paving stone** /ˈ·· ·/ *n* [C] one of the flat square pieces of stone that are used to make a hard surface to walk on

**pav·lo·va** /pævˈləʊvə‖pɑːvˈloʊ-/ *n* [C,U] a light cake made of MERINGUE, cream, and fruit

**paw¹** /pɔː‖pɒː/ *n* [C] **1** an animal's foot that has nails or CLAWS: *a lion's paw* **2** *informal* someone's hand: *Keep your filthy paws off me!*

**paw²** *v* [I,T] **1** if an animal paws a surface, it touches or rubs one spot repeatedly with its paw: [+ **at**] *The dog's pawing at the door again – let him out.* **2** *informal* to feel or touch someone in a rough or sexual way that is offensive: *First he drank too much, then he started pawing me.*

**paw·ky** /ˈpɔːki‖ˈpɒː-/ *adj especially ScotE* humorous in a quiet clever way that could be intended to be either funny or serious: *a pawky sense of humour*

**pawn¹** /pɔːn‖pɒːn/ *n* [C] **1** one of the eight smallest and least valuable pieces in the game of CHESS **2** someone who is used by a more powerful person or group: [+ **in**] *We're just pawns in the director's power game.*

**pawn²** *v* [T] to leave something valuable with a pawnbroker in order to borrow money from them

**pawn·bro·ker** /ˈpɔːnˌbrəʊkə‖ˈpɒːnˌbroʊkər/ *n* [C] someone whose business is to lend people money in exchange for valuable objects

**pawn·shop** /ˈpɔːnʃɒp‖ˈpɒːnʃɑːp/ *n* [C] a pawnbroker's shop

**paw·paw** /ˈpɔːpɔː‖ˈpɒːpɒː/ *n* [C] *especially BrE and CarE* the large yellow-green fruit of a tall tropical tree; PAPAYA

**pax** /pæks/ *interjection* a word used by children when they want to end an argument or fight

S1 W1 **pay¹** /peɪ/ *v past tense and past participle* **paid** /peɪd/
**1** ▶ **GIVE MONEY** ◀ [I,T] to give someone money for something you have bought, or for something they have done for you: *They ran off without paying.* | *Didn't pay 'em a penny, just asked 'em to do it.* | [+ **for**] *Mum and Dad paid for my driving lessons.* | **pay sb for sth** *When can you pay me for the work?* | **pay sb sth** *I paid her $200 for this painting.* | **pay sb to do sth** *Ray paid some kids to wash the car.* | **pay (in) cash** *You'd get a discount for paying cash.* | **pay by cheque/credit card** *May I pay by credit card?*
**2** ▶ **DEBT/BILL/TAX** ◀ [T] to pay money that you owe to a person, company etc: *I forgot to pay the gas bill!* | *How much tax did you pay last year?*
**3** ▶ **WAGE/SALARY** ◀ [I,T] to give someone money for the job they do: *How much do they pay you?* | *Home workers are very poorly paid.* | **pay sb $100 a day/£200 a week etc** *Programmers are paid about £200 a day.*
**4 pay attention (to)** to give your attention to something: *I'm sorry, I wasn't paying attention to what you were saying.*
**5 pay a call/visit on sb** or **pay sb a call/visit** to visit someone
**6 pay the penalty/price** to experience something unpleasant because you have done something wrong, made a mistake etc: **pay the price for (doing) sth** *You'll pay the price for drinking so much tomorrow.*
**7** ▶ **GOOD RESULT** ◀ [I] if a particular action pays, it brings a good result or advantage for you: *Crime doesn't pay.* | **it pays to do sth** *It usually pays to tell the truth.* | **it would/it might pay (you) to do sth** *It would pay you to ask if there are any jobs going at the London office.* | **pay dividends** *Getting some qualifications now will pay dividends in the long term.*
**8** ▶ **PROFIT** ◀ [I] if a shop or business pays, it makes a profit: *If the pub doesn't start to pay, we'll have to sell it.*
**9 pay sb a compliment** to say nice things about someone's appearance, behaviour etc: **pay sb the compliment of doing sth** *Gretta paid me the compliment of saying I was a good judge of character.*
**10 pay your respects (to sb)** *formal* to send polite greetings to someone or to visit them: **pay your last respects** (=go to someone's funeral)
**11 pay for itself** if something you buy pays for itself, it makes you save as much money as you bought it for: *A new boiler would pay for itself within two years.*
**12 pay your way** to pay for everything that you want without having to depend on anyone else for money
**13 pay through the nose (for sth)** *spoken* to pay far too much for something: *I had to pay through the nose for these tickets.*
**14 pay tribute to** to say how much you admire or respect someone or something: *Doctors paid tribute to her courage at the end.*
**15 pay court to sb** *old-fashioned* to treat someone, especially a woman, with great respect and admiration —see also **pay lip service to** (LIP SERVICE), **pay your dues** (DUE² (2))

**pay** sb/sth ↔ **back** *phr v* [T] **1** to give someone the money that you owe them; REPAY: **pay sb back** *Can you lend me £10 and I'll pay you back on Friday?* | **pay sth ↔ back** *We're paying back the loan over 15 years.* | **pay sb back sth** *Did I pay you back that £5?* **2** to make someone suffer for doing something wrong or unpleasant: **pay sb back for sth** *I'll pay Jenny back for what she did to me!*

**pay for** sth *phr v* [T] to suffer or be punished for something you have done: *These people should pay for their crimes.* | *You'll pay for that!* | **pay for doing sth** *I'll make her pay for ruining my chances.* | **pay dearly** *Nick's paid dearly for his unfaithfulness to his wife.*

**pay** sth ↔ **in/into** *phr v* [T] to put money in your bank account etc: *Did you remember to pay that cheque in?* | **pay sth into sth** *I've paid $250 into my account.*

**pay off** *phr v* **1** [T **pay** sth ↔ **off**] to give someone all the money you owe them: *I've paid off the balance on the dishwasher.* **2** [T **pay** sb ↔ **off**] to pay someone their wages and dismiss them from their job: *Two hundred workers have been paid off.* **3** [T **pay** sb ↔ **off**] to pay someone to keep quiet about something illegal or dishonest **4** [I] if a plan or something that you try to do pays off, it is successful: *They took a hell of a risk but it paid off.* —see also PAYOFF

**pay out** *phr v* **1** [I,T **pay** sth ↔ **out**] to pay a lot of money for something: *Why is it always me who has to pay out?* | **pay out sth for sth** *I paid out a lot of money for that car.* **2** [T **pay** sth ↔ **out**] to let a piece of rope be unwound —see also PAYOUT

**pay** sth ↔ **over** *phr v* to make an official payment of money: **pay sth over to** *The solicitor arranged for Clancy's share of the inheritance to be paid over to him.*

**pay up** *phr v* [I] to pay money that you owe, especially when you do not want to or you are late —see also PAID-UP

**USAGE NOTE: PAY**

GRAMMAR

You **pay** the cost of something: *pay $100/the bill/postage/the cost of removal | Will they pay my traveling expenses/accommodation costs?*

You **pay for** something you buy: *I'll pay for the tickets. | You'll have to pay for any stationery you use.* You also say **pay for** when both the cost and what is bought are mentioned: *She paid $200 for the use of the room.*

You **pay** a person etc: *Could you pay the taxi driver?* You also pay someone something, or pay something to someone: *He paid the assistant £30. | He has to pay half his salary to his ex-wife every month.*

You **pay by** cheque/credit card etc: *Can I pay by Visa?*

SPELLING

The past tense of **pay** is **paid** (NOT *payed*).

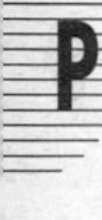

This graph shows how common the different grammar patterns of the verb **pay** are.

| Pattern | Approx. frequency |
|---|---|
| pay sth | ~57% |
| pay for | ~19% |
| pay sb | ~15% |
| pay | ~9% |
| pay to do sth | ~2% |
| other | ~1% |

10% 20% 30% 40% 50% 60%

Based on the British National Corpus and the Longman Lancaster Corpus

S1 W2 **pay²** *n* [U] **1** money that you are given for doing your job; SALARY: *Wayne gets his pay every Friday. | I like the work but the pay's terrible.* | **holiday/sick pay** (=money your employer gives you when you are on holiday or are ill) | **a pay rise/increase** *I've been promised a pay rise in January.* **2 in the pay of** someone who is in someone else's pay is working for them, often secretly: *an informer in the pay of the police*

**USAGE NOTE: PAY**

WORD CHOICE: **pay, salary, wages, fee, income**

Money given to someone in return for work is called **pay**: *Truck drivers are demanding higher pay. | a campaign against low pay*

A **salary** is paid to someone once a month, especially to professional people, managers etc and usually goes directly into their bank account: *a salary of $100,000 a year*

**Wages** are paid weekly, usually in the form of coins and notes, especially to people whose job is not professional, in management etc: *Wages at the cannery are very low.*

A **fee** is money that some professions charge for a particular service they have done: *doctor's/lawyer's fees*

**Income** means any money you receive regularly, from work or anywhere else: *Unearned income* (= money you get but not from work) *is taxed at a higher rate.*

**pay·a·ble** /ˈpeɪəbəl/ *adj* [not before noun] **1** a bill, debt etc that is payable must be paid: *payable in advance* **2 payable to** a cheque etc that is payable to someone has that person's name written on it and should be paid to them

**pay·bed** /ˈpeɪbed/ *n* [C] a hospital bed in a publicly owned hospital in Britain, used by someone who is paying to have better conditions, such as a private room

**pay·cheque** *BrE*, **paycheck** *AmE* /ˈpeɪ-tʃek/ *n* [C] **1** a cheque that pays someone's wages: *a weekly paycheque* **2** *especially AmE* the amount of wages someone earns; PAY PACKET *BrE*: *a nice fat paycheck*

**pay·day** /ˈpeɪdeɪ/ *n* [U] the day on which you get your wages: *When's payday?*

**pay·dirt** /ˈpeɪdɜːt‖-dɜːrt/ *n* [U] *AmE* **1 hit paydirt** *informal* to make a valuable or useful discovery **2** earth found to contain valuable minerals such as gold

**PAYE** /ˌpiː eɪ waɪ ˈiː/ *n* [U] pay as you earn; a system in Britain by which tax is taken away from your wages before you are paid

**pay·ee** /peɪˈiː/ *n* [C] *technical* the person to whom money, especially a cheque, should be paid

**pay en·ve·lope** /ˈ· ˌ···/ *n* [C] *AmE* an envelope containing your wages; PAY PACKET *BrE*

**paying guest** /ˌ·· ˈ· ·/ *n* [C] someone who lives in someone else's house with them and pays them rent; LODGER

**paying-in book** /ˌ·· ˈ· ·/ *n* [C] *BrE* a book of forms that you use when you pay money into your bank account

**paying-in slip** /ˌ·· ˈ· ·/ *n* [C] *BrE* a form that you use to pay money into your bank account; DEPOSIT SLIP *AmE*

**pay·load** /ˈpeɪləʊd‖-loʊd/ *n* **1** [C, U] the amount of goods or passengers carried by a vehicle or aircraft, for which payment is received **2** [C] the instruments and equipment carried in a SPACECRAFT: *The shuttle had a maximum payload of 65,000 pounds.* **3** [C] the amount of explosive that a MISSILE can carry

**pay·mas·ter** /ˈpeɪˌmɑːstə‖-ˌmæstər-/ *n* [C] **1** an official in a factory, the army etc, who gives people their wages **2** someone who pays someone else to do something, especially something illegal: *The assassin's paymasters were never identified.*

**pay·ment** /ˈpeɪmənt/ *n* **1** [C] an amount of money that has been or must be paid: *Discounts offered for cash payments | Tom's gotten into arrears with his mortgage payments.* | **make a payment** *Interest payments are made quarterly.* **2** [U] the act of paying: *We expect prompt payment. | payment by instalments* | **in payment of** (=to pay) *I enclose a cheque in full payment of my account.* | **on payment of** (=when an amount has been paid) *Any item can be reserved on payment of a small deposit.* **3** [U] someone's reward for doing something: [+ **for**] *All the payment I got for my troubles was insults.* **4 payment in kind** a way of paying for something with goods or services instead of money —see also BALANCE OF PAYMENTS, DOWN PAYMENT S2 W1

**pay·off** /ˈpeɪɒf‖-ɒːf/ *n* [C] *informal* **1** a payment that you make to someone in order to stop them from causing you any trouble, or when you make them leave their job: *A network of police payoffs was discovered. | The redundancies were bought by offering massive payoffs.* **2** the good result of a particular series of actions —see also **pay off**

**pay·o·la** /peɪˈəʊlə‖-ˈoʊlə/ *n informal, especially AmE* **1** [singular] a secret or indirect payment made to someone who uses their influence to make people buy what your company is selling —compare BRIBE² **2** [U] the practice of giving or taking these payments

**pay·out** /ˈpeɪ-aʊt/ *n* [C] *informal* a large payment of money in an insurance claim, competition etc or the act of making this payment: *a big payout on this month's lottery* —see also **pay out**

**pay pack·et** /ˈ· ˌ··/ *n* [C] *BrE* **1** the amount of money someone earns; PAYCHEQUE (2) **2** an envelope containing your wages; PAY ENVELOPE *AmE*

**pay phone** /ˈ· ·/ *n* [C] a public telephone that you can use when you put in a coin or a CREDIT CARD

**pay rise** /ˈ· ·/ *BrE*, **pay raise** *AmE n* [C] an increase in the amount of money you are paid for doing your job: *Some company directors have awarded themselves huge pay rises.*

**pay·roll** /ˈpeɪrəʊl‖-roʊl/ *n* **1** [C] a list of people who are employed by a company and the amount of wages each of them is paid: **be on the payroll** (=be employed by a company) *Nathan's still on the company payroll.* **2** [singular] the total amount of wages paid to all the people working for a particular company

**payroll tax** /ˈ·· ˌ·/ *n* [C,U] a tax that an employer must pay to the government in the US, and that is a PERCENTAGE of the total wages they pay

**pay set·tle·ment** /ˈ· ˌ···/ *n* [C] an agreement, after a long argument, between managers and a union, on how much workers should be paid

**pay·slip** /ˈpeɪslɪp/ *n* [C] a piece of paper that shows how much money an employed person has been paid and how much has been taken away for tax etc

**P.C.** /ˌpiː ˈsiː◂/ *n* [C] *BrE* police constable; a policeman of the lowest rank: *P.C. Williams | Two P.C.s were attacked.* —see also WPC

**PC¹** /ˌpiː ˈsiː◂/ *n* [C] a personal computer; a small computer that is used by one person at a time, in business or at home

**PC²** *adj* POLITICALLY CORRECT

**pcm** per calendar month; used when stating the amount of rent to be paid each month: *£500 pcm*

**PCP** /ˌpiː siː ˈpiː/ *n* [U] phencyclidine hydrochloride; an ANAESTHETIC that is also taken as an illegal drug

**pd** the written abbreviation of paid

**pdq** /ˌpiː diː ˈkjuː/ *adv slang* pretty damn quick; used to say that something should be done immediately: *If Jeff doesn't get back here pdq there's going to be trouble.*

**PDT** /ˌpiː diː ˈtiː/ the abbreviation of PACIFIC DAYLIGHT TIME

**PE** /ˌpiː ˈiː/ *n* [U] physical education; sport and physical activity taught as a school subject; PT *BrE*

**pea** /piː/ *n* [C] **1** a large round green seed that is cooked and eaten as a vegetable: *frozen peas | garden peas | pea soup* | **shell peas** (=take them out of their seed container) —see picture on page 414 **2** a plant that produces long green PODS that contain these seeds **3 like two peas in a pod** *informal* exactly the same in appearance, behaviour etc —see also SPLIT PEA, SWEET PEA

S2 W2 **peace** /piːs/ *n*
**1 ▶NO WAR◀ a)** [U] a situation in which there is no war between countries or in a country: **world peace** *a dangerous situation that threatens world peace* | **peace agreement/treaty etc** *the Geneva peace talks* | **be at peace with** *Germany has been at peace with France for fifty years.* **b)** [singular] a period of time in which there is no war: *a lasting peace* **c) peace movement/campaign etc** organized efforts to prevent war
**2 ▶AGREEMENT◀** [singular] an agreement that ends a war: *the Peace of Nijmegen | a negotiated peace*
**3 ▶NO NOISE◀** [U] a peaceful situation with no unpleasant noise: *A single gunshot shattered the peace of the May afternoon.* | **in peace** (=without being interrupted) *I wish you'd leave me in peace – I've got work to do.* | **peace and quiet** *We're going to the countryside for some peace and quiet.*
**4 ▶CALMNESS◀** [U] a feeling of calmness and lack of worry and problems: *the search for inner peace* | **peace of mind** (=to stop you from worrying) *Ann had to check the baby every few minutes for her own peace of mind.* | **at peace with yourself** (=calm and happy) *Lynn never seems to be at peace with herself.*
**5** [U] a situation in which there is no quarrelling between people who live or work together: *peace and stability in industrial relations* | **keep the peace** (=stop people from quarrelling, fighting, or causing trouble)
**6 disturb the peace** *law* to behave in a noisy or violent way: *Macklin was charged with disturbing the peace.* —see also BREACH OF THE PEACE, JUSTICE OF THE PEACE
**7 hold/keep your peace** to keep quiet even though there is something you would like to say: *In spite of John's provocative remarks, I held my peace.*
**8 make (your) peace with** to end your quarrel with someone, especially by telling them you are sorry: *Ann wanted to make her peace with her father before he died.*
**9 at peace** an expression meaning dead, used when you want to say this in a gentle way
**10 rest in peace** a prayer for someone who has died, said during a funeral service or written on a GRAVESTONE

**peace·a·ble** /ˈpiːsəbəl/ *adj* **1** a situation or way of doing something that is peaceable is calm, without any violence or fighting **2** someone who is peaceable dislikes arguing —**peaceably** *adv*: *The two tribes live peaceably together.*

**peace div·i·dend** /ˈ· ˌ···/ *n* [singular] the money saved on weapons and available for other purposes, when a government reduces its military strength

**peace·ful** /ˈpiːsfəl/ *adj* **1** quiet and calm without any worry or excitement: *We had a peaceful afternoon without the children.* | *into a deep and peaceful sleep* **2** without war: *a state of peaceful coexistence between nations* **3** deliberately avoiding any violence: *a peaceful demonstration* —**peacefully** *adv* —**peacefulness** *n* [U] S3

**peace·keep·ing** /ˈpiːskiːpɪŋ/ *adj* **peacekeeping force/troops etc** soldiers that are sent to a place where the people are fighting, to try to stop more violence

**peace-lov·ing** /ˈ· ˌ··/ *adj* believing strongly in peace rather than war

**peace·mak·er** /ˈpiːsmeɪkə‖-ər/ *n* [C] someone who tries to persuade other people or nations to stop fighting: *Eisenhower was anxious to play the role of peacemaker in his last year in office.*

**peace march** /ˈ· ·/ *n* [C] a march by people who are protesting against violence or military activities

**peace of·fer·ing** /ˈ· ˌ···/ *n* [C] *informal* something you give to someone to show them that you are sorry and want to be friendly, after you have annoyed or upset them: *I took along a box of chocolates as a peace offering.*

**peace pipe** /ˈ· ·/ *n* [C] a pipe which Native Americans use to smoke tobacco, which is shared in a ceremony as a sign of peace; PIPE OF PEACE

**peace·time** /ˈpiːstaɪm/ *n* [U] a period of time when a nation is not fighting a war —opposite WARTIME

**peach** /piːtʃ/ *n* **1** [C] a round fruit with soft yellow or red skin, that has sweet juicy flesh, and a large seed in its centre, or a tree that produces this fruit —see picture on page 413 **2** [U] a pale pinkish-orange colour —see picture on page 411 **3** [singular] *old-fashioned* someone or something that you think is attractive or like very much: *a peach of a hat* | *Jan's a real peach.* **4 a peaches and cream complexion** skin with an attractive pink colour

**Peach Mel·ba** /ˌpiːtʃ ˈmelbə/ *n* [C,U] half a peach served with ice cream and RASPBERRY juice

**pea·cock** /ˈpiːkɒk‖-kɑːk/ *n* [C] a large male bird which has long tail feathers that it can spread out, showing their beautiful blue and green colours and patterns

**peacock blue** /ˌ·· ˈ·◂/ *n* [U] a deep greenish-blue colour —**peacock blue** *adj*

**pea·fowl** /ˈpiːfaʊl/ *n* [C] a peacock or peahen

**pea green** /ˌ· ˈ·◂/ *n* [U] a light green colour, like that of PEAS —**pea green** *adj*

**pea·hen** /ˈpiːhen/ *n* [C] a large, brownish bird, the female peafowl

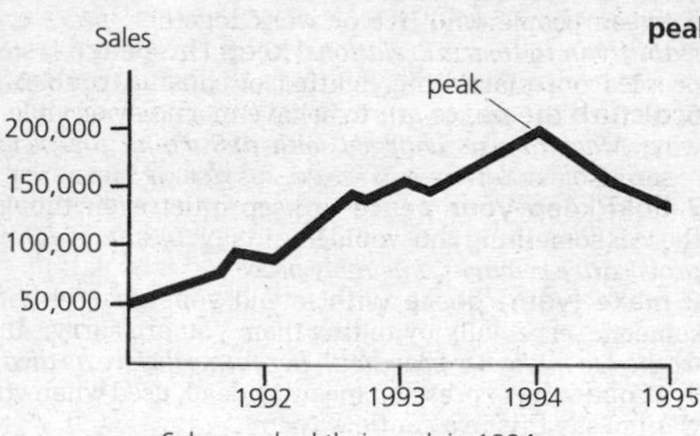

Sales reached their peak in 1994.

W3 **peak¹** /piːk/ *n* [C]
**1 ▶ TIME ◀** [usually singular] the time when something or someone is strongest, most successful, or best: *Her career was at its peak.* | *Sales have reached a new peak.* | **be at your peak/reach your peak** *Most athletes have reached their peak by the time they're 20.* —compare OFF-PEAK
**2 ▶ MOUNTAIN ◀ a)** the sharply pointed top of a mountain: *peaks covered with snow all the year round* —compare SUMMIT (1) —see picture on page 835 **b)** a whole mountain with a pointed top: *K2 is the world's highest peak.*
**3 ▶ POINT ◀** a part that curves to a point above a surface: *Whisk the egg whites until they form stiff peaks.*
**4 ▶ CAP ◀** the flat curved part of a cap that sticks out in front above your eyes —see picture at CAP¹

**peak²** *v* [I] to reach the highest point or level: *Sales peaked in August, then fell sharply.* | [+ **at**] *Around 1950 Chicago's population peaked at about 3.6 million.*

**peak³** *adj* **1 peak level/rate/value** the highest level etc of something: *The factory is running at peak productivity.* **2** *BrE* the peak time or period is when the greatest number of people are doing the same thing, using the same service etc: *the peak time for electricity consumption* | *Extra buses run at peak times.*

**peak·ed¹** /ˈpiːkɪ̈d/ *adj especially AmE* pale and ill; peaky *BrE*: *You're looking a bit peaked this morning.*

**peaked²** /piːkt/ *adj* a peaked cap has a flat curved part at the front above the eyes —see picture at CAP¹

**pea·ky** /ˈpiːki/ *adj informal especially BrE* pale or ill: *Jane's feeling a bit peaky today.*

**peal¹** /piːl/ *n* [C] **1** a sudden loud sound of laughter or thunder: [+ **of**] *Peals of laughter came from the other room.* **2** the sound of the loud ringing of bells: [+ **of**] *a joyous peal of bells* **3** *technical* **a)** a musical pattern made by ringing a number of bells one after the other **b)** a set of bells

**peal²** *v* also **peal out** [I] if bells peal, they ring loudly: *The bells pealed out across the churchyard.*

**pea·nut** /ˈpiːnʌt/ *n* **1** [C] a nut which grows in a soft shell under the ground and which can be eaten: *salted peanuts* **2 peanuts** [U] *informal* a sum of money that is so small that it is hardly worth mentioning: *The hotel workers get paid peanuts.*

**peanut but·ter** /ˌ·· ˈ··‖ˈ·· ˌ··/ *n* [U] a soft substance made from crushed peanuts, eaten on bread or used in cooking

**peanut gal·ler·y** /ˈ·· ˌ···/ *n* [C] *AmE humorous* the cheap rows of seats at the back of a theatre or cinema

S3 **pear** /peə‖per/ *n* [C] a sweet juicy fruit that has a round base and becomes thinner nearer the top, or the tree that produces this fruit —see also PRICKLY PEAR—see picture on page 413

**pearl** /pɜːl‖pɜːrl/ *n*
**1 ▶ JEWEL ◀** [C] **a)** a small round hard white object with a silvery shine, that is formed inside the shell of an OYSTER, and is very valuable as a jewel: *a string of pearls* | *a pearl necklace* **b)** an artificial copy of this jewel
**2 ▶ LIQUID ◀** [C] *literary* a small round drop of some liquid: *Pearls of dew sparkled on the grass.*
**3 ▶ HARD SUBSTANCE ◀** [U] a hard shiny, variously coloured substance formed inside some SHELLFISH, which is used for decorating objects; MOTHER-OF-PEARL: *a knife with a pearl handle*
**4 ▶ EXCELLENT THING/PERSON ◀** [C usually singular] someone or something that is especially good or valuable: *a pearl among women* | **a pearl beyond price** *Good health is a pearl beyond price.*
**5 cast pearls before swine** to give something valuable to someone who does not understand its value
**6 pearls of wisdom** an expression meaning wise remarks, often used jokingly to mean slightly stupid remarks: *Have you any more pearls of wisdom you'd like to share with us?*

**pearl bar·ley** /ˌ· ˈ··/ *n* [U] small grains of BARLEY that have been polished smooth

**pearl div·er** /ˈ· ˌ··/ *n* [C] someone who swims underwater in the sea, looking for shells that contain pearls

**pearl·y** /ˈpɜːli‖ˈpɜːrli/ *adj* like pearls or having the colour of pearls: *pearly white teeth*

**pearly gates** /ˌ·· ˈ·/ *n* [plural] *often humorous* the entrance to heaven

**pear-shaped** /ˈ· ·/ *adj* someone who is pear-shaped is larger around their waist and HIPS than around their chest

**peas·ant** /ˈpezənt/ *n* [C] **1** someone in a poor country or in former times, who does farm work on the piece of land where they live: *He was born into a peasant family during the 1930s.* **2** *informal* someone who does not have good manners or much education: *Don't be such a peasant!*

**peas·ant·ry** /ˈpezəntri/ *n* **the peasantry** all the peasants of a particular country

**pease pud·ding** /ˌpiːz ˈpʊdɪŋ/ *n* [U] *BrE* a dish made of dried PEAS, boiled with ham to make a thick yellow substance that is eaten with bread

**pea·shoot·er** /ˈpiːˌʃuːtə‖-ər/ *n* [C] a small tube used by children to blow small objects, especially dried PEAS, at someone or something

**pea soup·er** /ˌpiː ˈsuːpə‖-ər/ *n* [C] a very thick FOG

**peat** /piːt/ *n* **1** [U] a substance formed from decaying plants under the surface of the ground in some areas, which can be burned instead of coal, or mixed with soil to help plants grow well: *a peat bog* **2** [C] a piece of this used for burning on a fire —**peaty** *adj*: *brown peaty water*

**peb·ble** /ˈpebəl/ *n* [C] **1** a small smooth stone found on the beach or on the bottom of a river **2 you're not the only pebble on the beach** used to say that someone is not the only person who has to be considered or who deserves attention —**pebbly** *adj*: *a pebbly beach*

**peb·ble·dash** /ˈpebəldæʃ/ *n* [U] *BrE* a surface for the outside walls of houses, made of CEMENT with a lot of very small pebbles set into it —**pebbledash** *v* [T]

**pe·can** /pɪˈkæn, ˈpiːkən‖pɪˈkɑːn, pɪˈkæn/ *n* [C] a long thin nut with a dark red shell, or the tree that it grows on: *pecan pie*

**pec·ca·dil·lo** /ˌpekəˈdɪləʊ‖-loʊ/ *n* [C] a small unimportant thing that someone does wrong: *Bernard's wife had learnt to put up with his little peccadillos.*

**pec·ca·ry** /ˈpekəri/ *n* [C] a wild animal like a pig that lives in Central and South America

**peck¹** /pek/ *v* **1** [I, T] if a bird pecks something, it makes quick repeated movements with its beak to try to bite it: [+ **at**] *sparrows pecking at breadcrumbs* | **peck sth** *A bird flew down and pecked my hand.* | *It had pecked a hole in the bottom of its cage.* **2 peck sb on the cheek** to kiss someone quickly and lightly —see also HENPECKED
**peck at** sth ↔ *phr v* [T] to eat only a little bit of a meal because you are not hungry; **pick at** (PICK¹)

**peck²** *n* [C] **1 give sb a peck** to kiss someone quickly and lightly **2** an act of pecking **3** a measure of amount for dry substances such as fruit or grain

**peck·er** /ˈpekə‖-ər/ *n* [C] **1 keep your pecker up** *BrE spoken* used to tell someone to stay cheerful even when it is difficult to do so **2** *AmE slang* PENIS

**pecking or·der** /ˈ·· ˌ··/ *n* [C] *often humorous* the social system of a particular group of people or animals, in which each one knows who is more important and less important than themselves: *Patients seem to be very low down in the pecking order as far as making changes to hospital policy is concerned.*

**peck·ish** /ˈpekɪʃ/ *adj BrE informal* slightly hungry

**pecs** /peks/ *n* [plural] *informal* PECTORALS

**pec·tic** /ˈpektɪk/ *adj technical* containing pectin

**pec·tin** /ˈpektɪn/ *n* [U] *technical* a chemical substance like sugar that is found in some fruits and is important in making JAM [1] (1) and JELLY (1,2)

**pec·to·ral** /ˈpekt*ə*rəl/ *adj technical* of or connected with the chest: *pectoral muscles*

**pectoral fin** /ˌ··· ˈ·/ *n* [C] the FIN that is on the side of a fish's head and helps it to control the direction it swims in

**pec·to·rals** /ˈpektərəlz/ *n* [plural] your chest muscles: *strong men with bulging pectorals*

**pe·cu·li·ar** /pɪˈkjuːliə‖-liər/ *adj* **1** strange, unfamiliar, and a little surprising, especially in a way that is unpleasant or worrying: *This meat tastes peculiar.* | *It seems very peculiar that no one noticed Kay had gone.* **2 be peculiar to** if something is peculiar to a particular person, place, or situation, it is a feature that only belongs to that person etc: *The problem of racism is not peculiar to this country.* **3** behaving in a strange and slightly crazy way: *Auntie May's gone a bit peculiar lately.* **4 feel peculiar** *informal* to feel slightly ill

**pe·cu·li·ar·i·ty** /pɪˌkjuːliˈærɨti/ *n* **1** [C] something that is a feature of only one particular place, person, or situation: [+ **of**] *The lack of a written constitution is a peculiarity of the British political system.* **2** [C] a strange or unusual habit, quality etc: *It took some time for Theresa to get used to her husband's peculiarities.* **3** [U] the quality of being strange or unfamiliar

**pe·cu·li·ar·ly** /pɪˈkjuːliəli‖-ər-/ *adv* **1** especially: *a peculiarly difficult question* **2** in a strange or unusual way: *Theo had been behaving most peculiarly.* **3 peculiarly British/middle-class/Christian etc** something that is peculiarly British etc is a feature only of British people etc: *a peculiarly American phenomenon*

**pe·cu·ni·a·ry** /pɪˈkjuːniəri‖-nieri/ *adj formal* connected with or consisting of money: *a pecuniary advantage*

**ped·a·go·gi·cal** /ˌpedəˈgɒdʒɪk*ə*l‖-ˈgɑː-/ *adj technical* concerning teaching methods or the practice of teaching: *training in pedagogical skills* —**pedagogically** /-kli/ *adv*

**ped·a·gogue** /ˈpedəgɒg‖-gɑːg/ *n* [C] **1** a teacher who cares too much about rules **2** *old use* a teacher

**ped·a·go·gy** /ˈpedəgɒdʒi‖-goʊ-/ *n* [U] *technical* the practice of teaching or the study of teaching

**ped·al[1]** /ˈpedl/ *n* [C] **1** one of the two parts of a bicycle that you push round with your feet to make the bicycle go forward —see picture at BICYCLE[1] **2** a part in a car or on a machine that you press with your foot to control it: *the accelerator pedal* **3** a part on a piano or organ that you press with your foot to change the quality of the sound

**pedal[2]** *v* **pedalled, pedalling** *BrE*, **pedaled, pedaling** *AmE* [I, T] **1** [always + adv/prep] to ride a bicycle: [+ **up/along/down etc**] *Andrew pedalled up the road towards the town centre.* —see also SOFT PEDAL **2** to turn or push the pedals on a bicycle or other machine: *pedalling furiously on her exercise bike*

**pedal bin** /ˈ·· ·/ *n* [C] a container for waste that has a lid which is opened by pressing a pedal with your foot

**ped·ant** /ˈpednt/ *n* [C] someone who pays too much attention to rules and details: *She is something of a pedant when it comes to intellectual argument.* —**pedantry** *n* [U]

**pe·dan·tic** /pɪˈdæntɪk/ *adj* paying too much attention to rules and details: *He was meticulous, but never pedantic.* —**pedantically** /-kli/ *adv*

**ped·dle** /ˈpedl/ *v* [T] **1** to go from place to place, trying to sell something: *An old woman was peddling goods on a street corner.* | **peddle drugs** (=sell illegal drugs) **2** to try to get people to accept opinions, false information etc: *a magazine that peddles scandal and gossip* **3** *informal, especially AmE* to sell goods that are of low quality

**ped·dler** /ˈpedlə‖-ər/ *n* [C] **1** the American form of the word PEDLAR **2** *old-fashioned* someone who sells illegal drugs: *a dope peddler* —compare PUSHER

**ped·e·rast** /ˈpedəræst/ *n* [C] a man who has sex with a boy

**ped·es·tal** /ˈpedɨst*ə*l/ *n* [C] **1** the base on which a PILLAR or STATUE stands: *a Grecian bust on a pedestal* **2 pedestal basin/table** *especially BrE* a BASIN or table that is supported by a single COLUMN **3 put/place sb on a pedestal** to admire someone so much that you treat them or talk about them as though they are perfect: *You shouldn't put him on a pedestal – he doesn't deserve it.*

**pe·des·tri·an[1]** /pɨˈdestriən/ *n* [C] someone who is walking, especially in a street or other place used by cars —see picture on page 415

**pedestrian[2]** *adj* **1** ordinary and uninteresting and without any imagination: *a pedestrian description* | *a rather pedestrian student* **2 pedestrian walkway/footbridge etc** a path, bridge etc used by pedestrians

**pedestrian cross·ing** /·ˌ··· ˈ··/ *n* [C] *BrE* a special place for people to cross the road; CROSSWALK *AmE*

**pe·des·tri·a·nize** also **-ise** *BrE* /pɨˈdestriənaɪz/ *v* [T] to change a street or shopping area into a place where vehicles are not allowed —**pedestrianization** /pɨˌdestriənaɪˈzeɪʃ*ə*n‖-nə-/ *n* [U]

**pedestrian pre·cinct** /·ˌ··· ˈ··/ *BrE*, **pedestrian mall** /·ˌ··· ˈ·/ *AmE n* [C] a shopping area in the centre of a town where traffic cannot go

**pe·di·a·tri·cian** /ˌpiːdiəˈtrɪʃ*ə*n/ *n* [C] the American spelling of PAEDIATRICIAN

**pe·di·at·rics** /ˌpiːdiˈætrɪks/ *n* [U] the American spelling of PAEDIATRICS

**ped·i·cel** /ˈpedɪsel/ *n* [C] *technical* a long thin part of a plant below each flower

**ped·i·cure** /ˈpedɪkjʊə‖-kjʊr/ *n* [C, U] treatment for feet and toenails, to make them more comfortable or beautiful —**pedicurist** *n* [C]

**ped·i·gree[1]** /ˈpedɨgriː/ *n* [C, U] the past family, especially the parents, grandparents etc, of a person or animal, or an official written record of this

**pedigree[2]** *adj* [only before noun] a pedigree animal comes from a family that has been recorded for a long time and is considered to be of a very good breed: *a pedigree greyhound* —compare PUREBRED, THOROUGHBRED (1)

**ped·i·ment** /ˈpedɨmənt/ *n* [C] a three-sided piece of stone or other material placed above the entrance to a building, especially in the buildings of ancient Greece

**ped·lar** /ˈpedlə‖-ər/ *n* [C] *BrE* someone who used to walk from place to place selling small things; PEDDLER *AmE*

**pe·dom·e·ter** /pɨˈdɒmɨtə, pe‖-ˈdɑːmɪtər/ *n* [C] an instrument used for measuring how far you walk

**pe·do·phile** /ˈpiːdəfaɪl/ *n* [C] the American spelling of PAEDOPHILE

**pee[1]** /piː/ *v* [I] *informal* to pass liquid waste from your body; URINATE

**pee[2]** *n informal* **1** [singular] an act of passing liquid waste from your body: **go for a pee/have a pee** *Have I got time to go for a pee before we leave?* **2** [U] liquid waste passed from your body; URINE

**peek** /piːk/ *v* [I] to look quickly at something, especially something that you are not supposed to see: *The children were peeking from behind the wall.* —compare PEEP[1] —**peek** *n* [C] *I noticed Diane taking a quick peek at herself in the mirror.*

**peek·a·boo** /ˌpiːkəˈbuː/ *interjection, n* [U] a game played to amuse babies, in which you repeatedly hide your face and then show it again, or the word you say when you play this game

**peel¹** /piːl/ *v* **1** [T] to remove the skin from fruit or vegetables: *peeling potatoes* —see picture on page 834 **2 peel sth from/away/off etc** [T always + adv/prep] to remove the outer layer from something: *Jessie peeled the wrapper from the sweet.* **3** [I] **a)** to lose an outer layer or surface: *The walls were peeling with the damp.* **b)** if skin, paper, or paint peels, it comes off, usually in small pieces: *My skin always peels when I've been in the sun.* —see picture on page 1258 —see also **keep your eyes open/peeled** (EYE¹ (15))

**peel off** *phr v* **1** [I,T **peel** sth ↔ **off**] to take your clothes off: *The children peeled off their clothes and leapt into the pool.* **2** [I] to leave a moving group of vehicles, aircraft etc and go in a different direction: *The last two motorcycles peeled off from the convoy.*

**peel²** *n* [U] the outer layer of some fruits, especially the ones that you usually peel before you eat them: *orange peel*

**peel·er** /ˈpiːlə‖-ər/ *n* [C] **1** a special type of knife for removing the skin from fruit or vegetables —see picture on page 834 **2** *BrE old-fashioned* a police officer

**peel·ings** /ˈpiːlɪŋz/ *n* [plural] pieces of skin that have been removed from fruit or vegetables

**peep¹** /piːp/ *v* [I] **1** to look at something quickly and secretly, especially through a hole: [+ **into/through etc**] *I caught him peeping through the keyhole.* **2** [always + adv/prep] if something peeps from somewhere, it is just possible to see it: [+ **through/from etc**] *The sun peeped briefly through the clouds.* —compare PEEK, PEER²

**peep²** *n* [C] **1** a quick or secret look at something: **take a peep** *Mike had taken a peep at the answers.* **2 not hear a peep out of** *spoken* to not hear a sound from someone: *I don't want to hear a peep out of you until you've done your homework.* **3** *BrE* a word meaning the sound of a car's horn, used especially by or to children **4** a short weak high sound like the sound a mouse or a young bird makes

**peep·bo** /ˈpiːpbəʊ‖-boʊ/ *interjection, n* [U] PEEKABOO

**peep·ers** /ˈpiːpəz‖-ərz/ *n* [plural] *old-fashioned* your eyes

**peep·hole** /ˈpiːphəʊl‖-hoʊl/ *n* [C] a small hole in a door or wall that you can see through

**peeping Tom** /ˌpiːpɪŋ ˈtɒm‖-ˈtɑːm/ *n* [C] someone who secretly watches people, especially when they are undressing, having sex etc

**peep·show** /ˈpiːpʃəʊ‖-ʃoʊ/ *n* [C] **1** a type of show in which a man pays for a woman to take her clothes off while he watches **2** a box containing moving pictures that you look at through a small hole or LENS

**peer¹** /pɪə‖pɪr/ *n* [C] **1** someone of the same age, social class etc as you: *Children compete to win the approval of their peers.* | *The jury system gives you the right to be judged by your peers.* —see also PEER GROUP, PEER PRESSURE **2** a member of the British NOBILITY, who has the right to sit in the House of Lords —see also LIFE PEER

**peer²** *v* [I always + adv/prep] to look very carefully or hard, especially because you are having difficulty in seeing: [+ **at/across/through etc**] *Every few paces they stopped to peer ahead into the gloom.*

**peer·age** /ˈpɪərɪdʒ‖ˈpɪr-/ *n* **1 the peerage** all the British peers (PEER¹ (2)) considered as a group **2** [C] the rank of a British PEER¹ (2): *After ten years in the government she was given a peerage.*

**peer·ess** /ˈpɪərɪ̯s‖ˈpɪr-/ *n* [C] **1** a woman who is a member of the British NOBILITY and has the right to sit in the House of Lords; a female peer (PEER¹ (2)) **2** the wife of a British PEER¹ (2)

**peer group** /ˈ· ·/ *n* [C] a group of people, especially young people of the same age, social class etc as yourself: *Establishing good peer group relationships is very important.*

**peer·less** /ˈpɪələs‖ˈpɪr-/ *adj* better than any other: *Torvill and Dean's peerless performances in ice dancing*

**peer pres·sure** /ˈ· ˌ··/ *n* [C] a strong feeling that you must do the same things as other people of your age if you want them to like you: *Teenagers often start smoking because of peer pressure.*

**peeve** /piːv/ *n* [C] *informal* something that annoys you: **pet peeve** *Car alarms going off at night is one of my pet peeves.*

**peeved** /piːvd/ *adj informal* annoyed: *Ranulf felt peeved that she had not thanked him properly for his help.*

**peev·ish** /ˈpiːvɪʃ/ *adj* easily annoyed by small and unimportant things; bad-tempered: *The kids were peevish after so long in the car.* —**peevishly** *adv* —**peevishness** *n* [U]

**pee·wit** /ˈpiːwɪt/ *n* [C] a LAPWING

**pegs**

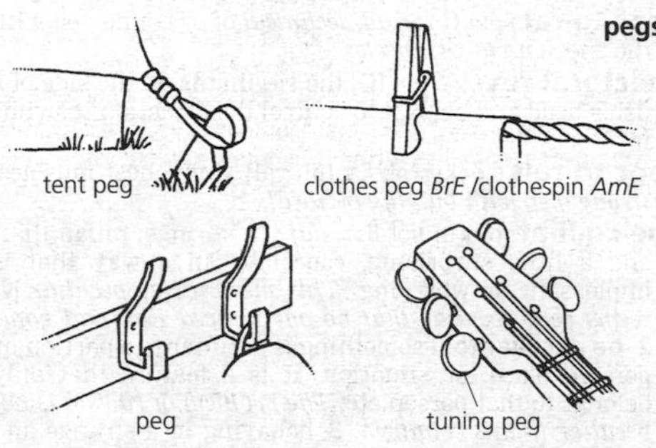


**peg¹** /peg/ *n* [C]

**1** ▸ **CLOTHES** ◂ **a)** a short piece of wood, metal etc fixed to a wall or door, used for hanging things on, especially clothes: *Hang your coat up on the peg.* **b)** *BrE* a small piece of plastic or wood used for fastening wet clothes to a line to dry; CLOTHES PEG **c) off the peg** *BrE* clothes that are off the peg are made to a standard size and have not been specially made to fit you; OFF-THE-RACK *AmE* —see also OFF-THE-PEG

**2 take/bring sb down a peg (or two)** to make someone realize that they are not as important or as good at something as they think they are: *It's time that young man was brought down a peg or two.*

**3** ▸ **FOR A TENT** ◂ a pointed piece of wood or metal that you push into the ground in order to keep a tent in the correct position

**4** ▸ **MUSICAL INSTRUMENT** ◂ a wooden screw used to tighten or loosen the strings of a VIOLIN, GUITAR etc; TUNING PEG

**5 a peg to hang sth on** something that is used as a reason or excuse when you are trying to prove or explain something

**6** ▸ **DRINK** ◂ *BrE old-fashioned* a small amount of strong alcoholic drink, especially WHISKY or BRANDY —see also **square peg in a round hole** (SQUARE¹ (11))

**peg²** **pegged, pegging** *v* [T] **1** to fasten something somewhere with a peg **2** to fix prices, wages etc at a particular level, or fix them in relation to something else: **peg sth to** *Most industrial countries stopped pegging their currencies to the US dollar in the early 1970s.* **3 have sb pegged as** *especially AmE* to regard someone's character in a particular way: *I never had you pegged as an idler.* **4 peg it** *AmE slang* to die

**peg away at** sth *phr v* [T not in passive] *BrE informal* to work hard and with determination: *Vicky's been pegging away at her books all week.*

**peg out** *phr v* **1** [I] *BrE informal* to die, or fall down because you are tired **2** [T **peg** sth ↔ **out**] *BrE* to fasten wet clothes to a washing line to dry **3** [T **peg** sth ↔ **out**] to mark a piece of ground with wooden sticks

**peg·board** /ˈpegbɔːd‖-bɔːrd/ *n* **1** [C] a small piece of board with holes in it, used to record the players' points in some games, especially card games **2** [U] thin board with holes in it, into which you can put PEGs or hooks to hang things on

**peg leg** /ˈ· ·/ *n* [C] *informal* an artificial leg, especially a wooden one

**pe·jo·ra·tive** /pɪˈdʒɒrətɪv‖-ˈdʒɔː-, -ˈdʒɑː-/ *adj formal* a word or expression that is pejorative expresses disapproval or criticism: *'Spinster' is a pejorative word for an unmarried woman.* —**pejoratively** *adv*

**peke** /piːk/ *n* [C] *informal* a pekinese

**pe·kin·ese** /ˌpiːkɪ̵ˈniːz◂/ *n* [C] a very small dog with a short flat nose and long silky hair —see picture at DOG[1]

**pe·lag·ic** /pɪ̵ˈlædʒɪk/ *adj technical* connected with or living in the deep sea, far from shore: *pelagic fish*

**pel·i·can** /ˈpelɪkən/ *n* [C] a large water bird that catches fish for food and stores them in a deep bag under its beak

**pelican cross·ing** /ˌ··· ˈ··/ *n* [C] a place on some roads in Britain, where someone who wants to cross the road can stop the traffic by pushing a button that makes TRAFFIC LIGHTS change to red —compare ZEBRA CROSSING

**pel·lag·ra** /pɪ̵ˈlægrə/ *n* [U] a disease caused by a lack of a type of B VITAMIN, that makes you feel tired and causes problems with your skin and CENTRAL NERVOUS SYSTEM

**pel·let** /ˈpelɪ̵t/ *n* [C] **1** a small ball of any soft substance, sometimes made by rolling it between your fingers **2** a small ball of metal made to be fired from a gun

**pell-mell** /ˌpel ˈmel◂/ *adv old-fashioned* rushing very quickly, and in a way that seems uncontrolled: *The children ran pell-mell out of school.*

**pel·lu·cid** /pɪ̵ˈluːsɪ̵d/ *adj literary* very clear; TRANSPARENT (1): *a pellucid stream* —**pellucidly** *adv*

**pel·met** /ˈpelmɪ̵t/ *n* [C] *BrE* a narrow piece of wood or cloth above a window that hides the rod that the curtains hang on; VALANCE *AmE*

**pelt**[1] /pelt/ *v* **1** [T] to attack someone by throwing a lot of things at them: **pelt sb with sth** *The Senator was pelted with rotten eggs.* **2 it is pelting down/it is pelting with rain** used to mean that it is raining very heavily **3** [I always + adv/prep] *informal* to run somewhere very fast: [+ **along/into/past etc**] *Three huge dogs came pelting out into the street.*

**pelt**[2] *n* [C] **1 a)** the skin of a dead animal with the fur or hair still on it **b)** the skin of a dead animal with the fur or hair removed and ready to be prepared as leather **2** the fur or hair of a living animal **3 (at) full pelt** moving as fast as possible: *Nancy drove her car at full pelt down the road.*

**pel·vic** /ˈpelvɪk/ *adj* in or connected with the pelvis

**pel·vis** /ˈpelvɪ̵s/ *n* [C] the large frame of bones at the base of your SPINE, to which your legs are joined —see picture at SKELETON (1)

**pem·mi·can** /ˈpemɪkən/ *n* [U] dried meat, beaten into small pieces and pressed into flat round shapes

pens

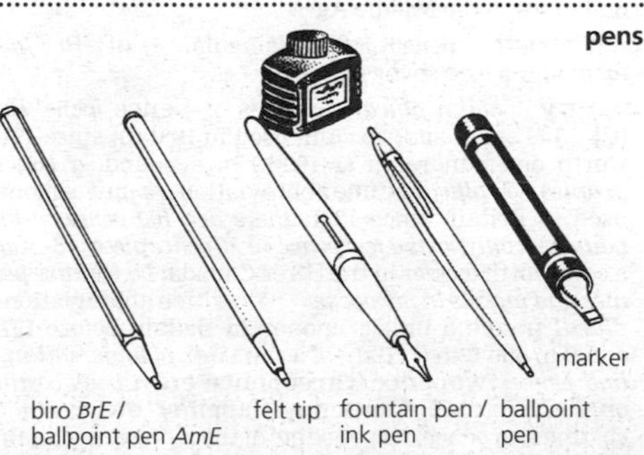


S2 **pen**[1] /pen/ *n* [C] **1** an instrument for writing or drawing with ink: *a ballpoint pen | a fountain pen | a felt-tip pen* **2** a small piece of land enclosed by a fence, used for keeping farm animals in: *a sheep pen* —see also PLAYPEN **3 put/set pen to paper** to begin to write **4** *AmE slang* PENITENTIARY; a prison

**pen**[2] *v* **penned, penning** [T] *formal* to write a letter or note with a pen

**pen** sb/sth ↔ **up/in** *phr v* [T] **1** to shut an animal in a small enclosed area **2 be penned in** to be restricted, as if you are being kept in a small place: *They were penned in watching TV with their parents all night.*

**pe·nal** /ˈpiːnl/ *adj* **1** [only before noun] connected with the legal punishment of criminals, especially in prisons: *penal reform | the penal system* | **penal colony/settlement** (=a special area of land where prisoners are kept) | **penal servitude** *law* (=a period of being kept in prison with hard physical work) **2** [only before noun] a penal offence can be punished by the law **3** very severe: *penal rates of taxation*

**penal code** /ˈ· ˌ·/ *n* [C] a system of laws and statements of the punishments for breaking those laws

**pe·nal·ize** also **-ise** *BrE* /ˈpiːnəl-aɪz‖ˈpiː-, ˈpe-/ *v* [T] **1** to treat someone unfairly or make them have a disadvantage: *The whole class is being penalized just because one student behaved badly. | Sales taxes penalize the consumer.* **2** to punish a team or player in sports by giving an advantage to the other team: *In one game the All Blacks were penalized for wasting time.* —**penalization** /ˌpiːnəlaɪˈzeɪʃən‖ˌpiːnələ-, ˌpe-/ *n* [U]

**pen·al·ty** /ˈpenlti/ *n plural* **penalties** [C] **1** a punishment for breaking a law, rule, or legal agreement: *No littering. Penalty $500.* | [+ **for**] *The penalty for murder was death.* | **impose a penalty** (=force someone to accept a penalty) *the highest penalty the court can impose* | **stiff/heavy penalty** (=a severe penalty) | **the death penalty** *Some MPs are calling for the death penalty to be brought back.* **2** something unpleasant that happens to you because of something unwise that you have done or because of the situation you are in: [+ **of**] *One of the penalties of being famous is the loss of privacy.* | **pay the penalty (for)** (=suffer the penalty for something) *They never insured their property and now they're paying the penalty for their foolishness.* **3** a disadvantage in sports given to a player or team for breaking a rule **4** a chance to kick the ball into the GOAL (3) in a game of football, given because the other team has broken a rule

**penalty ar·e·a** /ˈ··· ˌ···/ also **penalty box** /ˈ··· ˌ·/ *n* [C] the area in front of the GOAL (3) in football, in which the breaking of a rule means that the opposing team gets a PENALTY (4) —see picture on page 1264

**penalty clause** /ˈ··· ˌ·/ *n* [C] the part of a contract which says what someone will have to pay or do if they break the agreement, for example if they fail to complete work on time

**penalty kick** /ˈ··· ˌ·/ *n* [C] a penalty (PENALTY (4))

**penalty point** /ˈ··· ˌ·/ *n* [C] *BrE* a note made on a driver's LICENCE to show that they have done something wrong while they were driving

**penalty shoot-out** /ˌ··· ˈ· ·/ *n* [C] a series of penalty kicks used as a way of deciding which team has won a football game

**pen·ance** /ˈpenəns/ *n* **1** [C,U] the action of willingly making yourself suffer, especially for religious reasons, to show you are sorry for having done something wrong: **do penance (for)** *Bianca has confessed and done penance for her sins.* **2** [singular] something that you have to do but do not enjoy doing: *Visiting old Uncle Edgar had become more of a penance than a pleasure.*

**pence** /pens/ abbreviation **p** *BrE* the plural of PENNY (4): *a few pence | a 13 pence stamp*

**pen·chant** /ˈpɒnʃɒn, ˈpentʃənt‖ˈpentʃənt/ *n* [C] *French* a liking for something, especially something that is slightly disapproved of by other people: [+ **for**] *a penchant for fast cars*

**pen·cil**[1] /ˈpensəl/ *n* [C, U] **1** a narrow pointed wooden instrument, used for writing or drawing, containing a thin stick of a black or coloured substance: *written in* *pencil | drawn with a pencil | a pencil sketch* **2 a pencil of light** a narrow beam of light beginning from or ending in a small point —see also EYEBROW PENCIL

**pencil²** *v* **pencilled, pencilling** *BrE,* **penciled, penciling** *AmE* [T] to write something or make a mark with a pencil: *Mark pencilled a note to his wife.*

**pencil** sb/sth ↔ **in** *phr v* [T] to include someone or something in a list or an arrangement, knowing that this might have to be changed later: *Let's pencil in Friday at 10 for the meeting.*

**pencil push·er** /ˈ·· ˌ··/ *n* [C] *AmE* PEN PUSHER

**pencil sharp·en·er** /ˈ·· ˌ···/ *n* [C] a small thing with a blade inside, used for sharpening pencils

**pencil skirt** /ˈ·· ˌ·/ *n* [C] a long narrow straight skirt

**pen·dant, pendent** /ˈpendənt/ *n* [C] a piece of jewellery hanging from a thin chain that you wear around your neck: *a ruby pendant*

**pen·dent** /ˈpendənt/ *adj literary or technical* **1** hanging from something: *a pendent lamp* **2** sticking out beyond a surface: *pendent ledges of rocks*

**pend·ing¹** /ˈpendɪŋ/ *prep formal* while waiting for something, or until something happens: *A decision has been delayed pending further inquiries.*

**pending²** *adj* **1** [not before noun] *formal* not yet decided or settled: *As my divorce was pending, I had to stay where I was.* **2 pending file/tray** a container for keeping papers, letters etc that have not yet been dealt with **3** *formal* something that is pending is going to happen soon: *a pending criminal trial*

**pen·du·lous** /ˈpendjᵿləs‖-dʒə-/ *adj literary* hanging down loosely and swinging freely: *pendulous breasts* —**pendulously** *adv*

**pen·du·lum** /ˈpendjᵿləm‖-dʒə-/ *n* [C] **1** a rod with a weight at the bottom that swings regularly from side to side to control the working of a clock **2 the pendulum of opinion/fashion etc** something that tends to change regularly from one position to an opposite one: *The pendulum of public opinion has swung back.*

**pen·e·trate** /ˈpenᵻtreɪt/ *v*
**1 ▸ GO THROUGH ◂** [I,T] to enter something or pass through it, especially when this is difficult: *shells that penetrate thick armour plating* | [+ **into**] *Explorers penetrated into unknown regions.*
**2 ▸ BUSINESS ◂** [T] to start to sell things to an area or country, or to have an influence there: *Their goal is to penetrate undeveloped markets in the Third World.*
**3 ▸ ORGANIZATION ◂** [T] to get yourself accepted into a group or an organization in order to find out their secrets: *KGB agents had penetrated most of their intelligence services.*
**4 ▸ SEE THROUGH ◂** [T] to see into or through something even though it is difficult: *My eyes couldn't penetrate the gloom.*
**5 ▸ UNDERSTAND ◂ a)** [T] to succeed in understanding something: *Science has penetrated the mysteries of nature.* **b)** [I] *informal* to be fully understood by someone: *I heard what you said but it didn't fully penetrate.*
**6 ▸ SEX ◂** [T] *technical* if a man penetrates a woman, he puts his PENIS into her VAGINA when having sex —see also IMPENETRABLE —**penetration** /ˌpenᵻˈtreɪʃən/ *n* [U]: *the CIA's penetration of left wing organizations* —**penetrable** /ˈpenᵻtrəbəl/ *adj* —**penetrability** /ˌpenᵻtrəˈbɪlᵻti/ *n* [U]

**pen·e·trat·ing** /ˈpenᵻtreɪtɪŋ/ *adj* **1 penetrating look/eyes/gaze** a look etc which makes you feel uncomfortable and seems to see inside your mind: *an attempt to avoid her husband's penetrating gaze* **2** a penetrating sound is loud, clear, and often unpleasant: *a penetrating whistle* **3** showing an ability to understand things quickly and completely: *Parker had prepared some penetrating questions.* **4** spreading and reaching everywhere: *penetrating dampness* —**penetratingly** *adv*

**pen·e·tra·tive** /ˈpenᵻtrətɪv‖-treɪtɪv/ *adj* **1** able to get into or through something easily **2** showing an ability to understand things quickly and completely: *penetrative observations*

**pen friend** /ˈ· ·/ *n* [C] *BrE* someone you make friends with by writing letters, especially someone in another country whom you have never met; PEN PAL

**pen·guin** /ˈpeŋgwᵻn/ *n* [C] a large black and white Antarctic sea bird, which cannot fly but uses its wings for swimming

**pen·i·cil·lin** /ˌpenᵻˈsɪlᵻn/ *n* [U] a substance used as a medicine to destroy bacteria; an ANTIBIOTIC

**pe·nile** /ˈpiːnaɪl/ *adj technical* relating to the penis

**pe·nin·su·la** /pᵻˈnɪnsjᵿlə‖-sələ/ *n* [C] a piece of land almost completely surrounded by water but joined to a large mass of land —**peninsular** *adj*

**pe·nis** /ˈpiːnᵻs/ *n* [C] the outer sex organ of men and male animals that is used for urinating (URINATE) and in sexual activity

**pen·i·tent¹** /ˈpenᵻtənt/ *adj formal* feeling sorry because you have done something wrong, and intending not to do anything wrong again; REPENTANT: *He knelt and put his head on her knee like a penitent dog.* —**penitently** *adv* —**penitence** *n* [U]

**penitent²** *n* [C] someone who is doing religious PENANCE

**pen·i·ten·tial** /ˌpenᵻˈtenʃəl◂/ *adj formal* connected with being sorry for having done something wrong: *penitential journeys to famous shrines* —**penitentially** *adv*

**pen·i·ten·tia·ry** /ˌpenᵻˈtenʃəri/ *n* [C] a prison, especially in the US: *the North Carolina state penitentiary*

**pen·knife** /ˈpen-naɪf/ *n plural* **penknives** /-naɪvz/ [C] a small knife with blades that fold into the handle, usually carried in your pocket —see picture at KNIFE¹

**pen·man·ship** /ˈpenmənʃɪp/ *n* [U] *formal* the art of writing by hand, or skill in this art

**pen name** /ˈ· ·/ *n* [C] a name used by a writer instead of their real name; PSEUDONYM

**pen·nant** /ˈpenənt/ *n* [C] **1** a long narrow pointed flag used on ships or by schools, sports teams, etc **2 the pennant** the prize given to the best team in the American and National BASEBALL competitions

**pen·nies** /ˈpeniz/ *n* the plural of PENNY

**pen·ni·less** /ˈpenɪləs/ *adj* having no money: *The old lady died penniless.*

**pen·non** /ˈpenən/ *n* [C] a long narrow pointed flag, especially one carried on the end of a long pole by soldiers on horses in the Middle Ages

**pen·n'orth** /ˈpenəθ‖-ərθ/ *n* [singular + **of**] *BrE old-fashioned* a PENNYWORTH

**pen·ny** /ˈpeni/ *n plural* **pennies** or **pence** /pens/ *BrE* S1 [C] **1** a small BRONZE coin, used in Britain since 1971, worth one hundredth (1/100th) of a pound: *a bag of pennies* **2** *plural* **pence** abbreviation **p** a unit of money used in Britain since 1971: *there are 100 pence in one pound.* | *It only costs a few pence.* | *a 20 pence piece* **3** *AmE* a coin worth a CENT in the US or Canada: *I only have pennies and nickels in my pocket.* **4** written abbreviation **d** *plural* **pence** a unit of money in Britain before 1971, equal to one 12th (1/12th) of a SHILLING: *pounds, shillings and pence* | **twopence/threepence etc** *a book costing only sixpence* **5 fourpenny/sixpenny etc** worth or costing fourpence, sixpence etc of the money used in Britain before 1971: *a sixpenny piece* **6 not a penny** no money at all: *Not a penny of the money came to me.* | *She'll never get a penny from me.* **7 every penny** all of an amount of money: *You'd better pay it back – every penny!* **8 the/your last penny** the only money that is left: *She had given away her last penny.* **9 a penny for**

your thoughts/a penny for them *spoken* used to ask someone what they are thinking about when they are silent **10 the penny (has) dropped** *BrE informal* used to mean that someone has finally understood something that had been said **11 be two/ten a penny** *BrE* to be very cheap and easy to obtain, and therefore of little value: *Computer experts are two a penny nowadays.* **12 not have two pennies/half-pennies to rub together** *BrE informal* to be very poor **13 in for a penny, in for a pound** *BrE* used to mean that if something has been started, it should be finished, whatever the cost may be **14 turn up like a bad penny** *BrE* if someone you dislike turns up like a bad penny, they keep appearing in situations where they are not wanted —see also HALFPENNY, **spend a penny** (SPEND (5)), **cost a pretty penny** (PRETTY[1] (7))

**penny an·te** /ˈ·· ˌ··/ *adj AmE informal* involving very small sums of money: *his penny ante schemes to make money*

**penny can·dy** /ˈ·· ˌ··/ *n* [C,U] *AmE old-fashioned* a sweet that costs one cent for a piece

**penny dread·ful** /ˌ·· ˈ··/ *n* [C] *BrE* a cheap and badly written book about violent crime

**penny-far·thing** /ˌ·· ˈ··/ *n* [C] a bicycle with a very large front wheel and a very small back wheel, used in the late 19th century

**penny-half·penny** /ˌ·· ˈ··/ *n BrE* one and a half old pence

**penny-pinch·ing** /ˈ·· ˌ··/ *adj* unwilling to spend or give money —**penny pinching** *n* [U] —**penny pincher** *n* [C]

**penny whis·tle** /ˌ·· ˈ··/ *n* [C] a simple musical instrument shaped like a tube that you blow down

**pen·ny·worth** /ˈpenɪwəθ‖-wərθ/ *n* [singular + **of**] *old-fashioned* as much as you can buy with a penny

**pe·nol·o·gy** /piːˈnɒlədʒi‖-ˈnɑːl-/ *n* [U] the scientific study of the punishment of criminals and the operation of prisons —**penologist** *n* [C]

**pen pal** /ˈ· ·/ *n* [C] *especially AmE* someone you make friends with by writing letters, especially someone in another country whom you have never met; PEN FRIEND *BrE*

**pen push·er** /ˈ· ˌ··/ *n* [C] *BrE* someone who has a boring unimportant job in an office; PENCIL PUSHER *AmE*

S3 W2 **pen·sion¹** /ˈpenʃən/ *n* [C] an amount of money paid regularly by a government or company to someone who is officially considered to be too old or too ill to earn money by working: *They both have their pensions to live on now that they've retired.* | *a disability pension* | **draw a pension** *BrE* (=receive or collect a pension) | **pension rights/plan/scheme** *a company pension plan* | **occupational/company pension** (=one that you get from your former employer) | **old age pension** *BrE* (=paid regularly by the government to old people; SOCIAL SECURITY *AmE*)

**pension²** *v* [T] *BrE*

**pension** sb/sth ↔ **off** [T] **1** *informal* to make someone leave their job, especially because of old age or illness, and pay them a pension: *Jean was pensioned off at 55.* **2** *informal* to get rid of something because it is too old or not useful any more

**pension³** *n* [C] a house like a small hotel, where you can get a room and meals, in France or some other European countries —compare BOARDING HOUSE

**pen·sion·a·ble** /ˈpenʃənəbəl/ *adj* **1** giving someone the right to receive a pension: *a pensionable age* | *appointments that were not pensionable* **2 pensionable pay/salary** pay from which money is regularly taken for a pension

**pen·sion·er** /ˈpenʃənə‖-ər/ *n* [C] *BrE* someone who is receiving a pension, especially an OLD AGE PENSION

**pension fund** /ˈ·· ·/ *n* [C] a sum of money which is invested (INVEST (1)) and used to pay PENSIONS to those people who have regularly paid money into it

**pension plan** /ˈ·· ·/ *n* [C] a system by which your employer, insurance company etc provides you with a pension after you have made regular payments to them over many years —compare RETIREMENT PLAN

**pension scheme** /ˈ·· ·/ *n* [C] *BrE* a pension plan

**pen·sive** /ˈpensɪv/ *adj* thinking deeply about something and seeming a little sad: *Jan was pensive.* | *a pensive expression* —**pensively** *adv* —**pensiveness** *n* [U]

**penta-** /pentə/ *prefix* five: *a pentagon* (=shape with five sides)

**Pent·a·gon** /ˈpentəgən‖-gɑːn/ *n* **the Pentagon** the building in Washington DC from which the army, navy etc of the US are controlled, or the military officers who work in this building

**pen·ta·gon** *n* [C] a flat shape with five, usually equal, sides and five angles —**pentagonal** *adj*

**pen·ta·gram** /ˈpentəgræm/ *n* [C] a five-pointed star, used as a magic sign

**pen·tam·e·ter** /penˈtæmɪ̮tə‖-ər/ *n* [C] a line of poetry with five main beats —see also IAMBIC PENTAMETER

**pen·tath·lon** /penˈtæθlən/ *n* [singular] a sports event involving five different sports

**Pen·te·cost** /ˈpentɪkɒst‖-kɒːst, -kɑːst/ *n* [singular] **1** a Jewish religious holiday 50 days after Passover **2** the seventh Sunday after Easter when Christians celebrate the coming of the Holy Spirit; WHITSUN *BrE*

**Pen·te·cos·tal** /ˌpentɪˈkɒstəl◂‖-ˈkɒːs-,-ˈkɑːs-/ *adj* **1** belonging to or connected with a group of Christian churches with particular interest in the gifts of the HOLY SPIRIT **2** connected with the holiday of Pentecost

**Pen·te·cos·tal·ist** /ˌpentɪˈkɒstəlɪ̮st‖-ˈkɒːs-,-ˈkɑːs-/ *n* [C] someone who belongs to a Pentecostal church —**Pentecostalist** *adj* —**Pentecostalism** *n* [U]

**pent·house** /ˈpenthaʊs/ *n* [C] a very expensive and comfortable apartment or set of rooms built on top of a tall building: *a magnificent penthouse apartment*

**pent up** /ˌpent ˈʌp◂/ *adj* pent up emotions are not freely expressed: *She began to cry, letting her pent up grief come out.*

**pe·nul·ti·mate** /peˈnʌltɪ̮mɪ̮t, pə-/ *adj* [only before noun] *literary* next to the last: *the penultimate chapter*

**pe·num·bra** /pɪ̮ˈnʌmbrə/ *n* [C] *technical* a slightly dark area between full darkness and full light

**pe·nu·ri·ous** /pɪ̮ˈnjʊəriəs‖-ˈnʊr-/ *adj formal* very poor

**pen·u·ry** /ˈpenjʊ̮ri/ *n* [U] *formal* the state of being very poor; POVERTY: *families living in penury*

**pe·on** /ˈpiːən/ *n* [C] **1** *AmE usually humorous* someone who works at a boring or physically hard job for low pay **2** *AmE* someone in Mexico or South America who works as a kind of slave to pay his debts **3** an office messenger in India

**pe·o·ny** /ˈpiːəni/ *n* [C] a garden plant with large round flowers that are dark red, white, or pink

**peo·ple¹** /ˈpiːpəl/ *n* S1 W1

**1** [plural] persons: *Were there many people at the meeting?* | *Most people in our neighborhood drive to work.* | *a retirement home for elderly people* —see PERSON (USAGE)

**2 ▶ PEOPLE IN GENERAL ◀** [plural] people in general, or people other than yourself: *Sometimes people think we're sisters.* | *People enjoy reading about the rich and famous.* | **theatre/business etc people** *Computer people are notoriously bad at arithmetic.*

**3 the people** [plural] all the ordinary people in a country or a state who do not have special rank or position: *Abraham Lincoln spoke of 'government of the people, by the people, for the people'.* | *the common people* | **man of the people** *a politician who was regarded as a man of the people because his father had been a miner*

4 [C] a race or nation: *the national heritage of the American people|the peoples of Africa|The Chinese people share a common written language.* —see RACE[1] (USAGE)
**5 sb's people** [plural] **a)** the people that God, a king, or a leader rules or leads: *the exaltation of God's people* **b)** your parents, grandparents etc: *His people have lived in this valley for centuries.* **c)** *old-fashioned* your close relatives, especially parents: *Come home with me to meet my people.*
**6 of all people** *spoken* used to say that someone is the one person who you would not have expected to do something: *Why should he, of all people, get a promotion?|You of all people should have known better.*

**7** *AmE spoken* used to get the attention of a group of people: *Listen up, people!* —compare FOLK[2] (3) —see also LITTLE PEOPLE, PERSON

**people**[2] *v* **1 be peopled with/by** *literary* to be filled with people or things of a particular type: *Her little world was peopled with imaginary friends.* **2** [T] *technical* to live in a place; INHABIT: *the tribes who first peopled the peninsula*

**pep**[1] /pep/ *v* **pepped, pepping**
**pep** sb/sth ↔ **up** *phr v* [T] *informal* to make something or someone more active, interesting or full of energy: *You need something to pep you up – how about a drink?|Pep up the dish with some curry powder.*

**pep**[2] *n* [U] *informal* physical energy; VIGOUR: *His exercise routine keeps him full of pep.* —see also PEP TALK

S3 **pep·per**[1] /ˈpepə‖-ər/ *n* **1** [U] a grey or pale yellow powder used to add a slightly hot taste to food: *Pass the salt and pepper, please.* —see also BLACK PEPPER, WHITE PEPPER **2** a red powder like this, especially CAYENNE PEPPER or PAPRIKA **3** [C] a hollow red, green or yellow vegetable that is used in hot or cold dishes —see also BELL PEPPER, SWEET PEPPER —see picture on page 414

**pepper**[2] *v* [T] **1** to scatter things all over or all through something: **be peppered with** *a report peppered with statistics* **2** to hit something repeatedly with many bullets: **pepper sth with** *He peppered the side of the barn with buckshot.* **3** to add pepper to food

**pepper-and-salt** /ˌ··· ˈ·◂/ *adj* coloured with small areas of black and white mixed together: *a pepper-and-salt beard*

**pep·per·corn** /ˈpepəkɔːn‖ˈpepərkɔːrn/ *n* [C] the small dried fruit from a tropical plant which is crushed to make pepper

**peppercorn rent** /ˌ··· ˈ·/ *n* [C] *BrE* a very small amount of rent, much less than you would expect to pay

**pep·per mill** /ˈ·· ·/ *n* [C] a small piece of kitchen equipment which is used to crush peppercorns into pepper

**pep·per·mint** /ˈpepəˌmɪnt‖-ər-/ *n* **1** [U] a MINT plant with a strong taste which is often used in sweets and medicine **2** the taste of this plant: *peppermint candy* **3** [C] a sweet with the taste of peppermint

**pep·pe·ro·ni** /ˌpepəˈrəʊni‖-ˈroʊ-/ *n* [C,U] an Italian spicy dry SAUSAGE

**pepper pot** /ˈ·· ·/ *BrE*, **pepper shak·er** /ˈ·· ˌ··/ *AmE n* [C] a small container with little holes in the top used for shaking pepper onto food

**pep·per·y** /ˈpepəri/ *adj* **1** tasting of pepper **2** easily made angry; IRRITABLE

**pep pill** /ˈ· ·/ *n* [C] *informal* a PILL containing a drug that gives you more energy or makes you happier for a short time; STIMULANT (1)

**pep ral·ly** /ˈ· ˌ··/ *n* [C] *AmE* a meeting of all the students at a school before a sports event when CHEERLEADERS lead students in encouraging their team to win

**pep·sin** /ˈpepsɪ̈n/ *n* [U] a liquid in your stomach that changes food into a form that can be used by your body

**pep talk** /ˈ· ·/ *n* [C] *informal* a speech that is intended to encourage you to work harder, win a game etc: *The manager gave his team a pep talk at half time.*

**pep·tic ul·cer** /ˌpeptɪk ˈʌlsə‖-ər/ *n* [C] a sore painful place inside the stomach caused by the action of pepsin

**per** /pə· *strong* pɜː‖pər· *strong* pɜːr/ *prep* **1** for each: **per kilo/gallon/metre etc** (=for each kilo etc) *Apples are 60 cents per pound.|My car does about 12 miles per litre* (=for each litre of petrol).|**per head** (=for or by each person) *How much food should we allow per head?* **2 per hour/day/week etc** during each hour etc: *How many calls do you make per day?*|**miles/kilometres per hour** (=used for measuring speed) *a train travelling at 150 miles per hour* **3** according to: **as per sth** *work carried out as per your instructions* **4 as per usual** *spoken* used when something annoying happens which has often happened before: *Hardy was late, as per usual.* —see also PER ANNUM, PER CAPITA S3 W1

**per·ad·ven·ture** /ˌperədˈventʃə‖-ər/ *adv old use* **1** perhaps **2** by chance: *if peradventure we should meet*

**per·am·bu·late** /pəˈræmbjɡ̈leɪt/ *v* [I,T] *old-fashioned* to walk around or along a place without hurrying —**perambulation** /pəˌræmbjɡ̈ˈleɪʃən/ *n* [C,U]

**per·am·bu·la·tor** /pəˈræmbjɡ̈leɪtə‖-ər/ *n* [C] *old-fashioned especially BrE* a PRAM

**per an·num** /pər ˈænəm/ written abbreviation **p.a.** *adv formal* for or in each year: *a salary of $20,000 per annum*

**per·cale** /pəˈkeɪl‖pər-/ *n* [C,U] *AmE* cotton cloth, used especially for making sheets

**per cap·i·ta** /pə ˈkæpɪ̈tə‖pər-/ *adj, adv formal* for or by each person in a particular place: *What is the average per capita income in this country?*

**per·ceive** /pəˈsiːv‖pər-/ *v* [T not in progressive] **1** to understand or think of something in a particular way: **perceive that** *People now perceive that green issues are important to our future.*|**perceive sth as sth** *Holly began to perceive her father as a loser.*|**perceive sth to be sth** *The past is often perceived to be better than the present.*|**perceive what/where/who etc** *We were able to perceive where the problem lay.* **2** to notice something that is difficult to notice: *That morning, he perceived a change in Franca's mood.*|**perceive that** *Jill could just perceive that someone was inside the house.* W3

**percent**[1] also **per cent** *BrE* /pəˈsent‖pər-/ *adj, adv* **1 5 percent (5%)/10 percent (10%) etc** equal to 5, 10 etc parts out of a total that consists of 100 parts: *Leave the waitress a 15 percent (=15%) tip.* **2 a/one hundred percent** completely, totally: *I agree with you a hundred percent.* S3

**percent**[2] also **per cent** *BrE n* **5 percent (5%)/10 percent (10%) etc** an amount equal to 5, 10 etc parts out of a total that consists of 100 parts: *30 percent (=30%) of our profits|The bank charges interest at fourteen per cent (=14%).* S3 W3

**per·cen·tage** /pəˈsentɪdʒ‖pər-/ *n* **1** [C, U] *technical* an amount stated as if it is part of a whole which is 100: *"What percentage of school leavers go to university?" "About five per cent."*|**high/low percentage** *A high percentage of married women have part-time jobs.*|**in percentage terms** *The numbers are small, in percentage terms, but significant.* **2** [C usually singular] a share of profits: *She gets a percentage for every record sold.* **3 there is no percentage in** *informal* used to say that there is no advantage or profit in doing something W3

**per·cep·ti·ble** /pəˈseptɪ̈bəl‖pər-/ *adj formal* something that is perceptible can just be noticed, although it is small: *a barely perceptible sound|a small but perceptible change* —opposite IMPERCEPTIBLE —**perceptibly** *adv*

**per·cep·tion** /pəˈsepʃən‖pər-/ *n* **1** [C] the way you regard something and your beliefs about what it is like: *Parents' views influence their children's perceptions of the world.* **2** [U] the way that you notice things with your senses: *This drug alters perception.* **3** [U] the natural ability to understand or notice something quickly: *Ross shows unusual perception for a boy of his age.* W3

**per·cep·tive** /pə'septɪv‖pər-/ *adj approving* good at noticing and understanding what is happening or what someone is thinking or feeling: *a perceptive woman*| *perceptive comments* —**perceptively** *adv* —**perceptiveness** *n* [U]: *trust in their own powers of perceptiveness and intuition*

**perch¹** /pɜːtʃ‖pɜːrtʃ/ *n* [C] **1** a branch, stick, rod etc where a bird sits, especially in a bird cage **2** *informal* a high place where a person sits or where a building is placed: *From our perch on the hill, we can see the whole city.* **3** a fish that lives in lakes and rivers

**perch²** *v* **1 be perched on/upon/over etc** to be in a position on top of, or on the edge of something: *a house perched on a cliff above the town* **2 perch (yourself) on** to sit on top of, or on the edge of, something: *Linda perched herself on a bar stool.* **3** [I + **on**] if a bird perches on something, it flies down and sits on it

**per·chance** /pə'tʃɑːns‖pər'tʃæns/ *adv old use or literary* **1** perhaps **2** by chance: *Leave now, lest perchance he should find you.*

**per·cip·i·ent** /pə'sɪpiənt‖pər-/ *adj formal* quick to notice and understand things; PERCEPTIVE —**percipience** *n* [U]

**per·co·late** /'pɜːkəleɪt‖'pɜːr-/ *v* **1** [I always + adv/prep] if liquid, light etc percolates somewhere, it passes slowly through a material that has very small holes in it: [+ **through/down**] *Water percolated down through the rock.* **2** [I always + adv/prep] if information percolates among people, it is passed gradually from one person to another: [+ **through/down**] *News of the war percolated through to us after a few days.* **3 a)** [I] if coffee percolates, it is made in a special pot in which hot water is passed through crushed coffee beans **b)** [T] to make coffee by this method —**percolation** /ˌpɜːkə'leɪʃən‖ˌpɜːr-/ *n* [C,U]

**per·co·la·tor** /'pɜːkəleɪtə‖'pɜːrkəleɪtər/ *n* [C] a pot in which coffee is percolated

**per·cus·sion** /pə'kʌʃən‖pər-/ *n* **1** [U, singular] musical instruments, especially drums, that are played by being hit with an object such as a stick or hammer, or the group of people who play these instruments in an ORCHESTRA: *the percussion is too loud* **2** [U] the sound or effect of two things hitting each other with great force

**per·cus·sion·ist** /pə'kʌʃənɪst‖pər-/ *n* [C] someone who plays percussion instruments

**per di·em¹** /pə 'diːəm‖pər-/ *n* [C] *especially AmE* money paid by an employer to workers who are paid by the day: *What's the per diem for the job?*

**per diem²** *adv* happening every day or from one day to another: *We are paid per diem.*

**per·di·tion** /pə'dɪʃən‖pər-/ *n* [U] *formal* **1** punishment after death **2** *old use* complete destruction: *He had gambled his way to perdition.*

**per·e·gri·na·tion** /ˌperɪgrɪ'neɪʃən/ *n* [C] *literary or humorous* a long journey, especially in foreign countries: *His peregrinations took him to India and China.*

**per·e·grine fal·con** /ˌperɪgrɪn 'fɔːlkən‖-'fɒːl-, -'fɑːl-/ also **peregrine** *n* [C] a hunting bird with a black and white spotted front

**pe·remp·to·ry** /pə'remptəri/ *adj formal* **1** peremptory behaviour, speech etc is not polite or friendly and shows that the person speaking expects to be obeyed at once: *a peremptory tone of voice* **2** a peremptory command must be obeyed —**peremptorily** *adv*

**pe·ren·ni·al¹** /pə'reniəl/ *adj* **1 perennial problem/concern/struggle etc** a problem etc that people are concerned with all the time: *the film addresses the perennial theme of marital discord* **2** a plant that is perennial lives for more than two years —**perennially** *adv*

**perennial²** *n* [C] a plant that lives for more than two years —see also HARDY PERENNIAL

**per·e·stroi·ka** /ˌperɪ'strɔɪkə/ *n* [U] a Russian word meaning rebuilding, used to describe the policies of social, political, and economic change started by Mikhail Gorbachev in the former USSR

**per·fect¹** /'pɜːfɪkt‖'pɜːr-/ *adj* **1** of the very best possible kind or standard: *It's a perfect day for a picnic*|*a perfect example of Gothic architecture*|*a perfect marriage*| **the perfect crime** (=one in which the criminal is never discovered) *There is no such thing as the perfect crime.* **2** complete, without any faults or weaknesses: *a perfect performance*|*a perfect set of teeth*|*in perfect condition*|**nobody's perfect** *spoken* (=used when you are answering someone who has criticized you) *So I did the wrong thing! Well nobody's perfect.* **3** exactly right and just what is needed for a particular purpose; IDEAL¹ (1): *That's perfect! – just the way I wanted it to look.*| *"D'you want some more soup?" – "No, this is perfect."* (=enough; plenty)| *We've found the perfect actor to play the part.*|[+ **for**] *The house is perfect for our family.* **4** completely correct and accurate: *Your English is perfect.*|*a perfect copy of the original*|**perfect timing** (=when something happens at exactly the right time) *"Have you been waiting?" "No, it was perfect timing. I've just arrived."* **5 the perfect gentleman/wife/host** someone who behaves exactly as a typical gentleman etc ought to behave **6 a perfect stranger/fool/angel etc** complete stranger etc: *I felt a perfect idiot.* —see also PERFECTLY, **practice makes perfect** (PRACTICE (11)), PRESENT PERFECT, PAST PERFECT

S2 W2

**per·fect²** /pə'fekt‖pər-/ *v* [T] to make something perfect or as good as you are able to: *It's just a working model; we haven't perfected it yet.*

**per·fect³** /'pɜːfɪkt‖'pɜːr-/ *n technical* **the perfect** the form of a verb which shows a period of time up to and including the present, and in English is usually formed with 'have' and the past participle; PRESENT PERFECT —see also PAST PERFECT

**per·fec·ti·ble** /pə'fektɪbəl‖pər-/ *adj* something that is perfectible can be improved or made perfect —**perfectibility** /pəˌfektɪ'bɪlɪti‖pər-/ *n* [U]

**per·fec·tion** /pə'fekʃən‖pər-/ *n* [U] **1** the state of being perfect: **to perfection** (=perfectly) *the meat was cooked to perfection* **2** the process of making something perfect: *the perfection of his technique* **3** a perfect example of something: *Her performance was pure perfection.*

**per·fec·tion·ist** /pə'fekʃənɪst‖pər-/ *n* [C] someone who is not satisfied with anything unless it is completely perfect: *You did fine! Don't be such a perfectionist.* —**perfectionist** *adj* —**perfectionism** *n* [U]

**per·fect·ly** /'pɜːfɪktli‖'pɜːr-/ *adv* **1** in a perfect way: *She speaks English perfectly.*|*The colors match perfectly.* **2** a word meaning very or completely, used especially when you are annoyed about something: *We want to make our position perfectly clear!*| *You know perfectly well what I mean.*

S2 W3

**perfect par·ti·ci·ple** /ˌ·· '····/ *n* [C] the PAST PARTICIPLE

**perfect pitch** /ˌ·· '·/ *n* [U] the ability to correctly name any musical note that you hear, or to sing any note at the correct PITCH without the help of an instrument

**per·fid·i·ous** /pə'fɪdiəs‖pər-/ *adj literary* someone who is perfidious is disloyal and cannot be trusted; TREACHEROUS (1) —**perfidiousness** *n* [U]

**per·fi·dy** /'pɜːfɪdi‖'pɜːr-/ *n* [U] *literary* disloyalty to someone who trusts you; TREACHERY

**per·fo·rate** /'pɜːfəreɪt‖'pɜːr-/ *v* [T] **1** to make a hole or holes in something: *A broken rib had perforated her lung.* **2** [usually passive] to make a line of small holes in a piece of paper so that a part of it can be torn off easily —**perforated** *adj*: *a perforated sheet of paper*

**per·fo·ra·tion** /ˌpɜːfə'reɪʃən‖ˌpɜːr-/ *n* **1** [C usually plural] a small hole in something, or a line of holes made in a piece of paper so that it can be torn easily: *the perforations in a sheet of stamps* **2** [U] the making of a hole or holes in something

**per·force** /pə'fɔːs‖pər'fɔːrs/ *adv literary* because it is necessary: *He fell sick and had perforce to stay at home.*

S3 W2 **per·form** /pəˈfɔːm‖pərˈfɔːrm/ *v* **1** [I,T] to do something to entertain people, for example by acting a play, or playing a piece of music: *I've never seen 'Othello' performed so brilliantly.*|*Chris will be performing in public next week.* **2** [T] to do something such as a piece of work, a duty, or a ceremony, especially according to a usual or established method: *an operation performed by surgeons at Guy's Hospital*|*The advice service performs a useful function.*|**perform miracles** (=do things that seem impossible) **3 perform well/badly** to work or do something well, badly etc: *Our team performed very well on Saturday.*|*The car performs badly in the wet.*

S3 W1 **per·form·ance** /pəˈfɔːməns‖pərˈfɔːr-/ *n* **1 a)** [C] an act of performing a play or a piece of music: [+ **of**] *Stern's performance of the Bruch concerto*|**give a performance** *The orchestra will give two more performances this week.* **b)** an occasion on which a play, piece of music etc is performed: *This evening's performance will begin at 8.00 pm.* **2** [U] **a)** the act of doing a piece of work, duty etc: *the performance of his official duties* **b)** how well or badly you do a particular job or activity: *Jodie's performance in the exams was disappointing.* **3** [U] how well a car or other machine works: *The car's performance on mountain roads was impressive.*|*high-performance cars* (=very powerful cars) **4 a) a performance** *spoken* a process that takes too much time and effort: *What a performance!* **b)** an example of bad behaviour that involves angry shouting

**performance-re·lat·ed pay** /ˈ·ˌ·· ·ˌ··/ *n* [U] money that you earn which increases if you work well and decreases if you work badly

**per·form·er** /pəˈfɔːmə‖pərˈfɔːrmər/ *n* [C] **1** an actor, musician etc, who performs to entertain people: *circus performers* **2 skilful/brilliant/poor etc performer** someone who does a particular job or activity well or badly: **star performer** (=the best performer)

**performing arts** /ˌ·ˌ·· ˈ·/ *n* **the performing arts** arts such as dance, music, or DRAMA, which are performed to entertain people

**per·fume¹** /ˈpɜːfjuːm‖ˈpɜːr-/ *n* [C,U] **1** a liquid that has a strong pleasant smell, that you put on your skin or clothing to make yourself smell nice: *She never wears perfume.* **2** a sweet or pleasant smell: *the rose's heady perfume*

**per·fume²** /ˈpɜːfjuːm‖pərˈfjuːm/ *v* **1** *literary* to fill something with a sweet, pleasant smell: *The flowers in her garden perfumed the evening air.* **2** to put perfume on something: *Use lavender oil to perfume your handkerchiefs.* —**perfumed** *adj*: *perfumed soap*

**per·fum·er·y** /pəˈfjuːməri‖pər-/ *n* **1** [C] a place where perfumes are made or sold: *the store's perfumery counter* **2** [U] the process of making perfumes

**per·func·to·ry** /pəˈfʌŋktəri‖pər-/ *adj formal* **1** a perfunctory action is done quickly, and is only done because people expect it: *Olivia dismissed him with a perfunctory nod.*|*a perfunctory kiss on the cheek* **2** someone who is perfunctory does things in this way —**perfunctorily** *adv*: *The two men shook hands perfunctorily.*

**per·go·la** /ˈpɜːgələ‖ˈpɜːr-/ *n* [C] a structure made of posts built for plants to grow over in a garden

S2 W1 **per·haps** /pəˈhæps, præps‖pər-, præps/ *adv* **1** possibly; MAYBE: *This is perhaps her finest novel yet.*|*Perhaps she's next door.*|*"Do you think Mark's upset?" "Perhaps."*|**perhaps not** *"Do you think I dare ask him?" "Perhaps not."* **2** used to say that a number is only a guess: *The room was large, perhaps twenty feet square.* **3** *spoken* used to politely ask or suggest something: *I thought perhaps we'd have lunch in the garden.*|*Perhaps you'd like to join us?* **4** *spoken formal* used to say what you are going to do, or what someone else should do: *Perhaps in closing I could repeat a statement from our Chairman's opening address.* —see MAYBE (USAGE)

**per·il** /ˈperɪ̥l/ *n* **1** [U] *literary* great danger, especially of being harmed or killed: **in peril** *a prayer for those in peril on the sea* **2 the perils of a)** *literary* things that can cause great danger: *Cook faced the perils of the Atlantic seas.* **b)** things that might cause you problems in life: *Her mother had warned her about the perils of living alone.* **3 you do sth at your peril** used to warn someone that what they intend to do is very dangerous: *Those who ignore the gale warning do so at their peril.*

**per·il·ous** /ˈperɪ̥ləs/ *adj especially literary* very dangerous: *a perilous journey across the mountains* —**perilously** *adj*: *perilously close to the precipice* —**perilousness** *n* [U]

**pe·rim·e·ter** /pəˈrɪmɪ̥tə‖-ər/ *n* [C] **1** the border around an enclosed area such as a military camp: *the perimeter of the airfield*|*a perimeter fence* **2** the whole length of the border around an area or shape: *Calculate the perimeter of this rectangle.* —compare CIRCUMFERENCE

**pe·ri·na·tal** /ˌperɪ̥ˈneɪtl◂/ *adj technical* at or around the time of birth: *a high rate of perinatal mortality*

**pe·ri·od¹** /ˈpɪəriəd‖ˈpɪr-/ *n* [C] S3 W1

**1** ▶ **LENGTH OF TIME** ◀ a particular length of time with a beginning and an end: *Tomorrow's weather will be dry with sunny periods.*|*the period 1910–1917*|*a period of six weeks*|*a six-week period*|**trial period** (=a period of testing) *Helen has been taken on for a three month trial period.*

**2** ▶ **IN DEVELOPMENT** ◀ a particular period in the development of a country or a person: *Van Gogh's early period*

**3** ▶ **IN HISTORY** ◀ a particular period in history: *Which period are you studying?*

**4** ▶ **WOMAN** ◀ the MONTHLY flow of blood from a woman's body

**5** ▶ **DOT** ◀ *AmE* a DOT (.) in a piece of writing that shows the end of a sentence or an ABBREVIATION; FULL STOP *BrE* —see picture at PUNCTUATION MARK

**6** ▶ **FOR EMPHASIS** ◀ **period!** *AmE spoken* used to say that you have made a decision and that you do not want to discuss the subject any more: *I'm not going, period!*

**7** ▶ **SCHOOL** ◀ one of the equal parts that the school day is divided into; lesson: *What class do you have first period?*|*a double period of Science*

**period²** *adj* **period costume/furniture** clothes or furniture in the style of a particular time in history: *actors dressed in period costume*

**pe·ri·od·ic** /ˌpɪəriˈɒdɪk◂‖ˌpɪriˈɑː-/ also **periodical** *adj* [only before noun] happening repeatedly, usually at regular times: *periodic bouts of depression* —compare SPASMODIC (1) —**periodically** /-kli/ *adv*: *Teachers meet periodically to discuss progress.*

**pe·ri·od·i·cal** /ˌpɪəriˈɒdɪkəl‖ˌpɪriˈɑː-/ *n* [C] a magazine, especially one about a serious or technical subject, that comes out at regular times such as once a month

**periodic ta·ble** /ˌ···· ˈ··/ *n* [singular] a list of ELEMENTS (=simple chemical substances) arranged according to their ATOMIC STRUCTURE

**period pain** /ˈ··· ·/ *n* [U] pain that a woman gets when she has her PERIOD¹ (4); CRAMPS¹ (2) *AmE*

**period piece** /ˈ··· ·/ *n* [C] **1** something that was very modern when it was first made, written etc, but now seems old-fashioned **2** a typical example of something, such as a piece of furniture or work of art, from a particular period in history

**per·i·pa·tet·ic** /ˌperɪ̥pəˈtetɪk◂/ *adj formal* travelling from place to place, especially in order to do your job: *a peripatetic music teacher* —**peripatetically** /-kli/ *adv*

**pe·riph·e·ral¹** /pəˈrɪfərəl/ *adj* **1** connected to the main idea, question or activity, but much less important, and given much less attention: *Can we leave the peripheral issues till later?*|[+ **to**] *The love interest is peripheral*

to the main plot of the movie. **2** in the outer area of something or related to this area: *the city's peripheral suburbs* **3** peripheral equipment can be connected to a computer and used with it: *peripheral software* —**peripherally** *adv*

**peripheral**[2] *n* [C] a piece of equipment that is connected to a computer and used with it, for example a PRINTER[1]

**pe·riph·e·ry** /pəˈrɪfəri/ *n* **1** [C usually singular] the outer area or edge that surrounds a place: [+ **of**] *a residential area on the periphery of the city* —compare OUTSKIRTS **2 be on the periphery** to be only slightly involved in a group or activity: *extremists on the periphery of the animal rights movement*

**pe·riph·ra·sis** /pəˈrɪfrəsɪ̵s, -siːz/ *n plural* **periphrases** [C,U] *formal* **1** the unnecessary use of long words or phrases or unclear expressions **2** *technical* the use of AUXILIARY words instead of inflected (INFLECT (1)) forms —**periphrastic** /ˌperɪ̵ˈfræstɪk◂/ *adj*

**per·i·scope** /ˈperɪ̵skəʊp‖-skoʊp/ *n* [C] a long tube with mirrors fitted in it used to look over the top of something, especially to see out of a SUBMARINE

**per·ish** /ˈperɪʃ/ *v* **1** [I] *especially literary* to die, especially in a terrible or sudden way: *Hundreds perished when the ship went down.* **2** [I,T] *BrE, technical in AmE* if a material such as rubber or leather perishes, it decays and loses its natural strength **3 Perish the thought!** *spoken* used as a reply to an unacceptable idea or suggestion, to say that you hope this never happens

**per·ish·a·ble** /ˈperɪʃəbəl/ *adj* food that is perishable is likely to decay if it is not kept in the proper conditions: *perishable goods such as butter, milk, fruit and fish* —**perishables** *n* [plural]

**per·ished** /ˈperɪʃt/ *adj* **1** *BrE spoken* feeling very cold: *I wish I'd brought a jacket – I'm perished!* **2** *BrE, technical in AmE* material such as rubber that is perished has lost its strength and become useless: *The rubber hoses were found to be perished and had to be replaced.*

**per·ish·er** /ˈperɪʃə‖-ər/ *n* [C] *BrE old-fashioned* a child that behaves badly: *Come here, you little perisher!*

**per·ish·ing** /ˈperɪʃɪŋ/ *adj spoken especially BrE* **1** weather that is perishing is very cold: *It's really perishing this morning!* **2** feeling very cold: *Let's go indoors. I'm perishing!* **3** *old-fashioned* used to describe someone or something that is annoying you: *Tell those perishing kids to shut up!* —**perishingly** *adv*: *perishingly cold*

**per·i·style** /ˈperɪ̵staɪl/ *n* [C] *technical* a row of PILLARS around an open space in a building or the open space itself

**per·i·to·ni·tis** /ˌperɪ̵təˈnaɪtɪ̵s‖-tnˈaɪ-/ *n* [U] *technical* a poisoned and sore condition of the inside wall of your ABDOMEN (=part around and below your stomach)

**per·i·wig** /ˈperɪwɪg/ *n* [C] a white WIG with rolls or curls at the sides, worn in the 18th century

**per·i·win·kle** /ˈperɪwɪŋkəl/ *n* **1** [C] a small plant with light blue or white flowers that grows close to the ground **2** [C] a small sea animal that lives in a shell and can be eaten; WINKLE[2] **3** [U] a light blue colour

**per·jure** /ˈpɜːdʒə‖ˈpɜːrdʒer/ *v* [I] **perjure yourself** to tell a lie after promising to tell the truth in a court of law

**per·jur·er** /ˈpɜːdʒərə‖ˈpɜːrdʒərər/ *n* [C] someone who tells a lie after promising to tell the truth in a court of law

**per·ju·ry** /ˈpɜːdʒəri‖ˈpɜːr-/ *n* [C,U] the crime of telling a lie after promising to tell the truth in a court of law, or a lie told in this way: *Hall was found guilty of perjury.*

**perk**[1] /pɜːk‖pɜːrk/ *n* [C usually plural] something that you get legally from your work in addition to your wages such as goods, meals, or a car: *With all the perks, she's really earning over £20,000 a year.* | **one of the perks of the job** *I get a company car – it's one of the perks of the job.*

**perk**[2] *v* [I,T] *informal* to percolate (PERCOLATE (3))

**perk up** *phr v informal* **1** [I,T] to become more cheerful and interested in what is happening around you, or to make someone feel this way: *Zara perked up when her boyfriend's letter arrived.* | **perk sb ↔ up** *Have a cup of tea – that'll perk you up.* **2** [T **perk** sb/sth ↔ **up**] to make someone or something look brighter, neater etc: *You can soon perk the room up with a coat of paint.*

**perk·y** /ˈpɜːki‖ˈpɜːrki/ *adj informal* confidently cheerful and interested in what is happening around you: *You're very perky today!* —**perkily** *adv* —**perkiness** *n* [U]

**perm**[1] /pɜːm‖pɜːrm/ *n* [C] a process of putting curls into straight hair, by chemical treatment: *I'm going to have a perm to give my hair more body.*

**perm**[2] *v* [T] **1** to put curls into straight hair by means of a chemical treatment: *I'm having my hair permed today.* **2** *BrE* to choose and combine a number of football games from the list given in the FOOTBALL POOLS

**per·ma·frost** /ˈpɜːməfrɒst‖ˈpɜːrməfrɒːst/ *n* [U] a layer of soil, in very cold countries, that is always frozen

**per·ma·nence** /ˈpɜːmənəns‖ˈpɜːr-/ also **per·ma·nen·cy** /-nənsi/ *n* [U] the state of being permanent: *There's no feeling of permanence about our relationship.*

**per·ma·nent**[1] /ˈpɜːmənənt‖ˈpɜːr-/ *adj* continuing to exist for a long time or for all future time: *a paint that gives woodwork permanent protection against the weather* | *I need a permanent job.* | *Natalie seems to have a permanent grin on her face.* | **permanent fixture** (=someone or something that is always there) *Dan seems to have become a permanent fixture in her life now.* —compare TEMPORARY —**permanently** *adv*: *The accident left him permanently disabled.* 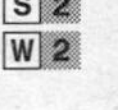

**permanent**[2] *n* [C] *AmE* a PERM[1]

**permanent wave** /ˌ··· ˈ·/ *n* [C] *formal* a PERM[1]

**permanent way** /ˌ··· ˈ·/ *n* [C] *BrE* a railway track and the stones and beams on which it is laid

**per·man·ga·nate** /pəˈmæŋgənɪ̵t‖pərˈmæŋgəneɪt/ also **permanganate of potash** *n* [U] a dark purple chemical compound used for killing BACTERIA

**per·me·a·ble** /ˈpɜːmiəbəl‖ˈpɜːr-/ *adj formal or technical* material that is permeable allows water, gas etc to pass through it: *a fine-grained permeable rock* —opposite IMPERMEABLE —**permeability** /ˌpɜːmiəˈbɪlɪ̵ti‖ˌpɜːr-/ *n* [U]

**per·me·ate** /ˈpɜːmieɪt‖ˈpɜːr-/ *v* **1** [I always + adv/prep, T] if liquid, gas etc permeates something, it enters it and spreads through every part of it: *Toxic chemicals may permeate the soil, threatening the environment.* | [+ **through/into**] *Water had permeated through cracks in the wall.* **2** [T] if ideas, beliefs, emotions etc permeate something, they are present in every part and have an effect on all of it: *A feeling of sadness permeates all his music.* —**permeation** /ˌpɜːmiˈeɪʃən‖ˌpɜːr-/ *n* [U]

**per·mis·si·ble** /pəˈmɪsɪ̵bəl‖pər-/ *adj formal* allowed by law or by the rules: *maximum permissible levels of radiation* —**permissibly** *adv*

**per·mis·sion** /pəˈmɪʃən‖pər-/ *n* [U] an act of officially allowing someone to do something: **permission to do sth** *I applied to the authorities for permission to cross the frontier.* | **give sb permission (to do sth)** *Who gave you permission to leave class early?* | **ask permission (from sb)** *If you want to take photographs, you must ask permission from the warden.* | **with your permission** *spoken* (–used to politely ask someone for permission to do something) *With your permission, I'll send a copy of this letter to the doctor.* —see also PLANNING PERMISSION S2 W3

**per·mis·sive** /pəˈmɪsɪv‖pər-/ *adj* allowing behaviour, especially sexual behaviour, that many other people disapprove of: *parents who are too permissive* | *the permissive society of the 1960s* —**permissiveness** *n* [U] *permissiveness in education* —**permissively** *adv*

**per·mit**[1] /pəˈmɪt‖pər-/ *v* **permitted, permitting** [T] W3 **1** *formal* to allow something to happen, especially by an official order or decision: *Smoking is only permitted in the public lounge.* | **permit sb sth** *You are not permitted access to confidential files.* | **permit sb to do sth** *I am afraid I cannot permit my daughter to marry you.* | **permit sth in/near etc** *Dogs are not permitted inside the shop.* **2** [I] to make it possible for something to happen: *I'll see you after the meeting, if time permits.* (=if it finishes early enough) | **weather permitting** (=if the weather is good enough) *We'll have a picnic in the woods, weather permitting.* **3** also **permit of** [T] *formal* to make something possible: *The facts permit of no other explanation.*

Frequencies of the verbs **let**, **allow** and **permit** in spoken and written English.

SPOKEN
let
allow
permit
WRITTEN
let
allow
permit
200 400 600 800 per million

Based on the British National Corpus and the Longman Lancaster Corpus

This graph shows that **let** is much more common in spoken English than **allow** and **permit**. **Allow** is more common in written English. **Permit** is a formal word meaning to officially let someone do something.

**per·mit²** /ˈpɜːmɪt‖ˈpɜːr-, pərˈmɪt/ *n* [C] an official written statement giving you the right to do something: *You're not allowed to park here unless you have a permit.* | **a travel/work/export etc permit** *The authorities may refuse to issue an export permit.* —see also WORK PERMIT

**per·mu·ta·tion** /ˌpɜːmjʊˈteɪʃən‖ˌpɜːr-/ *n* [C] one of the different ways in which a number of things can be arranged in order: *The six possible permutations of two letters chosen from ABC are AB, BA, CB, BC, AC, and CA.* —compare COMBINATION —**permute** *v* [T]

**per·ni·cious** /pəˈnɪʃəs‖pər-/ *adj formal* very harmful or evil, often in a way that you do not notice easily: *the pernicious effect of horror videos on children* | *a pernicious lie* —**perniciously** *adv* —**perniciousness** *n* [U]

**pernicious a·nae·mi·a** /ˌ·ˌ·· ·ˈ···/ *n* [U] *technical* a form of severe ANAEMIA (=too few red blood cells in the blood) that will kill the sick person if it is not treated

**per·nick·e·ty** /pəˈnɪkɪ̈ti‖pər-/ *BrE adj informal* **1** worrying too much about small and unimportant things; FUSSY (1); PERSNICKETY *AmE* **2** difficult to do because you have to deal with a lot of small objects; FIDDLY (1): *Changing this fridge lightbulb is a pernickety job.*

**per·o·ra·tion** /ˌperəˈreɪʃən/ *n* [C] *technical* **1** the last part of a speech, especially a part in which the main points are repeated **2** *formal* a long speech that sounds impressive but does not have much meaning

**per·ox·ide** /pəˈrɒksaɪd‖-ˈrɑːk-/ *n* [U] a chemical liquid used to make dark hair lighter or to kill BACTERIA

**peroxide blonde** /·ˌ·· ˈ·/ *n* [C] *old-fashioned* a woman who has changed the colour of her hair to very light yellow by using peroxide

**per·pen·dic·u·lar¹** /ˌpɜːpənˈdɪkjʊ̈lə◂‖ˌpɜːrpənˈdɪkjʊ̈lər◂/ *adj* **1** not leaning to one side or the other but exactly upright; VERTICAL¹ (1): *a perpendicular line* | *a perpendicular wall of rock* **2 be perpendicular to** if one line is perpendicular to another line, they form an angle of 90 degrees **3 Perpendicular** in the style of 14th and 15th century English churches which are decorated with straight, upright lines —**perpendicularly** *adv* —**perpendicularity** /ˌpɜːpəndɪkjʊ̈ˈlærɪ̈ti‖ˌpɜːr-/ *n* [U]

**perpendicular²** *n* **the perpendicular** an exactly upright position or line: *at an angle to the perpendicular*

**per·pe·trate** /ˈpɜːpɪ̈treɪt‖ˈpɜːr-/ *v* [T] *formal* to do something that is morally wrong or criminal: *crimes that have been perpetrated in the name of religion* —**perpetrator** *n* [C] *We'll bring the perpetrators to justice.* —**perpetration** /ˌpɜːpɪ̈ˈtreɪʃən‖ˌpɜːr-/ *n* [U] *the perpetration of crime*

**per·pet·u·al** /pəˈpetʃuəl‖pər-/ *adj* **1** continuing all the time without stopping, especially in a way that is worrying: *the perpetual noise of the machines* | *His wife lived in perpetual fear of his fiery temper.* **2** repeated many times in a way that annoys you: *Ella's perpetual moaning nearly drove me mad.* **3** *literary* permanent: *the perpetual snows of the mountaintops* —**perpetually** *adv*

**per·pet·u·ate** /pəˈpetʃueɪt‖pər-/ *v* [T] to make something continue to exist for a long time: *an education system that perpetuates the divisions in our society* —**perpetuation** /pəˌpetʃuˈeɪʃən‖pər-/ *n* [U]

**per·pe·tu·i·ty** /ˌpɜːpɪ̈ˈtjuːɪ̈ti‖ˌpɜːrpɪ̈ˈtuː-/ *n* **in perpetuity** *law* for all future time: *The community does not own land in perpetuity.*

**per·plex** /pəˈpleks‖pər-/ *v* [T usually passive] if something perplexes you, it makes you feel worried and confused because it is difficult to understand: *I was somewhat perplexed by his response.* | *a perplexing problem*

**per·plexed** /pəˈplekst‖pər-/ *adj* confused and worried by something that you do not understand: *She looked up at me with a perplexed stare.* —**perplexedly** /pəˈpleksɪ̈dli, -ˈplekstli‖pər-/ *adv*: *Florian was examining her perplexedly.*

**per·plex·i·ty** /pəˈpleksɪ̈ti‖pər-/ *n* **1** [U] the feeling of being confused or worried by something you cannot understand **2** [C usually plural] something that is complicated or difficult to understand: *moral perplexities*

**per·qui·site** /ˈpɜːkwɪ̈zɪt‖ˈpɜːr-/ *n* [C] *formal* a PERK¹

**per·ry** /ˈperi/ *n* [U] *especially BrE* an alcoholic drink made from PEARS

**per se** /ˌpɜː ˈseɪ‖ˌpɜːr ˈsiː, ˌpɜːr ˈseɪ, ˌper ˈseɪ/ *adv latin* a word meaning 'in itself' or 'by itself',used to say that something is being considered alone, not in connection with other things: *The music per se was not very good, but it did help to create the right atmosphere.*

**per·se·cute** /ˈpɜːsɪkjuːt‖ˈpɜːr-/ *v* [T] **1** to treat someone cruelly over a period of time, especially because of their religious or political beliefs: *Puritans left England to escape being persecuted.* **2** to deliberately cause trouble for someone by continually annoying them; HARASS: *Actors complained of being persecuted by the press.* —**persecutor** *n* [C] —**persecution** /ˌpɜːsɪˈkjuːʃən‖ˌpɜːr-/ *n* [C,U]: *the persecution of writers who criticize the government*

**persecution com·plex** /··ˈ·· ˌ··/ *n* [C] a mental illness in which someone believes that other people are continually trying to harm them

**per·se·ver·ance** /ˌpɜːsɪ̈ˈvɪərəns‖ˌpɜːrsɪ̈ˈvɪr-/ *n* [U] *approving* determination to keep trying to achieve something in spite of difficulties: *Beth has shown great perseverance in trying to overcome her handicap.*

**per·se·vere** /ˌpɜːsɪ̈ˈvɪə‖ˌpɜːrsɪ̈ˈvɪr/ *v* [I] *approving* to continue trying to do something in a very determined way in spite of difficulties: [+ **at/in/with**] *Rob keeps persevering in his efforts to learn French.* —**persevering** *adj*

**Per·sian¹** /ˈpɜːʃən, -ʒən‖ˈpɜːrʒən/ *n* **1** [U] the language of Iran; FARSI **2** [C] someone from Iran

**Persian²** *adj* from or connected with Iran, which used to be known as Persia: *a Persian carpet*

**Persian cat** /ˌ·· ˈ·/ *n* [C] a cat with long silky hair

**per·si·flage** /ˈpɜːsɪflɑːʒ‖ˈpɜːr-/ *n* [U] *formal* amusing talk, which usually includes laughing at other people

**per·sim·mon** /pəˈsɪmən‖pər-/ *n* [C] a soft orange-coloured fruit that grows in hot countries —see picture on page 413

**per·sist** /pəˈsɪst‖pər-/ *v* **1** to continue to do something, although this is difficult, or other people warn you not to do it: **persist in (doing) sth** *If you persist in causing trouble, the company may be forced to dismiss you.* | *"I'm* *sorry, I just don't think it's right," John persisted.* **2** [I] to continue to exist or happen: *Despite official denials, the rumours persisted.*

**per·sis·tent** /pə'sɪstənt‖pər-/ *adj* **1** continuing to do something, although this is difficult, or other people warn you not to do it: *Paul is amazingly persistent in trying to get Gina to go out with him.* | *Persistent attempts to interview Garbo were fruitless.* | **persistent offender** (=someone who continually breaks the law) **2** continuing to exist or happen, especially for longer than is usual or desirable: *the persistent bad weather* | *persistent headaches* —**persistently** *adv*: *He persistently called her at home.* —**persistence** *n* [U]

**per·snick·e·ty** /pə'snɪkəti‖pər-/ *adj AmE* PERNICKETY

S1 W1 **per·son** /'pɜːsən‖'pɜːr-/ *n* **1** [C] *plural* **people** a human being, especially considered as someone with their own particular character: *Tessa's a very intense person.* | *Hank's not the sort of person I find easy to talk to.* | *I like her as a person, but not as a boss.* | *What nice young people!* | *The person I need to speak to isn't here.* —see MAN[1] (USAGE) | **a city/cat etc person** (=someone who likes a particular thing or activity) *Are you one of those drama people?* **2 in person** if you do something in person, you do it by going somewhere yourself, not by letter or asking someone else to do it: *You have to go sign for it in person, they can't just mail it.* **3 businessperson/salesperson etc** someone who works in business, selling etc —see also CHAIRPERSON, SPOKESPERSON **4** [C] *plural* **persons** *formal or law* someone who is not known or not named: *Any person found trespassing will be prosecuted.* | *murder committed by a person or persons unknown* **5 about/on your person** *formal* on your body or hidden in your clothes: *Customs Officers found a gun concealed about his person.* **6 first/second/third person** one of the three special forms of verbs or PRONOUNS that show the speaker (first person), the one who is being spoken to (second person), or the one who is being spoken about (third person): *The third person singular of the verb 'go' is 'goes'.* | *'I', 'me', and 'we' are all first person pronouns.* —see also FIRST PERSON **7 in the person of** *formal* used before someone's name to emphasize that this is the person who represents a particular group: *I was met by the police in the person of Sergeant Black.* —see also MISSING PERSON, PERSON-TO-PERSON

**USAGE NOTE: PERSON**

GRAMMAR

The usual plural of **person** is **people**: *Only one person turned up.* | *A lot of people replied to our advert.* | *young people*

**People** meaning 'more than one person' is already plural and cannot form a plural with 's'. It always takes a plural verb: *Most people are basically honest.* | *People are dying of starvation every day* (NOT *...is dying*).

**People** meaning 'race' or 'nation' is countable and you can add 's' in the normal way: *the peoples of South East Asia*

**Persons** is very formal and used, for example, in official language: *He was murdered by a person or persons unknown.* You may also see it on offical notices: *This elevator may only carry eight persons.*

**per·so·na** /pə'səʊnə‖pər'soʊ-/ *n plural* **personae** /-niː/ [C] the way you behave when you are with other people, that makes them think that you are a particular type of person: *Joel has a very cheerful public persona but in private he's very different.*

**per·son·a·ble** /'pɜːsənəbəl‖'pɜːr-/ *adj* having an attractive appearance and a pleasant, polite way of talking and behaving: *a very personable young man*

**per·son·age** /'pɜːsənɪdʒ‖'pɜːr-/ *n* [C] *formal* **1** a famous or important person: *a royal personage* **2** a character in a play or book, or in history

**per·son·al**[1] /'pɜːsənəl‖'pɜːr-/ *adj* S1 W1
**1 ▶ DONE YOURSELF ◀** [only before noun] done, learned, or experienced by you yourself: *I know from personal experience that you can't trust Ralph.* | *The Mayor promised to give the matter his personal attention.* | *I'll take personal responsibility if this doesn't work.* | **personal contact** (=meeting and dealing with people yourself directly) *As you get promoted in a firm you lose that personal contact.*
**2 ▶ PRIVATE ◀** concerning only you, especially the private areas of your life: *May I ask you a personal question?* | *personal problems* | *personal letters* | *I'd tell you what's wrong, but it's a bit personal.* | **personal details** (=where you live, how old you are etc) *You will have to fill out a form giving your personal details.*
**3 ▶ YOUR OWN ◀** yours and no one else's: *Well, that's my personal view, anyway.* | *Modern art isn't to my personal taste.* | **my/their etc own personal** *They paid for everything and then he was given his own personal chaffeur to drive him home.* | **personal possessions/property/belongings** (=things belonging only to you) | **personal effects** *formal* (=small possessions) *personal effects scattered all around the wreckage of an aircraft*
**4 ▶ CRITICIZING ◀** involving rude or upsetting criticism of someone: *It's unprofessional to make such personal remarks.* | **get personal** *You don't have to get so personal!* | **(it's) nothing personal** *spoken* (=used to tell someone that you do not intend to be rude to them) *It's nothing personal, I just have to go home now.*
**5 personal friend** someone that you know well, especially a famous or important person: *Apparently the director is a personal friend of hers.*
**6 ▶ NOT OFFICIAL ◀** not concerned with your work, business, or official duties: *Please try not to make personal phone calls at work.* | **sb's personal life** *I don't answer questions about my personal life.*
**7 ▶ YOUR BODY ◀** [only before noun] concerning your body or the way you look: *Grant was always fussy about his personal appearance.* | *personal hygiene*
**8 personal touch** something you do to make something special, or that makes someone feel special: *It's those extra personal touches that make our service better.*
**9 personal development** the improvements in your character that come from your experiences in life: *the role of physical activities in the child's development*

**personal**[2] *n* [C] *AmE* a short advertisement put in a newspaper or magazine by someone who wants a friend or LOVER

**personal al·low·ance** /ˌ··· ·'··/ *n* [C] *BrE* the amount of money that you are allowed to earn each year before you start to pay INCOME TAX; EXEMPTION *AmE*

**personal as·sis·tant** /ˌ··· ·'··/ *n* [C] a PA; a special secretary who works for one person

**personal col·umn** /'··· ˌ··/ *n* [C] a part of a newspaper in which people can have private or personal messages printed

**personal com·pu·ter** /ˌ··· ·'··/ *n* [C] a PC; a small computer that is used by one person for business or at home

**personal i·den·ti·fi·ca·tion num·ber** /ˌ··· ····'·· ˌ··/ *n* [C] a PIN

**per·son·al·i·ty** /ˌpɜːsə'nælәti‖ˌpɜːr-/ *n* **1** [C,U] someone's character, especially the way they behave towards other people: *Iain has a very dynamic personality.* | *Childhood experiences have a strong influence on forming personality.* | **personality clash** (=when two people find it impossible to work together in a friendly way) **2** [U] the qualities that make someone interesting, friendly and enjoyable to be with: *The boss likes people with personality.* **3** [C] someone who is well known to the public, because they are often in the newspapers, on television etc: *a TV personality* | *a sports personality* **4 personalities** [plural] *BrE old-fashioned* unkind or rude remarks about someone's appearance, character etc: *Let's keep personalities out of the conversation, shall we!* **5** [C usually singular] the qualities which make a S3 W3

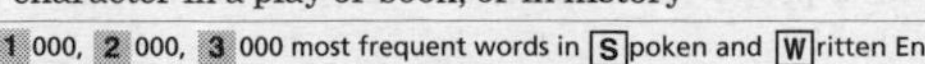

place or thing special: *It's partly the architecture which gives the town its personality.*

**personality cult** /ˌ··'···ˌ·/ *n* [C] the officially encouraged practice of giving too much admiration, praise, love etc to a political leader

**per·son·al·ize** also **-ise** *BrE* /ˈpɜːsənəlaɪz‖ˈpɜːr-/ *v* [T usually passive] **1** to put your name or INITIALS on something, or decorate it in your own way to show that it belongs to you: *Why not do something to personalize your office?* **2** to make something suitable for someone's particular needs or desires: *The bank is trying to personalize its service to customers.* **3** to change the subject of your remarks, arguments etc so that they are more concerned with personal matters or relationships than with facts: *In the later stages the campaign became highly personalized.* —**personalized** *adj* | *personalized license plates* —**personalization** /ˌpɜːsənəlaɪˈzeɪʃən‖ˌpɜːrsənələ-/ *n* [U]

S2 **per·son·al·ly** /ˈpɜːsənəli‖ˈpɜːr-/ *adv*
**1** ▸ **IN YOUR OPINION** ◂ [sentence adverb] *especially spoken* used to emphasize that you are only giving your own opinion about something: *Personally, I don't think much of the idea.*
**2** ▸ **DIRECTLY** ◂ doing or having done something yourself rather than through someone else: *I'm holding you personally responsible for this mess!* | *The managing director wrote personally to thank me.*
**3 take sth personally** to let yourself get upset or hurt by the things other people say or do: *Don't take it personally; she's rude to everyone.*
**4** ▸ **CRITICISM** ◂ directed against someone's character or appearance in an unpleasant way: *Sue didn't mean those criticisms personally you know.*
**5** ▸ **FRIEND** ◂ as a friend, or as someone you have met: *I don't know her personally, but I like her work.*

**personal or·ga·niz·er** /ˌ··· ˈ····/ *n* [C] a small book with loose sheets of paper, or a very small computer, for recording information, addresses, meetings etc

**personal pro·noun** /ˌ··· ˈ··/ *n* [C] *technical* a PRONOUN used for the person who is speaking, being spoken to, or being spoken about, such as 'I', 'you', and 'they'

**personal ster·e·o** /ˌ··· ˈ···/ *n* [C] a small CASSETTE PLAYER which you carry around with you and listen to through small HEADPHONES; WALKMAN

**personal stereo**

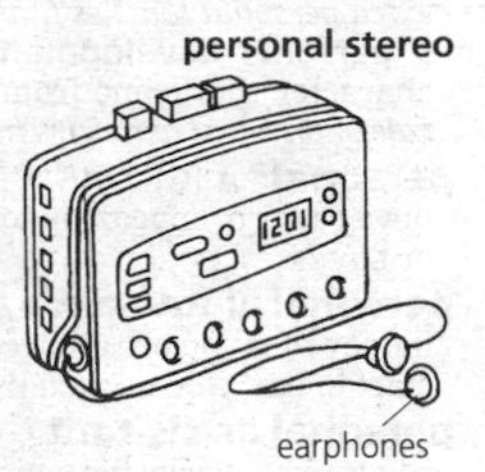


**persona non gra·ta** /pəˌsəʊnə nɒn ˈgrɑːtə‖pərˌsoʊnə nɑːn ˈgrætə/ *n* [U] *Latin* someone who is not acceptable to a government or not welcome in someone's house: *He was declared persona non grata.*

**per·son·i·fi·ca·tion** /pəˌsɒnɪfɪˈkeɪʃən‖pərˌsɑː-/ *n* **1 the personification of** someone who is a perfect example of a quality because they have a lot of it: *the personification of evil* **2** [C,U] the representation of a thing or a quality as a person, in literature or art: *the personification of Justice as a woman*

**per·son·i·fy** /pəˈsɒnɪfaɪ‖pərˈsɑː-/ *v* [T] **1** to think of or represent a quality or thing as a person: *Time is often personified as an old man with a scythe.* **2** to represent a particular quality or thing by having a lot of that quality or by being a typical example of that thing: *Our son is laziness personified.* | *The President seemed to personify American people in general.*

S3 W3 **per·son·nel** /ˌpɜːsəˈnel‖ˌpɜːr-/ *n* **1** [plural] the people who work in a company or organization, or in the army, navy etc: *medical personnel* | *All personnel are to receive security badges.* **2** [U] the department in an organization that appoints people to jobs and deals with their complaints, problems etc; HUMAN RESOURCES: *Fay finally decided to take her grievance to Personnel.*

**person-to-person** /ˌ··· ˈ··◂/ *adj* **person-to-person call** *AmE* a telephone call that is made to one particular person and does not have to be paid for if they are not there

**perspective**

a chessboard drawn in perspective

**per·spec·tive** /pəˈspektɪv‖pər-/ *n* **1** [C] a way of thinking about something which is influenced by the kind of person you are or by your experiences: [+ **on**] *His father's death gave him a whole new perspective on life.* | **from the perspective of** *The novel is written from the perspective of a child.* | **from a...perspective** *From a white male perspective, it's hard to understand oppression.* **2** [C,U] a sensible way of judging and comparing situations so that you do not imagine that something is more serious than it really is: *I think Viv's lost all sense of perspective.* | **get/keep sth in perspective** (=judge the importance of something correctly) **3** [U] a method of drawing a picture that makes objects look solid and shows distance and depth, or the effect this method produces in a picture: *Children's drawings often have no perspective.* | **in perspective/out of perspective** (=drawn with or without the effect of perspective) *The background is all out of perspective.* **4** [C] a view, especially one that stretches into the distance W

**per·spex** /ˈpɜːspeks‖ˈpɜːr-/ *n* [U] *BrE* a strong plastic material that can be seen through and is used instead of glass; PLEXIGLASS *AmE*

**per·spi·ca·cious** /ˌpɜːspɪˈkeɪʃəs◂‖ˌpɜːr-/ *adj formal* good at judging and understanding people and situations: *a perspicacious literary critic* | *a perspicacious remark* —**perspicaciously** *adv* —**perspicacity** /-ˈkæsɪti/ *n* [U]

**per·spi·ra·tion** /ˌpɜːspəˈreɪʃən‖ˌpɜːr-/ *n* [U] **1** liquid that appears on your skin when you are hot; SWEAT² (1) **2** the process of perspiring

**per·spire** /pəˈspaɪə‖pərˈspaɪr-/ *v* [I] to become wet on parts of your body, especially because you are hot or have been doing hard work; SWEAT¹ (1)

**per·suade** /pəˈsweɪd‖pər-/ *v* [T] **1** to make someone decide to do something, especially by repeatedly asking them or telling them reasons why they should do it: **persuade sb to do sth** *I finally managed to persuade her to go out for a drink with me.* | **persuade sb** *Leo wouldn't agree, despite our efforts to persuade him.* | **persuade sb into doing sth** *Don't let yourself be persuaded into buying things you don't really want.* **2** to make someone believe something or feel sure about something; CONVINCE: *I was persuaded by the sheer strength of this argument.* | **persuade sb of sth** *We finally persuaded Ben of the wisdom of this decision.* | **persuade sb (that)** *Carla failed to persuade us that she was innocent.*

**per·sua·sion** /pəˈsweɪʒən‖pər-/ *n* **1** the act or skill of persuading someone to do something: *After a little gentle persuasion, Debbie agreed to let us in.* | **powers of persuasion** (=skills used for persuading) **2** [C] *formal* a particular kind of belief, especially a political or religious one: *people of all political persuasions* **3** [singular] *formal* a strongly held belief or opinion: *It has always been my persuasion that capital punishment is wrong.* **4 of the ... persuasion** *formal or humorous* of a particular kind: *an artist of the modern persuasion*

**per·sua·sive** /pəˈsweɪsɪv‖pər-/ *adj* good at influencing other people to believe or do what you want: *They used* *some very persuasive arguments.* —**persuasively** *adv* —**persuasiveness** *n* [U]

**pert** /pɜːt‖pɜːrt/ *adj* **1** a girl or woman who is pert is amusing, but slightly disrespectful: *Angie gave him one of her pert little glances.* **2** clothing that is pert is neat and attractive in a cheerful way: *a pert little red hat set well back on her head* —**pertly** *adv* —**pertness** *n* [U]

**per·tain** /pə'teɪn‖pər-/ *v*
**pertain to** sth *phr v* [T] *formal* to be directly connected with something: *legislation pertaining to employment rights*

**per·ti·na·cious** /ˌpɜːtʃ'neɪʃəs◂‖ˌpɜːr-/ *adj formal* continuing to believe something or to do something in a very determined way; TENACIOUS —**pertinaciously** *adv* —**pertinacity** /-'næsʃti/ *n* [U]

**per·ti·nent** /'pɜːtʃnənt‖'pɜːr-/ *adj formal* directly concerned with something that is being considered: RELEVANT: *The investigator asked several highly pertinent questions.* | [+ **to**] *Your remarks are not pertinent to today's discussion.* —**pertinently** *adv* —**pertinence** *n* [U] —see also IMPERTINENT

**per·turbed** /pə'tɜːbd‖pər'tɜːrbd/ *adj* worried or annoyed because of something that has happened: *Fritz did not seem unduly perturbed when asked to change rooms.* —**perturbation** /ˌpɜːtə'beɪʃən‖ˌpɜːrtər-/ *n* [U] —**perturb** /pə'tɜːb‖pər'tɜːrb/ *v* [T]

**pe·ruse** /pə'ruːz/ *v* [T] *formal or humorous* to read something, especially in a careful way: *I'll give you the leaflet so you can peruse it at your leisure.* —**perusal** *n* [C,U]

**perv** /pɜːv‖pɜːrv/ *n* [C] *BrE spoken* a PERVERT —**pervy** *adj*

**per·vade** /pə'veɪd‖pər-/ *v* [T] if a feeling, idea, or smell pervades a place, it spreads through every part of it: *After the war a spirit of hopelessness pervaded the country.*

**per·va·sive** /pə'veɪsɪv‖pər-/ *adj* existing or spreading everywhere: *the pervasive influence of television* | **all-pervasive** (=extremely pervasive) *the all-pervasive mood of apathy* —**pervasiveness** *n* [U] —**pervasively** *adv*

**per·verse** /pə'vɜːs‖pər'vɜːrs/ *adj* continuing to behave in an unreasonable way, especially by deliberately doing the opposite of what people want you to do: *He gets some kind of perverse satisfaction from embarrassing people.* —**perversely** *adv* —**perverseness** *n* [U]

**per·ver·sion** /pə'vɜːʃən, -ʒən‖pər'vɜːrʒən/ *n* **1** [C,U] a type of sexual behaviour that is considered unnatural and unacceptable **2** [C,U] the process of changing something that is natural and good into something that is unnatural and wrong, or the result of such a change: *a perversion of the true meaning of democracy*

**per·ver·si·ty** /pə'vɜːsʃti‖pər'vɜːr-/ *n* [U] the quality of being perverse: *Max refused the money out of sheer perversity.*

**per·vert¹** /pə'vɜːt‖pər'vɜːrt/ *v* [T] **1** to change something in an unnatural and often harmful way: *Genetic scientists are often accused of perverting nature.* **2** to influence someone so that they begin to think or behave in an immoral way; CORRUPT² (1): *TV sex and violence perverts the minds of young children.* **3 pervert the course of justice** *law* to deliberately prevent a fair examination of the facts about a crime

**per·vert²** /'pɜːvɜːt‖'pɜːrvɜːrt/ *n* [C] someone whose sexual behaviour is considered unnatural and unacceptable: *What are you, some kind of pervert?*

**per·vert·ed** /pə'vɜːtʃd‖pər'vɜːr-/ *adj* **1** perverted ways of thinking and behaving, especially sexual behaviour, are unacceptable and unnatural **2** morally wrong or unnatural: *the perverted logic of Nazi propaganda*

**pe·se·ta** /pə'seɪtə/ *n* [C] the standard unit of money in Spain

**pes·ky** /'peski/ *adj informal especially AmE* annoying and causing trouble: *Those pesky kids!*

**pe·so** /'peɪsəʊ‖-soʊ/ *n* [C] the standard unit of money in Mexico, Colombia and Cuba

**pes·sa·ry** /'pesəri/ *n* [C] **1** a solid medicine or CONTRACEPTIVE chemical which is put into a woman's VAGINA **2** an instrument put into a woman's VAGINA to support her WOMB or as a CONTRACEPTIVE

**pes·si·mist** /'pesʃmɪst/ *n* [C] someone who always expects that the worst thing will happen: *Don't be such a pessimist – you're not going to fail.* —opposite OPTIMIST —**pessimism** *n* [U]

**pes·si·mis·tic** /ˌpesʃ'mɪstɪk◂/ *adj* expecting that bad things will happen in the future or that a situation will have a bad result: [+ **about**] *He remains deeply pessimistic about the peace process.* —opposite OPTIMISTIC —**pessimistically** /-kli/ *adv*

**pest** /pest/ *n* [C] **1** a small animal or insect that destroys crops or food supplies: *a chemical used in pest control* **2** *informal* an annoying person, especially a child: *Giles was being a thorough pest.*

**pes·ter** /'pestə‖-ər/ *v* [T] to annoy someone repeatedly, especially by asking them to do something: **pester sb for sth** *Beggars kept pestering us for money.* | **pester sb to do sth** *The kids have been pestering me to buy them new trainers.*

**pes·ti·cide** /'pestʃsaɪd/ *n* [C] a chemical substance used to kill insects and small animals that destroy crops

**pes·ti·lence** /'pestʃləns/ *n* [C,U] *literary* a disease that spreads quickly and kills large numbers of people

**pes·ti·lent** /'pestʃlənt/ also **pes·ti·len·tial** /ˌpestʃ'lenʃəl◂/ *adj* **1** *literary or humorous* extremely unpleasant and annoying **2** *old use* causing a pestilence

**pes·tle** /'pesəl, 'pestl/ *n* [C] a short stick with a heavy round end, used for crushing things in a MORTAR (=a special bowl) —see picture at LABORATORY

**pet¹** /pet/ *n* [C] **1** an animal such as a cat or a dog which you keep and look after at home: *Rabbits can make very good pets.* | *a pet tortoise* —see also TEACHER'S PET **2** *BrE spoken* a way of addressing someone who you like or love **3 be in a pet** *BrE old-fashioned* to be annoyed

**pet²** *v* [T] **1** to touch and stroke someone, especially a child or an animal, in a kind loving way: *Our cat loves being petted.* **2** to kiss and touch someone as part of a sexual activity —see also HEAVY PETTING

**pet³** *adj* **1 pet theory/project/subject** a plan, idea, or subject that you particularly like or are interested in **2 pet hate** *BrE* **pet peeve** *AmE* something that you strongly dislike because it always annoys you: *TV game shows are one of my pet hates.*

**pet·al** /'petl/ *n* [C] **1** the coloured part of a flower that is shaped like a leaf: *rose petals* | *Each of these flowers has seven petals.* **2 eight-petalled, blue-petalled etc** *BrE*, **-petaled** *AmE* having eight petals, blue petals etc

**pe·tard** /pʃ'tɑːd‖-ɑːrd/ *n* —see **be hoist with your own petard** (HOIST¹ (2))

**Peter** —see **rob Peter to pay Paul** (ROB (3))

**pet·er** /'piːtə‖-ər/ *v*
**peter out** *phr v* [I] to gradually become smaller or happen less often and then come to an end: *The road became narrower and eventually petered out.* | *Public interest in the environment is in danger of petering out.*

**pet·it bour·geois** /ˌpeti 'bʊəʒwɑː, -bʊə'ʒwɑː‖ˌpeti bʊr'ʒwɑː, pəˌtiː-/ *adj* another spelling of PETTY BOURGEOIS

**pe·tite** /pə'tiːt/ *adj* a woman who is petite is short and attractively thin

**petit four** /ˌpeti 'fɔə, -'fɔː‖-'fʊr, -'fɔːr/ *n* [C] *French* a small sweet cake or BISCUIT served with coffee

**pe·ti·tion¹** /pʃ'tɪʃən/ *n* [C] **1** a written request signed by a lot of people, asking someone in authority to do something or change something: [+ **against**] *They wanted me to sign a petition against experiments on animals.* | **draw up a petition** *Local residents have drawn up a petition to protest the hospital closure.* **2** an official letter to a law court, asking for a legal case to be considered: *She is threatening to file a petition for divorce.* **3** *formal* a formal prayer or request to someone in authority or to God or to a ruler

**petition²** *v* [I,T] **1** to ask the government or an organization to do something by sending it a petition: **petition sb to do sth** *Villagers petitioned the local authority to provide better bus services.* | [+ **against/for**] *Residents are petitioning against the new road.* **2** to make a formal request to someone in authority, to a court of law, or to God

**pe·ti·tion·er** /pɪ̈ˈtɪʃənə‖-ər/ *n* [C] **1** someone who writes or signs a petition **2** *law* someone who asks for their marriage to be legally ended

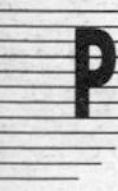

**petit mal** /ˌpeti ˈmæl/ *n* [U] *technical* a form of EPILEPSY which is not very serious —compare GRAND MAL

**pet name** /ˌ· ˈ·/ *n* [C] a name you call someone you like very much

**pet·rel** /ˈpetrəl/ *n* [C] a black and white sea bird; STORMY PETREL

**pet·ri·fied** /ˈpetrɪ̈faɪd/ *adj* **1** extremely frightened, especially so frightened that you cannot move or think: *She stood there, petrified at the thought of the crowds waiting outside.* **2 petrified wood/trees/insects etc** wood, trees etc that have changed into stone over a long period of time —**petrify** *v* [T] *My new boss absolutely petrifies me.* —**petrifaction** /ˌpetrɪ̈ˈfækʃən/ *n* [U]

**pet·ro·chem·i·cal** /ˌpetrəʊˈkemɪkəl‖-troʊ-/ *n* [C] a chemical substance obtained from PETROLEUM or natural gas: *the petrochemical industry*

**pet·ro·dol·lar** /ˈpetrəʊˌdɒlə‖ˈpetroʊˌdɑːlər/ *n* [C] a dollar earned by the sale of oil: *in search of petrodollars from Iran*

S3 **pet·rol** /ˈpetrəl/ *n* [U] *BrE* a liquid that is used to supply power to the engine of cars and other vehicles, which is obtained from PETROLEUM; GASOLINE *AmE*

**pet·ro·la·tum** /ˌpetrəˈleɪtəm/ *n* [U] *AmE* VASELINE

**petrol bomb** /ˈ·· ·/ *n* [C] *BrE* a simple bomb consisting of a bottle filled with petrol with a lighted cloth in the end

**pe·tro·le·um** /pɪ̈ˈtrəʊliəm‖-ˈtroʊ-/ *n* [U] oil that is obtained from below the surface of the Earth and is used to make petrol, PARAFFIN and various chemical substances: *petroleum-based products*

**petroleum jel·ly** /·ˌ··· ˈ··/ *n* [U] *especially BrE* VASELINE

**petrol sta·tion** /ˈ·· ˌ··/ *n* [C] *BrE* a place where you can take your car and fill it with petrol; GAS STATION *AmE*

**pet·ti·coat** /ˈpetikəʊt‖-koʊt/ *n* [C] **1** *especially BrE* a piece of women's underwear that hangs from your shoulders or waist; SLIP² (6) **2** a long skirt that was worn under a skirt or dress by women in the past

**pet·ti·fog·ging** /ˈpetiˌfɒgɪŋ‖-ˌfɑː-, -ˌfɔː-/ *adj BrE old-fashioned* **1** too concerned with small details **2** too unimportant to be worth considering

**pet·ti·ness** /ˈpetinɪ̈s/ *n* [U] behaviour and attitudes that are ungenerous and are too much concerned with unimportant matters: *the jealousy and pettiness of Hollywood*

**petting zoo** /ˈ·· ·/ *n* [C] *AmE* part of a zoo which has baby animals in it for children to touch

**pet·tish** /ˈpetɪʃ/ *adj* PETULANT —**pettishly** *adv* —**pettishness** *n* [U]

**pet·ty** /ˈpeti/ *adj* **1** a problem, detail, worry etc that is petty is small and unimportant: *He said he wasn't interested in petty details.* | *petty squabbles* **2** not generous and caring only about small unimportant things: *petty jealousy and spitefulness* —see also PETTINESS **3 petty tyrant/dictator etc** someone who is not really important but uses their power as if they were important: *Some petty bureaucrat wanted all the documents in triplicate.* **4 petty crime** a crime that is not serious, for example stealing things that have little value: **petty criminal/thief etc** *Big-time gangsters despise petty thieves.*

**petty bour·geois** /ˌ·· ˈ··‖ˌ·· ·ˈ·/ also **petit bourgeois** *adj* **1** paying too much attention to unimportant matters concerning social position, private possessions etc: *a petty bourgeois mentality* **2** belonging to the group of MIDDLE CLASS people who own small businesses, shops etc —**petty bourgeois** *n* [C]

**petty cash** /ˌ·· ˈ·/ *n* [U] an amount of money in coins or notes that is kept in an office for making small payments

**petty lar·ce·ny** /ˌ·· ˈ···/ *n* [U] *law* the crime of stealing things that are only worth a small amount of money

**petty of·fi·cer** /ˌ·· ˈ···◂/ *n* [C] an officer of low rank in the Navy —see table on page B4

**pet·u·lant** /ˈpetʃɡ̈lənt/ *adj* behaving in an impatient and angry way for no reason at all, like a child: *Kara stamped her foot and frowned petulantly.* —**petulantly** *adv* —**petulance** *n* [U]

**pe·tu·ni·a** /pɪ̈ˈtjuːniə‖pɪ̈ˈtuː-/ *n* [C] a garden plant which has pink, purple, or white TRUMPET-shaped flowers

**pew¹** /pjuː/ *n* [C] **1** a long wooden seat in a church **2 take a pew** *BrE spoken* used to invite someone to sit down

**pew²** *interjection AmE spoken* used when there is a very unpleasant smell; POOH *BrE*

**pew·ter** /ˈpjuːtə‖-ər/ *n* [U] **1** a grey metal made by mixing LEAD and TIN: *a pewter tankard* **2** objects made from this metal

**pey·o·te** /peɪˈəʊti‖-ˈoʊ-/ *n* **1** [U] a drug made from a Mexican CACTUS, which makes people imagine that strange things are happening to them; MESCALIN **2** [C] the plant that produces this drug

**pfen·nig** /ˈfenɪg/ *n* [C] a unit of money worth 1/100th of a German MARK² (8)

**PG** /ˌpiː ˈdʒiː/ *adj* parental guidance; a film that is PG may include parts that are unsuitable for children under 15: *Jurassic Park (PG)* —compare G, U, R, X-CERTIFICATE

**pH** /piː ˈeɪtʃ/ also **pH val·ue** /ˈ· ˈ· ˌ··/ *n* [singular] a number on a scale of 0 to 14 which shows how acid or ALKALINE a substance is

**phae·ton** /ˈfeɪtn‖ˈfeɪətn/ *n* [C] a light open carriage used in the past, usually pulled by two horses

**phag·o·cyte** /ˈfægəsaɪt/ *n* [C] a blood cell that protects your body by destroying harmful BACTERIA etc

**pha·lanx** /ˈfælæŋks‖ˈfeɪ-/ *plural* **phalanxes** *n* [C] **1** a large group of people who stand close together so that it is difficult to go through them: *A solid phalanx of policemen blocked the road.* **2** a group of soldiers who stand or move closely together in battle

**phal·lic** /ˈfælɪk/ *adj* like or related to the phallus: *phallic symbols*

**phal·lus** /ˈfæləs/ *n* [C] **1** a model of the male sex organ, used to represent sexual power **2** *technical* the male sex organ; PENIS

**phan·tas·m** /ˈfæntæzəm/ *n* [C,U] *literary* something that exists only in your imagination; an ILLUSION —**phantasmal** /fænˈtæzməl/ *adj*

**phan·tas·ma·go·ri·a** /ˌfæntæzməˈgɔːriə‖ˌfæntæz-/ *n* [C] *literary* a confused, changing, strange scene like something from a dream —**phantasmagorical** /-ˈgɒrɪkəl‖-ˈgɔː-/ *adj*

**phan·ta·sy** /ˈfæntəsi/ *n* [C,U] an old spelling of FANTASY

**phan·tom** /ˈfæntəm/ *n* [C] *literary* **1** a frightening and unclear image, especially of a dead person; GHOST¹ (1): **phantom horseman/hound/ship etc** *The phantom hound loomed suddenly out of the mist.* **2** something that exists only in your imagination: *the phantoms that troubled his dreams* **3** *humorous* used to describe an unknown person that you blame for something annoying: *The phantom pen stealer strikes again!*

**phantom preg·nan·cy** /ˌ·· ˈ···/ *n* [C] a medical condition in which a woman seems to be PREGNANT, but in fact is not

**pha·raoh** /ˈfeərəʊ‖ˈferoʊ/ *n* [C] a ruler of ancient Egypt

**phar·i·see** /ˈfærɪ̈siː/ *n* [C] **1** someone who pretends to be religious or to be concerned about morals **2 Pharisee** a member of a group of Jews who lived at the time of Christ and who believed in strictly obeying religious laws —**pharisaic** /ˌfærɪ̈ˈseɪ-ɪk/ *adj*

**phar·ma·ceu·ti·cal** /ˌfɑːməˈsjuːtɪkəl◂‖ˌfɑːrməˈsuː-/ *adj* concerned with the production of drugs and medicine: *the large pharmaceutical companies*

**phar·ma·ceu·ti·cals** /ˌfɑːməˈsjuːtɪkəlz‖ˌfɑːrməˈsuː-/ *n* [plural] drugs and medicines

**phar·ma·cist** /ˈfɑːməsɪ̈st‖ˈfɑːr-/ *n* [C] someone who is trained to prepare drugs and medicines and who works in a shop or in a hospital —compare CHEMIST

**phar·ma·col·o·gy** /ˌfɑːməˈkɒlədʒi‖ˌfɑːrməˈkɑː-/ *n* [U] the scientific study of drugs and medicines —**pharmacologist** *n* [C] —**pharmacological** /ˌfɑːməkəˈlɒdʒɪkəl◂‖ˌfɑːrməkəˈlɑː-/ *adj*

**phar·ma·co·poe·ia** /ˌfɑːməkəˈpiːə‖ˌfɑːr-/ *n* [C] *technical* an official book giving information about medicines

**phar·ma·cy** /ˈfɑːməsi‖ˈfɑːr-/ *n* **1** [C] *especially AmE* a shop or a part of a shop where medicines are prepared and sold: *an all-night pharmacy* **2** [U] the study or practice of preparing drugs and medicines

**phar·yn·gi·tis** /ˌfærɪnˈdʒaɪtɪ̈s/ *n* [U] a medical condition in which you have a sore swollen pharynx

**phar·ynx** /ˈfærɪŋks/ *n plural* **pharynxes** [C] the tube that goes from the back of your mouth to where the separate passages for food and air divide —see picture at RESPIRATORY

W2 **phase¹** /feɪz/ *n* [C] **1** a part of a process of development or growth: *a transitional phase before democratic elections are held* —compare STAGE¹ (1) **2 in phase/out of phase (with)** *BrE* working together in a way that produces the right effect, or not working together in this way: *The traffic lights were out of phase with each other.* **3** one of a fixed number of changes in the appearance of the moon or a planet when it is seen from the Earth

**phase²** *v* [T] to make something happen gradually in a planned way: *a phased withdrawal of military forces*

**phase** sth ↔ **in** *phr v* [T] to introduce something such as a new law, rule etc gradually: *The government is going to phase in the new pension system over the next five years.*

**phase** sth ↔ **out** *phr v* [T] to gradually stop using or providing something: *Leaded gas was phased out in the 1970s.*

**PhD** /ˌpiː eɪtʃ ˈdiː/ *n* [C] Doctor of Philosophy; a university degree of very high rank, above an MA or an MSc, which involves doing RESEARCH, or someone who has this degree: *Jacqueline Hope, PhD* —see also DOCTORATE

**pheas·ant** /ˈfezənt/ *n* [C, U] a large bird with a long tail, often shot for food, or the meat of this bird

**phe·no·bar·bi·tone** /ˌfiːnəʊˈbɑːbɪ̈təʊn‖ˌfiːnoʊˈbɑːrbɪ̈toʊn/ *BrE*, **phe·no·bar·bi·tal** /-bɪ̈tl‖-bɪ̈tɒːl/ *AmE n* [U] a powerful drug that helps you to sleep

**phe·nom·e·nal** /fɪˈnɒmɪ̈nəl‖-ˈnɑː-/ *adj* very unusual and impressive: *phenomenal strength* | *phenomenal economic growth* —**phenomenally** *adv*: *phenomenally successful*

W3 **phe·nom·e·non** /fɪˈnɒmɪ̈nən‖fɪˈnɑːmɪ̈nɑːn, -nən/ *n plural* **phenomena** [C] **1** something that happens or exists, especially something that is studied because it is not understood: [+ **of**] *the phenomenon of international terrorism* | *violent natural phenomena such as hurricanes* **2** something or someone that is very unusual because of a rare quality or ability that they have

**phew** /fjuː/ *interjection* used when you feel tired, hot, or RELIEVED

**phi·al** /ˈfaɪəl/ *n* [C] a small bottle, especially for liquid medicines: *a phial of morphine*

**Phi Be·ta Kap·pa** /ˌfaɪ ˌbiːtə ˈkæpə/ *n* [singular] an American society for university and college students who have reached a high level in their studies

**-phil** /fɪl/ *suffix* another form of the suffix -PHILE

**phi·lan·derer** /fɪ̈ˈlændərə‖-ər/ *n* [C] *old-fashioned* a man who has sex with many women, without intending to have any serious relationships —**philandering** *adj* —**philandering** *n* [U]

**phil·an·throp·ic** /ˌfɪlənˈθrɒpɪk◂‖-ˈθrɑː-/ *adj* a philanthropic person or institution gives money and help to people who are poor or in trouble —**philanthropically** /-kli/ *adv*

**phi·lan·thro·pist** /fɪ̈ˈlænθrəpɪ̈st/ *n* [C] a rich person who gives a lot of money to help poor people

**phi·lan·thro·py** /fɪ̈ˈlænθrəpi/ *n* [U] the practice of giving money and help to people who are poor or in trouble

**phi·lat·e·ly** /fɪ̈ˈlætəli/ *n* [U] the activity of collecting stamps for pleasure —**philatelic** /ˌfɪləˈtelɪk◂/ *adj* —**philatelist** /fɪ̈ˈlætəlɪst/ *n* [C]

**-phile** /faɪl/ *suffix* also **-phil** *(in nouns)* someone who likes something: *a bibliophile* (=who likes books) | *an Anglophile* (=who likes England or Britain)

**Phil·har·mon·ic** /ˌfɪləˈmɒnɪk◂, ˌfɪlhɑː-‖ˌfɪlərˈmɑː-, ˌfɪlhɑːr-/ *adj* used in the names of ORCHESTRAS

**-philia** /fɪliə/ *suffix (in nouns)* **1** *technical* a tendency to feel sexually attracted in a way that is not approved of, that may be part of a mental illness: *necrophilia* (=a sexual attraction to dead bodies) **2** *technical* a diseased or unhealthy tendency to do something: *haemophilia* (=a tendency to bleed) **3** a tendency to like something: *Francophilia* (=liking France)

**-philiac** /fɪliæk/ *suffix technical (in nouns)* **1** someone who feels sexually attracted in a way that is not approved of: *a necrophiliac* **2** someone who has a particular illness: *a haemophiliac*

**phi·lip·pic** /fɪ̈ˈlɪpɪk/ *n* [C] *literary* a strong angry speech publicly attacking someone

**phil·is·tine** /ˈfɪlɪ̈staɪn‖-stiːn/ *n* [C] someone who does not like or understand art, literature, music etc —**philistine** *adj* —**philistinism** *n* [U]

**phi·lol·o·gy** /fɪ̈ˈlɒlədʒi‖-ˈlɑː-/ *n* [U] the study of words and of the way words and languages develop —compare LINGUISTICS —**philologist** *n* [C] —**philological** /ˌfɪ̈ləˈlɒdʒɪkəl◂‖-ˈlɑː-/ *adj* —**philologically** /-kli/ *adv*

**phi·los·o·pher** /fɪ̈ˈlɒsəfə‖-ˈlɑːsəfər/ *n* [C] **1** someone who studies and develops ideas about the nature and meaning of existence and reality, good and evil etc: *Plato, Aristotle, and other Greek philosophers* **2** someone who thinks deeply about the world, life etc

**philosopher's stone** /ˌ·ˌ··· ˈ·/ *n* [singular] an imaginary substance that was thought in the past to have the power to change any other metal into gold

**phil·o·soph·i·cal** /ˌfɪləˈsɒfɪkəl◂‖-ˈsɑː-/ also **phil·o·soph·ic** /ˌfɪləˈsɒfɪk◂‖-ˈsɑː-/ *adj* **1** related to philosophy: *the philosophical writings of Sartre* **2** someone who is philosophical calmly accepts a difficult or unpleasant situation because they know it cannot be changed: [+ **about**] *Robert was surprisingly philosophical about losing his job.* —**philosophically** /-kli/ *adv*: *Marne took her defeat philosophically.*

**phi·los·o·phize** also **-ise** *BrE* /fɪ̈ˈlɒsəfaɪz‖-ˈlɑː-/ *v* [I + **about**] to make remarks about the nature and meaning of things as if you were a philosopher

**phi·los·o·phy** /fɪ̈ˈlɒsəfi‖-ˈlɑː-/ *n* **1** [U] the study of the nature and meaning of existence and reality, good and evil, etc **2** [C] one of the many systems of thought that has this study as its base: *the philosophy of Kant* **3** [C] a rule you follow in living your life, doing your job etc: *current management philosophy* —see also NATURAL PHILOSOPHY W3

**phil·tre** also **philter** *AmE* /ˈfɪltə‖-ər/ *n* [C] *literary* a magic drink or object that makes someone fall in love

**phiz·og** /ˈfɪzɒg‖-zɑːg/ *n* [C] *BrE old-fashioned* your face

**phle·bi·tis** /flɪˈbaɪtɪ̈s/ *n* [U] a swollen condition of the VEINS (=tubes that carry blood through your body)

**phlegm** /flem/ *n* [U] **1** the thick yellowish substance produced in your nose and throat, especially when you have a cold; MUCUS **2** unusual calmness in worrying, frightening, or exciting situations

**phleg·mat·ic** /flegˈmætɪk/ *adj* calm and not easily excited or worried: *Even the most phlegmatic individual would get stressed out under such pressure.* —**phlegmatically** /-kli/ *adv*

**phlox** /flɒks‖flɑːks/ *n* [C] **1** a tall garden plant with red, purple, or white flowers **2** *AmE* a low, spreading plant with pink or white flowers

**-phobe** /fəʊb‖foʊb/ *suffix (in nouns)* a person who dislikes or hates something: *an Anglophobe* (=someone who hates England or Britain) | *a xenophobe* (=someone who hates foreigners)

**pho·bi·a** /ˈfəʊbiə‖ˈfoʊ-/ *n* [C] a strong unreasonable fear of something: [+ **about**] *Owen has a phobia about heights.* —**phobic** *adj*

**-phobia** /fəʊbiə‖foʊ-/ *suffix (in nouns)* **1** a dislike or hatred of something: *Anglophobia* (=dislike of England or Britain) **2** *technical* a strong dislike or fear of something, that is unusual and may be part of a mental illness; a phobia: *claustrophobia* (=fear of being in a small enclosed space) | *aquaphobia* (=fear of water)

**-phobic** /fəʊbɪk‖foʊ-/ *suffix technical* **1** *(in nouns)* someone suffering from a particular phobia: *He's a claustrophobic.* **2** *(in adjectives)* suffering from or connected with a particular phobia: *I'm a bit agoraphobic.* —**-phobically** /fəʊbɪkli‖-foʊ/ *(in adverbs)*

**phoe·nix** /ˈfiːnɪks/ *n* [C] **1** a magic bird that is born from a fire according to ancient stories **2 rise like a phoenix from the ashes** to become successful again after seeming to have failed completely

**phon-** /fən; *strong* fəʊn, fɒn‖fən; *strong* foʊn, fɑːn/ *prefix* another form of the prefix PHONO-

**-phone** /fəʊn‖foʊn/ *suffix* **1** *in nouns* an instrument or machine connected with sound or hearing, especially a musical instrument: *earphones* (=for listening to a radio, etc) | *a saxophone* **2** *technical (in nouns)* someone who speaks a particular language: *a Francophone* (=who speaks French) **3** *(in adjectives)* speaking a particular language: *Francophone nations* (=where French is spoken)

S1 W2 **phone¹** /fəʊn‖foʊn/ *n* [C] **1** a telephone: *Could you answer the phone, please?* | *a long-distance phone call* | *What's your phone number?* | **by phone/over the phone** (=using a telephone) *I made a booking by phone.* **2** the part of a telephone into which you speak; RECEIVER (1): *Greg slammed down the phone angrily.* **3 be on the phone a)** to be making a telephone call: *Turn down the TV! I'm on the phone!* **b)** *BrE* to have a telephone in your home or office: *Are you on the phone?*

S1 **phone²** also **phone up** *v* [I,T] to speak to someone by telephone; TELEPHONE²: *Has Anna phoned yet?* | *I bet they'll phone up with some excuse.* | **phone sb (up)** *I phoned Jim up last night.* —see graph at TELEPHONE

**phone in** *phr v* [I,T] **1** to telephone the place where you work, especially to report something: *Why don't you phone in and say you are ill?* | **phone** sth ↔ **in** *How many salespeople have phoned in their figures so far?* **2** to telephone a radio or television show to give your opinion or ask a question: *We encourage viewers to phone in during the program.* —see also PHONE-IN

**phone book** /ˈ· ·/ *n* [C] a book that contains an alphabetical list of the names, addresses, and telephone numbers of all the people who have a telephone in a particular area; TELEPHONE DIRECTORY

**phone booth** /ˈ· ·/ *n* [C] *AmE* a small structure that is partly or completely enclosed, containing a public telephone

**phone box** /ˈ· ·/ *n* [C] *BrE* a small structure that is partly or completely enclosed, containing a public telephone

**phone·card** /ˈfəʊnkɑːd‖ˈfoʊnkɑːrd/ *n* [C] a plastic card that can be used in some public telephones instead of money

**phone-in** /ˈ· ·/ *n* [C] a radio or television programme in which you hear ordinary people expressing opinions or asking questions over the telephone

**pho·neme** /ˈfəʊniːm‖ˈfoʊ-/ *n* [C] *technical* the smallest unit of speech that can be used to make one word different from another word, such as the 'b' and the 'p' in 'big' and 'pig' —**phonemic** /fəˈniːmɪk/ *adj* —**phonemically** /-kli/ *adv*

**pho·ne·mics** /fəˈniːmɪks/ *n* [U] *technical* the study and description of the phonemes of languages

**phone-tap·ping** /ˈ· ˌ··/ *n* [U] the activity of listening secretly to other people's telephone conversations using special ELECTRONIC equipment

**pho·net·ic** /fəˈnetɪk/ *adj technical* **1** related to the sounds of human speech **2** using special signs, often different from ordinary letters, to represent the sounds of speech: *a phonetic alphabet* | *phonetic symbols*

**pho·net·ics** /fəˈnetɪks/ *n* [U] the science and study of speech sounds —**phonetician** /ˌfəʊnəˈtɪʃən‖ˌfoʊ-/ *n* [C]

**pho·ney** also **phony** *AmE* /ˈfəʊni‖ˈfoʊ-/ *adj informal* **1** false or not real, and intended to deceive someone; FAKE: *a phoney British accent* | *I gave the police a phoney address.* **2** someone who is phoney pretends to be good, clever, kind etc when they are not —**phoney** *n* [C] *Grant's such a phoney!* —**phoniness** *n* [U]

**phoney war** /ˌ·· ˈ·/ *n* [singular] a period during which a state of war officially exists but there is no actual fighting

**phon·ic** /ˈfɒnɪk, ˈfəʊ-‖ˈfɑː, ˈfoʊ-/ *adj technical* **1** related to sound **2** related to speech sounds

**phon·ics** /ˈfɒnɪks, ˈfəʊ-‖ˈfɑː-, ˈfoʊ-/ *n* [U] a method of teaching people to read in which they are taught to recognize the sounds that letters represent

**phono-** /fəʊnəʊ, -nə, fɒnə‖foʊnoʊ, -nə, fɑːnə/ *prefix* also **phon-** *technical* **1** concerning the voice or speech: *phonetics* (=science of speech sounds) **2** concerning sound: *a phonoreceptor* (=hearing organ)

**pho·no·graph** /ˈfəʊnəgrɑːf‖ˈfoʊnəgræf/ *n* [C] *AmE old-fashioned* a RECORD PLAYER

**pho·nol·o·gy** /fəˈnɒlədʒi‖ˈnɑː-/ *n* [U] *technical* the study of the system of speech sounds in a language, or the system of sounds itself —**phonologist** *n* [C] —**phonological** /ˌfəʊnəˈlɒdʒɪkəl◂‖ˌfoʊnəˈlɑː-/ *adj* —**phonologically** /-kli/ *adv*

**pho·ny** /ˈfəʊni‖ˈfoʊ-/ *adj* the usual American spelling of PHONEY

**phoo·ey** /ˈfuːi/ *interjection* used to express strong disbelief or disappointment

**phos·gene** /ˈfɒzdʒiːn‖ˈfɑːz-/ *n* [U] a poisonous gas used in war and in industry

**phos·phate** /ˈfɒsfeɪt‖ˈfɑːs-/ *n* [C,U] **1** one of the various forms of a SALT¹ (3) of PHOSPHORUS, widely used in industry **2** [usually plural] a substance containing a phosphate used for making plants grow better

**phos·pho·res·cence** /ˌfɒsfəˈresəns‖ˌfɑːs-/ *n* [U] a slight steady light that can only be noticed in the dark

**phos·pho·res·cent** /ˌfɒsfəˈresənt◂‖ˌfɑːs-/ *adj* shining slightly in the dark but producing little or no heat: *a strange phosphorescent light at night* —**phosphorescently** *adv*

**phos·pho·rus** /ˈfɒsfərəs‖ˈfɑːs-/ *n* [U] a poisonous yellowish ELEMENT (=simple substance) that starts to burn when brought out into the air —**phosphoric** /fɒsˈfɒrɪk‖fɑːsˈfɔː-, fɑːsˈfɑː-, ˈfɑːsfərɪk/ *adj*

**pho·to** /ˈfəʊtəʊ‖ˈfoʊtoʊ/ *n plural* **photos** [C] *informal* a photograph: *the family photo album* | **take a photo** *Let's take a photo of the hotel.* S W

**photo-** /fəʊtəʊ, -tə‖foʊtoʊ, -tə/ *prefix technical* **1** concerning light: *photosensitive paper* (=that changes when light acts on it) **2** concerning photography: *photojournalism* (=use of photographs in reporting news)

**photo booth** /ˈ·· ·/ *n* [C] a small structure in which you can sit to have photographs taken by a machine

**pho·to·cop·i·er** /ˈfəʊtəʊˌkɒpiə‖ˈfoʊtəˌkɑːpiər/ *n* [C] a machine that quickly makes photographic copies of documents —see picture on page 837

**pho·to·cop·y¹** /ˈfəʊtəʊˌkɒpi‖ˈfoʊtəˌkɑːpi/ *n* [C] a photographic copy, especially of something printed, written, or drawn: *Make three photocopies of the report, please.*

**photocopy²** *v* [T] to make a photographic copy of something: *Could you get this photocopied in the office?*

**pho·to·e·lec·tric** /ˌfəʊtəʊ-ɪˈlektrɪk◂‖ˌfoʊtoʊ-/ *adj* using an electrical effect that is controlled by light

**photoelectric cell** /ˌ····· ˈ·/ *n* [C] **1** an electronic instrument that changes light into electricity **2** an electronic instrument that uses light to start an electrical effect, often used in BURGLAR ALARMS

**photo fin·ish** /ˌ·· ˈ··/ *n* [C] the end of a race in which the leading runners finish so close together that a photograph has to be taken to decide which is the winner

**Pho·to·fit** /ˈfəʊtəʊfɪt‖ˈfoʊtoʊ-/ *n* [U] *BrE trademark* a way of making a picture of a face using a collection of photographs of parts of different faces, used to help the police catch a criminal

**pho·to·gen·ic** /ˌfəʊtəʊˈdʒenɪk◂, ˌfəʊtə-‖ˌfoʊtə- / *adj* always looking attractive in photographs: *Helen is very photogenic.*

S2 W2 **pho·to·graph¹** /ˈfəʊtəgrɑːf‖ˈfoʊtəgræf/ also **photo** *informal n* [C] a picture obtained by using a camera and film that is sensitive to light: *a passport photograph | wedding photographs | an old black-and-white photograph of the city* | **take a photograph** *Visitors are not allowed to take photographs inside the museum.* | **sb's photograph** (=a photograph of someone) *Did you see Leo's photograph in the newspaper?*

**photograph²** *v* **1** [T] to make a picture of someone or something by using a camera and film sensitive to light: *Michelle doesn't like being photographed.* **2 photograph well/badly** to always look attractive or unattractive in photographs

**pho·tog·ra·pher** /fəˈtɒgrəfə‖-ˈtɑːgrəfər/ *n* [C] someone who takes photographs, especially as a professional or as an artist: *a fashion photographer*

**pho·to·graph·ic** /ˌfəʊtəˈgræfɪk◂‖ˌfoʊ-/ *adj* **1** connected with photographs, using photographs, or used in producing photographs: *a photographic history of the West | photographic equipment* **2 photographic memory** the ability to remember exactly every detail of something you have seen —**photographically** /-kli/ *adv*

**pho·tog·ra·phy** /fəˈtɒgrəfi‖-ˈtɑː-/ *n* [U] the art, profession, or method of producing photographs or the scenes in films: *a documentary with marvellous wildlife photography*

**pho·ton** /ˈfəʊtɒn‖ˈfoʊtɑːn/ *n* [C] *technical* a unit of energy (ENERGY (2)) that carries light and has zero MASS

**photo-op·por·tu·ni·ty** /ˈ·· ··ˌ···/ *n* [C] a chance for someone such as a politician to be photographed for a newspaper in a way that will make them look good

**pho·to·sen·si·tive** /ˌfəʊtəʊˈsensɪ̈tɪv◂‖ˌfoʊtəˈsen-/ *adj* sensitive to the action of light, for example by changing colour or form: *photosensitive paper*

**pho·to·sen·si·tize** also **-ise** *BrE* /ˌfəʊtəʊˈsensɪ̈taɪz‖ˌfoʊtəˈsen-/ *v* [T] to make something photosensitive

**photo shoot** /ˈ·· ·/ *n* [C] an occasion during which a professional PHOTOGRAPHER takes pictures of a fashion model or an actor for advertisements

**pho·to·stat** /ˈfəʊtəstæt‖ˈfoʊ-/ *n* [C] *trademark* a type of machine used for making photographic copies, or the copy itself —**photostat** *v* [T] —**photostatic** /ˌfəʊtəˈstætɪk◂‖ˌfoʊ-/ *adj*

**pho·to·syn·the·sis** /ˌfəʊtəʊˈsɪnθɪ̈sɪ̈s‖ˌfoʊtəˈsɪn-/ *n* [U] the production by a green plant of special substances like sugar that it uses as food, caused by the action of sunlight on CHLOROPHYLL (=the green substance in leaves)

**phras·al** /ˈfreɪzəl/ *adj* consisting of or connected with a phrase or phrases

**phrasal verb** /ˌ·· ˈ·/ *n* [C] a group of words that is used like a verb and consists of a verb with an adverb or PREPOSITION, such as 'set off', 'look after', 'put up with'. In this dictionary phrasal verbs are marked *phr v.*

W3 **phrase¹** /freɪz/ *n* [C] **1** a group of words that together have a particular meaning, especially when they express the meaning well in a few words: *He said the President was – what was the phrase he used? – 'trigger happy'.* | *Mrs Thatcher was, in Gorbachev's phrase, 'the iron lady'.* **2** *technical* a group of words without a FINITE verb, especially when they are used to form part of a sentence, such as 'walking along the road' and 'a bar of soap' —compare CLAUSE (2), SENTENCE¹ (1) **3** a short group of musical notes that is part of a longer piece —see also **to coin a phrase** (COIN² (2)), **a turn of phrase** (TURN² (10))

**phrase²** *v* [T] **1** to express something in a particular way: *Criticisms were phrased in careful terms.* | *a politely-phrased refusal* **2** to perform music so as to produce the full effect of separate musical phrases

**phrase·book** /ˈfreɪzbʊk/ *n* [C] a book that explains phrases of a foreign language, for people to use when they travel to other countries

**phra·se·ol·o·gy** /ˌfreɪziˈɒlədʒi‖-ˈɑː-/ *n* [U] the way that words and phrases are chosen and used in a particular language or subject

**phras·ing** /ˈfreɪzɪŋ/ *n* [U] **1** the way that something is said: *I don't remember her exact phrasing.* **2** a way of playing music, reading poetry etc that separates the notes, words, or lines into phrases

**phre·nol·ogy** /frəˈnɒlədʒi‖-ˈnɑː-/ *n* [U] the study of the shape of the human head as a way of showing someone's character and abilities, which was popular especially in the 19th century —**phrenologist** *n* [C]

**phut** /fʌt/ *n* [singular] *BrE informal* **1 go phut** to stop working completely: *The microwave's gone phut.* **2** a sound like air suddenly escaping from something: *The engine gave a phut, and stopped.*

**phy·lum** /ˈfaɪləm/ *n plural* **phyla** /-lə/ [C] *technical* one of the main groups into which scientists divide plants, animals, and languages, above a CLASS

**physi-** /fɪzi/ *prefix* another form of the prefix PHYSIO-

**phys·ic** /ˈfɪzɪk/ *n* [C,U] *old use* medicine

**phys·i·cal¹** /ˈfɪzɪkəl/ *adj* S2 W1
**1** ▶**BODY NOT MIND**◀ related to someone's body rather than their mind or soul: *physical exercise | physical abuse | people with mental or physical disabilities*
**2** ▶**REAL/SOLID**◀ related to real objects or structures that can be touched, seen, felt, etc: *man's domination of his physical environment | They were kept in appalling physical conditions.*
**3** ▶**NATURAL**◀ related to or following natural laws: *There must be a physical explanation for the strange lights in the sky.*
**4** ▶**PERSON**◀ *informal* someone who is physical likes touching people a lot
**5** ▶**VIOLENT**◀ a word meaning violent, used to avoid saying this directly: *That was a very physical tackle!*
**6** ▶**SCIENCE**◀ [only before noun] a physical science is the part of an area of scientific study that is connected with PHYSICS: *physical chemistry* —see also PHYSICALLY

**physical²** also **physical ex·am·i·na·tion** /ˌ···· ····ˈ··/ *n* [C] a thorough examination of someone's body and general health by a doctor, especially to decide whether they are fit to do a particular job

**physical ed·u·ca·tion** /ˌ··· ··ˈ··/ *n* [U] sport and physical exercise taught as a school subject

**physical ge·og·ra·phy** /ˌ··· ·ˈ···/ *n* [U] the study of the Earth's surface and of its rivers, mountains etc rather than of the countries it is divided into —compare POLITICAL GEOGRAPHY

**physical jerks** /ˌ··· ˈ·/ *n* [plural] *BrE old-fashioned* physical exercises such as bending and stretching etc

**phys·i·cally** /ˈfɪzɪkli/ *adv* **1** in relation to the body rather than the mind or soul: *She is young and physically fit.* | *He's all right physically, but he's still very confused.* **2 physically impossible** not possible according to the laws of nature or what is known to be true: *Surely it's physically impossible to go a week without water?* S3

**physically chal·lenged** /ˌ··· ˈ··/ *adj especially AmE* a word meaning physically HANDICAPPED, used when you want to avoid offending people

**physical sci·ence** /ˌ··· ˈ··/ *n* [U] also **the physical sciences** [plural] the sciences, such as CHEMISTRY, PHYSICS etc, that are concerned with things that are not living

**phy·si·cian** /fɪ̇ˈzɪʃən/ *n* [C] *AmE formal* a doctor

**phys·i·cist** /ˈfɪzɪ̇sɪ̇st/ *n* [C] someone who studies or works in PHYSICS

**phys·ics** /ˈfɪzɪks/ *n* [U] the science concerned with the study of physical objects and substances, and of natural forces such as light, heat and movement

**phys·i·o** /ˈfɪziəʊ‖-zioʊ/ *n plural* **physios** [C] *informal* a PHYSIOTHERAPIST

**physio-** /fɪziəʊ, -ziə‖-zioʊ, -ziə/ *prefix* also **physi-** *technical* **1** concerning nature and living things: *physiology* (=study of how the body works) **2** physical: *physiotherapy* (=treatment using exercises etc)

**phys·i·og·no·my** /ˌfɪziˈɒnəmi‖-ˈɑː-, -ˈɑːg-/ *n* [C] *technical or humorous* the general appearance of a person's face

**phys·i·ol·o·gy** /ˌfɪziˈɒlədʒi‖-ˈɑː-/ *n* [U] **1** the science concerned with the study of how the bodies of living things work **2** the way the body of a person or an animal works and looks: *A newborn's physiology is not the same as an older baby's.* —compare ANATOMY —**physiologist** *n* [C] —**physiological** /ˌfɪziəˈlɒdʒɪkəl◂‖-ˈlɑː-/ *adj*: *The doctors could find no physiological cause for his illness.*

**phys·i·o·ther·a·pist** /ˌfɪziəʊˈθerəpɪ̇st‖-zioʊ-/ *n* [C] someone whose job is to give PHYSIOTHERAPY as a treatment for medical conditions

**phys·i·o·ther·a·py** /ˌfɪziəʊˈθerəpi‖-zioʊ-/ *n* [U] a treatment for illnesses and problems with muscles which uses special exercises, rubbing, heat etc

**phy·sique** /fɪ̇ˈziːk/ *n* [C] the shape and appearance of a human body, especially a man's body: *exercises designed to improve your physique*

**pi** /paɪ/ *n* [U] *technical* a number that is represented by the Greek letter (π) and is equal to the distance around a circle, divided by its width

**pi·a·nist** /ˈpiːənɪ̇st, ˈpjɑː-‖piˈænɪ̇st, ˈpiːə-/ *n* [C] someone who plays the piano, especially very well

S3 **pi·an·o¹** /piˈænəʊ‖-noʊ/ *n* [C] a large musical instrument that you play by sitting in front of it and pressing the KEYS (=narrow black and white bars)

**piano²** *adj, adv* played or sung quietly

**pi·a·no·la** /ˌpiːəˈnəʊlə‖-ˈnoʊ-/ *n* [C] a PLAYER PIANO

**piano stool** /·ˈ·· ·/ *n* [C] a small seat for sitting on while you play the piano

**pi·az·za** /piˈætsə‖-ˈɑːt-/ *n* [C] a public square (=large open area in a city) or market place, especially in Italy

**pic·a·dor** /ˈpɪkədɔː‖-dɔːr/ *n* [C] a man in a BULLFIGHT who rides a horse, and annoys and weakens the BULL by sticking a long spear into it

**pic·a·resque** /ˌpɪkəˈresk◂/ *adj* a picaresque story or NOVEL tells the adventures and travels of a character whose behaviour is not always moral but who is still likeable

**pic·a·yune** /ˌpɪkəˈjuːn/ *adj AmE* small and unimportant: *the picayune squabbling of party politicians*

**pic·ca·lil·li** /ˌpɪkəˈlɪli/ *n* [U] a hot-tasting sauce made with small pieces of vegetables and eaten with cold meat

**pic·co·lo** /ˈpɪkələʊ‖-loʊ/ *n plural* **piccolos** [C] a musical instrument that looks like a small FLUTE

S1 W1 **pick¹** /pɪk/ *v* [T]

**1 ▶ CHOOSE STH ◀** to choose someone or something good or suitable from a group or range of people or things: *Students have to pick three courses from a list of 15.* | *Let me pick a few examples at random.* | **pick your words** (=be careful about what you say) *Trevor was picking his words with great care.* | **pick sb as** *The group picked me as their spokesperson.* | **pick sb/sth for** *Harris was picked for the England team.* | **pick sb to do sth** *She has been picked to represent us in Rome.* —see also PICKED, **pick out** (PICK¹)

**2 ▶ FLOWERS/FRUIT ETC ◀** to pull off or break off a flower, fruit, nut etc from a plant or tree: *The cotton was picked by teams of men.* | *We picked some blackberries to eat on the way.* | **pick sb sth** *He picked her a single red rose.* | **pick a bunch/a basketful etc** *Amy picked a small bunch of wild flowers.* | **newly/freshly picked** *Runner beans should be eaten young and freshly picked.* | **go grape/strawberry etc picking** (=pick something either for your own use or as a part-time job)

**3 ▶ SMALL THINGS/PIECES ◀** to remove small things from something, or pull off small pieces of something: **pick sth from/off/out of** *Ahmed picked the melon pips from his teeth.* | *She was nervously picking bits of fluff off her sweater.* | **pick a hole in sth** (=make a hole in something by repeatedly pulling off small pieces of it)

**4 pick your teeth** to remove bits of food from between your teeth, with your fingers or something pointed

**5 pick your nose** to take MUCUS from your nose with your finger

**6 pick sth clean** to take all the meat from a bone

**7 pick your way through/across/among etc** to move slowly and carefully, choosing exactly where to put your feet down: *She picked her way between the piles of books.*

**8 pick and choose** to choose only the people or things you really like: *We can't pick and choose, we'll have to take what they give us.*

**9 pick a quarrel/fight (with sb)** to deliberately start a quarrel or fight with someone: *He got drunk one night and picked a quarrel with his girlfriend.*

**10 pick sb's brains** to ask someone who knows a lot about something for information and advice about it: *Have you got a minute? I need to pick your brains.*

**11 pick a lock (with)** to use something that is not a key to unlock a door, drawer etc: *She picked the lock with a hairpin.*

**12 pick holes (in)** to criticize a plan, an idea etc: *I had no trouble picking holes in her theory.* | *Stop picking holes! I bet you couldn't do any better.*

**13 pick sb's pocket** to quietly steal something from someone's pocket: *When all the fuss died down I found my pocket had been picked.* —see also PICKPOCKET

**14 pick a winner** *informal* an expression meaning to make a very good choice, sometimes used jokingly when you think someone has made a very bad choice

**15 pick sb/sth to pieces** *informal* to criticize someone or something very severely and in a very detailed way

**16 ▶ MUSICAL INSTRUMENT ◀** *AmE* to play a musical instrument by pulling at its strings with your fingers; PLUCK¹ (5) —see also **have a bone to pick with sb** (BONE¹ (2))

**pick at** sth *phr v* [T] **1** to eat something taking small bites and without much interest, for example because you feel unhappy: *He picked gloomily at his lamb chop.* **2** to touch something repeatedly with your fingers, often pulling it slightly: *The little boy was picking at his mother's sleeve, trying to get her attention.*

**pick** sb/sth ↔ **off** *phr v* [T] to shoot people or animals that are some distance away one at a time, by taking careful aim: *The sniper was picking off our men one by one.*

**pick on** sb/sth *phr v* [T] *spoken* **1** to choose someone to do an unpleasant job or blame someone for something, especially unfairly: *Why does the boss always pick on me?* | *You big bully – pick on someone your own size!* **2** to decide to choose someone or something: *First, pick on some daily task that you all share.*

**pick** sb/sth ↔ **out** *phr v* [T] **1** to choose someone or something carefully: *Pick out all the words in the poem that suggest despair.* **2** to recognize someone or something in a group of people or things: *It was easy to pick out Bob's father.* | *I could just pick out a few landmarks in the gloom.* **3 a)** if you pick out a shape, letter etc in a particular colour, you make it that colour so that it can be clearly seen: *Every name on the memorial was picked out in scarlet edged with gold.* **b)** if a light picks someone or something out, it shines directly on it: *The searchlight picked out a figure on the roof.* **4** to play a tune on a stringed musical instrument slowly or with difficulty: *He picked out a moody chord on his guitar.*

**pick over** sth ↔ *phr v* [T] to examine a group of small

things very carefully in order to choose the ones you want: *He turned the drawer upside-down and picked over the spilled contents.*

**pick through** sth *phr v* [T] to search through a pile or group of things, and take the one that you want

**pick up**

Steve is picking up the can.

Mom picked up her jacket from the dry cleaner's.

The truck driver picked up a hitchhiker.

**pick up** *phr v*
**1** ▶ **LIFT STH UP** ◀ [T **pick** sth ↔ **up**] to lift something up from a surface: *She kept picking up magazines and putting them down again.* | *My wife picks the baby up whenever it cries.* | *The phone rang and I picked it up.* | *The vacuum cleaner won't pick this stuff up.* | **pick sth up by sth** *The lioness picked up her cub by its neck.* | **bend/stoop (down) and pick sth up** *Seth bent to pick up the papers.* | **pick your feet up** (=used to tell someone to walk properly)
**2 pick yourself up** to get up from the ground after a fall: *Carol picked herself up and dusted herself off.*
**3** ▶ **TIDY STH** ◀ [T **pick** sth ↔ **up**] **a)** to put toys, magazines etc away neatly: *Please pick up your slippers.* **b)** *AmE* to make a place tidy: *Connie had made some effort to pick up the apartment.*
**4 pick up after sb** *informal especially AmE* to tidy things that someone else has left untidy: *Who wants to get married and spend their life picking up after some man?*
**5** ▶ **GET STH** ◀ [T **pick** sth ↔ **up**] *informal* **a)** to find or get something, especially unexpectedly: *I picked up a bug on holiday.* (=became ill) | *Hill only picked up four points fromt the two races.* | *We picked up some nice souvenirs.* | *Where can I pick up a cheap video camera?* **b)** to get or buy something, while you are going somewhere or doing something: *I picked up an evening paper on the way home.* | *For more details, pick up a leaflet in your local post office.*
**6** ▶ **COLLECT SB/STH** ◀ [T **pick** sth ↔ **up**] to collect someone who is waiting for you or something that you have left somewhere or need: *I'll pick my things up later.* | *She just dropped by to pick up her mail.* | *My husband will pick you up in the car.* | *Pick me up at 8.00.*
**7** ▶ **SKILL/INFORMATION ETC** ◀ [T **pick** sth ↔ **up**] to get a skill, language, habit, idea or piece of information by chance rather than by deliberately trying to get it: *"Where did you study Greek?" "I didn't, I just sort of picked it up when I lived there."* | *If you sing it several times, your children will begin to pick up the words.* | *There's a tip I picked up from a professional model.*
**8** ▶ **RADIO/RECORDING** ◀ if a machine picks up a sound, a movement or the presence of something, it is able to receive it, record it, or TRANSMIT (1) it: *The sensors pick up faint vibrations in the Earth.* | *I managed to pick up an American news broadcast.*
**9** ▶ **LET SB INTO A VEHICLE** ◀ [T **pick** sb ↔ **up**] to stop and let someone get into your car, boat etc: *They were picked up by a fishing boat.* | *It is an offence to pick up or set down a hitchhiker on a motorway.*
**10** ▶ **BECOME FRIENDLY WITH SB** ◀ [T **pick** sb ↔ **up**] to become friendly with someone you have just met because you find them sexually attractive: *I wish I could just go out and pick up a nice man.* | *Are you trying to pick me up?*
**11** ▶ **NOTICE STH** ◀ [T **pick** sth ↔ **up**] **a)** [U] to smell a slight smell or hear a quiet sound: *Then he picked up the even fainter aroma of apple pie.* | *The dogs picked up the scent and raced off.* **b)** to see something that you are looking for: *She picked up a flicker of movement just beyond the fence.* | *We picked up the car again within a block.* | **pick up the track/trail/traces** *Cody picked up the track of their horses but lost it again.*
**12** ▶ **START AGAIN** ◀ [I,T **pick** sth ↔ **up**] **a)** if a conversation, meeting etc picks up or if you pick it up, it starts again from the point where it was interrupted: **pick up where you left off** *informal: He left her for two years and then came back expecting to pick up where they had left off!* **b)** if you pick up a point or an idea that has been mentioned, you return to it and develop it further: *Tocqueville picks up this theme in his later works.*
**13** ▶ **IMPROVE** ◀ [I] **a)** if business, your social life etc picks up, it improves: *Trade is picking up nicely.* | *The economy is finally beginning to pick up again.* **b)** [T **pick** sb ↔ **up**] if a medicine, drink etc picks you up, it makes you feel better —see also PICK-ME-UP
**14 sb's speed/the wind/the beat etc picks up** if someone's speed etc picks up, it increases or grows stronger: *The breeze had now picked up considerably.*
**15 pick up speed/steam** to go faster: *The train was gradually picking up speed.*
**16 pick up the bill/tab (for sth)** *informal* to pay for something: *Why should the taxpayer pick up the tab for a private company's mistakes?*
**17** ▶ **A COLOUR** ◀ [T **pick** sth ↔ **up**] if a colour or a piece of furniture picks up the colour of something else, it has small amounts of that colour in it: *I like the way the curtains pick up the red and yellow in the rug.*
**18** ▶ **A CRIMINAL** ◀ [T **pick** sb ↔ **up**] if the police or another organized group of people pick someone up, they find them and take them somewhere, to answer questions or to be locked up: *The coastguard picked him up at Dover.* | *She was picked up on prostitution charges.*
**19 pick up the pieces (of sth)** if you pick up the pieces of a business, relationship etc that has gone seriously wrong, you try to get it back to the point where it was before: *Small agricultural communities are picking up the pieces after the long depression.*
**20 pick up the threads (of sth)** if you pick up the threads of a relationship, a way of life, or an idea that has been interrupted, you try to return to it again: *When I got home after the war it wasn't so easy to pick up the threads of my ordinary life again.*

**pick up on** *phr v* [T] **1** [**pick up on** sth] **a)** to notice something that other people do not notice: *It was very smart of you to pick up on the undercurrents between those two.* **b)** to notice something and react to it: *I was trying to indicate that I didn't want to go, but they didn't pick up on it.* **c)** to return to a point or an idea that has been mentioned and discuss it further: *Can I just pick up on your objections to the project?* **2** [**pick** sb **up on** sth] to criticize someone slightly for something they have said: *The Senator picked him up on his use of the word 'deception'.*

**pick²** *n* **1** [U] choice: **take your pick** (=choose) *You can have any one you like – take your pick!* | **have your pick of** (=to be able to choose any one of a group of things) *Sarah could have had her pick of any university in the country, but she chose her local college.* **2 the pick of sth** *informal* the best thing or things of a group: *It's the pick of this month's new movies.* | **the pick of the bunch** (=the best in the group) *It's not much good, but it's the pick of the bunch.* **3** [C] *AmE informal* someone or something that is chosen from among other people or things: *Reno was able to name his own pick for the Criminal Division.* **4** [C] a pickaxe: *He put his pick and shovel over his shoulder.* **5** [C] *AmE informal* a small, flat object for pulling at the strings of an instrument such as a GUITAR; PLECTRUM —see also ICE PICK

P

**pick·a·nin·ny** /ˌpɪkəˈnɪni/ *n* [C] word for a small African child, used in the past but now considered very offensive

**pick·axe** *BrE*, **pickax** *AmE* /ˈpɪk-æks/ *n* [C] a large tool used for breaking up roads, which consists of a curved iron bar with a sharp point on each end and a long handle

**picked** /pɪkt/ *adj* [only before noun] chosen as being very suitable for a particular job or purpose: *The assault group consisted of six picked men.* —see also HANDPICKED

**pick·er** /ˈpɪkə‖-ər/ *n* [C] **cotton picker/fruit picker etc** a person or machine that picks things, especially crops: *Orange pickers are on strike in California.*

**pick·et¹** /ˈpɪkʒt/ *n* [C] **1** also **picket line** a group or line of people who stand or march in front of a shop, factory, government building etc to protest about something or to stop people from going in during a STRIKE: *a picket on the steps of the Federal court building* | *None of the workers crossed the picket lines.* **2** one person in a picket: *The pickets persuaded some drivers not to enter the factory.* —see also FLYING PICKET **3** a soldier or a group of soldiers with the special duty of guarding a military camp: **picket duty** *Hanks, you're on picket duty tonight.*

**picket²** *v* **1** [I,T] to stand or march in front of a shop, factory, government building etc to protest about something or to stop people from going in during a STRIKE: *protesters picketing outside the White House gates* | **picket sth** *Miners picketed every pit for months.* **2** [T] to place soldiers around or near a place as guards

**picket fence** /ˈ·· ˌ·/ *n* [C] *AmE* a fence made up of a line of strong pointed sticks fixed in the ground —see picture on page 410

**pick·ings** /ˈpɪkɪŋz/ *n* [plural] *informal* **rich/easy pickings** money or profits that you can get easily: *There were rich pickings to be had if you played the stock market.*

**pick·le¹** /ˈpɪkəl/ *n* **1** [U] a strong-tasting liquid made with VINEGAR, used to preserve vegetables **2** [U] *BrE* a thick cold sauce eaten with food, made from pieces of vegetables preserved in VINEGAR: *sweet pickle* | *cheese and pickle sandwiches* **3** [C,U] *AmE* a CUCUMBER preserved in VINEGAR or salt water, or a slice of this: *Would you like pickle on your cheeseburger?* **4 be in a (pretty) pickle** *old-fashioned* to be in a difficult or confusing situation

**pickle²** *v* [T] to preserve food in VINEGAR or salt water: *pickled onions*

**pick·led** /ˈpɪkəld/ *adj old-fashioned informal* drunk

**pick-me-up** /ˈ· · ˌ·/ *n* [C] *informal* something that makes you feel more cheerful and gives you more energy, especially a drink or medicine

**pick·pock·et** /ˈpɪkˌpɒkʒt‖-ˌpɑːk-/ *n* [C] someone who steals things from people's pockets, especially in a crowd

**pick-up** /ˈ· ·/ *n* **1** [C] *especially AmE* a small open motor vehicle with low sides, used for carrying goods: *We used the pick-up to carry the lumber to the building site.* **2** [C] *informal* a stranger that you meet in a bar, at a party etc and spend a short time with, often in order to have sex **3** [U] *AmE* the rate at which a vehicle can increase its speed; ACCELERATION: *It was a tiny car, but it had good pick-up.* **4** [C] the part of a record player that receives and plays the sound from a record

**pick-up truck** /ˈ· · ˌ·/ *n* [C] *AmE* a PICK-UP (1)

**pick·y** /ˈpɪki/ *adj AmE informal* someone who is picky only likes very particular things: *a picky eater* | *She's so picky about her clothes.*

**picnic**

**pic·nic¹** /ˈpɪknɪk/ *n* [C] **1** an occasion when people take food and eat it outdoors, especially in the country: *We're having a picnic in the park this afternoon.* | *a picnic basket* (=for carrying food for a picnic) **2 be no picnic** *informal* to be difficult or unpleasant and need a lot of work: *Taking 60 kids to the museum will be no picnic!* **3 picnic lunch/supper** the food you take for a picnic: *Vera packed a picnic lunch and headed for the river.* **4** *BrE* the food you take for a picnic: *We'll take a picnic with us.*

**picnic²** *v* **picnicked, picnicking** [I] to have a picnic: *holidaymakers picnicking on the grass* —**picnicker** *n* [C]

**picnic ar·e·a** /ˈ·· ˌ···/ *n* [C] an area near a road where people in cars can stop and have a picnic

**pic·to·ri·al** /pɪkˈtɔːriəl/ *adj* related to paintings, drawings, or photographs

**pic·ture¹** /ˈpɪktʃə‖-ər/ *n* S W

**1 ▶ IMAGE ◀** [C] a painting, drawing, or photograph: *A picture of a waterfall hung on the wall.* | *Get the children to draw a picture of their dream house.* | *Gary got his picture in the papers.*

**2 ▶ SITUATION ◀** [singular] the general situation in a place, organization etc: *The general picture appears to be of low levels of union membership.* | *the wider political picture*

**3 ▶ DESCRIPTION ◀** [C usually singular] a description that gives you an idea of what something is like: [+ **of**] *Archaeologists are trying to build up a picture of life in Mayan cities.* | **paint a picture** (=describe something in a particular way) *Lee's film paints a bleak picture of life in the inner city.*

**4 ▶ TELEVISION ◀** [C usually singular] the image that appears on a television or cinema SCREEN: *Something's wrong with the TV – the picture is blurry.*

**5 ▶ MENTAL IMAGE ◀** [C usually singular] an image or memory that you have in your mind: *I still have a vivid picture of the first time I saw Paris.*

**6 take a picture** to use a camera to take a photograph: *Dad took a picture of us standing by a huge redwood tree.*

**7 put sb in the picture** to give someone information about something, so that they can understand it: *I've been away for a month so you'll have to put me in the picture.*

**8 get the picture** *especially spoken* to understand a situation: *"Her parents are separated and she's being raised by her sister." "I get the picture."*

**9 out of the picture** if someone is out of the picture, they are not involved in a situation: *"Is Pam still with Eric?" "No, he's out of the picture."*

**10 ▶ FILM ◀ a)** [C] a word meaning a film, used especially by people in the film industry: *It was voted the year's best picture.* **b) the pictures** *old-fashioned* the cinema: *Do you want to go to the pictures on Saturday?* | **be in pictures** (=act in films or work in making films)

**11 be the picture of health/innocence/despair etc** to look very healthy, innocent etc: *Head bowed and sobbing, she was the picture of misery.*

**12 the big picture** *AmE informal* a situation considered as a whole, rather than its details: *Try and get an idea of the big picture before you suggest any changes.*
**13 be/look a picture** *especially BrE* to be beautiful or unusual to look at: *Madge's garden is a picture in the summer.* —see also **pretty as a picture** (PRETTY² (8))

**picture²** *v* [T] **1** to imagine something, especially by creating an image in your mind: **picture sb/sth as sth** *Rob had pictured her as kind of serious, but she wasn't like that at all.* | **picture sb doing sth** *I really can't picture him skiing. He's so clumsy!* | **picture my surprise/horror/annoyance etc** (=used when saying how surprised, annoyed etc you were) *Picture my surprise on finding everyone had left!* **2** to show something or someone in a photograph, painting, or drawing: *The billboard pictured a handsome, thirtyish man smoking a cigarette.* **3** [often passive] to describe something clearly: *This situation is realistically pictured in the first chapter.*

**picture book** /ˈ·· ·/ *n* [C] a children's book that has a lot of pictures and usually a simple story

**picture card** /ˈ·· ·/ *n* [C] a FACE CARD

**picture pal·ace** /ˈ·· ˌ··/ *n* [C] *old-fashioned, especially BrE* a large building used for showing films to the public; CINEMA

**picture-per·fect** /ˌ·· ˈ··◂/ *adj AmE* exactly right in appearance or quality: *Doesn't the bride look picture-perfect?*

**picture post·card** /ˌ·· ˈ··/ *n* [C] *BrE* a POSTCARD with a photograph or picture on the front of it

**picture-postcard** /ˌ·· ˈ··◂/ *adj* [only before noun] *BrE* very pretty: *picture-postcard villages*

**picture rail** /ˈ·· ·/ *n* [C] a long narrow piece of wood fixed high on a wall, from which pictures can be hung

**pic·tur·esque** /ˌpɪktʃəˈresk◂/ *adj* **1** a place that is picturesque is pretty and interesting, especially in an old-fashioned way: *a picturesque New England village in the fall* **2** language that is picturesque uses unusual, interesting, or sometimes rude words to describe things: *He gave a picturesque account of his trip to New York.* **3** someone who is picturesque looks or behaves in an interesting, unusual, or slightly strange way: *a picturesque character with a long beard and a large pipe* —**picturesquely** *adv* —**picturesqueness** *n* [U]

**picture win·dow** /ˈ·· ˌ··/ *n* [C] a large window made of a single piece of glass

**pid·dle** /ˈpɪdl/ *v* [I] *informal* to URINATE
**piddle around** also **piddle about** *BrE phr v* [I] *informal* to waste time doing unimportant things —**piddle** *n* [U]

**pid·dling** /ˈpɪdlɪŋ/ *adj* small and unimportant: *I can't be bothered with all these piddling details.*

**pid·gin** /ˈpɪdʒɪ̆n/ *n* [C, U] **1** a language that is a mixture of two other languages and is used especially between people who do not speak each other's languages well **2 pidgin English/French etc** English, French etc that is either not very good or is mixed with the words or grammar of another language

2 **pie** /paɪ/ *n* [C, U] **1** a sweet food usually made with fruit baked inside a PASTRY covering: *apple pie* | *a slice of pie* —compare TART¹ (1) **2** *especially BrE* a food made of meat or vegetables baked in a PASTRY covering: *He bought a pie for lunch.* | *steak and kidney pie* **3 slice/share/piece of the pie** a share of something such as money, profits etc: *The smaller companies want a bigger share of the pie.* **4 pie in the sky** something good that someone is promising or suggesting, but which you do not think will happen: *The idea of full employment is just pie in the sky.* —see also MUD PIE, PIE CHART, **easy as pie** (EASY¹ (1)), **eat humble pie** (HUMBLE¹ (6)), **have a finger in every pie** (FINGER¹ (11)), **be as nice as pie** (NICE (5))

**pie·bald** /ˈpaɪbɔːld‖-bɒːld/ *adj* a piebald animal has large areas of skin of two different colours, usually black and white —**piebald** *n* [C]

**piece¹** /piːs/ *n* [C] 
**1 ▶ SEPARATE PART ◀** a part of something that has been separated, broken, or cut from the rest of it: *She cut the cake into 8 pieces.* | [+ **of**] *How many pieces of toast would you like?* | *pieces of broken glass* | **in pieces** (=broken into many pieces) *The vase had slipped and lay in pieces on the floor.*
**2 ▶ OBJECT ◀** a single thing of a particular type, often one that is part of a set of things: *Each piece of clothing had her name written in it.* | *Can I have another piece of paper?* | *a beautifully made piece of furniture* | **24-piece/60-piece etc** (=with 24, 60 etc pieces in the set) *an 80-piece orchestra*
**3 ▶ CONNECTED PART ◀** one of several different parts that must be joined together to make something: *Some of the jigsaw pieces are missing.* | **in pieces** (=separated into pieces) *The shelves are sold in pieces that you have to assemble.* | **take sth to pieces** (=separate it into pieces) *We'll have to take the whole engine to pieces to fix it.* | **come to pieces** (=be designed to be separated into pieces) *The table comes to pieces so it's easy to deliver.*
**4 piece of advice/information/gossip etc** some advice, information etc: *Let me give you a piece of advice – sell the car.* | *a juicy piece of gossip*
**5 piece of luck/stupidity/wilfulness etc** something lucky, stupid etc: *Finding that store sure was a piece of luck.*
**6 ▶ LAND ◀** an area of land: *The factory had been built on a piece of waste ground.*
**7 fall to pieces** to become very old and damaged: *All my clothes are falling to pieces.*
**8 go to pieces** to be so upset or nervous that you cannot think or behave normally: *We're looking for someone who won't go to pieces in a crisis.*
**9 smash/rip/tear sth to pieces** to damage something very severely: *The city had been shot to pieces in the air strike.* | *In a rage, I tore the letter to pieces.*
**10 pull/rip/tear sb to pieces** to criticize someone or their ideas very severely: *After she had finished speaking, Hayes tore her to pieces.*
**11 (all) in one piece** not damaged or injured: *Luckily the parcel arrived all in one piece.* | *The car was a wreck, but we got out in one piece.*
**12 give sb a piece of your mind** *informal* to tell someone that you are very angry with them
**13 be a piece of cake** *informal* to be very easy to do: *Learning to drive was a piece of cake for me.*
**14 a piece of the action** *informal* a share of the profits from a business activity, especially an illegal one
**15 be (all) of a piece a)** to be the same as something else: *The testimony was all of a piece with Mandeville's version of events.* **b)** to be the same in all parts: *The style of the book is all of a piece, both in illustrations and text.*
**16 ▶ MONEY ◀ a)** a coin of a particular value: **ten pence/fifty-cent etc piece** *Does anyone have change for a 50 pence piece?* **b)** *old use* a coin: *30 pieces of silver*
**17 ▶ ART/MUSIC ETC ◀** something that has been produced by an artist, musician, or writer: *The 1812 Overture is one of Tchaikovsky's finest pieces.*
**18 ▶ IN A NEWSPAPER ◀** a short written ARTICLE (2) in a newspaper or magazine: *Did you see that piece in the Observer about censorship?*
**19 ▶ IN GAMES ◀** a small object or figure used in playing games such as CHESS
**20 ▶ GUN ◀** *AmE slang* a small gun
**21 be a piece of shit/crap** *spoken* a rude way of saying that something is of very low quality: *Why did you buy that car? It's a piece of crap!*
**22 piece of ass** *AmE* an offensive expression meaning a woman, used by men when they are talking about sex
**23 a piece** *AmE old-fashioned* a short distance away: *The store is down the road a piece.* —see also MUSEUM

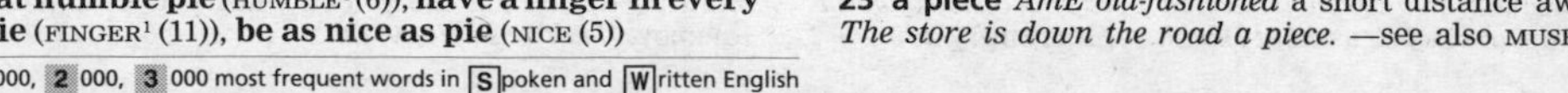

PIECE, PARTY PIECE, SET PIECE, **nasty piece of work** (NASTY[6]), **pick up the pieces** (PICK[1]), **say your piece** (SAY[1] (2)), **the villain of the piece** (VILLAIN (3))

**piece²** *v*

**piece** sth ↔ **together** *phr v* [T] **1** to use all the facts or information you have about a situation in order to understand it: *Police are still trying to piece together his movements before the murder.* **2** to put all the separate parts of an object into the correct order or position: *He was slowly piecing together torn fragments of a letter.*

**pi·èce de ré·sis·tance** /pi,es də rezi:'stɑ:ns/ *n* [C] *French* the best or most important thing or event in a series, especially when it comes after all the others: *The pièce de résistance was an enormous birthday cake with 21 candles.*

**piece·meal** /'pi:smi:l/ *adj* a process that is piecemeal happens slowly in separate unconnected stages and is not planned: *The airport had been developed in a piecemeal fashion.* —**piecemeal** *adv*: *The house was filled with odd furniture they'd bought piecemeal.*

**piece rate** /'· ·/ *n* [C] an amount of money that is paid for each thing a worker produces: *The piece rate was $2.00 per skirt.*

**pieces of eight** /,··· '·/ *n* [plural] silver coins used in the past in Spain

**piece·work** /'pi:swɜ:k‖-wɜ:rk/ *n* [U] work that is paid according to the number of things you complete or produce rather than the number of hours you work

**pie chart** /'· ,·/ *n* [C] a circle divided into several parts that shows how something such as an amount of money or the population is divided —see picture at CHART[1]

**pie crust** /'· ·/ *n* [C, U] the PASTRY (1) that is underneath and sometimes covering the meat or fruit in a PIE

**pied** /paɪd/ *adj* [only before noun] a pied animal, especially a bird, has two colours on its feathers or fur, usually black and white

**pied-à-terre** /,pjeɪd æ 'teə‖pi,ed ɑ: 'ter/ *n* [C] *French* a small apartment or house that is not your main home but which you own and stay in sometimes: *The Maines keep a pied-à-terre in London for theatre evenings.*

**pie-eyed** /,paɪ 'aɪd◂/ *adj old-fashioned* very drunk

**pier** /pɪə‖pɪr/ *n* [C] **1** a structure that is built out into the water so that boats can stop next to it: *The troop transport ship docked at Pier Five.* —compare JETTY **2** *especially BrE* a structure that is built out into the sea and has small buildings on it where people can eat, play games, and enjoy themselves: *Brighton pier | a concert on the pier* —compare BOARDWALK **3** a thick post of stone, wood, or metal used to support something such as a bridge

**pierce** /pɪəs‖pɪrs/ *v* [T] **1** to make a small hole in or through something using an object with a sharp point: *Maybe you can pierce another hole in your belt. | Steam the corn until it can easily be pierced by a fork.* **2 have your ears/nose etc pierced** to have a small hole made in your ears, nose etc so that you can wear jewellery **3** if sound, light, pain etc pierces something you can suddenly hear it, see it, or feel it: *The sun finally pierced the haze and the day was beautiful. | A sudden scream pierced the air.* **4 pierced ear/nose etc** a part of your body that has had small holes made in it so that you can wear jewellery

**pierc·ing** /'pɪəsɪŋ‖'pɪr-/ *adj*

**1 ▶ SOUND ◀** high, sharp, and usually unpleasant: *Raimundo grinned and let out a piercing whistle.*

**2 ▶ COLD/WIND ◀** very cold and seeming to cut through your clothes: *The wind whipped off the water with a piercing bite.*

**3 ▶ EYES/LOOK ◀** seeming to examine things and notice and understand more than other people would: *Her piercing brown eyes scanned their faces.*

**4 ▶ REMARK/QUESTION ◀** piercing questions, criticisms etc seem to notice and express the main point of something very clearly

**5 ▶ EMOTION ◀** affecting your emotions very much, especially in a sad way: *She had a piercing vision of what life would be like without David.* —**piercingly** *adv*

**pier·rot** /'pɪərəʊ‖'pi:əroʊ/ *n* [C] a CLOWN with white clothes and a white painted face

**pi·e·ty** /'paɪəti/ *n* [U] respect for God and religion, often shown in the way you behave —opposite IMPIETY —see also PIOUS

**pie·zo·e·lec·tric** /,pi:zəʊ-ɪ'lektrɪk◂, ,pi:tsəʊ-‖pi,eɪzoʊ-/ *adj* operated by electricity which is produced by pressure on a CRYSTAL

**pif·fle** /'pɪfəl/ *n* [U] *BrE old-fashioned* nonsense

**pif·fling** /'pɪflɪŋ/ *adj BrE old-fashioned* unimportant or useless: *Even these sums seem piffling in comparison.*

**pig¹** /pɪg/ *n* [C] S

**1 ▶ ANIMAL ◀** a farm animal that is usually pink or black and has short legs, a fat body, and a curved tail —see also GUINEA PIG (1)

**2 ▶ PERSON ◀** *spoken* **a)** someone who eats too much or eats more than their share: *Greedy pig, you ate all the candy!* **b)** someone who is very dirty or untidy: *How can you live in this mess? You're such a pig!* **c)** someone who is unpleasant or offensive: *You're a selfish pig.* | **male chauvinist pig** (=unpleasant man who thinks women are not equal to men)

**3 ▶ POLICE ◀** *slang* an insulting word meaning a police officer

**4 a pig (of a ...)** *BrE spoken* something that is very difficult or unpleasant to do: *Stripping wallpaper is a pig of a job.*

**5 make a pig's ear of** *BrE spoken* to do something very badly: *Jon's made a complete pig's ear of the decorating.* —see also **in a pig's eye** (EYE[1] (21))

**pig²** *v* [I, T] *BrE spoken* to eat a lot of food, even when you are not very hungry: *There's no ice cream left, Tony pigged the lot.*

**pig out** *phr v* [I] *informal* to eat a lot of food: *We pigged out on pizza and beer.*

**pi·geon** /'pɪdʒɪn/ *n* **1** [C] a grey bird with short legs that is common in cities **2 sb's pigeon** *BrE old-fashioned* something that a particular person is responsible for: *It's not my pigeon – someone else can deal with it.* —see also CARRIER PIGEON, CLAY PIGEON "SHOOTING", HOMING PIGEON S

**pigeon-chest·ed** /,·· '··◂‖'·· ,··/ *adj* someone who is pigeon-chested has a narrow chest that sticks out

**pi·geon·hole¹** /'pɪdʒɪnhəʊl‖-hoʊl/ *n* [C] **1** one of a set of small boxes built into a desk or into a frame on a wall, in which letters or papers can be put **2 put sb/sth into a pigeonhole** to have a very fixed idea about a person, activity etc, which is too simple and therefore unfair

**pigeonhole²** *v* [T] to consider a person, activity etc as belonging to a particular type or group, in a way that is too simple and therefore unfair; CATEGORIZE: *People tend to pigeonhole her just because she's a feminist.*

**pigeon-toed** /'·· ·/ *adj* someone who is pigeon-toed has feet that point inwards rather than straight forwards

**pig·ge·ry** /'pɪgəri/ *n* [C] *BrE* **1** a pig farm **2** a place where pigs are kept, usually with a building and an outdoor area; PIGSTY (1)

**pig·gish** /'pɪgɪʃ/ *adj* someone who is piggish eats too much or is dirty, or is unpleasant: *piggish behaviour* —**piggishly** *adv* —**piggishness** *n* [U]

**pig·gy¹** /'pɪgi/ *n* [C] **1** a word meaning a pig, used especially by or to children **2 piggy in the middle** *BrE* **a)** *informal* someone who is between two opposing groups or people and is unable to influence either side **b)** a game in which a ball is thrown between two people who try to prevent a third person in the middle from catching it; KEEP-AWAY *AmE*

**piggy²** *adj* **1** like a pig: *little piggy eyes* **2** *informal* wanting or taking more food than you really need; GREEDY: *Don't be so piggy, Ed.*

**pig·gy·back¹** /ˈpɪgibæk/ *n* [C] a ride on someone's back or shoulders: *Please, Uncle Jack, give me a piggy-back!* —**piggyback** *adv*

**piggyback**

**piggyback²** *v* [I] *AmE informal* to join or be joined with something that is larger, more important or more effective: [+ **on/onto**] *videos that simply piggyback onto the success of proven TV programs*

**piggy-bank** /ˈ·· ·/ *n* [C] a small container, usually in the shape of a pig, in which children can save coins

**pig·head·ed** /ˌpɪgˈhedɪ̵d◂/ *adj* determined to do things the way you want and refusing to change your mind, even when there are good reasons to do so; STUBBORN: *Stop being so pigheaded and admit that you were wrong!* —**pigheadedly** *adv* —**pigheadedness** *n* [U]

**pig i·ron** /ˈ· ˌ··/ *n* [U] a form of iron that is not pure, obtained directly from a BLAST FURNACE

**pig·let** /ˈpɪglɪ̵t/ *n* [C] a young pig

**pig·ment** /ˈpɪgmənt/ *n* [C,U] **1** a dry coloured powder that is mixed with oil, water etc to make paint **2** one of the natural substances in humans, plants, and animals that gives colour to skin, blood, hair etc

**pig·men·ta·tion** /ˌpɪgmənˈteɪʃən/ *n* [U] **1** the colouring of plant or animal cells caused by too much pigment **2** the colouring of living things: *Pigmentation is biologically inherited.*

**pig·my** /ˈpɪgmi/ *n* [C] another spelling of PYGMY

**pig·pen** /ˈpɪgpen/ *n* [C] *AmE* **1** a place where pigs are kept, usually with a building and an outdoor area; PIGSTY (1) **2** *informal* a very dirty or untidy place; PIGSTY (2)

**pig·skin** /ˈpɪgˌskɪn/ *n* **1** [U] leather made from the skin of a pig **2** [singular] *AmE informal* the ball used in American football: *tossing the pigskin around*

**pig·sty** /ˈpɪgstaɪ/ *n* [C] **1** a place where pigs are kept, usually with a building and an outdoor area **2** a very dirty or untidy place: *Clean up your room. It's a pigsty!*

**pig·swill** /ˈpɪgˌswɪl/ *n* [U] *BrE* **1** food that is given to pigs **2** tasteless or unpleasant food

**pig·tail** /ˈpɪgteɪl/ *n* [C] **1** one of two lengths of hair that have been pulled together on either side of the head and usually plaited (PLAIT¹), worn especially by very young girls: **in pigtails** *Jenny wore her hair in pigtails.* **2** all of the hair pulled to the back of the head and plaited so that it hangs down; BRAID¹ (2) *AmE* —compare BUNCH¹ (5), PLAIT², PONYTAIL —see picture at HAIRSTYLE

**pike** /paɪk/ *n* [C] **1** a large fish that eats other fish and lives in rivers and lakes **2** a TURNPIKE **3** a long-handled weapon used in the past by soldiers **4** *NEngE* a mountain or hill with a pointed top: *Scafell Pike*

**pike·man** /ˈpaɪkmən/ *n* [C] a soldier who fought in the past with a pike

**pike·staff** /ˈpaɪkstɑːf‖-stæf/ *n* [C] the long wooden handle of a pike (PIKE (3))

**pi·laff, pilaf** /ˈpiːlæf‖pɪˈlɑːf/ *n* [C,U] a pilau

**pi·las·ter** /pɪ̵ˈlæstə‖-ər/ *n* [C] a square COLUMN that sticks out partly beyond the wall of a building and is usually only a decoration

**pi·lau** /ˈpiːlaʊ‖pɪˈloʊ/ *n* [C,U] a dish made from rice mixed with vegetables and often meat: *mushroom pilau*

**pil·chard** /ˈpɪltʃəd‖-ərd/ *n* [C] a small fish that lives in the sea and can be eaten: *pilchards in tomato sauce*

S2 **pile¹** /paɪl/ *n*
**1** ▶ **LARGE AMOUNT/MASS** ◀ [C] **a)** a tidy collection of several things of the same kind placed on top of each other; STACK¹ (1): *We put the newspapers in piles on the floor.* | *The record I want is at the bottom of the pile.* | [+ **of**] *a pile of blankets* —compare HEAP¹ (1) **b)** a large mass of things collected together: *big pile of brushwood*
**2 a pile of** also **piles of** *informal* a lot of something: *I've got piles of work to do this evening.*
**3 at the bottom of the pile** in a very weak position in society or in an organization: *At the bottom of the pile are young people in their first jobs.*
**4** ▶ **CLOTH/CARPETS** ◀ [C,U] the soft surface of short threads on a CARPET or some types of cloth, especially VELVET: *a deep pile carpet* —compare NAP¹ (2)
**5** ▶ **POST** ◀ [C] a heavy post made of wood, stone, or metal, pushed into the ground as a support for a building, bridge etc
**6 make a/your pile** *informal* to make a lot of money: *He made his pile in the antiques business.*
**7** ▶ **BUILDING** ◀ [C] *especially BrE* a large tall old building or group of buildings: *They live in a rambling Victorian pile.*
**8** ▶ **MEDICAL** ◀ **piles** *BrE not technical* HAEMORRHOIDS

**pile²** *v* [T] **1** also **pile up** to make a pile by collecting things together; STACK² (1): *Ma stacked the cups and piled the plates.* | *We piled the books up on the table.* | **pile sth high** (=make a tall pile) *Clothes were piled high on the chair* **2** to fill something or cover a surface with a lot of something: *Anna piled spaghetti onto her plate.* | **be piled (high) with** *The cart was piled high with fruit and vegetables.*

**pile in/into** sth *phr v* [T] to go quickly into a place or vehicle in a disorganized way: *We all piled into the back of his car.*

**pile on** *phr v* [T] *informal* **1 pile on the praise/criticism etc** also **pile it on** to talk about something in a way that makes it seem much better or much worse than it really is; EXAGGERATE: *Mitch was really piling on the compliments!* | *It can't be that bad – Nellie tends to pile it on.* **2 pile on the agony** *BrE* to enjoy making something seem worse than it really is

**pile out** *phr v* [I] to quickly leave a place or get out of a vehicle in a rather disorderly way: [+ **of**] *As soon as the bell went the kids piled out of the building.*

**pile up** *phr v* [I,T] to become much larger in quantity or amount, or to make something do this; ACCUMULATE: *Work is really piling up.* | **pile sth ↔ up** *Greg has managed to pile up enormous debts.* —see also PILE-UP

**pile driv·er** /ˈ· ˌ··/ *n* [C] **1** a machine for pushing heavy posts into the ground **2** *informal* a very hard PUNCH² (1), especially in BOXING

**pile-up** /ˈ· ·/ *n* [C] *informal* a road traffic accident in which several vehicles crash into each other: *There had been several motorway pile-ups in the fog.*

**pil·fer** /ˈpɪlfə‖-ər/ *v* [I,T] to steal small amounts of things, or things that are not worth much, especially from the place where you work: *They'd been caught pilfering building materials from the construction site.* —**pilferer** *n* [C] —**pilfering** *n* [U]

**pil·grim** /ˈpɪlgrɪ̵m/ *n* [C] someone who travels a long way to a holy place for a religious reason: *pilgrims at Lourdes*

**pil·grim·age** /ˈpɪlgrɪ̵mɪdʒ/ *n* [C,U] **1** a journey to a holy place for religious reasons: *a pilgrimage to Mecca* **2** a journey to a place connected with someone or something famous: *Elvis Presley's home has become a place of pilgrimage.*

**Pilgrim Fa·thers** /ˌ·· ˈ··/ *n* **the Pilgrim Fathers** the group of English people who arrived to settle at Plymouth, Massachusetts in the US in 1620

**pill** /pɪl/ *n* **1** [C] a small solid piece of medicine, that you swallow whole: *He has to take pills to control his blood pressure.* | *sleeping pills* **2 the Pill** a pill taken regularly by some women in order to prevent them having babies: **on the Pill** *My doctor advised me to go on the Pill.* **3 sugar the pill** *BrE*, **sweeten the pill** *AmE* to do something to make an unpleasant job or situation less unpleasant for the person who has to accept it **4** *AmE informal* someone who annoys you, often a child: *Luke* S3

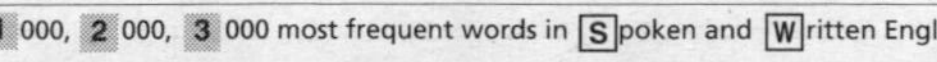

*can be a real pill sometimes.* —see also **a bitter pill (to swallow)** (BITTER[1] (7)), MORNING-AFTER PILL

**pil·lage** /ˈpɪlɪdʒ/ *v* [I,T] if an army pillages a place, it uses violence to steal from and damage a place that it has taken control of in a war; PLUNDER[1] —compare LOOT[2] —**pillage** *n* [U] —**pillager** *n* [C]

**pil·lar** /ˈpɪlə‖-ər/ *n* [C] **1 a)** a tall upright round post used as a support for a roof: *Huge pillars support the cathedral roof.* —see picture on page 410 **b)** a tall upright round post, usually made of stone, put up to remind people of an important person or event **2 pillar of the community/church etc** an active and important member of a group, organization etc **3** a very important part of a system of beliefs, especially religious beliefs: *These tenets are the pillars on which our faith is founded.* **4 be driven/passed from pillar to post** to go from one difficult situation to another without achieving much **5 pillar of dust/smoke/flame etc** a tall upright mass of dust, smoke, flame etc

**pillar box** /ˈ·· ·/ *n* [C] *old-fashioned* a large red tube-shaped box for posting letters that stands on streets in Britain —compare LETTERBOX (2)

**pill·box** /ˈpɪlbɒks‖-bɑːks/ *n* [C] **1** a small round box for holding pills (PILL (1)) **2** a small, strong, usually circular shelter with a gun inside it, built as a defence **3** also **pillbox hat** /ˌ·· ˈ·/ a small round hat for a woman

**pil·lion** /ˈpɪljən/ *n* [C] **1** a seat for a second person behind the driver of a motorcycle or a rider on a horse **2 ride pillion** to sit behind someone who is driving a motorcycle or riding a horse

**pil·lock** /ˈpɪlək/ *n* [C] *BrE slang* a very stupid person

**pil·lo·ry[1]** /ˈpɪləri/ *v* [T usually passive] if someone is pilloried, they are publicly criticized by a lot of people: *The education secretary was pilloried by the press for his latest proposals.*

**pillory[2]** *n* [C] a wooden frame with holes for the head and hands to be locked into, used in the past as a way of publicly punishing someone —compare **the stocks** (STOCK[1] (14))

S 3 **pil·low[1]** /ˈpɪləʊ‖-loʊ/ *n* [C] **1** a cloth bag filled with soft material, that you put your head on when you are sleeping —compare CUSHION[1] (1) **2** any object used to support your head while you are sleeping: *Paula used her rucksack as a pillow.* **3 pillow fight** a game in which children hit each other with pillows **4 pillow talk** *informal* conversation between lovers in bed

**pillow[2]** *v* [T] to rest your head somewhere, especially so that you can go to sleep: **pillow your head on sth** *Don fell asleep with his head pillowed on a sack.*

**pil·low·case, pillow case** /ˈpɪləʊkeɪs‖-loʊ-/ *n* [C] a cloth cover for a pillow

W 3 **pi·lot[1]** /ˈpaɪlət/ *n* [C] **1** someone who operates the controls of an aircraft or spacecraft: *an airline pilot* **2** someone with a special knowledge of a particular area of water, who is employed to guide ships across it: *a harbour pilot* **3** a television programme that is made in order to test whether people like it and would watch it **4 pilot test/project/scheme etc** a test that is done to see if an idea, product etc will be successful: *If the pilot survey goes well, we'll go into full production.* —see also AUTOMATIC PILOT

**pilot[2]** *v* [T] **1** to guide an aircraft, spacecraft, or ship as its pilot **2** to help someone to go to a place: **pilot sb toward/out etc** *He took my hand and piloted me through the corridors.* **3** to be responsible for making sure that a new law or plan is officially approved: **pilot sth through** *I'm relying on your skill in piloting this through Parliament.* **4** to test a new idea, product etc on people to find out whether it will be successful: *They are piloting parts of the book in language schools.*

**pilot light** /ˈ·· ·/ also **pilot burner** *n* [C] **1** a small gas flame that burns all the time and is used for lighting larger gas burners **2** a small electric light on a piece of electrical equipment that shows when it is turned on

**pilot of·fi·cer** /ˈ·· ˌ···/ *n* [C] a middle rank in the Royal Air Force, or someone who has this rank —see table on page B4

**pi·men·to** also **pimiento** /pɪ̯ˈmentəʊ‖-toʊ/ *n* [C,U] a small red PEPPER often used for putting inside OLIVES

**pimp** /pɪmp/ *n* [C] a man who makes money by controlling PROSTITUTES (=women who have sex with men for money) —**pimp** *v* [I]

**pim·per·nel** /ˈpɪmpənel‖-ər-/ *n* [C] a small wild plant with flowers that are blue, white, or especially red

**pim·ple** /ˈpɪmpəl/ *n* [C] a small raised red spot on your skin, especially on your face —see also GOOSE PIMPLES —**pimpled** *adj* —**pimply** *adj*

**PIN** /pɪn/ also **PIN num·ber** /ˈ· ˌ··/ *n* [C] Personal Identification Number; a number that you use when you get money from a CASHPOINT using a plastic card

**pins**

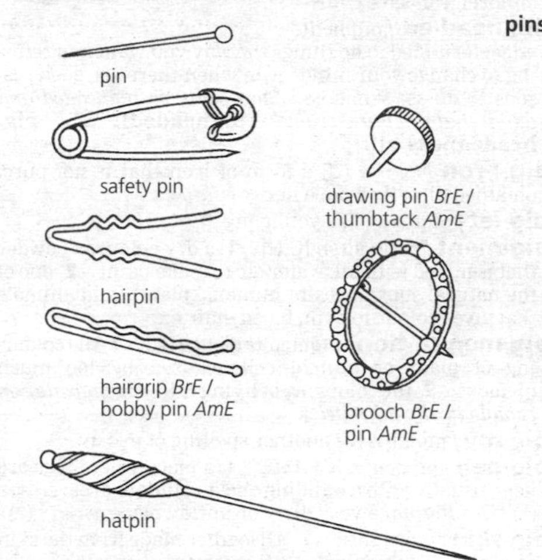


**pin[1]** /pɪn/ *n* [C] S 3

**1 ▸ FOR CLOTH ◂** a short thin piece of metal with a sharp point at one end, used especially for fastening together pieces of cloth while making clothes

**2 ▸ JEWELLERY ◂ a)** *AmE* an attractively shaped piece of metal, sometimes containing jewels, that you fasten to your clothes and wear as a decoration; BROOCH *BrE* **b)** *BrE* a short thin piece of metal with a decoration at one end, used as jewellery

**3 ▸ ELECTRICAL ◂** one of the pieces of metal that sticks out of an electric PLUG: *a three-pin plug*

**4 ▸ FOR SUPPORT ◂** a thin piece of metal or wood used as a support for something, or to fasten things together: *When I broke my leg, I had to have a pin inserted.*

**5 ▸ GAMES ◂** one of the bottle-shaped objects that you try to knock down in a game of BOWLING

**6 you could hear a pin drop** *spoken* used to say that it is very quiet and no one is speaking

**7 for two pins I'd ...** *BrE old-fashioned* used to say that you would like to do something to someone because they have annoyed you: *For two pins, I'd tell him to get lost.*

**8 pins** [plural] *BrE informal* legs —see also DRAWING PIN, PIN MONEY, PINS AND NEEDLES, ROLLING PIN, SAFETY PIN

**pin[2]** *v* **pinned, pinning 1** [T always + adv/prep] to fasten something somewhere, or to join two things together, using a pin: **pin sth together** *Pin the pieces together before sewing them.* | **pin sth to/on/onto** *Can you pin this to the notice board?* **2 pin your hopes on** to hope that something will happen or someone will help you, because all your plans depend on this: *Chris is pinning his hopes on getting into Yale.* **3 pin the blame on** to blame someone for something, often unfairly: *It's your fault – don't try to pin the blame on me!* **4** [T always + adv/prep] to make someone unable to move by putting a lot of pressure or weight on them: **pin sb to/under** *In* *the accident she was pinned under the car.* **5 pin your ears back!** *BrE spoken* used to tell someone to listen carefully

**pin** sb/sth ↔ **down** *phr v* [T] **1** to make someone give clear details or make a definite decision about something: *I've been trying to pin him down all week, but he won't say what's going on.* **2** to understand something clearly or be able to describe it exactly: *We know someone's been stealing, but it's difficult to pin down who it is.*

**pi·ña co·la·da** /ˌpiːnə kəˈlɑːdə/ *n* [C,U] an alcoholic drink made from COCONUT juice, PINEAPPLE juice, and RUM[1]

**pin·a·fore** /ˈpɪnəfɔː‖-fɔːr/ *n* [C] **1** also **pinafore dress** /ˈ··· ˌ·/ *BrE* a dress that does not cover your arms and under which you wear a shirt or BLOUSE; JUMPER (2) *AmE* **2** a loose piece of clothing that does not cover your arms, worn over your clothes to keep them clean

**pin·ball** /ˈpɪnbɔːl‖-bɒːl/ *n* [U] a game played on a machine with a sloping board down which a ball rolls, which the player has to prevent reaching the bottom

**pince-nez** /ˌpæns ˈneɪ, ˌpɪns-/ *n* GLASSES worn in the past that were held in position on the nose by a spring, instead of by pieces fitting round the ears

**pin·cer** /ˈpɪnsə‖-ər/ *n* **1** [C usually plural] one of the pair of claws (CLAW[1] (3)) that some SHELLFISH and insects have, used for holding and cutting food, and for fighting —see picture at LOBSTER **2 pincers** [plural] a tool made of two crossed pieces of metal used for holding things tightly —see picture at TOOL[1]

**pincer move·ment** /ˈ·· ˌ··/ *n* [C] a military attack in which two groups of soldiers come from opposite directions in order to trap the enemy between them

**pinch**[1] /pɪntʃ/ *v* **1** [T] to press a part of someone's flesh very tightly between your finger and thumb, especially so that it hurts: *Mum, he pinched me!* —see picture on page 1259 **2** [T] *informal* to steal something, especially something small or not very valuable: *Someone's pinched my coat!* **3** [I,T] if something you are wearing pinches you, it presses painfully on your flesh, because it is too tight: *Her head was aching and her new shoes pinched dreadfully.* **4 I had to pinch myself** *especially spoken* used to say that you needed to make sure a situation was real and that you were not imagining it **5 pinch and scrape** to be very careful about how much money you spend, because you do not have very much —see also PENNY-PINCHING **6** [T usually passive] *old-fashioned BrE* to ARREST [1] (1) someone

**pinch**[2] *n* **1 pinch of salt/pepper etc** a small amount of salt, pepper etc that you can hold between your finger and thumb: *Add a pinch of cayenne pepper.* **2** [C] an act of pressing someone's flesh between your finger and thumb: *She gave him a playful pinch.* **3 at a pinch** *BrE* **in a pinch** *AmE* if necessary in a particularly difficult or urgent situation: *We can squeeze one more person in the car, at a pinch.* | *In a pinch, I could manage $60.* **4 take sth with a pinch of salt** to not completely believe what someone says to you **5 feel the pinch** to have financial difficulties, especially because you are not making as much money as you used to make: *Local stores and businesses are beginning to feel the pinch.*

**pinched** /pɪntʃt/ *adj* a pinched face looks thin and unhealthy, for example because the person is ill, cold, or tired: *Years of working in the mine had left their faces pinched and haggard.*

**pinch-hit** /ˈ· ·/ *v* [I + **for**] *AmE* **1** to do something for someone else because they are unexpectedly not able to do it **2** to HIT[1] (4a) for someone else in BASEBALL (1) —**pinch-hitter** *n* [C] *Mark is sick — we're sending Jim as a pinch-hitter.*

**pin·cush·ion** /ˈpɪnˌkʊʃən/ *n* [C] a soft filled bag for sticking pins in until you need to use them

**pine**[1] /paɪn/ *n* **1** [C,U] a tall tree with long hard sharp leaves that do not fall off in winter: *a pine forest* **2** the soft pale-coloured wood of this tree, used to make furniture, floors etc: *a pine table*

**pine**[2] also **pine away** *v* [I] to gradually become weaker, less active, and less healthy, especially because you feel very unhappy: *After my grandfather died, my grandmother just pined away.*

**pine for** sth/sb *phr v* [T] to become unhappy or ill because you cannot be with someone you love or in a place you love: *She won't touch her food. I think she's pining for home.*

**pin·e·al gland** /ˈpɪniəl ˌglænd‖ˈpaɪn-/ *n* [C] a part of the brain that is thought to be sensitive to light in some way

**pine·ap·ple** /ˈpaɪnæpəl/ *n* [C,U] a large yellow-brown tropical fruit or its sweet juicy yellow flesh: *pineapple chunks* | *pineapple juice* —see picture on page 413

**pine·cone** /ˈpaɪnkəʊn‖-koʊn/ *n* [C] a fruit of the PINETREE

**pine mar·ten** /ˈ· ˌ··/ *n* [C] a small European animal that lives in forests

**pine nee·dle** /ˈ· ˌ··/ *n* [C] a leaf of the pinetree, that is thin and sharp like a needle

**pine·tree** /ˈpaɪnˌtriː/ *n* [C] a tall tree with long hard sharp leaves that do not fall off in winter; a PINE[1] (1)

**pine·wood** /ˈpaɪnwʊd/ *n* **1** [C] a forest of pinetrees **2** [U] the wood from a pinetree

**ping**[1] /pɪŋ/ *n* [C] a short high ringing sound: *The bell on the counter let out a sharp ping.*

**ping**[2] *v* **1** [I] to make a short high ringing sound **2** [I] *AmE* PINK[3]

**ping-pong** /ˈ· ·/ *n* [U] an indoor game played on a table top by two people with a small plastic ball and two BATS; TABLE TENNIS

**pin·head** /ˈpɪnhed/ *n* [C] the head of a pin

**pin·ion**[1] /ˈpɪnjən/ *v* **1** [T always + adv/prep] to hold or tie up someone's arms or legs very tightly, so that they cannot move freely: *Her arms were pinioned tightly behind her.* **2** [T usually passive] *technical* to cut off the big strong feathers from a bird's wings so that it cannot fly

**pinion**[2] *n* **1** [C] a small wheel, with teeth on its outer edge, that fits into a larger wheel and turns it or is turned by it —compare COGWHEEL **2** [C] *literary* a bird's wing **3** [C] *technical* the outer part of a bird's wing, where the strongest flying feathers grow

**pink**[1] /pɪŋk/ *adj* **1** pale red: *a wedding cake with pink and white icing* | *The western sky was glowing pink.* **2** [only before noun] a word used to talk about HOMOSEXUAL people: *a campaign aimed at the pink consumer* —see also **be tickled pink** (TICKLE[1] (3)) S2 W3

**pink**[2] *n* **1** [C,U] a pale red colour —see picture on page 411 **2** [C] a garden plant with pink, white, or red flowers **3 in the pink** *old-fashioned* in very good health

**pink**[3] *v* [I] *BrE* if a car engine pinks, it makes knocking sounds because it is not working properly; PING[2] *AmE*

**pink-col·lar** /ˌ· ˈ··◂/ *adj* **pink-collar jobs/workers/industries etc** *especially AmE* low-paid jobs done mainly by women, for example in offices and restaurants, or the women who do these jobs —compare WHITE-COLLAR, BLUE-COLLAR

**pink gin** /ˌ· ˈ·/ *n* [C,U] an alcoholic drink made of GIN and ANGOSTURA which gives it a pink colour

**pink·ie, pinky** /ˈpɪŋki/ *n* [C] *especially AmE or ScotE* the smallest finger of the human hand

**pink·ing shears** /ˈ·· ·/ also **pinking scissors** /ˈ·· ˌ··/ *n* [plural] a special type of scissors with blades that have V-shaped teeth, used for cutting cloth —see picture at SCISSORS

**pink·ish** /ˈpɪŋkɪʃ/ *adj* slightly pink: *a pinkish tinge*

**pink·o** /ˈpɪŋkəʊ‖-koʊ/ *n* [C] **1** *AmE* an insulting word for a SOCIALIST or COMMUNIST[2] (1) **2** *BrE* someone who supports LEFT WING ideas, but is not a strong believer in SOCIALISM —compare RED[1] (4) —**pinko** *adj*

**pink·y** /ˈpɪŋki/ *n* [C] a PINKIE

**pin mon·ey** /ˈ· ˌ··/ *n* [U] a small amount of money that you can spend on yourself rather than on necessary things

**pin·na·cle** /ˈpɪnəkəl/ *n* **1** [singular] the most successful, powerful, exciting etc part of something: [+ **of**] *By the age of 40, she had reached the pinnacle of her political career.* **2** [C] a pointed stone decoration, like a small tower, on a building such as a church or castle **3** [C] *especially literary* a high mountain top

**pin·nate** /ˈpɪneɪt/ *adj technical* a pinnate leaf is made of two rows of little leaves arranged opposite each other along a stem

**pin·ny** /ˈpɪni/ *n* [C] *BrE informal* a PINAFORE (2)

**pin·point¹** /ˈpɪnpɔɪnt/ *v* [T] **1** to say exactly what the facts about something really are: *This new report pinpoints the failings of the welfare system.* | **pinpoint what/how/why etc** *When children have learning difficulties, it's often difficult to pinpoint what the problem really is.* **2** to find or show the exact position of something: *The team went behind enemy lines to pinpoint the exact locations of missile launchers.*

**pinpoint²** *n* [C] **1** a very small point or dot of something: [+ **of**] *tiny pinpoints of light* **2 with pinpoint accuracy/precision** very exactly: *Radar can locate an underwater target with pinpoint accuracy.*

**pin·prick** /ˈpɪnˌprɪk/ *n* [C] **1** [C] a very small area or DOT of something: [+ **of**] *a pinprick of light* **2** a very small hole in something, similar to one made by a pin **3** something that slightly annoys you

**pins and nee·dles** /ˌ· · ˈ··/ *n* **1** [U] the uncomfortable prickly feeling you get in a part of your body when a full supply of blood comes back to it after having been partly blocked: **get pins and needles** *If you sit like that for too long you'll get pins and needles.* **2 be on pins and needles** *AmE* to be very nervous and unable to relax, especially because you are waiting for something important: *I wish Billy would give her a call. She's been on pins and needles all day.*

**pin·stripe** /ˈpɪnstraɪp/ *n* [C] **1** one of the thin light-coloured lines that forms a pattern on cloth against a darker background —see picture on page 839 **2 pinstripe suit** a man's suit made from cloth with a pinstripe pattern, worn especially by business people: *a navy-blue pinstripe suit* —**pin-striped** *adj*

S2 **pint** /paɪnt/ *n* **1** [C] a unit for measuring an amount of liquid, especially beer or milk, in the US and Britain. In the US a pint contains 16 ounces of liquid, and in Britain it contains 20 ounces: *Add two pints of water to the mixture.* | *half a pint of milk* —see table on page B2 **2** [C] *BrE* a pint of beer, especially one that you drink in a bar: *He's gone down the pub for a quick pint.* | *My dad remembers when a pint cost sixpence.* —compare HALF² (1)

**pin·ta·ble** /ˈpɪnˌteɪbəl/ *n* [C] *BrE* a machine for playing PINBALL on

**pin·to** /ˈpɪntəʊ‖-toʊ/ *n* [C] *AmE* a horse with irregular markings of two or more colours; PIEBALD *BrE*

**pinto bean** /ˈ·· ·/ *n* [C] a small light brown bean

**pint-size** /ˈ· ·/ also **pint-sized** *adj* [only before noun] small, and unimportant or unsatisfactory

**pin-up** /ˈ· ·/ *n* **1** [C] a picture of an attractive person, often a woman with not many clothes on, that is put up on a wall to be looked at and admired **2** [C] someone who appears in one of these pictures

**pin·wheel** /ˈpɪnwiːl/ *n* [C] *AmE* WINDMILL (2)

**pi·o·neer¹** /ˌpaɪəˈnɪə‖-ˈnɪr/ *n* **1** [C] one of the first people to do something that other people will later develop or continue to do: [+ **of**] *the pioneers of the Women's Liberation movement* | [+ **in**] *Hans Richter, a pioneer in experimental cinema* | **pioneer photographer/geologist etc** (=one of the first people to develop photography etc) **2** [C] one of the first people to travel to a new country or area and begin living there, farming etc: *the early pioneers of the Dakota territory*

**pioneer²** *v* [T] to be the first person to do, invent or use something: *The new cancer treatment was pioneered in the early eighties by Dr Sylvia Bannerjee.*

**pi·o·neer·ing** /ˌpaɪəˈnɪərɪŋ◂‖-ˈnɪr-/ *adj* [only before noun] introducing new and better methods or ideas for the first time: *the pioneering work of NASA scientists* | *his pioneering discoveries in the field of dynamics*

**pi·ous** /ˈpaɪəs/ *adj* **1** having strong religious beliefs, and showing this in the way you behave **2** pretending to have sincere religious feelings in order to make people think you are better than you really are: *Don't believe any of his pious talk.* **3 pious hope/wish** something that you want to be true or to happen, but that probably will not —see also PIETY —**piously** *adv* —**piousness** *n* [U]

**pip¹** /pɪp/ *n* [C] *BrE* **1** a small seed from a fruit such as an apple or orange **2** a high note that is part of a series of short sounds, used for example on the radio to show the time, or in the operation of public telephones; BEEP² (1) *AmE* **3** *old-fashioned* one of the stars on the shoulders of the coats of army officers that shows their rank **4 give sb the pip** *old-fashioned* to annoy someone

**pip²** **pipped, pipping** *v* [T] *BrE informal* **1 pip sb at the post** to beat someone at the last moment in a race, competition etc, when they were expecting to win: *I nearly got the job, but was pipped at the post by the other candidate.* **2** to beat someone in a race, competition etc, by only a small amount

**pi·pal** /ˈpiːpəl/ *n* [C] a large Indian tree

**pipe¹** /paɪp/ *n* [C] S2 W3

**1** ▶ **TUBE** ◀ a tube through which a liquid or gas flows, often under the ground: *A pipe had burst in the kitchen and flooded the floor.* | *Workmen were laying pipes under the road.* | *The pipe's blocked again!* | *a gas pipe*

**2** ▶ **FOR SMOKING** ◀ a thing used for smoking tobacco, consisting of a small tube with a container shaped like a bowl at one end: *Peters filled and lit his pipe.* | *pipe tobacco*

**3** ▶ **MUSIC** ◀ **a)** a simple musical instrument shaped like a tube and played by blowing **b)** one of the metal tubes through which air passes when an ORGAN (2) is played **c) the pipes** *BrE informal* BAGPIPES

**4 pipe dream** a hope, idea, plan etc that is impossible or will probably never happen: *Arsenal lost 4-0, making winning the league something of a pipe dream.*

**5 Put that in your pipe and smoke it!** *spoken* used to say that someone must accept what you have just said, even though they do not like it

**6 the pipes** BAGPIPES

**pipe²** *v*

**1** ▶ **SEND LIQUID/GAS** ◀ [T usually passive] to send a liquid or gas through a pipe to another place: *a piped water supply* | **pipe sth into/to** *Eighty per cent of sewage is piped directly into the sea.*

**2** ▶ **SPEAK/SING** ◀ [I,T] to speak or sing in a high voice: *A moorhen piped suddenly from the lake.*

**3** ▶ **MAKE MUSIC** ◀ [I,T] to make a musical sound using a pipe: *He piped a jaunty tune for us to dance to.*

**4** ▶ **FOOD** ◀ to decorate food, especially a cake, with thin lines of ICING or cream

**5 pipe sb aboard** *technical* to welcome someone important onto a ship by blowing a special whistle

**pipe down** *phr v* [I] *spoken* to stop talking or making a noise, and become calmer and less excited: *Pipe down! I'm trying to listen to the news.*

**pipe up** *phr v* [I] *informal* to begin to say something or start speaking, especially when you have been quiet until then: *The smallest child suddenly piped up with the answer.*

**pipe clean·er** /ˈ· ˌ··/ *n* [C] a length of wire covered with soft material, used to clean the inside of a tobacco pipe

**piped mu·sic** /ˌ· ˈ··/ *n* [U] quiet recorded music played continuously in shops, hotels, restaurants etc

**pipe fit·ter** /ˈ· ˌ··/ *n* [C] someone who puts in and repairs pipes for water, gas etc

**pipe·line** /ˈpaɪp-laɪn/ *n* [C] **1** a line of connecting pipes, often under the ground, used for taking gas, oil etc over long distances **2 be in the pipeline** if a plan, idea or event is in the pipeline, it is still being prepared, but it will happen or be completed soon: *We've made several changes lately, and there are more in the pipeline.*

**pipe of peace** /ˌ· · ˈ·/ *n* [C] a PEACE PIPE

**pip·er** /ˈpaɪpə‖-ər/ *n* [C] a musician who plays a PIPE[1] (3) or the BAGPIPES

**pipe rack** /ˈ· ·/ *n* [C] a small frame for holding several tobacco pipes

**pi·pette** /pɪˈpet‖paɪ-/ *n* [C] a thin glass tube for sucking up exact amounts of liquid, used especially in chemistry —see picture at LABORATORY

**pip·it** /ˈpɪpɪt/ *n* [C] a small brown or grey singing bird

**pip·pin** /ˈpɪpɪn/ *n* [C] a small sweet apple

**pip·squeak** /ˈpɪpskwiːk/ *n* [C] someone that you think is not worth attention or respect, especially because they are small or young: *Shut up, you little pipsqueak!*

**pi·quant** /ˈpiːkənt/ *adj* **1** having a pleasantly sharp taste or flavour: *a piquant tomato sauce* **2** interesting and exciting; INTRIGUING: *The disappearance of the letter made the situation all the more piquant.* —**piquantly** *adv* —**piquancy** *n* [U]

**pique**[1] /piːk/ *n* [U] **1** a feeling of being annoyed or upset, especially because someone has ignored you or made you look stupid: **a fit of pique** (=sudden anger) *Greta stormed off in a fit of pique.* **2** also **piqué** a type of material made of cotton, silk, or RAYON

**pique**[2] *v* **1** [T usually passive] to make someone feel annoyed or upset, especially by ignoring them or making them look stupid: **be/feel piqued** *We did feel a little piqued when nobody even bothered to ask us.* **2 pique your interest/curiosity** *especially AmE* to make you feel interested in something or someone

**pi·ra·cy** /ˈpaɪərəsi‖ˈpaɪrə-/ *n* [U] **1** the illegal copying and sale of books, TAPES, VIDEOS etc: *software piracy* **2** the crime of attacking and stealing from ships at sea

**pi·ra·nha** /pɪ̈ˈrɑːnjə, -nə/ *n* [C] a South American fish with sharp teeth that lives in rivers and eats flesh

**pi·rate**[1] /ˈpaɪərət‖ˈpaɪrət/ *n* [C] **1** someone who dishonestly copies and sells another person's work **2 pirate radio/TV (station)** illegal radio or television broadcasts, or the station sending them out: *a pirate channel* **3** someone who sails on the seas, attacking other boats and stealing things from them —**piratical** /paɪˈrætɪkəl, pɪ̈-/ *adj* —**piratically** /-kli/ *adv*

pirate

**pirate**[2] *v* [T] to illegally copy and sell another person's work such as a book, design, or invention —**pirated** *adj*: *pirated video tapes*

**pir·ou·ette** /ˌpɪruˈet/ *n* [C] a very fast turn made on one toe or the front part of one foot, especially by a BALLET dancer —**pirouette** *v* [I]

**pis·ca·to·ri·al** /ˌpɪskəˈtɔːriəl◂/ *adj formal* connected with fishing or fishermen

**Pis·ces** /ˈpaɪsiːz/ *n* **1** [singular] the twelfth sign of the ZODIAC, represented by two fish, and believed to affect the character and life of people born between February 21 and March 20: *Nick's a Pisces.* **2** [C] someone who was born between February 21 and March 20

**pish** /pɪʃ/ *interjection old use* used to express annoyance or impatience

**piss**[1] /pɪs/ *v* **1** [I] *informal* an impolite word meaning to URINATE **2 piss all over sb** *spoken* an impolite expression meaning to thoroughly defeat a person or a team **3 piss in the wind** *spoken* an impolite expression meaning to waste time or effort trying to do something that is impossible **4 be pissing (it) down (with rain)** *BrE informal* to rain very heavily: *By the time we got there, it was absolutely pissing down!* **5 piss yourself (laughing)** *BrE spoken* an impolite expression meaning to laugh uncontrollably: *When Michelle fell in that puddle we absolutely pissed ourselves.* **6 go piss up a rope!** *AmE spoken* a very impolite expression used to tell someone to go away **7 not have a pot to piss in** *AmE spoken* a very impolite expression meaning to be extremely poor

**piss about/around** *phr v BrE spoken* **1** [I] an impolite expression meaning to waste time doing stupid things with no purpose or plan: *Stop pissing about and get some work done!* **2** [T **piss** sb **about/around**] an impolite expression meaning to treat someone badly by not doing what you have promised to do, or by not being honest with them: *I wish he'd say yes or no – he's been pissing me around for weeks.*

**piss** sth ↔ **away** *phr v* [T] *spoken* a very impolite expression meaning to waste something very stupidly: *Jean inherited a load of money, but she pissed it all away.*

**piss off** *phr v* [I] *spoken* **1** [usually imperative] an offensive expression meaning to go away: *Why don't you just piss off and leave me alone!* **2** an offensive expression used to say no or to refuse to do something: *"Johnny, will you do the dishes?" "Piss off!"*

**piss** sb ↔ **off** *phr v* [T] *spoken* an impolite expression meaning to annoy someone very much: *It really pisses me off when my car won't start in the morning.*

**piss**[2] *n* **1** [singular] *spoken* an impolite word for an act of urinating (URINATE): **have/take a piss** *I need to have a piss.* **2** [U] *spoken* an impolite word meaning URINE **3 take the piss (out of sb/sth)** *BrE spoken* to make fun of someone, especially by copying them or trying to make them believe something untrue: *Stop taking the piss out of Dave!*|*£900 for that stereo? You're taking the piss!* **4 be on the piss** *BrE spoken* to be drinking a lot of alcohol: *"Where's Jo?" "Out on the piss somewhere."* **5 a piece of piss** *BrE spoken* something very easy: *That test was a piece of piss!* **6 full of piss and vinegar** *AmE spoken* full of energy

**piss**[3] *adv spoken* **piss poor/piss easy etc** an impolite expression meaning very poor, very easy etc: *"You'd make a piss-poor lawyer," he replied.*

**piss-ant**[1], **pissant** /ˈpɪsænt/ *adj* [only before noun] *AmE informal* an impolite word meaning of very low value, quality, or importance: *I get really fed up doing these piss-ant little jobs.*

**piss-ant**[2], **pissant** *n AmE informal* an impolite word meaning an annoying person with a weak character: *The stupid little piss-ant!*

**piss ar·tist** /ˈ· ˌ··/ *n* [C] *BrE informal* an impolite word for someone who drinks a lot of alcohol

**piss-ass** /ˈ· ·/ *adj AmE spoken* [only before noun] a very impolite word meaning not at all important, or very silly: *Seth thinks his piss-ass little job makes him somebody!*

**pissed** /pɪst/ *adj* **1** *BrE spoken* drunk: *They rolled in pissed at three in the morning.*|**pissed as a newt/pissed out of your head** (=extremely drunk) **2** *AmE spoken* an impolite word meaning annoyed, disappointed, or unhappy: *Oh God, I'm really pissed, I screwed up on my exam.*|[+ **with/at**] *Are you still pissed at me?* **3 pissed off** *especially BrE* annoyed, disappointed, or unhappy: [+ **with**] *I'm a bit pissed off with my job at the moment.*

**pis·ser** /ˈpɪsə‖-ər/ *n* [C] *spoken* **1** an impolite word meaning a difficult job or activity, or a bad or annoying situation: *"I'm grounded." "What a pisser."* **2** an impolite word meaning a toilet **3** *AmE* a very impolite word meaning a good situation: *I got the job! What a pisser!*

**piss·head** /ˈpɪshed/ *n* [C] *BrE spoken* an impolite word for someone who drinks a lot of alcohol

**piss·oir** /ˈpɪswɑː‖piːˈswɑːr/ *n* [C] *French* a public toilet

**piss-take** /ˈ· ·/ *n* [C usually singular] *BrE spoken* a joke in which you try to make fun of someone, for example by copying them or laughing at them —see also **take the piss out of** (PISS[2] (3))

**piss-up** /ˈ· ·/ *n* [C] *BrE spoken* an occasion when several people drink a lot of alcohol together: *I'm not going to the party – it sounds like just a piss-up to me.*

**pis·sy** /ˈpɪsi/ *adj spoken* an impolite word meaning small or unimportant and annoying

**pis·ta·chi·o** /pɪ̣ˈstɑːʃiəʊ‖pɪ̣ˈstæʃioʊ/ *plural* **pistachios** *n* [C] a small green nut: *pistachio ice cream*

**piste** /piːst/ *n* [C] a snow-covered slope which has been prepared for people to SKI[2] down

**pis·til** /ˈpɪstl/ *n* [C] *technical* the female seed-producing part of a flower

**pis·tol** /ˈpɪstl/ *n* [C] a small gun you can use with one hand

**pistol-whip** /ˈ· · ·/ *v* [I,T] to hit someone many times with a pistol

P

**pis·ton** /ˈpɪstən/ *n* [C] a part of an engine consisting of a short solid piece of metal inside a tube, that moves up and down to make the other parts of the engine move

**piston ring** /ˈ· · ·/ *n* [C] a circular metal spring used to stop gas or liquid escaping from between a piston and the tube that it moves in

**pit¹** /pɪt/ *n*
**1 ▶ HOLE ◀** [C] **a)** a hole in the ground, especially one made by digging: *Dig a pit and bury the rubbish in it.* | *a sand pit* | *a barbecue pit* **b)** a large hole in the ground from which stones or minerals have been dug: *a gravel pit*
**2 ▶ MARK ◀** [C] **a)** a small hollow mark in the surface of something: *There are tiny scratches and pits on the windshield.* **b)** a small hollow mark that is left on your face by some diseases, especially SMALLPOX
**3 ▶ MINE ◀** [C] a mine, especially a coal mine: *We have no choice but to close unprofitable pits.*
**4 ▶ UNTIDY PLACE ◀** [C] *spoken* a house or room that is dirty, untidy, or in bad condition: *No, we decided not to rent it – the place is an absolute pit!*
**5 be the pits** *usually spoken* used to say that something is extremely bad: *Rap music? That stuff is the pits!*
**6 in/at the pit of your stomach** if you feel nervous, frightened etc at the pit of your stomach, you experience these emotions strongly, often as an unpleasant feeling in your stomach: *a knot of fear in the pit of my stomach*
**7 ▶ CAR RACING ◀ the pit** *AmE*, **the pits** *BrE* the place beside the track in car RACES[1] (1) where cars can come in during a race to be quickly repaired
**8 ▶ IN A GARAGE ◀** [C] a hole in the floor of a garage that lets you get underneath a car to repair it
**9 ▶ IN FRUIT ◀** [C] *AmE* the single, large hard seed in some fruits; STONE[1] (4): *a peach pit*
**10 ▶ IN A THEATRE ◀** [C] **a)** an ORCHESTRA PIT **b)** *BrE old use* the seats at the back of the ground floor of a theatre
**11 the pit of despair/dismay/depression etc** *literary* a situation in which you feel extremely sad and without hope
**12 ▶ BUSINESS ◀** [C] *AmE* the area of a STOCK EXCHANGE where people buy and sell shares (SHARE[2] (5)); FLOOR[1] (8) *BrE*
**13 ▶ BODY PART ◀** [C] *AmE informal* an ARMPIT
**14 the pit** *biblical* HELL[1] (3): *cast into the pit of eternal damnation*

**pit²** *v past tense and past participle* **pitted 1 pit your wits against** to compete with someone or something in a situation in which you need all your intelligence: *Pit your wits against the Double or Dare computer!* **2** [T] *AmE* to take out the single, hard seed inside some fruits; STONE[1] (4) **3** [T usually passive] to put small marks or holes in the surface of something: *Heavy rain had pitted and blurred the trail.* —see also PITTED

**pit** sb/sth **against** sb/sth *phr v* [T] to test your strength, ability, power etc against someone else: *a chance to pit our strength against pro ball players*

**pit** sth ↔ **out** *phr v* [T] *AmE informal* to SWEAT so much that your clothes become wet under your arms

**pit·a bread** /ˈpɪtə bred‖ˈpiː-/ *n* [U] the American spelling of PITTA BREAD

**pit-a-pat** /ˈ· · ˌ·/ *adv informal* PITTER-PATTER —**pit-a-pat** *n* [singular]

**pit bull ter·ri·er** /ˌ· ·ˈ· · ·/ also **pit bull** /ˌ· ˈ·◂/ *n* [C] a small but extremely strong and sometimes violent fighting dog —see picture at DOG[1]

**pitch¹** /pɪtʃ/ *n* W3
**1 ▶ SPORTS FIELD ◀** [C] *BrE* a specially marked out area of ground on which a sport is played; FIELD[1] (4) *AmE*: *The crowd invaded the pitch at the end of the match.* | *a cricket pitch*
**2 ▶ STRONG FEELINGS ◀** [singular, U] the strength of your feelings or opinions about something: *Disagreement reached such a pitch that we thought a fight would break out.* | **at fever pitch** (=with a lot of excited feeling) *Speculation about the election was at fever pitch.*
**3 ▶ MUSIC ◀ a)** the highness or lowness of a musical note —see also PERFECT PITCH **b)** the ability of a musician to play or sing a note at exactly the correct pitch: *She's got good pitch.*
**4 ▶ SELLING ◀** [C] *informal* what a sales person says about a product to persuade people to buy it; SALES PITCH
**5 ▶ BASEBALL ◀** [C] a throw of the ball, or a way in which it can be thrown: *His first pitch went wide.*
**6 ▶ BLACK SUBSTANCE ◀** [U] a black, sticky substance that is used on roofs, the bottoms of ships etc to stop water coming through: **as black as pitch** (=very dark) —see also PITCH-BLACK, PITCH-DARK
**7 ▶ SHIP/AIRCRAFT ◀** [C] a backward and forward movement of a ship or an aircraft —compare ROLL[2] (4)
**8 ▶ SLOPE ◀** [singular, U] the degree to which a roof slopes
**9 ▶ STREET/MARKET ◀** [C] *BrE* a place in a public area where a street trader or entertainer goes to sell things or perform —see also **queer sb's pitch** (QUEER[3])

**pitch²** *v*
**1 ▶ THROW ◀** [T] to throw something with a lot of force, often aiming carefully: *Men slouched on the corner, pitching pennies.* | **pitch sth over/into/through etc** *Fran screwed up the letter and pitched it into the fire.*
**2 ▶ BALL GAMES ◀ a)** [I,T] to aim and throw a ball in BASEBALL —see picture on page 1263 **b)** [I] if a ball pitches in CRICKET or GOLF, it hits the ground **c)** [T] to hit the ball in a high curve in golf **d)** [T] to make the ball hit the ground when you are bowling (BOWL[2] (2)) in cricket
**3 ▶ FALL ◀** [I always + adv/prep, T always + adv/prep] to fall suddenly and heavily in a particular direction, or to make someone or something fall in this way: **pitch forward/backward/over etc** *Jim pitched forward as the train jerked to a halt.*
**4 ▶ SHIP/AIRCRAFT ◀** [I] if a ship or an aircraft pitches, it moves along with the back and front going up and down: *The old frigate pitched violently on the massive waves.* —compare ROLL[2] (4), YAW
**5 ▶ SET A LEVEL ◀** [T always + adv/prep] **a)** if you pitch an examination, explanation, speech etc at a particular level of difficulty, you make sure that it can be understood by people at that level: *Pitch the test at your average students' level of ability.* | *They're a young audience, so don't pitch it too high.* **b)** to set prices at a particular level: *Prices for the new hatchbacks are pitched very competitively.*
**6 ▶ MUSIC ◀** [T always + adv/prep] if you pitch your voice or another sound at a particular level, the sound is produced at that level: **pitch sth high/low etc** *This song is pitched too high for my voice.* —see also HIGH-PITCHED, LOW-PITCHED
**7 pitch camp/pitch a tent** to set up a tent or a camp for a short time: *We pitched our tents beside a stream.*
**8 ▶ BUSINESS DEALS ◀** [I,T] *informal, especially AmE* to try to make a business agreement, or to sell something by saying how good it is: *sales reps pitching the latest gadgets* | [+ **for**] *Jack's trying to pitch for a deal.*
**9 ▶ SLOPE ◀** [I always + adv/prep] to slope downwards: **pitch gently/steeply etc** *The roof pitches sharply to the rear of the house.* —see also PITCHED

**10 pitch sb a line/yarn** *AmE informal* to tell someone a story or give them an excuse that is difficult to believe: *She pitched me some yarn about a bomb scare on the metro.*

**pitch in** *phr v* [I] *informal* **1** to start to work eagerly as a member of a group: *If we all pitch in, we'll have it finished in no time.* **2** to add your help or support: **pitch in with sth** *The local council pitched in with the offer of a free van.* **3** to start to eat hungrily: *Pitch in – there's plenty for everyone.*

**pitch into** sb *phr v* [T] *spoken* to attack someone by hitting them or insulting them

**pitch up** *phr v* [I] *BrE spoken* to arrive somewhere; TURN UP: *Guess who just pitched up on Saturday night?*

**pitch-and-putt** /ˌ· · ˈ·/ *n* [U] *BrE* a game of GOLF played on a very small course

**pitch-black** /ˌ· ˈ·◂/ *adj* completely black or dark: *Night in the city is never pitch-black.*

**pitch·blende** /ˈpɪtʃblend/ *n* [U] a dark shiny substance dug from the earth, from which URANIUM and RADIUM are obtained

**pitch-dark** /ˌ· ˈ·◂/ *adj* completely dark

**pitched** /pɪtʃt/ *adj* a roof that is pitched is sloping rather than flat

**pitched bat·tle** /ˌ· ˈ··/ *n* [C] **1** an angry and usually long quarrel or argument: *We had a pitched battle with the council before they'd agree to repair the road.* **2** a battle between armies who have already chosen and prepared their positions —compare SKIRMISH[1] (1)

**pitch·er** /ˈpɪtʃə‖-ər/ *n* [C] **1** *AmE or BrE old-fashioned* a container for holding and pouring liquids with a handle and a SPOUT (=shaped part for pouring); JUG[1] (1): *a pitcher of water* —see picture at JUG[1] **2** *BrE* a large container for holding and pouring liquids, usually made of clay, with two handles **3** the player in BASEBALL who throws the ball —see picture on page 1263

**pitch·fork¹** /ˈpɪtʃfɔːk‖-fɔːrk/ *n* [C] an old-fashioned farm tool with a long handle and two long curved metal points, used especially for lifting HAY (=dried cut grass) —see picture at FORK[1]

**pitchfork²** *v* [T + **into/in/onto**] to put someone suddenly into a situation for which they are not properly prepared: *She was pitchforked into this predicament by her husband's early death.*

**pitch·out** /ˈpɪtʃaʊt/ *n* [C] a ball in BASEBALL that the PITCHER deliberately throws too far to the side for it to be hit

**pitch pine** /ˈ· ·/ *n* [C, U] a type of PINETREE that grows in North America, or the wood from this tree

**pit·e·ous** /ˈpɪtiəs/ *adj especially literary* expressing suffering and sadness in a way that makes you feel pity: *piteous sobs* —**piteously** *adv*

**pit·fall** /ˈpɪtfɔːl‖-fɒːl/ *n* [C] a problem or difficulty that is likely to happen in a particular job, course of action, or activity: *English spelling presents many pitfalls for foreign learners.* | **avoid a pitfall** *This little booklet will help you avoid the more obvious pitfalls of travelling alone.*

**pith** /pɪθ/ *n* [U] **1** a white substance just under the outside skin of oranges and similar fruit **2** a soft white substance that fills the stems of some plants **3 the pith of an argument/issue etc** the most important and necessary part of an argument etc

**pit·head** /ˈpɪt-hed/ *n* [C] the entrance to a coal mine and the buildings around it

**pith hel·met** /ˌ· ˈ··/ *n* [C] a large light hat worn especially in the past in hot countries, to protect your head from the sun; TOPEE —see picture at HELMET

**pith·y** /ˈpɪθi/ *adj* **pithy comments/saying/advice etc** strongly and cleverly stated, without wasting any words —**pithily** *adv* —**pithiness** *n* [U]

**pit·i·a·ble** /ˈpɪtiəbəl/ *adj formal* making you feel pity: *refugees living in pitiable conditions* —**pitiably** *adv*

**pit·i·ful** /ˈpɪtɪfəl/ *adj* **1** someone or something that is pitiful looks so sad and unfortunate that you feel very sorry for them: *The animals were a pitiful sight, in their small cages.* **2** not good enough to deserve respect or serious consideration: *You don't expect me to believe that pitiful excuse.* —**pitifully** *adv*: *pitifully thin*

**pit·i·less** /ˈpɪtɪləs/ *adj* **1** showing no pity; cruel: *a pitiless tyrant* **2** pitiless wind, rain, sun etc is very severe and shows no sign of changing: *the pitiless desert sun* —**pitilessly** *adv* —**pitilessness** *n* [U]

**pi·ton** /ˈpiːtɒn‖-tɑːn/ *n* [C] a piece of metal used in climbing, that you fix into the rock to hold the rope

**pit po·ny** /ˈ· ˌ··/ *n* [C] a small horse that was used in the past for moving coal in a mine

**pit prop** /ˈ· ·/ *n* [C] a support for the roof of an underground passage in a coal mine

**pit stop** /ˈ· ·/ *n* [C] **1** a time when you stop in the pits (PIT[1] (7)) during a car race to get more petrol or have repairs done **2 make a pit stop** *AmE informal* to stop when driving on a long journey, for food, petrol etc

**pit·ta bread** *BrE*, **pita bread** *AmE* /ˈpɪtə bred‖ˈpiːtə-/ *n* [C,U] a type of bread which is flat and hollow

**pit·tance** /ˈpɪtəns/ *n* [singular] a very small or unfairly small amount of money: *She gets paid a pittance.*

**pit·ted** /ˈpɪtɪd/ *adj* **1** having small marks or holes in the surface: *His skin was pitted like orange peel.* | [+ **with**] *The cylinders were pitted with corrosion.* **2** a pitted fruit has had the single, hard seed removed from it: *pitted cherries* | *pitted olives*

**pit·ter-pat·ter** /ˈpɪtə ˌpætə‖ˈpɪtər ˌpætər/ *adv* **go pitter-patter** to make a sound consisting of many quick light beats or sounds: *Anna's heart went pitter-patter as she opened the letter.* —**pitter-patter** *n* [singular] *the pitter-patter of rain on the roof*

**pi·tu·i·ta·ry** /pɪˈtjuːɪtəri‖pɪˈtuːɪteri/ also **pituitary gland** /·ˈ···· ˌ·/ *n* [C] the small organ at the base of your brain which produces HORMONES that control the growth and development of your body —**pituitary** *adj*

**pit·y¹** /ˈpɪti/ *n* **1 (it's a) pity** *spoken* used to show that you are disappointed about something and you wish things could have happened differently: [+ **(that)**] *Ralph's a really nice guy – pity he's not better looking.* | *It's a pity that Jan and George can't make it to the party.* | *Pity they didn't think of that earlier.* | **a pity to do sth** *It seems a pity to waste it.* | **what a pity** *"Did you know the concert was cancelled?" "No, what a pity."* | **a great pity** *There were very few locals at the meeting, which is a great pity.* **2** [U] sympathy for someone who is suffering or unhappy: *London's homeless need more than pity – they need practical help.* | *Poor man, she thought with pity, he's given up.* **3 for pity's sake** *spoken* used to show that you are very annoyed and impatient: *For pity's sake just shut up and let me drive!* **4 take pity on** to feel sorry for someone and do something to help them: *We walked on through the pouring rain until a kind driver took pity on us.* **5 more's the pity** *spoken* used after describing a situation, to show that you wish it was not true: *The new staff are all women, more's the pity.* **6 have pity on** *formal* to forgive someone or treat them sympathetically S3

**pity²** *v* [T not usually in progressive] to feel sorry for someone because they are in a very bad situation: *I pity anyone who has to feed a family on such a low income.* | *I pity Sophie having to live with that awful woman.*

**piv·ot¹** /ˈpɪvət/ *n* [C] **1** a fixed central point or pin on which something balances or turns **2** the one central thing that a whole plan depends on, and that everything is arranged around: [+ **of**] *The village chapel was the pivot of community life.*

**pivot²** *v* **1** [I,T] to turn or balance on a central point, or to make something do this: [+ **on**] *The table-top pivots on two metal pins.* **2** [I] to turn quickly on your feet so that you face in the opposite direction

**pivot on** sth *phr v* [T] to depend on or be planned around a particular event, or to have a particular idea as the central one: *This meeting with the board is crucial – our entire project pivots on it.*

**piv·ot·al** /ˈpɪvətəl/ *adj* **1 a pivotal event/role/moment etc** an event etc that has a very important effect on the way something develops: *Mandela's release was a pivotal event in South Africa's history.* | *The Small Business Act had a pivotal role in job creation.* **2** like or being a pivot: *a pivotal movement*

**pix** /pɪks/ *n* [plural] *slang* pictures or photographs

**pix·el** /ˈpɪksəl/ *n* [C] *technical* the smallest unit of an image on a computer SCREEN[1] (1)

**pix·ie, pixy** /ˈpɪksi/ *n* [C] an imaginary creature that looks like a very small human being, has magical powers, and likes to play tricks on people

S2 **piz·za** /ˈpiːtsə/ *n* [C,U] a thin flat round bread, baked with tomato, cheese, and sometimes vegetables or meat on top

**pizza par·lor** /ˈ·· ˌ··/ *n* [C] *AmE* a restaurant that serves pizza; PIZZERIA

**piz·zazz** /pəˈzæz/ *n* [U] *informal* an exciting strong quality or style: *This song and dance show needs more pizzazz.*

**piz·ze·ri·a** /ˌpiːtsəˈriːə/ *n* [C] a restaurant that serves pizza

**piz·zi·ca·to** /ˌpɪtsɪˈkɑːtəʊ‖-toʊ/ *n* [U] musical notes played by pulling on the strings (STRING[1] (4a)) of an instrument

**pj's** /ˌpiː ˈdʒeɪz/ *n* [plural] *AmE informal* PYJAMAS

**Pk** the written abbreviation of PARK

**pkt** the written abbreviation of PACKET

**Pl** the written abbreviation of PLACE

**pl** the written abbreviation of PLURAL

**plac·ard** /ˈplækɑːd‖-ərd/ *n* [C] a large notice or advertisement put up or carried in a public place: *The demonstrators carried placards attacking the government.*

**pla·cate** /pləˈkeɪt‖ˈpleɪkeɪt/ *v* [T] *formal* to make someone stop feeling angry; APPEASE: *I tried to placate her by offering to pay for the repairs.* —**placatory** /pləˈkeɪtəri, ˈplækətəri‖ˈpleɪkətɔːri/ *adv*: *placatory words* —**placation** /pləˈkeɪʃən/ *n* [U]

S1 W1 **place[1]** /pleɪs/ *n* [C]

① PLACE, POSITION, OR AREA
② TAKE PLACE
③ IN PLACE
④ FIRST/SECOND PLACE
⑤ OTHER MEANINGS

**place**

There are two places at the back.
There's still some room at the back.

### ① PLACE, POSITION, OR AREA

**1 ▶POINT/POSITION◀ a)** any area, point, or position in space: *This is the place where the accident happened.|Make sure you keep it in a safe place.|We kept moving from place to place.|The whole place was covered in dust.* **b)** a particular point in a larger area: *a sore place on my shoulder|There's a place on the wall where the paint's coming off.* —see POSITION (USAGE) —see graph at LOCATION

**2 ▶PLACE FOR DOING STH◀** a place that is used for, or is suitable for, a particular purpose or activity: **place to live/eat/park etc** *What they need is a decent place to live.|I couldn't find a place to park.|* **place for** *It's a great place for a vacation.|* **sth's place** (=where something is usually kept) *Put it back in its place when you've finished with it.*

**3 ▶BUILDING/TOWN/COUNTRY ETC◀** a particular place such as a shop, factory, town, or country: *They've just bought a little place in Wales.|We were living then in a place called Alberiga.|I got it at that big furniture place on the ring road.|a nice Korean place* (=restaurant) *on the corner*

**4 ▶SB'S HOUSE◀ your place/my place etc** *informal* the house, apartment, or room where you live, I live etc: *Do you want to come back to our place for coffee?*

**5 be no place for** to be a completely unsuitable place: *A damp bedsit was no place for a baby.*

**6 place of work** *formal* a factory, office etc where you work

**7 place of worship** *formal* a building such as a church, where people have religious ceremonies

### ② TAKE PLACE

**8 take place** to happen, especially after being planned or arranged: *The next meeting will take place on Thursday.|the changes taking place in Indian society*

**9 take the place of** to exist or be used instead of someone or something else; REPLACE: *Electric trains have now taken the place of steam ones.|No-one could take the place of her mother.*

**10 take second place to** to be less important than someone or something else: *Our personal wishes must take second place to the needs of the children.*

**11 take your place a)** to go to a particular position that you need to be in for an activity: *Take your places for the next dance.* **b)** to join, and form an important part of, a group of people or things: *This new work will take its place among the most important paintings of the century.*

### ③ IN PLACE

**12 in place** in the correct or usual position: *Have you got all the lights in place yet?*

**13 in place of** instead of: *In place of our advertised programme, we will be showing a film.*

**14 in sb's place a)** if you do something in someone's place, you do it because they were supposed to but could not: *Jane was ill, so I went to the conference in her place.* **b)** *spoken* used when talking about what you would do if you were in someone else's situation: *What would you do in my place?*

**15 in places** in some parts or areas, but not everywhere: *In places, there was even mould on the walls.*

### ④ FIRST/SECOND PLACE

**16 first/second/third etc place** first, second etc position in a race or competition: *I finished in fifth place.*

**17 in the first place a)** used to introduce a series of points in an argument, discussion etc: *Well, in the first place, I can't afford it, and in the second place I'm not really interested.* **b)** *spoken* used when talking about what was done, or should have been done, at the start of a situation: *I should never have gone in the first place!*

### ⑤ OTHER MEANINGS

**18 ▶AT COLLEGE ETC◀** an opportunity to take part in a course, activity, event etc: *He's been offered a place at York University.|There are only two places left on the word-processing course.*

**19 ▶ AVAILABLE SPACE ◀** a seat on a bus, room in a hotel etc that is available for someone to use: *There are still a few places left on the coach.*
**20 all over the place** *informal* **a)** everywhere: *There were policemen all over the place.* **b)** in a very untidy state: *Her hair was all over the place.*
**21 ▶ AT A TABLE ◀** a knife, fork, spoon, plate etc arranged on a table for one person to use: *Shall I lay places for five or for six?*
**22 put sb in their place** to show someone that they are not as clever or important as they think they are: *A few curt remarks from the chairperson soon put Bates in his place.*
**23 out of place a)** not suitable for a particular situation or occasion: *I felt completely out of place among all those smart rich people.* **b)** not in the correct or usual position: *Nothing was ever out of place in Kitty's house.*
**24 not your place** if it is not your place to do something, it is not your responsibility to do it, especially because you do not have enough power: *It's not my place to tell the directors what to do!*
**25 lose your place** to not know what point you had reached in a book, speech etc: *The lecturer seemed to have lost his place.*
**26 save/keep sb a place** to make sure that people do not sit in a particular chair that you want to save for someone else: *I might arrive a bit late, so could you save me a place?*
**27 have no place** *formal* to be completely unacceptable: *People with racist views have no place in this union.*
**28 fall into place a)** if things fall into place in your mind, you suddenly realize and understand what is really happening: *When I found out who he was, everything suddenly fell into place.* **b)** if plans or events fall into place, they start to happen in the way that you hoped they would: *Eventually I got a job, moved house, and my life began to fall into place.*
**29 be going places** *informal* to start becoming successful in your life: *He's really going places as an actor.*
**30 know your place** *often humorous* to behave in a way that shows that you know which people are more important than you: *I'll get back to the kitchen then – I know my place!* —see also DECIMAL PLACE, **have/take pride of place** (PRIDE[1] (6))

**USAGE NOTE: PLACE**

WORD CHOICE: **room, space, place, somewhere, anywhere**

The uncountable nouns **room** and **space** can both mean an empty area that can be used for any purpose: *Is there (any) room/space for me/us to sit down in here?| Is there room/space for more books on this shelf?| There's not enough room/space to move in here!*

**A place** or **a space** [C] is a single piece of space that can be used for something. However, **a place** in this sense often has a planned or official purpose, while **a space** may be unplanned and smaller: *I need a place to work* (= an office, a study, or desk). | *I need a space to work* (= a part of a room or table). You say *a public place* but usually *a parking space* (= for one car) and *an open/green space.*

In spoken English people often use **somewhere** or **anywhere**: *I can't find anywhere to park.| He's looking for somewhere to park his car.*

GRAMMAR

**Place** is singular, with the plural **places**: *I visited a lot of different places* (NOT *place*).

S3 **place**[2] *v*
W1 **1 ▶ POSITION ◀** [T always + adv/prep] to put something somewhere, especially with care: **place sth in/on/under etc** *He placed the book back on the shelf.| She had placed a tape recorder in front of her on the table.*
**2 ▶ SITUATION ◀** [T always + adv/prep] to put someone or something in a particular situation: *Her request places me in a very difficult position.*
**3 ▶ HOW IMPORTANT ◀** [T] to decide how good or important something is, as compared to something else: *Place the wines in order of preference.* | **place value/importance etc on sth** *The company places emphasis on training its staff.*
**4 ▶ IN A JOB ◀** [T] *formal* to find a suitable job for someone: *The agency had placed her with a local firm.*
**5 can't place sb** to be unable to remember why you recognize someone, what their name is etc: *I'm sure I've met that girl before somewhere, but I can't quite place her.*
**6 place a bet** to risk money by guessing the result of a future event
**7 place an order** to ask a shop or business to provide a product that you need: *We placed an order with Whiteley's for 200 shirts.*
**8 be placed to do sth/be placed for sth** to be in a situation where you have the ability or opportunity to do or have something: *You're better placed to arrange the meeting than I am.| How are you placed for money?* (=do you have enough money?)
**9 ▶ RACES ◀ a) be placed first/second etc** to be first, second etc in a race or competition **b)** [T] *BrE* if a horse is placed in a race, it comes second or third **c)** [I] *AmE* if a horse places in a race, it comes second

**pla·ce·bo** /plə'siːbəʊ‖-boʊ/ *n* [C] a substance given to a patient instead of medicine, without telling them it is not real, so that they get better because they think they are taking medicine: **placebo effect** (=the positive effect achieved by this)

**place card** /'· ·/ *n* [C] a small card with someone's name on it, put on a table to show where they are going to sit

**place kick** /'· ·/ *n* [C] a kick at a ball, especially in RUGBY or American football, when the ball is placed or held on the ground

**place mat** /'· ·/ *n* [C] a mat that you put on a table for each person who is eating there

**place·ment** /'pleɪsmənt/ *n* **1** [U] the act of finding a place for someone to live or work **2** [C] *especially BrE* a job, usually as part of a course of study, which gives you experience of a particular type of work **3** [C,U] the act of placing something in position

**pla·cen·ta** /plə'sentə/ *n* [C] a thick mass of flesh that joins an unborn child to its mother in the WOMB

**place set·ting** /'· ,··/ *n* [C] an arrangement of knives, forks, spoons, glasses etc to be used by one person

**plac·id** /'plæsɪ̈d/ *adj* **1** a placid person or animal does not easily get angry or excited: *He had a placid nature, well-suited to teaching.* **2** calm and peaceful: *The lake was placid and still under the moonlight.* —**placidly** *adv*: *Dobbs stood at the entrance, placidly smoking his pipe.* —**placidity** /plə'sɪdɪ̈ti/ *n* [U]

**pla·gia·ris·m** /'pleɪdʒərɪzəm/ *n* **1** [U] the act of using someone else's words, ideas, or work and pretending they are your own: *He was accused of plagiarism in his doctoral thesis.* **2** [C] an idea, phrase, story etc that has been copied from someone else's work, without stating that this is where it came from: *an article full of plagiarisms* —**plagiarist** *n* [C]

**pla·gia·rize** also **-ise** *BrE* /'pleɪdʒəraɪz/ *v* [I,T] to take words, ideas etc from someone else's work and use them in your work, as if they were your own ideas: *Half the ideas in his talk were plagiarized from an article I wrote last year.*

**plague**[1] /pleɪg/ *n* **1** [C,U] an attack of a disease that causes death and spreads quickly to a large number of people: *Europe suffered many plagues in the Middle Ages.* **2** [U] also **the plague** a very infectious disease that produces high fever and swellings on the body, and often leads to death, especially BUBONIC PLAGUE: *an outbreak of plague* —see also BLACK DEATH **3 a plague of rats/locusts etc** an uncontrollable and harmful increase in the numbers of a particular animal or insect **4 a plague on** *literary* used to show that you are extremely annoyed with someone or something —see also **avoid sb/sth like the plague** (AVOID (2))

**plague²** *v* [T usually passive] **1** to cause continual discomfort, suffering, or trouble to someone: *Nick was plagued by ill health throughout his short life.* | *street crime, riots, and other social problems plaguing our community* **2** [T] to annoy someone, especially by continually asking them for something: **plague sb with sth** *The kids have been plaguing me with questions.*

**P**

**plaice** /pleɪs/ *n plural* **plaice** [C,U] a flat sea fish that is a popular food

**plaid** /plæd/ **1** [U] thick cloth with a pattern of squares, especially of a type (TARTAN) originally from Scotland —see picture on page 839 **2** [C] a piece of plaid worn over the shoulder and across the chest by people from Scotland as part of their NATIONAL COSTUME

S2 W3 **plain¹** /pleɪn/ *adj*

**1 ► CLEAR ◄** very clear, and easy to understand or recognize; OBVIOUS (1): *He spoke in Russian, but his message was plain enough.* | **it is plain (that)** *It was plain that management policies would have to change.* | **as plain as day/as plain as the nose on your face** (=very clear) *Phil loves her – that's as plain as day.*

**2 ► SIMPLE ◄** without anything added or without decoration; simple: *a plain white blouse* | *It's just a plain wooden table but it looks just right in this room.* | *plain food* | *a plain gold wedding ring* —see picture on page 839

**3 ► HONEST ◄** showing clearly and honestly what you think about something, without trying to hide anything; FRANK¹ (1): *Let's have some plain, truthful answers.*

**4 make sth plain/make yourself plain** to state something very clearly, in a way that cannot be misunderstood: *They made their position plain from the start.* | *Let me make myself plain – we are not prepared to accept the deal as it stands.* —see also PLAINLY

**5 the plain truth/fact is** *especially spoken* used to say what you think is the simple and honest truth about a situation: *The plain truth is he's just not good enough.*

**6 plain stupidity/greed etc** stupidity etc, and nothing else: *His motive was plain greed.*

**7 ► NOT BEAUTIFUL ◄** a word meaning ugly or unattractive, often used because you want to avoid saying this directly: *Mrs Cookson was a rather plain woman.*

**8 ► PAPER ◄** plain paper does not have lines on it

**9 (just) plain Mr/Mrs etc** used to say that someone does not have a title, rank, or special name: *No, it's not Doctor, just plain Mister.*

**10 in plain English** simply or clearly expressed, especially without using technical language: *The computer system is explained in plain English.*

**11 in plain clothes** police officers in plain clothes are not wearing uniform

**12 be plain sailing** to be very easy to do or achieve —**plainness** *n* [U]

**plain²** *n* **1** also **plains** [C] a large area of flat dry land: *The grassy plain gave way to an extensive swamp.* | *the vast plains of central China* **2** [U] the ordinary stitch in knitting; KNIT (2)

**plain³** *adv* **plain stupid/wrong/rude etc** *informal* simply or completely stupid etc: *It's just plain crazy to spend all your pay as soon as you get it.*

**plain·chant** /ˈpleɪntʃɑːnt‖-tʃænt/ *n* [U] PLAINSONG

**plain choc·olate** /ˌ· ˈ··‖ˌ· ˈ···/ *n* [U] *BrE* chocolate made without milk and with very little sugar; DARK CHOCOLATE *AmE*

**plain-clothes** /ˌ· ˈ·◄/ *adj* plain-clothes police are police who wear ordinary clothes so that they can work without being recognised: *plain-clothes detectives*

**plain flour** /ˌ· ˈ·/ *n* [U] *BrE* flour that contains no BAKING POWDER: *sift 6 oz plain flour* —compare SELF-RAISING FLOUR

**plain·ly** /ˈpleɪnli/ *adv* **1** in a way that is easy to hear, see etc: *We could hear Tom's voice plainly over the noise of the crowd.* | *The mountains were plainly visible from our window.* **2** speaking honestly, and without trying to hide the truth: *She told him plainly that she had no intention of marrying him.* **3** if something is plainly true, necessary, correct etc it is easy to see that it is true etc; OBVIOUSLY [sentence adverb]: *Plainly an investigation into the tragedy would be necessary.* **4** simply or without decoration: *a plainly dressed young girl*

**plain sail·ing** /ˌ· ˈ··/ *n* [U] **be plain sailing** to be easy and not cause any trouble

**plain·song** /ˈpleɪnsɒŋ‖-sɔːŋ/ *n* [U] a type of old Christian church music in which a group of people sing a simple tune together, without musical instruments

**plain·spo·ken** /ˌpleɪnˈspəʊkən◄‖-ˈspoʊ-/ *adj* saying exactly what you think, especially in a way that people think is honest rather than rude

**plain·tiff** /ˈpleɪntɪf/ *n* [C] someone who brings a legal action against someone in a court of law; COMPLAINANT W

**plain·tive** /ˈpleɪntɪv/ *adj* a plaintive sound is high, like someone crying, and sounds sad: *the plaintive cry of the seagull* —**plaintively** *adv*

**plait¹** /plæt‖pleɪt/ *v* [T] *BrE* to twist 3 long pieces of hair, rope etc over and under each other to make one long piece; BRAID² *AmE*: *a plaited leather belt* | *She plaited her hair hurriedly.* —see picture at HAIRSTYLE

**plait²** *n* [C] *BrE* a length of something, especially hair, made by plaiting; BRAID¹ (2) *AmE*: *Jenni wore her hair in plaits.*

**plan¹** /plæn/ *n* [C] S W

**1 ► INTENTION ◄** something you have decided to do or achieve: *His plan is to get a degree in economics and then work abroad for a year.* | **sb's best plan** *BrE* (=the best course of action) *Your best plan would be to catch a taxi – it's much too far to walk.* | **change your plans/a change of plan** *There's been a change of plan – we're going on Monday instead.* | **have plans (for)** (=intend to do something) *We don't have any plans for the weekend – why don't you come over?* | **make plans (for)** (=prepare for something that you intend to do) *Julia's been busy making plans for her wedding.*

**2 ► METHOD/ARRANGEMENT ◄** a set of actions for achieving something in the future, especially one that has been considered carefully and in detail: *the government's five-year economic plan* | **plan for** *NASA announced plans for a new space station to be launched in 1998.* | **plan to do sth** *Have you heard about the plan to build a new science park?* | **keep to/stick to a plan** *If we keep to the plan the work should be completed in two weeks.* | **work out/draw up/devise a plan** *They devised a plan to reduce costs.* | **a plan falls through** (=it becomes impossible because something unexpected happens) | **go according to plan** (=happen in the way that was expected or arranged) *If everything goes according to plan the first stage will be completed by December.*

**3 ► MAP ◄** a drawing similar to a map, showing roads, towns, and buildings: *a street-plan of London*

**4 ► DRAWING ◄ a)** *technical* a drawing of a building, room, or machine as it would be seen from above, showing the shape, measurements, position of the walls etc —compare ELEVATION (4), SECTION¹ (6) —see also GROUND PLAN (1) **b)** a drawing that shows exactly how something will be arranged: *I have to organise a seating plan for the dinner.*

**5 plan of action/campaign** a series of actions that you plan to carry out in order to achieve a particular thing: *Get your team around a table and agree a plan of action to reach this season's targets.*

**6 Plan A** your first plan, which you will use if things happen as you expect

**7 Plan B** your second plan, which you can use if things do not happen as you expect

S1 W1 **plan²** *v* **planned, planning** **1** [I,T] to think carefully about something you want to do in the future, and decide exactly how you will do it: *We've been planning this visit for months – you can't cancel now.*| *The whole operation went exactly as planned.*|[+ **on**] *We hadn't planned on having so many guests – we'll never have enough food for them all!*| **plan ahead** (=make plans for a long time in the future) *Now that you're pregnant, you'll have to plan ahead.* **2** [T] to intend to do something, especially when you have definite plans for how you will do it: **plan to do sth** *Josie planned to work until she had saved enough money to go to nursing school.* **3** [T] to think about something you are going to make, and decide what it will be like; DESIGN²: *Planning a small garden is often difficult.*

**plan** sth ↔ **out** *phr v* [T] to plan something carefully, considering all the possible problems: *I'll get the maps so we can plan out our route.*

S2 W3 **plane¹** /pleɪn/ *n* [C]
**1** ▶ **AIRCRAFT** ◀ a vehicle that flies in the air and has wings and at least one engine; AEROPLANE *BrE*, AIRPLANE *AmE*: *The next plane to New York departs in 20 minutes.*| *It's quicker to go by plane.*
**2** ▶ **LEVEL** ◀ a level or standard of thought, conversation etc: *You can't really compare the two newspapers – they're on completely different intellectual planes.*
**3** ▶ **TOOL** ◀ a tool that has a flat bottom with a sharp blade in it, used for making wooden surfaces smooth —see picture at TOOL¹
**4** ▶ **TREE** ◀ a PLANE TREE
**5** ▶ **SURFACE** ◀ *technical* a completely flat surface in GEOMETRY

**plane²** *adj* [only before noun] *technical* completely flat and smooth: *a plane surface*

**plane³** *v* [T] to use a PLANE¹ (3) on a piece of wood to make it smooth: *He planed the edge of the door.*

**plane ge·om·e·try** /ˌ· ·ˌ···/ *n* [U] the study of lines, shapes etc that are TWO-DIMENSIONAL (=with measurements in only two directions, not three)

**plan·er** /ˈpleɪnə‖-ər/ *n* [C] an electric tool for making wooden surfaces smooth —see picture at TOOL¹

**plan·et** /ˈplænɪ̣t/ *n* [C] **1** a very large round object in space that moves around the sun or another star; Earth is a planet: *Mercury is the smallest of all the planets.*| *Is there life on other planets?*| *Planet Earth* **2 be (living) on another planet/what planet is sb on?** *spoken* humorous expressions used to say that someone's ideas are not at all practical or sensible **3 the planet** an expression meaning the world, used when talking about the environment: *the future of the planet* —**planetary** *adj*

**plan·e·tar·i·um** /ˌplænɪ̣ˈteəriəm‖-ˈter-/ *n* [C] a building where lights on a curved ceiling show the movements of planets and stars

**plane tree** /ˈ· ·/ *n* [C] a large tree with broad leaves that is often planted along streets; PLANE¹ (4)

**plan·gent** /ˈplændʒənt/ *adj literary* a plangent sound is loud and deep and sounds sad —**plangently** *adv* —**plangency** *n* [U]

**plank** /plæŋk/ *n* [C] **1** a long narrow, usually heavy piece of wooden board, used especially for making structures to walk on: *a small bridge made of planks* **2 plank of an argument/agenda/programme etc** one of the main features or principles of an argument etc: *The main plank of their election strategy is to reduce taxes on business.* —see also **walk the plank** (WALK¹ (12))

**plank·ing** /ˈplæŋkɪŋ/ *n* [U] planks when they are put together to make a floor

**plank·ton** /ˈplæŋktən/ *n* [U] the very small forms of plant and animal life that live in water, especially the sea, and are eaten by fish

**planned ob·so·les·cence** /ˌ· ··ˈ··/ *n* [U] the practice of making products that will soon become unfashionable or less advanced than the newest ones, so that people will have to buy new ones more often

**plan·ner** /ˈplænə‖-ər/ *n* [C] someone who plans something, especially someone whose job is to plan the way towns grow and develop

**planning per·mis·sion** /ˈ·· ·ˌ··/ *n* [U] official permission to build a new building or change an existing one

**plant¹** /plɑːnt‖plænt/ *n* S2 W1
**1** ▶ **LIVING THING** ◀ [C] a living thing that has leaves and roots and grows in earth, especially one that is smaller than a tree: *Don't forget to water the plants.*| *a potato plant*| *plant pots* —see also HOUSEPLANT
**2** ▶ **FACTORY** ◀ [C] a factory or building where an industrial process happens: *a huge chemical plant* —see also POWER PLANT

**3** ▶ **MACHINERY** ◀ [U] *BrE* heavy machinery that is used in industrial processes: *We are investing in new plant for the factory.*| *a plant hire business*
**4** ▶ **STH ILLEGAL** ◀ [C usually singular] something illegal or stolen that is hidden in someone's clothes or possessions to make them seem guilty
**5** ▶ **PERSON** ◀ [C] someone who is put somewhere or sent somewhere secretly to find out information

**plant²** *v* [T]
**1** ▶ **PLANTS/SEEDS** ◀ to put plants or seeds in the ground to grow: *to plant a tree*| *We've planted tomatoes and carrots in the garden.*
**2 plant a field/garden/area etc (with sth)** to plant seeds, plants, or trees in a field etc: *a hillside planted with fir trees*
**3** ▶ **PUT STH SOMEWHERE** ◀ [always + adv/prep] *informal* to put something firmly in or on something else: **plant sth in/on etc** *My grandmother planted a big wet kiss on my cheek.*| *She planted her feet firmly to the spot and refused to move.*
**4** ▶ **ILLEGAL GOODS** ◀ *informal* to hide stolen or illegal goods in someone's clothes, bags, room etc in order to make them seem guilty: **plant sth on sb** *Someone must have planted the drugs on her.*
**5 plant a bomb** *informal* to put a bomb somewhere: *Two men are accused of planting a bomb on the plane.*
**6** ▶ **PERSON** ◀ [T] to put or send someone somewhere, especially secretly, so that they can find out information: **plant sb in/at etc** *The police had planted undercover detectives at every entrance.*
**7 plant an idea/doubt/suspicion (in sb's mind)** to make someone begin to believe an idea, especially so that they do not realize it was you who gave them the idea

**plant** sth ↔ **out** *phr v* [T] to put a young plant into the soil outdoors, so that it has enough room to grow

**plan·tain** /ˈplæntɪ̣n/ *n* **1** [C,U] a kind of BANANA that is cooked before it is eaten, or the plant on which it grows —see picture on page 413 **2** [C] a common wild plant with small green flowers and wide leaves

**plan·ta·tion** /plænˈteɪʃən, plɑːn-‖plæn-/ *n* [C] **1** a large area of land in a hot country, where crops such as tea, cotton, and sugar etc are grown: *a rubber plantation* **2** a large group of trees grown to produce wood

**plant·er** /ˈplɑːntə‖ˈplæntər/ *n* [C] **1** a decorative container for growing plants in **2** someone who owns or is in charge of a plantation: *a tea planter* **3** a machine used for planting

**plaque** /plɑːk, plæk‖plæk/ *n* **1** [C] a piece of flat metal or stone with writing on it that is fixed to a building and reminds people of an event or person connected with the place: *The mayor unveiled a special commemorative plaque.* **2** [U] a substance which forms on your teeth, which BACTERIA can live and breed in

**plas·ma** /ˈplæzmə/ *n* [U] **1** the yellowish liquid part of the blood that contains blood cells **2** the living substance inside a cell; PROTOPLASM **3** a gas at a very high temperature inside stars, in flashes of electricity etc

**plas·ter¹** /ˈplɑːstə‖ˈplæstər/ *n* **1** [U] a substance used to cover walls and ceilings and give a smooth surface, consisting of LIME, water, and sand **2** [U] PLASTER OF PARIS **3** [C,U] *BrE* a piece of thin material that is stuck on to the skin to cover cuts and other small wounds; BANDAID *AmE* **4 in plaster** *BrE* if you have a leg, arm

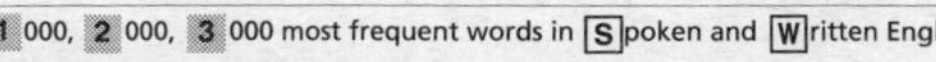
1 000, 2 000, 3 000 most frequent words in Spoken and Written English

etc in plaster you have a PLASTER CAST around a bone that is broken to keep it in place while it mends

**plaster²** *v* [T usually passive] **1** to spread or stick something all over a surface so that it is thickly covered: **plaster sth with sth** *Her face was plastered with make-up.* **2** to cover the pages of a newspaper with a particular story or report: *The news of the wedding was plastered all over the morning papers.* **3** to put wet plaster on a wall or ceiling **4** to make your hair lie flat or stick to your head: [+ **down/to etc**] *His hair was plastered to his forehead with sweat.*

**plaster** sth **over** *phr v* [T] to cover a hole or an old surface by spreading plaster over it

**plas·ter·board** /ˈplɑːstəbɔːd‖ˈplæstərbɔːrd/ *n* [U] board made of large sheets of cardboard held together with plaster, which is used to cover walls and ceilings

**plaster cast** /ˌ·· ˈ·, ˈ··· ·/ *n* [C] **1** a cover made from plaster of Paris used to keep a broken bone in place while it mends; CAST² (2) **2** a copy of a STATUE made of plaster of Paris

**plas·tered** /ˈplɑːstəd‖ˈplæstərd/ *adj* [never before noun] *informal* very drunk: *Chris was plastered after five beers.*

**plas·ter·er** /ˈplɑːstərə‖ˈplæstərər/ *n* [C] someone whose job is to cover walls and ceilings with PLASTER¹ (1)

**plaster of Par·is** /ˌplɑːstər əv ˈpærɪs‖ˌplæs-/ *n* [U] a quick-drying mixture of a white powder and water used for making plaster casts and to decorate buildings

S2 W2 **plas·tic¹** /ˈplæstɪk/ *n* **1** [C,U] a light strong material that is chemically produced, which can be made into different shapes when soft and is used to make many things: *children's toys made of plastic | the plastics industry* **2** [singular, U] *informal* small plastic cards that are used to pay for things instead of money; CREDIT CARDS: *"I haven't got any cash." "Don't worry, I'll stick it on the plastic."*

**plastic²** *adj* **1** made of plastic: *a plastic spoon | plastic bags* **2** *technical* a plastic substance can be formed into many different shapes and keeps the shape **3** something that is plastic looks or tastes artificial or unnatural: *plastic food | I hate that plastic smile of hers.*

**plastic art** /ˌ·· ˈ·/ *n* [C,U] *technical* art which shows things in ways in which they can be clearly seen, especially painting or SCULPTURE

**plastic bul·let** /ˌ·· ˈ··/ *n* [C] a large bullet made of hard plastic that is intended to injure but not kill, and is used for controlling violent crowds

**plastic ex·plo·sive** /ˌ·· ·ˈ··/ *n* [C,U] an explosive substance that can be shaped by hand, or a small bomb made from this

**plas·ti·cine** /ˈplæstɪsiːn/ *n* [U] *BrE trademark* a soft substance like clay made in many different colours, used by young children for making models or shapes

**plas·tic·i·ty** /plæˈstɪsɪti/ *n* [U] *technical* the quality of being easily made into any shape

**plastic mac** /ˌ·· ˈ·/ *n* [C] a cheap coat made of plastic, used to keep you dry in the rain

**plastic sur·ge·ry** /ˌ·· ˈ···/ *n* [U] the medical practice of changing the appearance of people's faces or bodies, either to improve their appearance or to repair injuries —**plastic surgeon** /ˌ·· ˈ··/ *n* [C]

**plastic wrap** /ˌ·· ˈ·/ *n* [U] *AmE* CLING FILM

**plat du jour** /ˌplɑː dʊ ˈʒʊə‖-ˈʒʊr/ *n* [C] *French* a dish that a restaurant prepares specially on a particular day in addition to its usual food

S2 W2 **plate¹** /pleɪt/ *n*

**1** ▶**FOOD**◀ **a)** [C] a flat and usually round dish that you eat from or serve food from: *The plates were piled high with rice. | a dinner plate |* **clear/empty your plate** (=eat everything on your plate) **b)** also **plateful** [C] the amount of food that is on a plate: [+ **of**] *He's eaten a whole plate of french fries.*

**2** ▶**SIGN**◀ **a)** [C] a flat piece of metal with words or numbers on it, for example on a door or a car: *The plate on the door said 'Dr Rackman'. | A plate below the statue indicated that it had been donated by the artist. |* **number/licence/registration plate** (=on a car) *Did anyone see the car's license plate?* —see also L-PLATE, NAMEPLATE **b) plates** [plural] the flat pieces of metal on a car which give information about who the car belongs to or which country it is from

**3 have a lot on your plate** *informal* to have a lot of problems to deal with or a lot of things to worry about

**4 hand sth to sb on a plate** *informal* to let someone have what they want without making them work to achieve it: *Liverpool virtually handed the game to United on a plate.*

**5** ▶**PROTECTIVE COVERING**◀ **a)** [C] *technical* one of the thin sheets of bone, horn etc that covers and protects the outside of an animal: *The reptile's body is covered with horny protective plates.* **b)** [C] a thin sheet of metal used to protect something: *steel plates used in the construction of ships*

**6** ▶**EARTH'S SURFACE**◀ [C] *technical* one of the very large sheets of rock that form the surface of the Earth —see also PLATE TECTONICS

**7** ▶**GOLD/SILVER ETC**◀ **a) gold/silver etc plate** ordinary metal with a thin covering of gold, silver etc **b)** [U] articles such as plates, cups, forks or knives made of gold or silver

**8** ▶**FOR COOKING**◀ [C] *especially BrE* a metal ring on an electric COOKER that you put pans on when cooking

**9** ▶**PICTURES/PHOTOS**◀ [C] **a)** a sheet of metal that has been cut or treated in some way so that words or pictures can be printed from its surface **b)** a picture in a book, printed on good-quality paper and usually coloured **c)** *technical* a thin sheet of glass used especially in the past in photography, with chemicals on it that are sensitive to light

**10** ▶**IN CHURCH**◀ **the plate** a small plate or container, used to collect money in a Christian church

**11** ▶**BASEBALL**◀ HOMEPLATE

**12** ▶**TEETH**◀ [C] **a)** a thin piece of plastic shaped to fit inside a person's mouth, into which false teeth are fixed **b)** a thin piece of plastic with wires fixed to it, that people wear to straighten their teeth; BRACE² (1)

**plate²** *v* [T] **be plated with a)** to be covered with a thin covering of gold, silver etc: *a beautiful necklace, plated with 22 carat gold |* **gold-plated/silver-plated** *a gold-plated bracelet* **b)** to be covered in sheets of a hard material such as metal or bone: *The ship had been heavily plated with protective sheets.*

**plat·eau** /ˈplætəʊ‖plæˈtoʊ/ *n plural* **plateaus** or **plateaux** /-təʊz‖-ˈtoʊz/ [C] **1** a large area of flat land that is higher than the land around it —see picture on page 835 **2** a period during which the level of cost, achievement etc does not change, especially after a period when it was increasing: *Inflation rates have reached a plateau. | learning plateaus among 14-year-olds*

**plate·ful** /ˈpleɪtfʊl/ *n* [C] all the food that is on a plate

**plate glass** /ˌ· ˈ·◂/ *n* [U] big pieces of glass made in large thick sheets for use especially in shop windows

**plate-lay·er** /ˈ· ˌ··/ *n* [C] *BrE* someone whose job is to make or repair railway tracks; TRACKLAYER *AmE*

**plate·let** /ˈpleɪtlɪt/ *n* [C] one of the very small plate-shaped cells in your blood that help it become solid when you bleed

**plate tec·ton·ics** /ˌ· ·ˈ··/ *n* [U] the study of the forming and movement of the large sheets of rock that lie under the surface of the Earth

**plat·form** /ˈplætfɔːm‖-fɔːrm/ *n* [C] W3

**1** ▶**TRAIN**◀ the raised place beside a railway track where you get on and off a train in a station: *The Edinburgh train will depart from platform six.*

**2** ▶**FOR SPEECHES**◀ a raised floor or stage for people to stand on when they are making a speech, performing etc: *He climbed on to the platform and began to address the crowd. | Please address your comments to the platform.* (=the people on the platform) | *a popular platform speaker*

**3** ▶**STRUCTURE**◀ a tall or high structure built so

that people can stand or work above the surrounding area: *an oil exploration platform*
**4 ▶ POLITICS ◀ a)** [usually singular] the main ideas and aims of a political party, especially the ones that they state just before an election: *He's running for mayor on a platform of low taxation.* —see also PLANK (2) **b)** a chance for someone to express their opinions, especially their political opinions: *The conference provides a platform for people on the left wing of the party.*
**5 ▶ BUS ◀** *BrE* the open part at the back of a DOUBLE-DECKER bus, where passengers get on and off the bus
**6 ▶ SHOES ◀** also **platform shoe** a shoe that has a thick layer of wood, leather etc underneath the front part and the heel
**7 ▶ COMPUTERS ◀** used to describe the type of computer system or SOFTWARE that you are using: *We're changing from an IBM to a Macintosh platform.*

**plat·form game** /ˈ·· ˌ·/ *n* [C] a computer game in which the action happens against a background that does not move

**plat·ing** /ˈpleɪtɪŋ/ *n* [U] a thin layer of metal that covers another metal surface: *gold plating*

**plat·i·num** /ˈplætɪ̥nəm/ *n* [U] a silver-grey metal that does not change colour or lose its brightness, used in making expensive jewellery and in industry. Platinum is an ELEMENT (1): *a platinum ring | jewellery made of platinum*

**platinum blonde** /ˌ··· ˈ·/ *n* [C] *informal* a young woman whose hair is a silver-white colour, especially one whose hair has been coloured with chemicals

**plat·i·tude** /ˈplætɪ̥tjuːd‖-tuːd/ *n* [C] a statement that has been made many times before and is not interesting or clever: *a typical politician's speech, full of platitudes* —**platitudinous** /ˌplætɪ̥ˈtjuːdɪ̥nəs◀‖-ˈtuː-/ *adj*

**pla·ton·ic** /pləˈtɒnɪk‖-ˈtɑː-/ *adj* a relationship that is platonic is just friendly or affectionate, not a sexual relationship —**platonically** /-kli/ *adv*

**pla·toon** /pləˈtuːn/ *n* [C] a small group of soldiers which is part of a COMPANY and is commanded by a LIEUTENANT

**plat·ter** /ˈplætə‖-ər/ *n* [C] **1** *especially AmE* a large plate from which food is served **2 chicken/seafood etc platter** chicken etc and other foods arranged on a plate and served in a restaurant **3** *BrE old use* a large plate, usually made of wood **4** *AmE old-fashioned* a RECORD[1] (3)

**plat·y·pus** /ˈplætɪ̥pəs/ *n* [C] a small, furry Australian animal that has a beak and feet like a duck, lays eggs, and gives milk to its young; DUCKBILLED PLATYPUS

**plau·dits** /ˈplɔːdɪ̥ts‖ˈplɒː-/ *n* [plural] *formal* praise and admiration: *Her performance won the plaudits of the critics.*

**plau·si·ble** /ˈplɔːzɪ̥bəl‖ˈplɒː-/ *adj* **1** a statement that is plausible is reasonable and seems likely to be true: *His explanation sounds fairly plausible to me.* **2** someone who is plausible is good at talking in a way that sounds reasonable and truthful, although they may in fact be lying: *a plausible rogue* —opposite IMPLAUSIBLE —**plausibly** *adv*: *It could plausibly be argued that these improvements are due to government policy.* —**plausibility** /ˌplɔːzɪ̥ˈbɪlɪ̥ti‖ˌplɒː-/ *n* [U]

S1 W1 **play[1]** /pleɪ/ *v*
**1 ▶ CHILDREN ◀** [I,T] when children play, they do things that they enjoy, often together or with toys: *The children ran off to play on the beach.* | **play sth** *The boys were playing soldiers.* | *I don't want to play that game!* | [+ **with**] *play with your new toys* | *He loves playing with his grandchildren.*
**2 ▶ SPORTS/GAMES ◀** [I,T] to take part in a game or sport: **play sth** *Do you play a lot of golf?* | *I enjoy playing chess.* | [+ **against**] *They're a terrible team to play against.* | [+ **for**] *He has played for England fifteen times now.* | **play sb** *She's playing Helen Evans in the semi-final.* (=playing against her)
**3 play a ball** to hit a ball in a game or sport: *She played the ball low, just over the net.*
**4 play games** to hide your real feelings or wishes in order to achieve something in a clever or secret way
**5 play the game** to behave in a fair and honest way
**6 ▶ MUSIC ◀** [I,T] **a)** to perform a piece of music on a musical instrument: *I've always wanted to learn to play the piano.* | *She tried to play a Bach Prelude.* | *Please play a tune on your concertina for me.* **b)** to produce music: *The bedside radio played softly.* | *I could hear a violin playing a waltz in the background.* | **play a record/tape/CD** (=produce music from it) *He just sits in his bedroom all day playing records.*
**7 ▶ THEATRE/ACTING ◀ a)** [T] to perform the actions and say the words of a particular character in a theatre performance: *He had always wanted to play Hamlet.* | **play a role/part** *The role of Mrs Goodfire was played by Jane Easton.* **b)** [I] if a play is playing at a particular theatre, it is being performed there: *'Macbeth' is now playing at the Theatre Royal in York.* **c)** [T] if actors play a theatre, they perform there in a play
**8 play a part/role in sth** to have an effect or an influence on something: *The press plays an important role in the life of a democracy.*
**9 ▶ PRETEND ◀** [linking verb] to behave as if you are a particular kind of person or have a particular feeling or quality, even though it is not true: **play dumb/dead etc** *The snake fools predators by playing dead.* | **play the idiot/the teacher etc** *If he is captured, he must play the idiot and reveal nothing.* | **play policeman/soldier etc** *These are ordinary people who think they'll play policeman for a while.* | **play the fool** (=behave in a silly way)
**10 play hard to get** to pretend that you are not sexually interested in someone so that they will become more interested in you
**11 ▶ BEHAVE ◀** [T always + adv/prep] to behave in a particular way in a situation in order to achieve the result or effect that you want: *We always discuss how the event will be played.* | **play it carefully/cool etc** *I think he might offer me the job, but I must play it carefully.* | **play (it) safe** (=avoid taking any risks) | **play it by ear** (=decide what to do according to the way a situation develops) *Let's just play it by ear.*
**12 play a joke/trick on sb** to do something to someone as a joke or trick: *I was trying to play a joke on you.*
**13 ▶ CARDS ◀** [T] to show a card in a game of cards by putting it down on the table: *She couldn't decide which card to play.* | *He played his ace and won the game.*
**14 play your cards right** to behave in a clever or skilful way in a situation so that you gain as much as possible from it: *If I play my cards right, I should do very well out of the deal.*
**15 play second fiddle (to sb)** to be in a lower position or rank than someone else
**16 play for time** to try to delay something so that you have more time to prepare for it or prevent it from happening: *He was playing for time until the others arrived.*
**17 ▶ SMILE ◀** [I always + adv/prep] if a smile plays over someone's lips, they smile quickly and only a little
**18 ▶ LIGHT ◀** [I always + adv/prep] if light plays on something, it shines on it and moves about on it: *She watched the sunlight playing on the water.*
**19 play the system** to use the rules of a system in a clever way, to gain advantage for yourself: *These accountants know how to play the tax system.*
**20 play the market** to risk money on the STOCK MARKET as a way of trying to earn more money
**21 play hooky** *AmE*/**play truant** *BrE* to stay away from school without permission
**22 play with fire** to do something that could have a very dangerous or harmful result
**23 play a hose/light on sth** to direct a HOSE or light towards something so that water or light goes onto it
**24 not play ball** to refuse to do something that someone else wants you to do: *She wanted Dean to lend her the money, but he wouldn't play ball.*
**25 play the field** to have sexual relationships with a lot of different people
**26 play sb for a sucker** *AmE* to show by the way that you

behave towards someone that you think they are stupid: *It seems to me they are playing me for a sucker in this hotel.* **27 play fast and loose with sb** *old-fashioned* to treat someone in a selfishly careless way

**play about/around with** sb/sth *phr v* [T] **1** to have a sexual relationship with someone that is not serious or not intended to last very long: *Her husband accused her of playing around with other men.* **2** to keep moving something around in your hands: *Stop playing around with that knife!*

**play along** *phr v* **1** [I + **with**] to pretend that you agree with someone's ideas because you want to gain an advantage for yourself or to avoid a quarrel **2** [T] **play sb along** to tell someone something that is not true because you need their help in some way

**play at** sth *phr v* [T] **1** if you play at doing something, you do not do it properly or seriously: *He just plays at being an artist.* **2** if children play at doctors, soldiers etc, they pretend to be doctors or soldiers **3 What is he/she etc playing at?** used when you do not understand what someone is doing or what they are trying to achieve: *What do you think you're playing at?|I don't know what on earth he's playing at.*

**play** sth ↔ **back** *phr v* [T] to play something that has been recorded on a machine so that you can listen to it or watch it: *I recorded my brother singing a song then played it back to him.*

**play** sth ↔ **down** *phr v* [T] to try to make something seem less important than it really is: *The government has tried to play down its defeat in the local elections.*

**play** sb **off against** sb *phr v* [T] if you play one person off against another, you encourage them to argue or quarrel with each other so that you can gain something

**play on** sth *phr v* [T] to use a feeling or an idea in order to gain an advantage for yourself: *They are playing on the fact that we don't like to appear ignorant.*

**play** sth ↔ **out** *phr v* [T] if you play out an event, you take part in it in a way that seems to have been planned or thought about before: *The weekend gives you a chance to play out your fantasies.|She watched the farce that was being played out before her.*

**play up** *phr v* **1** [T **play** sth ↔ **up**] if you play something up, you make it seem more important than it really is: *She knew the newspapers would try to play it up.* **2** [I,T **play** sb ↔ **up**] if children play up, they behave badly: *The children have really been playing up this afternoon.|I hope the kids don't play you up.* **3** [I,T **play** sb ↔ **up**] to hurt you or cause problems for you: *My leg's been playing me up recently.|The car's playing up again.*

**play up to** sb *phr v* [T] to behave in a very polite or kind way to someone because you want something from them: *politicians playing up to popular opinion*

**play with** sb/sth *phr v* **1** [T] to keep touching something or moving it about: *Stop playing with the light switch!* **2 play with the idea of doing sth** to consider the possibility of doing something: *I'm playing with the idea of writing a novel.* **3 play with yourself** to touch your own sex organs for pleasure **4 play with words** to use words in a clever or amusing way **5 have time/money to play with** to have extra time or money that is available to be used: *The budget is very tight; there isn't much money to play with.*

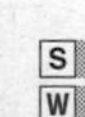

**play²** *n*

**1 ▶ THEATRE ◀** [C] a piece of writing performed in a theatre or on television or radio, consisting of speeches and conversations between several characters: *one of Shakespeare's best-known plays|When he retired, he wrote plays.*|**put on a play** (=perform a play) *The school will be putting on a play in the summer term.*

**2 ▶ AMUSEMENT ◀** [U] things that people, especially children, do for amusement rather than as work: *Soon Henry tired of his play, and wandered off along the beach.*|**at play** (=playing) *the happy laughter of children at play*|**in play** (=done only for amusement, not seriously) *She had hidden his books, in play.*

**3 ▶ ACTION IN A GAME OR SPORT ◀** [U] the actions that form part of a game or a sport: *The changes in rules were agreed upon before the next day's play began.|The match began on time, but rain stopped play after only an hour.|We have seen some very good play this afternoon.*

**4 in play/out of play** if a ball is in play or out of play, it is inside or outside the area allowed by the rules of the game: *He kicked the ball out of play.*

**5 bring sth into play** to use something or make it have an effect: *A whole complex system of muscles is brought into play for each movement of the body.*

**6 come into play** to be used or have an effect: *Several factors came into play to make this possible.*

**7 the play of light** the pattern made by light as it moves gently over a surface: *the play of light on the water*

**8 play on words** a use of a word that is interesting or amusing because it can be understood as having two very different meanings

**9 ▶ LOOSENESS ◀** [U] if there is some play in something, it is loose and can be moved: *There's too much play in that rope.*

**10 make a play for sth** to make an attempt to gain something: *He made a play for the leadership last year.*

**play·a·ble** /ˈpleɪəbəl/ *adj* **1** a piece of ground used for sports that is playable is in good condition and suitable for playing on **2** a piece of music that is playable is not too difficult to be played

**play-act·ing** /ˈ· ˌ··/ *n* [U] behaviour that is not serious or sincere but is made to look as if it is —**play-act** *v* [I]

**play·back** /ˈpleɪbæk/ *n* [C] *especially BrE* a recording of something that you play as soon as it is made, so that you can study it carefully; REPLAY² (2)

**play·bill** /ˈpleɪbɪl/ *n* [C] a printed notice advertising a play

**play·boy** /ˈpleɪbɔɪ/ *n* [C] a rich man who does no work and spends his time enjoying himself with beautiful women, fast cars etc: *a middle-aged playboy*

**play-by-play** /ˌ· · ˈ·◂/ *n* [C usually singular] *AmE* a report on what is happening in a game of sport, given at the same time as the game is being played

**Play-Doh** /ˈ· ·/ *n* [U] *trademark* a soft substance like clay made in many different colours, used by children for making models or shapes

**played-out** /ˌ· ˈ·◂/ *adj* **1** someone who is played-out is not as strong, powerful etc as they used to be **2** old-fashioned and no longer useful: *played-out ideas* —see also **play out** (PLAY¹)

**play·er** /ˈpleɪə‖-ər/ *n* [C] **1** someone who takes part in a game or sport: *a basketball player* **2** one of the important people or companies involved in a new or competitive type of business: *Murdoch is one of the major players in the multimedia industry.* **3** someone who plays a musical instrument **4** *old-fashioned* an actor —see also **key mover/player** (KEY²) S W

**player pi·an·o** /ˌ·· ·ˈ··/ *n* [C] a piano that is played by machinery, with the music controlled by a continuous roll of paper with holes cut into it for the notes —see also PIANOLA

**play·fel·low** /ˈpleɪˌfeləʊ‖-loʊ/ *n* [C] *old-fashioned* someone that you play with when you are a child

**play·ful** /ˈpleɪfəl/ *adj* **1** happily active and full of fun: *a playful little dog* **2** not intended in a serious way: *a playful kiss on the cheek|She tried to sound playful.* —**playfully** *adv* —**playfulness** *n* [U]

**play·go·er** /ˈpleɪˌgəʊə‖-ˌgoʊər/ *n* [C] someone who often goes to see plays

**play·ground** /ˈpleɪgraʊnd/ *n* [C] **1** a piece of ground for children to play on, especially at a school or in a park **2** a place where a particular group of people go to enjoy themselves: *the playground of the rich*

**play·group** /ˈpleɪgruːp/ *n* [C,U] *BrE* a kind of school where children aged 2–5 meet to learn and play; PRESCHOOL *AmE*: *Robert's at playgroup today.*

**play·house** /ˈpleɪhaʊs/ *n* [C] **1** a word meaning a theatre used in its name: *the Oxford Playhouse* **2** a small structure like a little house for children to play in

**playing card** /ˈ·· ·/ *n* [C] *formal* a CARD¹ (7)

**playing field** /ˈ·· ·/ *n* [C] a large piece of ground with particular areas marked out for playing football, cricket etc —see also LEVEL PLAYING FIELD

**play·mate** /ˈpleɪmeɪt/ *n* [C] *old-fashioned* someone who you play with when you are a child

**play-off** /ˈ· ·/ *n* [C] an additional game played to decide who will win after a game has ended with no winner

**play·pen** /ˈpleɪpen/ *n* [C] a frame made of bars or a net that provides an area for a small child to play safely in

**play·room** /ˈpleɪrʊm, -ruːm/ *n* [C] a room for children to play in

**play·school** /ˈpleɪskuːl/ *n* [C] *BrE* another word for PLAYGROUP

**play·thing** /ˈpleɪˌθɪŋ/ *n* [C] **1** a person that you treat like a toy, using them only for your own amusement and not caring about them: *I'm not just your plaything, you know.* | *Humanity has become the plaything of scientists, engineers and planners.* **2** *formal* a toy

**play·time** /ˈpleɪtaɪm/ *n* [U] a period of time at a school, when children can go outside and play

**play·wright** /ˈpleɪraɪt/ *n* [C] someone who writes plays

**pla·za** /ˈplɑːzə‖ˈplæzə/ *n* [C] **1** a public square or market place, especially in towns in Spanish-speaking countries **2** a group of shops and other business buildings in a town: *Central Plaza* —compare MALL

**plc** /ˌpiː el ˈsiː/ *n* PUBLIC LIMITED COMPANY; a large company in Britain which has shares that the public can buy: *Marks & Spencer plc*

**plea** /pliː/ *n* **1** [C] an urgent, serious or emotional request: **make a plea (for)** *The missing girl's parents made a desperate plea for her to contact them.* **2** [C usually singular] a statement by someone in a court of law saying whether they are guilty or not: **make/enter a plea** *Your Honor, we enter a plea of 'not guilty'.* **3** [singular] an excuse for something

**plea bar·gain·ing** /ˈ· ˌ···/ *n* [U] the practice of agreeing to admit in a court that one is guilty of a small crime, in exchange for not being charged with a more serious crime

**plead** /pliːd/ *v past tense* **pleaded** *or* **pled** /pled/ *especially AmE* **1** [I] to ask for something that you want very much, in a sincere and emotional way: *"Don't go!" Robert pleaded.* | [+ **for**] *The hostages' families pleaded for their safe return.* | **plead with sb to do sth** *Moira pleaded with her mother to let her go out.* | *a pleading voice* **2** [I,T not in passive] *law* to state in a court of law whether or not you are guilty of a crime: *You are charged with grand theft. How do you plead?* | **plead guilty/not guilty/innocent** *Henderson pled not guilty to the charge of murder.* | *The accused is mentally unstable, and unfit to plead.* —see graph at GUILTY **3 plead ignorance/illness/insanity etc** to give a particular excuse for your actions: *Well, if a cop stops you for speeding, you can always plead ignorance.* | *She left early, pleading a headache.* **4** [T] to speak or argue in support of something: **plead that** *Politicians pleaded that raising teachers' salaries would make the job more attractive.*

**plead·ing·ly** /ˈpliːdɪŋli/ *adv* if you say something pleadingly, or look at someone pleadingly, you speak to them or look at them as though you are asking them to do something in a sincere and emotional way

3 **pleas·ant** /ˈplezənt/ *adj* **1** enjoyable and making you
3 feel happy; nice: *Well, do have a pleasant weekend.* | *Nora! What a pleasant surprise to see you!* | *Yes, the cider's sweet, but it's pleasant.* **2** friendly, polite, and easy to talk to: *I know you don't like her, but at least try to be pleasant.* | *Nick seemed very pleasant on the phone.* **3** weather that is pleasant is dry and not too hot or cold: *It's overcast, but quite pleasant.* —opposite UNPLEASANT —**pleasantly** *adv: pleasantly surprised*

**pleas·ant·ry** /ˈplezəntri/ *plural* **pleasantries** *n* [C usually plural] a funny or not very serious remark, made in order to be polite: *A couple of old men stopped to exchange pleasantries in the street.*

**please¹** /pliːz/ *interjection* **1** used when you want to ask for something politely: *I'd like a cup of coffee, please.* | *Please can we go now?* | *"Would you like some more?" "Yes please."* **2** used to emphasize a request or wish: *"May I have some water?" "Please do."* | *Please don't be too long, because I have to go out soon.* | *Will you children please be quiet!* **3** used when you want to accept something that someone has offered you and show that you are grateful: *"Would you like a cup of tea?" "Please, I'd love one."* **4 Please!** *informal, often humorous* used to ask someone to stop behaving badly: *Alison! Please!* | *Please, John, this isn't the time to discuss it!* **5 please Sir/Mrs Towers etc** *spoken* used by children to get an adult's attention 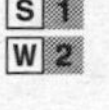

**please²** *v* [not in progressive] **1** [I,T] to make someone happy or satisfied: **please sb** *I only got married to please my parents.* | *The child is very eager to please.* | **be hard/easy etc to please** *Mark's a hard one to please.* —opposite DISPLEASE **2 please yourself a)** *spoken* used to tell someone that they can do whatever they like because you are annoyed and do not care what they do: *Well I'm going to the party – you can please yourself!* **b)** to do whatever you like because you do not have to obey anyone or follow any rules: *We don't have to be back in the hotel by any particular time, we can just please ourselves.* **3 as sb pleases a)** doing whatever you want to do: *He just does as he pleases and never thinks of anyone else.* **b)** *formal* used to tell someone that they will have to decide something and you do not mind what they do **4 whatever/however etc sb pleases** whatever, however etc someone wants: *They can appoint whoever they please.* **5 bold/cool as you please** *spoken* used to express surprise about someone's behaviour, when they have done something strange as if it is completely normal: *He was walking down the road carrying a rifle, as bold as you please.* **6 if you please a)** *formal* used to make a polite request: *Close the door, if you please.* **b)** *old-fashioned* used to say that you find something difficult to believe, or are very surprised or angry about it: *And now she says she needs yet another new dress, if you please!* **7 please God** used to express a very strong hope or wish: *They should have got back by now – please God they're OK.* W3

**pleased** /pliːzd/ *adj* **1** *especially BrE* happy or satisfied: *I was so pleased when they said they'd be able to stay another week.* | [+ **about**] *Are you pleased about the results?* | **pleased (with)** *Di seems pleased with her new car.* | **pleased (that)** *I'm pleased you decided to come.* | **very/really pleased** *We asked our lawyer to check the contract, and we're really pleased we did.* | **be pleased to hear/see/report etc** *I'm pleased to hear about your new job.* **2 be pleased to help/assist** to be very willing or happy to help: *If there's anything we can do, we'd be pleased to help.* **3 (I'm) pleased to meet you** *spoken* used as a polite greeting when you meet someone for the first time **4 pleased with yourself** feeling unreasonably proud or satisfied because you think you have done something clever: *She was looking very pleased with herself so I guessed she'd passed her driving test.* **5 not very pleased** *informal, often humorous* rather annoyed: *She wasn't very pleased when she found out about the dent in her car.* 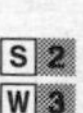

**pleas·ing** /ˈpliːzɪŋ/ *adj formal* **1** giving pleasure or enjoyment; pleasant: [+ **to**] *The painting is very pleasing to the eye.* **2** making you feel pleased and satisfied: *He has made pleasing progress in French this year.* —**pleasingly** *adv*

**plea·sur·a·ble** /ˈpleʒərəbəl/ *adj formal* enjoyable: *a pleasurable feeling of anticipation* —**pleasurably** *adv*

**plea·sure** /ˈpleʒə‖-ər/ *n* 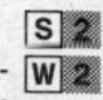
**1 ► ENJOYMENT ◄** [U] the feeling of happiness or satisfaction that you get from an experience you enjoy: *The children used to get a lot of pleasure out of that game when they were young.* | **give/bring pleasure** *Small gifts give*

*pleasure and don't cost much.* | **great pleasure** *a film that has given great pleasure to millions*
**2** ► **ENJOYABLE EXPERIENCE** ◄ [C,U] an activity or experience that you enjoy very much: *the simple pleasures of life* | **it is a pleasure to do sth** *It's been a great pleasure to meet you.*
**3 take pleasure in** to be pleased about and proud of something: *He took great pleasure in his grandchildren's achievements.*
**4 take pleasure in doing sth** to enjoy doing something bad to other people: *Charlie seems to take pleasure in bullying the younger kids.*
**5 (it's) my pleasure** *spoken* used when someone has thanked you for doing something and you want to say that you were glad to do it
**6 with pleasure** *spoken* used to say politely that you are happy to do something that someone has just asked you to do: *"Will you come?" "With pleasure madam."*
**7 have the pleasure of (doing) sth a)** *formal* to enjoy the experience of something: *I don't think I've had the pleasure of meeting your wife.* **b)** *humorous* used when you do not think something is enjoyable: *We had the pleasure of Rob's company last week.*
**8 at his/her Majesty's pleasure** *BrE law* if someone is put in prison at his or her Majesty's pleasure, there is no fixed limit to the time they have to spend there
**9 at your pleasure** if you can do something at your pleasure, you can do it when and as you want to
**10 sb's pleasure** *formal* what someone wants: *You can go there if that's your pleasure.*

**pleasure seek·er** /'·· ,··/ *n* [C] someone who does things just for enjoyment without considering other people

**pleat¹** /pliːt/ *n* [C] a flat narrow fold in cloth —see picture on page 840

**pleat²** *v* [T] to make a lot of flat narrow folds in a piece of cloth —**pleated** *adj*: *a pleated skirt*

**pleb** /pleb/ *n* [C usually plural] *informal or humorous* an insulting word meaning someone who is from a low social class: *Plebs like me can never aspire to such perfect manners.* —**plebby** *adj*

**plebe** /pliːb/ *n* [C] *AmE informal* a first year student at a military or naval college or university

**ple·be·ian** /plɪ'biːən/ *n* [C] **1** an insulting word for someone who is from a low social class **2** an ordinary person who had no special rank in ancient Rome —compare PATRICIAN —**plebeian** *adj*

**pleb·is·cite** /'plebɪ̈sɪ̈t‖-saɪt/ *n* [C,U] a system by which everyone in a country votes to decide a matter of national importance: *The choice of whether to join the federation was decided by plebiscite.* —compare REFERENDUM

**plec·trum** /'plektrəm/ *n* [C] a small thin piece of plastic, metal, or wood, that you hold and use for playing some stringed musical instruments such as a GUITAR; PICK² (5)

**pled** /pled/ *ScotE and AmE* the past tense and past participle of PLEAD

**pledge¹** /pledʒ/ *n* [C]
**1** ► **PROMISE** ◄ *formal* a firm promise or agreement, especially one made publicly or officially: *Industrial conflicts continued in spite of a no-strike pledge by the unions.* | **a pledge to do sth** *the government's pledge to make no deals with terrorists* | **fulfil a pledge** (=do what you promised) *Eisenhower fulfilled his election pledge to end the war in Korea.*
**2 sign/take the pledge** *old-fashioned* to promise never to drink alcohol, for religious or moral reasons
**3 a pledge of love/friendship etc** a serious promise of love etc made by two people
**4** ► **SOMETHING VALUABLE** ◄ something valuable that you leave with someone else as proof that you do what you have agreed to do, pay back what you owe etc: *She borrowed £50 and left her gold bracelet as a pledge.*
**5** ► **AT US COLLEGES** ◄ someone who has promised to become a member of a university FRATERNITY or SORORITY in the US but must pass a test before they can join

**pledge²** *v* [T] **1** to make a formal, usually public, promise that you will do something: **pledge to do sth** *They have pledged to fight any changes to the abortion laws.* | **pledge that** *The UK government has pledged that the wishes of the minority community in Northern Ireland will be respected.* | **pledge support/loyalty/solidarity etc** (=promise to give your support etc) **2** to make someone give a firm promise: *75% of members were pledged in advance to vote for the labor program.* | **pledge yourself to sth** *The Republicans pledged themselves to a tough stand against crime.* **3** to leave something with someone as a PLEDGE¹ (4) **4** to promise to become a member of a university FRATERNITY or SORORITY in the US

**pleis·to·cene** /'plaɪstəsiːn/ *adj* belonging to the period in the Earth's history that started about a million years ago and lasted about 800,000 years, when much of the Earth was covered with ice

**ple·na·ry** /'pliːnəri/ *adj* [only before noun] *formal* **1** a plenary meeting is one that is attended by everyone who has a right to attend: *The conference ended with a plenary debate.* **2** plenary power or authority is complete and has no limit: *The envoy was given plenary powers to negotiate with the rebels.* —**plenary** *n* [C]

**plen·i·po·ten·tia·ry** /,plenɪ̈pə'tenʃəri‖-ʃieri/ *n* [C] *formal or technical* someone who has full power to take action or make decisions, especially as a representative of their government in a foreign country —**plenipotentiary** *adj*: *plenipotentiary powers*

**plen·i·tude** /'plenɪ̈tjuːd‖-tuːd/ *n literary* **1** [U] completeness or fullness **2 a plenitude of** a large amount of something: *a plenitude of sunshine*

**plen·te·ous** /'plentiəs/ *adj poetic* plentiful —**plenteously** *adv* —**plenteousness** *n* [U]

**plen·ti·ful** /'plentɪfəl/ *adj* more than enough in quantity: *a plentiful supply of food and wine* | *Opportunities to practice the language are plentiful.* —**plentifully** *adv*

**plen·ty¹** /'plenti/ *pron* a large quantity that is enough or more than enough: *If you want some more chairs, there are plenty more in here.* | [+ **of**] *Make sure she eats well and gets plenty of fresh air.* | *You've got plenty of time.* | *I don't want any more work, I already have plenty to do.* —compare FEW, LOT 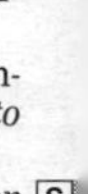

**plenty²** *adv informal* **1 plenty big enough, plenty bright enough etc** more than big enough, bright enough etc: *This apartment's plenty big enough for two.* **2** *AmE* to a large degree; a lot: *I sleep plenty, but I always wake up feeling tired.*

**plenty³** *n* [U] *formal* **1** a situation in which there is a large supply of something, especially something that is needed for life: *In years of plenty everyone has enough to eat.* **2 in plenty** in large supply; more than enough: *There was food and wine in plenty.* —see also HORN OF PLENTY

**ple·o·nas·m** /'pliːənæzəm/ *n* [C,U] *technical* the use of more words than are needed to express an idea: *The phrase 'an apple divided into two halves' is a pleonasm.* —**pleonastic** /,pliːə'næstɪk◂/ *adj*

**pleth·o·ra** /'pleθərə/ *n* **a plethora of** *formal* an amount of something that is larger than is needed or more than you can deal with: *a plethora of suggestions* | *a plethora of paperwork*

**pleu·ri·sy** /'plʊərɪ̈si‖'plʊr-/ *n* [U] a serious illness which affects your lungs, causing severe pain in your chest and sides

**plex·i·glass** /'pleksi,glɑːs‖-,glæs/ *n* [U] *AmE trademark* the name of a particular type of plastic, that is often just used to mean any plastic; PERSPEX *BrE*

**plex·us** /'pleksəs/ *n* —see SOLAR PLEXUS

**pli·a·ble** /'plaɪəbəl/ *adj* **1** easy to bend without breaking or cracking: *The clay should be moistened regularly to keep it soft and pliable.* **2** able and willing to change and accept new ideas and ways of doing things; ADAPTABLE: *The committee would benefit from having members who are more pliable.* **3** too easily influenced by other people —**pliability** /,plaɪə'bɪlɪ̈ti/ *n* [U]

**pli·ant** /ˈplaɪənt/ *adj* pliable —**pliantly** *adv* —**pliancy** *n* [U]

**pli·ers** /ˈplaɪəz‖-ərz/ *n* [plural] a small tool made of two crossed pieces of metal, used to hold small things or to bend and cut wire —see picture at TOOL[1]

**plight[1]** /plaɪt/ *n* [usually singular] a bad, serious, or sad condition or situation: *the plight of homeless children*

**plight[2]** *v* **plight your troth** *old use* to make a promise to someone that you will marry them

**plim·soll** /ˈplɪmsəl, -səʊl‖-səl, -soʊl/ *n* [C] a light shoe with a top made of thick cotton cloth and a flat rubber SOLE[1] (2) ; SNEAKER *AmE* —see picture at SHOE

**Plimsoll line** /ˈ·· ·/ also **Plimsoll mark** *n* [C] a line painted on the outside of a ship, showing the depth to which it can safely be allowed to float in the water when it is loaded

**plinth** /plɪnθ/ *n* [C] a square block, usually made of stone, that is used as the base for a PILLAR or STATUE

**Pli·o·cene** /ˈplaɪəsiːn/ *adj* belonging to the period in the Earth's history that started about thirteen million years ago and lasted about twelve million years

**plod** /plɒd‖plɑːd/ *v* **plodded, plodding** **1** [I always + adv/prep] to walk along slowly, especially with difficulty and great effort; TRUDGE[1] [+ **through/along etc**] *The children were plodding through the snow.* | *The mule plodded up the hill.* **2 plod on/along** to keep working steadily, especially at something that is uninteresting or difficult: *I'll just plod on for another hour or so.*

**plod·der** /ˈplɒdə‖ˈplɑːdər-/ *n* [C] someone who works slowly and is not very clever: *I've always been a bit of a plodder.*

**plonk[1]** /plɒŋk‖plɑːŋk, plɒːŋk/ *v* [T] *informal* **1** to put something down somewhere, especially noisily and carelessly: **plonk sth in/on etc** *Just plonk those bags anywhere in my room.* **2 plonk yourself (down)** to sit down heavily and then relax: *We plonked ourselves in front of the telly.*

**plonk[2]** *n* [U] *BrE informal* cheap wine

**plonk·er** /ˈplɒŋkə‖ˈplɑːŋkər, ˈplɒːŋ-/ *n* [C] *BrE slang* **1** a stupid person **2** a PENIS

**plop[1]** /plɒp‖plɑːp/ *n* [C] a sound like something solid dropping into liquid: *The soap fell into the bath with a loud plop.*

**plop[2]** *v* **plopped, plopping** **1** [I always + adv/prep] to fall somewhere making a sound like a plop: [+ **on/down etc**] *A few drops of rain began to plop on to the roof.* **2** [T] to put something into a liquid so that it makes a sound like a plop: [+ **into**] *I plopped a couple of ice cubes into the drink.* **3 plop (yourself) down** to sit down or lie down heavily: *She plopped down on a chair.*

**plo·sive** /ˈpləʊsɪv‖ˈploʊ-/ *n* [C] *technical* a CONSONANT sound that is made by completely stopping the flow of air out of your mouth and then suddenly letting it out, done, for example, when saying /b/ or /t/ —**plosive** *adj*

**plot[1]** /plɒt‖plɑːt/ *n* [C]
**1** ▶ **STORY/FILM** ◀ the set of connected events that a story, film etc is based on: *The plot of 'Twin Peaks' was so complicated that I couldn't follow it.*
**2** ▶ **PLAN** ◀ a secret plan, involving several people, to do something harmful or illegal: [+ **to**] *There have been rumors of a plot to overthrow the President.* | **hatch a plot** (=start making a plan)
**3 the plot thickens** *spoken humorous* used to say that events seem to be becoming more complicated and difficult to understand
**4** ▶ **PIECE OF LAND** ◀ **a)** a small piece of land for building or growing things on **b)** a piece of land that a particular family owns in a CEMETERY, in which members of the family are buried when they die
**5** ▶ **DRAWING** ◀ *AmE* a drawn plan of a building at ground level; GROUND PLAN

**plot[2]** *v* **plotted, plotting** **1** [I,T] to make a secret plan to harm a person or organization, especially a political leader or government: *We spent all week plotting our revenge.* | [+ **against**] *They were plotting against the government.* | **plot to do sth** *It was alleged that they had plotted to blow up the White House.* **2** [T] to draw a line or curve that shows facts, figures etc: *We plotted a graph to show the increase in sales figures this year.* **3** [T] to mark, calculate, or follow the position of a moving aircraft or ship: *He was already bent over the table, plotting a new course.* —**plotter** *n* [C]

**plough[1]** *usually* **plow** *AmE* /plaʊ/ *n* [C] **1** a large piece of farm equipment used to turn over the earth so that seeds can be planted **2 under the plough** used for growing crops **3 the Plough** *especially BrE* the group of seven bright stars seen only from the northern part of the world; BIG DIPPER (2) *AmE* —see also SNOW PLOUGH

**plough[2]** *usually* **plow** *AmE v* **1** [I,T] to turn over the earth using a plough so that seeds can be planted: *a ploughed field* **2** [I always + adv/prep] to move with a lot of effort or force: [+ **along/across etc**] *The ship ploughed slowly across the bay.*

**plough** sth ↔ **back** *phr v* [T] to put money that you have earned back into a business in order to make the business bigger and more successful: *Profits from ticket sales are ploughed back into further conservation projects.*

**plough into** sb/sth *phr v* [T] to hit something hard, especially while driving, because you are going too fast or not paying attention: *I ploughed into the car in front.*

**plough on** *phr v* [I] to continue doing something that is difficult or boring: *Julia ploughed on through the endless exam papers.*

**plough through** *phr v* [T] to read all of something, even though it is boring and takes a long time: *After ploughing through all those textbooks, it was a relief to read a novel.*

**plough** sth ↔ **up** *phr v* [T] to break up the surface of the ground by repeatedly travelling over it: *Horses plough up the paths and make them muddy for walkers.*

**plough·boy** /ˈplaʊbɔɪ/ *n* [C] *old use* a boy who led a horse that pulled a PLOUGH

**plough·man** /ˈplaʊmən/ *n* [C] *old use* a man whose job was to guide a PLOUGH that was being pulled by a horse

**plough·man's lunch** /ˌ·· ˈ·/ *n* [C] *BrE* a simple meal that people eat especially in PUBS, consisting of bread, cheese, onion, and PICKLE

**plough·share** *BrE usually* **plowshare** *AmE* /ˈplaʊʃeə‖-ʃer/ *n* [C] the broad curved metal blade of a PLOUGH, which turns over the soil

**plov·er** /ˈplʌvə‖-ər/ *n* [C] a small bird that lives near the sea

**plow** /plaʊ/ *n, v* the usual American spelling of PLOUGH

**ploy** /plɔɪ/ *n* [C] a clever method of getting an advantage, especially by deceiving someone: *His usual ploy is to pretend he's ill.* | *a cynical ploy to win votes*

**pluck[1]** /plʌk/ *v*
**1** ▶ **TAKE STH** ◀ [T] to take hold of something and remove it from somewhere by pulling it: **pluck sth from/off etc** *She bent forward to pluck a thread off the lapel of his jacket.*
**2 pluck up (the) courage** to force yourself to be brave and do something you are afraid of doing: *He finally plucked up enough courage to ask her out on a date.*
**3** ▶ **CHICKEN ETC** ◀ [T] to pull the feathers off a dead chicken or other bird before cooking it
**4** ▶ **FLOWER** ◀ *literary* to pick a flower or fruit: *Eve plucked an apple and offered it to Adam.*
**5** ▶ **MUSIC** ◀ [I,T] to pull sharply at the strings of a musical instrument: [+ **at**] *Someone was plucking at the strings of an old guitar.*
**6** ▶ **TAKE SB AWAY** ◀ [T always + adv/prep] to take someone away from a place or situation: **pluck sb from/off/away etc** *She was plucked from obscurity by a film producer.*
**7 pluck sth out of the air** to say or suggest a number, name etc that you have just thought of without thinking about it carefully: *I'm just plucking a figure out of the air here, but let's say it'll cost about $15,000.*

**8 pluck your eyebrows** to pull out hairs from the edges of your EYEBROWS

**pluck at** sth *phr v* [T] to pull something quickly and repeatedly with your fingers: *The little boy plucked at her sleeve.* | *Sally was staring into space, plucking nervously at her pearl choker.*

**pluck[2]** *n* [U] *old-fashioned* courage and determination: *I really admire him for cycling to Paris on his own – it must have taken a lot of pluck.*

**pluck·y** /ˈplʌki/ *adj* **pluckier, pluckiest** *informal* brave and determined: *It took guts to stand up to those bullies – she's a plucky kid.* —**pluckily** *adv* —**pluckiness** *n* [U]

S3 **plug[1]** /plʌg/ *n* [C]
**1 ▶ ELECTRICITY ◀ a)** a thing used for connecting a piece of electrical equipment to the main supply of electricity: *a two-pin plug* **b)** *BrE informal* a piece of plastic, usually on a wall, where electrical equipment is connected to the main electricity supply; SOCKET (1): *Make sure you turn the television off at the plug.* **c)** an object used for connecting a wire from one piece of electrical equipment such as a computer to another
**2 ▶ BATH ◀** a round flat piece of rubber or plastic used for stopping the water flowing out of a bath or SINK[2]
**3 ▶ ADVERTISEMENT ◀** *informal* an attempt to persuade people to buy a book, see a film etc, by talking about it publicly, especially on television or radio: **give sth a plug** *She appeared on all the talk shows to give her new book a plug.*
**4 ▶ IN AN ENGINE ◀** *informal* the part of a petrol engine that makes a SPARK and explodes the petrol mixture; SPARK PLUG: *Change the plugs every 10,000 miles.*
**5 pull the plug (on sth)** to prevent a plan or business from being able to continue, especially by deciding not to give it any more money: *We were doing fine until the bank pulled the plug on us.*
**6 ▶ PIECE ◀** a piece of something pressed tightly together: *a cotton wool plug* | *a plug of tobacco*
**7 ▶ FOR HOLDING SCREWS ◀** [C] a small plastic tube put in a hole to hold a screw tightly

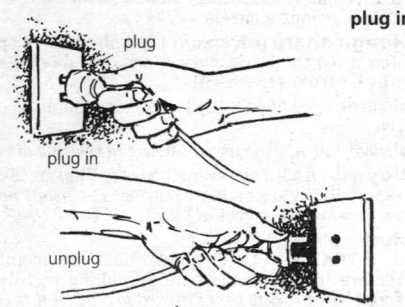

**plug in**

plug
plug in
unplug

**plug[2]** *v* [T]
**1** also **plug up** to fill or block a small hole: *I used cement to plug the holes in the plaster.* **2** to try to persuade people to buy a book, see a film etc by talking about it on television or radio: *Arnold was only on the show to plug his new movie.* **3 plug the gap/gaps** to provide more of something that is needed: *With so few trained doctors, paramedics were brought in to plug the gap.* **4** *AmE old-fashioned* to shoot someone

**plug away** *phr v* [I] to keep working hard at something: [+ **at**] *I'm sure if you keep plugging away at it, your English will improve.*

**plug** sth ↔ **in** *phr v* [T] to connect a piece of electrical equipment to the main supply of electricity, or to another piece of electrical equipment: *I don't think the antenna's plugged in right.*

**plug into** sth *phr v* [T] **1** to connect one piece of electrical equipment to another: **plug sth into sth** *The TV was plugged into the stereo system.* **2** to connect your computer to a big computer system

**plug·hole** /ˈplʌghəʊl‖-hoʊl/ *n* [C] *BrE* **1** a hole in a bath or SINK where water can flow out, which you can put a PLUG[1] (2) into; DRAIN[2] (1) *AmE* **2 go down the plughole a)** if work or effort goes down the plughole it is completely wasted: *Two years of hard work went right down the plughole.* **b)** if a business goes down the plughole, it fails

**plum[1]** /plʌm/ *n* **1** [C] a small round juicy fruit which is dark red or yellow and has a hard part in the middle, or the tree that produces this fruit: *stewed plums and custard* | *plum blossoms* —see picture on page 413 **2** [U] a dark red colour, like a plum —see also PLUM PUDDING

**plum[2]** *adj* **1 a plum job** *BrE informal* a good, well-paid, and often easy job that other people wish they had **2** having a dark red colour, like a plum

**plum·age** /ˈpluːmɪdʒ/ *n* [U] the feathers covering a bird's body: *the parrot's brilliant blue plumage*

**plumb[1]** /plʌm/ *v* [T] **1 plumb the depths of despair/misery/bad taste etc** to express a bad quality or feel an unpleasant emotion in a very extreme way: *When his wife left him Matt plumbed the very depths of despair.* **2** to succeed in understanding something completely; FATHOM[2]: *Psychologists are trying to plumb the deepest mysteries of the human psyche.*

**plumb** sth ↔ **in** *phr v* [T] to connect a piece of equipment such as a washing machine to the water supply

**plumb[2]** *adv* **1** [always + adv/prep] *informal* exactly: *The bullet hit him plumb between the eyes.* **2** *AmE informal, often humorous* completely: *I'm plumb tuckered out* (=very tired) | *The whole idea sounds plumb crazy to me.*

**plumb[3]** *adj technical* **1** exactly upright or level **2 out of plumb** not exactly upright or level

**plumb·er** /ˈplʌmə‖-ər/ *n* [C] someone whose job is to repair water pipes, baths, SINKs etc

**plumb·ing** /ˈplʌmɪŋ/ *n* [U] **1** the pipes that water flows through in a building: *We keep having problems with the plumbing.* **2** the work of fitting and repairing water pipes, baths etc

**plumb line** /ˈ· ·/ *n* [C] a piece of string with a piece of LEAD tied to one end, used for measuring the depth of water or for finding out if a wall is built exactly upright

**plume[1]** /pluːm/ *n* [C] **1** a small cloud of smoke, dust etc which rises up into the air: [+ **of**] *After the explosion, a plume of black smoke hung over the horizon.* **2** a large feather or bunch of feathers, especially one that is used as a decoration on a hat —see also NOM DE PLUME

**plume[2]** *v* **1** [T] if a bird plumes its feathers, it cleans them and makes them smooth **2 plume yourself on** *literary* to feel proud about a quality you have: *Meg plumed herself on her superior virtue.*

**plumed** /pluːmd/ *adj* [only before noun] having or decorated with feathers: *the knights' plumed helmets*

**plum·met** /ˈplʌmɪ̵t/ *v* [I] **1** to suddenly and quickly go down in value or amount: *House prices have plummeted.* **2** to fall very suddenly and quickly from a great height: *The plane plummeted towards the earth.* —compare PLUNGE[1]

**plum·my** /ˈplʌmi/ *adj* **1** a plummy British voice sounds very upper-class and old-fashioned: *the plummy Oxford tones of the newsreader* **2** tasting of or containing a lot of PLUMS

**plump[1]** /plʌmp/ *adj* **1** a word meaning pleasantly fat, often used when you want to avoid saying the word fat: *The nurse was a cheerful plump woman.* | *Dad's getting a bit plump – he needs to go on a diet.* —see picture on page 412 **2** having a full, round shape: *plump, soft pillows* | *plump juicy tomatoes* —compare CHUBBY, PORTLY —**plumpness** *n* [U] —see FAT[1] (USAGE)

**plump[2]** *v* **1 plump sth in/on etc** to put something down suddenly and carelessly: *Otto plumped a sheaf of papers on my desk and told me to get on with it.* | *You can* *plump the bags down anywhere you like.* **2 plump (yourself) down** to sit down suddenly and heavily

**plump for** sth *phr v* [T] *informal* to choose something after thinking carefully about it: *We finally plumped for a bottle of pink champagne.*

**plump** sth ↔ **up** *phr v* [T] to make CUSHIONS, PILLOWS etc bigger and softer by shaking them

**plum pud·ding** /ˌ· ˈ··/ *n* [C,U] *BrE* CHRISTMAS PUDDING

**plum to·ma·to** /ˈ· ·ˌ··/ *n* [C] a type of tomato which is shaped like a PLUM[1] (1) and is used in cooking

**plun·der[1]** /ˈplʌndə‖-ər/ *v* [I,T] to steal large amounts of money or property from somewhere, especially in a violent way that causes damage: *The rich provinces of Asia Minor were plundered by the invaders.|greedy tycoons who plunder their companies' pension funds|plundered treasures* —**plunderer** *n* [C]

**plunder[2]** *n* [U] **1** things that have been stolen during a violent attack, especially during a war: *Henry's army returned loaded down with plunder.* **2** the act of plundering: *the plunder of Africa by the European nations*

**plunge[1]** /plʌndʒ/ *v* **1** [I, T always + adv/prep] to move, fall, or be thrown suddenly forwards or downwards: [+ **off/into etc**] *Her car swerved and plunged off the cliff.*| **plunge to your death** *The rope broke and both the climbers plunged 500 feet to their death.*|**plunge sb/sth forward/through etc** *The car stopped suddenly and he was plunged forward through the windshield.* **2** [I] if a price, value, or rate plunges it suddenly goes down by a large amount: *The price of oil has plunged to a new low.* **3** [I] if a ship plunges, it moves violently up and down, usually because of high waves

**plunge in** *phr v* [I] to start talking, doing sth etc quickly and confidently, without worrying: *Zoe plunged in and started chatting happily.*

**plunge into** *phr v* [T] **1 plunge sth into sth** to push something firmly and deeply into something else: *Plunge the asparagus into boiling water.|Jill plunged her hands deep into her pockets.* **2 plunge sb/sth into sth** to make someone or something experience a particular type of situation, especially one that is difficult or unpleasant: *This latest scandal has plunged the Administration into controversy.|The hall was suddenly plunged into darkness.*|**be plunged into gloom/despair etc** (=suddenly experience great unhappiness) *The whole regiment was plunged into despair by this news.* **3 plunge into sth** to begin to do something suddenly, without thinking about the possible results: *Stuart was always plunging into risky ventures.*

**plunge[2]** *n*
**1 take the plunge** to decide finally to do something, especially after delaying it or worrying about it for a long time: *In 1990 Pam took the plunge and set up her own business.*
**2** ▶**DOWNWARD MOVEMENT**◀ [C usually singular] a sudden quick downward movement: *Without warning, the plane began a plunge towards the Earth.*
**3** ▶**INTO WATER**◀ [C usually singular] a DIVE[2] (1) or jump into water, or a quick swim: *Sue felt refreshed after a quick plunge in the lake.*
**4** ▶**DECREASE**◀ [C] a sudden large fall in the value of property, SHARES[2] (5) etc: *a dramatic plunge in house prices*

**plung·er** /ˈplʌndʒə‖-ər/ *n* [C] **1** a rubber cup on the end of a rod used for unblocking kitchen or bathroom pipes **2** *technical* a part of a machine that moves up and down **3** *AmE informal* someone who GAMBLES a lot

**plung·ing neck·line** /ˌ·· ˈ··/ *n* [C] a very low curve or V shape on the top edge of the front of a woman's dress

**plu·per·fect** /pluːˈpɜːfɪkt‖-ɜːr-/ *n* **the pluperfect** *technical* the PAST PERFECT tense of a verb

**plu·ral[1]** /ˈplʊərəl‖ˈplʊr-/ *n* [C] a word or form that shows you are talking about more than one object, person etc. For example, 'dogs' is the plural of 'dog'

**plural[2]** *adj* **1** a plural word or form shows you are talking about more than one object, person etc. For example 'we' is a plural pronoun **2** *formal* involving more than one person or thing or different kinds of people or things: *plural cultures|plural marriage*

**plu·ral·is·m** /ˈplʊərəlɪzəm‖ˈplʊr-/ *n* [U] *formal* **1** the principle that people of different races, religions, and political beliefs can live together peacefully in the same society **2** the holding of more than one job at a time, especially in the Church —**pluralist** *n* [C] —**pluralistic, pluralist** /ˌplʊərəˈlɪstɪk◂‖ˌplʊr-/ *adj*: *living in a pluralist society*

**plu·ral·i·ty** /plʊˈræl̩ti/ *n* **1** [C] *formal* a large number of different things: [+ **of**] *a plurality of cultures* **2** [C,U] *especially AmE technical* the largest number of votes in an election, especially when this is less than the total number of votes that all the other people or parties have received **3** [U] *technical* the state of being plural

**plus[1]** /plʌs/ *prep* **1** used when one number or amount is added to another: *Three plus six equals nine. (3 + 6 = 9)| The book has 250 pages, plus 28 pages of appendices.|All employees are paid $3 an hour plus $1.50 for time worked on the weekend.* **2** and also: *The unit deals with all lung and heart conditions, plus many other lesser ailments.* **3 plus four/six etc** *technical* four, six etc more than zero —opposite MINUS[1] S1 W2

**plus[2]** *n* [C] **1** *informal* something that gives you an advantage in a situation: *Knowledge of French and Spanish could be a plus in this job.* **2** a sign (+) showing that you should add two or more numbers together, or that a number is more than zero

**plus[3]** *adj* **1 plus factor/point** an advantage or favourable feature that something has: *Another plus point for the VHS system is that you can record three or four hours of material onto one tape.* **2 10/50 etc plus** more than a particular amount, number or level: *She earns $50,000 a year plus.|All the children in the class are six plus.* (=more than six years old) **3** [only before noun] greater than zero: *Daytime temperatures vary between minus 5° and plus 12°.*

**plus[4]** *conjunction* and also: *He's been studying for the exams all week, plus he's been working in a bar at night.|It's an old, draughty house. Plus the plumbing's not fixed yet.*

**plus fours** /ˌ· ˈ·/ *n* [plural] trousers with loose wide legs that are fastened just below the knee, worn by men especially in the 1920s when playing GOLF

**plush[1]** /plʌʃ/ also **plush·y** /ˈplʌʃi/ *adj informal* expensive, comfortable, and of good quality: *a plush hotel*

**plush[2]** *n* [U] silk or cotton cloth with a surface like short fur: *plush curtains*

**plus sign** *n* [C] the sign (+)

**Plu·to** /ˈpluːtəʊ‖-toʊ/ *n* [singular] the most distant PLANET, ninth in order from the Sun —see picture at SOLAR SYSTEM

**plu·toc·ra·cy** /pluːˈtɒkrəsi‖-ˈtɑːk-/ *n* [C] a ruling class of rich people, or a country ruled by such people, or a government that consists of them

**plu·to·crat** /ˈpluːtəkræt/ *n* [C] someone who has power because they are rich: *bloated plutocrats who exploit the workers* —**plutocratic** /ˌpluːtəˈkrætɪk◂/ *adj*

**plu·to·ni·um** /pluːˈtəʊniəm‖-ˈtoʊ-/ *n* [U] an element (=simple substance) that is used in the production of NUCLEAR power

**ply[1]** /plaɪ/ *v past tense and past participle* **plied** **1** [I always + adv/prep, T] *literary* if a vehicle or boat plies between two places or across a place it makes that journey regularly: [+ **between/across etc**] *Small fishing boats plied to and fro across the harbor.*|**ply sth** *a regular boat service that plies the lake* **2 ply your trade** *literary* to work at your job or business: *Flower sellers were plying their trade in the marketplace.* **3** [T] *old use or literary* to use or work skilfully with a tool **4 ply for hire** *BrE* if a taxi driver plies for hire, they drive around or wait somewhere looking for passengers

**ply** sb **with** sth *phr v* [T] **1** to keep giving someone large quantities of food and drink: *They plied us with sandwiches and mugs of strong coffee.* **2 ply sb with questions** to keep asking someone questions

**ply²** *n* [U] **two/three etc ply a)** used as a measurement of the thickness of thread, rope etc, according to the number of single threads it is made from **b)** used as a measurement of the thickness of plywood according to the number of thin sheets of wood it is made from

**Plym·outh Breth·ren** /ˌplɪməθ ˈbreðrən/ *n* [plural] a Christian organization that has very strict moral rules and is opposed to religious ceremony

**ply·wood** /ˈplaɪwʊd/ *n* [U] a material made of several thin sheets of wood stuck together to form a strong board

**PM** /ˌpiː ˈem/ *n* [C] *informal, especially BrE* the PRIME MINISTER: *an urgent meeting with the PM*

**pm** /ˌpiː ˈem/ *Latin* post meridiem; used after numbers expressing the time to show that it is after midday: *The meeting starts at 2.30 pm.*

**PMS** /ˌpiː em ˈes/ *n* [U] *AmE* premenstrual syndrome; unpleasant physical and emotional feelings felt by many women just before their PERIOD; PMT *BrE*

**PMT** /ˌpiː em ˈtiː/ *n* [U] *BrE* premenstrual tension; PMS *AmE*

**pneu·mat·ic** /njuːˈmætɪk‖nʊ-/ *adj* **1** *technical* filled with air: *pneumatic tyres* **2** worked by air pressure: *a pneumatic pump* —**pneumatically** /-kli/ *adv*

**pneumatic drill** /ˌ·ˌ·· ˈ·/ *n* [C] *especially BrE* a large powerful tool worked by air pressure which is used for breaking up hard materials, especially road surfaces; JACKHAMMER *AmE* —see picture at DRILL¹

**pneu·mo·ni·a** /njuːˈməʊniə‖nʊˈmoʊ-/ *n* [U] a serious disease of the lungs that makes it difficult for you to breathe

**PO** /ˌpiː ˈəʊ‖-ˈoʊ/ **1** the written abbreviation of POST OFFICE **2** the written abbreviation of PETTY OFFICER **3** the written abbreviation of POSTAL ORDER

**poach** /pəʊtʃ‖poʊtʃ/ *v*
**1** ▶ **COOK** ◀ [T] **a)** to cook eggs in a special pan over boiling water: *poached eggs on toast* **b)** to cook fish or meat in boiling water or other liquid: *Salmon is usually poached in a fish kettle.*
**2** ▶ **ANIMALS** ◀ [I,T] to catch or shoot animals, birds, or fish illegally, especially on private land without permission: *the poaching of elephants and the illegal trading of ivory*
**3** ▶ **PEOPLE/IDEAS** ◀ [I,T] **a)** to persuade someone to leave a team or company and join yours: *Foreign football clubs seem to be poaching all our best players.* **b)** to unfairly or illegally use someone else's ideas: *screenwriters poaching from literature*
**4 poach on sb's territory/preserve** to do something that is someone else's responsibility, especially when they do not want you to do it

**poach·er** /ˈpəʊtʃə‖ˈpoʊtʃər/ *n* [C] **1** someone who catches or shoots animals, birds, or fish on private land without permission **2** a pan with small containers shaped like cups for poaching eggs **3 poacher turned gamekeeper** *BrE* someone who was previously a criminal and now has responsibility for stopping crime

**PO Box** /ˌpiː əʊ ˈbɒks◂‖-oʊ ˈbɑːks◂/ *n* [C] a numbered box in a post office to which someone's mail can be sent and from which they can collect it: *For further information, write to PO Box 714, Key Largo, Florida.*

**pocked** /pɒkt‖pɑːkt/ *adj* covered with small holes or marks; POCKMARKED: *His face was pocked with scars.*

S2 W2 **pock·et¹** /ˈpɒkɪ̈t‖ˈpɑːkɪ̈t/ *n* [C]
**1** ▶ **IN CLOTHES** ◀ a small bag sewn onto or into a coat, trousers etc so that you can put things such as money or keys into it: *Joseph always stands with his hands in his pockets.* | **coat/trouser/jacket etc pocket** *The keys are in my coat pocket.* | **turn out your pockets** (=empty your pockets) —see picture on page 840
**2** ▶ **MONEY** ◀ the amount of money available for you to spend: *When will the new taxes start hitting people's pockets?.* | **suit every pocket** *We offer a range of repayment plans to suit every pocket.* | **from/out of your own pocket** (=using your own money instead of money from your company, the government etc) *The prince offered to pay for the restoration out of his own pocket.* | **have deep pockets** (=have a lot of money)
**3** ▶ **IN A BAG/DOOR ETC** ◀ a small bag or piece of material fastened to an object so that you can put small things into it: *All passengers should read the air safety card in the pocket of the seat in front.*
**4** ▶ **SMALL AREA/AMOUNT** ◀ **a)** a small area where the situation is very different from the area surrounding it: *Apart from a few pockets of resistance, the new government is firmly established.* | *a poor country dotted with pockets of wealth* **b)** a small amount of something that is different from what surrounds it: *The mine has a few remaining pockets of iron ore.*
**5 be/live in each other's pockets** *informal, especially BrE* if two people are in each other's pockets, they are together too much
**6 have sb/sth in your pocket a)** to be able to control someone such as a police officer or politician, by threatening them, paying them money etc: *a powerful organization with many local politicians in its pockets* **b)** to be very sure that you are going to win something such as a competition or election: *It looks like the Democrats have this election in their pockets already.*
**7 be out of pocket** *BrE informal* to have less money than you should have, after some form of exchange or business deal: *Unless you handle the deal carefully, you could be badly out of pocket.* | **£10/£50 etc out of pocket** *Selling the car so cheaply left her £100 out of pocket.*
**8 pick sb's pocket** to steal from someone by taking money from their pocket without them realizing
**9 put your hand in your pocket** to give money to someone who needs it or in order to help someone: *I hope everyone will put their hands in their pockets and give generously to the fund.*
**10** ▶ **FOR BALLS** ◀ a small net bag fastened to a BILLIARD or SNOOKER table which you have to hit the ball into —see also AIRPOCKET, **line your own pockets** (LINE² (4))

**pocket²** *v* [T] **1** to put something into your pocket: *Roy pocketed his wallet and car keys and left the house.* **2 a)** to steal money, especially money that you are responsible for: *The society's treasurer was accused of pocketing some of the profits.* **b)** to get money in a slightly dishonest way: *It's simple – we buy them for $5, sell them for $8, and pocket the difference.* **3** to hit a ball into a pocket in games such as BILLIARDS

**pocket³** *adj* [only before noun] small enough to be carried in your pocket: *a pocket dictionary*

**pocket bat·tle·ship** /ˌ·· ˈ···/ *n* [C] a fairly small fighting ship

**pock·et·book** /ˈpɒkɪ̈tbʊk‖ˈpɑː-/ *n* [C] **1** *AmE* a small flat case for holding papers and paper money; WALLET **2** a small NOTEBOOK **3** *AmE old-fashioned* a woman's HANDBAG, especially one without a STRAP¹

**pocket cal·cu·lat·or** /ˌ·· ˈ····/ *n* [C] a small piece of electronic equipment which you use to do calculations

**pock·et·ful** /ˈpɒkɪ̈tfʊl‖ˈpɑː-/ *n* [C] the amount that a pocket will hold: [+ **of**] *a pocketful of pebbles*

**pocket hand·ker·chief** /ˌ·· ˈ···/ *n* [C] *old-fashioned* a handkerchief made of cloth not of paper

**pocket-handkerchief** *adj informal, especially BrE* small and square in shape: *a pocket-handkerchief garden*

**pocket knife** /ˈ·· ·/ *n plural* **pocket knives** /-naɪvz/ [C] a small knife with one or more blades that fold into the handle —see picture at KNIFE¹

**pocket mon·ey** /ˈ·· ˌ··/ *n* [U] **1** *especially BrE* money given regularly to a child by its parents to spend on small things; ALLOWANCE (4) *AmE*: *Sophie spends her pocket money on sweets and magazines.* **2** *informal* a small amount of money that you can use to buy small things: *Gavin gives private lessons to earn himself a bit of pocket money.*

**pocket ve·to** /ˌ·· ˈ··/ *n* [C] a method used by the US President to stop a BILL (=proposal for a new law), by keeping it without signing it until Congress is no longer working

**pock·mark** /ˈpɒkmɑːk‖ˈpɑːkmɑːrk/ *n* [C] a hollow mark on someone's skin left by a disease such as SMALLPOX

**pock·marked** /ˈpɒkmɑːkt‖ˈpɑːkmɑːrkt/ *adj* covered with pockmarks; POCKED: *a pockmarked face*

**pod¹** /pɒd‖pɑːd/ *n* [C] **1** a long narrow seed container that grows on various plants, especially PEAS and beans: *a pea pod* **2** a part of a space vehicle that can be separated from the main part **3** a long narrow container for petrol or other substances, especially one carried under an aircraft wing **4** a container which holds the eggs of some types of insects

**pod²** *v* [T] to take beans, PEAS etc from their POD¹ (1) before cooking them

**podg·y** /ˈpɒdʒi‖ˈpɑː-/ *adj* another form of PUDGY

**po·di·a·trist** /pəˈdaɪətrɪ̈st/ *n* [C] *especially AmE* someone who looks after people's feet and treats foot diseases; CHIROPODIST *especially BrE* —**podiatry** *n* [U]

**po·di·um** /ˈpəʊdiəm‖ˈpoʊ-/ *n* [C] **1** a small raised area for a performer, speaker, or musical CONDUCTOR to stand on **2** *AmE* a tall sloping desk for putting an open book, notes for a speech etc on; LECTERN

**po·dunk** /ˈpəʊdʌŋk‖ˈpoʊ-/ *adj AmE informal* a podunk place is small and unimportant: *Brad comes from some podunk town east of the mountains.*

**p.o.ed** *adj AmE informal* very annoyed: *She was really p.o.ed when she didn't get the job.*

W3 **po·em** /ˈpəʊɪ̈m‖ˈpoʊ-/ *n* [C] a piece of writing arranged in patterns of lines and of sounds which often RHYME, expressing thoughts, emotions, and experiences in words that excite your imagination

**po·e·sy** /ˈpəʊɪ̈zi‖ˈpoʊɪ̈si/ *n* [U] *old use* poetry

W3 **po·et** /ˈpəʊɪ̈t‖ˈpoʊ-/ *n* [C] someone who writes poems

**po·et·as·ter** /ˌpəʊɪ̈ˈtæstə‖ˌpoʊɪ̈ˈtæstər/ *n* [C] *literary* someone who writes bad poems

**po·et·ess** /ˌpəʊɪ̈ˈtes◂‖ˈpoʊɪ̈tɪ̈s/ *n* [C] *old-fashioned* a female poet

**po·et·ic** /pəʊˈetɪk‖poʊ-/ also **poetical** /pəʊˈetɪkəl‖poʊ-/ *adj* **1** concerning poetry or typical of poetry: *poetic drama | poetic imagery* **2** having qualities of deep feeling or graceful expression: *Their dancing has a kind of poetic intensity.* —**poetically** /-kli/ *adv*

**poetic jus·tice** /·ˌ·· ˈ··/ *n* [U] a situation in which someone is made to suffer for something bad they have done, in a way that seems perfectly suitable or right: *After being bullied by her for so long, it struck me as poetic justice that she was now being victimized.*

**poetic li·cence** /·ˌ·· ˈ··/ *n* [U] the freedom to change facts, not to obey the usual rules etc, that is allowed to poets and other artists

**Poet Lau·re·ate** /ˌ·· ˈ···/ *n* [C] a poet who is appointed by the king or queen in Britain to write poems on important occasions

W3 **po·et·ry** /ˈpəʊɪ̈tri‖ˈpoʊ-/ *n* [U] **1** poems: *Wordsworth's poetry* **2** the art of writing poems: *the art of poetry* **3** *approving* a quality of beauty, grace, and deep feeling: *The way Martina moves around the court is sheer poetry.*

**po-faced** /ˌpəʊ ˈfeɪst◂‖ˌpoʊ-/ *adj BrE informal* having an unfriendly disapproving expression on your face: *That po-faced woman behind the bar refused to serve us.*

**po·go stick** /ˈpəʊgəʊ stɪk‖ˈpoʊgoʊ-/ *n* [C] a pole with a spring near the bottom and a bar which you can stand on while holding the top in order to jump about for fun

**pog·rom** /ˈpɒgrəm‖pəˈgrɑːm/ *n* [C] a planned killing of large numbers of people, especially Jews, usually done for reasons of race or religion

**poi·gnant** /ˈpɔɪnjənt/ *adj* making you feel sad or full of pity: *I was struck by the poignant contrast between his lively mind and his old frail body.* —**poignancy** *n* [U] —**poignantly** *adv*: *The road between Hué and Danang was poignantly named 'Street without Joy'.*

**poin·set·ti·a** /pɔɪnˈsetiə/ *n* [C] a tropical plant with groups of large bright red leaves that look like flowers

S1 W1 **point¹** /pɔɪnt/ *n*

**1** ▶ **IDEA** ◀ [C] a single fact, idea, or opinion that is part of an argument or discussion: *There was one point on which everyone agreed. | She had brought a list of points for discussion. | One important point must be borne in mind. | That's a very interesting point.* | **make a point** (=give a fact, idea, or opinion) *John made an interesting point about the role of the artist in society.* | **sb's point** *I agree with Jane's point that we need to look more closely at the costs.* | **make/prove your point** (=show that your idea or opinion is right) *He brought along a handful of documents to help prove his point.* | **the finer points** (=details that are difficult to understand) *the finer points of political theory*

**2** ▶ **MAIN MEANING/IDEA** ◀ **the point** the main idea in something that is said or done which gives meaning to all of it: **the point is ...** (=the most important thing is) *The point is that you should have told me where you were going.* | **beside the point** (=not important) *She is young, but that's beside the point.* | **come/get to the point** (=used to tell someone to reach the most important part of what they want to say) *I wish you would get to the point!* | **miss the point** (=not understand the main meaning of something) *Was I hearing him right, or had I completely missed the piont?* | **to the point** (=saying something important about the matter being dealt with) *The message was short and to the point.*

**3** ▶ **PLACE** ◀ [C] an exact place or position: *Line A crosses line B at point C. | a border crossing point*

**4** ▶ **IN TIME/DEVELOPMENT** ◀ [C] an exact moment, time, or stage in something's development: **at this point** *It was at this point the surgeon realized things were going wrong.* | **at this point in time** (=now) *It is impossible to give a definite answer at this point in time.* | **starting point** (=a time or stage from which something can start) *We can use this document as a starting point for our discussions.* | **to the point of** (=to a particular stage) *The beams had weakened to the point of being dangerous.* | **if it comes to the point** (=if a particular situation is reached when a decision has to be made) *If it comes to the point, I am prepared to resign over this.*

**5 boiling point/freezing point/melting point etc** the temperature at which something boils, freezes, melts etc

**6 the high/low point of** the best or worst stage, or best or worst moment of something: *The firework display was the high point of the evening. | This was the low point of his teaching career.*

**7 the point of no return** a stage in a process or activity when it becomes impossible to stop it or do something different

**8 be on the point of (doing) something** to be going to do something very soon: *I was on the point of leaving when the phone rang.*

**9** ▶ **QUALITY/FEATURE** ◀ [C] a particular quality or feature that something or someone has: *She tried to remind herself of his good points. | What are the points to look out for when buying a new computer?* | **the finer points of** (=the small details of quality) *He went on to educate us all on the finer points in choosing champagne.* | **it has its points** (=used to say that something has some good features or qualities) *It's not a car that I would buy, but it does have its points.* | **selling point** (=a feature that will help to sell sth) *The main selling point of the product is its price.* | **strong/weak point** (=a part of someone or something that is good or bad) *Neatness is not his strong point.*

**10** ▶ **PURPOSE** ◀ [U] the purpose or aim of something: *The whole point of this experiment is to show how the chemicals react in water.* | **there is no point** *I could see that there was no point in arguing with him.* | **not see the point** *I couldn't see the point of trying to explain.* | **what is the point?** *What was the point in working to pass exams if there were no jobs available?*

**11 up to a point** to some extent, but not completely: *I agree with you up to a point.*

**12** ▶ **SHARP END** ◀ [C] a sharp end of something: *a knife with a very sharp point*

**13 at the point of a gun/at gun point** if you do something at gun point, you do it while someone is pointing a gun towards you

**14 ▶ GAMES/SPORT ◀** [C] a unit used to show the score in a game or sport: *Steve Jones is 15 points ahead.* | **win/lose a point** *She lost three points for that fall.* | **beat sb on points/win on points** (=win a boxing match by gaining more points than your opponent rather than by defeating them completely)
**15 ▶ NUMBERS ◀** [C] a sign (.) used to separate a whole number from any decimals that follow it
**16 ▶ MEASURE ON A SCALE ◀** [C] a mark or measure on a scale: *The cost of living has risen by three percentage points.*
**17 ▶ SMALL SPOT ◀** [C] a very small spot: *The stars shone like tiny points of light in the sky.*
**18 ▶ DIRECTION ◀** [C] one of the marks on a COMPASS that shows direction: *the points of the compass*
**19 ▶ PIECE OF LAND ◀** [C] a long thin piece of land that stretches out into the sea
**20 ▶ ELECTRICITY ◀** [C] a piece of plastic with holes in it which is fixed to a wall and to which electrical equipment can be connected
**21 make a point (of doing sth)** to do something deliberately so that people notice: *I always make a point of introducing new members to the chairman.*
**22 ▶ RAILWAYS ◀ points** [plural] a piece of railway track that can be moved to allow a train to cross over from one track to another
**23 ▶ DANCING ◀ points** [plural] *technical* the ends of a dancer's feet, on which they balance when they are dancing in BALLET

Frequencies of the noun **point** in spoken and written English.

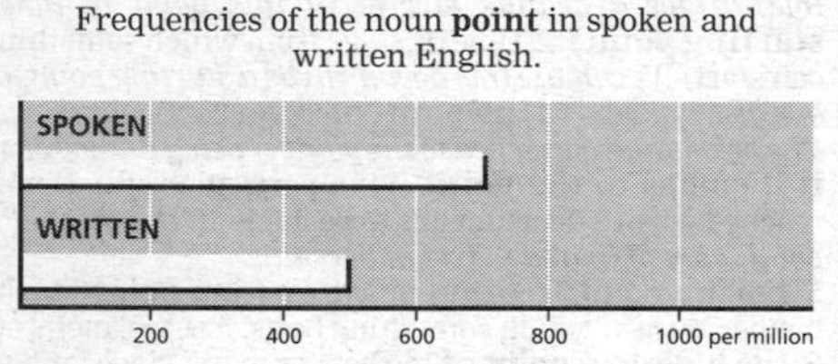


Based on the British National Corpus and the Longman Lancaster Corpus

This graph shows that the noun **point** is more common in spoken English than in written English. This is because it is used in a lot of common spoken phrases.

**point** (*n*) **SPOKEN PHRASES**

**24 what's the point?/there's no point** used to say that you do not think something is worth doing: *I could try to help but what's the point? He never listens to anyone.* | **what's the point in doing sth?/there's no point in doing sth** *There's no point in lying, I'll find out anyway.*
**25 I can't see any point in** used to say that you do not think something has any real purpose: *I've got no time for politics – I can't see any point in it.* | **I can't see any point in doing sth** *I can't see any point in going there when we can just call instead.*
**26 that's the point** used when emphasizing what the main fact, idea or purpose of something is: *It costs me more but it lasts much longer, you see. That's the point.* | **that's the whole point** *But that's the whole point – the richer you are, the more you should pay.*
**27 that's a good point** used when someone mentions an important fact or detail that you had not thought of: *"But how will you get there?" "That's a good point, I won't have the car, will I?"*
**28 that's not the point** used to tell someone that the fact or reason they are mentioning is not at all important: *Maybe you were trying to be helpful, but that's not the point, is it?*
**29 (that's) more to the point** used to say that a particular fact or reason is more important than the one that was just mentioned: *Yes, she has stolen the money, but why? That's more to the point.*
**30 I see your/his point** used to say that you can understand why someone has a particular idea or opinion: *He thought the meeting was a waste of time, and I could see his point.*
**31 I take your point** used to tell someone you accept that their idea or opinion is correct: *I take your point about that picture. It does look better here.*
**32 point taken** used to tell someone that you accept that you were wrong and they were right about something: *OK, point taken. I won't interfere any more.*
**33 you/they have a point** used to say that someone has an idea or opinion that is right: *Sue thinks it would be better to go by train, and I think she has a point.*
**34 not to put too fine a point on it** used when you are saying something in a very direct way that might upset someone: *She was being a real pain in the ass, not to put too fine a point on it.*

**point²** *v* S1 W1

**point**

**1 ▶ SHOW STH WITH YOUR FINGER ◀** [I] to show someone something by holding up one of your fingers or a thin object towards it: *"Look!" said a soldier, and pointed.* | *John leaned over her and pointed ahead.* | [+ **at**] *I could see him pointing at me and telling the other guests what I had said.* | [+ **to**] *He shook his head, and pointed to a gate at the bottom of the field.* | [+ **with**] *The driver pointed with his whip.*
**2 ▶ BE AIMED ◀** [I always + adv/prep] to be aimed in a particular direction: *The arrow always points north.* | [+ **at**] *There were TV cameras pointing at us.* | [+ **to**] *The hands of the clock pointed to a quarter past one.*
**3 ▶ AIM STH ◀** [T] to hold something so that it is aimed towards a person or thing: **point sth at** *I wish you'd stop pointing that gun at men.* | *Lionel had stood up and was pointing an accusing finger at his brother.*
**4 ▶ SHOW SB WHERE TO GO ◀** [T always + adv/prep] to show someone which direction they should go in: **point sb down/along/to etc** *The receptionist pointed her down the corridor to the manager's office.* | *He pointed Mrs Morel to a large armchair.*
**5 ▶ WALLS/BUILDINGS ◀** [T] to put new CEMENT between the bricks of a wall
**6 point your toes** to stretch the ends of your feet downwards when you are dancing
**7 point the finger at** to blame someone or say that they have done something wrong: *I don't want to point the finger at anyone in particular – I think we are all to blame for this.*
**8 point the way a)** to show the direction that something is in: *A line of buildings pointed the way to the village.* **b)** to show how something could change or develop successfully: *We feel that this report points the way forward for the water industry.*

**point** sth ↔ **out** *phr v* **1** [T] to show something to someone by pointing at it: *They walked into the car park and Cook pointed out his new car.* | *My mother pointed him out to me.* **2** [T] to tell someone something that they did not already know or had not thought about: *He pointed out the dangers of setting out without proper equipment.* | **point out that** *The officer pointed out that the story was somewhat hard to believe.* | **point sth out to sb** *Mr Rogers had pointed out to us that we should keep well away from the lake.*

**point to** sth *phr v* [T] to mention something because you think it is important: *Many politicians have pointed to the need for a written constitution.*

**point to/towards** sb/sth *phr v* [T] if something points to a fact, it makes it seem very likely that it is true: *All the evidence pointed to Blake as the murderer.*

**point** sth ↔ **up** *phr v* [T] *formal* to make something seem more important or more noticeable: *The latest economic figures point up the failure of the government's policies.*

**point-blank** /ˌ· ˈ·◂/ *adv* **1** if you say or refuse something point-blank, you do it directly and without trying to explain your reasons: *I told him point-blank that I did not want to be involved in the deal.* **2** a gun fired point-blank is fired very close to the person or thing it is aimed at: *Dodds fired both barrels point-blank at his former lover.* —**point-blank** *adj*: *shot at point-blank range*

**point du·ty** /ˈ· ˌ··/ *n* [U] *BrE* a police officer who is on point duty stands at a place where two roads cross and controls the traffic passing through

**point·ed** /ˈpɔɪntɪ̥d/ *adj* [usually before noun] **1** having a point at the end: *Poirot was a dapper little man with a pointed beard.* —see picture on page 412 **2 a pointed comment/look/remark** something you say or do in a deliberately direct and noticeable way, in order to show your annoyance or disapproval: *Mark's father made a pointed remark about his hair just as we were leaving.* —**pointedly** *adv*: *He looked at his watch pointedly. "Are you ready to go or not?"*

**point·er** /ˈpɔɪntə‖-ər/ *n* [C]
**1** ▶ **SHOWS NUMBER/DIRECTION ETC** ◀ a thin piece of metal that points to a number or direction on a piece of equipment, for example on a measuring instrument: *The pointer is halfway between 105 and 110 pounds.*
**2** ▶ **STICK** ◀ a long stick used to point at things on a map, board etc
**3** ▶ **ADVICE** ◀ a useful piece of advice or information that helps you do or understand something: [+ **on**] *Ralph gave me some pointers on my golf swing.*
**4** ▶ **SIGN** ◀ something that shows how a situation is developing, or is a sign of what might happen in the future: [+ **to**] *A pointer to the growing interest in healthy eating has been the rise in sales of fresh fish.*
**5** ▶ **DOG** ◀ a hunting dog that stands very still and points with its nose to where birds or animals are hiding

**poin·til·lis·m** /ˈpwæntɪlɪzəm, ˈpɔɪn-/ *n* [U] a style of painting popular in the late 19th century that uses small spots of colour all over the painting, rather than brush strokes —**pointillist** *adj* —**pointillist** *n* [C]

**point·less** /ˈpɔɪntləs/ *adj* **1** without any purpose or meaning: *a pointless waste of money* | *Life just seemed so pointless.* **2** not likely to have any useful result: *a pointless quarrel* | **it is pointless to do sth** *I think it would be pointless to discuss this issue again.* | **it is pointless doing sth** *It's pointless telling her to clean her room – she'll never do it.* —**pointlessly** *adv* —**pointlessness** *n* [U]

**point man** /ˈ· ·/ *n* [C] *AmE* a soldier who goes ahead of a group to see if there is any danger

**point of or·der** /ˌ· · ˈ··/ *n* [C] *formal* a rule connected with the organization of an official meeting: *One MP raised an objection on a point of order.*

**point of ref·e·rence** /ˌ· · ˈ···/ *n* [C] something you already know about that helps you understand a situation

**point of sale** /ˌ· · ˈ·◂/ *n* [C] the place or shop where a product is sold: *an advertising campaign in which posters and leaflets would be displayed at the point of sale*

**point of view** /ˌ· · ˈ·/ *n* [C] **1** a particular way of thinking about or judging a situation: *From a purely environmental point of view, this is not a good decision.* **2** someone's own personal opinion or attitude about something: *I respect your point of view, but I really don't agree with you.* | *My parents never seem to be able to see my point of view.*

**points·man** /ˈpɔɪntsmən/ *n* [C] *BrE* someone who operates the short RAILS that move so that a train can change from one set of tracks to another

**point-to-point** /ˌ· · ˈ·◂/ *n* [C] *BrE* a race for horses that goes across country areas

**poise¹** /pɔɪz/ *n* [U] **1** a calm, confident way of behaving, combined with an ability to control your feelings or reactions in difficult situations: *Travelling around Europe by herself seems to have given Louisa more poise and confidence.* **2** a graceful way of moving or standing, so that your body seems balanced and not awkward: *the poise of a dancer*

**poise²** *v* [T always + adv/prep] to put or hold something in a carefully balanced position, especially above something else: **poise sth over/above etc** *Benjamin poised the bottle over the second glass and glanced at Consuela to see if she wanted a drink.*

**poised** /pɔɪzd/ *adj* **1** [not before noun] not moving but ready to move or do something at any moment: [+ **for/on etc**] *She saw Matthew poised on the board for a swift, controlled racing dive.* | **poised to do sth** *He was waiting with the door open, poised to jump, as the train pulled into the station.* **2** [not before noun] completely ready to do or achieve something, and about to do it: **poised to do sth** *At this point, Spain was poised to become the dominant power in Europe.* **3** [not before noun] not moving and seeming to hang in the air: [+ **over/above etc**] *Noriko was holding her chopsticks poised in the air, as though waiting for me to say something.* | *Stanley's hand remained poised over the open box as the footsteps came closer.* **4** [not before noun] in a position in which two things have an equally strong influence: [+ **between**] *The tone of the book is poised between comedy and moral seriousness.* **5** behaving in a calm, confident way, and able to control your feelings and reactions: *Abbey walked to the microphone, poised and smiling.*

**poi·son¹** /ˈpɔɪzən/ *n* **1** [C,U] a substance that can cause death or serious illness if you eat it, drink it etc: *These fruits contain a deadly poison.* | *Joanna committed suicide by swallowing poison.* **2** [C,U] something such as an emotion or idea that makes you behave badly or become very unhappy: *Anger and hatred are poisons that destroy a person's emotional life.* **3 what's your poison?** *spoken* a humorous way of asking someone which alcoholic drink they would like —see also **one man's meat is another man's poison** (MEAT (8))

**poison²** *v* [T] **1** to harm or kill someone by giving them poison: *The whole family had been poisoned with strychnine.* **2** to add poison to something: *Germanicus feared that someone had poisoned his food.* | *poisoned arrows* **3** to make land, rivers, air etc impure, especially by the use of harmful chemicals: *We are poisoning our rivers with pesticides and toxic waste.* **4** to have very harmful and unpleasant effects on someone's mind and emotions: *Her father's tyranny had poisoned her childhood.* | *these violent videos that poison the minds of the young* **5 poison sb's mind against sb** to make someone dislike another person by saying bad and untrue things **6** *especially BrE* to infect a part of the body **7 poisoned chalice** an important job that someone is given, which is likely to cause them a lot of trouble —**poisoner** *n* [C]

**poison gas** /ˌ·· ˈ·/ *n* [U] gas that causes death or serious injury, used especially against an enemy in a war

**poi·son·ing** /ˈpɔɪzənɪŋ/ *n* [C,U] illness caused by swallowing, touching, or breathing in a poisonous substance: *Several cases of poisoning have been reported.* | **alcohol/mercury/radiation poisoning** (=caused by a particular substance) —see also FOOD POISONING

**poison i·vy** /ˌ·· ˈ··/ *n* [U] a bush or VINE that causes pain on your skin when you touch it

**poison oak** /ˌ·· ˈ·/ *n* [U] a North American plant that causes painful spots on your skin when you touch it

**poi·son·ous** /ˈpɔɪzənəs/ *adj* **1** containing poison or producing poison: *poisonous mushrooms* | *poisonous snakes* **2** full of unpleasant and unfriendly feelings: *There was a poisonous atmosphere in the household that made Bonita feel very uneasy.* **3** someone who is poisonous seems to get pleasure from causing arguments, unhappiness etc: *That poisonous bastard Lucett told Morris I was seeing his wife.* —**poisonously** *adv*

**poison-pen let·ter** /ˌ·· ˈ·· ˌ··/ *n* [C] a letter that is not signed and that says nasty and unpleasant things about the person it has been sent to

**poke¹** /pəʊk‖poʊk/ *v*

**1 ▶ WITH A FINGER/STICK ETC ◀** [T] to quickly push into something or someone with your finger, a stick, or something pointed: *Andy poked the fish to see if it was still alive.* | *Be careful with that umbrella, or you'll poke someone in the eye.* —see picture on page 1260

**2 ▶ THROUGH A SPACE/HOLE ◀ a)** [T always + adv/prep] to move or push something through a space or opening: *He poked his hands deep into his pockets.* | **poke your head around the door/through the window etc** *One of the nurses poked her head around the door.* **b) ▶ BE SEEN ◀** [I always + adv/prep] if something is poking through or out of something else, you can see part of it but not all of it: *Ella looked at the tiny face poking out of the wool blanket.* | *Weeds had started poking through the cracks in the path.*

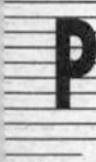

**3 poke a hole** to make a hole or hollow area in something by pushing something pointed into or through it: *Poke a hole in the dough and form it into a doughnut shape.*

**4 poke fun at** make fun of someone in an unkind way: *Some of the kids were poking fun at Judy because of the way she dressed.*

**5 poke your nose into** *informal* to take an interest or get involved in someone else's private affairs: *I don't want him poking his nose into our marriage.*

**6 poke the fire** to move coal or wood in a fire with a stick to make it burn better

**7 ▶ SEX ◀** [T] *slang taboo* to have sex with a woman

**poke around/about** *phr v* [I] *BrE informal* **1** to look for something by moving a lot of things around: *James began poking about in the cupboard, looking for the sugar.* **2** to try to find out information about other people's private lives, business etc, in a way that annoys them: *I don't want you poking around in my business.*

**poke at** sth *phr v* [T] to keep pushing something by making repeated movements with something pointed: *He was poking at the dust with his stick, making little patterns.*

**poke²** *n* **1 give sb/sth a poke** to quickly push your fingers, a stick etc into something or someone: *Vanessa gave me a poke in the ribs.* **2** [C] *AmE old-fashioned slang* a WALLET containing money

**pok·er** /ˈpəʊkə‖ˈpoʊkər/ *n* **1** [U] a card game that people usually play for money **2** [C] a metal stick used to move coal or wood in a fire to make it burn better

**poker-faced** /ˌ·· ˈ·◂/ *adj* showing no expression on your face: *Melanie waited poker-faced for their next offer.* —**poker face** *n* [singular]

**po·ker·work** /ˈpəʊkəwɜːk‖ˈpoʊkərwɜːrk/ *n* [U] pictures or patterns burned onto the surface of wood or leather with hot tools, or the art of making these pictures

**pok·ey** /ˈpəʊki‖ˈpoʊ-/ *n* [C] *AmE old-fashioned* a jail

**pok·y, pokey** /ˈpəʊki‖ˈpoʊ-/ *adj* **1** too small and not very pleasant or comfortable: *The whole family was crammed into two poky little rooms.* **2** *AmE* doing things very slowly, especially in a way that you find annoying: *I got behind some poky driver on the freeway.*

**pol** /pɒl‖pɑːl/ *n* [C] *AmE informal* a politician

**Po·lack** /ˈpəʊlæk‖ˈpoʊ-/ *n* [C] *AmE* an insulting word for someone from Poland

**po·lar** /ˈpəʊlə‖ˈpoʊlər/ *adj* **1** close to, or connected with the North Pole and the South Pole: *As our climate warms up, the polar ice caps will begin to melt.* **2** *technical* related to one of the POLES of a MAGNET **3 polar opposite/extreme** something exactly or completely opposite in character or nature

**polar bear** /ˌ·· ˈ·‖ˈ·· ·/ *n* [C] a large white bear that lives near the North Pole

**po·lar·ise** /ˈpəʊləraɪz‖ˈpoʊ-/ *v* a British spelling of POLARIZE

**po·lar·i·ty** /pəˈlærəti/ *n* [C,U] **1** *formal* the fact of people, opinions, or ideas being completely different or opposite to each other: [+ **between**] *the supposed polarity between the intellect and the emotions* **2** *technical* the state of having either a positive or negative electric charge

**po·lar·ize** also **-ise** *BrE* /ˈpəʊləraɪz‖ˈpoʊ-/ *v* [I,T] *formal* to divide into clearly separate groups with opposite beliefs, ideas, or opinions, or to make people do this: *a highly controversial issue that has polarized the country* | *Patterns of political support had become polarized between the north and south.* —**polarization** /ˌpəʊləraɪˈzeɪʃən‖ˌpoʊlərə-/ *n* [U]

**Po·lar·oid** /ˈpəʊlərɔɪd‖ˈpoʊ-/ *n trademark* **1** [C] a camera that uses a special film to produce a photograph very quickly **2** [C] a photograph taken with a Polaroid camera **3** [U] a special material which is put on the glass in SUNGLASSES, car windows etc to make the sun seem less bright **4 Polaroids** [plural] dark glasses with Polaroid material on them

**pole¹** /pəʊl‖poʊl/ *n* [C] W3

**1 ▶ STICK/POST ◀** a long stick or post usually made of wood or metal, often set upright in the ground to support something: *a telephone pole* | *a flagpole* | *The dusty curtains hung from unpolished brass poles.*

**2 ▶ NORTH/SOUTH POLE ◀** the most northern or most southern point on a PLANET, especially the Earth: *Amundsen's expedition was the first to reach the pole.*

**3 be poles apart** two people or things that are poles apart are as different from each other as it is possible to be: *Both brilliant pianists, Powell and Monk are poles apart in style.*

**4 ▶ OPPOSITE IDEAS/BELIEFS ◀** one of two situations, ideas, or opinions that are the complete opposite of each other: *We have the accumulation of wealth at one pole and poverty and misery at the other.*

**5 ▶ ELECTRICAL ◀ a)** one of two points at the ends of a MAGNET where its power is the strongest **b)** one of the two points at which wires can be fixed onto a BATTERY (1) in order to use its electricity

**6 ▶ IN THE SKY ◀** one of the two points in the sky, one to the north of the Earth and one to the south, around which the stars appear to turn

**Pole²** *n* [C] someone who comes from Poland

**pole³** *v* [I,T] to push a boat along in the water using a pole

**pole·axed** /ˈpəʊlækst‖ˈpoʊl-/ *adj* [not before noun] **1** *informal* very surprised and shocked: *I was poleaxed when I heard I'd passed the exam.* **2** unable to stand because something has hit you very hard: *The big Texan staggered and collapsed as if poleaxed.*

**pole·cat** /ˈpəʊlkæt‖ˈpoʊl-/ *n* [C] **1** a small dark brown wild animal that lives in northern Europe and can defend itself by producing an unpleasant smell **2** *AmE informal* a SKUNK

**po·lem·ic** /pəˈlemɪk/ *n formal or technical* **1** [C] a written or spoken statement that strongly criticizes or defends a particular idea, opinion, or person **2** [U] also **polemics** the practice or skill of making such statements: *Before long, the dispute had degenerated into heated polemics.*

**po·lem·i·cal** /pəˈlemɪkəl/ also **polemic** *adj formal or technical* using strong arguments to criticize or defend a particular idea, opinion, or person: *The health reforms were attacked in a highly polemical piece in the 'New Yorker'.* —**polemically** /-kli/ *adv*

**pole po·si·tion** /ˈ· ·ˌ··/ *n* [C,U] the front position at the beginning of a car or bicycle race

**Pole Star** /ˈ· ·/ *n* **the Pole Star** a star that is almost directly over the North Pole and that can be seen from the northern part of the world

**pole vault** /ˈ· ·/ *n* **the pole vault** the sport of jumping over a high bar using a long pole —**pole vaulter** *n* [C]

**po·lice¹** /pəˈliːs/ *n* [plural] **1 the police** an official organization whose job is to make sure that people obey the law, to catch criminals, and to protect people and S1 W1 property: *I heard the sound of a window breaking and called the police.|Accidents involving injuries must be reported to the police.|a police car* **2** the people who work for this organization: *Armed police surrounded the courthouse.|Several police were injured when violence broke out.* —see also MILITARY POLICE, SECRET POLICE

**police²** *v* [T] **1** to keep control over a particular area in order to make sure that laws are obeyed and people and property are protected, using a police or military force: *The army was brought in to police the riot-torn city.|new methods of policing the neighborhood* **2** to control a particular activity or industry by making sure that people follow the correct rules concerning what they do: *The agency was set up to police the nuclear power industry.* —**policing** *n* [U]: *policing in rural areas*

**police con·sta·ble** /ˌ·ˈ· ˈ···◂/ *n* [C] *BrE formal* a police officer of the lowest rank

**police court** /·ˈ· ·/ *n* [C,U] *AmE* a court of law for small crimes

**police de·part·ment** /·ˈ· ·ˌ··/ *n* [C] *AmE* the official police organization in a particular area or city

**police dog** /·ˈ· ·/ *n* [C] a dog trained by the police to find hidden drugs or catch criminals

**police force** /·ˈ· ·/ *n* [C] the official police organization in a country or area: *Marshall joined the police force in 1983.*

S 2 W 3 **po·lice·man** /pəˈliːsmən/ *n plural* **policemen** /-mən/ [C] a male police officer

**police of·fi·cer** /·ˈ· ˌ···/ *n* [C] a member of the police

**police state** /·ˈ· ·/ *n* [C] a country where the government strictly controls people's freedom to meet, write or speak about politics, travel where they like etc

**police sta·tion** /·ˈ· ˌ··/ *n* [C] the local office of the police in a town, part of a city etc

**po·lice·wom·an** /pəˈliːsˌwʊmən/ *n plural* **policewomen** /-ˌwɪmɪn/ [C] a female police officer

S 3 W 1 **pol·i·cy** /ˈpɒlɪ̈si‖ˈpɑː-/ *n* **1** [C,U] a course of action that has been officially agreed and chosen by a political party, business, or other organization: *the government's disastrous economic policies*|**[+ on]** *The company' operates a very strict policy on smoking.*|**defence/housing/foreign etc policy** *the President's new health policy*|**policy maker** (=someone who helps to decide what an organization's policies will be) **2** [C] a contract with an insurance company, or an official written statement giving all the details of such a contract: *You should obtain a separate policy covering valuable household items.* **3** [C,U] a particular principle that you believe in and that influences the way you behave: *Well, it's always been my policy not to talk behind people's backs.|You know what they say – honesty is the best policy.*

**po·li·o** /ˈpəʊliəʊ‖ˈpoʊlioʊ/ also **po·li·o·my·e·li·tis** /ˌpəʊliəʊmaɪəˈlaɪtɪ̈s‖ˌpoʊlioʊ-/ *technical n* [U] a serious infectious disease of the nerves in the SPINE, often resulting in permanent PARALYSIS (=complete inability to move particular muscles)

**pol·i sci** /ˌpɒli ˈsaɪ‖ˌpɑː-/ *n* [U] *AmE informal* political science

**pol·ish¹** /ˈpɒlɪʃ‖ˈpɑː-/ *v* [T] to make something smooth, bright, and shiny by rubbing it: *The floor had been polished to a satiny sheen.|It was my duty to polish the silver on Saturdays.* —**polisher** *n* [C] *an electric floor polisher* —**polishing** *n* [U] —see picture at CLEAN

**polish** sth ↔ **off** *phr v* [T] *informal* to finish food, work etc, quickly or easily: *At lunch, Rowan polished off six sandwiches!*

**polish** sb ↔ **off** *phr v* [T] *AmE informal* to kill or defeat someone: *Mather was polished off with a shotgun in another gangland killing.*

**polish** sth ↔ **up** *phr v* [T] **1** to improve a skill or an ability by practising it: *I need to polish up my Spanish before we go on vacation.* **2** to polish something

**polish²** *n* **1** [C,U] a liquid, powder, or other substance used for rubbing into a surface to make it smooth and shiny: *pine panelling gleaming with wax polish|furniture polish|shoe polish* —see also FRENCH POLISH **2** [U] a special quality of great skill and style in the way someone performs, writes, or behaves: *Carla's writing hs potential, but it lacks polish.* **3** [singular] a smooth shiny surface produced by polishing **4** [singular] an act of polishing a surface to make it smooth and shiny: *An occasional wipe and polish with a soft cloth will keep wall tiles looking good.* —see also SPIT AND POLISH

**Pol·ish³** /ˈpəʊlɪʃ‖ˈpoʊ-/ *adj* from or connected with Poland, its people, or their language

**Pol·ish⁴** *n* [U] the language of Poland

**pol·ished** /ˈpɒlɪʃt‖ˈpɑː-/ *adj* **1** shiny because of being rubbed, usually with polish: *highly polished boots* **2** a polished performance, piece of writing etc is done with great skill and style **3** polished social behaviour, speech etc is polite, confident, and graceful

**po·lit·bu·ro** /ˈpɒlɪtbjʊərəʊ‖ˈpɑːlɪ̈tbjʊroʊ/ *n* [C] the chief decision-making committee of a Communist party or Communist government

**po·lite** /pəˈlaɪt/ *adj* **1** behaving or speaking in a way that is correct for the social situation you are in, and showing that you are careful to consider other people's needs and feelings: *a polite refusal|What polite well-behaved children!*|**it is polite to do sth** *We left as soon as it was polite to do so.|It's not polite to talk with your mouth full.* —opposite RUDE (1), IMPOLITE **2** polite conversation, remarks etc are made because it is considered socially correct to do this: *a few polite remarks about the weather|Nathaniel's sexual exploits are hardly the subject of polite conversation.* **3 in polite society/circles/company** *often humorous* among people who are considered to have a good education and correct social behaviour: *You can't use words like that in polite company.* **4 just/only being polite** *spoken* saying something you may not really believe or think, in order to avoid offending someone: *I know Ian said he liked her singing, but he was just being polite.* —**politely** *adv* —**politeness** *n* [U] S 3

**pol·i·tic** /ˈpɒlɪ̈tɪk‖ˈpɑː-/ *adj formal* sensible and likely to bring advantage; PRUDENT: *It would not be politic to ignore the reporters.* —see also POLITICS, BODY POLITIC

**po·lit·i·cal** /pəˈlɪtɪkəl/ *adj* **1** [no comparative] connected with the government or public affairs of a country and its relations with other countries: *a loss of political freedom|a long period of political stability|The UN is seeking a political solution rather than a military one.|Cuba's political structure|one of the main political parties* **2** [no comparative] connected with the ideas, activities, or advantage of a particular party or group in politics: *a decision that was taken for purely political reasons|There were obvious political advantages in cutting taxes.|political propaganda* **3** [no comparative] a political offence or crime is harmful to a government: *the summary execution of a political offender* **4** interested in or active in politics: *Most students these days aren't very political.* **5 political football** *especially BrE* a difficult problem which opposing politicians argue about or which each side deals with in a way that will bring them advantage: *It is unfortunate that education has become something of a political football.* —see also POLITICALLY

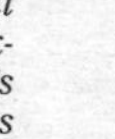

**political ac·tion com·mit·tee** /·ˌ··· ˈ·· ·ˌ··/ *n* [C] *AmE* an organization formed by a business, union, or INTEREST GROUP to help raise money so that people who support their ideas can try to be elected for Congress; PAC

**political a·sy·lum** /·ˌ··· ·ˈ··/ *n* [U] the right to remain safely in another country if you cannot live safely in your own because of the political situation there: *refugees seeking political asylum*

**political e·con·o·my** /·ˌ··· ·ˈ···/ *n* [U] the study of the way nations organize the production and use of wealth

**political ge·og·ra·phy** /·ˌ··· ·ˈ···/ *n* [U] the study of the way the Earth's surface is divided up into different countries, rather than the way it is marked by rivers, mountains etc

**po·lit·ic·ally** /pəˈlɪtɪkli/ *adv* in a political way: *Women were becoming more politically active.|a politically*

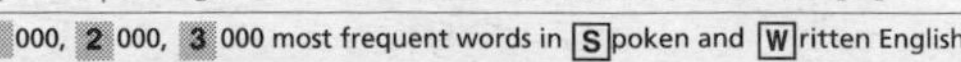

*motivated strike* [sentence adverb] *Politically, the organization was still very divided.*

**politically cor·rect** /ˌ‚··· ·'·/ *adj* language, behaviour, and attitudes that are politically correct are regarded as right and acceptable because they are careful to avoid offending women, black people, DISABLED people etc: *It's not politically correct to say 'handicapped' anymore.* —see also PC² —**political correctness** /ˌ‚··· ·'··/ *n* [U]

**political ma·chine** /ˌ‚··· ·'·/ *n* [singular] *AmE* the system used by people with the same political interests to make sure that political decisions bring advantage to themselves or to their group

**political pris·on·er** /ˌ‚··· '···/ *n* [C] someone who is put in prison because they oppose and criticize the government of their own country

**political sci·ence** /ˌ‚··· '··/ *n* [U] the study of politics and government —**political scientist** *n* [C]

W2 **pol·i·ti·cian** /ˌpɒlɪ'tɪʃən‖ˌpɑː-/ *n* [C] **1** someone who works in politics, especially an elected member of a parliament or similar institution **2** someone who is skilled at dealing with people or using the situation in an organization to bring advantage to themselves: *You really have to be a politician to succeed in this place.*

**po·li·ti·cize** also **-ise** *BrE* /pə'lɪtɪsaɪz/ *v* [T] to make something more political or more involved in politics: *an attempt to politicise the police*

**po·lit·i·cized** also **-ised** *BrE* /pə'lɪtɪsaɪzd/ *adj* having become involved in or interested in politics: *The public-sector unions are the most politicized.* —**politicization** /pəˌlɪtɪsaɪ'zeɪʃən‖-sə-/ *n* [U]

**pol·i·tick·ing** /'pɒlɪtɪkɪŋ‖'pɑː-/ *n* [U] political activity, usually done only for your own advantage: *the politicking behind the scenes at the party conference*

**po·lit·i·co** /pə'lɪtɪkəʊ‖-koʊ/ *n* [C] a disapproving word meaning a politician or someone who is active in politics: *east-coast politicos seeking Irish-American votes*

**politico-** /pəlɪtɪkəʊ‖-koʊ/ *prefix* political and: *politico-scientific*

S2 W2 **pol·i·tics** /'pɒlɪtɪks‖'pɑː-/ *n* **1** [U] ideas and activities that are concerned with the gaining and using of power in a country, city etc: *Most people are fairly cynical about politics.* | *She became quite active in student politics.* | [also + plural verb *BrE*] *Politics have always interested Anita.* **2** [U] the profession of being a politician: *Flynn retired from politics in 1986.* | **go into politics** (=become a politician) *Smith went into politics in his early twenties.* **3** [U] the activities of people in a group, organization etc that are concerned with gaining personal advantage: *Try not to get involved in office politics.* | *sexual politics* **4** [plural] someone's political beliefs and opinions: *I've always been open about my politics.* **5** [U] the study of political power and systems of government: *Tom is studying for a degree in politics.*

**pol·i·ty** /'pɒlɪti‖'pɑː-/ *n* [C,U] *formal* a particular form of political or government organization, or a condition of society in which political organization exists

**pol·ka** /'pɒlkə, 'pəʊlkə‖'poʊlkə/ *n* [C] a very quick, simple dance for people dancing in pairs, or a piece of music for this dance —**polka** *v* [I]

**polka dot** /'·· ·/ *n* [C] one of a number of DOTS (spots) that form a pattern, especially on material for clothing: *a white scarf with red polka dots* —**polka-dot** *adj*: *a polka-dot dress* —see picture on page 839

W3 **poll¹** /pəʊl‖poʊl/ *n* **1** [C] **a)** an attempt to find out what the public think about something, especially about a political subject, done by questioning a large number of people; OPINION POLL: *Another poll asked respondents if they favoured nuclear power.* | **carry out/conduct a poll** *MORI carried out a poll among senior managers to get their views on taxation.* **b)** a record of the result of this; OPINION POLL: *Recent polls show Labour well in the lead.* —see also DEED POLL, EXIT POLL, STRAW POLL **2 the poll** also **the polls** an election to choose a government or political representative: *a fourth successive defeat at the polls* | *The result of the poll won't be known until around midnight.* | **go to the polls** (=vote in an election) *It's only one more week until the country goes to the polls.* **3** [singular] the number of votes recorded at an election: *In most constituencies the largest party can pull 40% of the poll.* **4 the polls** *especially AmE* the place where you can go to vote in an election: *The polls won't close for another hour.*

**poll²** *v* [T] to try to find out what the public thinks about a subject by questioning a large number of people: *18% of the women we polled said their husbands had a drinking problem.*

**pol·lard¹** /'pɒləd, -lɑːd‖'pɑːlərd/ *n* [C] a tree that has had the top cut off to make the lower branches grow more thickly

**pollard²** *v* [T] to cut the top off a tree in order to make the lower branches grow more thickly —**pollarded** *adj*

**pol·len** /'pɒlən‖'pɑː-/ *n* [U] a fine powder produced by flowers, which is carried by the wind or by insects to other flowers of the same type making them produce seeds

**pollen count** /'·· ·/ *n* [C] a measure of the amount of pollen in the air, usually given as a guide for people who are made ill by it: *an unusually warm day with a very high pollen count*

**pol·li·nate** /'pɒlɪneɪt‖'pɑː-/ *v* [T] to make a flower or plant produce seeds by giving it pollen: *flowers pollinated by bees* —**pollination** /ˌpɒlɪ'neɪʃən/ *n* [U]

**poll·ing** /'pəʊlɪŋ‖'poʊ-/ *n* [U] the activity of voting in a political election: *Polling started at 8.00 this morning.* | **heavy/light polling** (=with many/few people voting)

**polling booth** /'·· ·/ *n* [C] *especially BrE* a small partly enclosed space in a polling station where you can vote secretly in an election; VOTING BOOTH *AmE*

**polling day** /'·· ·/ *n* [C] *BrE* the day on which people vote in an election

**polling sta·tion** /'·· ˌ··/ *especially BrE* **polling place** *AmE* *n* [C] the place where people go to vote in an election

**pol·li·wog, pollywog** /'pɒliwɒg‖'pɑːliwɑːg/ *n* [C] *AmE* a TADPOLE

**poll·ster** /'pəʊlstə‖'poʊlstər/ *n* [C] someone who prepares and asks questions to find out what people think about a particular subject

**poll tax** /'· ·/ *n* **1** [C] a tax of a fixed amount collected from every citizen of a country **2 the poll tax** a British tax of a fixed amount which was paid by each person during the late 1980s and early 1990s

**pol·lut·ant** /pə'luːtənt/ *n* [C,U] a substance that makes air, water, soil etc dangerously dirty, and is caused by cars, factories etc: *emissions of chemical pollutants*

**pol·lute** /pə'luːt/ *v* [T] **1** to make air, water, soil etc dangerously dirty and not suitable for people to use: *beaches polluted by raw sewage* | *industrial emissions that pollute the air* **2 pollute sb's mind** to give someone immoral thoughts and spoil their character: *fears that Lawrence's novels would pollute young minds* —**polluted** *adj*: *polluted rivers* —**polluter** *n* [C]

**pol·lu·tion** /pə'luːʃən/ *n* [U] **1** the process of making air, water, soil etc dangerously dirty and not suitable for people to use: *California's tough anti-pollution laws* | *chronic pollution of the atmosphere* **2** substances that make air, water, soil etc dangerously dirty: *industries and other sources of pollution* | *a national programme to cut sulphur dioxide pollution* W2

**Pol·ly·an·na** /ˌpɒli'ænə‖ˌpɑː-/ *n* [C usually singular] someone who is always cheerful and always thinks something good is going to happen

**po·lo** /'pəʊləʊ‖'poʊloʊ/ *n* [U] a game played between two teams of players riding horses, who hit a small ball with long-handled wooden hammers —see also WATER POLO

**pol·o·naise** /ˌpɒlə'neɪz‖ˌpɑː-/ *n* [C,U] a slow Polish dance popular in the 19th century, or the music for this dance

**polo neck** /'·· ·/ *n* [C] *BrE* a shirt or SWEATER with a high, close-fitting band around the neck that is rolled down;

TURTLENECK *AmE* —**polo-neck** *adj*: *a polo neck sweater* —see picture on page 840

**polo shirt** /'·· ·/ *n* [C] a shirt with short SLEEVES and a collar, made out of soft cotton material

**pol·ter·geist** /'pɒltəgaɪst‖'poʊltər-/ *n* [C] a spirit that makes objects move around and causes strange noises

**pol·troon** /pɒl'truːn‖pɑːl-/ *n* [C] *old use* a COWARD

**pol·y** /'pɒli‖'pɑːli/ *n* [C] *BrE informal* a POLYTECHNIC

**poly-** /pɒli‖pɑː-/ *prefix* many: *polysyllabic* (=with three or more SYLLABLES) | *polyandry*

**pol·y·an·dry** /ˌpɒli'ændri, 'pɒliændri‖ˌpɑːli'ændri/ *n* [U] *technical* the custom or practice of having more than one husband at the same time —compare BIGAMY, POLYGAMY —**polyandrous** /ˌpɒli'ændrə◂‖ˌpɑː/ *adj*

**pol·y·an·thus** /ˌpɒli'ænθəs‖ˌpɑː-/ *n* [C,U] a small garden plant with a group of round brightly-coloured flowers at the top of each stem

**pol·y·es·ter** /'pɒliestə, ˌpɒli'estə◂‖'pɑːliestər/ *n* [U] a man-made material used to make cloth

**pol·y·eth·y·lene** /ˌpɒli'eθəliːn‖ˌpɑː-/ *n* [U] *AmE* a strong light plastic used to make bags, sheets for covering food, small containers etc; POLYTHENE *BrE*

**po·lyg·a·my** /pə'lɪgəmi/ *n* [U] *technical* the custom or practice of having more than one husband or wife at the same time in a society where this is allowed —compare BIGAMY, MONOGAMY —**polygamous** *adj*

**pol·y·glot** /'pɒlɪglɒt‖'pɑːlɪglɑːt/ *adj formal* speaking or using many languages; MULTILINGUAL —**polyglot** *n* [C]

**pol·y·gon** /'pɒlɪgən‖'pɑːlɪgɑːn/ *n* [C] *technical* a flat shape with three or more sides —**polygonal** /pə'lɪgənəl/ *adj*

**pol·y·graph** /'pɒlɪgrɑːf‖'pɑːlɪgræf/ *n* [C] *technical* a piece of equipment that is used by the police to find out whether someone is telling the truth; LIE DETECTOR

**pol·y·he·dron** /ˌpɒlɪ'hiːdrən‖ˌpɑː-/ *n* [C] a solid shape with many sides

**pol·y·math** /'pɒlɪmæθ‖'pɑː-/ *n* [C] *formal* someone who has a lot of knowledge about many different subjects

**pol·y·mer** /'pɒlɪmə‖'pɑːlɪmər/ *n* [C] a chemical compound that has a simple structure of large MOLECULES

**pol·y·mor·phous** /ˌpɒlɪ'mɔːfəs◂‖ˌpɑːlɪ'mɔːr-/ also **pol·ymor·phic** /-fɪk◂/ *adj technical* having many forms, styles etc during different stages of growth or development

**pol·yp** /'pɒlɪ̣p‖'pɑː-/ *n* [C] **1** a very simple sea animal that has a body like a tube **2** a small lump that grows inside someone's body and is caused by an illness

**po·lyph·o·ny** /pə'lɪfəni/ *n* [U] a kind of music in which several different tunes or notes are sung or played together at the same time —**polyphonic** /ˌpɒlɪ'fɒnɪk◂‖ˌpɑːlɪ'fɑː-/ *adj*

**pol·y·pro·py·lene** /ˌpɒlɪ'prəʊpɪ̣liːn‖ˌpɑːli'proʊ-/ *n* [U] a hard light plastic material

**po·lys·e·mous** /pə'lɪsɪ̣məs, ˌpɒlɪ'siːməs‖-ˌpɑːl-/ *adj technical* a polysemous word has two or more different meanings —**polysemy** *n* [U]

**pol·y·sty·rene** /ˌpɒlɪ'staɪriːn◂‖ˌpɑː-/ *n* [U] *especially BrE* a soft light plastic material that prevents heat or cold from passing through it, used especially for making containers; STYROFOAM *AmE trademark*

**pol·y·syl·la·ble** /'pɒlɪˌsɪləbəl‖'pɑː-/ *n* [C] *technical* a word that contains more than three SYLLABLES —**polysyllabic** /ˌpɒlɪsɪ'læbɪk◂‖ˌpɑː-/ *adj*

**pol·y·tech·nic** /ˌpɒlɪ'teknɪk‖ˌpɑː-/ *n* [C] a kind of British college similar to a university, which provided training and degrees in many subjects, and existed until 1993

**pol·y·the·is·m** /'pɒlɪθiːɪzəm‖'pɑː-/ *n* [U] the belief that there is more than one god —compare MONOTHEISM —**polytheistic** /ˌpɒlɪθi'ɪstɪk◂‖ˌpɑː-/ *adj*

**pol·y·thene** /'pɒlɪ̣θiːn‖'pɑː-/ *n* [U] *BrE* a strong light plastic used to make bags, sheets for covering food, small containers etc; POLYETHYLENE *AmE*

**pol·y·un·sat·u·rate** /ˌpɒliʌn'sætʃərɪ̣t‖ˌpɑː-/ *n* [C] a FATTY ACID (=chemical that helps your body produce energy) that is POLYUNSATURATED

**pol·y·un·sat·u·ra·ted** /ˌpɒliʌn'sætʃəreɪtɪ̣d‖ˌpɑː-/ *adj* polyunsaturated fats or oils come from vegetables and plants, and are considered to be better for your health than animal fats —compare SATURATED FAT

**pol·y·u·re·thane** /ˌpɒlɪ'jʊərɪ̣θeɪn‖ˌpɑːlɪ'jʊr-/ *n* [U] a plastic used to make paints and VARNISH

**pom** /pɒm‖pɑːm/ *n* [C] *AustrE, NZE slang* an insulting word for an English person, especially one who has gone to live in Australia or New Zealand

**po·made** /pə'meɪd, pə'mɑːd‖poʊ'meɪd/ *n* [U] a sweet-smelling oily substance rubbed on men's hair to make it smooth, which was used especially in former times

**po·man·der** /pəʊ'mændə, pə'mæn-‖'poʊmændər/ *n* [C] a box or ball that contains dried flowers and HERBS and is used to make clothes or a room smell pleasant

**pom·e·gran·ate** /'pɒmɪ̣grænɪ̣t‖'pɑːmə-/ *n* [C] a round fruit that has a lot of small seeds, red juicy flesh, and a thick reddish skin

**pom·mel¹** /'pʌməl/ *n* [C] **1** the high, rounded part at the front of a SADDLE¹ (1) on a horse —see picture at HORSE¹ **2** the round end of a sword handle

**pommel²** *v* [T] *especially AmE* another spelling of PUMMEL

**pommel horse** /'·· ·/ *n* [C] a piece of equipment used in GYMNASTICS with two handles on top, which you hold onto and jump over

**pom·my** /'pɒmi‖'pɑː-/ *n* [C] *AustrE, NZE slang* a POM

**pomp** /pɒmp‖pɑːmp/ *n* [U] *formal* all the impressive clothes, decorations, music etc that are traditional for an important official or public ceremony: *all the usual pomp that surrounds occasions such as the royal wedding*

**pom·pom** /'pɒmpɒm‖'pɑːmpɑːm/ also **pom·pon** /-pɒn‖-pɑːn/ *n* [C] **1** a small woollen ball used as a decoration on clothing, especially hats **2** a large round ball of loose plastic strings connected to a handle, used by CHEERLEADERS —see picture at CHEERLEADER

**pom·pous** /'pɒmpəs‖'pɑːm-/ *adj* trying to make people think you are important, especially by using very formal and important-sounding words: *The principal gave a very pompous speech about 'the portals of learning'.* —**pompously** *adv* —**pompousness**, **pomposity** /pɒm'pɒsɪ̣ti‖pɑːm'pɑː-/ *n* [U]

**ponce¹** /pɒns‖pɑːns/ *n* [C] *BrE informal* **1** a PIMP **2** an offensive word meaning a man who is too concerned about his appearance

**ponce²** *v*

**ponce about/around** *phr v* [I] *BrE informal* **1** to waste time doing silly things: *At least I haven't been poncing about all day with theatre people.* **2** if a man ponces about, he behaves in a way that is thought to be how a woman behaves

**ponce off** sb *phr v* [T] *BrE* to ask someone to give you something such as a cigarette or drink without offering to pay: *I'd no money, you know, so I ponced off him.*

**pon·cho** /'pɒntʃəʊ‖'pɑːntʃoʊ/ *n plural* **ponchos** [C] **1** a coat consisting of one large piece of thick wool cloth like a BLANKET, with a hole in the middle for your head **2** *AmE* a coat that keeps out rain and is made of one large piece of material with a cover for your head

**ponc·y, poncey** /'pɒnsi‖'pɑː-/ *adj BrE informal* poncy clothes or behaviour are typical of a man who is too concerned about his appearance

**pond** /pɒnd‖pɑːnd/ *n* [C] **1** a small area of still water, especially one that has been artificially made: *a duck pond* **2 across the pond/on the other side of the pond** *informal* on the other side of the Atlantic Ocean in the US or in Britain S3

**pon·der** /'pɒndə‖'pɑːndər/ *v* [I,T] *formal* to spend time thinking carefully and seriously about a problem, a difficult question, or something that has happened: *Lisa pondered for a while before answering.* | [+ **on/over/about**] *As I pondered over the whole business, an idea struck me.* |

**ponder how/what/whether etc** *His critics might well ponder what would happen if he quit.* | **ponder sth** *Esteban sat pondering the state of his marriage.*

**pon·der·ous** /ˈpɒndərəs‖ˈpɑːn-/ *adj* **1** moving slowly or awkwardly because of being very big and heavy: *an elephant's ponderous walk* **2** boring and too serious: *a ponderous and difficult book, intended for experts* **3** very big and heavy: *Calvin's way was blocked by the ponderous body of his host.* —**ponderously** *adv* —**ponderousness** *n* [U]

**pone** /pəʊn‖poʊn/ *n* [U] *AmE informal* CORN PONE

**pong¹** /pɒŋ‖pɑːŋ/ *n* [C usually singular] *BrE informal* an unpleasant smell: *There's an awful pong in the fridge!*

**pong²** *v* [I] *BrE informal* to have a strong and unpleasant smell: *Ugh! Your socks really pong!* —**pongy** *adj*

**pon·iard** /ˈpɒnjəd‖ˈpɑːnjərd/ *n* [C] a small pointed knife used as a weapon in former times

**pon·tiff** /ˈpɒntɪ̠f‖ˈpɑːn-/ *n* [C] *technical* the POPE

**pon·tif·i·cal** /pɒnˈtɪfɪkəl‖pɑːn-/ *adj formal* **1** speaking as if you think your judgment or opinion is always right **2** connected with the POPE —**pontifically** /-kli/ *adv*

**pon·tif·i·cate¹** /pɒnˈtɪfɪ̠keɪt‖pɑːn-/ *v* [I] to give your opinion about something in a way that shows you think you are always right: [+ **about/on**] *He's always pontificating about the evils of modern society.*

**pon·tif·i·cate²** /pɒnˈtɪfɪkɪ̠t‖pɑːn-/ *n* [C] *technical* the position or period of being POPE

**pon·toon** /pɒnˈtuːn‖pɑːn-/ *n* [C] **1** *BrE* a card game, usually played for money; BLACKJACK *AmE* **2** one of several metal containers or boats that are fastened together to support a floating bridge **3** one of two hollow metal containers fastened to the bottom of a plane so that it can come down onto water and float

**pontoon bridge** /ˈ.ˈ. ./ *n* [C] a floating bridge which is supported by several pontoons

**po·ny** /ˈpəʊni‖ˈpoʊ-/ *n* [C] a small horse —see also PIT PONY, SHETLAND PONY

**po·ny·tail** /ˈpəʊniteɪl‖ˈpoʊ-/ *n* [C] hair tied in a bunch at the back of your head and falling like a horse's tail —see picture at HAIRSTYLE

**pony-trek·king** /ˈ.. ,../ *n* [U] *BrE* the activity of riding through the countryside on ponies; PACK TRIP *AmE*

**poo** /puː/ *n informal* **1** [U] a word meaning solid waste from your BOWELS, used especially by children; POOP¹ (3) *AmE* **2** [C usually singular] a word meaning the act of passing waste from your BOWELS, used especially by children; POOP¹ (4) *AmE* —**poo** *v* [I,T] *informal*

**pooch** /puːtʃ/ *n informal often humorous* [C] a dog

**poo·dle** /ˈpuːdl/ *n* [C] **1** a dog with thick curly hair —see picture at DOG¹ **2 be sb's poodle** *BrE humorous* if someone is another person's poodle, they always do what the other person tells them to do

**poof¹** /pʊf, puːf/ also **poof·ter** /ˈpʊftə, ˈpuːf-‖-ər/ *n* [C] *BrE* an offensive word for a HOMOSEXUAL man —**poofy** *adj* —compare POUF

**poof²** *interjection* **1** used when talking about something that happened suddenly: *Then poof! She was gone.* **2** used to show that you do not agree with or believe what someone has said: *Poof! He doesn't know what he's talking about.*

**pooh** /puː/ *interjection BrE spoken* used when there is a very unpleasant smell; PEW² *AmE*

**pooh-pooh** /,. ˈ./ *v* [T] *informal* to say that you think that an idea, suggestion, effort etc is silly or not very good: *Critics pooh-poohed the idea at first.*

S2 W2 **pool¹** /puːl/ *n*

**1** ▶ **WATER** ◀ [C] **a)** a SWIMMING POOL or PADDLING POOL: *Does the hotel have a pool?* | *an inflatable rubber wading pool* **b)** a small area of still water in a hollow place: *The children hunted for crabs in the pools between the rocks.* | *where the stream formed a shallow pool*

**2 a pool of water/blood/light etc** a small area of liquid or light on a surface: *Trautman lay unconscious in a pool of blood.* | *His desk lamp cast a pool of light on the documents.*

**3** ▶ **GAME** ◀ [U] a game in which you use a stick to knock numbered balls into holes around a table, which is often played in bars —compare SNOOKER

**4** ▶ **FOOTBALL** ◀ **the pools** a system in Britain in which people try to win money each week by guessing the results of football games

**5** ▶ **GROUP OF THINGS/PEOPLE** ◀ [C] **a)** a number of things or an amount of money that is shared by a group of people **b)** a group who are available to work when they are needed: *a pool of volunteers for community projects* —see also CAR POOL, GENE POOL, TYPING POOL

**pool²** *v* [T] to combine your money, ideas, skills etc with those of other people so that you can all use them: **pool your resources** *Investors agreed to pool their resources to develop the property.*

**pool hall** /ˈ. ./ *n* [C] *AmE* a building where people go to practise playing pool

**pool·room** /ˈpuːlruːm, -rʊm/ *n* [C] a room used for playing pool, especially in a bar

**poop¹** /puːp/ *n* **1** [C] *technical* the raised part at the back end of an old sailing ship **2 the poop** *AmE informal* the latest news about something that has happened, which is told to you unofficially by someone; LOWDOWN: *Come on, Dan, what's the poop? Are they hiring Collins?* **3** [U] *AmE informal* a word meaning solid waste from your BOWELS, used especially by children; POO (1) *BrE* **4** [singular] *AmE informal* a word meaning the act of passing waste from your BOWELS, used especially by children; POO (2) *BrE*

**poop²** *v AmE informal* [I,T] a word meaning to pass solid waste from your BOWELS, used especially by children; POO *BrE* —see also PARTY POOPER

**poop out** *phr v* [I] *AmE informal* **1** to stop trying to do something because you are tired, bored etc: *Ouida pooped out about halfway through the race.* **2** to decide not to do something you have already said you would do, because you are tired or not interested: **poop out on sb** *"Is Bill coming along?" "Nah, he's pooping out on us."*

**poop deck** /ˈ. ./ *n* [C] the floor on the raised part at the back of an old sailing ship

**pooped** /puːpt/ also **pooped out** /,. ˈ./ *adj* [not before noun] *AmE informal* very tired; EXHAUSTED (1)

**poop·er scoop·er** /ˈpuːpə ,skuːpə‖-pər ,skuːpər/ *n* [C] *informal* a small SPADE and a container, used by dog owners for removing their dogs' solid waste from the streets

**poo-poo** /ˈ. ./ *n* [U] POO

**poop sheet** /ˈ. ./ *n* [C] *AmE informal* written official instructions or information

**poor** /pɔː‖pʊr/ *adj* 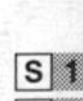

**1** ▶ **NO MONEY** ◀ having very little money and not many possessions: *Her family were so poor they couldn't afford to buy her new clothes.* | *Ethiopia is one of the poorest countries in the world.* | *a poor neighborhood*

**2 the poor** people who are poor: *state subsidies to help the poor buy basic foods*

**3** ▶ **NOT GOOD** ◀ not as good as it could be or should be; INFERIOR¹ (1): *Poor sanitation can lead to the spread of diseases.* | *The soil in this area is very poor.* | *poor rates of pay* | **poor hearing/eyesight/memory** *You'd better read it to me – my eyesight's pretty poor.*

**4 poor boy/girl/Joe etc** *especially spoken* used to show pity for someone because they are so unlucky, unhappy etc: *Poor kid, he's had a rough day.* | *I feel sorry for the poor horse with me riding it.* | **poor thing** *You poor thing, you've had a hard time of it, haven't you?* | **poor old** *Poor old Lou, having to work at weekends.*

**5** ▶ **NOT GOOD AT STH** ◀ not good at doing something: *a poor public speaker* | [+ **at**] *poor at spelling*

**6 make a poor job of** to do something badly: *The builders have made a really poor job of fixing our roof.*

**7** ▶ **HEALTH** ◀ someone whose health is poor is ill or

weak for a long period of time: **be in poor health** *My parents are both in rather poor health.*
**8 poor in sth** lacking things that people need: *fatty snacks that are poor in nutrients*
**9 poor loser** someone who behaves badly if they lose a game
**10 be a poor second/third etc** to finish a race, competition etc a long way behind the person ahead of you
**11 poor man's** *spoken often humorous* **a)** used to say that someone is like a very famous performer, writer etc but is not as good as they are: *He's a kind of poor man's Richard Gere.* **b)** used to say that something can be used for the same purpose as something else, and is much cheaper: *The abacus is the poor man's pocket calculator.*
**12 poor relation** someone or something that is not treated as well as other members of a group or is much less successful than they are: *Theatre musicians tend to be the poor relations of the musical profession.* —see also **be in bad/poor taste** (TASTE[1] (6)), POORLY, POORNESS

**poor boy** /ˈ· ·/ *n* [C] *AmE* a long bread roll that is cut open and filled with meat, cheese etc; SUBMARINE SANDWICH

**poor·house** /ˈpɔːhaʊs‖ˈpʊr-/ *n* [C] a building in former times where people could live and be fed, which was paid for with public money

**poor law** /ˈ· ·/ *n* **the Poor Law** a group of British laws which controlled the help given to poor people in former times

**poor·ly[1]** /ˈpɔːli‖ˈpʊrli/ *adv* badly: *poorly paid | Jana's doing poorly in school. | a poorly written article*

**poorly[2]** *adj* [not before noun] *informal especially BrE* ill: *Matt's wife's been feeling poorly.*

**poorly off** /ˌ·· ˈ·/ *adj* [not before noun] **1** someone who is poorly off does not have very much money **2 be poorly off for** to not have enough of something: *We have enough textbooks but we're poorly off for lab equipment.*

**poor·ness** /ˈpɔːnɪ̥s‖ˈpʊr-/ *n* [U] *formal* lack of skill or good qualities: [+ **of**] *the poorness of my German accent* —compare POVERTY

**poor-spir·it·ed** /ˌ· ˈ···◂/ *adj literary* having no confidence or courage —**poor-spiritedly** *adv*

**poo·tle** /ˈpuːtl/ *v* [I + **about/around**] *BrE spoken* to spend time pleasantly, doing things that are not very important

S3 **pop[1]** /pɒp‖pɑːp/ **popped, popping** *v*
**1 ▶ GO SOMEWHERE QUICKLY ◀** [I always + adv/prep] *spoken* to go somewhere quickly, suddenly, or unexpectedly: [+ **in/out/round/to etc**] *Could you pop round to the store for some bread? | Pat's just popped next door for ten minutes.*
**2 ▶ COME OUT OF STH ◀** [I always + adv/prep] to come suddenly or unexpectedly out of or away from something: [+ **out/off/up etc**] *A button popped off my shirt when I sneezed.* | **out/up popped** *The egg cracked open and out popped a tiny head.*
**3 ▶ PUT STH SOMEWHERE ◀** [T always + adv/prep] *informal* to put something somewhere quickly for a short time: **pop sth in/round/over etc** *I'll just pop these cakes into the oven. | Barry popped his head round the door to say hello.*
**4 ▶ SHORT SOUND ◀** [I,T] to make a short sound like a small explosion, or to make something make this sound: *Champagne corks were popping.* | **pop sth** *Please don't pop all the balloons before the party starts.*
**5 ▶ EARS ◀** [I] if your ears pop, you feel the pressure in them suddenly become less when you go quickly up or down in a plane, lift etc
**6 sb's eyes popped (out of their head)** used to say that someone looked extremely surprised or excited
**7 pop the question** *informal* to ask someone to marry you: *Hasn't Bill popped the question yet?*
**8 pop pills** *informal* to take PILLS too often
**9 pop your clogs** *BrE humorous* to die
**10 ▶ CORN ◀** [I,T] to cook corn until it swells and bursts open, or to be cooked in this way
**11 ▶ BORROWING MONEY ◀** [T] *BrE old-fashioned* to PAWN[2] something
**pop off** *phr v* [I] *informal* to die suddenly
**pop** sth ↔ **on** *phr v* [T] *spoken* **1** to quickly put on a piece of clothing: *Just pop this jacket on and we'll see if it fits.* **2** to quickly turn on a piece of electrical equipment: *Pop the kettle on, would you.*
**pop up** *phr v* [I] **1** to appear suddenly and unexpectedly: *Mushrooms tend to pop up overnight. | She popped up in Munich after all that time.* —see also POP-UP **2** to hit a ball into the air in a game of BASEBALL so that it only travels a short distance: *O'Malley popped up to first base.*

**pop[2]** *n* **1** [U] modern music that is popular with young people, and usually consists of simple tunes with a strong beat: **pop singer/concert/festival etc** *a pop record | pop culture* **2** [singular] *AmE informal* a word meaning your father, used especially to address him: *Can I borrow the car, Pop?* **3** [U] *informal* a sweet FIZZY drink such as LEMONADE; SODA (2) *AmE*: *a bottle of pop* **4** [C] a sudden short sound like a small explosion: *the pop of a champagne cork* | **go pop** (=make this sound) *The balloon went pop.* —see picture on page 1261 S3 W3

**pop[3]** the written abbreviation of POPULATION

**pop·a·dum, poppadum** /ˈpɒpədəm‖ˈpɑː-/ *n* [C] a large circular piece of very thin flat Indian bread cooked in oil

**pop art** /ˌ· ˈ·◂/ *n* [U] a kind of art that was popular in the 1960s, which shows ordinary objects, such as advertisements, or things you see in people's homes

**pop·corn** /ˈpɒpkɔːn‖ˈpɑːpkɔːrn/ *n* [U] a kind of corn that swells and bursts open when heated, and is usually eaten warm with salt or sugar

**Pope** /pəʊp‖poʊp/ *n* [C] **1** the leader of the Roman Catholic church: *The Pope will visit El Salvador this year. | Pope John XXIII* —see also PAPAL **2 Is the Pope (a) Catholic?** *informal humorous* used to say that something is clearly true or certain: *"Do you think they'll win?" "Is the Pope Catholic?"*

**pope's nose** /ˌ· ˈ·/ *n* **the pope's nose** *AmE, IrishE, ScotE* the piece of flesh at the tail end of a cooked bird, such as a chicken; PARSON'S NOSE *BrE*

**pop-eyed** /ˌ· ˈ·◂/ *adj informal* having your eyes wide open, because you are surprised or excited

**pop fly** /ˈ· ·/ *n* [C] a type of hit in BASEBALL in which the ball is hit straight up into the air and only travels a short distance —see picture on page 1263

**pop group** /ˈ· ·/ *n* [C] a group of people who sing and play POP MUSIC

**pop-gun** /ˈ· ·/ *n* [C] a toy gun that fires small objects, such as corks (CORK[1] (2)), with a loud noise

**pop·in·jay** /ˈpɒpɪ̥ndʒeɪ‖ˈpɑː-/ *n* [C] *old use* a young man who is too proud of his appearance

**pop·lar** /ˈpɒplə‖ˈpɑːplər/ *n* [C] a very tall straight thin tree

**pop·lin** /ˈpɒplɪ̥n‖ˈpɑːp-/ *n* [U] a strong shiny cotton cloth

**pop mu·sic** /ˈ· ˌ··/ *n* [U] modern music that is popular with young people and usually consists of simple tunes with a strong beat

**pop·o·ver** /ˈpɒpəʊvə‖ˈpɑːpoʊvər/ *n* [C] *AmE* a light, hollow cake made with eggs, milk, and flour

**pop·pa** /ˈpɒpə‖ˈpɑːpə/ *n* [singular] *AmE informal* father

**pop·pa·dum** /ˈpɒpədəm‖ˈpɑː-/ *n* [C] another spelling of POPADUM

**pop·per** /ˈpɒpə‖ˈpɑːpər/ *n* [C] *informal especially BrE* a small metal thing used for fastening a piece of clothing which consists of two parts, one of which is pressed into the hollow part of the other; SNAP[2] (6) —see picture at FASTENER

**pop·pet** /ˈpɒpɪ̥t‖ˈpɑː-/ *n* [C] *BrE spoken* a way of talking to or about a child or animal you are fond of: *Isn't he a poppet? | Come here, poppet.*

**pop·py** /ˈpɒpi‖-ˈpɑː-/ *n* [C] **1** a plant that has brightly coloured, usually red, flowers and small black seeds **2** a red colour —see picture on page 411

**pop·py·cock** /ˈpɒpikɒk‖ˈpɑːpikɑːk/ *n* [U] *old-fashioned* nonsense: *He's talking absolute poppycock!*

**pop·py·seed** /ˈpɒpisiːd‖ˈpɑː-/ *n* [U] the small black seeds of the poppy plant used in cakes, bread etc

**pop quiz** /ˈ· ·/ *n* [C] *AmE* a short test which is given without any warning in order to check that students have been studying

**pops** /pɒps‖pɑːps/ *adj* **pops concert/orchestra** *AmE* a concert or ORCHESTRA which performs CLASSICAL and popular music: *the Boston Pops Orchestra*

**Pop·si·cle** /ˈpɒpsɪkəl‖ˈpɑːp-/ *n* [C] *AmE trademark* a piece of ice, usually tasting of fruit, that you suck on a stick; ICE LOLLY *BrE*

**pop star** /ˈ· ·/ *n* [C] a famous and successful entertainer who plays or sings POP MUSIC

**pop·u·lace** /ˈpɒpjələs‖ˈpɑː-/ *n* [singular] *formal* the ordinary people who live in a country: *breaking the news to a joyful populace*

S2 W1 **pop·u·lar** /ˈpɒpjələ‖ˈpɑːpjələr/ *adj* **1** liked by a lot of people: *Hilary was popular at school.* | [+ **with**] *Video games are very popular with children.* | *a popular holiday resort* —opposite UNPOPULAR **2 popular belief/view/misconception** a belief etc that a lot of people have: **contrary to popular belief** *Contrary to popular belief, gorillas are basically shy, gentle creatures.* **3** [only before noun] popular entertainment, newspapers, programmes etc are intended to be suitable for ordinary people: *pilloried by the popular press* **4** [only before noun] done by a lot of people in a society, group etc: *popular protest* | *It was decided by popular vote.* **5 you'll be popular** *spoken* used when telling someone that other people will be annoyed with them: *You'll be popular when they find out you've lost their tickets.*

**pop·u·lar·i·ty** /ˌpɒpjəˈlærɪti‖ˌpɑː-/ *n* [U] the quality of being liked or supported by a large number of people: **gain in popularity** (=start to be liked by many people) *Western music is steadily gaining in popularity.* | *The president's popularity has declined considerably.*

**pop·u·lar·ize** /ˈpɒpjələraɪz‖ˈpɑː-/ also **-ise** *BrE v* [T] **1** to make something well known and liked: *Reggae music was popularized by Bob Marley in the 1970s.* **2** to make a difficult subject or idea easily understandable for ordinary people who have no special knowledge about it: *books aimed at popularizing modern science* —**popularization** /ˌpɒpjələraɪˈzeɪʃən‖ˌpɑːpjələrə-/ *n* [U]

**pop·u·lar·ly** /ˈpɒpjələli‖ˈpɑːpjələr-/ *adv* **popularly believed/thought/known etc** believed, thought, known etc by many people: *Vitamin C is popularly believed to prevent colds.*

**pop·u·late** /ˈpɒpjəleɪt‖ˈpɑː-/ *v* **be populated** if an area is populated by a particular group of people, they live there: [+ **by**] *The Central Highlands are populated mainly by peasant farmers.* | **densely/heavily/highly/thickly populated** (=a lot of people live in that place in relation to its size) *densely populated urban areas* | **thinly/sparsely populated** (=few people live in that place in relation to its size) *The northern islands are very sparsely populated.*

S2 W1 **pop·u·la·tion** /ˌpɒpjəˈleɪʃən‖ˌpɑː-/ *n* [U] **1** the number of people living in a particular area, country etc: *a city with a population of over two million* | *What is the population of Mexico?* **2** [C usually singular] all of the people who live in a particular area: *The whole population had turned out to welcome us home.* | *Most of the world's population don't get enough to eat.* | **the white/French/urban etc population** (=part of the group of people who live in a particular area who are white, French etc) *By the middle of the 19th century, the urban population of England exceeded the rural population.* **3 population explosion** a rapid increase in the population of an area or the whole planet **4 centre of population/population centre** a city, town etc: *far from most centres of population*

**pop·u·list** /ˈpɒpjəlɪst‖ˈpɑː-/ *adj* claiming to represent ordinary people: *a populist leadership* —**populist** *n* [C] —**populism** *n* [U] *the switch from Marxism to populism*

**pop·u·lous** /ˈpɒpjələs‖ˈpɑː-/ *adj formal* a populous area has a large population in relation to its size: *Hong Kong is one of the most populous areas in the world.* —**populousness** *n* [U]

**pop-up** /ˈ· ·/ *adj* **pop-up book/card/toaster etc** a book, card, TOASTER etc that is designed to make something suddenly spring out of it

**porce·lain** /ˈpɔːslɪn‖ˈpɔːrsəlɪn/ *n* [U] **1** a hard shiny white substance that is used for making expensive plates, cups etc **2** plates, cups etc made of this

**porch** /pɔːtʃ‖pɔːrtʃ/ *n* [C] **1** an entrance covered by a roof outside the front door of a house or church **2** *AmE* an open area with a floor and a roof, often made of wood, fixed to the side of a house on the ground floor; VERANDA: *sitting out on the porch* —see picture on page 410

**por·cu·pine** /ˈpɔːkjəpaɪn‖ˈpɔːr-/ *n* [C] an animal with long, sharp, needle-like parts growing all over its back and sides which it can make point upwards

**pore**[1] /pɔː‖pɔːr/ *n* [C] one of the small holes in your skin that liquid, especially SWEAT can pass through, or a similar hole in the surface of a plant: *Witch-hazel can help to unblock greasy pores.*

**pore**[2] *v*

**pore over** sth *phr v* [T] to read or look at something very carefully for a long time: *They expected to find him poring over his notes the night before the exam.*

**pork** /pɔːk‖pɔːrk/ *n* [U] **1** the meat from pigs: *pork chops* **2** *AmE slang* government money spent in a particular area in order to get political advantages

**pork bar·rel** /ˈ· ˌ··/ *n* [singular, U] *AmE slang* a government plan to increase the amount of money spent in a particular area in order to gain political advantage: *the pork barrel politics of military production contracts*

**pork·er** /ˈpɔːkə‖ˈpɔːrkər/ *n* [C] **1** a young pig that is made fat before being killed for food **2** *informal* an insulting word for a fat person **3** *slang* a lie

**pork pie** /ˌ· ˈ·◂/ *n* [C,U] *BrE* a small round PIE which contains pieces of cooked pork

**pork rinds** /ˌ· ˈ·/ *n* [plural] *AmE* SCRATCHINGS

**pork·y**[1] /ˈpɔːki‖ˈpɔːrki/ *adj informal* an insulting word meaning fat

**porky**[2] /ˈpɔːki‖ˈpɔːr-/ *n* [C] also **porky pie** /ˌ·· ˈ·/ *BrE slang* a lie

**porn** /pɔːn‖pɔːrn/ *n* [U] *informal* pornography: *the porn industry* | *computer porn is the latest threat* —see also HARD PORN, SOFT PORN

**porn·o** /ˈpɔːnəʊ‖ˈpɔːrnoʊ/ *adj* [usually before noun] *informal* PORNOGRAPHIC: *a porno movie*

**por·nog·ra·phy** /pɔːˈnɒgrəfi‖pɔːrˈnɑːg-/ *n* [U] **1** magazines, films etc that show sexual acts and images in a way that is intended to make people feel sexually excited: *a major campaign against pornography* **2** the treatment of sexual acts in pictures, film or writing in a way that is intended to make people feel sexually excited —**pornographer** *n* [C] —**pornographic** /ˌpɔːnəˈgræfɪk◂‖ˌpɔːr-/ *adj*: *The script was condemned as pornographic.* —**pornographically** /-kli/ *adv*

**po·rous** /ˈpɔːrəs/ *adj* porous rock or soil allows liquid, air etc to pass through slowly —**porousness** *n* [U]

**por·phy·ry** /ˈpɔːfəri‖ˈpɔːr-/ *n* [U] a type of hard dark red or purple rock containing CRYSTALS

**por·poise** /ˈpɔːpəs‖ˈpɔːr-/ *n* [C] a sea animal rather like a DOLPHIN, that swims in groups

**por·ridge** /ˈpɒrɪdʒ‖ˈpɑː-, ˈpɔː-/ *n* [U] **1** a soft breakfast food made by boiling OATMEAL (=crushed grain) in milk or water; OATMEAL *AmE* **2** *BrE slang* a period of time spent in prison: **do porridge** (=spend time in prison)

**port** /pɔːt‖pɔːrt/ *n* W2

**1** ▶ **WHERE SHIPS STOP** ◀ [C,U] a place where ships can load and unload people or things; HARBOUR[1]: **come into port/leave port** *The ferry was just about to leave port.* | **in port** *We're going to have two days ashore while the ship is in port.*

**2 ▶TOWN◀** [C] a town or city with a HARBOUR or DOCKS: *Britain's largest port | the Israeli port of Haifa*
**3 ▶WINE◀** [C,U] strong sweet Portuguese wine, usually drunk after a meal: *port and Stilton*
**4 ▶LEFT OF SHIP◀** [U] the left side of a ship or aircraft when you are looking towards the front: *on the port side* | **to port** *After the collision, the ship began leaning over to port.* —opposite STARBOARD
**5 ▶COMPUTER◀** [C] *technical* a part of a computer where you can connect another piece of equipment such as a PRINTER
**6 any port in a storm** *usually spoken* an expression meaning that you should take whatever help you can when you are in trouble, even if it has some disadvantages —see also FREE PORT, PORT OF ENTRY

**por·ta·ble** /ˈpɔːtəbəl‖ˈpɔːr-/ *adj* light and able to be carried or moved easily: *a portable typewriter* —**portable** *n* [C] *We swapped the colour television for a black and white portable.* —**portability** /ˌpɔːtəˈbɪlɪ̣ti‖ˌpɔːr-/ *n* [U]

**por·ta·crib** /ˈpɔːtəkrɪb‖ˈpɔːr-/ *n* [C] *AmE trademark* a small bed with handles in which a baby lies and can be carried; CARRYCOT *especially BrE* —see picture at BED[1]

**port·age** /ˈpɔːtɪdʒ‖ˈpɔːr-/ *n* [U] the act of carrying boats over land from one river to another

**Por·ta·kab·in** /ˈpɔːtəkæbɪ̣n‖ˈpɔːr-/ *n* [C] *trademark* a small hut that can be used as a temporary office, classroom etc, and can be moved by TRUCK

**por·tal** /ˈpɔːtl‖ˈpɔːrtl/ *n* [C usually plural] *literary* a tall and impressive gate or entrance to a building: *the carved Gothic portals of the college*

**port·cul·lis** /pɔːtˈkʌlɪ̣s‖pɔːrt-/ *n* [C] a strong iron gate that can be lowered over the entrance of a castle

**por·tend** /pɔːˈtend‖pɔːr-/ *v* [T] *literary* to be a sign that something is going to happen, especially something unpleasant: *strange events that portend some great disaster*

**por·tent** /ˈpɔːtent‖ˈpɔːr-/ *n* [C] *literary* a sign or warning that something is going to happen: [+ **of**] *This was a striking portent of things to come.* —compare OMEN

**por·ten·tous** /pɔːˈtentəs‖pɔːr-/ *adj* **1** *literary* events that are portentous are very important, especially because they show that something unpleasant is going to happen: *portentous events that boded ill* **2** trying to appear important and serious: *The book is portentous and badly edited.* —**portentously** *adv* —**portentousness** *n* [U]

**por·ter** /ˈpɔːtə‖ˈpɔːrtər/ *n* **1** [C] someone whose job is to carry travellers' bags at railway stations, airports etc: *I hailed a porter and then a cab.* **2** [C] *especially BrE* someone in charge of the entrance to a hotel, hospital etc **3** [C] someone whose job is to carry heavy goods at markets **4** [C] *AmE* someone whose job is to look after a sleeping carriage in a train **5** [U] *old-fashioned* a dark brown bitter beer

**por·ter·house steak** /ˌpɔːtəhaʊs ˈsteɪk‖ˌpɔːrtər-/ *n* [C,U] a thick, flat piece of high quality BEEF[1] (1)

**port·fo·li·o** /pɔːtˈfəʊliəʊ‖pɔːrtˈfoʊlioʊ/ *n* [C] **1** a large flat case used especially for carrying drawings, documents etc **2** a collection of drawings, paintings or other pieces of work by an artist, photographer etc **3** a collection of shares (SHARE[2] (5)) owned by a particular person or company: *an investment portfolio* **4** *formal, especially BrE* the area of responsibility of a particular government minister: *the foreign affairs portfolio*

**port·hole** /ˈpɔːthəʊl‖ˈpɔːrthoʊl/ *n* [C] a small round window on the side of a ship or plane: *a row of illuminated portholes*

**por·ti·co** /ˈpɔːtɪkəʊ‖ˈpɔːrtɪkoʊ/ *n* [C] a covered entrance to a building, consisting of a roof supported by PILLARS: *Above the portico is an commemorative plaque.*

**por·tion¹** /ˈpɔːʃən‖ˈpɔːr-/ *n* [C] **1** a part of something larger, especially a part that is different from the other parts: [+ **of**] *The front portion of the rocket breaks off.* | *The factory represents only a small portion of the company's interests.* **2** an amount of food for one person, especially served in a restaurant: *They're good-sized portions.* | [+ **of**] *Another portion of chips?* **3** [usually singular] a share of something, such as responsibility, blame, or profits that is divided between a small number of people: [+ **of**] *The other driver must bear a portion of the blame for the accident.* **4 sb's portion** *formal or literary* something that happens in your life that you cannot avoid; FATE (1): *Sorrow has always been her portion.*

**portion²** *v*
**portion** sth ↔ **out** *phr v* [T] to divide something into parts and give them to several people: **portion sth out among** *The money was portioned out among them.*

**port·ly** /ˈpɔːtli‖ˈpɔːr-/ *adj* someone who is portly, especially a rather old man, is fat and round: *a portly old gentleman* —**portliness** *n* [U]

**port·man·teau¹** /pɔːtˈmæntəʊ‖pɔːrtˈmæntoʊ/ *n* [C] *old-fashioned* a very large SUITCASE that opens into two parts

**portmanteau²** *adj* [only before noun] *formal* a portmanteau word is made by combining the sound and meaning of two other words: *'Edutainment' is a portmanteau word meaning education by entertainment.*

**port of call** /ˌ· · ˈ·/ *n* [C usually singular] **1** *informal* one of a series of places that you visit: *My next port of call was the City Records Department.* **2** a port where a ship stops on a journey from one place to another: *Our next port of call was Istanbul.*

**port of en·try** /ˌ· · ˈ··/ *n* [C] a place, such as a port or airport, where people or goods can enter a country

**por·trait¹** /ˈpɔːtrɪ̣t‖ˈpɔːr-/ *n* **1** [C] a painting, drawing, or photograph of a person: [+ **of**] *a portrait of Lenin* | *She's been commissioned to paint Andrew's portrait.* **2** [C] a description or representation of something: [+ **of**] *The article's portrait of Owen's career was very interesting.* **3** [U] *informal* portrait mode —see also SELF-PORTRAIT

**portrait²** *adj* a photograph, picture, book, or page that is portrait has the longer edges at the sides —opposite LANDSCAPE

**por·trai·ture** /ˈpɔːtrɪ̣tʃə‖ˈpɔːrtrɪ̣tʃər/ *n* [U] the art of painting or drawing pictures of people

**por·tray** /pɔːˈtreɪ‖pɔːr-/ *v* [T] **1** to describe or represent something or someone: *His most famous painting portrayed the death of Nelson.* | *Levi portrays the sheer horror of the concentration camps very powerfully.* **2 portray sb/sth as sth** to describe or show someone or something in a particular way, according to your opinion of them: *women portrayed as sex objects in Hollywood movies* | *Joan Crawford's daughter portrayed her as a maniac.* **3** to act the part of a character in a play: *She portrayed a doomed woman in the TV film 'Right to Die'.*

**por·tray·al** /pɔːˈtreɪəl‖pɔːr-/ *n* [C,U] the action of portraying someone or something: *Does the film give an accurate portrayal of life under Stalin?*

**Por·tu·guese** /ˌpɔːtʃʊ̣ˈgiːz◂‖ˌpɔːr-/ *n* [U] **1** the language of Portugal, Brazil, and some other countries: *Do you speak Portuguese?* **2 the Portuguese** the people of Portugal —**Portuguese** *adj*: *Portuguese wine*

**Portuguese man-of-war** /ˌ···· · ˈ·/ *n* [C] a very large JELLYFISH, which has long poisonous parts hanging down from its body

**pose¹** /pəʊz‖poʊz/ *v* **1 pose a problem/threat/challenge etc** to cause a problem, danger, difficulty etc: *Newton's challenge poses no threat to the leadership.* | *Rising unemployment is posing serious problems for the administration.* **2** [I,T] to sit or stand in a particular position in order to be photographed or painted, or to make someone do this: [+ **for**] *We posed for photographs after the graduation ceremony.* **3 pose a question** to ask a question, especially one that needs to be carefully thought about: *The first chapter poses the question: What constitutes a democracy?* **4 pose as sb** to pretend to be someone else, in order to deceive people: *Bryce was caught posing as a lawyer.* **5** [I] *especially BrE* to dress or behave like a fashionable, rich etc person in order to make other people notice you or admire you W3

**pose²** *n* [C] **1** the position in which someone stands or sits, especially in a painting, photograph etc: **in a pose** *a painting of the Duchess in a dramatic pose* | **strike a pose** (=stand or sit in a particular position) **2** *especially BrE* behaviour in which someone pretends to behave like a fashionable, rich, intelligent etc person in order to make other people notice them or admire them: **it's just a pose** *He's always talking about his deep interest in philosophy – it's just a pose.*

**pos·er** /ˈpəʊzə‖ˈpoʊzər/ *n* [C] **1** *informal* someone who tries to behave like a fashionable, rich, intelligent etc person to make people notice or admire them: *Kate's such a poser.* **2** *old-fashioned* a difficult question or problem

**po·seur** /pəʊˈzɜː‖poʊˈzɜːr/ *n* [C] *French* a POSER (1)

**posh** /pɒʃ‖pɑːʃ/ *adj* **1** a posh restaurant, hotel, car etc is expensive and looks as if it is used or owned by rich people: *a posh nightclub in Mayfair* **2** *BrE* behaving or speaking in a way which is typical of upper class people: *My mum has a really posh voice when she's on the phone.* —**posh** *adv*: *Doesn't he talk posh?*

**pos·it** /ˈpɒzɪt‖ˈpɑː-/ *v* [T] *formal* to suggest that a particular idea should be accepted as a fact; POSTULATE[1]: *positing the existence of even smaller particles*

S3 W1 **po·si·tion**[1] /pəˈzɪʃən/ *n*

**1** ▶ **STANDING/SITTING/POINTING ETC** ◀ [C] the way someone stands or sits, or the direction in which an object, SWITCH etc is pointing: *I had to work in an uncomfortable position, lying under the car.* | **a sitting/kneeling/standing position** *The prisoners were kept in a kneeling position.* | **a vertical/upright/horizontal position** *Make sure the container remains in an upright position.* | *She turned the switch to the 'on' position.*

**2** ▶ **SITUATION** ◀ [C usually singular] the situation that someone is in, or the situation concerning a particular subject: *What's the present position with regard to import restrictions?* | **in a good/strong/enviable etc position** *Reuters are now in an enviable position in the news and current affairs industry.* | **in your/her etc position** *I'm not sure what I'd do if I were in your position.* | **put sb in a difficult/awkward position** *You're putting me in rather a difficult position.*

**3** ▶ **LEVEL/RANK** ◀ [C] someone's or something's level or rank in a society or organization: [+ **in**] *the position of women in society* | **position of authority/influence** *You need to ask someone in a position of authority.* | **position of trust/responsibility** (=a position in which people depend on you to be honest or careful) | **abuse your position** (=use your authority wrongly)

**4** ▶ **OPINION** ◀ [C] an opinion or judgment on a particular subject, especially the official opinion of a government, party, or someone in authority; ATTITUDE: [+ **on**] *What's the party's position on tax reform?* | **take the position that** *The principal took the position that the students didn't need music classes.* | **reconsider your position** *The administration should reconsider its position.*

**5** ▶ **PLACE WHERE SB/STH IS** ◀ [C] the place where someone or something is, especially in relation to other objects and places: *I checked our position by the compass.* | *the position of the sun in the sky* | **a strategic position** (=one that is suitable for a particular purpose) *He placed himself in a strategic position next to the doorway.*

**6** ▶ **CORRECT PLACE** ◀ [U] the place where someone or something is supposed to be: **in position/out of position** *After the shelves were in position we realized we'd forgotten to paint them.* | *One of the legs was out of position.*

**7 take up (your) position** to move to a particular place so that you are ready to take part in a planned activity: *Police marksmen took up their positions around the bank.*

**8** ▶ **JOB** ◀ [C] your job: *Richard had to give up his position with the company.* | **hold a position** (=have a particular job) *She held the position of sales manager.* | **the position has been filled** (=the company has found someone to do the job) —see JOB[1] (USAGE)

**9 be in a position to do sth** to be able to do something because you have the ability, money, or power to do it: *When I know all the facts, I'll be in a position to advise you.*

**10 be in no position to do sth** to be unable to do something because you do not have the ability, money or power to do it: *While I'm unemployed, I'm in no position to support a family.*

**11 sb is in no position to talk** *spoken* used to say that someone should not criticize another person, because they have made the same mistakes

**12** ▶ **RACE/COMPETITION** ◀ [C,U] the place of someone or something in a race, competition, list etc: **2nd/3rd/4th position** *Alesi has moved up into 3rd position.*

**13** ▶ **SPORT** ◀ [C] the place where someone plays in a game of football, HOCKEY etc: *"What position do you play?"*

**14 be in a position of strength** to be in a situation in which you should be able to succeed or win: *workers bargaining from a position of strength*

**15 jockey/manoeuvre/jostle for position** to try to get an advantage over other people who are all trying to succeed in doing the same thing: *On the eve of the election the candidates were all jockeying for position.*

**16** ▶ **ARMY** ◀ [C] a place where an army has put soldiers, guns etc: *UN forces attacked Serb military positions around Sarajevo.*

**17** ▶ **SEX** ◀ [C] one of the ways in which two people can have sex: *Most people prefer face-to-face positions.*

**USAGE NOTE: POSITION**

WORD CHOICE: **place, position, location, spot, where**

**Place** is the usual word you use to talk about where something is or happens: *the place where I was born* | *one of the coldest places in the world*

**Position** is used to talk about the place where something is in relation to other things or places: *Plant the flowers in a sunny position.* | *a plan that shows the position of everything in the room*

**Location** is a more formal word for a place where someone works or lives, or where something is built. It may be used, for example, in business English or in advertising: *The company has found a new location for its offices.* | *a hotel in an extremely attractive location*

**Spot** is a more informal word used especially for a pleasant place: *This part of the beach is my favourite spot.*

In spoken English you usually use **where, anywhere, somewhere, someplace** etc instead of these words: *I'll show you where I was born.* | *She looked everywhere, but still couldn't find the letter.* | *Can we put the TV someplace else?* | *It depends on where they are from.*

**position**[2] *v* [T] to put something in a particular position: *Position the cursor before the letter you want to delete.*

**position pa·per** /ˈ··· ˌ··/ *n* [C] a written statement that shows how a department, organization etc intends to deal with something

**pos·i·tive** /ˈpɒzɪtɪv‖ˈpɑː-/ *adj* S2 W2

**1** ▶ **SURE** ◀ [not before noun] very sure, with no doubt at all that something is right or true: *"Are you sure?" "Positive."* | **positive (that)** *Are you absolutely positive you locked the door?* | [+ **of/about**] *It was definitely his fault – James was positive of that.*

**2** ▶ **CONFIDENT** ◀ believing that you will be successful or that a situation will have a good result: *You've got to be more positive about your work.* | **positive attitude/approach/outlook etc** *She started to have a more positive outlook on life.* | **think positive** *Think positive and all your problems will be solved.* —compare NEGATIVE[1] (2)

**3** ▶ **LIKELY TO BE SUCCESSFUL** ◀ showing that something is likely to succeed or improve: *All the signs are extremely positive – he'll be well again soon.*

**4** ▶ **AGREEMENT/SUPPORT** ◀ showing that someone agrees with you, supports what you are doing, and wants you to succeed: *The response we've had so far from*

*the public has been very positive.* | **positive criticism/feedback** (=criticism which includes praise for things done well, and encourages you to do better)
**5 positive proof/evidence/identification etc** proof, EVIDENCE etc that shows that there is no doubt that something is definitely true: *The fingerprints are positive proof that Elliott is the murderer.*
**6 ▶ SCIENTIFIC TEST ◀** showing signs of the chemical or medical condition that was being looked for: *The test results came back positive.* —opposite NEGATIVE[1] (4)
**7 ▶ GOOD/USEFUL ◀** having a good or useful effect: *At least something positive has come out of the situation.* | *a very positive experience*
**8 ▶ MORALLY GOOD ◀** [usually before noun] showing or encouraging someone, especially a child, to behave in a way that is morally good: *a positive social environment* | *positive role models*
**9 a positive miracle/delight/thrill etc** *spoken* used to emphasize how good, surprising, exciting etc something is: *It was a positive miracle that she survived.*
**10 ▶ MATHEMATICS ◀** *technical* a positive number is more than zero: *+ is the positive sign*
**11 ▶ ELECTRICITY ◀** [no comparative] *technical* having the type of electrical charge that is carried by PROTONS: *a positive charge* —opposite NEGATIVE[1] (5)
**12 positive pole** the end of a MAGNET which turns naturally towards the Earth
**13 ▶ BLOOD ◀** *technical* having RHESUS FACTOR in your blood —opposite NEGATIVE[1] (7) —**positiveness** *n* [U]

**positive di·scrim·i·na·tion** /ˌ··· ···ˈ··/ *n* [U] the practice of giving a certain number of jobs, places in universities etc to a group of people who are often treated unfairly because of their race or sex; AFFIRMATIVE ACTION

**pos·i·tive·ly** /ˈpɒzᵻtɪvli‖ˈpɑː-/ *adv* **1** *spoken* used to emphasize that something is true about someone or something, or when saying something surprising about them: *Gabi isn't pretty, she's positively beautiful!* | *Some patients positively enjoy being in hospital.* **2** *spoken* used to emphasize that you really mean what you are saying, especially when it may seem surprising: *This is positively the last time you'll hear me say this.* **3** in a way that shows you agree with something or want it to succeed: *The mayor spoke positively about the work that had been done so far.* **4 think positively** to believe that you are going to be successful or that a situation is going to have a good result **5** in a way that leaves no possibility of doubt: *Otto said quite positively that he would come.*
**6 positively charged** *technical* having the type of electrical charge that is carried by PROTONS

**pos·i·tiv·is·m** /ˈpɒzᵻtɪvɪzəm‖ˈpɑː-/ *n* [U] a kind of PHILOSOPHY that is based only on real facts which can be scientifically proved, rather than on ideas —**positivist** *n* [C]

**poss** /pɒs‖pɑːs/ **1** *BrE* the written abbreviation of possible: *Please send a photo if poss.* **2** the written abbreviation of POSSESSIVE[1] (3)

**pos·se** /ˈpɒsi‖ˈpɑːsi/ *n* [C] **1 a posse of** a large group of the same kind of people: *I was surrounded by a posse of photographers.* **2** a group of men gathered together by a SHERIFF (=local law officer) in the US in past times to help catch a criminal **3** *slang* someone's group of friends

W3 **pos·sess** /pəˈzes/ *v* [T not in progressive] **1** *formal* to own or have something, especially something valuable or important, something illegal, or an ability or quality: *Campbell was found guilty of possessing heroin.* | *The prison inmates possess a considerable degree of autonomy.* **2** *formal* a word meaning to own or have something, used especially when you are surprised that someone does not have something, or when saying that this is all they have: *I don't think Joe possesses a suit.* | *They used all the money they possessed.* **3 what (on earth) possessed you to...?** used to say that you cannot understand why someone did something stupid: *What on earth possessed her to do such a thing?* **4** *literary* if a feeling possesses you, you suddenly feel it very strongly and it affects your behaviour: *A sense of fear possessed him as he walked into the old house.*

**pos·sessed** /pəˈzest/ *adj* [not before noun] **1** if someone is possessed, their mind is controlled by an evil spirit: *Her family believed that she was possessed, and called in a priest.* | **like a man/possessed/like one possessed** (=violently or with a lot of energy) *He threw himself around like a man possessed.* **2 be possessed of** *literary* to have a particular quality, ability etc: *Charles was possessed of a sound intellect and a happy manner.* —see also SELF-POSSESSED

**pos·ses·sion** /pəˈzeʃən/ *n* W3
**1 ▶ STH YOU OWN ◀** [C usually plural] something that someone owns and keeps or uses themselves: *The police went through all the dead girl's possessions.* | *I packed my remaining possessions into the trunk.*
**2 ▶ STATE OF HAVING STH ◀** [U] *formal* the state of having or owning something, especially a valuable object, piece of information etc: **be in sb's possession** *The house has been in the family's possession since the 1500s.* | **be in possession of sth/have sth in your possession** (=have something) *She was found in possession of stolen goods.* | *I have in my possession a number of secret documents.* | **come into sb's possession** (=if something comes into your possession, you get it) *How did the painting come into your possession?* | **have possession of** (=to own or have something, after you have bought it or taken it from someone else) *The finance company now has possession of the house.*
**3 take possession of sth** if you take possession of a house, car, or valuable object, you get it after it has become yours: *We didn't take possession of the car until a few days after the auction.*
**4 ▶ DRUGS/GUN ◀** [U] *law* the crime of having illegal drugs or a gun with you or in your home: *He faces trial on charges of possession of a loaded firearm.*
**5 ▶ COUNTRY ◀** [C] a country controlled or governed by another country: *Britain's former overseas possessions*
**6 ▶ BALL ◀** [U] the state of having control of the ball in some sports: **get/lose possession** *Waddell gets possession, and he scores!*
**7 ▶ AMERICAN FOOTBALL ◀** [C] a period of time in American football when one team is playing OFFENSE[2] and has control of the ball
**8 ▶ EVIL SPIRITS ◀** [U] a situation in which someone's mind is being controlled by an evil spirit: *tales of possession and poltergeists and exorcisms*
**9 in (full) possession of your faculties/senses** able to think in a clear and intelligent way and not crazy, or affected by old age: *She's over 80 now, but she's still in full possession of all her faculties.*
**10 possession is nine-tenths of the law** used to mean that someone who has something is likely to keep it

**pos·ses·sive**[1] /pəˈzesɪv/ *adj* **1** wanting someone to have feelings of love or friendship only for you: *Men are very protective and sometimes possessive towards their daughters.* **2** unwilling to let other people use something you own: [+ **about**] *He's so possessive about his new car.* **3 possessive adjective/pronoun/form** used in grammar for words such as 'my', 'its', 'their' etc, which mean belonging to someone or something —**possessively** *adv* —**possessiveness** *n* [U]

**possessive**[2] *n* [C] *technical* a possessive adjective, pronoun, or form of a word

**pos·ses·sor** /pəˈzesə‖-ər/ *n* **be the proud possessor of** *often humorous* to have or own something: *He's now the proud possessor of two satellite dishes.*

**pos·si·bil·i·ty** /ˌpɒsᵻˈbɪlᵻti‖ˌpɑː-/ *n* **1** [C,U] something that may happen or may be true: [+ **of**] *the possibility of an enemy attack* | **a distinct/real possibility** (=something that is quite likely to happen) *A peace settlement now looks like a real possibility* | **there's a possibility (that)** (=used to say that you think something might happen or be TRUE): *There's always a possibility that he might go back to Seattle.* **2** [usually plural] something that gives you an opportunity to do what you want: [+ **for**] S2 W2

*The possibilities for improvement are endless.* | **a world of possibilities** (=many opportunities) *China's economic expansion has opened up a new world of possibilities for Western companies.* **3 exhaust all the possibilities** to try every possible way of doing something **4 have possibilities** if something has possibilities it could be made into something much better: *The house has great possibilities!* —see also **within the realms of possibility** (REALM (2))

S1 W1 **pos·si·ble¹** /ˈpɒsəbəl‖ˈpɑː-/ *adj* **1** able to be done or likely to happen or exist: *Accidents are always possible in this kind of situation.* | *Sony and Showscan are discussing possible joint projects.* | **it is possible to do sth** *Is it possible to predict what will happen in Russia?* | **it is possible (that)** (=used to say that you think something might happen or be true) *It's possible that she might have got lost on the way home.* | **it is possible for** (=used to say that someone is able to do something) *It should soon be possible for most people to work from home.* | **if (at all) possible** (=if it is possible to do it) *I want to avoid the rush hour traffic if possible.* **2 would it be possible** *spoken* used when asking politely if you can do or have something: **would it be possible (for sb) to do sth** *Would it be possible to have brown bread instead of white?* **3** acceptable or suitable: *This is only one of many possible answers to the problem of air pollution.* **4 as long/much/soon as possible** as long, soon, quickly etc as you can: *I need the money as soon as possible.* | *Sharon always does as little work as possible.* **5 the best/biggest/fastest possible** the best that can exist or be achieved: *Try to get the best possible price.* **6 where/wherever/whenever possible** every time you have an opportunity to do something: *I send a donation whenever possible.*

**possible²** *n* [C] someone or something that might be suitable or acceptable for a particular purpose: *Frank's a possible for the job.*

S1 W2 **pos·si·bly** /ˈpɒsəbli‖ˈpɑː-/ *adv* **1** used when saying that something may be true or likely, although you do not know exactly; perhaps: *"Are you coming with us tomorrow?" "Possibly. I'm not sure yet."* | *This novel is his most accessible, and possibly his most beautiful, book.* | **quite possibly** (=used to say that something is very likely) *"Do you think it was murder?" "Quite possibly."* **2 could you possibly/can you possibly** *spoken* used when making a polite request: *Could you possibly lend me another $20 till Monday?* **3** *spoken* used to say that you are very surprised or shocked by something, or you cannot understand it: **can/could sb possibly** *What on earth can she possibly mean?* | *How could anyone possibly do such a thing?* **4** used to emphasize that someone tried as hard as they could to achieve something: **do everything you possibly can/could** *Doctors did everything they possibly could to save the little boy's life.* **5 sb can't/couldn't possibly** used to say strongly that you refuse to do something or that someone cannot do something: *I can't possibly allow you to go home in this weather.*

**pos·sum** /ˈpɒsəm‖ˈpɑː-/ also **opossum** *especially BrE n* [C] **1** one of various types of small furry animals that climb trees and live in America or Australia **2 play possum** *informal* to pretend to be asleep or dead so that someone will not annoy or hurt you

**post-** /pəʊst‖poʊst/ *prefix* later than; after: *postwar* (=after a war) | *We'll have to postpone the meeting.* (=make it later) —compare ANTE-

S3 W3 **post¹** /pəʊst‖poʊst/ *n*
**1 ▶ POSTAL SYSTEM ◀ the post** *especially BrE* the official system for carrying letters, parcels etc from one place to another; MAIL¹ (1) *especially AmE*: *The letter must have got lost in the post.* | **be in the post** *Your cheque is in the post.* | **by post** *If you send the book by post it should get there by Friday.*
**2 put sth in the post** to send something to someone: *I'll put a copy in the post to you today.*
**3 ▶ COLLECTING/DELIVERING LETTERS ◀** [C,U] *especially BrE* the time when letters are collected or delivered, or the act of collecting or delivering them; MAIL *especially AmE* | **first/second post** (=the first collection or delivery of letters each day) *The parcel arrived in the second post.* | **catch/miss the post** *If you hurry, you should catch the last post.* —see also **by return (of) post** (RETURN² (8))
**4 ▶ LETTERS ◀** [U] *especially BrE* letters, parcels etc delivered to someone's house, office etc; MAIL¹ (2) *especially AmE*: *Was there any post for me today?*
**5 ▶ PIECE OF WOOD/METAL ◀** [C] a strong upright piece of wood, metal etc that is fixed into the ground, especially to support something: *a fence post*
**6 ▶ JOB ◀** [C] *formal especially BrE* a job, especially an important one; POSITION¹ (8): *She has been offered the post of ambassador to India.* | **take up a post** (=start doing an important job) *When he took up his present post at the BBC he was only 33.* | **resign (from) your post** *As a result of the scandal, Profumo was forced to resign his post.* —see JOB¹ (USAGE)
**7 ▶ SOLDIER/GUARD ETC ◀ sb's post** the place where someone is expected to be in order to do their duty: *The guard was punished for falling asleep at his post.*
**8 ▶ FOOTBALL/HOCKEY ETC ◀** [C] one of the two upright pieces of wood which players try to kick or hit the ball between in football, HOCKEY etc; GOALPOST
**9 ▶ RACE ◀ the post** also **the finishing post** the place where a race finishes, especially a horse race: *Dandyboy fell ten yards from the post.* —see also **as deaf as a post** (DEAF¹ (1)), **pip sb at the post** (PIP² (1)), **second-class post** (SECOND-CLASS (3)), LAST POST, STAGING POST, TRADING POST

**post²** *v* [T] S3
**1 ▶ LETTER ◀** *especially BrE* to send a letter, parcel etc by post; MAIL *AmE*: *She's just gone to post a letter.* | **post sb sth/post sth to sb** *I posted John the cheque last Friday.* | *I must post a card to Clara today.*
**2 keep sb posted** to keep telling someone the latest news about something: *Please, keep us posted about your financial situation, and let us know if we can help.*
**3 ▶ GUARD ◀** to send someone somewhere, to guard a building, check who enters or leaves a place, watch something etc; STATION²: *Two National Guardsmen had been posted at the gate.*
**4 ▶ JOB ◀** [usually passive] *especially BrE* to send someone to a different country or place to work for a company or to do a period of duty for the army, navy, or government; STATION² *AmE*: **post sb abroad/overseas etc** *Roger's been posted overseas for a few years.* | **post sb to** *Two years later he was posted to Buenos Aires.* —see JOB (USAGE)
**5 ▶ PUBLIC NOTICE ◀** also **post up** to put up a public notice about something on a wall or notice board: *The exam results were posted on the bulletin board yesterday.*
**6 be posted missing** if someone is posted missing, it is announced officially that they have disappeared

**post·age** /ˈpəʊstɪdʒ‖ˈpoʊs-/ *n* [U] the money charged for carrying a letter, parcel etc by post: *Please enclose $9.99, including $1.00 for postage.* | **postage and packing** (=charge for packing and sending something you have bought) *Yours for only £16.95 plus postage and packing!*

**postage me·ter** /ˈ·· ˌ··/ *n* [C] *AmE* a machine used by businesses which puts a mark on letters and packages to show that postage has been paid

**postage stamp** /ˈ·· ·/ *n* [C] *formal* a stamp

**post·al** /ˈpəʊstl‖ˈpoʊs-/ *adj* [only before noun] connected with the official system which takes letters from one place to another: *postal workers* | *an increase in postal charges*

**postal or·der** /ˈ·· ˌ··/ *n* [C] *BrE* an official paper that you buy at a post office as a safe way of sending money through the post: *a £2.00 postal order* —compare MONEY ORDER

**postal ser·vice** /ˈ·· ˌ··/ *n* [C] *especially AmE* the public service for carrying letters, parcels etc from one part of a country or the world to another

**postal vote** /ˈ·· ˌ·/ *n* [C] *BrE* a vote sent through the post, especially by someone who cannot be present to vote on the day of an election; ABSENTEE VOTE *AmE*

**post·bag** /ˈpəʊstbæg‖ˈpoʊst-/ *n BrE* **1** [singular] *informal* all the letters received by an important person, television programme etc on a particular occasion: *We've had an enormous postbag on the recent programme changes.* **2** [C] a bag for carrying letters, used by the person who delivers them; MAILBAG *AmE*

**post·box** /ˈpəʊstbɒks‖ˈpoʊstbɑːks/ *n* [C] *BrE* a box in a public place, into which you put letters you want to send; MAILBOX (2) *AmE* —see also LETTERBOX, PILLAR BOX

**post·card** /ˈpəʊstkɑːd‖ˈpoʊstkɑːrd/ *n* [C] a card that can be sent in the post without an envelope, especially one with a picture on it: *Don't forget to send us a postcard!*

**post·code** /ˈpəʊstkəʊd‖ˈpoʊstkoʊd/ *n* [C] *BrE* a group of letters or numbers which shows the exact area where a house is, so that letters, parcels etc can be delivered more quickly; ZIP CODE *AmE*

**post·date** /ˌpəʊstˈdeɪt‖ˌpoʊst-/ *v* [T] **1** to write a cheque with a date that is later than the actual date, so that it cannot be used or become effective until that time **2** to happen, live, or be made later in history than something else: *The mosaic postdates this period, although the style is quite similar.* —compare ANTEDATE, BACKDATE

**post doc** /ˌ· ˈ·/ *n* [C] *informal especially AmE* someone who is studying after they have finished their PHD

**post doc·tor·al** /ˌ· ˈ···◂/ *adj* connected with study done after a PHD

S3 **post·er** /ˈpəʊstə‖ˈpoʊstər/ *n* [C] a large printed notice, picture, or photograph, used to advertise something or as a decoration: *the bedroom wall was covered in posters*

**poste res·tante** /ˌpəʊst ˈrestɒnt‖ˌpoʊst resˈtɑːnt/ *n* [U] *BrE* a post office department which keeps letters for people who are travelling, until they arrive to collect them; GENERAL DELIVERY *AmE*

**pos·te·ri·or**[1] /pɒˈstɪəriə‖pɑːˈstɪriər/ *n* [C] *humorous* the part of the body you sit on; BOTTOM[1] (7): *plonking his substantial posterior down on the bench*

**posterior**[2] *adj* [only before noun] *technical* near or at the back of something: *the posterior end of the abdomen* —opposite ANTERIOR (1)

**pos·ter·i·ty** /pɒˈsterɪ̈ti‖pɑː-/ *n* [U] people who will live after you are dead: **preserve sth for posterity** *We must preserve these songs for posterity.*

**poster paint** /ˈ·· ·/ *n* [C,U] *BrE* brightly coloured paint that contains no oil, used especially by children to paint pictures

**post-free** /ˌ· ˈ·◂/ *adv BrE* a letter sent post-free has no charge for the person who sends it; POSTPAID *AmE* —**post-free** *adj*

**post-grad** /ˌ· ˈ·◂/ *n* [C] *informal* a postgraduate —**post-grad** *adj*

**post·grad·u·ate**[1] /ˌpəʊstˈgrædjuɪ̈t‖ˌpoʊstˈgrædʒuɪ̈t/ *n* [C] **1** *especially BrE* someone who is studying at a university to get a MASTER'S DEGREE or a PHD; GRADUATE[1] *AmE* **2** *AmE* someone who is studying after finishing a PHD

**postgraduate**[2] *adj* **1** *BrE* connected with studies done at a university after completing a first degree; GRADUATE[2] *AmE*: *postgraduate qualifications* **2** *AmE* connected with studies done after completing a PHD

**post-haste** /ˌ· ˈ·/ *adv literary* very quickly: *departing poste-haste*

**post hoc** /ˌ· ˈ·/ *adj formal* a post hoc explanation, argument etc make a connection between two events that have happened simply because one happened after the other: *spurious post hoc analyses of the causes of the war*

**post horn** /ˈ· ·/ *n* [C] a horn used in the 18th and 19th centuries as a warning by people riding on a carriage

**post·hu·mous** /ˈpɒstjʊ̈məs‖ˈpɑːstʃə-/ *adj* happening after someone's death, or given to someone or printed after their death —**posthumously** *adv*: *The medal was awarded posthumously.*

**post·ie** /ˈpəʊsti‖ˈpoʊ-/ *n* [C] *informal* a POSTMAN

**post-in·dus·tri·al** /ˌ· ·ˈ···◂/ *adj* connected with the period in the late 20th century when the older types of industry became less important, and computers became more important: *work patterns in post-industrial society*

**post·ing** /ˈpəʊstɪŋ‖ˈpoʊs-/ *n* [C] *especially BrE* the act of sending someone to a place to do their job, especially a soldier: [+ **to**] *still waiting for a posting to France*

**Post-it** /ˈ· ·/ *n* [C] *trademark* a small piece of sticky coloured paper, used for leaving notes to people

**post·man** /ˈpəʊstmən‖ˈpoʊst-/ *n plural* **postmen** /-mən/ [C] *especially BrE* someone whose job is to collect and deliver letters; MAILMAN *AmE*

**post·mark** /ˈpəʊstmɑːk‖ˈpoʊstmɑːrk/ *n* [C] an official mark made on a letter, parcel etc that shows the place and time it was sent —**postmark** *v* [T] *The letter was postmarked Iowa.*

**post·mas·ter** /ˈpəʊstˌmɑːstə‖ˈpoʊstˌmæstər/ *n* [C] the person who is in charge of a post office

**post·mis·tress** /ˈpəʊstmɪstrɪ̈s‖ˈpoʊst-/ *n* [C] a woman who is in charge of a post office

**post-mod·ern·is·m** /ˌ· ˈ····/ *n* [U] a style of building, painting etc which uses an unusual mixture of old and new styles and was popular in the 1980s —**post-modernist** *adj*: *a post-modernist painting* —**post-modernist** *n* [C]

**post-mor·tem** /ˌpəʊstˈmɔːtəm‖ˌpoʊstmɔːr-/ *n* [C] **1** also **postmortem examination** *formal* an examination of a dead body to discover why the person died; AUTOPSY: *The post-mortem revealed that Mills had been strangled.* **2** an examination of a plan or event that failed, in order to discover why it failed: *a post-mortem on the company's poor results*

**post·na·tal** /ˌpəʊstˈneɪtl◂‖ˌpoʊst-/ *adj technical* connected with the time after a baby is born: *postnatal care* —compare ANTENATAL, PRENATAL

**postnatal de·pres·sion** /ˌ··· ·ˈ··/ *n* [U] an illness in which a woman feels DEPRESSED (1) after her baby has been born

**post of·fice** /ˈ· ˌ··/ *n* **1** [C] a place where you can buy stamps, send letters and parcels etc **2 the Post Office** *BrE* the national organization which is responsible for collecting and delivering letters: *a Post Office van*

**post office box** /ˈ· ·· ˌ·/ *n* [C] *formal* a PO BOX

**post·paid** /ˌpəʊstˈpeɪd◂‖ˌpoʊst-/ *adv AmE* a letter sent postpaid has no charge for the person sending it; POST-FREE *BrE* —**postpaid** *adj*

**post·pone** /pəʊsˈpəʊn‖poʊsˈpoʊn/ *v* [T] to change an event, action etc to a later time or date: *The match had to be postponed.* | **postpone sth until** *We're postponing our holiday until we have some more money.* | **postpone doing sth** *Gail and Jim have decided to postpone having a family for a while.* —**postponement** *n* [C,U]

**post·pran·di·al** /ˌpəʊstˈprændiəl◂‖ˌpoʊst-/ *adj formal* happening just after dinner: *a postprandial nap*

**post·script** /ˈpəʊsˌskrɪpt‖ˈpoʊs-/ written abbreviation **PS** *n* [C] **1** a message written at the end of a letter below the place where you sign your name: *The postscript at the end said, 'See you soon'.* **2** something that you add at the end of a story or account that you have been telling someone: *an interesting postscript to this tale*

**post-trau·mat·ic stress dis·or·der** /ˌ· ··ˈ·· ···/ *n* [U] *technical* a mental illness which can develop after a very bad experience such as a plane crash

**pos·tu·late**[1] /ˈpɒstjʊ̈leɪt‖ˈpɑːstʃə-/ *v* [T] *formal* to suggest that something might have happened or be true: [+ **that**] *One theory postulates that the ancient Filipinos came from India and Persia.* —**postulation** /ˌpɒstjʊ̈ˈleɪʃən‖ˌpɑːstʃə-/ *n* [C,U]

**pos·tu·late**[2] /ˈpɒstjʊ̈lɪ̈t‖ˈpɑːstjə-/ *n* [C] *formal* something believed to be true, but not proven, on which an argument or scientific discussion is based: *the basic postulates of Marxism*

**pos·ture**[1] /ˈpɒstʃə‖ˈpɑːstʃər/ *n* **1** [C,U] the position you hold your body in when you sit or stand: *Poor posture can* *lead to muscular problems in later life.* **2** [singular] the way you behave or think in a particular situation: *the administration's posture towards China*

**posture²** *v* [I] **1** to stand or behave in a way that you hope will make other people notice and admire you: *Alexi stood posturing in front of the mirror.* **2** to pretend to have a particular opinion or attitude: *pseudo-intellectual posturing* —**posturing** *n* [C,U]

**post-vi·ral syn·drome** /ˌ· ˌ·· ˈ··/ *n* [U] an illness that lasts for a long time and causes weakness, tiredness, and pain in your muscles; ME

**post-war** /ˌ· ˈ·◂/ *adj* [only before noun] happening or existing after a war, especially the Second World War: *economic conditions in post-war Britain* —**post-war** *adv* —compare PRE-WAR

**po·sy** /ˈpəʊzi‖ˈpoʊ-/ *n* [C] *especially literary* a small BUNCH of flowers: *a posy of African violets*

S2 W3 **pot¹** /pɒt‖pɑːt/ *n*

**1** ▶ **TEA/COFFEE** ◀ [C] a container with a handle and a small tube for pouring, used to make tea or coffee

**2** ▶ **COOKING** ◀ [C] a container used for cooking which is round, deep, and usually made of metal: *The sink was full of dirty pots and pans.*

**3** ▶ **STORING FOOD** ◀ [C] a glass or clay container used for storing food: *a jam pot* | *a pot of honey*

**4** ▶ **FOR A PLANT** ◀ [C] a container for a plant, usually made of plastic or baked clay

**5** ▶ **BOWL** ◀ [C] a dish, bowl, plate or other container that is made by shaping clay and then baking it

**6** **have pots of** *BrE informal* to have a lot of something, especially money: *Julie's Dad's got pots of money!*

**7** **go to pot** *informal* if something such as a place or an organization goes to pot, it becomes much worse because no one is interested in looking after it or making it work: *This government has let the whole country go to pot.*

**8** ▶ **DRUG** ◀ [U] *old-fashioned* MARIJUANA

**9** ▶ **STOMACH** ◀ [singular] *informal* a large rounded stomach that sticks out; POTBELLY

**10** ▶ **CARD GAMES** ◀ **the pot** all the money that people have risked in a game of cards, especially POKER (1)

**11** **the pot calling the kettle black** *informal* used to say that you should not criticize someone for a fault that you also have

**12** **take a pot at** *informal* to shoot at something without aiming carefully —see also CHAMBER POT, MELTING POT

**pot²** *v* **potted, potting** [T] **1** to shoot at animals in order to kill them: *Giles was out with his gun, potting rabbits.* —see also POT SHOT **2** to put a plant in a pot filled with soil —see also POTTED (1) **3** [T] to hit a ball into one of the bags at the edge of the table in games such as BILLIARDS, POOL¹ (3), and SNOOKER

**pot** sth↔ **on** *phr v* [T] *BrE* to move a plant into a large pot because it has grown too big for the pot it is in

**po·ta·ble** /ˈpəʊtəbəl‖ˈpoʊ-/ *adj formal* water that is potable is suitable for drinking

**pot·ash** /ˈpɒtæʃ‖ˈpɑː-/ *n* [U] a sort of potassium used especially in farming to make the soil better

**po·tas·si·um** /pəˈtæsiəm/ *n* [U] a silver-white soft metal that is an ELEMENT (1) and usually exists in compounds formed with other substances

S2 **po·ta·to** /pəˈteɪtəʊ‖-toʊ/ *n plural* **potatoes** **1** [C,U] a round white vegetable with a brown skin, that grows as a root: *mashed potato* | *roast potatoes* —see picture on page 414 **2** [C] a plant that has potatoes growing at its roots —see also SWEET POTATO

**potato chip** /ˈ·ˈ·· ·/ *n* [C] *AmE* a thin piece of fried potato which is sold in packets; CRISP¹ *BrE*

**potato peel·er** /ˈ·ˈ·· ˌ··/ *n* [C] a small tool like a knife, used for removing the skin of a potato

**pot·bel·lied** /potˈbelid‖ˈpɑːt-/ *adj* having a large stomach that sticks out: *naked potbellied children begging for food*

**pot·bel·ly** /ˈpɒtˌbeli‖ˈpɑːt-/ *n* [C] a large round stomach that sticks out

**pot·boil·er** /ˈpɒtˌbɔɪlə‖ˈpɑːtˌbɔɪlər/ *n* [C] a book that is written quickly to make money

**pot·bound** /ˈpɒtbaʊnd‖ˈpɑːt-/ *adj BrE* a plant that is potbound cannot grow any more because its roots have grown to fill the pot it is in; ROOTBOUND *AmE*

**po·teen** /pəˈtʃiːn, -ˈtiːn/ *n* [U] Irish WHISKY made secretly and illegally to avoid paying tax

**po·ten·cy** /ˈpəʊtənsi‖ˈpoʊ-/ *n* [U] **1** the power that an idea, argument, action etc has to influence people: *The spectre of mass unemployment had lost none of its political potency.* **2** the strength of the effect of a drug, medicine, alcohol etc on your mind or body: *a high potency drug* **3** the ability of a man to have sex

**po·tent** /ˈpəʊtənt‖ˈpoʊ-/ *adj* **1** having a powerful effect or influence on your body or mind: *a particularly potent cider* | *The film is full of potent images of war.* **2** powerful and effective: *a potent new weapons system* —**potently** *adv* —see also IMPOTENT

**po·ten·tate** /ˈpəʊtənteɪt‖ˈpoʊ-/ *n* [C] *literary* a ruler with direct power over his people: *Eastern potentates*

**po·ten·tial¹** /pəˈtenʃəl/ *adj* [only before noun] a potential customer, problem, effect etc is not a customer, problem etc yet, but may become one in the future: *The agents were eager to impress potential buyers.* | *a potential threat to national security* S3 W2

**potential²** *n* [U] **1** the possibility that something will develop in a certain way, or have a particular effect: [+ **for**] *The potential for abuse in such a system is enormous.* | *sales potential* (=the amount of something that is likely be sold) **2** natural ability that could develop to make you very good at something: *a young player with great potential* | **have/show potential** (=to be likely to be successful) | **achieve/fulfil/realize your potential** (=succeed in doing as well as you possibly can) *We want each student to realize their full potential.* **3** *technical* the difference in VOLTAGE between two points on an electrical CIRCUIT (4) W3

**po·ten·ti·al·i·ty** /pəˌtenʃiˈæləti/ *n* [C,U] *formal* the possibility that something may develop in a particular way

**po·ten·tial·ly** /pəˈtenʃəli/ *adv* [+ adj/adv] something that is potentially dangerous, useful etc is not actually dangerous etc at the present time but is likely to become so: *I knew that I was in a potentially dangerous situation.* | *The benefits of computerised ordering are potentially very great.*

**pot·ful** /ˈpɒtfʊl‖ˈpɑːt-/ *n* [C] the amount that a pot can contain

**pot·head** /ˈpɒthed‖ˈpɑːt-/ *n* [C] *informal* someone who smokes a lot of MARIJUANA

**pot·hold·er** /ˈpɒthəʊldə‖ˈpɑːthoʊldər/ *n* [C] a piece of thick material used for holding hot cooking pans

**pot·hole** /ˈpɒthəʊl‖ˈpɑːthoʊl-/ *n* [C] **1** a hole in the surface of a road that makes driving difficult or dangerous: *swerving to avoid the potholes* **2** a long hole that goes deep under the ground, formed by natural processes —**potholed** *adj*

**pot·hol·ing** /ˈpɒtˌhəʊlɪŋ‖ˈpɑːtˌhoʊl-/ *n* [U] the sport of climbing down inside holes under the ground —**pothole** *v* [I] —**potholer** *n* [C]

**po·tion** /ˈpəʊʃən‖ˈpoʊ-/ *n* [C] **1** *literary* a drink intended to have a special or magic effect on the person who drinks it: *a love potion* **2** *humorous* a medicine, especially one that seems strange, old-fashioned, or unnecessary: *treating herself with pills and potions*

**pot luck** /ˌ· ˈ·/ *n* **take pot luck** **a)** to choose something without knowing very much about it and hope that it will be what you want: *We hadn't booked a hotel so we had to take pot luck.* **b)** to have a meal at someone's home in which you eat whatever they have available: *I'm not sure what there is in the fridge – you'll have to take pot luck.*

**pot·luck** /ˌpɒtˈlʌk◂‖ˌpɑːt-/ *n AmE* a meal made up of dishes of food brought by many different people

**pot plant** /ˈ· ·/ *n* [C] **1** *BrE* a plant that is grown indoors in a pot as a decoration; POTTED PLANT *AmE* **2** *informal* a MARIJUANA plant

**pot·pour·ri** /pəʊˈpʊri‖ˌpoʊpʊˈriː/ *n* **1** [U] a mixture of pieces of dried flowers and leaves kept in a bowl to make a room smell pleasant **2** [C] a mixture of things that are not usually put together, for example different pieces of music or writing: *a pot-pourri of literary styles*

**pot roast** /'· ·/ *n* [C] a dish that consists of a piece of meat cooked in a pan with potatoes or other vegetables

**pot·sherd** /'pɒt-ʃɜːd‖'pɑːt-ʃɜːrd/ *n* [C] *technical* a piece of a broken clay pot from long ago: *Roman coins and potsherds*

**pot shot** /'· ·/ *n* **take a pot shot at** to shoot at someone or something without aiming very carefully

**pot·ted** /'pɒtɪd‖'pɑː-/ *adj* [only before noun] **1** a potted plant grows indoors in a pot: *a potted palm* **2 a potted history/version** *especially BrE* a short explanation or description of something that gives only the main facts: *short potted histories of all the teams in the league* **3** *BrE* potted meat or fish has been made into a PASTE for spreading on bread

**potted plant** /,·· '·/ *n* [C] a plant that is grown indoors in a pot as a decoration; POT PLANT *BrE*

**pot·ter¹** /'pɒtə‖'pɑːtər/ *n* [C] **1** someone who makes pots, dishes etc out of clay —see also POTTERY **2 have a potter/go for a potter** *spoken* to move around a place in a slow unhurried way

**potter²** also **potter about/around** *v* [I] *BrE* to spend time doing pleasant things that are not important without hurrying; PUTTER² *AmE*: *I spent the morning pottering about in the garden.* —**potterer** *n* [C]

**potter's wheel** /,·· '·/ *n* [C] a special round flat object that spins around very fast, onto which wet clay is placed so that it can be shaped into a pot

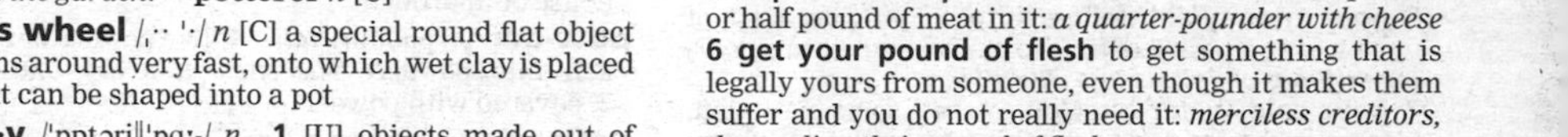

**pot·ter·y** /'pɒtəri‖'pɑː-/ *n* **1** [U] objects made out of baked clay: *a fine collection of medieval pottery* **2** [U] clay that has been shaped and baked in order to make pots, dishes etc: *a pottery dish* **3** [U] the activity of making pots, dishes etc out of clay: *Pottery and basket-making were usually done by the women.*|*a pottery class* **4** [C] a factory where pottery objects are made

**pot·ting shed** /'·· ·/ *n* [C] *BrE* a small building, usually made of wood, where garden tools, seeds etc are kept

**pot·ty¹** /'pɒti‖'pɑːti/ *adj BrE informal* **1** crazy or silly: *What a potty idea!*|**drive sb potty** (=make someone crazy) *Your radio is driving me potty.* **2 potty about** extremely interested in something, or liking someone very much: *Gemma's potty about riding.*|*He's completely potty about her.* —**pottiness** *n* [U]

**potty²** *n* [C] **1** *informal* a container shaped like a bowl, used by very young children as a toilet **2 go to the potty** an expression meaning to go to the toilet, used by or to children

**potty-train** /'·· ·/ *v* [T] to teach a child to use a potty or toilet —**potty-training** *n* [U] —**potty-trained** *adj*

**pouch** /paʊtʃ/ *n* [C] **1** a small leather bag used for keeping things such as tobacco or money in: *a rucksack with pouches on the sides* **2** a pocket of skin which KANGAROOS use for carrying their babies **3** a fold of skin like a bag which animals such as SQUIRRELS have inside each cheek to carry and store food **4** *AmE* an area of loose skin under someone's eyes

**pouf** /pʊf, puːf/ *n* [C] *BrE* **1** a round soft piece of furniture used to sit on or rest your feet on; HASSOCK *AmE* **2** *BrE informal* an insulting word for a male HOMOSEXUAL —compare POOF¹

**pouffe** /puːf/ *n* [C] *BrE* a POUF¹ (1)

**poul·ter·er** /'pəʊltərə‖'poʊltərər/ *n* [C] *BrE old fashioned* someone who sells poultry

**poul·tice** /'pəʊltɪs‖'poʊl-/ *n* [C] something that is put on someone's skin to make it less swollen or painful, often made of bread and milk

**poul·try** /'pəʊltri‖'poʊl-/ *n* **1** [plural] birds that are kept on farms for supplying eggs and meat: *large-scale poultry farms* **2** [U] meat from birds such as chickens, ducks etc

**pounce** /paʊns/ *v* [I] to suddenly jump on an animal or person after waiting to attack them: *crouching, ready to pounce*|[+ **on**] *The cat pounced on an unsuspecting mouse.* —**pounce** *n* [C]

**pounce on** sb/sth *phr v* [T] **1** to notice a mistake and immediately criticize or disagree with it: *The boss was quick to pounce on any error in her work.* **2** to accept an offer or invitation eagerly

**pound¹** /paʊnd/ *n* S1 W2

**1** ▶ **WEIGHT** ◀ written abbreviation **lb** [C] a unit for measuring weight, equal to 16 OUNCES or about 0.454 kilograms: *a pound of apples*|*Moira weighs about 130 pounds.*|*The grapes cost $2 a pound.* —see table on page B2

**2** ▶ **MONEY** ◀ [C] **a)** written abbreviation £ the standard unit of money in Britain, which is divided into 100 pence: *a five pound note*|*They spent over a thousand pounds on their holiday.*|*a multi-million pound business* **b)** the standard unit of money in various other countries, such as Egypt and the Sudan **c)** a coin or note worth this amount: *Can you change a pound?*

**3 the pound** the value of British money in relation to the money of other countries: *There was pressure on the pound in the foreign exchange markets.*

**4** ▶ **PLACE** ◀ [C] a place where lost dogs and cats, or cars that have been illegally parked, are kept until the owner claims them

**5 a quarter/half pounder** a HAMBURGER with a quarter or half pound of meat in it: *a quarter-pounder with cheese*

**6 get your pound of flesh** to get something that is legally yours from someone, even though it makes them suffer and you do not really need it: *merciless creditors, demanding their pound of flesh*

**7 a 3-pounder/24-pounder etc** **a)** animal, or fish that weighs 3 pounds, 24 pounds etc **b)** a gun that fires a SHELL¹ (2) that weighs 3 pounds, 24 pounds etc

**pound²** *v*

**1** ▶ **HIT** ◀ [I,T] to hit something several times, making a lot of noise: [+ **against/on**] *A heavy sea pounded against the pier.*|**pound sth** *Thomas pounded the door with his fist.*

**2** ▶ **MOVE** ◀ [I always + adv/prep] to walk or run quickly with heavy, loud steps: [+ **along/through/down**] *He pounded up the stairs in front of her.*

**3** ▶ **HEART** ◀ [I] if your hearts pounds, it beats very quickly: *Patrick rushed to the door, his heart pounding with excitement.*

**4** ▶ **BREAK** ◀ [T] to hit something many times with a tool in order to break it into pieces or make it flat: *Pound the almonds and mix with breadcrumbs.*

**5** ▶ **MUSIC** ◀ also **pound out, pound away** [T] to play music loudly by hitting your piano, drum etc very hard: *Mrs. Jones pounded out the hymns on the old piano.*

**6** ▶ **ARMY** ◀ [T] to attack a place continuously for a long time with bombs or shells (SHELL¹ (2)): *Enemy forces have been pounding the city for over two months.*

**7 pound the beat** *BrE* if a policeman pounds the beat, he walks regularly around the area he is responsible for

**pound·age** /'paʊndɪdʒ/ *n* [U] *technical* **1** an amount charged for every pound in weight, or for every British £1 in value **2** *informal* weight: *trying to shed that extra poundage*

**pound cake** /'· ·/ *n* [C] *AmE* a heavy cake made from flour, sugar, and butter

**pound·ing** /'paʊndɪŋ/ *n* **1** [singular, U] the action or the sound of something repeatedly hitting a surface very hard, or of your heart beating: *The pounding of hooves was getting nearer.* **2 take a pounding** **a)** to be completely defeated: *Our football team took a real pounding.* **b)** to be hit many times by a lot of bombs or shells (SHELL¹ (2))

**pound ster·ling** /,· '··/ *n* [singular] *technical* the standard unit of money in Britain, which is divided into 100 pence

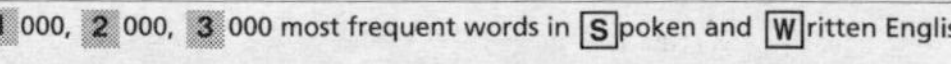

**pour** /pɔː‖pɔːr/ *v*

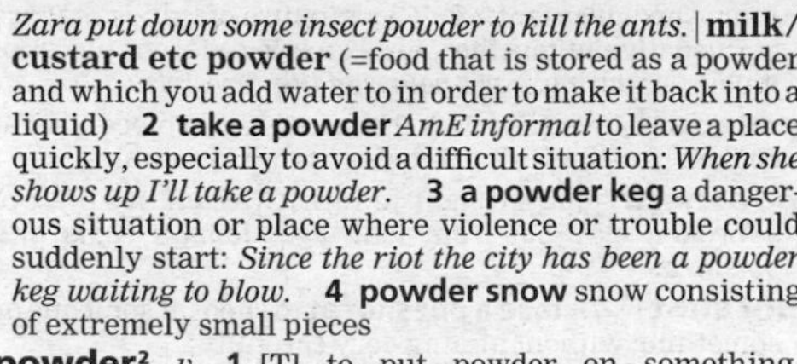


**1 ▶ LIQUID ◀** [T] to make a liquid or a substance such as salt or sand flow out of or into a container: **pour sth into/out/down etc** *Kim poured some water into a glass.* | *You might as well pour the oil down the drain.* | **pour sb sth** *Why don't you pour yourself another drink?*
**2 ▶ TEA ◀** also **pour out** [I] *BrE* to fill cups with tea: *Shall I pour or will you?*
**3 ▶ LIQUID/SMOKE ◀** [I always + adv/prep] to flow quickly and in large amounts: [+ **from/down/out**] *Smoke was pouring out of the chimney.*
**4 ▶ ARRIVE/LEAVE ◀** [I always + adv/prep] if people or things pour into or out of a place, a lot of them arrive or leave at the same time: [+ **into/from/through**] *The men poured into the hall for the meeting.* | *Offers of help poured in from all over the country.*
**5 ▶ RAIN ◀** also **pour down** [I] to rain heavily without stopping: *The rain poured down endlessly.* | **it's pouring/it poured** *It poured all night.* | **It's pouring rain/hail etc** *AmE*: *It's pouring rain out there!*
**6 pour money/aid/dollars into** to provide a lot of money over a period of time to pay for something: *pouring millions of dollars into education*
**7 pour cold water over/on** to spoil someone's plan, idea or keenness to do something by criticizing them: *pouring cold water on suggestions that he might resign*
**8 pour oil on troubled waters** to try to stop a quarrel by talking to people and making them calmer
**9 pour scorn on** to say that something or someone is stupid and not worth considering: *The press is pouring scorn on the 'do nothing' Congress.*
**10 pour well** if a container pours well, you can pour liquid easily from it
**11 pour it on** *informal* to tell someone about a situation in a way that makes it seem much worse than it really is, in order to make them feel sorry for you: *She was really pouring it on.*

**pour** sth ↔ **out** *phr v* [T] if you pour out your thoughts, feelings etc, you tell someone everything about them, especially because you feel very unhappy: **pour sth out to sb** *Liam poured out his feelings of loneliness to Laura.* | **pour out your heart/soul** (=tell someone all your feelings including your most secret ones)

**pout** /paʊt/ *v* [I,T] to push out your lips because you are annoyed or to look sexually attractive: *The child pouted, cried, and went into a tantrum.* —**pout** *n* [C] —**pouty** *adj*

W3 **pov·er·ty** /ˈpɒvəti‖ˈpɑːvərti/ *n* **1** [U] the situation or experience of being poor: **dire/abject/grinding poverty** (=very bad poverty) *Thousands of children live in dire poverty.* **2 the poverty line/level** the income below which a person or a family is officially considered to be very poor and in need of help: *More than 20% of American families now live below the poverty line.* **3** [singular, U] *formal* a lack of a particular quality: [+ **of**] *a surprising poverty of imagination* —compare POORNESS

**poverty-strick·en** /ˈ··· ˌ··/ *adj* extremely poor and having problems because of this: *a poverty-stricken area*

**poverty trap** /ˈ··· ˌ·/ *n* [C] a situation in which a poor person will not get any advantage from taking a job because they would then lose their payments from the government

**POW** /ˌpiː əʊ ˈdʌbəljuː‖-oʊ-/ *n* [C] a PRISONER OF WAR: *Thousands of POWs died in the camps.*

**pow** /paʊ/ *interjection* used to represent the sound of a gun firing, an explosion, or someone hitting another person hard, especially in children's COMICS

**pow·der¹** /ˈpaʊdə‖-ər/ *n* **1** [C,U] a dry substance in the form of very small grains: *Grind the sugar into a powder.* | *Zara put down some insect powder to kill the ants.* | **milk/custard etc powder** (=food that is stored as a powder and which you add water to in order to make it back into a liquid) **2 take a powder** *AmE informal* to leave a place quickly, especially to avoid a difficult situation: *When she shows up I'll take a powder.* **3 a powder keg** a dangerous situation or place where violence or trouble could suddenly start: *Since the riot the city has been a powder keg waiting to blow.* **4 powder snow** snow consisting of extremely small pieces

**powder²** *v* **1** [T] to put powder on something, especially your skin: *Dana took out her compact and began powdering her cheeks.* **2 be powdered with** to be covered with small pieces of something: *Their shoulders were powdered with snow.* **3 powder your nose** an expression meaning to go to the TOILET, used by women to avoid saying this directly

**powder blue** /ˌ·· ˈ·◂/ *n* [U] pale blue: *a powder blue dress*

**pow·dered** /ˈpaʊdəd‖-ərd/ *adj* **1** produced or sold in the form of a powder: *powdered milk* **2** covered with powder: *powdered hair*

**powder puff** /ˈ·· ·/ *n* [C] a small piece of soft material used by women to spread POWDER on their face or body

**powder room** /ˈ·· ·/ *n* [C] **1** an expression meaning a toilet for women in a theatre, hotel, restaurant etc, used to avoid saying this directly **2** *AmE* a small room with a toilet and WASHBASIN next to the main living room in a house or apartment

**pow·der·y** /ˈpaʊdəri/ *adj* **1** like powder or easily broken into powder: *The snow was dry and powdery.* **2** covered with powder

**pow·er¹** /ˈpaʊə‖paʊr/ *n* 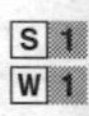
**1 ▶ CONTROL ◀** [U] the ability or right to control people or events: *We all felt that the chairman had too much power.* | *He was motivated by greed, envy, and the lust for power.* | [+ **over**] *She has a lot of power over the people in her team.* | **power struggle** (=a situation in which groups or leaders try to defeat each other and get complete control) *engaged in a bitter power struggle against Chairman Sir George Scott*
**2 ▶ CONTROL OF A COUNTRY ◀** [U] the position of having political control of a country or government: **be in power** *The dictator had been in power for seven years.* | **come/rise to power** (=start having political control) *De Gaulle came to power in 1958.* | **return to power** *The Labour Party returned to power after 13 years.* | **get into power** *If the Social Democrats got into power, they would change the whole system of local government.* | **take/sieze power** *The Communists seized power in 1962.* | **lose power** *Left-wing parties lost power in several European countries last year.*
**3 ▶ INFLUENCE ◀** [U] the ability to influence people or give them strong feelings: [+ **of**] *We were stunned by the power of his speech.* | *the immense power of television*
**4 ▶ RIGHT/AUTHORITY ◀** [C,U] the right or authority to do something: *The police have been given special powers to help them in the fight against terrorism.* | **the power to do sth** *She was the one who had the power to hire or fire people.* | **the power of** *The chairman has the power of veto on all decisions.*
**5 ▶ ABILITY ◀** [C,U] a natural or special ability to do something: [+ **of**] *After the accident she lost the power of speech.* | **the power to do sth** *Local people believe that the plant has the power to cure all kinds of ailments.*
**6 earning/purchasing/bargaining power** the ability to earn money, buy things etc: *Average earning power has shot up by more than 50%.*
**7 student power/black power/parent power etc** the political or social influence that an organized group has: *another victory for student power*
**8 ▶ STRENGTH ◀** [U] the strength of something such as an explosion, animal or natural force and its ability to move or destroy things: *the sheer power and majesty of the elephant* | *the power of the explosion*
**9 ▶ ENERGY ◀** [U] energy that can be used to make a machine work or to make electricity: **nuclear/wind/**

**solar etc power** *Many people are opposed to the use of nuclear power.* | **under its own power** (=without help from another machine, ship etc) *The cruiser was able to leave port under its own power.* | **lose/run out of power** *It keeps losing power when I take a sharp bend.*
**10 ► ELECTRICITY ◄** [U] electricity that is used in houses, factories etc: *She plugged the machine in and switched the power on.* | *Power is provided by a small 9 volt battery.* | **power cut/failure/outage** (=a short time when the electricity supply is not working) *Parts of the country have had power cuts because of the storms.*
**11 ► STRONG COUNTRY ◄** [C] a country that is strong and important, or has a lot of military strength: *Egypt is still an important power in the Middle East.* | **world power** (=a very important country that can influence events in different parts of the world)
**12 air/sea power** ships or aircraft that help an army in the air or on the sea: *The outcome will be decided by air power.*
**13 be in sb's power** to be in a situation in which someone has complete control over you
**14 be in sb's power to do sth** if it is in someone's power to do something, they have the authority or ability to do it: *It is not in my power to tell you the results of the exam.*
**15 be beyond/outside sb's power to do sth** if it is beyond someone's power to do something, they do not have the authority or ability to do it: *I am afraid it is beyond my power to do what you are asking.*
**16 do everything in your power** to do everything that you are able or allowed to do: *The ambassador promised to do everything in his power to get the hostages released.*
**17 do sb a power of good** *BrE informal* to make someone feel more healthy, happy, and hopeful about the future: *It looks as if your holiday has done you a power of good.*
**18 the powers of good/evil** spirits or magical forces that are believed to influence events in a good or evil way
**19 ► MATHEMATICS ◄** [C] if a number is increased to the power of three, four, five etc, it is multiplied by itself three, four, five etc times
**20 high-powered/low-powered etc** having a motor that is very powerful, not very powerful etc: *irresponsible young men in high-powered sports cars*
**21 a power in the land** *old-fashioned* someone who has a lot of power and influence in a country
**22 the power behind the throne** someone who is able to secretly control and influence decisions made by the leader or government of a country, but does not have an official government position themselves
**23 the powers that be** *informal* the unknown people who have important positions of authority and power, and whose decisions affect your life: *The powers that be have decided that smoking is a Bad Idea.*
**24 be on a power trip** *informal* to be enjoying the new power or authority that you have been given, in a way that other people find unpleasant —see also STAYING POWER, BALANCE OF POWER, HIGH-POWERED

**power²** *v* **1** [T usually passive] to supply power to a vehicle or machine: *The motor is powered by a solar battery.* **2** [I + adv/prep] to move powerfully and quickly: [+ **through/up/down**] *His strong body powered through the water.* **3 battery-powered/nuclear-powered etc** working or moving by means of power from a BATTERY, NUCLEAR energy etc: *an atomic-powered ship* —see also HIGH-POWERED

**power³** *adj* **1** driven by a motor: *power tools* **2** *informal* showing that you are important in a business organization: *a power lunch*

**power base** /ˈ·· ·/ *n* [C] an area or group of people whose support gives a politician or leader their power: *Texas remained Johnson's political power base.*

**pow·er·boat** /ˈpaʊəbəʊt‖ˈpaʊərboʊt/ *n* [C] a powerful MOTORBOAT that is used for racing

**power bro·ker** /ˈ·· ˌ··/ *n* [C] someone who controls who should have political power in an area

**power cut** /ˈ·· ·/ *n* [C] a period of time when there is no electricity supply

**power dres·sing** /ˈ·· ˌ··/ *n* [U] a way of dressing in which the colour and style of your clothes is intended to emphasize how important your job is: *Eighties power dressing at its brashest*

**power drill** /ˈ·· ·/ *n* [C] a tool for making holes that works by electricity

**pow·er·ful** /ˈpaʊəfəl‖ˈpaʊr-/ *adj* W2

**1 ► IMPORTANT ◄** a powerful person, organization, group etc is able to control and influence events and other people's actions: *The president is the most powerful man in America and probably the world.* | *a powerful consortium of European companies*
**2 ► AFFECTING SB'S FEELINGS/IDEAS ◄** having a strong effect on someone's feelings or on the way they think: *Jealousy is such a powerful emotion.* | *a powerful speech* | *The film uses a powerful blend of images and words.* | **powerful reasons/arguments** (=reasons that make you think that something must be true)
**3 ► MACHINE/WEAPON ETC ◄** a powerful machine, engine, weapon etc works very effectively and quickly or with great force: *a new generation of more powerful PCs* | *The Jaguar XJ12 features a powerful 24 valve engine.*
**4 ► MEDICINE ◄** a powerful medicine or drug has a very strong effect on your body: *The drug is a thousand times more powerful than LSD.*
**5 ► PHYSICALLY STRONG ◄** physically strong: *Jed was a powerful, well-built man.* | *powerful jaws that can kill in seconds*
**6 ► TEAM/ARMY ETC ◄** a powerful team, army etc is very strong and can easily defeat other teams or armies: *The Allies had assembled a powerful fighting force.*
**7 ► LIGHT/SOUND/TASTE/SMELL ◄** very strong, bright, loud etc: *The alarm emits a powerful high-pitched sound.*
**8 ► EXPLOSION/KICK/PUNCH ETC ◄** a powerful blow, explosion etc hits someone with a lot of force or has a lot of force: *an explosion ten times more powerful than Hiroshima* | *a powerful header just over the bar* —**powerfully** *adv*: *Christie is very powerfully built.* —see also ALL-POWERFUL

**pow·er·house** /ˈpaʊəhaʊs‖ˈpaʊr-/ *n* [C] *informal* **1** an organization or place that produces a lot of ideas and has a lot of influence: *In the 60s, MIT was an intellectual powerhouse.* **2** someone who is very strong and has a lot of energy: *a powerhouse of a man*

**pow·er·less** /ˈpaʊələs‖ˈpaʊr-/ *adj* [not before noun] unable to stop or control something because you do not have the power, strength, or legal right to do so: **powerless to do sth** *The fire was so big that firefighters were powerless to prevent it from spreading.* | [+ **against**] *The Hungarians were powerless against the might of the Red Army.* —**powerlessly** *adv* —**powerlessness** *n* [U]

**power line** /ˈ·· ·/ *n* [C] a large wire carrying electricity above or under the ground: *overhead power lines*

**power of at·tor·ney** /ˌ·· · ·ˈ··/ *n* [C,U] *law* the legal right to do things for another person in their personal or business life, or a document giving this right

**power plant** /ˈ·· ·/ *n* [C] **1** *technical* the machine or engine that supplies power to a factory, plane, car etc **2** *AmE* a building where electricity is produced to supply a large area; POWER STATION

**power point** /ˈ·· ·/ *n* [C] *especially BrE* a place on a wall where electrical equipment can be connected to the electricity supply; SOCKET

**power pol·i·tics** /ˈ·· ˌ···/ *n* [U] the use or threat of armed force in international politics: *mere pawns in a game of international power politics*

**power sta·tion** /ˈ·· ˌ··/ *n* [C] a building where electricity is produced to supply a large area

**power steer·ing** /ˈ·· ˌ··/ *n* [U] a system for steering (STEER¹ (1)) a vehicle which uses power from the vehicle's engine and so needs less effort from the driver

**power tool** /ˈ·· ·/ *n* [C] a tool that works by electricity

**pow-wow** /ˈ· ·/ *n* [C] **1** *humorous* a meeting or discussion **2** a meeting or council of Native Americans

**pox** /pɒks‖pɑːks/ *n old use* **1 the pox** the disease SYPHILIS **2** [U] the disease SMALLPOX **3 a pox on** *old use* used to show that you are angry or annoyed with someone —see also CHICKENPOX

**pox·y** /ˈpɒksi‖ˈpɑː-/ *adj BrE slang* used to show that you do not like someone or something: *Keep your poxy money.*

**pp** **1** the written abbreviation of pages: *See pp 15 – 17.* **2** written before the name of another person when you are signing a letter for them

**PPS** /ˌpiː piː ˈes/ *n* [C] **1** a note added after a PS in a letter or message **2** Parliamentary Private Secretary; a member of the British parliament who is appointed to help a minister

**PR** /ˌpiː ˈɑː‖-ˈɑːr/ *n* [U] **1** PUBLIC RELATIONS; the work of persuading people to think that a company or organization is a good one: *a leading PR agency in the city | It's not very good for your PR, is it?* **2** PROPORTIONAL REPRESENTATION

**prac·ti·ca·ble** /ˈpræktɪkəbəl/ *adj* an idea or way of doing something that is practicable is able to be used successfully in a particular situation: *The only practicable course of action is to sell the company.* —**practicably** *adv* —**practicability** /ˌpræktɪkəˈbɪlɪ̣ti/ *n* [U]

S3 W2 **prac·ti·cal¹** /ˈpræktɪkəl/ *adj*
**1** ▶ **CONCERNED WITH REAL SITUATIONS** ◀ concerned with real situations and events rather than ideas: *How much practical experience do you have of working with computers? | a practical knowledge of simple medicine | Most of the things you learn at school have no practical value in the real world.* —compare THEORETICAL
**2** ▶ **SENSIBLE** ◀ sensible and basing your decisions on what is possible and what will really work: *Be practical! We can't afford the car and the vacation!* —opposite IMPRACTICAL (1)
**3** ▶ **LIKELY TO WORK** ◀ practical plans, methods, advice etc are likely to succeed or be effective in a situation: *The only practical solution is to sell the company. | The agency provides practical advice and support to pregnant teenagers.* | **practical alternative** (=another way of doing something that is likely to work) —opposite IMPRACTICAL (1)
**4** ▶ **USEFUL** ◀ designed to be useful rather than attractive: *Majorie always gets us practical Christmas presents – last year we got a kettle.*
**5** ▶ **SUITABLE** ◀ suitable for a particular purpose or for normal life: *I always wanted a Ferrari, but it's not a very practical car. | Jeans would be the most practical thing to wear.* —opposite IMPRACTICAL (1)
**6** ▶ **GOOD AT REPAIRING/MAKING THINGS** ◀ good at repairing or making things: *I'm not very practical – I don't know the first thing about cars.*
**7 a practical certainty/disaster/sell-out etc** something that is almost certain, almost a DISASTER etc: *Sampras looks a practical certainty to win Wimbledon this year.*
**8 for/to all practical purposes** used when saying what the real effect of a situation is: *For all practical purposes the federation no longer exists.*

**practical²** *n* [C] *BrE* a lesson or examination in science, cooking etc in which you have to do or make something yourself rather than write or read about it: *We have chemistry practicals after Christmas.*

**prac·ti·cal·i·ty** /ˌpræktɪˈkælɪ̣ti/ *n* **1 practicalities** [plural] the real facts of a situation rather than ideas about how it might be: *concerned with the practicalities of planning lessons and courses* **2** [U] how suitable an idea, method, or plan is for a situation, and whether or not it will work: *doubts about the practicality of your suggestion* **3** [U] the quality of being sensible and basing your plans on what you know will work

**practical joke** /ˌ··· ˈ·/ *n* [C] a trick that is intended to give someone a surprise or shock and make other people laugh —**practical joker** *n* [C]

**prac·ti·cally** /ˈpræktɪkli/ *adv* **1** *especially spoken* almost: *The hall was practically empty. | Practically all my friends are gay.* **2** in a sensible way which takes account of problems: *"But how can we pay for it?" said John practically.*

**prac·tice** /ˈpræktɪ̣s/ *n* 
**1 a)** ▶ **A SKILL** ◀ [U] regular activity that you do in order to improve a skill: *It takes hours of practice to learn to play the guitar. | With a little more practice you should be able to pass your test.* **b)** [C] a period of time you spend training to improve your skill in doing something: *choir practice | We have two rugby practices a week.*
**2 in practice** used when saying what really happens rather than what should happen or what people think happens: *In practice women receive much lower wages than their male colleagues.*
**3** ▶ **CUSTOM** ◀ [C] something that you do often because of your religion or your society's tradition: *religious beliefs and practices* | **the practice of doing sth** *The Navy has abandoned the practice of serving rum to the men.* —see HABIT (USAGE)
**4** ▶ **STH DONE OFTEN** ◀ [C,U] something that people do often, especially a particular way of doing something: *the widespread practice of under-declaring taxable income | unsafe sexual practices | dangerous working practices*
**5** ▶ **DOCTOR/LAWYER** ◀ [C] the work of a doctor or lawyer or the place where they work: **medical/legal practice** *Mary Beth had a busy legal practice in Los Angeles.* —see also GENERAL PRACTICE, PRIVATE PRACTICE
**6 common/standard/general/normal practice** the usual and accepted way of doing something: *In Scandinavian countries it is common practice for the husband to stay at home to look after the baby.*
**7 good/bad practice** an example of a good or very bad way of doing something, especially in a particular job: *It's not considered good practice to reveal clients' names.*
**8 be out of practice** to have not done something for a long time so that you are unable to do it well
**9 be in practice** if you are in practice you have practised something regularly and are able to do it well
**10 put sth into practice** if you put an idea, plan etc into practice, you start to use it and see if it is effective: *The hard part is putting it all into practice.*
**11 practice makes perfect** used to say that if you do an activity regularly, you will become very good at it

**prac·tise** *BrE*, **practice** *AmE* /ˈpræktɪ̣s/ *v* **1** [I,T] to do an activity regularly in order to improve your skill or to prepare for a test: 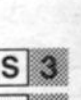 **practise (doing) sth** *John's practising the violin. | Today we're going to practise parking.* | **practise for sth** *She's practising for her driving test.* | **practise sth on sb** *Everybody wants to practise their English on me.* | **practise hard** (=practise a lot) *If you practise hard you might be the next Carl Lewis.* **2** [T] to use a particular method or custom: *Polyandry is still practised in some parts of the world.* **3** [I,T] to work as a doctor or lawyer: [+ **as**] *Gemma is now practising as a dentist.* | **practise sth** *He went on to practise law.* **4** [T] if you practise a religion, system of ideas etc, you live your life according to its rules **5 practise what you preach** to do the things that you advise other people to do: *The Green candidate should practise what she preaches and sell her car.*

**prac·tised** *BrE*, **practiced** *AmE* /ˈpræktɪ̣st/ *adj* **1** someone who is practised in a particular job or skill is good at it because they have done it many times before: *a practised hunter* | **practised in (doing) sth** *Kate became practised in the art of disguising her emotions.* | **to the practised eye** (=to someone who has seen something many times and knows a lot about it) **2** [only before noun] a practised action has been done so often that it now seems very easy: *With practised ease he slit open the sack.*

**prac·tis·ing** *BrE*, **practicing** *AmE* /ˈpræktɪ̣sɪŋ/ *adj* **1 a practising Catholic/Muslim/Jew etc** someone who follows the rules and customs of a particular religion **2 a practising doctor/lawyer/teacher etc** someone who is working as a doctor, lawyer etc: *Few practising teachers have time for such research.*

W3 **prac·ti·tion·er** /præk'tɪʃənə‖-ər/ *n* [C] **1 medical/legal practitioner** someone who works as a doctor or a lawyer **2** someone who regularly does a particular activity: *skilful public relations practitioners* | [+ **of**] *a practitioner of Taoist philosophy* —see also GENERAL PRACTITIONER

**prae·sid·i·um** /prɪ'sɪdiəm, -'zɪ-/ *n* [C] another spelling of PRESIDIUM

**prag·mat·ic** /præg'mætɪk/ *adj* dealing with problems in a sensible, practical way instead of strictly following a set of ideas: *a pragmatic approach to politics* —**pragmatically** /-kli/ *adv*

**prag·mat·ics** /præg'mætɪks/ *n* [U] *technical* the study of how words and phrases are used with special meanings in particular situations

**prag·ma·tis·m** /'prægmətɪzəm/ *n* [U] a way of dealing with problems in a sensible, practical way instead of following a set of ideas: *conditioned more by political pragmaticism than religious zeal* —**pragmatist** *n* [C]

**prai·rie** /'preəri‖'preri/ *n* [C] a wide open area of land in North America which is covered in grass or wheat

**prairie dog** /'·· ·/ *n* [C] a small animal with a short tail, which lives in holes on the prairies

**praise**[1] /preɪz/ *v* [T] **1** to say that you admire and approve of someone or something, especially publicly: *The play was praised by the critics when it was first shown on Broadway.* | **praise sb/sth for sth** *The Mayor praised the rescue team for their courage.* | **praise sb/sth highly** *a highly praised novel* | **praise sb/sth to the skies** (=to praise someone or something very much) **2** to give thanks to God and show your respect to him, especially by singing in a church **3 God/Heaven be praised** also **Praise the Lord** used to say that you are pleased something has happened and thank God for it

**praise**[2] *n* [U] **1** words that you say or write in order to praise someone or something: **be full of praise for** (=praise something a lot) *Mrs. George was full of praise for her nurses' caring attitude.* | **high praise** (=a lot of praise) *Bork received high praise for his efforts to cut spending.* | **win praise** (=receive praise) *The film has won praise from audiences and critics alike.* **2** the expression of respect and thanks to God: *Let us give praise unto the Lord.* **3 praise be!** *old-fashioned* used when you are very pleased about something that has happened —see also **sing sb's praises** (SING (5))

**praise·wor·thy** /'preɪzwɜːði‖-ɜːr-/ *adj* deserving praise, especially when not completely successful: *the Italian team's praiseworthy attempts to reach a draw* —**praiseworthiness** *n* [U]

**pra·line** /'prɑːliːn/ *n* [C,U] a sweet food made of nuts cooked in boiling sugar

**prams**

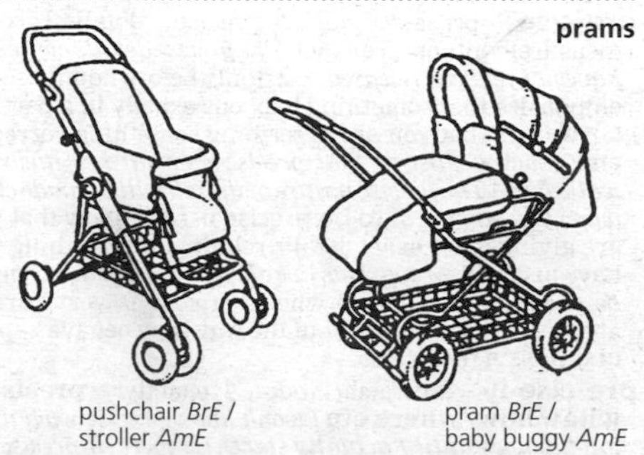

pushchair *BrE* / stroller *AmE*

pram *BrE* / baby buggy *AmE*

S3 **pram** /præm/ *n* [C] *BrE* a small vehicle with four wheels in which a baby can lie down while being pushed; BABY CARRIAGE *AmE* —compare BUGGY (3)

**prance** /prɑːns‖præns/ *v* [I] **1** [always + adv/prep] to walk moving your body in a confident way in order to make people notice and admire you: [+**around/in/up**] *Leo's always prancing around as if he owns the place.* **2** if a horse prances, it moves with high steps

**prang** /præŋ/ *v* [T] *BrE informal* to damage a vehicle in an accident —**prang** *n* [C]

**prank** /præŋk/ *n* [C] a trick, especially one which is played on someone to make them look silly: *a childish prank*

**prank·ster** /'præŋkstə‖-ər/ *n* [C] someone who plays tricks on people to make them look silly

**prat** /præt/ *n* [C] *BrE informal* a stupid person: *Don't be such a prat.* —**prattish** *adj*

**prate** /preɪt/ *v* [I + **on/about**] *old-fashioned* to talk in a meaningless, boring way about something

**prat·fall** /'prætfɔːl‖-fɒːl/ *n* [C] an embarrassing accident or mistake: *another one of the Vice-President's pratfalls*

**prat·tle** /'prætl/ *v* [I] to talk continuously about silly and unimportant things: **prattle on (about)** *What's Sarah prattling on about?* —**prattle** *n* [U] —**prattler** *n* [C]

**prawn** /prɔːn‖prɒːn/ *n* [C] a small pink SHELLFISH that is used for food: *a prawn salad sandwich*

**pray**[1] /preɪ/ *v* [I,T] **1** to speak to God in order to ask for help or give thanks: *They went to the mosque to pray.* | [+ **for**] *Let us pray for peace.* | [+ **to**] *Martha prayed to God every night.* | **pray sth** *"Dear Lord, show me my duty," she prayed.* **2** to wish or hope very strongly that something will happen: **pray that** *Paul was praying that no one had noticed his absence.* | [+ **for**] *We're praying for a fine day tomorrow.* S3

**pray**[2] *adv* [sentence adverb] *old-fashioned* used when politely asking a question or telling someone to do something: *Pray be seated.* | *And who, pray, is this?*

**prayer** /preə‖prer/ *n* **1** [C] words that you say when praying to God, especially a fixed form of words: *We all had to say our prayers before going to bed.* | [+ **for**] *a prayer for the deceased* **2** [U] the act of praying or the regular habit of praying: *the power of prayer* | *a prayer meeting* | **in prayer** (=praying) *The congregation knelt in prayer.* **3** [C] a wish or hope that something will happen: *Nadia's one prayer is that the children won't suffer.* **4 prayers** [plural] a regular religious meeting in a church, school etc, at which people pray together: *Prayers are at 9 o'clock.* **5 not have a prayer** *informal* to have no chance of succeeding: *I hadn't done any work for the exam, and I knew I didn't have a prayer.* **6 sb's prayers are answered** *informal* used to say that someone has got something that they wanted very much: *I thought all my prayers were answered when I got that job.* —see also LORD'S PRAYER S3 W3

**prayer book** /'· ·/ *n* [C] a book containing prayers used in some Christian church services

**prayer mat** /'· ·/ also **prayer rug** *n* [C] a small mat which Muslims kneel on when praying

**prayer wheel** /'· ·/ *n* [C] a piece of wood or metal that is shaped like a drum and turns around on a pole, on which prayers are written, used in Tibet

**pray·ing man·tis** /,·· '··/ *n* [C] a large insect that eats other insects

**pre-** /priː/ *prefix* **1** before someone or something: *prewar* (=before a war) **2** in preparation: *a prearranged signal* | *Preset the video.* —compare ANTE-

**preach** /priːtʃ/ *v* **1** [I,T] to give a talk in public about a religious subject, especially about the correct moral way for people to behave: [+ **to/on/about**] *Christ began preaching to large crowds.* | **preach sth** *The pastor preached a sermon on brotherly love.* **2** [T] to talk about how good or important something is and try to persuade other people about this: **preach the virtues of** *Imran's always preaching the virtues of a healthy outdoor life.* **3** [I] to give someone advice in a way that they think is boring or annoying: *I'm sorry, I didn't mean to preach.* **4 preach to the converted** to talk about what you think is right or important to people who already have the same opinions as you —see also **practise what you preach** (PRACTISE (5))

**preach·er** /ˈpriːtʃə‖-ər/ *n* [C] someone who gives talks at religious meetings but who is not actually a priest

**preach·y** /ˈpriːtʃi/ *adj informal* trying too much to persuade people to accept a particular opinion

**pre·am·ble** /priˈæmbəl‖ˈpriːæmbəl/ *n* [C] *formal* a statement at the beginning of a book, document, or talk, explaining what it is about: **without preamble** (=immediately and without any explanation) *"Murder," he said, without preamble. "No doubt about it."*

**pre·arranged** /ˌpriːəˈreɪndʒd◂/ *adj* planned in advance: *At a prearranged signal, everyone stood up.* —**prearrangement** *n* [U]

**pre·car·i·ous** /prɪˈkeəriəs‖-ˈker-/ *adj* **1** a precarious situation or state is likely to become very dangerous: *The refugees live a precarious existence in shanty towns.* | *a precarious peace* **2** someone or something precarious is likely to fall —**precariously** *adv*: *a cup of tea balanced precariously on her knee* —**precariousness** *n* [U]

**pre·cast** /ˌpriːˈkɑːst◂‖-ˈkæst◂/ *adj* precast CONCRETE is already formed into blocks ready for use to make buildings

**pre·cau·tion** /prɪˈkɔːʃən‖-ˈkɒː-/ *n* [C usually plural] something you do in order to prevent something dangerous or unpleasant from happening: *Fire precautions were neglected.* | *elaborate precautions to avoid detection* | [+ **against**] *You should save your work often as a precaution against computer failure.* | **take the precaution of doing sth** *I took the precaution of insuring my camera.*

**pre·cau·tion·a·ry** /prɪˈkɔːʃənəri‖-ˈkɒːʃəneri/ *adj* **precautionary measures/steps etc** things that you do in order to prevent something dangerous or unpleasant from happening: *The ward will be closed for a week as a precautionary measure.*

W3 **pre·cede** /prɪˈsiːd/ *v* [T] *formal* **1** to happen or exist before something or someone or to come before something else in a series: *The numbers on the license plate are preceded by a letter.* | *He was a much stronger leader than the man who preceded him.* (=was leader before him) **2** to go somewhere before someone else: *John preceded his guests into the lounge.* **3** to say or write something as an introduction to a speech, book etc: *The author preceded his speech with a few words of welcome.*

**pre·ce·dence** /ˈpresɪ̣dəns/ *n* [U] **1** **take/have precedence over** to be considered more important than someone or something else and therefore come or be done before them: *Saving the child's life took precedence over everything else.* **2** the relative importance of different things or people and the need to deal with the most important first, then the second most important, and so on: **in order of precedence** *Arrange the tasks in order of precedence.*

**pre·ce·dent** /ˈpresɪ̣dənt/ *n* **1** [C] an action or official decision which can be used to give legal support to later actions or decisions: **set/create a precedent** *The invasion of Panama set a dangerous precedent.* **2** [C,U] something of the same type that has happened or existed before: [+ **for**] *Is there any precedent for this?* | **without precedent** (=never happening before) *An epidemic on this scale is without precedent.* **3** [U] the way that things have always been done: **break with precedent** (=to do something in a new way)

**pre·ced·ing** /prɪˈsiːdɪŋ/ *adj* [only before noun] *formal* happening or coming before the time, place, or part mentioned: *We made more money this month than in the whole of the preceding quarter.* —opposite FOLLOWING

**pre·cept** /ˈpriːsept/ *n* [C] *formal* a rule on which a way of thinking or behaving is based: *basic moral precepts*

**pre·cinct** /ˈpriːsɪŋkt/ *n* **1** [C] *AmE* an area within a town or city that has its own police force, local government representatives etc: *the 44th Precinct* **2** [C] *AmE* the main police station in a particular area of a town or city: *Book him and take him down to the precinct.* **3** [C] **shopping/pedestrian precinct** *BrE* an area of a town where people can walk and cars are not allowed **4** **precincts** [plural] the area that surrounds an important building: *the precincts of the cathedral*

**pre·ci·os·i·ty** /ˌpreʃiˈɒsɪ̣ti‖-ˈɑː-/ *n* [U] *literary* the attitude of being too concerned about style or detail in your writing or speech, so that it sounds unnatural

**pre·cious¹** /ˈpreʃəs/ *adj* **1** precious memories or possessions are important to you because they are connected with people you like or events in your life: *The doll is very precious to me because it was my mother's.* **2** something that is precious is valuable and important and should not be wasted or used without care: *Don't waste precious time talking to him, he's not worth it.* **3** rare and worth a lot of money: *a precious jewel* **4** [only before noun] *spoken* used to show that you are annoyed that someone seems to care too much about something: *Your precious career is becoming more important than your family.* **5** someone who is precious is formal and unnatural because they are trying too hard to be perfect —**preciously** *adv* —**preciousness** *n* [U]

**precious²** *adv informal* **precious little/few** very little or very few: *He has precious little experience of computing.*

**precious met·al** /ˌ·· ˈ··/ *n* [C,U] a rare and valuable metal such as gold or silver

**precious stone** /ˌ·· ˈ·/ *n* [C] a rare and valuable jewel such as a DIAMOND or an EMERALD¹ —compare SEMI-PRECIOUS

**pre·ci·pice** /ˈpresɪ̣pɪ̣s/ *n* [C] a very steep side of a high rock, mountain or cliff: *towards the edge of the precipice*

**pre·cip·i·tate¹** /prɪ̣ˈsɪpɪ̣teɪt/ *v* **1** [T] *formal* to make something serious happen more quickly than was expected; HASTEN: *The economic crisis was precipitated by the US's inability to deal with the budget deficit.* **2** [T] to force someone or something into a particular state or condition: *The rise in the value of oil precipitated a world economic crisis.* **3** **precipitate sb somewhere** *formal* to make someone fall forwards or downwards with great force **4** [I,T + **out**] *technical* to separate a solid substance from a liquid by chemical action, or to be separated in this way

**pre·cip·i·tate²** /prɪ̣ˈsɪpɪ̣tɪ̣t/ *n* [C,U] *technical* a solid substance that has been chemically separated from a liquid

**precipitate³** *adj formal* done too quickly, especially without thinking carefully enough —**precipitately** *adv*

**pre·cip·i·ta·tion** /prɪ̣ˌsɪpɪ̣ˈteɪʃən/ *n* **1** [C,U] *technical* rain, snow etc that falls on the ground, or the amount of rain, snow etc that falls **2** [C,U] *technical* a chemical process in which a solid substance is separated from a liquid **3** [U] *formal* the act of doing something too quickly in a way that is not sensible

**pre·cip·i·tous** /prɪ̣ˈsɪpɪ̣təs/ *adj* **1** dangerously high or steep: *A precipitous path led down the cliff.* **2** PRECIPITATE³ —**precipitously** *adv* —**precipitousness** *n* [U]

**pré·cis** /ˈpreɪsiː‖preɪˈsiː/ *n plural* **précis** /ˈpreɪsiːz‖preɪˈsiːz/ [C] a statement which gives the main ideas of a piece of writing, speech etc: *a concise and accurate précis* —**précis** *v* [T]

**pre·cise** /prɪˈsaɪs/ *adj* **1** precise details, costs, measurements etc are exact: *The precise details of the sale have not yet been released.* **2** [only before noun] used to emphasize that something happens exactly in a particular way or that you are describing something correctly and exactly: *Just at that precise moment her husband walked in.* | *The precise nature of the job will be made clear when you start.* **3** **to be precise** used to show that you are giving more exact details relating to something you have just said: *My parents live abroad – in North Borneo to be precise.* **4** someone who is precise is very careful about small details or about the way they behave —**preciseness** *n* [U] W3

**pre·cise·ly** /prɪˈsaɪsli/ *adv* **1** exactly: **precisely what/how/where etc** *I won't know precisely what the job involves until I actually start.* | *Be there at precisely 4 o'clock.* **2** used to emphasize that a particular thing is completely true or correct: *I didn't go precisely because I thought he might be there.* | *She's precisely the kind of person we're looking for.* **3** *spoken* used to say that you S2 W3 agree completely with someone: *"Roberts should resign." "Precisely."*

**pre·ci·sion¹** /prɪˈsɪʒən/ *n* [U] the quality of being very exact

**precision²** *adj* [only before noun] **1** made or done in a very exact way: *precision grinding* **2 precision tool/instrument** a precision tool or instrument is used for making or measuring something in a very exact way

**pre·clude** /prɪˈkluːd/ *v* [T] *formal* to prevent something or make something impossible: **preclude sb from doing something** *Age alone will not preclude him from standing as a candidate.* —**preclusion** /-ˈkluːʒən/ *n* [U]

**pre·co·cious** /prɪˈkəʊʃəs‖-ˈkoʊ-/ *adj often spoken* a precocious child behaves more like an adult than a child, for example by asking difficult and intelligent questions: *At school he revealed precocious talents a a painter and writer.* —**precociously** *adv* —**precociousness** also **precocity** /prɪˈkɒsɨti‖-ˈkɑː-/ *n* [U]

**pre·cog·ni·tion** /ˌpriːkɒgˈnɪʃən‖-kɑːg-/ *n* [U] *formal* the knowledge that something will happen before it does

**pre·con·ceived** /ˌpriːkənˈsiːvd◂/ *adj* [only before noun] preconceived ideas, opinions etc are formed before you really have enough knowledge or experience: *preconceived notions about art*

**pre·con·cep·tion** /ˌpriːkənˈsepʃən/ *n* [C] a belief or opinion you have already formed before you know the actual facts: *widely held but largely unexamined preconceptions about girls' attitudes towards science*

**pre·con·di·tion** /ˌpriːkənˈdɪʃən/ *n* [C] something that must happen or exist before something else can happen: **[+ of/for]** *A ceasefire is a precondition for talks.*

**pre·cooked** /ˌpriːˈkʊkt◂/ *adj* precooked food has been partly or completely cooked in advance so that it can be quickly heated up later —**precook** *v* [T]

**pre·cur·sor** /prɪˈkɜːsə‖-ˈkɜːrsər/ *n* [C] *formal* something that happened or existed before something else and influenced its development: **[+ of/to]** *a precursor of modern jazz*

**pre·date** /priːˈdeɪt/ *v* [T] to happen or exist earlier in history than something else: *The kingdom predates previously known African cultures by over 3,000 years.*

**pred·a·tor** /ˈpredətə‖-ər/ *n* [C] **1** an animal that kills and eats other animals **2** someone who tries to use another person's weakness to get advantages

**pred·a·to·ry** /ˈpredətəri‖-tɔːri/ *adj* **1** a predatory animal kills and eats other animals for food **2** trying to use someone's weakness to get advantages for yourself: *predatory share-buying by large foreign companies*

**pre·de·ces·sor** /ˈpriːdɨsesə‖ˈpredɨsesər/ *n* [C] **1** someone who had your job before you started doing it: *The President inherited his economic problems from his predecessor.* **2** a machine, system etc that existed before another one in a process of development: *The Julian calendar was more accurate than its predecessor.* —opposite SUCCESSOR

**pre·des·ti·na·tion** /prɪˌdestɨˈneɪʃən, ˌpriːdes-/ *n* [U] the belief that God has decided everything that will happen and that people cannot change this

**pre·des·tined** /prɪˈdestɨnd/ *adj* something that is predestined is certain to happen because it has been decided by God or FATE: **predestined to do sth** *All our plans seemed predestined to fail.*

**pre·de·ter·mined** /ˌpriːdɪˈtɜːmɨnd‖-ɜːr-/ *adj formal* if something is predetermined, it has been formed or arranged before it happens, and does not happen by chance: *The colour of your eyes is predetermined by those of your parents.* | *a predetermined location* —**predetermination** /ˌpriːdɪtɜːmɨˈneɪʃən‖-ɜːr/ *n* [U]

**pre·de·ter·min·er** /ˌpriːdɪˈtɜːmɨnə‖-ˈtɜːrmɨnər/ *n* [C] *technical* a word that is used before a DETERMINER (=a word such as 'the', 'that', 'his' etc). In the phrases 'all the boys' and 'both his parents', the words 'all' and 'both' are predeterminers

**pre·dic·a·ment** /prɪˈdɪkəmənt/ *n* [C] a difficult or unpleasant situation in which you do not know what to do, or you have to make a difficult choice: *There is no painless way out of America's current economic predicament.*

**pred·i·cate¹** /ˈpredɪkɨt/ *n* [C] the part of a sentence that makes a statement about the subject, such as 'swim' in 'Fishes swim' and 'is an artist' in 'She is an artist' —compare SUBJECT¹ (5)

**pred·i·cate²** /ˈpredɨkeɪt/ *v* [T] *formal* **be predicated on** to be based on something as the reason for doing something else: *The company's decision to take on more staff was predicated on the belief that the recession was over.*

**pre·dic·a·tive** /prɪˈdɪkətɪv‖ˈpredɨkeɪ-/ *adj* a predicative adjective or phrase comes after a verb, for example 'happy' in the sentence 'She is happy.' —**predicatively** *adv*

**pre·dict** /prɪˈdɪkt/ *v* [T] to say that something will happen or that something will happen in a particular way: *Economists are predicting a fall in interest rates.* | **predict (that)** *The report predicted that more jobs would be lost in the coal industry.* | **predict whether/what/how etc** *It is difficult to predict what the long-term effects of the accident will be.* S3 W3

**pre·dic·ta·ble** /prɪˈdɪktəbəl/ *adj* **1** if the result of something is predictable, you know what it will be before it happens: *The outcome of these experiments is not always entirely predictable.* **2** behaving or happening in the way that you expect, especially when this seems boring or annoying: *I used to be interested in politics, but now it's all getting very predictable.* | *You're just so predictable!* —**predictably** *adv* [sentence adverb] *Predictably it was the demonstrators who were blamed for the violence.* —**predictability** /prɪˌdɪktəˈbɪlɨti/ *n* [U]

**pre·dic·tion** /prɪˈdɪkʃən/ *n* [C,U] something that you say is going to happen, or the act of saying what you think is going to happen: **[+ of]** *Earlier predictions of a Republican victory began to look increasingly unlikely.* | **make a prediction** *I'd find it very hard to make a prediction.* —**predictive** /-tɪv/ *adj*

**pre·di·gested** /ˌpriːdaɪˈdʒestɨd, ˌpriːdɨ-/ *adj* predigested new information etc has been put in a simple form and explained so that it is easy to understand

**pre·di·lec·tion** /ˌpriːdɪˈlekʃən‖ˌpredlˈek-/ *n* [C] *formal* if you have a predilection for something, especially something rather unusual, you like it very much

**pre·dis·pose** /ˌpriːdɪsˈpəʊz‖-ˈpoʊz/ *v* [T] to make someone more likely to behave or think in a particular way or suffer from a health problem

**pre·dis·posed** /ˌpriːdɪsˈpəʊzd‖-ˈpoʊzd/ *adj* **predisposed to/towards** tending to behave in a particular way, or to have a particular health problem: *Men are more likely to be predisposed towards violence than women.*

**pre·dis·po·si·tion** /ˌpriːdɪspəˈzɪʃən/ *n* [C] a tendency to behave in a particular way or suffer from a particular illness: **[+ to/towards]** *a predisposition towards seasickness*

**pre·dom·i·nance** /prɪˈdɒmɨnəns‖-ˈdɑː-/ *n* **1** [singular] if there is a predominance of one type of person or thing in a group, there are more of that type than of any other type: **[+ of]** *the predominance of white people in the audience* **2** [U] someone or something that has predominance has the most power or importance in a particular group or area: *The company has finally achieved predominance in Asia.*

**pre·dom·i·nant** /prɪˈdɒmɨnənt‖-ˈdɑː-/ *adj* more powerful, more common, or more easily noticed than others: *the predominant group in society*

**pre·dom·i·nant·ly** /prɪˈdɒmɨnəntli‖-ˈdɑː-/ *adv* mostly or mainly: *The city's population is predominantly Irish.*

**pre·dom·i·nate** /prɪˈdɒmɨneɪt‖-ˈdɑː-/ *v* [I] **1** to have the most importance or influence, or to be most easily noticed: *The views of the leftwing have tended to predominate within the party.* **2** if one type of person or thing predominates in a group or area, there are more of this type than any other: *Pine trees predominate on the west coast.*

**pree·mie** /ˈpriːmi/ *n* [C] *AmE informal* a PREMATURE (2) baby

**pre·em·i·nent** /priˈemənənt/ *adj* much more important, more powerful, or much better than any others of its kind: *Hollywood's pre-eminent role in the film industry* —**pre-eminently** *adv* —**pre-eminence** *n* [U]

**pre·empt** /priˈempt/ *v* [T] to make what someone has planned to do or say unnecessary or ineffective by saying or doing something first: *I didn't want to pre-empt what you were about to say.* —**pre-emption** /-ˈempʃən/ *n* [U]

**pre·emp·tive** /priˈemptɪv/ *adj* a pre-emptive action is done to harm someone else before they can harm you, or to prevent something bad from happening: **pre-emptive strike/attack** *a series of pre-emptive strikes on guerilla bases* —**pre-emptively** *adv*

**preen** /priːn/ *v* **1** [I,T] if a bird preens or preens itself, it cleans itself and makes its feathers smooth using its beak **2** [I] to look proud because of something you have done **3 preen yourself a)** to spend a lot of time in front of a mirror making yourself look tidier and more attractive **b)** to be very pleased with yourself

**pre·ex·ist** /ˌpriːɪgˈzɪst/ *v* [I, T] *formal* to exist before something else: *Inform your doctor of any pre-existing medical condition, eg, diabetes.* —**pre-existing** *adj*

**pre·fab** /ˈpriːfæb‖ˌpriːˈfæb/ *n* [C] *informal* a small prefabricated building

**pre·fab·ri·cate** /priːˈfæbrɪkeɪt/ *v* [T] to make the parts of a building, ship etc in a factory in standard sizes, so that they can be fitted together somewhere else —**prefabricated** *adj*: *a prefabricated building* **prefabrication** /priːˌfæbrɪˈkeɪʃən/ *n* [U]

**pref·ace¹** /ˈprefəs/ *n* [C] an introduction at the beginning of a book or speech

**preface²** *v* [T] *formal* to say or do something before the main part of what you are going to say: *I'd like to preface my remarks by saying a little about myself.*

**pref·a·to·ry** /ˈprefətəri‖-tɔːri/ *adj formal* forming a preface or introduction: *a few prefatory remarks*

**pre·fect** /ˈpriːfekt/ *n* [C] **1** an older student in some British schools, who has special duties and helps to control younger students **2** a public official in France, Italy etc who is responsible for a particular area

**pre·fec·ture** /ˈpriːfektʃʊə‖-tʃər/ *n* [C] a large area which has its own local government in France, Italy, Japan etc: *Saitama prefecture*

S2 **pre·fer** /prɪˈfɜː‖-ˈfɜːr/ *v* **preferred, preferring** [T not in
W2 progressive] **1** to like someone or something more than someone or something else: *"What kind of music do you like?" "These days I prefer classical music"* | **prefer sb/sth to sb/sth** *I much prefer dogs to cats.* | **prefer to do sth** *Many people living in cities would actually prefer to live in the country.* | **prefer doing sth** *Chantal prefers travelling by train.* **2 would prefer** if you would prefer to do something, you want to do it more than another thing you could do instead, or that you are doing now: **would prefer to do sth** *We would prefer to live in the US, but I can't get a visa.* **3 I would prefer it if** *spoken* **a)** used to say that you wish a situation was different: *Of course, I'd prefer it if I didn't have to do so much work.* **b)** used when telling someone politely not to do something: *I'd prefer it if you didn't smoke in front of the children.* **4 prefer charges** *law* to make an official statement that someone has done something illegal

**pref·e·ra·ble** /ˈprefərəbəl/ *adj* better or more suitable: **preferable to (doing) sth** *I think France would be preferable to Majorca in August.* | **infinitely preferable** (=much better or much more suitable) *Leah finds novels infinitely preferable to poetry.* —**preferably** *adv* | *Can you tidy your room please – preferably today?*

W3 **pref·e·rence** /ˈprefərəns/ *n* **1** [C,U] if you have a preference for something, you like it more than another thing: **have a preference** *We could eat Chinese, Italian, or Indian – do you have any preference?* | **have a preference for** *I must admit I have a preference for younger men.* | **have no strong/particular preference** (=not prefer one thing more than anything else) | **express a preference** (=say that you like one person or thing more than others) *I asked her where she wanted to go on vacation, but she didn't express any preference.* **2** [C] the thing that you like best in a group of things: *Taste both drinks and make a note of your preference.* **3 give/show preference to** to treat someone more favourably than you treat other people: *In allocating housing, preference is given to those who have young children.* **4 in preference to** if you choose one thing in preference to another, you choose it instead because you think it is better: *Many people choose the train in preference to driving.*

**pref·e·ren·tial** /ˌprefəˈrenʃəl◂/ *adj* [only before noun] preferential treatment, rates etc are deliberately different in order to give an advantage to particular people: *preferential credit terms* —**preferentially** *adv*

**pre·fer·ment** /prɪˈfɜːmənt‖-ɜːr-/ *n* [U] *formal* appointment to a more important job

**pre·fig·ure** /ˌpriːˈfɪgə‖-gjər/ *v* [T] *formal* to be a sign that shows that something will happen later —**prefiguration** /ˌpriːfɪgəˈreɪʃən‖-gjə-/ *n* [C,U]

**pre·fix¹** /ˈpriːfɪks/ *n* [C] **1** a group of letters that is added to the beginning of a word to change its meaning and make a new word, such as 'un' in 'untie' or 'mis' in 'misunderstand' —compare AFFIX, SUFFIX **2** a title such as 'Ms' or 'Dr' used before someone's name

**prefix²** *v* [T] **1** to add a prefix to a word, name or set of numbers **2** *formal* to say something before the main part of what you have to say

**preg·nan·cy** /ˈpregnənsi/ *n* [C,U] the condition of being pregnant or the period of time when a woman is pregnant: *This drug should not be taken during pregnancy.* | *her third pregnancy* | *teenage pregnancies*

**preg·nant** /ˈpregnənt/ *adj* **1** having an unborn baby S3
growing inside your body: *On the same day I started the job I found out I was pregnant.* | **twenty weeks/three months etc pregnant** *She went skiing when she was 7 months pregnant!* | **get pregnant** *It came as a shock – I thought I was too old to get pregnant.* | **get sb pregnant** (=make a woman pregnant by having sex with her) *I didn't mean to get her pregnant.* | **fall pregnant** *old-fashioned* (=become pregnant) | **heavily pregnant** (=having a baby inside your body that is almost ready to be born) **2 a pregnant pause/silence** a pause or silence which is full of meaning or emotion, even though no one says anything: *Dave's outburst was followed by a pregnant pause.* **3 pregnant with** *formal* containing a lot of a quality or feeling: *Every phrase in this poem is pregnant with meaning.*

**pre·heat** /ˌpriːˈhiːt/ *v* [T] to heat an OVEN to a particular temperature before it is used to cook something: *Preheat the oven to 375°.*

**pre·hen·sile** /prɪˈhensaɪl‖-səl/ *adj technical* a prehensile tail, foot etc can curl round things and hold on to them

**pre·his·tor·ic** /ˌpriːhɪˈstɒrɪk◂‖-ˈstɔː-, -ˈstɑː-/ *adj* **1** connected with the time in history before anything was written down: *prehistoric burial grounds* | *prehistoric animals* **2** *often humorous* very old-fashioned: *Keith's ideas about educating girls are positively prehistoric.* —**prehistorically** /-kli/ *adv*

**pre·his·to·ry** /priːˈhɪstəri/ *n* [U] the time in human history before anything was written down

**pre·judge** /ˌpriːˈdʒʌdʒ/ *v* [T] to form an opinion about someone or something before you know or have considered all the facts: *Try not to prejudge the issue.* —**prejudgment** *n* [C,U]

**prej·u·dice¹** /ˈpredʒədəs/ *n* **1** [C,U] an unreasonable dislike and distrust of people who are different from you in some way, especially because of their race, sex, religion etc: *Women still have to face a great deal of prejudice in the workplace.* | [+ **against**] *Prejudice against black people is common in many parts of America.* |

**racial/sexual prejudice** (=prejudice against people who belong to a different race or sex) *victims of racial prejudice* **2** [U] **to the prejudice of** *formal* having a harmful effect or influence on something else: *Harry continued to smoke, to the prejudice of his health.* **3 without prejudice** *law* without harming or affecting something else

**prejudice²** *v* [T] **1** to influence someone so that they have an unfair or unreasonable opinion about someone or something: **prejudice sb against sth** *My own schooldays prejudiced me against all formal education.* | **prejudice sth/sb in sb's favour** *Johnson's pleasant manner prejudiced the jury in his favour.* **2** to have a bad effect on your opportunities, chances etc of succeeding in doing something: *I don't want to do anything that would prejudice my chances of getting the job.*

**prej·u·diced** /ˈpredʒədəst/ *adj* **1** having an unreasonable dislike of a particular group of people who are different from you in some way, especially because they belong to a different race, sex, or religion: [+ **against**] *He denied being prejudiced against black people.* **2** having an unreasonable dislike of something: [+ **against**] *I don't know why they're all so prejudiced against the idea.*

**prej·u·di·cial** /ˌpredʒəˈdɪʃəl◂/ *adj formal* having a bad effect on something

**prel·ate** /ˈprelət/ *n* [C] *technical* a BISHOP, CARDINAL, or other important priest in the Christian church

**pre·lim·i·na·ry¹** /prɪˈlɪmənəri‖-neri/ *adj* [only before noun] happening before something that is more important, often in order to prepare for it: *the preliminary rounds of the competition.* | *a preliminary draft* | [+ **to**] *Speeches are preliminary to the real debate.*

**preliminary²** *n* [C usually plural] **1** something that is done first, to introduce or prepare for something else: *After the usual preliminaries, we made a start on the food.* **2 the preliminaries** the first part of a competition, when it is decided who will go on to the main competition

**pre·lit·e·rate** /priːˈlɪtərət/ *adj technical* a society that is preliterate has not developed a written language —compare ILLITERATE

**prel·ude** /ˈpreljuːd/ *n* [C] **1 be a prelude to** if an event is a prelude to a more important event, it happens just before it and makes people expect it: *The fighting in the streets may be a prelude to more serious trouble.* **2** *technical* a short piece of music for piano or ORGAN **3** a short piece of music at the beginning of a large musical piece: *Chopin's preludes*

**pre·mar·i·tal** /priːˈmærətəl/ *adj* happening or existing before marriage: *premarital sex* —**premaritally** *adv*

**pre·ma·ture** /ˈpremətʃə, -tʃʊə, ˌpreməˈtʃʊə‖ˌpriːməˈtʃʊər◂/ *adj* **1** happening before the natural or proper time: *His premature death at the age of 32 is a great loss.* | *premature ageing of the skin* **2** a premature baby is born before the usual time of birth: *a premature birth* | *The baby was six weeks premature.* **3** done too early or too soon: *I think your criticism of the new law is a bit premature, as we don't yet know all the details.* —**prematurely** *adv*: *The baby was born prematurely.*

**pre·med·i·tat·ed** /priːˈmedəteɪtəd‖prɪ-/ *adj* a premeditated crime or attack is planned in advance and done deliberately: *The defense claim that the killing was not premeditated.*

**pre·med·i·ta·tion** /priːˌmedəˈteɪʃən‖prɪ-/ *n* [U] the act of thinking about something and planning it before you actually do it: *cold-blooded premeditation*

**pre·men·stru·al** /priːˈmenstruəl/ *adj technical* happening just before a woman's PERIOD (=the time each month when blood flows from her body)

**premenstrual syndrome** /·,··· ˈ··/ **premenstrual tension** *BrE n* [U] the tiredness, headache, bad temper etc experienced by many women in the days before their PERIOD¹ (4)

**prem·i·er¹** /ˈpremiə‖prɪˈmɪr/ *n* [C] a PRIME MINISTER: *the Irish Premier*

**premier²** *adj formal* [only before noun] best or most important: *the Shelbourne, one of Dublin's premier hotels*

**prem·i·ere**, **première** /ˈpremieə‖prɪˈmɪr/ *n* [C] the first public performance of a film or play: **world premiere** (=the first performance in the world) *Spielberg's new movie gets its world premiere tonight.* —**premiere** *v* [I,T] | *Her film was premiered in New York.*

**prem·i·ere·ship** /ˈpremiəʃɪp‖prɪˈmɪrʃɪp/ *n* [C,U] the period when someone is PRIME MINISTER

**prem·ise** /ˈpreməs/ *n* [C] **1 premises** the buildings and land that a shop, restaurant, company etc uses: *We hope to be moving to new premises shortly.* | *business premises* | **off the premises** *The manager escorted him off the premises.* | **on the premises** *No food or drink is to be consumed on the premises.* **2** also **premiss** *BrE* a statement or idea that you accept as true and use as a base for developing other ideas: *American justice works on the premise that an accused person is innocent until they are proved guilty.* W3

**pre·mi·um** /ˈpriːmiəm/ *n* **1** [C] the cost of insurance, especially the amount to pay each year: *Insurance premiums are set to rise again.* | *the annual premium* **2** [U] *especially AmE* HIGH-OCTANE (=good quality petrol) **3 premium quality** very high quality: *premium quality British potatoes* **4** [C] an additional amount of money, above a standard rate or amount: *Farmers are being offered a premium for organically grown vegetables.* | *premium payments for weekend work* **5 at a premium a)** if something is at a premium, there is little of it available or it is difficult to get: *Foldaway furniture is the answer where space is at a premium.* **b)** if something is sold at a premium, it is sold at a higher price than usual **6 put/place a premium on** to consider one quality as being much more important than others: *The new management puts a premium on efficiency.* **7 premium prices** prices that are higher than usual, especially because there is not much of something available

**premium bond** /ˈ··· ,·/ *n* [C] a document that you buy from the government in Britain, giving you the chance to win a large prize each month

**pre·mo·ni·tion** /ˌpreməˈnɪʃən, ˌpriː-/ *n* [C] a strange and unexplainable feeling that something, especially something unpleasant, is going to happen: **have a premonition** *When Anne didn't arrive, Paul had a premonition that she was in danger.* | [+ **of**] *a premonition of death*

**pre·mon·i·to·ry** /prɪˈmɒnətəri‖-ˈmɑːnətɔːri/ *adj formal* giving a warning that something unpleasant is going to happen: *a disease with few premonitory symptoms*

**pre·na·tal** /ˌpriːˈneɪtl◂/ *adj* [only before noun] concerning unborn babies and the care of PREGNANT women; ANTENATAL *BrE*: *prenatal care* —compare POSTNATAL —**prenatally** *adv*

**pre·oc·cu·pa·tion** /priːˌɒkjəˈpeɪʃən‖-ˌɑːk-/ *n* **1** [singular, U] a strong interest in something, usually because you are worried about it, with the result that you do not pay attention to other things: [+ **with**] *the Bundesbank's preoccupation with keeping down inflation* **2** [C] something that you give all your attention to: *Brad's main preoccupations were eating and sleeping.*

**pre·oc·cu·pied** /priːˈɒkjəpaɪd‖-ˈɑːk-/ *adj* thinking about something a lot, with the result that you do not pay attention to other things: *I tried to speak to Bella, but she seemed a little preoccupied.* | [+ **with**] *Rod's completely preoccupied with all the wedding preparations at the moment.*

**pre·oc·cu·py** /priːˈɒkjəpaɪ‖-ˈɑːk-/ *v* [T] *formal* if something preoccupies someone, they think or worry about it a lot: *Something's been preoccupying you – what is it?*

**pre·or·dain** /ˌpriːɔːˈdeɪn‖-ɔːr-/ *adj* [not before noun] *formal* if something is preordained, it is certain to happen in the future because God or FATE has decided it

**prep¹** /prep/ *n* [U] *BrE informal* school HOMEWORK

**prep² prepped, prepping** *v* [T] *AmE informal* **1** to prepare someone for an operation or an examination **2** to prepare food for cooking in a restaurant

**prep³** *n* [C] the written abbreviation of PREPOSITION

**pre·packed** /ˌpriːˈpækt◂/ also **pre·pack·aged** /-ˈpækɪdʒd◂/ *adj* prepacked or prepackaged food or other goods are already wrapped or are sold ready to use: *prepacked fresh fruit and vegetables*

**pre·paid** /ˌpriːˈpeɪd◂/ *adj* a prepaid envelope does not need a stamp because the cost of posting it has already been paid by the person who will receive it

S2 W3 **prep·a·ra·tion** /ˌprepəˈreɪʃən/ *n* **1** [U] the act or process of preparing something: [+ **for**] *Business training is a good preparation for any career.* | [+ **of**] *Richard's currently involved in the preparation of the budget.* | **in preparation for** (=in order to prepare for something) *Justin had opened several bottles of wine in preparation for the party.* | **be in preparation** (=being prepared) *Plans for the new school are now in preparation.* **2 preparations** [plural] arrangements for something that is going to happen: [+ **for**] *preparations for the Queen's visit* | **make preparations** *The army is making preparations for a full-scale invasion.* **3** [C] a medicine, COSMETIC etc: *a new preparation for cleansing the skin*

**pre·par·a·to·ry** /prɪˈpærətəri‖-tɔːri/ *adj* **1** [only before noun] done in order to get ready for something: *preparatory talks to clear the way for a peace settlement* **2 preparatory to** *formal* before something else and in order to prepare for it: *The partners held several meetings preparatory to signing the agreement.*

**preparatory school** /·ˈ···· ·/ *n* [C] **1** a private school in Britain for children between the ages of 8 and 13 **2** a private school in the US that prepares students for college

S1 W1 **prepare** /prɪˈpeə‖-ˈper/ *v*
**1 ▶ MAKE STH READY ◀** [T] to make something such as a machine, a place, or a piece of writing ready to be used: *Mansell's team were up all night preparing the car for the race.* | *I'd better go upstairs and prepare her room.* | *Have you prepared your speech yet?*
**2 ▶ MAKE PLANS/ARRANGEMENTS ◀** [I,T] to make plans or arrangements for something that will happen in the future: *Olympus is preparing to launch a new range of cameras.* | [+ **for**] *We only heard about the meeting yesterday, so we haven't started preparing for it yet.* | **prepare sth** *They've prepared a special surprise party for him.* | *The airlines have prepared contingency plans in case the strike goes ahead.* | **prepare to do sth** *Her parents were busy preparing to go on holiday.*
**3 ▶ MAKE YOURSELF READY ◀** [T] to make yourself mentally or physically ready for something that you expect to happen soon: **prepare yourself (for)** *Prepare yourself for a shock.* | *They prepared themselves for a long wait.* | *Can you just give me a couple more moments to prepare myself?* | **prepare for action** *The captain told the men to prepare for action.*
**4 ▶ TRAINING/EXPERIENCE ◀** [T] to provide someone with the training, skills, experience etc that they will need to do something or to deal with an unpleasant situation: **prepare sb for sth** *a course that prepares students for English examinations* | *Schools should do more to prepare children for the world of work.* | **prepare sb to do sth** *Nothing in his life had prepared him for this ordeal.*
**5 ▶ FOOD ◀** [T] to make food or a meal ready to eat: *Prepare the sauce while the pasta is cooking.* | **prepare sth for sb** *John's preparing supper for us.* | **prepare sb sth** | *Helen had prepared us a wonderful meal.*
**6 prepare the way for/prepare the ground for** to provide the conditions that make it possible for something to be achieved, or for someone to succeed in doing something: *Curie's research prepared the way for the work of modern nuclear scientists.*
**7 ▶ MEDICINE/CHEMICAL ◀** [T] to make a medicine or chemical ready to be used, usually by mixing several substances: *Preparing herbal medicines requires a lot of skill and knowledge about different kinds of herbs.*

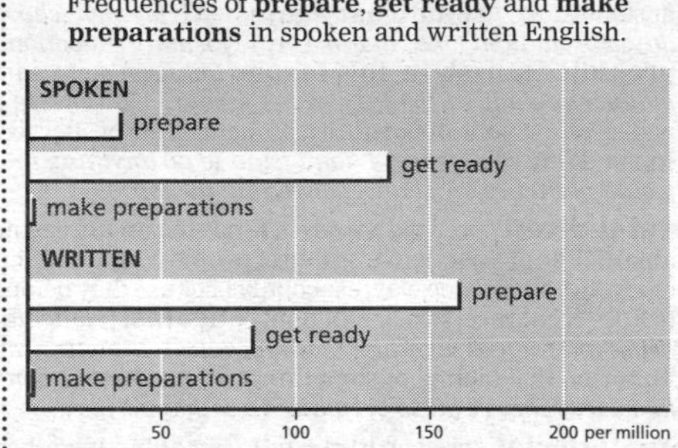


Frequencies of **prepare**, **get ready** and **make preparations** in spoken and written English.

Based on the British National Corpus and the Longman Lancaster Corpus

This graph shows that **get ready** is more common in spoken English than **prepare** or **make preparations**. However, in written English, **prepare** is the most common of the three. **Make preparations** is the least common in both spoken and written English. It is less general, and suggests making a lot of arrangements for something that is going to happen.

**pre·pared** /prɪˈpeəd‖-ˈperd/ *adj* S2
**1 be prepared to do sth** to be willing to do something, especially something difficult or something that you do not usually do: *You have to be prepared to take risks in this kind of work.* | *How much is she prepared to pay?*
**2 I'm not prepared to do sth** *spoken* used when saying strongly that you refuse to do something: *I'm not prepared to sit here and listen to this rubbish!*
**3 ▶ READY TO DEAL WITH STH ◀** [not before noun] ready to do something or deal with a situation because you were expecting it to happen or because you have made careful and thorough preparations: [+ **for**] *I wasn't prepared for all their questions.* | **well/badly prepared** *Luckily we were well prepared for the storm.* | **ill-prepared** (=not prepared to deal with a difficult situation) *The country was ill-prepared to fight another war.* | **be prepared for the worst** (=expect that something very bad may happen and be ready for it) *There was no news and we were prepared for the worst.*
**4 ▶ READY TO BE USED ◀** [not before noun] arranged and ready to be used: *The boss is due any minute – is everything prepared?* | **get sth prepared** *By the time we'd got all our stuff prepared it was time to go on stage*
**5 ▶ MADE EARLIER ◀** planned, made, or written at an earlier time: *The president read out a prepared statement.* | **hastily prepared** (=prepared very quickly because you were not expecting something) *Hastily prepared arrangements were made to welcome the new visitor.*

**pre·pared·ness** /prɪˈpeədnɪ̈s, -ˈpeərɪ̈d-‖-ˈperəd-, -ˈperd-/ *n* [U] the state of being ready for something: *the country's lack of military preparedness*

**pre·pon·de·rance** /prɪˈpɒndərəns‖-ˈpɑːn-/ *n formal* **a preponderance of** if there is a preponderance of people or things of a particular type in a group, there are more of that type than of any others: *There is a preponderance of female students in the music department.*

**pre·pon·de·rant** /prɪˈpɒndərənt‖-ˈpɑːn-/ *adj formal* main or most important —**preponderantly** *adv*

**pre·pon·de·rate** /prɪˈpɒndəreɪt‖-ˈpɑːn-/ *v* [I] *formal* to be more important or frequent than something else

**prep·o·si·tion** /ˌprepəˈzɪʃən/ *n* [C] a word that is used before a noun, PRONOUN, or GERUND to show that word's connection with another word, such as 'of' in 'a house made of wood', and 'by' in 'We open it by breaking the lock' —**prepositional** *adj* **prepositionally** *adv*

**prepositional phrase** /ˌ····ˈ·/ *n* [C] *technical* a phrase consisting of a preposition and the noun following it, such as 'in bed' or 'on the table'

**pre·pos·sess·ing** /ˌpriːpəˈzesɪŋ◂/ *adj formal* looking attractive or pleasant: *a prepossessing smile*

**pre·pos·ter·ous** /prɪˈpɒstərəs‖-ˈpɑːs-/ *adj formal* **1** completely unreasonable; ABSURD: *The whole idea sounds absolutely preposterous!* **2** extremely unusual and silly: *Look at that preposterous car!* —**preposterously** *adv* —**preposterousness** *n* [U]

**prep·py** /ˈprepi/ *adj AmE informal* typical of students who go to expensive private schools in the US, especially by dressing very neatly: *preppy clothes*

**prep school** /ˈ· ·/ *n* [C] *informal* a PREPARATORY SCHOOL

**pre·pu·bes·cent** /ˌpriːpjuːˈbesənt◂/ *adj formal* concerned with the time just before a child reaches PUBERTY

**pre·quel** /ˈpriːkwəl/ *n* [C] a book, television programme, etc that tells you what happened before the story that is told in a popular book or film

**Pre-Raph·ae·lite** /priːˈræfəlaɪt/ *n* [C] a member of a group of late 19th century English painters and artists —**Pre-Raphaelite** *adj*

**pre·re·cord** /ˌpriːrɪˈkɔːd‖-ˈkɔːrd/ *v* [T] to record music, a radio programme etc on a machine so that it can be used later —**prerecorded** *adj*: *prerecorded videos* —**prerecording** *n* [C,U]

**pre·req·ui·site** /priːˈrekwɪ̈zɪ̈t/ *n* [C] *formal* something someone must have before they can be allowed to do something, or which must exist before something else can happen: [+ **for/to/of**] *A reasonable proficiency in English is a prerequisite for the course.*

**pre·rog·a·tive** /prɪˈrɒgətɪv‖-ˈrɑː-/ *n* [C, usually singular] a right that someone has because of their importance or position: *the royal prerogative*

**pres** **1** the written abbreviation of present **2** the written abbreviation of president

**pres·age** /ˈpresɪdʒ, prɪ̈ˈseɪdʒ/ *v* [T] *literary* to be a warning or a sign that something is going to happen especially something bad: *A chill breeze blows, presaging winter.* —**presage** *n* [C]

**Pres·by·te·ri·an** /ˌprezbɪ̈ˈtɪəriən◂‖-ˈtɪr-/ *n* [C] a member of the Presbyterian church, one of the largest churches in the US and the national church of Scotland —**Presbyterian** *adj* —**Presbyterianism** *n* [U]

**pres·by·ter·y** /ˈprezbɪ̈təri‖-teri/ *n* [C] **1** a local court or council of the Presbyterian church or the area controlled by that church **2** a house in which a Roman Catholic priest lives **3** the eastern part of a church, behind the area where the CHOIR (=trained singers) sit

**preschool** /ˈpriː skuːl/ *n* [C] *AmE* a school for young children between two and five years of age, where they learn such things as numbers, colours, and letters; **nursery school** (NURSERY (2)) *BrE*

**pre-school** /ˌpriː ˈskuːl◂/ *adj* connected with the time in a child's life before they are old enough to go to school: *a pre-school playgroup*

**pre-school·er** /ˌpriː ˈskuːlə‖-ər/ *n* [C] *AmE* a child who does not yet go to school

**pre·sci·ent** /ˈpreʃiənt/ *adj formal* able to imagine or know what will happen in the future —**prescience** *n* [U]

**pre·scribe** /prɪˈskraɪb/ *v* [T] **1** to say what medicine or treatment a sick person should have: **prescribe sb sth** *If these don't work I may have to prescribe you something stronger.* | **prescribe sth for sth** *one of the most commonly prescribed drugs for treating depression* **2** to state officially what someone can and cannot do, or what should be done in a particular situation: *What punishment does the law prescribe for this crime?* | **prescribe who/how/what etc** *You have no right to prescribe how others should behave.*

**pre·scribed** /prɪˈskraɪbd/ *adj* decided by a rule: *a prescribed number of hours*

**pre·script** /ˈpriːˌskrɪpt/ *n* [C] *formal* an official order or rule

**pre·scrip·tion** /prɪˈskrɪpʃən/ *n* **1** [C] a piece of paper on which a doctor writes what medicine a sick person should have, so that they can get it from a PHARMACIST **2** [C] a particular medicine or treatment ordered by a doctor for a sick person: *Prescriptions used to be free when the National Health Service started.* | **prescription charges** (=the fixed amount of money you have to pay in Britain for drugs which your doctor has ordered) **3 on prescription** a drug that you get on prescription can only be obtained with a written order from the doctor —compare **over the counter** (COUNTER[1] (2)) **4** [C usually singular] an idea or suggestion about how to make a situation, activity etc successful: [+ **for**] *Her prescription for the advancement of women was education.* **5** [U] the act of prescribing a medicine or drug

**pre·scrip·tive** /prɪˈskrɪptɪv/ *adj* **1** stating or ordering how something should be done or what someone should do: *prescriptive teaching methods* **2** *technical* stating how a language should be used, rather than describing how it is used: *prescriptive grammar* —**prescriptively** *adv*

**prescriptive right** /·,·· ˈ·/ *n* [C] *law* a right that has existed for so long that it is as effective as a law

**pres·ence** /ˈprezəns/ *n* **1** [U] the state of being present in a particular place: *Your presence is requested at the club meeting on Friday.* | [+ **of**] *The police scientists detected the presence of poison in the dead woman's blood.* —opposite ABSENCE (1) **2 in sb's presence** with someone or in the same place as them: *John never seemed at ease in my presence.* | *The police will only interview a child in the presence of an adult.* **3** [U] the ability to impress people and make them believe you: *a man of great presence* **4** [singular] a group of people from another country, an army, or the police, who are in a place to watch and influence what is happening: *the American presence in the war zone* | *a strong police presence at the march* **5** [C usually singular] a spirit or influence that cannot be seen but is felt to be near: *They felt a strange presence in the deserted house.* **6 make your presence felt** to have a strong and obvious effect on the people around you or the situation you are in: *Since Webb joined the team he has really made his presence felt.* S3 W2

**presence of mind** /ˌ··· ˈ·/ *n* [U] the ability to deal with a dangerous situation calmly and quickly: **have the presence of mind to do sth** *Luckily Isabel had the presence of mind to take down the car's registration number.*

**pres·ent[1]** /ˈprezənt/ *adj* **1 be present a)** to be in a particular place: *How many people were present at the meeting yesterday?* | *small amounts of gas present in the atmosphere* **b)** to be felt strongly or remembered for a long time: *The memory of her brother's death a year ago is still present in her mind.* **2** [only before noun] happening or existing now: *What is your present address?* | *Usually I'd advise you to wait, but in the present situation I think it's best to act without delay.* **3** [only before noun] *technical* related to a verb that shows an existing state or action: *'He wants' and 'They are coming' are examples of verbs in the present tense.* **4 all present and correct** *BrE* also **all present and accounted for** *AmE* used to say that everyone who is supposed to be in a place, at a meeting etc is now here **5 present company excepted** used when you are saying something rude about someone to tell the people you are with that you do not mean to include them in the statement: *Women are never satisfied with anything! Present company excepted, of course.* —see also PRESENTLY

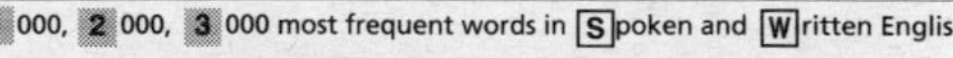

Frequencies of **present** (*adj*), **now** and **at the moment** in spoken and written English.

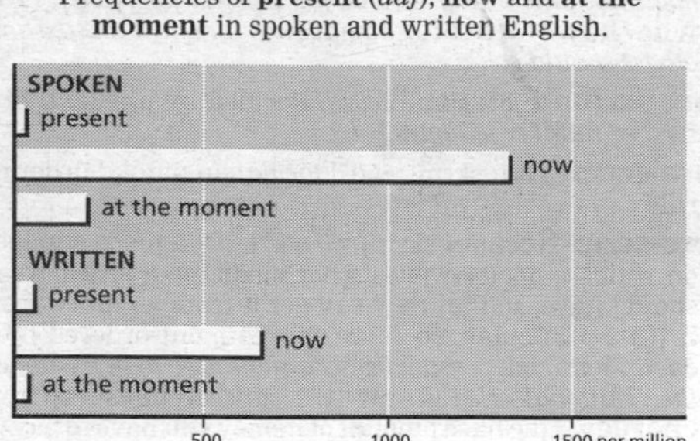


Based on the British National Corpus and the Longman Lancaster Corpus

This graph shows that **now** is much more common than **present** and **at the moment** in both spoken and written English. **At the moment** is more common in spoken English than in written English. **Present** is the least common of the three. It is formal, and is only used before a noun, for example in expressions such as 'the present situation', 'the present leader' etc.

S2 W1 **pres·ent²** /prɪˈzent/ *v* [T]
**1 ▶ GIVE ◀** to give something to someone, especially at a formal or official occasion: **present sb with sth** *David's manager presented him with the award for best sales in the region.*
**2 ▶ CAUSE STH TO HAPPEN ◀** to cause something to happen or exist: *Slippery floors in the work area present a hazard to employees.* | **present sb with sth** *His resignation presents us with a tricky situation.* | **present a problem/difficulty** *This equation should present no problems if you know some basic trigonometry.*
**3 ▶ SHOW ◀** to offer or show information about something in a particular way: *The movie presents its characters in a way that I find difficult to believe in.* | *Tobacco companies are trying to present a more favorable image.*
**4 ▶ A SPEECH ◀** to give a speech in which you offer an idea, plan etc to be considered or accepted: **present sth to sb** *The team is presenting its report to the board on Tuesday.*
**5 ▶ DOCUMENT/TICKET ◀** to show something such as an official document or ticket to someone in an official position: *You must present your passport to the customs officer.*
**6 ▶ THEATRE/CINEMA ◀** to give a performance in a theatre, cinema, etc, or broadcast a programme on television or radio: *This evening PBS presents the first of a six-part historical drama about the Civil War.*
**7 ▶ TELEVISION/RADIO ◀** *BrE* if you present a television or radio programme, you introduce its different parts: *Tonight's edition of Newsnight, presented by Jeremy Paxman.*
**8 sth presents itself** if a situation, opportunity etc presents itself, it suddenly happens or exists: *As soon as the opportunity presents itself, I'm going to talk to Mr. Boyer about that job.*
**9 ▶ FORMALLY INTRODUCE SB ◀** to introduce someone formally, especially to someone of a very high rank: *I was presented to the Queen in 1964.*
**10 present arms** a command to soldiers to hold their weapons upright in front of their bodies as a greeting to a person of high rank
**11 present your apologies/compliments etc** *formal* used to greet someone, apologize to them etc very politely: *Mrs. Gottlieb presents her apologies and regrets she will not be able to attend.*

**pres·ent³** /ˈprezənt/ *n* [C] something you give someone on a special occasion or to thank them for something; gift: *One of my Japanese students gave me a beautiful fan as a present.* | **birthday/Christmas present** *Christmas presents under the tree*

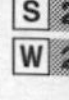

**present⁴** *n* [singular] **1** the time that we are experiencing now: *You have to stop worrying about the past and start thinking about the present!* | **no time like the present** (=used to say that if you are going to do something at all, you should do it now) *"I was thinking of asking Maura to marry me." "Do it! There's no time like the present!"* **2** *technical* the form of a verb that shows what exists or is happening now —see also HISTORIC PRESENT **3 at present** at this time; now: *Ms. Hellman is busy at present, can she ring you later?* —see PRESENTLY (USAGE)

**pre·sen·ta·ble** /prɪˈzentəbəl/ *adj* tidy and attractive enough to be introduced or shown to someone: *a presentable piece of work* | **make yourself presentable** *I must go and make myself presentable before the guests arrive.* —**presentably** *adv*

S2 W3 **pre·sen·ta·tion** /ˌprezənˈteɪʃən‖ˌpriːzen-, -zən-/ *n*
**1 ▶ PROOF ◀** [C,U] the act of showing someone something so that it can be checked or considered: [+ **of**] *On presentation of the relevant identity documents you may collect your property.*
**2 ▶ APPEARANCE ◀** [U] the way in which something is said, offered, shown, explained etc to others: *This word processor is excellent for presentation and layout of complex documents.* | *The presentation of food can be as important as the taste.*
**3 ▶ PRESENT PRIZE ◀** [C] the act of giving someone a prize or present at a formal ceremony: [+ **of**] *The presentation of prizes will begin at three o'clock.*
**4 ▶ TALK ◀** [C] an event at which a new product or idea is described and explained: **give a presentation** *I've been asked to give a short presentation on the aims of the project.*
**5 ▶ PERFORMANCE ◀** [C] the act of performing something in front of an audience: [+ **of**] *There are two presentations of the cabaret every night.*
**6 ▶ BABY ◀** [C,U] *technical* the position in which a baby is lying in its mother's body just before it is born: *a breech presentation* —**presentational** *adj*

**presentation cop·y** /ˌ··ˈ·· ˌ··/ *n* [C] a book that is given to someone, especially by the writer or PUBLISHER

**pres·ent-day** /ˌprezənt ˈdeɪ◀/ *adj* modern or existing now: *present-day Sicily*

**pre·sent·er** /prɪˈzentə‖-ər/ *n* [C] *BrE* someone who introduces the different parts of a television or radio show; ANNOUNCER *AmE*: *radio presenter, Libby Purves*

**pre·sen·ti·ment** /prɪˈzentɪ̬mənt/ *n* [C] *formal* a strange and uncomfortable feeling that something is going to happen; PREMONITION [+ **of**] *a presentiment of danger*

**pres·ent·ly** /ˈprezəntli/ *adv formal* **1** in a short time; soon: *The doctor will be here presently.* | *Presently a bell rang and they all trooped into school.* **2** *especially AmE and ScotE* now; at this time: *Scientists are presently working on identifying the cause of the disease.*

**USAGE NOTE: PRESENTLY**

UK-US DIFFERENCE

In both British and American English **presently** can mean the same as **soon**, but is a little old-fashioned: *If you take a seat, the doctor will see you presently.*

In American English, and formal British English, it can also be used to mean 'at the present time' or to talk about something that is happening now: *He is presently living in Seoul.* | *District councils are presently making good progress on the development plans.*

**present par·ti·ci·ple** /ˌ·· ˈ····/ *n technical* a PARTICIPLE that is formed in English by adding 'ing' to the verb, as in 'sleeping'. It can be used in COMPOUND¹ (4) forms of the verb to show PROGRESSIVE tenses, as in 'she's sleeping', or as an adjective, as in 'the sleeping child'

**present per·fect** /ˌ·· ˈ··/ *n technical* the form of a verb that shows a period of time up to and including the present, formed in English with the present tense of the verb 'have', as in 'he has gone' and a PAST PARTICIPLE

**pres·er·va·tion** /ˌprezəˈveɪʃən‖-zər-/ *n* [U] **1** the act of keeping something unharmed or unchanged: [+ **of**] *The police are responsible for the preservation of law and order.* **2** the degree to which something has remained unchanged or unharmed by weather, age etc: *The old building is in a good state of preservation.* —see also SELF-PRESERVATION

**pres·er·va·tion·ist** /ˌprezəˈveɪʃənɪ̵st‖-zər-/ *n* [C] *especially AmE* someone who works to prevent historical places, buildings etc from being destroyed

**preservation or·der** /··ˈ·· ˌ··/ *n* [C] *especially BrE* an official order that something, especially a tree or building, must be preserved and not damaged

**pre·ser·va·tive** /prɪˈzɜːvətɪv‖-ɜːr-/ *n* [C,U] a chemical substance that is used to stop food or wood from decaying

W3 **pre·serve¹** /prɪˈzɜːv‖-ɜːrv/ *v* [T] **1** to save something or someone from being harmed or destroyed: *I think these traditional customs should be preserved.* | *The wreck was preserved by the muddy sea bed.* | **preserve sb/sth from sth** *They were determined to preserve their leader from humiliation.* **2** to store food for a long time after treating it so that it will not decay: *figs preserved in brandy* **3** to make something continue without changing: *The Baroness had managed to preserve her good looks.* —see also WELL-PRESERVED —**preservable** *adj*

**preserve²** *n* **1** [C, U] a substance made from boiling fruit or vegetables with sugar, salt, or VINEGAR **2** [singular] an activity that is only suitable or allowed for a particular group of people: *Banking used to be a male preserve.* | [+ **of**] *Gardening is sometimes considered the preserve of the elderly.* **3** [C] an area of land or water that is kept for private hunting or fishing

**pre-set** /priːˈset/ *present participle* **pre-setting** *past tense and past participle* **pre-set** *v* [T] to set a piece of electrical equipment, so that it will start to work

**pre-shrunk** /ˌpriːˈʃrʌŋk◂/ *adj* clothes that are pre-shrunk are made to SHRINK (=became smaller when washed) before they are sold: *pre-shrunk Levis*

**pre·side** /prɪˈzaɪd/ *v* [I] to be in charge of a formal ceremony, meeting etc: *They could find no clergyman who would agree to preside at the funeral.*

**preside over** *phr v* [T] **1** to be in charge of a situation over which you do not have much control: *The president found himself presiding over the worst economic depression in the history of the US.* **2** to be the head of a company or organization **3** to be in charge of a meeting or a formal meal

**pres·i·den·cy** /ˈprezɪ̵dənsi/ *n* [C] **1** the job of president: *Roosevelt was elected four times to the presidency of the US.* **2** the period of time for which a person is president: *During his presidency he undertook a great initiative towards world peace.*

S2 W1 **pres·i·dent** /ˈprezɪ̵dənt/ *n* [C] **1** the official leader of a country that does not have a king or queen: *the President of France* | *President Kennedy* **2** the person in charge of a club, college, government department etc **3** *AmE* the head of a business, bank etc: *the president of General Motors*

**president-e·lect** /ˌ··· ·ˈ·/ *n* [singular] someone who has been elected as a new president, but who has not yet started the job

**pres·i·den·tial** /ˌprezɪ̵ˈdenʃəl◂/ *adj* connected with a president: *a presidential election* | *the party's presidential candidate*

**pre·sid·i·um, praesidium** /prɪˈsɪdiəm, -ˈzɪ-/ *n plural* **presidia** [C] a committee chosen to represent a large political organization, especially in a COMMUNIST country

S2 W2 **press¹** /pres/ *n*

**1** ▶**NEWS**◀ **a)** [U] also **the press** people who write reports for newspapers, radio, or television: *the freedom of the press* [also + plural verb *BrE*]: *In August the press are desperate for news.* | *press photographers* **b)** [singular, U] reports in newspapers and on radio and television: *To judge from the press, the concert was a great success.* | *press clippings* | **press coverage** (=the reports written about something in newspapers)

**2 get/be given a bad press** to be criticized in the newspapers or on radio or television: *The police have been getting a bad press in the last few months.*

**3 get/be given a good press** to be praised in the newspapers or on radio or television: *Our recycling policy is getting a good press.*

**4** ▶**PRINTING**◀ [C] **a)** a business that prints and sometimes also sells books: *the Clarendon Press* **b)** also **printing press** a machine that prints books, newspapers, or magazines

**5 trouser/flower/wine press** a piece of equipment used to put weight on something to make it flat or to force liquid out of it: *You can still buy old cheese presses in some areas.*

**6** ▶**PUSH**◀ a light steady push against something small: *Give the button another press.*

**7 go to press** if a newspaper, magazine, or book goes to press, it is printed

**8** ▶**CROWD**◀ a crowd of people pushing against each other

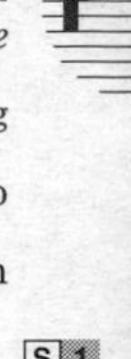

S1 W2 **press²** *v*

**1** ▶**AGAINST STH**◀ [T always + adv/prep] to push something firmly against a surface: *The little boys pressed their noses against the glass.* | *Viv tried to press himself back against the wall.* | *The old man pressed a coin into her hand.*

**2** ▶**BUTTON**◀ [T] to push something with your finger to make a machine start, a bell ring etc: *What happens if I press the reset button?*

**3** ▶**CLOTHES**◀ [T] to make clothes smooth using heat; IRON: *I'll need to press my suit.*

press

**4** ▶**CROWD**◀ [I always + adv/prep] to move in a particular direction by pushing: *The crowds pressed around her, hoping for her autograph.*

**5** ▶**PERSUADE**◀ [T] to try hard to persuade someoneto do something: *Please don't press me on this point, I have no more to say.* | **press sb to do sth** *Katie pressed me to stay a little longer.* | **press sb for sth** *The bank is pressing us for a quick decision.*

**6** ▶**FOR JUICE**◀ [T] to put a heavy weight on something to get liquid from it: *The grapes must be pressed to extract the juice.*

**7** ▶**MAKE STH FLAT**◀ [T] to put pressure or a weight on something to make it flat: *pressing flowers*

**8** ▶**HOLD SB/STH CLOSE**◀ [T] to hold someone or something close to you because you feel upset, are protecting them etc: **press sb/sth to you** *Prue pressed the photograph to her chest and wept.*

**9 press sb's hand/arm** to hold someone's hand or arm tightly for a short time, to show friendship, sympathy etc: *Frank pressed my hand warmly when we met.*

**10 press charges** to say officially that someone has done something illegal and must go to court: *Police are often reluctant to press charges in such cases.*

**11** ▶**CLAIM/STATEMENT**◀ [T] to continue to try to make someone accept a claim or statement that you are making: *We shall not press our claim for compensation.* | *I don't want to press the point, but we are late.*

**12 press sb/sth into service** to use someone or something not completely suitable, because of an unexpected problem: *My scarf was pressed into service as a bandage.*

**13 press sth home a)** to push something into its place: *Jane slammed the door and pressed the bolt home.* **b)** to repeat or emphasize something, so that people remember it: *We must press home the case for action.*

**14 press home your advantage** to try to succeeed completely, using an advantage that you have gained
**15 press the flesh** *humorous* to shake hands with a lot of people: *politicians pressing the flesh*
**16 ▶ RECORD ◀** [T] to make a copy of a GRAMOPHONE record etc

**press** (sb) **for** sth *phr v* [I,T] to keep asking for something or to try hard to achieve something: *The firm is pressing me for a decision on their offer.* | *We must continue to press for full equality.*

**press on** *phr v* **1** [I] also **press ahead** to continue doing something, especially working, in a determined way: [+ **with**] *Shall we stop here, or press on to the next town?* | *Let's press on with our work.* **2** [T **press** sth **on** sb] to try hard to give something to someone, so that it is hard for them to refuse it: **press sth on sb** *Nick was pressing yet another drink on me.*

P

**press a·gent** /ˈ· ˌ··/ *n* [C] someone whose job is to supply photographs or information about a particular actor, musician etc to newspapers, radio or television —**press agency** *n* [C]

**press bar·on** /ˈ· ˌ··/ *n* [C] *informal, especially BrE* someone who owns and controls one or more important national newspapers

**press box** /ˈ· ·/ *n* [C] an enclosed area at a sports ground used by people from newspapers, radio, or television

**press con·fer·ence** /ˈ· ˌ···/ *n* [C] a meeting at which someone makes an official statement to people who write news reports and answers questions: *The Green Party held a press conference the next day.*

**press corps** /ˈ· ·/ *n* [C] a group of people who write news reports, at a place where something important is happening

**press cut·ting** /ˈ· ˌ··/ also **press clipping** *n* [C] a short piece of writing or a picture, cut out from a newspaper or magazine

**pressed** /prest/ *adj* **be pressed for time/money etc** to not have enough time, money etc: *I'm a bit pressed for time – could you call back tomorrow?*

**press gal·le·ry** /ˈ· ˌ···/ *n* [C] an area above or at the back of a hall, used by news reporters

**press-gang**[1] /ˈ· ·/ *n* [C] a group of sailors employed in the past to take men away by force to join the navy

**press-gang**[2] *v* [T] **press-gang sb into doing sth** *informal* to force someone to do something: *I was press-ganged into doing the dishes.*

**pre·ssie, prezzie** /ˈprezi/ *n* [C] *BrE spoken* a present: *Did you get some nice pressies?*

**press·ing**[1] /ˈpresɪŋ/ *adj* **1** needing to be discussed or dealt with very soon; URGENT: *There is a pressing need for reform in this area.* **2** demanding something in a way that is hard to refuse: *a pressing invitation* —**pressingly** *adv*

**pressing**[2] *n* [C] **1** a number of GRAMOPHONE records made at one time **2** an act of pressing

**press·man** /ˈpresmæn/ *plural* **pressmen** /-men/ *n* [C] *BrE informal* someone who writes news reports

**press of·fice** /ˈ· ˌ··/ *n* [C] the office of an organization or government department which gives information to the newspapers, radio, or television —**press officer** *n* [C]

**press re·lease** /ˈ· ·ˌ·/ *n* [C] an official statement giving information to the newspapers, radio, or television

**press sec·re·ta·ry** /ˈ· ˌ····/ *n* [C] a secretary to an important organization or person, who gives information about them to the newspapers, radio, or television

**press-stud** /ˈ· ·/ *n* [C] *BrE* a small metal FASTENER for a piece of clothing, in which one part is pressed into a hollow part in the other; SNAP[2] (6) *AmE*

**press-up** /ˈ· ·/ *n* [C] *especially BrE* a type of exercise in which you lie facing the ground, and push your body up with your arms; PUSH-UP *especially AmE*

S1 W1 **pres·sure**[1] /ˈpreʃə‖-ər/ *n*
**1 ▶ FORCE ◀** [U] the act of force or weight being put on to something: *The pressure of the water turns the wheel.* | *factors such as temperature and pressure*
**2 ▶ STRENGTH ◀** [C,U] the strength of the force or weight put on something: **high/low pressure** *The gas containers burst at high pressures.* | *Low atmospheric pressure often brings rain.* —see also BLOOD PRESSURE
**3 ▶ STRONG ◀** [U] an attempt to persuade someone by using influence, arguments, or threats: [+ **for**] *pressure for change inside the party* | **pressure to do sth** *There was great pressure to conform to existing standards.* | **under pressure from** *John only agreed to go under pressure from his parents.* | **be/come under pressure (to do sth)** *The company is under pressure to improve pay and conditions.* | **give in to pressure** (=agree to do something that someone has persuaded you to do) | **put pressure on** (=to try to persuade someone to do something because it is their duty.) *Their parents were putting pressure on them to get married.* | **exert pressure on/bring pressure to bear on** *formal*: *Special interest groups can bring great pressure to bear on legislation.*
**4 problems/demands** [C,U] conditions of work or a way of living that cause anxiety or difficulties: *Paul changed jobs because he couldn't stand the pressure* | [+ **on**] *There are a lot of pressures on young people today.* | **under pressure** *You need to be able to work accurately under pressure.* | **pressure of work** *Lou couldn't stay long because of pressure of work.*
**5 pile on the pressure** to increase the amount of pressure on someone: *Just when she was at her weakest, Martin started piling on the emotional pressure.*

**pressure**[2] *v* [T] to try to make someone do something by making them feel it is their duty to do it; PRESSURIZE *BrE* **pressure sb into doing sth** *I've been pressured into helping with the decorating.* | **pressure sb to do sth**

**pressure cook·er** /ˈ·· ˌ··/ *n* [C] a tightly covered cooking pot in which food is cooked very quickly by the pressure of hot steam

**pres·sured** /ˈpreʃəd‖-ərd/ *adj* feeling worried, or making you feel worried because of the number of things you have to do; PRESSURIZED (2) *BrE*: *This is the most pressured job I've ever had.*

**pressure group** /ˈ·· ·/ *n* [C] a group or organization that tries to influence the opinions of ordinary people and persuade the government to do something: *environmental pressure groups* —see also INTEREST GROUP

**pressure point** /ˈ·· ·/ *n* [C] **1** a point on the body where an ARTERY (=a tube that carries blood) that runs near a bone can be pressed and closed off, to stop blood loss **2** a place on the body that is massaged (MASSAGE[2] (1)) or used in treatments such as REFLEXOLOGY or ACUPUNCTURE **3** a place or situation that may involve trouble or problems: *a pressure point for racial tension*

**pres·sur·i·za·tion** /ˌpreʃəraɪˈzeɪʃən‖-rə-/ *n* [U] the quality of being (PRESSURIZED (1) or the degree to which something is pressurized

**pres·sur·ize** also **-ise** /ˈpreʃəraɪz/ *v* [T] *BrE* to try to make someone do something by making them feel it is their duty to do it; PRESSURE[2] **pressurize sb into doing sth** *They would have enjoyed the party more if they hadn't been pressurised into going.* | **pressurize sb to do sth** *Normally apathetic members were pressurized to vote.*

**pres·sur·ized** also **-ised** *BrE* /ˈpreʃəraɪzd/ *adj* **1** containing air that has controlled pressure: *a pressurized container* | *pressurised high altitude aircraft* **2** *BrE* feeling worried or making you feel worried, because of the amount of things you have to do; PRESSURED: *today's pressured society*

**pres·tige** /preˈstiːʒ/ *n* [U] **1** the respect and importance a person, organization, or profession has, because of their high position in society, or the quality of their work: *striving for prestige, status and power* | *The teaching profession has lost the prestige it used to have.* **2 prestige car/position/neighbourhood etc** a car etc that is expensive and important-looking in a way that other people admire —compare STATUS (2)

**pres·ti·gious** /preˈstɪdʒəs‖-ˈstiː-, -ˈstɪ-/ *adj* admired as one of the best and most important: *a prestigious job* | *a prestigious award*

**pres·to**[1] /ˈprestəʊ‖-toʊ/ *adj, adv technical* played or sung very quickly

**presto²** *n* [C] *technical* a piece or section of music played or sung very quickly

**presto³** *interjection spoken* used when you show someone something unbelievable or magical; HEY PRESTO *BrE*: *And presto! The rabbit disappears.*

**pre·stressed** /ˌpriː ˈstrest◂/ *adj* pre-stressed CONCRETE has been made stronger by having wires put inside it

S1 W3 **pre·su·ma·bly** /prɪˈzjuːməbli‖-ˈzuː-/ *adv* [sentence adverb] used to say that you think something is likely to be true: *If you're eating beforehand, presumably you won't want to go to a restaurant.* | *Presumably you've all seen this notice now.*

S3 **pre·sume** /prɪˈzjuːm‖-ˈzuːm/ *v* **1** [T] to think you can be sure of something because it is likely, although there is no proof: *Each of you will make a speech, I presume?* | **presume (that)** *I presume we'll be there by six o'clock.* | **presume sb/sth to be sb/sth** *From the way they talked I presumed them to be married.* | **be presumed to do sth** *The temple is presumed to date from the first century BC.* **2** [T] to accept something as true until it is proved untrue, especially in law: *We must presume innocence until we have evidence of guilt.* | **be presumed dead/innocent etc** *Their nephew was missing, presumed dead.* **3** [I] *formal* to behave without respect or politeness by doing something that you have no right to do: **presume to do sth** *Are you presuming to tell me how to treat my family?* **4** [T usually in present tense] *formal* to accept something as being true and base something else on it; PRESUPPOSE: *The statement that everyone is free presumes equality of opportunity.* | **presume that** *Our recommendations presume that a capable person is in charge.*

**presume on/upon** sth *phr v* [T] *formal* to use someone's kindness, or a relationship, to ask them for more than you should: *I felt it would be presuming on our friendship to ask him to lend me that much money.*

**pre·sump·tion** /prɪˈzʌmpʃən/ *n* **1** [C] an act of thinking that something is true because it is very likely: *the presumption that she would leave* **2** [U] disrespectful or impolite behaviour that shows you are too confident: *Ryan's presumption in telling her when they would meet* **3** [C,U] *law* the act of thinking something is true because it is very likely, although there is no certain proof: *the presumption of innocence*

**pre·sump·tive** /prɪˈzʌmptɪv/ *adj formal or technical* based on a reasonable belief about what is likely to be true: *a presumptive diagnosis* —**presumptively** *adv* —see also HEIR PRESUMPTIVE

**pre·sump·tu·ous** /prɪˈzʌmptʃuəs/ *adj* showing disrespect as a result of being too confident: *She found Conrad charming but rather presumptuous.* —**presumptuously** *adv* —**presumptuousness** *n* [U]

**pre·sup·pose** /ˌpriːsəˈpəʊz‖-ˈpoʊz/ *v* [T] *formal* **1** to depend on something that is thought to be true; ASSUME **presuppose that** *The plans presuppose that people usually respond to calls for help.* **2** to depend on something in order to exist or be true: *Every form of human society presupposes some kind of division of labour.*

**pre·sup·po·si·tion** /ˌpriːsʌpəˈzɪʃən/ *n formal* **1** [C] something that someone thinks is true without proof; ASSUMPTION [+ **that**] *the presupposition that crime is just another form of sickness* **2** [U] the act of thinking something is true without proof

**pre·teen** /ˌpriːˈtiːn◂/ *adj* connected with, or made for children who are 11 or 12 years old: *preteen clothing* —**preteen** *n* [C] *AmE*

**pre·tence** also **pretense** *AmE* /prɪˈtens‖ˈpriːtens/ *n* [singular, U] **1** an attempt to pretend that something is true: [+ **that**] *Susie abandoned the pretence that she didn't want to go to the party.* | **keep up the pretence of being/doing sth** *How long are you going to keep up the pretence of being ill?* | **under (the) pretence of sth** *John waited for her under pretence of tying his shoelaces.* | **make a pretence of doing sth** *Tollitt made no pretence of hiding his surprise.* **2 under/on false pretences** if you do something under false pretences, you do it by pretending that something is true: *Mellors obtained credit under false pretences.* **3 no pretence to superiority/faith/education etc** no claim that you are SUPERIOR¹ (4) etc: *a simple man, with little pretence to education*

**pre·tend¹** /prɪˈtend/ *v* **1** [I,T] to behave as if something is true when in fact you know it is not: *We're not really sisters; we were just pretending.* | **pretend (that)** *The candidate pretended she had worked for a newspaper before.* | **pretend to do sth** *Sarah pretended to be cheerful and said nothing about the argument.* | **pretend sth** *Dennis often pretends deafness when you ask him an awkward question.* **2** [T, usually in questions and negatives] to claim that something is true, especially something that cannot be shown to be true: **pretend (that)** *I can't pretend I understand these technical terms.* (=I admit I do not understand them) **pretend to sth** *I can't pretend to much expertise in computing.* **3** [I,T] to imagine something is true as a game: **pretend (that)** *Let's pretend we're on the moon.* S2 W3

This graph shows how common the different grammar patterns of the verb **pretend** are.

| | |
|---|---|
| pretend (that) | |
| pretend to do sth | |
| pretend | |
| pretend to | |
| pretend sth | |
| other | |

10% 20% 30% 40% 50% 60%

Based on the British National Corpus and the Longman Lancaster Corpus

**pretend²** *adj* a word meaning imaginary, used especially by or with children: *We sang songs around a pretend campfire.*

**pre·tend·ed** /prɪˈtendɪd/ *adj* false or unreal, in spite of seeming to be true or real: *pretended sorrow*

**pre·tend·er** /prɪˈtendə‖-ər/ *n* [C] someone who claims a right to be king, leader etc, that many people do not accept: *the pretender to the English throne*

**pre·tense** /prɪˈtens‖ˈpriːtens/ *n* [singular, U] an American spelling of PRETENCE

**pre·ten·sion** /prɪˈtenʃən/ *n* [C usually plural] an attempt to seem richer, more important etc than you really are: [+ **to**] *a man with pretensions to grandeur* | *an area with upper-class pretensions*

**pre·ten·tious** /prɪˈtenʃəs/ *adj* trying to seem more important, clever etc than you really are —opposite UNPRETENTIOUS: *It's pretentious of him to keep the complete works of Proust on full display.* | *a pretentious movie* —**pretentiously** *adv* —**pretentiousness** *n* [U]

**pret·er·ite** also **preterit** *AmE* /ˈpretərɪt/ *n* **the preterite** *technical* the tense or verb form that expresses a past action or condition —**preterite** *adj*

**pre·ter·nat·u·ral** /ˌpriːtəˈnætʃərəl◂‖-tər-/ *adj formal* **1** beyond what is usual or normal: *He felt possessed of a preternatural strength and fearlessness.* **2** strange, mysterious, and unnatural: *twisted images emerging through the preternatural green light* —**preternaturally** *adv* | *preternaturally strong*

**pre·text** /ˈpriːtekst/ *n* [C] a reason given for an action, in order to hide the real intention; EXCUSE² (1,2) [+ **for**] *The riots were used as a pretext for banning all political activity.* | **on/under the pretext of doing sth** *Tom called at her apartment on the pretext of asking for a book.* —see EXCUSE² (USAGE)

**pret·ti·fy** /ˈprɪtɪfaɪ/ *v* [T] to change something with the intention of making it pretty, but often with the effect of spoiling it: *The new owners have prettified the house.*

**pret·ty¹** /ˈprɪti/ *adv* [+ adj/adv] *spoken* **1** fairly, though not completely: *I'm pretty sure he'll say yes.* | *Life on the farm was pretty tough.* —see RATHER (USAGE) **2** very: *It's pretty hard to see how we'll manage.* **3 pretty well** also **pretty much** very nearly; almost: *I'd say that's* S2 W3 *pretty well impossible.* | *"How is he feeling today?" "Pretty much the same."* **4 pretty near** *especially AmE* almost: *That bout of pneumonia pretty near killed Roy.* —see also **be sitting pretty** (SIT[6])

S3 W3 **pretty[2]** *adj* **prettier, prettiest** **1** a woman or child who is pretty is good-looking in an ordinary way: *Susan's certainly a pretty girl, but I wouldn't call her beautiful.* | *Maria looks much prettier with her hair cut short.* **2** something that is pretty is pleasant to look at or listen to without being very beautiful or impressive: *a pretty dress* | *a pretty tune* | *What a pretty little garden!* **3** a boy who is pretty looks attractive in a way that is typical of a girl: *She said, "Oh Nick's the pretty one really."* **4 not a pretty sight** *often humorous* very unpleasant to look at: *After a night's drinking, Al was not a pretty sight.* **5 not just a pretty face** *humorous spoken* to have qualities or abilities as well as an attractive appearance: *I'm not just a pretty face, you know!* **6 come to a pretty pass** *old-fashioned* used to say that a very bad situation has developed: *Things have come to a pretty pass, if you can't say what you think without causing a fight.* **7 cost a pretty penny** *old-fashioned* to cost a lot of money **8 pretty as a picture** very pretty **9 pretty pretty** *BrE* spoilt by too much pretty decoration —**prettily** *adv*: *Charlotte sang very prettily.* **prettiness** *n* [U]

**pret·zel** /ˈpretsəl/ *n* [C] a hard salty BISCUIT or CRACKER (1) baked in the shape of a stick or a loose knot

**pre·vail** /prɪˈveɪl/ *v* [I] *formal* [not in progressive] **1** if a belief, custom etc prevails, it exists among a group of people: [+ **in/among etc**] *Belief in magic still prevails in some rural parts of the country.* **2** if someone or their ideas prevail, they win an argument or fight after a long time: [+ **over**] *The military finally prevailed over the civilian resistance movement.* | *Justice prevailed in the end.*

**prevail on/upon** sb *phr v* [T] *formal* to persuade someone: **prevail on sb to do sth** *David was prevailed upon to propose a vote of thanks.*

**pre·vail·ing** /prɪˈveɪlɪŋ/ *adj* [only before noun] **1** existing or accepted in a particular place or at a particular time; CURRENT[1]: *the prevailing state of education* | *prevailing trends* **2 prevailing wind** a wind that blows over a particular area most of the time

**prev·a·lent** /ˈprevələnt/ *adj* common at a particular time or in a particular place: [+ **in/among etc**] *Solvent abuse is especially prevalent among younger teenagers.* | *prevalent attitudes* —**prevalence** *n* [U]

**pre·var·i·cate** /prɪˈværɪkeɪt/ *v* [I] to try to hide the truth by not answering questions directly —**prevarication** /prɪˌværɪˈkeɪʃən/ *n* [C,U]

S2 W1 **pre·vent** /prɪˈvent/ *v* [T] to stop something from happening, or stop someone from doing something: *The rules are intended to prevent accidents.* | **prevent sb/sth (from) doing sth** *Lacey has a back injury that may prevent him from playing in tomorrow's game.* —**preventable** *adj*

**pre·ven·ta·tive** /prɪˈventətɪv/ *adj* another form of the word PREVENTIVE: *preventative measures*

**pre·ven·tion** /prɪˈvenʃən/ *n* [U] the act of preventing something, or the actions that you take in order to prevent something happening: [+ **of**] *the prevention of war* | **crime/accident prevention** *Accident prevention is one of the main aims of the campaign.*

**pre·ven·tive** /prɪˈventɪv/ also **preventative** *adj* [only before noun] intended to prevent something you do not want to happen, such as illness, or crime: *preventive health programs* | **preventive actions/measures** (=actions intended to stop something happening or a situation getting worse) *Simple preventive measures will reduce the risk of infection.* —**preventively** *adv* —**preventatively** *adv*

**preventive de·ten·tion** /ˌ·ˌ·· ·ˈ··/ *n* [U] *BrE law* a system in which people who are guilty of many crimes are kept in prison for a long time

**preventive medi·cine** /ˌ·ˌ·· ˈ···‖·ˌ·· ˈ···/ *n* [U] medical treatment, advice, and health education that is designed to prevent disease happening rather than cure it

**pre·verb·al** /ˌ· ˈ··◂/ *adj* [only before noun] happening before a child has learned to speak: *the pre-verbal stages*

**pre·view** /ˈpriːvjuː/ *n* [C] **1** an occasion when you can see a film, play etc before it is shown to the public: **sneak preview** *a sneak preview of his new play* **2** an advertisement for a film or television programme that often consists of short parts from it; TRAILER (3) *BrE*

**pre·vi·ous** /ˈpriːviəs/ *adj* **1** [only before noun] happening or existing before the event, time, or thing that is being mentioned: *a better result than we've had in previous years* | *She has two children from a previous marriage.* | **previous experience** *Do you have any previous experience of this kind of work?* | **previous offences/convictions** (=things that a criminal has done, or been judged guilty of, before) **2 a bit previous** *BrE informal* done before the right or sensible time: *It's a bit previous to ask for the money before they've done the job.* **3 previous to sth** before a particular time or event: *There were almost no women MPs previous to 1945.* S1 W1

**pre·vi·ous·ly** /ˈpriːviəsli/ *adv* before the present time: *The world record was previously held by a Spanish athlete.* | **two days/three years etc previously** *The car was now worth twice what we'd paid for it six months previously.* S3 W2

**pre·vi·sion** /ˌpriːˈvɪʒən/ *n* [C,U] *formal* something you see in your mind or knowledge you have of an event before it happens —compare PREMONITION

**pre-war** /ˌ· ˈ·◂/ *adj, adv* happening or existing before a war, especially the First or Second World Wars: *conditions in pre-war Europe* —compare POST-WAR

**prey[1]** /preɪ/ *n* **1** [U] an animal that is hunted and eaten by another animal or by a person: *a tiger stalking its prey* **2 bird/beast of prey** a bird or animal which lives by killing and eating other animals: *falcons and other birds of prey* **3 be/fall prey to sth** to be unable to avoid being affected by something unpleasant: *During the long wait she was prey to all sorts of doubts and anxieties.* **4** [U] someone who can easily be deceived or influenced: *Some salesmen consider young housewives easy prey.*

**prey[2]** *v*

**prey on** sb/sth *phr v* [T] **1** if an animal or bird preys on another animal or bird it hunts and eats it: *Cats prey on birds and mice.* **2** to try to influence or deceive weaker people: *religious cults that specialize in preying on young people* **3 prey on your mind** to make you worry continuously: *The accident has been preying on my mind all week.*

**prez·zie** /ˈprezi/ *n* [C] *BrE spoken* another spelling of PRESSIE

**price[1]** /praɪs/ *n* S1 W1

**1** ▶ **MONEY** ◀ [C,U] the amount of money for which something is sold, bought, or offered: *Fuel prices are rising steadily.* | [+ **of**] *Can you tell me what the price of a new window would be?* | *They agreed on a price of £2000 for the car.* | **high/low price** *You can get cars in Europe at very low prices.* | **price increase/rise** *Experts say that price rises will be gradual.* | **right price** *We don't have to sell to the first buyer, we can wait for the right price.* | **at a good/fair etc price** *You can get a three-course meal at a fairly reasonable price.* | **half/full price** *I bought these jeans half price in the sale.* | **in price** *Videos vary in price depending on the make.* —see also ASKING PRICE, COST[1] (USAGE), COST PRICE, LIST PRICE, MARKET PRICE

**2 at a price** **a)** used to say that you can buy something, but only if you pay a lot of money: *You can get goat's cheese at the local delicatessen – at a price!* **b)** used to say that something can be achieved, but that it involves something unpleasant: *She was finally made senior executive, but at what price!*

**3 at any price** if you want to do something at any price you are determined to do it, even if it is very difficult: *She was determined to have a child at any price.*

**4 not at any price** used to say that you would never sell

something, or do something, even for a lot of money: *Sorry, that painting's not for sale at any price.*
**5 put a price on sth a)** to say how much something costs: *Could you put a price on the damage the storm caused?* **b)** to give something a financial value: *You just can't put a price on their fighting spirit.*
**6 the price of success/freedom etc** the unpleasant or unwelcome things that you must suffer in order to be successful, free etc: *Monroe paid the ultimate price of success, dying alone in her room.*
**7 What price fame/glory etc?** *usually spoken* used to say that it is possible that it was not worth achieving something good, because too many bad things have happened as a result: *Homeless widows and orphans viewing tonight's carnage may well ask, what price political independence?*
**8 ▶AT HORSE RACE◀** [C] the chance that a horse will win a race expressed in numbers; ODDS (4): *"What price are you offering on "Lucky Shot?" "Seven to four."*
**9 be above/beyond/without etc price** to be extremely valuable or important
**10 a price on sb's head** a reward for catching or killing someone: *running scared with a price on his head*
**11 everyone has their price** used to say that you can persuade people to do anything if you give them what they want —see also **cheap at the price** (CHEAP[1] (8)), **name your price** (NAME[2] (7)), **pay the price** (PAY[1] (6))

This graph shows some of the words most commonly used with the noun **price**.

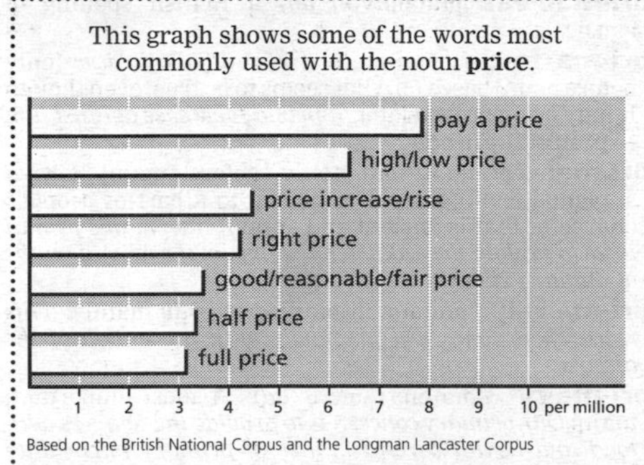


Based on the British National Corpus and the Longman Lancaster Corpus

**price²** *v* [T] **1** [usually in passive] to fix the price of something that is for sale: *a moderately priced apartment* | **be priced at** *The tennis rackets are priced at £75 each.* **2** to put the price on goods to show how much they cost **3** to compare the prices of things: *We spent Saturday morning pricing microwaves.* **4 price yourself out of the market** to demand too much money for the services or goods that you are selling

**price con·trol** /ˈ· ·,·/ *n* [U] a system in which the government sets the prices of things;

**price fix·ing** /ˈ· ,··/ *n* [U] **1** a system in which the government sets the prices of things; PRICE CONTROL **2** an agreement between producers and sellers of a product to fix its price at a high level

**price in·dex** /ˈ· ,··/ *n* [C] a system of numbers by which the prices of goods can be compared with what they were in the past —see also RETAIL PRICE INDEX

**price·less** /ˈpraɪsləs/ *adj* **1** so valuable that it is difficult to give a financial value: *priceless antiques* **2** a quality or skill that is priceless is extremely important or useful: *The ability to motivate people is a priceless asset.* **3** *informal* extremely funny or silly: *The look on his face when I walked in was priceless.*

**price list** /ˈ· ·/ *n* [C] a list of prices for things being sold

**pric·es and in·comes pol·i·cy** /,·· · ˈ·· ,···/ *n* [C] government actions to prevent prices and incomes increasing, in order to stop or limit INFLATION

**price sup·port** /ˈ· ·,·/ *n* [U] a system in which the government keeps the price of a product at a fixed level by giving the producer money or buying the product itself

**price tag** /ˈ· ·/ *n* [C] **1** a small ticket showing the price of something **2** the amount that something costs: *It's difficult to put a price tag on such a project.*

**price war** /ˈ· ·/ *n* [C] a period when two or three companies reduce the prices of what they sell, all trying to get the most customers

**pric·ey, pricy** /ˈpraɪsi/ *adj* **pricier, priciest** *informal* expensive: *New books are pretty pricey nowadays.*

**prick**

**prick¹** /prɪk/ *v* **1** [T] to make a small hole in something, using a sharp point: *Prick the pastry lightly with a fork.* | **prick yourself/prick your finger** *Ouch! I've pricked my finger with the needle.* **2** [I,T] to feel an unpleasant stinging feeling on your skin, or to make someone feel this: **prick sth** *The coarse material was beginning to prick my whole body.* —see also PRICKLE² (1) **3 prick sb's conscience** to make someone feel guilty or ashamed: *a documentary that should prick the consciences of the comfortable middle classes* **4 prick (up) its ears** if an animal pricks up its ears it raises them and points them towards a sound: *The rabbit stopped suddenly, pricking up its ears.* **5 prick (up) your ears** to listen carefully because you have heard something interesting: *Jay pricked up his ears when I mentioned vacation.* **6 prick the bubble (of sth)** to make someone see the uncomfortable truth of a situation

**prick** sth **out** *phr v* [T] to place a young plant in a specially prepared hole

**prick²** *n* [C]
**1 ▶PAIN◀** a slight pain you get when something sharp goes into your skin: *Don't worry, it's just a little needle prick.*
**2 ▶SMALL HOLE◀ a)** a small hole made by a sharp point in your skin or the surface of something: *A sample of blood was drawn from a prick in the skin.* **b)** an act of pricking something: *Give the sausages a prick.* —see also PINPRICK
**3 ▶SEX ORGAN◀** *slang taboo* a PENIS
**4 ▶PERSON◀** *slang taboo* a stupid unpleasant man
**5 prick of conscience** an uncomfortable feeling that you have done something wrong
**6 a prick of light** a small point or circle of light

**prick·le¹** /ˈprɪkəl/ *n* [C] **1** a long thin sharp point on the skin of some plants and animals **2** a stinging feeling on your skin: *prickles of perspiration*

**prickle²** *v* **1** [T] to give someone a stinging feeling on their skin: *The bush prickled the back of his legs.* **2** [I] if your skin prickles it begins to sting or feel cold because you are very frightened, angry etc: *The skin on the back of her neck prickled as she heard the door creak open.* | **prickle with anger/excitement etc** (=to feel strong anger, excitement etc) *She spoke brusquely, prickling with an increasing dislike of Damien Flint.*

**prick·ly** /ˈprɪkli/ *adj* **1** covered with prickles: *Prickly brambles grew on either side of the path.* **2** *informal* someone who is prickly gets annoyed or offended easily: *Fiona's in a very prickly mood this morning.* **3** something prickly makes you feel a small stinging sensation on your skin: *a prickly woollen sweater* | **a prickly feeling** *I've got a prickly feeling in my leg.* **4** causing problems, disagreements, and difficulties: *Nuclear power is still a prickly issue.* —**prickliness** *n* [U]

**prickly heat** /ˌ·· ˈ·/ *n* [U] a skin condition caused by strong sunlight that consists of uncomfortable red spots on the skin

**prickly pear** /ˌ·· ˈ·/ *n* [C,U] a kind of CACTUS with yellow flowers, or the fruit of this plant

**pric·y** /ˈpraɪsi/ *adj* another spelling of PRICEY

S3 W3 **pride¹** /praɪd/ *n* [U]

**1 ▶ FEELING OF PLEASURE ◀** a feeling of satisfaction and pleasure in what you have done, or in what someone connected with you has done: **show/feel/take pride in (doing)sth** *The employees all show great pride in their company.*|*She takes pride in doing a job well.*|**show/feel/take (a) pride in sth** *Scott takes a great pride in his appearance.*|**a glow of pride** (=pride that is very clearly shown)|**with pride** *They talked about their son with obvious pride.*
**2 ▶ RESPECT ◀** a feeling that you like and respect yourself and that you deserve to be respected by other people: **hurt sb's pride** *Don't offer her money, you'll hurt her pride.*|**give sb their pride back** *Getting a job gave Sam his pride back.*
**3 ▶ TOO MUCH PRIDE ◀** a feelng that you are better than other people because you are cleverer, more important etc: *His pride would not allow him to ask for help.*
**4 sb's pride and joy** someone or something that someone is very proud of, and that is important to them: *The garden is my father's pride and joy.*
**5 the pride of a)** the thing or person that the people in a particular place are most proud of: *Wigan's rugby team was the pride of the town.* **b)** the best thing in a group: *This Japanese sword is the pride of my collection.*
**6 have/take pride of place** to have the most important position in a group: *A huge birthday cake took pride of place on the table.*
**7 swallow your pride/put your pride in your pocket** to forget your feelings of pride and do something that seems necessary, although you do not want to do it: *Jerry swallowed his pride and apologised.*
**8** a group of lions: *A young lion had strayed some distance from the pride.*

**pride²** *v* **pride yourself on sth** to be especially proud of something that you do well, or of a quality that you have: *The school prides itself on its academic record.*

W3 **priest** /priːst/ *n* [C] **1** someone who is specially trained to perform religious duties and ceremonies in the Christian church **2** a man with religious duties and responsibilities in some non-Christian religions

**USAGE NOTE: PRIEST**

WORD CHOICE: **priest, clergyman, clergy, minister, pastor, chaplain, padre**

A **priest** is someone in charge of the prayers, services etc for the people who attend a particular church, especially in the Roman Catholic Church.

A priest in a Protestant church is often called a **minister**, and this is the most usual word in American English. A **vicar** is a priest who is in charge of a church in the Church of England. In the US **pastor** is also used for someone in charge of a particular church in the Protestant religion.

More general words for priests include **the clergy, clergymen**, or a **clergyman**: *talks between education chiefs and the clergy*|*She married an impoverished clergyman.*

A priest who looks after the religious needs of an organization such as a university, hospital, or prison is a **chaplain**. A priest who looks after the religious needs of soldiers in the army, navy etc, is also called a **chaplain**, but can also be called a **padre**.

**priest·ess** /ˈpriːstes/ *n* [C] a woman with religious duties and responsibilities in some non-Christian religions

**priest·hood** /ˈpriːsthʊd/ *n* **1 the priesthood** the job or position of a priest: *He decided to enter the priesthood.* **2** [C,U] all the priests of a particular religion or country

**priest·ly** /ˈpriːstli/ *adj* connected with a priest: *priestly garments*

**prig** /prɪg/ *n* [C] someone who obeys moral rules very carefully, and shows in an annoying way that they think they are better than other people —**priggish** *adj* —**priggishness** *n* [U]

**prim** /prɪm/ *adj* **1** very formal and careful in the way you behave, and easily shocked by anything rude: *a prim and studious manner*|**prim and proper** *Andy's much too prim and proper to enjoy your jokes.* **2** small and neat: *a prim apron* —**primly** *adv* —**primness** *n* [U]

**pri·ma bal·le·ri·na** /ˌpriːmə bæləˈriːnə/ *n* [C] the main woman dancer in a BALLET company

**pri·ma·cy** /ˈpraɪməsi/ *n* [U] *formal* the state of being the most important thing or person: **[+ over]** *the primacy of practical skill over theoretical knowledge*

**prima don·na** /ˌpriːmə ˈdɒnə‖-ˈdɑːnə/ *n* [C] **1** the most important woman singer in an OPERA company **2** someone who thinks that they are very good at what they do, and demands a lot of attention, admiration etc from other people: *In my view, football players are a bunch of over-paid pampered prima donnas.*

**pri·mae·val** /praɪˈmiːvəl/ *adj* a British spelling of PRIMEVAL

**pri·ma fa·cie** /ˌpraɪmə ˈfeɪʃi‖-ʃə/ *adj Latin law* [only before noun] based on what seems to be true, even though it may be disproved later: *a prima facie case against him* —**prima facie** *adv*

**pri·mal** /ˈpraɪməl/ *adj* [only before noun] *formal* **1** primal feelings seem to belong to a part of people's character that is ancient and animal-like: *man's primal urge to explore the unknown* **2** basic: *the primal truths of human existence*

**pri·ma·ri·ly** /ˈpraɪmərəli‖praɪˈmerəli/ *adv* mainly: *This research is concerned primarily with prevention of the disease.* W3

**pri·ma·ry¹** /ˈpraɪməri‖-meri/ *adj* **1** most important; main: *Our primary concern is to provide the refugees with food and health care.*|*a matter of primary importance* **2 primary school/teacher/level etc** concerning the education of children between five and eleven years old; ELEMENTARY (3) *AmE*: *a primary teacher*|*at primary level* **3** happening or developing before other things S3 W2

**primary²** *n* [C] **1** *technical* one of the longest feathers on a bird's wing **2** a primary election

**primary col·our** /ˌ··· ˈ··/ *n* [C] one of the three colours red, yellow, and blue, which you can mix together to make any of the other colours

**primary e·lec·tion** /ˌ··· ·ˈ··/ *n* [C] an election in the US at which members of a political party in one area vote to decide who will be their party's CANDIDATE for a political position

**primary health care** /ˌ··· ˈ· ·/ also **primary med·i·cal care** /ˌ··· ˈ··· ·/ *n* [U] the medical care that someone receives first when they become ill or have an accident

**primary school** /ˈ··· ˌ·/ *n* [C] *BrE* a school for children between five and eleven years old in England and Wales; ELEMENTARY SCHOOL *AmE*

**primary stress** /ˌ··· ˈ·/ *n* [C,U] *technical* the strongest force given in speech to a part of a long word, like the force given to 'pri' in 'primary'. It is shown in this dictionary by the mark (ˈ).

**Pri·mate** /ˈpraɪmɪ̣t/ *n* [C] the most important and powerful priest in a country or an area, especially in the Church of England; ARCHBISHOP

**pri·mate** /ˈpraɪmeɪt/ *n* [C] a member of the group of MAMMALS that includes humans and monkeys

**prime¹** /praɪm/ *adj* [only before noun] **1** most important: *Smoking is the prime cause of heart disease.*|*Our prime concern is getting the economy back on its feet.*

2 of the very best quality or kind: *The hotel is in a prime location overlooking the valley.*|*prime cuts of beef* **3 be a prime candidate/target etc** to be the person or thing that is most suitable or most likely to be chosen for a particular purpose: *The railways are a prime candidate for privatization.* **4 prime example** a very typical example of something: *Sherlock Holmes is the prime example of the great detective.*

**prime²** *n* **1 be in your prime/be in the prime of life** to be at the time in your life when you are strongest and most active: **past your prime** *Sadly I think the team are past their prime.*|**be cut off in your prime** (=die when you are in your prime) **2** [C] a PRIME NUMBER

**prime³** *v* [T] **1** [usually passive] to prepare someone for a situation so that they know what to do: *I felt fully primed by the day of the meeting.*|**prime sb to do sth** *The witness had been primed to say nothing about the car.*|**prime sb for sth** *primed for action* **2** to prepare a gun or mine so that it can fire or explode **3** to put a special layer of paint on a surface, to prepare it for the next layer **4 prime the pump** to encourage a business, industry, or activity to develop by putting money or effort into it

**prime cost** /ˌ· ˈ·/ *n* [C,U] the actual cost of producing something as opposed to money spent on selling it, renting factories etc —compare OVERHEAD² (1)

**prime fac·tor** /ˌ· ˈ··/ *n* [C] a number that can be divided only by itself and the number one, and is a FACTOR of another number: *7 is a prime factor of 21.*

**Prime Me·rid·i·an** /ˌ· ·ˈ···/ *n* the imaginary line drawn from north to south on the earth, from which east and west are measured in degrees on a map

**Prime Min·is·ter** /ˌ· ˈ···/ abbreviationPM *n* [C] the chief minister and leader of the government in some countries with a parliamentary system of government

**prime mov·er** /ˌ· ˈ··/ *n* [C] **1** someone who has great influence in the development of something important: *She's one of the prime movers in the Republican movement.* **2** *technical* a natural force, such as wind or water, that can be used to produce power

**prime num·ber** /ˌ· ˈ··/ *n* [C] a number that can be divided only by itself and the number one

**prim·er¹** /ˈpraɪmə‖-ər/ *n* **1** [C,U] paint that is spread over the bare surface of wood, metal etc before the main covering of paint is put on **2** [C] a tube containing explosive, used to fire a gun, explode a bomb etc **3** [C] *BrE old-fashioned* a beginner's book in a school subject

**pri·mer²** /ˈpraɪmə‖ˈprɪmər/ *n* [C]*AmE* a set of basic instructions: *a primer of good management*

**prime rate** /ˈ· ˌ·/ *n* [C] the lowest rate of interest at which money can be borrowed, which banks offer to their largest customers —compare BASE RATE

**prime rib** /ˌ· ˈ·/ *n* [singular, U] a piece of good quality BEEF that is cut from the chest of the animal

**prime time** /ˈ· ˌ·/ *n* [U] *especially AmE* the time in the evening when the greatest number of people are watching television

**pri·me·val** also **primaeval** *especially BrE* /praɪˈmiːvəl/ *adj* **1** belonging to the earliest period in the existence of the universe or the Earth: *Primeval clouds of gas formed themselves into stars.* **2** very ancient: *primeval forests* **3** primeval emotions or attitudes are very strong, and seem to come from a part of people's character that is ancient and animal-like

**prim·i·tive¹** /ˈprɪmɪ̈tɪv/ *adj* **1** belonging to a society that has a very simple way of life, without modern industries and machines: *primitive tools made from stones and animal bones*|*primitive art* **2** belonging to an early stage of the development of humans, or of plants or animals: *primitive man*|*a primitive fish* **3** very simple when compared to modern things: *primitive machinery*|*The house was primitive, with an earthen floor and mud walls.* **4** old-fashioned and uncomfortable: *Conditions at a lot of our football stadiums are primitive.* —**primitively** *adv* —**primitiveness** *n* [U]

**primitive²** *n* **1** someone who comes from a simple society and is not used to modern machines and modern ways of life **2** a painter who paints simple pictures like those of a child **3** a painter or SCULPTOR of the time before the Renaissance

**pri·mo·gen·i·ture** /ˌpraɪməʊˈdʒenɪ̈tʃə‖-moʊˈdʒenɪ̈tʃər/ *n* [U] *technical* the system by which property owned by a man goes to his eldest son after his death

**pri·mor·di·al** /praɪˈmɔːdiəl‖-ˈmɔːr-/ *adj formal* **1** existing at the beginning of time or the beginning of the Earth: *the primordial seas* **2** in the simplest form: *primordial passions* **3 primordial soup** the mixture of substances, gases etc thought to have existed before the beginning of life on Earth —**primordially** *adv*

**primp** /prɪmp/ *v* [I,T] to make yourself look attractive by arranging your hair, putting on MAKE-UP etc: *primping in front of the mirror*

**prim·rose** /ˈprɪmrəʊz‖-roʊz/ *n* **1** [C] a small wild plant with light yellow flowers, or the flower from this plant **2** [U] primrose yellow **3 the primrose path** *literary* a way of life full of pleasure that harms the soul

**primrose yel·low** /ˌ·· ˈ··◂/ *n* [U] a light yellow colour —**primrose yellow, primrose** *adj*

**prim·u·la** /ˈprɪmjɡ̈lə/ *n* [C] a plant of the primrose family with brightly coloured flowers

**Pri·mus** /ˈpraɪməs/ also **primus stove** /ˈ·· ·/ *n* [C] *trademark BrE* a small STOVE (=a piece of equipment for cooking) that burns oil and can be easily carried around

**prince** /prɪns/ *n* [C] **1** the son of a king or queen, or one of their close male relatives: *Prince Albert* **2** a male ruler of a small country or state: *Prince Rainier of Monaco* **3** the best man in a group: **the prince of/a prince among** *a prince among waiters* **4 merchant prince** someone who has become very rich in business W3

**Prince Charm·ing** /ˌ· ˈ··/ *n* [C] *informal or humorous* a perfect man who a young girl might dream about meeting

**prince con·sort** /ˌ· ˈ··/ *n* [C] a title sometimes given to the husband of a ruling queen

**prince·dom** /ˈprɪnsdəm/ *n* [C usually singular] *formal* a country ruled by a prince; PRINCIPALITY

**prince·ly** /ˈprɪnsli/ *adj* **1 princely sum** an expression meaning a large amount of money, often used jokingly to mean a very small amount of money: *My Dad offered me the princely sum of ten pence to wash his car!* **2** *formal* fine, splendid, or generous;: *a princely gift*|*a princely man* **3** belonging to or connected with a prince: *the princely states*

**Prince of Wales** /ˌprɪns əv ˈweɪlz/ *n* **the Prince of Wales** a title given to the first son of a British king or queen

**prin·cess** /ˌprɪnˈses◂‖ˈprɪnsəs/ *n* [C] **1** a close female relation of a king and queen, especially a daughter: *Princess Anne* **2** the wife of a prince: *Princess Diana*

**prin·ci·pal¹** /ˈprɪnsɪ̈pəl/ *adj* [only before noun] most important; main: *My principal source of income is teaching.*|*The principal character in the book is called Scarlett.* —see also PRINCIPALLY W2

**principal²** *n* **1** [singular] *technical* an amount of money lent to someone, put into a business etc, on which INTEREST is paid **2** [C] *AmE* someone who is in charge of a school; HEAD TEACHER *BrE* **3** [C] *especially BrE* someone who is in charge of a universitiy, college, or school **4** [C] the main performer in a play, group of musicians etc **5** [C often plural] a person for whom you are acting as a representative, especially in business: *I will have to consult my principals before I can give you an answer on that.*

**principal boy** /ˌ··· ˈ·/ *n* [C] *BrE* the main male character in a PANTOMIME, usually played by a young woman

**prin·ci·pal·i·ty** /ˌprɪnsɪ̈ˈpælɪ̈ti/ *n* [C] **1** a country ruled by a PRINCE **2 the Principality** *BrE* Wales

**prin·ci·pally** /ˈprɪnsɪ̥pli/ *adv* mainly: *The money is principally invested in government stock.*

**principal parts** /ˌ··· ˈ·/ *n* [plural] *technical* the parts of a verb from which other parts are formed in English; the INFINITIVE, past tense, present participle, past participle

S3 **prin·ci·ple** /ˈprɪnsɪ̥pəl/ *n*
W1 **1 ▶ MORAL RULE ◀ a)** [C,U] a moral rule or set of ideas which makes you behave in a particular way: *She resigned on a matter of principle.* | **the principle of the thing** *spoken*: *You shouldn't just take the car without asking, it's the principle of the thing.* | **on principle** (=because of a moral rule you follow) *I don't eat meat on principle.* | **on the principle that** *We charge no fees on the principle that education should be available for all.* **b)** strong ideas about what is morally right or wrong, that you try to follow in everything you do: *He has no principles; he'll do anything, as long as it's profitable.* | **against sb's principles** (=morally wrong to that person)
**2 ▶ RULES OF A PROCESS ◀ a)** [C] a rule which explains the way something such as a machine works, or which explains a natural force in the universe: *the principle of the internal combustion engine* | *Archimedes' principle* **b) principles** *plural* the general rules on which a skill, science etc is based: *Einstein's theories form the basic principles of modern physics.* | **first principles** (=the most important and basic rules)
**3 ▶ BELIEF ◀** [C] a belief that is accepted as a reason for an action, way of thinking etc: *the principle of free markets*
**4 man/woman of principle** someone who has strong ideas about what is morally right or wrong
**5 in principle a)** if something is possible in principle, there is no good reason why it should not happen, but it has not actually happened yet: *In principle you are entitled to a financial grant, but they're difficult to claim.* **b)** if you agree in principle, you agree about a general plan or idea without the details: *The scheme seems O.K. in principle, but I'd like to know more details.*

**prin·ci·pled** /ˈprɪnsɪ̥pəld/ *adj* **1** having a strong belief about what is morally right and wrong: *a principled woman* **2** based on truths, beliefs or morals: *a principled distinction between physical and emotional injury*

S2 **print¹** /prɪnt/ *v*
W3 **1 a) ▶ WORDS BY MACHINE ◀** [I,T] to produce words, numbers, or pictures on paper, using a machine which puts ink onto the surface: *That's what your letter's going to look like when it's printed.* | *Press this key to print a copy of the text.* | **print sth on/across** *the address printed on the form* | **print sth in** *The menu was printed in Japanese and English.* | *The word 'scandal' was printed in bold type.* | **be printed with** *cards printed with his name and address* | **a printed card/acknowledgement/text etc** *You will receive a printed acknowledgement of your payment.* | **the printed page/word** (=language in printed form) **b)** [I] to be printed by a computer: *The document will print as it appears on the screen.*
**2 ▶ BOOKS/NEWSPAPERS ◀** [T] to produce many copies of a book, newspaper etc in printed form: *the first cookery book to be printed in America*
**3 ▶ IN A NEWSPAPER ◀** [T] to print a letter, speech etc in a newspaper, magazine etc; PUBLISH: *The Telegraph has printed numerous articles criticising these sales techniques.* | *If you print that, I'll sue you.*
**4 ▶ ON A SCREEN ◀** also **print sth out** [I,T] if a computer prints words and numbers on a screen it puts them there: *An error message is printed and the program ends.*
**5 ▶ PHOTOGRAPH ◀** [T] to produce a photograph from a photographic film: *The pictures have to be developed and printed.*
**6 ▶ CLOTH ◀** [T] to decorate cloth with a pattern put all over its surface by a machine: **printed with** *a new sari printed with brown and violet flowers*
**7 print money** if a government prints money, it produces too many bank notes in order to pay for something
**8 a licence to print money** a way of making a lot of money easily: *This policy is a scandal – it's a licence to print money!*
**9 ▶ WRITE ◀** [I,T] to write words by hand without joining the letters: *Please print your name* | **print sth in** *a thin brown envelope with the address printed in capitals*
**10 ▶ MARK ◀** [T] to make a mark on a surface or in a soft substance by pressing something on to it: *The mark of the man's shoe was clearly printed in the mud.*

**print** sth ↔ **off/out** *phr v* [T] to produce a printed copy of a computer document: *Once you've designed your poster, you can print off as many copies as you like.*

**print²** *n* W3
**1 ▶ BOOKS/NEWSPAPERS ◀** [U] writing that has been printed in books, newspapers etc: *The information is available in many forms including print, microfilm, and CD-ROM.* | **in print** (=printed in a book, newspaper etc) *He believed everything he saw in print.* | **see your name in print** *a politician who likes to see his name in print* | **get into print** (=be printed) *It was the first of his stories to get into print.* | **get sth into print** (=have your work printed) | **print unions/workers** (=those involved in printing newspapers, books etc)
**2 be out of print** if a book is out of print, it is no longer being printed and you cannot buy new copies: *This volume is now out of print.*
**3 be in print** if a book is in print new copies of it are still being printed: *Her book is still in print, a hundred years after its original publication.*
**4 ▶ LETTERS ◀** [U] the letters in which something is printed: *books with large print for elderly people* | *This printer can produce high quality print.*
**5 the small/fine print** the details of a legal document, often in very small writing: *You should always read the small print before signing anything.*
**6 ▶ MARK ◀** [C] a mark made on a surface or in a soft substance by something that has been pressed onto it: *His feet left prints in the soft soil.* | *The children had decorated the walls with hand prints.*
**7 prints** [plural] the marks made by the pattern of lines on the ends of your fingers; FINGERPRINTS
**8 ▶ CLOTH ◀** [C,U] cloth, especially cotton, on which a coloured pattern has been printed: **a print dress/blouse** *She stood there in her print dress and white apron.*
**9 ▶ PATTERN ◀** [C] the pattern printed on a piece of cloth: *The curtains were green with a print of sunflowers.*
**10 ▶ PHOTOGRAPH ◀** [C] a photograph in the form of a picture that has been produced from a film: *You get three sets of prints, plus a free film.*
**11 ▶ PICTURE ◀** [C] a picture that has been printed from a small sheet of metal or block of wood, or a copy of a painting produced by photography

**prin·ta·ble** /ˈprɪntəbəl/ *adj* suitable to be printed and read by everyone: *Her remarks were scarcely printable* (=were very rude). —compare UNPRINTABLE

**printed cir·cuit** /ˌ·· ˈ··/ *n* [C] a set of connections between points in a piece of electrical equipment which uses a thin line of metal, not wire, to CONDUCT (=carry) the electricity

**printed mat·ter** /ˈ·· ˌ··/ *n* [U] printed articles, such as advertisements, that can be sent by post at a cheap rate

**print·er** /ˈprɪntə‖-ər/ *n* [C] **1** a machine which is connected to a computer and makes a printed record of computer information —compare PRINTING PRESS **2** someone employed in the trade of printing W3

**printer's ink** /ˈ··· ·/ *n* [U] printing ink

**print·ing** /ˈprɪntɪŋ/ *n* **1** [U] the act or process of making a book, magazine, etc by pressing or copying letters or photographs onto paper: *the invention of printing* | *a printing error* **2** [C] an act of printing a number of copies of a book: *the third printing*

**printing ink** /ˈ·· ·/ *n* [U] a type of ink that dries very quickly and is used in printing books and newspapers etc

**printing press** /ˈ·· ·/ also **printing machine** /ˈ·· ·ˌ·/ *n* [C] a machine that prints newspapers, books etc; press

**print·out** /ˈprɪntˌaʊt/ *n* [C,U] a sheet or length of paper with printed information on it, produced by a computer

3 **pri·or¹** /ˈpraɪə‖praɪr/ *adj* **1 prior to** *formal* before: *All the arrangements should be completed prior to your departure.* | *Guests can relax in the lounge prior to entering the theatre.* **2 prior warning/notice/discussion etc** a warning etc happening before something else happens: *The bomb exploded without any prior warning.* **3 prior agreement/arrangment etc** an arrangement made before the present situation: *Under a prior agreement the company will sell the land in ten years time.* | **a prior engagement** *formal* (=something you have planned to do) *I won't be at the meeting as I have a prior engagement.*

**prior²** *n* [C] **1** the man in charge of a PRIORY **2** the priest next in rank to the person in charge of an ABBEY

**pri·or·ess** /ˈpraɪərɪ̈s/ *n* [C] the woman in charge of a PRIORY

**pri·o·ri·tize** also **-ise** *BrE* /praɪˈɒrɪ̈taɪz‖-ˈɔːr-/ *v* [T] **1** to put several things, problems etc in order of importance, so that you can deal with the most important ones first: *Prioritize your tasks to ensure maximum efficiency.* **2** to deal with one thing first, because it is the most important: *The public wants to see the fight against crime prioritized.* —**prioritization** /praɪˌɒrɪ̈taɪˈzeɪʃən‖-ˌɔːrɪ̈tə-/ *n* [U]

2 2 **pri·or·i·ty** /praɪˈɒrɪ̈ti‖-ˈɔːr-/ *n* **1** [C] the thing that you think is most important and that needs attention before anything else: *First let's decide what our priorities are.* | *Manufacturers are making safety a design priority.* | **top/high/low priority** (=important or unimportant thing) *Women's issues are often seen as a low priority.* **2 have/take/get priority** also **be given priority** to be considered most important and dealt with before anything or anyone else: *If medical supplies are short, children will be given priorty.* | [+ **over**] *Roosevelt decided that the war in Europe would take priority over the war in the Pacific.* **3 get your priorities right** used to tell someone they should consider the most important things first: *Peter should get his priorities right and spend more time with his family.*

**pri·o·ry** /ˈpraɪəri/ *n* a Christian religious house or group of MONKS or NUNS, (=men or women living a religious life) which is smaller and less important than an ABBEY

**prise** /praɪz/ *v* [T] a British spelling of PRIZE³ (2)

**pris·m** /ˈprɪzəm/ *n* [C] **1** a transparent block of glass that breaks up white light into different colours **2** *technical* a solid object with matching ends and several sides which are the same width all the way up

**pris·mat·ic** /prɪzˈmætɪk/ *adj* **1** using or containing a PRISM: *a prismatic compass* **2** a prismatic colour is very clear and bright

2 2 **pris·on** /ˈprɪzən/ *n* **1** [C,U] a large building where people are kept as a punishment for a crime, or while waiting to go to court for their TRIAL¹ (1): *a maximum security prison* | *Forbes will be released from prison next week.* | **in prison** (=being kept in prison) *Bates was sentenced to three years in prison.* | **prison cell** (=a room where prisoners are locked up) | **prison sentence** (=the length of time someone has to stay in prison) | **send sb to prison** (=to officially order someone to be in prison) *Dow was sent to prison for six years for rape.* | **put sb in prison** *He will be put in prison for a very long time.* **2** [U] the system of sending people to be kept in a prison: *I don't believe that prison deters criminals from offending.*

**prison camp** /ˈ‥ ·/ *n* [C] a special prison in which PRISONERS OF WAR are kept

3 2 **pris·on·er** /ˈprɪzənə‖-ər/ *n* [C] **1** someone who is kept in a prison as a punishment for a crime: *The prisoners are allowed an hour's exercise every day.* **2** someone who is taken by force and kept somewhere, for example during a war: *enemy prisoners* | *political prisoners* | **hold/keep sb prisoner** *The guerillas kept her prisoner for three months.* | **take sb prisoner** *The captain was taken prisoner by enemy soldiers.*

**prisoner of con·science** /ˌ‥· · ˈ‥/ *n* [C] someone who is put in prison because of their political ideas

**prisoner of war** /ˌ‥· · ˈ·/ *n* [C] a soldier, member of the navy etc who is caught by the enemy during a war and kept as a prisoner

**prison vis·i·tor** /ˌ‥ ˈ‥·/ *n* [C] someone who visits prisoners in Britain to help them

**pris·sy** /ˈprɪsi/ *adj informal* behaving very correctly and easily shocked by anything rude: *"She's not a very nice girl," Jinny said in her prissy little voice.* —**prissily** *adv* —**prissiness** *n* [U]

**pris·tine** /ˈprɪstiːn/ *adj* extremely fresh or clean: *the pristine whiteness of newly fallen snow* | **in pristine condition** (=in the same condition as when it was made) *a '68 Volvo in pristine condition*

**prith·ee** /ˈprɪði/ *interjection old use* please

**priv·a·cy** /ˈprɪvəsi, ˈpraɪ-‖ˈpraɪ-/ *n* [U] **1** the state of being able to be alone, and not seen or heard by other people: *With seven people squashed in one house, you don't get much privacy.* **2** the state of being free from public attention: *each individual's right to privacy*

**pri·vate¹** /ˈpraɪvɪ̈t/ *adj* S1 W1

**1 ▶ NOT FOR EVERYONE ◀** only for use by one particular person or group, not for everyone: *a private road* | *private property*

**2 ▶ SECRET ◀ a)** private feelings, information, or opinions are personal or secret and not for other people to know about: *What I told you was private – I thought you would respect that.* **b)** a private meeting, conversation etc involves only a small number of people, and is not for other people to know about: *a peace deal hammered out in a series of private talks*

**3 ▶ NOT GOVERNMENT ◀** [only before noun] not connected with, owned by, or paid for by the government: *a private hospital* | *private pension plans* | **go private** *BrE* (=pay for medical treatment instead of getting it free at a public hospital)

**4 ▶ NOT PART OF YOUR WORK ◀** separate from and not connected with your work or your official position: *The president is paying a private visit to Europe.* | **private life** (=the parts of your life not connected with your job or your public life, especially your relationships) *I never discuss my private life in interviews.*

**5 ▶ QUIET PLACE ◀** quiet and without lots of people: *Is there a private corner where we can have a talk?*

**6 ▶ PERSON ◀** [only before noun] a private person is one who likes being alone, and does not talk much about their thoughts or feelings: *Although he spends a lot of time in the public eye, he is really a very private man.*

**7 private joke** a joke made between friends, family members etc that other people do not understand —see also PRIVATELY

**private²** *n* **1 in private** without other people being present: *I have something to tell you, but I'll speak to you about it in private.* **2** [C] a soldier of the lowest rank —see table on page B3 **3 privates** [plural] *informal* PRIVATE PARTS

**private de·tec·tive** /ˌ‥ ·ˈ‥/ *n* [C] someone who can be employed to look for information or missing people, or to follow people and report on what they do

**private ed·u·ca·tion** /ˌ‥ ‥ˈ‥/ *n* [U] education provided for money, rather than free education provided by the government

**private en·ter·prise** /ˌ‥ ˈ‥·/ *n* **1** [U] the economic system in which private businesses are allowed to compete freely with each other, and the government does not control industry —see also PRIVATE SECTOR **2** [C] a business established by an individual person or group

**pri·va·teer** /ˌpraɪvəˈtɪə‖-ˈtɪr/ *n* [C] **1** an armed ship in former times that was not in the navy but attacked and robbed enemy ships carrying goods **2** someone who commanded or sailed on a ship of this kind

**private eye** /ˌ‥ ˈ·/ *n* [C] *informal* a PRIVATE DETECTIVE

**private in·come** /ˌ‥ ˈ‥/ *n* [C] money that someone gets regularly, not from working but because they own part of a business or have money which earns INTEREST¹ (4)

**private in·ves·ti·gat·or** /ˌ·· ˈ·ˌ···/ *n* [C] a PRIVATE DETECTIVE

**private law** /ˈ·· ˌ·/ *n* [U] *law* the part of the law concerned with ordinary people, private property, and relationships

**pri·vate·ly** /ˈpraɪvɪ̱tli/ *adv* **1** with no one else present: *Could I speak to you privately?* **2** if you feel or think something privately, you do not tell anyone about it [sentence adverb] *Privately, Prue felt that the whole exercise was a waste of time.* **3** *especially BrE* using or involving private rather than government institutions: *Both children are privately educated.* | *a privately-owned company*

**private medi·cine** /ˌ·· ˈ··‖ˌ·· ˈ···/ *n* [U] *BrE* the system in which medical treatment and advice is not provided by the government but is paid for by the person who needs it, or by their insurance company —compare NHS

**private mem·ber** /ˌ·· ˈ··/ *n BrE* [C] a member of parliament who is not a minister in the government

**private member's bill** /ˌ·· ˈ·· ˌ·/ *n* [C] a law introduced to the British parliament by a member of parliament who is not a minister in the government

**private parts** /ˌ·· ˈ·/ *n* [plural] an expression meaning 'sex organs', used when you want to avoid naming them directly

**private pa·tient** /ˌ·· ˈ··/ *n* [C] *BrE* someone who pays for medical treatment or advice, rather than receiving it free through the government's system

**private prac·tice** /ˌ·· ˈ··/ *n* [U] **1** the business of a professional person that is independent of a bigger or government controlled organization: *Richard set up in private practice.* **2** *AmE* the business of a professional person, especially a doctor, who works alone rather than with others

**private school** /ˌ·· ˈ·/ *n* [C] a school not supported by government money, where education must be paid for by the parents of the children

**private sec·re·ta·ry** /ˌ·· ˈ····/ *n* [C] a secretary who is employed to help one person, especially with CONFIDENTIAL business

**private sec·tor** /ˌ·· ˈ··◂/ *n* **the private sector** the industries and services in a country that are owned and run by private companies, and not by the state or government: *pay increases in the private sector* | *private sector employers* —compare PUBLIC SECTOR

**private sol·dier** /ˌ·· ˈ··/ *n* [C] *formal* a soldier of the lowest rank; PRIVATE² (2)

**private view** /ˌ·· ˈ·/ also **private view·ing** /ˌ·· ˈ··/ *n* [C] an occasion when a few people are invited to see a show of paintings before the rest of the public

**pri·va·tion** /praɪˈveɪʃən/ *n* [C,U] *formal* a lack or loss of the things that everyone needs, such as food, warmth, and shelter: *Despite the privations of wartime she managed to keep the children healthy.*

**pri·vat·ise** /ˈpraɪvɪ̱taɪz/ *v* a British spelling of PRIVATIZE

**pri·vat·i·za·tion** also **-isation** *BrE* /ˌpraɪvətaɪˈzeɪʃən‖-tə-/ *n* [C, U] the act of privatizing something

**pri·vat·ize** also **-ise** *BrE* /ˈpraɪvətaɪz/ *v* [T] to sell an organization, industry, or service that was previously controlled and owned by a government —compare NATIONALIZE

**priv·et** /ˈprɪvɪ̱t/ *n* [U] a bush with leaves that stay green all year, often grown to form a HEDGE

W3 **priv·i·lege** /ˈprɪvɪ̱lɪdʒ/ *n* **1** [C] a special advantage that is given only to one person or group of people: *Don't forget that using the car is a privilege, not a right!* | **the privilege of (doing) sth** *the privilege of having an office of my own* **2** [U] a situation in which people who are rich or of a high social class have many more advantages than other people: *an outdated system based on aristocratic privilege* **3** [singular] something that you are lucky to have the chance to do, and that you enjoy very much: **the privilege of doing sth** *Ladies and gentlemen, I have the great privilege of introducing our speaker for tonight.* | *It was a privilege to hear her play.* **4** [C,U] the right to do or say something which might not normally be acceptable without being punished, especially in parliament: **a breach of privilege** (=a breaking of the rules about what a member of parliament can do or say)

**priv·i·leged** /ˈprɪvɪ̱lɪdʒd/ *adj* **1** having a special advantage or a chance to do something that most people cannot do: **privileged to do sth** *Francis felt privileged to work for such a man.* | *Recently I was privileged to view his private collection.* **2** having advantages because of your wealth, social position etc: **the privileged few** *Only the privileged few were able to afford university then.* **3** *law* privileged information does not have to be given even if a court of law asks for it

**priv·y¹** /ˈprɪvi/ *adj* **1** **privy to** sharing in the knowledge of facts that are secret: *Colby was privy to the committee's decisions.* **2** *old use* secret and private —**privily** *adv*

**privy²** *n* [C] *old use* a toilet, especially one outside a house

**Privy Coun·cil** /ˌ·· ˈ··/ *n* **the Privy Council** a group of important people in Britain who advise the king or queen on political affairs —**Privy Councillor** *n* [C]

**Privy Purse** /ˌ·· ˈ·/ *n* **the privy purse** money given by the British government to the king or queen for their personal use

**prize¹** /praɪz/ *n* [C] **1** something that is given to someone who is successful in a competition, race, game of chance etc: *First prize was a weekend for two in Paris.* | [+ **for**] *Festival judges awarded 'Victims' the prize for the best feature film.* | **win a prize** *Hundreds of cash prizes to be won!* | **prize winner** *a list of prize winners* | **award (sb) a prize** (=decide who will have a prize) **2** something that is very valuable to you or that it is very important to have: *Toulouse was a rich prize, and the Count's army fought hard to keep it.* **3** **(there are) no prizes for guessing sth** *spoken* used to say that it is very easy to guess something: *No prizes for guessing who told you that!* **4** an enemy ship caught at sea in the past, or the goods it contained S W

**prize²** *adj* [only before noun] **1** good enough to win a prize or to have won a prize: *a herd of prize cattle* —see also PRIZE-WINNING **2** **prize money** money that is given to the person who wins a competition, race etc **3** **a prize idiot/fool** *informal* a complete IDIOT, fool etc **4** best, most important, or most useful: *The resource centre is one of our prize assets.*

**prize³** *v* [T] **1** [often passive] to think that someone or something is very important or valuable: *a necklace which his mother had prized* **2** [T always + adv/prep] also **prise** *BrE* to move or lift something, by pushing it away from something else; PRY (2) *AmE*: **prize sth off/up/apart etc** *Eventually we prized the lid off with a knife.*

**prize** sth **out** *phr v* [T] to get information from someone with difficulty or by using force: **prize sth out of sb** *It took an hour to prize the address out of him.*

**prized** /praɪzd/ *adj* extremely important or valuable to someone: **prized possession** *Nathaniel's bicycle is his most prized possession.*

**prize day** /ˈ· ·/ *n* [C] *BrE* an occasion when prizes are given to pupils who have done well in particular subjects

**prize·fight** /ˈpraɪzfaɪt/ *n* [C] **1** a public BOXING match, in which two men fight each other with bare hands, in order to win money **2** *AmE* a professional BOXING match —**prizefighter** *n* [C] —**prizefighting** *n* [U]

**prize-win·ning** /ˈ· ˌ··/ *adj* [only before noun] a prize-winning film, book etc has won a prize: *a prize-winning science reporter*

**PRO** /ˌpiː ɑːr ˈəʊ‖-ˈoʊ/ *n* [C] a public relations officer; someone whose job is to supply information about an organization, so that people have a good opinion of it —see also PR (1)

**pro-** /prəʊ‖proʊ/ *prefix* **1** in favour of or supporting something: *pro-American* | *the pro-abortion lobby* —compare ANTI- **2** *technical* doing a job instead of someone: *the pro-vice-chancellor*

**pro¹** /prəʊ‖proʊ/ *n* [C] **1** a PROFESSIONAL (=someone

who earns money because they are good at a particular sport or skill) **2** *informal* also **old pro** someone who has had a lot of experience with a particular type of situation: *Ben's an old pro at this type of thing – leave it to him.* **3 the pros and cons** the advantages and disadvantages of something: *the pros and cons of owning your own home* **4** *BrE informal* a PROSTITUTE —see also PRO FORMA, PRO RATA

**pro²** *prep* if you are pro an idea, plan, suggestion etc, you support it and hope that it will succeed: *As a party, they had always been pro nuclear power.*

**pro³** *adj informal* PROFESSIONAL | **turn/go pro** (=become pro) *Both skaters turned pro last year.*

**pro·ac·tive** /ˌ· ˈ··/ *adj* able to change events rather than react to them, and make things happen: *a pro-active approach to staffing requirements*

**pro-am** /ˌprəʊ ˈæm◂‖ˌproʊ-/ *n* [C] a competition, especially in GOLF, for PROFESSIONALS (=people who play for money) and AMATEURS (=people who play just for pleasure) —**pro-am** *adj*

**prob·a·bil·i·ty** /ˌprɒbəˈbɪl̩ti‖ˌprɑː-/ *n* **1** [singular, U] how likely it is that something will happen, exist, or be true: [+ **of**] *very little probability of finding it again* | **there is a strong probability that** *There is a very strong probabililty that she will make a full recovery.* | **the probability is that** (=it is likely that) *If you can answer these questions, the probability is that you'd be good at the job.* **2 in all probability** an expression meaning very probably, used especially when you are making a judgment about something: *There will, in all probability, be parts that you do not understand.* **3** [C] something that is likely to happen or exist: *A peace agreement now seems a real probability.* **4** the mathematically calculated chance that something will happen: *a probability of one in four*

**prob·a·ble¹** /ˈprɒbəbəl‖ˈprɑː-/ *adj* likely to exist, happen, or be true: *A victory doesn't seem very probable at this stage.* | **it is probable that** *It seems highly probable that they'll have to move house.* | **probable result/outcome/effect etc** *The new building will go ahead at a probable cost of £2.5 million.* —opposite IMPROBABLE

**probable²** *n* [C] someone who is likely to be chosen for a team, to win a race etc

S1 W1 **prob·a·bly** /ˈprɒbəbli‖ˈprɑː-/ *adv* [sentence adverb] used to say that something is likely to happen, likely to be true etc: *I probably still have my old army pictures.* | *Probably the best way to learn Spanish is by actually going to live in Spain.* | *"Do you think you'll return to work after the baby?" "Yeah, probably."* | **very/most probably** *She most probably thinks she's right when she says things like that.*

**pro·bate¹** /ˈprəʊbeɪt, -b̩t‖ˈproʊbeɪt/ *n* [U] *law* the legal process of deciding that someone's WILL² (2) has been properly made and can be carried out

**probate²** *v* [T] *AmE law* to prove that a WILL² (2) is legal

**pro·ba·tion** /prəˈbeɪʃən‖proʊ-/ *n* [U] **1** a system that allows some criminals not to go to prison, if they behave well and see a PROBATION OFFICER (=special adviser) regularly, for a fixed period of time: *The court fined Kevin and gave him two years' probation.* | **(put sb) on probation** *Mike was put on probation for stealing a car.* **2** a period of time, during which someone who has just started a job is tested to see whether they are suitable for what they are doing: *After six months' probation, Helen became a permanent member of staff.* | **on probation** *I'm on probation for another month yet.* **3** *AmE* a fixed period of time in which you must improve your work or behave well so that you will not have to leave your job: **(put sb) on probation** *I'm afraid I have no choice but to put you on probation.* —**probationary** *adj*: *a probationary period* | *probationary teachers*

**pro·ba·tion·er** /prəˈbeɪʃənə‖proʊˈbeɪʃənər/ *n* [C] **1** someone who has recently started a job, especially nursing or teaching, and who is being tested to see whether they are suitable for it **2** someone who has broken the law, and has been put on probation **3** someone who is being tested to see if they are suitable to be a member of a church or religious group

**probation of·fi·cer** /·ˈ·· ˌ···/ *n* [C] someone whose job is to watch, advise, and help people who have broken the law and are on probation

**probe¹** /prəʊb‖proʊb/ *v* [I, T] **1** to ask questions in order to find things out, especially things that other people do not want you to know: [+ **into**] *I don't want to probe too deeply into your personal affairs.* | **probe sth** *a report probing the official's involvement with drug dealing* **2** to look for something or examine something, using a long thin instrument: *Jules probed the mud gingerly with a stick.* —**probing** *adj*: *probing questions* —**probingly** *adv*

**probe²** *n* [C] **1** a long thin metal instrument that doctors and scientists use to examine parts of the body **2** a SPACE PROBE **3** an expression meaning a very thorough INQUIRY into something, used by newspapers: *a police corruption probe*

**pro·bi·ty** /ˈprəʊb̩ti‖ˈproʊ-/ *n* [U] *formal* complete honesty: *I have always found Bentner to be a model of probity in our dealings.*

**prob·lem** /ˈprɒbləm‖ˈprɑː-/ *n* [C] S1 W1

**1 ▶ DIFFICULTY ◀** a situation that causes difficulties: *There was rarely any problem in motivating the students to study.* | **have a problem with** *I've been having a few problems with the car.* | **a drug/crime problem** *tough new measures to combat the drug problem* | **pose a problem** *The shortage of trained staff poses a serious problem.* | **solve a problem** *a policy that will solve the unemployment problem* —see TROUBLE (USAGE)

**2 no problem** *spoken* **a)** used to say that you are very willing to do something: *"Could you make the booking in her name?" "Yes, no problem."* | *No problem! I'd love to show you around.* **b)** used after someone has said thank you or said that they are sorry: *"Thanks so much for all your help." "Oh, no problem!"*

**3 that's your problem** *spoken* used to tell someone to deal with their own problem or situation by themselves: *If you can't get yourself there on time, that's your problem.*

**4 it's/that's not my problem** *spoken* used to say you do not care about a problem someone else has: *"Your brother's under a lot of pressure." "That's not my problem."*

**5 What's your problem?** *spoken* used to ask someone what is wrong, in a way that is not sympathetic, and shows that you think they are being unreasonable: *Look, what's your problem? I've never seen you act like this!*

**6 a problem child/family/drinker etc** a child etc who behaves in a way that is difficult for other people to deal with

**7 Do you have a problem with that?** *spoken* used to ask someone why they oppose you or disagree with you, in a way that shows you think they are wrong

**8 ▶ QUESTION ◀** a question, especially one connected with numbers or facts, that must be answered: *The teacher gave them 20 mathematical problems.*

**prob·lem·at·ic** /ˌprɒbləˈmætɪk◂‖ˌprɑː-/ *adj* full of problems and difficult to deal with: *The situation might become slightly problematic as more people are involved.* —**problematically** /-kli/ *adv*

**problem page** /ˈ·· ·/ *n* [C] a page in a magazine where letters about personal problems are printed, and answers are suggested

**problem-solv·ing** /ˈ·· ˌ··/ *n* [U] finding ways of doing things, or finding answers to problems: *Involve the class in a problem-solving activity.*

**pro bo·no pub·li·co** /prəʊ ˌbəʊnəʊ ˈpʊblɪkəʊ‖proʊ ˌboʊ-noʊ ˈpuːblɪkoʊ/ also **pro bono** *adj Latin* used to descibe work that someone, especially a lawyer, does without getting paid for it: *Some law firms will take on pro bono cases when possible.*

**pro·bos·cis** /prəˈbɒs̩s‖-ˈbɑː-/ *n* [C] *plural* **proboscises** /-s̩siːz/ **1** a long thin tube that forms part of the mouth of some insects and worms **2** the long thin nose of certain animals, such as the elephant

**pro·ce·du·ral** /prəˈsiːdʒərəl/ *adj formal* connected with a procedure, especially in a law court

S3 W2 **pro·ce·dure** /prəˈsiːdʒə‖-ər/ *n* **1** [C] the correct or normal way of doing something: [+ **for**] *What's the procedure for renewing your car tax?* | **correct/proper/standard procedure** *A lie-detector test is standard procedure.* **2** [U] the accepted method and order of doing things, especially in an official meeting, a law case etc: *Too much time was spent arguing about procedure.*

S3 W3 **pro·ceed** /prəˈsiːd/ *v* [I] **1** to continue to do something that has already been started: *The work is proceeding according to plan.* | [+ **with**] *Travis paused to consult his notes, then proceeded with his questions.* | [+ **to**] *We can now proceed to the main business of the meeting.* **2 proceed to do sth** an expression meaning to do something next, used especially about something annoying or surprising: **proceed to do sth** *Patrick said he liked my work, and then proceeded to tell me everything was wrong with it!* **3** [always +adv/prep] *formal* to move in a particular direction: [+ **in/to etc**] *Passengers for the Miami flight should proceed to gate 25.* —see also PROCEEDS

**proceed against** sb *phr v* [T] *law* to begin a legal case against someone

**proceed from** sth *phr v* [T not in passive] *formal* to happen or exist as a result of something: *diseases that proceed from poverty*

W2 **pro·ceed·ings** /prəˈsiːdɪŋz/ *n* [plural] **1** also **proceeding** [C] an event or series of actions, especially an unusual or annoying one: *We watched the proceedings in the street from the window.* **2** actions taken in a law court or in a legal case: *Legal proceedings can be enormously expensive.* **3** the official records of meetings: *the proceedings of the London Historical Society*

**pro·ceeds** /ˈprəʊsiːdz‖ˈproʊ-/ *n* [plural] the money that has been gained from doing something or selling something: *We sold the business and bought a retirement condo with the proceeds.*

S2 W1 **pro·cess**[1] /ˈprəʊses‖ˈprɑː-/ *n* [C] **1** a series of natural developments or events that produce gradual change: *Coal was formed out of dead forests by a slow process of chemical change.* | *the digestive process* **2** a series of actions that someone takes in order to achieve a particular result: *Teaching him to read was a slow process.* | *the electoral process* | **by a process of elimination** (=by proving that no other possibility is true) *The identity of the dead man was established by a process of elimination.* **3 be in the process of doing sth/be in process** to have started doing something and not yet be finished: *The company is in the process of moving to new offices.* | *New guidelines are in process.* **4** a system or a treatment of materials that is used to produce goods: *an advanced industrial process* **5 in the process** while you are doing something or something is happening: *Katie jumped out of the tree, spraining her ankle in the process.* **6** *technical* a legal case, considered as a series of actions —see also DUE PROCESS

**process**[2] *v* [T] **1** to treat food or some other substance by adding substances to give it colour, keep it fresh etc: *processed cheese* **2** to print a picture from a photographic film **3** to deal with a document: *Your application for a mortgage is being processed.* **4** to put information into a computer to be examined —see also DATA PROCESSING, WORD PROCESSOR

**pro·cess**[3] /prəˈses/ *v* [I always + adv/prep] to move in a procession, or to move very slowly and seriously

**processed food** /ˌ·· ˈ·/ *n* [U] food that has been specially treated before it is sold, in order to make it look more attractive or last longer

**pro·ces·sion** /prəˈseʃən/ *n* [C] **1** a line of people or vehicles moving slowly as part of a ceremony: *the funeral procession* | *a carnival procession* | **in procession** *They marched in procession to the Capitol Building.* **2** several people or things of the same kind, appearing or happening one after the other: [+ **of**] *a never-ending procession of unwelcome visitors*

**pro·ces·sion·al** /prəˈseʃənəl/ *adj* [only before noun] connected with or used during a procession: *Flags lined the processional route.*

**pro·ces·sor** /ˈprəʊsesə‖ˈprɑːsesər/ *n* [C] the central part of a computer that does the calculations needed to deal with the information it is given; CENTRAL PROCESSING UNIT —see also FOOD PROCESSOR

**pro-choice** /ˌ· ˈ·/ *adj* someone who is pro-choice believes that women have a right to ABORTION, and uses this word to describe their views: *pro-choice activists*

**pro·claim** /prəˈkleɪm‖proʊ-/ *v* [T] *formal* **1** to say publicly that something important is true or exists: *Their religion encouraged them to proclaim their faith.* | *A national holiday was proclaimed.* | **proclaim sb sth** *His son was immediately proclaimed king.* **2** to show something clearly or be a sign of something: *The two gold stripes on Tanya's uniform proclaimed her seniority.*

**proc·la·ma·tion** /ˌprɒkləˈmeɪʃən‖ˌprɑː-/ *n* **1** [C] an official public statement about something that is important: *the country's proclamation of independence* | *a royal proclamation* **2** [U] the act of stating something officially and publicly

**pro·cliv·i·ty** /prəˈklɪvəti‖proʊ-/ *n* [C + **to/towards/for**] *formal* a strong liking for something or natural tendency to do something, especially something bad: *The child shows no proclivity towards aggression as far as I can see.*

**pro·con·sul** /prəʊˈkɒnsəl‖proʊˈkɑːn-/ *n* [C] someone who governed a part of the ancient Roman Empire —**proconsular** /-ˈkɒnsjələ‖-lɑnsələr/ *adj*

**pro·con·su·late** /prəʊˈkɒnsjələt‖proʊˈkɑːnsəl-/ also **pro·con·sul·ship** /-ˈkɒnsəlʃɪp‖-ˈkɑːn-/ *n* [C] the rank of a proconsul, or the time during which someone was a proconsul

**pro·cras·ti·nate** /prəˈkræstəneɪt/ *v* [I] *formal* to delay doing something that you ought to do, usually because you do not want to do it: *Stop procrastinating – just go and tell her.* —**procrastination** /prəˌkræstəˈneɪʃən/ *n* [U]

**pro·cre·ate** /ˈprəʊkrieɪt‖ˈproʊ-/ *v* [I,T] *formal or technical* to produce children or baby animals —**procreation** /ˌprəʊkriˈeɪʃən‖ˌproʊ-/ *n* [U]

**proc·tor**[1] /ˈprɒktə‖ˈprɑːktər/ *n* [C] **1** a university officer, especially at Oxford or Cambridge, whose duties include making sure that students keep the rules **2** *AmE* someone who watches students in an exam to make sure that they do not cheat

**proctor**[2] *v* [T] *AmE* to watch students in an exam to make sure that they do not cheat; INVIGILATE *BrE*

**pro·cu·ra·tor fis·cal** /ˌ···· ˈ··/ *n* [C] an official in Scotland who decides whether someone should be sent to court for a TRIAL[1] (1)

**pro·cure** /prəˈkjʊə‖proʊˈkjʊr/ *v formal* **1** [T] to obtain something, especially something that is difficult to get: **procure sb sth/procure sth for sb** *Somehow he had procured us an invitation.* **2** [I,T] *old-fashioned* to provide a PROSTITUTE for someone —**procurable** *adj* —**procurement** *n* [U] —**procurer** *n* [C]

**prod**[1] /prɒd‖prɑːd/ *v* **prodded, prodding** [I,T] **1** to push or press something with your finger or a pointed object; POKE[1] (1): *She prodded me sharply in the ribs.* | [+ **at**] *Theo prodded at the dead snake.* —see picture on page 1260 **2** to strongly encourage someone to do something: *She's not lazy, but she needs prodding.* | **prod sb into (doing) sth** *We just need something to prod them into action.*

**prod**[2] *n* [C usually singular] **1** a sudden pressing or pushing movement, using your finger or a pointed object; POKE[2]: *Jerry gave me a sharp prod in the back.* **2 give sb a prod** to encourage or remind someone to do something: *You'll need to give him a prod to get him to clean his room.* **3** an instrument used for prodding something: *a cattle prod*

**prod·i·gal**[1] /ˈprɒdɪgəl‖ˈprɑː-/ *adj* **1** tending to waste what you have, especially money: *a prodigal lifestyle* | [+ **of/with**] *Don't be so prodigal of your time.* **2** *formal* giving or producing large amounts of something; LAVISH:[1] (1) *a prodigal feast* | [+ **of**] *The garden was filled with blossom and prodigal of scent.* —**prodigally** *adv* —**prodigality** /ˌprɒdɪˈgælɪ̥ti‖ˌprɑː-/ *n* [U]

**prodigal**[2] *n humorous* someone who spends money carelessly and wastes their time

**pro·di·gious** /prəˈdɪdʒəs/ *adj* extremely or surprisingly large or powerful: *a prodigious feat* —**prodigiously** *adv*

**prod·i·gy** /ˈprɒdɪdʒi‖ˈprɑː-/ *n* [C] **1** a young person who is extremely clever or good at doing something: *a mathematical prodigy* | **a child/infant prodigy** *Mozart was a child prodigy.* **2** something strange and wonderful: [+ **of**] *prodigies of endurance*

1 **pro·duce**[1] /prəˈdjuːs‖-ˈduːs/ *v*
1 **1 ▶NATURALLY◀** [T] to grow something or make it naturally: *Canada produces high-quality wheat.* | *The pancreas produces insulin in the body.* | *More sun produces riper grapes.*
**2 ▶RESULT◀** [T] to make something happen or develop, or have a particular result or effect: *New medicines are producing remarkable results in the treatment of cancer.* | *a remark which produced howls of protest* | *courses designed to produce better teachers*
**3 ▶SHOW◀** [T] to show, bring out, or offer something so it can be seen or considered: *When challenged, he suddenly produced a gun.* | *She produced no evidence in support of her argument.*
**4 ▶WITH SKILL◀** [T] to make something using skill and imagination: *In this play Eliot produces some of his most expressive poetry.* | *Diane produced a fantastic meal.*
**5 ▶GOODS◀** [I,T] to make things to be sold: *The factory produces an incredible 100 cars per hour.* | *Gas can be produced from coal.* —see also MASS-PRODUCED
**6 ▶PLAY/FILM◀** [T] to control the preparation of a play, film etc and then show it to the public: *Jane's play was produced at a London theatre.* —see also PRODUCER (2)
**7 ▶BABY◀** [T] to have a baby: *Anthea felt pressure from the family to produce a son.*
**8 ▶MATHS◀** [T] *technical* to lengthen or continue a line to a point, in GEOMETRY —see also PRODUCTION

**prod·uce**[2] /ˈprɒdjuːs‖ˈproʊduːs/ *n* [U] something that has been produced, especially by growing or farming: *agricultural produce* | *mangoes labelled 'produce of India'* —see PRODUCTION (USAGE)

3 **pro·duc·er** /prəˈdjuːsə‖-ˈduːsər/ *n* [C] **1** a person, company, or country that makes or grows goods, foods, or materials: [+ **of**] *England is a producer of high quality wool.* | **a coffee/wine/car etc producer** *one of the world's largest beef producers* —compare CONSUMER **2** someone who has general control of the preparation of a play, film, or broadcast, but who does not direct the actors: *Ned's been the news producer at Channel 7 for some time now.* —see PRODUCTION (USAGE)

1 **prod·uct** /ˈprɒdʌkt‖ˈprɑː-/ *n* **1** [C,U] something useful
1 that is made in a factory, grown, or taken from nature: *A product with a strong brand name is very important for good sales.* | *investing in product development* | *Demand for products like coal and steel is declining.* | *I'm allergic to dairy products.* —see PRODUCTION (USAGE) **2 the product of a)** someone whose behavior, opinions etc can be explained by their experiences: *Although he reacted violently against the society of his day, Nietsche's philosophy is a direct product of the Germany of that time.* **b)** something that is a result of someone's actions or of good or bad conditions: *Today's housing problems are the product of years of neglect.* **3** [C] *technical* the number you get by multiplying two or more numbers in MATHEMATICS: [+ **of**] *The product of 3 times 5 is 15.* **4** [C] *technical* a new chemical compound produced by chemical action

1 **pro·duc·tion** /prəˈdʌkʃən/ *n* **1** [U] the process of mak-
1 ing or growing things to be sold as products, or the amount that is produced: *The production of consumer goods has increased throughout the world.* | *Smoking is banned in the factory's production areas.* | **production costs/manager/process etc** *Production costs for the plane were too high.* | **go into (full) production** (=begin to be produced in large numbers) *The prototype engines never went into production* **2** [U] the act or process of making something new, or of bringing something into existence: *The skin's natural production of oil slows down as we get older.* **3** [C] something produced by skill or imagination, especially a play, film, or broadcast: *the new Shakespeare production at the Arts Theatre* **4** [U] the act of showing something: *Entrance is permitted only on production of a ticket.* **5 make a production (out) of sth** *informal* to do something in a way that takes more effort than is necessary: *They only want a sandwich, Bella, don't make a production out of it!*

**USAGE NOTE: PRODUCTION**

WORD CHOICE: **production, product, produce, producer**.

**Production** [U] is the process in which things are made, usually with the help of people, or in a factory: *We need to increase production* (NOT *the production*). | *mass production of computers*

A **production** [C] is a play, film etc made for the theatre, television, or radio etc: *a new production of 'King Lear'*

A **product** [C] is something that is made to be sold, often in a factory, or a natural substance like wood, coal etc that is taken from the ground or land to sell: *Glaxo produces a lot of pharmaceutical products.* | *food products such as cakes and ketchup* | *The country's main products are timber, coal and sugar.* **Product** can also be used to show where something is made, for example on a whiskey bottle you might see: *Product of Scotland*

In business, selling and advertising language, a wider range of things are beginning to be called products. For example a life insurance company might call the services it sells its products.

**Produce** [U] (which is pronounced differently from the verb) is a general word for food grown, especially on farms, and sold without being changed much: *He works in the produce section at the local supermarket.*

If a person, company or country produces something, they are a **producer** [C]: *Brazil, the world's most important producer of coffee.*

**production line** /ˈ·ˈ·· ·/ *n* [C] an arrangement of machines and workers in a factory where each worker or machine does one job in the making of a product and it is then passed on to the next worker or machine; ASSEMBLY LINE

**production num·ber** /·ˈ·· ˌ··/ *n* [C] a scene in a MUSICAL involving many people singing and dancing

**production plat·form** /·ˈ·· ˌ··/ *n* [C] a large piece of equipment standing on very long legs, used for getting oil out of the ground under the sea; OIL RIG

**pro·duc·tive** /prəˈdʌktɪv/ *adj* **1** producing or achieving a lot: *Most of us are more productive in the morning.* | *productive land* | *a productive meeting* (=having useful results) —opposite UNPRODUCTIVE **2** producing goods, crops, or wealth: *Increased demand means developing more productive capacity in the factory.* **3 productive of sth** *formal* causing or producing something: *Few ideas have been more productive of controversy than the redistribution of wealth.* —**productively** *adv* —**productiveness** *n* [U]

**pro·duc·tiv·i·ty** /ˌprɒdʌkˈtɪvɪ̥ti, -dək-‖ˌprɑː-/ *n* [U] the rate at which goods are produced, and the amount produced, compared with the work, time, and money needed to produce them: *Management is always seeking ways to increase worker productivity.* | *a productivity bonus*

**prof** /prɒf‖prɑːf/ *n* [C] **1** *informal* a PROFESSOR **2 Prof** the written abbreviation of PROFESSOR

**pro·fane**[1] /prəˈfeɪn/ *adj* **1** showing disrespect for God or for holy things, using rude words, or religious words wrongly: *a profane action | uttering profane curses* **2** *formal* not religious, ordinary or holy but dealing with human life: *sacred and profane art* —opposite SACRED —**profanely** *adv*

**profane**[2] *v* [T] *formal* to treat something holy in a disrespectful way —**profanation** /ˌprɒfəˈneɪʃən‖ˌprɑː-/ *n* [C,U]

**pro·fan·i·ty** /prəˈfænəti/ *n plural* **profanities** [C,U] **1** rude words, or religious words used wrongly **2** an act of showing disrespect for God or for holy things

P

**pro·fess** /prəˈfes/ *v* [T] *formal* **1** [T] to make a claim about something, especially a false one: **profess to do sth** *Leon professes to love his son, but he shows precious little evidence of it.* | **profess to be sth** *Tusker professed to be an expert on Islamic art.* **2** to declare a personal feeling or belief openly and freely: *Rodin always professed his admiration for Greek and Gothic sculpture.* | **profess yourself (to be) sth** *The composer professed himself to be delighted with the way we played his work.* **3** [T] to have a religion or belief: *Matt professed no religion.*

**pro·fessed** /prəˈfest/ *adj* [only before noun] *formal* **1** clearly stating what you believe: *a professed atheist* **2** pretended, rather than real or sincere: *Holly's professed uncertainty* —**professedly** /prəˈfesədli/ *adv*

S3 W3 **pro·fes·sion** /prəˈfeʃən/ *n* [C] **1** a job that needs special education and training: *What made you choose law as a profession?* —see JOB (USAGE) **2 by profession** as your job: *Castillo is a social worker by profession.* **3** all the people in a particular profession [also + plural verb *BrE*]: *The medical profession are divided on the main causes of heart attacks.* **4** a declaration of your belief, opinion, or feeling: *His speech was simply a profession of old-fashioned socialism.* **5 the oldest profession** *humorous* the job of being a PROSTITUTE

S2 W1 **pro·fes·sion·al**[1] /prəˈfeʃənəl/ *adj*
**1** ►**JOB**◄ [only before noun, no comparative] connected with a job that needs special education and training: *What professional qualifications does he have? | on the basis of professional advice*
**2** ►**WELL TRAINED**◄ showing that someone has been well trained and is good at their work: *This business plan looks very professional. | a more professional approach to work*
**3** ►**PAID**◄ [no comparative] doing a job, sport or activity for money: *a professional tennis player | a professional army* | **turn professional** (=start to do something as a job) —compare AMATEUR[1] (1)
**4** ►**TEAM/EVENT**◄ [no comparative] done by or connected with people who are paid: *Jim's the manager of a professional hockey team. | The golf tournament is a professional event.* —compare AMATEUR[1] (1)
**5 professional person/man/woman etc** someone who works in a profession, or who has an important position in a company or business: *We'd prefer to rent the house to a professional couple.*
**6 a professional liar/complainer etc** *humorous* someone who lies or complains too much
**7 professional foul** *BrE* a FOUL (=a rule broken in a sport) done deliberately to gain some advantage

W3 **professional**[2] *n* [C] **1** someone who earns money by doing a job, sport, or activity that many other people do just for enjoyment: *Hurd signed as a professional in 1978.* —compare AMATEUR[2] **2** someone who works in a job that requires special education and training: *the relationship between health professionals and patients* **3** someone who has a lot of experience and does something very skilfully: *You read that like a real professional.* **4 tennis/golf/swimming etc professional** someone who is very good at a sport and is employed by a private club to teach its members

**pro·fes·sion·al·is·m** /prəˈfeʃənəlɪzəm/ *n* [U] **1** the skill and high standards of behaviour expected of a professional person: *The success of the orchestra is due to the professionalism of its members.* **2** the practice of using professional players in sports

**pro·fes·sion·al·ly** /prəˈfeʃənəli/ *adv* **1** as part of your work: *Many foreign students will go on to use their English professionally.* **2** in a way that shows high standards and good training: *Where did you learn to ski so professionally?* **3** as a paid job rather than just for enjoyment: *a chance to play football professionally*

**pro·fes·sor** /prəˈfesə‖-ər/ *n* [C] **1** *especially BrE* a teacher of the highest rank in a university department; FULL PROFESSOR *AmE*: *Thank you, Professor Barclay, for your comments. | my science professor | a professor of history* **2** *AmE* a teacher at a university or college: *Ted's a college professor. | Professor, can I ask you a question?* —see also ASSISTANT PROFESSOR, ASSOCIATE PROFESSOR **3** a title taken by some people who teach various skills: *Madame Clara, professor of dancing*

**USAGE NOTE: PROFESSOR**

BRITISH AND AMERICAN ENGLISH

In many countries all university teachers are called **professor**. In Britain **professor** is used only for members of the highest rank of university teachers: *a research professor | Professor Leech is in charge of the department here.* Lower ranks in a university are **lecturer**, **senior lecturer**, and **reader**.

In the US many more university teachers are called **professor**, which is used of any full member of the teaching staff of a university or college. There are three specific ranks: **associate professor**, **assistant professor**, and **full professor**.

School teachers are never called professors in English.

**pro·fes·so·ri·al** /ˌprɒfəˈsɔːriəl◂‖ˌprɑː-/ *adj* connected with the job of a professor, or considered typical of a professor: *His speech was clipped and precise – almost professorial.* —**professorially** *adv*

**pro·fes·sor·ship** /prəˈfesəʃɪp‖-sər-/ *n* [C] the job or position of a university or college professor: *a professorship in Japanese*

**prof·fer** /ˈprɒfə‖ˈprɑːfər/ *v* [T] *formal* **1** to offer something to someone, especially by holding it out in your hands: *Sarah sipped from the glass proffered by the attendant.* | **proffer sb sth** *Poirot proffered him a cigarette.* **2** to give someone advice, an explanation, etc: *the proffered invitation* —**proffer** *n* [C]

**pro·fi·cien·cy** /prəˈfɪʃənsi/ *n* [U] a high standard of ability and skill: [+ **in**] *a high level of proficiency in grammar*

**pro·fi·cient** /prəˈfɪʃənt/ *adj* able to do something well or skilfully: [+ **in/at**] *Martha's proficient in Swedish. | a proficient typist* —**proficiently** *adv*

**pro·file**[1] /ˈprəʊfaɪl‖ˈproʊ-/ *n* [C] **1** a side view of someone's head: *Dani has a lovely profile.* | **in profile** *I only saw her face in profile.* **2** a short description that gives important details about a person, a group of people, or a place: [+ **of**] *The company has an employee profile of everyone working for them. | We need a profile of the area: population, main roads, water supplies, etc.* **3 have a high profile/give sth a high profile** to be noticed by many people, or to make something get a lot of attention: *Jack runs a department with a high public profile.* **4 keep a low profile** to behave quietly and avoid doing things that will make people notice you **5** an edge or shape of something seen against a background: *the sharp profile of the western foothills against the sky* W

**profile**[2] *v* [T] to write or give a short description of someone or something: *The new editor was profiled in the Sunday paper.*

**pro·fil·ing** /ˈprəʊfaɪlɪŋ‖ˈproʊ-/ *n* **offender profiling** the process of studying a crime, especially a murder, and making judgments about the character of the person who did it

**prof·it**[1] /ˈprɒfət‖ˈprɑː-/ *n* **1** [C,U] money that you gain by selling things or doing business: *They sold the business* S W *and bought a yacht with the profits.* | *The profit each day from the snack bar is usually around $500.* | **make (a) profit** *The telephone companies are making handsome profits every day.* (=very large ones) | **at a profit** *They sold their house at a huge profit.* | **clear profit** *Suzanne made a clear profit of £200 on the car sale* | **net profit** (=after tax etc is paid) | **gross profit** (=before tax etc is paid) | **bring sth into profit** (=gain money from it) **2** [U] an advantage that you gain from doing something: *reading for profit and pleasure* —see also NON-PROFITMAKING

**profit²** *v* [T] *formal* to be useful or helpful to someone: *It will profit you nothing to follow his example.*

**profit by/from** sth *phr v* [T] to learn from something that happens, or get something good from a situation: *My wardrobe definitely profited from having a stylish older sister.*

**prof·it·a·bil·i·ty** /ˌprɒfɪ̈təˈbɪlɪ̈ti‖ˌprɑː-/ *n* [U] the state of producing a profit, or the degree to which a business or activity is profitable: *a decline in company profitability*

**prof·i·ta·ble** /ˈprɒfɪ̈təbəl‖ˈprɑː-/ *adj* producing a profit or a useful result: *The advertising campaign proved very profitable.* | *a highly profitable business* | *a profitable afternoon* —opposite UNPROFITABLE —**profitably** *adv*

**profit and loss ac·count** /ˌ·· · ˈ· ·ˌ·/ *n* [C] a financial statement showing a company's income, spending, and profit over a particular period

**prof·i·teer** /ˌprɒfɪ̈ˈtɪə‖ˌprɑːfɪ̈ˈtɪr/ *n* [C] someone who makes unfairly large profits, especially by selling things at very high prices when they are difficult to get: *black market profiteers* —**profiteer** *v* [I] —**profiteering** *n* [U]

**pro·fit·e·role** /prəˈfɪtərəʊl‖-roʊl/ *n* [C] *BrE* a small round PASTRY with a sweet filling and chocolate on the top

**prof·it·less** /ˈprɒfɪ̈tləs‖ˈprɑː-/ *adj* not making a profit, or not worth doing —**profitlessly** *adv*

**profit mar·gin** /ˈ·· ˌ··/ *n* [C] the difference between the cost of producing something and the price you sell it at

**profit shar·ing** /ˈ·· ˌ··/ *n* [U] a system by which all the people who work for a company share in its profits

**prof·li·gate¹** /ˈprɒflɪ̈gɪ̈t‖ˈprɑː-/ *adj formal* **1** wasting money in a silly and careless way: *profligate spending of the taxpayer's money* **2** behaving in an immoral way and not caring about it at all —**profligacy** *n* [U]

**profligate²** *n* [C] *formal* someone who is prolifigate

**pro for·ma** /prəʊ ˈfɔːmə‖proʊ ˈfɔːr-/ *adj adv Latin* if something is approved, accepted etc pro forma, this is part of the usual way of doing things, but does not involve any actual choice or decision: *pro forma approval*

**pro forma in·voice** /· ˌ·· ˈ··/ *n* [C] a bill sent to a customer to show what a price would be if he made an order; QUOTATION

**pro·found** /prəˈfaʊnd/ *adj* **1** showing strong, serious feelings: *I owe you a profound apology.* **2** having a strong influence or effect: *The mother's behavior has a profound impact on the developing child.* **3** showing great knowledge and understanding: *a profound remark* | *Jenner is a profound thinker.* **4** *literary* deep or far below the surface of something: *Her work engages something profound in the human psyche.* **5** *technical* complete: *profound deafness* —**profoundly** *adv*: *profoundly disturbing news*

**pro·fun·di·ty** /prəˈfʌndɪ̈ti/ *n formal* **1** [U] the quality of knowing and understanding a lot, or having strong, serious feelings: *a young woman of extraordinary profundity* | *Fairy tales have a profundity absent in most children's literature.* **2** [C usually plural] something that someone says that shows this quality: *The profundities of his speech were lost on the young audience.*

**pro·fuse** /prəˈfjuːs/ *adj* **1** given, flowing, or growing freely and in large quantities: *profuse tears* **2** too eager or generous with your praise, thanks etc: [+ **in**] *Stella was profuse in her thanks.* —**profusely** *adv*: *sweating profusely in the heat* —**profuseness** *n* [U]

**pro·fu·sion** /prəˈfjuːʒən/ *n* [singular, U] a supply or amount that is almost too large: [+ **of**] *The house was overflowing with a profusion of strange ornaments.* | **in profusion** *Corn marigolds grow in profusion in the fields.*

**pro·gen·i·tor** /prəʊˈdʒenɪ̈tə‖proʊˈdʒenɪ̈tər/ *n* [C] *technical* **1** a person or animal that lived a long time ago, to whom someone or something living now is related; ANCESTOR **2** *formal* someone who first thought of an idea a long time ago; PRECURSOR: [+ **of**] *a progenitor of modern music*

**prog·e·ny** /ˈprɒdʒɪ̈ni‖ˈprɑː-/ *n* [U] **1** *technical or formal* the DESCENDANTS of a person, animal, or plant form, or the things that can develop from something else: *The drug-resistant cells' progeny are also drug-resistant.* **2** *old-fashioned or humorous* someone's children: *Sarah with her numerous progeny*

**pro·ges·ter·one** /prəʊˈdʒestərəʊn‖proʊˈdʒestəroʊn/ *n* [U] a female sex HORMONE that is produced by a woman when she is going to have a baby and is also used in CONTRACEPTIVE drugs

**prog·na·thous** /prɒgˈneɪθəs‖prɑːg-/ *adj technical* with a jaw that sticks out more than the rest of your face

**prog·no·sis** /prɒgˈnəʊsɪ̈s‖prɑːgˈnoʊ-/ *n plural* **prognoses** [C] **1** *technical* a doctor's opinion of how an illness or disease will develop: *The doctor's prognosis for Mum wasn't hopeful.* —compare DIAGNOSIS **2** *formal* a judgement about the future based on information or experience: [+ **of**] *a hopeful prognosis of the country's future development*

**prog·nos·ti·cate** /prɒgˈnɒstɪ̈keɪt‖prɑːgˈnɑː-/ *v* [T] to say what will happen, or to be a sign of what will happen —**prognostication** /prɒgˌnɒstɪ̈ˈkeɪʃən‖prɑːgˌnɑː-/ *n* [C,U]

**pro·gram¹** /ˈprəʊgræm‖ˈproʊ-/ *n* [C] **1** a set of instructions given to a computer to make it perform an operation: *a new program for forecasting sales figures* **2** the American spelling of PROGRAMME 

**program²** *v* **programmed, programming** [T] **1** to give a computer a set of instructions that it can use to perform a particular operation: **program sth to do sth** *Scientists are trying to program computers to think in the same way as humans.* **2** the American spelling of programme —see also PROGRAMMER

**pro·gram·ma·ble** /ˈprəʊgræməbəl‖ˈproʊ-/ *adj* able to be controlled by a computer or electronic program: *a programmable heating system*

**pro·gramme¹** *BrE*, **program** *AmE* /ˈprəʊgræm‖ˈproʊ-/ *n* [C] **1** an important plan, especially one organized by a government or large organization: *a United Nations programme to control the spread of AIDS* | *the US space program* **2** a show or performance on television or radio, especially one that is played regularly: *Northern Exposure is my favorite TV program.* | [+ **about**] *There's a programme on about organic gardening.* **3** a set of planned activities in education or training, with a specific purpose: *Stanford University's MBA program* | *Lucy's new fitness programme includes a 5 mile jog every morning.* **4** a printed description of what will happen at a play, concert etc and of the people who will be performing **5** the planned order of activities or events at a performance or meeting; SCHEDULE¹ (1) *The next race on today's programme is the King George V Handicap.* **6** a series of actions done in a particular order by a machine such as a washing machine: *The light goes off when it finishes its program.* —see also PROGRAM¹ 

**programme²** *BrE*, **program** *AmE* *v* [T] **1 be programmed** to be made to behave or think in a particular way because of the influence of a society, group, or situation: [+ **to**] *Are girls programmed at an early age not to be interested in science subjects?* **2** to set a machine to operate in a particular way: *I've programmed the video to come on at ten.* —see also PROGRAM¹ **3** to arrange for something to happen as part of a series of planned events or activities: *What's programmed for this afternoon?*

**programmed course** /ˌ·· ˈ·/ *n* [C] a course of study that is part of programmed learning

**programmed learn·ing** /ˌ·· ˈ··/ *n* [U] a method of learning in which the subject to be learned is divided into small parts, and you have to get one part right before you can go on to the next

**programme mu·sic** *BrE*, **program music** *AmE* /ˈ·· ˌ··/ *n* [U] descriptive music which uses sound to suggest a story, picture etc

**pro·gram·mer** /ˈprəʊgræmə‖ˈproʊgræmər/ *n* [C] someone whose job is to write computer PROGRAMS

**pro·gram·ming** /ˈprəʊgræmɪŋ‖ˈproʊ-/ *n* [U] **1** the activity of writing PROGRAMS for computers: *programming languages* **2** television or radio programmes, or the activity of producing them: *nearly 200 hours of sports programming*

S2 W2 **pro·gress¹** /ˈprəʊgres‖ˈprɑː-/ *n* **1** [U] the process of getting better at doing something, or getting closer to finishing or achieving something: [+ **of/on/towards**] *Nico had been candid with Stern about the progress of the investigation.* | *tests designed to monitor the student's progress* **2 make progress a)** to get better at doing something or come closer to finishing or achieving something: *Nick has made good progress with his studies this year.* | *I'm afraid we're not making much progress.* **b)** to move towards a place: *By nighttime we had still made very little progress.* **3** [U] change towards a better society because of developments in science or fairer methods of social organization: *the great march of progress* **4 in progress** *formal* happening now, and not yet finished: *No Talking. Examination in Progress.* **5** [U] slow or difficult movement towards a place: *We watched with apprehension their progress across the face of the cliff.* **6** [C] *old use* a journey, especially by a king or queen

**progress²** *v* [I] **1** to develop over a period of time and become something better or more complete: *Work on the ship progressed quickly.* | *I asked the nurse how my son was progressing.* | [+ **to**] *Cindy has progressed to reading on her own.* **2** if an activity or situation progresses, it continues to happen or develop gradually: *As the meeting progressed, Nina grew more and more bored.* **3** to move forward slowly: *Our taxi seemed to be progressing with agonizing slowness.* **4** to move on from doing one thing to doing another: [+ **to**] *We started with a bottle of wine, and then progressed to whisky.* —compare REGRESS

**pro·gres·sion** /prəˈgreʃən/ *n* **1** [U] a gradual process of change or development: *They offer rapid career progression.* | **progression from sth to sth** *The progression from infection to disease can take up to 7 years.* **2** [U] movement towards a goal or particular place: *the river's stately progression towards the Gulf of Mexico* **3** a number of things coming one after the other —see also ARITHMETIC PROGRESSION, GEOMETRIC PROGRESSION

**pro·gres·sive¹** /prəˈgresɪv/ *adj* **1** supporting new or modern ideas and methods, especially in politics and education: *a progressive administration* | *progressive and forward-looking policies* **2** happening or developing gradually over a period of time: *the progressive elimination of rural poverty* | *Britain's progressive decline as a world power* **3** the progressive form of a verb is used to show that an action or activity is continuing to happen, and is shown in English by the verb 'be', followed by a PRESENT PARTICIPLE, as in 'I was waiting for the bus' —**progressively** *adv*: *The situation became progressively worse.* —**progressiveness** *n* [U]

**progressive²** *n* [C] someone with modern ideas who wants to change things

**progressive tax** /ˌ·· ˈ·/ *n* [singular] a tax that takes a larger PERCENTAGE of money from people with higher incomes than from people with lower incomes —compare REGRESSIVE TAX

**progress re·port** /ˈ·· ·ˌ·/ *n* [C] a statement about how something, especially work, is advancing or developing

**pro·hib·it** /prəˈhɪbɪt‖proʊ-/ *v* [T] **1** to officially stop an activity by making it illegal or against the rules: *Smoking is strictly prohibited inside the factory.* | **prohibit sb from doing sth** *Nuclear powers are prohibited from selling this technology.* **2** to make something impossible or prevent it from happening: *High costs had prohibited the building work from being completed.*

**pro·hi·bi·tion** /ˌprəʊhɪˈbɪʃən‖ˌproʊ-/ *n* **1** [U] the act of officially stopping something by law: [+ **of**] *prohibition of the sale of firearms* **2** [C] an order stopping something: [+ **on/against**] *a prohibition on Sunday trading* **3 Prohibition** the period from 1919 to 1933 in the US when the production and sale of alcoholic drinks was forbidden by law

**pro·hi·bi·tion·ist** /ˌprəʊhɪˈbɪʃənɪst‖ˌproʊ-/ *n* [C] someone who supported Prohibition —**prohibitionism** *n* [U]

**pro·hib·i·tive** /prəˈhɪbɪtɪv‖proʊ-/ *adj* **1** prohibitive prices are so high that they prevent people from buying something: *The cost of land in Tokyo is prohibitive.* **2** a prohibitive tax or rule prevents people from doing things: *a prohibitive tax on imports* —**prohibitively** *adv*: *prohibitively expensive*

**pro·hib·i·to·ry** /prəˈhɪbɪtəri‖proʊˈhɪbɪtɔːri/ *adj* intended to stop something

**proj·ect¹** /ˈprɒdʒekt‖ˈprɑː-/ *n* [C] **1** an important and carefully planned piece of work, that is intended to build or produce something new, or to deal with a problem: *the Channel Tunnel project* | *a long-term project to help the homeless* **2** a part of a school course that involves careful study of a particular subject over a period of time: [+ **on**] *We're doing a project on pollution.* **3** also **the projects** *AmE informal* a HOUSING PROJECT S W

**pro·ject²** /prəˈdʒekt/ *v*

**1** ► **CALCULATE** ◄ [T] to calculate the size, amount, or rate of something as it will be in the future, using the information you have now: *The company projected an annual growth rate of 3%.* | *projected sales forecasts*

**2** ► **STICK OUT** ◄ [I,T] to stick out beyond an edge or surface: [+ **out/from/through etc**] *The huge guns projected outwards from the deck of the ship.*

**3** ► **FILM** ◄ [T] to make the picture of a film, photograph etc appear in a larger form on a SCREEN¹ (2) or flat surface

**4** ► **YOURSELF** ◄ [T] to make other people have a particular idea about you: **project an image** *Regina always projects an image of quiet self-confidence* | **project yourself** *You'll need to project yourself well in the interview.*

**5** ► **FEELING** ◄ [T] *technical* to avoid dealing with your own feelings by imagining that someone else is feeling them: **project sth on/onto sb** *You're projecting your insecurity onto me.*

**6** ► **PLAN** ◄ **be projected** to be planned to happen in the future: *A visit by President Clinton is projected for March.*

**7** ► **THROW** ◄ [T] *technical* to throw something up or forward with great force

**8** ► **PICTURE** ◄ *technical* **a)** to make a picture of a solid object on a flat surface **b)** to make a map using this method

**9 project yourself into the future/past etc** to imagine that you are in the future, past etc: *I kept trying to project myself back into a time when I thought those kind of parties were fun.*

**10 project your voice** to speak clearly and loudly so that you can be heard by everyone in a big hall or room

**pro·jec·tile** /prəˈdʒektaɪl‖-tl/ *n* [C] an object that is thrown or is fired from a weapon, such as a bullet, stone, or SHELL¹ (2,3) —**projectile** *adj*

**pro·jec·tion** /prəˈdʒekʃən/ *n* **1** [C] a calculation of the amount or rate of something as it will be in the future, which is used for making official plans: [+ **of**] *projections of declining natural gas production* **2** [C] a statement about what will happen, based on information available now: *Early projections show a three point lead for the Socialists.* **3** [C] *formal* something that sticks out from S a surface: *small projections of weathered rock on the hillside* **4** [U] the act of projecting a film or picture: *projection equipment* **5** [U] *technical* the act of imagining that someone else is feeling what you are in fact feeling **6** [C] *technical* an image of something that has been projected, especially an image of the world's surface on a map —see also MERCATOR PROJECTION

**pro·jec·tion·ist** /prəˈdʒekʃənɪst/ *n* [C] someone whose job is to operate the projector in a cinema

**pro·jec·tor** /prəˈdʒektə‖-ər/ *n* [C] a piece of equipment that makes a film appear on a SCREEN[1] (2a) or a flat surface

**pro·lapse** /ˈprəʊlæps, prəʊˈlæps‖proʊˈlæps, proʊ-/ *n* [C] *technical* the falling down or slipping of an inner part of your body, such as the WOMB, from its usual position

**prole** /prəʊl‖proʊl/ *n* [C] *BrE informal* an insulting word for a working class person

**pro·le·tar·i·an** /ˌprəʊlɪˈteəriən◂‖ˌproʊlɪˈter-/ *adj* concerning or involving the proletariat

**pro·le·tar·i·at** /ˌprəʊlɪˈteəriət‖ˌproʊlɪˈter-/ *n* **the proletariat** the class of workers who own no property and work for wages, especially in factories, building things etc

**pro-life** /ˌ· ˈ·/ *adj* someone who is pro-life is opposed to ABORTION and uses this word to describe their views

**pro-lif·er** /ˌ· ˈ··/ *n* [C] a member of a pro-life group

**pro·lif·e·rate** /prəˈlɪfəreɪt/ *v* [I] if something proliferates it increases rapidly and spreads to many different places: *Self-help groups have proliferated all over London.*

**pro·lif·e·ra·tion** /prəˌlɪfəˈreɪʃən/ *n* **1** [singular, U] a rapid increase in the amount or number of something: [+ **of**] *the proliferation of nuclear weapons | a proliferation of cafes and restaurants* **2** [U] *technical* the very fast growth of new parts of a living thing, such as cells or BUDS

**pro·lif·ic** /prəˈlɪfɪk/ *adj* **1** a prolific artist, writer etc produces many works of art, books etc **2** an animal or plant that is prolific produces many babies or many other plants **3** *literary* existing in large numbers: *the prolific bird life* —**prolifically** /-kli/ *adv*

**pro·lix** /ˈprəʊlɪks‖proʊˈlɪks/ *adj formal* a prolix piece of writing has too many words and is boring

**PROLOG** /ˈprəʊlɒg‖ˈproʊlɔːg, -lɑːg/ *n* [U] *trademark* a computer language that is similar to human language

**pro·logue** /ˈprəʊlɒg‖ˈproʊlɔːg, -lɑːg/ *n* [C usually singular] **1** the introduction to a play, a long poem etc **2** *literary* an act or event that leads to a much more important event —compare EPILOGUE

**pro·long** /prəˈlɒŋ‖-ˈlɔːŋ/ *v* [T] **1** to deliberately make something such as a feeling or activity last longer: *I was trying to think of some way to prolong the conversation.* **2** **prolong the agony** *informal* to delay telling someone something that they very much want to know: *There's no point in prolonging the agony. The situation won't get any better.*

**pro·lon·ga·tion** /ˌprəʊlɒŋˈgeɪʃən‖ˌproʊlɔːŋ-/ *n* **1** [U] the act of making something last longer **2** [C + **of**] something added to another thing which makes it longer

**pro·longed** /prəˈlɒŋd‖-ˈlɔːŋd/ *adj* continuing for a long time: *a prolonged absence*

**prom** /prɒm‖prɑːm/ *n* [C] **1** *AmE* a formal dance party for HIGH SCHOOL students, often held at the end of a school year **2** *BrE informal* a PROMENADE (1) **3** *BrE informal* a PROMENADE CONCERT

**prom·e·nade** /ˌprɒməˈnɑːd◂, ˈprɒmənɑːd‖ˌprɑːməˈneɪd◂/ *n* [C] **1** *BrE* a wide road next to the beach where people can walk for pleasure **2** *old-fashioned* a walk for pleasure in a public place

**promenade con·cert** /ˌ··ˈ· ˌ··, ˈ··· ˌ··/ *n* [C] *BrE* a concert at which many of the listeners stand rather than sit

**promenade deck** /ˌ··ˈ· ·, ˈ··· ˌ·/ *n* [C] the upper level of a ship where people can walk for pleasure

**prom·i·nence** /ˈprɒmɪnəns‖ˈprɑː-/ *n* **1** [U] the fact of being important and well-known: **come to/gain prominence** (=become important and well-known) *Gandhi first came to prominence in South Africa in the 1920s.* **2** **give sth prominence/give prominence to sth** to put something in a position where it is easily noticed because you think it is important: *The topic didn't deserve the prominence it was given.* **3** *formal* a part or place that is higher or larger than what is around it

**prom·i·nent** /ˈprɒmɪnənt‖ˈprɑː-/ *adj* **1** [C] well-known and important: *a prominent Russian scientist* | **play a prominent role** *Mandela played a prominent role in the early years of the ANC* **2** something that is prominent is large and sticks out: *a prominent nose* **3** **a prominent place/position** somewhere that is easily seen and is usually used for things that are important: *The Kaiser's photo displayed in a prominent position on the piano*

**pro·mis·cu·ous** /prəˈmɪskjuəs/ *adj* **1** having sex with a lot of people: *Single men were the most promiscuous group.* **2** *old use* made of many different parts **3** *old use* not choosing carefully; INDISCRIMINATE —**promiscuously** *adv* —**promiscuity** /ˌprɒmɪˈskjuːɪti‖ˌprɑː-/ *n* [U]

**prom·ise**[1] /ˈprɒmɪs‖ˈprɑː-/ *v* **1** [I,T] to tell someone that you will definitely do something or that something will happen: **promise (that)** *Hurry up, we promised that we wouldn't be late.* | **promise sb (that)** *You promised me the car would be ready on Monday.* | **I/we promise** *"Promise me you won't do anything stupid." "I promise."* | **promise to do sth** *The children have promised to give us a hand with the packing.* | **promise sb sth** (=promise to give someone something) *The company promised us a bonus this year.* | **Promise?** *spoken* (=used to ask if someone promises) *"I'll be back by 1.00." "Promise?" "Yes! Don't worry."* | **promise sth to sb** *I can't give you the book – I've promised it to Ian.* | **as promised** (=at the time or place that is promised) *Here you are – one new watch as promised.* | **I promise you** *spoken* (=I warn you) *I promise you, the work won't be easy.* **2** [T] to make you expect that something will happen: **promise to be** *Tonight's meeting promises to be a difficult one | dark clouds promising showers later* **3** **promise sb the moon/the earth** to promise to give someone something that is impossible for you to give **4** **I can't promise anything** *spoken* used to tell someone that you will try to do what they want, but may not be able to: *I'll try my best, but I can't promise anything.* S 2 W 2

**promise**[2] *n* **1** [C] a statement that you will definitely do something or that something will definitely happen: *I'll never lie to you again. That's a promise.* | [+ **of**] *a promise of help* | **a promise to do sth** *They've given a promise to introduce equal pay for women.* | [+ **that**] *I kept thinking of my mother's promise that she'd read me the story if I was good.* | **keep/break a promise** (=to do or fail to do something you promised) *Don't make promises you can't keep.* | *You broke your promise to give up smoking.* **2** [U] signs that something or someone will be good or successful: *a young man full of promise* | [+ **of**] *the promise of future profits* | **show promise** (=to be likely to become very good) *My son shows great promise as a chess player.* S 3 W 3

**Promised Land** /ˌ·· ˈ·/ *n* [singular] **1** a situation or condition that you have wanted for a long time because it will bring you happiness and security: *the promised land of full employment* **2** the land of Canaan, which was promised by God to Abraham and his people in the Bible

**prom·is·ing** /ˈprɒmɪsɪŋ‖ˈprɑː-/ *adj* showing signs of being successful in the future: *a promising career in law | a promising young actor* —**promisingly** *adv*

**prom·is·so·ry note** /ˈprɒmɪsəri ˌnəʊt‖ˈprɑːmɪsɔːri ˌnoʊt/ *n* [C] a document promising to pay money before a particular date

**pro·mo** /ˈprəʊməʊ‖ˈproʊmoʊ/ *plural* **promos** *n* [C] *informal* a short film that advertises an event or product

**prom·on·to·ry** /ˈprɒməntəri‖ˈprɑːməntɔːri/ *n* [C] a high long narrow piece of land which goes out into the sea —see picture on page 835

**pro·mote** /prəˈməʊt‖-ˈmoʊt/ *v* [T] **1** to help something

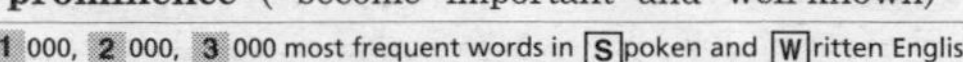

to develop and be successful: *a meeting to promote trade between Taiwan and the U.K.*|*Fertilizer promotes leaf growth.* **2** [usually passive] to give someone a better, more responsible job in a company: **promote sb to sth** *Helen was promoted to senior manager.* —opposite DEMOTE **3** to make sure people know about a new product, film etc by offering it at a reduced price or advertising it on television **4** to be responsible for arranging a large public event such as a concert or a sports game **5** to try to persuade people to believe or support an idea or way of doing things: *a passionate speech promoting equality* **6 be promoted** if a sports team is promoted, they play in a different group of better teams the next year —opposite RELEGATE (2)

**pro·mot·er** /prəˈməʊtə‖-ˈmoʊtər/ *n* [C] **1** someone who arranges and advertises concerts or sports events **2** someone who tries to make people believe or support an idea or way of doing things: *promoters of solar energy*

S3 W3 **pro·mo·tion** /prəˈməʊʃən‖-ˈmoʊ-/ *n* **1** [C,U] a move to a more important job or rank in a company or organization: *I want a job with good promotion prospects.*|[**+ to**] *Your promotion to Senior Editor is now official.* **2** [C,U] an activity intended to help sell a product, or the product that is being promoted: *a winter sales promotion* **3** [U] the activity of persuading people to support an idea or way of doing things: *the promotion of equal opportunities* **4** [U] the activity of helping something develop and succeed: *the promotion of technology development centers* **5** [U] a move by a sports team from playing in one group of teams to playing in a better group —opposite **relegation** (RELEGATE (2))

**pro·mo·tion·al** /prəˈməʊʃənəl‖-ˈmoʊ-/ *adj* promotional films, events etc are made or organized to advertise something: *a series of interviews and promotional appearances*

**prompt**[1] /prɒmpt‖prɑːmpt/ *v* **1** [T] to make someone decide to do something, especially something that they had been thinking of doing: **prompt sb to do sth** *Her situation prompted me to do something about getting a new job.* **2** to make people say or do something as a reaction: *What prompted that remark?* **3** [T] to help a speaker who pauses, by suggesting how to continue: *"I can't decide...." said Beatrice. "Decide what?" prompted Marlon.* **4** [I,T] to remind an actor or actress of the next words in a speech

**prompt**[2] *adj* **1** done quickly, immediately, or at the right time: *prompt delivery of your purchases* **2** [not before noun] someone who is prompt arrives at the right time or does something on time: *Lunch is at two. Try to be prompt.*|*Grandma is always prompt in answering letters.* —**promptly** *adv*: *The performance begins promptly at nine o' clock.* —**promptness** *n* [U]

**prompt**[3] *adv informal* happening at the exact time: *We're meeting at 6.30 prompt, so don't be late.*

**prompt**[4] *n* [C] **1** a word or words said to an actor in a play, to help them remember what to say **2** a sign on a computer screen which shows that the computer has finished one operation and is ready to begin the next: *When you see the 'C' prompt type 'WP'.*

**prompt·er** /ˈprɒmptə‖ˈprɑːmptər/ *n* [C] someone who tells actors in a play what words to say when they forget

**proms** /prɒmz‖prɑːmz/ *n BrE informal* **the proms** a series of PROMENADE CONCERTS

**prom·ul·gate** /ˈprɒməlgeɪt‖ˈprɑː-/ *v* [T] **1** to spread an idea or belief to as many people as possible **2** to make a new law come into effect by announcing it officially —**promulgator** *n* [C] —**promulgation** /ˌprɒməlˈgeɪʃən‖ˌprɑː-/ *n* [U]

**pron** the written abbreviation of PRONOUN

**prone** /prəʊn‖proʊn/ *adj* **1** likely to do something or suffer from something, especially something bad or harmful: [**+ to**] *Some plants are prone to a particular disease.*|**prone to do sth**|*Kids are all prone to eat junk food.*|**strike-prone/accident-prone etc** *I never saw a girl more accident-prone.* **2** *formal* lying down with the front of your body facing down: *Colley lay prone in his bunk.* —compare PROSTRATE[1] (1) —**proneness** *n* [U]

**prong** /prɒŋ‖prɒːŋ/ *n* [C] **1** a thin sharp point of something such as a fork that has several points: *a pitchfork with three huge prongs* **2 two-pronged, three-pronged etc a)** having two, three etc prongs **b)** a two-pronged or three-pronged attack is made on two or three parts of something at the same time **3** *AmE slang* a PENIS (=male sexual organ)

**pro·nom·i·nal** /prəʊˈnɒmɪ̣nəl‖proʊˈnɑː-/ *adj technical* related to or used like a PRONOUN —**pronominally** *adv*

**pro·noun** /ˈprəʊnaʊn‖ˈproʊ-/ *n* [C] a word that is used instead of a noun or noun phrase, such as 'he' instead of Peter or instead of 'the man' —see also DEMONSTRATIVE PRONOUN, PERSONAL PRONOUN

**pro·nounce** /prəˈnaʊns/ *v* **1** [T] to make the sound of a letter, word etc, especially in the correct way: *How do you pronounce your name?* **2** to officially state that something is true: **pronounce sb/sth (to be) sth** *The victim was pronounced dead on arrival.*|*I now pronounce you man and wife.* **3** [I,T + **on/against**] *law* to give a legal judgment **4 pronounce on/upon sth** to state your opinion about a subject, especially when you do not really know much about it: *I don't want to listen to him pronounce on wine all night.* **5 pronounce sentence** *law* if a judge pronounces sentence, he or she tells the court what kind of punishment a criminal will have

**pro·nounce·a·ble** /prəˈnaʊnsəbəl/ *adj* a word, name etc that is pronounceable is easy to say —opposite UNPRONOUNCEABLE

**pro·nounced** /prəˈnaʊnst/ *adj* very strong or noticeable: *a pronounced Polish accent*|*a pronounced effect in reducing crime* —**pronouncedly** /prəˈnaʊnsɪ̣dli/ *adv*

**pro·nounce·ment** /prəˈnaʊnsmənt/ *n* [C] *formal* an official public statement: *the Pope's latest pronouncement on birth control*

**pron·to** /ˈprɒntəʊ‖ˈprɑːntoʊ-/ *adv spoken* quickly or immediately: *Bring that hose over here, pronto!*

**pro·nun·ci·a·tion** /prəˌnʌnsiˈeɪʃən/ *n* **1** [C,U] the way in which a language or a particular word is pronounced: *Make sure you give each word its correct pronunciation.* **2** [singular, U] a particular person's way of pronouncing a word or words

**-proof** /pruːf/ *suffix* **1** *(in adjectives)* treated or made so as not to be harmed by something, or to protect people against something: *a bulletproof car*|*an ovenproof dish* (=that cannot be harmed by heat) **2** *(in verbs)* to treat or make something so that it cannot be harmed by something, or gives protection against it: *to soundproof a room* (=so that sound cannot get into or out of it)

**proof**[1] /pruːf/ *n* **1** [C,U] facts, information, documents etc that prove something is true: [**+ of**] *Bring a passport as proof of identity.*|[**+ (that)**] *Do you have any proof that this man stole your bag?*|**conclusive proof** (=that cannot be doubted)|**proof positive** (=definite proof) **2** [C] *technical* a printed copy of a piece of writing used to find and remove mistakes before the final printing is done: *Can you check these proofs?* **3** [C] a photograph that is used as a test copy before an official copy is made **4** [C] **a)** a test in MATHEMATICS of the correctness of a calculation **b)** a list of reasons that shows a THEOREM (=statement) in GEOMETRY to be true **5 the proof of the pudding (is in the eating)** used to say that you can only know whether something is good or bad after you have tried it **6** [U] *technical* the standard strength of some kinds of alcoholic drink compared with that of PROOF SPIRIT: *This gin is 15% under proof.* **7 put sth to the proof** to test the quality or strength of something 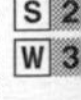

**proof**[2] *adj* **1 waterproof/bulletproof etc** something that is waterproof etc will not let water etc through it or into it: *a soundproof room* **2 child-proof/vandal-proof** not easily affected or damaged by someone or something: *a child-proof latch on the cupboard* **3 be proof against** to be too strong or good to be affected by something bad: *a faith that is proof against temptation*

**4 30° proof/40° proof etc** *BrE*, also **30 proof/40 proof etc** *AmE* whisky, bourbon etc that has a particular proof contains a specific amount of alcohol

**proof**[3] *v* [T usually passive] to treat a material with a substance in order to protect it against water, oil etc: [+ **against**] *climbing gear proofed against water*

**proof·read** /'pruːfˌriːd/ *past tense and past participle* **proofread** /-red/ *v* [I,T] to read through something written or printed in order to correct any errors in it —**proofreader** *n* [C]

**proof spir·it** /ˌ· '··/ *n* [U] a standard mixture of alcohol and water with which the strength of some acoholic drinks is compared for the purposes of taxation

**prop**[1] /prɒp‖prɑːp/ *v* **propped, propping** [T always + adv/prep] to support something by leaning it against something, or by putting something else under, next to, or behind it: **prop sth against/on** *He propped his bike against a tree.* | **prop sth open** *Give me something to prop the door open.*

**prop** sth ↔ **up** *phr v* [T] **1** to prevent something from falling by putting something against it or under it: *The builders are trying to prop up the crumbling walls of the church.* **2** if a government props up another government it helps it with financial or military support so that it can continue to exist **3 prop yourself up** to stand or sit straight by leaning against something

**prop**[2] *n* [C] **1** an object placed under or against something to hold it in a position —see also PIT PROP **2** a small object such as a book, weapon etc used by actors in a play or film **3** *informal* a short form of the word PROPELLER **4** something or someone that helps you to feel strong, or that an idea or system needs in order to exist: *The big house and the car were all props to his ego.*

**prop·a·gan·da** /ˌprɒpə'gændə‖ˌprɑː-/ *n* [U] false or partly false information used by a government or political party to make people agree with them: *pure Fascist propaganda* | *a propaganda film* | **propaganda campaign** (=an organised plan to spread propaganda) —**propagandize** also **ise** *BrE v* [I,T] —**propagandist** *n* [C]

**prop·a·gate** /'prɒpəgeɪt‖'prɑː-/ *v formal* **1** [I,T] to grow and produce new plants or to make a plant do this: *a species that propagates by spores* | *You can propagate these plants by root cuttings.* **2** [T] to spread an idea, belief etc to many people: *The group started a magazine to propagate its ideas.* **3** [T] if an animal, insect, or CELL etc propagates itself or is propagated, it increases in number by reproducing; REPRODUCE (1) —**propagation** /ˌprɒpə'geɪʃən‖ˌprɑː-/ *n* [U]

**prop·a·gat·or** /'prɒpəgeɪtə‖'prɑːpəgeɪtər/ *n* [C] **1** someone who spreads ideas, beliefs etc **2** a covered box of soil in which seeds are planted to grow quickly

**pro·pane** /'prəʊpeɪn‖'proʊ-/ *n* [U] a colourless gas used for both cooking and heating

**pro·pel** /prə'pel/ *v* **propelled, propelling** [T] to move, drive, or push something forward: *old ships propelled by steam* | *a rocket-propelled grenade* —see also PROPULSION

**pro·pel·lant**, **propellent** /prə'pelənt/ *n* [C,U] **1** an explosive for firing a bullet or ROCKET[1] **2** gas pressed into a small space in a container of liquid, which pushes out the liquid when the pressure is taken away —**propellant** *adj*

**pro·pel·ler** /prə'pelə‖-ər/ *n* [C] a piece of equipment consisting of two or more blades that spin around, that makes an aircraft or ship move

**pro·pel·ling pen·cil** /ˌ·,·· '··/ *n* [C] *BrE* a pencil made of plastic or metal, in which the stick of the LEAD can be pushed out as it is used up; MECHANICAL PENCIL *AmE*

**pro·pen·si·ty** /prə'pensɪ̈ti/ *n* [C] *formal* a natural tendency to behave in a particular way: **a propensity to do sth** *the male propensity to fight* | **a propensity for (doing) sth** *The child shows a propensity for disrupting class.*

**prop·er**[1] /'prɒpə‖'prɑːpər/ *adj* **1** [only before noun, no comparative] *especially BrE* right, suitable, or correct: *She needs proper medical attention.* | *Put that back in its proper place.* | *I went through the proper process, I wrote to my MP.* **2** socially or legally correct and acceptable: *I don't feel that it would be proper for me to give you that information.* | **be only (right and) proper** *It's only right and proper that Shari apologize for what she said!* **3** [only before noun] *BrE spoken* real: *Can't you get a proper job?* | *Try to eat proper meals instead of chips and baked beans.* **4** [only after noun] according to the real, most exact meaning of the word: *Monkeys proper only began to evolve thirty five million years ago.* **5 proper to sth a)** *formal* belonging to one particular type of thing: *the reasoning abilities proper to our species* **b)** natural or normal in a particular place or situation: *dressed in a way that was proper to the occasion* **6** [only before noun] *BrE spoken* complete: *He's made a proper fool of himself this time!* | *You're in a proper old mess.* **7** very polite, and careful to do what is socially correct: *Andrew's behaviour was so proper that she couldn't help laughing.* —see also PROPERLY

**proper**[2] *adv especially BrE spoken* **1** used by some people to mean PROPERLY, although most people think that this is incorrect: *Why don't you talk proper?* **2 good and proper** completely: *Tom drove the car into a wall and wrecked it good and proper.*

**proper frac·tion** /ˌ·· '··/ *n* [C] a FRACTION such as $\frac{3}{4}$ in which the number above the line is smaller than the one below it —compare IMPROPER FRACTION

**prop·er·ly** /'prɒpəli‖'prɑːpərli/ *adv* **1** correctly, or in a way that is considered right: *Make sure the job is done properly.* | *He never explains anything properly.* | *Granny will be there, so behave properly.* **2** *especially BrE informal* completely; thoroughly: *Is that cake properly defrosted?* **3** really; in fact: *Documents which properly belong to the family were taken away by the authorities.* | **properly speaking** *especially BrE* (=really) *He's not a policeman at all, properly speaking.* **4** used to say that someone was right to do something: **quite/very/perfectly properly** *She told me, perfectly properly, that it was no business of mine.* S1 W2

**proper noun** /ˌ·· '·/ also **proper name** *n* [C] a noun such as 'James', 'New York', or 'China' that is the name of one particular thing and is spelt with a CAPITAL[2] (3) letter —see also NOUN

**prop·er·tied** /'prɒpətid‖'prɑːpər-/ *adj* [only before noun] owning a lot of property or land: *the propertied classes*

**prop·er·ty** /'prɒpəti‖'prɑːpər-/ *n plural* **properties** **1** [U] the thing or things that someone owns: *That's my personal property! Leave it alone!* | *Some of the stolen property was found in Mason's house.* **2** [U] land, buildings, or both together: *Property prices have shot up recently.* **3** [C] a word meaning a building, a piece of land, or both together, used especially by lawyers or ESTATE AGENTS: *Several properties on this street are for sale.* **4** [C] a quality or power that belongs naturally to something: *a herb with healing properties* | *One of the most important properties of gold is its malleability.* **5** [U] ownership of land, goods etc: *a belief in the idea of communal property* —see also LOST PROPERTY, REAL PROPERTY S2 W1

**property de·vel·op·er** /'··· ˌ,···/ *n* [C] someone who makes money by buying land and building on it

**property tax** /'··· ˌ·/ *n* [C,U] a tax based on the value of someone's house

**proph·e·cy** also **prophesy** *AmE* /'prɒfɪ̈si‖'prɑː-/ *n plural* **prophecies** **1** [C] a statement that something will happen in the future, especially one made by someone with religious or magic powers: [+ **that**] *The prophecy that David would become king was fulfilled.* **2** [U] the making of statements about what will happen in the future —see also **self-fulfilling prophecy** (SELF-FULFILLING)

**proph·e·sy**[1] /'prɒfɪ̈saɪ‖'prɑː-/ *v* **prophesies, prophesying, prophesied** [I,T] to use religious or magical knowledge to say what will happen in the future;

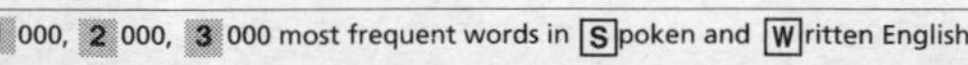

FORETELL: [+ **that**] *The soothsayer prophesied that the war would be won.* | **prophesy who/what/how etc** *He even prophesied how the crops would fail.*

**proph·e·sy²** /ˈprɒfəsi‖ˈprɑː-/ *n* [C] an American spelling of prophecy

**proph·et** /ˈprɒfɪ̈t‖ˈprɑː-/ *n* [C] **1** a man whom people in the Christian, Jewish, or Muslim religion believe has been sent by God to lead them and teach them their religion **2 the Prophet** Muhammad, who formed the Muslim religion: *followers of the Prophet* **3 the Prophets** the Jewish holy men whose writings form part of the OLD TESTAMENT, or the writings themselves **4 prophet of doom/disaster** someone who believes that bad or unpleasant things will happen in the future **5** someone who introduces and teaches a new idea: [+ **of**] *Rontgen was regarded as the prophet of the new materialism.*

**proph·et·ess** /ˌprɒfɪ̈ˈtes‖ˈprɑːfɪ̈təs/ *n* [C] a woman whom people believe has been sent by God to lead them

**pro·phet·ic** /prəˈfetɪk/ *adj* correctly saying what will happen in the future: *Nick's remark proved prophetic two months later.* —**prophetically** /-kli/ *adv*

**pro·phet·i·cal** /prəˈfetɪkəl/ *adj* like a prophet, or related to the things a prophet says or does

**pro·phy·lac·tic¹** /ˌprɒfɪ̈ˈlæktɪk◂‖ˌprɑː-/ *adj technical* intended to prevent disease

**prophylactic²** *n* [C] *technical* **1** something used to prevent disease **2** *AmE often humorous* a CONDOM

**pro·phy·lax·is** /ˌprɒfɪ̈ˈlæksɪ̈s‖ˌprɑː-/ *n* [C,U] *technical* a treatment for preventing disease

**pro·pin·qui·ty** /prəˈpɪŋkwɪ̈ti/ *n* [U + **of** / **to**] *formal* the fact of being near someone or something, or of being related to someone

**pro·pi·ti·ate** /prəˈpɪʃieɪt/ *v* [T] *formal* to make someone who has been unfriendly or angry with you feel more friendly by doing something to please them —**propitiation** /prəˌpɪʃiˈeɪʃən/ *n* [U]

**pro·pi·ti·a·to·ry** /prəˈpɪʃiətəri‖-tɔːri/ *adj formal* intended to please someone and make them feel less angry and more friendly: *a propitiatory gift of flowers*

**pro·pi·tious** /prəˈpɪʃəs/ *adj formal* good and likely to bring good results: *a propitious moment* | [+ **for**] *Conditions after the 1905 revolution were propitious for stable development.* —**propitiously** *adv*

**pro·po·nent** /prəˈpəʊnənt‖-ˈpoʊ-/ *n* [C] someone who supports something or persuades people to do something; ADVOCATE² (1): [+ **of**] *Steinem has always been a strong proponent of women's rights.* —compare OPPONENT (2)

**proportion**

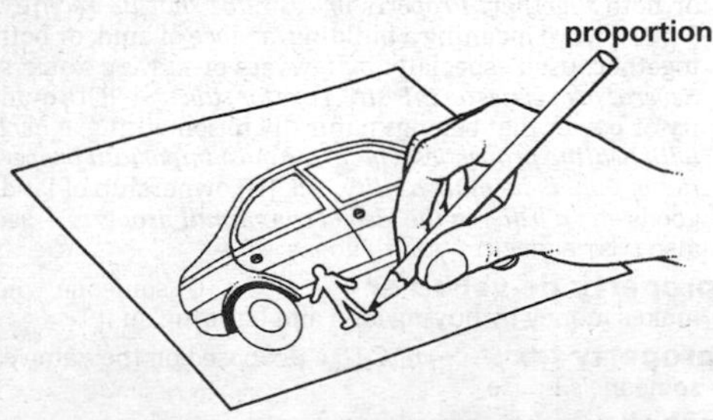

The car is out of proportion to the man.

S2 W2 **pro·por·tion¹** /prəˈpɔːʃən‖-ˈpɔːr-/ *n*
**1 ▶ AMOUNT ◀** [C] a part or share of a larger amount: **proportion of sth to sth** *The proportion of men to women in the population has changed in recent years.* | [+ **of**] *Quite high proportions of their incomes are spent on fuel.*
**2 ▶ NUMBER ◀** [C] a number of people or things, considered as a part or share of a larger number: [+ **of**] *Far higher proportions of part-time workers have no health insurance at all.* | [also + plural verb *BrE*] *A large proportion of the people are illiterate.*
**3 ▶ RELATIONSHIP ◀** [C, U] the relationship between the amounts, numbers, or sizes of different things that go together to form a whole: *eating the right foods in the right proportions* | **proportion of sth to sth** *The proportion of men to women has changed in recent years.* | **the proportion of** *Make salad dressing in the proportion of three parts oil to one part vinegar.*
**4 ▶ ATTRACTIVENESS ◀** [U] **a)** the correct relationship between the size, shape and position of the different parts of something, which gives it an attractive appearance: *Builders must learn about scale and proportion.* | **in proportion** *Reduce the drawing so that all the elements stay in proportion.* **b)** the correct relationship between the size or shape of something and the place where it is: **out of proportion (to/with)** *They've built a house that's completely out of proportion with the size of the lot.*
**5 in proportion (to/with sth)** according to a particular relationship in size, amount etc: *If you use a whole pineapple, increase the other ingredients in proportion.* | *Tax is then calculated in proportion to what you earn.*
**6 in proportion (to sth)** when you compare sizes, amounts etc: *Her feet are small in proportion to her height.*
**7 ▶ SIZE/IMPORTANCE ◀ proportions** [plural] the size and shape of something, or the degree to which something is important: *a building of classic proportions* | *It may reduce the task to more manageable proportions.* | **immense/huge/massive etc proportions** *an ecological tragedy of enormous proportions* | **epic/heroic/mythic proportions** *For most of us, Scott was a hero of mythic proportions.* | **crisis/epidemic etc proportions** *a fall in silk prices of catastrophic proportions*
**8 keep things in proportion** to react to a situation sensibly, and not think that it is worse or more serious than it really is: *Try to keep things in proportion; you won't die if you don't get the job.* —see also PERSPECTIVE²
**9 get/blow things (all) out of proportion** to react to a situation as if it is worse or more serious than it really is
**10 out of (all) proportion (to sth)** a reaction, result, emotion etc that is out of proportion is too strong or great, compared to the situation in which it happens: *The fear of violent crime has now risen out of all proportion to the actual risk.*
**11 sense of proportion** the ability to judge what is most important in a situation: **keep/lose a sense of proportion** *You can protest by all means, but keep a sense of proportion.*
**12 ▶ MATHEMATICS ◀** [U] *technical* equality in the mathematical relationship between two sets of numbers, as in the statement '8 is to 6 as 32 is to 24'

**proportion²** *v* [T usually passive] *formal* **1 well/badly/beautifully etc proportioned** having a size and shape that is either pleasant or unpleasant to look at, or is either right or wrong for its use: *a well proportioned room* | *long, beautifully proportioned legs* **2** to make something stay in a particular relationship with something else according to size, amount, position etc: **proportion sth to sth** *Allowances for expenditure have been proportioned to your income.*

**pro·por·tion·al** /prəˈpɔːʃənəl‖-ˈpɔːr-/ *adj* something that is proportional to something else stays in a correct or suitable relationship to the other thing in size, amount, importance etc: [+ **to**] *Carlow will have to pay an amount of compensation proportional to the damage he did.* —**proportionally** *adv*

**proportional rep·re·sen·ta·tion** /ˌ·ˌ··· ···ˈ··/ *n* [U] PR; a system of voting in elections by which all political parties are represented in the government according to the number of votes they receive in the whole country

**pro·por·tion·ate** /prəˈpɔːʃənɪ̈t‖-ˈpɔːr-/ *adj* something that is proportionate to something else stays in a correct or suitable relationship to the other thing in size, amount, importance etc: *The decline in production was* *offset by a proportionate increase in federal aid.* —opposite DISPROPORTIONATE —**proportionately** *adv*

S3 W1 **pro·pos·al** /prəˈpəʊzəl‖-ˈpoʊ-/ *n* **1** [C,U] a plan or suggestion which is made formally to an official person or group, or the act of making it: *Clinton is facing a battle to get Congress to accept his budget proposals.* | **proposal to do sth** *The proposal to build a new bypass is meeting with stiff opposition.* | **proposal that** *The company had to put forward a proposal that layoffs be considered.* see PROPOSE (USAGE) **2** [C] the act of asking someone to marry you

S3 W2 **pro·pose** /prəˈpəʊz‖-ˈpoʊz/ *v*

**1** ▶ **PLAN** ◀ [T] *formal* to suggest something as a plan or course of action: *Lyle proposed large cuts in the training budget.* | **propose that** *Hansen has proposed that I become his business partner.* | *the proposed budget cuts*

**2** ▶ **AT A MEETING** ◀ [T] to formally suggest a course of action at a meeting and ask people to vote on it: *I propose the admission of Peter King as a new member.* | **propose a motion** (=formally suggest a plan at a meeting) | **propose sb** (=formally suggest someone for an official position) *Mrs Banks has been proposed for the position of Treasurer.*

**3** ▶ **THEORY** ◀ [T] to suggest an idea, method etc as an answer to a scientific question or as a better way of doing something: *His theory proposes the existence of black holes in the universe.*

**4** ▶ **MARRIAGE** ◀ **a)** [I] to ask someone to marry you, especially in a formal way: [+ **to**] *Shaun proposed to me only six months after we met.* **b) propose marriage** *formal* to ask someone to marry you

**5 propose a toast to sb** also **propose sb's health** to formally ask a group of people at a social event to join you in wishing someone success, happiness, etc, while raising a glass of wine and then drinking from it

**6** ▶ **INTEND** ◀ [T] *formal* to intend to do something: **propose to do sth** *How do you propose to explain your long absence?* | **propose doing sth** *Just how do you propose paying for all this?* —**proposer** *n* [C]

**USAGE NOTE: PROPOSE**

WORD CHOICE: **propose, intend, suggest, proposal, suggestion, let's, why don't we**

**Propose** followed by the *to* form of a verb is a more formal way of saying you intend to do something: *What are you proposing to do with that old car of yours?*

**Propose** followed by a noun means that you are formally suggesting something should be considered: *propose a motion/solution/course of action etc*

**Propose** followed by a *that* clause has a similar meaning to **suggest**: *I propose/suggest that we buy a new car* (=I think that this is what we should do).

**Propose** followed by the *ing* form of a verb may have either of the above senses.

The difference between **suggest** and **propose** is that **propose** is more formal and often means that you have already thought about what you are proposing. But you may **suggest** an idea without a lot of careful thought: *At the meeting conservationists proposed a different route for the highway.* | *As we came out of the theater, Jean suggested a Chinese meal.*

With similar differences you can also make a **proposal** or a **suggestion**: *the committee's proposal to raise local taxes* | *George's suggestion that we go skating tonight*

In spoken English people do not usually say **I suggest that** but rather **Let's** or **Why don't we?**: *Let's go for a Chinese meal.* | *Why don't we get a new car?*

GRAMMAR

You **propose** or **suggest** something always **to** someone: *He proposed a business deal to her* (NOT *He proposed her a business deal* or *He proposed her to a business deal*). Also you would say: *I suggested to her that we go to the disco* (NOT *I suggested her that we go to the disco).*

**Suggest** is not used with the *to* form of the verb: *He suggested leaving/that we leave* (NOT *He suggested to leave*).

**proposed** /prəˈpəʊzd‖-ˈpoʊz/ *adj* a proposed charge, arrangement etc is one that has been formally suggested to an official person or group: *How will the proposed study be carried out?* | *The proposed site has several drawbacks.* W3

**prop·o·si·tion¹** /ˌprɒpəˈzɪʃən‖ˌprɑː-/ *n* [C]

**1** ▶ **JUDGMENT** ◀ a statement that consists of a carefully considered opinion or judgment: *Marx accepted several of the key propositions developed by Adam Smith.* | **proposition that** *We were asked to discuss the proposition that women are satisfied with less money.*

**2** ▶ **SUGGESTION** ◀ an offer or suggestion, especially in business or politics: *I'll consider your proposition and let you know.* | *We have a proposition to make.*

**3 an attractive/interesting/practical etc proposition** something that is an attractive etc idea, especially in business or politics: *The newest software makes computerized recruitment an attractive proposition.*

**4** ▶ **MATHEMATICS** ◀ *technical* a word used in GEOMETRY meaning something that must be proved, or a question to which the answer must be found

**5** ▶ **SEX** ◀ a statement that you would like to have sex with someone which avoids saying this to them directly

**6** ▶ **LAW** ◀ also **Proposition** a suggested change or addition to the law of a state of the US, which citizens vote on —**propositional** *adj*

**proposition²** *v* [T] to suggest to someone that they have sex with you: *prostitutes propositioning the passers-by*

**pro·pound** /prəˈpaʊnd/ *v* [T] *formal* to suggest an idea, explanation etc for other people to consider

**pro·pri·e·ta·ry** /prəˈpraɪətəri‖-teri/ *adj formal* **1** a proprietary medicine, cleaning liquid etc is one that is sold under a TRADE NAME **2** proprietary behaviour makes it seem that you think you own something or someone: *Arnold wrapped his arm around his fiancée with a proprietary air.* **3 proprietary information** information about a company's products, methods etc which is known only to people who work for the company

**pro·pri·e·tor** /prəˈpraɪətə‖-ər/ *n* [C] *formal* an owner of a business: *Echenard was proprietor of the famous Hotel du Louvre.* —**proprietorial** /prəˌpraɪəˈtɔːriəl/ *adj* —**proprietorially** *adv*

**pro·pri·e·tress** /prəˈpraɪətrɪ̣s/ *n* [C] *old-fashioned* a woman who owns a business

**pro·pri·e·ty** /prəˈpraɪəti/ *n formal* **1** [singular, U] correctness of social or moral behaviour, especially between men and women or between people of different social ranks, age etc: *Jonathan behaved with the utmost propriety on our first date.* **2 the proprieties** the accepted rules of correct social behaviour: *strict in observing the proprieties* —see also IMPROPRIETY

**pro·pul·sion** /prəˈpʌlʃən/ *n* [U] *technical* **1** the force that drives a vehicle forward **2 jet propulsion** the use of engines which push out hot gases to make an aircraft fly —**propulsive** /-sɪv/ *adj*: *propulsive force*

**pro ra·ta** /ˌprəʊ ˈrɑːtə‖proʊˈreɪtə/ *adj technical* a payment or share that is pro rata is calculated according to exactly how much of something is used, how much work is done, etc —**pro rata** *adv*

**pro·rate** /prəʊˈreɪt‖proʊ-/ *v* [T] *AmE* to calculate a charge, price, etc according to the actual amount of service received rather than by a standard sum

**pro·rogue** /prəʊˈrəʊg, prə-‖proʊˈroʊg, prə-/ *v* [T] *technical* to leave any unfinished business of a PARLIAMENT to be dealt with at the next meeting —**prorogation** *n* [U]

**pros** /prəʊz‖proʊz/ *n* [plural] —see **the pros and cons** (PRO¹ (3))

**pro·sa·ic** /prəʊˈzeɪ-ɪk, prə-‖proʊ-, prə-/ *adj* boring, ordinary, or lacking in imagination: *a prosaic writing style* |

*People said he'd been a pirate, but the truth was more prosaic.* —**prosaically** /-kli/ *adv*

**pro·sce·ni·um** /prəˈsiːniəm, prəʊ-‖prə-, proʊ-/ *n* [C] **1** the part of a theatre stage which comes forward beyond the curtain **2 proscenium arch** the arch at the front of a theatre stage where a curtain can be lowered

**pro·sciut·to** /prəʊˈʃuːtəʊ‖proʊˈʃuːtoʊ/ *n* [U] uncooked, dried, Italian HAM (=salted meat) which is eaten in very thin pieces

**pro·scribe** /prəʊˈskraɪb‖proʊ-/ *v* [T] **1** *formal* to try to stop the existence of something such as a political organization **2** *old use* to state publicly that a citizen is no longer protected by the law —**proscription** /-ˈskrɪpʃən/ *n* [C,U]

**prose** /prəʊz‖proʊz/ *n* **1** [U] written language in its usual form, as opposed to poetry: *Gilbert's clear, simple prose* **2** [C] *BrE* a student's exercise in which you translate a piece of writing into a foreign language

**pros·e·cute** /ˈprɒsɪkjuːt‖ˈprɑː-/ *v* **1** [I,T] to officially say that someone is guilty of a crime and must be judged by a court of law: *Shoplifters will be prosecuted.* | **prosecute sb for sth** *Buxton's being prosecuted for assault.* | *If payment is not received by 1 March we'll be forced to prosecute.* **2** [I,T] to represent someone in court as their lawyer, when they are bringing a criminal charge against someone else —compare DEFEND (6) **3** [T] *formal* to continue doing something: *We cannot prosecute the investigation further.*

**prosecuting at·tor·ney** /ˈ····ˌ··/ *n* [C usually singular] *AmE* a DISTRICT ATTORNEY

W3 **pros·e·cu·tion** /ˌprɒsɪˈkjuːʃən‖ˌprɑː-/ *n* **1** [C,U] the process or act of bringing a charge against someone for a crime, or of being judged for a crime in a court of law: *The evidence is now sufficient to bring a prosecution against him.* | *I want immunity from prosecution before I give you any names.* **2 the prosecution** the lawyers who represent the person bringing a criminal charge against someone in a court of law: *the chief witness for the prosecution* —compare DEFENCE (5) **3** [U] *formal* the doing of something that is your job: *the prosecution of her duties*

**pros·e·cu·tor** /ˈprɒsɪkjuːtə‖ˈprɑːsɪkjuːtər-/ *n* [C] a lawyer who represents the person who is bringing a criminal charge against someone

**pros·e·lyte** /ˈprɒsəlaɪt‖ˈprɑː-/ *n* [C] *formal* someone who has recently been persuaded to join a religious group, political party etc; CONVERT[2]

**pros·e·lyt·ize** also **-ise** *BrE* /ˈprɒsələtaɪz‖ˈprɑː-/ *v* [I,T] *formal* to try to persuade someone to join a religious group, political party etc, especially in a way that people find offensive —**proselytizer** *n* [C]

**pros·o·dy** /ˈprɒsədi‖ˈprɑː-/ *n* [U] the rules for arranging the patterns of sounds and beats in poetry, or the study of these rules —**prosodic** /prəˈsɒdɪk‖-ˈsɑː-/ *adj*

S2 W2 **pros·pect¹** /ˈprɒspekt‖ˈprɑː-/ *n* **1** [C,U] a possibility that something which you hope for will happen soon: [+ **of**] *There's little prospect of employment, I'm afraid.* | [+ **for**] *There are good prospects for growth in the retail sector.* | **every prospect** (=a strong posssibility) | *Peace talks start today with every prospect of success.* **2** [singular] something that is possible or is likely to happen in the future: [+ **of**] *The prospect of marriage terrified Alice.* | *a depressing prospect* **3 prospects** [plural] chances of future success: *You can't marry a man with no job and no prospects!* **4** [C] a person, job, plan etc that has a good chance of success in the future: *Reg was the brightest schoolboy rugby prospect in years.* **5** [C usually singular] *formal* a view of a wide area of land, especially from a high place: *a fine prospect across the valley* **6 in prospect** *formal* likely to happen in the near future

**pro·spect²** /prəˈspekt‖ˈprɑːspekt/ *v* [I + **for**,] [T] to examine an area of land or water, in order to find gold, silver, oil etc

**pro·spec·tive** /prəˈspektɪv/ *adj* [only before noun] **1** likely to do a particular thing or achieve a particular position: **prospective employee/candidate/buyer etc** *I'm meeting a prospective buyer for the house today.* **2** likely to happen: **prospective costs/career/changes etc** *What are the prospective returns from an investment of $10,000 over five years?*

**pro·spec·tor** /prəˈspektə‖ˈprɑːspektər/ *n* [C] someone who looks for gold, minerals, oil etc

**pro·spec·tus** /prəˈspektəs/ *n* [C] **1** a small book that advertises a college, university, new business etc **2** a formal statement giving details of a future event in business, such as the sale of shares (SHARE² (5))

**pros·per** /ˈprɒspə‖ˈprɑːspər/ *v* **1** [I] to be successful and become rich: *My father was no longer prospering in business.* **2** [I] to grow and develop in a healthy way; THRIVE: *The children seemed to prosper under their care.* **3** [T] *old use* to make something succeed

**pro·sper·i·ty** /prɒˈsperəti‖prɑː-/ *n* [U] a condition of having money and everything that is needed for a good life: *an era of unparalleled peace and prosperity*

**pros·per·ous** /ˈprɒspərəs‖ˈprɑː-/ *adj* successful and rich: *working for a strong, prosperous and united Europe* —**prosperously** *adv*

**pros·tate** /ˈprɒsteɪt‖ˈprɑː-/ also **prostate gland** *n* [C] the organ in the male body that produces a liquid in which SPERM (=seeds) are carried

**pros·the·sis** /prɒsˈθiːsəs‖prɑːs-/ *plural* **prostheses** /-siːz/ *n* [C] *technical* an artificial leg, tooth, or other part of the body which takes the place of a missing part

**pros·ti·tute¹** /ˈprɒstətjuːt‖ˈprɑːstətuːt/ *n* [C] **1** someone, especially a woman, who earns money by having sex with people who pay for it **2 male prostitute** a man who earns money in this way

**prostitute²** *v* [T] **1** *formal* to use your skills, abilities etc in a way that does not show their true value, in order to earn money: *Olivier never prostituted his acting talent by appearing in TV commercials.* **2 prostitute yourself a)** to have sex in return for money **b)** to do unpleasant work just to get money

**pros·ti·tu·tion** /ˌprɒstəˈtjuːʃən‖ˌprɑːstəˈtuːʃən/ *n* [U] **1** the work of prostitutes: *an alarming rise in teenage prostitution* **2** *formal* the use of your skill, ability etc, in a way that does not show its true value

**pros·trate¹** /ˈprɒstreɪt‖ˈprɑː-/ *adj* **1** lying on your front with your face towards the ground, for example because you are injured, or are praising God —compare PRONE (2) **2** so shocked, upset etc that you can no longer do anything: [+ **with**] *Judy was prostrate with grief after her father's death.*

**pro·strate²** /prəˈstreɪt‖ˈprɑːstreɪt/ *v* [T] **1 prostrate yourself** to lie on your front with your face towards the ground as an act of praise or a sign of obedience **2 be prostrated** *formal* to have lost all your strength, courage, or energy: *prostrated by illness* —**prostration** /prɒˈstreɪʃən‖prɑː-/ *n* [C,U]

**pros·y** /ˈprəʊzi‖ˈproʊ-/ *adj* a prosy style of writing or speech is boring and shows no imagination —**prosily** *adv* —**prosiness** *n* [U]

**prot-** /prəʊt‖proʊt/ *prefix* another form of the prefix PROTO-

**pro·tag·o·nist** /prəʊˈtægənəst‖proʊ-/ *n* [C] **1** one of the main supporters of a new aim or policy, especially a social one: [+ **of**] *Ogden was one of the earliest protagonists of educational reform.* **2** *formal* the most important character in a play, film, or story **3** *formal* someone who is in a competition, battle, or struggle: *the protagonists in America's 'software wars'* —compare ANTAGONIST

**pro·te·an** /ˈprəʊtiən, prəʊˈtiːən‖ˈproʊtiən, proʊ-/ *adj literary* having the ability to change continually in appearance or behaviour

**pro·tect** /prəˈtekt/ *v* [T] **1** to keep someone or something safe from harm, damage, or illness: **protect sb/sth from sth** *Try to protect your skin from the sun.* | *Kids should be protected from all that violence.* | **protect sth** *laws protecting the rights of disabled people* | *I have to* S2 W2 *protect my reputation.* | **protect sb/sth against** *a natural camouflage that protects them against predators* | [+ **against**] *locks to protect against burglars* **2** [usually passive] to keep something such as an old building or a rare animal safe from harm or destruction, by means of special laws **3** to help the industry and trade of your own country by taxing foreign goods —see also PROTECTIONISM, PROTECTIVE —**protected** *adj*: *Spotted owls are a protected species.*

S2 W2 **pro·tec·tion** /prəˈtekʃən/ *n* **1** [U] the act of protecting or state of being protected: *You're guaranteed police protection if you testify in court.* | [+ **against**] *Take these vitamins daily for protection against minor infections.* | **give/offer/provide protection** (=protect) | *Helen's thin coat gave little protection against the cold.* **2** [U] the promise of payment from an insurance company if something bad happens: *Our Five-Star Policy offers complete protection in case of fire.* **3** [singular] something that protects: [+ **against**] *Wear a bullet-proof vest as a protection against snipers.* **4** [U] protection money

**pro·tec·tion·is·m** /prəˈtekʃənɪzəm/ *n* [U] the system of helping your country's trade, especially by taxing foreign goods —**protectionist** *adj* —**protectionist** *n* [C]

**protection mon·ey** /·ˈ·· ˌ··/ *n* [U] money paid to criminals to stop them from damaging your property

**protection rack·et** /·ˈ·· ˌ··/ *n* [C] *informal* a system in which criminals demand money from you to stop them from damaging your property

**pro·tec·tive** /prəˈtektɪv/ *adj* **1** [only before noun] used or intended for protection: *protective clothing* | *protective legislation* | *a protective layer of varnish* **2** wanting to protect someone from harm or danger, often in a way that unintentionally restricts their freedom: [+ **towards/of**] *I can't help feeling protective towards my kids.* **3** intended to give an advantage to your own country's industry: *a protective tariff on imports of foreign cars* —**protectively** *adv* **protectiveness** *n* [U]

**protective cus·to·dy** /·ˌ·· ˈ···/ *n* [U] a situation in which the police make you stay somewhere to protect you from other people

**pro·tec·tor** /prəˈtektə‖-ər/ *n* [C] something or someone that protects: *He sees himself as her protector.*

**pro·tec·tor·ate** /prəˈtektərɪ̣t/ *n* [C] a country that is protected and controlled by a more powerful country, especially in the areas of defence and foreign affairs

**prot·é·gé** /ˈprɒtəʒeɪ‖ˈproʊ-/ *n* [C] a young person who is guided and helped by someone who has influence, power, or more experience

**prot·é·gée** /ˈprɒtəʒeɪ‖ˈproʊ-/ *n* [C] a young woman who is guided and helped by someone who has influence, power, or more experience

W2 **pro·tein** /ˈprəʊtiːn‖ˈproʊ-/ *n* [C,U] one of the many substances that exist in food such as meat, eggs, and beans, which help your body to grow and keep it strong and healthy

**pro tem** /ˌprəʊ ˈtem‖ˌproʊ-/ also **pro tem·po·re** /-ˈtempəreɪ/ *Latin adj, adv* happening now but only for a short time: *a pro tem committee of nine men*

W3 **pro·test¹** /ˈprəʊtest‖ˈproʊ-/ *n* **1** [C,U] a strong complaint that shows you disagree with, or are angry about something that you think is wrong or unfair: *a written protest alleging police brutality* | *I turned off the TV, despite loud protests from the kids.* | [+ **against**] *American flags were burned as a protest against US intervention.* | *a protest song* | **in protest** (=as a way of making a protest) *Seven prisoners are on hunger strike in protest against their treatment.* | *the protest movements of the 1960s* | **a storm of protest/wave of protest** (=a lot of angry protest) *The price rises caused a storm of protest.* **2** [C] an occasion when people come together in public to express disapproval or opposition to something: *Student protests swept across the nation's campuses.* **3 without protest** calmly and without complaining: *Ben accepted his punishment without protest.* **4 under protest** unwillingly, and with the feeling that you have been unfairly treated: *I only signed the document under protest.*

**pro·test²** /prəˈtest/ *v* **1** [I,T] to say or do something publicly to show that you disagree with, or are angry about something that you think is wrong or unfair: [+ **against/at/about**] *Someone has to keep protesting against human rights violations.* | *I heard him protesting loudly as the medics took him away.* | *"Let me go!" Sarah protested angrily.* | **protest sth** *AmE*: *a large crowd protesting the war* **2** [T] to state very firmly that something is true, especially when other people do not believe you: **protest that** *Even if Mandy protests that she's not drunk, don't let her drive.* | **protest your innocence** (=keep saying that you are innocent)

**Prot·es·tant** /ˈprɒtɪ̣stənt‖ˈprɑː-/ *n* [C] a member of a part of the Christian church that separated from the Roman Catholic church in the 16th century —**Protestant** *adj* —**Protestantism** *n* [U]

**prot·es·ta·tion** /ˌprɒtɪ̣ˈsteɪʃən ˌprəʊ-‖ˌprɑː-, ˌproʊ-/ *n formal* [C + **of**] a strong statement saying that something is true, especially when other people say it is not

**pro·test·er** /prəˈtestə‖-ər/ *n* [C] someone who takes part in a public activity to show their opposition to something

**proto-** /prəʊtəʊ, -tə‖proʊtoʊ, -tə/ *prefix* also **prot-** *technical* first in time or order, before other things of the same kind are developed; original: *the huge protogalaxy from which all the galaxies developed*

**pro·to·col** /ˈprəʊtəkɒl‖ˈproʊtəkɔːl, -kɑːl/ *n* **1** [U] the system of rules on the correct and acceptable way to behave on official occasions: *a breach of diplomatic protocol* **2** [C] *technical* a method for connecting computers so that they can exchange information

**pro·ton** /ˈprəʊtɒn‖ˈproʊtɑːn/ *n* [C] a very small piece of matter that carries POSITIVE electricity and that together with a NEUTRON forms the NUCLEUS (=central part) of an atom —see also ELECTRON

**pro·to·plas·m** /ˈprəʊtəplæzəm‖ˈproʊ-/ *n* [U] *technical* the colourless substance that forms the cells of plants and animals

**pro·to·type** /ˈprəʊtətaɪp‖ˈproʊ-/ *n* [C] the first form that a new design of a car, machine etc has: [+ **of/for**] *a complete working prototype of the new model*

**pro·to·zo·a** /ˌprəʊtəˈzəʊə‖ˌproʊtəˈzoʊə/ *n* [plural] very small living things that only have one cell

**pro·to·zo·an** /ˌprəʊtəˈzəʊən‖ˌproʊtəˈzoʊən/ also **pro·to·zo·on** /-ˈzəʊɒn‖-ˈzoʊɑːn/ *n* [C] a single member of the protozoa —**protozoan** *adj*

**pro·trac·ted** /prəˈtræktɪ̣d/ *adj* lasting a long time, especially longer than usual, or necessary: *the likelihood of an ugly and protracted guerilla war* —**protract** *v* [T] —**protraction** /-ˈtrækʃən/ *n* [U]

**pro·trac·tor** /prəˈtræktə‖proʊˈtræktər/ *n* [C] an instrument usually in the shape of a half-circle, used for measuring and drawing angles

**pro·trude** /prəˈtruːd‖proʊ-/ *v* [I] to stick out from somewhere: *protruding eyes* | [+ **from**] *A pair of shoes protruded from under the bed.*

**pro·tru·sion** /prəˈtruːʒən‖proʊ-/ *n* **1** [C] something that protrudes **2** [U] the act of protruding

**pro·tu·be·rance** /prəˈtjuːbərənt‖-ˈtuː-/ *n* [C] *formal* something that sticks out from the surface of something else

**pro·tu·be·rant** /prəˈtjuːbərənt‖-ˈtuː-/ *adj* curving outwards from a surface —**protuberantly** *adv*

**proud** /praʊd/ *adj* S2 W3
**1** ▶**PLEASED**◀ feeling pleased with your achievements, family, country etc because you think they are very good: *You should see them with the baby – they're so proud!* | [+ **of**] *Jane's very proud of her new car.* | **proud (that)** *We are proud that a pupil from our school has won a prize.* | **proud to do/be sth** *She was proud to be part of such a prestigious project.* —see also HOUSEPROUD

**2 ▶ TOO PROUD ◀** thinking that you are more important, skilful etc than you really are: *Proud and boastful, Jaggers was typical of the young brokers.*
**3 ▶ REFUSE HELP ◀** having so much respect for yourself that you will not let other people help you when you are in a difficult situation: *My grandfather's penniless, but he's too proud to ask for help.*
**4 do sb proud a)** *informal* to provide a lot of good food, drink etc when people are visiting you or celebrating something: *Clare did us proud last Christmas.* **b)** to make people feel proud of you by doing something well: *Congratulations Bobby, you've done us proud!*
**5 as proud as a peacock** feeling very pleased with yourself because you have done something well
**6 ▶ IMPRESSIVE ◀** *literary* tall and impressive: *the proud cathedral spire* —see also PRIDE[1] —**proudly** *adv*

S2 W1 **prove** /pruːv/ *v past tense* **proved** *past participle* **proved** *also* **proven** /ˈpruːvən/ *especially AmE*
**1 ▶ SHOW THE TRUTH ◀** [T] to show that something is true by providing facts, information etc: *Evidence has been found that proves his innocence.* | **prove (that)** *It is impossible to prove that God exists.* | **prove sb wrong/innocent etc** *It would give me great pleasure to prove Sam wrong.* —see also DISPROVE
**2 ▶ BE SOMETHING ◀** [linking verb, T] if someone or something proves difficult, helpful etc, you find out that this is what they are like: *Working from home proved a real advantage after my son was born.* | **prove to be sth** *Your computing experience should prove to be useful.*
**3 prove yourself** to show how good you are at something by trying hard to do it well: *When I started the job, I felt I had to prove myself.*
**4 ▶ BREAD ◀** [I] if DOUGH (=unbaked bread mixture) proves, it rises and becomes light because of the YEAST in it
**5 ▶ LAW ◀** [T] *law* to show that a WILL has been made properly —**provable** *adj* —**provably** *adv*

**prov·en[1]** /ˈpruːvən, ˈprəʊvən‖ˈproʊvən, ˈpruːvən/ *adj* **1** [usually before noun] tested and shown to be true: *a woman of proven ability* **2 not proven** an expression used in Scottish law when a court cannot decide definitely that someone is guilty of a crime

**proven[2]** /ˈpruːvən/ *especially AmE* a past participle of PROVE

**prov·e·nance** /ˈprɒvənəns‖ˈprɑː-/ *n* [U] *formal* the place where something originally came from: *a rug of Iranian provenance*

**prov·en·der** /ˈprɒvɪ̈ndə‖ˈprɑːvɪ̈ndər/ *n* [U] *old-fashioned* dry food for horses and cattle

**prov·erb** /ˈprɒvɜːb‖ˈprɑːvɜːrb/ *n* [C] a short well-known statement that contains advice about life in general

**pro·ver·bi·al** /prəˈvɜːbiəl‖-ɜːr-/ *adj* **1 the proverbial** used when describing something using a well-known expression: *This was not the proverbial free lunch!* **2** well-known by a lot of people: *It was a level of corruption which became proverbial.* **3** connected with a proverb: *a proverbial saying* —**proverbially** *adv*

S1 W1 **pro·vide** /prəˈvaɪd/ *v* [T] **1** to make sure that someone gets what they need, especially by giving it to them: **provide sth for sb** *The hotel provides a shoe-cleaning service for guests.* | **provide sb with sth** *a project designed to provide young people with work* | **provide sth** *I'll provide the food if you bring the wine.* **2** to produce a useful result, opportunity etc: *We are hoping the enquiry will provide an explanation for the accident.* | **provide sb with sth** *This has provided police with a vital clue.* **3 provide that** *formal* if a law or rule provides that something must happen, it states that it must happen
**provide against** sth *phr v* [T] *formal* to make plans in order to deal with a bad situation that might happen
**provide for** sb/sth *phr v* [T] **1** to give someone the things they need, such as money, food etc: *Without work, how can I provide for my children?* **2** *formal* to make plans in order to deal with something that might happen in the future: *The policy provides for a 60% increase in traffic.* **3** *formal* if a law or rule provides for something, it makes doing that thing possible

**pro·vid·ed** /prəˈvaɪdɪ̈d/ also **provided that** *conjunction* used to say that something will only be possible if something else happens or is done: *I don't mind Guy coming with us, provided he pays for his own meals.* S3 W2

**Prov·i·dence, providence** /ˈprɒvɪ̈dəns‖ˈprɑː-/ *n* [singular, U] a force that some people believe controls our lives, especially because it is what God wants

**prov·i·dent** /ˈprɒvɪ̈dənt‖ˈprɑː-/ *adj formal* careful and sensible, especially by saving money for the future —opposite IMPROVIDENT —**providently** *adv*

**prov·i·den·tial** /ˌprɒvɪ̈ˈdenʃəl◂‖ˌprɑː-/ *adj formal* happening just when you need it; LUCKY: *To Robyn, it seemed a providential opportunity to make the break with Charles.* —**providentially** *adv*

**pro·vid·er** /prəˈvaɪdə‖-ər/ *n* [C] someone who provides something, especially someone who supports a family

**pro·vid·ing** /prəˈvaɪdɪŋ/ also **providing that** *conjunction* used to say that something will only be possible if something else happens or is done: *Sure you can borrow the car, providing you get it back to me before 10 o'clock.* S2

**prov·ince** /ˈprɒvɪ̈ns‖ˈprɑː-/ *n* **1** also **Province** [C] one of the large areas into which some countries are divided: *Sichuan is China's most populous province.* **2 the provinces** *especially BrE* the parts of a country that are not near to the capital city **3 sb's province** a subject that someone knows a lot about or something that they are responsible for: *Sales forecasts are outside my province – talk to the Sales Manager.* **4** an area that an ARCHBISHOP (=a priest of the highest rank) is responsible for —compare DIOCESE W3

**pro·vin·cial[1]** /prəˈvɪnʃəl/ *adj* **1** connected with the parts of a country that are not near the capital city: *a small provincial town* **2** a provincial attitude shows that you are unwilling to accept new ideas or to think about things in new ways —**provincially** *adv*

**provincial[2]** *n* [C] someone who comes from the parts of a country that are not near the capital city

**pro·vin·cial·is·m** /prəˈvɪnʃəlɪzəm/ *n* [U] the attitude of not wanting to accept new ideas and not being interested in new things

**prov·ing ground** /ˈ·· ·/ *n* [C] **1** a place or situation in which something new is tried out or tested: *High-crime areas make ideal proving grounds for new officers.* **2** an area for scientific testing, especially of vehicles

**pro·vi·sion[1]** /prəˈvɪʒən/ *n* **1** [C,U] the act of providing something that someone needs: [+ **of**] *Many women would welcome the provision of childcare facilities at work.* | [+ **for**] *provision for people with disabilities* S3 W1
**2 make provision for** to make plans for future needs: *Ralph wanted to make proper provision for his children.*
**3 provisions** food supplies, especially for a journey
**4** [C] a condition in an agreement or law: *Let me set out the main provisions of the contract.*

**provision[2]** *v* [T] to provide someone or something with a lot of food and supplies, especially for a journey

**pro·vi·sion·al** /prəˈvɪʒənəl/ *adj* **1** intended to exist for only a short time and likely to be changed in the future: *a provisional government* —compare TEMPORARY **2** provisional offers, arrangements etc are not yet definite but should become definite in the future: *We accept a provisional bookings by phone.* —**provisionally** *adv*

**provisional li·cence** /ˌ··· ˈ··/ *n* [C] *BrE* an official document that you need when you are learning to drive; LEARNER'S PERMIT *AmE*

**pro·vi·so** /prəˈvaɪzəʊ‖-zoʊ/ *n* [C] *plural* **provisos** a condition that you ask for before you will agree to something: *The only proviso is that your vacation has to be for a minimum of five nights.*

**prov·o·ca·tion** /ˌprɒvəˈkeɪʃən‖ˌprɑː-/ *n* [C,U] an action or event that makes someone angry or that is intended to do this: *It was a vicious attack, with absolutely no provocation.*

**pro·voc·a·tive** /prəˈvɒkətɪv‖-ˈvɑː-/ *adj* **1** provocative behaviour, remarks etc are intended to make people angry or to cause a lot of discussion: *Some would say he wrote a deliberately provocative book.* **2** provocative clothes, movements etc are intended to make someone sexually excited —**provocatively** *adv*

**pro·voke** /prəˈvəʊk‖-ˈvoʊk/ *v* [T] **1** to cause a sudden reaction that is often very extreme or unpleasant: *The decision to invade provoked storms of protest in the UN.* | **provoke sb to do sth** *It's the first time an article has provoked me to write in to the newspaper.* **2** to try to make someone angry by doing or saying things that you know annoy them: **provoke sb into doing sth** *Don't let him provoke you into losing your temper!*

**Prov·ost** also **provost** /ˈprɒvəst‖ˈproʊvoʊst/ *n* [C] **1** a person in charge of a college in a British university **2** *AmE* an important university official **3** the leader of a Scottish town council —compare MAYOR **4** the main priest in a group of priests connected with a CATHEDRAL in Britain

**pro·vost court** /prəˈvəʊ kɔːt‖ˈproʊvoʊ kɔːrt/ *n* [C] a type of military court

**provost mar·shal** /prəˌvəʊ ˈmɑːʃəl‖ˌproʊvoʊ ˈmɑːr-/ *n* [C] an officer who is in charge of military police

**prow** /praʊ/ *n* [C] *especially literary* the front part of a ship or boat

**prow·ess** /ˈpraʊəs/ *n* [U] *formal* great skill at doing something: *Peregrines are known for their hunting prowess.*

**prowl**[1] /praʊl/ *v* **1** [I,T] if an animal prowls, it moves around an area quietly, especially because it is hunting another animal **2** [I,T] if someone prowls, they move around an area quietly, especially because they are involved in some criminal activity: *gangs prowling the streets* **3** [I always + adv/prep] to walk around a place because you do not have anything to do: [**+around/about**] *Kim prowled restlessly around the room.*

**prowl**[2] *n* [singular] **1 be on the prowl** to be moving around quietly looking for something or someone: *police cars on the prowl* **2** an act of prowling

**prowl·er** /ˈpraʊlə‖-ər/ *n* [C] someone who follows people or waits near their home, especially at night, and frightens or harms them: *If you think there is a prowler outside, don't go out to check – call the police.*

**prox·i·mate** /ˈprɒksəmət‖ˈprɑːk-/ *adj formal* **1** nearest in time, order, or family relationship **2** a proximate cause is a direct one —**proximately** *adv*

**prox·im·i·ty** /prɒkˈsɪməti‖prɑːk-/ *n* [U] *formal* nearness in distance or time: [**+ to**] *Proximity to a good school is important.* | **in close proximity** (=very near)

**prox·y** /ˈprɒksi‖ˈprɑːksi/ *n* [C] **1** someone that you choose to represent you, especially to vote for you **2 by proxy** if you do something by proxy, you arrange for someone else to do it for you

**proxy vote** /ˈ·· ˌ·/ *n* [C] a vote you make by officially sending someone else to vote for you

**prude** /pruːd/ *n* [C] someone who is too easily shocked by anything connected with sex

**pru·dence** /ˈpruːdəns/ *n* [U] a sensible and careful attitude that makes you avoid unnecessary risks

**pru·dent** /ˈpruːdənt/ *adj* sensible and careful, especially by trying to avoid unnecessary risks: *It might be prudent to get a virus detector for the network.* —opposite IMPRUDENT —**prudently** *adv*

**pru·den·tial** /pruːˈdenʃəl/ *adj old-fashioned* PRUDENT —**prudentially** *adv*

**prud·er·y** /ˈpruːdəri/ *n* [U] prudish behaviour

**prud·ish** /ˈpruːdɪʃ/ *adj* too easily shocked by things connected with sex —**prudishly** *adv* —**prudishness** *n* [U]

**prune**[1] /pruːn/ *v* [T] **1** also **prune back** to cut some of the branches of a tree or bush to make it grow better: *I need to prune the roses this weekend.* **2** also **prune down** to get rid of the unnecessary parts of something: *The essay's too long, you need to prune it down.*

**prune**[2] *n* [C] a dried PLUM, usually cooked before eating

**pruning hook** /ˈ·· ·/ *n* [C] a knife that is shaped like a hook and is usually on a long pole, used for cutting branches off trees

**pru·ri·ent** /ˈprʊəriənt‖ˈprʊr-/ *adj formal* too strongly interested in sex —**pruriently** *adv* —**prurience** *n* [U]

**Prus·sian blue** /ˌprʌʃən ˈbluː/ *n* [U] a deep blue colour —**Prussian blue** *adj*

**prus·sic ac·id** /ˌprʌsɪk ˈæsəd/ *n* [U] a very poisonous acid

**pry** /praɪ/ *v present participle* **prying** *past tense* **pried** **1** [I] to try to find out details about someone else's private life in an impolite way: *I don't wish to pry, but is it true that you're having problems at home?* **2** [T always + adv/prep] *especially AmE* to force something open, or force it away from something else; PRISE[3] (2): **pry sth open/away etc** *We finally managed to pry open the door with a screwdriver.* **3 away from prying eyes** in private, where people cannot see: *I'd like to show you something, away from prying eyes.*

**PS** /ˌpiː ˈes/ *n* [C] a note added at the end of a letter, giving more information: *She added a PS asking me to send her some money.* | *Best wishes, Julie. PS If Thursday is not convenient, let me know.*

**psalm** /sɑːm‖sɑːm, sɑːlm/ *n* [C] a song or poem praising God

**psalm·ist** /ˈsɑːməst‖ˈsɑːm-, ˈsɑːlm-/ *n* [C] someone who has written a psalm

**psal·ter** /ˈsɔːltə‖ˈsɒːltər/ *n* [C] a book containing the psalms from the Bible, often with music, for use in a church

**psal·ter·y** /ˈsɔːltəri‖ˈsɒːl-/ *n* [C] an ancient musical instrument with strings stretched over a board

**pse·phol·o·gy** /seˈfɒlədʒi‖siːˈfɑː-/ *n* [U] the study of how people vote in elections —**psephologist** *n* [C]

**pseud** /sjuːd‖suːd/ *n* [C] *BrE informal* someone who pretends to know a lot about art, literature etc —**pseudy** *adj*

**pseudo-** /sjuːdəʊ‖suːdoʊ/ *prefix* not real; false: *pseudo-intellectuals* (=who pretend to be clever) | *He says astrology's just a pseudoscience.*

**pseu·do·nym** /ˈsjuːdənɪm‖ˈsuːdənɪm/ *n* [C] an invented name used by someone, especially a writer, instead of their real name: *Charlotte Bronte wrote under the pseudonym of Currer Bell.* —**pseudonymy** /sjuːˈdɒnəmi‖suːˈdɑː-/ *n* [U]

**pseu·don·y·mous** /sjuːˈdɒnəməs‖suːˈdɑː-/ *adj* written or writing under a pseudonym: *the pseudonymous writer of the 'Insider' column* —**pseudonymously** *adv*

**pshaw** /pʃɔː‖ʃɒː/ *interjection old-fashioned* used to express annoyance, disapproval, or disagreement

**pso·ri·a·sis** /səˈraɪəsəs/ *n* [U] an illness which makes your skin dry, red, and FLAKY (=coming off in small bits)

**psst** /ps/ *interjection* used to attract someone's attention without other people noticing: *Psst! There's someone coming!*

**PST** /ˌpiː es ˈtiː/ the abbreviation of PACIFIC STANDARD TIME

**psych** /saɪk/ *v*

**psych** sb/sth ↔ **out** *phr v* [T] *informal* to do or say things that will make your opponent in a game or competition feel nervous or confused, so that it is easier for you to win: *Leonard stared hard at Duran before the fight, trying to psych him out.*

**psych** sb **up** *phr v* [T] *informal* **1 psych yourself up** to prepare yourself mentally before doing something so that you feel confident: [**+ for**] *So George, tell us how the players psych themselves up for the big game.* **2 be psyched up** also **be psyched** *especially AmE* to be mentally prepared for an event and excited about it

**psych-** /saɪk/ *prefix* another form of the prefix PSYCHO-

**psy·che** /ˈsaɪki/ *n* [C usually singular] *technical or formal* someone's mind, or their basic nature, which controls their attitudes and behaviour: *The image of the independent pioneer lies at the heart of the American psyche.*

**psy·che·del·ic** /ˌsaɪkəˈdelɪk◂/ *adj* **1** psychedelic drugs such as LSD make you HALLUCINATE (=see things that do not really exist) **2** psychedelic art, clothing etc has complicated patterns of strong bright colours, shapes etc —**psychedelically** *adv*

**psy·chi·at·ric** /ˌsaɪki'ætrɪk◂/ *adj* connected with the study and treatment of mental illness: *He'll have to undergo psychiatric treatment at the hospital.* | *psychiatric unit* —**psychiatrically** /-kli/ *adv*

**psychiatric hospital** /·'·· ˌ···/ *n* [C] a hospital where people with mental illnesses are treated

**psy·chi·a·trist** /saɪ'kaɪətrɪ̣st‖sə-/ *n* [C] a doctor trained in the treatment of mental illness —compare PSYCHOLOGIST

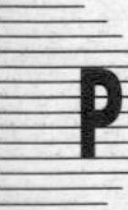

**psy·chi·a·try** /saɪ'kaɪətri‖sə-/ *n* [U] the study and treatment of mental illnesses

**psy·chic¹** /'saɪkɪk/ *adj* [no comparative] **1** also **psychical** /'saɪkɪkəl/ connected with mysterious events involving the power of the human mind: *psychic phenomena* | *psychic research* **2** having the ability to know what other people are thinking or what will happen in the future: *How did you know I was here? You must be psychic!* —compare CLAIRVOYANT **3** also **psychical** affecting the mind rather than the body: *psychic disorders* —**psychically** /-kli/ *adv*

**psychic²** *n* [C] someone who has mysterious powers, especially the ability to receive messages from dead people

**psy·cho** /'saɪkəʊ‖-koʊ/ *n* [C] *informal* someone who is likely to suddenly behave in a violent or crazy way

**psycho-** /saɪkəʊ, -kə‖-koʊ, kə/ *prefix* also **psych-** *technical* concerning the mind, as opposed to the body: *psychotherapy* (=treatment of the mind)

**psy·cho·a·nal·y·sis** /ˌsaɪkəʊ-ə'næləṣəṣ‖-koʊ-/ *n* [U] a way of treating someone who is mentally ill by talking to them about their past life, feelings etc, in order to find out the hidden causes of their problems —**psychoanalytic** /ˌsaɪkəʊ-ænə'lɪtɪk◂‖-koʊænl'ɪtɪk◂/ **psychoanalytical** /-tɪkəl/ *adj*: *psychoanalytic dream interpretation* —**psychoanalytically** /-kli/ *adv*

**psy·cho·an·a·lyst** /ˌsaɪkəʊ'ænəl-ạst‖-koʊ-/ *n* [C] someone who is trained in psychoanalysis

**psy·cho·an·a·lyze** *BrE* also **-ise** /ˌsaɪkəʊ'ænəlaɪz‖-koʊ-/ *v* [T] to treat someone by psychoanalysis

**psy·cho·bab·ble** /'saɪkəʊˌbæbəl‖-koʊ-/ *n* [U] *informal* the language that sounds scientific but is often annoying, that some people use when talking about their emotional problems

**psy·cho·bi·ol·o·gy** /ˌsaɪkəʊbaɪ'ɒlədʒi‖-koʊbaɪ'ɑː-/ *n* [U] the study of the body in relation to the mind

**psy·cho·drama** /'saɪkəʊˌdrɑːmə‖-koʊˌdrɑːmə,-ˌdræmə/ *n* [C] a way of treating mental illness in which people are asked to act in a situation together to help them understand their emotions

**psy·cho·ki·ne·sis** /ˌsaɪkəʊkaɪ'niːsạs‖-koʊkạ-/ *n* [U] the moving of solid objects using only the power of the mind, which some people believe is possible —**psychokinetic** /-kaɪ'netɪk◂‖-kạ'ne-/ *adj* **psychokinetically** /-kli/ *adv*

W3 **psy·cho·log·i·cal** /ˌsaɪkə'lɒdʒɪkəl◂‖-'lɑː-/ *adj* **1** connected with the way that people's minds work and the way that this affects their behaviour **2** illness, fears etc that are psychological are in someone's mind and are not real: *Max says he's got some sort of virus, but I'm sure it's psychological.* **3 psychological warfare** [U] behaviour intended to make your opponents less confident **4 the psychological moment** *informal* the exact time in a situation when you have the best chance to achieve what you want —**psychologically** /-kli/ *adv*: *psychologically disturbed* | *Psychologically* (=from a psychological point of view) *it's a good idea to praise a child for their efforts.*

**psy·chol·o·gist** /saɪ'kɒlədʒạst‖-'kɑː-/ *n* [C] someone who is trained in psychology: *child psychologists* —compare PSYCHIATRIST

W3 **psy·chol·o·gy** /saɪ'kɒlədʒi‖-'kɑː-/ *n* **1** [U] the study of the mind and how it works: *educational psychology* **2** [C,U] the usual way in which a particular person or group thinks and reacts: *the psychology of the mob* **3** [U] *informal* knowledge of the way that people think, that makes you able to control what they do: *Use a bit of psychology. Tell them you think they'd do it better!*

**psy·cho·met·ric** /ˌsaɪkəʊ'metrɪk◂‖-koʊ-/ *adj* for measuring mental abilities and qualities: *psychometric tests*

**psy·cho·path** /'saɪkəpæθ/ *n* [C] someone who has a serious and permanent mental illness that makes them behave in a violent or criminal way —compare SOCIOPATH —**psychopathic** /ˌsaɪkə'pæθɪk◂/ *adj*: *a psychopathic personality* —**psychopathically** /-kli/ *adv*

**psy·cho·sis** /saɪ'kəʊsạs‖-'koʊ-/ *n plural* **psychoses** /-siːz/ [C,U] a serious mental illness that can change your character and make you unable to behave in a normal way —see also PSYCHOTIC

**psy·cho·so·mat·ic** /ˌsaɪkəʊsə'mætɪk◂‖-kəsə-/ *adj* **1** a psychosomatic illness is caused by fear or anxiety rather than by any physical problem **2** concerned with the relationship between the mind and physical illness —**psychosomatically** /-kli/ *adv*

**psy·cho·ther·a·py** /ˌsaɪkəʊ'θerəpi‖-koʊ-/ *n* [U] the treatment of mental illness, for example DEPRESSION, by talking to someone and discussing their problems rather than using drugs or medicine —**psychotherapist** *n* [C]

**psy·chot·ic** /saɪ'kɒtɪk‖-'kɑː-/ *adj* suffering from psychosis: *psychotic behaviour* —**psychotic** *n* [C] —**psychotically** /-kli/ *adv*

**pt** /ˌpiː 'tiː/ **1** the written abbreviation of PART: *Pt. II, Chapter 7, p. 157* **2** the written abbreviation of PAYMENT **3** the written abbreviation of PINT: *Add 1 pt stock.* **4** the written abbreviation of POINT **5** often **Pt** the written abbreviation of PORT (1): *Pt Moresby*

**PT** *n* [U] *especially BrE* physical training; organized games, physical exercises etc at school: *a PT instructor* | *PT lessons at school* —compare GYM (2)

**PTA** /ˌpiː tiː 'eɪ/ *n* [C] Parent-Teacher Association; an organization of parents and teachers that tries to help and improve a particular school: *an active member of the PTA* —compare PTO²

**Pte** *BrE* the written abbreviation of PRIVATE² (2): *Pte Larry Grossman*

**pter·o·dac·tyl** /ˌterə'dæktɪl‖-tl, -tɪl/ *n* [C] a type of large flying animal that lived many millions of years ago

**PTO¹** /ˌpiː tiː 'əʊ‖-'oʊ/ *BrE* please turn over; written at the bottom of a page to tell the reader to look at the next page

**PTO²** *n* [C] *especially AmE* Parent-Teacher Organization; an organization of parents and teachers that tries to help and improve a particular school

**Ptol·e·ma·ic sys·tem** /ˌtɒlạ'meɪ-ɪk ˌsɪstạm‖ˌtɑːl-/ *n* [singular] the old system of belief that the Earth was at the centre of the universe, with the sun, stars and PLANETS moving around it

**pto·maine** /'təʊmeɪn, təʊ'meɪn‖'toʊmeɪn, toʊ-/ *n* [C,U] a poisonous substance formed by BACTERIA in decaying food

**pty** the written abbreviation of PROPRIETARY, used in Australia, New Zealand, and South Africa after the name of a business company: *Australian Wine Growers Pty*

**pub** /pʌb/ *n* [C] a building in Britain where alcohol can be bought and drunk: *Do you fancy going to the pub?* | *a pub lunch* —compare BAR² (1) S W

**pub-crawl** /'· ˌ·/ *n* [C] *informal, especially BrE* a visit to several pubs, one after the other, during which you have a drink in each pub: *a Saturday night pub-crawl*

**pu·ber·ty** /'pjuːbəti‖-ər-/ *n* [U] the stage of physical development during which you change from a child to an adult able to have children

**pu·bes·cent** /pjuː'besənt/ *adj* a pubescent boy or girl is going through puberty

**pu·bic** /'pjuːbɪk/ *adj* [only before noun] related to or near to the sexual organs: *pubic hair*

1 **pub·lic¹** /ˈpʌblɪk/ *adj*
1 **1 ▶ ORDINARY PEOPLE ◀** [no comparative] connected with all the ordinary people in a country, who are not members of the government or do not have important jobs: *The law was changed as a result of public pressure.* | **in the public interest** (=helpful or useful to ordinary people) *Publishing this story was definitely in the public interest.* | **public outcry** (=strong objections from many people) *New taxes provoked a public outcry.*
**2 ▶ FOR ANYONE ◀** [no comparative] available for anyone to use: *a public telephone* | *a public beach* | *proposals to ban smoking in public places*
**3 ▶ GOVERNMENT ◀** [no comparative] connected with the government and with the services it provides for people: **public money** *Simply pumping public money into the railways is not the answer.* | **public office** (=the job of being part of a government) *We do not believe he is fit for public office.* —see also PUBLIC SERVICE
**4 ▶ KNOWN ABOUT ◀** [no comparative] known about by most people: **make sth public** (=tell everyone) *The name of the victim has not been made public.* | **be public knowledge** (=not secret) *It's public knowledge that Ann has an alcohol problem.* | **in the public eye/view** (=on television, radio etc a lot because you are famous) | **public figure** (=famous person)
**5 ▶ NOT HIDDEN ◀** intended for anyone to know, see or hear: *Demands for a public investigation have been ignored.* | **public display of grief/affection etc** (=showing your emotions so that everyone can see)
**6 ▶ PLACE WITH A LOT OF PEOPLE ◀** a public place usually has a lot of people in it: *Don't talk about it here; this place is too public.*
**7 public life** work that you do, especially for the government, that makes you well-known to many people: *Judge Carson retired from public life in 1944.*
**8 public image** the character or attitudes that a famous person, organization etc is thought by most people to have: *Marilyn tried hard to protect her public image.* | *Violence doesn't help the game's public image.*
**9 go public a)** to tell everyone about something that was secret: *We have all the evidence, so now we can go public!* **b)** to become a PUBLIC COMPANY
**10 public appearance** a visit by a famous person in order to make a speech, advertise something etc
**11 public property a)** something that is provided for anyone to use, and is usually owned by the government: *Two demonstrators were charged with damaging public property.* **b)** *informal* something that everyone has a right to know about: *When you're a TV star you're public property it seems!*
**12 public enemy number one** the criminal, problem etc that is considered the most serious threat to people's safety: *Drugs have become public enemy number one.* —compare PRIVATE¹ —**publicly** *adv*: *publicly humiliated*

2 **public²** *n* **1 the public** ordinary people who do not
2 belong to the government or have any special position in society: *The castle is open to the public daily.* | [also + plural verb in *BrE*] *The public are not interested in this issue.* | **the general public** *Our special offer is not available to the general public.* **2 in public** if you do something in public you do it where anyone can see: *Her husband was always nice to her in public.* —opposite **in private** (PRIVATE² (1)), —see also **wash your dirty linen in public** (WASH¹ (6)) **3** [singular, U] the people who like listening to a particular singer, reading a particular writer etc: *A star has to try to please her public.* | [also + plural verb in *BrE*] *Today's theatre-going public are very demanding.*

**public ac·cess** /ˌ·· ˈ··/ *n* [U] the right of ordinary people to go onto particular areas of land or read particular documents: [+ **to**] *public access to information*

**public access chan·nel** /ˌ·· ˈ·· ˌ··/ *n* [C] a television CHANNEL provided by CABLE¹ (3) television companies in the US on which anyone can broadcast

**public-ad·dress sys·tem** /ˌ·· ·ˈ· ˌ··/ *n* [C] a PA (1)

**public af·fairs** /ˌ·· ·ˈ·/ *n* [plural] events and questions, especially political ones, which have an effect on most people: *a public affairs programme on TV*

**pub·li·can** /ˈpʌblɪkən/ *n* [C] *formal, especially BrE* someone who is in charge of a PUB

**pub·li·ca·tion** /ˌpʌbləˈkeɪʃən/ *n* **1** [U] the action of making a book available for sale, or the time at which you do this: *The book is ready for publication.* **2** [C] a book, magazine etc: *a monthly publication* **3** [U] the act of making something known to the public: *the publication of the election results* W2

**public bar** /ˌ·· ˈ·/ *n* [C] *BrE* a room with plain furniture in a PUB, hotel etc where you can buy drinks

**public com·pa·ny** /ˌ·· ˈ···/ *n* [C] *BrE* a company that offers its SHARES for sale on the STOCK EXCHANGE; PUBLIC CORPORATION *AmE*

**public con·ve·nience** /ˌ·· ·ˈ··/ *n* [C] *BrE* a small building with toilets in it, provided for anyone to use

**public cor·po·ra·tion** /ˌ·· ··ˈ··/ *n* [C] **1** *AmE* a company that offers its SHARES for sale on the STOCK EXCHANGE ; PUBLIC COMPANY *BrE* **2** *BrE* a government or organization that controls a business

**public de·fend·er** /ˌ·· ·ˈ··/ *n* [C] *AmE* a lawyer who is paid by the government to defend people in court, because they cannot pay for themselves —compare DISTRICT ATTORNEY

**public do·main** /ˌ·· ·ˈ·/ *n law* **in the public domain** a play, idea etc that is in the public domain is available for anyone to perform or use

**public ex·pen·di·ture** /ˌ·· ·ˈ···/ *n* [U] the money that the government spends on public services

**public foot·path** /ˌ·· ˈ··/ *n* [C] *BrE* a path that everyone has the right to use

**public fund·ing** /ˌ·· ˈ··/ also **public funds** /ˌ·· ˈ·/ *n* [U] money that the government gives to support organizations or events

**public health** /ˌ·· ˈ·/ *n* [U] **1** health care provided by the government, including medical care and public cleaning services **2** the health of all the people in an area: *a danger to public health*

**public hol·i·day** /ˌ·· ˈ···/ *n* [C] a special day when people do not go to work and shops do not open

**public house** /ˌ·· ˈ·/ *n* [C] *BrE formal* a PUB

**public hous·ing** /ˌ·· ˈ··/ *n* [U] *AmE* houses or apartments built by the US government for poor people —compare COUNCIL HOUSE

**public in·quiry** /ˌ·· ·ˈ··‖ˌ·· ˈ···, ˌ·· ·ˈ··/ *n* [C] an official attempt to find out the cause of something, especially an accident

**pub·li·cist** /ˈpʌbləsəst/ *n* [C] someone whose job is to make sure that people find out about a new product, film, book etc or about what a famous person is doing

**pub·lic·i·ty** /pʌˈblɪsəti/ *n* [U] **1** the attention that someone or something gets from newspapers, television etc: *The case has received massive publicity.* | **bad/adverse publicity** (=publicity that makes you look bad) | **publicity stunt** (=something that is only done to get publicity) **2** the business of making sure that people know about a new product, film etc or what a particular famous person is doing: *Who's going to do the show's publicity?* | **publicity campaign** (=a series of activities intended to give something publicity) S2 W3

**pub·li·cize** also **-ise** *BrE* /ˈpʌbləsaɪz/ *v* [T] to give information about something to the public, so that they know about it: *Schools need to publicize their exam results.* | **well-/widely/highly publicized** (=receiving a lot of attention) *the well-publicized financial difficulties that Rochford has faced*

**public lend·ing right** /ˌ·· ˈ·· ·/ *n* [C] a system in Britain by which writers are paid if their books are borrowed from public libraries

**public li·bra·ry** /ˌ·· ˈ···/ *n* [C] a building where people can go to read or borrow books without having to pay

**public lim·it·ed com·pa·ny** /ˌ·· ˌ··· ˈ···/ also **plc** *n* [C] a British company owned by at least two people and whose shares (SHARE² (5)) are available to everyone

**public nui·sance** /ˌ·· ˈ··/ *n* [C] **1** *law* an action that is harmful to everyone: *He committed a public nuisance by blocking the road.* **2** a person who does things that annoy a lot of people

**public o·pin·ion** /ˌ·· ·ˈ··/ *n* [U] the opinions or beliefs that ordinary people have about a particular subject: *The government is bowing to public opinion on this issue.*

**public own·er·ship** /ˌ·· ˈ···/ *n* [U] businesses, property etc in public ownership are owned by the state: *The steel and coal industries were taken into public ownership.*

**public pros·e·cu·tor** /ˌ·· ˈ····/ *n* [C] a British lawyer who works for the government, and tries to prove in a court of law that someone has done something illegal —compare DISTRICT ATTORNEY

**public re·la·tions** /ˌ·· ·ˈ··/ *n* **1** [U] PR; the work of explaining to the public what an organization does, so that they will understand it and approve of it: *a public relations officer in a big oil company* **2** [plural] the relationship between an organization and the public: *Helping the theatre would be good for public relations.*

**public relations ex·er·cise** /ˌ··ˈ·· ˌ··/ *n* [C] something that an organization does just to make itself popular, rather than because it is the right thing to do: *The conference was largely a public relations exercise.*

**public school** /ˌ·· ˈ·/ *n* [C] **1** a private British school, paid for by parents, where children usually live as well as study **2** a free local school, especially in the US and Scotland, controlled and paid for by the government —compare PRIVATE SCHOOL

**public sec·tor** /ˌ·· ˈ··/ *n* [singular] the industries and services in a country that are owned and run by the government: *a job in the public sector | public sector employees* —compare PRIVATE SECTOR

**public serv·ant** /ˌ·· ˈ··/ *n* [C] someone who works for the government, especially someone who is elected

**public serv·ice** /ˌ·· ˈ··/ *n* **1** [C usually plural] a service or product that a government provides, such as electricity, TRANSPORT, etc: *What the people want is decent, local public services.* **2** [C] a service provided to people because it will help them, and not for profit: *This directory is provided as a public service to the community.* **3** [singular, U] the government or its departments: *a career in public service*

**public service an·nounce·ment** /ˌ·· ˈ·· ·ˌ··/ *n* [C] *especially AmE* a special message on television or radio, giving information about an important subject

**public speak·ing** /ˌ·· ˈ··/ *n* [U] the activity of making speeches in public: *a clear voice, used to public speaking*

**public spend·ing** /ˌ·· ˈ··/ *n* [U] the money that the government spends on public services: *We must cut public spending or impose higher taxes.*

**public-spir·it·ed** /ˌ·· ˈ····◂/ *adj* willing to do what is helpful for everyone in society: *decent, public-spirited people*

**public tel·e·vi·sion** /ˌ·· ˈ····, ˌ·· ··ˈ··/ *n* [U] a television service in the US which is paid for by the government, by large companies, and by the public

**public trans·port** /ˌ·· ˈ··/ *BrE*, **public trans·por·ta·tion** /ˌ·· ··ˈ··/ *AmE n* [U] bus services, train services etc, provided for everyone to use

**public works** /ˌ·· ˈ·/ *n* [plural] buildings, roads, PORTS etc provided and built by the government

S3 W1 **pub·lish** /ˈpʌblɪʃ/ *v* **1** [I,T] to arrange the writing, production and sale of a book, magazine etc: *Her second novel was published in July.* | *We publish education books.* **2** [T] if a book, magazine etc publishes a letter, article etc, it prints it for people to read: *We can't publish all the letters we receive.* **3** [T usually passive] to make official information such as a report available for everyone to read: *The latest unemployment figures will be published tomorrow.* **4** [I,T] if a writer or musician publishes their work, they arrange for it to be printed and sold

W3 **pub·lish·er** /ˈpʌblɪʃə‖-ər/ *n* [C] a person or company whose business is to arrange the writing, production and sale of books, newspapers etc

**pub·lish·ing** /ˈpʌblɪʃɪŋ/ *n* [U] the business of producing books and magazines: *Tony wants to get a job in publishing.* | *a new publishing house* —see also **desktop publishing** (DESKTOP (2))

**puce** /pjuːs/ *adj* dark brownish purple —**puce** *n*

**puck** /pʌk/ *n* [C] a hard flat circular piece of rubber that you hit with the stick in the game of ICE HOCKEY

**puck·er** /ˈpʌkə‖-ər/ also **pucker up** *v* [I,T] **1** if your mouth puckers or if you pucker it, the lips are pulled tightly together: *Her mouth puckered up and she started to cry.* **2** [I] if cloth puckers, it gets lines or folds in it and is no longer flat —**pucker** *n* [C] —**puckered** *adj*

**puck·ish** /ˈpʌkɪʃ/ *adj literary* showing that you are amused by other people, and like to make jokes about them: *a puckish grin* —**puckishly** *adv*

**pud** /pʊd/ *n* [C, U] *BrE informal* a PUDDING

**pud·ding** /ˈpʊdɪŋ/ *n* **1** [C,U] a hot sweet dish, made from cake, rice, bread etc with fruit, milk or other sweet things added: *another helping of rice pudding | bread and butter pudding* **2** [C,U] a thick sweet creamy dish, usually made with milk, eggs, sugar, and a little flour, and served cold: *chocolate pudding* **3** [C,U] *BrE* any sweet dish served at the end of a meal: *There's ice-cream for pudding.* —see also DESSERT **4** [C,U] *BrE* a boiled dish that is not sweet, made of a mixture of flour, fat etc, with meat or vegetables inside: *steak and kidney pudding* **5** [C] *BrE informal* someone who is fat and stupid —see also BLACK PUDDING, CHRISTMAS PUDDING, MILK PUDDING, PLUM PUDDING, YORKSHIRE PUDDING **the proof of the pudding is in the eating** (PROOF[1] (5)) 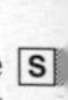

**pudding ba·sin** /ˈ·· ˌ··/ *n* [C] *BrE* **1** a deep round dish in which puddings are cooked **2** a way of cutting someone's hair so that it is in the shape of an upside down bowl

**pud·dle** /ˈpʌdl/ *n* [C] a small pool of water, especially rainwater, on a path, road etc: *Children splashed through the puddles.*

**pu·den·dum** /pjuːˈdendəm/ *n plural* **pudenda** /-də/ [C] *old-fashioned* the sexual organs, especially of a woman

**pudg·y** /ˈpʌdʒi/ *adj* rather fat: *pudgy fingers* —**pudginess** *n* [U]

**pueb·lo** /ˈpwebləʊ‖-loʊ/ *n* [C] *Spanish* a small town, especially in the south west US

**pu·er·ile** /ˈpjʊəraɪl‖-ˈpjʊrəl/ *adj formal* puerile jokes, remarks etc are silly and stupid; CHILDISH: *He's got such a puerile sense of humour.* —**puerility** /pjʊˈrɪləti/ *n* [U]

**pu·er·per·al** /pjuːˈɜːpərəl‖-ˈɜːr-/ *adj technical* happening while giving birth to a child or in the period after this: *puerperal depression*

**puff**[1] /pʌf/ *v* **1** [I] to breathe quickly and with difficulty after running, carrying something heavy etc: *Catherine was puffing loudly as she carried the box into the room.* | [+ **up/along etc**] *Duncan passed me, puffing up the hill.* —see also **huff and puff** (HUFF[1] (1)) **2** [I, T] to breathe in and out while smoking a cigarette, pipe etc: **puff at/on sth** *Dr Foulger paused to puff on his pipe before answering.* **3 a)** [T always + adv/prep] to blow smoke or steam out of something: *Don't puff smoke into my face.* **b)** [I] if smoke or steam puffs from somewhere, it comes out in little clouds: *Steam puffed out of the chimney* **4** [I always + adv/prep] if a steam train puffs along, it moves while sending out little clouds of steam: *By now we were puffing along at a good speed.*

**puff** sth ↔ **out** *phr v* [T] **puff out your cheeks/chest** to make your cheeks etc bigger by filling them with air: *George puffed out his chest proudly*

**puff up** *phr v* **1** [I, T **puff** sth ↔ **up**] to become bigger by increasing the amount of air inside, or to make something bigger in this way: *Bake for 25-30 minutes until the souffle puffs up about 5cm | Birds puff up their feathers to keep warm.* **2** [I] if your eye, face etc puffs up, it swells painfully because of injury or infection: *My eye had puffed up because of a mosquito bite.* **3** [T **puff** sb **up**] to make someone feel very pleased or proud

**puff**[2] *n* [C] **1** the action of taking the smoke from a cigarette etc into your lungs: [+ **at**] *a puff at a cigarette* | **have/take a puff** *"May I have just one puff?" "Sure, I* *thought you didn't smoke."* **2** a sudden small movement of wind, air, or smoke [+ **of**] *puffs of smoke coming from the chimney|The water was calm and there wasn't even a puff of wind.* —see picture on page 416 **3 cheese/cream/lemon puff** a piece of light PASTRY (2) with a soft mixture inside **4 get your puff back** *BrE informal* to be able to breathe normally again after doing something that made you breathe very hard **5 out of puff** *BrE informal* breathing hard and very tired: *He only has to climb the stairs and he's out of puff!*

**puff·ball** /ˈpʌfbɔːl‖-bɒːl/ *n* [C] a type of round FUNGUS that bursts to release its seeds

**puffed** /pʌft/ *adj* [not before noun] *BrE informal* breathing quickly because you have been using lots of energy

**puffed sleeve** /ˌ· ˈ·/ *n* [C] a short sleeve that is wider in the middle than at each end

**puffed up** /ˌ· ˈ·◂/ *adj* behaving in a way that shows you are too proud: *All these pompous, puffed up television pundits make me sick.*

**puffed wheat** /ˌ· ˈ·/ *n* [U] grains of wheat that have been cooked to make them very light and are eaten with milk

**puf·fin** /ˈpʌfɪ̵n/ *n* [C] a North Atlantic seabird with a black and white body and a large brightly coloured beak

**puff pas·try** /ˌ· ˈ··/ *n* [U] a kind of very light PASTRY with a lot of air in it

**puff·y** /ˈpʌfi/ *adj* **puffier, puffiest** puffy eyes, faces, or cheeks are swollen —**puffiness** *n* [U]

**pug** /pʌg/ *n* [C] a small fat short-haired dog with a wide flat face and a short flat nose

**pu·gi·lis·m** /ˈpjuːdʒɪ̵lɪzəm/ *n* [U] *formal* the sport of BOXING (=fighting with your hands)

**pu·gi·list** /ˈpjuːdʒɪ̵lɪ̵st/ *n* [C] *formal* a BOXER (=a sportsman who fights with his hands)

**pug·na·cious** /pʌgˈneɪʃəs/ *adj formal* very eager to quarrel or fight with people —**pugnaciously** *adv* —**pugnacity** /pʌgˈnæsɪ̵ti/ *n* [U]

**puke¹** /pjuːk/ also **puke up** *v* [I,T] *informal* **1** to bring food back up from your stomach through your mouth; VOMIT **2 it makes me puke!** *informal* used to say that something makes you very angry or annoyed: *It makes me puke when I hear rich people complaining about taxes!*

**puke²** *n* [U] *informal* food brought back up from your stomach through your mouth; VOMIT²

**puk·ey**, **puky** /ˈpjuːki/ *adj slang* very unpleasant or unattractive

**puk·ka** also **pukha** /ˈpʌkə/ *adj especially IndE, PakE* **1** very good **2** real, or properly made: *It can't compete with pukka racing cars.* **3** *humorous* too formal

**pul·chri·tude** /ˈpʌlkrɪ̵tjuːd‖-tuːd/ *n* [U] *formal* beauty, especially of a woman

S1 W1 **pull¹** /pʊl/ *v*

**1 ▶ MOVE STH TOWARDS YOU ◀** [I,T] to use your hands to make something move towards you or in the direction that you are moving: *Help me move the piano; you push and I'll pull.* | **pull sth** *I pulled the handle and it just snapped off!* | **pull sth into/away from/over etc** *Pull the chair nearer to the fire.* | **pull sth open/shut** *Ally tried to pull the drawer open.* | **pull hard** *They pulled hard on the rope.* —see picture on page 415

**2 ▶ PUT ON/TAKE OFF ◀** [T always + adv/prep] to put on or take off clothing, usually quickly: *Ted pulled his socks on.* | *pulling off her hat and coat*

**3 ▶ MOVE YOUR BODY ◀** [T always + adv/prep] **a)** to move your arm or your whole body away from someone or something that is holding it or touching it: **pull sth away/off/out of etc** *She pulled her arm out of his grasp.* **b)** to hold onto something and use force to move your body: **pull yourself up/through etc** *Harry pulled himself up onto the wall.*

**4 ▶ CARRIAGE/TRAIN ◀** [T usually passive] if horses or a railway ENGINE pull a carriage etc, they make it move along behind them

**5 ▶ USE A CONTROL ◀** [T] to move a control such as a SWITCH² (1) or TRIGGER towards you to make a piece of equipment work: *She raised the gun, and pulled the trigger.*

**6 ▶ REMOVE ◀** [T always + adv/prep] to use force to take something out of the place where it is fixed or held: **pull sth out/up/away** *Gemma pulled the cork from the bottle.*

**7 ▶ SMOKE ◀** [T always + adv/prep] to take smoke from a cigarette, pipe etc into your lungs: **pull on/at sth** *Todd sat thinking, pulling on his pipe.*

**8 ▶ MUSCLE ◀** [T] to injure one of your muscles by stretching it too much during physical activity; STRAIN² (4): *Paul pulled a muscle trying to lift the freezer.*

**9 ▶ CROWD/VOTES ETC ◀** [T] if an event, performer etc pulls crowds or a politician pulls a lot of votes, a lot of people come to see them or vote for them: *The big match pulled an enormous crowd.* | *She's unlikely to pull many votes.* | **pull the punters** *informal* (=attract customers)

**10 ▶ SEXUALLY ATTRACT ◀** [I,T] *BrE spoken* to attract someone in order to have sex with them: *Ken's hoping to pull the girls with his flashy new car.*

**11 ▶ GUN/KNIFE ◀** [T] to take out a gun or knife ready to use it: **pull sth on sb** *He suddenly pulled a gun on me.*

**12 ▶ BEER ◀** [T] *especially BrE* to get beer out of a BARREL by pulling a handle: *to pull a pint*

**13 ▶ CAR ◀** [I] if a car pulls to the left or right as you are driving, it moves in that direction because of a mechanical problem: *The car seems to be pulling to the left.*

**14 pull sb's leg** to tell someone something that is not true, as a joke

**15 pull the other one (it's got bells on)** *spoken* used to tell someone that you think they are joking or not telling the truth: *A racing driver? Pull the other one!*

**16 pull a fast one** *spoken* to deceive someone: *He was trying to pull a fast one when he told you he'd paid.*

**17 ▶ SUCCEED ◀** [T] *slang, especially AmE* to do something illegal or dishonest such as a crime or trick: *The gang have pulled another bank robbery.* | *What are you trying to pull?*

**18 pull the curtains/the blind** to open or close curtains or a BLIND: *Could you just pull the blind, please?*

**19 ▶ HORSE ◀** [I] if a horse pulls it struggles and presses hard against the piece of metal in its mouth

**20 pull sb's licence** *informal* to take away someone's DRIVING LICENCE because they have done something wrong

**21 pull a punch** to deliberately hit someone with less force than you could do, so that it hurts less —see also **not pull any punches** (PUNCH² (7))

**22 ▶ CRICKET/GOLF ◀** [I,T] *technical* to hit the ball in CRICKET or GOLF so that it does not go straight but moves to one side

**23 ▶ ROW A BOAT ◀** [I,T] to make a boat move by using OARS —see also PUSH¹ —see also **pull/make a face** (FACE¹ (2)), **pull your finger out** (FINGER¹ (7)), **pull rank (on)** (RANK¹ (5)), **pull the rug (out) from under sb's feet** (RUG (3)), **pull your socks up** (SOCK¹ (3)), **pull strings** (STRING¹ (7)), **pull your weight** (WEIGHT¹ (13)), **pull the wool over sb's eyes** (WOOL (4))

**pull ahead** *phr v* [I] if one vehicle pulls ahead of another it gets in front of it by moving faster

**pull** sb/sth **apart** *phr v* [T] **1** to separate people or animals when they are fighting **2** to make someone feel very unhappy: *The constant rows were pulling her apart.*

**pull at** sth *phr v* [T] **1** to take a hold of something and pull it several times: *The child pulled at his mother's coat.* **2** to take smoke from a pipe or cigarette into your lungs: *He pulled at his pipe a couple of times.* **3** *old-fashioned* to take a long drink from a bottle or glass

**pull away** *phr v* [I] **1 a)** to start to drive away from a place where you had stopped: *Matt jumped onto the bus just as it was pulling away.* **b)** to drive or run more quickly than another vehicle or person and leave them behind you: **pull away from sth/sb** *Nkoku is pulling away from the other runners.* **2** to move backwards quickly when someone is trying to touch you or hold you: *I tried to kiss her but she pulled away.*

**pull down** *phr v* [T] **1** [**pull** sth↔ **down**] to destroy a building that is no longer used: *The old chapel is dangerous and will have to be pulled down.* **2 pull down a menu** to make a computer PROGRAM show you a list of the things it can do **3** [**pull** sb **down**] *AmE* to make someone less healthy or successful: *Her problems over the last few months have really pulled her down.*

**pull in** *phr v* **1** [I] if a train pulls in, it arrives at a station **2** [I] if a car or a driver pulls in they move to the side of the road and stop: *She pulled in to let the ambulance pass.* —compare **pull over** (PULL[1]), —see also PULL-IN **3** [T **pull** sb ↔ **in**] if a police officer pulls someone in, they take them to a police station because they think they may have done something wrong **4** [T **pull** sth ↔ **in**] *informal* if you pull in a lot of money you earn it **5** [T **pull** sb/sth **in**] if an event, a show etc pulls in a lot of people they go to see it: *'Les Miserables' has been pulling in huge crowds in New York.*

**pull off** *phr v* [T] *informal* **1** to succeed in doing something difficult: **pull sth ↔ off** *They gave you the money! How did you pull that off?* **2** if a car pulls off a road it turns into a smaller road or entrance: **pull off sth** *We pulled off the road to get some food.*

**pull out** *phr v* **1** [I] if a train pulls out it leaves a station —compare **pull away** (PULL[1]) **2** [I] **a)** to drive onto a road from another road, or after you have stopped at the side: *Don't pull out! There's something coming.* **b)** to drive over to a different part of the road, especially where the traffic is moving faster, in order to OVERTAKE (1): *That truck pulled straight out in front of me.* —see picture on page 415 **3** [I,T **pull** sb/sth ↔ **out**] to get out of a bad situation or dangerous place, or order someone else to do so: *Jim saw that the firm was going to be ruined, so he pulled out.* | *Most of the troops have been pulled out.* —see also **pull out all the stops** (STOP[2] (6))

**pull over** *phr v* [I,T **pull** sth/sb **over**] to stop the vehicle you are driving at the side of the road, or order someone else to do so: *The policeman signalled to him to pull over.*

**pull through** also **pull round** *phr v* [I,T **pull** sb **through**] **1** to stay alive after you have been very ill or badly injured, or help someone do this: *His injuries are severe but he's expected to pull through.* —compare **bring through** (BRING) **2** to succeed even though you have had a lot of difficulties, or help someone do this: *Margaret had real problems, but the teacher pulled her through.*

**pull together** *phr v* **1** [I] if a group of people pull together, they all work hard to achieve something: *If we all pull together, we'll finish on time.* **2 pull yourself together** to force yourself to stop behaving in a nervous, frightened, or disorganized way: *Stop behaving like a baby! Pull yourself together.* **3** [T **pull** sth **together**] to improve something by organizing it more effectively: *We need an experienced manager to pull the department together.*

**pull up** *phr v* **1** [I] to stop the vehicle that you are driving: *Don pulled up at the red light and we stopped behind him.* —see picture on page 415 **2 pull up a chair/stool etc** to get a chair and sit down next to someone who is already sitting **3** [T **pull** sb **up**] to stop someone who is doing something wrong and tell them you do not approve: [**+on**] *I felt I had to pull her up on her lateness.* **4 pull sb up short/pull sb up with a jerk** if something pulls you up short it makes you stop and think about whether you are doing the right thing: *Jan's unexpected criticism pulled me up short.*

**pull²** *n*
**1** ▶ **ACT OF PULLING** ◀ [C] an act of using force to move something towards you or in the same direction that you are moving: *Give the rope a good pull.* —compare TUG[1]
**2** ▶ **FORCE** ◀ [C usually singular] a strong force such as GRAVITY, that makes things move in a particular direction: *gravitational pull of the moon*
**3** ▶ **EMOTIONAL** ◀ [C usually singular] a strong feeling that you want to go to a particular place or person: *The old sailor still felt the pull of the sea.*
**4** ▶ **CLIMB** ◀ [singular] *BrE old-fashioned* a difficult climb up a steep road: *It was a long pull up that hill.*
**5** ▶ **INFLUENCE** ◀ [singular, U] *informal* special influence that gives you an unfair advantage: *His family's name gives him a lot of pull in this town.*
**6** ▶ **SMOKE** ◀ [C] an act of taking the smoke from a cigarette, pipe etc into your lungs: *She took a long pull on her cigarette.*
**7** ▶ **DRINK** ◀ [C] an act of taking a long drink of something: *Brett took a good pull at his beer.*
**8** ▶ **HANDLE** ◀ [C] a rope or handle that you use to pull something: *a bell-pull*
**9** ▶ **CRICKET/GOLF** ◀ [C] a way of hitting the ball in CRICKET (2) or GOLF so that it does not go straight, but moves to one side

**pul·let** /ˈpʊlɪ̈t/ *n* [C] a young chicken during its first year of laying eggs

**pul·ley** /ˈpʊli/ *n* [C] a piece of equipment consisting of a wheel over which a rope or chain is pulled to lift heavy things

**pull-in** /ˈ· ·/ *n* [C] *BrE informal* a place by the side of a road where vehicles can stop and drivers can buy food and drinks

**Pull·man** /ˈpʊlmən/ *n* [C] a very comfortable train carriage, especially one that you can sleep in, or a train made up of these carriages

**pull-on** /ˈ· ·/ *adj* [only before noun] a pull-on shirt, dress etc does not have any buttons, so you pull it on over your head

**pull-out** /ˈ· ·/ *n* [C] **1** part of a book or magazine that can be removed and is like a separate small book: *a 16-page pull-out on cake decorating* **2** the act of an army, business, etc leaving a particular place or area of activity: *The pull-out of troops will begin after the treaty is signed.*

**pull·o·ver** /ˈpʊlˌəʊvə‖-ˌoʊvər/ *n* [C] a piece of WOOLLEN clothing without buttons that you wear on the top half of your body; SWEATER, JUMPER (1) *BrE*

**pull-up** /ˈ· ·/ *n* [C] *AmE* an exercise in which you use your arms to pull yourself up towards a bar above your head

**pul·mo·na·ry** /ˈpʊlmənəri, ˈpʌl/ *adj technical* connected with the lungs or having an effect on the lungs

**pulp¹** /pʌlp/ *n* [U] **1** a very soft substance that is almost liquid: **boil/cook sth to a pulp** *First, boil the vegetables to a pulp.* **2** the soft inside part of a fruit or vegetable: *Halve the melon and scoop out the seeds and pulp.* **3** wood or other substances from plants that are used for making paper **4** books, magazines, films etc that are of poor quality or are badly written **5 beat sb to a pulp** *informal* to hit someone until they are seriously injured **6** part of the inside of a tooth —**pulpy** *adj*

**pulp²** *adj* [only before noun] pulp magazines, stories etc are of poor quality and are often about sex and violence: *pulp novels* | *pulp fiction*

**pulp³** *v* [T] **1** to beat or crush something until it becomes so soft that it is almost liquid: *pulped apples* **2** to make books or newspapers into paper

**pul·pit** /ˈpʊlpɪt/ *n* [C] a raised, box-like structure at the front of a church, from which the priest speaks

**pulp·wood** /ˈpʌlpwʊd/ *n* [U] crushed wood that is used to make paper

**pul·sar** /ˈpʌlsɑː‖-sɑːr/ *n* [C] an object that is far away in space and like a star, that produces a regular radio signal

**pul·sate** /pʌlˈseɪt‖ˈpʌlseɪt/ *v* [I] **1** to make sounds or movements that are strong and regular like a heart beating: *The thumping, pulsating music shook the kitchen walls.* **2** *literary* to be strongly affected by a powerful emotion or feeling: [**+ with**] *The whole city seemed to be pulsating with excitement.*

**pul·sa·tion** /pʌlˈseɪʃən/ *n* **1** [C] *especially technical* a beat of the heart or any regular beat that can be measured **2** [U] pulsating movement

**pulse**[1] /pʌls/ *n* **1** [C usually singular] **a)** the regular beat that can be felt, for example at your wrist, as your heart pumps blood around your body: *I checked his pulse – he was still alive.* **b)** also **pulse rate** the number of these beats per minute: **take/feel sb's pulse** (=to count how many times someone's heart beats in a minute, usually by feeling their wrist) *The nurse took my pulse – it was faster than normal.* | **your pulse quickens/races** (=it gets faster because you are excited, nervous etc) **2** [C] an amount of sound, light, or electricity that continues for a very short time: *emitting pulses of sound at around 200 cycles per second* **3 pulses** [plural] seeds such as beans, PEAS, and LENTILS that can be eaten **4** [C,U] a strong regular beat as in music, or on a drum —see also **have/keep your finger on the pulse** (FINGER[1] (12))

**pulse**[2] *v* [I] **1** to move or flow with a steady rapid beat or sound: *the blood pulsing through his veins* | *coloured lights pulsing in time with the music* **2** if a feeling or emotion pulses through someone, they feel it very strongly: *excitement pulsing through the crowd*

**pul·ver·ize** also **-ise** *BrE* /ˈpʌlvəraɪz/ *v* [T usually passive] **1** to crush something into a powder **2** *informal* to completely defeat someone —**pulverization** /ˌpʌlvəraɪˈzeɪʃən‖-rə-/ *n* [U]

**pu·ma** /ˈpjuːmə/ *n* [C] a COUGAR

**pum·ice** /ˈpʌmɪ̈s/ also **pumice stone** /ˈ·· ·/ *n* **1** [U] very light silver-grey rock that has come from a VOLCANO, and is used as a powder for cleaning **2** [C] a piece of this stone used for rubbing your skin to clean it or make it soft

**pum·mel** /ˈpʌməl/ **pummelled, pummelling** *BrE*, **pummeled, pummeling** *AmE* *v* [T] **1** to hit someone or something many times quickly with your FISTS (=closed hands) *She flew at him and pummelled his chest.* **2** *informal* to completely defeat someone at a sport

3 **pump**[1] /pʌmp/ *n* **1** [C] a machine for forcing liquid or gas into or out of something: **water/air/beer etc pump** (=for moving water/air etc) | **hand/foot pump** (=operated by your hand or foot) —see picture at BICYCLE | **petrol pump/gas pump** (=for putting petrol or gas into cars) —see also STOMACH PUMP —see picture at BICYCLE[1] **2** [C usually plural] *BrE* a flat light shoe for dancing, exercise etc: *a pair of ballet pumps* **3** [C usually plural] *especially AmE* a woman's plain shoe that does not fasten —see picture at SHOE[1] **4** [C usually plural] *BrE* a shoe made of CANVAS (=thick cloth) with rubber on the bottom, used for sports: *Don't forget your pumps for PE.* **5** [C] an act of pumping **6 all hands to the pumps** used to say that everyone must work hard because a very difficult job has to be done —see also HEAT PUMP, **prime the pump** (PRIME[3] (4)), PARISH PUMP

**pump**[2] *v* **1** [T always + adv/prep] to make liquid or gas move in a particular direction with a pump: **pump sth into/out of/through etc** *The fire department are still pumping floodwater out of the cellars.* | **pump gas** *AmE* (=put petrol into your car at a petrol station) **2** also **pump away** [I] to move very quickly in and out or up and down: *My heart was pumping fast.* **3** also **pump away** [I] to operate a pump: *He pumped away furiously.* **4** [T] to bring a supply of water, oil etc to the surface from under the ground **5** [I always + adv/prep] when a liquid pumps from somewhere, it comes out in sudden small amounts: [+ **from/out of etc**] *The blood was pumping from the wound in his thigh.* **6** [T] *informal* to ask someone a lot of questions, in order to find out something: **pump sb for sth** *I tried to pump him for information about their other contacts.* **7 pump sb full of sth** to put a lot of drugs into someone's body: *athletes pumped full of steroids* **8 pump iron** *informal* to do exercises by lifting heavy weights **9 have your stomach pumped** to have the contents of your stomach removed by a pump, after swallowing something harmful

**pump** sth **into** sb/sth *phr v* [T] **pump bullets into sb/sth** *informal* to shoot someone several times

**pump out** *phr v* **1** [I,T] if something such as music, information, or a supply of products is pumped out or pumps out, a lot of it is produced: *There's a huge amount of propaganda pumped out by the food industry.* | *Music pumped out from the loudspeakers overhead.* **2** [T **pump** sth ↔ **out**] to remove liquid from something using a pump: *You'll have to pump the boat out.*

**pump** sth ↔ **up** *phr v* [T] **1** to fill a tyre, AIRBED etc with air until it is correctly filled; INFLATE (1) **2** to increase the value, amount etc of something: *The US was able to pump up exports.* **3 pump up the music/volume etc** *slang* to play music louder

**pump** sb ↔ **up** [T] to increase someone's excitement, interest etc: *He was really pumped up before the game.*

**pump-ac·tion** /ˈ· ··/ *adj* **a pump action shotgun/hairspray etc** a SHOTGUN etc that is operated by pulling or pressing part of it in or out

**pum·per·nick·el** /ˈpʌmpənɪkəl‖ˈpʌmpər-/ *n* [U] a heavy dark brown bread

**pump·kin** /ˈpʌmpkɪ̈n/ *n* **1** [C,U] a very large orange fruit that grows on the ground, or the inside of this fruit: *pumpkin pie* —see picture on page 414 **2** [singular] *AmE* a way of addressing someone you love

**pump room** /ˈ· ·/ *n* [C] a room at a SPA where you can go to drink the water

**pun**[1] /pʌn/ *n* [C] an amusing use of a word or phrase that has two meanings, or of words with the same sound but different meanings, for example: *Seven days without water make one weak.* (=1 week)

**pun**[2] *v* **punned, punning** [I + **on**] to make a pun

**punch**[1] /pʌntʃ/ *v* [T] **1** to hit someone or something hard with your FIST (=closed hand) **punch sb in/on sth** *Gallacher swung round and punched me hard in the stomach.* | **punch sb/sth** *I punched the wall in anger.* | **punch the air** (=to make a movement like a punch, to show that you are very pleased about something) —see picture on page 1259 **2** to make a hole in something using a metal tool or other sharp object: **punch a ticket/card etc** *The guard punched my ticket.* | **punch a hole in/through sth** *These bullets can punch a hole through 20mm steel plate.* **3** to push a button or key on a machine: *Sally punched the eighth floor button and the doors shut.* **4** *AmE* to move cattle from one place to another **5 punch holes in an argument/idea etc** *BrE* to disagree with someone's idea or plan and show what is wrong with it **6 punch the clock** *AmE informal* to record the time that you start or finish work by putting a card into a special machine **7 punch sb's lights out** *AmE informal* to hit someone hard in the face S3

**punch in** *phr v* **1** [I] *AmE* to record the time that you arrive at work, by putting a card into a special machine; CLOCK IN **2** [T **punch** sth ↔ **in**] to put information into a computer by pressing buttons or keys

**punch out** *phr v AmE* [I] **1** to record the time that you leave work, by putting a card into a special machine; CLOCK OUT **2** [T **punch** sb **out**] to hit someone so hard that they fall over

**punch**[2] *n* **1** [C] a quick strong hit made with your FIST (=closed hand): **punch in/on etc** *a punch in the kidneys* | **throw a punch** (=aim a punch at someone) **2** [U] a strong, effective quality in the way that you express things that makes people interested: *The speech was O.K. but it had no real punch.* **3** [C] a metal tool for cutting holes or for pushing something into a small hole: *a hole punch* **4** [C,U] a drink made from fruit juice, sugar, water, and usually some alcohol: *a bowl of rum punch* **5 as pleased as Punch** very happy: *He's as pleased as Punch about the baby.* **6 beat sb/sth to the punch** *informal* to do or get something before someone else **7 not pull any punches** *informal* to express your disapproval very clearly, without trying to hide what you feel: *He wasn't pulling any punches! He said my work was 'pathetic'.* —see also **pack a (hard) punch** (PACK[1] (10))

**Punch and Ju·dy show** /ˌpʌntʃ ən ˈdʒuːdi ʃəʊ‖-ʃoʊ/ *n* [C] a traditional type of entertainment for children, especially at British SEASIDE towns, that uses PUPPETS

**punch·bag** /ˈpʌntʃbæg/ *BrE*, **punching bag** *AmE* /ˈ· · ·/ *n* [C] **1** a heavy leather bag hung from a rope, that is punched for exercise **2 use sb as a punchbag** *BrE informal* to hit or punch someone

**punch ball** /ˈ· ·/ *n* [C] a large leather ball that is fixed on a spring and is punched for exercise

**punch bowl** /ˈ· ·/ *n* [C] a large bowl in which punch (=a mixed drink) is served

**punch-drunk** /ˈ· ·/ *adj* **1** *informal* very confused, especially because you have had continuous bad luck or have been treated badly **2** a BOXER who is punch-drunk is suffering brain damage from being hit too much

**punched card** /ˌ· ˈ·/ also **punch card** /ˈ· ·/ *n* [C] a card with a pattern of holes in it that was used in the past for putting information into a computer

**punch line** /ˈ· ·/ *n* [C] the last few words of a joke or story, that make it funny or surprising

**punch-up** /ˈ· ·/ *n* [C] *BrE informal* a fight: *Two people are to appear in court after a punch-up at their London home.*

**punch·y** /ˈpʌntʃi/ *adj* a punchy piece of writing or speech is very effective because it expresses ideas clearly in only a few words: *a punchy article* —**punchiness** *n* [U]

**punc·til·i·ous** /pʌŋkˈtɪliəs/ *adj formal* being very careful to behave correctly and keep exactly to rules: *Jimmy was always most punctilious about repaying any loans.* —**punctiliously** *adv* —**punctiliousness** *n* [U]

**punc·tu·al** /ˈpʌŋktʃuəl/ *adj* arriving, happening etc at exactly the time that has been arranged: *She's always very punctual for appointments.* | *the punctual payment of invoices* —**punctually** *adv*: *The meeting began punctually at nine o'clock.* —**punctuality** /ˌpʌŋktʃuˈælɪ̈ti/ *n* [U]

**punc·tu·ate** /ˈpʌŋktʃueɪt/ *v* **1** [T] to divide written work into sentences, phrases etc using COMMAS, FULL STOPS etc **2 be punctuated by/with sth** to be interrupted many times with something such as a noise: *silence occasionally punctuated by laughter*

**punc·tu·a·tion** /ˌpʌŋktʃuˈeɪʃən/ *n* [U] the marks used in dividing a piece of writing into sentences, phrases etc

**punctuation mark** /ˌ··ˈ·· ·/ *n* [C] a sign, such as a COMMA or QUESTION MARK, that is used in dividing a piece of writing into sentences, phrases etc

**punctuation marks**

| | |
|---|---|
| . | full stop *BrE* / period *AmE* |
| , | comma |
| ; | semi-colon |
| : | colon |
| ? | question mark |
| ! | exclamation mark *BrE*/ exclamation point *AmE* |
| ( ) | brackets |
| " " | quotation marks |

**punc·ture**¹ /ˈpʌŋktʃə‖-ər/ *n* [C] **1** *BrE* a hole made accidentally in a tyre, so that air comes out of it; FLAT² (2) *AmE*: *I'm sorry I'm late; I had a puncture.* | *to mend a puncture* **2** a small hole made by a sharp point

**puncture**² *v* **1** [T] to make a small hole through the surface of something, especially in a tyre: *A nail on the road punctured one of my tyres.* | *Puncture some holes in the cover.* **2** [I] if a ball, tyre etc punctures, it gets a small hole in it so that gas or air comes out: *The ball punctured on the holly bush.* **3** [T] to suddenly destroy a feeling or belief, making someone feel unhappy, silly, or confused: *The shocking news finally punctured his smug complacency.*

**pun·dit** /ˈpʌndɪ̈t/ *n* [C] someone who knows a lot about a particular subject, and is often asked for their opinions on it: *political pundits*

**pun·gent** /ˈpʌndʒənt/ *adj* **1** a pungent taste or smell is strong and sharp: *the pungent aroma of garlic* **2** pungent remarks or writing criticize something in a very direct and clever way: *a few typically pungent remarks from Senator Moynihan* —**pungently** *adv* —**pungency** *n* [U]

**pun·ish** /ˈpʌnɪʃ/ *v* [T] **1** to make someone suffer because they have done something wrong or broken the law: *Some people believe that smacking is not an acceptable way to punish a child.* | *In some countries women who have abortions can be punished by imprisonment.* | **punish sb for (doing) sth** *Ewing was hauled before the Football Association to be punished for misconduct.* **2** if you punish a crime you punish anyone who is guilty of it: *Vandalism will be severely punished.* **3 punish yourself (for sth/for doing sth)** to blame yourself for something: *The accident wasn't your fault; stop punishing yourself.*

**pun·ish·a·ble** /ˈpʌnɪʃəbəl/ *adj* a punishable act may be punished by law, especially in a particular way: *a punishable offence* | [+ **by**] *Murder is punishable by death.*

**pun·ish·ing**¹ /ˈpʌnɪʃɪŋ/ *adj* **punishing schedule/workload/journey etc** a SCHEDULE etc that is so long or difficult that it makes you tired and weak: *a punishing regime of exercise and diet* —**punishingly** *adv*

**punishing**² *n* **take a punishing** *informal* to suffer rough or damaging treatment: *The car took a real punishing on the journey.*

**pun·ish·ment** /ˈpʌnɪʃmənt/ *n* **1** [C] a way in which someone or something is punished: [+ **for**] *I sent Alex to bed early as a punishment for breaking the window.* | *You know the punishment for treason, don't you?* | **a harsh/severe punishment** (=one that makes someone suffer a lot) **2** [U] the act of punishing someone or the process of being punished: *We are determined that the terrorists will not escape punishment.* **3** [U] *informal* rough treatment; damage: *With five children in the house, the furniture has to take a lot of punishment.* —see also CAPITAL PUNISHMENT, CORPORAL PUNISHMENT W

**pu·ni·tive** /ˈpjuːnɪ̈tɪv/ *adj* **1 punitive taxes/price increases etc** taxes etc that are so severe that people find it very difficult to pay: *The new Bill enables people to sue and win punitive damages for discrimination.* **2** | **punitive actions/measures/damages etc** actions etc that are intended to punish someone: *plans to take punitive action against terrorists* —**punitively** *adv*

**punk** /pʌŋk/ *n* **1** also **punk-rock** /ˌ· ˈ·/ [U] a type of loud violent music popular in the late 1970s and the 1980s: *great punk bands like the Sex Pistols and X-Ray spex* **2** also **punk-rocker** [C] someone who dresses like people who follow punk rock, with brightly-coloured hair, chains and pins and torn clothing: *Marilyn was a punk in '79.* | *punk hairstyles* **3** [C] *AmE slang* a young man or a boy who fights and breaks the law: *You little punk!* **4** [U] *AmE* a substance that burns without a flame and is used to light FIREWORKS etc

**pun·kah** /ˈpʌŋkə/ *n* [C] *especially IndE, PakE* a FAN¹ (2) hung across a room and swung backwards and forwards by pulling a rope, especially in the past

**pun·kin** /ˈpʌŋkɪ̈n/ *n* [C] *AmE* another spelling of PUMPKIN (2)

**pun·net** /ˈpʌnɪ̈t/ *n* [C] *BrE* a small square basket in which soft fruits such as strawberries (STRAWBERRY) are sold, or the amount contained in one of these

**pun·ster** /ˈpʌnstə‖-ər/ *n* [C] someone who makes PUNS (=jokes involving two words that sound similar)

**punt**¹ /pʌnt/ *n* **1** [C] a long narrow river-boat with a flat bottom and square ends, that is moved by pushing a long pole against the bottom of the river **2** [singular] the act of going out in a punt: *Let's go for a punt.* **3** [C] in American football, a long kick that you make after dropping the ball from your hands **4** [C] *BrE informal* money that you risk on the result of something such as a race; a BET **5 take a punt** *informal* to make a guess when you do not have full enough information to make a proper decision

**punt²** *v* **1** [I,T] in American football, to drop the ball from your hands and kick it: *He punted the ball forty yards.* —see picture on page 1263 **2** [I,T] to go or take someone on a river by punt: *We were punting up the river.*

**punt·er** /ˈpʌntə‖-ər/ *n* [C] **1** *BrE informal* someone who makes a BET (=risks money) on the result of a horse race etc: *a regular punter* **2** *BrE informal* someone who uses a product or a service; customer: *You've got to try to please the punters.* **3** the player who punts the ball in American football

**pu·ny** /ˈpjuːni/ *adj* **1** small, thin, and weak: *a puny little guy* **2** unimpressive and ineffective: *my own puny attempts at humour* —**puniness** *n* [U]

**pup¹** /pʌp/ *n* [C] **1** a young dog; a PUPPY: *a spaniel pup* **2** a young SEAL¹ (1) or OTTER: *seal pups* **3** *old-fashioned* an insulting word for a young man who is rude or too confident: *Don't you threaten me, you young pup!* **4 be sold a pup** *BrE old-fashioned* to be tricked into buying something that is worthless or useless

**pup²** *v* [I] *technical* to give birth to pups

**pu·pa** /ˈpjuːpə/ *n plural* **pupas** or **pupae** /-piː/ [C] an insect in the middle stages of its development when it is protected inside a special cover —**pupal** *adj*: *in the pupal stage*

**pu·pate** /pjuːˈpeɪt‖ˈpjuːpeɪt/ *v* [I] *technical* to become a pupa

S2 W1 **pu·pil** /ˈpjuːpəl/ *n* [C] **1** *especially BrE* someone who is being taught, especially a child: *This school has about 500 pupils.* | *I teach private pupils on Wednesdays.* **2** the small black round area in the middle of your eye —see picture at EYE¹

**pup·pet** /ˈpʌpɪt/ *n* [C] **1** a model of a person or animal that you can move by pulling wires or strings, or by putting your hand inside it: *a puppet show* **2** a person or organization that has lost their independent position and allows someone else to control them: *She's just a puppet of the management.* | **puppet government/regime** (=a government controlled by a more powerful country or organization)

**pup·pe·teer** /ˌpʌpɪˈtɪə‖-ˈtɪr/ *n* [C] someone who performs with puppets

S3 **pup·py** /ˈpʌpi/ *n* [C] **1** a young dog **2** *old-fashioned* a young man who is rude or too confident

**puppy fat** /ˈ·· ·/ *n* [U] *BrE informal* fat that children have on their bodies that they usually lose as they get older

**puppy love** /ˈ·· ·/ *n* [U] a young boy's or girl's love for someone, which people do not regard as serious: *It's only puppy love; he'll grow out of it.*

**pur·blind** /ˈpɜːblaɪnd‖ˈpɜːr-/ *adj formal or literary* stupid or dull

S3 W3 **pur·chase¹** /ˈpɜːtʃɪs‖ˈpɜːr-/ *v* [T] **1** *formal* to buy something, especially something big or expensive: *a loan to purchase a new car* **2** *literary* to gain something but only by losing something else: *They purchased life at the expense of honour.* —**purchasable** *adj*

S3 W3 **purchase²** *n* **1** [C, U] *formal* the act of buying something: *Fill in the date of purchase.* | *The company spent a lot on expansion including the purchase of a large warehouse.* | **make a purchase** (=buy something) —see also HIRE PURCHASE —see graph at BUY **2** [C usually plural] *formal* something that has been bought: *Do you wish us to deliver your purchases?* **3 on special purchase** being sold at a cheaper price than usual: *These boots are on special purchase.* **4** [singular, U] *formal* a firm hold with your hands or feet: *I tried to gain a purchase on the narrow ledge.*

**purchase price** /ˈ·· ·/ *n* [singular] *formal* the price that has to be paid if you want to buy something: *We need to borrow 80% of the purchase price.*

**pur·chas·er** /ˈpɜːtʃɪsə‖ˈpɜːrtʃɪsər/ *n* [C] *formal* the person who buys something

**purchasing pow·er** /ˈ··· ˌ··/ *n* [U] **1** the amount of money that a person or group has available to spend compared to other people: *Widespread wage rises result in increased purchasing power.* **2** the value of a unit of money considered in terms of how much you can buy with it: *The purchasing power of the dollar has declined.*

**pur·dah** /ˈpɜːdə, -dɑː‖ˈpɜːr-/ *n* [U] **1** the custom, especially among Muslim people, according to which women stay in their home or cover their faces so that they cannot be seen by men **2 in purdah a)** women who are in purdah live according to this custom **b)** staying away from other people

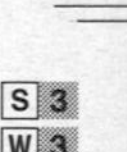

**pure** /pjʊə‖pjʊr/ *adj* S3 W3

**1** ► **NOT MIXED** ◄ not mixed with anything else: *Is this sweater made of pure wool?* | *The cocaine was 95% pure.* | *The purest form of the southern accent can be heard in Tennessee.*

**2 pure chance/greed/hell etc** complete chance etc: *By pure chance my boss was flying on the same plane as me.* | *"How was the exam?" "Pure hell!"* | *a work of pure genius* | *the pure thrill of living*

**3** ► **CLEAN** ◄ clean, without anything harmful or unhealthy: *The air by the sea is pure and healthy.* | *pure drinking water*

**4** ► **WITHOUT EVIL** ◄ having no evil ideas or plans, especially no sexual thoughts or experience; INNOCENT¹ (4): *a pure young girl* | *I'm sure he had the purest of motives.*

**5** ► **COLOUR** ◄ clear and not mixed with other colours: *a cloudless sky of the purest blue*

**6** ► **SOUND** ◄ very clear and beautiful to hear: *a pure note* | *a lovely pure soprano*

**7** ► **ART** ◄ a pure form of art is done exactly according to an accepted standard or pattern

**8 as pure as the driven snow** an expression meaning morally perfect, often used jokingly to describe someone who is not like this at all

**9 pure and simple** *especially spoken* used to say that there is only one reason for something: *The mistake was due to carelessness, pure and simple.*

**10 pure science/mathematics etc** work done in science etc in order to increase our knowledge of it rather than to make practical use of it: *pure and applied research* —compare APPLIED —see also IMPURE, PURELY, PURIFY, PURITY —**pureness** *n* [U]

**pure·blood·ed** /ˌpjʊəˈblʌdɪd◄‖ˌpjʊr-/ *adj* with parents, grandparents etc from only one group or race of people, with no mixture of other groups

**pure·bred** /ˈpjʊəbred‖ˈpjʊr-/ *adj* coming from only one breed of animal with no mixture of other breeds: *purebred Irish wolfhounds* —compare PEDIGREE², THOROUGHBRED (1) —**purebred** *n* [C]

**pu·ree**, **purée** /ˈpjʊəreɪ‖pjʊˈreɪ/ *n* [C,U] food that is boiled or crushed until it is a soft mass that is almost liquid: *apple puree* | *tomato puree* —**puree, purée** *v* [T]

**pure·ly** /ˈpjʊəli‖ˈpjʊrli/ *adv* **1** completely and only, without anything else being involved: *a decision that was taken for purely political reasons* | *I bumped into Sally purely by chance.* **2 purely and simply** used to emphasize that only one reason or purpose is involved in a situation or decision: *I can tell you now, I'm doing it purely and simply for the money.* S2 W3

**pur·ga·tive** /ˈpɜːgətɪv‖ˈpɜːr-/ *n* [C] a medicine or food that makes your BOWELS empty themselves —**purgative** *adj*: *Figs often have a purgative effect.*

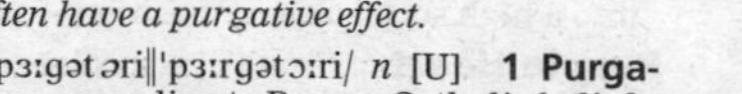

**pur·ga·tory** /ˈpɜːgətəri‖ˈpɜːrgətɔːri/ *n* [U] **1 Purgatory** a place where, according to Roman Catholic beliefs,

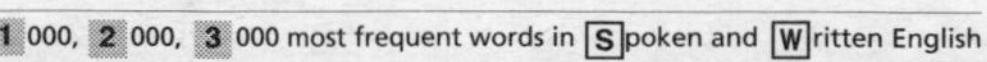

the souls of dead people must suffer for the bad things they did, until they are pure enough to enter heaven **2** *humorous* a place, situation, or time when you suffer a lot: *It's purgatory listening to Ben trying to play the violin!* —**purgatorial** /ˌpɜːɡəˈtɔːriəl◂‖ˌpɜir-/ *adj*

**purge[1]** /pɜːdʒ‖pɜːrdʒ/ *v* [T] **1** to force your opponents or people who disagree with you to leave an organization or place, often by using violence: **purge sth of sb/sth** *an attempt to purge the region of ethnic minorities* | **purge sb/sth from sth** *purging dissidents from the party* **2** *literary* to get rid of your bad feelings such as hatred: **purge sb/sth of sth** *It took her months to purge herself of her feelings of guilt.* | **purge sth from sth** *You must purge this hatred from your soul.* **3** *old-fashioned* to take a medicine to clear all the waste from your BOWELS

**purge[2]** *n* [C] **1** an action to remove your opponents or people who disagree with you from an organization or place, often using violence: *The new president carried out a purge of disloyal army officers.* | *the Stalinist purges of the 1930s* **2** *old-fashioned* a medicine that clears all the waste from your BOWELS

**pu·ri·fi·ca·tion** /ˌpjʊərɪ̇fɪ̇ˈkeɪʃən‖ˌpjʊr-/ *n* [U] **1** a process that removes the dirty or unwanted parts from something: *a water purification plant* **2** acts or ceremonies to remove evil from someone: *ritual purification*

**pu·ri·fy** /ˈpjʊərɪ̇faɪ‖ˈpjʊr-/ *v* **purified, purifying** [T] **1** to remove the dirty or unwanted parts from something: *The liquid is purified by passing it through charcoal.* **2** to get rid of evil from your soul —**purifier** *n* [C] *a water purifier*

**pur·ist** /ˈpjʊərɪ̇st‖ˈpjʊr-/ *n* [C] someone who has very strong ideas about what is correct, for example in matters of grammar, art, or music: *The purists won't like it but opera on TV certainly brings in the audiences.* —**purism** *n* [U]

**pu·ri·tan** /ˈpjʊərɪ̇tən‖-ˈpjʊr-/ *n* [C] **1** someone who has very strict moral standards and thinks that pleasure is unnecessary or wrong **2 Puritan** a member of a Protestant religious group in the 16th and 17th centuries, who wanted to make religion simpler —**puritan** also **Puritan** *adj*: *a Puritan background* | *puritan beliefs*

**pu·ri·tan·i·cal** /ˌpjʊərɪ̇ˈtænɪkəl◂‖ˌpjʊr-/ *adj* having extreme attitudes about religion and moral behaviour: *a puritanical father who wouldn't let his children watch television* —**puritanically** /-kli/ *adv*

**pu·ri·tan·is·m** /ˈpjʊərɪ̇tənɪzəm‖ˈpjʊr-/ *n* [U] **1** a way of living according to very strict rules, especially concerning religion and moral behaviour **2 Puritanism** the beliefs and practices of the Puritans

**pu·ri·ty** /ˈpjʊərɪ̇ti‖ˈpjʊr-/ *n* [U] the quality or state of being pure: *Strict controls are needed to ensure the purity of herbal drugs.* —opposite IMPURITY

**purl[1]** /pɜːl‖pɜːrl/ *v* [I,T] to use the purl stitch when you KNIT (=make clothes from wool)

**purl[2]** *n* [U] one of the types of stitches that you use when you KNIT (=make clothes from wool)

**pur·lieus** /ˈpɜːljuːz‖ˈpɜːrluːz/ *n* [plural] *literary* the area in and around a place

**pur·loin** /pɜːˈlɔɪn, ˈpɜːlɔɪn‖-ɜːr-/ *v* [T] *formal or humorous* to steal or borrow something without permission: *Marek managed to purloin a copy of the house key.*

**pur·ple** /ˈpɜːpəl‖ˈpɜːr-/ *n* [U] **1** a dark colour that is a mixture of red and blue —see picture on page 411 **2 purple with rage/purple in the face etc** very red in the face as a result of being angry or embarrassed **3 purple passage/prose/patch** a piece of writing that has a grander style **4 born to the purple** *literary* born into a high social class or position —**purple** *adj*

**Purple Heart** /ˌ·· ˈ·/ *n* [C] a special MEDAL given to US soldiers who have been wounded in battle

**purple heart** *n* [C] *informal* a PILL containing an illegal drug that gives you a feeling of energy and excitement

**pur·plish** /ˈpɜːplɪʃ‖ˈpɜːr-/ *adj* slightly purple: *purplish blue*

**pur·port[1]** /pɜːˈpɔːt‖pɜːrˈpɔːrt/ *v* [I,T] **purport to be/be purported to be** *formal* to claim to be something, and give the impression that it is true, even if it is not: *The letter is purported to be a secret agreement between the president and the general.*

**pur·port[2]** /ˈpɜːpɔːt, -pət‖ˈpɜːrpɔːrt/ *n* [U] *formal* the general meaning of what someone says: [+ **of**] *The purport of her remarks was clear.*

**pur·pose[1]** /ˈpɜːpəs‖ˈpɜːr-/ *n* S W

**1 ▶ WHAT STH IS SUPPOSED TO DO ◀** [C] the thing that an event, process, or activity is supposed to achieve, or the job that something is supposed to do —see REASON[1] (USAGE): [+ **of**] *The purpose of this meeting is to elect a new committee.* | *What is the purpose of the little red button?* | **the purpose of doing sth** *The sole purpose of conducting a business is to make money.* | **serve a purpose** (=have a particular purpose, or help you achieve a purpose) *The discussion serves a twin purpose – instruction and feedback.* | *No useful purpose will be served by re-opening the murder enquiry.*

**2 on purpose** deliberately: *Jack's been really annoying me and I think he's doing it on purpose.*

**3 ▶ PLAN ◀** [C] *formal* an intention or a plan: *Tom went for a walk, with no definite purpose in mind.* | **purpose in doing sth** *My main purpose in setting up the experiment was to obtain fresh data.*

**4 ▶ AIM ◀** [U] the feeling of having an aim in life: *I need to find meaning and purpose in my life.*

**5 for all practical purposes** also **for all intents and purposes** used to say that something may not exactly be true but it is true in general: *She became for all practical purposes, a director of the company.*

**6 for the purposes of** used to say that someone or something will be considered in a particular way in a discussion, document etc: *For tax purposes you will be treated as a married couple.*

**7 serve its purpose** if something serves its purpose, it does what you intended it to do: *Our holiday had served its purpose; we both felt thoroughly relaxed.*

**8 to good purpose/to no purpose** *formal* with good results or with no results: *Clara has used her musical talents to good purpose.*

**9 to the purpose** *old-fashioned* useful or helpful —see also **accidentally on purpose** (ACCIDENTALLY (2)), PURPOSELY, CROSS-PURPOSES

**purpose[2]** *v* [T] *old use* to intend to do something: *Drake purposed to voyage around the globe.*

**purpose-built** /ˌ·· ˈ·◂/ *adj BrE* designed and made for a particular purpose: *purpose-built toilets for disabled people*

**pur·pose·ful** /ˈpɜːpəsfəl‖ˈpɜːr-/ *adj* having a clear aim or purpose; determined: *a purposeful man who wouldn't worry about who he hurt* —**purposefully** *adv* —**purposefulness** *n* [U]

**pur·pose·less** /ˈpɜːpəsləs‖ˈpɜːr-/ *adj* not having a clear aim or purpose: *a purposeless existence on the streets of London* —**purposelessly** *adv* —**purposelessness** *n* [U]

**pur·pose·ly** /ˈpɜːpəsli‖ˈpɜːr-/ *adv formal* deliberately: *a purposely provocative comment*

**purr** /pɜː‖pɜːr/ *v* **1** [I] if a cat purrs, it makes a soft, low sound in its throat to show that it is pleased: *A big grey tom cat sat in his lap purring contentedly.* **2** [I] if the engine of a vehicle or machine purrs, it works perfectly and makes a quiet smooth sound: *The big Bentley purred along the wide road.* **3** [I,T] if someone purrs, they speak in a soft, low, and SEXY voice: *"Are you doing anything tonight?" she purred.* —**purr** *n* [C]

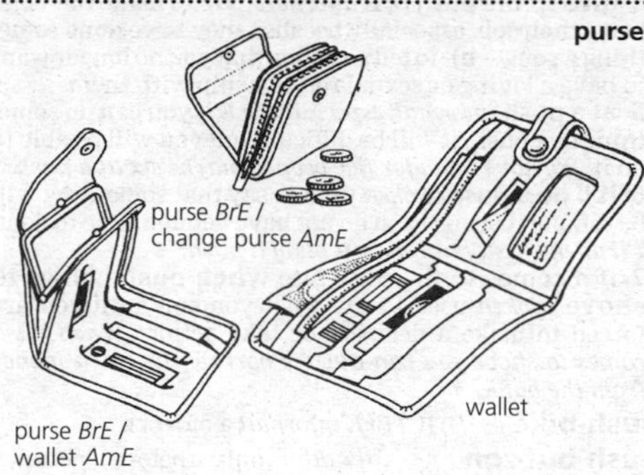


3 **purse¹** /pɜːs‖pɜːrs/ *n* **1** [C] *BrE* a small container for keeping coins in, made of leather, cloth, plastic etc, used especially by women; CHANGE PURSE *AmE*: *She took a pound coin out of her purse.|Hayley snapped her purse shut.* **2** [C] *BrE* a small flat leather container divided into parts for keeping paper money, cards, coins etc in, and used especially by women; WALLET *AmE*: *Check my purse. I think I've only got a twenty pound note.* **3** [C] *AmE* a bag, often made of leather, in which a woman carries her money and personal things; HANDBAG *BrE*: *She reached in her purse and took out a mirror.* —see picture at BAG¹ **4** [singular] *formal* the amount of money that a person, organization, or country has available to spend: *It was an expense that my purse could not afford.*|**the public purse** (=money controlled by a government) *These defence commitments are a continuing drain on the public purse.* **5** [C] the amount of money given to someone who wins a BOXING match **6 hold/control the purse strings** to control the money in a family, company etc: *Maureen definitely holds the purse strings.*

**purse²** *v* **purse your lips** to bring your lips together tightly into a small circle, especially to show disapproval or doubt: *Mrs Biddell pursed her lips and stared.*

**purs·er** /ˈpɜːsə‖ˈpɜːrsər/ *n* [C] an officer who is responsible for the money on a ship and is also in charge of the passengers' rooms, comfort etc

**pur·su·ance** /pəˈsjuːəns‖pərˈsuː-/ *n* **in pursuance of** *formal* **a)** with the aim of doing or achieving something: *Staff voted to take industrial action in pursuance of a better deal.* **b)** during the process of doing or achieving something

3 2 **pur·sue** /pəˈsjuː‖pərˈsuː/ *v* [T] **1** to continue doing an activity or trying to achieve something over a long period of time: *Kristin pursued her acting career with great determination.* **2 pursue the matter/argument/question** to continue trying to ask about, find out about, or persuade someone about a particular subject: *Janet did not dare pursue the matter too far.* **3** to chase or follow someone or something, in order to catch them, attack them etc: *Briggs ran across the field with one officer pursuing him.* **4** to keep trying to persuade someone to have a relationship with you

**pur·su·er** /pəˈsjuːə‖pərˈsuːər/ *n* [C] someone or something that is chasing you: *Luckily, Joey managed to outrun his pursuers.*

**pur·suit** /pəˈsjuːt‖pərˈsuːt/ *n* **1** [singular] the act of trying to achieve something in a determined way: [+ **of**] *the right of all people to the pursuit of liberty and happiness*|**in pursuit of** (=while trying to get) *I'm always amazed at the things people do in pursuit of love.* **2** [U] the act of chasing or following someone: **in pursuit** (=following behind) *There were no fewer than four police cars in pursuit.*|**in hot pursuit** (=following close behind) *The quarterback sprinted toward the end zone with Jansen in hot pursuit.* **3** [C usually plural] *formal* an activity such as a sport or HOBBY, which you spend a lot of time doing: *She immersed herself in academic pursuits.*

**pu·ru·lent** /ˈpjʊərələnt‖ˈpjʊr-/ *adj technical* containing or producing PUS —**purulence** *n* [U]

**pur·vey** /pɜːˈveɪ‖pɜːr-/ *v* [T + **to**] *formal* to supply goods, services, or information to people

**pur·vey·or** /pɜːˈveɪə‖pɜːrˈveɪər/ *n* [C usually plural] *formal* someone who supplies information, goods, or services to people, especially as a business: *purveyors of farmyard fresh poultry*

**pur·view** /ˈpɜːvjuː‖ˈpɜːr-/ *n* **within/outside the purview of** *formal* within or outside the limits of someone's job, activity, or knowledge: *This matter comes within the purview of the Department of Health.*

**pus** /pʌs/ *n* [U] a thick yellowish liquid produced in an infected part of your body: *Pus was oozing out of the wound.*

**push¹** /pʊʃ/ *v* S1 W2

**1** ▶ **MOVE** ◀ [I,T] to make someone or something move by using your hands, arms, shoulders etc to put pressure on them: *It's still stuck – you'll have to push harder.|When I give the signal, I want you all to push.*|**push sb/sth** *Johnson was penalised for pushing another player.*|**push sb/sth up/across/away etc** *They were trying to push me into the water.|He pushed away his plate when he had finished.*|**push the door open/shut** *I slowly pushed the door open.* —see picture on page 1260

**2** ▶ **BUTTON/SWITCH** ◀ [I,T] to press a button, SWITCH etc, especially in order to make a piece of equipment start working: *You just push that button there, and the coffee comes out here.*

**3** ▶ **TRY TO GET PAST SB** ◀ [I, T always + adv/prep] to use your hands, arms, shoulders etc to make someone move, especially so that you can get past them: *There's no need to push. There are enough tickets for everyone.*|**push past/through** *Jackson pushed past the journalists and escaped in his limousine.*|**push your way towards/across etc** *She pushed her way to the front of the crowd.*

**4** ▶ **ENCOURAGE/PERSUADE** ◀ [T] to encourage or persuade someone to do something that they do not want to do: **push sb to do sth** *Her husband keeps pushing her to accept the job.*|**push sb into doing sth** *My parents pushed me into going to college.*

**5** ▶ **WORK HARD** ◀ [T] to make someone work very hard: *The teachers don't seem to push these kids very hard.*|**push yourself** *He's been pushing himself too much.*

**6** ▶ **DRUGS** ◀ [T] *informal* to sell illegal drugs —see also PUSHER

**7** ▶ **ADVERTISE** ◀ **a)** [T] *informal* to try to sell more of a product by advertising it a lot

**8** ▶ **IDEAS/OPINIONS** ◀ [T] to try to make people accept your ideas or opinions, especially by talking about them a lot: *I wish you'd stop pushing all this political rubbish.*

**9 push the boat out** *BrE informal* to spend a lot of money on something because you want to make sure that it is enjoyable, successful etc

**10 push your luck/push it** *informal* to stupidly do something again, taking a risk that you will avoid problems because you have done it successfully before: *Look, just don't push it! I've had about enough of your criticism!*

**11 push sth to the back of your mind** to try to forget about an unpleasant feeling or situation: *I think you should push all these doubts to the back of your mind.*
**12 push the point** *old-fashioned* to keep trying to make someone accept your opinion in a way that they find annoying —see also PULL[1], PUSHED, PUSHING

**push ahead** *phr v* [I] to continue with a plan or activity, especially in a determined way: [+ **with**] *After careful consideration they decided to push ahead with the deal.*

**push along** *phr v* [I] *spoken* to leave a place: *It's getting late, I think we should be pushing along.* —see also **push off** (PUSH[1])

**push** sb **around** also **push** sb **about** *BrE phr v* [T] to give someone orders in a rude or threatening way: *Who do you think you're pushing around? Do it yourself.*

**push** sth ↔ **aside** *phr v* [T] to try to forget about something, especially something unpleasant, so that you can give your attention to what you are doing: *You just have to try and push these negative thoughts aside.*

**push** (sb) **for** sth *phr v* [T] to keep asking for something or trying to persuade people to do something, because you believe it is important or necessary: *People living near the airport are pushing for new restrictions on night flights.* | *I'll have to push you for a decision.*

**push forward** *phr v* **1** [I] to continue moving towards a place, in spite of difficulties: *As the army pushed forward, the death toll mounted.* **2 push yourself forward** to try to make other people notice you: *If she's going to do well at school, she'll have to push herself forward more.*

**push in** *phr v* [I] **1** to give advice, join in a conversation etc when you are not really involved: *No, it didn't seem like you were pushing in or anything, just trying to help.* **2** *BrE informal* to rudely and unfairly join a line of people, in front of other people who were already waiting

**push off** *phr v* [I] **1** *spoken, especially BrE* used to tell someone rudely to go away **2** *old-fashioned* to leave a place —see also **push along** (PUSH[1]) **3** if a boat pushes off from the shore, it moves away from it

**push on** *phr v* [I] **1** to continue travelling somewhere, especially after you have had a rest: *It was getting dark but we decided to push on a little further.* **2** to continue doing an activity: [+ **with**] *I'd better push on with my homework.*

**push** sb/sth ↔ **over** *phr v* [T] to make someone or something fall to the ground by pushing them: *Several people had been pushed over in the rush for bargains.*

**push** sth ↔ **through** *phr v* [T] to get a new law officially accepted: *The White House made every effort to push the policy through Congress.*

**push** sth ↔ **up** *phr v* [T] **1** to make the amount, number, or value of something increase: *The war has pushed up oil prices.* —compare **push down** (PUSH[1]) **2 be pushing up (the) daisies** *humorous* to be dead

**push**[2] *n*
**1** ▶ **PUSHING MOVEMENT** ◀ [C] the act of pushing or pressing something: *With a gentle push, the car started moving down the slope.* | **give sb/sth a push** *He gave her a push to see if she was awake.* | *If the door's stuck, just give it a push.* | **at the push of a button** (=used to emphasize how easy a machine is to use) *The liquidizer is marvellous, creating tasty soups at the push of a button.*
**2** ▶ **ENCOURAGEMENT** ◀ [singular] a small amount of encouragement, persuasion, or help from someone else: *It looked like she would never go, but all she needed was a gentle push.*
**3** ▶ **ATTACK/ATTEMPT** ◀ **a)** [C] a planned military attack into the area where the enemy is: *The army has made another big push into enemy territory.* **b)** [C] a determined and well-planned attempt to gain an advantage over your opponents in business, advertising etc: *The company has recently made a big push into the Japanese market.*
**4 give sb the push** *BrE informal* **a)** to make someone leave their job, especially because they have done something wrong **b)** to tell someone that you no longer want to have a loving or sexual relationship with them
**5 at a push** *informal, especially BrE* if you can do something at a push, it will be difficult, but you will be able to do it: *We have room for five people, maybe six at a push.*
**6 it'll be a push** *spoken* used to say that something will be difficult because you do not have enough time to do it: *I'll do my best, but it'll be a bit of a push.*
**7 if it comes to the push** also **when push comes to shove** *spoken* used to say what you can do if you are forced to make a decision or take action: *When push comes to shove you can always borrow the extra money from the bank.*

**push-bike** /ˈ· ·/ *n* [C] *BrE informal* a BICYCLE

**push-but·ton** /ˈ· ˌ··/ *adj* [only before noun] **1** operated by pressing a button with your finger: *The old car had a push-button starter.* **2** using computers or electronic equipment rather than traditional methods: *push-button warfare* | *the push-button piloting of a ship*

**push·cart** /ˈpʊʃkɑːt‖-kɑːrt/ *n* [C] a large flat container like a box with wheels, used especially by people who sell goods in the street

**push·chair** /ˈpʊʃ-tʃeə‖-tʃer/ *n* [C] *BrE* a small folding seat on wheels, in which a young child sits and is pushed along; STROLLER *AmE* —compare BABY CARRIAGE —see picture at PRAM

**pushed** /pʊʃt/ *adj* [not before noun] *informal* **1 be pushed for** to have difficulty finding enough time, money etc: *I'm always rather pushed for money at the end of the month.* **2** too busy: *I'd love to help, but I'm a bit pushed at the moment.* **3 be (hard) pushed to do sth** to have a lot of difficulty doing something: *You'll be hard pushed to find someone to type your essay for you now.*

**push·er** /ˈpʊʃə‖-ər/ *n* [C] *informal* someone who sells illegal drugs —compare PEDDLER (2) —see also PEN-PUSHER

**push·ing** /ˈpʊʃɪŋ/ *prep* **be pushing 18/30/60 etc** *usually spoken* to be nearly 18, 30, 60 years old etc: *Sheila must be pushing 40 by now.*

**push·o·ver** /ˈpʊʃˌəʊvə‖-ˌoʊvər/ *n informal* **be a pushover a)** to be easy to persuade, influence, or defeat: *Duncan will soon see that I'm no pushover.* | [+ **for**] *Mr Wasco is a pushover for blondes with green eyes.* **b)** to be very easy to do or win: *The exam was a pushover.*

**push-start** /ˈ· ·/ *v* [T] to push a vehicle in order to make the engine start —**push-start** *n* [C]

**push-up** /ˈ· ·/ *n* [C] *AmE* an exercise in which you lie on the floor on your front and push yourself up with your arms; PRESS-UP *BrE*

**push·y** /ˈpʊʃi/ *adj* so determined to succeed and to get what you want that you behave in a way that seems rude: *a pushy salesman* —**pushily** *adv* —**pushiness** *n* [U]

**pu·sil·lan·i·mous** /ˌpjuːsɪ̍ˈlænɪ̍məs/ *adj formal* frightened of taking even small risks —**pusillanimously** *adv* —**pusillanimity** /ˌpjuːsɪ̍ləˈnɪmɪ̍ti/ *n* [U]

**puss** /pʊs/ *n* [usually singular] **1** *informal* a name for a cat, or a way of calling a cat: *Come here, puss, puss, puss!* **2** *AmE slang* face: *a smack in the puss*

**pus·sy** /ˈpʊsi/ *n* [C] **1** also **pussy cat** /ˈ·· ·/ an informal word for a cat, used especially by or to children **2** *taboo* a woman's sex organs **3** *AmE informal* an insulting word for a man who is weak or not brave

**pus·sy·foot** /ˈpʊsifʊt/ also **pussyfoot around/about** *v* [I] *informal* to be too careful and frightened to do something, such as taking firm decisions or telling someone exactly what you think: *Stop pussyfooting around, and tell me what he said!*

**pussy wil·low** /ˈ·· ˌ··/ *n* [C,U] a tree with white flowers that are soft like fur

**pus·tule** /ˈpʌstjuːl‖-tʃuːl/ *n* [C] *technical* a small raised spot on your skin containing PUS (=a thick yellow liquid)

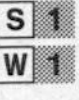

**put** /pʊt/ *v past tense* **put** *present participle* **putting**

① MOVE STH
② CHANGE SB'S SITUATION
③ SAY/EXPRESS
④ ASK FOR AN ANSWER/DECISION
⑤ ADD STH
⑥ SEND SB SOMEWHERE
⑦ PUT RIGHT/STRAIGHT
⑧ STOP/END STH
⑨ IN ORDER OF IMPORTANCE/QUALITY
⑩ OTHER MEANINGS
⑪ WRITE

**① MOVE STH**
**1** [T always + adv/prep] to move something from one place or position into another, especially using your hands: **put sth in/on/there etc** *Put those bags on the table.* | *You should put your hand over your mouth when you cough.* | *I can't remember where I put my keys.*

**② CHANGE SB'S SITUATION**
**2** [T always + adv/prep] to change someone's situation: *This was the shot that put Sampras into the semifinal.* | **put sb in an awkward position** (=make someone's situation difficult or embarrassing) *Paul's resignation has put us in an awkward position.* | **put sb out of a job/out of work** (=make them lose their job) *Pit closures have put thousands of miners out of a job.* | **put sb in a bad mood** (=make them feel annoyed) *The long delay had put us all in a bad mood.*
**3 put sb in command/charge/control** to give someone authority over a group, activity, organization etc: *Tom Pendlebury has been put in charge of the project.*

**③ SAY/EXPRESS**
**4** [T always + adv/prep] to express something using words in a particular way: **put sth well/cleverly/succinctly etc** *I thought her arguments were quite cleverly put.* | *Well, since you put it like that, I can't really refuse.* | **as sb puts it** (=used to repeat what someone else has said) *Long-term planning is a waste of time because – as Keynes puts it – in the long term we're all dead.* | **put sth into words** (=express a feeling or idea)
**5 to put it bluntly** *spoken* used to tell someone that you are going to say exactly what you think: *To put it bluntly, Robert's just not good enough for the job.*
**6 to put it mildly** *spoken* used to say that a situation is actually worse than the way you are describing it: *We are, to put it mildly, in a mess.*
**7 how can I put it?** *spoken* used when what you are going to say might sound unpleasant or impolite: *Derek's – how shall I put it – not very attractive.*
**8 to put it another way** used when trying to explain something in a different way and make it clearer: *Money makes money. To put it another way, the greater the investment, the greater the profit.*

**④ ASK FOR AN ANSWER/DECISION**
**9** [T] to ask a question, especially when you want to get someone's opinion about something: *After the break, you will be able to put your questions to the panel.* | **put it to sb** *I put it to you, Mr President, that these measures will not solve the problem of violent crime.*
**10 put a proposition/proposal/case to** to tell someone or a group of people about something and ask them to agree to it or make a decision about it

**⑤ ADD STH**
**11** [T] to add something: *Put a little romance into your life.* | *Just put a little more expression into it.*
**12** [T] to make money available to be used in a business, or add it to something such as a bank account

**⑥ SEND SB SOMEWHERE**
**13** [T always + adv/prep] to arrange for or order someone to go to a place for a particular purpose: **put sb in/on etc** *Putting troops into Rwanda is not an option.*
**14 put sb on a train/plane etc** to take someone to a plane, train etc to start a journey

**⑦ PUT RIGHT/STRAIGHT**
**15 put sb straight/right** to tell someone the true facts when they have made a mistake that annoys you: *Let me put you straight on one thing, Andy's not a thief.*
**16 put sth straight** to make something look clean and tidy: *It took us all weekend to put the garden straight.*
**17 put sth right** to make a situation better, especially after someone has made a mistake or behaved badly: *I'll put it right at once.*

**⑧ STOP/END STH**
**18 put a stop to/put an end to** to stop an activity that is harmful or unacceptable: *There's too much money being wasted, and it's time we put a stop to it.*
**19 put paid to** *BrE* to spoil and end your hopes or plans completely: *A car accident put paid to his chances of taking part in the race.*

**⑨ IN ORDER OF IMPORTANCE/QUALITY**
**20** [T always + adv/prep] to consider something as having a particular level of importance or quality: **put sb as/among/in etc** *I'd put Porto amongst the top ten European teams.* | **put sth first/before** *The job's important to him, but he puts his family first.*

**⑩ OTHER MEANINGS**
**21 put sth into action/effect/practice** to start using a plan, idea, knowledge etc: *James was keen to put some of the things he had learned into practice.*
**22 put pressure on a)** to make someone's situation difficult **b)** to try to make someone do something
**23 put energy/work/enthusiasm etc into** to use a lot of energy etc when you are doing an activity: *I hope the show's a success – they've put so much work into it.*
**24 put sth behind you** to try to forget about an unpleasant event or experience and think about the future: *The team must put Saturday's defeat behind them and concentrate on tonight's game.*
**25 ▶THROW◀** to throw a SHOT (=a heavy metal ball) in a sports competition
**26 put it there** *spoken* used to tell someone to put their hand in yours, either as a greeting or after making an agreement with them: *$500? OK, it's a deal. Put it there!*

**⑪ WRITE**
**27** [T] to write something or to make a mark with a pen or pencil: **put sth in/on/under** *Put your name at the top of each answer sheet.* —see also **put your finger on** (FINGER[1] (4)), **put your foot down** (FOOT[1] (10)), **put your foot in it** (FOOT[1] (12)), **put sth to good use** (USE[2] (4)), **put your back into it** (BACK[1] (19))

**put about** *phr v* **1** [T **put** sth ↔ **about**] *BrE informal* to give other people news or information, especially when it is unpleasant or untrue: **put it about that** *Someone's been putting it about that she's splitting up with her husband.* **2 put yourself about** *BrE informal* to have sexual relationships with a lot of

[continued on next page]

[continued from previous page]
different people **3** [I,T] *technical* if a ship puts about or if you put it about, it changes direction

**put across** *phr v* [T] **1** [**put** sth↔ **across**] to explain your ideas, beliefs, policies etc in a way that people can understand: *The union representative put her argument across very effectively.* **2 put yourself across** to communicate effectively, so that people have a clear idea of your character, your ideas etc: *Sue's never been very good at putting herself across at interviews.*

**put** sth↔ **aside** *phr v* [T] **1** to try to stop thinking about a problem, quarrel, or disagreement, because you want to achieve something: *The UN has called on the warring factions to put aside their differences.* **2** to save money regularly, usually for a particular purpose: *We're trying to put aside a few hundred dollars every month toward our vacation.* **3** to put down something you are reading or working with, in order to start doing something else: *Charles put aside his newspaper and got up to answer the door.* **4** to keep a period of time free in order to be able to do something: *Try to put aside an hour each day for exercise.*

**put** sth **at** sth *phr v* [T] to calculate and state an amount, someone's age etc, without trying to be very exact: *Official estimates put the damage at over $10 million.*

**put** sb/sth **away** *phr v* [T] **1** [**put** sth↔ **away**] to put something in the place where it is usually kept: *Let me just put these files away.* **2** [**put** sb **away**] *informal* to put someone in a prison or in a mental hospital: *He was put away for five years for armed robbery.* **3** [**put** sth↔ **away**] *informal* to eat or drink a lot: *It's amazing the amount that child can put away.* **4** [**put** sth↔ **away**] to save money: *My Grandfather had put away over £50,000.*

**put back** *phr v* **1** [T **put** sth ↔ **back**] to arrange for an event to start at a later time or date; POSTPONE: *The meeting has been put back to next Thursday.* **2** [T **put** sth ↔ **back**] to delay a process or activity by a number of weeks, months etc: *This fire could put back the opening date by several weeks.* **3 put a clock/a watch back** to make a clock or watch show an earlier time —see also **put the clock back** (CLOCK[1] (4))

**put** sth ↔ **by** *phr v* [T] to save money regularly in order to use it later: *We're trying to put a little by each month for a new car.*

**put down** *phr v*
**1** ► **CRITICIZE** ◄ [T **put** sb ↔ **down**] to keep criticizing someone in front of other people: *I hate the way Dave puts me down the whole time.* | **put yourself down** *"I don't stand a chance of getting the job." "Don't be silly, you mustn't put yourself down."*
**2** ► **PAY** ◄ [T **put** sth ↔ **down**] to pay part of the total cost of something, so that you can pay the rest later: *How much could you afford to put down on a house?*
**3** ► **WRITE** ◄ [T **put** sth ↔ **down**] *BrE* to write something, especially a name or number on a piece of paper or on a list: *I'll just put your phone number down in my book.*
**4** ► **KILL** ◄ [T **put** sth ↔ **down**] to kill an animal without causing it pain, usually because it is old or ill: *We had to have the dog put down.*
**5 put the phone down** to put the RECEIVER back onto the telephone when you have finished speaking to someone: **put the phone down on sb** (=to suddenly end a telephone conversation)
**6 put down a revolution/revolt/rebellion etc** to stop a REVOLUTION (2) etc by using force: *Military police were called in to put down the riot.*
**7** ► **STOP A VEHICLE** ◄ [T **put** sb **down**] *BrE* to stop a vehicle so that passengers can get off at a particular place: *Just put me down at the gate.*
**8** ► **AIRCRAFT** ◄ [I,T] if an aircraft puts down or if a pilot puts it down, it lands: *The engine failed and the plane put down in the sea.*
**9** ► **BABY** ◄ [T **put** sb **down**] to put a baby in its bed: *We try to put Amy down at six every evening.*
**10 I couldn't put it down** *spoken* used to say that you found a book, game etc extremely interesting: *Once I'd started reading it I just couldn't put it down.*
**11 put down a motion/an amendment** to suggest a subject, plan, change in the law etc for a parliament or committee to consider

**put** sb **down as** sth *phr v* [T] to guess what someone is like or what they do, without having much information about them: *They'd already put me down as a good-for-nothing young artist.*

**put** sb **down for** sth *phr v* [T] **1** to put someone's name on a list so that they can take part in an activity, join an organization etc: *We've put Simon's name down for nursery school.* **2 put sb down for £5/£20 etc** *especially BrE* to write someone's name on a list with an amount of money that they have promised to give

**put** sth **down to** sth *phr v* [T] **1** to explain the reason for something, especially when you are only guessing: *I put Jane's moodiness down to the stress she was under.* **2 put it down to experience** used to tell someone not to feel too upset by failure, but to learn something useful from it: *Everyone gets rejected from time to time; put it down to experience.*

**put** sth ↔ **forth** *phr v* [T] **put forth leaves/shoots/roots etc** *literary* if a tree or bush puts forth leaves etc it begins to grow them

**put** sb/sth ↔ **forward** *phr v* [T] **1** to suggest a plan, proposal etc, especially in order to start discussions about something that needs to be decided: *The working party has put forward a good case for moving to a new site.* | *the theories put forward by Dr. Kesner* **2** to arrange for an event to start at an earlier time or date: *The men's final has been put forward to 1:30.* **3 put a clock/watch forward** to make a clock or watch show a later time **4 put yourself/sb's name forward** to suggest formally that you or someone else should be considered for a particular job, membership of an organization etc: *We put Joe's name forward to serve on the local council.*

**put in** *phr v*
**1** ► **EQUIPMENT** ◄ [T **put** sth ↔ **in**] to fix a piece of equipment into your home so that it is ready to be used: *We decided to have a new bathroom put in.*
**2** ► **TIME/ENERGY** ◄ [T **put** sth ↔ **in**] to spend time or use energy working or practising something: *You have to put in a lot of effort to learn a new language.*
**3** ► **SAY STH** ◄ [T **put** sth ↔ **in**] to interrupt someone in order to say something: *"I'm sure Daniel's the best man for the job." Mrs Weevers put in.*
**4 put in a claim/request** to officially make a claim or request: *She put in a claim for damage to the photographs.*
**5** ► **ELECT** ◄ [T **put** sb ↔ **in**] to elect a politician or political party
**6 put in an appearance** to go to a social event, meeting etc for a short time: *I don't really want to go to the party, but I'd better put in an appearance.*
**7** ► **SHIP** ◄ [I] if a ship puts in, it enters a port

**put in for** sth *phr v* [T] to make a formal request for something: *It's time you put in for a pay increase.*

**put** sb/sth ↔ **off** *phr v* [T] **1** to arrange to do something at a later time or date, especially because there is a problem, difficulty etc: *The meeting's been put off till next week.* | **put off doing sth** *We'll have to put off going on vacation until you're better.* **2** to delay meeting someone, paying someone etc because you do not want to do it until later: *I just don't have the money right now – I'll have to put him off for another week.* | *I managed to put Ron off with a promise to pay him next week.* **3** to delay doing something until later because you do not want to do it now: *You really ought to write to her. You can't just keep putting it off.* **4** to make you dislike something or not want to do something: *The job sounded interesting but the idea of moving house again put me off.* | *Don't be put off by the title – it's a really good book.* | **put sb off (doing) sth** *This lousy weather is enough to put anyone off camping.* **5** to make it difficult for someone to do something, by preventing them from thinking clearly about what they are doing: *The photographers put McEnroe off his game.* | *Stop* *giggling! You're putting me off.* **6** to let someone leave a vehicle at a particular place: *I'll put you off at the bottom of the street.*

**put** sth ↔ **on** *phr v* [T]
**1 ▶ CLOTHES ◀** [**put** sth ↔ **on**] to put a piece of clothing on your body: *Put your coat on before you go outside.*|*I'll have to put my glasses on; I can't read the sign from here.*
**2 ▶ ON SKIN ◀** [**put** sth ↔ **on**] to put MAKE-UP, cream etc on your skin: *It takes Julie about half an hour to put her make-up on every morning.*
**3 ▶ LIGHT/HEAT ETC ◀** [**put** sth ↔ **on**] to make a light or a piece of electrical or gas equipment start working by pressing or turning a button: *Shall I put the kettle on?*
**4 ▶ MUSIC ◀** to put a record, TAPE or CD into a machine and start playing it
**5 ▶ PRETEND ◀** [**put** sth ↔ **on**] to pretend to have a certain feeling, opinion, way of speaking etc especially in order to get attention: *Sheila's not really that upset; she's just putting it on.*|*He always puts on that posh voice when he's on the phone.*
**6 put on weight/12 lbs/4 kg etc** to become fatter and heavier: *Rosie's put on five kilos since she quit smoking.*
**7 ▶ PLAY/SHOW ETC ◀** [**put** sth ↔ **on**] to arrange or perform a show, concert, play etc: *We're putting on a concert to raise money for famine victims.*
**8 ▶ COOK ◀** [**put** sth ↔ **on**] to start cooking something: *Robbie will be home in ten minutes; I'd better put the potatoes on.*
**9 put on a bus/train/coach** *BrE* to provide a bus or train in order to take people somewhere: *British Rail will be putting on extra trains for football fans.*
**10 you're putting me on!** *spoken, especially AmE* used to tell someone that you think they are joking: *"They offered me a raise at work." "You're putting me on! How much?"*
**11 ▶ ADD ◀** [**put** sth **on** sth] to add an amount of money or tax onto the cost of something: *The new tax could put another ten cents on the price of gas.*
**12 ▶ RISK MONEY ◀** [**put** sth **on** sth] to risk an amount of money on the result of a game, race etc: *We put £50 on Brazil to win the Cup.*
**13 put on a brake** to make a vehicle stop or slow down by pressing a PEDAL or handle

**put** sb **onto** sb/sth *phr v* [T] *informal* to give someone information about something interesting or usefulthat they did not know about: *Barbara put us onto this fantastic French restaurant in Baltimore.*

**put out**

Joan put the fire out.

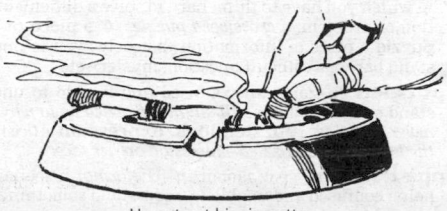

He put out his cigarette.

**put out** *phr v*
**1 put out a fire/cigarette etc** to make a fire etc stop burning —see FIRE[1] (USAGE)
**2 put out a light/lamp** to make a light stop working by pressing or turning a button
**3 feel/be put out** to feel upset or offended: *We were a little put out at not being invited to the wedding.*
**4 ▶ MAKE WORK ◀** [T **put** sb ↔ **out**] to make extra work or cause problems for someone: *Will it put you out if I bring another guest?*
**5 put yourself out** to make an effort to do something that will help someone: *Fred rarely puts himself out on other people's behalf.*
**6** [T **put** sth ↔ **out**] to put something outside the house: *Remember to put the cat out before you go to bed.*| **put the rubbish/garbage out** (=put dirty or unwanted things outside your house to be taken away)| **put the washing out** (=put clothes outside to dry)
**7 put your tongue out** to push your tongue out of your mouth, especially as a rude sign to someone
**8 put your back/knee/shoulder etc out** to injure part of your body, especially by stretching it too much: *I put my knee out playing tennis yesterday.*
**9 put your hand/foot/arm out** to stretch your hand etc forward: *Jimmy put his foot out and tripped me up.*
**10 ▶ MAKE UNCONSCIOUS ◀** [T **put** sb **out**] to make someone unconscious before a medical operation
**11 put out information/statistics/a statement etc** to produce information etc for people to read or listen to: *The police department has put out a statement apologizing for its officers' conduct.*
**12 ▶ PRODUCE STH ◀** to produce radio signals, print magazines, broadcast programmes etc
**13 put out feelers/antennae** to try to discover information or opinions by listening to people or watching what is happening: *It might be worth putting feelers out to see if there are any jobs going in Paul's school.*
**14 ▶ SHIP ◀** [I] if a ship puts out, it starts to sail
**15 ▶ HAVE SEX ◀** [I] *AmE slang* if a woman puts out, she has sex with a man
**16** [T **put** sb **out**] to end a BATTER's innings in BASEBALL by, for example, catching the ball that they have hit

**put** sth ↔ **over** *phr v* [T] **1** to communicate an idea or feeling: *The course is designed to help you put over your ideas more effectively.* **2 put one over on** *informal* to deceive someone into believing something untrue or accepting something that is useless: *They think they've found a way to put one over on the welfare office.*

**put through** *phr v* [T] **1** [**put** sb/sth ↔ **through**] to connect someone to someone else on the telephone: *One moment please, I'm just trying to put you through.* **2 put sb through school/college/university** to pay for someone to study at school or college: *Andrew's parents insisted on putting him through medical school.* **3** [**put** sb **through** sth] to make someone do something unpleasant or difficult: *We put all new recruits through a rigorous week-long training programme.*|**put sb through it** *They really put me through it at that job interview.* **4** [**put** sth ↔ **through**] to do what is necessary in order to get a plan or suggestion accepted or approved: *Production will start up again when these changes have been put through.*

**put** sth **to** sb *phr v* [T] **1** to ask someone a question or make a suggestion to them: *Can I put a question to the speaker?* **2** to offer a group of people something such as a proposal or plan which they can accept or reject: *The latest offer will be put to the negotiating committee this afternoon.*|**put sth to the vote** (=get people to vote on it) *Let's put the motion to the vote.* **3 put sb to trouble/inconvenience etc** [usually in questions and negatives] to make someone do something that will cause them trouble or inconvenience

[continued on next page]

[continued from previous page]
**4 put your name/signature to** to sign a letter, document etc saying that you agree with what is written in it

**put** sth ↔ **together** *phr v* [T] **1** to prepare or produce something by collecting pieces of information, ideas etc: *We're putting together an anthology of war poetry.* | *It took all morning to put the proposal together.* **2** to make a machine, model etc by joining all the different parts: *I can't work out how to put this table together.* **3 more ... than the rest put together** used when comparing two sets of people or things to say that one set contains more than the total of all the other sets: *Italy scored more points than the rest of the group put together.*

**put up** *phr v*
**1 ► BUILD ◄** [T **put** sth ↔ **up**] to build a wall, fence, or tall building: *They're putting up several new office blocks in the centre of town.*
**2 ► ON A WALL ◄** [T **put** sth ↔ **up**] to put a picture, notice etc on a wall so that people can see it: *The exam results will be put up on Friday afternoon.*
**3 ► INCREASE ◄** [T **put** sth ↔ **up**] to increase the cost or value of something: *Our landlord keeps threatening to put the rent up.*
**4 ► LET SB STAY ◄** [T **put** sb ↔ **up**] to let someone stay in your house and give them meals: *They agreed to put two foreign students up over the summer.*
**5 ► STAY SOMEWHERE ◄** [I always + adv/prep] *especially BrE* to stay in a place for a short time: [+ **at/in/with**] *We can put up at a hotel for the night.*
**6 put up a fight/struggle/resistance** to show great determination to oppose something or get out of a difficult situation: *Gina put up a real fight to overcome the disease.*
**7 put up money/$3 million/£50** to give an amount of money for a particular purpose: *An anonymous donor put up $50,000 for the new science lab.*
**8 ► ELECTIONS ◄** [T **put** sb ↔ **up**] to suggest someone as a suitable person to be elected to a position: *They're putting Tom Sackville up as a candidate in the next elections.*
**9 put up a proposal/argument/case etc** to explain a suggestion or idea so that other people can think about it or discuss it: *If you can put up a good enough case, the board will provide the finance.*

**put** sb **up to** sth *phr v* [T] to encourage someone to do something stupid or dangerous: *It's not like Martha to play practical jokes; someone must have put her up to it.*

**put up with** sb/sth *phr v* [T] to accept an unpleasant situation or person without complaining: *I don't know how you put up with their constant quarrelling.* | *You see what I have to put up with!*

**pu·ta·tive** /ˈpjuːtətɪv/ *adj* [only before noun] *formal* believed or accepted by most people: *the putative father of her child*

**put-down** /ˈ· ·/ *n* [C usually singular] something you say that is intended to make someone feel stupid or unimportant; SNUB[2]: *Some feminists see the put-downs girls experience as the means by which men control women.* —see also **put down** (PUT)

**put-on** /ˈ· ·/ *n* [C usually singular] *AmE informal* something you say or do to try to make someone believe something that is not true

**pu·tre·fac·tion** /ˌpjuːtrəˈfækʃən/ *n* [U] *formal* the process of decay in a dead animal or plant, especially when it smells very bad

**pu·tre·fy** /ˈpjuːtrəfaɪ/ *v* [I,T] *formal* if a dead animal or plant putrefies, it decays and smells very bad

**pu·tres·cent** /pjuːˈtresənt/ *adj formal* beginning to decay and smell very bad: *putrescent fish* —**putrescence** *n* [U]

**pu·trid** /ˈpjuːtrəd/ *adj* **1** dead animals, plants, or parts of the body that are putrid are decaying and smell very bad **2** *informal* very unpleasant: *a putrid smell*

**putsch** /pʊtʃ/ *n* [C] a secretly planned attempt to remove a government by force: *the communist putsch of 1948*

**putt** /pʌt/ *n* [C] a light hit intended to move a GOLF BALL a short distance along the ground towards the hole —**putt** *v* [I,T] —see picture on page 1264

**put·tee** /ˈpʌti‖pʌˈtiː/ *n* [C usually plural] a long piece of cloth that is wrapped around the leg from the knee down, worn as part of an army uniform in the past

**put·ter[1]** /ˈpʌtə‖-ər/ *n* a kind of GOLF CLUB (=stick) to hit the ball a short distance towards or into the hole —see picture on page 1264

**putter[2]** *v* [I always + adv/prep] **1** *AmE* to spend time doing things that are not very important in a relaxed way; POTTER[2] *BrE*: *I puttered around for a while, tidying up the kitchen.* **2** *AmE* to walk or move slowly and without hurrying; POTTER[2] *BrE* **3** *informal* to make the low repeating sound that a vehicle makes when it is moving slowly

**put·ting** /ˈpʌtɪŋ/ *n* [U] a simple game of GOLF played on putting greens in Britain

**putting green** /ˈ·· ·/ *n* [C] **1** one of the smaller smooth areas of grass on a GOLF COURSE where you hit the ball into the hole **2** *BrE* a smooth area of grass with many holes in it for playing a simple type of GOLF

**put·ty** /ˈpʌti/ *n* [U] **1** a soft substance that dries hard and is used to fix glass into window frames **2 be putty in sb's hands** to be easily controlled or influenced by someone

**put-up job** /ˈ· · ˌ·/ *n* [C usually singular] *informal* an attempt to trick someone by secretly arranging for something to happen: *There were rumors that the kidnapping of Miletti was a put-up job.*

**put-up·on** /ˈ· ·ˌ·/ *adj* [not before noun] *informal* someone who feels put-upon thinks that other people are treating them unfairly by expecting them to do too much

**putz** /pʌts/ *n* [C] *AmE informal* **1** someone, especially a man, who is stupid, annoying, and unpleasant **2** *taboo* a PENIS

**puz·zle[1]** /ˈpʌzəl/ *v* [T] **1** to confuse someone or make them feel slightly anxious because they do not understand something: *What puzzles me is how the burglar got into the house without setting off the alarm.* **2** [I, T] to think for a long time about something because you cannot understand or solve it: [+ **over/about**] *I've been sitting here puzzling about what to do.* | **puzzle your head over** *I've been puzzling my head over this problem for weeks.*

**puzzle** sth ↔ **out** *phr v* [T] to solve a confusing or difficult problem by thinking about it carefully: *I've been trying to puzzle out why she's so upset.*

**puzzle[2]** *n* [C] **1** [usually singular] something that is difficult to understand or explain: *These computers are a puzzle to me.* **2** a game or toy that has a lot of pieces that you have to fit together —see also JIGSAW (1) **3** a game in which you have to think hard to solve a difficult question or problem: *a crossword puzzle* **4 a piece of the puzzle** a piece of information that helps you to understand part of a difficult question, mystery etc

**puz·zled** /ˈpʌzəld/ *adj* confused and unable to understand something: *I'm still slightly puzzled as to why she never called us.* | **puzzled look/expression** *Alice read the letter with a puzzled expression on her face.*

**puz·zle·ment** /ˈpʌzəlmənt/ *n* [U] *formal* a feeling of being confused and unable to understand something

**puz·zler** /ˈpʌzlə‖-ər/ *n* [C] *informal* something that is difficult to understand or explain

**puz·zling** /ˈpʌzlɪŋ/ *adj* confusing and difficult to understand or explain: *The children showed a puzzling lack of curiosity about the new baby.*

**PVC** /ˌpiː viː ˈsiː◂/ *n* [U] a type of plastic

**pvt** *AmE* the written abbreviation of PRIVATE, the lowest military rank in the army; PTE *BrE*

**pw** the written abbreviation of per week: *Rent is £55 pw.*

**PWA** /ˌpiː dʌbəljuː ˈeɪ/ *n* [C] person with AIDS; someone who has the disease AIDS

**PWR** /ˌpiː dʌbəljuː ˈɑː‖-ˈɑːr/ *n* [C] pressurized water reactor; a type of NUCLEAR REACTOR for producing electricity

**PX** /ˌpiː ˈeks/ *n* [C] a special shop for food and other supplies on a US military base —compare NAAFI

**pyg·my**, **pigmy** /ˈpɪgmi/ *n* [C] **1** also **Pygmy** a person belonging to a race of very small people, especially one of the tribes of central Africa **2 pygmy rabbit/hippo/elephant etc** a very small type of rabbit, HIPPO etc

**py·ja·mas** *especially BrE* also **pajamas** *especially AmE* /pəˈdʒɑːməz‖-ˈdʒæ-, -ˈdʒɑː-/ *n* [plural] **1** a soft, loose pair of trousers and a top that you wear in bed: *a pair of striped pyjamas* **2 pyjama party** a party where all the guests are asked to wear pyjamas **3** loose trousers that are tied around the waist, worn by Muslim men or women —**pyjama** *adj*: *pajama bottoms*

**py·lon** /ˈpaɪlən‖-lɑːn, -lən/ *n* [C] **1** one of the tall metal structures that supports wires carrying electricity across the country **2** *AmE* one of a set of plastic CONES placed on a road to control traffic and protect people working there **3** a tall structure or post used to support something heavy or to help guide aircraft to land

**PYO** *BrE* the abbreviation of 'pick your own', used by farms that let people pick their own fruit and vegetables

**py·or·rho·ea** *BrE* also **pyorrhea** *especially AmE* /ˌpaɪəˈriːə/ *n* [U] a DISEASE of your GUMS that makes your teeth become loose

**pyr·a·mid** /ˈpɪrəmɪd/ *n* [C] **1** a large stone building with four TRIANGULAR (=3 sided) walls that slope in to a point at the top, especially in Egypt and Central America **2** [usually singular] a system or organization in which a small number of people have power or influence over a much larger number of people: *different levels of the management pyramid* **3** a pile of objects that have been put into the shape of a pyramid: [+ **of**] *a pyramid of oranges* **4** a pyramid-shaped object —**pyramidal** /ɪˈræmɪdl/ *adj* —see picture at SHAPE[1]

**pyramid sel·ling** /ˈ··· ˌ··/ *n* [U] a system of selling things in which someone buys the right to sell a particular kind of goods and then sells these goods to lots of other people, who sell them to others, especially in their houses

**pyre** /paɪə‖paɪr/ *n* [C] a high pile of wood on which a dead body is placed to be burned in a funeral ceremony

**Py·rex** /ˈpaɪreks/ *n* [U] *trademark* a special type of strong glass that does not break at high temperatures and is used for making cooking dishes

**py·ri·tes** /paɪˈraɪtiːz‖pə-/ *n* [U] a compound of SULPHUR with a type of metal, usually iron, or iron and COPPER: *iron pyrites* —see also FOOL'S GOLD

**py·ro·ma·ni·a** /ˌpaɪrəʊˈmeɪniə‖-rə-/ *n* [U] *technical* a mental illness that gives you a strong desire to start fires

**py·ro·ma·ni·ac** /ˌpaɪrəʊˈmeɪniæk‖-rə-/ *n* [C] **1** *technical* someone who suffers from the mental illness of pyromania **2** *informal humorous* someone who enjoys making and watching fires

**py·ro·tech·nics** /ˌpaɪrəʊˈteknɪks‖-rə-/ *n* **1** [plural] *formal or technical* a public show of FIREWORKS **2** [U] *technical* the skill or business of making FIREWORKS **3** [plural] an impressive show of someone's skill as a public speaker, musician etc —**pyrotechnic** *adj*

**Pyr·rhic vic·to·ry** /ˌpɪrɪk ˈvɪktəri/ *n* [C] a victory in which the person who wins suffers so much that the victory was hardly worth winning

**py·thon** /ˈpaɪθən‖-θɑːn, -θən/ *n* [C] a large tropical snake that kills animals for food by winding itself around them and crushing them

**pyx** /pɪks/ *n* [C] a small container in which the holy bread used for the Christian ceremony of COMMUNION (2) is kept

**Q, q** /kjuː/ *plural* **Q's, q's** *or* **Qs, qs** *n*[C] the 17th letter of the English alphabet

**q** the written abbreviation of question

**QC** /ˌkjuː ˈsiː/ *n* [C] Queen's Counsel; a BARRISTER (=type of lawyer) of high rank in the British legal system

**QED** /ˌkjuː iː ˈdiː/ the abbreviation of the Latin phrase quod erat demonstrandum, used to say that a fact, event etc proves that what you say is true

**qr** the written abbreviation of QUARTER

**qt** the written abbreviation of QUART

**q.t.** /ˌkjuː ˈtiː/ *n* **on the q.t.** *informal* secret or secretly

**Q-tip** /ˈkjuː tɪp/ *n* [C] *AmE trademark* a COTTON BUD

**qua** /kweɪ, kwɑː‖kwɑː/ *prep Latin formal* used to show you are talking about the main character or the general idea of something: *Money, qua money, cannot provide happiness.*

**quack¹** /kwæk/ *v* [I] to make the sound that ducks make

**quack²** *n* [C] *informal* **1** someone who pretends to have medical knowledge or skills: *a quack doctor* **2** *BrE* a doctor: *You'd better go and see the quack with that burn.* **3** [C] a word used especially by or to children to mean the sound a duck makes

**quack·er·y** /ˈkwækəri/ *n* [U] the activities of someone who pretends to have medical knowledge or skills

**quad** /kwɒd‖kwɑːd/ *n* [C] **1** a square open area with buildings all around it, especially in a school or college **2** a short form of QUADRUPLET

**quadr-** /kwɒdr‖kwɑːdr/ *prefix* another form of the prefix QUADRI-

**quad·ran·gle** /ˈkwɒdræŋgəl‖ˈkwɑː/ *n* [C] **1** a square open area with buildings all around it **2** *technical* a flat shape that has four straight sides

**quad·rant** /ˈkwɒdrənt‖ˈkwɑː-/ *n* [C] **1** a quarter of a circle —see picture at SHAPE¹ **2** an instrument for measuring angles, used when sailing or when looking at the stars

**quad·ra·phon·ic, quadrophonic** /ˌkwɒdrəˈfɒnɪk◂‖ˌkwɑːdrəˈfɑː-/ *adj* using a system of sound recording, broadcasting etc in which sound comes from four different SPEAKERS at the same time —compare MONO², STEREO²

**quad·rat·ic e·qua·tion** /kwɒˌdrætɪk ɪˈkweɪʒən‖kwɑː-/ *n* [C] *technical* an EQUATION such as $ax^2+bx+c=y$, which includes numbers or quantities multiplied by themselves

**quadri-** /kwɒdrɪ‖kwɑː-/ *prefix* also **quadru-** /kwɒdrʊ‖-kwɑː-/ **quadr-** /kwɒdr‖kwɑːdr/ four; four times: *quadrilateral* (=with four straight sides) | *a quadruped* (=an animal with four legs)

**quad·ri·lat·er·al** /ˌkwɒdrɪˈlætərəl◂‖ˌkwɑː-/ *n* [C] a flat shape with four straight sides —**quadrilateral** *adj*

**qua·drille** /kwəˈdrɪl‖kwɑː-/ *n* [C] a dance, popular especially in the 19th century, in which the dancers form a square

**qua·dril·lion** /kwɒˈdrɪljən‖kwɑː-/ *number* **1** *BrE* the number one followed by 24 zeros **2** *AmE* the number one followed by 15 zeros

**quad·ro·phon·ic** /ˌkwɒdrəˈfɒnɪk◂‖ˌkwɑːdrəˈfɑː-/ *adj* another spelling of QUADRAPHONIC

**quadru-** /kwɒdrʊ‖kwɑː-/ *prefix* another form of the prefix QUADRI-

**quad·ru·ped** /ˈkwɒdrʊped‖ˈkwɑːdrə-/ *n* [C] *technical* an animal that has four legs —compare BIPED

**quad·ru·ple¹** /ˈkwɒdrʊpəl, kwɒˈdruː-‖kwɑːˈdruː-/ *v* [I,T] to increase and become four times as big or as high or make something increase in this way: *Food prices quadrupled during the war.* | *The company has quadrupled its profits in just three years.*

**quadruple²** *adj, predeterminer* **1** four times as big or as many: *The subjects were given quadruple the normal dosage of the drug.* **2** having four parts —**quadruple** *adj*

**quad·ru·plet** /ˈkwɒdrʊplɪt‖kwɑːˈdruːp-/ *n* [C] one of four babies born at the same time to the same mother

**quaff** /kwɒf, kwɑːf‖kwɑːf, kwæf/ *v* [T] *literary* to drink a lot of something quickly: *wedding guests quaffing champagne*

**quag·mire** /ˈkwægmaɪə, ˈkwɒg-‖ˈkwægmaɪr/ *n* [C usually singular] **1** an area of soft wet muddy ground: *In the rainy season the roads become a quagmire.* **2** a difficult or complicated situation: *Public housing regulations are a legislative quagmire.*

**quail¹** /kweɪl/ *n* **1** [C] a small bird like a PARTRIDGE **2** [U] the meat of a quail

**quail²** *v* [I] *literary* to be afraid; TREMBLE: [+ **at**] *She quailed visibly at the sight of the grim prison walls.*

**quaint** /kweɪnt/ *adj* unusual and attractive, especially in an old-fashioned way: *one of those quaint British traditions*

**quake¹** /kweɪk/ *v* [I] **1** to shake or tremble, usually because you are very frightened: [+ **with**] *Quaking with fear, I reached for the phone to call the police.* **2 quake in your boots** *informal* to feel very afraid **3** if the earth, a building etc quakes, it shakes violently: *The explosion made the whole house quake.*

**quake²** *n* [C] an EARTHQUAKE

**Quak·er** /ˈkweɪkə‖-ər/ *n* [C] a member of the Society of Friends, a Christian religious group that opposes all violence, has no priests or ceremonies, and holds its religious meetings in silence —**Quaker** *adj*

**qual·i·fi·ca·tion** /ˌkwɒlɪfɪˈkeɪʃən‖ˌkwɑː-/ *n* **1** [C usually plural] an examination that you have passed, especially at school or university: *Eva had excellent academic qualifications, but no work experience.* | *a teaching qualification* | **paper qualifications** (=official qualifications rather than experience or personal qualities) **2** [C] a skill, personal quality, or type of experience that makes you suitable for a particular job or position: [+ **for**] *The status of barrister provides a qualification for various public appointments.* | **qualification to do sth** *Isobel has all the right qualifications to become a good manager.* **3** [C, U] something that you add to a statement to limit its effect or meaning: *The committee expressed support for our plans but with certain qualifications.* **4** [U] the achievement of reaching the necessary standard to enter a sports competition, or passing examinations for a particular job: *On qualification you can expect to find work abroad.* | *We need to beat Poland to ensure qualification for the World Cup finals.* S2 W3

**qual·i·fied** /ˈkwɒlɪfaɪd‖ˈkwɑː-/ *adj* **1** having suitable knowledge, experience, or qualifications, especially for a particular job: *a qualified accountant* | *highly qualified engineering staff* | **qualified to do sth** *He's qualified to teach in elementary school, but not in high school.* | *It's a complex legal matter and I don't feel qualified to give an opinion.* **2** qualified agreement, approval etc is limited in some way, because you do not completely agree or approve: *The Gann Report received qualified approval from the colleges.* S3

**qual·i·fi·er** /ˈkwɒlɪfaɪə‖ˈkwɑːlɪfaɪr/ *n* [C] **1** someone who has reached the necessary standard for entering a competition **2** a game that you have to win in order to be able to take part in a competition: *Rosenthal looks set to miss tomorrow's World Cup qualifier in Helsinki.* **3** *technical* a word or phrase that limits or adds to the meaning of another word or phrase

**qual·i·fy** /ˈkwɒlɪfaɪ‖ˈkwɑː-/ *v* S2 W3
**1** ▶ **PASS EXAMS** ◀ [I] to pass an examination or reach the standard of knowledge or skill that you need in order to do something: [+ **as**] *Olga recently qualified*

*as a pilot.* | *After qualifying, doctors spend at least two years working in hospitals.*
**2 ▶ HAVE A RIGHT ◀** [I] to have the right to claim something: [+ **for**] *You may be able to qualify for unemployment benefit.*
**3 ▶ MAKE SB SUITABLE ◀** [T] if your knowledge or ability qualifies you to do something, it makes you a suitable person to do it: **qualify sb for sth** *Fluency in three languages qualifies her for work in the European Parliament.* | **qualify sb to do sth** *Our four-week course will qualify you to teach English overseas.*
**4 ▶ HAVE THE RIGHT QUALITIES ◀** [I] to have all the necessary qualities to be considered to be a particular thing: [+ **as**] *I don't think that really qualifies as an answer.* | *Does photography qualify as an art form?*
**5 ▶ SPORT ◀** [I] to reach the necessary standard to enter or continue in a competition or sports event: *If the French team wins, it will qualify for a place in the finals.*
**6 ▶ ADD SOMETHING ◀** [T] to add to something that has already been said, in order to limit its effect or meaning; MODIFY: *Could I just qualify that last statement?*

**qual·i·ta·tive** /ˈkwɒlɪ̣tətɪv‖ˈkwɑːlɪ̣teɪ-/ *adj* connected with the quality or nature of something: *a qualitative study of educational services* —compare QUANTITATIVE

S1 W1 **qual·i·ty¹** /ˈkwɒlɪ̣ti‖ˈkwɑː-/ *n* **1** [C] something such as courage, intelligence, or loyalty that people may have as part of their character: *You need special personal qualities to work as a nurse.* | *Bravery was never a quality that I noticed in Gerald.* **2** [C] something such as size, colour, feel or weight that makes one thing different from other things: *The analysis looks at the physical and chemical qualities of the sample.* **3** [C,U] the degree to which something is good or bad: *The higher the price the better the quality.* | *The recent hot, humid weather is affecting air quality.* | **high quality** (=very good) *high quality ingredients* **4** [U] a high standard: *Remember, it's quality we're aiming for so don't rush the job.* | **of quality** *an actor of real quality* **5 quality of life** the satisfaction in your life that comes from having good health, comfort, good relationships etc, rather than from money **6 a man/lady of quality** *old-fashioned* a man or woman of high social rank

**quality²** *adj* [only before noun] **1** *especially BrE* a word meaning very good, used especially by people who are trying to sell something: *We provide quality rented accommodation for professional people.* | *quality childcare at prices people can afford* | *quality double glazing* **2 quality newspapers/press/journalism** *BrE* newspapers etc aimed at educated readers

**quality as·sur·ance** /ˈ··· ·ˌ··/ *n* [U] management of the quality of goods or services so that they stay at a good standard

**quality con·trol** /ˈ··· ·ˌ·/ *n* [U] the practice of checking goods as they are produced to make sure that their quality is good enough —**quality controller** *n* [C]

**quality time** /ˈ··· ˌ·/ *n* [U] the time that you spend giving someone your full attention, especially time spent with your children after work

**qualm** /kwɑːm‖kwɑːm, kwɑːlm/ *n* [C usually plural] a feeling/slight worry because you are not sure that what you are doing is right: *Despite my qualms, I took the job.* | **have no qualms about** (=not be worried) *He seemed to have no qualms about breaking the speed limit.*

**quan·da·ry** /ˈkwɒndəri‖ˈkwɑːn-/ *n* **be in a quandary (about/over)** to be unable to decide what to do about a difficult problem or situation: *The city council is in a quandary over whether to raise taxes or not.*

**quan·go** /ˈkwæŋgəʊ‖-goʊ/ *n plural* **quangos** [C] an independent organization in Britain, started by the government but with its own legal powers

**quan·ta** /ˈkwɒntə‖ˈkwɑːn-/ the plural of QUANTUM

**quan·ti·fi·er** /ˈkwɒntɪ̣faɪə‖ˈkwɑːntɪ̣faɪr/ *n* [C] *technical* a word or phrase such as 'much', 'few' or 'a lot of' that is used with a noun to show quantity

**quan·ti·fy** /ˈkwɒntɪ̣faɪ‖ˈkwɑːn-/ *v* [T] to measure something and express it as a number, especially something that is difficult to measure: *Life has got worse for a lot of people, but in ways that are hard to quantify.* —**quantifiable** *adj* | *The damage caused by pollution is not easily quantifiable.* **quantification** /ˌkwɒntɪ̣fɪ̣ˈkeɪʃən‖kwɑːn-/ *n* [U]

**quan·ti·ta·tive** /ˈkwɒntɪ̣tətɪv‖ˈkwɑːntɪ̣teɪ-/ *adj* connected with amounts rather than with the quality or nature of something: *quantitative estimates* | *quantitative chemical analysis* —compare QUALITATIVE —**quantitatively** *adv*

**quan·ti·ty** /ˈkwɒntɪ̣ti‖ˈkwɑːn-/ *n* **1** [C] also **quantities** [plural] an amount of something that can be counted or measured: [+ **of**] *microscopic quantities of heroin* **2** [U] amount: [+ **in**] *Your work has improved in quantity and quality this term.* **3** also **quantities** [plural] a large amount or number: [+ **of**] *Quantities of arms were discovered hidden in the trucks.* | **in quantity** (=in large amounts) *It's a lot cheaper if you buy it in quantity.* —see also **unknown quantity** (UNKNOWN¹ (4))

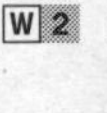

**quantity sur·vey·or** /ˈ··· ·ˌ··/ *n* [C] someone whose job is to calculate the amount of materials that will be needed to build something, how long it will take to build etc and what it will cost

**quan·tum** /ˈkwɒntəm‖ˈkwɑːn-/ *n* /-tə/ *plural* **quanta** /-tə/ *technical* an amount of energy in NUCLEAR PHYSICS, which varies from the next possible smaller or larger amount by a specific degree

**quantum leap** /ˌ·· ˈ·/ also **quantum jump** *AmE* *n* [C] a very large and important improvement: *This discovery is a quantum leap for medical science.*

**quantum me·chan·ics** /ˌ·· ·ˈ··/ *n* [U] the study of the way that atoms and smaller pieces of MATTER¹ (30) behave

**quantum the·o·ry** /ˈ·· ˌ···/ *n* [singular] the idea that energy, especially light, travels in separate pieces and not in a continuous form

**quar·an·tine¹** /ˈkwɒrəntiːn‖ˈkwɔː-/ *n* [U] a period of time when a person or animal is kept apart from others in case they are carrying a disease: **in quarantine** (=being kept somewhere in a period of quarantine)

**quarantine²** *v* **quarantined, quarantining** [T often passive] to put a person or animal in quarantine

**quark** /kwɑːk, kwɔːk‖kwɔːrk, kwɑːrk/ *n* [C] **1** *technical* one of the smallest known amounts of MATTER¹ (30) that forms part of an atom **2** [U] a type of German soft cheese

**quar·rel¹** /ˈkwɒrəl‖ˈkwɔː-, ˈkwɑː-/ *n* [C] **1** an angry argument, often about something that is not important: [+ **with**] *She got into a silly quarrel with the other children.* | [+ **about/over**] *What was the quarrel all about?* | **pick a quarrel (with)** (=deliberately start a quarrel) *He seems to enjoy picking a quarrel with everyone he meets.* **2** a reason or subject for disagreement: *Is there any quarrel between those two that I should know about?* **3 have no quarrel with** *formal* to have no reason to dislike someone or disagree with an idea, decision etc: *We have no quarrel with the court's verdict.*

**quarrel²** *v* **quarrelled, quarrelling** *BrE*, **quarreled, quarreling** *AmE* [I] to have an argument: *I wish you two would stop quarrelling.* | [+ **with**] *They're forever bickering and quarrelling with each other.* | [+ **about**] *We're not going to quarrel about a few dollars.*

**quarrel with** sth *phr v* [T] to disagree with something or complain about something: *Few of us can quarrel with the idea of more choice and more competition.*

**quar·rel·some** /ˈkwɒrəlsəm‖ˈkwɔː-, ˈkwɑː-/ *adj* someone who is quarrelsome seems to like quarrelling: *a quarrelsome tone in his voice* —**quarrelsomeness** *n* [U]

**quar·ry¹** /ˈkwɒri‖ˈkwɔː-, ˈkwɑː-/ *n* [C] **1** a place where large amounts of stone, sand etc are dug out of the ground: *a slate quarry* —compare MINE² (1) **2** [singular] the person or animal that you are hunting or chasing: *The police saw the empty room and knew their quarry had escaped.*

**quarry²** *v* [T] to dig out stone, sand etc from a quarry: [+ **from**] *It was built with stones quarried from Portland.*

**quart** /kwɔːt‖kwɔːrt/ *n* [C] **1** a unit used for measuring liquids and some dry goods —see table on page B2 **2 put a quart into a pint pot** *BrE informal* to try to do more than you have time or space for

S1 W2 **quar·ter¹** /ˈkwɔːtə‖ˈkwɔːrtər/ *n*
**1 ▶AMOUNT◀** [C] one of four equal or almost equal parts into which something can be divided: *Cut it into quarters.* | [+ **of**] *a quarter of a mile* | *in the last quarter of the 19th century* | *They're firing almost a quarter of the workforce.* | *It's about a page and a quarter.*
**2 ▶PART OF AN HOUR◀** [C] one of the four periods of 15 minutes into which each hour can be divided: *I'll meet you in three-quarters of an hour.* (=in 45 minutes) | **quarter to** *BrE*/**quarter of** *AmE* (=15 minutes before the hour) *It's a quarter of two.* (=1:45) | **quarter past** *BrE*/**quarter after** *AmE* (=15 minutes after the hour) *a quarter past ten* (=10:15)
**3 ▶MONEY◀** [C] a coin in the US and Canada, worth 25 cents

**4 ▶THREE MONTHS◀** [C] a period of three months, used especially in connection with bills, wages, and income: *The company's profits rose by 11% in the first quarter of the year.* —see also QUARTERLY¹
**5 ▶PART OF A CITY◀** [C] an area of a town or city where a particular kind of people typically live or work: *the student quarter* | *We took a rented house in the Creole quarter of New Orleans.*
**6 ▶HOME◀ quarters** [plural] a house or rooms where you can live, especially in the army: *staff quarters* | **married quarters** (=where soldiers with wives live)
**7 in/from ... quarters** in or from different groups of people: *Offers of financial help came from the most unexpected quarters.* | *There were doubts in many quarters about the country's ability to repay the debt.*
**8 all quarters of the Earth/globe** *literary* everywhere in the world
**9 give no quarter** *old use* to show no pity towards someone, especially an enemy whom you have defeated: *It was a fight to the death, with no quarter given.*
**10 ▶WEIGHT◀** [C] *BrE* a unit for measuring weight, equal to 28 pounds or about 13 kilos
**11 ▶AT COLLEGE◀** [C] *AmE* a period of 10 to 12 weeks into which a teaching year is divided in some American colleges and universities: *What classes are you taking this quarter?*
**12 ▶SPORT◀** [C] one of the four equal periods of time into which games of some sports are divided
**13 ▶MOON◀** [C] the period of time twice a month when you can see a quarter of the moon's surface
**14 ▶MEAT◀** [C] a large piece of meat from a large animal, including one of its legs: *a quarter of beef* —see also **at close quarters** (CLOSE² (2))

**quarter²** *v* [T] **1** to cut or divide something into four parts: *Quarter the tomatoes and place them round the dish.* **2** *old use* to provide soldiers, workers etc with a place to sleep and eat: *Our forces were quartered in tents on the edge of the woods.*

**quar·ter·back¹** /ˈkwɔːtəbæk‖ˈkwɔːrtər-/ *n* [C] **1** the player in AMERICAN FOOTBALL who directs the team's attacking play and passes the ball to the other players at the start of each attacking move **2 Monday morning quarterback** *AmE* someone who gives advice on something only after it has happened

**quarterback²** *v AmE* **1** [I] to play in the position of quarterback in AMERICAN FOOTBALL **2** [T] *informal* to organize or direct an activity, event etc: *She quarterbacked the new sales campaign.*

**quarter day** /ˈ‥ ·/ *n* [C] *BrE* a day which officially begins a three-month period of the year, and on which payments are made, for example at the STOCK EXCHANGE

**quar·ter·deck** /ˈkwɔːtədek‖ˈkwɔːrtər-/ *n* [C] the back part of the upper DECK (=floor level) of a ship, used mainly by officers

**quar·ter·fi·nal** /ˌkwɔːtəˈfaɪnl‖ˌkwɔːrtər-/ *n* [C] one of the set of four games near the end of a competition, whose winners play in the two SEMIFINALS

**quarter horse** /ˈ‥ ˌ·/ *n* [C] a strong horse in the US, bred to run short races, usually of a quarter of a mile

**quar·ter·ly¹** /ˈkwɔːtəli‖ˈkwɔːrtər-/ *adj, adv* produced or happening four times a year: *quarterly accounts* | *a quarterly newsletter*

**quarterly²** *n* [C] a magazine that is produced four times a year

**quar·ter·mas·ter** /ˈkwɔːtəˌmɑːstə‖ˈkwɔːrtərˌmæstər/ *n* [C] **1** a military officer in charge of providing food, uniforms etc **2** a ship's officer in charge of signals and guiding the ship on the right course

**quarter note** /ˈ‥ ·/ *n* [C] *AmE* a musical note which continues for a quarter of the length of a WHOLE NOTE; CROTCHET *BrE* —see picture at MUSIC

**quarter ses·sions** /ˈ‥ ˌ‥/ *n* [plural] an English law court in former times, which has been replaced by the Crown Court

**quar·ter·staff** /ˈkwɔːtəstɑːf‖ˈkwɔːrtərstæf/ *n* [C] a long wooden pole used as a weapon, especially in former times

**quar·tet** /kwɔːˈtet‖kwɔːr-/ *n* [C] **1** four singers or musicians who perform together: *He's the trombonist in a jazz quartet.* **2** a piece of music written for four performers **3** four people or things of the same type: *The same quartet of characters appears in another of her novels.* —compare QUINTET, TRIO

**quar·to** /ˈkwɔːtəʊ‖ˈkwɔːrtoʊ/ *n* [C] *technical* **1** the size of paper, or the paper itself, produced by folding a large sheet of paper twice, to produce four sheets: *quarto sheets of paper* **2** a book with pages of quarto size

**quartz** /kwɔːts‖kwɔːrts/ *n* [U] a hard mineral substance, used in making electronic watches and clocks: *a quartz gold watch*

**qua·sar** /ˈkweɪzɑː‖-ɑːr/ *n* [C] *technical* a very bright, very distant object similar to a star

**quash** /kwɒʃ‖kwɑːʃ, kwɒːʃ/ *v* [T] *formal* **1** to officially state that a judgement or decision is no longer legal or correct: *The judge quashed the decision of the lower court.* **2** to use force to end protests or disobedience: *quash a rebellion*

**quasi-** /kwɑːzi, kweɪzaɪ/ *prefix* **1** in some ways; partly: *the chairman's quasi-judicial role* (=acting in some ways like a judge) **2** false or pretended: *quasi-scientific ideas*

**quat·er·cen·te·na·ry** /ˌkwætəsenˈtiːnəri‖ˌkwɑːtərsenˈte-/ *n* [C] the day or year exactly 400 years after a particular event: *the quatercentenary of Shakespeare's birth*

**quat·rain** /ˈkwɒtreɪn‖ˈkwɑː-/ *n* [C] a group of four lines in a poem

**qua·ver¹** /ˈkweɪvə‖-ər/ *v* [I,T] if your voice quavers, it shakes as you speak, especially because you are nervous: *"Please help me," he quavered.* —**quavery** *adj*

**quaver²** *n* [C] **1** *BrE* a musical note which continues for an eighth of the length of a SEMIBREVE; EIGHTH NOTE *AmE* —see picture at MUSIC **2** a shaking sound in your voice

**quay** /kiː‖keɪ/ *n* [C] a place where boats can be tied up or can stop to load and UNLOAD: *a quay lined with fishing boats*

**quay·side** /ˈkiːsaɪd/ *n* [C] the area next to a quay: *people strolling along the quayside* | *a quayside restaurant*

**quea·sy** /ˈkwiːzi/ *adj* feeling that you are going to VOMIT: *The sea got rougher, and I began to feel a little queasy.* —**queasiness** *n* [U]

**queen¹** /kwiːn/ *n* [C] S2 W2
**1 ▶RULER◀** also **Queen a)** the female ruler of a country: *Elizabeth II became Queen of England in 1952.* **b)** the wife of a king
**2 ▶CARD◀** a playing card with a picture of a queen on it: *the queen of hearts*
**3 ▶HOMOSEXUAL◀** *informal* an insulting word for a male HOMOSEXUAL, especially one who behaves like a woman

**4 queen bee** a woman who behaves as if she is the most important person in a place
**5 the queen of** a woman who is regarded as the best at a particular activity or in a particular field: *Tammy Wynette, the queen of country music.*
**6 ▶ INSECT ◀** a large female BEE, ANT etc, which lays the eggs for a whole group
**7 ▶ CHESS ◀** the most powerful piece in the game of CHESS —see also BEAUTY QUEEN, DRAG QUEEN, MAY QUEEN

**queen²** *v* [T] **1 queen it over** *informal* to behave in an annoying way as if you are more important than other people **2** *technical* to change a PAWN¹ (1) into a queen in the game of CHESS

**queen·ly** /ˈkwiːnli/ *adj* suitable for or like a queen: *She gave a queenly wave as she rode past.*

**Queen Moth·er** /ˌ· ˈ··/ *n* [singular] the mother of the ruling king or queen

**Queen's Coun·sel** /ˌ· ˈ··/ *n* a QC

**Queen's En·glish** /ˌ· ˈ··/ *n BrE* **speak the Queen's English** to speak very correctly and in a way that is typical of people who belong to the highest social class —see also KING'S ENGLISH

**Queen's ev·i·dence** /ˌ· ˈ···/ *n BrE* **turn Queen's evidence** if a criminal turns Queen's evidence, they agree to help the police, law courts etc to catch other criminals by giving them information —see also EVIDENCE¹, KING'S EVIDENCE, STATE'S EVIDENCE

**queen-size** /ˈ· ·/ *adj especially AmE* a queen-size bed, sheet etc is larger than the standard size for a bed for two people —compare DOUBLE BED, KING-SIZE, SINGLE¹ (4)

**queer¹** /kwɪə‖kwɪr/ *adj* **1** *old-fashioned* strange or difficult to explain: *This orange tastes queer.* | *She gave a queer laugh.* **2** *informal* a word meaning HOMOSEXUAL, considered offensive when used by people who are not homosexual **3** *BrE* ill or sick: *I'm feeling a little queer – I think I'll go and lie down.* **4 queer in the head** *old-fashioned* talking or behaving strangely; crazy **5 be in queer street** *BrE old-fashioned* to owe people money —**queerly** *adv*: *queerly shaped* —**queerness** *n* [U]

**queer²** *n* [C] *informal* an insulting word for a HOMOSEXUAL

**queer³** *v* **queer sb's pitch** *BrE informal* to spoil someone's plans or chance to do something

**queer bash·ing** /ˈ· ˌ··/ *n* [U] *informal* physical violence against people because they are HOMOSEXUAL

**quell** /kwel/ *v* [T] *formal* **1** to bring an end to a violent situation especially when people are protesting: **quell a riot/revolt/disturbance etc** *They needed more troops to quell the ever-rising tide of rioting.* **2** to reduce unpleasant feelings, especially of doubt or worry: *I thought about the advantages of the deal, trying to quell a growing sense of unease.*

**quench** /kwentʃ/ *v* [T] **1 quench your thirst** to stop yourself from feeling thirsty: *Iced tea really quenches your thirst.* **2 quench a fire** to make a fire stop burning

**quer·u·lous** /ˈkwerʊləs/ *adj formal* complaining all the time in an annoying way: *"But why can't I go?" he said in a querulous tone.* —**querulously** *adv* —**querulousness** *n* [U]

**que·ry¹** /ˈkwɪəri‖ˈkwɪri/ *n* [C] a question you ask to get information, or to check that something is true or correct: *We will answer any queries by letter.*

**query²** *v* [T] **1** to express doubt that something is true or correct: [+ **whether**] *I'd query whether these figures are reliable.* **2** [T] to ask a question: *"What time are we leaving?" queried Mrs Evans.*

**quest** /kwest/ *n* [C] *especially literary* a long search for something such as truth or knowledge: [+ **for**] *the quest for enlightenment* —**quest** *v* [I] *to quest after the truth*

**ques·tion¹** /ˈkwestʃən/ *n* [C]
**1 ▶ ASKING FOR INFORMATION ◀** a sentence or phrase that asks for information: **ask (sb) a question** *They asked me a lot of questions about my work experience.* | *May I ask a question?* | **answer a question** *Answer three out of five questions on the exam paper.* | *Does anyone have any questions?* —see ASK (USAGE)
**2 ▶ SUBJECT/PROBLEM ◀** a subject or problem that needs to be settled, discussed, or dealt with; ISSUE¹ (1): *Several questions had still not been resolved.* | *This brings us to the question of government funding.* | **the question is** *The question is, do I take the job in Japan, or stay here?*
**3 ▶ DOUBT ◀** a feeling of doubt about something: **raise questions about** *This incident raises further questions about the effectiveness of airport security.* | **there is no question** (=there is no doubt) *He's by far the best, there's no question about it.* | **open to question** (=likely or able to be doubted) *The wisdom of this policy is open to question.*
**4 without question a)** without any doubt: *Marilyn was, without question, a very beautiful woman.* **b)** if you obey an order without question, you obey immediately and do not complain at all
**5 there's no question of** used to say that there is no possibility of something happening: *There is no question of the government holding talks with terrorists.*

**6 in question** the things, people etc in question are the ones that are being discussed or talked about: *The goods in question had been stolen.*
**7 be a question of** used when you are giving the most important fact, part, or feature or something: *Dance is a question of control and creative expression.* | *I would love to come, but it's a question of time.*
**8 out of the question** not possible or not allowed: *You can't go to the wedding in that old shirt – it's quite out of the question.*
**9 it's just a question of** *spoken* used to say that something is easy or not complicated: *It's just a question of putting in a couple of screws.*
**10 pop the question** *informal humorous* to ask someone to marry you: *Simon finally plucked up the courage to pop the question.*
**11 good question!** *spoken* used to show that you do not know the answer to a question: *"How can we afford this?" "Good question!"* —see also **leading question** (LEADING¹ (4)), **rhetorical question** (RHETORICAL (1)), **beg the question** (BEG (5)), **call into question** (CALL¹ (21))

**question²** *v* [T] S2 W3 **1** to ask someone questions to find out what they know about something, especially about a crime: *We're taking them in for questioning.* | **question sb about** *The police questioned him about the missing $10,000.* | **question sb closely** (=ask them a lot of difficult questions to find out exactly what they know) **2** to have doubts about something or tell someone about these doubts: *Are you questioning the truth of what I'm saying?* | *It makes me question the whole basis of the research.*

**ques·tion·a·ble** /ˈkwestʃənəbəl/ *adj* **1** not definitely true or correct: *The report's conclusions are questionable because the sample used was very small.* **2** behaviour or actions that are questionable seem likely to be dishonest or wrong: *business deals of a rather questionable kind*

**ques·tion·er** /ˈkwestʃənə‖-ər/ *n* [C] someone who is asking a question, for example in a public discussion

**ques·tion·ing** /ˈkwestʃənɪŋ/ *adj* a questioning look or expression shows that you have doubts about something or need some information: *the questioning eyes of a child* —**questioningly** *adv*

**question mark** /ˈ·· ·/ *n* [C] **1** the mark (?) that is used at the end of a sentence to show that it asks a question —see picture at PUNCTUATION MARK **2 a question mark over** if there is a question mark over something, there is a possibility that it will not be be successful or will not continue to exist: *A big question mark hangs over the company's future.*

**questionmas·ter** /ˈ·· ˌ··/ *n* [C] *BrE* the person who asks the questions in a QUIZ game

**ques·tion·naire** /ˌkwestʃəˈneə, ˌkes-‖-ˈner/ *n* [C] a written set of questions which you give to a large number of people in order to collect information: **fill in/complete a questionnaire** (=answer all the questions in it)

**question tag** /ˈ·· ·/ *n* [C] *technical* a phrase such as 'isn't

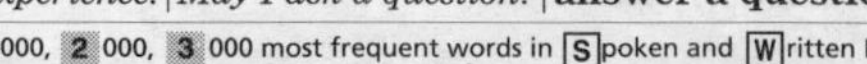

it?', 'won't it?', or 'does she?' that you add to the end of a statement to make it a question or to check that someone agrees with you: *You're from Hamburg, aren't you?*

**question time** /'·· ·/ *n* [U] the period of time in a parliament when ministers answer questions from members of the parliament

S3 **queue¹** /kjuː/ *n* [C] *BrE* **1** a line of people waiting to enter a building, buy something etc, or a line of vehicles waiting to move; LINE¹ (22) *AmE* —see picture at PUSH IN: *The queue for the cinema went right round the building.* | *We were stuck in a queue for half an hour.* | **jump a queue** (=go unfairly to the front of a queue instead of waiting) **2** *technical* a list of jobs that a computer has to do in a particular order; ORDER¹ (12) *AmE*: *the print queue* —see also **the dole queue** (DOLE¹ (5))

**queue²** *v past tense and past participle* **queued** *present participle* **queuing** or **queueing** also **queue up** [I] *BrE* to form or join a line of people or vehicles waiting to do something or go somewhere; **line up** (LINE²) *AmE*: *The post office was really busy – we had to queue for ages to get served.* | [+ **for**] *people queuing for tickets*

**queue-jump** /'· ·/ *v* [I] *BrE informal* to go unfairly to the front of a queue, instead of waiting

**quib·ble¹** /'kwɪbəl/ *v* [I + **over/about**] to argue about small points or details that are completely unimportant: *Don't quibble about the money – just pay what she asks.*

**quibble²** *n* [C] a small complaint or criticism about something very unimportant: *I have just one quibble – there's a spelling mistake here.*

**quiche** /kiːʃ/ *n* [C,U] a flat open piece of PASTRY (1) filled with a mixture of eggs, cheese, vegetables etc

S1 W2 **quick¹** /kwɪk/ *adj*

**1 ▶ SHORT TIME ◀** continuing or existing for only a short time: *I just have to make a quick phone call.* | *John had a quick meal and then went out again.* | *That was quick! I thought you'd be another hour.*

**2 ▶ FAST ◀** moving or happening fast: *She walked with short, quick steps.* | *A series of quick changes take place as the chemicals bond.*

**3 ▶ SOON ◀** happening very soon, without any delay: *We've put the house on the market and we're hoping for a quick sale.*

**4 ▶ CLEVER ◀** able to learn and understand things fast: *That child's a really quick learner.* | **a quick study** *AmE slang* (=a student who is clever and learns quickly)

**5 be quick** to hurry: *If you want to come with me you'll have to be quick – I'm leaving in ten minutes.* | **be quick about it** *Just bring me that book, and be quick about it.*

**6 be quick to do sth** to react quickly to what someone says or does: *You're always very quick to criticize my ideas – let's hear yours!*

**7 be quick on the draw/uptake** to quickly understand a situation or what someone tells you, so that you know what you have to do

**8 a quick one/half/pint** *especially BrE informal* a drink that you have in a hurry: *Let's stop for a quick one before the train comes.*

**9 have a quick temper** to get angry very easily

**10 a quick fix** *informal* a repair to something or an answer to a problem that will work only for a short time —see also QUICKLY —**quickness** *n* [U]

**quick²** *interjection* used to tell someone to hurry or come quickly: *Quick! We'll miss the bus!* | *Come on! Quick!*

S3 **quick³** *adv* quickly; fast: *Come back quick – something terrible has happened!* | **quick as a flash** *informal* (=very quickly) *Quick as a flash she replied "That's not what I've heard!"*

**quick⁴** *n* [U] **1 cut sb to the quick** if a remark or criticism cuts you to the quick, it makes you very upset **2 the quick** the sensitive flesh under your fingernails and toenails: *Her nails were bitten to the quick.* **3 the quick and the dead** *old use* all people, including those who are alive and those who are dead

**quick-change ar·tist** /,· '· ,··/ *n* [C] an entertainer who can change their clothes or appearance very quickly

**quick·en** /'kwɪkən/ *v* [I,T] **1** to become quicker or make something quicker: *the quickening pace of technological change* | **quicken your pace** (=walk faster) *Ray glanced at his watch and quickened his pace.* | **your heart/pulse quickens** (=your heart beats faster because you are afraid, excited etc) *Val caught sight of Rob and felt her heart quicken.* **2** *formal* if a feeling quickens, or if something quickens it, it becomes stronger or more active: *This policy served only to quicken anti-government feeling.* **3** *old use or literary* to come alive or make something come alive

**quick·en·ing** /'kwɪkənɪŋ/ *n* [U] the first movements of a baby that has not been born yet

**quick·fire** /'kwɪkfaɪə‖-faɪr/ *adj* quickfire conversation, speech etc is very fast and full of clever or amusing remarks: *He's full of quickfire patter and smooth gestures.*

**quick·freeze** /'kwɪkfriːz/ *v* [T] to freeze food very quickly so that it keeps all its taste; FLASHFREEZE *AmE*

**quick·ie** /'kwɪki/ *n* [C] *informal* **1** something done or made quickly and easily: *This recipe is a favourite quickie for when I'm in a hurry.* **2** *humorous* a sexual act done in a hurry —**quickie** *adj*: *a quickie divorce*

**quick·lime** /'kwɪk-laɪm/ *n* [U] a white substance obtained by burning LIMESTONE

**quick·ly** /'kwɪkli/ *adv* **1** fast: *She checked nothing was coming and walked quickly across the road.* | *Quickly, John, we don't have much time.* **2** after only a very short time: *I realized fairly quickly that this wasn't going to be easy.* **3** for a short time: *I'll just quickly nip into that shop.* S1 W1

**quick march** /,· '·/ *interjection* used as a command to tell a group of soldiers to march quickly

**quick·sand** /'kwɪksænd/ also **quicksands** *plural n* [C,U] wet sand that is dangerous because it pulls you down into it if you try to walk on it

**quick·sil·ver** /'kwɪk,sɪlvə‖-ər/ *n* [U] *old use* MERCURY (=a metal that is liquid at normal temperatures)

**quick·step** /'kwɪkstep/ *n* [C] a dance with fast movements of the feet, or the music for this dance

**quick-tem·pered** /,· '··◂/ *adj* easily becoming angry: *Our young men were quick-tempered and likely to do rash things.*

**quick-wit·ted** /,· '··◂/ *adj* able to understand things quickly and give quick, clever replies —**quickwittedness** *n* [U]

**quid** /kwɪd/ *n plural* **quid** [C] *BrE informal* **1** one pound in money; £1: *She earns at least 600 quid a week.* **2 be quids in** to make a profit, especially a good profit: *We'll be quids in if we get this contract.* S2

**quid pro quo** /,kwɪd prəʊ 'kwəʊ‖-proʊ 'kwoʊ/ *n* [C] something that you give or do in exchange for something else, especially when this arrangement is not official: [+ **for**] *The quid pro quo is that we pay them a very low rent.*

**qui·es·cent** /kwi'esənt, kwaɪ-/ *adj formal* not developing or doing anything, especially when this is only a temporary state —**quiescently** *adv* —**quiescence** *n* [U]

**qui·et¹** /'kwaɪət/ *adj* S2 W2

**1 ▶ NO NOISE ◀** not making much noise: *We'll have to be quiet so as not to wake the baby.* | *The engine is 20% quieter than its nearest rival's.* | **(as) quiet as a mouse** (=very quiet)

**2 quiet!/be quiet!** *spoken* used to tell someone, rather rudely, to stop talking or making noise

**3 ▶ PEACEFUL ◀** a quiet place or time is one where there is not much activity and there are not many people: *I'd love to go on holiday somewhere where it's nice and quiet.* | **quiet day/weekend** *a quiet weekend at home*

**4 ▶ NOT SPEAKING ◀ a)** not saying much or not saying anything: *You're very quiet, Mom – is anything the matter?* **b)** someone who is quiet does not usually talk very much: *"What's she like?" "Oh, quiet – but friendly enough."*

**5 ▶ NOT BUSY ◀** if business is quiet, there are not many customers: *August is a quiet time of year for the retail trade.*

**6 keep quiet** to not say anything, because you do not know anything or because you do not want to tell a secret: *I didn't know anything about it so I just kept quiet.*
**7 keep sth quiet/keep quiet about sth** to keep information secret: *You're getting married? You kept that quiet!*
**8 keep sb quiet** to stop someone from talking, complaining, or causing trouble: *I gave the children some candy to keep them quiet.*
**9 have a quiet word (with)** *especially BrE* to talk to someone privately when you want to criticize them or tell them about something serious: *I'll have a quiet word with Brian about his behaviour.* —see also QUIETLY —**quietness** *n* [U]

**quiet²** *n* [U] **1** quietness; calmness: *the quiet of the churchyard* | **peace and quiet** *I've had an awful day – now I just want some peace and quiet.* **2** silence: *Can I have quiet please!* **3 on the quiet** *informal* without telling anyone; secretly: *We found out he'd been doing some freelance work on the quiet.*

**qui·et·en** /ˈkwaɪətn/ also **quiet** *AmE v* **1** also **quieten down** [I,T] to become less noisy or less active, or to make someone or something do this: *The chatter quietened briefly when she came into the room.* | *Things tend to quieten down after the Christmas rush.* **2** [T] to make someone feel less frightened or worried

**qui·et·is·m** /ˈkwaɪətɪzəm/ *n* [U] *formal* a calm state in which you accept situations and do not have any desire to change them

S3 W3 **qui·et·ly** /ˈkwaɪətli/ *adv* **1** without making much noise: *Peter spoke so quietly I could hardly hear him.* **2** in a way that does not attract attention: *They have quietly gathered enough support to challenge the leadership.* **3 quietly confident/optimistic** *especially BrE* fairly confident of success, but without talking proudly about it

**qui·e·tude** /ˈkwaɪətjuːd‖-tuːd/ *n* [U] *formal* calmness, peace, and quiet

**qui·e·tus** /kwaɪˈiːtəs, kwiˈeɪtəs‖kwaɪˈiːtəs/ *n* [singular] *formal* **1** death **2** the end of something

**quiff** /kwɪf/ *n* [C] *BrE* a part of a man's hair style where the hair stands up at the front above his forehead

**quill** /kwɪl/ *n* [C] **1** a bird's feather, especially a large one, including the stiff, hard part at the base which joins to the bird's body **2** also **quill pen** a pen made from a large bird's feather, used in past times **3** a thing like a thin, sharp stick that grows on some animals such as a PORCUPINE, in order to protect them

**quilt** /kwɪlt/ *n* [C] **1** a warm thick cover for a bed, made of cloth filled with something such as feathers **2** *especially AmE* a thin cloth cover used on a bed to make it look attractive

**quilt·ed** /ˈkwɪltɪ̣d/ *adj* quilted cloth or clothing has been made thicker and warmer by having a special layer of material stitched into it: *a quilted bath robe*

**quilt·ing** /ˈkwɪltɪŋ/ *n* [U] the work of making a quilt, or the material and stitches that you use

**quin** /kwɪn/ *n* [C] *BrE informal* a QUINTUPLET

**quince** /kwɪns/ *n* [C, U] a hard, yellowish fruit like a large apple, used for making JELLY —see picture on page 413

**quin·ine** /ˈkwɪniːn‖ˈkwaɪnaɪn/ *n* [U] a drug used for treating fevers, especially MALARIA

**quinine wa·ter** /ˈ·· ˌ··/ *n* [U] *AmE* a bitter-tasting drink often mixed with strong alcoholic drinks such as GIN

**quint** /kwɪnt/ *n* [C] *AmE informal* a QUINTUPLET

**quin·tes·sence** /kwɪnˈtesəns/ *n* **the quintessence of sth** *formal* a perfect type or example of something: *John is the quintessence of good manners.*

**quin·tes·sen·tial** /ˌkwɪntɪ̣ˈsenʃəl◂/ *adj* being a perfect example of a particular type of person or thing: *'Guys and Dolls' is the quintessential American musical.* —**quintessentially** *adv* | *a quintessentially English rural scene*

**quin·tet** /kwɪnˈtet/ *n* [C] **1** five singers or musicians who perform together **2** a piece of music written for five performers —compare QUARTET, SEXTET, TRIO

**quin·tu·plet** /ˈkwɪntjʊplɪ̣t, kwɪnˈtjuːp-‖kwɪnˈtʌp-/ *n* [C] one of five babies born to the same mother at the same time —compare QUADRUPLET, SEXTUPLET

**quip** *v* [I] to say something short clever and amusing: *"Practice makes perfect," quipped Peter when he saw Janet trying to ski.* —**quip** *n* [C]

**quire** /kwaɪə‖kwaɪr/ *n* [C] *technical* 24 sheets of paper

**quirk** /kwɜːk‖kwɜːrk/ *n* [C] **1** something strange that happens by chance: **quirk of fate/history etc** (=something that happens by chance and influences later events) *By a quirk of fate, he left just before the bomb exploded.* **2** a strange habit or feature of someone's character: *one of her many annoying little quirks.*

**quirk·y** /ˈkwɜːki‖ɜːr-/ *adj* strange and unusual, in an unexpected way: *The music was a quirky mixture of jazz and classical violins.* —**quirkily** *adv* —**quirkiness** *n* [U]

**quis·ling** /ˈkwɪzlɪŋ/ *n* [C] someone who helps an army or enemy country that has taken control of his own country

**quit** /kwɪt/ *v past tense and past participle* **quit** *also* **quitted** *BrE present participle* **quitting** **1** [I,T] *informal, especially AmE* to leave a job, school etc, especially because you are annoyed or unhappy: *I'm tired of being treated like this. I quit.* | *Her husband had to quit because of ill health.* | **quit school/your job etc** *She quit school at 17 and left home.* **2** [T] *informal especially AmE* to stop doing something bad or annoying: *Quit it Robby, or I'll tell mom!* | **quit doing sth** *I wish you'd all quit complaining.* **3 be quit of** *formal* to be finished with something that was causing you problems **4** [T] *old use* to leave a place

**quite** /kwaɪt/ *predeterminer, adv* **1** [+ adj/adv] *especially BrE* fairly: **quite big/tall etc** *The restaurant does great food and the prices are quite reasonable.* | *I got a letter from Sylvia quite recently.* | **quite a big sth/a tall sth etc** *He's quite a good soccer player really.* | **quite a lot/a few etc** *We managed to get quite a lot of information for the survey.* —see RATHER (USAGE) **2 quite good/funny etc** *AmE* very good, funny etc: *The food was quite good!* **3 quite a lot/bit/few** large number or amount: *She must have left here, oh, quite a few years ago.* **4 not quite why/what/where etc** not exactly why, what, where etc: *I must admit, the play wasn't quite what we expected.* **5 not quite** not completely: *They weren't quite ready so we waited in the car.* **6 quite a/quite some** used to describe something that is unusually good, long, interesting etc: *That was quite a party you had last night.* | *That makes quite a noise, doesn't it?* | *He ran quite some distance before he found a public telephone.* **7** [+ adj/adv] *BrE* very or completely: *It's one thing driving a car but a lorry is quite different.* | *That's quite ridiculous!* | **quite the best/the worst etc** *It was quite the most interesting museum I've ever visited.* **8 I'm not quite sure** used to say that you are not certain about something: *I'm not quite sure what her second name is.*

Frequencies of the adverb **quite** in spoken and written English.

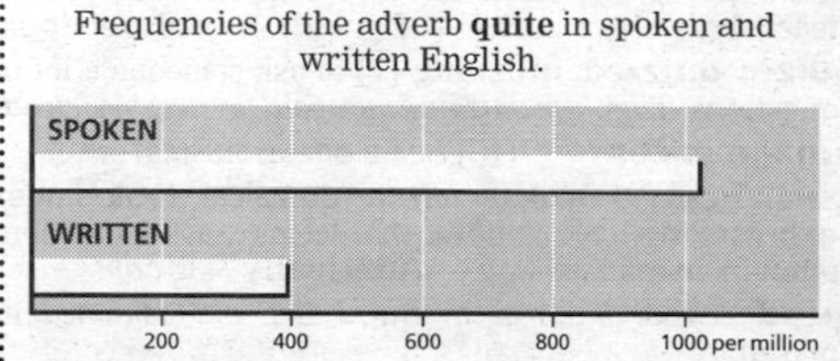


Based on the British National Corpus and the Longman Lancaster Corpus

This graph shows that the adverb **quite** is much more common in spoken English than in written English. This is because it is used a lot in spoken English to emphasize amounts, sizes etc or to emphasize how good, bad etc something is. It is also used in a lot of common spoken phrases.

**quite** (*predeterminer, adv*) **SPOKEN PHRASES**

**9 quite right** *BrE* used to show that you strongly agree with someone: *"Why should they get paid more* *than us?" "Quite right, it's completely unfair."* **10 quite like** *BrE* to like something, but not very much: *Well, I quite like maths, but I don't like the teacher.*|*It's funny, but he quite likes it after all.* **11 that's quite all right** used to reply to someone that you do not mind what they are doing: *"I hope I'm not disturbing you." "That's quite all right."* **12 I'm quite happy to do something** *BrE* used to say that you are very willing to do something: *If they want to come in and discuss it, I'd be quite happy to meet them.* **13 quite frankly/honestly** *BrE* used when you are giving a very direct or honest opinion: *Well, quite frankly, I've never heard such rubbish in all my life!* **14 quite/quite so** *BrE formal* used to show that you agree with what someone is saying: *"They really should have thought of this before." "Yes, quite."* **15 quite enough** *especially BrE* used when you are annoyed with what someone is saying or doing and you want them to stop: *I've heard quite enough about your problems. What about mine?* **16 quite something** *especially BrE* used to say that someone or something is very impressive: *You should have come to the Carnival, it was quite something, I can tell you.*

**quits** /kwɪts/ *adj informal* **1 be quits (with)** to be in an equal situation with someone again, especially because you have paid them what you owed: *You pay for the taxi, and that'll make us quits.*|*If I win the next game, we'll be quits.* **2 call it quits a)** to agree that a debt or argument is settled: *Just give me $20 and we'll call it quits.* **b)** to agree to stop doing something: *Let's just paint this door then call it quits for the day.*

**quit·tance** /ˈkwɪtəns/ *n* [C] *law* a statement saying that someone no longer has to do something such as paying back money that they owe

**quit·ter** /ˈkwɪtə‖-ər/ *n* [C] *informal* someone who does not have the determination or courage to finish something that is difficult

**quiv·er**[1] /ˈkwɪvə‖-ər/ *v* [I] to tremble slightly, especially because you feel angry, excited, or upset: *Suddenly the child's mouth began to quiver, and he burst into tears.*|[+ **with**] *quivering with rage*

**quiver**[2] *n* [C] **1** a slight trembling: *I felt a quiver of excitement run through me.* **2** a long case for carrying ARROWS

**qui vive** /ˌkiː ˈviːv/ *n* **on the qui vive** taking special care to notice things; watching closely

**quix·ot·ic** /kwɪkˈsɒtɪk‖-ˈsɑː-/ *adj* having ideas that are not practical and plans based on unreasonable hopes of improving the world: *a silly quixotic proposal*

**quiz**[1] /kwɪz/ *n plural* **quizzes** [C] **1** a competition in which you have to answer questions: **sports/news/general knowlege etc quiz** (=a quiz about sports, news etc) *a quiz show on TV* **2** a short test that a teacher gives to a class: *a biology quiz* —see also POP QUIZ

**quiz**[2] *v* **quizzed, quizzing** [T] to ask someone a lot of questions: *They kept quizzing me about my new boyfriend.*

**quiz·mas·ter** /ˈ· ˌ··/ *n* [C] *BrE* a QUESTION-MASTER

**quiz·zi·cal** /ˈkwɪzɪkəl/ *adj* **a quizzical look/smile/expression** a look, smile etc that seems to ask a question, often in an amused way —**quizzically** /-kli/ *adv*

**quod** /kwɒd‖kwɑːd/ *n* **in quod** *BrE old-fashioned* in prison

**quoit** /kwɔɪt, kɔɪt/ *n* **1 quoits** [U] a game in which you throw rings over a small upright post **2** [C] a ring used in the game of quoits

**quon·dam** /ˈkwɒndəm, -dæm‖ˈkwɑːn-/ *adj formal* connected with an earlier time: *my quondam tutor*

**Quon·set hut** /ˈkwɒnset ˌhʌt‖ˈkwɑːn-/ *n* [C] *AmE trademark* a building that is shaped like half a tube and is made of iron sheets

**quo·rate** /ˈkwɔːrɪ̈t/ *adj technical* a meeting that is quorate has a quorum present —opposite INQUORATE

**Quorn** /kwɔːn‖kwɔːrn/ *n* [U] *BrE trademark* a vegetable substance that can be used in cooking instead of meat

**quo·rum** /ˈkwɔːrəm/ *n* [C usually singular] the smallest number of people who must be present at a meeting for official decisions to be made

**quo·ta** /ˈkwəʊtə‖ˈkwoʊ-/ *n* [C] **1** the amount or share of something that you think is normal or that is officially expected: *Salesmen selling over the quota receive a $1000 bonus.* **2** a limit, especially an official limit, on the number or amount of something that is allowed in a particular period: *Most countries have an immigration quota.*|*a strict quota on imports*|*I think I've had my quota of coffee for the day.*

**quo·ta·ble** /ˈkwəʊtəbəl‖ˈkwoʊ-/ *adj* a quotable remark or statement is interesting and noticeable, especially because it is clever or amusing

**quo·ta·tion** /kwəʊˈteɪʃən‖kwoʊ-/ *n* **1** [C] a sentence or phrase, from a book, speech etc which you repeat in a speech or piece of writing because it is interesting, amusing etc: *a quotation from the Bible*|*a dictionary of quotations* **2** [C] a written statement of exactly how much money a piece of work will cost: *Could you give us a quotation for fixing the roof?* —compare ESTIMATE[2] (2) **3** [U] the act of quoting something that someone else has written or said

**quotation mark** /·ˈ·· ·/ *n* [C usually plural] one of a pair of marks (" ") or (' ') that show the beginning and end of reported speech or of a quoted word or phrase; INVERTED COMMA *BrE* —see picture at PUNCTUATION MARK

**quote**[1] /kwəʊt‖kwoʊt/ *v* **1** [I,T] to repeat exactly what someone else has said or written: **quote (sth) from sth** *She quoted from a newspaper article.*|**quote sb as saying sth** *The President himself was quoted as saying he would veto the bill.*|**don't quote me (on this)** (=used to show that what you are saying is not an official statement) *Don't quote me on this, but the company is in deep trouble.*|**quote sb/sth** *To quote an old saying, every dog has his day.* **2** [T] to mention an example of something to support what you are saying **3** [T] to tell a customer the price you will charge them for a service or product: *They quoted us $800 for car repairs.* —compare ESTIMATE[1] **4 quote ... unquote** *spoken* used at the beginning and end of a quoted word or phrase to emphasize that it is exactly correct S2 W3

**quote**[2] *n* [C] *informal* **1** a QUOTATION **2 in quotes** words that are in quotes are between a pair of QUOTATION MARKS S2

**quoth** /kwəʊθ‖kwoʊθ/ *v* [T] *old use* **quoth I/he/she etc** a way of saying 'I said', 'he said' etc

**quo·tid·i·an** /kwəʊˈtɪdiən‖kwoʊ-/ *adj old use* daily; ordinary

**quo·tient** /ˈkwəʊʃənt‖ˈkwoʊ-/ *n* [C] *technical* the number which is obtained when one number is divided by another

**Qu·r'an** /kɔːˈrɑːn, kə-‖kəˈræn, -ˈrɑːn/ *n* **the Qur'an** another spelling of KORAN (=the holy book of Islam)

**q.v.** *Latin* quod vide; used to tell readers to look in another place in the same book for a piece of information

**qwert·y** /ˈkwɜːti‖ˈkwɜːrti/ *adj BrE* a qwerty KEYBOARD on a computer or TYPEWRITER has the keys arranged in the usual way, with Q,W,E,R,T, and Y on the top row

**R¹, r** /ɑː‖ɑːr/ *plural* **R's, r's** the 18th letter of the English alphabet —see also **three** (THREE (2))

**R²** **1** *AmE* the written abbreviation of Republican Party: *Steve Gunderson (R)* **2** the written abbreviation of REX OR REGINA the Latin words for king or queen: *Elizabeth R* **3** the written abbreviation of river, used especially on maps **4** *AmE* used to show that a film may not be watched by children under 17

**rab·bi** /ˈræbaɪ/ *n* [C] a Jewish priest

**rab·bin·i·cal** /rəˈbɪnɪkəl/ *adj* connected with the writings or teaching of rabbis

S 3 **rab·bit¹** /ˈræbɪ̈t/ *n* **1** [C] a common small animal with long ears and soft fur, that lives in a hole in the ground **2** [U] the fur or meat of a rabbit

**rabbit²** *v* **rabbitted, rabbitting 1 rabbit on** [I] *informal, especially BrE* to talk continuously, especially in an uninteresting or annoying way **2 go rabbitting** to hunt or shoot rabbits

**rabbit hutch** /ˈ·· ·/ *n* [C] a wooden CAGE for pet rabbits

**rabbit punch** /ˈ·· ·/ *n* [C] a quick hit on the back of the neck, made with the side of the hand

**rabbit war·ren** /ˈ·· ˌ··/ *n* [C] **1** an area under the ground where wild rabbits live in their holes **2** a building or place with a lot of narrow passages or streets where you can easily get lost

**rab·ble** /ˈræbəl/ *n* [singular] **1** a noisy crowd of people who are likely to cause trouble: *Their army was nothing more than an undisciplined rabble.* **2** used about a group of people that you do not respect: *How can you hang out with that rabble in the bar each night?*

**rabble-rous·er** /ˈ·· ˌ··/ *n* [C] someone who tries to make a crowd of people angry and violent, especially in order to achieve political aims —**rabble-rousing** *adj*: *a rabble-rousing speech* —**rabble-rousing** *n* [U]

**rab·id** /ˈræbɪ̈d/ *adj* **1** having very extreme and unreasonable opinions, especially about politics; FANATICAL: *rabid right-wingers* **2** suffering from rabies: *a rabid dog*

**ra·bies** /ˈreɪbiːz/ *n* [U] a disease that kills animals and people, that you can catch if you are bitten by an infected dog etc

**rac·coon, racoon** /rəˈkuːn, ræ-‖ræ-/ *n* **1** [C] a small North American animal that lives in trees, and has a long tail with black and white rings on it **2** [U] the thick fur of a raccoon

S 2 W 2 **race¹** /reɪs/ *n*
**1 ▶SPORT◀** [C] a competition in which each competitor tries to run, drive etc fastest and finish first: *She came fifth in the race.* | *a swimming race*
**2 ▶PEOPLE◀ a)** [C] one of the main groups that humans can be divided into according to the colour of their skin and other physical features: *people of all races and creeds* **b)** [U] the fact of belonging to one of these groups: *The law forbids discrimination on the grounds of race or religion.* | *a person of mixed race* **c)** [C] a group of people with the same customs, history, language etc: *the Nordic races* —see also HUMAN RACE
**3 ▶GET/DO STH FIRST◀** [C usually singular] a situation in which one group of people tries to obtain or achieve something before another group does: **race to do sth** *the race to develop a nuclear bomb* | [+ **for**] *an international race for power and prestige* | **the race is on** (=people are competing to do something) *The race is on to find a cure for AIDS.*
**4 ▶HORSE RACE◀ the races** an occasion when horse races are held: *a day out at the races* | *Doncaster Races*
**5 a race against time** an attempt to finish doing something very important fast
**6 ▶ANIMAL/PLANT◀** [C] *technical* a type of animal or plant —see also ARMS RACE

> **USAGE NOTE: RACE**
>
> WORD CHOICE: **race, nation, people, state, tribe**
>
> A **race** is a very large group of human beings of the same colour and/or physical type: *different races and nationalities*
>
> A **nation** is a group of people who share the same history and usually a language, and often live in the same area or independent country: *the Indian nations of North America* | *the Scottish nation*
>
> A race or a nation may also be called a **people** [C]. This is sometimes considered to be a more acceptable word than race: *the peoples of Asia* | *the Jewish people*
>
> A **state** is either a politically independent country, or one of the political parts that makes up a country: *the Polish state* | *the state of California* States can often contain people of different races or nations.
>
> A **tribe** is a social group, smaller than a nation, that shares the same customs and usually the same language, and often follows an ancient or traditional way of life: *the tribes living in the Amazon region*

**race²** *v*
**1 ▶SPORT◀ a)** [I,T] to compete against someone or something in a race: [+ **against**] *She'll be racing against some of the world's top athletes.* | **race sb to/back/there** *I'll race you to the end of the road.* **b)** [T] to use an animal or a vehicle to compete in a race: *Prouteau was racing a Ferrari in the Formula One championships.* | *young horses that had never been raced*
**2 ▶MOVE QUICKLY◀** [I always + adv/prep, T always + adv/prep] to move very quickly or make someone or something move very quickly: [+ **out/home/into**] *I had to race back home for my umbrella.* | *I watched as her eyes raced over the page.* | **race sb to/back/there** *The sick woman was raced to the hospital.*
**3 ▶TIME◀ race by/past** if time races by, it passes very quickly: *The seconds went racing past.*
**4 ▶HEART/MIND ETC◀** [I] if your heart, PULSE¹ (1), or mind races, it works harder and faster than usual, especially because you are ill or anxious: *My heart started racing at the sound of approaching footsteps.*
**5 ▶ENGINE◀** [I] if an engine races, it runs too fast

**race car** /ˈ· ·/ *n* [C] *AmE* a RACING CAR

**race·card** /ˈreɪskɑːd‖-kɑːrd/ *n* [C] *BrE* a programme giving the races, times, and horses at a horse racing event

**race·course** /ˈreɪs-kɔːs‖-kɔːrs/ *n* [C] **1** *BrE* a track, usually covered with grass, around which horses race; RACETRACK (2) *AmE* **2** *AmE* a track around which runners, cars etc race

**race·go·er** /ˈreɪsgəʊə‖-goʊər/ *n* [C] someone who goes regularly to horse races

**race·horse** /ˈreɪshɔːs‖-hɔːrs/ *n* [C] a horse specially bred and trained for racing

**race meet·ing** /ˈ· ˌ··/ *n* [C] *BrE* an occasion when horse races are held at a particular place

**race re·la·tions** /ˈ· ·ˌ··/ *n* [plural] the relationship that exists between people from different countries, religions etc who are living in the same place: *The result of the trial could have a damaging effect on race relations in the city.*

**race ri·ot** /ˈ· ˌ··/ *n* [C] violent behaviour, such as fighting and attacks on property, caused by hatred between people of different races

**race·track** /ˈreɪs-træk/ *n* [C] **1** a track around which runners, cars etc race **2** *AmE* a track, usually covered with grass, around which horses race; RACECOURSE (1) *BrE*

**ra·cial** /ˈreɪʃəl/ *adj* **1** [only before noun] connected with the relationships between different races of people: *an appeal for racial and religious tolerance|racial conflict|* **racial discrimination** (=unfair treatment of people because of their race)| **racial prejudice** (=the belief that other races are not as good or as intelligent as your own race)| **racial harassment** (=insulting or annoying someone because of their race) **2** connected with the various races that humans can be divided into: *a broad range of racial and ethnic groups|people of different racial origin* —**racially** *adv*: *Police officers believe the attack was racially motivated.*

**ra·cial·is·m** /ˈreɪʃəlɪzəm/ *n* [U] *BrE old-fashioned* RACISM —**racialist** *n*, *adj*

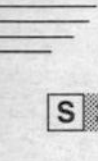

**rac·ing¹** /ˈreɪsɪŋ/ *n* [U] **1** the sport of racing horses: *watching the racing on television|* **racing results/tips/paper etc** *today's racing results* **2 car/bicycle/greyhound etc racing** the sport of racing cars etc

**racing²** *adj* [only before noun] designed or bred for racing: *racing pigeons|a racing yacht*

**racing car** /ˈ·· ·/ *n* [C] *BrE* a car that is specially designed for car races; RACE CAR *AmE*

**ra·cis·m** /ˈreɪsɪzəm/ *n* [U] **1** unfair treatment of people, or violence against them, because they belong to a different race from your own: *the ugly face of racism rearing its head again in Europe* **2** the belief that different races of people have different characters and abilities, and that the qualities of your own race are the best

**rac·ist** /ˈreɪsɪst/ *n* [C] someone who believes that people of their own race are better than others, and who treats people from other races unfairly and sometimes violently: *white racists* —**racist** *adj*: *racist attitudes*

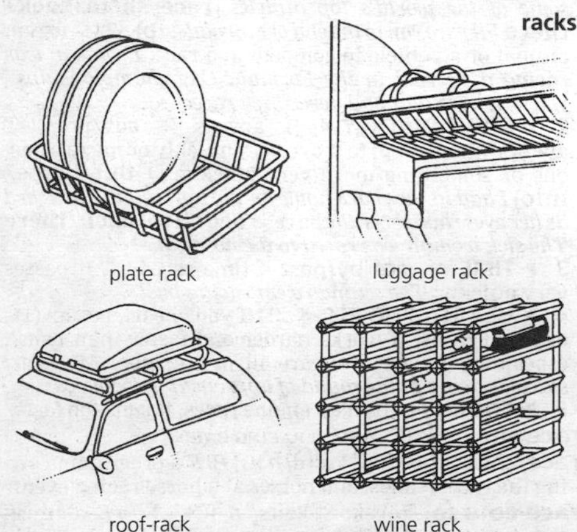


**rack¹** /ræk/ *n* [C] **1** a frame or shelf, usually with bars or hooks, for holding things on: *The dishes are on the plate rack.|a magazine rack* —see also LUGGAGE RACK, ROOF-RACK **2 the rack** a piece of equipment used in the past to make people suffer severe pain by stretching their bodies **3 on the rack** suffering severe pain or anxiety **4 go to rack and ruin** to gradually get into a very bad condition as a result of not being looked after: *The old farmhouse had gone to rack and ruin.* **5** *AmE* a three-sided frame used for arranging the balls at the start of a game of SNOOKER¹ or POOL¹ (3) **6 a rack of lamb/pork** *BrE* a fairly large piece of meat from the side of an animal

**rack²** *v* **1** [T usually passive] to make someone suffer great mental or physical pain: **be racked by/with** *She was racked by feelings of guilt.|He lay on the ground racked with pain.* **2 rack your brain(s)** to think very hard or for a long time: *I really had to rack my brains to remember his name.*

**rack** sth ↔ **up** *phr v* [T] *informal* **1** *AmE* to gradually get points, votes etc, especially in a competition or election: *The team racked up enough points to win the NFL title.* **2** *AmE* to damage or ruin something: *That motorcycle accident really racked up his leg.* **3** to make the value, amount, or level of something go up: *High interest rates have racked up the pound.*

**rack·et¹** /ˈrækɪt/ *n* **1** [singular] *informal* a loud noise: *They're making a hell of a racket downstairs.* —see NOISE¹ (USAGE) **2** [C] *informal* a dishonest way of obtaining money, such as by threatening people or selling them illegal goods: **drugs/gambling/smuggling etc racket** *He runs a numbers racket on the side.* —see also PROTECTION RACKET **3** also **racquet** [C] a BAT¹ (2b) used for hitting the ball in games such as tennis: *a tennis racket* —see pictures at SQUASH and TENNIS **4 rackets** also **racquets** [U] a fast ball game for two or four players, played with rackets and a hard ball on an indoor court

**racket²** *v* [I always + adv/prep] to make a lot of noise as you move around: [+ **around/about etc**] *racketing about upstairs*

**rack·e·teer** /ˌrækɪˈtɪə‖-ˈtɪr/ *n* [C] someone who is involved in a dishonest method of obtaining money

**rack·e·teer·ing** /ˌrækɪˈtɪərɪŋ‖-ˈtɪr-/ *n* [U] obtaining money dishonestly by means of a carefully planned system: *Keating is awaiting trial on fraud and racketeering charges.*

**rack·et·y** /ˈrækɪti/ *adj informal* making a lot of noise: *a rackety old typewriter*

**rac·on·teur** /ˌrækɒnˈtɜː‖-kɑːnˈtɜːr/ *n* [C] someone who is good at telling stories in an interesting and amusing way

**ra·coon** /rəˈkuːn, ræ-‖ræ-/ *n* [C] another spelling of RACCOON

**rac·quet·ball** /ˈrækɪtbɔːl‖-bɔːl/ *n* [U] a game for two or four players, popular in the US, played in an enclosed court and following the rules of HANDBALL (1)

**rac·y** /ˈreɪsi/ *adj* speech or writing that is racy is exciting and entertaining: **racy jokes/humour/stories** (=connected with sex) —**racily** *adv* —**raciness** *n* [U]

**ra·dar** /ˈreɪdɑː‖-ɑːr/ *n* [C,U] a method of finding the position of things such as planes or MISSILES by sending out radio waves: *The missile was identified using radar.|a radar screen*

**radar trap** /ˈ·· ·/ *n* [C] a method or set of equipment that uses radar to catch drivers who are going faster than the legal speed

**rad·dled** /ˈrædld/ *adj* **1** *BrE* looking old or tired **2** *AmE* confused or anxious

**ra·di-** /reɪdi/ *prefix* another form of the prefix RADIO-

**ra·di·al¹** /ˈreɪdiəl/ *adj* arranged in a circular shape with bars, lines etc coming from the centre: *radial street patterns*

**radial²** *n* [C] *informal* a RADIAL TYRE

**radial tyre** *BrE*, **radial tire** *AmE* /ˌ··· ˈ·/ *n* [C] a car tyre with wires inside the rubber that go completely around the wheel to make it stronger and safer

**ra·di·ance** /ˈreɪdiəns/ *n* [U] **1** great happiness, or energy that shows in the way someone looks: *the unmistakeable radiance of youth* **2** a soft light that shines from or onto something

**ra·di·ant** /ˈreɪdiənt/ *adj* **1** full of happiness and love, in a way that shows in your face, eyes etc: *a radiant smile* | [+ **with**] *radiant with joy* **2** [only before noun] very bright: *a radiant blue sky* **3** *technical* [only before noun] radiant heat, energy etc is sent out by radiation —**radiantly** *adv*: *radiantly beautiful*

**ra·di·ate** /ˈreɪdieɪt/ *v* **radiated, radiating 1** [I always + adv/prep, T] if something radiates light or heat, or if light or heat radiates from something, it is sent out in all directions: *The log fire radiated a warm cosy glow.* | [+ **down/from/away etc**] *Warmth radiated down from the tin roof.* **2** [I, T] if someone radiates a feeling or quality, or if it radiates from them, they show it or feel it in a way that is easy to notice: *She radiated energy and self-confidence.* | [+ **from**] *Sexual magnetism radiated from him.* **3** to spread out from a central point: [+ **from/to**] *A system of roads radiates from the town centre.*

**ra·di·a·tion** /ˌreɪdiˈeɪʃən/ *n* [U] **1** a form of energy that comes especially from NUCLEAR reactions, which is very harmful to living things if present in large amounts: *an escape of low-level radiation from the nuclear power plant* | *lethal doses of radiation* **2** energy in the form of heat or light sent out as beams that you cannot see: *electromagnetic radiation* | *sun cream that filters out harmful ultraviolet radiation* **3** the radiating of heat, light etc

**radiation sick·ness** /·ˈ·· ˌ··/ *n* [U] an illness caused by your body receiving too much radiation

**ra·di·a·tor** /ˈreɪdieɪtə‖-ər/ *n* [C] **1** a thing used for heating a room, consisting of a flat hollow metal container fixed to a wall, through which hot water passes **2** the part of a car or aircraft which stops the engine from getting too hot —see picture at ENGINE (1)

W3 **rad·i·cal¹** /ˈrædɪkəl/ *adj* **1** a radical change has a lot of important effects: *radical alterations to the original script* | *a radical reform of the tax system* **2** radical opinions, ideas, leaders etc support thorough and complete social or political change: *the radical views of the left wing of the party* **3** related to the central or most important qualities of something; FUNDAMENTAL: *a radical questioning of basic Communist tenets* | *radical differences between the two groups* **4** *AmE slang* very good or enjoyable: *That was one radical party last night!* —**radically** /-kli/ *adv*

**radical²** *n* [C] someone who wants thorough and complete social and political change —**radicalism** *n* [U]

**rad·i·i** /ˈreɪdiaɪ/ *n* the plural of RADIUS

**ra·di·o-** /reɪdiəʊ‖-dioʊ/ *prefix* also **radi- 1** *technical* **a)** concerning waves of force, eg light, sound, or radio waves: *radiopaque* (=which waves will not pass through) **b)** using radio waves: *a radiotelephone* (=working without wires) | *radiopaging* (=calling people by radio) **2** concerning RADIOACTIVITY: *radiochemistry* (=the study of RADIOACTIVE chemicals)

S1 W2 **ra·di·o¹** /ˈreɪdiəʊ‖-dioʊ/ *n* **1 a)** [C] a piece of electronic equipment which you use to listen to programmes that are broadcast, such as music and news: *turn on the radio* | *listening to the radio in the car* | **on the radio** (=broadcast on a radio) *an interesting program on the radio this morning* **b) the radio** programmes that are broadcast on the radio, considered in general: *I don't really listen to the radio much.* **c)** [U] the sending or receiving of programmes by radio: *Radio was a powerful medium during the war years, keeping up people's morale.* **2** [U] the activity of making and broadcasting programmes which can be heard on a radio: *David Jason worked in radio before TV.* | **local/national radio** (=programmes or companies broadcasting for a local area, or for the whole country) | **radio programme/show/drama etc** *John Peel's late-night radio show* **3 a)** [C] a piece of electronic equipment, for example on a plane or ship, which can send and receive spoken messages **b)** [U] the sending or receiving of these messages: *We've lost radio contact.*

**radio²** *v* [I,T] to send a message using a radio: *The ship radioed for help.* | *Radio London for permission to land.*

**ra·di·o·ac·tive** /ˌreɪdiəʊˈæktɪv◂‖-dioʊ-/ *adj* containing RADIATION (=a form of energy that can harm living things) *a highly radioactive material* | *radioactive contamination*

**radioactive dat·ing** /ˌ····· ˈ··/ *n* [U] *AmE* a scientific method of calculating the age of a very old object by measuring the amount of a certain substance in it; CARBON DATING *BrE*

**radioactive waste** /ˌ····· ˈ·/ *n* [U] harmful radioactive substances that remain after energy has been produced in a NUCLEAR REACTOR

**ra·di·o·ac·tiv·i·ty** /ˌreɪdiəʊækˈtɪvɪti‖-dioʊ-/ *n* [U] **1** a quality that certain substances have which makes them send out RADIATION (=a form of energy that can harm living things) **2** the energy which is produced in this way: *Workers were exposed to high levels of radioactivity.*

**radio bea·con** /ˈ··· ˌ··/ *n* [C] a tower that sends out radio signals to help aircraft stay on the correct course

**ra·di·o·car·bon dat·ing** /ˌreɪdiəʊkɑːbən ˈdeɪtɪŋ‖-dioʊkɑːr-/ *n* [U] *formal* CARBON DATING

**radio-cas·sette play·er** /ˌ··· ·ˈ· ˌ··/ *n* [C] a piece of electronic equipment that contains both a radio and a CASSETTE PLAYER

**radio-con·trolled** /ˌ··· ·ˈ·◂/ *adj* **a radio-controlled aircraft/vehicle/vessel** controlled from far away using radio signals

**ra·di·o·gram** /ˈreɪdiəʊgræm‖-dioʊ-/ *n* [C] **1** *BrE* a piece of furniture, popular in the 1950s, which contained a radio and a record player **2** a message sent by radio

**ra·di·og·ra·pher** /ˌreɪdiˈɒgrəfə‖-ˈɑːgrəfər/ *n* [C] someone whose job is to take X-RAY photographs of the inside of someone's body, or who treats people for illnesses using an X-RAY machine

**ra·di·og·ra·phy** /ˌreɪdiˈɒgrəfi‖-ˈɑːg-/ *n* [U] the taking of X-RAY photographs of the inside of someone's body for medical purposes

**ra·di·ol·o·gist** /ˌreɪdiˈɒlədʒɪst‖-ˈɑː-/ *n* [C] a hospital doctor who is trained in the use of RADIATION to treat people

**ra·di·ol·o·gy** /ˌreɪdiˈɒlədʒi‖-ˈɑː-/ *n* [U] the study and medical use of RADIATION

**radio-tel·e·phone** /ˌ··· ˈ···/ *n* [C] a telephone, used especially in cars, that works by sending and receiving radio signals

**radio tel·e·scope** /ˌ··· ˈ···/ *n* [C] a very large piece of equipment that collects the RADIO WAVES that come from stars and other objects in space

**ra·di·o·ther·a·py** /ˌreɪdiəʊˈθerəpi‖-dioʊ-/ *n* [U] the treatment of illnesses using RADIATION —**radiotherapist** *n* [C]

**radio wave** /ˈ··· ˌ·/ *n* [C usually plural] a form of electric energy that can move through air or space

**rad·ish** /ˈrædɪʃ/ *n* [C] a small vegetable whose red or white root is eaten raw and has a strong SPICY taste —see picture on page 414

**ra·di·um** /ˈreɪdiəm/ *n* [U] a rare metal that is RADIOACTIVE and is used in the treatment of diseases such as CANCER

**ra·di·us** /ˈreɪdiəs/ *n plural* **radii** /-diaɪ/ [C] **1** the distance from the centre to the edge of a circle: *The radius of the throwing circle should be 1.5 metres.* **2 within a 10 mile/200 metre etc radius** within a distance of 10 miles, 200 metres in all directions from a particular place: *All vegetation was destroyed within a 2km radius of the volcano.* **3** a line drawn straight out from the centre of a circle to its edge —see picture at CIRCLE¹ **4** *technical* the outer bone of the lower part of your arm —see picture at SKELETON¹

**ra·don** /ˈreɪdɒn‖-dɑːn/ *n* [U] a RADIOACTIVE gas that can be dangerous in large amounts

**rad·waste** /ˈrædweɪst/ *n* [U] *AmE* RADIOACTIVE WASTE

R

**RAF** /ˌɑːr eɪ ˈef‖ræf/ *n* the Royal Air Force; the British AIRFORCE

**raf·fi·a** /ˈræfiə/ *n* [U] a soft substance like string that comes from the leaves of a PALM tree and is used for making baskets, hats, MATS etc

**raf·fish** /ˈræfɪʃ/ *adj literary* behaving or dressing in a confident and cheerful way that shows no concern for what other people think but is still attractive: *a raffish air about him which some women found appealing* —**raffishly** *adv* —**raffishness** *n* [U]

S3 **raf·fle¹** /ˈræfəl/ *n* [C] a kind of competition or game in which people buy numbered tickets and can win prizes

**raffle²** also **raffle off** *v* [T] to offer something as a prize in a raffle

**raft¹** /rɑːft‖ræft/ *n* [C] **1** a flat floating structure, usually made of pieces of wood tied together, used as a boat **2** a flat floating structure that you can sit on, jump from etc when you are swimming **3 a (whole) raft of** *spoken, especially AmE* a large number of things or large amount of something: *He has a whole raft of camera equipment.* **4** a small flat rubber boat filled with air, used if a boat sinks or a plane crashes into the sea

**raft²** *v* [I, T] to travel by raft or carry things by raft

**raf·ter** /ˈrɑːftə‖ˈræftər/ *n* [C usually plural] one of the large sloping pieces of wood that form the structure of a roof

**rag¹** /ræg/ *n*

**1** ▶ **CLOTH** ◀ [C,U] a small piece of old cloth, for example one used for cleaning things: *Can I use this piece of rag for the car?* | *an oily old rag*

**2 in rags** wearing old torn clothes: *an old beggar dressed in rags*

**3 go from rags to riches** to become very rich after starting your life very poor

**4** ▶ **NEWSPAPER** ◀ [C] *informal* a newspaper that you think is of low quality: *The Evening News is just a provincial rag.*

**5** ▶ **MUSIC** ◀ [C] a piece of RAGTIME music: *Georgia Rag*

**6** ▶ **STUDENTS' EVENT** ◀ [C] *BrE* an event organized by students every year in order to make money for people who are poor, sick etc: *rag week*

**7** ▶ **TRICK** ◀ [C] *BrE old-fashioned* a trick played on someone as a joke: *They did it as a rag.* —see also **glad rags** (GLAD (6)), **like a red rag to a bull** (RED¹ (6)), **lose your rag** (LOSE¹ (6))

**rag²** *v* **ragged, ragging** [T] *BrE old-fashioned* to laugh at someone or play tricks on them

**ra·ga** /ˈrɑːgə/ *n* [C] **1** a piece of Indian music based on an ancient pattern of notes **2** one of the ancient patterns of notes that are used in Indian music

**rag·a·muf·fin** /ˈrægəˌmʌfɪn/ *n* [C] *literary* a dirty young child wearing torn clothes

**rag-and-bone-man** /ˌ· · ˈ· ·/ *n* [C] *BrE* a man who goes around the streets buying and collecting old clothes and other things that people no longer want

**rag·bag** /ˈrægbæg/ *n* **a ragbag of** a confused mixture of things that do not seem to go together or make sense: *a ragbag of ill-thought-out measures to help the homeless*

**rag doll** /ˌ· ˈ·‖ˈ· ·/ *n* [C] a soft DOLL¹ (1) made of cloth

**rage¹** /reɪdʒ/ *n* [C,U] **1** a strong feeling of uncontrollable anger: *His letter had filled her with rage and disappointment.* | **in a rage** *She stormed out of the room in a rage.* | **fly into a rage** (=suddenly become very angry) *Major Sanderson instantly flew into a terrible rage.* | **shaking/trembling/quivering with rage** *Blake sprang to his feet, his face trembling with rage.* **2 be (all) the rage** *informal* to be very popular and fashionable: *Platform shoes were all the rage then.* **3 a rage for** *old-fashioned* a very popular fashion: *There was a great rage for open sports cars at that time.*

**rage²** *v* [I] **1** if something rages, such as a battle, a disagreement, or a storm, it continues with great violence or strong emotions: *Controversy over the scandal is still raging.* | *Outside a great storm was raging.* **2** | [+ at/about/against] to feel very angry about something and show this in the way you behave or speak: *Margo raged against the unfairness of the situation.*

**rag·ga** /ˈrægə/ *n* [U] a form of popular music from the West Indies

**rag·ged** /ˈrægɪd/ *adj*

**1** ▶ **CLOTHES** ◀ also **raggedy** *especially AmE* torn and in bad condition: *A beggar was dozing on a pile of ragged blankets.* | *piles of raggedy old books*

**2** ▶ **PEOPLE** ◀ wearing clothes that are old and torn: *a group of ragged children*

**3** ▶ **UNEVEN** ◀ also **raggedy** not straight or neat, but with rough uneven edges: *a ragged hedge*

**4** ▶ **TIRED** ◀ *informal* tired after using a lot of effort: *The walkers looked pretty ragged by the end of the day.* | **run sb ragged** (=make them do a lot of work)

**5** ▶ **PERFORMANCE** ◀ a ragged performance, shout etc is one that people are not doing together or properly: *He gave a somewhat ragged performance, I thought.* | *a ragged cheer*

**6 be on the ragged edge** *AmE informal* to be feeling very tired or upset —**raggedly** *adv*: *raggedly dressed* —**raggedness** *n* [U]

**rag·ing** /ˈreɪdʒɪŋ/ *adj* **1** [only before noun] raging feelings and emotions are extremely strong: *a raging thirst* | *raging jealousy* **2 a raging headache/toothache etc** a very bad pain in your head etc **3 raging stream/torrent/waters** water that flows fast and violently

**rag·lan** /ˈræglən/ *adj* **1 raglan coat/sweater etc** a coat etc which has arms that are joined in a sideways line from the arm to the neck **2 raglan sleeve** an arm of a coat etc joined in this way

**ra·gout** /ræˈguː, ˈræguː‖ræˈguː/ *n* [C, U] *French* a mixture of vegetables and meat boiled together; STEW¹ (1)

**rag·tag** /ˈrægtæg/ *adj* **1** *informal* looking untidy, poor, and dirty: *a ragtag bunch of kids* **2 ragtag and bobtail** *old-fashioned* a crowd of untidy, poor people

**rag·time** /ˈrægtaɪm/ *n* [U] a type of music and dancing that has a strong beat and was popular in the US in the early part of this century

**rag trade** /ˈ· ·/ *n* **the rag trade** *BrE* the business of making and selling clothes, especially women's clothes

**rag·weed** /ˈrægwiːd/ *n* [U] a North American plant that produces a substance which causes HAY FEVER

**rag·wort** /ˈrægwɜːt‖-wɜːrt/ *n* [U] a common plant with yellow flowers, and leaves with uneven edges

**raid¹** /reɪd/ *n* [C] **1** a short attack on a place by soldiers, planes, or ships, intended to cause damage but not take control: [+ **on**] *a bombing raid on the railway line* | *cross-border raids* | **carry out/launch/make a raid** *Aircraft are carrying out raids on enemy ships.* **2** a sudden visit by the police searching for something illegal: *Following this morning's raid, three people have been charged with possessing illegal drugs.* | **police raid** *a police raid on a club* | **dawn raid** (=carried out very early in the morning) **3** an attack by criminals on a bank or similar place: *a bank raid* | [+ **on**] *raids on post offices in the area* | **carry out a raid** *Armed robbers carried out a raid on the Gateway Bank last night.* **4** *technical* an attempt by a company, to buy enough SHARES in another company to take control of it —see also AIR RAID

**raid²** *v* [T] **1** if police raid a place, they go there suddenly to search for something illegal: *Suspected drug dealers' homes were raided.* **2** to make a sudden armed attack on a place: *Vikings raided settlements on the east coast.* | **a raiding party** (=group taking part in an attack) **3** to take or steal a lot of things from a place: *She raided Jim's cash-box.* | *Animal-rights activists got in and raided the laboratories.* | **raid the larder/refrigerator** *humorous* (=take food from your family's kitchen because you are hungry) —see also RAM-RAIDING —**raider** *n* [C]

**rail¹** /reɪl/ *n* **1** [C] a bar that is fixed along or around something, especially to stop you from falling: *Mrs* S2 W2 

*Kellow held tightly onto the rail as she climbed the stairs.* **2** [C] a bar that you use to hang things on: *a clothes rail* | *a towel rail fixed to the bathroom door* **3** [C] one of the two long metal tracks fixed to the ground that trains move along **4** [U] travelling by train: *I prefer to go by rail.* | *rail travel* **5 go off the rails** *informal* to start behaving in a strange or socially unacceptable way: *At 17 he suddenly went off the rails and started stealing.*

**rail**[2] *v* **1** [T] to enclose or separate an area with rails: [+ **off/in**] *The police railed off the area where the accident happened.* **2** [I] *formal* to complain angrily about something, especially something that you think is very unfair: [+ **against/at**] *railing against injustice*

**rail·ing** /ˈreɪlɪŋ/ *n* [C usually plural] one of the metal bars in a fence that is made of a series of upright bars: *Jimmy somehow got his head stuck in the railings*

**rail·le·ry** /ˈreɪləri/ *n* [U] *formal* friendly joking about someone: *affectionate raillery*

**rail·road**[1] /ˈreɪlrəʊd‖-roʊd/ *n* [C] *AmE* **1** a railway: *The supplies were sent on the railroad.* **2 the railroad** all the work, equipment etc connected with a train system: *He had taken a job as a ticket agent on the railroad.*

**railroad**[2] *v* [T] to force or persuade someone do something without giving them enough time to think about it: **railroad sb into doing sth** *The workers were railroaded into signing the agreement.*

S2 W2 **rail·way** /ˈreɪlweɪ/ *n* [C] *BrE* **1** [C] a method of travelling or moving things around by train; RAILROAD[1] (1) *AmE* **2 the railway/the railways** all the work, equipment etc connected with a train system; the RAILROAD[1] (2) *AmE*: *working on the railways*

**railway line** /ˈ·· ·/ *n* [C] *BrE* **1** one of the two metal tracks fixed to the ground that trains move along **2** a part of the railway system that connects two places: *an old disused railway line*

**railway sta·tion** /ˈ·· ˌ··/ *n* [C] *BrE* the place where trains stop for passengers to get on and off; RAILROAD STATION *AmE*

**rai·ment** /ˈreɪmənt/ *n* [U] *literary* clothes

S2 W2 **rain**[1] /reɪn/ *n* **1** [U] water that falls in small drops from clouds in the sky: *Rain is forecast for tomorrow.* | *We've had 5 inches of rain in two days!* | *We got caught in the rain and I'm soaked through.* | **it looks like rain** *spoken* (=it is probably going to rain) *It looks like rain, so let's go inside.* | **heavy/light rain** (=a large or small amount) *There will be heavy rain in most parts of the country.* | **pour with rain** *BrE* (=to rain very hard) *It was pouring with rain as we set off.* —see picture on page 836 **2 the rains** a period in the year when there is a lot of rain in tropical countries; MONSOON: *The rains have started early this year.* **3 be (as) right as rain** *spoken* to be healthy, especially after you have been ill or had a bad experience **4 (come) rain or shine** *spoken* whatever happens or whatever the weather is like: *Don't worry. We'll be there – rain or shine.* **5 under a rain of arrows/blows etc** being hit by many arrows etc at the same time —see also ACID RAIN —**rainless** *adj*

**rain**[2] *v* **1** [I] if it rains, drops of water fall from clouds in the sky: *Oh no! It's raining again!* | *It was raining hard.* **2 be rained off** *BrE*/**be rained out** *AmE* if an event or activity is rained off or rained out, it has to stop because there is too much rain: *We were supposed to go to a double header but it was rained out.* **3 it never rains but it pours** *spoken* used to say that as soon as one thing goes wrong, a lot of other things go wrong as well **4 it's raining cats and dogs** *spoken* it is raining very hard

**rain down** *phr v* [I,T] if something rains down, or is rained down, it falls in large quantities: *Tears rained down her cheeks.* | *The falling chimney rained down dust and stones.*

**rain·bow** /ˈreɪnbəʊ‖-boʊ/ *n* [C] a large curve of different colours that can appear in the sky when there is both sun and rain

**rain check** /ˈ· ·/ *n* **1 take a rain check (on)** *informal, especially AmE* used to say that you will do something in the future but not now: *"Care for a drink?" "I'll take a rain check – I figure you'd like to be alone."* **2** [C] *AmE* a ticket for an outdoor event, such as a sports game, that you can use again if it rains and the action stops

**rain·coat** /ˈ· ·/ *n* [C] a coat that you wear when it is raining —see picture at COAT[1]

**rain drop** /ˈ· ·/ *n* [C] a single drop of rain

**rain·fall** /ˈreɪnfɔːl‖-fɒːl/ *n* [C,U] the amount of rain that falls on an area in a particular period of time: *an area with very low rainfall*

**rain for·est** /ˈ· ˌ··/ *n* [C] a tropical forest with tall trees that are very close together, growing in an area where it rains a lot: *environmental groups campaigning against the destruction of the rain forest*

**rain gauge** /ˈ· ·/ *n* [C] an instrument that is used for measuring the amount of rain

**rain·proof** /ˈreɪnpruːf/ *adj* able to keep rain out: *a rain-proof jacket*

**rain·storm** /ˈreɪnstɔːm‖-ɔːrm/ *n* [C] a sudden heavy fall of rain

**rain·wa·ter** /ˈreɪnwɔːtə‖-wɒːtər, -wɑː-/ *n* [U] water that has fallen as rain

**rain·y** /ˈreɪni/ *adj* **1 rainy day/afternoon/weather etc** a day etc when it rains a lot **2 save it for a rainy day** to save something, especially money, for a time when you will need it

**raise**[1] /reɪz/ *v* [T] S2 W1

**1 ▶MOVE◀ a)** to move or lift something to a higher position, place, or level: *Can you raise your arm above your head?* | *They're thinking of raising the ceiling in the kitchen.* | *The teacher raised his finger to his lips for silence.* **b)** to move or lift something into an upright position: *The bridge can be raised in the middle to allow ships through.* **c)** to move your eyes or face so that you are looking upwards: *She raised her eyes from the newspaper when he came in.* **d)** also **raise up** to lift the upper part of your body from a lying position: *She raised herself up on her arms and looked around sleepily.*

**2 ▶INCREASE◀** to increase an amount, number, or level: *We have no plans to raise taxes at present.* | *The reaction is started by raising the temperature to 140°C.*

**3 ▶IMPROVE◀** to improve the quality or standard of something: *Better training will raise the efficiency of the workforce.*

**4 ▶CHILDREN◀** *especially AmE* to look after your children and help them grow; BRING UP *BrE*: *Many women return to work after raising their families.* | **raise sb (as) a Catholic/Muslim etc** *His parents raised him as a Protestant.* | **born and raised** *She was born and raised a country girl.* | **be raised on** *These kids are raised on a diet of junk food.*

**5 ▶FARMING◀** to grow plants or keep cows, pigs etc so that they can be used as food: *raise wheat/pigs*

**6 raise hopes/consciousness/awareness etc** to make people more hopeful etc: *The peace talks have raised hopes for the hostages' release.* | *The conference is intended to raise people's awareness of AIDS.*

**7 ▶EMOTION/REACTION◀ a)** to cause a particular emotion or reaction: *His long absence is beginning to raise fears for his safety.* | *His jokes barely raised a laugh.* **b)** to try to show a particular feeling or emotion although you do not really feel it: *She felt so sad, she couldn't even raise a smile.*

**8 raise a question/objection/point etc** to begin to talk or write about a question etc that you want to be considered: *A number of objections were raised at the meeting.* | *This raises important issues about security.*

**9 ▶COLLECT MONEY/PEOPLE◀ a)** to collect money, support etc so that you can use it to help people: *We are raising money to pay for a new hospital ward.* **b)** *old-fashioned* to collect together a group of people, especially soldiers: *The king raised a vast army.*

**10 a) raise your eyebrows (at)** to show surprise, doubt, disapproval etc by moving your EYEBROWS upwards: *Chuck raised his eyebrows at her, not knowing*

*what to say.* **b) raise eyebrows** if something raises eyebrows it surprises people: *The story raised a few eyebrows in the media world.*
**11 ▶VOICE◀ raise your voice** to speak loudly or shout because you are angry: *Don't raise your voice to me, young man!* | **raised voices** *We could hear raised voices coming from the bar.*
**12 raise your glasses** *spoken* used to tell a group of people to celebrate something by holding up their glasses and drinking from them: *Ladies and gentlemen, will you raise your glasses to the bride and groom.*
**13 raise the spectre of sth** *literary* to make you aware of something frightening: *The continuing violence has raised the spectre of civil war.*
**14 ▶DEAD PERSON◀** *Biblical* to make someone who has died live again: *Jesus raised Lazarus from the grave.*
**15 ▶WAKE SB◀** *literary* to wake someone who is difficult to wake: *Try as he might he could not raise her.*
**16 raise the alarm** to warn people about danger: *A passerby raised the alarm before the fire got out of control.*
**17 raise a siege/embargo** *formal* to allow goods to go in and out of a place again after they have been stopped by force or by a law
**18 ▶CARD GAME◀** to make a higher BID than an opponent in a card game: *I'll raise you $100.*
**19 ▶SPEAK TO SB◀** to speak to someone on a piece of radio equipment: *They finally managed to raise him at Miller's sheep farm.*

**20 ▶BUILD◀** *formal* to build something such as a MONUMENT
**21 raise hell/Cain a)** *informal* to behave in an angry and threatening way: *I'll raise hell with whoever is responsible for this mess.* **b)** *especially AmE* to behave in a wild, noisy way that upsets other people: *The kids next door were raising hell last night.*
**22 raise the roof** to make a very loud noise when singing, celebrating etc
**23 raise your hand** *especially AmE* to put your arm in the air to show that you want something: *Raise your hand if you know the answer.*
**24 raise 2/4/10 etc to the power of 2/3/4 etc** *technical* to multiply a number by itself a particular number of times: *2 raised to the power of 3 (=$2^3$) is 8.*

**USAGE NOTE: RAISE**

WORD CHOICE: **raise, lift, increase, rise, bring up, rear, grow, improve**

People or other forces **raise** things to a higher position, though in informal language **lift** is usually used: *The crane raised/lifted the whole house.* In a court of law you may hear: *Raise the book in your right hand.*

People, governments etc **raise** or **increase** the price, cost, or amount of something: *The government is raising the tax on cigarettes again.* | *Heavy traffic is raising/increasing the level of pollution in the town.*

When things or prices move upwards on their own, they **rise**: *The balloon rose slowly from the ground.* | *the problem of rising inflation* | *Industrial production looks set to rise in the new year.*

You can also **raise** children, meaning you look after them as they grow up. This sense is more common in American English than in British English, where **bring up** is the more usual expression.

In both British and American English it is common either to **raise** or **bring up** a point, question etc in a discussion.

Again, especially in American English you may **raise** cattle or wheat on a farm. More generally, and in British English, you **rear** cattle and **grow** wheat, flowers, or vegetables.

When you are talking about making something better, people often use either **raise** or **improve**: *I'm working hard to raise/improve my TOEFL score.* | *Women still need to raise/improve their position in society* (NOT *raise up*).

When something gets better on its own you can use **rise** or **improve**: *Standards are rising/improving.*

The noun **raise** means a pay increase and is American English. In British English you say: *He got a (pay) rise.*

Otherwise the noun is always **rise**: *a rise in house prices/standards* | *the rise of the Roman Empire*

GRAMMAR

The past tense of **rise** is **rose**, the perfect tense is **have risen** (NOT *raised*).

**raise²** *n* [C] *AmE* an increase in the money you earn; RISE² (2) *BrE*

**rai·sin** /ˈreɪzən/ *n* [C] a dried GRAPE (=the fruit that wine is made from)

**rai·son d'êt·re** /ˌreɪzɒn ˈdetrə‖-zoʊn-/ *n* [C] *French* the reason something exists, why someone does something etc: *Commerce was the main raison d'être of the town.*

**Raj** /rɑːdʒ/ *n* [singular] **the (British) Raj** the rule of the British government in India before India became independent in 1947

**ra·jah**, **raja** /ˈrɑːdʒə/ *n* [C] the king or ruler of an Indian state —see also RANEE

**rake¹** /reɪk/ *n* **1** [C] a gardening tool with a row of metal teeth at the end of a long handle, used for making soil level, gathering up dead leaves etc **2** [C] *old-fashioned* a man who behaves in an unacceptable way, having many sexual relationships, drinking too much alcohol etc **3** [C] a tool used by a CROUPIER for gathering in the money at a table where games are played for money **4** [singular] the angle of a slope: *the rake of the stage*

**rake²** *v* **1** [I,T] to move a rake across a surface in order to make the soil level, gather dead leaves etc: [+ **over/up**] *She raked over the soil to loosen the weeds.* **2** [I always + adv/prep] to search a place very carefully for something: [+ **through/around/about**] *I've been raking through my drawers looking for those tickets.* **3** [T] to point something such as a gun, camera, or strong light, so that it covers a wide area, by slowly moving it from one side to another: *The searchlight raked the open ground around the prison.* **4 rake a fire/ashes/coals** to push a stick backwards and forwards in a fire in order to remove ashes **5 rake your fingers/nails** to pull your fingers or nails through something or across a surface: *Ken raked his fingers through his hair.*

**rake** sth ↔ **in** *phr v* [T] *informal* to earn a lot of money without trying very hard: *Lou's been raking in the dollars since he opened his business.* | **rake it in** *If someone opened a burger bar, they'd really rake it in.*

**rake** sth ↔ **up** *phr v* [T] *informal* **1** also **rake together** to collect things or people together for a purpose, but with difficulty: *Karen has had real problems raking up enough players for the volleyball game.* | *Between them they could only rake together $300.* **2** to talk about something from the past that people would prefer you not to mention: *Don't rake up that old quarrel again!*

**rake-off** /ˈ· ·/ *n* [C] *informal* a dishonest share of profits: *The taxi driver gets a rake-off from the hotel.*

**rak·ish** /ˈreɪkɪʃ/ *adj* **1 at a rakish angle** if you wear a hat at a rakish angle, you do not wear it straight, and this makes you look relaxed and confident **2** *old-fashioned* a rakish man behaves in an unacceptable way, having many sexual relationships, wasting money, drinking too much alcohol etc —**rakishly** *adv* —**rakishness** *n* [U]

**ral·ly¹** /ˈræli/ *v* **rallied, rallying 1** [I,T] to come together or bring people together to support an idea, a political party etc: *Margaret Thatcher's speech had the effect of rallying the party faithful.* | [+ **to**] *Fellow Republicans rallied to the President's defense.* | **rallying point** (=an idea, event etc that makes people come together to support something they believe in) *The demonstration was a rallying point for students fighting for lower rents.* | **rallying cry** (=a word or phrase used to unite people in support of an idea) **2** [I] to become stronger again after a period of weakness or defeat: *Towards the end of the race, Cram rallied and won in style.* | *Stock prices rallied this afternoon after earlier falls.*

**rally round** *phr v* [I,T] *informal* if a group of people rally round, they all try to help you in a difficult situation: *Her friends all rallied round when she was ill.*

**rally²** *n* [C] **1** a large public meeting, especially one that is held outdoors to support a political idea, protest etc: *a big anti-abortion rally* **2** a car race on public roads: *the Monte Carlo Rally* **3** a series of hits of the ball between players in games like tennis

**RAM** /ræm/ *n* [C,U] Random Access Memory; the memory in a computer system that is used as a temporary store for information, usually the software that organizes the DATA

**ram¹** /ræm/ *v* **rammed, ramming** [T] **1** to run or drive into something very hard: *I was waiting at the traffic lights when a car rammed me from behind.* **2** [always + adv/prep] to push something into a position using great force: **ram sth into/down** *First, you'll have to ram the posts into the ground.* **3 ram sth down sb's throat** to try to make someone accept an idea or opinion by continually repeating it, especially when they are not interested

**ram** sth ↔ **home** *phr v* [T] to make sure someone fully understands something by emphasizing it and by providing a lot of examples, proof etc: *He rammed his points home with graphic pictures of neglect.*

**ram²** *n* [C] **1** an adult male sheep —compare EWE **2** a BATTERING RAM **3** *technical* a machine that hits something again and again to force it into a position

**Ram·a·dan** /ˈræmədæn, -dɑːn, ˌræməˈdɑːn, -ˈdæn/ *n* [U] the ninth month of the Muslim year, during which Muslims are not allowed to eat or drink during the day while it is light

**ram·ble¹** /ˈræmbəl/ *v* [I] **1** [always + adv/prep] to go on a walk for pleasure: **[+ through/along etc]** *We rambled through the woods.* **2** to talk in a very confused way so that other people find it hard to understand you: *The fever was getting worse and he was starting to ramble.* **3** a plant that rambles grows in all directions

**ramble on** *phr v* [I] to talk or write for a long time in a way that other people find boring: *He rambled on about his trip to Paris.*

**ramble²** *n* [C] a long walk for pleasure: *We went on a ramble in the Peak District.*

**ram·bler** /ˈræmblə‖-ər/ *n* [C] **1** *BrE* someone who goes on rambles **2** a rose bush that rambles

**ram·bling** /ˈræmblɪŋ/ *adj* **1** a building that is rambling has an irregular shape and covers a large area: *a large rambling house on the hillside* **2** speech or writing that is rambling is very long and does not seem to have any clear organization or purpose: *a long and rambling letter*

**ram·bunc·tious** /ræmˈbʌŋkʃəs/ *adj AmE humorous* RUMBUSTIOUS: *a weekend with three rambunctious kids* —**rambunctiously** *adv* —**rambunctiousness** *n* [U]

**ram·e·kin** /ˈræmɪ̈kɪ̈n, ˈræmkɪ̈n/ *n* [C] a small dish in which food for one person can be baked and served

**ram·ie** /ˈræmi/ *n* [C,U] a plant from which cloth is made

**ram·i·fi·ca·tion** /ˌræmɪ̈fɪ̈ˈkeɪʃən/ *n* [C usually plural] *formal* **1** an additional result of something you do, which may not have been clear when you first decided to do it: *The environmental ramifications of the road-building program had not been considered.* **2** a part of a system or structure that has many parts

**ram·i·fy** /ˈræmɪ̈faɪ/ *v* [I] *rare* to spread outwards and to form a system or network

**ramp** /ræmp/ *n* [C] **1** *AmE* a road for driving onto or off a large main road; SLIP ROAD *BrE*: *Take the Lake Drive ramp at Charles Street.* **2** a slope that has been built to connect two places that are at different levels: *Ramps are needed at exits and entrances for wheelchair users.* **3** *BrE* a change in the level between two parts of a road where repairs are being done **4** a raised part on some roads, designed to make traffic drive more slowly; HUMP

**ram·page¹** /ræmˈpeɪdʒ, ˈræmpeɪdʒ/ *v* [I] to rush about in groups wildly or violently: **[+ about/through]** *football fans rampaging through the streets*

**rampage²** *n* **on the rampage** rushing about in a wild and violent way, often causing damage: *gangs of youths on the rampage*

**ram·pant** /ˈræmpənt/ *adj* **1** something bad that is rampant, such as crime or disease, is widespread and difficult to control: *The country faces famine and rampant disease.* | *rampant inflation* **2** a plant that is rampant grows and spreads uncontrollably: *rampant garden weeds* **3** *technical* an animal drawn in HERALDRY that is rampant is standing on its two back legs —**rampantly** *adv*

**ram·part** /ˈræmpɑːt‖-ɑːrt/ *n* [C usually plural] a wide pile of earth or a stone wall built to protect a castle or city in the past

**ram-raid·ing** /ˈ· ··/ *n* [U] *BrE informal* the crime of driving a car into a shop window in order to steal goods from the shop —**ram-raider** *n* [C]

**ram·rod** /ˈræmrɒd‖-rɑːd/ *n* [C] **1 stiff/straight as a ramrod** sitting or standing with your back straight and your body stiff **2** a stick for pushing GUNPOWDER into an old-fashioned gun, or for cleaning a small gun

**ram·shack·le** /ˈræmʃækəl/ *adj* a ramshackle building or vehicle is in bad condition and in need of repair: *a ramshackle old farmhouse*

**ran** /ræn/ the past tense of RUN

**ranch** /rɑːntʃ‖ræntʃ/ *n* [C] **1** a very large farm in the western US and Canada where sheep, cattle, or horses are bred **2** *AmE* a farm that produces a particular product: *a fruit ranch* **3** a RANCH HOUSE

**ranch·er** /ˈrɑːntʃə‖ˈræntʃər/ *n* [C] someone who owns or works on a ranch: *a cattle rancher*

**ranch house** /ˈ· ·/ *n* [C] *AmE* **1** a house built on one level, usually with a roof that does not slope much —see picture on page 170 **2** a house on a ranch in which the rancher lives

**ranch·ing** /ˈrɑːntʃɪŋ‖ˈræn-/ *n* [U] work on a ranch

**ran·cid** /ˈrænsɪ̈d/ *adj* oily or fatty food that is rancid smells or tastes unpleasant because it is no longer fresh: *rancid butter* —**rancidity** /rænˈsɪdɪ̈ti/ *n* [U]

**ran·cour** *BrE*, **rancor** *AmE* /ˈræŋkə‖-ər/ *n* [U] *formal* a feeling of hatred, especially when you cannot forgive someone: *He spoke openly about the war without a trace of rancour.* —**rancorous** *adj* —**rancorously** *adv*

**rand** /rænd/ *n plural* **rand** [C] the standard unit of money in South Africa

**R and B** /ˌɑːr ən ˈbiː/ *n* [U] rhythm and blues; a style of popular music that is a mixture of BLUES and JAZZ

**R and D** /ˌɑːr ən ˈdiː/ *n* [U] research and development; the part of a business concerned with studying new ideas and planning new products

**ran·dom** /ˈrændəm/ *adj* **1** happening or chosen without any definite plan, aim, or pattern: *a random sample* | *random drug testing of athletes* | *A few random shots were fired.* **2 at random** in a random way: *The killer appears to have selected his victims at random.* —**randomly** *adv*: *7 randomly chosen numbers* —**randomness** *n* [U]

**random ac·cess mem·o·ry** /ˌ·· ˈ·· ˌ···/ *n* [C,U] RAM

**R and R** /ˌɑːr ənd ˈɑː‖-ˈɑːr/ *n* [U] *AmE* rest and relaxation; a holiday given to people in the army, navy, etc after a long period of hard work or during a war

**rand·y** /ˈrændi/ *adj BrE informal* full of sexual desire: *She was feeling very randy.* —**randiness** *n* [U]

**ra·nee, rani** /ˈrɑːni, rɑːˈniː/ *n* [C] the queen or princess of an Indian state —see also RAJAH

**rang** /ræŋ/ the past tense of RING

**range¹** /reɪndʒ/ *n* S1 W1

**1** ▶ **GROUP** ◀ [singular] a number of things which are all different but of the same general type: **[+ of]** *an interesting range of books and videos* | *The drug is effective*

*against a range of bacteria.* | *We teach the full range of ballroom dances.* | **wide/broad/whole range of** *We have students from a wide range of backgrounds.*
**2 ▸ LIMITS/AMOUNTS ◂** [singular] the limits within which amounts, quantities, ages etc can vary: **age/price etc range** *toys suitable for children in the pre-school age range* | **in the range (of)** *I would expect a salary in the range of $25,000 to $30,000.* | **beyond/out of sb's range** (=more than someone's limit on price, age etc) *The price of the house is well beyond our range.*
**3 ▸ POWER/RESPONSIBILITY ETC ◂** [singular] the area of power, responsiblity, or activities that a person or organization has; SCOPE: **the range of** *The range of his power was immense.* | **within/outside the range of** *These issues fall outside the range of the enquiry.*
**4 ▸ PRODUCTS ◂** [C] a set of similar products made by a particular company or available in a particular shop: *The coconut shampoo is the best in the range.* | [+ **of**] *a new range of kitchenware* | **top of the range** (=best) *a new top of the range racing bike*
**5 ▸ DISTANCE ◂ a)** [singular, U] the distance within which something can be seen or heard: [+ **of**] *The transmitter has a range of 10,000 miles.* | **within range** (=near enough to reach, hear etc) *By now the ship was within range of enemy radar.* | **out of range** (=too far away to reach, hear etc) *He was relieved that the others were out of range of his mother's penetrating voice.* | **at close range** (=very near) *You can see the animals at very close range.* **b)** [singular, U] the distance over which a particular weapon can hit things: *the gun's range* | [+ **of**] *missiles with a range of 500 miles* | **within range** (=near enough to hit) | **out of range** (=too far away to hit) *I ducked down to get out of range of the gunshots.* | **at close/short/point-blank range** (=from very close) *Both men had been shot at point-blank range.* | **long/short range missile** *The destroyer was equipped with short range missiles.* **c)** [C] the distance which a vehicle such as an aircraft can travel before it needs more petrol etc: [+ **of**] *The VR126 has a range of 2000 miles.*
**6 ▸ MUSIC ◂** [C usually singular] all the musical notes that a particular singer or musical instrument can make: *As the child grew older, his vocal range changed.*
**7 ▸ MOUNTAINS ◂** [C] a group of mountains or hills, usually in a line: *a village in the foothills of the Karakoram range*
**8 ▸ WEAPONS TESTING ◂** [C] an area of land where you can test weapons or practise using them: *a rifle range* | *a missile testing range*
**9 ▸ GRASS LAND ◂** [C,U] *AmE* a large area of grass land used by cattle
**10 ▸ COOKING ◂** [C] *especially AmE* **a)** a COOKER **b)** *BrE* a place in a kitchen where there is a fire for cooking, used in the past —see also FREE-RANGE

W3 **range²** *v*
**1 ▸ INCLUDE ◂ a)** [I always + adv/prep] if prices, levels, temperatures etc range from one amount to another, they include both those amounts and anything in between: **range from sth to sth** *There were 120 students whose ages ranged from 10 to 18.* | **range between sth and sth** *The population of these cities ranges between 3 and 5 million inhabitants.* | **range in age/size etc** (=include many different ages, sizes etc) *The shoes range in price from $25 to $100.* **b)** [I always + adv/prep] to include a range of different feelings, actions etc: **range from sth to sth** *Their reactions ranged from anger to humiliation.* | *US intervention has taken many forms, ranging from supplying medicines to full-scale air strikes.*
**2 ▸ INCLUDE MANY SUBJECTS ◂** [I] to deal with a wide range of subjects or ideas in a book, speech, conversation etc: **range (widely) over** *His lectures ranged widely over a variety of topics.* —see also WIDE-RANGING
**3 range yourself with/against** to publicly state your agreement with, or opposition to, a particular group's beliefs and ideas: *Police rounded up any individuals who had ranged themselves against the authorities.*
**4 ▸ ARRANGE ◂** [T always + adv/prep] to put things in a particular order or position: **range sth on/along/against etc** *Cups and plates neatly ranged on her shelves.*
**5 ▸ MOVE AROUND ◂** [I always + adv/prep] to move around in an area of land; wander: [+ **over/through**] *Cattle ranged over the pastures in search of food.*

**range·find·er** /ˈreɪndʒˌfaɪndə‖-ər/ *n* [C] an instrument for finding the distance of an object when firing a weapon or taking photographs

**rang·er** /ˈreɪndʒə‖-ər/ *n* [C] **1** someone whose job is to look after a forest or area of countryside: *a wildlife ranger* **2** a police officer in North America in past times, who rode through country areas **3** a COMMANDO (=a specially trained soldier) **4** a girl who belongs to a part of the Guide Association in Britain, for girls between the ages of 14 and 19 —compare GUIDE¹ (4)

**ra·ni** /ˈrɑːni, rɑːˈniː/ *n* a RANEE

**rank¹** /ræŋk/ *n* W3
**1 ▸ POSITION IN ARMY/ORGANIZATION ◂** [C,U] the position or level that someone holds in an organization, especially in the police or armed forces: *promotion to the rank of General* | **high/senior/low/junior rank** *Bates is very young to hold such a senior rank.*
**2 the ranks a)** all the members of the armed forces who are not officers: **be reduced to the ranks** (=be punished by no longer being an officer) | **rise from the ranks** (=become an officer after being an ordinary soldier) **b)** the people who belong to an organization or to a group: *The pay freeze led to a lot of discontent in the ranks.* | *The Christian Democrats now face opposition from within their own ranks.* | **join the ranks of** (=become a member of a group) *She was forced to join the ranks of the self-employed.*
**3 close ranks** if the people in a group close ranks, they join together to support each other against other people: *At the first hint of trouble their family closes ranks.*
**4 break ranks a)** to stop supporting a group that you are a member of **b)** if soldiers break ranks, they do not stay in line: *the police broke ranks and used their batons indiscriminately*
**5 pull rank (on)** *informal* to use your authority over someone to make them do what you want, especially unfairly: *You may just have to pull rank and tell them they have to do it.*
**6 ▸ LINE ◂** [C] **a)** a line of people or things: **rank after rank/rank upon rank** *On the shelves were rank after rank of liquor bottles.* **b)** a line of soldiers, police officers etc, standing side by side
**7 of the first rank** of the highest quality: *Emily Dickinson is a poet of the first rank.*
**8 ▸ SOCIAL CLASS ◂** [C, U] someone's position in society: *people of all ranks in society*
**9 ▸ TAXI ◂** [C] a place where taxis wait in a line to be hired; TAXI RANK

**rank²** *v* **1 a)** [I always + adv/prep, not in progressive] to have a particular position in a list of people or things that are put in order of quality or importance: [+ **among/as/with**] *This recession ranks as one of the worst in recent times.* **b)** [T often passive] to decide the position of someone or something on a list based on quality or importance: **be ranked fourth/number one etc** *Agassi was at that time ranked sixth in the world.* | **rank sb/sth in order** *Rank them in order of ability.* **2** [T] *AmE* to have a higher rank than someone else; OUTRANK: *A general ranks a captain.* **3** [T often passive] to arrange things in a regular order: *There were several pairs of riding boots ranked neatly in the hall.*

**rank³** *adj* **1** having a very strong and unpleasant smell or taste: *rank tobacco* **2** [only before noun] complete; total: *a rank beginner at the job* | *rank disobedience* | **rank outsider** (=person or animal that is not expected to win) *The Olympic champion was beaten by a rank outsider.* **3** a plant that is rank is too thick and has spread everywhere —**rankly** *adv* —**rankness** *n* [U]

**rank and file** /ˌ· · ˈ·◂/ *n* **the rank and file** the ordinary members of an organization rather than the leaders: *The* *rank and file of the party had lost confidence in the leadership.*

**rank·ing¹** /ˈræŋkɪŋ/ *n* [C] a position on a scale that shows how good someone or something is when compared with others: *In the last two years, she has moved steadily up the world rankings.*

**ranking²** *adj* [only before noun] a ranking person has a high position in an organization or is one of the best at an activity: *a ranking member of the department*

**ranking of·fi·cer** /ˈ·· ˌ···/ *n* [singular] the officer in a group who has the highest rank

**ran·kle** /ˈræŋkəl/ *v* [I] if something rankles, you still remember it angrily because it upset you or annoyed you a lot: *a bitter dispute that still rankled months afterwards*

**ran·sack** /ˈrænsæk/ *v* [T] **1** to search a place very thoroughly: *She's ransacking the desk drawers for old family photos.* **2** to go through a place stealing things and causing damage: *Houses were wrecked and ransacked by wandering gangs of soldiers.*

**ran·som¹** /ˈrænsəm/ *n* [C] **1** an amount of money paid to free someone who is held as a prisoner: *The kidnappers were demanding a ransom of $25,000.* **2 hold sb to ransom a)** to put someone in a situation where they are forced to agree to your demands: *The management will not allow the strikers to hold them to ransom.* **b)** to keep someone prisoner until money is paid

**ransom²** *v* [T] to set someone free by paying a ransom

**rant** /rænt/ *v* [I] to talk or complain in a loud, excited, and rather confused way because you feel strongly about something: *ranting on about the way his boss treats him* | **rant and rave** (=rant continuously) *I see the tabloids are all ranting and raving about Fergie's skiing trip.*

**rap¹** /ræp/ **rapped, rapping** *v*
**1 ▶ HIT ◀** [I,T] to hit or knock something quickly and lightly: *She rapped the table with her pen and called for silence.* | [+ **at/on**] *rapping loudly on the door*
**2 ▶ SAY ◀** also **rap out** [T] to say something loudly, suddenly, and in a way that sounds angry: *Captain Blake rapped out an order.*
**3 ▶ CRITICIZE ◀** [T] a word meaning to criticize someone angrily used in newspapers: *a film rapped by critics for its excessive violence*
**4 ▶ MUSIC ◀** [I] to say the words of a RAP² (2)
**5 ▶ CONVERSATION ◀** [I] *old-fashioned* to talk in an informal way to friends; CHAT
**6 rap sb over the knuckles** to criticize someone, often officially, for something they have done wrong: *schools rapped over the knuckles for their failure to improve examination results*

**rap²** *n*
**1 ▶ KNOCK ◀** [C] a quick light hit or knock: *We heard a sharp rap on the door.*
**2 ▶ MUSIC ◀** [C, U] a type of popular music in which the words of a song are not sung, but spoken in time to music with a steady beat
**3 ▶ CRIME ◀** *AmE informal* **a)** a statement by the state that someone is responsible for a serious crime; CHARGE¹ (4): **murder rap/drunk driving rap** *He's in police custody facing a murder rap.* **b)** time spent in prison as punishment for a crime: **beat the rap** (=escape punishment)
**4 take the rap (for sth)** to be blamed or punished for a mistake or crime, especially unfairly: *It didn't worry him that someone else would have to take the rap for his greed.*
**5 ▶ CRITICISM ◀ a rap on/over the knuckles** *informal* strong criticism for something you have done wrong: *The New York Post received an official rap over the knuckles for the way it reported the story.*
**6 ▶ NOT FAIR ◀ a bum rap** *AmE slang* unfair treatment or punishment

**ra·pa·cious** /rəˈpeɪʃəs/ *adj formal* taking everything that you can, especially by using violence: *a rapacious band of robbers* —**rapaciously** *adv* —**rapaciousness** *n* [U] —**rapacity** /rəˈpæsɪ̈ti/ *n* [U]

**rape¹** /reɪp/ *v* [T] to force someone to have sex, especially by using violence: *Burgess will be in court today, accused of raping a fifteen-year old girl.*

**rape²** *n* **1** [C,U] the crime of forcing someone to have sex, especially by using violence: *He was charged with the attempted rape of a female colleague.* | *a rape victim* —see also DATE RAPE, RAPIST **2** [singular] sudden unnecessary destruction, especially of the environment: *The timber companies are carrying out a systematic rape of our forests.* **3** [U] a European plant with yellow flowers, grown as animal food and for its oil

**rap·id** /ˈræpɪ̈d/ *adj* done or happening very quickly and in a very short time: *The patient made a rapid recovery.* | *a period of rapid population growth* —**rapidly** *adv*: *the rapidly changing world of computer technology* —**rapidity** /rəˈpɪdɪ̈ti/ *n* [U] | *Their debts mounted with alarming rapidity.* W3

**rapid-fire** /ˈ·· ·/ *adj* **1** rapid-fire questions, jokes etc are said quickly one after another **2** a rapid-fire gun can fire shots quickly one after another

**rap·ids** /ˈræpɪ̈dz/ *n* [plural] part of a river where the water looks white because it is moving very fast over rocks; WHITEWATER *AmE*

**rapid tran·sit sys·tem** /ˌ·· ˈ·· ˌ··/ also **rapid transit** *n* [C] *AmE* a system for moving people quickly around a city using trains; SUBWAY

**ra·pi·er** /ˈreɪpiə‖-ər/ *n* [C] a long thin sword with two sharp edges —see picture at SWORD

**rap·ine** /ˈræpaɪn‖ˈræpɪ̈n/ *n* [U] *literary* the taking away of property by force; PLUNDER² (2)

**rap·ist** /ˈreɪpɪ̈st/ *n* [C] a man who has forced someone to have sex, especially by using violence

**rap·pel** /ræˈpel/ *v* [I] *AmE* to ABSEIL —**rappel** *n* [C]

**rap·per** /ˈræpə‖-ər/ *n* [C] someone who speaks the words of a RAP² (2) (=type of popular music) *world-famous rapper, Ice T*

**rap·port** /ræˈpɔː‖-ɔːr/ *n* [singular, U] friendly agreement and understanding between people: [+ **between/with**] *She's established a good rapport with her new colleagues.*

**rap·proche·ment** /ræˈprɒʃmɒŋ, ræˈprəʊʃ-‖ˌræprouʃˈmɑːŋ/ *n* [singular, U] *formal* the establishment of a good relationship between two countries or groups of people, after a period of unfriendly relations: *the signs of a rapprochement between the two countries*

**rap·scal·lion** /ræpˈskæljən/ *n* [C] *old use* someone who behaves badly, but whom you still like

**rap sheet** /ˈ· ·/ *n* [C] *AmE informal* a list kept by the police of someone's criminal activities

**rapt** /ræpt/ *adj* **1** *AustrE informal* very pleased and happy **2** *literary* so interested in something that you do not notice anything else: *looks of rapt attention*

**rap·ture** /ˈræptʃə‖-ər/ *n* [U] **1** great excitement and happiness: *He stared with rapture at his baby son.* **2 go into raptures** to express great pleasure and happiness about something: [+ **over/about/at**] *She went into raptures about the climate, the food, the spring flowers.*

**rap·tu·rous** /ˈræptʃərəs/ *adj formal* expressing great happiness or admiration: *the audience leapt to their feet in rapturous applause* | *A rapturous reception awaited the winning team.* —**rapturously** *adv*

**rare** /reə‖rer/ *adj* **1** not seen or found very often, or not happening very often: *This species of plant is becoming increasingly rare.* | *We only went to the cinema on very rare occasions.* | **it is rare to do sth** *It is rare to find such an interesting group of people.* | **it is rare for sb/sth to do sth** *It's very rare for her to miss a day at school.* **2** meat that is rare has only been cooked for a short time and is still red: *I like my steak rare.* **3** [only before noun] *BrE old-fashioned* unusually good or extreme: *We had a rare old time at the party.* **4** air that is rare has less oxygen than usual because it is in a high place —see also RARELY, RARITY —**rareness** *n* [U]

> **USAGE NOTE: RARE**
>
> WORD CHOICE: **rare, uncommon, scarce, infrequent, unusual, rarely, scarcely**
>
> Things that do not exist in large numbers or amounts, are **uncommon**: *an uncommon name/ species of birds.* **Rare** things are uncommon, and often valuable: *a rare hand-crafted book cover|He collects rare coins.*
>
> Things that you need and are difficult to find or get, though they may at other times be available, are **scarce**: *Food is scarce in the refugee camps.|Parking spaces are scarce on Saturdays.*
>
> Events that do not happen often are **infrequent** or **rare**: *Opportunities for promotion are rare/ infrequent in this company.|the infrequent letters from her son|the rare sight of a deer grazing*
>
> It is unusual and rather formal to say: *It is not rare to...* People usually say **uncommon** or **unusual** or try to avoid using two negatives completely. For example, this sentence is perfectly acceptable: *It's not unusual to see tears at a wedding.* But you could say instead: *You often see tears at a wedding.*
>
> **Rarely** means 'not often' but **scarcely** means 'hardly', or only 'just': *I rarely visit Houston* (NOT *scarcely*, though you could say *'scarcely ever'*).|*The train leaves in an hour —we've scarcely got time to pack.*

R

**rare earth** /ˌ· ˈ·/ *n* [C] one of a group of rare metal substances

**rar·e·fied** /ˈreərɪ̈faɪd‖ˈrer-/ *adj* **1** *often humorous* rarefied ideas, opinions etc can only be understood by, or only involve, one small group of people: *the rarefied atmosphere of international diplomacy* **2** rarefied air is the air in high places, which has less oxygen than usual

W2 **rare·ly** /ˈreəli‖ˈrerli/ *adv* not often: *She very rarely complains.|This method is rarely used in modern laboratories.* —see RARE (USAGE) —see picture at FREQUENCY

**rar·ing** /ˈreərɪŋ‖ˈrer-/ *adj* **1 raring to go** very eager to start an activity: *They woke up early and were raring to go.* **2 raring to do sth** very eager to do something: *The children were raring to get out into the snow.*

**rar·i·ty** /ˈreərɪ̈ti‖ˈrer-/ *n* **1 be a rarity** to not happen or exist very often: *The village was so remote that visitors were a rarity.* **2** [C] something that is valuable or interesting because it is rare: *He had picked up all kinds of rarities on his travels.* **3** [U] the quality of being rare: *Such stamps are expensive because of their rarity.*

**ras·cal** /ˈrɑːskəl‖ˈræs-/ *n* [C] **1** *humorous* a child who behaves badly but whom you still like: *You little rascal! Where have you hidden my shoes?* **2** *old-fashioned* a dishonest man —**rascally** *adj old use*: *a rascally trick*

**rash¹** /ræʃ/ *adj* doing something too quickly, without thinking carefully about whether it is sensible or not: *Don't go making any rash decisions about your future!|It was rather rash of you to lend them your car.* —**rashly** *adv*: *I rashly agreed to look after the children.* —**rashness** *n* [U] *Strangely, it was his rashness which attracted me.*

**rash²** *n* [C] **1** a lot of red spots on someone's skin, caused by an illness: *She had a nasty rash on her arms.*| **come/break out in a rash** *My mother comes out in a rash if she eats seafood.*|**heat rash/nettle rash/ nappy rash etc** (=a rash caused by heat etc) *The baby's got nappy rash again.* **2 a rash of** *informal* a large number of unpleasant events, changes etc within a short time: *a sudden rash of unofficial strikes*

**rash·er** /ˈræʃə‖-er/ *n* [C] *BrE* a thin piece of BACON or HAM¹ (1): *a rasher of streaky bacon* —see picture on page 416

**rasp¹** /rɑːsp‖ræsp/ *v* **1** [I,T] to make a rough unpleasant sound, like that of two surfaces rubbing together: *metal rasping against stone|They could hear Peter's rasping breath as he fell to the ground.* **2** [T] to rub a surface with something rough —**raspingly** *adv*

**rasp²** *n* **1** [singular] an unpleasant noise, like the sound of two rough surfaces rubbing together: *With a rasp of steel, they drew their swords.|the rasp of a saw* **2** [C] a metal tool with a rough surface, like a FILE¹ (5), used for shaping wood or metal

**rasp·ber·ry** /ˈrɑːzbəri‖ˈræzberi/ *n* [C] **1** a soft sweet red berry, or the bush that this berry grows on: *raspberry jam* —see picture on page 413 **2** *informal* a rude sound made by putting your tongue out and blowing: **blow a raspberry** *BrE*/**give a raspberry** *AmE* (=to make this sound)

**Ras·ta** /ˈræstə/ *n* [C] *informal* a Rastafarian

**Ras·ta·fa·ri·an** /ˌræstəˈfeəriən◂‖-ˈfer-/ *n* [C] someone who believes in a religion that is popular in Jamaica, which has Haile Selassie as its religious leader, and has the belief that black West Indians will return to Africa —**Rastafarian** *adj* —**Rastafarianism** *n* [U]

**Ras·ta·man** /ˈræstəmæn/ *n* [C] *informal* a male Rastafarian

**rat¹** /ræt/ *n* [C] **1** an animal that looks like a large mouse with a long tail: *rat poison* **2** *spoken* someone who has been disloyal to you or deceived you: *But you promised to help us, you rat!* **3 look like a drowned rat** to look very wet and uncomfortable **4 like rats deserting the sinking ship** used to describe people who leave a company, organization etc when it is in trouble —see also RAT RACE, RATS, RAT TRAP, **smell a rat** (SMELL¹ (7))

**rat²** *v* **ratted, ratting** [I] *informal* to be disloyal to someone, especially by telling someone in authority about something wrong that person has done: [+ **on**] *They'll kill you if they find out you've ratted on them!*

**rat-arsed** /ræt-ɑːrst/ *adj BrE slang* extremely drunk

**rat-a-tat** /ˌræt ə ˈtæt/ also **rat-a-tat-tat** /ˌ· · · ˈ·/ *n* [singular] the sound of knocking, especially on a door

**rat·bag** /ˈrætbæg/ *n* [C] *BrE, AustrE informal* an unpleasant person

**ratch·et** /ˈrætʃɪ̈t/ *n* [U] a machine part consisting of a wheel or bar with teeth on it, which allows movement in only one direction

ratchet

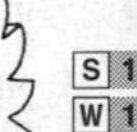

S1 W1 **rate¹** /reɪt/ *n* [C]

**1 ▶ SPEED ◀** the speed at which something happens over a period of time: *Our money was running out at an alarming rate.|Children learn at different rates.*|[+ **of**] *the rate of economic growth*

**2 ▶ AMOUNT ◀** the number of times something happens or the number of examples of something within a certain period: **birth/unemployment/divorce/ crime rate** *The divorce rate rose from 20,000 in 1961 to 150,000 in 1985.*|**high/low rate of** *high rates of unemployment*|**success/failure rate** (=the number of times that something succeeds or fails) *Penicillin has a high success rate in bacterial infections.*

**3 ▶ MONEY ◀** a charge or payment fixed according to a standard scale: *The sports centre has reduced rates for students.|Nurses are demanding higher rates of pay.*| **hourly/weekly rate** (=the amount paid per hour/ week) *What's the hourly rate for cleaning?*|**the going rate** (=the usual amount paid for work) *I'm told $20 an hour is the going rate for private tuition.*

**4 at this rate** *spoken* used to say what will happen if things continue to happen in the same way as now: *At this rate we won't even be able to afford a holiday.*

**5 at any rate** *spoken* used when you are stating one definite fact in a situation that is uncertain or unsatisfactory: *Well, at any rate, we won't starve!|They've had technical problems – at any rate that's what they told me.*

**6 first-rate/second-rate/third-rate** of good, bad, or very bad quality: *a cheap third-rate motel*
**7 at a rate of knots** *BrE informal* very quickly: *Jack's getting through the ironing at a rate of knots!*
**8 rates** [plural] a local tax, paid before 1990 by owners of buildings in Britain —see also BASE RATE, EXCHANGE RATE, INTEREST RATE

**rate²** *v*
**1 ▶JUDGE THE QUALITY◀ a)** [T] to think that someone or something has a particular quality, value, or standard: **be rated (as) sth** *Lewis is currently rated the world's No. 1 athlete.* | *She is generally rated as one of the best modern poets.* | **rate sb/sth highly** (=think they are very good or important) *The company seems to rate him very highly.* **b)** [I] to be considered as having a particular quality, value, or standard: [+ **as**] *Becker rates as one of the finest players of his generation.*
**2 ▶THINK SB/STH IS GOOD◀** [T] *BrE informal* to think that someone or something is very good: *I know they're your favourite team, but I just don't rate them.*
**3 ▶DESERVE◀** [T] *informal, especially AmE* to deserve: *They rate a big thank-you for all their hard work.* | **rate a mention** (=be important enough to be in the news) *a local incident that didn't rate a mention in the national press*
**4 ▶FILMS◀ be rated G/U/PG/X** if a film is rated G, U etc it is officially judged to be suitable or unsuitable for children —see also X-RATED
**5 ▶ANGRY◀** [I,T] *old use* to speak angrily to someone; BERATE

**rate·a·ble val·ue, ratable value** /ˌreɪtəbəl ˈvæljuː/ *n* [C] a value given to buildings in Britain before 1990 in order to calculate how much local tax the owner should be charged

**rate of ex·change** /ˌ· · ·ˈ·/ *n* [C] the EXCHANGE RATE

**rate of re·turn** /ˌ· · ·ˈ·/ *n* [singular] a company's profit for a year, expressed as a PERCENTAGE of the money that the company has spent during the year

**rate·pay·er** /ˈreɪtpeɪə‖-ər/ *n* [C] *BrE* someone who pays taxes that are used to provide local services

**rat fink** /ˈ· ·/ *n* [C] *AmE informal* someone who you trusted who has given information to the police or done something else wrong

S1 W1 **ra·ther** /ˈrɑːðə‖ˈræðər/ *predeterminer, adv* **1** [+ adj/adv] quite; fairly: *I was rather surprised to see him with his ex-wife.* | *He was limping rather badly as he walked off the field.* | *It's not too big for you at all. I rather like the way it fits you.* | **rather a big hat/a tall man etc** *Simon's always been rather a difficult person to get along with.* | **rather too big/too tall etc** *They spoke rather too quietly to be heard at the back of the hall.* **2 would rather** if you would rather do or have something, you would prefer to do it or have it: *I suppose I could lend it to them but I'd rather not.* | *To be honest, I'd rather have a quiet night in front of the TV.* | **would rather do sth than do sth** *I'd rather die than ask him for his autograph.* | **would rather sb did sth** *We'd rather you didn't smoke in our home.* **3 rather than a)** more than or to a greater degree than someone or something else: *The parents should be blamed rather than the children.* | *I think you'd call it a lecture rather than a talk.* **b)** instead of someone or something else: *Rather than squeezing your own oranges, have you tried buying packs of orange juice?* **4 or rather** used to correct something that you have said, or give more specific information: *You have to be sixteen for cheap tickets – or rather under sixteen.* **5 not...but rather...** used to say that someone does not do something but does something else instead: *The committee does not deal with individual correspondence, but rather discusses issues in its newsletter.* **6 Rather!** *spoken BrE old-fashioned* used to agree with someone

**USAGE NOTE: RATHER**

WORD CHOICE: **fairly, quite, pretty, rather, kind of**

You use **fairly** or **quite** to describe something that is neither good nor bad: *The weather was fairly cold* (=more than a little cold, but not extremely cold). | *The movie was quite good* (=more than a little good).

**Rather** is fairly formal, and is especially used in British English. It often suggests that something is bad or unsuitable: *It's rather cold* (=colder than I would like). | *I was driving rather fast* (=a little too fast).

British English speakers often use **rather** about things they like very much: *Yes I painted it myself - I'm rather pleased with it.*

**Pretty** is the most usual way of saying 'fairly' or 'very' in American English, and is used in British English as well. It is more common in spoken English than in writing: *Charlie's Restaurant is pretty good, especially if you want somewhere cheap.* | *You'd better wear a coat — it's pretty cold out.*

GRAMMAR

Note that you say: *a rather/fairly/pretty long road* but *quite a long road.*

Of these four words, only **rather** can be used with comparative forms: *I'd prefer a rather shorter hairstyle.*

**Rather** is not used before *than* when you are comparing people or things: *Books are more interesting than TV* (NOT *Books are interesting rather than TV*). But it is used when you are using adjectives to compare: *TV is relaxing rather than interesting.*

**Rather** can only be used to mean **prefer** in the phrase **I/he would rather** followed by the base form of a verb or a clause: *They'd rather walk* (NOT *they rather to walk/walking/a walk*). | *I'd rather not answer that question.*

**rat·i·fy** /ˈrætɪ̈faɪ/ *v* [T] to make a written agreement official by signing it: *The government delayed ratifying the treaty.* —**ratification** /ˌrætɪ̈fɪ̈ˈkeɪʃən/ *n* [U] | *an attempt to delay ratification of the treaty*

**rat·ing** /ˈreɪtɪŋ/ *n* **1** [C] a level on a scale that shows how good, important, popular etc someone or something is: *The President's popularity rating is low according to recent opinion polls.* **2 the ratings** a list that shows which films, television programmes etc are the most popular: *The new comedy series shot up to the top of the ratings in the first week.* **3** [singular] a letter that shows whether or not a film is suitable for children: *The Godfather had an X-rating when it was first shown in 1972.* **4** [C] a SAILOR in the British navy who is not an officer **5** [C] the class in which a ship or machine is placed, according to its size —see also CREDIT RATING

**ra·ti·o** /ˈreɪʃiəʊ‖ˈreɪʃoʊ/ *n* [C] *plural* **ratios** a relationship between two amounts that is represented by a pair of numbers showing how much greater one amount is than the other: **the ratio of sth to sth** *The ratio of nursing staff to doctors is 2:1.* —compare PROPORTION¹ S3 W3

**ra·tion¹** /ˈræʃən‖ˈræ-, ˈreɪ-/ *n* **1** [C] a fixed amount of something such as food or petrol that you are allowed to have, when there is not much available: *the weekly meat ration* **2 rations** [plural] the food that is given to a soldier or member of a group each day: *The expedition had sufficient rations to last them another five days.* **3 have had your ration of** to have had as much of something as you would expect or consider to be fair: *We've had more than our ration of bad luck this year.*

**ration²** *v* [T] **1** to control the supply of something such as food or petrol by allowing people to have only a fixed amount of it: *Petrol was rationed during the war.* **2** to

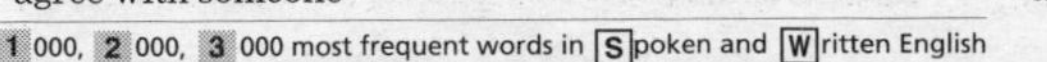

allow someone to have only a small amount of something because there is not enough: **ration sb to sth** *We were rationed to two eggs a week.* —**rationing** *n* [U]

**ration** sth ↔ **out** *phr v* [T] to give out supplies of something in small amounts: *They rationed out the remaining water as fairly as they could.*

**ra·tion·al** /ˈræʃənəl/ *adj* **1** based on clear, practical or scientific reasons: *It can't have just disappeared! There must be a perfectly rational explanation.* **2** sensible and able to make decisions based on intelligent thinking rather than on emotion: *rational behaviour | We should be able to sort this out like rational human beings!* —**rationally** *adv*: *Scientific training makes you think rationally.* —**rationality** /ˌræʃəˈnælɪ̈ti/ *n* [U] —opposite IRRATIONAL

**ra·tio·nale** /ˌræʃəˈnɑːl‖-ˈnæl/ *n* [C,U] *formal* the reasons and principles on which a decision, plan, belief etc is based: *The rationale behind introducing this technique is that it will substantially speed up our work.*

**ra·tion·al·ist** /ˈræʃənəlɪ̈st/ *n* [C] someone who bases their opinions and actions on intelligent thinking, rather than on emotion or religious belief —**rationalism** *n* [U] —**rationalist, rationalistic** /ˌræʃənəˈlɪstɪk◂/ *adj*

**ra·tion·al·ize** also **-ise** *BrE* /ˈræʃənəlaɪz/ *v* [I,T] **1** to find or invent a reasonable explanation for your behaviour or attitudes: *Tony was still trying to rationalize his decision to leave his wife and children.* **2** *especially BrE* to make a business system more effective by getting rid of unnecessary staff, equipment etc —**rationalization** /ˌræʃənəlaɪˈzeɪʃən‖-lə-/ *n* [C,U] *Rationalization is a word management use when they are sacking people.*

**rat race** /ˈ· ·/ *n* [U] **the rat race** the unpleasant situation in business, politics etc in which people are continuously competing against each other for success: *Paul went off to a Greek island to escape from the rat race.*

**rats** /ræts/ *interjection* used as an expression of annoyance: *Oh rats! I've left my purse at home.*

**rat·tan** /rəˈtæn/ *n* [U] the plant from which WICKER furniture is made

**rat-tat** /ˌræt ˈtæt/ *n* [singular] RAT-A-TAT

**rat·ted** *v* **get ratted** *BrE slang* to get extremely drunk

**rat·tle**[1] /ˈrætl/ *v* **1** [I,T] to shake, or make something shake, with quick repeated knocking noises: *The windows rattled in the wind. | The beggar was rattling coins in an old mug.* **2** [I] to move quickly, making a rattling noise: **[+ along/past/over etc]** *The cart rattled along the stony road.* **3** [T] *informal* to make someone lose confidence or become nervous: *Keep calm – don't let yourself get rattled. | It was an old trick of his – rattling people by getting their names wrong.* **4 rattle sb's cage** *spoken humorous* to make someone feel angry or annoyed: *Who rattled your cage?* —see also SABRE-RATTLING

**rattle around** *phr v* [I] *informal* to be in a house, office etc that is bigger then you need it to be: *We rattle around a bit now that the children have all left.*

**rattle** sth ↔ **off** *phr v* [T] to say something quickly and easily, from memory: *He rattled off the poem.*

**rattle on** *phr v* [I] *informal* to talk quickly for a long time, about things that are not interesting: *Nancy would rattle on for hours about her grandchildren.*

**rattle through** sth *phr v* [T] *informal* to do something very quickly because you want to finish it as soon as possible: *She rattled through her speech in five minutes.*

**rattle**[2] *n* **1** [singular] the noise that you hear when the parts of something knock against each other: **[+ of]** *the rattle of chains* **2** [C] a baby's toy that makes this noise **3** [C] a wooden instrument that makes a loud knocking noise, used by people watching football games —see also DEATH RATTLE

**rat·tler** /ˈrætlə‖-ər/ *n* [C] *informal* a rattlesnake

**rattle·snake** /ˈrætlsneɪk/ *n* [C] a poisonous American snake that makes a noise like a rattle with its tail

**rat·tling** /ˈrætlɪŋ/ *adj, adv old-fashioned* **a rattling good yarn/story** a very good or interesting story: *He tells a rattling good story.*

**rat trap** /ˈ· ·/ *n* [C] *AmE informal* a dirty old building that is in very bad condition

**rat·ty** /ˈræti/ *adj* **1** *BrE informal* bad-tempered; IRRITABLE **2** *AmE informal* in bad condition; SHABBY: *a ratty old sofa* **3** like a rat

**rau·cous** /ˈrɔːkəs‖ˈrɒː-/ *adj* a raucous voice is unpleasantly loud: *raucous shouts from the street* —**raucously** *adv*: *They laughed raucously.* —**raucousness** *n* [U]

**raunch·y** /ˈrɔːntʃi‖ˈrɒː-/ *adj informal* sexually exciting or intended to make you think about sex: *a raunchy dance* —**raunchily** *adv* —**raunchiness** *n* [U]

**rav·age** /ˈrævɪdʒ/ *v* [T often passive] to destroy, ruin, or damage something very badly; DEVASTATE (1): **be ravaged by sth** *The population was ravaged by cholera.*

**rav·ag·es** /ˈrævɪdʒɪ̈z/ *n* **the ravages of war/time/disease etc** the damage or destruction caused by something such as war, disease, storms etc: *The ravages of drink were clear in the dark rings under his eyes.*

**rave**[1] /reɪv/ *v* [I] **1** to talk in an angry, uncontrolled way: **[+ at]** *Dad raved at me for hours about how irresponsible I'd been.* **2** to talk in a crazy way that is impossible to understand, especially because you are very ill **3 rave about/over** to talk in a very excited way about something, saying how much you admire or enjoy it: *After the game people raved about Tommy Craig's performance.* —see also **rant and rave** (RANT), RAVING

**rave**[2] *adj* **rave reviews/notices** newspaper articles that praise something a lot, for example a play or film: *His last film got rave reviews in the British press.*

**rave**[3] *n* [C] **1** a very large party held in an empty building in Britain, at which young people dance and sometimes take illegal drugs: **rave scene/band/culture etc** (=a scene etc that is connected with raves) **2** *especially AmE* a piece of writing in a newspaper, magazine etc that praises a film, play, or performance very much —see also RAVE-UP

**rav·el** /ˈrævəl/ *v* **ravelled, ravelling** *BrE*, **raveled, raveling** *AmE* [I] **1** if something made from wool or cloth ravels, the threads in it become separated from one another **2** if threads ravel, they become knotted and twisted —compare UNRAVEL

**ra·ven**[1] /ˈreɪvən/ *n* [C] a large shiny black bird with a large black beak

**raven**[2] *adj* [only before noun] raven hair is black and shiny

**raven-haired** /ˌ·· ˈ·◂/ *adj literary* having shiny black hair

**rav·e·ning** /ˈrævənɪŋ/ *adj literary* ravening animals are extremely hungry: *a ravening beast*

**rav·e·nous** /ˈrævənəs/ *adj* extremely hungry: *Have a sandwich – you must be ravenous!* —**ravenously** *adv*

**rav·er** /ˈreɪvə‖-ər/ *n* [C] *BrE informal* someone who goes to a lot of parties and has many sexual partners

**rave-up** /ˈ· ·/ *n* [C] *BrE informal* a noisy party where people drink and dance a lot

**ra·vine** /rəˈviːn/ *n* [C] a deep narrow valley with steep sides: *21 killed as bus swerves into ravine*

**rav·ing** /ˈreɪvɪŋ/ *adj informal* **1** talking or behaving in a crazy way: *a raving lunatic* | **raving mad** *informal especially BrE* (=completely crazy) **2 raving beauty/success** someone who is very beautiful or something that is very successful

**rav·ings** /ˈreɪvɪŋz/ *n* [plural] things someone says that are crazy and have no meaning: *Sometimes in his ravings he talks about a super-intelligent pig.*

**rav·i·o·li** /ˌræviˈəʊli‖-ˈoʊli/ *n* [U] small squares of PASTA filled with meat —see picture at PASTA

**rav·ish** /ˈrævɪʃ/ *v* [T] *literary* **1** to RAPE a woman **2 be ravished** to feel great pleasure when you look at or listen to something: *I was ravished by her beauty.*

**rav·ish·ing** /ˈrævɪʃɪŋ/ *adj* very beautiful: *ravishing good looks* —**ravishingly** *adv*: *a ravishingly pretty young woman*

W3 **raw¹** /rɔː‖rɒː/ *adj*
**1** ▶ **FOOD** ◀ not cooked: *raw meat|raw carrot*
**2** ▶ **INFORMATION** ◀ **raw data/statistics etc** information that has not been arranged, checked, or prepared for use
**3** ▶ **SKIN** ◀ a part of your body that is raw is red and sore: *My hands were raw with cold.*
**4** ▶ **MATERIALS** ◀ raw cotton, sugar, wool etc are in their natural state and have not yet been prepared for use —see also RAW MATERIALS
**5** ▶ **NOT EXPERIENCED** ◀ not experienced or not yet fully trained: *Most of our soldiers were raw recruits.*
**6 touch/hit a raw nerve** to upset someone by something you say: *In mentioning his departure I knew I had touched a raw nerve.*
**7 get a raw deal** to be unfairly treated: *Women tend to get a raw deal when it comes to pay.*
**8** ▶ **WEATHER** ◀ very cold and wet: *A raw wind chilled him to the bone.*
**9** ▶ **EMOTIONS/QUALITIES** ◀ raw emotions or qualities are strong and natural, but not completely developed or controlled: *Katie was surprised by her own raw courage and endurance.|the singer's raw, husky voice*
**10** ▶ **LANGUAGE** ◀ *AmE informal* containing a lot of sexual details
**11** ▶ **DESCRIPTIONS** ◀ giving the unpleasant facts, without trying to make them seem more acceptable: *a raw account of poverty in the cities* —**rawness** *n* [U]

**raw²** *n* **1 life/nature in the raw** the way humans or animals live in their natural state including all the violence and cruelty: *Her films portray nature in the raw.* **2 in the raw** *AmE informal* not wearing any clothes: *She sunbathes in the raw.* **3 catch/touch sb on the raw** *BrE* to say or do something that upsets someone

**raw·hide** /ˈrɔːhaɪd‖ˈrɒː-/ *n* [U] natural leather that has not been specially treated

**raw ma·te·ri·als** /ˌ· ˈ····/ *n* [plural] materials such as coal, oil etc, in their natural state, before being treated in order to make things

**ray** /reɪ/ *n* [C] **1** [often plural] a narrow beam of light from the sun or from something such as a lamp: *the sun's rays|*[+ **of**] *Rays of light filtered through the pine trees.* **2** *technical* a beam of heat, electricity, or other form of ENERGY (2): *a gun that fires invisible rays* —see also COSMIC RAY, GAMMA RAY, X-RAY **3 ray of hope/light/comfort etc** something that provides a small amount of hope or happiness in a difficult situation: *If only I could see some ray of hope for the future.* **4 ray of sunshine** *informal* an expression meaning someone or something that makes a situation seem better: *Little Annie was an unexpected ray of sunshine in her life.* **5** a large flat sea fish with a long pointed tail

**ray gun** /ˈ· ·/ *n* [C] an imaginary gun in SCIENCE FICTION stories that fires rays which kill people

**ray·on** /ˈreɪɒn‖-ɑːn/ *n* [U] a smooth material used for making clothes

**raze** /reɪz/ *v* [T] to completely destroy a town or building: **raze sth to the ground** (=destroy it so that nothing is left) *houses that had been razed to the ground in the war*

**ra·zor** /ˈreɪzə‖-ər/ *n* [C] **1** a sharp instrument used for removing hair, especially from a man's face: *an electric razor* **2 be on a razor edge** to be in a dangerous position where a mistake could be very dangerous: *Politically we are on a razor edge. Whatever judgment we make could have dire consequences.*

**razors**

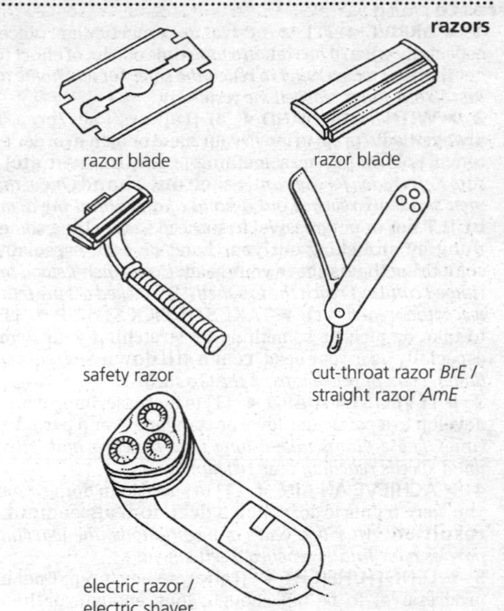


**razor blade** /ˈ·· ·/ *n* [C] a small flat blade with a very sharp cutting edge used in a SAFETY RAZOR —see picture at RAZOR

**ra·zor-sharp** /ˌ·· ˈ·◂/ *adj* **1** very sharp: *a razor-sharp hunting knife* **2** very intelligent: *his razor-sharp wit*

**razz** /ræz/ *v* [T] *AmE spoken* to make a joke about someone that is insulting or makes them feel embarrassed; TEASE¹ (1): *The kids were razzing Tom about Jenny.*

**raz·zle** /ˈræzəl/ *n* **go on the razzle** *BrE slang* to go somewhere such as to a party to enjoy yourself

**razzle-daz·zle** /ˌ·· ˈ··/ *n* [U] *informal* **1** a lot of activity that is intended to be impressive and excite people **2** *AmE informal* a complicated series of actions intended to confuse your opponent, especially in American football

**razz·ma·tazz** /ˌræzməˈtæz/ also **raz·za·ma·tazz** /ˌræzəməˈtæz/ *n* [U] *informal* busy or noisy activity that is intended to attract people's attention: *all the razzmatazz surrounding presidential elections*

**RC** /ˌɑː ˈsiː‖ˌɑːr-/ the abbreviation of Roman Catholic

**Rd** the written abbreviation of Road, used in addresses

**-rd** /d‖rd/ *suffix* forms written ORDINAL numbers with 3: *the 3rd* (=third) *of June|his 53rd birthday*

**RDA** /ˌɑː diː ˈeɪ‖ˌɑːr-/ *n* [singular] Recommended Daily Allowance; the amount of substances such as VITAMINS or MINERALS that you should have each day

**'re** /ə‖ər/ the short form of 'are': *We're ready to go but they're not.*

**RE** /ˌɑːr ˈiː/ *n* [U] Religious Education; a school subject in Britain

**re-** /riː/ *prefix* **1** again: *They're rebroadcasting the play.* **2** again in a new and better way: *You'd better re-write that letter.* **3** back to a former state: *After years of separation they were finally reunited.*

**re¹** /riː/ *prep* used especially in business letters to introduce the subject that you are going to write 'about': *re your enquiry of the 19th October*

**re²** /reɪ/ *n* [singular] the second note in a musical SCALE¹ (8) according to the SOL-FA system

**reach¹** /riːtʃ/ *v*

**1** ▶ **ARRIVE** ◀ [T] to arrive at a particular place, especially when it has taken a long time or a lot of effort to get there: *It was a relief to reach the safety of our home at last.* | *Your letter reached me yesterday.*

**2** ▶ **WITH YOUR HAND** ◀ **a)** [I always + adv/prep, T always + adv/prep] to move your hand or arm in order to touch, hold, or pick up something: [+ **for/in/over etc**] *I saw Kelly reach for the gun.* | **reach out a hand** *One of the men suddenly reached out a hand and grabbed my arm.* **b)** [I,T not in progressive] to succeed in touching something by stretching out your hand or arm, especially something that is above your head: *Even when I stood on tiptoe I couldn't reach the top shelf.* | *We picked all the fruit we could reach.* **c)** ▶ **TAKE STH/PICK STH UP** ◀ [T] to take or pick up something by stretching your arm, especially over your head: **reach sth down** *She reached down a can of peaches from the top shelf.*

**3** ▶ **LEVEL/STANDARD** ◀ [T] to increase, improve, or develop to a particular level or standard over a period of time: *These plants take a long time to reach maturity.* | *wind speeds reaching over 100 mph*

**4** ▶ **ACHIEVE AN AIM** ◀ [T] to succeed in doing what you were trying to do: **reach a decision/agreement/result etc** *After two years of negotiations, the warring parties have finally reached a settlement.*

**5** ▶ **LENGTH/HEIGHT** ◀ [I always + adv/prep, T not in progressive] to be big enough, long enough, or high enough to get to a particular point or level: *The flood waters reached the lower floor of the houses.* | **reach as far as/down to** *Her skirt reaches down to her ankles.*

**6** ▶ **SPEAK TO SB** ◀ [T] to speak to someone or leave a message for them, especially by telephone; CONTACT²: *Here's my phone number, in case you need to reach me.*

**7** ▶ **BE SEEN/HEARD BY SB** ◀ [T] if a message, television programme etc reaches a lot of people, they hear it or see it: *The sales campaign reached a target audience of 12,000 women.*

**8 reach for the stars** to aim for something that is very difficult to achieve

**USAGE NOTE: REACH**

WORD CHOICE: **reach, arrive, get to, achieve, catch**

To **arrive** somewhere is to come to it after travelling: *Sam usually arrives home from work at 5.15.* | *What time does the train arrive?*

**Reach** suggests more time or effort is involved: *At last we reached the base camp.*

In spoken English people usually use **get to**: *You can easily get to the city centre from here.* If a train, bus, plane etc arrives, you say **get in**: *The bus gets in at four-thirty.* Note that you **get/arrive/reach etc home** (NOT **to home**).

You may **reach** a standard or level, especially through your own efforts, but **achieve** is often a better word: *I want to reach/achieve a good level of English* | *He achieved his aim in life — to write a book* (NOT *reached*).

If you get to a bus, train etc just in time, you **catch** it: *You'd better hurry if you want to catch that bus.*

GRAMMAR

You **reach** a place (NOT **reach at** or **reach to** it): *He reached Tokyo at 5 am.*

You **arrive at** a particular place, town, or building: *We arrived at the station at midnight.* | *What time will they arrive at his house?*

You **arrive in** a country or a big city: *arrive in London/Tokyo/France*

Sometimes you do not need a preposition at all: *When will they arrive there/here/home?*

**reach²** *n* **1** [singular, U] the distance that you can stretch out your arm to touch something: *a boxer with a long reach* | **out of reach/beyond reach** *The cat jumped away, out of his reach.* | **within reach** *Adjust the car seat so that all the controls are within reach.* **2** [singular, U] the limit to which someone or something can have a power or influence: **beyond the reach of** *He lives in Paraguay, beyond the reach of the British authorities.* **3 within (easy) reach of** within a distance that you can easily travel: *All the main tourist attractions are within easy reach of the hotel.* **4** [C] a straight part of a river between two bends

reach

The oranges are out of Tim's reach / beyond Tim's reach.

**re·act** /riˈækt/ *v* [I] **1** to behave in a particular way because of something that has happened or something that has been said to you: [+ **to**] *How did Wilson react to your idea?* | *He reacted angrily to accusations of disloyalty.* | **react by doing sth** *Ellie reacted by marching out of the room.* —see also OVERREACT **2** *technical* if a chemical substance reacts, it changes when it is mixed with another chemical substance: [+ **with/on**] *An acid reacts with a base to form a salt.* **3** to become ill when you take a particular drug, eat a particular kind of food etc: [+ **to**] *The patient reacted badly to penicillin.* —compare RESPOND S3 W3

**react against** sth *phr v* [T] to show that you dislike someone else's rules or way of doing something by deliberately doing the opposite: *Feminists reacted against the limitations of women's traditional roles.*

**re·ac·tion** /riˈækʃən/ *n* S2 W2

**1** ▶ **TO A SITUATION/EVENT** ◀ [C,U] something that you feel or do that is a result of something that has happened to you or been said to you: *What was Jeff's reaction when you told him about the job?* | [+ **to**] *Her parents' reaction to the news was surprisingly calm.* | **mixed reaction** (=people react in different ways) *The pay offer brought a mixed reaction from union members.* | **gut reaction** (=what you immediately feel before you have time to think) *My gut reaction to her story was disbelief!*

**2** ▶ **ABILITY** ◀ **reactions** [plural] your ability to move quickly when something dangerous happens suddenly: **quick/slow reactions** *In motor racing the drivers need to have very quick reactions.*

**3** ▶ **TO FOOD/DRUGS** ◀ [C] a bad effect, such as illness, caused by food that you have eaten or a drug that you have taken: *an allergic reaction* | [+ **to**] *Some people experience a mild reaction to the drug.*

**4** ▶ **SCIENCE** ◀ [C,U] **a)** a chemical change that happens when two or more chemical substances are mixed together; CHEMICAL REACTION **b)** a physical force that is the result of an equally strong physical force in the opposite direction —see also NUCLEAR REACTION

**5** ▶ **CHANGE** ◀ [singular] a change in people's attitudes, behaviour, fashions etc that happens because they disapprove of what was done in the past: [+ **against**] *The attitudes of this generation are a reaction against the selfish values of the 1980s.*

**6** ▶ **TIRED/SAD** ◀ [singular] a sudden feeling of weakness, tiredness, or unhappiness that you sometimes get after a lot of activity: *Bridget seems depressed; I think she's suffering a reaction after all the excitement.*

**7** ▶ **AGAINST CHANGE** ◀ [U] *formal* strong and unreasonable opposition to all social and political changes: *The revolution was defeated by the forces of reaction.* —see also CHAIN REACTION

**re·ac·tion·a·ry** /riˈækʃənəri‖-ʃəneri/ *adj* strongly and unreasonably opposed to social or political change: *The* *new measures were opposed by reactionary elements within the party.* —**reactionary** *n* [C]

**re·ac·ti·vate** /ri'æktɪveɪt/ *v* [T] to make something start working again, or to start a process again

**re·ac·tive** /ri'æktɪv/ *adj* **1** reacting to events or situations rather than starting something new: *Many businesses follow a reactive strategy rather than initiating new products.* **2** *technical* a reactive chemical substance changes when it is mixed with another chemical substance

**re·ac·tor** /ri'æktə‖-ər/ *n* [C] a NUCLEAR REACTOR

The teacher is reading out the list of successful students.

S1 W1 **read**[1] /riːd/ *v past tense and past participle* **read** /red/

**1 ▶ WORDS/BOOKS ◀** [I,T] to look at written words and understand what they mean: *Tom could read by the time he was four.* | **read sth** *Read the instructions carefully before you start.* | *I'm sorry, I can't read your handwriting.* | *I can read Spanish but I can't speak it very well.* | *I've read a lot of Agatha Christie.* | *reading the paper*

**2 ▶ INFORMATION ◀** [I,T not in progressive] to find out information from books, newspapers etc: *You can't believe everything you read in the papers.* | [+ **about/of**] *Did you read about that terrible car crash?* | *I read of his death in the local newspaper.* | **read (that)** *Simon was amazed when he read that Sally had won a literary prize.*

**3 ▶ READ AND SPEAK ◀** [I,T] to say the written words in a book, newspaper etc so that people can hear them: **read sb sth** *Daddy, will you read me a story?* | **read to sb** *Our mother reads to us every evening.* | **read (sth) aloud** *He glanced at the letter and began to read it aloud.*

**4 ▶ MUSIC/MAPS/SIGNS ETC ◀** [T] to look at signs, pictures etc and understand what they mean: *He plays the flute well but can't actually read music.* | *map reading*

**5 ▶ UNDERSTAND STH IN A PARTICULAR WAY ◀** [T] to choose to understand a situation, remark, etc in one of several possible ways: **read sth as** *I read her reply as a refusal.* | *The poem can be read as a protest against war.* | **read sth well/accurately** (=understand something correctly) *Reagan's speech showed that he had accurately read the mood of Congress.*

**6 ▶ HAVE A PARTICULAR FORM/MEANING ◀** [I not in progressive] if words read in a particular way, they have a particular form, or produce a particular effect when you read them: *The first sentence read: "If I should die before you receive this letter..."* | *The name should read 'Benson', not 'Fenton'.* | **read well/awkwardly etc** (=be easy or difficult to read and understand) *The report reads well, but it doesn't cover the most important points.*

**7 read sth as sth/for sth read sth** used to tell someone to replace a wrong number or word with the correct one: *Please read £50 as £15.* | *For 'November'* (=instead of November) *on line 6, read 'September'.*

**8 ▶ MEASURING ◀** [T] **a)** to look at the number or amount shown on a measuring instrument: *Read the meter and tell me how much electricity we've used.* **b)** if a measuring instrument reads a particular number, it shows that number: *The thermometer read 46 degrees.*

**9 ▶ AT UNIVERSITY ◀** [T] *BrE* to study a subject at a university: *I read history at Cambridge.*

**10 take it as read (that)** **a)** *especially BrE* to feel certain that something is true without having proof; ASSUME: *You can take it as read that the press will support our opponents.* **b)** to accept a report, statement etc as correct and complete without reading or hearing it: *We'll have to take the secretary's report as read.*

**11 read between the lines** to guess someone's real feelings from something they say or write: *Reading between the lines, I'd say Robert's got a lot of problems.*

**12 read sb's mind/thoughts** to guess what someone else is thinking: *As if he had read her mind, he stood up and offered her his seat.*

**13 read sb like a book** to know someone so well that you immediately know what they are thinking or feeling

**14 read sb's palm** to look carefully at someone's hand, in order to find out about their future: *Have you ever had your palm read?*

**15 read sb's lips** to understand what someone is saying by watching the way their lips move —see also LIP-READ

**16 ▶ COMPUTER ◀** [T] *technical* if the DISK DRIVE of a computer reads information from a DISK, it takes the information and puts it into the computer's memory

**17 do you read me?** *spoken* used to ask someone whether they fully understand what you are saying: *I do not want this to happen again! Do you read me?*

**18 well-read/widely-read** having read a lot of books and gained a lot of knowledge: *She is an intelligent, well-read human being.*

**19 widely-read/little-read etc** read by a lot of people, few people etc: *Jon Naughton's widely-read column in the Observer.* —see also READING, **read (sb) the riot act** (RIOT[1] (4))

**read for** sth *phr v* [T] **1** *BrE old-fashioned* to study a subject in order to get a university degree: *She's reading for a degree in physics.* **2** to perform the part of a particular character from a play, as a test of your ability to act in the play; AUDITION[2]

**read** sth **into** sth *phr v* [T] to think that a situation, action etc has a meaning or importance that it does not really have: *It was only a casual remark. I think you're reading too much into it.*

**read** sth ↔ **out** *phr v* [T] to say the words that are written in a message, list etc, so that people can hear: *He opened the envelope and read out the name of the winner.*

**read** sth ↔ **through/over** *phr v* [T] to read something carefully from beginning to end in order to check details or find mistakes: *Read the contract over carefully before you sign it.*

**read** sth ↔ **up** also **read up on** sth *phr v* [T] *informal* to read a lot about something because you will need to know about it: *I'll have to read up on the tax laws before the meeting tomorrow.*

**read**[2] *n* [singular] **1** *BrE informal* an act of reading something, or time spent doing this: *have a nice quiet read* **2 a good read** something that you enjoy reading: *It's not great literature, but it's a good read.*

**rea·da·ble** /'riːdəbəl/ *adj* **1** interesting or enjoyable to read, and easy to understand: *a very readable account of their research into genetics* **2** writing or print that is readable is clear and easy to read; LEGIBLE —**readibility** /ˌriːdə'bɪləti/ *n* [U] —opposite UNREADABLE —see also MACHINE-READABLE

**re·ad·dress** /ˌriːə'dres/ *v* [T] *BrE* to FORWARD[3] (1)

**read·er** /'riːdə‖-ər/ *n* [C] **1** someone who reads a particular book, newspaper etc: *At this point in the novel, the reader still does not know the hero's true identity.* | *a Guardian reader* **2** someone who reads a lot, or reads in a particular way: *an avid reader* | *Susan isn't much of a reader* (=does not read a lot). | **a fast/slow reader** *I'm not a very fast reader, but I do like novels.* **3** an easy book to help children learn to read, to help people learn a foreign language etc **4 Reader** a teacher in a British university who has the rank just below PROFESSOR: *Reader in Sociology at Bristol* —see also MIND READER —see PROFESSOR (USAGE) S3 W2

**read·er·ship** /'riːdəʃɪp‖-ər-/ *n* [C,U] **1** the people who read a particular newspaper or magazine: *The magazine*

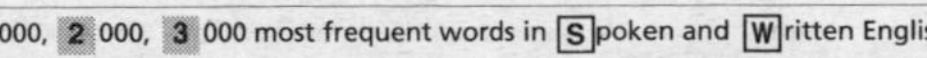

*has a readership of 60,000.* **2** the job that a Reader has in a British university: *a readership in linguistics*

W3 **read·i·ly** /ˈredɪli/ *adv* **1** quickly and easily: *Computers make data readily available to users.* **2** quickly, willingly, and without complaining: *He readily obeyed.*

**read·i·ness** /ˈredinɪs/ *n* **1** [U] a state of being prepared and ready for what is going to happen: **in readiness (for)** *They stacked the firewood in readiness for the evening campfire.* **2** [singular, U] willingness to do something: **readiness to do sth** *the UN's readiness to intervene in the civil war*

W2 **read·ing** /ˈriːdɪŋ/ *n*
**1** ▶ **THE ACTIVITY/SKILL** ◀ [U] the activity of understanding written words: *Children are taught reading and writing in their first years at school.*
**2** ▶ **UNDERSTANDING** ◀ [C] your opinion of what a particular statement, situation, event etc means; INTERPRETATION: *What's your reading of this response?*
**3** ▶ **BOOKS** ◀ [U] the books, articles etc that you read: *Her main reading seems to be mystery novels.* | **light reading** (=books that are easy and enjoyable)
**4** ▶ **TO A GROUP** ◀ [C] **a)** an occasion when a piece of literature is read to a group of people: *a poetry reading* **b)** a piece of literature or part of the Bible that is read to a group of people: *The first reading is from Corinthians I, Chapter 3.*

**5** ▶ **MEASUREMENT** ◀ [C] a number or amount shown on a measuring instrument: **take a reading** *Thermometer readings were taken every two hours.*
**6** ▶ **THE ACT OF READING STH** ◀ [singular] the act of reading something: *Even a casual reading of the text gives you an idea of the theme.*
**7** ▶ **IN PARLIAMENT** ◀ [C] one of the three occasions in the British Parliament or the US Congress, when a BILL (=suggested new law) is read and discussed: *the second reading of the Industrial Relations Bill*
**8 make good/interesting/boring etc reading** to be enjoyable, interesting etc to read: *Your report made fascinating reading.*

**re·ad·just** /ˌriːəˈdʒʌst/ *v* **1** [I] to get used to a new situation, job or way of life: [+ **to**] *Soldiers struggled to readjust to life outside the army.* **2** [T] to make a small change to something or to its position: *The unemployment figures need to be readjusted to allow for people on training programmes.* —**readjustment** *n* [C,U]

**read-only mem·o·ry** /ˌ· ·· ˈ···/ *n* [C,U] ROM

**read-out** /ˈ· ·/ *n* [C] a record of information that has been produced by a computer, shown on a SCREEN or in print: *This program gives you a read-out of all the areas where sales have increased.* —compare PRINT-OUT

**read·y**[1] /ˈredi/ *adj*
**1** ▶ **PREPARED** ◀ [not before noun] prepared for what you are going to do: *Come on. Aren't you ready yet?* | **ready to do sth** *Everything's packed, and we're ready to leave.* | [+ **for**] *I don't want to take the test yet; I'm not ready for it.* | **get ready** *I need about half an hour to get ready, so I'll see you at six.* | **make ready** *formal* (=prepare to start doing something) | **ready for anything** *I felt strong, fit, and ready for anything.* | **ready and waiting** *When the right opportunity came, she was ready and waiting.* | **ready for (the) off** *spoken* (=ready to go somewhere) *Right, I'm ready for the off.* | **when you're ready** *spoken* (=used to tell someone that you are ready for them to start doing something) | **ready when you are** *spoken* (=used to tell someone that you are ready to do what you have arranged to do together) | **ready to roll** *spoken* (=ready to start an activity, journey etc) —see graph at PREPARE
**2** ▶ **FOR IMMEDIATE USE** ◀ [not before noun] something that is ready can be used or eaten immediately: *When will supper be ready?* | *The peaches are ripe and ready to eat.* | [+ **for**] *Is everything ready for the exhibition?* | **get sth ready** *We must get the house ready for the new tenants.* | **have sth ready** *Next time, I had my answer ready.* | **ready cooked/mixed etc** (=already cooked or mixed, and ready to be eaten or used)
**3 be ready for a drink/meal/holiday etc** *spoken* to need or want a drink, meal etc as soon as possible: *You must be ready for a drink after all that hard work.*
**4 be ready to cry/drop etc** *informal* to be so upset or tired that you feel you will cry, fall down etc: *By the end of that walk, we were ready to drop.*
**5** ▶ **WILLING** ◀ willing and quick to do or give something: [+ **with**] *She's always ready with an excuse.* | **ready to do sth** *You're too ready to criticize.* | *They were wonderful neighbours – always ready to help in a crisis.*
**6** ▶ **QUICK** ◀ [only before noun] quick or without delay: *a ready answer* | *This system gives readier access to the data.* | **a ready wit** (=the ability to think quickly of clever, amusing things to say)
**7 ready money/cash** money that can be spent at once in coins or notes: *He was only willing to sell it for ready cash.*
**8 ready, steady, go!** *BrE spoken* used to tell people to start a race —see also READILY, READINESS, **rough and ready** (ROUGH[1] (13))

**ready**[2] *n* **1 at the ready** *especially BrE* available to be used immediately: *The crowd stood around, cameras at the ready.* **2 the readies** *BrE slang* money that is available to be used immediately: *I'm trying to scrape together the readies to pay for a trip to Hong Kong.*

**ready**[3] *v* [T] *formal* to make something ready

**ready-made** /ˌ·· ˈ·◂/ *adj* [only before noun] **1** already prepared, and ready to be used immediately: *ready-made bolognese sauce* **2** convenient and immediately available for you to use: *The rain gave us a ready-made excuse to stay at home.* **3** ready-made opinions or ideas have been copied from someone else **4** READY-TO-WEAR

**ready-to-wear** /ˌ·· · ˈ·◂/ *adj old-fashioned* ready-to-wear clothes are made in standard sizes, not made specially to fit one person

**re·af·firm** /ˌriːəˈfɜːm‖-ɜːrm/ *v* [T] to formally state an intention, belief etc again, especially as an answer to a question or doubt: *The conference overwhelmingly reaffirmed its commitment to nuclear disarmament.* | [+ **that**] *The statement reaffirmed that the government would never make concessions to terrorists.* —**reaffirmation** /ˌriːæfəˈmeɪʃən‖-fər-/ *n* [C,U]

**re·af·for·es·ta·tion** /ˌriːəfɒrɪˈsteɪʃən‖-fɔː, -fɑː-/ *BrE technical n* [U] REFORESTATION

**re·a·gent** /riˈeɪdʒənt/ *n* [C] *technical* a substance that shows that another substance in a compound exists, by causing a chemical REACTION (4a)

**real**[1] /rɪəl/ *adj* S1 W1
**1** ▶ **NOT ARTIFICIAL** ◀ something that is real is actually what it seems to be and not false, artificial or pretended: *Is that ring made of real gold?* | *He calls himself Peter Jones, but it's not his real name.* | *He's never shown any real regret.* | **the real thing/the real McCoy** *I don't like reproductions. It has to be the real thing or nothing.* | *This is the real McCoy – genuine malt whisky.*
**2** ▶ **NOT IMAGINARY** ◀ actually existing and not just imagined: *The children know that Santa Claus isn't a real person.* | **very real danger/possibility/risk etc** *There is a very real danger of an explosion.* | **in real life** *That kind of thing only happens in films, not in real life.* | **in the real world** (=in actual situations where people have to deal with practical problems) *idealistic theories that don't work in the real world*
**3** ▶ **TRUE** ◀ actual and true, not what people think or say: *John later told me the real reason for his absence.*
**4** ▶ **PROPER** ◀ [only before noun] having all the right qualities that you expect a particular kind of thing or person to have: *Now he's what I'd call a real man.* | *The next day we had our first real meeting.*
**5 a real idiot/beauty/disaster etc** *spoken* used to emphasize how stupid, beautiful, terrible etc someone or something is: *You're a real idiot!* | *Our marriage was a real disaster!* | *Thanks – you've been a real help.*
**6 no real chance/hope/reason etc** if there is no real chance etc, there is almost no chance: *There's no real hope of Rod passing this examination.*

**7 ► MOST IMPORTANT ◄** the real questions, problems etc are the most important ones: *The government has failed to deal with the real issues.*
**8 real income/costs/value etc** income etc that is calculated after including in the calculation the general decrease in the value of money: *a 2% annual growth in real income* | **in real terms** (=calculated in this way) *In real terms, the value of their wages has fallen.*
**9 for real** *spoken, especially AmE* seriously, not pretending: *After two trial runs we did it for real.*
**10 get real!** *spoken, especially AmE* used to tell someone that they are being very silly or unreasonable
**11 are you for real?** *AmE spoken* used when you are very surprised by or disapprove of what someone has done or said

**real²** *adv AmE spoken* very: *I'm real sorry!* | *He's real smart.*

**real es·tate** /ˈ· ·ˌ·/ *n* [U] *especially AmE* **1** property in the form of land or houses **2** the business of selling houses or land

**real estate a·gent** /ˈ· ·· ˌ··/ *AmE n* [C] someone whose job is to sell houses or land for other people; ESTATE AGENT

**re·a·lign** /ˌriːəˈlaɪn/ *v* [T] **1** to arrange something differently in relation to something else: *You'll have to realign your text columns if you change the typeface.* **2** to change the aims and relationships that a political party or other organization has: *an attempt to realign the relationship between the state and private business*

**re·a·lign·ment** /ˌriːəˈlaɪnmənt/ *n* [C, U] **1** a change in the way two or more things are organized, so that they have a different relationship to each other: **[+ of]** *a realignment of political parties* **2** the process of arranging parts of something so that they return to their correct positions in relation to each other: *the realignment of broken bones*

**rea·lis·m** /ˈrɪəlɪzəm/ *n* [U] **1** the ability to accept and deal with situations in a practical way, without being influenced by feelings or false ideas **2** also **Realism** the style of art and literature in which everything is shown or described as it really is in life —**realist** *n* [C]

S3 **rea·lis·tic** /rɪəˈlɪstɪk/ *adj* **1** judging and dealing with situations in a practical way according to what is actually possible: *It's just not realistic to expect a promotion so soon.* | *a realistic estimate of the costs* | **be realistic** (=think in a sensible, practical way) *Come on, be realistic – you can't just afford it!* —opposite UNREALISTIC **2** pictures, models, plays etc that are realistic show things as they are in real life: *Her drawings aren't very realistic.* | *a realistic television drama*

**rea·lis·tic·ally** /rɪəˈlɪstɪkli/ *adv* **1** in a practical way and according to what is actually possible: *You have to look realistically at the options available.* | [sentence adverb] *Realistically, we can't expect things to improve before the end of next year.* **2** in a way that shows or describes things as they are in real life: *She told the ghost story so realistically that they were terrified.*

S2 W2 **re·al·i·ty** /riˈælɪti/ *n* **1** [U] things that actually happen or are true, not things that are imagined or thought about: *She can't tell the difference between fantasy and reality.* | *Books can be an escape from reality.* **2 in reality** used to say something is different from what people think: *Henry always seems so self-confident, but in reality he's extremely shy.* **3 become a reality** to actually happen: *Marilyn's dream of being a film star became a reality.* **4 the reality/realities of** what actually happens in a situation, rather than what you think might happen: *They were unprepared for the reality of city life.* | **harsh realities** *the harsh realities of unemployment* **5 the reality is that** used to say that the truth about a situation is very different from what people say: *They keep saying we'll get the money, but the reality is that there's none left.*

**re·aliz·a·ble** also **realisable** *BrE* /ˈrɪəlaɪzəbəl/ *adj* **1** possible to achieve: *realizable goals* **2** in a form that can be changed into money: *realizable value*

**re·a·li·za·tion** also **realisation** *BrE* /ˌrɪəlaɪˈzeɪʃən‖-lə-/ *n* [singular, U] **1** the act of understanding something that you had not noticed before: **[+ that]** *the realization that changes were needed in the organization* **2** the act of achieving what you had planned, hoped, or aimed for: **[+ of]** *the realisation of happiness* **3** **[+ of]** the act of changing something into money by selling it

**rea·lize** also **-ise** *BrE* /ˈrɪəlaɪz/ *v* [T not usually in progressive] S1 W1
**1 ► KNOW STH'S IMPORTANCE ◄** to know and understand the importance of something: **realize (that)** *Do you realize that you're an hour late?* | **realize who/what/how etc** *I realize how much she means to you.* | **realize sth** *None of us realised the danger we were in.*
**2 ► KNOW STH NEW ◄** to start to know something that you had not noticed before: **realize (that)** *I suddenly realized he was crying.* | *Later, we realized that we'd met before in Paris.* | **realize who/what/how etc** *I realized then how hungry I was.* | **realize sth** *Tim didn't realize his mistake until the next day.*
**3 realize an ambition/hope/goal etc** *formal* to achieve something that you were hoping to achieve: *She has finally realized her ambition of becoming a teacher.*
**4 sb's worst fears were realized** used to say that the thing that you were afraid of actually happened: *My worst fears were realized when I saw the exam questions.*
**5 ► MONEY ◄ a)** to obtain an amount of money, especially by selling something: *The initial campaign has realized $5000 in cash and pledges.* | **realize a profit on sth** *We realized a profit on the house.* **b)** to change something that you own into money, especially by selling it: *We were obliged to realize most of our assets.*

**real·ly** /ˈrɪəli/ *adv* S1 W1
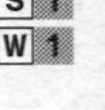
**1 ► THE REAL SITUATION ◄** used when you are saying what is actually the truth of a situation, rather than what people might wrongly think: *What really happened?* | *Oliver was not really her cousin.* | *You are pretending to be annoyed, but you're not really.*
**2 ► DEFINITELY ◄** *especially spoken* used to emphasize something you are saying: *You ought really to have asked me first.* | *I really don't mind.* | *I'm absolutely fine, Dad – really.*
**3 ► VERY MUCH ◄** very much; extremely: *really nice* | *His letter really irritated her.* | *It doesn't really matter, does it?*

Frequencies of the adverb **really** in spoken and written English.

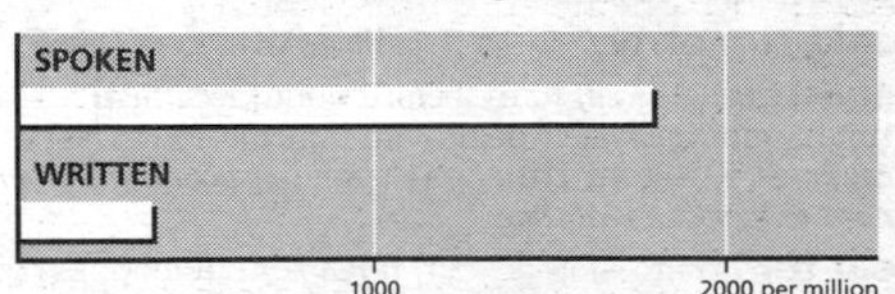


Based on the British National Corpus and the Longman Lancaster Corpus

This graph shows that the adverb **really** is much more common in spoken English than in written English. This is because it is used a lot in spoken English to emphasize what you are saying. It also has some special uses as a reply in conversation and is used in some common spoken phrases.

**really** (*adv*) **SPOKEN PHRASES**

**4 really? a)** used to show that you are surprised by what someone has said: *"There are something like 87 McDonalds in Hong Kong." "Really?"* **b)** used in conversation to show that you are listening to or interested in what the other person is saying: *"I think we might go to the Grand Canyon in June." "Oh, really?"* **c)** *AmE* used to express agreement: *"It's a pain having to get here so early." "Yeah, really!"* **d)** *especially BrE*

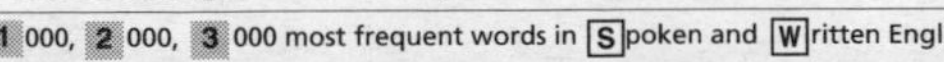

used to express disapproval: *Really, Larry, you might have told me!*
**5 not really** used to say 'no' or 'not completely': *"Do you want to come along?" "Not really."*
**6 I don't really know** used to say that you are not certain about something: *I don't really know what he's up to. I haven't heard from him for ages.*
**7 I really don't know** used to say that you definitely do not know something, especially when someone has asked you about it: *I can't answer that, I really don't know.*
**8 really and truly** used to emphasize a statement or opinion: *Really and truly, I think you should tell him.*

**USAGE NOTE: REALLY**

UK-US DIFFERENCE

**Really** with an adjective or adverb meaning 'very' is common in British English, and is the usual word in American English: *I'm really fed up with this job.*

In informal spoken American English **real** is often used: *That's a real nice car.*

GRAMMAR

**Really** meaning 'very' must go immediately before the adjective it strengthens: *He's a really nice man* (=a very nice man).|*I think she's really stupid.*

**Really** in other positions usually emphasises that what you are saying is true even though it might not seem to fit: *He's really a nice man* (=he is nice, though you might not think so): *She uses lots of long words, but really she's pretty stupid.*

**Really** is usually used before a verb but not immediately after it (except after the verb **to be**): *It's really cold in here.*|*She doesn't really know what to do.*

SPELLING

Remember there are two 'l's' in **really**.

**realm** /relm/ *n* [C] **1** a general area of knowledge, interest, or thought: *the spiritual realm*|[+ **of**] *the realm of human history* **2 within the realms of possibility** possible: *Such a thing is not within the realms of possibility.* **3** *literary* a country ruled over by a king or queen **4 the Realm** *formal* the United Kingdom: *the defence of the Realm*

**re·al·pol·i·tik** /reɪˈɑːlpɒlɪtiːk‖-pɑː-/ *n* [U] politics based on practical situations and needs rather than on moral principles or ideas

**real prop·er·ty** /ˌ· ˈ···/ *n* [U] *law* REAL ESTATE (1)

**real-time** /ˈ· ·/ *adj* [only before noun] *technical* a real-time computer system deals with information as fast as it receives it —**real time** *n* [U] *Airline booking systems need to work in real time.*

**real·tor** /ˈrɪəltə, -tɔː‖-ər, -ɔːr/ *n* [C] *AmE* a REAL ESTATE AGENT

**ream[1]** /riːm/ *n* [C] **1 reams** [plural] *informal* a large amount of writing on paper: [+ **of**] *reams of notes* **2** *AmE* 500 pieces of paper **3** *BrE* 480 pieces of paper

**ream[2]** *v* [T] **1** *AmE informal* to treat someone badly, especially by cheating **2** *technical* to make a hole larger

**re·an·i·mate** /riːˈænɪmeɪt/ *v* [T] *formal* to give someone or something new strength or the energy to start again

**reap** /riːp/ *v* [I,T] **1** to cut and gather a crop of grain **2 reap the benefit/reward/profit (of)** to get something good as a result of what you have done: *Don't let others reap the benefits of your research.* —**reaper** *n* [C] —see also GRIM REAPER —compare HARVEST[2]

**re·ap·pear** /ˌriːəˈpɪə‖-ˈpɪr/ *v* [I] to appear again after not being seen for some time: *They felt tense, knowing that he might reappear at any time.* —**reappearance** *n* [C,U]

**re·ap·praise** /ˌriːəˈpreɪz/ *v* [T] to examine something again in order to consider whether you should change your opinion of it: *The time had come to reappraise their economic strategy.* —**reappraisal** *n* [C,U]

**rear[1]** /rɪə‖rɪr/ *n* **1 the rear** the back part of an object, vehicle or building, or a position at the back of an object or area: *a garden at the rear of the house*|*The engine is in the rear.* —compare FRONT[1] (2) **2** [C] *informal* the part of your body which you sit on; BOTTOM[1] (7) **3 bring up the rear** to be at the back of a line of people or in a race: *Bringing up the rear is the smallest yacht in the race.*

**rear[2]** *v* **1** [T] to look after a person or animal until they are fully grown: *She's reared a large family.*|*cattle rearing* —see RAISE[1] (USAGE) **2** also **rear up** [I] if an animal rears, it rises upright on its back legs: *The horse reared and threw me off.* —compare BUCK[2] (1) **3 be reared on** to be given a particular kind of food, books, entertainment etc regularly while you are a child: *reared on a diet of potatoes* **4 rear its ugly head** if a problem or difficult situation rears its ugly head, it appears and is impossible to ignore: *Scandal rears its ugly head again.*

**rear[3]** *adj* [only before noun] at or near the back of something: *the rear door of the car*|*knock at the rear entrance*

**rear ad·mi·ral** /ˌ· ˈ···◂/ *n* [C] a high rank in the navy —see table on page B4

**rear·guard** /ˈrɪəgɑːd‖ˈrɪrgɑːrd/ *n* **fight a rearguard action a)** to make a determined effort to prevent a change that you think is bad, although it seems too late to stop it: *A rearguard action is being fought against the sale of the land for business development.* **b)** if an army fights a rearguard action, it defends itself at the back against an enemy that is chasing it

**re·arm** /riːˈɑːm‖-ˈɑːrm/ *v* [I,T] to obtain weapons again or provide someone else with new weapons: *If we're going to fight we must rearm.*|**rearm sb with sth** *They rearmed their allies with modern missiles.* —**rearmament** *n* [U]

**rear·most** /ˈrɪəməʊst‖ˈrɪrmoʊst/ *adj* [only before noun] furthest back; last: *the rearmost carriage of the train*

**re·ar·range** /ˌriːəˈreɪndʒ/ *v* [T] **1** to change the position or order of things: *Let's rearrange the furniture and have the desk by the window.* **2** to change the time of a meeting etc —**rearrangement** *n* [C,U]

**rear·view mir·ror** /ˌrɪəvjuː ˈmɪrə‖ˌrɪrvjuː ˈmɪrər/ *n* [C] a mirror in a car etc that lets the driver see the area behind —see picture on page 409

**rear·ward** /ˈrɪəwəd‖ˈrɪrwərd/ *adj* in or towards the back of something —**rearwards** also **rearward** *adv*

**rea·son[1]** /ˈriːzən/ *n* S1 W1
**1** ▶ **CAUSE** ◀ [C] the cause or explanation for something that has happened or that someone has done: *The reason I bought one was that it was so cheap.*|**reason (that)** *The only reason I went was that I wanted to meet your friends.*|**reason why** *We'd like to know the reason why she didn't accept the job.*|[+ **for**] *I can see no reason for their behaviour.*|**give a reason** (=explain) *She just left without giving any reason.*|**for personal/health etc reasons** *She wants to change her job for purely personal reasons.*|**for reasons of** *The main tower has been closed for reasons of safety.*|**by reason of** *formal*: *He was found not guilty by reason of insanity.*|**for some reason** *especially spoken* (=for a reason that you do not know or cannot understand) *They've decided to change all our job titles, for some reason.*|**have your reasons** *spoken* (=have a secret reason for doing something) *"Why did you tell him?" "Oh, I had my reasons."*|**for reasons best known to yourself** (=for reasons that other people do not understand) *For reasons best known to herself, she's sold the house and left the country.* —see EXCUSE[3] (USAGE)
**2** ▶ **GOOD OR FAIR REASON** ◀ [U] a fact that makes it right or fair for someone to do something: **reason to do sth** *I have no reason to believe that Grant's death was not an accident.*|*There is no reason to panic.*|**have every reason to do sth** (=have very good reasons for doing something) *Under the circumstances we had every reason to be suspicious.*|**be no reason to do sth** *I know I'm late, but that's no reason to shout at me.*|**with (good) reason**

(=not stupidly or unnecessarily) *Natalie was alarmed by the news, and with reason.*
**3 all the more reason to do sth** *spoken* used to say that what has just been mentioned is an additional reason for doing what you have suggested: *"She's going on holiday soon." "All the more reason to ask her today."*
**4 ▶ GOOD JUDGMENT ◀** [U] sensible judgment and understanding: *There's reason in what he says.* | **listen to reason** (=be persuaded by someone's sensible advice) *We keep telling her why it won't work, but she just won't listen to reason.* | **see reason** (=accept advice and make a sensible decision) *They tried to make him see reason.*
**5 within reason** within sensible limits: *You can go anywhere you want, within reason.*
**6 go/be beyond all reason** to be more than is acceptable or reasonable: *Their demands go beyond all reason.*
**7 ▶ ABILITY TO THINK ◀** [U] the ability to think, understand and form judgments that are based on facts: *The power of reason separates us from other animals.* | **lose your reason** *old-fashioned* (=become mentally ill)
**8 no reason** *spoken* used when someone asks you why you are doing something and you do not want to tell them: *"Why d'you want to go that way?" "Oh, no reason."* —see also **without rhyme or reason** (RHYME[1] (4)), **it stands to reason** (STAND[1] (40))

**USAGE NOTE: REASON**

WORD CHOICE: **cause, reason, purpose**

A **cause** is anything that produces a result, often not a person: *the causes of inflation* | *the cause of the accident*

A **reason** explains something, often after it has happened or been done: *There was no reason for the attack.* | *There are several reasons why the plan won't work.* | *Give me one good reason.*

A **purpose** is what you hope to achieve by something you do, and is intentional: *Their purpose is to attract attention to environmental issues.*

GRAMMAR

**Reason** is often followed by **for**, **that**, or **why**: *What's the reason for all this noise?* (NOT the reason **of** or **to**) | *the reason that/why he left* (NOT *the reason because/how he left...*). It is also possible to leave out **that**: *the reason he left*

The nature of a **reason** is usually described in a *that* clause: *The reason for the party was that it was Sue's birthday.* In spoken English you may also hear *because* used, though this is considered to be incorrect by many speakers: *The reason for the party is because it's Sue's birthday.*

**Purpose** is often followed by **of** or **in**: *The purpose of the trip/of my coming is to see the President* (NOT *the purpose why I'm coming*). | *My purpose in coming is to see the President* (NOT *of/for coming...*).

People usually say *For this reason/purpose...* (NOT *from/because of this reason..., in/on this purpose* or *for this cause*).

**reason²** *v* **1** [T] to form a particular judgment about a situation after carefully considering the facts: **reason (that)** *We reasoned that the terrorists would not negotiate unless we made some concessions.* **2** [I] to think and make judgements: *the ability to reason*

**reason** sth **out** *phr v* [T] to find an explanation or solution to a problem, by thinking of all the possibilities: *Let's reason this out instead of quarrelling.*

**reason with** sb *phr v* [T] to talk to someone in order to try to persuade them to be more sensible: *I tried to reason with her but she locked herself in the bathroom, crying.*

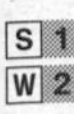
**rea·son·a·ble** /ˈriːzənəbəl/ *adj* **1** fair and sensible: *Be reasonable – you can't expect her to do all the work on her own!* | *a reasonable request* | **it is reasonable to do sth** *It's reasonable to suppose that prices will come down soon.* —opposite UNREASONABLE **2** fairly good, but not especially good: *She has a reasonable chance of doing well in the exam.* **3** a reasonable amount is not too much or too many: *They let a reasonable amount of time pass before visiting him again.* **4** prices that are reasonable seem fair because they are not too high: *good quality furniture at reasonable prices* —see CHEAP² (USAGE) **5 beyond reasonable doubt** *law* if something is proved beyond reasonable doubt, it is shown to be almost certainly true —**reasonableness** *n* [U]

**rea·son·a·bly** /ˈriːzənəbli/ *adv* **1** [+adj/adv] to a satisfactory degree, although not completely: *The car is in reasonably good condition.* | *I was reasonably happy with the results.* **2** in a way that is right or fair: *He can't reasonably be expected to have known that.* **3** in a sensible and reasonable way: *Despite her anger, she had behaved very reasonably.*

**rea·soned** /ˈriːzənd/ *adj* [only before noun] based on careful thought, and therefore sensible: *a reasoned approach to the problem*

**rea·son·ing** /ˈriːzənɪŋ/ *n* [U] a process of thinking carefully about something in order to make a judgement: *logical reasoning* | **the reasoning behind** *What is the reasoning behind this proposal?*

**re·as·sur·ance** /ˌriːəˈʃʊərəns‖-ˈʃʊr-/ *n* **1** [U] help or advice that makes you feel less worried or frightened about a problem: *Martin always looked to his sister for reassurance.* **2** [C] a remark or statement that makes someone feel calmer about something that is worrying them: *The patient needed repeated reassurances.*

**re·as·sure** /ˌriːəˈʃʊə‖-ˈʃʊr/ *v* [T] to make someone feel calmer and less worried or frightened about a problem or situation: *I was reassured by their offer of support.* | **reassure sb (that)** *They apologized and reassured us that the matter would be dealt with immediately.* —see INSURE (USAGE)

**re·as·sur·ing** /ˌriːəˈʃʊərɪŋ◂‖-ˈʃʊr-/ *adj* making you feel less worried or frightened: *It's reassuring to know that there's always someone around to help.* —**reassuringly** *adv*: *She smiled reassuringly at the newcomers.*

**re·bar·ba·tive** /rɪˈbɑːbətɪv‖-ɑːr-/ *adj formal* very unattractive or offensive: *Karajan has been subject to rebarbative questioning and criticism.*

**re·bate** /ˈriːbeɪt/ *n* [C] an amount of money that is paid back to you when you have paid too much tax, rent etc: *In the end I managed to claim a tax rebate.*

**reb·el¹** /ˈrebəl/ *n* [C] **1** someone who opposes or fights against people in authority: *Anti-government rebels have seized the radio station.* | *rebel soldiers* **2** someone who refuses to do things in the normal way, or the way that other people want them to: *Tom has always been the rebel of the family.* | *a teenage rebel*

**re·bel²** /rɪˈbel/ *v* **rebelled, rebelling** [I] to oppose or fight against someone in a position of authority: [+ **against**] *the story of a teenager who rebels against his father* | *those who had rebelled against the government*

**re·bel·lion** /rɪˈbeljən/ *n* [C,U] **1** an organised attempt to change the government, or other authority, using violence: *an armed rebellion* | [+ **against**] *a rebellion against the military regime* | **put down/crush a rebellion** (=use violence to stop it) **2** active opposition to someone in authority: *a rebellion by right-wing members of the party* | [+ **against**] *a clear rebellion against parental control* —compare REVOLUTION (2)

**re·bel·lious** /rɪˈbeljəs/ *adj* **1** deliberately disobeying: *rebellious teenagers* | *rebellious behaviour* **2** fighting against the government of your country: *rebellious warlords* —**rebelliously** *adv* —**rebelliousness** *n* [U]

**re·birth** /ˌriːˈbɜːθ‖-ɜːrθ/ *n* [singular] *formal* a change by which an important idea, feeling, or organization becomes active again: *The 1980s saw a rebirth of conservative thinking.* | *spiritual rebirth*

**re·boot** /ˌriːˈbuːt/ *v* [I,T] if you reboot a computer, or if it reboots, you start it up again after it has stopped working: *Try rebooting the machine and see what happens.*

**re·born** /ˌriːˈbɔːn‖-ɔːrn/ *adj* [not before noun] *literary* **1** having become active again after being inactive: *Our hopes of success were reborn when we received thousands*

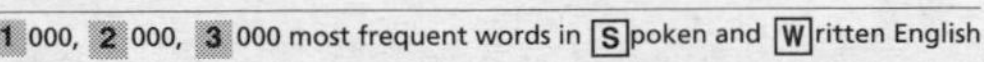

*of letters of support.* **2 be reborn** to be born again, especially according to some beliefs, ancient stories etc

**re·bound¹** /rɪˈbaʊnd/ *v* **1** [I] if a ball or other moving object rebounds, it moves quickly back through the air, after hitting something: [+ **off**] *The ball rebounded off the wall and I caught it.* **2** [I] if prices, values etc rebound, they increase again after decreasing: *Share prices rebounded today after last week's losses.* **3** [I,T] *technical* to catch a BASKETBALL after a player has tried unsuccessfully to get a point

**rebound on/upon** sb *phr v* [T not in passive] if a harmful action rebounds on someone, it has a bad effect on the person who did it

**re·bound²** /ˈriːbaʊnd/ *n* **1 on the rebound** **a)** someone who is on the rebound is upset or confused because a romantic relationship they had has ended: *He married Victoria on the rebound, after Louise left him.* **b)** a ball that rebounds is moving back through the air after hitting something: *I caught the ball on the rebound.* **2** [C] *technical* an act of catching a BASKETBALL after a player has tried unsuccessfully to get a point

**re·buff** /rɪˈbʌf/ *n* [C] *formal* an unkind or unfriendly answer to a friendly suggestion or offer of help; SNUB²: *Every attempt Yves made to befriend her met with a rebuff.* —**rebuff** *v* [T] | *Brady rebuffed all her suggestions.*

R

**re·build** /ˌriːˈbɪld/ *past tense and past participle* **rebuilt** /-ˈbɪlt/ *v* [T] **1** to build something again, after it has been damaged or destroyed: *Most of the houses you see were rebuilt after the Great Fire.* **2** to make something strong and successful again: *The first priority is to rebuild the area's manufacturing industry.*

**re·buke** /rɪˈbjuːk/ *v* [T] *formal* to speak to someone severely, about something they have done wrong: **rebuke sb for doing sth** *Father Cary rebuked her for using bad language.* —**rebuke** *n* [C,U] *a stern rebuke*

**re·but** /rɪˈbʌt/ *v* **rebutted, rebutting** [T] *formal* to prove that a statement or a charge made against you is false; REFUTE —**rebuttal** *n* [C]

**re·cal·ci·trant** /rɪˈkælsɪ̈trənt/ *adj formal* refusing to do what you are told to do, even after you have been punished: *recalcitrant children* —**recalcitrantly** *adv* —**recalcitrance** *n* [U]

S3 W2 **re·call¹** /rɪˈkɔːl‖-ˈkɒːl/ *v* [T]

**1 ▶ REMEMBER STH ◀** [not in progressive] to deliberately remember a particular fact, event, or situation from the past, especially in order to tell someone about it: **recall that** *I seem to recall that Barry was with us at the time.* | **recall doing sth** *I don't recall ever meeting her.* | **recall what/how/where etc** *Afterwards Olivia could not recall what they had talked about.* | **as I recall** *spoken* (=used when you are telling someone what you remember about a past situation) *As I recall, it was you who suggested this idea in the first place.*

**2 ▶ PERSON ◀** to officially tell someone to come back from a place where they have been sent: [+ **from**] *The Ambassador was recalled from Washington.*

**3 ▶ PRODUCT ◀** if a company recalls one of its products, it asks you to return it because there may be something wrong with it: *The B Series cars have been recalled to the manufacturers due to an engine fault.*

**4 ▶ ON A COMPUTER ◀** to bring information back onto the screen of a computer

**5 ▶ BE SIMILAR TO ◀** if something recalls something else, it makes you think of it because it is very similar: *a style of film-making that recalls Alfred Hitchcock* —**recallable** *adj*

**re·call²** /rɪˈkɔːl, ˈriːkɔːl‖-ɒːl/ *n* **1** [U] the ability to remember something that you have learned or experienced: **powers of recall** (=ability to remember) | **total recall** (=the ability to remember everything) | **instant recall** (=the ability to remember a fact immediately) **2** [singular, U] a command telling someone to return from a place where they have been officially sent: [+ **of**] *the recall of all Allied seamen to their own countries* **3 beyond/past recall** impossible to bring back or remember

**re·cant** /rɪˈkænt/ *v* [I,T] *formal* to say publicly that you no longer have a political or religious belief that you had before: *Galileo was forced to recant his belief in the Copernican theory.* —**recantation** /ˌriːkænˈteɪʃən/ *n* [C,U]

**re·cap** /ˈriːkæp‖, riːˈkæp/ *v* **recapped, recapping** [I,T] to repeat the main points of something that has just been said; short for RECAPITULATE: *Let me just recap what's been said so far.* —**recap** /ˈriːkæp/ *n* [C]

**re·ca·pit·u·late** /ˌriːkəˈpɪtʃɪ̈leɪt/ *v* [I,T] *formal* to repeat the main points of something that has just been said —**recapitulation** /ˌriːkəpɪtʃɪ̈ˈleɪʃən/ *n* [C,U]

**re·cap·ture** /riːˈkæptʃə‖-ər/ *v* [T] **1** to bring back the same feelings or qualities that you experienced in the past: *an attempt to recapture our childhood innocence* **2** to catch a prisoner or animal that has escaped: *They travelled only at night, to avoid being recaptured by the enemy.* **3** to take control of a piece of land again by fighting for it —**recapture** *n* [U]

**re·cast** /ˌriːˈkɑːst‖ˌriːˈkæst/ *v past tense and past participle* **recast** [T] **1** to give something a new shape or a new form of organization: *an attempt to recast the statement in less formal language* **2** to give parts in a play or film to different actors —**recasting** *n* [C,U]

**rec·ce** /ˈreki/ *n* [C,U] *informal* RECONNAISSANCE

**recd** the written abbreviation of received (RECEIVE)

**re·cede** /rɪˈsiːd/ *v* [I] **1** if something you can see or hear recedes, it gets further and further away until it disappears: [+ **into**] *footsteps receding into the distance* **2** if a memory, feeling, or possibility recedes, it gradually goes away: *As the threat of attack receded, village life returned to normal.* **3** if water recedes, it moves back from an area that it was covering: *Flood waters finally began to recede in November.* **4** if your hair recedes, you gradually lose the hair at the front of your head: **receding hairline** *Ian is getting self-conscious about his receding hairline.* —see picture on page 412 **5 receding chin** a chin that slopes backwards

**re·ceipt** /rɪˈsiːt/ *n* **1** [C] a written statement that you give to someone, showing that you have received money or goods from them: *Keep all your receipts for work-related expenses.* | **make out a receipt** (=write a receipt) **2** [U] *formal* the act or fact of receiving something: [+ **of**] *Receipt of benefits is permitted for up to 12 months.* | **be in receipt of** *formal* (=to have received something) *We are now in receipt of your letter of the 17th.* | **on/upon receipt of** *formal* (=when you have received something) *On receipt of your instructions, we will dispatch the goods.* **3 receipts** [plural] *technical* the money that a business, bank, or government receives: *total revenue receipts of $18.4 million* S2

**re·ceive** /rɪˈsiːv/ *v* [T] S1 W1

**1 ▶ BE GIVEN STH ◀** to be officially given something: *We have received numerous complaints about the airport noise.* | **receive sth from sb** *In 1962 she received an honorary doctorate from Harvard.* | *You may be entitled to receive assistance from the state.* —see OBTAIN (USAGE)

**2 ▶ BE SENT STH ◀** *formal* to get a letter, message, telephone call etc: *Yes, Anne received your letter Monday.* | *By the time the police received the call it was too late.*

**3 ▶ TREATMENT ◀** *formal* if you receive a particular type of treatment, an injury etc, it is done to you or it happens to you: *The victim received injuries from which he has since died.* | *a cancer patient receiving radiation therapy*

**4 ▶ IDEAS/INFORMATION ◀** [usually passive] to react in a particular way to a suggestion, idea, or piece of information: *Edith's plans were very well received by the board.* | *He did not receive the news very cheerfully.*

**5 be on the receiving end (of)** to be the person who is most affected by someone else's actions, usually in an unpleasant way: *I'm the one who's always on the receiving end of his bad moods.*

**6 ▶ PEOPLE ◀** *formal* to officially accept someone as a guest or member of a group: *She only receives guests on Sundays.* | **receive sb into sth** *Tessa was later received into the Church.*

**7 ▶ BY RADIO ◀ a)** if a radio or television receives radio waves or other signals, it makes them become sounds or pictures **b)** to be able to hear a radio message that someone is sending: *"Are you receiving me?" "Receiving you loud and clear!"*

Frequencies of the verbs **receive** and **get** in spoken and written English.

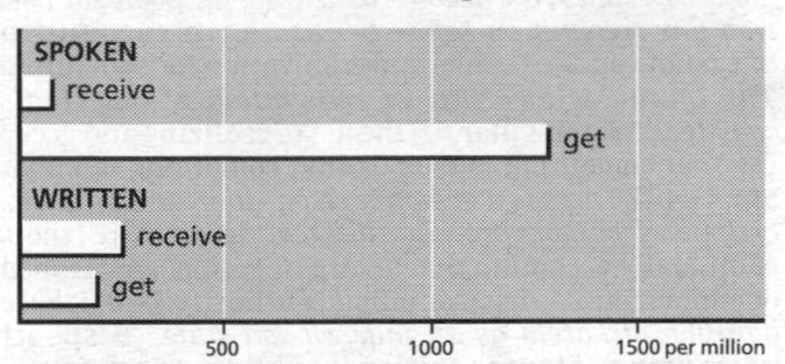


Based on the British National Corpus and the Longman Lancaster Corpus

This graph shows that it is much more usual in spoken English to use **get** rather than **receive**, which is more formal and is therefore more common in written English.

**re·ceived** /rɪˈsiːvd/ *adj* [only before noun] *formal* accepted or considered to be correct by most people: *Sonntag's articles challenged received notions about photography.* | **received wisdom** (=the opinions most people have about what is true) *The received wisdom in Washington is that the Defense Secretary will resign.*

**Received Pro·nun·ci·a·tion** /ˌ·ˌ· ···ˈ··/ *n* [U] RP

**re·ceiv·er** /rɪˈsiːvə‖-ər/ *n* [C]
**1 ▶ TELEPHONE ◀** the part of a telephone that you hold next to your mouth and ear: *Cory slammed down the receiver and stormed out of the room.*
**2 ▶ BUSINESS ◀** someone who is officially in charge of a business or company that is BANKRUPT (=has no money): *The business is in the hands of the receivers.*
**3 ▶ STOLEN PROPERTY ◀** someone who buys and sells stolen property
**4 ▶ RADIO ◀** *formal* a radio or television
**5 ▶ AMERICAN FOOTBALL ◀** a player in American football who is in a position to catch the ball

**re·ceiv·er·ship** /rɪˈsiːvəʃɪp‖-vər-/ *n* [U] **go into receivership** if a person or business goes into receivership, they are controlled by the official receiver (RECEIVER (2)) because they have no money

**re·ceiv·ing** /rɪˈsiːvɪŋ/ *n* [U] the crime of buying and selling stolen goods

S2 W1 **re·cent** /ˈriːsənt/ *adj* having happened or begun to exist only a short time ago: *recent developments in medicine* | *my recent visit to China* | *In recent years, terrorism has become a greater threat.* —**recentness** *n* [U]

S1 W1 **re·cent·ly** /ˈriːsəntli/ *adv* not long ago: *I've only recently started learning French.* | *Jerry lived in Cairo until quite recently.* | *a recently published biography*

**re·cep·ta·cle** /rɪˈseptəkəl/ *n formal* a container for putting things in: *Please dispose of waste in the appropriate receptacle.*

W3 **re·cep·tion** /rɪˈsepʃən/ *n* **1** [C usually singular] a particular type of welcome for someone, or a particular type of reaction to their ideas, work etc: *If you spoke their language you'd get a friendlier reception.* | *Vaughan's play met with a mixed reception from the critics.* **2** [C] a large formal party to celebrate an event or to welcome someone: *a wedding reception* | *A champagne reception will be held in honour of the ambassador's visit.* **3** [U] **a)** the desk or office where visitors arriving in a hotel or large organization go first: *Please leave your key at the reception desk.* **b)** *BrE* the area around or in front of this desk or office; LOBBY[1] (1): *I'll wait for you in reception.* **4** [U] the quality of radio or television signals that you receive: *listeners complaining about poor reception*

**re·cep·tion·ist** /rɪˈsepʃənɪst/ *n* [C] someone whose job is to welcome and deal with people arriving in a hotel or office building, visiting a doctor etc

**reception room** /-ˈ·· ·/ *n* [C] *BrE* a word, used especially by people who sell houses, for a room, especially a LIVING-ROOM, in a private house that is not a kitchen, bedroom, or bathroom: *The house has three bedrooms, a large kitchen and two reception rooms.*

**re·cep·tive** /rɪˈseptɪv/ *adj* willing to consider new ideas or listen to someone else's opinions: *You might find them in a more receptive mood tomorrow.* | [+ **to**] *receptive to new ideas and values* —**receptively** *adv* —**receptiveness** also **receptivity** /ˌriːsepˈtɪvɪti/ *n* [U]

**re·cess[1]** /rɪˈses, ˈriːses‖ˈriːses, rɪˈses/ *n* **1** [C,U] a time for rest during the working day or year, especially in parliament, law courts etc: *Parliament's summer recess* | *After Slater's testimony, the judge called a recess.* **2** [U] *AmE* a short period of time between lessons at a school when children can go outdoors and play; BREAK[2] (1c) *BrE*: *The older kids were picking on Richie at recess.* **3** [C] a space in the wall of a room for shelves, cupboards etc **4 the recesses of** the inner hidden parts of something: *the deep recesses of the cave*

**re·cess[2]** /rɪˈses‖ˈriːses, rɪˈses/ *v* [I] *especially AmE* to take a recess (RECESS[1] (1))

**re·cessed** /rɪˈsest‖ˈriːsest, rɪˈsest/ *adj* fitted into a part of a wall that is further back than the rest of the wall: *a recessed bookshelf*

**re·ces·sion** /rɪˈseʃən/ *n* [C] a period of time during which there is less trade, business activity, and wealth than usual S2 W3

**re·ces·sive** /rɪˈsesɪv/ *adj technical* a recessive physical feature is passed to children from their parents only if both parents have this feature in their GENES

**re·charge** /ˌriːˈtʃɑːdʒ‖-ɑːr-/ *v* [T] **1** to put a new supply of electricity into a BATTERY (1) **2 recharge your batteries** get back your strength and energy again: *I'm going to spend a week in the mountains to recharge my batteries.* —**rechargeable** *adj* —**recharge** /ˈriːtʃɑːdʒ‖-ɑːr-/ *n* [C]

**re·cher·ché** /rəˈʃeəʃeɪ‖rəˈʃer-, rəʃerˈʃeɪ/ *adj formal* a recherché subject, idea, word etc is uncommon and has been chosen to make people admire your knowledge

**re·cid·i·vist** /rɪˈsɪdɪvɪst/ *n* [C] *technical* a criminal who keeps doing things that are illegal, even after they have been punished —**recidivism** *n* [U]

**re·ci·pe** /ˈresɪpi/ *n* [C] **1** a set of instructions for cooking a particular type of food: [+ **for**] *a recipe for tomato soup* | *a recipe book* **2 be a recipe for** to be likely to cause a particular result: *The fact that four different companies are writing the software sounds like a recipe for disaster to me.* S3

**re·cip·i·ent** /rɪˈsɪpiənt/ *n formal* someone who receives something: [+ **of**] *the recipient of the Nobel Peace Prize*

**re·cip·ro·cal** /rɪˈsɪprəkəl/ *adj formal* a reciprocal arrangement or relationship is one in which two people or groups do or give the same things to each other: *Such treaties provide reciprocal rights and obligations.* —compare MUTUAL —**reciprocally** /-kli/ *adv*

**re·cip·ro·cate** /rɪˈsɪprəkeɪt/ *v* **1** [I,T] to do or give something, because something similar has been done or given to you: *I cannot accept his generosity – I am not in a position to reciprocate.* **2** [T] to feel the same about someone as they feel about you: *Kara had fallen in love with Dan, but her affection was not reciprocated.* —**reciprocation** /rɪˌsɪprəˈkeɪʃən/ *n* [U]

**re·ci·pro·ci·ty** /ˌresɪˈprɒsɪti‖-ˈprɑː-/ *n* [U] *formal* a situation in which two people, groups, or countries give each other similar kinds of help or special rights

**re·cit·al** /rɪˈsaɪtl/ *n* [C] **1** a performance of music or poetry, usually given by one performer: *a piano recital* | [+ **of**] *a recital of operatic arias* **2** *formal* a spoken description of a series of events: [+ **of**] *Fred launched into a long recital of his adventures.*

**re·ci·ta·tion** /ˌresɪˈteɪʃən/ *n* [C,U] an act of saying a poem, piece of literature etc that you have learned, for people to listen to: *recitations from Shakespeare*

**re·ci·ta·tive** /ˌresɪ̩tə'tiːv/ *n* [C,U] *technical* a speech set to music sung by one person that continues the story of an OPERA (=musical play) between the songs

**re·cite** /rɪ'saɪt/ *v* **1** [I,T] to say a poem, piece of literature etc that you have learned, for people to listen to: *a poem I had to recite at school* **2** [T] to tell someone a series or list of things: *Don't encourage him, or he'll recite the whole family history!* —**reciter** *n* [C]

**reck·less** /'rekləs/ *adj* not caring or worrying about the possible bad or dangerous results of your actions: *reckless driving | a reckless adventurer | a reckless waste of money* —**recklessly** *adv* —**recklessness** *n* [U]

S2 W3 **reck·on** /'rekən/ *v* [T not in progressive] **1** *spoken* to think that something is a fact, or have a particular opinion about something: **reckon (that)** *Wayne reckons we ought to call her. | Do you reckon they'll get married?* **2** to guess a number or amount, without calculating it exactly: **reckon how much/how many etc** *How much do you reckon she earns?* | **reckon sth to be sth** *The likely cost of the system is reckoned to be about £10,000.* | **be reckoned in thousands/millions** *Her personal fortune is reckoned in millions.* **3** *formal* to think that someone or something is a particular kind of person or thing: **be reckoned to be sth** *Julia is often reckoned to be the most beautiful woman in Hollywood.* | **reckon sb among/as** *I reckon him among my friends.* **4** *formal* to calculate an amount: *My pay is reckoned from the first of the month.*

**reckon** sth ↔ **in** *phr v* [T] to include something when you are calculating: *Have you reckoned in the cost of postage?*

**reckon on** sth *phr v* [T] to expect something to happen when you are making plans: **reckon on doing sth** *We didn't reckon on spending so much on repairs.*

**reckon** sth ↔ **up** *phr v* [T] *old-fashioned* to add up an amount, cost etc, in order to get a total: *Can you reckon up the money we've made?*

**reckon with** sb/sth *phr v* [T] **1 not reckon with** to not consider a possible problem when you are making plans: *We hadn't reckoned with the possibility that it might rain.* **2 sb/sth to be reckoned with** something or someone that is powerful and must be regarded seriously as a possible opponent, competitor, danger etc: *The principal was certainly a woman to be reckoned with.* **3 have sb/sth to reckon with** to have to deal with someone or something powerful: *Any invader would have the military might of NATO to reckon with.*

**reckon without** sb/sth *phr v* [T] *BrE* to not consider a possible problem when you are making plans: *We had reckoned without the difficulty of selling the house.*

**reck·on·ing** /'rekənɪŋ/ *n* **1** [U] calculation that is based on a careful guess rather than on exact knowledge: *By my reckoning it must be 60 km from here to the coast.* **2** [C] *old use* a bill: *We paid our reckoning and left.* **3 day of reckoning** the time when the results of your actions or behaviour become clear and start to affect you, especially in a bad way —see also DEAD RECKONING

**re·claim** /rɪ'kleɪm/ *v* [T] **1** to officially ask for something to be given back to you: *You may be entitled to reclaim some tax.* **2** to make an area of desert, MARSH (=wet land), etc suitable for farming or building **3** to obtain useful products from waste material: *metal reclaimed from old cars in junkyards* —**reclamation** /ˌreklə'meɪʃən/ *n* [U] | *land reclamation*

**re·cline** /rɪ'klaɪn/ *v* **1** [I] *formal* to lie or lean back in a relaxed way: [+ **in/on**] *a girl reclining on a deck chair* **2** [I,T] if you recline a seat or if it reclines, the back of the seat is lowered, so that you can lean back in it: *reclining seats*

**re·cluse** /rɪ'kluːs‖'rekluːs/ *n* [C] someone who chooses to live alone, and does not like seeing or talking to other people: *The guy was a recluse – a defrocked priest, so people said.* —**reclusive** /rɪ'kluːsɪv/ *adj*

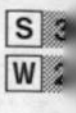

S3 W2 **rec·og·ni·tion** /ˌrekəg'nɪʃən/ *n* **1** [U] the act of knowing someone or something because you have known or learned about them in the past: *Years later, she passed me in the street without even the smallest sign of recognition.* | **beyond/out of all recognition** (=having become impossible to recognize) | *His face was bruised and swollen almost beyond recognition.* **2** [singular, U] public admiration and thanks for someone's work or achievements: *Despite a life devoted to helping the poor, she never won any recognition before her death.* | **in recognition of** (=show public thanks and admiration for something) | *This medal is awarded in recognition of outstanding courage.* **3** [singular, U] the act of realizing and accepting that something is true or that something is important: [+ **of**] *There is a growing recognition among doctors of the need for more preventative treatment.* **4** [U] the act of officially accepting that an organization, government, document etc has legal or official authority: [+ **of**] *the recognition of Latvia as an independent state* **5 speech/voice/image etc recognition** the ability of a computer to recognize voices, shapes etc

S1 W1 **rec·og·nize** also **-ise** *BrE* /'rekəgnaɪz, 'rekən-/ *v* **1** [T not in progressive] to know who someone is or what something is, because you have seen, heard, experienced, or learned about them in the past: *She was humming a tune I didn't recognize.* | *Saleha came home so thin and weak her own children hardly recognized her.* | *You shouldn't go yourself. You'll be recognised.* | *It was malaria, but Dr Lee hadn't recognized the symptoms.* **2** [T] to officially accept that an organization, government, document etc has legal or official authority: *The management recognizes three main trade unions.* | *British medical qualifications are recognized in Canada.* | **recognize sth as** *The US has not recognized the Cuban government since 1961.* **3 be recognized as** to be thought of as being important or very good by a lot of people: *Lawrence's novel was eventually recognized as a work of genius.* | **recognized expert/authority** *a recognized authority on the teaching of English* **4** [T] to accept and admit, often unwillingly, that something is true: **recognize (that)** *We recognize that this is an unpleasant choice to have to make.* | **recognize what/how/who etc** *Do you think he recognized how foolish he looks?* **5** [T] to officially and publicly thank someone for something they have done, by giving them a special honour —**recognizable** /'rekəgnaɪzəbəl, -kən-, ˌrekəg'naɪ-/ *adj* —**recognizably** *adv*

**re·coil¹** /rɪ'kɔɪl/ *v* [I] **1** to move back suddenly and quickly from something you dislike or are frightened of: [+ **from**] *She recoiled from his touch as if she had been slapped.* **2** to feel such a strong dislike of a particular situation that you want to avoid it: [+ **from**] *Rigby tends to recoil from making difficult decisions.* **3** if a gun recoils, it suddenly moves backwards after it has been fired

**re·coil²** /'riːkɔɪl/ *n* [singular, U] the sudden backward movement of a gun after being fired

**rec·ol·lect** /ˌrekə'lekt/ *v* [T] *old-fashioned* to be able to remember something, especially by deliberately trying to remember: *As far as I recollect, I have never owned a black suit.* | **recollect how/when/what etc** *Davenport tried to recollect when he had last used his car.* | **recollect that** *One witness recollected that the visitor had arrived by the side door.* | **recollect doing sth** *I recollect seeing Ryder some years ago in Bonn.*

**rec·ol·lec·tion** /ˌrekə'lekʃən/ *n formal* **1** [U] an act of remembering something, especially something you try to remember: **have no recollection** (=not remember) *I have no recollection of ever having received the money.* | **to the best of my recollection** (=used when you are unsure if you remember correctly) *To the best of my recollection, she drives a Mercedes.* **2** [C] something from the past that you remember: *His earliest recollection was a great branch of lilac hanging outside the window.*

S3 W2 **rec·om·mend** /ˌrekə'mend/ *v* [T] **1** to advise someone to do something, especially because you have special knowledge of a situation or subject: *The Senate Foreign*

*Relations Committee recommended ratification of the treaty despite public opinion.* | **recommend that** *Doctors recommend that all children should be immunized against measles.* | **recommend doing sth** *The manufacturers recommend changing the oil after 500 km.* | **strongly recommend** *Graham's father strongly recommended sending the boy to school in England.* | **recommended limit/dosage/allowance etc** *It is dangerous to exceed the recommended dosage.* **2** to praise something or someone, or suggest them for a particular purpose or job: *I recommend the butter chicken – it's delicious.* | *Can you recommend a good lawyer?* | **recommend sth to sb** *Oh, that book? Karen recommended it to me.* | **recommend sth for** *My mother always recommends the market for fresh fruit and veg.* | **recommend sb for** *I would recommend Mr Bryant for the position of Assistant Manager.* | **highly/thoroughly recommend** *That new restaurant in town is highly recommended.* **3 sth has much/little/nothing to recommend it** used to say that something has many, few, or no good qualities: *As a tourist resort the place doesn't have anything to recommend it.*

W3 **rec·om·men·da·tion** /ˌrekəmenˈdeɪʃən/ *n* **1** [C] official advice given to someone, especially about what to do: **make a recommendation** *The committee made a number of recommendations for improving safety standards.* **2** [U] the action of suggesting to someone that they should choose a particular thing or person that you think is very good: **on sb's recommendation** *On Hawley's recommendation five officers were court martialled.* **3** [C] *especially AmE* a formal letter or statement saying that someone would be a suitable person to do a job, take a course of study etc

**rec·om·pense¹** /ˈrekəmpens/ *v* [T] *formal* to give someone a payment for trouble or losses that you have caused them, or a reward for their efforts to help you: **recompense sb for sth** *We hope this payment will go some way to recompense you for any incovenience we may have caused.* —compare COMPENSATE (2)

**recompense²** *n* [singular, U] *formal* something that you give to someone for trouble or losses that you have caused them, or as a reward for their help: [+ **for**] *£1,000 isn't really much recompense for all they've been through.* —compare COMPENSATION (1)

**rec·on·cile** /ˈrekənsaɪl/ *v* **1** [T] if you reconcile two ideas, situations, or facts you accept or show that they can exist together and are not directly opposed to each other: **reconcile sth with sth** *She could never reconcile his violent temper with his pacifist ideals.* | **reconcile accounts** (=to make two sets of figures add up to the same) **2 be reconciled (with)** to have a good relationship again with someone after you have quarrelled with them: *After 20 years of silence, he was finally reconciled with his family.*

**reconcile** sb **to** sth *phr v* [T] to make someone able to accept a difficult or unpleasant situation: **reconcile yourself to sth** *We watch the character as he tries to reconcile himself to the idea of his own death.*

**rec·on·cil·i·a·tion** /ˌrekənsɪliˈeɪʃən/ *n* [singular, U] a situation in which two people, countries etc become friendly with each other again after quarrelling: *All our attempts at reconciliation have failed.* | [+ **between**] *There seemed little hope of reconciliation between the two superpowers.* | **spirit of reconciliation** *a new spirit of reconciliation in the negotiations*

**rec·on·dite** /ˈrekəndaɪt, rɪˈkɒn-‖ˈrekən-, rɪˈkɑːn-/ *adj* [only before noun] *formal* recondite information, knowledge etc is not known about or understood by many people

**re·con·di·tion** /ˌriːkənˈdɪʃən/ *v* [T] to repair something, especially an old machine, so that it works like a new one —**reconditioned** *adj*: *a reconditioned engine*

**re·con·nais·sance** /rɪˈkɒnɪ̮səns‖rɪˈkɑː-/ *n* [C,U] the military activity of sending soldiers and aircraft to find out about the enemy's forces: *a reconnaissance mission*

**re·con·noi·tre** *BrE*, **reconnoiter** *AmE* /ˌrekəˈnɔɪtə‖ˌriːkəˈnɔɪtər/ *v* [I,T] to try to find out the position and size of your enemy's army, for example by flying planes over land where their soldiers are

**re·con·sid·er** /ˌriːkənˈsɪdə‖-ər/ *v* [I,T] to think again about something you have decided, with the possibility that you might change your mind: *I have received your letter of resignation but I want you to reconsider your decision.* —**reconsideration** /ˌriːkənsɪdəˈreɪʃən/ *n* [U]

**re·con·sti·tute** /riːˈkɒnstɪ̮tjuːt‖riːˈkɑːnstɪ̮tuːt/ *v* **1** [T] to bring something, especially an organization, back into existence in a different form: **reconstitute sth as** *remnants of the old regiments reconstituted as the New Model Army* **2 reconstituted milk/eggs etc** milk powder etc to which water has been added in order to change it back into the form it was in before it was dried —**reconstitution** /ˌriːkɒnstɪ̮ˈtjuːʃən‖-kɑːnstɪ̮ˈtuː-/ *n* [U]

**re·con·struct** /ˌriːkənˈstrʌkt/ *v* [T] **1** to produce a complete description or copy of something that happened by collecting together pieces of information: *Police are trying to reconstruct the events of last Friday.* **2** to build something again after it has been destroyed or damaged

**re·con·struc·tion** /ˌriːkənˈstrʌkʃən/ *n* **1** [U] the work that is done after a war to repair the damage that was caused to a country's buildings, industry etc: *Reconstruction of the town began in 1948.* **2** [C usually singular] a copy of something that does not exist any more: [+ **of**] *a reconstruction of a Native American village* **3** [C] a short film made using actors that tries to show how a real event happened: *Police are broadcasting a reconstruction of the crime.*

**rec·ord¹** /ˈrekɔːd‖-ərd/ *n* S1 W1

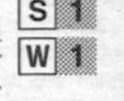

**1 ▶ INFORMATION ◀** [C] information about an event or series of events that is written down or stored on computer, film etc so that it can be looked at in the future: *medical records* | [+ **of**] *records of births, marriages, and deaths* | **keep a record** (=write down details of things as they happen) *Keep a record of any money you pay out.* | **the biggest/lowest/highest etc on record** (=the biggest etc that has ever been recorded) *Today saw some of the hottest temperatures on record.* | **place/put sth on record** (=include something in the official records) *I ask the court to place on record the fact that my client cooperated with the police.*

**2 ▶ HIGHEST/BEST EVER ◀** [C] the fastest speed, longest distance, highest or lowest level etc that has ever been reached, especially in sport: **break a record** (=do something faster, better etc than the previous record) *Kenoco Oil's half-yearly profits broke all records.* | **hold a record** (=be the person who has achieved the fastest speed, the greatest distance etc) | **set a record** (=achieve a new record) *The Americans set a new world record in the sprint relay.* | **record level/figure/sales etc** (=the highest level etc that has ever been reached) *a record level of unemployment* | **an all-time record** (=the best that has ever been achieved)

**3 ▶ MUSIC ◀** a round flat piece of plastic with a hole in the middle that music and sound is stored on: *the disc jockey who plays your favourite records*

**4 ▶ SB'S PAST BEHAVIOUR ◀** [singular] the known facts about someone's past behaviour and how successful, good, or bad they have been: *Laporte's service record in Indochina* | **good/bad record** *The country has a fairly good record on human rights.* | **sb's record on** *Senator Donegan asked the President to justify his record on welfare.* | **criminal record** (=a list made by the police of someone's crimes) *He'll never get a job if they find out about his criminal record.* | **sb's track record** (=how successful someone has been up to now) *The company has a good track record in the export trade.*

**5 off the record** if what you are telling someone is off the record, it is unofficial: *I'd like to emphasize that anything said here is strictly off the record.*

**6 be/go on record as saying** to be known to have said something publicly or officially: *She's on record as saying she thinks men and women should live separate lives.*

**7 for the record** *spoken* used to mean that you want

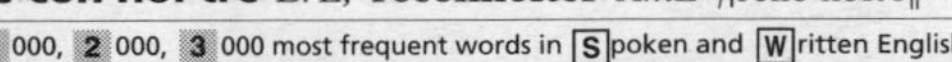

people to remember what you are now saying: *Let me just state for the record, that until yesterday my client had never seen Mr Rigati before.*
**8 put/set the record straight** to tell people the truth about something, because you want to make it very clear that what they believe is not true: *The director gave an interview to the newspapers to set the record straight.*

S3 W2 **re·cord²** /rɪˈkɔːd‖-ɔːrd/ *v* **1** [T] to write information down or store it in a computer or on film so that it can be looked at in the future: *The expedition recorded over 500 new species of plants.* | *Make sure you record the numbers of tickets you sell.* | **record that** *An official report records that at least half the nation's monuments are in need of repair.* **2** [I,T] to store music, sound, television programmes etc on TAPE or DISCS so that people can listen to them or watch them again: *Are you going to record tonight's concert?* | *The group has just recorded a new album.* | *Is the machine still recording?* | *recording their conversation* **3** [T] if an instrument records the size, speed, temperature etc of something, it measures it and keeps that information: *Wind speeds of up to 100 kph have been recorded.*

**record-break·ing** /ˈ·· ˌ··/ *adj* [only before noun] higher, faster etc than anything similar ever achieved: *his record-breaking flight across the Atlantic*

**re·cord·er** /rɪˈkɔːdə‖-ˈkɔːrdər/ *n* **1** [C] **cassette recorder/tape recorder/video recorder etc** a piece of electrical equipment that records music, films etc **2** [C] a simple musical instrument that you play by blowing straight down it **3** a judge in a city court, in some areas of Britain and the US

**record-hold·er** /ˈ·· ˌ··/ *n* [C] the person who has achieved the fastest speed, the longest distance etc in a sport: *the current world record-holder for the discus throw*

W3 **re·cord·ing** /rɪˈkɔːdɪŋ‖-ɔːr-/ *n* [C] **1** a piece of music or speech or a broadcast that has been recorded: [+ **of**] *Have you heard the new recording of Mozart's Requiem?* **2 recording studio/equipment etc** a studio etc used for recording music or sounds

**record li·bra·ry** /ˈ·· ˌ···/ *n* [C] a place where lots of musical recordings are stored for people to borrow

**record play·er** /ˈ·· ˌ··/ *n* [C] a piece of equipment for playing records or music —compare STEREO¹

**re·count¹** /rɪˈkaʊnt/ *v* [T] *formal* to tell someone a story or describe a series of events

**re·count²** /ˈriːkaʊnt/ *n* [C] a process of counting votes again: *I demand a recount!* —**recount** /riːˈkaʊnt/ *v* [T]

**re·coup** /rɪˈkuːp/ *v* [T] to get back an amount of money you have lost or spent: *Finance companies have managed to recoup some of the losses they made during the recession.* | **recoup yourself** (=to get money for yourself after you have lost some) *Landlords recouped themselves by charging higher rents for their other properties.*

**re·course** /rɪˈkɔːs‖ˈriːkɔːrs/ *n formal* **have recourse to** to use something to help you when you are in a difficult situation: **without recourse to** (=without having to use something) *We hope to solve this problem without recourse to further borrowing.*

W2 **re·cov·er¹** /rɪˈkʌvə‖-ər/ *v*
**1 ▶ GET BETTER ◀** [I] **a)** to get better after an illness, accident, shock etc: *After a few days of fever, he began to recover.* | [+ **from**] *My boss is recovering from a heart attack.* **b)** if something recovers after a period of trouble or difficulty, it returns to its normal condition: *After this war, the country will take a long time to recover.*
**2 ▶ STH STOLEN/LOST ETC ◀** [T] to get back something that was taken from you, lost, or almost destroyed: *Police have so far failed to recover the stolen jewellery.* | *A number of bodies were recovered from the wreckage.*
**3 ▶ MONEY ◀** [T] to get back the same amount of money that you have spent or lost; RECOUP: *The company hopes to recover the cost of developing their new product.*
**4 ▶ ABILITIES/SENSES ◀** [T] to get back an ability, a sense, or control over your feelings, movements etc: *It was some hours before she recovered consciousness.* | **recover yourself** (=control yourself again after being upset, embarrassed etc) *It took Mom a few minutes to recover herself, but then she was back in control again.* | **recover your balance** (=stop yourself from falling) —**recoverable** *adj*

**re·cov·er²** /ˌriː ˈkʌvə‖-ər/ *v* [T] to put a new cover on a piece of furniture

**re·cov·er·y** /rɪˈkʌvəri/ *n* **1** [singular, U] a process of getting better after an illness, injury etc: [+ **from**] *She made a quick recovery from the flu.* **2** [singular, U] the process of becoming stronger or more successful again after a difficult period: *Hopes of economic recovery are fading.* **3** [U] the act of getting something back: [+ **of**] *The recovery of the car from the lake took two hours.* W3

**recovery pro·gram** /·ˈ··· ˌ··/ *n* [C] *AmE* a course of treatment for people who are addicted (ADDICT (1)) to drugs or alcohol

**recovery room** /·ˈ···· ·/ *n* [C] a room in a hospital where people first wake up after their operation

**rec·re·ant** /ˈrekriənt/ *n* [C] *old use* someone who is disloyal and lacks courage

**re·cre·ate** /ˌriːkriˈeɪt/ *v* [T] to make something from the past exist again or seem to exist again: *Scientists are trying to recreate these conditions.* —**recreation** /ˌriːkriˈeɪʃən/ *n* [C,U]

**rec·re·a·tion** /ˌrekriˈeɪʃən/ *n* [C,U] an activity that you do for pleasure or amusement: *His only recreations are drinking beer and watching football.* | *a recreation center* —**recreational** *adj*: *recreational facilities*

**recreational ve·hi·cle** /·ˌ··· ˈ···/ *n* [C] *AmE* an RV

**recreation ground** /·ˈ··· ·/ *n* [C] *BrE* an area of public land used for sports and games

**recreation room** /·ˈ··· ·/ *n* [C] **1** a public room, for example in a hospital, used for social activities or games **2** *AmE* a room in a private house, where you can relax, play games etc

**re·crim·i·na·tion** /rɪˌkrɪmɪˈneɪʃən/ *n* [C usually plural, U] a situation in which people blame each other, or what they say when they are blaming each other: *Bitter accusations and recriminations followed the disaster.*

**rec room** /ˈrek ruːm, -rʊm/ *n* [C] *AmE informal* a RECREATION ROOM (2)

**re·cru·des·cence** /ˌriːkruːˈdesəns/ *n* [usually singular] *formal* a sudden return or reappearance of something, especially something bad or unpleasant: [+ **of**] *a worrying recrudescence of urban violence*

**re·cruit¹** /rɪˈkruːt/ *v* **1** [I,T] to find new people to work in a company, join an organization, do a job etc: *We're having difficulty recruiting enough properly qualified staff.* **2 a)** [I,T] to get people to join the army or navy: *Most of the men in the village were recruited that day.* **b)** [T] to form a new army in this way **3** [T] *informal* to persuade someone to do something for you: **recruit sb to do sth** *I recruited three of my friends to help me move everything to the new apartment.* —**recruitment** *n* [U]

**recruit²** *n* [C] **1** someone who has just joined the army, navy, or air force: **raw recruit** (=one who is completely untrained) **2** someone who has recently joined an organization, group of people etc: *The society was always trying to find ways of attracting new recruits.*

**rec·tal** /ˈrektəl/ *adj technical* related to the RECTUM

**rec·tan·gle** /ˈrektæŋgəl/ *n* [C] a shape that has four straight sides and four 90° angles at the corners. Usually two of the sides are longer than the other two —compare SQUARE¹ (1) —see picture at SHAPE¹

**rec·tan·gu·lar** /rekˈtæŋgjʊlə‖-ər/ *adj* having the shape of a rectangle

**rec·ti·fi·er** /ˈrektɪfaɪə‖-ər/ *n* [C] *technical* an instrument that changes the flow of an electrical current in a wire —see also RECTIFY

**rec·ti·fy** /ˈrektɪfaɪ/ *v* **rectified, rectifying** [T] **1** *formal* to correct something that is wrong: *I did my best to rectify the situation, but the damage was already done.* | *Please rectify the mistake at once.* **2** *technical* to make alcohol pure **3** *technical* to change an ALTERNATING CURRENT (=flow of electricity backwards and forwards along a wire) to a DIRECT CURRENT (=flow in only one direction) —**rectifiable** *adj* —**rectification** /ˌrektɟfɟ'keɪʃən/ *n* [C,U] —see also RECTIFIER

**rec·ti·lin·e·ar** /ˌrektɟ'lɪniə◂‖-ər◂/ *adj technical* formed or moving in a straight line or consisting of straight lines

**rec·ti·tude** /'rektɟtjuːd‖-tuːd/ *n* [U] *formal* honesty and moral correctness

**rec·to** /'rektəʊ‖-toʊ/ *n* [C] *technical* a page on the right-hand side of a book —**recto** *adj* —opposite VERSO

**rec·tor** /'rektə‖-ər/ *n* [C] **1** a priest in the Church of England or the Episcopal Church who is responsible for an area from which he receives his income directly —compare VICAR **2** the person in charge of certain colleges and schools, especially in Scotland

**rec·to·ry** /'rektəri/ *n* [C] a house where the rector of the local church lives, or used to live

**rec·tum** /'rektəm/ *n* [C] *technical* the lowest part of your BOWELS —see picture at DIGESTIVE SYSTEM

**re·cum·bent** /rɪ'kʌmbənt/ *adj formal* lying down on your back or side: *a full-length portrait of the recumbent warrior*

**re·cu·pe·rate** /rɪ'kjuːpəreɪt, -'kuː-/ *v* **1** [T] to get better again after an illness or injury: *The doctor sent her to the Sea View Rest Home to recuperate.*|[+ **from**] *A good night's sleep was all I needed to recuperate from the stresses of the day.* **2** [T] to get back money that you have spent or lost in business: *We've recuperated our losses.* —**recuperation** /rɪˌkjuːpə'reɪʃən, -ˌkuː-/ *n* [U]

**re·cu·pe·ra·tive** /rɪ'kjuːpərətɪv, -'kuː-‖-pəreɪtɪv/ *adj* helping you to get better again after an illness: *a recuperative vacation*

**re·cur** /rɪ'kɜː‖-ɜːr/ *v* [I] **recurred, recurring** **1** if something, especially something bad or unpleasant, recurs, it happens again: *There is a danger that the disease may recur in later life.*|*a recurring nightmare* **2** *technical* if a number or numbers after a DECIMAL POINT recur, they are repeated forever in the same order

**re·cur·rence** /rɪ'kʌrəns‖-'kɜːr-/ *n* [C,U] *formal* an occasion when something that has happened before, happens again: [+ **of**] *Measures must be taken to stop a recurrence of last night's violence.*

**re·cur·rent** /rɪ'kʌrənt‖-'kɜːr-/ *adj* happening or appearing repeatedly: *recurrent minor illnesses*|*a recurrent theme in Eliot's poetry* —**recurrently** *adv*

**re·cy·cla·ble** /ˌriː'saɪkləbəl/ *adj* used materials or substances that are recyclable can be recycled —**recyclable** *n* [usually plural] *AmE*

**re·cy·cle** /ˌriː'saɪkəl/ *v* [I,T] to put used objects or materials through a special process, so that they can be used again: *We take all our bottles and newspapers to be recycled.* —**recycled** *adj*: *recycled paper*

**re·cy·cling** /ˌriː'saɪklɪŋ/ *n* [U] the process of treating things such as paper or steel so that they can be used again: *Recycling is important to help protect our environment.*

S1 W1 **red¹** /red/ *adj* **redder, reddest**
**1 ▶COLOUR◀** having the colour of blood or fire: *We painted the door bright red.*|*a beautiful red rose*
**2 ▶HAIR◀** hair that is red has an orange-brown colour
**3 ▶SKIN◀** skin that is red is a bright pink colour, usually only for a short time: *Her cheeks were red with excitement.*
**4 ▶POLITICS◀** *informal* COMMUNIST or extremely LEFT-WING
**5 be as red as a beetroot** *BrE*/**beet** *AmE* to have a very red face, usually because you are embarrassed
**6 like a red rag to a bull** *BrE* very likely to make someone angry or upset: *Just mentioning his ex-wife's name was like a red rag to a bull.*
**7 roll out the red carpet/give sb the red carpet treatment** to give special treatment to someone important who is visiting you: *He's our best customer, so make sure you give him the red carpet treatment.*
**8 a red cent** [usually in negatives] *AmE informal* a very small amount of money: *They'll never be able to pay that – they don't have a red cent!*|*not worth a red cent* —**redness** *n* [U] —see also **paint the town red** (PAINT² (6))

**red²** *n* **1** [C,U] the colour of blood or fire: *Red is often used as a danger sign.*|*the reds and yellows of the fall trees*|*The corrections were marked in red.* (=in red ink) —see picture on page 411 **2** [C,U] red wine: *a nice bottle of red* **3** [C] *informal* a slightly insulting word for someone who has COMMUNIST or very LEFT-WING ideas or opinions **4 see red** to become very angry: *The way he treated that dog just made me see red.* **5 in the red** *informal* owing more money than you have: *These car payments are going to put me into the red again.* —compare **be in the black** (BLACK² (4))

**red ad·mi·ral** /ˌ· '···/ *n* [C] a type of BUTTERFLY that has black wings with bright red marks on them

**red a·lert** /ˌ· ·'·/ *n* [C usually singular] a warning of sudden very great danger: *Evacuate the building – this is a red alert!*|**be on red alert** (=be ready to deal with a danger) *All the hospitals have been put on red alert.*

**red blood cell** /ˌ· '· ·/ also **red cor·pus·cle** /ˌ· '···/ *n* [C] one of the cells in your blood that carry oxygen to every part of your body —compare WHITE BLOOD CELL

**red-blood·ed** /ˌ· '··◂/ *adj* a red-blooded man is strong and full of sexual energy

**red·breast** /'redbrest/ *n* [C] *poetic* a ROBIN

**red·brick** /'redbrɪk/ *adj* a redbrick university is one of the British universities built in the late 19th or early 20th century —compare OXBRIDGE

**red card** /ˌ· '·/ *n* [C] a piece of red card held up by the REFEREE in a football match, to show that a player has done something against the rules and will not be allowed to play for the rest of the game —see picture on page 1264

**red·coat** /'redkəʊt‖-koʊt/ *n* [C] a British soldier during the 18th and 19th centuries

**Red Cres·cent** /ˌ· '··/ *n* [singular] an organization in Muslim countries that helps people who are suffering as a result of war, floods, disease etc

**Red Cross** /ˌ· '·/ *n* [singular] an international organization that helps people who are suffering as a result of war, floods, disease etc

**red·cur·rant** /ˌred'kʌrənt◂‖-'kɜːr-/ *n* [C] a very small red fruit that grows on bushes in northern Europe —compare BLACKCURRANT

**red·den** /'redn/ *v* [I,T] to become red, or make something red: *Lynn's face reddened at this description of herself.*

**red·dish** /'redɪʃ/ *adj* slightly red: *reddish-brown lipstick*

**re·dec·o·rate** /riː'dekəreɪt/ *v* [I,T] *BrE* to put new paint or paper on the walls of a room —**redecoration** /riːˌdekə'reʃən/ *n* [U]

**re·deem** /rɪ'diːm/ *v* [T] *formal*
**1 ▶IMPROVE STH◀** to make something less bad: *Olivier's performance redeemed what was otherwise a second-rate play.*|**redeeming feature** (=the one good thing about someone or something that is unpleasant) *a brutal man, whose one redeeming feature was his honesty*
**2 ▶FREE SB◀** to free someone from the power or evil, especially in the Christian religion: *Christ came to Earth to redeem us from our sins.* —see also REDEEMER
**3 redeem yourself** to do something that will improve what other people think of you, after you have behaved badly or failed: *She was trying desperately to redeem herself after last week's embarrassing mistake.*
**4 redeem a promise/pledge/obligation etc** *formal* to do what you promised to do: *The government found itself unable to redeem its election pledges.*
**5 ▶GET MONEY FOR STH◀** to exchange a piece of paper representing an amount of money for the money that it is worth: *Redeem this coupon for 20p off your next jar of coffee.*|*Bonus shares can be redeemed until 31st July.*

6 ►**GET STH BACK**◄ to buy something back which you had left with someone in order to borrow money from them: *I was finally able to redeem my watch from the pawnbrokers.* —**redeemable** *adj*

**Re·deem·er** /rɪˈdiːmə‖-ər/ *n* [singular] *literary* **the Redeemer** Jesus Christ

**re·demp·tion** /rɪˈdempʃən/ *n* [U] **1** the state of being freed from the power of evil, believed by Christians to be made possible by Jesus Christ **2 past/beyond redemption** too bad to be saved, repaired, or improved **3** *technical* the exchange of shares (SHARE[2] (5)), bonds (BOND[1] (1)) etc for money —**redemptive** /-tɪv/ *adj*

**re·de·ploy** /ˌriːdɪˈplɔɪ/ *v* [T] to move someone or something to a different place or job: *Army tanks were redeployed elsewhere in the region.* —**redeployment** *n* [U]

**re·de·vel·op** /ˌriːdɪˈveləp/ *v* [T] to make an area more modern by putting in new buildings or changing the old ones: *The old docks are being redeveloped as a business park.* —**redevelopment** *n* [C,U]

**red eye** /ˈ· ·/ *n* [U] *AmE informal* **1** a plane that makes a journey at night: *I took the red-eye to LA.* **2** cheap WHISKY

**red-faced** /ˌ· ˈ·◄/ *adj* embarrassed or ashamed: *The election result left them rather red-faced.*

**red gi·ant** /ˌ· ˈ··/ *n* [singular] a star that is near the middle of its life, and is larger and less solid than the sun

**red-hand·ed** /ˌ· ˈ··◄/ *adj* **catch sb red-handed** to catch someone at the moment when they are doing something wrong: *Earl was caught red-handed taking money from the register.*

**red·head** /ˈredhed/ *n* [C] someone who has red hair

**red her·ring** /ˌ· ˈ··/ *n* [C] a fact or idea that is not important but is introduced to take your attention away from the points that are important

**red-hot** /ˌ· ˈ·◄/ *adj* **1** metal that is red-hot is so hot that it shines red: *The poker glowed red-hot in the fire.* **2** *informal* very hot: *Be careful with those plates – they're red-hot.* **3** *informal* extremely active or exciting: *a red-hot news story | red-hot enthusiasm*

**re·dial** /ˌriːˈdaɪəl/ *v* [I,T] to DIAL a telephone number again

**Red In·di·an** /ˌ· ˈ···/ *n* [C] a word for a Native American, that is now usually considered offensive

**re·di·rect, re-direct** /ˌriːdaɪˈrekt, -dɪ̆-/ *v* [T] **1** to send something in a different direction, or use something for a different purpose: *She was good at redirecting the children's energy into something useful. | redirecting funds to other departments* **2** *BrE* to send someone's letters to their new address from an address that they have left; FORWARD[3] (1)

**re·dis·trib·ute** /ˌriːdɪˈstrɪbjuːt/ *v* [T] to give something to each member of a group so that it is divided up in a different way than it was before: *an attempt to redistribute the country's wealth more fairly* —**redistribution** /ˌriːdɪstrɪ̆ˈbjuːʃən/ *n* [U]

**red-let·ter day** /ˌ· ˈ·· ·/ *n* [C] *informal* a day when something special happens that makes you very happy

**red-light dis·trict** /ˌ· ˈ· ˌ··/ *n* [C] the area of a town or city where there are many PROSTITUTES (=women who have sex for money)

**red meat** /ˌ· ˈ·/ *n* [U] dark coloured meat such as BEEF or LAMB —compare WHITE MEAT

**red·neck** /ˈrednek/ *n* [C] *AmE informal* a man who lives in a country area of the US, is uneducated, and may have strong unreasonable opinions —**redneck** *adj*

**re·do** /riːˈduː/ *v* [T] *past tense* **redid** /-ˈdɪd/ *past participle* **redone** /-ˈdʌn/ to do something again: *You'll have to redo this piece of work. | We're having the kitchen redone* (=decorated again) *professionally.*

**red·o·lent** /ˈredəl-ənt/ *adj formal* **1 redolent of** making you think of something: *a style redolent of the sixties* **2** smelling strongly of something: *The air was redolent with roses.* —**redolence** *n* [U]

**re·doub·le** /riːˈdʌbəl/ *v* [T] **redouble your efforts** to greatly increase your effort as you try to do something: *The musicians laughed and redoubled their efforts to keep up with the singer.*

**re·doub·ta·ble** /rɪˈdaʊtəbəl/ *adj literary* someone who is redoubtable is a person you respect or fear: *He was not looking forward to facing the redoubtable Mrs Macclesfield.*

**re·dound** /rɪˈdaʊnd/ *v* **redounded to sb's fame/credit/honour etc** *formal* to make someone more famous, more respected etc: *glorious deeds that redound to the honour of our country*

**red pep·per** /ˌ· ˈ··/ *n* **1** [C] a red vegetable which you can eat raw or use in cooking; CAPSICUM: *stuffed red peppers* **2** [U] a hot tasting red powder used in cooking; CAYENNE

**re·dress**[1] /rɪˈdres/ *v* [T] *formal* **1** to correct something that is wrong or unfair: *redressing the racial inequalities of society today* **2 redress the balance** to make a situation fair or equal when it has been unfair or unequal: *If one species breeds too much, the theory says a new epidemic will arise to redress the balance.*

**re·dress**[2] /rɪˈdres‖ˈriːdres/ *n* [U] *formal* money that someone pays you because they have caused you harm, or damaged your property; COMPENSATION (1): *The only hope of redress is in a lawsuit.*

**red·skin** /ˈredˌskɪn/ *n* [C] *old use* a word for a Native American, that is now considered to be offensive

**red tape** /ˌ· ˈ·/ *n* [U] official rules that seem unnecessary and prevent things from being done quickly and easily: *a procedure surrounded by bureaucracy and red tape*

**re·duce** /rɪˈdjuːs‖rɪˈduːs/ *v* **1** [T] to make something smaller or less in size, amount, or price: *We were hoping that they would reduce the rent a little.* | **reduce sth by half/ten percent etc** *The workforce has been reduced by half.* | [+ **to**] *All the shirts were reduced to £10.* —see also REDUCTION **2** [I] *especially AmE* to become thinner by losing weight **3** [T] if you reduce a liquid or it reduces, you boil it or it boils until there is less of it **4 in reduced circumstances** *old-fashioned* poorer than you were before **5** [T] *old use* to take control of a place by using military force

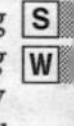

**reduce** sb/sth **to** sth *phr v* [T] **1 reduce sb to tears/silence etc** to make someone cry, be silent etc: *David's extraordinary reply reduced me to silence.* **2 reduce sb to doing sth** to force someone into a particular kind of behaviour or way of life: *Eventually Charlotte was reduced to begging on the streets.* **3** to change something into a shorter simpler form: *The report can be reduced to three main points.* **4 reduce sth to rubble/ashes etc** to destroy something, especially a building, completely **5 reduce sb to the ranks** to make an army officer an ordinary soldier

**re·duc·tion** /rɪˈdʌkʃən/ *n* **1** [C,U] the fact of something becoming or being made smaller: [+ **in**] *a slight reduction in the price of oil | strategies for noise reduction* | **make a reduction** (=sell something more cheaply) *We can make a reduction if you buy in bulk.* **2** [C] a smaller copy of a photograph, map, or picture —opposite ENLARGEMENT (1)

**re·dun·dan·cy** /rɪˈdʌndənsi/ *n* **1** [C,U] *BrE* a situation in which someone has to leave their job, because they are no longer needed: *The closure of the export department resulted in over 100 redundancies. | 2,000 workers now face redundancy.* **2** [U] a situation in which something is not used because something similar or the same already exists **3** [C,U] *technical* the quality of containing additional parts that will make a system work if other parts fail

**redundancy pay** /ˈ···· ˌ·/ *n* [U] *BrE* money you get from your employer when you are made redundant; SEVERANCE PAY *AmE*

**re·dun·dant** /rɪˈdʌndənt/ *adj* **1** *BrE* if you are redundant your employer no longer has a job for you: **make sb redundant** *Seventy factory workers were made redundant in the resulting cuts.* **2** not necessary because something else does the same thing: *The word gradually* *became redundant and dropped out of the language.* —**redundantly** *adv*

**re·du·pli·cate** /rɪˈdjuːplɪ̈keɪt‖rɪˈduː-/ *v* [T] *formal* to repeat a part of something, especially part of a word —**reduplication** /rɪˌdjuːplɪ̈ˈkeɪʃən‖-ˌduː-/ *n* [C,U]

**red·wood** /ˈredwʊd/ *n* [C,U] a very tall tree that grows in California, or the wood from this tree

**reed** /riːd/ *n* [C] **1** a type of tall plant like grass that grows in wet places: *Reeds grew in clumps all along the river bank.* **2** a thin piece of wood that is fixed into a musical instrument such as an OBOE or CLARINET, and produces a sound when you blow over it

**re-ed·u·cate** /riːˈedjʊ̈keɪt‖-dʒə-/ *v* [T] to teach someone to think or behave in a different way: *Young criminals must above all be re-educated.*

**reed·y** /ˈriːdi/ *adj* **1** a voice that is reedy is high and unpleasant to listen to **2** a place that is reedy has a lot of reeds growing there

**reef¹** /riːf/ *n* [C] a line of sharp rocks, often made of CORAL, or a raised area of sand near the surface of the sea: *The ship was wrecked on a reef.* | *the Great Barrier Reef*

**reef²** also **reef in** *v* [T] *technical* to tie up part of a sail in order to make it smaller

**ree·fer** /ˈriːfə‖-ər/ *n* [C] *old-fashioned* a cigarette containing the drug MARIJUANA

**reef knot** /ˈ· ·/ *n* [C] *especially BrE* a double knot that cannot come undone easily; SQUARE KNOT *AmE*

**reek¹** /riːk/ *v* [I] **1** to smell strongly and unpleasantly of something: *This room absolutely reeks.* | [+ **of**] *His breath reeked of garlic.* **2** to seem to be strongly connected with something bad or unpleasant: [+ **of**] *The whole business reeks of dishonesty.*

**reek²** *n* [singular] a strong unpleasant smell: *a reek of tobacco and beer*

**reel¹** /riːl/ *n* [C] **1 a)** *BrE* a round object onto which thread, wire, fishing line, cinema film etc can be wound: *a cotton reel* —compare BOBBIN **b)** the amount that one of these objects will hold: *Have you got another reel of film?* **2** one of the parts of a cinema film that is contained on a reel: *a scene from the final reel of 'High Noon'* **3** a quick and cheerful Scottish or Irish dance, or the music for this

**reel²** *v* **1** also **reel back** [I] to step backwards suddenly and almost fall over, especially after being hit or getting a shock: *Diane reeled back in amazement.* | *A punch in his stomach sent him reeling.* **2** [I] to feel very shocked or confused: *All these statistics make my head reel.* | [+ **from**] *The party is still reeling from its recent election defeat.* **3** [I] to seem to go around and around: *The room reeled before my eyes and I fainted.* **4** [T always + adv/prep] to make something move on or off a reel by winding it: *He reeled in his fishing line.* **5** [I always + adv/prep] to walk in an unsteady way, moving from side to side as if you are drunk: *Captain Banks came reeling up the street.*

**reel** sth ↔ **off** *phr v* [T] *informal* to repeat a lot of information quickly and easily: *Jack reeled off a list of names.*

**re-e·lect** /ˌriː ɪˈlekt/ *v* [T] to elect someone again —**re-election** /-ˈlekʃən/ *n* [C,U] *Barnes is seeking re-election.*

**re-en·try** /riˈentri/ *n* [C,U] an act of entering a place again: *The shuttle made a successful re-entry into the Earth's atmosphere.*

**reeve** /riːv/ *n* [C] **1** the president of a modern Canadian town council **2** an English law officer in former times

**ref¹** /ref/ *n* [C] *BrE informal* a REFEREE

W2 **ref²** the written abbreviation of REFERENCE

**re·fec·to·ry** /rɪˈfektəri/ *n* [C] *BrE* a large room in a school, college etc where meals are served and eaten; CAFETERIA *AmE*

S1 W1 **re·fer** /rɪˈfɜː‖-ɜːr/ *v* **referred, referring**

**refer to** *phr v* [T] **1** [**refer to** sb/sth] to mention or speak about someone or something: *We agreed never to refer to the matter again.* | *Although she didn't mention any names, everyone knew who she was referring to.* | **refer to sth/sb as** *Johnson referred to the discovery as a major breakthrough in medical science.* **2** [**refer to** sth] to look at a book, map, piece of paper etc, for information: *Complete the exercise without referring to a dictionary.* | *Let me just refer to my notes for the exact figures.* **3** [**refer to** sth/sb] if a statement, number etc refers to someone or something, it is about that person or thing: *The figures in the left-hand column refer to our sales abroad.* **4** [**refer** sb/sth **to** sb/sth] to send someone or something to another place or person for information, advice, or a decision: *My complaint was referred to the manufacturers.* | *Professor Watson referred me to an article she had written on the subject.* | *My doctor is referring me* (=is sending me for treatment) *to a dermatologist.* —see also CROSS-REFER

**re·fer·a·ble** /rɪˈfɜːrəbəl/ *adj* [+ **to**] *formal* something that is referable to something else can be related to it

**ref·er·ee¹** /ˌrefəˈriː/ *n* [C] **1** someone who is in charge of a game in sports such as football, BASKETBALL, or BOXING —compare UMPIRE¹ —see picture on page 1264 **2** *BrE* someone who provides information about you when you are trying to get a job: *His headmaster agreed to act as his referee.* **3** someone who is asked to settle a disagreement: *an independent referee*

**referee²** *v* **refereed, refereeing** [I,T] to be the referee for a game

**ref·er·ence** /ˈrefərəns/ *n* **1** [C,U] something you say or write that mentions another person or thing: [+ **to**] *There is no direct reference to her own childhood in the novel.* | **make reference to** *Winston made no reference to what had happened.* | **a passing reference (to)** (=a quick mention) *a speech about the economy without even a passing reference to the problem of unemployment* **2** [C,U] the act of looking at something for information: *Use this dictionary for easy reference.* | **for future reference** (=to have information in the future) *Keep their price list on file for future reference.* **3 with reference to** *formal* used to say what you are writing or talking about, especially in business letters: *With reference to your recent advertisement, I am writing to request further details.* **4** [C] **a)** a letter written by someone who knows you well, usually to a new employer, giving information about you: **take up references** (=get references) *We will need references from your former employers.* **b)** a person who provides information about your character and abilities: *Ask your teacher to act as one of your references.* **5** [C] **a)** a note that tells you where the information that is used in a book, article etc comes from: *a list of references at the end of the article* **b)** a number that tells you where you can find the information you want in a book, on a map etc: *map reference SG49* —see also CROSS-REFERENCE, FRAME OF REFERENCE, **terms of reference** (TERM¹ (18)) S3 W1

**reference book** /ˈ··· ·/ *n* [C] a book such as a dictionary or ENCYCLOPAEDIA that you look at to find information

**reference li·bra·ry** /ˈ··· ˌ···/ *n* [C] a public place where books are stored, where you can use the books but cannot take them away

**ref·e·ren·dum** /ˌrefəˈrendəm/ *n* [C,U] *plural* **referenda** or **referendums** an occasion when everyone in a country votes in order to make a decision about a particular subject: **hold a referendum** *A referendum was held on whether abortion should be made legal.*

**re·fer·ral** /rɪˈfɜːrəl/ *n* [C,U] *formal* an act of sending someone or something to another place for help, information, a decision etc: *the referral of the case to the Court of Appeal*

**re·fill¹** /ˌriːˈfɪl/ *v* [T] to fill something again: *I'll just refill the coffee pot.* —**refillable** *adj*: *a refillable lighter*

**re·fill²** /ˈriːfɪl/ *n* [C] **1** a container filled with something such as ink or petrol that you use to fill or replace the empty container in your pen, CIGARETTE LIGHTER etc: *I must buy some refills for my pen.* **2** *spoken* another drink to refill your glass: *Would you like a refill?*

**re·fine** /rɪˈfaɪn/ *v* [T] **1** to improve a method, plan, system etc by gradually making slight changes to it: *The current structure will be retained and refined.* **2** to make a substance pure using an industrial process: *the petroleum refining industry*

**re·fined** /rɪˈfaɪnd/ *adj* **1** [no comparative] a substance that is refined has been made pure by an industrial process: *refined oil | refined white sugar* **2** someone who is refined is polite and seems to be well-educated or to belong to a high social class: *a refined way of speaking* **3** a method or process that is refined has been improved to make it more effective —opposite UNREFINED

**re·fine·ment** /rɪˈfaɪnmənt/ *n* **1** [C] an addition or improvement to an existing product, system etc: *The new car has a number of refinements such as an air bag and a catalytic converter.* **2** [U] the quality of being polite and well-educated, in a way that is typical of someone from a high social class: *a woman of great refinement* **3** [U] the process of improving something: [+ **of**] *the continued refinement of existing systems* **4** [U + **of**] the process of making a substance pure

**re·fin·e·ry** /rɪˈfaɪnəri/ *n* [C] a factory where something such as metal, sugar, or oil is refined: *an oil refinery*

**re·fit** /ˌriːˈfɪt/ *v* **refitted, refitting** [I, T] to make a ship ready to be used again, by doing repairs and putting in new machinery: *We sailed into port to refit.* —**refit** /ˈriːfɪt/ *n* [C,U] | *The yacht needs a refit.*

**re·flate** /riːˈfleɪt/ *v* [I,T] *technical* to increase the supply of money in a country or system, in order to encourage trade: *measures to reflate the economy*

**re·fla·tion** /riːˈfleɪʃən/ *n* [U] *technical* the process of increasing the amount of money being used in a country in order to increase trade —**reflationary** *adj* —compare DEFLATION, INFLATION (1)

S2 W1 **re·flect** /rɪˈflekt/ *v* **1** [T] if a surface reflects light, heat, sound, or an image, it throws back the light etc that hits it: *White clothes are cooler because they reflect the heat.* | *The moon reflects the sun's rays.* | **be reflected in** *She could see her face reflected in the water.* **2** [T not usually in progressive] to show or be a sign of a particular situation or feeling: *The low value of the dollar reflects growing concern about the US economy.* | **be reflected in** *The growing conflict has been reflected in the paper's editorial section.* | **reflect who/what/how etc** *Does this letter reflect how you really feel?* **3** [I, T] to think carefully about something, or to express your thoughts: [+ **on**] *Take some time to reflect on your future plans.* | **reflect that** *I reflected that there wasn't much point in continuing with my plans now that Al was gone.*

**reflect on/upon** *phr v* [T] to influence people's opinion of someone or something, especially in a bad way: **reflect on sb/sth** *an economic record that reflects badly on government policy* | *If my children are rude, that reflects on me as a parent.*

**reflecting tel·e·scope** /ˈ‧‧ ˌ‧‧‧/ *n* [C] an instrument for seeing distant objects that reflects an image in a mirror to make it bigger —compare REFRACTING TELESCOPE

reflection

S3 W3 **re·flec·tion** /rɪˈflekʃən/ *n* **1** [C] an image reflected in a mirror or similar surface: *We looked at our reflections in the lake.* **2** [C,U] careful thought, or an idea or opinion based on this: *A moment's reflection will show the stupidity of this argument.* | [+ **on**] *It was interesting to hear her reflections on the situation in the Far East.* | **on reflection** (=used to say that you have thought more about something, and changed your opinion) *At first I thought her ideas were crazy, but on reflection, I realize there was some truth in what she said.* **3** [C] something that shows the effects of, or is a sign of, a particular situation: [+ **of**] *The rising crime rate is a reflection of an unstable society.* | *His speech was an accurate reflection of the public mood.* **4 be a reflection on** to show someone's character, abilities, work etc in an unfavourable way: *The students bad grades are no reflection on the teachers, but they do say something about the tests.* **5** [U] the fact of light, heat, sound or an image being reflected

**re·flec·tive** /rɪˈflektɪv/ *adj* **1** thinking quietly: *in a reflective mood* **2** a reflective surface reflects (REFLECT (1)) the light

**re·flec·tor** /rɪˈflektə‖-ər/ *n* [C] **1** a small piece of plastic that is fastened to a bicycle or piece of clothing, so that it can be seen more easily at night —see picture at BICYCLE **2** a surface that reflects light

**re·flex** /ˈriːfleks/ *n* [C] **1** a sudden movement that your muscles make as a natural reaction to a physical effect: *The doctor checked my reflexes.* **2 reflexes** [plural] the natural ability to react quickly and well to sudden situations: *A tennis player needs to have good reflexes.* **3** also **reflex action** something that you do when you react to a situation without thinking: *His hand went to his gun in a reflex action.*

**re·flex·ive** /rɪˈfleksɪv/ *adj technical* a reflexive verb or PRONOUN shows that the action in a sentence affects the person or thing that does the action —**reflexive** *n* [C]

**re·flex·ol·o·gy** /ˌriːflekˈsɒlədʒi‖-ˈsɑː-/ *n* [U] a kind of ALTERNATIVE MEDICINE in which areas of the feet are touched or rubbed in order to cure a medical problem

**re·for·est·a·tion** /riːˌfɒrɪ̈ˈsteɪʃən‖-ˌfɔː-‖-ˌfɑː-/ *n* [U] the practice of planting trees in order to grow a forest for industrial use or to improve the environment —**reforest** /riːˈfɒrɪ̈st‖-ˈfɔː-, -ˈfɑː-/ *v* [I,T]

**re-form** /ˌriːˈfɔːm‖-ɔːrm/ *v* [I,T] **1** to start to exist again or to make something start to exist again: *At the end of the year the company re-formed, and began trading again.* **2** to form into lines again, or to make soldiers do this: *The platoon re-formed, ready to attack.*

**re·form¹** /rɪˈfɔːm‖-ɔːrm/ *v* **1** [T] to change a system, law, organization etc so that it operates in a fairer or more effective way: *plans to reform the tax system* **2** [I,T] to change your behaviour and become a better person, or to make someone do this: **be a reformed character** *Harry's a reformed character since he stopped taking drugs.* | **reformed criminal/sinner/alcoholic etc** (=someone who is no longer a criminal etc)

**reform²** *n* [C,U] a change made to a system or organization, in order to improve it remove unfairness etc: *educational reform* | [+ **of**] *a radical reform of the legal system* W

**ref·or·ma·tion** /ˌrefəˈmeɪʃən‖-fər-/ *n* **1** [C,U] an improvement made by changing something a lot **2 the Reformation** the religious changes in Europe in the 16th century, that resulted in the Protestant churches being established

**re·for·ma·to·ry** /rɪˈfɔːmətəri‖rɪˈfɔːrmətɔːri/ *n* [C] *AmE or old use* a special school where young people who have broken the law are sent; COMMUNITY HOME *BrE*

**re·form·er** /rɪˈfɔːmə‖-ɔːrmər/ *n* [C] someone who tries to improve a system, law, or society: *a great social reformer*

**re·form·ist** /rɪˈfɔːmɪ̈st‖-ɔːr-/ *adj* wanting to change systems or situations, especially in politics —**reformist** *n* [C]

**reform school** /ˈ‧‧ ‧/ *n* [C] *AmE* a REFORMATORY

**re·fract** /rɪˈfrækt/ *v* [T] *technical* to make light change direction when passing through glass or water —**refraction** /rɪˈfrækʃən/ *n* [U]

**refracting tel·e·scope** /ˌ·ˈ·· ˌ···/ *n* [C] an instrument for seeing distant objects that refracts images by passing them through a LENS (=a piece of glass)

**re·frac·to·ry** /rɪˈfræktəri/ *adj formal* disobedient and difficult to deal with or control

**re·frain¹** /rɪˈfreɪn/ *v formal* to not do something that you want to do: [+ **from**] *Kindly refrain from smoking.*

**refrain²** *n* [C] **1** part of a song that is repeated, especially at the end of each VERSE **2** *formal* a remark or idea that is often repeated: *Our proposal met with the constant refrain that the company could not afford it.*

**re·fresh** /rɪˈfreʃ/ *v* **1** [T] to make someone feel less tired or less hot: *He refreshed himself with a glass of beer.* | *A shower will refresh you.* **2 refresh sb's memory** to make someone remember something: *I looked at the map to refresh my memory of the route.* **3 refresh sb's drink** *AmE spoken* to add more of an alcoholic drink to someone's glass: *Can I refresh your drink?* **4** [I,T] *technical* to provide computer OUTPUT again; UPDATE¹ (1): *This display will not refresh until you repeat the command.* —**refreshed** *adj* | *After a good sleep he awoke refreshed.*

**re·fresh·er course** /·ˈ·· ·/ *n* [C] a training course that teaches you about new developments in a particular subject or skill, especially one that you need for your job

**re·fresh·ing** /rɪˈfreʃɪŋ/ *adj* **1** making you feel less tired or less hot: *a long refreshing drink* | *The breeze was refreshing after the stuffy classroom.* **2** pleasantly different from what is familiar and boring: *It made a refreshing change to talk to someone new.* —**refreshingly** *adv*

**re·fresh·ment** /rɪˈfreʃmənt/ *n* **1 refreshments** [plural] small amounts of food and drink that are provided at a meeting, sports event etc: *Refreshments will be served after the meeting.* **2** [U] food and drink in general: *We worked all day without refreshment.* | **liquid refreshment** *humorous* (=alcoholic drink) **3** [U] the experience of being made to feel less tired or hot

**re·fri·ge·rant** /rɪˈfrɪdʒərənt/ *n* [C] *technical* a substance used in refrigeration systems

**re·fri·ge·rate** /rɪˈfrɪdʒəreɪt/ *v* [T] to make something such as food or liquid cold in order to preserve it: *refrigerate the mixture overnight* —**refrigeration** /rɪˌfrɪdʒəˈreɪʃən/ *n* [U] | *Meat must be kept under refrigeration.*

**re·fri·ge·ra·tor** /rɪˈfrɪdʒəreɪtə‖-ər/ *n* [C] *BrE formal* or *AmE* a special cupboard kept cold by electricity, in which you store food and drink; FRIDGE —see picture on page 883

**re·fuel** /ˌriːˈfjʊəl/ *v* **refuelled, refuelling** *BrE*, **refueled, refueling** *AmE* **1** [I,T] to fill a vehicle or plane with FUEL before continuing a journey: *We stopped in Dubai to refuel.* **2** [T] to make feelings, emotions, or ideas stronger: *The news has refuelled speculation about whether there might be something illegal going on.*

**ref·uge** /ˈrefjuːdʒ/ *n* [C] a place that provides protection or shelter from danger: *a refuge for battered wives* | [+ **from**] *a refuge from the storm* | **take/seek refuge in sth** (=look for or find safety somewhere) *During the frequent air-raids people take refuge in their cellars.*

W3 **ref·u·gee** /ˌrefjʊˈdʒiː/ *n* [C] someone who has been forced to leave their country, especially during a war: *Refugees were streaming across the border.* | *a refugee camp*

**re·ful·gent** /rɪˈfʌldʒənt‖rɪˈfʊl-/ *adj literary* very bright —**refulgence** *n* [U]

**re·fund¹** /ˈriːfʌnd/ *n* [C] a sum of money that is given back to you: *You can apply for a refund of your travel costs.*

**re·fund²** /rɪˈfʌnd/ *v* [T] to give someone their money back, especially because they are not satisfied with the goods or services they have paid for: *I took the radio back, and they refunded my money.* —compare REIMBURSE

**re·fur·bish** /ˌriːˈfɜːbɪʃ‖-ɜːr-/ *v* [T] **1** to thoroughly repair and improve a building by painting and cleaning it **2** to change and improve a plan, idea or skill —**refurbishment** *n* [C,U]

**re·fus·al** /rɪˈfjuːzəl/ *n* [C,U] **1** an act of saying or showing that you will not do something that someone has asked you to do: **refusal to do sth** *His refusal to pay the fine got him into trouble.* | **point-blank refusal** (=an immediate direct refusal) **2** an act of not accepting something that is being offered to you: [+ **of**] *They couldn't understand Raymond's refusal of a scholarship to Yale.* **3 give sb first refusal** to let someone decide whether they want to buy a house, car etc that you are selling before you offer it to other people

**re·fuse¹** /rɪˈfjuːz/ *v* **1** [I] to say or show that you will not do something that someone has asked you to do: *I'm sure if you ask her to help you, she won't refuse.* | **refuse to do sth** *I refuse to take part in anything that's illegal.* | **flatly refuse/refuse point blank** (=refuse very firmly and directly) *Mother flatly refused to go back into the hospital.* **2** [I, T] to say no to something that you have been offered; DECLINE¹ (4): *Mrs Sutton refused a second piece of cake.* | *Their offer is too good to refuse.* **3** [T] to not give or allow someone something that they want: **refuse sb sth** *The US authorities refused him a visa.* S2 W1

**USAGE NOTE: REFUSE**

WORD CHOICE: **agree to, accept, refuse, reject, decline, turn down, deny**

**Refuse, reject, decline, turn down** all mean that you do not do something that someone has asked you to do (opposite: **agree to**), or do not take something that you are **offered** (opposite: **accept**).

You can **refuse** an invitation, application, offer, permission, or you can **refuse to** say or do something: *She refused to come with us.*

More strongly, you **reject** an application, idea, proposal, offer, improvement, or plan: *The Greens rejected the proposals for the new road.* | *Her first novel was rejected by over 30 publishers.*

You **decline** an invitation, offer, or to give permission by saying or writing something rather than doing something. This word is less strong but more formal and polite: *The Senator has declined all our invitations to an open debate on the matter.*

Less formally, you can **turn down** an invitation, application, suggestion, offer, or plan: *He turns down all offers of help.*

You can also **deny** someone permission, an opportunity, or their rights. But usually if you **deny** something especially something wrong that someone has said you have done, you say it is not true: The sentence *She denied working for the enemy*, means *She said she was not working for the enemy* (NOT *She refused to work for the enemy*).

**ref·use²** /ˈrefjuːs/ *n* [U] *formal* waste material; RUBBISH¹ (1): *a refuse dump* | *declining standards in housing maintenance, refuse collection and street lighting*

**re·fute** /rɪˈfjuːt/ *v* [T] *formal* **1** to prove that a statement or idea is not correct: *an attempt to refute Moore's theories* **2** to say that a statement is wrong or unfair: *She refuted the allegations of malpractice.* —**refutable** *adj* —**refutation** /ˌrefjʊˈteɪʃən/ *n* [C,U]

**reg.** /redʒ/ an abbreviation of REGISTRATION | **L reg./M reg. etc** *BrE* (=to say what the age of a car is according to the year when it was registered)

**re·gain** /rɪˈgeɪn/ *v* [T] **1** to get something back, especially an ability or quality that you have lost: *The family never quite regained its former influence.* | **regain consciousness** (=wake up after being unconscious) | **regain control (of)** *Government forces have regained control of some areas.* | **regain your balance** (=stop yourself from falling) **2** *literary* to reach a place again

**re·gal** /ˈriːgəl/ *adj formal* typical of a king or queen and therefore usually impressive: *a regal manner* | *a ceremony of regal splendour* —**regally** *adv* | *She held out her hand regally.*

**re·gale** /rɪˈgeɪl/ *v*
**regale** sb **with** sth *phr v* to entertain someone with something, especially stories: *Bailey regaled the customers with tales of our exploits.*

**re·ga·li·a** /rɪˈgeɪliə/ *n* [U] traditional clothes and decorations, used at official ceremonies: *the royal regalia*

S3 **re·gard¹** /rɪˈgɑːd‖-ɑːrd/ *n formal*
**1 ▶ RESPECT ◀** [U] respect for someone or something: [+ **for**] *She has so little regard for him, she is unlikely to follow his advice.*|**hold sb/sth in high regard** (=admire and respect them very much) *a teacher who is held in high regard by his colleagues*
**2 ▶ ATTENTION ◀** [U] *formal* attention or consideration that is shown towards someone or something: [+ **for**] *He has no regard for her feelings.*|[+ **to**] *a report that pays scant regard to the facts of the case*
**3 as regards** used to introduce the subject you are going to talk or write about: *As regards environmental issues, the government will enforce existing regulations.*
**4 in this regard** *formal* used to connect what you are going to say with something you have just mentioned: *Progress is slow. In this regard, lack of funds is a factor.*
**5 with/in regard to** *formal* used to say what particular subject you are talking or writing about: *With regard to future oil supplies, the situation is uncertain.*

**6 ▶ GREETING ◀ regards** [plural] good wishes: *My husband sends his regards.*|**with kind/best/warm regards** (=used to end a letter in a friendly but rather formal way)
**7 ▶ LOOK ◀** [singular] *literary* a long look without moving your eyes

S2 W1 **regard²** *v* [T] **1** [not in progressive] to think about someone or something in a particular way: **regard sb/sth as sth** *Paul seems to regard sex as sinful and immoral.*|*Edith wore strange clothes and was widely regarded as eccentric.*|**regard sb with admiration/fear/concern etc** *Sue regarded the others with fear and jealousy.*|**regard sb well/badly etc** *a work of art that is highly regarded by the experts* **2** *formal* to look at someone or something, especially in a particular way: *I stood back a little and regarded him coldly.* **3** *formal* to pay attention to something: *You must regard the safety regulations.*

S3 **re·gard·ing** /rɪˈgɑːdɪŋ‖-ɑːr-/ *prep formal* a word used especially in business letters to introduce the subject you are writing about: *Regarding your recent inquiry...*

**re·gard·less** /rɪˈgɑːdləs‖-ɑːr-/ *adv* **1** if you continue doing something regardless, you do it in spite of difficulties or opposition: *You get a lot of criticism but you just have to carry on regardless.* **2 regardless of** without being affected by different situations, problems etc: *equal treatment for all, regardless of race, religion, or sex*|*All our proposals were rejected regardless of their merits.*

**re·gat·ta** /rɪˈgætə/ *n* [C] a sports event at which there are races for rowing boats or sailing boats

**Regency¹** /ˈriːdʒənsi/ *adj* Regency buildings, furniture etc are from or in the style of the period 1811-1820 in Britain

**re·gen·cy²** *n* [C,U] a period of government by a REGENT (=person who governs instead of a king or queen)

**re·gen·e·rate** /rɪˈdʒenəreɪt/ *v* [T] *formal* to make something develop and grow strong again: *Given time the forest will regenerate itself.*|*The Marshall Plan sought to regenerate the shattered Europe of 1947.* —**regenerative** /-nərətɪv/ *adj: a regenerative process* —**regeneration** /rɪˌdʒenəˈreɪʃən/ *n* [U] *a new strategy for urban regeneration*

**re·gent** /ˈriːdʒənt/ *n* [C] someone who governs instead of a king or queen ruling who is ill, absent, or still a child —**regent** *adj* [only after noun] *the Prince Regent*

**reg·gae** /ˈregeɪ/ *n* [U] a kind of popular music from the West Indies with a strong regular beat

**re·gi·cide** /ˈredʒɪsaɪd/ *n formal* **1** [U] the crime of killing a king or queen **2** [C] someone who does this

W2 **re·gime** /reɪˈʒiːm/ *n* [C] **1** a government that has not been elected in fair elections: *The regime has liquidated all its opponents.* **2** a particular system of government or management, especially one you disapprove of: **the old/new regime** (=the previous or present system of government)|**the Thatcher/Eisenhower/Faulkner etc regime** (=the government of Thatcher etc) **3** a regimen

**re·gi·men** /ˈredʒɪmɪn/ *n* [C] *formal* a special plan of food, exercise etc that is intended to improve your health

**re·gi·ment¹** /ˈredʒɪmənt/ *n* [C] **1** a large military group usually consisting of several BATTALIONS: *the Royal Sussex Regiment* **2** a large number of people, animals, or things: *a whole regiment of ants*

**re·gi·ment²** /ˈredʒɪment/ *v* [T usually passive] to organize and control people firmly and usually too strictly: *the regimental routine of boarding school* —**regimentation** /ˌredʒɪmenˈteɪʃən/ *n* [U]|*institutional regimentation*

**re·gi·ment·al** /ˌredʒɪˈmentl◂/ *adj* connected with a regiment: *the regimental band*

**Re·gi·na** /rɪˈdʒaɪnə/ *n Latin* **1** used as a title in official writing after the name of the ruling British queen: *Elizabeth Regina* **2** used to mean the governing power of the state in the title of a British law case when a queen is ruling: *the case of Frankland v. Regina* (=Frankland against the government) —compare REX

**re·gion** /ˈriːdʒən/ *n* [C] **1** a fairly large area of a country or of the world, usually without exact limits: *oil fields in the Appalachian region of the US*|*The invaders occupied important coastal regions.*|*America's main ally in this region* —see AREA (USAGE) **2** a particular part of someone's body: *a pain in the lower back region* **3 (somewhere) in the region of** used to describe an amount of time, money, etc without being exact: *The school received a grant somewhere in the region of £2,500.* **4 the regions** the parts of a country that are away from the capital city: *Government policy is to relocate jobs from the capital to the regions.* S W

**re·gion·al** /ˈriːdʒənəl/ *adj* connected with a particular region: *regional cooking*|*regional alliances such as Nato* S W

**re·gion·al·is·m** /ˈriːdʒənəlɪzəm/ *n* [U] loyalty to a particular region of a country and the desire for it to be more politically independent

**re·gis·ter¹** /ˈredʒɪstə‖-ər/ *n* S W
**1 ▶ OFFICIAL LIST ◀** [C] an official list containing the names of all the people, organizations, or things of one particular type: *a civil register of births, deaths and marriages*|*children on the 'at risk' register*
**2 ▶ OFFICIAL BOOK ◀** [C] a book kept for a special purpose, such as in a church or REGISTRY OFFICE, which a man and woman sign after their marriage ceremony: *the school attendance register*
**3 ▶ MUSIC ◀** [C] *technical* the range of musical notes that someone's voice or a musical instrument can reach
**4 ▶ LANGUAGE STYLE ◀** [C,U] *technical* the words, style, and grammar used by speakers and writers in a particular situation or in a particular type of writing: *the correct register for a formal social situation*
**5 ▶ BUSINESS MACHINE ◀** [C] a CASH REGISTER
**6 ▶ HEATING CONTROL ◀** [C] *AmE* a movable metal plate that controls the flow of air in a HEATING OR COOLING system

**register²** *v* W
**1 ▶ ON A LIST ◀ a)** [T] to record a name or details about someone or something in an official list: *We are registering the baby's birth this morning.*|*The tanker is registered in Rotterdam.*|**be registered (as) unemployed/disabled etc** (=be on an official list of a particular group) **b)** [I] to put your name on an official list, for example when you arrive at a hotel, join a course of study etc: [+ **for**] *How many students have registered for English classes?*
**2 ▶ SHOW A FEELING ◀** [T] to show or express a feeling: *Her face registered shock and anger.*
**3 ▶ STATE YOUR OPINION ◀** [T] *formal* to officially state your opinion about something so that everyone

knows what you think or feel: *The delegation registered their protests at the White House meeting.*
**4 ▶ REALIZE ◀** [I usually in negatives, T] if something registers, or if you register it, you notice it or realize it and then remember it: *She must have told me her name, but it just didn't register.*|*I'd been standing there for several minutes before he registered my presence.*
**5 ▶ MEASUREMENT ◀** [I,T] if an instrument registers an amount or if an amount registers on it, the instrument shows or records that amount: *The thermometer registered 98.6°.*
**6 ▶ MAIL ◀** [T] to send a parcel, letter etc by REGISTERED POST: *Did you register the parcel?*

**registered nurse** /ˌ··· ˈ·/ also **RN** *n* [C] someone who has been trained and is officially allowed to work as a nurse

**registered of·fice** /ˌ··· ˈ··/ *n* [C] the office of a company in Britain, to which all letters and official documents must be sent

**registered post** /ˌ··· ˈ·/ *n* [U] *BrE* a way of insuring something that you send by post in case it gets lost or damaged; REGISTERED MAIL *AmE*

**register of·fice** /ˈ··· ˌ··/ *n* [C] a REGISTRY OFFICE

**re·gis·trar** /ˌredʒɪ̇ˈstrɑː◂‖ˈredʒɪ̇strɑːr/ *n* [C] **1** someone who is in charge of official records, for example in a REGISTRY OFFICE or in a college **2** a British hospital doctor who has finished their training but is of a lower rank that a CONSULTANT (2)

3 **re·gis·tra·tion** /ˌredʒɪ̇ˈstreɪʃən/ *n* **1** [U] the act of recording names and details on an official list: *Student registration is the first week in September.*|**[+ of]** *the registration of motor vehicles* **2** [C] *AmE* an official piece of paper containing details about a motor vehicle and the name of its owner

**registration doc·u·ment** /·ˈ·· ˌ···/ *n* [C] *BrE* an official piece of paper containing details about a motor vehicle and its owner

**registration num·ber** /·ˈ·· ˌ··/ *n* [C] *BrE* the official set of numbers and letters shown on the front and back of a motor vehicle on the NUMBER PLATE

**registration plate** /·ˈ·· ˌ·/ *n* [C] *AustrE, NZE* the metal plate on the front and back of a motor vehicle, which has a special number on it; NUMBER PLATE *BrE*, LICENSE PLATE *AmE*

**re·gis·try** /ˈredʒɪ̇stri/ *n* [C] a place where all the information used by an organization is kept

**registry of·fice** /ˈ··· ˌ··/ *n* [C] a local government building in Britain where you can get married, and where births, marriages, and deaths are officially recorded

**re·gress** /rɪˈgres/ *v* [I] *technical* to go back to an earlier and worse condition, or to a less developed way of behaving: *The patient had regressed to a state of childish dependency.* —**regression** /rɪˈgreʃən/ *n* [U] —**regressive** *adj*

**regressive tax** /·ˈ·· ˌ·/ *n* [C] a tax that has less effect on the rich than on the poor

**re·gret¹** /rɪˈgret/ *v* [T] **1** to feel sorry about something you have done and wish you had not done it: **regret doing sth** *She deeply regretted losing her temper.*|**[+ that]** *He regrets that he never went to college.*|**regret sth** *It's a great opportunity, Mr Jarvis – you'll never regret it.*|**bitterly/deeply regret** (=regret something very much) *It was a stupid decision and I bitterly regret it.*|**live to regret sth** (=regret something later) *I'm afraid this is a decision that he'll live to regret.*|**you'll regret it** *spoken* (=used when threatening someone) *You'd better not tell the police, or you'll regret it.* **2** [not in progressive] *formal* to be sorry and sad about a situation: *The management regrets any inconvenience caused to its customers.*|**I regret that** *formal* (=used to politely say that you cannot do something) *I regret that I will be unable to attend.*|**I regret to say/inform/tell** (=used when you are going to give someone bad news) *I regret to inform you that your contract will not be renewed.*

**USAGE NOTE: REGRET**
GRAMMAR
**Regret** is often followed by an *ing* form of a verb, not often by the *to* form unless it is related to something that is about to be said. So if you say: *I regret to tell you this, but I just crashed the car*, you mean *I'm sorry, but I crashed the car*. Compare this with: *I regret telling you I crashed the car*. This means *I'm sorry I told you I crashed the car*.
You **regret** something (NOT **regret about/for something**).

**regret²** *n* [C,U] **1** sadness that you feel about something because you wish it had not happened or that you had not done it: **[+ at]** *The company expressed deep regret at the accident.*|*Jason detected a note of regret in her voice.*|**with (great/deep) regret** *With great regret they abandoned the idea of rebuilding the kitchen.*|**have no/few regrets** (=not feel sorry about something that you have done) *Hetty felt no regrets about her decision to leave home.* **2 much to my regret** *formal* used to say that you are sorry about something: *Much to our regret, we will be unable to attend your wedding.* **3 give/send your regrets** *formal* to say that you are unable to go to a meeting, accept an invitation etc: *My father was ill and had to send his regrets.*

**re·gret·ful·ly** /rɪˈgretfəli/ *adv* **1** feeling sad because you do not want to do what you are doing: *She looked at her watch and turned regretfully towards home.* **2** [sentence adverb] used to talk about a situation that you wish was different or that you are sorry about: *Regretfully we cannot cater for small children or pets.* —**regretful** *adj*

**re·gret·ta·ble** /rɪˈgretəbəl/ *adj* something that is regrettable makes you feel sorry or sad because it has unpleasant results: *Most workers regarded the strike as a regrettable necessity.*|*It is a regrettable fact that our hearing fails as we grow old.*

**re·gret·ta·bly** /rɪˈgretəbli/ *adv* used when you consider the existing situation to be unsatisfactory [sentence adverb] *Regrettably, the patients weren't asked for their opinion.* [+ adj/adv] *Some of the students are regrettably ignorant of contraception.*

**re·group** /ˌriː ˈgruːp/ *v* [I,T] to form new groups or form groups again, or to make people do this: *The Russians retreated, needing to regroup their forces.*

**reg·u·lar¹** /ˈregjɪ̇lə‖-ər/ *adj* S2 W2
**1 ▶ EQUAL SPACES ◀** a regular series of things has the same amount of time or space between each thing and the next: *His breathing was slow and regular.*|**at regular intervals** *Plant the seeds at regular intervals.*
**2 ▶ EVERY DAY/WEEK ETC ◀** [usually before noun] happening or doing something many times and often at the same times every day, month, year etc: *I really miss the security of a regular pay cheque.*|**on a regular basis** *It has always been our policy to review staff productivity on a regular basis.*|**regular as clockwork** (=at exactly the same time every day, week etc) *He phones us every Sunday at six, regular as clockwork.*
**3 ▶ OFTEN ◀** [only before noun] happening or doing something very often: **regular customer/visitor** *Old Joe is one of the bar's regular customers.*
**4 ▶ USUAL ◀** [only before noun] normal or usual: *Driving the van was a change from his regular duties.*
**5 ▶ SHAPE ◀** evenly shaped with parts or sides of equal size: *a regular hexagon*|*He had strong, regular teeth.*|*regular features* (=an evenly shaped face)
**6 ▶ NORMAL ◀** [only before noun] *especially AmE* of a normal or standard size: *a regular coke*
**7 ▶ ORDINARY ◀** *especially AmE* ordinary, without any special feature or qualities: *Regular teachers just don't have the training to deal with problem children.*
**8 ▶ FRIENDLY ◀** *AmE* nice and friendly: *a regular guy*
**9 be/keep regular** *informal* **a)** to get rid of waste from your BOWELS often enough to be healthy **b)** a woman who is regular has her MENSTRUAL PERIOD at the same time each month

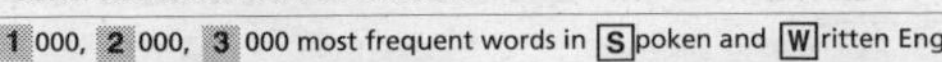

**10 ▶GRAMMAR◀** *technical* a regular verb or noun changes its forms in the same way as most verbs or nouns; the verb 'dance' is regular but 'be' is not

**11 ▶EMPHASIZING◀** [only before noun] *informal* used to emphasize what you think someone is like: *The child's so bossy – a regular little dictator!*

**12 regular soldier/army/troops etc** having a permanent job in the army —**regularity** *n* [U]

**regular**[2] *n* **1** [C] *informal BrE* a customer who goes to the same shop, bar etc very often: *The barman knows all the regulars by name.* **2** [C] a soldier whose permanent job is in the army **3** [U] *AmE* petrol that contains LEAD —compare UNLEADED

**reg·u·lar·ize** also **-ise** *BrE* /ˈregjʊləraɪz/ *v* [T] to make a situation that has existed for some time legal or official —**regularization** /ˈregjʊləraɪˈzeɪʃən‖-lərə-/ *n* [U]

S3 W3 **reg·u·lar·ly** /ˈregjʊləli‖-ərli/ *adv* **1** at regular times, for example every day, week, or month: *The club meets regularly once a fortnight.* **2** often: *I am regularly invited to give talks about my time in Nepal.* **3** evenly arranged or shaped: *a fence with regularly spaced vertical posts*

**reg·u·late** /ˈregjʊleɪt/ *v* [T] **1** to control an activity or process, especially by rules: *There are strict rules regulating the use of chemicals in food.* **2** to make a machine work at a particular speed, temperature etc; ADJUST: *You can regulate the thermostat by turning this little dial.*

S2 W2 **reg·u·la·tion**[1] /ˌregjʊˈleɪʃən/ *n* **1** [C] an official rule or order: **building/planning/safety etc regulations** *The company is very strict on enforcing health and safety regulations.* | **rules and regulations** *There are too many rules and regulations governing small businesses.* **2** [U] control over something, especially by rules: *the regulation of public spending*

**regulation**[2] *adj* [only before noun] used or worn because of a rule or custom: *regulation uniforms*

**reg·u·la·tor** /ˈregjʊleɪtə‖-ər/ *n* [C] **1** an instrument for controlling the temperature, speed etc of something **2** someone who makes sure that, or makes it possible for, a system to operate properly or fairly: *Oftel, the official telecommunications regulator*

**reg·u·la·to·ry** /ˌregjʊˈleɪtəri‖ˈregjʊlətɔːri/ *adj formal* having the purpose of controlling an activity or process, especially by rules

**re·gur·gi·tate** /rɪˈgɜːdʒɪteɪt‖-ɜːr-/ *v formal* **1** [I,T] to bring food that you have already swallowed, back into your mouth: *Some birds and animals regurgitate food to feed their young.* **2** [T] to repeat facts, ideas etc that you have read or heard without thinking about them yourself —**regurgitation** /rɪˌgɜːdʒɪˈteɪʃən‖-ɜːr-/ *n* [U]

**re·hab** /ˈriːhæb/ *n* [U] *AmE* the process of curing someone who has an alcohol or drugs problem: *a rehab program* | **in rehab** *She's been in rehab for a week.* —**rehab** *v* [T]

**re·ha·bil·i·tate** /ˌriːhəˈbɪlɪteɪt/ *v* [T] **1** to help someone to live a healthy, useful, or active life again after they have been seriously ill or in prison: *a special unit for rehabilitating stroke patients* **2** to improve a building or area so that it returns to the good condition it was in before **3** to make people think that someone is good again after a period when they thought that person was bad: *President Nixon seems to have been rehabilitated in the US.* —**rehabilitation** /ˌriːhəbɪlɪˈteɪʃən/ *n* [U]

**re·hash** /riːˈhæʃ/ *n* [C] something such as a piece of writing or a film which is really a copy of an earlier one, although some things have been changed to make it seem new: *just a rehash of the original 1959 version* —**rehash** /ˈriːhæʃ/ *v* [T] | *He keeps rehashing the same old speech.*

**re·hears·al** /rɪˈhɜːsəl‖-ɜːr-/ *n* [C,U] a period or a particular occasion when all the people in a play, concert etc practise it before a public performance —see also DRESS REHEARSAL

**re·hearse** /rɪˈhɜːs‖-ɜːrs/ *v* **1** [I,T] to practise or make people practise something such as a play or concert in order to prepare for a public performance: *The musicians were rehearsing until 2 o'clock in the morning.* **2** [T] to practise something that you plan to say to someone: *Sandy rehearsed her resignation speech.* **3** [T] *formal* to repeat an opinion that has often been expressed before

**re·heat** /ˌriːˈhiːt/ *v* [T] to make a meal or drink hot again

**re·house** /ˌriːˈhaʊz/ *v* [T] to put someone in a new or better home: *All flood victims will be rehoused as soon as possible.*

**Reich** /raɪk, raɪx/ *n German* **the Third Reich** the German state between 1933 and 1945

**reign**[1] /reɪn/ *n* [C] **1** the period of time during which someone is king or queen: *the reign of Queen Victoria* **2** a period during which something is the most powerful or most important feature of a place: *the reign of Stalinism in Russia* | **reign of terror** (=when a government kills many of its political opponents)

**reign**[2] *v* [I] **1** to be the king or queen: *George VI reigned from 1936 to 1952.* **2** *literary* to be the most important feature of a place at a particular time: *Anarchy reigned for many months.* **3 the reigning champion** the most recent winner of a competition: *the reigning Wimbledon champion*

**re·im·burse** /ˌriːɪmˈbɜːs‖-ɜːrs/ *v* [T] *formal* to pay money back to someone who has had to spend the money because of their work: **reimburse sb for sth** *The company will reimburse you for any costs incurred on the course.* —**reimbursement** *n* [C,U]

**rein**[1] /reɪn/ *n* [C] **1** also **reins** [plural] a long narrow band of leather that is fastened around a horse's head in order to control it —see picture at HORSE[1] **2 give (full/free) rein to** to allow an emotion or feeling to be expressed freely: *He gave free rein to his imagination and produced a brilliant piece of writing.* **3 give sb (a) free rein** to give someone complete freedom to do a job in whatever way they choose **4 keep a tight rein on sb/sth** to control something strictly: *The finance director keeps a tight rein on spending.* **5 take/hand over the reins** to take or give someone control over an organization or country: *Who'll take over the reins while the boss is in hospital?*

**rein**[2] *v*

**rein** sth ↔ **in** *phr v* [T] **1** to start to control a situation more strictly: *The government is reigning in public expenditure.* **2** to make a horse go more slowly by pulling on the reins

**re·in·car·nate** /ˌriːɪnˈkɑːneɪt‖-ɑːr-/ *v* **be reincarnated** to be born again in another body after you have died

**re·in·car·na·tion** /ˌriːɪnkɑːˈneɪʃən‖-ɑːr-/ *n* **1** [U] the belief that after someone dies their soul lives again: *Hindus believe in reincarnation.* **2** [C] the person or animal that a reincarnated person has become: *She thinks she is a reincarnation of Cleopatra.*

**rein·deer** /ˈreɪndɪə‖-dɪr/ *n plural* **reindeer** [C] a large DEER with long wide horns: *Herds of reindeer graze on the tundra.*

**re·in·force** /ˌriːɪnˈfɔːs‖-ˈfɔːrs/ *v* [T] **1** to give support to an opinion, idea, or feeling, and make it stronger: *Conclusions from the report have been reinforced by more recent studies.* **2** to make part of a building, structure, piece of clothing etc stronger: *The sea wall is being reinforced with tons of cement.* **3** to make a group of people, especially an army, stronger by adding people, equipment etc W

**reinforced con·crete** /ˌ··· ˈ··/ *n* [U] CONCRETE with metal RODS in it, used to make buildings stronger

**re·in·force·ment** /ˌriːɪnˈfɔːsmənt‖-ˈfɔːrs-/ *n* **1** [U] the act of making something stronger **2 reinforcements** [plural] more soldiers who are sent to an army to make it stronger: *The Spanish soon returned with reinforcements and firearms.*

**re·in·state** /ˌriːɪnˈsteɪt/ *v* [T] to put someone back into a job or position of authority that they had before: *The manager had been unfairly dismissed, and he was duly reinstated.* —**reinstatement** *n* [C,U]

**re·in·sure** /ˌriːɪnˈʃʊə‖-ˈʃʊr/ *v* [T] *technical* to share the insurance of something between two or more companies, so that there is less risk for each —**reinsurance** *n* [U]

**re·invent** /ˌriːɪnˈvent/ *v* [T] **1** to produce an idea that is based on something that existed in the past **2 reinvent the wheel** *informal* to waste time trying to find a way of doing something when someone else has already discovered the best way to do it

**re·is·sue** /ˌriːˈɪʃuː, -ˈɪsjuː‖-ˈɪʃuː/ *v* [T] to produce a record, book etc again, after it has not been available for some time: *CBS reissued 'Lady in Satin'.* —**reissue** *n* [C]

**re·it·e·rate** /riːˈɪtəreɪt/ *v* [T] *formal* to repeat a statement or opinion in order to make your meaning as clear as possible: **reiterate that** *Let me reiterate that we have absolutely no plans to increase taxation.* —**reiteration** /riːˌɪtəˈreɪʃən/ *n* [C,U]

2 **re·ject**[1] /rɪˈdʒekt/ *v* [T]
2 **1 ▶ OFFER/SUGGESTION ◀** to refuse to accept an offer, suggestion, or request: *Sarah rejected her brother's offer of help.* —see REFUSE[1] (USAGE)
**2 ▶ NOT EMPLOY ◀** to refuse to accept someone for a job, course of study etc: *Ian was rejected by the army because of his bad eyesight.*
**3 ▶ PRODUCT ◀** to throw away something that has just been made, because its quality is not good enough: *We have very strict quality control, so anything that is imperfect is rejected.*
**4 ▶ BELIEF ◀** to decide that you do not believe in something: *The present generation has largely rejected the beliefs of its parents.*
**5 ▶ ORGAN ◀** if your body rejects an organ, such as a heart, after a TRANSPLANT operation, it produces substances that attack that organ
**6 ▶ NOT LOVED ◀** to refuse to give someone any love or attention: *She was six months pregnant and feeling fat and rejected.* —**rejection** /-ˈdʒekʃən/ *n* [C,U] | *Above all, Phillips feared rejection and loneliness.* | *China's rejection of the 1987 proposals*

**re·ject**[2] /ˈriːdʒekt/ *n* [C] a product that has been rejected because there is something wrong with it

**re·jig** /riːˈdʒɪg/ *BrE*, **re·jig·ger** /riːˈdʒɪgə‖-ər/ *AmE v* **rejigged, rejigging** [T] *informal* to arrange or organize something in a different way, especially in order to make it better, more suitable, more useful etc: *Many of his songs are rejigged versions of old Hooker numbers.* —**rejig** /ˈriːdʒɪg/ *n* [singular]

**re·joice** /rɪˈdʒɔɪs/ *v* [I] *literary* to feel or show that you are very happy: [**+ at/over**] *His family rejoiced at the news.*

**rejoice in** sth *phr v* [T] **1** to be very happy about something: *We rejoiced in our good fortune.* **2** *BrE humorous* to have a name or title that is silly or amusing: *He rejoices in the name of Pigg.*

**re·joic·ing** /rɪˈdʒɔɪsɪŋ/ also **rejoicings** [plural] *n* [U] *literary* a situation in which a lot of people behave in a very happy way because they have had good news: [**+ at/over**] *There was great rejoicing over the victory.*

**re·join**[1] /ˌriːˈdʒɔɪn/ *v* [T] **1** to go back to a group of people that you were with before: *Crystal went to rejoin her friends in the lounge.* **2** to join an organization again: *In 1938 he rejoined the Socialists.* **3** to join two things together again: *The cables need to be rejoined.*

**re·join**[2] /rɪˈdʒɔɪn/ *v* [T] *formal* to say something in reply, especially rudely or angrily

**re·join·der** /rɪˈdʒɔɪndə‖-ər/ *n* [C] *formal* a reply, especially a rude one: *A smart rejoinder only occurred to me later.*

**re·ju·ve·nate** /rɪˈdʒuːvəneɪt/ *v* [T] **1** to make an organization effective again, for example by bringing in new ideas: *The Party was rejuvenated by an influx of younger members.* **2** [usually passive] to make someone look or feel young and strong again —**rejuvenation** /rɪˌdʒuːvəˈneɪʃən/ *n* [singular, U]

**re·kin·dle** /riːˈkɪndl/ *v* [T] **1** to make someone have a particular feeling, thought etc again: *a chance to rekindle an old friendship* **2** to light a fire or flame again

**re·laid** /ˌriːˈleɪd/ past tense and past participle of RELAY[3]

**re·lapse** /rɪˈlæps/ *v* [I] **1** to become ill again after you have seemed to improve **2** to start to behave badly again or become less active: [**+ into**] *Clara relapsed into her usual sulky manner.* —**relapse** /rɪˈlæps‖ˈriːlæps/ *n* [C,U] | *she's had an unexpected relapse*

**re·late** /rɪˈleɪt/ *v* **1** [I,T] to show or prove a connection between two or more things: *The police are still trying to relate the two pieces of evidence.* | **relate sth to** *The report seeks to relate the rise in crime to an increase in unemployment.* **2** [T] *formal* to tell someone about events that have happened to you or to someone else: *Witnesses to the same crime related the events completely differently.* **3** [I] *AmE spoken* to feel that you understand someone's problem, situation etc: *"I'm just swamped with work right now." "Yeah, I can relate."*  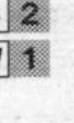

**relate to** sb/sth *phr v* [T] **1** to be concerned with or be about a particular subject: *This relates to something I mentioned earlier.* **2** to be directly connected with and affected by something: *The cost relates directly to the amount of time spent on the project.* **3** to be able to have a good relationship with people because you understand their feelings and behaviour: *Laurie finds it difficult to relate to children.* **4** *informal* to feel that you understand or sympathize with a particular idea or situation: *I can really relate to that song.*

**re·lat·ed** /rɪˈleɪtɪ̣d/ *adj* **1** connected in some way: *drug abuse and other related issues.* | [**+ to**] *The heart attack could be related to his car crash last year.* | **drug/stress-related** *stress-related illness* **2** [not before noun] connected by a family relationship: *Catriona and I are related.* | [**+ to**] *I am related to Simon by marriage.* **3** animals, plants, languages etc that are related belong to the same group —**relatedness** *n* [U] 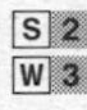

**re·la·ting to** /rɪˈleɪtɪŋ tuː/ *prep* about; relating: *documents relating to immigration laws*

**re·la·tion** /rɪˈleɪʃən/ *n* 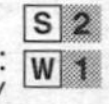
**1 ▶ FAMILY ◀** [C] a member of your family; relative: *We have relations in Canada and Scotland.* | **close/distant relation** *Diane's a distant relation of mine – a third cousin, I think.* | **no relation** (=not a relative) *His name's Johnson too – no relation.* —see also BLOOD RELATION, **poor relation** (POOR (12)) —see RELATIONSHIP (USAGE) 
**2 ▶ BETWEEN PEOPLE/COUNTRIES ◀ relations** [plural] **a)** official connections between companies, countries etc: *Canada and Italy established diplomatic relations in 1970.* **b)** the way in which people or groups of people behave towards each other: [**+ between**] *Relations between workers and management have improved recently.*
**3 in relation to** used to talk about something that is connected with or compared with the thing you are talking about: *Women's earnings are still very low in relation to men's.*
**4 ▶ CONNECTION ◀** [C,U] a connection between two or more things: **bear no relation to** (=have no connection with and be completely different from something) *The retail price bears no relation to the price the farmer receives.*
**5 have (sexual) relations (with)** *old-fashioned* to have sex with someone

**re·la·tion·al** /rɪˈleɪʃənəl/ *adj technical* a relational word is used as part of a sentence but without a meaning of its own, for example the word 'have' in 'I have gone'. —compare NOTIONAL

**relational da·ta·base** /·ˌ··· ˈ···/ *n* [C] *technical* a computer DATABASE that allows a user to find and work with the same information in many different ways

**re·la·tion·ship** /rɪˈleɪʃənʃɪp/ *n* **1** [C] the way in which two people or two groups behave towards each other: [**+ between**] *an improved relationship between the police and local people* | [**+ with**] *We have a good working relationship with the managers.* **2** [C,U] the way in which two or more things are connected and affect each other: [**+ between**] *the relationship between poor housing and health problems* **3** [C] a situation in which two people spend time together or live together, and have romantic or sexual feelings for each other: *I just don't feel* S1 W1

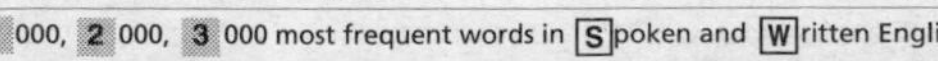

*I'm ready for a relationship right now.* **4** [U] the way in which you are related to someone in your family

> **USAGE NOTE: RELATIONSHIP**
>
> WORD CHOICE: **relationship, relations, relation, connection**
>
> A **relationship with** someone or something is usually close, and may involve strong feelings: *Jane's stormy relationship with her husband. What kind of relationship does she have with her mother?*
>
> **Relations** between people, groups, countries etc are often about working together or communicating: *Relations between industrialists and environmentalists have improved recently.* Relations is a more official word: *friendly relations in the workplace/between East and West*
>
> A **relation** or **relationship to** someone or something, like a **connection**, is usually about a simple fact: *Jane's relationship to/connection with Jeff is that he is her uncle/boss.* | *What relation has temperature to humidity?*
>
> A **relationship between** people and other people or things may be either close and full of emotion, or simply a matter of fact: *the relationship between bosses and workers* | *What's the relationship between temperature and humidity?*

S3 W3 **rel·a·tive¹** /ˈrelətɪv/ *n* [C] a member of your family; RELATION (1): *visits from friends and relatives at Christmas*

W2 **relative²** *adj* **1** having a particular quality when compared with something else: **relative peace/comfort/safety etc** *an atmosphere of relative calm after the riots* | **relative merits/costs/values etc** (=the advantages, costs etc of two or more things that are compared with each other) *discussing the relative merits of various sports cars* | **it's all relative** (=used to mean it cannot be judged on its own but must be compared with others) *You think you're poor, but look at people in really poor countries – it's all relative.* **2 relative to** connected with a particular subject: *facts relative to this issue*

**relative clause** /ˌ··· ˈ·/ *n* [C] *technical* a part of a sentence that has a verb in it, and is joined to the rest of the sentence by 'who', 'which', 'where' etc, for example, the phrase 'who lives next door', in the sentence 'The man who lives next door is a doctor'.

S2 W2 **rel·a·tive·ly** /ˈrelətɪvli/ *adv* **1 relatively easy/few/cheap** fairly easy etc compared with other things: *The drug has relatively few known side effects.* **2 relatively speaking** used when comparing something with all similar things: *Relatively speaking, it's not important.*

**relative pro·noun** /ˌ··· ˈ··/ *n* [C] *technical* a PRONOUN such as 'who', 'which', or 'that' by which a relative clause is connected to the rest of the sentence

**rel·a·tiv·i·ty** /ˌreləˈtɪvəti/ *n* [U] the relationship in PHYSICS between time, space, and MOTION (=movement) according to Einstein's THEORY

**re·launch** /ˈriːlɔːntʃ‖-lɒːntʃ/ *n* [C] a new effort to sell a product that is already on sale —**relaunch** /riːˈlɔːntʃ‖-ˈlɒːntʃ/ *v* [T]

S3 W3 **re·lax** /rɪˈlæks/ *v*

**1** ▶ **REST** ◀ [I,T] to feel calm and comfortable and stop worrying, or to make someone do this: *After a hard day's work, relax in the swimming pool.* | *Relax – I'm sure the kids will be back any minute.* | **relax sth/sb** *A nice hot bath should help to relax you.*

**2** ▶ **LOOSEN** ◀ [I,T] if you relax a part of your body or it relaxes, it becomes less stiff or less tight: *Gentle exercise can relax stiff shoulder muscles.*

**3 relax your hold/grip a)** to hold something less tightly than before: *Molassi relaxed his grip on my arm.* **b)** to become less strict in the way you control something: *It seemed unlikely that Britain would willingly relax her grip on the territories.*

**4 relax rules/controls/regulations etc** to make rules etc less strict: *Hughes believes that immigration controls should not be relaxed.*

**5 relax your vigilance/concentration etc** to reduce the amount of attention you give to something

**re·lax·a·tion** /ˌriːlækˈseɪʃən/ *n* **1** [C,U] a way of resting and enjoying yourself: *I play the piano for relaxation.* | *Playing golf is one of Bruce's favorite relaxations.* **2** [U] the process of making rules on the control of something less strict: [+ **of**] *a relaxation of government controls*

**re·laxed** /rɪˈlækst/ *adj* **1** feeling calm and comfortable and not worried: *Gail was lying in the sun looking very relaxed and happy.* **2** a situation that is relaxed is comfortable and informal: *a relaxed atmosphere*

**re·lax·ing** /rɪˈlæksɪŋ/ *adj* making you feel relaxed: *a relaxing afternoon in the garden*

**re·lay¹** /ˈriːleɪ/ *n* **1 in relays** if people do something in relays, several small groups of them do it, one group after another, so that the activity is continuous **2** [C] a relay race **3** [C,U] a piece of electrical equipment that receives radio or television signals and sends them on

**re·lay²** /ˈriːleɪ‖rɪˈleɪ, ˈriːleɪ/ *v past tense and past participle* **relayed** [T] **1** to pass a message from one person or place to another: **relay sth to sb** *He quickly relayed this news to the other members of staff.* **2** to send out radio or television signals by relay: *The concert will be relayed at 9 p m.*

**re·lay³** /ˌriːˈleɪ/ *v past tense and past participle* **re-laid** /-ˈleɪd/ [T] to lay something such as a CARPET¹ (1) again

**relay race** /ˈ·· ˌ·/ *n* [C] a running or swimming race between two or more teams in which each member of the team takes part one after another

**release¹** /rɪˈliːs/ *v* [T] S W

**1** ▶ **LET SB FREE** ◀ to let someone go free: *The hostages were released in November 1988.* | **release sb from** *They decided to release the bird from its cage.*

**2** ▶ **STOP HOLDING** ◀ to stop holding something that you have been holding tightly or carefully: *The man finally released her arm.* | **release your grasp/grip/hold (on)** *The noise made him release his grasp.*

**3** ▶ **MAKE PUBLIC** ◀ to let news or official information be known and printed: *The new trade figures have just been released.*

**4** ▶ **MACHINERY** ◀ to allow part of a piece of machinery or equipment to move from the position in which it is fixed: *Don't forget to release the handbrake.*

**5** ▶ **FEELINGS** ◀ to express or get rid of feelings such as anger or worry: *Physical exercise is a good way of releasing tension.*

**6** ▶ **FILM/RECORD** ◀ to make a record or film available for people to buy or see

**7** ▶ **CHEMICAL** ◀ to let a substance flow out: *Adrenalin is released in moments of danger.*

**8** ▶ **FROM A DUTY** ◀ to allow someone not to do their duty or work: **release sb from** *She was released from her teaching duties to attend the funeral.*

**9** ▶ **WEAPON** ◀ to make a weapon fly or fall: *The missiles were released from a height of four thousand metres.*

**re·lease²** *n* 

**1** ▶ **FROM PRISON** ◀ [singular, U] the act of allowing someone to go free or being allowed to go free: *She went to the Governor to beg for her son's release.* | [+ **from**] | *Simon has obtained early release from prison.*

**2** ▶ **FEELINGS** ◀ [U] **a)** freedom to show or express your feelings: *Music has always provided me with a form of emotional release.* **b)** a feeling that you are free from the worry or pain that you have been suffering: *that wonderful feeling of release when the examinations are over*

**3** ▶ **RECORD/FILM** ◀ [C] a new record or film: *the band's latest release*

**4 on (general) release** if a film, record etc is on release it has recently become possible to see or buy it

**5** ▶ **OFFICIAL STATEMENT** ◀ [C] an official statement that is made available to be printed or broadcast —see also PRESS RELEASE

**6** ▶ **CHEMICALS** ◀ [U] the act of letting a chemical,

gas etc flow out of its usual container: *the slow release of toxic waste into the rivers*
**7 ▶ MAKING STH AVAILABLE ◀** [U] the act of making something available: *October 22nd is the date set for the report's release.*
**8 ▶ ON A MACHINE ◀** [C] a handle, button etc that can be pressed to allow part of a machine to move

**rel·e·gate** /ˈrelɪgeɪt/ *v* [T] **1** *formal* to give someone or something a less important position than before: *Academic excellence seems to have been relegated to a role of secondary importance.* **2 be relegated (to)** *especially BrE* if a sports team is relegated, it is moved into a lower DIVISION —**relegation** /ˌrelɪˈgeɪʃən/ *n* [U]

**re·lent** /rɪˈlent/ *v* [I] to change your attitude and become less severe or cruel towards someone: *She finally relented and let him borrow the car.*

**re·lent·less** /rɪˈlentləs/ *adj* **1** someone who is relentless never stops being strict, cruel, or determined: [+ **in**] *a regime that was relentless in its persecution of dissidents* **2** something unpleasant that is relentless continues without ever stopping or getting less severe: *the relentless fury of the waves | a relentless struggle for power* —**relentlessly** *adv* | *Kate listened to the rain beating relentlessly against the window.*

S2 W2 **rel·e·vant** /ˈreləvənt/ *adj* directly connected with the subject or problem being discussed or considered: *For further information see the relevant chapters in the users' manual.* | [+ **to**] *These issues are directly relevant to the needs of slow learners.* —opposite IRRELEVANT —**relevance** also **relevancy** *n* [U] | *What you say has no relevance to the subject.* —**relevantly** *adv*

**re·li·a·ble** /rɪˈlaɪəbəl/ *adj* someone or something that is reliable can be trusted or depended on: *She may forget – she's not very reliable.* | *a reliable source of information* —opposite UNRELIABLE —**reliably** *adv* | *We are reliably informed that fighting has broken out between the two factions.* —**reliability** /rɪˌlaɪəˈbɪləti/ *n* [U]

**re·li·ance** /rɪˈlaɪəns/ *n* **1** [singular, U] the state of being dependent on something: [+ **on**] *our country's reliance on imported oil* **2 place reliance on** *formal* to trust someone or something

**re·li·ant** /rɪˈlaɪənt/ *adj* **be reliant on/upon** to depend on someone or something: *In my view she's far too reliant on her parents for financial support.* —see also SELF-RELIANT

**rel·ic** /ˈrelɪk/ *n* **1** [C] an old object or custom that reminds people of the past: *their crisp white uniforms, a relic of British colonial rule | She cleared up the glasses, the only relics of the previous night's party.* **2** [C] a part of the body or clothing of a holy person which is kept after their death because it is thought to be holy: *the sacred relics of John the Baptist* **3 relics** [plural] *old use* someone's dead body

S2 W2 **re·lief** /rɪˈliːf/ *n*
**1 ▶ COMFORT ◀** [singular, U] a feeling of comfort when something frightening, worrying, or painful has ended or has not happened: *I felt a huge surge of relief and happiness.* | **be a relief** *In a way it was a relief to know exactly what we were up against.* | **to your relief** (=making you feel relief) *To our great relief the children all arrived home safely.* | **what a relief!** | *"The boss didn't realize you were late." "What a relief!"* | **a sigh of relief** | *The men went away and she heaved a sigh of relief.*
**2 ▶ REDUCTION OF PAIN ◀** [U] the reduction of pain or unhappy feelings: **pain relief** *the various methods of pain relief available to women in labor* | [+ **of**] *the relief of suffering* | [+ **from**] *Tranquillizers provide only temporary relief from depression.*
**3 ▶ HELP ◀** [U] money, food, clothes etc given to people who are poor or hungry: *a relief fund for refugees*
**4 ▶ MONEY ◀** [U] *especially AmE* money given by the government to help people who are poor, old, unemployed etc; BENEFIT[1] (2) *BrE*
**5 ▶ REPLACE SB ◀** [C] a person or group of people that replaces another one and does their duty after they have finished: *the relief for the military guard | a relief driver*
**6 the relief of** the act of freeing a town when it has been surrounded by an enemy: *the relief of Mafeking*
**7 ▶ DECORATION ◀** [C] a shape or decoration that is raised above the surface it is on
**8 ▶ STICKING OUT ◀ in relief** a shape or decoration that is in relief sticks out above the rest of the surface it is on: **in high/low relief** (=sticking out a lot or a little)
**9 stand out in bold/stark/sharp relief** to be very different from everything around and therefore very easy to notice: *The tree stood out in stark relief against the snow.*
**10 light/comic relief** a funny moment during a serious film, book, or situation: *There wasn't much in the way of light relief on the radio.*
**11 ▶ MAP ◀ in relief** if you show a part of the Earth's surface in relief, you show the differences in height between different parts of it —see also TAX RELIEF

**relief map** /ˈ·ˌ· ·/ *n* [C] a map with the mountains and high parts shown differently from the low parts, especially by being printed in a different colour

**re·lieve** /rɪˈliːv/ *v* [T] S3
**1 ▶ PAIN/PROBLEM ◀** to make a pain, problem, unpleasant feeling less severe: *Drugs helped to relieve the pain.* | *Volunteers were recruited to relieve the acute labour shortage.* | *Adults often swear in order to relieve their feelings.* —see graph at PAIN[1]
**2 relieve the boredom/monotony etc** to make something less dull and boring: *I went for a walk to relieve the boredom of the day.*
**3 relieve yourself** a polite expression meaning to URINATE
**4 ▶ REPLACE SB ◀** to replace someone when they have completed their duty or when they need a rest: *The guard will be relieved at midnight.*
**5 ▶ A TOWN ◀** to free a town which an enemy has surrounded

**relieve** sb **of** sth *phr v* [T] **1** *formal* to help someone by taking something from them, especially a job they do not want to do or something heavy that they are carrying: *Jessie could relieve you of some of the chores.* | *A tall gentleman kindly offered to relieve her of her suitcase.* **2 relieve sb of their post/duties/command etc** *formal* to take away someone's job because they have done something wrong: *After the defeat General Meyer was relieved of his command.* **3** *humorous* to steal something from someone: *A couple of guys I met in the bar relieved me of my wallet.*

**re·lieved** /rɪˈliːvd/ *adj* feeling happy because you are no longer worried about something: *She looked immensely relieved when she heard this news.* | **relieved to see/hear/know sth** *His mother was relieved to see him eating properly again.* | [+ **that**] *I feel so relieved that I haven't got to take that wretched exam again.*

**re·li·gion** /rɪˈlɪdʒən/ *n* **1** [U] people's belief in the life of the spirit and usually in one or more gods: *The theme was the relationship between religion and literature.* | **get religion** *informal* (=suddenly become interested in religion in a way that seems strange to other people) *He got religion in a big way when he was at college.* **2** [C] a particular system of this belief and all the ways of expressing your love for your god, ceremonies, and duties that are connected with it: *Islam and Buddhism are two of the great religions of the world.* | *the Christian religion* | **practise a religion** (=take part in the ceremonies and obey the rules of a religion) **3** [singular] an activity or area of interest which is extremely or unreasonably important in your life: *Football was a religion in my family.* S2 W2

**re·li·gious** /rɪˈlɪdʒəs/ *adj* **1** connected with religion in general or with a particular religion: *I don't go along with her religious beliefs.* | *a religious ceremony* **2** believing strongly in your religion and obeying its rules carefully: *a deeply religious person* S2 W2

**re·li·gious·ly** /rɪˈlɪdʒəsli/ *adv* **1** if you do something religiously, you are always very careful to do it: *I was religiously following all the instructions.* **2** in a way that is connected with religion

R

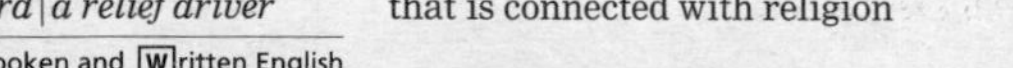

**re·lin·quish** /rɪˈlɪŋkwɪʃ/ *v* [T] *formal* to let someone else have your position, power, or rights, especially unwillingly: *The Duke was obliged to relinquish all rights and claims to the territory.* | **relinquish sth to sb** *He refused to relinquish sovereignty to his son.* | **relinquish your hold/grip on sth** | *Richard stubbornly refused to relinquish his hold on the family business.*

**rel·i·qua·ry** /ˈrelɨkwəri‖-kweri/ *n* [C] a container for religious objects that are connected with holy people

**rel·ish¹** /ˈrelɪʃ/ *v* [T] to enjoy an experience or the thought of something that is going to happen: *Peter didn't really relish the thought of spending Christmas at his in-laws.* | *He spoke calmly, relishing the chance to infuriate his boss.*

**relish²** *n* **1** [U] great enjoyment of something: *There was a certain relish in his voice as he announced the news.* | **with (great) relish** | *She looked forward with relish to the prospect of going abroad for the first time.* **2** [C,U] a SAUCE eaten with food which adds taste to it: *tomato relish*

**re·live** /ˌriːˈlɪv/ *v* [T] to experience something again that happened in the past, or to remember or imagine it very clearly: *We often find ourselves reliving our schooldays when we meet up.*

**rel·lo** /ˈreləʊ‖-loʊ/ *n* [C] *AustrE spoken* a relative: *We're having the rellos over.*

**re·load** /ˌriːˈləʊd‖-ˈloʊd/ *v* [I,T] to put another bullet into a gun, film into a camera, or PROGRAM into a computer: *Reload the pistol, quick!*

**re·lo·cate** /ˌriːləʊˈkeɪt‖riːˈloʊkeɪt/ *v* [I,T] if a group of people or a business relocates, or is relocated, they move to a different place: [**+ to**] *A lot of firms are relocating to the North of England.* | **relocate sb/sth to** *The residents were relocated to temporary accommodation.* —**relocation** /ˌriːləʊˈkeɪʃən‖-loʊ-/ *n* [U]

**re·luc·tant** /rɪˈlʌktənt/ *adj* slow and unwilling: *She gave a reluctant smile.* | **reluctant to do sth** *She seemed reluctant to join in the discussion.* —**reluctance** *n* [singular, U] *He answered these questions with a certain reluctance.* —**reluctantly** *adv*: *Reluctantly, he agreed.*

S2 W2 **re·ly** /rɪˈlaɪ/ *v*

**rely on/upon** sb/sth *phr v* [T] **1** to trust someone or something to do what you need or expect them to do: **rely on sb/sth to do sth** *I think we can rely on Derek not to tell anyone.* | **rely on sb/sth doing sth** *You can't just rely on your parents lending you the money.* | **rely on sb/sth for sth** *Tim always relies on his wife for advice on clothes* **2** to depend on something in order to continue to live or exist: **rely on sth/sb for** *They have to rely on the river for their water.*

S1 W1 **re·main** /rɪˈmeɪn/ *v* **1** [I always + adv/prep, linking verb] to continue to be in the same state or condition: *Would the audience please remain seated?* | *'La Strada' remains one of Fellini's best films.* | *The Government remained in power for twelve years.* **2** [I] *formal* to stay in the same place without moving away: [**+ at/in/with etc**] *She remained at home to look after the children.* **3** [I] to continue to exist, after others have gone or been destroyed: *Little of the original architecture remains.* | *What remains of the original art collection is now in the city museum.* **4** [I] to be left after other things have been dealt with: **remain to be done** *Several points remain to be settled.* | **it only remains for me to say/thank etc** (=used to introduce the last remark in a speech or meeting) *It only remains for me to thank our hosts.* | **the fact remains** (=used to say that a particular fact cannot be ignored) *I know Benson has a PhD but the fact remains he has no practical experience.* **5 it remains to be seen** *spoken* used to say that it is still uncertain whether something will happen or is true: *It remains to be seen whether or not the operation was successful.* —see also REMAINING

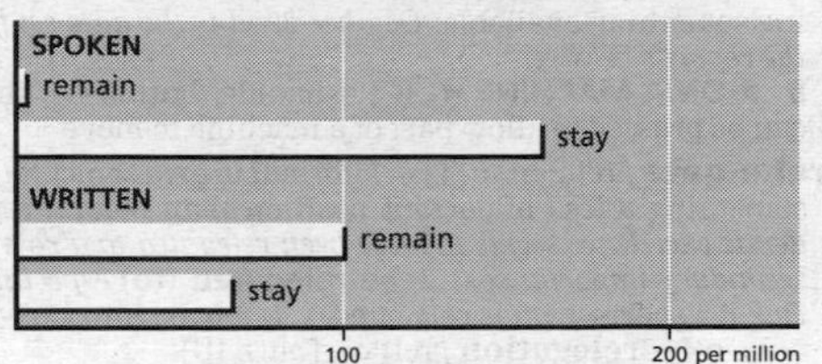


Based on the British National Corpus and the Longman Lancaster Corpus

This graph shows that it is much more usual in spoken English to use **stay** rather than **remain**, which is formal when used in this meaning and is therefore more common in written English.

**re·main·der** /rɪˈmeɪndə‖-ər/ *n* **the remainder** the part of something that is left after everything else has gone or been dealt with: *Please pay half the money now and the remainder when you receive the goods.* | [**+ of**] *The remainder of the class should use this time for study.*

**re·main·ing** /rɪˈmeɪnɪŋ/ *adj* [only before noun] the remaining people or things are those that are left when the others have gone, been used, or been dealt with: *The few remaining guests were in the kitchen finishing off the wine.* | *The only remaining question is whether we can raise the money.*

**re·mains** /rɪˈmeɪnz/ *n* [plural] **1 the remains (of)** the parts of something that are left after the rest has been destroyed or has disappeared: *He ate the remains of the casserole hungrily.* | *the extensive Roman remains* (=of ancient buildings) *at Arles* **2** the body of someone who has died: *Her remains are buried in Westminster.*

**re·make¹** /ˌriːˈmeɪk/ *v past tense and past participle* **remade** /-ˈmeɪd/ [T] **1** to film a story or record a tune again: *The band has just remade an old Frank Sinatra hit.* **2** to build or make something again

**re·make²** /ˈriːmeɪk/ *n* [C] a record or film that has the same music or story as one that was made before

**re·mand¹** /rɪˈmɑːnd‖rɪˈmænd/ *v* [T usually passive] *BrE* to send someone back from a court of law, to wait for their TRIAL¹ (1) | **be remanded in custody** (=be kept in prison until your TRIAL¹ (1))

**remand²** *n* [U] the period of time that someone spends in prison before their TRIAL¹ (1): *remand prisoners* | *a remand centre* | **be on remand** (=in prision waiting for you TRIAL¹ (1)): *Evans committed suicide while on remand in Parkhurst prison.*

**remand home** /ˈ·· ·/ also **remand cen·tre** /ˈ·· ˌ··/ *n* [C] *BrE* a place where young criminals are kept while waiting for a TRIAL¹ (1)

**re·mark¹** /rɪˈmɑːk‖-ɑːrk/ *n* **1** [C] something that you say when you express an opinion or say what you have noticed: **make/pass a remark** *She could hear the other girls making rude remarks about her.* **2 (worthy) of remark** *old use* important enough to be noticed: *Nothing of remark has happened since you left.*

**remark²** *v* [T + **that**] to say something, especially about something you have just noticed: *"That's a lovely shirt you're wearing," she remarked.* | **remark that** *Her father remarked that it was time to leave.*

**remark on/upon** sth *phr v* [T] to notice that something has happened and say something about it: *Everyone remarked on his absence.*

**re·mar·ka·ble** /rɪˈmɑːkəbəl‖-ɑːr-/ *adj* unusual or surprising and therefore deserving attention or praise: *She has made remarkable progress.* | *a remarkable coincidence* | [**+ about**] *There's nothing particularly remarkable about the landscape.* | [**+ for**] *Finland is remarkable for its large number of lakes.*

**re·mar·ka·bly** /rɪˈmɑːkəbli‖-ɑːr-/ *adv* unusually; noticeably [+ adj/adv] *She plays the violin remarkably well for a child of her age.* [sentence adverb] *Remarkably, all of the passengers survived the crash.*

**re·mar·ry** /ˌriːˈmæri/ *v* [I,T] to marry again: *Widowed in 1949, Mrs Hayes never remarried.* —**remarriage** /riːˈmærɪdʒ/ *n* [C]

**re·mas·ter** /riːˈmɑːstə‖-ˈmæstər/ *v* [T] *technical* to use a computer to make a better musical recording from the original: *digital remastering*

**re·me·di·a·ble** /rɪˈmiːdiəbəl/ *adj formal* able to be put right or cured

**re·me·di·al** /rɪˈmiːdiəl/ *adj* **1** aimed at correcting a fault in something, or curing a problem with someone's health: *Some remedial work needs to be done on the foundations.*|*remedial care for head injuries* **2 remedial course/class/teacher etc** a special course etc that helps students who have more difficulty in learning than others: *a remedial program for helping teenagers with basic comunication skills*

3 **rem·e·dy¹** /ˈremɪ̈di/ *n* [C] **1** a way of dealing with a problem or making an unsatisfactory situation better: *Is Government intervention the appropriate remedy?*|[+ **for**] *The law doesn't provide a remedy for this kind of injustice.* **2** a medicine to cure an illness or pain that is not very serious: *an excellent remedy for period pains* **3 beyond/past/without remedy** *formal* if a situation is beyond remedy nothing can be done to make it better: *She felt as if her marital problems were beyond remedy.*

**remedy²** *v* [T] to deal with a problem or improve a bad situation: *The company should act quickly to remedy these grievances.*

1 **re·mem·ber** /rɪˈmembə‖-ər/ *v*
1 **1** [I,T] ▶ **THE PAST** ◀ to have a picture in your mind of people, events, places etc from the past: **remember sb/sth** *Do you remember Rosa Davies?*|*Mr Wilson has lived on our street for as long as I can remember.*|**remember (that)** *I remember you two couldn't stand each other at first!*|**remember sb doing sth** *I remember my father bringing home a huge Christmas tree.*|**remember sb as sth** *I remember Clive as an irritable but tremendously creative man.*|**remember doing sth** *I remember meeting her at a party once.*|**remember well/clearly** *"Do you remember a guy called Casey?" "Sure, I remember him well."*|**vaguely/dimly/scarcely remember** (=not remember well) *I vaguely remember reading something about her husband in the paper.*|**remember correctly/rightly** *They had three children, if I remember rightly.*|**distinctly/vividly remember** *I distinctly remember telling you to be home by 10 o'clock.*
**2** ▶ **INFORMATION/FACTS** ◀ [I,T] to bring information or facts that you know into your mind: *What did I do with my car keys? Oh, I remember, I left them on the kitchen table.*|*I can't remember her phone number.*|[+ **that**] *I suddenly remembered that I'd left the stove on.*|**remember what/how/why etc** *I'm trying to remember whether I said six or seven o'clock.*
**3** ▶ **TO DO/GET SOMETHING** ◀ [I,T] to remember something that you must do, get, or bring: **remember to do sth** *Did you remember to get the bread?*|*Remember to close the windows before you go out.*|**remember sth** *I do hope he remembered the wine.*|*The thing to remember is to keep stirring the sauce.*
**4** ▶ **KEEP STH IN MIND** ◀ to keep a particular fact about a situation in your mind: [+ **that**] *You must remember that we didn't have cars in those days.*
**5** ▶ **HONOUR THE DEAD** ◀ to think about someone who has died with special respect, often in a ceremony: *On this day we remember the dead of two world wars.*
**6 be remembered for sth/as sth** to be famous for something important that you once did: *Bobby Moore will always be remembered as captain of the England squad in 1966.*
**7** ▶ **GIVE SB A PRESENT** ◀ [T] to give someone a present on a particular occasion: *She always remembers me at Christmas.*|**remember sb in your will** (=arrange for someone to have something of yours after you die)
**8 remember me to sb** used to ask someone to give a greeting from you to someone else

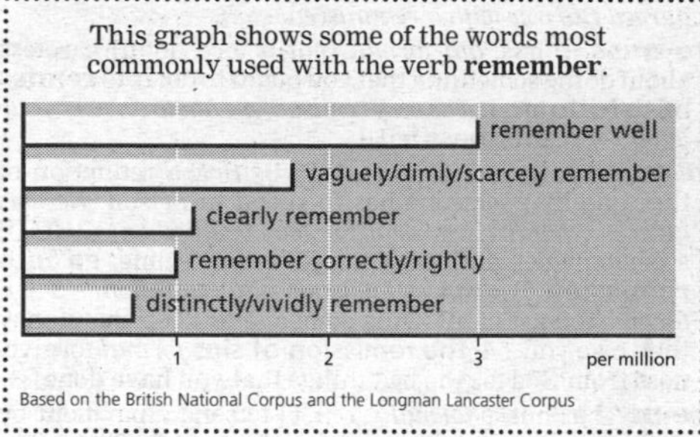


**re·mem·brance** /rɪˈmembrəns/ *n* **1 in remembrance of sb** in order to remember and give honour to someone who has died: *a service in remembrance of those killed in the war* **2** [C,U] *formal* a memory that you have of a person or event: *fond remembrances*

**Remembrance Day** /ˈ·ˌ·· ·/ also **Remembrance Sunday** /ˌ·ˌ·· ˈ··/ *n* the Sunday nearest to November 11th, when a ceremony is held in Britain to remember people who were killed in the two world wars

**re·mind** /rɪˈmaɪnd/ *v* [T] **1** to make someone remember something that they must do: *I must pay the gas bill. I'll put it here to remind me.*|**remind sb about sth** *Will you remind me about that appointment?*|**remind sb to do sth** *"Remind me to buy stamps." "OK."*|**remind sb (that)** *I'll just call Sylvia to remind her that we are meeting at 8.*|**that reminds me** *spoken* (=used when something has just made you remember something you were going to say or do) *Oh, that reminds me, I saw Jenny in town today.*|**remind sb what/how/when etc** *Remind me what to do, I haven't used this machine for ages.*|**remind yourself (to do sth)** *Find some way of reminding yourself to answer letters.* **2** to make someone remember someone that they knew or something that happened in the past: **remind sb of sth** *Hearing that song always reminds me of a certain night in Santa Cruz.*|**remind sb what/how etc** *The letter reminded me what a jerk Jim could be.* **3 Don't remind me** *spoken* used in a joking way when someone has mentioned something that embarrasses or annoys you: *"We've got a test tomorrow." "Don't remind me!"* **4 let me remind you/may I remind you** *spoken formal* used to add force to a warning or criticism: [+ **that**] *Let me remind you that you are expected to arrive on time.* S1 W2

**remind** sb **of** sb/sth *phr v* [T not in progressive] to seem similar to someone or something else: *The view reminded her of Scotland.*|*Corinne reminds me of myself when I was her age.*

**re·mind·er** /rɪˈmaɪndə‖-ər/ *n* **1** [C] something that makes you notice something or understand it better: [+ **of**] *a reminder of the dangers of drinking and driving*|[+ **about**] *Kids need constant reminders about crossing roads safely.*|**be a reminder that** *Occasional bursts of gunfire are a reminder that the battle isn't over yet.*|**serve as a reminder** (=be a reminder) *The President's bodyguards serve as a reminder that he's no ordinary guy out for a walk.* **2** [C] something that reminds you of something that happened or existed in the past: [+ **of**] *Her disability remains as a perpetual reminder of the war years.* **3** something, for example a letter, that reminds you to do something which you might have forgotten

**rem·i·nisce** /ˌremɪ̈ˈnɪs/ *v* [I] to talk or think about pleasant events in your past: [+ **about**] *We walked on, reminiscing about the old days.*

**rem·i·nis·cence** /ˌremɪ̈ˈnɪsəns/ *n* [C,U often plural] a spoken or written story about events that you remember: [+**of/about**] *reminiscences of the war* —compare MEMOIR

**rem·i·nis·cent** /ˌremɪ̈ˈnɪsənt/ *adj* **1 reminiscent of**

reminding you of something: *written in a style strongly reminiscent of Virginia Woolf's novels* **2** [only before noun] thinking about the past: *"Those were the days," agreed Barrow with a reminiscent sigh.*

**re·miss** /rɪˈmɪs/ *adj formal* [not before noun] careless about doing something that you ought to do: **it is remiss of sb to do sth** *It was very remiss of me not to answer your letter.* —**remissness** *n* [U]

**re·mis·sion** /rɪˈmɪʃən/ *n* **1** [C,U] *BrE* a reduction of the time that someone has to spend in prison: *He was given six months' remission for good behaviour.* **2** [C,U] a period when an illness improves for a time: **go into remission** *The cancer has gone into remission.* **3** [U] *formal* the act of allowing someone to keep the money they owe you **4 the remission of sins** *formal* forgiveness from God for the bad things that you have done

**re·mit¹** /rɪˈmɪt/ *v formal* **1** [I,T] to send a payment by post: *Please remit payment by cheque.* **2** [T] to free someone from a debt or punishment —compare UNREMITTING

**remit** sth **to** sb/sth *phr v* [T] *formal* to send a proposal, plan, or problem back to someone for them to make a decision about

**re·mit²** /ˈriːmɪt‖rɪˈmɪt, ˈriːmɪt/ *n* [singular, U] *BrE formal* the particular piece of work that someone has been officially asked to deal with: *It is not part of our remit to criticize government policy.*

**re·mit·tance** /rɪˈmɪtəns/ *n* **1** [C] *formal* an amount of money that you send by post to pay for something **2** [U] the act of sending money by post: **on remittance of** (=when the money has been sent) *We will forward the goods on remittance of £10.*

**re·mit·tent** /rɪˈmɪtənt/ *adj formal* a remittent fever or illness is severe for short periods but improves between those times

**rem·nant** /ˈremnənt/ *n* [C] **1** [usually plural] a small part of something that remains after the rest of it has been used, destroyed, or eaten: *The remnants of a meal stood on the table.* **2** a small piece of cloth left from a larger piece and sold cheap

**re·mod·el** /ˌriːˈmɒdl‖ˌriːˈmɑːdl/ **remodelled, remodelling** *BrE* **remodeled, remodeling** *AmE v* [T] to change the shape or appearance of something: *He was in a terrible accident, and had to have his jaw remodelled.*

**re·mon·strance** /rɪˈmɒnstrəns‖rɪˈmɑːn-/ *n* [C,U] *formal* a complaint or protest: *loud cries of remonstrance*

**rem·on·strate** /ˈremənstreɪt‖rɪˈmɑːn-/ *v* [I] *formal* to tell someone that you strongly disapprove of something they have said or done: [+ **with/against**] *They only stopped teasing after Evans remonstrated with them.* —**remonstrative** /rɪˈmɒnstrətɪv‖-ˈmɑːn-/ *adj*

**re·morse** /rɪˈmɔːs‖-ɔːrs/ *n* [U] a strong feeling of being sorry that you have done something very bad: *When he saw tears in her eyes, he was full of remorse for what he had said.* —**remorseful** *adj* —**remorsefully** *adv*

**re·morse·less** /rɪˈmɔːsləs‖-ˈmɔːr-/ *adj* **1** something unpleasant or threatening that is remorseless continues to happen and seems impossible to stop: *Their coats gave little protection against the remorseless Baltic winds.* **2** cruel, and not caring how much other people are hurt: *Within a few years, our country had been taken over by remorseless European settlers.* —**remorselessly** *adv* | *Stray soldiers were remorselessly hunted down and shot.* —**remorselessness** *n* [U]

**re·mort·gage** /ˌriːˈmɔːgɪdʒ‖-ɔːr-/ *v* [T] to borrow money by having a second MORTGAGE¹ (1) on your house, or increasing the one you have

W3 **re·mote¹** /rɪˈməʊt‖-ˈmoʊt/ *adj* **1** far away in space or time: *remote stars* | *something from the remote past, dimly remembered* | **a remote ancestor** (=someone related to you, who lived a long time ago) **2** far from towns: *As a westerner I was a strange sight in this remote spot.* **3** very different from something: [+ **from**] *It was so alien, so remote from anything he had ever known.* **4 a remote chance/possibility** a very slight chance or possibility: [+ **that**] *There's a remote chance that you will catch him before he leaves.* **5** unfriendly, and not interested in people: *She was quiet and remote, and had an annoying air of superiority.* **6 not have the remotest idea** used to emphasize the fact that you know nothing about something: [+ **what/where/who etc**] *Miranda hasn't the remotest idea where he's gone.* —**remoteness** *n* [C]

**remote²** *n* [C] *spoken* REMOTE CONTROL

**remote con·trol** /ˌ·ˌ· ·ˈ·/ *n* **1** [C] a thing you use for controlling a piece of electrical or electronic equipment without having to touch it, for example for turning a television on or off **2** [U] the process of controlling equipment from a distance, using radio or electronic signals —**remote-controlled** *adj*

**re·mote·ly** /rɪˈməʊtli‖-ˈmoʊt-/ *adv* **not remotely interested/similar/possible etc** not at all interested, similar etc

**remote sens·ing** /·ˌ· ˈ··/ *n* [U] the use of SATELLITES to obtain pictures and information about the Earth

**re·mould¹** /ˈriːməʊld‖-moʊld/ *n* [C] an old tyre with a new surface, that you can use again

**re·mould²** /ˌriːˈməʊld‖-ˈmoʊld/ *v* [T] *formal* to change an idea, system, way of thinking etc: *They don't want to destroy the EC, but remould it in a more appropriate form.*

**re·mount** /ˌriːˈmaʊnt/ *v* [I,T] to get onto a horse, bicycle etc again

**re·mov·a·ble** /rɪˈmuːvəbəl/ *adj* easy to remove: *The chair has a removable cover for easy cleaning.*

**re·mov·al** /rɪˈmuːvəl/ *n* [C,U] **1** the act of taking something away: *We'll arrange for the removal of this rubbish as soon as possible.* | *stain removal* **2** the process of taking furniture from your old house to your new one: **removal company/man etc** *The removal men have been in and out all day.* 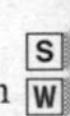

**removal van** /·ˈ·· ·/ *n* [C] *BrE* a large VAN used for moving furniture from one house to another; MOVING VAN *AmE*

**re·move** /rɪˈmuːv/ *v* 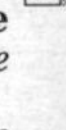

**1 ▶ TAKE AWAY ◀** [T] to take something away from the place where it is: *Do not remove this notice.* | **remove sth from** *Reference books may not be removed from the library.*

**2 ▶ CLOTHES ◀** [T] to take off a piece of clothing: *He removed his hat and gloves.*

**3 ▶ GET RID OF ◀** [T] to get rid of something: *an operation to remove a tumour* | *These reforms will not remove poverty and injustice.*

**4 be far removed from** to be very different from something: *Life in the army was far removed from the comfort of his parents' home.*

**5 removed from** *old use* hidden from someone or something

**6 ▶ FROM A JOB ◀** [T] to force someone out of an important position or dismiss them from a job: [+ **from**] *The governor was removed from office, pending an investigation.*

**7 ▶ PLACE ◀** [I] *old use* to go to live or work in another place: [+ **from/to**] *Our office has removed from Boston to New York.*

**8 cousin once/twice etc removed** the child, GRANDCHILD etc of your COUSIN, or your cousin's father, grandfather etc

**re·mov·er** /rɪˈmuːvə‖-ər/ *n* [C,U] **paint/nail-varnish/stain etc remover** a substance that removes paint marks etc

**REM sleep** /ˈrem sliːp/ *n* [U] a period during sleep when there is rapid movement of the eyes, thought to be a sign that you are dreaming

**re·mu·ne·rate** /rɪˈmjuːnəreɪt/ *v* [T] *formal* to pay someone for something they have done for you —**remuneration** /rɪˌmjuːnəˈreɪʃən/ *n* [C,U] *Our company offers a competitive remuneration package, including a company car.*

**re·mu·ne·ra·tive** /rɪˈmjuːnərətɪv‖-nəreɪtɪv/ *adj formal* making a lot of money —**remuneratively** *adv*

**Re·nais·sance**[1] /rɪˈneɪsəns‖ˈrenəˌsɑːns/ *n* **1 the Renaissance** the period of time in Europe between the 14th and 17th centuries when the art, literature, and ideas of ancient Greece were discovered again, examined, and developed **2 Renaissance art/furniture/architecture etc** art, furniture etc belonging to the Renaissance period

**renaissance**[2] *n* [singular] a new interest in a particular form of art, music etc, that has not been fashionable

**re·nal** /ˈriːnl/ *adj* [only before a noun] *technical* concerning the kidneys (KIDNEY (1)): *acute renal failure*

**re·name** /riːˈneɪm/ *v* [T] [usually passive] to give something a new name: **rename sth sth** *Myddleton Way was renamed Allende Avenue.*

**re·nas·cent** /rɪˈnæsənt/ *adj* [only before a noun] *formal* becoming popular, strong, or important again: *Voters are flooding back to the renascent Labour Party.*

**rend** /rend/ *past tense and past participle* **rent** /rent/ *v* [T] *literary* to tear or break something violently into pieces

**ren·der** /ˈrendə‖-ər/ *v* **1 render sth useless/render sb harmless etc** to make someone or something useless etc: *New laws have rendered this kind of assistance virtually impossible.* **2 render an apology/an explanation/a service etc** *formal* to say sorry to someone, give someone an explanation. etc: **for services rendered** (=in payment for something you have done) **3** [T] to express or present something in a particular way: **render sth as sth** *Through her art, she attempts to render feelings as colors.* | **render sth in sth** *Children soon learn to render their thoughts in speech.* **4 render sth into English/Russian/Chinese etc** *old use* to translate something into English, Russian etc **5** [T] *technical* to spread PLASTER[1] (1) or CEMENT on the surface of a wall

**render** sth ↔ **down** *phr v* [T] to melt fat until it is pure

**render** sth↔ **up** *phr v* [T] *old use* to give something to someone, especially to a ruler or enemy

**ren·der·ing** /ˈrendərɪŋ/ *n* [U] **1** *BrE* the way a play or piece of music is performed; RENDITION (1): *her passionate rendering of Elgar's cello concerto* **2** a material made mainly of CEMENT and sand, used to protect the outside walls of buildings

**ren·dez·vous**[1] /ˈrɒndʒvuː, -deɪ-‖ˈrɑːndeɪ-/ *n plural* **rendezvous 1** [C] an arrangement to meet at a particular time and place: [+ **with**] *a midnight rendezvous with Jose* **2** [C usually singular] a place where two or more people have arranged to meet: *We arrived early at the rendezvous.* **3** [C] a popular place for people to meet: *The bar is a regular rendezvous for media people.*

**rendezvous**[2] *v* [I + **with**] to meet someone as you have arranged

**ren·di·tion** /renˈdɪʃən/ *n* **1** [U] the way a play or piece of music is performed; RENDERING (1) *BrE* **2** [C] a TRANSLATION of a piece of writing: *an English rendition of a Greek poem*

**ren·e·gade** /ˈrenɪgeɪd/ *n especially literary* someone who joins an opposing side in a war, in politics etc: *a renegade, who had once been a leader of the Party* | **renegade soldiers/troops etc** *At the meeting were several renegade Communists.*

**re·nege** /rɪˈniːg, rɪˈneɪg‖rɪˈnɪg, rɪˈniːg/ *v* [I] *formal* **renege on an agreement/a deal etc** to not do something you have promised or agreed to do: *Why has the government reneged on its commitment to the welfare program?*

**re·new** /rɪˈnjuː‖rɪˈnuː/ *v* [T] **1** to arrange for a contract, membership of a club etc to continue: *I must remember to renew the car insurance.* **2** to replace something that is old or broken with something new: *The window frames will have to be renewed.* **3** to begin to do something again, after a period of rest: **renew an attack** *The naval attack was renewed the next morning.* | **renew a friendship/acquaintance etc** (=start a relationship again) **4 renew a book** to arrange to borrow a library book for a further period of time —see also RENEWED

**re·new·a·ble** /rɪˈnjuːəbəl‖rɪˈnuː-/ *adj* **1** a renewable contract, ticket etc can be made to continue after the date on which it ends: *The permit is renewable after 12 months.* **2** something that is renewable can be replaced by natural processes or good management, so that it is never used up: **renewable energy/resources** *Sun, wind and waves provide renewable sources of energy.*

**re·new·al** /rɪˈnjuːəl‖-ˈnuː-/ *n* **1** [singular, U] an act of renewing something: [+ **of**] *a renewal of interest in late Victorian culture* **2 inner city/urban renewal** the process of bringing new jobs, industry, homes etc to the poor areas of large towns

**re·newed** /rɪˈnjuːd‖-ˈnuːd/ *adj* **1 renewed interest/vigour/enthusiasm etc** interest etc that increases again after not being very strong: *renewed concern about the effects of acid rain* **2** [not before noun] feeling healthy and relaxed again, after feeling ill or tired

**ren·net** /ˈrenɪt/ *n* [U] a substance used for making milk thicker in order to make cheese

**re·nounce** /rɪˈnaʊns/ *v* [T] **1** to publicly say that you will no longer keep something, or stay in an important position, because you no longer have the right to it: *The only course left to Nixon was to renounce the presidency.* | **renounce a claim** *James II renounced all claims to the English throne.* **2** to publicly say that you no longer believe in or support something: *Writers and artists were called upon to renounce all bourgeois values.* —see also RENUNCIATION

**ren·o·vate** /ˈrenəveɪt/ *v* [T] to repair and paint a building so that it is in good condition again: *They are living in temporary accommodation while their apartment is being renovated.* —**renovation** /ˌrenəˈveɪʃən/ *n* [U]

**re·nown** /rɪˈnaʊn/ *n* [U] fame and admiration, that you get because of some special skill or something that you have done: [+ **as**] *At college, I'd acquired some renown as a football player.* | **win renown** *She eventually won international renown with her film 'Dispute'.*

**re·nowned** /rɪˈnaʊnd/ *adj* known and admired by a lot of people, especially for some special skill, achievement, or quality: **be renowned for** *The region is renowned for its fine Persian rugs.* | **be renowned as** *Goldman was renowned as a journalist and author.* | **renowned footballer/statesman/architect etc** *The lecture will be delivered by renowned Marxist historian, Jeff Davies.* —see FAMOUS (USAGE)

**rent**[1] /rent/ *v* **1** [I,T] to regularly pay money to live in a house or room that belongs to someone else, or to use something that belongs to someone else: **rent sth from sb** *We rent our apartment from an old retired couple.* | *Nick's been renting for five years now, and he can't afford to buy.* | *a rented video recorder* —see HIRE[1] (USAGE) **2** [T] also **rent ↔ out** to let someone live in a house, room etc that you own, in return for money: *If you can't sell your house, why don't you think about renting it?* | **rent sth out to sb** *She rents out her flat to students.* **3** [T] *especially AmE* to pay money for the use of something for a short period of time; HIRE[1] (1) *BrE*: *Why don't we rent a boat for the afternoon?* **4** [I + **at/for**] if a house rents at or rents for a particular amount of money, that is how much someone pays in order to use it **5 rent-a-crowd/mob etc** people who are willing to take part in a protest about something, even if they do not feel strongly about it

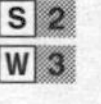

**rent**[2] *n* **1** [C,U] the money that someone pays for the use of a room, a house etc that belongs to someone else: **high/low rent** *Office rents are extremely high in this part of London.* | **pay the rent** *I don't earn enough to pay the rent, let alone run a car.* | **raise the rent/raise rents** (=make someone pay more rent) —see COST[1] (USAGE) **2** [C,U] *especially AmE* an amount of money paid for the use of a car, boat etc that belongs to someone else **3** [C] a large tear in cloth, or a hole shaped like a tear in something: *There were huge rents all down the side of the sofa.*

**rent**[3] the past tense and past participle of REND

**rent·al** /ˈrentl/ *n* **1** [C usually singular] the money that you pay to use a car, television, tools etc over a period of time: *£20 of this telephone bill is for line rental.* **2** [C,U] an arrangement by which you rent something: *TV rentals | rental costs | a video rental shop* **3** [C] *AmE* the act of renting something such as a car or house: *Car rental is expensive in Ohio.* | **rental car** *We had a rental car when we were on vacation.* | **rentals** (=houses for renting) *Are there any summer rentals in this area?*

**rent book** /ˈ· ·/ *n* [C] a small book used to record the amounts and dates of someone's rent payments

**rent boy** /ˈ· ·/ *n* [C] *BrE* a young man who has sex with other men in return for money; a male PROSTITUTE

**rent·ed** /ˈrentɪ̣d/ *adj* **rented accommodation/housing/apartment etc** houses etc that people pay rent for: *financial aid for families living in rented accommodation*

**rent-free** /ˌ· ˈ·◂/ *adj, adv* without payment of rent: *He lives there rent-free.* | *rent-free accommodation*

**rent re·bate** /ˈ· ˌ· ·/ *n* [C] *BrE* money that some people get from local government to help them pay their rent

**rent strike** /ˈ· ·/ *n* [C] a time when all the people living in a group of houses or apartments refuse to pay their rent, as a protest against something

**re·nun·ci·a·tion** /rɪˌnʌnsiˈeɪʃən/ *n* [C,U] *formal* a decision not to keep a particular set of beliefs, way of life, power, or object: **[+ of]** *Eastern Europe's renunciation of Communism.* | *The life of a monk is one of renunciation.*

**re·o·pen** /riˈəʊpən‖-ˈoʊpən/ *v* **1** [I,T] if a theatre, restaurant etc reopens or is reopened, it opens again after being closed **2** [I,T] if you reopen a discussion or law case, or if it reopens, you begin it again after it has stopped: *A report from medical scientists has reopened the debate on tobacco advertising.* **3** [T] if a government reopens the border of their country, they allow people to pass through it again after it has been closed

**re·or·der** /riˈɔːdə‖-ˈɔːrdər/ *v* [I,T] **1** to order a product again: *Stock levels are getting low – we need to reorder.* **2** to change things or put them in a more suitable order: *The whole system needs reordering.*

**re·or·gan·ize** also **-ise** *BrE* /riːˈɔːgənaɪz‖-ˈɔːr-/ *v* [I,T] to arrange or organize something in a new way: *I've reorganized my room so there's space for my new bookcase.* —**reorganization** /riˌɔːgənaɪˈzeɪʃən‖-ɔːrgənə-/ *n* [U]

**rep** /rep/ *n* **1** [C] *informal* a SALES REPRESENTATIVE **2** [C] *informal* someone who speaks officially for a company or organization; REPRESENTATIVE² (1): *You need to speak to the union rep.* **3** [C] *informal* a REPERTORY theatre or company **4** [U] *informal* REPERTORY **5** [C] *AmE informal* a REPUTATION **6 Rep a)** the written abbreviation of REPUBLICAN **b)** the written abbreviation of REPRESENTATIVE

**re·paid** /rɪˈpeɪd/ *v* the past tense and past participle of REPAY

S3 **re·pair¹** /rɪˈpeə‖-ˈper/ *v* [T] **1** to fix something that is damaged, broken, or not working properly: *I'll have to get the car repaired.* | *to repair a broken fence* **2** *formal* to do something to remove the harm that your mistake or wrong action has caused: *How can I repair the wrong I have done her?* —see also IRREPARABLE

**repair to** sth *phr v* [T] *old-fashioned* to go to a place: *Shall we repair to the drawing room?*

S3 W3 **repair²** *n* **1** [C,U] an act of repairing something: *The garage is carrying out repairs on my car.* | **be in need of repair** | *The church roof was badly in need of repair.* | **under repair** (=being repaired) *The road is under repair.* | **beyond repair** (=so damaged that it cannot be mended) *My watch was crushed beyond repair.* | **repair work** (=work to repair something) **2 in good/bad/poor repair** in good or bad condition: *Many of our major roads are in bad repair.* **3** [C] place on something that has been repaired: *The repair on the table top can hardly be seen.* —**repairer** *n* [C]

**re·pair·a·ble** /rɪˈpeərəbəl‖-ˈper-/ *adj* able to be repaired

**rep·a·ra·ble** /ˈrepərəbəl/ *adj formal* a reparable loss is one that you can get back in some way —opposite IRREPARABLE

**rep·a·ra·tion** /ˌrepəˈreɪʃən/ *n* **1 reparations** [plural] money paid by a defeated country after a war, for all the deaths, injuries, and damage it has caused **2** [C,U] *formal* payment made to someone for damage, loss, or injury that you have caused them in the past: **make reparation (to sb) for sth** *No reparation has been made to African countries for the damage of the slave trade.*

**rep·ar·tee** /ˌrepɑːˈtiː‖ˌrepərˈtiː/ *n* [U] conversation which is very fast and full of clever amusing remarks

**re·past** /rɪˈpɑːst‖rɪˈpæst/ *n* [C] *formal or humorous* a meal

**re·pat·ri·ate** /riːˈpætrieɪt‖riːˈpeɪ-/ *v* [T] **1** to send someone back to their own country: *At the end of the war, prisoners were repatriated.* **2** to send profits or money you have earned back to your own country

**re·pay** /rɪˈpeɪ/ *v* **repaid** /-ˈpeɪd/, **repaying** [T] **1** to pay back money that you have borrowed: *The loan must be repaid with interest.* | **repay sb sth** *Jenny repaid her parents the £1000 they lent her.* **2** to reward someone for helping you: **repay sb for sth** *How can I ever repay you for what you've done?* | **repay sb's kindness/generosity etc** *He wanted to repay their kindness, and took them out for a meal.* **3 repay your effort** to seem worth the time you have spent

**re·pay·a·ble** /rɪˈpeɪəbəl/ *adj* money that is repayable at a certain time has to be repaid by that time: *Mortgages are usually repayable over 25 years.*

**re·pay·ment** /rɪˈpeɪmənt/ *n* **1** [U] the act of paying back money: *The rate of repayment is based on your income.* **2** [C] an amount of money that you pay back: *mortgage repayments of about £330 per month*

**re·peal** /rɪˈpiːl/ *v* [T] if a government repeals a law it officially ends that law: *It's high time this grossly unfair law was repealed.* —**repeal** *n* [U] | *the repeal of the prohibition laws*

**re·peat¹** /rɪˈpiːt/ *v* S W

**1 ▶ STATE AGAIN ◀** [T] to say or write something again: *Can you repeat your question?* | **repeat that** *Steven repeated patiently that he was busy.* —see SAY¹ (USAGE)

**2 ▶ DO AGAIN ◀** [T] to do something again: *Repeat the treatment twice a day if necessary.* | *Anyone who gets less than 45% will have to repeat the test.*

**3 ▶ ACHIEVE STH AGAIN ◀** [T] to achieve the same results, or the same high level of performance: *Other scientists are trying to repeat these results.* | *Can he repeat his success of 1993?*

**4 ▶ LEARN ◀** [T] to say something you have learned: *Sandra repeated the poem hesitantly.* | **repeat after sb** *Repeat after me: amo, amas, amat...*

**5 ▶ TELL STH YOU HEAR ◀** [T] to say something that you have heard someone else saying: *Don't repeat this to anyone but I think Derek's got a new girlfriend.*

**6 repeat yourself** to say something that you have already said without realizing that you have done it: *Mrs Fardell repeats herself a bit, but she's very good for 85.*

**7 ▶ BROADCAST ◀** [T often passive] to broadcast a television or radio programme again: *'Omnibus' will be repeated at 10 o'clock on Tuesday.*

**8 ▶ FOOD ◀** [I + **on**] *informal* if food repeats on you, its taste keeps coming back into your mouth after you have eaten it

**9 sth doesn't bear repeating** used to say that you do not want to repeat what someone has said, especially because it is rude: *Her comments about her ex-husband just don't bear repeating!*

**10 history repeats itself** used to say that an event is like something that happened before

**repeat²** *n* [C] **1** a television or radio programme that has been broadcast before: *There's nothing but repeats on the TV tonight.* **2** an event very like something that happened before: **[+ of]** *The England-Holland match was basically a repeat of last year's game at Wembley.* | **repeat performance** (=something bad that happens again) *Last year's holiday was a disaster – we don't want a repeat performance this year.* **3 repeat order** a supply of the same products to a customer who has ordered them before **4 repeat prescription** *BrE* an order for medicine that you have had before, which you can get without seeing your doctor **5** *technical* the sign at the end of a line of written music that tells the performer to play the music again, or the act of playing the music again

**re·peat·ed** /rɪˈpiːtɪ̈d/ *adj* [only before noun] done or happening again and again: *repeated calls for change | repeated failure*

**re·peat·ed·ly** /rɪˈpiːtɪ̈dli/ *adv* many times: *Graham was repeatedly warned by the doctors to not work so hard.*

**re·peat·er** /rɪˈpiːtə‖-ər/ *n* [C] *technical* a repeating gun or clock

**re·peat·ing** /rɪˈpiːtɪŋ/ *n* [C] **1** a repeating gun can be fired several times without being loaded again **2** a repeating watch or clock can be made to repeat the last STRIKE (=sound made at an hour or quarter of an hour)

**re·pel** /rɪˈpel/ *v* **repelled, repelling** **1** [T] if something repels you, you want to avoid it because you do not like it: *Her heavy make-up and cheap scent repelled him.* **2** [T] to fight a group or military force and make them stop attacking you: *repel invaders | repel an attack* **3** [T] to keep something or someone away from you: *Fire repels wild animals.* **4** [I,T] *technical* if two things repel each other they push each other away with an electrical force

**re·pel·lent¹** /rɪˈpelənt/ *adj* **1** nasty or very unpleasant: *Stories about famous villains can be both repellent and fascinating.* **2 water repellent** water repellent material does not let water pass through it

**repellent², repellant** *n* [C,U] a substance that keeps insects away: *mosquito repellent*

**re·pent** /rɪˈpent/ *v* [I,T] **1** a word meaning to be sorry for something you have done, used especially in a religious context: [+ **of**] *Repent of your sins and you will be forgiven.* **2** *formal* to be sorry for something and to wish you had not done it: **repent doing sth** *I began to repent parting with you.* | **repent sth** *He repented his decision.*

**re·pen·tance** /rɪˈpentəns/ *n* [U] the state of being sorry for something you have done

**re·pen·tant** /rɪˈpentənt/ *adj formal* sorry for something wrong that you have done —opposite UNREPENTANT —**repentantly** *adv*

**re·per·cus·sion** /ˌriːpəˈkʌʃən‖-pər-/ *n* **1 repercussions** [plural] the results of an action or event, especially a bad one, that continue to have an effect for some time, in complicated and unexpected ways: *The break-up of communism has had world-wide repercussions.* **2** [C] *technical* a sound or force coming back after it hits something

**rep·er·toire** /ˈrepətwɑː‖-pərtwɑːr/ *n* [C usually singular] **1** all of the plays, pieces of music etc, that a performer or group has learned and can perform **2** the total number of things that someone or something is able to do: *the behavioral repertoire of newborn infants*

**rep·er·to·ry** /ˈrepətəri‖ˈrepərtɔːri/ *n* **1** [U] a type of theatre work in which actors perform different plays on different days, instead of doing the same play for a long time: *a repertory company* **2** [C] a repertoire

**rep·e·ti·tion** /ˌrepɪ̈ˈtɪʃən/ *n* **1** [U] doing the same thing many times: [+ **of**] *his constant repetition of the same old jokes | In my day, everything was learned by repitition.* **2** [C] something that is done again: [+ **of**] *I don't want a repetition of this incident.*

**rep·e·ti·tious** /ˌrepɪ̈ˈtɪʃəs◂/ *adj* saying the same thing several times: *a boring, repetitious style*

**re·pet·i·tive** /rɪˈpetɪ̈tɪv/ *adj* done many times in the same way: *She hated the tedious, repetitive household tasks.* —**repetitively** *adv*

**repetitive strain in·ju·ry** /ˌ·ˌ··· ˈ· ˌ···/ *n* [U] *technical* RSI; pains in your hands, arms etc caused by doing the same hand movements very many times

**re·phrase** /ˌriːˈfreɪz/ *v* [T] to express something in different words so that its meaning is clearer or more acceptable: *OK. Let me rephrase the question.*

S2 W1 **re·place** /rɪˈpleɪs/ *v* [T] **1** to start doing something instead of another person, or being used instead of another thing: *I'm replacing Sue on the team. | These PCs replace the old system network.* **2** to remove someone from their job or something from its place, and put a different person or thing there: *Well, if he can't manage he'll have to be replaced.* | **replace sth with sth** *They're replacing the old windows with double glazing.* **3** to get something new to put in the place of something that has been broken, stolen etc: *I'll replace the vase I broke as soon as possible.* **4** to put something back in its correct place: *He replaced the book on the shelf.* —**replaceable** *adj*

**re·place·ment** /rɪˈpleɪsmənt/ *n* **1** [U] the act of replacing something, often with something newer, better etc: *Those tyres are badly in need of replacement.* **2** [C] someone or something that replaces another person or thing: [+ **for**] *It will be difficult to find a replacement for Ted.* | **replacement car/bulb/battery** *We'll need a replacement bulb for the hall light.* W3

**re·play¹** /ˌriːˈpleɪ/ *v* [T] **1** to play a game of sport again: *The game ended in a draw and will be replayed on Wednesday.* **2** to play something again that has been recorded: *We replayed all the romantic bits of the video.*

**re·play²** /ˈriːpleɪ/ *n* [C] **1** a game of sport that is played again: *Milan won the semi-final replay 3–0.* **2** a piece of action in a game of sport seen on television, that is immediately shown again: *You can see on the replay that the goalkeeper was clearly fouled.* **3** *informal* something that is done exactly as it was before: *a replay of the same mistakes*

**re·plen·ish** /rɪˈplenɪʃ/ *v* [T + **with**] *formal* to fill something again or put new supplies into something —**replenishment** *n* [U]

**re·plete** /rɪˈpliːt/ *adj* [not before noun] **1** *formal* fully supplied with something: [+ **with**] *a book replete with diagrams* **2** *old-fashioned* so full of food or drink that you want no more —**repletion** /rɪˈpliːʃən/ *n* [U]

**rep·li·ca** /ˈreplɪkə/ *n* [C] a very good copy, especially of a painting or other work of art: [+ **of**] *The model was an exact replica of the Taj Mahal.*

**rep·li·cate** /ˈreplɪ̈keɪt/ *v* [T] *formal* to do or make something again, so that you get the same result or make an exact copy —**replication** /ˌreplɪ̈ˈkeɪʃən/ *n* [C, U]

**re·ply¹** /rɪˈplaɪ/ *v* **1** [I,T] to answer someone by saying or writing something: *I asked Clive where he was going but he didn't reply.* | [+ **to**] *You must reply to Dennis's letter soon.* | **reply that** *I can only reply that I did not realise what was happening.* | *"That's what I expected," replied Mandy.* —see ANSWER¹ (USAGE) **2** [I] to react to an action by doing something else: [+ **to/with**] *The terrorists replied to their threats with violence.* 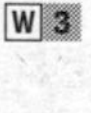

**reply²** *n* [C] **1** something that is said, written, or done as a way of replying: [+ **to**] *We've had 60 replies to our advertisement so far.* | **make no reply** (=not reply) *I asked him if I could help, but he made no reply.* | *The only reply was a burst of gunfire.* **2 in reply to** *formal* as a way of replying to something: *I am writing in reply to your letter of 1st June.* **3 without reply** if a sports team gets a number of points or goals (GOAL (2)) without reply, their opponents get no points 

**reply-paid** /ˌ· ˈ·◂/ *adj* a reply-paid envelope has had the cost of a stamp already paid by the person who sent it

**re·po man** /ˈriːpəʊ mæn‖-poʊ/ *n* [C] *informal* someone whose job is to REPOSSESS (=take away) cars that have not been paid for

**re·port¹** /rɪˈpɔːt‖-ɔːrt/ *n* **1** [C] a written or spoken description of a situation or event, giving people the information they need: *the chairman's report* | [+ **on/of**] *police reports of the accident* **2** [C] a piece of writing in a newspaper about something that is happening, or part of a television or radio news programme: *We're getting reports from the scene of the fighting.* | *a weather report* **3** [C] an official piece of writing that carefully considers a particular subject, and is often written by a group of people: [+ **on/of**] *a recent report on child abuse* —see graph at NEWS **4** [C, U] things people say that may or S2 W1

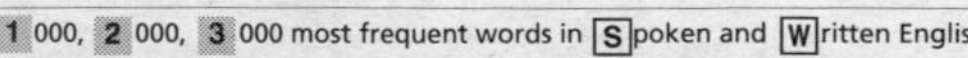

may not be true; RUMOUR: *According to reports he's not coming back.* **5** *BrE* [C] a written statement by teachers about a child's work at school, sent to their parents; REPORT CARD *AmE*: *Dad promised me a new bike if I got a good report.* **6** [C] *formal* the noise of an explosion or shot: *a loud report*

S3 W1 **report²** *v*
**1 ▶ NEWS ◀** [I,T] to give people information about recent events, especially in newspapers and on television and radio: *This is Gavin Williams, reporting from the United Nations in New York.* | **report sth** *We aim to report the news as fairly as possible.* | **[+ on]** *The Post sent her to Bangladesh to report on the floods.* | **report that** *The newspapers reported that he had died in a car accident.* | **report doing sth** *They reported having seen the remains of the body.* | **be reported to be** *He is reported to have been driving whilst drunk.*
**2 ▶ JOB/WORK ◀** [I,T] to tell someone about what has been happening, or what you are doing as part of your job: **report (to sb) on** *Come back next week to report on your progress.* | *Anything to report, Sergeant?*
**3 ▶ PUBLIC STATEMENT ◀** [T] to officially give information to the public: *Scientists are due to report the first step towards the development of an AIDS vaccine.*
**4 ▶ CRIME/ACCIDENT ◀** [T] to tell the police or someone in authority that an accident or crime has happened: *I'd like to report a theft.* | **report sth to sb** *All accidents must be reported to the safety officer.* | **report sb/sth missing** *The plane was reported missing in heavy fog.*
**5 ▶ COMPLAIN ◀** [T] to complain about someone to people in authority: *Robert reported Guy for smoking in school.* | **report sb to sb** *Kevin was eventually reported to the police.*
**6 ▶ ARRIVAL ◀** [I] to go somewhere and officially state that you have arrived: **[+ to]** *All visitors must report to the site office.*
**7 report sick** to officially tell your employers that you cannot come to work because you are ill
**report back** *phr v* [I,T] to bring or send back an account of something: **[+ to]** *Find out and report back to me quickly.* | **report back that** *The soldiers reported back that enemy forces were moving towards the border.*
**report to** sb *phr v* [T] to be responsible to someone at work and be managed by them: *The accountants report to the Deputy Financial Director.*

**re·port·age** /rɪˈpɔːtɪdʒ, ˌrepɔːˈtɑːʒ‖-ɔːr-/ *n* [U] **1** the particular style of reporting used in newspapers, radio or television **2** the act of reporting news

**report card** /-ˈ· ·/ *n AmE* a written statement by teachers about a child's work at school, sent to their parents; REPORT *BrE*

**re·port·ed·ly** /rɪˈpɔːtɪ̇dli‖-ɔːr-/ *adv* [sentence adverb] according to what people say: *He is reportedly not intending to return to this country.*

**reported speech** /ˌ·· ˈ·/ *n* [U] the style of speech or writing used to report what someone says without repeating their actual words; INDIRECT SPEECH —compare DIRECT SPEECH

S3 **re·port·er** /rɪˈpɔːtə‖-ˈpɔːrtər/ *n* [C] someone who writes about events for a newspaper, radio, or television —compare JOURNALIST —see also COURT REPORTER

**re·pose¹** /rɪˈpəʊz‖-ˈpoʊz/ *n* [U] *formal* a state of calm or comfortable rest —**reposeful** *adj*

**repose²** *v formal* **1** [I] if something reposes in a place it is put there: **[+ on]** *Two small glasses reposed on the tray.* **2** [I] if someone reposes somewhere they rest there **3 repose your trust/hope etc in sb** to trust someone to help you

**re·pos·i·to·ry** /rɪˈpɒzɪ̇təri‖rɪˈpɑːzɪ̇tɔːri/ *n* [C] **1** a place where things are stored in large quantities: *a furniture repository* **2** *formal or humorous* a person or book that gives a lot of information: *Matthew is a repository of football statistics.*

**re·pos·sess** /ˌriːpəˈzes/ *v* [T] to take back cars, furniture, or property from people who cannot pay for them as they had arranged: *Eventually the bailiffs came to repossess the flat.* —**repossession** /-ˈzeʃən/ *n* [C,U]

**rep·re·hend** /ˌreprɪˈhend/ *v* [T] *formal* to express disapproval of a person or an action

**rep·re·hen·si·ble** /ˌreprɪˈhensɪ̇bəl/ *adj formal* reprehensible behaviour is bad and deserves criticism: **[+ of]** *It was really reprehensible of you to leave such young children alone.*

S W **rep·re·sent** /ˌreprɪˈzent/ *v*
**1 ▶ SPEAK FOR SB ◀** [T] **a)** to speak officially for another person or group of people, giving their opinions and taking action for them: *Mr Kobayashi was chosen to represent the company at the conference.* | *He was represented in court by a famous criminal lawyer.* **b)** to say or do something that expresses the feelings, opinions etc of a group of people: *The protesters represented only a small section of public opinion.*
**2 be represented** to have sent someone from your group to a meeting, ceremony etc: *All the local societies and clubs were represented in the parade.*
**3 represent an improvement/an obstacle/a challenge etc** *formal* used to say that something should be thought of as a particular thing: *This essay represents a considerable improvement on your recent work.*
**4 ▶ GOVERNMENT ◀** [T] to be the member of a parliament or other law making institution, such as the Congress, for a particular area: *Does Kathryn Walker still represent Worcester?* | *He represents the 8th Congressional District of Illinois.*
**5 ▶ A SIGN ◀** [T] to be a sign or mark that shows the position of a particular thing, especially on a map or plan; SYMBOLIZE: *The red lines on the map represent railways.*
**6 ▶ SHOW STH ◀** [T] to be a picture or STATUE of something: *This painting represents the first settlers arriving in America.*
**7 represent yourself as** to say that you are something that you are not: *They represented themselves as the party of low taxation.*
**8 represent sb as** to describe someone in a particular way, so that people have a particular opinion of them: *Shakespeare represents Richard III as a black-hearted villain.*

**re-pre·sent** /ˌriː prɪˈzent/ *v* [T] to give, offer, or send something again, especially an official document: *The phone company re-presented the bill for payment.*

S W **rep·re·sen·ta·tion** /ˌreprɪzenˈteɪʃən/ *n* **1** [U] the state of having representatives to speak, vote, or make decisions for you: *Minority groups need more effective parliamentary representation.* | *Paul appeared in court without any representation.* —see also PROPORTIONAL REPRESENTATION **2** [U] the act of representing someone or something **3** [C] a painting, sign etc that shows or describes something else: *This painting is a representation of a storm at sea.* **4 representations** [plural] *especially BrE* official complaints made in a formal way: **make representations about/to** *A group of students made representations to the college about bad accommodation.*

**rep·re·sen·ta·tion·al** /ˌreprɪzenˈteɪʃənəl/ *adj* a representational painting or style of art shows things as they actually appear in real life —compare ABSTRACT¹ (3)

**Rep·re·sen·ta·tive** /ˌreprɪˈzentətɪv◂/ *n* [C] a member of the House of Representatives, the Lower House of Congress in the United States

**representative¹** *adj* **1** like other members of the same group; typical: **[+ of]** *Are your opinions representative of the views of all the students?* **2** a representative system of government allows everyone to express their opinions by voting for representatives: *Change is needed if we are to have a fully representative democracy.*

S W **representative²** *n* [C] **1** a person who has been chosen to speak, vote, or make decisions for someone else: **[+ of]** *an elected representative of the people* **2 Representative** a member of the House of Representatives, the Lower House of Congress in the United States —see also SALES REPRESENTATIVE

**re·press** /rɪˈpres/ *v* [T] **1** to stop yourself expressing a feeling: *I could hardly repress my laughter.* **2** to control a group of people by force —compare SUPPRESS (1)

**re·pressed** /rɪˈprest/ *adj* having feelings or desires that you do not allow yourself to express: *a repressed child | I was boiling over with repressed anger.*

**re·pres·sion** /rɪˈpreʃən/ *n* **1** [U] very strong control of feelings or desires which you are ashamed of, until you no longer know that you have them: *years of sexual repression* **2** [U] cruel and severe control of a large group of people: *fleeing from repression* **3** [C] an act of repressing people, or a feeling that is repressed

**re·pres·sive** /rɪˈpresɪv/ *adj* a repressive system of government or law is severe and cruel: *a repressive regime, which imprisoned thousands | an old-fashioned and repressive education system* —**repressively** *adv* —**repressiveness** *n* [U]

**re·prieve¹** /rɪˈpriːv/ *v* [T usually passive] to officially stop a prisoner from being killed as a punishment

**reprieve²** *n* [C] an official order stopping the killing of a prisoner as a punishment: *A last minute reprieve saved him.*

**rep·ri·mand** /ˈreprɪmɑːnd‖-mænd/ *v* [T] to tell someone officially that something they have done is very wrong: *The military court reprimanded him for failing to do his duty.* —**reprimand** *n* [C] | *a severe reprimand*

**re·print¹** /ˌriːˈprɪnt/ *v* [I,T] if a book is reprinted or reprints, more copies are printed because the first ones have been sold

**re·print²** /ˈriːprɪnt/ *n* [C] an act of printing a book again because all the copies of it have been sold

**re·pri·sal** /rɪˈpraɪzəl/ *n* [C,U] also **reprisals** [plural] an act of violence or other strong reaction, to punish your enemies or opponents for something they have done: *They didn't tell the police for fear of reprisal.* | **in reprisal (for)** *prisoners killed in reprisal for the raid*

**re·prise** /rɪˈpriːz/ *n* [C] the repeating of all or part of a piece of music, film etc

**re·proach¹** /rɪˈprəʊtʃ‖-ˈproʊtʃ/ *n formal* **1** [U] blame or disapproval for the things you have done: *"Are you going already?" he cried, his voice full of reproach.* | **beyond/above reproach** *formal* (=impossible to criticize; perfect) *His behaviour throughout this affair has been beyond reproach.* **2** [C] a remark that expresses criticism or disapproval: *Her question was clearly a reproach.* **3 a reproach to** something that makes a person, society etc feel bad or ashamed; DISGRACE¹: *These derelict houses are a reproach to the city.*

**reproach²** *v* [T] **1** *formal* to blame or criticize someone in a way that shows you are disappointed, but not angry: **reproach sb for/with sth** *She reproached me for my lack of foresight.* | **reproach sb for doing sth** *Jake reproached her bitterly for abandoning him.* **2 reproach yourself** to feel guilty about something that you think you are responsible for: *You've got nothing to reproach yourself for – it was his own decision.*

**re·proach·ful** /rɪˈprəʊtʃfəl‖-ˈproʊtʃ-/ *adj* a reproachful look, remark etc shows that you are criticizing someone or blaming them: *She shot me a reproachful glance.* —**reproachfully** *adv*

**rep·ro·bate** /ˈreprəbeɪt/ *n* [C] *formal or humorous* someone who behaves in an immoral way: *an old reprobate who spent all his money on gin*

**re·pro·cess** /riːˈprəʊses‖-ˈprɑː-/ *v* [T] to treat a waste substance so that it can be used again

**re·pro·duce** /ˌriːprəˈdjuːs‖-ˈduːs/ *v* **1** [I,T] if a plant or animal reproduces, or reproduces itself, it produces young plants or animals: *Fish reproduce by laying eggs.* **2** [T] to make a photograph or printed copy of something: *This edition reproduces the original text in full.* **3** [T] to make something that is just like something else, or make something happen again in the same way as it happened the first time: *British scientists have so far been unable to reproduce these results.* | *They try to reproduce the exact sounds of early music.* —**reproducible** *adj*

**re·pro·duc·tion** /ˌriːprəˈdʌkʃən◂/ *n* **1** [U] the act or process of producing young animals or plants: *Reproduction may not take place in poor conditions.* **2** [U] the act of producing a copy of a book, picture, piece of music etc: *Unauthorized reproduction of this publication is strictly forbidden.* | *high quality sound reproduction* **3** [C] a copy of a work of art, piece of furniture etc: *a cheap reproduction of a famous painting* | **reproduction furniture/chairs etc** *a reproduction Louis XIV table*

**re·pro·duc·tive** /ˌriːprəˈdʌktɪv◂/ *adj* [only before noun] **1** connected with the process of producing young animals or plants: *the human reproductive system* **2** connected with the copying of books, pictures, music etc: *the reproductive quality of audio tape*

**re·proof** /rɪˈpruːf/ *n formal* **1** [U] blame or disapproval: *She felt the reproof of her father's gaze.* **2** [C] a remark that blames or criticizes someone: *a sharp reproof*

**re·prove** /rɪˈpruːv/ *v* [T] *formal* to criticize someone for something that they have done: **reprove sb for doing sth** *I was reproved for wasting good paper.*

**re·prov·ing** /rɪˈpruːvɪŋ/ *adj formal* expressing criticism of something that someone has done: *There was a reproving tone in her voice.* —**reprovingly** *adv*

**rep·tile** /ˈreptaɪl‖ˈreptl/ *n* [C] **1** a type of animal such as a snake or LIZARD whose blood changes according to the temperature around it, and that usually lays eggs **2** *informal* someone who is unpleasant or cannot be trusted: *That reptile must have told the police!*

**rep·til·i·an¹** /repˈtɪliən/ *adj* like a reptile or connected with reptiles

**reptilian²** *n* [C] *technical* a reptile

**re·pub·lic** /rɪˈpʌblɪk/ *n* [C] a country governed by elected representatives of the people, and led by a president, not a king or queen —compare MONARCHY W2

**re·pub·li·can¹** /rɪˈpʌblɪkən/ *adj* **1** connected with or supporting a system of government that is not led by a king or queen and is elected by the people **2 Republican** connected with or supporting the Republican Party (=one of the two main political parties in the US) **3 Republican** connected with or supporting political parties that want Northern Ireland to become part of the Republic of Ireland, not part of the United Kingdom —**republicanism, Republicanism** *n* [U]

**republican²** *n* [C] **1** someone who believes in government by elected representatives only, with no king or queen **2 Republican** a member or supporter of the Republican Party in the US **3 Republican** someone from Northern Ireland who believes that Northern Ireland should become part of the Republic of Ireland, not the United Kingdom

**re·pu·di·ate** /rɪˈpjuːdieɪt/ *v* [T] *formal* **1** to refuse to accept something; REJECT¹ (1): *He repudiated all offers of friendship.* **2** to state formally that something is untrue or incorrect: *I repudiate emphatically any suggestion that I have acted dishonourably.* **3** *old-fashioned* to state that you no longer have any connection with someone, especially a relative; DISOWN **4** to refuse to pay a debt —**repudiation** /rɪˌpjuːdiˈeɪʃən/ *n* [U]

**re·pug·nance** /rɪˈpʌgnəns/ *n* [U] *formal* a strong feeling of dislike for something very unpleasant or morally wrong: *They shrank back from what they saw, with looks of repugnance etched on their faces.*

**re·pug·nant** /rɪˈpʌgnənt/ *adj formal* very unpleasant and offensive: *I find his political beliefs completely repugnant.*

**re·pulse¹** /rɪˈpʌls/ *v* [T] *formal* **1** to defeat a military attack: *They attacked with cavalry but were repulsed.* **2** if something or someone repulses you, you feel they are very unpleasant: *The very thought of his cold clammy hands repulsed me.* —see also REPULSIVE (1) **3** to refuse an offer of friendship or help in a way that is rude

**repulse²** *n* [singular] **1** *formal* the act of rudely refusing when someone offers to help you or be your friend **2** *technical* the defeat of a military attack

**re·pul·sion** /rɪˈpʌlʃən/ *n* **1** [singular, U] a feeling that you want to avoid something or move away from it, because it is very unpleasant **2** [U] *technical* the electric or MAGNETIC force by which one object pushes another one away from it —opposite ATTRACTION

**re·pul·sive** /rɪˈpʌlsɪv/ *adj* **1** very unpleasant: *What a repulsive man!* **2** *technical* repulsive forces push objects away from each other —**repulsively** *adv* —**repulsiveness** *n* [U]

**rep·u·ta·ble** /ˈrepjətəbəl/ *adj* respected for being honest or for doing good work: *a very reputable firm* —**reputably** *adv*

W3 **rep·u·ta·tion** /ˌrepjəˈteɪʃən/ *n* [C] **1** the opinion that people have about a particular person or thing because of what has happened in the past: [+ **for**] *a reputation for honesty and efficency* | [+ **as**] *She had already begun to establish a reputation as a writer.* | **a good/bad reputation** *This restaurant has a very good reputation.* | **win/earn/establish a reputation as** *His approach had won him a reputation as a tough manager.* **2 live up to your reputation** to behave in the way that people expect: *Martin lived up to his reputation and arrived late.* **3 live up to its reputation** to be at least as bad or good as people had thought: *a mountain that lived up to its fearsome reputation*

**re·pute** /rɪˈpjuːt/ *n* [U] *formal* **1** reputation: **of good/evil/international etc repute** *a man of good repute* **2** a good reputation: *a hotel of some repute*

**re·put·ed** /rɪˈpjuːtəd/ *adj* [only before noun] according to what most people say or think, but not definitely: *the reputed billionaire Pablo Escobar* | **be reputed to be/do sth** *She is reputed to be extremely wealthy.*

**re·put·ed·ly** /rɪˈpjuːtədli/ *adv* [sentence adverb] according to what most people say or think: *The committee had reputedly spent over $3000 on 'business entertainment'.*

S2 W2 **re·quest**[1] /rɪˈkwest/ *n* **1** [C] a polite or formal demand for something: [+ **for**] *They have made an urgent request for international aid.* | **request that** *He ignored the neighbours' requests that he should make less noise.* | **at sb's request** (=because they asked you to) *I telephoned her in Paris, at Staunton's request.* | **on request** (=when you ask for it) *Further details will be sent on request.* | **by request** (=because someone has especially asked for it) *There were no flowers at the funeral, by request.* | **any requests?** *spoken* (=used to ask people if they want anything) *I'm going to the bar – any requests?* **2** [C] a piece of music that is played on the radio because someone has asked for it

S3 **request**[2] *v* [T] **1** *formal* to ask for something politely or formally: *I wrote them a letter, officially requesting permission to proceed.* | **request that** *The staff immediately requested that he reconsider his decision.* | **request sb to do sth** *All club members are requested to attend the annual meeting.* **2** to ask for a particular piece of music to be played on the radio: *This song was requested by Mrs Simpson of Potters Bar.*

**USAGE NOTE: REQUEST**

WORD CHOICE: **ask (for), request, demand**

**Ask** is the usual word for speaking or writing to someone in order to get something done: *I asked one of my friends to help me.* You use **ask for** when you are trying to get something: *I asked for help.*

**Request** is more formal and official. Also if you **request** something, often you have the right to get what you are asking for: *The letter politely requested that Miss Willis present herself for interview the next day.* | *The government has requested a meeting with community leaders.*

**Demand** is even stronger. If you **demand** something, you feel strongly that you have the right to it: *I demand to see the manager!*

GRAMMAR

You **request** something (NOT **request for** sth). But you do use **for** with the noun: *requests for money* (NOT *requests of money*).

**req·ui·em** /ˈrekwiəm, ˈrekwiem/ also **requiem mass** /ˌ··· ˈ·/ *n* [C] **1** a Christian religious ceremony of prayers for someone who has died **2** a piece of music written for this ceremony

**re·quire** /rɪˈkwaɪə‖-ˈkwaɪr/ *v* [T not in progressive] **1** if a problem, or situation requires particular action it makes it necessary: *It's a matter that requires very careful handling.* | *What's required is a complete reorganization of the system.* **2** to need something: *These plants require moist soil at all times.* **3** [usually passive] to officially demand that people do something, because of a law or rule: **require sb to do sth** *You are required by law to wear seat belts.* | [+ **that**] *Regulations require that students attend at least 90% of the lectures.* | **the required standard/level/period etc** *You have not yet reached the required standard to pass grade 3.* **4** *formal* used to ask someone what they need: *Is there anything further you require, sir?* S W

Frequencies of the verbs **require** and **need** in spoken and written English.

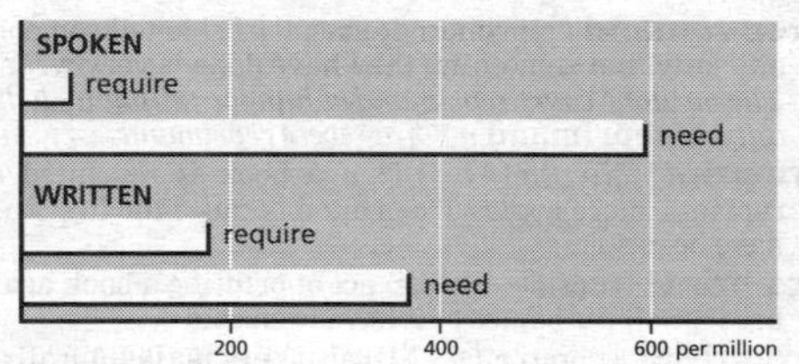


Based on the British National Corpus and the Longman Lancaster Corpus

This graph shows that **need** is much more common than **require** in both spoken and written English. **Require** is more formal than **need** and is therefore more common in written English than in spoken English.

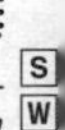

**re·quire·ment** /rɪˈkwaɪəmənt‖-ˈkwaɪr-/ *n* [C] **1** something that is needed or asked for: *The refugees' main requirements are food and shelter.* | **meet a requirement** (=have what is necessary) *The new computer system will meet all our requirements.* **2** something that a college, employer etc says you must have: *The minimum requirement was a degree in engineering.*

**req·ui·site** /ˈrekwəzət/ *adj formal* needed for a particular purpose: *He lacks the requisite qualifications.*

**req·ui·sites** /ˈrekwəzəts/ *n* [plural] *formal* a word meaning things that are needed for a particular purpose, used especially in shops: *The airport shops sells toilet requisites.*

**req·ui·si·tion**[1] /ˌrekwəˈzɪʃən/ *v* [T] to officially demand to have something, especially so that it can be used by an army: *Troops had requisitioned houses in the town.*

**requisition**[2] *n* [C,U] an official demand to have something, usually made by an army or military authority

**re·quit·al** /rɪˈkwaɪtl/ *n* [U] *formal* **1** payment for something done or given **2** something that you do to harm someone who has harmed you

**re·quite** /rɪˈkwaɪt/ *v* [T] *formal* to give or do something in return for something done or given to you in the past

**re·re·lease** /ˌriː rɪˈliːs/ *v* [T] if a record or film is re-released, it is produced and sold for a second time, usually with small changes —**re-release** /ˈriː rɪliːs/ *n* [C]

**re·route** /ˌriːˈruːt‖-ˈruːt,-ˈraʊt/ *v* [T] to send vehicles in a different direction from the normal one

**re·run**[1] /ˈriːrʌn/ *n* [C] **1** a film or old television programme that is being shown again **2** something that happens in the same way as something that happened before: *The government wants to avoid a rerun of last year's currency crisis.* **3** a race or competition that is held again

**re·run²** /riːˈrʌn/ *v* [T] **1** to show a film or recorded television programme again **2** to arrange for a race or competition to be held again

**re·sched·ule** /ˌriːˈʃedjuːl‖-ˈskedʒʊl, -dʒəl/ *v* [T] **1** to arrange for something to happen at a different time, because the time you had planned is no longer convenient: *The press conference had to be rescheduled for March 19.* **2** *technical* to arrange for a debt to be paid back later than was originally agreed

**re·scind** /rɪˈsɪnd/ *v* [T] to officially end a law, decision, or agreement that has been made in the past

rescue

**res·cue¹** /ˈreskjuː/ *v* [T] to save someone or something from a situation of danger or harm: *Hundreds are still in the water, waiting to be rescued.* | **rescue sb/sth from** *She died trying to rescue her children from the blaze.* | *a final attempt to rescue the company from ruin* —**rescuer** *n* [C]

**rescue²** *n* [C] an occasion when someone or something is rescued from danger: *a daring rescue at sea* | **rescue team/attempt/bid etc** *A rescue team is trying to reach the trapped miners.* | **come to the rescue** (=help someone in danger or difficulty) *His father came to his rescue and lent him the money.*

2 1 **re·search¹** /rɪˈsɜːtʃ, ˈriːsɜːtʃ‖-ɜːr-/ *n* [U] also **researches** [plural] **1** serious study of a subject, that is intended to discover new facts or test new ideas: **[+into/on]** *research into the causes of cancer* | **research project/student/grant etc** *Alison is a research student in our lab.* **2** the activity of finding information about something that you are interested in or need to know about: **do research** *I'm doing some research for an article about student life.* | *I've done some research – it looks as if the train will be fastest.* —see also MARKET RESEARCH, R AND D

**re·search²** /rɪˈsɜːtʃ‖-ɜːr-/ *v* [T] **1** to study a subject in detail, especially in order to discover new facts or test new ideas: *He's researching the effects of aerosols on the environment.* **2** to supply all the necessary facts and information for something: *This book has been very well researched.* —**researcher** *n* [C]

**research and de·vel·op·ment** /ˌ.. . ˈ..., ˌ.. . . ˈ...‖/ *n* [U] R AND D

**re·sell** /ˌriːˈsel/ *v past tense and past participle* **resold** /-ˈsəʊld‖-ˈsoʊld/ [T] to sell something that you have bought: *The retailer resells the goods at a higher price.*

**re·sem·blance** /rɪˈzembləns/ *n* [C,U] a SIMILARITY between two things, especially in the way they look: **[+ between]** *You can see the resemblance between Susan and her sister.* | **bear a resemblance to** (=look like) *He bears a remarkable resemblance to Kurt Russell.*

**re·sem·ble** /rɪˈzembəl/ *v* [T not in progressive or passive] to look like, or be similar to, someone or something: **closely resemble** *Mick closely resembled his father.*

**re·sent** /rɪˈzent/ *v* [T] to feel angry or upset about a situation or about something that someone has done, especially because you think that it is not fair: **resent doing sth** *He resents having to get my permission first.* | **greatly/strongly/bitterly resent** *She greatly resented her brother's refusal to help.*

**re·sent·ful** /rɪˈzentfəl/ *adj* feeling angry and upset about something that you think is unfair: **[+ of/at/about etc]** *His daughters became increasingly resentful of his authority.* —**resentfully** *adv* | *"You should have told me," said Marion resentfully.* —**resentfulness** *n* [U]

**re·sent·ment** /rɪˈzentmənt/ *n* [U] a feeling of anger because something has happened that you think is unfair

**res·er·va·tion** /ˌrezəˈveɪʃən‖-zər-/ *n* **1** [C] an arrangement made so that a place is kept for you in a hotel, restaurant, plane etc; BOOKING (1) | **make a reservation** *Customers are advised to make seat reservations well in advance.* **2** [C,U] a feeling of doubt because you do not agree completely with a plan, idea, or suggestion: **have/express reservations (about)** *I had serious reservations about his appointment as captain.* | **without reservation** (=completely) *We condemn their actions without reservation.* **3** [C] an area of land in the US kept separate for Native Americans to live on: *a Navajo reservation* **4** [C] *especially AmE* an area of land where wild animals can live without being hunted; RESERVE: *a game reservation* —see also CENTRAL RESERVATION S3

**re·serve¹** /rɪˈzɜːv‖-ɜːrv/ *v* [T] **1** to arrange for a place in a hotel, restaurant, plane etc to be kept for you: *Do you have to reserve tickets in advance?* | *I'd like to reserve a table for two.* **2** to keep something so that it can be used by a particular person or for a particular purpose: **reserve sth for sb** *These seats are reserved for the elderly and disabled.* | *Reserve a little of the mixture to sprinkle over the top of the pie.* **3** to use or show something only in one particular situation: **reserve sth for** *a tone of voice she usually reserved for dealing with officials* **4 reserve the right to do sth** *formal* an expression meaning that you will do something if you think it is necessary, used especially in notices or official documents: *The management reserves the right to refuse admission.* W3



**reserve²** *n* **1** [C] also **reserves** *plural* an amount of something kept for future use, especially for difficult or dangerous situations: **[+ of]** *reserves of food* | *an inner reserve of strength* **2 in reserve** ready to be used if needed unexpectedly: *We always keep some money in reserve, just in case.* **3** [U] a quality in someone's character that makes them not like expressing their emotions or talking about their problems: *His characteristic detachment and reserve made it difficult to guess his thoughts.* **4** [C] someone who will play in a sports team if one of the other players is injured or ill **5** [C] a price limit below which something will not be sold, especially in an AUCTION **6** [U] also **reserves** a military force that a country has in addition to its usual army

**re·served** /rɪˈzɜːvd‖-ɜːr-/ *adj* **1** unwilling to express your emotions or talk about your problems: *Ellen was a shy, reserved girl.* **2** kept specially to be used by one particular person: *I'm sorry, but this seat's reserved.* | *reserved parking spaces* | **[+ for]** *The front row is reserved for the family of the bride.* **3 all rights reserved** used at the end of printed or recorded material to show that it is illegal to copy it without special permission —**reservedly** /rɪˈzɜːvɪ̣dli‖-ɜːr-/ *adv* —**reservedness** *n* [U] —see also UNRESERVED

**reserve price** /ˈ.. ./ RESERVE² (5)

**re·serv·ist** /rɪˈzɜːvɪ̣st‖-ɜːr-/ *n* [C] a soldier in the reserve (RESERVE² (6)), who is trained to fight and may join the professional army during a war

**res·er·voir** /ˈrezəvwɑː‖-ərvwɑːr, -vɔːr/ *n* [C] **1** a lake, especially an artificial one, where water is stored before it is supplied to people's houses **2** a large amount of something that has not yet been used: *She found she had reservoirs of unexpected strength.* **3** *technical* a place where something, such as liquid, is kept before it is used —see picture at ENGINE

**re·set¹** /ˌriːˈset/ *v past tense and past participle* **reset** *present participle* **resetting** [T] **1** to change a clock, control etc so that it shows a different time or number **2** to put a broken bone back into its correct place: *The doctor reset the fracture.* **3** to load an OPERATING SYSTEM for a small computer from a DISK into the computer's memory; BOOT² (2) **4** to put a jewel into a new piece of jewellery

5 to write a new set of questions for an examination 6 *technical* to make new pages from which to print a book: *The book had to be reset because there were so many mistakes in the first printing.* —**reset** *n* [C,U]

**re·set²** /ˈriːset/ *adj* a reset button is used to make a machine or instrument ready to work again

**re·set·tle** /riːˈsetl/ *v* **1** [I,T] to go to live in a new country or area, or help people to do this: *Many Ugandan Asian families resettled in Canada.*|*tribesmen who were forcibly resettled by the government* **2** [T] to start using an area again as a place to live: *The area was resettled in the latter half of the century.* —**resettlement** *n* [U]

**re·shuf·fle¹** /riːˈʃʌfəl/ *v* [T] *BrE* to change around the jobs of the people who work in an organization, especially in government: *The Prime Minister reshuffled his cabinet.*

**re·shuffle²** /riːˈʃʌfəl, ˈriːʃʌfəl/ *n* [C] *BrE* the act of changing around the jobs of people who work in an organization, especially in a government: *a Cabinet reshuffle*

**re·side** /rɪˈzaɪd/ *v* [I always + adv/prep] *formal* to live in a particular place

**reside in** sth/sb *phr v* [T not in passive] *formal* **1** to be present in something: *For Fellini, the poetry of cinema resides primarily in movement.* **2** also **reside within** sth/sb if a power, right etc resides in something or someone, it belongs to them

**res·i·dence** /ˈrezɪdəns/ *n* **1** [C] *formal* **a)** a house, especially a large one **b)** the place where an AMBASSADOR (=important representative from a foreign country) lives **2** [U] **a)** the state of living in a place **b)** permission to live somewhere permanently **3 in residence a)** *formal* living in a place or present there **b)** a student who is in residence is at their university **4 artist/poet/playwright etc in residence** an artist etc who has been officially chosen by a college or other institution to work there and to help the students **5 take up residence** *fomal* to start live in a place: *He's taken up residence in an old castle.* —see also HALL OF RESIDENCE

**res·i·dent¹** /ˈrezɪdənt/ *adj* **1** *formal* living in a place: [+ **in**] *Many retired British people are now resident in Spain.* **2** [only before noun] living or working in a particular place or institution: *a resident tutor* **3** [only before noun] *humorous* belonging to a particular group: *He's our resident expert on computer games.*

S2 W3 **resident²** *n* [C] **1** someone who lives or stays in a place such as a house or hotel: *Only residents can drink in the hotel bar.* **2** *AmE* a doctor working at a hospital where he is being trained; REGISTRAR (2) *BrE*

W3 **res·i·den·tial** /ˌrezɪˈdenʃəl◂/ *adj* **1** a residential part of a town consists of private houses, with no offices or factories: *a quiet residential street* **2** living at a place while you are doing something, or in order to do something: **a residential job/course/patient etc** *a residential school for the deaf*|*a weekend residential course*

**residential care** /ˌ····ˈ·/ *n* [U] a system of professional care for people who are too old or ill to look after themselves at home

**residential treat·ment fa·ci·li·ty** /ˌ····ˈ···ˌ···/ *n* [C] *AmE technical* an expression meaning a MENTAL HOSPITAL, used because you want to avoid saying this directly

**resident phy·si·cian** /ˌ···ˈ··/ *n AmE* a RESIDENT² (2)

**residents' as·so·ci·a·tion** /ˈ·····ˌ··/ *n* [C] an association of people who meet to discuss the problems and needs of the area where they live

**re·sid·u·al** /rɪˈzɪdʒuəl/ *adj* [only before noun] *formal* remaining after a process, event etc is finished: *There was still some residual unrest after the rebellion had been crushed.*|**residual income** (=the money left from what you earn after you have paid your taxes)

**res·i·due** /ˈrezɪdjuː‖-duː/ *n* [C] **1** *technical* a substance that is left after a chemical process: *a sticky residue in the bottom of the test-tube* **2** the part of something that is left after the rest has gone or been taken away: [+ **of**] *The residue of his estate goes to his daughter.*

W **re·sign** /rɪˈzaɪn/ *v* [I,T] **1** to officially and permanently leave your job or position because you want to: [+ **from**] *She's just resigned from the committee.*|**resign your post/position** *The manager was forced to resign his post after allegations of corruption.* **2 resign yourself to sth/to doing sth** to make yourself accept something that is unpleasant but cannot be changed: *You must resign yourselves to waiting a bit longer.* —see also RESIGNED

W **res·ig·na·tion** /ˌrezɪgˈneɪʃən/ *n* **1** [C,U] the act of resigning, or a written statement to say you are doing this: *You have the choice between resignation and dismissal.*|**hand in your resignation/tender your resignation** (=resign) *Guess what? Roy's handed in his resignation.* **2** [U] the act of calmly accepting a situation that cannot be changed though it is unpleasant: *She accepted her fate with resignation.*

**re·signed** /rɪˈzaɪnd/ *adj* **1** a resigned look, sound etc shows that you are making yourself accept something that you do not like: *a resigned look on her face*|*He sounded resigned and dejected.* **2 be resigned to sth/to doing sth** to accept a situation that you do not like, but cannot change: *Isabelle seems resigned to the fact that she's dying.* —**resignedly** /rɪˈzaɪnɪdli/ *adv*

**re·sil·i·ence** /rɪˈzɪliəns/ also **re·sil·i·en·cy** /-liənsi/ *n* [U] **1** the ability to return quickly to your usual health or state of mind after suffering an illness, difficulties etc: *resilience of character* **2** the ability of a substance to return to its former shape when pressure is removed; FLEXIBILITY

**re·sil·i·ent** /rɪˈzɪliənt/ *adj* **1** someone who is resilient quickly becomes healthy or happy again after an illness, difficulty, change etc: *I wouldn't worry – kids are very resilient.* **2** a resilient substance returns to its former shape when pressure is removed —**resiliently** *adv*

**res·in** /ˈrezɪn/ *n* **1** [U] a thick sticky liquid that comes out of some trees **2** [C] an artificial plastic substance that is produced chemically and used in industry —**resinous** *adj*

W **re·sist** /rɪˈzɪst/ *v* **1** [T] to try to prevent change or prevent yourself being forced to do something: *Demonstrators today violently resisted attempts to evict them from the building.*|*I was in their power, and knew it was pointless to resist.* **2** [I,T] to oppose or fight someone or something: *The city resisted the enemy onslaught for two weeks.* **3** [I,T usually in negatives] to stop yourself having something that you like very much or doing something that you want to do: **cannot resist sth/doing sth** *I just can't resist chocolates.*|*I couldn't resist sneaking a look at her diary.*|**hard/impossible to resist** *It's hard to resist an invitation like that.*|**resist the temptation/impulse etc** *She resisted the temptation to tell him what she really thought.* **4** [T] to not be changed or harmed by something: *A balanced diet will increase your ability to resist infection.* **5 resist arrest** to try to prevent the police from taking you to the police station —**resistable** *adj*

S W **re·sist·ance** /rɪˈzɪstəns/ *n*

**1 ▶ AGAINST CHANGE ◀** [singular, U] a refusal to accept new ideas or changes: *When you introduced computerized billing, was there much resistance from consumers?*|[+ **to**] *There has been a lot of resistance to this new law.*

**2 ▶ FIGHTING ◀** [singular, U] fighting against someone or something that is attacking you: **put up/offer resistance** (=resist) *The defenders put up strong resistance.*

**3 ▶ AGAINST INFECTION/ILLNESS ◀** [singular, U] the natural ability of an animal or plant to stop diseases from harming it: *Vitamins can build up your resistance to colds and flu.*

**4 wind resistance/air resistance etc** the degree to which a moving object, such as a car or plane, is made to move more slowly by the air it moves through

**5 ▶ ELECTRICITY ◀** [U] the degree to which a substance can stop an electric current passing through

**6 the resistance** an organization that secretly fights

against an enemy that now controls their country: *Mitterand was in the French Resistance during the war.*
**7 take the line of least resistance** to do the easiest thing in a difficult situation
**8 ▶ EQUIPMENT ◀** [C] a RESISTOR —see also PASSIVE RESISTANCE

**re·sis·tant** /rɪˈzɪstənt/ *adj* **1** not damaged or affected by something: [+ **to**] *This type of flu is resistant to antibiotics.* **2** opposed to something and wanting to prevent it happening: [+ **to**] *The Club is resistant to any form of change.* **3 heat-resistant/fire-resistant** something that is heat-resistant etc will not be damaged by heat etc

**re·sis·tor** /rɪˈzɪstə‖-ər/ *n* [C] a piece of wire or other material used for increasing electrical resistance

**re·sit** /ˌriːˈsɪt/ *v past tense and past participle* **resat**, *present participle* **resitting** [T] *especially BrE* to take an examination again —**resit** /ˈriːsɪt/ *n* [C]

**re·skill·ing** /ˌriː ˈskɪlɪŋ/ *n* [U] *BrE* the teaching of new work skills, especially to unemployed people

**res·o·lute** /ˈrezəluːt/ *adj* doing something in a very determined way because you have very strong beliefs, aims etc —opposite IRRESOLUTE —**resolutely** *adv*: *She resolutely resisted his amorous advances.* —**resoluteness** *n* [U]

3 **res·o·lu·tion** /ˌrezəˈluːʃən/ *n*
**1 ▶ DECISION ◀** [C] a formal decision or statement agreed on by a group of people, especially after a vote: *The resolution was passed by a two-thirds majority.*
**2 ▶ SOLUTION ◀** [singular, U] the act of finding a way to deal with a difficulty: *The lawyer's advice led to the resolution of this problem.*
**3 ▶ DETERMINATION ◀** [U] *approving* the quality of having strong beliefs and determination
**4 ▶ PROMISE ◀** [C] a promise to yourself to do something: **make a resolution** *Carol made a resolution to work hard at school this year.* | **New Year's resolution** (=a resolution made on January 1st) *a New Year's resolution to stop smoking* —compare RESOLVE²
**5 ▶ CLEARNESS ◀** [C,U] the power of a television, camera, MICROSCOPE etc to give a clear picture of things, or a measure of this: *a high resolution microscope*

3 **re·solve¹** /rɪˈzɒlv‖rɪˈzɑːlv, rɪˈzɒːlv/ *v* **1** [T] to find a satisfactory way of dealing with a problem or difficulty; settle: *negotiations to resolve the dispute* | *There weren't enough beds, but the matter was resolved by George sleeping on the sofa.* **2** [I,T] to make a definite decision to do something: **resolve to do sth** *After the divorce she resolved never to marry again.* | **resolve that** *Mary resolved that she would try to work harder.* **3** [I,T] to make a formal decision, especially by voting: **resolve to do sth** *The Senate resolved to accept the President's budget proposals by 70 votes to 30.* **4** [T] to separate something into its different parts
**resolve** sth **into** sth *phr v* [T] **1** *technical* to separate or become separated into parts: *This mixture will resolve into two separate compounds.* **2 resolve itself into** to gradually change into something else; become: *The argument resolved itself into an uneasy truce.*

**resolve²** *n* [U] *formal* strong determination to succeed in doing something: *His encouragement and support strengthened our resolve.*

**res·o·nance** /ˈrezənəns/ *n* **1** [U] the deep, loud, continuing quality of a sound: *the resonance of his voice* **2** [C,U] *formal* the special meaning that something has for you because it is connected with your own experiences **3** [C,U] *technical* sound that is produced or increased in an object by sound waves from another object

**res·o·nant** /ˈrezənənt/ *adj* **1** a resonant sound is deep, loud, clear, and continues for a long time **2 resonant with** filled with a particular sound: *The air was resonant with the shouts of children.* **3** *technical* resonant materials increase any sound produced inside them —**resonantly** *adv*

**res·o·nate** /ˈrezəneɪt/ *v* [I] **1** to make a deep, loud, clear sound that continues for a long time **2** to make a sound that is produced as a reaction to another sound
**resonate with** sth *phr v* [T] **1** *formal* to be full of a particular meaning or feeling: *Literature that resonates with biblical imagery.* **2** to be full of a sound: *a hall resonating with laughter*

**res·o·na·tor** /ˈrezəneɪtə‖-ər/ *n* [C] a piece of equipment for making the sound louder in a musical instrument

**re·sort¹** /rɪˈzɔːt‖-ɔːrt/ *n* **1** [C] a place where people often go for holidays: **seaside/beach/mountain etc resort** *a seaside resort south of Tokyo* | **resort hotel/beach/town** *Jan and Matt run a small resort hotel in Vermont.* **2 as a last resort/in the last resort** used to say what you will do if everything else fails: *As a last resort we could borrow more money on the house.* | **of last resort** (=used when everything else has failed) *a weapon of last resort* **3 have resort to** *formal* to do something bad or extreme because you cannot think of any other solution: *It may be necessary to have resort to force.* **4** [C] *AmE* a hotel for people on holiday W3

**resort²** *v*
**resort to** sth *phr v* [T] to use something or do something that is bad, in order to succeed or deal with a problem: *When polite requests failed Paul resorted to threats.* | **resort to doing sth** *Sally resorted to stealing when her money ran out.*

**re·sound** /rɪˈzaʊnd/ *v* [I] **1** if a place resounds with a sound it is full of it; ECHO¹ (2) [+ **with/to**] *The hall resounded with laughter and cheering.* **2** if a sound such as a musical note resounds, it continues loudly and clearly for quite a long time: [+ **through/around etc**] *a horn resounding through the forest*

**re·sound·ing** /rɪˈzaʊndɪŋ/ *adj* **1** [only before noun] a resounding noise is so loud that it seems to continue for a few seconds: *The vase fell to the floor with a resounding crash.* **2 resounding success/victory/defeat etc** a very great or complete success, etc, that many people know about: *The show, Five Guys Named Moe, was a resounding success.* —**resoundingly** *adv*

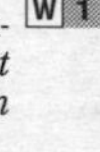

**re·source¹** /rɪˈzɔːs, -ˈsɔːs‖ˈriːsɔːrs/ *n*
**1 ▶ OIL/COAL ETC ◀** [C often plural] something such as land, minerals, or natural energy that exists in a country and can be used to increase its wealth: *Canada's vast mineral resources* | **natural resources** *a country rich in natural resources*
**2 ▶ MONEY/PROPERTY ETC ◀ resources** [plural] all the money, property, skills etc that you have available: *We must make the best possible use of our limited financial resources.* | *resources for research and development* | **pool your resources** (=put together all the resources that each of you can provide)
**3 ▶ PERSONAL QUALITIES ◀ resources** [plural] personal qualities, such as courage and a strong mind, that you need to deal with a difficult situation: **inner resources** *Martin has inner resources that will see him through this crisis.* —see also HUMAN RESOURCES
**4 ▶ EDUCATIONAL ◀** [C] something such as a book, film, or picture used by teachers or students to provide information: *resources for learning* | *a valuable new computer resource* | **resource room/centre etc** (=a room, building etc where resources are kept)
**5 ▶ PRACTICAL ABILITY ◀** [U] *formal* ability in dealing with practical problems; RESOURCEFULNESS: *a man of great resource*

**re·source²** /rɪˈzɔːs, -ˈsɔːs‖-ˈsɔːrs/ *v* [T] *technical* to provide money or other resources for something: *The program failed because it wasn't adequately resourced.*

**re·source·ful** /rɪˈzɔːsfəl, -ˈsɔːs-‖-ɔːr-/ *adj approving* good at finding ways of dealing with practical problems: *a resourceful woman who could cope in almost any circumstances* —**resourcefully** *adv* —**resourcefulness** *n* [U]

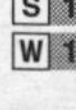

**re·spect¹** /rɪˈspekt/ *n*
**1 ▶ ADMIRATION ◀** [U] admiration for someone, especially because of their personal qualities, knowledge or skill: [+ **for**] *I have the greatest respect for Jane's*

*judgment.* | **win/earn/gain the respect of** *With his decisive handling of the dispute, he had won the respect of everyone.* | **command the respect of** (=have and deserve someone's respect) *Dr Weiss commands the respect of all who know him.* —opposite DISRESPECT
**2 with (the greatest) respect/with (all) due respect** *spoken formal* used to politely introduce an expression of disagreement: *With respect, sir, I think you're quite wrong.*
**3 ▶ CONSIDERATION ◀** [U] an attitude of regarding something or someone as important so that you are careful not to harm them, treat them rudely etc: [+ **for**] *Out of respect for the wishes of her family, the affair was not reported in the newspapers.* | *children who show no respect for authority* | **treat sb/sth with respect** *Old people deserve to be treated with more respect.*
**4 ▶ FOR DANGER ◀** [U] a careful attitude towards something or someone that is dangerous: [+ **for**] *Forbes has always shown a healthy respect for the treacherous currents of the Yangtze.*
**5 in one respect/in some respects/in every respect** used to say that something is true in one way, in some ways, or in every way: *In many respects the new version is not so good as the old one.* | *Aunt Arabella is very stubborn. Kim takes after her in that respect.*
**6 ▶ GREETINGS ◀ respects** [plural] *formal* polite greetings: **give/send your respects** *Give my respects to your wife.* | **pay your respects** (=make a polite visit) *I've come to pay my respects to the countess.*
**7 pay your last respects (to)** to go to someone's funeral
**8 in respect of** *formal* **a)** concerning or in relation to: *This is especially true in respect of the United Kingdom.* **b)** an expression meaning in payment for, used in business letters: *The builder will be paid £300 in respect of the work already done.*
**9 with respect to** *formal* used to introduce a new subject, or to return to one that has already been mentioned: *With respect to your other proposals, I am not yet able to give you our decision.* —see also SELF-RESPECT

**respect²** *v* [T] **1** [not in progressive] to admire someone because they have high standards and good personal qualities such as fairness and honesty: *He's not the most popular teacher, but the students respect him.* | *John had always respected Matthew's opinion.* | **respect sb for** *Molly always told us exactly what she thought, and we respected her for that.* **2** to be careful not to do anything against someone's wishes, rights etc: *I promise to respect your wishes.* | *The President is expected to respect the constitution.*

**re·spec·ta·bil·i·ty** /rɪˌspektəˈbɪlɪ̈ti/ *n* [U] the quality of being considered morally correct and socially acceptable: *The couple exuded an air of quiet respectability.*

**re·spec·ta·ble** /rɪˈspektəbəl/ *adj* **1** having standards of behaviour, appearance etc that are socially acceptable and approved of: *a respectable married woman* | *nice children from respectable homes* | *Let's make you look a bit more respectable before you go out.* **2** *informal* good or satisfactory: *a respectable income* | *Her exam results were respectable, although not brilliant.* —**respectably** *adv* —**respectableness** *n* [U]

**re·spect·ed** /rɪˈspektɪ̈d/ *adj* admired by many people because of your work, achievements etc: *a highly respected journalist*

**re·spect·er** /rɪˈspektə‖-ər/ *n* [C] **be no respecter of persons** to be equally harmful towards all people whether they are rich or poor, important or ordinary: *Disease is no respecter of persons.*

**re·spect·ful** /rɪˈspektfəl/ *adj* feeling or showing respect: *The soldiers bowed their heads in respectful silence as the funeral procession went by.* —opposite DISRESPECTFUL —**respectfully** *adv* —**respectfulness** *n* [U]

**re·spec·tive** /rɪˈspektɪv/ *adj* [only before noun] people's respective jobs, houses, families etc are the various ones that each of them has: *The two friends said goodbye and went their respective ways.*

 **re·spec·tive·ly** /rɪˈspektɪvli/ *adv* each separately in the order mentioned: *My two sons, Adam and Alexander, are five and nine respectively.*

**res·pi·ra·tion** /ˌrespɪ̈ˈreɪʃən/ *n* [U] *technical* the process of breathing —see also ARTIFICIAL RESPIRATION

**res·pi·ra·tor** /ˈrespɪ̈reɪtə‖-ər/ *n* [C] a piece of equipment that you wear over your nose and mouth to help you breathe in a place where there is gas, smoke etc

**the human respiratory system**

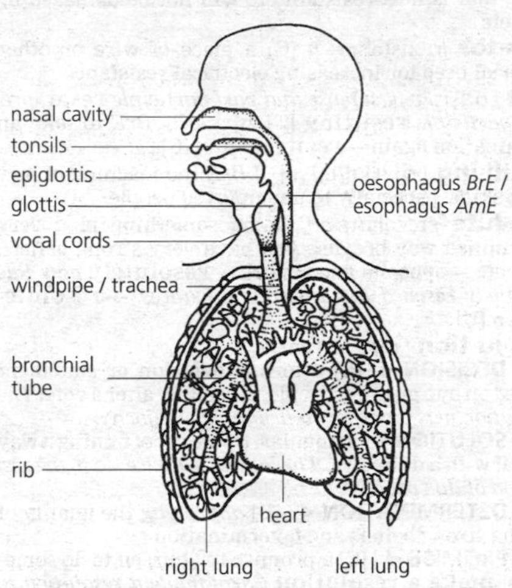


**re·spi·ra·to·ry** /rɪˈspɪrətəri, ˈrespɪ̈reɪtəri, rɪˈspaɪərə-‖ˈrespərətɔːri, rɪˈspaɪrə-/ *adj formal or technical* connected with breathing: *respiratory diseases* | *the respiratory system*

**res·pite** /ˈrespɪt, -paɪt‖-pɪt/ *n* [singular, U] **1** a short time when something unpleasant stops happening, so that the situation is temporarily better: [+ **from**] *a welcome respite from the constant pressure of work* | **without respite** *The noise went on all night without even a moment's respite.* **2** a short period of delay before you have to do something that is unpleasant: *We have a few days' respite before we need to pay the rent.*

**re·splen·dent** /rɪˈsplendənt/ *adj formal* very beautiful, bright and shining in appearance: *the resplendent colours of the New England woods in the fall* —**resplendence** *n* [U] —**resplendently** *adv* | *resplendently dressed in shimmering silk robes*

**re·spond** /rɪˈspɒnd‖rɪˈspɑːnd/ *v* **1** [I] to react to something that has been said or done: [+ **to**] *Clive responded to my suggestion with a laugh.* | **respond by doing sth** *The US responded by sending troops into Laos.* —see ANSWER¹ (USAGE) **2** [I,T + **that**] to say or write something as a reply: *He responded that he would be pleased to attend.* | [+ **to**] *No one has yet responded to our complaints.* **3** [I] to improve as a result of a particular kind of treatment: [+ **to**] *Her cancer failed to respond to treatment.* | *Most children respond well to individual attention in class.*

**re·spon·dent** /rɪˈspɒndənt‖rɪˈspɑːn-/ *n* [C] **1** *formal* someone who answers questions **2** *law* someone who has to defend their own case in a law court, especially in a DIVORCE case —compare CO-RESPONDENT

**re·sponse** /rɪˈspɒns‖rɪˈspɑːns/ *n* **1** [C,U] something that is done as a reaction to something that has happened or been said: *The attack provoked an angry response.* | [+ **to**] *a sympathetic response to our appeal for help* | **in response to** (=as a response to) *The law was passed in response to public pressure.* **2** [C] something that is said or written as a reply: *His question failed to get a response* *from any of the students.* **3** [C] a part of a religious service that is spoken or sung by the people as an answer to a part that is spoken or sung by the priest

S2 W1 **re·spon·si·bil·i·ty** /rɪˌspɒnsɪ̈ˈbɪlɪ̈ti‖rɪˌspɑːn-/ *n*
**1 ▶ IN CHARGE ◀** [U] a duty to be in charge of or look after something, so that you make decisions and can be blamed if something bad happens: *She was given promotion and more responsibility.* | **have responsibility for** *The Health Minister has overall responsibility for Britain's hospitals.* | **take responsibility for** (=agree to be in charge of something or someone) *My husband took full responsibility for organizing the trip.* | **assume responsibility for** *formal* (=agree to be in charge of) *Richard assumed responsibility for his brother's children.* | **accept responsibility for** *The management accepts no responsibility for cars left in the car park.*
**2 ▶ DUTY ◀** [C] a duty that you have, especially because you are in charge of something: *The head of a large company has many responsibilities.* | **have a responsibility to do sth** *Every citizen has a responsibility to vote.* | **it is sb's responsibility to do sth** *It is your responsibility to check that all doors and windows are locked.* | **moral responsibility** (=a duty to do something because it is morally right)
**3 ▶ BLAME ◀** [U] blame for something bad that has happened: **accept/take responsibility** *We refuse to accept responsibility for the breakdown of negotiations.*
**4 sense of responsibility** an ability to behave sensibly so that you can be trusted to do the right thing: *Parents need to encourage a sense of responsibility in their children.*
**5 a responsibility to sb** a duty to help or serve someone because of your work, position in society etc: *A doctor's first responsibility is to her patients.*
**6 do sth on your own responsibility** to do something without being told to do it or officially allowed to do it
**7 claim responsibility (for)** to officially state that you are the person or organization that did something, especially an act of TERRORISM (=violence in order to get political power)

S2 W2 **re·spon·si·ble** /rɪˈspɒnsɪ̈bəl‖rɪˈspɑːn-/ *adj*
**1 ▶ GUILTY ◀** [not before noun] if someone is responsible for an accident, mistake, crime etc, it is their fault or they can be blamed: [+ **for**] *The police arrested those responsible for the burglaries.* | *When he loses his temper, he isn't responsible for his actions.* | *If any of the children got hurt, I should feel responsible.* | **hold sb responsible (for)** (=blame someone for something) *I shall hold you personally responsible for anything that goes wrong.*
**2 ▶ IN CHARGE OF ◀** [not before noun] having a duty to be in charge of or to look after someone or something: [+ **for**] *Each commissioner is responsible for a department.* | *They're not my children, but I still feel responsible for them.*
**3 responsible job/position/post** a job in which the ability to make good judgments and decisions is needed
**4 ▶ SENSIBLE ◀** sensible and able to make good judgments so that you can be trusted: *You can leave the children with Stuart – he's very responsible.* —opposite IRRESPONSIBLE
**5 be responsible to** if you are responsible to someone, that person is in charge of your work and you must explain your actions to them: *In the US, cabinet members are directly responsible to the president.*
**6 ▶ CAUSE ◀** if something is responsible for a change, problem, event etc, it causes it: [+ **for**] *Social changes are responsible for many of our modern problems.*

**re·spon·si·bly** /rɪˈspɒnsɪ̈bli‖rɪˈspɑːn-/ *adv* in a sensible way which makes people trust you: *Can I rely on you to behave responsibly while I'm away?*

**re·spon·sive** /rɪˈspɒnsɪv‖rɪˈspɑːn-/ *adj* **1** ready to react in a useful or helpful way: [+ **to**] *We try to be responsive to the needs of the customer.* **2** easily controlled, and reacting quickly in the way that you want: *a car with very responsive steering* | *The disease is not proving responsive to treatment.* **3** willing to give answers or show your feelings about something: *I tried to get him talking but he wasn't very responsive.* —**responsively** *adv* —**responsiveness** *n* [U] —opposite UNRESPONSIVE

**re·spray** /ˌriːˈspreɪ/ *v* [T] to change the colour of a car by putting new paint on it —**respray** /ˈriːspreɪ/ *n* [C]

**rest¹** /rest/ *n* S1 W1
**1 the rest** what is left after everything else has been used, dealt with, killed etc: *I got half way through reciting the poem and couldn't remember the rest.* | *At least four of the enemy were killed and the rest fled.* | [+ **of**] *He'll be in a wheelchair for the rest of his life.*
**2 ▶ RELAXING ◀** [C,U] a period of time when you are not doing anything tiring and you can relax or sleep: *The doctor says I need complete rest.* | *You'll feel much better after a good night's rest.* | **have/take a rest** *You must be tired. Why don't you take a rest?* | **well-earned rest** (=rest that you deserve because you have been working hard)
**3 put/set sb's mind at rest** to make someone feel less anxious or worried: *I managed to set his mind at rest about my safety.*
**4 come to rest a)** to stop moving: *The car braked sharply, coming to rest on the edge of the cliff.* **b)** if your eyes come to rest on something, you stop looking around and look at that one thing
**5 give it a rest!** *BrE spoken* used to tell someone to stop talking about something because they are annoying you: *Oh, give it a rest! I don't want to hear about your job!*
**6 at rest a)** *technical* not moving: *Measure the mass of an object at rest.* **b)** an expression meaning dead, used to avoid upsetting someone: *He now lies at rest in the churchyard.*
**7 lay/put sth to rest** to get rid of a false idea or belief by showing that it is not true: *At last these dangerous rumours have been put to rest.*
**8 and all the rest of it** *BrE spoken* used at the end of a short list to mean other things of a similar type: *They accused me of being unreliable, irresponsible, and all the rest of it.*
**9 for the rest** *BrE* used to introduce a short final remark at the end of a speech or piece of writing: *For the rest, we can only guess the effect of these changes.*
**10 and the rest!** *BrE spoken* used to emphasize in a humorous way that a number or amount is really much higher than someone thinks: *"I'd say she's about 40." "Yeah, and the rest!"*
**11 lay sb to rest** an expression meaning to bury someone, used when you want to avoid saying this directly: *She was laid to rest in the graveyard behind the church.*
**12 ▶ IN MUSIC ◀** [C] **a)** a period of silence of a particular length in a piece of music **b)** a written sign that shows how long the period of silence should be
**13 ▶ SUPPORT ◀** [C] a support that you can rest your arm, head etc on

**rest²** *v* S3 W3
**1 ▶ RELAX ◀** [I] to stop working or doing an activity for a time and sit down or lie down to relax: *If you're tired, we'll stop and rest for a while.*
**2 rest your feet/legs/eyes etc** to stop using a part of your body because it is feeling sore or tired
**3 ▶ GIVE SUPPORT ◀** [T always + adv/prep] to support an object or part of your body by putting it on or against something: **rest sth against/on etc** *Rest your head on my shoulder.*
**4 ▶ LIE/LEAN ON ◀** [I always + adv/prep] to lie or lean on something for support: [+ **against/on etc**] *The ladder rested against the wall.* | *She sat with her elbows resting on the table.*
**5 let the matter rest** also **let it rest** to stop discussing or dealing with something: *We could go on arguing but I think we'd better let the matter rest.*
**6 rest assured (that)** *formal* used to tell someone not to worry, because what you say about a situation is true: *You can rest assured that I will never tell anyone.*
**7 will not rest until** if you will not rest until something

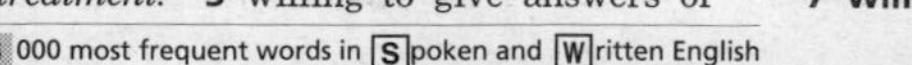

happens, you will not be satisfied until it happens: *We will not rest until the murderer is found.*
**8 ► LIE BURIED ◄** [I always + adv/prep] a word meaning to lie buried, used when you do not want to say this directly: *My mother rests beside my father in the family graveyard.* | **last/final resting place** (=the place where someone is buried) *He decided Rome, where he had been so happy, would be his final resting place.* | **rest in peace** (=often written on a grave)
**9 rest on your laurels** to be satisfied with what you have done, so that you do not make any further effort
**10 I rest my case** *spoken* **a)** *formal* used by a lawyer when they have finished trying to prove something in a court of law **b)** *humorous* used when something happens or is said which proves that you were right

**rest on/upon** sth *phr v* [T not in progressive] **1** *formal* to depend on or be based on something: *Success in management ultimately rests on good judgment.* **2** if your eyes rest on something, you look at it

**rest with** sb *phr v* [T not in progressive] if a decision rests with someone, they are responsible for it: *The final decision rests with the President.*

**rest a·r·ea** /ˈ· ˌ···/ *n* [C] *especially AmE* a place near a road where you can stop and rest, go to the toilet etc

**re·state** /ˌriːˈsteɪt/ *v* [T] to say something again in a different way, so that it is clearer or more strongly expressed: *He restated the question.* —**restatement** *n* [C,U]

S3 W2 **res·tau·rant** /ˈrestərɒnt‖-rənt, -rɑːnt/ *n* [C] a place where you can buy and eat a meal: *an expensive fish restaurant*

**restaurant car** /ˈ···· ·/ *n* [C] a carriage on a train where meals are served; DINING CAR

**res·tau·ra·teur** /ˌrestərəˈtɜː‖-ˈtɜːr/ also **res·tau·ran·teur** /ˌrestərɒnˈtɜː‖-rɑːnˈtɜːr/ *n* [C] someone who owns and manages a restaurant

**rest·ed** /ˈrestɪ̈d/ *adj* [not before noun] feeling healthier, stronger, or calmer because you have had time to relax: *We came back feeling rested and ready for work.*

**rest·ful** /ˈrestfəl/ *adj* peaceful and quiet, making you feel relaxed: *restful music* —**restfully** *adj*

**rest home** /ˈ· ·/ *n* [C] a place where old or sick people can live and be looked after

**res·ti·tu·tion** /ˌrestɪ̈ˈtjuːʃən‖-ˈtuːʃən/ *n* [U] *formal* the act of giving back something that was lost or stolen to its owner, or of paying for damage: **make restitution** *The court ordered him to make full restitution to the family.*

**res·tive** /ˈrestɪv/ *adj* unable to keep still, especially because you are impatient or bored: *The children were becoming restive from sitting at the dinner table so long.* —**restively** *adv* —**restiveness** *n* [U]

**rest·less** /ˈrestləs/ *adj* **1** unable or unwilling to keep still, especially because you are nervous or bored: *The children had been indoors all day and were getting restless.* **2** unwilling to stay in one place, and always wanting new experiences: *After a few weeks in Marseille, I grew restless and decided to take a ship to Corsica.* **3 restless night** a night during which you cannot sleep or rest —**restlessly** *adj* —**restlessness** *n* [U]

**re·stock** /ˌriːˈstɒk‖ˌriːˈstɑːk/ *v* [I,T + **with**] to bring in more supplies to replace those that have been used

**res·to·ra·tion** /ˌrestəˈreɪʃən/ *n* [C,U] **1** the act of thoroughly repairing something such as an old building or a piece of furniture so that it looks the same as it did when it was first made: *a fund for the restoration of historic buildings* **2** the act of bringing back a law, tax, or system of government: [+ **of**] *They're fighting for the restoration of democratic rights.* | *the restoration of the monarchy in Spain* **3 the Restoration** the return of Charles II to become King of England in 1660, and the period afterwards: **Restoration comedy/drama** (=plays written during this time in England) **4** the act of officially giving something back to its former owner: *an attempt to secure the restoration of their lands*

**re·sto·ra·tive¹** /rɪˈstɔːrətɪv/ *adj formal* making you feel healthier or stronger: *the restorative power of long walks*

**restorative²** *n* [C] *humorous* a drink, especially an alcoholic one, that makes you feel better

**re·store** /rɪˈstɔː‖-ɔːr/ *v* [T] W

**1 ► FORMER SITUATION ◄** to make something return to its former level or condition: *So far all attempts to restore normal relations between the two countries have failed.* | **restore sth to sth** *The government promises to restore the economy to full strength.*
**2 restore hope/confidence/calm etc** to make a person or group feel hopeful, confident, calm etc again: *a victory that restored the team's confidence*
**3 restore order** to make people stop fighting and breaking the law: *Police were called in to restore order.*
**4 ► REPAIR ◄** to repair an old building, piece of furniture, or painting etc so that it is in its original condition: *The church was carefully restored after the war.*
**5 ► GIVE STH BACK ◄** *formal* to give back to someone something that was lost or taken from them: **restore sth to sb** *In 1972 a treaty restored Okinawa to Japan.*
**6 restore sb's sight/hearing etc** to make someone able to see, hear etc again: *an operation to restore his hearing*
**7 ► BRING BACK A LAW ◄** to bring back a law, tax, right etc: *a campaign to restore the death penalty*
**8 restore sb to power/the throne** *formal* to give back power to a king, queen, or president

**re·stored** /rɪˈstɔːd‖-ɔːrd/ *adj* [not before noun] feeling better and healthier: *restored by the mountain freshness*

**re·strain** /rɪˈstreɪn/ *v* [T] **1** to prevent someone from doing something harmful or stupid: **restrain sb from doing sth** *I had to restrain her from running out into the street after him.* | **restrain yourself (from)** *She could hardly restrain herself from hitting Walt.* **2** to control or limit something that is tending to increase: *Price rises restrain consumer spending.*

**re·strained** /rɪˈstreɪnd/ *adj* **1** behaviour that is restrained is calm and controlled and does not show your real feelings: *a restrained and cool-headed response to their unfair criticisms* **2** not too brightly coloured or decorated: *The decor was subtle and restrained.*

**re·straint** /rɪˈstreɪnt/ *n* **1** [U] the ability not to do something that you very much want to do, because you know it is more sensible not to do it: *The police were commended for their restraint in handling the disturbances.* | **show/exercise restraint** *I think he showed great restraint, considering how she treated him.* **2** [C usually plural, U] a rule or principle that limits people's activity or behaviour: [+**on**] *restraints on public spending* | *moral restraints on sexual behaviour* | **impose restraints** (=make rules to control something) *The government imposed restraints on the export of military hardware.* | **wage restraint** (=agreement not to demand or pay large wage increases) **3** [U] *formal* physical force used to stop someone from moving freely, especially because they are likely to be violent: *the proper use of physical restraint to control dangerous prisoners* **4** [C] a SEAT BELT

**re·strict** /rɪˈstrɪkt/ *v* [T] S W

**1 ► SIZE/AMOUNT/RANGE ◄** to limit or control the size, amount, or range of something: *The new law restricts the sale of hand guns.* | **restrict sth to** *The speaker restricted her remarks to* (=only talked about) *the health care proposals.*
**2 ► MOVEMENT/ACTIVITY ◄** to limit someone's actions or movements: *The cramped living conditions severely restricted the children's opportunities for play.*
**3 restrict yourself to** to allow yourself to have only a particular amount of something, or do only a particular type of activity: *I'm restricting myself to two cigarettes a day.* | *Journalists should restrict themselves to reporting the facts.*

**re·strict·ed** /rɪˈstrɪktɪ̈d/ *adj* **1** small or limited in size, area, or amount: *It's difficult trying to work in such a restricted space.* **2** limited or controlled, especially by laws or rules: *Press freedom is severely restricted.* | [+ **to**] *The sale of alcohol is restricted to* (=can only be sold to) *people over the age of 18.* | *restricted access for large* *vehicles* **3** limited in what you can do, or in your movements: *A stroke left her with restricted movement in her right leg.*|**restricted life** (=limited in your experiences) *Many women lead very restricted lives, staying at home and bringing up children.* **4** a restricted area or document can only be seen or used by a particular group of people because it is secret or dangerous: *No Entry – restricted area for army personnel only.* **5 be restricted to** to only affect a limited area, group etc: *The damage is restricted to the left side of the brain.*

S2 W3 **re·stric·tion** /rɪˈstrɪkʃən/ *n* **1** [C often plural] a rule or system that limits or controls what you can do or what is allowed to happen: [+ **on**] *restrictions on immigration from Mexico into the US*|**impose/place restrictions on sth** *The 1986 law imposed new financial restrictions on private companies.*|**raise/lift a restriction** (=remove a restriction) *Speed restrictions were lifted once the roadworks were completed.* **2** [U] the act of restricting the size, amount, or range of something

**re·stric·tive** /rɪˈstrɪktɪv/ *adj* tending to restrict your activity too much: *restrictive trade legislation*|*Rimbaud found life in Charleville too restrictive.*

**restrictive clause** /·,·· ˈ·/ also **restrictive rel·a·tive clause** /·,·· ,··· ˈ·/ *n* [C] *technical* a part of a sentence that says which person or thing is meant. For example in 'the man who came to dinner', the phrase 'who came to dinner' is a restrictive clause

**restrictive prac·ti·ces** /·,·· ˈ···/ *n* [plural] **1** unreasonable limits that one TRADE UNION puts on the kind of work that members of other trade unions are allowed to do **2** an unfair trade agreement between companies that limits the amount of competition there is

**rest room** /ˈ· ·/ *n* [C] *AmE* a room with a toilet, in a place such as a restaurant or cinema

**re·struc·ture** /,riːˈstrʌktʃə‖-ər/ *v* [T] to change the way in which something such as a government, business, or system is organized: *The school curriculum has been restructured to include more science.*

S1 W1 **re·sult¹** /rɪˈzʌlt/ *n*

**1 ▶ HAPPENING BECAUSE OF STH ◀** [C,U] something that happens or exists because of something that happened before: [+ **of**] *One result of the cold weather has been a sharp increase in our heating bill.*|*Ken's illness is the result of an accident at work.*|**as a result (of)** (=because of something that has happened) *As a result of the pilots' strike, all flights have had to be cancelled.*|**with the result that** *Sara wasn't at school last week, with the result that she missed an important test.*|**be a direct result (of)** (=caused by one thing only) *High unemployment is a direct result of the recession.*|**end/final/net result** (=the result at the end of a long process) *The net result of all these changes is that people will pay more tax.* —see THUS (USAGE)

**2 ▶ SPORTS/ELECTIONS ◀** [C] the final number of points, votes etc at the end of a competition, game, or election: *The election results were announced at midnight.*|*the football results*

**3 ▶ SCIENTIFIC TESTS ◀** [C] the answers that are produced by a scientific study or test: *Results show that men are twice as likely to suffer from stress as women.*|*We should have the result of your blood test tomorrow.*

**4 ▶ EXAMINATIONS ◀** [C] *BrE* the mark you get in an examination: *When do we get our exam results?*

**5 ▶ SUCCESS ◀ results** [plural] things that happen successfully because of your efforts: **get results** (=succeed in getting what you want) *If the program doesn't get results, it should be dropped.*

**6 ▶ BUSINESS ◀ results** [plural] a company's results are the accounts that show how successful it has been over a period of time, usually a year

**7 get a result** *BrE informal* to win a victory in a sports match: *We didn't play well but at least we got a result.*

W3 **result²** *v* [I] to happen or exist as a result of something: [+ **from**] *problems resulting from past errors*

**result in sth** *phr v* [T not in passive] to make something happen; cause: *an accident that resulted in the death of two passengers*

**re·sul·tant** /rɪˈzʌltənt/ *adj* [only before noun] *formal* happening or existing as a result of something: *a growing economy and its resultant benefits*

**re·sume¹** /rɪˈzjuːm‖rɪˈzuːm/ *v* **1** [I,T] *formal* to start doing something again after a pause or interruption: *They were silent, then Billy resumed his story.*|*Let us resume where we left off.* **2** if an activity or process resumes, it starts again after a pause: *Work resumed on the following day.* **3 resume your seat/place/position** *formal* to go back to the seat, place, or position where you were before: *Everyone resumed their seats for the second half of the performance.*

**re·su·me², résumé** /ˈrezjʊmeɪ, ˈreɪ-‖,rezʊˈmeɪ/ *n* [C] **1** [+ **of**] a short account of something such as an article or speech, that gives the main points but no details **2** *AmE* a short written account of your education and your previous jobs that you send to an employer when you are looking for a new job; CV *BrE*

**re·sump·tion** /rɪˈzʌmpʃən/ *n* [singular, U] *formal* the act of starting an activity again after a pause: [+ **of**] *the resumption of underground nuclear testing*

**re·sur·face** /,riːˈsɜːfɪ̀s‖-ɜːr-/ *v* **1** [I] to appear again: *Old rivalries began to resurface.* **2** [I] to come back up to the surface of the water **3** [T] to put a new surface on a road

**re·sur·gence** /rɪˈsɜːdʒəns‖-ɜːr-/ *n* [singular, U] the appearance again and growth of a belief or activity, especially one that is harmful or undesirable: [+ **of**] *a resurgence of racial violence*|[+ **in**] *a resurgence in the popularity of 60s music* —**resurgent** *adj*

**res·ur·rect** /,rezəˈrekt/ *v* [T] to start an old practice, custom, belief etc again after it has not existed for a long time: *Old theories about the origin of the universe have been resurrected.*

**res·ur·rec·tion** /,rezəˈrekʃən/ *n* [U] **1** also **Resurrection** the return of Jesus Christ to life after his death after being crucified (CRUCIFY), which is one of the main beliefs of the Christian religion **2** also **Resurrection** the return of all dead people to life at the end of the world **3** a situation in which an idea, custom, feeling etc is brought back into existence: *a resurrection of old jealousies*

**re·sus·ci·tate** /rɪˈsʌsɪ̀teɪt/ *v* [T] to make someone breathe again or become conscious after they have almost died —**resuscitation** /rɪ,sʌsɪ̀ˈteɪʃən/ *n* [U] —see also CPR

**re·tail¹** /ˈriːteɪl/ *n* [U] the sale of goods in shops to customers, for their own use and not for selling to anyone else: *goods for retail only*|**retail trade/business etc** *workers in the retail trade*|**retail outlet** (=a shop) —compare WHOLESALE¹

**retail²** /rɪˈteɪl/ *v* **1** [I,T] *technical* to sell goods in a shop: *The product is retailed through a big chain of furniture stores.* **2 retail at $5/£20 etc** *technical* to be sold at a particular price in shops: *This wine retails at £6.95 a bottle.* **3** [T] *formal* to tell people about something, especially about other people's private affairs: *Who is responsible for retailing these rumours?*

**retail³** *adv* from a shop: *We bought it retail.*

**re·tail·er** /ˈriːteɪlə‖-ər/ *n* [C] someone who sells things in a shop; SHOPKEEPER

**re·tail·ing** /ˈriːteɪlɪŋ/ *n* [U] the business of selling goods to the public in shops: *People who work in retailing are often badly paid.*|*retailing organizations*

**retail park** /ˈ·· ·/ *n* [C] *BrE* a special area outside a town with many large shops and space for cars to park

**retail price in·dex** /,·· ˈ· ,··/ abbreviation **RPI** *n* [singular] an official system of numbers that shows changes in the cost of living in Britain each month, based on the price of goods and services bought by an average person —see also CONSUMER PRICE INDEX

**re·tain** /rɪˈteɪn/ *v* [T] *formal* **1** to keep something or continue to have something: *A copy of the invoice should be retained by the Accounts Department.*|*It's important that the elderly should retain a sense of dignity.*|*a heavy* 

*soil that retains water* —see also RETENTION (1) **2** to keep facts in your memory **3** to make sure that you will have someone's help or services, by paying for them before you actually have them: *They decided to retain their lawyer at their own expense.* | **retaining fee** (=money paid to keep someone working for you)

**re·tain·er** /rɪˈteɪnə‖-ər/ *n* [C] **1** an amount of money paid to someone, especially a lawyer, for work that they are going to do **2** a reduced amount of rent that you pay for a room, flat etc when you are not there, so that it will still be available when you return **3** *old use* a servant, especially one who has always worked for a particular person or family: *an old and trusted family retainer*

**re·take¹** /ˌriːˈteɪk/ *v* [T] **1** to get control of an area again in a war: *Rebels have retaken the city.* **2** to take an examination again because you have previously failed it **3** to film or photograph something again

**re·take²** /ˈriːteɪk/ *n* [C] **1** an act of filming or photographing something again: *They had to do several retakes before the director was satisfied.* **2** *BrE* an examination or test that you take again because you failed it

**re·tal·i·ate** /rɪˈtælieɪt/ *v* [I] to do something bad to someone because they have done something bad to you: **retaliate by doing sth** *When the police started to arrest people, some of the demonstrators retaliated by throwing stones.*

**re·tal·i·a·tion** /rɪˌtæliˈeɪʃən/ *n* [U] action against someone who has done something bad to you: *the threat of retaliation* | **in retaliation for** *Union leaders are threatening strike action in retaliation for the recent pay cuts.*

**re·tal·i·a·to·ry** /rɪˈtæliətəri‖-tɔːri/ *adj formal* done against someone because they have harmed you: *retaliatory raids*

**re·tard¹** /rɪˈtɑːd‖-ɑːrd/ *v* [T] *formal* to delay the development of something, or to make something happen more slowly than expected: *Cold weather retards the growth of many plants.* —**retardation** /ˌriːtɑːˈdeɪʃən‖-ɑːr-/ *n* [U]

**re·tard²** /ˈriːtɑːd‖-ɑːrd/ *n* [C] *slang* an offensive word meaning a stupid person

**re·tard·ed** /rɪˈtɑːdɪd‖-ɑːr-/ *adj* less intelligent than other people because of slower mental development: *a special programme for retarded children* | *mentally retarded*

**retch** /retʃ/ *v* [I] to try to VOMIT, or feel as if you are going to vomit when you do not: *Like someone drowning, she fought for air, gasping and retching.*

**retd** the written abbreviation for RETIRED; used after the name of a former military officer

**re·tell** /ˌriːˈtel/ *v* [T] *past tense and past participle* **retold** /-ˈtəʊld‖-ˈtoʊld/ to tell a story again, often in a different way or in a different language

**re·ten·tion** /rɪˈtenʃən/ *n* [U] **1** *formal* the act of keeping something: [+ **of**] *Committee members voted for the retention of the existing voting system.* **2** *technical* the ability or tendency of something to hold liquid, heat etc within itself **3** the ability to keep something in your memory: *powers of retention*

**re·ten·tive** /rɪˈtentɪv/ *adj* a retentive memory or mind is able to hold facts and remember them —**retentively** *adv* —**retentiveness** *n* [U]

**re·think** /ˌriːˈθɪŋk/ *v past tense and past participle* **rethought** /-ˈθɔːt‖-ˈθɒːt/ [I,T] to think about a plan or idea again in order to decide if any changes should be made: *an opportunity to rethink our campaign strategy* —**rethink** /ˈriːθɪŋk/ *n* [singular]

**ret·i·cent** /ˈretɪsənt/ *adj* unwilling to talk about what you feel or what you know: *She's naturally reticent, even with some of her closest friends.* | [+ **about**] *Mr Jamieson was very reticent about the reasons for his decision.* —**reticence** *n* [U] —**reticently** *adv*

**re·tic·u·la·ted** /rɪˈtɪkjʊleɪtɪd/ *adj technical* forming or covered with a pattern of squares and lines that looks like a net —**reticulation** /rɪˌtɪkjʊˈleɪʃən/ *n* [C,U]

**ret·i·na** /ˈretɪnə/ *n* [C] the area at the back of your eye that receives light and sends an image of what you see to your brain —see picture at EYE¹

**ret·i·nue** /ˈretɪnjuː‖-nuː/ *n* [C] a group of helpers or supporters who are travelling with an important person: *visiting Congressmen and all their retinue*

**re·tire** /rɪˈtaɪə‖-ˈtaɪr/ *v* S2 W3

**1** ▶ **FROM WORK** ◀ **a)** [I] to stop work at the end of your working life: *He retired when he was 65.* | [+ **from**] *After retiring from the army it took William a long time to adjust to civilian life.* | **retire early** (=retire before the usual age) **b)** [T usually passive] to dismiss someone and pay them a PENSION, especially because of illness: *The manager was retired on half salary.*

**2** ▶ **TO A QUIET PLACE** ◀ [I] *formal* to go away to a quiet place: *He often retires to his country home to work on his book.* | *The jury has retired to consider its verdict.*

**3** ▶ **FROM A GAME** ◀ [I] to stop competing in a game or race because you are losing or injured: *He was forced to retire from the competition due to a leg injury.*

**4** ▶ **TO BED** ◀ [I] *literary* to go to bed

**5** ▶ **ARMY** ◀ [I] to move back from a battle after being defeated: *The army retired to regroup for a fresh attack.* —compare RETREAT¹ (2)

**re·tired** /rɪˈtaɪəd‖-ˈtaɪrd/ *adj* having stopped working, usually because of your age: *a retired teacher* | *Both my parents are retired now.*

**re·tir·ee** /rɪˌtaɪəˈriː‖-ˌtaɪˈriː/ *n* [C] *AmE* someone who has stopped working, usually because of their age

**re·tire·ment** /rɪˈtaɪəmənt‖-ˈtaɪr-/ *n* S2 W3 **1** [C,U] the act of retiring from your job, or the time when you do this: *June's colleagues arranged a surprise party for her retirement.* | **retirement present/party etc** (=a present, party etc for someone who is retiring) | **on retirement** (=from the time when you retire) *On retirement you will receive a small pension.* | **take early retirement** (=retire at an earlier age than usual) | **retirement age** (=the age when people usually stop working) **2** [singular, U] the period after you have retired: *a long and happy retirement* | *a retirement pension*

**retirement plan** /-ˈ··· ·/ *n* [C] *AmE* a system for saving money for your retirement, especially if you will not receive money from your employer —compare PENSION PLAN

**re·tir·ing** /rɪˈtaɪərɪŋ‖-ˈtaɪrɪŋ/ *adj* **1** not wanting to be with other people, especially people you do not know; SHY¹ (1): *As a child, Elizabeth was very retiring.* **2 the retiring president/manager/director etc** a president etc who is soon going to leave their job

**re·tool** /ˌriːˈtuːl/ *v* **1** [T] *AmE informal* to organize something in a new way: *The College Board has retooled the admission exams.* **2** [I,T] to change or replace the machines or tools in a factory

**re·tort¹** /rɪˈtɔːt‖-ɔːrt/ *v* [T] to reply quickly, in an angry or humorous way: *"It's all your fault!" he retorted.*

**retort²** *n* [C] **1** a short and angry or humorous reply: *He was about to make a jovial retort, but stopped.* **2** a bottle with a long narrow bent neck, used for heating chemicals

**re·touch** /ˌriːˈtʌtʃ/ *v* [T] to improve a picture or photograph by painting over marks or making other small changes: *postcards that have been retouched to cover the grey skies*

**re·trace** /rɪˈtreɪs, riː-/ *v* [T] **1** to go back the way you have come: **retrace your steps** *After about fifty paces, he turned around and began to retrace his steps.* **2** to repeat exactly the same journey that someone else has made: *We shall be retracing the route taken by Marco Polo.* **3** to find out about a series of past actions or events: *Detectives are hoping to retrace her movements.*

**re·tract** /rɪˈtrækt/ *v* **1** [T] to make an official statement saying that something which you said previously is not true; WITHDRAW (3): *He confessed to the murder but later retracted his statement.* **2** [I,T] if part of a machine or an animal's body retracts or is retracted, it moves back into the main part: *Cats can retract their claws.*

**re·tract·a·ble** /rɪˈtræktəbəl/ *adj* **1** a retractable part of something can be pulled back into the main part: *a knife with a retractable blade* **2** having a retractable part: *a retractable ball-point pen*

**re·trac·tion** /rɪˈtrækʃən/ *n* **1** [C] an official statement saying that something which you said previously is not true: *The newspaper was forced to publish a retraction of all its allegations.* **2** [U] the act of retracting something

**re·train** /ˌriːˈtreɪn/ *v* [I,T] to learn or to teach someone the skills that are needed to do a different job: *Staff are being retrained to use the new machinery.* —**retraining** *n* [U] | *a retraining programme for unemployed miners*

**re·tread¹** /ˈriːtred/ *n* [C] **1** a retreaded tyre **2** *AmE informal* something that is made or done again, with a few changes added: *retreads of old TV shows* **3** *AmE informal* someone who has been trained to do work which is different from what they did before

**re·tread²** /ˌriːˈtred/ *v* [T] to put a new rubber surface on an old tyre

**re·treat¹** /rɪˈtriːt/ *v* [I]

**1** ▶ **MOVE BACK** ◀ **a)** to walk back and away from someone or something because you are afraid or embarrassed: *He saw her and retreated, too shy to speak to her.* | [+ **to/from etc**] *Perry lit the fuse and retreated to a safe distance.* **b)** if an area of water, snow or land retreats, it gradually gets smaller: *The flood waters are slowly retreating.*

**2** ▶ **OF AN ARMY** ◀ to move away from the enemy after being defeated in battle: *The rebels retreated, pursued by government troops.*

**3** ▶ **CHANGE YOUR MIND** ◀ to change your mind about a promise you have publicly made or about a principle you have stated, because the situation has become too difficult: [+ **from**] *Current economic problems have forced the government to retreat from its pledge to cut taxes.*

**4** ▶ **TO A QUIET PLACE** ◀ to go away to a place that is quiet or safe: [+ **from/into/to**] *After the noise of the city he was glad to retreat to his hotel room.*

**5 retreat into yourself/your thoughts etc** to ignore what is happening around you and give all your attention to your private thoughts

**retreat²** *n*

**1** ▶ **MOVEMENT BACK** ◀ [singular, U] a movement back and away from someone or something, because you are afraid, embarrassed etc: **beat a retreat** (=walk away quickly) *Jim beat a hasty retreat when he saw his wife's mother at the door.*

**2** ▶ **CHANGE OF INTENTION** ◀ [singular, U] an act of changing your mind about a promise you publicly made or a principle you stated, because the situation has become too difficult: *a retreat from hard-line policies*

**3** ▶ **OF AN ARMY** ◀ [C,U] a movement away from the enemy after a defeat in battle: *Napoleon's retreat from Moscow.* —opposite ADVANCE² (3) | **be in full retreat** (=be retreating fast and continuously) | **sound the retreat** (=give a loud signal for retreat)

**4** ▶ **PLACE** ◀ [C] a place you can go to that is quiet or safe: *von Mulne's retreat in the mountains*

**5** ▶ **THOUGHT AND PRAYER** ◀ [C,U] a period of time that you spend praying or studying religion in a quiet place: *They go on retreat twice a year.*

**re·trench** /rɪˈtrentʃ/ *v* [I] if a government or organization retrenches, it spends less money —**retrenchment** *n* [C,U] *a government policy of retrenchment*

**re·tri·al** /ˌriːˈtraɪəl, ˈriːtraɪəl‖ˌriːˈtraɪəl/ *n* [C] a process of judging a law case in court again: *The jury was dismissed and the judge ordered a retrial.*

**ret·ri·bu·tion** /ˌretrəˈbjuːʃən/ *n* [singular, U] severe punishment that is deserved: [+ **for**] *retribution for terrorist attacks* | **divine retribution** (=punishment from God) | **mete out retribution** (=give retribution) —**retributive** /rɪˈtrɪbjətɪv/ *adj*: *retributive justice*

**re·triev·al** /rɪˈtriːvəl/ *n* [U] **1** *technical* the process of getting back information from a computer system: *information retrieval* | *a retrieval system* **2** [U] the act of getting back something you have lost or left somewhere **3 be beyond/past retrieval** if a situation is beyond retrieval, it has become so bad that it cannot be made right again

**re·trieve** /rɪˈtriːv/ *v* **1** [T] *formal* to find something and bring it back: **retrieve sth from** *I went back to the locker room to retrieve my jacket.* | *The wreckage of the crashed plane was retrieved from the ocean.* **2 retrieve your losses** get back money equal to what you lost **3** [T] *technical* to get back information that has been stored in the memory of a computer **4 retrieve a situation** to make a situation satisfactory again after there has been a serious mistake or problem: *She tried to apologise but it was already too late to retrieve the situation.* **5** [I,T] if a dog retrieves, it finds and brings back birds and small animals its owner has shot —**retrievable** *adj*

**re·triev·er** /rɪˈtriːvə‖-ər/ *n* [C] a type of dog that can be trained to retrieve birds that its owner has shot

**retro-** /retrəʊ, -trə‖-troʊ, -trə/ *prefix* **1** back towards the past: *retroactive legislation* (=which has an effect on things already done) | *in retrospect* (=looking back at what has happened) **2** back towards an earlier and worse state: *a retrograde step* | *to retrogress* **3** backwards: *a retro-rocket* (=that fires backwards, opposite to the direction of travel)

**ret·ro¹** /ˈretrəʊ‖-troʊ/ *adj* deliberately using styles of fashion or design from the recent past: *retro clothing stores*

**retro²** *n* [C] *AmE informal* a RETROSPECTIVE

**ret·ro·ac·tive** /ˌretrəʊˈæktɪv◂‖-troʊ-/ *adj formal* a law or decision that is retroactive is effective from a particular date in the past: *a retroactive pay increase* —see also RETROSPECTIVE¹ —**retroactively** *adv*

**ret·ro·flex** /ˈretrəfleks/ *adj technical* a retroflex speech sound is made with the end of your tongue pointing backwards and upwards

**ret·ro·grade** /ˈretrəgreɪd/ *adj formal* involving a return to an earlier and worse situation: **a retrograde step** *Privatisation is seen as a retrograde step.*

**ret·ro·gress** /ˌretrəˈgres/ *v* [I + **to**] *formal* to go back to an earlier and worse state —**retrogression** /-ˈgreʃən/ *n* [U]

**ret·ro·gres·sive** /ˌretrəˈgresɪv◂/ *adj formal* returning to an earlier and worse situation: *a retrogressive idea* | *retrogressive change* —**retrogressively** *adv*

**ret·ro·spect** /ˈretrəspekt/ *n* [U] **in retrospect** thinking back to a time in the past, especially with the advantage of knowing more now than you did then: *In retrospect, it was the wrong time to set up a new company.* | *My teenage years seem happier in retrospect than they were.*

**ret·ro·spec·tion** /ˌretrəˈspekʃən/ *n* [U] *formal* thought about the past

**ret·ro·spec·tive¹** /ˌretrəˈspektɪv◂/ *adj* **1** a law or decision that is retrospective is effective from a particular date in the past; RETROACTIVE: *retrospective legislation* **2** concerned with or thinking about the past: *in a retrospective mood*

**retrospective²** *n* [C] a show of the work of an ARTIST, that includes all the kinds of work they have done

**re·try** /ˌriːˈtraɪ/ *v* [I] to judge a law case again in court

**ret·si·na** /retˈsiːnə/ *n* [U] a Greek wine that tastes of the RESIN (=juice) of certain trees

**re·turn¹** /rɪˈtɜːn‖-ɜːrn/ *v* 

**1** ▶ **GO BACK** ◀ [I] to go back to a place where you were before, or come back from a place where you have just been: [+ **to**] *Conor did not return to Ireland until 1937.* | [+ **from**] *When Alice returned from university, she was a changed person.* | **return home** *We got lost, returning home well after midnight.* | **never to return** *formal*: *500 airmen flew from these airfields, never to return.*

**2** ▶ **GIVE BACK** ◀ [T] to give something back to its owner, or put something back in its place: *We lent them our lawnmower and they never returned it!* | **return sth to sb/sth** *I have to return some books to the library.*

**3** ▶ **FEELING/PROBLEM** ◀ [I] if a feeling, problem,

quality etc returns, it starts to exist again or to have an effect again: *If the pain returns, take two of the tablets every four hours.*|[+ **to**] *Stability will only return to the region when the civil war ends.*
**4 ▶START AGAIN◀** [I] to go back to an activity, job etc that you were doing before you stopped or were interrupted; RESUME[1] (1) [+ **to**] *Nicholas looked up, grinned, then returned to his newspaper.*|**return to work** *Most mothers return to full-time work within twelve months.*
**5 ▶DISCUSS AGAIN◀** [I] to start discussing or dealing with a subject that you have already mentioned, especially in a piece of writing: [+ **to**] *I shall return to the subject of inflation in chapter five.*|*Returning to sanctions, do you think they will really be effective?*
**6 ▶REACT◀** [T] to do something or give something to someone because they have given the same thing to you: *I smiled at her but she refused to return my smile.*|*You never returned my call!*|**return fire** (=shoot back at someone shooting at you) *The enemy returned our fire.*
**7 ▶BALL◀** [T] to send the ball back to your opponent in a game such as tennis
**8 ▶ELECT◀** [T usually passive] *BrE* to elect someone to a political position, especially to represent you in parliament: *Durrant was returned with an increased majority.*
**9 return a verdict** if a JURY return their VERDICT, they say whether someone is guilty or not
**10 ▶PROFIT◀** [T] if an INVESTMENT returns a particular amount of money, that is how much profit it produces: *Government bonds return around 10%.*
**11 ▶TAX◀** [T] *formal* to give a particular amount as the answer to an official question concerning tax

Frequencies of **return, get/go/come back**, and **get/go/come home** in spoken and written English.

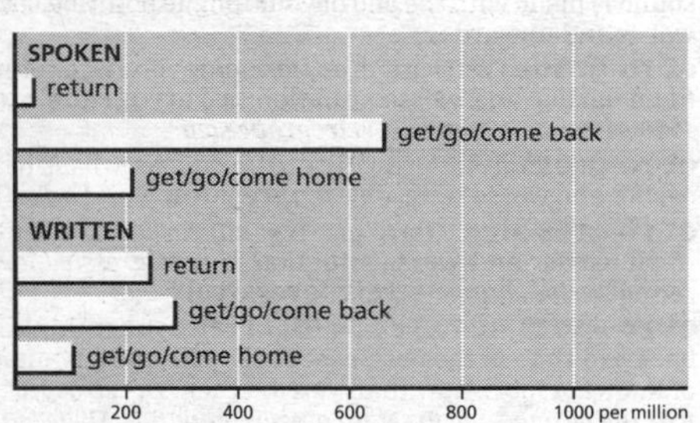


Based on the British National Corpus and the Longman Lancaster Corpus

This graph shows that is much more usual in spoken English to use **get/go/come back** or **get/go/come home** rather than **return**. **Return** is much more common in written English than in spoken English.

S2 W2 **return[2]** *n*
**1 ▶GOING BACK◀** [singular, U] the act of returning from somewhere, or your arrival back in the place where you started from: *We're all looking forward to your return!*|**on/upon your return** (=when you return) *On his return from Germany he was promoted to Colonel.*
**2 ▶OF A FEELING/PROBLEM◀** [U] the fact of something such as a problem, feeling, or activity starting to happen or exist again: [+ **of**] *the return of nationalism to Eastern Europe*
**3 ▶GIVING BACK◀** [U] the act of giving, putting, or sending something back: *The family are demanding the return of the dowry.*|*a return of prisoners*
**4 ▶TO AN ACTIVITY◀** [singular] returning to an activity, job, or way of life: [+ **to**] *the idea of a return to a simpler, more natural way of life*|**a return to work** (=after stopping work as a protest) *an end to the strike and an immediate return to work*
**5 ▶PROFIT◀** [U] also **returns** [plural] the amount of profit that you get from something: *The company returns over the last three years have been spectacular.*|**return on investment/capital/sales** *£10,000! That's not a bad return on our investment, is it?*
**6 in return (for)** in exchange for, or as payment for something: *I'd like to buy you a meal in return for all your hospitality.*|*She gave us food and clothing and asked for nothing in return.*
**7 ▶STATEMENT◀** [C] a statement giving information in reply to an official question: **tax return** *Have you sent in your tax return yet?*
**8 by return (of post)** *BrE* if you reply to a letter by return, you send your reply almost immediately
**9 ▶TICKET◀** [C] *BrE* a ticket for a trip from one place to another and back again; ROUND TRIP *AmE* —compare SINGLE[2] (4) —see also DAY RETURN
**10 many happy returns** *BrE* used to greet someone on their birthday
**11 ▶COMPUTER◀** [U] the control that you press on a computer or TYPEWRITER after you have finished the line you are writing: *Key in your file name and press return.* —see also **the point of no return** (POINT[1] (7))

**return[3]** *adj* **return ticket/fare** a ticket for, or the price charged for, a trip from one place to another and back again; ROUND-TRIP *AmE* —compare SINGLE[1] (6)

**re·turn·a·ble** /rɪˈtɜːnəbəl‖-ɜːr-/ *adj* **1** returnable bottles, containers etc can be given back to the shop, often to be used again **2** *formal* something such as money or an official paper that is returnable must be given or sent back: *a returnable deposit*

**re·turn·er** /rɪˈtɜːnə‖-ˈtɜːrnər/ *n* [C] *BrE* someone who goes back to work after a long time away, especially a woman who left work to look after her children

**returning of·fi·cer** /·ˈ·· ˌ···/ *n* [C] the official in each town or area of Britain who arranges an election to Parliament and announces the result

**Reu·ben sand·wich** /ˌruːbɪn ˈsænwɪdʒ‖-ˈsændwɪtʃ/ *n* [C] an American SANDWICH made with SALT BEEF, Swiss cheese and SAUERKRAUT

**re·u·nify** /riːˈjuːnɪfaɪ/ *v* [T] to join the parts of something together again, especially a country that was divided —compare REUNITE —**reunification** /riːˌjuːnɪfɪˈkeɪʃən/ *n* [U] *the reunification of Germany*

**re·u·nion** /riːˈjuːnjən/ *n* **1** [U] the state of being brought together again after a period of being separated: [+ **with**] *Joseph's eventual reunion with his brother.* **2** [C] a social meeting of people who have not met for a long time, especially people who were at school or college together: *our college reunion.*

**re·u·nite** /ˌriːjuːˈnaɪt/ *v* [I,T usually passive] to come together again or bring people together again: **be reunited with** *reunited with his family*

**re·use** /ˌriːˈjuːz/ *v* [T] to use something again: *Disposable syringes are not to be reused.* —**reusable** *adj* —**reuse** /ˌriːˈjuːs/ *n* [U]|*the reuse of derelict urban land*

**Rev** also **Revd** *BrE* the written abbreviation of Reverend; a title used before the name of a minister of the Christian church: *the Rev D Macleod*

**rev[1]** /rev/ *n* [C] *informal* a complete turn of a wheel or engine part, used as a unit for measuring the speed of an engine; REVOLUTION (4)

**rev[2]** also **rev up** *v* **revved, revving** [I,T] if you rev an engine, or if an engine revs, you make it work faster: *the sound of a car revving up in the driveway*

**re·val·ue** /riːˈvæljuː/ *v* [T] **1** to examine something again in order to calculate its present value: *I'm having all my grandmother's jewelry revalued to see if I need to insure it.* **2** to increase the value of a country's money in relation to that of other countries: *The dollar has just been revalued.* —compare DEVALUE —**revaluation** /riːˌvæljuːˈeɪʃən/ *n* [C,U]

**re·vamp** /riːˈvæmp/ *v* [T] *informal* to arrange something in a new way so that it appears to be better although often there is no real improvement: *They've revamped the whole exam system.* —**revamp** /ˈriːvæmp/ *n* [C]|*an amazing revamp of her stage personality*

**Revd** *BrE* a British spelling of REV

S3 W1 **re·veal** /rɪˈviːl/ *v* [T] **1** to show something that was previously hidden: *The curtains opened to reveal a darkened stage.* **2** to make known something that was previously secret or unknown: *The newspaper story revealed a cover-up of huge proportions.* | **reveal (that)** *He revealed that he had been in prison twice before.*

**re·veal·ing** /rɪˈviːlɪŋ/ *adj* **1** a remark or event that is revealing shows you something interesting or surprising about a situation or someone else's character: *Some of her comments during the interview were very revealing.* **2** revealing clothes allow parts of your body to be seen which are usually kept covered: *a very revealing dress*

**re·veil·le** /rɪˈvæli‖ˈrevəli/ *n* [singular, U] a special tune played as a signal to wake soldiers in the morning, or the time at which it is played

**rev·el** /ˈrevəl/ *v* **revelled, revelling** *BrE*, **reveled, reveling** *AmE* [I] *old use* to spend time dancing, eating, drinking etc, especially at a party —**revel** *n* [C usually plural] *their drunken revels*

**revel in** sth *phr v* [T] to enjoy something very much, especially praise, popularity, or something that other people do not expect you to enjoy: *He seems to be revelling in all the attention he's getting.* | *revelling in their embarrassment*

**rev·e·la·tion** /ˌrevəˈleɪʃən/ *n* **1** [C] a surprising fact about someone or something that is made known and was previously secret: *revelations in the papers about a government scandal* **2 be a revelation** *informal* to be surprisingly good, enjoyable, or useful: *Alice Walker's novel was a real revelation to me.* **3** [U] the act of suddenly making known a surprising fact that had previously been secret **4** [C,U] an event, experience etc that is considered to be a message from God

**rev·ell·er** *BrE*, **reveler** *AmE* /ˈrevələ‖-lər/ *n* [C usually plural] someone who is having fun singing, dancing etc in a noisy way: *drunken revellers in Trafalgar Square on New Year's Eve*

**rev·el·ry** /ˈrevəlri/ *n plural* **revelries** [U] wild noisy dancing, eating, drinking etc

**re·venge**¹ /rɪˈvendʒ/ *n* [U] **1** something you do in order to punish someone who has harmed or offended you: **[+ for]** *Hamlet was seeking revenge for his father's murder.* | **get/take revenge (on)** *He took revenge on his employers by setting fire to the factory.* | **be out for revenge** (=be trying to get your revenge) | **in revenge** (=to punish someone) *a bomb attack in revenge for the imprisonment of the terrorists* **2 get your revenge** to defeat someone who has previously defeated you in a sport —**revengeful** *adj*

**revenge**² *v* [T] **revenge yourself on/be revenged on** *formal* to punish someone who has harmed you: *his unconscious desire to be revenged on her for her disloyalty*

W2 **rev·e·nue** /ˈrevənjuː‖-nuː/ also **revenues** *plural n* [U] **1** money that a business or organization receives over a period of time, especially from selling goods or services: *advertising revenue* **2** money that the government receives from tax —see also INLAND REVENUE, INTERNAL REVENUE SERVICE

**re·ver·be·rate** /rɪˈvɜːbəreɪt‖-ɜːr-/ *v* [I] **1** if a loud sound reverberates, it is heard many times as it is sent back from different surfaces, so that the room or building where it is seems to shake: **[+ through/around/along etc]** *The sound of a train passing reverberated through the house.* **2** if an event, action, or idea reverberates, it has a strong effect over a wide area: *His death shocked the whole country and reverberated far beyond its boundaries.*

**re·ver·be·ra·tion** /rɪˌvɜːbəˈreɪʃən‖-ɜːr-/ *n* **1** [C usually plural] a severe effect that is caused by a particular event: *The reverberations of the energy crisis are felt especially by the car industry.* **2** [C,U] a loud sound that hits a surface and is heard again and again: *the deep reverberation of the bass drum*

**re·vere** /rɪˈvɪə‖-ˈvɪr/ *v* [T] *formal* to respect and admire someone or something very much: *a much revered teacher*

**rev·e·rence**¹ /ˈrevərəns/ *n* **1** [U] *formal* great respect and admiration for someone or something: **[+ for]** *You should show proper reverence for the national flag.* **2 your/his reverence** *old use* used when speaking to or about a priest: *The visitors have arrived, your reverence.*

**reverence**² *v* [T] *old use* to revere someone or something

**Rev·e·rend**¹ /ˈrevərənd/ *n* a title of respect used before the name of a minister of the Christian church: *the Reverend John Graham*

**reverend**² *adj* [only before noun] *old use* deserving respect

**Reverend Moth·er** /ˌ··· ˈ··/ *n* [C] a title of respect for the woman in charge of a CONVENT; MOTHER SUPERIOR

**rev·e·rent** /ˈrevərənt/ *adj formal* showing respect and admiration: *They sat in reverent silence.* —**reverently** *adv* | *He kissed her hand reverently.*

**rev·e·ren·tial** /ˌrevəˈrenʃəl◂/ *adj formal* showing respect: *He spoke of the dead man in reverential tones.* —**reverentially** *adv* | *They treated him reverentially.*

**rev·e·rie** /ˈrevəri/ *n* [C,U] a state of imagining or thinking about pleasant things, that is like dreaming: *She was startled out of her reverie by the door bell.*

**re·vers·al** /rɪˈvɜːsəl‖-ɜːr-/ *n* [C,U] **1** a change to an opposite arrangement, process or course of action: *There has been a dramatic reversal of government policy.* **2** [C] a failure or other problem that prevents you from being able to do what you want: *In spite of setbacks and reversals, his business was at last making money.*

**re·verse**¹ /rɪˈvɜːs‖-ɜːrs/ *v*

**1 ▶ CHANGE STH ◀** [T] to change something, such as a decision, judgment, or process so that it is the opposite of what it was before: *The court of appeal reversed the original verdict and set the prisoner free.* | *What can we do to reverse the present trend of falling sales?*

**2 ▶ CAR ◀** [I,T] if a car or its driver reverses, they go backwards: **[+ out/into etc]** *a car reversing out of a driveway* | *Before you reverse, make sure there are no pedestrians behind you.* | **reverse a car/bus etc** (=make it reverse) —see picture on page 415

**3 ▶ CHANGE THE ORDER ◀** [T] to change round the usual order of the parts of something: *They reversed the normal order for the ceremony and started with prayers.*

**4 ▶ TURN STH OVER ◀** [T] to turn something over, so as to show the back of it: *Reverse the paper in the printer.*

**5 reverse the charges** *BrE* to make a telephone call which is paid for by the person you are telephoning; CALL COLLECT *AmE* —**reversible** *adj*: *This coat is reversible, you can wear it inside out.* —**reversibility** *n* [U]

**reverse**²

**1 ▶ THE OPPOSITE ◀ the reverse** the exact opposite of what has just been mentioned: *The economic situation is certainly improving, although recent trade figures suggest the reverse.* | **quite the reverse** (=completely the opposite) *I was not happy – quite the reverse, I was seething with anger.*

**2 go into reverse** if a trend or process goes into reverse, it starts to happen in the opposite way: *a danger that the movement towards democracy will go into reverse*

**3 ▶ IN A CAR ◀** [U] the control in a vehicle that makes it go backwards; REVERSE GEAR | **into/in reverse** *Put the car into reverse.*

**4 ▶ A DEFEAT ◀** [C] *formal* a defeat or a problem that delays your plans; SETBACK: *Losing the Senate vote was a serious reverse for the President.*

**5 ▶ OTHER SIDE ◀** [singular] the less important side or the back of an object that has two sides: *Is there a pattern on the reverse of the cloth?*

**6 ▶ OF A COIN ◀** [singular] the side of a coin that does not show a person's head: *The British ten-pence piece has a lion on the reverse.*

**reverse**³ *adj* [only before noun] **1 reverse order/procedure/process etc** the opposite order etc to what is usual or to what has just been stated: **in reverse order**

R

*Re-assemble the parts in reverse order.* **2 the reverse side** the back of something: *Sign the check on the reverse side.*

**reverse dis·crim·i·na·tion** /ˌ· ·ˌ···ˈ·· / *n* [U] the practice of giving unfair treatment to a group of people who usually have advantages, in order to be fair to the group of people who were unfairly treated in the past —compare POSITIVE DISCRIMINATION

**reverse gear** /ˌ· ˈ·/ *n* [U] the control in a vehicle that makes it go backwards

**reversing light** /·ˈ·· ˌ·/ *n* [C] a light on the back of a car which comes on when the car is going backwards —see picture on page 409

**re·ver·sion** /rɪˈvɜːʃən‖rɪˈvɜːrʒən/ *n* [singular, U] *formal* **1** a return to a former, usually bad, condition or habit: [+ **to**] *the danger of a reversion to tribal warfare in the region* **2** *law* the return of property to a former owner

**re·vert** /rɪˈvɜːt‖-ɜːrt/ *v*

**revert to** sb/sth *phr v* [T] **1** to go back to a former condition or habit, especially one that was bad: *As soon as they stopped farming, the land reverted to wilderness.* | *He had reverted to lazing in bed and coming in late to work.* | **revert to type** (=return to your former type of behaviour) **2** to return to an earlier subject of conversation: *I'd like to revert to the first point you made.* **3** *law* if land or a building reverts to someone, it becomes the property of its former owner again

**re·vet·ment** /rɪˈvetmənt/ *n* [C] *technical* a surface of stone or other building material added for strength to a wall that holds back loose earth, water etc

S3 W2 **re·view¹** /rɪˈvjuː/ *n* **1** [C,U] an act of carefully examining and considering a situation or process: *The Department of Agriculture ordered an urgent review of pesticide safety.* | *a review of progress in computer science over the last 20 years* | **under review** (=being examined and considered) *Nuclear weapons systems are currently under review.* | **come up for review** (=come to the time when there is supposed to be a review) *The ban on whaling came up for review in 1990.* **2** [C] an article in a newspaper or magazine that gives an opinion about a new book, play, film etc: *Her latest novel got good reviews in the press.* **3** [U] the work of writing these: *He sent her an offprint of the article for review.* | **review copy** (=a copy of a book etc sent to a magazine or newspaper for review) **4** [C] an official show of the army, navy etc in the presence of a king, president, or officer of high rank: *a naval review* **5** [C] a REVUE

W3 **review²** *v* **1** [T] to examine, consider and judge a situation or process carefully: *Government spending has been reviewed to try and reduce the budget deficit.* **2** [I,T] to write an article judging a new book, play, film etc: *Bernstein sometimes reviewed classical music in the 'Post'.* | **be well reviewed** (=be praised by reviewers) **3** [T] to officially examine a group of soldiers, ships etc at a military show: *The President will review the soldiers on parade.* **4** [T] *AmE* to look again at something quickly, such as school work, notes of lessons, or a report, etc —compare REVISE (2)

**re·view·er** /rɪˈvjuːə‖-ər/ *n* [C] someone who writes about new books, plays etc in a newspaper or magazine

**re·vile** /rɪˈvaɪl/ *v* [T] to express hatred of someone or something: *The President was now reviled by the very Party he had helped to lead.* —**reviler** *n* [C]

**re·vise** /rɪˈvaɪz/ *v* **1** [T] to change your opinions, plans etc because of new information or ideas: *I've revised my opinion of Bill – he's much more intelligent than I thought.* | *Our original forecast of this year's profits has now been revised upwards.* (=we think profits will be higher) | **revised estimate** (=a calculation that has been changed to make it more accurate) *Are there any questions on the revised estimates of the budget?* **2** [I,T] *BrE* to study lessons or notes again, in order to learn them before an examination: *She's still got a lot of revising to do before the exam.* **3** [T] to change a piece of writing by adding new information, making improvements, or correcting mistakes: *Eliot revised his American lectures for publication.* | **revised edition** (=a new and improved form or copy of a book) *a revised edition of the encyclopedia* —compare REVIEW² —**reviser** *n* [C]

**re·vi·sion** /rɪˈvɪʒən/ *n* **1** [C,U] the process of changing something, especially a piece of writing, in order to improve it by correcting it or including new information or ideas: *His lecture needs a lot of revision.* | **be subject to revision** (=be considered for possible change) *The department budget is subject to monthly revision.* **2** [C] a piece of writing that has been improved and corrected **3** [U] *BrE* the work of studying lessons, notes etc again in order to learn them: *I'll have to do some revision before my exam.*

**re·vi·sion·is·m** /rɪˈvɪʒənɪzəm/ *n* [U] ideas which are changing away from the main beliefs of a political system, especially a Marxist system —**revisionist** *adj* —**revisionist** *n* [C] *revisionist writings*

**re·vis·it** /ˌriːˈvɪzɪt/ *v* [T] **1** to return to a place you once knew well: *They revisited the town where he grew up.* **2** to come back to in order to discuss again: *OK, so we need to revisit this proposal as soon as the budget position is clearer.* **3 revisited** an event, fashion etc revisited is something else very like it that reminds you of it: *a music festival that was essentially Woodstock revisited*

**re·vi·tal·ize** also **-ise** *BrE* /riːˈvaɪtəlaɪz/ *v* [T] to put new strength or power into something: *They hope to revitalize the neighborhood by providing better housing.* —**revitalization** /riːˌvaɪtəlaɪˈzeɪʃən‖-tl-ə-/ *n* [U]

**re·vi·val** /rɪˈvaɪvəl/ *n* **1** [C,U] a process of something becoming active or strong again: *The Roosevelt administration wanted to stimulate an economic revival.* | [+ **of**] *the revival of old fears and jealousies* **2** [C,U] the fact of something becoming popular again: [+ **of**] *the revival of Buddhism in China* | *Opera is enjoying a revival.* **3** [C] a new production of a play that has not been recently performed: *a revival of 'West Side Story'* **4** [C] a REVIVAL MEETING

**re·vi·val·is·m** /rɪˈvaɪvəlɪzəm/ *n* [U] an organized attempt to make a religion more popular —**revivalist** *adj*

**revival meet·ing** /·ˈ·· ˌ··/ *n* [C] a public religious meeting with music, famous speakers etc, that is intended to make people interested in Christianity

**re·vive** /rɪˈvaɪv/ *v* **1** [I,T] to become or make someone conscious, healthy, or strong again: *The doctors revived her with injections of glucose.* | *The plant will revive if you water it.* **2** [T] to come back or bring something back into existence or popularity: *Helen's trip home has revived memories of her childhood.* | *reviving old customs*

**re·viv·i·fy** /riːˈvɪvɪfaɪ/ *v* [T] *formal* to give new life and health to someone or something: *the aim was to strengthen, revivify and revitalise the Labour Party*

**rev·o·ca·tion** /ˌrevəˈkeɪʃən/ *n* [C,U] the act of revoking a law, decision etc

**re·voke** /rɪˈvəʊk‖-ˈvoʊk/ *v* [T] to officially state that a law, decision, contract etc is no longer effective; CANCEL: *Their work permits have been revoked.*

**re·volt¹** /rɪˈvəʊlt‖-ˈvoʊlt/ *v* **1** [I] if a group of people revolt, they take strong and often violent action against the government, usually with the aim of taking power away from them; REBEL²: *George III's repressive measures forced the Colonies to revolt.* **2** [I] to refuse to accept someone's authority or obey rules, laws etc: [+ **against**] *Public opinion will revolt against any further increase in taxes.* **3** [T] if something revolts you, it is so unpleasant that it makes you feel sick and shocked: **be revolted by/at** *We were revolted by their cruelty.* —see also REVULSION

**revolt²** *n* **1** a refusal to accept someone's authority or obey rules, laws etc: *The President faces a Senate revolt.* | *a child's revolt against rigid, oppressive parents* **2** strong and often violent action by a lot of people against their ruler or government: [+ **against**] *an armed revolt against a tyrannical regime* | **in revolt** *The peasants rose* *up in armed revolt.* **3** a feeling of being sick and very shocked at something unpleasant: *a sense of revolt at the bloody scenes*

**re·volt·ing** /rɪˈvəʊltɪŋ‖-ˈvoʊl-/ *adj* extremely unpleasant; DISGUSTING: *the revolting taste of sour milk | His leering glances were revolting to her.* —**revoltingly** *adv | Your socks are revoltingly dirty.*

S3 W2 **rev·o·lu·tion** /ˌrevəˈluːʃən/ *n* **1** [C] a complete change in ways of thinking, methods of working etc: *Computer technology has caused a revolution in business practices.* —see also INDUSTRIAL REVOLUTION **2** [C,U] a time of great, usually sudden, social and political change, especially the changing of a ruler or political system by force: *the French Revolution | social inequalities that led to revolution* —see also COUNTER-REVOLUTION **3** [C,U] one complete circular movement, or continued circular movement, around a fixed point: [+ **round/around**] *The Earth makes one revolution round the sun each year.* **4** one complete circular spinning movement, made by something such as a wheel fixed on a central point: *a speed of 100 revolutions per minute* —see also REVOLVE

**rev·o·lu·tion·a·ry**[1] /ˌrevəˈluːʃənəri◂‖-ʃəneri◂/ *n* [C] someone who joins in or supports a political or social revolution: *socialist revolutionaries*

**revolutionary**[2] *adj* **1** completely new and different, especially in a way that leads to great improvements: *The new cancer drug is a revolutionary breakthrough.* **2** [only before noun] connected with a political or social revolution: *a revolutionary leader*

**rev·o·lu·tion·ize** also **-ise** *BrE* /ˌrevəˈluːʃənaɪz/ *v* [T] to completely change the way people think or do things, especially because of a new idea or invention: *New metal alloys have revolutionized car manufacture.*

**re·volve** /rɪˈvɒlv‖rɪˈvɑːlv/ *v* [I,T] to spin around or make something spin around, on a central point; ROTATE (1): *The metal disc revolves at high speed.* | **revolve sth** *Revolve the drum to get all the clothes out of the dryer.*

**revolve around** sth *phr v* [T not in passive] **1** [not in progressive] to have something as a main subject or purpose: *The story revolves around a young girl who runs away from home. | Her life seems to revolve around her career.* | **think the world revolves around you** *informal* (=think that you are more important than anyone or anything else) **2** to move in circles around something: *The moon revolves around the Earth.*

**re·volv·er** /rɪˈvɒlvə‖rɪˈvɑːlvər/ *n* [C] a small gun which has a revolving container for bullets, so that several shots can be fired without having to put more bullets in

**re·volv·ing** /rɪˈvɒlvɪŋ‖-ˈvɑːl-/ *adj* a revolving object is designed so that it turns with a circular movement: *a revolving stage in the theatre*

**revolving door** /ˌ·ˌ·· ˈ·/ *n* [C] a type of door in the entrance of a large building, that goes round and round as people go through it

**re·vue** /rɪˈvjuː/ *n* [C] a show in a theatre, that includes songs, dances, and jokes about recent events

**re·vul·sion** /rɪˈvʌlʃən/ *n* [U] a strong feeling of shock and very strong dislike: *News of the atrocities produced a wave of anger and revulsion.*

W3 **re·ward**[1] /rɪˈwɔːd‖-ˈwɔːrd/ *n* **1** [C,U] something that you receive because you have done something good or helpful: [+ **for**] *She received a crystal decanter as a reward for her services. | $100 was a poor reward for all my work!* **2** [C] an amount of money that is offered to someone who finds something that was lost or gives the police information: *A reward was offered for the return of the jewels.* **3 be its own reward** if something that you do is its own reward, it makes you feel happy and satisfied: *Working for a good cause can be its own reward.*

**reward**[2] *v* [T] to give something to someone because they have done something good or helpful: *How can I reward your kindness?* | **reward sb with sth** *Larry complimented her and was rewarded with a smile.* | **reward sb for sth** *She was generously rewarded for her work.*

**re·ward·ing** /rɪˈwɔːdɪŋ‖-ɔːr-/ *adj* making you feel happy and satisfied because you feel you are doing something useful or important, even if you do not earn much money: *Teaching can be a very rewarding career.*

**re·wind** /riːˈwaɪnd/ to make a CASSETTE TAPE or VIDEO go backwards so as to see or hear it again

**re·wire** /ˌriːˈwaɪə‖-ˈwaɪr/ *v* [T] to put new electric wires in a building, machine, light etc

**re·word** /ˌriːˈwɜːd‖-ˈwɜːrd/ *v* [T] to say or write something again in different words, in order to make it easier to understand or more suitable: *Let me reword my question.*

**re·work** /ˌriːˈwɜːk‖-ˈwɜːrk/ *v* [T] to make changes in music or a piece of writing, in order to use it again

**re·write** /ˌriːˈraɪt/ *v past tense* **rewrote** /-ˈrəʊt‖-ˈroʊt/ *past participle* **rewritten** /-ˈrɪtn/ [T] to change something that has been written, especially in order to improve it, or because new information is available: *Rewrite the passage in your own words.* —**rewrite** /ˈriːraɪt/ *n* [C] | *Software packages may need complete rewrites to match new hardware.*

**Rex** /reks/ *n Latin* **1** a title used in official writing after the name of a king, when the king's name has been written in Latin: *Henricus Rex* **2** *law* a word meaning the state, used in the names of law cases in Britain when a king is ruling: *Rex v Jones*

**rhap·so·dize** also **-ise** *BrE* /ˈræpsədaɪz/ *v* [I] to talk about something in an eager, excited, and approving way: [+ **about/over**] *rhapsodizing about the aroma of the mountain forests*

**rhap·so·dy** /ˈræpsədi/ *n* [C] **1** a piece of music that is written to express emotion, and does not have a regular form **2** an expression of eager and excited approval: *listening to Miss Duval's rhapsodies about Venice*

**rhe·o·stat** /ˈriːəstæt/ *n* [C] a piece of equipment that controls the loudness of a radio or the brightness of an electric light, by limiting the flow of electric current

**Rhe·sus fac·tor** /ˈriːsəs ˌfæktə‖-tər/ *n* [singular] *technical* a substance whose PRESENCE (RHESUS POSITIVE) or absence (RHESUS NEGATIVE) in the red blood cells may have dangerous effects for some babies or when a person receives blood from another person

**rhesus mon·key** /ˈriːsəs ˌmʌŋki/ *n* [C] a small monkey from northern India that is often used in medical tests

**rhet·o·ric** /ˈretərɪk/ *n* [U] **1** language used to persuade or influence people, especially by politicians: *the rhetoric of their political rallies* **2** speech or writing that sounds impressive, but is not actually sincere or very useful: *Positive action is better than rhetoric.* **3** the art of speaking or writing to persuade or influence people

**rhe·tor·i·cal** /rɪˈtɒrɪkəl‖-ˈtɔː-, -ˈtɑː-/ *adj* **1 rhetorical question** a question that you ask as a way of making a statement, without expecting an answer, such as 'Who knows what might happen?' **2** using speech or writing in special ways in order to persuade people or to produce an impressive effect: *impassioned rhetorical phrases* —**rhetorically** /-kli/ *adv*

**rhet·o·ri·cian** /ˌretəˈrɪʃən/ *n* [C] *formal* someone who is trained or skilful in the art of persuading or influencing people through speech or writing

**rheu·mat·ic** /ruːˈmætɪk/ *adj* **1** connected with rheumatism: *a rheumatic condition of the joints* **2** suffering from rheumatism

**rheumatic fe·ver** /ˌ·ˌ·· ˈ··/ *n* [U] a serious infectious disease that causes fever, swelling in your joints, and sometimes damage to your heart

**rheu·mat·ick·y** /ruːˈmætɪki/ *adj informal* rheumatic

**rheu·mat·ics** /ruːˈmætɪks/ *n* [plural] *informal especially BrE* rheumatism

**rheu·ma·tis·m** /ˈruːmətɪzəm/ *n* [U] a disease that makes your joints or muscles painful and stiff

**rheu·ma·toid ar·thri·tis** /ˌruːmətɔɪd ɑːˈθraɪtɪs‖-ɑːr-/ *n* [U] a disease that continues for many years, and makes your joints painful and stiff, and often makes them lose their proper shape

**RH fac·tor** /ˌɑːr ˈeɪtʃ ˌfæktə‖-tər/ *n* [C] the RHESUS FACTOR

**rhine·stone** /ˈraɪnstəʊn‖-stoʊn/ *n* [C,U] a jewel made from glass or a transparent rock that is intended to look like a diamond

**rhi·no** /ˈraɪnəʊ‖-noʊ/ *n plural* **rhinos** [C] *informal* a rhinoceros

**rhi·no·ce·ros** /raɪˈnɒsərəs‖-ˈnɑː-/ *n* [C] a large heavy African or Asian animal with thick skin and either one or two horns on its nose

**rhi·no·plas·ty** /ˈraɪnəʊˌplæsti‖-noʊ-/ *n* [U] PLASTIC SURGERY on your nose —**rhinoplastic** /ˌraɪnəʊˈplæstɪk◂‖-noʊ-/ *adj*

**rhi·zome** /ˈraɪzəʊm‖-zoʊm/ *n* [C] *technical* the thick stem of some plants such as the IRIS, which lies flat along the ground with roots and leaves growing from it

**rho·do·den·dron** /ˌrəʊdəˈdendrən‖ˌroʊ-/ *n* [C] a bush with bright flowers which keeps its leaves in winter

**rhom·boid**[1] /ˈrɒmbɔɪd‖ˈrɑːm-/ *n* [C] *technical* a shape with four sides whose opposite sides are equal; PARALLELOGRAM —see picture at SHAPE[1]

**rhomboid**[2] also **rhom·boid·al** /rɒmˈbɔɪdl‖rɑːm-/ *adj technical* shaped like a rhombus

**rhom·bus** /ˈrɒmbəs‖ˈrɑːm-/ *n* [C] *technical* a shape with four equal straight sides, especially one that is not a square —see picture at SHAPE[1]

**rhu·barb** /ˈruːbɑːb‖-ɑːrb/ *n* **1** [U] a plant with broad leaves and a thick red stem that can be eaten **2** [U] *spoken* a word used by actors to make a sound like many people talking **3** [C] *AmE old-fashioned* a noisy argument

**rhyme**[1] /raɪm/ *n* **1** [C] a short poem or song, especially for children, using words that rhyme —see also NURSERY RHYME **2** [C] a word that rhymes with another word, for example 'fold' and 'cold': [+ **for**] *I can't find a rhyme for 'orange'.* **3** [U] the use of words that rhyme in poetry, especially at the ends of lines: *Shakespeare sometimes wrote in rhyme.* **4 without rhyme or reason** in a way that cannot be reasonably explained: *Joe's moods change without rhyme or reason.*

**rhyme**[2] *v* [not in progressive] **1** [I] if two words or lines of poetry rhyme, they end with the same sounds, including a vowel: [+ **with**] *'House' rhymes with 'mouse'.* | **rhyming couplet** (=two lines of poetry that end in words that rhyme) **2** [T] to put two or more words together to make them rhyme: [+ **with**] *You can't rhyme 'box' with 'backs'.*

**rhyming slang** /ˌ‥ ˈ·/ *n* [U] a way of talking, used especially by COCKNEYS (=people from east London), in which you use words or phrases that rhyme with the words you mean, instead of using the normal words. For example, 'plates of meat' is rhyming slang for 'feet'.

**rhyth·m** /ˈrɪðəm/ *n* [C,U] **1** a regular repeated pattern of sounds or movements: *the exciting rhythms of African drum beats* | *the rhythm of your heartbeat* **2** a regular pattern of changes: *the rhythm of the seasons*

**rhythm and blues** /ˌ‥ · ˈ·/ *n* [U] R AND B (=a type of music)

**rhyth·mic** /ˈrɪðmɪk/ also **rhyth·mic·al** /-ɪkəl/ *adj* having rhythm: *the rhythmic thud of the bass drum* —**rhythmically** /-kli/ *adv* | *tapping rhythmically on the table*

**rhythm meth·od** /ˈ‥ ˌ‥/ *n* [singular] a method of BIRTH CONTROL which depends on having sex only at a time when the woman is not likely to become PREGNANT

**rhythm sec·tion** /ˈ‥ ˌ‥/ *n* [C] the part of a band that provides a strong RHYTHM with drums and other similar instruments

**ri·al** /riˈɑːl‖riˈɒːl, -ˈɑːl/ *n* [C] a RIYAL

**rib**[1] /rɪb/ *n* [C] **1** one of the 12 pairs of curved bones that surround your chest: *He broke a rib in the accident.* —see picture at RESPIRATORY **2** a piece of meat that includes an animal's rib: *barbecued ribs* **3** a curved piece of wood, metal etc that is used as part of the structure of something such as a boat or building —see also PRIME RIB, SPARERIBS **dig sb in the ribs** (DIG[1] (5))

**rib**[2] *v* **ribbed, ribbing** [T] *informal* to make jokes and laugh at someone so that you embarrass them, but in a friendly way: *Tony's always ribbing me about my accent.*

**rib·ald** /ˈrɪbəld/ *adj* ribald songs, remarks, riddles, or jokes are humorous, rude and usually about sex

**rib·ald·ry** /ˈrɪbəldri/ *n* [U] ribald songs, remarks, or jokes

**ribbed** /rɪbd/ *adj* having a pattern of raised lines: *ribbed stockings*

**rib·bing** /ˈrɪbɪŋ/ *n* [U] **1** friendly jokes and laughter about someone that embarrasses them: *Jake always took some ribbing about his lack of hair.* **2** a pattern of raised lines in knitting (KNIT (1))

**rib·bon** /ˈrɪbən/ *n*

**1 ▶ SILK ◀** [C,U] a long narrow piece of cloth used to tie things or as a decoration: *a red ribbon in her hair*

**2 ▶ STH NARROW ◀** [singular] something that is long and narrow: *a ribbon of shining water*

**3 be cut/torn to ribbons** to be very badly damaged by being cut or torn in many places: *Her feet were cut to ribbons on the rocks.* | **be in ribbons** (=be badly torn in many places) *His coat was in ribbons.*

**4 ▶ PRIZE ◀** [C] *AmE* a small arrangement of coloured ribbon in the form of a flat flower, that is given as a prize in a competition; ROSETTE: **blue ribbon** (=the first prize)

**5 ▶ MILITARY HONOUR ◀** [C] a piece of ribbon with a special pattern or colours on it, worn to show that you have received a military honour

**6 ▶ INK ◀** a long narrow piece of cloth or plastic with ink on it that is used in a TYPEWRITER

**ribbon de·vel·op·ment** /ˈ‥ ˌ‥‥/ *n* [U] *BrE* long lines of houses along the side of the main roads leading out of a city, or the practice of arranging houses in this way

**rib cage** /ˈ· ·/ *n* [C] the structure of RIBS around your lungs, heart, and other organs

**ri·bo·fla·vin** /ˌraɪbəʊˈfleɪvɪn‖ˌraɪbə-/ *n* [U] *technical* VITAMIN B2, a substance that exists in meat, milk, and some vegetables, and that is important for your health

**rice** /raɪs/ *n* [U] **1** a food that consists of small white or brown grains that you boil in water until they become soft enough to eat: *a tasty sauce served with rice or pasta* **2** the plant that produces this grain

**rice pad·dy** /ˈ· ˌ‥/ *n* [C] a field in which rice is grown

**rice pa·per** /ˈ· ˌ‥/ *n* [U] **1** a thin paper made especially in China and used by painters there **2** a similar type of thin paper that can be eaten, which is used in cooking

**rice pud·ding** /ˌ· ˈ‥/ *n* [U] a sweet dish made of rice, milk, and sugar cooked together

**rich** /rɪtʃ/ *adj* 

**1 ▶ WEALTHY ◀** **a)** having a lot of money or valuable possessions: *one of the richest women in America* | *He got rich by making money on the stock market.* | *a rich and powerful nation* **b) the rich** people who have a lot of money and possessions: *tax laws that benefit the rich*

**2 ▶ LARGE AMOUNT ◀** having or containing a lot of something: [+ **in**] *Citrus fruits are rich in vitamin C.* | **oxygen-rich/nutrient-rich/protein-rich etc** (=containing a lot of oxygen etc) *Pregnant women should eat protein-rich foods.*

**3 ▶ FULL OF INTEREST ◀** full of interesting or important events, ideas etc: *the rich literary tradition of England* | [+ **in**] *a story that was rich in detail*

**4 ▶ SMELL ◀** having a strong pleasant smell: *The rich scent of the pine trees was heavy in the air.*

**5 ▶ COLOUR ◀** having a beautiful strong colour: *stained glass dyed a rich blue*

**6 ▶ FOOD ◀** containing foods such as butter, cream, and eggs, which make you feel full very quickly: *a rich fruit cake*

**7 ▶ MUSIC/SOUNDS ◀** having a pleasant low sound: *the rich tone of a cello*

**8 ▶ SOIL/LAND ◀** good for growing plants in; FERTILE (1): *Cotton grew well in the rich, black soil.*

**9 ▶ CLOTH/JEWELLERY ETC ◀** expensive and beautiful: *She stroked the rich velvet of the dress enviously.*

**10 that's rich (coming from him/you etc)** used to say that what someone has said is unreasonable and that

they are criticizing you for doing something that they do themselves: *Ron told me I was disloyal. That's pretty rich coming from a married man.*
**11 ► PETROL ◄** having too much petrol mixed with the air, so that a car's engine does not operate smoothly

**rich·es** /ˈrɪtʃɨz/ *n* [plural] *especially literary* expensive or beautiful possessions and large amounts of money: *the riches he had brought back from his travels*

**rich·ly** /ˈrɪtʃli/ *adv* **1 richly decorated/embroidered etc** beautifully and expensively decorated etc: *a cloak richly embroidered with gold thread* **2 richly coloured** having beautiful strong colours: *the richly coloured mosaic* **3 richly deserve** to completely deserve something such as success or punishment: *They got the punishment they so richly deserved.* **4** in large amounts: *He was richly rewarded for his services.*

**rick¹** /rɪk/ *n* [C] a large pile of STRAW or grass that is kept in a field until it is needed

**rick²** *v* [T] *BrE* to twist and slightly injure your back, neck, ANKLE etc: *He whirled around so quickly he ricked his neck.*

**rick·ets** /ˈrɪkɨts/ *n* [U] a disease that children get in which their bones become soft and bent, caused by a lack of VITAMIN D

**rick·et·y** /ˈrɪkɨti/ *adj* a rickety piece of furniture or part of a building is in such bad condition that it looks as if it will break if you use it: *an old rickety wooden chair* —see picture on page 1258

**rick·shaw** /ˈrɪkʃɔː‖-ʃɒː/ *n* [C] a small vehicle used in South East Asia for carrying one or two passengers, that is pulled by someone walking or riding a bicycle

**ric·o·chet¹** /ˈrɪkəʃeɪ/ *v* [I] if a moving object, such as a bullet or stone, ricochets, it changes direction when it hits a surface at an angle: [**+ off**] *Bullets ricocheted off the boulders around him.*

**ricochet²** *n* [C] **1** something such as a bullet or a stone that has ricocheted **2** an act of ricocheting

S1 **rid¹** /rɪd/ *adj* **1 get rid of a)** to throw away something you do not want or use any more: *It's time we got rid of all these old toys.* **b)** to take action so that you no longer have something unpleasant that you do not want: *I can't get rid of this cough.* | *He opened the windows to get rid of the smell of stale tobacco.* **c)** to make someone leave because you do not like them or because they are causing problems: *I had to get rid of my assistant because he was habitually late.* **2 be rid of** to have got rid of something or someone so that they are not there to worry or annoy you: *The clerical part of his job was tedious, and he was glad to be rid of it.* | **be well rid of** *especially spoken* (=be lucky to be rid of) *You're well rid of her, she's nothing but trouble.*

**rid²** *v past tense* **rid** or **ridded** *past participle* **rid** *present participle* **ridding**

**rid** sb/sth **of** sth *v* [T] **1** to remove something or someone that is bad or harmful from a place, organization etc: *A huge vaccination program rid the world of smallpox.* **2 rid yourself of sth** to take action so that you do not have a feeling, thought, or problem that was causing you trouble any more: *She's trying to rid herself of a dependence on drugs.*

**rid·dance** /ˈrɪdns/ *n* [U] **good riddance** *spoken* a rude way of saying you are glad someone has left: *"Jim's left." "Well, good riddance," said Faye. "I never liked him."*

**-ridden** /rɪdn/ *suffix (in adjectives)* **1** feeling too much of a strong emotion: *her guilt-ridden dreams* **2** too full of something: *mosquito-ridden swamps*

**rid·dle¹** /ˈrɪdl/ *n* [C] **1** a question that is deliberately very confusing and usually has a humorous or clever answer: *Solve this riddle—What is black and white and red all over? Answer—An embarrassed zebra.* **2** a mysterious action, event, or situation that you do not understand and cannot explain: *The origins of the Basque language remain a riddle.* | *the riddle of the universe* **3** a large wire container with holes in it used to separate earth from stones

**riddle²** *v* [T] **1** to shake the coal etc in a fire or push it about with a stick, in order to remove ashes **2** to make a lot of small holes in something

**rid·dled** /ˈrɪdld/ *adj* **1 riddled with** very full of something, especially something bad or unpleasant: *awful concrete apartment blocks, riddled with damp* | *an isolated village community, riddled with prejudice* **2 riddled with holes** full of small holes: *The wall of the fort was riddled with bullet holes.* | *streets riddled with potholes*

**ride¹** /raɪd/ *v past tense* **rode** /rəʊd‖roʊd/ *past particple* **ridden** /ˈrɪdn/ S2 W2
**1 ► ANIMAL ◄** [I,T] to sit on an animal, especially a horse, and make it move along: *She learnt to ride when she was seven.* | **ride away/across/back etc** *He rode away across the marshes.* | **ride sth** *I've never ridden a horse.* | **ride on sth** *She arrived riding on a white horse.* | **go riding** *I go riding every Saturday.* | **ride a race** *I rode a good number of races last season.* | **ride a winner** (=ride a horse that wins a race) *I rode my first winner last year.* | **ride the countryside/range** *AmE* (=to travel on a horse across the countryside) *They rode the countryside in search of her.*
**2 ► BICYCLE/MOTORBIKE ◄** [I always + adv/prep,T] to travel on a bicycle or MOTORBIKE **ride away/down/to etc** *They mounted their bikes and rode off.* | **ride sth** *She rode her bicycle to school every day.* | **ride on sth** *Can I ride on your bike?*
**3 ► VEHICLE ◄** [I always + adv/prep, T] *especially AmE* to travel in a bus, car, or other vehicle: **ride in/on sth** *It was the first time they had ridden in a train.* | *I ride in cabs whenever I can.* | **ride to/into/back etc** *We got onto the bus and rode into San Francisco.* | **ride a bus** *AmE*: *Ann rode a bus for the rest of the distance.*
**4 ride on sb's shoulders/back** if a child rides on someone's shoulders or back, they are carried in that way: *He was tired so he rode on his father's shoulders.*
**5 ► IN A LIFT ◄** [I always + adv/prep, T] *especially AmE* to travel up or down in a lift: **ride up/down** *I walked to the elevator and rode back down.* | **ride sth** *When the elevator arrived he rode it down to his floor.*
**6 ► IN WATER ◄ a)** [I always + adv/prep] to move or float on the water: *The smaller boat was lighter and rode higher in the water.* | **ride at anchor** *There was a large ship riding at anchor in the bay.* **b) ride a wave** to float on a wave and move forward with it: *The sea was full of surfboarders riding the waves.*
**7 be riding high** to feel very happy and confident: *They were riding high on their election victory.*
**8 let sth ride** *spoken* to take no action about something that is wrong or unpleasant: *He made a derogatory remark, but I let it ride.*
**9 ride roughshod over** to ignore someone else's feelings or ideas because you have the power or authority to do this: *He was accused of riding roughshod over his colleagues' proposals.*
**10 ► ANNOY SB ◄** [T] *AmE spoken* to annoy someone by repeatedly criticizing them or asking them to do things: *Stop riding her – she's doing her best.*
**11 ride a punch/blow** to move back slightly when someone hits you, so that you are not hit with so much force: *He managed to ride the punch.*
**12 be riding for a fall** *informal* to be doing something unwise which could result in failure: *I had a feeling he was riding for a fall, and tried to tell him so.*

**ride** sb ↔ **down** *phr v* [T] to knock someone down when you are riding on a horse: *They were almost ridden down by the cavalry.*

**ride on** sth *phr v* [T] if someone's success or the respect that they get is riding on something, it depends on it: *He knew he had to win – his reputation was riding on it.*

**ride** sth ↔ **out** *phr v* **1** [T] if a ship rides out a storm, it manages to keep floating until the storm has ended **2** [T] if you ride out a difficult situation, you are not badly harmed by it: *The company was deeply involved in the scandal, but managed to ride it out successfully.*

**ride up** *phr v* [I] if a skirt rides up, it moves upwards so that it is no longer covering your body properly

R

S3 **ride²** *n* [C]
**1 ▶ JOURNEY ◀** a journey on a horse or bicycle, or in a vehicle: *It was a lovely morning for a ride.* | [+ **in/on**] *a ride in the director's personal car* | **go for a ride** *Let's go for a ride in the countryside.* | **have a ride** *Can I have a ride on your motorbike?* | **take sb for a ride** *Shall I take you for a ride in my car?* | **give sb a ride** *A man gave me a ride back to Harrisburg.* | **a car/lorry/train etc ride** *He was exhausted after the coach ride from Manchester.* | **get a (free) ride** *I managed to get a free ride down to the station.* | **hitch a ride** *She hitched a ride into town.*
**2 give sb a rough ride** *informal* to make a situation difficult or unpleasant for someone in authority: *The journalists gave the Prime Minister a pretty rough ride.*
**3 take sb for a ride** *spoken* to trick someone, especially in order to get money from them: *I'd just begun to realise he was taking me for a ride.*
**4 come/go along for the ride** *spoken* to join what other people are doing just for pleasure, not because you are seriously interested in it: *I had nothing better to do, so I thought I'd go along for the ride.*
**5 have/be in for a bumpy ride** *informal* to have or be likely to have difficulties or problems
**6 ▶ MACHINE ◀** a large machine that people ride on for pleasure at a FAIR: *The rides are exciting, but very expensive.*
**7 ▶ PATH ◀** a path that is suitable for horses but not for cars: *a grassy ride*

**rid·er** /ˈraɪdə‖-ər/ *n* [C] **1** someone who rides a horse, bicycle etc **2** a statement that is added, especially to an official decision or judgment: *The rider stated that paragraph 27 applied only to foreign imports.*

**ridge¹** /rɪdʒ/ *n* [C] **1** a long area of high land, especially at the top of a mountain: *a windswept ridge* —see picture on page 835 **2 a)** a line of something that rises above a surface: *a ridge of boulders* | *a sandy ridge* **b)** a long narrow raised part of a surface: *The ridges on the soles give the shoes a better grip.* **3 a ridge of high pressure** *technical* a long area of high ATMOSPHERIC pressure

**ridge²** *v* [T] to make a ridge or ridges in something

**ridged** /rɪdʒd/ *adj* something that is ridged has ridges on its surface: *gnarled, ridged bark*

**rid·i·cule¹** /ˈrɪdɪ̣kjuːl/ *n* [U] unkind laughter or remarks intended to make someone or something seem stupid: *He used his acute brain and mischievous wit to riducule Tory MPs.* | **be held up to ridicule** (=be publicly made to look stupid) *In 'The Lord of the Flies', Piggy had become an object of ridicule, ignored by the other boys.* | **an object of ridicule** (=a person or thing that everyone laughs at and regards as stupid)

**ridicule²** *v* [T] to laugh at a person, idea, institution etc: *My ideas were ridiculed by the rest of the team.*

S2 **ri·dic·u·lous** /rɪˈdɪkjɪ̣ləs/ *adj* silly or unreasonable: *She looked absolutely ridiculous in those trousers.* | *"I'm too scared to go on my own." "Oh, don't be ridiculous!"* | **it is ridiculous that** *It's ridiculous that we have to wait six weeks.* —**ridiculously** *adv* —**ridiculousness** *n* [U]

**rid·ing** /ˈraɪdɪŋ/ *n* [U] the sport or activity of riding horses

**rife** /raɪf/ *adj* **1** [not before noun] if something bad or unpleasant is rife, it is very common: *Violent crime is rife in our inner cities.* —see also **run rife** (RUN¹ (37)) **2 rife with** full of something bad or unpleasant: *The streets were rife with rumors of the President's resignation.*

**riff** /rɪf/ *n* [C] a repeated series of notes in popular or JAZZ music: *whistling a Scott Joplin riff*

**rif·fle** /ˈrɪfəl/ also **riffle through** *v* [T] *informal* to quickly turn over the pages of a book, magazine etc

**riff-raff** /ˈrɪf ræf/ *n* [U] an insulting word for people who are noisy, badly-behaved, or of low social class: *She seemed to have invited most of the local riff-raff.*

**ri·fle¹** /ˈraɪfəl/ *n* [C] a gun with a long BARREL (=tube-shaped part) which you hold up to your shoulder

**rifle²** *v* [T] **1** also **rifle through** to search quickly through a cupboard, drawer etc: *He rifled through his pockets for a coin.* **2** to steal things from a place: *The warehouse's entire stock was rifled.*

**rifle range** /ˈ·· ·/ *n* [C] a place where people practise shooting with rifles

**rift** /rɪft/ *n* [C] **1** a situation in which two people or groups have begun to dislike or distrust each other, usually caused by a serious disagreement: *The government has been weakened by internal rifts.* **2** a crack or narrow opening in a large mass of rock, cloud etc

**rift val·ley** /ˈ· ˌ··/ *n* [C] a valley with very steep sides, formed by the cracking and moving of the Earth's surface

**rig¹** /rɪg/ *v* **rigged, rigging** [T] **1** to arrange or influence an election, competition etc in a dishonest way so that you get the result that you want: *She claimed the election was rigged.* **2** [usually passive] to provide a ship with ropes, sails etc: *a fully-rigged vessel*

**rig** sb ↔ **out** *phr v* [T] *informal* to dress someone in special or unusual clothes: *They had rigged the little boy out in a sailor suit.*

**rig** sth ↔ **up** *phr v* [T] *informal* to make equipment, furniture etc quickly from objects that you find around you: *We rigged up a simple shower at the back of the cabin.*

**rig²** *n* [C] **1** a large structure in the sea used for getting oil from the ground under the sea **2** the way in which a ship's sails and MASTS are arranged **3** *informal* a large TRUCK: *driving the rig down to Baltimore* **4** *AmE informal* a set of equipment for a special purpose: *the photographer's camera and all the rest of his rig* **5** *old-fashioned* a set of clothes —see also LIGHTING RIG

**rig·a·ma·role** /ˈrɪgəmərəʊl‖-roʊl/ *n* [C] an American spelling of RIGMAROLE

**rig·a·to·ni** /ˌrɪgəˈtəʊni‖-ˈtoʊni/ *n* [U] a type of PASTA in the shape of short tubes —see picture at PASTA

**rig·ging** /ˈrɪgɪŋ/ *n* [U] all the ropes, chains etc that hold up a ship's sails —see picture at YACHT

**right¹** /raɪt/ *adj* S1 W1
**1 ▶ TRUE/CORRECT ◀** based on true facts; correct: *Is that the right time?* | *Yes. $6.47 is the right answer.* | *New research has proved their theories right.* | **be right about** *You were right about the party – it was awful.* | **half right** (=partly but not completely right) *Well, you're half right – he's not actually an actor, but he does work in the theatre.*
**2 ▶ CORRECT/NORMAL ◀** in the position, order or state which is correct or where something works best: *This diagram's not right!* | **put sth right** (=change something so that it is correct or works properly) *You'll have to call a plumber to put the machine right.*
**3 that's right** *spoken* **a)** used to agree with what someone says or to answer 'yes' to a question: *"Is this Piccadilly Circus?" "That's right, mate."* | *"...and before you know it, it's too late." "That's right, that's right."* **b)** used when you are telling someone that you are angry about what they are doing: *That's right! Just go out and leave me to do the dishes as usual!*
**4 ▶ SIDE ◀** [only before noun] **a)** concerning or belonging to the right side of your body, which has the hand that most people write with: *Raise your right arm.* | *My right shoe pinches.* —opposite LEFT¹ (1) **b)** on the same side of something as your right side: *Take the next right turn.* | *the right bank of the river* —opposite LEFT¹ (2)
**5 ▶ SUITABLE ◀** most suitable for a particular occasion or purpose: *This is definitely the right decision for the company.* | **be right for/be the right person for** *Floella is the right person for that job.* | **be right for sb/be the right person for sb** (=to be a suitable partner for someone) *Elaine and Stu are so right for each other!*
**6 ▶ MORALLY ◀** an action that is right is morally correct: **right to do sth** *Do you think I was right to report them to the police?* | *It can't be right to keep lying to your husband.* | **it's only right** (=anything else would not be right) *It's only right that the children get an equal share.* | **it is right that** *I think it's right that the people who work hardest should earn the most.* —opposite WRONG¹ (4)
**7 ▶ TOTAL ◀** [only before noun] *BrE spoken* used to emphasize how bad someone or something is: *He sounds*

*like a right idiot!*|*Don't go in there, it's a right rip-off.*| **right royal** (=extremely special in a way that is suitable for a king, queen etc) *a right royal welcome*
**8 things are not right** used to say that there are problems connected with a relationship or situation: *Things haven't been right between Carl and me for a while now.*
**9 be in the right place at the right time** to seem to always be in the place where something useful becomes available or is being offered: *Being a news photographer is all about being in the right place at the right time.*
**10 ▶ HEALTHY ◀** *spoken* healthy: *I haven't been feeling right all day.*|**put sb right** (=make someone feel healthy again) *A week's rest will put you right again.* —see also **put sb right/straight** (PUT (15))
**11 not right in the head/not in your right mind** *usually humorous* crazy: *If he thinks he can get to the Olympics, he's not in his right mind!*
**12 (as) right as rain** *informal* completely healthy, especially after an illness: *The doctor says I'll be as right as rain in a couple of days.*
**13 ▶ SOCIALLY ◀** *BrE* the right people, places, schools etc are considered to be the best or most important: *Sonia's always careful to be seen with the right people.*
**14 right you are/righto/righty ho** *BrE spoken* used to agree with what someone is saying or telling you to do: *"Shut the door, will you?" "Righto."*
**15 am I right in thinking (that)** *spoken* used when you think that something is true, but you are not completely sure: *Am I right in thinking that you come from Australia?*

Frequencies of the word **right** in spoken and written English.

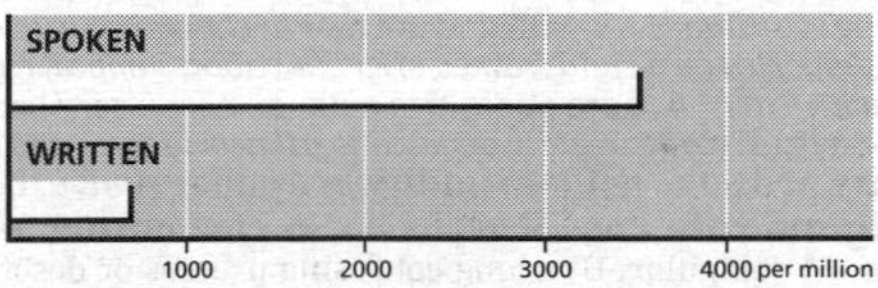


Based on the British National Corpus and the Longman Lancaster Corpus

This graph shows that the word **right** is much more common in spoken English than in written English. This is because it has several uses as an interjection in conversations.

**right** (*adj*) **SPOKEN USES**

**16** *BrE* used to get someone's attention so that you can tell them something: *Right! Open your books on page 16.*
**17** *BrE* used to say you are ready to do something: *Right, let's go!*
**18** *especially BrE* used to say 'yes' to a suggestion or order: *"Come over tomorrow." "Right, OK, see you then."*
**19** used to agree with what someone says: *"I mean, why shouldn't she go out with him if she wants to?" "Yeah, right."*
**20** used as a question to ask if what you have said is correct: *We're leaving at 10.30, right?*
**21** used to check that someone is understanding what you are saying: *So I went into the bar, right, and I saw the manager, right, and I said......*

S1 W1 **right²** *adv*
**1 right at/behind/in front of** exactly in a particular position or place: *She was standing right in the middle of the room.*|*There's the house, right in front of you.*
**2 ▶ IMMEDIATELY ◀** immediately and without any delay: **right now/away/after** *I'll find the address for you right away.*|*It's on right after the 6:30 news.*|**right off the bat** *AmE* (=without much thought) *Kay wrote the answers down right off the bat.*
**3 ▶ CORRECTLY ◀** correctly: *We guessed right – they'd already gone.*
**4 ▶ DIRECTION/SIDE ◀** towards the direction or side that is on the right: *Turn right at the crossroads.* —opposite LEFT²
**5 right along/through/into/around etc** all the way along, through etc: *Go right to the end of the road.*|*I haven't read the book right through yet.*
**6 be right behind sb** *spoken* to completely support someone in their ideas or in what they are trying to achieve
**7 I'll be right with you/right there** *spoken* used to ask someone to wait because you are coming very soon: *"Lunch is ready!" "I'll be right there."*
**8 be right up there (with)** *informal* to be as good or as important as the very best: *As far as I'm concerned he's right up there with Bob Dylan.*
**9 right, left and centre** *BrE* **right and left** *AmE* everywhere or in every way: *We're losing money right, left and centre.*

**right³** *n* 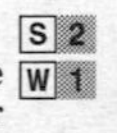
**1 ▶ ALLOWED ◀** [C usually singular] if you have the right to do something you are morally, legally, or officially allowed to do it: **right to do sth** *We have a constitutional right to defend ourselves.*|*Everyone should have the right to live in peace.*|**be within your rights (to do sth)** (=be morally or legally allowed to do something) *You'd be well within your rights to take him to court.*|**as of right** *formal* (=because it is their right) *Every shareholder will receive an invitation as of right.*
**2 have a right to be annoyed/upset/angry** to have a good or understandable reason for being annoyed, upset etc: *You had every right to be angry with them.*
**3 have no right to do sth** used to say that someone's actions are completely unreasonable or unfair: *You have no right to treat us like this – we are innocent.*
**4 the right a)** the side of your body that has the hand that most people write with, or this side of anything else: *Take the first turning on the right.*|*On your right, you can see the Houses of Parliament.*|*Take two steps to the right.* **b)** also **the Right** [singular] political parties or groups such as the CONSERVATIVES in Britain or the REPUBLICANS in the US, which strongly support the CAPITALIST economic system
**5 rights** [plural] the freedom and advantages that everyone should be allowed to have: *We must stand up and fight for our rights!*|*a denial of basic human rights*|**women's/workers' rights etc** *New legislation is gradually taking away workers' rights.*|**equal rights** (=the same rights for everyone, whatever their sex, race, or social position) —see also CIVIL RIGHTS, HUMAN RIGHTS
**6 ▶ CORRECT BEHAVIOUR ◀** [U] behaviour that is generally agreed to be morally correct: *You're old enough to know what's right.*|*Some of these kids don't seem to know the difference between right and wrong.*
**7 be in the right** to have the best reasons, arguments etc in a disagreement with someone else: *Both sides are convinced that they are in the right.*
**8 by rights** *spoken* used to describe what should happen if things are done fairly or correctly: *By rights Jenkins should have had a promotion by now.*
**9 in your own right** without depending on anyone or anything else: *Elizabeth II is Queen in her own right.*
**10 put sth/sb to rights** to make a place, person, or situation return to normal again: *This medicine will soon put you to rights.*|*It took ages to put the room to rights again.*
**11 the rights and wrongs of** all the different reasons for and against something: *I'm not interested in the rights and wrongs of the system, I just want my money back!*
**12 do right by** *old-fashioned* to do what is morally correct for someone: *I mean to do right by her.*
**13 ▶ HIT ◀** [C] a hit using your right hand: *He got me with a right on the jaw.* —**rightness** *n* [U] —see also **two wrongs don't make a right** (WRONG³ (5))

**right⁴** *v* [T] **1 right a wrong** to do something to prevent an unjust situation from continuing **2** to put something back into the state or situation that it should be in: *We must try to right the balance between taxation and government spending* **3** to put something, especially a boat, back into its correct upright position: *I finally managed to right the canoe.*

**right an·gle** /ˈ· ˌ··/ *n* [C] **1** an angle of 90°, like the angles at the corners of a square —see picture at ANGLE[1] **2 be at right angles (to sth)** if two things are at right angles, they make a 90° angle where they touch —**right angled** *adj*: *a right-angled triangle*

**right·eous** /ˈraɪtʃəs/ *adj* **1 righteous indignation/anger etc** strong feelings of anger when you think a situation is not morally right or fair: *"You should have asked me first" said Corrine, full of righteous indignation.* **2** *formal* morally good and fair: *a righteous and loving God* —see also SELF-RIGHTEOUS —**righteously** *adv* —**righteousness** *n* [U]

**right field** /ˈ· ·/ *n* **1** [C] one of the main areas of the playing field in BASEBALL —opposite LEFT FIELD **2** [U] the position of someone who plays in this area

**right·ful** /ˈraɪtfəl/ *adj* [only before noun] *formal* according to what is legally and morally correct: *Every effort was made to return the purse to its rightful owner.*|*the rightful heir to the throne* —**rightfully** *adv*|*the lands that are rightfully yours* —**rightfulness** *n* [U]

**right-hand** /ˈ· ·/ *adj* [only before noun] on the right side of something: *Get into the right-hand lane.*|*It's on the right-hand side.* —opposite LEFT-HAND

**right-hand drive** /ˌ· · ˈ·/ *adj* [only before noun] a right-hand drive vehicle is one in which the driver sits on the right —opposite LEFT-HAND DRIVE

**right-hand·ed** /ˌ· ˈ··◂/ *adj* **1** a right-handed person uses their right hand for writing, throwing etc **2** a right-handed tool is designed for right-handed people: *right-handed scissors* —opposite LEFT-HANDED —**right-handed** *adv*

**right-hand·er** /ˌ· ˈ··/ *n* [C] **1** someone who uses their right hand for writing, throwing etc **2** a hit with your right hand —opposite LEFT-HANDER

**right-hand man** /ˌ· · ˈ·/ *n* [singular] the person who supports and helps you the most, especially in your job

**Right Hon** the written abbreviation of Right Honourable

**Right Hon·our·a·ble** /ˈ· ˌ····/ *adj* used when formally announcing or talking about lords or important government ministers in Britain: *the Right Honourable Giles Williams MP*

**right·ist** /ˈraɪtɪst/ *adj* supporting RIGHT-WING ideas or groups —opposite LEFTIST —**rightist** *n* [C] —**rightism** *n* [U]

**right·ly** /ˈraɪtli/ *adv* **1** for a good or sensible reason: *The audience was rightly outraged at this suggestion.*| **quite rightly** *BrE*: *She insisted, quite rightly, that we all put our seat belts on.* **2** correctly: *As she rightly pointed out, this will do nothing to solve the problem.*| **if I remember rightly** *spoken*: *If I remember rightly, Ray's parents emigrated shortly after the war.* **3 rightly or wrongly** used to say that whatever you think of someone's action, this is what they did: *Rightly or wrongly, the Italians decided to withdraw from the competition.* **4 and rightly so** *spoken* used to say that a decision or action you have just described is fair and morally right: *Bryan was punished, and rightly so.* **5 I can't rightly say/don't rightly know** *spoken* used to say that you are not sure whether something is correct or not

**right-mind·ed** /ˌ· ˈ··◂/ *adj* a right-minded person has opinions, principles, or standards of behaviour that you approve of: *All right-minded people will support us.* —**right-mindedness** *n* [U]

**right of ap·peal** /ˌ· · ·ˈ·/ *n plural* **rights of appeal** [C] *law* the legal right to ask for a court's decision to be changed

**right-of-cen·tre** /ˌ· · ˈ··◂/ *adj* supporting ideas and aims that are between the centre and the right in politics —opposite LEFT-OF-CENTRE

**right of way** /ˌ· · ˈ·/ *n* **1** [U] the right to drive into or across a road before other vehicles: *I never know who has right of way at this junction.* **2** [C] *plural* **rights of way a)** the right to walk across someone else's land: *We have a right of way across his field to our house.* **b)** a path that people have the right to use: *Private property – no right of way.*

**right on** /ˌ· ˈ·◂/ *adj* **1** *BrE* someone who is right on or has right on opinions, supports social justice, equal rights etc: *It's one of those annoyingly right on magazines about the environment.* **2** *AmE* someone is right on when they say something that is correct or that you completely agree with: *Jodie was right on with that remark.*

**rights is·sue** /ˈ· ˌ··/ *n* [C] *technical* an offer of company SHARES (=part of the company you can own) at a cheaper price than usual, to people who own some already

**right-think·ing** /ˌ· ˈ··◂/ *adj* a right-thinking person has opinions, principles or standards of behaviour that you approve of: *Any right-thinking woman would agree.*

**right·ward** /ˈraɪtwəd‖-wərd/ *adj* on or towards the right: *a rightward glance* —opposite LEFTWARD

**right·wards** /ˈraɪtwədz‖-wərdz/ *especially BrE*, usually **rightward** *AmE adv* on or towards the right —opposite LEFTWARDS

**right wing** /ˌ· ˈ·◂/ *n* **the right wing** political groups that believe very strongly in the CAPITALIST economic system: *The party is dominated by its right wing.* —**right-wing** *adj*|*right-wing views* —**right-winger** *n* [C]|*a prominent right-winger in the party* —opposite LEFT WING

**ri·gid** /ˈrɪdʒɪd/ *adj* **1** rigid methods, systems etc are very strict and difficult to change: *Betty's finding it hard to keep to the school's rigid rules.*|*the rigid discipline of army life* **2** someone who is rigid is very unwilling to change their ideas: *He's very rigid and old fashioned.*|*rigid attitudes* **3** stiff and not moving or bending: *a tent supported on a rigid framework*|*The rabbit stopped, rigid with fear.* **4 bore sb rigid** to make someone very bored —**rigidly** *adv*: *rigidly opposed to all new ideas* —**rigidity** /rɪˈdʒɪdɪti/ *n* [U] —**rigidify** /rɪˈdʒɪdɪfaɪ/ *AmE v* [I,T]

**rig·ma·role** /ˈrɪgmərəʊl‖-roʊl/ also **rigamarole** *AmE* *n* **1** [singular, U] a long confusing process or description: *Omar went into this rigmarole about how he lost his passport.* **2** [U] a long confusing series of actions that seems silly: *I had to go through the whole rigmarole of kissing the Bible and swearing to tell the truth.*

**rig·or** /ˈrɪgə‖-ər/ *n* [U] the American spelling of RIGOUR

**rig·or mor·tis** /ˌrɪgə ˈmɔːtɪs, ˌraɪgɔː-‖ˌrɪgər ˈmɔːr-/ *n* [U] *Latin* the condition in which someone's body becomes stiff after they die

**rig·or·ous** /ˈrɪgərəs/ *adj* **1** careful, thorough, and exact: *rigorous safety checks* **2** very severe or strict: *rigorous army training* —**rigorously** *adv*

**rig·our** *BrE*, **rigor** *AmE* /ˈrɪgə‖-ər/ *n* [U] **1 the rigours of** the problems and unpleasant conditions of a difficult situation: *all the rigours of a Canadian winter* **2** *BrE formal* strictness or severity of a punishment: *He deserves to be punished with the full rigour of the law.* **3** great care and thoroughness in making sure that something is correct: *Their research seems to me to be lacking in rigour.*

**rig-out** /ˈ· ·/ *n* [C] *BrE informal* a set of clothes: *You can't go out in that rig-out!* —see also **rig out** (RIG[1])

**rile** /raɪl/ *v* [T] *informal* to make someone extremely angry: *It really riled her to think that Henry was lying.*

**Ri·ley** /ˈraɪli/ *n* **lead the life of Riley** *BrE informal* to have enough money to do what you like: *Barbara's been leading the life of Riley since that lottery win.*

**rim**[1] /rɪm/ *n* [C] **1** the outside edge of something circular: *the rim of a glass*|*Fit the tyre round the rim of the wheel.* **2 gold-rimmed/red-rimmed etc** with a gold, red etc rim: *gold-rimmed spectacles* —**rimless** *adj*|*Annie wore rimless glasses.*

**rim**[2] **rimmed, rimming** *v* [T] *literary* to be around the edge of something: *Trees rimmed the lake.*

**rime** /raɪm/ *n* [U] *literary* FROST (=powdery ice)

**rind** /raɪnd/ *n* [C,U] **1** the thick outer skin of some types of fruit, such as oranges: *grated lemon rind* —compare PEEL² **2** the thick outer skin of some foods, such as BACON or cheese

S1 W2 **ring¹** /rɪŋ/ *n*
**1 ▶ JEWELLERY ◀** [C] a piece of jewellery that you wear on your finger: *a diamond ring* (=decorated with diamonds) —see also ENGAGEMENT RING, WEDDING RING —see picture at JEWELLERY
**2 ▶ CIRCLE ◀** [C] **a)** a circular line or mark: *Martha had dark rings round her eyes from too many sleepless nights.* **b)** an object in the shape of a circle: *curtain rings|piston rings|Slice the onions into rings.* **c)** a group of people or things arranged in a circle: *A ring of armed troops surrounded the building.*
**3 ▶ BELLS ◀** [C] the sound made by a bell or the act of making this sound: *He gave several loud rings at the door.* —see picture on page 1261
**4 give sb a ring** *BrE informal* to make a telephone call to someone: *I'll give you a ring later in the week.*
**5 ▶ CRIMINALS ◀** [C] a group of people who illegally control a business or criminal activity: **drugs/spy ring** *Police suspect a drug ring may be operating in the area.|revelations of a massive spy ring*
**6 have a ring of truth** to seem likely to be true: *Mrs Datchet's story had a ring of truth about it.*
**7 have a familiar ring** if something has a familiar ring, you feel that you have heard it before: *Jerry's excuse had a strangely familiar ring.*
**8 run rings around** *informal* to be able to do something much better than someone else can: *My five-year-old can run rings around me on the computer.*
**9 ▶ COOKING ◀** [C] *especially BrE* one of the circular areas on top of a COOKER that is heated by gas or electricity —see picture on page 833
**10 ▶ SPORT/ENTERTAINMENT ◀ a)** a small square area surrounded by ropes, where people BOX or WRESTLE **b)** a large circular area surrounded by seats at a CIRCUS **c) the ring** the sport of BOXING: *He retired from the ring at 34.*

S1 W2 **ring²** *v past tense* **rang** /ræŋ/ *past participle* **rung** /rʌŋ/
**1 ▶ BELL ◀ a)** [T] to make a bell make a sound: *I rang the doorbell but no-one came.* **b)** [I] if a bell rings, it makes a noise: *At that moment, the bell rang for lunch.* **c)** [I] to ring a bell to call someone to serve you: [+ **for**] *Ring for service.*
**2 ▶ SOUNDS ◀** [I] **a)** to make a high continuous sound: *Tap the glass gently, and you'll hear it ring.* **b)** your ears ring after you have been somewhere very noisy or heard a loud sound: *The explosion made our ears ring.* **c)** *literary* if a place rings with a sound it is full of that sound: *The courtyard rang with the sound of horses' hooves.*
**3 ▶ TELEPHONE ◀ a)** [I,T] *BrE* to make a telephone call to someone; CALL¹ (7) *especially AmE*: *I rang you yesterday but you weren't in.|Ring 192 for information.|*[+ **for**] *Sally rang for a taxi.* —see TELEPHONE (USAGE) **b)** [I] if a telephone rings, it makes a sound to show that someone is phoning you: *The phone hasn't stopped ringing all day.*
**4 ring a bell** *informal* if something rings a bell, you think you have heard it before: *Her name rings a bell but I can't remember her face.*
**5 not ring true** if something does not ring true, you do not believe it, even though you are not sure why: *It was a clever excuse but it didn't really ring true.*
**6 ring the changes** to make changes to something, not because it needs changing but just in order to make it more interesting, more attractive etc: *It's easy to ring the changes in your living room with some new cushion covers.*
**7 ring hollow** if words ring hollow, you do not feel that they are true or sincere: *Their expressions of sympathy rang hollow.*
**8 ring in your ears** if a sound or remark rings in your ears, you seem to continue to hear it after it has finished: *She went out, his cruel laughter ringing in her ears.*
**ring back** *phr v* [I,T **ring** sb **back**] *BrE* to telephone someone again, for example because you were not available when they telephoned you: *John rang, and he wants you to ring him back.*
**ring in** *phr v* **1** [I] *BrE* to telephone the place where you work: *Jane's rung in to say she'll be late.* **2 ring in the New Year** to celebrate the beginning of the New Year by ringing church bells
**ring off** *phr v* [I] *BrE* to end a telephone call: *He rang off without giving his name.*
**ring out** *phr v* **1** [I] a voice, bell etc that rings out is loud and clear: *The sound of a shot rang out.* **2 ring out the Old Year** to celebrate the end of the year by ringing church bells
**ring round** *phr v* [I,T] *BrE* to make telephone calls to a group of people, in order to organize something, find out information etc: *I'll ring round to see whether anyone's interested in coming with us.*
**ring** sth/sb ↔ **up** *phr v* **1** [I,T **ring** sb ↔ **up**] *BrE* to telephone someone: *I'll ring the manager up tomorrow.* **2** [T **ring** sth ↔ **up**] to press buttons on a CASH REGISTER to record how much money is being put inside: *The cashier rang up $300 by mistake.*

**ring³** *v past tense and past participle* **ringed** [T] **1** to surround something: *Police marksmen ringed the office block.|***ring sth with** *Her fair hair was ringed with light.* **2** to draw a circular mark around something: *Ring the mistakes in red.* **3** to put a metal ring around a bird's leg

**ring·er** /ˈrɪŋə‖-ər/ *n* [C] someone who rings church bells or hand bells —see also **dead ringer** (DEAD¹ (24))

**ring·fence** /ˈrɪŋfens/ *v* [T] to decide officially that something, especially money, can only be used for a particular purpose: *Ok, so this £20,000 is ringfenced as the training budget.*

**ring fin·ger** /ˈ· ˌ··/ *n* [C] the finger that you traditionally wear your WEDDING RING on

**ring·ing** /ˈrɪŋɪŋ/ *adj* a ringing sound or voice is loud and clear: *"Come here!" he commanded, in ringing tones.*

**ring·lead·er** /ˈrɪŋˌliːdə‖-ər/ *n* [C] someone who leads a group that is doing something illegal or wrong: *Police arrested the ringleaders but let the others go free.*

**ring·let** /ˈrɪŋlɪt/ *n* [C] a long curl of hair that hangs down

**ring-pull** /ˈ· ·/ *n* [C] the ring on the top of a can of drink that you pull to open it

**ring road** /ˈ· ·/ *n* [C] *BrE* a road that goes around a large town to keep the traffic away from the centre; BELTWAY *AmE*

**ring·side** /ˈrɪŋsaɪd/ *n* [singular] **1** the area nearest to the performance in a CIRCUS, BOXING match etc **2 ringside seat** a seat very near to the performers in a CIRCUS, BOXING match etc

**ring span·ner** /ˈ· ˌ··/ *n* [C] *BrE* a tool with a circular end that fits over a NUT to make it tighter or looser; BOX END WRENCH *AmE* —see picture at TOOL¹

**ring·worm** /ˈrɪŋwɜːm‖-wɜːrm/ *n* [U] a skin infection that causes red rings, especially on your head

**rink** /rɪŋk/ *n* [C] **1** a specially prepared area of ice for skating (SKATE²) **2** a special area with a smooth surface where you can go around on ROLLER SKATES

**rink·y-dink** /ˈrɪŋki dɪŋk/ *adj AmE informal* cheap and of bad quality

**rinse¹** /rɪns/ *v* [T] **1** to wash clothes, dishes etc quickly with water, especially running water, and without soap: *Let me just rinse my hands.|Rinse the vegetables under a cold tap.* **2** to wash something in clean water in order to remove soap from it: *Rinse your hair thoroughly to get all the shampoo out.* **3** to remove soap, dirt etc from something by washing it quickly with water: **rinse sth out/away/off etc** *I tried to rinse the mud off under the tap.* **4** to put colour into your hair
**rinse** sth ↔ **out** *phr v* [T] to wash something in clean water, especially to remove soap from it: *Don't forget to rinse out your swimsuit.*

**rinse²** *n* **1 give sth a rinse** to rinse something: *I'll just*

R

*give this shirt a quick rinse.* **2** [C,U] a product you use to change the colour of your hair or to make it more shiny: *a blue rinse for grey hair*

S3 **ri·ot¹** /ˈraɪət/ *n* **1** [C] a situation in which a large crowd of people are behaving in a violent and uncontrolled way especially when they are protesting about something: *The army were called in to put down the riot.* | **race riot** (=between people of different races) *Ethnic tensions led to a massive race riot.* **2 a riot of colour** something with many different bright colours: *The garden is a riot of colour in May.* **3 run riot a)** if people run riot, they behave in a violent, noisy, and uncontrolled way: *Demonstrators are running riot through the town.* **b)** if your imagination, thoughts etc run riot, you cannot control them **c)** if a plant runs riot, it grows very quickly **4 read (sb) the riot act** *often humorous* to give someone a strong warning that they must stop causing trouble: *If the kids don't settle down soon, I'll go up and read them the riot act.* **5** [singular] *old-fashioned* someone or something that is very funny or enjoyable: *Sally's a riot when she's had a few drinks!* | **have a riot** (=have a lot of fun) *"How was the party?" "Oh, we had a riot!"*

**riot²** *v* [I] if a crowd of people riot, they behave in a violent and uncontrolled way, for example by fighting the police and damaging cars or buildings: *Students were rioting in the streets.* —**rioting** *n* [U] —**rioter** *n* [C]

**ri·ot·ous** /ˈraɪətəs/ *adj* **1** wild, exciting, and uncontrolled: *riotous drinking and singing* **2** uncontrolled, noisy, and perhaps dangerous: **riotous behaviour** *BrE: Steve was arrested for riotous behaviour the night before his wedding.* —**riotously** *adv* —**riotousness** *n* [U]

**riot po·lice** /ˈ·· ˌ·/ *n* [U] police whose job is to stop riots: *The riot police used tear gas to control the mob.*

**RIP** /ˌɑːr aɪ ˈpiː/ the written abbreviation of Rest in Peace (=words written on a stone over a grave)

**rip¹** /rɪp/ **ripped, ripping** *v* **1** [I,T] to tear something or be torn quickly and violently: *I've ripped my skirt on a nail.* | *The sails ripped under the force of the wind.* | **rip sth open** (=open something by tearing it) *Impatiently, Sue ripped the letter open.* —see picture on page 1258 **2** [T always + adv/prep] to remove something quickly and violently, using your hands: **rip sth out/off/away/down** *We've had to rip down all the old wallpaper.* **3 rip sth/sb to shreds a)** to destroy something or damage it badly by tearing it in many places: *Jill's kitten is ripping her sofa to shreds.* **b)** to strongly criticize someone, or their opinions, remarks, behaviour etc: *My argument was ripped to shreds at once.* **4 let rip** *informal* to speak or behave violently or emotionally: [+ **at/about**] *Mom really let rip about the state of my room.* **5 let sth rip** *informal* to make a car, boat etc go as fast as it can: *Put your foot on the gas and let her rip!*

**rip off** *phr v* [T] *spoken* **1** [**rip** sb ↔ **off**] to charge someone too much money for something: *They really ripped us off at that hotel!* **2** [**rip off** sth] to steal something: *Somebody's ripped off my bike!* —see also RIP-OFF

**rip through** sth *phr v* [T] to move through a place quickly and with violent force: *A huge explosion ripped through the courthouse.*

**rip** sth ↔ **up** *phr v* [T] to tear something into several pieces: *Pru ripped his photo up into tiny bits.*

**rip²** *n* [C] a long tear or cut: *There was a rip in the tire caused by a sharp stone.*

**rip·cord** /ˈrɪpkɔːd‖-kɔːrd/ *n* [C] **1** the string that you pull to open a PARACHUTE **2** the string that you pull to let gas out of a BALLOON

**ripe** /raɪp/ *adj* **1** ripe fruit or crops are fully grown and ready to eat: *Those apples aren't ripe yet.* —opposite UNRIPE **2 be ripe for** to be in a suitable condition for something, especially for some kind of change: *The land was ripe for industrial development.* **3 the time is ripe (for)** used to say it is a very suitable time for something to happen: *The time was ripe for a challenge to the government.* **4 ripe old age** if you live to a ripe old age, you are very old when you die: *Grandad lived to the ripe old age of 94.* **5** ripe cheese has developed a strong taste and is ready to eat **6** a ripe smell is strong and unpleasant: *The office was so hot that we all smelled rather ripe by the end of the day.* **7** *BrE informal* rude but amusing: *I thought his language was a bit ripe.* —**ripeness** *n* [U]

**rip·en** /ˈraɪpən/ *v* [I,T] to become ripe or to make something ripe: *The tomatoes quickly ripened in the hot weather.*

**rip-off** /ˈ· ·/ *n* [C] *informal* something that is unreasonably expensive: *Five pounds for a coffee? What a rip-off!* —see also **rip off** (RIP¹)

**ri·poste¹** /rɪˈpɒst, rɪˈpəʊst‖rɪˈpoʊst/ *n* [C] **1** *formal* a quick, clever, and amusing reply: *a suitably witty riposte* **2** *technical* a quick return stroke with a sword in FENCING (=the sport of fighting with swords)

**riposte²** *v* **1** [I,T] *formal* to reply quickly and cleverly **2** [I] *technical* to make a riposte in FENCING

**rip·ple¹** /ˈrɪpəl/ *v* **1** [I,T] to move in small waves, or to make something move in this way: *Arnie's muscles rippled as he carried the huge crates.* | *Look how the breeze is rippling the long grass.* **2** [I always + adv/prep] to pass from one person to another like a wave: **ripple around/through etc** *Excitement rippled around the courtroom.* | *A thrill of pleasure rippled through me.* **3** [I] to make a noise like water that is flowing gently: *The water rippled over the stones.* | *a rippling brook*

**ripple²** *n* **1** [C] a small low wave on the surface of a liquid: *The wind made ripples on the surface of the pond.* —see picture at REFLECTION **2 a ripple of applause/laughter etc** a sound that gets gradually louder and softer: *A ripple of laughter ran through the audience.* **3 a ripple of shock/unease/nervousness etc** a feeling that spreads through a person or a group because of something that has happened: *A ripple of shock ran around the meeting.* **4** [C] a shape or pattern that looks like a wave: *ripples on the sand* **5 raspberry ripple/chocolate ripple etc** a type of ICE CREAM that has different coloured bands of fruit, chocolate etc in it **6 ripple effect** a situation in which one action causes another, which then causes a third, etc

**rip-roar·ing** /ˌ· ˈ··◂/ *adj informal* **1 rip-roaring success** a very big success: *The new musical looks set to become a rip-roaring success.* **2** noisy, exciting, and uncontrolled: *Micky had a rip-roaring time spending his first wage packet.* | **rip-roaring drunk** (=very drunk)

**rip·snort·er** /ˌrɪpˈsnɔːtə‖-ˈsnɔːrtər/ *n* [C] *old-fashioned* something very exciting: *The roller coasters there are real ripsnorters.*

**rise¹** /raɪz/ *v past tense* **rose** /rəʊz‖roʊz/ *past participle* **risen** /ˈrɪzən/ [I] S2 W1

**1 ▶INCREASE◀** to increase in number, amount or value: *House prices are likely to rise towards the end of this year.* | **rise by 10%/$3/a large amount etc** *Sales rose by 20% over the Christmas period.* | **rise dramatically/sharply** (=increase greatly) *The number of people seeking asylum in the United Kingdom has risen sharply from five thousand a year in 1988 to over thirty thousand in 1990.* | **rise steadily** (=increase slowly but continuously) *The divorce rate has risen steadily since the 1950s.* | **rising prices/unemployment etc** *Rising crime has driven many families out of down-town areas.* | **rise and fall** *Populations rise and fall in response to the availability of food.* | **... and rising** *The unemployment level is twelve percent and rising.* —see RAISE¹ (USAGE)

**2 ▶GO UPWARDS◀** to go upwards: *The polar ice caps will melt and the sea level will rise* | *Smoke rose from the chimney.* | *The road rises steeply from the village.*

**3 ▶STAND◀** *especially written* to stand up: *Mick McGrath rose and shouted. "Right, lads! Five minutes to finish your beer and then let's go."* | **rise from the table/your chair etc** *Charlotte rose from the table and went over to the window.* | **rise to your feet** *He rose to his feet and tapped on the table as if he was going to speak.*

**4 ▶BECOME SUCCESSFUL◀** to become important, powerful, successful or rich: [+ **from**] *Damascus had*

*risen from a provincial centre of commerce to the capital of the world's greatest empire.* | [+ **to**] *He had entered the army as a boy and risen to the rank of colonel by 1914.* | **rise to the top** *The people who rise to the top in politics are usually the most ruthless.* | **rise to fame** *The Beatles rose to fame in the early 60s.* | **rise to power** *Mussolini rose to power in Italy in 1922.*
**5 ▶ VOICE/SOUND ◀ a)** to be heard: [+ **from**] *The sound of children playing rose from the street.* | **rise above sth** (=be louder than something) *He could hear the rhythm of chanting voices rising above the sound of the traffic.* **b)** to become louder or higher: *Her voice rose with anger and emotion: "I trusted you!"*
**6 ▶ SUN/MOON/STAR ◀** to appear in the sky: *The sun rose and the sea turned gold.*
**7 ▶ EMOTION ◀** if a feeling or emotion rises, you feel it more and more strongly: *I felt panic rising, and my heart banged loudly in my chest.* | *rising excitement* | **sb's spirits rise** (=they become much happier) *Our spirits rose when we heard of the ship's safe return.*
**8 ▶ BE TALL ◀** to be very tall: *Snow-capped mountains rose in the distance.* | **rise above** (=be much taller than) *The tower rose above the surrounding trees.*
**9 rise from** if something tall rises from a place, its base is in that place: *Spiro was pointing at a gentle curve of hill-side that rose from the glittering sea.*
**10 ▶ BREAD/CAKES ETC ◀** if bread, cakes etc rise they become bigger because they contain YEAST or as they are baked
**11 ▶ BED ◀** *literary* to get out of bed in the morning
**12 ▶ AGAINST A GOVERNMENT/ARMY ◀** also **rise up** if a large group of people in a country rise, they try to defeat the government or army that is controlling them: *The Russian people rose in rebellion in 1917.*
**13 rise to the occasion/challenge** to deal successfully with a difficult situation or problem
**14 rise to sth** if you rise to a remark, you reply to it rather than ignoring it, especially because it has made you angry: *She refused to rise to his sexist remarks.*
**15 rise from the dead/grave** to come alive after having died: *On the third day Jesus rose from the dead.*
**16 rise through the ranks** to start working for an organization in a low-paid job, and to gradually improve your position, until you get a very important, well-paid job: *She had risen through the ranks, having joined the company as a secretary after she graduated from high school.*
**17 rise from the ranks** to become an officer in the army after having been an ordinary soldier
**18 rise out of sth** to be caused by sth or begin with sth: *The quarrel had risen out of a misunderstanding.* | *All this fuss and extravagance rose out of a sudden whim to please his small, first-born son*
**19 ▶ COURT/PARLIAMENT ◀** if court etc rises, that particular meeting is formally finished
**20 all rise** *spoken formal* used to tell people to stand up at the beginning of a meeting of a court of law
**21 rise and shine** *spoken humorous* used to tell someone to wake up and get out of bed
**22 ▶ RIVER ◀** if a river rises somewhere, it begins there: *The River Rhine rises in Switzerland.*
**23 ▶ WIND ◀** if the wind rises, it becomes stronger: *battling against the rising gale*

**rise above** *phr v* [T] **1** to deal with an insult or unpleasant situation without letting yourself become upset by it: *Her name was splashed across the newspapers every day, but somehow she managed to rise above it.* **2** to be morally good or wise enough to be able to avoid something that you should not do: *We must rise above the desire for power, personal advancement and material gain.* **3** to be of a higher standard than other things that are similar: *The novel is spirited and witty, but rarely rises above the level of pulp fiction.* **4** to have the knowledge and wisdom to understand and realize things that other people do not notice: *A true historian seeks the truth: he rises above his own race and writes for mankind.* **5** to improve your situation by becoming more successful, rich or important: *I was ambitious and wanted to rise above such a life.*

**rise against** *phr v* [T] **1** if a group of people rise against the government, king etc they try to defeat them so that they can control the country: *Rebels rose in discontent against the government and began killing people indiscriminately.* **2** *literary* to be very angry and upset by something: *His whole heart rose against this.*

**rise²** *n* W2
**1 ▶ INCREASE ◀** [C] an increase in number, amount or value: *We have sold 120,000 cars this year, a 20% rise on 1988.* | [+ **in**] *In the last ten years we have seen a three per-cent rise in serious and fatal accidents on our roads.* | **rise in costs/prices/taxes etc** *A rise in taxes will be necessary if we are to improve our education system.* | **rent/price rise** *Tenants face a 20% rent rise.* | **rise and fall** *the rise and fall of the temperature during the day*
**2 ▶ WAGES ◀** [C] *BrE* an increase in wages; RAISE² *AmE*: *After you've worked here for one year you get a rise.* | **pay rise** *The railworkers were offered a 3% pay rise.*
**3 ▶ SUCCESS/POWER ◀** [singular] the achievement of importance, success or power: [+ **of**] *The fifteenth century saw the rise of a new social class – the merchant class.* | *the rise of facism in Italy* | **rise to power** *Thatcher's rise to power in the late 70s* | **rise to fame** *the band's sudden rise to fame took everyone by surprise.* | **rise and fall** *the rise and fall of the Roman Empire*
**4 give rise to sth** *especially written* to be the reason why something, especially something bad or unpleasant happens: *Two phenomena are giving rise to world-wide concern – mass unemployment and mass migration into cities.* | *The President's absencehas given rise to speculation about his health.*
**5 ▶ SLOPE ◀** [C] an upward slope: *There's a slight rise in the road just before our house.*
**6 get a rise out of sb** to make someone become annoyed or embarrassed by making a joke about them: *You can always get a rise out of Peter by teasing him about his age.* —see also HIGH RISE

**ris·er** /ˈraɪzə‖-ər/ *n* [C] **1 early/late riser** someone who usually gets out of bed very early or very late **2** *technical* the upright part of a step on a set of stairs

**ris·i·ble** /ˈrɪzǩbəl/ *adj formal* something that is risible is so stupid that it deserves to be laughed at: *a risible suggestion* —**risibility** /ˌrɪzǩˈbɪlǩti/ *n* [U]

**ris·ing¹** /ˈraɪzɪŋ/ *n* [C] a sudden attempt by a large group of people to violently remove a government or ruler

**rising²** *adj* **1** [only before noun] becoming more important or famous: *a rising young actor* **2 rising five/six etc** nearly five, six etc years old **3 the rising generation** young people who will soon be old enough to vote, have jobs etc

**rising damp** /ˌ·· ˈ·/ *n* [U] *BrE* a condition where water comes up from the ground and gets into the walls of a building

**risk¹** /rɪsk/ *n* S2 W1
**1 ▶ POSSIBILITY OF BAD RESULT ◀** [C, U] the possibility that something bad, unpleasant, or dangerous may happen: *If you're considering starting a business, think carefully about the risks involved.* | [+ **of**] *the risk of serious injury* | **reduce/increase the risk of** *Wear rubber gloves to reduce the risk of infection.* | [+ **that**] *There was some risk that fire would break out again.* | **a calculated risk** (=a risk you think will have a good result) *It was a calculated risk to appoint a man without management experience to such a senior post.* | **an element of risk** (=some risk, but not much) *There's an element of risk in any kind of investment.* | **it's worth the risk** *I never walk home alone at night – it's not worth the risk.*
**2 take a risk** to decide to do something even though you know it may have bad results: *The fuel tank could blow up, but that's a risk we'll have to take.*
**3 at risk** be in a situation where you may be harmed: *We must stop these rumours; the firm's reputation is at risk.* | **be at risk of** *People with fair skins are more at risk of*

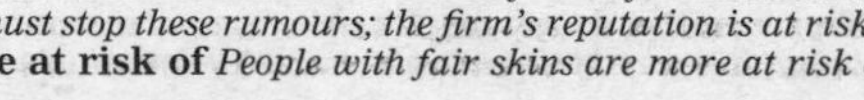

*skin cancer.* | **put sb/sth at risk** *I've no respect for a man who would put his children at risk like that.*

**4 run a risk** to be in a situation where there is a risk of something bad happening to you: *Anyone travelling without a passport runs the risk of being arrested.*

**5 at the risk of doing sth** used when you think that what you are going to say or do may have a bad result, may offend or annoy people etc: *At the risk of sounding stupid, can I ask a simple question?*

**6 at your own risk** if you do something at your own risk, you do it even though you understand the possible dangers and have been warned about them: *You leave valuables in the classroom at your own risk.*

**7 ▶ CAUSE OF DANGER ◀** [C] something or someone that is likely to cause harm or danger: [**+ to**] *Polluted water supplies are a risk to public health.* | **health risk** (=something likely to harm people's health) *Meat from the infected animals is regarded as a serious health risk.* | **fire risk** (=something that could cause a dangerous fire) *The tyre dump is a major fire risk.* | **security risk** (=someone who may tell important secrets to an enemy country)

**8 ▶ INSURANCE/BUSINESS ◀** [C] a person or business judged according to the danger involved in giving them insurance or lending them money: **a good/bad/poor risk** *a good credit risk* | *Drivers under 21 are regarded as poor risks by insurance companies.*

The graph shows some of the words most commonly used with the noun **risk**.

take a risk
at risk
reduce/increase the risk
high risk
run a risk
low risk
health/fire/safety risk
1 2 3 4 5 6 7 per million

Based on the British National Corpus and the Longman Lancaster Corpus

**risk²** *v* [T] **1** to put something in a situation in which it could be lost, destroyed, or harmed: *When children start smoking, they don't realize that they're risking their health.* | **risk sth on sth** *You'd be crazy to risk your money on an investment like that!* | **risk your life** *Martina risked her life to save her dog from the fire.* | **risk your neck** *informal* (=do something very dangerous in order to help someone) *I'm not going to risk my neck just to save a common criminal.* | **risk life and limb** (=do something very dangerous) *Why risk life and limb jumping out of a plane with a parachute on your back?* **2** to get into a situation where something unpleasant may happen to you: **risk defeat/death/dismissal etc** *The government risks an embarrassing defeat if it calls an election now.* | **risk being defeated/killed/dismissed etc** *Workers who broke the strike risked being attacked when they left the factory.* **3** to do something that you know may have dangerous or unpleasant results: **risk doing sth** *Are you prepared to risk traveling without an armed guard?* | **risk it** *spoken*: *You could slip out of school between classes, but I wouldn't risk it.*

**risk man·age·ment** /ˈ· ˌ···/ *n* [U] a system to prevent or reduce dangerous accidents or mistakes

**risk-tak·ing** /ˈ· ˌ··/ *n* [U] the practice of doing things that involve risks in order to achieve something —**risk-taker** *n* [C]

**risk·y** /ˈrɪski/ *adj* involving a risk that something bad will happen; rather dangerous: *It's risky to go out so soon after being ill.* | *a risky investment* | **a risky business** (=a dangerous action or situation) *Buying a secondhand car is a risky business.* —**riskily** *adv* —**riskiness** *n* [U]

**ri·sot·to** /rɪˈzɒtəʊ‖-ˈsɔːtoʊ/ *n plural* **risottos** [C,U] a hot meal made from rice mixed with cheese, vegetables, or pieces of meat

**ris·qué** /ˈrɪskeɪ‖rɪˈskeɪ/ *adj* a joke, remark etc that is risqué is slightly shocking, especially because it is about sex

**ris·sole** /ˈrɪsəʊl‖-soʊl/ *n* [C] cooked meat cut into very small pieces mixed with potato or bread, and cooked in hot fat

**rite** /raɪt/ *n* [C] **1** a ceremony that is always performed in the same way, usually for religious purposes: *funeral rites* | *satanic rites* | **perform a rite** *a traditional rite that was performed at harvest time* **2 rite of passage** a special ceremony or action that is a sign of a new stage in someone's life, especially when a boy starts to become a man **3 last rites** final prayers or religious ceremonies for someone who is dying: *A priest came to give him the last rites.*

**rit·u·al¹** /ˈrɪtʃuəl/ *n* [C,U] **1** a ceremony that is always performed in the same way, in order to mark an important religious or social occasion: *the ritual of communion in the Christian Church* | **perform a ritual** *The shaman performed the ritual on the young boy.* **2** something that you do regularly and in the same way each time: *The children performed the bedtime ritual of washing and brushing their teeth.*

**ritual²** *adj* [only before noun] **1** done as part of a rite or ritual: *ritual dances* **2** done in a fixed and expected way, but without real meaning or sincerity: *The police issued the usual ritual apology.* —**ritually** *adv*

**rit·u·al·is·tic** /ˌrɪtʃuəˈlɪstɪk◂/ *adj* ritualistic words, types of behaviour etc always follow the same pattern, especially because they form part of a ritual: *ritualistic incantations* | *I got tired with the boring, almost ritualistic weekly meetings.* —**ritualistically** /-kli/ *adv*

**ritz·y** /ˈrɪtsi/ *adj informal* fashionable and expensive: *a ritzy restaurant*

**ri·val¹** /ˈraɪvəl/ *n* [C] **1** a person, group, or organization that you compete with in sport, business, a fight etc: *He left the government to become her most formidable rival.* | [**+ for**] *The two girls were rivals for Jack's attention.* | **rival company/nation/team etc** *Sheena left her job and went to work for a rival company.* | **arch-rival** (=main rival) *Hanover High School was our arch-rival in football.* **2** something that is equally as good or important as something else: **rival claim/explanation/argument etc** *The court listened to the rival explanations in turn.* | **have no/few rivals** (=be better than all others or most others)

**rival²** *v* **rivalled, rivalling** *BrE*, **rivaled, rivaling** *AmE* [T] to be as good or important as someone or something else: *The college's facilities rival those of Harvard and Yale.* —see also UNRIVALLED

**ri·val·ry** /ˈraɪvəlri/ *n* [C,U] continuous competition: *a fierce rivalry between the two basketball teams*

**riv·en** /ˈrɪvən/ *adj formal* split violently apart: *a community riven by religious differences*

**riv·er** /ˈrɪvə‖-ər/ *n* [C] **1** a natural and continuous flow of water in a long line across a country into the sea: *the Mississippi River* | *We swam to a large rock in the middle of the river.* | **river bank** (=the land at the side of a river) *We ate our lunch on the river bank.* | **mouth of the river** (=where a river joins the sea) | **up river** (=in the opposite direction from the way the river is flowing) *a ship sailing up river* | **down river** (=in the same direction as the way the river is flowing) **2** a large amount of moving liquid: [**+ of**] *a river of hot lava flowing from the volcano* —see also **sell sb down the river** (SELL¹ (12))

**river ba·sin** /ˈ·· ˌ··/ *n* [C] an area from which all the water flows into the same river

**river bed** /ˈ···/ *n* [C] the ground over which a river flows

**riv·er·side** /ˈrɪvəsaɪd‖-ər-/ *n* [singular] the land on the banks of a river: *We had a picnic by the riverside.* | **riverside path/cottage etc** *a riverside inn*

**rivet¹** *v* **1 be riveted on/to** if your attention is riveted on something, you are so frightened or so interested that you keep looking at it: *Barnes watched in terror, his eyes riveted on the huge tiger.* **2 be riveted to the spot** to be so shocked or frightened that you cannot move **3** [T] to fasten something with rivets

**riv·et²** /ˈrɪvɪ̣t/ *n* [C] a metal pin used to fasten pieces of metal together

**riv·et·ing** /ˈrɪvɪ̣tɪŋ/ *adj* **1** something that is riveting is so interesting or exciting that you cannot stop watching it or listening to it: *a riveting performance* **2** *humorous* used when you do not really think something is interesting at all: *What a riveting conversation!*

**ri·vi·e·ra** /ˌrɪviˈeərə‖-ˈerə/ *n* **the Riviera** a warm coast that is popular with people who are on holiday, especially the Mediterranean coast of France

**riv·u·let** /ˈrɪvjə̣lɪ̣t/ *n* [C] a very small stream of liquid, especially water: *Rivulets of sweat ran down his face.*

**ri·yal, rial** /riˈɑːl‖riˈɔːl, -ˈɑːl/ *n* [C] the standard unit of money in Saudi Arabia and other Arab countries

**RN** /ˌɑːr ˈen/ **1** Royal Navy; the British navy: *Captain Anstruther, RN* **2** REGISTERED NURSE

**RNA** /ˌɑːr en ˈeɪ/ *n* [U] an important chemical that exists in all living cells

**roach** /rəʊtʃ‖roʊtʃ/ *n* **1** *AmE informal* a COCKROACH **2** a European fish similar to a CARP **3** *slang* the part of a MARIJUANA cigarette that you suck smoke through

**road** /rəʊd‖roʊd/ *n* **1** [C,U] a specially prepared hard surface for cars, buses, bicycles etc to travel on: *a busy road | at the end of the road |* **up/down/along the road** (=further along the road) *We live just down the road.* | **by road** (=driving) *It takes three hours by road.* | **main road** *Take the main road out of town and turn left at the first light.* | **side road** (=a small road that is not used much) | **dirt road** *especially AmE* (=a road without a hard surface) | **road accident/repairs/user etc** *He was killed in a road accident.* | **road sense** (=knowledge about how to behave sensibly near traffic) *Kids of that age have no road sense.* | **road safety** (=how to be safe when driving or walking on roads) *a road safety campaign* —see STREET (USAGE) **2 Road** written abbreviation **Rd** used in addresses after the names of roads: *65 Maple Road* **3 on the road a)** travelling in a car, especially for long distances: *I've been on the road since 5:00 a.m. this morning.* **b)** if a group of actors or musicians is on the road they are travelling from place to place giving performances **c)** if your car is on the road, you have paid for the repairs, tax etc necessary for you to legally drive it: *It costs a lot of money to keep these old cars on the road.* **4 on the road to success/recovery/peace etc** developing in a way that will result in success etc: *It was this deal that set him on the road to his first million.* **5 go down a road** *informal* to follow a particular course of action: *You could move your pension to a private scheme, but I wouldn't advise going down that road.* **6 one for the road** *spoken* a last alcoholic drink before you leave a party, PUB etc **7 get out of the road!** *BrE spoken* a rude way of telling someone to move —see also **the end of the road** (END¹ (18)), **hit the road** (HIT¹ (16))

**road·block** /ˈrəʊdblɒk‖ˈroʊdblɑːk/ *n* [C] **1** a place where the police are stopping traffic: *Roadblocks were set up after two prisoners escaped from the county jail.* **2** *AmE* something that stops the progress of a plan: *mental roadblocks that get in the way of success*

**road hog** /ˈ· ·/ *n* [C] *informal* someone who drives too fast without thinking about other people's safety

**road·house** /ˈrəʊdhaʊs‖ˈroʊd-/ *n* [C] *AmE* a restaurant or bar on a main road outside a city

**road·ie** /ˈrəʊdi‖ˈroʊ-/ *n* [C] *informal* someone whose job is moving equipment for musicians

**road man·a·ger** /ˈ· ˌ···/ *n* [C] someone who makes arrangements for entertainers when they are travelling

**road rage** /ˈ· ·/ *n* [U] violence and angry behaviour by car drivers towards other car drivers: *a road rage attack*

**road·runner** /ˈrəʊdrʌnə‖ˈroʊdrʌnər/ *n* [C] a small bird that runs very fast

**road·show** /ˈrəʊdʃəʊ‖ˈroʊdʃoʊ/ *n* [C] *BrE* a group that travels around the country giving performances for entertainment or advertising

**road·side** /ˈrəʊdsaɪd‖ˈroʊd-/ *n* [singular] the edge of the road: **roadside cafe/pub etc** (=next to a road)

**road·sign** /ˈrəʊdsaɪn‖ˈroʊd-/ *n* [C] a sign next to a road, that gives information to drivers

**road tax** /ˈ· ·/ *n* [C,U] a tax in Britain that the owner of a vehicle must pay in order to drive it on the roads

**road test** /ˈ· ·/ *n* [C] a test to check that a vehicle is in good condition and safe to drive —**roadtest** *v* [T]

**road·way** /ˈrəʊdweɪ‖ˈroʊd-/ *n* [singular] the part of the road used by vehicles

**road·work** /ˈrəʊdwɜːk‖ˈroʊdwɜːrk/ *n* **roadworks** [plural] *BrE* repairs that are being done to a road

**road·wor·thy** /ˈrəʊdˌwɜːði‖ˈroʊdwɜːr-/ *adj* a vehicle that is roadworthy is in good condition and safe enough to drive —**roadworthiness** *n* [U]

**roam** /rəʊm‖roʊm/ *v* **1** [I,T] to walk or travel, usually for a long time, with no clear purpose or direction: [+ **over/around/about etc**] *herds of wild deer roaming freely over the hills* | **roam the streets/hills etc** *You shouldn't let your children roam the streets.* **2** [I + **over**] if your eyes roam over something, you look slowly at all parts of it: *His eyes roamed over the bookshelves.*

**R**

**roan** /rəʊn‖roʊn/ *n* [C] a horse of a particular colour, especially light brown —**roan** *adj*

**roar¹** /rɔː‖rɔːr/ *v* **1** [I] to make a deep, very loud noise: *We heard a lion roar.* **2** [T] to say or shout something in a deep, powerful voice: *"Get out of my house!" he roared.* **3** [I] also **roar with laughter** *especially BrE* to laugh loudly and continuously: *When Charlie's trousers fell down, the audience roared.* **4** [I always + adv/prep] if a vehicle roars somewhere, it moves very quickly and noisily: [+ **past/down etc**] *There was a cloud of dust as a truck roared past.*

**roar²** *n* [C] **1** a deep, loud noise made by an animal such as a LION, or by someone's voice: *A roar of approval came from the crowd.* **2** a continuous loud noise, especially made by a machine or a strong wind: *the roar of the traffic*

**roaring** /ˈrɔːrɪŋ/ *adj* **1** [only before noun] making a deep, very loud, continuous noise: *the roaring wind and waves* **2 roaring fire** a roaring fire burns with a lot of flames and heat **3 do a roaring trade (in)** *BrE informal* to sell a lot of something very quickly **4 be a roaring success** *BrE* to be extremely successful: *The new musical has been a roaring success.* **5 roaring drunk** *BrE* very drunk and noisy

**roast¹** /rəʊst‖roʊst/ *v* **1** [I,T] to cook something, such as meat, in an OVEN or over a fire —see picture on page 833 **2** [I,T] to heat nuts, coffee, beans etc quickly in order to dry them and give them a particular taste: *dry-roasted peanuts* **3** [T] *informal* to strongly criticize or make insulting remarks about someone or something: *Her first play got roasted by the critics.*

**roast²** *n* [C] **1** a large piece of roasted meat —see also POT ROAST **2** *AmE* an occasion at which people celebrate a special event in someone's life by telling funny stories or giving speeches about them: *We're going to have a roast for Jack when he retires.* **3 hot dog roast/oyster roast etc** *AmE* an outdoor party at which food is cooked on an open fire

**roast³** *adj* [only before noun] roasted: *roast chicken*

**roast·ing¹** /ˈrəʊstɪŋ‖ˈroʊs-/ also **roasting hot** /ˌ·· ˈ·◂/ *adj informal* very hot, especially so that you feel uncomfortable: *a roasting hot day | I'm absolutely roasting in this suit.*

**roasting²** *n* **give sb a roasting** *informal especially BrE* to talk angrily to someone in order to tell them that you disapprove of their behaviour

**rob** /rɒb‖rɑːb/ *v* **robbed, robbing** [T] **1** to steal money or property from a person, bank etc: *The gang tried to rob a bank using a sawn-off shotgun.* | **rob sb of sth** *Mrs* S3

*Clegg was severely beaten and robbed of all her possessions.* | *The company director robbed pensioners of millions.* —see STEAL[1] (USAGE) —see picture at STEAL[1] **2 rob sb/sth of sth** to take away an important quality, ability etc from someone or something: *Being bullied has robbed Duane of his self-confidence.* **3 rob Peter to pay Paul** to take money away from someone or something that needs it in order to pay someone else or use it for something else **4 I was robbed!** *spoken* used when you think that you were beaten unfairly in a sport **5 rob the cradle** *AmE humorous* to have a sexual relationship with someone who is a lot younger than you; CRADLE-SNATCH *BrE*

**rob·ber** /ˈrɒbə‖ˈrɑːbər/ *n* [C] someone who steals money or property: *a bank robber*

**robber bar·on** /ˌ·· ˈ··, ˈ·· ˌ··/ *n* [C] a powerful man who used force to get money, land etc, for example a businessman in US in the 19th century who made a lot of money in a dishonest way

**rob·ber·y** /ˈrɒbəri‖ˈrɑː-/ *n* [C,U] the crime of stealing things from a bank, shop etc, especially using violence: *Police are investigating a series of bank robberies in South Wales.* | **armed robbery** (=robbery using a gun) *a 10 year prison sentence for armed robbery* —see also **daylight robbery** (DAYLIGHT (2))

**robe**[1] /rəʊb‖roʊb/ *n* [C] **1** also **robes** a long loose piece of clothing, especially one worn for official ceremonies: *a priest's robes* **2** *especially AmE* a long loose piece of clothing that you wear over your night clothes or after a bath; DRESSING GOWN *especially BrE* —see also BATHROBE

**robe**[2] *v formal* **1 be robed in** to be dressed in a particular way: *The hostess looked very glamorous, robed in emerald velvet.* **2 robe yourself** *literary* to put on your clothes

**rob·in** /ˈrɒbɪ̣n‖ˈrɑː-/ *n* [C] **1** a common small European bird with a red breast and brown back **2** a North American bird like a European robin, but larger

**ro·bot** /ˈrəʊbɒt‖ˈroʊbɑːt, -bət/ *n* [C] **1** a machine that can move and do some of the work of a person, and is usually controlled by a computer: *cars built by robots* **2** someone who works or behaves like a machine, without having thoughts or feelings —**robotic** /rəʊˈbɒtɪk‖roʊˈbɑː-/ *adj*

**ro·bo·tics** /rəʊˈbɒtɪks‖ˈroʊbɑː-/ *n* [U] the study of how robots are made and used

**ro·bust** /rəˈbʌst, ˈrəʊbʌst‖rəˈbʌst, ˈroʊ-/ *adj* **1** a robust person is strong and healthy: *a robust 85-year-old* **2** a robust object is strong and not likely to break: *a six-foot giant who seemed likely to flatten even the most robust of deckchairs* **3** a robust system, organization etc is strong and not likely to have problems: *The US economy is now much more robust.* **4** behaving or speaking in a strong and determined way: *a typically robust performance by the former Prime Minister* —**robustly** *adj* —**robustness** *n* [U]

S2 W2 **rock**[1] /rɒk‖rɑːk/ *n*
**1 ▶ STONE ◀ a)** [U] stone, or a type of stone that forms part of the Earth's surface: *To build the tunnel, they had to cut through 500 feet of solid rock.* | **rock formation** (=a shape made naturally from rock) *the rock formations of the Arizona desert* **b)** [C] a piece of stone, especially a large one: *Kim sat down on a rock.* **c) rocks** [plural] a line of rock under or next to the sea: *A ship had been driven onto the rocks during the storm.*
**2 ▶ MUSIC ◀** [U] also **rock music** a type of popular modern music with a strong loud beat, played using GUITARS and drums: *a rock concert* | *rock veteran, Eric Clapton*
**3 as solid/steady as a rock a)** very strongly built or well supported and not likely to break or fall **b)** someone who is as solid or steady as a rock is very strong and calm in difficult situations and you can depend on them —see also ROCK-SOLID
**4 be on the rocks** *informal* a relationship or business that is on the rocks is having a lot of problems and is likely to fail soon: *Tim's marriage is on the rocks.*
**5 scotch/vodka etc on the rocks** an alcoholic drink that is served with ice but no water
**6 ▶ SWEET FOOD ◀** [U] *BrE* a hard sweet food made in long round pieces: *a stick of Blackpool rock*
**7 ▶ JEWEL ◀** [C usually plural] *informal* a DIAMOND or other jewel
**8 be (stuck) between a rock and a hard place** to have a choice between two things, both of which are unpleasant
**9 get your rocks off** *slang* if a man gets his rocks off, he has sex

**rock**[2] *v* **1** [I,T] to move gently backwards and forwards or from side to side, or to make something do this: *Paul sat gently rocking the child in his arms.* | *The waves made the boat rock from side to side.* | **rock with laughter** *Jim rocked with laughter when he heard what had happened.* **2** [T] to make the people in a place or organization feel very shocked or surprised: *In 1970, the city of Newark was rocked by a major scandal.* **3 rock the boat** *informal* to cause problems for other members of a group by criticizing something or trying to change the way something is done: *A lot of people didn't really agree with the policy, but they didn't want to rock the boat.* **4** [T] if an explosion, or EARTHQUAKE (=violent movement of the earth) rocks an area, it makes it shake

**rock and roll** /ˌ· · ˈ·/ *n* [U] ROCK 'N' ROLL

**rock bot·tom** /ˌ· ˈ··◂/ *n* **hit/reach rock bottom** *informal* to become as unhappy or unpleasant as it is possible to be: *My personal life had hit rock bottom.*

**rock-bottom** *adj* a rock-bottom price is as low as it can possibly be: *bargain holidays at rock-bottom prices*

**rock cake** /ˈ· ·/ also **rock bun** *n* [C] *BrE* a small hard cake with a rough surface that has dried fruit in it

**rock climb·ing** /ˈ· ˌ··/ *n* [U] the sport of climbing up very steep rock surfaces such as the sides of mountains —**rock climber** *n* [C]

**rock-crys·tal** /ˈ· ˌ··/ *n* [U] pure natural QUARTZ (=a very hard mineral) that is transparent

**rock·er** /ˈrɒkə‖ˈrɑːkər/ *n* [C] **1** one of the curved pieces of wood fixed to the bottom of a ROCKING CHAIR, that allows it to move backwards and forwards if you push it **2 be off your rocker** *spoken* to be crazy **3** a member of a group of young people in Britain in the 1960s who wore leather JACKETS, rode MOTORCYCLES, and listened to ROCK 'N' ROLL music —compare MOD **4** a ROCKING CHAIR

**rock·e·ry** /ˈrɒkəri‖ˈrɑː-/ *n* [C] part of a garden where there are rocks with small plants growing between them

**rock·et**[1] /ˈrɒkɪ̣t‖ˈrɑː-/ *n* [C] **1** a vehicle used for travelling or carrying things into space, which is shaped like a big tube **2** a similar object used as a weapon, especially one that carries a bomb: *anti-tank rockets* **3** a small tube fixed to a stick, that contains explosive powder and is used as a FIREWORK **4 give sb a rocket** *BrE informal* to criticize someone angrily because they have done something wrong

**rocket**[2] *v* [I] **1** also **rocket up** if a price or amount rockets, it increases quickly and suddenly: *Interest rates rocketed.* **2** [always + adv/prep] to move somewhere very fast: [+ **through/along etc**] *The train rocketed through the tunnel.* **3** [always + adv/prep] to achieve a successful position very quickly: [+ **to**] *Their new album rocketed to number one in the charts.*

**rocket launch·er** /ˈ·· ˌ··/ *n* [C] a weapon like a tube used for firing military rockets into the air

**rock·fall** /ˈrɒkˌfɔːl‖ˈrɑːkˌfɒːl/ *n* [C] a pile of rocks that are falling or have fallen

**rock gar·den** /ˈ· ˌ··/ *n* [C] a ROCKERY

**rock-hard** /ˌ· ˈ·◂/ *adj* **1** extremely hard: *The bread was stale and rock-hard.* **2** *BrE humorous* strong and not afraid of anyone

**rock·ing chair** /ˈ·· ·/ *n* [C] a chair that has two curved pieces of wood fixed under it, so that it moves backwards and forwards —see picture at CHAIR[1]

**rocking horse** /ˈ·· ·/ *n* [C] a wooden horse for children that moves backwards and forwards when you sit on it

**rock mu·sic** /ˈ· ˌ··/ *n* [U] a type of popular modern music with a strong loud beat, played using GUITARS and drums

**rock 'n' roll** /ˌrɒk ən ˈrəʊl‖ˌrɑːk ən ˈroʊl/ *n* [U] a style of music that was very popular in the 1950s, and has a strong loud beat: *Elvis, the kind of rock 'n' roll*

**rock pool** /ˈ· ·/ *n* [C] *BrE* a small pool of water between rocks by the sea; TIDE POOL *AmE*

**rock salt** /ˈ· ·/ *n* [U] a kind of salt which is obtained from under the ground

**rock-sol·id** /ˌ· ˈ··◂/ *adj* **1** very strong so that you can depend on it **2** very hard and not likely to break

**rock-stead·y** /ˌ· ˈ··◂/ *adj* very strong or very calm: *rock-steady nerves*

**rock·y** /ˈrɒki‖ˈrɑːki/ *adj* **1** covered with rocks or made of rock: *the rocky hills of New England* **2** *informal* a relationship or situation that is rocky is difficult and may not continue or be successful: *The company faces a rocky road ahead.* —**rockiness** *n* [U]

**ro·co·co** /rəˈkəʊkəʊ‖rəˈkoʊkoʊ/ *adj* rococo buildings and furniture have a lot of curly decoration and were fashionable in Europe in the 18th century

**rod** /rɒd‖rɑːd/ *n* [C] **1** a long thin pole or bar: *The walls are reinforced with steel rods.* **2** a long thin pole used with a line and hook for catching fish: *a fishing rod* **3 make a rod for your own back** to do something that will cause trouble for you in the future —see also HOT ROD, **rule sb/sth with a rod of iron** (RULE[2] (6))

**rode** /rəʊd‖roʊd/ the past tense of RIDE[1]

**ro·dent** /ˈrəʊdənt‖ˈroʊ-/ *n* [C] one of a group of small animals with long sharp front teeth, such as rats or rabbits

**ro·de·o** /ˈrəʊdiəʊ, rəʊˈdeɪ-əʊ‖ˈroʊdioʊ, roʊˈdeɪ-oʊ/ *n plural* **rodeos** [C] a type of entertainment in which COWBOYS ride wild horses, and catch cattle with ropes

**roe** /rəʊ‖roʊ/ *n* [C,U] fish eggs eaten as a food

**roe deer** /ˈ· ·/ *n* [C] a small European and Asian DEER that lives in forests

**roent·gen, röntgen** /ˈrɒntgən‖ˈrentgən/ *n technical* the international measure for X-RAYS

**ro·ger[1]** /ˈrɒdʒə‖ˈrɑːdʒər-/ *interjection* used in radio conversations to say that a message has been understood

**roger[2]** *v* [T] *BrE slang taboo* to have sex with someone

**rogue[1]** /rəʊg‖roʊg/ *n* [C] **1** *often humorous* a man or boy who behaves badly or causes trouble, but who you like in spite of this: *What's the little rogue done now, I wonder?* | *a lovable rogue* **2** *old-fashioned* a man who is dishonest and has a bad character: **rogues' gallery** (=a group of bad people) —**roguery** *n* [U]

**rogue[2]** *adj* [only before noun] **1** a rogue person or organization does not follow the usual rules or methods and often causes trouble **2** a rogue wild animal lives apart from the main group and is often dangerous

**rogu·ish** /ˈrəʊgɪʃ‖ˈroʊ-/ *adj* someone with a roguish expression or smile looks amused, especially because they have done something slightly dishonest or wrong —**roguishly** *adv* —**roguishness** *n* [U]

**rois·ter** /ˈrɔɪstə‖-ər/ *v* [I] *old-fashioned* to behave in a cheerful, rough, noisy way —**roisterer** *n* [C]

W3 **role** /rəʊl‖roʊl/ *n* [C] **1** the way in which someone or something is involved in an activity or situation, and how much influence they have on it: **play a leading/major/key role** (=be important in making changes happen) *Mandela played a leading role in ending apartheid in South Africa.* | *China's growing role in Hong Kong's economy* | *the role of diet in the prevention of diseases such as cancer* **2** the character played by an actor in a play or film: **play a role** (=act a role) *Matthews plays the role of a young doctor suspected of murder.* | **the lead/leading role** (=the most important role) | **minor role** (=an unimportant role) **3** the position that someone has in society, in an organization etc, or the way they are expected to behave in a relationship with someone else: *Women are often forced into a supportive role.* | **role reversal** (=a situation in which two people, especially a man and a woman, take each other's roles)

**role mod·el** /ˈ· ˌ··/ *n* [C] someone whose behaviour, attitudes etc people try to copy because they admire them

**role-play** /ˈ· ·/ *n* [C,U] an exercise in which you behave in the way that someone else would behave in a particular situation, especially to help you learn something: *the use of role-play in the classroom* —**role-play** *v* [I,T]

**roll[1]** /rəʊl‖roʊl/ *v* S1 W3

**1** ▶ **ROUND OBJECT** ◀ [I always + adv/prep, T] if something that is round rolls or if you roll it, it moves along a surface by turning over and over: *The ball rolled into the street.* | **roll sth** *Maybe we can roll the log to the middle of the campsite.*

**2** ▶ **PERSON/ANIMAL** ◀ [I always + adv/prep] to turn your body over one or more times while lying down: *The dog had been rolling in mud puddles.* | *Ralph rolled onto his stomach.*

**3** ▶ **STH WITH WHEELS** ◀ [I always + adv/prep, T always + adv/prep] to move on wheels, or make something that has wheels move: [+ **into/forwards/past etc**] *We watched as the bus rolled slowly backwards down the hill.* | **roll sth to/around/by etc** *The waitress rolled the dessert cart over to our table.*

**4** ▶ **PAPER/STRING ETC** ◀ [T] also **roll up** to bend or wind something such as paper, string etc into the shape of a tube or ball: *Harry rolled the newspaper and put a rubber band around it.* | *Roll the yarn into a ball.*

**5** ▶ **DROP OF LIQUID** ◀ [I always + adv/prep] to move over a surface smoothly without stopping: [+ **down/onto**] *Tears rolled down her cheeks.*

**6** ▶ **WAVES/CLOUDS** ◀ [I always + adv/prep] to move in a particular direction: [+ **into/towards etc**] *Mist rolled in from the sea.* | *waves rolling onto the beach*

**7 roll your eyes** to move your eyes round and upwards, especially in order to show that you are annoyed: *Marta rolled her eyes as Will started to tell another stupid joke.*

**8** ▶ **GAME** ◀ [I,T] if you roll DICE, you throw them as part of a game

**9** ▶ **SHIP/PLANE** ◀ [I] if a ship or plane rolls, it leans one way and then another with the motion of the water or air

**10** ▶ **MAKE STH FLAT** ◀ [T] to make something flat by moving something heavy over it: *Roll the pie crust flat with a rolling pin.*

**11** ▶ **WALK** ◀ [I always + adv/prep] to walk in a rather uncontrolled way, moving your body from side to side, usually because you are drunk: *We rolled out of the bar at about 3:00 that morning.*

**12** ▶ **SOUND** ◀ [I] if drums or THUNDER[1] (1) roll, they make a long low series of sounds

**13** ▶ **MACHINE/CAMERA** ◀ [I] if a machine such as a film camera or a PRINTING PRESS rolls, it operates: *Quiet! The cameras are rolling!*

**14 (all) rolled into one** if something is several different things rolled into one, it includes qualities of all those things: *Mum was cook, chauffeur, nurse, and entertainer all rolled into one.*

**15 get rolling** if a plan, business etc gets rolling, it starts operating: *When the business gets rolling, we'll have more time to think about other things.*

**16 roll a cigarette** to make your own cigarette, using loose tobacco and special paper: **roll your own** (=make your own cigarettes) *It's cheaper to roll your own.*

**17 roll out of bed** *informal* to get out of bed: *I finally rolled out of bed about noon.*

**18 be rolling in the aisles** if people in a theatre, cinema etc are rolling in the aisles, they are laughing a lot

**19 be ready to roll** *spoken especially AmE* used to say you are ready to do something: *OK, everything's in the car. Is everybody ready to roll?*

**20 roll on** *BrE* used to say that you wish a time or event would come quickly: *Roll on the weekend!*

**21** ▶ **ATTACK** ◀ [T] *AmE* to rob someone, especially when they are drunk and asleep: *punks on the streets rolling drunks for small change*

**22 roll your r's** to pronounce the sound /r/ using your tongue in a way that makes the sound very long

**23 a rolling stone gathers no moss** used to say that

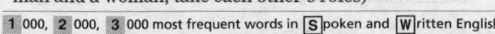

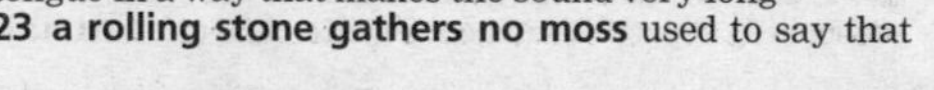

someone who often changes jobs, etc does not have any real relationships or responsibilities —see also **set/start/keep the ball rolling** (BALL[1] (9)), **heads will roll** (HEAD[1] (52)), **be rolling in it** (ROLLING (3))

**roll around/round** *phr v* [I] if something that happens regularly rolls around, it happens again: *By the time autumn rolled around, we still hadn't finished painting the house.*

**roll away** *phr v* [I always + adv/prep] if countryside rolls away, it is full of small hills as far as you can see: *green pastures rolling away into the distance*

**roll** sth ↔ **back** *phr v* [T] **1** to force your opponents in a war to move back from their position **2** to reduce the influence or power of a system, government etc, especially because it has too much power: *Dulles saw communism as something evil to be rolled back, not just contained.* **3** *AmE* to reduce the price of something: *the administration's promise to roll back taxes*

**roll** sth ↔ **down** *phr v* [T] **roll a window down** to open a car window

**roll in** *phr v* [I] **1** to happen or arrive in large numbers or quantities: *Pleas for help were made to the public, and the money came rolling in.* **2** to arrive later than usual or expected without seeming to be worried: *Chris finally rolled in at about 4:00 am.* **3** if clouds, mist etc roll in, they begin to cover an area of the sky or land: *Fog rolled in from the sea.*

**roll** sth ↔ **out** *phr v* [T] **1** to make something flat and thin by pushing a special tube shaped object over it: *Roll out the pastry.* —see picture on page 834 **2** to make something flat and straight on the ground, after it has been rolled into a tube shape: *Roll out your sleeping bag inside the tent.* **3 roll out the red carpet** to make special preparations for an important visitor

**roll over** *phr v* **1** [I] to turn your body round once so that you are lying in a different position: *Ben rolled over and kissed her.* **2** [T] **roll** sb/sth **over** to turn someone's body over on the ground: **roll sb onto** *The guards rolled him over onto his front.*

**roll up** *phr v* **1 roll your sleeves/trousers up** to turn the ends of your sleeves etc over several times so that they are shorter **2 roll your sleeves up** to start doing a job even though it is difficult or unpleasant: *We're just going to have to roll our sleeves up and get on with it.* **3 roll a window up** to close the window of a car **4** [I] to arrive somewhere, especially late or unexpectedly: *Brad and Debbie rolled up in their new convertible at about 9:00.* **5 roll up!** *BrE spoken* used to call people to come and watch or buy things at a CIRCUS (1), FAIR[2] (1) etc

**roll**[2] *n*

**1 ▶ PAPER/FILM/MONEY ETC ◀** [C] a piece of paper, film, money that has been rolled into the shape of a tube: [+ **of**] *a roll of film* | *8 rolls of toilet paper for $1.99* | *Dusty pulled a huge roll of $100 bills from his pocket.*

**2 ▶ BREAD ◀** [C] a small round LOAF of bread for one person: *Put the rolls on the table.* | **ham/cheese etc roll** *BrE* (=one that is filled with ham, cheese etc)

**3 ▶ PHYSICAL MOVEMENT ◀** [C] **a)** the action of moving by rolling your body: *a young horse having a roll in the field* **b)** a movement done, often as part of a sport, by rolling on the ground in a controlled way with your body curled: *tumblers doing rolls and handstands at the circus*

**4 ▶ SHIP/PLANE ◀** [C] the movement of a ship or plane when it leans from side to side with the motion of the water or air

**5 ▶ SKIN/FAT ◀** [C + **of**] a thick layer of skin or fat, usually just below your waist

**6 roll of drums/guns/thunder** a long low, fairly loud sound made by drums etc

**7 be on a roll** *informal* to be having a lot of success with what you are trying to do

**8 ▶ GAME ◀** [C] the action of throwing DICE as part of a game: *It's your roll, Rob.*

**9 ▶ LIST OF NAMES ◀** an official list of names, especially of people at a meeting, in a class etc: **call/take the roll** (=say the list of names to check that everyone on it is there)

**10 roll in the hay** *informal* an act of having sex with someone

**roll bar** /ˈ· ·/ *n* [C] a strong metal bar over the top of a car, intended to protect the people inside if the car turns over

**roll-call** /ˈ· ·/ *n* [C,U] the act of reading out an official list of names to check who is there

**rolled gold** /ˌ· ˈ·/ *n* [U] a thin layer of gold on the surface of another metal; FILLED GOLD *AmE*

**rolled oats** /ˌ· ˈ·/ *n* [plural] *especially BrE* a kind of oats (OATS (1)), used for making PORRIDGE

**roll·er** /ˈrəʊlə‖ˈroʊlər/ *n* [C] **1** a tube-shaped piece of wood, metal etc that can be rolled over and over, used in a machine for crushing, printing etc **2** a large tube-shaped piece of stone, metal etc that you roll over the surface of grass or roads to make them smooth: *a garden roller* **3** a long, powerful wave: *great Atlantic rollers* **4** a tube-shaped piece of metal or wood, used for moving heavy things that have no wheels **5** a small tube-shaped piece of metal or plastic that you wrap your hair around to make it curl **6** a ROLLS-ROYCE

**roller blades** /ˈ·· ·/ *n* [plural] special boots with a single row of wheels fixed under each boot

**roller blind** /ˈ·· ·/ *n* [C] *BrE* a piece of cloth or other material that can be rolled up and down to cover a window —see picture at BLIND[3]

**roller coaster**

**roller coast·er** /ˈ·· ˌ··/ *n* [C] **1** a track with sudden steep slopes and curves, which people ride on for excitement in special small carriages **2** a situation that is impossible to control, because it keeps changing very quickly: *Their relationship was a continual emotional roller coaster.*

**roller skate** /ˈ·· ·/ *n* [C] a special boot with four wheels fixed under it —**roller-skate** *v* [I] —**roller skating** *n* [U]

**roller tow·el** /ˈ·· ˌ··/ *n* [C] a cloth you use for drying your hands, which is joined together at the ends and wound around a bar of wood or metal

**rol·lick·ing**[1] /ˈrɒlɪkɪŋ‖ˈrɑː-/ *adj* [only before noun] *old-fashioned* noisy and cheerful: *a rollicking song*

**rollicking**[2] *n* **give sb a rollicking** *BrE informal* to criticize someone angrily for something they have done

**roll·ing** /ˈrəʊlɪŋ‖ˈroʊ-/ *adj* **1** [only before noun] rolling hills have many long gentle slopes **2** if you have a rolling walk, you move from side to side as you walk **3 be rolling in it** *informal* to be extremely rich: *If James can afford that car, he must be rolling in it!*

**rolling mill** /ˈ·· ·/ *n* [C] a factory or machine in which metal is rolled into large, flat, thin pieces

**rolling pin** /ˈ·· ·/ *n* [C] a long tube-shaped piece of wood used for making PASTRY flat and thin before you cook it

**rolling stock** /ˈ·· ·/ *n* [U] all the trains, carriages etc that are used on a railway

**roll·mop** /ˈrɒlmɒp‖ˈrɑːlmɑːp/ *n* [C] a HERRING that has been rolled up and preserved in VINEGAR

**roll of hon·our** /ˌ· · ˈ··/ *n* [C] *BrE* a list of the names of people who are officially praised, especially because they were brave in battle; HONOR ROLL *AmE*

**roll-on** /ˈ· ·/ *n* [C] **1** also **roll-on de·o·dor·ant** /ˌ· · ˈ··· ·/ a bottle which contains liquid that you rub under your arms in order to stop your SWEAT[2] (1) from smelling unpleasant **2** a woman's GIRDLE (=type of underwear) that you pull on in one piece, worn in the past

**roll-on roll-off** /ˈ· · ˌ· ·/ *adj* [only before noun] *BrE* a roll-on roll-off ship is one that vehicles can drive straight on and off: *a roll-on roll-off car ferry*

**Rolls-Royce** /ˌrəʊlz ˈrɔɪs◂‖ˌroʊlz-/ *n* [C] *trademark* **1** a very expensive and comfortable car made by a British company **2** *BrE informal* something that is regarded as the highest quality example of a particular type of product; CADILLAC *AmE*: *the Rolls-Royce of video recorders*

**roll-top desk** /ˌ· · ˈ·/ *n* [C] a desk that has a cover that you roll back when you open it

**roll-up** /ˈ· ·/ *n* [C] *BrE* a cigarette that you make yourself

**roly-poly[1]** *adj* a roly-poly person is round and fat

**ro·ly-po·ly[2]** /ˌrəʊli ˈpəʊli◂‖roʊli ˈpoʊ-/ *n* [C,U] a British sweet food made of JAM[1] (1) that is rolled up inside PASTRY

**ROM** /rɒm‖rɑːm/ *n* [U] read-only memory; the part of a computer where permanent instructions and information are stored —compare RAM

**Ro·man** /ˈrəʊmən‖ˈroʊ-/ *adj* **1** connected with ancient Rome or the Roman Empire **2** connected with the city of Rome —**Roman** *n* [C]

**roman** *n* [U] *technical* the ordinary style of printing that uses small upright letters, like the style used for printing these words —compare ITALICS

**Roman al·pha·bet** /ˌ·· ˈ···/ *n* [singular] the alphabet used in English and many other European languages, which begins with the letters A, B, C

**Roman Cath·o·lic** /ˌ·· ˈ···◂/ *adj* belonging to or connected with the part of the Christian religion whose leader is the Pope —**Roman Catholic** *n* [C] —**Roman Catholicism** /ˌ·· ·ˈ····/ *n* [U]

**ro·mance[1]** /rəʊˈmæns, ˈrəʊmæns‖roʊˈmæns, ˈroʊ-/ *n* **1** [C] an exciting and often short relationship between two people who love each other: **a whirlwind romance** (=one that happens very suddenly and quickly) **2** [U] love, or a feeling of being in love: *The romance had gone out of their relationship.* **3** [U] the feeling of excitement and adventure that is connected with a particular place, activity etc: *the romance of life in the Wild West* **4** [C] a story about the love between two people **5** [C] a story that has brave characters and exciting events: *a Medieval romance*

**romance[2]** *v* [I] to describe things that have happened in a way that makes them seem better or more important than they really were: [+ **about**] *an old man romancing about the past*

**Romance lan·guage** /ˈ· ˈ···/ *n* [C] a language that comes from Latin, for example French or Spanish

**Ro·man·esque** /ˌrəʊməˈnesk◂‖ˌroʊ-/ *adj* in the style of building that was popular in Western Europe in the 11th and 12th centuries, and had many round ARCHes and thick PILLARS

**Roman law** /ˌ·· ˈ·/ *n* [U] *law* CIVIL LAW

**Roman nose** /ˌ·· ˈ·/ *n* [C] a nose that curves out near the top —see picture on page 412

**roman nu·mer·al** /ˌ·· ˈ···/ *n* [C] a number in a system first used in ancient Rome that uses the combinations of the letters I, V, X, L, C, D, and M

**Romano-** /rəmɑːnəʊ‖-noʊ/ *prefix* **1** connected with ancient Rome; Roman **2** ancient Roman and: *Romano-British art*

**ro·man·tic[1]** /-rəʊˈmæntɪk, rə-‖roʊ-, rə-/ *adj*
**1** ▶ **SHOWING LOVE** ◀ showing strong feelings of love: *"Tom always sends me red roses on my birthday." "How romantic!"*
**2** ▶ **CONNECTED WITH LOVE** ◀ connected with feelings of love or with a loving relationship: *It's not a romantic relationship – they're just business partners.*
**3** ▶ **BEAUTIFUL** ◀ beautiful in a way that affects your emotions and makes you think of love or adventure: *a romantic village nestling at the foot of the mountains*
**4** ▶ **NOT PRACTICAL** ◀ not practical, and basing your actions too much on an imagined idea of the world: *romantic notions about becoming a famous actress*
**5** ▶ **STORY/FILM** ◀ a romantic story or film is about love: *a romantic comedy*
**6 Romantic art/literature etc** art or literature that is based on the ideas of romanticism —**romantically** /-kli/ *adv*

**romantic[2]** *n* [C] **1** someone who shows strong feelings of love and likes doing things that are connected with love such as buying flowers, presents etc: *Oh, Andy, you're such a romantic!* **2** someone who is not practical, and bases their ideas too much on an imagined idea of the world: *an incurable romantic* **3** also **Romantic** a writer, painter etc, whose work is based on romanticism

**ro·man·ti·cis·m, Romanticism** /rəʊˈmæntɪ̈sɪzəm, rə-‖roʊ, rə-/ *n* [U] a way of writing or painting that was popular in the late 18th and early 19th century, in which feelings and wild natural beauty were considered more important than anything else

**ro·man·ti·cize** also **-ise** *BrE* /rəʊˈmæntɪ̈saɪz, rə-‖roʊ, rə-/ *v* [T] to talk or think about things in a way that makes them seem more romantic or attractive than they really are: *a rather romanticized picture of life in the war*

**Ro·ma·ny** /ˈrəʊməni‖ˈrɑː-/ *n* **1** [C] a GIPSY **2** [U] the language of the GIPSY people

**ro·me·o, Romeo** /ˈrəʊmiəʊ‖ˈroʊmioʊ/ *n* [C] *often humorous* a man who tries to attract all the women he meets in a ROMANTIC[1] (1) or sexual way: *the office Romeo*

**romp[1]** /rɒmp‖rɑːmp/ *v* [I] **1** [always + adv/prep] to play in a noisy way, especially by running, jumping etc: [+ **around/about**] *They could hear the children romping around upstairs.* **2 romp home** if someone or something, especially a horse in a race, romps home, they win the race or competition easily
**romp through** sth *phr v* [T] *BrE informal* to succeed in doing or finishing something quickly and easily

**romp[2]** *n* [C] **1** *informal* a piece of amusing entertainment which has a lot of exciting scenes: *Branagh's new film is an enjoyable romp.* **2** *BrE humorous* a word for sexual activity, used especially by newspapers **3** an occasion when people play noisily and roughly

**romp·ers** /ˈrɒmpəz‖ˈrɑːmpərz/ *n* [plural] a piece of clothing for babies, made like a top and trousers joined together

**ron·do** /ˈrɒndəʊ‖ˈrɑːndoʊ-/ *n plural* **rondos** [C] a piece of music in which the main tune is repeated several times

**rönt·gen** /ˈrɒntgen‖ˈrentgən/ *n* [C] another spelling of ROENTGEN

**rood** /ruːd/ *n* [C] *old use or technical* a Christian cross, usually in a church

**rood screen** /ˈ· ·/ *n* [C] a decorated wooden or stone wall in a Christian church, that divides the part where the CHOIR (=singers) sit from the part where other people sit

**roof[1]** /ruːf‖ruːf, rʊf/ *n* [C] S3 W2
**1** ▶ **OF A BUILDING** ◀ the outside surface or structure on top of a building, vehicle, tent etc: *Our roof used to leak whenever it rained.* | *We can probably strap the cases to the roof of her car.* —see picture on page 410
**2** ▶ **OF A PASSAGE** ◀ the top of a passage under the ground; CEILING (1): *Soon, the whole tunnel roof was collapsing on top of the miners.*
**3 a roof over your head** somewhere to live: *I may not have a job, but at least I've got a roof over my head.*
**4 go through the roof** *informal* **a)** also **hit the roof** to suddenly become very angry: *Put that back before Dad sees you and hits the roof!* **b)** if a price, cost etc goes through the roof, it increases to a very high level

5 ▶ **OF YOUR MOUTH** ◀ the hard upper part of the inside of your mouth
6 **under the same roof/under one roof** in the same building or home: *We enjoy each other's company, but we can't live under the same roof or we argue all the time.*
7 **under my/her etc roof** in your home: *As long as you live under this roof, young man, you'll do as your mother says.*
8 **the roof falls in/caves in** *AmE informal* if the roof falls in or caves in, something bad suddenly happens to you when you do not expect it
9 **red-roofed/slate-roofed etc** having a roof that is red, made of SLATE[1] (2) etc —see also **raise the roof** (RAISE[1] (22)), SUNROOF

**roof**[2] *v* [T usually passive] to put a roof on a building: **be roofed with** *a cottage, roofed with the local slate*
**roof** sth ↔ **in/over** *phr v* [T] to cover an open space by putting a roof over it: *We're going to roof in the yard to make a garage.*

**roof·ing** /ˈruːfɪŋ‖ˈruːf-, ˈrʊf-/ *n* [U] stones, tiles (TILE[1] (2)) etc for making or covering roofs

**roof-rack** /ˈ· ·/ *n* [C] *BrE* a metal frame fixed on top of a car and used for carrying bags, cases etc; LUGGAGE RACK *AmE* —see picture at RACK[1]

**roof·top** /ˈruːftɒp‖ˈruːftɑːp, ˈrʊf-/ *n* [C] the upper surface of a roof: *the view across the rooftops* —see also **shout sth from the rooftops** (SHOUT[1] (3))

**rook**[1] /rʊk/ *n* [C] **1** a large black European bird like a CROW[1] (1) **2** one of the pieces in a game of CHESS; CASTLE

**rook**[2] *v* [T] *old-fashioned* to cheat someone, especially to get their money

**rook·e·ry** /ˈrʊkəri/ *n* [C] a group of NESTS made by rooks

**rook·ie** /ˈrʊki/ *n* [C] **1** *especially AmE* someone who has just started doing a job and has little experience: *rookie cops* **2** *AmE* someone who is in their first year of playing a professional sport: *a rookie out of Georgia Tech*

S1 W1 **room**[1] /ruːm, rʊm/ *n*
1 ▶ **IN A BUILDING** ◀ [C] a part of the inside of a building that has its own walls, floor and ceiling: **bathroom/dining room/meeting room etc** (=a room used for washing, eating etc) *The meeting room's upstairs on your right.* | *We could hear someone laughing in the next room.* | *It's bedtime – you'd better go up to your room.* | *I'm staying at the Arosa Hotel – Room 348.* | **single/double room** (=a room in a hotel for one person or for two) —see PLACE[1] USAGE
2 ▶ **SPACE** ◀ [U] enough space for a particular purpose: **there's room in** *I'd like to bring the children if there's room in the car.* | **there's room for** *There's not enough room in the fridge for all this food.* | **there's room to do sth** *There wasn't really room to lie down comfortably.* | **have room (for sth)** *Do you have room for another book in your bag?* | *Have you got room for some dessert?* (=can you eat some?) | **make room (for sth)** *I'll just clear out the cupboard to make room for your stuff.* | **leave room (for sth)** (=make sure there is enough room for something) *Leave room for people to get past.* | **take up room** (=use a lot of space) *That old wardrobe takes up too much room.* | **leg-room/head-room** (=space for your legs or head in a vehicle) *You have more leg-room if you travel first class.* | **there's not enough room to swing a cat** *informal* (=used to say that there is very little space in a room) —see also ELBOW-ROOM
3 ▶ **OPPORTUNITY** ◀ [U] the chance to do the things that you want to do or need to do: [+ **for**] *There's little room for innovation.* | **room to do sth** *Children need to have room to develop their natural creativity.* | **room for manoeuvre** (=freedom to change your plans or decisions) *The strict export regulations left us no room for manoeuvre.*
4 ▶ **POSSIBILITY** ◀ [U] the possibility that something may exist or will happen: **room for doubt** *The evidence left no room for doubt – Brooks was guilty.*
5 **there's room for improvement** used to say that someone's work or performance is not perfect and needs to be improved
6 **one-roomed/two-roomed etc** having one room, two rooms etc
7 ▶ **APARTMENT** ◀ **rooms** [plural] *old-fashioned especially BrE* two or more rooms that you rent in a building, or stay in at a college —see also FRONT ROOM, LIVING ROOM, SITTING ROOM

**room**[2] *v* [I] *AmE* **1 room with sb** to share a room with someone at college **2** [+ **in**] to rent and live in a room somewhere

**room and board** /ˌ· · ˈ·/ *n* [U] *AmE* a room to sleep in and food: *I pay $1200 a quarter for room and board.*

**room·er** /ˈruːmə, ˈrʊm-‖-ər/ *n* [C] *AmE* someone who pays rent to live in a house with it's owner LODGER *BrE*

**room·ful** /ˈruːmfʊl, ˈrʊm-/ *n* [C] a large number of things or people that are all together in one room: [+ **of**] *It's too intimidating to read my poetry to a roomful of strangers.*

**rooming house** /ˈ··· ·/ *n* [C] *AmE* a house where you can rent a room to live in; LODGING HOUSE *BrE*

**room·mate** /ˈruːmˌmeɪt, ˈrʊm-/ *n* [C] **1** someone who you share a room with, especially at college: *Ben and I were roommates at university.* **2** *AmE* someone you share a room, apartment, or house with; FLATMATE *BrE*: *I hate the way my roommate never does the dishes.*

**room ser·vice** /ˈ· ˌ··/ *n* [U] a service provided by a hotel, by which food, drink etc can be sent to a guest's room

**room tem·pe·ra·ture** /ˈ· ˌ····/ *n* [U] the normal temperature inside a house

**room·y** /ˈruːmi/ *adj* a house, car etc that is roomy is large and has a lot of space inside it —**roominess** *n* [U]

**roost**[1] /ruːst/ *n* [C] a place where birds rest and sleep —see also **rule the roost** (RULE[2] (5)

**roost**[2] *v* [I] **1** if a bird roosts, it rests or sleeps somewhere **2 sb's chickens come home to roost** used to say that someone's past mistakes are causing problems for them now

**roost·er** /ˈruːstə‖-ər/ *n* [C] *especially AmE* a male chicken; COCK[1] (1) *BrE*

**root**[1] /ruːt/ *n* [C] S3 W2
1 ▶ **PLANT** ◀ the part of a plant or tree that grows under the ground and gets water from the soil: *Be careful not to damage the roots when repotting.* | *tree roots* —see picture at GERMINATE
2 ▶ **CAUSE OF A PROBLEM** ◀ the main cause of a problem: *Money is the root of all evil.* | **be/lie at the root of** (=be the cause of a problem) *Often allergies are at the root of a lot of the problems.* | **get to the root of** (=find out the cause of a problem) | **root cause** (=the main reason for a problem)
3 ▶ **OF A CUSTOM/TRADITION** ◀ **roots** the origins of a custom or TRADITION that has continued for a long time: **has its roots in** *Jazz has its roots in the folk songs of the southern states of the US.*
4 ▶ **OF AN IDEA/BELIEF** ◀ the main part of an idea or belief which all the other parts come from: **be/lie at the root of** *Foucault is challenging the very root of 20th century liberalism.*
5 ▶ **FAMILY CONNECTION** ◀ **sb's roots** your connection with a place because you were born there, or your family used to live there: *Naita has come to Ghana in search of her roots.*
6 **put down roots** if you put down roots somewhere, you start to feel that this place is your home and to have relationships with the people there
7 ▶ **TOOTH/HAIR ETC** ◀ the part of a tooth, hair etc that fixes it to the rest of your body
8 **take root a)** if an idea takes root, people begin to accept or believe it: *The concepts of democracy and free trade are finally beginning to take root.* **b)** if a plant takes root, it starts to grow where you have planted it
9 **have a (good) root round** *informal especially BrE* to search for something by moving other things around
10 **root and branch** if you destroy something root and branch, you get rid of it completely and permanently because it is bad
11 ▶ **LANGUAGE** ◀ *technical* the basic part of a word

which shows its main meaning, to which other parts can be added: *The suffix 'ness' can be added to the root 'cold' to form the word 'coldness'.* —compare STEM[1] (4)
**12 ▶ MATHEMATICS ◀** *technical* a number that when multiplied by itself a certain number of times, equals the number that you have: *2 is the fourth root of 16.* —see also CUBE ROOT, SQUARE ROOT, GRASS ROOTS

**root**[2] *v*
**1 ▶ SEARCH ◀** [I always + adv/prep] to search for something by moving things around: [+ **through/in/around**] *"Hang on a second," said Leila, rooting through her handbag for a pen.* | [+ **for**] *pigs rooting for food*
**2 ▶ PLANT ◀ a)** [I] to grow roots: *New shrubs will root easily in summer.* **b)** [T usually passive] to fix a plant firmly by its roots: *The bush was too firmly rooted in the hard earth to dig up easily.* | **root itself** *Clumps of thyme had rooted themselves between the rocks.* —see also **deeply rooted** (DEEPLY (5))
**3 be rooted in** to have developed from something and be strongly influenced by it: *policies that are rooted in Marxist economic theory*
**4 be rooted to the spot** to be so shocked, surprised, or frightened that you cannot move
**root for** sb *phr v* [T] *informal* **1** to give support and encouragement to someone in a competition, test or difficult situation, because you want them to succeed: *Good luck – we'll all be rooting for you!* **2** *especially AmE* to support a sports team or player by shouting and cheering: *We'll all be rooting for the Dallas Cowboys in the Superbowl.*
**root** sth ↔ **out** *phr v* [T] **1** to find out where a particular kind of problem exists and get rid of it: *Racism cannot be rooted out without strong government action.* **2** *informal* to find something by searching for it: *I'll try and root out something suitable for you to wear.*
**root** sth ↔ **up** *phr v* [T] to dig or pull a plant up with its roots

**root beer** /ˈ· ·/ *n* [C,U] a sweet, non-alcoholic drink made from the roots of some plants, drunk especially in the US

**root·bound** /ˈruːtbaʊnd/ *adj AmE* a plant that is rootbound cannot grow any more because its roots have filled the pot it is growing in; POTBOUND *BrE*

**root crop** /ˈ· ·/ *n* [C] a vegetable or plant that is grown so that its root parts can be used

**root·le** /ˈruːtl/ also **rootle around/about** *v* [I] *BrE informal* to search for something by moving many other things around

**root·less** /ˈruːtləs/ *adj* having nowhere that you feel is really your home: *a rootless existence on the street* —**rootlessness** *n* [U]

**root vege·ta·ble** /ˈ· ˌ···/ *n* [C] a vegetable such as a potato or CARROT that grows under the ground —see picture on page 414

S3 W3 **rope**[1] /rəʊp‖roʊp/ *n* **1** [C,U] very strong, thick string, made by twisting together many threads of NYLON or other material: *They tied up the prisoner with rope.* | *a bell rope* **2 know the ropes** to know how to do all the parts of a job, deal with a system etc, because you have a lot of experience of it **3 show sb the ropes** to teach someone how to do a job or deal with a system: *This is Shirley's first day, so will you show her the ropes?* **4 be on the ropes** *informal* to be in a very bad situation, in which you are likely to be defeated **5 give sb plenty of rope** to give someone a lot of freedom to do something in the way they want to do it **6 give sb enough rope to hang themselves** to give someone freedom to do what they want to do, because you think they will cause problems for themselves **7 be at the end of your rope** *especially AmE* to have no more PATIENCE or strength left to deal with a problem or a difficult situation **8 the rope** *old-fashioned* HANGING as a punishment **9 the ropes** the rope fence that surrounds an area used for BOXING or WRESTLING **10 a rope of pearls** PEARLS on a string, worn around your neck as jewellery —see also JUMP ROPE, **money for old rope** (MONEY (16))

**rope**[2] *v* **1** [T always + adv/prep] to tie things together using rope: **rope sth to sth** *Harvey roped his horse to a nearby tree.* | **rope sb/sth together** *Two firemen roped themselves together and plunged into the lake.* **2** [T] *AmE* to catch an animal using a circle of rope
**rope** sb ↔ **in** *phr v* [T] *informal* to persuade someone to help you in a job, or to join in an activity, especially when they do not want to: **rope sb in to do sth** *I've roped Dad in to help with the entertainment.* | **rope sb into doing sth** *Have you been roped into selling tickets?*
**rope** sth ↔ **off** *phr v* [T] to surround an area with ropes, especially in order to separate it from another area: *Last night police roped off the area of the find.*

**rope lad·der** /ˈ· ˌ··/ *n* [C] a LADDER made of two long ropes connected by wooden pieces that you stand on

**rop·ey, ropy** /ˈrəʊpi‖ˈroʊ-/ *adj BrE informal* **1** in bad condition or of bad quality: *We stayed in a really ropey hotel.* **2** slightly ill: *I'm feeling a bit ropey this morning.*

**ro-ro** /ˈrəʊ rəʊ‖ˈroʊ roʊ/ *n* [C] *BrE informal* a ROLL-ON ROLL-OFF ship

**Ror·schach test** /ˈrɔːʃɑːk test‖ˈrɔːr-/ *n* [C] a method of testing someone's character, by making them say what spots of ink with various shapes look like

**ro·sa·ry** /ˈrəʊzəri‖ˈroʊ-/ *n* **1** [C] a string of BEADS *used by Roman Catholics for counting prayers* **2 the Rosary** the set of prayers that are said by Roman Catholics while counting rosary BEADS

**ro·sé** /ˈrəʊzeɪ‖roʊˈzeɪ/ *n* [U] pink wine

**rose**[1] /rəʊz‖roʊz/ *n* S3 W3
**1 ▶ FLOWER ◀** [C] a flower that has a pleasant smell, and is usually red, pink, white, or yellow, or the bush that this grows on
**2 ▶ COLOUR ◀** [U] a pink colour —see picture on page 411
**3 not all roses** also **not a bed of roses** *informal* if a job or situation is not all roses, it is not always pleasant and there are often difficult things to deal with
**4 put the roses back in sb's cheeks** *informal* to make someone look healthy again
**5 be coming up roses** *informal* be happening or developing in the best possible way
**6 not come out of sth smelling of roses** *informal* to have been involved in a situation that makes you seem dishonest, so that people stop trusting you
**7 ▶ FOR WATER ◀** [C] a circular piece of metal with holes in it, that is fitted to the end of a pipe or WATERING CAN so that liquid comes out in several thin streams
**8 ▶ LIGHT ◀** [C] *technical* the circular object from which an electric CEILING light hangs

**rose**[2] *adj* having a pink colour

**rose**[3] the past tense of RISE[1]

**ro·se·ate** /ˈrəʊziət‖ˈroʊ-/ *adj poetic* pink

**rose·bud** /ˈrəʊzbʌd‖ˈroʊz-/ *n* [C] the flower of a rose before it opens

**rose bush** /ˈ· ·/ *n* [C] the plant that roses grow on

**rose-col·oured** *BrE*, **rose-colored** *AmE* /ˈ· ··/ *adj* **1** having a pink colour **2** a rose-coloured idea of what something is like shows that you think something is more pleasant than it really is, because you do not notice anything unpleasant: **see sth through rose-coloured/rose-tinted spectacles** (=never notice bad things)

**rose hip** /ˈ· ·/ *n* [C] the small red fruit of some kinds of rose bush, used in medicines and juices: *rose hip syrup*

**rose·ma·ry** /ˈrəʊzməri‖ˈroʊzmeri/ *n* [U] leaves that have a strong, pleasant smell and are used in cooking, or the bush that these come from

**rose-tint·ed** /ˈ· ··/ *adj especially BrE* ROSE-COLOURED

**ro·sette** /rəʊˈzet‖roʊ-/ *n* [C] **1** a circular BADGE made of coloured RIBBON that is given to the winner of a competition or that people in Britain wear to show support for a particular football team or political party **2** a shape like a round flat flower that has been made in stone or wood

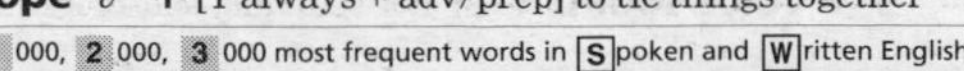

**rose·wa·ter** /ˈrəʊzˌwɔːtə‖ˈroʊzˌwɒːtər, -ˌwɑː-/ *n* [U] a liquid made from roses, used for its pleasant smell

**rose·wood** /ˈrəʊzwʊd‖ˈroʊz-/ *n* [U] a hard dark red wood, used for making expensive furniture

**ros·in** /ˈrɒzɪn‖ˈrɑː-/ *n* [U] a solid, slightly sticky substance that you rub on the BOW of a VIOLIN etc, to keep it moving correctly on the strings —**rosin** *v* [T]

**ros·ter¹** /ˈrɒstə‖ˈrɑːstər-/ *n* [C] a list of people's names showing the jobs they must do and the times when they must do them: *a duty roster*

**roster²** *v* [T] to put someone's name on a roster

**ros·trum** /ˈrɒstrəm‖ˈrɑː-/ *n* [C] a small PLATFORM (=raised area) that you stand on when you are making a speech or conducting (CONDUCT¹ (2)) musicians

**ros·y** /ˈrəʊzi‖ˈroʊ-/ *adj* **1** pink: *rosy cheeks* **2** seeming to offer hope of success or happiness: *The future is beginning to look much rosier.*|*rosy optimism*|**paint a rosy picture of** (=describe a situation in a way that makes it seem much better than it really is) —**rosiness** *n* [U]

**rot¹** /rɒt‖rɑːt/ *v* **1** [I, T] to decay by a gradual natural process, or to make something do this: *Sugar rots your teeth.*|*the stench of rotting eggs* **2 rot in jail/prison etc** to get into a bad mental or physical condition because you have been forced to stay in a place such as a prison: *As far as they're concerned we can rot in jail.*

**rot²** *n* [U] **1 stop the rot** *informal* to stop a bad situation from getting worse and worse: *If Leeds don't stop the rot soon they can say goodbye to a top eight team ranking.* **2 the rot set in** *informal* used to say that a situation starts to get worse, and nothing could stop this process **3** the natural process of decaying or the part of something that has decayed **4** *BrE old-fashioned* nonsense: *You do talk rot!* —see also DRY ROT

**ro·ta** /ˈrəʊtə‖ˈroʊ-/ *n* [C] *BrE* a list that shows when each person in a group must do a particular job: *a cleaning rota*

**ro·ta·ry¹** /ˈrəʊtəri‖ˈroʊ-/ *adj* **1** turning in a circle around a fixed point, like a wheel: *the rotary movement of the helicopter blades* **2** having a main part that does this: *a rotary engine*

**rotary²** *n* [C] *AmE* a ROUNDABOUT

**Rotary Club** /ˈ··· ˌ·/ *n* **the Rotary Club** an organization of business people in a town who work together to raise money for people who are poor or sick

**ro·tate** /rəʊˈteɪt‖ˈroʊteɪt/ *v* **1** [I,T] to turn around a fixed point, or to make something do this: *a rotating blade* **2** [I, T] if a job rotates, or if people rotate jobs, they each do the jobs for a fixed period of time, one after the other: *The chairmanship of the committee rotates annually.*|*We usually rotate the worst jobs, so that no one gets stuck with them.* **3** [T] *technical* to regularly change the crops grown on a piece of land, in order to preserve the quality of the soil

**ro·ta·tion** /rəʊˈteɪʃən‖roʊ-/ *n* **1** [U] the action of turning around a fixed point: [+ **about/around/on**] *the rotation of the Earth on its axis* **2** [C] one complete turn around a fixed point: *The blades spin at 100 rotations per minute.* **3 in rotation a)** if a group of people do something in rotation they do it one after the other in a regular order: *The four were Area Board chairmen, serving in rotation.* **b)** if a group of things are used in rotation they are used one after the other in a regular order: *It's good practice to use three balls in rotation in cold weather.* **4** [U] the practice of changing regularly from one thing to another, or regularly changing the person who does a particular job **5 crop rotation** *technical* the practice of regularly changing the crops that are grown on a piece of land, in order to preserve the quality of the soil —**rotational** *adj*

**rote** /rəʊt‖roʊt/ *n* [U] *formal* a method of learning that involves repeating something until you remember it, without having to understand it: **learn (sth) by rote** *old-fashioned grammar teaching and learning by rote*

**rot·gut** /ˈrɒtgʌt‖ˈrɑːt-/ *n* [U] *informal* strong cheap low-quality alcohol

**ro·tis·ser·ie** /rəʊˈtɪsəri‖roʊ-/ *n* [C] a piece of equipment for cooking meat by turning it around and around on a metal rod

**ro·tor** /ˈrəʊtə‖ˈroʊtər/ *n* [C] *technical* **1** a part of a machine that turns around on a fixed point **2** also **rotor blade** the long flat part on top of a HELICOPTER that turns around and around

**rot·ten¹** /ˈrɒtn‖ˈrɑːtn/ *adj* **1** badly decayed: *rotten fruit*|*the smell of rotten eggs*|*The wood was completely rotten.* **2** *informal* very nasty or unpleasant: *What rotten weather!*|*It's a rotten thing to do.* **3** *informal* a word meaning very bad at doing something, or very badly done, used especially when you feel annoyed about this: *He's a rotten driver.* **4 feel rotten a)** to feel ill **b)** to feel unhappy and guilty about something: [+ **about**] *I felt rotten about having to fire him.* **5 a rotten apple** one bad person who has a bad effect on all the others in a group —**rottenly** *adv* —**rottenness** *n* [U]

**rot away** *phr v* [I,T] to decay completely and disappear or break into small pieces, or to make something do this: *In places the timbers have rotted away.*

**rotten²** *adv informal* **1 spoil sb rotten** to treat someone too well or too kindly, especially a child: *Melanie's beautiful, wilful, and she's been spoiled rotten all her life.* **2 fancy sb rotten** *BrE humorous* to be extremely attracted to someone in a sexual way

**rot·ter** /ˈrɒtə‖ˈrɑːtər/ *n* [C] *BrE old-fashioned* an unpleasant person who treats other people badly

**rott·wei·ler** /ˈrɒtvaɪlə,-waɪlə‖ˈrɑːtwaɪlər/ *n* [C] **1** a type of strong and dangerous dog, often used as a guard dog **2 rottweiler politics/tendencies etc** *humorous* politics etc in which politicians attack each other in a very determined way

**ro·tund** /rəʊˈtʌnd‖roʊ-/ *adj humorous* having a fat round body —**rotundity** *n* [U]

**ro·tun·da** /rəʊˈtʌndə‖roʊ-/ *n* [C] a round building or hall, especially one with a DOME (=a round bowl-shaped roof)

**rou·ble, ruble** /ˈruːbəl/ *n* [C] the standard unit of money in the former USSR

**rouge** /ruːʒ/ *n old-fashioned* [U] pink or red powder or cream that women put on their cheeks —**rouge** *v* [T]

**rough¹** /rʌf/ *adj* S2 W3

**1 ▶ NOT SMOOTH ◀** having an uneven surface: *Her hands were rough from hard work.*|*A rough track led to the farm.*|*rough grass* —opposite SMOOTH¹ (1)

**2 ▶ NOT EXACT ◀** not exact or not containing many details APPROXIMATE: *This is just a rough sketch but it gives you the idea.*|*a rough translation*|**a rough idea** *Could you give me a rough idea what time you'll be home?*|**at a rough guess** *spoken* (=without being at all certain or exact) *At a rough guess, I'd say he was about 45.*|**a rough estimate** *I can only give you a rough estimate of the cost at this stage.* —see graph at IDEA

**3 ▶ NOT GENTLE ◀** using force or violence: *Rugby is a very rough game.*|*A stroller should be easy to fold and capable of withstanding rough treatment.*

**4 ▶ TOWN/AREA ETC ◀** a rough area is a place where there is a lot of violence or crime: *a rough part of town*

**5 ▶ HAVING A LOT OF PROBLEMS/DIFFICULTIES ◀** [usually before noun] a rough period is one in which you have a lot of problems or difficulties: *Don't be too angry with her – she's had a very rough time of it lately.*|*I've had a really rough day.*|**go through a rough patch** (=experience problems or difficulties)|**give sb/sth a rough ride** (=a very difficult time) *The bill may have gotten through the House but it's in for a rough ride in the Senate.*

**6 ▶ UNFAIR/UNLUCKY ◀** unfair or unlucky: **it's rough on sb** *It's rough on him, losing his job like that.*|*Two burglaries in one week? That's a bit rough!*

**7 ▶ WEATHER/SEA ◀** with strong wind or storms: *In the evening we were sick, it was a very rough crossing.*

**8 ▶ NOT COMFORTABLE ◀** uncomfortable, with difficult conditions: *a rough, pioneering way of life*

**9 ▶ VOICE/SOUND ◀ a)** not sounding soft or gentle,

and often rather unpleasant or angry: *the rough voices of the workmen* **b)** having an unpleasant sound, especially because there is something wrong with a machine: *The clutch sounds rough, better get it checked.*
**10 ► SIMPLE/NOT WELL MADE ◄** simple and often not very well made: *We constructed a rough shelter using whatever materials we could find.*
**11 feel rough** *informal* to feel ill: *I think I'd better go to bed – I'm feeling pretty rough.*
**12 look rough** *informal* to look untidy, dirty, or unhealthy: *We had been travelling for two days, and must have looked pretty rough.*
**13 rough and ready** simple, but just good enough for a particular purpose
**14 rough justice** punishment that is severe or unfair
**15 a rough night** a night when you did not sleep well
**16 rough stuff** *spoken* violent behaviour
**17 a bit of rough** *BrE humorous* someone from a lower social class than you, with whom you have a sexual relationship
**18 give sb the rough side of your tongue** *BrE old-fashioned* to speak angrily to someone **—roughness** *n* [U] —see also ROUGH DIAMOND, ROUGH PAPER, ROUGHLY

**rough²** *n* **1 take the rough with the smooth** to accept the bad things in life as well as the good ones **2** [C] a picture drawn very quickly, not showing all the details **3 the rough** uneven ground with long grass on a GOLF course —see picture on page 1264 **4 in rough** *BrE* if you write or draw something in rough, you do it without paying attention to details or tidiness: *It's best to work in rough first, and then write it out neatly.* —see also DIAMOND IN THE ROUGH

**rough³** *v* **rough it** *informal* to live for a short time in conditions that are not very comfortable: *Let's just take the tent – I don't mind roughing it for a bit.*
**rough** sth ↔ **in** *phr v* [T] to add something to a picture, without showing all the exact details: *If you look here you can see another angle for the arm roughed in.*
**rough** sth ↔ **out** *phr v* [T] to draw or write something, without showing all the exact details: *Iain was peering at a diagram the engineer had roughed out on his notepad.*
**rough** sb ↔ **up** *phr v* [T] *informal* to attack someone and hurt them by hitting them

**rough⁴** *adv* **1 sleep rough** *BrE* to sleep outside with nothing to protect you from the weather: *sleeping rough on the street* **2 play rough** to play in a fairly violent way —see also **cut up rough** (CUT¹)

**rough·age** /ˈrʌfɪdʒ/ *n* [U] a substance contained in some foods that helps your BOWELS to work; DIETARY FIBRE: *Wholemeal bread is a valuable source of roughage.*

**rough-and-tum·ble** /ˌ· · ˈ··/ *n* **1** [singular, U] noisy rough behaviour when playing or fighting, especially by children **2** [U] the usual busy, noisy, or rough way in which a particular activity takes place: *the rough-and-tumble of politics*

**rough·cast** /ˈrʌfkɑːst‖-kæst/ *n* [U] a rough surface on the outside of a building, made of PLASTER¹ (1) mixed with little stones or broken shells **—roughcast** *adj*

**rough di·a·mond** /ˌ· ˈ···/ *n* [C] *informal* someone who seems rude, rough, or unfriendly, but is actually kind and generous; DIAMOND IN THE ROUGH *AmE*

**rough·en** /ˈrʌfən/ *v* [I,T] to become rough, or to make something rough

**rough-hewn** /ˌ· ˈ·◄/ *adj* rough-hewn wood or stone has been roughly cut and its surface is not yet smooth

**rough-house¹** /ˈ· ·/ *n* [singular] *BrE old-fashioned* a noisy fight, usually without weapons

**rough·house²** *v* [I] *AmE* to play roughly or fight; WRESTLE (1): *Either stop roughhousing or play outside!*

S2 **rough·ly** /ˈrʌfli/ *adv* **1** not exactly; about: *There were roughly 200 people there.*|*How much have you got, roughly?*|*Azaleas flower at roughly the same time each year.*|**roughly speaking** (=used when saying something without giving exact details or information) *Roughly speaking, I'd say we need about $500.* —see graph at APPROXIMATELY **2** not gently or carefully: *Alan dropped the cat roughly to the floor.*

**rough·neck** /ˈrʌfnek/ *n* [C] **1** a member of a team of people who make or operate an OIL-WELL **2** *informal especially AmE* someone who usually behaves in a rough, rude, or angry way

**rough pa·per** /ˌ· ˈ··/ *n* [U] *BrE* paper that is used for writing or drawing things that will later be changed or copied more neatly

**rough·shod** /ˈrʌfʃɒd‖-ʃɑːd/ *adj* **ride roughshod over** to behave in a way that ignores other people's feelings or opinions

**rou·lette** /ruːˈlet/ *n* [U] a game in which a small ball is spun around on a moving wheel, and people try to win money by guessing which hole it will fall into —see also RUSSIAN ROULETTE

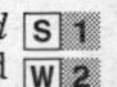
**round¹** /raʊnd/ *adj* **1** shaped like a circle: *a round table*|*Jamie's eyes grew round with delight.* **2** shaped like a ball: *a plant with small round berries* **3** fat and curved: *Charlie had a chubby face and round cheeks.* **4** a round number is a whole number, often ending in 0: *Let's make it a round £50 I owe you.*|**a round hundred/dozen etc** (=a complete hundred etc) **5 in round figures** not expressed as an exact number but as the nearest 10, 100, 1000 etc: *In round figures, the expected profit is about £600 million.* —see also ROUNDLY, **a square peg in a round hole** (SQUARE² (11)), **—roundness** *n* [U]

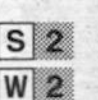
**round²** *adv* [only after verb] *especially BrE* **1** if something moves round, it moves in a circular movement: *It is water moving through the mechanism which pushes the wheel round.*|**round and round** *He stared at the washing machine, just watching the clothes go round and round.* **2** if something such as a group of people or things are round something, they surround that thing: *If you'll all gather round we'll begin the experiment.*|**all round** *The garden had a fence all round to keep out dogs.* **3** to many people or in many parts of a place, a room etc: *Please, come in, let me show you round.*|*Would someone hand the drinks round please.*|**all round** *It was a beautiful room, with cushions scattered all round.*|**enough to go round** (=enough for everyone) *Do you think there are enough seats to go round?* **4** in the opposite direction: *When he turned round I recognised him immediately.* **5** if you go round, you do not go the most direct way to get somewhere: *I don't mind driving round by the market on my way to the station.* **6 the wrong/the other/the opposite etc way round a)** facing the wrong, other, opposite etc direction: *You're wearing your T-shirt the wrong way round.* **b)** in the wrong, other, opposite etc order: *You got it the wrong way round. She left him, he didn't walk out on her!* **7 round about** about a particular time or amount: *It's a coincidence that all his grandparents died round about the same time.* **8 change/switch etc round** to change the position that things are in so that they are in each other's places: *The dartboard was at the back, but they've changed things round.* **9** *informal* to or in someone's house: *I'm inviting the neighbours round for a drink.*|*Sally left a note saying she'd be round at her cousin's house.* **10 (just) round the corner** not very far away at all: *She could walk, it's only round the corner.* **11 go round the shops/pub etc** to go to the shops etc: *I could go round the village and see if something's still open.* **12 go round (and round) in circles** to not make progress at something such as trying to solve a problem **13 2 metres/12 feet etc round** having a CIRCUMFERENCE of 2 metres, 12 feet etc **14 the first/second etc time round** the first, second, etc time that you do something: *Who says marriage is better the second time round?* —see also ALL-ROUND —compare AROUND

**round³** *prep especially BrE* **1** if something moves round something, it moves around it in a circular movement: *The earth goes round the sun.*|*The lions slowly circled round the gazelle, waiting to pounce.* —see picture on page 1257 **2** surrounding or covering something: *sitting round the table*|*Why have you got a bandage round*

*your wrist?* **3** if you go round something you do not go the most direct way to get somewhere: *You'll have to go right round the roadworks to get there.* **4** at or to the other side of something: *Suddenly the thief disappeared round the corner.* | *There must be another entrance round the back of the house.* **5** to or in all parts of a place: *Let me show you round the castle.* | *travelling round Europe* **6** a way round a difficult situation or problem is a way to solve it or avoid it: *We'll have to leave earlier – there's no other way round it!* **7 round here** in the place, area of a town etc where you are now: *Do you live round here?* | *There must be a pen round here somewhere.* **8** at about a particular time: *It must have been round midnight when I heard the scream.* —compare AROUND —see also **round the clock** (CLOCK[1] (6))

**USAGE NOTE: ROUND**

WORD CHOICE: **round, around, about**

In many contexts, **round** and **around** have the same meaning in British English, though American speakers do not use **round** in this way: *The price was somewhere round three thousand (BrE).* | *The price was somewhere around three thousand.*

In British English, you can use **round** for describing a circular movement: *The satellite travelled right round the Earth.* Americans would always use **around** in this meaning: *The satellite traveled right around the Earth.* The same is true when you use **around** and **round** to mean moving to different places: *He's travelling round the world for a few years (BrE).* | *He's traveling around the world for a few years.* Both **round** and **around** are correct in British English, although **round** is slightly less formal.

British English speakers often use **about** instead of **around** in some meanings: *Stop fooling about, you two.* | *"Where's my bag?" "It must be about somewhere."*

Both British and American speakers use **about** to mean 'approximately': *He's about six feet tall.*

**round**[4] *n* [C]
**1** ▶ **SERIES** ◀ a number or set of events that are connected: [+ **of**] *For Jodie, life was a continual round of parties.* | *the next round of arms talks*
**2** ▶ **FOOD/NEWSPAPERS/LETTERS ETC** ◀ a regular visit to a number of houses, offices etc to deliver or sell things: **paper/milk round etc** (=a job in which you deliver newspapers, milk etc to people's houses)
**3** ▶ **VISITS** ◀ **rounds** the usual visits that someone, especially a doctor, regularly makes as part of their job: **be (out) on your rounds** *I'm sorry; the doctor is out on her rounds till 3 o'clock.*
**4 do the rounds of** to go around from one place to another, often looking for work: *Daniela's doing the rounds of the theatrical agents.*
**5 do the rounds** *informal* also **go the rounds** *BrE* if an illness or piece of news does the rounds, it is passed on from one person to another: *There's a nasty kind of flu doing the rounds this winter.*
**6** ▶ **ALCOHOL** ◀ if you buy a round of drinks in a bar, you buy drinks for all the people in your group: **it's my/your etc round** (=used to say that you or another person should buy drinks for all the other people in your group) *What are you having? It's my round.*
**7 round of applause** a period when people are clapping (CLAP[1] (1)) to show that they enjoyed a performance
**8 round of sandwiches** *especially BrE* SANDWICHES made from two whole pieces of bread
**9 round of toast** *especially BrE* one whole piece of bread that has been toasted (TOAST[2] (2))
**10** ▶ **GOLF** ◀ a complete game of GOLF
**11** ▶ **BOXING** ◀ one of the periods of fighting in a boxing (BOX[2] (1)) or wrestling (WRESTLE (1)) match that are separated by short rests: *Bruno was knocked out in the second round.*
**12** ▶ **COMPETITION** ◀ one of the stages in a sports competition, especially in tennis or football: *Did Sampras get through to the third round?*
**13** ▶ **GUN SHOT** ◀ a single shot from a gun, or a bullet for one shot: *I've only got ten rounds of ammunition left.*
**14** ▶ **CIRCLE** ◀ something that has a circular shape: *Slice the potatoes into rounds.*
**15** ▶ **SONG** ◀ a song for three or four singers, in which each one sings the same tune, starting at different times
**16 the daily round** the things that you have to do every day: *the daily round of cooking and cleaning*
**17 in the round** a play that is performed in the round is performed on a central stage surrounded by the people watching it

**round**[5] *v* [T] **1** to go round something such as a bend or the corner of a building: *The Ferrari rounded the bend at top speed.* **2** to make something into a round shape: *Jenny rounded her lips and blew him a kiss.*

**round** sth ↔ **down** *phr v* [T] to reduce an exact figure to the nearest whole number —compare **round up**

**round** sth ↔ **off** *phr v* [I,T] **1** to do something as a way of ending an event, performance etc in a suitable or satisfactory way: **round sth ↔ off with** *Fresh strawberries would round the meal off nicely.* **2** [T] to take the sharp edges off something: *Round off the corners with a pair of scissors.* **3** to change an exact figure to the nearest whole number

**round on** sb/sth *phr v* [T] to suddenly turn and attack someone when they do not expect it, physically or with words: *Then, for no reason at all, she rounded on me and started screaming.*

**round out** *phr v* [T] to make an experience more thorough or complete: **round sth ↔ out** *Denise decided to round out her education with a year in Paris.*

**round** sb/sth ↔ **up** *phr v* [T] **1** to find a particular group of people and force them to go to prison: *The government's opponents are being rounded up and thrown in jail.* **2** to find and gather together a group of people or things: *See if you can round up a few friends to help you!* —see also ROUND-UP (1) **3** to increase an exact figure to the next highest whole number —compare **round down** **4** to finish a meeting or other event by doing something: *Frances likes to round up a speech with a joke.*

**round·a·bout**[1] /ˈraʊndəbaʊt/ *n* [C] *BrE* **1** a raised circular area which cars drive around, used where three or more roads join; TRAFFIC CIRCLE *AmE* **2** round structure which children sit on while people push it around and around; MERRY-GO-ROUND *AmE* **3** a MERRY-GO-ROUND (1) —see also **swings and roundabouts** (SWING[2] (8))

**roundabout**[2] *adj* not done in the shortest, most direct way possible: *a roundabout route to avoid the worst of the traffic* | *It was a roundabout way of telling us to leave.*

**round·ed** /ˈraʊndɪ̣d/ *adj* having a round shape; curved —see also WELL-ROUNDED

**roun·ders** /ˈraʊndəz‖-ərz/ *n* [singular] a British ball game, similar to BASEBALL, in which players hit the ball and then run around the edge of an area

**Round·head** /ˈraʊndhed/ *n* [C] someone who supported Parliament against the King in the English Civil War in the 17th century —compare CAVALIER

**round·ly** /ˈraʊndli/ *adv* **roundly condemn/criticize etc** (=criticize someone strongly and severely) *All the major parties roundly condemned the attack.*

**round rob·in** /ˌ· ˈ··/ *n* [C] **1** a competition in which every player or team plays against each of the other players or teams **2** a letter expressing opinions or complaints, signed by many people and sent as a form of protest

**round-shoul·dered** /ˌ· ˈ··◂/ *adj* having shoulders that are bent forwards or slope downwards

**round-ta·ble** /ˌ· ˈ··◂/ *adj* [only before noun] a round-table discussion or meeting is one in which everyone can talk about things in an equal way

**round-the-clock** /ˌ· · ˈ·◂/ *adj* [only before noun] all the time, both day and night: *He'll need round-the-clock hospital care.* —see also **round the clock** (CLOCK[1] (6))

**round trip** /ˌ· ˈ·/ *n* [C] a journey to a place and back again: *The round trip took just over an hour.*

**round-trip** /ˌ· ˈ·◂/ *adj AmE* a round-trip ticket includes the journey to a place and back again; RETURN[2] (9) *BrE*

**round-up** /ˈ· ·/ *n* [C] **1** an occasion when people, or animals, of a particular type are all brought together, often using force: *a round-up of suspected drug-dealers* **2** a short description of the main parts of the news, on the radio or on television —see also **round up** (ROUND[5])

**rouse** /raʊz/ *v* **1 raise sb (from their sleep/slumbers)** to wake someone up with difficulty because they are sleeping deeply **2** [T] to make someone start doing something, especially when they have been too tired or unwilling to do it: **rouse sb into action** *The commander tried to rouse them all into action.* | **rouse yourself** *When Alice finally roused herself, she realized Harold was already home.* **3** [T] to make someone feel a particular emotion, such as hope or fear —compare AROUSE

**roused** /raʊzd/ *adj* [not before noun] angry: **when roused** *When roused, he could be quite violent.*

**rous·ing** /ˈraʊzɪŋ/ *adj* a rousing song, speech etc makes people feel excited and eager to do something

**roust** /raʊst/ *v* [T] *AmE* to make someone move from a place: *Go roust the kids, it's time we went.*

**rous·ta·bout** /ˈraʊstəbaʊt/ *n* [C] *especially AmE* a man who does work for which he needs to be strong but not skilled, especially in a port, an OILFIELD, or a CIRCUS (1)

**rout[1]** /raʊt/ *v* [T] to defeat someone completely in a battle, competition, or election

**rout[2]** *n* [singular] a complete defeat in a battle, competition or election: **put sb to rout** *literary* (=defeat them completely in a battle)

W2 **route[1]** /ruːt‖ruːt, raʊt/ *n* [C] **1** the way from one place to another, especially a way that is regularly used and can be shown on a map: **[+ to/from]** *What's the best route to Cambridge?* | **take/follow a route** (=use a route) *We weren't sure about which route we should take.* **2** a road, railway, or imaginary line along which vehicles often travel: *The London-New York route is the busiest.* | *Is your office on a bus route?* **3** a way of doing something or achieving a particular result: *the surest route to disaster* | *his route to fame and fortune* **4 Route 66, 54 etc** used to show the number of a main road in the US: *Take Route 95 through Connecticut.* —see also EN ROUTE, SNOW ROUTE, TRADE ROUTE

**route[2]** *v* [T] to send something or someone using a particular route: **[+ through/by]** *They had to route the goods through Germany.* —see also RE-ROUTE

**route march** /ˈ· ·/ *n* [C] a long march done by soldiers when they are training

W3 **rou·tine[1]** /ruːˈtiːn/ *n* **1** [C,U] the usual or normal way in which you do things: *John's departure had upset their daily routine.* | *Mark longed to escape from the same old familiar routine.* | **a break in the routine** (=a change from what you normally do) **2** [C] a set of steps learned and practised by a dancer for a public performance **3** [C] *technical* a set of instructions given to a computer so that it will do a particular operation —**routinize** /ruːˈtiːnaɪz, ˈruːtiːnaɪz/ *v* [T] *AmE*

**rou·tine[2]** /ˌruːˈtiːn◂/ *adj* **1** | **routine questions/examination/visit etc** (=usual questions etc that are not concerned with any kind of serious problem) *It's just a routine medical examination, nothing to get worried about.* | *a routine visit to the dentist* **2** ordinary and boring: **routine jobs/tasks** *What's more, routine jobs make people less motivated.*

**rou·tine·ly** /ruːˈtiːnli/ *adv* if something is routinely done, it is usually done as part of the normal process of working, doing a job etc

**roux** /ruː/ *plural* **roux** /ruːz/ *n* [C,U] a mixture of flour, butter, and milk that is used for making SAUCES

**rove** /rəʊv‖roʊv/ *v* [I] **1** to travel from one place to another: **roving reporter** (=someone who works for a newspaper or television company, and moves from place to place) **2** if someone's eyes rove, they look continuously from one part of something to another: **[+ around/over]** *Benedict's eyes roved boldly over her sleeping body.* **3 have a roving eye** *old-fashioned* to be always looking for a chance to have romantic relationships

**rov·er** /ˈrəʊvə‖ˈroʊvər/ *n* [C] *literary* someone who travels around from place to place

**row[1]** /rəʊ‖roʊ/ *n* [C] **1** a line of things or people next to each other: **[+ of]** *a row of houses* | *rows of trees* | *Plant the seedlings in parallel rows.* | **in a row** (=next to each other) *On a long table, place the containers in a row.* | *The children were asked to stand in a row.* | **row upon row** (=many rows) *row upon row of shelves stacked with books* **2** a line of seats in a theatre or cinema: *We sat in the front row.* **3 three/four etc times in a row** happening a number of times in exactly the same way or with the same result: *She won four times in a row.* **4 go for a row** to take a short journey in a ROWING BOAT

**row[2]** /raʊ/ *n BrE* **1** [C] an angry argument that lasts a short time, especially between people who know each other well: *The news caused a terrible family row.* | **have a row (with sb)** *Those two are always having rows.* **2** [C] a situation in which people disagree strongly about important public matters; CONTROVERSY: **[+ about/over]** *The Prime Minister is at the centre of a new row over government secrecy.* **3** [singular] a loud unpleasant noise that continues for a long time: *Stop that row – I'm trying to get to sleep!*

**row[3]** /rəʊ‖roʊ/ *v* **1** [I,T] to make a boat move across water using OARS (=long poles that are flat at the end): **[+ away/towards/across]** *She rowed across the lake.* **2** [I] to be able to make a boat move in this way, or to do this as a sport: *Jenny used to row at college.*

**row[4]** /raʊ/ *v* [I + **about**] *BrE* to argue in an angry way

**row·an** /ˈrəʊən, ˈraʊən/ *n* [C] a small tree that has bright red berries

**row·boat** /ˈrəʊbəʊt‖ˈroʊboʊt/ *n* [C] *AmE* a small boat that you move through the water with OARS (=long poles that are flat at the end); ROWING BOAT *BrE*

**row·dy[1]** /ˈraʊdi/ *adj* behaving in a noisy, rough way that is likely to cause arguments and fighting: *a rowdy group of soccer fans* —**rowdily** *adv* —**rowdiness** *n* [U]

**rowdy[2]** *n* [C, usually plural] *old-fashioned* someone who behaves in a rough noisy way

**row house** /ˈrəʊ haʊs‖ˈroʊ-/ *n* [C] *AmE* a house that is part of a line of houses that are joined to each other; TERRACED HOUSE *BrE* —see picture on page 410

**row·ing** /ˈrəʊɪŋ‖ˈroʊ-/ *n* [U] the sport or activity of making a boat move through water with OARS

**rowing boat** /ˈrəʊɪŋ bəʊt‖ˈroʊɪŋ boʊt/ *n* [C] *BrE* a small boat that you move through the water with OARS (=long poles that are flat at the end) ; ROWBOAT *AmE*

**row·lock** /ˈrɒlək; *technical* ˈrəʊlɒk‖ˈrɑːlək; *technical* ˈroʊlɑːk/ *n* [C] *BrE* one of the U-shaped pieces of metal that holds the OARS of a rowing boat; **oarlock** *AmE*

**roy·al[1]** /ˈrɔɪəl/ *adj* [only before noun] **1** connected with or belonging to a king or queen: *the royal chapel at Versailles* —compare REGAL **2** very impressive, as if done for a king or queen: *a royal welcome* —see also **right royal** (RIGHT[1] (7)) **3** *informal* used to emphasize how bad something or someone is: *She's a royal pain in the neck!* **4 the royal 'we'** *BrE* the use of the word 'we' instead of 'I', by the Queen or King —**royally** *adv*

**royal[2]** *n* [C] *informal* a member of a royal family

**royal as·sent** /ˌ·· ˈ··/ *n* [U] the signing of a law by the British king or queen after it has been decided by Parliament, so that it officially becomes law

**royal blue** /ˌ·· ˈ·◂/ *n* [U] a strong, bright blue colour —**royal blue** *adj* —see picture on page 411

**royal com·mis·sion** /ˌ·· ·ˈ··/ *n* [C] a group of people who make suggestions about a subject that the British government thinks may need new laws

**royal flush** /ˌ·· ˈ·/ *n* [C usually singular] a set of cards that someone has in a card game, which are the five most important cards in a SUIT (=one of the four different types of card)

**Royal High·ness** /ˌ·· ˈ··/ *n* [C] **your/his/her Royal Highness** used when speaking about or to a royal person, especially a prince or princess

**roy·al·ist** /ˈrɔɪəlɪ̣st/ *n* [C] someone who supports a king or queen, or believes that a country should be ruled by kings or queens —**royalist** *adj*

**royal pre·rog·a·tive** /ˌ·· ·ˈ···/ *n* [singular, U] the special rights that a king or queen has

**roy·al·ty** /ˈrɔɪəlti/ *n* **1** [U] members of a royal family **2 royalties** [plural] payments made to the writer of a book or piece of music

**RP** /ˌɑː ˈpiː‖ˌɑːr-/ *n* [U] Received Pronunciation; the form of British pronunciation that many educated people in Britain use, and that is thought of as the standard form

**rpm** /ˌɑː piː ˈem‖ˌɑːr-/ revolutions per minute; a measurement of the speed at which an engine or RECORD PLAYER turns

**RR** /ˌɑːr ˈɑː‖-ɑːr/ rural route; used in addresses in country areas of the US, to show which mail delivery area a letter should go to

**RSI** /ˌɑːr es ˈaɪ/ *n* [U] repetitive strain injury; pain in your hands, arms etc caused by doing the same movements very many times, especially when typing (TYPE² (2))

**RSVP** /ˌɑːr es viː ˈpiː/ *French* used on invitations to ask someone to reply

**Rt Hon** the written abbreviation of RIGHT HONOURABLE

S3 **rub¹** /rʌb/ **rubbed, rubbing** *v* **1** [I,T] to move your hand, a cloth etc over a surface while pressing against it: *Kolchinsky nodded and then rubbed his eyes wearily.* | *She began rubbing her hair with a towel.* | *You'll have to rub harder if you want to get it clean.* —see picture on page 1259 **2** [T] to make something press against something else and move it around: **rub sth against/on** *Celia's cat purred loudly, rubbing against her legs.* | **rub sth together** *We tried to make a fire by rubbing two pieces of wood together.* **3** [I] to move around while pressing against another surface, often causing pain, damage etc: [+ **against/on**] *These shoes are too tight – they keep rubbing on my heels.* **4** [T always + adv/prep] to put a substance into or onto the surface of something by pressing it and moving it about with your hand, a cloth etc: **rub sth on/into/over/ etc** *Can you rub some sun cream on my back for me, please?* **5 rub it in** *informal* to remind someone about something they want to forget, especially because they are embarrassed about it: *Look, I know I should have been more careful, but there's no need to keep rubbing it in.* **6 rub shoulders with** *informal* to spend time with rich or famous people: *As a reporter he gets to rub shoulders with all the big names in politics and the media.* **7 rub salt into the wound** *informal* to make a bad situation even worse for someone **8 rub sb's nose in it/in the dirt** *informal* to keep reminding someone about something they did wrong or failed to do, especially in order to punish them **9 rub sb up the wrong way** *informal* to annoy someone by the way you behave towards them: *I don't know what it is about Paula, but she really rubs me up the wrong way.* **10 be rubbing your hands** *informal* to be pleased because something has happened which gives you an advantage, especially because something bad has happened to someone else **11 not have two pennies/halfpennies to rub together** *BrE humorous* to not have any money

**rub along** *phr v* [I + **with/together**] *BrE* to have a friendly relationship with someone

**rub down** *phr v* [T] **1** [**rub** sth ↔ **down**] to make a surface dry or smooth by rubbing it with a cloth or SANDPAPER **2** [**rub** sb **down**] **a)** to MASSAGE (=rub their muscles) someone, especially after hard exercise **b)** [**rub** sb/sth **down**] to dry a person or animal by rubbing them with a cloth, TOWEL etc —see also RUBDOWN

**rub off** *phr v* [**rub** (sth ↔) **off**] **1** [I,T] to remove something from a surface by rubbing it, or to come off a surface because of being rubbed: *Be careful not to rub off the paint.* **2** [I] if a feeling, quality, or habit rubs off on someone, they start to have it because they are with another person who has it: [+ **on**] *His enthusiasm shines through and seems to rub off on everyone else.*

**rub** sb/sth **out** *phr v* [T] **1** *BrE* to remove writing, a picture etc from a surface by rubbing it with a piece of rubber, a cloth etc; ERASE (2) *especially AmE*: *You might as well rub the whole thing out and start over.* **2** *AmE old-fashioned* to murder someone

**rub²** *n* **1 give sb/sth a rub** to rub something or MASSAGE² (1) someone for a short time: *Give the table a good rub with a damp cloth.* **2 there's/here's the rub** used when saying that a particular problem is the reason why a situation is so difficult

**rub·ber** /ˈrʌbə‖-ər/ *n*

**1 ▸ MATERIAL ◂** [U] a substance used to make tyres, gloves, boots etc, which is made from the juice of a tropical tree or artificially: *a rubber ball*

**2 ▸ FOR REMOVING MARKS ◂** *BrE* **a)** a thing you use for removing pencil marks; ERASER **b)** a thing you use for cleaning marks from a BLACKBOARD: ERASER

**3 ▸ SEX ◂** [C] *AmE informal* a CONDOM

**4 ▸ SHOE ◂** [C usually plural] *AmE old-fashioned* a rubber shoe that you wear over an ordinary shoe when it rains or snows; GALOSH *BrE*

**5 ▸ SERIES OF GAMES ◂** [C] a series of games of BRIDGE (=a card game) or CRICKET (2)

**6 ▸ FOR STANDING ON/IN ◂** [C] the piece of white rubber where the PITCHER (=person who throws the ball) stands in a BASEBALL game

**rubber band** /ˌ·· ˈ·/ *n* [C] a thin circular piece of rubber used for fastening things together; ELASTIC BAND *BrE*

**rubber boot** /ˈ·· ·/ *n* [C] a tall boot made of rubber that keeps your feet and the lower part of your legs dry; WELLINGTON *BrE* —see picture at BOOT¹

**rubber bul·let** /ˌ·· ˈ··/ *n* [C] a bullet made of rubber that is not intended to seriously hurt or kill people, but is used to control violent crowds

**rubber check** /ˌ·· ˈ·/ *n* [C] *AmE informal* a cheque that the bank refuses to accept because the person who wrote it does not have enough money

**rubber din·ghy** /ˌ·· ˈ··/ *n* [C] a small rubber boat that is filled with air

**rub·ber·neck** /ˈrʌbənek‖-ər-/ *v* [I] *informal especially AmE* to look around at something, especially something such as an accident while you are driving past: *tourists rubbernecking at the White House* —**rubbernecker** *n* [C]

**rubber plant** /ˈ·· ·/ *n* [C] a plant with large, shiny, dark green leaves that is often grown indoors

**rubber stamp** /ˌ·· ˈ·/ *n* [C] a small piece of rubber with a handle, used for printing dates or names on paper

**rubber-stamp** /ˌ·· ˈ·/ *v* [T] to give official approval to something without really thinking about it: *Democrats in Congress refused to rubber-stamp the Reagan program.*

**rub·ber·y** /ˈrʌbəri/ *adj* **1** looking or feeling like rubber: *The meat was rather rubbery.* **2** if your legs or knees are rubbery, they feel weak or unsteady

**rub·bing** /ˈrʌbɪŋ/ *n* [C] a copy of a shape or pattern made by rubbing WAX, CHALK etc onto a piece of paper laid over it: *a brass rubbing*

**rubbing al·co·hol** /ˈ·· ˌ···/ *n* [U] *AmE* a type of alcohol used for cleaning wounds or skin; SURGICAL SPIRIT *BrE*

**rub·bish¹** /ˈrʌbɪʃ/ *n* [U] *especially BrE* **1** food, paper etc that is no longer needed and has been thrown away; GARBAGE (1) *AmE*: *The dustmen collect the rubbish on Thursdays.* **2** *informal* objects, papers etc that you no longer use and should throw away: *I must clear some of* S3 *the rubbish from my desk.* **3** *informal* an idea, statement, etc that is rubbish is silly or wrong and does not deserve serious attention; nonsense: *Oh, don't talk such rubbish!* | **a load of (old) rubbish** *I reckon all this stuff about re-incarnation is a load of rubbish.* | **rubbish!** *spoken* (=used to tell someone that what they have just said is completely wrong) **4** *informal* a film, book etc that is rubbish is very bad: *the usual Hollywood rubbish*

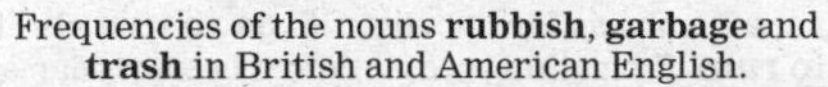
Frequencies of the nouns **rubbish**, **garbage** and **trash** in British and American English.

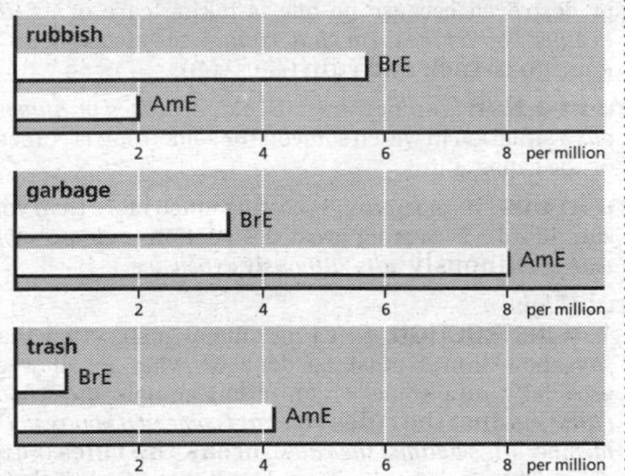


Based on the British National Corpus and the Longman Lancaster Corpus

In British English **rubbish** is commonly used to mean something that is no longer needed and has been thrown away, or something that is very bad in quality or does not deserve serious attention. In American English **garbage** and **trash** are commonly used for these meanings. **Trash** is only used in British English to mean something, especially a book, film etc that is of very bad quality.

**rubbish²** *v* [T] *BrE* to say something is bad or useless

**rubbish³** *adj BrE informal* not skilful at a particular activity: *They're a rubbish football team.*

**rub·bish·y** /ˈrʌbɪʃi/ *adj BrE informal* silly or of a very low quality; TRASHY: *rubbishy magazines*

**rub·ble** /ˈrʌbəl/ *n* [U] broken stones or bricks from a building or wall that has been destroyed

**rub·down** /ˈrʌbdaʊn/ *n* [C] **1** *especially AmE* if you give someone a rubdown, you rub their body to make them relaxed, especially after exercise; MASSAGE¹ **2** if you give a surface a rubdown, you rub it to make it smooth or clean —see also **rub down** (RUB¹)

**rube** /ruːb/ *n* [C] *AmE slang* someone, usually from the country, who has no experience of other places and thinks in a simple way

**Rube Gold·berg** /ˌruːb ˈgəʊldbɜːg‖-ˈgoʊldbɜːrg/ *adj AmE* a Rube Goldberg machine etc is very complicated and impractical, in an amusing way; HEATH ROBINSON *BrE*

**ru·bel·la** /ruːˈbelə/ *n* [U] *technical* an infectious disease that causes red spots on your body, and can damage an unborn child; GERMAN MEASLES

**Ru·bi·con** /ˈruːbɪkən, -kɒn‖-kɑːn/ *n* **cross the Rubicon** to do something that will have extremely important effects in the future and that you cannot change

**ru·bi·cund** /ˈruːbɪkənd/ *adj literary* someone who is rubicund is fat and has a red face

**ru·ble** /ˈruːbəl/ *n* [C] another spelling of ROUBLE

**ru·bric** /ˈruːbrɪk/ *n* [C] *formal* a set of instructions or an explanation in a book, examination paper etc

**ru·by** /ˈruːbi/ *n* **1** [C] a red jewel **2** [U] the colour of this jewel

**ruck¹** /rʌk/ *n* [C] **1 the ruck** ordinary events or people, which seem rather boring compared to the lives of rich or famous people: *She dreamed of getting out of the ruck and becoming a famous singer.* **2** a group of RUGBY players trying to get the ball when it is lying on the ground

**ruck²** *v*
**ruck** (sth) ↔ **up** *phr v* [I,T] if a piece of cloth rucks up, or if you ruck it up, it forms folds in an untidy way: *Your coat's all rucked up at the back.*

**ruck·sack** /ˈrʌksæk/ *n* [C] *especially BrE* a bag used for carrying things on your back, especially by people on long walks; BACKPACK¹

**ruck·us** /ˈrʌkəs/ *n* [singular] *informal especially AmE* a noisy argument or confused situation; RUMPUS: *drunken fraternity boys raising a ruckus at 3 in the morning*

**ruc·tions** /ˈrʌkʃənz/ *n* [plural] *informal especially BrE* complaints and comments because many people are annoyed about a situation

**rud·der** /ˈrʌdə‖-ər/ *n* [C] a flat part at the back of a ship or aircraft that can be turned in order to control the direction in which it moves —see picture at YACHT

**rud·der·less** /ˈrʌdələs‖-dər-/ *adj* without a leader who can make decisions: *a company left rudderless by the resignation of its CEO*

**rud·dy** /ˈrʌdi/ *adj* **1** a ruddy face looks pink and healthy: *ruddy cheeks* **2** a word used instead of BLOODY when saying strongly that you are annoyed with someone or something: *I wish that ruddy dog would stop barking!* **3** *literary* red: *The fire cast a ruddy glow over the room.* —**ruddiness** *n* [U] —**ruddy** *adv*

**rude** /ruːd/ *adj* **1** speaking or behaving in a way that is not polite and is likely to offend or annoy people: *Don't be so rude to your father!* | *a rude remark* | *I didn't mean to be rude, but I had to leave early.* | **it is rude to do sth** *It's rude to stare.* —see graph at IMPOLITE **2** rude jokes, words, songs etc are about sex **3 a rude awakening** a situation in which you suddenly realize something unpleasant **4 in rude health** *BrE* very healthy **5** *literary* made in a simple, basic way: *a rude wooden hut* —**rudely** *adv* —**rudeness** *n* [U]

**ru·di·men·ta·ry** /ˌruːdʒˈmentəri◂/ *adj* **1** a rudimentary knowledge or understanding of a subject is very simple and basic: *a rudimentary knowledge of Japanese* **2** rudimentary equipment, methods, systems etc are very basic and not advanced: *The classroom equipment is pretty rudimentary.* **3 a rudimentary tail/wing/eye** a part of an animal that has only developed into a very simple form

**ru·di·ments** /ˈruːdʒmənts/ *n* [plural] *formal* the most basic parts of a subject, which you learn first: [+ **of**] *the rudiments of tennis*

**rue** /ruː/ *v* [T] *literary* to wish that you had not done something; REGRET¹ (1): **rue the day (that)** *She learned to rue the day she had met Henri.*

**rue·ful** /ˈruːfəl/ *adj* feeling or showing that you wish you had not done something: *a rueful smile* —**ruefully** *adv*

**ruff** /rʌf/ *n* [C] **1** a stiff circular white collar, worn in Europe in the 16th century **2** a circle of feathers or fur around the neck of an animal or bird

**ruf·fi·an** /ˈrʌfiən/ *n* [C] *old-fashioned* a violent man, involved in crime: *a gang of ruffians* —**ruffianly** *adj*

**ruf·fle¹** /ˈrʌfəl/ *v* [T] **1** also **ruffle up** to make a smooth surface uneven: *Birds ruffle up their feathers for warmth.* **2** to offend or upset someone slightly: **ruffle sb's feelings/pride etc** *Louise's sharp comments had ruffled his pride.* | **get ruffled** *Some of the audience were shouting, and the speaker began to get ruffled.* | **ruffle sb's feathers** (=upset or annoy someone slightly)

**ruffle²** *n* [C] a band of thin cloth sewn in folds as a decoration around the edge of something such as a collar

**rug** /rʌg/ *n* [C] **1** a piece of thick cloth or wool that is smaller than a CARPET and is put on the floor as decoration —compare MAT¹ **2** *BrE* a large piece of material that you can wrap around yourself, especially when you are travelling **3 pull the rug (out) from under sb's feet** *informal* to suddenly take away something that someone was depending on to achieve what they wanted **4** *humorous especially AmE* a TOUPEE

S3 W3 **rug·by** /ˈrʌgbi/ also **rugby foot·ball** /ˌ·· ˈ··/ *n* [U] a type of football played with an OVAL (=egg-shaped) ball that you can catch and carry in your hands

**Rugby League** /ˌ·· ˈ·/ *n* [U] a type of rugby played by teams of players who are usually paid for playing

**Rugby U·nion** /ˌ·· ˈ··/ *n* [U] a type of rugby played by teams of 15 players

**rug·ged** /ˈrʌgʒd/ *adj* **1** land that is rugged is rough and uneven: *rugged terrain | a rugged coastline* **2** a rugged car or piece of equipment etc is strongly built and not likely to break easily; STURDY **3** a man who is rugged is good-looking and has strong features which are often not perfect: *Ann admired his rugged good looks.* **4** rugged behaviour is confident and determined but not always polite —**ruggedly** *adv* **ruggedness** *n* [U]

**rug·ger** /ˈrʌgə‖-ər/ *n* [U] *BrE informal* Rugby Union

S3 **ru·in¹** /ˈruːʒn/ *v* [T] **1** to spoil or destroy something completely: *The rain ruined our holiday. | My new white dress was totally ruined!* —see DESTROY (USAGE) **2** to make someone lose all their money: *Jefferson was ruined by the law suit.* —**ruined** *adj* [only before noun]: *ruined houses*

**ruin²** *n* **1** [U] a situation in which you have lost all your money, your social position, or the good opinion that people had about you: **lead to sb's ruin** *Joe's rashness led ultimately to his ruin.* | **be on the road to ruin** (=be doing something that will make you lose your money, position etc) | **be on the brink of ruin** (=be about to lose all your money or your position) *With the collapse of grain prices, small farmers are on the brink of financial ruin.* **2 be the ruin of** *humorous* to make someone lose all their money, their good health, the good opinion that other people have about them etc: *Drinking was the ruin of him.* **3** [C] also **ruins** [plural] the part of a building that is left after the rest has been destroyed: *an interesting old ruin | the ruins of a bombed-out office block* **4 the ruins of** the parts of something such as an organization, system, or set of ideas that remain after the rest have been destroyed: *the ruins of the Welfare State in post-Thatcher Britain* **5 be/lie in ruins a)** if a building is in ruins it has fallen down or been badly damaged: *The castle now lies in ruins.* **b)** if someone's life, hopes, plans, or an organization is in ruins, they are having great problems and cannot continue: *After the war the Japanese economy lay in ruins.* **6 go to ruin** also **fall into ruin** if something goes to ruin it becomes damaged or destroyed because no one is taking care of it: *His brother had let the farm go to ruin.* —see also MOTHER's RUIN, **go to rack and ruin** (RACK¹ (4))

**ru·in·a·tion** /ˌruːʒˈneɪʃən/ *n* [U] *old-fashioned or humorous* a situation in which someone or something is ruined, or the cause of this

**ru·in·ous** /ˈruːʒnəs/ *adj* **1** costing much more than you can afford **2** causing great destruction: *ruinous civil war* —**ruinously** *adv*: *ruinously expensive*

**rule¹** /ruːl/ *n* S2 W2

**1** ▶ **INSTRUCTION** ◀ [C] an official instruction that says how things must be done or what is allowed, especially in a game, organization, or job: *the school rules* | **against the rules** *You can't come in if you're not a member – it's against the rules.* | **break the rules** (=disobey) *There's a penalty if you break the rules.* | **stick to the rules** (=obey) *I'm not going to play if you won't stick to the rules!* | **bend/stretch the rules** (=say that on this occasion someone does not have to obey a particular rule) *We might be able to bend the rules just this one time.* | **the rules that govern sth** (=the rules that say how something should be done) *changes to the rules governing international athletics* | **rules and regulations** *I'm sick of all their petty rules and regulations.* | **hard and fast rule** (=clear and definite rule) *There are no hard and fast rules about what to wear to classes.* | **unwritten rule** (=something that people usually expect you to do) *an unwritten rule concerning being late for work* | **rules are rules** *spoken* (=used to tell someone that rules must be obeyed)

**2** ▶ **BEHAVIOUR** ◀ [C] the way of behaving that is accepted as right by most people: *the rules of etiquette*

**3** ▶ **OF GRAMMAR/OF A SYSTEM** ◀ [C] a statement about what is usually allowed in the grammar of a language, or according to a particular system: *English grammar has very few rules that cannot be broken.*

**4** ▶ **GOVERNMENT** ◀ [U] the government of a country by a particular group of people or using a particular system: *an end to over 200 years of French rule | rule by a social elite* | **under sb's rule** (=when someone is the leader of a country) *Britain prospered under Elizabeth's rule.* | **foreign rule** (=government by foreigners) | **majority rule** (=government by the political party that most people have voted for) *majority rule in South Africa* | **the rule of law** (=a situation in which the people in a country obey the laws) *The rule of law had broken down and the army was sent in to restore order.*

**5** ▶ **CONTROL** ◀ [U] a system for controlling a group of people: [+ **by**] *rule by the gun*

**6 as a (general) rule** used to say that something usually happens or is usually true: *As a rule most students finish their coursework by the end of May.*

**7 be the rule** used to say that something is the usual situation: *It tends to be the rule that boys are more interested in cars than girls.*

**8 sth is the exception, not the rule** used to say that something is unusual: *You do get some women in managerial positions, but it's the exception rather than the rule.*

**9 rule of thumb** a rough method of calculation, based on practical experience: *As a rule of thumb, you'll pay £10 a month for each £100 you borrow.*
**10 the rule is** *spoken* used when advising someone what to do in a particular situation: *The rule is: if you feel any pain you should stop exercising immediately.*
**11 make it a rule (to do sth)** to try to make sure that you always do something: *I generally make it a rule to be up by 7.*
**12 ▶ FOR MEASURING ◀** [C] *old-fashioned* RULER (2) —see also GOLDEN RULE, GROUND RULES, HOME RULE, SLIDE RULE, **work to rule** (WORK[1] (30))

**rule[2]** *v*
**1 ▶ GOVERNMENT ◀** [I,T] to have the official power to control a country and the people who live there: *Queen Victoria ruled England for 64 years.* | [**+ over**] *Alexander the Great ruled over a large empire.*
**2 ▶ CONTROL/INFLUENCE ◀** [T] if a feeling or desire rules someone it has a powerful and controlling influence on their actions: *the passion for power and success which rules her life*
**3 ▶ COURT/LAW ◀** [I always + adv/prep, T] to make an official decision about something, especially a legal problem: **rule that** *The judge ruled that she should have custody.* | [**+ on**] | *The Supreme Court has yet to rule on the case.* | **rule in favour of** *The tribunal ruled in her favour.* —see also RULING[1]
**4 let your heart rule your head** to make decisions based on what you feel not what you think
**5 rule the roost** *informal* to be the most powerful person in a group: *It's his wife who rules the roost in their house.*
**6 rule sb with a rod of iron** to control a group of people in a very severe way
**7 sb rules** an expression, often written on walls, used to say that the team, GANG etc mentioned is better than anyone else: *Arsenal rules OK.* | *Midland High rules!*
**8 ▶ DRAW A LINE ◀** [T] to draw a line using a ruler or other straight edge: *Rule a line under each answer.*
**9 be ruled by sb** *old-fashioned* to do what someone else tells you to do —see also OVERRULE

**rule** sth/sb ↔ **out** *phr v* [T] **1** to decide that something is not possible or suitable: *The police have ruled out suicide.* **2** to make it impossible for something to happen: *The mountainous terrain rules out most forms of agriculture.*

**rule·book** /ˈruːlbʊk/ *n* **1 go by the rulebook** *informal* to obey exactly the rules about how something should be done: *If we went by the rule book I'd have to report this conversation.* **2** [C] a book of rules, especially one that is given to workers in a job

**ruled** /ruːld/ *adj* ruled paper has parallel lines printed across it

**rul·er** /ˈruːlə‖-ər/ *n* [C] **1** someone such as a King or Queen who has official power over a country or area **2** a flat narrow piece of plastic, metal etc with straight edges, that you use for measuring things or drawing straight lines: *a 12-inch ruler*

**rul·ing[1]** /ˈruːlɪŋ/ *n* [C **+ on**] an official decision, especially one made by a court

**ruling[2]** *adj* [only before noun] **1** the ruling group in a country or organization is the group that controls it **2 sb's ruling passion** the thing that interests someone more than anything else: *the martial arts are Sandy's ruling passion*

**rum[1]** /rʌm/ *n* [C,U] a strong alcoholic drink made from sugar, or a glass of this drink

**rum[2]** *adj old-fashioned* unusual or strange

**rum·ba** /ˈrʌmbə/ *n* [C,U] a popular dance from Cuba, or the music for this dance

**rum·ble[1]** /ˈrʌmbəl/ *v* **1** [I] to make a series of long low sounds, especially a long distance away from you: *We could hear thunder rumbling in the distance.* **2** [I always + adv/prep] to move slowly while making this sound: [**+ along/past etc**] *A tank rumbled past.* **3** if your stomach rumbles, it makes a noise, especially because you are hungry **4** [T] *informal especially BrE* to find out what someone is secretly intending to do: *We've been rumbled; someone must have told the police.*

**rumble[2]** *n* [singular] a series of long low sounds: *the rumble of distant gunfire*

**rum·bling** /ˈrʌmblɪŋ/ *n* **1 rumblings** comments that show that people are starting to become annoyed, or that a difficult situation is developing: *rumblings of discontent* **2** [C usually singular] a rumbling noise

**ru·mi·nant** /ˈruːmɪnənt/ *n* [C] *technical* an animal such as a cow that has several stomachs and eats grass

**ru·mi·nate** /ˈruːmɪneɪt/ *v* [I] **1** *formal* to think for a long time about something: [**+ about/on etc**] *He sat ruminating on the answer he'd been given.* **2** *technical* if animals such as cows ruminate, they bring food back into their mouths from their stomachs and CHEW it again —**rumination** /ˌruːmɪˈneɪʃən/ *n* [C,U]

**rum·mage[1]** /ˈrʌmɪdʒ/ *v* [I always + adv/prep] also **rummage around** to search for something by moving things around in a careless way: [**+ in/through etc**] *Looks like someone's been rummaging around in my desk.*

**rummage[2]** *n* **1 have a rummage** *informal* to rummage **2** [U] *especially AmE* old clothes, toys etc that you no longer want; JUMBLE[1] (2) *BrE*

**rummage sale** /ˈ·· ·/ *n* [C] *AmE* an event at which old clothes, toys etc are sold as a way of getting money, for example to help a school or church; JUMBLE SALE *BrE*

**rum·my** /ˈrʌmi/ *n* [U] a simple card game

**ru·mour** *BrE*, **rumor** *AmE* /ˈruːmə‖-ər/ *n* [U] information that is passed from one person to another and which may or may not be true, especially about someone's personal life or about an official decision: [**+ about/of**] *I've heard all sorts of rumors about him and his secretary.* | [**+ that**] *There's a rumour going around that Eddie's bankrupt.* | **rumour has it (that)** (=there is a rumour that) *Rumour has it that Jean's getting married again.*

**ru·moured** *BrE*, **rumored** *AmE* /ˈruːməd‖-ərd/ *adj* if something is rumoured to be true, people are saying secretly or unofficially that it may be true: **it is rumoured that** *It was rumoured that Johnson had been poisoned.* | **be rumoured to be sth** *She was rumored to be a millionaire.* | **widely rumoured** *a young man widely rumoured to be her lover*

**ru·mour·mon·ger** *BrE*, **rumormonger** *AmE* /ˈruːməˌmʌŋgə‖-mərˌmɑːŋ, -ˌmʌŋgər-/ *n* [C] someone who tells other people rumours

**rump** /rʌmp/ *n* **1** [C] the part of an animal's back that is just above its legs **2 rump steak** meat that comes from this part of a cow **3** [C] *humorous* the part of your body that you sit on; BOTTOM[1] (7) **4** *BrE* [singular] the part of a group or government that remains after most of the other members have left

**rum·ple** /ˈrʌmpəl/ *v* [T] to make hair, clothes etc less tidy —**rumpled** *adj*: *rumpled sheets*

**rum·pus** /ˈrʌmpəs/ *n* [singular] *informal* a lot of noise, especially made by people quarrelling: *There's a real rumpus going on upstairs.*

**rumpus room** /ˈ·· ·/ *n* [C] *AmE* a room in a house that is used by the family for games, parties etc

**rump·y pump·y** /ˌrʌmpi ˈpʌmpi/ *n* [U] *BrE humorous* sexual activity

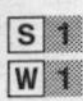

# run[1] /rʌn/ *v past tense* ran /ræn/ *past participle* run *present participle* running

① MOVE QUICKLY ON FOOT
② CONTROL/BE IN CHARGE OF
③ MACHINES/SYSTEMS
④ CARS/TRAINS/BOATS ETC
⑤ WATER/LIQUIDS
⑥ CONTINUE
⑦ HAPPEN/TAKE PLACE
⑧ TOUCH/RUB A SURFACE
⑨ THOUGHTS/FEELINGS
⑩ ROADS/FENCES ETC
⑪ COLOUR/PAINT
⑫ NOT ENOUGH/NONE LEFT
⑬ BECOME UNCONTROLLED
⑭ DO/ARRANGE STH
⑮ OTHER MEANINGS

## ① MOVE QUICKLY ON FOOT

**1** [I] to move quickly on foot by moving your legs more quickly than when you are walking: *I had to run to catch the bus.* | *Two youths were killed when running to help people injured in the bomb blast.* [+ adv/prep] *Each morning we ran down to the harbour to see the previous night's catch.* | **run for cover** (=run in order to find shelter or protection) *Suddenly shots rang out, and we had to run for cover.* | **run for your life** (=in order to avoid being killed) *Hundreds ran for their lives from the burning building.*

**2** ▶ **IN A RACE** ◀ **a)** [I,T] to take part in a running race: *I'd never run a marathon before.* | [+ **in**] *Are you running in the 100 metres?* **b)** [T] to hold a race: *The Derby will be run at 3 o'clock.*

**3 run for it** *spoken* to run as quickly as possible in order to escape: *Police – quick, run for it!*

**4 run and fetch/get/do sth** *spoken* used to ask a child to get or do something quickly for you: *Run and tell your father supper's ready.*

**5 run along** *spoken* used to tell a child to go away: *Run along now, all of you, I'm busy.*

## ② CONTROL/BE IN CHARGE OF

**6** [T] to control or be in charge of a company, an organization, or system: *For a while, she ran a restaurant in Boston.* | *Many people belong to a pension scheme run by their employers.* | **well/badly run** (=organized efficiently/inefficiently) *A well-run company should not have problems of this kind.* | **state-run** (=controlled and paid for by the state) *a state-run airline* —see CONTROL[1] (USAGE)

**7 run sb's life** *informal* to keep telling someone what they should do all the time, in a way that they find annoying: *Don't try to run my life!*

## ③ MACHINES/SYSTEMS

**8** ▶ **MACHINES** ◀ [I] if a machine runs, it operates: *Don't touch the engine while it's running.* | **run on electricity/gas/unleaded petrol etc** (=get its power from electricity etc) | **run smoothly** (=operate with all its parts working exactly as they should) *My car's not running too smoothly at the moment.*

**9** ▶ **COMPUTERS** ◀ [I,T] to operate a computer PROGRAM[1] (1): *The RS8 system runs both Unix and MPX-32.*

**10 up and running** working fully and correctly: *The new system won't be up and running until next week.*

## ④ CARS/TRAINS/BOATS ETC

**11** ▶ **PUBLIC TRANSPORT** ◀ **a)** if a bus, train etc service runs, it takes people from one place to another at fixed times of the day: *The buses don't run on Sundays.* **b)** [T] if someone runs a bus, train etc service, they make it operate: *They're running special trains to and from the exhibition.*

**12** ▶ **FAST/OUT OF CONTROL** ◀ [I always + adv/prep] to move too fast or in an uncontrolled way: [+ **into/down/through etc**] *The truck ran downhill at a frightening speed.* | *Her car ran into a tree.*

**13 run aground/ashore** if a ship runs aground, it cannot move because the water is not deep enough: *An oil tanker has run aground near the Valdez oil terminal.*

**14 run a car** to pay for all the things that are needed to keep a car working: *I can't really afford to run a car.*

**15 run sb home/to the station etc** *informal* to take someone somewhere in your car: *Shall I run you home?*

## ⑤ WATER/LIQUIDS

**16** [I always + adv/prep] to flow in a particular direction or place: [+ **down/along etc**] *Big tears ran down Stephanie's face.* | *A stream ran through the garden.*

**17** ▶ **TAP** ◀ [I] if a TAP (=thing for controlling the supply of water) is running, there is water coming out of it: *Did you leave the kitchen faucet running?*

**18 run a bath** to fill a bath with water: **run sb a bath** *Could you run me a nice hot bath while I finish my meal?*

**19** ▶ **SB'S NOSE** ◀ [I] if someone's nose is running, liquid is flowing out of it

## ⑥ CONTINUE

**20** ▶ **OFFICIAL PAPERS** ◀ [I] to continue to be officially able to be used for a particular period of time: *The contract runs for a year.* | *My car insurance only has another month to run.*

**21** ▶ **PLAY/FILM** ◀ [I] to continue being performed regularly in one place: *The play ran for two years.*

**22** ▶ **STORY/ACCOUNT ETC** ◀ [I] to continue in a particular way: *I forget now how the story runs.*

**23 run its course** to continue in the expected way until finished: *Wait until the illness has run its course.*

**24 this one will run and run** *BrE humorous* used to say that you think a problem, joke etc will continue for a long time

## ⑦ HAPPEN/TAKE PLACE

**25** [I] to happen or take place, especially in the way that was intended: **run according to plan** (=happen in the way that you had planned) *So far, it had all run exactly according to plan.* | **run smoothly** (=happen with no unexpected problems) *Her job is to ensure university catering runs smoothly.*

## ⑧ TOUCH/RUB A SURFACE

**26** [T always + adv/prep] to move or rub something lightly along a surface: **run sth down/through/along** *Charles ran his fingers through her hair.*

## ⑨ THOUGHTS/FEELINGS

**27** [I always + adv/prep] if thoughts or feelings run through you, you experience them suddenly: [+ **through/down etc**] *The same thought kept running through his mind.* | *I felt a sharp pain run down my leg.*

**28 be running high** if feelings are running high, people are becoming angry or upset about something: *Feelings at the game were running high.*

## ⑩ ROADS/FENCES ETC

**29** [I always + adv/prep] to exist in a particular place

or continue in a particular direction: [+ **along/through etc**] *The road runs along a valley.*

**⑪ COLOUR/PAINT**

**30** [I] if colour runs, it spreads from one area of cloth to another, when the cloth is wet: *The colour ran when I washed your red shirt, and now all your socks are pink!*
**31** [I] if paint runs, it moves onto an area where you did not intend it to go

**⑫ NOT ENOUGH/NONE LEFT**

**32 be running short (of sth)** to have very little of something left: *I'm running short of cash – do you think you could lend me some?*
**33 time is running short** used to say that there is little time left: *Time was already running short.*
**34 be running low (on sth)** to have very little left of something that you normally keep a supply of: *We're running low on fuel again.*
**35 run dry** if a river or WELL (=hole in the ground for getting water) runs dry, there is no water left in it: *The drought was so severe that even the well ran dry.*

**⑬ BECOME UNCONTROLLED**

**36 run wild** to behave in an uncontrolled way: *Since their mother left, those children have been running wild.*
**37 run rife** to spread quickly in an uncontrolled way: *Disease is running rife in the shanty towns.*
**38 run riot** **a)** if people run riot, they start to behave in a violent or uncontrolled way: *Angry demonstrators ran riot through the town.* **b)** if feelings run riot, they increase quickly in a way that you cannot control: *Let your imagination run riot.*

**⑭ DO/ARRANGE STH**

**39 run a check/test on** to arrange for something or someone to be checked or tested: *A check had to be run on all participants, for security reasons.* | *We'd better run a test on all the equipment before we begin.*
**40 run an errand** **a)** to go to a shop, office etc in order to buy, do, or get something for someone else: *a boy running errands for his mother* **b)** *AmE* to go to a shop, office etc to buy or get something that you need: *I have a few errands to run downtown.*

**⑮ OTHER MEANINGS**

**41 ▶ IN AN ELECTION ◀** [I] to try to be elected in an election; STAND[1] (41): [+ **for**] *Bob Dole's running for President.* | [+ **against**] *The Democrats chose Mondale to run against Reagan.*
**42 ▶ HOLE IN CLOTHES ◀** [I] if a hole in TIGHTS, STOCKINGS etc runs, it gets bigger in a straight line
**43 run drugs/guns** to bring drugs or guns into a country illegally in order to sell them —see also DRUG RUNNER, GUN-RUNNING
**44 run a story/feature/article** to print a story etc in a newspaper or magazine: *The editor decided at the last minute not to run the story.*
**45 run in the family** if something such as a quality, disease, or skill runs in the family, many people in that family have it: *Karen's very good at music too – it runs in the family.*
**46 run a temperature/fever** to have a body temperature that is higher than normal, because you are ill: *She's running a temperature of a 102°.*
**47 run a mile** *informal* to try very hard to avoid a situation, person, or place, because you find them frightening or embarrassing: *She's so shy that if a man ever spoke to her I think she'd run a mile!*
**48 be running late** to be doing everything later than planned or expected: *They were running late, so I didn't get interviewed until nearly 4 o'clock.*
**49 be running scared** to have become worried about the power of an enemy or opponent: *Their new software has the competition running scared.*
**50 come running** **a)** *informal* to respond in a very eager way when someone asks or tells you to do something: *He thinks he's only got to crook his finger and I'll come running.* **b)** *especially spoken* to ask someone for help, advice, or sympathy when you have a problem: [+ **to**] *Well I warned you, so don't come running to me when it all goes wrong!*
**51 run your eyes over** *informal* to look quickly at something: *Could you run your eyes over my report before I turn it in?*
**52 run that by me again** *spoken* used to ask someone to explain something again, because you did not completely understand —see also RUNNING, **run amok** (AMOK), **make your blood run cold** (BLOOD[1] (5)), **run counter to sth** (COUNTER[3]), **cut and run** (CUT[1] (30)), **run a risk** (RISK[1] (4)) **run deep** (DEEP[1] (5)), **run sb/sth to earth** (EARTH[1] (13)), **run to fat** (FAT[2] (6)), **run the gauntlet** (GAUNTLET (5)), **run sb to ground** (GROUND[1] (22)), **run rings around** (RING[1] (8)), **run to seed** (SEED[1] (3))

**run across** sb/sth *phr v* [T] to meet or find someone or something by chance: *I ran across an old friend last week.*

**run after** sb/sth *phr v* [T] **1** to chase someone or something: *Her dog was running after a rabbit.* **2** *informal* to try to get someone's attention, especially because you are sexually attracted to them **3** *spoken* to do many small jobs for someone, like a servant: *I can't keep running after you all day!*

**run around** *phr v* [I] **1** to run in an area, without a definite direction or purpose: *The children were running around in the garden.* **2 run around with sb** to spend a lot of time with someone, especially in a way that other people disapprove of: *Is it true that she's been running around with an older man?* **3** *informal* to be very busy doing many small jobs: *At fifty, I didn't want to be running around making bottles and changing diapers.* —see also RUN-AROUND

**run away** *phr v* [I] **1** to leave a place, especially secretly, in order to escape from someone or something: [+ **from**] *Toby ran away from home at the age of 14.* | *They ran away together to get married.* —see also RUNAWAY **2** to try to avoid a problem or difficult situation because it is unpleasant or embarrassing: *You've got to stop running away, and learn to face your problems.*

**run away with** sb/sth *phr v* [T] **1 run away with you** if your feelings, ideas etc run away with you, they start to control how you behave because you can no longer think in a sensible way: *Don't let your imagination run away with you!* **2** to leave a place secretly or illegally with someone else: *He ran away with the boss's wife.* **3 run away with the idea/impression that** *spoken* to think that something is true when it is not: *Don't run away with the idea that this is going to be easy!* **4** *informal* to win a competition or sports game very easily: *The Reds ran away with the championship.* **5** to steal something: *They found that the treasurer had run away with the proceeds.*

**run down** *phr v* **1** [T **run** sb/sth ↔ **down**] to drive into a person or animal and kill or injure them: *Their daughter was run down by a car just outside their house.* **2** [T **run** sb/sth ↔ **down**] *informal* to say things that are rude, unpleasant, or unfair about someone or something: *Paula's jealous of you – that's why she keeps running you down.* | *Don't run yourself down!* **3** [I] if a clock, machine, BATTERY etc runs down, it has no more power and stops working **4** [T **run** sth ↔ **down**] to let a company, organization etc gradually become smaller or stop working: *The coal industry is being slowly run down.* **5** [T **run** sb/sth ↔ **down**] to find someone or something after searching for a long time: *I finally ran him down at his new office in Glendale.* —see also RUNDOWN, RUN-DOWN

**run** sb/sth ↔ **in** *phr v* [T] **1** *old-fashioned* if the police run a criminal in, they catch them; ARREST[1] (1) **2** if you run in a new car, you drive it slowly and carefully at first

**run into** sb/sth *phr v* [T] **1** to hit someone or something with a car or other vehicle: *His car skidded and ran into a lamp-post.* **2** *informal* to meet someone by chance: *Guess who I ran into in town today!*

[continued on next page]

[continued from previous page]
**3 run into difficulties/problems/debt etc** to start to experience difficulties: *After a promising start, the company ran into trouble.* **4 run into hundreds/thousands etc** to reach an amount of several hundred, several thousand etc: *By now they had debts running into thousands of pounds.* **5** if something such as a word, colour etc runs into another word, colour etc, it joins it or mixes with it so that it is difficult to separate them **6 run sth into the ground a)** to use something so much that you destroy it: *We ran that Chevrolet right into the ground.* **b)** to talk about a subject so much that there is nothing more left to say

**run off** *phr v* **1** [I] to leave a place or person in a way that people disapprove of: *Amy's husband had run off and left her with two children to bring up.* **2** [T **run** sth ↔ **off**] to quickly print several copies of something: *Shall I run off some more of those notices for you on the photocopier?* **3** [T **run** sth ↔ **off**] to write a speech, poem, piece of music etc quickly and easily: *He could run off a comedy monologue in half an hour.* **4 be run off your feet** to be so busy that you do not have time to stop or rest **5 run off at the mouth** *AmE informal* to talk too much **6** [T **run** sth ↔ **off**] to get rid of weight by running: *I'm trying to run off some of my excess fat!*

**run off with** sth/sb *phr v* [T] *informal* **1** to go away somewhere with someone, because you are having a sexual relationship that people do not approve of: *Liz shocked us all by running off with a married man.* **2** to take something without permission: *Then I found that he had run off with all my savings.*

**run on** *phr v* [I] to continue happening for longer than expected or planned: *The lecture ran on until 11 o'clock.*

**run out** *phr v* **1** [I] to use all of something and not have any of it left: [+ **of**] *The truck's run out of gas again.* **2** [I] if food, money etc runs out, there is none left: *Our supplies soon ran out.* | *My patience was running out.* **3** [I] if an agreement, official document etc runs out, it reaches the end of the period when it is officially allowed to continue; EXPIRE (1): *My contract runs out in September.*

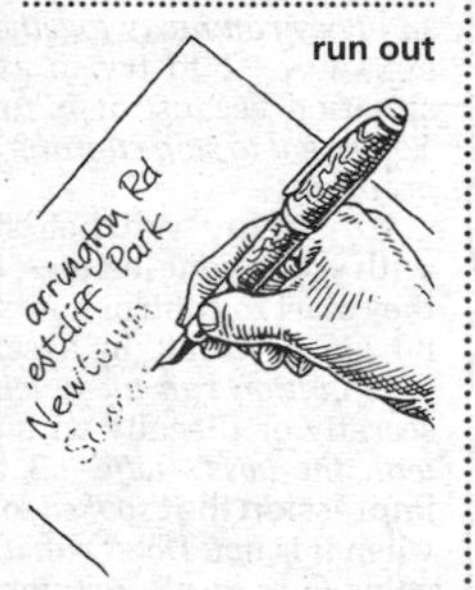


**4 run out on** to leave someone, when you should not: *He ran out on his second wife two years later.* **5 run out of steam** *informal* also **run out of gas** *AmE* to have no energy or eagerness left for something that you are trying to do: *The whole team seemed to have run out of gas.* **6 run sb out of town** *old-fashioned* to force someone to leave a place, because they have done something wrong **7** [T **run** sb ↔ **out**] to end a player's INNINGS in CRICKET (2) by hitting the stumps (STUMP[1] (4)) with the ball while they are running

**run over** *phr v* **1** [T **run** sb/sth ↔ **over**] to hit someone or something with a car or other vehicle, and drive over them: *He was run over by a bus and killed.* **2** [T **run over** sth] to explain or practise something again: *Could we just run over the section on verbs again?* **3** [T **run over** sth] to think about a series of events, possibilities etc: *I ran over the options in my mind.* **4** [I] also **run over time** to continue past the arranged time: *The meeting ran over, and I was late for lunch.* **5** [I] if a container runs over, there is so much liquid inside that some flows out; OVERFLOW

**run through** *phr v* [T] **1** [**run through** sth] to repeat something so that you remember it or get better at it: *Let's run through the first scene again.* **2** [**run through** sth] to read, look at, or explain something quickly: *I'll just run through the figures with you.* **3** [**run through** sth] to be present in many parts of something or continue through it, for example in an artist's work or in a society: *This theme runs through the whole book.* | *a fundamental problem running right through our society* **4** [**run** sb **through**] *literary* to push a sword completely through someone —see also RUN-THROUGH

**run to** sth *phr v* [T] **1** to reach a particular amount: *The damages awarded by the court could easily run to one billion pounds.* **2** *BrE* to be enough money to pay for something, or have enough money for it: *My wages won't run to a new car.*

**run** sth ↔ **up** *phr v* [T] **1 run up a bill/expenses/debts** to use a lot of something or borrow a lot of money, so that you will have to pay a lot of money: *She ran up an enormous phone bill.* **2** to make something, especially clothes, very quickly: *I ran this dress up in a single evening.* **3** to raise a flag on a pole

**run up against** sth/sb *phr v* [T] to have to deal with unexpected problems or a difficult opponent: *We ran up against some unexpected opposition.*

S2 W2 **run**[2] *n*

**1 ▶ON FOOT◀** [C] a period of time spent running, or a distance that you run: *a 5-mile run* | **go for a run** (=for exercise or pleasure) *She usually goes for a run before breakfast.* | **break into a run** (=start running) *He was still following me, and in a panic I broke into a run.* | **at a run** (=running) *Sarah left the house at a run.*

**2 be on the run a)** to be trying to escape or hide, especially from the police: *A dangerous criminal is on the run in the bay area of the city.* **b)** if an army or an opponent is on the run, they may soon be defeated

**3 make a run for it** to suddenly start running, in order to escape: *One of the prisoners made a run for it.*

**4 in the long run** later in the future, not immediately: *The less you rely on painkillers now, the better it will be for your health in the long run.*

**5 in the short run** in the near future: *Economies like these save money in the short run, but in the end you'll be no better off.*

**6 a run of good/bad luck** several lucky or unlucky things happening quickly after each other: *Losing my job was the start of a run of bad luck that year.*

**7 a run of failures/wins/strikes etc** a series of failures, wins etc: *The company has had a run of spectacularly successful years.*

**8 a run on** a situation in which lots of people suddenly buy a particular product: *There's been a big run on ice-cream during this hot weather.*

**9 have the run of** to be allowed to use a place when and how you want: *I had the run of the house for the afternoon.*

**10 in the normal run of events** used when saying what usually happens: *In the normal run of events, I would never have gone there.*

**11 have a (good) run for your money** *informal* if you have a good run for your money, you have succeeded in doing something for an unusually long time or you have been unusually successful: *He lived to be 92, so I think he had a good run for his money.*

**12 give sb a good run for their money** to play well in a competition or sports game, so that your opponent has to use all their skill and effort to defeat you: *They beat us, but we certainly gave them a good run for their money.*

**13 ▶ILLNESS◀ the runs** *informal* DIARRHOEA (=an illness that makes you need to go to the toilet often)

**14 ▶PLAY/FILM◀** [C] a continuous series of performances of a play, film etc in the same place: *His first play had a three-month run in the West End.*

**15 ▶JOURNEY◀** [singular] **a)** a journey by train, ship, TRUCK etc, made regularly between two places: *It's*

*only a 55-minute run from London to Brighton.* **b)** *informal* a short journey in a car, for pleasure: *Let's take the car out for a run.*
**16** ▶ **FOR ANIMALS** ◀ [C] an enclosed area where animals such as chickens or rabbits are kept
**17** ▶ **SPORT** ◀ [C] a point won in CRICKET or BASEBALL
**18** ▶ **SKI-ING** ◀ [C] a sloping area of land that you can SKI down: *They don't let beginners go on the higher runs.*
**19** ▶ **IN CLOTHES** ◀ *AmE* [C] a line of torn stitches in TIGHTS, STOCKINGS etc; LADDER[1] (3) *BrE*
**20** ▶ **BANK** ◀ [singular] an occasion when lots of people all take their money out of a bank at the same time
**21 run on the dollar/pound etc** a situation in which a lot of people sell dollars etc and the value goes down
**22** ▶ **MUSIC** ◀ [C] a set of notes played or sung quickly up or down a SCALE in a piece of music
**23** [C] ▶ **CARD GAMES** ◀ a set of cards with numbers in a series, held by one player —see also DRY RUN, DUMMY RUN, FUN RUN, MILK RUN, TRIAL RUN

**run·a·bout** /ˈrʌnəbaʊt/ *n* [C] *informal* a small car used for short journeys

**run-a·round** /ˈ· ·ˌ·/ *n* **give sb the run-around** *informal* to deliberately avoid giving someone a definite answer, especially when they are asking you to do something: *Every time we ask the landlord about fixing the roof, he gives us the run-around.* —see also **run around** (RUN[1])

**run·a·way**[1] /ˈrʌnəweɪ/ *adj* [only before noun] **1** a runaway vehicle or animal has gone out of control **2 runaway success/inflation etc** success, INFLATION etc that happens quickly or uncontrollably: *The film was a runaway success.* **3** a runaway person has left the place where they are supposed to be: *a runaway child*

**runaway**[2] *n* [C] someone, especially a child, who has left home without telling anyone and does not intend to come back —see also **run away** (RUN[1])

**run·down** /ˈrʌndaʊn/ *n* [C usually singular] **1** a quick report or explanation of an idea, situation etc: **give sb a rundown on** *Someone give Charlie a quick rundown on what we've done so far.* **2** [singular] the process of making a business or industry smaller and less important

**run-down** /ˌ· ˈ·◂/ *adj* **1** a building or area that is run-down is in very bad condition: *a run-down inner-city area* **2** [not before noun] someone who is run-down is tired and not healthy: *You look a bit run-down – maybe you need a rest.*

**rune** /ruːn/ *n* [C] *technical* **1** one of the letters of the alphabet used in the past by people in Northern Europe **2** a magic song or written sign —**runic** *adj*

**rung**[1] /rʌŋ/ the past tense of RING[2]

**rung**[2] *n* [C] **1** one of the bars that form the steps of a ladder **2** *informal* a particular level or position in an organization or system: *on the highest rung of the salary scale* **3** a bar between two legs of a chair

**run-in** /ˈ· ·/ *n* [C] an argument or disagreement, especially with someone in an official position: **have a run-in with** *Michael got drunk and had a run-in with the police.*

**run·ner** /ˈrʌnə‖-ər/ *n* [C] **1** someone who runs as a sport: *a long-distance runner* **2** someone who walks or runs from place to place carrying messages, especially in former times **3 do a runner** *BrE* to leave somewhere quickly in order to avoid paying for something or having to meet someone: *By the time the police got there, the boys had done a runner.* **4** one of the two thin pieces of metal that a SLEDGE has, or the single piece of metal under a SKATE[1] (1) **5** the bar of wood or metal that a drawer or curtain slides along **6** *technical* a stem with which a plant such as a STRAWBERRY spreads itself along the ground **7** a long narrow piece of cloth or CARPET —see also DRUG RUNNER, FRONT-RUNNER

**runner-bean** /ˌ·· ˈ·/ *n* [C] *BrE* a vegetable that grows as a long green POD (=seed container) on a climbing plant —see picture on page 414

**runner-up** /ˌ·· ˈ·/ *n plural* **runners-up** [C] the person or team that comes second in a race or competition

**run·ning**[1] /ˈrʌnɪŋ/ *n* [U] **1** the act or sport of running: **running shoes/track etc** *New facilities including a pool and a running track.* **2 the running of** the way in which a business, home, organization etc is managed or organized: *Brian took over the running of the company while his father was away.* **3 be in the running/out of the running** to have some hope or no hope of winning a race or competition: *Bruno is still in the running for the world title.* **4 make (all) the running** *BrE informal* **a)** to be the person who makes most of the suggestions in a relationship, plan, activity etc **b)** to be in a competition, race, election etc

**running**[2] *adj* [only before noun] **1 running water** **a)** water that comes from a TAP[1] (1): *Disease spreads fast in villages where there is no running water.* **b)** water that is flowing or moving: *Many fish prefer running water.* **2 running repairs** small repairs that you do to a machine to keep it working **3 running total** a total that is continually increased as new costs, amounts etc are added: *Keep a running total of your expenses as you go along.* **4 running commentary** a spoken description of an event, especially a race or game, made while the event is happening: *a running commentary on the basketball game* **5 running battle/argument** an argument that continues or is repeated over a long period of time **6 running sore** a sore area on your skin, that has liquid coming out of it **7 in running order** a machine that is in running order is working correctly **8 the running order** the order in which the different parts of an event have been arranged to take place: *changes in the running order for the teachers' conference*

**running**[3] *adv* **three years/five times etc running** for three years etc without a change or interruption: *Sylvie has won the poetry prize for the fourth year running.*

**running costs** /ˈ·· ·/ *n* [plural] the amount of money that is needed to operate an organization, system etc

**running jump** /ˌ·· ˈ·/ *n* [C] **1** a jump made by running up to the point at which you leave the ground **2 take a running jump** *spoken* used to tell someone to go away and stop annoying you: *If he hassles you again tell him to take a running jump!*

**running mate** /ˈ·· ·/ *n* [C usually singular] the person who someone who is trying to become president, leader etc chooses to help them in an election: *Al Gore was Bill Clinton's running mate in the 1992 election.*

**run·ny** /ˈrʌni/ *adj informal* **1** something, especially a food, that is runny is not solid or thick enough: **go runny** (=become runny) *The butter had gone runny in the heat.* **2** a runny nose, runny eyes etc have liquid coming out of them, usually because you have a cold

**run-off** /ˈ· ·/ *n* **1** [C] a second competition or election that is arranged to decide the winner when two competitors get an equal number of points or votes the first time —compare PLAY-OFF —see also **run off** (RUN[1]) **2** [U] *technical* rain or other liquid that flows off the land into rivers: *nitrogen-rich run-off from agricultural land*

**run-of-the-mill** /ˌ· · · ˈ·◂/ *adj* not special or interesting in any way; ordinary: *a run-of-the-mill performance*

**run-on sen·tence** /ˈ· · ˌ··/ *n* [C] *especially AmE* a sentence that has two main CLAUSES without connecting words or correct PUNCTUATION

**runt** /rʌnt/ *n* [C] **1** the smallest and least developed baby animal of a group born at the same time: *the runt of the litter* **2** *informal* a small, unpleasant or unimportant person

**run-through** /ˈ· ·/ *n* [C] a short practice before a performance, test etc: *a final run-through of the play*

**run-up** /ˈ· ·/ *n* **1 the run-up to** the period of time just before an important event: *the run-up to the 1992 election* **2** [C] the act of running, or the distance that you run, before you kick a ball, jump over a pole etc

**run·way** /ˈrʌnweɪ/ *n* [C] **1** a long specially prepared hard surface like a road on which aircraft land and take off **2** *AmE* a long narrow part of a stage that stretches out into the area where the AUDIENCE sits

**ru·pee** /ruːˈpiː/ *n* [C] the standard unit of money in India, Pakistan, and some other countries

**rup·ture¹** /ˈrʌptʃə‖-ər/ *n* **1** [C,U] an occasion when something suddenly breaks apart or bursts: *the rupture of a blood vessel* **2** [C] a situation in which two countries or groups of people suddenly disagree and often end their relationship with each other: *the rupture between the two religious communities* **3** [C,U] a medical condition in which an organ of the body sticks out through the wall of muscle that normally surrounds it; HERNIA

**rupture²** *v* **1** [I,T] to break or burst, or make something break or burst: *A pipeline carrying crude oil has ruptured.* **2 rupture yourself** to cause a RUPTURE¹ (3) in your body

W2 **ru·ral** /ˈrʊərəl‖ˈrʊr-/ *adj* **1** happening in or connected with the countryside, not the city: *a peaceful rural setting | rural bus routes* **2** like the countryside or reminding you of the countryside: *It's very rural round here isn't it?* —opposite URBAN

**rural de·liv·er·y** /ˌ·· ·ˈ···/ *n* RD

**rural route** /ˈ·· ·/ *n* RR

**ruse** /ruːz‖ruːs, ruːz/ *n* [C] a clever trick used to deceive someone: *It dawned on me that this was only a ruse, done to gain time.*

S2 W3 **rush¹** /rʌʃ/ *v*

**1 ▶ MOVE QUICKLY ◀** [I always + adv/prep] to move very quickly, especially because you need to be somewhere very soon: **[+ out/past/through/along etc]** *We rushed home to find out what had happened to Julie. | One of the pipes burst and water came rushing out.*

**2 ▶ DO STH QUICKLY ◀** [I,T] to do something too quickly, especially so that you do not have time to do it carefully or well: *There's plenty of time – we don't need to rush.* | **rush sth** *You shouldn't rush this sort of work.*

**3 rush to do sth** to do something eagerly and without delay: *Fans rushed to buy tickets as soon as they went on sale.*

**4 ▶ TAKE/SEND URGENTLY ◀** [T always + adv/prep] to take or send something somewhere very quickly, especially because of an unexpected problem: *The Red Cross rushed medical supplies to the war zone.* | **rush sb somewhere** *Dan was rushed to the hospital with serious head injuries.*

**5 ▶ MAKE SB HURRY ◀** [T] to try to make someone do something more quickly than they want to: *I'm sorry to rush you, but we need a decision by Friday.* | **rush sb into doing sth** *Don't let them rush you into signing the contract.*

**6 ▶ ATTACK ◀** [T] to attack someone suddenly and in a group: *They rushed the guard and stole his keys.*

**7 ▶ AMERICAN UNIVERSITIES ◀** *AmE* **a)** [T] to give parties for students, have meetings etc, in order to decide whether to let them join a FRATERNITY or SORORITY (=type of club) **b)** [I,T] to go through the process of trying to be accepted into these clubs

**8 ▶ AMERICAN FOOTBALL ◀** [I,T] to carry the ball forward —see also RUSHED

**rush about/around** *phr v* [I] to try to do a lot of things in a short period of time: *I was rushing around all morning trying to get everything ready for the trip.*

**rush into** sth *phr v* [T] to get involved in something without taking enough time to think carefully about it: **rush into things** *spoken*: *He's asked me to marry him, but I don't want to rush into things.*

**rush** sth ↔ **out** *phr v* [T] to make a new product, book etc available for sale very quickly

**rush** sth ↔ **through** *phr v* [T] to deal with official or government business, more quickly than usual: *The legislation was rushed through parliament.*

**rush²** *n*

**1 ▶ FAST MOVEMENT ◀** [singular] a sudden fast movement of things or people: *Someone shouted 'fire!', and there was a rush towards the door.* | **in a rush** *her words came out in a rush | a sudden rush of wind*

**2 ▶ HURRY ◀** [singular, U] a situation in which you need to hurry: *There's always such a rush to get things done.* | **there's no rush** *spoken* (=there is no need to hurry) *There's no rush. We don't have to leave till 10.30.* | **do sth in a rush** (=do something quickly, especially so that it is not done well) *It all seems to have been decided in such a rush.* | **be in a rush** *I'm sorry, I can't talk now – I'm in kind of a rush.*

**3 ▶ BUSY PERIOD ◀ the rush** the time in the day, month, year etc when a place or group of people are particularly busy: *The café is quiet until the lunchtime rush begins. | the Christmas rush* —see also RUSH HOUR

**4 ▶ PEOPLE WANTING STH ◀** [singular] a situation in which a lot of people suddenly try to do or get something: **[+ on]** *a rush on swimsuits in the hot weather* | **rush to do sth** *There was a big rush to get tickets for the football game.* —see also GOLD RUSH

**5 ▶ PLANT ◀** [C] a type of tall grass that grows in water, often used for making baskets, mats etc

**6 ▶ FEELING ◀ a)** [C] *informal* a strong, usually pleasant feeling that you get from taking a drug or from doing something exciting: *Playing in front of a packed house was a real rush.* **b) rush of excitement/panic etc** a sudden very strong feeling of excitement etc: *I felt a rush of excitement as she walked through the door.*

**7 ▶ FILM ◀ rushes** [plural] the first prints of a film before it has been edited (EDIT (1)); DAILY³ (3) *AmE*

**8 ▶ AMERICAN STUDENTS ◀** [singular] *AmE* the time when students in American universities who want to join a FRATERNITY or SORORITY (=type of club) go to a lot of parties: *rush week | a rush party*

**rushed** /rʌʃt/ *adj* **1** done very quickly or too quickly, because there was not enough time: *a rather rushed meeting* **2 be rushed off your feet** *especially BrE* to be so busy that you do not have time to stop or rest

**rush hour** /ˈ· ·/ *n* [C,U] the time of day when the roads, buses, trains etc are most crowded, because people are travelling to or from work: *heavy rush hour traffic*

**rusk** /rʌsk/ *n* [C] *especially BrE* a hard sweet dry bread for babies to eat

**rus·set** /ˈrʌsɪ̣t/ *n* [U] *especially literary* a reddish-brown colour —**russet** *adj* —see picture on page 411

**Rus·sian¹** /ˈrʌʃən/ *n* **1** [U] the language of Russia **2** [C] someone from Russia

**Russian²** *adj* from or connected with Russia

**Russian rou·lette** /ˌ·· ··ˈ·/ *n* [U] a game in which you risk killing yourself by shooting at your head with a gun that has a bullet in only one of six CHAMBERS

**rust¹** /rʌst/ *n* [U] **1** the reddish-brown substance that forms on iron and steel when they get wet: *There were large patches of rust on the car.* **2** a plant disease that causes reddish-brown spots —see also RUSTPROOF, RUSTY

**rust²** *v* [I,T] to become covered with rust or make something become covered in rust: *a rusted old basketball hoop*

**rust away** *phr v* [I] to be gradually destroyed by rust

**rus·tic¹** /ˈrʌstɪk/ *adj* **1** simple, old-fashioned, and not spoiled by modern developments, in a way that is typical of the countryside: *The village had a certain rustic charm.* **2** [only before noun] roughly made from wood: *a rustic chair* —**rusticity** *n* [U]

**rustic²** *n* [C] *literary or humorous* someone from the country, especially a farm worker

**rus·tle¹** /ˈrʌsəl/ *v* **1** [I,T] if leaves, papers, clothes etc rustle, or if you rustle them, they make a noise as they rub against each other: *Stop rustling that newspaper!* **2** [T] to steal farm animals such as cattle, horses, or sheep

**rustle** sth ↔ **up** *phr v* [T] *informal* to find or make something quickly, especially food or a meal: *I'll rustle up a couple of steaks on the barbecue.*

**rustle²** *n* [singular] the noise made when something rustles: *a rustle of leaves* —see picture on page 1261

**rus·tler** /ˈrʌslə‖-ər/ *n* [C] someone who steals farm animals such as cattle, horses, or sheep

**rust·proof** /ˈrʌstpruːf/ *adj* metal that is rustproof will not RUST

**rust·y** /ˈrʌsti/ *adj* **1** metal that is rusty is covered in RUST[1] (1): *a rusty nail* —see picture on page 1258 **2** if someone's skill in a particular activity or subject is rusty, it is not as good as it used to be, because they have not practised it for a long time: *My French is very rusty these days.* —**rustiness** *n* [U]

**rut** /rʌt/ *n* **1** [C] a deep narrow track left in soft ground by a wheel **2 in a rut** living or working in a situation that never changes, so that you feel bored: **be stuck in a rut** *I was stuck in a rut, and decided to look for a new job.* **3 the rut** *technical* the period of the year when some male animals, especially DEER, are sexually active

**ru·ta·ba·ga** /ˌruːtəˈbeɪgə/ *n* [C] *AmE* a large round yellow vegetable; SWEDE *BrE* —see picture on page 414

**ruth·less** /ˈruːθləs/ *adj* **1** so determined to get what you want that you do not care if you have to hurt other people in order to do it: *a ruthless dictator | a ruthless disregard for basic human rights* **2** determined and firm when taking unpleasant decisions: *We'll have to be ruthless if we want to eliminate this kind of time-wasting.* —**ruthlessly** *adv* —**ruthlessness** *n* [U]

**rut·ted** /ˈrʌtɨd/ *adj* a surface that is rutted has deep narrow tracks in it left by the wheels of vehicles: *a rutted dirt road*

**RV** /ˌɑː ˈviː‖ˌɑːr-/ *n* [C] *AmE* recreational vehicle; a large vehicle, usually with cooking equipment and beds in it, that a family can use for travelling or camping

**Rx.** *AmE* the written abbreviation of PRESCRIPTION (1)

**rye** /raɪ/ *n* [U] **1** a type of grain that is used for making bread and WHISKY: *rye bread* **2** also **rye whis·key** /ˌ· ˈ··/ *AmE* a type of American WHISKY made from rye: *rye and Coke*

**rye·grass** /ˈraɪgrɑːs‖-græs/ *n* [U] a type of grass that is grown as food for animals

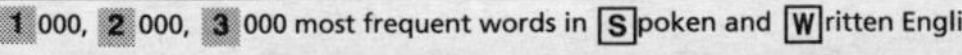

**S, s** /es/ *plural* **S's, s's** *n* [C] **1** the 19th letter of the English alphabet **2** the written abbreviation of south or southern

**-s** /z, s/ *suffix* **1** forms the plural of nouns: *a cat and two dogs* **2** forms the third person singular of the present tense of most verbs: *he plays | she sits* **3** *especially AmE* forms adverbs meaning during a particular time: *Do you work Sundays?* (=regularly each Sunday) | *Summers we go to the seaside.*

**-s'** /z, s/ *suffix* forms the possessive case of plural nouns: *the girls' dresses* (=the dresses belong to the girls)

**-'s¹** /z, s/ **1** the short form of 'is': *John's here.* | *What's that?* | *She's writing a letter.* **2** the short form of 'has': *Polly's gone out.* | *A spider's got eight legs.* **3** a short form of 'does' used in questions after who, what etc and that many people think is incorrect: *How's he plan to do it?* —compare -'D **4** a short form of 'us' used only in 'let's'

**-'s²** *suffix* **1** forms the possessive case of singular nouns, and of plural nouns that do not end in -s: *my sister's husband* | *Mary's generosity* | *yesterday's lesson* | *the children's bedroom* | *the man in the corner's coat* (=the coat belonging to the man in the corner) **2** *BrE* the shop or home of someone: *I bought it at the baker's* (=at the baker's shop) | *I met him at Mary's* (=at Mary's house)

**S & L** /ˌes ənd ˈel/ *n* [C] *informal* SAVINGS AND LOAN ASSOCIATION

**sab·ba·tar·i·an** /ˌsæbəˈteəriən◂‖-ˈter-/ *n* [C] someone who strongly believes that the Sabbath should be a holy day on which people do not work —**sabbatarian** *adj*

**Sab·bath** /ˈsæbəθ/ *n* **1 the Sabbath a)** Sunday, considered as a day of rest and prayer by most Christian churches **b)** Saturday, considered as a day of rest and prayer in the Jewish religion **2 keep/break the Sabbath** to obey or not obey the religious rules of this day

**sab·bat·i·cal** /səˈbætɪkəl/ *n* [C,U] a period when someone, especially someone in a university job, stops doing their usual work in order to study or travel: **be on sabbatical** *Dr Watson's not here at the moment, she's on sabbatical.* —**sabbatical** *adj*: *a sabbatical year*

**sa·ber** /ˈseɪbə‖-ər/ *n* [C] the usual American spelling of SABRE

**sa·ble¹** /ˈseɪbəl/ *n* [C,U] an expensive fur used to make coats etc, or the small animal that this fur comes from

**sable²** *adj poetic* black or very dark

**sab·o·tage¹** /ˈsæbətɑːʒ/ *v* [T] **1** to secretly damage or destroy equipment, vehicles etc that belong to an enemy or opponent, so that they cannot be used: *Every single fighter plane had been sabotaged.* **2** to deliberately spoil someone's plans because you do not want them to succeed: *Her father sabotaged her acting ambitions by refusing to pay for her to go to drama school.*

**sabotage²** *n* [U] damage that has been done deliberately to equipment, vehicles etc in order to prevent an enemy or opponent from using them: *This is no accident – it's a deliberate act of sabotage.*

**sab·o·teur** /ˌsæbəˈtɜː‖-ˈtɜːr/ *n* [C] someone who deliberately damages, destroys, or spoils someone else's property or activities, in order to prevent them from doing something —see also HUNT SABOTEUR

**sa·bre** *BrE*, **saber** *AmE* /ˈseɪbə‖-ər/ *n* [C] **1** a light pointed sword with one sharp edge used in FENCING **2** a heavy sword with a curved blade, used in more former times —see picture at SWORD

**sabre-rat·tling** /ˈ·· ˌ··/ *n* [U] threats to use military force, especially when you do not think they are very frightening or serious

**sac** /sæk/ *n* [C] *technical* a part inside a plant or animal that is shaped like a bag and contains liquid or air

**sac·cha·rin** /ˈsækərɨn/ *n* [U] a chemical substance that tastes sweet and is used instead of sugar in drinks

**sac·cha·rine** /ˈsækəriːn/ *adj formal* too romantic in a way that seems silly and insincere: *a saccharine love story*

**sac·er·do·tal** /ˌsæsəˈdəʊtl◂, ˌsækə-‖-sərˈdoʊ-, -kər-/ *adj technical* connected with or belonging to a priest

**sach·et** /ˈsæʃeɪ‖sæˈʃeɪ/ *n* [C] a small plastic or paper package containing a liquid or powder: *a sachet of shampoo* —see picture at CONTAINER

**sack¹** /sæk/ *n* **1** [C] **a)** a large bag made of strong rough cloth or strong paper, used for storing or carrying flour, coal, vegetables etc: *a sack of potatoes* **b)** also **sackful** the amount that a sack can contain **2 get the sack/give sb the sack** *BrE informal* to be dismissed from your job or to dismiss someone from their job: *He got the sack for stealing.* | *They've never actually given anyone the sack.* **3 hit the sack** *spoken* to go to bed: *It's one o'clock – time to hit the sack I think.* **4 in the sack** *informal* in bed

**sack²** *v* [T] **1** *BrE informal* to dismiss someone from their job; FIRE² (2) *especially AmE*: *She was sacked for organizing a union.* **2** to knock down the QUARTERBACK¹ (1) in American football **3** if an army sacks a place they go through it destroying or stealing things, and attacking people

**sack out** *phr v* [I] *AmE informal* to go to sleep: *He sacked out on the sofa.*

**sack·cloth** /ˈsæk-klɒθ‖-klɔːθ/ also **sacking** /ˈsækɪŋ/ *n* [U] **1** rough cloth for making sacks **2 wear sackcloth and ashes** to behave in a way that shows everyone you are sorry about something you have done wrong

**sack race** /ˈ· ·/ *n* [C] a race in which the competitors, usually children, have to jump forwards with both legs inside a SACK¹ (1a)

**sac·ra·ment** /ˈsækrəmənt/ *n* [C] **1 the Sacrament** the bread and wine that is eaten at Christian ceremonies **2** one of the important Christian ceremonies, such as marriage or COMMUNION (2) —**sacramental** /ˌsækrəˈmentl◂/ *adj*

**sa·cred** /ˈseɪkrɨd/ *adj* **1** connected with a god or religion: *sacred painting* | *a sacred vow* **2** greatly respected, or believed to be holy: *Cows are sacred to Hindus.* | *Human life is sacred.* **3** extremely important to you, especially in a way that other people think is silly or annoying: *He thinks his parking space is sacred.* **4 is nothing sacred?** *spoken* used to express shock when something you think is valuable or important is being changed or harmed: *They're putting a tax on books – is nothing sacred?* —**sacredly** *adv* —**sacredness** *n* [U]

**sacred cow** /ˌ·· ˈ·/ *n* [C] a belief that is so important to some people that they will not let anyone criticize it

**sac·ri·fice¹** /ˈsækrɨfaɪs/ *n* **1** [C,U] something valuable that you decide not to have, in order to get something that is more important: *the need for economic sacrifice* | **make sacrifices** *My parents were forever reminding me of the sacrifices they made to give me an education.* **2** [C,U] the act of offering something to a god, especially in former times by killing an animal or a person in a religious ceremony: **make a sacrifice** *It was common to make sacrifices to the gods to ensure a good harvest.* **3** [C] an object or animal that is offered to a god in a ceremony of sacrifice: **human sacrifice** (=a person killed as a sacrifice) **4** *literary* **the final/supreme sacrifice** the act of dying while you are fighting for a principle

**sacrifice²** *v* **1** [T] to willingly stop having something you want or doing something you like in order to get something more important: **sacrifice sth for** *It's not worth sacrificing your health for your career.* | **sacrifice sth to do sth** *He sacrificed a promising career to look after his handicapped daughter.* **2** [I,T] to offer something or someone to a god as a sacrifice

**sac·ri·fi·cial** /ˌsækrɪ̇ˈfɪʃəl◂/ *adj* connected with or offered as a sacrifice: *a sacrificial gift* —**sacrificially** *adv*

**sac·ri·lege** /ˈsækrɪ̇lɪdʒ/ *n* [C,U] **1** the act of treating something holy in a way that does not show respect **2** *spoken* the act of treating something badly when someone else thinks it is very important: *You recorded over his Jimi Hendrix tapes? That's sacrilege!* —**sacrilegious** /ˌsækrɪ̇ˈlɪdʒəs◂/ *adj* —**sacrilegiously** *adv*

**sac·ris·tan** /ˈsækrɪ̇stən/ *n* [C] *technical* someone whose job is to take care of the holy objects in a church

**sac·ris·ty** /ˈsækrɪ̇sti/ *n* [C] *technical* a small room in a church where holy cups and plates are kept, and where priests put on their ceremonial clothes; VESTRY (1)

**sac·ro·sanct** /ˈsækrəʊsæŋkt‖-roʊ-/ *adj* something that is sacrosanct is considered to be so important that no one is allowed to criticize or change it: *Weekends are sacrosanct in our family so I never take any work home.*

S2 W3 **sad** /sæd/ *adj*
**1** ▶ **UNHAPPY** ◀ unhappy, but especially because something unpleasant has happened to you or someone else: *What's the matter with him? He looks so sad.* | **be sad to do sth** *I was sad to see them go in the end.* | **[+ about]** *I was glad to be going home, but sad about the friends I was leaving behind.* | **sad smile/face/expression etc** *There was such a sad look in her eyes.* —opposite HAPPY (1)
**2** ▶ **STH THAT MAKES YOU SAD** ◀ a sad event, situation etc makes you feel unhappy: *A special meeting was called to announce the sad news of his death.* | **sad book/song/film etc** *What a sad movie! I cried all the way through.* | **it is sad that** *It's sad that James can't be with us.* | **it is sad to see/hear etc** *It was sad to see all that food going to waste.* | **sad time/day/moment etc** *This is a sad day for all of us.*
**3** ▶ **NOT SATISFACTORY** ◀ [only before noun] a sad situation is very bad or unacceptable: **sad state of affairs** (=bad situation) *It's a sad state of affairs when you can't go out at night for fear of being attacked.* | **the sad fact is (that)** *spoken*: *The sad fact is that prejudice and discrimination still exist.* | **sad to say** *spoken*: *Sad to say, we never found them.*
**4** ▶ **LONELY** ◀ a sad person or someone who has a sad life seems lonely and unhappy and you feel sorry for them: *She's a sad character – I don't think she has any friends at all.* | **sad case** (=someone you feel sorry for)
**5** ▶ **BORING** ◀ *spoken slang* used to say that someone or something is boring and unfashionable: *I think Carole's a bit of a sad name. Oh, sorry, is your mum called Carole?* | **sad bastard** *Get a life, you sad bastard.*
**6 sadder but wiser** having learned something from an unpleasant experience: *He came out of the relationship sadder but wiser.* —**sadness** *n* [singular, U] —see also SADLY

**sad·den** /ˈsædn/ *v* [T often passive] *formal* to make someone feel sad or disappointed: *Dorothea was saddened by his sudden change of heart.* | **it saddens sb** *It saddened him to think that the others no longer trusted him.*

**sad·dle**[1] /ˈsædl/ *n* **1** [C] a seat made of leather that is put on a horse's back so that someone can ride it —see picture at HORSE[1] **2** [C] a seat on a bicycle or a MOTORCYCLE —see picture at BICYCLE[1] **3 be in the saddle** *informal* **a)** to be in a position in which you have power or authority: *He's been in the saddle for 30 years now, and it's time he retired.* **b)** to be riding a horse: *They were weary after many hours in the saddle.*

**saddle**[2] *v* [T] to put a saddle on a horse
**saddle up** *phr v* [I,T] to put a saddle on a horse: *We saddled up and rode quickly back to the farm.*
**saddle** sb **with** sth *phr v* [T] to give someone a difficult or boring job: *It's his party, but I've been saddled with organizing the whole thing!*

**saddle bag** /ˈ·· ·/ *n* [C] a bag for carrying things that is fixed to the saddle on a horse or bicycle

**sad·dler** /ˈsædlə‖-ər/ *n* [C] someone who makes saddles and other leather products, or a shop where these are sold

**sad·dler·y** /ˈsædləri/ *n* [U] **1** goods made by a saddler **2** the art of making saddles and other leather goods

**saddle shoe** /ˈ·· ·/ *n* [C] *AmE* a shoe that has a toe and heel of one colour, with a different colour in the middle

**saddle-sore** /ˈ·· ·/ *adj* [not before noun] feeling stiff and sore after riding a horse or bicycle

**sa·dhu** /ˈsɑːduː/ *n* [C] a Hindu holy man who lives a very simple life

**sa·dis·m** /ˈseɪdɪzəm/ *n* [U] **1** the practice of getting pleasure from being cruel to someone: *New recruits were treated with ruthless sadism.* **2** the practice of getting sexual pleasure from hurting someone

**sa·dist** /ˈseɪdɪ̇st/ *n* [C] someone who enjoys being cruel to other people

**sa·dis·tic** /səˈdɪstɪk/ *adj* cruel and enjoying making other people suffer: *He took a sadistic delight in humiliating her.* —**sadistically** /-kli/ *adv*

**sad·ly** /ˈsædli/ *adv* **1** in a way that shows that you are sad: *Peter shook his head sadly and turned away.* **2** [sentence adverb] unfortunately: *Sadly, they just can't be trusted.* **3** in a way that makes you sad: *He was a popular man and will be sadly missed.* | *We were sadly disappointed.* **4 sadly lacking/neglected etc** in a way that seems bad or wrong: *The garden was beautiful once, but it has been sadly neglected.* **5 be sadly mistaken** to be completely wrong about something: *If you think you'll get any money from him, you're sadly mistaken.*

**sa·do·mas·o·chis·m** /ˌseɪdəʊˈmæsəkɪzəm‖-doʊ-/ *n* [U] the practice of getting sexual pleasure from hurting someone or being hurt —**sadomasochist** *n* [C] —**sadomasochistic** /ˌseɪdəʊmæsəˈkɪstɪk◂‖-doʊ-/ *adj*

**sae** /ˌes eɪ ˈiː/ *BrE* **1** stamped addressed envelope; an envelope that you put your name, address, and a stamp on, so that someone else can send you something **2** self-addressed envelope; an envelope that you put your own name and address on —see also SASE

**sa·fa·ri**[1] /səˈfɑːri/ *n* [C] a trip through countryside in Africa, that you go on to watch wild animals: **go/be on safari** *They spent their vacation on safari in Kenya.*

**safari**[2] *adj* **safari suit/jacket** a suit or JACKET (1) that is made of light-coloured material, usually with a belt and two pockets on the chest

**safari park** /ˈ··· ·/ *n* [C] an enclosed area of land where wild animals are kept, so that people can drive round and look at them

**safe**[1] /seɪf/ *adj* S2 W2
**1** ▶ **NOT CAUSING HARM** ◀ not likely to cause any physical injury or harm: *Flying is one of the safest forms of travel.* | *the safe disposal of radioactive waste* | *Don't go too near the edge – it isn't safe.* | **it is safe to do sth** *Is it safe to swim here?* | **[+ for]** *Parents want play-areas that are safe for their children.*
**2** ▶ **NOT IN DANGER** ◀ [not before noun] not in danger of being lost, harmed, or stolen: *Will you feel safe in the house on your own?* | **[+ from]** *We were safe from attack in the shelter.* | **keep sth safe** *I'm trusting you with these documents – so make sure you keep them safe.* | **safe and sound** (=unharmed, especially after being in danger) *The missing children were found safe and sound.*
**3** ▶ **PLACE** ◀ a safe place is one where something is not likely to be stolen or lost: *Keep the receipt in a safe place.*
**4 safe journey/arrival/return etc** a journey etc that ends safely: *They prayed for their father's safe return.* | **safe journey** *spoken* (=what you say to someone when they start a long journey)
**5** ▶ **NO RISK** ◀ not involving any risk and very likely to succeed: *a safe investment* | *a safe method of contraception* | **(as) safe as houses** (=completely safe)
**6** ▶ **SUBJECT** ◀ a subject of conversation that is safe is not likely to upset anyone or make people argue: *I kept to safe subjects, like the weather.*
**7 better (to be) safe than sorry** *spoken* used to say that it is better to be careful now, even if this takes time, effort

etc, so that nothing bad will happen later: *I've checked all the safety harnesses – better safe than sorry!*
**8 to be on the safe side** *spoken* to do something especially carefully in order to avoid an unpleasant situation: *I'd take an umbrella, just to be on the safe side.*
**9 be in safe hands** to be with someone who will look after you very well: *I've needed to know my kids were in safe hands.*
**10 a safe pair of hands** someone you can trust to do a difficult job without making mistakes —**safely** *adv*: *Drive safely!* | *I think we can safely assume that she will pass the exam.* —see also **play it safe** (PLAY[1] (11)), **a safe bet/a sure bet** (BET[2] (6)), **safe seat** (SEAT[1] (5))

**safe**[2] *n* [C] a strong metal box or cupboard with special locks where you keep money and valuable things

**safe con·duct** /ˌ· ˈ··/ *n* [C,U] official protection for someone when they are passing through a dangerous area: *This letter should guarantee you safe conduct through the war zone.*

**safe-de·pos·it box** /ˈ· ·ˌ·· ˌ·/ *n* [C] a SAFETY DEPOSIT BOX

**safe·guard**[1] /ˈseɪfgɑːd‖-gɑːrd/ *v* [T] to protect something from harm or damage: *New regulations were introduced to safeguard the environment.* | **safeguard sth against** *a program for safeguarding the computer system against viruses*

**safeguard**[2] *n* [C] a rule, agreement etc that is intended to protect someone or something from possible dangers or problems: *The law contains important safeguards to protect housebuyers.* | [+ **against**] *safeguards against the exploitation of children*

**safe ha·ven** /ˌ· ˈ··/ *n* [C] a place where someone can go to in order to escape from possible danger or attack

**safe house** /ˌ· ˈ·/ *n* [C] a house where someone can hide when their enemies are looking for them

**safe·keep·ing** /ˌseɪfˈkiːpɪŋ/ *n* [U] **1 for safekeeping** if you put something somewhere for safekeeping, you put it in a place where it will not get damaged, lost, or stolen **2 be in sb's safekeeping** to be in a position or situation where someone is looking after you

**safe sex** /ˌ· ˈ·/ *n* [U] ways of having sex that reduce the risk of the spread of AIDS and other sexual diseases, especially by using a CONDOM

S3 W2 **safe·ty** /ˈseɪfti/ *n*
**1 ▶ NOT IN DANGER ◀** [U] the state of being safe from danger or harm: *The company seemed totally unconcerned about the safety of its workers.* | **in safety** (=without any danger) *Spectators could watch the launch in complete safety.* | **for safety's sake** (=in order to be safe) *We travelled in pairs, for safety's sake.*
**2 sb's safety** how safe someone is in a particular situation: *The boy has now been missing for 5 days and there are fears for his safety.* | **for sb's own safety** *For your own safety please do not smoke inside the plane.*
**3 ▶ NOT DANGEROUS ◀** [U] the state of not being dangerous or likely to cause harm or injury: *Some scientists expressed concern over the safety of the test.* | **safety measures/precautions/checks** (=things that are done in order to make sure that something is safe) *The accident would never have happened if the correct safety procedures had been followed.* | **road safety** (=safety of people using the roads) *Police are visiting schools as part of their latest road safety campaign.*
**4 ▶ SAFE PLACE ◀** [U] a place where you are safe from danger: **the safety of** *When the shelling began people fled to the safety of the city.* | **lead/take sb to safety** *Fire fighters led the children to safety.* | **reach safety** *We were relieved to reach dry land and safety.*
**5 safety in numbers** *spoken* used to say that a dangerous or unpleasant situation is better if there are a lot of people with you
**6 ▶ SPORT ◀** [C] *technical* a way of getting two points in American football by making the other team put the ball down in its own GOAL (3)

**safety belt** /ˈ·· ·/ *n* [C] a SEAT BELT

**safety catch** /ˈ·· ·/ *n* [C] a lock on a gun that stops it from being fired accidentally

**safety cur·tain** /ˈ·· ˌ··/ *n* [C] a thick curtain at the front of a theatre stage that prevents fire from spreading

**safety-de·pos·it box** /ˈ·· ·ˌ·· ˈ·/ *n* [C] a small box used for storing valuable objects, usually kept in a special room in a bank

**safety glass** /ˈ·· ·/ *n* [U] strong glass that breaks into very small pieces that are not sharp, used for example in car windows

**safety is·land** /ˈ·· ˌ··/ *n* [C] *AmE* a TRAFFIC ISLAND

**safety lamp** /ˈ·· ·/ *n* [C] a special lamp used by MINERS, that has a flame which will not make underground gases explode

**safety match** /ˈ·· ·/ *n* [C] a match that can only be lit by rubbing it along a special surface on the side of its box

**safety net** /ˈ·· ·/ *n* [C] **1** a large net used to catch someone who is performing high above the ground if they fall **2** a system or arrangement that exists to help you if you have serious problems or get into a difficult situation: *a safety net of welfare payments for the poor*

**safety pin** /ˈ·· ·/ *n* [C] a wire pin with a cover that its point fits into so that it cannot hurt you —see picture at PIN[1]

**safety ra·zor** /ˈ·· ˌ··/ *n* [C] a RAZOR that has a cover over part of the blade to protect your skin —see picture at RAZOR

**safety valve** /ˈ·· ·/ *n* [C] **1** something you do that allows you to express strong feelings such as anger without doing any harm: *Exercise provided him with a good safety valve from pressure at work.* **2** a part of a machine that allows gas, steam etc to be let out when the pressure becomes too great

**saf·fron** /ˈsæfrən/ *n* [U] **1** bright orange powder that is used in cooking to give food a special taste and colour: *saffron rice* **2** a bright orange-yellow colour

**sag**[1] /sæg/ **sagged, sagging** *v* [I] **1** to sink or bend downwards and away from the usual position: *The branch sagged under the weight of the apples.* | *His shoulders sagged dejectedly.* **2** to become weaker or less valuable: *attempts to revive the sagging economy* | *My morale sagged still further.*

**sag**[2] *n* [singular, U] a downward bending or sinking movement or position: *a sag in a mattress*

**sa·ga** /ˈsɑːgə/ *n* [C] **1** a long story, especially one that continues over a period of many years: *an absorbing family saga* **2** *informal* a long and complicated series of events or a description of this: *I had to listen to a great long saga about her medical problems.* **3** one of the stories written about the Vikings of Norway and Iceland

**sa·ga·cious** /səˈgeɪʃəs/ *adj formal* able to understand and judge things very well; WISE[1] (2) —**sagaciously** *adv*

**sa·ga·ci·ty** /səˈgæsəti/ *n* [U] *formal* good judgment and understanding; WISDOM

**sage**[1] /seɪdʒ/ *n* **1** [U] a plant with grey-green leaves that are used in cooking **2** [C] *literary* someone, especially an old man, who is very wise

**sage**[2] *adj literary* very wise, especially as a result of a lot of experience: *sage advice* —**sagely** *adv*

**sage·brush** /ˈseɪdʒbrʌʃ/ *n* [U] a small plant that is very common in the western US

**sag·gy** /ˈsægi/ *adj informal* having a shape that sinks or drops downwards: *The mattress was rather saggy in the middle.*

**Sa·git·tar·i·us** /ˌsædʒəˈteəriəs‖-ter-/ *n* **1** [singular] the ninth sign of the ZODIAC, represented by an animal that is half-horse and half-human, and believed to affect the character and life of people born between November 22 and December 21 **2** [C] someone who was born between November 22 and December 21

**sa·go** /ˈseɪgəʊ‖-goʊ/ *n* [U] a white food substance used to make sweet dishes with milk

**sahib** /sɑːb‖ˈsɑː-ɪb/ *n* [C] *IndE & PakE* used as a title of respect for a man in India, especially in former times,: *Good morning, sahib!*

**said¹** /sed/ the past tense and past participle of SAY¹

**said²** *adj* [only before noun] *law or humorous* used when giving more information about someone or something that has just been mentioned: *The said weapon was later found in the defendant's home.*

S3 **sail¹** /seɪl/ *v* **1** [I always +adv/prep] to travel across an area of water in a boat or ship: *the first Europeans to sail across the Atlantic | Three tall ships sailed past.* **2** [I,T] to direct or control the movement of a boat or ship: *The captain sailed his ship safely through the narrow passage. | My father taught me to sail when I was 14.* **3** [I] to start a journey by boat or ship: *We sail at dawn.* | [+ **for**] *They're sailing for Antigua next week.* **4** [I always +adv/prep] to move quickly and smoothly through the air: *At that moment a ball came sailing over the fence and landed in my lap.* **5** [I always +adv/prep] to move forwards gracefully and confidently: *Penelope sailed into the room, her dress billowing behind her.* **6 sail close to the wind** to do or say something that is nearly wrong, illegal, or dishonest: *You're sailing a bit close to the wind with that remark.* —see also **sail/fly under false colours** (FALSE (10))

**sail through** *phr v* [I,T] to succeed very easily in a test, examination etc

**sail²** *n* [C] **1** a large piece of strong cloth fixed onto a boat, so that the wind will push the boat along: *a yacht with white sails* | **hoist/lower the sails** (=put the sails up or down) **2 set sail** to begin a journey by boat or ship: *The following week the 'Queen Elizabeth' set sail for Jamaica.* **3 under sail** *literary* moving along on a ship or boat that has sails

**sail·board** /ˈseɪlbɔːd‖-bɔːrd/ *n* [C] a flat board with a sail, that you stand on in the sport of WIND-SURFING

**sail·boat** /ˈseɪlbəʊt‖-boʊt/ *n* [C] *AmE* a small boat with one or more sails

**sail·ing** /ˈseɪlɪŋ/ *n* **1** [U] the sport or activity of travelling in or directing a small boat with sails: *Sylvia had always enjoyed sailing.* **2** [C] a time when a ship leaves a port: *Luckily, there was another sailing at 2 o'clock.* —see also PLAIN SAILING

**sailing boat** /ˈ·· ·/ *n* [C] *BrE* a small boat with one or more sails

**sailing ship** /ˈ·· ·/ *n* [C] a large ship with sails

**sail·or** /ˈseɪlə‖-ər/ *n* [C] **1** someone who works on a ship **2** someone who travels in a boat: **bad/good sailor** (=someone who does or does not feel sick when they are in a boat)

**sailor suit** /ˈ·· ·/ *n* [C] a blue and white suit that looks like an old-fashioned sailor's uniform, worn by children

**saint** /seɪnt/ *n* [C] **1** someone who is given a special honour by the Christian church after they have died, because they were very good or holy: *Saint Patrick* **2** *informal* someone who is extremely good, kind, or patient: *His wife must have been a saint to put up with him for all those years.* **3 the patience of a saint** a very large amount of patience: *You need the patience of a saint for this job.*

**saint·ed** /ˈseɪntɨd/ *adj* **1** having been made a saint by the Christian church **2** *old-fashioned* used when talking about a dead person **3 my sainted aunt!** *old-fashioned spoken* used to express surprise or shock

**saint·hood** /ˈseɪnthʊd/ *n* [U] the state of being a saint

**saint·ly** /ˈseɪntli/ *adj* seeming to be completely good and honest, with no faults: *a doctor who had led a saintly and blameless life* —**saintliness** *n* [U]

**saint's day** /ˈ· ·/ *n* [C] the day of the year when the Christian church remembers a particular saint

**saith** /seθ/ *biblical* says

S2 W3  **sake¹** /seɪk/ *n* [U] **1 for the sake of** in order to help, improve, or please someone or something: *He moved to the seaside for the sake of his health. | I only went for Kay's sake.* | **for sb's own sake** (=because it will be good for them) *I hope he's told her the truth for his own sake.* **2 for the sake of it** if you do something for the sake of it, you do it because you want to and not for any particular reason: *I'm sure she agrees with you really – she just likes arguing for the sake of it.* **3 for the sake of argument** *spoken* if you say something for the sake of argument, what you say may not be true but it will help you to have a discussion: *Let's say, just for the sake of argument, that you've got £200 to invest.* **4 for God's/Christ's/goodness'/Heaven's etc sake** *spoken* **a)** used when you are telling someone how important it is to do something or not to do something: *For goodness sake, don't tell him that!* **b)** used to show that you are angry or annoyed: *What's the matter now, for God's sake?* —see GOD (USAGE)

**sa·ke²** /ˈsɑːki/ *n* [U] a Japanese alcoholic drink made from rice, served in small cups, usually warm

**sa·laam** /səˈlɑːm/ *v* [I] to bend forwards and put your hand against your forehead, as a polite greeting in some Eastern countries —**salaam** *n* [C]

**sal·a·ble** /ˈseɪləbəl/ *adj* another spelling of SALEABLE

**sa·la·cious** /səˈleɪʃəs/ *adj formal* expressing too much unpleasant sexual detail: *salacious jokes* —**salaciously** *adv* —**salaciousness** *n* [U]

**sal·ad** /ˈsæləd/ *n* [C,U] **1** a mixture of raw vegetables, especially LETTUCE, CUCUMBER, and TOMATO: *a cheese salad | Would you like some salad with your pasta? | a salad bowl* | **toss a salad** (=mix it all together, usually with a DRESSING) **2** raw or cooked food cut into small pieces and served cold: *potato salad*

**salad cream** /ˈ·· ·/ *n* [U] *BrE* a thick light-coloured liquid, similar to MAYONNAISE, that you put on salad

**salad days** /ˈ·· ·/ *n* [plural] *old-fashioned* the time of your life when you are young and not very experienced

**salad dress·ing** /ˈ·· ˌ··/ *n* [C,U] a liquid mixture made from oil and VINEGAR, for putting on salads

**sal·a·man·der** /ˈsæləmændə‖-ər/ *n* [C] a small animal similar to a LIZARD

**sa·la·mi** /səˈlɑːmi/ *n* [C,U] a large SAUSAGE with a strong taste, that is eaten cold

**sal·a·ried** /ˈsælərid/ *adj* receiving money every month for the work you do, rather than for every week or every hour: *salaried workers*

**sal·a·ry** /ˈsæləri/ *n* [C,U] money that you receive as payment from the organization you work for, usually paid to you every month: **be on a salary of** (=be earning a particular amount) *She's on a salary of £16,000.* —compare WAGE¹ (1) —see PAY (USAGE) W3

**sale** /seɪl/ *n* S2 W1

**1 ▶ ACT OF SELLING ◀** [C,U] the act of giving property, food, or other goods to someone in exchange for money: [+ **of**] *The use and sale of marijuana remains illegal. | The house sale was completed in two weeks.* | **make a sale** (=sell something) *Every time Harvey makes a sale he gets $50 commission.* | **lose a sale** (=not sell something that you were going to sell) *Rather than lose a sale, car salesmen will often bring down the price.*

**2 for sale** available to be bought: *Excuse me, are these for sale? | There was a "for sale" sign in the yard.* | **put sth up for sale** (=to make something, especially a house, available to be bought) *Reluctantly, they put the family home up for sale.*

**3 ▶ LOWER PRICES ◀** [C] a period of time when shops sell their goods at lower prices than usual: *Marsdon's department store is having a sale this week.* | **the sales** *BrE* (=when all the shops have a sale) | **the January/summer/autumn etc sales** *I picked up some real bargains in the January sales this year.*

**4 ▶ EVENT ◀** [C] an event at which things are sold to the person who offers the highest price; AUCTION¹: *a sale of 17th century paintings*

**5 sales a)** [plural] the total number of products that a company sells during a particular period of time: *We grossed more than $500,000 in sales last year.* | **sales figures/targets etc** *We've already reached our sales*

*targets for this year.* **b)** [U] the part of a company that deals with selling products: *She found a job in sales.|a sales manager*
**6 sales drive/campaign** an effort made by a company to try to increase the number of products it sells
**7 sales pitch/talk** the things that someone says when they are trying to persuade you to buy something
**8 on sale a)** available to be bought in a shop: *Stephen King's new novel will go on sale next week.* **b)** *especially AmE* available to be bought at a lower price than usual: *I could only afford to buy the CD player because it was on sale.*
**9 (on) sale or return** if a shop buys something on sale or return, it can return the goods that it is unable to sell —see also BILL OF SALE, JUMBLE SALE, POINT OF SALE

**sale·able, salable** /ˈseɪləbəl/ *adj* something that is saleable can be sold, or is easy to sell: *a saleable commodity* —**saleability** /ˌseɪləˈbɪləti/ *n* [U]

**sale of work** /ˌ· · ˈ·/ *n* [C] *BrE* an event at which people sell things they have made, especially in order to get money for a good purpose

**sale·room** /ˈseɪlrʊm, -ruːm/ *n* [C] *BrE* a room where things are sold by AUCTION²

**sales·clerk** /ˈseɪlzklɑːk‖-klɜːrk/ *n* [C] *AmE* someone who sells things in a shop; SHOP ASSISTANT *BrE*

**sales·girl** /ˈseɪlzgɜːl‖-gɜːrl/ *n* [C] *old-fashioned* a young woman who sells things in a shop

**sales·man** /ˈseɪlzmən/ *n plural* **salesmen**/-mən/ [C] a man whose job is to persuade people to buy his company's products

S

**sales·per·son** /ˈseɪlzpɜːsən‖-pɜːr-/ *n* [C] someone whose job is selling things

**sales rep·re·sen·ta·tive** /ˈ· ··ˌ···/ also **sales rep** /ˈ· ·/ *n* [C] someone who travels around, usually within a particular area, selling their company's products

**sales slip** /ˈ· ·/ *n* [C] *AmE* a small piece of paper that you are given in a shop when you buy something; RECEIPT (1)

**sales tax** /ˈ· ·/ *n* [C,U] *AmE* a tax that you have to pay in addition to the cost of something you are buying —compare VAT

**sales·wom·an** /ˈseɪlzˌwʊmən/ *n plural* **saleswomen** /-ˌwɪmɪn/ [C] a woman whose job is selling things

**sa·li·ent** /ˈseɪliənt/ *adj formal* the salient points or features of something are the most important or most noticeable parts of it: *The salient features of his plan are summarized in this report.* —**salience** *n* [U]

**sa·line¹** /ˈseɪlaɪn/ *adj* containing or consisting of salt: *saline solution* —**salinity** /səˈlɪnəti/ *n* [U]

**saline²** *n* [U] a special mixture of water and salt

**sa·li·va** /səˈlaɪvə/ *n* [U] the liquid that is produced naturally in your mouth

**salivary gland** /ˈ····· ˌ·/ *n* [C] a part of your mouth that produces saliva

**sal·i·vate** /ˈsæləveɪt/ *v* [I] to produce more saliva in your mouth than usual, especially because you see or smell food —**salivation** /ˌsæləˈveɪʃən/ *n* [U]

**sal·low** /ˈsæləʊ‖-loʊ/ *adj* sallow skin looks slightly yellow and unhealthy: *a sallow complexion* —**sallowness** *n* [U]

**sal·ly¹** /ˈsæli/ *n* [C] **1** an amusing clever remark **2** a sudden quick attack and return to a position of defence

**sally²** *v*
**sally forth** *phr v* [I] *old-fashioned* to leave somewhere that is safe in order to do something that you expect to be difficult or dangerous: *Each morning they sallied forth in search of jobs.*

**salm·on** /ˈsæmən/ *n* **1** [C] *plural* **salmon** a large fish with silver skin and pink flesh that lives in the sea but swims up rivers to lay its eggs **2** [U] this fish eaten as food

**sal·mo·nel·la** /ˌsælməˈnelə/ *n* [U] a kind of BACTERIA in food that makes you ill

**sal·on** /ˈsælɒn‖səˈlɑːn/ *n* [C] **1** a shop where you can get your hair cut etc: *a beauty salon* **2** a shop where fashionable and expensive clothes are sold **3** a room in a very large house where people can meet and talk **4** a regular meeting of famous people at which they talk about art, literature, or music, popular in 18th century France

**sa·loon** /səˈluːn/ *n* [C] **1** a public place where alcoholic drinks were sold and drunk in the western US in the 19th century **2** *BrE* a car that has a separate enclosed space for your bags etc; SEDAN *AmE* **3** a large comfortable room where passengers on a ship can sit and relax

**saloon bar** /·ˈ· ·/ *n* [C] *BrE* a comfortable room in a PUB

**sal·sa** /ˈsælsə‖ˈsɑːl-/ *n* [U] **1** a type of Latin American dance music **2** a SAUCE (1) made from onions, tomatoes (TOMATO) and chillies (CHILLI (2)) that you put on Spanish or Mexican food

**salt¹** /sɔːlt‖sɒːlt/ *n* **1** [U] a natural white mineral that is added to food to make it taste better or to preserve it; SODIUM CHLORIDE *technical*: *Try to reduce the amount of salt you use.|a pinch of salt*|**table salt** (=very small grains of salt you use in cooking)|**sea salt** (=large grains of salt made by drying sea water)|**rock salt** (=salt in a solid form rather than in grains) **2 the salt of the earth** someone who is ordinary, but good and honest **3 take sth with a pinch/grain of salt** *informal* to not completely believe what someone tells you because you know that they do not always tell the truth **4** [C] *technical* a type of chemical substance —see also BATH SALTS, EPSOM SALTS, SMELLING SALTS, OLD SALT, **rub salt into sb's wounds** (RUB¹ (7)), **not worth his salt** (WORTH¹ (9))

**salt²** *v* [T] **1** to add salt to food to make it taste better **2** also **salt down** to add salt to food to preserve it **3** to put salt on the roads to prevent them from becoming icy
**salt** sth ↔ **away** *phr v* [T] to save money for the future, especially dishonestly by hiding it

**salt³** *adj* [only before noun] **1** preserved by salt: *salt pork* **2 salt water** water that contains salt, especially naturally in the sea **3** consisting of salt water: *a salt lake*

**salt cel·lar** /ˈ· ˌ··/ *n* [C] *BrE* a small container for salt; SALT SHAKER *AmE*

**salt·pe·tre** *BrE*, **saltpeter** *AmE* /ˌsɔːltˈpiːtə‖ˌsɒːltˈpiːtər/ *n* [U] a substance used in making GUNPOWDER (=powder that causes explosions) and matches

**salt shak·er** /ˈ· ˌ··/ *n* [C] *AmE* a small container for salt

**salt truck** /ˈ· ·/ *n* [C] *AmE* a large vehicle that puts salt or sand on the roads in winter to make them less icy; GRITTER *BrE*

**salt·wa·ter** /ˈsɔːltˌwɔːtə‖-ˌwɒːtər, -ˌwɑː-/ *adj* [only before noun] living in salty water or in the sea: *saltwater fish*

**salt·y** /ˈsɔːlti‖ˈsɒːlti/ *adj* **1** tasting of or containing salt **2** *old-fashioned* a story, joke, or conversation that is salty is amusing and often about sex

**sa·lu·bri·ous** /səˈluːbriəs/ *adj formal* a place that is salubrious is pleasant and healthy to be in: *They've moved to a more salubrious part of town.*

**sal·u·ta·ry** /ˈsæljətəri‖-teri/ *adj* a salutary experience is unpleasant but teaches you something

**sal·u·ta·tion** /ˌsæljəˈteɪʃən/ *n formal* **1** [C] a word or phrase used at the beginning of a letter or speech, such as "Dear Mr. Smith" **2** [C,U] something you say or do when greeting someone

**sa·lute¹** /səˈluːt/ *v* **1** [I,T] to move your right hand to your head in order to show respect to an officer in the army, navy etc **2** [T] *formal* to praise someone for the things they have achieved, especially publicly: **salute sb as** *James Joyce was saluted as the greatest writer of the 20th century.* **3** [T] *old-fashioned* to greet someone in a polite way, especially by moving your hand or body

**salute²** *n* **1** [C] an act of raising your right hand to your head as a sign of respect, usually done by a soldier to an officer **2** [C] an occasion when guns are fired into the air in order to show respect for someone important:

*a 21-gun salute* **3** [C,U] *formal* a movement made to greet someone with your hand or head

**sal·vage¹** /ˈsælvɪdʒ/ *v* [T] **1** to save something from a situation in which other things have already been damaged, destroyed, or lost: **salvage sth from** *We managed to salvage a few photo albums from the fire.* **2** to do something to make sure that you do not fail completely or lose something completely: *They brought on Christiansen in a last-minute attempt to salvage the game.*|*Is there still a chance of salvaging their marriage?*|**salvage your reputation** (=do something so that you do not lose people's respect)

**salvage²** *n* [U] **1** the act of saving things from a situation in which other things have already been damaged, destroyed, or lost: *a salvage operation* **2** things that have been saved in this way

S3 **sal·va·tion** /sælˈveɪʃən/ *n* [U] **1** the state of being saved from evil or death in the Christian religion **2** something that prevents danger, loss, or failure: **be the salvation of** *The recent rain will be the salvation of this year's wheat crop.*

**Salvation Ar·my** /·ˌ·· ˈ··/ *n* **the Salvation Army** a Christian organization that tries to help poor people

**salve¹** /sælv, sɑːv‖sæv/ *n* [C,U] a substance that you put on sore skin to make it less painful

**salve²** *v* [T] *formal* **salve your conscience** if you do something to salve your conscience, you do it to make yourself feel less guilty: *Buying his wife flowers helped to salve his conscience.*

**sal·ver** /ˈsælvə‖-ər/ *n* [C] a large metal plate used for serving food or drink at a formal meal: *a silver salver*

**sal·vo** /ˈsælvəʊ‖-voʊ/ *n* [C usually singular] *formal* **1** [+ **of**] the firing of several guns during a battle or as part of a ceremony **2 opening salvo** the first in a series of questions, statements etc that you use to try to win an argument: *In his opening salvo against the education practices of the 1960s, Stein mentioned several important studies.* **3** sudden laughter, APPLAUSE etc from many people at the same time

**Sa·mar·i·tan** /səˈmærɪ̣tən/ also **good samaritan** *n* [C] someone who helps you when you have problems

**sam·ba** /ˈsæmbə/ *n* [C,U] a fast dance from Brazil, or the type of music played for this dance

S1 W1 **same¹** /seɪm/ *adj* [only before a noun] **1 the same person/place/thing etc a)** one particular person, thing etc and not a different one: *He is in the same chair every evening.*|*I'll never make the same mistake again.*|[+ **as**] *It's hard to believe she's the same age as Brian.*|**this same person/that same thing etc** *It is those same people who voted for the Democrats who now complain about their policies.* **b)** used to say two or more people, things etc are exactly like each other; IDENTICAL: *It was so embarrassing! Both women were wearing the same dress.*|*It's the same kind of work, just a different department.*|[+**as**] *He gets the same pay as me but he gets his own office.*|**just/exactly the same** *If you can ride a push-bike then riding a motorbike is exactly the same thing. It's a question of balance.*|**much the same** (=almost the same) *The furniture is made in much the same way as it was over 200 years ago.* **2** used to say that a particular person or thing does not change: *Her perfume has always had the same effect on me.*|*He's the same old Peter, moody and irritable.* **3 at the same time** if two things happen at the same time they both happen together: *Kate and I both went to live in Spain at the same time.* **4 the very same/the self same** used when you are surprised that someone or something is the same person or thing and not a different one: *It is hard to believe it was in the very same house that Shakespeare wrote his plays.* **5 amount/come to the same thing** to have the same result or effect: *It doesn't matter whether she was happy to leave or not – it amounts to the same thing. We need a new secretary.* **6 the same old story/excuse etc** *informal* something that you have heard many times before: *It's the same old story – his wife didn't really love him.* **7 same difference** *spoken especially AmE* used to say that different actions, behaviour etc have the same result or effect: *"I could mail the letter tomorrow morning or send a fax." "Same difference, it'll still not get there on time."* **8 by the same token** in the same way, or for the same reasons: *I realise that he hasn't come up with any new ideas, but by the same token we haven't needed any.* **9 be in the same boat** to be in the same difficult situation that someone else is in

**USAGE NOTE: SAME**

GRAMMAR

Remember that **same** almost always has *the* or *this/that* etc before it: *They wear the same clothes every day* (NOT *They wear same clothes*).|*People are the same all over the world*|*That very same day, Trisha phoned him.*

In informal spoken English you will hear **same** used with *the* left out, but this is not considered correct in writing: *"I thought the game was really good" "Same here"*|*"What would you like?" "Same again please."*

When you are comparing, you always say that one thing is **the same as** another: *Bob dresses just the same as his father did.*|*I go to the same college as you* (NOT *...to the same college with*).

**same²** *pron* **1 the same a)** used to say that two or more people or things are exactly like each other: *The coins may look the same but one's a forgery.*|*Thanks for your help – I'll do the same for you one day.* **b)** used to say that a particular person or thing does not change: *"How's your wife?" "About the same, thanks."*|*Now that Sam's retired, things just won't be the same.* **2 (and the) same to you!** *spoken* used as a reply to a greeting or as an angry reply to a rude remark.: *"Happy Christmas!" "And the same to you Ben."* **3 just/all the same** in spite of a particular situation, opinion etc: *I realise she can be very annoying, but I think you should apologise all the same.* **4 same here** *spoken* used to say that you feel the same way as someone else: *"I'm absolutely exhausted." "Same here!"* **5 (the) same again** used to ask for another drink of the same kind **6 more of the same** used to mean a person, thing etc like the one just mentioned: *He has produced a string of thrillers, and this movie is just more of the same.* —see also **all the same to sb** (ALL² (11), **one and the same** (ONE³ (7))

**same³** *adv* **1 the same (as)** in the same way: *"Rain" and "reign" are pronounced the same even though they are spelt differently.*|*Everyone had to dress the same as a well known historical figure.* **2 same as sb** *spoken* just like someone else: *I have my pride, same as anyone else.*

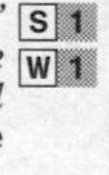

**same·ness** /ˈseɪmnɪ̣s/ *n* [U] a boring lack of variety, or the quality of being very similar to something else

**same·y** /ˈseɪmi/ *adj informal* boring and having very little variety: *His novels tend to be very samey.*

**sa·mo·sa** /sæˈməʊsə‖-ˈmoʊ-/ *n* [C] a type of Indian food made from meat or vegetables covered in thin PASTRY (1) and cooked in hot oil

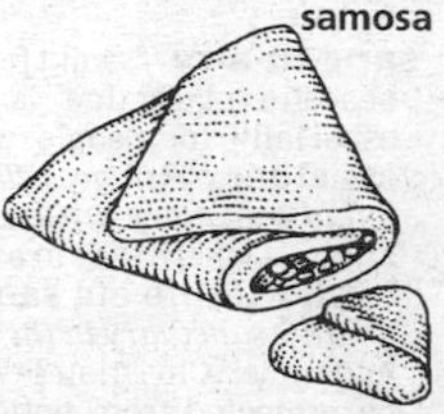
samosa

**sam·o·var** /ˈsæməvɑː‖-vɑːr/ *n* [C] a large metal container used in Russia to boil water for making tea

**sam·pan** /ˈsæmpæn/ *n* [C] a small boat used in China and Southeast Asia

**sam·ple¹** /ˈsɑːmpəl‖ˈsæm-/ *n* [C] **1** a small part or amount of something that is examined in order to find out something about the whole: *They took a blood sample to test for hepatitis.*|[+ **of**] *I'd like to see some samples of your work.* **2** a small amount of a product that people can try S3 W2 in order to find out what it is like: [+ **of**] *samples of a new shampoo* **3** a group of people who have been chosen to give information or answers to questions: *The sample consisted of 344 elementary and secondary school teachers.* | **random sample** (=one in which you choose people without knowing anything about them) *Out of a random sample of drivers, 21% had been involved in an accident in the previous year.* | **representative sample** (=one that is planned to include several different types of people) *a nationally representative sample of over 4500 elderly persons*

**sample²** *v* [T] **1** to taste food or drink in order to see what it is like —see TASTE (USAGE) **2** [often passive] to choose some people from a larger group in order to ask them questions or get information from them: *18% of the adults sampled admitted having had problems with alcohol abuse.* **3** to try an activity, go to a place etc in order to see what it is like: *Here's your chance to sample the delights of country life.*

**sam·pler** /ˈsɑːmplə‖ˈsæmplər/ *n* [C] a piece of cloth with different stitches on it, made to show how good someone is at sewing

**sam·u·rai** /ˈsæmʊraɪ/ *n* [C] *plural* **samurai** a member of a powerful military class in Japan in former times —**samurai** *adj*: *a samurai sword*

**san·a·to·ri·um** /ˌsænəˈtɔːriəm/ *n* [C] a kind of hospital for sick people who are getting better but still need rest and a lot of care

**sanc·ti·fy** /ˈsæŋktɪ̆faɪ/ *v* [T] **1** to make something socially or religiously acceptable or to give something official approval: *sexual roles that are sanctified by marriage* **2** to make something holy —**sanctification** /ˌsæŋktɪ̆fɪ̆ˈkeɪʃən/ *n* [U]

**sanc·ti·mo·ni·ous** /ˌsæŋktɪ̆ˈməʊniəs◂‖-ˈmoʊ-/ *adj formal* behaving as if you are morally better than other people, in a way that is annoying: *sanctimonious politicians preaching to everyone about family values* —**sanctimoniously** *adv* —**sanctimoniousness** *n* [U]

**sanc·tion¹** /ˈsæŋkʃən/ *n* **1** **sanctions** [plural] official orders or laws stopping trade, communication etc with another country, as a way of forcing its leaders to make political changes: [+ **against**] *US sanctions against Cuba* | **impose sanctions on** (=start using sanctions) | **lift sanctions** (=stop using sanctions) **2** [U] official permission, approval, or acceptance: *It emerged that the aide had acted without White House sanction.* **3** [C] a form of punishment that can be used if someone disobeys a rule or law

**sanction²** *v* [T] *formal* **1** to officially accept or allow something: *The church refused to sanction the king's second marriage.* **2** **be sanctioned by** to be made acceptable by something: *a barbaric custom, but one sanctioned by long usage*

**sanc·ti·ty** /ˈsæŋktɪ̆ti/ *n* [U] **1** **the sanctity of life/marriage etc** the quality that makes life, marriage etc so important that it must be respected and preserved: *the sanctity of the Constitution* **2** *formal* the holy or religious character of a person or place: *an aura of sanctity*

**sanc·tu·a·ry** /ˈsæŋktʃuəri,-tʃəri‖-tʃueri/ *n* **1** [C, U] a peaceful place that is safe and provides protection, especially for people who are in danger: **find/seek sanctuary** *Refugees fleeing from the advancing army found sanctuary in Geneva.* **2** [C] an area for birds or animals where they are protected and cannot be hunted: **bird/wildlife etc sanctuary** *The park is the largest wildlife sanctuary in the US.* **3** [U] the right that people had under Christian law, especially in former times, to be protected from police, soldiers etc by staying in a church **4** [C] the part of a religious building that is considered to be the most holy **5** [C] *AmE* the room where religious services take place

**sanc·tum** /ˈsæŋktəm/ *n* [C] **1** **inner sanctum** *often humorous* a place or room that only a few important people are allowed to enter **2** a holy place inside a temple

W3 **sand¹** /sænd/ *n* [U] **1 a)** a substance consisting of very small pieces of rocks and minerals, that forms beaches and deserts: *footprints in the sand* **b)** this substance when it is found in soil, used in building etc: *a mixture of sand and cement* **2** **sands** [plural] *BrE* an area of beach: *miles of golden sands* **3** **the sands of time** *literary* moments of time that pass quickly

**sand²** *v* **1** [I,T] also **sand down** to make a surface smooth by rubbing it with SANDPAPER or using a special piece of equipment **2** [T] to put sand on a frozen road to make it safer

**san·dal** /ˈsændl/ *n* [C] a light shoe that is fastened onto your foot by leather bands and worn in warm weather —see picture at SHOE¹

**san·dal·wood** /ˈsændlwʊd/ *n* [U] pleasant-smelling wood from a Southern Asian tree, or the oil from this wood

**sand·bag** /ˈsændbæg/ *n* [C] a bag filled with sand used for protection against floods, explosions etc

**sand·bank** /ˈsændbæŋk/ *n* [C] a raised area of sand in a river, ocean etc

**sand bar** /ˈ· ·/ *n* [C] a long pile of sand in a river or the ocean formed by the movement of the water

**sand·blast** /ˈsændblɑːst‖-blæst/ *v* [T] to clean or polish metal, stone, glass etc with a machine that sends out a powerful stream of sand

**sand·box** /ˈsændbɒks‖-bɑːks/ *n* [C] *especially AmE* a special area of sand for children to play in; SANDPIT *BrE*

**sand·cas·tle** /ˈsændˌkɑːsəl‖-ˌkæ-/ *n* [C] a small model of a castle made out of sand by children playing on a beach

**sand dune** /ˈ· ·/ *n* [C] a hill formed of sand in a desert or near the sea —see picture on page 835

**sand·er** /ˈsændə‖-ər/ also **sanding ma·chine** /ˈ· · ˌ·/ *n* [C] an electric tool with a rough surface that moves very quickly, used for making surfaces smooth

**sand fly** /ˈ· ·/ *n* [C] a small fly that bites people and lives on beaches

**sand·man** /ˈsændmæn/ *n* [singular] an imaginary man who is supposed to make children go to sleep

**sand·pa·per¹** /ˈsændˌpeɪpə‖-ər/ *n* [U] strong paper covered on one side with sand or a similar substance, used for rubbing wood in order to make the surface smooth

**sandpaper²** *v* [T] to rub something with sandpaper

**sand·pip·er** /ˈsændˌpaɪpə‖-ər/ *n* [C] a small bird with long legs and a long beak that lives around muddy or sandy shores

**sand·pit** /ˈsændˌpɪt/ *n* [C] *BrE* a special area of sand for children to play in SANDBOX *AmE*

**sand·stone** /ˈsændstəʊn‖-stoʊn/ *n* [U] a type of soft yellow or red rock often used in buildings

**sand·storm** /ˈsændstɔːm‖-ɔːrm/ *n* [C] a storm in the desert in which sand is blown around by strong winds

**sand·trap** /ˈsændtræp/ *n* [C] *AmE* a hollow place on a GOLF course, filled with sand, from which it is difficult to hit the ball; BUNKER (3) *BrE* —see picture on page 1264

**sand·wich¹** /ˈsænwɪdʒ‖ˈsændwɪtʃ, ˈsænwɪtʃ/ *n* **1** [C] S3 two pieces of bread with cheese, meat, egg etc between them: *I've brought sandwiches for lunch today.* | *a ham sandwich* **2** [C] *BrE* a cake consisting of two layers with JAM¹ (1) and cream between them —see also CLUB SANDWICH, OPEN SANDWICH

**sandwich²** *v* [T] **be sandwiched between** to be in a very small space between two other things: *The car was sandwiched between two big trucks.*

**sandwich board** /ˈ· · ·/ *n* [C] two boards with advertisements on them that hang in front and behind someone who is paid to walk around in public

**sandwich course** /ˈ· · ·/ *n* [C] *BrE* a course of study at a college or university that includes periods spent working in industry or business

**sand·y** /ˈsændi/ *adj* **1** covered with sand: *My towel's all sandy!* | **sandy beach** *BrE* (=one that is made of sand not stones) **2** hair that is sandy is a yellowish-brown —**sandiness** *n* [U] —see picture on page 835

**sane** /seɪn/ *adj* **1** able to think in a normal and reasonable way —opposite INSANE **2** reasonable and based on sensible thinking: *a sane solution to a delicate problem* **3 keep sb sane** to stop someone from thinking about their problems and becoming upset —**sanely** *adv* —see also SANITY

**sang** /sæŋ/ the past tense of SING

**sang-froid** /ˌsɒŋ ˈfrwɑː‖ˌsɑːŋ-/ *n* [U] courage and the ability to keep calm in dangerous or difficult situations: *The British, once renowned for their stiff upper lip and sang-froid, were now regarded as a nation of hooligans.*

**san·gri·a** /sæŋˈgriːə, sæn-, ˈsæŋgriə/ *n* [U] a Spanish drink made from red wine, fruit, and fruit juice

**san·gui·na·ry** /ˈsæŋgwɪ̈nəri‖-neri/ *adj formal* involving violence and killing: *a bitter and sanguinary war*

**san·guine** /ˈsæŋgwɪ̈n/ *adj formal* **1** cheerful and hopeful about the future; CONFIDENT: *We are less sanguine about the prospects for peace since the row at the UN.* **2** red and healthy looking: *a sanguine complexion* —**sanguinely** *adv*

**san·i·tar·i·um** /ˌsænɪ̈ˈteəriəm‖-ˈter-/ *n* [C] an American spelling of SANATORIUM

**san·i·ta·ry** /ˈsænɪ̈təri‖-teri/ *adj* **1** [only before noun] connected with health, especially with the removal of dirt, infection, or human waste: *After examining the sanitary arrangements, they ordered the whole place to be disinfected.* **2** clean and not involving any danger to your health —opposite INSANITARY

**sanitary pad** /ˈ···· ˌ·/ also **sanitary tow·el** /ˈ···· ˌ··/ *BrE*, also **sanitary napkin** *AmE* —*n* [C] a piece of soft material that a woman wears between her legs during her PERIOD[1] (4)

**san·i·ta·tion** /ˌsænɪ̈ˈteɪʃən/ *n* [U] the protection of public health by removing and treating waste, dirty water etc

**sanitation work·er** /ˌ··ˈ·· ˌ··/ *n* [C] *AmE formal* someone who removes waste material that people put outside their houses

**san·i·tize** also **-ise** *BrE* /ˈsænɪ̈taɪz/ *v* [T] **1** to make news, literature etc less offensive by taking out anything unpleasant, with the result that it is not complete or interesting: *The film is a highly sanitized version of his life, making no mention of his many affairs.* **2** to clean something thoroughly, removing dirt and BACTERIA

**san·i·ty** /ˈsænɪ̈ti/ *n* [U] **1** the ability to think in a normal and sensible way: *I took a vacation by myself to try to regain my sanity.* **2** the condition of being mentally healthy: *The man's story became stranger and stranger, and I began to doubt his sanity.* —opposite INSANITY

**sank** /sæŋk/ the past tense of SINK

**San·skrit** /ˈsænskrɪt/ *n* [U] an ancient language of India

**sans ser·if** /ˌsæn ˈserɪ̈f, ˌsænz-/ *n* [U] *technical* a style of printing in which letters have no SERIF

**San·ta Claus** /ˈsæntə klɔːz‖ˈsænti klɒːz, ˈsæntə-/ also **Santa** *n* [singular] an imaginary old man with red clothes and a long white BEARD who, children believe, brings them presents at Christmas; FATHER CHRISTMAS *BrE*

**sap[1]** /sæp/ *n* **1** [U] the watery substance that carries food through a plant **2** [C] *AmE informal* a stupid person who is easy to deceive or treat badly **3 feel the sap rising** *humorous* to begin to feel full of energy, especially in a sexual way

**sap[2]** *v* **sapped, sapping** [T] to gradually weaken or destroy something: **sap sb's courage/energy/strength** *Her long illness was gradually sapping Charlotte's strength.*

**sa·pi·ent** /ˈseɪpiənt/ *adj literary* very wise —**sapiently** *adv* —**sapience** *n* [U]

**sap·ling** /ˈsæplɪŋ/ *n* [C] a young tree

**sap·per** /ˈsæpə‖-ər/ *n* [C] *BrE* a soldier whose job involves digging and building

**sap·phic** /ˈsæfɪk/ *adj literary* LESBIAN

**sap·phire** /ˈsæfaɪə‖-faɪr/ *n* [C,U] a transparent bright blue jewel

**sap·py** /ˈsæpi/ *adj* **1** *AmE* expressing love and emotions in a way that seems silly; SOPPY (1) *BrE*: *a sappy song* **2** full of SAP (=liquid in a plant)

**sap·ro·phyte** /ˈsæprəfaɪt/ *n* [C] a kind of plant that eats substances that were once living —**saprophytic** /ˌsæprəˈfɪtɪk/ *adj*

**sap·wood** /ˈsæpwʊd/ *n* [U] the younger outer wood in a tree, that is paler and softer than the wood in the middle

**sar·a·band** /ˈsærəbænd/ *n* [C] a slow piece of music based on a type of 17th century dance

**Sar·a·cen** /ˈsærəsən/ *n* [C] *old use* a word for a Muslim, used in the Middle Ages

**Sa·ran Wrap** /səˈræn ræp/ *n* [U] *AmE trademark* thin transparent plastic used for wrapping food; CLINGFILM *BrE*

**sar·cas·m** /ˈsɑːkæzəm‖ˈsɑːr-/ *n* [U] a way of speaking or writing that involves saying the opposite of what you really mean in order to make an unkind joke or to show that you are annoyed: **heavy scarcasm** (=very clear sarcasm) *She was an hour late. "Good of you to arrive on time," George said, with heavy sarcasm.*

**sar·cas·tic** /sɑːˈkæstɪk‖sɑːr-/ *adj* saying things that are the opposite of what you mean in order to make an unkind joke or to show that you are annoyed: *a sarcastic remark* —**sarcastically** /-kli/ *adv*

**sar·coph·a·gus** /sɑːˈkɒfəgəs‖sɑːrˈkɑː-/ *n* [C] a decorated stone box for a dead body, used in ancient times

**sar·dine** /ˌsɑːˈdiːn◂‖ˌsɑːr-/ *n* **1** [C] a small young fish that is often packed in flat metal boxes **2 be packed like sardines** to be crowded tightly together in a small space: *commuters packed like sardines on the evening train*

**sar·don·ic** /sɑːˈdɒnɪk‖sɑːrˈdɑːnɪk/ *adj* speaking or smiling in an unpleasant way, that shows you do not have a good opinion of someone or something: *Brett raised a sardonic eyebrow.* —**sardonically** /-kli/ *adv*

**sa·ree** /ˈsɑːri/ *n* [C] another spelling of sari

**sarge** /sɑːdʒ‖sɑːrdʒ/ *n* [singular] *spoken* SERGEANT

**sa·ri** /ˈsɑːri/ *n* [C] a long piece of cloth that you wrap around your body, worn especially by women from India

sari

**sar·ky** /ˈsɑːki‖ˈsɑːr-/ *adj BrE informal* SARCASTIC

**sar·nie** /ˈsɑːni‖ˈsɑːr-/ *n* [C] *BrE informal* a SANDWICH

**sa·rong** /səˈrɒŋ‖səˈrɒːŋ, səˈrɑːŋ/ *n* [C] a loose skirt consisting of a long piece of cloth wrapped around your waist

**sarsa·pa·ril·la** /ˌsɑːspəˈrɪlə‖ˌsæs-/ *n* [U] a sweet non-alcoholic drink made from the root of the SASSAFRAS plant

**sar·to·ri·al** /sɑːˈtɔːriəl‖sɑːr-/ *adj formal* connected with men's clothes or how they are made: **sartorial elegance** *a man of great sartorial elegance* —**sartorially** *adv*

**SAS** /ˌes eɪ ˈes/ *n* [singular] Special Air Service; a British military force that is specially trained to do secret and dangerous work

**SASE** /ˌes eɪ es ˈi/ *n* [C] *AmE* self-addressed stamped envelope; an envelope that you put your name, address, and a stamp on, so that someone else can send you something

**sash** /sæʃ/ *n* [C] **1** a long piece of cloth that you wear around your waist like a belt: *a party dress with a blue sash* **2** a long piece of cloth that you wear over one shoulder and across your chest as a sign of a special honour: *a sash with the words Miss USA* **3** a wooden frame that has a sheet of glass fixed into it to form part of a window

**sa·shay** /sæ'ʃeɪ/ *v* [I always + adv/prep] *informal* to walk in a confident way moving your body from side to side, especially so that people look at you: *Olivia sashayed down the catwalk.*

**sash win·dow** /'· ,··/ *n* [C] a window consisting of two frames that you open by sliding one up or down, behind or in front of the other

**sass** /sæs/ *v* [T] *AmE informal* to talk in a rude way to someone you should respect: *Don't you sass me young lady!*

**sas·sa·fras** /'sæsəfræs/ *n* [C,U] a small Asian or North American tree, or the pleasant-smelling roots of this tree used in food and drink

**Sas·se·nach** /'sæsənæk/ *n* [C] *ScotE* a word meaning an English person, used as a joke or to show disapproval

**sas·sy** /'sæsi/ *adj AmE* **1** a child who is sassy is rude to someone they should respect **2** a woman who is sassy behaves in a way that is intended to be attractive to men

**Sat** a written abbreviation SATURDAY

**sat** /sæt/ the past tense and past participle of SIT

**Sa·tan** /'seɪtn/ *n* [singular] the Devil, considered to be the main evil power and God's opponent

**sa·tan·ic** /sə'tænɪk/ *adj* **1** connected with practices that treat the Devil like a god: *satanic rites* **2** extremely cruel or evil: *satanic laughter* —**satanically** /-kli/ *adv*

**sat·an·is·m** /'seɪt ənɪzəm/ *n* [U] the practice of respecting the Devil as if he were a god —**satanist** *n* [C] —**satanist** *adj*

**sat·ay sauce** /,sæteɪ 'sɔːs‖,sɑːteɪ 'sɒːs/ *n* [U] a thick liquid made with PEANUTS and used to give a special taste to meat

**satch·el** /'sætʃəl/ *n* [C] a leather bag that you carry over your shoulder, used especially in the past by children for carrying books to school —see picture at BAG[1]

**sate** /seɪt/ *v* [T] *literary* **be sated (with)** to have had enough or more than enough of something to satisfy you

**sat·el·lite** /'sætḷlaɪt/ *n* [C] **1** a machine that has been sent into space and goes around the Earth, moon etc, used for radio, television, and other electronic communication: *the launch of a communications and weather satellite* | **by satellite** (=using a satellite) *This broadcast comes live by satellite from New York.* **2** a moon that moves around a PLANET: *The moon is a satellite of the Earth.* **3 a)** a country, town, or organization that is controlled by or is dependent on another larger one: **satellite country/town/suburb** (=one that has developed next to a large city)

**satellite dish** /'··· ,·/ *n* [C] a large circular piece of metal that receives special television signals so that you can watch satellite television

satellite dish

**satellite tel·e·vi·sion** /,··· '····, ,···'··/ also **satellite TV** /,··· ·'·/ *n* [U] television programmes that are broadcast using satellites in space

**sa·ti·ate** /'seɪʃieɪt/ *v* [T usually passive] *literary* to satisfy a desire or need for something such as food or sex, especially so that you feel you have had too much —**satiated** *adj*: *Zeke lay on the couch, satiated after his meal.* —**satiety** /sə'taɪəti/ *n* [U]

**sat·in[1]** /'sætḷn‖'sætn/ *n* [U] a type of cloth that is very smooth and shiny

**satin[2]** *adj* having a smooth shiny surface

**sat·in·wood** /'sætḷnwʊd‖'sætn-/ *n* [C,U] an East Indian tree, or the hard smooth wood that comes from this tree

**sat·in·y** /'sætḷni‖'sætni/ *adj* smooth, shiny, and soft

## ● ● ● ● Position and Direction ● ● ● ●

*The prepositions below refer to the picture opposite.*

" Good Afternoon Ladies and Gentlemen. Welcome to the 6th national cycle race.

It's turning into quite a day! **All about / around** me people are leaning **over**① the barriers to get a good view of the race. Local residents are hanging **out**② of their windows, and **beyond** the spectators, traffic is **at**③ a standstill.

The police are out in full force. There's a police motorbike **next to / beside / alongside**④ the cyclists, a policewoman leaning **on**⑤ the barriers, and a helicopter **overhead**⑥.

Not far **from** me, **in / among** the crowd I can see last year's champion with his daughter **on**⑦ his shoulders. And **off** to the right, there are a number of fans pushing their way **through**⑧ the crowd **to / towards** the front.

**Across**⑨ the finishing line **in** first place comes number thirty four. Directly **in front**⑩ of me photographers are trying to get shots of the winner, and just **below / beneath / underneath**⑪ me jubilant fans are cheering.

**On / to**⑫ the left of the new champion, cycling **past** the photographers is number sixty one. Then, **behind**⑬ the leaders, **in** a red helmet is De Kosten **from** Belgium who is racing **towards / in the direction of** the finishing line. Chasing **after**⑭ him are numbers ninety two and a hundred and five, and at this very moment a small group of cyclists have just come **round**⑮ the corner **into** view. "

POLICE
6
3
15
2
4
14
13
11
1
12
61
34
10
FINISH
9
8
7
5
Jupiter

cracked plaster
broken windowpane
rusty window frame
tattered curtains
peeling paintwork
leaky pipe
frayed cushions
faded sofa
wilted flowers
torn spine
dusty table top
ripped cover
dog-eared pages
chipped cup
worm-eaten table
threadbare rug
rickety chair
crumpled paper
stained carpet

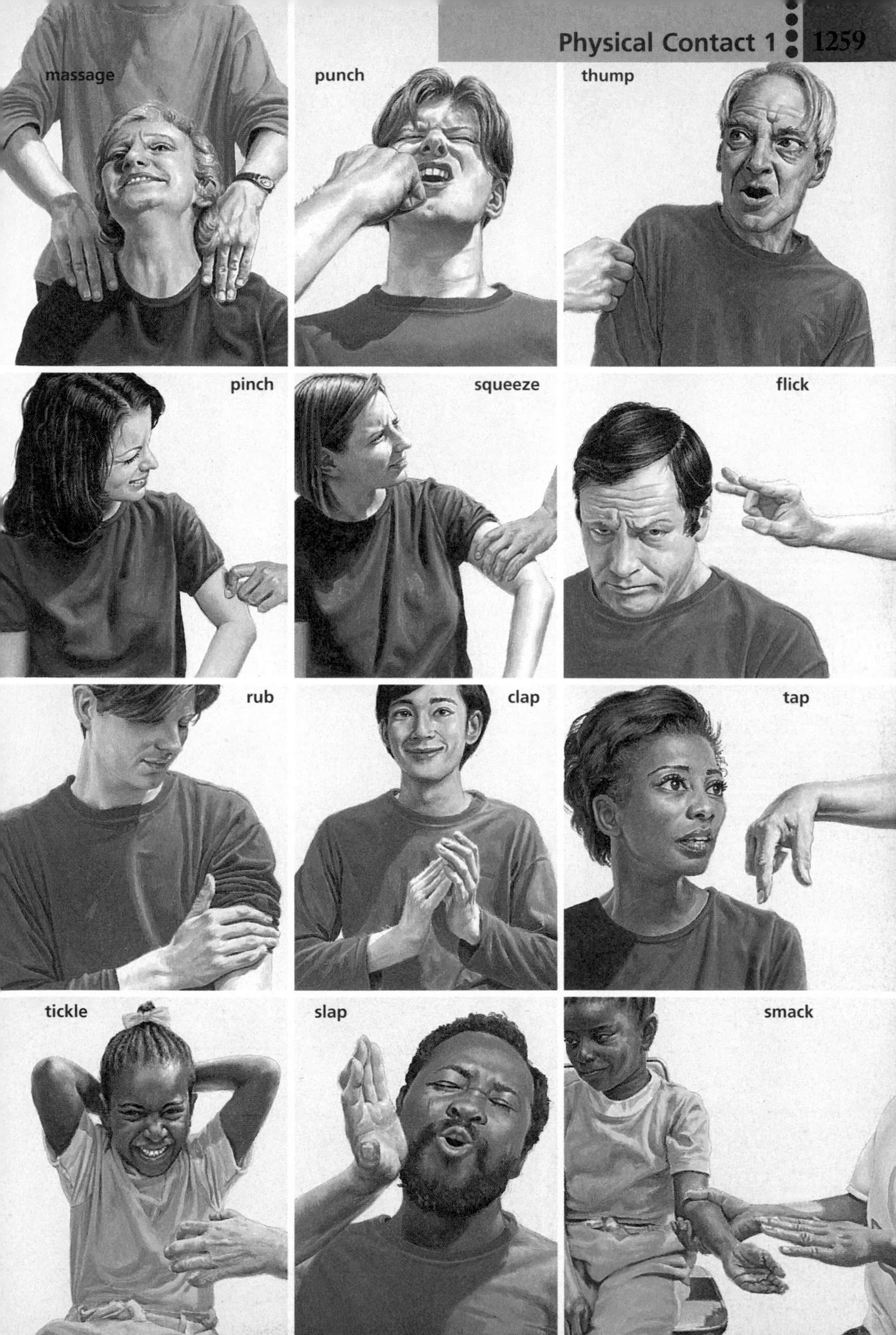
massage
punch
thump
pinch
squeeze
flick
rub
clap
tap
tickle
slap
smack

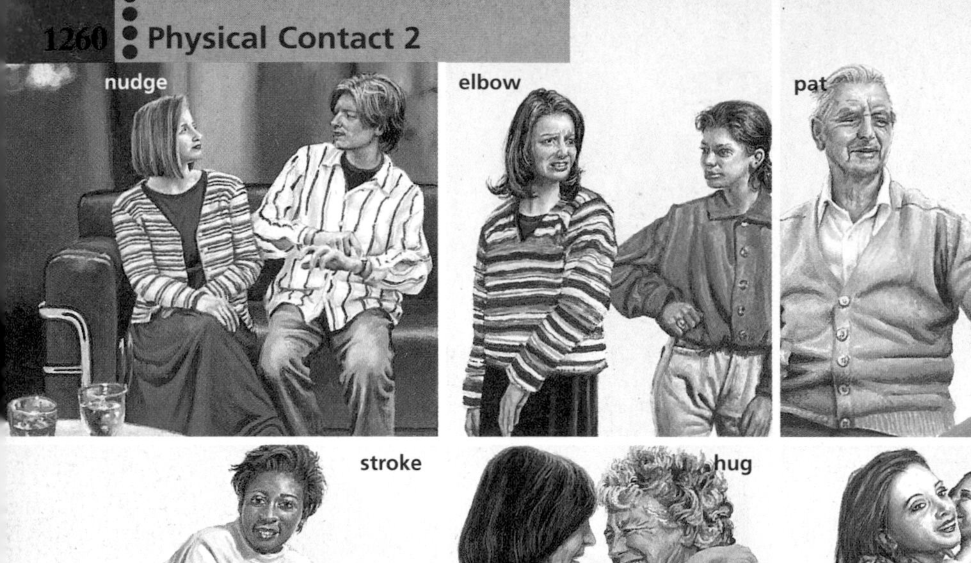

nudge

elbow

pat

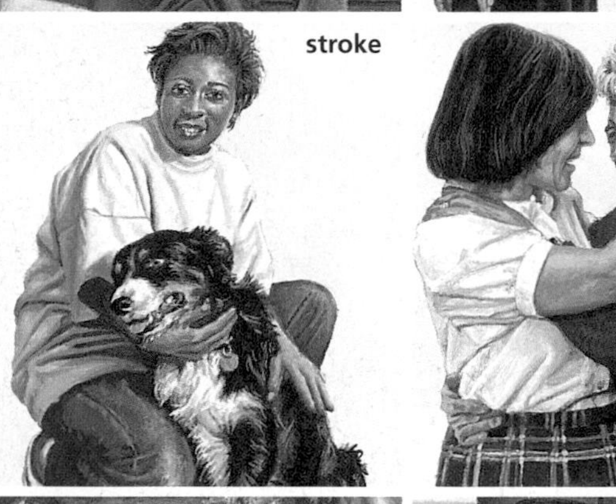

stroke

hug

cuddle

feel

frisk

pull / drag

prod / poke

push / shove

chop

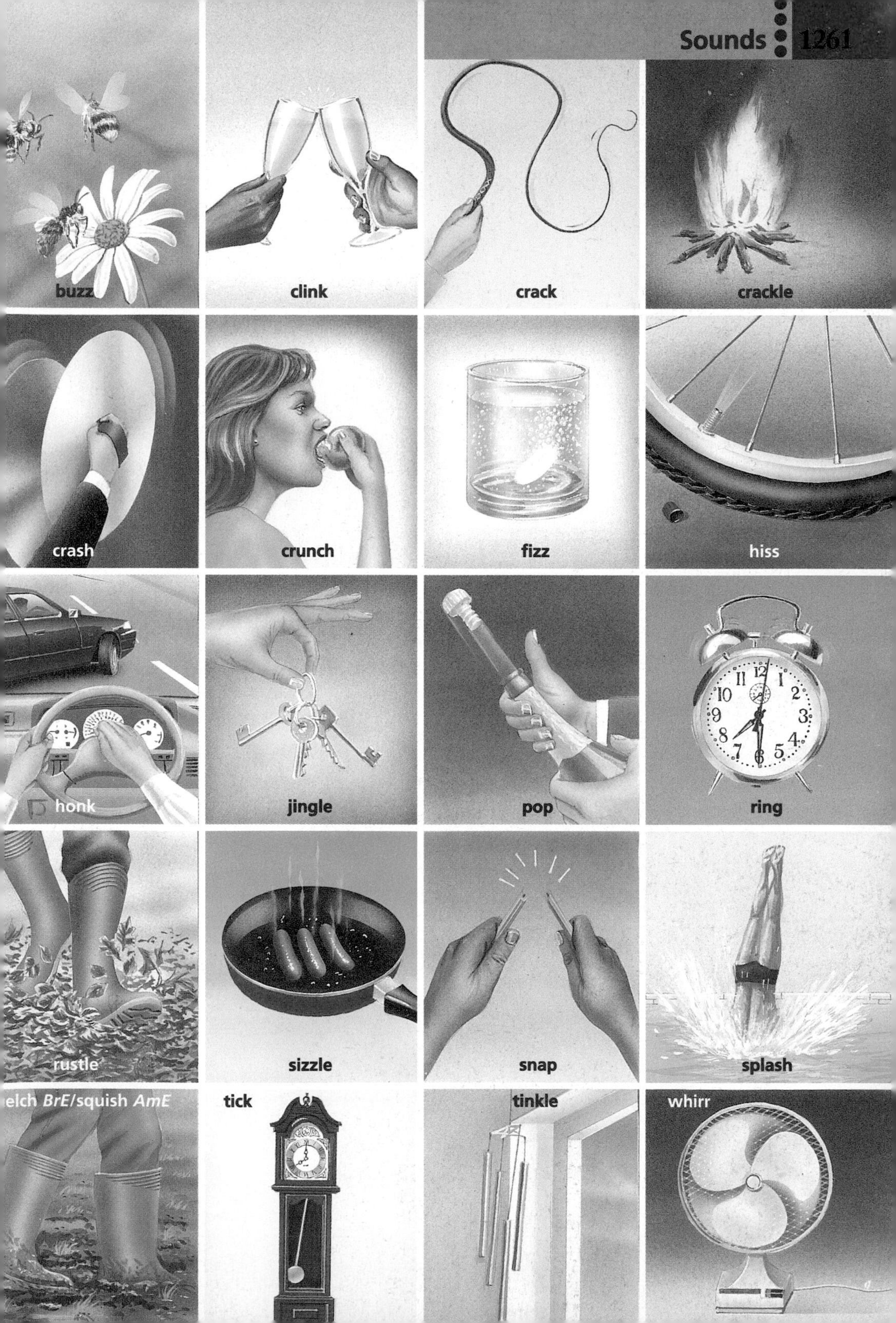
buzz
clink
crack
crackle
crash
crunch
fizz
hiss
honk
jingle
pop
ring
rustle
sizzle
snap
splash
elch BrE/squish AmE
tick
tinkle
whirr

Liz **crept** upstairs trying not to wake her parents.

She **tiptoed** along the landing.

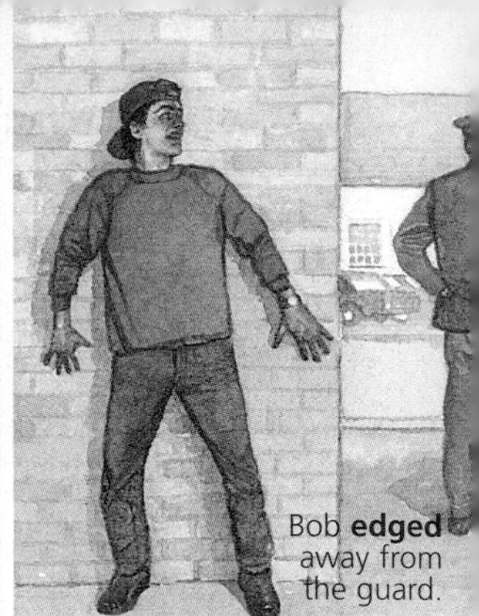
Bob **edged** away from the guard.

Garcia **limped** off in agony.

Granny **shuffled** across the room.

She **trudged** home with the shopping.

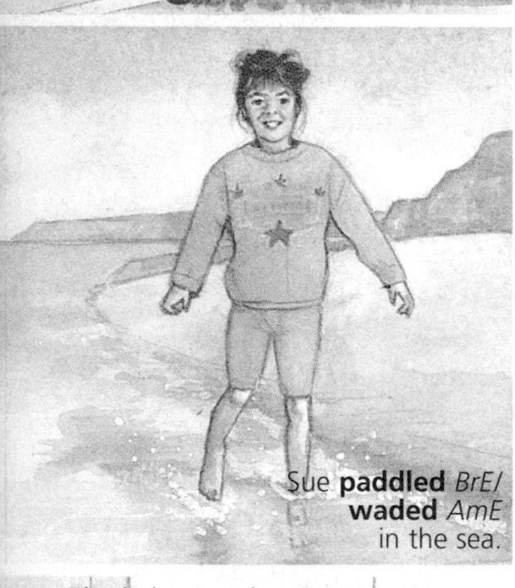
Sue **paddled** *BrE*/ **waded** *AmE* in the sea.

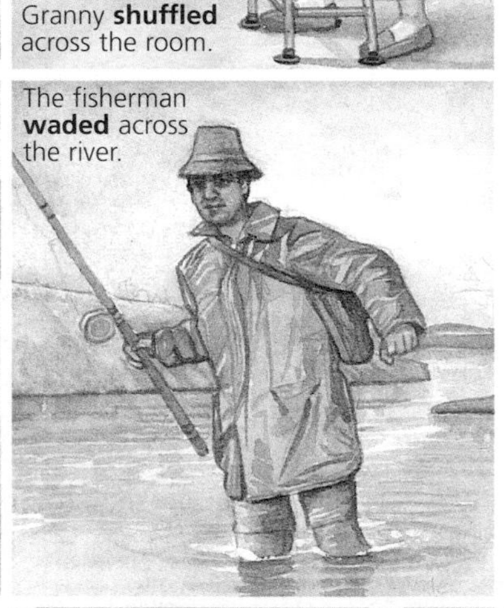
The fisherman **waded** across the river.

He **paced** up and down waiting for news.

The baby stood and **tottered** forwards.

He **staggered** under the weight of the box.

We took a **stroll** in the park.

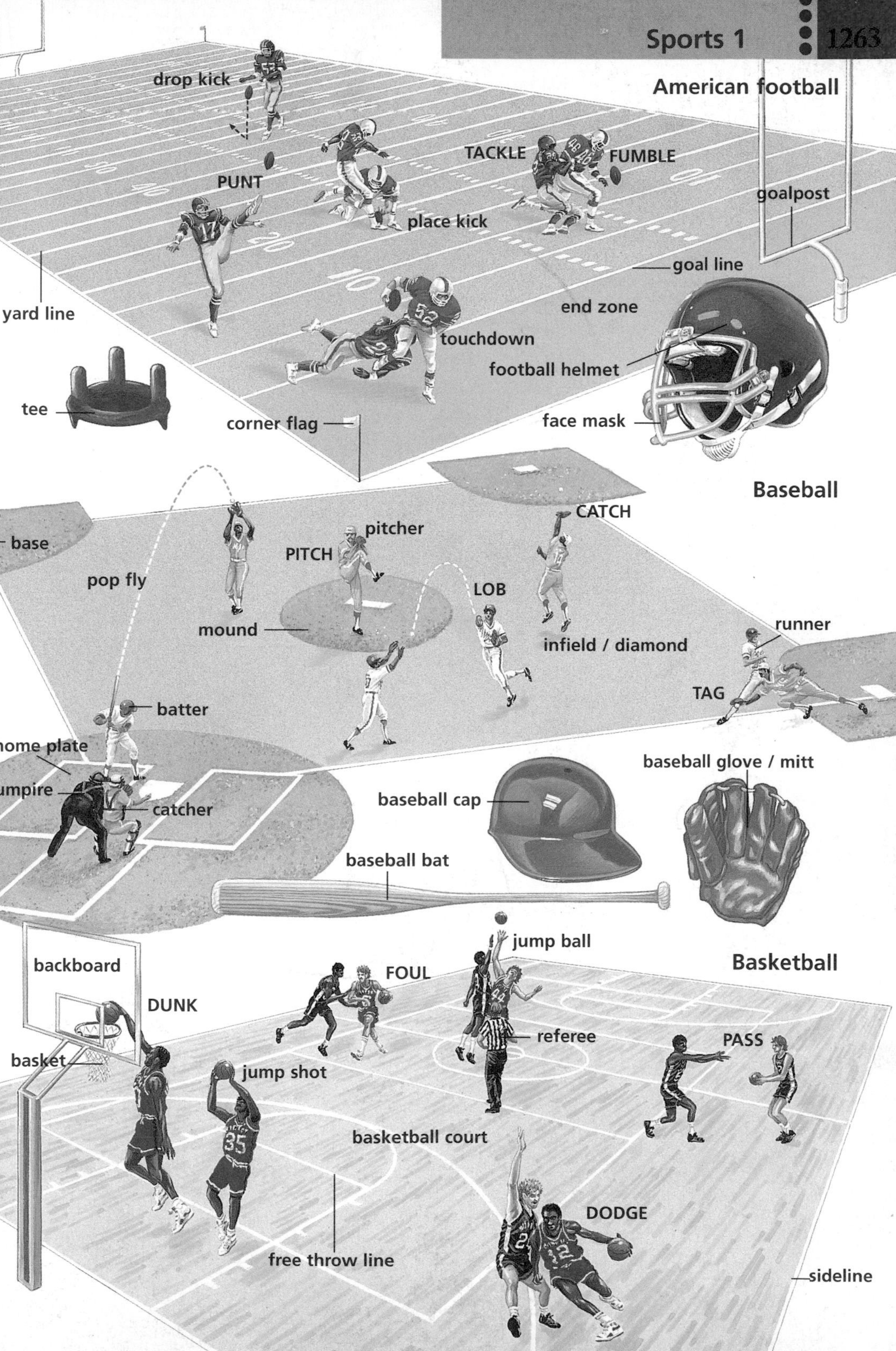
American football
drop kick
TACKLE
FUMBLE
PUNT
goalpost
place kick
goal line
yard line
end zone
touchdown
football helmet
tee
corner flag
face mask
Baseball
CATCH
base
pitcher
PITCH
pop fly
LOB
runner
mound
infield / diamond
TAG
batter
home plate
baseball glove / mitt
umpire
baseball cap
catcher
baseball bat
jump ball
backboard
Basketball
FOUL
DUNK
referee
PASS
basket
jump shot
basketball court
DODGE
free throw line
sideline

Badminton
net
overarm
MISS
smash
forehand volley
service court
underarm
serve
umpire
short service line
long service line
(doubles)
backhand
string
shaft
grip / handle
long service
line (singles)
shuttlecock
badminton racket
Football / Soccer
linesman
red card
SEND OFF
obstruction
HEAD
DRIBBLE
crossbar
penalty spot
TACKLE
SHOOT
throw-in
SAVE
goal
penalty area
goalkeeper /
goalie
corner
caddie
Golf
bunker BrE/
sand trap AmE
rough
fairway
headcover
PUTT
green
follow - through
golf
clubs
hole BrE/ cup AmE
tee
DRIVE
putter
iron
wood
golf
cart

**sat·ire** /ˈsætaɪə‖-taɪr/ *n* **1** [U] a way of talking or writing about something, for example politics and politicians, in which you deliberately make them seem funny so that people will see their faults: *the characteristic use of satire in Jonson's work* **2** [C] a play, book, story etc written in this way: *a political satire* —**satirical** /səˈtɪrɪkəl/ *adj* —**satiric** *adj* —**satirically** /-kli/ *adv*

**sat·i·rist** /ˈsætɪrɪst/ *n* [C] someone who writes satire

**sat·ir·ize** also **-ise** *BrE* /ˈsætɪraɪz/ *v* [T] to use satire to make people see someone or something's faults: *a play satirizing the fashion industry*

S3 W3 **sat·is·fac·tion** /ˌsætɪsˈfækʃən/ *n* **1** [C,U] a feeling of happiness or pleasure because you have achieved something or got what you wanted: *She got great satisfaction from helping people learn.* | *a sigh of deep satisfaction* | **job satisfaction** (=enjoyment of your job) —opposite DISSATISFACTION **2** [U] fulfilment of a need, demand, claim, desire etc: *the satisfaction of public demand* | *sexual satisfaction* **3** [U] *formal* a reply to a complaint that you have made: **get satisfaction** *I got no satisfaction from the customer complaints department.* **4 have/get the satisfaction of doing sth** to get a small amount of pleasure from a situation that is unsatisfactory in other ways: *Well, at least you'll get the satisfaction of knowing you were right.* **5 to sb's/sth's satisfaction a)** if something is explained, proved etc to someone's satisfaction, they now accept and believe it **b)** if a situation, arrangement etc is to someone's satisfaction, they are pleased with it: *Finally we got the furniture arranged to her satisfaction.*

**sat·is·fac·to·ry** /ˌsætɪsˈfæktəri◂/ *adj* **1** good enough for a particular situation or purpose: *Reicher could not provide a satisfactory excuse for his absence.* | *None of the solutions was entirely satisfactory.* **2** making you feel pleased and happy: *a satisfactory conclusion* —**satisfactorily** *adv* —opposite UNSATISFACTORY

S3 **sat·is·fied** /ˈsætɪsfaɪd/ *adj* **1** pleased because something has happened in the way that you want, or because you have achieved something: *a satisfied smile* | [**+ with**] *I'm not really satisfied with the way he cut my hair.* —opposite DISSATISFIED **2** feeling sure that something is right or true: [**+ that**] *The police weren't satisfied that Boyet was telling the truth.* **3 satisfied?** *spoken* used to show that someone has annoyed you by asking too many questions or making too many demands: *Okay, okay, I'll go over there and ask him this afternoon. Satisfied?* —see also SELF-SATISFIED

S2 W2 **sat·is·fy** /ˈsætɪsfaɪ/ *v* [T] **1** to please someone by providing enough of what they want: *Nick felt that nothing he did would satisfy his boss.* **2 satisfy a request, desire, need etc** to provide what someone has asked for, what they need etc: *Just to satisfy my curiosity, how much did it cost?* | *The salad just didn't satisfy her hunger.* **3** *formal* to make someone feel sure that something is right or true; CONVINCE: **satisfy sb of sth** *Jackson tried to satisfy me of his innocence.* **4** *formal* to be good enough for a particular purpose, standard etc: *You have not yet satisfied all the conditions for admission.* **5** *formal* to find the correct answer to an EQUATION (1) in mathematics, etc

**sat·is·fy·ing** /ˈsætɪsfaɪ-ɪŋ/ *adj* **1** making you feel pleased and happy, especially because you have got what you wanted: **it is satisfying to do sth** *After all he'd put me through, it was very satisfying to see him begging for once.* **2** food that is satisfying makes you feel that you have eaten enough: *a satisfying meal* —**satisfyingly** *adv*

**sat·su·ma** /sætˈsuːmə/ *n* [C] a fruit that looks like a small orange, and has no seeds

**sat·u·rate** /ˈsætʃəreɪt/ *v* [T] **1** *formal* to make something very wet; SOAK[1] (2): *Water poured through the hole, saturating the carpet.* **2** to put a large number of people or things into a particular place, especially so that you could not add any more: *The area was saturated with police to prevent further trouble.* **3 saturate the market** to offer so much of a product for sale that there is more than people want to buy **4** *technical* to mix as much of a solid into a chemical mixture as possible

**sat·u·rat·ed** /ˈsætʃəreɪtɪd/ *adj* **1** extremely wet: *By the time I arrived home, I was completely saturated.* | [**+ with**] *saturated with sweat* **2** *technical* if a chemical mixture is saturated, it has had as much of a solid mixed into it as possible

**saturated fat** /ˌ···· ˈ·/ *n* [C,U] a kind of fat from meat and milk products that is thought to be less healthy than other kinds of fat from vegetables or fish

**sat·u·ra·tion** /ˌsætʃəˈreɪʃən/ *n* [U] **1** the act or result of making something completely wet **2 saturation bombing** a military attack in which a whole area is bombed **3 saturation coverage** a situation in which a particular event is given so much attention by newspapers, television etc that everyone has heard about it: *The trial was given saturation coverage by the press.* **4** *technical* the state of a chemical mixture that has reached its SATURATION POINT (2)

**saturation point** /··ˈ·· ·/ *n* [C usually singular] **1** a situation in which no more people or things can be added because there are already too many: *The number of summer tourists in the area has now reached saturation point.* **2** *technical* the state that a chemical mixture reaches when it has had as much of a solid substance mixed into it as possible

**Sat·ur·day** /ˈsætədi‖-ər-/ *n* [C,U] the day between Friday and Sunday. In Britain, Saturday is considered the sixth day of the week, and in the US it is considered the seventh day of the week: **on Saturday** *We went for a picnic on Saturday.* | *Deats always goes home on Saturdays.* | **last/next Saturday** *I saw Sally last Saturday at the Mall.* | **on a Saturday** *My birthday is on a Saturday this year.*

**Sat·urn** /ˈsætən‖-ərn/ *n* [singular] the PLANET that is sixth in order from the sun and is surrounded by large rings —see picture at SOLAR SYSTEM

**sat·ur·na·li·a** /ˌsætəˈneɪliə‖-tər-/ *n* [C] *literary* an occasion when people enjoy themselves in a very wild and uncontrolled way

**sat·ur·nine** /ˈsætənaɪn‖-ər-/ *adj literary* looking sad and serious, especially in a threatening way: *Goebbel's lean saturnine face had the hypnotic power of a swaying cobra.*

**sat·yr** /ˈsætə‖-ər/ *n* [C] a god in ancient Greek literature, represented as half human and half goat

**sauce** /sɔːs‖sɒːs/ *n* **1** [C,U] a thick cooked liquid that is served with food to give it a particular taste: **tomato/chocolate etc sauce** *pasta with tomato sauce* **2** [U] *BrE old-fashioned* rude remarks made to someone that you should respect: *Less of your sauce, my girl!*

**sauce boat** /ˈ· ·/ *n* [C] a container that has a handle and is shaped like a boat, used for serving sauce with a meal

**sauce·pan** /ˈsɔːspæn, -pən‖ˈsɒːs-/ *n* [C] a deep round metal container with a handle that is used for cooking —see picture at PAN[1]

**sau·cer** /ˈsɔːsə‖ˈsɒːsər/ *n* [C] a small round plate that curves up at the edges that you put a cup on —see also FLYING SAUCER

**sauc·y** /ˈsɔːsi‖ˈsɒːsi/ *adj* **1** *especially BrE* saucy pictures, jokes etc are about sex in a way that is amusing but not shocking: *saucy postcards* **2** slightly rude, in a way that is amusing: *a saucy remark* —**saucily** *adv* —**sauciness** *n* [U] —see also SAUCE (2)

**sau·er·kraut** /ˈsaʊəkraʊt‖-ər-/ *n* [U] a German food made from CABBAGE (=a round green vegetable) that has been left in salt so that it tastes sour

**sau·na** /ˈsaʊnə, ˈsɔːnə‖ˈsaʊnə/ *n* [C] **1** a room that is heated to a very high temperature by hot air, where people sit because it is considered healthy **2** a period of time when you sit or lie in a room like this: **have/take a sauna** *I have a sauna and massage every week.*

**saun·ter** /ˈsɔːntə‖ˈsɒːntər/ *v* [I always + adv/prep] to walk in a slow unhurried way, that makes you look confident or proud: *Will came sauntering down the road with his hands in his pockets.* —**saunter** *n* [singular]

S3 **saus·age** /ˈsɒsɪdʒ‖ˈsɒː-/ *n* [C,U] **1** [C] a small tube of skin filled with a mixture of meat, SPICES etc, eaten hot or cold: *pork sausages* **2 not a sausage!** *BrE old-fashioned, informal* nothing at all: *"Have you heard from Tom yet?" "No, not a sausage!"*

**sausage dog** /ˈ·· ·/ *n* [C] *BrE informal* a DACHSHUND

**sausage meat** /ˈ·· ·/ *n* [U] the soft meat mixture that is used to make sausages

**sausage roll** /ˌ·· ˈ·/ *n* [C] *BrE* a piece of sausage meat inside a tube of PASTRY

**sau·té** /ˈsəʊteɪ‖soʊˈteɪ/ *v* [T] to cook something quickly in a little hot oil or fat: *Sauté the potatoes for 5 minutes.*

**sav·age¹** /ˈsævɪdʒ/ *adj* **1** very cruel and violent: *a savage dog|The punishment seemed too savage.* **2** criticizing someone or something very severely: **savage attack/criticism etc** *an unexpectedly savage attack on the President's record* **3** very severe and harmful: *savage pay cuts* **4** [only before noun] *old-fashioned* an insulting way of describing a person or group from a country where the way of living seems very simple and undeveloped; PRIMITIVE¹ (1) —**savagely** *adv* —**savageness** *n* [U]

**savage²** *n* [C] *old-fashioned* an insulting word for someone from a country where the way of living seems very simple and undeveloped: *This culture flourished while Europeans were still savages living in caves.*

**savage³** *v* [T] **1** if an animal savages someone, it attacks and bites them, causing serious injuries: *savaged by a mad dog* **2** to criticize someone or something very severely: *The play was savaged by the critics.*

S

**sav·ag·e·ry** /ˈsævɪdʒəri/ *n* [C,U] extremely cruel and violent behaviour: *He used to beat the boy with great savagery.*

**sa·van·na, savannah** /səˈvænə/ *n* [C,U] a large flat area of grassy land in a warm part of the world

**sav·ant** /ˈsævənt‖səˈvɑːnt, sæ-/ *n* [C] *literary* someone who knows a lot about a particular subject

S1 W1 **save¹** /seɪv/ *v*

**1** ▶ **FROM HARM/DANGER** ◀ [T] to make someone or something safe from danger, harm, or destruction: *Thousands of lives have been saved by this drug.*|**save sb/sth from** *He saved his friend from drowning.*|*The sudden fall in interest rates saved the company from bankruptcy.*

**2** ▶ **MONEY IN A BANK** ◀ also **save up** [I,T] to keep money so that you can use it later, especially when you gradually add more money over a period of time: **[+ for]** *I'm saving up for a new car.*|*So far, I've saved about £500.* —see also SAVER

**3** ▶ **NOT WASTE** ◀ [T] to use less money, time, energy etc so that you do not waste any: *We'll save a lot of time if we go by car.*|*modern energy-saving devices*|**save sb sth** *Reserving a seat in advance could save you $10.*

**4** ▶ **TO USE LATER** ◀ [T] to keep something so that you can use or enjoy it in the future: *Let's save the rest of the cake for later.*|*He saved his strength for the end of the race.*

**5** ▶ **COLLECT** ◀ also **save** sth ↔ **up** [T] to keep all the objects of a particular kind that you can find, so that they can be used for a special purpose: *She always saved foreign stamps for her grandson's album.*|*I'm saving up tokens for a free set of wine glasses.*

**6** ▶ **HELP TO AVOID** ◀ [T] to help someone by making it unnecessary for them to do something unpleasant or inconvenient: **save sb sth** *If you could lend me £5, it would save me a trip to the bank.*|**save sb doing sth** *A brush with a long handle will save you having to bend down.*|**save sb the trouble/bother (of doing sth)** *I'll wash up and save you the trouble of doing it later.*

**7** ▶ **KEEP FOR SB** ◀ [T] to stop people from using something so that it is available for someone else: **save sb sth** *Will you save me a seat on the bus?*|**save sth for sb** *We'll save some dinner for you if you're late.*

**8 save sb's life** to prevent someone from dying: *Surgeons operated in an attempt to save her life.*

**9 you saved my life** *spoken* used to thank someone who has got you out of a difficult situation or solved a problem for you: *Thanks again for the loan – you really saved my life.*

**10 save sb's skin/neck/bacon etc** *informal* to make it possible for someone to escape from an extremely difficult or dangerous situation: *He lied in court to save his skin.*

**11 save the day** to make a situation end successfully when it seemed likely to end badly: *Frank saved the day by offering to drive us all there.*

**12 save face** to do something that will stop you looking stupid or feeling embarrassed —see also FACE-SAVING

**13 saving grace** the one good thing that makes someone or something acceptable: *Beautiful photography was the saving grace of an otherwise awful film.*

**14 not be able to do sth to save your life** *informal* to be completely unable to do something: *He couldn't paint to save his life!*

**15 save your breath** *spoken* used to tell someone that it is not worth saying anything, because nothing they say will make any difference to the situation

**16 save sb from themselves** to prevent someone from doing something that is likely to harm them in the end

**17** ▶ **SPORT** ◀ [T] to stop the other side from getting a GOAL (2) in a sport such as football, HOCKEY etc —see picture on page 1264

**18** ▶ **COMPUTER** ◀ [I,T] to make a computer keep the work that you have done on it: *Don't forget to save before you close the file.*

**19** ▶ **RELIGION** ◀ [I,T] in the Christian church, to free someone from the power of evil and SIN: *Jesus came to save sinners.*

**save on** sth *phr v* [T] to avoid wasting something by using as little as possible of it: *We use a wood stove to save on electricity.*

**save²** *n* [C] an action by the GOALKEEPER in football, HOCKEY etc that prevents the other team from getting a GOAL (2)

**save³** also **saving** *prep formal* except for: *She answered all the questions save one.*|**[+that]** *I agree with you, save that you've got one or two details wrong.*

**sav·er** /ˈseɪvə‖-ər/ *n* [C] *especially BrE* someone who saves money in a bank or BUILDING SOCIETY|**regular saver** (=someone who usually saves money with a particular bank etc) *Regular savers can benefit from a 3% annual bonus.*

**savi·ng** /ˈseɪvɪŋ/ *n* **1 savings** [plural] all the money that you have saved, especially in a bank **2** [C usually singular] an amount of something that you have not used or spent: *This amount represents a considerable saving over last year's expenditure.* **3** [U] the act of keeping money so that you can use it later —see also SAVE¹ (2) W

**savings ac·count** /ˈ·· ·ˌ·/ *n* [C] a bank account that pays INTEREST¹ (4) on the money you have in it

**savings and loan as·so·ci·a·tion** /ˌ·· · ˈ· ··ˌ··/ *n* [C] *AmE* a business that lends money, usually so that you can buy a house, and into which you pay money to be saved; BUILDING SOCIETY *BrE*

**savings bank** /ˈ·· ·/ *n* [C] a bank that encourages people to save small amounts of money

**savings bond** /ˈ·· ·/ *n* [C] *technical* a BOND¹ (1) sold by the US government that cannot be sold from one person to another

**sa·viour** *BrE*, **savior** *AmE* /ˈseɪvjə‖-ər/ *n* **1** [C usually singular] someone or something that saves you from a difficult or dangerous situation **2** [singular] in the Christian religion, a word for Jesus Christ

**sav·oir-faire** /ˌsævwɑː ˈfeə‖-wɑːr ˈfer/ *n* [U] the ability to do or say the right things, especially in social situations: *famous in diplomatic circles for his savoir -faire*

**sa·vo·ry** /ˈseɪvəri/ *n* **1** [U] a plant used in cooking to add taste to meat, beans etc **2** [C] the American spelling of SAVOURY

**sa·vour**[1] *BrE*, **savor** *AmE* /ˈseɪvə‖-vər/ *v* [T] to make an activity or experience last as long as you can, because you are enjoying every moment of it: *She sipped her wine, savouring every drop.* —see TASTE (USAGE)

**savour of** sth *phr v* [T] *formal* to seem to have a small amount of a quality that people do not like: *radical ideas savouring of revolution*

**savour**[2] *BrE*, **savor** *AmE* —*n* [singular, U] *formal* **1** a taste or smell, especially one that is pleasant **2** interest and enjoyment: *Life seemed to have lost its savour for him.*

**sa·vour·y**[1] *BrE*, **savory** *AmE* /ˈseɪvəri/ *adj* **1** *BrE* having a taste that is not sweet **2** having a pleasant and attractive smell or taste: *A savoury smell of stew came from the kitchen.* **3 not very savoury/none too savoury etc** something that is not savoury seems unpleasant or morally unacceptable: *This hotel doesn't have a very savoury reputation.*

**savoury**[2] *BrE*, **savory** *AmE* —*n* [C] a small amount of salty food, sometimes served at the end of a formal meal

**sa·voy** /səˈvɔɪ/ *n* [C] a type of CABBAGE (=round green vegetable) with curled leaves

**sav·vy** /ˈsævi/ *n* [U] *informal* practical knowledge and ability —**savvy** *adj AmE*: *I just wasn't savvy enough in high school to keep up.*

**saw**[1] /sɔː‖sɒː/ the past tense of SEE

**saw**[2] *n* [C] **1** a tool that has a flat blade with a row of V-shaped metal pieces, used for cutting wood —see picture at TOOL[1] **2** *old use* a well-known wise statement; PROVERB

**saw**[3] *v past tense* **sawed** *past participle* **sawn** /sɔːn‖sɒːn/ *especially BrE*, **sawed** *especially AmE* [I,T] to cut something using a saw: *We had to saw the board in half.* | [+ **through**] *He sawed through a power cable by mistake.*

**saw at** sth *phr v* [T] to cut something with a repeated backwards and forwards movement: *He sawed at the loaf with a blunt knife.*

**saw** sth ↔ **off** *phr v* [T] to remove something by cutting it off with a saw: *One branch was dead and needed to be sawn off.*

**saw** sth ↔ **up** *phr v* [T] to cut something into many pieces, using a saw: *I sawed up the tree for firewood.*

**saw·bones** /ˈsɔːbəʊnz‖ˈsɒːboʊnz/ *n* [C] *AmE informal* a doctor or SURGEON

**saw·buck** /ˈsɔːbʌk‖ˈsɒː-/ *n* [C] *AmE old-fashioned* a $10 note

**saw·dust** /ˈsɔːdʌst‖ˈsɒː-/ *n* [U] very small pieces of wood that are left when you cut wood with a SAW[2] (1)

**saw·mill** /ˈsɔːmɪl‖ˈsɒː-/ *n* [C] a factory where logs are cut into boards using a machine

**sawn-off shot·gun** /ˌ· · ˈ· ·/ *BrE*, **sawed-off shotgun** *AmE* —*n* [C] a SHOTGUN that has had its BARREL (=long thin part) cut short

**sawyer** /ˈsɔːjə‖ˈsɒːjər/ *n* [C] *old use* someone whose job is sawing wood

**Sax·on** /ˈsæksən/ *n* [C] a member of the German race that came to live in England in the 5th century —**Saxon** *adj*

**sax·o·phone** /ˈsæksəfəʊn‖-foʊn/ *n* [C] also **sax** /sæks/ *informal* a metal musical instrument with a single REED (2), used mostly in JAZZ and dance music

**sax·oph·o·nist** /sækˈsɒfənɪst‖ˈsæksəfoʊnɪst/ *n* [C] someone who plays the saxophone

**say**[1] /seɪ/ *v past tense and past participle* **said** /sed/ *3rd person singular present tense* **says**

S1 W1

① USE WORDS
② WRITING/NUMBERS
③ MEAN/SHOW
④ GENERAL OPINION
⑤ SUGGEST/SUPPOSE
⑥ SPOKEN PHRASES
⑦ OTHER MEANINGS

**① USE WORDS**

**1 ▶WORD/SOUND◀** [T] to pronounce a word or sound: *"What did you say?"* | *"I'm so tired" she said.* | **say hello/goodbye etc** *She left without even saying goodbye.* —see SPEAK (USAGE)

**2 ▶THOUGHT/OPINION◀** [I only in questions and negatives, T] to express a thought, opinion, explanation etc in words: *Don't believe anything he says.* | *"Why did she leave?" "I don't know – she didn't say."* | **thing to say** *What a ridiculous thing to say!* | **say (that)** *Adam says he's thirsty.* | *I always said that you'd do okay in the end, didn't I?* | **say how/why/who etc** *Did she say what happened?* | *The doctor couldn't say how long it would take.* | **say yes/no (to)** (=agree or refuse) *Can I go, Mum? Oh please say yes!* | **say so/not** *"Do you think they're happy?" "I wouldn't say so."* | **sth to say** *Does anyone else have anything to say?* | *I couldn't think of anything to say to him.* | **say (you're) sorry** *Look, I've said I'm sorry – what more do you want?* | **say a few words** (=make a short speech) *I'd just like to say a few words about the schedule.* | **say your piece** (=say what you want to say) *OK, you've said your piece – now shut up.*

**3 say to yourself** to think something: *So I said to myself "It's time I left."*

**4 ▶TELL SB TO DO STH◀** [T not in progressive] to tell someone to do something: **say to do sth** *Nina said to meet her at 4.30.*

**5 ▶RULES◀** [T] to state what people are allowed to do: **say (that)** *The law says you can't sell alcohol on a Sunday afternoon.* | *Mom says we're not allowed to talk to strangers.*

**6 say your prayers/say grace etc** [T] to speak the fixed set of words that form a prayer etc: *Have you said your prayers?*

**7 say sth to sb's face** *informal* to make an unpleasant or criticizing remark to the person that the remark is about: *If you're going to make comments about my work, at least have the courage to say them to my face!*

**8 say sth you shouldn't** *informal* to say something that is embarrassing or secret: *Oh dear, have I said something I shouldn't again?* —see also **say a mouthful** (MOUTHFUL (4))

**② WRITING/NUMBERS**

**9** [T not in passive] to give information in written words, numbers, or pictures: *The clock in the hall said it was 7.30.* | *What does this word say?* | *Well that's what Sue said in her letter.* | **say (that)** *It said in the paper that there were no survivors.* | **say to do sth** *The label says to take one before meals.* | **say who/what/how etc** *Does it say in the instructions how much you should use?*

**③ MEAN/SHOW**

**10 ▶NOT DIRECTLY◀** [T] to suggest what you

[continued on next page]

[continued from previous page]
mean in an indirect way: *What do you think the writer is saying in this passage?* | *So what you're saying is, there's none left.* | **say (that)** *Are you saying I'm fat?*

**11 ▶ SHOW CHARACTER/QUALITIES ◀** [T] to show what someone or something's real character or qualities are: **say a lot about** (=show something very clearly) *The fact that he returned the money says a lot about his character.* | **say a lot for** (=show that someone or something has a lot of good qualities) *It says a lot for Jayne that she had the sense not to tell them.* | **not say much for** (=show that something is not of a high standard or quality) *These results don't say much for the quality of the teaching.*

**12 ▶ HAVE MEANING ◀** [T] to have or show a meaning that someone can understand: *Most modern art doesn't say much to me.*

### ④ GENERAL OPINION

**13** [T] to express an opinion that a lot of people have: *Well, you know what they say – blood's thicker than water.* | **they say (that)** (=people think that) *They say he's been all round the world.* | **(be) said to do sth** *She's said to be the richest woman in the world.* | **it is said (that)** *It is said that he was a spy during the war.*

### ⑤ SUGGEST/SUPPOSE

**14** [T usually in imperative] to suggest or suppose that something might happen or might be true: *I say we should forget the whole thing.* | **let's/just say (that)** *Let's say your plan fails, then what?* | *Just say you won the lottery – what would you do?*

Frequencies of the verb **say** in spoken and written English.

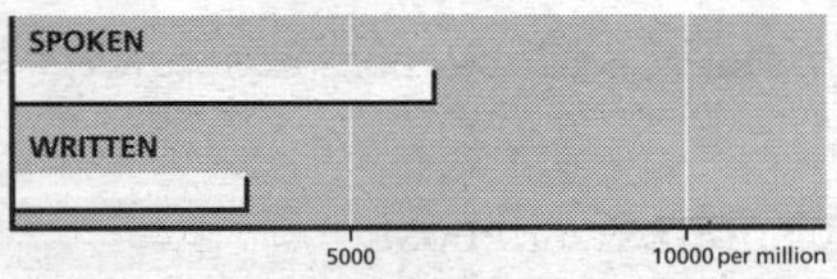


Based on the British National Corpus and the Longman Lancaster Corpus

This graph shows that the verb **say** is much more common in spoken English than in written English. This is because it is used in a lot of common spoken phrases.

### ⑥ SPOKEN PHRASES

**15 I must say** used when you want to emphasize what you are saying: *Well, that's clever, I must say!* | *I must say it made me jump.*

**16 I can't say (that)** used to say that you definitely do not think or feel something: *I can't say I envy her being married to him!*

**17 having said that** used before saying something that makes the opinion you have just given seem less strong: *Hannah didn't do a very good job, but having said that, I don't think I could have done any better.*

**18 say no more** used to show that you understand what someone means, although it has not been said directly: *"I saw him leaving her flat at 6.30 this morning." "Say no more!"*

**19 enough said** used to say that something is clear, and does not need to be explained any further

**20 I'd rather not say** used when you do not want to tell someone something: *"So what are your plans now?" "I'd rather not say at the moment."*

**21 you can say that again!** used to say that you completely agree with someone: *"Gosh, it's hot today." "You can say that again!"*

**22 say when** used to ask someone to tell you when to stop doing something, especially pouring them a drink

**23 who says?** used to say that you do not agree with a statement, opinion etc: *Who says I have to retire at 60?*

**24 who can say?** used to say that nobody knows the answer to a question: *Who can say whether they'll ever find a cure?*

**25 who's to say?** used to say that your judgment of a situation might not be correct, because you can never be sure what will happen in the future: *But who's to say that she won't do better than him in the end?*

**26 what do you say?** used to ask someone if they agree with a suggestion: *We could go into partnership; what do you say?* | **what do you say we do sth?** *What do you say we all go to a movie?* | **what do/would you say to (doing) sth?** *What would you say to a meal out?*

**27 you don't say!** used to show that you are not at all surprised by what someone has just told you

**28 say the word** used to tell someone they have only to ask and you will do what they want: *Just say the word and I'll get rid of her.*

**29 I'll say this for him/her etc** used when you want to mention something good about someone, especially when you have been criticizing them: *I will say this for Tom – at least he's consistent.*

**30 say what you like** *especially BrE* used when giving an opinion that you are sure is correct, even if the person you are talking to might disagree with you: *Say what you like, she's a very good mother.*

**31 whatever you say** used to tell someone that you agree to do what they want, accept their opinion etc, especially because you do not want an argument

**32 can't say fairer than that** *BrE* used to say that you have given the best offer that you can: *I'll give you £25 for it; I can't say fairer than that.*

**33 you said it! a)** used when someone says something that you agree with, although you would not have actually said it yourself: *"I was always stubborn as a kid." "You said it!"* **b)** *AmE* used to say that you agree with someone: *"Let's go home." "You said it! I'm tired."*

**34 what have you got to say for yourself?** used to ask someone for an explanation when they have done something wrong: *Late again? What have you got to say for yourself?*

**35 that's not saying much** used to emphasize that something is not very strange or unusual: *She's taller than me, but I'm only 5 foot 2, so that isn't saying much.*

**36 when all's said and done** used to remind someone about an important point that they should remember: *When all is said and done, he's only nine years old – don't expect too much.*

**37 I wouldn't say no (to)** used to say that you would like something, and would accept it you were offered it: *I wouldn't say no to a cup of coffee.*

**38 I say** *old-fashioned* **a)** *BrE* used to get someone's attention: *I say, could you pass me that book?* **b)** used to show you are slightly interested, angry etc: *"My husband's ill today." "I say! I'm sorry to hear that."*

### ⑦ OTHER MEANINGS

**39 go without saying** used to say that something is so clear that it does not really need to be stated: *It goes without saying that I'll return the money afterwards.*

**40 to say the least** used to say that you could have described something, criticized someone etc a lot more severely than you have: *Jane could have been more considerate, to say the least.*

**41 that is to say** used before describing what you mean in more detail: *Let's do as he suggested, that is to say, you fly down and I'll bring the car.*

**42 that's not to say** used to make it clear that something is not true, when you think someone might think that it is: *That's not to say that I agree with what you're doing, of course.*

**43 not to say** *especially BrE* used to show that you could have used a stronger word to describe something: *It would be silly, not to say mad, to sell your car.*

**44 say £45/100 years/Tuesday etc** used to suggest a possible example, amount etc when discussing

something: *They must owe say $2,000 in rent.* | *Can you come to dinner? Say, 7.30?*
**45 there's no saying how/what/when etc** used to say that it is impossible to know something: *There's no saying what he'll do next.*
**46 nothing/something/not much etc to be said for** used to say that there are a lot of, not many etc good reasons for doing something: *There's a lot to be said for taking a few days off now and then.* | *It was a strange plan, with very little to be said for it.*
**47 to say nothing of** used to say that you have described only some of the bad points about something: *It was a complete waste of time, to say nothing of all the stress and bother!*
**48 have something to say about** to be angry about something: *If you don't do your homework your father will have something to say about it!*
**49 have a lot to say for yourself** someone who has a lot to say for themselves talks all the time
**50 what sb says goes** used to emphasize who is in control in a situation: *My wife wants to go to Italy this year, and what she says goes!* —see also **wouldn't say boo to a goose** (BOO[2] (3)), **easier said than done** (EASY[2] (6)), **no sooner said than done** (SOON (4))

**USAGE NOTE: SAY**
WORD CHOICE: **say, tell, repeat, give, tell sb about/of, talk about/of, speak about/of**
In general, you **say** words **to** someone, but what you **tell** someone is facts, information etc: *I said hello/sorry/thanks/a few words to her* (NOT *told her 'Hello'*) | *I told her the reason/the truth/a lie/a story/a joke* (NOT *said*).
You usually only use **say** with the actual words that are spoken: *He said, "Open the door"*. Only **tell** can be used to report commands: *He told me to open the door.*
There are special verbs for **say**ing certain things: *I asked "Where is it?"* (less often *I said ...*) | *I'd like to welcome you* (NOT usually *say welcome*). | *He congratulated her* (=said 'Congratulations!'). | *She explained why she had done it* (=said why she had done it). If you **say** something **again**, you **repeat** it.
With some kinds of information **give** is more usual than **tell**: *He gave (us) his opinion/some advice/the details/a lot of information/an order/a message.*
You usually **tell** someone **about**, **talk about** or **speak about** (formal) people, things etc that are not themselves information: *He told us about Harvey/the accident* (NOT *said the accident to us*). | *I'm here to talk about the school/the school fair on Friday* (NOT *tell you the fair*).
**Of** can be used instead of **about** with these verbs, but this can sound old-fashioned or literary: *a story that tells of a frog* (you would usually just say *a story about a frog*)
GRAMMAR
**Say** cannot have a person as its object. The person you are speaking to can be mentioned as well, but only after *to*: *She said goodbye to her parents.* (NOT *She said her parents goodbye.*) *I said to them 'What do you need?'* | *Celia once said to me that her husband tended to be violent.*
However, where the object is a *that* clause, and you want to mention the person you are talking to as well, people often use **tell**, which can have a person as object: *You used to tell me that he was a nice person.* With a *wh-* clause in indirect speech **tell** is far more common: *Tell me what you need* (NOT: *Say to me what you need*).
Where the object is a clause and you do not want to mention the person you are talking to it is usual to use **say**: *Call us to say when you'll arrive* (NOT *to tell when*).
In spoken English *that* is often left out of the *that* clause: *Tell me it's not true!* | *I said I was sorry.*
**Tell** (but not **say**) can be followed by *to* forms of verbs: *He told us to do it* (NOT *said to us to do it*). However, there must be an object noun as well (NOT *He told to do it*).
**Tell** (unlike **say**) is not usually followed immediately by *to* and a noun: *I'll tell my parents the truth/tell the truth to my parents* (NOT *...tell to my parents the truth*).
**Say** and **tell** can both be used with **about**, but usually you use it with an object as well: *Let me say something about my family.* | *Sally was telling us all about the party.* In informal spoken English you will quite often hear things like: *I've already said about that!* | *You were saying about Harvey?* but some people would consider these to be incorrect. More often people use other verbs here: *I've already talked about my family.*

**say²** *n* [singular, U] **1** the right to take part in deciding something: [**+ in**] *The workers had no say in how the factory was run.* | *Don't I have any say in the matter?* **2 have/say your say** *informal* to have the opportunity to give your opinion about something: *Mark always has to have his say, even if he knows nothing about the subject.*

**say³** *interjection AmE informal* used to express surprise, or to introduce an idea you have just had: *Say, haven't I seen you before somewhere?*

**say·ing** *n* [C] **1** a well-known short statement that expresses an idea most people believe is true and wise —compare PROVERB **2 as the saying goes** used to introduce a particular phrase that people often say: *One thing led to another as the saying goes.* W3

**say-so** *n* [singular] *informal* **1** someone's permission: *Without his say-so, you can't leave the hospital.* **2 on sb's say-so** based on someone's personal statement without any proof: *Why should I believe it on your say-so?*

**S-bend** /ˈes bend/ *n* [C] *BrE* **1** a bend in a road in the shape of an 'S' that can be dangerous to drivers; S-CURVE *AmE* **2** part of a waste pipe in the shape of an 'S' that keeps bad smells out of a building

**scab** /skæb/ *n* [C] **1** a hard layer of dried blood that forms over a cut or wound while it is getting better **2** an insulting word for someone who works while the other people in the same factory, office etc are on STRIKE² (1) —**scab** *v* [I]

**scab·bard** /ˈsjæbəd‖-ərd/ *n* [C] a metal or leather cover for the blade of a knife or sword; SHEATH (1)

**scab·by** /ˈskæbi/ *adj* **1** scabby skin is covered with scabs: *scabby knees* **2** *BrE* a word meaning nasty or unpleasant, used especially by children

**sca·bies** /ˈskeɪbiz/ *n* [U] a skin disease caused by very small insects

**sca·brous** *adj literary* rude or shocking, especially in a sexual way: *The film is a joy – hilariously funny and unremittingly scabrous.*

**scads** /skædz/ *n* [plural] *informal* large numbers or quantities of something: *scads of money*

**scaf·fold** /ˈskæfəld,-fəʊld‖-fəld,-foʊld/ *n* [C] **1** a structure built next to a building or high wall, for workmen to stand on while they build, repair, or paint the building **2** a structure with a raised stage used for killing criminals by hanging them or cutting off their heads **3** *AmE* a structure that can be moved up and down to help people work on high buildings; CRADLE¹ (5) *BrE*

**scaf·fold·ing** /ˈskæfəldɪŋ/ *n* [U] poles and boards that are built into a structure for workmen to stand on when they are working next to a high wall on the outside of a building

**scal·a·wag** /ˈskæləwæg/ *n* [C] the usual American spelling of SCALLYWAG

**scald¹** /ˈskɔːld‖skɒːld/ *v* [T] to burn your skin with hot liquid or steam: *Mind you don't scald yourself with that kettle!*

**scald²** *n* [C] a burn caused by hot liquid or steam

**scald·ing** /ˈskɔːldɪŋ‖ˈskɒːl-/ *adj* **1** extremely hot: *a cup of scalding tea* **2** scalding criticism is very severe

S3 W2 **scale¹** /skeɪl/ *n*

**1 ▶SIZE/LEVEL◀** [singular, U] the size or level of something, or the amount that something is happening or being done: [+ **of**] *The scale of the pollution problem was much worse than scientists had predicted.* | **large/small etc scale** *There has been development on a massive scale since 1980.* | *a large-scale research project*

**2 ▶RANGE◀** [C usually singular] the whole range of different types of people, things, ideas etc, from the lowest level to the highest: *At the other end of the scale are the super-rich.* | *Fish are lower down the evolutionary scale.*

**3 ▶MEASURING INSTRUMENT◀ scales** [plural] also **scale** *AmE* **a)** a machine for weighing people or objects: *the bathroom scales* —see picture on page 833 **b)** a piece of equipment with two dishes used especially in the past for weighing things by comparing them to a known weight —see also **tip the balance/scales** (TIP² (8))

**4 ▶MEASURING SYSTEM◀** [C] a system for measuring the force, speed, amount etc of something: *Earthquakes are measured on the Richter scale.* | *the company pay scale*

**5 on a scale of 1 to 10** *spoken* used when you are asking someone to say how good they think something is: *On a scale of 1 to 10, how do you rate his performance?*

**6 ▶MEASURING MARKS◀** [C] a set of marks with regular spaces between them on a tool or instrument used for measuring: *a ruler with a metric scale* | *the scale on a thermometer*

**7 ▶MAP/MODEL◀** [C,U] the relationship between the size of a map, drawing, or model and the actual size of the place or thing that it represents: *a scale of 1:250 000* | *What's the scale of this map?*

**8 ▶MUSIC◀** [C] a series of musical notes moving upwards or downwards in PITCH² (3) with fixed distances between each note

**9 ▶FISH◀** [C usually plural] one of the small flat pieces of skin that cover the bodies of fish, snakes etc —see picture at FISH¹

**10 ▶TEETH◀** [U] a white substance that forms on your teeth

**11 ▶WATER PIPES◀** [U] a white substance that forms around the inside of hot water pipes or containers in which water is boiled

**12 the scales fell from my eyes** *literary* used to say that you suddenly realized what had been clear to other people —see also FULL-SCALE

**scale²** *v* [T] **1** to climb to the top of something that is high and difficult to climb: *Rescuers had to scale a 300m cliff to reach the injured climber.* **2** to remove the SCALES (=skin) from a fish —compare DESCALE

**scale** sth ↔ **down** *phr v* [T] *BrE*, **scale** sth ↔ **back** *AmE* to reduce the size of an organization, plan etc so that it operates at a lower level: *Both companies have announced plans to scale back auto production next year.*

**sca·lene tri·an·gle** /ˌskeɪliːn ˈtraɪæŋgəl/ *n* [C] a flat shape with three angles and three sides of unequal length —see picture at SHAPE¹

**scal·lion** /ˈskæljən/ *n* [C] *AmE* a young onion with a small round end and a long green stem; SPRING ONION *BrE*

**scal·lop¹** /ˈskɒləp‖ˈskɑː-/ *n* [C] **1** a small sea creature that has a hard flat shell made of two parts that fit together **2** [usually plural] one of a row of small curves decorating the edge of clothes, curtains etc

**scallop²** also **scollop** *v* [T] **1** to decorate something by making the edge into a row of small curves **2** to bake something in a cream or cheese SAUCE (1): *scalloped potatoes*

**scal·ly·wag** /ˈskæliwæg/ *especially BrE*, also **scalawag** *AmE n* [C] *humorous* someone, especially a child, who causes trouble but not in a serious way

**scalp¹** /skælp/ *n* [C] **1** the skin on your head **2** *informal* a clear sign that you have completely defeated someone else: *The public were calling for his scalp.*

**scalp²** *v* [T] **1** *AmE informal* to buy tickets for an event and sell them again at a much higher price **2** to cut off a dead enemy's scalp as a sign of victory

**scal·pel** /ˈskælpəl/ *n* [C] a small very sharp knife used by doctors in operations —see picture at KNIFE¹

**scal·per** /ˈskælpə‖-ər/ *n* [C] *AmE* a person who makes money by buying tickets for an event and selling them again at a very high price; TOUT² (1) *BrE*

**scal·y** /ˈskeɪli/ *adj* **1** an animal, such as a fish, that is scaly is covered with small flat pieces of hard skin **2** scaly skin is dry and rough —**scaliness** *n* [U]

**scam** /skæm/ *n* [C] *slang* a clever but dishonest plan, usually to get money

**scamp** /skæmp/ *n* [C] *old-fashioned* a child who has fun by tricking people: *Come back here with my hat, you young scamp!*

**scam·per** /ˈskæmpə‖-ər/ *v* [I always + adv/prep] to run with quick short steps, like a child or small animal: [+ **in/out/off etc**] *Giggling, the children scampered back to the house.*

**scam·pi** /ˈskæmpi/ *n BrE* **1** [plural] large PRAWNS (=sea creature that can be eaten) **2** [U] *BrE* PRAWNS covered in BATTER and cooked in oil: *scampi and chips*

**scan¹** /skæn/ *v* **scanned, scanning** **1** [T] to examine an area carefully, because you are looking for a particular person or thing: *He scanned the horizon ahead, but there was no sign of the convoy.* | [+ **for**] *The police scanned the whole area but found no trace of her body.* **2** also **scan through** [I,T] to read something quickly in order to understand its main meaning or to find some particular information: *I scanned the page quickly for her name.* **3** [T] if a machine scans an object or a part of your body, it passes a BEAM¹ (16) of ELECTRONS over it to produce a picture of what is inside: *All luggage has to be scanned at the airport.* —see also SCANNER (1) **4** [T] if a machine or instrument scans an area it searches it with RADAR or SONAR: *The ship scanned the area ahead for enemy submarines.* **5** *technical* **a)** [I] poetry that scans has a correct regular pattern of beats **b)** [T] to find or show a regular pattern of beats in a poem or line of poetry —see also SCANSION

**scan²** *n* [C] **1** the act of scanning something **2** a test done by a SCANNER (=special machine for producing a picture) *a brain scan* **3** an image of an unborn baby, produced by a SCANNER: *The scan showed the baby was normal.*

**scan·dal** /ˈskændl/ *n* **1** [C,U] behaviour or events, often involving famous people, that are considered to be immoral or shocking: *a sex scandal involving several government officials* | *Some newspapers thrive on spreading gossip and scandal.* | **a scandal breaks** (=becomes known to everyone) *They had already left the country when the scandal broke.* **2 be a scandal** *spoken* to be very shocking or unacceptable: *The price of beef these days is an absolute scandal!*

**scan·dal·ize** also **-ise** *BrE* /ˈskændəl-aɪz/ *v* [T usually passive] to do something that shocks people very much: *The entire village was scandalized by the affair.*

**scan·dal·mon·ger** /ˈskændəlˌmʌŋgə‖-ˌmɑːŋgər, -ˌmʌŋ-/ *n* [C] someone who tells people untrue and shocking things about someone else —**scandalmongering** *n* [U]

**scan·dal·ous** /ˈskændələs/ *adj* completely unfair and wrong: *a scandalous waste of public money* | *It's scandalous that you still haven't been paid!* —**scandalously** *adv*

**Scan·di·na·vi·an** /ˌskændʒˈneɪviən◂/ *n* [C] someone from the area of Northern Europe that consists of Norway, Sweden, Denmark, and usually Finland and Iceland —**Scandinavian** *adj*: *Scandinavian languages*

**scan·ner** /ˈskænə‖-ər/ *n* [C] **1** a machine that passes a BEAM[1] (16) of ELECTRONS over something in order to produce a picture of what is inside: *An electronic scanner was passed over the package.* —see picture on page 837 **2** a piece of computer equipment that copies an image from paper onto the SCREEN[1] (1)

**scan·sion** /ˈskænʃən/ *n* [U] the pattern of regular beats in poetry, or the marks you write to represent this

**scant** /skænt/ *adj* [only before noun] not enough: **scant attention/regard/consideration** *I paid scant attention to all my father's warnings.*

**scant·y** /ˈskænti/ *adj* not big enough for a particular purpose: *a scanty bikini* —**scantily** *adv*: *scantily clad models*

**-scape** /skeɪp/ *suffix (in nouns)* a wide view of a particular area, especially in a picture: *the impressive cityscape of New York* | *some old Dutch seascapes* (=pictures of the sea)

**scape·goat** /ˈskeɪpgəʊt‖-goʊt/ *n* [C] someone who is blamed for something bad that happens, even if it is not their fault: *He claimed he had been made a scapegoat for the administration's failures.* —**scapegoat** *v* [T]

**scap·u·la** /ˈskæpjələ/ *n* [C] *technical* one of the two flat bones on each side of your upper back; SHOULDER-BLADE —see picture at SKELETON

**scar[1]** /skɑː‖skɑːr/ *n* [C] **1** a permanent mark that is left after you have had a cut or wound —see picture on page 412 **2** a permanent emotional or mental effect caused by an upleasant experience: **leave scars** *The trauma of her mother's death had left deep scars.* **3** an ugly permanent mark on something: *The old mines are a scar on the rural landscape.* **4** *BrE* a cliff on the side of a mountain

**scar[2]** *v* **1 be scarred** to have a permanent mark on your skin because of a cut or wound: *His hands were badly scarred by the fire.* **2** [T] if an unpleasant experience scars you, it has a permanent effect on your character or feelings: **be scarred for life** (=never completely recover from an unpleasant experience) *She's likely to be scarred for life by the attack.* **3** [I] also **scar over** if a wound scars, it becomes healthy but leaves a permanent mark on your skin

**scar·ab** /ˈskærəb/ also **scarab bee·tle** /ˈ·· ˌ··/ *n* [C] a large black BEETLE (=insect with a hard shell) or a representation of this

**scarce[1]** /skeəs‖skers/ *adj* **1** if food, clothing, water etc is scarce, there is not enough of it available: *Fruit was always scarce in winter, and cost a lot.* —see RARE (USAGE) **2 make yourself scarce** *informal* to leave a place, especially in order to avoid an unpleasant situation

**scarce[2]** *adv literary* scarcely

**scarce·ly** /ˈskeəsli‖ˈsker-/ *adv* **1** almost not or almost none at all: *Parts of the city had scarcely changed since we were last there.* | **scarcely any/ever** *There's scarcely any coffee left.* | **can/could scarcely** *It was getting dark and she could scarcely see in front of her.* | **scarcely a word/moment/day etc** *Scarcely a day goes by when I don't think of him.* —see RARE (USAGE) **2** only just: **have scarcely done sth when** *Scarcely had I opened the door when the dog came running in.* —see ALMOST (USAGE) **3** definitely not or almost certainly not: *This is scarcely the place to talk about your personal problems.*

**scar·ci·ty** /ˈskeəsəti‖ˈsker-/ *n* [singular, U + **of**] a situation in which there is not enough of something: *the present scarcity of labour*

**scare[1]** /skeə‖sker/ *v* **1** [T] to make someone feel frightened: *Ignore him, he's just trying to scare us.* | **scare the hell/life/shit out of sb** (=scare someone very much) *You scared the hell out of me jumping out like that!* **2** [I] to become frightened: *I don't scare easily you know!*

**scare** sb ↔ **into** *phr v* [T] to make someone do something by frightening them or threatening them: **scare sb into doing sth** *Some parents try to scare their children into behaving well.*

**scare** sb/sth ↔ **off/away** *phr v* [T] **1** to make someone or something go away by frightening them: *We lit fires to scare away the wolves.* **2** to make someone uncertain or worried so that they do not do something they were going to do: *Rising prices are scaring off many potential customers.*

**scare up** sth *phr v* [T] *AmE informal* to make something although you have very few things to make it from: *Let me see if I can scare up something for you to eat.*

**scare[2]** *n* **1** [singular] a sudden feeling of fear: **give sb a scare** *That car only just missed me – it gave me a real scare!* **2** [C] a situation in which a lot of people become frightened about something: *a bomb scare* | *An escape of radioactive gas caused a major scare.*

**scare·crow** /ˈskeəkrəʊ‖ˈskerkroʊ/ *n* [C] an object made to look like a person that a farmer puts in a field to frighten birds

**scared** /skeəd‖skerd/ *adj* frightened of or nervous about something: [+ **of**] *I've always been scared of dogs.* | *Don't be scared of asking if you need any help.* | **scared (that)** *I was scared that they might tell the police.* | **scared to do sth** *Janice lay on the floor trembling, too scared to move.* | **scared stiff/scared to death/scared out of your wits** (=extremely frightened) *I was scared stiff at the thought of having to make a speech.* S 3

**scare·dy-cat** /ˈskeədikæt‖ˈsker-/ *n* [C] *informal* an insulting word for someone who is easily frightened, used especially by children

**scare·mon·ger·ing** /ˈskeəˌmʌŋgərɪŋ‖ˈskerˌmɑːŋ-, -ˌmʌŋ-/ *n* [U] the practice of deliberately making people worried or nervous, especially in order to get a political or other advantage: *Jackson publicly accused the anti-nuclear lobby of scaremongering.* —**scaremonger** *n* [C]

**scare sto·ry** /ˈ· ˌ··/ *n* [C] a report, especially in a newspaper, that makes a situation seem more serious or worrying than it really is

**scare tac·tics** /ˈ· ˌ··/ *n* [plural] methods of persuading people to do something by frightening them: *Employers had used scare tactics to force a return to work.*

**scare·y** /ˈskeəri‖ˈskeri/ *adj* another spelling of SCARY

**scarves**

**scarf[1]** /skɑːf‖skɑːrf/ *n* [C] *plural* **scarfs** *or* **scarves** /skɑːvz‖skɑːrvz/ **1** a long narrow piece of material that you wear around your neck to keep it warm **2** a square piece of material that a woman wears over her head or around her neck

**scarf[2]** also **scarf down/up** *v* [I,T] *AmE slang* to eat something very quickly and noisily; SCOFF (2) *BrE*

**scar·i·fy** /ˈskeərəfaɪ, ˈskærəfaɪ‖ˈsker-, ˈskær-/ *v* [T] **1** to break and make loose the surface of a road or field using a pointed tool **2** *technical* to make small cuts on an area of skin using a sharp knife **3** *literary* to criticize someone very severely

**scar·let** /ˈskɑːlət‖-ɑːr-/ *adj* bright red —**scarlet** *n* [U] —see picture on page 411

**scarlet fe·ver** /ˌ·· ˈ··/ *also* **scar·la·ti·na** /ˌskɑːləˈtiːnə‖ˌskɑːr-/ *n* [U] a serious infectious illness that causes a sore throat and red spots on your skin

**scarlet pim·per·nel** /ˌ·· ˈ···/ *n* [C] a small wild plant with bright red flowers

**scarlet wom·an** /ˌ·· '··/ *n* [C] *old-fashioned* a woman who has sexual relationships with many different people

**scarp** /skɑːp‖skɑːrp/ *n* [C] *technical* a line of natural cliffs

**scar·per** /'skɑːpə‖'skɑːrpər/ *v* [I] *BrE informal* to run away: *Those kids scarpered without paying their bill!*

**scarves** /skɑːvz‖skɑːrvz/ the plural of SCARF[1]

**scar·y, scarey** /'skeəri‖'skeri/ *adj informal* frightening: *a scary movie*

**scat**[1] /skæt/ *interjection* used to tell a child or an animal to go away: *Go on, scat! And don't come back!*

**scat**[2] *n* [U] a style of JAZZ[1] (1) singing, in which the voice is made to sound like a musical instrument

**scath·ing** /'skeɪðɪŋ/ *adj* scathing remarks, comments etc criticize someone or something very severely: *The newspapers were extremely scathing about him.* | *scathing criticism* —**scathingly** *adv*

**scat·o·lo·gic·al** /ˌskætə'lɒdʒɪkəl◂‖-'lɑː-/ *adj formal* too interested in or connected with human waste, in a way that is unpleasant: *scatological humor* —**scatology** /skæ'tɒlədʒi‖-'tɑː-/ *n* [U]

**scat·ter** /'skætə‖-ər/ *v* **1** [T] to throw or drop a lot of things over a wide area in an irregular way: **scatter sth over/on/around** *Books lay scattered all over the floor.* | **scatter sth with sth** *The sky was scattered with stars.* **2** [I,T] if a group of people scatter, or if something scatters them, everyone suddenly moves in different directions, especially to escape danger: *There was a sudden crack of gunfire and the crowd scattered in all directions* **3 be scattered to the four winds** *literary* to be broken up or separated and lost —see also SCATTERED, SCATTERING

**scat·ter·brain** /'skætəbreɪn‖-ər-/ *n* [C] someone who often forgets or loses things because they do not think in a practical way: *Don't tell me you've lost your glasses again, you scatterbrain!* —**scatterbrained** *adj*

**scat·tered** /'skætəd‖-ərd/ *adj* spread over a wide area or over a long period of time: *houses scattered across the hillside* | **scattered showers** (=used in weather reports to say there will be some short periods of rain)

**scat·ter·ing** /'skætərɪŋ/ *n* [C] a small number of things or people spread out over a large area: [+ **of**] *a largely Catholic country with a scattering of Protestant communities*

**scat·ty** /'skæti/ *adj BrE informal* someone who is scatty often forgets or loses things because they are not sensible or practical —**scattiness** *n* [U]

**scav·enge** /'skævɪ̈ndʒ/ *v* [I,T] **1** if an animal scavenges, it eats anything that it can find: *dogs scavenging from the dustbins* **2** if someone scavenges, they search through things that other people do not want for food or useful objects: [+ **for**] *a man scavenging for food in piles of garbage* —**scavenger** *n* [C]

**sce·na·ri·o** /sɪ̈'nɑːriəʊ‖-'næ-, -'ne-/ *n plural* **scenarios** [C] **1** a situation that could possibly happen but has not happened yet: *Try to imagine a scenario where only 20% of people have a job.* | **worst-case/nightmare scenario** (=the worst possible situation) *the nightmare scenario of a radiation leak* **2** a written description of the characters, place, and things that will happen in a film, play etc

S2 W2 **scene** /siːn/ *n*

**1** ► **PLAY/FILM** ◄ [C] **a)** part of a play during which there is no change in time or place: *Hamlet, Act 5 Scene 2* **b)** a single piece of action that happens in one place in a film, book etc: *Some of the more violent scenes are very disturbing.* | *a love scene*

**2** ► **VIEW/PICTURE** ◄ [C] a view of a place as you see it, or as it appears in a picture: *a peaceful country scene* | *a painter of street scenes*

**3** ► **ACCIDENT/CRIME** ◄ [singular] the place where an accident, crime etc happened: [+ **of**] *the scene of the crime* | **on/at the scene** *Investigators are now at the scene, searching for clues to the cause of the explosion.* | *Journalists were on the scene within minutes of the crash.*

**4 the gay/fashion/political etc scene** a particular set of activities and the people who are involved in them: *Keith is heavily involved in the London theatre scene.* | *the drugs scene*

**5** ► **ARGUMENT** ◄ [C] a loud angry argument, especially in a public place: *a terrible scene that ended with Rachel running out of the restaurant in tears* | *There were angry scenes in parliament today.* | **make a scene** *If you don't sit down and stop making a scene, I'm leaving!*

**6** ► **SITUATION** ◄ [C] all the things that are happening in a place, and the effect or situation that they cause: [+ **of**] *The burning building was a scene of panic as everyone ran to get out.* | *a scene of perfect peace and harmony*

**7 bad scene** *AmE informal* a difficult or unpleasant situation: *We realized by the looks on their faces that we had walked into a bad scene.*

**8 not your scene** *informal* not the type of thing you like: *Loud discos aren't really my scene.*

**9 behind the scenes** secretly, while other things are happening publicly: *Most important political decisions are made behind the scenes.*

**10 set the scene a)** to provide the conditions in which an event can happen: *The government seems unaware that these policies are setting the scene for social unrest.* **b)** to describe the situation before you begin to tell a story

**11 be/come on the scene** to be or become involved in a situation, activity etc: *By then, there was a boyfriend on the scene.* —see also **a change of air/climate/scenery** (CHANGE[2] (3)), **steal the scene/show/limelight** (STEAL[1] (3))

**sce·ne·ry** /'siːnəri/ *n* [U] **1** the natural features of a particular part of a country, such as mountains, forests, deserts etc: *The best part of the trip was the scenery. It was fantastic.* **2** the painted background, furniture etc used on a theatre stage

**sce·nic** /'siːnɪk/ *adj* surrounded by views of beautiful countryside: *Let's take the scenic route home.* —**scenically** /-kli/ *adv*

**scent**[1] /sent/ *n* **1** [C] a pleasant smell that something has: *the scent of roses* **2** [C] the smell of a particular animal or person that some other animals, for example dogs, can follow: **on the scent** (=following this smell) *The hounds were soon on the stag's scent.* **3 throw/put sb off the scent** to give someone false information to prevent them from catching you or discovering something: *The gang changed car to throw the police off the scent.* **4** [C,U] *especially BrE* a liquid that you put on your skin to make it smell nice; PERFUME[1] (1)

**scent**[2] *v* **1** [T] if an animal scents another animal or a person, it knows that they are near because it can smell them: *The deer scented our presence and ran back into the forest.* **2 scent fear/danger/victory etc** *literary* to feel sure that something is going to happen: *We scented danger and decided to leave.*

**scent·ed** /'sentɪ̈d/ *adj* having a particular smell, especially a pleasant one: [+ **with**] *an air freshener scented with spring flowers*

**scent·less** /'sentləs/ *adj* without a smell

**scep·ter** /'septə‖-tər/ *n* [C] the American spelling of SCEPTRE

**scep·tic** *BrE*, **skeptic** *AmE* /'skeptɪk/ *n* [C] someone who does not believe things unless they have definite proof: *A lot of my friends believe in astrology, but I'm a sceptic myself.*

**scep·ti·cal** *BrE*, **skeptical** *AmE* /'skeptɪkəl/ *adj* tending to doubt or not believe what other people tell you: [+ **about**] *Many scientists remain skeptical about the value of this research program.* —**sceptically** /-kli/ *adv*

**scep·ti·cis·m** *BrE*, **skepticism** *AmE* /'skeptɪ̈sɪzəm/ *n* [U] a sceptical attitude: *The government's claim that the country is now coming out of recession is being treated with deep scepticism.*

**scep·tre** *BrE*, **scepter** *AmE* /'septə‖-ər/ *n* [C] a short decorated stick carried by kings or queens at ceremonies

3 3 **sched·ule¹** /ˈʃedjuːl‖ˈskedʒʊl, -dʒəl/ *n* [C] **1** a plan of what someone is going to do and when they are going to do it: **full schedule** (=busy schedule) *I've got a very full schedule today.*|**tight schedule** (=including a lot of things that must be done in a short time) *Our production schedule is so tight that we may have to take on extra staff.*|**ahead of/on/behind schedule** (=before, at, after the planned time) *We finished the project three weeks ahead of schedule.* **2** *AmE* a list that shows the times that buses, trains etc leave or arrive at a particular place; TIMETABLE¹ (1) *BrE* **3** a formal list of something, for example prices: *a schedule of postal charges*

**schedule²** *v* [T] [usually passive] to plan that something will happen at a particular time: [+ **for**] *The meeting has been scheduled for this afternoon.*|**be scheduled to do sth** *The new airport is scheduled to open just before Christmas.*|**scheduled flight** (=a plane service that flies at the same time every day or every week)

**sche·ma** /ˈskiːmə/ also **sche·ma·ta** /ˈskiːmətə/ *n* [C] *technical* a plan showing only the important parts of something; DIAGRAM

**sche·mat·ic** /skiːˈmætɪk, skɪ-/ *adj* in the form of a basic plan or arrangement: *a schematic outline*|*a schematic diagram of DNA*

**sche·ma·tize** *also* **-ise** *BrE* /ˈskiːmətaɪz/ *v* [T] to arrange something in a system

1 **scheme¹** /skiːm/ *n* [C] **1** *BrE* an official plan that is intended to help people in some way, for example by providing education or training: *a government training scheme for the unemployed*|*a pension scheme* **2** a clever plan, especially to do something bad or illegal: *another one of his dumb schemes for making money* **3** a system that you use to organize information, ideas etc: *classification scheme*|**colour scheme** (=the way the colours have been organized in a room) **4 be in the scheme of things** to be part of the way things generally happen, or are organized: *It was seen as a medium-sized company in the general scheme of things.*

**scheme²** *v* [I] to secretly make clever and dishonest plans to get or achieve something: **scheme to do sth** *He spent the next two years bitterly scheming to get his revenge.*|**scheme against sb** *She became convinced that her family was scheming against her.* —**schemer** *n* [C]

**scher·zo** /ˈskeətsəʊ‖ˈskertsoʊ/ *n* [C] a cheerful piece of music played quickly and happily —**scherzo** *adj, adv*

**schis·m** /ˈsɪzəm, ˈskɪzəm/ *n* [C,U] the separation of a group into two groups, caused by a disagreement about its aims and beliefs, especially in the Christian church

**schis·mat·ic** /sɪzˈmætɪk, skɪz-/ *adj* related to or connected with schism

**schist** /ʃɪst/ *n* [U] *technical* a type of rock that naturally breaks apart into thin flat pieces

**schiz·o** /ˈskɪtsəʊ‖-soʊ/ *n* [C] *slang* a SCHIZOPHRENIC

**schiz·oid** /ˈskɪtsɔɪd/ *adj* **1** *technical* typical of schizophrenia **2** *informal* quickly changing between opposite opinions or attitudes

**schiz·o·phre·ni·a** /ˌskɪtsəʊˈfriːniə, -sə-‖-soʊ-, -sə-/ *n* [U] a serious mental illness in which someone's thoughts and feelings become separated from what is really happening around them

**schiz·o·phren·ic¹** /ˌskɪtsəʊˈfrenɪk◂, -sə-‖-soʊ-, -sə-/ *adj* **1** *technical* typical of or connected with schizophrenia **2** *informal* quickly changing from one opinion, attitude etc to another

**schizophrenic²** *n* [C] someone who has schizophrenia

**schlep** /ʃlep/ *v* [T] *AmE informal* to carry or pull something heavy: [+ **down/out/along etc**] *I schlepped his bag all the way to the airport and he didn't even thank me.*

**schlep around** *phr v* [I] to spend your time lazily doing nothing useful

**schmaltz·y** /ˈʃmɔːltsi, ˈʃmæltsi‖ˈʃmɒːltsi, ˈʃmɑːltsi/ *adj informal especially AmE* a schmaltzy piece of music, book etc deals with emotions such as love and sadness in a way that seems silly and insincere: *a schmaltzy love song* —**schmaltz, schmalz** *n* [U]

**schmooze** /ʃmuːz/ *v* [I] *AmE informal* to talk about unimportant things: *drinking and schmoozing after filming was done*

**schmuck** /ʃmʌk/ *n* [C] *AmE informal* a stupid person

**schnapps** /ʃnæps/ *n* [U] a strong alcoholic drink

**schnit·zel** /ˈʃnɪtsəl/ *n* [C,U] a small piece of VEAL covered with small pieces of bread and cooked in oil

**schnook** /ʃnʊk/ *n* [C] *AmE informal* a stupid person

**schnoz·zle** /ˈʃnɒzəl‖ˈʃnɑː-/ *n* [C] *AmE humorous* a nose

**schol·ar** /ˈskɒlə‖ˈskɑːlər/ *n* [C] **1** someone who knows a lot about a particular subject, especially one that is not a science subject: *a Latin scholar* **2** *informal* a clever and well-educated person: *I'm afraid I'm not much of a scholar.* **3** someone who has been given a SCHOLARSHIP (=money) to study at a school or college: *a Rhodes scholar* **4** *literary or BrE old use* a child who is at school

**schol·ar·ly** /ˈskɒləli‖ˈskɑːlərli/ *adj* **1** concerned with serious study of a particular subject: *a scholarly journal* **2** someone who is scholarly spends a lot of time studying, and knows a lot about a particular subject

**schol·ar·ship** /ˈskɒləʃɪp‖ˈskɑːlər-/ *n* **1** [C] an amount of money that is given to someone by an educational organization to help pay for their education **2** [U] the knowledge, work, or methods involved in serious studying: *Her latest publication is a fine piece of scholarship.*

**scho·las·tic** /skəˈlæstɪk/ *adj* [only before noun] *formal* **1** connected with schools or teaching: *scholastic books* **2** connected with scholasticism

**scho·las·ti·cis·m** /skəˈlæstɪ̣sɪzəm/ *n* [U] a way of studying thought, especially religious thought, based on things written in ancient times

**school¹** /skuːl/ *n* S1

**1 ▶ WHERE CHILDREN LEARN ◀** [C] a place where children are taught: *Which school do you go to?*|*There are several good schools in the area*|**school bus/building etc** *the school hall*|**to/from school** *Mum takes us to school every morning.* W1

**2 ▶ TIME AT SCHOOL ◀** [U] **a)** a day's work at school: *School begins at 8.30.*|**before/after school** *I'll see you after school.* **b)** the time during your life when you go to a school: *After two years of school, he still couldn't read.*|**start/leave school** *She started school when she was four.*|*I left school two years ago.*

**3 ▶ UNIVERSITY ◀** **a)** [C,U] *AmE* a university, or the time when you study there: *Where did you go to school?*|**law/medical/graduate etc school** *After two years of medical school, I thought I knew everything.* **b)** [C] a department that teaches a particular subject at a university: [+ **of**] *the School of Oriental Languages*

**4 ▶ ONE SUBJECT ◀** [C] a place where a particular subject or skill is taught: *a language school in Brighton*|*the Pastern Riding School*|[+ **of**] *Amwell School of Motoring*

**5 at school** **a)** in the school building: *I can get some work done while the kids are at school.* **b)** *BrE* attending a school, rather than being at college or university or having a job: *We've got two children at school, and one at university.*

**6 in school** **a)** in the school building: *Sandra's not in school today – she's not well.* **b)** *AmE* attending a school or university as opposed to having a job: *Are your boys still in school?*

**7 ▶ ART ◀** [C] a number of people who are considered as a group because of their style of work: *the Impressionist school*

**8 school of thought** an opinion or way of thinking about something that is shared by a group of people: *There are two schools of thought on drinking red wine with fish.*

**9 of the old school** having old-fashioned values or qualities, especially good ones: *an officer of the old school*

**10 ▶ SEA ANIMALS ◀** [C] a large group of fish, WHALES¹ (1), DOLPHINS etc that are swimming together: [+ **of**] *a school of whales*

**11 the school of hard knocks** *old-fashioned* the difficult or unpleasant experiences you have in life

**school²** *v* [T] *old-fashioned* to train or teach someone: **be schooled in sth** *a young lady schooled in all the usual accomplishments*

**school board** /ˌ· ˈ·/ *n* [C] a group of people, including some parents, who are elected to govern a school or group of schools in the US

**school·boy** /ˈskuːlbɔɪ/ *n* [C] *especially BrE* **1** a boy attending school **2 schoolboy humour** jokes that are silly and rude but not offensive

**school·child** /ˈskuːltʃaɪld/ *n plural* **schoolchildren** /ˈskuːltʃɪldrən/ [C] a child attending school

**school·day** /ˈskuːldeɪ/ *n* [C] **1** a day of the week when children are usually at school **2 schooldays** the time of your life when you go to school

**school dis·trict** /ˈ· ˌ··/ *n* [C] an area in one state of the US that includes a number of schools which are governed together

**school friend** /ˈ· ·/ *n* [C] *especially BrE* a friend who goes to the same school as you

**school·girl** /ˈskuːlgɜːl‖-gɜːrl/ *n* [C] *especially BrE* a girl attending school

**school gov·ern·or** /ˌ· ˈ···/ *n* [C] a member of a group of people in Britain who are elected to make decisions about how a school should be managed

**school·house** /ˈskuːlhaʊs/ *n* [C] a school building, especially for a small village school

**school·ing** /ˈskuːlɪŋ/ *n* [U] school education

**school·kid** /ˈskuːlkɪd/ *n* [C] *informal* a child attending school

**school-leav·er** /ˈ· ˌ··/ *n* [C] *BrE* someone who leaves school, especially when they are looking for a job rather than going to college, university etc: *a shortage of jobs for school-leavers*

**school·marm** /ˈskuːlmɑːm‖-mɑːrm/ *n* [C] a woman who is considered to be old-fashioned, strict, and easily shocked —**schoolmarmish** *adj*

**school·mas·ter** /ˈskuːlˌmɑːstə‖-ˌmæstər/ *n* [C] *especially BrE* a male teacher, especially in a PRIVATE SCHOOL (=one that parents pay to send their children to)

**school·mate** /ˈskuːlmeɪt/ *n* [C] someone who goes or went to the same school as you

**school mis·tress** /ˈ· ˌ··/ *n* [C] *especially BrE* a female teacher, especially in a PRIVATE SCHOOL (=one that parents pay to send their children to)

**school·room** /ˈskuːlruːm, -rʊm/ *n* [C] a room used for teaching in a small school

**school·teach·er** /ˈskuːlˌtiːtʃə‖-ər/ *n* [C] a TEACHER

**school tie** /ˌ· ˈ·/ *n* [C] **1** a special tie with a particular colour or pattern that children wear at some schools in Britain **2 the old school tie** *BrE informal* the unofficial system by which people who went to the same school, especially an expensive one, help each other to gain important positions later in their lives.

**school·work** /ˈskuːlwɜːk‖-wɜːrk/ *n* [U] work done for or during school classes

**schoo·ner** /ˈskuːnə‖-ər/ *n* [C] **1** a fast sailing ship with two sails **2** a large tall glass for SHERRY or beer

**schwa** /ʃwɑː/ *n* [C] *technical* a vowel typically heard in parts of a word that are spoken without STRESS¹ (4), such as the "a" in "about"

**sci·at·ic** /saɪˈætɪk/ *adj technical* connected with the hips (HIP¹ (1))

**sci·at·i·ca** /saɪˈætɪkə/ *adj* pain in the lower back, hips (HIP¹ (1)) and legs

S1 W1 **sci·ence** /ˈsaɪəns/ *n* **1** [U] knowledge about the world, especially based on examination and testing, and on facts that can be proved: *Science has taught us how atoms are made up.* | *The computer is one of the marvels of modern science.* | *developments in science and technology* **2** [U] the study of science: *a degree in science* **3** [C] a particular part of science, for example BIOLOGY, CHEMISTRY, or PHYSICS: *the physical sciences* —see also NATURAL SCIENCE, SOCIAL SCIENCE, **blind sb with science** (BLIND² (4))

**science fic·tion** /ˌ·· ˈ··/ *n* [U] a kind of writing in which imaginary future developments in science and their effect on life are described

**science park** /ˈ·· ·/ *n* [C] an area where there are a lot of companies or organizations that do scientific work

**sci·en·tif·ic** /ˌsaɪənˈtɪfɪk◂/ *adj* **1** [no comparative] about or connected with science, or using its methods: *scientific discoveries* | *scientific proof* **2** *informal* done very carefully, using an organized system: *We do keep accounts for the business, but we're not very scientific about it.* —**scientifically** /-kli/ *adv* S W

**sci·en·tist** /ˈsaɪəntɪ̈st/ *n* [C] someone who works or is trained in science S W

**sci·en·tol·ogy** /ˌsaɪənˈtɒlədʒi‖-ˈtɑː-/ *n* [U] a religion which says that Christ was only one of several important teachers

**sci-fi** /ˌsaɪ ˈfaɪ◂/ *n* [U] *informal* SCIENCE FICTION

**scim·i·tar** /ˈsɪmɪ̈tə‖-ər/ *n* [C] a sword with a curved blade —see picture at SWORD

**scin·til·la** /sɪnˈtɪlə/ *n* [singular] **not a scintilla of truth/evidence etc** not even the smallest amount of truth etc: *There isn't a scintilla of evidence to prove it.*

**scin·til·late** /ˈsɪntɪ̈leɪt/ *v* [I] *literary* to shine with small quick flashes of light; SPARKLE¹ (1) —**scintillation** /ˌsɪntɪ̈ˈleɪʃən/ *n* [U]

**scin·til·lat·ing** /ˈsɪntɪ̈leɪtɪŋ/ *adj* interesting, clever, and amusing: *scintillating conversation*

**sci·on** /ˈsaɪən/ *n* [C] **1** *technical* a living part of a plant that is cut off, especially for fixing onto another plant **2** *literary* a young member of a famous or important family: *scions of wealthy East coast families*

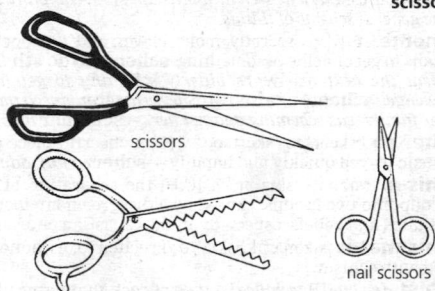

**scissors**

scissors

nail scissors

pinking shears *BrE* / pinking scissors *AmE*

**scis·sors** /ˈsɪzəz‖-ərz/ *n* [plural] a tool for cutting paper, made of two sharp blades and a handle with two holes for your fingers: *a pair of scissors*

**scle·ro·sis** /sklɪ̈ˈrəʊsɪ̈s‖-ˈroʊ-/ *n* [C,U] *technical* a disease that causes an organ or soft part of your body to become hard —**sclerotic** /sklɪ̈ˈrɒtɪk‖-ˈrɑː-/ *adj* —see also MULTIPLE SCLEROSIS

**scoff** /skɒf‖skɒːf, skɑːf/ *v* **1** [I] to laugh at a person or idea, and talk about them in a way that shows you think they are stupid: [+ **at**] *They scoffed at the idea that anything could be changed.* **2** [T] *BrE informal* to eat something very quickly: *Who's scoffed all the cake?*

**scold¹** /skəʊld‖skoʊld/ *v* [T] to angrily criticize someone, especially a child, about something they have done: *As kids we were always getting scolded by the local farmer.* —**scolding** *n* [C,U]

**scold²** *n* [C] *old use* a woman who often complains or criticizes

**scol·lop** /ˈskɒləp‖ˈskɑː-/ *n* [C] another spelling of SCALLOP

**sconce** /skɒns‖skɑːns/ *n* [C] an object that is fixed to a wall and holds CANDLES or electric lights

**scone** /skɒn, skəʊn‖skoʊn, skɑːn/ *n* [C] a small round, soft cake sometimes containing dried fruit: *scones and cream*

**scoop¹** /skuːp/ *n* [C] **1** a round deep spoon for holding or serving food such as corn, flour, or ICE CREAM: *an icecream scoop* **2** also **scoopful** an amount of food removed with this kind of spoon: [+ **of**] *three scoops of ice cream* **3** an important or exciting news story that is printed in one newspaper before any of the others know about it: *Royal Diary Scoop!* **4** a very big profit that a company makes **5 what's the scoop?** *spoken especially AmE* used to ask someone for information or news about something

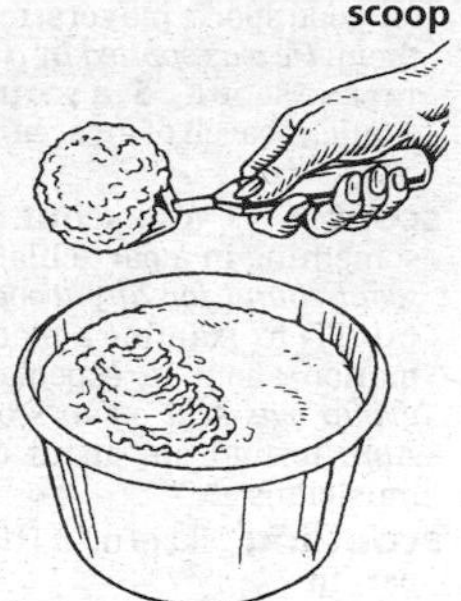
**scoop**

**scoop²** *v* [T] **1** to pick something up with a scoop, a spoon, or with your curved hand: [+ **up/out/off etc**] *She scooped up a handful of sand.* | *Scoop out the seeds from the melon.* **2** to be the first newspaper to print an important news report: *The Daily News scooped the other papers by revealing the prince's marriage plans.*

**scoop neck** /ˌ. ˈ.◂/ *n* [C] a round, quite low neck on a woman's TOP —see picture on page 840

**scoot** /skuːt/ *v* [I] *informal* to leave a place quickly and suddenly: *There's the bus now – I'd better scoot!*

**scoot·er** /ˈskuːtə‖-ər/ *n* [C] **1** a type of small less powerful MOTORBIKE —see picture at MOTORBIKE **2** a child's vehicle with two small wheels, an upright handle, and a narrow board that you stand on with one foot, while the other foot pushes against the ground

3 **scope¹** /skəʊp‖skoʊp/ *n* [U] **1** the range of things that a subject, activity, book etc deals with: *a repertoire of extraordinary scope* **beyond/within the scope of** *The politics of the country is really beyond the scope of a tourist book like this.* | **widen/broaden the scope of** (=include more things) *an attempt to broaden the scope of the inquiry* **2** the opportunity to do or develop something: [+ **for**] *Is there much scope for initiative in this job?*

**scope²** *v* [T]

**scope** sth/sb **out** *phr v* [T] *AmE old-fashioned* to look at something or someone to see what they are like: *Let's scope out that new club tonight.*

**scorch¹** /skɔːtʃ‖skɔːrtʃ/ *v* **1** [I,T] if you scorch something, or if it scorches, its surface burns slightly and changes colour: *The walls had been blackened and scorched by the fire.* | *I scorched my new shirt with the iron.* **2** [T] if strong heat scorches plants, it dries them and kills them: *All the grass had been scorched brown.* **3** [T] if strong heat scorches you, it burns you: *The hot sand scorched our feet.* **4** [I always + adv/prep] *BrE informal* to travel extremely fast: [+ **along/down/across etc**] *A car came scorching down the fast lane at 110 miles an hour.*

**scorch²** *n* **1** [C] a mark made on something where its surface has been burnt **2** [U] brown colouring on plants caused by some plant diseases

**scorched earth pol·i·cy** /ˌ. . ˈ. ˌ.../ *n* [C] the destruction by an army of everything useful in an area, especially crops, so that the land cannot be used by an enemy

**scorch·er** /ˈskɔːtʃə‖ˈskɔːrtʃər/ *n* [C usually singular] *informal* an extremely hot day: *Phew, what a scorcher!*

**scorch·ing** /ˈskɔːtʃɪŋ‖ˈskɔːr-/ *adj* extremely hot: *scorching sun* | **scorching hot** *a scorching hot day*

3 **score¹** /skɔː‖skɔːr/ *n* [C]

2 **1 ▶ IN A GAME ◀** the number of points that each team or player has won in a game or competition: **the score** *What's the score?* | **keep (the) score** (=make a record of the score) *Is anybody keeping score?* | **final score** *The final score was Everton 2, Spurs 4.*

**2 ▶ MUSIC ◀** a written or printed copy of a piece of music, especially for a large group of performers: *a vocal score* | *Who wrote the score for the movie?*

**3 ▶ IN A TEST ◀** *AmE* the number of points a student has earned for correct answers in a test

**4 on that score** *spoken* concerning the particular thing you have just mentioned: *As for the cost, you don't need to worry on that score.*

**5 know the score** *informal* to know the real facts of a situation, including any unpleasant ones: *John won't do anything risky – he knows the score.*

**6 settle a score** to do something to harm or hurt someone who has harmed or hurt you in the past: *Jack came back after five years to settle some old scores.*

**7 ▶ MARK ◀** a mark that has been cut onto a surface with a sharp tool: *deep scores in the wood*

**score²** *v* W2

**1 ▶ WIN POINTS ◀** [I,T] to win a point in a sport, game, or competition: *Arsenal scored in the final minute of the game.* | **score a goal/point/run** *Which player has scored the most runs this season?*

**2 ▶ RECORD POINTS ◀** [I] to record the number of points someone has in a game or competition as it is played: *Will you score for us?*

**3 ▶ GIVE POINTS ◀** [T] **a)** to give someone a particular number of points in a game or competition: **score sb 6/8 etc** *The Canadian judge scored her 15.* **b)** to be worth a particular number of points in a game or competition: *A bull's-eye scores 50 points.*

**4 score points** also **score off sb** to argue with someone in order to prove that you are better than they are

**5 ▶ SUCCEED ◀** [I,T] *informal* to be very successful in something you do: *Atwood has scored again with another popular book.* | **score a success** *The Green party scored some successes in the north west.*

**6 ▶ HAVE SEX ◀** [I] *slang* to have sex with someone you have just met: *Did you score, then?*

**7 ▶ PAPER ◀** [T] to mark a line on a piece of paper, using a sharp instrument: *Scoring the paper first makes it easier to fold.*

**8 ▶ MUSIC ◀** [usually passive] to arrange a piece of music for a group of instruments or voices

**9 ▶ GET DRUGS ◀** [I,T] *slang* to manage to buy or get illegal drugs

**score** sth ↔ **out/through** *phr v* [T] to draw a line through something that has been written

**score³** *number* **1** *old use* twenty **2 scores of** a lot of: *scores of people in line for food*

**score·board** /ˈskɔːbɔːd‖ˈskɔːrbɔːrd/ *n* [C] a board on which the points won in a game are recorded

**score·card** /ˈskɔːkɑːd‖ˈskɔːrkɑːrd/ *n* [C] a printed card used by someone watching a sports match or race to record what happens

**scor·er** /ˈskɔːrə‖-ər/ *n* [C] **1** also **scorekeeper** someone who keeps an official record of the points won in a sports game **2** a player who wins a point or GOAL (2) **3 high/low scorer** someone who gets a large or small number of points in a test

**scorn¹** /skɔːn‖skɔːrn/ *n* [U] the feeling that someone or something is stupid, old-fashioned, or not as good as other people or things; CONTEMPT: [+ **for**] *They had nothing but scorn for their working-class parents.* | **pour scorn on** *Davis poured scorn on the proposal.*

**scorn²** *v* [T] to refuse to accept ideas, suggestions etc because you think they are stupid, old-fashioned, or unreasonable: *Most young people today scorn the idea that virginity is important.* | **scorn to do sth** (=refuse to do something, because you think it is not good enough) *She scorned to hide away like a coward.*

**scorn·ful** /ˈskɔːnfəl‖ˈskɔːrn-/ *adj* feeling or showing scorn: *a scornful look* | [+ **of**] *They remained scornful of all our attempts to find a solution.* —**scornfully** *adv*

**Scor·pi·o** /ˈskɔːpiəʊ‖ˈskɔːrpioʊ/ *n* **1** [singular] the eighth sign of the ZODIAC, represented by a SCORPION, and believed to affect the character and life of people born between October 23 and November 21 **2** [C] someone who was born between October 23 and November 21

**scor·pi·on** /ˈskɔːpiən‖-ɔːr-/ *n* [C] a tropical animal like an insect with, a curving tail and a poisonous sting

scorpion

**Scot** /skɒt‖skɑːt/ *n* [C] someone from Scotland

**scotch** /skɒtʃ‖skɑːtʃ/ *v* [T] to stop something happening by firmly doing something to prevent it: *British delegates soon scotched any idea of a deal.*|**scotch a rumour** (=stop people saying something untrue)

**Scotch¹** *n* [C,U] a strong alcoholic drink made in Scotland, or a glass of this

**Scotch²** *adj* SCOTTISH

**Scotch broth** /ˌ· ˈ·/ *n* [U] thick soup made from vegetables, meat and BARLEY (=type of grain)

**Scotch egg** /ˌ· ˈ·/ *n* [C] a cooked egg covered with meat and small pieces of bread

**Scotch mist** /ˌ· ˈ·/ *n* [C,U] thick mist with light rain

**Scotch pan·cake** /ˌ· ˈ··/ *n* [C] a small round flat cake

**Scotch tape** /ˌ· ˈ·, ˈ· ·/ *n* [U] *AmE trademark* sticky thin transparent material used for sticking light things together; SELLOTAPE *BrE trademark*

**scotch tape** *v* [T] *AmE* to stick things together with Scotch tape; SELLOTAPE *BrE*

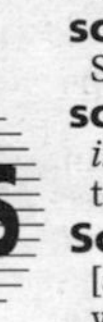

**scot-free** /ˌskɒtˈfriː‖ˌskɑːt-/ *adv* **get away/off scot-free** *informal* to avoid being punished although you deserve to be

**Scot·land Yard** /ˌskɒtlənd ˈjɑːd‖ˌskɑːtlənd ˈjɑːrd/ *n* [singular] *BrE* the part of the London police that deals with serious crimes, or their main office

**Scots** /skɒts‖skɑːts/ *adj* Scottish

**Scots·man** /ˈskɒtsmən‖ˈskɑːts-/ *n* [C] a man who comes from Scotland

**Scots·wom·an** /ˈskɒtsˌwʊmən‖ˈskɑːts-/ *n* [C] a woman who comes from Scotland

**Scot·tish** /ˈskɒtɪʃ‖ˈskɑːtɪʃ/ *adj* from or belonging to Scotland

**scoun·drel** /ˈskaʊndrəl/ *n* [C] *old-fashioned* a bad or dishonest man: *a charming scoundrel, without morals*

**scour** /skaʊə‖skaʊr/ *v* [T] **1** to search very carefully and thoroughly through an area, a document, etc: *A team of detectives is scouring the countryside.* **2** also **scour out** to clean something very thoroughly by rubbing it with a rough material: *The pans really needed to be scoured.* —see picture at CLEAN² **3** also **scour out** to form a hole by continuous movement over a long period: *Over the years, the stream had scoured out a round pool in the rock.* —**scour** *n* [singular]

**scour·er** /ˈskaʊərə‖ˈskaʊr-/ *n* [C] a small ball of wire or rough plastic for cleaning cooking pots and pans

**scourge¹** /skɜːdʒ‖skɜːrdʒ/ *n* [C] **1** something that causes a lot of harm or suffering: [+ **of**] *The scourge of apartheid has finally ended.* **2** a WHIP used to punish people in former times

**scourge²** *v* [T] **1** to cause a lot of harm or suffering to a place or group of people: *a country scourged by disease and war* **2** to hit someone with a whip as punishment in former times

**scouring pad** /ˈ·· ·/ *n* [C] a scourer

**Scouse** /skaʊs/ *n* [U] *BrE* **1** the way of speaking that is typical of people from Liverpool **2** a thick soup with meat, potatoes, and vegetables —**Scouse** *adj*

**Scous·er** /ˈskaʊsə‖-ər/ *n* [C] someone from Liverpool

**scout¹** /skaʊt/ *n* [C] **1 a) the scouts** an organization for young boys that teaches them practical skills **b)** also **boy scout** a boy who is a member of this organization **2** *AmE* also **girl scout** a girl who is a member of an organization for girls that teaches them practical skills; GUIDE *BrE* **3** a soldier, plane etc that is sent to search the area in front of an army, get information about the enemy: *He sent three scouts ahead to take a look at the bridge.* **4** someone whose job is to look for good sports players, musicians etc in order to employ them: *He was spotted by a scout at the age of 13.* —see also TALENT SCOUT **5 a scout round/around** *BrE informal* a quick search of an area: *I'll have a scout round to see if I can find it.*

**scout²** *v* **1** also **scout round/around** [I] to look for something in a particular area: [+ **for**] *I want you all to scout round for any wood you can find.* **2** also **scout out** [T] to examine a place or area in order to get information about it, especially in a military situation: *A group was sent off to scout out the area ahead.* **3** [T] *AmE* to find out about the abilities of sports players, musicians etc

**scout·ing** /ˈskaʊtɪŋ/ *n* [U] the activities that scouts take part in

**scout·mas·ter** /ˈskaʊtˌmɑːstə‖-ˌmæstər/ *n* [C] a man who is the leader of a group of scouts (SCOUT¹ (1a))

**scowl¹** /skaʊl/ *v* [I + **at**] to look at someone in an angry way

scowl

**scowl²** *n* [C] an angry or disapproving expression on someone's face

**Scrab·ble** /ˈskræbəl/ *n* [U] *trademark* a game in which players try to make words from the separate letters they have

**scrab·ble** *v* [I **always + adv + prep**] to try to find something by feeling with your fingers, especially quickly among a lot of other things: [+ **around/about etc**] *She was scrabbling through her pockets for a cigarette.*

**scrag end** /ˌ· ˈ·/ also **scrag** *n* [U] *BrE* the bony part of a sheep's neck, that is sometimes boiled for soup

**scrag·gly** /ˈskræɡəli/ *adj AmE informal* growing in a way that looks uneven and in bad condition: *his scraggly unwashed hair*

**scrag·gy** /ˈskræɡi/ *adj* too thin and bony: *scraggy wrists*

**scram** /skræm/ *v* [I usually in imperative] *informal* to leave a place very quickly, especially so that you do not get caught: *Scram, you two!*

**scram·ble¹** /ˈskræmbəl/ *v*

**1** ▶ **CLIMB** ◀ [I always + adv/prep] to climb up or over something with difficulty, using your hands to help you: [+ **up/down/back etc**] *We scrambled up a rocky slope.*

**2 scramble to your feet** to stand up quickly and awkwardly: *He scrambled to his feet, blushing furiously.*

**3** ▶ **COMPETE** ◀ [I] to struggle or compete with other people to get or reach something: [+ **for**] *People were scrambling madly for shelter.*

**4** ▶ **INFORMATION/MESSAGE** ◀ [T] *technical* to use special equipment to mix messages, radio signals etc into a different form, so that they cannot be understood by other people, especially an enemy: *A magnetic field will scramble the information on a computer disk.*

**5 scramble an egg** to cook an egg by mixing the white and yellow parts together and heating it

**6 scramble sb's brains** *informal* to make someone unable to think clearly or reasonably: *This girl has taken enough drugs to completely scramble her brains.*

**7** ▶ **AIRCRAFT** ◀ [I] *technical* if a military plane scrambles, it goes up into the air very quickly in order to escape or to attack an enemy

**scramble²** *n* **1** [singular] a difficult climb in which you have to use your hands to help you: *a rough scramble over boulders* **2** [singular] a situation in which people compete with and push each other in order to get what they want: [+ **for**] *a scramble for the best seats*|**a**

**scramble to do sth** *a scramble to pick up the scattered coins* **3** [singular] a situation in which something has to be done very quickly, with a lot of rushing around: **mad scramble** *It was a mad scramble trying to get things ready in time.* **4** [C] a MOTORCYCLE race over rough ground

**scrambled egg** /ˌ·· ˈ·/ *n* [C,U] egg cooked in a pan after the white and yellow parts have been mixed together

**scram·bler** /ˈskræmblə‖-ər/ *n* [C] a machine that mixes up a radio or telephone message so that it cannot be understood without special equipment

**scrap¹** /skræp/ *n*

**1** ▶ **PAPER/CLOTH** ◀ [C] a small piece of paper, cloth etc: [+ **of**] *He wrote his address on a scrap of paper and gave it to me.* | *a quilt made out of scraps of old fabric* —see picture on page 416

**2** ▶ **OLD OBJECTS** ◀ [U] materials or objects that are no longer used for the purpose they were made for, but can be used again in another way: *The car was eventually sold for scrap.* | **scrap metal** (=metal from old cars, machines etc that is melted and used again)

**3** ▶ **FOOD** ◀ **scraps** [plural] pieces of food that are left after you have finished eating: *They fed the dog on scraps.*

**4** ▶ **INFORMATION** ◀ [C] a small piece of information, truth etc: [+ **of**] *There wasn't a single scrap of evidence to connect him with the murder.* | *scraps of news*

**5 not make a scrap of difference** *informal* to not change a situation at all: *Nothing I said made a scrap of difference.*

**6** ▶ **FIGHT** ◀ [C] *informal* a short fight or argument: *The girls have scraps over their toys sometimes, but nothing serious.*

**scrap²** *v* **scrapped, scrapping 1** [T] to decide not to use a plan or system because it is not practical: *We've decided to scrap the whole idea of renting a car.* **2** [T] to get rid of an old machine, vehicle etc, and use its parts in some other way: *The navy's biggest aircraft carrier is being scrapped this year.* **3** [I] *informal* to have a short fight or argument

**scrap·book** /ˈskræpbʊk/ *n* [C] a book with empty pages where you can stick pictures, newspaper articles, or other things you want to keep

**scrape¹** /skreɪp/ *v* **1** [T] to remove something from a surface, using the edge of a knife, stick etc: *Scrape the carrots and slice them thinly.* | **scrape sth away/off etc** *I tried to scrape some of the mud off my boots.* | *We scraped away several layers of old varnish.* | **scrape sth clean** *The plates had all been scraped clean.* **2** [I always + adv/prep,T] to rub against a rough surface in a way that causes slight damage or injury, or to make something do this: [+ **on/against etc**] *The car exhaust was hanging down and scraping the ground.* | **scrape sth on/against etc** *I scraped my knee painfully on the concrete.* **3** [I,T] to make an unpleasant noise by rubbing roughly against a surface: *Chairs scraped loudly as they stood up.* | **scrape (sth) on/down/against etc** *Her fingernails scraped down the blackboard.* **4 scrape home** *especially BrE* to win a race, election, or competition by a very small amount: *Johnson scraped home just milliseconds ahead of Lewis.* **5 scrape a hole** to make a hole or hollow place in the ground by rubbing the surface **6 scrape (the bottom of) the barrel** *informal* to have to use something even though it is not very good because there is nothing better available —see also **bow and scrape** (BOW¹ (4)), **pinch and scrape** (PINCH¹ (5)), **scrape/scratch a living** (LIVING¹ (1))

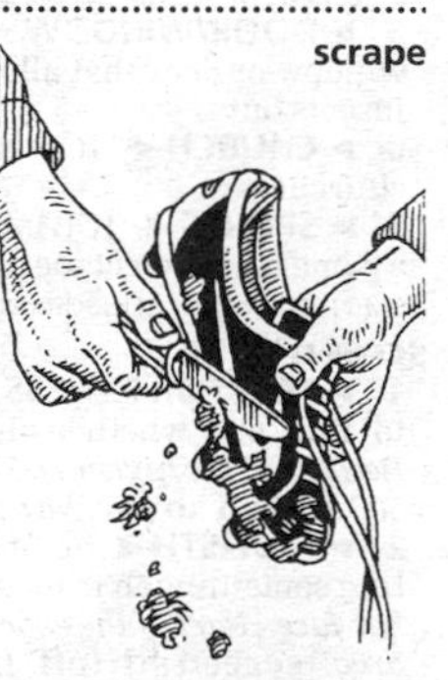


**scrape by** *phr v* [I] **1** to have just enough money to live: *They just managed to scrape by on Fred's tiny salary.* **2** *especially AmE* to only just succeed in passing an examination or dealing with a difficult situation

**scrape in/into** *phr v* [I,T] to only just succeed in getting a job, place at university, position in government etc: *He just scraped into college.* | *Labour scraped in by a small majority.*

**scrape through** *phr v* [I,T] to only just succeed in passing an examination or dealing with a difficult situation: *Dani just scraped through her exams.*

**scrape** sth ↔ **together/up** *phr v* [T] to get enough money for a particular purpose, when this is difficult: *She scraped together the last of her savings to buy the cottage.*

**scrape²** *n* **1** [singular] the unpleasant noise made when one surface rubs roughly against another: *We heard the scrape of a chair downstairs and then footsteps.* **2** [C] a situation that is difficult or slightly dangerous: *He got himself into all sorts of scrapes as a boy.* **3** [C] a mark or slight injury caused by rubbing against a rough surface: *We came away from the accident with only a few cuts and scrapes.*

**scrap·er** /ˈskreɪpə‖-ər/ *n* [C] a tool used to remove something from a surface by rubbing: *a paint scraper*

**scrap·heap** /ˈskræphiːp/ *n* **1 throw sb/sth on the scrapheap** *informal* to get rid of someone or something because you no longer think they are useful, in a way that seems unfair: *Twenty years of loyal service and they're throwing him on the scrapheap!* **2** [C] a pile of unwanted things, especially pieces of metal

**scra·pie** /ˈskreɪpi/ *n* [U] a serious disease that sheep get

**scrap·ings** /ˈskreɪpɪŋz/ *n* [plural] small pieces that have been scraped from a surface

**scrap pa·per** /ˈ· ˌ··/ *n* [U] *BrE* paper, often paper that has already been used on one side, that you use for making notes, lists etc; SCRATCH PAPER *AmE*

**scrap·ple** /ˈskræpl/ *n* [U] *AmE* food made from pieces of meat mixed together with CORNMEAL

**scrap·py** /ˈskræpi/ *adj* **1** untidy or badly organized: *a scrappy, badly written report* | *a scrappy bit of paper* **2** *AmE informal* always wanting to argue or fight

**scratch¹** /skrætʃ/ *v*

**1** ▶ **RUB YOUR SKIN** ◀ [I,T] to rub your skin with your nails, especially because it itches (ITCH¹ (1)): *Try not to scratch those mosquito bites.*

**2** ▶ **MAKE A MARK** ◀ [T] to rub something sharp or rough against a hard surface so that it makes a thin mark: *Mind you don't scratch the table with those scissors!*

**3** ▶ **MAKE A CUT** ◀ [I,T] to make a small cut by pulling something sharp against someone's skin: *I scratched my hand on a blackberry bush.* | *Be careful. That cat scratches.*

scratch

**4** ▶ **MAKE A NOISE** ◀ [I always + adv/prep] to make a noise by rubbing something with a sharp or pointed object: *The dog kept scratching at the door to be let in.*

**5** ▶ **REMOVE STH** ◀ [T always + adv/prep] to remove something from a surface by rubbing it with something sharp: **scratch sth off/away etc** *I scratched away a little of the paint with my fingernail.*

**6** ▶ **STOP PLANNING** ◀ [T] to stop planning to do something because it is no longer possible or practical: *I guess we can scratch that idea.*

**7 scratch the surface** to deal with only a very small part of a subject: *In this essay I can only hope to scratch the surface of the topic.*

**8 scratch your head** *informal* to think hard about a

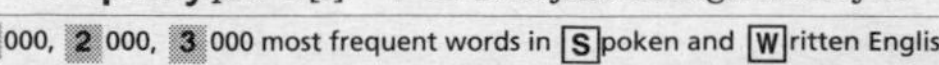

difficult question or problem: *The last question really had us scratching our heads.*
**9 ▶ REMOVE FROM RACE ◀** [I,T] to remove someone from a race or competition before it begins
**10 up to scratch** if something is up to scratch it is good enough: *Kaari's French isn't up to scratch* **you scratch my back, I'll scratch yours** *spoken* used to say that you will help someone if they agree to help you —see also **scrape/scratch a living** (LIVING[1] (1))

**scratch** sth↔ **out** *phr v* [T] to draw a line through a word, in order to remove it: *Philippa's name had been scratched out.*

**scratch²** *n*
**1 ▶ MARK OR CUT ◀** [C] a thin mark or cut on the surface of something or on someone's skin: *a scratch on the car door*
**2 from scratch** if you do or start something from scratch, you begin it without using anything that existed or was prepared before: *It was years since I'd learnt any German, and I really had to start again from scratch.*
**3 not come/be up to scratch** to not be good enough for a particular standard: *His schoolwork really hasn't been up to scratch lately.*
**4 ▶ SOUND ◀** [C] a sound made by something sharp or rough being rubbed on a hard surface: *I could hear the scratch of the dog's claws on the floor.*
**5 have a scratch** to rub part of your body with your nails
**6 it's only/just a scratch** *spoken* used to say that you are not seriously hurt or injured
**7 without a scratch** if you escape from a dangerous situation without a scratch, you are not injured at all

**8 ▶ MUSIC ◀** [U] a type of popular music produced by stopping a record while it is playing and moving it with your hands to make a sound

**scratch³** *adj* [no comparative] **1** a scratch team, game, side etc is put together in a hurry, using anyone that is available **2** a scratch player in a sport does not have a HANDICAP (=officially arranged disadvantage)

**scratch·ings** /ˈskrætʃɪŋz/ *n* [plural] *BrE* small pieces of pig's skin that have been cooked in hot fat and are eaten cold; PORK RINDS *AmE*

**scratch·pad** /ˈskrætʃpæd/ *n* [C] *especially AmE* several sheets of cheap paper joined together at the top or side, used for writing notes or lists

**scratch pa·per** /ˈ· ˌ··/ *n* [U] *AmE* paper, often paper that has already been used on one side, that you use for making notes, lists etc; SCRAP PAPER *BrE*

**scratch test** /ˈ· ·/ *n* [C] a medical test that involves cutting someone's skin slightly and putting a substance on it to see how their body reacts

**scratch·y** /ˈskrætʃi/ *adj* **1** scratchy clothes or materials feel rough and uncomfortable **2** a scratchy record makes a lot of unpleasant noises because it is old or damaged —**scratchiness** *n* [U]

**scrawl¹** /skrɔːl‖skrɒːl/ *v* [T] to write in a careless and untidy way, so that your words are not easy to read

**scrawl²** *n* [singular] something written in an untidy careless way, or an untidy careless way of writing

**scraw·ny** /ˈskrɔːni‖ˈskrɒː-/ *adj* thin, unattractive, and looking weak: *a scrawny kid in jeans and a T-shirt*

**scream¹** /skriːm/ *v* **1** [I] to make a loud high noise with your voice because you are hurt, frightened, excited etc: *Shots rang out, and people started screaming.* | *a screaming baby* | [+ **with/in**] *The woman lay there, screaming with pain.* | **scream with laughter** (=laugh very loudly in a high voice) **2** also **scream out** [I,T] to shout something in a very loud high voice because you are angry or frightened: *"Get out!" she screamed.* | [+ **for**] *I screamed for help.* | [+ **at**] *Calm down and stop screaming at me!* | **scream insults/abuse etc** *Lola screamed insults at him as he left.* **3** [T] to make a very loud high noise: *The police car approached, its siren screaming.*

**scream (out) at** sb *phr v* [I] *informal* if something such as a very bright colour or a mistake screams at you, it is very noticeable and annoying

**scream²** *n* [C] **1** a loud high sound made with your voice because you are very frightened, angry, hurt, or excited: *Her screams could be heard all down the block.* | **scream of laughter/terror etc** *There were screams of excitement when he finally walked on stage.* | **let out a scream** *He let out a scream of terror.* **2** a very loud high sound: *The scream of the jet taking off drowned Ryan's response.* **3 be a scream** [I] *informal* used to describe someone or something that is very funny: *We went to the party dressed as twins. It was a scream!*

**scream·ing·ly** /ˈskriːmɪŋli/ *adv* **screamingly funny** extremely funny

**scree** /skriː/ *n* [C] an area of small loose broken rocks on the side of a mountain: *a scree slope* —see picture on page 835

**screech** /skriːtʃ/ *v* **1** [I,T] to make a very unpleasant, high noise with your voice, especially because you are angry: [+ **at**] *She screeched at me to take off my muddy shoes.* **2** [I] if a vehicle or its wheels screech, they make a high loud unpleasant noise: *The train's wheels screeched and clattered as it drew out of the station.*
**3 screech to a halt/stop/standstill:** if a vehicle screeches to a halt, it stops very suddenly, so that the wheels make a loud unpleasant noise —**screech** *n* [singular] *a screech of tires*

**screen¹** /skriːn/ *n*
**1 ▶ TELEVISION/COMPUTER ◀** [C] the flat glass part of a television or computer: *This popular show will be back on your screens in the autumn.* | **on screen** (=on a computer screen) *It's easy to change the text on screen before printing it.* S W
**2 ▶ CINEMA ◀ a)** [C] the large white surface that pictures are shown on in a cinema **b)** [singular, U] films in general: *The play was adapted for the screen.*
**3 ▶ MOVABLE WALL ◀** [C] a kind of wall that can be moved around, used to divide one part of a room from another: *The nurse put a screen around my bed.*
**4 ▶ HIDE OR PROTECT ◀** [C usually singular] something or someone that protects or hides someone or something else: *We planted these bushes as a screen, as the shed is so ugly.* | *It turned out that the used car business was just a screen for his drug-dealing activities.*
**5 ▶ DOOR/WINDOW ◀** [C] a wire net put in front of a window or door that allows air into the house but keeps insects out
**6 ▶ CHURCH ◀** [C] a decorative wall in some churches
**7 ▶ SPORTS ◀** [C] *AmE* a player or group of players in a game who protect the player who has the ball —see also SMOKESCREEN, SUNSCREEN

**screen²** *v* [T]
**1 ▶ TEST FOR ILLNESS ◀** to do tests on a lot of people to find out whether they have a particular illness: *Because of the higher risks, we try to screen all women over 50.* | **screen sb for** *We were all screened for hepatitis.*
**2 ▶ HIDE STH ◀** to hide or protect something by putting something in front of it: [+ **off**] *A large hat screened her face.* | *Part of the room was screened off as a reception area.* | **screen sth (off) from** | *The house is screened from the road by a row of trees.*
**3 ▶ TEST EMPLOYEES ◀** to examine or test people to make sure that they will be loyal to your company, organization etc: *All applicants are screened for security.*
**4 ▶ PROTECT SB ◀** to protect someone who is involved in dishonest or illegal activities: *He had been screening his business partner during the fraud investigation.*
**5 ▶ TELEVISION ◀** to show a film or television programme

**screen** sth ↔ **out** *phr v* [T] **1** to prevent something harmful from entering or passing through: *Sun lotions screen out damaging ultraviolet light.* **2** to decide that someone or something is not suitable for a job, position etc

**screen door** /ˈ· ˌ·/ *n* [C] *AmE* a door outside the main door, that will let air in but keep insects out

**screen·ing** /ˈskriːnɪŋ/ *n* **1** [C,U] the showing of a film or television programme: *a screening of Spielberg's new movie* **2** [U] tests done to make sure that someone does not have a particular disease: *screening for breast cancer* **3** [U] tests or checks done to make sure that someone or something is suitable for a particular purpose

**screen·play** /ˈskriːnpleɪ/ *n* [C] a story written for film or television: *her first screeplay, an adaptation of Austen's 'Sense and Sensibility'*

**screen print·ing** /ˈ· ˌ··/ *n* [U] a way of printing pictures by pushing paint or ink through a specially prepared cloth onto paper

**screen test** /ˈ· ˌ·/ *n* [C] an occasion when someone is filmed while performing, in order to see if they are suitable to act in a film

**screen·writ·er** /ˈskriːnˌraɪtə‖-ər/ *n* [C] someone who writes plays for film or television

**screws**

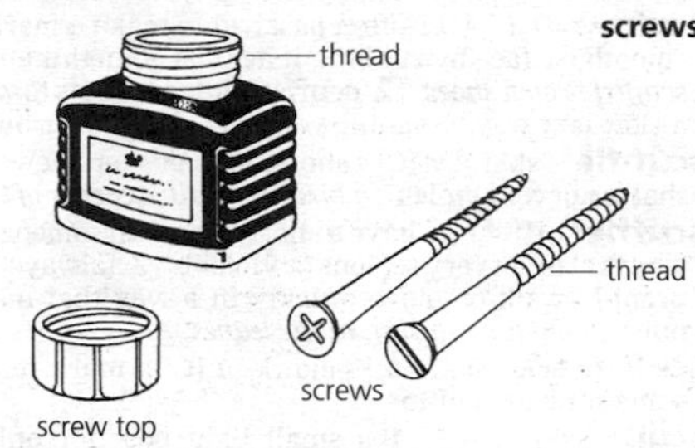


**screw¹** /skruː/ *n* **1** [C] a thin pointed piece of metal that you push and turn in order to fasten pieces of metal or wood together: *Tighten the screws on the plug.* **2** [C] *slang taboo* an act of having sex **3 have a screw loose** *informal often humorous* to be slightly crazy **4 put/tighten the screws on sb** *informal* to force someone to do something by threatening them **5** [C] *BrE slang* a word for a prison officer, used especially by prisoners **6 a screw of tobacco/tea etc** *BrE old-fashioned* a small amount of tobacco, tea etc in a twisted paper packet

**screw²** *v* **1** [T always + adv/prep] to fasten one object to another using a screw: **screw sth into/onto/to sth** *Screw the socket into the wall.* | *The bar stools were screwed to the floor.* **2** [T always + adv/prep] to fasten or close something by turning it until it cannot be turned anymore: **screw sth on/together etc** *Don't forget to screw the cap back onto the toothpaste.* **3** [I,T] *taboo* to have sex with someone **4 screw you/him/that etc** *spoken taboo* used to show that you are very angry with someone: *"Screw you" he yelled.* **5** [T always + adv/prep] to twist paper or cloth into a small round shape: **screw sth (up) into sth** *She screwed the letter up into a ball and threw it in the bin.* **6** [T often passive] *informal* to cheat someone or treat them in a dishonest way, especially to get money from them: *They really screwed you in that nightclub, charging £10 for a drink.* | **screw sb for** *They screwed us for $60 in the end.* —see also **have your head screwed on (straight)** (HEAD¹ (28))

**screw around** *phr v* [I] *taboo* to have sex with a lot of different people

**screw up** *phr v* **1 screw your eyes/face up** to move the muscles in your face in a way that makes your eyes seem narrow: *He screwed up his eyes against the bright light.* **2** [I] *informal* to make a bad mistake or do something very stupid: *I really screwed up, didn't I?* **3** [T **screw** sth ↔ **up**] *informal* to spoil something such as a plan, by doing something stupid: *Breaking my ankle really screwed up our holiday plans!* **4** [T **screw** sb ↔ **up**] *informal* to make someone feel very unhappy, confused, or anxious, especially for a long time: *It really screwed her up when her mother died.* —see also SCREWED UP **5 screw up your courage** to try to be brave enough to do something you are very nervous about: *I screwed up my courage and went over to talk to her.*

**screw·ball** /ˈskruːbɔːl‖-bɒːl/ *n* [C] *informal especially AmE* someone who seems very strange or crazy

**screw·driv·er** /ˈskruːˌdraɪvə‖-ər/ *n* [C] **1** a tool with a narrow blade at one end that you use for turning screws —see picture at TOOL¹ **2** an alcoholic drink made from VODKA and orange juice

**screwed up** /ˌ· ˈ·◂/ *adj informal* unhappy or anxious because you have had bad experiences in the past: *sexually and emotionally screwed up*

**screw top** /ˌ· ˈ·◂/ *n* [C] a cover that you twist onto the top of a bottle or other container —**screw-top** *adj*

**screw·y** /ˈskruːi/ *adj informal* an idea, plan, etc that is screwy seems strange or crazy: *The whole thing sounds pretty screwy to me!*

**scrib·ble¹** /ˈskrɪbəl/ *v* **1** [T] to write something quickly and untidily: *I scribbled his phone number in my address book.* **2** [I] to draw marks that have no meaning: *Don't scribble on the desk like that!*

**scribble²** *n* **1** [U] also **scribbles** meaningless marks or pictures, especially done by children **2** [singular, U] untidy writing that is difficult to read

**scrib·bler** /ˈskrɪbələ‖-ər/ *n* [C] *informal* a writer, especially an unimportant one

**scribe** /skraɪb/ *n* [C] someone employed to copy things in writing, especially before printing was invented

**scrim·mage** /ˈskrɪmɪdʒ/ *n* **1** [C] *informal* a fight **2** [U] a practice game of football, BASKETBALL etc

**scrimp** /skrɪmp/ *v* [I] to try to save as much money as you can even though you have very little: **scrimp and save** *We had to scrimp and save to pay for the holiday.*

**scrip** /skrɪp/ *n* [U] an official piece of paper, especially a SHARE that is instead of money or a DIVIDEND: *scrip dividend* | *scrip issue*

**script** /skrɪpt/ *n* **1** [C] the written form of a speech, play, film etc: *Galton and Simpson wrote some excellent comedy scripts.* **2** [C,U] the set of letters used in writing a language; ALPHABET: *Arabic script* **3** [C] *BrE* a piece of work written by a student in an examination **4** [singular, U] *formal* writing done by hand, especially with the letters of the words joined

**script·ed** /ˈskrɪptɪ̈d/ *adj* a speech or broadcast that is scripted has been written down before it is read

**scrip·tur·al** /ˈskrɪptʃərəl/ *adj* connected with or based on the Bible

**scrip·ture** /ˈskrɪptʃə‖-ər/ *n* **1** also **the (Holy) Scriptures** [U] the Bible **2** [C,U] the holy books of a particular religion: *Buddhist scriptures* **3** [U] *old-fashioned* the study of the Bible, taught as a school subject

**script·writ·er** /ˈskrɪptˌraɪtə‖-ər/ *n* [C] someone who writes SCRIPTS for films, television etc

**scrof·u·la** /ˈskrɒfjɪ̈lə‖ˈskrɒː-, ˈskrɑː-/ *n* [U] a disease that makes the organs in your neck swell up —**scrofulous** *adj*

**scroll¹** /skrəʊl‖skroʊl/ *n* [C] **1** a long piece of paper that can be rolled up, and is used as an official document **2** a decoration shaped like a roll of paper

**scroll²** *v* [I,T] to move information on a computer screen up or down so that you can read it: [+ **up/down**] *Could you scroll down a few lines?*

**scroll·work** /ˈskrəʊlwɜːk‖ˈskroʊlwɜːrk/ *n* [U] *technical* decoration in the shape of scrolls

**scrooge** /skruːdʒ/ *n* [C] *informal* someone who hates spending money: *My landlord's a real scrooge.*

**scro·tum** /ˈskrəʊtəm‖ˈskroʊ-/ *n plural* **scrota** /-tə/ *or* **scrotums** [C] the bag of flesh that contains the TESTICLES of men and male animals

**scrounge¹** /skraʊndʒ/ *v* [I,T] *informal* to get money or something you want by asking other people for it rather than by paying for it yourself: **scrounge (sth) off/from sb** *I managed to scrounge some money off my dad.* —**scrounger** *n* [C]

**scrounge²** *n* **be on the scrounge** *BrE informal* to be trying to get money or things you want by asking other people for them

**scrub¹** /skrʌb/ *v* **1** [I,T] to rub something hard, especially with a stiff brush in order to clean it: *She was down on her hands and knees scrubbing the floor.* | [+ **at**] *Tom scrubbed at the stain but it wouldn't come out.* —see picture at CLEAN² **2** [T] *informal* to decide not to do something that you had planned: *We had to scrub our plans for a party.*

**scrub** sth ↔ **out** *phr v* [T] to clean the inside of a place or object thoroughly: *Prisoners must scrub their cells out once a week.*

**scrub up** *phr v* [I] to wash your hands and arms before doing a medical operation

**scrub²** *n* **1** [U] low bushes and trees that grow in very dry soil **2 give sth a scrub** *especially BrE* to clean something by rubbing it hard

**scrub·ber** /ˈskrʌbə‖-ər/ *n* [C] **1** *BrE* an offensive word for PROSTITUTE (=a woman who has sex for money) **2** a plastic or metal object you use to clean pans

**scrubbing brush** /ˈ··· ·/ *especially BrE*, **scrub brush** /ˈ· ·/ *AmE* —*n* [C] a stiff brush that you use for cleaning things —see picture at BRUSH¹

**scrub·by** /ˈskrʌbi/ *adj* **1** covered by low bushes: *scrubby terrain* **2** *informal* looking dirty and untidy: *a scrubby schoolboy*

**scrub·land** /ˈskrʌblənd/ *n* [U] land that is covered with low bushes

**scruff** /skrʌf/ *n* **1 by the scruff of the neck** if you hold a person or animal by the scruff of their neck, you hold the flesh, fur, or clothes at the back of the neck **2** [C] *BrE informal* someone who looks untidy or dirty

**scruf·fy** /ˈskrʌfi/ *adj* dirty and untidy: *a scruffy old pair of jeans* —**scruffily** *adv* —**scruffiness** *n* [U]

**scrum¹** /skrʌm/ *n* **1** [C] a particular arrangement of players in the game of RUGBY **2** [singular] *BrE informal* a crowd of people who are all pushing each other to try and get something: *There was the usual scrum for tickets when the box office opened.*

**scrum²** *v*

**scrum down** *phr v* [I] to form a scrum during a game of RUGBY

**scrum·half** /ˌskrʌmˈhɑːf‖-ˈhæf/ *n* [C] a player in RUGBY who has to put the ball into the SCRUM¹ (1)

**scrum·mage** /ˈskrʌmɪdʒ/ *n* [C] a SCRUM¹ (1)

**scrump** /skrʌmp/ *v* [T] *BrE old-fashioned* to steal fruit, especially apples, from trees

**scrump·tious** /ˈskrʌmpʃəs/ *adj informal* food that is scrumptious tastes very good: *a scrumptious chocolate dessert*

**scrum·py** /ˈskrʌmpi/ *n* [U] *BrE* a strong alcoholic drink made from apples

**scrunch** /skrʌntʃ/ *v* [I] *informal* if stones or other objects scrunch under your feet, they make a noisy sound when you walk on them: *The pebbles scrunched as we walked along the beach.*

**scrunch** sth ↔ **up** *phr v* [T] to crush and twist something into a small round shape: *I scrunched up the letter and threw it in the bin.*

**scru·ple¹** /ˈskruːpəl/ *n* [C usually plural] a belief about right and wrong that prevents you from doing something bad: *Atkins was a ruthless man with few moral scruples.* | **without scruple** (=without caring about the effects your actions may have on other people) *They made thousands of families homeless without scruple.*

**scruple²** *v* **not scruple to do sth** *literary* to be willing to do something even though it may have harmful or unpleasant effects: *I did not scruple to tell him what I thought.*

**scru·pu·lous** /ˈskruːpjələs/ *adj* **1** careful to be honest and fair: *Mr Samuel has always been most scrupulous in his dealings with us.* —opposite UNSCRUPULOUS **2** done very carefully so that every detail is correct: *scrupulous attention to detail* —**scrupulously** *adv*: *scrupulously clean* —**scrupulousness** *n* [U]

**scru·ti·neer** /ˌskruːtəˈnɪə‖-ˈnɪr/ *n* [C] *BrE* an official who examines or counts votes in an election

**scru·ti·nize** also **-ise** *BrE* /ˈskruːtənaɪz/ *v* [T] to examine someone or something very thoroughly and carefully: *James scrutinized the painting closely.*

**scru·ti·ny** /ˈskruːtəni/ *n* [U] careful and thorough examination of someone or something: **careful/close scrutiny** *Close scrutiny of the document showed it to be a forgery.* | **under scrutiny** *Diana resented her private life being under such public scrutiny.*

**scu·ba div·ing** /ˈskuːbə ˌdaɪvɪŋ/ *n* [U] the sport of swimming under water while breathing through a tube connected to a container of air on your back

**scud** /skʌd/ *v* [I always + adv/prep] *literary* if clouds scud past, they move quickly across the sky

**scuff** /skʌf/ *v* **1** [T often passive] to make a mark on a smooth surface by rubbing it against something rough: *scuffed brown shoes* **2 scuff your feet/heels** to walk in a slow lazy way, dragging your feet along the ground

**scuf·fle¹** /ˈskʌfəl/ *n* [C] a short fight between a few people that is not very violent: *a brief scuffle in a corner of the bar*

**scuffle²** *v* [I] **1** to have a short fight with someone, in a way that is not very serious or violent **2** [always + adv/prep] to walk or move quickly in a way that makes a noise: *a mouse scuffling in the leaves*

**scuff·mark** /ˈskʌfmɑːk‖-mɑːrk/ *n* [C] a mark made on something by scuffing

**scull¹** /skʌl/ *n* [C] **1** a small light boat for only one person **2** one of the OARs that you use when you are sculling a boat

**scull²** *v* [I,T] to ROW³ (1) a small light boat, especially a boat that is only for one person

**scul·le·ry** /ˈskʌləri/ *n* [C] a room next to the kitchen, especially in a large old house, where cleaning jobs are done

**scul·lion** /ˈskʌljən/ *n* [C] *old use* a boy employed to work in a kitchen

**sculpt** /skʌlpt/ *v* [T often passive] **1** to make a solid object that represents someone or something, by shaping stone, wood, clay etc **2** to make something into a particular shape as a result of a natural process, for example the movement of a river

**sculp·tor** /ˈskʌlptə‖-ər/ *n* [C] someone who makes sculptures

**sculp·ture** /ˈskʌlptʃə‖-ər/ *n* **1** [U] the art of making solid objects representing people or animals out of stone, wood, clay etc: *a talent for sculpture* **2** [C,U] the objects produced in this form of art: *an interesting abstract sculpture*

**sculp·tured** /ˈskʌlptʃəd‖-tʃərd/ *adj* **1 sculptured features/beauty/muscles etc** features etc that have a clear shape as if they had been made by an artist **2** [only before noun] decorated with sculptures: *a sculptured pedestal*

**scum** /skʌm/ *n* **1** [singular, U] an unpleasant substance that forms on the surface of a liquid: *The pond was covered with green scum.* **2** [C] *plural* **scum** *spoken* an unpleasant nasty person: *Don't you ever dare say that again you scum!* | **scum of the earth** (=the worst people you can imagine) —**scummy** *adj*

**scum·bag** /ˈskʌmbæg/ *n* [C] *spoken* an unpleasant person

**scup·per¹** /ˈskʌpə‖-ər/ *v* [T] *BrE* **1** [usually passive] *informal* to ruin someone's plans or chances of success: *The recent terrorist attacks have scuppered any chance of a peace settlement.* **2** to deliberately sink your own ship

**scupper²** *n* [C] *technical* a hole in the side of a ship that allows water to flow back into the sea

**scur·ri·lous** /ˈskʌrələs‖ˈskɜːr-/ *adj formal* scurrilous remarks, articles etc contain damaging and untrue statements about someone —**scurrilously** *adv* —**scurrilousness** *n* [U]

**scur·ry** /ˈskʌri‖ˈskɜːri/ *v* [I always + adv/prep] to move quickly with short steps: [+ **along/past/across**] *A beetle scurried across the path.* —**scurry** *n* [singular, U]

**S-curve** /ˈes kɜːv‖-kɜːrv/ *n* [C] *AmE* a bend in the road in the shape of an 'S', that can be dangerous to drivers; S-BEND *BrE*

**scur·vy** /ˈskɜːvi‖ˈskɜːr-/ *n* [U] a disease caused by not eating foods such as fruit and vegetables that contain vitamin C (VITAMIN (2))

**scut·tle¹** /ˈskʌtl/ *v* **1** [I always + adv/prep] to move quickly with short steps: [+ **along/past/down**] *I caught sight of Miss Rawlings scuttling down the corridor.* **2** [T] to sink a ship by making holes in the bottom, especially in order to prevent it being used by an enemy

**scuttle²** *n* [C] a container for carrying coal

**scut·tle·butt** /ˈskʌtlbʌt/ *n* [U] *AmE informal* stories about other people's personal lives, especially containing things that are unkind and untrue about them

**scuz·zy** /ˈskʌzi/ *adj informal* unpleasant and dirty

**scythe** /saɪð/ *n* [C] a farming tool that has a long curved blade fixed to a long wooden handle, and is used to cut grain or long grass

**SE** the written abbreviation of SOUTHEAST or SOUTHEASTERN

S3 W1 **sea** /siː/ *n* **1** [singular] *especially BrE* the large area of salty water that covers much of the earth's surface: OCEAN: *You don't often get the chance to swim in the sea in England – it's too cold!* | **rough/calm sea** (=with or without large waves) *The sea was calm and there was no breeze.* | **by sea** (=on a ship) *I sent my luggage ahead of me by sea.* | **by the sea** (=on the coast) *She lives in a little cottage by the sea.* | **at sea** *Life at sea was never easy and he was always pleased to be back home.* | **put to sea** (=start a journey on the sea) | **the open sea** (=far away from land) | **lost at sea** (=drowned) **2** [C] a large area of salty water that is mostly enclosed by land: *the Mediterranean Sea* **3 a sea of** a large number of something: *A sea of faces stared up at me from the audience.* **4 be (all) at sea** to be confused or not sure what to do: *I'm all at sea with this maths homework.* **5 the seas** *literary* the sea, used especially when you are not talking about a particular ocean: **across the seas** (=far away) *She was born in a northern land far, far across the seas.* **6** [C] one of the broad plains on the moon and Mars

**sea a·nem·o·ne** /ˈ· ·ˌ···/ *n* [C] a brightly-coloured sea animal that sticks onto rocks and looks like a flower

**sea bed** /ˈ· ·/ *n* [singular] the land at the bottom of the sea

**sea·bird** /ˈsiːbɜːd‖-bɜːrd/ *n* [C] a bird that lives near the sea and finds food in it

**sea·board** /ˈsiːbɔːd‖-bɔːrd/ *n* [C] the part of a country that is near the sea: *the eastern seaboard of the US*

**sea·borne** /ˈsiːbɔːn‖-bɔːrn/ *adj* carried on or arriving in ships: *the threat of a seaborne invasion*

**sea breeze** /ˈ· ·/ *n* [C] a light wind that blows from the sea onto the land

**sea cap·tain** /ˈ· ˌ··/ *n* [C] the CAPTAIN of a ship

**sea change** /ˈ· ·/ *n* [singular] a very big change in something: *a sea change in public opinion*

**sea dog** /ˈ· ·/ *n* [C] *literary or humorous* someone with a lot of experience of ships and sailing

**sea·far·ing** /ˈsiːˌfeərɪŋ‖-ˌfer-/ *adj* [only before noun] **1** connected with the life and activities of a sailor: *a story from my seafaring days* **2** having strong connections with ships and the sea, especially because of international trade: **seafaring nation/country** *The Danes are an ancient seafaring nation.* —**seafarer** *n* [C]

**sea·food** /ˈsiːfuːd/ *n* [U] animals from the sea that you can eat, especially SHELLFISH

**sea·front** /ˈsiːfrʌnt/ *n* [C usually singular] *especially BrE* the part of a town where the shops, houses etc are next to the beach: *a hotel right on the seafront*

**sea·go·ing** /ˈsiːˌgəʊɪŋ‖-ˌgoʊ-/ *adj* [only before noun] built to travel on the sea: *a seagoing yacht*

**sea·gull** /ˈsiːgʌl/ *n* [C] a common grey and white bird that lives near the sea

**sea·horse** /ˈsiːhɔːs‖-hɔːrs/ *n* [C] a small sea fish with a head and neck that look like those of a horse

**seal¹** /siːl/ *n* [C] S3

**1 ▶ ANIMAL ◀** a large sea animal that eats fish and lives around coasts or on floating pieces of ice **2 ▶ OFFICIAL MARK ◀** a mark that has a special design and shows the legal or official authority of a person or organization: *a black book stamped with the Presidential Seal*

seal

**3 ▶ ON CONTAINERS/PIPES ◀ a)** a piece of rubber or plastic that keeps air, water, dirt etc out of something: *Do not use this product if the inner seal is broken.* **b)** a piece of WAX¹ (1), paper, wire etc that you have to break in order to open something

**4 seal of approval** if you give something your seal of approval, you say that you approve of it, especially officially: *All we need now is the chairman's seal of approval.*

**5 set the seal on** to make something definite or complete: *A last-minute goal set the seal on Tottenham's victory.*

**6 seal of friendship/success/victory etc** something that makes your friendship stronger, your success more certain etc

**seal²** *v* **1** also **seal up** [T] to close an entrance or a container with something that stops air, water etc from coming in or out of it: *The windows have been sealed up for years.* **2** [T] to close an envelope, pack etc by using something sticky to hold its edges in place: *Don't seal the envelope yet.* **3 my lips are sealed** *spoken* used to say that you are not going to tell someone something **4 seal sb's fate** to make something, especially something bad, sure to happen: *He was about to say the words that would seal my fate for ever.* **5 seal a friendship/promise/agreement etc** to do something that makes a friendship, promise etc more formal or definite

**seal** sth ↔ **in** *phr v* [T] to stop what something contains from getting out: *Fry the meat quickly to seal in the flavor.*

**seal** sth ↔ **off** *phr v* [T] to stop people entering an area or building, because it is dangerous: *Following a bomb warning, police have sealed off the whole area.*

**sea lane** /ˈ· ·/ *n* [C] a fixed path across the sea that ships regularly use

**seal·ant** /ˈsiːlənt/ *n* [C,U] a layer of paint, polish etc that is put on the surface of something to protect it from air, water etc

**sealed** /siːld/ *adj* shut with something that prevents air, water etc from getting in or out: *Keep all dressings in a sealed sterile pack.*

**sea legs** /ˈ· ·/ *n* [plural] **find/get your sea legs** to begin to be able to walk normally, not feel ill etc when you are travelling on a ship

**seal·er** /ˈsiːlə‖-ər/ *n* **1** [C,U] a layer of paint, polish etc put on the surface of something to protect it from air, water etc **2** [C] a person or ship that hunts seals (SEAL¹ (1))

**sea lev·el** /ˈ· ˌ··/ *n* [U] the average height of the sea, used as a standard for measuring other heights and depths, such as the height of a mountain: **above/below sea level** *1000m above sea level*

**seal·ing** /ˈsiːlɪŋ/ *n* [U] the hunting or catching of seals (SEAL¹ (1))

**sealing wax** /ˈ·· ·/ *n* [U] a red substance that melts and becomes hard again quickly, used for sealing (SEAL² (2)) letters, documents etc

**sea li·on** /ˈ· ˌ··/ *n* [C] a large type of SEAL¹ (1)

**seal·skin** /ˈsiːlˌskɪn/ *n* [U] the skin or fur of some types of SEAL¹ (1), used for making leather or clothes

**seam** /siːm/ *n* [C] **1** a line where two pieces of cloth, leather etc have been stitched together: *a split in the seam of his jeans* —see picture on page 840 **2** a layer of a mineral, especially coal, under the ground: **a rich seam** (=one that contains a lot of high quality coal) **3** a line where two pieces of metal, wood etc have been joined together **4 be coming/falling apart at the seams a)** if a plan, organization etc is coming or falling apart at the seams, so many things are going wrong with it that it will probably fail: *Her whole life was threatening to come apart at the seams.* **b)** if a piece of clothing etc is coming or falling apart at the seams, the stitches on it are coming unfastened **5 be bursting at the seams** if a room or building is bursting at the seams, it is so full of people that hardly anyone else can fit into it

**sea·man** /ˈsiːmən/ *plural* **seamen** /-mən/ *n* [C] **1** a sailor on a ship or in the navy who is not an officer: *a merchant seaman* —see table on page B4 **2** someone who has a lot of experience of ships and the sea

**sea·man·ship** /ˈsiːmənʃɪp/ *n* [U] the skills and knowledge that an experienced sailor has

**seamed** /siːmd/ *adj* [only before noun] **1** having a seam: *seamed stockings* **2** a seamed surface has many deep lines on it: *A gentle smile spread over her old, seamed face.*

**sea mile** /ˈ· ·/ *n* [C] a unit for measuring distance at sea that is slightly longer than a land mile, and equals 1853 metres; NAUTICAL MILE

**sea mist** /ˈ· ·/ *n* [U] a mist on land that comes in from the sea

**seam·less** /ˈsiːmləs/ *adj* **1** not having any seams (SEAM (1)): *seamless stockings* **2** something seamless is done or happens so smoothly that you cannot tell where one thing stops and another begins: *I see the piece very much as a flowing, seamless whole.*

**seam·stress** /ˈsiːmstrɪs, ˈsem-‖ˈsiːm-/ *n* [C] *old-fashioned* a woman whose job is SEWING and making clothes

**seam·y** /ˈsiːmi/ *adj* involving unpleasant things such as crime, violence, poverty, or immorality: **seamy side (of sth)** *the seamy side of the film industry*

**se·ance** /ˈseɪɑːns, -ɒns‖ˈseɪɑːns/ *n* [C] a meeting where people try to talk to or receive messages from the spirits of dead people

**sea·plane** /ˈsiːpleɪn/ *n* [C] a plane that can take off from and land on the surface of the sea

**sea·port** /ˈsiːpɔːt‖-pɔːrt/ *n* [C] a large town on or near a coast with a HARBOUR¹ that big ships can use

**sea pow·er** /ˈ· ˌ··/ *n* **1** [U] the size and strength of a country's navy **2** [C] a country with a powerful navy

**sear¹** /sɪə‖sɪr/ *v* **1** [I always + adv/prep, T] to burn something with a sudden powerful heat: *The choking fumes seared their lungs* **2** [T] to cook the outside of a piece of meat, quickly at a high temperature, in order to keep its juices in **3** [I always + adv/prep] to have a very strong sudden and unpleasant effect on you: [+ **into/onto/on**] *The scene will be forever seared onto my memory.*

**sear²** *adj literary* another spelling of SERE

S3 W2 **search¹** /sɜːtʃ‖sɜːrtʃ/ *n* **1** [C usually singular] an attempt to find someone or something: [+ **for**] *Bad weather is hampering the search for survivors* | **in search of** (=looking for) *Mario went off in search of some matches.* | **call off a search** (=stop looking for someone or something) | **carry out a search** *Security guards will be carrying out a search of the premises.* | **house-to-house search** (=one that involves searching every house or building in an area) | **strip search** (=an official search in which you must take off all of your clothes) **2** [singular] an attempt to find a solution to a problem or an explanation for something: *the search for the meaning of life* **3 search and rescue** the process of searching for someone who is lost and who may need medical help, for example in the mountains or at sea

**search²** *v* W3

**1** ▶ **LOOK FOR** ◀ [I,T] to spend time looking for someone or something: *Rescue workers searched all night in the hope of finding more survivors.* | [+ **for**] *a mother bird searching for food* | **search sth for sth** *Detectives are out searching the yard for clues* | **search through sth** (=look for something among papers in a drawer etc) | **search in/under/around etc** *"Two beers, please," Patricia ordered, searching in her purse.*

**2** ▶ **PERSON** ◀ [T] to look in someone's pockets, clothes etc in order to find something, especially drugs or weapons: *Visitors to the prison are thoroughly searched before they are allowed in.*

**3** ▶ **SOLUTION/EXPLANATION ETC** ◀ [I] to try to find a solution to a problem, an explanation for something etc: [+ **for**] *Scientists are still searching for a cure for the disease.*

**4 Search me!** *spoken* used to tell someone that you do not know the answer to a question: *"So where's she gone tonight then?" "Search me!"*

**5** ▶ **EXAMINE** ◀ [T] to examine something very carefully in order to find something out: *Anya searched his face anxiously.*

**search** sth ↔ **out** *phr v* [T] to find or discover something by searching: *We were too tired to search out extra blankets.*

Frequencies of **search, look for** and **try to find** in spoken and written English.

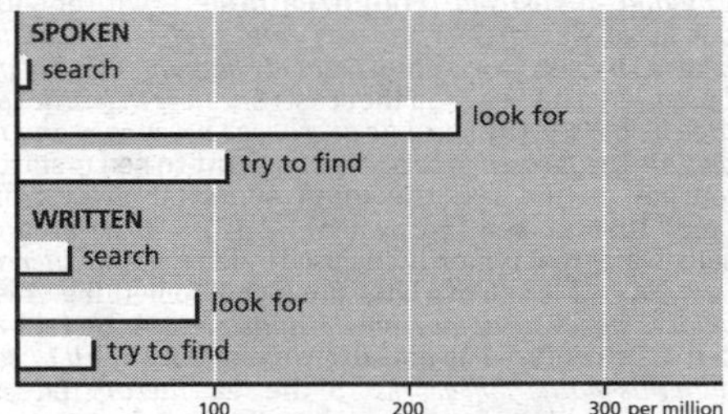


Based on the British National Corpus and the Longman Lancaster Corpus

This graph shows that the expressions **look for** and **try to find** are much more common in both spoken and written English than the verb **search**. **Look for** and **try to find** are used in a very general way. **Search** is used when someone, often a group of people, spends time looking for something or someone in a careful, organized way. It is more common in written English than in spoken English.

**search·ing** /ˈsɜːtʃɪŋ‖ˈsɜːr-/ *adj* [only before noun] **1 searching look/glance** a look from someone who is trying to find out as much as possible about someone's thoughts and feelings **2 searching examination/investigation/analysis** an examination etc that looks throroughly at all the facts —**searchingly** *adv*

**search·light** /ˈsɜːtʃlaɪt‖ˈsɜːr-/ *n* [C] a powerful light that can be turned in any direction, used for finding people, vehicles etc in the dark

**search par·ty** /ˈ· ˌ··/ *n* [C] a group of people organized to look for someone who is missing or lost

**search war·rant** /ˈ· ˌ··/ *n* [C] a legal document that gives the police official permission to search a building, for example in order to look for stolen goods

**sear·ing** /ˈsɪərɪŋ‖ˈsɪr-/ *adj* **1** searing heat is extremely hot **2** searing pain is severe and feels like a burn: *a searing pain behind the eyes* **3** searing words or attitudes are very severe and critical: *an expression of deep, searing contempt*

**sea·scape** /ˈsiːskeɪp/ *n* [C] a picture or painting of the sea

**sea ser·pent** /ˈ· ˌ··/ *n* [C] an imaginary large snake-like animal that people used to think lived in the sea

**sea·shell** /ˈsiːʃel/ *n* [C] the shell of some types of sea animal

**sea·shore** /ˈsiːʃɔː‖-ʃɔːr/ *n* **the seashore** the land along the edge of the sea, usually consisting of sand and rocks —compare BEACH, SEASIDE

**sea·sick** /ˈsiːˌsɪk/ *adj* feeling very ill because of the movement of a boat or ship —**seasickness** *n* [U]

**sea·side** /ˈsiːsaɪd/ *n* **the seaside** *especially BrE* an area or town along the edge of the sea, especially a place you go to have a holiday or to enjoy yourself: **seaside resort** (=where a lot of people go for their holidays) —see SHORE[1] (USAGE)

3 **sea·son¹** /ˈsiːzən/ *n*
1 **1 ▶ IN A YEAR ◀** [C] one of the four main periods in a year; spring, summer, autumn, or winter
**2 ▶ USUAL TIME FOR STH ◀** [singular] a period of time in a year when something happens most often or when something is usually done: **rainy/dry/wet etc season** (=when there is a lot of rain etc) | **growing/raspberry/asparagus etc season** (=when particular plants are growing) | **hunting/shooting/fishing etc season** (=when you can do that sport) | **mating/breeding season** (=when animals breed) | **football/basketball etc season** (=when a sport is officially played) | **tourist season** *AmE*, **holiday season** *BrE* (=the time of year when people come to a particular place for a holiday) | **high/peak season** (=the time of year when a place is most busy, especially a holiday place) | **low/off/slack season** (=the time of year when a place or company is not busy) | **the holiday season** *AmE* (=Thanksgiving, Christmas, and New Year's)
**3 be in season a)** if vegetables or fruit are in season, it is the time of year when they are ready to eat **b)** if a female animal is in season, she is ready to MATE[2] (1)
**4 out of season a)** if vegetables or fruit are out of season, it is not the time of year when they would normally become ready to eat **b)** if you travel or stay somewhere out of season, you do it at the time of year when most people do not
**5 ▶ FASHION ◀** [C] a time during which particular designs of clothes are produced and sold and are considered to be fashionable: *The Paris season began in May.*
**6 ▶ FILMS ETC ◀** [singular] a time during which a series of films, television programmes etc is shown, especially ones made by the same person or about the same subject: *a new season of comedy on BBC1*
**7 season's greetings** used especially on greetings cards to say that you hope someone has a happy Christmas
**8 the season of good will** the time around Christmas —see also CLOSE SEASON, OPEN SEASON, SILLY SEASON

**season²** *v* [T] **1** to add salt, pepper etc to something you are cooking to make it taste better **2** to make wood hard and ready to use by gradually drying it

**sea·so·na·ble** /ˈsiːzənəbəl/ *adj formal* **1** suitable for the time of year **2** coming or happening at a suitable time —**seasonably** *adv*

**sea·son·al** /ˈsiːzənəl/ *adj* **1** usually happening or available during a particular season: *a pie made with seasonal fruits* | **seasonal norm** *BrE* (=the average weather conditions for a particular season) **2** happening or needed only at a particular time of year: **seasonal workers/labour/employment etc** *seasonal jobs in the tourist industry*

**sea·son·ally** /ˈsiːzənəli/ *adv* according to what is usual for a particular season: **seasonally adjusted figures** *BrE* (=figures, especially about the number of unemployed people, that are changed according to what usually happens at a particular time of year)

**sea·soned** /ˈsiːzənd/ *adj* **1 seasoned traveller/campaigner/veteran etc** a very experienced traveller etc **2** seasoned food has salt, pepper etc added: **well seasoned/highly-seasoned** (=with a strong taste)

**sea·son·ing** /ˈsiːzənɪŋ/ *n* [C,U] salt, pepper, spices (SPICE[1] (1)) etc that add a more interesting taste to food

**season tick·et** /ˈ·· ˌ··‖ˌ·· ˈ··/ *n* [C] a ticket for several journeys, performances, games etc that costs less than you would pay altogether if you paid for each journey etc separately: **season ticket holder** (=someone who owns a season ticket)

**seat¹** /siːt/ *n* 
**1 ▶ PLACE TO SIT ◀** [C] a place where you can sit, for example a chair: *Excuse me, can you tell us where our seats are?* | *a 150-seat airliner* | **have/take a seat** *spoken* (=used to politely invite someone to sit down) *If you'd like to take a seat, the doctor will see you shortly.* | **back/front seat** (=the seats in the back or front of a car etc) | **passenger seat** (=the seat next to the driver in a car) | **take your seat** (=sit down in your seat) *The judge hurried in and took his seat.* | **reserve a seat** (=pay for a theatre seat before you go) —see picture at THEATRE
**2 ▶ PART OF A CHAIR ◀** [C usually singular] the flat part of a chair etc that you sit on: *Don't put your feet on the seat!*
**3 seat of your trousers/pants** the part of your trousers that you sit on
**4 two-seater/three-seater etc** a vehicle or piece of furniture with two seats, three seats etc
**5 ▶ OFFICIAL POSITION ◀** [C] a position as a member of a government or a group that makes official decisions: *a seat on the board of directors* | **win/lose a seat** *The Tories won 419 seats in the last election.* | **a safe seat** (=a position held by a political party that is not likely to be lost in an election)
**6 seat of learning/government etc** *formal* a place, usually a city, where a university or government is based
**7 take a back seat** to let someone else make the important decisions
**8 be on the edge of your seat** to be waiting excitedly to see what happens next
**9 do sth by the seat of your pants** to do something by using only your own skill and experience, without any help from anyone or anything else
**10 be in the driving seat** *BrE* also **be in the driver's seat** *especially AmE* to control everything that happens in an organization, relationship, or situation
**11 be in the hot seat** to be in a position in which you have to make important decisions or answer a lot of difficult questions
**12 ▶ ON A HORSE ◀** [singular] *technical* the way someone sits on a horse: *Sally's got a good seat.*
**13 ▶ HOUSE ◀** [C] a home of a rich, important family in the countryside **family/country seat** —see also **back-seat driver** (DRIVER (2)), LOVESEAT, WINDOW SEAT

**seat²** *v* [T]
**1 be seated a)** to be sitting down: *Paul was seated at the head of the table with his wife next to him.* **b)** *spoken formal* used to politely invite people to sit down: *Please be seated so we can begin the meeting.*
**2 remain/stay seated** to stay in your seat: *Remain seated until the aircraft has come to a complete stop.*
**3 seat yourself beside/in/on etc** *formal* to sit down somewhere
**4 ▶ ARRANGE WHERE PEOPLE SIT ◀** [always + adv/prep] to arrange for someone to sit somewhere: **seat sb beside/on/near etc** *Whatever you do, make sure you don't seat Alan and Pat next to each other.* —see SIT (USAGE) —see picture on page 838
**5 ▶ HOLD A NUMBER OF PEOPLE ◀** [not in progressive] if a room, vehicle, table etc seats a certain number of people, it has enough seats for that number: *The new stadium seats 60,000.*
**6 ▶ FIT STH SOMEWHERE ◀** *technical* to fit something, tightly into a space that is specially made for it

**seat belt** /ˈ· ·/ *n* [C] a strong belt fastened to the seat of a car or plane which you fasten around yourself to prevent yourself being thrown out of your seat in an accident —see picture on page 409

**seat·ing** /ˈsiːtɪŋ/ *n* [U] **1** all the seats in a theatre, cinema etc: **seating capacity** (=the number of people that can fit in a theatre, cinema etc) **2** a way of arranging seats, or a plan of who will sit in them: **seating plan/arrangements etc** *Do you have a seating plan for the dinner guests?*

**sea ur·chin** /ˈ· ˌ··/ *n* [C] a small round sea animal that has a hard shell, sometimes with sharp points

**sea·wall** /ˌsiːˈwɔːl‖ˈsiːwɒːl/ *n* [C] a wall built along the edge of the sea to stop the water from flowing over an area of land

**sea·ward** /ˈsiːwəd‖-wərd/ *adj* facing or directed towards the sea: *the seaward side of the town* | **seaward wind/breeze** (=going towards the sea)

**sea·wards** /ˈsiːwədz‖-wɜːrdz/ also **seaward** *adv* towards the sea

**sea·way** /ˈsiːweɪ/ *n* [C] **1** a line of travel regularly used by ships on the sea **2** a river or CANAL (1) used by ships to go from the sea to places that are not on the coast

**sea·weed** /ˈsiːwiːd/ *n* [U] a common plant that grows in the sea

**sea·wor·thy** /ˈsiːwɜːði‖-ɜːr-/ *adj* a ship that is seaworthy is safe and in good condition —**seaworthiness** *n* [U]

**se·ba·ceous** /səˈbeɪʃəs/ *adj technical* related to a part of the body which produces special oils: *sebacious glands*

**sec** /sek/ *n* [C] *spoken* **1** a very short time: **hang on a sec/hold on a sec/just a sec etc** (=used to ask someone to wait a short time) *"Is Clive there, please?" "Hold on a sec, I'll go and see."* | **in a sec** (=very soon) *I'll be with you in a sec.* **2** the written abbreviation of SECRETARY

**sec·a·teurs** /ˈsekətɜːz‖ˌsekəˈtɜːrz/ *n* [plural] *BrE* large, very strong sharp scissors that you use for cutting plant stems; CLIPPERS (1) *AmE*

**se·cede** /sɪˈsiːd/ *v* [I] *formal* to formally leave an organization, especially because there has been a disagreement about its aims etc: [ + **from**] *By 1861, 11 states had seceded from the Union.* —**secession** *n* [singular, U]

**se·clude** /sɪˈkluːd/ *v* [T] *formal* to keep yourself or someone else away from other people

**se·clud·ed** /sɪˈkluːdɪ̣d/ *adj* **1** a secluded place is private and quiet because it is a long way from other places and people: *We eventually came to a secluded farmhouse.* **2 a secluded life/existence** a way of living that is quiet and private because you do not see many people

**se·clu·sion** /sɪˈkluːʒən/ *n* **1** [U] the state of being private and away from other people: **live/dwell/rest etc in seclusion** *The Emperor lived in utter seclusion behind the walls of the Forbidden City.* | **the seclusion of** *Writers are attracted to the peace and seclusion of the area.* **2** [singular, U] an act of keeping yourself or someone else alone and away from other people: **keep sb in seclusion** *In some societies, women are still kept in seclusion.* | **be in seclusion** (=be in a situation where you will not or cannot see or speak to other people)

**sec·ond¹** /ˈsekənd/ *number* **1** 2nd; the person, thing, event etc after the first one: *His second goal was from a penalty.* | *a second year student at University* | *In the second of a series of programmes we look at the role of women in industry.* | **the second largest/biggest etc** (=the one after the largest, the biggest etc) *Dalton is the second tallest boy in the class.* | **come/finish second** (=be the one after the winner of a race or competition) **2 second home/car etc** another home, car etc besides the one you use most of the time **3 be/come a poor second** to not be as good, interesting etc as something else: *Once you've tasted real vanilla, the artificial stuff is a poor second.* **4 every second year/person/thing etc** the second, then the fourth year etc: *Only water the plants every second day.* **5 be second only to sth** to be the most important thing, the best thing etc, apart from one other particular thing: *Colin's career was second only to his family.* **6 be second to none** to be the best: *As a singer, Ella Fitzgerald was second to none.*

S1 W2 **second²** *n* **1** [C] a unit for measuring time that is equal to 1/60 of a minute: **for 5/20/30 etc seconds** *Hold your breath for four seconds.* | **take 5/20/30 etc seconds** *The whole operation takes about twenty seconds.* **2** [C] *especially spoken* a very short period of time: **a few seconds** *Just wait there for a few seconds.* | **within seconds** (=after a few seconds) *Within seconds Cassie called me back.* | **just a second** *spoken* (=wait a moment) *Just a second and I'll come and help.* | **in a matter of seconds** (=in a very short time) —see also SPLIT SECOND **3 seconds** [plural] **a)** *informal* another serving of the same food after you have eaten your first serving: *Does anyone want seconds?* **b)** clothes or other goods that are sold cheaply in shops because they are not perfect —compare SECOND-HAND **4** [C] someone who helped and supported someone who was fighting in a DUEL¹ (1) or other organized fight in former times

**second³** [sentence adverb] used to add another piece of information to what you have already said or written; SECONDLY: *Firstly the church is a place of worship and second, is somewhere the community can congregate.*

**second⁴** *v* [T] to formally support a suggestion or plan made by another person in a meeting: **second a motion/proposal/amendment etc** *Who'll second the motion?*

**second⁵** /sɪˈkɒnd‖-ˈkɑːnd/ *v* [T] *BrE* to send someone to do someone else's job for a short time: **second sb to** *Jill's been seconded to the marketing department while David's away.* —see also SECONDMENT

**sec·ond·a·ry** /ˈsekəndəri‖-deri/ *adj* **1 secondary education/schooling/teaching etc** the education, teaching etc of children between the ages of 11 and 16 **2** not as important or urgent as something else: *a secondary role* | **be of secondary importance/be a secondary consideration** *Getting there's the main thing – how we get there is a secondary consideration.* | **be secondary to** *Social skills shouldn't necessarily be seen as secondary to academic achievement.* **3** coming after or developing from something else of the same type: *The danger isn't from the disease itself, but from secondary infections that might occur.* —**secondarily** *adv* W

**secondary mod·ern** /ˌ···· ˈ··/ *n* [C] a type of school that existed in Britain until the 1960s, where children who were thought not to be the most intelligent were sent —compare COMPREHENSIVE SCHOOL, GRAMMAR SCHOOL

**secondary school** /ˈ···· ˌ·/ *n* [C] a school for children between the ages of 11 and 16 or 18 —compare ELEMENTARY SCHOOL, PRIMARY SCHOOL

**secondary stress** /ˌ···· ˈ·/ *n* [C,U] *technical* the second strongest STRESS¹ (4) given in speech to part of a word or sentence, and shown in this dictionary by the mark ˌ

**second base** /ˌ·· ˈ·/ *n* [singular] the second place you have to run to in games such as BASEBALL

**second best¹** /ˌ·· ˈ·◂/ *adj* not quite as good as the best thing of the same type: *Allie was the second best shooter on the team.*

**second best²** *n* [U] something that is not as good as the best: *I've never been able to accept second best.*

**second child·hood** /ˌ·· ˈ··/ *n* [U] **be in your second childhood** a polite expression meaning that an old person is behaving and thinking like a small child because their mental abilities are not as good as they used to be

**second class** /ˌ·· ˈ·/ *n* **1** [U] a way of delivering mail in Britain that is cheaper and slower than sending things by FIRST CLASS (2) mail: **send sth second class** *If you send it second class, it won't get there till the end of the week.* **2** [U] the system in the US for delivering newspapers, magazines, advertisements etc **3** [U] a way of travelling, especially on a train, that is cheaper but not as comfortable as FIRST CLASS (1) travel: **travel second class** *Are you travelling first or second class?* **4** [singular] a level of a university degree in Britain that is below the top level

**second-class** /ˌ·· ˈ·◂/ *adj* **1** [only before noun] considered to be less important than other people or things: **second-class citizen** (=someone who is not as important as other people in society) *Why should children be* *treated like second-class citizens?* **2 second-class carriage/compartment/ticket etc** connected with cheaper and less comfortable travel on a train: *Two second-class tickets, please.* **3 second-class mail/post/stamp etc** connected with posting things more cheaply and slowly —compare FIRST CLASS

**second cous·in** /ˌ·· ˈ··/ *n* [C] a child of a COUSIN (1) of one of your parents

**second-de·gree** /ˌ·· ·ˈ··◂/ *adj* **second-degree burn/burns** *technical* the second most serious form of burn

**second-guess** /ˌ·· ˈ·/ *v* [T] **1** to try to say what will happen or what someone will do before they do it **2** *AmE* to criticize something after it has already happened

**second hand** /ˈ·· ˌ·/ *n* [C] the pointer that shows seconds on a clock or watch

**second-hand** /ˌ·· ˈ·◂/ *adj* not new, and used by someone else before you: *When I was a kid I hated wearing second-hand clothes.* | **get/buy sth second-hand** *They get all their furniture second-hand.*

**second-hand shop** /ˌ·· ˈ· ·/ *n* [C] a shop where you can buy cheap second-hand goods, especially clothes

**second-in-com·mand** /ˌ·· · ·ˈ·/ *n* [C] the person who has the next highest rank to the person who has the highest rank, especially in a military organization

**second lan·guage** /ˌ·· ˈ··/ *n* [C usually singular] a language that you speak in addition to the language you learned as a child

**second lieu·ten·ant** /ˌ·· ·ˈ··/ *n* [C] a middle rank in several of the US and British military forces, or someone who has this rank —see table on page B4

W3 **sec·ond·ly** /ˈsekəndli/ *adv* [sentence adverb] used to introduce the second fact, reason, subject etc that you want to talk about: *First we must establish exactly what happened. Secondly, we must try to find out why.*

**se·cond·ment** /sɪˈkɒndmənt‖-ˈkɑːnd-/ *n* [singular, U] *especially BrE* a period of time that you spend away from your usual job, either doing another job or studying: **be on secondment from** *He's not at the university permanently – he's on secondment.*

**second na·ture** /ˌ·· ˈ··/ *n* [U] **be second nature (to sb)** something that is second nature to you is something you have done so often that you do it almost without thinking: *Wearing a seatbelt is second nature to most drivers.*

**second per·son** /ˌ·· ˈ··/ *n technical* a form of a verb or PRONOUN that is used to show the person you are speaking to. For example, "you" is a second person PRONOUN, and "you are" is the second person singular and plural of the verb "to be" —compare FIRST PERSON, THIRD PERSON

**second-rate** /ˌ·· ˈ·◂/ *adj* [usually before noun] not very good: *second-rate artists*

**second sight** /ˌ·· ˈ·/ *n* [U] the ability to know what will happen in the future, or to know about things that are happening somewhere else

**second-string** /ˌ·· ˈ·◂/ *adj* [only before noun] *AmE* not regularly part of a team, group etc, but sometimes taking someone else's place in it

**second thought** /ˌ·· ˈ·/ *n* **1 on second thoughts** *BrE*, **on second thought** *AmE spoken* used to say that you have changed your mind about something: *I'll have a coffee please. Oh no, on second thought, make it a beer.* **2 have second thoughts** to change your mind, or start having doubts about something: *You're not having second thoughts, are you?*

**second wind** /ˌsekənd ˈwɪnd/ *n* [singular] a new feeling of energy that you get when you have been working or exercising very hard and had thought you were too tired to continue: **get your second wind** *OK, let's go – you should have got your second wind by now.*

**se·cre·cy** /ˈsiːkrəsi/ *n* [U] **1** the process of keeping something secret, or the state of being kept a secret: *I must stress the need for absolute secrecy about the project.* **2 be sworn to secrecy** if you have been sworn to secrecy by someone, you have promised them that you will not repeat what they have told you: *I really can't tell you, I've been sworn to secrecy.*

**se·cret¹** /ˈsiːkrɪ̈t/ *adj* **1** known about by only a few people and kept hidden from others: **secret passage/hideout/hiding place etc** *Rosie took them to a secret hideout in the woods.* | **secret diplomacy/negotiations/meetings etc** *She's had secret meetings with him behind your back.* | **keep sth secret** *They kept their marriage secret until last year.* —see also TOP SECRET **2** [only before a noun] secret feelings or actions are ones that you do not want other people to know about: *I still have my secret fears about his intentions.* | **a secret admirer** *Did you know you had a secret admirer?* | **a secret drinker/smoker** *the watery eyes of a secret drinker* **3 secret about sth** liking to keep things secret; SECRETIVE —**secretly** *adv*: *They were secretly married last week.* S3 W3

**secret²** *n* [C] **1** something kept hidden or known about by only a few people: *Our plans must remain a secret.* | **keep a secret** (=not tell a secret to anyone) *Can you keep a secret?* | **let sb in on the secret** (=tell someone a secret) | **closely-guarded secret** (=one that is carefully kept) **2 the secret of** a particular way of achieving a good result, that is the best or only way: *the secret to making good bread* | **the secret of success** *What do you think is the secret of her success?* **3 in secret** in a private way or place that other people do not know about: *Lilian cried in secret, afraid to tell anyone.* **4 make no secret of** to make your opinions about something clear: *Howard made no secret of his disappointment.* **5 the secrets of nature/the universe etc** the things no one yet knows about nature etc S3 W3

**secret a·gent** /ˌ·· ˈ··/ *n* [C] someone whose job is to find out and report on the military and political secrets of other countries

**sec·re·tar·i·al** /ˌsekrɪ̈ˈteəriəl‖-ˈter-/ *adj* connected with the work of a secretary: *a secretarial course*

**sec·re·tar·i·at** /ˌsekrɪ̈ˈteəriət‖-ter-/ *n* [C] a government office or the office of an international organization with a SECRETARY (2) or SECRETARY-GENERAL who is in charge: *the United Nations Secretariat in New York*

**sec·re·ta·ry** /ˈsekrɪ̈təri‖-teri/ *n* [C] **1** someone who works in an office typing (TYPE² (1)) letters, keeping records, arranging meetings etc: *Julie works as a secretary in a lawyer's office.* | *You can ring my secretary to make an appointment.* **2 a)** a British government official, such as a minister or someone who has a high rank in a department: *the Foreign Secretary* | **Secretary of State** *the Secretary of State for Home Affairs* | **Permanent Secretary** (=someone in charge of a government department) **b)** an official who is chosen by the president of the US, who is in charge of a large government department: *the Secretary of the Treasury* | **Secretary of State** (=the person who deals with American relations with other countries) **c)** a British government representative, below the rank of AMBASSADOR: *the First Secretary at the British Embassy* **3** an official of an organization who keeps records, writes official letters etc: *secretary of the Wilton Tennis Club* S3 W1

**secretary gen·e·ral** /ˌ···· ˈ···/ *n* [C] the most important official in charge of a large organization, especially an international organization: *the UN Secretary General*

**se·crete** /sɪˈkriːt/ *v* [T] *technical* **1** if a part of an animal or plant secretes a substance, it produces it: *Hormones are secreted by various glands.* —see also EXCRETE **2** *formal* to hide something: *McCready secreted the package inside his donkey-jacket.*

**se·cre·tion** /sɪˈkriːʃən/ *n* **1 a)** [C,U] *technical* a substance, usually liquid, produced by part of a plant or animal **b)** [U] the production of this material: *the secretion of enzymes* **2** [U] *formal* the act of hiding something

**se·cre·tive** /ˈsiːkrɪ̈tɪv, sɪˈkriːtɪv/ *adj* someone who is secretive likes to keep their thoughts, intentions or actions hidden from others: *Everyone was very secretive*

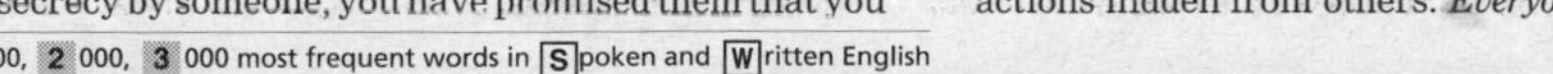

*about their earnings.* —**secretively** *adv* —**secretiveness** *n* [U]

**secret po·lice** /ˌ·· ·'·/ *n* **the secret police** a police force controlled by a government, that secretly tries to defeat the political enemies of that government

**secret ser·vice** /ˌ·· '··/ *n* [singular] **1** a British government organization that uses SECRET AGENTS to obtain secret information about other countries **2** a US government department dealing with special kinds of police work, especially protecting the President

**sect** /sekt/ *n* [C] a group of people with their own particular set of beliefs and practices, especially within or separated from a larger religious group: *an early, ascetic Christian sect*

**sec·tar·i·an** /sek'teəriən‖-'ter-/ *adj* **1 sectarian violence/conflict/murder etc** violence etc that is connected with the strong feelings between people of different religious groups **2** *especially AmE* supporting a particular religious group and its beliefs: *a sectarian journal* —**sectarianism** *n* [U]

S1 W1 **sec·tion¹** /'sekʃən/ *n*
**1 ▶ PLACE/OBJECT ◀** [C] one of the parts that something, such as an object or place is divided into: [+ **of**] *The spoons go in the front section of the drawer.* | *one of the older sections of Philadelphia* | *Decorate the torte with orange sections.* | *the back section of the plane*
**2 ▶ GROUP OF PEOPLE ◀** [C] a separate group within a larger group of people: [+ **of**] *a large section of the American public* | **all sections of the community** (=everyone in a particular place)
**3 ▶ ORGANIZATION/INSTITUTION ◀** [C] one of the parts of an organization, institution, department etc: *all the salespeople in my section* | *the reference section of the library* | **brass/woodwind etc section** (=the part of an orchestra that plays those instruments)
**4 ▶ FITTING TOGETHER ◀** [C] one of the parts of something that you fit together: *You buy the bookcase in sections and assemble it.*
**5 ▶ BOOK/NEWSPAPER/REPORT ◀** [C] a separate part of something that is written, such as a book or newspaper: *Who has the sports section?* | *in the final section of this chapter*
**6 ▶ SIDE/TOP VIEW ◀** [C,U] a picture that shows what a building, part of the body etc would look like if it were cut from top to bottom or side to side: **in section** *Here's the outside view, and here are the floors in section.*
**7 ▶ MEDICAL/SCIENTIFIC ◀** *technical* **a)** [C,U] a medical operation that involves cutting **b)** [C] a very thin flat piece that is cut from skin, a plant etc to be looked at under a microscope
**8 ▶ PART OF A TOWN ◀** [C] *AmE* a part of a town in the western US that is one mile square
**9 ▶ MATHEMATICS ◀** [C] *technical* the shape that is made when a solid figure is cut by a flat surface in mathematics: *conic sections* —see also CROSS-SECTION

**section²** *v* [T] *technical* **1** to cut a SECTION from skin, a plant, or a shape in mathematics etc **2** to draw a SECTION¹ (6) of something such as a house **3** to cut a part of the body in a medical operation

**section** sth ↔ **off** *phr v* [T] to divide an area into parts, by making a dividing line between them: *The vegetable plots were sectioned off by a low wall.*

**sec·tion·al** /'sekʃənəl/ *adj* **1** made up of sections that can be put together or taken apart: *a six-foot sectional sofa* **2** limited to one particular group or area within a larger group: *different sectional interests each seeking to represent working women* **3** connected with a SECTION¹ (6): *a sectional view of the new building*

**sec·tion·al·is·m** /'sekʃənəlɪzəm/ *n* [U] too much loyalty towards your own political or social group

W1 **sec·tor** /'sektə‖-ər/ *n* [C] **1** a part of an area of activity, especially of business, trade etc: [+ **of**] *the agricultural sector of the economy* | *understaffing in all sectors of the educational system* | **public/private sector** (=business controlled by the government or by private companies) **2** one of the parts into which an area is divided for a purpose, especially for military reasons: *Planes searched a broad sector of the Indian Ocean.* **3** *technical* an area in a circle enclosed by two straight lines drawn from the centre to the edge —see picture at SHAPE¹

**sec·u·lar** /'sekjʊ̈lə‖-ər/ *adj* **1** not connected with or controlled by a church or other religious authority: *secular education* | *our modern secular society* **2** a secular priest lives among ordinary people, rather than with other priests in a MONASTERY

**sec·u·lar·is·m** /'sekjʊ̈lərɪzəm/ *n* [U] a system of social organization that keeps out all forms of religion —**secularist** *n* [C]

**sec·u·lar·ize** also **-ise** *BrE* /'sekjʊ̈ləraɪz/ *v* [T] to remove the control or influence of religious groups from a society or an institution —**secularization** /ˌsekjʊ̈lərаɪ'zeɪʃən‖-rə-/ *n* [U]

**se·cure¹** /sɪ'kjʊə‖-kjʊr/ *v* [T] **1** to get or achieve something that will be permanent, especially after a lot of effort: *UN negotiators are still trying to secure the release of the hostages.* | *a deal to secure the company's future* **2** to make something safe from being attacked, harmed, or lost: [+ **against**] *Extra men will be needed to secure the camp against attack.* **3** to fasten or tie something firmly in a particular position: *a tent secured with heavy wooden pegs* | **secure sth to sth** *John secured the boat firmly to the jetty.* **4** to legally promise that if you cannot pay back money you have borrowed, you will give the lender goods or property of the same value instead: *a secured loan* W2

**secure²** *adj* S3
**1 ▶ PERMANENT/CERTAIN ◀** a situation that is secure is one that you can depend on because it is not likely to change: *There is no such thing as a secure job these days.* | *a secure source of funds* | **on secure ground** (=when you know exactly what to do or say)
**2 ▶ SAFE PLACE ◀ a)** locked or guarded so that people cannot get in or out, or steal anything: *Make sure the doors and windows are secure before you leave.* **b)** safe from and protected against attacks: [+ **from**] *The southern border is secure from enemy shelling.*
**3 ▶ SAFE FEELING ◀** feeling safe and protected from danger: *I'll feel more secure with a burglar alarm.*
**4 ▶ CONFIDENT ◀ a)** feeling confident about yourself and your abilities: *a secure and happy child* —opposite INSECURE (1) **b)** feeling confident and certain about a situation and not worried that it might change: *We're waiting to have kids until we're financially secure.* | **secure in the knowledge that** *Myles relaxed, secure in the knowledge that they wouldn't find him.*
**5 ▶ FIRMLY FIXED ◀** firmly fixed, tied, or fastened: *Are you sure that shelf is secure?*

**se·cure·ly** /sɪ'kjʊəli‖-'kjʊr-/ *adv* tied, fastened etc tightly, especially in order to make something safe: **securely locked/fastened/tied etc** *Make sure the saddle is securely buckled so it doesn't come loose.*

**se·cu·ri·ty** /sɪ'kjʊərɪ̈ti‖-'kjʊr-/ *n* W1
**1 ▶ PUBLIC/GOVERNMENT SAFETY ◀** [U] things that are done in order to keep someone or something safe: *For reasons of security, all luggage must be searched.* | **security measures/checks/procedures etc** *Strict security measures were in force during the President's visit.* | **national/state security** (=protection of a country from attack or harm) | **tight security** (=careful protection using a lot of soldiers, police etc) | **security man/guard** (=someone employed to protect a person or building) | **security forces/operations etc** (=those whose job is to protect a country, sometimes used to avoid saying military) *the UN Security Forces* | **security firm** (=a company that provides protection for other people's property, money etc) | **maximum security prison** (=for very dangerous prisoners, from which it is very difficult to escape) | **high security** (=carefully protected or made safe)

2 ▶ **PROTECTION FROM BAD SITUATIONS** ◀ [U] **a)** the state of being protected from the bad things that could happen to you: **job security** (=not being in danger of losing your job)|**financial security** (=knowing you have enough money to pay for the things you need) *This plan can offer your family financial security in the event of your death.* **b)** ▶ **STH THAT PROTECTS YOU** ◀ something that protects you from the bad things that could happen to you: [+ **against**] *Does your insurance provide enough security against illness?*|[+ **of**] *the security of a loving family*
3 ▶ **GUARDS** ◀ [U] the department of a company which deals with the protection of its buildings and equipment: *I'll have to report this to Security.*
4 ▶ **BORROWING MONEY** ◀ [U] something such as property that you promise to give someone if you cannot pay back money you have borrowed from them: **put sth up as security** *She had to put up her house as security on the loan.*
5 ▶ **SAFETY FROM HARM** ◀ [U] how safe something is from being lost, stolen, or damaged: *If you're worried about their security, put your jewels in the hotel safe.*
6 **securities** [plural] stocks (STOCK[1] (3)) or shares (SHARE[2] (5))

**security blank·et** /·'··· ,··/ *n* [C] a BLANKET[1] (1), soft toy etc that a child likes to hold and touch to comfort themselves

**security clear·ance** /·'··· ,··/ *n* [C,U] official permission for someone to see secret documents etc, or to enter a building, after a strict checking process

**security guard** /·'···,·/ *n* [C] someone whose job is to guard a building or a vehicle carrying money

**security light** /·'···,·/ *n* [C] a light that turns on when someone tries to enter a dark building or area —see picture on page 410

**security risk** /·'···,·/ *n* [C] someone who cannot be trusted by a government and who therefore is not allowed to do particular jobs

**security ser·vice** /·'··· ,··/ *n* [C] a government organization that protects a country's secrets against enemy countries or protects the government against attempts to take away its power

**se·dan** /sɪ'dæn/ *n* [C] *AmE and AustrE* a large car that has a separate enclosed space for your bags etc; SALOON (2) *BrE*

**sedan chair** /·,· '·/ *n* [C] a seat on two poles with a cover around it on which an important person was carried in former times

**se·date[1]** /sɪ'deɪt/ *adj* **1** moving in a slow and rather formal way: *a sedate procession* **2** peaceful, ordinary, and not very exciting: *a sedate seaside town on the South Coast* —**sedately** *adv* —**sedateness** *n* [U]

**sedate[2]** *v* [T often passive] to make someone sleepy or calm by giving them drugs

**se·da·tion** /sɪ'deɪʃən/ *n* [U] the use of drugs to make someone sleepy or calm: **under (heavy) sedation** *I couldn't speak to her as she was still under sedation.*

**sed·a·tive** /'sedətɪv/ *n* [C] a drug used to make someone sleepy or calm

**sed·en·ta·ry** /'sedəntəri‖-teri/ *adj formal* **1** a sedentary job is done while sitting down, and without moving around very much **2** a sedentary group of people tend always to live in the same place; SETTLED: *a sedentary population*

**sedge** /sedʒ/ *n* [U] a plant like grass that grows in groups on low wet ground

**sed·i·ment** /'sedɪ̣mənt/ *n* [singular, U] solid matter that settles at the bottom of a liquid: *a brownish sediment at the bottom of the tank* —see picture on page 835

**sed·i·men·ta·ry** /,sedɪ̣'mentəri◂/ *adj* made of the solid matter that settles at the bottom of the sea, rivers, lakes etc: *sedimentary rock*|*sedimentary deposits*

**sed·i·men·ta·tion** /,sedɪ̣men'teɪʃən,-mən-/ *n* [U] the natural process by which small pieces of rock, earth etc settle at the bottom of the sea etc and form a solid layer

**se·di·tion** /sɪ'dɪʃən/ *n* [U] *formal* speech, writing, or actions intended to encourage people to disobey a government: *Leading communists were charged with sedition.*

**se·di·tious** /sɪ'dɪʃəs/ *adj formal* intended to illegally encourage people to disobey the government: *a seditious speech* —**seditiously** *adv*

**se·duce** /sɪ'dju:s‖-'du:s/ *v* [T often passive] **1** to persuade someone to have sex with you, especially someone who is younger than you or in a weaker position than you: *The head lecturer here was sacked for seducing female students.* **2** to make someone want to do something by making it seem very attractive or interesting to them: **seduce sb into doing sth** *Jim was seduced into leaving the company by the offer of higher pay.* —**seducer** *n* [C]

**se·duc·tion** /sɪ'dʌkʃən/ *n* **1** [C,U] an act of persuading someone to have sex with you for the first time: *The seduction scene in Act 2 of the Opera.* **2** [C usually plural] something that strongly attracts people, but often has a bad effect on their lives: *the seduction of money*

**se·duc·tive** /sɪ'dʌktɪv/ *adj* **1** someone who is seductive is sexually attractive: *She had a low, seductive voice.* **2** something that is seductive is very interesting or attractive to you, in a way that persuades you to do something you would not usually do: *the seductive power of advertising* —**seductively** *adv*: *She smiled seductively at him across the table.* —**seductiveness** *n* [U]

**sed·u·lous** /'sedjɪ̣ləs‖'sedʒə-/ *adj formal* hard working and determined: *a sedulous worker* —**sedulously** *adv*

**see**

Karen was blindfolded so she couldn't see anything.

They looked at the paintings.

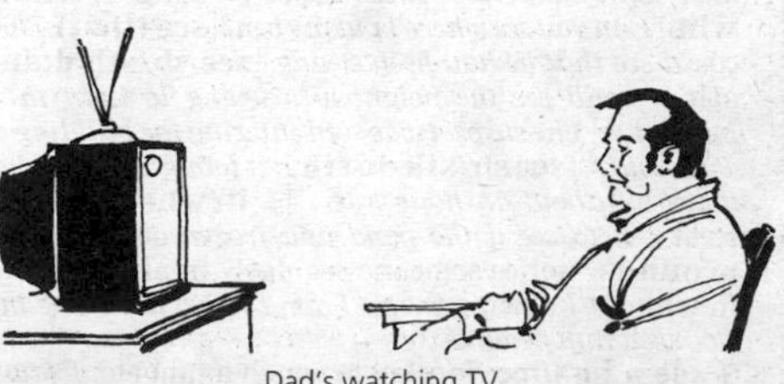
Dad's watching TV.

S1 W1

## see¹ /siː/ *v past tense* saw /sɔː‖sɒː/ *past participle* seen /siːn/

① UNDERSTAND/REALIZE
② WITH YOUR EYES
③ FIND OUT
④ GOODBYE
⑤ VISIT/MEET
⑥ CONSIDER
⑦ FUTURE
⑧ IMAGINE
⑨ MAKE SURE
⑩ EXPERIENCE
⑪ GO WITH SB
⑫ OTHER MEANINGS

### ① UNDERSTAND/REALIZE

**1** [I,T] to understand or realize something: *I can see that you're not very happy with the situation.|Seeing his distress, Louise put her arm around him.*|[+ **why/what/who** etc] *"Ann's really fed up." "I can see why!"*|**see what sb means** *usually spoken* (=understand what someone is saying) *Do you see what I mean?*|**see the point** (=understand the reason for something) *I can't see the point of learning Latin when you're never going to use it.*|**see both sides** (=understand both opinions in a discussion or argument)|**not see that it matters** (=not think something is important) *The recipe says to use fresh cream, but I can't see that it matters.*|**not see the joke** (=not understand why something is funny) *Ian laughed politely even though he couldn't see the joke.*|**not see reason/sense** (=realize you are being silly or unreasonable) *I've tried to explain that we can't afford it, but he just won't see reason.*

**2 I see** *spoken* used to show that you are listening to what someone is telling you and that you understand it: *"You turn this dial to control the central heating." "Oh, I see."*

**3 you see** *spoken* used when you are explaining something to someone: *The shop's open till 8 you see, so I can pick some stuff up after work.|You see the thing is I'm really busy right now.*

**4 see** *spoken* used to check that someone is listening and understands what you are explaining to them: *You mix the flour and eggs like this, see.*

**5 see sth for what it is/see sb for what they are** to realize that someone or something is not as good or pleasant as they seem

**6 not see the wood for the trees** also **not see the forest for the trees** *AmE* to be unable to understand something because you are looking too much at small details rather than the whole thing

### ② WITH YOUR EYES

**7 ▶ ABILITY TO SEE ◀** [I,T not in progressive] to be able to use your eyes to look at things and know what they are: *I can't see a thing without my glasses!*|**not see to do sth** *It's so dark I can hardly see to do my work.*

**8 ▶ NOTICE/EXAMINE ◀** [T not in progressive] to notice, examine, or recognize someone or something by looking: *Can I see your ticket, please.|You see a lot of men with long hair these days.*|[+ **where/what/who**] *Can you see where I put my pen?*|**see (that)** *They could see that he had been crying.*|**see sb/sth doing sth** *I could see the neighbours trying to light their barbecue.|The suspect was seen entering the building at 1500 hours.*|**see sb/sth do sth** *Pat thought he saw her drive off about an hour later.*|[+ **if/whether**] *Nick went out to see if the pond had frozen over.*|**see sb around** (=notice someone regularly in places you go to without knowing them) *I don't know his name but I've seen him around.*

**9 see a film/movie/play** to watch a film etc: *I saw a really good movie last night.*

**10 ▶ TELEVISION ◀** [T not in progressive] to watch a particular programme on television: *Did you see the game last night?*

**11 ▶ FIND INFORMATION ◀** [T only in imperative] used to tell you where you can find information: *See p.58.|See press for details.*|**see above/below** *The results are shown in Table 7a (see below).*

**12 be seen** to look at or be noticed by people who are important in society: *Royal Ascot is the place to be seen.*

**13 be seen to be doing sth** to make sure that other people notice you working hard or doing something good: *The government must be seen to be doing something about the rise in violent crime.*

### ③ FIND OUT

**14** [T] to find out information or a fact: [+ **what/when/who/how** etc] *Can you see who's at the door.*|[+ **if/whether**] *Sharon! See if there's any beer in the fridge!|an experiment to see whether the new material melts at high temperatures*|**see for yourself** (=used to tell someone to look at something so that they can find out if it is true) *If you don't believe me, see for yourself.*

**15 see what sb/sth can do** *spoken* **a)** to find out if you can deal with a situation or problem: [+ **about**] *I'll see what I can do about speeding up the process.* **b)** to find out how good someone or something is at what they are supposed to be able to do: *Let's take the Porsche out to the racetrack and see what it can do!*

### ④ GOODBYE

**16 see you!** *spoken* used to say goodbye when you know you will see someone again: **see you tomorrow/at 3/Sunday etc** *See you Friday – your place at 8:30.*|**see you in a bit** *BrE* (=see you soon)|**see you in a while** (=see you soon) *AmE*|**(I'll) be seeing you!** (=see you soon)

**17 see you around** *spoken* used to say goodbye to someone when you have not made a definite arrangement to meet again

**18 see you later** *spoken* used to say goodbye to someone when you are going to see them again soon or later in the same day

### ⑤ VISIT/MEET

**19 ▶ VISIT/MEET SB ◀** [T] to visit or meet someone: *We're going to see Lucy after work.*|**see you** (=I will meet you) *See you at 8 at Bear's Place.*

**20 ▶ HAVE A MEETING ◀** [T] to have an arranged meeting with someone: *Mr Thomas is seeing a client at 2:30.*|**see sb about sth** (=see someone to discuss something) *I have to see my teacher about my grades.*

**21 ▶ BY CHANCE ◀** [T, not in progressive] to meet someone by chance: *I saw Penny in town today.*

**22 ▶ SPEND TIME WITH SB ◀** [T] to spend time with someone: *Do you still see any of your old college friends?*|**see a lot of sb** (=see someone often) *She's been seeing a lot of John recently.*|**see more/less of sb**

(=see someone more or less often) *They've seen much more of each other since Dan moved to London.*
**23 ▶ HAVE A VISIT ◀** [T] to have a visit from someone: *She's too sick to see anyone at the moment.*
**24 be seeing sb** to be having a romantic relationship with someone: *Is she seeing anyone at the moment?*

**⑥ CONSIDER**
**25 see sb/sth as sth** to consider something to be a particular thing or to have a particular quality: *Jake saw any man who spoke to his wife as a potential threat.* | **be seen as sth** *America is seen as the land of opportunity.*
**26 ▶ CONSIDER STH IN A PARTICULAR WAY ◀** [T always + adv/prep] to regard or consider something in a particular way: *He sees things differently now that he's in management.* | **as sb sees it** (=according to someone's opinion of a situation) *As they see it, I'm the one to blame.* | **the way I see it** *spoken*: *Well, the way I see it, nothing's really going to change around here.* | **see fit (to do sth)** (=consider an action to be right and sensible) *You must do whatever you see fit.*
**27 seeing that** considering that: *She writes very well seeing that English isn't her first language.*
**28 (be) seen against sth** to be considered together with something else: *The unemployment data must be seen against the backdrop of world recession.*

**⑦ FUTURE**
**29** [I,T] to find out about something in the future: [+ **if/whether**] *It will be interesting to see whether Glenn gets the job.* | [+ **how/what/when etc**] *I might come – I'll see how I feel tomorrow.* | **we'll see** *spoken* (=used when you do not want to make a decision immediately) *"Can we go to the zoo, Dad?" "We'll see."* | **I'll/we'll have to see** (=used when you cannot make a decision immediately) *I don't know if I can lend you that much – I'll have to see.* | **wait and see** *spoken*: *We'll just have to wait and see.* | **see how it goes/see how things go** *usually spoken* (=used when you are going to do something and will deal with problems as they appear) | **you'll see** *spoken* (=used to tell someone that something will happen in the way you have described it) *I'll do better than any of them, you'll see.*
**30 see sth coming** to realize that there is going to be a problem before it actually happens: *We should really have seen this mess coming.*

**⑧ IMAGINE**
**31** [T not in progressive] to form a picture of something or someone in your mind; IMAGINE (31): *He could see a great future for her in music.* | **can't see sth** (=think that something is unlikely to happen or be true) *Stuart thinks the car will go, but I can't see it myself.* | **see sb as sth** (=be able to imagine someone being something) *I just can't see her as a ballet dancer.*
**32 be seeing things** to imagine that you see something which is not really there: *There's no one there – you must have been seeing things.*

**⑨ MAKE SURE**
**33** [T not in progressive] to make sure or check that something is done correctly: **see that** *It's up to you to see that the job's done properly.* | **see to it** (=make sure that something is done) *Don't worry – I'll see to it.*
**34 ▶ WARNING ◀** [T, only in imperative] used as a warning that something is important and must be done: **see (that)** *Please see that the room is straightened up before you leave.*

**⑩ EXPERIENCE**
**35 ▶ PERSON ◀** [T not in progressive] to have experience of something: *We've seen some good times together, Dave and I.* | **have seen it all (before)** (=to have experienced something before, especially so that there is nothing else for you to learn about it) —see also **(been there), seen that, done that** (BEEN (3))
**36 ▶ TIME/PLACE ◀** [T] if a time or place has seen a particular event or situation, it happened or existed in that time or place: *This year has seen a big increase in road accidents.*

**⑪ GO WITH SB**
**37 see sb across the road** to help someone to cross a road safely
**38 see sb home** to go with someone when they go home to make sure that they are safe: *Wait a minute! I'll get Nick to see you home.*
**39 see sb to the door** to go to the door with someone when they leave your house, to say goodbye to them

**⑫ OTHER MEANINGS**
**40 let me see/let's see** *spoken* used to show that you are trying to remember something: *Let me see...where did I put that letter?*
**41 seeing as/how/that** *spoken* an expression meaning because, used especially when a situation makes you decide or suggest something that you had not intended: *Seeing as you're going into town, can you get a few things for me?* | **seeing (as) it's you** *humorous* (=used to say that you are treating someone especially well because you like them)
**42 I don't see why not** *spoken* used to say yes in answer to a request: *"Can we go to the park?" "I don't see why not."*
**43 have seen better days** *informal* to be in a bad condition: *This coat has seen better days.*
**44 see the back of sb** *spoken* used to say that you will be happy when someone leaves because you do not like them: *I can't wait to see the back of him.*
**45 see the last of sb/sth** to not see someone or something again because they have gone or are finished: *By Friday we should be seeing the last of the rain for a while.*
**46 see the light a)** to realize that something is true **b)** to have a special experience that makes you believe in a religion **c)** also **see the light of day** to exist or first appear: *The book that she had planned to write never saw the light of day.*
**47 I'll see what I can do** *spoken* used to say that you will try to help someone: *Leave the ones you haven't done with me, and I'll see what I can do.*
**48 see your way (clear) to** *spoken* to be able and willing to help someone: *I think I could see my way to lending you a little.*
**49 see sb coming (a mile off)** *spoken* to recognize that someone will be easy to trick or deceive: *You paid £500 for that! They must have seen you coming!*
**50 not see beyond the end of your nose** to be so concerned with yourself and what you are doing that you do not realize what is happening to other people around you
**51 see sb right** *BrE spoken* to make sure that someone is properly rewarded: *Just do this for me and I'll see you right.*
**52 ▶ GAME OF CARDS ◀** to risk the same amount of money as your opponent in a CARD[1] (7) game

**see about** sth *phr v* [T] **1** to make arrangements or deal with something: *I'd better see about dinner.* | **see about doing sth** *Claire's gone to see about getting tickets for that concert.* **2 we'll have to see about that** *spoken* used to say that you do not know if something will be possible: *"The school trip's really cheap and Dad says I can go." "We'll have to see about that!"* **3 we'll soon see about that** *spoken* used to say that you intend to stop someone doing something they are planning to do

**see around** also **see round** *BrE phr v* [T] to visit a place and walk around looking at it: *Would you like to see around the old castle?*

**see in** *phr v* **1** [T **see** sth ↔ **in** sb/sth] to notice a particular quality in someone or something that makes you like them: *He saw a gentleness in Susan.* | **not know what sb sees in sb** *spoken* (=not know why someone likes someone) *I really don't know what she sees in him!* **2** [T **see** sb **in**] to show a visitor the way when they arrive at a building: *Will you see the*

[continued on next page]

[continued from previous page]
*guests in when they arrive?* **3** [I] to be able to see into someone's house: *Close the curtains so that no one can see in while I dress.* **4 see in the new year** to celebrate the beginning of a new year

**see** sb/sth **off** *phr v* [T] **1** to go to an airport, train station etc to say goodbye to someone: *I think they've gone to the airport to see their daugher off.* **2** to chase someone away, or make someone leave an area: *Security guards saw him off the premises.* **3** to defend yourself successfully in a fight or battle, or beat an opponent in a game: **see off the competition** *They saw off the competition to become the nation's number one bestseller.* **4** *BrE slang* to kill someone

**see** sb/sth **out** *phr v* [T] **1** to go to the door with someone to say goodbye to them when they leave: **I'll see myself out** *spoken* (=used to tell someone they do not have to come to the door with you) **2** to continue to do something until it finishes, even if you do not like doing it: *I don't enjoy the course but I'll see it out.*

**see over** sth *phr v* [T] *BrE* to examine something large such as a house, especially when you are considering buying it

**see through** *phr v* [T] **1** [**see through** sth] to recognize the truth about something that is intended to deceive you: *I could see through his lies.* **2** [**see through** sb] to know what someone is really like, especially what their bad qualities are **3** [**see** sth **through**] to continue doing something, especially something difficult or unpleasant, until it is finished: *Martin felt sick with nerves, but was determined to see the thing through.* **4** [**see** sb **through** sth] to give help and support to someone during a difficult time: *I've given him a sedative; that should see him through the night.*

**see to** sb/sth *phr v* [T] to deal with something or do something for someone: *We'll have to see to that window – the wood's rotten.* | **have/get sth seen to** *You should get that tooth seen to by a dentist.* | **see to it that** *Will you see to it that this letter gets mailed today?* —see also **not see sb for dust** (DUST[1] (6)), **it remains to be seen** (REMAIN (5)), **see red** (RED[2] (4)), **see the colour of sb's money** (COLOUR[1] (12)), **wouldn't be seen dead** (DEAD[1] (17))

Frequencies of the verb **see** in spoken and written English.

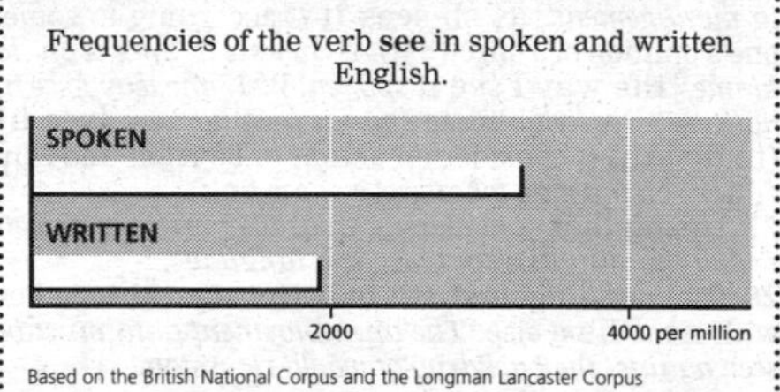


Based on the British National Corpus and the Longman Lancaster Corpus

This graph shows that the verb **see** is much more common in spoken English than in written English. This is because it is used in a lot of common spoken phrases.

**see²** *n* [C] *technical* an area governed by a BISHOP (1)

S3 W3 **seed¹** /siːd/ *n plural* **seeds** or **seed** **1 a)** [C,U] a small, hard object produced by plants, from which a new plant of the same kind grows: *sunflower seeds* | **plant/sow seeds** (=put them into the ground) *Plant the seeds in sandy soil, about 10 cm apart.* | **grow sth from seed** (=grow a plant from a seed, rather than planting it when it is already partly grown) **b)** [U] a quantity of seeds: *grass seed* **2** *AmE* [C] one of the small hard objects in a fruit such as an apple or orange, from which new fruit trees grow; PIP[1] (1) *BrE* **3 go/run to seed a)** if a plant or vegetable goes or runs to seed, it starts producing flowers and seeds as well as leaves **b)** if a person goes or runs to seed, they become unattractive, fat, or unhealthy especially because of getting old or lazy **4 the seeds of sth** something that makes a new situation start to grow and develop: *the seeds of victory* | **sow (the) seeds of doubt/destruction/rebellion etc** (=do or say something which makes a bad feeling or situation develop and become a much more serious problem) *Sectarian agitators did much to sow the seeds of discontent among the people.* **5 number one/number three etc seed** [C] a tennis player who is given a particular position according to how likely they are to win a competition: *He's been top seed for the past two years.* **6** *biblical or humorous* SEMEN or SPERM **7** [U] *biblical* the group of people who have a particular person as their father, grandfather etc, especially when they form a particular race

**seed²** *v* **1** [T] to remove seeds from fruit: *seeded raisins* **2** [T usually passive] to give a tennis player a particular position, according to how likely they are to win a competition: *seeded fourth at Wimbledon* **3** [T often passive] to plant seeds in the ground **4** [I] to produce seeds

**seed·bed** /ˈsiːdbed/ *n* [C] **1** an area of ground where young plants are grown from seeds before they are planted somewhere else **2** a place or condition that encourages something, especially a bad situation, to develop: [**+ of**] *The city's slums were a seedbed of rebellion.* —see also HOTBED

**seed cap·i·tal** /ˈ· ˌ···/ *n* [U] the money you have to start a new business with

**seed·ling** /ˈsiːdlɪŋ/ *n* [C] a young plant grown from seed

**seed pearl** /ˈ· ·/ *n* [C] a very small and often imperfect PEARL

**seed·y** /ˈsiːdi/ *adj informal* **1** a seedy person or place looks dirty or poor, and is often involved in or connected with illegal, immoral, or dishonest activities: *a bunch of seedy characters* **2** *old-fashioned informal* feeling slightly ill —**seediness** *n* [U]

**see·ing** /ˈsiːɪŋ/ *conjunction spoken* because a particular fact or situation is true: **seeing (that)** *We could have a joint party, seeing that your birthday is the same day as mine.* | **seeing as** *I won't stay long, seeing as you're busy.* S3

**seeing eye dog** /ˌ·· ˈ· ˌ·/ *n* [C] *AmE* a dog trained to guide blind people; GUIDE DOG

**seek** /siːk/ *v past tense and past participle* **sought** /sɔːt‖ sɒːt/ W1

**1 ▶ LOOK FOR ◀** [I,T] **a)** a word meaning to look for something that you need such as a job or friendship, used especially in newspapers and advertisements: *Virgo woman seeks Scorpio man.* | *new graduates seeking employment* **b)** *formal* to look for the answer to a question or problem

**2 ▶ TRY TO GET ◀** [T] *formal* to try to achieve or get something: *Do you think the President will seek reelection?* | *We only seek justice, not revenge.* | **seek to do sth** *We are always seeking to improve productivity.* | **attention-seeking/publicity-seeking** (=trying to attract people's attention) *a publicity-seeking stunt*

**3 ▶ ASK FOR ◀ seek (sb's) advice/help/assistance etc** *formal* to ask someone for advice or help: *If the symptoms persist, seek medical advice.* —see REQUEST[2] (USAGE)

**4 seek your fortune** *literary* to go to another place hoping to gain success and wealth: *Young William went to America to seek his fortune.*

**5 ▶ MOVE TOWARDS ◀** [T] to move naturally towards something or into a particular position: *Water seeks its own level.* —see also HEAT-SEEKING, HIDE AND SEEK, SELF-SEEKING, SOUGHT-AFTER

**seek** sb/sth ↔ **out** *phr v* [T] to look very hard for someone or something, especially someone who is avoiding you or hiding from you: *Our mission is to seek out the enemy and destroy them.*

**seek·er** /ˈsiːkə‖-ər/ *n* [C] someone who is trying to find or get something: **job-seeker/asylum-seeker** *a brilliant politician and a ruthless power-seeker*

S 1 W 1 **seem** /siːm/ *v* [linking verb, not in progressive] **1** to appear to be a particular thing or to have a particular quality, feeling, or attitude: *Dinah didn't seem very sure.* | **seem to sb** *Larry seemed pretty angry to me.* | *"How did she seem to you?" "Kind of upset."* | **seem like** *Well, it seemed like a good idea at the time.* | **sb/sth seems a** *That seems a risky thing to try.* | **not be what he/she/it etc seems** *Things aren't always what they seem.* **2** to appear to exist or be true: **seem to** *I seem to have lost my car keys.* | **it seems to sb (that)** *It seems to me you don't have much choice.* | **It seems (that)/it would seem (that)** *It would seem that someone left the building unlocked.* | **it seems like** *It seems like only yesterday that Tommy was born.* | **it seems as if/as though** *It seemed as though she didn't have a friend in the world.* | **so it seems** (=it appears to be true) *"So Bill's leaving her?" "So it seems."* **3** to appear to be happening or to be doing something: **seem to do sth** *The rainbow seemed to end on the hillside.* | **seem like** *It seemed like the whole town had come to the show.* **4 can't/couldn't seem to do sth** used to say that you have tried to do something but cannot do it: *I just can't seem to get it into his head that he has to plan things better.*

**seem·ing** /ˈsiːmɪŋ/ *adj* [only before noun] *formal* appearing to be something, especially when this is not actually true; APPARENTLY: *It was a seeming piece of good luck which later led to all kinds of trouble.*

**seem·ing·ly** /ˈsiːmɪŋli/ *adv* **1** appearing to be something when this is not actually true; APPARENT: *The road was dusty and seemingly endless.* **2** *sentence adverb* according to the facts as you know them: *There is seemingly nothing we can do to stop the plans going ahead.*

**seem·ly** /ˈsiːmli/ *adj old-fashioned* suitable for a particular situation or social occasion, according to accepted standards of behaviour: *It would be more seemly to keep quiet about it in front of the guests.* —opposite UNSEEMLY —**seemliness** *n* [U]

**seen** /siːn/ the past participle of SEE

**seep** /siːp/ *v* [I always + adv/prep] to flow slowly through small holes or spaces: [+ **in/into/through etc**] *Whenever it rained water started seeping in.*

**seep·age** /ˈsiːpɪdʒ/ *n* [singular, U] a gradual flow of liquid through small spaces or holes: *Looks like a seepage problem in your basement.*

**seer** /sɪə‖sɪr/ *n* [C] *especially literary* someone who can see into the future and say what will happen

**seer·suck·er** /ˈsɪəˌsʌkə‖ˈsɪrˌsʌkər/ *n* [U] a light cotton cloth with an uneven surface and a pattern of lines

**see·saw**[1] /ˈsiːsɔː‖-sɒː/ *n* [C] a piece of equipment that children play on, made of a board that is balanced in the middle, so that when one end goes up the other goes down

**seesaw**[2] *v* [I] to move repeatedly from one state or condition to another and back again: *seesawing emotions*

**seethe** /siːð/ *v* [I] if a place is seething with people, insects etc there are a lot of them all moving quickly in different directions: *seething with ants* | *a seething mass of people*

**seeth·ing** /ˈsiːðɪŋ/ *adj* extremely angry, but unable or unwilling to show it: *By the time we got home, David was seething.*

**see-through** /ˈ· ·/ *adj* a see-through piece of clothing is made of cloth that you can see through —compare TRANSPARENT (1): *This dress is completely see-through when it's wet!*

**seg·ment** /ˈsegmənt/ *n* [C] **1** a part of something that is in some way different from or affected differently from the whole: *A large segment of the public is against the new tax.* **2** a part of a fruit, flower or insect that naturally divides into parts: *the segments of an orange* —see picture on page 416 **3** *technical* a part of a circle separated from the rest of the circle by a straight line across it —see picture at SHAPE[1] **4** *technical* the part of a line between two points

**seg·men·ta·tion** /ˌsegmenˈteɪʃən,-mən-/ *n* [U] the act of dividing something or to be divided into smaller parts

**seg·ment·ed** /segˈmentɪ̌d/ *adj* made up of separate parts that are connected to each other

**seg·re·gate** /ˈsegrɪgeɪt/ *v* [T often passive] to separate one group of people from others, especially because they are of a different race, sex or religion: *Blacks were segregated from whites in churches, schools and colleges.*

**seg·re·gat·ed** /ˈsegrɪgeɪtɪ̌d/ *adj* a segregated school or other institution can only be attended by members of one sex, race etc: *a segregated audience* —compare INTEGRATED

**seg·re·ga·tion** /ˌsegrɪˈgeɪʃən/ *n* [U] the practice of keeping people of different races or religions apart and making them live, work, or study separately: *The US Supreme Court ruled in 1954 that segregation in schools was unconstitutional.* —compare INTEGRATION

**sei·gneur** /seˈnjɜː‖seɪˈnɜːr/ *n* [C] someone who owned land in a FEUDAL system

**seis·mic** /ˈsaɪzmɪk/ *adj technical* connected with or caused by EARTHQUAKES or powerful explosions: *an increase in seismic activity*

**seis·mo·graph** /ˈsaɪzməgrɑːf‖-græf/ *n* [C] an instrument that measures and records the movement of the earth during an EARTHQUAKE

**seis·mol·o·gy** /saɪzˈmɒlədʒi‖-ˈmɑː-/ *n* [U] the scientific study of EARTHQUAKES —**seismologist** *n* [C]

**seize** /siːz/ *v* **1** [T] to take hold of something suddenly and violently: *He seized my hand and dragged me away from the window.* | **seize sth from sb** *Maggie seized the letter from her and began to read out loud.* **2** [T] to take control of a place suddenly and quickly, using military force: **seize power/seize control (of)** *The rebels have seized power in a violent coup.* **3** [T] if the police or government officers seize something, they take away illegal goods such as drugs or guns **4 seize a chance/opportunity (with both hands)** to quickly and eagerly do something when you have the chance to **5 be seized with terror/desire etc** to suddenly be affected by an extremely strong feeling: *I was seized with a sudden desire to laugh out loud.* **6** [T] to suddenly catch someone and make sure they cannot get away: *The gunmen were seized in a military style operation.* W 3

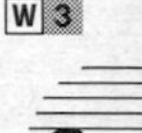

**seize on/upon** sth *phr v* [T] to suddenly become very interested in an idea, excuse, what someone says etc: *Margot seized on the excuse to get out of choir practice.*

**seize up** *phr v* [I] **a)** if an engine or part of a machine seizes up, its moving parts stop working and can no longer move, for example because of lack of oil **b)** if a part of your body, such as your back, seizes up you suddenly cannot move it and it is very painful

**sei·zure** /ˈsiːʒə‖-ər/ *n* **1** [U] the act of suddenly taking control or possession of something: *the Fascist seizure of power in 1922* **2** [C] a sudden attack of an illness, for example a HEART ATTACK: *an epileptic seizure*

**sel·dom** /ˈseldəm/ *adv* very rarely: *She seldom reads newspapers.* —see picture at FREQUENCY

**se·lect**[1] /sɪ̌ˈlekt/ *v* [T] to choose something by carefully thinking about which is the best, most suitable etc: *I selected four postcards and handed them to the cashier.* | **select sb to do sth** *Simon's been selected to represent us at the conference in Rio.*

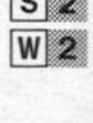

**select**[2] *adj formal* **1** a select group of people or things is a small special group that has been carefully chosen: *The information was only given to a select group of reporters.* | *select cuts of beef* **2** only lived in, visited, or used by a small number of rich people; EXCLUSIVE[1] (1): *a select apartment block*

**select com·mit·tee** /·ˌ· ·ˈ··/ *n* [C] a small group of politicians and advisers from various parties that has been chosen to examine a particular subject

**se·lec·tion** /sɪ̌ˈlekʃən/ *n* **1** [U] the careful choice of a particular person or thing from among a group of similar people or things: *the process of jury selection* | **make a selection** *Please make your selections and move along.*

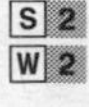

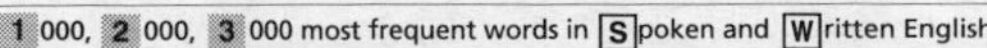

2 [C] something that has been chosen from among a group of things: [+ **from**] *a program of selections from Gilbert and Sullivan* **3** [C usually singular] a collection of things of a particular type, especially of things that are for sale; RANGE: [+ **of**] *a fine selection of perfumes* —see also NATURAL SELECTION

**se·lec·tive** /sə̇ˈlektɪv/ *adj* **1** careful about what you choose to do, buy, allow etc: [+ **about**] *We're very selective about what we let the children watch on TV.* **2** affecting or concerning the best or most suitable people or things from a larger group: *the selective breeding of horses* —**selectively** *adv* —**selectivity** /sə̇ˌlekˈtɪvə̇ti/ *n* [U]

**se·lec·tor** /sə̇ˈlektə‖-ər/ *n* [C] **1** *BrE* a member of a committee that chooses the best people for something such as a sports team **2** *technical* a piece of equipment that helps you find the right thing, for example the correct GEAR[1] (1) in a car

**se·le·ni·um** /sə̇ˈliːniəm/ *n* [U] a poisonous ELEMENT (1) that is not a metal and is used in some electrical instruments to make them sensitive to light

S2 W3 **self** /self/ *n plural* **selves** /selvz/ **1** [C usually singular] the type of person you are, your character, your typical behaviour etc: **sb's usual/normal self** *Sid was not his usual smiling self.* | **be/look/feel (like) your old self** (=be the way you usually are again, especially after having been ill, unhappy etc) *Howard was beginning to feel like his old self again.* | **sb's true self** (=what someone is really like, rather than what they pretend to be like) **2 sb's sense of self** someone's consciousness of being a separate person, different from other people **3 be a shadow/ghost of your former self** to not be at all like the cheerful, healthy, strong etc person that you used to be **4** [U] *spoken* your own desires and satisfaction rather than anyone else's: *It's always self, self, self! You never think of anyone else!* **5** [U] a word written in business letters, on cheques etc meaning yourself

S3 **self-** /self/ *prefix* **1** by yourself or by itself: *He's self-taught.* (=he taught himself) | *self-propelled* **2** of, to, with, for, or in yourself or itself: *a self-addressed envelope* (=which you address to yourself) | *a self-portrait* (=a picture that you have drawn or painted of yourself) | *self-restraint*

**self-ab·ne·ga·tion** /ˌ· ··ˈ··/ *n* [U] *formal* a lack of interest in your own needs and desires; ABNEGATION

**self-ab·sorbed** /ˌ· ·ˈ·◂/ *adj* concerned only with yourself and the things that affect you: *I wouldn't worry – teenagers always seem totally self-absorbed.* —**self-absorption** *n* [U]

**self-ad·dressed** /ˌ· ·ˈ·◂/ *adj* a self-addressed envelope has the sender's address on it so that it can be sent back to them —see also SAE, SASE

**self-ad·he·sive** /ˌ· ·ˈ··◂/ *adj* a self-adhesive envelope, BANDAGE etc has a sticky surface and does not need liquid or glue to make it stay closed

**self-ap·point·ed** /ˌ· ·ˈ··◂/ *adj* thinking that you are the best person to lead other people or represent their wishes and opinions, especially when you are not: *a self-appointed guardian of morality*

**self-as·sem·bly** /ˌ· ·ˈ··◂/ *adj* sold as separate parts that you put together yourself at home

**self-as·ser·tive** /ˌ· ·ˈ··◂/ *adj* very confident and not shy about saying what you think or want —**self-assertiveness** *n* [U] —**self-assertion** *n* [U]

**self-assurance** /ˌ· ·ˈ··/ confidence and the belief that you are able to deal with people and problems easily

**self-as·sured** /ˌ· ·ˈ·◂/ *adj* calm and confident about what you are doing: *His air of self-assured confidence made him a born leader.* —**self-assurance** *n* [U]

**self-a·ware·ness** /ˌ· ·ˈ··/ *n* [U] knowledge and understanding of yourself: *Personal doubts often serve to focus self-awareness.*

**self-ca·ter·ing** /ˌ· ˈ···/ *adj BrE* a self-catering holiday is one where you stay in a place where you can cook your own food —**self-catering** *n* [U]

**self-cen·tred** *BrE*, **self-centered** *AmE* /ˌ· ˈ··◂/ *adj* paying so much attention to yourself that you do not notice what is happening to other people; SELFISH —**self-centredness** *n* [U]

**self-con·fessed** /ˌ· ·ˈ·◂/ *adj* [only before noun] admitting that you have a particular quality, especially one that is bad: *a self-confessed television addict*

**self-con·fi·dent** /ˌ· ˈ···/ *adj* sure that you can do things well, that people like you, that you are attractive etc, and not shy or nervous in social situations —**self-confidently** *adv* —**self-confidence** *n* [U]

**self-con·gra·tu·la·tion** /ˌ· ···ˈ··/ *n* [U] behaviour that shows in an annoying way that you think you have done very well at something —**self-congratulatory** /ˌ· ···ˈ···‖ˌ· ·ˈ·····/ *adj*: *a smug, self-congratulatory smile*

**self-con·scious** /ˌ· ˈ··/ *adj* **1** worried and embarrassed about what you look like or what other people think of you: *I hate wearing glasses – they make me feel self-conscious.* | [+ **about**] *Jerry's pretty self-conscious about his weight.* **2** self-conscious art, writing etc shows that the artist etc is too aware of how the public will react to them: *self-conscious art-house movies* —**self-consciously** *adv* —**self-consciousness** *n* [U]

**self-con·tained** /ˌ· ·ˈ·◂/ *adj* **1** something that is self-contained is complete in itself, and does not need other things or help from somewhere else to make it work: *a self-contained database package* **2** someone who is self-contained tends not to be friendly or show their feelings **3** *BrE* a self-contained FLAT[2] (1) has its own kitchen and bathroom

**self-con·tra·dic·to·ry** /ˌ· ··ˈ···/ *adj* containing two opposite statements or ideas that cannot both be true

**self-con·trol** /ˌ· ·ˈ·/ *n* [U] the ability to behave calmly and sensibly even when you feel very excited, angry etc: *Greater self-control is the simple answer to most people's eating problems.* —**self-controlled** *adj*

**self-de·cep·tion** /ˌ· ·ˈ··/ *n* [U] the act of making yourself believe something is true when it is not: *He was unwilling to admit that the visionary idea was sheer self-deception.* —**self-deceptive** *adj*

**self-de·feat·ing** /ˌ· ·ˈ··◂/ *adj* causing exactly the same problems and difficulties that you are trying to prevent or deal with

**self-de·fence** *BrE*, **self-defense** *AmE* /ˌ· ·ˈ·/ *n* [U] **1** something you do to protect yourself or your property: **in self-defence** (=to protect yourself) *I swear, I shot him in self-defense.* **2** skills that you learn to protect yourself if you are attacked: *a self-defence class for women*

**self-de·ni·al** /ˌ· ·ˈ··/ *n* [U] the practice of not doing or having the things you enjoy, either because you cannot afford it, or for moral or religious reasons —**self-denying** *adj*

**self-dep·re·cat·ing** /ˌ·ˈ····/ *adj* trying to make your own abilities or achievements seem unimportant: *self-deprecating humour*

**self-des·truct** /ˌself dɪˈstrʌkt◂/ *v* [I] if something such as a bomb self-destructs, it destroys itself, usually by exploding —**self-destruct** *adj*: *a self-destruct mechanism*

**self-des·truc·tion** /ˌ· ·ˈ··/ *n* [U] the practice of deliberately doing things that are likely to seriously damage or kill you: **be bent on self-destruction** (=be determined to damage or destroy yourself) —**self-destructive** *adj*: *self-destructive behaviour*

**self-de·ter·min·a·tion** /ˌ· ···ˈ··/ *n* [U] the right of the people of a particular country to govern themselves and to choose the type of government they will have

**self-dis·ci·pline** /ˌ· ˈ···/ *n* [U] the ability to make yourself do the things you know you ought to do, without someone making you do them: *I just wonder if I've got enough self-discipline to finish the course.* —**self-disciplined** *adj*

**self-doubt** /ˌ· ˈ·/ *n* [U] the feeling that you and your abilities are not good enough

**self-drive** /ˌ· ˈ·◂/ *adj* [only before noun] *BrE* a self-drive car is one that you have hired (=paid for) to drive yourself

**self-ed·u·cat·ed** /ˌ· ˈ····◂/ *adj* having taught yourself by reading books etc, rather than learning things in school

**self-ef·fac·ing** /ˌ· ·ˈ··◂/ *adj* not wanting to attract attention to yourself or your achievements, especially because you are not socially confident: *He was loved for his skill and also his self-effacing modesty.* —**self-effacement** *n* [U]

**self-em·ployed** /ˌ· ·ˈ·◂/ *adj* working for yourself and not employed by a company: **go self-employed** (=become self-employed) | **the self-employed** (=people who are self-employed) *pension plans for the self-employed* —**self-employment** *n* [U]

**self-es·teem** /ˌ· ·ˈ·/ *n* [U] the feeling that you are someone who deserves to be liked, respected, and admired: *Teachers need to help build up their students' sense of self-esteem.* | **low self-esteem** (=not much self-esteem)

**self-ev·i·dent** /ˌ· ˈ···◂/ *adj* clearly true and needing no more proof; OBVIOUS (1): *self-evident truths*

**self-ex·am·in·a·tion** /ˌ· ···ˈ··/ *n* [U] **1** careful thought about whether your actions and your reasons for them are right or wrong **2** the practice of checking parts of your body for early signs of some illnesses

**self-ex·plan·a·to·ry** /ˌ· ·ˈ····/ *adj* clear and easy to understand without needing further explanation: *Messages displayed as a result of user error are self-explanatory.*

**self-ex·pres·sion** /ˌ· ·ˈ··/ *n* [U] the expression of your feelings, thoughts, ideas etc, especially through activities such as painting, writing, or acting etc: *The curriculum needs room for creative self-expression.* —**self-expressive** *adj*

**self-ful·fil·ling** /ˌ··ˈ··◂/ *adj* **self-fulfilling prophecy** a statement about what is likely to happen in the future that becomes true because you expected it to happen and therefore changed your behaviour

**self-gov·ern·ing** /ˌ· ˈ···/ *adj* a country or organization that is self-governing is controlled by its own members rather than by someone from another country or organization: *a self-governing trust*

**self-gov·ern·ment** /ˌ· ˈ···/ *n* [U] the government of a country by its own citizens, without people from other countries having any control or influence

**self-help** /ˌ· ˈ·/ *n* [U] the use of your own efforts to deal with your problems instead of depending on other people: **self-help group** (=a group of people with a particular illness or problem who help each other)

**self·hood** /ˈselfhʊd/ *n* [U] *technical* the knowledge of yourself as an independent person separate from others

**self-im·age** /ˌ· ˈ··/ *n* [C] the idea you have of your own abilities, physical appearance, and character: *Bullies often have a poor self-image.*

**self-im·port·ance** /ˌ· ·ˈ··/ *n* [U] the attitude that shows you think you are more important than other people

**self-im·por·tant** /ˌ· ·ˈ··◂/ *adj* behaving in a way that shows you think you are more important than other people: *a self-important, pompous little man* —**self-importantly** *adv*

**self-im·posed** /ˌ· ·ˈ·◂/ *adj* a self-imposed rule, condition, responsibility etc is one that you have made yourself accept, and which no one has asked you to accept: *five years of self-imposed exile in Bolivia*

**self-in·dul·gence** /ˌ· ·ˈ··/ *n* [singular, U] the act of allowing yourself to have or do something that you enjoy but do not need: *My one self-indulgence is expensive coffee.*

**self-in·dul·gent** /ˌ· ·ˈ··◂/ *adj* allowing yourself to have or do things you enjoy but do not need, especially if you do this too much —**self-indulgently** *adv*

**self-in·flict·ed** /ˌ· ·ˈ··◂/ *adj* self-inflicted pain, problems, illnesses etc are those you have caused yourself: *It cannot be a self-inflicted blow, so it must be murder.*

**self-in·terest** /ˌ· ˈ··/ *n* [U] consideration only of what is best for you rather than other people: *His offer was motivated solely by self-interest.* —**self-interested** *adj*

**self·ish** /ˈselfɪʃ/ *adj* caring only about yourself and not about other people: *How can you be so selfish?* | *selfish motives* —**selfishly** *adv* —**selfishness** *n* [U]

**self-knowl·edge** /ˌ· ˈ··/ *n* [U] an understanding of your own character, your reasons for doing things etc

**self·less** /ˈselfləs/ *adj* caring about other people more than about yourself: *selfless devotion to their work* —**selflessly** *adv* —**selflessness** *n* [U]

**self-made** /ˌ· ˈ·◂/ *adj* a self-made man or woman has become successful and rich by their own efforts, and did not have advantages like money or a high social position when they started: *a self-made millionaire*

**self-o·pin·ion·at·ed** /ˌ· ·ˈ····◂/ *adj* always believing that your own opinions and ideas are always right and that everyone else should always agree with you

**self-pit·y** /ˌ· ˈ··/ *n* [U] the feeling of being sorry for yourself because you have been unlucky or you think people have treated you badly: *Stop wallowing in your own self-pity and do something about it!* —**self-pitying** *adj*

**self-por·trait** /ˌ· ˈ··/ *n* [C] a drawing, painting, or description that you do of yourself

**self-pos·sessed** /ˌ· ·ˈ·◂/ *adj* calm, confident, and in control of your feelings, even in difficult or unexpected situations —**self-possession** *n* [U]

**self-pres·er·va·tion** /ˌ· ··ˈ··/ *n* [U] protection of yourself in a threatening or dangerous situation: *the instinct for self-preservation*

**self-pro·claimed** /ˌ· ·ˈ·◂/ *adj* having given yourself a position or title without the approval of other people: *a self-proclaimed champion of the working class*

**self-rais·ing flour** /ˌ· ·· ˈ·/ *n* [U] *BrE* a type of flour that contains BAKING POWDER; SELF-RISING FLOUR *AmE*

**self-reg·u·la·to·ry** /ˌ· ˈ·····/ also **self-regulating** /ˌ· ˈ····/ *adj* a self-regulatory system, industry, or organization is one that controls itself, rather than having an independent organization or laws to make sure that rules are obeyed —**self-regulation** /ˌ· ··ˈ··/ *n* [U]

**self-re·li·ant** /ˌ· ·ˈ··◂/ *adj* able to decide what to do by yourself, without depending on the help or advice of other people: *Hong Kong must prepare to be more self-reliant for growth in the 1990s.* —**self-reliance** *n* [U]

**self-re·spect** /ˌ· ·ˈ·/ *n* [U] a feeling of being happy about what you are, what you do, and what you believe in: *It's difficult to keep your self-respect when you have been unemployed for a long time.*

**self-re·spect·ing** /ˌ· ·ˈ··◂/ *adj* [only before noun] having respect for yourself and your abilities and beliefs: **no self-respecting ... would do sth** *No self-respecting actor would appear in a porn movie.*

**self-re·straint** /ˌ· ·ˈ·/ *n* [U] the ability not to do or say something you very much want to, because you know this is more sensible: **exercise self-restraint** *Police officers must learn to exercise self-restraint.*

**self-right·eous** /ˌ· ˈ··◂/ *adj* proudly sure that your beliefs, attitudes, and morals are good and right, in a way that annoys other people: *That's the most unfair, self-righteous statement I've ever heard!* —**self-righteously** *adv* —**self-righteousness** *n* [U]

**self-ris·ing flour** /ˌ· ··ˈ·/ *n* [U] *AmE* a type of flour that contains BAKING POWDER; SELF-RAISING FLOUR *BrE*

**self-rule** /ˌ· ˈ·/ *n* [U] the government of a country or part of a country by its own citizens

**self-sac·ri·fice** /ˌ· ˈ···/ *n* [U] the act of doing without things you want, need, or care about in order to help someone else —**self-sacrificing** *adj*

**self·same** /ˈ· ·/ *adj* [only before noun] *literary* exactly the same: *two great victories on the self-same day*

**self-sat·is·fied** /ˌ· ˈ···/ *adj* too pleased with yourself and what you have done: *He seemed as smug and self-satisfied as his father* —**self-satisfaction** /ˌ· ··ˈ··/ *n* [U]

**self-seek·ing** /ˌ· ˈ··◂/ *adj* doing things only because they will give you an advantage that other people do not have: *a self-seeking politician*

**self-serv·ice** /ˌ· ˈ··◂/ *adj* a self-service restaurant, shop etc is one in which you get things for yourself and then pay for them —**self-service** *n* [U]

**self-start·er** /ˌ· ˈ··/ *n* [C] someone who is able to work successfully on their own without needing other people's help or a lot of instructions

**self-styled** /ˈ· ·/ *adj* [only before noun] having given yourself a title or position without having a right to it: *a self-styled professor*

**self-suf·fi·cient** /ˌ· ·ˈ··◂/ *adj* providing all the things you need without help from outside: *In those days the farm was largely self-sufficient.* —**self-sufficiency** *n* [U]

**self-sup·port·ing** /ˌ· ·ˈ··◂/ *adj* able to earn enough money to support yourself: *The business will soon become self-supporting.*

**self-taught** /ˌ· ˈ·◂/ *adj* having learned a skill or subject by yourself, rather than in a school: *a self-taught accountant*

**self-willed** /ˌ· ˈ·◂/ *adj* very determined to do what you want, even when this is unreasonable: *a wild and self-willed child* —**self-will** *n* [U]

**self-wind·ing** /ˌselʃ ˈwaɪndɪŋ◂/ *adj* a self-winding watch is one that you do not have to WIND[3] to make it work

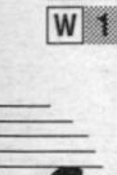

S1 W1 **sell**[1] /sel/ *v past tense and past participle* **sold** /səʊld‖soʊld/

**1 ► GIVE STH FOR MONEY ◄** [I,T] to give something to someone in exchange for money: *If you offer them another thousand, I think they'll sell.* | **sell sth for £100/$50/30p etc** *Toni's selling her car for £700.* | **sell sb sth/sell sth to sb** *I'm not selling you my shares!* | *The vase was sold to an American buyer.* | **sell sth** *Now he regrets selling all his old records.* | **sell sth at a profit/loss** (=making or losing money on a sale) —opposite BUY
**2 ► MAKE STH AVAILABLE ◄** [T] to offer something for people to buy: *Do you sell cigarettes?* | *a job selling advertising space*
**3 sell at/for £100/$50/30p** to be offered for sale at a particular price: *Smoke alarms sell for as little as five pounds.*
**4 ► MAKE STH ATTRACTIVE ◄** [I,T] to make people want to buy something: *Scandal sells newspapers.* | **sell sb sth/sell sth to sb** (=persuade someone that they want to buy something) *You have to go out and really sell the stuff, Leo.*
**5 ► SELL A LOT ◄** [I] to be bought by people in large numbers: *Tickets for the concert just aren't selling.* | **sell well/badly** *Anti-age creams always sell well.*
**6 sell like hotcakes** to sell quickly and in large amounts
**7 ► IDEA/PLAN ◄** [I,T] to try to make someone accept a new idea or plan, or to become accepted: *It's all right for Washington, but will it sell in small-town America?* | **sell sb sth/sell sth to sb** *Just try selling taxes to the voters* | **be sold on (doing) sth/be sold on the idea** (=think an idea or plan is very good) *Joe's completely sold on the concept – he thinks it's brilliant.*
**8 sell yourself a)** to be able to make yourself seem impressive to other people: *If you want a promotion, you've got to sell yourself better.* **b)** to do something that is against your principles in exchange for money or some other advantage
**9 sell sb/sth short** to not give someone or something the praise, attention, or reward that they deserve: *You're selling yourself short – tell them about all your qualifications.*
**10 sell your body** to have sex with someone for money
**11 sell your soul (to the devil)** to do something bad in exchange for money, power etc
**12 sell sb down the river** to do something that harms a group of people who trusted you to help them, in order to gain money or power for yourself
**13 sell your support/vote** *AmE* to give your support or vote to the person who will give you the biggest financial advantage

**sell off** *phr v* [T] **1 sell** sth ↔ **off** to try to get rid of things that no one seems to want to buy by selling them cheaply: *Looks like they're trying to sell off a bunch of junk.* **2** to sell something because you need the money: *After the war we were forced to sell off part of the farm.* **3** to sell all or part of an industry or company

**sell out** *phr v* **1 be/have sold out** if a shop sells out of something, it has no more of that particular thing left to sell: *Sorry, we're sold out.* | **have sold out of sth** *We've completely sold out of those shirts in your size, sir.* **2** [I] if a product, tickets, places at a concert etc sell out, they are all sold and there are none left: *Wow! Those scarves sold out fast.* | **be sold out** *Tonight's performance is completely sold out.* **3** [I,T] to not keep to your beliefs or principles in order to get more money, a comfortable life, or a political advantage: *Ex-hippies who've sold out and become respectable businessmen.* **4** [I] [+ **to**] to sell your business or your share in a business: *Wyman says he'll sell out if business doesn't pick up.*

**sell up** [I,T] *especially BrE* to sell most of what you own, especially your house or your business: *Liz decided to sell up and move abroad.*

**sell**[2] *n* [singular] *BrE informal* something you have been tricked into buying or doing that disappoints you: *What a sell! It's only plastic that looks like wood.* —see also HARD SELL, SOFT SELL

**sell-by date** /ˈ· · ˌ·/ *n* [C] *BrE* **1** the date stamped on a food product, after which it should not be sold; EXPIRATION DATE *AmE* **2 be past its sell-by date** *informal* if an idea, method, system etc is past its sell-by date it has become no longer useful or interesting

**sell·er** /ˈselə‖-ər/ *n* [C] **1** someone who sells something —opposite BUYER **2 good/bad etc seller** a product that sells well, badly etc —see also BEST-SELLER

**seller's mar·ket** /ˌ·· ˈ··/ *n* [singular] a situation in which there is not much of a particular product available for sale, so prices tend to be high —opposite BUYER'S MARKET

**sell·ing** /ˈselɪŋ/ *n* [U] the job and skill of persuading people to buy things; sales (SALE (5b)): *a career in selling*

**selling point** /ˈ·· ·/ *n* [C] something about a product that will make people want to buy it: *The computer's two main selling points are that it's cheap and portable.*

**selling price** /ˈ·· ·/ *n* [C] the price at which something is actually sold —compare ASKING PRICE

**sell-off** /ˈ· ·/ *n* [C] *BrE* the act of selling an industry, especially one that the government owns, to private buyers: *fears that services will be cut after the sell-off*

**Sel·lo·tape** /ˈseləteɪp,-loʊ-‖-lə-,-loʊ-/ *n* [U] *BrE trademark* sticky thin clear material in a long narrow length that is used for sticking things together; SCOTCH TAPE *AmE*: *a roll of sellotape* —**sellotape** *v* [T]

**sell-out** /ˈ· ·/ *n* [singular] **1** a performance, sports game etc, for which all the tickets have been sold **2** *informal* a situation in which someone has not done what they promised to do or were expected to do by the people who trusted them: *a political sell-out*

**sel·vage, selvedge** /ˈselvɪdʒ/ *n* [C] the edge of a piece of cloth, made strong in such a way that the threads will not come out

**selves** /selvz/ the plural of SELF

**se·man·tic** /sɪˈmæntɪk/ *adj* connected with the meanings of words —**semantically** /-kli/ *adv*: *'Purchase' and 'buy' are semantically the same.* (=they mean the same thing)

**se·man·tics** /sɪˈmæntɪks/ *n* [U] **1** the study of the meaning of words and other parts of language **2 the semantics of** *technical* the meaning of a word or piece of writing

**sem·a·phore** /ˈseməfɔː‖-fɔːr/ *n* [U] a system of sending messages using two flags, that you hold in different positions to represent letters and numbers

**sem·blance** /ˈsembləns/ *n* **1 semblance of** a condition or quality that is similar to another one: *The herbs slow the heart and give the body a semblance of death.* **2** a condition or quality that is at least slightly like another one: **some semblance of** *The troops were called in to bring some semblance of order to the riot-torn city.*

**se·men** /ˈsiːmən/ *n* [U] the liquid produced by the male sex organs in humans and animals that contains SPERM

**se·mes·ter** /sɨˈmestə‖-ər/ *n* [C] one of the two periods into which a year at high schools and universities is divided, especially in the US —compare TERM[1] (9)

**sem·i** /ˈsemi/ *plural* **semis** *n* [C] **1** *BrE informal* a house that is joined to the one next to it to form a pair; DUPLEX (1) *AmE*: *a two-bedroomed semi* **2** *informal* a SEMIFINAL **3** *AmE* a very large heavy vehicle consisting of two connected parts, that carries goods over long distances; JUGGERNAUT (1) *BrE*

**semi-** /semi/ *prefix* **1** exactly half: *a semicircle* **2** partly but not completely: *in the semidarkness|a semi-invalid|semi-literate people* **3** happening, appearing etc twice in a particular period: *a semi-weekly visit|a semi-annual publication* —compare BI-

**semi-au·to·mat·ic** /ˌ·· ··ˈ··◂/ *adj* a semi-automatic weapon moves each new bullet into position ready for you to fire, so that you can fire the next shot very quickly —**semi-automatic** *n* [C]

**sem·i·breve** /ˈsemibriːv/ *n* [C] *BrE* a musical note which continues as long as two MINIMS; WHOLE NOTE *AmE* —see picture at MUSIC

**sem·i·cir·cle** /ˈsemiˌsɜːkəl‖-ɜːr-/ *n* [C] **1** half a circle —see picture at SHAPE[1] **2** a group arranged in a curved line, as if on the edge of half a circle: *Get the kids to sit in a semicircle.* —**semicircular** /ˌsemiˈsɜːkjɡlə◂‖-ˈsɜːrkjɡlər◂/ *adj*

**sem·i·co·lon** /ˌsemiˈkəʊlən‖ˈsemiˌkoʊlən/ *n* [C] a PUNCTUATION MARK (;) used to separate independent parts of a sentence or list —see picture at PUNCTUATION MARK

**sem·i·con·duc·tor** /ˌsemikənˈdʌktə‖-ər/ *n* [C] a substance, such as SILICON, that allows some electric currents to pass through it and is used in electronic equipment for this purpose —compare CONDUCTOR (3)

**sem·i·de·tached** /ˌsemidɪˈtætʃt◂/ *adj BrE* a semi-detached house is joined to another house by one shared wall —compare DETACHED (2) TERRACED HOUSE —see picture on page 410

**sem·i·fi·nal** /ˌsemiˈfaɪnl◂/ *n* [C] one of a pair of sports games, whose winners then compete against each other to decide who wins the whole competition: *The world chess championship semifinal at Linares, Spain.*

**sem·i·fi·nal·ist** /ˌsemiˈfaɪnəl-ɨst/ *n* [C] a person or team that competes in a semifinal

**sem·i·nal** /ˈsemɨnəl/ *adj* **1** *formal* a seminal book, piece of music etc is new and important, and influences the way in which literature, music etc develops in the future: *Barry Commoner's seminal 1970s book on ecology.* **2** [only before noun] *technical* producing or containing SEMEN: *seminal fluid*

**sem·i·nar** /ˈsemɨnɑː‖-nɑːr/ *n* [C] a class in which a small group of students meet to study or talk about a particular subject: *a Shakespeare seminar*

**sem·i·na·ry** /ˈsemɨnəri‖-neri/ *n* [C] **1** a college for training priests or ministers **2** *old-fashioned* a school

**sem·i·ot·ics** /ˌsemiˈɒtɪks‖-ˈɑːt-/ also **sem·i·ol·o·gy** /ˌsemiˈɒlədʒi‖-ˈɑːl-/ *n* [U] *technical* the way in which people communicate through signs and images, or the study of this —**semiotician** /ˌsemiəˈtɪʃən/, **semiologist** /ˌsemiˈɒlədʒɨst‖-ˈɑl-/ *n* [C] —**semiotic** *adj*

**sem·i·pre·cious** /ˌsemiˈpreʃəs◂/ *adj* a semiprecious jewel or stone is valuable, but not as valuable as a DIAMOND, RUBY etc

**semi-pro·fes·sion·al** /ˌ·· ·ˈ···◂/ *adj* **semi-professional player/footballer/musician etc** someone who is paid for doing a sport etc, but does not do it as their main job

**sem·i·qua·ver** /ˈsemiˌkweɪvə‖-ər/ *n* [C] *BrE* a musical note which continues for a sixteenth of the length of a SEMIBREVE; SIXTEENTH NOTE *AmE* —see picture at MUSIC

**semi-skilled** /ˌ·· ˈ·◂/ *adj* **a)** a semi-skilled worker is not highly skilled or professional, but needs some skills for the job they are doing **b)** a semi-skilled job is one that you need some skills to do, but you do not have to be highly skilled

**semi-skimmed** /ˌ·· ˈ·◂/ *n* [U] *BrE* milk that has had about half the fat removed; TWO PERCENT MILK *AmE*

**Se·mite** /ˈsiːmaɪt‖ˈsem-/ *n* [C] someone who belongs to the race of people that includes Jews, Arabs and, in ancient times, Babylonians, Assyrians etc —see also ANTI-SEMITISM

**Se·mit·ic** /sɨˈmɪtɪk/ *adj* **1 a)** belonging to the race of people that includes Jews, Arabs and, in ancient times, Babylonians, Assyrians etc **b)** belonging to or connected with any of the languages of these people **2** another word for JEWISH

**sem·i·tone** /ˈsemitəʊn‖-toʊn/ *n* [C] *BrE* the difference in PITCH[2] (3) between any two notes that are next to each other on a piano; HALF STEP *AmE*

**sem·i·trop·i·cal** /ˌsemiˈtrɒpɪkəl◂‖-ˈtrɑː-/ *adj* SUBTROPICAL

**semi-vo·wel** /ˈ·· ˌ··/ *n* [C] *technical* a sound made in speech that sounds like a vowel, but is in fact a consonant, like /w/

**sem·i·week·ly** /ˌsemiˈwiːkli◂/ *adj, adv* appearing or happening twice a week: *a semiweekly paper*

**sem·o·li·na** /ˌseməˈliːnə/ *n* [U] **1** grains of crushed wheat, used especially in making sweet dishes and PASTA **2** a sweet dish made with these grains and milk

**Sem·tex** /ˈsemteks/ *n* [U] *trademark* a powerful explosive often used illegally to make bombs

**sen·ate**, **Senate** /ˈsenɨt/ *n* **1** [singular] one of the two parts of the government that has the power to make laws, in countries such as the US, Australia, and France, which is smaller than the other part but has a higher rank: *The Senate may veto this year's spending bill.* **2** [singular] the highest level of government in ancient Rome **3** [C] the governing council at some universities

**sen·a·tor**, **Senator** /ˈsenətə‖-tər/ *n* [C] a member of a senate: *Senator Kennedy* —**senatorial** /ˌsenəˈtɔːriəl◂/ *adj*: *senatorial duties*

**send** /send/ *v past tense and past participle* **sent** /sent/ S1 W1
**1 ▶ BY POST/RADIO ETC ◀** [T] to arrange for something to go or be taken to another place, especially by post: **send sb a letter/message/card** *Honestly, I get tired of sending Christmas cards.* | **send sth to** *Send your bill to the above address.* | **send sth by post/sea/air etc** *It will get there quicker if you send it by airmail.* | **send a letter/message/card** *I sent her a message to say that I'd be late.* | **send a signal** *Radio signals were sent into deep space.* | **send sth back/up/over etc** *I've ordered some coffee to be sent up here.*
**2 ▶ SEND SB TO DO STH ◀** [T] to tell someone to go somewhere, usually so that they can do something for you there: *Who sent you?* | *Richard couldn't come so he sent his sister instead.* | **send sb to** *The United Nations will send troops to the region.* | **send sb around/over/home etc** *At noon the principal sent everyone home.* | **send sb to do sth** *I sent Jean to go get some more butter.*
**3 ▶ SEND SB TO STAY SOMEWHERE ◀** [T always + adv/prep] to arrange for someone to go somewhere and spend some time there: **send sb to** *I'd never send my kids to boarding school.* | *People get sent to jail for doing stuff like that!* | **send sb on sth** *We want to send you on a short management course.*
**4 send your love/regards/best wishes etc** to ask someone to give your greetings, good wishes etc to someone else: *Mother sends her love.*
**5 ▶ AFFECT SOMEONE ◀** [T] to affect someone's feelings or condition: **send sb to/into** *His boring speeches always send me to sleep.* | **send sb** (=make them feel extremely happy) *Oh, doesn't his music just send you?*
**6 send sb/sth flying/sprawling/reeling etc** to make someone or something move quickly through the air: *The explosion sent glass flying everywhere.*
**7 send out/up/forth etc** to make something come out of itself: *The fire was sending up thick clouds of smoke.*

S

**8 send word** to tell someone something by sending them a letter or message: **send word (to sb) that** *Somebody should send word that Rhoda's ill.* | **send word through sb** *Send word through Davies that we need more supplies.*
**9 send sb packing** also **send sb about their business** *informal* to tell someone who is not wanted that they must leave at once

**send away** *phr v* **1** [T **send** sb ↔ **away**] to send someone to another place: *I was sent away to school at the age of seven.* **2 send away for sth** to order something to be sent to you by post: *Send away for your free poster.*

**send** sth ↔ **back** *phr v* to return something to where it came from: *The steak was completely raw so I sent it straight back.*

**send down** *phr v* **1** [T **send** sth ↔ **down**] to make something lose value: *Reports of the company's bad trading figures sent its share prices down.* **2** [T **send** sb **down**] *BrE informal* to send someone to prison: *Do you think he'll be sent down for it?* **3 be sent down** *BrE* to be told to leave a university because of bad behaviour

**send for** sb/sth *phr v* [T] **1** to ask or order someone to come to you by sending them a message: *Should I send for a doctor?* | **send for help** *Quick – go send for help.* **2** to ask or order that something be brought or sent to you: *We'll have to send for the spare parts.*

**send** sth ↔ **in** *phr v* [T] **1** to send something, usually by post, to a place where it can be dealt with: *I sent in a couple of job applications last week.* **2** to send soldiers, police etc somewhere to deal with a very difficult or dangerous situation: *It's time to send in the troops.*

**send off** *phr v* **1** [T **send** sth ↔ **off**] to send something somewhere by post: *I sent off the check this morning.* **2 send off for sth** to order something to be sent to you by post: *I'd better send off for an application form.* **3** [T **send** sb ↔ **off**] to send someone to another place: *We sent the kids off to their grandparents this morning.* **4** [T **send** sb ↔ **off**] *BrE* to order a sports player to leave the field because they have broken the rules —see picture on page 1264

**send** sth ↔ **on** *phr v* [T] **1** *especially BrE* to send someone's letters or possessions to their new address from their old address; FORWARD[3] (1) *AmE*: *My flatmate said she'd send on all my post.* **2** to send something that has been received to another place so that it can be dealt with: *The data is then sent on to the Census Bureau.*

**send out** *phr v* **1** [T **send** sth/sb ↔ **out**] to send something from a central point to various other places: *Make sure you send out the invitations in good time.* | *Search parties were sent out to look for survivors.* **2** [**send** sth ↔ **out**] to broadcast or produce a signal, light, sound etc: *The ship is sending out an SOS signal.* **3 send out for sth** to ask a restaurant or food shop to deliver food to you at home or at work: *Halfway through the meeting we sent out for sandwiches.*

**send up** *phr v* [T **send** sth/sb ↔ **up**] **1** to make something increase in value: *The shortage is bound to send prices up.* **2** *BrE informal* to show how silly something is by copying it in a very funny way: *The film sends up all those Hollywood disaster movies.*

**send·er** /ˈsendə‖-ər/ *n* [C] the person who sent a particular letter, package, message etc: **Return to Sender** (=stamped on a parcel when it could not reach the person it was sent to)

**send-off** /ˈ· ·/ *n* [C] *informal* a party or other occasion when people gather together to say goodbye to someone who is leaving: **give sb a good send-off** *We gave her a really good send-off.*

**send-up** /ˈ· ·/ *n* [C] *BrE informal* the act of copying someone or something in a way that makes them look funny or silly: [+ **of**] *a brilliant send-up of Clint Eastwood*

**se·nes·cent** /sɪ̆ˈnesənt/ *adj technical* becoming old and showing the effects of getting older: *a senescent industry* —**senescence** *n* [U]

**se·nile** /ˈsiːnaɪl/ *adj not technical* mentally confused or behaving strangely, because of old age: *The poor old lady's getting senile: she hardly recognizes me now.* —**senility** /sɪˈnɪlɪ̆ti/ *n* [U]

**senile de·men·tia** /ˌ·· ·ˈ··/ *n* [U] a medical condition that can affect the minds of old people

**Se·ni·or** /ˈsiːniə‖-ər/ written abbreviation **Sr.** *AmE*, **Snr** *BrE* —*adj* [only after noun] *especially AmE* used after a man's name to show that he is the older of two men who have the same name and come from the same family: *John J. Wallace, Sr.*

**senior[1]** *adj* **1** [only before noun] older: *Senior pupils have certain privileges.* **2** having a higher position or rank: *a very senior officer* | [+ **to**] *Only one manager is senior to me now.* | **senior partner** (=the more important person in a business partnership) —compare JUNIOR[2] W2

**senior[2]** *n* [C] **1 be two/five/ten etc years sb's senior** to be two, five, ten etc years older than someone: *Her husband was nine years her senior.* —opposite JUNIOR[1] (1) **2** *AmE* a student in their last year of HIGH SCHOOL or university: *Jen will be a senior this year.* —compare FRESHMAN, JUNIOR[1] (4), SOPHOMORE **3** *CanE* a SENIOR CITIZEN

**senior cit·i·zen** /ˌ··· ˈ···/ *n* [C] an old person, especially someone who is over 60, or who is RETIRED —see OLD (USAGE)

**senior high school** /ˌ··· ˈ· ·/ also **senior high** /ˌ··· ˈ·/ *n* [C] *AmE* a school in the US for students between 14 and 18 —compare JUNIOR HIGH SCHOOL

**se·ni·or·i·ty** /ˌsiːniˈɒrɪ̆ti‖-ˈɔː-, -ˈɑː-/ *n* [U] **1** the situation of being older or higher in rank than someone else: *Her seniority finally earned her some respect.* **2** official advantage that you have because of the length of time you have worked in a company or organization: *Workers with less than 5 years' seniority may be laid off.*

**sen·na** /ˈsenə/ *n* [U] a tropical plant with a fruit that is often used to make a medicine to help your bowels (BOWEL (1)) work

**sen·sa·tion** /senˈseɪʃən/ *n* **1** [U] the ability to feel, especially through your sense of touch: *Jerry realized with alarm that he had no sensation in his legs.* **2** [C,U] a feeling that you get from one of your five senses, especially the sense of touch: *a tingling sensation in the skin* | [+ **of**] *a strange sensation of weightlessness* **3** [C] a feeling that is hard to describe, caused by a particular event, experience, or memory: **sensation (that)** *The fog gave me the strange sensation that I was alone in the world.* **4 a sensation** extreme excitement or interest, or someone or something that causes this: *News of their engagement created a great sensation.*

**sen·sa·tion·al** /senˈseɪʃənəl/ *adj* **1** very interesting and exciting: *The effect of the discovery was sensational.* | *a sensational result* **2** intended to interest, excite, or shock people, in a way that you disapprove of or find unpleasant: *sensational press coverage of the divorce* **3** *informal* very good or impressive: *You look sensational in that dress!* —**sensationally** *adv*

**sen·sa·tion·al·is·m** /senˈseɪʃənəlɪzəm/ *n* [U] a way of reporting events or stories that makes them seem as strange, exciting, or shocking as possible, and in a way that people disapprove of —**sensationalist** *adj*: *a sensationalist magazine article on teenage sex*

**sen·sa·tion·al·ize** also **-ise** *BrE* /senˈseɪʃənəlaɪz/ *v* [T] to deliberately make something seem as strange, exciting, or shocking as possible, in a way that people disapprove of: *a sensationalized account of the trial*

S1 W1

## **sense¹** /sens/ *n*

① JUDGMENT/UNDERSTANDING
② A FEELING
③ MAKE SENSE
④ SEE/SMELL/TOUCH ETC
⑤ SKILL/ABILITY
⑥ MEANING
⑦ CRAZY/SILLY
⑧ OTHER MEANINGS

### ① JUDGMENT/UNDERSTANDING

**1** [U] good understanding and judgment, especially about practical things: **have the sense to do sth** *You should have had the sense to turn off the electricity before touching the wires.* —see also COMMON SENSE

**2 there is no sense in (doing) sth** *spoken* used to say that it is not sensible to do something: *There's no sense in getting upset about it now.*

**3 talk sense** *spoken* to say things that are reasonable or sensible: **talk sense!** (=used when you are annoyed with someone for saying something silly) *Oh talk sense, Stuart, we couldn't possibly go without the car.*

**4 talk/knock some sense into sb** to try to persuade someone to stop behaving in a way that you think is silly: *He says he's dropping out of school – will you try and talk some sense into him?*

**5 see sense** to realize that you are being silly and unreasonable: *I hope Jack sees sense before it's too late.*

**6 bring sb to their senses** to make someone think or behave in a reasonable and sensible way: *I hope she fails. That'll bring her to her senses.*

**7 come to your senses** to realize that what you are doing is not sensible: *One day he'll come to his senses and see what a fool he's been.*

### ② A FEELING

**8** [C] a feeling about something: **[+ of]** *The whole affair left me with a sense of complete helplessness.* | *A new sense of urgency had entered into their negotiations.* | **have the sense that** *I don't know why, but I had the sense that he was lying.*

### ③ MAKE SENSE

**9 make sense a)** to have a clear meaning that is easy to understand: *Read this and tell me if it makes sense.* **b)** to have a good reason or explanation: *It just doesn't make sense – why would she do a thing like that?* **c)** to be a sensible thing to do: *It makes sense to save money while you can.*

**10 make sense of sth** to understand something, especially something difficult or complicated: *Can you make any sense of this article at all?*

### ④ SEE/SMELL/TOUCH ETC

**11** [C] one of the five natural powers of sight, hearing, feeling, taste, and smell, that give us information about the things around us: **sense of smell/taste/touch etc** *a poor sense of smell.* | **the five senses** (=all of the senses) | **the senses** (=several or all of the five senses) *combinations of flavors, textures, and color to delight the senses* —see also SIXTH SENSE

### ⑤ SKILL/ABILITY

**12** [singular] a natural ability to judge something: **sense of direction/rhythm/timing etc** *I'll probably get lost – I haven't got a very good sense of direction.* | **dress/clothes sense** *He has no dress sense at all.* (=does not know what clothes look good)

### ⑥ MEANING

**13** [C] the meaning of a word, phrase, sentence etc: *I'm using the word 'family' in its broadest sense.* | *In this dictionary the different senses of a word are marked by numbers.* | **in every sense of the word** (=using all possible meanings of this word) *He's a gentleman in every sense of the word.*

**14 the sense of sth** the basic meaning of something

### ⑦ CRAZY/SILLY

**15 take leave of your senses** to start to behave in an unreasonable or silly way: *You're challenging him to a fight? Have you taken leave of your senses?*

**16 be out of your senses** to behave in a way that other people think is unreasonable and possibly risky

### ⑧ OTHER MEANINGS

**17 sense of humour** *BrE*, **sense of humor** *AmE* the ability to understand or enjoy things that are funny, or to make people laugh: *I like Michelle – she's got a really good sense of humour.*

**18 in no sense** used to emphasize that something is definitely not true: *In no sense does this excuse their actions.*

**19 in a very real sense** used to emphasize the fact that something is definitely true: *In a very real sense, we can say that education is the most vital of all resources.*

**20 sense of occasion:** a feeling or understanding that an event or occasion is very serious or important

**21 in a sense/in one sense/in some senses etc** in one particular way, but without considering all the other facts or possibilities: *In some senses this may be true, but it's not really relevant.* | *In a sense, I think he likes being responsible for everything.*

**22 regain your senses** *old-fashioned* to stop feeling FAINT¹ (3) or unwell: *Out in the fresh air, she quickly regained her senses.*

**sense²** *v* [T] **1** if you sense something, you feel that it exists or is true, without being told or having proof: *The horse sensed danger and stopped.* | *I could sense her growing irritation.* | **sense (that)** *I sensed that there was someone in the room with me.* | **sense what/how/who etc** *Hugo had already sensed how unhappy she was.* **2** if a machine senses something, it discovers and records it: *an electronic device used for sensing intruders*

**sense·less** /ˈsensləs/ *adj* **1** happening or done for no good reason or with no purpose: *the senseless death of a young girl* | *senseless violence* **2** unconscious: *They beat him senseless, and left him for dead.* —**senselessly** *adv* **senselessness** *n* [U]

**sense or·gan** /ˈ· ˌ··/ *n* [C] a part of your body through which you see, smell, hear, taste, or feel something

**sen·si·bil·i·ty** /ˌsensəˈbɪləti/ *n plural* **sensibilities** **1 wound/offend sb's sensibilities** to offend someone by being rude or unpleasant etc: *It wounded her delicate sensibilities to be addressed in such a vulgar manner.* **2** [U] the ability to understand feelings, especially those expressed in literature or art: *Basil was above all a person of sensibility and perception.*

**sen·si·ble** /ˈsensəbəl/ *adj* **1** reasonable, practical, and able to judge things well: *I think that's a very sensible suggestion.* | *Surely it would be sensible to get a second opinion.* | *Come now, be sensible.* **2 sensible clothes/shoes** *especially BrE* clothes or shoes that are practical, comfortable, and strong rather than attractive or fashionable **3 sensible of sth** *old-fashioned* knowing or recognizing something: *He was sensible of the*

*trouble he had caused.* **4** *formal* noticeable: *a sensible increase in temperature* —**sensibly** *adv*: *Sensibly, Barbara had brought an umbrella.*

S3 W3 **sen·si·tive** /ˈsensɪ̣tɪv/ *adj*
**1 ▶ UNDERSTANDING PEOPLE ◀** able to understand other people's feelings and problems: *Underneath all that macho stuff, he's really a sensitive guy.* | [+ **to**] *We must be sensitive to the community's needs.* —opposite INSENSITIVE
**2 ▶ EASILY OFFENDED ◀** easily hurt, upset, or offended by things that people say: *Don't be so sensitive – I wasn't criticizing you!* | [+ **about**] *Lara's very sensitive about her figure.* | **sensitive soul** (=someone who is easily upset by small or unimportant things) —see also HYPERSENSITIVE
**3 ▶ COLD/PAIN ETC ◀** able to feel physical sensations, especially pain, more than usual: *Make sure you protect sensitive areas of your skin with a good suncream.* | **be sensitive to sth** *Ruth is very sensitive to cold.*
**4 ▶ ART/MUSIC ETC ◀** able to understand or express yourself through art, music, literature etc: *a sensitive musician* | *a very sensitive performance*
**5 ▶ SITUATIONS/SUBJECTS ◀** a situation or subject that is sensitive needs to be dealt with very carefully because it may offend people or make them angry: *Sorry I didn't realize it was such a sensitive issue.*
**6 ▶ HEAT/LIGHT ETC ◀** able to measure or react to very small changes in heat, light etc: *We need a more sensitive thermometer for this.* | **highly sensitive** (=very sensitive) *a highly sensitive electronic camera* | [+ **to**] *film that is sensitive to ultraviolet light.* | **light-sensitive/heat-sensitive etc** *light-sensitive photographic paper* —**sensitively** *adv* —**sensitivity** /ˌsensɪ̣ˈtɪvɪ̣ti/ also **sensitiveness** /ˈsensɪ̣tɪvnɪ̣s/ *n* [U]

**sen·si·tiv·i·ties** /ˌsensɪ̣ˈtɪvɪ̣tiz/ *n* [plural] someone's feelings and the fact that they could be upset or offended: *The sensitivities of the black community were largely ignored.*

**sen·si·tize** also **-ise** *BrE* /ˈsensɪ̣taɪz/ *v* **1** [T usually passive] to give someone some experience of a particular problem or situation so that they can notice it and understand it easily: **sensitize sb to sth** *Her upbringing had sensitized her to discrimination.* **2** [T] *technical* to treat a material or a piece of equipment so that it will react to physical or chemical changes: *sensitized photographic paper* —**sensitization** /ˌsensɪ̣taɪˈzeɪʃən‖-tə-/ *n* [U]

**sen·sor** /ˈsensə‖-ər/ *n* [C] *technical* a piece of equipment used for discovering the presence of light, heat, sound etc, especially in small amounts

**sen·so·ry** /ˈsensəri/ *adj* connected with or using your senses of sight, hearing, smell, taste or touch: *sensory stimuli* | *sensory deprivation* —see also ESP (1)

**sen·su·al** /ˈsenʃuəl/ *adj* **1** connected with the feelings of your body rather than your mind: *purely sensual pleasures* **2** interested in or making you think of physical pleasure, especially sexual pleasure: *sensual lips* | *a sensual woman* —**sensuality** /ˌsenʃuˈælɪ̣ti/ *n* [U] **sensually** *adv*

**sen·su·al·ist** /ˈsenʃuəlɪ̣st/ *n* [C] someone who is only interested in physical pleasure

**sen·su·ous** /ˈsenʃuəs/ *adj* **1** pleasing to your senses: *the sensuous feeling of silk on her skin* **2** full of powerful images or sounds that suggest physical pleasure: *sensuous music* —**sensuously** *adv* —**sensuousness** *n* [U]

**sent** /sent/ the past tense and past participle of SEND

S1 W2 **sen·tence[1]** /ˈsentəns/ *n* [C] **1** a group of words that usually contains a subject and a verb, expresses a complete idea or asks a question, and that, when written in English, begins with a capital letter and ends with a FULL STOP[1] (1) **2** a punishment that a judge gives to someone who has been declared guilty of a crime: *a six year prison sentence* | **heavy/light sentence** (=long or short time in prison) | **life sentence** (=very long time in prison) *a life sentence for murder* | **death sentence** (=punishment by death) | **serve a sentence** (=spend time in prison as a punishment) **3 pass/pronounce sentence** to officially state what a punishment will be

**sentence[2]** *v* [T often passive] if a judge sentences someone found guilty of a crime, they officially and legally give them a punishment: [+ **to**] *Sanchez was sentenced to three years in prison for his part in the crime.*

**sentence ad·verb** /ˈ·· ˌ··/ *n* [C] an adverb that expresses an opinion about the whole sentence that contains it

**sen·ten·tious** /senˈtenʃəs/ *adj formal* saying clever things about morality or the way people should behave: *sententious remarks* —**sententiously** *adv*

**sen·tient** /ˈsenʃənt/ *adj formal or technical* having feelings and knowing that you exist: *Man is a sentient being.*

**sen·ti·ment** /ˈsentɪ̣mənt/ *n* **1** [C,U] *formal* an opinion or feeling you have about something: *It is my sentiment that we should vote against the motion.* | **popular sentiment** (=what most people think) | **my/your sentiments** *I share your sentiments entirely.* **2** [U] feelings of pity, love, sadness etc that are often considered to be too strong or not suitable for a particular situation: *There's no place for sentiment in business!*

**sen·ti·ment·al** /ˌsentɪ̣ˈmentl◂/ *adj* **1** someone who is sentimental is too easily affected by emotions such as love, sympathy, sadness etc: *There's nothing wrong with being a little sentimental!* **2** based on or connected with your feelings rather than on practical reasons: **for sentimental reasons/purposes** *I only keep these old photos for sentimental reasons.* **3 sentimental value** if something has sentimental value, it is not worth much money, but it is important to you because it reminds you of someone you love or a happy time in the past: *The stolen rings were of great sentimental value to the owner.* **4** a story, film, book etc that is sentimental deals with emotions such as love and sadness in a way that seems silly and insincere: *I enjoyed the movie but the ending was too sentimental.* —**sentimentally** *adv*

**sen·ti·men·tal·ist** /ˌsentɪ̣ˈmentl-ɪ̣st/ *n* [C] someone who behaves or writes in a sentimental way —**sentimentalism** *n* [U]

**sen·ti·men·tal·i·ty** /ˌsentɪ̣menˈtælɪ̣ti/ *n* [U] the quality of being sentimental

**sen·ti·ment·al·ize** also **-ise** *BrE* /ˌsentɪ̣ˈmentl-aɪz/ *v* [I,T] to speak, write or think about something in a way that mentions only the good or happy things about something, but not the bad things: *a sentimentalized account of life during the war* | [+ **about/over**] *Listen to Albert sentimentalizing about his childhood again.*

**sen·ti·nel** /ˈsentɪnəl/ *n* [C] *old-fashioned* a sentry

**sen·try** /ˈsentri/ *n* [C] a soldier standing outside a building as a guard

**sentry box** /ˈ·· ·/ *n* [C] a tall narrow shelter with an open front where a soldier can stand while guarding a building

**se·pal** /ˈsepəl/ *n* [C] *technical* one of the small leaves directly under a flower

**sep·a·ra·ble** /ˈsepərəbəl/ *adj* two things that are separable can be separated or considered separately: *Supply and demand are not easily separable.* —opposite INSEPARABLE —**separably** *adv* —**separability** /ˌsepərəˈbɪlɪ̣ti/ *n* [U]

**sep·a·rate[1]** /ˈsepərɪ̣t/ *adj* **1** things, places, buildings etc that are separate are not joined to each other or touching each other: *separate bedrooms* | *The poor travelled in a separate carriage.* | [+ **from**] *Keep the fish separate from the other food.* **2** ideas, information, activities etc that are separate are not connected or do not affect each other in any way: *two separate problems* | [+ **from**] *He tries to keep his professional life completely separate from his private life.* **3** different: *This word has 3 separate meanings.* | *She's been warned on three separate occasions that her work is not good enough.* **4 go your separate ways a)** to finish a relationship with someone, especially a romantic relationship **b)** to start travelling in a different direction from someone you have been travelling with —**separately** *adv*: *They did arrive together, but I think they left separately.* S2

S2 W2 **sep·a·rate²** /ˈsepəreɪt/ *v*
**1 ▶ BE BETWEEN ◀** [T often passive] if something separates two places or two things, it is between them so that they are not touching each other or connected with each other: *The two towns are separated by a river.* | *Seventeen years had separated them.*
**2 ▶ DIVIDE ◀** [I,T] to divide or split into different parts, or layers, or to make something do this: *Here's a trick to keep your salad dressing from separating.* | [+ **from**] *At this point the satellite separates from its launcher.* | **separate sth into** *It would help if we separated this stuff into three different piles.* | **separate eggs** (=divide the white part from the yellow part)
**3 ▶ STOP LIVING TOGETHER ◀** [I] to start to live apart from your husband, wife or sexual partner: *It's the children who suffer when their parents separate.*
**4 ▶ RECOGNIZE DIFFERENCE ◀** [T] to recognize that one idea is different from another, and to deal with each idea alone: [+ **from**] *It's not always easy to separate cause from effect.*
**5 ▶ MOVE APART ◀** [I T] to move apart, or make people move apart: [+ **from**] *We had to separate Philip and Jason because they were talking all the time.*
**6 ▶ MAKE SB/STH DIFFERENT ◀** [T + **from**] to be the thing that makes someone or something different from other similar people or things: *What is it that you think separates her from the other applicants?*
**7 separate the men from the boys** *informal* to do something that makes it clear which people are brave or strong and which are not: *The climb through the mountains will definitely separate the men from the boys.*
**8 separate the sheep from the goats** also **separate the wheat from the chaff** to separate the good things from the bad things
**separate** sth ↔ **out** *phr v* [I,T] if part of something separates out or is separated out, it becomes separate from the other parts

**sep·a·rat·ed** /ˈsepəreɪtɪd/ *adj* not living with your husband, wife or sexual partner any more: *David and I have been separated for six months but we're not divorced yet.*

**sep·a·rates** /ˈsepərɪts/ *n* [plural] women's clothing, such as skirts, shirts, and trousers, that can be worn in different combinations

**sep·a·ra·tion** /ˌsepəˈreɪʃən/ *n* **1** [C,U] a period of time that two or more people spend apart from each other: *Their separation lasted over 20 years.* **2** [C] a situation in which a husband and wife agree to live apart even though they are still married —compare DIVORCE¹ (1) **3** [U] the act of separating or the state of being separate

**sep·a·ra·tist** /ˈsepərətɪst/ *n* [C] a member of a group in a country that wants to establish a new separate country with its own government —**separatism** *n* [U]

**sep·a·ra·tor** /ˈsepəreɪtə‖-ər/ *n* [C] a machine for separating liquids from solids, or cream from milk

**se·pi·a** /ˈsiːpiə/ *n* [U] **1** a dark reddish brown colour **2 sepia photograph/print** a photograph, picture etc, especially an old one, that is this colour **3** an ink used for drawing which has this colour

**sep·sis** /ˈsepsɪs/ *n* [U] *technical* an infection in part of the body, in which PUS is produced

**Sep·tem·ber** /sepˈtembə‖-ər/ written abbreviation **Sept** *n* [C,U] the ninth month of the year, between August and October: **in September (1998/2000 etc)** *The project is due to finish in September.* | **last/next September** *We haven't seen each other since last September.* | **on September 6th** (also **on 6th September** *BrE*): *The meeting will be on September 6th.* (spoken as: *on the sixth of September* or *on September the sixth* or *(AmE) on September sixth*)

**sep·tet** /sepˈtet/ *n* [C] **1** a group of seven singers or musicians who perform together **2** a piece of music written for seven performers

**sep·tic** /ˈseptɪk/ *adj especially BrE* a wound or part of your body that is septic is infected with BACTERIA: *a septic finger*

**sep·ti·cae·mi·a** *BrE*, **septicemia** *AmE* /ˌseptɪˈsiːmiə/ *n* [U] *technical* a serious condition in which infection spreads from a small area of your body through your blood; BLOOD POISONING

**septic tank** /ˈ‥ ˌ·/ *n* [C] a large container kept under ground used for putting human body waste into

**sep·tu·a·ge·nar·i·an** /ˌseptʃuədʒɪˈneəriən‖-ˈner-/ *n* [C] someone who is between 70 and 79 years old

**se·pul·chral** /sɪˈpʌlkrəl/ *adj* **1** *literary* sad, serious and slightly frightening: *a sepulchral voice* **2** *technical* related to burying dead people

**sep·ul·chre** *BrE*, **sepulcher** *AmE* /ˈsepəlkə‖-kər/ *n* [C] *old use* a small room or building in which the bodies of dead people were put

**se·quel** /ˈsiːkwəl/ *n* **1** [C] a book, film, play etc that continues the story of an earlier one, usually written or made by the same person **2** [C usually singular] an event that happens as a result of something that happened before

**se·quence** /ˈsiːkwəns/ *n* **1** [C,U] a series of related events, actions etc which have a fixed order and usually lead to a particular result: **sequence of events** *the sequence of events leading up to the war* **2** [C,U] the order that events or actions happen in, or are supposed to happen in: **in/out of sequence** (=in or out of order) *Please check that the page numbers are in sequence.* **3** [C] one part of a story, film etc that deals with a single subject or action: *the dream sequence at the beginning of Ryder's film* W2

**se·quenc·ing** /ˈsiːkwənsɪŋ/ *n* [U] *formal* the arrangement of things into an order, especially events or actions

**se·quen·tial** /sɪˈkwenʃəl/ *adj formal* connected with or happening in a sequence —**sequentially** *adv*

**se·ques·ter** /sɪˈkwestə‖-ər/ *v* [T] **1** to force a group of people, such as a JURY, to stay away from other people **2** to sequestrate

**se·ques·tered** /sɪˈkwestəd‖-ərd/ *adj literary* a sequestered place is quiet and far away from people

**se·ques·trate** /sɪˈkwestreɪt, ˈsiːkwɪ-/ *v* [T usually passive] to take property away from the person it belongs to because they have not paid their debts —**sequestration** /ˌsiːkwɪˈstreɪʃən/ *n* [C,U]

**se·quin** /ˈsiːkwɪn/ *n* [C] a small shiny round flat piece of metal that you SEW onto clothing for decoration —**sequined, sequinned** *adj*

**se·quoi·a** /sɪˈkwɔɪə/ *n* [C] a tree from the western US that can grow to be 100 metres in height

**se·ra·glio** /sɪˈrɑːljəʊ‖-joʊ/ *n* [C] a HAREM

**ser·aph** /ˈserəf/ *plural* **seraphs** also **seraphim** /-rəfɪm/ *n* [C] one of the ANGELS that protects the seat of God, according to the Bible

**se·raph·ic** /sɪˈræfɪk/ *adj literary* extremely beautiful or pure, like an ANGEL

**sere** /sɪə‖sɪr/ *adj literary* very dry

**ser·e·nade¹** /ˌserɪˈneɪd/ *n* [C] **1** a song that a man performs for the woman he loves, especially standing below her window at night **2** a piece of gentle music

**serenade²** *v* [T] if you serenade someone, you sing or play music to them to show them that you love them

**ser·en·dip·i·ty** /ˌserənˈdɪpɪti/ *n* [U] *literary* the natural ability to make interesting or valuable discoveries by accident

**se·rene** /sɪˈriːn/ *adj* **1** someone who is serene is very calm and relaxed: *Mother sat in the evening sunlight, serene and beautiful.* **2** a place or situation that is serene is very peaceful: *a serene summer night* —**serenely** *adv* —**serenity** /sɪˈrenɪti/ *n* [U]

**serf** /sɜːf‖sɜːrf/ *n* [C] someone in former times who lived and worked on land that they did not own and who had to obey the owner of this land —compare SLAVE¹ (1)

**serf·dom** /ˈsɜːfdəm‖ˈsɜːrf-/ *n* [U] the state of being a serf

**serge** /sɜːdʒ‖sɜːrdʒ/ *n* [U] strong, usually WOOLLEN cloth

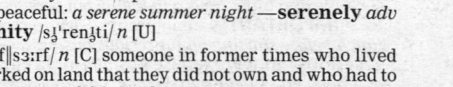

**ser·geant** /ˈsɑːdʒənt‖ˈsɑːr-/ *n* [C] a low rank in the army, air force, police etc, or someone who has this rank —see table on page B4

**sergeant-at-arms** /ˌ·· · ˈ·/ *n* [C] a SERJEANT-AT-ARMS

**sergeant ma·jor** /ˌ·· ˈ··◂/ *n* [C] a military rank —see table on page B4

**se·ri·al**[1] /ˈsɪəriəl‖ˈsɪr-/ *n* [C] a story that is broadcast or printed in several separate parts on television, in a newspaper etc: *a six-part serial*

**serial**[2] *adj* [only before noun] **1** arranged or happening one after the other in the correct order: *placed in serial order|serial processing on a computer* **2 serial killings/murders** killings or murders that are done in the same way one after the other —**serially** *adv*

**se·ri·al·ize** also **-ise** *BrE* /ˈsɪəriəlaɪz‖ˈsɪr-/ *v* [T often passive] to print or broadcast a story in several separate parts: *His book was first serialized in The New Yorker.* —**serialization** /ˌsɪəriəlaɪˈzeɪʃən‖ˌsɪriələ-/ *n* [U]

**serial ki·ller** /ˈ··· ˌ··/ *n* [C] someone who has killed several people, one after the other and in the same way

**serial num·ber** /ˈ··· ˌ··/ *n* [C] a number put on things that are produced in large quantities so that each one is slightly different: *serial numbers on dollar bills*

S2 W1 **se·ries** /ˈsɪəriːz‖ˈsɪr-/ *n plural* **series** [C] **1** [singular] several events or actions of the same kind that happen one after the other but that are not connected: [+ **of**] *There's been a whole series of accidents on this stretch of road recently* **2** a group of events that are connected and have a particular result: *a strange series of events that led to his death* **3** a set of television or radio programmes in which each one tells the next part of a story or deals with the same kind of subject: *a new comedy series* **4** a group of events or actions of the same kind that are planned to happen one after another in order to achieve something: *It'll have to undergo a series of tests.|a series of lectures on the subject of biotechnology* **5 in series** *technical* being connected so that electricity passes though the parts of something electrical in the correct order

**ser·if** /ˈserɪf/ *n* [C] a short flat line at the top or bottom of some printed letters —see also SANS SERIF

S1 W1 **se·ri·ous** /ˈsɪəriəs‖ˈsɪr-/ *adj*

**1** ▶ **SITUATION/PROBLEM** ◀ a serious situation, problem, accident etc is extremely bad or dangerous: *a serious illness|How serious do you think the situation is?*| **serious crime** *The number of serious crimes has increased dramatically in the last year.*

**2 be serious a)** if someone is serious about something, they say what they really mean and are not joking or pretending: [+ **about**] *I stopped laughing when I realized Jen was serious about it.*|**I'm serious!** *spoken* (=used to emphasize that something is important) *I'm serious, Kerry. You'd better listen!*|**deadly serious** (=extremely serious) **b)** *spoken* used to tell someone that what they have just said is silly or impossible: *"We could make it from here to Florida if we drove all night." "Be serious! It's a three day drive."*|**you can't be serious!** *"I thought I'd try to fix the car myself." "You can't be serious!"*

**3** ▶ **CAREFUL** ◀ careful and thorough: *I think this matter needs serious consideration.|a serious article*

**4** ▶ **ROMANTIC RELATIONSHIP** ◀ a serious romantic relationship is intended to continue for a long time: *Oo, sounds like it's serious!*|[+ **about**] *Are you really serious about her then?*|**serious boyfriend/girlfriend** *Don't even think about Peter. He has a serious girlfriend.*

**5** ▶ **PERSON** ◀ someone who is serious is always very sensible and quiet: *He's a nice guy, but very serious.*

**6** ▶ **IMPORTANT** ◀ important: *They agreed to have lunch before starting on the serious business.*

**7 serious money/exercise etc** *informal* a large amount of money etc: *I'll have to do some serious exercise before I can fit into that dress.*

**8** ▶ **VERY GOOD** ◀ [only before noun] *informal* very good and often expensive: *He's got some serious stereo equipment!*

**9** ▶ **SPORT/ACTIVITY** ◀ [only before noun] someone very interested in something, and spending a lot of time doing it: *a serious golfer|Any serious student of psychology should read this article.*

**10** ▶ **WORRIED/UNHAPPY** ◀ seeming slightly worried or unhappy: *You look serious. What's wrong?* —**seriousness** *n* [U]

**se·ri·ous·ly** /ˈsɪəriəsli‖ˈsɪr-/ *adv* S2 W2 **1** in a serious way: *I think it's about time we talked seriously about our relationship.|Is she seriously ill?|I'm seriously concerned about Ben.* **2 take sb/sth seriously** to believe that someone or something is worth paying attention to or should be respected: *No-one's likely to take Laurie seriously.|Don't joke with Linda, she takes everything far too seriously.*|**never take anything seriously** *It's infuriating that he never takes anything seriously.* **3 seriously?** *spoken* used to ask someone if they really mean what they have just said: *Quit your job? Seriously?* **4 seriously** *spoken* [sentence adverb] used to show that what you say next is not a joke: *Seriously though, I really think Toby likes you!*

**ser·jeant-at-arms, sergeant-at-arms** /ˌsɑːdʒənt ət ˈɑːmz‖ˌsɑːrdʒənt ət ˈɑːrmz/ *n* [C] an officer of a British law court or parliament whose job is to keep meetings quiet enough to be useful

**ser·mon** /ˈsɜːmən‖ˈsɜːr-/ *n* [C] **1** a religious talk given as part of a Christian church service, usually based on a part of the Bible: **preach a sermon** *Pastor Grisson preached a sermon on evangelism.* **2** *informal* a talk in which someone tries to give you unwanted moral advice; LECTURE[1] (2)

**ser·mon·ize** also **-ise** *BrE* /ˈsɜːmənaɪz‖ˈsɜːr-/ *v* [I] to give a lot of unwanted moral advice in a serious way

**ser·pent** /ˈsɜːpənt‖ˈsɜːr-/ *n* [C] **1** *literary* a snake, especially a large one **2 the Serpent** the evil snake in the Garden of Eden according to the Bible

**ser·pen·tine** /ˈsɜːpəntaɪn‖ˈsɜːrpəntiːn/ *adj* twisting or winding like a snake: *the serpentine course of the river*

**ser·rat·ed** /sɪˈreɪtɪd, se-/ *adj* **serrated knife/edge** with a sharp edge made of a row of connected V shapes like teeth —**serration** /-ˈreɪʃən/ *n* [C,U]

**ser·ried** /ˈserid/ *adj* [no comparative] *literary* pressed closely together; CROWDED

**se·rum** /ˈsɪərəm‖ˈsɪr-/ *n* [C,U] **1** a liquid containing substances that fight infection, that is put into a sick person's blood —compare VACCINE **2** *technical* the watery part of blood or the liquid from a plant —**serous** *adj*

**ser·vant** /ˈsɜːvənt‖ˈsɜːr-/ *n* [C] 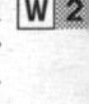 **1** someone who is paid to clean someone's house, cook for them, answer the door etc **2 servant of sth/sb** someone who is controlled by someone or something: *Are we the masters or the servants of computers?* —see also CIVIL SERVANT

**serve**[1] /sɜːv‖sɜːrv/ *v* S1 W1

**1** ▶ **FOOD/DRINK** ◀ [I,T] to give someone food or drink as part of a meal: *What kind of wine should we serve?*|**serve sth with sth** *Serve the dish with rice and a green salad.*|**serve sb** *Why aren't you out there serving the guests?*|**serve sth hot/cold etc** *delicious served hot or cold*|**serve breakfast/lunch/dinner** *Breakfast is served between 7 and 9 a.m.*|**serving spoon/dish** (=one used to serve food) —see picture on page 838

**2 serve two/three/four etc** if food serves two, three etc people, there is enough for that number of people: *One large fish should serve two to three people.*

**3** ▶ **BE USEFUL/HELPFUL** ◀ [I,T] to be useful or helpful for a particular purpose or reason: **serve as sth** *The old couch had to serve as a guest bed.*|**serve sb well** *Her talent for selling will serve her well in the future.*|**serve sb's needs** *We don't get enough aid to serve our needs.*|**serve a purpose** *If you haven't got a crate, a large cardboard box will serve the purpose.|Sure, you could phone her, but what purpose would that serve?*

**4** ▶ **DO A HELPFUL JOB** ◀ [I,T] to spend a period of time doing a job, especially one that helps the organization: *The school board members serve a two-year term.*|[+

**in]** *He returned to Greece to serve in the army.* | **[+ on]** *Annette serves on various local committees.* | **[+ as]** *Martin served as ambassador to Burma in the '60s.* | **serve sb/sth** *And let's not forget the women who served their country in the war.*
**5 ▶ HAVE AN EFFECT ◀** [I,T] to have a particular effect or result: **serve to do sth** *Let that serve to demonstrate what happens if you don't pay attention.* | **serve (sb) as sth** *The pictures only served as a reminder of happier times.*
**6 ▶ SHOP/RESTAURANT ◀** [I,T] to help the customers in a shop, restaurant etc, especially by bringing them the things that they want: *The waitress doesn't seem to want to serve us.* | *Are you being served?*
**7 ▶ PROVIDE STH ◀** [T] to provide a group of people with something that is necessary or useful: *water mains to serve the new homes in the area*
**8 ▶ PRISON ◀** [T] to spend a particular period of time in prison: **serve a sentence** *Fox had served an eighteen-month sentence for burglary.* | **serve time** (=spend time in prison)
**9 it serves sb right** *spoken* used to say that you think someone deserves it if something unpleasant happens to them, because they have been stupid or unkind: *"Ouch! She pinched me!" "Serves you right, teasing her like that."*
**10 ▶ SPORT ◀** [I,T] to start playing in a game such as tennis or VOLLEYBALL by throwing the ball up in the air and hitting it to your opponent —see picture on page 1264
**11 serve an apprenticeship** to learn a job or skill by working for a fixed period of time for someone who has a lot of experience
**12 serve a summons/writ etc** to officially send or give someone a written order to appear in a court of law
**13 ▶ CHURCH ◀** [I] to help a priest during the EUCHARIST —see also **if my memory serves me (right/well/correctly)** (MEMORY (4))

**serve** sth ↔ **out** *phr v* [T] **1** to continue doing something until the end of a fixed period of time: *Dillon's served out nearly all his sentence.* **2** *BrE* to put food onto plates: *Serve out the rice, will you?*

**serve** sth ↔ **up** *phr v* [T] to put food onto plates so that people can eat it

**serve²** *n* [C] the action in a game such as tennis or VOLLEYBALL in which you throw the ball in the air and hit it to your opponent

**serv·er** /ˈsɜːvə‖ˈsɜːrvər/ *n* [C] **1** a special spoon or tool for putting a particular kind of food onto a plate: *salad servers* **2** a player who hits a ball to begin a game in tennis, VOLLEYBALL etc **3 a)** the main computer on a NETWORK¹ (4), that controls all the others **b)** one of the computers on a network that provides a special service: **file/print/mail server** *All important data is stored on a central file server.* **4** someone who helps a priest during the EUCHARIST

**ser·ve·ry** /ˈsɜːvəri‖ˈsɜːr-/ *n* [C] *BrE* the part of a restaurant where people get food to take back to their tables

## ser·vice¹ /ˈsɜːvɪ̵s‖ˈsɜːr-/ *n*

① FOR THE PUBLIC
② HELP
③ WORK DONE FOR SB
④ ARMY/NAVY ETC
⑤ OTHER MEANINGS

### ① FOR THE PUBLIC

**1 public services** [C often plural] things such as education, hospitals, banks etc that are provided for the public to use: *the decline in public services in recent times* | **the welfare/medical/social etc service** (=services provided especially by the government) | **police/fire/ambulance etc service** *He joined the police service at the age of 18.*
**2 jury/military/community etc service** something that ordinary people can be asked to do for the public as a public duty or as a punishment: *You're lucky you were only sentenced to community service.*

### ② HELP

**3** [singular, U] help that you give to someone: **be of service** (=help someone) *Don't thank me – I'm glad to be of service.* | **do sb a service** (=do something to help someone) *Oh, thanks, it'll be doing me a service.* | **provide a service** (=provide help for someone) | **for services rendered** *formal* (=for help that you have given)
**4 ▶ SHOP/HOTEL ETC ◀** [U] the help that people who work in a shop, restaurant, bar etc give you: *What was the service in that new restaurant like?* | **customer service** *For refunds, please go to the customer service counter.*
**5 ▶ ORGANIZATION ◀** [C] an organization that provides advice and help, for example with legal or personal problems: *a careers information service*
**6 be at your service** *formal or humorous* if someone or something is at your service, they are available to help you in some way if you need them: *My secretary and library are at your service.*
**7 press sb/sth into service** to persuade someone to help you, or use something to help you do something: *We pressed Georgie's old bike into service.*

### ③ WORK DONE FOR SB

**8 ▶ EMPLOYMENT ◀** [plural, U] the work you do for a person or organization: **20/30 years etc of service** *Brian's retiring after 25 years of loyal service to the company.* | **services to sb** (=work, especially successful work, you have done for someone) *an award for services to the printing industry* | **public service** (=work done for the public or the government)
**9 ▶ SERVANT ◀** [U] the job of working as a servant in someone's house, especially in former times: **be in service** (=be working as a servant in someone's house) | **domestic service** (=the job of working for someone in their house)
**10 ▶ BUSINESS ◀** [C] a business that provides help or does jobs for people rather than producing things: *the export of both manufactured goods and services* | **a babysitting/press-cutting/ironing etc service** *She's set up a dog-walking service in her local area.* —see also SERVICE INDUSTRY
**11 ▶ GOVERNMENT ◀** [C usually singular] an organization that works directly for a government: *the diplomatic service* | *the foreign service*

### ④ ARMY/NAVY ETC

**12 the services** a country's military forces, especially considered as a job: *I'm not sure what I'll do, maybe join the services.*
**13 (be on) active service** to be actually fighting in a battle or war while you are in the army, navy etc

### ⑤ OTHER MEANINGS

**14 ▶ RELIGION ◀** [C] a formal religious ceremony, for example in church: **hold/conduct a service** (=be the person in charge of a service) *The Reverend James Wilkins will conduct the service.* | **marriage/**

[continued on next page]

[continued from previous page]
**funeral/christening etc service** *a memorial service for the disaster victims*
**15 ▶ SPORT ◀** [C] an act of hitting a ball through the air in order to start a game, for example in tennis: *It's your service.*
**16 services** *BrE* a place near a MOTORWAY where you can stop and have a meal or drink, or buy food, petrol etc: *How far is it to the next services?* —see also SERVICE STATION
**17 ▶ CAR/MACHINE ◀** [C] an examination and repair of a machine or car to keep it working properly: *I'm getting the bus home – my car's in for a service.*
**18 ▶ PLATES ETC ◀ dinner/tea service** a set of matching plates, bowls, cups etc
**19 ▶ BUS/TRAIN ◀** [C usually singular] a regular journey made by a bus, train, boat etc to a particular place or at a particular time: *the 8:15 service to Cambridge* —see also LIP SERVICE

**service²** *v* [T] **1** to examine a machine or vehicle and fix it if necessary: *I'm having the car serviced next week.* **2** to provide people with something they need or want: *city departments that service the local communities* **3** *technical* to pay the INTEREST¹ (4) on a debt

**service³** *adj* **service stairs/elevator etc** stairs etc that are only for the use of people working in a place, rather than the public

**ser·vice·a·ble** /ˈsɜːvɪ̣səbəl‖ˈsɜːr-/ *adj* ready or suitable to be used for a particular purpose: *serviceable shoes* —**serviceability** /ˌsɜːvɪ̣səˈbɪlɪ̣ti‖ˌsɜːr-/ *n* [U]

**service a·re·a** /ˈ·· ˌ···/ *n* [C] *BrE* a place where you can stop on a MOTORWAY that has petrol, food, toilets etc

**service charge** /ˈ·· ˌ·/ *n* [C] **1** *BrE* an amount of money that is added to a bill in a restaurant and given to the waiters **2** an amount of money paid to the owner of a block of FLATS for services such as cleaning the stairs

**service club** /ˈ·· ˌ·/ *n* [C] *AmE* a usually national organization made of smaller local groups in which members do things to help their COMMUNITY

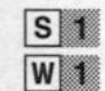

**service in·dus·try** /ˈ·· ˌ···/ *n* [C,U] an industry that provides a service such as insurance, bank accounts, or advertising rather than a product

**ser·vice·man** /ˈsɜːvɪ̣smən‖ˈsɜːr-/ *n plural* **servicemen** /-mən/ [C] a man who is a member of the military

**service sta·tion** /ˈ·· ˌ··/ *n* [C] a place that sells petrol, food, etc

**ser·vice·wom·an** /ˈsɜːvɪ̣sˌwʊmən‖ˈsɜːr-/ *n plural* **servicewomen** /-ˌwɪmɪn/ [C] a woman who is a member of the military

**ser·vi·ette** /ˌsɜːviˈet‖ˌsɜːr-/ *n* [C] *BrE & CanE* a NAPKIN —see picture on page 838

**ser·vile** /ˈsɜːvaɪl‖ˈsɜːrvəl, -vaɪl/ *adj* **1** too eager to obey someone without questioning them: *a servile attitude* **2** connected with SLAVES or with being a slave —**servilely** *adv* —**servility** /sɜːˈvɪlɪ̣ti‖sɜːr-/ *n* [U]

**serv·ing** /ˈsɜːvɪŋ‖ˈsɜːr-/ *n* [C] an amount of food that is enough for one person; HELPING: *How many servings does the recipe make?*

**ser·vi·tor** /ˈsɜːvɪ̣tə‖ˈsɜːrvɪ̣tər/ *n* [C] *old use* a male servant

**ser·vi·tude** /ˈsɜːvɪ̣tjuːd‖ˈsɜːrvɪ̣tuːd/ *n* [U] the condition of being a SLAVE or being forced to obey someone else: *The legislation of 1781 abolished penal servitude in Bohemia.* —see also PENAL SERVITUDE

**ses·a·me** /ˈsesəmi/ *n* [U] a tropical plant grown for its seeds and oil and used in cooking —see also OPEN SESAME

**ses·sion** /ˈseʃən/ *n* [C] **1** a meeting or period of time used for a particular purpose, especially by a group of people: *a drinking session* | *question-and-answer sessions* | *a jazz session* **2** a formal meeting or group of meetings of an organisation, especially a court or parliament: **in session** *the noise of Parliament in session* **3 sessions a)** PETTY SESSIONS **b)** QUARTER SESSIONS S3 W2

S1 W1

## set¹ /set/ *v past tense and past participle* **set**

① PUT DOWN
② START STH HAPPENING
③ DECIDE/ESTABLISH
④ JOB/STH TO DO
⑤ MAKE READY
⑥ MUSIC/BOOKS
⑦ WANT/NOT WANT
⑧ OTHER MEANINGS

### ① PUT DOWN

**1 ▶ PUT ◀** [T always + adv/prep] to carefully put something down somewhere, especially something that is difficult to carry: **set sth down/on etc** *She set the tray down on a table next to his bed.*

### ② START STH HAPPENING

**2 set sth on fire/alight/ablaze** to make something start burning: *Crowds of youths started overturning cars and setting them on fire.*
**3 set the pattern/tone/trend** to happen or do something in a particular way that is then repeated many times or which continues for a long time: *Gabriel's style set the trend for the scores of rock videos that followed.*
**4 set in motion/progress/train** to make something start happening, especially by means of an official order: *The govenment is to set in motion a wide-ranging review of defence spending.*

### ③ DECIDE/ESTABLISH

**5 set a time/date/price etc** to decide that something should happen at a particular time, cost a particular amount of money etc: *Have you set a date for the wedding?*
**6 set guidelines/standards/conditions/limits etc** to officially establish rules, standards etc for doing something: *standards of hygiene set by the Health Department*
**7 set a precedent** if an event or action sets a precedent, it shows people a way of doing something which they can use or copy: *If her claim against her employers is successful, it could set a legal precedent.*

### ④ JOB/STH TO DO

**8 set sb a task/challenge/goal etc** to decide that someone should try and achieve something, especially something that needs a lot of effort: *Wilkins then set himself the task of tagging all the birds on the island.* | **set yourself to do sth** *She had set herself to write a novel.*
**9 ▶ GIVE SB A PIECE OF WORK ◀** [T] *BrE* to give someone a piece of work to do, especially a student in your class or someone who works for you: **set sb sth** *Mr. Phipps set us an essay on the origins of the French Revolution.*
**10 ▶ EXAMINATION ◀** [T] *BrE* to invent questions

for students to answer, especially in an examination: *Whoever set the questions obviously didn't know much about physics.*

**11 set to work** to start doing something in a determined way, especially something that is difficult and needs a lot of effort: **set to work to do sth** *They set to work to paint the outside of the building.* | [+ **on**] *Davies is about to set to work on a second book.*

**12 set sb to work** to make someone start doing a particular kind of work for you: **set sb to work doing sth** *Before dawn Harry had set them to work collecting firewood for breakfast.*

**13 set sb/sth doing sth** to make someone start doing something or make something start happening: *Her last remark had set me thinking.* | *The wind set the trees rustling.*

## ⑤ MAKE READY

**14 ▶ MOVE PART OF A MACHINE/CLOCK ETC ◀** [T] to move part of a machine, clock etc so that it is in a particular position and is ready to be used: *Have you set the alarm?* | **set sth to/at** *Just set the dial to 'hot wash' and press the 'on' button.*

**15 set the table** to arrange plates, knives, cups etc on a table so that it is ready for a meal

**16 set a trap a)** to make a trap ready to catch an animal **b)** to invent a plan to show that someone is doing something wrong: *The FBI set a trap for the Congressmen it believed were taking bribes.*

## ⑥ MUSIC/BOOKS

**17 ▶ FILM/PLAY/STORY ◀** [T usually passive] if a film, play, story etc is set in a place or period, it happens there or at that time: *The novel is set in France in the early 19th century.*

**18 ▶ PRINTING ◀** to make the words and letters of a book, newspaper etc ready to be printed: *In those days books had to be set by hand.*

**19 set sth to music** to write music for a story or a poem, so that it can be sung

## ⑦ WANT/NOT WANT

**20 set your mind/sights/heart on sth** to be determined to achieve something or decide that you definitely want to have it: *Once Sharon sets her mind on something, she usually gets what she wants.*

**21 set yourself against** to be determined that you do not want something to happen or you do not want to take part in something: *Angie seems to have set herself against the idea completely.*

## ⑧ OTHER MEANINGS

**22 set a record** to run a race in a faster time than anyone else, jump further than anyone else, win a competition more times than anyone else etc: *The Kenyan runner set a new Olympic Record in the 3000 metres.*

**23 ▶ SUN ◀** [I] if the sun sets, it moves close to the horizon and then goes below it

**24 set an example** to behave in a way that shows other people how to behave: *Teachers should set an example for their students.*

**25 set sb straight/right** to tell someone the right way to do something or the true facts about something: [+ **on**] *I set him right on one or two points of procedure.* —see also **set the record straight** (STRAIGHT[2] (7))

**26 set sth right** to deal with any problems, mistakes etc: *I wish you'd been here – you could easily have set things right.*

**27 set sb free/loose** to allow someone to be free, or to allow a dangerous person to escape: *Brian Keenan and the other hostages were finally set free.*

**28 set great store by/set a high value on** to consider something to be very important: *At my old school they set great store by athletic achievements.*

**29 ▶ LIQUID/GLUE/CEMENT ETC ◀** [I] to become hard and solid: *How long does it take for the glue to set?*

**30 ▶ BONE ◀ a)** [T] if you set a broken bone, you move the broken ends so that they are in the right place to grow together again **b)** [I] if a broken bone sets, it joins together again

**31 ▶ HAIR ◀** [T] to arrange someone's hair while it is wet so that it has a particular style when it dries

**32 be set into** to be fixed into the surface of something: *a large brick fireplace which was set into the wall*

**33 be set with gems etc** to be decorated with jewels: *a gold bracelet set with rubies*

**set about** *phr v* [T] **1** to start doing something, especially something that needs a lot of time and effort **set about doing sth** *She set about clearing up after the party.* **2** to deal with something in a particular way: *I think you're setting about the problem in the wrong way.* **3** *especially literary* to attack someone by hitting and kicking them: *They set about him with their fists.*

**set against** *phr v* [T] **1** [**set** sb **against** sb] to make someone start to fight or quarrel with another person, especially a person who they had friendly relations with before: *The bitter civil war has set brother against brother.* **2** [**set** sth **off against** sth] to consider something in relation to another thing, especially when that other thing is very important: *The recent improvement in output has to be set against increased labour costs.* **3 set sth (off) against tax** to make an official record of the money you have spent on something connected with your job, in order to reduce the amount of tax you have to pay

**set apart** *phr v* [T] **1** [**set** sb/sth **apart**] to make someone or something different and often better than other people or things: *It is man's ability to think which sets him apart from other animals.* **2** [**set** sth **apart**] to keep something for a special purpose and only use it for that purpose: *Regular times should be set apart for seeing patients.*

**set** sth ↔ **aside** *phr v* [T] **1** to keep something, especially money or time, for a special purpose and only use it for that purpose: [+ **for**] *Try to set aside at least an hour each day for learning new vocabulary.* | *a room that had been set aside for visitors* **2** to decide that you will not be influenced by a particular feeling, belief, or principle, because something else is more important: *Congress ought to set aside its political differences to pass a health care bill.* **3** to declare that a previous legal decision or agreement no longer has any effect: *The judge set aside the verdict of the lower court.*

**set back** *phr v* [T] **1** [**set** sb/sth ↔ **back**] to delay the progress or development of something, or delay someone from finishing something: *The cultural revolution set back the modernization of China by many years.* **2** [**set** sb **back**] *informal* to cost someone a lot of money: *The new laptop from Toshiba will set you back a cool $2000.*

**set down** *phr v* [T] **1** [**set** sth ↔ **down**] to write about something so that you have a record of it: *I wanted to set my feelings down on paper.* **2** [**set** sth ↔ **down**] to establish how something should be done in an official set of rules or an official document: *The club rules are set down in its constitution.* **3** [**set** sb ↔ **down**] *BrE* to stop a car, bus etc and allow someone to get out: *The driver set her down at the station.*

**set forth** *phr v* **1** [T **set** sth ↔ **forth**] *formal* to write or talk about an idea, argument, or set of figures: *Rousseau set forth his theories on education in his book 'Emile'.* **2** [I] *literary* to begin a journey: *They were about to set forth on a voyage into the unknown.*

**set in** *phr v* [I] if something sets in, especially something unpleasant, it begins and seems likely to continue for a long time: *Winter seems to be setting in early this year.* | *A period of further economic decline set in during the 1930s.*

**set off** *phr v* **1** [I] to start to go somewhere: *I wanted to set off early in order to avoid the traffic.* | *The old man set off down the path towards the river.* **2** [T **set** sth ↔ **off**] to make something start happening or make people suddenly start doing something, especially when you do not intend to do so: *The incident*

[continued on next page]

set off

She set off early in the morning.

The burglar set the alarm off.

[continued from previous page]
*set off a chain of events which resulted in the outbreak of World War I.* | *News of the deal set off a flurry of activity on Wall Street.* **3** [T **set** sth ↔ **off**] to make something such as an alarm system start operating, especially when you do not intend to do so: *The high winds set off a lot of car alarms.* **4** [T **set** sth ↔ **off**] to make a bomb explode, or cause an explosion: *The slightest movement would have set off the device and blown us all sky high.* **5** [T **set** sth ↔ **off**] if a piece of clothing, colour, decoration etc sets something off, it makes it look attractive: *a stylish beige dress, set off by a blue jacket and scarf* **6** [T **set** sb **off**] to make someone start laughing, crying, or talking about something: *Don't mention anything about weddings – you'll only set her off again.*

**set on** *phr v* [T] [**set** sb **on/onto** sb] to make people or animals attack someone: *The farmer threatened to set his dogs on them if they didn't get off his land.* | **be set on/upon by sb** (=be suddenly attacked by people or animals) *He was set on by a gang of hooligans as he was leaving the bar.*

**set out** *phr v* **1** [I] to start a journey, especially a long journey: *Columbus and his crew set out from Europe in 1492.* | [+ **for**] *We packed our rucksacks and set out for the hills.* **2 set out to do sth** to start doing something or making plans to do something in order to achieve a particular result: *She deliberately set out to poison her husband.* | **set out with the intention of doing sth** *They set out with the intention of becoming the number one team in the league.* **3** [T **set** sth ↔ **out**] to write or talk about something such as a group of facts, ideas, or reasons, especially in a clearly organized way: *He set out the reasons for his decision in his report.* | *The guidelines are set out in paragraph two.* **4** [T **set** sth ↔ **out**] to put a group of things down and arrange them in order: *Aunti Lou set out the dinner on the table.* **5 set out on a career/course of action** to start a particular kind of job or start doing something in a particular way: *My nephew is just setting out on a career in journalism.*

**set to** *phr v* [I] *BrE* to start doing something eagerly and with a lot of effort and determination: *If we all set to, we can finish the cleaning in half an hour*

**set up** *phr v*
**1 ▶ COMPANY/ORGANIZATION ETC ◀** [I,T] to start a company, organization, committee etc; ESTABLISH: **set sth ↔ up** *The Race Relations Board was originally set up in 1965.* | *They want to set up their own import-export business.* | **set up as** (=start your own business as) *John used his inheritance to set up as a graphic designer.* | **set up shop/set up in business** (=begin operating a business) *We mortgaged our house and set up shop with the money from that.*
**2 ▶ ARRANGE/ORGANIZE ◀** [T **set** sth ↔ **up**] to make the necessary arrangements so that something can happen, such as a meeting, an event, or a system for doing something: *I'll get my secretary to set up a working lunch for us.* | *There was a lot of work involved in setting up the festival.* | *We need to set up emergency procedures to deal with this sort of problem.*
**3 ▶ EQUIPMENT ◀** [I,T] to prepare the equipment that will be needed for an activity so that it is ready to be used: *The next band was already setting up on the other stage.* | **set** sth ↔ up *Does anyone know how to set up this generator?* | *Why don't you set up the Monopoly game while I finish washing the dishes?*
**4 ▶ BUILD/PUT UP ◀** [T **set** sth ↔ **up**] to place or build something such as a sign or STATUE somewhere: *The army has set up road blocks round the city.*
**5 set up home/house** to start living in your own home, especially with someone else, instead of living with your parents: *Lucy and Paul are thinking of setting up house together.*
**6 set up camp a)** to put up a tent or group of tents in a place so that you can stay there: *We set up camp near the shore of the lake.* **b)** *informal* to move all your things to a place so that you can start to live or work there: *She's set up camp in my office.*
**7 ▶ MAKE SB SEEM GUILTY ◀** [T **set** sb ↔ **up**] *informal* to deliberately make other people think that someone has done something wrong, or illegal: *The four terrorists claimed they had been set up by the police.*
**8 ▶ HEALTHY/FULL OF ENERGY ◀** [T **set** sb **up**] to make you feel healthy and full of energy: | **set sb up for the day** *A good breakfast will set you up for the day.*
**9 set sb up for life** *informal* if something sets you up for life, it provides you with enough money for the rest of your life: *In a few more years you should be set up for life.*
**10 ▶ START HAPPENING ◀** [T **set up** sth] *especially technical* to make a condition or a process start happening: *If one reactor has a meltdown, it could set up a chain reaction.* | *Stimulation of the sensory receptors sets up neural activity.*
**11 ▶ NOISE ◀ set up a commotion/din/racket etc** to start making a loud, unpleasant noise: *At this, the two babies set up a tremendous howling.*

S1 W1 **set²** *n*
**1 ▶ GROUP OF THINGS ◀** [C] a group of things that form a whole: *a chess set* | [+ **of**] *a set of tools* | *We are now facing a whole new set of problems.*
**2 ▶ TELEVISION/RADIO ◀** [C] a television, or a piece of equipment for receiving radio signals: *a colour television set* —see also CRYSTAL SET
**3 ▶ STAGE ◀** [C] the scenery, furniture etc that is put on a stage to represent where the action of the play is taking place: *The play wasn't that good but the set was impressive.*
**4 ▶ FILM ◀** [C] a place where a film or television programme is acted and filmed: *Everyone must be on the set to start filming at eight o'clock.*
**5 ▶ SPORT ◀** [C] one part of a game such as tennis or VOLLEYBALL: *Agassi won the second set 6 – 4.*
**6 ▶ MUSIC ◀** [C] a series of songs performed by one band or singer as part of a concert
**7 ▶ HAIR ◀** [singular] an act of arranging your hair in a particular style when it is wet: **a shampoo and set** (=washing the hair and arranging it in a style)

**8 ▶ PEOPLE ◀** [singular] a group of people with similar interests: *Joanna got in with a rather wild set at college.* —see also JET SET
**9 ▶ FIRMNESS ◀** [singular] the state of becoming firm or solid: *You'll get a better set if you use gelatine.*
**10 ▶ PART OF BODY ◀** [C] the way in which you are sitting, standing etc, especially when you look stiff: [+ **of**] *From the set of her shoulders it was obvious that Sue was exhausted.*
**11 ▶ STUDENTS ◀** [C] *BrE* a group of children who have the same level of ability in a subject at school: *Adam's in the top set for maths.*
**12 ▶ MATHS ◀** [C] *technical* a collection of numbers etc in MATHEMATICS: *The set (x,y) has two members.*
**13 ▶ ONION ◀** [C] a small brown root planted in order to grow onions: *onion sets*

**set**[3] *adj*
**1 ▶ PLACED ◀** being in the position that is mentioned: *a town set on a hill | Diane had very deep-set eyes. | a house set back from the road*
**2 ▶ WAGE/TIME ◀** a set time, amount etc is fixed and cannot be changed: *We pay a set amount each week.*
**3 a set book/text etc** *BrE* a book that must be studied for an examination —see also SET[1] (10)
**4 a set menu/meal** *BrE* a set meal has a fixed price and includes a combination of foods that the restaurant suggests
**5 be set on/upon/against** to be very determined about something: *Nina's very set on going to this party.* | **be dead set on/upon/against** *The government's dead set against the plan.*
**6 have your heart set on sth** to be determined to do something: *She's got her heart set on going to France this summer.*
**7 ▶ READY ◀** [only after noun] *informal* someone who is set for something is prepared for it: **set for sth** *Are you all set for the journey?* | **set to do sth** *I was all set to leave when the phone rang.* | **get set** (=get ready) *"On your marks – get set – go!" said the starter.* | **all set** *Okay, I'm all set, let's get going.*
**8 set smile/teeth/jaw** a set smile etc shows that you are not happy about something or are determined to do something: *Gloria greeted her guests with a set smile.*
**9 set opinions/beliefs etc** set opinions or beliefs are ones you are not likely to change
**10 be set in your ways** to be used to doing the same things every day: *Uncle's 80 now and very set in his ways.*
**11 set to (do sth)** likely to do something: *The temperature is set to drop very low tonight. | This issue is set to cause the government serious embarrassment.*

**set·back** /ˈsetbæk/ *n* [C] something that delays or prevents progress, or makes things worse than they were: *The recent crime figures are a major setback for the law and order reforms.* —see also **set back** (SET[1])

**set piece** /ˌ· ˈ·◂/ *n* [C] part of a play, piece of music, painting etc that follows a well-known formal pattern or style, and is often very impressive: *The trial scene at the end of the play is a classic set piece.*

**set·square** /ˈsetskweə‖-skwer/ *n* [C] a flat piece of plastic or metal with three sides and one right angle, used for drawing or testing angles; TRIANGLE (4)

**set·tee** /seˈtiː/ *n* [C] a long seat with a back and usually with arms, for more than one person to sit on; SOFA

**set·ter** /ˈsetə‖-ər/ *n* [C] **1** a long-haired dog often trained to find where animals or birds are so they can be shot **2** someone who does a particular job, or who does things that other people copy: **exam setter/trap setter/fashion setter etc** (=someone who gives exams, puts out traps etc) —see also **set the pattern/tone/trend** (SET[1] (3)), TRENDSETTER

W2 **set·ting** /ˈsetɪŋ/ *n* [C usually singular] **1** all the things that surround someone or something at a particular time, including the events that happen, their environment, or the people they are with: *an old farm house in a beautiful setting | children brought up in a privileged setting* **2** the place or time that the action of a book, film etc happens: *Canberra is the setting for his latest novel.* **3** [C] the position in which you fix the controls on a machine or instrument: *The freezer's already on its highest setting.* **4** [C] the metal that holds a stone in a piece of jewellery, or the way the stone is fixed: *a diamond ring in a gold setting* **5** [C] music that is written to go with a poem, prayer etc **6 the setting of the sun** *literary* the time when the sun goes down —see also PLACE SETTING

**set·tle**[1] /ˈsetl/ *v* S2 W2
**1 ▶ MAKE COMFORTABLE/SAFE ◀ a)** [I always + adv/prep, T always + adv/prep] to put yourself or someone else in a comfortable position: [+ **back/into/down**] *Mel settled back in his chair and closed his eyes.* | **settle yourself** *Kari had already settled herself in a corner where she could watch.* **b)** to put something carefully in a particular place so that it stays there: *Lee settled the cup on the saucer.*
**2 ▶ MOVE DOWN/STAY ◀** [I] **a)** if dust, snow etc settles it comes down and stays in one place: [+ **on/in**] *snow settling on the roofs | The sediment will settle in the bottle after a few days.* **b)** if a bird, insect etc settles it flies down and rests on something: [+ **on**] *A fly settled on the plate of cookies.*
**3 ▶ END AN ARGUMENT ◀** [I,T] to end an argument by agreeing on something: [+ **with**] *It looks like they're finally going to settle with the railroad.* | **settle a quarrel/argument/dispute etc** *There's only one way to settle the dispute, and they know it.* | **settle out of court** (=come to an agreement to avoid going to a court of law) | **settle your differences** (=agree to stop arguing with someone)

**4 ▶ DECIDE ◀** [T] to decide on something, especially so that you can make definite arrangements: **settled (that)** *It was settled that Jim would visit us on the weekend.* | **It is settled** (=it is now decided) *It's settled then. I'll go back to the States in June.* | **That settles it!** (=this is enough information for a decision to be made) *Carol's only 15? That settles it. We are not taking her with us.*
**5 ▶ PAY MONEY ◀** [T] to pay money that is owed: **settle a bill/account/claim** *We expect you to settle your account in full each month. | These insurance companies take forever to settle a claim.*
**6 ▶ TAKE CARE OF DETAILS ◀** [T] to put all the details of a piece of business into order and deal with them, for example before you travel or because you may die soon: **settle the details** (=deal with the details of a plan, agreement etc) | **settle your affairs** (=put your personal business in order) | **settle an estate** (=deal with the way someone's property is divided after they die)
**7 ▶ QUIET/CALM ◀** [I,T] to become quiet or calm, or to make someone or something quiet or calm: *When the children had settled, Miss Brown gave out the new reading books.* | **settle your nerves/stomach** (=stop your nerves or stomach from being upset) *A little soda should settle your tummy.*
**8 ▶ LIVE IN A PLACE ◀ a)** [I] to go to live in a new place, and stay there: *After returning from abroad they settled in Chicago.* **b)** [T] to go to a new place where there are few people and start to live there: *Jamestown was already settled when the Pilgrims came to America.*
**9 ▶ A FEELING/QUALITY ◀** [I always + adv/prep] if a quality or feeling settles over a place or on someone it has a strong effect: [+ **over/on**] *Despair seemed to settle on him and he could hardly work. | A velvety silence settled over the room.*
**10 settle a score/account** to do something to hurt or cause trouble for someone because they have harmed or offended you: *She's got a few old scores to settle with him.*
**11 ▶ SINK ◀** [I] if something such as a building or the ground settles it sinks slowly to a lower level: *The crack in the wall is caused by the ground settling.*
**12 ▶ LOOK ◀** [I] if your eyes settle on someone or

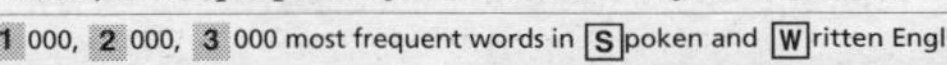

something you look at them carefully for a period of time: [+ **on**] *The teacher's steely eyes settled on Bobby.*
**13 ▶ EXPRESSION ◀** [I] if a particular expression settles on your face, it stays there: *His face settled into a severe frown.*
**14 ▶ FOOD ◀** [I] if something you eat settles, it is digested (DIGEST[1] (1)) well: *Give your lunch a chance to settle.*

**settle down** *phr v* **1** [I,T **settle** sb **down**] to stop talking or behaving in an excited way, or to make someone do this: *Everybody settle down so we can hear the story.* | *Sheila seems to have settled down more since school started.* **2** [I] to start living in a place with the intention of staying there, especially after you have travelled a lot: *They'd like to see her daughter settle down, get married, and have kids.* **3** [I,T] to start giving all of your attention to a job, activity etc: [+ **to**] *They settled down to a serious discussion over coffee.* | **settle yourself down** *Sally sighed, and settled herself down to listen.*

**settle for** sth *phr v* [T not in passive] to accept or agree to something, especially something that is less than what you want: *We've no TV and have had to settle for hearing the news on the radio.* | *They want $3000 for their car and won't settle for anything less.* | *You'll have to settle for a cheaper car.*

**settle in/into** *phr v* **1** [I,T **settle** sb **in**] to become used to a new home, job, surroundings etc or to help someone do this: *Are you settling in OK?* | *It takes a few months to settle into life at college.* **2** [I] to make yourself comfortable and prepare to stay somewhere for a period of time: [+ **for**] *They settled in for a long wait in the airport lounge.*

**settle on/upon** *phr v* [T] **1** [**settle on** sth/sb] to decide or agree on something: *They haven't settled yet on a name for the baby.* **2** [**settle** sth **on** sb] *BrE formal* to make a formal arrangement to give money or property to someone: *She settled a small yearly sum on each of her children.*

**settle up** *phr v* **1** [I] to pay what you owe on an account or bill: [+ **with**] *I'll settle up with the bartender and we can leave.* **2** [I] if two or more people settle up, they agree on a final arrangement for paying money, dividing property etc: *It's time we settled up. What do I owe you?*

**settle²** *n* [C] a long wooden seat with a high back that usually has a hollow place for storing things under the seat

**set·tled** /ˈsetld/ *adj* **1** unlikely to change; fixed: *They lead a settled life.* | *The community has firm and settled ideas on this question.* **2 feel/be settled** to feel comfortable about living or working in a particular place: *I'd work better if I felt more settled in my job.*

W2 **set·tle·ment** /ˈsetlmənt/ *n*
**1 ▶ OFFICIAL AGREEMENT ◀** [C,U] an official agreement or decision that ends an argument between two sides: **reach/achieve a settlement** *failure to reach a settlement in the trade war* | **negotiated/political/peaceful etc settlement** (=made after discussions are held, political decisions taken etc) | **divorce/peace/financial etc settlement** (=the agreement about what the two sides will do after a divorce, after fighting stops etc) *Martin lost the house in their divorce settlement.* | **out-of-court settlement** (=money you pay or things you agree to do to prevent someone going to court)
**2 ▶ GROUP OF HOUSES ◀** [C] a group of houses and buildings where people live, in an area where no group lived before: *a Bronze Age settlement* | *Wrangell is Alaska's second oldest settlement.*
**3 ▶ NEW AREA/PLACES ◀** [U] the movement of a new population into a place to live there: [+ **of**] *the settlement of the American West*
**4 ▶ PAYMENT ◀** [C,U] the payment of money that you owe someone: **in settlement** *a $1000 check in settlement*
**5 ▶ GIFT ◀** [C,U] a formal gift of money or property: **on/upon** *He made a handsome settlement on his daughter when she married.*
**6 ▶ SINKING ◀** [U] the slow sinking of a building, the ground under it etc; SUBSIDENCE

**set·tler** /ˈsetlə‖-ər/ *n* [C] someone who goes to live in a new place where there are few people: *early settlers in Australia*

**set-to** /ˈ· ·/ *n* [C usually singular + **with**] *informal* a short fight or quarrel —see also **set to** (SET[1])

**set-up** /ˈ· ·/ *n* [C usually singular] **1** a way of organizing or arranging something: *a less traditional classroom set-up* | *He has a nice little set-up, with a studio at the back and gallery space at the front.* **2** all the parts that work together in a system, for example in a computer system **3** *informal* a dishonest plan that tricks you: *How do I know this isn't a set-up?* —see also **set up** (SET[1])

**sev·en** /ˈsevən/ *number* **1** 7 **2 the seven year itch** *humorous* the idea that after seven years of being married, people feel less satisfied with their relationship —**seventh** *number* —see also **at sixes and sevens** (SIX (3))

**sev·en·teen** /ˌsevənˈtiːn◂/ *number* 17

**sev·enth** /ˈsevənθ/ *n* **1** [C] one of seven equal parts of something **2 be in seventh heaven** *informal* to be extremely happy: *He's in seventh heaven when he's watching football.*

**sev·en·ty** /ˈsevənti/ *number* **1** 70 **2 the seventies** the years from 1970 to 1979 **3 in your seventies** aged between 70 and 79: **in your early/late seventies** (=below or above 75) **4 in the seventies** if the temperature is in the seventies, it is between 70° and 79° FAHRENHEIT —**seventieth** *adj*

**seventy-eight** /ˌ··· ˈ·/ *n* [C] an old-fashioned record that is played by being turned 78 times a minute

**sev·er** /ˈsevə‖-ər/ *v formal* **1** [I,T] to cut through something, separating it into two parts, or to become severed in this way: *Martin's hand was severed in the accident.* | *a severed rope* **2** [T] to end a relationship with someone, or a connection with something: *severing family ties* —see also SEVERANCE PAY —**severance** *n* [U]

**sev·er·al¹** /ˈsevərəl/ *quantifier* a number of people or things that is more than a few, but not a lot: *I visited him in Kansas several times.* | *several million dollars* | *Several people have volunteered to go.* | [+ **of**] *Several of us think it's a bad idea.* S1 W1

**several²** *adj* [only before noun, no comparative] *formal or literary* different and separate; RESPECTIVE: *They shook hands and went their several ways.* —**severally** *adv*: *These issues can be considered severally, or as a whole.*

**sev·er·ance pay** /ˈ···· ·/ *n* [U] money you get when you leave a company because your employer no longer has a job for you

**se·vere** /səˈvɪə‖-ˈvɪr/ *adj* S3
**1 ▶ VERY BAD ◀** very bad, or serious enough for you to worry about: *severe injuries to the head and neck* | *severe depression* | *a severe setback to hopes of peace* —see graph at PAIN[1] W2
**2 ▶ WEATHER ◀** severe weather conditions are extremely hot, cold, dry etc and are unpleasant or dangerous: *the severest winter since 1948* | *severe flooding*
**3 ▶ STRICT ◀** someone who is severe is very strict and demands that rules of behaviour are obeyed or standards are followed: *Don't be so severe with the children.*
**4 ▶ EXTREME ◀** criticism or punishment that is severe is extreme, and intended to prevent more crimes or bad behaviour: *Drug smuggling continues to flourish despite the severe sentences of the courts.* | *a report containing severe criticism of the company's actions*
**5 ▶ UNFRIENDLY ◀** disapproving or unfriendly: *a severe expression*
**6 ▶ PLAIN ◀** plain and simple in style with little or no decoration; AUSTERE: *The town hall of Bruges is less severe but equally imposing.* —**severity** *n* [C,U] *We didn't realize the severity of her illness.* | *"You can't leave now," he said with some severity.*

**se·vere·ly** /səˈvɪəli‖-ˈvɪr-/ *adv* **1** very badly or to a great degree: *a severely damaged building* | *severely disabled* |

*His movements are severely restricted.* **2** in a strict way: *Parents don't punish their children so severely these days.* **3** in a way that shows you disapprove greatly: *"Stop behaving like a fool!" she said severely.* **4** in a plain simple style with little or no decoration: *severely dressed*

**sew** /səʊ‖soʊ/ *v past tense* **sewed** *past participle* **sewn** /səʊn‖soʊn/ also **sewed** *AmE* [I,T] to use a needle and thread to join pieces of cloth together to make or repair clothes or fasten something such as a button to them: *I learned to sew at school.* | **sew sth on sth** *Can you sew a patch on my jeans?*

**sew** sth ↔ **up** *phr v* [T] **1** to close or repair something by sewing it: *Could you sew up this hole in my trousers?* **2** [usually passive] *informal* to finish a business agreement or plan and get the result you want: *Bob reckons the deal should be sewn up in a week.* **3** [usually passive] to gain control over a situation so that you are sure to win or gain something: *It seems like the Democrats have the election all sewn up.*

**sew·age** /ˈsjuːɪdʒ, ˈsuː-‖ˈsuː-/ *n* [U] the mixture of waste from the human body and used water that is carried away from houses by sewers: *Chlorine is used in sewage treatment.*

**sewage farm** /ˈ··· ·/ *BrE*, **sewage plant** *AmE n* [C] a place where sewage is treated to stop it being harmful

**sew·er** /ˈsjuːə, ˈsuːə‖ˈsuːər/ *n* [C] a pipe or passage under the ground that carries away waste material and used water from houses and factories

**sew·er·age** /ˈsjuːərɪdʒ, ˈsuː-‖ˈsuː-/ *n* [U] the system by which waste material and water is carried away in sewers and then treated to stop it being harmful

**sew·ing** /ˈsəʊɪŋ‖ˈsoʊ-/ *n* [U] **1** the activity or skill of making or repairing clothes or decorating cloth with a needle and thread **2** something you have sewn or are going to sew: *Imogen sighed and picked up her sewing.*

**sewing ma·chine** /ˈ·· ·ˌ·/ *n* [C] a machine for stitching cloth or clothes together

S1 W2 **sex¹** /seks/ *n* **1** [U] the activity in which a male and female join their sexual organs in order to create babies, or for pleasure: *All you see on TV is sex and violence these days.* **2** **have sex** when two people have sex they take part in an activity that involves contact between their sexual organs: *Would you have sex with someone on your first date?* **3** [U] the male or female nature of a person, animal, or plant: *Please put your name, age, and sex at the top of the form.* | *You can now tell the sex of a baby before it is born.* **4** [C] the two sexes are the two groups of male and female people, animals etc: **the opposite sex** (=the group that you are not in) *He's terrified of the opposite sex.* | **sex discrimination** (=unfair treatment because of which sex you are) *She's prosecuting the company for sex discrimination.* **5** **single-sex school/college etc** *BrE* a school etc for either males or females, but not for both together

**sex²** *v* [T] *technical* to find out whether an animal is male or female

**sex·a·ge·na·ri·an** /ˌseksədʒɪˈneəriən‖-ˈner-/ *n* [C] *formal* someone who is between 60 and 69 years old —**sexaganarian** *adj*

**sex ap·peal** /ˈ· ··/ *n* [U] the quality of being sexually attractive: *He's a nice guy – but he's got no sex appeal!*

**sex change** /ˈ· ·/ *n* [C usually singular] a medical operation or treatment which changes someone's body so that they look like someone of the other sex

**sex drive** /ˈ· ·/ *n* [C usually singular] someone's ability or need to have sex regularly

**sex ed·u·ca·tion** /ˈ· ··ˌ··/ *n* [U] education in schools about the physical processes and emotions involved in sex

**sex·is·m** /ˈseksɪzəm/ *n* [U] the belief that women are weaker, less intelligent, and less important than men: *The book gives a range of examples of sexism in education.*

**sex·ist** /ˈseksɪst/ *adj* **1** believing that women are weaker, less intelligent, and less important than men **2** resulting from or connected with this belief: *sexist attitudes* —**sexist** *n* [C]

**sex·less** /ˈseksləs/ *adj* **1** not sexually attractive; not SEXY **2** neither male nor female; NEUTER¹ (1)

**sex life** /ˈ· ·/ *n* [C] someone's sexual activities: *Jim's too busy to have much of a sex life.*

**sex-linked** /ˈ· ·/ *adj technical* an illness or medical condition that is sex-linked is caused by the GENES of only one sex and so is passed to children by parents of that sex

**sex ma·ni·ac** /ˈ· ˌ···/ *n* [C] someone who always wants to have sex, thinks about it all the time, and is unable to control these feelings

**sex ob·ject** /ˈ· ˌ··/ *n* [C] someone you consider only as a means of satisfying your sexual desire rather than as a whole person

**sex of·fend·er** /ˈ· ·ˌ··/ *n* [C] someone who is guilty of a crime related to sex

**sex·ol·o·gy** /sekˈsɒlədʒi‖-ˈsɑː-/ *n* [U] the study of sexual behaviour, especially among humans —**sexologist** *n* [C]

**sex or·gan** /ˈ· ˌ··/ *n* [C] a part of the body concerned with the production of children, such as the PENIS or VAGINA

**sex·ploi·ta·tion** /ˌseksplɔɪˈteɪʃən/ *n* [U] *informal* a word meaning the use of sex in films and magazines in order to make money, used by people who think this is wrong

**sex·pot** /ˈsekspɒt‖-pɑːt/ *n* [C] *informal* a word meaning a sexually attractive woman, that many women think is offensive

**sex shop** /ˈ· ·/ *n* [C] *BrE* a shop selling goods, magazines etc related to sex and sexual activities

**sex sym·bol** /ˈ· ˌ··/ *n* [C] someone who represents society's idea of what is sexually attractive: *sex symbols such as Madonna and Tom Cruise*

**sex·tant** /ˈsekstənt/ *n* [C] a tool for measuring angles between stars in order to calculate the position of your ship or aircraft

**sex·tet** /seksˈtet/ *n* [C] **1** a group of six singers or musicians performing together **2** a piece of music for six performers: *Brahm's sextet in B flat*

**sex·ton** /ˈsekstən/ *n* [C] someone who takes care of a church building, and sometimes rings the bells and digs graves

**sex·tu·plet** /sekˈstjuːplɪt‖-ˈstʌ-/ *n* [C] one of six people who are born at the same time and have the same mother

**sex·u·al** /ˈsekʃuəl/ *adj* **1** connected with sex: *a disease passed on by sexual contact* | *sexual relationships* | *sexual desire* **2** connected with the social relationships between men and women: *sexual politics* **3** connected with the way people or animals have babies: *sexual reproduction* —**sexually** *adv*: *sexually experienced* | *sexually attractive* S2 W2

**sexual har·ass·ment** /ˌ··· ˈ···, ˌ··· ··ˈ··/ *n* [U] unwelcome touching or remarks about sex from someone, especially if you are expected to accept this to make progress in your job

**sexual in·ter·course** /ˌ··· ˈ···/ *n* [U] *formal* the act of two people having sex with each other

**sex·u·al·i·ty** /ˌsekʃuˈælɪti/ *n* [U] the things people do and feel that are connected with their desire or ability to have sex: *Sexuality was never discussed.* | **male/female sexuality** *a study of male sexuality*

**sex·u·al·ly trans·mit·ted dis·ease** /ˌ···· ·ˌ·· ··ˈ·/ *n* [C,U] STD; a disease that is passed on through sexual intercourse, such as AIDS, HERPES etc

**sex·y** /ˈseksi/ *adj* **sexier, sexiest** **1** sexually exciting or attractive: *Oh, don't you think he's sexy?* | *a sexy picture* **2** *informal* exciting to think about or use: *Constitutional change is not a sexy issue.* | *sexy computer software* —**sexily** *adv* —**sexiness** *n* [U] —see BEAUTIFUL (USAGE)

**SF** /ˌes ˈef/ *adj* the abbreviation of SCIENCE FICTION

**Sgt** the written abbreviation of SERGEANT

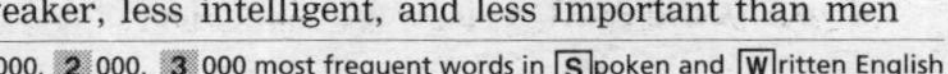

S3 **sh** /ʃ/ *interjection* used to tell someone to be quiet: *Sh! I'm trying to sleep.*

**shab·by** /ˈʃæbi/ *adj* **1** untidy and in a bad condition from being used for a long time: *a shabby suit|shabby hotel rooms* **2** wearing clothes that are old and worn: *a shabby tramp* **3** unfair and unkind: *That's a shabby way to treat someone.|a shabby trick* —**shabbily** *adv* —**shabbiness** *n* [U]

**shack¹** /ʃæk/ *n* [C] a small building that has not been built very well: *a tin shack*

**shack²** *v*

**shack up** *phr v* [I] *informal* to start living with someone who you have sex with but are not married to: **shack up together/with** *Last I heard, they were shacked up together in Croydon.*

**shack·le¹** /ˈʃækəl/ *n* [C] **1 the shackles of slavery/convention etc** *literary* the limits put on your freedom and happiness by SLAVERY etc **2** one of a pair of metal rings joined by a chain that are used for fastening together a prisoner's hands or feet

**shackle²** *v* [T] **1** to put many limits on what someone can do: *Industrial progress is being shackled by a mass of regulations.* **2** to put shackles on someone

**shad** /ʃæd/ *n* [C,U] a north Atlantic fish used for food

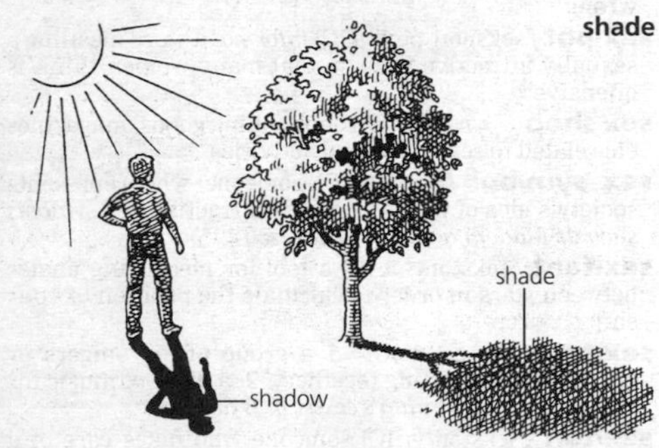

**shade¹** /ʃeɪd/ *n*

**1** ▸ **SLIGHT DARKNESS** ◂ [U] slight darkness or shelter from the direct light of the sun made by something blocking it: *a plant that likes a lot of shade*|**in the shade** *Let's find a table in the shade.|It's 35°C in the shade.*|**in the shade of a tree/wall etc** *sitting in the shade of a large oak tree* —compare SHADOW¹ (1)

**2** ▸ **FOR BLOCKING LIGHT** ◂ [C] **a)** something you use to reduce or block light: **lampshade/eyeshade** (=over a lamp, or above your eyes) **b)** *AmE* a BLIND³ (1)

**3 shades** [plural] *informal* SUNGLASSES

**4** ▸ **IN A PICTURE** ◂ [U] the dark places in a picture: **light and shade** *using light and shade to mould figures*

**5** ▸ **COLOUR** ◂ [C] a particular kind of red, green, blue etc: [+ **of**] *a wonderful shade of pink*

**6 shade of meaning/opinion/feeling etc** a meaning etc that is slightly different from other ones; NUANCE: *various shades of opinion in the party*

**7 a shade** *formal* very slightly: *Ken was just a shade too honest about his feelings.*

**8 shades of** used to say that something reminds you of someone or something else, especially when you would rather forget: *Huh. Shades of my poorer days.*

**9 put sth in the shade** to be so good or impressive that other similar things or people seem much less important or interesting: *Well Arthur, your choir puts our little town chorus in the shade.*

**10** *literary* the spirit of a dead person; GHOST¹ (1)

**11 have it made in the shade** *AmE informal* to be extremely rich

**shade²** *v* [T] **1** to protect something from direct light: *See, the yucca plant's being shaded by that tree.*|**shade your eyes/face etc** *Shading her eyes, Anita scanned the horizon.* **2** also **shade in** to make part of a picture or drawing darker: *You still need to shade in that bit there.*

**shade into** sth *phr v* [T] if one thing shades into another, it is impossible to tell where one stops and another starts: *Sea shades into sky at the horizon.|Right and wrong often shade into each other.*

**shad·ing** /ˈʃeɪdɪŋ/ *n* **1** [U] the areas of a drawing or painting that have been made to look darker **2 shadings** [plural] slight differences between things, situations, or ideas

**shad·ow¹** /ˈʃædəʊ‖-doʊ/ *n* W2

**1** ▸ **DARKNESS** ◂ [U] also **shadows** *plural* darkness caused by something preventing light from entering a place: **in shadow** *The room was half in shadow.*|**in the shadows** *a thief lurking in the shadows* —see picture at SHADE¹

**2** ▸ **DARK SHAPE** ◂ [C] a dark shape that someone or something makes on a surface when they are between that surface and the light: *Look how long our shadows are!*|**in the shadow of** (=under something, where its shadow will sometimes fall) *We buried Mama in the shadow of the old elm.*

**3 cast a shadow over/on** *literary* **a)** to make a dark shape appear on a surface by being between that surface and the light: *The house cast long shadows on the lawn.* **b)** to make something seem less attractive or impressive: *After that, a shadow was cast over his reputation.*

**4 without/beyond a shadow of a doubt** without any doubt at all: *Without a shadow of a doubt he's the most talented player we've ever had.*

**5 be in sb's shadow** to be less happy and successful than you could be because someone else gets noticed much more: *Kate grew up in the shadow of her film star sister.*

**6 be a shadow of your former self** to be so unhappy that you seem like a different person

**7 shadows under sb's eyes** small dark areas under someone's eyes that show they are tired

**8 sb's shadow** someone who follows someone else everywhere they go —see also **afraid of your own shadow** (AFRAID (4)), FIVE O'CLOCK SHADOW

**shadow²** *v* [T] **1** to follow someone closely in order to watch what they are doing: *Detectives shadowed them for weeks, collecting evidence.* **2** [usually passive] *literary* to cover something with a shadow, or make it dark: *a shadowed alley*

**shadow³** *adj* **1 shadow chancellor/foreign secretary etc** the politician in the main opposition party in the British parliament who would become CHANCELLOR (1) etc if their party was in government, and who is responsible for speaking on the same subjects **2 shadow cabinet** the group of politicians in the British parliament who would become ministers if their party was in government

**shadow box·ing** /ˈ·· ˌ··/ *n* [U] fighting with an imaginary opponent, especially as training for BOXING

**shadow pup·pet** /ˈ·· ˌ··/ *n* [C] a flat PUPPET that makes special shapes on a wall when you shine a light behind it

**shad·ow·y** /ˈʃædəʊi‖-doʊ-/ *adj* **1** mysterious and difficult to know anything about: **shadowy figure** *Anastasia Romanov is a shadowy figure.* **2** full of shadows, or difficult to see because of shadows: *a shadowy room*

**shad·y** /ˈʃeɪdi/ *adj* **1** protected from the sun or producing shade: *the shady side of the street|shady trees* **2** probably dishonest or illegal: *a shady character|She's been involved in some shady deals.*

**shaft¹** /ʃɑːft‖ʃæft/ *n* S3

**1** ▸ **HANDLE** ◂ [C] a long handle on a tool, SPEAR etc —see picture on page 1264

**2** ▸ **PASSAGE** ◂ [C] a passage which goes up through a building or down into the ground, so that someone or something can get in or out: **mine/elevator/ventilation shaft** *a 300-foot elevator shaft*

**3 shaft of light/sunlight** [C] a narrow beam of light

**4** ▸ **ENGINE PART** ◂ [C] a thin long piece of metal in

an engine or machine that turns and passes on power or movement to another part of the machine
**5 ► FOR A HORSE ◄** [C usually plural] one of a pair of poles between which a horse is tied to pull a vehicle
**6 shaft of wit** [C] *literary* a clever amusing remark, especially an unkind one
**7 ► ARROW ◄** [C] *literary* an ARROW (1)
**8 give sb the shaft** *AmE slang* to treat someone unfairly, for example by dismissing them from their job without a good reason

**shaft²** *v* [T] *slang* to treat someone unfairly, especially by dishonestly getting money from them: *We really got shafted in that computer deal.*

**shag¹** /ʃæg/ *adj* **shag carpet/rug** a CARPET¹ (1) or RUG (1) with a rough surface made from long threads of wool

**shag²** *n* **1** [C] *BrE taboo* an act of having sex with someone **2** [C] a large black sea bird **3** [U] strong-tasting TOBACCO with thick leaves cut into small thin pieces

**shag³** *v* [I,T] *BrE taboo* to have sex with someone

**shagged** /ʃægd/ also **shagged out** /,· '·/ *adj BrE slang taboo* very tired: *I'm not going – I'm too shagged!*

**shag·gy** /'ʃægi/ *adj* **1** shaggy hair or fur is long and untidy: *a shaggy black beard* **2** having shaggy hair: *a shaggy sheepskin coat* —**shagginess** *n* [U]

**shaggy dog sto·ry** /,·· '·,··/ *n* [C] a long joke that often ends in a silly or disappointing way

**Shah** /ʃɑː/ *n* [C] the title of the kings of Iran, used in the past

S3 W2 **shake¹** /ʃeɪk/ *past tense* **shook** /ʃʊk/ *past participle* **shaken** /'ʃeɪkən/ *v*
**1 ► MOVEMENT ◄** [I] to move up and down or from side to side with quick repeated movements: *His hand shook as he signed the paper.* | *The ground was shaking beneath their feet.* | **shake with anger/fear/laughter etc** (=be so angry, frightened etc that you cannot stop shaking) | **shake like a leaf** (=shake a lot, especially because you are very nervous or frightened) *What's the matter? You're shaking like a leaf.*

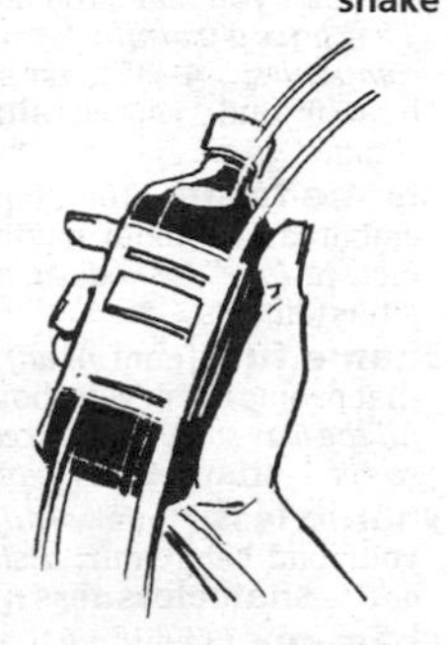
shake

**2 ► SHAKE STH ◄** [T] to make something or someone move up and down or from side to side with quick repeated movements: *The blast shook windows five miles away.* | **shake sth onto/out/over etc** *Shake the sand out of your shoes.*
**3 ► SHAKE SB ◄** [T] to hold someone by their shoulders and push and pull them backwards and forwards roughly, especially because you are angry with them: *She was being such a brat, I felt like shaking her.*
**4 shake your head** to move your head from side to side as a way of saying no: *He didn't reply, but just shook his head.*
**5 shake hands (with)** also **shake sb's hand/shake sb by the hand** to move someone's hand up and down with your own hand as a greeting or as a sign you have agreed something: *Wilkinson shook my hand warmly.*
**6 shake on it** *spoken* to agree on a decision or business agreement by shaking hands: *Let's shake on it.*
**7 be shaken** to feel very shocked and upset: *Kerrie was so shaken by the attack that she still won't go out alone.*
**8 shake sb's confidence/faith/belief** to make someone feel less confident, less sure about their beliefs etc
**9 shake your fist** to show that you are angry by holding up and shaking your tightly closed hand
**10 ► VOICE ◄** [I] if your voice shakes it sounds nervous or uncertain: *Reg's voice shook with rage.*
**11 shake a leg** *spoken* used to tell someone to start doing something now: *C'mon you guys, shake a leg! We haven't got all day.*
**12 shake in your shoes/boots** *informal* to be very nervous: *I was shaking in my shoes – I thought he'd give me the sack.*

**shake down** *phr v* **1** [I] *BrE informal* to get used to a new situation that you are working or living in **2** [T **shake** sb **down**] *AmE informal* to get money from someone by using threats **3** [T **shake** sb/sth ↔ **down**] *AmE informal* to search a person or place thoroughly **4** [T **shake** sth ↔ **down**] *BrE* to test a ship or plane under real conditions —see SHAKEDOWN **5** [I + **in/on etc**] *BrE informal* to sleep on the floor, on a seat etc, instead of in a proper bed

**shake** sb ↔ **off** *phr v* **1** [T **shake** sth ↔ **off**] to get rid of an illness, problem etc: *I can't seem to shake off this cold.* **2** [T] to escape from someone who is chasing you

**shake** sth ↔ **out** *phr v* [T] to shake a cloth, a bag, a sheet etc so that any small pieces of dirt, dust etc come off: *Shake the crumbs out of the tablecloth.*

**shake** sb/sth ↔ **up** *phr v* [T] **1** [T **shake** sb ↔ **up**] to give someone a very unpleasant shock, so that they feel very upset and frightened: *Seeing that accident really shook me up.* —see also SHAKEN **2** [T] to make changes to an organization in order to make it more effective —see also SHAKEUP

**shake²** *n* **1** [C] an act of shaking: **give sth a shake** *Give the bottle a good shake before you pour.* | **shake of the head** (=a movement of the head from side to side to say no) *She just refuses with a smile and a shake of the head.* **2 the shakes** *not technical* a nervous shaking of your body caused by illness, fear, too much alcohol etc: **get the shakes** *As soon as they left I started getting the shakes.* **3 in a couple of shakes/two shakes** *informal* very soon: *We'll be back in a couple of shakes.* **4 no great shakes** *spoken* not very skilful: *He's no great shakes, but he's better that the last chef they had.* **5** [C] *AmE* a cold drink made from milk that tastes of fruit, chocolate etc; MILK SHAKE **6 fair shake** *AmE informal* fair treatment: *Dave didn't get his fair shake – everyone else had the chance of an interview.*

**shake·down** /'ʃeɪkdaʊn/ *n* **1** [C] *AmE informal* the act of getting money from someone by using threats **2** [C] *AmE informal* a thorough search of a place or a person **3** [C] a final test of a boat, plane etc before it is put into general use: *a shakedown flight* **4** [singular] *BrE informal* a place prepared as a bed on the floor, on a seat etc

**shak·en** /'ʃeɪkən/ also **shaken up** *adj* [not usually before noun] upset, shocked, or frightened: *"How's Jacob?" "Pretty shaken up, but nothing's broken."*

**shake·out** *n* /'ʃeɪkaʊt/ **1** [C usually singular] a situation in which several companies fail because they cannot compete with stronger companies in difficult economic conditions **2** [C] a SHAKEUP

**shak·er** /'ʃeɪkə‖-ər/ *n* [C] **1** a container with holes in the lid, used to shake sugar etc onto food: *a salt shaker* **2** also **cocktail shaker** a container in which drinks are mixed **3** a small container for shaking DICE¹ (1) —see also **movers and shakers** (MOVER (4))

**Shakes·pea·re·an** /ʃeɪk'spɪəriən‖-'spɪr-/ *adj* [only before noun] **1** in the style of Shakespeare: *an almost Shakespearean richness of language* **2** connected with the work of Shakespeare: *a famous Shakespearean actor*

**shake·up** /'ʃeɪkʌp/ *n* [C] a process by which an organization makes a lot of big changes in a short time to improve its effectiveness: *a huge shakeup of the education system*

**shak·y** /'ʃeɪki/ *adj* **1** weak and unsteady because of old age, illness or shock: *shaky voice* | **be shaky on your feet** (=not able to walk very well) *Grandad was a little shaky on his feet after the accident.* **2** not thorough, complete, or certain: *My knowledge of history is a little shaky.* | *shaky evidence* **3** not firm or steady: *shaky foundations* —**shakily** *adv* —**shakiness** *n* [U]

**shale** /ʃeɪl/ *n* [U] a smooth soft rock which breaks easily into thin flat pieces

**shall** /ʃəl; *strong* ʃæl/ *modal verb negative short form* **shan't** **1 I/we shall** used to express what you will do S3 W1 in the future: *We shall be away next week.*|*I shall have finished it by Friday.* **2 shall I/we?** *BrE* used to make a suggestion, or ask a question that you want the other person to decide about: *Shall I open the window?*|*What shall I get for dinner?*|*Shall we say 6 o'clock, then?* **3 you/he/she/they shall** *formal or old-fashioned* used to describe what will happen to someone, especially when you are saying that it is very definite: *They shall be judged only by God.*|*I said you could go, and so you shall.* **4 we shall see** *spoken* used when you do not know what will happen in the future, or when you do not want to give someone a definite answer **5** *formal* used in official documents to show a law, command, promise etc: *All payments shall be made by the end of the month.*

**shal·lot** /ʃəˈlɒt‖ʃəˈlɑːt/ *n* [C] a vegetable like a small onion

**shal·low¹** /ˈʃæləʊ‖-loʊ/ *adj* **1** something that is shallow has only a short distance from the bottom to the surface: *a shallow river*|*the shallow end of the swimming pool*|*a shallow grave* —see picture at LOW¹ **2** not interested in or showing any understanding of important or serious matters: *a shallow argument*|*If he's only interested in your looks, that just shows how shallow he is.* **3 shallow breathing** breathing that only takes in small amounts of air —**shallowly** *adv* —**shallowness** *n* [U]

**shallow²** *v* [I] to become shallow

**shal·lows** /ˈʃæləʊz‖-loʊz/ *n* **the shallows** an area of shallow water: *We could see fish darting about in the shallows.*

**Sha·lom** /ʃæˈlɒm‖ʃæˈloʊm/ *interjection* a Jewish word used to say hello or goodbye

**shalt** /ʃəlt; *strong* ʃælt/ *v* **thou shalt** *old use* you shall

**sham¹** /ʃæm/ *n* **1** [singular] an attempt to deceive people by pretending something is true or good, especially when it is easy to see that it is not: *These so-called democratic reforms are a complete sham.* **2** [singular] someone who pretends to be something they are not, especially to gain an advantage or sympathy: *He was bogus, a sham, an imposter!* **3** [U] behaviour or actions intended to deceive people by pretending that something is true or good

**sham²** *adj* [only before noun] made to appear real in order to deceive people; false: *sham jewellery*

**sham³** *v* [I,T] to pretend to be upset, ill etc to gain sympathy or an advantage: *She's not ill, she's only shamming.*

**sha·man** /ˈʃɑːmən/ *n* [C] someone with religious authority in some tribes, who is believed to be able to talk to spirits, cure illnesses etc —**shamanism** *n* [U]

**sham·ble** /ˈʃæmbəl/ *v* [I always + adv/prep] to walk slowly and awkwardly, dragging your feet in a tired, weak, or lazy way: **[+ along/ past/out etc]** *The old man shambled out of the room muttering to himself.*| **shambling gait** (=a shambling way of walking)

**sham·bles** /ˈʃæmbəlz/ *n informal* **a shambles a)** an event or situation that is a complete failure because it has not been organized or planned properly: **be (in) a shambles** *By 1985 the economy was in a shambles.*|**make a shambles of sth** *Potts, you made a complete shambles of that speech.* **b)** a place where there is a lot of damage, destruction, and confusion: *This kitchen is a shambles!*

**sham·bol·ic** /ʃæmˈbɒlɪk‖-ˈbɑː-/ *adj informal* lacking organization or planning: *The way they run this place is totally shambolic.*

S 2 **shame¹** /ʃeɪm/ *n* **1** [U] the uncomfortable feeling of being guilty and embarrassed that you have when you have done something wrong: *a deep sense of shame*|**to your shame** (=making you feel ashamed) *She realized to her shame that she had forgotten Nina's birthday.*|**hang/bow your head in shame** (=look downwards and avoid looking at other people because you feel ashamed) **2 it's a shame (that)/what a shame!** *spoken* used to say that a situation is disappointing, and you wish things had happened differently: *It's a shame you have to leave so soon.*|*Oh it's raining. What a shame!* **3 Shame on you!** *spoken* used to tell someone that they should feel shame because of something they have done **4** [U only in questions and negatives] the ability to feel shame: *How could you do such a thing? Have you no shame?* **5 put sb/sth to shame** *informal* to be so much better than someone or something else that it makes the other thing seem very bad or ordinary: *His cooking puts mine to shame.* **6** [U] loss of honour and respect: **there is no shame in sth** (=it should not make you feel ashamed) *There's no shame in being poor.*|**bring shame on sb** *You've brought shame on this family.*

**USAGE NOTE: SHAME**

WORD CHOICE: **shame, embarrassment, ashamed, feel silly, embarrassed**

**Shame** is an uncomfortable feeling you have when you have done something wrong, and you feel that people will no longer respect you. If you make a mistake this may cause **embarrassment**, but not usually **shame** because **shame** is much stronger.

**Ashamed** (adj) is not quite so strong, but still not usually used about unimportant or accidental things: *I couldn't think of anything to say and felt silly/embarrassed* (NOT *ashamed*). However, someone might be **ashamed** if they are caught cheating in a test, for example, because they have done something morally wrong.

**shame²** *v* **1 shame sb** to make someone feel ashamed: *It shames me to say it, but I lied.* **2 shame sb into doing sth** to force someone to do something by making them feel ashamed: *His wife shamed him into handing the money back.* **3** [T] to be so much better than someone else that you make them seem bad or feel embarrassed: *They have a training record that would shame most other companies.* **4** [T] make someone feel that they have lost honour and respect: **shame sb** *Your cowardice has shamed us all.*

**shame·faced** /ˌʃeɪmˈfeɪst◂/ *adj* looking ashamed or embarrassed about having behaved badly: *"You really blew it, Ian." He nodded, shamefaced.* —**shamefacedly** /-ˈfeɪsɪ̈dli/ *adv*

**shame·ful** /ˈʃeɪmfəl/ *adj* shameful behaviour is so bad that people think you should be ashamed of it: *It's shameful the way some people treat their pets.*|*a shameful family secret* —**shamefully** *adv* —**shamefulness** *n* [U]

**shame·less** /ˈʃeɪmləs/ *adj* not seeming to be ashamed of your bad behaviour: *a shameless liar* —**shamelessly** *adv* —**shamelessness** *n* [U]

**sham·my** /ˈʃæmi/ *n* [C] a piece of soft leather used for cleaning and polishing glass or metal; CHAMOIS²

**sham·poo¹** /ʃæmˈpuː/ *n* **1** [C,U] a liquid soap for washing your hair **2** [C,U] a liquid used for cleaning carpets (CARPET¹ (1)) **3** [C] an act of shampooing or having your hair shampooed: *$21 for a shampoo, cut, and blow-dry*

**shampoo²** *v* [T] to wash something with shampoo

**sham·rock** /ˈʃæmrɒk‖-rɑːk/ *n* [C] a small plant with three green leaves on each stem that is the national EMBLEM of Ireland

**shan·dy** /ˈʃændi/ *n* [C,U] a drink made of beer mixed with LEMONADE (2), or a glass of this drink

**shang·hai** /ʃæŋˈhaɪ/ *v* [T + **into**] to trick or force someone into doing something unwillingly: *I got shanghaied into organizing the kids' party.*

**shank** /ʃæŋk/ *n* **1** [C] a straight narrow part of a tool or object that connects the two ends: *the shank of a key* **2** [C,U] a piece of meat cut from the leg of an animal **3** [C usually plural] *old use* the part of a person's or animal's leg between the knee and ANKLE —see picture at HORSE¹

**shan't** /ʃɑːnt‖ʃænt/ *especially BrE* the short form of 'shall not': *I shan't see you again.*

**shan·ty** /ˈʃænti/ *n* [C] **1** a small, roughly built hut made from thin sheets of wood, TIN¹ (1), plastic etc that very poor people live in **2 sea shanty** a song sung by sailors in former times, as they did their work

**shan·ty·town** /ˈʃæntiˌtaʊn/ *n* [C] an area in or near a town where people live in shanties

**shapes**

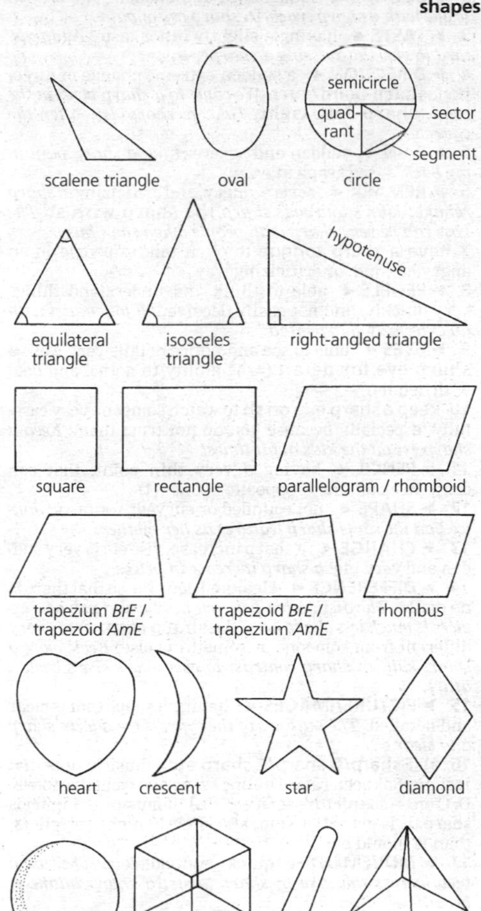


S2 W2 **shape¹** /ʃeɪp/ *n*
**1 ▶ OUTER FORM ◀ a)** [C,U] the outer form of something, that you see or feel: *What shape is the table – round or oval?* | *You can recognize a tree by the shape of its leaves.* | **round/square etc in shape** *The eyeball is almost spherical in shape.* | **lose its shape** (=become the wrong shape) *His battered old hat had completely lost its shape.* | **out of shape** (=having become the wrong shape) *Meryl's sweater had stretched completely out of shape.* | **in the shape of** (=having the same shape as something) *She was wearing a pin in the shape of a bird.* **b)** [C] a particular shape, or thing that is that shape: *OK Katie, which of these shapes are triangles?*
**2 ▶ THING NOT SEEN CLEARLY ◀** [C] a thing or person that you cannot see clearly enough to recognize: *A large shape loomed up out of the mist.*
**3 ▶ CHARACTER OF STH ◀** [singular] a particular combination of qualities and features that something has: **the shape of** *the shape of British politics today* | *Dr Singh was responsible for the final shape of the report.* | **in any shape or form** (=of any kind) *We will not tolerate racism in any shape or form.* | **the shape of things to come** (=an example of the way things will develop in the future)
**4 in the shape of** used to explain what something consists of: **sth comes in the shape of** *Help came in the shape of a $10,000 loan from his parents.*
**5 in good/bad/poor shape a)** in a good or bad condition: *Considering how old the car is, it's not in bad shape.* **b)** in a good or bad state of health or physical FITNESS (1): *After three months without any exercise or training the champion's in poor shape.*
**6 in shape/out of shape** in a good or bad state of health or physical FITNESS (1): **get (yourself) into shape** *I've got to get into shape before summer.*
**7 knock/lick sb into shape** *informal* to make someone better so that they reach the necessary standard: *Some of them lack experience, but we'll soon knock them into shape.*
**8 take shape** to develop into a clear and definite form: *An idea was beginning to take shape in his mind.*
**9 in/of all shapes and sizes** of many different types: **come in all shapes and sizes** *Domestic pets come in all shapes and sizes.*

**shape²** *v* [T] **1** to influence something such as a belief, opinion etc and make it develop in a particular way: *People's political beliefs are often shaped by what they read in the newspapers.* **2** to make something have a particular shape, especially by pressing it: **shape sth into sth** *Shape the dough into small balls.* S3

**shape up** *phr v* [I] *informal* **1** to make progress and improve in the way you want: *The new recruits are shaping up nicely.* **2** to improve your behaviour or work: *If you don't shape up, I'll have to contact your parents.* **3 shape up or ship out** *AmE spoken* used to tell someone that if they do not improve they will be made to leave a place or their job

**shaped** /ʃeɪpt/ *adj* having a particular shape: **egg-shaped/V-shaped etc** *an L-shaped living room* | **be shaped like** *The building was shaped like a giant pyramid.*

**shape·less** /ˈʃeɪpləs/ *adj* **1** not having a clear or definite shape: *Why should fat women have to wear baggy, shapeless dresses?* **2** something such as a book or a plan that is shapeless does not seem to have a clear structure —**shapelessly** *adv* —**shapelessness** *n* [U]

**shape·ly** /ˈʃeɪpli/ *adj* having a body that has an attractive shape: *shapely curved legs* —**shapeliness** *n* [U]

**shard** /ʃɑːd‖ʃɑːrd/ also **sherd** *n* [C] a sharp piece of broken glass, metal etc

**share¹** /ʃeə‖ʃer/ *v* S1 W1
**1 ▶ USE EQUALLY ◀** [I,T] to have or use something that other people also have or use at the same time: *We don't have enough books for everyone, so you'll have to share.* | **share sth** *The last bus had gone, so the three of us shared a taxi.* | **share sth with sb** *I shared a room with her at college.* | **shared house/flat** *BrE* (=with people not related to each other living in it) —see BETWEEN (USAGE)
**2 ▶ LET SB USE STH ◀** [T] to let someone have or use something that belongs to you: *Even as a kid he'd never share his toys.* | **share sth with** *I shared my lunch with a few hungry pigeons.*
**3 ▶ DIVIDE ◀** also **share** sth ↔ **out** [T] to divide something between two or more people: **share sth between/among sb** *At his death, his property was shared out between his children.*
**4 ▶ SAME INTEREST/OPINION ETC ◀** [T] to have the same opinion, experience, feeling etc as someone else: *I share your concern about this.* | **share in sth** *His daughters did not share in his happiness.* | **share sth with sb** *Stubbornness was a characteristic he shared with his mother.* | **share an interest** (=have the same interest in something as someone else)
**5 ▶ RESPONSIBILITY ◀** [T] to be equally responsible for doing something, paying for something etc: *I own the house, but we share the bills.* | *We all share some blame for the mess-up.*
**6 ▶ TELL SB STH ◀** [I,T] to tell other people about an idea, secret, problem etc: *It's always better to share your worries.* | **share sth with sb** *Are you going to share the joke with us?* | **share** *especially AmE: If you feel the need to share we're all listening.*

**7 share and share alike** *spoken* used to say that you should share things fairly and equally between everyone

S1 W1 **share²** *n*
**1** ▶ **PART OF STH** ◀ [singular] the part of something that belongs to you, or that should be paid for or done by you: [+ **of/in**] *I gave them my share of the bill and left.* | *a share in the profits* | **do your share** (=do your part of a job, duty etc that you share with other people) *I do my share of the housework.*
**2 flat/house share** *BrE* a situation in which people who are not related to each other live together
**3 your (fair) share a)** as much or more of something as you could reasonably expect to have: *She's had more than her fair share of bad luck this year.* | *You've sure had your share of problems, haven't you?* **b)** as much as everyone else: *Don't worry – you'll get your fair share.* | *I've made my share of mistakes.*
**4 share in** your part in an activity, event etc: *Employees are always given a share in decision-making.*
**5** ▶ **FINANCIAL** ◀ [C] one of the equal parts into which the ownership of a company is divided: [+ **in**] *He decided to sell his shares in Allied Chemicals.* | **share offer/issue** (=a time when shares in a company are sold or begin to be sold) —compare STOCK¹ (3)
**6** ▶ **FARM TOOL** ◀ [C] *old-fashioned* a PLOUGHSHARE —see also **the lion's share** (LION (3)), TIMESHARE —**sharing** *n* [U]

**share·crop·per** /ˈ·ˌ··/ *n* [C] *especially AmE* a farmer who uses someone else's land, and gives the owner half the crop in return

**share·hold·er** /ˈʃeəˌhəʊldə‖ˈʃerˌhoʊldər/ *n* [C] *especially BrE* someone who owns shares in a business; STOCKHOLDER *especially AmE*: *Shareholders have been told to expect an even lower result for 1995.*

**share in·dex** /ˈ· ˌ··/ *n* [C] *technical* an official and public list of SHARE² (5) prices

**share·ware** /ˈʃeəweə‖ˈʃerwer/ *n* [U] free or cheap computer SOFTWARE that is produced by small companies

**sha·ri·a, sheria** /ʃəˈriːə/ *n* [U] a system of religious laws followed by Muslims

**shark** /ʃɑːk‖ʃɑːrk/ *n* [C] **1** *plural* **shark** or **sharks** a large fish with several rows of very sharp teeth that is sometimes considered to be dangerous to humans **2** *informal* someone who cheats other people out of money —see also LOAN SHARK

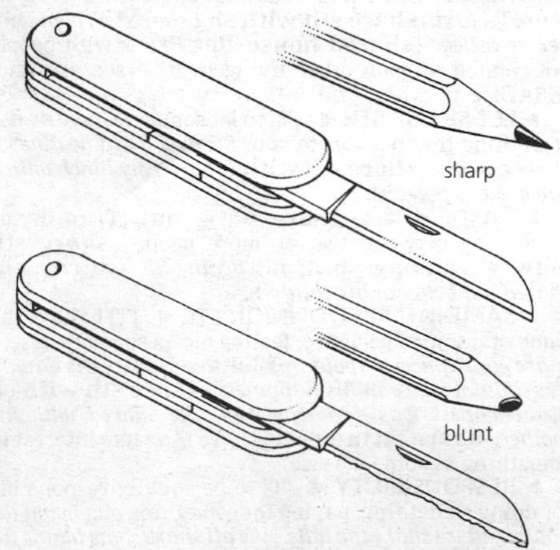


S3 W2 **sharp¹** /ʃɑːp‖ʃɑːrp/ *adj*
**1** ▶ **ABLE TO CUT** ◀ having a very thin edge or point that can cut things easily: *Peel the apples using a sharp knife.* | *The metal was jagged with lots of sharp edges.* | **razor sharp** (=very sharp) —opposite BLUNT¹ (1)
**2** ▶ **SOUNDS** ◀ loud, short, and sudden: *The branch broke with a sharp crack.* | *a sharp cry of pain*
**3** ▶ **TASTE** ◀ having a slightly bitter taste: *Add mustard to give the dressing a sharper taste.*
**4** ▶ **DIRECTION** ◀ a sudden extreme change of direction: **sharp bend/turn** *We came to a sharp bend in the road.* | **sharp left/right** *Take a sharp left after the church.*
**5** ▶ **PAIN** ◀ sudden and severe: *I felt a sharp pain in my back.* —see graph at PAIN¹
**6** ▶ **REMARK** ◀ severe, angry, and criticizing: *a sharp rebuke* | *John's tone was sharp.* | **be sharp with sb** *The boss can be very sharp with people when she's busy.*
**7 have a sharp tongue** to often talk to people in an angry, unkind, or criticizing way
**8** ▶ **PEOPLE** ◀ able to think and understand things very quickly, and not easily deceived: *a journalist with an extremely sharp mind*
**9** ▶ **EYES** ◀ able to see and notice details very well: **a sharp eye for detail** (=the ability to notice and deal with details)
**10 keep a sharp eye on sb** to watch someone very carefully, especially because you do not trust them: *Keep a sharp eye on the kids at all times!*
**11** ▶ **PENCIL** ◀ having a very thin point, that can draw an exact line —opposite BLUNT¹ (1)
**12** ▶ **SHAPE** ◀ not rounded or curved; ANGULAR: *Janice had the same sharp features as her mother.*
**13** ▶ **CHANGE** ◀ a sharp increase, rise etc is very sudden and very big: *a sharp increase in prices*
**14** ▶ **DIFFERENCE** ◀ clear and definite, so that there is no doubt: *The distinction between public and private services is much less sharp here.* | **in sharp contrast** (=very different from someone or something else) *Keele wore a smart suit, in sharp contrast to everyone's else's casual attire.*
**15** ▶ **PICTURE/IMAGES** ◀ having a shape that is clear and detailed: *The outlines of the cypress trees were sharp and clear.*
**16 a) F sharp/D sharp/C sharp etc** a musical note that is sharp has been raised by one SEMITONE from the note F, D, C etc —see picture at MUSIC **b)** if music or singing is sharp, it is played or sung at a slightly higher PITCH² (3) than it should be
**17** ▶ **MOVEMENT** ◀ quick and sudden: *The wind blew across the lake in sharp gusts.* | *a sharp intake of breath*
**18** ▶ **FEELINGS** ◀ very strong and unexpected: *I was left with a sharp sense of disappointment.*
**19 sharp practice** behaviour, especially in business, that is dishonest but not illegal
**20 a sharp frost** a very cold severe FROST¹ (1)
**21 be on the sharp end of sth** to experience the worst effects of something: *We were always on the sharp end of clients' complaints.*
**22 sb looks sharp** *AmE* if someone looks sharp, they are dressed well and attractively; SMART¹ (2) *especially BrE*: *Tod looked really sharp in his tux.* —**sharpness** *n* [U] —see also SHARPLY

**sharp²** *adv* **1 at ten-thirty/2 o'clock etc sharp** at exactly 10.30, 2.00 etc: *We're meeting at 10 o'clock sharp.* **2 sharp left/right** if you turn sharp left or right, you make a sudden change of direction to the left or right: *You turn sharp right at the crossroads.* **3 look sharp** *spoken* **a)** *BrE* used to tell someone to do something quickly: *If you look sharp you might catch him before he leaves for London.* **b)** *especially AmE* used to warn someone about something: *Look sharp, the boss is coming!* **4** played or sung at a slightly higher PITCH² (3) than is correct

**sharp³** *n* [C] **1** a musical note that has been raised one SEMITONE above the note written **2** the sign (♯) in a line of written music used to show this —see picture at MUSIC

**sharp-eared** /ˌ· ˈ·◂/ *adj* able to hear very well

**sharp·en** /ˈʃɑːpən‖ˈʃɑːr-/ *v* **1** [I,T] to become sharper or make something sharper: *Sharpen all your pencils before* *the test.|The light grew brighter and the shadows sharpened.* **2** [T] to make a feeling stronger and more urgent: *These latest moves have sharpened fears of a military conflict.*

**sharpen** sth ↔ **up** *phr v* [T] to improve something so that it is up to the necessary standard, quality etc: *We need more rehearsals to sharpen up the dance routine.*

**sharp·en·er** /ˈʃɑːpənə, ˈʃɑːpnə‖ˈʃɑːrpənər, ˈʃɑːrpnər/ *n* [C] a tool or machine for sharpening pencils, knives etc

**sharp·er** /ˈʃɑːpə‖ˈʃɑːrpər/ *n* [C] *old-fashioned* someone who cheats or is dishonest

**sharp-eyed** /ˌ· ˈ·◂/ *adj* able to see very well and notice small details: *My sharp-eyed mother had already spotted him.*

**sharp·ish** /ˈʃɑːpɪʃ‖ˈʃɑːr-/ *adv BrE spoken* quickly: *We'd better leave pretty sharpish if we want to catch that bus.*

W3 **sharp·ly** /ˈʃɑːpli‖ˈʃɑːr-/ *adv*
**1** ▶ **SPEAK/LOOK** ◀ in a severe and disapproving way: *"What do you mean by that?" Paul asked sharply.|I glanced at her sharply, but said nothing.*|**sharply critical** (=very critical and disapproving)
**2** ▶ **CHANGE** ◀ if something rises, falls etc sharply, it rises or falls quickly and suddenly: *Prices have risen sharply over the last few months.*
**3** ▶ **MOVE** ◀ quickly and suddenly: *She heard a noise behind her and turned around sharply.*
**4** ▶ **SHOW DIFFERENCES** ◀ clearly and definitely: *Opinion is sharply divided.*
**5 sharply contrasted/contrasting** very different: *His aggressive behaviour contrasted sharply with the mild manners of his brother.*

**sharp-wit·ted** /ˌ· ˈ··◂/ *adj* able to think and react very quickly

**shat** /ʃæt/ the past tense and past participle of SHIT[2]

**shat·ter** /ˈʃætə‖-ər/ *v* **1** [I,T] to break suddenly into very small pieces, or to make something break in this way: **[+ into]** *The plate hit the floor, and shattered into tiny bits.*|**shatter sth** *A stone shattered the window.* **2** [T] to make someone feel diaspointed by showing or proving that someone's hopes or beliefs are impossible or wrong: *Hopes of a peace agreement were shattered today when talks broke down again.*|**shatter sb's illusions** *A few weeks in a tiny damp room soon shattered his illusions about university life.*

**shat·tered** /ˈʃætəd‖-ərd/ *adj* [not before noun] **1** very shocked and upset: *I wasn't just disappointed, I was absolutely shattered.* **2** *BrE informal* very tired; EXHAUSTED (1): *By the time we got home we were both shattered.*

**shat·ter·ing** /ˈʃætərɪŋ/ *adj* **1** very shocking and upsetting: *shattering news from home* **2** *BrE informal* making you very tired

**shat·ter·proof** /ˈʃætəpruːf‖-tər-/ *adj* glass that is shatterproof is specially designed so that it will not form sharp dangerous pieces if it is broken

S3 **shave**[1] /ʃeɪv/ *v* **1** [I,T] to cut off hair very close to the skin, especially from the face: *I washed and shaved, then hurried out of the house.|His hands shake so badly his wife has to shave him.*|**shave your head/legs/armpits etc** *Once Jenni shaved her head for a bet.* **2** [T] to touch something slightly as you pass it; SCRAPE[1] (2): *The car just shaved the wall as we went round the corner.*

**shave** sth↔ **off** *phr v* [T] **1** to remove hair by shaving: *They made me shave off my beard when I joined the army.* **2** to remove very thin pieces from the surface of something, using a knife or other cutting tool: *I had to shave a few millimetres off the bottom of the door to make it shut.* **3** to reduce an amount or number very slightly: *She's shaved half a second off the world record.*

**shave**[2] *n* **1** [C usually singular] an act of shaving your face: *He looked as if he needed a shave.*|**have a shave** *I'll just have a shave before we go.* **2 a close shave a)** a situation in which you only just avoid an accident or something bad **b)** a shave that cuts the hair very close to your face

**shav·en** /ˈʃeɪvən/ *adj* with all the hair shaved off: *his shaven head* —see also CLEAN-SHAVEN, UNSHAVEN

**shav·er** /ˈʃeɪvə‖-ər/ *n* [C] a tool used for shaving, especially a small electric machine —compare RAZOR

**shav·ing bag** /ˈ···/ *n* [C] *AmE* a TOILET BAG —see picture at BAG[1]

**shaving brush** /ˈ·· ·/ *n* [C] a brush used for spreading soap or shaving cream over your face when you shave

**shaving cream** /ˈ·· ·/ *n* [U] a mixture made of soap, used for putting on your face when you shave

**shaving foam** /ˈ·· ·/ *n* [U] a special cream that you put on your face when you shave

**shav·ings** /ˈʃeɪvɪŋz/ *n* [plural] very thin pieces, especially of wood, cut from a surface with a sharp blade: *a pile of wood shavings on the floor*

**shawl** /ʃɔːl‖ʃɒːl/ *n* [C] a piece of soft cloth, in a square or TRIANGULAR shape, that is worn around the shoulders or head, especially by women: *an embroidered shawl*

**she-** /ʃiː/ *prefix* female: *a she-goat|a she-devil* (=evil woman)

**she**[1] /ʃi; *strong* ʃiː/ *pron* [used as the subject of a verb] S1
**1 a)** a woman or girl who has been mentioned already, W1 or who the person you are talking to already knows about: *What did she say when you told her?|Why don't you ask Beth – she's got plenty of money.|I saw you talking to that girl. Who is she?* **b)** a female animal who has been mentioned already **2 a)** used to talk about a boat or ship: *The QE2 docked at Portsmouth Harbour where she will spend the next few months being refurbished.* **b)** used to talk about a country **c)** used to talk about a vehicle or machine that you are very fond of

**she**[2] /ʃiː/ *n* [singular] *informal* a female: *What a beautiful child! Is it a he or a she?*

**sheaf** /ʃiːf/ *plural* **sheaves** /ʃiːvz/ *n* [C + **of**] **1** a bunch of wheat, corn etc tied together after it has been cut **2** several pieces of paper held or tied together

**shear** /ʃɪə‖ʃɪr/ *v past tense* **sheared** *past participle* **sheared** *or* **shorn** /ʃɔːn‖ʃɒːn/ **1** [T] to cut the wool off a sheep **2 be shorn of** to have something valuable or important taken away from you: *Shorn of all real power by the new laws, the deputy soon resigned.* **3** also **shear off, shear away** [I,T] *technical* to break apart because of a sideways or twisting force **4** [T] *literary* to cut off someone's hair

**shear·er** /ˈʃɪərə‖ˈʃɪrər/ also **sheep shearer** *n* [C] someone who cuts the wool off sheep

**shears** /ʃɪəz‖ʃɪrz/ *n* [plural] a heavy tool for cutting, like a big pair of scissors: **a pair of shears** *Sam was trimming the hedge with a pair of garden shears.*

**sheath** /ʃiːθ/ *plural* **sheaths** /ʃiːðz/ *n* [C] **1** a cover for the blade of a knife or sword **2** *BrE* CONDOM **3** a close-fitting part of a plant or animal that acts as a protective covering

**sheathe** /ʃiːð/ *v* [T] **1** to put a knife or sword into a sheath: *He sheathed his sword.* **2** to be enclosed in a protective outer cover: **be sheathed in/with** *The nuclear reactor is sheathed with lead.*

**sheath·ing** /ˈʃiːðɪŋ/ *n* [C usually singular] a protective outer cover, for example for a building or a ship

**sheath knife** /ˈ· ·/ *n* [C] a knife with a fixed blade that does not fold, that is carried in a sheath

**sheaves** /ʃiːvz/ the plural of SHEAF

**she·bang** /ʃɪˈbæŋ/ *n* **the whole shebang** *informal, especially AmE* the whole thing: *It's a big project, and she's in charge of the whole shebang.*

**she·been** /ʃɪˈbiːn/ *n* [C] *informal, especially IrishE* a place where alcoholic drinks are sold illegally

**she'd** /ʃid; *strong* ʃiːd/ **1** the short form of 'she had': *She'd already gone when we got there.* **2** the short form of 'she would': *She'd like to come with us.*

**shed**[1] /ʃed/ *n* [C] **1** a small building, often made of S3 wood, used especially for storing things: *We had a tool*

S

*shed in our back yard.|a cattle shed|a garden shed* **2** a large industrial building where work is done, large vehicles are kept or machinery is stored etc

**shed²** *v* [T] *past tense and past participle* **shed** *present participle* **shedding**
**1 ▶ LIGHT ◀** if something sheds light, it lights the area around it: *The lamp shed a yellow glow onto the desk.*
**2 ▶ DROP/FALL OFF ◀ a)** to drop something or allow it to fall: *He strode across the bathroom, shedding wet clothes as he went.* **b)** if an animal sheds skin or hair or a plant sheds leaves etc, they fall off as part of a natural process: *Deciduous trees shed their leaves in autumn.|As it grows, a snake will regularly shed its skin.*
**3 ▶ GET RID OF ◀** to get rid of something that you no longer need or want: *The company is planning to shed about a quarter of its workforce.|I shed my inhibitions and joined the dancing.*|**shed pounds/stones** (=get thinner by losing several pounds etc) *I'd like to shed a few pounds.*
**4 shed light on** to make something easier to understand, by providing new or better information: *We're hoping his letter will shed some light on the mystery.*
**5 ▶ WATER ◀** if something sheds water, the water flows off its surface, instead of sinking into it
**6 shed blood** to kill or injure people, especially during a war or a fight: *Too much blood has already been shed in this conflict.* —see also BLOODSHED
**7 shed tears** *especially literary* to cry: *She had not shed a single tear during the funeral.*
**8 shed its load** *BrE* if a vehicle sheds its load, the goods it is carrying accidentally fall off

**sheen** /ʃiːn/ *n* [singular, U] a soft smooth shiny appearance; LUSTRE (1): *Her hair had a lovely coppery sheen.*

S2 W3 **sheep** /ʃiːp/ *n* [C] *plural* **sheep** **1** a grass-eating farm animal that is kept for its wool and its meat: *Sheep were grazing on the hillside.|a sheep farmer*|**a flock of sheep** (=a group of sheep) —see also LAMB **2** [often plural] someone who does not think independently, but follows what everyone else does or thinks **3 separate the sheep from the goats** to find out which people are intelligent, skilful, successful etc, and which are not: *This test should really separate the sheep from the goats.* **4 make sheep's eyes at** *old-fashioned* to look at someone in a way that shows you love them —see also **black sheep, count sheep** (COUNT¹ (2)), **a wolf in sheep's clothing** (WOLF¹ (2))

**sheep-dip** /ˈ· ·/ *n* [C,U] a chemical used to kill insects that live in sheep's wool, or a special bath in which this chemical is used

**sheep dog** /ˈ· ·/ *n* [C] **1** a dog that is trained to control sheep **2** *informal* a dog of a type that is often used for this, usually a COLLIE —see also OLD ENGLISH SHEEPDOG

**sheep·fold** /ˈʃiːpfəʊld‖-foʊld/ *n* [C] an area of land with a fence or wall around it, used for keeping sheep in

**sheep·ish** /ˈʃiːpɪʃ/ *adj* uncomfortable or embarrassed because you know that you have done something silly or wrong: *Richard was looking sheepish.* —**sheepishly** *adv*: *She grinned sheepishly.* —**sheepishness** *n* [U]

**sheep·pen** /ˈ· ·/ *n* [C] a small area of ground with a fence around it, used for keeping sheep together for a short time

**sheep·skin** /ˈʃiːpˌskɪn/ *n* [C,U] the skin of a sheep with the wool still on it: *a sheepskin coat*

**sheer¹** /ʃɪə‖ʃɪr/ *adj* **1 sheer luck/happiness/stupidity etc** luck, happiness etc with no other feeling or quality mixed with it: *It was sheer bliss not having to get up.|sheer hypocrisy* **2 the sheer weight/size etc of** used to emphasize how heavy, big etc something is: *The sheer size of the country makes communications difficult* **3** a sheer drop, cliff, slope etc is very steep and almost VERTICAL¹ (1): *There was a sheer drop from to the sea 200 feet below.* **4** sheer NYLON, silk etc is very thin and fine, so that it is almost transparent: *sheer stockings*

**sheer²** *adv* straight up or down in an almost VERTICAL¹ (1) line: *The mountains rise sheer from the sea.*

**sheer³** *v* [I] **sheer off/away** to change direction suddenly, especially in order to avoid something: *The boat sheered away and headed out to sea again.*

**sheet** /ʃiːt/ *n* [C] **1** a large piece of thin cotton or NYLON cloth that you put on a bed to lie on or lie under: **change the sheets** (=put clean sheets on a bed) **2** a thin flat piece of something such as paper, glass, or metal, that usually has four sides: [+ **of**] *I picked up a clean sheet of paper and began to write.|a sheet of glass* —see picture on page 416 **3** a large flat area of something such as ice or water spread over a surface: *A sheet of ice covered the lake.* **4** a sheet of rain or fire is a very large moving mass of it: *The rain was coming down in sheets.* **5** *technical* a rope or chain that controls the angle between a sail and the wind on a ship —see also BAKING SHEET, BALANCE SHEET, **as white as a sheet** (WHITE¹ (2)), **clean sheet** (CLEAN¹ (10))  S2 W2

**sheet an·chor** /ˈ· ˌ··/ *n* [C] **1** a ship's largest ANCHOR¹ (1), used only in times of danger **2** someone or something that you depend on very much in a difficult or dangerous situation

**sheet·ing** /ˈʃiːtɪŋ/ *n* [U] cloth or other material that is made into sheets, or used in the form of a sheet: *The roof was covered in plastic sheeting.|cotton sheeting*

**sheet light·ning** /ˌ· ˈ··, ˈ· ˌ··/ *n* [U] a type of LIGHTNING that appears as a sudden flash of brightness covering a large area of sky —compare FORKED LIGHTNING

**sheet met·al** /ˈ· ˌ··/ *n* [U] metal in the form of thin sheets

**sheet mu·sic** /ˈ· ˌ··, ˌ· ˈ··/ *n* [U] music that is printed on single sheets and not fastened together inside a cover

**sheikh, sheik** /ʃeɪk‖ʃiːk/ *n* [C] **1** an Arab chief or prince **2** a Muslim religious leader or teacher

**sheikh·dom, sheikdom** /ˈʃeɪkdəm‖ˈʃiːk-/ *n* [C] a place that is governed by an Arab chief or prince

**shei·la** /ˈʃiːlə/ *n* [C] *AustrE or NZE slang* a young woman

**shek·el** /ˈʃekəl/ *n* [C] **1** the standard unit of money in Israel **2 shekels** [plural] *humorous* money

**shelf** /ʃelf/ *n plural* **shelves** /ʃelvz/ **1** [C] a long flat narrow board fixed onto a wall or in a frame or cupboard, used for putting things on or storing things on: *Put it back on the top shelf.|shelves of books|supermarket shelves* **2** [C] a narrow surface of rock shaped like a shelf, especially underwater **3 off the shelf** available to be bought immediately without having to be specially designed or ordered: *off-the-shelf computer software packages* —compare OFF-THE-PEG **4 be (left) on the shelf a)** *old-fashioned* considered to be too old to get married **b)** if a plan, idea etc is left on the shelf it is not used or considered —see also SHELVE¹ S3 W3

**shelf life** /ˈ· ·/ *n* [singular] the length of time that food, chemicals etc can be kept in a shop before they become too old to sell: *Chocolate has a shelf life of 9 months.*

**she'll** /ʃil; *strong* ʃiːl/ the short form of 'she will': *She'll be back in a minute.*

**shells**

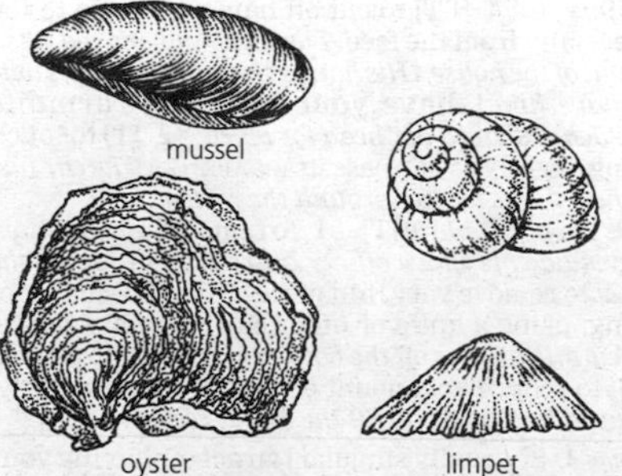


**shell¹** /ʃel/ *n* **1** [C] **a)** a hard outer part that covers or protects a nut, egg, or seed and some types of animal: *a*  W3

*snail shell* **b)** the shell of a small sea animal such as a COCKLE or MUSSEL especially one that is lying on a beach **2** [C] a metal container, like a large bullet, which is full of an explosive substance and is fired from a large gun: *We ran for cover as shells dropped all around us.* **3** [C] *especially AmE* a metal tube containing a bullet and an explosive substance used in a gun; CARTRIDGE (1) **4** [C] the outside structure of something, especially the part of a building that remains when the rest of it has been destroyed **5 come out of your shell** to become less shy and more confident and willing to talk to people: *She's really come out of her shell since she went to college.*

**shell²** *v* [T] **1** to fire shells at something: *Opposition forces have been shelling the town since yesterday.* **2** to remove something such as beans or nuts from a shell or a POD¹ (1): *Josie was shelling peas on the verandah.*

**shell out** *phr v* [T] *informal* to pay a lot of money for something, especially unwillingly: *If you want the repairs done right, you'll have to shell out at least $800.*

**shel·lac** /ʃə'læk/ *n* [U] a kind of transparent paint for protecting or hardening surfaces

**shel·lack·ing** /ʃə'lækɪŋ/ *n* [singular] *AmE informal* a situation in which you are severely defeated or criticized: *The Chargers got a shellacking in the Superbowl.*

**shell·fire** /'ʃelfaɪə‖-faɪr/ also **shell·ing** /'ʃelɪŋ/ *n* [U] the firing of large guns at a place: **come under shellfire** (=have these guns fired at you) *The city came under heavy shellfire.*

**shell·fish** /'ʃel,fɪʃ/ *plural* **shellfish** *n* **1** [C,U] a sea or water animal that does not have a BACKBONE, but has a shell: *Lobsters and oysters are shellfish.* **2** [U] such animals as a type of food: *Do you like shellfish?*

**shell shock** /'· ·/ *n* [U] *old-fashioned* a type of mental illness caused by the shock of fighting in a war or battle

**shell shocked** /'· ·/ *adj* **1** *informal* feeling tired confused or anxious because of a recent difficult experience: *I think she's a bit shell-shocked after her exams.* **2** mentally ill because of the terrible experiences of war

**shell suit** /'· ·/ *n* [C] *BrE* a light brightly-coloured piece of clothing consisting of trousers and a JACKET (1), that fit tightly at the wrists and at the bottom of the legs

**shel·ter¹** /'ʃeltə‖-ər/ *n* **1** [U] a place to live, considered as one of the basic needs of life: *They are in desperate need of food, clothing and shelter.* **2** [U] protection, from danger or from wind, rain, hot sun etc: **the shelter of** *We eventually reached the shelter of the caves.* | *They grow well in the shelter of big oak trees.* | **take shelter** *The men took shelter in a bombed-out farmhouse.* | **run for shelter** *All around me, people were running for shelter.* | **give sb shelter** (=protect them, especially from the weather or from danger) —see also TAX SHELTER **3** [C] a building or an area with a roof over it that protects you from the weather or from danger: *a shelter for the homeless* | *We tried to fix up a shelter from the rain.* | **air-raid shelter** (=to protect people from bombs dropped by planes) | **bus shelter** (=a small structure with a roof where you wait for a bus)

**shelter²** *v* **1** [T] to provide a place where someone or something is protected, especially from the weather or from danger: *Collins was arrested for sheltering enemy soldiers.* | **shelter sb/sth from** *Plant herbs next to a wall to shelter them from the wind.* **2** [I] to stay in or under a place where you are protected from the weather or from danger: [+ **from**] *We sat in the shade, sheltering from the sun.*

**shel·tered** /'ʃeltəd‖-ərd/ *adj* **1 a sheltered life/childhood/existence etc** a life etc in which someone has been too protected from difficult or unpleasant experience: *Marian's sheltered upbringing had left her unprepared for such extreme poverty.* **2** a place that is sheltered is protected from extreme weather conditions: *a sheltered valley* **3 sheltered accommodation/housing** *BrE* a place for people to live who cannot fully look after themselves where help is provided if they need it: *sheltered accommodation for the elderly*

**shelve** /ʃelv/ *v* **1** [T] to decide not to continue with a plan, idea etc, although you might continue with it at a later time: *We had to shelve the new building plans due to lack of funding.* **2** [I always + adv/prep] land that shelves is at a slight angle: [+ **up/down/towards etc**] *The garden shelves gently towards the sea.* **3** [T] to put something on a shelf, especially books

**shelves** /ʃelvz/ the plural of SHELF

**shelv·ing** /'ʃelvɪŋ/ *n* **1** [U] wood, metal etc used for shelves **2** a set of shelves fixed to a wall

**she·nan·i·gans** /ʃɪ̈'nænɪgənz/ *n* [plural] *informal* **1** bad behaviour that is not very serious; MISCHIEF **2** slightly dishonest activities

**shep·herd¹** /'ʃepəd‖-ərd/ *n* [C] someone whose job is to take care of sheep

**shepherd²** *v* [T always + adv/prep] to lead or guide a group of people somewhere, making sure that they go where you want them to go: **shepherd sb into/out/towards etc** *I don't enjoy those tours where you're always being shepherded around some old ruins.*

**shep·herd·ess** /'ʃepədes‖-ərdɪ̈s/ *n* [C] a woman or girl whose job is to take care of sheep

**shepherd's pie** /,·· '·/ *n* [U] a baked dish made of small pieces of cooked meat covered with cooked potato

**sher·bet** /'ʃɜːbət‖'ʃɜːr-/ *n* **1** [C] *AmE* a frozen sweet made with water, fruit, milk and the white part of an egg **2** [U] *BrE* a powder that is eaten as a sweet

**sherd** /ʃɜːd‖ʃɜːrd/ *n* [C] another spelling of SHARD

**sher·iff** /'ʃerɪ̈f/ *n* [C] **1** an elected law officer of a COUNTY in the US **2** also **High Sheriff** the chief officer of the King or Queen in a COUNTY of England and Wales, who has mostly ceremonial duties **3** the chief judge in a DISTRICT (2) or COUNTY in Scotland

**sheriff's court** /'·· ,·/ *n* [C] the lower court of law in Scotland, dealing with CIVIL (3) and criminal cases

**Sher·pa** /'ʃɜːpə‖'ʃɜːr-/ *n* [C] a Himalayan person who is often employed to guide people through mountains

**sher·ry** /'ʃeri/ *n* [C, U] a pale or dark brown strong wine, originally from Spain

**she's** /ʃiz; *strong* ʃiːz/ **1** the short form of 'she is' **2** the short form of 'she has'

**Shet·land po·ny** /,ʃetlənd 'pəuni‖-'pouni/ *n* [C] a small strong horse with long rough hair

**shew** /ʃəu‖ʃou/ *v* [I,T] an old spelling of SHOW

**shh** /ʃ/ *interjection* used to tell people to be quiet: *Shh! I can't hear what he's saying.*

**Shi·a, Shiah** /'ʃiːə/ *n* **1 the Shiah** the Shiite branch of the Muslim religion **2** [C] a Shiite

**shi·a·tsu** /ʃi'ɑːtsuː/ *n* [U] a Japanese form of MASSAGE (=pressing and rubbing someone's body) used to prevent or treat physical or emotional problems

**shib·bo·leth** /'ʃɪbəleθ‖-lɪ̈θ/ *n* [C] *formal* an old idea, custom or principle that you think is no longer important or suitable for modern times

**shields**

**shield¹** /ʃiːld/ *n* [C] **1 a)** a thing that soldiers used consisting of a broad piece of metal or leather **b)** also **riot shield** a piece of equipment made of strong plastic, used by the police to protect themselves against angry crowds **2** something in the shape of a shield, wide at the top and curving to a point at the bottom, that is used for a COAT OF ARMS, a prize in sport etc **3** something that protects a person or thing against harm or damage: *the ozone layer, the shield that protects the Earth from the Sun's harmful rays*

**shield²** *v* [T] to protect someone or something from being harmed, or damaged: *Women will often lie to shield even the most abusive partner.* | **shield sb/sth from sth** *He held up his hands, shielding his eyes from the sun.* | *import tariffs that shield firms from foreign competition*

W3 **shift¹** /ʃɪft/ *v*
**1 ▶ MOVE ◀ a)** [I,T] to move from one place or position to another, or make something do this: *Jonas stood and listened, shifting uncomfortably from one foot to another.* | *The sun had shifted around to the west.* | *She shifted her gaze from me to Bobby with a look of suspicion.* **b)** [T] *informal* to move something, especially by picking it up and carrying it: *Give me a hand to shift these chairs.*
**2 shift attention/emphasis/focus** to change a situation, discussion etc by giving special attention to one idea or subject instead of to a previous one: *The president is shifting the focus of the debate to foreign policy issues.* | **attention/emphasis/focus shifts** *Under these new arrangements, the emphasis has shifted from state provision to personal responsibility.*

**3 ▶ COSTS/SPENDING ◀** [T always + adv/prep] to change the way that money is paid or spent: *This simply shifts the cost of medical insurance from employer to employee.* | *the need to shift more resources towards the alleviation of poverty*
**4 ▶ OPINIONS ◀** [I,T] to change your opinions or beliefs, especially about political matters: *Opinion in the country was beginning to shift to the right.* | *shifting attitudes towards marriage* | **shift your ground** (=change your opinion) *The government shifted its ground, and gradually lent its support to African nationalism.*
**5 shift the blame/responsibility** to make someone else responsible for something, especially for something bad that has happened: *It was a blatant attempt to shift the responsibility for the crime on to the victim.*
**6 ▶ DIRT/MARKS ◀** [T] *BrE* to remove dirt or marks from a surface or piece of clothing: *a new washing powder that will shift any stain*
**7 ▶ IN A CAR ◀** [I,T] *especially AmE* to change the gears (GEAR¹ (1)) when you are driving: *I shifted into second gear.*

**shift²** *n* [C] **1** a change in the way people think about something, in the way something is done etc: **[+ from/to]** *a major shift from manufacturing to service industries* | **[+ in]** *a shift in emphasis from defense spending to civilian spending* | **a marked shift** (=a very noticeable change) *There has been a marked shift in attitudes towards homosexuality.* **2 a)** one of the periods during each day and night when workers in a factory, hospital etc are at work: **do/work a shift** *I usually work the night shift, which is from 10 at night till 6 in the morning.* | *Do you do shift work?* **b)** the workers who work during one of these periods **3 a)** a simple straight loose-fitting woman's dress **b)** *old use* a similar piece of clothing worn as underwear **4** the KEY¹ (3) on a computer or TYPEWRITER that you press to print a capital letter: *To run the spellchecker, press SHIFT and F7.* **5** *old use* a clever trick or method

**shift key** /ˈ· ·/ *n* [C] the KEY¹ (3) on a KEYBOARD that you press to make a capital letter

**shift·less** /ˈʃɪftləs/ *adj* lazy and seeming to have no interest in working hard or trying to succeed: *my shiftless nephew, who was never any good* —**shiftlessly** *adv* —**shiftlessness** *n*

**shift·y** /ˈʃɪfti/ *adj informal* looking dishonest and slightly nervous: *a shifty-looking little man* | *shifty eyes* —**shiftily** *adv* —**shiftiness** *n* [U]

**Shi·ite** /ˈʃiː-aɪt/ *n* a member of one of the two main branches of the Muslim religion —compare SUNNI —**Shiite** *adj*

**shil·ling** /ˈʃɪlɪŋ/ *n* [C] **1** a coin used in Britain until 1971, worth 12 old pence and 1/20 of £1 **2** a unit of money used in Kenya, Uganda, and Somalia

**shil·ly-shal·ly** /ˈʃɪli ˌʃæli/ *v* [I] *informal* to waste time or take too long to make a decision

**shim·mer** /ˈʃɪmə‖-ər/ *v* [I] to shine with a soft light that looks as if it shakes slightly: *The lake shimmered in the moonlight.* —**shimmer** *n* [U] *the shimmer of the desert air in the midday heat*

**shin¹** /ʃɪn/ *n* [C] the front part of your leg between your knee and your foot —see picture at BODY

**shin²** *v* [I] **shin up/shin down** to climb up or down a tree, pole etc by using your hands and legs, especially quickly; SHINNY *AmE*: *to shin up the drainpipe*

**shin·bone** /ˈ· ·/ *n* [C] the front bone in your leg below your knee; TIBIA —see picture at SKELETON

**shin·dig** /ˈʃɪndɪɡ/ *n* [C] *old-fashioned* a noisy party

**shine¹** /ʃaɪn/ *v past tense and past participle* **shone** /ʃɒn‖ʃoʊn/ S3 **1** [I] to produce light: *At last the sun was shining after weeks of rain.* | **[+ in/on]** *That lamp's shining in my eyes.* **2** [I] to look bright and shiny: *a big basket of shining fish of every shape and size* | *I want you to clean this kitchen until it shines.* **3** [T] to hold or point a lamp, light etc so that the light from it goes in a particular direction: **shine sth into/across/onto etc** *Shine the flashlight over here so that I can see what I'm doing.* **4** [I] if your eyes shine, or your face shines, you have an expression of happiness: *"I passed!" exclaimed Rufus, his eyes shining.* **5** [I not in progressive] to be very good at something: **[+ in/at]** *He really shines in history.*
**shine through** *phr v* [I] if a quality that someone has shines through, you can easily see that they have it: *What shines through in all her work is her enthusiasm for life.*

**shine²** *past tense and past participle* **shined** *v* [T] to make something bright by rubbing it; polish

**shine³** *n* **1** [singular, U] the brightness that something has when light shines on it: *The old table has a beautiful shine.* **2** [singular] an act of making something bright by polishing it: **give sth a shine** *Give your shoes a good shine before you go.* **3 take a shine to** *informal* to like someone very much when you have only just met them —see also **(come) rain or shine** (RAIN¹ (4))

**shin·gle** /ˈʃɪŋɡəl/ *n* **1** [C,U] one of many small thin pieces of building material, especially wood, used to cover a roof or wall **2** [U] small round pieces of stone on a beach: *shingle glistening with broken shells* —see picture on page 835 **3 hang out your shingle** *AmE* to start your own business, especially as a doctor or lawyer

**shin·gles** /ˈʃɪŋɡəlz/ *n* [U] a disease caused by an infection of the nerve endings, which produces painful red spots

**shin·ing** /ˈʃaɪnɪŋ/ *adj* [only before noun] excellent in a way that is easy to see: **a shining example of** *O'Reilly was a shining example of courage on the battlefield.*

**shin·ny** /ˈʃɪni/ *v* [I] *AmE* **shinny up/down** to SHIN²

**Shin·to** /ˈʃɪntəʊ‖-toʊ/ also **Shin·to·is·m** /ˈʃɪntəʊɪzəm‖-toʊ-/ *n* [U] the ancient religion of Japan that has gods who represent various parts of nature, and gives great importance to people who died in the past

**shin·y** /ˈʃaɪni/ *adj* smooth and bright: *a shiny polished table* | *shiny hair* | *a big shiny limousine* —**shininess** *n* [U] —see picture at SLIP¹

**-ship** /ʃɪp/ *suffix (in nouns)* **1 a)** the state of having a particular position or job: *Full membership* (=being a full member) *of the club costs $35.* | *professorship* (=the job of PROFESSOR) **b)** the time during which this lasts: *their long friendship* | *during his premiership* **2** the art or skill of a particular person: *her peerless musicianship | a work of great scholarship* —see also -MANSHIP **3** the whole group of a particular group: *a magazine with a readership of 9000* (=with 9000 readers) **4** forms part of certain titles: *your ladyship*

S2 W2 **ship¹** /ʃɪp/ *n* [C] **1** a large boat used for carrying people or goods across the sea: *a cruise ship | a merchant ship* | **by ship** *Most of the island's supplies are brought in by ship.* **2** a large SPACECRAFT or aircraft **3 ships that pass in the night** people who meet for a short time and then never meet again **4 when your ship comes in** used when you are wishing that something will suddenly happen to make you rich: *When my ship comes in, I'll quit work and travel around the world.*

**ship²** *past tense* **shipped** *present participle* **shipping** *v* [T] **1** to send or carry something by ship: **ship sth out/to etc** *I'm flying over to the States and having my car shipped out later.* **2** to deliver goods or make them available for people to buy: *The new Windows software was announced in April and they're planning to ship it in October.* **3** to order someone to go somewhere: **ship sb off/out etc** *As soon as the doctor saw her, he shipped her straight off to the hospital. | I was in Heidelberg at the time, about to be shipped out to Vietnam.* **4 ship water** if a boat ships water, water comes into it over its sides **5 ship oars** to stop rowing and to bring the OARS into the boat —see also **shape up or ship out** (SHAPE² (3))

**ship·board** /ˈʃɪpbɔːd‖-bɔːrd/ *n* [U] **on shipboard** on a ship

**ship·build·er** /ˈʃɪpˌbɪldə‖-ər/ *n* [C] a company that makes ships —**shipbuilding** *n* [U] *an old shipbuilding town*

**ship·load** /ˈʃɪpləʊd‖-loʊd/ *n* [C] the amount of goods or people a ship can carry: **[+ of]** *A shipload of new cars has just arrived.*

**ship·mate** /ˈʃɪpmeɪt/ *n* [C] a SAILOR*'s* shipmate is another sailor who is working on the same ship

**ship·ment** /ˈʃɪpmənt/ *n* [C,U] a load of goods sent by sea, road, or air, or the act of sending them: **[+ of]** *The goods are now ready for shipment. | a large shipment of grain*

**ship·per** /ˈʃɪpə‖-ər/ *n* [C] a company that sends goods to places by ship

**ship·ping** /ˈʃɪpɪŋ/ *n* [U] **1** ships considered as a group: *The port is closed to all shipping.* **2** all the ships belonging to a particular country: *Israeli shipping was excluded from the Straits of Tiran.* **3** the delivery of goods, especially by ship

**shipping fore·cast** /ˈ·· ˌ··/ *n* [C] *BrE* a radio broadcast that says what the weather will be like at sea

**shipping lane** /ˈ·· ˌ·/ *n* [C] an officially approved path of travel that ships must follow

**ship's chand·ler** /ˌ· ˈ··/ *n* [C] someone who sells equipment for ships

**ship·shape** /ˈʃɪpʃeɪp/ *adj* [not before noun] neat and clean: *Let's get this house shipshape.*

**ship-to-shore** /ˌ· · ˈ·◂/ *adj* providing communication between a ship and people on land: *ship-to-shore radio*

**ship·wreck¹** /ˈʃɪp-rek/ *n* [U] the destruction of a ship in an accident: *The survivors of the shipwreck were flown to land by helicopter.*

**shipwreck²** *v* **be shipwrecked** to have been sailing in a ship that has had a serious accident and can no longer sail: *Beatty was shipwrecked off the coast of Africa.*

**ship·wright** /ˈʃɪp-raɪt/ *n* [C] someone who builds or repairs ships

**ship·yard** /ˈʃɪp-jɑːd‖-jɑːrd/ *n* [C] a place where ships are built or repaired

**shire** /ʃaɪə‖ʃaɪr/ *n* [C] **1 the shires** the country areas in the central part of England **2** *BrE old use* a COUNTY

**shire horse** /ˈ· ·/ *n* [C] a type of large powerful horse used for pulling large loads

**shirk** /ʃɜːk‖ʃɜːrk/ *v* [I,T] to deliberately avoid doing something you should do, because you are lazy: *a salesman who was fired for shirking* | **shirk your responsibilities/duties/obligations** | *Are you accusing me of shirking my responsibilities?* —**shirker** *n* [C]

**shirt** /ʃɜːt‖ʃɜːrt/ *n* [C] **1** a piece of clothing that covers the upper part of your body and your arms, usually has a collar, and is fastened at the front by buttons: *I have to wear a shirt and tie to work.* —see picture on page 840 **2 keep your shirt on** *spoken* used to tell someone who is becoming angry that they should stay calm **3 have the shirt off someone's back** *informal* to take everything that someone owes you, without showing any sympathy **4 put your shirt on sth** *BrE* to risk all your money on something —see also STUFFED SHIRT S2 W3

**shirt·front** /ˈʃɜːtfrʌnt‖ˈʃɜːrt-/ *n* [C] the part of a shirt that covers your chest

**shirt·sleeves** /ˈʃɜːtsliːvz‖ˈʃɜːrt-/ *n* **in (your) shirtsleeves** wearing a shirt but no JACKET (1): *It was 90° and the men were in their shirtsleeves.*

**shirt tail** /ˈ· ·/ *n* [C] the part of a shirt that is below your waist and is usually inside your trousers

**shirt·waist·er** /ˈʃɜːtˌweɪstə‖ˈʃɜːrtˌweɪstər/ *BrE*, **shirtwaist** /ˈʃɜːtweɪst‖ˈʃɜːrt-/ *AmE n* [C] a woman's dress in the style of a long shirt

**shirt·y** /ˈʃɜːti‖ˈʃɜːr-/ *adj BrE informal* bad-tempered, angry, and rude: *Phil got a bit shirty when I tried to tell him he was wrong.*

**shish ke·bab** /ˈʃɪʃ kɪ̆ˌbæb‖-ˌbɑːb/ *n* [C] small pieces of meat that are put on a long thin metal stick and cooked

**shit¹** /ʃɪt/ *n taboo, especially spoken* S2

**1 shit!/oh shit!** used to express anger, fear, or disappointment: *Shit! I've left my purse at home.*

**2 ▶ BODY WASTE ◀** [U] solid waste that comes out of your body from your BOWELS: *Mind that dog shit!*

**3 have/get the shits** to have or get DIARRHOEA

**4 ▶ STH UNPLEASANT/BAD QUALITY ◀** [U] something that is useless or very bad quality: *Their apartment is full of cheap modern shit. | What's that shit you're reading?*

**5 ▶ STUPID/UNTRUE TALK ◀** [U] something that you think is stupid or untrue: *You expect me to believe that shit?* | **full of shit** (=saying things that are stupid or not true) *You're full of shit, Rudy. All this stuff about money and cars is just to impress the girls.*

**6 ▶ PERSON ◀** [C] someone who is very unpleasant and treats other people badly: *You don't want to get involved with Colin – he's a complete shit.*

**7 in deep shit** also **in the shit** *BrE* in a lot of trouble: *Pete's in deep shit because his wife's found out that he lied to her.*

**8 not give/care a shit** to not care at all about something: *I don't give a shit what you think!*

**9 feel like shit** to feel very ill: *I woke up with a hangover, and felt like shit for the rest of the day.*

**10 beat/kick the shit out of** to beat or kick someone very violently: *I'll beat the shit out of you!*

**11 give sb shit** to insult someone or criticize them: *She's always giving me shit about my clothes and stuff.*

**12 the shit hit the fan** used to say that there will be a lot of trouble when someone finds out about something: *He'll be back this afternoon, and that's when the shit will really hit the fan.* —see also **scare the shit out of** (SCARE¹ (1)), **tough shit** (TOUGH¹ (6))

**shit²** *v past tense and past participle* **shit** or **shat** /ʃæt/ *taboo, especially spoken* **1** [I] to pass solid waste out of your body from your BOWELS **2 shit yourself** to feel very worried or frightened: *I'm absolutely shitting myself about the test next week.* **3** [T] *AmE* to tell someone something that is untrue: *Are you shitting me?*

**shit³** *adj taboo, spoken* **1** *especially BrE* very bad: *Jim is shit at football. | It's a really shit job.* **2 be up shit creek** to be in a very difficult or dangerous situation

**shite** /ʃaɪt/ *n BrE, spoken* another word for SHIT¹ (1)

**shit-faced** /ˈ· ·/ *adj taboo, spoken* very drunk

**shit-for-brains** /ˌ· · ˈ·/ *n* [C] *taboo* someone who is very stupid

**shit hole** /ˈ· ·/ *n* [C] *taboo, spoken* a place that is very dirty and unpleasant: *They live in a total shit hole.*

**shit-hot** /ˌ· ˈ·◂/ *adj taboo, spoken* extremely good

**shit·less** /ˈʃɪtləs/ *adj* **scare sb shitless** *taboo, spoken* to make someone feel very frightened

**shit stir·rer** /ˈ· ˌ··/ *n taboo, especially BrE* [C] someone who deliberately makes trouble for other people

**shit·ty** /ˈʃɪti/ *adj taboo, spoken* very bad, unpleasant, or nasty: *Dave's been in a shitty mood all morning.*

**shiv·er¹** /ˈʃɪvə‖-ər/ *v* [I] to shake slightly because you are cold or frightened: *The children stood outside shivering.* | [+ **with**] *Juanita was shivering with cold.*

**shiver²** *n* [C] **1** a slight shaking movement of your body caused by cold or fear: *A shiver ran through her at the thought of Worrel's ugly face.* **2 give you the shivers** *informal* to make you feel afraid: *Snakes give me the shivers.* **3 send shivers (up and) down your spine** *informal* to make you feel very frightened or excited: *A sudden scream from outside sent shivers down his spine.* **4 shivers** [plural] *literary* one of the very small pieces into which something breaks when it is hit or dropped

**shiv·er·y** /ˈʃɪvəri/ *adj* trembling or shaking because of cold, fear, or illness: *He felt shivery and nauseous.*

**shoal** /ʃəʊl‖ʃoʊl/ *n* [C] **1** a large group of fish swimming together **2** a small hill of sand just below the surface of water that makes it dangerous for boats

S2 W2 **shock¹** /ʃɒk‖ʃɑːk/ *n*
**1 ▶ SHOCKING EVENT/SITUATION ◀** [C usually singular] an unexpected and unpleasant event, situation, or piece of news that surprises and upsets you: *It was a real shock to hear that the factory would have to close.* | **come as a shock** (=be a shock) *We knew Rob had cancer, but it still came as a shock when he died.*
**2 ▶ UNEXPECTED UNPLEASANT FEELING ◀** [singular U] the feeling of surprise and disbelief you have when something very unpleasant happens unexpectedly: *I was numb with shock when I found out Graham was having an affair.* | **get a shock** *They'll get a shock when they get this bill.* | **in a state of shock** (=extremely shocked by something and unable to think or react normally) *Several hours after we had heard we were still in a state of shock that Cobain was dead.*
**3 ▶ MEDICAL ◀** [U] a medical condition in which someone looks pale and their heart and lungs are not working correctly, usually after a sudden very unpleasant experience: **suffer from shock** *Several witnesses were taken to hospital suffering from shock.* | **in (a state of) shock** *Paul's in shock, but otherwise his injuries are not serious.*
**4 ▶ ELECTRICITY ◀** also **electric shock** [C] a sharp, painful feeling caused by a dangerous flow of electricity passing through your body: **get a shock** *I got a shock off the toaster this morning.*
**5 ▶ SHAKING ◀** [C,U] violent shaking caused for example by an explosion or EARTHQUAKE etc: *The shock of the explosion was felt miles away.* —see also SHOCK WAVE
**6 a shock of hair** a very thick mass of hair —see also SHOCKED, SHELL SHOCK, TOXIC SHOCK SYNDROME

**USAGE NOTE: SHOCK**

WORD CHOICE: **shock, surprise, shocking**

**Shock** and **shocking** are both fairly strong words and you may have to think whether they are the words you really need to express your meaning.

If something **is, comes as**, or **gives you** a **shock** it is unexpected and often very bad: *It came as a great shock to hear she was leaving home.*|*He'll be OK once he gets over the shock.*

A **surprise** is something that is unexpected, but is not necessarily bad: *What a nice surprise! I didn't even think you were in the country!*|*It was quite a surprise to know I was actually good at drawing.*

Something that is **shocking** is extremely bad, often in an offensive or immoral way: *shocking violence.* So you would not use **shocking** to describe, for example, your first day at school, or something that was simply an unpleasant surprise.

**shock²** *v* **1** [T] to make someone feel very surprised and upset, and unable to believe what has happened: *The murder of such a young child deeply shocked the whole community.* | **it shocks sb to do sth** *It shocked me to think how close we had come to being killed.* **2** [I,T] to make someone feel very offended, by talking or behaving in an immoral or socially unacceptable way: *He seems to enjoy shocking people.* | *Just ignore all their bad language – they only do it to shock.* **3** [T] to give an electric shock to someone

**shock³** *adj* [only before noun] a word meaning very surprising, used especially in newspapers: *England's shock defeat by Luxembourg in last night's game*

**shock ab·sorb·er** /ˈ· ·ˌ··/ *n* [C] a piece of equipment connected to each wheel of a vehicle to make travelling more comfortable

**shocked** /ʃɒkt‖ʃɑːkt/ *adj* **1** feeling surprised and upset by something very unexpected and unpleasant: [+ **at**] *We were shocked at their terrible working conditions.* | **shocked to see/hear/learn etc** *I was very shocked to hear of Brian's death.* **2 a shocked silence** a situation in which no one speaks because they are all very shocked: *A shocked silence greeted Helen's announcement that she was pregnant.* S3

**shock·er** /ˈʃɒkə‖ˈʃɑːkər/ *n* [C] *informal* a film, news story etc that shocks you: *TV star in drugs shocker!*

**shock·ing** /ˈʃɒkɪŋ‖ˈʃɑː-/ *adj* **1** very offensive or upsetting: *The book was originally thought to be too shocking to publish.* **2** *BrE informal* very bad: *It's shocking, the way he treats his wife.* —**shockingly** *adv* S3

**shocking pink** /ˌ·· ˈ·◂/ *n* [U] a very bright pink colour —**shocking pink** *adj*

**shock·proof** /ˈʃɒkpruːf‖ˈʃɑːk-/ *adj* a watch, machine etc that is shockproof is designed so that it is not easily damaged if it is dropped or hit

**shock tac·tics** /ˈ· ˌ··/ *n* [plural] methods of achieving what you want by deliberately shocking someone

**shock treat·ment** /ˈ· ˌ··/ also **shock ther·a·py** /ˈ· ˌ···/ *n* [U] treatment of mental illness using powerful electric shocks

**shock wave** /ˈ· ·/ [plural] *n* **1 shock waves** strong feelings of shock that people feel when something bad happens unexpectedly: *The stock market crash sent shock waves through the financial community.* **2** [C,U] a very strong wave of air pressure or heat from an explosion, EARTHQUAKE etc

**shod** /ʃɒd‖ʃɑːd/ the past tense and past participle of SHOE²

**shod·dy** /ˈʃɒdi‖ˈʃɑːdi/ *adj* **1** made or done cheaply or carelessly: *shoddy workmanship* **2** unfair and dishonest: *a shoddy trick* —**shoddily** *adv* —**shoddiness** *n* [U]

**shoe¹** /ʃuː/ *n* [C] **1** something that you wear to cover your feet, made of leather or some other strong material: *Children grow out of shoes very quickly.* | *high heeled shoes* | *a pair of tennis shoes* —compare BOOT¹ (1), SANDAL, SLIPPER **2** a curved piece of iron that is nailed onto a horse's foot; HORSESHOE **3 be in sb's shoes** to be in someone else's situation, especially a bad one: *I'm glad I'm not in his shoes with all those debts to pay off.* | *If I were in your shoes, I'd tell Jan to get lost!* **4 step into/fill sb's shoes** to do a job that someone else used to do, and do it as well as they did: *It'll be hard to find someone to fill Pete's shoes.* **5 if the shoe fits (, wear it)** *AmE spoken* used to say that if a remark that has been made about you is true, then you should accept it: *"Are you saying I'm a fool?" "If the shoe fits..."* S2 W3

**shoe²** *v* [T] *past tense* **shod** /ʃɒd‖ʃɑːd/ *present participle* **shoeing 1 well/badly/elegantly etc shod** *especially literary* wearing good, bad etc shoes **2** to put a shoe on a horse

**shoe·horn, shoe-horn** /ˈʃuːhɔːn‖-hɔːrn/ *n* [C] a curved piece of metal or plastic that you can put inside the back of a shoe when you put it on, to help your heel go in easily

**shoe·lace** /ˈʃuːleɪs/ *n* [C] a thin piece of material, like string, that goes through holes in the front of your shoes and is used to fasten them: *Tie your shoelaces or you'll trip.*

**shoe·mak·er** /ˈʃuːmeɪkə‖-ər/ *n* [C] someone who makes shoes and boots; COBBLER (2)

**shoe·shine stand** /ˈ·· ˌ·/ *n AmE* a place, often in the street, where you pay to have your shoes polished

**shoe·string** /ˈʃuːˌstrɪŋ/ *n* **1 on a shoestring** *informal* if you do something on a shoestring, you do it without spending much money: *The program was run on a shoestring for years until they found a sponsor.* | *a movie that was made on a shoestring budget* **2** *AmE* a shoelace

**shoe·tree** /ˈʃuːtriː/ *n* [C] an object shaped like a shoe that you put inside a shoe so that it keeps its shape

**sho·gun** /ˈʃəʊgʌn‖ˈʃoʊ-/ *n* [C] a military leader in Japan until the middle of the 19th century

**shone** /ʃɒn‖ʃoʊn/ the past tense and past participle of SHINE

**shoo¹** /ʃuː/ *interjection* used to tell a child or an animal to go away

**shoo²** *v* [T always + adv/prep] to make a child or animal go away, especially because they are annoying you: **shoo sb out/away etc** *He shooed the kids out of the kitchen.*

**shoo-in** /ˈ· ·/ *n* [C] *AmE informal* someone who is expected to win a race, election etc easily

**shook** /ʃʊk/ the past tense of SHAKE

**shoot¹** /ʃuːt/ *v past tense and past participle* **shot** /ʃɒt‖ʃɑːt/ S2 W2

① GUNS/WEAPONS
② SPORT
③ SPEAK/TALK/ASK
④ QUICK/SUDDEN
⑤ OTHER MEANINGS

**① GUNS/WEAPONS**

**1 ▶ KILL/INJURE ◀** [T] to deliberately kill or injure someone using a gun: *Lincoln was shot while watching a play in Ford's Theater.* | **shoot sb in the leg/head etc** *He had been shot in the back while trying to escape.* | **shoot sb dead** *They were shot dead in their home by armed robbers.* | **shoot (sb) on sight** (=shoot as soon as you see someone) *The guards have orders to shoot intruders on sight.*

**2 ▶ FIRE A GUN ◀** [I,T] to fire a weapon at someone, or make a weapon fire: *I'm coming out with my hands up, don't shoot.* | **shoot at** (=try to shoot someone) *We spent the afternoon shooting at pigeons on the roof.* | **shoot bullets/arrows etc** *It's only a toy – it doesn't shoot real bullets.* | **shoot a gun/rifle etc** *I learned to shoot a revolver when I was a child.* | **shoot to kill** (=shoot at someone with the intention of killing them, because they are considered very dangerous) *The police were told to shoot to kill.*

**3 ▶ BIRDS/ANIMALS ◀** [I,T] to shoot and kill animals or birds as a sport: *They spent the weekend in Scotland shooting grouse.*

**② SPORT**

**4** [I,T] to kick or throw a ball in a sport such as football or BASKETBALL towards the place where you can get a point: *Magic turned and shot the ball, making a 3*

[continued on next page]

[continued from previous page]
*pointer in the final second.* | [+ **at**] *The striker shot at goal and missed.* —see picture on page 1264
**5 shoot pool/billiards etc** *AmE informal* to play a game such as POOL [1] (3) or BILLIARDS

### ③ SPEAK/TALK/ASK

**6 shoot questions at** to ask someone a lot of questions very quickly: *The lawyer shot a series of rapid questions at Hendrickson.*
**7 shoot your mouth off** *informal* to talk about something that you should not talk about or that you know nothing about: *Don't go shooting your mouth off, now.*
**8 shoot the bull/shoot the breeze** *AmE informal* to have an informal conversation about unimportant things: *Cal and I were sitting on the porch shooting the breeze.*
**9 ▶ SHOOT! ◀** *AmE spoken* used to tell someone to start speaking: *"Shoot, Ward," Richards said, "ask anything you want."*

### ④ QUICK/SUDDEN

**10 ▶ MOVE QUICKLY ◀** [I always + adv/prep, T always + adv/prep] to move quickly in a particular direction, or to make something move in this way: [+ **past/along etc**] *She shot past me and ran into the house.* | *Flames were shooting skyward.* | **shoot sth up/in/along etc** *The fountains shoot water at the walls of the pool.*
**11 shoot to fame/stardom etc** to suddenly become very successful: *Their new album shot straight to the top of the album charts.*

**12 ▶ PAIN ◀** [I always + adv/prep] if pain shoots through your body, you feel it going quickly through it: [+ **through/along**] *A spasm of pain suddenly shot along his arm.* | **shooting pains** (=continuous short pains passing through your body) *shooting pains in your back*
**13 shoot a look/glance (at)** to look at someone quickly, especially so that other people do not see, to show them how you feel: *Jack shot an anxious look at his mother.*

### ⑤ OTHER MEANINGS

**14 ▶ PHOTOGRAPH ◀** [I,T] to take photographs or make a film of something: *When one of the actors died, they had to shoot the final scene again.*
**15 ▶ PLANTS ◀** [I] if a plant shoots, a new part of it starts to grow, especially a new stem and leaves
**16 ▶ LOCK ON A DOOR ◀** to move the BOLT on a door so that it is in the locked or unlocked position
**17 shoot!** *AmE spoken* used to show that you are annoyed or disappointed about something: *Shoot! I knew this would happen.*
**18 shoot yourself in the foot** to say or do something stupid that will cause you a lot of trouble: *Glen really shot himself in the foot shouting at his boss like that.*
**19 shoot the lights** *BrE informal* to keep driving even though the traffic lights say you should stop
**20 shoot your bolt** *BrE*, also **shoot your wad** *AmE informal* to have used all of your money, power, energy etc —see also SHOT[2], **blame/shoot the messenger** (MESSENGER (2))

**shoot down**

**shoot** sb/sth ↔ **down** *phr v* [T] **1** to destroy an enemy plane while it is flying: *Rhodes's plane was shot down over France.* **2** to kill someone with a gun, especially someone who cannot defend themselves: *They are accused of shooting down unarmed demonstrators.* **3 shoot sb/sth down (in flames)** *informal* to tell someone that what they are saying or suggesting is wrong or stupid: *Another of my great ideas shot down in flames!*
**shoot for/at** sth *phr v* [T] *informal, especially AmE* to try to achieve a particular aim, especially one that is very difficult: *Management is shooting for a 50% increase in sales in the next financial year.*
**shoot off** *phr v* [I] *BrE informal* to leave quickly or suddenly: *Sorry, but I'll have to shoot off before the end of the meeting.*
**shoot through** *phr v* [I] *informal especially AustrE* **1** to leave a place, especially very quickly **2** to die
**shoot up** *phr v* **1** [I] to quickly increase in number or amount: *Prices have certainly shot up recently.* | *Supermarkets are shooting up all over the area.* **2** [I] to grow taller very quickly: *Your son's really shot up since we last saw him.* **3** [T **shoot** sb/sth ↔ **up**] to injure or damage someone or something by shooting them with bullets: *The building was so badly shot up it was unrecognizable.* **4** [I,T] *slang* to take illegal drugs by using a needle

**shoot²** *n* [C] **1** the part of a plant that that comes up above the ground when it is just beginning to grow —see picture at GERMINATE **2** an occasion when someone takes photographs or makes a film: *One of the models is on a shoot for that new perfume Passion.* **3** an occasion when people shoot birds or animals for sport, or the area of land where they do this

**shoot·er** /ˈʃuːtə‖-ər/ *n* [C] *informal* a word meaning a gun, used especially in films about COWBOYS or criminals

**shoot·ing** /ˈʃuːtɪŋ/ *n* **1** [C] a situation in which someone is injured or killed by a gun: *politically-motivated shootings* **2** [U] the sport of shooting animals and birds: *the shooting season*

**shooting gal·le·ry** /ˈ·· ˌ···/ *n* [C] **1** a place where people shoot guns at objects to win prizes **2** *AmE slang* a large empty building in a city, where people buy drugs and INJECT (1) them

**shooting match** /ˈ·· ·/ *n* **the whole shooting match** *spoken* the whole of a situation, or an event that is the best or most complete of its kind: *We're having a big church wedding with bridesmaids, a pageboy – the whole shooting match.*

**shooting star** /ˌ·· ˈ·/ *n* [C] a small piece of rock or metal from space, that burns brightly as it falls towards the Earth; METEOR

**shooting stick** /ˈ·· ·/ *n* [C] a pointed stick with a top that opens out to form a seat that you use when doing outdoor sports —see picture at STICK²

**shoot-out** /ˈ· ·/ *n* [C] **1** a fight using guns to settle an argument **2** a PENALTY SHOOT-OUT

**shop¹** /ʃɒp‖ʃɑːp/ *n* S1 W1
**1 ▶ PLACE WHERE YOU BUY THINGS ◀** [C] **a)** *BrE* a building or part of a building where things are sold to the public; STORE *AmE*: *The shops in town close at 5.30.* | **toy shop/pet shop etc** *Have you seen that new shoe shop?* **b)** a small shop that sells one particular type of thing: *a candle shop* —see also BUCKET SHOP, CORNER SHOP, COFFEE SHOP
**2 ▶ MAKING/REPAIRING THINGS ◀** [C] a place where things are made or repaired: *After assembly, the cars go to*

*the paint shop to be painted.* | *a repair shop* —see also SHOP FLOOR, SHOP STEWARD
**3 ▶ SCHOOL SUBJECT ◀** [U] *AmE* a subject taught in schools that shows students how to use tools and machinery to make things out of wood and metal
**4 set up shop** *informal* to start a business
**5 shut up shop** *informal* to close a shop or business, either temporarily or permanently
**6 talk shop** *informal* to talk about things that are connected to your work, especially in a way that other people find boring: *I'm fed up with you two talking shop.*
**7 all over the shop** *BrE spoken* **a)** scattered around untidily: *There were bits of paper all over the shop.* **b)** confused and disorganized: *I'm all over the shop this morning.*
**8 ▶ GO SHOPPING ◀** [singular] *BrE spoken* an occasion when you go shopping, especially for food and other things you need regularly: *doing the weekly shop*

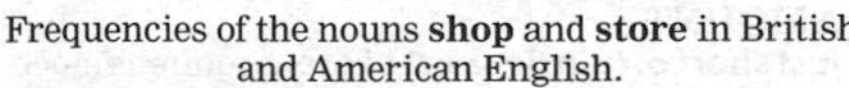

Frequencies of the nouns **shop** and **store** in British and American English.

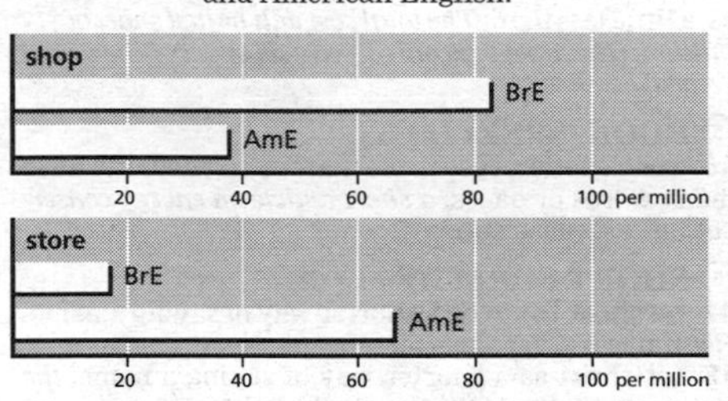


Based on the British National Corpus and the Longman Lancaster Corpus

This graph shows that when talking about a building where things are sold, **shop** is the usual word in British English and **store** is the usual word in American English. Americans use **shop** to mean a small shop where one particular type of thing is sold. In British English **store** is used to mean a very large shop that sells many different types of things, and is usually used in the expression **department store**.

S 2 **shop²** *v* **shopped, shopping** **1** [I] to go to one or more shops to buy things: **[+ for]** *I was shopping for a new dress, but couldn't find anything I liked.* —see also WINDOW-SHOP **2 go shopping a)** *BrE* to go to one or more shops to buy things, often for enjoyment **b)** *especially AmE* to go to shops to buy clothes **3** [T] *BrE informal* to tell the police about someone who has done something illegal: *He was shopped by his ex-wife.* —**shopper** *n* [C]

**shop around** *phr v* [I] to compare the price and quality of different things before you decide which to buy: *Shop around before you decide which insurance policy to take out.*

**shop as·sis·tant** /ˈ· ·ˌ··/ *BrE n* [C] someone whose job is to help customers in a shop; SALESCLERK *AmE*

**shop·fit·ting** /ˈʃɒpˌfɪtɪŋ‖ˈʃɑːp-/ *n* [U] *BrE* the business of putting equipment in shops such as shelves, containers etc —**shopfitter** *n* [C]

**shop floor** /ˌ· ˈ·◂/ *n* **the shop floor** *BrE* **1** the area in a factory where the ordinary workers do their work: *The chairwoman started her working life on the shop floor.* **2** the ordinary workers in a factory, not the managers

**shop front** /ˈ· ·/ *n* [C] the outside part of a shop that faces the street; STOREFRONT *AmE*

**shop·keep·er** /ˈʃɒpˌkiːpə‖ˈʃɑːpˌkiːpər/ *n* [C] *especially BrE* someone who owns or is in charge of a small shop; STOREKEEPER *AmE*

**shop·lift** /ˈʃɒpˌlɪft‖ˈʃɑːp-/ *v* [I] to take something from a shop without paying for it —**shoplifter** *n* [C] *Shoplifters will be prosecuted.*

**shop·lift·ing** /ˈʃɒpˌlɪftɪŋ‖ˈʃɑːp-/ *n* [U] the crime of stealing things from shops, for example by hiding them in your bag, or under your clothes

**shop·per** /ˈʃɒpə‖ˈʃɑːpər/ *n* [C] someone who buys things in shops: *The streets were crowded with shoppers.*

**shop·ping** /ˈʃɒpɪŋ‖ˈʃɑː-/ *n* [U] **1** the activity of going to shops to buy things: *Shopping is now a major leisure industry.* **2 do the shopping** *BrE* to go shopping to buy food and other things you need regularly: *We always do our shopping on Fridays.* **3** *BrE* the things that you have just bought from a shop: *Do you need some help carrying your shopping?* S 2 W 3

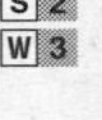

**shopping cen·tre** *BrE*, **shopping center** *AmE* /ˈ·· ˌ··/ *n* [C] a group of shops built together in one area, often under one roof

**shopping mall** /ˈ·· ·/ *n* [C] *AmE* a large, specially built covered area where there are a lot of shops; MALL

**shopping pre·cinct** /ˈ·· ˌ··/ *n* [C] *BrE* an area in a town where there are a lot of shops and where cars are not allowed

**shop-soiled** /ˈ· ·/ *adj BrE* **1** something that is shop-soiled is slightly damaged or dirty because it has been in a shop for a long time; SHOPWORN *AmE* **2** an idea that is shop-soiled is no longer interesting because it has been discussed many times before: *the same old shop-soiled arguments*

**shop stew·ard** /ˌ· ˈ··/ *n* [C] a worker who is elected by members of a TRADE UNION in a factory or other business to represent them in dealing with managers

**shop·walk·er** /ˈʃɒpwɔːkə‖ˈʃɑːpwɒːkər/ *n* [C] *especially BrE* someone who is employed in a large shop to help the customers and watch the other workers to make sure they are working properly

**shop·worn** /ˈʃɒpwɔːn‖ˈʃɑːpwɔːrn/ *adj AmE* SHOP-SOILED

**shore¹** /ʃɔː‖ʃɔːr/ *n* **1** [C,U] the land along the edge of a large area of water, such as an ocean or lake: *We could see a boat about a mile from shore.* | *the shores of the Mediterranean* | **on shore** (=away from a ship) *We had a couple of hours on shore.* **2 these shores/British shores/our shores etc** *especially literary* a particular country that has a border on the sea: *Millions of immigrants flocked to these shores in the 19th century.* —see also ASHORE, OFFSHORE, ONSHORE

**shore²** *v*

**shore** sth ↔ **up** *phr v* [T] **1** to support a wall with large pieces of wood, metal etc to stop it from falling down: *The roof had been shored up with old timbers.* **2** to help or support something that is likely to fail or is not working well: *attempts to shore up the struggling economy*

**USAGE NOTE: SHORE**

WORD CHOICE: **shore, bank, coast, seaside, beach**

The usual word for the land at the edge of a sea or lake is **shore**: *At night he would stand on the shore and gaze out to sea.* | *There was a little cabin on the opposite shore.*

The edges of a river are its **banks**.

When you are talking about a country, or a large area of a country, you call the land next to the sea the **coast**: *the Atlantic coast of Spain* | *I could tell from his clothes that he was from the West Coast.*

In British English the **seaside** is the area by the sea considered as a place of enjoyment: *a holiday at the seaside.* In American English you are more likely to use **beach**: *In summer, my mother used to take me to the beach.* But you can also use **beach** in both British and American English for the flat land right at the edge of the sea, that is covered by water some of the time: *They walked hand in hand along the beach.*

**shorn** /ʃɔːn‖ʃɔːrn/ *v* the past participle of SHEAR

## short¹ /ʃɔːt||ʃɔːrt/ *adj*

① LENGTH/HEIGHT/DISTANCE
② TIME
③ NOT ENOUGH
④ AMOUNT
⑤ BOOK/SPEECH ETC
⑥ SHORT FORM OF
⑦ PRONUNCIATION
⑧ OTHER MEANINGS

### ① LENGTH/HEIGHT/DISTANCE

**1** measuring a small amount in distance or length: *a short corridor with two rooms on each side|a short skirt|It's a short drive from the airport.|Anita had her hair cut short.* —see picture on page 412

**2 ▶PERSON◀** someone who is short is of less than average height: *a short plump woman*

**3 be 3 feet/10 miles/2 metres short of** to have not quite reached a place you are trying to get to: *Our car broke down two miles short of the town.*

### ② TIME

**4** happening or continuing for only a little time or for less time than usual: *a short meeting|I'm afraid there will be a short delay.|Morris gave a short laugh.|I've only been living in Brisbane a short time.|Some people have short memories, don't they?*|**a short space of time** *Both her parents died within a short space of time.*

**5 at short notice** *BrE* also **on short notice** *AmE* with very little warning that something is going to happen: *The party was arranged at very short notice.|I can't make it Friday. It's a bit short notice I'm afraid.*

**6 in the short term** during the period of time that is not very far into the future: *Interest rates are unlikely to fall in the short term.* —see also SHORT-TERM

**7 in short order** in a short time and without delay: *All the tents were put up in short order.*

**8 make short work of** *informal* to finish something quickly and easily, especially a meal or a job: *The kids made short work of the sandwiches.*

**9 short and sweet** *spoken* not taking a long time and less boring or unpleasant than you expected: *They won't listen to a long lecture, so just keep it short and sweet.*

### ③ NOT ENOUGH

**10 a)** not having enough of something you need: **be short of** *I'm a little short of money at the moment.|Your little girl's not short of confidence, is she?*|**be 5p/$10 etc short** *Have you all paid me? I'm still about $9 short.* **b) be short** if time, money etc is short, there is not as much of it as you need: *Money was short in those days. We had to get by on $30 a week.|It'll be difficult – time and resources are short.*

**11 be in short supply** if something is in short supply, there is not enough of it available: *Gasoline was in short supply just after the war.*

**12 be (a bit/rather) short** *BrE* to not have much money: *Could you lend me £5? I'm a bit short tonight.*

**13 be short on** *informal* to have less of something than you should have: *Sometimes I think he's a little short on common sense.*

**14 give sb short measure** to give someone less than the correct amount of something, especially in a shop

### ④ AMOUNT

**15 just short of/a little short of etc** not quite as much as; a little less than: *The total cost will be just short of $17 million.|Her time was only 2 seconds short of the world record.*

### ⑤ BOOK/SPEECH ETC

**16** a book, letter, speech etc that is short does not have many words or pages: *a short article on energy conservation* —see also SHORT STORY

### ⑥ SHORT FORM OF

**17 be short for** to be a shorter way of saying a name: *Her name is Alex, short for Alexandra.*

**18 for short** as a shorter way of saying a name: *the Reformed Electoral System (or the RES for short)*

### ⑦ PRONUNCIATION

**19** *technical* a short vowel is pronounced quickly and without being emphasized: */æ/, as in 'cat', is a short vowel.*

### ⑧ OTHER MEANINGS

**20 be short with** to speak to someone using very few words, in a way that seems rude or unfriendly: *Sorry I was short with you on the phone this morning – I was being hassled by the kids.*

**21 give sb/sth short shrift** to not give much attention or sympathy to someone: *Her suggestions were given short shrift by the chairman.*|**get short shrift** *My warnings, as usual, got short shrift.*

**22 have a short temper** to get angry very easily

**23 nothing/little short of** used to emphasize that something is very good, very surprising etc: *Brigitte's recovery seemed nothing short of a miracle.*

**24 draw/get the short straw** to be given something difficult or unpleasant to do, especially when other people have been given something better

**25 life's too short** *spoken* used to say that something is too unimportant to worry about or spend time on —**shortness** *n* [U]

**short²** *adv* **1 be running short** if you are running short of something, or if something is running short, it is being used up and there will soon not be enough left: *We're running short of coffee again.|Our supplies of beer were running short.|Let's go – time's running short.* **2 stop short** to suddenly stop speaking or stop what you are doing, for example because something has surprised you or you have just thought of something **3 stop short of doing sth** to almost do something but decide against actually doing it: *Paula stopped just short of accusing me of lying.* **4 pull/bring sb up short** to make someone suddenly stop moving or stop what they are doing: *The sight of the gun in her hand pulled me up short.* **5 cut sb short** to stop someone before they have finished speaking, by interrupting them: *I was halfway through my explanation when Walter cut me short.* **6 cut sth short** to suddenly bring something to an end before it has properly finished: *His death at the age of 38 cut short a brilliant career.* **7 fall short of** to be less than the result, level, or standard that you expect or to fail to achieve something you are hoping for: *The appeal for money has fallen well short of its target.|I'm afraid the results fell short of our expectations.* **8 go short (of)** to have less food, money etc than you need: *She made sure that her children never went short.* **9 short of (doing) sth** without actually doing something: *Short of locking her in her room, he couldn't really stop her from seeing Jack.* **10 be taken short/be caught short** *BrE informal* to have a sudden strong need to go to the toilet

**short³** *n* **1 in short** used when you want to say, in just a few words, what is the most important point about a situation: *In short, he is a liar.* **2 shorts** [plural] **a)** short trousers ending at or above the knees: *a pair of tennis shorts* **b)** *especially AmE* men's UNDERPANTS **3** [C]

*BrE informal* a strong alcoholic drink, drunk in a small glass **4** [C] *informal* a short film shown before the main film at a cinema **5** [C] *informal* a SHORT CIRCUIT: *a short in the system*

**short**[4] *v* [I,T] *informal* to SHORT-CIRCUIT, or make something do this: *Maybe the battery has shorted.*

**short·age** /ˈʃɔːtɪdʒ‖ˈʃɔːr-/ *n* [C,U] a situation in which there is not enough of something that people need: [+ **of**] *a shortage of skilled labour* | **water/gasoline/bread etc shortage** *water shortages in the summer*

**short back and sides** /ˌ· · · ˈ·/ *n* [singular] *BrE* a way of cutting a man's hair so that it is very short at the back and sides of his head and slightly longer on top

**short·bread** /ˈʃɔːtbred‖ˈʃɔːrt-/ *n* [U] a hard, sweet BISCUIT made with a lot of butter

**short·cake** /ˈʃɔːtkeɪk‖ˈʃɔːrt-/ *n* [U] **1** *BrE* thick shortbread **2** *AmE* cake over which a sweet fruit mixture is poured

**short-change** /ˌ· ˈ·/ *v* [T often passive] **1** to treat someone unfairly by not giving them what they deserve: *When the band only played for 15 minutes the fans felt they had been short-changed.* **2** to give back too little money to someone who has paid for something by giving more than the exact price

**short cir·cuit** /ˌ· ˈ··/ *n* [C] the failure of an electrical system caused by bad wires or a fault in a connection in the wires

**short-circuit** *v* **1** [I, T] to have a short circuit or cause a short circuit in something **2** [T] to get something done without going through the usual long methods: *I short-circuited the whole process by a simple telephone call.*

**short·com·ing** /ˈʃɔːtˌkʌmɪŋ‖ˈʃɔːrt-/ *n* [C usually plural] a fault in someone's character or abilities, or in a product, system etc, that makes something less successful or effective than it should be: *In spite of all her shortcomings, she's still the best teacher the school has.* | *The present system, whatever its shortcomings, has worked well for several years.* | [+ **in**] *The inspection revealed some serious shortcomings in our safety procedures.*

**short·crust pas·try** /ˌʃɔːtkrʌst ˈpeɪstri‖ˌʃɔːrt-/ *n* [U] a kind of PASTRY (1) made with half as much fat as flour

**short cut** /ˌ· ˈ·, ˈ· ·‖ˈ· ·/ *n* [C] **1** a quicker, more direct way of going somewhere than the usual one: *We were late for the game, but found a short cut through the fields.* | **take a short cut** *Carlos decided to take a short cut home.* **2** a quicker way of doing something: [+ **to**] *There aren't really any short cuts to learning English.*

**short·en** /ˈʃɔːtn‖ˈʃɔːrtn/ *v* [I,T] to become shorter or make something shorter: *The days are shortening now.* | **shorten sth** *They're talking about shortening the working week.* —opposite LENGTHEN

**short·en·ing** /ˈʃɔːtnɪŋ‖ˈʃɔːrt-/ *n* [U] fat made from vegetable oil that you mix with flour when making PASTRY (1)

**short·fall** /ˈʃɔːtfɔːl‖ˈʃɔːrtfɒːl/ *n* [C] the difference between the amount you have and the amount you need or expect: *severe crop shortfalls* | [+ **in/of**] *a shortfall in staffing levels* | *a shortfall of about £1 million*

**short·hand** /ˈʃɔːthænd‖ˈʃɔːrt-/ *n* [U] **1** a fast method of writing using special signs or shorter forms to represent letters, words, and phrases: **in shorthand** *The reporter took notes in shorthand.* —compare LONGHAND **2 be shorthand for** to be a shorter but less clear way of saying something: *He's been 'relocated', which is shorthand for 'given a worse job a long way away'.*

**short·hand·ed** /ˌʃɔːtˈhændɪ̯d◂‖ˌʃɔːrt-/ *adj* having fewer helpers or workers than you need: *We'll be shorthanded next month as five of my staff will be on holiday.*

**shorthand typ·ist** /ˌ·· ˈ··/ *n* [C] *BrE* someone whose job is to use shorthand to write down what someone else says and then TYPE[2] (1) a copy of it; STENOGRAPHER *especially AmE*

**short-haul** /ˈʃɔːthɔːl‖ˈʃɔːrthɒːl/ *adj* a shorthaul aircraft or flight travels a fairly short distance

**short·ie** /ˈʃɔːti‖ˈʃɔːr-/ *adj* [only before noun] *informal* a shortie coat or JACKET (1) etc is one that is shorter than the usual size —see also SHORTY

**short list**[1] /ˈ· ·/ *n* [C] *BrE* a list of the most suitable people for a job, chosen from all the people who were first considered

**short-list**[2] *v* [T usually passive] *BrE* to put someone on a short list for a job: **short-list sb for** *She's been short-listed for the sales director's job.*

**short-lived** /ˌʃɔːt ˈlɪvd◂‖ʃɔːrt ˈlaɪvd◂/ *adj* lasting only a short time: *Our happiness was short-lived.*

**short·ly** /ˈʃɔːtli‖ˈʃɔːrt-/ *adv* **1** soon: *Ms Jones will be back shortly.* | **shortly before/after** *The accident happened shortly before midday.* **2** speaking impatiently: *"I've explained that already," Rod said shortly.* W3

**short-or·der cook** /ˌ· ·· ˈ·/ *n* [C] *AmE* someone in a restaurant kitchen who makes the food that can be prepared easily or quickly

**short·range** /ˌ·ˈ·◂/ *adj* **1** designed to travel or operate only within a short distance: *a shortrange missile* **2 shortrange plan/goal/forecast etc** concerned only with the period that is not very far into the future: *shortrange plans*

**short-sheet** /ˈ· ·/ *v* [T] *AmE* to fold the top sheet on a bed so that no one can get into it, as a trick; APPLE PIE BED

**short-sight·ed** /ˌ· ˈ··◂/ *adj* **1** *especially BrE* unable to see objects clearly unless they are very close; NEARSIGHTED *especially AmE* —opposite LONGSIGHTED **2** not considering the possible effects of something that seems to save time, money, or effort at the moment: *a short-sighted policy of stopping investment in training* —opposite FAR-SIGHTED —**short-sightedly** *adv* —**short-sightedness** *n* [U]

**short-staffed** /ˌ· ˈ·◂/ *adj* having fewer than the usual or necessary number of workers: *We'll try to get the order through by Monday, but we're very short-staffed at the moment.*

**short·stop** /ˈʃɔːtstɒp‖ˈʃɔːrtstɑːp/ *n* [C] a player in BASEBALL who tries to stop any balls that are hit between second and third BASE[1] (8)

**short sto·ry** /ˌ· ˈ··/ *n* [C] a short written story about imaginary situations, usually containing only a few characters

**short-tem·pered** /ˌ· ˈ··◂/ *adj* **1** easily becoming angry or impatient: *Roger's back pain is making him pretty short-tempered these days.* **2** angry and impatient: *a short-tempered reply*

**short-term** /ˌ· ˈ·◂/ *adj* [usually before noun] continuing for only a short time, or concerned only with the period that is not very far into the future: *The treatment may bring short-term benefits to Aids sufferers.* | *Most of the staff are on short-term contracts.* —opposite LONG-TERM —**short-term** *adv*

**short-term·is·m** /ˌ· ˈ···/ *n* [U] a way of planning or thinking that is concerned only with what gives you advantage now, rather than what might happen in the future: *short-termism in the banking world* —**short-termist** *adj*

**short time** /ˌ· ˈ·◂/ *n* **be on short time** *BrE* a factory or office that is on short time is operating for less than the usual number of hours or days: *Workers were put on short time because raw materials were scarce.*

**short wave** /ˌ· ˈ·◂/ *n* [U] radio broadcasting on waves of less than 60 metres in length, which can be sent around the world —see also LONG WAVE, MEDIUM WAVE

**short·y** /ˈʃɔːti‖ˈʃɔːrti/ *n* [C] an insulting name for someone who is not very tall

## shot¹ /ʃɒt‖ʃɑːt/ *n*

① GUNS/SHOOTING
② SPORT
③ FILM/PHOTOGRAPHS
④ ATTEMPT/GUESS
⑤ OTHER MEANINGS

### ① GUNS/SHOOTING

**1 fire a shot** to fire a gun: *He pulled out his rifle and fired three shots.*
**2 take a shot at** to try to kill or injure someone by firing a gun at them: *Someone took a shot at him as he was getting out of his car.*
**3 ▶ SOUND ◀** [C] the sound of a gun being fired: *Where were you when you heard the shot?*
**4 ▶ BULLETS ◀** [U] **a)** small metal balls for shooting from a SHOTGUN **b)** *old use* large metal balls for shooting from a CANNON¹
**5 a good shot/bad shot** someone who can shoot a gun well, badly etc: *Sergeant Cooper is an excellent shot.*

### ② SPORT

**6** [C] an attempt to throw, kick, or hit the ball towards the place where you can get a point: *Shaw made the shot and turned to run down the court.*|*Good shot!*
**7** [C] a heavy metal ball that competitors try to throw as far as possible in the sport of SHOT PUT
**8 a 10 to 1 shot/50 to 1 shot etc** a horse, dog etc in a race, whose chances of winning are expressed as numbers that show the ODDS

### ③ FILM/PHOTOGRAPHS

**9** [C] a photograph: *I managed to get some good shots of the carnival.*
**10** [C] the view of something in a film, television programme, or photograph that is produced by having the camera in a particular position: *In the opening shot we see Garfield at his desk reading.*

### ④ ATTEMPT/GUESS

**11** [C] *informal* an attempt to do something or achieve something: **[+ at]** *This will be his second shot at the championship.*|**have a shot (at sth)** *I decided to have a shot at decorating the house myself.*
**12 a long shot** an attempt or guess at something that is not very likely to be successful, but is still worth trying: *It's a long shot, but if we hurry we might still find her.*
**13 a shot in the dark** an attempt to guess something without having any facts or definite ideas: *My answer to the last question was a complete shot in the dark.*

### ⑤ OTHER MEANINGS

**14 ▶ DRINK ◀** [C] a small amount of a strong alcoholic drink: **[+ of]** *He poured himself another shot of whiskey.*
**15 ▶ DRUG ◀** [C] *AmE* an INJECTION of a drug (=when it is put into the body with a needle): *Have you had your typhoid and cholera shots?*
**16 ▶ REMARK ◀** [C] an angry remark: **a parting shot** (=something you say as you are leaving) *Carl turned for one parting shot: "You marry him, then!"*|**a cheap shot** (=an unnecessarily rude remark)
**17 big shot** an important or powerful person, especially in business: *a big shot in the record business*
**18 like a shot** if you do something like a shot, you do it very quickly and eagerly: *If he asked me to go to Africa with him, I'd go like a shot!*
**19 a shot in the arm** something that makes you more confident or more successful: *The latest opinion poll has given the Socialists a much needed shot in the arm.*
**20 a shot across the bows** *especially BrE* something you say or do to warn someone about what might happen if they fail to do want you want them to do —see also **call the shots** (CALL¹ (25)), MUG SHOT, **not by a long chalk/shot** (LONG¹ (15))

**shot²** *adj* [not before noun] **1 be shot** to be in bad condition because of being used too much or treated badly: *My back tires are shot. I'll have to get new ones before we go.*|**shot to pieces** *After a long day of exams, my nerves were shot to pieces.* **2 be/get shot of** *informal* to get rid of someone or something: *I don't care how nice the house is any more. I just want to be shot of it.* **3 be shot through with** *formal* **a)** if a piece of cloth is shot through with a colour, it has very small threads of that colour woven into it: *a fine silk shot through with gold threads* **b)** to have a lot of a particular quality or feeling: *a charming collection of stories, shot through with a gentle humour*

**shot³** *v* the past tense and participle of shoot

**shot·gun** /ˈʃɒtgʌn‖ˈʃɑːt-/ *n* [C] a long gun fired from the shoulder, especially one used for killing birds or animals

**shotgun wed·ding** /ˌ·· ˈ··/ *n* [C] a wedding that has to take place immediately because the woman is going to have a baby

**shot put** /ˈ· ·/ *n* [singular] a sporting competition in which you throw a heavy metal ball as far as you can —**shot putter** *n* [C] *an Olympic shot putter*

S1 W1 **should** /ʃəd; *strong* ʃʊd/ *modal verb* [negative short form **shouldn't**] **1** used to show that something is the best thing to do because it is morally right, fair, honest etc: *He should learn to be more polite.*|*What you should have done is call the police.*|*I have no sympathy for him. He shouldn't accept bribes.*|*"I don't care what people think." "Well, you should."* **2** used to show that something is the best thing to do because it helps you, is good for you etc.: *The leaflet tells you what you should do if the power fails.*|*Why shouldn't I smoke if I want to?*|*I think he should have tried to get some more qualifications before applying for the job.* **3** used to show what the correct or expected amount, situation etc is, especially when it is not correct or not what is expected: *Eat noodles the way they should be eaten, with chopsticks.*|*What do you mean there are only ten tickets? There should be twelve.* **4** used to say that something will probably be good, bad, interesting etc: *It should be a good movie – its reviews were very good.*|*With her talent and experience, she should do well for herself.* **5** used after 'that' in some expressions showing an opinion or feeling: *It's odd that he should react in this way.*|*The residents demanded that there should be an official inquiry.* **6 should it rain/should there be a problem etc** if it rains, if there is a problem etc: *Should anyone phone, tell them I'm in conference.* **7** *formal, especially BrE* used after 'I' or 'WE' in conditional sentences: *I should stay in bed if I were you.*|*I should be surprised if he came.* **8** *formal especially BrE* used after 'IF' to emphasize that something might or might not happen: *If the wound should become inflamed do not hesitate to call me.* **9** used in reported speech to mean SHALL: *I promised I should be back by midnight.* **10 what should happen but/who should appear but etc** *especially humorous* used to show that you were surprised when something happened, a particular person appeared etc: *Just at that moment who should walk in but old Jim himself.* **11 I should worry/he should care etc** *humorous* used to mean the opposite of what you seem to be saying: *With all his money, he should worry about giving the waiter a tip!* **12 I should have thought** *spoken* *especially BrE* used as a polite or joking way of showing that you disagree with what someone has said: *"Why isn't it working?" "I should have thought that was obvious."* **13 I should like** *formal, especially BrE* used to say politely that you want something: *"Will you require anything else?" "Yes, I should like a dry martini."* **14 I should think** used to say what you believe or expect to be true: *I shouldn't think there'll be a problem parking at that time of night.* **15 I should think so/not** *spoken* used to strongly agree with what someone has said: *"I'm not going out tonight." "I should think not, with so much work to do!"*

S2 W2 **shoul·der¹** /ˈʃəʊldə‖ˈʃoʊldər/ *n* [C]
**1 ▶ BODY PART ◀** one of the two parts of the body at each side of the neck where the arm is connected: *Put a shawl around your shoulders in case you get cold.* | **shrug your shoulders** (=raise them to show that you do not know something or do not care) *Keith just shrugged his shoulders and said it wasn't his problem.* —see pictures at BODY, HORSE¹
**2 ▶ CLOTHES ◀** the part of a piece of clothing that covers your shoulders: *a jacket with padded shoulders*
**3 ▶ MEAT ◀** the upper part of the front leg of an animal that is used for meat: *a shoulder of pork*
**4 a shoulder to cry on** someone who gives you sympathy: *Ben is always there when I need a shoulder to cry on.*
**5 shoulder to shoulder** working together to achieve the same thing: *We worked shoulder to shoulder for five years in that hell-hole.*
**6 stand shoulder to shoulder with** to completely share someone's opinions about something and support them in what they are doing
**7 on sb's shoulders** if a difficult or unpleasant responsibility is on someone's shoulders, they are the person that has that responsibility: *The duty of informing the children's parents fell on the shoulders of Sergeant Flynn.* | *The blame rests squarely on Jim's shoulders.*
**8 put your shoulder to the wheel** to start to work with great effort and determination
**9 ▶ ROAD-SIDE ◀** *AmE* an area of ground beside a road where drivers can stop their cars if they are having trouble —see also HARD SHOULDER, SOFT SHOULDER —see picture on page 415
**10 ▶ MOUNTAIN ◀** a rounded part of a mountain just below the top —see also **cry on sb's shoulder** (CRY¹ (4)), **give sb the cold shoulder** (COLD¹ (8)), **have a chip on your shoulder** (CHIP¹ (5)), **rub shoulders with** (RUB¹ (6)), **head and shoulders above the rest** (HEAD¹ (50)), **straight from the shoulder** (STRAIGHT² (9))

**shoulder²** *v* **1** [T] **shoulder a responsibility/duty/cost etc** to accept a difficult or unpleasant responsibility, duty etc: *The residents are being asked to shoulder the costs of the repairs.* **2** [T] to lift something onto your shoulder to carry it: *They shouldered the boat and took it down to the river.* **3 shoulder your way through/into etc** to move through a large crowd of people by pushing with your shoulder: *She shouldered her way through the onlookers.* **4 shoulder arms** an order given to a soldier telling him to hold his weapon against his shoulder

**shoulder bag** /ˈ·· ·/ *n* [C] a bag that hangs from your shoulder

**shoulder blade** /ˈ·· ·/ *n* [C] one of the two flat bones on each side of your back SCAPULA —see picture at SKELETON

**shoulder-high** /ˌ·· ˈ·◂/ *adj, adv* as high as your shoulder: *shoulder-high grass*

**shoulder-length** /ˈ·· ˌ·/ *adj* shoulder-length hair hangs down to your shoulders —see picture on page 412

**shoulder pad** /ˈ·· ·/ *n* [C] a thick flat piece of material that is fixed under the shoulders of a piece of clothing to make your shoulders look bigger

**shoulder strap** /ˈ·· ·/ *n* [C] **1** a long narrow piece of material on a piece of women's clothing that goes over the shoulder **2** a long narrow piece of material fixed to a bag etc so that you can carry it over your shoulder

**should·n't** /ˈʃʊdnt/ *v* the short form of 'should not'

**shouldst** /ʃədst; *strong* ʃʊdst/ *v old use* the second person singular form of the verb SHOULD

**shout¹** /ʃaʊt/ *v* **1** [I, T] to say something very loudly: *There's no need to shout, I'm not deaf!* | *We could hear them shouting for help.* | *"Watch out!" she shouted, as the car started to move.* | **shout at sb** *I wish you'd stop shouting at the children.* | **shout sth at sb** *He'll be writing on the blackboard and the kids will all be shouting at him.* | **shout yourself hoarse** (=make your voice rough and weak by shouting a lot) **2** to call out loudly, for example because you are angry or in pain: *My brother shouted in pain as the ball hit him.* **3 shout sth from the rooftops** to tell everyone about something because you want everyone to know about it: *But she was in love, and she wanted to shout the fact from the rooftops.* **4 be all over bar the shouting** *BrE spoken* used to say that something is almost finished and there is no doubt what the result will be: *The kids were arrested and pleaded guilty. It was all over bar the shouting.*

**shout** sb ↔ **down** *phr v* [T] to shout in order to prevent someone from being heard: *Unpopular speakers were shouted down by the crowd.*

**shout out** *phr v* [I **shout** sth ↔ **out**] to say something suddenly in a loud voice: *Don't shout out the answer in class, put up your hand.*

**shout²** *n* **1** [C] a loud call expressing anger, pain, excitement etc: *a warning shout* | *shouts of delight from the football crowd* | **give a shout** *Tom gave a shout of triumph as he realized he'd won.* **2 give sb a shout** *spoken* to go and find someone and tell them something: *Give me a shout when you're ready to go.* **3 sb's shout** *AustrE or BrE informal* someone's turn to buy drinks: *It's my shout. Same again?*

S3 **shove¹** /ʃʌv/ *v* **1** [I,T] to push someone or something, in a rough or careless way, using your hands or shoulders: **shove sb aside/into etc** *Secret Service men shoved people aside to make way for the President.* | **shove sb/sth** *Stop shoving me or I'll tell the teacher!* | **pushing and shoving** (=pushing with your body, especially in a crowd) *There was no trouble at the rally apart from a little pushing and shoving.* —see picture on page 1260 **2** [T always + adv/prep] to put something somewhere carelessly or without thinking much: **shove sth into/under etc** *Let's shove everything into the closet just for now.* **3 shove up/over** *spoken, especially BrE* to move along on a seat to make space for someone else: *Shove up mate, there's no room to sit down here.* —see also **when push comes to shove** (PUSH² (7))

**shove off** *phr v* [I] **1** *spoken* used to tell someone rudely or angrily to go away: *Shove off! I'm busy.* **2** to push a boat away from the land, usually with a pole

**shove²** *n* [C] a strong push: **give sth a shove** *We gave the door one good shove and it came open.*

**shov·el¹** /ˈʃʌvəl/ *n* [C] **1** a tool with a rounded blade and a long handle used for moving earth, stones etc —compare SPADE (1) **2** a part of a large vehicle or machine used for moving or digging earth

**shovel²** *v* **shovelled, shovelling** *BrE*, **shoveled, shoveling** *AmE* [I,T] **1** to lift and move earth, stones etc with a shovel: *The workmen shovelled loads of gravel onto the road.* | **shovel the driveway/sidewalk etc** *AmE* (=shovel snow from a road or path) *Chris, I asked you two days ago to shovel the front path.* **2 shovel sth into/onto etc** to put something into a place quickly: *He was shovelling spaghetti into his mouth.*

**shov·el·ful** /ˈʃʌvəlfʊl/ *n* [C] the amount of coal, snow, earth etc that you can carry on a shovel

S1 W1 **show¹** /ʃəʊ‖ʃoʊ/ *v past tense* **showed** *past participle* **shown** /ʃəʊn‖ʃoʊn/
**1 ▶ PROVE ◀** [T] to provide facts or information that make it clear that something is true or that something exists: **show (that)** *The latest poll clearly shows that most voters are unaware of this.* | *As her record plainly shows, Wyler is one of the world's all-time great players.* | **show how/what** *Her experience shows how easily young women can get into trouble abroad.* | **show sth**

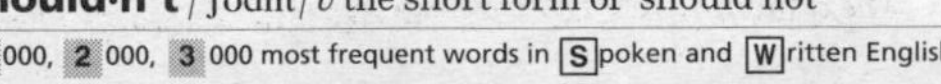

*Recent events in Somalia show the futility of war.* | *Statistics show a marked rise in nitrogen levels at this point.* | **show sb/sth to be** *formal*: *He later showed himself to be an excellent chess player.* | **it just shows/it just goes to show** *spoken* (=when a bad experience you have been talking about proves something) *And he took everything she had. It just goes to show, you should never trust a stranger.* —see graph at INDICATE

**2** ▶ **SHOW YOUR FEELINGS ETC** ◀ [T] to let your feelings, attitudes, or personal qualities be clearly seen in the way you behave, the way you look etc: *She's never shown much interest in my work.* | *I think it shows great determination on her part.* | *He showed his agreement by a slight nod.* | **show how/what etc** *I was determined not to show how upset I was.*

**3** ▶ **INFORMATION/MEASUREMENTS ETC** ◀ [T not usually in progressive] **a)** if a picture, map etc shows something, you can see it on the picture, map etc: *This diagram shows the correct position of the gear lever.* | *a useful chart showing all the flights coming into and out of Paris* **b)** if a clock or other measuring instrument shows a time, a number etc, you can see that time etc on it: *The victim's watch showed five minutes past two.*

**4** ▶ **LET SB SEE** ◀ [T] to let someone see something, for example by holding it out so that they can look at it: **show sb sth** *Jackie showed the official her passport.* | **show sth to sb** *Show your ticket to the man at the entrance.* | **show sth** *All passes must be shown on entering the building.*

**5** ▶ **TELL/EXPLAIN STH** ◀ [T] **a)** to tell someone how to do something, by explaining it to them, often by doing it yourself so that they can see you: **show sb how to do sth** *I showed him how to work the coffee machine.* | **show sb sth** *Show her the right way to do it.* **b)** to tell someone where a place or thing is, for example by pointing to it: **show sb sth** *I'll show you the exact spot where it happened.* | **show sb where** *Could you show me where I can put my coat?*

**6** ▶ **GUIDE SB** ◀ [T always + adv/prep] to go with someone and guide them to a place: **show sb to/in/out/around** *Goodbye, Mrs Davies. My secretary will show you out.* (=out of the office or building) | **show sb sth** *Come on out, and I'll show you the garden* —see also **show** sb ↔ **around, show** sb **over** sth —see LEAD[1] (USAGE)

**7** ▶ **CAN BE SEEN** ◀ **a)** [I] if something shows it is easy to see: *His happiness showed in his face.* | *Don't worry about that tiny stain; it won't show.* **b)** [T] if material shows dirt or a mark, it is easy to see the dirt or mark on it: *That light jacket will show the slightest crease.*

**8** ▶ **FILM** ◀ **a)** [I] if a film is showing at a cinema, you can see it there **b)** [T] if a cinema shows a film, it makes it available for people to see: *The local movie theater is showing Tom Cruise's latest picture.* —see also SHOWING

**9 have something/nothing etc to show for** if you have something to show for your efforts, hard work etc, you have achieved something as a result of them: *Is that all you've got to show for a whole week's work?*

**10 show a profit/loss** if a company shows a profit or loss, it makes a financial profit or loss

**11 show your hand** to make your true power or intentions clear, especially after you have been keeping them secret: *She needed to be cautious, and not show her hand too soon.*

**12 show your face** if you will not show your face somewhere, you will not go there because you have a good reason to feel ashamed or embarrassed about being there: *He wouldn't dare show his face in here after the way he behaved last week!*

**13** ▶ **ART/PICTURES** ◀ [T often passive] to put a collection of paintings or other works of art in one place so that people can come and see them: *Her recent sculptures are being shown at the Hayward Gallery.*

**14** ▶ **ANIMAL** ◀ [T] to put an animal into a competition with other animals

**15** ▶ **ARRIVE** ◀ [I] *informal, especially AmE* to arrive at the place where someone is waiting for you; show up: *I came to meet Hank, but he never showed.*

**16 ... and it shows** *spoken* used to say that something, especially something bad, is very clear to see: *"I did the whole report in only two days!" "And it shows!"*

**17 I'll show him/them etc** *spoken* used to say that you will prove to someone that you are better, more effective etc than they think you are: *They're convinced I'm going to fail, but I'll show them!*

**18 show sb in a good/bad etc light** if an action shows you in a good or bad light, it makes people have a good or bad opinion about you: *a decision which does not show Roosevelt in a particularly favourable light*

**19 show sb the door** to make it clear that someone is not welcome and should leave

**20 show sb who's boss** *informal* to prove to someone who is threatening your authority that you are more powerful than they are: *Don't let your horse pull his head down – show him who's boss.*

**21 show the way** if you show the way for other people, you do something new that others then try to copy: *In the 70s Panderm showed the way with its revolutionary new techniques.*

**22 show a leg!** *BrE spoken* used to tell someone to get out of bed

**23 show a clean pair of heels** *BrE old-fashioned informal* to run away very fast

**show** sb ↔ **around** (sth) *phr v* [T] to go around a place with someone when they first arrive there, to show them what is interesting, useful etc: *Pat will show you around the building so you can meet everyone.* | *We were shown around by an elderly guide.*

**show off** *phr v* **1** [I] to try to impress people and make them admire your abilities, achievements, or possessions: *Pay no attention to Susan – she's just showing off.* **2** [T **show** sth ↔ **off**] to show something to a lot of people because you are very proud of it: *Peter was keen to show off his new car.* **3** [T **show** sth ↔ **off**] if one thing shows off something else, it makes the other thing look especially attractive: *The white dress showed off her dark skin beautifully.*

**show** sb **over** sth *phr v* [T] *especially BrE* to guide someone through an interesting building or a house that is for sale: *Our company chairman showed the Prime Minister over the new plant.*

**show** sb ↔ **round** (sth) *phr v BrE* to SHOW AROUND

**show up** *phr v* **1** [I] *informal* to arrive, especially at the place where someone is waiting for you: *I was almost asleep when Chris finally showed up.* **2** [T **show** sth ↔ **up**] to make it possible to see or notice something that was not clear before: *The sunlight showed up the cracks in the wall.* | *These riots show up the deficiencies in police training.* **3** [I] to be easy to see or notice: *The subtitles won't show up against such a light background.* | *A lot of bugs showed up when I ran the program.* **4** [T **show** sb ↔ **up**] to make someone feel embarrassed by behaving in a stupid or unacceptable way when you are with them: *Why must you always show me up at these occasions?*

**show**[2] *n* S1 W1

**1** ▶ **PERFORMANCE** ◀ [C] an entertaining performance, especially one that includes singing, dancing, or jokes: *She is appearing in a show on Broadway.* | *Cowan's one-man show opens on April 16th* —see also FLOOR SHOW

**2** ▶ **TV/RADIO** ◀ a programme on television or on the radio: *She's been in a lot of popular TV shows.* | *comedy shows* | **chat/talk show** (=a show on which well-known people talk about their lives, work etc) | **game show** (=a show in which people play games for prizes) | **quiz show** (=a show in which people compete to answer questions)

**3** ▶ **A COLLECTION OF THINGS** ◀ [C] an occasion when a lot of similar things are brought together in one place so that people can come and look at them, or so that they can compete against each other; EXHIBITION: **flower/dog etc show** *The annual pet show takes place in August.* | *Are you entering your pony in the show?* | **fashion/air etc show** *We have a stand at the 1996 travel show.* | *exhibits at the Motor Show* | **hold/put on/stage a show** *The gallery is holding a major show of her work next month.*

**4 be on show** to be shown to the public: *The painting will be on show until the end of the month.* | *Frink's works will go on show next week.*
**5 ► FEELINGS/QUALITIES ◄ a show of** [C] something that shows what something is like, how someone feels etc; DISPLAY OF: *a little show of bad temper* | **a show of strength/force** *Their army staged a big military parade as a show of strength.*
**6** [singular, U] something you do to pretend to other people that something is true; PRETENCE: [+ **of**] *"Oh, no. I don't mind," she said, with a show of cheerfulness.* | **make a show of/put on a show of** *I made a show of interest, but I didn't really care what happened.* | **for show** *We went through a marriage ceremony, but it was all for show, to convince the authorities.*
**7 ► EVENT /SITUATION ◄** *informal singular* a place or situation where something is being done or organized: **run the show** (=be in charge of something) *Who's running this show, you or me?*
**8 put up a good/poor etc show** *informal* to perform, play etc well or badly: *Our team put up a pretty good show, but we lost in the end.*
**9 let's get this show on the road** *spoken* used to tell people it is time to start working or start a journey
**10 (jolly) good show** *BrE old-fashioned spoken* used to express your approval of something —see also **steal the show** (STEAL[1] (3))

**show**[3] *adj* **show-house/-flat** *BrE* a house or apartment that has been built and filled with furniture to show buyers what similar new houses or apartments look like

**show and tell** /ˌ· · ˈ·/ *n* [U] an activity for school children in which they bring an object to school and tell the other children about it: *Ramona brought in a fossil for show and tell.*

**show·biz** /ˈʃəʊbɪz‖ˈʃoʊ-/ *n* [U] *informal* SHOW BUSINESS

**show busi·ness** /ˈ· ˌ··/ also **showbiz** *informal n* [U] the entertainment industry, for example television, films, popular theatre etc: *Some of the biggest names in show business will be at the gala.*

**show·case** /ˈʃəʊkeɪs‖ˈʃoʊ-/ *n* [C] **1** an event or situation that is designed to show the good qualities of a person, organization, product etc: [+ **for**] *The new musical is a good showcase for her talents.* **2** a glass box containing objects for people to look at in a shop, at an art show etc —**showcase** *v* [T]

**show·down** /ˈʃəʊdaʊn‖ˈʃoʊ-/ *n* [C usually singular] a meeting, argument, fight etc that will settle a disagreement or competition that has continued for a long time: *Sunday's game will be a showdown between the two leading teams.* | [+ **with**] *a showdown with the striking auto workers*

S2 **show·er**[1] /ˈʃaʊə‖-ər/ *n* [C]
**1 ► FOR WASHING IN ◄** a thing that you stand under to wash your whole body: *Why does the phone always ring when I'm in the shower?*
**2 ► ACT OF WASHING ◄** an act of washing your body while standing under a shower: *I need a shower.* | **take a shower** *especially AmE* **have a shower** *especially BrE*: *Nick rolled out of bed, took a shower and got dressed.*
**3 ► RAIN ◄** a short period of rain or snow: *Heavy showers are forecast in the hills tomorrow.* | *a snow shower*
**4 ► THINGS IN THE AIR ◄** a lot of small, light things falling or appearing together: [+ **of**] *Peter kicked the fire and sent up a shower of sparks.*
**5 ► PARTY ◄** *especially AmE* a party at which presents are given to a woman who is going to get married or have a baby: *We're having a shower for Sherri on Friday.* | *a baby shower*
**6 ► PEOPLE ◄** *BrE informal* a group of stupid or lazy people

**shower**[2] *v* **1** [I] to wash your whole body while standing under a shower **2** [I always + adv/prep, T] to scatter a lot of small light things onto a person or place, or to be scattered in this way: [+ **down/over/upon**] *Volcanic dust showered down on the onlookers.* | **shower sb/sth with** *The branches of the trees showered me with snow.* | **shower sth down/over/on** *Thousands of leaflets were showered over occupied France.* **3** to generously give someone a lot of things: **shower sb with sth** *When he left the school, his students showered him with presents.* | **shower sth on/upon sb** *Childless herself, she'd shower my kids with toys.*

**shower cap** /ˈ·· ·/ *n* [C] a plastic hat that keeps your hair dry in a shower

**shower gel** /ˈ·· ·/ *n* [U] *BrE* a type of liquid soap that you use to wash yourself in a shower

**show·er·proof** /ˈʃaʊəpruːf‖ˈʃaʊər-/ *adj* showerproof clothes keep you dry in light rain but not in heavy rain

**show·er·y** /ˈʃaʊəri/ *adj* raining frequently for short periods: *a showery day*

**show·girl** /ˈʃəʊgɜːl‖ˈʃoʊgɜːrl/ *n* [C] one of a group of women who sing or dance in a musical show

**show·ing** /ˈʃəʊɪŋ‖ˈʃoʊ-/ *n* **1** [C] an occasion when a film, art show etc can be seen or looked at, especially a special occasion that people are invited to: *a private showing of the film 'King Kong'* **2** [singular] something that shows how well or how badly you are doing: **a good/poor showing** *Their poor showing in the mid-term elections is being blamed on the President.* | **on sb's present/current showing** (=judging by the way they are performing now) *On our present showing, we're unlikely to get into the finals.*

**show jump·ing** /ˈ· ˌ··/ *n* [U] a sport in which horses with riders have to jump a series of fences as quickly and skilfully as possible —**show jumper** *n* [C]

**show·man** /ˈʃəʊmən‖ˈʃoʊ-/ *n plural* **showmen** /-mən/ [C] someone who is good at entertaining people and getting a lot of public attention: *In politics it helps to be a bit of a showman.*

**show·man·ship** /ˈʃəʊmənʃɪp‖ˈʃoʊ-/ *n* [U] skill at entertaining people and getting public attention

**shown** /ʃəʊn‖ʃoʊn/ the past participle of SHOW

**show-off** /ˈ· ·/ *n* [C] *informal* someone who always tries to show how clever or skilled they are so that other people will admire them: *Don't be such a show-off!*

**show of hands** /ˌ· · ˈ·/ *n* [singular] a vote taken by counting the raised hands of the people at a meeting: *The dispute was settled with a show of hands.*

**show·piece** /ˈʃəʊpiːs‖ˈʃoʊ-/ *n* [C usually singular] something that an organization, government etc wants people to see, because it is a very good or successful example: *The modern languages department is the showpiece of the university.* | *a showpiece factory*

**show·place** /ˈʃəʊpleɪs‖ˈʃoʊ-/ *n* [C] a place which is open to the public because of its beauty, historical interest etc

**show·room** /ˈʃəʊrʊm, -ruːm‖ˈʃoʊ-/ *n* [C] a large room where you can look at things that are for sale such as cars or electrical goods: *a car showroom*

**show-stop·ping** /ˈ· ˌ··/ *adj* a show-stopping performance is extremely good or impressive: *his show-stopping performance as Stanley Kowalski* —**showstopper** *n* [C]

**show tri·al** /ˈ· ˌ··/ *n* [C] an unfair TRIAL[1] (1) that is organized by a government for political reasons, not in order to find out whether someone is guilty: *Inadequacies of the Soviet system that made such show trials necessary.*

**show·y** /ˈʃəʊi‖ˈʃoʊi/ *adj* something that is showy is very colourful, big, expensive etc, especially in a way that attracts people's attention: *a showy car* —**showily** *adv* —**showiness** *n* [U]

**shrank** /ʃræŋk/ the past tense of SHRINK

**shrap·nel** /ˈʃræpnəl/ *n* [U] small pieces of metal from a bomb, bullet etc that are scattered when it explodes: *Robert suffers from an old shrapnel wound.*

**shred**[1] /ʃred/ *n* **1** [C] a small thin piece that is torn or cut roughly from something: [+ **of**] *a shred of cloth* | *shreds of dried coconut* | **tear/rip/cut sth to shreds** *Jackie was so mad with Tom she tore all his letters to shreds.* —see picture on page 416 **2 in shreds a)** torn in many places: *My scarf was in shreds after the dog had played with it.* **b)** completely ruined: *Simon went home* *with his career in shreds.* **3** [singular] a very small amount: **not a shred of proof/evidence/doubt** (=not at all) | *There's not a shred of evidence to convict him.*

**shred²** *v* **shredded, shredding** [T] **1** to cut or tear something into small thin pieces: *Coleslaw is made with shredded cabbage.* **2** to put a document into a shredder: *By the time the police got there the files had all been shredded.*

**shred·der** /ˈʃredə‖-ər/ *n* [C] a machine that cuts documents into small pieces so that no one can read them

**shrew** /ʃruː/ *n* [C] **1** a very small animal like a mouse with a long pointed nose **2** *old use* an unpleasant woman who always argues and disagrees with people

**shrewd** /ʃruːd/ *adj* **1** good at judging what people or situations are really like, especially in a way that makes you successful in business, politics etc: *Martin's a shrewd judge of character.* | *a shrewd businesswoman* **2** well judged and likely to be right: *At a shrewd guess, I'd say Henry is going to leave his job.* | **have a shrewd idea** (=have an opinion about something that is probably correct) —**shrewdly** *adv*: *"Were you jealous of her?" asked Sara shrewdly.* —**shrewdness** *n* [U]

**shrew·ish** /ˈʃruːɪʃ/ *adj old use* a shrewish woman is one who always argues and disagrees with people

**shriek¹** /ʃriːk/ *v* [I] **1** to make a very high, loud sound: *Judith suddenly shrieked and looked to see what had bitten her.* | **shriek with joy/pain/fright etc** *Everyone was shrieking with laughter in the bar.* **2** [T] to say something in a high, loud voice because you are excited, afraid, or angry: *Anne stood in the doorway shrieking abuse at him.*

**shriek²** *n* [C] a loud high sound made because you are frightened, excited, angry etc: [+ **of**] *a shriek of terror* | **with a shriek** *Miss Lavish, with a shriek of dismay, dragged her backwards.*

**shrill¹** /ʃrɪl/ *adj* **1** a shrill sound is very high and unpleasant; PIERCING (1): *He heard the shrill voice of a woman in the next room.* | *a shrill whistle* **2** shrill words express repeated, often unreasonable complaints or criticism: *We use quiet persuasion rather than shrill denunciation.* —**shrillness** *n* [U] —**shrilly** /ˈʃrɪl-li, ˈʃrɪli/ *adv*

**shrill²** *v* **1** *especially literary* [I] to produce a very high and unpleasant sound: *The telephone shrilled twice.* **2** [T] to say something in a very high voice: *"Shame!" she shrilled.*

**shrimp** /ʃrɪmp/ *n* [C] **1 a)** *BrE* a small pink sea creature that you can eat, with ten legs and with a soft shell **b)** *AmE* a creature like this, but bigger; PRAWN *AmE* **2** *humorous* someone who is very small

**shrimp cock·tail** /ˌ· ˈ··/ *n* [C,U] *AmE* shrimps without their shells in a red sauce, eaten before the main part of a meal; PRAWN COCKTAIL *BrE*

**shrimp·ing** /ˈʃrɪmpɪŋ/ *n* [U] the activity of fishing for shrimps

**shrine** /ʃraɪn/ *n* [C] **1** a place that is connected with a holy event or holy person, and that people visit to pray **2** a place that people visit and respect because it is connected with a famous person or event: *Elvis's home has become a shrine for his fans.*

**shrink¹** /ʃrɪŋk/ *v past tense* **shrank** /ʃræŋk/ *past participle* **shrunk** /ʃrʌŋk/ **1** [I,T] to become smaller or to make something smaller through the effects of heat or water: *Hot water shrinks woollen clothes.* | *Will it shrink if I wash it?* —see also PRE-SHRUNK, SHRUNKEN **2** [I,T] to become smaller in amount, size or value: *The number of students has shrunk from 120 to 70.* | *The shrinking pound damages the tourist trade.* **3** [I always + adv/prep] *especially literary* to move back and away from something, especially because you are frightened: [+ **back/away/from**] *Jenny shrank back against the wall in horror.*

**shrink from** sth *phr v* [T] to avoid doing something difficult or unpleasant: *I will not shrink from my duties.* | **shrink from doing sth** *The Prime Minister is unlikely to shrink from making tough decisions.*

**shrink²** *n* [C] *informal humorous* a PSYCHOANALYST or PSYCHIATRIST

**shrink·age** /ˈʃrɪŋkɪdʒ/ *n* [C] the act of shrinking, or the amount that something shrinks: *a further shrinkage in the size of the workforce*

**shrink·ing vi·o·let** /ˌ·· ˈ···/ *n* [C] *humorous* someone who is very shy

**shrink-wrapped** /ˌ· ˈ·◂/ *adj* goods that are shrink-wrapped are wrapped tightly in plastic —**shrink-wrap** *n* [U]

**shriv·el** /ˈʃrɪvəl/ also **shrivel up** *v* **shrivelled, shrivelling** *BrE*, **shriveled, shriveling** *AmE* [I,T] if something shrivels or is shrivelled, it becomes smaller and its surface is covered in lines because it is very dry or old: *The grapes are left out in the sun to shrivel up and become raisins.* —**shrivelled** *adj*: *Mrs Carey was a tiny, shrivelled old lady.*

**shroud¹** /ʃraʊd/ *n* [C] **1** a cloth that is wrapped around a dead person's body before it is buried **2** something that hides or covers something: *The fog rolled in, and a grey shroud covered the city.* | [+ **of**] *A shroud of silence surrounded the general's death.*

**shroud²** *v* **1 be shrouded in mist/smoke etc** to be covered and hidden by mist, smoke etc: *The black streets were shrouded in fog.* **2 be shrouded in mystery/secrecy etc** to be mysterious, secret etc: *The origins of this ritual are shrouded in mystery.*

**Shrove Tues·day** /ˌʃrəʊv ˈtjuːzdi‖ˌʃroʊv ˈtuːz-/ *n* [C,U] the day before the first day of the Christian period of Lent, when people traditionally eat PANCAKES

**shrub** /ʃrʌb/ *n* [C] a small bush with several woody stems

**shrub·be·ry** /ˈʃrʌbəri/ *n* [C,U] shrubs planted close together in a group, or a part of a garden where shrubs grow

**shrug¹** /ʃrʌg/ *v* [I,T] to raise and then lower your shoulders in order to show that you do not know something or do not care about something

**shrug** ↔sth **off** *phr v* [T] to treat something as unimportant and not worry about it: *We can't just shrug these objections off.*

**shrug²** *n* [C usually singular] a movement of your shoulders upwards and then downwards again

**shrunk** /ʃrʌŋk/ the past tense and past participle of SHRINK

shrug

**shrunk·en** /ˈʃrʌŋkən/ *adj* [usually before noun] having become smaller or been made smaller: *a shrunken old woman*

**shtick, schtick** /ʃtɪk/ *n* [U] *AmE* the style of humour that a particular actor or COMEDIAN typically uses

**shuck** /ʃʌk/ *v* [T] *AmE* to remove the outer cover of a vegetable such as corn or PEAS, or the shell of OYSTERS or CLAMS

**shuck off** *phr v* [T] *AmE informal* to take off a piece of clothing: *She shucked off her jacket and ran upstairs.*

**shucks** /ʃʌks/ *interjection AmE old-fashioned* used to show you are a little disappointed about something

**shud·der¹** /ˈʃʌdə‖-ər/ *v* [I] **1** to shake uncontrollably for a short time because you are frightened, or cold, or because you think something is very unpleasant: [+ **at**] *He touched Ralph's bare shoulder and Ralph shuddered at the human contact.* **2** if a vehicle or machine shudders, it shakes violently: *The train shuddered to a halt.* **3 I shudder to think** used to say that you do not want to think about something because it is too unpleasant: *I shudder to think what they'll say when they see the mess the house is in.*

**shudder at** *phr v* [T] to think that something is very bad or unpleasant: *Modern doctors shudder at treatments such as bleeding people with leeches.*

**shudder²** *n* [C usually singular] a shaking movement: *The building gave a sudden shudder.*

**shuf·fle¹** /ˈʃʌfəl/ *v* **1** [I always + adv/prep] to walk very slowly and noisily, without lifting your feet off the ground: [+ **along/towards/down etc**] *The old man shuffled along the sidewalk.* | *The class came shuffling in from the playground.* —see picture on page 1262 **2** [T] to move something such as papers into a different order or into different positions: *Jack sat nervously shuffling the papers around on his desk.* **3** [I,T] to mix PLAYING CARDS around into a different order before playing a game with them: *Is it my turn to shuffle?* **4 shuffle your feet** to move your feet slightly, especially because you are bored or embarrassed: *Malcolm shuffled his feet and apologized again.* **—shuffler** *n* [C] —see also RESHUFFLE¹

**shuffle²** *n* **1** [singular] a slow walk in which you do not lift your feet off the ground **2** [C] the act of mixing cards into a different order before playing a game

**shuf·fle·board** /ˈʃʌfəlbɔːd‖-bɔːrd/ *n* [U] a game played in the US in which you use a long stick to push a flat round object towards an area with numbers on it

**shuf·ti** /ˈʃʊfti/ *n* **have a shufti** *BrE spoken* to have a quick look at something

**shun** /ʃʌn/ *v* [T] to avoid someone or something deliberately: *a shy woman who shunned publicity* | *Victims of the disease found themselves shunned by society.*

**shunt¹** /ʃʌnt/ *v* [T] **1** to move a train or railway carriage onto a different track **2** to move someone or something to another place, especially in a way that seems unfair: **shunt sb off/around/aside etc** *Smith was shunted off to one of the company's smaller offices.*

**shunt²** *n* [C] an act of moving a train or railway carriage to a different track

**shush** /ʃʊʃ/ *v* **1 shush!** *spoken* used to tell someone, especially a child, to be quiet: *"Shush!" said Jerry. "Not so loud."* **2** [T] to tell someone to be very quiet, especially by putting your fingers against your lips or by saying 'shush': *He started to cry and Francesca shushed him.*

1 2 **shut¹** /ʃʌt/ *v past tense and past participle* **shut** *present participle* **shutting** **1** [I,T] to close something, or to become closed: *The door shut with a bang.* | *She lay down on her bed and shut her eyes.* | *Laruelle put the jewels back and shut the lid of the box.* —see OPEN² (USAGE) **2 shut sth in the door/drawer etc** to shut a door etc against something so that it gets trapped there: *Watch out! You're going to get the cat's tail shut in the door.* **3 shut your mouth/trap/face!** *spoken* used to rudely and angrily tell someone to stop talking **4 shut it!** *BrE spoken* used to tell someone rudely and angrily to stop talking **5** [I,T] *especially BrE* to stop being open to the public for a short time or permanently; CLOSE¹ (3): *The post office shuts at 5 o'clock.* | *He lost his job when they shut the factory.* **6 shut your eyes/ears to** to refuse deliberately to notice or pay attention to something: *You simply can't shut your eyes to the truth of the matter.* **7 shut your ears to** to deliberately not listen to something: *He could not shut his ears to the cries and groans coming from inside the room.*

**shut** sb/sth ↔ **away** *phr v* [T] **a)** to put someone or something in a place away from other people where they cannot be seen **b) shut yourself away** to stay at home or go somewhere quiet, so that you can be alone: *She shut herself away in her room to work on her novel.*

**shut down** *phr v* **1** [I,T] if a company, factory, large machine etc shuts down or is shut down, it stops operating: *There's a rumor going around that the plant is shutting down next year.* | *The printing press had been shut down for servicing.* **2** [T **shut** sb ↔ **down**] *AmE informal* to prevent an opposing team or player from playing well or getting points: *We all knew that if we wanted to win we'd have to shut down Bobby Mitchell.*

**shut** sb **in** *phr v* [T] to put or keep someone in a room and stop them from getting out: *The children would be shut in the dormitory at night.*

**shut off** *phr v* **1** [I,T] if a machine, tool etc shuts off or if you shut it off, it stops operating: *The machine shuts off automatically if it gets too hot.* | **shut** sth ↔ **off** *I let the engine run for a minute and then shut it off.* **2** [T **shut** sth ↔ **off**] to prevent goods or supplies from being available or being delivered: *a strike that closed the mines and shut off coal supplies* **3 shut yourself off** to avoid meeting and talking to other people: [+ **from**] *After her last movie, Garbo shut herself off from the world.* **4 be shut off from** to be separated from other people or things, especially so that you are not influenced by them: *The valley is completely shut off from the modern world by a range of high mountains.*

**shut** sb/sth **out** *phr v* [T] **1** [**shut** sb ↔ **out**] to deliberately not let someone join you in an activity or share your thoughts and feelings: *I felt I was being shut out from all the family's affairs.* | *How can I help you if you just keep shutting me out all the time?* **2** [**shut** sb/sth ↔ **out**] to prevent someone or something from entering a place: *Paula packed the bottom of the doors with blankets to shut out the draught.* | *heavy curtains that shut out the sunlight* **3** [**shut** sth ↔ **out**] to stop yourself from thinking about or noticing something, so that you are not affected by it: *When she's reading, she seems to be able to shut out the rest of the world.* **4** [**shut out** sb] *AmE* to defeat an opposing team and prevent them from getting any points: *The Chicago Bears shut out the Broncos.*

**shut up** *phr v* **1 shut up!** *spoken* used to tell someone rudely to stop talking: *Oh, shut up! I don't want to hear your excuses.* | [+ **about**] *We know you won, but just shut up about it, okay!* **2** [T **shut** sb **up**] to make someone stop talking or be quiet: *The only way to shut Philippa up was to give her something to eat.* **3** [T **shut up** sb] to keep someone in a place away from other people, and prevent them from leaving: *I've had a terrible cold and been shut up in my room for a week.* **4** [T **shut** sth ↔ **up**] to close a shop, room etc so that people cannot get into it: *Bernadette cleaned the attic and then shut it up for another year.* **5 shut up shop** *informal BrE* to close a business or stop working, at the end of the day or permanently

**shut²** *adj* [not usually before noun] **1** not open; closed: *Is the door shut properly?* | *He sat with his eyes shut.* | **blow/slam/bang shut** *The door slammed shut behind him.* | **pull/kick/slide etc sth shut** *Jenny pulled the window shut.* **2** *BrE* not open for business; closed *AmE*: *It's 6.30 pm and the banks are shut.* | [+ **for**] *The first four hotels we tried were shut for the winter.*

**shut·down** /ˈʃʌtdaʊn/ *n* [C] the closing of a factory, business, or piece of machinery: *the shutdown of several power stations*

**shut-eye** /ˈ· ·/ *n* [U] *informal* sleep: *I've got to get some shut-eye.*

**shut-in** /ˈ· ·/ *n* [C] *AmE* someone who is ill or DISABLED and cannot leave their house very easily: *visiting the sick and shut-ins*

**shut-out** /ˈ· ·/ *n* [C] *AmE* a game in which one team is prevented by the other from getting any points

**shut·ter** /ˈʃʌtə‖-ər/ *n* [C] **1** [usually plural] one of a pair of wooden or metal covers on the outside of a window that can be closed to keep light out or prevent thieves from coming in —see picture on page 410 **2** a part of a camera that opens for a very short time to let light onto the film **3 put up the shutters** *BrE informal* to close a business at the end of the day or permanently

**shut·ter·bug** /ˈʃʌtəbʌg‖-ər-/ *n* [C] *AmE informal* someone who likes to take a lot of photographs

**shut·tered** /ˈʃʌtəd‖-ərd/ *adj* with closed shutters, or having shutters: *A gust of wind shook the shuttered windows.*

**shut·tle¹** /ˈʃʌtl/ *n* [C] **1** a plane, bus, or train that makes regular short journeys between two places: *He took the Washington-New York shuttle.* **2** a SPACECRAFT that can fly into space and return to Earth, and can be used more than once; SPACE SHUTTLE **3 shuttle service** a plane, bus, or train service that goes regularly between two places that are fairly near each other: *There's a shuttle service from the city center to the airport.* **4** a pointed tool used in weaving, to pass a thread over and under the threads that form the cloth **5 shuttle diplomacy** international talks, for example to make a peace agreement, carried out by someone who travels between countries and talks to members of the governments

**shuttle**[2] *v* **1** [I always + adv/prep] to travel frequently between two places: [+ **between/back and forth**] *Susan shuttles between Rotterdam and London for her job.* **2** [T] to move people from one place to another place that is fairly near: *The passengers were shuttled to the hotel by bus.*

**shut·tle·cock** /ˈʃʌtlkɒk‖-kɑːk/ *n* [C] a small light object that you hit over the net in the game of BADMINTON; BIRDIE[1] (3) *AmE* —see picture on page 1264

**shy**[1][I] /ʃaɪ/ *adj* **1** nervous and embarrassed about talking to other people, especially people you do not know: *Billy's very shy with adults, but he's fine with other children.* | *a shy smile* | **painfully shy** (=extremely shy) *At 15, I was painfully shy.* | **be too shy to do sth** *I needed a ride home but was too shy to ask anyone.* | **go all shy** *spoken* (=suddenly become very shy) *Look, she's gone all shy – stop teasing her!* **2** unwilling to do something or get involved in something: [+ **about/of**] *Men are often shy about sharing their problems.* | *Madonna is certainly not shy of publicity.* **3** [not before noun] *especially AmE* less than the amount needed: [+ **of**] *He was only 30 votes shy of the number he needed for the nomination.* **4 fight shy of (doing) sth** to avoid doing something or getting involved in something: *He fought shy of an open quarrel.* **5** shy animals get frightened easily and are unwilling to come near people —see also **once bitten twice shy** (BITE[1] (13)), CAMERA-SHY —**shyly** *adv*: *"I have a question," she said, shyly stroking Ralph's arm.* —**shyness** *n* [U]

**shy**[2] *v* **1** if a horse shies, it makes a sudden movement away from something because it is frightened **2** [T] *old-fashioned* to throw a ball or other object at something

**shy away from** sth *phr v* [T] to avoid doing something because you are not confident enough or you are worried or nervous about it: *They criticized the leadership, but shied away from a direct challenge.*

**shys·ter** /ˈʃaɪstə‖-ər/ *n* [C] *AmE informal* a dishonest person, especially a lawyer or politician

**Si·a·mese cat** /ˌsaɪəmiːz ˈkæt/ *n* [C] a type of cat that has blue eyes, short grey or brown fur, and a dark face

**Siamese twin** /ˌ··· ˈ·/ *n* [C usually plural] one of two people who are born joined to each other

**sib·ilant**[1] /ˈsɪbɪ̣lənt/ *adj formal* making or being an "s" or "sh" sound: *a sibilant, fluttering voice*

**sibilant**[2] *n* [C] *technical* a sibilant sound such as /ʃ/ in English

**sib·ling** /ˈsɪblɪŋ/ *n* [C] **1** *formal* a brother or sister **2 sibling rivalry** competition between brothers and sisters for their parents' attention or love

**sib·yl** /ˈsɪbɪl, -bəl/ *n* [C] one of a group of women in the ancient world who were thought to know the future

**sic**[1] /sɪk/ *adv Latin* used after a word that you have copied in order to show that you know it was not spelled or used correctly: *We had seen several signs that said 'ORANGE'S (sic) FOR SALE'.*

**sic**[2] *v* [T] *AmE informal* **1** to tell a dog to attack someone: *He sicced his dog on me.* **2 sic 'em!** *spoken* used to tell a dog to attack someone

S1 W3 **sick**[1] /sɪk/ *adj*

**1** ▶ **ILL** ◀ suffering from a disease or illness: *Where's Sheila – is she sick?* | *a sick child* | **get sick** *AmE* (=become ill) *At the last minute I got sick and couldn't go.* | **sick as a dog** (=very sick) *Pete's at home in bed, sick as a dog.* | **be off sick** (=be away from work or school because you are ill) *I was off sick for four days with the flu.* | **call in sick** (=telephone to say you are not coming to work because you are ill) *You have to call in sick before 9.30.* | **take sick** *old-fashioned* (=become ill) *He took sick and died a week later.* —see graph at ILL[1]

**2 be sick** to bring food up from your stomach through your mouth; VOMIT: *The cat's been sick on the carpet.* | *You'll be sick if you eat any more of that chocolate!* | **violently sick** (=suddenly and severely sick) *I was violently sick the last time I ate prawns.*

**3 feel sick** also **be/feel sick to your stomach** to feel as if you are going to VOMIT: *As soon as the ship started moving I began to feel sick.* —see also CARSICK, SEASICK, TRAVEL-SICK

**4 be sick (and tired) of** also **be sick to death of** to be angry and bored with something that has been happening for a long time: *I'm really sick of housework!* | *We're getting sick and tired of listening to them argue all the time.*

**5 be worried sick/be sick with worry** to be extremely worried: *Why didn't you tell me you were coming home late? I've been worried sick!*

**6 make me/you sick** *spoken* **a)** to make you feel very angry: *People like you make me sick!* **b)** *spoken humorous* to make someone feel jealous: *You make me sick with your 'expenses paid' holidays!*

**7** ▶ **STRANGE/CRUEL** ◀ **a)** someone who is sick does things that are strange and cruel, and seems mentally ill: *I keep getting obscene phone calls from some sick pervert.* | *a sick mind* **b)** sick stories, jokes etc deal with death and suffering in a cruel or unpleasant way: *Did you see that film 'Brain Dead'? Sick, isn't it?* | *Has he told you his sick joke about the undertaker?*

**8 sick as a parrot** *BrE spoken humorous* extremely disappointed: *"How did you feel when you missed that penalty?" "Sick as a parrot."*

**9 sick at heart** *literary* very unhappy, upset, or disappointed about something: *I was sick at heart to think that I would never see the place again.*

**USAGE NOTE: SICK**

WORD CHOICE: **sick, vomit, throw up, ill, not well, unwell, something wrong with**

In spoken British English to **be sick** is more often used to mean 'to throw up the contents of the stomach through the mouth' than 'to be generally ill': *If you eat too many sweets you'll be sick.* The more formal word in British and American English is **vomit**, and a less formal word is **throw up**.

If you are talking about general illness, especially when you do not say exactly what illness it is, you would usually use **ill** in British English, and **sick** in American English: *She's been ill for several days now.* | *You'll end up getting sick if you don't get more rest.* In British and American English you can also use **not well**: *Diana hasn't been feeling very well lately.*

**Ill** usually has a stronger meaning than **not well**. You may be **not well** because of a bad cold but **ill** with cancer. **Unwell** is a more formal word for **not well** or **ill**.

Before a noun **sick** always means 'generally not well' (**ill** and **unwell** are not usually used before a noun): *He's gone to visit his sick mother.*

When you want to talk about a particular part of the body that is hurt or has a disease you can say there is **something wrong with**...: *Tommy can't play today – there's something wrong with his knee* (NOT *He has a sick knee|he is sick with his knee*).

SPELLING

Note that **homesick** is written as one word.

**sick**[2] *n* **1 the sick** people who are ill: *The sick and wounded were allowed to go free.* **2** [U] *BrE informal* VOMIT

**sick**[3] *v*

**sick** sth ↔ **up** *phr v* [T] *BrE informal* to bring up food from your stomach; VOMIT[1]

**sick·bay** /ˈsɪkbeɪ/ *n* [C] a room on a ship, in a school etc where there are beds for people who are sick

**sick·bed** /ˈsɪkbed/ *n* [C usually singular] the bed where a sick person is lying: *The president carried on working from his sickbed.*

**sick·en** /ˈsɪkən/ *v* **1** [T] to make you feel shocked and angry, especially because you strongly disapprove of something: *The idea of organized dog fights sickens me.*|*All decent people should be sickened by such a pointless waste of lives.* **2 be sickening for something** *spoken especially BrE* to start to have an illness and show signs of having it: *I think Tommy must be sickening for something, the way he's been moping around.* **3** [I] *old-fashioned* to gradually become very ill: *The older people just sickened and died as food supplies ran low.*

**sicken of** sth *phr v* [T] to lose your desire for something or your interest in it: *He finally sickened of the endless round of parties and idle conversation.*

**sick·en·ing** /ˈsɪkənɪŋ, ˈsɪknɪŋ/ *adj* **1** very shocking, annoying, or upsetting; DISGUSTING: *Local police said it was one of the most sickening attacks they had come across.*|*their sickening hypocrisy* **2 a sickening thud/crash** an unpleasant sound that makes you think someone has been injured or something has been broken: *His head hit the floor with a sickening thud.* **3** *BrE spoken* making you feel jealous: *"Helen's just bought herself a new BMW." "God, how sickening!"* —**sickeningly** *adv*

**sick·ie** /ˈsɪki/ *n* [C] *AustrE & BrE informal* a day when you say that you are ill and do not go to work, even though you are not really ill

**sick·le** /ˈsɪkəl/ *n* [C] a tool with a blade in the shape of a hook, used for cutting wheat or long grass

**sickle-cell a·nae·mi·a** *BrE*, **sickle-cell anemia** *AmE* /ˌ·· ·ˈ···/ *n* [U] a serious illness that mainly affects black people, in which the blood cells change shape, causing weakness and fever

**sick·ly** /ˈsɪkli/ *adj* **1** weak, unhealthy, and often ill: *a sickly child*|*a sickly pallor to his face* **2** a sickly smell, taste etc is unpleasant and makes you feel sick: *the sickly odor of rotting garbage*

**sick·ness** /ˈsɪknɪs/ *n* **1** [U] the state of being ill; ILLNESS: *an insurance policy against long-term sickness and injury*|*working days lost due to sickness* **2** [U] the feeling that you are about to bring up food from your stomach; NAUSEA: *A wave of sickness came over him.*| **morning sickness** (=sickness that some women get when they are going to have a baby)|**travel/car/sea/air sickness** (=sickness that some people get while travelling) **3** [C] a particular illness: *They died within a few days of each other, probably from a sickness like the plague.* **4** [U] the serious problems and weaknesses of a social, political, or economic system: *He said the idea of 'success' was part of the sickness of Western cultures.*

**sickness ben·e·fit** /ˈ·· ˌ···/ *n* [U] *BrE* money paid by the government to someone who is too sick to work

**sick note** /ˈ· ·/ *n* [C] *BrE* a note written by your doctor or your parents saying that you were too sick to go to work or school; EXCUSE² (5) *AmE*

**sick·o** /ˈsɪkəʊ‖-koʊ/ *n* [C] *slang especially AmE* someone who gets pleasure from things that most people find unpleasant or upsetting: *There's plenty of twisted sickos out there who are into kiddie porn.*

**sick-out** /ˈ· ·/ *n* [C] *AmE* a STRIKE (=protest about pay or working conditions) in which all the workers at a company say they are sick and stay home on the same day

**sick pay** /ˈ· ·/ *n* [U] money paid by an employer to a worker who cannot work because of illness

**sick·room** /ˈsɪk-rʊm, -ruːm/ *n* [C] a room where someone who is sick can go to lie down

## side¹ /saɪd/ *n* [C]

S1 W1

① PLACE/AREA/POSITION
② DIRECTION
③ SUBJECT/SITUATION
④ IN A QUARREL/WAR/SPORT
⑤ PEOPLE
⑥ SUPPORT
⑦ OTHER MEANINGS

### ① PLACE/AREA/POSITION

**1 ▶ PART OF AN AREA ◀** one of the two areas that are on either the left or the right of an imaginary line, or on either the left or the right of a border, wall, river etc: *Drive on the left-hand side of the road.*|*a scar on the right side of his face*|*Fuel is cheaper on the French side of the border.*|*The south side of town is pretty run-down.*| **the far/other side** (=the area furthest from you or opposite you) *I could just see Rita on the far side of the square.*|**to one side (of)** *Off to one side was a small wooden shed.*

**2 ▶ NEXT TO ◀** [usually singular] the place or area directly next to someone or something, on the right or the left: *Put the table on the left side of the couch.*|*Stand on this side of me so Dad can get a photo.*|**by/at sb's side** (=beside them) *Tyler's daughter walked at his side.*|**side by side** (=next to each other) *Two bottles stood side by side on the shelf.*|*We walked along the beach, side by side.*|**on either side** (=on the left side and the right) *On either side of the front gates stood a tall tree.*

**3 ▶ EDGE ◀** the part of an object or area that is furthest from the middle, at or near the edge: *a little store by the side of the highway*|*a triangle with unequal sides*|*Jack sat down heavily on the side of the bed.*| **roadside/lakeside etc** *a charming hotel on the riverside* —see also SEASIDE

**4 ▶ OF A BUILDING/OBJECT/VEHICLE ETC ◀** a surface of something that is not its front, back, top, or bottom: *There's an entrance at the side of the building.*|*The lifeboat was lowered over the ship's side.*|*Someone ran into the side of my car.*|*Scrape the batter from the sides of the bowl.*

**5 ▶ MOUNTAIN/VALLEY ETC ◀** one of the sloping areas of a hill, mountain etc: *an old cave in the side of the valley*|**hillside/mountainside etc** *sheep grazing on the steep hillside*

**6 ▶ FLAT SURFACE ◀** one of the flat surfaces of something: *Which side of the box do you put the label on?*|*A cube has six sides.*

**7 ▶ OF A THIN OBJECT ◀** one of the two surfaces of a thin flat object: *Write only on one side of the paper.*|*I'll paint the other side of the fence tomorrow.*|*Try playing side A of the tape.*

**8 three-sided/four-sided etc** with three sides, four sides etc: *a five-sided shape* —see also ONE-SIDED

**9 steep-sided/bare-sided etc** with a particular type of side: *a sheer-sided gorge*|*a huge flat-sided rock*

**10 ▶ PAGE ◀** *BrE* a page of writing on one side of a piece of paper: *How many sides have we got to write?*

### ② DIRECTION

**11 from side to side** moving continuously, first in one direction then in the other: *The rope bridge swung from side to side in a terrifying manner.*

**12 from all sides** from every direction: *Planes were attacking us from all sides.*

**13 on all sides/on every side** in every direction: *We*

[continued on next page]

[continued from previous page]
*were surrounded on all sides by a wall of flames.* | *Gunfire erupted on every side.*

### ③ SUBJECT/SITUATION

**14** one part or feature of a subject, problem, or situation, especially when compared with another part: *Tell me your side of the story.* | *We expect you to keep your side of the bargain.* | **all/both sides** *Try to look at all sides of the issue.* | **technical/financial/social etc side** *She takes care of the financial side of the business.* | **serious/funny etc side** *Can't you see the funny side of all this?*

### ④ IN A QUARREL/WAR/SPORT

**15** one of the people, groups, or countries opposing each other in a quarrel, war etc: *fighting on the Bosnian side in the civil war* | *My sympathy lay on the side of the rebels.* | **take sides** (=choose to support a particular person or opinion) *I'm sorry, but I'm not taking sides on this one.* | **be on sb's side** (=agree with someone and support them) *Thank God at least you're on my side.* | **whose side are you on?** *spoken* (=used when someone is arguing against you when they should be supporting you)
**16 ▶ IN SPORT ◀** [also + plural verb *BrE*] *BrE* a sports team: *He plays for the Welsh side.*

### ⑤ PEOPLE

**17 ▶ PART OF SB'S CHARACTER ◀** [usually singular] one part of someone's character, especially when compared with another part: *One side of me is cautious, and another side says go ahead and do it!* | *It was a side of Shari I hadn't seen before.* | **emotional/romantic/funny etc side** *Jeff does have his romantic side, honestly!*
**18 ▶ PART OF YOUR BODY ◀** the part of your body from your shoulder to the top of your leg: *He had a scar running right the way down his side.*
**19 ▶ OF A FAMILY ◀** the parents, grandparents etc of your mother or your father: *Ken is Scottish on his mother's side.*

### ⑥ SUPPORT

**20 not leave sb's side** to always be with someone and look after them: *Promise me you'll never leave her side.*
**21 side by side** closely together with each other and helping each other: *We've worked side by side for years.*

### ⑦ OTHER MEANINGS

**22 on the high side/the heavy side etc** *spoken* a little too high, too heavy etc: *Ooh, the price is a bit on the high side, isn't it?* | *The sheets are still a little on the damp side.*
**23 on the side: a)** in addition to your regular job: *Freelancing can help you make a little money on the side.* —see also SIDELINE[1] (1) **b)** dishonestly or illegally: *Simms didn't seem the type to have a lover on the side.* —see also **a bit on the side** (BIT[1] (21)) **c)** food that is served on the side is ordered with the main dish in a restaurant, but is not usually part of that dish: *Could I have waffles with an egg on the side?*
**24 have sth on your side** to have an advantage that increases your chances of success: *Greg has youth on his side, he'll recover.* | *We've got the law on our side.*
**25 get on the right/wrong side of sb** *informal* to make someone very pleased with you or very angry with you: *Be careful not to get on the wrong side of her.*
**26 let the side down** *BrE informal* to behave in a way that makes things difficult for your family, team etc, or makes them embarrassed: *I'm disappointed in you, Alex, you've really let the side down.*
**27 ▶ TV STATION ◀** [usually singular] *BrE informal* a television station; CHANNEL[1] (1): *What's on the other side?*
**28 a side of beef/bacon** one half of an animal's body, cut along the BACKBONE and bought for food
**29 put/leave/set sth to one side** to save something to be dealt with or used later: *Let's leave that question to one side for now.* | *Put a little money to one side each week.*
**30 on the right/wrong side of 30, 40 etc** *spoken* younger or older than 30, 40 etc
**31 take etc sb to one side** to take someone away from other people for a short time for a private talk: *Maybe you can quietly take Pam to one side and ask about Henry.*
**32 on the wrong/right side of the law** *informal* breaking/not breaking the law: *OK, do it, but keep on the right side of the law!*
**33 this side of** without going as far as: *It's the best Chinese food this side of Peking.*
**34 criticize/scold/curse sb up one side and down the other** *AmE spoken* criticize someone, treat them unkindly etc without worrying about how they feel —see also FLIP SIDE, **to be on the safe side** (SAFE[1] (8)), **split your sides** (SPLIT[1] (9)), **two sides of the same coin** (COIN[1] (4)), **the other side of the coin** (COIN[1] (3)), **get out of bed (on) the wrong side** (BED[1] (9)), **err on the side of caution** (ERR (1))

**side²** *adj* [only before noun] **1** in or on the side of something: **a side door/panel etc** *Hannah slipped out through a side exit.* **2** from the side of something: *Can you get a side view?* **3 side street/road etc** a street, road etc that is smaller than a main street but is often connected to it: *He'd found a nice quiet side street off San Vincente.*

**side³** *v* [I] to support or argue against a person or group in a quarrel, fight etc: **[+ with/against]** *Frank sided with David against their mother.*

**side·arm** /ˈsaɪd-ɑːm‖-ɑːrm/ *n* [C often plural] a weapon carried or worn at someone's side, for example a gun or sword

**side·board** /ˈsaɪdbɔːd‖-bɔːrd/ *n* **1** [C] a long low piece of furniture usually in a DINING ROOM, used for storing plates, glasses etc **2 sideboards** *BrE* sideburns

**side·burns** /ˈsaɪdbɜːnz‖-bɜːrnz/ *n* [plural] hair grown down the sides of a man's face in front of his ears —see picture on page 412

**side·car** /ˈsaɪdkɑː‖-kɑːr/ *n* [C] a seat, often enclosed, that is joined to the side of a MOTORCYCLE and has a separate wheel

**side dish** /ˈ· ·/ *n* [C] a small amount of food such as a SALAD that you eat with a main meal

**side ef·fect** /ˈ· ·ˌ·/ *n* [C] **1** an effect that a drug has on your body in addition to curing pain or illness: *a natural remedy with no harmful side effects* **2** an unexpected or unplanned result of a situation or event: *These policy changes could have beneficial side effects for the whole economy.*

**side is·sue** /ˈ· ˌ··/ *n* [C] *especially BrE* a subject or problem that is not as important as the main one, and may take people's attention away from the main subject: *We mustn't let the meeting get bogged down in side issues.*

**side·kick** /ˈsaɪdˌkɪk/ *n* [C] *informal* someone who spends time with or helps another person, especially when that person is more important than they are: *He starred as Sherlock Holmes' bumbling sidekick Watson.*

**side·light** /ˈsaɪdlaɪt/ *n* [C] *BrE* one of the two small lights next to the main front lights on a car; PARKING LIGHT *AmE* —see picture on page 409

**side·line¹** /ˈsaɪdlaɪn/ *n* **1** [C] an activity that you do as well as your main job or business in order to earn more money: *Zoe does a bit of freelance photography as a sideline.* **2 on the sidelines** not taking part in an activity even though you want to or should do: *A severe knee injury put him on the sidelines for the rest of the season.* | *You can't stay on the sidelines for ever; it's time you got involved.* **3 sidelines** [plural] the area just outside the lines that form the edge of a sports field: *Beckenbauer stood on the sidelines shouting instructions to his team.* —see picture at TENNIS **4** [C] a line at the side of a sports field, which shows where the players are allowed to play

**sideline²** *v* **be sidelined** to be unable to play in a game because you are injured, or unable to take part in something because you are not as good as someone else: *Baggio was once again sidelined through injury.*

**side·long** /ˈsaɪdlɒŋ‖-lɒːŋ/ *adj* **1 a sidelong look/glance** a way of looking at someone by moving your eyes to the side, especially so that it seems secret, dishonest, or disapproving: *He stole a sidelong glance at the woman sitting next to him.* **2 a sidelong look at** an unusual and often humorous way of considering a subject: *The book takes a sidelong look at life in Hollywood.* —**sidelong** *adv*

**side-on** /ˌ· ˈ·◂/ *adj* coming from one side rather than from in front or behind: *a side-on collision* —**side-on** *adv*

**side or·der** /ˈ· ˌ··/ *n* [C] a small amount of food ordered in a restaurant to be eaten with a main meal but served on a separate dish: *a side order of onion rings*

**si·der·e·al** /saɪˈdɪəriəl‖-ˈdɪr-/ *adj technical* related to or calculated using the stars: *the sidereal day*

**side-sad·dle** /ˈ· ˌ··/ *adv* **ride/sit side-saddle** to ride or sit on a horse with both legs on the same side of the horse

**side·show** /ˈsaɪdʃəʊ‖-ʃoʊ/ *n* [C] **1** a separate small part of a FAIR ² (1) or CIRCUS (1) , where you pay to play games or watch a performance **2** an event that is much less important or serious than another one: *The initial conflict was a mere sideshow compared with the World War that followed.*

**side·split·ting** /ˈsaɪdˌsplɪtɪŋ/ *adj* extremely funny: *He told some sidesplitting jokes.*

**side·step** /ˈsaɪdstep/ *v* **1 sidestep a problem/issue/question** to avoid doing something that will cause you difficulty or inconvenience, such as dealing with a difficult problem: *The report simply sidesteps the environmental issues.* **2** [I,T] to step quickly sideways to avoid being hit or walking into someone —**sidestep** *n* [C]

**side·swipe¹** /ˈsaɪdswaɪp/ *n* **take a sideswipe at** to criticize someone or something while you are talking about something different: *At the end of the speech he couldn't resist taking a sideswipe at his former boss.*

**sideswipe²** *v* [T] *AmE* to hit the side of a car with another car so that the two sides touch quickly: *She was going too fast and sideswiped a parked car.*

**side·track¹** /ˈsaɪdtræk/ *v* [T usually passive] to make someone stop doing what they should be doing, or stop talking about what they started talking about, by making them interested in something else: **get sidetracked** *Don't get too sidetracked by the audience's questions.*

**sidetrack²** *n* [C] *AmE* a short railway track connected to a main track

**side·walk** /ˈsaɪdwɔːk‖-wɒːk/ *n* [C] *AmE* a hard surface or path at the side of a street for people to walk on; PAVEMENT *BrE* —see graph at PAVEMENT —see picture on page 410

**sidewalk art·ist** /ˈ·· ˌ··/ *n* [C] *AmE* someone who draws pictures on a sidewalk, hoping that people will give them money; PAVEMENT ARTIST *BrE*

**side·ways** /ˈsaɪdweɪz/ *adv* **1** to or towards one side: *A strong gust of wind blew the car sideways into the ditch.* **2** with the side, rather than the front or back, facing forwards: *They brought the piano sideways through the front door.* —**sideways** *adj*: *a furtive sideways glance*

**side-wheel·er** /ˈsaɪd ˌwiːlə‖-ər/ *n* [C] *AmE* an old-fashioned type of ship which is pushed foward by a pair of large wheels at the sides; PADDLE STEAMER *BrE*

**sid·ing** /ˈsaɪdɪŋ/ *n* [C] a short railway track connected to a main track, where trains are kept when they are not being used

**si·dle** /ˈsaɪdl/ *v* [I always + adv/prep] to walk towards something or someone slowly and quietly, as if you do not want to be noticed: **[+ up/towards/along]** *A woman in dark glasses sidled up to us and asked if we wanted to buy a watch.*

**siege** /siːdʒ/ *n* [C,U] **1** a military operation during which an army surrounds a place and tries to gain control of it by stopping supplies of food, weapons etc from reaching it: *The siege lasted almost four months.* | **lay siege to** (=start a siege) *In June 1176 King Richard laid siege to Limoges.* | **raise a siege** (=end it) **2** a situation in which the police surround a building to try and force the people inside to come out: **lay siege to** *When the scandal broke, dozens of journalists laid seige to Mellor's apartment.* **3 be under siege a)** to be surrounded by an army in a seige **b)** to be continually criticized, or attacked by questions, problems, threats etc: *The TV station has been under siege from irate viewers phoning in to complain.* **4 siege mentality** the feeling among a group of people that they are surrounded by enemies and must do everything they can to protect themselves

**si·en·na** /siˈenə/ *n* [U] a type of earth that is dark yellow, used to make paint

**si·er·ra** /siˈerə/ *n* [C] a row or area of sharply pointed mountains

**si·es·ta** /siˈestə/ *n* [C] a short sleep in the afternoon, especially in warm countries: **take/have a siesta** *The stores all close after lunch when everyone takes a siesta.*

**sieve¹** /sɪv/ *n* [C] **1 a)** a round wire kitchen tool with a lot of small holes, used for separating solid food from liquid or small pieces of food from large pieces **b)** a round wire tool for separating small objects from large objects **2 have a memory like a sieve** *informal* to forget things easily

**sieve²** *v* [T] to put flour or other food through a sieve

**sieve** sth ↔ **out** *phr v* [T] to separate solid objects from liquid or smaller objects from larger ones by using a sieve: *sieve out the seeds from the raspberry jam* —see picture on page 834

**sift** /sɪft/ *v* [T] **1** to put flour, sugar etc through a sieve or similar container in order to remove large pieces **2** also **sift through** to examine information, documents etc carefully in order to find something out or decide what is important and what is not: *Police are sifting through the evidence in the hope of finding more clues.*

**sift** sth ↔ **out** *phr v* [T] to separate something from other things: **[+ from]** *It's hard to sift out the truth from the lies in this case.*

**sift·er** /ˈsɪftə‖-ər/ *n* [C] a container with a lot of small holes in the top used for shaking flour, sugar etc onto things

**sigh¹** /saɪ/ *v* [I] **1** to breathe in and out making a long sound, especially because you are bored, disappointed, tired etc: *"Well, there's nothing we can do about it now," she sighed.* | **sigh heavily/deeply** *Frankie stared out of the window and sighed deeply.* | **[+ with]** *He sighed with despair at the thought of all the opportunities he had missed.* **2** if the wind sighs, it makes a long sound like someone sighing: *The wind sighed in the trees.* **3 sigh for sth** to be sad because you are thinking about a pleasant time in the past: *Emilia sighed for her lost youth.*

**sigh²** *n* [C] an act or sound of sighing: **[+ of]** *She settled down in her chair with a long sigh of relief.* | **breathe/give/heave/let out a sigh of relief** *We all heaved a sigh of relief when we heard they were safe.*

**sight¹** /saɪt/ *n* S2 W2

**1 ► ABILITY TO SEE ◄** [U] the physical ability to see: *Anne's sight is very good for someone of her age.* | *He has no sight in his right eye, but his left eye is fine.* | **lose your sight** (=become blind) *She had lost her sight in a riding accident.*

**2 ► ACT OF SEEING ◄** [singular, U] the act of seeing something: *The crowd was waiting for a sight of the Queen.* | **at the sight of** *I always faint at the sight of blood.* | **catch sight of** (=suddenly see or notice something) *Sheila caught sight of her own face in one of the shop windows.* | **be hidden from sight** *The house is hidden from sight behind trees.* | **on sight** (=as soon as you see someone) *soldiers trained to shoot on sight* | *Jo disliked him on sight.* | **at first sight** (=the first time you see someone) *We fell in love with the cottage at first sight.*

**3 ▶ THING YOU SEE ◀** [C] **a)** something you can see, especially something unusual, beautiful etc: *Tourists are a familiar sight in this part of the city.|the rare sight of a fox|all the sounds and sights of the forest|* **a sorry sight** *often humorous* (=something you see that makes you feel sad or sympathetic) *Fiona was a sorry sight in her wet clothes.* **b) the sights** [plural] famous or interesting places that tourists visit: *In the afternoon, you'll have a chance to relax or to go and see the sights.* —see also SIGHTSEEING

**4 in/within sight a)** inside the area that you can see: *When we got to the beach, there wasn't a soul in sight.|If you don't lock up the food, they'll eat everything in sight.* **b)** likely to happen soon: *Six months from the start of the strike, there is still no end in sight.|Peace is now in sight.*

**5 out of sight a)** outside the area that you can see: *Karen waved until the car was out of sight.* **b)** *old-fashioned slang* extremely good: *The skiing there is out of sight!*

**6 be within sight of a)** to be in the area where you can see something: *We camped within sight of the lake.* **b)** to be in a position where you will soon be able to get something or achieve something: *Dan was now within sight of the championship.*

**7 lose sight of a)** to forget to think about or deal with something important: *It's easy to lose sight of the real issue.|Never lose sight of the fact that you have a lot of talent.* **b)** to stop being able to see something or someone: *I lost sight of him in the crowd.*

**8 come into sight/disappear from sight etc** to appear or disappear: *Soon the train came into sight.*

**9 not let sb out of your sight** to make sure that someone stays near you: *Since the accident, Donna hasn't let the children out of her sight.*

**10 be sick of/hate/can't stand the sight of** to dislike someone or something very much: *Alan and Sam can't stand the sight of each other.*

**11 a sight for sore eyes** *spoken* **a)** someone or something that you feel very happy to see **b)** *BrE* someone or something that is very unattractive or very funny to look at

**12 set your sights on** to decide that you want something and will make a determined effort to achieve it: *I was still young then, and my sights were set on a acting career.*

**13 come in sight of** to arrive at a position from which you can see a particular place, building etc: *At last they came in sight of the city.*

**14 at first sight** when you first start considering something: *The results of the tests were, at first sight, surprising.*

**15 a sight more/a sight better etc** *spoken* a lot more etc: *You'd earn a damn sight more if you got a proper qualification.*

**16 be a sight/look a sight** to look very funny or stupid, or very untidy or unpleasant: *We'd had an all-night party, and the place looked a bit of a sight.*

**17 ▶ GUN ◀** [C often plural] the part of a gun or other weapon that guides your eye when you are aiming at something —see picture at GUN[1]

**18 out of sight, out of mind** used to say that you will soon forget someone if you do not see them for a while: *I pestered him continuously: I wasn't going to allow myself to become a case of out of sight, out of mind.* —see also **know sb by sight** (KNOW[1] (16))

**sight²** *v* [T] to see something from a long distance away, or see something you have been looking for: *The sailors gave a shout of joy when they sighted land.|Several rare birds have been sighted in the area.*

**sight·ed** /ˈsaɪtɪd/ *adj* someone who is sighted can see, and is not blind: **partially sighted** (=having limited ability to see) —see also CLEAR-SIGHTED, FAR-SIGHTED, LONGSIGHTED, SHORT-SIGHTED

**sight·ing** /ˈsaɪtɪŋ/ *n* [C] an occasion on which something is seen, especially something rare or something that people are hoping to see: *Several people in the area have reported sightings of UFOs.*

**sight·less** /ˈsaɪtləs/ *adj literary* blind

**sight-read** /ˈsaɪt riːd/ *v past tense and past participle* **sightread** /-red/ [I,T] to play or sing written music when you look at it for the first time, without practising it first —**sight-reader** *n* [C] —**sight-reading** *n* [U]

**sight·see·ing** /ˈsaɪtˌsiːɪŋ/ *n* [U] the act of visiting famous or interesting places, especially as tourists: **go sightseeing** *We bought souvenirs and then went sightseeing.*

**sight·se·er** /ˈsaɪtˌsiːə‖-ər/ *n* [C] someone, especially a tourist, who is visiting a famous or interesting place

**signs**



**sign¹** /saɪn/ *n* S W

**1 ▶ STH THAT PROVES STH ◀** [C] an event, fact etc that shows that something is happening or that something is true; INDICATION: **sign of** *The tests can detect early signs of disease.|* **sign that** *Exports have risen by 20%, a sign that the economy is improving.|* **a sure sign** (=clear proof) *You know Eric, if he won't eat, it's a sure sign that he's in love again!|* **telltale sign** (=a sign that is easy to recognize, usually of something bad) *telltale signs of drug abuse.|* **show signs of** *For the first time she was beginning to show signs of her age.|* **every sign of** (=clear signs of) *They showed every sign of being willing to cooperate.* —see graph at INDICATE

**2 there's no sign of a)** if there is no sign of something, you cannot see anything which shows that it exists or has happened: *The police looked all around the house, but there was no sign of a struggle.* **b)** if there is no sign of someone, you cannot see them anywhere, or they have not arrived when you expected them to: *Jerry kept looking out of the window, but there was still no sign of her.*

**3 ▶ MOVEMENT OR SOUND ◀** [C] a movement, sound etc that you make in order to tell someone to do something or give them information; GESTURE[1] (1): **give/make a sign** *Nobody move until I give the sign.|* **[+ that]** *Bruce made a sign that he was ready to leave.|* **sign for sb to do sth** *Three short blasts on the whistle was the sign for us to begin.*

**4 ▶ GIVES INFORMATION ◀** [C] a piece of paper, metal etc in a public place, with words or drawings on it that give people information, warn them not to do something etc: *road signs|a no smoking sign*

**5 ▶ PICTURE/SYMBOL ◀** [C] a picture, shape etc that has a particular meaning; SYMBOL: *For some reason the computer can't display the dollar sign.*

**6 ▶ STAR SIGN ◀** [C] also **star sign** a group of stars, representing one of 12 parts of the year, that some people believe influences your behaviour and your life: *I'm a Scorpio – what sign are you?*

**7 ▶ LANGUAGE ◀** [U] a language that uses hand movements instead of spoken words, used by people who cannot hear; SIGN LANGUAGE

**8 sign of life** a movement that shows that someone is

alive, or something that shows that there are people in a particular place: *We entered the building with caution but strangely there was no sign of life.*

**9 sign of the times** something that shows how bad society has become: *So many houses have burglar alarms nowadays. It's a sign of the times I suppose.*

**10 the sign of the Cross** the hand movement that some Christians make in the shape of a cross, to show respect for God or to protect themselves from evil

S3 W3 **sign²** *v* **1** [I,T] to write your SIGNATURE on a letter or document to show that you wrote it, agree with it: *Sign here please.* | **sign sth** *You forgot to sign the check!* | *Over a hundred people have signed the petition.* | *a signed photo of Paul McCartney* | **sign your name** *The artist had signed his name in the corner of the painting.* **2 sign an agreement/treaty etc** to show formally that you agree to do something, by signing a legal document: *Both presidents signed the treaty as part of the new peace plan.* | **sign sth with sb** *France has just signed a new trade deal with Japan.* **3** [T] if an organization such as a football team or music company signs someone, that person signs a contract agreeing to work for it: *CBS Records had signed her back in 1988 on a three-album contract.* **4** [I] to try to tell someone something or ask them to do something by using signs and movements: **sign to sb to do sth** *He was desperately signing to me to not mention anything about Jack.* | **sign for sb to do sth** *She signed for us to go inside.* —see graph at INDICATE **5 all signed and sealed** with all the necessary legal documents agreed and signed: *It'll all be signed and sealed by Friday, you can move in then.* **6** [I,T] to use SIGN LANGUAGE: *The whole performance was signed* (=translated into sign language) *by a local interpreter.* —**signer** *n* [C]

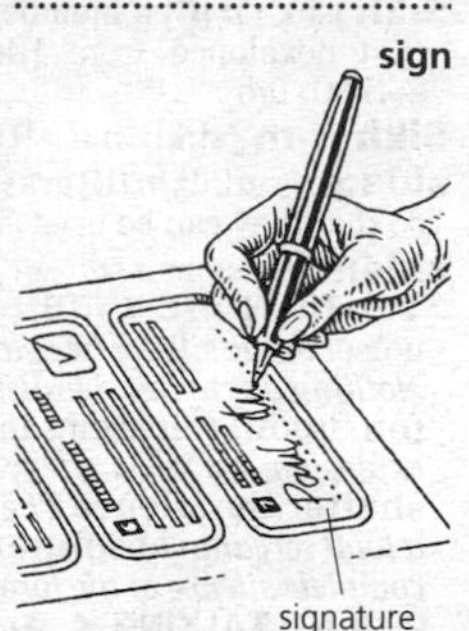


**sign** sth ↔ **away** *phr v* [T] to sign a document that gives your property or legal right to someone else: *She had signed away all claims to the house.*

**sign for** sth *phr v* [T] **1** to sign a document to prove that you have received something: *This is a registered letter, someone will have to sign for it.* **2 sign for Liverpool/Arsenal etc** *BrE* to sign a contract agreeing to play for a particular football team

**sign in** *phr v* **1** [I] to write your name on a form, in a book etc when you enter a place such as a hotel, office or club: *Remember to sign in at reception.* **2** [T **sign** sb ↔ **in**] to write someone else's name in a book so that they are allowed to enter a club that you are a member of

**sign off** *phr v* [I] **1** *informal* to end a radio or television programme by saying goodbye **2** to finish an informal letter by writing your name at the end of it: *It's getting late so I'll sign off now. Love, John.*

**sign on** *phr v* **1** [I,T] to sign a document agreeing to work for someone, especially as a soldier, sailor etc, or to persuade someone to do this: *He signed on as a soldier in the US army.* | **sign sb ↔ on** *I went to the local recruiting office and was signed on for three years.* **2** [I] *BrE* to state officially that you are unemployed by signing a form, so that you can get money from the government

**sign out** *phr v* **1** [I] to write your name in a book when you leave a place such as a hotel, office or club **2** [T **sign** sth ↔ **out**] to write your name on a form or in a book to show that you have taken or borrowed something: *Bernstein signed out a company car and drove to the meeting.*

**sign** sth ↔ **over** *phr v* [T] to sign an official document that gives your property or rights to someone else: [+ **to**] *When he became ill, he signed his property in France over to his son.*

**sign up** *phr v* **1** [T usually passive] if someone is signed up by an organization, they sign a contract agreeing to work for that organization: *Several well-established researchers have been signed up for the project.* **2** [I] to arrange to take part in a course of study: [+ **for**] *I'm thinking of signing up for the philosophy course this term.* | **sign up to do sth** *Over half the people who signed up to do engineering were women.*

**sign with** sth *phr v* [T] **1** *AmE* to sign a contract agreeing to play for a particular sports team **2** to sign a contract agreeing that a particular company has the right to record and sell your music

**sig·nal¹** /ˈsɪgnəl/ *n* [C] **1** a sound or action that you make in order to give information to someone or tell them to do something: **signal (for sb) to do sth** *A bell began to ring, the 8 o'clock signal to start work.* | *When he closes his book, it's a signal for everyone to stand up.* | **give a signal** *Don't start yet – wait for me to give the signal.* | **at a signal (from sb)** *At a signal from their leader the worshippers knelt to pray.* | **danger signal/warning signal etc** *A red flag is often used as a danger signal.* —see also SMOKE SIGNAL **2** an event or action that shows what someone feels or what is likely to happen: **signal that** *Gorbachev's speech was a signal that major changes were on the way.* | **a clear signal** *The opinion poll is a clear signal that voters do not support the President's foreign policy.* | **danger signal/warning signal** *Rapid breathing is a danger signal and you should call your doctor.* | **send/give a signal** *This will send the wrong signal to potential investors.* **3** a series of light waves, sound waves etc that carry an image, sound, or message, such as is used in radio or television: **send out/transmit a signal (to)** *The signal was sent out to our troops immediately.* | **receive/pick up a signal** *Astronomers have been picking up faint signals that may be from a distant planet.* **4** a piece of equipment with coloured lights, used on a railway to tell train drivers whether they can continue or must stop: **signal failure** (=when these lights do not work) *The report confirmed that signal failure had been the cause of the accident.* S3 W2

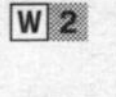

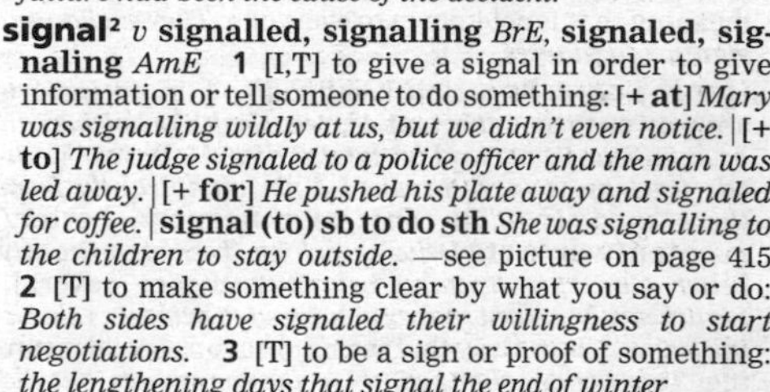

**signal²** *v* **signalled, signalling** *BrE*, **signaled, signaling** *AmE* **1** [I,T] to give a signal in order to give information or tell someone to do something: [+ **at**] *Mary was signalling wildly at us, but we didn't even notice.* | [+ **to**] *The judge signaled to a police officer and the man was led away.* | [+ **for**] *He pushed his plate away and signaled for coffee.* | **signal (to) sb to do sth** *She was signalling to the children to stay outside.* —see picture on page 415 **2** [T] to make something clear by what you say or do: *Both sides have signaled their willingness to start negotiations.* **3** [T] to be a sign or proof of something: *the lengthening days that signal the end of winter*

**signal³** *adj* [only before noun] *formal* important: **signal achievement/success/failure etc** *Getting the health care bill passed was a signal personal triumph for the President.*

**signal box** /ˈ·· ·/ *n* [C] *BrE* a small building near a railway from which the signals and tracks are controlled; SIGNAL TOWER *AmE*

**sig·nal·ize** *also* **-ise** *BrE* /ˈsɪgnəlaɪz/ *v* [T usually passive] *formal* to be a clear sign of something: *a quaint tradition that signalizes our attainment of learning*

**sig·nal·ly** /ˈsɪgnəli/ *adv formal* very noticeably: *These principles are signally lacking in modern society.*

**sig·nal·man** /ˈsɪgnəlmən/ *n plural* **signalmen** /-mən/ [C] **1** *especially BrE* someone whose job is to control railway signals **2** a member of the army or navy who is trained in signalling

**signal tow·er** /ˈ·· ˌ··/ *n* [C] *AmE* a building next to a railway track from which signals and tracks are controlled; SIGNAL BOX

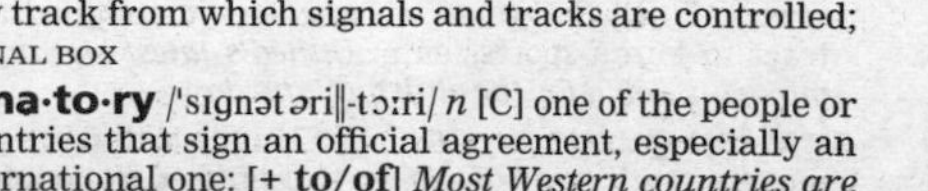

**sig·na·to·ry** /ˈsɪgnətəri‖-tɔːri/ *n* [C] one of the people or countries that sign an official agreement, especially an international one: [+ **to/of**] *Most Western countries are signatories of this treaty.*

**sig·na·ture** /ˈsɪgnətʃə‖-ər/ *n* [C] your name written in the way you usually write it, for example at the end of a letter or contract or on a cheque: *I couldn't read his signature.* | *a petition with four thousand signatures* | **put your signature to/on** (=sign something to show that you agree with it) —see picture at SIGN

**signature tune** /ˈ··· ˌ·/ *n* [C] a short piece of music used at the beginning and end of a television or radio programme

**sig·net** /ˈsɪgnɪ̵t/ *n* [C] a metal object used for printing a small pattern in WAX[1] (1) as an official SEAL

**signet ring** /ˈ·· ·/ *n* [C] a ring that has a signet on it

W2 **sig·nif·i·cance** /sɪgˈnɪfɪkəns/ *n* [singular, U] **1** the meaning of a word, sign, action etc, especially when this is not immediately clear: [+ **of**] *Could you explain the significance of this part of the contract?* | **the full/real/true significance** *It was only later that we realized the true significance of his remark.* **2** the importance of an event, action etc, especially because of the effects or influence it will have in the future: [+ **of**] *It is impossible to over-estimate the significance of this major discovery.* | [+ **for**] *a judgment that has long-term significance for the rights of disabled people* | **be of great/major/little significance** *So far, research has not produced anything of very great significance.*

S3 W1 **sig·nif·i·cant** /sɪgˈnɪfɪkənt/ *adj* **1** having an important effect or influence, especially on what will happen in the future: *His most significant political achievement was the abolition of the death penalty.* | *Please inform us if there are any significant changes in your plans.* | **highly significant** (=very significant) *a highly significant discovery that might eventually lead to a vaccine* | [+ **for**] *The result is highly significant for the future of the province.* | **it is significant that** *Police believed it was significant that he had recently opened a bank account abroad.* **2** large enough to be noticeable or have noticeable effects: *A significant number of drivers fail to keep to speed limits.* | *A background in computing will give you a significant advantage.* **3** a significant look, smile etc has a special meaning that is not known to everyone: *They exchanged significant glances.*

S3 W2 **sig·nif·i·cant·ly** /sɪgˈnɪfɪkəntli/ *adv* **1** in an important way or to an important degree: *Health problems can be significantly reduced by careful diet.* | [+ **from**] *Methods used by younger teachers differ significantly from those used by older ones.* | **significantly better/greater/worse etc** *Delia's work has been significantly better since her training course.* [sentence adverb] | *Significantly, no newspaper has dared to print this shocking story.* **2** in a way that seems to have a special meaning: *Tom nodded significantly at the suggestion, but did not comment.*

**sig·nif·i·ca·tion** /ˌsɪgnɪ̵fɪ̵ˈkeɪʃən/ *n* [C] *formal* the intended meaning of a word

**sig·ni·fy** /ˈsɪgnɪ̵faɪ/ *v* [not in progressive] **1** [T] to represent, mean, or be a sign of something: *Some tribes use special facial markings to signify status.* | **signify that** *Recent changes in climate may signify that global warming is starting to have an effect.* **2** [T] *formal* to make a wish, feeling, or opinion known by doing something: **signify that** *With a gesture Mr Bosch signified that the three representatives could depart.* | **signify sth (to sb)** *He turned away from her slightly to signify his indifference.* **3** [I] to be important enough to have an effect on something: *These figures don't really signify in the overall results.*

**sign·ing** /ˈsaɪnɪŋ/ *n* **1** [U] the act of signing something such as an agreement or contract: *The club was excited about the signing of these two Argentinian football stars.* **2** [C] *BrE* someone who has just signed a contract to join a sports team: *United's latest signing will make his debut for the club on Saturday.*

**sign lan·guage** /ˈ· ˌ··/ *n* [C,U] a language that uses hand movements instead of spoken words, used by people who cannot hear

**sign·post[1]** /ˈsaɪnpəʊst‖-poʊst/ *n* [C] a sign on a road showing directions and distances: *The signpost said 'Bedford 3 miles'.* | [+ **to**] *Just follow the signposts to Padua.*

**signpost[2]** *v* [T] *BrE* **1 be well/badly signposted** to be clearly or unclearly marked by signposts: *The village isn't very well signposted so it's quite hard to find.* **2** to show something clearly so that everyone will notice and understand it: *They have signposted their conclusions in the report.*

**Sikh** /siːk/ *n* [C] a member of an Indian religious group that developed from Hinduism in the 16th century —**Sikh** *adj*

**Sikh·is·m** /ˈsiːkɪzəm/ *n* [U] the religion of the Sikhs

**si·lage** /ˈsaɪlɪdʒ/ *n* [U] grass or other plants cut and stored so that they can be used as winter food for cattle

**si·lence[1]** /ˈsaɪləns/ *n* W

**1** ▶ **NO NOISE** ◀ [U] complete absence of sound or noise: *In the silence he heard a faint clicking noise.* | [+ **of**] *Nothing disturbed the silence of the night.* | **silence falls (on/upon)** (=it begins to be completely quiet) *After the explosion, an eerie silence fell upon the scene.* | **break/shatter the silence** *The silence was suddenly broken by a loud scream.* | **absolute/complete/dead silence** *the complete silence of the forest at night*

**2** ▶ **NO TALKING** ◀ **a)** [C,U] complete quiet because no one is talking, or a period of complete quiet: *There was a long silence before anyone answered.* | *She raised her hand and waited for silence.* | *"Silence!" thundered the judge.* | **in silence** (=not saying anything) *We walked back to the house in silence.* | **embarrassed/awkward/stunned etc silence** *There was a moment's embarrassed silence.* | **stony silence** (=when someone has said something very shocking or unreasonable) *Their suggestion was met with a stony silence.* **b)** [U] failure or refusal to discuss something or answer questions about something: [+ **on**] *The government's silence on such an important issue seems very strange.* | **take sb's silence for/as** (=think that someone's silence has a particular meaning) *She took his silence as an agreement.*

**3** ▶ **NO COMMUNICATION** ◀ [C,U] failure to write a letter to someone, telephone them etc: *After two years of silence he suddenly got in touch with us again.*

**4 reduce sb to silence** to speak to someone so angrily, rudely etc that they are too shocked or upset to reply: *This stinging criticism reduced me to silence for the rest of the meeting.*

**5 a one-minute silence/two-minute silence etc** a period of time in which everyone stops talking as a sign of honour and respect towards someone who has died

**silence[2]** *v* [T] **1** to make someone stop talking, or stop something making a noise: *"Just a minute," she snapped, silencing him with a look of hatred.* **2** to make someone stop expressing opposition or criticisms: *Opponents of the regime were silenced by threats of violence.* | *a brilliant new book that silenced her critics*

**si·lenc·er** /ˈsaɪlənsə‖-sər/ *n* [C] **1** a thing that is put on the end of a gun so that it makes less noise when it is fired **2** *BrE* a piece of equipment that is connected to the EXHAUST[2] (1) of a vehicle to make its engine quieter; MUFFLER (2) *AmE*

**si·lent** /ˈsaɪlənt/ *adj* W

**1** ▶ **NOT SPEAKING** ◀ **a)** not saying anything: *Phil was silent for a moment as he thought about his reply.* | **fall silent** (=become quiet) *The crowd fell silent when the President appeared.* **b)** not talking much to other people: *Nate was in his late teens, a silent and self-contained boy.* | **the strong silent type** (=a man who looks strong and does not talk very much)

**2** ▶ **NOT COMMUNICATING** ◀ failing or refusing to talk about something or express an opinion: [+ **on/about**] *The company is suspiciously silent about its plans for cutting costs.* | **remain silent** *The prisoner remained silent when questioned.*

**3** ▶ **QUIET** ◀ without any sound, or not making any sound: *In the early morning the village was completely silent.* | *At last the guns were silent.*

4 ▶ **FILMS** ◀ a silent film is a cinema film with no sound, of the type made before about 1927: *silent movies*
5 ▶ **LETTER** ◀ a silent letter in a word is not pronounced and does not have a sound. *The 'w' in 'wreck' is silent.*
6 **silent as the grave** completely silent, often in a way that seems mysterious —**silently** *adv*

**silent ma·jor·i·ty** /ˌ·· ·ˈ···/ *n* **the silent majority** all the people in a country who are not politically active, whose opinions are believed to represent the ideas that most ordinary people have

**silent part·ner** /ˌ·· ˈ··/ *n* [C] *AmE* someone who owns part of a business but is not actively involved in the way it operates; SLEEPING PARTNER *BrE*

**sil·hou·ette** /ˌsɪluˈet/ *n* [C] a dark image, shadow, or shape, seen against a light background: *The silhouette of the cathedral could be seen against the dawn sky.* —**silhouetted** *adj*: *tall chimney stacks silhouetted against the orange flames.*

**sil·i·ca** /ˈsɪlɪkə/ *n* [U] a chemical compound that exists naturally as sand, QUARTZ, and FLINT, used in making glass

**sil·i·cate** /ˈsɪlɪkeɪt, -kɪ̈t/ *n* [C,U] *technical* one of a group of common solid mineral substances

**sil·i·con** /ˈsɪlɪkən/ *n* [U] *technical* a simple substance that is not a metal, and exists naturally in large quantities combined with other metals, minerals etc

**silicon chip** /ˌ··· ˈ·/ *n* [C] a CHIP[1] (4) (=in a computer)

**sil·i·cone** /ˈsɪlɪ̈kəʊn‖-koʊn/ *n* [U] one of a group of chemicals that are not changed by heat or cold and are used in making types of rubber, oil, and RESIN (2)

**silicone im·plant** /ˌ··· ˈ··/ *n* [C] a piece of silicone that is put into the body, especially into a woman's breasts to make them larger

**sil·i·co·sis** /ˌsɪlɪ̈ˈkəʊsɪ̈s‖-ˈkoʊ-/ *n* [U] an illness of the lungs caused by breathing SILICA, common among people who work in mines etc

**silk** /sɪlk/ *n* **1** [U] a thin, smooth, soft cloth made from very thin thread which is produced by a silkworm: *a silk shirt | a dress made of the finest silk* **2** [C] *BrE law* a KC or QC (=type of important lawyer) | **take silk** (=become a KC or QC) **3 silks** *technical* the coloured shirts worn by JOCKEYS (=people who ride horses in races)

**silk·en** /ˈsɪlkən/ *adj literary* **1** soft, smooth, and shiny like silk: *her silken hair* **2** made of silk: *a silken handkerchief*

**silk screen** /ˈ· ·/ also **silk screen print·ing** /ˌ· · ˈ··/ *n* [U] a way of printing by forcing paint or ink onto a surface through a stretched piece of cloth

**silk·worm** /ˈsɪlkwɜːm‖-wɜːrm/ *n* [C] a type of MOTH whose young produces silk thread

**silk·y** /ˈsɪlki/ *adj* **1** soft, smooth and shiny, like silk: *silky fur* **2** a silky voice is gentle, and is used especially when someone is trying to persuade you to do something —**silkily** *adv* —**silkiness** *n* [U]

**sill** /sɪl/ *n* [C] **1** the narrow shelf at the base of a window frame **2** the part of a car frame at the bottom of the doors: *You've got a lot of rust on your sills.*

**sil·la·bub** /ˈsɪləbʌb/ *n* [C,U] SYLLABUB

3 **sil·ly**[1] /ˈsɪli/ *adj* **1** not sensible, showing bad judgment: *This may sound like a silly question, but what is the point of this exercise?* | **a silly thing to do/say** *I left my keys at home, which was a pretty silly thing to do.* —see SHAME[1] (USAGE) **2** stupid in a childish or embarrassing way: *I wish you kids would stop being so silly. | a silly hat | I hate their parties – we always end up playing silly games.* **3** *spoken* not serious or practical: *They served us coffee in these silly little cups. | Try making a silly offer – they might just accept it.* **4 bore sb silly** *informal* to make someone extremely bored **5 drink yourself silly** *informal* to get very drunk —**silliness** *n* [U]

**silly**[2] *n* [singular] *spoken* used to tell someone that you think they are being stupid: *No, silly, I didn't mean that!*

**silly bil·ly** /ˈ·· ˌ··/ *n* [C] *spoken* used to tell someone, especially a child, that they are behaving in a silly way

**silly sea·son** /ˈ·· ˌ··/ *n* **the silly season** *BrE informal* a period in the summer when newspapers print stories that are not very serious because there is not much political news

**si·lo** /ˈsaɪləʊ‖-loʊ/ *n* [C] **1** a tall structure like a tower that is used for storing grain, winter food for farm animals etc **2** a large structure under the ground from which a large MISSILE can be fired

**silt**[1] /sɪlt/ *n* [U] moving sand, mud, soil etc that is carried in water and then settles at a bend in a river, an entrance to a port etc

**silt**[2] *v*
**silt up** *phr v* [I,T] to fill or become filled with silt: *The old harbour silted up years ago.*

**sil·van** /ˈsɪlvən/ *adj* SYLVAN

**sil·ver**[1] /ˈsɪlvə‖-ər/ *n* **1** [U] a shiny, whitish, valuable metal that is used to make jewellery, knives, coins etc, and is a chemical ELEMENT **2** [U] spoons, forks, dishes etc that are made of silver or a similar metal: *As kitchen-maid, it was my job to polish the silver.* **3** [U] the colour of silver **4** [C] *informal* a SILVER MEDAL **5** [U] *BrE old-fashioned* coins that are made partly or completely of silver —see also **be born with a silver spoon in your mouth** (BORN[2] (11)), **every cloud has a silver lining** (CLOUD[1] (7)) S3

**silver**[2] *adj* **1** made of silver: *a silver teapot* **2** coloured silver: *a silver Mercedes*

**silver**[3] *v* [T] *technical* to cover a surface with a thin shiny silver coloured surface in order to make a mirror

**silver an·ni·ver·sa·ry** /ˌ·· ··ˈ···/ *n* [C] SILVER WEDDING ANNIVERSARY

**silver birch** /ˌ·· ˈ·/ *n* [C,U] a type of BIRCH tree that has a silvery-white TRUNK and branches

**silver dol·lar** /ˌ·· ˈ··/ *n* [C] a former US one dollar coin, that is now very valuable

**sil·ver·fish** /ˈsɪlvəfɪʃ‖-ər-/ *n plural* **silverfish** or **silverfishes** [C] a small silver-coloured insect that is found in houses and sometimes damages paper or cloth

**silver foil** /ˌ·· ˈ·/ *n* [U] *BrE* FOIL (=very thin sheets of metal)

**silver ju·bi·lee** /ˌ·· ˈ···/ *n* [C] *especially BrE* the date that is exactly 25 years after the date of an important public event, especially a CORONATION: *the Queen's Silver Jubilee*

**silver med·al** /ˌ·· ˈ··/ *n* [C] a MEDAL made of silver that is given to the person who finishes second in a race or competition

**silver pa·per** /ˌ·· ˈ··◂/ *n* [U] *BrE* paper that is shiny like metal on one side, used especially for wrapping food

**silver plate** /ˌ·· ˈ·◂/ *n* [U] metal with a thin covering of silver —**silver-plated** *adj*: *a silver-plated candlestick*

**silver screen** /ˌ·· ˈ·/ *n* **the silver screen** *old-fashioned* the film industry, especially of Hollywood: *stars of the silver screen*

**sil·ver·smith** /ˈsɪlvəˌsmɪθ‖-ər-/ *n* [C] someone who makes things out of silver

**silver-tongued** /ˌ·· ˈ·◂/ *adj especially literary* good at talking to people and persuading them

**sil·ver·ware** /ˈsɪlvəweə‖-vərwer/ *n* [U] **1** objects made of silver, especially knives, spoons, dishes etc **2** *AmE* knives, spoons and forks made of any metal —see picture on page 838

**silver wed·ding an·ni·ver·sa·ry** /ˌ·· ˈ·· ··ˌ···/ *n* [C] the date that is exactly 25 years after the date of a wedding

**sil·ver·y** /ˈsɪlvəri/ *adj* **1** shiny and silver in colour: *the silvery light of the moon* **2** *especially literary* having a pleasant, light, musical sound: *peals of silvery laughter*

**sim·i·an** /ˈsɪmiən/ *adj technical* connected with or similar to a monkey or APE[1] (1) —**simian** *n* [C]

**sim·i·lar** /ˈsɪmələ, ˈsɪmɪlə‖-ər/ *adj* **1** almost the same but not exactly the same: *We have similar tastes in music. | students of roughly similar abilities | These two signatures are so similar it's very difficult to tell them apart. | I saw* S1 W1 *something similar in yesterday's 'Times'.* | [+ **to**] *My opinions on the matter are similar to Kay's.* **2** [no comparative] *technical* exactly the same in shape but not size: *Similar triangles have equal angles.* —see also SIMILARLY

W 2 **sim·i·lar·i·ty** /ˌsɪmɪ̈ˈlærɪ̈ti/ *n* **1** [U] the fact of being similar to something else, or the degree to which two or more things are similar to each other; RESEMBLANCE: [+ **between**] *a striking similarity between the two designs* | [+ **to**] *What I like about his poetry is its similarity to Wordsworth's.* | *The stories show some similarity to parts of the Old Testament.* **2** [C] a way in which things or people are similar: *The police say there are some similarities between the two attacks.* | [+ **in**] *When studying children and other young animals we can see similarities in their behaviour.*

**sim·i·lar·ly** /ˈsɪmɪ̈ləli‖-ərli/ *adv* in a similar way: **similarly situated/expressed/inclined etc** *This idea is similarly expressed in his most recent book.* | [sentence adverb] *Men must wear a jacket and tie. Similarly, women must wear a skirt or dress and not trousers.*

**sim·i·le** /ˈsɪmɪ̈li/ *n* **1** [C] an expression that describes something by comparing it with something else, using the words 'as' or 'like', for example 'as white as snow' **2** [U] the use of expressions like this

**sim·mer¹** /ˈsɪmə‖-ər/ *v* **1** [I,T] to cook something slowly in water that is gently boiling: *A pot was simmering on the stove.* **2** [I] if you are simmering or your emotions are simmering, you feel anger, hate, love etc very strongly, and can only just prevent yourself from expressing it: *Passions were simmering underneath the surface.* | [+ **with**] *The crowd was simmering with rage by the time the defendant arrived in court.* **3 simmer down!** *spoken* used to tell someone to be less excited, angry etc: *Simmer down, Holly – it won't help to lose your temper.*

**simmer²** *n* [singular] the condition of simmering: *Bring the vegetables to a simmer.*

**sim·nel cake** /ˈsɪmnəl ˌkeɪk/ *n* [C] *BrE* a cake made with dried fruit, that is traditionally eaten at Easter

**sim·pat·i·co** /sɪmˈpætɪkəʊ‖-koʊ/ *adj AmE informal* **1** someone who is simpatico is easy to like **2** in agreement: *He and I are simpatico about a lot of things.*

**sim·per** /ˈsɪmpə‖-ər/ *v* [I] to smile in a silly, annoying way: *Betsy simpered coyly at him as she spoke.* —**simper** *n* [C] —**simperingly** *adv*

S 1 W 1 **sim·ple** /ˈsɪmpəl/ *adj*

**1** ▶ **PLAIN** ◀ without a lot of decoration or unnecessary things added: *a simple dress* | *simple but delicious food* | *a building constructed in a simple, classic style*

**2** ▶ **EASY** ◀ not difficult or complicated: *I'm sure there's a perfectly simple explanation.* | *a simple but effective solution to the problem* | **it's not as simple as that** *spoken* (=used to say that something is not as easy as someone thinks it is) *I wish we could offer you more money but I'm afraid it's not as simple as that.*

**3** ▶ **ONLY** ◀ [only before noun] not complicated or involving anything else: *Completing the race is not just a simple matter of physical fitness.* | *We can't do it, for the simple reason that we don't have enough time.* | **the simple truth/fact is** (=used to emphasize the truth about something) *The simple truth is, he isn't good enough for the job.* | **pure and simple** (=without any other reason or feature) *Their motive was greed, pure and simple.*

**4** ▶ **NOT HAVING MANY PARTS** ◀ consisting of only a few necessary parts: *Bacteria are simple forms of life.* | *A knife is a simple tool.*

**5** ▶ **ORDINARY** ◀ honest and ordinary and not special in any way: *Joe was just a simple farmer.*

**6 the simple life** *informal* life without all the problems of the modern world, especially life in the countryside, without too many possessions, or modern machines

**7** ▶ **UNINTELLIGENT** ◀ [not before noun] not intelligent: *I'm afraid old Luke's a bit simple.*

**simple frac·ture** /ˌ·· ˈ··/ *n* [C] *technical* a broken or cracked bone that does not cut through the flesh that surrounds it —compare COMPOUND FRACTURE

**simple in·terest** /ˌ·· ˈ···/ *n* [U] INTEREST¹ (4) that is calculated on the sum of money that you first invested (INVEST (1)), and does not include the interest it has already earned —compare COMPOUND INTEREST

**simple-mind·ed** /ˌ·· ˈ··◂/ *adj* unable to understand complicated things, and not showing much understanding of the world: *a simple-minded desire for a return to the past*

**sim·ple·ton** /ˈsɪmpəltən/ *n* [C] *old-fashioned* someone who has a very low level of intelligence

**sim·pli·ci·ty** /sɪmˈplɪsɪ̈ti/ *n* [U] the quality of being simple, especially when this is attractive or useful: *Mona wrote with a beautiful simplicity of style.* | *For the sake of simplicity, the tax form is divided into three sections.* | **be simplicity itself** (=be very simple) *The plan was simplicity itself – how could she have misunderstood?*

**sim·pli·fy** /ˈsɪmplɪ̈faɪ/ *past tense and past participle* **simplified** *v* [T] to make something easier or less complicated: *an attempt to simplify the tax laws* | *Try to simplify your explanation for the children.* —see also OVERSIMPLIFY —**simplified** *adj*: *a simplified version of Chinese script* —**simplification** /ˌsɪmplɪ̈fɪ̈ˈkeɪʃən/ *n* [C,U]

**sim·plis·tic** /sɪmˈplɪstɪk/ *adj* treating difficult subjects in a way that is too simple: *a naive and simplistic approach to economic policy* —**simplistically** /-kli/ *adv*

**sim·ply** /ˈsɪmpli/ *adv* **1** only: *Some students lose marks simply because they don't read the question properly.* | *Simply fill in the coupon and take it to your local store.* | *It isn't simply a question of money.* **2** in a way that is easy to understand: *Try to express yourself more simply.* | **to put it simply** (=to explain things in a simple way) *To put it simply, the tax cuts mean the average worker will be about 3% better off.* **3** used to emphasize what you are saying: *What a simply wonderful idea!* | *This piece of work simply isn't good enough.* | **quite simply** *It is, quite simply, the most ridiculous idea I've ever heard.* **4** in a plain and ordinary way, without spending much money: *We had to live very simply on my father's small salary.* S W

**sim·u·la·crum** /ˌsɪmjʊ̈ˈleɪkrəm/ *n* [C + **of**] *formal* an image of something

**sim·u·late** /ˈsɪmjʊ̈leɪt/ *v* [T] **1** to make or produce something that is not real but has the appearance of being real: *a machine that simulates conditions in space* | *A sheet of metal can be shaken to simulate thunder.* **2** *formal* to pretend to have a feeling; FEIGN: *We tried to simulate surprise.*

**sim·u·lat·ed** /ˈsɪmjʊ̈leɪtɪ̈d/ *adj* not real, but made to look, feel etc like a real thing, situation, or feeling: *simulated leather* | *a simulated nuclear explosion*

**sim·u·la·tion** /ˌsɪmjʊ̈ˈleɪʃən/ *n* **1** [C,U] an activity or situation that produces conditions which are not real, but have the appearance of being real, used especially for testing something: *a computer simulation used to train airline pilots* | [+ **of**] *an audio-visual simulation of the beginning of the universe* **2** [U] the act or process of simulating something

**sim·u·la·tor** /ˈsɪmjʊ̈leɪtə‖-ər/ *n* [C] a piece of equipment used for training people by letting them feel what real conditions are like, for example in an aircraft: *a flight simulator*

**sim·ul·cast** /ˈsɪməlkɑːst‖ˈsaɪməlkæst/ *v* [T usually passive] *AmE* to broadcast a programme on television and radio at the same time —**simulcast** *n* [C]

**sim·ul·ta·ne·ous** /ˌsɪməlˈteɪniəs◂‖ˌsaɪ-/ *adj* happening or done at exactly the same time: *a simultaneous broadcast of the concert on TV and radio* | **simultaneous translation** (=immediate translation of what someone is saying as they are speaking) —**simultaneously** *adv*: *two pictures taken simultaneously from different camera angles* —**simultaneity** /ˌsɪməltəˈniːɪ̈ti‖ˌsaɪ-/ *n* [U]

**sin¹** /sɪn/ *n* **1** [C,U] disobedience to God, or an offence against God or religious laws: *The Bible says adultery is a sin.* | *the sin of pride* | *the Christian concept of sin* | **commit a sin** (=do something that breaks a religious law) S

**2** [singular] *informal* something that you strongly disapprove of: *It's a sin the way they waste all this money.*| **commit a sin** *I had committed the unforgivable sin of forgetting her birthday.*| **it's a sin to do sth** *It'd be a sin to evict them just because they haven't paid their rent.* **3 live in sin** *old-fashioned* if two people live in sin they live together in a sexual relationship without being married **4 as miserable/ugly/guilty as sin** *spoken* very unhappy, ugly, guilty etc **5 for my sins** *spoken especially BrE* an expression used to suggest jokingly that something is like a punishment: *I'm the local party organizer, for my sins.* —see also SINFUL, **cover/hide a multitude of sins** (MULTITUDE (3)), ORIGINAL SIN, —**sinless** *adj*

**sin[2]** *v* **sinned, sinning** [I] **1** to break God's laws: [+ **against**] *He has sinned against God.* **2 be more sinned against than sinning** *old fashioned* used to say that someone should not be blamed for what they have done wrong, because they have been badly treated by other people

**sin[3]** *technical* the written abbreviation of SINE

1 **since[1]** *conjunction* [used with the present perfect and the
1 past perfect tenses] **1** at a time after a particular time or event in the past: *In the 12 months since I last wrote to you a lot has happened to me.*|*I can't have seen him since 1983.*|*It's been years since I enjoyed myself so much.* **2** during the period of time after a particular time or event in the past: *Since he started that diet he's lost over 20 lbs in weight.*| **ever since** *We've been friends ever since we met at school.* **3** used to give the reason for something: *I'll be forty next month, since you ask.*|*Since you are unable to answer perhaps we should ask someone else.*

2 **since[2]** *prep* [used with the present perfect and the past
2 perfect tenses] **1** at a time in the past after a particular time or event: *They haven't met since the wedding last year.*|*Since the end of the war over a dozen hostages have been released.* —compare FOR[1] (8) **2** for the whole of a long period of time after a particular time or event in the past: *Since the day we met I have known he was not to be trusted.*| **ever since** *Ever since the war she's been able to feed a whole family with a few potatoes and eggs.* **3 since when?** *spoken* used in questions to show surprise, anger etc: *Have you checked this bill? Since when does £42 plus £5 service charge come to £48?*

3 **since[3]** /sɪns/ *adv* [used with the present perfect and the past perfect tenses] **1** at a time in the past after a particular time or event: *He husband died over ten years ago but she has since remarried.*|*I've since forgotten what our argument was about.*|*He walked out of that door last Tuesday and no one's seen him since.* **2** for the whole of a long period of time after a particular time or event in the past: *The accident happened four years ago and she has hardly spoken since.*| **ever since** *We came to the UK in 1974 and have lived here ever since.* **3 long since** if something has long since happened, it happened a long time ago: *I've long since forgiven her for what she did.*

**USAGE NOTE: SINCE**

WORD CHOICE: **since (prep/conj), from, after, from...to/till/until, for**

**Since** is mainly used where you want to talk about a state or activity that started at some time in the past and has continued to the time when you are speaking: *I've been here since ten o'clock this morning.*|*The place had completely changed since I went there three years ago* (NOT *It has changed since three years/three years before*).

**From** or **after** may be used to show the starting points of periods of time where you do not use **since**. For example: *I hope they'll be friends from now on* (NOT *since now on*), means I hope they will be friends from now and into the future. *She was very unhappy for a while after leaving home* (NOT *since*) means that she was unhappy from a period of time in the past until a later time in the past.

**From...to/until/till** is used where you want to give both ends of a period of time during which some state existed or some activity was being done. This construction can go with most tenses of the verb: *I was here from ten till two.*|*From 1990 to the present he's had no regular job* (NOT *since 1990 to the present*).|*She works from sunrise until sunset.*

**For** is used where you want to give the length of a period of time, but do not need to say exactly when it started or finished. It goes with all tenses of verbs: *We lived there for a long time.*|*She's only staying for a week.* When you use **for** with the present perfect tense, it gives a period of time that ends at the time of speaking: *I've been waiting for two hours* (NOT *since two hours*).

In spoken English the **for** is often left out: *I've been here two hours.*|*She's only staying a week.*

GRAMMAR

The point of time with **since** may be shown by a clause, which may contain a verb in the simple past: *He's been ill ever since he arrived.*

The point of time with **since** may also be shown less exactly, by mentioning a period of time that ended in the past: *He's been working here since last week/the 60s* (= he started at some time during the 60s).|*Since I was a kid I've wanted to visit Disney World.*

A **since** clause may also itself cover the whole period from a point in the past to the time of speaking: *Since she's been living here she's made a lot of friends.*

However, as in all the above examples, the main verb in any clause with **since** usually has to be in one of the perfect tenses. Compare also: *Yesterday Bobby told me he hadn't eaten since Tuesday* (= between Tuesday and yesterday he did not eat anything).

Non-perfect tenses are used only in particular situations, for example where you are talking about the length of time itself: *It's two weeks since I've seen you* (NOT *...since I haven't seen you*).|*It seems like months since you last paid me.* Note also: *Since the car accident she can't walk properly* (= she hasn't been able to walk properly).

**sin·cere** /sɪnˈsɪə‖-ˈsɪr/ *adj* **1** a feeling, belief, statement etc that is sincere is honest and true, and based on what you really feel and believe; GENUINE (1): *sincere admiration*|*a sincere desire to find out the truth* **2** someone who is sincere is honest and says what they really feel or believe: *He was gentle and sincere by nature.*|[+ **in**] *They were completely sincere in their beliefs.* —opposite INSINCERE

**sin·cere·ly** /sɪnˈsɪəli‖-ˈsɪr-/ *adv* **1** in a sincere way: *I sincerely hope I'll see her again.*|*a sincerely held belief* **2 sincerely/yours sincerely** an expression used to end a formal letter that you have begun by addressing someone by name

**sin·cer·i·ty** /sɪnˈserɪ̣ti/ *n* [U] **1** the quality of honestly believing something or really meaning what you say: *I don't doubt her sincerity, but I think she's got her facts wrong.* **2 in all sincerity** *formal* very sincerely: *May I say in all sincerity that your support has been most valuable.*

**sine** /saɪn/ *n* [C] *technical* the FRACTION (2) calculated for an angle by dividing the length of the side opposite it in a TRIANGLE with a RIGHT ANGLE by the length of the side opposite the RIGHT ANGLE —compare COSINE, TANGENT (3)

**si·ne·cure** /ˈsaɪnɪkjʊə, ˈsɪn-‖-kjʊr/ *n* [C] a job which you get paid for even though you do not have to do very much

**si·ne qua non** /ˌsɪni kwɑː ˈnəʊn‖-ˈnɑːn/ *n* [singular] *Latin formal* something that you must have, or which must exist, for something else to be possible: [+ **for/of**] *The control of inflation is a sine qua non for economic stability.*

**sin·ew** /ˈsɪnjuː/ *n* [C,U] **1** *not technical* a long strong piece of TISSUE (3) in your body that connects a muscle to a bone **2** [usually plural] *literary* a means of strength or support: *the sinews of our national defense*

**sin·ew·y** /ˈsɪnjuːi/ *adj* having strong muscles: *a big man with long, sinewy arms*

**sin·ful** /ˈsɪnfəl/ *adj* **1** *literary or biblical* morally wrong or guilty of doing something morally wrong: *a sinful man | Even within marriage they believed it was sinful to seek pleasure in sex.* **2** very wrong or bad: *a sinful waste of taxpayers' money* —**sinfully** *adv*

S1 W2 **sing** /sɪŋ/ *v past tense* **sang** /sæŋ/ *past participle* **sung** /sʌŋ/ **1** [I,T] to produce musical sounds, songs etc with your voice: *Sophie's been singing in the church choir for years.* | **sing a song/tune etc** *We all enjoy singing carols at Christmas.* | **sing sb a song/tune etc** *Come on, sing us a song!* | **sing to sb** *She walked along, singing to herself.* **2 sing sb to sleep** to sing to a baby or child until they go to sleep **3** [I] if birds sing, they produce high musical sounds: *I awoke to hear the birds singing outside my window.* **4** [I always + adv/prep] to make a high, continuous, ringing sound: **[+ on]** *A kettle was singing on the stove.* | **[+ past/by etc]** *An enemy bullet sang past my ear.* **5 sing sb's praise(s)** to praise someone very much: *Diane really admires you – she's always singing your praises.* **6** [I] *slang* to tell someone or the police everything you know about a crime, especially a crime you were involved in yourself: *We'll soon make him sing.* **7** [I + **of**, T] *literary* to praise someone in poetry

**sing along** *phr v* [I] to sing with someone else who is already singing: *Sing along if you know the words.*

**sing out** *phr v* [I,T] *informal* to sing or shout out clearly and loudly: *If you see anything that looks interesting, sing out.*

**sing up** *phr v* [I] to sing more loudly: *Sing up, boys, I can't hear you!*

**sing·a·long** /ˈsɪŋəlɒŋ‖-lɔːŋ/ *n* [C] *AmE* an informal occasion when people sing songs together; SINGSONG *BrE*

**singe¹** /sɪndʒ/ *v* [I,T] to burn something slightly on its surface or edge, or to be burned in this way: *If the iron's too hot it'll singe your shirt.*

**singe²** *n* [C] a mark made by burning something slightly

S3 **sing·er** /ˈsɪŋə‖-ər/ *n* [C] someone who sings, especially as a profession: *an opera singer | a pop singer*

**singer-song·writ·er** /ˌ·· ˈ···/ *n* [C] someone who writes songs and sings them

**Sing·ha·lese** /ˌsɪŋəˈliːz◂/ *n, adj* SINHALESE

S2 W1 **sin·gle¹** /ˈsɪŋgəl/ *adj*

**1** ▶ **ONE** ◀ [only before noun] only one: *A single tree gave shade from the sun.* | *They won the game by a single point.* | *Write your answer on a single sheet of paper.* | **not a single** (=not even one) *We didn't get a single reply to our advertisement.*

**2** ▶ **SEPARATE** ◀ [only before noun] considered on its own: *the highest price ever paid for a single work of art* | **the single most/biggest/greatest etc** *Cigarette smoking is the single most important cause of lung cancer.* | *The single biggest problem we face is apathy.* | **every single word/day etc** *There's no need to write down every single word I say.*

**3** ▶ **PEOPLE** ◀ **a)** not married: *changes in the tax rate for single people* **b)** not involved in a romantic relationship: *I never meet any attractive single men!* —see also SINGLE PARENT

**4 single bed/room etc** meant for or used by one person only: *You have to pay extra for a single room.* —compare DOUBLE¹ (4) —see picture at BED¹

**5** ▶ **NOT DOUBLE** ◀ having only one part, quality etc, as opposed to having two or more: *Use double, not single, thread to reinforce the seams.* | *A single flower has only one set of petals.* | *a single-sex school* (=either for boys or for girls, but not both)

**6** ▶ **TICKET** ◀ *BrE* a single ticket etc is for a trip from one place to another but not back again; ONE-WAY —compare RETURN³ —see also SINGLY

**single²** *n* [C] **1** a musical record that has only one short song on each side: *Have you heard their latest single?* **2 a)** a single RUN² (17) in CRICKET (2) **b)** a hit that allows the person who is hitting the ball to reach first BASE¹ (8) in BASEBALL **3 singles** a game, especially in tennis, played by one person against another: *I prefer singles – you get more exercise.* | *Who won the women's singles?* —compare **doubles** (DOUBLE² (5)), | **singles bar/club/night** (=a bar, club etc intended for people who are not married or involved in a romantic relationship) **4** *BrE* a ticket for a trip from one place to another but not back again: *A single to Oxford, please.* —compare RETURN² (9) **5** *AmE* a one dollar BILL¹ (3): *Anybody have five singles?*

**single³** *v*

**single** sb/sth ↔ **out** *phr v* [T] to choose someone or something from among a group of similar people or things, especially in order to praise them or criticize them: *His article starts by singling out the five key goals of US foreign policy.* | **single sb out for praise/blame etc** *The report singles out Mr Clarke and Mr Heseltine for special criticism.*

**single-breast·ed** /ˌ·· ˈ··◂/ *adj* a single-breasted suit has a JACKET with only one set of buttons at the front —compare DOUBLE-BREASTED —see picture on page 840

**single cream** /ˌ·· ˈ·/ *n* [U] thin cream that can be poured —compare DOUBLE CREAM *BrE*; HEAVY CREAM *AmE*

**single cur·ren·cy** /ˌ·· ˈ···/ *n* [C] a unit of money that is shared by several different countries: *paving the way for monetary union and a single currency in Europe*

**Single Eu·ro·pe·an Mar·ket** /ˌ·· ˌ···· ˈ··/ *n* [singular] the unrestricted movement of goods and services between the countries of the European Union

**single fig·ures** /ˌ·· ˈ··/ *n* **in single figures** any number below 10: *Interest rates have stayed in single figures for over a year now.*

**single file** /ˌ·· ˈ·/ *n* [U] moving in a line, with one behind another: *We walked in single file across the narrow bridge.* —**single file** *adv*: *kids shuffling single file down the hall*

**single-hand·ed** /ˌ·· ˈ··◂/ *adj* [only before noun] done by one person without help from anyone else: *a single-handed voyage across the Atlantic* —**single-handed, single-handedly** *adv*: *She rebuilt the house single-handed.*

**single hon·ours** /ˌ·· ˈ··/ *n* [U] a university degree course in Britain in which only one main subject is studied —compare JOINT HONOURS

**single lane road** /ˌ·· · ˈ·/ *n* [C] *AmE* a road that is only wide enough for one car to go along it

**single mar·ket** /ˌ·· ˈ··/ *n* [singular] the SINGLE EUROPEAN MARKET

**single-mind·ed** /ˌ·· ˈ··◂/ *adj* someone who is single-minded has one clear aim and works very hard to achieve it: *Molly worked with single-minded determination, letting nothing distract her.* —**single-mindedly** *adv* —**single-mindedness** *n* [U]

**sin·gle·ness** /ˈsɪŋgəlnɪs/ *n formal* **singleness of purpose** [U] great determination when you are working to achieve something

**single par·ent** /ˌ·· ˈ··/ *n* [C] a mother or father who looks after their children on their own, without a partner

**sin·glet** /ˈsɪŋglɪt/ *n* [C] *BrE* a piece of clothing without SLEEVES that is worn as underwear or as a light shirt when playing some sports

**single track road** /ˌ·· · ˈ·/ *n* [C] *BrE* a road that is only wide enough for one car to go along it

**sin·gly** /ˈsɪŋgli/ *adv* one at a time; separately: *The children walked along the beach singly or in groups of two or three.*

**sing·song** /ˈsɪŋsɒŋ‖-sɔːŋ/ *n* [C] **1** [C] *BrE* an informal occasion when people sing songs together; SINGALONG *AmE*: *There was a bit of a singsong at the pub.*

2 [singular] a way of speaking in which your voice repeatedly rises and falls: *She talked in a strange sing-song.* —**singsong** *adj*: *a singsong voice*

**sin·gu·lar**[1] /ˈsɪŋgjʊlə‖-ər/ *adj* **1** a singular noun, verb, form etc is used when writing or speaking about one person or thing: *If the subject is singular, use a singular verb.* **2** *formal* very great or very noticeable: *a woman of singular beauty*|*He showed a singular lack of tact in the way he handled the situation.* **3** *literary* very unusual or strange: *a singular novel by an eccentric writer*

**singular**[2] *n* [C] the form of a word used when writing or speaking about one person or thing

**sin·gu·lar·i·ty** /ˌsɪŋgjʊˈlærɪ̌ti/ *n* **1** [C] *technical* **a)** another word for a BLACK HOLE **b)** a set of events that do not obey the usual laws of nature, especially the events that happened at the BIG BANG (=beginning of the universe) **2** [U] *old-fashioned* strangeness

**sin·gu·lar·ly** /ˈsɪŋgjʊləli‖-lərli/ *adv formal* **1** very noticeably: *a singularly beautiful woman*|*a singularly unsuccessful attempt to gain publicity* **2** *old-fashioned* in an unusual way; strangely

**Sin·ha·lese** /ˌsɪnhəˈliːz◂/ *n* [C] **1** a person from one of the groups of people who live in Sri Lanka **2** one of the languages of Sri Lanka —**Sinhalese** *adj*

**sin·is·ter** /ˈsɪnɪ̌stə‖-ər/ *adj* making you feel that something evil, wrong, or illegal is happening or will happen: *a sinister figure lurking in the shadows*|*a sinister looking mask*|*Was it all a cover-up for more sinister activities?*

3 **sink**[1] /sɪŋk/ *past tense* **sank** /sæŋk/ or **sunk** /sʌŋk/ *past participle* **sunk** *v*

**1 ► IN WATER ◄ a)** [I] to go down below the surface of water, mud etc: *The Titanic sank after hitting an iceberg.*|*If you put it in water, will it float or sink?*|*The heavy guns sank up to their barrels in the mud.* **b)** [T] to damage a ship so badly that it sinks: *Three ships were sunk that night by enemy torpedoes.*

**2 ► MOVE LOWER ◄** [I] **a)** to move downwards to a lower level: *It was several days before the flood waters sank and life returned to normal.*|*Her head sank onto her chest as she dozed off in her chair.* **b)** to fall down or sit down heavily, especially because you are very tired and weak: **[+ into/on/down etc]** *Sinking down on the bed, she tried to collect her thoughts.*|**sink to your knees** (=fall into a kneeling position) *The prisoner sank to his knees, begging for mercy.*

**3 ► SUN/MOON ◄** [I] to move downwards in the sky, and disappear from sight: *The sun was sinking behind the coconut palms.*

**4 ► CHANGE/GET WORSE ◄** [I always + adv/prep] to gradually pass into a different state, especially one that is worse: **sink into crisis/despair/decay etc** *The Soviet economy was sinking deeper and deeper into crisis.*|*neglected buildings sinking into decay*|**be sinking fast** (=getting weaker and about to die) *By this time, she was sinking fast and there was little we could do for her.*

**5 ► LOWER AMOUNT/VALUE ◄** [I] to go down in amount or value: *The population had sunk to a few dozen families.*|*efforts by the central banks to prop up the sinking dollar*

**6 ► QUIET ◄** [I] if your voice sinks you start talking more quietly: *Holmes's voice sank as he revealed the truth about the murders.*|**sink into silence** *moaning and crying out in pain, and finally sinking into silence.*

**7 your heart sinks/your spirits sink** to lose hope or confidence, especially when you feel unable to do everything that you have to do: *The journey seemed never-ending, and her spirits sank lower.*|*I realized, with a sinking heart, that I had forgotten to post that vital letter.*

**8 that sinking feeling** *informal* the unpleasant feeling that you get when you suddenly realize that something bad is going to happen: *I had that sinking feeling you get when you know you've made a huge mistake.*

**9 be sunk a)** *informal* to be in a situation when you are certain to fail or have a lot of problems: *If we can't find a taxi we'll really be sunk.* **b) be sunk in gloom/misery/apathy etc** to be so unhappy, tired etc that you feel completely unable to improve your situation: *He wandered around aimlessly all day, then returned home sunk in gloom.*

**10 sink without trace a)** if a ship sinks without trace, it sinks and no one knows where it has sunk **b)** if someone sinks without trace, they disappear mysteriously and you never hear about them again: *Actors who quarrelled with their studios just seemed to sink without trace.*

**11 sink so low/sink to doing sth** to be dishonest enough or selfish enough to do something very bad or unfair: *Cheating his own sister – how could he have sunk so low?*

**12 sink your teeth/claws/knife etc into sth** to put your teeth or something sharp into someone's flesh, into food etc: *The dog sank its teeth into my arm.*

**13 sink a well/hole/mine etc** to dig a deep hole in the ground

**14 ► MONEY ◄** [T] to lend or spend a lot of money on a business, in the hope of making more money in the future; INVEST: **sink sth in/into** *They had sunk most of their savings into a property venture.*

**15 ► BALL ◄** [T] to hit a ball into a hole in games such as GOLF or SNOOKER

**16 sink your differences** to agree to stop arguing and forget about your disagreements, especially in order to unite and oppose someone else

**17 sink or swim** to suceed or fail without help from anyone else: *They don't give you a lot of guidance – you're just left to sink or swim, really.*

**18 ► DRINK ◄** [T] *BrE informal* to drink alcohol, especially in large quantities: *We sank a few pints at the pub first.*

**sink in** *phr v* [I] if information, facts etc sink in, you gradually understand them or realize their full meaning: *For a moment her words didn't sink in.*|*The stupidity of what I had done began to sink in with an awful finality.*

**sink**[2] *n* [C] **1** *BrE* a large open container, especially in a kitchen, that you fill with water and use for washing dishes etc: *Dirty plates were piled high in the sink.* —see picture on page 833 **2** *AmE* an open container in a kitchen or bathroom that you can fill with water and use for washing yourself, washing dishes etc —see also **everything but the kitchen sink** (EVERYTHING (6))

**sinker** —see **hook, line and sinker** (HOOK[1] (7))

**sinking fund** /ˈ·· ˌ·/ *n* [C] *technical* money saved regularly by a business to pay for something in the future

**sin·ner** /ˈsɪnə‖-ər/ *n* [C] *especially biblical* someone who has sinned (SIN) by not obeying God's laws

**Sinn Fein** /ˌʃɪn ˈfeɪn/ *n* [singular] an Irish political organization that wants Ireland to become a united republic

**Sino-** /saɪnəʊ‖-noʊ/ *prefix* **1** of China; Chinese **2** Chinese and: *Sino-Japanese trade*

**si·nol·o·gy** /saɪˈnɒlədʒi‖-ˈnɑː-/ *n* [U] *technical* the study of Chinese language, history, literature etc

**sin·u·ous** /ˈsɪnjuəs/ *adj* smoothly curving and twisting, like the movements of a snake: *a dance with sinuous movements*|*the river's sinuous course*

**si·nus** /ˈsaɪnəs/ *n* [C] one of the hollow spaces filled with air in the bones of your face that have an opening in your nose

**sip**[1] /sɪp/ *v* [I,T] to drink something slowly, taking very small mouthfuls: *She was sitting at the bar sipping a Martini.*|**[+ at]** *Kruger sipped at his whisky thoughtfully.*

**sip**[2] *n* [C] a very small amount of a drink: **take a sip (of)** *George took another sip of coffee.*

**si·phon**[1]**, syphon** /ˈsaɪfən/ *n* [C] **1** a bent tube used for getting liquid out of a container, by holding the other end of the tube at a lower level than the container **2** also **soda siphon** *BrE* a kind of bottle for holding SODA WATER that is forced out of the bottle using gas pressure

**siphon**[2]**, syphon** *v* [T always + adv/prep] **1** to remove liquid from a container by using a siphon: **siphon sth off/out/into etc** *I siphoned some gasoline out of the* *tank.* **2** to dishonestly take money from a business, account etc to use it for a purpose for which it was not intended: **siphon sth off/from etc** *Corrupt officials had been siphoning off public funds for private business ventures.|I later found she had siphoned thousands of dollars from our bank account.*

W3 **sir** /sə; *strong* sɜːǁsər; *strong* sɜːr/ *n* **1** *spoken* a way of addressing a man, for example a male customer in a shop or a military officer that shows respect: *"Report back to me in an hour, sergeant." "Yes, sir."|Can I help you, sir?* —compare MADAM (1) *BrE*; MA'AM *AmE* **2** *AmE spoken* used to get the attention of a man whose name you do not know: *Sir! You dropped your wallet!* —compare MA'AM **3 Dear Sir** used at the beginning of a formal letter to a man **4 Sir** a title used before the first name of a KNIGHT or BARONET: *Sir James Wilson|Sir Jasper* **5** *BrE spoken* used by children at school as a way of addressing or talking about a male teacher: *Sir, I've forgotten my homework.|Look out – sir's coming back!* —compare MISS² (2) **6 no sir!** also **no siree!** *AmE old-fashioned spoken* used to emphasize that you do not want something, will not accept something etc: *I will not have that man in my home, no sir!*

**sire¹** /saɪəǁsaɪr/ *n* **1** *old use* a way of addressing a king: *The people await you, sire.* **2** [C usually singular] *technical* the father of a four-legged animal, especially a horse

**sire²** *v* [T] **1** to be the father of an animal, especially a horse: *a stallion that has sired several race winners* **2** *old-fashioned or humorous* to be the father of a person

**si·ren** /ˈsaɪərənǁˈsaɪr-/ *n* [C] **1** a piece of equipment that makes very loud warning sounds, used on police cars, fire engines etc: *police sirens wailing in the distance* **2 siren voices/call/song** *literary* encouragement to do something that sounds very attractive, but will have bad results: *The government must ignore the siren voices calling for a cut in interest rates.* **3** a word used especially in newspapers meaning a woman who is very attractive but also dangerous to men: *Hollywood sirens like Marilyn Monroe* **4 the Sirens** a group of women in ancient Greek stories, whose beautiful singing made sailors sail towards them into dangerous water

**sir·loin** /ˈsɜːlɔɪnǁˈsɜːr-/ also **sirloin steak** /ˌ·· ˈ·/ *n* [C,U] expensive meat cut from a cow's lower back

**si·roc·co** /sɪˈrɒkəʊǁ-ˈrɑːkoʊ/ *n* [C] a hot wind blowing from the desert of North Africa across to southern Europe

**sir·rah** /ˈsɪrə/ *n old use* an angry and disrespectful way of addressing a man

**sis** /sɪs/ *n spoken especially AmE* used when speaking to your sister

**sis·sy, cissy** /ˈsɪsi/ *n* [C] *informal* a boy that other boys dislike because he prefers doing things that girls enjoy: *David played with dolls and used to get called a sissy by the other kids.* —**sissy** *adj*

S1 W1 **sis·ter** /ˈsɪstəǁ-ər/ *n* [C] **1** a girl or woman who has the same parents as you: *Janet and Abigail are sisters.|He has three sisters and two brothers.* —see picture at FAMILY **2** also **Sister** *BrE* a nurse in charge of a hospital WARD¹ (1): *I'm feeling a bit better today, Sister.|the night sister* **3** also **Sister** a NUN: *Good morning, Sister Mary.* **4 sister company/organization/ship etc** a company etc that belongs to the same group or organization: *the Daily Express and its sister paper the Daily Star* **5** *AmE spoken* a way of addressing a woman, used especially by African Americans **6** a word used by women to talk about other women and to show that they have feelings of friendship and support towards them: *We have to support our sisters in southern Africa.*

**sis·ter·hood** /ˈsɪstəhʊdǁ-ər-/ *n* **1** [U] a special, loyal relationship among women who share the same ideas and aims, especially among FEMINISTS **2** [C] a group of women who live a religious life together

**sister-in-law** /ˈ·· · ˌ·/ *plural* **sisters-in-law** or **sister-in-laws** *n* [C] **1** the sister of your husband or wife **2** your brother's wife **3** the wife of the brother of your husband or wife —see picture at FAMILY

**sis·ter·ly** /ˈsɪstəliǁ-ər-/ *adj* typical of a loving sister: *sisterly affection* —**sisterliness** *n* [U]

**sit**

**sit** /sɪt/ *v past tense and past participle* **sat** /sæt/ *present participle* **sitting** S W

**1 ▶ IN A CHAIR ETC ◀ a)** [I] to be on a chair or seat, or on the ground, with the top half of your body upright and your weight resting on your BUTTOCKS: **[+on/in/by etc]** *sitting in a comfortable armchair|We all sat around the campfire and sang songs.|She's the girl that sits next to me in my math class.*|**sit at a desk/table etc** (=sit facing it) *Harry sat at his desk and stared out of the window.*|**sit doing sth** *We sat watching TV for a while.*|**sit still** *I wish you children would sit still for 5 minutes.* **b)** [I always+adv/prep] to get to a sitting position after you have been standing up: *Jim walked over and sat beside her.* **c)** [T always + adv/prep] to make someone sit down or help them to sit down: **sit sb down/on/in etc** *I sat him down in the armchair by his bed.*

**2 ▶ OBJECTS/BUILDINGS ETC ◀** [I always + adv/prep] to lie or be placed in a particular position: **[+on/in etc]** *"Where's my coat?" "It was sitting on the bottom of the stairs last time I saw it."|a village sitting on the side of a hill|When I got to work I found a huge bunch of flowers sitting on my desk.*

**3 ▶ DO NOTHING ◀** [I always +adv/prep] to stay in one place for a long time, especially sitting down, doing nothing useful or helpful: *I spent half the morning sitting in a traffic jam.|Well, I can't sit here chatting all day.|She just sits there complaining all day.*

**4 ▶ COMMITTEE/PARLIAMENT ETC ◀** [I] **a)** to be a member of a committee, parliament, or other official group: **[+in/on]** *She sits on several government committees.|Their father sits in the National Assembly.* **b)** to have a meeting in order to carry out official business: *The council only sits once a month.|The court will sit until all the evidence has been heard.*

**5 sit tight a)** to stay where you are and not move: *If your car breaks down, just sit tight and wait for the police.* **b)** to stay in the same situation, and not change your mind and do anything new: *We're advising all our investors to sit tight till the market improves.*

**6 be sitting pretty** to be in a very good or favourable position: *With profits up by over 80%, the company is sitting pretty.*

**7 sit in judgment on/over** to give your opinion about whether someone has done something wrong, especially when you have no right to do this

**8 sit on sb's tail** to drive very close behind a car, especially because you are waiting for a chance to pass it **9 ▶ANIMAL/BIRD◀** [I always + adv/prep] **a)** to be in, or get into, a resting position, with the tail end of the body resting on a surface: *The cat likes to sit on the wall outside the kitchen.* **b)** if a bird sits on its eggs, it covers them with its body to make the eggs HATCH **10 ▶PICTURE/PHOTO◀** [I + **for**] to sit somewhere so that you can be painted or photographed **11 ▶LOOK AFTER◀** [I + **for**] to look after a baby or child while its parents are out; BABYSIT **12 ▶EXAMS◀** [I + **for,** T] *BrE* to take an examination: *Tracy's sitting her GCSEs this year.*

**sit around/about** *phr v* [I] to spend a lot of time sitting and doing nothing very useful: *We used to just sit around for hours talking about the meaning of life.*

**sit back** *phr v* [I] **1** to settle yourself in a comfortable chair and relax: *You sit back and watch TV – I'll wash up.* **2** to relax and make no effort to get involved in something or influence what happens: *Don't just sit back and wait for new business to come to you.|All we have to do now is sit back and watch the checks roll in.*

**sit down** *phr v* [I] **1** to be in a sitting position or get into a sitting position: *Come over here and sit down !|If you work sitting down, you need to take plenty of exercise.|* **sit yourself down** *spoken*: *Come in Sally, sit yourself down.* **2 sit down and ...** to try to solve a problem or deal with something that needs to be done, by giving it all your attention: *I think we need to sit down and analyse these figures properly.|Maybe if you sat down and talked it through you could reach an agreement.*

**sit in** *phr v* [I] **1** to be present at a meeting but not take an active part in it: [+ **on**] *Do you mind if I sit in on some of the interviews?* **2** to do a job, go to a meeting etc instead of the person who usually does it: [+ **for**] *This is Alan James sitting in for Suzy Williams on the mid-morning show.* **3** to take part in a SIT-IN (=kind of protest)

**sit on** sth *phr v* [T] *informal* to delay dealing with something: *I sent my application about six weeks ago and they've just been sitting on it.*

**sit** sth ↔ **out** *phr v* [T] to stay where you are until something finishes, especially something boring or unpleasant: *We forced ourselves to sit the play out.|rich businessmen who had sat the war out comfortably in South Africa*

**sit through** sth *phr v* [T] to attend a meeting, performance etc, and stay until the end, even if it is very long and boring: *As a councillor, you have to sit through endless planning meetings.*

**sit up** *phr v* **1** [I] to be in a sitting position or get into a sitting position after you have been lying down: *By the time I got there he was sitting up in bed and reading a book.|At this, Faye sat up and flung aside the bed covers.* **2** [T **sit** sb **up**] to help someone to sit after they have been lying down **3** [I] to sit in a chair with your back up straight: *Just sit up straight and stop slouching.* **4** [I] to stay up very late: *Sometimes we just sit up and watch videos all night.* **5 make sb sit up (and take notice)** to do something surprising or impressive that makes someone pay attention to you: *a fantastic performance that made all the critics sit up and take notice*

**USAGE NOTE: SIT**

WORD CHOICE: **sit, sit at/in front of/on/in, sit down, seat, be seated**

You **sit at** a table, piano, or desk (unless you choose to **sit on** them!), and also **at** a computer or the controls of a car or plane. However, you sit **in front of** the television or the fire (though you can also sit *by* or *around* a fire).

You **sit on** something that has a flat, level surface such as the floor, the grass, a simple chair or seat, a bench, or a bed.

You **sit in** a tree, long grass, a car, a room, a corner, an armchair, the driving seat of a car.

When you are talking about the action of moving from standing to sitting, it is more common to use **sit down** rather than **sit** on its own: *They quietly sat down again* (NOT usually *sat again*). *Please sit down!* You usually only say *Sit!* to a dog.

Note that **seat** as a verb is only transitive, is a little formal, and is used in these ways: *This hall will seat 100 people* (=has seats for 100 people).|*They seated us at the front* (=put us in seats at the front).

**Be seated** is a formal expression for **sit down**. At a formal dinner for example, you might hear: *Please be seated* (=please sit down).

**sit·com** /ˈsɪtkɒm‖-kɑːm/ *n* [C,U] a popular type of television or radio entertainment consisting of a series of amusing stories about the same set of characters

**sit-down** /ˈ· ·/ *adj* **1 sit-down meal/dinner/lunch etc** a meal served to people sitting at a table: *a sit-down meal for 20 people* **2 sit-down strike/protest** a protest in which people sit down, especially to block a road or other public place, until their demands are listened to

**site¹** /saɪt/ *n* [C] **1** a place where something important or interesting happened: *an archaeological site*|[+ **of**] *the site of the Battle of Waterloo* **2** an area of ground where something is being built or will be built: *a construction site*|[+ **of**] *the site of a proposed missile base* **3 camp/camping/caravan site** *especially BrE* a piece of ground where you can camp 

**site²** *v* **be sited** be placed or built in a particular place: [+ **in/near etc**] *The new factory is to be sited in Fort Collins.*

**sit-in** /ˈ· ·/ *n* [C] a type of protest in which people refuse to leave the place where they work or study until their demands are agreed to: **hold/stage a sit-in** *Students staged a sit-in to protest about experimentation on animals.*

**sit·ter** /ˈsɪtə‖-ər/ *n* [C] **1** someone who sits or stands somewhere so that someone else can paint them or take photographs of them **2** *especially AmE* a BABYSITTER

**sit·ting** /ˈsɪtɪŋ/ *n* [C] **1** one of the times when a meal is served in a place where there is not enough space for everyone to eat at the same time: *The first sitting is at 12:30, and the second is at 1:30.* **2** an occasion when you have yourself painted or photographed **3** a meeting of a law court or parliament **4 at/in one sitting** during one continuous period when you are sitting in a chair: *I sat down and read the whole book in one sitting.*

**sitting duck** /ˌ·· ˈ·/ *n* [C] someone who is easy to attack or easy to cheat: *Out in the open, the soldiers were sitting ducks for enemy fire.*

**sitting mem·ber** /ˌ·· ˈ··/ *n* [C] *BrE* someone who is a member of a parliament at the present time: *the sitting member for Newbury*

**sitting room** /ˈ·· ·/ *n* [C] *especially BrE* the room in a house where you sit, relax, watch television etc; LIVING ROOM

**sitting ten·ant** /ˌ·· ˈ··/ *n* [C] *BrE* someone who lives in a rented house or flat, especially when this gives them legal rights to stay there

**sit·u·ate** /ˈsɪtʃueɪt/ *v* [T] *formal* to describe or consider something as being part of something else or connected with something else: **situate sth in** *Freud situates the origins of these anxieties in the subconscious.*

**sit·u·at·ed** /ˈsɪtʃueɪtɪ̣d/ *adj* **1 be situated** to be in a particular place or position: *a small town situated just south of Cleveland*|**beautifully/conveniently/pleasantly situated** *All the apartments are beautifully situated overlooking the beach.* **2 be well/badly situated** to be in a particular situation: *Microsoft is well situated to exploit this new market.*

S1 W1 **sit·u·a·tion** /ˌsɪtʃuˈeɪʃən/ *n* [C] **1** a combination of all the things that are happening and all the conditions that exist at a particular time in a particular place: *In the present situation, I wouldn't advise you to sell your house.* | *You're putting me in a very awkward situation.* | *I'd better go and see the boss and explain the situation.* | *With no rain for three months and food supplies running out, the situation here is getting desperate.* | **the economic/political/financial situation** *In view of the company's financial situation, there will be no salary increases this year.* | **fire situation/crisis situation etc** *especially spoken*: *We are unlikely to have a full-employment situation this year.* | **no-win situation** (=a situation which will end badly, whichever choice you make) **2** a word meaning the kind of area where a building is situated, used especially by people who sell or advertise buildings: *The house is in a charming situation, on a wooded hillside.* **3** *old-fashioned* a job: *She managed to get a situation as a parlour maid.*

**situation com·e·dy** /ˌ.... ˈ.../ *n* [C,U] *formal* a SITCOM

**Situations Va·cant** /ˌ.... ˈ../ *n* [singular] *BrE* the title of the part of a newspaper where jobs are advertised

**sit-up** /ˈ. ./ *n* [C] an exercise in which you sit up from a lying position, while keeping your feet on the floor

**six** /sɪks/ *number* **1** 6 **2 it's six of one and half a dozen of the other** *spoken* used to say there is not much difference between two possible choices, situations etc **3 at sixes and sevens** *BrE informal* disorganized and confused: *When the visitors arrived we were still at sixes and sevens.* **4** a hit in the game of CRICKET, worth six runs (RUN² (17)), in which the ball goes beyond the edge of the playing area before touching the ground —**sixth** *number*: *our sixth child*

S

**six·fold** /ˈsɪksfəʊld‖-foʊld/ *adv* by six times as much or as many: *Burglaries have increased sixfold.* —**sixfold** *adj*: *a sixfold increase in teenage pregnancies*

**six-foot·er** /ˌ. ˈ../ *n* [C] *informal* someone who is at least six feet (1.83 metres) tall

**six-pack** /ˈ. ./ *n* [C] six CANS or bottles of a drink, especially beer, sold together as a set: *There's a six-pack in the fridge.*

**six·pence** /ˈsɪkspəns/ *n* [C, U] a small silver-coloured coin worth six old pennies (PENNY), used in Britain until 1971, or this amount of money

**six-shoot·er** /ˈ. ˌ../ *n* [C] *old-fashioned, especially AmE* a small gun holding six bullets

**six·teen** /ˌsɪkˈstiːn◂/ *number* 16 —**sixteenth** *number*

**six·teenth** /ˌsɪkˈstiːnθ◂/ *n* [C] one of sixteen equal parts of something

**sixteenth note** /ˈ.. ˌ./ *n* [C] *AmE* a musical note which continues for a sixteenth of the length of a WHOLE NOTE; SEMIQUAVER *BrE* —see picture at MUSIC

**sixth** /sɪksθ/ *n* [C] one of six equal parts of something: *About one sixth of the children admitted to taking drugs.*

**sixth form** /ˈ. ./ *n* [C] the highest level in the British school system, for students, usually aged between 16 and 18, who are preparing to take A LEVELS (=the highest level of exams) —**sixth former** *n* [C]

**sixth form col·lege** /ˈ. . ˌ../ *n* [C] a type of school in Britain for students over the age of 16

**sixth sense** /ˌ. ˈ./ *n* [singular] a special feeling or ability to know things without using any of your five ordinary senses such as your hearing or sight: *A sixth sense told me that I was in danger.*

**six·ties** /ˈsɪkstiz/ *n* [plural] **1 the sixties** also **the '60s** the years from 1960 to 1969 **2 in your sixties** aged from 60 to 69: **early/late sixties** *I'd say she was in her late sixties.* **3** the numbers from 60 to 69, especially when used to measure temperature: **the low sixties/the upper sixties** *a fine spring day with the temperature in the upper sixties* (=about 68 or 69 degrees)

**six·ty** /ˈsɪksti/ *number* 60 —**sixtieth** *number*

**sixty-four-thou·sand-dol·lar ques·tion** /ˌ.. . ˌ. ˌ.. ˈ../ *n* [singular] *informal* the most important question, which you do not know the answer to: *But will they accept the offer? That's the sixty-four-thousand-dollar question.*

**siz·a·ble** /ˈsaɪzəbəl/ *adj* another spelling of SIZEABLE

S W **size**¹ /saɪz/ *n*

**1** ▶ **HOW BIG** ◀ [C,U] how big or small something is: *The American states vary enormously in size and population.* | *The firm underestimated the size of the market for their new product.* | **be the size of** (=be the same size as) *There were rats the size of cats.* | *He's a small boy, about John's size.* | *Their apartment is half the size of ours.* | **that size/this size** (=as big as that/this) *In a class this size, there are bound to be a few trouble-makers.* | **in all/different/various shapes and sizes** *They make these replacement windows in all shapes and sizes.* | **full size** (=the biggest size that something usually is) *He's quite a big dog, but he's still not full size yet.* | **be a good/fair/nice size** (=be fairly big) *The garden's a pretty good size.* | *It's a nice size bedroom.*

**2** ▶ **VERY BIG** ◀ [U] the fact of being very big: *You should have seen the size of their car!* | **sheer size** *What offends people is the sheer size of these pay increases.*

**3** ▶ **CLOTHES/GOODS** ◀ [C] one of a set of standard measures according to which clothes and other goods are produced and sold: *These shoes are one size too big.* | *The shirts come in three sizes, small, medium, and large.* | **size 8/16 etc** *I take size 10 shoes.*

**4 large-sized/medium-sized etc** large in size etc: *a medium-sized car* | **bite-sized** (=small enough to be eaten easily) *Cut the meat into bite-sized chunks.*

**5 try sth for size** to try something, especially clothing, to see if it is the right size for you

**6 to size** if you cut, make, or prepare something to size, you make it the right size for a particular use: *Cut the tile to size and fix it to the wall with adhesive.*

**7 that's about the size of it** *spoken* used to agree that what someone has said about a situation is a good or correct way of describing it

**8** ▶ **GLUE** ◀ [U] a thick sticky liquid used for giving stiffness and a shiny surface to paper, cloth etc —see also **cut sb down to size** (CUT¹), **try sth for size** (TRY)

**size**² *v* [T] **1** to sort things according to their size: *Shrimp are sized for canning into large, medium and small.* **2** to cover or treat something with SIZE¹ (8)

**size** sth/sb ↔ **up** *phr v* [T] to look at or consider a person or situation and make a judgment about them: *It only took a few seconds for her to size up the situation.*

**size·a·ble, sizable** /ˈsaɪzəbəl/ *adj* fairly large: *a sizeable cash payment*

**siz·zle** /ˈsɪzəl/ *v* [I] to make a sound like water falling on hot metal: *The steak was sizzling on the barbecue.* —**sizzle** *n* [singular] —see picture on page 1261

**siz·zler** /ˈsɪzələ‖-ər/ *n* [C] *informal* a very hot day: *Yesterday was a real sizzler!*

**siz·zling** /ˈsɪzəlɪŋ/ *adj especially AmE* very hot: *It's sizzling in the sun.*

**SJ** a written abbreviation used after a priest's name, to show that he is a JESUIT

**ska** /skɑː/ *n* [U] a kind of popular music from the West Indies with a fast regular beat, similar to REGGAE

**skag, scag** /skæg/ *n* [U] *slang* HEROIN

**skate**¹ /skeɪt/ *n* **1** [C] one of a pair of boots with metal blades on the bottom, for moving quickly on ice; ICE-SKATE² **2** [C] one of a pair of boots or frames with small wheels on the bottom, for moving quickly on flat smooth surfaces; ROLLER SKATE **3** [C,U] *plural* **skate** *or* **skates** a large flat sea fish that can be eaten **4 get/put your skates on** *BrE spoken* used to tell someone to hurry: *Put your skates on, or you'll be late for school.*

**skate**² *v* [I] **1** to move on skates: *The children skated on the frozen pond.* **2 be skating on thin ice** *informal* to be doing something that may get you into trouble —**skater** *n* [C]

**skate over/around** sth *phr v* [T] to avoid mentioning a problem or subject, or not give it enough attention:

The President was accused of skating over the issue of the homeless.

**skate·board** /ˈskeɪtbɔːd‖-bɔːrd/ *n* [C] a short board with two small wheels at each end, which you can stand on and ride as a sport —**skateboarding** *n* [U]

**skat·ing** /ˈskeɪtɪŋ/ *n* [U] the activity or sport of moving on skates: **go skating** *Zelda's going skating in the afternoon.*

**skating rink** /ˈ·· ˌ·/ *n* [C] a place or building where you can SKATE² (1)

**ske·dad·dle** /skɪˈdædl/ *v* [I] *spoken humorous* to leave a place quickly, especially because you do not want to be caught

**skeet shoo·ting** /ˈskiːt ˌʃuːtɪŋ/ *n* [U] *AmE* the sport of shooting at clay objects that have been thrown into the air; CLAY PIGEON SHOOTING *BrE*

**skein** /skeɪn/ *n* [C] a long loosely wound piece of thread, wool, or YARN¹ (1)

**skel·e·tal** /ˈskelʒtəl/ *adj* like a skeleton or connected with a skeleton: *the skeletal bodies of the starving people*

**skeleton**

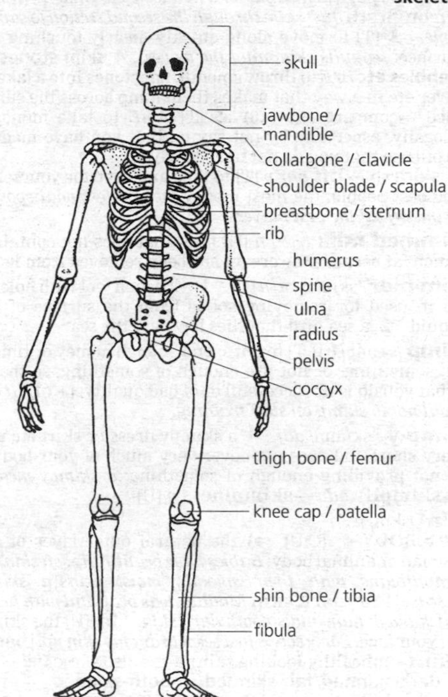


**skel·e·ton** /ˈskelʒtən/ *n* [C]
**1 a)** ▶**BONES**◀ the structure consisting of all the bones in a human or animal body: *the human skeleton* **b)** a set of these bones or a model of them, fixed in their usual positions, used for example by medical students
**2** ▶**MAIN PART**◀ the most important parts of something, to which more detail can be added later: **[+ of]** *It is just a skeleton of the report, showing the three basic points.*
**3** ▶**THIN**◀ *informal* an extremely thin person or animal: *The prisoners were just skeletons.*
**4 a skeleton in the cupboard/closet** *informal* an embarrassing or unpleasant secret about something that happened to you in the past
**5 skeleton staff/service** only enough to keep an operation or organization running: *British Rail is operating a skeleton service on Christmas Day.*

**skeleton key** /ˈ··· ·/ *n* [C] a key made to open a number of different locks

**skep·tic** /ˈskeptɪk/ *n* [C] the American spelling of SCEPTIC

**skep·ti·cal** /ˈskeptɪkəl/ *adj* the American spelling of SCEPTICAL

**skep·ti·ci·sm** /ˈskeptʒsɪzəm/ *n* [C,U] the American spelling of SCEPTICISM

**sketch¹** /sketʃ/ *n* [C] **1** a simple, quickly-made drawing that does not show much detail: *First she makes a sketch of a scene and then she paints it.* **2** a short humorous scene on stage, television etc that is part of a larger show: *Her TV programme is made up of a series of comic sketches.* **3** a short written or spoken description: *a brief sketch of the main weaknesses of the British economy*

**sketch**

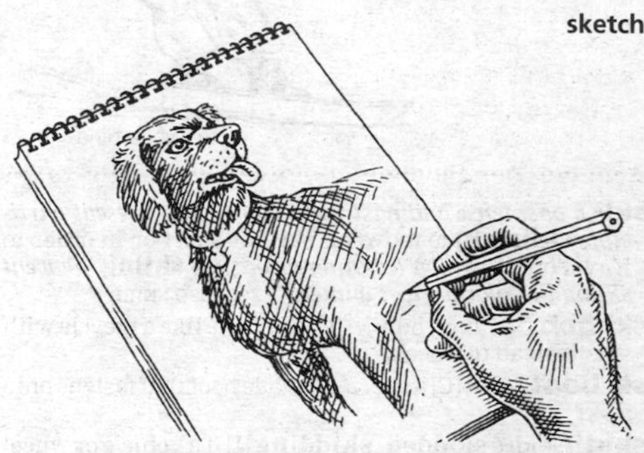

**sketch²** *v* [I,T] to draw a sketch of something
**sketch in** sth *phr v* [T] to add more information about something: *I'd like to sketch in a few details for you.*
**sketch** sth ↔ **out** *phr v* [T] to describe something in a general way giving the basic ideas: *We're having a meeting to sketch out a new business plan.*

**sketch·pad** /ˈsketʃpæd/ also **sketch·book** /ˈsketʃbʊk/ *n* [C] a number of sheets of paper fastened together for drawing on

**sketch·y** /ˈsketʃi/ *adj* not thorough or complete, and not having enough details to be useful: *We were only able to provide the police with sketchy details.* —**sketchily** *adv*

**skew¹** /skjuː/ *v* [T] to affect a test or an attempt to get information in a way that makes the results incorrect: *All the people we questioned lived in the same area, which had the effect of skewing the figures.*

**skew²** *adj* not straight

**skew·bald** /ˈskjuːbɔːld‖-bɒːld/ *n* [C] a horse with large white and brown shapes on it —**skewbald** *adj*

**skewed** /skjuːd/ *adj* **1** an opinion, piece of information, result etc that is skewed is incorrect, especially because you do not know all the facts: *The results of a telephone poll will always be skewed since those who do not have phones are obviously excluded.* **2** something that is skewed is not straight and is higher on one side than the other: *The picture on the wall was slightly skewed.*

**skew·er¹** /ˈskjuːə‖-ər/ *n* [C] a long metal or wooden stick for putting through pieces of meat while cooking them

**skewer²** *v* [T] to make a hole through a piece of food, an object etc with a skewer or with something similar: *Grant skewered bits of meat and put them on the barbecue.* —see picture on page 834

**skew-whiff** /ˌ· ˈ·◂/ *adj BrE informal* not straight: *The top of the bookcase is skew-whiff.*

**ski¹** /skiː/ *n plural* **skis** [C] **1** one of a pair of long thin narrow pieces of wood or plastic that you fasten to your boots and use for moving on snow **2** a piece of strong material shaped like a ski under a small vehicle so that it can travel on the snow

**ski²** *v past tense and past participle* **skied** *present participle* **skiing** [I] to move on skis for sport or in order to travel on snow: *I'm learning to ski.* | **go skiing** *We went skiing in Colorado last winter.* —see also SKIER

**ski·bob** /ˈskiːbɒb‖-bɑːb/ *n* [C] a vehicle like a bicycle with skis instead of wheels

**ski boot** /ˈ· ·/ *n* [C] a specially made boot that fastens onto a ski

**skid¹** /skɪd/ *v* **skidded, skidding** [I] if a vehicle or wheel skids, it suddenly slides sideways and you cannot control it: *The wheels of the truck skidded on the wet snow.*

**skid²** *n* **1** [C] a sudden uncontrollable sliding movement of a vehicle: *She could hear the skid of the car as it went around the corner.* | **go into a skid** (=start skidding) *He slammed on the brakes and we went into a long skid.* | **skid marks** *The only sign of the crash were the skid marks on the road.* **2 on the skids** *informal* being in a situation that is bad and getting worse: *He's been on the skids since losing his job.* **3 put the skids under** *informal* to make it likely or certain that something will fail: *The recession put the skids under his plans for starting a new business.* **4** [C] a part that is underneath some aircraft used in addition to wheels for landing on: *helicopter skids* **5** [usually plural] a piece of wood that is put under a heavy object to lift or move it

**skid·pan** /ˈskɪdpæn/ *n* [C] *BrE* a special slippery surface where drivers can practise controlling skidding cars

**skid row** /ˌskɪd ˈrəʊ‖-ˈroʊ/ *n* [U] **be on skid row** *informal* if someone is on skid row, they drink too much and have no job, nowhere to live etc

**ski·er** /ˈskiːə‖-ər/ *n* [C] someone who skis (SKI²)

**skies** /skaɪz/ *n* the plural form of SKY

**skiff** /skɪf/ *n* [C] a small light boat for one person

**skif·fle** /ˈskɪfəl/ *n* [U] *especially BrE* a type of popular music played in the 1950s and often using instruments made by the players themselves

**ski·ing** /ˈskiːɪŋ/ *n* [U] the sport of moving down hills or across the countryside in the snow, wearing SKIS

**ski jump** /ˈ· ·/ *n* [C] **1** a competition in which people wearing SKIS jump off a cliff at the bottom of a slope to see how far they can go through the air **2** a steep slope ending in a cliff, used for ski jump competitions

**skil·ful** *BrE*, usually **skillful** *AmE* /ˈskɪlfəl/ *adj* **1** good at doing something, especially something that needs special ability or training: *a skillful team player* **2** made or done very well and cleverly: *her skilful handling of a difficult problem* | *the skilful use of sound effects* —**skilfully** *adv*

**ski lift** /ˈ· ·/ *n* [C] a piece of equipment that carries SKIERS up to the top of a slope

**skill** /skɪl/ *n* [C,U] an ability to do something well, especially because you have learned and practised it: *Reading and writing are two different skills.* | *You need computing skills for that job.* | [+ **at/in**] *I admired his skill at driving.* | **with great skill/with a lot of skill** *The whole team played with great skill and determination.* S W

**skilled** /skɪld/ *adj* **1** someone who is skilled has the training and experience that is needed to do something well: *Skilled craftsmen, such as carpenters, bricklayers, etc are in great demand.* | **highly skilled** *a highly skilled negotiator* | [+ **at/in**] *She's very skilled at dealing with members of the public.* **2** work that is skilled needs special abilities or training in order to do it: *Bricklaying is very skilled work.* —opposite UNSKILLED

**skil·let** /ˈskɪlɪ̣t/ *n* [C] a flat heavy cooking pan with a long handle —see picture at PAN¹

**skill·ful** /ˈskɪlfəl/ *adj* an American spelling of SKILFUL

**skim** /skɪm/ *v* **skimmed, skimming** **1** [T] to remove floating fat or solids from the surface of a liquid: **skim sth off/from** *After simmering the meat and vegetables skim the fat from the surface.* **2** [I,T] to read something quickly to find the main facts or ideas in it: *She skimmed the sports page to find out who had won the game.* | **skim through sth** *Just skim through the second section to save time.* **3** [T] to move along quickly, nearly touching a surface: *seagulls skimming the waves* **4 skim stones/pebbles etc** *BrE* to throw smooth, flat stones into a lake, river etc in a way that makes them jump across the surface —compare SKIP¹ (8) **5** [T] *AmE* to take money illegally, especially by not saying that you have made profits so that you do not have to pay tax

**skim** sb ↔ **off** *phr v* [T] to take and keep for yourself the best people, the most money etc: *Professional sport skims off all the best players.*

**skimmed milk** /ˌ· ˈ·/ *n* [U] milk that does not contain much fat because the cream has been removed from it

**skim·mer** /ˈskɪmə‖-ər/ *n* [C] **1** a kitchen tool with holes in it, used for removing solids from the surface of a liquid **2** a sea bird that flies low over the sea

**skimp** /skɪmp/ *v* [I,T] to not spend enough money or time on something, or not use enough of something, so that what you do is unsuccessful or of bad quality: [+ **on**] *It's vital not to skimp on staff training.*

**skimp·y** /ˈskɪmpi/ *adj* **1** a skimpy dress or skirt etc is very short and does not cover very much of your body **2** not providing enough of something: *a skimpy meal* —**skimpily** *adv* —**skimpiness** *n* [U]

**skin¹** /skɪn/ *n* S W

**1** ▶ **BODY** ◀ [C,U] **a)** the natural outer layer of a human or animal body: *Babies have beautifully soft skin.* | *amphibians with their smooth, moist skins* | *a skin disease* | **fair/dark skin** *Madhur was beautiful with her thick black hair and smooth dark skin.* **b)** [U] the skin on your face: *Some soaps just seem to dry my skin up.* | **bad skin** (=unhealthy-looking skin) —see also SKINCARE

**2 dark-skinned/fair-skinned/smooth-skinned etc** having dark skin, smooth skin etc: *If you are very fair-skinned you should avoid going in the sun too much.* —see also **have a thick skin** (THICK¹ (11))

**3** ▶ **ANIMAL SKIN** ◀ [C,U] the skin of an animal, used as leather, fur etc: *a tiger skin* | *a sheepskin jacket*

**4** ▶ **FOOD** ◀ [C,U] **a)** the natural outer cover of some fruits and vegetables: *banana skins* | *onion skin* **b)** the outer cover of a SAUSAGE **c)** a thin solid layer that forms on the top of a liquid when it gets cold or is left uncovered: *Cover the soup to stop a skin from forming.*

**5 by the skin of your teeth** *informal* if you do something by the skin of your teeth, you only just succeed in doing it: *We woke up late and caught the plane by the the skin of our teeth.*

**6 get under sb's skin** *informal* if someone gets under your skin, they annoy you, especially by the way they behave: *What really gets under my skin is people who push straight to the front of the line.*

**7 be skin and bone** *informal* to be extremely thin in a

way that is unattractive and unhealthy: *Tania was all skin and bone when she got back from her world tour.*
**8 it's no skin off my nose** *spoken* used to say that you do not care what someone else thinks or does because it does not affect you: *Well, I offered to help out, but if she doesn't want me to it's no skin off my nose!* —see also **save sb's skin** (SAVE[1] (10)), **jump out of your skin** (JUMP[1] (4))

**skin²** *v* **skinned, skinning** [T] **1** to remove the skin from an animal, fruit, or vegetable: *Add the tomatoes, skinned and sliced.* **2** to hurt yourself by rubbing off some skin: *She skinned her knee when she fell off her bike.* **3 skin sb alive** *humorous* to punish someone very severely: *I'll skin him alive if I get hold of him!* **4** *AmE informal* to completely defeat someone: *The football team really skinned Watertown last year.*
**skin up** *phr v* [I] *BrE slang* to make a cigarette with MARIJUANA in it

**skin·care** /ˈskɪnkeə‖-ker/ *adj* skincare products are intended to improve the condition of your skin, especially the skin on your face —**skincare** *n* [U]

**skin-deep** /ˌ· ˈ·◂/ *adj* [not before noun] something that is skin-deep seems to be important or real, but in fact it is not because it only affects the way things appear: *Beauty is only skin deep.*

**skin-div·ing** /ˈ· ˌ··/ *n* [U] the sport of swimming under water with light breathing equipment but without a protective suit —**skin-diver** *n* [C]

**skin·flint** /ˈskɪnˌflɪnt/ *n* [C] *informal* someone who hates spending money or giving it away; MISER

**skin·ful** /ˈskɪnfʊl/ *n* **have a skinful** *BrE spoken* to drink a lot of alcohol and become drunk

**skin·graft** /ˈskɪngrɑːft‖-græft/ *n* [C] a medical operation in which healthy skin is removed from one part of your body and used on another to replace burned or damaged skin

**skin·head** /ˈskɪnhed/ *n* [C] a young man who has hair that is cut very short, especially one who behaves violently: *a gang of noisy skinheads*

S3 **skin·ny** /ˈskɪni/ *adj informal* very thin, especially in a way that is unattractive: *Some supermodels are far too skinny.* —see THIN (USAGE)

**skinny-dip·ping** /ˈ·· ˌ··/ *n* [U] *informal* swimming with no clothes on

**skint** /skɪnt/ *adj* [not before noun] *BrE informal* having no money, especially for a short time: *I'm skint at the moment.*

**skin-tight** /ˌ· ˈ·◂/ *adj* clothes that are skin-tight fit tightly against your body: *skin-tight jeans*

**skip¹** /skɪp/ *v*
**1** ▶**MOVEMENT**◀ [I] to move forwards with quick steps and jumps: [+ **across/along etc**] *Maria skipped along at her mother's side.*
**2** ▶**NOT DO STH**◀ [T] *informal* to not do something that you usually do or that you should do: *Children who skip breakfast often don't concentrate as well as others.* | *He skipped chemistry class three times last month.*
**3** ▶**NOT DEAL WITH**◀ [I, T] to leave something out, or not do something that would normally be the next thing you deal with: *I decided to skip the first two chapters.* | [+ **to**] *Let's skip to the last item on the agenda.* | [+ **over**] *I suggest we skip over the details and get to the main point.*
**4** ▶**CHANGE SUBJECTS**◀ [I always + adv/prep] to go from one subject to another in no fixed order: [+ **about/around/to etc**] *It was a badly organized talk – he just kept skipping around from one idea to another.*
**5** also **skip rope** *AmE* [I] to jump over a rope as you pass it over your head and under your feet as a game
**6 skip town/skip the country** to leave a place suddenly and secretly, especially to avoid being punished or paying debts: *Martin skipped the country with £5000.*
**7 skip it!** *spoken* used to say angrily that you do not want to talk about something: *"Sorry, what were you saying?" "Oh, skip it!"*
**8 skip rocks/stones** *AmE* to throw smooth, flat stones into a lake, river etc in a way that makes them jump across the surface —compare SKIM (4)
**9 skip a year/grade** to start a new school year in a class that is one year ahead of the class you would normally enter
**10 sb's heart skips a beat** used to say that someone is very excited, surprised, or frightened: *His heart skipped a beat when he realized Mattie was there.*
**skip out** also **skip off** *phr v* [I] to leave suddenly and secretly, especially in order to avoid being punished or paying money: *Martha skipped out without paying her bill.* | **skip out on** *AmE* (=leave someone when they need you) *Joel skipped out on his wife when she was 8 months pregnant.*

**skip²** *n* [C] **1** a quick light stepping and jumping movement **2** *BrE* a large container for bricks, wood and similar heavy waste; DUMPSTER *AmE*

**ski pants** /ˈ· ·/ *n* [plural] tight trousers with a band of cloth that goes under your foot, worn by women

**ski plane** /ˈ· ·/ *n* [C] an aircraft that has skis (SKI[1] (2)) for landing on snow, instead of wheels

**ski pole** /ˈ· ·/ *n* [C] one of two pointed short poles used for balancing and for pushing against the snow when skiing (SKI²)

**skip·per¹** /ˈskɪpə‖-ər/ *n* [C] *informal* **1** the person in charge of a ship **2** the leader of a sports team

**skipper²** *v* [T] *informal* to be in charge of a ship, sports team etc

**skipping rope** /ˈ·· ˌ·/ *n* [C] *BrE* a long piece of rope with handles that children use for jumping over; JUMP ROPE *AmE*

**skirl** /skɜːl‖skɜːrl/ *v* [I] to make a high sharp sound: *A seagull skirled overhead.* —**skirl** *n* [singular]

**skir·mish¹** /ˈskɜːmɪʃ‖ˈskɜːr-/ *n* [C] **1** a fight between small groups of soldiers, ships etc, especially one that happens away from the main part of a battle **2** a short argument, especially between political opponents: *Bates was sent off after a skirmish with the referee.*

**skirmish²** *v* [I + **with**] to be involved in a short fight or argument —**skirmisher** *n* [C]

**skirt¹** /skɜːt‖skɜːrt/ *n* [C] **1** a piece of outer clothing worn by women and girls, which hangs down from the waist like the bottom part of a dress: *She wore a white blouse and a plain black skirt.* —compare DRESS[1] (1) —see picture on page 840 **2** also **skirts** [plural] the part of a dress or coat that hangs down from the waist **3 the skirts of a forest/hill/village etc** the outside edge of a forest etc **4 a bit of skirt** *BrE informal* an offensive expression meaning an attractive woman

**skirt²** also **skirt around** *v* [T] **1** to go around the outside edge of a place or area: *The old footpath skirts around the village.* **2** to avoid talking about an important subject, especially because it is difficult or embarrassing: *a disappointing speech that skirted around all the main issues*

**skirting board** /ˈ·· ·/ *n* [C,U] *BrE* a long narrow piece of wood that is fixed along the bottom of the walls in a room; BASEBOARD *AmE* —see picture on page 410

**ski run** /ˈ· ·/ *n* [C] a marked track on a slope for skiing (SKI²)

**skit** /skɪt/ *n* [C] a short humorous performance or piece of writing that shows how silly something is by copying it: [+ **on**] *They did a skit on beauty contests.*

**skit·ter** /ˈskɪtə‖-ər/ *v* [I] to run very quickly and lightly, like a small animal

**skit·tish** /ˈskɪtɪʃ/ *adj* **1** a horse or other animal that is skittish easily gets excited or frightened **2** a person who is skittish is not very serious, and their feelings, behaviour, and opinions keep changing —**skittishly** *adv* —**skittishness** *n* [U]

**skit·tle** /ˈskɪtl/ *n* **1 skittles** [U] a British game in which a player tries to knock down objects shaped like bottles by rolling a ball at them **2** [C] one of the objects you roll the ball at in the game of skittles —see also **not all beer and skittles** (BEER (3))

**skive** /skaɪv/ also **skive off** *v* [I] *BrE informal* to avoid work or school by staying away or leaving without permission —**skiver** *n* [C]

**skiv·vies** /ˈskɪviz/ *n* [plural] *AmE* a man's underwear

**skiv·vy¹** /ˈskɪvi/ *n* [C] *BrE humorous* a servant who does only the dirty unpleasant jobs in a house: *You iron your shirt – I'm not your skivvy.*

**skivvy²** *v* [I] *BrE* to do all the dirty unpleasant jobs in a house, as if you were a servant

**skul·dug·ge·ry** /ˌskʌlˈdʌɡəri/ *n* [U] *often humorous* secretly dishonest or illegal activity: *Some skulduggery no doubt went on during the election.*

**skulk** /skʌlk/ *v* [I always + adv/prep] to hide or move about secretly, trying not to be noticed, especially when you are intending to do something bad: [+ **about/around/in etc**] *He was still skulking around outside when they left the building.*

**skull** /skʌl/ *n* [C] **1** the bones of a person's or animal's head —see picture at SKELETON **2 sb can't get it into their (thick) skull** *spoken* to be unable to understand something very simple: *He can't seem to get it into his skull that I'm just not interested in him.*

**skull and cross·bones** /ˌ· · ˈ··/ *n* [singular] **1** a picture of a human skull with two bones crossed below it, used in former times on the flags of PIRATE¹ (3) ships **2** a picture of a human skull with two bones crossed below it, used on containers to show that what is inside is very dangerous

**skull cap** /ˈ· ·/ *n* [C] a simple close-fitting cap for the top of the head, worn sometimes by priests or Jewish men

**skunk¹** /skʌŋk/ *n* [C] a small black and white North American animal that produces a strong unpleasant smell if it is attacked

**skunk²** *v* [T] *AmE informal* to defeat a player or team very easily

**skunk cab·bage** /ˈ· ˌ··/ *n* [C,U] a large North American plant similar to a CABBAGE, with an unpleasant smell

S2 W2 **sky** /skaɪ/ *n* [singular, U] **1** the space above the earth where clouds and the sun and stars appear: *The rocket shot up into the sky.* | *The sky turned dark just before the storm.* | **a patch/strip etc of sky** *There's a patch of blue sky between the clouds.* | **a blue/cloudy etc sky** (=used to describe how the sky looks at a particular time) *The sun blazed down from a clear blue sky.* **2 skies** a word meaning sky, used especially when describing the weather: *a land of blue skies and warm sunshine* | **the skies** *The skies were filled with scudding clouds.* | *the crowded skies above our major airports* **3 the sky's the limit** *spoken* used to say that there is no limit to what someone can achieve, spend, win etc —see also **pie in the sky** (PIE (4)), **praise sb/sth to the skies** (PRAISE¹ (1))

**sky-blue** /ˌ· ˈ·◂/ *n* [U] the bright blue colour of a clear sky —**sky-blue** *adj* —see picture on page 411

**sky·cap** /ˈskaɪkæp/ *n* [C] *AmE* someone who carries passengers' cases at an airport

**sky·div·ing** /ˈskaɪˌdaɪvɪŋ/ *n* [U] the sport of jumping from an aircraft and falling through the sky before opening a PARACHUTE —**sky-diver** *n* [U]

**sky-high** /ˌ· ˈ·◂/ *adj informal* extremely high: *If this thing explodes we'll be blown sky-high.* —**sky-high** *adv* —see also **blow sth sky-high** (BLOW¹ (19))

**sky·lark** /ˈskaɪlɑːk‖-lɑːrk/ *n* [C] a small bird that sings while flying high in the sky

**sky·light** /ˈskaɪlaɪt/ *n* [C] a window in the roof of a building

**sky·line** /ˈskaɪlaɪn/ *n* [C] the shape made by hills or buildings against the sky

**sky·rock·et** /ˈskaɪˌrɒkɪt‖-ˈrɑː-/ *v* [I] *informal* to increase suddenly and greatly: *The trade deficit has skyrocketed.*

**sky·scrap·er** /ˈskaɪˌskreɪpə‖-ər/ *n* [C] a very tall modern city building

**sky·wards** /ˈskaɪwədz‖-wərdz/ *adv* up into the sky or towards the sky: *The bird soared skywards.*

**slab** /slæb/ *n* [C] **1** a thick flat four-sided piece of a hard material such as stone: *The patio was made of stone slabs.* —see picture on page 416 **2 a slab of cake/chocolate etc** a large flat piece of cake etc **3 on the slab** *slang* lying dead in a hospital or MORTUARY

**slack¹** /slæk/ *adj* **1** not taking enough care or making enough effort to do things right: *Tollitt blundered with a slack header towards the goalkeeper.* | *The report criticized airport security as 'disgracefully slack'.* **2** with less business activity than usual: *Business is slack just now.* **3** hanging loosely, or not pulled tight: *The fan belt is a little slack.* | *a slack mouth* | *Keep the rope slack till I say 'pull'.* —**slackly** *adv* —**slackness** *n* [U]

**slack²** *n* **1** [C] money, space, or people that an organization has, but does not need: *There is very little slack in the training budget for this year.* **2 take up the slack a)** to make a rope tighter **b)** to do something that needs to be done because someone else is no longer doing it: *We're relying on Walters to take up the slack while Gonzalez is gone.* **3** [U] looseness in the way that something such as a rope hangs or is fastened **4 slacks** [plural] *old-fashioned* trousers **5** [U] coal in very small pieces

**slack³** also **slack off** *v* [I] to make less of an effort than usual or be lazy in your work

**slack·en** /ˈslækən/ also **slacken off** *v* [I, T] **1** to gradually become slower, weaker, less active etc, or to make something do this: *The heavy rain showed no signs of slackening off.* | **slacken your pace/speed** (=go or walk more slowly) *Once outside the gates, I slackened my pace.* **2** to make something looser or to become looser: *Just slacken the screws a little.* —opposite TIGHTEN

**slack·er** /ˈslækə‖-ər/ *n* [C] someone who is lazy and does not do all the work they should

**slag¹** /slæɡ/ *n* **1** [U] light waste material rather like glass, which is left when metal is obtained from rock **2** [C] *BrE slang* an insulting word for a woman, used to suggest that she has had a lot of sexual partners —**slaggy** *adj*

**slag²**

**slag** sb ↔ **off** *phr v* [T] *BrE informal* to talk about someone in a very critical way, especially when they are not there: *He's always slagging her off behind her back.*

**slag heap** /ˈ· ·/ *n* [C] *especially BrE* a pile of waste material at a mine or factory

**slain** /sleɪn/ *v* the past participle of SLAY

**slake** /sleɪk/ *v* [T] *literary* **1 slake your thirst** to drink so that you are not THIRSTY any more **2** to satisfy a desire

**sla·lom** /ˈslɑːləm/ *n* [U] a race for people on SKIS or in CANOES down a winding course marked by flags

**slam¹** /slæm/ *v* **slammed, slamming**

**1 ▶ DOOR/GATE ◀** [I,T] if a door, gate etc slams, or if someone slams it, it shuts with a loud noise: *Please don't slam the door.* | *We could hear people shouting and doors slamming in the house next door.* | **slam shut** *A door slammed shut in the distance.*

**2 ▶ PUT STH SOMEWHERE ◀** [T always + adv/prep] to put something on or against a surface with a fast violent movement: **slam sth/on/down etc** *Henry slammed the phone down and walked angrily out of the room.*

**3 slam on the brakes** to make a car stop very suddenly

**4 ▶ CRITICIZE STH ◀** [T] a word used especially in newspapers, meaning to criticize something strongly: *The government's amnesty for tax-dodgers was slammed today by opposition leaders.* | **slam sb for sth** *The television company was slammed by the media for its portrayal of a gang rape.*

**5 slam the door in sb's face a)** to shut a door hard when someone is trying to come in **b)** to rudely refuse to meet someone or talk to them

**slam into** sth *phr v* [T] to drive or move very fast

towards something and hit it: *The car slammed into a lamp-post.*

**slam²** *n* [C usually singular] the noise or action of a door or gate slamming —see also GRAND SLAM

**slam dunk** /ˈ· ·/ *v* [I, T] to put a ball through the net in BASKETBALL using a lot of force —**slam dunk** *n* [C]

**slam·mer** /ˈslæmə‖-ər/ *n* **in the slammer** *slang* in prison: *He was thrown in the slammer.*

**slan·der¹** /ˈslɑːndə‖ˈslændər/ *n* **1** [C] a false spoken statement about someone that is intended to damage the good opinion that people have **2** [U] the legal offence of making a statement of this kind: *The doctor was awarded record damages against her partners for slander.* —compare LIBEL¹ —**slanderer** *n* [C]

**slander²** *v* [T] to say untrue things about someone in order to damage other people's good opinion of them

**slan·der·ous** /ˈslɑːndərəs‖ˈslæn-/ *adj* a slanderous statement about someone is untrue, and is intended to damage other people's good opinion of them: *slanderous allegations*

**slang** /slæŋ/ *n* [U] very informal language that includes new and sometimes rude words, especially words used only by particular groups of people such as criminals, schoolchildren, or people who take drugs: *schoolboy slang* | **a slang word/expression/term** *'Screw' is a slang word used by prisoners to mean prison officer.* —**slangy** *adj*: *slangy expressions*

**slanging match** /ˈ·· ˌ·/ *n* [C] *BrE informal* an angry argument in which people insult each other: *They got into a bit of a slanging match in the pub.*

**slant¹** /slɑːnt‖slænt/ *v* [I] to slope or move in a sloping line: *slanting handwriting* | *The sun's rays slanted through the trees.* —**slantingly** *adv*

**slant²** *n* **1** a sloping position or angle: *a steep slant* | **at/on a slant** *Set the pole at a slant.* **2** a way of writing about or thinking about a subject that shows strong support for a particular opinion or set of ideas: *The editorial had an anti-union slant.* | *The report provides a new slant on important environmental issues.*

**slant·ed** /ˈslɑːntɪ̣d‖ˈslæn-/ *adj* **1** providing facts or information in a way that unfairly favours one opinion, one side of an argument etc; BIASED: **[+ towards]** *The survey was heavily slanted towards the ruling party.* **2** sloping to one side

S 2 **slap¹** /slæp/ *v* **slapped, slapping** **1** [T] to hit someone quickly with the flat part of your hand: *Do you think it's OK to slap children if they're really rude?* | **slap sb on the back** (=hit them on the back in a friendly way) —see picture on page 1259 **2** [T always + adv/prep] to put something down noisily on a surface, especially when you are angry: **slap sth on/down** *I slapped the report down on his desk and told him to do it again.* **3** [I] to hit a surface, making a sound like someone being slapped noisily: **[+ against]** *Small waves slapped against the jetty.*

**slap** sb **down** *phr v* [T] to unfairly and unkindly criticize someone so that they lose confidence

**slap** sth ↔ **on** *phr v* [T] *informal* **1** to put or spread something quickly or carelessly onto a surface: *She rushed upstairs and slapped on some make-up.* **2** to suddenly announce a new charge, tax etc, especially unfairly or without warning: *Many tour operators slap on supplements for single people.*

**slap²** *n* [C] **1** a quick hit with the flat part of your hand: **give sb a slap** *Julia gave Roy a friendly slap on the cheek.* **2 a slap in the face** an action that seems to be deliberately intended to offend or upset someone, especially someone who has tried very hard to do something: *When I wasn't promoted it felt like such a terrible slap in the face.* **3 a slap on the wrist** *informal* a punishment that is not very severe

**slap³** /slæp/ also **slap-bang** /ˌ· ˈ·/ *adv informal* hitting something very hard, especially when you are running, driving etc: **[+ into]** *I ran slap-bang into a lamp-post.*

**slap·dash** /ˈslæpdæʃ/ *adj* careless and done too quickly: *a very slapdash piece of work*

**slap·hap·py** /ˈslæpˌhæpi/ *adj* cheerfully careless and likely to make mistakes

**slap·per** /ˈslæpə‖-ər/ *n* [C] *BrE slang* a sexually immoral woman, or a woman who remains strong and cheerful in spite of a difficult life

**slap·stick** /ˈslæpˌstɪk/ *n* [U] humorous acting in which the performers fall over, throw things at each other etc

**slap-up** /ˈ· ·/ *adj* **slap-up meal/dinner etc** *BrE informal* a very large enjoyable meal

**slash¹** /slæʃ/ *v* **1** [I always + adv/prep, T] to violently cut or try to cut something with a knife, sword etc: *Most of the seats on the train had been slashed by vandals.* | **[+ at/through]** *Alan was slashing at the snake with a huge stick.* | **slash your way through** (=make a path through something by slashing) *They had to slash their way through thick undergrowth.* | **slash your wrists** (=deliberately cut your wrists with the intention of killing yourself) **2** [T often passive] a word used especially in newspapers and advertising meaning to greatly reduce an amount, price etc: *Over the last year the workforce has been slashed by 50%.*

**slash²** *n* [C] **1** a quick movement that you make with a sword, knife etc in order to cut someone or something **2** also **slash mark** a line (/) used in writing to separate words, numbers, or letters **3** a long narrow wound or a long narrow cut in a piece of material: *He staggered into hospital with slashes across his face.* **4 have/take a slash** *BrE spoken* an impolite expression meaning to URINATE

**slat** /slæt/ *n* [C] a thin flat piece of wood, plastic etc used especially in furniture —**slatted** *adj*: *a slatted bench*

**slate¹** /sleɪt/ *n*

**1** ▶ **ROCK** ◀ [U] a dark grey rock that can easily be split into flat thin pieces: *a slate mine*

**2** ▶ **ON A ROOF** ◀ [C] one of the small pieces of slate or similar material used for covering roofs: *There were several slates missing from the roof.*

**3 slate blue/grey** a dark grey or blue colour

**4** ▶ **POLITICS** ◀ [C] *especially AmE* a list of people that voters can choose in an election or that are being considered for an important job

**5 put sth on the slate** *BrE old-fashioned* to arrange to pay for something later, especially food or drink: *Two whiskies, and could you put them on the slate!*

**6** ▶ **FOR WRITING ON** ◀ [C] a small board in a wooden frame used for writing on in schools in former times —see also **a clean slate** (CLEAN¹ (10)), **wipe the slate clean** (WIPE¹ (6))

**slate²** *v* [T] **1** *BrE informal* to criticize a book, film etc severely, especially in a newspaper: *Donkin's most recent novel has been slated by the critics.* **2 be slated** *especially AmE* **a)** to be expected to succeed in getting a particular position or job: **be slated to be/do sth** *Rogers is slated to be the Democratic candidate.* **b)** to be expected or planned to happen at a time in the future: **be slated for** *The office buildings are slated for demolition next June.* —**slated** *adj*

**slath·er** /ˈslæθə‖-ər/ *v* [T] *AmE* to cover something with a thick layer of a soft substance: *toast slathered with butter*

**slat·tern** /ˈslætən‖-ərn/ *n* [C] *old-fashioned* a dirty untidy woman —**slatternly** *adj*

**slaugh·ter¹** /ˈslɔːtə‖ˈslɒːtər/ *v* [T] **1** to kill large numbers of people in a cruel or violent way: *Hundreds of innocent civilians were slaughtered.* —see KILL¹ (USAGE) **2** to kill an animal for food **3** *informal* to defeat an opponent by a large number of points: *We got slaughtered 110 – 54.*

**slaughter²** *n* [U] **1** the act of killing large numbers of people in a cruel or violent way **2** the act of killing animals for food

**slaugh·ter·house** /ˈslɔːtəhaʊs‖ˈslɒːtər-/ *n* [C] a building where animals are killed

**slave¹** /sleɪv/ *n* [C] **1** someone who is legally owned by another person and works for them for no money: *accusing her mother of treating her like a slave* **2 be a**

**slave to/of** to be completely influenced by something so that you cannot make your own decisions: *A lot of kids nowadays are slaves of fashion.* **3 slave driver** *informal* someone who makes people work extremely hard: *She knew the girls called her a slave driver behind her back.*

**slave²** *v* [I always + adv/prep] to work very hard with little time to rest: [+ **away/over/for**] *I've been slaving away for hours to get this report finished.* | **slaving away over a hot stove** (=a humorous way of saying you are cooking)

**slave la·bour** *BrE,* **slave labor** *AmE* /ˌ· ˈ··/ *n* [U] **1** *informal* work for which you are paid an unreasonably small amount of money: *£2 an hour! That's slave labour!* **2** work done by SLAVES or the people who do this work: *The Pyramids were largely built by slave labour.*

**slav·er¹** /ˈslævə‖-ər/ *v* [I] to let SALIVA (=liquid produced inside your mouth) come out of your mouth, especially because you are hungry: *The dog started slavering at the sight of the bone.*

**slaver over** sth *phr v* [T] *informal* to be very excited about something, especially in an unpleasant or stupid way: *slavering over the parked Ferrari out front*

**slav·er²** /ˈsleɪvə‖-ər/ *n* [C] *old use* **1** someone who sells slaves **2** a ship for slaves

**sla·ve·ry** /ˈsleɪvəri/ *n* [U] **1** the system of having slaves: *the abolition of slavery* **2** the condition of being a slave: **sell sb into slavery** (=to sell someone as a SLAVE)

**slave trade** /ˈ· ·/ *n* [singular] the buying and selling of slaves, especially Africans who were taken to America

**slav·ish** /ˈsleɪvɪʃ/ *adj* **slavish imitation/devotion etc** behaviour or actions that show that you cannot make your own decisions about what you should do: *a slavish devotion to duty* —**slavishly** *adv* —**slavishness** *n* [U]

**slaw** /slɔː‖slɒː/ *n* [U] *AmE* a cold dish made with CABBAGE, CARROTS, and onions; COLESLAW

**slay** /sleɪ/ *v past tense* **slew** /sluː/ *past participle* **slain** /sleɪn/ [T] **1** *literary* a word meaning to kill someone, often used in newspaper reports; MURDER² (1): *Thousands were slain in the battle.* **2** *AmE informal* to amuse someone a lot: *That guy really slays me!* —**slayer** *n* [C]

**sleaze** /sliːz/ *n* **1** [U] immoral behaviour, especially involving sex or dishonesty: *the sleaze factor in US politics* **2** also **sleazebag** *slang especially AmE* someone who is immoral or cannot be trusted

**slea·zy** /ˈsliːzi/ *adj* **1 sleazy hotel/bar etc** a hotel etc that looks dirty and cheap **2** someone who is sleazy is immoral or unpleasant: *sleazy business associates* —**sleaziness** *n* [U]

**sledge¹** /sledʒ/ *BrE,* **sled** /sled/ *AmE* —*n* [C] a vehicle for travelling over snow with two long narrow pieces of wood or metal fixed under it

**sledge²** *BrE,* **sled** *AmE* —*v* [I] to travel or ride on a sledge

**sledge·ham·mer** /ˈsledʒˌhæmə‖-ər/ *n* [C] a large heavy hammer

**sleek¹** /sliːk/ *adj* **1** sleek hair or fur is straight, shiny, and healthy-looking: *The cat had sleek black fur.* **2** a vehicle or other object that is sleek has a smooth attractive shape: *the sleek lines of the new Mercedes* **3** someone who is sleek looks rich, but you feel that you cannot trust them: *sleek executive types in their expensive suits* —**sleekly** *adv* —**sleekness** *n* [U]

**sleek²** *v* [T always + adv/prep] to make hair or fur smooth and shiny by putting water or oil on it: **sleek sth back/down etc** *His hair was sleeked back with oil.*

S1 W2 **sleep¹** /sliːp/ *v past tense and past participle* **slept** /slept/ **1 ▶ REST ◀** [I] to rest your mind and body by being asleep: *I normally sleep on my back.* | *You're welcome to stay if you don't mind sleeping on the floor.* | **sleep well/soundly** *Did you sleep well?* | **sleep like a log/top** *informal* (=sleep very well) | **sleep late** (=sleep until late in the morning) *We usually sleep late on Sundays.* | **not sleep a wink** (=not sleep at all) *I didn't sleep a wink all night.* | **sleep the night** *BrE* (=sleep at someone else's house for the night) *We talked till late and then Bob ended up sleeping the night.*
**2 sleep rough** *BrE* to sleep outdoors in uncomfortable conditions, especially because you have no money
**3 sleep on it** *informal* to not make a decision about something important until the next day: *Why don't you sleep on it and give me your final reply tomorrow?*
**4 sleep tight** *spoken* used especially to children before they go to bed to say that you hope they sleep well: *Good night, sweetheart. Sleep tight!*
**5 ▶ NUMBER OF PEOPLE ◀** [T] to have enough beds for a particular number of people: **sleep two/four/six etc** *The villa will sleep four easily.*
**6 let sleeping dogs lie** to deliberately avoid mentioning a problem or argument that you had in the past, so that you do not cause any problems: *She decided to let sleeping dogs lie and not to ask her son about the missing money.*
**7 ▶ BE QUIET AT NIGHT ◀** [I] *literary* if a village, house etc sleeps it is night time and very quiet: *While the house slept, he crept downstairs and out of the front door.*

**sleep around** *phr v* [I] *informal* to be too willing to have sex with a lot of different people

**sleep in** *phr v* [I] to sleep later than usual in the morning: *They like to sleep in on Saturdays.* —compare OVERSLEEP

**sleep** sth ↔ **off** *phr v* [T] to sleep until you do not feel ill any more, especially after drinking too much alcohol: *sleeping off the effects of last night's party*

**sleep over** *phr v* [I] to sleep at someone's house for a night: *If you don't want to drive, you're welcome to sleep over.*

**sleep through** *phr v* **1** [T **sleep through** sth] to sleep while something is happening and not be woken by it: *How did you manage to sleep through that thunderstorm?* **2** [I] to sleep continuously for a long time: *I slept right through till lunchtime.*

**sleep together** *phr v* [I] *informal* to have sex: *I'm sure those two are sleeping together.*

**sleep with** sb *phr v* [T] *informal* to have sex with someone, especially someone you are not married to: *It's common knowledge that he's sleeping with his secretary.*

**sleep²** *n* S2 W3
**1 ▶ AT NIGHT ◀** [U] the natural state of being asleep: *I didn't get much sleep last night.* | *Try and get some sleep before the journey.* | **get to sleep** (=succeed in sleeping) *I had terrible trouble getting to sleep last night.* | **in your sleep** (=while you are sleeping) *She sometimes talks in her sleep.* | **send sb to sleep** (=make someone sleep) *The combination of warmth and music sent him to sleep.* | **sing/rock sb to sleep** (=sing to a baby until it sleeps or gently move it)
**2 ▶ PERIOD OF SLEEPING ◀** [singular] a period of sleeping: *I usually have a sleep after lunch.* | **a light/deep sleep** *She was woken from a deep sleep by a ring at the door.* | **a good night's sleep** (=a night when you sleep well and after which you feel healthy and active)
**3 go to sleep a)** to start sleeping: *I went to sleep at 9 o'clock and woke up at 6.* **b)** *informal* if a part of your body goes to sleep, you cannot feel it for a short time because it has not been getting enough blood
**4 don't lose sleep over it** *spoken* used to tell someone not to worry about something
**5 put sb/sth to sleep a)** to give drugs to a sick animal so that it dies without too much pain **b)** *informal* to make someone unconscious before an operation by giving them drugs
**6 can do sth in your sleep** *informal* to be able to do something very easily, especially because you have done it many times before
**7 ▶ IN YOUR EYES ◀** [U] *informal* a substance that forms in the corners of your eyes while you are sleeping

**sleep·er** /ˈsliːpə‖-ər/ *n* [C] **1 a) a heavy sleeper** someone who does not wake easily **b) a light sleeper** someone who wakes easily **2** someone who is asleep **3** a train with carriages that have beds for passengers to sleep in, or a bed on this kind of train **4** *especially BrE* a heavy piece of wood or CONCRETE supporting a railway track; TIE[1] (7) *AmE* **5** *BrE* a small ring worn in your ear —see picture at JEWELLERY **6** *AmE* a film, book etc which is successful but not immediately

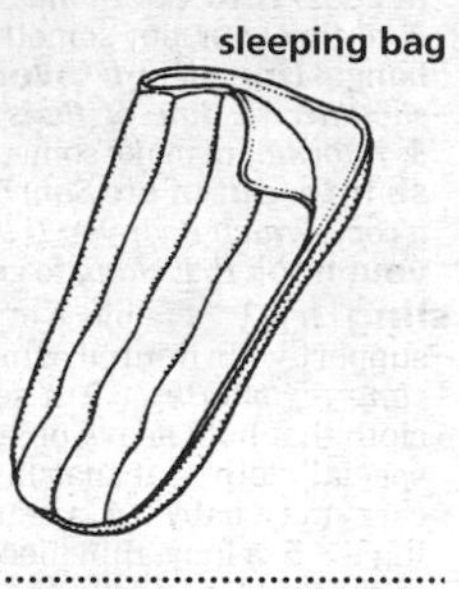


**sleeping bag** /ˈ·· ·/ *n* [C] a large warm bag for sleeping in, especially when camping

**sleeping car** /ˈ·· ·/ *n* [C] a part of a train with beds for passengers

**sleeping draught** /ˈ·· ·/ *n* [C] *old use* a special drink which makes you sleep

**sleeping part·ner** /ˌ·· ˈ··/ *n* [C] *BrE* someone who owns part of a business but is not actively involved in operating it; SILENT PARTNER *AmE*

**sleeping pill** /ˈ·· ·/ *n* [C] a PILL which helps you to sleep

**sleeping po·lice·man** /ˌ·· ·ˈ··/ *n* [C] *BrE* a narrow raised part in a road which makes traffic go slowly; SPEED BUMP

**sleeping sick·ness** /ˈ·· ˌ··/ *n* [U] a serious African disease that causes extreme tiredness, fever and makes you lose weight

**sleep·less** /ˈsliːpləs/ *adj* unable to sleep: **sleepless night** *David spent a sleepless night wondering what to do.* —**sleeplessly** *adv* —**sleeplessness** *n* [U]

**sleep·o·ver** /ˈsliːpəʊvə‖-oʊvər/ *n* [C] *AmE* a party for children in which they stay the night at someone's house

**sleep·walk·er** /ˈsliːpˌwɔːkə‖-ˌwɒːkər/ *n* [C] someone who walks while they are sleeping —**sleepwalk** *v* [I] —**sleep-walking** *n* [U]

**sleep·y** /ˈsliːpi/ *adj* **1** tired: *The warmth from the fire made her feel sleepy.* **2** a sleepy town or village is very quiet and not much happens there —**sleepily** *adv* —**sleepiness** *n* [U]

**sleep·y·head** /ˈsliːpihed/ *n* [C] *spoken* someone, especially a child, who looks as if they want to go to sleep: *Come on sleepyhead, wake up!*

**sleet** /sliːt/ *n* [U] snow and rain which falls when it is very cold —**sleet** *v* [I] —**sleety** *adj* —see picture on page 836

**sleeve** /sliːv/ *n* [C] **1** the part of a piece of clothing which covers your arm or part of your arm: *a dress with long sleeves* —see picture on page 840 **2 long-sleeved/short-sleeved etc** having sleeves that are long or short **3 have something up your sleeve** *informal* to have a secret plan or idea that you are going to use later: *Come on, what have you got up your sleeve?* **4** *especially BrE* a stiff envelope for keeping a record in; JACKET (3) *AmE* **5** *technical* a tube that surrounds a machine part —see also **laugh up your sleeve** (LAUGH[1] (13))

**sleeve·less** /ˈsliːvləs/ *adj* a sleeveless jacket, dress etc has no sleeves

**sleigh** /sleɪ/ *n* [C] a large vehicle pulled by animals, used for travelling over snow

**sleight of hand** /ˌslaɪt əv ˈhænd/ *n* [U] **1** the use of clever tricks and dishonesty to achieve something **2** quick skilful movement with your hands, especially when performing magic tricks

**slen·der** /ˈslendə‖-ər/ *adj* **1** thin and graceful: *She had a long slender neck.* | *a row of slender columns* —see THIN (USAGE) **2** not enough to be useful, helpful, or effective: **slender chance/hope** *The company now only has a slender hope of survival.* | **by/with a slender majority** *The Republicans won by a slender majority.* —**slenderness** *n* [U]

**slept** /slept/ the past tense and past participle of SLEEP

**sleuth** /sluːθ/ *n* [C] *old-fashioned* someone who tries to find out information about a crime; DETECTIVE

**slew[1]** /sluː/ *v* [I, T always + adv/prep] to turn or swing suddenly and violently, or to make something do this: [+ **around/sideways**] *I lost control of the car and it slewed sideways into the ditch.*

**slew[2]** the past tense of SLAY

**slew[3]** *n* **a slew of** *informal* a large number of: *We've got a whole slew of difficulties.*

**slice[1]** /slaɪs/ *n* **1** [C] a flat piece of bread, meat etc cut from a larger piece *a slice of bread and butter* | *Cut the pork into thin slices.* —see picture on page 416 **2** [C] a part or share of something good: *Everyone wanted a slice of the profits.* **3** [C] a kitchen tool used for lifting and serving pieces of food —see also FISH SLICE **4 a)** [U] a spinning movement of the ball in sports such as tennis and golf, which makes it move to one side rather than straight ahead **b)** [C] a way of hitting the ball which makes it do this **5 a slice of life** a description or image in a film, play, or book which shows life as it really is —see also **a slice of the cake** (CAKE[1] (7))

**slice[2]** *v* **1** also **slice up** [T] to cut meat, bread etc into thin flat pieces: *Could you slice the joint for me?* —see picture on page 834 **2** [I always + adv/prep, T] to cut something easily with one long movement of a sharp knife or edge: [+ **into/through**] *The blade's so sharp it could easily slice through your finger.* | **slice sth in two/in half etc** **3** [I always + adv/prep, T] to move quickly and easily through something such as water or air, or to make something do this: [+ **through/into**] *The speedboat sliced through the waters of the lake.* **4** [T] to hit the ball in sports such as tennis or golf so that it spins sideways instead of moving straight forward **5 any way you slice it** *AmE spoken* whatever way you choose to consider the problem

**slice** sth↔ **off** *phr v* [T] to cut something with one long movement of a sharp knife etc so that it becomes separate: *With one blow of his sword, Igor sliced off the man's head.*

**sliced bread** /ˌ· ˈ·/ *n* [U] **1** bread that is sold already cut into slices **2 the best thing since sliced bread** *informal* to be new and very helpful, useful etc: *He reckons his new word processor is the best thing since sliced bread.*

**slick[1]** /slɪk/ *adj* **1** using clever talk to persuade people but in a way that does not seem sincere or honest: *a slick salesman* **2** a slick film, programme etc is cleverly made and attractive but contains no important or interesting ideas: *the usual slick Hollywood stuff* **3** *informal* working or moving very smoothly, skilfully and effectively: *a slick operation* | *He got round the defender using some slick footwork.* **4** smooth and slippery: [+ **with**] *He felt his hands grow slick with sweat.* **5** *AmE old-fashioned* very good or attractive —**slickly** *adv* —**slickness** *n* [U]

**slick[2]** *n* [C] **1** an area of oil on the surface of water or on a road; OIL SLICK **2** *AmE* a magazine printed on good quality paper with a shiny surface, usually with a lot of colour pictures; GLOSSY MAGAZINE[2] (1) *especially BrE* **3** a smooth car tyre used for racing

**slick[3]** *v*

**slick** sth ↔ **down/back** *phr v* [T] to make hair or fur smooth and shiny by using oil, water etc: *His hair was slicked back, as was the fashion then.*

**slick·er** /ˈslɪkə‖-ər/ *n* [C] *AmE* a coat made to keep out the rain —see also **city slicker**

**slide[1]** /slaɪd/ *v past tense and past participle* **slid** /slɪd/ W3 **1** [I,T] to move smoothly over a surface while continuing to touch it, or to make something move in this way: [+ **along/across/down etc**] *The kids were sliding on the ice.* | **slide sth across/along etc** *Peter slid his glass across the table.* **2** [I, T always + adv/prep] to move somewhere quietly without being noticed, or to move something in this way: [+ **into/out of etc**] *Daniel slid out of the room when no one was looking.* | **slide sth into/out of etc** *She slid a gun into her pocket.* **3** [I] if prices etc slide, they become lower: *When will the government* *take action to support the sliding pound?* **4 let sth slide** to let a situation get gradually worse, without trying to stop it: *Simon had really let things slide and the house was a mess.*

**slide²** *n*
**1 ▶ FOR CHILDREN ◀** [C] a large structure for children to slide down at a PLAYGROUND
**2 ▶ FOR HAIR ◀** [C] a small metal or plastic object that holds your hair in place
**3 ▶ MOVEMENT ◀** [singular] a sliding movement across a surface: *The car went into a slide on the surface.*
**4 ▶ PICTURE ◀** [C] a small piece of film in a frame that shows a picture on a SCREEN¹ (2a) when you shine light through it: *Don't you want to see my slides of Korea?*
**5 ▶ PRICE/AMOUNT ◀** [singular] a fall in prices, amounts etc: *a slide in living standards*
**6 ▶ IN SCIENCE ◀** [C] a small piece of thin glass used for holding something when you look at it under a MICROSCOPE —see picture at LABORATORY
**7 ▶ MUSIC ◀** [C] a part of a machine or musical instrument, such as the U-shaped tube of a TROMBONE
**8 ▶ EARTH/SNOW ◀** [C] *AmE* a sudden fall of earth, stones, snow etc down a slope —see also LANDSLIDE

**slide rule** /ˈ· ·/ *n* [C] an old-fashioned instrument that looks like a ruler with a middle part that slides, used for calculating

**sliding door** /ˌ·· ˈ·/ *n* [C] a door that slides open rather than swinging from one side

**sliding scale** /ˌ·· ˈ·/ *n* [C] a system for paying tax, wages etc in which the rates that you pay VARY according to changing conditions

S2 W3 **slight¹** /slaɪt/ *adj* **1** not serious or not important: *a slight headache|a slight improvement|There's been a slight change of plan.*|**not the slightest chance/doubt/difference etc** (=no chance, doubt etc at all) *It doesn't make the slightest difference whether we discuss it today or tomorrow.|"What were they talking about?" "I haven't the slightest idea."* **2** thin and delicate: *a slight figure in a red dress*

**slight²** *v* [T] to offend someone by treating them rudely or without respect: *Denver felt slighted when no one called him back.* —**slighting** *adj*: *slighting remarks*

**slight³** *n* [C] *formal* a remark or action that offends someone: [+ **on/to**] *Jane took your comment as a slight on her work.*

S1 W2 **slight·ly** /ˈslaɪtli/ *adv* **1 slightly different/older/worried etc** a little bit different, older etc: *a slightly different attitude|Alison is slightly older than the others.|"Are you worried about him?" "Just slightly."* **2 slightly-built** having a thin and delicate body

S3 **slim¹** /slɪm/ *comparative* **slimmer** *superlative* **slimmest** *adj* **1** someone who is slim is attractively thin: *a slim waist* —see THIN (USAGE) **2 slim chance/hopes etc** very little chance etc of getting what you want: *There's a slim chance someone may have survived.* **3** thinner than usual or less than usual: *a slim volume of poetry|the slimmest of majorities*

**slim²** *v* **slimmed, slimming 1** [I] to make yourself thinner by eating less, taking a lot of exercise etc: *I'm going to start slimming after Christmas.* **2** [I,T] also **slim down** to reduce the size or number of something: *It was decided to slim down the workforce.* —**slimmer** *n* [C]

**slime** /slaɪm/ *n* [U] **1** a thick slippery substance that looks or smells unpleasant **2** a slippery substance that comes from the bodies of SNAILs and slugs (SLUG¹ (1))

**slim·line** /ˈslɪmlaɪn/ *adj* **1** a slimline drink has fewer CALORIES than the normal type **2** a slimline piece of equipment is smaller or thinner than others of the same type: *a slimline dishwasher*

**slim·ming** /ˈslɪmɪŋ/ *n* [U] the activity of trying to make yourself thinner by eating less, taking exercise etc: **slimming club/magazine/foods etc** *I've found a good slimming plan.*

**slim·y** /ˈslaɪmi/ *adj* **1** covered with slime: *slimy mud* **2** *informal* unpleasantly friendly in order to get something for yourself: *a slimy manner* —**sliminess** *n* [U]

**sling¹** /slɪŋ/ *v past tense and past participle* **slung** /slʌŋ/ [T always + adv/prep] **1** to throw something roughly or with a lot of force: *Sling me the keys, will you?*|**sling sth across/into etc** *Fiona slung her bag across the room.* **2** to throw or put something somewhere so that it can hang: **sling sth on/over etc** *He slung his coat over his shoulder.|A line of flags was slung between the trees.* **3** *informal* to make someone leave or go to a place: **sling sb into/out of etc** *Sam was slung into jail for punching a cop.|Watch it, or you'll be slung out of school.* **4 sling your hook** *BrE slang* to go away —see also MUDSLINGING

**sling²** *n* [C] **1** a piece of cloth tied around your neck to support your injured arm or hand: *She had her arm in a sling for months.* **2** a set of ropes or strong pieces of cloth that hold heavy objects to be lifted or carried **3** a special cloth seat that fastens over your shoulders for carrying a baby **4** a cloth band on a weapon for carrying it **5** a long, thin piece of rope with a piece of leather in the middle, used in the past as a weapon for throwing stones

**sling·back** /ˈslɪŋbæk/ *n* [C] a kind of woman's shoe that is open at the back and has a band going round the heel —see picture at SHOE¹

**sling·shot** /ˈslɪŋʃɒt‖-ʃɑːt/ *n* [C] *AmE* a small stick in the shape of a Y with a thin band of rubber, used by children to throw stones; CATAPULT¹ (2) *BrE*

**slink** /slɪŋk/ *past tense and past participle* **slunk** /slʌŋk/ *v* [I always + adv/prep] to move somewhere quietly and secretly, especially because you are afraid or ashamed: [+ **away/off/back etc**] *I saw you slinking off early!*

**slink·y** /ˈslɪŋki/ *adj* a slinky dress etc is smooth and tight and shows the shape of your body: *a slinky black dress*

**slip**

**slip¹** /slɪp/ *v* **slipped, slipping** S3 W2
**1 ▶ SLIDE ◀** [I] to accidentally slide a short distance quickly or to fall by sliding: *Suddenly, Frank slipped and fell over the edge.|My foot slipped and I nearly fell.* —see also SLIPPERY
**2 ▶ MOVE QUICKLY ◀** [I always + adv/prep] to move quickly, smoothly, or secretly: **slip out/through/by etc** *Nobody saw her slip silently out.|The weeks slipped slowly by.|The terrorists had slipped through the airport's security net.*
**3 ▶ PUT STH SOMEWHERE ◀** [T] to put something somewhere or give someone something quietly, secretly, or smoothly: **slip sth around/into/through etc** *I slipped a note into his hand under the table.|I slipped the Mercedes into gear.*|**slip sb sth** *Jerry slipped the waiter £5 to get them a good table.*
**4 ▶ LOSE YOUR HOLD ◀** [I always + adv/prep] if something that you are holding slips, it falls because it is difficult to hold or was not held firmly: *The soap slipped out of my hand.|The knife slipped and cut my finger.*
**5 ▶ GET WORSE ◀** [I] to become worse or lower than before: *Profits have slipped slightly this year.|You must be slipping – you never used to miss a shot like that.*

**6 slip your mind/memory** if something slips your mind you forget to do something: *I'm sorry I missed your birthday; it completely slipped my mind.*
**7 let sth slip (through your fingers) a)** to not take an opportunity, offer etc: *You're not going to let a chance like that slip through your fingers, are you?*
**8 slip a disc** to suffer an injury when one of the connecting parts between the bones in your back moves out of place
**9 ▶ GET FREE ◀** [T] to get free from something that was holding you: *The dog slipped his collar and ran away.*
**10 let (it) slip (that)** to say something without meaning to, when you had wanted it to be a secret: *Leila let slip that she's thinking about leaving the company.*
**11 slip through the net** if someone or something slips through the net, they are not caught or dealt with by the system that is supposed to catch them or deal with them: *homeless people slip through the social security net*

**slip into** sth *phr v* [T] **1** to put clothes on quickly: *I'll just slip into something more comfortable.* **2 slip into sleep/unconsciousness etc** to gradually fall asleep, become unconscious etc: *Granny slipped into a coma and died peacefully that night.*

**slip** sth ↔ **off** *phr v* [T] to take clothes off quickly: *Slip off your shirt and I'll take your blood pressure.*

**slip** sth ↔ **on** *phr v* [T] to put clothes on quickly: *Amanda slipped her robe on.*

**slip out** *phr v* [I] if something slips out, you say it without really intending to: *I'm sorry I spoilt your surprise. It just slipped out.*

**slip out of** sth *phr v* [T] to take clothes off quickly: *Keith slipped out of his jacket.*

**slip** sth **over on** sb *phr v* [T] *informal, especially AmE* to play a clever trick on someone

**slip up** *phr v* [I] to make a mistake: *The office slipped up and the letter was never sent.* —see also SLIP-UP

**slip²** *n*
**1 ▶ PAPER ◀** [C] a small or narrow piece of paper: [+ **of**] *Rosie marked her place with a slip of paper.*
**2 ▶ MISTAKE ◀** [C] a small mistake: *If you make a slip, rub it out neatly.*
**3 a slip of the tongue/pen** something that you say when you meant to say something else: *'Jim' was a slip of the tongue; I meant to say 'John'.* —see also FREUDIAN SLIP
**4 give sb the slip** *informal* to manage to escape from someone who is chasing you: *Bates gave the police the slip.*
**5 ▶ SLIDE ◀** [C] an act of sliding a short distance or of falling by sliding
**6 ▶ WOMAN'S CLOTHES ◀** [C] a piece of clothing that a woman wears under her clothes, and which hangs from her shoulders or her waist
**7 a slip of a girl/boy etc** *old-fashioned* a small thin young person: *He was only a slip of a lad.*
**8 ▶ CRICKET ◀** [C usually plural] a part of the field where players stand, trying to catch the ball in CRICKET
**9 ▶ CLAY ◀** [U] clay that is almost liquid and is used for making pots

**slip case** /ˈ· ·/ *n* [C] a hard cover for putting a book in

**slip co·ver** /ˈ· ,··/ *n* [C] *AmE* **1** a paper cover for a book; DUST JACKET **2** a loose cloth cover for furniture

**slip·knot** /ˈslɪpnɒt‖-nɑːt/ *n* [C] a knot that you can make tighter or looser by pulling one of its ends

**slip-on** /ˈ· ·/ *n* [plural] shoes without a fastening that you can slide onto your feet —**slip-on** *adj*: *slip-on shoes*

**slip·page** /ˈslɪpɪdʒ/ *n* [C,U] the amount by which something slips, or the act of slipping

**slipped disc** /,· ˈ·/ *n* [C usually singular] a painful injury caused when one of the connecting parts between the bones in your back moves out of place

**slip·per** /ˈslɪpə‖-ər/ *n* [C] a light soft shoe that you wear at home —see picture at SHOE¹

**slip·per·y** /ˈslɪpəri/ *adj* **1** something that is slippery is difficult to hold, walk on etc because it is wet or GREASY: *Be careful! The floor's very slippery.* **2** *informal* someone who is slippery cannot be trusted and usually manages to avoid being punished: **slippery customer** (=someone you cannot trust) *I wouldn't lend him any money, he's a real slippery customer.* **3 be on the slippery slope** *BrE informal* to have begun a process or habit which is hard to stop and which will develop into something extremely bad: *Once you start taking soft drugs you're on the slippery slope to becoming an addict.* —**slipperiness** *n* [U]

**slip·py** /ˈslɪpi/ *adj informal* a slippy surface or object is difficult to hold, walk on etc because it is wet or GREASY

**slip road** /ˈ· ·/ *n* [C] *BrE* a road for driving onto or off a MOTORWAY; RAMP (1) *AmE* —see picture on page 415

**slip·shod** /ˈslɪpʃɒd‖-ʃɑːd/ *adj* done too quickly and carelessly: *a slipshod piece of work*

**slip·stream** /ˈslɪpstriːm/ *n* [singular] the area of low air pressure just behind a fast-moving vehicle

**slip-up** /ˈ· ·/ *n* [C] a careless mistake that spoils a process or plan: *We should have informed you, I'm sorry for the slip-up.*

**slip·way** /ˈslɪpweɪ/ *n* [C] a sloping track that is used for moving boats into or out of the water

**slit¹** *v* /slɪt/ *past tense and past participle* **slit** *present participle* **slitting** [T] to make a straight narrow cut in cloth, paper, skin etc: **slit sth open** (=open it by slitting it) *Guy slit open the envelope.* | **slit sb's throat** (=kill someone with a knife)

**slit²** *n* [C] a long straight narrow cut or hole: *light shining through a slit in the door* | *a skirt with a slit up the side*

**slith·er** /ˈslɪðə‖-ər/ *v* [I always + adv/prep] to slide smoothly across a surface, twisting or moving from side to side: [+ **through/across etc**] *snakes slithering through the grass* | *He slithered down the muddy bank into the water.*

**slith·er·y** /ˈslɪðəri/ *adj* unpleasantly slippery

**sliv·er** /ˈslɪvə‖-ər/ *n* [C] a very small thin pointed piece of something that has been cut or broken off something: *a sliver of glass* | *a sliver of cake* —see picture on page 416

**sliv·o·vitz** /ˈslɪvəvɪts, ˈsliː-/ *n* [U] a strong alcoholic drink made in SE Europe from PLUMS

**slob** /slɒb‖slɑːb/ *n* [C] *informal* someone who is lazy, dirty, untidy, or rude: *Come on, get up and do something you big slob!*

**slob around** *phr v* [I] *BrE slang* to spend time doing nothing and being lazy

**slob·ber** /ˈslɒbə‖ˈslɑːbər/ *v* [I] to let SALIVA (=the liquid produced by your mouth) come out of your mouth and run down: *I hate dogs that slobber everywhere.*

**slobber over** sth/sb *phr v* [T] to keep saying how much you love someone in a way that embarrasses or annoys other people: *They keep slobbering over each other.*

**slob·ber·y** /ˈslɒbəri‖ˈslɑː-/ *adj* a slobbery kiss or mouth is unpleasantly wet

**sloe** /sləʊ‖sloʊ/ *n* [C] a small bitter fruit like a PLUM

**sloe gin** /,· ˈ·/ *n* [U] an alcoholic drink made with SLOES, GIN, and sugar

**slog¹** /slɒg‖slɑːg/ *v informal* **1 slog (away) at** *especially BrE* also **slog through** to work hard at something without stopping, especially when the work is boring or difficult: *I've been slogging away at this essay for days.* | *all those books we had to slog through at school* | **slog your guts out** *informal* (=work extremely hard) *slogging their guts out to get it finished on time* **2** [I always + adv/prep] to make a long hard journey somewhere, especially on foot: [+ **down/up/through etc**] *We slogged up the hill with the wind blowing against us.* **3 slog it out** *BrE* to fight or argue about something until one side wins

**slog²** *n* [singular] **1** *BrE informal* a piece of work that takes a lot of time and effort and is usually boring: *It was a bit of a slog addressing all those envelopes.* **2** a long period of tiring walking: *a long hard slog uphill*

**slo·gan** /ˈsləʊgən‖ˈsloʊ-/ *n* [C] a short easily-remembered phrase used by an advertiser, politician etc: *demonstrators chanting anti-racist slogans | We need an advertising slogan for the new campaign.*

**sloop** /sluːp/ *n* [C] a small sailing ship with one central MAST (=pole for sails)

**slop¹** /slɒp‖slɑːp/ *v* **slopped, slopping** **1** [I always + adv/prep] if liquid in a container slops, it moves around or over the edge in an uncontrolled way: [+ **around/about/over**] *The water slopped around in the bucket.* **2** [T] to make liquid do this: **slop sth over/into etc** *He slopped his beer all over her skirt.* **3** [T] *AmE* to feed slop to pigs

**slop about** *phr v* [I] *BrE informal* **1** to spend time being lazy: *We spent the day slopping about the house.* **2** to play or move around in mud, dirty water etc

**slop out** *phr v* [I] when prisoners slop out, they empty their toilet buckets —**slopping-out** *n* [U]

**slop²** also **slops** *plural n* [U] **1** food waste that is used to feed animals **2** *BrE* liquid waste from food or drinks: *Empty all your slops into the bucket over there.* **3** *BrE* dirty water or URINE **4** food that is too soft and tastes bad: *They served up some kind of slop I just couldn't eat.*

W3 **slope¹** /sləʊp‖sloʊp/ *n* **1** [C] a piece of ground or a surface that slopes: *walking slowly up a steep slope* | **a gentle slope** (=a slope that is not steep) **2** [singular] the angle at which something slopes in relation to a flat surface: *a slope of 30 degrees*

**slope²** *v* [I] if the ground or a surface slopes, it is higher at one end than the other: [+ **up/down/away etc**] *The land slopes down to the sea.*

**slope off** *phr v* [I] *BrE informal* to leave somewhere quietly and secretly, especially when you are avoiding work: *Mike's always sloping off when it's time to do the dishes.*

**slop·py** /ˈslɒpi‖ˈslɑːpi/ *adj* **1** not done carefully or thoroughly: *This piece of work is very sloppy.* | *sloppy writing* **2** sloppy clothes are loose-fitting, untidy, or dirty: *a sloppy old sweater* **3** expressing your feelings of love too strongly and in a silly way: *He keeps sending me sloppy letters.* **4** not solid enough: *sloppy jelly* —**sloppily** *adv* —**sloppiness** *n* [U]

**sloppy joe** /ˌslɒpi ˈdʒəʊ‖ˌslɑːpi ˈdʒoʊ/ *n* [C] **1** *AmE* a kind of food, made from BEEF with SPICES added and served on a BUN (2) **2** *BrE* a big loose-fitting SWEATER

**slosh** /slɒʃ‖slɑːʃ/ *v* **1** [I always + adv/prep] if a liquid in a container sloshes around, it moves against the sides of its container in an uncontrolled way: [+ **around/about**] *Water sloshed about in the bottom of the boat.* **2** [T always + adv/prep] to make a liquid do this: **slosh sth around/about** *Joe sloshed the whisky around in his glass.* **3** [I always + adv/prep] to walk through water or mud noisily: [+ **through/about**] *sloshing through the mud* **4** [T] *BrE slang* to hit someone; PUNCH¹ (1)

**sloshed** /slɒʃt‖slɑːʃt/ *adj* [not before noun] *informal* drunk: *He was already well sloshed when we got there.*

**slot¹** /slɒt‖slɑːt/ *n* [C] **1** a long narrow hole made in a surface, especially for putting something into: *Place your coins in the slot slowly.* **2** a short period of time allowed for one particular event on a programme or timetable: *a regular ten-minute slot on the breakfast show* | *landing slots at Heathrow Airport*

slot

**slot²** *v* **slotted, slotting** [I always + adv/prep] to go into a slot, or to make something do this: [+ **in**] *The disc slots in at the front.* | **slot sth together** (=fit together) *You buy the bookshelf in pieces and then slot them together yourself.*

**slot in** *phr v* [I,T] *informal* to find a time or a place for someone or something in a plan, organization etc: **slot sb/sth** ↔ **in** *We should be able to slot the meeting in before lunch.*

**sloth** /sləʊθ‖sloʊθ/ *n* **1** [C] an animal of Central and South America that moves very slowly, has grey fur, and lives in trees **2** [U] *formal* laziness: *combination of sloth and boredom*

**sloth·ful** /ˈsləʊθfəl‖ˈsloʊθ-/ *adj formal* lazy or not active —**slothfully** *adv* —**slothfulness** *n* [U]

**slot ma·chine** /ˈ· ·ˌ·/ *n* [C] **1** a machine used for playing a game that starts when you put money into it **2** *BrE* a machine that you buy cigarettes, food, or drink from; VENDING MACHINE

**slotted spat·u·la** /ˌ·· ˈ···/ *n AmE* a FISH SLICE

**slotted spoon** /ˌ·· ˈ·/ *n* [C] a large spoon with holes in it

**slouch¹** /slaʊtʃ/ *v* [I] to stand, sit, or walk with a slouch: *Stop slouching, it's not good for your back.* | *I slouched in my chair.* —**slouchingly** *adv*

**slouch²** *n* **1** [singular] a way of standing, sitting, or walking with your shoulders bent forward that makes you look tired or lazy **2 be no slouch (at)** *informal* to be very good or skilful at something: *She's certainly no slouch where organization is concerned.*

**slough¹** /slʌf/ *v*

**slough** sth ↔ **off** *phr v* [T] **1** *technical* to get rid of a dead outer layer of skin **2** *literary* to get rid of a feeling, belief etc: *He was unable to slough off the stigmatizing label of criminal.*

**slough²** /slaʊ‖sluː, slaʊ/ *n* **1** [C] an area of land covered in deep dirty water or mud **2 a slough of despair/troubles etc** *literary* a bad situation or condition that you cannot get out of easily: *He soon became the forgotten man and was able to return to his slough of despondency.*

**slov·en·ly** /ˈslʌvənli/ *adj* lazy and untidy and not caring about your appearance: *The landlady was fat and slovenly.* —**slovenliness** *n* [U]: *a man with shabby clothes and a general air of slovenliness*

**slow¹** /sləʊ‖sloʊ/ *adj* 

**1 ▶ MOVE ETC ◀** not moving, being done, or happening quickly: *a slow train* | *a slow, smoochy dance at the end of the evening* | *The computer's just so slow today, isn't it?*

**2 ▶ LONG TIME ◀** **a)** taking a long time or a longer time than usual: *With the fog and ice, our journey was very slow.* | *It's quite a slow process.* **b)** taking too long, especially because of someone being unwilling: *a slow response to our requests for help* | **slow to recognize/see/follow etc** *Our companies have been very slow to react to foreign competition.*

**3 ▶ CLOCK ◀** [not before noun] if a clock is slow it is showing a time earlier than the correct time: **ten minutes/five minutes etc slow** *The station clock was five minutes slow.*

**4 ▶ LARGE ROAD ◀** [only before noun] the slow lane on a large road is not intended for fast-moving vehicles

**5 ▶ BUSINESS ◀** if business or trade is slow, there are not many customers or not much is sold

**6 ▶ STUPID ◀** not good or quick at understanding things: *Sometimes he can be rather slow.* | *helping the slower pupils* | **slow off the mark/slow on the uptake** (=not good at understanding things) —**slowly** *adv*: *The time passed slowly* | *slowly gathering speed as we rolled downhill*

**slow²** *v* [I,T] also **slow up** to become slower or make something slower: *The train slowed as it went around the bend.* | *Business slows up at this time of year.* —see picture on page 415 

**slow down** *phr v* **1** [I,T **slow** sth ↔ **down**] to become slower or make something slower: *Motorists should slow down and take extra care in foggy conditions.* | *My aching knee was beginning to slow me down.* **2** [I] to become less active or busy than you usually are: *You're sixty, it's time you slowed down a bit.*

**slow³** *adv* slowly —see also GO-SLOW

**slow burn** /ˌ· ˈ·/ *n* **do a slow burn** *AmE informal* to slowly get angry: *Tony fumbled the ball and I could see the coach do a slow burn.*

**slow·coach** /ˈsləʊkəʊtʃ‖ˈsloʊkoʊtʃ/ *n* [C] *BrE informal* someone who moves or does things too slowly; SLOWPOKE *AmE*: *Come on slowcoach, hurry up!*

**slow·down** /ˈsləʊdaʊn‖ˈsloʊ-/ *n* **1** [C usually singular] a reduction in activity or speed: *a slowdown in the US economy* **2** [C] *AmE* a period when people deliberately work slowly in order to protest about something

**slow mo·tion** /ˌ· ˈ··/ *n* [U] movement on film shown at a slower speed than it really happened: **in slow motion** *Let's show that goal again in slow motion.*

**slow pitch** /ˈ· ·/ *n* [U] *AmE* a game like SOFTBALL, played by mixed teams of men and women

**slow·poke** /ˈsləʊpəʊk‖ˈsloʊpoʊk/ *n* [C] *AmE informal* SLOWCOACH

**slow-wit·ted** /ˌ· ˈ··◂/ *adj* not good at understanding things: *He was a big, slow-witted man who would hurt no-one.*

**slow-worm** /ˈ· ·/ *n* [C] a small European LIZARD with no legs, which looks like a small snake

**sludge** /slʌdʒ/ *n* [U] **1** soft thick mud, especially at the bottom of a liquid **2** the solid substance that is left when SEWAGE (=the liquid waste from houses, factories etc) has been cleaned **3** thick dirty oil in an engine —**sludgy** *adj*

**slug¹** /slʌg/ *n* [C] **1** a small slow-moving creature with a soft body like a SNAIL but without a shell **2** [C] *AmE informal* a bullet **3** *informal* a small amount of a strong alcoholic drink: *a slug of brandy* **4** [C] *AmE informal* a piece of metal shaped like a coin used to illegally get a drink, ticket etc from a machine

**slug²** *v* [T] **1** *informal* to hit someone hard with your closed hand: *I stood up and he slugged me again.* **2** to hit a ball hard **3 slug it out** if two people slug it out, they fight by hitting each other hard

**slug·ger** /ˈslʌgə‖-ər/ *n* [C] *informal AmE* a BASEBALL player who hits the ball very hard

**slug·gish** /ˈslʌgɪʃ/ *adj* moving or reacting more slowly than normal: *I always feel sluggish first thing in the morning.|the company's sluggish sales performance* —**sluggishly** *adv*: *The stream flows sluggishly through the fields.* —**sluggishness** *n* [U]

**sluice¹** /sluːs/ *n* [C] a passage for water to flow through, with a special gate which can be opened or closed to control it

**sluice²** *v* **1** [T] to wash something with a lot of water: **sluice sth out/down** *Can you sluice out the cow shed?*| **sluice sth over/into etc** *I sluiced water over the wound.* **2** [I + **out/over**] if water sluices somewhere, a large amount of it suddenly flows there

**slum¹** /slʌm/ *n* **1** [C] a house or an area of a city that is in very bad condition, where very poor people live: **the slums** (=a slum area) *He grew up in the East London slums.* **2** [singular] *informal* a very untidy place

**slum²** *v* **slum it/be slumming** *informal often humorous* to spend time in conditions that are much worse than you are used to: *If we're going to travel for 6 months we'll have to slum it most of the time.*

**slum·ber¹** /ˈslʌmbə‖-ər/ *v* [I] *literary* to sleep

**slumber²** *n* also **slumbers** [singular, U] *literary* sleep: *He passed into a deep slumber.*

**slumber par·ty** /ˈ·· ˌ··/ *n* [C] *AmE* a children's party when a group of children sleep at one child's house

**slum·lord** /ˈslʌmlɔːd‖-lɔːrd/ *n* [C] *AmE* someone who owns houses in a very poor area and charges high rents for buildings that are in bad condition

**slum·my** /ˈslʌmi/ *adj* a slummy area is one where very poor people live and the buildings are in bad condition: *a little junk shop in the slummy quarter of the town*

**slump¹** /slʌmp/ *v* **1** [I] to suddenly go down in price, value, or number: *Sales slumped by 20% last year.* **2 be slumped** to be sitting with your body leaning completely backwards or forwards, because you are tired or unconscious: [+ **in/against**] *a drunk slumped against the wall* **3** [I] to suddenly fall down or sit down because you feel weak or become unconscious: [+ **back/over/on**] *His head slumped on his chest.|Father slumped back in his chair.*

**slump²** *n* **1** a sudden fall in prices, sales, profits etc: [+ **in**] *a slump in agricultural prices* **2** a period when there is a big reduction in trade so that many companies have to close and many people lose their jobs: *the slump in the late 80s* **3** *especially AmE* a period when a player or team does not play well: *The Dodgers have been in a slump for the last three weeks.*

**slung** /slʌŋ/ *v* the past tense and past participle of SLING

**slunk** /slʌŋk/ *v* the past tense and past participle of SLINK

**slur¹** /slɜː‖slɜːr/ *v* **1** [I,T] to speak unclearly without separating your words or sounds correctly: **slur your words/speech** *He was obviously drunk and slurring his words.* **2** [T] to criticize someone or something unfairly **3** [T] to play a group of musical notes smoothly together —**slurred** *adj*: *slurred speech*

**slur²** *n* **1** [C] an unfair criticism that is intended to make people dislike someone or something: [+ **on**] *a slur on my reputation* **2** [singular] an unclear way of speaking in which the words are not separated: *the slur in his voice* **3** [C] a curved line written over musical notes to show they must be played together smoothly

**slurp** /slɜːp‖slɜːrp/ *v* [I,T] to drink a liquid while making a noisy sucking sound: *Don't slurp your soup!* —**slurp** *n* [C usually singular]: *He drank his coffee with a slurp.*

**slur·ry** /ˈslʌri‖ˈslɜːri/ *n* [U] a mixture of water and mud, coal, or animal waste

**slush** /slʌʃ/ *n* **1** [U] partly melted snow **2** [U] *informal* feelings or stories that seem silly because they are too concerned with love and romantic subjects: *And don't give us that slush about your children just to make us feel sorry for you!* **3** [C,U] *especially AmE* a drink made with crushed ice and a sweet liquid: *cherry slush* —**slushy** *adj*: *a slushy movie*

**slush fund** /ˈ· ·/ *n* [C] a sum of money kept for dishonest purposes, especially by a politician

**slut** /slʌt/ *n* [C] **1** an offensive word for a woman who has had many sexual partners: *Get out of here you slut!* **2** an offensive word for a lazy untidy woman —**sluttish** *adj*: *a dress that was nasty and sluttish* —**sluttishness** *n* [U]

**sly** /slaɪ/ *adj* **1** very clever in the way that you use tricks and dishonesty to get what you want: *The way he did it was really sly.* **2 sly smile/glance/wink etc** a smile, look etc shows that you are hiding something you know from other people: *She gave me a sly look.* **3 on the sly** *informal* secretly, especially when you are doing something that you should not do: *They'd been seeing each other on the sly for months.* —**slyly** *adv* —**slyness** *n* [U]

**smack¹** /smæk/ *v* [T] **1** to hit a child with your hand in order to punish them: *To bed now, or I'll smack your bottom!* —see picture on page 1259 **2** to hit something against something else so that it makes a short loud noise: **smack sth against/into etc** *He smacked his fist against his palm.* **3 smack your lips** to make a short loud noise with your lips because you are hungry **4** *BrE informal* to hit someone hard with your closed hand; PUNCH¹ (1): *Say that again and I'll smack you!*

**smack of** sth *phr v* [T] if something smacks of dishonesty, desperation etc it seems to contain some of that quality: *I don't want to say anything that smacks of disloyalty.*

**smack²** *n* **1** [C] **a)** a hit made with your hand held flat, especially to punish a child: *Quiet, or I'll give you a smack!* **b)** *BrE informal* a hard hit with your closed hand; PUNCH² (1) **2** [C] a short loud noise caused especially when something hits something else **3 give sb a smack on the lips/cheek** *informal* to kiss someone **4 have a smack at** *BrE informal* to try to do something **5** [U] *slang* HEROIN (=a dangerous illegal drug) **6** [C] a small fishing boat

**smack³** *adv informal* **1** exactly or directly in the middle or in front of something: **smack in the middle/in**

**front of etc** *There was a hole smack in the middle of the floor.* | **smack-bang** *BrE* **/smack-dab** *AmE*: *The plane was stuck there, smack-dab in the middle of the lake!* **2** if something moves smack into or against something, it hits it with a lot of force, making a loud noise: *The car ran smack into the side of the bus.*

**smack·er** /ˈsmækə‖-ər/ *n* [C] *slang* **1** a pound or a dollar: *It cost me fifty smackers.* **2** also **smack·er·oo** /ˌsmækəˈruː/ a loud kiss

S1 W1 **small¹** /smɔːl‖smɒːl/ *adj*
**1 ▶ SIZE ◀** not large in size or amount: *He's a small man, only five feet tall.* | *Luxembourg is one of the smallest countries in Europe.* | *No, not that one – the small one with the red handle!* | *a smaller increase in the inflation rate than last year* —see LITTLE¹ (USAGE)
**2 ▶ UNIMPORTANT ◀** a small problem, job, mistake etc is unimportant or easy to deal with: *Your work is good, but I found a number of small mistakes.* | *It's a small matter but worth mentioning.*
**3 ▶ YOUNG CHILD ◀** a small child is young: *She's married with three small children.*
**4 small farmer/dealer/business** a farmer, business etc that does not involve large amounts of money: *Most of the land in this region belongs to small farmers.*
**5 ▶ LETTER ◀** small letters are the smaller of the two forms that we use, for example 'b' rather than 'B'
**6 a conservative with a small 'c'/a pacifist with a small 'p' etc** *informal* someone who believes in the principles you have mentioned, but not very strongly
**7 small fortune** a lot of money: *That dress must have cost you a small fortune.*

**8 make sb feel small** to do something to make someone feel stupid, unimportant, or ashamed: *She was always laughing at me and making me feel small.*
**9 in a/some small way** if something helps, affects, influences etc it has an effect but not an important one: *It was good to feel we had helped in some small way.*
**10 ▶ VOICE ◀** a small voice is quiet and soft: *"I don't want to stay here." she said in a small voice.*
**11 small beer** *BrE* / **small potatoes** *AmE* someone or something that is not at all important: *Parking fines? Pretty small beer compared with some of the things he's done in the past.*
**12 small fry** *informal* **a)** unimportant people or things: *Of course no one bothers about small fry like us.* **b)** *AmE* children: *I've sent the small fry out to play in the yard.* —**small** *adv*: *He writes so small I can't read it.* —**smallness** *n* [U]

**small²** *n* **1 the small of your back** the lower part of your back where it curves **2 smalls** [plural] *BrE old-fashioned informal* underwear

**small ad** /ˈ· ·/ *n* [C] *BrE* an advertisement put in a newspaper by someone who wants to buy or sell something; WANT AD *AmE*

**small arms** /ˈ··‖ˌ·ˈ·/ *n* [plural] guns that are held in one or both hands for firing

**small change** /ˌ· ˈ·/ *n* [U] money in coins of low value: *Do you have any small change?*

**small claims court** /ˌ· ˈ· ˈ·/ *n* [C] a court where people can try to get back small amounts of money from other people or from companies when they think it has been taken unfairly

**smallest room** /ˌ·· ˈ·/ *n* [singular] *BrE* the room where the toilet is, used to avoid the word toilet

**small·hold·ing** /ˈsmɔːlˌhəʊldɪŋ‖ˈsmɒːlˌhoʊld-/ *n* [C] *BrE* a piece of land used for farming that is smaller than an ordinary farm —**small-holder** *n* [C]

**small hours** /ˈ· ·/ *n* [plural] **the small hours** the early morning hours, between about one and four o'clock: *We stayed up talking into the small hours.*

**small in·tes·tine** /ˌ· ·ˈ··/ *n* [singular] the long tube that food goes through after it has gone through your stomach —see picture at DIGESTIVE SYSTEM

**small·ish** /ˈsmɔːlɪʃ‖ˈsmɒːl-/ *adj especially BrE* fairly small: *a smallish town* | *She's smallish with red hair.*

**small-mind·ed** /ˌsmɔːlˈmaɪndɪ̆d◂‖ˌsmɒːl-/ *adj* too concerned with the small problems and details of your life, so that you do not think about what is really important; PETTY (1): *a greedy, bigoted and small-minded man* —**small-mindedness** *n* [U] —compare NARROW-MINDED

**small·pox** /ˈsmɔːlpɒks‖ˈsmɒːlpɑːks/ *n* [U] a serious disease that causes spots which leave marks on your skin

**small print** /ˈ· ˌ·/ *n* [U] all the details in a contract or agreement which contain many rules and restrictions: *Always read the small print before you sign anything.*

**small-scale** /ˌ· ˈ·◂/ *adj* small in size: *a small-scale study*

**small screen** /ˈ· ˌ·/ *n* [singular] television: *a film made for the small screen*

**small talk** /ˈ· ·/ *n* [U] polite friendly conversation about unimportant subjects: *small talk about the weather*

**small-time** /ˌ· ˈ·◂/ *adj* **small-time crook/gangster etc** a criminal who is not very successful —**small-timer** *n* [C]

**small-town** /ˈ· ·/ *adj* [only before noun] **1** connected with a small town: *a small-town lawyer* **2** *especially AmE* not very interested in anything new or different: *small-town attitudes*

**smarm·y** /ˈsmɑːmi‖-ɑːr-/ *adj* polite in an insincere way that you think is unpleasant: *He fooled us with his soft smarmy ways.*

**smart¹** /smɑːt‖smɑːrt/ *adj* S3 W2
**1 ▶ CLEVER ◀** *especially AmE* **a)** intelligent: *The smart kids get good grades and go off to college.* | *Some smart lawyer got him out of jail.* **b)** trying to seem clever in a disrespectful way: *Don't get smart with me, young man.*
**2 ▶ WELL-DRESSED ◀** *BrE* wearing neat attractive clothes and having a generally tidy appearance: *Chris was looking very smart in his new grey suit.*
**3 ▶ FASHIONABLE ◀** *BrE* fashionable or used by fashionable people: *one of Bonn's smartest restaurants*
**4 ▶ QUICK ◀** a smart movement is done quickly and with force: *a smart blow on the head.* | **at a smart pace** (=fairly fast) *The horse set off at a smart pace.*
**5 ▶ EXCELLENT ◀** *BrE old-fashioned* excellent —**smartly** *adv*: *smartly dressed women* | *He turned smartly and walked away* —**smartness** *n* [U]

**smart²** *v* **1** to be upset because someone has hurt your feelings or offended you: **be smarting from** *She was still smarting from the insult.* **2** [I] if a part of your body smarts, it hurts with a stinging pain: *My eyes were smarting from the smoke.*

**smart³** *n* [singular] **1** a feeling that you have when you are upset and offended by something **2** a stinging pain **3 smarts** [U] *AmE informal* intelligence: *If she had any smarts, she'd get rid of the guy.*

**smart al·eck** /ˈsmɑːt ˌælɪ̆k‖ˈsmɑːrt-/ *n* [C] *informal* someone who always says clever things or always has the right answer in a way that is annoying

**smart arse** /ˈ· ·/ *BrE*, also **smart ass** *AmE* —*n* an impolite word for a smart aleck: *He got in trouble with the teacher for being such a smart ass in class.* —**smart-arse** also **smart-ass** *adj*: *smart-arse remarks*

**smart bomb** /ˈ· ·/ *n* [C] a bomb that is fired from an aircraft and guided by a computer

**smart card** /ˈ· ·/ *n* [C] a small plastic card with an electronic part that records and remembers information

**smart·en** /ˈsmɑːtn‖ˈsmɑːr-/ *v*
**smarten up** *phr v especially BrE* **1** also **smarten yourself up** [I] to make yourself look neat and tidy: *You'd better smarten yourself up a bit before the interview.* **2** [T] **smarten** sth ↔ **up** to make something look neater: *a coat of paint to smarten the room up*

**smart·y·pants** /ˈsmɑːtipænts‖ˈsmɑːr-/ *n* [C] *humorous* someone who always says clever things or always has the right answer, in a slightly annoying way

**smash¹** /smæʃ/ *v* **1** [I, T] to break into many small pieces violently or noisily, or to make something do this by dropping, throwing, or hitting it: *I dropped the plate and it smashed.* | *He used a chair to smash the window.* **2** [I always + adv/prep, T always + adv/prep] to hit an object or surface violently, or to make something do this: **smash sth against/down/into** *Larry smashed his fist down on the table.* **3** [T] to destroy something such as a political system or criminal organization: *The French police claim to have smashed a massive drugs racket.* **4** [T] to hit a high ball in tennis etc with a strong downward action —see picture on page 1264

**smash** sth ↔ **down** *phr v* [T] to hit a door, wall etc violently so that it falls to the ground

**smash** sth ↔ **in** *phr v* [T] to hit something so violently that you break it and make a hole in it: **smash sb's face/head in** *informal* (=hit someone hard in the face or head) *He had threatened to smash Jo's head in if he ever went there again.*

**smash** sth ↔ **up** *phr v* [T] to deliberately damage or destroy something: *A gang of thugs came into the bar and smashed the place up.* —see also SMASH-UP

**smash²** *n* **1** [singular] the loud sound of something breaking: [+ **of**] *We heard the smash of plates breaking in the kitchen.* **2** [C] a hard downward shot in tennis or similar games **3** [C] *BrE* a serious road or railway accident

**smash-and-grab** /ˌ· · ˈ·/ *adj* **smash-and-grab raid** the act of robbing a shop by breaking the window and stealing valuable goods —**smash and grab** *n* [C]

**smashed** /smæʃt/ *adj* [not before noun] *informal* very drunk or affected by a drug: *She's smashed out of her mind.*

**smash·er** /ˈsmæʃə‖-ər/ *n* [C] *BrE old-fashioned* someone that you think is very attractive, or something that is very good: *It's a beautiful boat – a real smasher!*

**smash hit** /· ˈ·/ *n* [C] a very successful new play, book, film etc: *This film is going to be a smash hit.*

**smash·ing** /ˈsmæʃɪŋ/ *adj BrE old-fashioned* very good: *We had a smashing holiday.*

**smash-up** /ˈ· ·/ *n* [C] a serious road or railway accident

**smat·ter·ing** /ˈsmætərɪŋ/ *n* [C + **of**] **1** a small number or amount of something: *a smattering of rain* **2 have a smattering of** [not in progressive] to have a small amount of knowledge about a subject, especially a foreign language

**smear¹** /smɪə‖smɪr/ *n* [C] **1** a dirty or oily mark on something: *There were smears of chocolate on Charlie's shirt.* **2** a SMEAR TEST **3** an attempt to harm someone by spreading untrue stories about them —**smeary** *adj*

**smear²** *v*

**1** ► **SPREAD** ◄ [T always + adv/prep] to spread a liquid or soft substance over a surface, especially carelessly or untidily: **smear sth with** *The tablecloth was smeared with jam, crayon and berry-juice.* | **smear sth on/over etc** *Elaine smeared sun tan lotion liberally on her body.*

**2** ► **DIRTY** ◄ [T] to make something dirty or oily; SMUDGE: *Careful! You'll smear my shirt!*

**3** ► **UNCLEAR** ◄ [I,T] to become unclear or make something unclear by rubbing it: *Several words were smeared and I couldn't read them.*

**4** ► **TELL LIES** ◄ [T] to spread an untrue story about someone in order to harm them: *an attempt to smear the party leadership*

**5** ► **PAINT** ◄ [I] if a substance such as paint smears when something touches it, it spreads over parts of a surface where it should not be: *Don't lean on the wall or the paint will smear.*

**smear cam·paign** /ˈ· ·ˌ·/ *n* [C] a deliberate plan to tell untrue stories about someone, especially a politician etc in order to harm them

**smear test** /ˈ· ·/ *n* [C] a medical test in which cells from the entrance to a woman's WOMB (=the place where a baby grows) are examined under a microscope; CERVICAL SMEAR

S2 W3 **smell¹** /smel/ *n* **1** [C] the quality that people and animals recognize by using their nose: *Some flowers have a stronger smell than others.* | *The wine has a light, lemony smell.* | [+ **of**] *I opened the window to get rid of the smell of beer and cigarettes.* —compare AROMA, FRAGRANCE **2** [C] an unpleasant smell: *Pooh! What a smell!* —compare ODOUR, STINK² (1) **3** [U] the ability to notice or recognize smells: *A mole finds its food by smell alone.* | **sense of smell** *Blind people often have an excellent sense of smell.* **4** [C usually singular] an act of smelling something: *Have a smell of this cheese; does it seem all right?*

**smell²** *v past tense and past participle* **smelled** *especially AmE*, **smelt** /smelt/ *BrE* S2 W3

**1** ► **A PARTICULAR SMELL** ◄ [I always + adv/prep; linking verb + adj] to have a particular smell: **smell nice/good/spicy etc** *That soup smells delicious!* | *a sweet-smelling flower* | [+ **of**] *The car smelled of leather and wood.* | **smell like** *It smells like a hospital in here – has anyone been using disinfectant?*

**2** ► **UNPLEASANT** ◄ [I] to have an unpleasant smell: *His breath smells.* | *We must clean out the bird-cage – it's starting to smell.*

**3** ► **RECOGNIZE A SMELL** ◄ [T] to notice or recognize a particular smell: *I think I smell gas!* | **smell that** *I could smell that the milk wasn't fresh.*

**4** ► **PUT YOUR NOSE NEAR STH** ◄ [T] to put your nose near something to discover what kind of smell it has; SNIFF¹ (2): *Diane smelled his breath to see if he'd been drinking.*

**5** ► **ABILITY TO SMELL** ◄ [I] to have the ability to notice and recognize smells: *I've got a cold and I can't smell.*

**6 smell trouble/danger etc** to feel that something bad is going to happen: *He smelt trouble and got up to leave.*

**7 smell a rat** *informal* to guess that something wrong or dishonest is happening: *They know we hate them and will smell a rat if we try to be nice to them.*

**8 smell fishy** if a story, excuse etc smells fishy, you think it is likely to be untrue: *Max can't be working late again! It smells very fishy to me.*

**9** ► **SEEM** ◄ [linking verb] *informal* to seem: **smell wrong/odd/worrying etc** *Sarah's description of events didn't smell right to me.*

**smell** sb/sth ↔ **out** *phr v* [T] **1** to find something by smelling: *The hounds smelt out a fox.* **2** *informal* to find something such as trouble or violence because you have a natural ability to do this: *Wherever the fighting is, Sergeant Cooper can smell it out.* **3** to make a place smell unpleasant: *That fish is smelling the kitchen out.*

**smelling salts** /ˈ·· ·/ *n* [plural] a strong-smelling chemical that you hold under someone's nose to make them conscious again

**smell·y** /ˈsmeli/ *adj* **smellier, smelliest** having an unpleasant smell: *smelly socks* —**smelliness** *n* [U]

**smelt¹** /smelt/ *BrE* a form of the past tense and past participle of SMELL

**smelt²** *v* [T] to melt a rock that contains metal in order to remove the metal

**smelt³** *n* [C] a small fish

**smid·gin**, **smidgen** /ˈsmɪdʒɪn/ *n* [singular] *informal* a small amount of something, especially food: *"More cheese?" "Just a smidgin, please."*

**smile¹** /smaɪl/ *v* S3 W1

**1** [I] to have or make a smile on your face: **smile at sb** *Joanna was smiling at us in a friendly way.* | *Neil smiled to himself, thinking about how he had tricked them.*

**2 smile at sth** to be amused by something, often without showing it: *Graham smiled at his colleague's suggestion.*

**3** [T] to say or express something with a smile: *"So this is your secret weapon" he smiled.* | *She smiled a welcome.* —compare GRIN¹ (1)

**4 be all smiles** to look very happy and to behave in a friendly way

**5 smile to think/see/remember etc** to be amused when you think about something, see something etc: *When I look back at my youth I smile to think how naive I was.*

**6** ► **LUCK/FORTUNE** ◄ [T] *especially literary* if luck or FORTUNE smiles on you, you have very good luck —**smilingly** *adv*: *Melissa smilingly reached for a cigarette.*

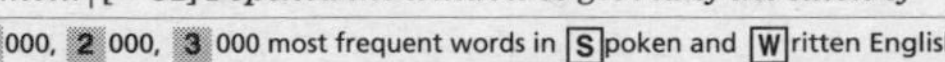

S2 W2 **smile²** *n* [C] an expression on your face in which your mouth curves upwards to show that you are happy, amused, friendly, etc: *George had a big smile on his face.* | *"Hello," he said with a smile.* | **give sb a smile** *Tracy gave the girl a warm smile.*

**smirk** /smɜːk‖smɜːrk/ *v* [I + **at**] to smile in an unpleasant way that shows that you are pleased by someone else's bad luck: *They smirked knowingly at each other across the table.* —**smirk** *n* [C]: *Wipe that smirk off your face – there's nothing funny about it!*

**smite** /smaɪt/ *v past tense* **smote** /sməʊt‖smoʊt/ *past participle* **smitten** /ˈsmɪtn/ [T + **down**] **1** *old use* to hit something hard **2** *biblical* to destroy, attack, or punish someone

**smith** /smɪθ/ *n* [C] **1** someone who makes and repairs things made of iron; BLACKSMITH **2 goldsmith/silversmith etc** someone who makes things from gold, silver etc

**-smith** /smɪθ/ *suffix* [in nouns] a maker of something: *a gunsmith* (=someone who makes guns) | *a wordsmith* (=someone who works with words, for example a JOURNALIST) —see also -SMITH

**smith·e·reens** /ˌsmɪðəˈriːnz/ *n* [plural] **smash sth to smithereens** *informal* to completely destroy something by breaking it into very small pieces

**smith·y** /ˈsmɪði‖-θi, -ði/ *n plural* **smithies** [C] a place where iron objects such as HORSESHOES were made and repaired in the past

**smit·ten** /ˈsmɪtn/ *v* **1** the past participle of SMITE **2 be smitten (with sb/sth)** to suddenly feel that you love someone or like something very much: *The young man was smitten with Miranda and her charms.* | **be smitten with a desire to do sth** (=want to do it very much) *She was smitten with a sudden desire to be rich like them.*

**smock** /smɒk‖smɑːk/ *n* [C] **1** a piece of clothing like a long, loose shirt, worn epecially by women who are PREGNANT (=going to have a baby) **2** a piece of clothing like a coat, worn by artists, hospital workers etc

**smock·ing** /ˈsmɒkɪŋ‖ˈsmɑː-/ *n* [U] a type of decoration made on cloth by pulling the cloth into small regular folds held tightly with stitches

**smog** /smɒg‖smɑːg, smɒːg/ *n* [U] brown unhealthy air caused by smoke from cars and factories in cities

S3 W3 **smoke¹** /sməʊk‖smoʊk/ *n* **1** [U] grey gas that is produced by something burning: *Clouds of black smoke belched from the building.* | *cigarette smoke* **2** [C usually singular] an act of smoking a cigarette etc: *a cup of coffee and a smoke* **3** [C] *slang* a cigarette or drugs that are smoked **4 the Smoke** *BrE, AustrE* London or any large town or city **5 go up in smoke** *informal* if your plans go up in smoke, you cannot do what you intended to do **6 there's no smoke without fire** *spoken* used to say that if something bad is being said about someone, it is probably partly true —**smokeless** *adj*

S2 W2 **smoke²** *v* **1** [I,T] to suck or breathe in smoke from a cigarette, pipe etc: *I haven't smoked for over two years.* **2** [T] to breathe in smoke from burning an illegal drug: *smoking dope* **3** [I] if something smokes it has smoke coming out of it: *a smoking chimney* **4** [I] if a fire smokes it lets too much smoke into a room **5** [T] to give fish and meat a special taste by hanging it in smoke

**smoke** sb/sth ↔ **out** *phr v* [T] **1** to fill a place with smoke to force someone or something to come out **2** to discover who is causing a particular problem and force them to make themselves known: *an attempt to smoke out and defeat the subversive forces in government*

**smoke a·larm** /ˈ· ·ˌ·/ also **smoke detector** /ˈ· ·ˌ··/ *n* [C] a piece of electronic equipment which warns you when there is smoke or fire in a building —see picture at ALARM¹

**smoke bomb** /ˈ· ·/ *n* [C] something that you throw that lets out clouds of smoke, used by police to control crowds

**smoked** /sməʊkt‖smoʊkt/ *adj* **smoked salmon/bacon/sausage etc** fish, meat etc that has been left in smoke to give it a special taste

**smoked glass** /ˌ· ˈ·/ *n* [U] glass that is a dark grey colour

**smoke-free** /ˌ· ˈ·◂/ *adj* **smoke-free area/zone etc** a place where you are not allowed to smoke

**smok·er** /ˈsməʊkə‖ˈsmoʊkər/ *n* [C] **1** someone who smokes cigarettes, CIGARS etc: **heavy smoker** (=someone who smokes a lot) **2** a railway carriage in which smoking is allowed

**smoke·screen** /ˈsməʊkskriːn‖ˈsmoʊk-/ *n* [C] **1** something that you do or say to hide your real plans or actions: *All that stuff about being a businessman was just a smokescreen to hide his criminal activities.* **2** a cloud of smoke produced so that it hides soldiers, ships etc during a battle

**smoke sig·nal** /ˈ· ˌ··/ *n* [C] a message sent out to people who are far away, using the smoke from a fire

**smoke·stack** /ˈsməʊkstæk‖ˈsmoʊk-/ *n* [C] a tall CHIMNEY at a factory or on a ship

**smokestack in·dus·try** /ˈ·· ˌ···/ *n* [C usually plural] *especially AmE* a big traditional industry such as car-making or coal-mining

**smok·ing** /ˈsməʊkɪŋ‖ˈsmoʊk-/ *n* [U] the habit or activity of breathing in tobacco smoke from a cigarette, pipe etc: *The sign says 'No Smoking'.* | **give up smoking** (=stop) *I gave up smoking nearly ten years ago.* —see also PASSIVE SMOKING S2

**smoking jack·et** /ˈ·· ˌ··/ *n* [C] a type of man's JACKET (1)

**smoking room** /ˈ·· ·/ *n* [C] a room where smoking is allowed in a building such as a hotel or factory

**smok·y** /ˈsməʊki‖ˈsmoʊ-/ *adj* **1** filled with smoke: *a smoky room* **2** producing too much smoke: *a smoky old diesel engine* **3** having the taste, smell, or appearance of smoke: *his smoky green eyes* —**smokiness** *n* [U]

**smol·der** /ˈsməʊldə‖ˈsmoʊldər/ *v* [I] the American spelling of SMOULDER

**smooch** /smuːtʃ/ *v* [I + **with**] *informal* if two people smooch, they kiss and hold each other in a romantic way

**smooch·y** /ˈsmuːtʃi/ *adj BrE informal* a smoochy song is slow and romantic

**smooth¹** /smuːð/ *adj* W3

**1** ▶ **FLAT** ◀ a smooth surface is completely flat and even: *The stone steps had been worn smooth by centuries of visitors.* —opposite ROUGH¹ (1)

**2** ▶ **SOFT** ◀ skin or fur that is smooth is soft and pleasant to touch, and your hand moves easily over it: *Sheila stroked the cat's silky smooth fur.* | *as smooth as a baby's bottom*

**3** ▶ **LIQUID** ◀ a liquid mixture that is smooth is thick but with no big pieces in it: *Beat the eggs and flour until they are smooth.* —opposite LUMPY

**4** ▶ **GRACEFUL** ◀ [only before noun] a smooth movement, style, way of doing something etc is graceful and has no sudden awkward changes: *Swing the tennis racquet in one smooth motion.* —opposite JERKY¹

**5** ▶ **WITHOUT PROBLEMS** ◀ a system, operation, or process that is smooth operates well and without problems: *contributing to the smooth running of the company* —see also **go smoothly** (SMOOTHLY (2))

**6** ▶ **PLEASANT TASTE** ◀ a drink such as WHISKY or beer that is smooth is not bitter but tastes pleasant and is easy to swallow

**7** ▶ **POLITE** ◀ someone who is smooth is polite, confident, and relaxed, but does not seem sincere: *I never trust these smooth salesmen.*

**8** ▶ **COMFORTABLE** ◀ a journey that is smooth is comfortable because the plane does not shake, or the sea is not rough: *We had a smooth crossing on the boat.* | *a smooth flight* —opposite BUMPY —see also SMOOTHLY, SMOOTH-TALKING —**smoothness** *n* [U]

**smooth²** *v* [T] **1** also **smooth out** to make something such as paper or cloth flat by moving your hands across it: *They smoothed out the map on the table and planned their route.* **2** also **smooth down** to make something that is raised flat by moving your hands across it: *Angela smoothed her hair down neatly.* **3** also **smooth down** to take away the roughness from the surface of wood, clay etc: *You have to smooth it before you varnish it.* **4** [always +adv/prep] to rub a liquid, cream, etc gently over a surface or into a surface: **smooth sth into/over** *She smoothed suntan lotion over her legs.* **5 smooth the way** to make it easier for something to happen, by dealing with any problems first: *an agreement smoothing the way to an eventual merger*

**smooth** sth ↔ **away** *phr v* [T] to get rid of problems or difficulties easily: *A few objections have to be smoothed away before we can start the project.*

**smooth** sth ↔ **over** *phr v* [T] to make problems or difficulties seem less important: *Sally managed to smooth over the bad feelings between them.*

**smooth·ie, smoothy** /ˈsmuːði/ *n* [C] *informal* someone who is good at persuading people, but does not seem to be sincere: *Yuk! What a smoothie!*

**smooth·ly** /ˈsmuːðli/ *adv* **1** in a smooth way **2 go smoothly** if a planned event, piece of work etc goes smoothly, there are no problems to spoil it: *It'll take about three hours, if everything goes smoothly.*

**smooth talk·ing** /ˌ· ˈ··/ *adj* a smooth-talking person is good at persuading people and saying nice things but you do not trust them: *a smooth-talking salesman*

**smor·gas·bord** /ˈsmɔːɡəsbɔːd‖ˈsmɔːrɡəsbɔːrd/ *n* [C,U] a meal in which people serve themselves from a large number of different dishes

**smote** /sməʊt‖smoʊt/ the past tense of SMITE

**smoth·er** /ˈsmʌðə‖-ər/ *v* **1** [T always + adv/prep] **smother sth with/in** to cover the whole surface of something with something else: **smother sth with/in** *a delicious sponge cake smothered in chocolate | He smothered her with kisses.* **2 smother your anger/irritation** to hide your feelings: *struggling to smother her jealousy* **3 smother sb with love/kindness etc** to express your feelings for someone too strongly, so that your relationship with them cannot develop normally **4** [T] to kill someone by putting something over their face to stop them breathing: *One night she took a pillow and smothered him.* **5** [T] to make a fire stop burning by preventing air from reaching it **6** [T] to get rid of anyone who opposes you: *They ruthlessly smother all opposition.*

**smoul·der** *BrE*, **smolder** *AmE* /ˈsməʊldə‖ˈsmoʊldər/ *v* [I] **1** if something such as wood smoulders, it burns slowly without a flame: *a smouldering log* **2** if someone smoulders or if their feelings smoulder, they have strong feelings that they do not express: *He sensed a smouldering hostility towards him.* | **smoulder with passion/anger** *The workforce were smouldering with discontent.*

**smudge¹** /smʌdʒ/ *n* [C] a dirty mark: *There's a smudge of grease on your chin.* —**smudgy** *adj*

smudge

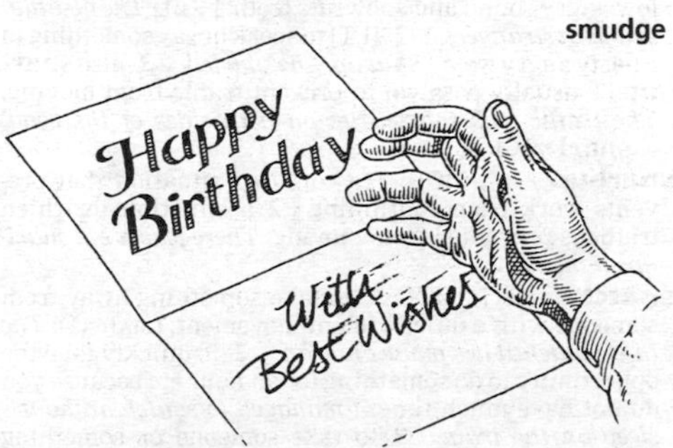


**smudge²** *v* **1** [T] to make writing, painting etc become unclear by touching or rubbing it: *Don't touch it! You'll smudge the ink.* **2** [I] if ink, writing etc smudges, its edges become unclear because it has been touched or rubbed **3** [T] to make a dirty mark on a surface: *Someone had smudged the paper with their greasy hands.*

**smug** /smʌɡ/ *adj* **smugger, smuggest** showing too much satisfaction with your own cleverness or success: *"I knew I'd win," she said with a smug smile. | What are you looking so smug about?* —**smugly** *adv Simon sat back smugly as Gould left the room.* —**smugness** *n* [U]: *his unbearable smugness*

**smug·gle** /ˈsmʌɡəl/ *v* [T] **1** to take something or someone illegally from one country to another: **smuggle sth into/out of** *They caught her trying to smuggle drugs into France.* | **smuggle sth through customs** (=to illegally take something past the officials who check what is being brought into the country) **2** *informal* to take something or someone secretly to a place where they are not allowed to be: *He managed to smuggle his notes into the examination.*

**smug·gler** /ˈsmʌɡlə‖-ər/ *n* [C] someone who takes something illegally from one country to another: *a drug smuggler*

**smug·gling** /ˈsmʌɡəlɪŋ/ *n* [U] the crime of taking things illegally from one country to another: *a diamond-smuggling operation*

**smut** /smʌt/ *n* **1** [U] books, stories, talk etc that offend some people slightly because they are about sex: *I won't have smut like that in my house!* **2** [C,U] dirt or SOOT (=black powder produced by burning), or a piece of this

**smut·ty** /ˈsmʌti/ *adj* **smuttier, smuttiest** **1** books, stories etc that are smutty offend some people slightly because they are about sex: *smutty jokes* **2** marked with small pieces of dirt or SOOT —**smuttiness** *n* [U] —**smuttily** *adv*

**snack** /snæk/ *n* **1** [C] a small amount of food that is eaten between main meals or instead of a meal: *I only had time to grab a quick snack.* | **snack food** (=food, such as PEANUTS or POPCORN that is intended to be eaten as a snack) **2 snacks** [plural] small things to eat that are provided at a party, meeting etc

**snack bar** /ˈ· ·/ *n* [C] a place where you can buy snacks: *Let's get a chilli dog at the snack bar.*

**snaf·fle** /ˈsnæfəl/ *v* [T] *BrE informal* to take something quickly, especially when it is rude or unfair to do this

**sna·fu** /snæˈfuː/ *n* [singular] *AmE informal* a situation in which a plan does not happen in the way it should: *What a snafu! Three of the contestants didn't even show up!*

**snag¹** /snæɡ/ *n* [C] **1** a disadvantage or problem, especially one that is not very serious: *It's an interesting job. The only snag is that it's not very well paid.* **2 a)** a sharp part of something that holds or cuts things that touch it **b)** a tear in something made by getting it stuck on a snag

**snag²** *v* **snagged, snagging** [T] **1** to damage something such as a piece of clothing by getting it stuck on something: *Oh damn! I've snagged my stockings.* **2** *AmE informal* to try to get someone to notice you, especially when you want help: *I'll try to snag the waiter next time he comes by.*

**snail** /sneɪl/ *n* [C] **1** a small soft creature that moves very slowly and has a hard shell on its back **2 at a snail's pace** extremely slowly

snail

**snail mail** /ˈ· ·/ *n* [U] *humorous* an expression meaning letters that are sent by post, used especially by people who send computer messages

**snake¹** /sneɪk/ *n* [C]  **1** an animal with a long thin body and no legs, that often has a poisonous bite **2** an insulting word meaning someone who cannot be trusted **3 snake in the grass** *informal* someone who pretends to be your friend but does something to harm you

**snake²** *v* [I always + adv/prep] if a river, road, train, or line snakes somewhere, it moves in long, twisting curves: [+ **along/past/down etc**] *The road snaked* *along the valley far below.* | **snake its way through/into etc** *The train was snaking its way through the mountains.*

**snake·bite** /ˈsneɪkbaɪt/ *n* **1** [C,U] the bite of a poisonous snake **2** [C] *BrE* an alcoholic drink that is half LAGER and half CIDER

**snake charm·er** /ˈ· ˌ··/ *n* [C] someone who entertains people by controlling snakes by playing music to them

**snakes and lad·ders** /ˌ· · ˈ··/ *n* [U] *BrE* a children's game played on a board in which you can move forwards and upwards along pictures of LADDERS or go downwards and backwards along pictures of snakes; CHUTES AND LADDERS *AmE*

**snake·skin** /ˈsneɪkˌskɪn/ *n* [U] the skin of a snake used to make shoes, bags etc: *snakeskin shoes*

**snak·y** /ˈsneɪki/ *adj* moving or lying in twisting curves: *a snaky road*

W3 **snap¹** /snæp/ *v*

**1** ▶ **BREAK** ◀ [I,T] if something snaps, or if you snap it, it breaks with a sudden sharp noise: *Pablo felt the second blow on his collar bone and heard it snap.* | *The impact must have snapped the cable.* | **snap sth off** *Patricia snapped a twig off.* | **snap sth in two/in half etc** (=break it into two pieces) *The teacher snapped the chalk in two and gave me a piece.*

**2** ▶ **MOVE (STH) SUDDENLY** ◀ [I always + adv/prep, T always + adv/prep] to move into a particular position suddenly, making a short sharp noise, or to make something move like this: **snap together/back etc** *The pieces just snap together like this.* | *The sails would be flat one minute, then snap and billow out with the wind the next.* | **snap open/shut** *She snapped her briefcase shut.*

**3** ▶ **SAY STH ANGRILY** ◀ [I,T] to say something quickly in an angry or annoyed way: *He laughed. "What's so funny?" I snapped.* | [+ **at**] *He was jumpy and aggressive, and snapped at Walter for no reason.* | **snap sb's head off** *BrE* (=say something in a very angry way) *I told her I was going to be late and she nearly snapped my head off!*

**4** ▶ **ANIMAL** ◀ [I] if an animal such as a dog snaps, it tries to bite you: [+ **at**] *Boxer was snapping at his ankles.*

**5** ▶ **PHOTOGRAPH** ◀ [T] to take a photograph: *wandering around Paris, snapping all the landmarks*

**6 snap your fingers** to make a short, sharp noise by moving one of your fingers quickly against your thumb, for example in order to get someone's attention

**7** ▶ **BECOME ANGRY ANXIOUS ETC** ◀ [I] to suddenly stop being able to control your anger, anxiety, or other feelings in a difficult situation: *I was handling the stress OK but then suddenly I just snapped.*

**8** ▶ **MIND** ◀ *old-fashioned* if your mind snaps, you become mentally ill

**9 snap to it** also **snap it up** *AmE spoken* used to tell someone to hurry and do something immediately: *Come on, snap to it, get that room cleaned up!*

**10 snap to attention** if soldiers snap to attention, they suddenly stand very straight —see also SNAP-ON

**snap** sth ↔ **on/off** *phr v* [T] to turn a light on or off

**snap out of** sth *phr v* [T not in passive] **snap out of it** to stop being sad or upset and make yourself feel better: *Chantal's been depressed for days. I wish she'd snap out of it.*

**snap** sb/sth ↔ **up** *phr v* [T] **1** to buy something immediately, especially because it is very cheap: *If you see one for under $100, you should snap it up.* **2** to eagerly take an opportunity to have someone as part of your company, team etc: *They needed a good quarterback and would have snapped him up if they'd had a chance.*

**snap²** *n*

**1** ▶ **SOUND** ◀ [singular] a sudden loud sound, especially made by something breaking or closing: *I shut the book with a snap, and put it away.* —see picture on page 1261

**2** ▶ **PHOTOGRAPH** ◀ [C] *informal especially BrE* a photograph taken by someone who is not a professional photographer: *holiday snaps*

**3 be a snap** *AmE informal* to be very easy to do: *The test was a snap.*

**4 a snap of your fingers** a sudden sound made by quickly moving one of your fingers against your thumb

**5** ▶ **GAME** ◀ [U] a card game in which players put down one card after another and try to be the first to shout 'snap' when there are two cards that are the same

**6** ▶ **CLOTHES FASTENER** ◀ [C] *AmE* a small metal fastener on clothes that works by pressing two parts together —see also BRANDY SNAP, COLD SNAP —see picture at FASTENER

**snap³** *adj* **snap judgment/decision** a judgment or decision made quickly and without enough thought or preparation: *I hate making snap decisions.*

**snap⁴** *interjection* **1** *BrE spoken* used when you see two things that are exactly the same: *Hey, snap! I've got a dress just like that!* **2** *spoken* said in the game of snap when two cards that are the same are put down

**snap·drag·on** /ˈsnæpˌdrægən/ *n* [C] a garden plant with white, red, or yellow flowers

**snap-on** /ˈ· ·/ *adj* [only before noun] a snap-on part of a toy or tool can be fastened on and removed easily

**snap·per** /ˈsnæpə‖-ər/ *n* [C] a type of fish that lives in warm seas, often used as food

**snap·pish** /ˈsnæpɪʃ/ *adj* bad-tempered: *Children are often spiteful and snappish.* —**snappishly** *adv* —**snappishness** *n* [U]

**snap·py** /ˈsnæpi/ *adj* **1** quick to react in an angry way **2** a snappy title or phrase is short, clever and easy to remember **3 make it snappy** also **look snappy** *informal* used to tell someone to hurry: *Get me a drink and make it snappy.* **4** *BrE informal* snappy clothes are attractive and fashionable: *a snappy suit* | **a snappy dresser** (=someone who wears fashionable clothes) —**snappily** *adv* —**snappiness** *n* [U]

**snap·shot** /ˈsnæpʃɒt‖-ʃɑːt/ *n* [C] **1** an informal photograph: *holiday snapshots* **2** a piece of information that quickly gives you an idea of what the situation is like at a particular time: *The US balance sheet provides a snapshot of what Americans own and owe.*

**snare¹** /sneə‖sner/ *n* [C] **1** a trap for catching an animal, especially one that uses a wire or rope to catch the animal by its foot **2** *literary* something that is intended to trick someone and get them into a difficult situation

**snare²** *v* [T] **1** to catch an animal by using a snare **2** to deceive someone so that they cannot escape from a difficult situation

**snare drum** /ˈ· ·/ *n* [C] a small flat drum that makes a hard continuous sound when you hit it

**snarl** /snɑːl‖snɑːrl/ *v* **1** [I] if an animal snarls it makes a low angry sound and shows its teeth: [+ **at**] *The alsatian snarls at strangers.* **2** [I,T] to speak or say something in a nasty angry way: *"Shut up," he snarled.* **3** also **snarl up** [T usually passive] to prevent traffic from moving: *The traffic was snarled up on both sides of the road.* —**snarl** *n* [C]

**snarl-up** /ˈ· ·/ *n* [C] **1** a confused situation that prevents work from continuing **2** a situation in which traffic is prevented from moving: *There was a big snarl-up on the M1.*

**snatch¹** /snætʃ/ *v* [T] **1** to take something away from someone with a quick violent movement; GRAB¹ (1): *The thief snatched her purse and ran.* **2** to quickly take the opportunity to do something for an hour etc because you do not have much time: *I managed to snatch an hour's sleep on the train.* **3** to take someone or something away from a place by force: *Vargas was snatched from his home by two armed men.*

**snatch at** sth *phr v* [T] to quickly put out your hand to try to take or hold something: *Jessie snatched at the bag but I pulled it away.*

**snatch²** *n* [C] **1 a snatch of conversation/music/song etc** a short and incomplete part of a conversation, song etc that you hear **2 in snatches** for short periods: *I only slept in snatches during the night.* **3** | [+ **with**] a quick movement with your hand in order to take or hold something or someone

**snatch squad** /ˈ· ˌ·/ *n* [C] a group of policemen who go quickly into a crowd to ARREST[1] (1) people

**snaz·zy** /ˈsnæzi/ *adj informal* clothes that are snazzy are bright , fashionable, and attractive: *a snazzy red jacket* —**snazzily** *adv*

**sneak[1]** /sniːk/ *v past tense and past participle* **sneaked** /sniːkt/ **snuck** /snʌk/ *AmE* **1** [I always + adv/prep] to go somewhere secretly and quietly in order to avoid being seen or heard: [+ **in/past/around etc**] *They managed to sneak past the guard on the gate.* **2** [T always + adv/prep] to hide something and take it somewhere secretly: **sneak sth through/by/past etc** *I'm going to try and sneak these bottles of wine through Customs.* **3 sneak a look/glance at** to look at something quickly and secretly, especially something that you are not supposed to see **4** [T] *informal* to quickly and secretly steal something unimportant or of little value: **sneak sth from** *We used to sneak cigarettes from Dad to smoke in the garden.*

**sneak on** sb *phr v* [T] *informal* to tell someone such as a parent or teacher about something that another person has done wrong, because you want to cause trouble for that person: *Adrian's not popular because he's always sneaking on other kids.*

**sneak up** *phr v* [I] to come near someone very quietly, so that they do not see you until you reach them: [+ **on/behind etc**] *Don't sneak up on me like that! You gave me quite a shock.* —see also **sneak preview** (PREVIEW[1])

**sneak[2]** *n* [C] *BrE informal* a child who is disliked because they tell adults about bad things that other children have done wrong

**sneak·er** /ˈsniːkə‖-ər/ *n* [C] *especially AmE* a type of light soft shoe with a rubber SOLE (=bottom) used for sports —see picture at SHOE[1]

**sneak·ing** /ˈsniːkɪŋ/ *adj* **1 have a sneaking admiration/affection etc for** to have a secret feeling of admiration etc for someone **2 have a sneaking suspicion/feeling (that)** to have a slight feeling that someone has done something wrong without being sure: *I have a sneaking suspicion he throws away my letters without even reading them.*

**sneak·y** /ˈsniːki/ *adj* doing things in a secret and dishonest or unfair way: *That was really sneaky, hiding his wallet!* —**sneakily** *adv*

**sneer[1]** /snɪə‖snɪr/ *v* [I,T] to smile or speak in a very unkind way that shows you have no respect for someone or something: [+ **at**] *Bob always sneers at my taste in clothes.* —**sneering** *adj*: *a sneering letter* —**sneeringly** *adv*

**sneer[2]** *n* [C] an unkind smile or remark that shows you have no respect for something or someone

**sneeze[1]** /sniːz/ *v* [I] **1** if you sneeze, air suddenly comes from your nose, making a noise, for example when you have a cold: *The baby keeps sneezing – she must be getting a cold.* **2 not to be sneezed at** *spoken* good enough to be considered carefully: *An offer of £900 is not to be sneezed at.*

**sneeze[2]** *n* [C] an act or sound of sneezing

**snick** /snɪk/ *v* [T] *BrE* to make a small cut or mark on something; NICK[2] (1) —**snick** *n* [C]

**snick·er** /ˈsnɪkə‖-ər/ *v* [I] *AmE* to laugh quietly, and often unkindly, at something which is not supposed to be funny; SNIGGER *BrE* —**snicker** *n* [C]

**snide** /snaɪd/ *adj informal* making unkind criticisms, often in a clever, indirect way: **snide remarks/comments** *She's always making snide remarks about Marco's pronunciation.* —**snidely** *adv*

**sniff[1]** /snɪf/ *v*
**1 ▶ BREATHE NOISILY ◀** [I] to breathe air into your nose noisily, especially in short breaths: *Stop sniffing – why can't you blow your nose?*
**2 ▶ SMELL ◀** [I,T] to breathe air in through your nose in order to smell something: *He opened the milk and sniffed it.* | [+ **at**] *The dog was sniffing at the dead bird*
**3** [T] to say something in a proud complaining way: *"I expected something much better," she sniffed.*
**4 not to be sniffed at** *spoken* good enough to be considered carefully: *An 8% salary increase is not to be sniffed at.*
**5** [T] to take a harmful drug through your nose: *sniffing cocaine* —see also GLUE SNIFFING

**sniff out** sth *phr v* [T] **1** to discover or find something by its smell: *They've got dogs at the customs for sniffing out drugs.* **2** *informal* to find out something: *Vic's been asking questions, trying to sniff out where you went last night.*

**sniff[2]** *n* [C] an act or sound of sniffing

**sniffer dog** /ˈ· · ·/ *n* [C] a dog that has been trained to find drugs or explosives by using its sense of smell

**snif·fle[1]** /ˈsnɪfəl/ *v* [I] to sniff repeatedly to stop liquid from running out of your nose, especially when you are crying or you have a cold: *For goodness sake, stop sniffling!*

**sniffle[2]** *n* an act or sound of sniffling: **have the sniffles** (=keep sniffing)

**sniff·y** /ˈsnɪfi/ *adj BrE informal* having a disapproving attitude towards something or someone especially because you think they are not good enough for you: *Don't get sniffy, he's a friend of mine!*

**snif·ter** /ˈsnɪftə‖-ər/ *n* [C] **1** *AmE* a special glass for drinking BRANDY —see picture at GLASS[1] **2** *BrE old-fashioned* a small amount of an alcoholic drink

**snig·ger** /ˈsnɪgə‖-ər/ *v* [I] *BrE* to laugh quietly, and often unkindly, at something which is not supposed to be funny; SNICKER *AmE*: [+ **at**] *What are you sniggering at? This is a serious poem.* —**snigger** *n* [C]

**snip[1]** /snɪp/ *n* [C] **1** a quick small cut with scissors **2 be a snip** *BrE informal* to be surprisingly cheap: *At £20 for a dozen, they're a snip.* —see CHEAP (USAGE)

**snip[2]** *v* [I,T] to cut something by making quick cuts with scissors: *I hurriedly snipped the string and untied the parcel.* | **snip sth off** (=remove it by snipping) *Snip the ends of the beans off before you cook them.* —see picture on page 834

**snipe[1]** /snaɪp/ *v* [I] **1** to shoot from a hidden position at unprotected people **2** to criticize someone in a nasty way: [+ **at**] *I wish you two would stop sniping at each other.* —**sniping** *n* [U]

**snipe[2]** *n* [C] **1** a bird with a very long thin beak that lives in wet areas, and is often shot for sport **2** *AmE* someone who is strongly disliked

**snip·er** /ˈsnaɪpə‖-ər/ *n* [C] someone who shoots at unprotected people from a hidden position: *Edwards was shot and killed by snipers*

**snip·pet** /ˈsnɪpɪ̍t/ *n* [C] **snippet of information/news etc** a small piece of information etc: *We'd welcome any odd snippets of information you might pick up.*

**snip·py** /ˈsnɪpi/ *adj AmE informal* quick to show that you are angry or offended, or that you will not obey someone

**snit** /snɪt/ *n* **be in a snit** *AmE informal* to be unreasonably annoyed about something: *Martha's in a snit because I used her omelet pan.*

**snitch[1]** /snɪtʃ/ *v informal* **1** [I + on] to tell someone such as a parent or teacher about something that another person has done wrong becuase you want to cause trouble for that person **2** [T] to quickly steal something unimportant or of little value

**snitch[2]** *n* [C] **1** *informal* someone who is disliked because he or she tells a parent or teacher about something wrong that another person has done **2** *BrE humorous* a nose

**sniv·el** /ˈsnɪvəl/ *v* **snivelled, snivelling** *BrE*, **sniveled, sniveling** *AmE* [I] to behave or speak in a weak complaining way, especially when you are crying: *I warned you – so don't come snivelling back to me when it all goes wrong!*|*a snivelling coward*

**snob** /snɒb‖snɑːb/ *n* [C] **1** someone who thinks they are better than people from a lower social class and dislikes being with them or doing the things they do: *John wouldn't go to a football match, he's too much of a snob.* **2 intellectual snob** someone who thinks they are too intelligent to enjoy ordinary forms of entertainment **3 music/wine etc snob** someone who knows a lot about music, wine etc and thinks their opinions are better than other people's **4 snob value/appeal** something that has snob value is liked by people who think they are better than other people: *A Rolls-Royce has snob appeal.*

**snob·be·ry** /ˈsnɒbəri‖ˈsnɑːb-/ *n* [U] **1** the feelings and behaviour of snobs **2 inverted snobbery** a type of snobbery in which people of a low social class think they are better than people of a higher social class

**snob·bish** /ˈsnɒbɪʃ‖ˈsnɑː-/ also **snob·by** /ˈsnɒbi‖ˈsnɑːbi/ *adj* having attitudes, behaviour etc that are typical of a snob —**snobbishly** *adv* —**snobbishness** *n* [U]

**snog** /snɒg‖snɑːg/ *v* **snogged, snogging** [I,T] *BrE informal* if two young people snog, they kiss each other, especially for a long time —**snog** *n* [C usually singular]

**snook** /snuːk‖snʊk, snuːk/ *n* —see **cock a snook** (COCK² (4))

**snoo·ker¹** /ˈsnuːkə‖ˈsnʊkər/ *n* [U] a game played on a special table covered in green cloth, in which two people hit coloured balls into holes at the sides and corners of the table with CUES (=long sticks)

**snooker²** *v* [T, often passive] *BrE informal* to make it impossible for someone to do what they want to do: *If the council refuses our planning application, we're snookered.*

**snoop** /snuːp/ *v* [I] to try to find out about someone's private affairs by secretly looking in their house, examining their possessions etc: [**+ around/about**] *I caught him snooping around in my office.* —**snoop** *n* [singular] **snooper** *n* [C]

**snoot** /snuːt/ *n* [C] *AmE informal* your nose

**snoot·y** /ˈsnuːti/ *adj informal* rude and unfriendly, because you think you are better than other people: *snooty neighbours* —**snootily** *adv* —**snootiness** *n* [U]

**snooze** /snuːz/ *v* [I] *informal* to have a short, light sleep: *Dad was snoozing in a deckchair.* —**snooze** *n* [C]

**snore¹** /snɔː‖snɔːr/ *v* [I] to breathe noisily through your mouth and nose while you are asleep: *Bill's snoring is driving me nuts.*

**snore²** *n* [C] the noise you make when you snore

**snor·kel¹** /ˈsnɔːkəl‖ˈsnɔːr-/ *n* [C] **1** a tube that allows a swimmer to breathe air under water **2** a piece of equipment that allows a SUBMARINE to take in air when it is under water

**snorkel²** *v* [I] to swim under water using a snorkel —**snorkelling** *BrE*, **snorkeling** *AmE*— *n* [U]

**snort¹** /snɔːt‖snɔːrt/ *v* **1** [I,T] to express anger, impatience, or amusement by breathing air noisily through your nose: *"Certainly not," he snorted.*|[**+ with**] *She snorted with contempt at the suggestion.* **2** [I] to make a loud noise by forcing air out through your nose: *The horse snorted and stamped its hoof impatiently.* **3** [T] *slang* to take drugs by breathing them in through your nose: *snorting cocaine*

**snort²** *n* [C] **1** a loud sound made by breathing through your nose, especially to show anger, impatience, or amusement: *a snort of laughter* **2** a small amount of a drug that is breathed in through the nose: *a snort of cocaine*

**snot** /snɒt‖snɑːt/ *n informal* **1** [U] an impolite word for the thick MUCUS (=liquid) produced in your nose **2** [C] someone who is SNOTTY (1)

**snot-nosed** /ˈ· ·/ *adj AmE informal* an impolite word used to describe children who are not very clean: *that snot-nosed kid next door*

**snot·ty** /ˈsnɒti‖ˈsnɑːti/ *adj informal* **1** thinking that you are more important than other people: *I won't be told what to do by some snotty little clerk!* **2** wet and dirty with MUCUS

**snotty-nosed** /ˈ·· ·/ *adj BrE informal* SNOTTY (2)

**snout** /snaʊt/ *n* **1** [C] the long nose of some kinds of animals, such as pigs **2** [C] *BrE informal* a criminal who gives information about other criminals to the police

**snow¹** /snəʊ‖snoʊ/ *n* **1** [U] water frozen into soft white FLAKES (=pieces) that fall from the sky in cold weather and cover the ground: *mountain peak covered with snow*|*roads blocked by deep snow*|*melting snow* —see picture on page 836 **2** [C] a period of time in which snow falls: *one of the heaviest snows this winter* **3** [U] *slang* COCAINE S3 W3

**snow²** *v* **1 it snows** if it snows, snow falls from the sky: *It snowed all night.*|*Look! It's snowing!* **2** [T] *AmE informal* to persuade someone to believe or support something, especially by lying to them: *I was completely snowed by his Southern charm.* **3 be snowed in/up** to be unable to travel from a place because so much snow has fallen there: *We were snowed in for three days last winter.* **4 be snowed under (with sth)** to have more work than you can deal with

**snow·ball¹** /ˈsnəʊbɔːl‖ˈsnoʊbɒːl/ *n* [C] **1** a ball of snow that children make and throw at each other: *a snowball fight* **2 not have a snowball's chance in hell** *informal* to have no chance at all

**snowball²** *v* [I] if a plan, problem, business etc snowballs it grows bigger at a faster and faster rate: *Once the contest became popular, it quickly snowballed into an all-day event with TV coverage.*

**snow·bird** /ˈsnəʊbɜːd‖ˈsnoʊbɜːrd/ *n* [C] *AmE informal* someone, especially an old person, who moves to a warmer place every winter

**snow blind·ness** /ˈ· ˌ··/ *n* [U] eye pain and difficulty in seeing things, caused by looking at snow in bright sunlight —**snow blind** *adj*

**snow-blow·er** /ˈ· ˌ··/ *n* [C] *especially AmE* a machine which clears snow from roads by blowing it away

**snow·board** /ˈsnəʊbɔːd‖ˈsnoʊbɔːrd/ *n* [C] a long wide board made of plastic, which people use to travel over snow for sport —**snowboarder** *n* [C] —**snowboarding** *n* [U] —see picture at SKI²

**snow·bound** /ˈsnəʊbaʊnd‖ˈsnoʊ-/ *adj* blocked or prevented from leaving a place by large amounts of snow: *snowbound traffic*

**snow-capped** /ˈ· ·/ *adj literary* snow-capped mountains are covered in snow at the top

**snow chains** /ˈ· ·/ *n* [plural] a set of chains that are fixed around the wheels of a car so that it can drive over snow without slipping

**snow·drift** /ˈsnəʊˌdrɪft‖ˈsnoʊ-/ *n* [C] a deep mass of snow piled up by the wind

**snow·drop** /ˈsnəʊdrɒp‖ˈsnoʊdrɑːp/ *n* [C] a European plant with a small white flower which appears in early spring

**snow·fall** /ˈsnəʊfɔːl‖ˈsnoʊfɒːl/ *n* [C, U] the amount of snow that falls, or the amount that falls in a particular period of time: *an average snowfall of eight centimetres a year*|*Heavy snow falls are forecast.*

**snow·field** /ˈsnəʊfiːld‖ˈsnoʊ-/ *n* [C] a wide area of land that is always covered in snow

**snow·flake** /ˈsnəʊfleɪk‖ˈsnoʊ-/ *n* [C] a small soft flat piece of frozen water that falls as snow

**snow job** /ˈ· ·/ *n* [singular] *AmE informal* an act of persuading someone to believe or support something, especially by lying to them

**snow line** /ˈsnəʊlaɪn‖ˈsnoʊ-/ *n* **the snow line** the level above which snow on a mountain never melts —see picture on page 835

**snow·man** /ˈsnəʊmæn‖ˈsnoʊ-/ *n* [C] a figure of a person made of snow, made especially by children

**snow·mo·bile** /ˈsnəʊməbiːl‖ˈsnoʊmoʊ-/ *n* [C] a small vehicle with a motor that moves over snow or ice easily

**snow pea** /ˈ· ·/ *n* [C] *AmE* a kind of PEA whose POD (=cover) and seeds you can eat; MANGETOUT *BrE*

**snow plough** *BrE*, **snow plow** *AmE* /ˈ· ·/ *n* [C] a vehicle or piece of equipment for pushing snow off roads, railways etc

**snow route** /ˈ· ·/ *n* [C] *AmE* an important road in a city that cars must be removed from when it snows, so that it can be cleared of snow

**snow·shoe** /ˈsnəʊʃuː‖ˈsnoʊ-/ *n* [C] one of a pair of wide flat frames which you attach to your shoes, so that you can walk on snow without sinking

**snow·storm** /ˈsnəʊstɔːm‖ˈsnoʊstɔːrm/ *n* [C] a storm with strong winds and a lot of snow

**snow·suit** /ˈsnəʊsuːt, -sjuːt‖ˈsnoʊsuːt/ *n* [C] a warm piece of clothing that covers the whole of a child's body

**snow tire** /ˈ· ·/ *n* [C] *AmE* a special car tyre used when driving on snow or ice.

**snow-white** /ˌ· ˈ·◂/ *adj* pure white

**snow·y** /ˈsnəʊi‖ˈsnoʊi/ *adj* **1** full of snow or snowing: *Today it will be snowy in many areas.* **2** *literary* pure white: *snowy hair* —**snowiness** *n* [U]

**Snr** the written abbreviation of SENIOR, used after someone's name: *James Taylor, Snr*

**snub¹** /snʌb/ *v* **snubbed, snubbing** [T] to treat someone rudely, especially by intentionally ignoring them when you meet: *Mayor Koch snubbed the Giants and refused to offer them a victory parade.*

**snub²** *n* [C] an act of snubbing someone: *Still smarting from the snub, he stalked from the room.*

**snub³** *adj* a snub nose is short and flat and points slightly upwards

**snub-nosed** /ˌ· ˈ·◂/ *adj* having a snub nose that points slightly upwards

**snuck** /snʌk/ *AmE* past tense and past participle of SNEAK

**snuff¹** /snʌf/ *v* **1** also **snuff out** [T] to put out a CANDLE flame by pressing the burning part with your fingers or covering it with a snuffer **2** [I,T] if an animal snuffs, it breathes air into its nose noisily in order to smell something; SNIFF¹ (2) **3 snuff it** *BrE informal* to die

**snuff** sth **out** *phr v* [T] to suddenly end something, especially someone's life: *a young life snuffed out*

**snuff²** *n* [U] a type of tobacco in powder form, which people suck in through their noses: *a pinch of snuff*

**snuff·er** /ˈsnʌfə‖-ər/ *n* [C] a tool with a small bell-shaped end on a handle for putting out CANDLES

**snuf·fle** /ˈsnʌfəl/ *v* [I] to breathe noisily through your nose making low sounds: *pigs snuffling round*

**snug¹** /snʌg/ *adj* **snugger, snuggest** **1** a room or space that is snug is small, warm, and comfortable and makes you feel protected: *a snug little sitting-room with a log fire burning* **2** someone who is snug feels comfortable, happy, and warm: *The kids were soon tucked up snug in their beds.* **3** clothes that are snug fit closely —**snugly** *adv* —**snugness** *n* [U]

**snug²** *n* [C] *BrE* a small comfortable room in a PUB

**snug·gle** /ˈsnʌgəl/ *v* [I always + adv/prep] *informal* to settle into a warm comfortable position: [+ **up/down/into etc**] *Let's snuggle up together and watch TV.*

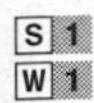

**so¹** /səʊ‖soʊ/ *adv* **1 a) so big/tall etc** [+adj/adv] used to describe how big, tall etc something is, especially when it is very big or very tall: *Why does life have to be so complicated?*|*It was so embarrassing – everyone was standing there looking at us!*|*I've never seen so many people attend this church before.*|**so tall a man/so high a mountain etc** *(formal)*: *I've never seen so beautiful a baby before.* —see SUCH (USAGE) **b) worry/talk etc so** *formal* to worry, talk etc a great deal: *I wish he wouldn't fuss so – it makes me feel nervous.* **2 so tall/big etc (that)** used when you mean that because someone or something is very tall, big etc, something happens or someone does something: *He was so fat he couldn't get through the door.*|*You couldn't hear yourself think, the music was so loud.*|**so tall etc as to be sth** *The statement was so ambiguous as to be totally meaningless.* **3** used to talk about an idea, suggestion, situation etc that has been mentioned before: *"Will I need my umbrella?" "I don't think so."*|*He seemed to be very understanding, more so than I expected.* **4 so would John/so do I/so is he etc** used to add a positive statement to one that has just been mentioned: *If you're going to take the day off then so will I.*|*Frank adores dogs and so does his wife.* **5 not so tall/big etc as..** not as tall, big etc as something else: *You know, Harry's not so clever as I first thought.* —see also **as/so far as** (FAR¹ (3)), **as/so long as** (LONG² (6)), —see AS (USAGE) **6 so as to do sth** in order to do something: *Credit has been arranged so as to spread the payments over a 10 month period.*|*So as not to cause offence many of the mourners stood at the back of the church.* **7 so many/much a)** a particular amount, number, level, degree etc: *There's only so much you can do with hair this fine.* **b)** used to say that something is the same as something else that is worse: *Teenage magazines are just so much wasted paper.* **8 (just) as...so...** used to compare two people or things, when they are the same: *Just as the French love their wine, so the English love their beer.* **9** used when you are being polite to mean 'very': *I'm so pleased to meet you at last.*|**ever so** *BrE*: *The children are ever so excited. It's the first time they've been to Disneyland.* **10** *formal* therefore: *The passport was found to have passed its expiry date and so to be void.* —see THUS (USAGE) —see also **and so on/forth** (AND), **even so** (EVEN¹ (4)), **so far** (FAR¹ (25)), **so far as possible** (FAR¹ (26)), **so much for** (MUCH² (12)), **just so** (JUST¹ (29))

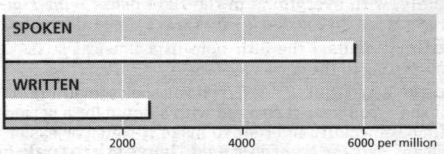

Frequencies of the word **so** in spoken and written English.

| | 2000 | 4000 | 6000 per million |
|---|---|---|---|
| SPOKEN | | | |
| WRITTEN | | | |

Based on the British National Corpus and the Longman Lancaster Corpus

This graph shows that the word **so** is much more common in spoken English than in written English. This is because it has special uses in spoken English and is used in some common spoken phrases.

**SO** *(adv)* **SPOKEN USES AND PHRASES**

**11 so a)** used to get someone's attention, especially in order to ask them a question: *So, how long do you think you'll be staying in England?* **b)** used to check that you have understood something: *So let me get this straight. You two aren't actually married then?* **c)** used to show that you do not think something is important: *So, I lied. They can't put me in prison for that!* **d)** used to show that you have found something out about someone: *So! You've got a new girlfriend, huh?* **e)** used with a movement of your hand to show how big, high etc something or someone is: *Oh, he must be about so tall.* **f)** also **like so** used when you are showing someone how to do something using your hands, feet etc: *Fold the material, so, and push the needle through.* **g)** used when asking a question about what has just been said: *"I've decided to leave." "So what are you going to do?"* **12 so she is/so they are etc** used to agree with something that has just been mentioned and that you had not noticed or had forgotten: *"Don't forget your brother is coming round for dinner." "So he is. I'd better get some food in."* **13 so what?** used to show that you do not think that something that has been mentioned is important: *Yeah, I do smoke. So what?* **14 so long!** *AmE* used to say goodbye **15 so be it** used to show that you do not agree with someone's decision but you will accept it anyway: *If you're sure you want to sell your car, then so be it!* **16 I do so/it is so etc** *AmE* used especially by

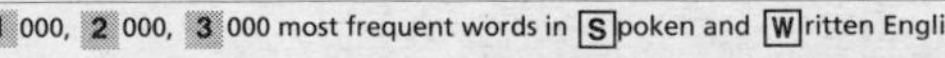

children to say that something is true, can be done etc when someone else says that it is not, can not etc: *"You can't swim." "I can so."* **17 so I see** used to say that you know that what someone is telling you is true because you can see that it is: *"I broke my leg." "So I see. How did it happen?"* **18 so much the better** used to say that if something happens it will make the situation even better than it already is: *Katie's coming with us and if you join in too, so much the better.* **19 so help me** used to say that you are determined to do something bad to someone, even though you know it is wrong: *One more word and so help me I'll kill you!*

**so²** *conjunction* **1** used to give the reason why something happens, why someone does something etc: *I heard a noise so I got out of bed and turned the light on.* | *There was no food in the house so we rang out for a pizza.* **2 so (that) a)** in order to make something happen, something possible etc: *So that everyone can see, will the taller children stand at the back.* | *The vase had been put on top of the cupboard so it wouldn't get broken.* **b)** used to say that something happens as a result of something else: *Many contestants later failed drug tests, so that the race had to be rerun.*

**so³** *adj* [not before noun] **1 be so** *especially spoken* to be true or correct: *The newspapers claim she killed him in self defence but that just isn't so.* | *"Bill says that you appeared in court last week" "Is that so? Well let me tell you one or two things about Bill."* **2 more so/less so/too much so** phrases in which 'so' is used instead of repeating an adjective that you have mentioned before: *Bill is very popular and Ted is even more so.* | *Jerry is very honest, maybe too much so.* **3 be just/exactly so** to be arranged tidily, with everything in the right place: *With Tim, if everything isn't just so he can't relax.* —see also so-so

**so⁴** *n* [singular] the fifth note in a musical SCALE¹ (8) according to the SOL-FA system

S 3 **soak¹** /səʊk‖soʊk/ *v* **1** [I,T] if you soak something or let it soak, you keep it covered with a liquid for a period of time, especially in order to make it softer or easier to clean: *Soak the beans overnight.* | **leave sth to soak** *Just leave the dishes to soak; I'll wash them later.* | **soak sth off/out** (=remove it by soaking) *Soak the label off the jar.* **2** [I always + adv/prep, T] to make something completely wet, or to become completely wet: [**+ through/into etc**] *If the ink soaks through the paper, it'll stain the table underneath.* | **soak sth** *The rain came suddenly and soaked all the washing.* **3** [I] to spend a long time taking a bath **4** [T] *informal* to make someone pay too much money in prices or taxes: *Soak the rich seems to be the policy of all socialist governments*

**soak** sth ↔ **up** *phr v* [T] **1** if something soaks up a liquid, it takes the liquid into itself: *He used a towel to soak up the blood.* **2** to learn something quickly and easily: *That child just soaks up information.* **3 soak up the sun** to sit outside for a long time enjoying the sun

**soak²** *n* [C] **1** a long and enjoyable time spent in the bath: *a good long soak after shopping all day* **2** an act of soaking something: **give sth a soak** *Give the towels a good soak, they're very dirty.* **3 an old soak** *BrE humorous* someone who is often drunk

**soaked** /səʊkt‖soʊkt/ *adj* [not before noun] **1** very wet or wearing very wet clothes: *The rain's coming on heavier – we're going to get soaked.* | **soaked through** (=completely wet) *Get those clothes off; they're soaked right through!* | **soaked to the skin** (=wearing clothes that are completely wet) **2 be soaked in** to be full of a particular quality: *a city soaked in history*

**soak·ing¹** /ˈsəʊkɪŋ‖ˈsoʊ-/ also **soaking wet** /ˌ·· ˈ·◂/ *adj* very wet: *You're soaking! Come in and dry off.*

**soaking²** *n* [C] a SOAK² (2)

**soaking sol·u·tion** /ˈ·· ·ˌ··/ *n* [C,U] a liquid that you keep CONTACT LENSES in when you are not wearing them

**so-and-so** /ˈ· · ˌ·/ *n plural* **so-and-sos 1** [U] an expression meaning a particular person or thing, used when you do not give their name: *They're always gossiping about so-and-so having an affair with so-and-so* —compare SUCH AND SUCH **2** [C] a word meaning a very unpleasant or unreasonable person, used to avoid saying a stronger word, such as BASTARD: *Peter can be a real so-and-so at times.*

**soap¹** /səʊp‖soʊp/ *n* **1** [U] the substance that you use to wash your body: *Wash thoroughly with soap and water.* | *a bar of soap* —compare DETERGENT **2** [C] *informal* a television or radio story about the daily lives of the same group of people, which is broadcast regularly; SOAP OPERA S 3

**soap²** *v* [T] to rub soap on or over someone or something: *Will you soap my back for me?*

**soap·box** /ˈsəʊpbɒks‖ˈsoʊpbɑːks/ *n* **get on your soapbox** *informal* to tell people your own strong opinions about something loudly and forcefully: *Don't mention politics, or Burt will be back on his soapbox again.*

**soap·flakes** /ˈsəʊpfleɪks‖ˈsoʊp-/ *n* [plural] small thin pieces of soap used for washing delicate clothes

**soap op·e·ra** /ˈ· ˌ···/ *n* [C] a SOAP¹ (2)

**soap pow·der** /ˈ· ˌ··/ *n* [U] *BrE* a powder that is made from soap and other chemicals, used for washing clothes

**soap·stone** /ˈsəʊpstəʊn‖ˈsoʊpstoʊn/ *n* [U] a soft stone that feels like soap

**soap·suds** /ˈsəʊpsʌdz‖ˈsoʊp-/ *n* [plural] the mass of small BUBBLES formed on top of soapy water

**soap·y** /ˈsəʊpi‖ˈsoʊpi/ *adj* **1** containing soap: *warm soapy water* **2** like soap: *This cheese is kind of soapy-tasting.* **3** *BrE informal* so pleasant that it seems false: *Joan reads those awful soapy romances.* —**soapiness** *n* [U]

**soar** /sɔː‖sɔːr/ *v* [I]

**1 ▶AMOUNTS/PRICES ETC◀** to increase quickly to a high level: *The temperature soared to 90 degrees.* | *Health care costs continue to soar.*

**2 ▶IN THE SKY◀ a)** to fly, especially very high up in the sky, floating on air currents **b)** to go quickly upwards to a great height: *The rocket soared into orbit.*

**3 ▶SPIRITS/HOPES◀** if your spirits or hopes soar, you begin to feel very happy or hopeful: *Adam's smile sent her spirits soaring.*

**4 ▶LOOK TALL◀** [not in progressive] if buildings, trees, towers etc soar they look very tall and impressive: *Here the cliffs soar 500 feet above the sea.* —**soaring** *adj*: *a soaring skyscraper* | *soaring crime figures*

**sob** /sɒb‖sɑːb/ *v* **sobbed, sobbing 1** [I] to cry noisily while breathing in short, sudden bursts: *Josie flung herself on the bed, sobbing.* **2** also **sob out** [T] to say something or tell someone something while you are sobbing: *Joshua sobbed out the whole sad story.* —**sob** *n* [C]: *loud sobs* —**sobbingly** *adv*

**so·ber¹** /ˈsəʊbə‖ˈsoʊbər/ *adj* **1** not drunk: *I've never seen him sober.* | **as sober as a judge** (=completely sober) **2** having a serious attitude to life: *a sober and intelligent young man* **3** plain and not at all brightly coloured: *a sober grey suit* —**soberly** *adv*

**sober²** *v* also **sober down** [I,T] to become or make someone become more serious in behaviour or attitude: *Diane sobered down a lot as she got older.*

**sober** sb ↔ **up** *phr v* [I,T] to gradually become or make someone become less drunk: *A cup of black coffee might sober you up.*

**so·ber·ing** /ˈsəʊbərɪŋ‖ˈsoʊ-/ *adj* making you feel very serious: *a sobering thought* | *The news had a sobering effect.*

**so·bri·e·ty** /səˈbraɪəti/ *n* [U] *formal* behaviour that shows a serious attitude to life

**so·bri·quet** /ˈsəʊbrɪkeɪ‖ˈsoʊ-/ also **soubriquet** *n* [C] *literary* an unofficial title or name; NICKNAME

**sob sto·ry** /ˈ· ˌ··/ *n* [C] *informal* a story, especially one that is untrue, that someone tells you in order to make you feel sorry for them: *She had some sob story about her cat getting run over.*

**Soc.** the written abbreviation of SOCIETY (3)

**so-called** /ˌ· ˈ·◂/ *adj* [only before noun] a word used to W 3 describe someone or something that has been given a name that you think is wrong: *The so-called expert on international affairs turned out to be a research student.*

**soc·cer** /ˈsɒkə‖ˈsɑːkər/ *n* [U] a word for the game of FOOTBALL (1) used so that it is not confused with AMERICAN FOOTBALL or RUGBY *BrE* —see picture on page 1264

**so·cia·ble¹** /ˈsəʊʃəbəl‖ˈsoʊ-/ *adj* someone who is sociable enjoys being with other people: *a pleasant, sociable couple* —opposite UNSOCIABLE —**sociably** *adv* —**sociability** /ˌsəʊʃəˈbɪləti‖ˌsoʊ-/ *n* [U]

**sociable²** *n* [C] *AmE old-fashioned* a SOCIAL²

S2 W1 **so·cial¹** /ˈsəʊʃəl‖ˈsoʊ-/ *adj*
1 ▶ **SOCIETY** ◀ concerning human society and its organization, or the quality of people's lives: *Various social issues, such as unemployment and education, were discussed.* | *social trends* | *demands for social change*
2 ▶ **RANK** ◀ related to the position in society that you have, according to your job, family, wealth etc: *social status* | *a wide circle of friends from different social backgrounds* | **social class** (=a group of people who have the same social position) *every social class, from manual workers to aristocrats* | **social mobility** (=ability to move into a higher social class)
3 ▶ **MEETING PEOPLE** ◀ related to the way you meet people and form relationships: **social skills** (=ability to meet people easily and deal well with them) *College gives you an opportunity to develop your social skills.* | **social contacts** (=people you meet outside work) | **social graces** (=attractive manners, behaviour etc when you meet people)
4 ▶ **WITH FRIENDS** ◀ related to the time you spend with your friends for enjoyment: **social life** (=activities with your friends) *You sure seem to have a busy social life these days!* | **social club/evening/gathering etc** (=a club or occasion at which people can enjoy being together) | **social drinking** (=drinking alcohol with your friends)
5 ▶ **ANIMALS** ◀ forming groups or living together in their natural state: *Elephants are social animals.* —see also ANTI-SOCIAL, SOCIABLE, UNSOCIAL —**socially** *adv*: *socially acceptable behaviour* | *Do you and your colleagues ever meet socially?*

**social²** *n* [C] *old-fashioned* a planned informal party for the members of a group, club or church

**social climb·er** /ˌ·· ˈ··/ *n* [C] someone who tries to get accepted into a higher social class by becoming friendly with people who belong to that class

**social de·moc·ra·cy** /ˌ·· ·ˈ···/ *n* [U] **1** a political and economic system based on socialism combined with DEMOCRATIC principles, such as personal freedom and government by elected representatives **2** [C] a country with a government based on this system —**social democrat** /ˌ·· ˈ···/ *n* [C]

**social di·sease** /ˈ·· ·ˌ·/ *n* [C] an expression meaning VENEREAL DISEASE, used to avoid saying this directly

**social en·gi·neer·ing** /ˌ·· ··ˈ··/ *n* [U] the practice of making changes in the law in order to change society according to a political idea.

**so·cial·is·m** /ˈsəʊʃəl-ɪzəm‖ˈsoʊ-/ *n* [U] a system of political beliefs and principles whose main aims are that everyone should have an equal opportunity to share wealth and that industries should be owned by the government —compare CAPITALISM, COMMUNISM

**so·cial·ist¹** /ˈsəʊʃəl-əst‖ˈsoʊ-/ *adj* **1** based on socialism or connected with a political party that supports socialism: *socialist principles* | *the socialist manifesto* **2** a socialist country or government has a political system based on socialism

**socialist²** *n* [C] someone who believes in socialism

**so·cia·lite** /ˈsəʊʃəl-aɪt‖ˈsoʊ-/ *n* [C] someone who is well known for going to many fashionable parties: *He's married to some rich Miami socialite.*

**so·cial·i·za·tion** /ˌsəʊʃəl-aɪˈzeɪʃən‖ˌsoʊʃələ-/ *n* [U] the process by which people, especially children, are made to behave in a way that is acceptable in their society: *the socialization of young offenders*

**so·cial·ize** also **-ise** *BrE* /ˈsəʊʃəl-aɪz‖ˈsoʊ-/ *v* **1** [I] to spend time with other people in a friendly way: [+ **with**] *I enjoy socializing with my students after class.* **2** [T] *technical* to train someone to behave in a way that is acceptable in the society they are living in

**socialized medi·cine** /ˌ··· ˈ··‖ˌ··· ˈ···/ *n* [U] *AmE* medical care provided by a government and paid for through taxes

**social sci·ence** /ˌ·· ˈ··/ *n* **1** [U] the study of people in society, which includes history, politics, ECONOMICS, SOCIOLOGY and ANTHROPOLOGY **2** [C] one of these subjects —compare NATURAL SCIENCE —**social scientist** *n* [C]

**social se·cu·ri·ty** /ˌ·· ·ˈ···/ *n* [U] **1** *BrE* government money that is paid to people who are unemployed, old, ill etc; WELFARE (3) *AmE*: **be on social security** (=be receiving money from the government) **2 Social Security** a system of insurance run by the American government, into which workers make regular payments, and which provides money when they are unable to work, especially because they are old —compare NATIONAL INSURANCE

**social serv·ice** /ˌ·· ˈ··‖ˈ·· ˌ··/ *n* **1** [C] a service that is necessary for society to work properly and is provided by the government or supported by government money: *Should the railways make a profit or should they be run as a social service?* **2 social services** [plural] *especially BrE* the special services provided by a government or local council to help people who have particular problems: *Cuts in social services have been widespread.*

**social stud·ies** /ˈ·· ˌ··/ *n* [plural] the study of people in society; SOCIAL SCIENCE

**social work** /ˈ·· ·/ *n* [U] work done by government or private organizations to improve bad social conditions and help people with particular social problems

**social work·er** /ˈ·· ˌ··/ *n* [C] someone who is employed in SOCIAL WORK

**so·ci·e·tal** /səˈsaɪətl/ *adj technical* related to a particular society: *societal attitudes*

**so·ci·e·ty** /səˈsaɪəti/ *n* S1 W1
1 ▶ **PEOPLE IN GENERAL** ◀ [U] people in general, considered in relation to the structure of laws, organizations etc that makes it possible for them to live together: *Society has a right to expect people to obey the law.* | **a danger to society** *He should be locked up; he's a danger to society!*
2 ▶ **A PARTICULAR GROUP** ◀ [C,U] a particular large group of people who share laws, organizations, customs etc: *Britain is a multi-racial society.* | *Drug abuse is one of the problems confronting modern Western society.* | **the consumer society** *Is greed a product of the consumer society?* | **the affluent society** *Shopaholics are a new problem, born of the affluent society.* | **polite society** (=people who think they have the highest standards of behaviour)
3 ▶ **CLUB** ◀ [C] an organization or a club with members who share similar interests, aims etc: *the university film society* | *the Law Society*
4 ▶ **UPPER CLASS** ◀ [U] the fashionable group of people who are rich and belong to the upper class: *a society wedding* | **high society** (=the richest, most fashionable etc people) | **be introduced into society** (=to begin to attend the fashionable events organized by this group)
5 ▶ **COMPANY** ◀ [U] *formal* the companionship of other people: *Jacob shunned the society of others, preferring to be alone.* —see also BUILDING SOCIETY, FRIENDLY SOCIETY

**socio-** /səʊsiəʊ, -siə, səʊʃiəʊ, -ʃiə‖soʊsioʊ, -siə, soʊʃioʊ, -ʃiə/ *prefix technical* **1** concerning society; social: *sociology* (=study of society) **2** social and: *sociopolitical*

**so·ci·o·ec·o·nom·ic** /ˌsəʊsiəʊekəˈnɒmɪk, ˌsəʊʃiəʊ-, -iːkə-‖ˌsoʊsioʊekəˈnɑː-, ˌsoʊʃioʊ-, -iːkə-/ *adj* based on a

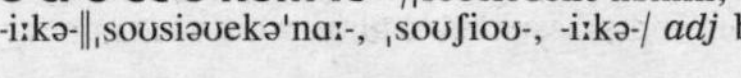

combination of social and economic conditions —**socio-economically** /-kli/ *adv*

**so·ci·ol·o·gy** /ˌsəʊsiˈɒlədʒi, ˌsəʊʃi-‖ˌsoʊsiˈɑːl-, ˌsoʊʃi-/ *n* [U] the scientific study of societies and the behaviour of people in groups —compare ANTHROPOLOGY, ETHNOLOGY, SOCIAL SCIENCE —**sociologist** *n* [C] —**sociological** /ˌsəʊsiəˈlɒdʒɪkəl,ˌsəʊʃi-ʃ,soʊsiəˈlɑː-,ˌsoʊʃi-/ *adj*: *a sociological study of the working class* —**sociologically** /-kli/ *adv*

**so·ci·o·path** /ˈsəʊsiəˌpæθ,ˈsəʊʃi-‖ˈsoʊ-/ *n* [C] *technical* someone whose behaviour towards other people is considered unacceptable, strange, and possibly dangerous —**sociopathic** /ˌsəʊsiəˈpæθɪk◂,ˌsəʊʃi-‖ˌsoʊ-/ *adj*

S3 **sock¹** /sɒk‖sɑːk/ *n* [C] **1** a piece of clothing made of soft material that you wear on your foot inside your shoe: *a pair of cotton socks* **2 give sb/sth a sock** *informal* to hit someone or something very hard, especially with your hand closed **3 pull your socks up** *BrE informal* to make an effort to improve your behaviour or your work: *If you don't pull your socks up, you'll fail the exam.* **4 put a sock in it** *BrE informal* used to tell someone in a joking way to stop talking **5 knock sb's socks off** *AmE informal* to surprise someone very much: *When I saw all the people there, it knocked my socks off!*

**sock²** *v* [T] **1** *informal* to hit someone very hard: *He socked the intruder on the jaw.* **2 sock it to sb** *old-fashioned* to tell someone something in a direct and forceful way: *Go on, sock it to him!*

**sock in** *phr v* [T] *AmE* **be socked in** if an airport, road, or area is socked in, it is very difficult to see far because of bad fog, snow, or rain

**sock·e·roo** /ˌsɒkəˈruː‖ˌsɑːk-/ *n* [singular] *AmE informal* something that is very successful and impressive: *That was one sockeroo of a firework show!*

**sock·et** /ˈsɒkɪt‖ˈsɑː-/ *n* [C] **1** a piece of plastic with holes in it, which is fixed into a wall and which you can connect electrical equipment to: *Don't let the baby stick her fingers in the socket.* **2** a hollow part of a structure into which something fits: *Kendrick grabbed my arm, nearly pulling it out of its socket.*

**sock·ing** /ˈsɒkɪŋ‖ˈsɑː-/ *adv* **socking great** *BrE spoken* extremely big: *a socking great hole in the floor*

**sock·o** /ˈsɒkəʊ‖ˈsɑːkoʊ/ *adj AmE informal* very impressive or strong

**sod¹** /sɒd‖sɑːd/ *n* **1** [C] *BrE informal* an impolite word meaning a stupid or annoying person, especially a man: *Get up, you lazy sod!* **2 be a sod** *BrE informal* an impolite expression meaning to be very difficult: *That door's a sod to open.* **3 poor sod** *BrE spoken* an impolite expression meaning someone you feel sorry for, or have no respect for: *The poor sod's wife left him.* **4** [C,U] a piece of earth or the layer of earth with grass and roots growing in it

**sod²** *v* [T only in imperative or infinitive] *BrE spoken* **1 sod it/that** used to rudely express anger or great annoyance at something or someone: *Sod it, I've missed the train.* | *"He thinks you should apologize." "Well, sod that!"* **2** used to say rudely that something is not important: *Sod the job, I'm going home.* **3 sod off** used to tell someone rudely to go away: *Just tell him to sod off.*

**so·da** /ˈsəʊdə‖ˈsoʊ-/ *n* **1** [C,U] water containing bubbles (BUBBLE¹ (1)) of gas that is added to alcoholic drinks: *Do you want soda in your Scotch?* **2** [U] a sweet drink filled with gas: *a bottle of orange soda* **3** [C] *AmE* an ICE-CREAM SODA **4** [U] a compound of SODIUM in powder form that is used for cooking or cleaning: *baking soda*

**soda foun·tain** /ˈ·· ˌ··/ *n* [C] *AmE old-fashioned* a place in a shop at which drinks, ice cream etc are served

**sod all** /· ˈ·/ *n* [U] *BrE informal* an impolite expression meaning nothing at all: *I got sod all from the deal.*

**soda si·phon** /ˈ·· ˌ··/ *n* [C] a special type of bottle from which SODA WATER is forced out in a fast stream by gas pressure

**soda wa·ter** /ˈ·· ˌ··/ *n* [U] water with bubbles (BUBBLE¹ (1)) of gas in it that is added to alcoholic drinks

**sod·den** /ˈsɒdn‖ˈsɑːdn/ *adj* very wet and heavy: *the sodden ground* | *sodden clothing*

**sod·ding** /ˈsɒdɪŋ‖ˈsɑː-/ *adj BrE informal* an impolite word used to emphasize that you are angry: *This sodding computer's crashed again!*

**so·di·um** /ˈsəʊdiəm‖ˈsoʊ-/ *n* [U] a silver-white metal that is an ELEMENT (=simple substance) and only exists naturally in combination with other substances

**sodium bi·car·bo·nate** /ˌ··· ·ˈ···/ *n* [U] a white powder used in baking to make cakes etc lighter

**sodium chlo·ride** /ˌ··· ˈ··/ *n* [U] *technical* salt

**sod·o·mite** /ˈsɒdəmaɪt‖ˈsɑː-/ *n* [C] *old use* a word meaning someone who practices sodomy

**sod·o·my** /ˈsɒdəmi‖ˈsɑː-/ *n* [U] *old use or law* a sexual act in which a man puts his sex organ into someone's ANUS, especially that of another man

**Sod's law** /ˌ· ˈ·/ *n* [U] *BrE humorous* the natural tendency for things to go wrong whenever possible: *It's Sod's law that the car breaks down when you need it most.*

**so·fa** /ˈsəʊfə‖ˈsoʊ-/ *n* [C] a comfortable seat with raised arms and a back, wide enough for two or three people; SETTEE

**sofa bed** /ˈ·· ·/ *n* [C] a sofa which can be changed into a bed

**soft** /sɒft‖sɒːft/ *adj* S2 W2

**1** ▶ **NOT HARD** ◀ **a)** not hard or firm, but easy to press: *a soft pillow* | *My feet sank into the soft ground.* | **get/go soft** *Cook the onions until they go soft.* **b)** less hard than average: *a soft lead pencil* | *a soft cheese*

**2** ▶ **NOT ROUGH** ◀ having a surface that is smooth and pleasant to touch: *a baby's soft skin* | *The fur was soft to the touch.*

**3** ▶ **NOT LOUD** ◀ a soft sound, voice, or music is quiet and pleasant to listen to: *a whisper so soft that I could hardly hear it* | *a soft accent*

**4** ▶ **NOT BRIGHT** ◀ [only before noun] soft colours or lights are pleasant and relaxing because they are not too bright: *Soft lighting creates a romantic atmosphere.* | *The room was a soft peach colour.*

**5** ▶ **VIOLENT** ◀ gentle and without much force: *a soft breeze*

**6** ▶ **TOO EASY** ◀ *informal* a soft job, life etc is too easy and does not involve much work or hard physical work: *Mike's landed himself a soft job in the stores.* | **soft option** (=a choice that allows you to avoid difficulties or hard work) *The computer course isn't a soft option – it's pretty tough.* | *If you agree, you're taking the soft option.*

**7** ▶ **NOT STRICT** ◀ someone who is soft seems weak because they are not strict enough with other people: *If you give way, the kids'll think you're soft.* | **be soft on** *No politician wants to seem soft on crime.* | **take a soft line** (=not be strict enough) *Courts have been taking too soft a line with young offenders* —opposite TOUGH

**8** ▶ **WATER** ◀ not containing much LIME¹ (3) so that it forms bubbles (BUBBLE¹ (1)) from soap easily

**9** ▶ **PHYSICAL CONDITION** ◀ *informal* having a body that is not in a strong physical condition, because you do not do enough exercise: *He'd got soft after all those years in a desk job.*

**10 have a soft spot for** to be fond of someone even when they do not behave well: *She's always had a soft spot for Grant.*

**11 a soft touch** *informal* someone from whom you can easily get money, because they are kind or easy to deceive: *The children regard their aunt as a bit of a soft touch.*

**12** ▶ **STUPID** ◀ *BrE* stupid or silly: *You must be soft if you think I'll give you fifty quid!*

**13 soft in the head** *old-fashioned* very stupid or crazy

**14 be soft on** *old-fashioned* to be sexually attracted to someone —**softly** *adv*: *She stroked his head softly.* | *Music played softly in the background.* —**softness** *n* [U]

**soft·ball** /ˈsɒftbɔːl‖ˈsɒːftbɒːl/ *n* **1** [U] a game similar to BASEBALL but played on a smaller field with a slightly larger and softer ball **2** [C] a special ball used to play this game

**soft-boiled** /ˌ· ˈ·◂/ *adj* an egg that is soft-boiled is boiled long enough for the white part to become solid, but not the yellow part in the centre —compare HARD-BOILED

**soft cop·y** /ˈ· ˌ··/ *n* [U] *technical* information stored in a computer's memory or shown on a SCREEN [1] (1) rather than printed on paper —compare HARD COPY

**soft cur·ren·cy** /ˌ· ˈ···/ *n* [C,U] money of a particular country that may fall in value and is difficult to exchange for the money of a country that is economically stronger

**soft drink** /ˈ· ·/ *n* [C] a cold drink that does not contain alcohol

**soft drug** /ˌ· ˈ·/ *n* [C] an illegal drug such MARIJUANA that is not considered to be harmful

**soft·en** /ˈsɒfən‖ˈsɔː-/ *v* [I,T] **1** to become softer or make something softer: *Choose a good moisturizer to soften and protect your skin | Cook until the onion has softened.* **2** if your attitude softens, or if something softens it, it becomes less strict and more sympathetic: *The British position on textile imports is softening. | Local police have softened their attitude towards young people who live on the streets* **3 soften the blow/impact etc** to make the effect of something less severe: *The minister may try to soften the blow of pay freezes by announcing a cut in interest rates.* **4** if your expression or voice softens, or if something softens it, you look or sound kinder and more gentle: *His voice softened when he spoke to her.* —opposite HARDEN (2)

**soften** sb/sth ↔ **up** *phr v* [T] **1** *informal* to be nice to someone before you ask them to do something so that they will be ready to help you: *You'll have to soften Alison up before you ask to borrow her car.* **2** to make an enemy's defences weaker so that they will be easier to attack, especially by bombing them

**soft·en·er** /ˈsɒfənə‖ˈsɔːfənər/ *n* [C] a substance that you add to water to make clothes feel soft after washing: *a fabric softener* —see also WATER SOFTENER

**soft fo·cus** /ˌ· ˈ··◂/ *n* [U] the arrangement of a photographic LENS (2) in a camera so that the edge of the object that is being photographed is not clear

**soft fruit** /ˌ· ˈ·/ *n* [C,U] *especially BrE* small fruit that you can eat that has no hard skin: *Strawberries and raspberries are soft fruit.*

**soft fur·nish·ings** /ˌ· ˈ···/ *n* [plural] *BrE* things such as curtains, chair covers etc that are made of cloth and are used in decorating a room

**soft·heart·ed** /ˌsɒftˈhɑːtɪ̈d◂‖ˌsɔːftˈhɑːr-/ *adj* easily affected by feelings of pity or sympathy for other people: *Paul's really kind and softhearted.*

**soft·ie** /ˈsɒfti‖ˈsɔːf-/ *n* [C] another spelling of SOFTY

**soft land·ing** /ˌ· ˈ··/ *n* [C] a situation in which a SPACECRAFT comes down onto the ground gently and without any damage

**softly-softly** /ˌ·· ˈ··/ *adj BrE* **softly-softly approach** a way of dealing with something or someone which involves being very patient and careful: *I think we need to adopt a softly-softly approach with Mike.*

**softly-spok·en** /ˌ·· ˈ··/ *adj* another form of the word SOFT-SPOKEN

**soft pal·ate** /ˌ· ˈ··/ *n* [C] the soft part of the back of the top of your mouth

**soft ped·al** /ˌ· ˈ··/ *v* [T] *informal* to make something seem less important or less urgent than it really is

**soft porn** /ˌ· ˈ·/ *n* [U] magazines, pictures etc that show sexual acts and images in a way that is intended to be sexually exciting, but which are not of the most offensive type —compare HARD PORN

**soft sell** /ˌ· ˈ·◂/ *n* [singular] a way of advertising or selling things that involves gently persuading people to buy something in a friendly and indirect way compare HARD SELL

**soft shoul·der** /ˌ· ˈ··/ *n* [C] ground at the edge of a road that is too soft to drive on — compare HARD SHOULDER

**soft-soap** /ˈ· ·/ *v* [T] *informal* to say nice things to someone in order to persuade them to do something, change their mind etc: *Don't think you can soft-soap me!* —**soft soap** *n* [U]

**soft-spok·en** /ˌ· ˈ··◂/ *adj* having a pleasant gentle voice

**soft toy** /ˌ· ˈ·/ *n* [C] *BrE* a toy for young children made of cloth and filled with soft material; STUFFED ANIMAL *AmE*

**soft·ware** /ˈsɒftweə‖ˈsɔːftwer/ *n* [U] the sets of PROGRAMS (=instructions) that you put into a computer when you want it to do particular jobs: *She loaded the new software. | word processing software* —compare HARDWARE (1) W2

**soft·wood** /ˈsɒftwʊd‖ˈsɔːft-/ *n* [C,U] wood from trees such as PINE [1] (2) and FIR that is cheap and easy to cut, or a tree with this type of wood —compare HARDWOOD

**soft·y, softie** /ˈsɒfti‖ˈsɔːfti/ *n* [C] *informal* someone who is too easily affected by feelings of pity or sympathy, or who is too easily persuaded: *He's a big softy.*

**sog·gy** /ˈsɒgi‖ˈsɑːgi/ *adj* unpleasantly wet and soft: *The ground was soggy from the rain. | The bottom of the pie has gone all soggy.* —**soggily** *adv* —**sogginess** *n* [U]

**soh** /səʊ‖soʊ/ *n* [singular,U] another spelling of SO[4]

**So·Ho** /ˈsəʊˌhəʊ‖ˈsoʊˌhoʊ/ *n* Small Office; Home Office; an expression referring to electronic office systems, including especially E-MAIL: *SoHo accounting software*

**soi·gné, soignée** *fem* /ˈswɑːnjeɪ‖swɑːnˈjeɪ/ *adj formal* dressed or arranged fashionably and with care: *a soignée divorcee in her forties*

**soil[1]** /sɔɪl/ *n* **1** [C,U] the top layer of the earth in which plants grow: *an area of rich soil | The bush grows well in a sandy soil.* —see LAND[1] (USAGE) **2 the soil** *literary* farming as a job or way of life: *They make their living from the soil.* **3 on British soil/French soil etc** *formal* in Britain, in France etc: *The crime was committed on American soil.* **4 sb's native soil** *literary* your own country —see also NIGHT SOIL W2

**soil[2]** *v* [T] **1** *formal* to make something dirty, especially with waste from your body **2 not soil your hands** to not do something because you consider it too dirty, unpleasant, or dishonest: *I wouldn't soil my hands with such a devious scheme.* —**soiled** *adj*: *soiled diapers*

**soi·ree, soirée** /ˈswɑːreɪ‖swɑːˈreɪ/ *n* [C] *old-fashioned* a formal evening party, often including a performance of music

**soj·ourn** /ˈsɒdʒɜːn‖ˈsoʊdʒɜːrn/ *n* [C] *literary* a short period of time that you stay in a place that is not you home: *a brief sojourn in Europe* —**sojourn** *v* [I]

**sol** /sɒl‖soʊl/ *n* [singular, U] SO[4]

**sol·ace[1]** /ˈsɒlɪ̈s‖ˈsɑː-/ *n* **1** [U] *formal* a feeling of emotional comfort at a time of great sadness or disappointment: **seek/find solace in** *After the death of her son, Val found solace in the church.* **2 be a solace to** to bring a feeling of comfort and calmness to someone, when they are sad or disappointed: *Mary was a great solace to me after Arthur died.*

**solace[2]** *v* [T] *literary* to give emotional comfort to someone; CONSOLE[1]

**so·lar** /ˈsəʊlə‖ˈsoʊlər/ *adj* **1** connected with the sun **2** using the power of the sun's light and heat: *solar energy*

**solar cell** /ˌ·· ˈ·/ *n* [C] a piece of equipment for producing electric power from sunlight

**so·lar·i·um** /səʊˈleəriəm‖soʊˈler-/ *n* [C] **1** a place with SUNBEDS (=beds with special lamps) where you can get an artificial SUNTAN: *The hotel has a solarium and sauna.* **2** a room, usually enclosed by glass, where you can sit in bright sunlight

**solar pan·el** /ˌ·· ˈ··/ *n* [C] a piece of equipment, usually on a roof, that uses the heat of the sun to heat water or to make electricity

**solar plex·us** /ˌsəʊlə ˈpleksəs‖ˌsoʊlər-/ *n* [singular] *not technical* the front part of your body below your chest

**solar system**

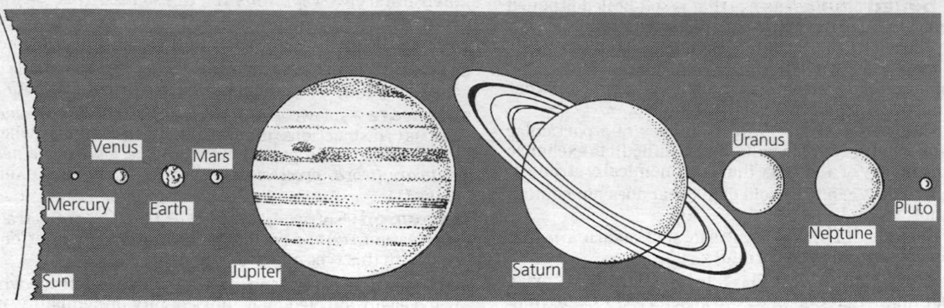


**solar sys·tem** /ˈ·· ˌ··/ *n* **1 the solar system** the sun and the PLANETS that go around it **2** [C] this kind of system around another star

**solar year** /ˌ·· ˈ·/ *n* the period of time which the Earth travels around the Sun, equal to just over 365 days

**sold** /səʊld‖soʊld/ the past tense and past participle of SELL

**sol·der¹** /ˈsɒldə, ˈsəʊl-‖ˈsɑːdər/ *n* [U] a soft metal, usually a mixture of lead and tin, which can be melted and used to join two metal sufaces, wires etc

**solder²** *v* [T] to join or repair metal surfaces with solder

**soldering i·ron** /ˈ··· ˌ··/ *n* [C] a tool which is heated, usually by electricity, for melting and putting on solder

S2 W2 **sol·dier¹** /ˈsəʊldʒə‖ˈsoʊldʒər/ *n* [C] a member of the army of a country, especially someone who is not an officer

**soldier²** *v*

**soldier on** *phr v* [I] *especially BrE* to continue working in spite of difficulties: *He doesn't like the job, but he'll soldier on until they can find a replacement.*

**sol·dier·ing** /ˈsəʊldʒərɪŋ‖ˈsoʊl-/ *n* [U] the life or job of a soldier

**sol·dier·ly** /ˈsəʊldʒəli‖ˈsoʊldʒərli/ *adj* typical of a good soldier

**soldier of for·tune** /ˌ··· ˌ· ˈ··/ *n* [C] *literary* someone who works as a soldier for anyone who will pay him; MERCENARY

**sol·dier·y** /ˈsəʊldʒəri‖ˈsoʊl-/ *n* [singular, U] *literary* a group of soldiers of a particular, usually bad, kind

**sold-out** /· ˈ·◂/ *adj* a concert, performance etc that is sold-out has no more tickets left

W3 **sole¹** /səʊl‖soʊl/ *adj* [only before noun] **1** the sole person, thing etc is the only one: *the sole American in the room* **2** a sole duty, right, responsibility etc is one that is not shared with anyone else: *Derek has sole responsibility for sales in Eire.*

**sole²** *n* **1** [C] the bottom surface of your foot, especially the part you walk or stand on: *The soles of his feet were caked in mud.* —see picture at FOOT¹ **2** [C] flat bottom part of a shoe, not including the heel —see picture at SHOE¹ **3 thick-soled/leather-soled etc** having soles that are thick, made of leather etc **4** [C,U] a flat fish that is often used for food —see also LEMON SOLE

**sole³** *v* [T usually passive] to put a new sole on a shoe

**so·le·cis·m** /ˈsɒlɪsɪzəm‖ˈsɑː-/ *n* [C] *formal* **1** something that is different from what is considered polite behaviour: *a social solecism* **2** a mistake in grammar

**sole·ly** /ˈsəʊl-li‖ˈsoʊl-/ *adv* not involving anything or anyone else; only: *Scholarships are given solely on the basis of financial need.* | *I shall hold you solely responsible for anything that goes wrong.*

**sol·emn** /ˈsɒləm‖ˈsɑː-/ *adj* **1** very serious in behaviour or style: *a solemn expression* | *solemn music* **2 solemn promise/pledge/word etc** a promise that is made very seriously and with no intention of breaking it: *I'll never be unfaithful again. I give you my solemn word.* **3** a solemn ceremony is performed in a very serious way —**solemnly** *adv* —**solemness** *n* [U]

**so·lem·ni·ty** /səˈlemnɪti/ *n* **1** [U] the quality of being serious in behaviour or manner: *the solemnity of a great religious occasion* **2 solemnities** [plural] the ceremonies of an important and serious occasion: *He was buried with all the solemnities befitting a monarch.*

**sol·em·nize** also **-ise** *BrE* /ˈsɒləmnaɪz‖ˈsɑː-/ *v* **solemnize a marriage** *formal* to perform a wedding ceremony in a church —**solemnization** /ˌsɒləmnaɪˈzeɪʃən‖ˌsɑːləmnə-/ *n* [U]

**sol-fa** /ˌsɒl ˈfɑː‖ˌsoʊl-/ *n* [U] the system in which the notes of the musical SCALE¹ (8) are represented by seven short words DO, RE, MI etc, used especially in singing

**so·li·cit** /səˈlɪsɪt/ *v* **1** [I] to offer to have sex with someone in exchange for money: *She was arrested for soliciting.* **2** [I,T] *formal* to ask someone for money, help, or information: **solicit sth from sb** *The governor sent two officials to Mexico City to solicit aid from the President.* **3** [T] *AmE* to sell something by taking orders for a product or service, usually by going to people's houses or businesses —**solicitation** /səˌlɪsɪˈteɪʃən/ *n* [C,U]

**so·lic·i·tor** /səˈlɪsɪtə‖-tər/ *n* [C] a type of lawyer in Britain who gives advice, does the necessary work when property is bought and sold, and defends people, especially in the lower courts of law —compare ADVOCATE² (2), BARRISTER —see LAWYER (USAGE) 

**so·lic·i·tor gen·e·ral** /·ˌ··· ˈ···/ *n* [C] the government law officer next in rank below the ATTORNEY GENERAL

**so·lic·i·tous** /səˈlɪsɪtəs/ *adj formal* anxiously caring about someone's safety, health, or comfort: [+ **of/for/about**] *Mary was always solicitous of my health.* —**solicitously** *adv* —**solicitousness** *n* [U]

**so·lic·i·tude** /səˈlɪsɪtjuːd‖-tuːd/ *n* [U + **for**] *formal* anxious and eager care for someone's health, safety etc

**sol·id¹** /ˈsɒlɪd‖ˈsɑː-/ *adj* 

**1 ▶ FIRM/HARD ◀** having a firm shape, and usually hard: *Even the milk was frozen solid.* | *After wading through the marshes we were glad to be on solid ground.* | **solid food(s)** *The baby isn't old enough to eat solid foods yet.*

**2 ▶ STRONGLY MADE ◀** strong and well made: *good, solid furniture* | **as solid as a rock** (=very solid) *The frame looks quite flimsy, but in fact it's as solid as a rock.*

**3 ▶ VALUABLE WORK ◀** well done and of real practical value: *five years of solid achievement* | *a good solid education*

**4 ▶ DEFINITE FACTS ◀** [only before noun] based on real facts; definite: *We need some solid evidence to prove our case.*

**5 solid basis/foundation** a strong principle on which

something is based: *Our relationship is built on a solid foundation of mutual trust.*
**6 ▶HONEST AND RESPECTED◀** respected because you are honest and people can depend on you to behave well: *a respectable solid citizen | a firm with a solid reputation*
**7 solid gold/silver/oak etc** consisting completely of gold: *a solid gold cup*
**8 ▶NOT HOLLOW◀** having no holes or spaces inside: *a solid rubber ball | a shrine carved out of the solid rock* —see picture at HOLLOW[1]
**9 ▶LOYAL◀** giving loyal support that you can depend on: *a solid supporter of the Clinton administration*
**10 ▶CONTINUOUS◀** *informal* without any pauses: *The lecture lasted two solid hours.* | **five hours/two weeks solid** *On Saturday I went to bed and slept fourteen hours solid.*
**11 ▶CLOSE TOGETHER◀** very close together without any spaces in between: *The road was blocked by a solid mass of protesters.* | *a solid line of traffic stretching away into the distance*
**12 ▶GEOMETRY◀** *technical* having length, width, and height; THREE-DIMENSIONAL: *A sphere is a solid figure.*
**13 ▶IN AGREEMENT◀ be solid** *BrE* to be in complete agreement: *The workers are 100% solid on this issue.* | [+ **for/against**] *The members were solid against the idea.* —**solidly** *adv*: *solidly built* —**solidness** *n* [U]

**solid**[2] *n* **1** [C] a firm object or substance that has a fixed shape, unlike a gas or liquid: *Water changes from a liquid to a solid when it freezes.* **2 solids a)** [plural] food that is not liquid: *He's still too ill to eat solids* **b)** [C] *technical* the part of a liquid which has the qualities of a solid when it is separated from the SOLVENT[2]: *milk solids* **3** *technical* a shape which has length, width, and height

**sol·i·dar·i·ty** /ˌsɒlɪ̣ˈdærɪ̣ti‖ˌsɑː-/ *n* [U] loyalty and general agreement between all the people in a group, or between different groups because they all have a shared aim: *an appeal for workers' solidarity* | [+ **with**] *The rail workers will strike to show their solidarity with the miners.*

**solid fu·el** /ˌ·· ˈ··/ *n* [C] a solid substance such as coal that is burnt to produce heat or power

**so·lid·i·fy** /səˈlɪdɪ̣faɪ/ *v* **1** [I,T] to become solid or make something solid: *The volcanic lava solidifies as it cools.* **2** [T] to make an agreement, plan, attitude etc firmer and less likely to change: *The two countries signed a treaty to solidify their alliance.* —**solidification** /səˌlɪdɪ̣fɪ̣ˈkeɪʃən/ *n* [U]

**so·lid·i·ty** /səˈlɪdɪ̣ti/ *n* [U] **1** the strength or hardness of something: *the solidity of the stone walls* **2** the quality of something that is permanent and can be depended on: *the solidity and respectability of bourgeois institutions*

**solid-state** /ˌ·· ˈ·◂/ *adj* **1** a solid-state electrical system uses TRANSISTORS **2** solid-state PHYSICS is concerned with the qualities of solid substances, especially the way in which they CONDUCT[1] (3) electricity

**sol·i·dus** /ˈsɒlɪ̣dəs‖ˈsɑː-/ *n plural* **solidi** /-daɪ/ [C] an OBLIQUE[2]

**so·lil·o·quy** /səˈlɪləkwi/ *n* [C,U] a speech in a play in which a character talks to himself or herself so that the audience knows their thoughts —compare MONOLOGUE —**soliloquize** /-kwaɪz/ *v* [I]

**sol·ip·sis·m** /ˈsɒlɪ̣psɪzəm‖ˈsoʊ-, ˈsɑː-/ *n* [U] the idea that only the SELF exists or can be known

**sol·i·taire** /ˌsɒlɪ̣ˈteə‖ˌsɑːlɪ̣ˈter/ *n* **1** [C] a single jewel or a piece of jewellery with a single jewel in it, especially a large diamond **2** [U] a game played by one person with small wooden or plastic pieces on a board **3** [U] *AmE* a game of cards for one person; PATIENCE (4) *BrE*

**sol·i·ta·ry**[1] /ˈsɒlɪ̣təri‖ˈsɑːlɪ̣teri/ *adj* **1** [only before noun] a solitary person or thing is the only one you can see in a place: *a solitary tree in the middle of the field* **2** spending a lot of time alone, usually because they like being alone: *a solitary man who never spoke to anyone.* —see ALONE[1] (USAGE) **3** done or experienced without anyone else around: *a long, solitary walk across the moors* **4 not a solitary word/thing etc** if there is not a solitary thing or person, there is not even one: *He followed her round without a solitary word.* —**solitarily** *adv* —**solitariness** *n* [U]

**solitary**[2] *n* **1** [U] *informal* solitary confinement **2** [C] someone who lives completely alone; HERMIT

**solitary con·fine·ment** /ˌ···· ·ˈ··/ *n* [U] an additional punishment for a prisoner in which they are kept alone and are not allowed to see anyone else

**sol·i·tude** /ˈsɒlɪ̣tjuːd‖ˈsɑːlɪ̣tuːd/ *n* [U] the state of being alone especially when this is what you enjoy: *She wished for the solitude of her house on the lake.*

**so·lo**[1] /ˈsəʊləʊ‖ˈsoʊloʊ/ *adj* **1** done alone without anyone else helping you: *Ridgeway's solo voyage across the Atlantic* | **go solo** (=start doing something on your own) **2** related to or played as a musical solo: *a solo passage for viola* —**solo** *adv*: *When did you first fly solo?*

**solo**[2] *n plural* **solos** [C] **1** a piece of music for one performer —compare DUET **2** a job or performance that is done alone, especially an aircraft flight

**so·lo·ist** /ˈsəʊləʊɪ̣st‖ˈsoʊloʊ-/ *n* [C] a musician who performs a solo

**sol·stice** /ˈsɒlstɪ̣s‖ˈsɑːl-/ *n* [C] the time of either the longest or the shortest day of the year —compare EQUINOX

**sol·u·ble** /ˈsɒljʊ̈bəl‖ˈsɑː-/ *adj* **1** a soluble substance can be dissolved (DISSOLVE (1)) in a liquid: *soluble aspirin* **2** *formal* a problem that is soluble, can be solved —opposite INSOLUBLE —**solubility** /ˌsɒljʊ̈ˈbɪlɪ̣ti‖ˌsɑː-/ *n* [U]

**so·lu·tion** /səˈluːʃən/ *n* **1** [C] a way of solving a problem or dealing with a difficult situation: *The best solution would be for them to separate.* | [+ **to/for**] *There are no simple solutions to the problem of overpopulation.* | **find a solution** *Both sides are trying to find a peaceful solution.* **2** [C] the correct answer to a problem in an exercise or competition: [+ **to**] *The solution to last week's puzzle is on page 12.* **3** [C,U] a liquid mixed with a solid or gas, usually without a chemical change: *a weak sugar solution* 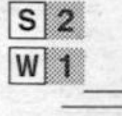

**solve** /sɒlv‖sɑːlv/ *v* [T] **1** to find or provide a way of dealing with a problem: *Charlie thinks money will solve all his problems.* **2** to find the correct answer to a problem or the explanation for something that is difficult to understand: *solving a mathematical equation* | **solve a crime/mystery/case** *The police haven't been able to solve the murder yet.* —**solvable** *adj* 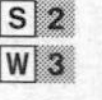

**sol·vent**[1] /ˈsɒlvənt‖ˈsɑːl-/ *adj* having enough money to pay your debts: *I have to wait until my paycheck arrives before I'm solvent again.* —opposite INSOLVENT —**solvency** *n* [U]

**solvent**[2] *n* [C,U] a liquid that is able to turn a solid substance into liquid

**solvent a·buse** /ˈ·· ·ˌ·/ *formal n* [U] the habit of breathing in gases from glues or similar substances in order to get a pleasant feeling; GLUE-SNIFFING

**som·bre** *BrE*, **somber** *AmE* /ˈsɒmbə‖ˈsɑːmbər/ *adj* **1** sad and serious; GRAVE[2] (1): *They sat in sombre silence.* | *a sombre expression* | *on the sombre occasion of his mother's funeral* **2** dark and without any bright colours: *a suit of sombre grey* —**sombrely** *adv* —**sombreness** *n* [U]

**som·bre·ro** /sɒmˈbreərəʊ‖sɑːmˈbreroʊ/ *n plural* **sombreros** [C] a Mexican hat for men that is tall with a wide, round BRIM[1] (1) turned up at the edges —see picture at HAT

**some**[1] /səm; *strong* sʌm/ *determiner* **1** a number of people or things or an amount of something, when the exact number or amount is not stated: *I need some apples for this recipe.* | *My mother has inherited some land in western Australia.* | *They're looking for someone with some experience.* | *The doctor gave her some medicine for her cough.* **2** a number of people or things or an amount of something but not all: *Some people believe in life after death.* | *She's been so depressed that some days she can't get out of bed in the morning.* **3** used to mean a person or thing, when you do not know or say exactly which: *There must be some reason for her behaviour.* | *Some women came up to me and told me we'd been to school together.* | *Can you give me some idea of the cost?* **4** a fairly large S1 W1 number of people or things or a fairly large amount of something: *Some days later I read that he had died.* | *It was some time before they managed to turn the alarm off.* | *The donation went some way towards paying for the damage.* **5 some friend/help! etc** *especially spoken* used, especially when you are annoyed, to mean someone has not been friendly, helpful etc: *"Surely you can have a day off soon?" "Some hope with this new boss!"* **6** used to say that something was very good or very impressive: *That was some party last night!* | *Some speech you made last night Tom!* **7 some...or other/another** *informal* used to show that you are not certain exactly which person, thing or place and do not think it matters: *Just give him some excuse or other.* | *I think he's staying with some friends or another in Wales.*

**some²** /sʌm/ *pron* **1** a number of people or things or an amount of something, when the exact number or amount is not stated: *I've made a pot of coffee. Would you like some?* | *"Do you know where the screws are?" "Yes, there are some in the garage."* | *People gave plenty of suggestions and we used some in the new show.* **2** a number of people or things or an amount of something but not all: *Some say it was an accident but I don't believe it.* | *Many of the exhibits were damaged in the fire and some were totally destroyed.* | [+ **of**] *Some of his jokes were very rude indeed.* **3 and then some** *informal especially AmE* and more: *"They say he earns $40,000." "Yes, and then some!"*

**some³** *adv* **1 some 10 people/50%/£100 etc** an expression meaning about 10 people, 50%, £100 etc: *She gained some 25 pounds in weight during pregnancy.* **2** *AmE* a fairly or a little: *"Are you feeling better today?" "Some, I guess."* **3 some little/some few** a fairly large number or amount of something: *We travelled some little way before noticing that Bradley wasn't with us.* **4 some more** an additional number or amount of something: *Would you like some more cake?*

**-some¹** /səm/ *suffix (in adjectives)* **1** causing or producing something: *a troublesome boy* (=who causes trouble) **2** liking to do something: *a quarrelsome woman* (=who likes to quarrel) | *frolicsome* **3** describes someone or something that can be treated in a particular way, or that you would like to treat in that way: *a cuddlesome baby* (=that you would like to hold in your arms)

**-some²** *suffix (in nouns)* a group of a particular number, especially in a game: *a golf foursome* (=four people playing GOLF together)

S1 W3 **some·bod·y¹** /ˈsʌmbɒdi, -bədi‖-bɑːdi, -bədi/ *pron* used to mean a person, when you do not know, or do not say who the person is: *There's somebody waiting to see you.* | *Somebody's car alarm kept me awake all night.* | **somebody new/different etc** *We need somebody neutral to sort this out.* | **somebody else** (=a different person) *If you can't make it, we can always invite somebody else.* | **or somebody** (=or someone similar) *"Who was at the door?" "It was a priest or somebody wanting to talk about religion."*

**somebody²** *n* **be somebody** to be or feel important: *She was the first teacher who'd made Paul feel like he was somebody.*

**some·day** /ˈsʌmdeɪ/ *adv* at an unknown time in the future especially a long time in the future: *Maybe someday I'll be rich!*

S2 W2 **some·how** /ˈsʌmhaʊ/ *adv* **1** in some way, or by some means, although you do not know how: *Don't worry, we'll get the money back somehow.* | **somehow or other** *Maybe we could glue it together somehow or other.* **2** for some reason that is not clear: *Somehow, I just don't think it'll work.*

S1 W1 **some·one¹** /ˈsʌmwʌn/ *pron* used to mean a person, when you do not know, or do not say, who the person is: *What would you do if someone tried to rob you in the street?* | *Will someone please explain what's going on.* | **someone new/different etc** *We'll make an appointment as soon as we find someone suitable.* | **someone else** (=a different person) *They noticed someone else in the water.* | **or someone** (=or someone similar) *You have to get a doctor or someone to sign as a witness.*

**someone²** *n* **be someone** to be or feel important

**some·place** /ˈsʌmpleɪs/ *adv especially AmE* somewhere: *I must have left my jacket someplace.*

**som·er·sault** /ˈsʌməsɔːlt‖-ərsɒːlt/ *n* [C] a movement in which someone rolls or jumps forwards or backwards so that their feet go over their head before they stand up again: **do/turn a somersault** *Lana turned a somersault in midair.* —**somersault** *v* [I]: *The car somersaulted twice before coming to a stop.*

**some·thing** /ˈsʌmθɪŋ/ *pron* [not usually in questions or negatives] S1 W1 **1** used to mean a particular thing when you do not know its name, do not know exactly what it is etc: *There's something in my eye.* | *Sarah said something about coming over later.* | **something new/old etc** *It's a good little car but I'm looking for something faster.* | **something else** (=something different) *The house was too small so they decided to look for something else.* —see SOME (USAGE) **2 there is something about** used to say that a person, situation etc has a quality or feature that you recognize but you cannot say exactly what it is: *There's something about America that I find really exciting.* | **there is something unusual/strange etc about** *There was always something a little sad about her.* **3 do something** to do something in order to deal with a problem or difficult situation: *Don't just stand there – do something!* | **do something about sth** *Can't you do something about that smell!* **4 it's (quite/really) something** used to say that something should be admired because it is impressive: *Running your own company at age 21 is really something!* **5 something like 100/two thousand etc** aproximately 100, two thousand etc: *Something like 80% of the population has no running water.* **6 something of a** used like 'rather' to emphasize the effect of something, the seriousness of something etc: *He has made something of a name for himself in the world of tennis.* **7 be something of a gardener/an expert etc** to know a lot about something or to be very good at something: *Charlie's always been something of an expert on architecture.* **8 have something of** to have a few of the same features or qualities that someone else has: *It was clear that Jenkins had inherited something of his father's brilliance.* **9 there's something in** used to admit that someone's words are true or their ideas are successful etc: *They had to concede that there was something in his teaching methods.* **10 have/be something to do with** to be connected with or related to a particular person or thing, but you are not sure in what way: *I don't know much about his work, but I know it's something to do with animals.* **11 thirty-something/forty-something etc** *especially humorous* used to say that someone is aged between 30 and 39, between 40 and 49 etc when you do not know exactly **12 a little something** a small or cheap gift: *I got you a little something from my holiday.*

Frequencies of the word **something** in spoken and written English.

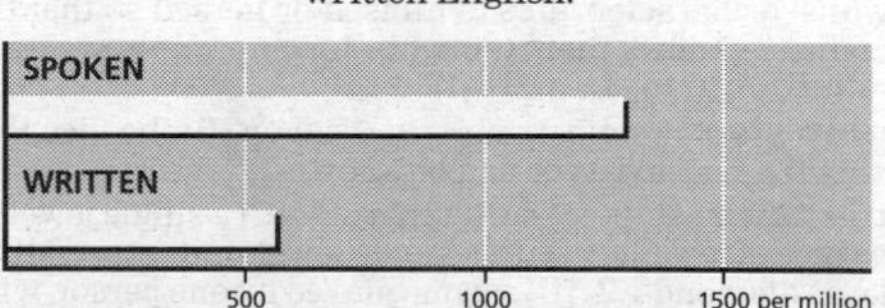


Based on the British National Corpus and the Longman Lancaster Corpus

This graph shows that the word **something** is much more common in spoken English than in written English. This is because it is used in a lot of common spoken phrases.

**something** (*pron*) **SPOKEN PHRASES**

**13 or something** used when you cannot remember or do not want to give another example of something you are mentioning: *Here's some money. Get yourself a* *sandwich or something.* | *Her name was Judith, or Julie or something.* **14 something like that** used when you cannot remember or do not want to say something exactly: *She works in sales or promotion, something like that.* **15 there's something wrong with** used to say that something is not working properly: *There's something wrong with my car so I had to get the bus.* **16 something to eat/drink** some food or a drink: *Would you like something to drink?* | *We had something to eat after the show.* **17 something to do** an activity or task: *If you're looking for something to do, why not clean up the kitchen?* **18 sixty something/John something etc** used when you cannot remember the rest of a number or name: *It cost over a hundred pounds. A hundred and twenty something it was.* **19 that's something** used to say that there is one thing that you should be glad about: *At least we have some money left. That's something, isn't it?*

**some·time**[1] /ˈsʌmtaɪm/ *adv* at a time in the future or in the past, although you do not know exactly when: *We'll take a vacation sometime in September.* | *Our house was built sometime around 1900.* —see picture at FREQUENCY

**sometime**[2] *adj* [only before noun] *formal* former: *Sir Richard Marsh, the sometime chairman of British Rail*

S1 W1 **some·times** /ˈsʌmtaɪmz/ *adv* on some occasions but not all: *Sometimes I stay late in the library after class.* —see picture at FREQUENCY

**some·way** /ˈsʌmweɪ/ *adv AmE informal* SOMEHOW (1)

S2 W2 **some·what** /ˈsʌmwɒt‖-wɑːt/ *adv* **1** more than a little but not very: *The price is somewhat higher than I expected.* **2 more than somewhat** *BrE formal* very much: *His behaviour displeased me more than somewhat.*

S1 W2 **some·where** /ˈsʌmweə‖-wer/ *adv* [not usually in questions or negatives] **1** in or to a place, but you do not say or know exactly where: *My car keys are around here somewhere.* | **somewhere to live/to sleep etc** *There must be somewhere to eat cheaply in this town.* | **somewhere safe/different etc** *Is there somewhere safe where I can leave my bike?* | **somewhere else** *Go and play somewhere else – I'm trying to work.* | **or somewhere** (=or a similar place) *We could hold the meal at Giorgio's or somewhere.* —see PLACE[1] (USAGE) **2 somewhere around/between etc** a little more or a little less than a particular number or amount; APPROXIMATELY: *We now have somewhere in the region of 500 firefighters in this area alone.* **3 be getting somewhere** to be making progress: *Well, that's a problem solved! At last I feel we're getting somewhere.*

**som·nam·bu·list** /sɒmˈnæmbjʊlɪst‖sɑːm-/ *n* [C] *formal* someone who walks while they are asleep —**somnambulism** /sɒmˈnæmbjʊlɪzəm‖sɑːm-/ *n* [U]

**som·no·lent** /ˈsɒmnələnt‖ˈsɑːm-/ *adj literary* **1** almost starting to sleep **2** making you want to sleep: *a somnolent summer's afternoon* —**somnolence** *n* [U]

S1 W1 **son** /sʌn/ *n* **1** [C] someone's male child: *Her son Sean was born in 1983.* | *They have three sons and a daughter.* —see also **like father like son** (FATHER[1] (7)) —see picture at FAMILY **2** [singular] used by an older person as a friendly way to address a boy or young man: *What's your name, son?* **3 the Son** Jesus Christ; the second member of the group that includes God the Father and the HOLY SPIRIT **4 my son** used by a priest to address a man or boy **5** [C usually plural] *literary* a man from a particular place or country, or a man who has a particular job: *sons of Britain who fell in battle* —see also **favourite son** (FAVOURITE[1] (2))

**so·nar** /ˈsəʊnɑː, -nə‖ˈsoʊnɑːr, -nər/ *n* [U] equipment on a ship or SUBMARINE that uses sound waves to find out the position of objects under the water

**so·na·ta** /səˈnɑːtə/ *n* [C] a piece of music with three or four parts that is written for a piano, or for a piano and another instrument

**son et lu·mi·ère** /ˌsɒn eɪ ˈluːmieə‖ˌsɑːn eɪ luːmˈjer/ *n* [singular, U] *especially BrE* a performance that tells the story of a historical place or event using lights and recorded sound

**song** /sɒŋ‖sɔːŋ/ *n* S2 W2

**1 ▶ MUSIC WITH WORDS ◀ a)** [C] a short piece of music with words for singing: *The students played guitars and sang folk songs.* | *a pop song on the radio* **b)** [U] songs in general: *He's doing research into popular song.* | **burst/break into song** (=suddenly start singing) *Patty must be in love – she keeps bursting into song!*

**2 ▶ BIRDS ◀** [C,U] the musical sounds made by birds: *the song of the lark*

**3 for a song** very cheaply: *He bought the house for a song five years ago.*

**4 a song and dance about a)** *BrE* if you make a song and dance about something you complain too much about it in a way that seems unnecessary: *There's no need to make such a song and dance about a little scratch on the car.* **b)** *AmE* a very complicated explanation or excuse for something you have done: *She gave us a long song and dance about why she hadn't sent the order on time.*

**song·bird** /ˈsɒŋbɜːd‖ˈsɔːŋbɜːrd/ *n* [C] a bird that can make musical sounds

**song·book** /ˈsɒŋbʊk‖ˈsɔːŋ-/ *n* [C] a book with the words and music of many songs

**song·ster** /ˈsɒŋstə‖ˈsɔːŋstər/ *n* [C] *literary* **1** someone who sings and sometimes writes songs **2** a songbird

**song·writ·er** /ˈsɒŋˌraɪtə‖ˈsɔːŋˌraɪtər/ *n* [C] someone who writes the words and usually the music of a song

**son·ic** /ˈsɒnɪk‖ˈsɑː-/ *adj technical* connected with sound, SOUND WAVES, or the speed of sound

**sonic boom** /ˌ·· ˈ·/ also **sonic bang** *BrE n* [C] the loud sound like an explosion, that an aircraft makes when it starts to travel faster that the speed of sound

**son-in-law** /ˈ· · ˌ·/ *n* [C] the husband of your daughter —compare DAUGHTER-IN-LAW —see picture at FAMILY

**son·net** /ˈsɒnɪt‖ˈsɑː-/ *n* [C] a poem with fourteen lines which RHYME with each other in a fixed pattern: *Shakespeare's sonnets*

**son·ny** /ˈsʌni/ *n* [singular] *old-fashioned spoken* used when speaking to a boy or young man who is much younger than you: *Now you just listen to me, sonny.*

**Sonny Jim** /ˌsʌni ˈdʒɪm/ *n BrE old-fashioned or humorous* used as a friendly way of speaking to someone, especially a man

**son of a bitch, sonofabitch** /ˌsʌnəvə ˈbɪtʃ/ *n spoken especially AmE* **1** [C] an impolite expression meaning a man or object that you are very angry or annoyed with: *That son of a bitch isn't going to get away with this!* **2 son of a bitch!** an impolite expression of annoyance: *Son of a bitch! The car won't start!* **3 be a son of a bitch** to be very difficult: *Getting the new tire on was a real son of a bitch.*

**son of a gun** /ˌ· · · ˈ·/ *n* [C] *AmE old-fashioned spoken* **1** a man that you are annoyed with: *That son of a gun didn't show up to fix the washer again today.* **2** *humorous* a man you like or admire: *John, you old son of a gun, where have you been?* **3** *humorous* an object that is difficult to deal with: *The sofa was huge, and we couldn't get the son of a gun to fit through the door!* **4 son of a gun!** used to express surprise

**Son of God** /ˌ· · ˈ·/ *n* [singular] used by Christians to mean Jesus Christ

**so·nor·ous** /ˈsɒnərəs, səˈnɔːrəs‖səˈnɔːrəs, ˈsɑːnərəs/ *adj* having a pleasantly deep loud sound: *a sonorous voice* —**sonorously** *adv* —**sonorousness** *n* [U]

**soon** /suːn/ *adv* **1** in a short time from now, or a short time after something else happens: *It will be dark soon.* | *David arrived back from Paris sooner than I expected.* | *They wanted to climb to the top, but they soon abandoned this idea.* | **[+ after]** *Paula was pregnant soon after their honeymoon.* | **how soon** (=how quickly) *How soon can you finish the report?* | **as soon as possible** (=as quickly as possible) *Try and get the car fixed as soon as possible.* | S1 W1

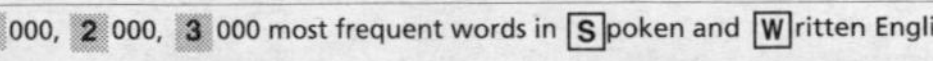

**as soon as you can** *I'll come over to your place as soon as I can.* | **all too soon** (=much sooner than you would like) *Children grow up all too soon.* | **the sooner the better** (=used to say that it is important that something should happen very soon) *The sooner you answer Jack's letter the better.* | **the sooner ... the sooner** (=used to say that if something happens soon, then something that you want will happen soon afterwards) *The sooner I get this work done, the sooner I can go home.* **2 as soon as** immediately after something has happened: *I came as soon as I heard the news.* **3 no sooner had ... than** used to say that something happened almost immediately after something else: *No sooner had he sat down than the phone rang.* **4 no sooner said than done** used to say that you will do something immediately **5 sooner or later** used to say that something is certain to happen at some in the future, though you cannot be sure exactly when: *She's bound to find out sooner or later.* **6 not a moment too soon/none too soon** almost too late, and when you thought that something was not going to happen in time: *"The doctor's here!" "And not a moment too soon!"* **7 would sooner do sth** if you would sooner do something, you would much prefer to do it, especially instead of something that seems unpleasant: *I'd sooner die than marry you!* **8 would (just) as soon** used to say that you would prefer to do something or would prefer something to happen: *I'd just as soon you didn't drive the car while I'm gone.*

**soot** /sʊt/ *n* [U] black powder that is produced when something is burnt: *There was a lot of soot up the chimney.* —**sooty** *adj*

**soothe** /suːð/ *v* [T] **1** to make someone feel calmer and less anxious, upset, or angry: *Rocking often soothes a crying baby.* **2** to make a pain less severe: *I bought some lozenges to soothe my sore throat.* —**soothing** *adj*: *gentle, soothing music* —**soothingly** *adv*

**sooth·say·er** /ˈsuːθˌseɪə‖-ər/ *n* [C] *old use* someone who is believed to be able to say what will happen in the future

**sop[1]** /sɒp‖sɑːp/ *n* [C usually singular] something not very important or valuable that you offer to someone to prevent them from complaining or getting angry about something: [+ **to**] *The company agreed to inspect the river regularly, as a sop to the environmental lobby.*

**sop[2]** *v* **sopped, sopping**

**sop** sth ↔ **up** *phr v* [T] to remove liquid from a surface by using a piece of cloth that takes the liquid into itself: *Jesse sopped up the spilled drink with a towel.*

**so·phis·ti·cate** /səˈfɪstɪ̡keɪt/ *n* [C] someone who is sophisticated

W3 **so·phis·ti·cat·ed** /səˈfɪstɪ̡keɪtɪ̡d/ *adj* **1** having a lot of experience of life, good judgment about socially important things such as art, fashion etc: *a play that will only appeal to a sophisticated audience* | *a suave, sophisticated Frenchman* **2** a sophisticated machine, system, method etc is very cleverly designed and very advanced and often works in a complicated way: **highly sophisticated** *highly sophisticated weapons systems* **3** having a lot of knowledge and experience of difficult or complicated subjects and therefore able to understand them well: *British voters today are much more sophisticated than they were in the 60's* —**sophistication** /səˌfɪstɪ̡ˈkeɪʃən/ *n* [U]: *social institutions that show a high level of sophistication*

**soph·ist·ry** /ˈsɒfɪ̡stri‖ˈsɑː-/ *n formal* **1** [U] the clever use of reasons or explanations that seem correct but are really false, in order to deceive people **2** [C] a reason or explanation used like this

**soph·o·more** /ˈsɒfəmɔː‖ˈsɑːfəmɔːr/ *n* [C] *AmE* someone who is in their second year of study at a college or HIGH SCHOOL

**soph·o·mor·ic** /ˌsɒfəˈmɒrɪk◂‖ˌsɑːfəˈmɔːrɪk◂, -ˈmɑː-/ *adj AmE formal* childish and not very sensible

**sop·o·rif·ic** /ˌsɒpəˈrɪfɪk‖ˌsɑː-◂/ *adj formal* making you feel ready to sleep: *His voice had an almost soporific effect.* —**soporifically** /-kli/ *adv*

**sopped** /sɒpt‖sɑːpt/ *adj AmE* very wet

**sop·ping** /ˈsɒpɪŋ‖ˈsɑː-/ also **sopping wet** /ˌ.. ˈ.◂/ *adj* very wet: *My shoes were sopping.*

**sop·py** /ˈsɒpi‖ˈsɑːpi/ *adj BrE informal* **1** expressing romantic feelings of love or sadness in a way that seems silly or weak; SAPPY (1) *AmE*: *a soppy film* **2 be soppy about** to be very fond of someone or something, in a way that seems silly to other people: *She's soppy about dogs.*

**so·pra·no** /səˈprɑːnəʊ‖-ˈprænoʊ/ *n* [C] **1** a woman, girl, or young boy whose singing voice is very high: *the famous soprano Kiri Te Kanawa* **2** a type of SAXOPHONE that can produce very high notes —**soprano** *adj, adv*: *She sings soprano.*

**sor·bet** /ˈsɔːbeɪ‖ˈsɔːrbɪ̡t/ *n* [C,U] a frozen sweet food made of fruit juice, sugar, and water; WATER ICE, SHERBET *AmE*

**sor·cer·er** /ˈsɔːsərə‖ˈsɔːrsərər/ *n* [C] a man who uses magic and receives help from evil spirits, especially in stories

**sor·cer·ess** /ˈsɔːsərɪ̡s‖ˈsɔːr-/ *n* [C] a woman who uses magic and receives help from evil spirits, especially in stories

**sor·cer·y** /ˈsɔːsəri‖ˈsɔːr-/ *n* [U] magic that uses the power of evil spirits: *a cult practicing sorcery and witchcraft*

**sor·did** /ˈsɔːdɪ̡d‖ˈsɔːr-/ *adj* **1** involving immoral or dishonest behaviour: *sordid political motives* | **sordid details** *She revealed all the sordid details of her affair with Pascal.* **2** very dirty and unpleasant; SQUALID (1): *a sordid little room at the top of the house*

**sore[1]** /sɔː‖sɔːr/ *adj* **1** a part of your body that is sore is painful and often red because of a wound or infection or because you have used a muscle too much: *My legs were really sore after aerobics last week.* | *a sore finger* | **a sore throat** *Val woke up with a sore throat and a temperature of 102°.* **2** [not before noun] *informal, especially AmE* upset, angry, and annoyed, especially because you have not been treated fairly: *He was still sore because I didn't call him back on Friday night.* | [+ **at/about**] *Don't be sore at me. I was going to tell you, I just forgot.* **3 a sore point/spot** something that is likely to make someone upset or angry when you talk about it: *His lack of education has always been a sore point with him.* **4** [only before noun] used to emphasize how serious, difficult etc something is: *Inner city schools are in sore need of extra funds.* —see also **be like a bear with a sore head** (BEAR[2] (4)), **a sight for sore eyes** (SIGHT[1] (11)), **stick out like a sore thumb** (STICK[1]) S3

**sore[2]** *n* [C] a painful, often red, place on your body caused by a wound or infection: *They were starving and covered with sores.* —see also COLD SORE, BEDSORE

**sore·head** /ˈsɔːhed‖ˈsɔːr-/ *n* [C] *AmE informal* someone who is unpleasant or angry in an unreasonable way

**sore·ly** /ˈsɔːli‖ˈsɔːrli/ *adv* very much or very seriously: **sorely tempted** (=extremely tempted) *I was sorely tempted to just walk away from him after his rudeness.*

**sor·ghum** /ˈsɔːgəm‖ˈsɔːr-/ *n* [U] a type of grain that is grown in tropical areas

**so·ror·i·ty** /səˈrɒrɪ̡ti‖səˈrɔː-/ *n* [C] a club for women students at an American university

**sor·rel** /ˈsɒrəl‖ˈsɔː-, ˈsɑː-/ *n* [U] a plant with leaves that taste sour that is used in cooking

**sor·row[1]** /ˈsɒrəʊ‖ˈsɑːroʊ, ˈsɔː-/ *n* **1** [U] a feeling of great sadness, usually because someone has died or because something terrible has happened to you: *He expressed his sorrow at my father's death.* **2** [C] an event or situation that makes you feel great sadness: *the family's joys and sorrows* **3 more in sorrow than in anger** in a way that shows you are sad or disappointed rather than angry about a particular situation —see also **drown your sorrows** (DROWN (4))

**sorrow[2]** *v* [I] *formal* to feel or express sorrow

**sor·row·ful** /ˈsɒrəʊfəl‖ˈsɑːroʊ-,ˈsɔː-/ *adj literary* very sad: *an old woman with a sorrowful expression* —**sorrowfully** *adv* —**sorrowfulness** *n* [U]

S1 W2 **sor·ry** /ˈsɒri‖ˈsɑːri, ˈsɔːri/ *adj*
**1 ▶ ASHAMED ◀** [not before noun] feeling ashamed or unhappy about something bad you have done: **be sorry about** *We're sorry about all the mess, Mom.* | **be sorry (that)** *Casey was sorry he'd gotten so angry at the kids over nothing.* | **say (you are) sorry** *Go say you are sorry to your sister for hitting her, Larry.* | **sorry for** *Tell Barbara you're sorry for pulling her hair.* | **say sorry** *especially BrE*: *Say sorry to your mother, Andrew.*
**2 be/feel sorry for** to feel pity or sympathy for someone because something bad has happened to them: **feel/be sorry for** *Tina was sorry for Pat; she seemed so lonely.* | *I've got no sympathy for him, but I feel sorry for his wife.* | **feel sorry for yourself** (=feel unhappy and pity yourself) *It's no good feeling sorry for yourself. It's all your own fault.*
**3 ▶ DISAPPOINTED ◀** [not before noun] feeling sad about a situation or about something you have done, and wishing you had not done it or the situation was different: *You'll be sorry if your father catches you!* | **be sorry (that)** *Brigid was always sorry she hadn't kept up her piano lessons.* | *I'm sorry you didn't enjoy the meal.* | **be sorry to do sth** *We were sorry to miss your concert.* | *I won't be sorry to leave this place.* | **be sorry to hear/learn/see** *I was sorry to hear about your accident.*
**4 ▶ VERY BAD ◀** [only before noun] very bad, especially in a way that makes you feel pity or disapproval: **sorry sight** *Milly was a sorry sight, dirty and dishevelled, by the time she got home.* | **sorry state of affairs** *It's a sorry state of affairs when a sick old lady has to wait three hours to see a doctor.*

Frequencies of the word **sorry** in spoken and written English.

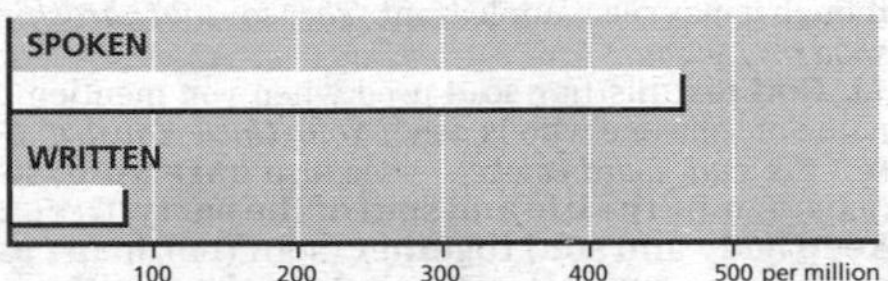

Based on the British National Corpus and the Longman Lancaster Corpus

This graph shows that the word **sorry** is much more common in spoken English than in written English. This is because it has special uses in spoken English and is used in some common spoken phrases.

**sorry** (*adj*) **SPOKEN USES AND PHRASES**

**5 sorry/I'm sorry a)** used to tell someone that you feel ashamed and unhappy about something bad you have done to them: *I'm sorry. I didn't mean to hurt you. Please forgive me.* | **[+ about]** *Sorry about that. I'll buy you a new one.* | **I'm sorry (that)** *I'm so sorry that I missed your birthday. I just completely forgot.* **b)** used as a polite way of excusing yourself in a social situation: *I'm sorry, did I step on your foot?* | *It's about ten miles, sorry, kilometres from here.* | **sorry (that)** *Sorry we're a bit late – we got lost.* | **sorry to do sth** *I'm sorry to bother you, but Ms. Duggan is on the line.* —see EXCUSE[1] (USAGE) **c)** used to politely disagree with someone: *I'm sorry, Alex, but you've got your figures wrong.*
**6 sorry?** *especially BrE* used to ask someone to repeat something that you have not heard properly; PARDON[1] (1): *Sorry? What was that again?* | *"Like a drink?" "Sorry?" "I said, would you like a drink?"*
**7 you'll be sorry** used to tell someone they will regret what they have done: *You'll be sorry when I tell your Dad about this.* | **you'll be sorry (that)** *One day you'll be sorry that you didn't study harder at school.*
**8 I'm sorry to say** used to say that you are disappointed that something has happened: *I wrote to them several times but they never replied, I'm sorry to say.*

S1 W1 **sort**[1] /sɔːt‖sɔːrt/ *n*
**1 ▶ TYPE ◀** [C] *especially BrE* a group or class of people, things etc that have similar qualities or features; type: **[+ of]** *What sort of shampoo do you use?* | **all sorts of** (=a lot of different types of things) *soup flavoured with all sorts of herbs* | **of this/that sort** *On expeditions of this sort you have to be prepared for trouble.* | **of some sort/some sort of** (=of an unknown type) *Her pupils were dilated as if she was on some sort of drug.* | **of one sort or another** (=of various sorts) *Violence of one sort or another is a fact of life in modern cities.* —see KIND[1] (USAGE)
**2 a sort of** *especially BrE* used when describing someone or something in a not very exact way: *The walls are a sort of greeny-blue colour.*
**3 of sorts/of a sort** used when something is of a particular type but is not a very good example of it: *I taught myself to type and got a job of sorts.*
**4 ▶ PERSON ◀** [singular] *BrE* someone who has a particular type of character, and is therefore likely to behave in a particular way: *Iain's never even looked at another woman. He's not the sort.* | **a good/bad sort** *old-fashioned*: *Jane's not a bad sort, she's just a bit careless.*
**5 out of sorts** feeling a little ill or upset: *Louise went back to work feeling rather out of sorts after their row.*
**6 ▶ COMPUTER ◀** [singular] if a computer does a sort, it puts things in a particular order —compare KIND[1]

Frequencies of the noun **sort** in spoken and written English.

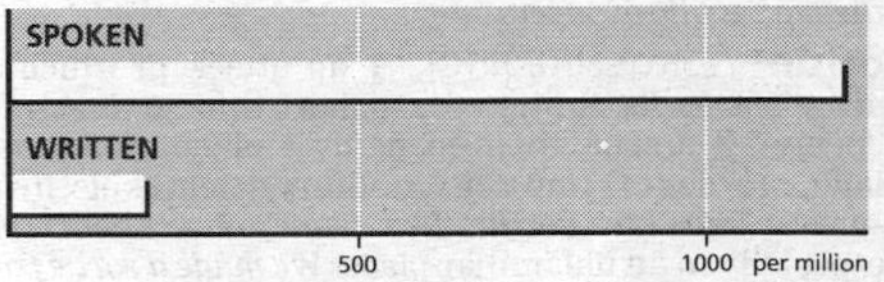

Based on the British National Corpus and the Longman Lancaster Corpus

This graph shows that the noun **sort** is much more common in spoken English than in written English. This is because it is used in a lot of common spoken phrases.

**sort** (*n*) **SPOKEN PHRASES**

**7 sort of a)** used to say that something is partly true but does not describe the exact situation: *I sort of like him, but I don't know why.* | *"Were you disappointed?" "Well, yes, sort of. But it didn't matter really."* **b)** *especially BrE* used when you are not sure you are using the best word to describe something: *Then they started sort of chanting, you know, like singing and shouting at the same time.* **c) sort of price/time/speed etc** *especially BrE* a price etc that is within a certain range: *What sort of time were you thinking of starting?* | *That's the sort of price I was looking for.*
**8 sort of thing** *especially BrE* used when you are not giving an exact description or list of something: *Just keep away from drink, drugs, that sort of thing.* | *We could just stay here and pass the time, sort of thing.*
**9 sort of like** *especially BrE* used when you are trying to describe something but cannot think of the exact words: *It was sort of like really strange and mysterious, walking round this empty building.*
**10 all sorts** *especially BrE* a lot of different types of things: *They play pop, rock, jazz, soul, all sorts in there.* | **[+ of]** *I like all sorts of food, I'm not fussy.*
**11 it takes all sorts (to make a world)** *BrE* used to say that you think someone is behaving in a strange or crazy way: *He goes climbing up cliffs without ropes or anything? Oh well, it takes all sorts.*
**12 what sort of...?** *especially BrE* used when you are angry about what someone has said or done: *What sort of time do you call this to come in?*
**13 nothing of the sort** *especially BrE* used to say angrily that something is not true or that someone should not do something: *"I'm going to watch T.V." "You'll do nothing of the sort."*

S1 **sort²** *v* **1** [T] to put things in a particular order or arrange them in groups according to size, rank, type etc: *The eggs are sorted according to size.* | **sort sth into** *The teacher sorted the children into teams.* **2 be sorted** *BrE spoken* if something such as a problem is sorted, you have dealt with it in a satisfactory way: **get sth sorted** (=repaired) *We need to get the washing machine sorted.* | **get yourself sorted** (=deal with all your problems)

**sort** sb/sth **out** *phr v* [T] **1** to organize something that is mixed up or untidy: *I must sort out my clothes for tomorrow.* **2** to separate something from a group: *I've sorted out the papers that can be thrown away.* **3 sort itself out** if something sorts itself out, it stops being a problem without you having to do anything: *Our financial problems should sort themselves out in a week or two.* **4** *especially BrE* to deal with problems: *There's been a mistake. I'll try to sort things out and call you back.* | **get sth sorted out** *I want to get everything sorted out before we leave.* | **sort yourself out** (=deal with all your problems and difficulties) *I'm staying with a friend until I manage to sort myself out.* **5** *BrE* to make someone stop doing something annoying or unpleasant, especially by punishing them: *If he bothers you again I'll soon sort him out.*

**sort through** sth *phr v* [T] to look for something among a lot of similar things, especially when you arrange these things into an order: *Vicky swiftly sorted through a pile of papers.*

**sor·tie¹** /ˈsɔːti‖ˈsɔːrti/ *n* [C] **1** an attack in which an army leaves its position for a short time to attack the enemy **2** a short flight made by a plane over enemy land, in order to bomb a city, military defences etc: *flying sorties into the Pacific war zone* **3** a short trip, especially to an unfamiliar place: *We made a sortie from our hotel to the open-air market.* **4** an attempt at doing something: *The article marked my first sortie into print.*

**sortie²** *v* [I] to make a short attack on an enemy's position or a flight over enemy land

**sorting of·fice** /ˈ·· ˌ··/ *n* [C] a place where letters and packages are put into groups according to where they have to be delivered

**sort-out** /ˈ· ·/ *n* [singular] *BrE informal* an act of tidying a room, desk etc and getting rid of the things you do not need: *These cupboards need a good sort out.*

**SOS** /ˌes əʊ ˈes‖-oʊ-/ *n* [singular] **1** used as a signal calling for help by a ship or a plane that is in danger **2** an urgent message that someone is in trouble and needs help: *This is an SOS for a Mr. Tucker, whose mother is seriously ill.* —compare MAYDAY

**so-so** /ˈ· ·/ *adj, adv spoken* neither very good nor very bad; average: *"How was the party?" "Oh, so-so."*

**sot** /sɒt‖sɑːt/ *n* [C] *old-fashioned* someone who is drunk all the time

**sot·tish** /ˈsɒtɪʃ‖ˈsɑː-/ *adj old-fashioned* stupid and often drunk —**sottishness** *n* [U]

**sot·to vo·ce** /ˌsɒtəʊ ˈvəʊtʃi‖ˌsɑːtəʊ ˈvoʊ-/ *adv formal* in a very quiet voice, so that other people cannot easily hear: *"No, it was Daniel," she continued, sotto voce.*

**sou** /suː/ *n* [singular] *BrE old-fashioned* a very small amount of money: *He didn't have a sou.*

**sou·bri·quet** /ˈsuːbrɪkeɪ/ *n* [C] another spelling of SOBRIQUET

**souf·flé** /ˈsuːfleɪ‖suːˈfleɪ/ *n* [C,U] a baked dish that is very light and is made with egg whites and often cheese or fruit

**sough** /sʌf, saʊ/ *v* [I] *literary* if the wind soughs, it makes a soft sound when passing through trees —**sough** *n* [U]

**sought** /sɔːt‖sɒːt/ the past tense and past participle of SEEK

**sought-af·ter** /ˈ· ˌ··/ *adj* wanted by a lot of people but rare or difficult to get: **much/highly sought-after** *Bryce became a much sought-after defense lawyer.*

**souk** /suːk/ *n* [C] a market in an Arab country

**soul** /səʊl‖soʊl/ *n* S3 W3

**1 ▶ SPIRIT ◀** [C] the SPIRITUAL part of a person that is believed to continue to exist after they die: *A prayer was said for the souls of those who had died in the accident.*

**2 ▶ INNER CHARACTER ◀** [singular] the part of a person that contains their true character, where their deepest thoughts and feelings come from: *Deep down in her soul she knew she could never marry him.*

**3 ▶ PERSON ◀** [C] a person: *Betty's a happy soul with a ready smile.* | **not a (living) soul** (=no one) *I won't tell a living soul.* | **not a soul to be seen** *There wasn't a soul to be seen in the park.* | **poor old soul** *The poor old soul had fallen and broken her hip.*

**4 ▶ POPULATION ◀ souls** [plural] *literary* people, considered as the population of a place: *a village with a population of 300 souls*

**5 ▶ SENSE OF BEAUTY ◀** [U] **a)** the ability to be emotionally affected by great art, music, or literature: *My brother doesn't appreciate poetry – he has no soul.* **b)** the quality of sincere human feelings that makes a painting, piece of music, performance etc attractive: *Her performance was technically perfect, but it lacked soul.*

**6 ▶ SPECIAL QUALITY ◀** [U] the special quality or part that gives something its true character: **[+ of]** *Basho's poems capture the true soul of old Japan.*

**7 be the soul of discretion etc** to always be extremely careful to keep secrets: *You can trust Leon, he's the very soul of discretion.*

**8 ▶ MUSIC ◀** [U] SOUL MUSIC

**9 bless my soul/upon my soul** *old-fashioned spoken* used to express surprise

**10 be good for the soul** *humorous* if something is good for the soul, it is good for you and you should do it, even though it may seem unpleasant: *They say that hardship is good for the soul.*

**11 God rest his/her soul** used when you mention the name of someone who is dead: *Your Uncle Edward, God rest his soul, loved cricket.* —see also **bare your soul** (BARE² (2)), **be the life and soul of the party** (LIFE (32)), **keep body and soul together** (BODY (14)), **heart and soul** (HEART (2)), **sell your soul (to the devil)** (SELL¹ (11)), SOUL MUSIC

**soul broth·er** /ˈ· ˌ··/ *n* [C] *AmE informal* an expression meaning a black man, used especially by young black people in the 1960s and 1970s

**soul-des·troy·ing** /ˈ· ·ˌ··/ *adj* something soul-destroying is extremely boring or makes you feel unhappy: *the soul-destroying monotony of routine jobs*

**soul food** /ˈ· ·/ *n* [U] *AmE* food that is typically cooked and eaten by black people in the Southern US

**soul·ful** /ˈsəʊlfəl‖ˈsoʊl-/ *adj* expressing deep, usually sad emotions: *a soulful look* —**soulfully** *adv* —**soulfulness** *n* [U]

**soul·less** /ˈsəʊl-ləs‖ˈsoʊl-/ *adj* lacking attractive qualities that make human beings happy: *a soulless city of grey concrete and steel* —**soullessly** *adv* —**soullessness** *n* [U]

**soul mate** /ˈ· ·/ *n* [C] someone you have a close relationship with because you share the same emotions and interests

**soul mu·sic** /ˈ· ˌ··/ *n* [U] a type of popular music that often expresses deep emotions, usually performed by black singers and musicians; SOUL (8)

**soul-search·ing** /ˈ· ˌ··/ *n* [U] careful examination of your thoughts and feelings because you are very worried about whether or not it is normally right to do something: *After much soul-searching, I decided to resign.*

**soul sis·ter** /ˈ· ˌ··/ *n* [C] *AmE informal* an expression meaning a black woman, used especially by young black people in the 1960s and 1970s

**sound¹** /saʊnd/ *n* S1 W1

**1 ▶ SENSATION ◀** [U] something that you hear, or what can be heard: *strange sounds coming from the next room* | **[+ of]** *the sound of voices* | **not make a sound**

(=keep quiet) *Don't make a sound, any of you!* | *Light travels faster than sound.* | *a vowel sound* —see NOISE[1] (USAGE)
**2 ► TV/RADIO ◄** [U] **a)** the sound produced by a television or radio broadcast, a film etc: *We apologize for the loss of sound during that report.* | *a sound engineer* **b)** the loudness of a television, radio, film etc: *Turn the sound down will you?*
**3 by the sound of it/things** judging from what you have heard or read about something: *By the sound of it, her problems are worse than we thought.*
**4 not like the sound of** to feel worried by something that you have heard or read: *I don't like the sound of this. How long has she been missing?*
**5 sounds** [plural] *BrE spoken* music, especially on a record, CASSETTE etc: *Have you got any sounds?*

S1 W2 **sound[2]** *v*
**1 ► SEEM ◄** [linking verb] if something or someone sounds good, bad, strange etc, that is how they seem to you when you hear or read about them: **sound like** *Serge's idea sounds like fun.* | **sound good/bad/awful etc** *Istanbul sounds really exciting.* | *Sue sounds a strange person.* | *£50 sounds about right.* | **it sounds as if/as though** *It sounds to me as if he needs professional help.*
**2 ► VOICE ◄** [linking verb] to seem to show a particular quality with your voice: **sound tired/cheerful/awful etc** *Josie didn't sound very keen when I spoke to her.* | **sound as if/as though** *You sound as if you've got a cold.*
**3 ► MAKE A NOISE ◄** [I,T] if something sounds or if you sound it, it makes a noise: *The bell sounded for dinner.* | **sound sth** *Sound your horn to warn other drivers.*
**4 sound the alarm** to warn people of danger
**5 ► PRONOUNCE ◄** [T usually passive] *technical* to make the sound of a letter in a word: *The 's' in 'island' is not sounded.*
**6 ► MEASURE DEPTH ◄** [T] *technical* to measure the depth of the sea, a lake etc —see also SOUNDINGS (2)
**sound off** *phr v* [I] **1** *informal* to express strong opinions about something especially when you are complaining angrily: **sound off about** *Philip's always sounding off about the environment.* **2** *AmE* if soldiers sound off they shout out their names to show that they are present
**sound** sb/sth ↔ **out** *phr v* [T] to talk to someone in order to find out what they think about a plan or idea: *I think I ought to sound him out about it before doing anything.* | *We'd like to sound out your ideas on the new project.*

W3 **sound[3]** *adj*
**1 ► WELL-JUDGED ◄** sensible and likely to produce the right results: **sound advice/judgement/reasons** *Ted'll always give you sound advice.* | *an environmentally sound policy* | *a sound investment* —opposite UNSOUND
**2 ► PERSON ◄** someone who is sound can be depended on to make good decisions and give good advice: *a sound person to have on a committee* | **[+ on]** *Brown is not altogether sound on matters of finance.* —opposite UNSOUND
**3 ► THOROUGH ◄** complete and thorough: *a sound knowledge of the European market*
**4 ► IN GOOD CONDITION ◄** in good condition and not damaged in any way: *The bodywork's sound but the engine needs replacing.* | **sound as a bell** (=in perfect condition)
**5 ► HEALTHY ◄** physically or mentally healthy: **sound as a bell** (=in perfect health) | **of sound mind** *law* (=not mentally ill) *Dorothy contested the will, saying that Mr. Palmer had not been of sound mind when it was drawn up.*
**6 ► SLEEP ◄** sound sleep is deep and peaceful: **sound sleeper** (=someone who always sleeps well)
**7 ► PUNISHMENT ◄** severe and thorough: *a sound beating* —**soundness** *n* [U]

**sound[4]** *adv* **sound asleep** deeply asleep

**sound bar·ri·er** /ˈ· ˌ···/ *n* **the sound barrier** the sudden increase in the pressure of air against an aircraft when it reaches the speed of sound: **break the sound barrier** (=go faster than the speed of sound) *Chuck Yeager flew the first jet to break the sound barrier.*

**sound bite** /ˈ· ·/ *n* [C] a very short part of a speech or statement, especially one made by a politician, that is broadcast on radio or television

**sound check** /ˈ· ·/ *n* [C] the process of checking that all the equipment needed for broadcasting or recording is working properly

**sound ef·fects** /ˈ· ·ˌ·/ *n* [plural] sounds produced artificially for a radio or television broadcast, a film etc

**sounding board** /ˈ·· ·/ *n* **1** [C] someone you discuss your ideas with in order to try them out: **[+ for]** *Ivan uses his secretary as a sounding board.* **2** [C] a board that is placed behind someone who is speaking to a large group of people so that they can be heard more easily

**sound·ings** /ˈsaʊndɪŋz/ *n* [plural] **1** careful or secret questions that you ask someone to find out what they think about something: **take soundings** *We're taking soundings to find out how people feel about the changes.* **2** measurements you make to find out how deep water is

**sound·less** /ˈsaʊndləs/ *adj* without any sound —**soundlessly** *adv*: *Theo crept soundlessly into the room.* —**soundlessness** *n* [U]

**soundly** /ˈsaʊndli/ *adv* **1** if you sleep soundly, you sleep deeply and peacefully: *The baby slept soundly all night.* **2 soundly beaten/whipped/defeated** completely defeated or severely punished: *The Green candidate was soundly beaten.*

**sound·proof[1]** /ˈsaʊndpruːf/ *adj* a soundproof wall, room etc is one that sound cannot pass through or into

**soundproof[2]** *v* [T] to make something soundproof

**sound sys·tem** /ˈ· ˌ··/ *n* [C] a very large STEREO system, especially one that includes the equipment a band needs to control its sound at a performance

**sound·track** /ˈsaʊndtræk/ *n* [C] **1** the recorded music from a film **2** the band near the edge of a piece of film where the sound is recorded

**sound wave** /ˈ· ·/ *n* [C] the form that sound takes when it travels

**soup[1]** /suːp/ *n* **1** liquid cooked food often containing small pieces of meat, fish, or vegetables: *chicken noodle soup* **2 be in the soup** *informal* to be in trouble: *If Dad catches you you'll be in the soup.* S3

**soup[2]** *v*
**soup** sth ↔ **up** *phr v* [T] *informal* to improve something by making it bigger, more attractive, or more exciting: *software programs to soup up the office E-mail*

**soup·çon** /ˈsuːpsɒn‖-sɑːn/ *n* [singular] *French, formal or humorous* a small amount of something: *It needs a soupçon more salt.*

**souped-up** /ˌ· ˈ·◂/ *adj* a souped-up car has been made more powerful, especially by adding special parts to the engine: *a souped-up Mustang*

**soup kitch·en** /ˈ· ˌ··/ *n* [C] a place where people with no money and no homes can get free food

**soup spoon** /ˈ· ·/ *n* [C] a round spoon that is used for eating soup —see picture at SPOON[1]

**sour[1]** /saʊə‖saʊr/ *adj* **1** having a sharp acid taste that stings your tongue, like the taste of a LEMON: *sour, tangy apples* | *Sprinkle a little sugar over the strawberries if they are sour.* —compare BITTER[1] (4), SWEET[1] (1) **2** milk or other food that is sour is not fresh and has an unpleasant taste because it has fermented (FERMENT[1]): **turn/go sour** (=become sour) *In warm weather, milk can go sour in just a few hours.* **3** unfriendly or looking bad-tempered: *Rob gave me a sour look.* | **sour-faced** *a sour-faced old man* **4 sour grapes** the attitude of someone who pretends to dislike something that they really want, because they cannot have it **5 turn/go sour** *informal* if a relationship or plan turns or goes sour, it becomes less enjoyable, pleasant, or satisfactory: *As time went by their marriage turned sour.* —**sourly** *adv* —**sourness** *n* [U]

**sour²** *v* [I,T] **1** if a relationship or someone's attitude sours, of if something sours it, it becomes unfriendly or unfavourable: *An unhappy childhood has soured her view of life.* **2** if milk sours or something sours it, it begins to have an unpleasant sharp taste

S2 W1 **source¹** /sɔːs‖sɔːrs/ *n* [C] **1** a thing, place, activity etc that you get something from: *They get their money from various sources.* | [+ **of**] *Milk is a very good source of calcium.* | *For me, music is a great source of enjoyment.* | **at source** *Is your pension taxed at source?* (=before it is paid to you) **2** the cause of something, especially a problem, or the place where it starts: [+ **of**] *We've found the source of the trouble – a faulty connection.* | *Two players have the same name, which has been the source of some confusion.* **3** a person, book, or document that supplies you with information: *List all your sources at the end of the essay.* | **reliable sources** *I've heard from reliable sources that the company is in trouble.* **4** the place where a stream or river starts

**source²** *v* [T] to find out where something can be obtained from

**source code** /ˈ· ·/ *n* [U] *technical* a computer PROGRAM¹ that can be read by someone who knows the language it is written in —compare MACHINE CODE

**sour cream** /ˌ· ˈ·/ *also* **soured cream** *BrE n* [U] cream which has been made sour by adding a kind of BACTERIA

**sour·dough** /ˈsaʊədəʊ‖ˈsaʊərdoʊ/ *n* [U] *AmE* uncooked DOUGH (=bread mixture) that is left to FERMENT¹ before being used to make bread: *sourdough bread*

**sour·puss** /ˈsaʊəpʊs‖ˈsaʊr-/ *n* [C] *humorous* a BAD-TEMPERED person, who always complains and is never satisfied

**sou·sa·phone** /ˈsuːzəfəʊn‖-foʊn/ *n* [C] a very large musical instrument made of metal, which you blow into, used especially in marching bands

**souse** /saʊs/ *v* [T] to put something in water or pour water over something, making it completely wet

**soused** /saʊst/ *adj* **1** soused fish has been preserved in water, salt, and VINEGAR: *soused herrings* **2** *informal* drunk: *He was so soused he couldn't even write his name.*

S1 W2 **south¹, South** /saʊθ/ written abbrevation **S** *n* [singular, U] **1** the direction that is at the bottom of a map of the world, below the EQUATOR, and is on the right of someone facing the rising sun: *I'm lost; which direction is South?* | **from/towards the south** *winds blowing from the south* | **to the south (of)** *Gatwick airport is a few miles to the south of London.* | **in the south** *A strange star appeared in the south.* **2** **the south** the southern part of a country: *There'll be showers in the south tomorrow.* | *the South of France* **3** **the South** the southern states of the US: *the cotton fields of the South*

**south²** *adj* [only before noun] **1** in the south or facing the south: *The south side of the building gets a lot of sun.* | *South America* **2** a south wind comes from the south

**south³** *adv* **1** towards the south: *The swallows fly south in the winter.* | *The garden faces south so it gets a lot of sun.* **2** **down south** *BrE informal* in or to the southern part of England: *We moved down south about five years ago.* **3** **go south** *AmE informal* if a situation, organization, or set of standards goes south, it becomes very bad although it was once very good: *Seems like all our moral standards have just gone south.*

**south·bound** /ˈsaʊθbaʊnd/ *adj* travelling or leading towards the south: *southbound traffic*

**south·east¹** /ˌsaʊθˈiːst◂/ *n* [U] **1** the direction that is exactly between south and east **2** **the southeast** the southeastern part of a country —**southeast** *adv*: *The road runs southeast.*

**southeast²** *adj* [only before noun] **1** a southeast wind comes from the southeast **2** in the southeast of a place: *the southeast quarter of the city*

**south·east·er** /ˌsaʊθˈiːstə‖-ər/ *n* [C] a strong wind or storm coming from the southeast

**south·east·er·ly** /ˌsaʊθˈiːstəli‖-ər-/ *adj* **1** towards or in the southeast: *Snow will spread to southeasterly regions tonight.* **2** a southeasterly wind comes from the southeast

**south·east·ern** /ˌsaʊθˈiːstən‖-ərn/ *adj* in or from the southeast part of a country

**south·east·ward** /ˌsaʊθˈiːstwəd‖-wərd/ *adj* going towards the southeast: *in a southeastward direction* —**southeastwards, southeastward** *adv*

**south·er·ly** /ˈsʌðəli‖-ər-/ *adj* **1** in the south or towards the south: *Tara walked in a southerly direction.* **2** a southerly wind comes from the south

**south·ern** /ˈsʌðən‖-ərn/ *adj* in or from the south part of the world or of a country: *southern Italy* | *the southern hemisphere* | *a strong southern accent* S2 W2

**South·ern·er** /ˈsʌðənə‖-ərnər/ *n* [C] someone who lives in or comes from the southern part of a country

**Southern Lights** /ˌ·· ˈ·/ *n* [plural] bands of coloured light in the night sky, seen in the most southern parts of the world

**south·ern·most** /ˈsʌðənməʊst‖-ərnmoʊst/ *adj* furthest south: *the southernmost tip of the island*

**south·paw** /ˈsaʊθpɔː‖-pɒː/ *n* [C] someone who uses their left hand more than their right hand, especially a PITCHER (3) in BASEBALL or a BOXER

**South Pole** /ˌ· ˈ·/ *n* **the South Pole** the most southern point on the Earth's surface, and the land around it —see also MAGNETIC POLE, NORTH POLE —see picture at EARTH¹

**south·ward** /ˈsaʊθwəd‖-wərd/ *adj* going towards the south: *the southward journey*

**south·wards** /ˈsaʊθwədz‖-wərdz/ also **southward** *adv* towards the south: *The ship sailed southwards.*

**south·west¹** /ˌsaʊθˈwest◂/ *n* [U] **1** the direction that is exactly between south and west **2** **the southwest** the southwestern part of a country —**southwest** *adv*: *We headed southwest.*

**southwest²** *adj* [only before noun] **1** a southwest wind comes from the southwest **2** in the southwest of a place: *down in the southwest corner of France*

**south·west·er** /ˌsaʊθˈwestə‖-ər/ also **sou'wester** *n* [C] a strong wind or storm from the southwest

**south·west·er·ly** /ˌsaʊθˈwestəli‖-ərli/ *adj* **1** towards or in the southwest **2** a southwesterly wind comes from the southwest

**south·west·ern** /ˌsaʊθˈwestən‖-ərn/ *adj* in or from the southwest part of a country

**south·west·ward** /ˌsaʊθˈwestwəd‖-wərd/ *adj* going towards the southwest: *in a southwestward direction* —**southwestwards, southwestward** *adv*

**sou·ve·nir** /ˌsuːvəˈnɪə, ˈsuːvənɪə‖-ɪər/ *n* [C] an object that you keep to remind yourself of a special occasion or a place you have visited: [+ **of**] *I bought a model of the Eiffel Tower as a souvenir of Paris.* | *a souvenir shop* | *a souvenir programme from the Gala Concert*

**sou'west·er** /saʊˈwestə‖-ər/ *n* [C] **1** a hat made of shiny material that keeps the rain off, with a wide piece at the back that covers your neck **2** a SOUTHWESTER

**sove·reign¹** /ˈsɒvrɪ̠n‖ˈsɑːv-/ *n* [C] **1** *formal* a king or queen **2** a former British gold coin worth £1

**sovereign²** *adj* **1** having the highest power in a country: *Most European monarchs no longer have sovereign control.* **2** a sovereign country or state is independent and governs itself: *The UN was designed as an association of sovereign states.* **3** **sovereign remedy** *old-fashioned* an excellent way of curing all kinds of illnesses and problems

**sove·reign·ty** /ˈsɒvrɪ̠nti‖ˈsɑːv-/ *n* [U] **1** complete freedom and power to govern: *the sovereignty of Parliament* **2** the power that an independent country has to govern itself

**So·vi·et** /ˈsəʊviət, ˈsɒ-‖ˈsoʊ-, ˈsɑː-/ *adj* from or connected with the former USSR (Soviet Union) or its people

**soviet** *n* [C] an elected council in a Communist country

**sow**[1] /səʊ‖soʊ/ *past tense* **sowed** *past participle* **sown** /səʊn‖soʊn/ *or* **sowed** *v* **1** [I,T] to plant or scatter seeds on a piece of ground: *Sow the seeds in late March.* | **sow sth with sth** *We're sowing the field with grass.* **2 sow the seeds of** to do something that will cause a bad situation in the future: *repressive policies that are sowing the seeds of future conflicts* —**sower** *n* [C]

**sow**[2] /saʊ/ *n* [C] a fully grown female pig —opposite BOAR

**sown** /səʊn‖soʊn/ the past participle of sow

**sox** /sɒks‖sɑːks/ *n* [plural] an American spelling of socks, used especially in advertising

**soy** /sɔɪ/ *also* **soy·a** /ˈsɔɪə/ *n* [U] soy beans

**soy bean** /ˈ· ·/ *also* **soya bean** /ˈ· · ·/ *n* [C] the bean of an Asian plant from which oil and food containing a lot of PROTEIN is produced

**soy sauce** /ˌ· ˈ·‖ˈ· ·/ *n* [U] a dark brown liquid that is used especially in Japanese and Chinese cooking

**soz·zled** /ˈsɒzəld‖ˈsɑː-/ *adj BrE humorous* drunk

**spa** /spɑː/ *n* [C] **1** a place that has a spring of mineral water that people believe makes you healthy: *the spas of Germany* **2** *AmE* a bath or pool that sends currents of hot water around you; JACUZZI

S1 W1 **space**[1] /speɪs/ *n*

**1 ► AMOUNT OF SPACE ◄** [U] the amount of an area, room, container etc that is empty or available to be used: *There's space for a table and two chairs.* | *How much space is there on each disk?* | **make space** *I'm trying to make space for all Tom's canoeing gear.* | **leave space** *Leave enough space for the suitcases.* | **closet/cupboard/office space** *There's plenty of closet space in our new apartment.* | **sense/feeling of space** (=the feeling that a room has plenty of space) *Mirrors give a sense of space.* —see PLACE[1] (USAGE)

**2 ► PIECE OF SPACE ◄** [C,U] an area, especially one used for a particular purpose: *a parking space* | *There was just an empty space where the book had been.* | **clear a space** *Lucy cleared a space on her desk for her new computer.*

**3 ► BETWEEN EARTH AND STARS ◄** [U] the area outside the Earth's air where the stars and PLANETS are: *space travel* | **outer space** (=far away in space) *creatures from outer space*

**4 ► ALL AROUND EVERYTHING ◄** [U] all of the space in which everything exists, and in which everything has a position or direction: *the exact point in space where two lines meet* | *beyond the dimensions of space and time*

**5 ► BETWEEN THINGS ◄** [C] an empty space between two things, or between two parts of something; GAP[1] (1): *The children hid in the space between the wall and the shed.*

**6 ► TIME ◄ a) in/during the space of** within a particular period of time: *Mandy had four children in the space of four years.* **b) a short space of time** a short period of time during which a lot of things happen: *It's amazing how well we knew each other after such a short space of time.*

**7 ► EMPTY LAND ◄** [C, U] land, or an area of land that has not been built on: **open space** *a pleasant town centre with plenty of open space* | **wide open spaces** *the wide open spaces of the prairies*

**8 ► IN WRITING ◄** [C] **a)** an empty space between written or printed words, lines etc **b)** the width of a typed letter of the alphabet: *The word 'the' takes up three spaces.* **c)** a place provided for you to write your name or other information on a document, piece of paper etc: *Please write any comments in the space provided.*

**9 ► IN A NEWSPAPER ◄** [U] the amount of space in a newspaper, magazine or book that is used for a particular subject: *Endless space has been devoted to Princess Di.*

**10 ► FREEDOM ◄** [U] the freedom to do what you want or do things on your own, especially in a relationship with someone else: *I've split up with Phil because I need more space.*

**11 look/stare into space** to look straight in front of you without looking at anything in particular, usually because you are thinking: *What's wrong with Jenny? She's just been staring into space all day.* —see also BREATHING SPACE

**space**[2] *v* also **space out** **1** [T always + adv/prep] to arrange objects or events so that they have equal spaces or periods of time between them: **space sth ↔ out/along etc** *Try to space out your classes and study in between.* | *Space the desks one metre apart.* | **be evenly spaced** (=with equal spaces) **2** also **space out** [I] *AmE informal* to stop paying attention and just look in front of you without thinking, especially because you are bored or because you have taken drugs: *I was so tired I just spaced out, completely unable to concentrate.* —see also SPACED OUT

**space-age** /ˈ· ·/ *adj informal* very modern: *This space-age device can remember up to 100 phone numbers.*

**space bar** /ˈ· ·/ *n* [C] the part at the bottom of a TYPEWRITER that you press to make a space

**space ca·det** /ˈ· ·ˌ·/ *n* [C] *informal* someone who forgets things, does not pay attention, and often behaves strangely: *I like her, but she's kind of a space cadet.*

**space cap·sule** /ˈ· ˌ··/ *n* [C] the part of a space vehicle that carries people into space to obtain information and then comes back to Earth

**space·craft** /ˈspeɪs-krɑːft‖-kræft/ *n* [C] a vehicle that is able to travel in space

**spaced out** /ˌ· ˈ·◄/ *adj informal* not fully conscious of what is happening around you, for example because you are extremely tired or because you have taken drugs: *JD looked spaced out, face flushed, hair in disarray.* —see also **space** (SPACE[2] (2))

**space heat·er** /ˈ· ˌ··/ *n* [C] a small machine for heating a room

**space·man** /ˈspeɪsmæn/ *n plural* **spacemen** /-men/ [C] **1** *informal* a man who travels into space; ASTRONAUT **2** someone in stories who visits the Earth from another world: *little green spacemen from Mars*

**space probe** /ˈ· ·/ *n* [C] a SPACECRAFT without people in it, that is sent into space to collect information about the conditions there and send it back to Earth: *a space probe investigating Jupiter*

**space·ship** /ˈspeɪsˌʃɪp/ *n* [C] a vehicle for carrying people through space, especially in stories

**space shut·tle** /ˈ· ˌ··/ *n* [C] a vehicle that is designed to go into space and back to Earth several times to do experiments and carry people

**space sta·tion** /ˈ· ˌ··/ *n* [C] a large SPACECRAFT that stays above the Earth and is a base for people travelling in space or for scientific tests: *Mir, the Soviet space station orbiting earth*

**space·suit** /ˈspeɪs-suːt, -sjuːt‖-suːt/ *n* [C] a special suit for wearing in space, that covers and protects your whole body and provides an air supply

**space-time con·tin·u·um** /ˌ· ˈ· ·ˌ···/ *n* [U] *technical* the universe considered as having four measurements: length, width, depth, and time

**space·walk** /ˈspeɪswɔːk‖-wɒːk/ *n* [C] the act of moving around outside a spacecraft while in space, or the time spent outside it

**space·wom·an** /ˈspeɪsˌwʊmən/ *n plural* **spacewomen** /-ˌwɪmɪn/ [C] *informal* a woman who travels into space; ASTRONAUT

**space·y** /ˈspeɪsi/ *adj informal* behaving as though you are not fully conscious of what is happening around you: *June is pretty spacey; I'd never let her take care of the kids.* —**spacey** *adv*: *Dan acts kind of spacey.*

**spac·ing** /ˈspeɪsɪŋ/ *n* [U] the amount of space between each printed letter, word, or line on a page: **single spacing** (=lines with no empty lines between them) | **double spacing** (=lines with one empty line between each one)

**spa·cious** /ˈspeɪʃəs/ *adj* a spacious house, room etc is large and has plenty of space to move around in: *a spacious, comfortably furnished living room* —**spaciously** *adv* —**spaciousness** *n* [U]

**spack·le** /ˈspækl/ *n* [U] *AmE* a substance used to fill holes in walls, that becomes very hard when it dries

**spade** /speɪd/ *n* **1** [C] a tool for digging that has a long handle and a broad metal blade you push into the ground **2** [C] a PLAYING CARD belonging to the set of cards that have one or more black shapes that look like pointed leaves printed on them: *the queen of spades* **3 call a spade a spade** to say exactly what you think is true, without trying to be polite **4 in spades** *informal especially Am E* to a much greater degree, or in a much greater amount, than you expected: *It may have been tough, but Ginny's effort was repaid in spades.* **5** [C] *old-fashioned* a very offensive word for a black person

**spade·work** /ˈspeɪd-wɜːk‖-wɜːrk/ *n* [U] hard work that has to be done in preparation before something can happen: *Credit must go to the researchers, who did a lot of the spadework.*

**spa·ghet·ti** /spəˈgeti/ *n* [U] a type of PASTA in very long thin pieces, that is cooked in boiling water —compare MACARONI, TAGLIATELLE, VERMICELLI —see picture at PASTA

**spaghetti west·ern** /ˌ·· ˈ··/ *n* [C] a film about American COWBOYS in the Wild West, especially one made in Europe by an Italian director

**spake** /speɪk/ *biblical or poetic* a past tense of SPEAK

**Spam** /spæm/ *n* [U] *trademark* a type of inexpensive CANNED meat made mainly of PORK

**spam** *v* [I,T] *technical* sending copies of the same information to many different groups on the INTERNET: *spamming the newsgroups*

**span¹** /spæn/ a past tense of SPIN

**span²** *n* [C] **1** the length of time over which someone's attention, life etc continues: *A four-year-old's concentration span is usually about 10 minutes.* **2** a period of time between two dates or events: *Over a span of ten years, the company has made great strides.* **3** the part of a bridge, ARCH¹ (1) etc that goes across from one support to another **4** the distance from one side of something to the other: *a bird with a large wing span*

**span³** *v* **spanned, spanning** [T] **1** to include all of a period of time: *a career spanning four decades* **2** to include all of a particular space or area: *The Mongol Empire spanned much of Central Asia.* **3** if a bridge spans an area of water it goes from one side to the other

**span·gle¹** /ˈspæŋgəl/ *v* [T] to cover something with shiny spots: **be spangled with** *His mackintosh was spangled with drops of rain.* —**spangled** also **spangly** *adj*: *acrobats in spangled tights*

**spangle²** *n* [C] a small piece of shiny metal or plastic sewn on to clothes to give them a shining effect; SEQUIN

**Spang·lish** /ˈspæŋglɪʃ/ *n* [U] *especially AmE* a mixture of the Spanish and English languages

**Span·iard** /ˈspænjəd‖-ərd/ *n* [C] a Spanish person

**span·iel** /ˈspænjəl/ *n* [C] a type of dog with long ears that hang down —see picture at DOG¹

**Span·ish¹** /ˈspænɪʃ/ *adj from or* connected with Spain

**Spanish²** *n* [U] the language of Spain and parts of South America

**Spanish fly** /ˌ·· ˈ·/ *n* [U] a substance made from dried insects, that is supposed to be an APHRODISIAC (=drug causing sexual excitement)

**Spanish ome·lette** /ˌ·· ˈ··/ *n* [C] a thick OMELETTE made with cooked vegetables

**spank** /spæŋk/ *v* [T] to hit a child, on their bottom with your open hand —compare SMACK¹ —**spanking, spank** *n* [C,U]: *If you don't stop that noise, you'll get a spanking.*

**spank·ing¹** /ˈspæŋkɪŋ/ *adj old-fashioned* **at a spanking pace/rate** very fast: *They started walking at a spanking rate.*

**spanking²** *adv old-fashioned* **spanking new/clean etc** very new, clean etc: *a spanking new car*

**span·ner** /ˈspænə‖-ər/ *n* [C] **1** *BrE* a metal tool that fits over a nut (NUT¹ (2)) and is used for turning it to make it tight or to undo it; WRENCH² (3) *AmE* —see also RING SPANNER —see picture at TOOL¹ **2 put/throw a spanner in the works** *BrE informal* to unexpectedly do something that prevents a plan or process from continuing or succeeding: *He won't lend us the money? Well, that really puts a spanner in the works.*

**spar¹** /spɑː‖spɑːr/ *v* **sparred, sparring** [I] **1** to practise BOXING with someone: *He once sparred with Mike Tyson.* **2** to argue with someone but not in an unpleasant way: *gentle sparring between the generations*

**spar²** *n* [C] a thick pole, especially one used on a ship to support sails or ropes —compare MAST (1)

**spare¹** /speə‖sper/ *adj* **S2**

**1 ► ADDITIONAL ◄ spare key/bulb/battery etc** a key etc that you have in addition to the ones you normally use, so that it is available if another is needed

**2 ► AVAILABLE ◄** not being used by anyone and available to be used: *Have you got any spare boxes?*

**3 spare time** time when you are not working: *What do you do in your spare time?*

**4 spare change** coins of little value that you do not need and can give to other people: *Do you have any spare change for the phone?*

**5 be going spare** *spoken* if something is going spare it is available for you to have or use: *I'll have some of that cake if it's going spare.*

**6 ► THIN ◄** *literary* tall and thin: *an old man with a spare wiry frame*

**7 go spare** *BrE informal* to become very angry or worried: *Dad would go spare if he knew I'd stayed out all night.*

**spare²** *v* [T] **S3**

**1 ► GIVE ◄** if you can spare something, you can give it to someone because you are not using it or do not need it: *I can't spare the time.* | *We're too busy to spare anyone to help you right now.* | **spare sb sth** *Could you spare me £5?*

**2 money/time to spare** if you have time, money etc to spare, there is some left in addition to what you have used or need: *We had an hour to spare so we looked round the shops.* | *They got there with seconds to spare.*

**3 spare sb trouble/difficulty/pain etc** to prevent someone from having to experience something difficult or unpleasant: *They did what they could to spare him any pain.*

**4 spare a thought for** to think about another person who is in a worse situation than they are: *Spare a thought for Nick, who's doing his exams while we lie in the sun.*

**5 spare no expense** to spend as much money as necessary to make something really good and not worry about the cost: *Janet's parents spared no expense on her wedding.*

**6 spare sb the details** to not tell someone all the details about something, because it is unpleasant or boring

**7 ► NOT DAMAGE OR HARM ◄** to not damage or harm someone or something even though other people or things are being damaged, killed or destroyed: *Only the children were spared.*

**8 spare sb's feelings** to avoid doing something that would upset someone: *We carefully avoided mentioning Cathy's break-up to spare her feelings.*

**9 spare sb's blushes** *BrE* to avoid doing something that would embarrass someone

**spare³** *n* **1** [C] an additional thing of a particular kind that you keep so that it is available: *If the fuse has gone, the spares are kept in the garage.* **2** [C] a SPARE TYRE (1) **3 spares** [plural] *BrE* new parts for vehicles or machines

**spare part** /ˌ· ˈ·/ *n* [C] a new part for a vehicle or machine, that is used to replace a part that is damaged or broken

**spare-part sur·ge·ry** /ˌ· · ˈ···/ *n* [U] *informal* an operation to put an artificial organ, or an organ from a dead person, into the body of a living person

**spare·ribs** /ˈspeəˌrɪbz‖ˈsper-/ *n* [plural] the ribs (RIB[1] (2)) of a pig and the meat on them served as a food

**spare room** /ˌ· ˈ·/ *n* [C] a bedroom in your house, that is kept for guests to use when they come to stay

**spare tyre** *BrE*, **spare tire** *AmE* /ˌ· ˈ·/ *n* [C] **1** an additional wheel with a tyre on it, that you keep in a car for use if another tyre gets damaged **2** *humorous* a large ring of fat around someone's waist

**spar·ing** /ˈspeərɪŋ‖ˈsper-/ *adj* using or giving only a little of something; FRUGAL: [+ **with**] *There's not much shampoo left, so be sparing with it.* | [+ **in**] *The critics were sparing in their praise.* —**sparingly** *adv*: *Apply the glue sparingly.*

**spark**[1] /spɑːk‖spɑːrk/ *n*
**1** ▶ **FIRE** ◀ [C] a very small bit of brightly burning material produced by a fire or by hitting or rubbing together two hard objects: *In a gas leak, any small spark will cause an explosion.* | *a shower of sparks from the fire*
**2** ▶ **ELECTRICITY** ◀ [C] a flash of light caused by electricity passing across a space
**3 spark of interest/excitement/anger etc** a small amount of a feeling or quality, that can be noticed in someone's expression or behaviour: *Meg's eyes lacked their usual spark of humour.*
**4** ▶ **INTELLIGENCE/ENERGY** ◀ [U] a quality of intelligence or energy that makes someone successful or fun to be with: *Ali has plenty of spark and wit.*
**5** ▶ **CAUSE** ◀ [C] a small action or event that quickly causes trouble or violence: *Hani's murder was the spark that started the riot.*
**6 sparks fly** if sparks fly between two people, they argue angrily: *Sparks were flying at the Conroy's last night!*

**spark**[2] *v* **1** also **spark off** [T] to be the cause of trouble or violence: *a minor incident that sparked off the conflict* **2** [T] to start someone's interest in something: *Going to an exhibition sparked Chris's interest in photography.* **3** [I] to produce sparks of fire or electricity **4** [I] *AmE old-fashioned* to pay special attention to someone you are sexually attracted to

**sparking plug** /ˈ·· ·/ *n* [C] *BrE* a SPARK PLUG

**spar·kle**[1] /ˈspɑːkəl‖ˈspɑːr-/ *v* [I] **1** to shine in small bright flashes: *The diamond ring sparkled in the sunlight.* **2** if someone's eyes sparkle, they shine brightly, especially because the person is happy or excited: [+ **with**] *Ron's eyes sparkled with excitement.* —see also SPARKLING

**sparkle**[2] *n* [C,U] **1** a bright shiny appearance, with tiny points of flashing light **2** a quality that makes something seem interesting and full of life: *The dialogue doesn't have much sparkle.*

**spar·kler** /ˈspɑːklə‖ˈspɑːrklər/ *n* [C] **1** a FIREWORK in the shape of a thin stick, that gives off sparks of fire as you hold it in your hand **2 sparklers** [plural] *informal* diamonds

**spark·ling** /ˈspɑːklɪŋ‖ˈspɑːr-/ *adj* **1** shining brightly with points of flashing light: *a sparkling lake* **2** a sparkling drink has bubbles (BUBBLE[1] (1)) of gas in it: *a sparkling wine* **3** full of life and intelligence: *sparkling wit*

**spark plug** /ˈ· ·/ *n* [C] *technical* a part in a car engine that produces an electric SPARK[1] (2) to make the petrol mixture start burning

**spark·y** /ˈspɑːki‖ˈspɑːr-/ *adj* full of life and energy: *a sparky debating partner*

**sparring match** /ˈ·· ·/ *n* [C] a friendly argument that is not serious

**sparring part·ner** /ˈ·· ˌ··/ *n* [C] **1** someone you practise BOXING with **2** someone you regularly have friendly arguments with

**spar·row** /ˈspærəʊ‖-roʊ/ *n* [C] a small brown bird, very common in many parts of the world

**sparse** /spɑːs‖spɑːrs/ *adj* existing only in small amounts: *sparse vegetation* | *Data on fatal accidents are sparse and difficult to obtain.* —**sparsely** *adv*: *a sparsely populated area* —**sparseness** *n* [U]

**spar·tan** /ˈspɑːtn‖-ɑːr-/ *adj* spartan conditions or ways of living are simple and without any comfort: *spartan accommodation* | *adjusting to the spartan life of boarding school*

**spas·m** /ˈspæzəm/ *n* [C] **1** a sharp pain when your muscles suddenly become tighter in an uncontrolled way **2 a spasm of grief/laughter/coughing** a sudden strong feeling or reaction that lasts for a short period

**spas·mod·ic** /spæzˈmɒdɪk‖-ˈmɑː-/ *adj* **1** happening for short irregular periods, not continuously: *spasmodic bursts of energy* **2** like or connected with a muscle spasm —**spasmodically** /-kli/ *adv*

**spas·tic** /ˈspæstɪk/ *adj* **1** *slang* an offensive word meaning stupid or lacking in skill, used especially by children **2** *old-fashioned* having CEREBRAL PALSY, a disease that prevents control of the muscles —**spastic** *n* [C]

**spat**[1] /spæt/ the past tense and past participle of SPIT

**spat**[2] *n* **1** [C] *informal* a short unimportant quarrel: *It's just your normal, average sibling spat.* **2** [plural] special pieces of cloth worn in former times by men above their shoes and fastened with buttons

**spate** /speɪt/ *n* **1 a spate of** a large number of similar unpleasant things that happen in a short period of time: *a spate of burglaries* **2 in spate** a river, stream etc that is in spate, is very full and flowing very fast

**spa·tial** /ˈspeɪʃəl/ *adj technical* concerning the position, size, shape etc of things —**spatially** *adv*

**spat·ter** /ˈspætə‖-ər/ *v* **1** [T] to scatter or throw small amounts of mud, dirt etc all over a surface: **spatter sb/sth with** *a passing car spattered with mud* | **spatter sth on/over etc** *Grey flicked his brush spattering paint over my shirt.* **2** [I] if liquid spatters on a surface, drops of it fall or are thrown on it: [+ **on**] *The first drops of rain spattered on the stones.* —**spatter** *n* [C]

**spat·u·la** /ˈspætjʊlə‖-tʃələ/ *n* [C] **1** a kitchen tool with a wide flat blade used for spreading, mixing, or lifting soft substances **2** *BrE* a small instrument with a flat surface, used by doctors to hold your tongue down so that they can examine your throat

**spawn**[1] /spɔːn‖spɒːn/ *v* **1** [I,T] if a fish or FROG spawns it produces eggs in large quantities together **2** [T] to make a series of things happen or start to exist: *the massive bureaucracy spawned by these programs*

**spawn**[2] *n* [U] the eggs of a fish, FROG etc laid together in a soft mass

**spay** /speɪ/ *v* [T] to remove part of the sex organs of a female animal so that it is not able to have babies

**speak** /spiːk/ *v past* **spoke** /spəʊk‖spoʊk/ *past participle* **spoken** /ˈspəʊkən‖ˈspoʊ-/ S1 W1
**1** ▶ **IN CONVERSATION** ◀ [I always + adv/prep] to talk to someone about something or have a conversation: **speak to sb about sth** *I intend to speak to the manager about the way I have been treated.* | *I know her by sight but not to speak to* (=not well enough to talk to her). | **speak with** *especially AmE*: *Sally would like to speak with you for a minute.* | **speak of** *formal*: *It was the first time she had ever spoken of marriage.* —see SAY[1] (USAGE)
**2** ▶ **SAY WORDS** ◀ [I] to use your voice to produce words: *I was so shocked I couldn't speak.* | [+ **to**] *John! Speak to me! Are you alright?*
**3** ▶ **A LANGUAGE** ◀ [T not in progressive] to be able to speak a particular language: *Do you speak English?* | **not speak a word of** (=not speak it at all) *He doesn't speak a word of French.* | **French-speaking/Italian-speaking etc** *a German-speaking secretary*
**4** ▶ **FORMAL SPEECH** ◀ [I] to make a formal speech: *Diana's been invited to speak at the annual conference.* | **speak in favour of/against** (=support or oppose) *Only one MP spoke against the bill.* —see also SPEAKER
**5 be not speaking/not be on speaking terms** if two people are not speaking they will not be polite or talk to each other, especially because they have quarrelled
**6** ▶ **EXPRESS IDEAS/OPINIONS** ◀ [T] to say something that expresses your ideas or opinions: *Not a word*

*was spoken about the whole affair.* | **speaking as a parent/teacher/democrat etc** *Speaking as a parent, I would like to see more discipline in schools.* | **speak well/badly/ill of** (=say good or bad things about someone) *It's wrong to speak ill of the dead.* | **speak highly of** (=praise someone) *I'm so pleased to meet you – my wife has always spoken very highly of you.* | **speak your mind** (=tell people exactly what you think, even if it offends them) *She's very direct, the kind of person who believes in speaking their mind.*

**7 generally/personally/technically speaking** used when you are expressing a general, personal etc opinion: *Generally speaking, rural schools provide a better environment for the students.*

**8 speak out of turn** to say something when you do not have the right or authority to say it: *I hope I haven't spoken out of turn – I didn't know it was supposed to be a secret.*

**9 none/nothing to speak of** not large or important enough to mention: *There's been no rain to speak of-only a few drops.*

**10 so to speak** used when you are saying something in words that do not have their usual meaning: *We all learned this theory, so to speak, at our mother's knee.*

**11 speak volumes** to express something very clearly, without using words: *Mary could not express the high hopes she had for her daughter, but her actions spoke volumes.*

**speak for** sb/sth *phr v* [T] **1** to express the feelings, thoughts, or beliefs of a person or group of people: *I think I speak for everyone here when I say we wish you all the best.* **2 speak for yourself** *spoken* used to tell someone that you do not have the same opinion as they do: *"We were all bored in that lecture." "Speak for yourself! I liked it."* **3 be spoken for** if something or someone is spoken for, it has already been promised to someone else: *The first 300 cars off the production line have already been spoken for.* **4 speak for itself/themselves** to show something so clearly that no explanation is necessary: *1994 has been a very good year for us – the figures speak for themselves.* —see also **actions speak louder than words** (ACTION (15)), **in a manner of speaking** (MANNER (4))

**speak of** sth *phr v* [T] *literary* to show clearly that something happened or that it exists: *The lush vegetation spoke of a richer, damper climate.*

**speak out** *phr v* [I] to publicly speak in protest about something, especially when protesting could be dangerous: [+ **about/against**] *Five students who had spoken out against the regime were arrested.*

**speak to** sb *phr v* [T] *informal* to talk to someone who has done something wrong, to tell them not to do it again: *Joe was late again today, you'll have to speak to him.*

**speak up** *phr v* [I] **1** used to ask someone to speak louder: *Speak up, please, I can't hear you.* **2** to express your opinion freely and clearly: *"Is that wise?" Isidore spoke up, gathering courage.* **3 speak up for** to speak in support of someone: *It's about time someone spoke up for single mothers.*

**USAGE NOTE: SPEAK**

WORD CHOICE: **speak, talk, discuss, describe, say**

**Speak** is a little formal and often gives the idea that one person is saying more than any others in a conversation: *He won't listen to me – will you speak to him?* | *Could you speak a little louder please?*

**Talk** is over twice as frequent in spoken English and usually suggests that two or more people are having a conversation: *We stayed up all night talking.* | *Are you two talking about me?*

If you **talk about** something with someone, for example, in order to reach a decision, you **discuss** it: *The boss wants to discuss next year's budget at the meeting.* You can **discuss** or **describe** something either in speech or in writing.

In British English **speak with** and **talk with** often mean a longer more formal talk than **speak to** or **talk to**, but in American English they are used more generally.

Compare **speak** a language and **speak in** a language: *Catherine may speak Greek* means either 'she may know Greek' or 'she knows Greek and may use it on this occasion': *'Catherine may speak in Greek'* means only the second of these.

GRAMMAR

When **speak** is transitive, its object is usually a language: *What's she speaking* (=what language)? | *I don't speak a word of Thai* (NOT *talk*). You **say** other things: *What's she saying?* (=what words?). Note that you say *I didn't say it/anything/those things* (NOT *speak it* etc). | *I gave my opinion* (NOT *spoke* my opinion). But you would sometimes say: *She spoke the truth* (=told the truth).

In writing **talk** is rarely transitive and can take only a few objects: *He's talking nonsense/business.* Otherwise you need to say **talk about**: *She talked about her childhood for a long time.* In informal spoken English, however, you will hear things like: *We're talking big bucks!* (=there is a lot of money involved in this situation) or: *They're talking cars again* (=they are talking about cars).

When it is transitive neither **talk** nor **speak** can have a person as its object: *I spoke to him yesterday* (NOT *spoke him*). | *They should talk to each other more* (NOT *talk each other*).

See also **say** (WORD CHOICE).

**-speak** /spiːk/ *suffix (in nouns)* the special language, especially slang words or words that are difficult to understand, used in a particular business or activity: *computerspeak*

**speak·eas·y** /ˈspiːkˌiːzi/ *n* [C] a place in the US in the 1920's and 1930's where you could buy alcohol illegally

**speak·er** /ˈspiːkə‖-ər/ *n* [C] **1** someone who makes a speech, usually at a meeting: *Our speaker tonight is Mr Pearson.* | **after-dinner speaker** (=someone who makes a speech after a formal meal) **2 French speaker/English speaker etc** someone who speaks French etc **3** the part of a radio or record player where the sound comes out **4 the Speaker** an official who controls discussions in a parliament 

**speaking tube** /ˈ· · ·/ *n* [C] a pipe through which people in different rooms can talk to each other

**spear¹** /spɪə‖spɪr/ *n* [C] **1** a pole with a sharp pointed blade at one end, used as a weapon in the past **2** a thin pointed stem of a plant, shaped like a spear: *asparagus spears*

**spear²** *v* [T] **1** to push or throw a spear into something, especially in order to kill it: *The huntsmen were spearing fish from the river.* **2** to push a pointed object, usually a fork, into something, so that you can pick it up

**spear·head¹** /ˈspɪəhed‖ˈspɪr-/ *v* [T] to lead an attack or organized action: *Ross spearheaded a campaign to improve sales.*

**spearhead²** *n* [C usually singular] a person or group of people who lead an attack or organized action: *The group became the spearhead of the labor union movement.*

**spear·mint** /ˈspɪəˌmɪnt‖ˈspɪr-/ *n* [U] **1** a fresh MINT¹ (1) taste, often used in sweets: *spearmint chewing gum* **2** the MINT¹ (2) plant that this taste comes from

**spec** /spek/ *n BrE informal* **1 on spec** if you do something on spec, you do it without being sure that you will get what you are hoping for: *I sent in an application on spec.* **2 specs** [plural] glasses (GLASS¹ (3)) to help you see

**spe·cial¹** /ˈspeʃəl/ *adj* **1** not ordinary or usual but different in some way and often better or more important: *a special case, deserving special treatment* | *diabetics on a special diet* | **special occasion** (=an important social 

event) *I keep this suit for special occasions.* | **anything special** *spoken*: *Are you doing anything special for Christmas?* | **special edition** (=a special type of car, watch etc produced only for a short time) **2 special offer** a low price charged for a product for a short time: *There's a special offer on this shampoo – two for the price of one.* **3** particularly important to someone and deserving attention, love etc: *Rob's a special friend of mine.* | *a wonderful teacher who made every child feel special* **4** unusually good: *I'd like you to try some of this whisky. It's rather special.* | **nothing special** (=not particularly good) *"What was the food like?" "Nothing special."* **5** more than usual: *Take special care on the roads tonight – it's icy* —see ESPECIALLY (USAGE).

**special**[2] *n* [C usually singular] **1** something that is not usual or ordinary, and is made or done for a special purpose: *a two-hour television special on famine in Africa* **2** *informal, especially AmE* a lower price than usual for a particular product for a short period of time: *The supermarket has a special on chicken.* | **on special** *Breyer's ice cream is on special this week.* **3** *ScotE* a type of beer

**special a·gent** /ˌ·· ˈ··/ *n* [C] *AmE* someone who works for the FBI

**Special Branch** /ˈ·· ˌ·/ *n* [U] a department of the British police force that deals with political crimes or crimes affecting the safety of the government, for example TERRORISM

**special con·sta·ble** /ˌ·· ˈ···/ *n* [C] someone in Britain who has an ordinary job, but is sometimes employed as a police officer when the police need more help

**special de·liv·e·ry** /ˌ·· ·ˈ···/ *n* [C, U] a service that delivers a letter or package very quickly

**special ed·u·ca·tion** /ˌ·· ··ˈ··/ *n* [U] the education of children who have particular physical problems or learning problems

**special ef·fect** /ˌ·· ·ˈ·/ *n* [C] an unusual image or sound in a film or television programme that has been produced artificially: *the amazing special effects in 'Jurassic Park'*

**special forc·es** /ˌ·· ˈ··/ *n* [plural] soldiers who have been specially trained to fight against GUERRILLA or TERRORIST groups

**special in·terest group** /ˌ·· ˈ·· ˌ·/ *n* [C] a group of people who all share the same aims

**spe·ci·al·ism** /ˈspeʃəlɪzəm/ *n* **1** [U] the practice of limiting your interests or activities to particular subjects **2** [C] an activity or subject that you know a lot about

S3 **spe·cial·ist** /ˈspeʃəl̥ɪst/ *n* [C] **1** someone who knows a
W3 lot about a particular subject, or is very skilled at it: [+ **in**] *a specialist in African history* **2** a doctor who knows more about one particular type of illness or treatment than other doctors: *a heart specialist*

**spe·ci·al·i·ty** /ˌspeʃiˈæl̥ɪti/ *n plural* **specialities** [C] *BrE* **1** a kind of food that is always very good in a particular restaurant or area; SPECIALTY (1) *AmE*: *Try the mushroom pâté – it's our speciality.* **2** a subject or skill that you know a lot about or have a lot of experience of; SPECIALTY (2) *AmE*: *Preston's speciality was night photography.*

S3 **spe·cial·ize** also **-ise** *BrE* /ˈspeʃəlaɪz/ *v* [I] to limit all or most of your study, business etc to a particular subject or activity: [+ **in**] *After qualifying, Zelda decided to specialize in contract law.* —**specialization** /ˌspeʃəlaɪˈzeɪʃən‖-lə-/ *n* [C,U]

**spe·cial·ized** also **-ised** *BrE* /ˈspeʃəlaɪzd/ *adj* trained, designed, or developed for a particular purpose or type of work: *Don't try repairing it yourself – it requires specialized knowledge.* | **highly specialized** (=very specialized) *a highly specialized field of study*

**special li·cence** /ˌ·· ˈ··/ *n* [C,U] special permission given by the Church of England for a marriage to take place at a time or place not usually allowed

**spe·cial·ly** /ˈspeʃəli/ *adv* **1** for one particular purpose, and only for that purpose: *I had this dress made specially for the wedding.* **2** *especially spoken* much more than usual, or much more than other people or things ESPECIALLY: *We specially wanted to visit Disneyland.* —see ESPECIALLY (USAGE)

**special needs** /ˌ·· ˈ·/ *n* [plural] needs that someone has because they have mental or physical problems: *children with special needs*

**special school** /ˈ·· ˌ·/ *n* [C] a school for children with physical problems or problems with learning

**spe·cial·ty** /ˈspeʃəlti/ *n* [C] *especially AmE* **1** a kind of food that is always very good in a particular area or restaurant; SPECIALITY (1) *BrE*: *Our specialty is clam chowder.* **2** a subject or job that you know a lot about or have a lot of experience of; SPECIALITY (2) *BrE*: *Johnson's specialty is Medieval European history.*

**spe·cies** /ˈspiːʃiːz/ *n plural* **species** [C] a group of animals or plants which are all similar and can breed together to produce young animals or plants of the same kind as them: **endangered species** (=one that may soon no longer exist) *This type of rattlesnake has been declared an endangered species.* W3

**spe·cif·ic**[1] /spl̥ˈsɪfɪk/ *adj* **1** [only before noun] a specific thing, person, or group is one particular thing etc: *Is this game meant for a specific age-group?* **2** detailed and exact: *Una gave us very specific instructions.* | *You said you live in the West Country, could you be a bit more specific?* **3 specific to** *formal* limited to, or affecting only one particular thing: *a disease specific to horses* S1 W1

**specific**[2] *n* **1 specifics** [plural] particular details that must be decided exactly: **get down to/go into specifics** *I can't go into specifics at this time, but I can tell you that we have an agreement.* **2** [C] *technical* a drug that has an effect only on one particular DISEASE

**spe·cif·ic·ally** /spl̥ˈsɪfɪkli/ *adv* **1** concerning or intended for one particular type of person or thing only: *a video specifically aimed at teenagers* **2** in a detailed or exact way: *I specifically asked you not to do that!* **3** [sentence adverb] used when you are adding more exact information: *Tom's hoping to move to Spain, or more specifically, Barcelona.* S2 W3

**spe·ci·fi·ca·tion** /ˌspesl̥fl̥ˈkeɪʃən/ *n* **1** [C usually plural] a detailed instruction about how something should be designed or made: *a car manufactured according to exact specifications* | **job specification** (=detailed description of what a job involves) **2** [C] a clear statement of what is needed or wanted: *Any student can apply for a loan, the only specification being that you must be in full-time education.*

**specific grav·i·ty** /·ˌ·· ˈ···/ *n* [U] *technical* the weight of a substance divided by the weight of the amount of water that would fill the same space

**spe·ci·fy** /ˈspesl̥faɪ/ *v* **specified, specifying** [T] to state something in an exact and detailed way: *Names and numbers were not specified.* | **specify who/what/how etc** *Did you specify where the new work station has to go?* | **specify that** *The rules clearly specify that competitors must not accept payment.* W3

**spe·ci·men** /ˈspesl̥ml̥n/ *n* [C] **1** a small amount or piece of something that is taken from a plant or animal, so that it can be tested or examined: *a zoological specimen* | [+ **of**] *The doctor will need a specimen of your blood.* **2** a single example of something: *a very fine specimen of 12th century glass* **3** *humorous* a person you are describing in a particular way, usually in an unpleasant way: *Who's that revolting specimen your daughter's going out with?*

**spe·cious** /ˈspiːʃəs/ *adj formal* seeming to be true or correct, but actually false: *a specious argument* —**speciously** *adv* —**speciousness** *n* [U]

**speck** /spek/ *n* [C] a very small mark, spot, or piece of something: *The boat was soon just a speck on the horizon.* —see picture on page 416

**speck·le** /ˈspekəl/ *n* [plural] small marks or spots covering a background of a different colour

**speck·led** /ˈspekəld/ *adj* covered with many small marks or spots: *speckled eggs* —see picture on page 839

**spec·ta·cle** /ˈspektəkəl/ *n* [C] **1** a very impressive show or scene: *The military parade was a magnificent spectacle.* **2** [usually singular] an unusual thing or situation to be seen or noticed: [+ **of**] *the curious spectacle of a cat actually chasing a dog* **3 make a spectacle of yourself** to behave in a way that is likely to make other people notice you and laugh at you **4 spectacles** *plural formal* two pieces of round glass in a frame, worn in front of your eyes to help you to see clearly; glasses (GLASS[1] (3)) —see also **see the world through rose-coloured spectacles** (ROSE-COLOURED (2))

**spec·tac·u·lar[1]** /spek'tækjələ‖-ər/ *adj* **1** very impressive and exciting: *a spectacular fireworks display* **2** unusually great or large: *His new show is a spectacular success.* —**spectacularly** *adv*

**spectacular[2]** *n* [C] an event or performance that is very large and impressive: *a television spectacular*

**spec·tate** /spek'teɪt‖'spekteɪt/ *v* [I] to watch a sports event

**spec·ta·tor** /spek'teɪtə‖'spekteɪtər/ *n* [C] someone who is watching an event or game: *The match attracted over 40,000 spectators.*

**spectator sport** /·'·· ,·‖'··· ,·/ *n* [C] a sport that people go and watch

**spec·ter** /'spektə‖-ər/ *n* [C] the American spelling of SPECTRE

**spec·tra** /'spektrə/ the plural of SPECTRUM

**spec·tral** /'spektrəl/ *adj* **1** *literary* connected with or like a spectre: *a spectral apparition* **2** *technical* connected with or made by a SPECTRUM

**spec·tre** *BrE*, **specter** *AmE* /'spektə‖-ər/ *n* **1 the spectre of** something that people are afraid of because it may affect them soon: *the spectre of unemployment* **2** [C] *literary* a GHOST

**spec·tro·scope** /'spektrəskəʊp‖-skoʊp/ *n* [C] an instrument used for forming and looking at spectra (SPECTRUM (2)) —**spectroscopy** /spek'trɒskəpi‖-'trɑː-/ *n* [U] —**spectroscopic** /,spektrə'skɒpɪk◂‖-'skɑː-/ *adj*

**spec·trum** /'spektrəm/ *n plural* **spectra** /-trə/ [C] **1** a complete range of opinions, ideas, situations etc, going from one extreme to its opposite: *Our speakers tonight come from both ends of the political spectrum.* | [+ **of**] *a wide spectrum of opinion* **2** the set of bands of coloured light into which a beam of light may be separated by passing it through a PRISM **3** a complete range of radio, sound etc waves: *the electromagnetic spectrum*

**spec·u·late** /'spekjəleɪt/ *v* **1** [I,T] to think or talk about the possible causes or effects of something without knowing all the facts or details: [+ **on/about**] *We can only speculate about why he did it.* | **speculate that** *George began to speculate that the two events might be linked.* **2** [I] to buy goods, property, shares (SHARE[2] (5)) in a company etc hoping that you will make a large profit when you sell them: [+ **in**] *Ned had speculated in gold and lost heavily.* —**speculator** *n* [C] | *property speculators*

**spec·u·la·tion** /,spekjə'leɪʃən/ *n* [C,U] **1** the act of guessing without knowing all the facts about something, or the guesses that you make: [+ **about**] *increased speculation about the possibility of tax cuts* | **speculation that** *There is some speculation that the president was aware of the situation.* | **pure speculation** (=speculation that is not based on any facts) *The jury should disregard the witness's last statement as pure speculation.* | **wild/idle speculation** (=speculation that is unlikely to be true) **2** the act of trying to make a profit by speculating (SPECULATE[2]): *property speculation*

**spec·u·la·tive** /'spekjələtɪv‖-leɪ-/ *adj* **1** based on guessing, not on information or facts: *These figures are, at best, speculative.* **2** bought or done in the hope of making a profit later: *speculative investments* —**speculatively** *adv*

**sped** /sped/ the past tense and past participle of SPEED

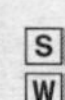

**speech** /spiːtʃ/ *n* **1** [C] a talk, especially a formal one about a particular subject, given to a group of people: *an election speech* | **give/make/deliver a speech** *Dr Ozu made a brilliant speech about the need for change.* **2** [U] the ability to speak: *Only humans are capable of speech.* | **power of speech** (=the ability to speak) *brain damage resulting in the loss of the power of speech* | **speech impediment** (=a physical or nervous problem that affects your speech) **3** [U] spoken language rather than written language: *In speech we use a smaller vocabulary than in writing.* | **freedom of speech** (=the right to say whatever you want) **4** [U] the particular way in which someone speaks: *Bob's speech was slurred, and he sounded drunk.* **5** [C] a set of lines that an actor must say in a play: *Hamlet's longest speech* —see also DIRECT SPEECH, FIGURE OF SPEECH, INDIRECT SPEECH, PART OF SPEECH, REPORTED SPEECH, **speech bubble** (BUBBLE[1] (3))

**speech day** /'· ·/ *n* [C] an occasion held once a year in some British schools, when prizes are given to children

**spee·chi·fy** /'spiːtʃɪfaɪ/ *v* [I] *informal* to make speeches in order to seem important: *speechifying about the dishonesty of politicians*

**speech·less** /'spiːtʃləs/ *adj* unable to speak because you feel very angry, upset etc: [+ **with**] *speechless with rage.* —**speechlessly** *adv* —**speechlessness** *n* [U]

**speech marks** /'· ·/ *n* [plural] the marks (" ") or (' ') that show when someone starts speaking and when they stop

**speech syn·the·siz·er** /'· ,····/ *n* [C] a computer system that produces sounds like human speech

**speech ther·a·py** /,· '···, '· ,···/ *n* [U] treatment that helps people who have difficulty in speaking properly —**speech therapist** *n* [C]

**speed[1]** /spiːd/ *n* S1 W2

**1 ▸ OF MOVEMENT ◂** [C,U] how fast something moves or travels: *What speed are we doing?* | *Police are advising motorists to reduce speed.* | **pick up/gather speed** (=gradually start to travel faster) *Once outside the station, the train began to pick up speed.* | **a speed of 60 mph/80 kph etc** *a truck traveling at a speed of 50 mph* | **at top/full speed** (=as fast as possible) *Forster was bundled into a waiting car and driven away at top speed.* | **at high/low speed** (=very fast or very slow) *a metal disc revolving at high speed* | **at breakneck speed** (=dangerously fast) | **at speed** *formal* (=fast) *The bus was already travelling at speed.*

**2 ▸ OF ACTION ◂** [U] the rate at which something happens or is done: *Everyone was surprised by the speed of events.* | **with speed** *formal* (=quickly) *The government acted with speed and efficiency.* | **reading/operating speed** (=the speed at which a person reads or a machine operates)

**3 ▸ PHOTOGRAPHY ◂** [C] **a)** the degree to which photographic film is sensitive to light **b)** the time it takes for a camera SHUTTER (2) to open and close: *a shutter speed of 1/250 second*

**4 ▸ DRUG ◂** [U] *slang* an illegal drug that makes you very active; AMPHETAMINE

**5 five-speed/ten-speed etc** having five etc gears (GEAR[1] (1)): *a five-speed gearbox*

**speed[2]** *v past* **sped** /sped/ *also* **speeded** **1** [I always + adv/prep] to go quickly: [+ **along/by/off etc**] *The robbers sped off in their getaway car.* **2** [T always + adv/prep] take someone or something somewhere very quickly: **speed sb to/away/back etc** *Security guards sped her to a waiting helicopter.* **3 be speeding** to be driving faster than the legal limit: *I got caught speeding on Route 40 yesterday.* S3

**speed by** *phr v* [I] if time speeds by, it seems to pass very quickly: *The weeks sped by and soon it was time to go back to school.*

**speed up** *phr v* [I,T] to move or happen faster or make something move or happen faster: *We'd better speed up if we want to be on time.* | **speed sth ↔ up** *The new system will speed up the registration process.*

**speed·boat** /'spiːdbəʊt‖-boʊt/ *n* [C] a small boat with a powerful engine designed to go fast

**speed bump** /'· ·/ *n* [C] a narrow raised part across a road that forces traffic to go slowly

**speed·ing** /'spiːdɪŋ/ *n* [U] the offence of driving faster than the legal limit: *Liz was found guilty of speeding and fined £50.*

**speed lim·it** /ˈ· ˌ··/ *n* [C] the fastest speed allowed by law on a particular piece of road: *a 30 mph speed limit*

**speed·om·e·ter** /spɪˈdɒmɪ̣tə, spiː-‖-ˈdɑːmɪ̣tər/ *n* [C] an instrument in a vehicle that shows how fast it is going —see picture on page 409

**speed read·ing** /ˈ· ˌ··/ *n* [U] the skill of reading very quickly

**speed skat·ing** /ˈ· ˌ··/ *n* [U] the sport of racing on ice wearing ICE SKATES

**speed trap** /ˈ· ·/ *n* [C] a place on a road where police wait to catch drivers who are going too fast

**speed·way** /ˈspiːdweɪ/ *n* [U] **1** the sport of racing MOTORCYCLES or cars on a special track **2** [C] a special track for this sport

**speed·well** /ˈspiːdwel/ *n* [U] a small European wild plant with light blue or white flowers

**speed·y** /ˈspiːdi/ *adj* **1** happening or done quickly or without delay: *We hope you make a speedy recovery.* | *The accusations brought a speedy denial.* **2** a speedy car goes fast —**speedily** *adv* —**speediness** *n* [U]

**spe·le·ol·o·gy** /ˌspiːliˈɒlədʒi‖-ˈɑːl-/ *n* [U] *technical* **1** the sport of walking and climbing in CAVES **2** the scientific study of CAVES —**speleologist** *n* [C] —**speleological** /ˌspiːliəˈlɒdʒɪkəl◂‖-ˈlɑː-/ *adj*

S2 **spell**[1] /spel/ *v past tense and past participle* **spelt** /spelt/ *especially BrE*, **spelled** *especially AmE* **1** [I,T] to form a word by writing or naming the letters in the correct order: *"How do you spell your name?" "S-M-Y-T-H."* | **can spell** (=be good at spelling words correctly) *I used to fail exams because I couldn't spell.* | **spell sth wrong/wrongly** *You've spelled my name wrong.* **2** [T not in passive] if letters spell a word, they form it: *B-O-O-K spells 'book'.* **3 spell trouble/disaster/danger etc** if a situation or action spells trouble etc, it makes you expect trouble etc: *Such a scandal could spell disaster for the government.* **4** [T] *AmE & AustrE* to do someone else's work for them for a short period so that they can rest: *Can I spell you at the wheel?*

**spell** sth ↔ **out** *phr v* [T] **1** to show how a word is spelled by writing or saying the letters separately in the right order: *"Could you spell that out for me?" "F-A-H-E-R-T-Y"* **2** to explain something clearly and in detail: **spell out how/what etc** *Will the Minister spell out exactly how he intends to finance these tax cuts?* **3** to write a word in its complete form instead of using an ABBREVIATION: *If you are using initials for the title of a group, be sure to spell them out at least once in your article.*

**spell**[2] *n* [C] **1** a piece of magic that someone does or the special words or ceremonies used in doing it: **put a spell on/cast a spell over** (=do a piece of magic to change something) *The wizard had put a spell on the city to send all its people to sleep.* | **break the spell** (=stop the spell from working) | **under a spell** *The frog was really a handsome young prince under a spell.* **2** a period of a particular kind of activity, weather etc, usually a short period: *After a brief spell in the army I returned to teaching.* | [+ **of**] *a spell of bad luck* | **a cold/wet/dry spell** *Do you remember that foggy spell we had in April?* **3** a power that attracts and influences you so strongly that it completely controls your feelings: **be/fall under sb's spell** *Maya fell under his spell within minutes of meeting him.* **4** a very short period of feeling ill: *a dizzy spell*

**spell·bind·ing** /ˈspelbaɪndɪŋ/ *adj* extremely interesting and holding your attention completely: *a spellbinding tale* —**spellbinder** *n* [C]

**spell·bound** /ˈspelbaʊnd/ *adj* extremely interested in something you are listening to: **hold sb spellbound** *The storyteller held his audience spellbound.*

**spell-check·er** /ˈ· ˌ··/ *n* [C] a computer PROGRAM that checks what you have written and makes your spelling correct —**spell-check** *v* [I,T]

**spel·ler** /ˈspelə‖-ər/ *n* [C] **1 good/bad/poor speller** someone who is good or bad at spelling words correctly **2** *AmE* a book for teaching spelling

**spell·ing** /ˈspelɪŋ/ *n* **1** [U] the act of spelling words correctly or the ability to do this: *Her spelling has improved.* **2** [C] the way in which a word is spelled: *What's the American spelling of 'colour'?* S2

**spelling bee** /ˈ·· ·/ *n* [C] *AmE* a competition in which the winner is the one who spells the most words correctly

**spelt** /spelt/ *especially BrE* the past tense and past participle of SPELL

**spe·lunk·ing** /spɪ̣ˈlʌŋkɪŋ/ *n* [U] *AmE* the sport of walking and climbing in CAVES —**spelunker** *n* [C]

**spend** /spend/ *past tense and past participle* **spent** /spent/ *v* S1 W1

**1 ▶ MONEY ◀** [I,T] to use your money to buy or pay for things: **spend money/£5/$10/a lot** *I spent so much money this weekend!* | **spend money etc on sth** *More money should be spent on health and education.* | **spend money etc on sb** (=buy things for someone) *Cecilia spends far too much money on those spoilt kids of hers.* | **money well spent** (=a sensible way of spending money) *The repairs cost a lot, but it's money well spent.*

**2 ▶ TIME ◀** [T] to pass or use time: **spend time in/with etc** *We'll have to spend the night in a hotel.* | *I want to spend more time with my family.* | **spend time doing sth** *Much of my time is spent studying financial reports.*

**3 spend the night with** to stay for the night and have sex with someone

**4 ▶ FORCE/EFFORT ◀** [T] *literary* to use all of something: *The storm had spent its force.*

**5 spend a penny** *BrE spoken* an expression meaning to URINATE, used when you want to avoid saying this directly: *I need to spend a penny – where are the loos?*

**spend·er** /ˈspendə‖-ər/ *n* [C] someone who spends money: **big spender** (=someone who regularly spends very large amounts of money)

**spend·ing** /ˈspendɪŋ/ *n* [U] the amount of money spent, especially by a government or organization: **government/public/defence spending** *a reduction in government spending on defense*

**spending mon·ey** /ˈ·· ˌ··/ *n* [U] money that you have available to spend on your own personal pleasures: *$25 a week in spending money*

**spend·thrift** /ˈspendˌθrɪft/ *n* [C] someone who spends money carelessly, even when they do not have a lot of it

**spent**[1] /spent/ the past tense and past participle of SPEND

**spent**[2] *adj* **1** already used, and now empty or useless: *spent cartridges* **2 be a spent force** if a political idea or organization is spent force, it no longer has any power or influence: *Socialism had become a spent political force in the country.* **3** *literary* extremely tired

**sperm** /spɜːm‖spɜːrm/ *n* **1** *plural* **sperm** *or* **sperms** [C] a cell produced by the sex organs of a male animal, which is able to join with the female egg to produce a new life **2** [U] the liquid from the male sex organs that these cells swim in; SEMEN

**sper·ma·cet·i** /ˌspɜːməˈseti‖-ɜːr-/ *n* [U] a solid oily substance found in the head of the SPERM WHALE and used in making skin creams, CANDLES etc

**sper·ma·to·zo·on** /ˌspɜːmətəˈzəʊɒn‖ˌspɜːrmətəˈzoʊən/ *n plural* **spermatozoa** /-ˈzəʊə‖-ˈzoʊə/ [C] *technical* a sperm

**sperm bank** /ˈ· ·/ *n* [C] a place where SEMEN is kept to be used in medical operations to help women to become PREGNANT

**sper·mi·cide** /ˈspɜːmɪ̣saɪd‖ˈspɜːr-/ *n* [C,U] a cream or liquid that kills SPERMS, used while having sex to prevent the woman from becoming PREGNANT —**spermicidal** /ˌspɜːmɪ̣ˈsaɪdl◂‖ˌspɜːr-/ *adj*: *spermicidal jelly*

**sperm whale** /ˈ· ·/ *n* [C] a large WHALE, hunted for its oil, fat and SPERMACETI

**spew** /spjuː/ *v* **1** *also* **spew out/forth** [I always + adv/prep,T] to flow out of something in large quantities, or to make something flow out in this way: [+ **from/into/**

over] *Lava spewed from the volcano.* | **spew sth (out)** *The burst pipe was spewing out dirty water.* **2** also **spew up** [I,T] *BrE informal* to VOMIT

**SPF** /ˌes piː ˈef/ Sun Protection Factor; a number on a bottle of SUNTAN cream that tells you how much protection it gives you from the sun: *SPF 25*

**sphag·num** /ˈsfægnəm/ *n* [C,U] *technical* a type of MOSS

**sphere** /sfɪə‖sfɪr/ *n* [C] **1** a ball shape: *The Earth is not a perfect sphere.* —see picture at SHAPE **2** a particular area of activity, work, knowledge etc: *His reputation lies in the scientific sphere.* **3 sphere of influence** a person or country's sphere of influence is the area where they have power to change things

**-sphere** /sfɪə‖sfɪr/ *suffix technical (in nouns)* the air surrounding the Earth at a particular height: *the stratosphere*

**spher·i·cal** /ˈsferɪkəl/ *adj* having the shape of a sphere

**sphe·roid** /ˈsfɪərɔɪd‖ˈsfɪr-/ *n* [C] *technical* a shape that is similar to a ball, but not a perfect sphere

**sphinc·ter** /ˈsfɪŋktə‖-ər/ *n* [C] *technical* a muscle that surrounds a passage in your body, and can tighten in order to close it: *the anal sphincter*

**sphinx** /sfɪŋks/ *n* [C] an ancient Egyptian image of a lion with a human head lying down

**spic, spik** /spɪk/ *n* [C] *AmE* a very offensive word meaning a Spanish-speaking American

**spice¹** /spaɪs/ *n* **1** [C,U] one of the various types of powder or seed, taken from plants, that you put into food you are cooking to give it a special taste: *Indian spices such as cumin and saffron* **2** [singular, U] interest or excitement that is added to something: *They need gossip to add a bit of spice to their dull lives.* —see also **variety is the spice of life** (VARIETY¹ (5))

**spice²** *v* [T] **1** also **spice up** to add interest or excitement to something: *an essay that needs spicing up* **2** to add spice to food [+ **with**]: *baked apples spiced with cinnamon and nutmeg*

**spick-and-span** /ˌspɪk ən ˈspæn/ *adj* a room, house etc that is spick-and-span is completely clean and tidy

**spic·y** /ˈspaɪsi/ *adj* **1** food that is spicy has a pleasantly strong taste, and gives you a pleasant burning feeling in your mouth: *pasta with a spicy tomato sauce* **2** a story that is spicy is slightly shocking or rude: *a spicy rumour* —**spicily** *adv* —**spiciness** *n* [U]

**spi·der** /ˈspaɪdə‖-ər/ *n* [C] a small creature with eight legs which makes networks of thread for catching insects

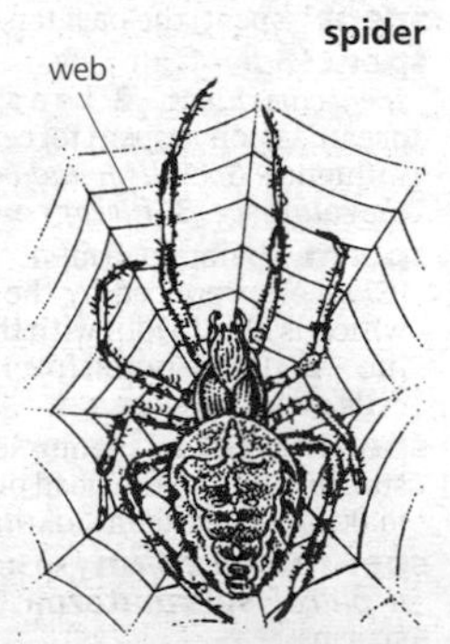

spider

**spi·der·web** /ˈspaɪdəweb‖-dər-/ *n* [C] *AmE* a very fine network of sticky threads made by a spider to catch insects; COBWEB *BrE*

**spi·der·y** /ˈspaɪdəri/ *adj* writing that is spidery is untidy with long thin lines

**spiel** /ʃpiːl, spiːl/ *n* [C,U] *informal* fast talk that the speaker has used many times before and that is intended to persuade people to buy something: *the salesman's spiel*

**spif·fing** /ˈspɪfɪŋ/ *adj BrE old-fashioned* excellent

**spif·fy** /ˈspɪfi/ *adj informal especially AmE* very neat and fashionable: *A spiffy little red car.*

**spig·ot** /ˈspɪgət/ *n* [C] **1** a TAP¹ (1,2) in a large container that controls the flow of liquid from it **2** *especially AmE* an outdoor TAP¹ (1)

**spik** /spɪk/ *n* [C] another spelling of SPIC

**spike¹** /spaɪk/ *n* [C] **1** something long and thin with a sharp point, especially a pointed piece of metal: *spikes along the top of a fence* **2 spikes** [plural] metal points on the bottom of a shoe used for running, or the shoe itself —see picture at STUD¹ **3** *technical* a sharp point on a GRAPH **4** *technical* the head of a plant that produces grain such as corn or wheat

**spike²** *v* [T] **1** to push a sharp point into something: *a guy spiking litter and putting it in a garbage bag* **2** to add a strong alcoholic drink to a weak or non-alcoholic one: [+ **with**] *Bill's drink had been spiked with vodka.* **3** to prevent someone from saying something or printing something in a newspaper: *A clumsy attempt to spike rumours of a cabinet split.* **4 spike sb's guns** *BrE* to spoil an opponent's plans

**spik·y** /ˈspaɪki/ *adj* **1** having long sharp points: *a spiky cactus* **2** hair that is spiky is stiff and stands up on top of your head —see picture on page 412 **3** *BrE informal* easily offended or annoyed —**spikiness** *n* [U]

**spill¹** /spɪl/ *past tense and past participle* **spilt** /spɪlt/ *especially BrE* **spilled** *especially AmE v* **1** [I,T] if you spill a liquid or if it spills, it accidentally flows over the edge of a container: **spill sth down/on/over** *Oh no! I've spilt coffee all down my shirt!* | [+ **on/over**] *He slipped and the wine spilled all over the carpet.* **2** [I always + adv/prep] if people spill out of somewhere, they move out in large groups: [+ **out/into/onto etc**] *Crowds from the theatre were spilling onto the street.* **3 spill the beans** *informal* to tell something that someone else wanted you to keep a secret **4 spill your guts** *AmE* to tell someone everything you know about something, especially because you are upset: *some drunk spilling his guts to me at the bar* **5 spill blood** *literary* to kill or wound people —see also **cry over spilt milk** (CRY¹ (5)) S3

spill

**spill over** *phr v* [I] if a problem or bad situation spills over, it spreads and begins to affect other places, people etc: [+ **into**] *There is a danger that the conflict will spill over into neighbouring towns.*

**spill²** *n* **1** [C,U] an act of spilling something or an amount of something that is spilled: **oil spill** *The oil spill in Alaska threatens ecological catastrophe.* **2** [C] a piece of wood or twisted paper for lighting lamps, fires etc **3** [C] *old-fashioned* a fall from a horse, bicycle etc

**spil·lage** /ˈspɪlɪdʒ/ *n* [C,U] a SPILL² (1)

**spill·way** /ˈspɪlweɪ/ *n* [C] a passage for water to flow over or around a DAM (=wall for holding back water)

**spilt** /spɪlt/ *especially BrE* the past tense and past participle of SPILL

**spin¹** /spɪn/ *past tense and past participle* **spun** /spʌn/ *v* S3

spin

**1** ▶ **TURN AROUND** ◀ [I,T] to turn around and around very quickly, or to make something do this: *The ice skater was spinning faster and faster.* | *spin the roulette wheel* | **spin (sth/sb) around** *Liz spun around on her heel to face me.*

**2** ▶ **WOOL/COTTON** ◀ [I,T] to make cotton, wool etc into thread by twisting it: *The wool is spun into thread and then woven.*

**3** ▶ **WET CLOTHES** ◀ [T] to get water out of clothes using a machine after you have washed them

**4** ▶ **INSECT** ◀ [T] if a SPIDER or insect spins a WEB (1) or COCOON, it produces thread to make it

**5 sb's head spins** if your head spins, you feel as if you

might FAINT because you are shocked, excited, or drunk: *My head was spinning with all this new information.*
**6 spin a story/yarn/line** [T] to tell someone a story that is not true in order to deceive them: *beggars spinning hard-luck stories*
**7 ▶ DRIVE ◀** [I always + adv/ prep] to drive or travel quickly: [**+ past/along etc**] *Barbara waved as she spun past in her new sportscar.*

**spin** sth↔ **off** *phr v* [T] **1** to produce a new television programme using characters from another programme: *'The Rifleman' spun off another new series, 'Wanted Dead or Alive.'* **2** to form a separate and partly independent company from parts of an existing company: *The company spun off its financial services division in 1988.*

**spin** sth↔ **out** *phr v* [T] **1** to make something continue for longer than is necessary: *I'm paid by the hour, so I spin the work out as long as I can.* **2** to use money, food etc as carefully and slowly as possible because you do not have very much of it: [**+ over**] *I've only got £10 left, so we'll have to spin it out over the whole week.*

**spin²** *n*
**1 ▶ TURNING ◀** [C] an act of turning around quickly: *the spin of a top | The dance ended with a dramatic spin.*
**2 ▶ CAR ◀** [C] *informal* a short trip in a car for pleasure: *Let's go for a spin in the country.*
**3 ▶ BALL ◀** [U] if you put spin on a ball in a game such as tennis or CRICKET (2) , you deliberately make the ball turn very quickly so that it is difficult for your opponent to hit
**4 fall/go into a (flat) spin a)** to become very confused and anxious: *The sudden fall on the stock-market sent brokers into a spin.* **b)** if an aircraft goes into a spin it falls suddenly, turning around and around
**5 ▶ WET CLOTHES ◀ give sth a spin** *BrE* to turn clothes around very fast in a machine to remove water from them
**6 ▶ INFORMATION ◀** [singular] *informal especially AmE* a way of providing information that makes it seem to be favourable for a particular person or political party: *trying to put a positive spin on the economic figures*
**7 ▶ SCIENCE ◀** [singular] a quality of an ELEMENTARY PARTICLE that influences its behaviour with other particles —see also SPIN DOCTOR

**spi·na bif·i·da** /ˌspaɪnə ˈbɪfɪ̣də/ *n* [U] a serious condition in which a person's SPINE is split down the middle from birth, leaving their SPINAL CORD unprotected

**spin·ach** /ˈspɪnɪdʒ, -ɪtʃ‖-ɪtʃ/ *n* [U] a vegetable with large dark green leaves —see picture on page 414

**spin·al** /ˈspaɪnl/ *adj* belonging to or affecting your SPINE (1): *spinal injuries*

**spinal col·umn** /ˈ·· ˌ··/ *n* [C] *technical* your SPINE (1)

**spinal cord** /ˌ·· ˈ·/ *n* [C] the thick string of nerves enclosed in your SPINE (1) by which messages are sent to and from your brain

**spin·dle** /ˈspɪndl/ *n* [C] **1** a part of a machine shaped like a stick, around which something turns **2** a round pointed stick used for twisting the thread when you are spinning wool

**spin·dly** /ˈspɪndli/ *adj* long and thin in a way that looks weak: *spindly legs*

**spin doc·tor** /ˈ· ˌ··/ *n* [C] *informal* someone whose job is to give information to the public in a way that gives the best possible advantage to a politician or organization: *The White House spin doctors are hard at work explaining the President's about-face on taxes.*

**spin-dry·er** /ˌ· ˈ··/ *n* [C] *especially BrE* a machine that removes most of the water from washed clothes by spinning them around and around very fast —**spin-dry** *v* [T]

**spine** /spaɪn/ *n* [C] **1** the row of bones down the centre of your back that supports your body and protects your SPINAL CORD —see picture at SKELETON **2** a stiff sharp point on an animal or plant: *cactus spines* **3** the part of a book that the pages are fastened onto

**spine-chil·ling** /ˈ· ˌ··/ *adj* a spine-chilling story or film is very frightening in a way that people enjoy —**spine-chiller** /ˈspaɪnˌtʃɪlə‖-ər/ *n* [C]

**spine·less** /ˈspaɪnləs/ *adj* **1** lacking courage and determination: *a bunch of spineless do-gooders* **2** without a spine: *spineless creatures such as jellyfish* —**spinelessly** *adv* —**spinelessness** *n* [U]

**spi·net** /spɪˈnet‖ˈspɪnɪ̣t/ *n* [C] a musical instrument of the 16th and 17th centuries, which is played like a piano

**spin·na·ker** /ˈspɪnəkə‖-kər/ *n* [C] a sail with three points at the front of a boat, used when the wind is directly behind —see picture at YACHT

**spin·ner** /ˈspɪnə‖-ər/ *n* [C] **1** someone whose job is to make thread by twisting cotton, wool etc **2** a BOWLER in a game of CRICKET (2) who throws the ball with a spinning action **3** a thing used for catching fish that moves around and around when pulled through the water —see also MONEY-SPINNER

**spin·ney** /ˈspɪni/ *n* [C] *BrE* a small area of trees and bushes

**spinning jen·ny** /ˈspɪnɪŋ ˌdʒeni/ *n* [C] an industrial machine used in the past for making cotton, wool etc into thread

**spinning wheel** /ˈ·· ·/ *n* [C] a simple machine consisting of a wheel on a frame that people used in their homes in the past for making cotton, wool etc into thread

**spin-off** /ˈ· ·/ *n* [C] **1** an unexpected but useful result of something, that happens in addition to the intended result: *Laser research has had important spin-offs for eye surgery.* —see also **spin off** (SPIN¹) **2** a television programme involving characters that were previously in another programme or film: *'Maude' was a spin-off from 'All in the Family'.* **S**

**spin·ster** /ˈspɪnstə‖-ər/ *n* [C] *old-fashioned* an unmarried woman, usually one who is no longer young and seems unlikely to marry —**spinsterhood** *n* [U]

**spin the bot·tle** /ˌ· · ˈ··/ *n* [U] a game in which people sitting in a circle spin a bottle in the middle and when the bottle stops spinning and points to someone, that person must do something, such as kissing another person

**spin·y** /ˈspaɪni/ *adj* having a lot of spines (SPINE (2)): *a spiny gorse bush*

**spi·ral¹** /ˈspaɪərəl‖ˈspaɪr-/ *adj* in the form of a continuous line or curve that winds around a central point, moving further away from it all the time: *a spiral watch spring* —**spirally** *adj*

**spiral²** *n* [C] **1** a spiral curve **2** a process, usually a harmful one, in which something gradually but continuously rises, falls, gets worse etc: *Shipbuilding entered a spiral of decline.* | **upward/downward spiral** *a vicious downward spiral of debt* **3 inflationary spiral** a situation where wages and prices rise continuously because the level of INFLATION (1) is high

spiral

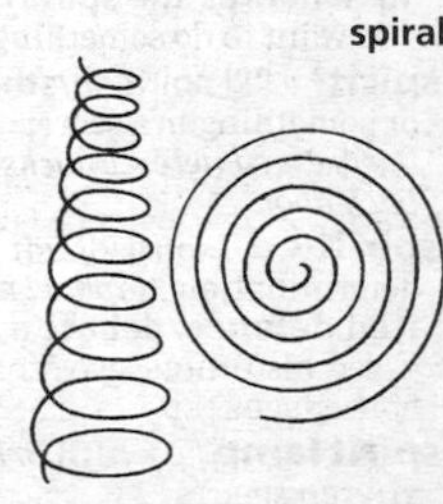

**spiral³** *v* **spiralled, spiralling** *BrE*, **spiraled, spiraling** *AmE* [I] **1** [always + adv/prep] to move in a continuous curve that gets nearer to or further from its central point as it goes round: [**+ to/around etc**] *The damaged plane spiralled to the ground.* **2** if debt or the cost of something spirals, it increases quickly and uncontrollably: *the spiraling cost of legal services*

**spiral stair·case** /ˌ·· ˈ··/ *n* [C] a set of stairs arranged in a circular pattern so that they go around a central point as they get higher

**spire** /spaɪə‖spaɪr/ *n* [C] a roof that rises steeply to a point on top of a tower, especially on a church

**spir·it¹** /ˈspɪrɪ̣t/ *n* S3 W2
**1 ▶ INNER PART ◀** [singular, U] an inner part of

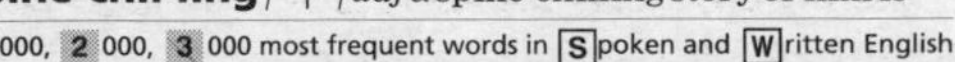

someone that includes their thoughts and feelings, and is thought of as making them what they are: *His spirit was untameable.* | *strong in spirit* | **independent/proud/free etc spirit** (=a person with a particular type of character) *a toddler already showing an independent spirit*
**2 ▶ SOUL ◀** [C] the part of someone that is believed to continue to live after they have died: *Although Laurie is dead, I can feel his spirit with me.* —compare SOUL (1)
**3 ▶ DEAD PERSON ◀** [C] a dead person who is believed to have returned to this world and has strange or magical powers; GHOST[1] (1): *Some people believe that evil spirits can be removed by exorcism.*
**4 ▶ HAPPY/SAD ◀ spirits** [plural] the way someone feels at a particular time, for example if they are cheerful or sad: **be in good/low spirits** (=be happy or sad) | **be in high spirits** (=be excited) *We started our journey in high spirits.* | **keep sb's spirits up** (=make sure someone does not become less cheerful) | **raise/lift sb's spirits** (=make someone feel happier and more hopeful) *long, hot summer days that lift the spirits* | **sb's spirits lift/sink** (=become more or less cheerful) *My spirits sank when I saw the mess they'd left.*
**5 in spirit** you say you will be somewhere in spirit or with someone in spirit, when you cannot be with them but are thinking about them: *I can't come to your wedding but I'll be there in spirit.*
**6 ▶ DRINK ◀** [C usually plural] **a)** *especially BrE* a strong alcoholic drink such as WHISKY or BRANDY **b)** *BrE* liquid such as alcohol, used for cleaning
**7 get into the spirit/enter into the spirit** *BrE* to start to feel as happy, excited etc as the people around you: *Judith couldn't really enter into the spirit of the occasion.*

**8 ▶ ATTITUDE ◀** [singular] the attitude that you have towards something: *You've got to approach this meeting in the right spirit.* | *a true spirit of friendship*
**9 ▶ DETERMINATION ◀** [U] *approving* courage, energy, and determination: *Our team played with great spirit.* | **fighting spirit** (=brave determination) | **break sb's spirit** (=make someone lose their courage and determination) *slaves whose spirits had been broken*
**10 that's the spirit** *spoken* used to express approval of someone's behaviour or attitude
**11 team/community/public etc spirit** a strong feeling of belonging to a particular group and wanting to help them
**12 the spirit of the age/times** the set of ideas, beliefs, and aims that are typical of a particular period in history
**13 when/as the spirit moves you** when you feel that you want to do something

**spirit[2]** *v* [T] **spirit sb/sth away/off** to remove someone or something in a secret or mysterious way: *At the end of the press conference Jackson was spirited away through a back door.*

**spir·it·ed** /ˈspɪrɪ̣tɪ̣d/ *adj approving* having energy and determination: *Raphael is so young and spirited.* | **a spirited defence/debate** *a spirited defence of her decisions* —see also HIGH-SPIRITED, LOW-SPIRITED, MEAN-SPIRITED, PUBLIC-SPIRITED

**spirit lamp** /ˈ· · ·/ *n* [C] *BrE* a small lamp that burns METHYLATED SPIRITS

**spir·it·less** /ˈspɪrɪ̣tləs/ *adj* **1** having no energy or determination **2** not cheerful —**spiritlessness** *n* [U]

**spirit lev·el** /ˈ·· ˌ··/ *n* [C] a tool for testing whether a surface is level; LEVEL[1] (11) *AmE*

**spir·i·tu·al[1]** /ˈspɪrɪ̣tʃuəl/ *adj* **1** connected with your spirit rather than with your body or mind: *As a priest I'm responsible for your spiritual welfare.* | *spiritual values* **2** connected with religion: *the spiritual authority of the church* **3 spiritual home** a place where you feel you belong because you share the ideas and attitudes of that society —**spiritually** *adj*

**spiritual[2]** *n* [C] a religious song of the type sung originally by the black people of the US

**spir·i·tual·is·m** /ˈspɪrɪ̣tʃʊlɪzəm/ *n* [U] the belief that dead people may send messages to living people, usually through a MEDIUM (=someone with special powers) —**spiritualist** *n* [C] —**spiritualistic** /ˌspɪrɪ̣tʃʊˈlɪstɪk◂/ *adj*

**spir·i·tu·al·i·ty** /ˌspɪrɪ̣tʃuˈælɪ̣ti/ *n* [U] the quality of being interested in religion or religious matters

**spir·i·tu·ous** /ˈspɪrɪ̣tʃuəs/ *adj* [only before noun] *technical* containing alcohol

**spit[1]** /spɪt/ *past tense and past participle* **spat** /spæt/ also **spit** *AmE; present participle* **spitting** *v*
**1 ▶ LIQUID FROM YOUR MOUTH ◀** [I] to blow a small amount of SALIVA (=the liquid in your mouth) out of your mouth: [+ **at/on**] *Mom, Judy spit at me!* | *Kevin cleared his throat and spat on the path.* | *Don't get too close to the camels – they spit!*
**2 ▶ FOOD ETC ◀** [T] to force something out of your mouth: *spit blood* | **spit sth out** *Ian was chewing on some gristle but was too polite to spit it out.*
**3 ▶ RAIN ◀ be spitting** to rain very lightly: *You don't need an umbrella, it's only spitting.*
**4 ▶ SAY STH ◀** [T] also **spit out** to say something quickly in a very angry way: *"Don't even think of taking it!" she spat.*
**5 spit it out** *spoken* used to ask someone to tell you something that they seem too frightened or embarrassed to say: *Come on Jean, spit it out!*
**6 ▶ SMALL PIECES ◀** [I] to send out small bits of something, for example fire or hot oil, into the air: *sausages spitting in a pan* | *The van drove off, gravel spitting from under the wheels.*
**7 ▶ CAT ◀** [I] if a cat spits it makes short, angry sounds
**8 be within spitting distance** *spoken* to be very close to where you are
**9 I could just spit** *spoken* used to say that you are very angry or annoyed

**spit[2]** *n* **1** [U] the watery liquid that is produced in your mouth; SALIVA **2** [C] a long thin stick that you put through meat to turn it and cook it over a fire **3** [C] a long narrow piece of land that sticks out into the sea, a river etc —see picture on page 835 **4 be the (dead) spit of** *BrE spoken* to look exactly like someone else: *Sam is the dead spit of his dad.* **5 spit and polish** *informal* thorough cleaning and polishing **6 spit and sawdust** *BrE spoken* a spit and sawdust PUB is rough, dirty and simple in style

**spit·ball** /ˈspɪtbɔːl‖-bɔːl/ *n* [C] *AmE* a small piece of paper that children put in their mouth and then throw at each other

**spite[1]** /spaɪt/ *n* **1 in spite of** without being prevented by something; DESPITE: *We went out in spite of the rain.* | **in spite of the fact that** *Kelly loved her husband in spite of the fact that he drank too much.* **2** [U] a feeling of wanting to hurt or upset people, for example because you are JEALOUS or think you have been unfairly treated: **out of spite** (=because of spite) *She broke it just out of spite.* | **pure/sheer spite** (=spite and nothing else) **3 in spite of yourself** if you do something in spite of yourself, you do it although you did not expect or intend to do it W3

**spite[2]** *v* [T only in infinitive] to deliberately annoy or upset someone: *The neighbours throw things over the garden wall just to spite us.* —see also **cut off your nose to spite your face** (CUT[1])

**spite·ful** /ˈspaɪtfəl/ *adj* deliberately nasty to someone in order to hurt or upset them: *What I can't forgive is that it was such a spiteful thing to do.* —**spitefully** *adv* —**spitefulness** *n* [U]

**spit·fire** /ˈspɪtfaɪə‖-faɪr/ *n* [C] someone, especially a woman, who becomes angry very easily

**spitting im·age** /ˌ·· ˈ··/ *n* **be the spitting image of sb** to look exactly like someone else

**spit·tle** /ˈspɪtl/ *n* [U] *old-fashioned* the liquid in your mouth; SPIT[2] (1)

**spit·toon** /spɪˈtuːn/ *n* [C] a container used to SPIT[1] (1) into

**spiv** /spɪv/ *n* [C] *BrE old-fashioned* a man who gets money from small dishonest business deals

**splash**[1] /splæʃ/ *v* **1** [I] if a liquid splashes, it hits or falls on something noisily or it moves noisily: [+ **against/on/over**] *Great drops of rain splashed on the window.* **2** [T always + adv/prep] to make someone or something wet with a lot of small drops of water or other liquid: **splash sth on/over/with etc sth** *Shivering, he splashed cold water on his face and washed his hands.* **3** also **splash about/around** [I] to make water fly up in the air with a loud noise by hitting it or by moving around in it: *Maggie watched the children splashing about in the pool.* **4** [T] *informal* if a newspaper splashes a story or picture over its pages, it makes it very large and easy to notice

**splash down** *phr v* [I] if a SPACECRAFT splashes down it deliberately lands in the sea —see also SPLASHDOWN

**splash out on sth** *phr v* [T] *informal* to spend a lot of money on something: *We splashed out on a new kitchen.*

**splash**[2] *n* **1** [C] the sound of a liquid hitting something or being moved around quickly: *Rachel fell into the river with a loud splash.* —see picture on page 1261 **2** [C] a mark made by a liquid splashing onto something else: *There were splashes of paint all over my clothes.* **3 a splash of colour** small area of bright colour **4 make a splash** *informal* to do something that gets a lot of public attention: *Russell's new show made a big splash in New York.* **5** [singular] *especially BrE* a small amount of liquid added to a drink: *Just a splash of milk in my coffee, please.*

**splash**[3] *adv informal* with a splash: *You should have seen Rex – he jumped splash into the lake!*

**splash·back** /ˈsplæʃbæk/ *BrE*, **splashboard** /ˈsplæʃbɔːd‖-bɔːrd/ *AmE n* [C] the area of a bathroom or kitchen wall that is behind TAPS and covered in tiles (TILE[1] (1))

**splash·down** /ˈsplæʃdaʊn/ *n* [C, U] a landing by a SPACECRAFT in the sea

**splash guard** /ˈ· ·/ *n* [C] *AmE* a flat piece of rubber hanging behind the wheel of a vehicle to prevent mud being thrown up; MUDFLAP *BrE*

**splash·y** /ˈsplæʃi/ *adj AmE* big, bright and very easy to notice; FLASHY

**splat**[1] /splæt/ *n* [singular] *informal* a noise like something wet hitting a surface hard

**splat**[2] *v* **splatted, splatting** [I, T] to make a noise like something wet hitting a surface, or to make something make this noise: [+ **against**] *Big raindrops splatted against the windscreen.*

**splat·ter** /ˈsplætə‖-ər/ *v* [I, T] to cover something with small drops of liquid: *Mud splattered the hem of her kimono.*

**splay** /spleɪ/ also **splay out** *v* [I, T] if fingers or legs splay or are splayed, they spread further apart, often in a way that looks strange: *He sat sturdily on the floor, legs splayed apart.*

**splay foot·ed** /ˌ· ˈ··◂/ *adj* having very flat wide feet

**spleen** /spliːn/ *n* **1** [C] an organ near your stomach that controls the quality of your blood —see picture at DIGESTIVE **2** [U] *formal* anger: **vent your spleen on sb** (=get angry with someone)

**splen·did** /ˈsplendɪ̣d/ *adj formal* **1** excellent or very fine: *a splendid person|a splendid suggestion* **2** beautiful and impressive: *There are some splendid villas near Rome.|a splendid view of the port* —**splendidly** *adv*: *Joe and my father are getting along splendidly.*

**splen·dif·e·rous** /splenˈdɪfərəs/ *adj BrE informal humorous* splendid

**splen·dour** *BrE*, **splendor** *AmE* /ˈsplendə‖-ər/ *n* **1** [U] impressive beauty and richness, usually in a large building or large place: *the gothic splendor of the cathedral* **2 splendours** [plural] impressive, beautiful, rich features, especially of a large building or place: *the splendours of Versaillles*

**sple·net·ic** /splɪ̣ˈnetɪk/ *adj literary* bad-tempered and often angry

**splice**[1] /splaɪs/ *v* [T] **1** to join the ends of two pieces of rope, film etc so that they form one continuous piece **2 get spliced** *BrE informal* to get married

**splice**[2] *n* [C] the act of joining the ends of two things together, or the place where this join has been made

**splic·er** /ˈsplaɪsə‖-ər/ *n* [C] a machine for joining pieces of film or recording TAPE [1] (1a) neatly together

**splint** /splɪnt/ *n* [C] a flat piece of wood, metal etc, used for keeping a broken bone in position while it mends

**splin·ter**[1] /ˈsplɪntə‖-ər/ *n* [C] a small sharp piece of wood, glass, or metal, that has broken off a larger piece: *I've got a splinter in my finger.*|[+ **of**] *splinters of glass* —**splintery** *adj*: *splintery plywood* —see picture on page 416

**splinter**[2] *v* [I,T] if something such as wood splinters, or you splinter it, it breaks into thin sharp pieces: *Soft wood splinters easily.*

**splinter group** /ˈ·· ˌ·/ also **splinter or·ga·niz·a·tion** /ˈ·· ···ˌ··/ *n* [C] a group of people that has separated from a political or religious organization because they have different ideas etc: *Green Realignment, a splinter group of the British Green Party*

**split**[1] /splɪt/ *v past tense and past participle* **split** *present participle* **splitting** 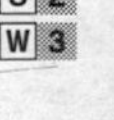

**1 ▶ INTO GROUPS ◀** also **split up** [I,T] if a group of people splits or is split, it divides into two or more groups, because one group strongly disagrees with the other: *The issue of women's ordination is splitting the church.*|[+ **over/on**] *The party split over segregation.*| **be split on/over** *The National Defense Committee is split over the use of military force.*

**2 ▶ INTO PARTS ◀** also **split up** [I,T] to divide or separate something into different parts, or to be divided into different parts: [+ **into**] *Each district was split up into a number of sub-divisions.|At the end of the bridge the expressway split into two roads.*

**3 ▶ BREAK OR TEAR ◀** [I,T] if something splits or if you split it, it tears or breaks along a straight line: *Harry split his trousers climbing over the fence.*|[+ **open**] *One of the pumpkins had split open.*|**split (sth) in two/half** *The board had split in two.*|**split (sth) down/across/along etc** *He split the stone down the middle.*

**4 ▶ SHARE ◀** [T] to divide something into separate parts so that two or more people each get a part: **split sth between** *Profits will be split between three major charities.*|**split sth three/four etc ways** (=into three, four, or more equal parts) *I think we should split what's left three ways.*|**split the bill/cost** *It's only fair to split the cost of the bills.*

**5 ▶ INJURE ◀** also **split open** [T] to cut someone's head or lip, by hitting them: *The poor guy had his head split right open.*

**6 ▶ LEAVE ◀** [I] *slang* to leave quickly: *They grabbed her purse and split.*

**7 split hairs** to argue that there is a difference between two things, when the difference is really too small to be important: *Let's stop splitting hairs and get back to the main issue.*

**8 split the difference** to agree on an amount that is exactly between two amounts that have been mentioned: *You want $20, I'm offering $10. Why don't we split the difference?*

**9 split your sides** to laugh very hard

**split off** *phr v* **1** [I] to completely separate from a group: [+ **from**] *The ancestors of this animal split off from the rest and established themselves as an independent species.* **2** [I,T] to break something away from something so that it is completely separate, or to break off in this way: *Huge boulders had split off and rolled down the mountainside.*

**split on** sb *phr v* [T] *informal especially BrE* to tell someone in authority about something wrong that someone else has done: *You wouldn't split on a pal would you?*

**split up** *phr v* **1** [I] to end a marriage or relationship: *Steve's parents split up when he was four.*|[+ **with**] *Jackie's splitting up with her boyfriend.* **2** [I,T] to divide into groups: *Please don't split up when we get to the*

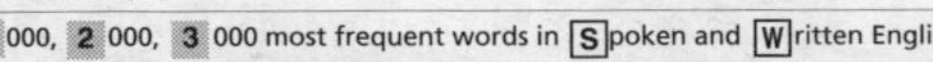

*museum.* | **split sth ↔ up** *The teacher split up the class into three groups.* **3** [T **split** sth ↔ **up**] to divide or separate something into different parts: *The article is easier to read if you split it up into sections.*

**split²** *n* [C] **1** a long straight hole caused when something breaks or tears: *a split in the seat of his trousers* **2** a serious disagreement that divides an organization or group of people into smaller groups: *Arguments over admitting women to the club may lead to a split.* **3** the part of something you receive when something, especially money, is shared: **a three-way/four-way etc split** (=a share of something that is divided equally between three, four etc people) **4** *informal* a difference between two things, ideas etc: *the split between ideals and reality* **5 do the splits** to spread your legs wide apart so that your legs touch the floor along their whole length —see also BANANA SPLIT

**split ends** /ˌ· ˈ·/ *n* [plural] a condition of someone's hair in which the ends have split into several parts

**split in·fin·i·tive** /ˌ· ·ˈ···/ *n* [C] a phrase in which you put an adverb or other word between 'to' and an INFINITIVE, as in 'to easily win'. Some people think this is incorrect English

**split-lev·el** /ˌ· ˈ··◂/ *adj* a split-level house, room or building has floors at different heights in different parts

**split pea** /ˌ· ˈ·◂/ *n* [C] a dried PEA split into its two halves

**split per·son·al·i·ty** /ˌ· ··ˈ···/ *n* [C] *not technical* a condition in which someone has two very different ways of behaving; SCHIZOPHRENIA

**split ring** /ˌ· ˈ·/ *n* [U] a metal ring, used for keeping keys on, that can be opened to allow the keys to be put on or taken off

**split screen** /ˌ· ˈ·◂/ *n* [C] a method used in films and on television screen (SCREEN¹ (1,2)) to show different scenes or pieces of information at the same time: *a split-screen movie*

**split sec·ond** /ˌ· ˈ··◂/ *n* **a split second** an extremely short period of time: *I just turned round for a split second and she vanished!* —**split-second** *adj*: *a split-second decision*

**split shift** /ˌ· ˈ·/ *n* [C] a period of work that is divided into two or more parts on the same day: *Chefs work a split shift.*

**split tick·et** /ˌ· ˈ··/ *n* [C] a vote in US elections in which the voter has voted for some CANDIDATES of one party and some of the other party —**split-ticket** *adj*: *split-ticket voting*

**split·ting** /ˈsplɪtɪŋ/ *adj* a splitting HEADACHE is very bad

**splodge** /splɒdʒ‖splɑːdʒ/ *n* [C] *informal* a large mark of mud, paint etc with an irregular shape: *a splodge of ketchup on his shirt* —**splodgy** *adj*

**splosh** /splɒʃ‖splɑːʃ/ *v* [I always + adv/prep] *BrE informal* to make a noise by falling into or moving through water; SPLASH¹ —**splosh** *n* [C] *a discreet splosh as the eel-fisherman cast off*

**splotch** /splɒtʃ‖splɑːtʃ/ *n* [C] a SPLODGE

**splurge** /splɜːdʒ‖splɜːrdʒ/ *v* [I] *informal* to spend more money than you can usually afford: *Let's splurge and take a cab.* —**splurge** *n* [C]

**splut·ter** /ˈsplʌtə‖-ər/ *v* [I] **1** to talk quickly in short confused phrases, especially because you are angry or surprised: *"But ...But ...I can't believe...how could you?" she spluttered.* | [+ **with**] *Katie was spluttering with rage.* **2** to make short sharp noises, like someone spitting (SPIT¹ (1)): *Bill was coughing and spluttering.* | *The boat's engine spluttered and stopped.* —**splutter** *n* [C]

**spoil** /spɔɪl/ *past tense and past participle* **spoiled** *or* **spoilt** /spɔɪlt/ *BrE v*

**1 ▶ RUIN STH ◀** [T] to have a bad effect on something so that it is no longer attractive, enjoyable, useful etc: *The countryside has been spoiled by the new freeway.* | *Don't spoil your sister's birthday by crying at her party.* | **spoil everything** (=completely ruin someone's plan) *Mom arrived home just then, which spoiled everything.* —see also **spoil/ruin your appetite** (APPETITE (1)) —see DESTROY (USAGE)

**2 ▶ FOOD ◀** [I] to start to decay: *Food will spoil if the temperature in your freezer rises above 8°C.*

**3 ▶ CHILD ◀** [T] to give a child whatever they want, or let them do what they want, with the result that they behave badly: **spoil sb with sth** *Jimmy's grandmother spoils him with toys and candy.*

**4 ▶ TREAT KINDLY ◀** [T] to look after someone in a way that is kind or too kind: *You know you're spoiling me with all this good cooking.* | **spoil yourself** *Go on, spoil yourself. Have another piece of cake.*

**5 ▶ VOTING PAPER ◀** [T] to mark a BALLOT PAPER wrongly so that your vote is not included

**6 be spoiling for a fight/argument** to be very eager to fight or argue with someone —see also SPOILS, SPOILER

**spoil·age** /ˈspɔɪlɪdʒ/ *n* [U] *technical* waste resulting from something being spoiled

**spoiled** /spɔɪld/ *usually* **spoilt** *BrE adj* **1** someone, especially a child, who is spoiled is rude and behaves badly because their parents have always given them what they want and allowed them to do what they want: **spoiled brat** (=spoiled, annoying child) | **spoiled rotten** (=very spoiled) **2 be spoilt for choice** *BrE* to have so many good things to choose from that you cannot decide which one to choose

**spoil·er** /ˈspɔɪlə‖-ər/ *n* [C] **1** a piece of an aircraft wing that can be lifted up to slow the plane down **2** a raised part on a racing car that stops the car lifting off the road at high speeds **3** a book, article etc that is produced to take attention away from another similar book and spoil its success **4** *AmE* a person or team that spoils another's winning record

**spoils** /spɔɪlz/ *n* [plural] *formal or literary* **a)** things taken by an army from a defeated enemy, or things taken by thieves: *the spoils of war* | *dividing up the spoils* **b)** profits gained through political power

**spoil·sport** /ˈspɔɪlspɔːt‖-spɔːrt/ *n* [C] *informal* someone who spoils other people's fun: *Don't be a spoilsport, Richard. We can't play without you.*

**spoilt** /spɔɪlt/ *adj* another form of the word SPOILED

**spoke¹** /spəʊk‖spoʊk/ the past tense of SPEAK

**spoke²** *n* [C] **1** one of the thin metal bars which connect the outer ring of a wheel to the centre, especially on a bicycle —see picture at BICYCLE¹ **2 put a spoke in sb's wheel** to prevent someone from doing something they have planned: *I feel like telling the press everything. That'd put spoke in their wheel.*

**-spoken** /spəʊkən‖spoʊ-/ *suffix (in adjectives)* speaking in a particular way: *a softly-spoken girl* (=who speaks quietly)

**spok·en¹** /ˈspəʊkən‖ˈspoʊ-/ the past participle of SPEAK

**spoken²** *adj* **1 spoken English/language** the form of language that you speak rather than write **2 quietly/softly/well-spoken** speaking in a quiet, educated etc way **3 be spoken for** *informal* **a)** if something is spoken for, you cannot buy it because it is being kept for someone else **b)** if someone is spoken for, they are married or already have a serious relationship with someone

**spokes·man** /ˈspəʊksmən‖ˈspoʊks-/ *n plural* **spokesmen** /-mən/ [C] someone who has been chosen to speak officially for a group, organization or government: *a White House spokesman* | [+ **for**] *a spokesman for victims' families* W2

**spokes·per·son** /ˈspəʊksˌpɜːsən‖ˈspoʊksˌpɜːr-/ *n plural* **spokespeople** /-piːpəl/ [C] a word meaning spokesman or spokeswoman which some people use because they think that 'spokesman' should not be used for both sexes

**spokes·wom·an** /ˈspəʊksˌwʊmən‖ˈspoʊks-/ *n plural* **spokeswomen** /-ˌwɪmɪn/ [C] a woman who has been chosen to speak officially for a group, organization, or government

**spo·li·a·tion** /ˌspəʊliˈeɪʃən‖ˌspoʊ-/ *n* [U] *formal* the violent or deliberate destruction or spoiling of something: *the spoliation of the environment*

**sponge¹** /spʌndʒ/ *n* **1** [C,U] a piece of a soft natural or artificial substance full of small holes, which can suck up liquid and is used for washing: *The physio ran onto the field with a wet sponge.* **2** [C] a simple sea creature from which natural sponge is produced **3** [singular] *especially BrE* an act of washing something with a sponge: *Give my back a quick sponge, would you?* **4** [C] a SPONGER **5** [C,U] *BrE* SPONGE CAKE

**sponge²** *v* **1** also **sponge down** [T] to wash something with a wet cloth or sponge: *Sponge down the walls before you paint them.* **2** [T always + adv/prep] to remove liquid or a mark with a wet cloth or sponge: **sponge sth off/out/up** *Wendy tried to sponge the wine off her dress.* **3** [I] to get money, free meals etc from other people, without doing anything for them: *Right-wing politicians accuse the poor of sponging.* | **sponge off sb** *Carl's been sponging off his family ever since he left college.*

**sponge bag** /ˈ· ·/ *n* [C] *BrE* a small bag for carrying the things that you need to wash with

**sponge bath** /ˈ· ·/ *n* [C] an act of washing your whole body with a wet cloth when you cannot use a BATHTUB or SHOWER¹ (1)

**sponge cake** /ˈ· ·/ *n* [C,U] a light cake made from eggs, sugar, and flour but usually no fat

**sponge pud·ding** /ˌ· ˈ··/ *n* [C] *BrE* a food made of eggs, butter, flour and sugar which is eaten hot

**spon·ger** /ˈspʌndʒə‖-ər/ *n* [C] someone who gets money, free meals etc, from other people and does nothing for them

**spong·y** /ˈspʌndʒi/ *adj* soft and full of holes that contain air or liquid like a SPONGE¹ (1): *The earth was soft and spongy underfoot.* —**sponginess** *n* [U]

**spon·sor¹** /ˈspɒnsə‖ˈspɑːnsər/ *n* [C] **1** a person or company that pays for a show, broadcast, sports event etc in exchange for the right to advertise at that event: *the Championship's sponsor, Martell Cognac* **2** someone who agrees to give someone else money for a CHARITY (2) if they walk, run, swim etc a particular distance **3** someone who officially agrees to help someone else, or to be responsible for what they do: *You need a sponsor to get a working visa.* **4** someone who officially introduces or supports a proposal for a new law **5** a GODPARENT

**sponsor²** *v* [T] **1** to give money to a sports event, theatre etc: *The bank is sponsoring a sports day for children in the area.* **2** to agree to give someone money for CHARITY if they walk, run, etc a particular distance: *I've sponsored Alison $1 for every mile in the walkathon.* **3** to officially support a proposal for a new law

**spon·sored** /ˈspɒnsəd‖ˈspɑːnsərd/ *adj* **sponsored walk/swim etc** *BrE* an event in which many people walk, swim etc a particular distance in order to collect money for a CHARITY (2)

**spon·sor·ship** /ˈspɒnsəʃɪp‖ˈspɑːnsər-/ *n* [U] support, usually financial support for an activity or event: *The expedition is looking for sponsorship from one of the major banks.*

**spon·ta·ne·ous** /spɒnˈteɪniəs‖spɑːn-/ *adj* happening or done without being planned or organized, but because you suddenly feel you would like to do it: *The crowd gave a spontaneous cheer when the result was announced.* —**spontaneously** *adv* —**spontaneousness, spontaneity** /ˌspɒntəˈniːɪ̈ti, -ˈneɪɪ̈ti‖ˌspɑːn-/ *n* [U]

**spontaneous com·bus·tion** /ˌ··· ·ˈ··/ *n* [U] burning caused by chemical changes inside something rather than by heat from outside

**spoof** /spuːf/ *n* [C] a funny book, play, film etc that copies a serious or important one and makes it seem silly: [+ **of/on**] *'A Five Minute Hamlet' is an amusing spoof of Shakespeare's most famous play.* —**spoof** *v* [T]

**spook¹** /spuːk/ *n* [C] *informal* **1** a GHOST¹ (1) **2** *slang* a SPY¹: *Yup. He was a real live CIA spook.*

**spook²** *v* [T] *informal especially AmE* to frighten someone: *You've really spooked me with that story about plane crashes.*

**spook·y** /ˈspuːki/ *adj informal* strange or frightening in a way that makes you think of ghosts (GHOST¹ (1)): *a spooky old house with creaking stairs*

**spool** /spuːl/ *n* [C] **1** an object shaped like a wheel that you wind electric wire, recording TAPE¹ (1a), photographic film etc around **2** *AmE* a REEL¹ (1a): *Don't forget to rewind the spool.*

**spoons**

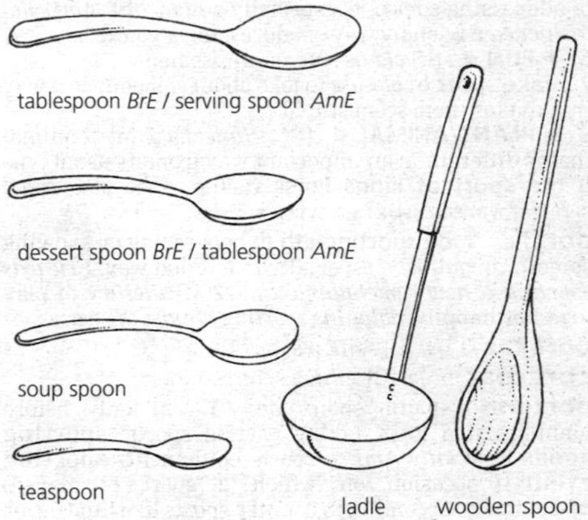

**spoon¹** /spuːn/ *n* [C] **1** a thing used for eating, cooking, or serving food, consisting of a small bowl-shaped part and a long handle **2** a SPOONFUL —see also **be born with a silver spoon in your mouth** (BORN² (11)), DESSERTSPOON, GREASY SPOON, SOUP SPOON, WOODEN SPOON

**spoon²** *v* [T] to pick up or move food with a spoon: [+ **into/on**] *Spoon the mixture into glasses.*

**spoo·ner·is·m** /ˈspuːnərɪzəm/ *n* [C] a phrase in which the speaker makes the mistake of exchanging the first sounds of two words, with a funny result, for example 'sew you to a sheet' for 'show you to a seat'

**spoon-feed** /ˈ· ·/ *v past tense and past participle* **spoon-fed/-fed** [T] **1** to give too much information and help to someone: *Spoon-feeding students does not help them remember things.* **2** to feed someone, especially a baby, with a spoon

**spoon·ful** /ˈspuːnfʊl/ *n* [C] the amount that a SPOON will hold: [+ **of**] *Two spoonfuls of sugar, please.*

**spoor** /spɔː, spʊə‖spɔːr, spʊr/ *n* [C] the track of foot marks or FAECES (=solid waste) left by a wild animal

**spo·rad·ic** /spəˈrædɪk/ *adj* happening often but not regularly; INTERMITTENT: *sporadic fighting in the west of the city* —**sporadically** /-kli/ *adv*

**spore** /spɔː‖spɔːr/ *n* [C] a cell like a seed, produced by some plants such as MUSHROOMS, and by some very simple animals, which is able to develop into a new plant or animal

**spor·ran** /ˈspɒrən‖ˈspɔː-, ˈspɑː-/ *n* [C] a special bag made of leather or fur, worn in front of a KILT by a Scotsman

**sport¹** /spɔːt‖spɔːrt/ *n* 
**1 ▶ GAMES ◀ a)** [C] a physical activity in which people compete against each other: *My favourite sports are tennis and swimming.* | *I was never any good at sports when I was young.* | **spectator sport** (=one which is watched by large groups of people) *Football is one of the most popular spectator sports.* **b)** [U] *BrE* sports in

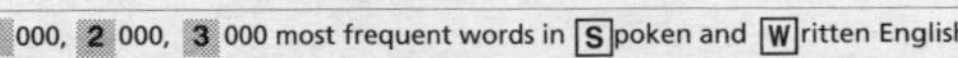

general: *Here's news about today's sport.* | *Why is there so much sport on TV?*
**2** ▶ **HUNTING** ◀ [C] a country outdoor activity such as hunting or fishing: **blood sports** (=sports that involve killing animals)
**3 sports** [plural] *BrE* an occasion when people compete in running, jumping, throwing etc: **school/county sports** *The school sports are usually held in July.*
**4** ▶ **HELPFUL PERSON** ◀ also **good sport** *old-fashioned* a helpful cheerful person who lets you enjoy yourself and never complains when there is trouble: *His Mum will let us have a party. She's a good sport.* | **be a sport** (=used when asking someone to help you) *Be a sport and lend me your bike.*
**5** ▶ **MAN/BOY** ◀ *spoken* **a)** *AustrE* a friendly way of addressing someone, especially a man **b)** *AmE old-fashioned* a friendly way of addressing a young boy
**6** ▶ **FUN** ◀ [U] *old use* fun or amusement
**7 make sport of** *old-use* to joke about someone in a way that makes them seem stupid
**8** ▶ **PLANT/ANIMAL** ◀ [C] *technical* a plant or animal that is different in an important way from its usual type
**9 the sport of kings** horse racing —see also FIELD SPORTS, WINTER SPORTS, WATER SPORTS

**sport²** *v* **1 be sporting sth** to be wearing or showing something publicly, especially in a proud way: *Eric was sporting a new camel-hair coat.* **2** [I] *literary* to play together happily: *dolphins sporting amidst the waves*

**sport car** /ˈ· ·/ *n* [C] *AmE* a SPORTS CAR

**sport coat** /ˈ· ·/ *n* [C] *AmE* a SPORTS JACKET

**sport·ing** /ˈspɔːtɪŋ‖ˈspɔːr-/ *adj* **1 a)** [only before noun] related to or taking part in sports: **sporting goods** *especially AmE* (=sports equipment) | **sporting event** (=occasion on which a sport is played) **b)** related to or joining in country sports like hunting or horse racing: *the sporting gentry* **2** *BrE* fair and generous, especially in sports: **it is sporting of sb** *It was sporting of him to admit that his last shot was out.* **3 a sporting chance** a fairly good chance of succeeding or winning: *Neil has a sporting chance of getting in the football team.* —**sportingly** *adv*

**spor·tive** /ˈspɔːtɪv‖ˈspɔːr-/ *adj literary* enjoying fun and making jokes in a friendly way; PLAYFUL —**sportively** *adv* —**sportiveness** *n* [U]

**sport jack·et** /ˈ· ˌ··/ *n* [C] *AmE* a SPORTS JACKET

**sports** /spɔːts‖spɔːrts/ *adj* [only before noun] **1** connected with sport or used for sport: *a sports field* | *sports equipment* | *sports clubs* **2** on the subject of sport: *When I buy a newspaper, I always read the sports page first.* | *a sports commentator on television*

**sports car** /ˈ· ·/ *n* [C] a low fast car, often with a roof that can be folded back or removed

**sports·cast** /ˈspɔːtskɑːst‖ˈspɔːrtskæst/ *n* [C] *AmE* a television broadcast of a sports match —**sportscaster** *n* [C]

**sports cen·tre** /ˈ· ˌ··/ *n* [C] *BrE* a building where many different types of indoor sports are played

**sports coat** /ˈ· ·/ *n* [C] a SPORTS JACKET

**sports day** /ˈ· ·/ *n* [C] *especially BrE* a day on which the children at a school have sports competitions; FIELD DAY (2) *AmE*

**sport shirt** /ˈ· ·/ *n* [C] *AmE* a SPORTS SHIRT

**sports jack·et** /ˈ· ˌ··/ *n* [C] a man's comfortable JACKET (1), usually made of TWEED, worn on informal occasions

**sports·man** /ˈspɔːtsmən‖ˈspɔːrts-/ *plural* **sportsmen** /-mən/ *n* [C] a man who plays several different sports, especially outdoor sports —see also SPORTSWOMAN

**sports·man·like** /ˈspɔːtsmənlaɪk‖ˈspɔːrts-/ *adj* behaving in a fair, honest, and polite way when competing in sports: *gentlemanly and sportsmanlike behaviour*

**sports·man·ship** /ˈspɔːtsmənʃɪp‖ˈspɔːrts-/ *n* [U] behaviour that is fair, honest and polite in a game or sports competition: **good/bad sportsmanship** *We try to teach the kids good sportsmanship.*

**sports schol·ar·ship** /ˈ· ˌ···/ *n* [C] money given to some college students in America to pay for all or part of their education because they are good enough to play for one of the college's sports teams

**sports shirt** /ˈ· ·/ *n* [C] a shirt for men that is worn on informal occasions

**sports·wear** /ˈspɔːtsweə‖ˈspɔːrtswer/ *n* [U] **1** clothes that are worn to play sports or when you are relaxing **2** *AmE* clothes that are suitable for informal occasions

**sports·wom·an** /ˈspɔːtsˌwʊmən‖ˈspɔːrts-/ *n plural* **sportswomen** /-ˌwɪmɪn/ [C] a woman who plays many different sports, especially outdoor sports

**sport·y** /ˈspɔːti‖ˈspɔːrti/ *adj informal* **1** designed to look attractive in a bright informal way: *a sporty jacket and skirt* **2** *especially BrE* good at and fond of sport: *I'm not a very sporty person.* —**sportiness** *n* [U]

**spot¹** /spɒt‖spɑːt/ *n* [C] 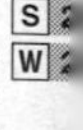
**1** ▶ **PLACE** ◀ a particular place or area, especially a pleasant place where you spend time: *an ideal spot for a picnic* | *We walked along the beach looking for a spot to sit.* | **camping/swimming/holiday spot** (=a place that is suitable for a particular activity) *We found several good camping spots by the river.* | **the exact/very/same spot** (=the exact place where something happens) | **a sunny/shady spot** *These plants grow best in a sunny spot.* —see POSITION (USAGE) —see graph at LOCATION
**2** ▶ **AREA** ◀ a usually round area on a surface, that is a different colour or is rougher, smoother etc than the rest: *Dalmatian dogs have white coats with black or brown spots.* | [+ **of**] *Her pink suit made a bright spot of colour against the white steps.*
**3** ▶ **MARK** ◀ a small mark on something, especially one that is made by a liquid: *There are a lot of grease spots on the shirt.* | *spots of paint on the carpet*
**4 on the spot** if you do something on the spot, you do it immediately, often without thinking about it very carefully: *He bought the car on the spot.* | *The police could give you an on the spot fine.*
**5 be on the spot** to be in the place where something is happening: *As the man on the spot, Coen was in a position to take vital decisions.*
**6** ▶ **MARK ON SKIN** ◀ **a)** a small round red area on someone's skin that shows that they are ill: *I was covered in spots when I had measles.* **b)** *BrE* a small raised red mark on someone's skin, especially on their face; PIMPLE: *This cream clears up teenage spots in days.*
**7** ▶ **POSITION** ◀ a position in a competition, event, television programme etc: *The Bulldogs earned a spot in the semi-finals.* | *A bluegrass band has the second spot on the program.* | **guest spot** (=part of a television or radio programme showing someone who does not usually appear on the programme) *a guest spot on the Johnny Carson show*
**8 run/dance/hop etc on the spot** to run etc in one place, without moving forwards or around the area
**9 weak spot: a)** a point at which someone or something is not very good: *He'd look at my work and immediately find every weak spot.* **b)** *AmE* if someone has a weak spot for something, they like it very much
**10 put sb on the spot** to deliberately ask someone a question that is difficult or embarrassing to answer: *Reporters put the governor on the spot with questions about his involvement in the bribery scandal.*
**11 in a spot** *informal* in a difficult situation: **put sb in a spot** *You've put us in one hell of a spot by telling them that, you know.*
**12 bright spot** something that is good in a bad situation: **the one/only bright spot** *Being able to visit my folks was the one bright spot of the vacation.*
**13 a spot of** *BrE informal* a small amount of something: *I could do with a spot of whisky.* | **a spot of bother** (=a small amount of trouble)
**14** ▶ **ON CLOTH** ◀ **spots** *BrE* small round areas that form a pattern on a piece of cloth; POLKA DOTS: *a dark blue dress with white spots*
**15 spots of rain** *BrE* a few drops of rain
**16** ▶ **LIGHT** ◀ a SPOTLIGHT¹ (1)

**17 five-spot/ten-spot etc** *AmE spoken* a piece of paper money worth five dollars, ten dollars etc
**18 ▶ ADVERTISEMENT ◀** a short radio or television advertisement, especially one for a politician: *a 30-second spot on the local radio station* —see also BEAUTY SPOT, BLACK SPOT, BLIND SPOT, **not change your spots** (CHANGE[1] (1)), G-SPOT, **high point/spot** (HIGH[1] (13)), **hit the spot** (HIT[1] (27)), **hot spot** (HOT[1] (27), **knock spots off** (KNOCK[1] (13)), **be rooted to the spot** (ROOT (10)), **have a soft spot for** (SOFT (10)), TROUBLE SPOT

S 3 **spot²** *v* [T]
**1 ▶ NOTICE ◀** to notice something, especially something that is difficult to see, or that you are looking for: *Luckily, the enemy planes were spotted early.* | *I spotted a break in the fence and headed towards it.* | **spot sb doing sth** *Meg spotted someone coming out of the building.* | **difficult/easy to spot** *Dick's very tall, so he's easy to spot in a crowd.*
**2 ▶ RECOGNIZE ◀** to recognize the good or bad qualities in someone or something: *You must learn to spot trouble ahead and prevent it.* | **spot sb's potential** *Island Records were the first to spot his potential.*
**3 be spotted** to have small round marks on the surface: [+ **with**] *The floor was spotted with paint.*
**4 ▶ GAME ◀** *AmE* to give the other player in a game an advantage: **spot sb sth** *He spotted me six points and he still won.*

**spot³** *adj technical* for buying or paying immediately, not at some future time: **spot cash/price** *They won't take credit; they want spot cash.* | *What's the spot price for oil?*

**spot check** /ˌ· ˈ·‖ˈ· ˌ·/ *n* [C] a quick examination of a few things or people from a group, to check whether everything is correct or satisfactory: *spot checks by customs officers*

**spot·less** /ˈspɒtləs‖ˈspɑːt-/ *adj* **1** completely clean: *Joe's house is spotless.* **2 spotless reputation/record/character** a completely honest and good character: *Before his arrest, the suspect's record was spotless.* —**spotlessly** *adv* —**spotlessness** *n* [U]

**spot·light¹** /ˈspɒtlaɪt‖ˈspɑːt-/ *n* **1 a)** [C] a light with a very bright beam which can be directed at someone or something —see picture at LIGHT[1] **b)** [singular] the round area of light made by this beam on the ground, stage etc: *Step into the spotlight so we can see you!* **2 be in the spotlight** to receive a lot of attention in the newspapers, on television etc: *Now that he's entered politics he is constantly in the spotlight.*

**spotlight²** *v past tense and past participle* **spotlighted** *or* **spotlit** [T] **1** to direct attention to someone or something: *The article spotlights the problems of the homeless.* **2** to shine a strong beam of light on something —**spotlit** /ˈspɒtlɪt‖ˈspɑːt-/ *adj*

**spot-on** /ˌ· ˈ·◂/ *adj, adv BrE informal* exactly right: *Judith is always spot-on with her advice.*

**spot·ted** /ˈspɒtɪ̣d‖ˈspɑː-/ *adj* [usually before noun] having small round marks or DOTS on the surface: *red and white spotted pyjamas* —see picture on page 839

**spotted dick** /ˌ·· ˈ·/ *n* [U] a boiled PUDDING (1) with CURRANTS which is eaten in Britain

**spot·ter** /ˈspɒtə‖ˈspɑːtər/ *n* [C] **bird/train etc spotter** *especially BrE* someone who spends time watching birds, trains etc

**spot·ty** /ˈspɒti‖ˈspɑːti/ *adj* **1** *BrE informal* having spots on your face: *a spotty youth* **2** *AmE* good only in some parts, but not in other parts; PATCHY

**spouse** /spaʊs, spaʊz/ *n* [C] *formal* a husband or wife

**spout¹** /spaʊt/ *n* [C] **1** a small tube or pipe on a container that you pour liquid out through **2 a spout of water/blood etc** a sudden strong stream of liquid which comes out of somewhere very fast: *The whale blew a spout of water into the air.* —see also **water spout** **3 up the spout** *BrE informal* **a)** if someone's plans have gone up the spout, they cannot succeed: *Her chances of studying medicine have gone up the spout.* **b)** completely wrong: *His calculations are completely up the spout.* **c)** *old-fashioned* going to have a baby; PREGNANT

**spout²** *v* **1 a)** [I always + adv/prep] if liquid or fire spouts from somewhere, it comes out very quickly in a powerful stream: [+ **from**] *Blood was spouting from the wound in her arm.* **b)** [T] to send out liquid or flames very quickly in a powerful stream: *a volcano spouting lava* **2** also **spout off** [I,T] *informal* to talk a lot about something in a boring way, especially without thinking about what you are saying: [+ **about**] *I'm tired of listening to Jim spouting about politics.* | **spout (off) sth** *It's no use spouting theories about education if you've never actually taught anyone.* **3** [I] if a WHALE spouts it sends out a stream of water from a hole in its head

**sprain** /spreɪn/ *v* [T] to damage a joint in your body by suddenly twisting it: *I fell down the steps and sprained my ankle.* —**sprain** *n* [C]

**sprang** /spræŋ/ the past tense of SPRING

**sprat** /spræt/ *n* [C] a small European HERRING

**sprawl¹** /sprɔːl‖sprɒːl/ *v* **1** also **sprawl out** [I always + adv/prep] to lie or sit with your arms or legs stretched out in a lazy or careless way: [+ **in/on etc**] *He just sprawls out in his chair and expects me to bring his dinner.* | **be sprawled out** *The students were sprawled out on the grass.* | **send sb sprawling** (=hit someone with such force that they fall over) **2** [I always + adv/prep] if buildings or a town sprawl, they spread out over a wide area in an untidy and unattractive way: *An industrial estate sprawled across the valley.*

**sprawl²** *n* [singular] **1** a large area of buildings that are spread out in an untidy and unattractive way: *a vast sprawl of industrial development* | **urban sprawl** *Los Angeles' huge urban sprawl* **2** [singular] a position in which you have your arms or legs stretched out in a lazy or careless way

**spraw·ling** /ˈsprɔːlɪŋ‖ˈsprɒːl-/ *adj* spreading over a wide area in an untidy or unattractive way: *a sprawling metropolis*

**spray¹** /spreɪ/ *v* **1** [T] to make a stream of small drops of liquid come out of a small tube or several small holes: **spray sb with sth** *She sprayed herself with perfume.* | **spray sth on/over sth** *Vandals had sprayed graffiti on the walls.* | **spray crops/plants** (=cover them with liquid to protect them from insects or disease) **2** [I always + adv/prep] if liquids or small bits spray somewhere they are quickly scattered through the air: [+ **over/around/from etc**] *Grass started spraying from the blades of the lawn mower.* **3 spray (sb/sth with) bullets** to shoot many bullets from a gun quickly: *Gunmen sprayed the crowd with bullets.* S 3

**spray**

**spray²** *n*
**1 ▶ LIQUID ◀** [C,U] liquid which is forced out of a special container in a stream of very small drops: **hair spray** (=spray which you put on your hair to keep it tidy) | **insect spray** (=spray used for killing insects)
**2 ▶ A CAN ◀** [C] a can or other container with a special tube which forces liquid out in a stream of small drops: *Avoid sprays that contain harmful CFCs.*
**3 ▶ FROM THE SEA ◀** [U] water in very small drops blown from the sea or a wet surface: *A thunderous plume of spray leapt half-way up the cliff.*
**4 ▶ BRANCH ◀** [C] a small branch from a tree or plant used for decoration: [+ **of**] *sprays of holly*
**5 ▶ FLOWERS/JEWELS ◀** [C] an attractive arrangement of flowers or jewels
**6 a spray of bullets/dust etc** a lot of very small objects or bits moving quickly through the air

**spray can** /ˈ· ·/ *n* [C] a can from which paint is sprayed

**spray·er** /ˈspreɪə‖-ər/ *n* [C] a piece of equipment used for spraying liquid, especially to protect crops from insects or disease

**spray gun** /ˈ· ·/ *n* [C] a piece of equipment held like a gun, which sprays liquid in very small drops

**spray paint** /ˈ· ·/ *n* [U] paint that is sprayed from a can —**spray-paint** *v* [I,T]

S2 W2 **spread¹** /spred/ *v past tense and past participle* **spread**
**1 ▶ OPEN OR ARRANGE ◀** also **spread** sth ↔ **out** [T] to open something so that it covers a bigger area, or arrange a group of things, so that they cover a flat surface: **spread sth on** *Let's spread the map out on the floor.*|**spread sth over/across etc** *She spread the towel over the radiator to dry.*|*The market women had spread out their goods on the pavement.*
**2 ▶ DISEASE/FEELING/PROBLEM/FIRE ◀** [I,T] to increase, or be increased, and affect more and more people or affect a larger area: *The fire spread very quickly.*|[+ **through/to/across etc**] *Cholera is spreading through the refugee camps at an alarming rate.*|**spread sth** *She's the sort of woman who enjoys spreading bad feeling.*
**3 ▶ INFORMATION/IDEAS ◀ a)** [I] to become known about or used by people more and more: *News of the explosion spread swiftly.*|[+ **to/through/over etc**] *Buddhism spread to China from India.*|**the word spread** (=the news became known by more and more people) *The word spread that Louise had resigned.*|**spread like wildfire** (=become known very quickly) **b)** [T] to tell a lot of people about something: **spread lies/rumours/gossip** *Andy loves spreading rumours about his colleagues.*|**spread the word** *Can you spread the word that the meeting is at 10.30?*

**4 ▶ PEOPLE/PLANTS/ANIMALS ◀** [I always + adv/prep] to begin to live or grow in other areas or countries: **throughout/over etc** *The Moors spread all over Southern Spain.*
**5 ▶ SOFT SUBSTANCE ◀ a)** [T] to put a soft substance onto a surface in order to cover it: **spread sth on/over** *He spread plaster on the walls.*|**spread sth with sth** *Spread the toast thinly with butter.* —see picture on page 834 **b)** [I] to be soft enough to be put onto a surface in order to cover it: *If you warm up the butter it'll spread more easily.*
**6 ▶ COVER A LARGE AREA ◀ a)** also **spread out** [I always + adv/prep] to cover or stretch over a large area: [+ **across/over etc**] *Leafy branches spread above her forming a canopy.* **b) be spread across/over etc** to exist or be present over a large area: *The population is fairly evenly spread across the country.*
**7 spread (out) your legs/arms/fingers etc** to push your legs, fingers arms etc as far apart as possible
**8 ▶ DO STH GRADUALLY ◀** also **spread** sth ↔ **out** [T] to do something gradually over a period of time: **spread sth over sth** *Could I spread the repayments over a longer period?*
**9 ▶ WORK/RESPONSIBILITY/MONEY ◀** [T] to share work, responsibility, or money among several people: *The work will be spread across the departments.*|**spread the load/burden** *If we type five pages each that should help spread the load.*
**10 ▶ EXPRESSION ◀** [I always + adv/prep] to gradually cover all of someone's face: [+ **across/over**] *A mischievous grin spread over her face.*
**11 spread seeds/manure/fertilizer** to scatter seeds, MANURE etc on the ground
**12 spread your wings** to start to have an independent life: *A year spent studying abroad should allow him to spread his wings a bit.*
**13 spread its wings** if a bird or insect spreads its wings it stretches them wide
**14 spread a/the table (with)** *old-fashioned* to put food and drink on a table

**spread out** *phr v* **1** [I] if a group of people spread out, they move apart from each other so that they cover a wider area: *The detective ordered the officers to spread out and search the surrounding fields.* **2** [T **spread** sth ↔ **out**] to open something out or arrange a group of things on a flat surface: *Sue spread out her notes on the kitchen table and began to write.* **3** [I] to cover or stretch over a large area: *A lush green valley spread out below us.* **4** [T **spread** sth ↔ **out**] to do something gradually over a period of time: *You can spread out the cost over a year.*

**spread²** *n*
**1 ▶ INCREASE ◀** [singular] the increase in the area, or number of people, affected by something, or in the number of people who do something: **the spread of** *the spread of liberal ideas in the 19th century*
**2 ▶ SOFT FOOD ◀** [C,U] a soft food which you spread on bread: **cheese/chocolate etc spread** (=cheese, chocolate etc in a soft form)
**3 ▶ LARGE MEAL ◀** [singular] *informal* a large meal for several guests on a special occasion: *She organized a marvellous spread for the soiree afterwards.*
**4 ▶ RANGE ◀** [singular] a range of people or things: *We have a good spread of ages in the department.*
**5 double-page spread/centre spread** a special article or advertisement in a newspaper or magazine, which covers two pages or covers the centre pages
**6 ▶ HAND/WINGS ◀** [U] the area covered when the fingers of a hand, or a bird's wings, are fully stretched
**7 a spread of land/water** an area of land or water
**8 ▶ FARM ◀** [C] *AmE* a large farm or RANCH
**9 ▶ MONEY ◀** *technical* the difference between the buying price and the selling price of shares (SHARE² (5)) on the STOCK EXCHANGE —see also MIDDLE-AGED SPREAD

**spread·ea·gled** /spredˈiːgəld‖ˈsprediːgəld/ *adj* lying with arms and legs stretched out: *He lay spreadeagled on the bed.*

**spread·sheet** /ˈspredʃiːt/ *n* [C] *technical* a kind of computer PROGRAM that can show and calculate information about sales, taxes, profits etc

**spree** /spriː/ *n* [C] a short period of time doing something that you enjoy, especially spending money or drinking: **go (off) on a spree** *He's gone off on a drinking spree with his friends.*|**a shopping/spending etc spree** *I'm going on a shopping spree to cheer myself up.*

**sprig** /sprɪg/ *n* [C] a small stem or part of a branch with leaves or flowers on it: [+ **of**] *a sprig of parsley*

**spright·ly** /ˈspraɪtli/ *adj* an old person who is sprightly is still active and full of energy —**sprightliness** *n* [U]

**spring¹** /sprɪŋ/ *n* S2 W2
**1 ▶ SEASON ◀** [C,U] the season between winter and summer when leaves and flowers appear: *It was a cold, sunny day in early spring*|*the spring of 1933*|*spring flowers*
**2 ▶ BED/CARS ETC ◀ a)** [C usually plural] something, usually a twisted piece of metal, that will return to its previous shape after it has been pressed down **b)** [U] the ability of a chair, bed etc to return to its normal shape after being pressed down: *There's not much spring in this old sofa.*
**3 ▶ WATER ◀** [C] a place where water comes up naturally from the ground: *The islands are renowned for their thermal springs and sulphur baths.*
**4 with a spring in your step** if you walk with a spring in your step, you move quickly and cheerfully
**5 ▶ SUDDEN JUMP ◀** [singular] a sudden quick movement or jump in a particular direction

**spring²** *v past tense* **sprang** /spræŋ/ *also* **sprung** /sprʌŋ/ *AmE, past participle* **sprung**
**1 ▶ MOVE SUDDENLY ◀** [I always + adv/prep] to move suddenly and quickly in a particular direction, especially by jumping: [+ **out of/from/towards etc**] *Tom sprung out of bed and rushed to the window.*|*A kitten sprang from under the bush.*|**spring to your feet** (=stand up suddenly)
**2 ▶ EXPRESSION/TEARS ◀** [I always + adv/prep] to appear suddenly on someone's face or in their eyes: [+ **into/to**] *Tears sprang into her eyes as she started telling them what had happened.*
**3 ▶ MOVE BACK ◀** [I always + adv/prep] to move

quickly back again after being pushed downwards or sideways: [+ **back/up**] *The branch sprang back and hit him in the face.*
**4 spring to mind** if someone or something springs to mind you immediately think of them: *Nobody's name actually springs to mind as an ideal candidate.*
**5 spring into action** also **spring to life** to suddenly become active: *The whole town would spring into action at carnival time.*
**6 spring into existence** to suddenly begin to exist: *A lot of small businesses sprang into existence during the 1980s.*
**7 spring open/shut** to open or close suddenly and quickly: *The lid of the box sprang open.*
**8 spring a trap** **a)** if an animal springs a trap, it makes the trap move and catch it **b)** to make someone say or do something by tricking them
**9 spring a leak** if a boat or a container springs a leak, it begins to let liquid in or out through a crack or hole
**10 spring to sb's defence** to quickly defend someone who is being criticized: *Charlene sprang immediately to her son's defence.*
**11 spring to attention** if soldiers spring to attention they stand suddenly upright
**12 spring a surprise** to make something unexpected or unusual happen
**13 ▶ PRISON ◀** [T] *informal* to help someone escape from prison: *A gangland boss was recently sprung from Dartmoor prison.*

**spring from** *phr v* [T] *spoken* **1** to be caused by something: *Her rudeness to other people springs from a basic insecurity.* **2 where did you/she etc spring from?** used to express surprise when you suddenly see someone who you thought was somewhere else

**spring** sth **on** sb *phr v* [T] to tell someone some news that surprises or shocks them

**spring up** *phr v* [I] to suddenly appear or start to exist: *Fast-food restaurants are springing up all over town.* | *A strong wind seemed to have sprung up from nowhere.*

**spring·board** /ˈsprɪŋbɔːd‖-bɔːrd/ *n* [C] **1** something that helps you to start doing something, especially by giving you ideas abut how to do it: [+ **for**] *Teachers can use these ideas as a springboard for planning their own lessons.* **2** a strong board for jumping on or off, used when diving (DIVE[1] (1)) or doing GYMNASTICS

**spring·bok** /ˈsprɪŋbɒk‖-bɑːk/ *n* [C] a small DEER that can run fast and lives in South Africa

**spring break** /ˌ· ˈ·/ *n* [C] *AmE* a holiday from college or university in the spring, that is usually two weeks long

**spring chick·en** /ˌ· ˈ··/ *n* [C] **she's/you're no spring chicken** *humorous* used to say that someone is no longer young

**spring-clean** /ˌ· ˈ·◂/ *v* [I,T] to clean a house thoroughly, usually once a year: **do the spring-cleaning** *Judith's busy doing the spring-cleaning.* —**spring-clean** *n* [singular] *BrE*

**spring fe·ver** /ˌ· ˈ··/ *n* [U] a sudden feeling of energy and wanting to do something new and exciting that you have in the spring

**spring on·ion** /ˌ· ˈ··/ *n* [C] *BrE* a strong-tasting onion with a small white round part and a long green stem, usually eaten raw; SCALLION, GREEN ONION *AmE*

**spring roll** /ˌ· ˈ·‖ˈ· ·/ *n* [C] a type of Chinese food consisting of a piece of rolled PASTRY filled with vegetables and sometimes meat and cooked in oil; EGG ROLL *AmE*

**spring tide** /ˌ· ˈ·/ *n* [C] a large rise and fall in the level of the sea at the time of the NEW MOON and the FULL MOON

**spring·time** /ˈsprɪŋtaɪm/ *n* [U] the time of the year when it is spring: *Paris in the springtime.*

**spring train·ing** /ˌ· ˈ··/ *n* [U] *AmE* the period during which a BASEBALL team gets ready for competition

**spring·y** /ˈsprɪŋi/ *adj* **1** something that is springy comes back to its former shape after being pressed or walked on: *The turf felt springy underfoot.* **2 springy step/walk** a way of walking which is quick and full of energy —**springily** *adv* —**springiness** *n* [U]

**sprin·kle**[1] /ˈsprɪŋkəl/ *v* **1** [T] to scatter small drops of liquid or small pieces of something: **sprinkle sth on/over sth** *She sprinkled perfume on the pillow.* | **sprinkle sth with sth** *Sprinkle the pasta with cheese.* —see picture on page 834 **2 be sprinkled with jokes/quotations etc** to be full of jokes etc: *Dr Krowik's conversation was liberally sprinkled with literary allusions.*
**3 it is sprinkling** *AmE* if it is sprinkling, it is raining lightly

**sprinkle**[2] *n* [singular] **1** a sprinkling: *Add a sprinkle of salt.* **2** *AmE* a light rain

**sprin·kler** /ˈsprɪŋklə‖-ər/ *n* [C] **1** a piece of equipment with holes, used for scattering water on grass or soil **2** a piece of equipment with holes that is on a ceiling and scatters water if there is a fire

**sprin·kling** /ˈsprɪŋklɪŋ/ *n* **a sprinkling of** a small quantity or amount of something: *The hilltops were covered with a sprinkling of snow.*

**sprint**[1] /sprɪnt/ *v* [I] to run very fast for a short distance: [+ **along/across/up etc**] *Bill sprinted up the steps.*

**sprint**[2] *n* **1** [singular] a short period of running very fast: **put on a sprint/make a sprint** (=run very quickly for a short distance) **2** [C] a short race in which the runners run very fast over a very short distance: *the 100 metre sprint*

**sprint·er** /ˈsprɪntə‖-ər/ *n* [C] someone who runs in fast races over short distances: *sprinter Linford Christie*

**sprite** /spraɪt/ *n* [C] **1** a FAIRY (1), especially one who is graceful or who likes playing tricks on people **2** an image produced by a special type of computer, that is drawn in layers to look real

**spritz** /sprɪts/ *v* [T] *AmE* to SPRAY a liquid in short bursts: *Spritz a little water on the fern every day.* —**spritz** *n* [C] *a spritz of hair spray*

**spritz·er** /ˈsprɪtsə‖-ər/ *n* [C,U] a drink made with SODA WATER and white wine

**sprock·et** /ˈsprɒkɪ̣t‖ˈsprɑː-/ *n* [C] **1** also **sprocket wheel** a wheel with a row of teeth (TOOTH (2)) for fitting into and turning a bicycle chain or a photographic film with holes **2** one of the teeth on a wheel of this kind

**sprog** /sprɒg‖sprɑːg/ *n* [C] *BrE humorous* a child or baby

**sprout**[1] /spraʊt/ *v* **1** [I] if leaves or BUDS sprout they appear and begin to grow **2** [I,T] if vegetables, seeds, or plants sprout they start to produce SHOOTS, or BUDS: *Keep the tray away from direct sunlight until the seeds begin to sprout.* | **sprout sth** *The plant had sprouted a few flower stalks.* **3** also **sprout up** [I always + adv/prep] to appear suddenly in large numbers: [+ **in/throughout**] *Office blocks seem to be sprouting up everywhere.* **4** [T] to grow suddenly, or grow something suddenly, especially hair, horns, or wings: *Jim seemed to have sprouted a beard overnight.*

**sprout**[2] *n* [C] **1** a small green vegetable like a very small CABBAGE; BRUSSELS SPROUT **2** a new growth on a plant; SHOOT[2] (1) **3** [usually plural] *AmE* an ALFALFA seed which has grown a stem and is eaten **4** *AmE* a BEANSPROUT

**spruce**[1] /spruːs/ *n* [C,U] a tree that grows in northern countries and has short leaves shaped like needles

**spruce**[2] *v*

**spruce up** *phr v* [I,T] *informal* to make yourself or something look neater and tidier: *I'll just go upstairs and spruce up a bit before dinner.* | **spruce sb/sth ↔ up** *We need to spruce the house up a bit before we sell it.*

**spruce**[3] *adj* neat and clean: *Mr Bailey was looking very spruce in a white linen suit.* —**sprucely** *adv*

**sprung**[1] /sprʌŋ/ a past tense and the past participle of SPRING

**sprung**[2] *adj* supported or kept in shape by SPRINGS: *a sprung mattress*

**spry** /spraɪ/ *adj* a spry old person is active and cheerful: *a spry ninety-year old* —**spryly** *adv*

**spud** /spʌd/ *n* [C] *informal* a POTATO

**spume** /spjuːm/ *n* [U] *literary* FOAM[1] (1) that forms on the top of waves when the sea is rough

**spun** /spʌn/ the past tense and past participle of SPIN

**spunk** /spʌŋk/ *n* [U] **1** *informal* courage **2** *BrE slang* SEMEN —**spunky** *adj*: *Clare's a spunky team captain.*

**spur[1]** /spɜː‖spɜːr/ *n* [C] **1** a sharp pointed object on the heel of a rider's boot which is used to encourage a horse to go faster **2** a fact or event that makes you try harder to do something: *Did your father's success act as a spur when you started in business?* **3 do sth on the spur of the moment** to do something suddenly, without thinking about it before you do it: *On the spur of the moment she picked up the phone and called Mike.* —see also SPUR-OF-THE-MOMENT **4** a piece of high ground which sticks out from the side of a hill or mountain **5** a railway track or road that goes away from a main line or road **6** the stiff sharp part that sticks out from the back of a male chicken's leg

**spur[2]** *v* **spurred, spurring** **1** also **spur on** [T] to encourage someone to try harder in order to succeed: **spur sb (on) to** *It's unlikely that harsh criticism will spur a child on to greater efforts.* | **spur sb into action** (=to make someone start doing something) **2** [T] to make an improvement or change happen faster: *Lower taxes would spur investment and help economic growth.* **3** [I,T] to encourage a horse to go faster, especially by pushing it with special points on the heels of your boots

**spu·ri·ous** /ˈspjʊəriəs‖ˈspjʊr-/ *adj* **1** a spurious statement, argument etc, is not based on facts or good reasoning and is likely to be incorrect: *a cosy and entirely spurious view of family life* **2** insincere: *spurious sympathy* —**spuriously** *adv* —**spuriousness** *n* [U]

**spurn** /spɜːn‖spɜːrn/ *v* [T] *especially literary* to refuse to accept something or to have a relationship with someone, espeically because you are too proud: *She spurned all offers of help.* | *a spurned lover*

**spur-of-the-mo·ment** /ˌ· · · ˈ··◂/ *adj* [only before noun] a spur-of-the-moment decision or action is made or done suddenly without planning

**spurt[1]** /spɜːt‖spɜːrt/ *v* **1** [I] if liquid or flames spurt from something they pour out of it quickly and suddenly: [+ **from/out of**] *Water began spurting from a hole in the pipe.* **2** [T] to send out liquid or flames **3** [I always + adv/prep] to move somewhere very quickly: [+ **towards/across**] *He spurted towards the finishing line.*

**spurt[2]** *n* [C] **1** a sudden pouring out of liquid or flames: [+ **of**] *The fire sent up spurts of flame.* | **in spurts** (=quickly for short periods) *The water came out of the tap in short spurts.* **2** a short sudden increase of activity, effort, or speed: [+ **of**] *a sudden spurt of academic progress* | **put on a spurt** (=to suddenly move more quickly for a short period) *Eric put on a spurt to try and catch up with the others.* | **in spurts** (=in sudden short periods of effort) *I tend to work in spurts.*

**sput·ter** /ˈspʌtə‖-ər/ *v* **1** [I] to make several sudden soft sounds like someone spitting (SPIT[1] (1)): *The engine began sputtering as the car climbed the hill.* **2** [I,T] to talk quickly in short confused phrases, especially because you are angry or shocked; SPLUTTER (1)

**spu·tum** /ˈspjuːtəm/ *n* [U] *technical* liquid in your mouth which you have coughed up from your lungs

**spy[1]** /spaɪ/ *n* [C] someone whose job it is to find out secret information about another country, organization, or group: *a British spy in World War II* | *a spy film*

**spy[2]** *v* **1** [I] to secretly collect information about an enemy country or an organization you are competing against: [+ **on**] *He was charged with spying on top-secret naval bases.* **2 spy on sb** to watch someone secretly: *Jean's always spying on the neighbours.* **3** [T] *especially literary* to suddenly see someone or something, especially after searching for them: *Ellen suddenly spied her friend in the crowd.*

**spy** sth ↔ **out** *phr v* [T] **1** to secretly find out information about something **2 spy out the land** to secretly find out more information about a situation before deciding what to do

**spy·glass** /ˈspaɪglɑːs‖-glæs/ *n* [C] a small TELESCOPE used by sailors in the past

**sq** the written abbreviation of SQUARE

**squab·ble** /ˈskwɒbəl‖ˈskwɑː-/ *v* [I] to quarrel continuously about something unimportant: [+ **about/over**] *The kids are still squabbling about whose turn it is to wash the dishes.* —**squabble** *n* [C]

**squad** /skwɒd‖skwɑːd/ *n* [C] **1** a group of players from which a team will be chosen for a particular sports event: *the Italian World Cup squad* **2** the police department responsible for dealing with a particular kind of crime: **drugs/fraud/vice squad** *Officers of the narcotics squad raided the club.* **3** a small group of soldiers working together as a unit: *a drill squad* **4** *AmE* a group of CHEERLEADERS —see also DEATH SQUAD, FIRING SQUAD, FLYING SQUAD W3

**squad car** /ˈ· ·/ *n* [C] a car used by police on duty; PATROL CAR: *He was bundled into the back of a squad car.*

**squad·dy, squaddie** /ˈskwɒdi‖ˈskwɑː-/ *n* [C] *BrE informal* a soldier who is not an officer

**squad·ron** /ˈskwɒdrən‖ˈskwɑː-/ *n* [C] a military force consisting of a group of aircraft or ships: *a squadron of bombers*

**squadron lead·er** /ˈ··· ˌ··/ *n* [C] an officer in the British AIRFORCE below a WING COMMANDER

**squal·id** /ˈskwɒlɪ̈d‖ˈskwɑː-/ *adj* **1** dirty and unpleasant because of a lack of care or money: *How can anyone live in such squalid conditions?* | *a tiny squalid apartment* **2** involving low moral standards or dishonesty; SORDID (1): *a squalid tale of sex and corruption* —see also SQUALOR —**squalidly** *adv* —**squalidness** *n* [U]

**squall[1]** /skwɔːl‖skwɒːl/ *n* [C] a sudden strong wind, especially one that brings rain or snow: *A violent squall sank both ships.*

**squall[2]** *v* [I] if a baby or child squalls, it cries noisily

**squal·ly** /ˈskwɔːli‖ˈskwɒːli/ *adj* squally rain or snow comes with sudden strong winds: *squally showers*

**squal·or** /ˈskwɒlə‖ˈskwɑː‖ˈskwɒːlər, ˈskwɑː-/ *n* [U] the condition of being SQUALID: *The refugees are forced to live in squalor.*

**squan·der** /ˈskwɒndə‖ˈskwɑːndər/ *v* [T] to spend money or use your time carelessly on things that are not useful: **squander sth on** *They squandered millions on that film.* —**squanderer** *n* [C]

**square[1]** /skweə‖skwer/ *adj* S2 W3

**1 ▶ SHAPE ◀** having four straight equal sides and 90° angles at the corners: *a square flower bed*

**2 ▶ ANGLE ◀** forming a 90° angle: *a square corner* | *a square jaw* | *square shoulders*

**3 square metre/mile etc** an area of measurement equal to a square with sides a metre long, a mile long etc: *about four square meters of ground* | *There isn't a café within a square mile of here.*

**4 5 feet/2 metres etc square** having the shape of a square with sides that are 5 feet, 2 metres etc long: *The room is six metres square.*

**5 ▶ LEVEL ◀** parallel with a straight line: [+ **with**] *I don't think the shelf is square with the floor.*

**6 a square deal** honest and fair treatment from someone, especially in business: *I try to give my workers a square deal, decent wages, and a clean room.* —see also **hit sth fair and square** (FAIR[3] (2)), **tell sb fair and square** (FAIR[3] (3))

**7 a square meal** a good satisfying meal

**8 be all square** to have the same number of points as your opponent in a competition: *The teams were all square at the end of the first half.*

**9 (all) square** *informal* if two people are square they do not owe each other any money: *Here's your £10 back, that makes us square.*

**10 ▶ UNFASHIONABLE ◀** *old-fashioned* boring and unfashionable

**11 a square peg in a round hole** *informal* someone who

is in a job or situation that is not suitable for them —**squareness** *n* [U]

S 2 **square²** *n* [C]
**1 ▶ SHAPE ◀ a)** a shape with four straight equal sides with 90° angles at the corners: *First of all, draw a square.* —see picture at SHAPE¹ **b)** a piece of something in this shape: [+ **of**] *a square of cloth* —see picture on page 416
**2 ▶ IN A TOWN ◀ a)** a broad open area in the middle of a town usually in the shape of a square, or the buildings surrounding it: *There's a market in the square every Tuesday.* **b) Square** used in addresses: *She lives in Hanover Square.*
**3 be back to square one** to be back in exactly the same situation that you started from, so that you have made no progress: *Police have released the suspect and are now back to square one.*
**4 ▶ NUMBER ◀** the result of multiplying a number by itself: *The square of 4 is 16.* —see also SQUARE ROOT
**5 ▶ IN A GAME ◀** a space on a board used for playing a game such as CHESS
**6 ▶ PERSON ◀** *old-fashioned* someone who is boring because they are not interested in the newest styles of music, clothes etc
**7 ▶ TOOL ◀** a flat tool with a straight edge, often shaped like an L, used for drawing or measuring 90° angles —see also SETSQUARE
**8 be on the square** *old-fashioned* to behave or speak honestly: *Are you really on the square?*

**square³** *v* [T]
**1 ▶ MULTIPLY ◀** to multiply a number by itself
**2 ▶ IN A COMPETITION ◀** to win the same number of points or games as your opponent: *India won the second match to square the series at one each.*
**3 ▶ PAY SB MONEY ◀** to pay money to someone in an official position, so that they do what you want: *We'll have to square a few goverment officials, if we're going to get this scheme approved.*
**4 square your shoulders** to push back your shoulders with your back straight, usually to show your determination
**5 ▶ MAKE STH STRAIGHT ◀** to make something straight or parallel
**6 square the circle** to attempt something impossible

**square** sth ↔ **away** *phr v* [T usually passive] *AmE* to finish something, especially by putting the last details in order: *Get your work squared away before you leave.*

**square off** *phr v* [T] **1** [T **square** sth ↔ **off**] to make something square with straight edges **2** [I] *AmE* to get ready to fight someone

**square up** *phr v* **1** [I] to pay money that you owe: *I'll pay for the drinks and you can square up later.* **2** [I] *BrE* to get ready to fight someone **3** [T **square up to** sb/sth] to deal with a difficult situation or person in a determined way: *I admire the way she squared up to the problem.*

**square with** *phr v* **1** [I,T not in progressive] if you square two ideas, statements etc with each other or if they square with each other they can be accepted together even though they seem different: *Ben's story doesn't square with Jane's version.* | **square sth with sth** *How do you square fighting in a war, with being a Christian?* | **square sth with your conscience** (=make yourself believe that what you are doing is morally right) **2** [T **square** sth **with** sb] to arrange something with someone by persuading them to agree to it or allow it: *I'll take the day off if I can square it with my boss.*

**square⁴** *adv* [only after verb] **1** directly and firmly; SQUARELY: | **square in the eye** *Look him square in the eye and say no.* **2** [+ **to**] at 90° to a line; SQUARELY (2)

**square-bash·ing** /ˈ· ˌ··/ *n* [U] *BrE informal* practice in marching as part of military training

**square brack·ets** /ˌ· ˈ··/ *n* [plural] *BrE* a pair of BRACKETS [ ], used for enclosing information —see picture at PUNCTUATION MARK

**squared** /skweəd‖skwerd/ *adj* **1** divided into squares or marked with squares: *squared paper* **2 3/9/10 etc squared** the number 3, 9 etc mulitiplied by itself: *3 squared equals 9.*

**square dance** /ˈ· ·/ *n* [C] a type of COUNTRY DANCE in which four pairs of dancers face each other in a square

**square knot** /ˈ· ·/ *n* [C] *AmE* a double knot that will not come undone easily; REEF KNOT

**square·ly** /ˈskweəli‖ˈskwer-/ *adv* [only after verb] **1** directly and firmly; SQUARE⁴ (1): *He turned and faced her squarely.* **2** completely and with no doubt: *The report puts the blame squarely on the government.* **3** straight on something and centrally; SQUARE⁴ (2): *Dr Soames jammed his hat squarely on his head.* **4** at 90° to a line; SQUARE⁴ (2)

**square-rigged** /ˌ· ˈ·◂/ *adj* a ship that is square-rigged has its sails set across it and not along its length

**square root** /ˌ· ˈ·/ *n* [C] the square root of a number is the number which, when multiplied by itself, equals that number: *The square root of nine is three.*

**squar·ish** /ˈskweərɪʃ‖ˈskwer-/ *adj* shaped almost like a square

**squash¹** /skwɒʃ‖skwɑːʃ, skwɒːʃ/ *v* **1** [T] to press something into a flat shape, often breaking or damaging it: *I don't want my hat getting squashed in your bag.* | *Hey! You're squashing me!* **2** [I always + adv/prep, T always + adv/prep] to push yourself or something else into a space that is too small: [+ **into**] *Seven of us squashed into the car.* **3** [T] *informal* to use your power or authority to stop something that is causing trouble; QUASH

squash

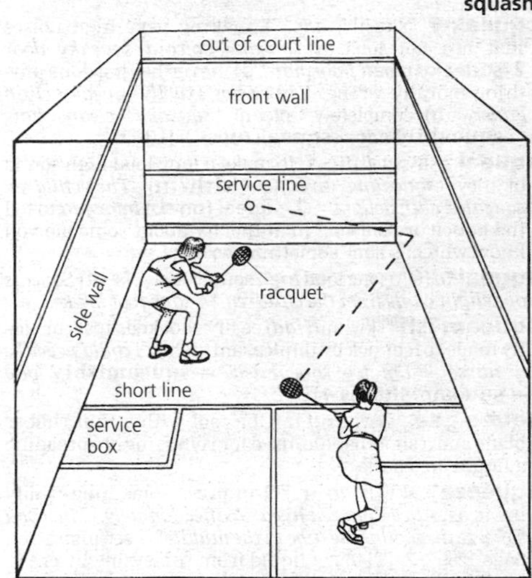

a squash court

**squash²** *n* **1** [U] a game played by two people who use rackets (RACKET¹ (3)) to hit a small rubber ball against the four walls of a square court **2 it's a squash** *spoken* used to say that there is not enough space for everyone to fit comfortably in: *Sorry it's a squash with six in the car.* **3** [C,U] one of a group of large vegetables with solid flesh and hard skins, such as PUMPKINS and ZUCCHINI —see picture on page 414 **4** [U] *BrE* a drink made from fruit juice, sugar, and water

**squashed** /skwɒʃt‖skwɑːʃt, skwɒːʃt/ *adj* broken or made flat by being pressed hard: *a bag of squashed tomatoes*

**squash rack·ets** /ˈ· ˌ··/ *n* [U] SQUASH² (1)

**squash·y** /ˈskwɒʃi‖ˈskwɑːʃi, ˈskwɒːʃi/ *adj* soft and full of liquid: *squashy overripe tomatoes* —**squashiness** *n* [U]

**squat**[1] /skwɒt‖skwɑːt/ *v* **squatted, squatting** [I] **1** also **squat down** to sit with your knees bent under you, your bottom off the ground, and balancing on your feet: [+ **on/behind/in etc**] *Parsons squatted down beside the footprints to get a better look.* —see picture at CROUCH **2** to live in a building or on a piece of land without permission and without paying rent: *There are people squatting in the house next door.*

**squat**[2] *adj* unattractively short and thick or low and wide: *squat stone cottages roofed in slate*

**squat**[3] *n* **1** [C] a squatting position **2** [singular] *BrE* a house that people are living in without permission and without paying rent: *She lives in a draughty squat in Camden.*

**squat·ter** /ˈskwɒtə‖ˈskwɑːtər/ *n* [C] someone who lives in an empty building or on a piece of land without permission and without paying rent: *crudely built squatters' shacks*

**squaw** /skwɔː‖skwɒː/ *n* [C] *old use* a word for a Native American woman, which many people think is offensive

**squawk** /skwɔːk‖skwɒːk/ *v* [I] **1** if a bird squawks, it makes a loud sharp angry sound: *Behind her a peacock squawked.* **2** *informal* to complain loudly and angrily —**squawk** *n* [C]

**squeak**[1] /skwiːk/ *v* [I] **1** to make a very short high noise or cry that is not loud: *I can hear mice squeaking in the walls.*|*a squeaking hinge* **2** [always + adv/prep] *informal* to succeed, win, or pass a test by a very small amount so that you only just avoid failure: [+ **through/by**] *She only just squeaked through her maths test.*

**squeak**[2] *n* [C] a very short high noise or cry: *a squeak of alarm*

**squeak·y** /ˈskwiːki/ *adj* **1** making very high noises that are not loud: *a squeaky voice*|*a squeaky door* **2 squeaky clean** *informal* **a)** never having done anything morally wrong: *You're not exactly squeaky clean either.* **b)** completely clean: *squeaky clean hair* —**squeakily** *adv* —**squeakiness** *n* [U]

**squeal**[1] /skwiːl/ *v* [I] **1** to make a long loud high sound or cry: *squealing tires*|[+ **with/in**] *The children squealed with delight.* **2 squeal (on sb)** *informal* to tell the police or someone in authority about someone you know who has done something wrong

**squeal**[2] *n* [C] a long loud high sound or cry: [+ **of**] *Squeals of delight came from the children.*|*a squeal of brakes*

**squeam·ish** /ˈskwiːmɪʃ/ *adj* easily shocked, upset or easily made to feel sick by unpleasant sights: *I could never be a nurse – I'm too squeamish.* —**squeamishly** *adv* —**squeamishness** *n* [U]

**squee·gee** /ˈskwiːdʒiː/ *n* [C] a tool with a thin rubber blade and a short handle, used for removing or spreading a liquid on a surface

**squeeze**[1] /skwiːz/ *v* **1** [T] to press something firmly inwards: *Alice squeezed his arm affectionately.*|*Must you squeeze the toothpaste tube in the middle?* —see picture on page 1259 **2** [T] to get liquid from something by pressing it: **squeeze sth out** *Try to squeeze a bit more out of the tube.*|**squeeze sth on/onto sth** *Squeeze a bit of lemon onto the fish.* —see picture on page 834 **3** [I always + adv/prep,T always + adv/prep] to try to make something fit into a space that is too small, or to try to get into such a space: [+ **into/through/past/between**] *Five of us squeezed into the back seat of the car.*|*Move your chair and I'll try to squeeze past.*|**squeeze sth into** *You'll never squeeze yourself into that dress.* **4 squeeze sth out of sb** to force someone to tell you something: *See if you can squeeze more information out of them.* **5 squeeze sb out (of sth)** to make it difficult for someone to continue in business, by attracting their customers: *It's the big operators squeezing the independents out of the market.* **6** [T] to manage to do something although you are very busy: **squeeze sth in/into** *How do you manage to squeeze so much into one day?*|**squeeze sb in** (=have time to see them) *I can squeeze you in at four o'clock.* **7 squeeze in/into/through** to succeed, win, or pass a test by a very small amount so that you only just avoid failure **8** [T] to strictly limit the amount of money that is available to a company or organization: *The failure of the levy has squeezed the school district's budget.*

**squeeze**[2] *n* **1 a (tight) squeeze** a situation in which there is only just enough room for things or people to fit somewhere: *It'll be a squeeze with six people in the car.* **2** [C] an act of pressing something firmly, usually with your hands: **give sb/sth a squeeze** *Marty gave her hand a little squeeze.* **3 a squeeze of lemon/lime etc** a small amount of juice obtained by squeezing a piece of fruit —see picture on page 416 **4 a squeeze** a situation in which wages, prices, borrowing money etc are strictly controlled: *a credit squeeze* **5 put the squeeze on sb** *informal* to try to persuade someone to do something **6 your/her/his main squeeze** *AmE informal* someone's BOYFRIEND or GIRLFRIEND

**squeeze·box** /ˈskwiːzbɒks‖-bɑːks/ *n* [C] *informal* an ACCORDION

**squeez·er** /ˈskwiːzə‖-ər/ *n* [C] a small tool for squeezing juice from fruit such as LEMONS

**squelch** /skweltʃ/ *v* [I] **1** to make a sucking sound by walking in soft wet mud [+ **through/along/up**] *We squelched up the sodden path.* —see picture on page 1260 **2** [T] *AmE* to stop something such as an idea from continuing to develop or spread: *Such rigid teaching methods only serve to squelch kids' creativity.* —**squelch** *n* [C]

**squelch·y** /ˈskweltʃi/ *adj* squelchy mud or ground is soft and wet and makes a sucking noise when you walk on it

**squib** /skwɪb/ *n* [C] **1** a small exploding FIREWORK **2** *literary* a short amusing piece of writing that attacks someone —see also **damp squib** (DAMP[1] (2))

**squid** /skwɪd/ *plural* **squid** *or* **squids** *n* [C] a sea creature with a long body and ten arms around its mouth

**squidg·y** /ˈskwɪdʒi/ *adj BrE* soft and wet, like thick mud

**squif·fy** /ˈskwɪfi/ *adj BrE old-fashioned* slightly drunk

**squig·gle** /ˈskwɪgəl/ *n* [C] a short irregular line in writing or drawing that curls and twists: *I can't read the signature, it's just a squiggle.* —**squiggly** *adj*: *squiggly lines*

**squint**[1] /skwɪnt/ *v* [I] **1** to look at something with your eyes partly closed in order to see better: *Anna squinted in the sudden bright sunlight.*|[+ **at**] *Squinting at the target, Mark took careful aim.* **2** [not in progressive] to have a squint

**squint**[2] *n* [singular] **1** a condition of your eye muscles that makes each eye look in a different direction **2 have/take a squint at sth** *informal* to look at something

**squire** /skwaɪə‖skwaɪr/ *n* [C] **1** the man who in the past owned most of the land around a country village in England **2** a young man in the Middle Ages who learned how to be a KNIGHT[1] (1) by serving one **3** *BrE spoken* used by some men to address a man when they do not know his name

**squirm** /skwɜːm‖skwɜːrm/ *v* [I] **1** to twist your body from side to side because you are uncomfortable or nervous: *Stop squirming so I can finish doing your hair!* **2** to feel very embarrassed or ashamed: [+ **with**] *Greg turned red, squirming with guilt.* —**squirm** *n* [singular]

**squir·rel**[1] /ˈskwɪrəl‖ˈskwɜːrəl/ *n* [C] a small animal with a long furry tail that climbs trees and eats nuts

**squirrel**[2] *v* [T + **away**] *especially AmE* to keep something in a safe place to use later

**squir·rel·y** /ˈskwɪrəli‖ˈskwɜː-/ *adj AmE informal* unable to stay still; RESTLESS

**squirt**[1] /skwɜːt‖skwɜːrt/ *v* [I,T] **1** [I,T] if you squirt liquid or if it squirts, it is forced out of a narrow hole in a thin fast stream: *Water's squirting from about five different leaks.*|**squirt sth** *Squirt some oil in the lock.* **2** [T] to hit or cover someone or something with a thin fast stream of liquid: **squirt sb/sth with sth** *Mom! Chad's squirting me with the hose!*

**squirt**[2] *n* [C] **1** a fast thin stream of liquid —see picture on page 416 **2 little squirt** *spoken* an insulting word for a short person, especially someone who is annoying you: *You're just an ignorant little squirt.*

**squirt gun** /ˈ· ·/ *n* [C] *AmE* a WATER PISTOL

**squish** /skwɪʃ/ *v* **1** [I always + adv/prep] to make a soft sucking sound by moving in or through something soft and wet like mud —see picture on page 1261 **2** [I,T] *AmE informal* to SQUASH¹ something, or to become squashed

**squish·y** /ˈskwɪʃi/ *adj* soft and wet or full of liquid: *squishy mud* —**squishiness** *n* [U]

**Sr** *BrE*, **Sr.** *AmE* **1** [only after noun] the written abbreviation of SENIOR: *Douglas Fairbanks, Sr.* **2** [only before noun] the written abbreviation of SEÑOR: *Sr Lopez* **3** the written abbreviation of Sister, used in front of the name of a NUN: *Sr Bernadette* **4** *BrE* the written abbreviation of Sister, used in front of the name of a nurse

**SS** /ˈes es/ [only before noun] the abbreviation of STEAMSHIP

S3 **ssh** /ʃ/ *interjection* used to ask for silence or less noise: *Ssh! You'll wake everybody up.*

**St** *BrE* also **St.** **1** [only after noun or adjective] the written abbreviation of street: *Wall St.* | *Church St* **2** the written abbreviation of SAINT: *St Luke's Gospel* **3 st** the written abbreviation of STONE¹ (6)

**-st** /st/ *suffix* **1** forms written ORDINAL numbers with 1: *the 1st* (=first) *prize* | *my 21st birthday* **2** *old use or biblical* another form of the suffix -EST (2): *thou dost* (=you do)

**stab¹** /stæb/ *v* **stabbed, stabbing** **1** [T] to push a knife into someone or something: **stab sb to death** *Smith was found stabbed to death in a burning car.* | **stab sb in the heart/arm etc** *Luca stabbed her in the thigh with a breadknife.* **2** [I,T] to make quick pushing movements with your finger or something pointed; JAB¹ **3 stab sb in the back** to do something that harms someone who likes and trusts you; BETRAY —see also STABBING

**stab²** *n* [C] **1** an act of stabbing or trying to stab someone: *severe stab wounds* | [+ **at**] *He made a vicious stab at me with a broken bottle.* **2 a stab of fear/disappointment/pain etc** a sudden sharp feeling of fear etc: *A quick stab of excitement ran through him.* **3 have/make a stab at (doing) sth** *informal* to try to do something **4 a stab in the back** an attack from someone you thought was a friend: *One of them smiles in your face while the other one stabs you in the back.*

**stab·bing¹** /ˈstæbɪŋ/ *adj* a stabbing pain is sharp and sudden, as if it had been made by a knife: *stabbing headaches*

**stabbing²** *n* [C] a crime in which someone is stabbed

**sta·bil·i·ty** /stəˈbɪləti/ *n* [U] **1** the condition of being strong, steady and not changing: [+ **of**] *the stability of the dollar* | *a long period of political stability* **2** *technical* the ability of a substance to stay in the same state —opposite INSTABILITY

**sta·bil·ize** also **-ise** *BrE* /ˈsteɪbəlaɪz/ *v* [I,T] to become firm, steady or unchanging, or to make something firm or steady: *The patient's condition has now stabilized.* —**stabilization** /ˌsteɪbəlaɪˈzeɪʃən‖-lə-/ *n* [U]

**sta·bil·iz·er** also **-iser** *BrE* /ˈsteɪbəlaɪzə‖-ər/ *n* [C] **1** a chemical that helps something such as a food to stay in the same state **2** a piece of equipment that helps make something such as an aircraft, ship, or bicycle steady

W3 **sta·ble¹** /ˈsteɪbəl/ *adj* **1** steady and not likely to move or change: *Be careful, that ladder isn't stable.* | *a stable marriage* | *a politically stable country* **2** calm, reasonable, and not easy to upset: *Norman's a bit neurotic, but his wife's a very stable person.* **3** *technical* a stable substance tends to stay in the same chemical or ATOMIC state —opposite UNSTABLE —see also STABILITY —**stably** *adv*

**stable²** *n* [C] **1** *BrE* a building where horses are kept **2** *AmE* a building where horses, cattle etc are kept **3 a)** a group of racing horses that has one owner or trainer **b)** a group of people working for the same company or with the same trainer: *actors from the same Hollywood stable* **4 shut/close the stable door after the horse has bolted** to try to prevent something when it is too late, and harm has already been done

**stable³** *v* [T] to put or keep a horse in a stable

**sta·ble·boy** /ˈsteɪbəlbɔɪ/ also **stable lad** /ˈ·· ·/ *BrE*, **sta·ble·man** /ˈsteɪbəlmæn/ *AmE n* [C] a man or boy who works in a stable and looks after horses

**sta·ble·mate** /ˈsteɪbəlmeɪt/ *n* [C] something or someone that is like other things or people: *ambient music and its stablemate techno*

**sta·bles** /ˈsteɪbəlz/ *n* [plural] a stable or a group of stables

**sta·bling** /ˈsteɪblɪŋ/ *n* [U] space for horses to be stabled

**stac·cat·o** /stəˈkɑːtəʊ‖-toʊ/ *adv* when music is played staccato the notes are cut short and do not flow smoothly —compare LEGATO —**staccato** *adj*

**stack¹** /stæk/ *n* [C] **1** a neat pile of things one on top of the other: [+ **of**] *a stack of papers* | *stacks of dishes waiting to be washed* **2** a large pile of grain, grass etc that is stored outside —see also HAYSTACK **3 a stack of/stacks of** *informal especially BrE* a large amount: *Mr. Truman has stacks of money.* **4** a tall chimney **5 the stacks** a part of a library where books are stored close together **6** a temporary store of information on a computer —see also **blow your top/stack** (BLOW¹ (20))

**stack²** *v* **1** also **stack up** [I,T] to form a neat pile or make things into a neat pile: *These chairs are designed to stack easily.* | **stack sth** *Stack the books up against the wall.* | *a stacking hi-fi system* **2** [T usually passive] to put piles of things on a place or in a place: [+ **with**] *The floor was stacked with boxes.* **3 have the odds stacked against you** *informal* to be at a great disadvantage: *The home team can't win; the odds are stacked against them.* **4 stack the cards** *BrE* **stack the deck** *AmE informal* to arrange cards dishonestly in a game **5** also **stack up** [I,T] if aircraft stack or are stacked around an airport, they are made to fly around it until they can land

**stack up** *phr v* [I] *informal* to have a particular appearance when compared with something else: [+ **against**] *How does their product stack up against our own?*

**stacked** /stækt/ *adj informal* an offensive word meaning having large breasts

**stack sys·tem** /ˈ· ˌ··/ *n* [C] an arrangement of equipment for playing music, in which one piece stands on top of another

**stack-up** /ˈ· ·/ *n* [C] a situation in which several aircraft are flying around an airport waiting to land

**sta·di·um** /ˈsteɪdiəm/ *n plural* **stadiums** or **stadia** /-diə/ [C] a building for sports, consisting of a field surrounded by rows of seats: *a baseball stadium*

**staff¹** /stɑːf‖stæf/ *n* S2 W2

**1 ▶ WORKERS ◀ a)** [C, also + plural verb *BrE*] the people who work for an organization, especially a school or business: *The school's staff is excellent.* | *We now employ a staff of 25.* | **member of staff** *Complaints by members of staff about sick pay.* | **on the staff** (=being a member of staff) *It's good to have you on staff.* **b)** [plural] the members of such a group: *Andrea's in charge of about 20 staff.* | *complaints by members of staff about sick pay* | *a special car park for senior staff* | **on the staff** (=being a member of staff) *It's good to have you on the staff.*

**2 ▶ STICK ◀** [C] *plural* **staves** /steɪvz/ **a)** *old use* a long thick stick to help you walk **b)** a long thick stick that an official holds in some ceremonies

**3 ▶ FLAG ◀** [C] a pole for flying a flag on; FLAGPOLE

**4 ▶ MUSIC ◀** [C] the set of five lines that music is written on; STAVE¹ (1)

**5 the staff of life** *literary* a basic food, especially bread —see also GENERAL STAFF, GROUND STAFF

**staff²** *v* [T usually passive] to provide the workers for an organization: *The refuge is staffed mainly by volunteers.* —see also OVERSTAFFED, UNDERSTAFFED —**staffing** *n* [U] *staffing levels*

**staff nurse** /ˈ· ˌ·/ *n* [C] a British hospital nurse whose rank is just below a sister's (SISTER (2))



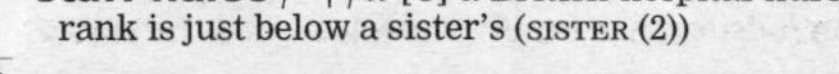

**staff of·fi·cer** /ˈ· ˌ···/ *n* [C] an officer who helps a military commander of a higher rank

**staff ser·geant** /ˈ· ˌ··/ *n* [C,U] a lower rank in the army or the US Air Force or Marines, or someone who has this rank —see table on page B4

**stag** /stæg/ *n* [C] **1** a fully grown male DEER **2** *BrE* someone who buys shares (SHARE² (5)) in a new company, hoping to sell them quickly and make a profit **3 go stag** *AmE informal* if a man goes stag he goes to a party without a woman —see also STAG NIGHT, STAG PARTY

S1 W1 **stage¹** /steɪdʒ/ *n*

**1 ▶ TIME/STATE ◀** [C] a particular time or state that something reaches as it grows or develops: *The plan is still in its early stages.* | *the different stages of a child's development* | **at this stage** *It would be unwise to comment at this stage of the negotiations.* | **stage by stage** (=gradually) | **at a later stage** *The design may well be modified at a later stage.* —compare PHASE¹ (1), STEP¹ (4)

**2 ▶ THEATRE ◀** [C] the raised floor in a theatre on which plays are performed: **on stage** *She is on stage for most of the play.* | **stage left/right** (=from the left or right side of the stage) —see picture at THEATRE

**3 ▶ ACTING ◀ the stage** acting as a profession: **go on the stage** (=become an actor)

**4 take centre stage/be at the centre of the stage** to have everyone's attention, or to be very important: *Sally just loves to take center stage.* | *The hostage question has returned to the centre of the stage.*

**5 ▶ PLACE ◀** [singular] a place where something important happens: *Geneva has been the stage for many such conferences.* | *the European political stage*

**6 set the stage for** to prepare for something or make something possible: *Will this agreement merely set the stage for another war?*

**7 he's/she's going through a stage** *informal* used to say that someone young will soon stop behaving badly or strangely —see also LANDING STAGE

**stage²** *v* [T] to organize an event that people will come to see, or that you hope many people will notice: *We hope to stage four plays this season.* | *They'll be staging a Hockney exhibition.* | **stage a strike/demonstration/sit-in etc** *School teachers are staging a protest against the cuts.*

**stage·coach** /ˈsteɪdʒkəʊtʃ‖-koʊtʃ/ *n* [C] a closed vehicle pulled by horses that in former times carried passengers who paid to go to a particular place

**stage di·rec·tion** /ˈ· ·ˌ··/ *n* [C] a written instruction to an actor to do something in a play

**stage door** /ˌ· ˈ·◂/ *n* [C] the side or back door in a theatre, used by actors and theatre workers

**stage fright** /ˈ· ·/ *n* [U] nervousness felt by someone who is going to perform in front of a lot of people

**stage·hand** /ˈsteɪdʒhænd/ *n* [C] someone who works on a theatre stage, getting it ready for a play or for the next part of a play

**stage-man·age** /ˈ· ˌ··/ *v* [T] *informal* to organize a public event, such as a meeting, in a way that will give you the result that you want: *The press conference was cleverly stage-managed.*

**stage man·ag·er** /ˈ· ˌ···/ *n* [C] someone in charge of a theatre stage during a performance

**stage name** /ˈ· ˌ·/ *n* [C] a name used by an actor instead of his or her real name

**stage·struck** /ˈsteɪdʒstrʌk/ *adj* loving to see plays, or wanting very much to become an actor

**stage whis·per** /ˌ· ˈ··/ *n* [C] **1** an actor's loud WHISPER that other actors on the stage seem not to hear **2** a loud WHISPER that is intended to be heard by everyone: *"What's going on?" I demanded in a stage whisper.*

**stage·y** /ˈsteɪdʒi/ *adj* another spelling of STAGY

**stag·fla·tion** /stægˈfleɪʃən/ *n* [U] an economic condition in which there is INFLATION (=a continuing rise in prices) but many people do not have jobs and businesses are not doing well

**stag·ger¹** /ˈstægə‖-ər/ *v* **1** [I always + adv/prep] to walk or move unsteadily, almost falling over: [**+ away/into/down etc**] *The old man staggered drunkenly to his feet.* | *Marcus came staggering through the door with his groceries.* —see picture on page 1262 **2** [T usually passive] to make someone feel very surprised or shocked: *What staggered us was the sheer size of her salary.* **3** [T] to arrange people's working hours, holidays etc so that they do not all begin and end at the same time **4** [T] to start a race with each runner at a different place on a curved track

**stagger²** *n* [C usually singular] an unsteady movement of someone who is having difficulty in walking

**stag·gered** /ˈstægəd‖-ərd/ *adj* [not before noun] very surprised at something that has happened to you, or some news that you have heard that is hard to believe: [**+ by/at**] *I was staggered by the size of the phone bill.* | **staggered to hear/see/find etc** *We were staggered to find that we were not entitled to any money.*

**stag·ger·ing** /ˈstægərɪŋ/ *adj* very surprising, shocking, and almost unbelievable: *The cost was a staggering $10 million.* —**staggeringly** *adv*: *a staggeringly high phone bill*

**stag·ing** /ˈsteɪdʒɪŋ/ *n* **1** [C,U] the activity or art of performing a play: *a modern-dress staging of 'Hamlet'* **2** [U] movable boards and frames for standing on

**staging a·re·a** /ˈ·· ˌ···/ *n* [C] a place where soldiers meet and where military equipment is gathered before it is moved to another place

**staging post** /ˈ·· ·/ *n* [C] a place where a stop is regularly made on a long journey: *Bahrain is a staging post on the flight from Britain to Australia.* —compare STOPOVER

**stag·nant** /ˈstægnənt/ *adj* **1** stagnant water or air does not move or flow and often smells bad: *a stagnant pond* **2** not changing, developing, or making progress; inactive: *Industrial output has remained stagnant.* —**stagnancy** *n* [U] —**stagnantly** *adv*

**stag·nate** /stægˈneɪt‖ˈstægneɪt/ *v* [I] to stop developing or making progress: *a stagnating economy* | *I don't want to spend the rest of my life stagnating in that office.* —**stagnation** /stægˈneɪʃən/ *n* [U] *economic stagnation*

**stag night** /ˈ· ·/ *n* [C] *BrE* the night before a man's wedding, which he spends with his male friends, drinking or having a party

**stag par·ty** /ˈ· ˌ··/ *n* [C] a party for men only, especially on the night before a man's wedding

**stag·y, stagey** /ˈsteɪdʒi/ *adj* behaviour that is stagy is not natural and is like the way an actor behaves on a stage: *a very stagy manner* —**stagily** *adv*

**staid** /steɪd/ *adj* serious, old-fashioned, and boring in the way you live, dress, or work: *a staid old bachelor* | *staid attitudes* —**staidly** *adv* —**staidness** *n* [U]

**stain¹** /steɪn/ *v* **1** [I,T] to accidentally make a mark on something, especially one that cannot be removed, or to be marked in this way: [**+ with**] *teeth stained with nicotine from years of smoking* | *Pale carpets stain too easily.* —see picture on page 1258 **2** [T] to change the colour of something, especially something made of wood, by using a special chemical or DYE **3 stain sb's name/honour/reputation etc** *literary* to damage the good opinion that people have about someone

**stain²** *n* **1** [C] a mark that is difficult to remove, especially one made by a liquid such as blood, coffee, or ink: *There's a big stain on your tie.* | **blood/ink/wine etc stain** *How do you get wine stains out of a tablecloth?* **2** [C,U] a chemical for darkening something, especially wood **3 a stain on sb's character/reputation etc** something that makes people think that someone has done something wrong or illegal

**stained glass** /ˌ· ˈ·◂/ *n* [U] glass of different colours used for making pictures and patterns in windows, especially in a church

**stain·less** /ˈsteɪnləs/ *adj literary* without any sign of illegal or immoral behaviour: *a lady of beauty, rank and stainless reputation*

**stainless steel** /ˌ·· ˈ·/ *n* [U] a type of steel that does not RUST: *stainless steel cutlery*

S2 W3 **stair** /steə‖ster/ *n* **1 stairs** [plural] a set of steps built for going from one level of a building to another: **up/down the stairs** *Jerry ran up the stairs.* | **the top/head of the stairs** *Kate was standing at the top of the stairs.* | **the foot of the stairs** (=the bottom) | **a flight of stairs** (=between two floors of a building) *The attic's up five flights of stairs.* —see also DOWNSTAIRS, UPSTAIRS² —see picture on page 410 **2** [C] one of the steps in a set of stairs: *Lucy sat down on the bottom stair.* **3** [C] *especially literary* a set of stairs: *a steep winding stair to the tower.* **4 below stairs** *old-fashioned BrE* in the servants' part of a large house, in the past

**stair·case** /ˈsteəkeɪs‖ˈster-/ *n* [C] a set of stairs inside a building with its supports and the side parts that you hold on to

**stair·way** /ˈsteəweɪ‖ˈster-/ *n* [C] a staircase, especially a large or impressive one

**stair·well** /ˈsteəwel‖ˈster-/ *n* [C] the space going up through all the floors of a building, where the stairs go up

W3 **stake¹** /steɪk/ *n*
**1 ▶ SHARP POST ◀** [C] a pointed piece of wood, metal etc that is pushed into the ground to hold a rope, mark a particular place etc
**2 the stake** a post to which a person was tied in former times to be killed by being burnt: **burn sb at the stake** *Witches were often burnt at the stake.*
**3 have a stake in** to have an important part or share in a business, plan etc so that you will gain if it succeeds: *a 33% stake in the business* | *I just don't feel I have a stake in the country's future.*
**4 be at stake** if something that you value very much is at stake, you will lose it if a plan or action is not successful: *If we lose the contract, hundreds of jobs are at stake.*
**5 (be prepared to) go to the stake for/over sth** to take great risks to protect or defend an idea, belief etc: *That's my opinion, but I wouldn't go to the stake for it.*
**6 ▶ RISK ◀** [C usually singular] money risked on the result of something, especially a horse race; BET² (1)
**7 stakes** [plural] money that people risk on the result of a game, race, etc, all of which is taken by the winner: *We're playing for very high stakes here.*
**8 play for high stakes a)** to risk a lot of money in a game **b)** to be in a situation where you gain or lose a lot
**9 the popularity/fashion etc stakes** a situation that can be considered as if it were a competition: *Ben wouldn't score very highly in the popularity stakes.*
**10 pull up stakes** *AmE*, **up stakes** *BrE informal* to leave your job or home: *We're going to pull up stakes and move to Montana.*

**stake²** *v* [T] **1** to risk money on a race or competition: *Hargreave staked his whole fortune on one card game.* **2** to risk losing something that is valuable or important to you, if a plan or action is not successful: **stake sth on sb/sth** *The President is staking his reputation on these trade talks.* | *I've staked all my hopes on you.* **3** also **stake up** to fasten or strengthen something with stakes: *Those young trees will have to be staked.* **4** also **stake off** to mark or enclose an area of ground with stakes: *The muddiest corner of the field has been staked off.* **5 stake (out) a claim** to say publicly that you think you have a right to have or own something: *Joe staked his claim to the land where he found the gold.*

**stake** sth ↔ **out** *phr v* [T] *informal* to watch a place secretly and continuously: *The vice squad have been staking out the club for weeks.* —**stakeout** *n* [C]

**stake·hold·er** /ˈsteɪkˌhəʊldə‖-ˌhoʊldər/ *n* [C] **1** someone chosen to hold the money that is risked by people on a race, competition etc and to give all of it to the winner **2** someone, usually a lawyer, who takes charge of a property during a quarrel or a sale

**stal·ac·tite** /ˈstæləktaɪt‖stəˈlæktaɪt/ *n* [C] a sharp pointed object hanging down from the roof of a CAVE, which is formed gradually by water that contains minerals as it drops slowly from the roof

**stal·ag·mite** /ˈstæləgmaɪt‖stəˈlægmaɪt/ *n* [C] a sharp pointed object coming up from the floor of a CAVE, formed by drops from a stalactite

**stale¹** /steɪl/ *adj* **1** bread or cake that is stale is no longer fresh or good to eat: **go stale** *This loaf has gone stale.* **2** air that is stale is not fresh or pleasant **3** news or jokes that are stale are no longer interesting or exciting: *the same stale old jokes we've all heard before* **4** someone who is stale has no new ideas, interest, or energy, because they have been doing the same thing for too long: **feel/get/go stale** *I'm getting stale in this job – I need a change.* —**staleness** *n* [U]

**stale²** *v* [I] *formal* to become less interesting or exciting

**stale·mate** /ˈsteɪlmeɪt/ *n* [C,U] **1** a situation in which it seems impossible to settle an argument or disagreement, and neither side can get an advantage; DEADLOCK: *The discussions with the miners' union ended in stalemate.* **2** a position in CHESS in which neither player can win —**stalemate** *v* [T]

**stalk¹** /stɔːk‖stɒːk/ *n* [C] **1** a long narrow part of a plant that supports leaves, fruits, or flowers; stem: *celery stalks* **2** a thin upright object: *a microphone on a short stalk* **3 eyes out on stalks** *BrE informal* if your eyes are out on stalks you are surprised or shocked

**stalk²** *v* **1** [T] to follow a person or animal quietly in order to catch or kill them: *a tiger stalking its prey* | *We know the rapist stalks his victims at night.* **2** [I always + adv/prep] to walk in a proud or angry way, with long steps: [+ **out/off/away**] *Yvonne turned and stalked out of the room in disgust.*

**stalk·er** /ˈstɔːkə‖ˈstɒːkər/ *n* [C] a criminal who follows a woman over a period of time in order to force her to have sex, or kill her

**stalk·ing** /ˈstɔːkɪŋ‖ˈstɒː-/ *n* [U] the crime of following someone over a period of time in order to force them to have sex or kill them

**stalking horse** /ˈ·· ˌ·/ *n* [C] someone or something that hides someone's true purpose, especially a politician who says he wants his leader's job when the real plan is that another, more important politician should get it

**stall¹** /stɔːl‖stɒːl/ *n* **1** [C] a table or a small shop with an open front, especially outdoors, where goods are sold: *a market stall* **2** [C] an enclosed area in a building for an animal **3** [C usually singular] an occasion when an engine stops working: *The plane went into a stall.* **4** [C usually plural] a seat in a row of fixed seats for priests and singers in some larger churches: *choir stalls* **5 shower/toilet stall** a small enclosed private area for washing or using the toilet **6 the stalls** *BrE* the seats on the main level of a theatre or cinema: *a good seat in the front row of the stalls* —see picture at THEATRE S2

**stall²** *v* **1** [I,T] if an engine stalls or you stall it, it stops because there is not enough power or speed to keep it going: *Stupid car! It always stalls on hills.* | **stall sth** *An inexperienced pilot may easily stall a plane.* **2** [I] *informal* to deliberately delay because you are not ready to do something, answer questions etc: *Quit stalling and answer my question!* **3** [T] *informal* to make someone wait or stop something from happening until you are ready: *Maybe we can stall the sale until the prices go up.* | *Dad's coming! Stall him for a minute while I hide this.*

**stall·hold·er** /ˈstɔːlˌhəʊldə‖ˈstɒːlˌhoʊldər/ *n* [C] *BrE* someone who rents and keeps a market stall

**stal·lion** /ˈstæljən/ *n* [C] a male horse kept for breeding —compare MARE

**stal·wart¹** /ˈstɔːlwət‖ˈstɒːlwərt/ *n* [C] someone who works hard and is loyal to a particular organization or set of ideas: *Conservative party stalwarts*

**stalwart²** *adj* **1 stalwart supporter/ally etc** a very loyal and strong supporter etc **2** *formal* strong in appearance —**stalwartly** *adv*

**sta·men** /ˈsteɪmən/ *n* [C] *technical* the male part of a flower that produces POLLEN

**stam·i·na** /ˈstæmɪ̣nə/ *n* [U] physical or mental strength that lets you continue doing something for a long time without getting tired: *You need stamina to be a long-distance runner.*

**stam·mer¹** /ˈstæmə‖-ər/ *v* [I,T] to speak or say something with a lot of pauses and repeated sounds, either because you have a speech problem, or because you are nervous, excited etc: *Whenever he was angry he would begin to stammer slightly.* —compare STUTTER¹ (1) —**stammerer** *n* [C] —**stammeringly** *adv*

**stammer²** *n* [C usually singular] a speech problem which makes someone speak with a lot of pauses and repeated sounds: *He's got a bad stammer.*

S2 **stamp¹** /stæmp/ *n* [C]

**1** ▶ **MAIL** ◀ also **postage stamp** *formal* a small piece of paper that you buy and stick onto an envelope or package before posting it: *a 29-cent stamp* | **a sheet/book of stamps** (=set of stamps that you buy)

**2** ▶ **TOOL** ◀ a tool for pressing or printing a mark or pattern onto a surface, or the mark made by this tool: *a date stamp* | *a passport stamp*

**3 the stamp of sth** if something has the stamp of a particular quality, it clearly has that quality: **bear the stamp of sth** *The speech bore the stamp of authority.*

**4** ▶ **PAYMENT** ◀ *BrE* a small piece of paper that is worth a particular amount of money and is bought and collected for something over a period of time: *television licence stamps*

**5** ▶ **TAX** ◀ a piece of paper for sticking to some official papers to show that British tax has been paid

**6** ▶ **IN A SHOP** ◀ a TRADING STAMP

**7 a man/woman of his/her stamp** *formal* someone with a particular kind of character: *I wouldn't trust a man of his stamp.*

**8** an act of stamping, especially with your foot: *an angry stamp*

S1 W1 **stamp²** *v*

**1** ▶ **FOOT** ◀ [I] to lift your foot off the ground and put it down hard on something: [+ **on**] *Marta shrieked and started stamping on the cockroach.* | **stamp around** (=walk this way) *Just because you're mad you don't have to stamp around like that.*

**2 stamp your foot** to lift your foot off the ground and bring it down again very hard because you are angry: *"I will not!" yelled Bert, and stamped his foot.*

**3 stamp your feet** to keep lifting each foot and bringing it down again very hard, to make a noise or because you are cold: *She stood at the bus stop stamping her feet to keep warm.*

**4** ▶ **MAKE A MARK** ◀ [T] to put a pattern, sign or letters on something using a special tool: **stamp sth on sth** *Stamp the date on all the letters.* | **stamp sth with sth** *Your passport must be stamped with your entry date.*

**5 stamp on sb/sth** *informal* to use force or your authority to stop someone from doing something, or stop something from happening: *Roberts stamped on every suggestion we made and then decided to end the project.*

**6** ▶ **AFFECT SB/STH** ◀ [T] to have an important or permanent effect on someone or something: **be stamped on sb's memory** *That awful experience is indelibly stamped on my memory.* | **stamp sb with sth** *His army years had stamped him with an air of brisk authority.*

**7 stamp sb as sth** to show that someone has a particular type of character: *The latest scandal clearly stamped her as a liar.*

**8** ▶ **MAIL** ◀ [T] to stick a stamp onto a letter, parcel etc

**stamp** sth ↔ **out** *phr v* [T] **1** to prevent something bad from continuing: *We aim to stamp out poverty in our lifetimes.* **2** to put out a fire by stepping hard on the flames **3** to make a shape or object by pressing hard on something using a machine or tool

**stamp du·ty** /ˈ· ˌ··/ *n* [U] a tax that must be paid in Britain on particular legal documents that have to be officially checked

**stamped ad·dressed en·ve·lope** /ˌ· ·ˌ· ˈ···/ *n* [C] *BrE* an SAE; an envelope with your name, address and a stamp on it, which you send to a person or organization so that they can send you information; SELF-ADDRESSED *AmE*

**stam·pede¹** /stæmˈpiːd/ *n* [C] **1** a sudden rush of frightened animals **2** a sudden rush by a lot of people, all wanting to do the same thing or go to the same place: *stampede of producers offering her roles in their films* **3** *AmE* an entertainment event at which COWBOYS show their skills, and there are competitions, dancing etc —compare RODEO

**stampede²** *v* [I,T] **1** if animals stampede, they suddenly start running together, because they are frightened: *a herd of stampeding buffalo* **2 be/get stampeded** to be made frightened or worried so that you do something too quickly: [+ **into**] *Don't get stampeded into any rash decisions.*

**stamp·ing ground** /ˈ··· ·/ *n* [C] **sb's stamping ground** a favourite place where someone often goes

**stance** /stɑːns‖stæns/ *n* [C usually singular] **1** an opinion that is stated publicly: [+ **on**] *an uncompromising stance on nuclear disarmament* | **take/adopt a stance** *The President has adopted a tough stance on terrorism.* **2** a position in which you stand, especially when doing a particular activity: *a good relaxed stance is essential when skiing* —compare POSTURE¹ (1)

**stanch** /stɑːntʃ‖stɒːntʃ, stɑːntʃ/ *v* [T] an American spelling of STAUNCH²

**stan·chion** /ˈstɑːntʃən‖ˈstæn-/ *n* [C] a strong upright bar used to support something

S1 W1 **stand¹** /stænd/ *v past tense and past participle* **stood** /stʊd/

① BE UPRIGHT
② CAN'T STAND
③ ACCEPT/BEAR
④ IN A PARTICULAR STATE/SITUATION
⑤ CONTINUE/NOT CHANGE
⑥ NOT MOVED OR USED
⑦ FEELINGS/OPINIONS
⑧ LEVEL/AMOUNT/VALUE/HEIGHT
⑨ BE RESPONSIBLE
⑩ LAW
⑪ BE PROUD/INDEPENDENT
⑫ COULD STAND
⑬ OTHER MEANINGS

① **BE UPRIGHT**

**1** [I] to support yourself on your feet in an upright position: *It looks like we'll have to stand – there are no seats left.* | *Can you see any better from where you're standing?* | **stand and do sth** *Diane stood and waved until his car was gone.* | **stand still** (=not move) *Stand still and let me wipe your face.* | **stand there** (=stand and not do anything) *Don't just stand there – help me!* | **stand on your toes/stand on tiptoe** (=support yourself on your toes) *If you stand on tiptoe you can just about reach it.* —see also STANDSTILL, **stand up**

**2** ▶ **STAND SOMEWHERE TO DO STH** ◀ [I always

+ adv/prep] to take a particular position or do something in particular while standing: *Everybody stand in a circle.* | *You don't need to stand closer to the microphone.* | [+ **at/beside/by etc**] *Ouida, you stand at the door and greet people.* | **stand on sth** *We used to get in trouble for standing on the seats.* | **stand somewhere doing sth** *They just stood there laughing.* | **stand back/aside** (=step backwards or sideways) *Stand back and give her some air!* | **stand clear (of)** (=move away) *Stand clear of the doors, please.*

**3 ▶ RISE ◀** also **stand up** [I,T] to rise to an upright position, or to make someone do this: *Suddenly, everyone stood up and cheered.* | *Please stand and face the judge.* | *Come on, stand up and say something.* | **stand sb (up) on sth** *Stand Molly up on a chair so she can see.*

**4 ▶ ON A BASE ◀** [I, T always + adv/prep] to stay upright on a base or on an object, or to put something there: *Few houses were left standing after the tornado.* | *A green lamp stood on the leather-topped desk.* | *There's a parking lot where the theater once stood.* | **stand sth on/in/over etc** *Can you stand that pole in the corner for now?*

**5 stand to attention** if soldiers stand to attention, they stand very straight and stiff to show respect

**6 stand on your head/hands** to support yourself on your head or hands, with your feet in the air

**7 stand in line** *AmE* to wait to be able to do something until the people ahead of you have done it; queue up (QUEUE[2]) *BrE*: *Gail has men standing in line wanting to go out with her.*

**8 stand fast/stand firm/stand your ground** to refuse to be forced to move backwards

### ② CAN'T STAND

**9** [T] *usually spoken* to not like someone or something at all, or think that something is extremely unpleasant: *I can't stand whiskey.* | **can't stand the sight of** *I'm so mad, I can hardly stand the sight of him.* | **can't stand to see/hear/do etc** *I can't stand to see good food going to waste.* | **can't stand seeing/hearing/doing etc** *Lily can't stand working in an office.* | **can't stand sb/sth doing** *I can't stand people dropping litter.* —see also **stand for** (STAND[1]), **can't bear sth/sb** (BEAR[1] (1))

### ③ ACCEPT/BEAR

**10** [T] to be able to accept or deal well with a difficult situation; TOLERATE: *I've had about as much as I can stand of your arguing!* | *I don't know if I can stand the waiting any longer.* | **stand sb doing sth** *How can you stand Marty coming home late all the time?* | **not stand any nonsense** *Get up to bed, and I won't stand any nonsense.* —see graph at BEAR

**11 ▶ BE GOOD ENOUGH ◀** [T] to be done or made well enough to be successful, strong, or useful for a long time: **stand close examination** (=be proved to be correct, well made etc) *I suspect Murray's theory won't stand close examination.* | **stand the test of time** (=stay strong) *It's nice to see their marriage has stood the test of time.*

**12 if you can't stand the heat, get out of the kitchen** used to say that you should leave a job or situation if you cannot deal with its difficulties

### ④ IN A PARTICULAR STATE/SITUATION

**13** [I always + adv/prep, linking verb] to be in, stay in, or get into a particular state: *Court stands adjourned until 2 p.m.* | **as sth stands** *The law, as it stood, favoured the developers.* | **the way things stand/as things stand** (=used when talking about the state that a situation has reached) *I'm not too thrilled with the way things stand at the moment.* | **where/how do things stand?** (=used to ask what is happening in a situation) *Where do things stand in terms of the budget?* | **stand united/divided** (=agree or disagree completely) *The committee stands divided on this issue.* | **stand prepared/ready to do sth** (=be prepared to do something whenever it is necessary) | **stand together** (=stay united) *If we all stand together, they can't beat us.* | **stand in awe of sb** (=admire them, be afraid of them, or both)

### ⑤ CONTINUE/NOT CHANGE

**14 stand alone** to continue to do something alone, without help from anyone else: *Harper stood alone in his refusal to sell to the railroad.*

**15 ▶ STILL EXIST ◀** [I not in progressive] to continue to exist, be correct, or be VALID: *My offer of a place to stay still stands.* | *The court of appeal has ruled that the conviction should stand.*

**16 stand still** to not change or progress at all although time has passed: *Nothing stands still in the computer industry.* | **time stands still** *Going back home, it's as if time has stood still and I'm ten years old.*

**17 stand your ground/stand firm/stand fast** also **stand your guns** *AmE* to refuse to change your opinions, intentions, or behaviour: *Stand your ground, don't let them talk you into anything you don't want.* | [+ **on/against**] *I call on you as citizens to stand firm against racism!*

**18 stand pat** *AmE informal* to refuse to change a decision, plan etc: [+ **on**] *Harry's standing pat on his decision to fire Janice.*

### ⑥ NOT MOVED OR USED

**19** [I, linking verb] to stay in a particular position, place, or state without being moved or used: *The car's been standing in the garage for weeks.* | **stand empty/idle** (=not being used) *scores of derelict houses standing empty*

**20 ▶ LIQUID ◀** [I] a liquid that stands does not flow or is not made to move: *standing pools of marsh water*

### ⑦ FEELINGS/OPINIONS

**21 know how/where you stand (with sb)** to know how someone feels about you: *Yvonne may be blunt, but you always know where you stand with her.*

**22 where sb stands** someone's opinion about something, or the official rule about something: [+ **on**] *The voters want to know where you stand on abortion.*

**23 from where I stand** according to what you know or feel: *Well from where I'm standing, it seems like she's being unreasonable.*

**24 I stand corrected** *spoken formal* used to admit that your opinion or something that you just said was wrong

### ⑧ LEVEL/AMOUNT/VALUE/HEIGHT

**25** [I always + adv/prep] to be at a particular level or amount: [+ **at**] *Inflation currently stands at four percent.* | *Your bank balance stands at $720.92.*

**26** [I always + adv/prep] to have a particular rank or position when compared to similar things or people: *I know your son stands high on the list of suitable candidates.* | **stand in relation to** *How do their sales stand in relation to those of similar firms?*

**27** [I always + adv/prep, linking verb] *usually written* to be a particular height: **stand four feet etc (high)/stand 20 metres etc (tall)** *The Eiffel Tower stands 300m high.*

### ⑨ BE RESPONSIBLE

**28** [linking verb] to take a particular responsibility: **stand guard (over)** *If you stand guard over our stuff, I'll run get the tickets.* | **stand bail** (=pay money as a promise that someone will return to a court to be judged) | **stand surety** (=be responsible for the results if someone else does not do what they promise to)

### ⑩ LAW

**29 stand trial** to be brought to a court of law to have your case examined and judged: [+ **for**] *Gresham will stand trial for murder.*

**30 stand accused** to be the person in a court of law who is being judged for a crime: *Vincent Amis, you stand accused of murder.*

### ⑪ BE PROUD/INDEPENDENT

**31 stand on your own (two) feet** to be able to earn what you need without help from others: *I'll think of*

[continued on next page]

[continued from previous page]
*him as equal when he's learnt to stand on his own two feet.*
**32 stand tall** *AmE* to be proud and feel ready to deal with anything
**33 stand on your dignity** to demand to be treated with respect: *Never one to stand on her dignity, Eva joined in with the fun.*

## ⑫ COULD STAND

**34** used to say very directly that it would be a good idea for someone to do something or for something to happen: **sb could stand to do sth** *You could stand to lose a few pounds.* | **sth could stand another look/more attention etc** (=it ought to be looked at more closely) *Your report could stand another read-through for typos.*
**35 I could stand sth** *AmE spoken humorous* used to say that you would like something: *I could stand another piece of pie!*

## ⑬ OTHER MEANINGS

**36 stand a chance/hope (of doing sth)** to be likely to be able to do something or to succeed: *You'll stand a better chance of getting a job with a degree.* | **not stand a chance** *I'm afraid she doesn't stand a chance.* | **stand little chance** (=not be likely to succeed) *The bill stands little chance of becoming law.*
**37 stand to gain/lose/win etc** to be likely to do or have something: *We stand to make a lot of money from the merger.*
**38 do sth standing on your head** to do something easily: *Get Anne to help – she can fix things like that standing on her head.*
**39 stand on your head to do sth** to make a great effort to do something: *You won't find me standing on my head to help him any more.*

**40 it stands to reason** used to say that something should be completely clear to anyone who is sensible: *If the thefts are all in the same area, it stands to reason it's the same kids doing it.*
**41 ►ELECTION◄** [I] to try to become elected to a council, parliament etc: *Who's standing for the Democrats in the 44th district?* —see also **stand against**
**42 stand in sb's way/path** to prevent someone from doing something: *If you really want to marry Liam, I'm not going to stand in your way.*
**43 stand sb in good stead** to be very useful to someone when needed: *Now that I'm emigrating to the United States, my being able to speak English should stand me in good stead.*
**44 stand sb a drink/meal etc** to pay for something as a gift to someone; TREAT[1] (5): *Come on, Jack, I'll stand you a drink if you like.*
**45 not stand on ceremony** to not worry about the formal rules of polite behaviour: *Don't stand on ceremony – if you want a drink, have one.*
**46 stand or fall by/on** to depend on something for success: *The whole project must stand or fall on the quality of its research.*
**47 stand sth on its head** to show that a belief, idea etc is completely untrue: *Galileo's discovery stood medieval thought on its head.*
**48** [I + **on/in**] *BrE* to accidentally step on or in something: *Mind you don't stand on Fluffy's tail.* —see also **make sb's hair stand on end** (HAIR (6)), **leave sb standing** (LEAVE[1] (31)), **not have a leg to stand on** (LEG[1] (8))

**stand against** sb/sth *phr v* [T] to oppose a person, organization, plan, decision etc: *If we don't stand against the cutbacks, they'll cut even more next year.*

**stand around** *phr v* [I] to stand somewhere and not do anything: *It's too cold to stand around out here – I'm going back inside.*

**stand by** *phr v* **1** [T] to not do anything to help someone or prevent something from happening: *We are not prepared to stand by and let them close our schools.* **2** [T **stand by** sth] to keep a promise, agreement etc, or to declare that something is still true: *I stand by what I said earlier.* **3** [T **stand by** sb] to stay loyal to someone and support them, especially in a difficult situation: *Wes needs to know we'll always stand by him.* **4** [I] to be ready to do something if necessary: **be standing by** *A rescue boat is always standing by in case of trouble.* | [+ **for**] *Stand by for the countdown.* | **stand by to do sth** *Stand by to cue the commercial.* —see also BYSTANDER, STANDBY

**stand down** *phr v* **1** [I] to agree to leave your position or to stop trying to be elected, so that someone else can have a chance: *I'm prepared to stand down in favor of a younger candidate.* —see also **step down** (STEP[2]) **2** [I] to leave the WITNESS BOX in court **3** [I, T **stand** sb ↔ **down**] *BrE* to send a soldier away from work after they have done their work for the day, or to stop working for the day; **go off duty** (DUTY (3))

**stand for** sth *phr v* [T] **1** if a letter, number or sign stands for something, it represents it as a short form of a word, name, or idea: *"My name is Dean E. Beller." "What does the E stand for?"* **2** [usually in questions and negatives] to allow something to continue to happen without complaining about it or trying to stop it: *We will not stand for this sort of behavior, young man!* | **stand for being** *I won't stand for being treated like a child.* **3** to support a particular set of ideas, values, or principles: *I want to know what she stands for before I'll vote for her.*

**stand in** *phr v* [I] to temporarily do someone else's job: [+ **for**] *Can you stand in for Meg while she's on vacation?* —see also STAND-IN

**stand out** *phr v* [I] **1** to be very easy to see or notice by looking or sounding different from other things or people: *I think black lettering will stand out best on a yellow sign.* | **stand out in a crowd** *Well, that dress will make you stand out in a crowd!* **2 stand out a mile** to be very clear or noticeable: *They thought no one knew but it stood out a mile they were interested in each other.* **3** to be clearly better or the best: **stand out as** *Among mystery writers, P D James stands out as a superior storyteller.* | [+ **from/among/above**] *Nathan stands out from the rest of the singers.* —see also STANDOUT

**stand out against** sth *phr v* [T] to be strongly opposed to an idea, plan etc: *We must stand out against bigotry.*

**stand over** sb *phr v* [T] to stand very close behind someone and watch as they work to make sure they do nothing wrong: *I can't concentrate with him standing over me like that.*

**stand to** *phr v* [I, T **stand** sb ↔ **to**] *BrE* to order a soldier to move into a position so that they are ready for action, or to move into this position

**stand up** *phr v* **1** [I usually in progressive] to stand: *Boy am I tired, I've been standing up all day.* | **stand up straight** *Stand up straight, boy, don't slouch!* **2** [I always + adv/prep] to stay healthy in a difficult environment or in good condition after a lot of hard use: [+ **to**] *The trees stood up pretty well to the frosts this winter.* **3** [I] to be proved to be true, correct, useful etc when tested: **stand up under/to** *stand up under close scrutiny* | **stand up in court** (=be successfully proved in a court of law) *Without a witness, the charges will never stand up in court.* **4** [T **stand** sb **up**] *informal* to not meet someone after you have promised to do something with them: *I was supposed to go to a concert with Kyle on Friday, but he stood me up.* **5 stand up and be counted** to make it very clear what you think about something when this is dangerous or might cause trouble for you —see also STAND-UP

**stand up for** sb/sth *phr v* [T] to support or defend a person or idea when they are being attacked: *It's time we stood up for our rights.* | *Didn't anyone stand up for James and say it wasn't his fault?*

**stand up to** sb/sth *phr v* [T] to refuse to accept unfair treatment from a person or organization: *He'll respect you more if you stand up to him.*

**stand²** *n* **1 ▶ FOR SUPPORT ◀** [C] a piece of furniture or equipment for supporting something: *a music stand|an umbrella stand|Can we put another microphone stand here?*| **coat-stand/hat-stand** (=for hanging coats or hats on) **2 ▶ FOR SELLING ◀** [C] a small structure used for selling or showing things; STALL¹ (1): *a hotdog stand|Come by our stand at the exhibition and see the new products.* —see also NEWSSTAND **3 ▶ OPINION/ATTITUDE ◀** [C usually singular] a position or opinion that you state firmly and publicly: **take a stand (on)** *The Labour Party has not taken a stand on the political position of the monarchy.* **4 ▶ SPORTS GROUND ◀** [C] also **stands** *plural* a building where people stand or sit to watch the game at a sports ground —see also GRANDSTAND **5 ▶ OPPOSE/DEFEND ◀** [C] a strong effort to defend yourself or to oppose something: **make a stand** *In February 1916 the French army made a stand at Verdun.*|**make/mount a stand against** *Somebody's got to make a stand against the parish council.* **6 ▶ SPORTS GAME ◀** [C] the period of time in which two batsmen (BATSMAN) are playing together in a game of CRICKET (2) , or the points that they get **7 the stand** *AmE* a WITNESS BOX: **take the stand** *Will the next witness please take the stand?* —see also ONE-NIGHT STAND

**stand·a·lone** /ˈstændələʊn‖-loʊn/ *adj technical* a stand-alone computer works on its own without being part of a NETWORK¹ (4)

S3 W2 **stan·dard¹** /ˈstændəd‖-ərd/ *n* **1 ▶ LEVEL OF QUALITY ◀** [C often plural, U] a level of quality, skill, ability or achievement by which someone or something is judged, that is considered to be necessary or acceptable in a particular situation: *The airline has rigorous safety standards.*|[+ **of**] *Inspections are meant to ensure the standard of teaching is acceptable.*|**(of a) high/low standard** *Our students achieve very high standards of musical ability.|Articles of a low standard will not be accepted.*|**set a standard** (=decide what people are expected to do) *The International Atomic Energy Agency sets standards for the industry.*|**meet/reach/attain a standard** *They have to reach a certain standard or they won't pass.*|**to standard** (=well enough) *completing work to standard and on time*|**maintain standards** (=keep them the way they are) *After his early success, Cameron was unable to maintain such high standards.*|**above/below standard** (=better than usual, or not good enough) *The accommodation here is really below standard.*|**up to standard** (=good enough) *Your recent work just hasn't been up to standard.*|**raise/lower a standard** *We're not about to lower our standards just to make a cheaper product.*|**let standards fall/drop/slip** (=allow them to get worse) *On no account must we let standards slip.*
**2 ▶ COMPARING ◀** [C usually plural] the ideas of what is good or normal that someone uses to compare one thing with another: **by sb's standards** *They were all pretty excitable by our quiet English standards.*|**by any standard(s)** (=by anyone's opinion or values) *It's a deprived area by any standard.*
**3 ▶ MORAL RULE ◀** [C usually plural] rules for behaviour based on an idea of what is morally good and right: *Nobody could live up to his standards.*
**4 ▶ MEASUREMENT ◀** [C] a fixed official rule for measuring weight, purity, value etc: *an official government standard for the purity of silver*
**5 ▶ SONG ◀** [C] a popular song that has been sung by many different singers
**6 ▶ FLAG ◀** [C] a flag used in ceremonies: *the royal standard*
**7 ▶ MILITARY POLE ◀** [C] a pole with a picture or shape at the top carried in the past at the front of an army —see also DOUBLE STANDARD, LIVING STANDARD

This graph shows some of the words most commonly used with the noun **standard**.

| Collocation | Frequency (per million) |
|---|---|
| high standard | ~6.7 |
| set a standard | ~3.4 |
| meet a standard | ~2.9 |
| to standard | ~1.4 |
| low standard | ~1.3 |
| maintain standards | ~1.2 |
| reach/attain a standard | ~1.0 |

Axis: 2, 4, 6, 8, 10 per million

Based on the British National Corpus and the Longman Lancaster Corpus

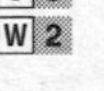
**standard²** *adj* **1** accepted as normal or usual: *We paid them the standard rate for the job.*|**standard practice/procedure** (=the usual way of doing things) *Searching luggage at airports is now standard practice.* **2** regular and usual in shape, size, quality etc: *We make shoes in standard and wide sizes.|All these vans are made to a standard design.* **3** a standard book, work, author etc is read by everyone studying a particular subject **4 standard English/spelling/pronunciation etc** *BrE* the form of English, spelling, pronunciation etc that most people in Britain use, and that is not limited to one area or group of people —see also NON-STANDARD, SUBSTANDARD

**standard-bear·er** /ˈ·· ˌ··/ *n* [C] **1** an important leader in a moral argument or political group **2** a soldier who carried the STANDARD (=flag) at the front of an army

**standard de·duc·tion** /ˌ·· ·ˈ··/ *n* [C usually singular] *AmE* a fixed amount of the money you earn that you do not have to pay tax on

**standard de·vi·a·tion** /ˌ·· ··ˈ··/ *n* [C] *technical* a number in statisics (STATISTIC (1)) that shows how widely members of a mathematical set vary from the average set

**standard-is·sue** /ˌ·· ˈ··◂/ *adj* included in ordinary military equipment

**stan·dard·ize** also **-ise** *BrE* /ˈstændədaɪz‖-ər-/ *v* [T] to make all the things of one particular type the same as each other: *Attempts to standardize English spelling have never been successful.* —**standardization** /ˌstændədaɪˈzeɪʃən‖-dərdə-/ *n* [U]

**standard lamp** /ˈ·· ·/ *n* [C] *BrE* a tall lamp that stands on the floor; FLOOR LAMP *AmE* —see picture at LIGHT¹

**standard of liv·ing** /ˌ··· ˈ··/ *n* [C usually singular] the amount of wealth, comfort, and things that can be bought that a particular person, group, country etc has: *a nation with a high standard of living*

**standard time** /ˌ·· ˈ·/ *n* [singular] the time to which all clocks in a particular area of the world are set

**stand·by, stand-by** /ˈstændbaɪ/ *n* **1** [C] something that is kept ready so that it can be used when needed: *Powdered milk is a good standby in a emergency.|The hospital has a standby generator.* **2 on standby** ready to help immediately if you are needed: *A special team of police were kept on standby.* **3** [U] the condition of being ready to travel on a plane if there are any seats left when it is ready to leave: *a cheap standby ticket*|**on standby** *All the seats are taken, but we can put you on standby.* **4** [C] someone or something that you can always depend on or that will always be suitable: *It's useful to have a little black dress as a standby.* —see also **stand by** (STAND¹)

**stand-in** /ˈ· ·/ *n* [C] **1** someone who does the job or takes the place of someone else for a short time: *Gilbert failed to find a stand-in and so could not go to their dinner party.* **2** someone who takes the place of an actor for some scenes in a film —see also **stand in** (STAND¹)

**stand·ing¹** /ˈstændɪŋ/ *adj* [only before noun]

1 permanently agreed or arranged: *You have to pay standing charges whether or not you use the service.* | **standing invitation** (=permission to visit someone whenever you like) **2 standing order(s) a)** an agreement to pay for something regularly from your bank account **b)** a permanent rule that a committee, council etc follows when it meets **3** done from a standing position: *The runners set off from a standing start.* | **standing ovation** (=when people stand up to CLAP[1] (1) after a performance) **4 standing joke** something that happens often and that people make jokes about: *My spelling mistakes had become a standing joke in the office.*

**standing**[2] *n* [U] **1** someone's rank or position in a system, organization, society etc, based on what other people think of them: *The scandal will certainly damage the Governor's standing in the polls.* | **high/low standing** *a lawyer of high standing* **2 of five/many etc years' standing** used to show the time during which something such as an agreement has existed: *an arrangement of several years' standing*

**standing ar·my** /ˌ·· ˈ··/ *n* [C] a professional, permanent army, rather than one that has been formed for a war

**standing com·mit·tee** /ˈ·· ˌ···/ *n* [C] a group of people chosen by the British parliament or the US Congress to consider possible new laws

**standing or·der** /ˌ·· ˈ··/ *n* [C,U] an arrangement by which a bank pays a fixed amount of money from your account every month, year etc —compare DIRECT DEBIT

**standing room** /ˈ·· ·/ *n* [U] space for standing in a theatre, sports ground etc: **standing room only** (=no seats are left)

**stand·off** /ˈstændɒf‖-ɔːf/ *n* [C] a situation in which neither side in a fight or battle can gain an advantage

**stand-of·fish** /ˌstænd ˈɒfɪʃ‖-ˈɔːf-/ *adj informal* rather unfriendly and formal: *She was cold and stand-offish.* —**stand-offishly** *adv* —**stand-offishness** *n* [U]

**stand·out** /ˈstændaʊt/ *n* [C] *AmE* someone who is better at doing something or more attractive than other people in a group: *In that class, Mary's a standout.* —**standout** *adj: a standout performance*

**stand·pipe** /ˈstændpaɪp/ *n* [C] a pipe that provides water in a public place in the street

**stand·point** /ˈstændpɔɪnt/ *n* [C usually singular] a way of thinking about people, situations, ideas etc; POINT OF VIEW: *the feminist standpoint* | [+ **of**] *Let's look at this from the standpoint of the voters.*

**stand·still** /ˈstændˌstɪl/ *n* [singular] a situation in which there is no movement or activity at all: **come to a standstill/bring sth to a standstill** *Strikers brought production to a standstill.* | **at a standstill** *Traffic was at a standstill on the freeway.*

**stand-up**[1], **standup** /ˈstændʌp/ *adj* [only before noun] **1** stand-up COMEDY involves one person telling jokes as a performance: *a stand-up comedian* **2** done or intended to be used by people who are standing up: *We had a stand-up buffet.* **3** a stand-up fight, argument etc is loud and violent: *If it came to a stand-up fight, I wouldn't have a chance.* **4** able to stay upright: *a photo in a stand-up frame* | *a stand-up collar* —see also **stand up**

**stand-up**[2] also **standup** *n* [U] stand-up COMEDY: **do stand up** *Mark used to do stand up at Roxy's bar.*

**stank** /stæŋk/ the past tense of STINK

**stan·za** /ˈstænzə/ *n* [C] a group of lines in a repeated pattern forming part of a poem

**sta·ple**[1] /ˈsteɪpəl/ *n* [C] **1** a small piece of thin wire that is pushed into sheets of paper and bent over to hold them together **2** a small U-shaped piece of metal with pointed ends, used to hold something in place **3** a food that is needed and used all the time: *staples like flour and rice* **4** *technical* the main product that is produced in a country: *Bananas and sugar are the staples of Jamaica.*

**staple**[2] *v* [T] to fasten two or more things together with a staple

**staple**[3] *adj* [only before noun] **1** forming the greatest or most important part of something: *Oil is Nigeria's staple export.* | *a staple ingredient of comedy* **2 staple diet a)** the food that you normally eat: *They live on a staple diet of rice and vegetables.* **b)** something that is always being produced, seen, bought etc: *television's staple diet of soap operas and quiz shows* **3** used all the time: *Marty's staple excuses*

**staple gun** /ˈ·· ·/ *n* [C] a tool used for putting strong staples into walls

**sta·pler** /ˈsteɪplə‖-ər/ *n* [C] a tool used for putting staples into paper

**star**[1] /stɑː‖stɑːr/ *n* [C]

**1** ▶ **IN THE SKY** ◀ a burning mass of gases in space that can be seen at night as a point of light in the sky: *I lay on my back and looked up at the stars.* —see also FALLING STAR, SHOOTING STAR

**2** ▶ **PERFORMER** ◀ **a)** a famous and successful performer in entertainment or sport: **film/movie star** *There were pictures of film stars all over the walls.* | **pop star** (=famous popular music singer) | **big star** (=very famous performer) *By the age of twenty she was already a big star.* | **star quality** (=something that makes you seem special, and likely to be a star) | **rising star** (=someone who is becoming successful and famous) *a rising star in the music world* **b)** someone who acts the part of the main character in a film or play: *The star of his next movie was an unknown young actress.* | **the star part** (=the most important part in a film or play) | **child star** (=a child who has an important part in a film) | **the star of the show** (=the person who gives the best performance in a play, film etc) —see also STAR[2]

**3** ▶ **SHAPE** ◀ **a)** a shape with four or more points which is supposed to look like a star in the sky: *A five-pointed star is called a pentagram.* —see picture at SHAPE[1] **b)** a mark in this shape, used to draw attention to something written; ASTERISK **c)** a piece of cloth or metal in this shape, worn to show someone's rank or position

**4** ▶ **HOTELS/RESTAURANTS** ◀ a mark used in a system for judging the quality of hotels and restaurants: **three-star/four-star/five-star** *a two-star bed and breakfast*

**5 the stars a)** *informal* a HOROSCOPE (=description of what will happen to you in the future) that is printed in newspapers or magazines: **read your stars** *I never read my stars – I don't believe any of it anyway.* **b)** *literary* a force that controls what will happen in the future; FATE (2): **written in the stars** (=decided by this) —see also STAR-CROSSED

**6** ▶ **SUCCESSFUL PERSON** ◀ *informal* someone who is particularly successful at a job, course of study etc: *I was the star of my village because I won a place at the school in Nayoumi.* | **a star player/performer/salesman etc** *the Academy's star pupil* | **shining star** (=very successful person)

**7 you're/she's a star!** *informal* used to say that someone is very good at something or thank someone for helping you

**8 star turn** the main or best performer or event in a performance: *Our star turn was a fire-eating act.*

**9 star attraction** the most interesting person or thing, that most people want to see

**10 see stars** to see flashes of light, especially because you have been hit on the head: *I felt a little dizzy and could see stars.*

**11 have stars in your eyes** to imagine that something you want to do is much more exciting or attractive than it really is —see also STARRY-EYED

**12 four star (petrol)** *BrE* high quality petrol that has lead (LEAD[3] (1)) in it —see also EVENING STAR, FOUR-STAR GENERAL, FIVE-STAR GENERAL, MORNING STAR, **guiding star** (GUIDING), **born under a lucky/unlucky star** (BORN (10)), **reach for the stars** (REACH[1] (8)), **thank your lucky stars** (THANK (6))

**star**[2] **starred, starring** *v* **1** [I] to act the part of the main character in a film or play: [+ **in**] *She will star in the Los Angeles production of 'Phantom' this year.* **2** [T] if a film or play stars someone, that person acts the part of the main character: *a film starring Meryl Streep* **3 starring role** the most important acting part in a film, play etc **4** to put an ASTERISK (=a star-shaped mark) next to something written: *The starred items will be available from July.*

**star·board** /ˈstɑːbəd‖ˈstɑːrbərd/ *n* [U] the side of a ship or aircraft that is on your right when you are facing forwards —**starboard** *adj* —opposite PORT (4)

**starch¹** /stɑːtʃ‖stɑːrtʃ/ *n* **1** [U] a white substance that has no taste and forms an important part of foods such as grain, rice, and potatoes **2** [C, U] a food that contains this substance: *Avoid fatty foods and starches.* **3** [U] a substance that is mixed with water and is used to make cloth stiff

**starch²** *v* [T] to make cloth stiff, using starch: *a starched white tablecloth*

**star cham·ber** /ˌ· ˈ··/ *n* [C] a group of people that meets secretly and makes decisions that are important or judgements that are severe

**starch·y** /ˈstɑːtʃi‖ˈstɑːr-/ *adj* **1** containing a lot of STARCH¹ (1): *starchy foods* **2** very formal and correct in your behaviour: *Not knowing what to say or do he became stiff and starchy.* —**starchily** *adv* —**starchiness** *n* [U]

**star-crossed** /ˈ· ·/ *adj literary* star-crossed lovers can never be happy because their situation prevents them from being together

**star·dom** /ˈstɑːdəm‖ˈstɑːr-/ *n* [U] the situation of being a famous performer: *Her triumphs were clouded by the loneliness of stardom.* | **shoot/rise to stardom** (=become famous very quickly)

**star·dust** /ˈstɑːdʌst‖ˈstɑːr-/ *n* [U] *literary* an imaginary magic substance like shiny powder

S3 W2 **stare¹** /steə‖ster/ *v* [I] **1** to look at something or someone for a long time without moving your eyes: [+ **out**] *Stop staring out of the window and do some work!* | [+ **at**] *What are you staring at?* | **stare into space** (=look for a long time at nothing) —see GAZE¹ (USAGE) **2 be staring sb in the face a)** *informal* to be very clear and easy to see; be OBVIOUS: *The solution is staring you in the face.* **b)** to seem impossible to avoid: *Defeat was staring us in the face.* —see also **stark staring mad** (STARK² (2))

**stare** sb **out** *BrE*, **stare** sb **down** *AmE phr v* [T] to look at someone for so long that they start to feel uncomfortable and look away

**stare²** *n* [C] a long steady look or a way of staring: *a disapproving stare* | *She ignored the stares of everyone around her.* | **hold sb's stare** (=not look away when someone is staring at you)

**star·fish** /ˈstɑːˌfɪʃ‖ˈstɑːr-/ *n* [C] a flat sea animal that has five arms forming the shape of a star

**star·fruit** /ˈstɑːˌfruːt‖ˈstɑːr-/ *n* [C] a pale green fruit that has a shape similar to a star

**star·gaz·er** /ˈstɑːˌgeɪzə‖ˈstɑːrˌgeɪzər/ *n* [C] **1** someone who studies ASTRONOMY or ASTROLOGY **2** someone with ideas or plans that are impossible or not practical —**stargazing** *n* [U]

**star jump** /ˈ· ·/ *n* [C usually plural] *BrE* one of a series of exercise jumps that you do from a standing position with your arms and legs pointing out at each side; JUMPING JACK

**stark¹** /stɑːk‖stɑːrk/ *adj* **1** very simple and severe in appearance: *In the cold dawn light the castle looked stark and forbidding.* | *the stark beauty of the New Mexico desert* **2** unpleasantly clear and impossible to avoid; HARSH: | **stark reality** *The film shows the stark realities of life in the slums.* | **stark choice** *The Tories are facing a stark choice between cutting the deficit and maintaining benefits.* **3** [only before noun] complete; total: *Jerry's eyes were wide open with a look of stark terror.* | **in stark contrast to** (=completely opposite) *Their poverty was in stark contrast to the luxury all around them.* —**starkly** *adv* —**starkness** *n* [U]

**stark²** *adv* **1 stark naked** *informal* not wearing any clothes at all; completely NAKED **2 stark raving mad** also **stark staring mad** *BrE* completely crazy

**stark·ers** /ˈstɑːkəz‖ˈstɑːrkərz/ *adj* [not before noun] *BrE informal* not wearing any clothes; NAKED

**star·less** /ˈstɑːləs‖ˈstɑːr-/ *adj* with no stars showing in the sky

**star·let** /ˈstɑːlɪt‖ˈstɑːr-/ *n* [C] a young actress who plays small parts in films and is hoping to become famous

**star·light** /ˈstɑːlaɪt‖ˈstɑːr-/ *n* [U] the light that comes from the stars, often considered to be romantic

**star·ling** /ˈstɑːlɪŋ‖ˈstɑːr-/ *n* [C] a greenish black bird that is very common in Europe

**star·lit** /ˈstɑːˌlɪt‖ˈstɑːr-/ *adj literary* made brighter by stars: *a starlit night*

**Star of Da·vid** /ˌstɑːr əv ˈdeɪvɪd/ *n* [C usually singular] a star with six points that is strongly connected with Judaism or the state of Israel

**star·ry** /ˈstɑːri/ *adj* having many stars: *a starry winter sky*

**starry-eyed** /ˌ·· ˈ·◂/ *adj informal* happy and hopeful about things in a way that is silly or UNREALISTIC: *a starry-eyed optimist*

**Stars and Stripes** /ˌ· · ˈ·/ *n* [singular] *AmE* the flag of the US

**star sign** /ˈ· ·/ *n* [C] one of the twelve signs of the ZODIAC (=the system that uses people's birth dates to say what will happen to them in the future)

**Star-Span·gled Ban·ner** /ˌ· ·· ˈ··/ *n* [singular] **1** the NATIONAL ANTHEM (=national song) of the US **2** *AmE literary* the flag of the US

**star-stud·ded** /ˈ· ˌ··/ *adj* including many famous performers: *a star-studded cast*

**start¹** /stɑːt‖stɑːrt/ *v* S2 W2

**1** ▶ **BEGIN DOING STH** ◀ [I,T] to begin doing something: **start doing sth** *I've just started learning German.* | *We'd better start getting dressed soon.* | **start to do sth** *When Tom heard this he started to laugh uncontrollably.* | *Things started to go wrong after we reached Cairo.* | *Damn! It's just started to rain.* | **start sth** *Haven't you started that book yet?* | *There was so much to do we didn't know where to start.* | *Do start,* (=begin to eat a meal) *or it'll go cold.* | [+ **from**] *Starting from point A draw a straight line down to point B.* | **start (off) with** (=deal with something as the first part of an activity) *Decorating the place was going to be a major job, and we decided to start with the kitchen.* | **start (off) by doing** *Start by melting the butter in the frying pan.* | **start again** (=begin doing something again) *Billy was afraid to say anything in case she started crying again.* | **get started** (=start doing something, especially when you have not been able to do anything yet, or have been lazy) *We better get started if we want to finish this job by midday.* | **start from scratch** (=start a job or activity from the beginning) *They had to start from scratch redecorating the house.* | **start afresh/anew** (=start doing something again better or differently) *Lisa saw the new job as a chance to start afresh.* —see graph at COMMENCE

**2** ▶ **BEGIN HAPPENING** ◀ also **start off** [I,T] to begin happening or make something begin happening: *Do you know what time the match starts?* | [+ **in**] *The marathon race starts in the city centre.* | **start sth** *The avalanche was started by a rockfall on the higher slopes.* | **start sb doing sth** *The conversation he overheard had started him thinking.* | **start with** *The festivities started with a huge fireworks display.* | **starting from now/tomorrow/next week etc** *You have two minutes to answer the following questions starting from now.* | **get started** (=start happening, especially after a delay) *The match finally got started at 2.30 p.m.*

**3 to start with a)** used when talking about the beginning of a situation, especially when it changes later: *I felt nervous to start with, but soon began to relax.* **b)** used to

emphasize the first of a list of facts or opinions you are stating: *We're not going on holiday this year; to start with we haven't got the money and then there's still a lot we need to do on the house.* —see FIRSTLY (USAGE)
**4 ▶ PERIOD OF TIME ◀** [I always + adv/prep, T always + adv/prep] if a fixed period of time starts in a certain way, or you start it in a certain way, it begins in that way: [+ **badly/well**] *The season started badly for United when they lost their first three matches.* | **start sth with/on etc** *Jerome always starts the day with a cup of coffee and a cigarette.*
**5 be back where you started** to have failed to do what you have been trying to do: *Liz hasn't got his address, so we're back where we started.*
**6 ▶ JOB/SCHOOL ◀** [I,T] to begin a new job, or to begin going to school, college etc: *The sales manager phoned this morning to ask if I could start next week.* | **start school/college/work** *Simon's starting school in September.*
**7 ▶ JOURNEY ◀** also **start off/out** [I] to begin a journey: *We'll have to start early to get to Edinburgh by midday.* | [+ **from**] *We start out from Harlow at seven.*
**8 ▶ LIFE/PROFESSION ◀** also **start off/out** [I always + adv/prep, T always + adv/prep] to begin your life or profession in a certain way: [+ **as/in**] *Rob started off as a salesman and now he's managing director.* | **start sth** *We started married life living in a caravan.*
**9 ▶ ROAD/RIVER ◀** [I always + adv/prep] if a river, road etc starts somewhere it begins in that place: [+ **in/at**] *The Mississippi starts in Minnesota.*

**10 ▶ CAR ◀** also **start up** [I,T] if you start a car or engine or if it starts, it begins to work: *The car wouldn't start this morning.* | **get the car/engine started** *He couldn't get his motorbike started.*
**11 ▶ PRICES ◀** [I always + adv/prep] if prices start at or from a particular figure, that is the lowest figure at which you can get or buy something: [+ **at/from**] *Prices for bed and breakfast start at £15 a night.*
**12 ▶ BUSINESS/CLUB ◀** also **start up** [T] to make something begin to exist: *Sally decided to start up a club for single mums in the neighbourhood.* | **start a business/company/firm** *Bruno started his own plumbing business when he was only 24.*
**13 start a family** to have your first baby: *At 34 she thought it was about time they started a family.*
**14 start a fire** to deliberately cause a fire
**15 start a fight/argument etc** to deliberately cause a fight, argument etc: *Don't let him drink too much – he'll only start a fight with someone.*
**16 start a rumour** to tell other people something, usually something unpleasant or untrue: *She wondered who could have started such a vicious rumour.*
**17 Don't (you) start!** *BrE spoken* used to tell someone to stop complaining, arguing or annoying you: *"Mum, I don't like this ice-cream." "Oh, don't you start!"*
**18 you started it !** *spoken* used to tell someone that they caused an argument or problem: *"Stop arguing with me Dave!" "It was you who started it."*
**19 start something/anything** to begin causing trouble: *I was worried in case my mate Ronnie started anything.*
**20 ▶ MOVE SUDDENLY ◀** [I] to move your body suddenly, especially because you are surprised or afraid: *A loud knock at the door made her start.* | [+ **from**] *Emma started from her chair and rushed to the window.*
**21 ▶ LIQUID ◀** [I always + adv/prep] if a liquid or substance starts from somewhere, it comes out quickly: *Blood started from the wound.*
**22 start young** to begin doing something when you are young: *"Marcia's only ten and she's already got a boyfriend." "Yes, they start young nowadays!"*

**start off** *phr v* **1** [I,T] to begin happening or make something begin happening: **start sth ↔ off** *Richard started the discussion off by telling us about his experiences in Africa.* | *The match started off at a fast and furious pace.* **2** [I] to begin a journey: *What time will we have to start off in the morning?* **3** [I] to move in a particular direction: *The bus started off slowly up the road.* **4** [T **start** sb ↔ **off**] to help someone begin an activity: *I tried to start the children off by giving them ideas for things to write about.* **5** [T **start** sb ↔ **off**] *informal* to make someone get angry, or start laughing, by saying something: *Don't mention Steve's name to Jenny; it'll only start her off!* | **start sb off doing sth** *David's remarks started the girls off giggling.*

**start** sb **on** sth *phr v* [T] to make someone start doing something regularly, especially because it will be good for them: *We started Gemma on solid foods when she was four months old.*

**start on** sth *phr v* [T] to begin doing something or using something: *Let's start on the wine shall we?* | *I guess it's time we started on the packing.*

**start on at** sb *phr v* [T] to begin criticizing someone or complaining to them about something: *Ray's wife started on at him about how he spent too much time in the pub.*

**start over** *phr v* [I] *AmE* to start doing something again from the beginning, especiallly because you want to do it better: *If you make a mistake when you're keying, just press delete and start over.*

This graph shows how common the different grammar patterns of the verb **start** are.

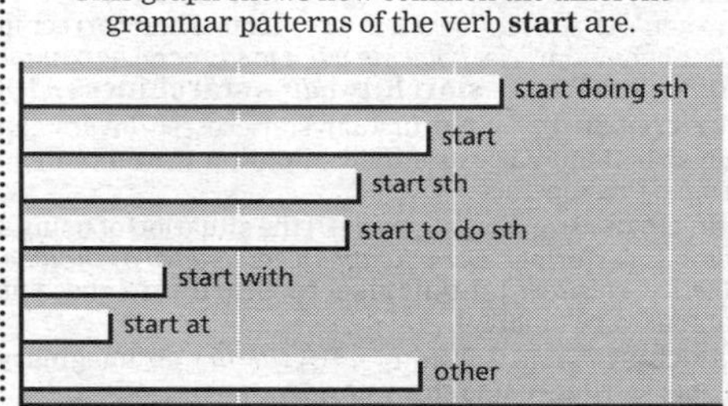


**start²** *n* S W
**1 ▶ OF AN ACTIVITY/EVENT ◀** [C usually singular] the beginning of an activity or event or the point at which it starts to develop: [+ **of**] *This fighting marked the start of more widespread civil unrest.* | *We arrived late and missed the start of the film.* | **(right) from the start** *We've had problems with this project right from the start.* | **from start to finish** *The concert was a fiasco from start to finish.* | **get off to a good/bad start** (=begin well or badly) *Chelsea got off to a good start, beating their opponents 5-0.*
**2 ▶ OF A PERIOD OF TIME ◀** [C usually singular] the beginning of a fixed period of time: **the start of the year/day/season** *The start of the season was marred by the awful weather.* | **get off to a good/bad start** *The day got off to a bad start when I missesd the train.*
**3 make a start (on sth)** to begin doing something: *I guess it's time I made a start on the housework.*
**4 ▶ SPORT ◀ the start** the place where a race begins: *The horses were all lined up at the start.*
**5 ▶ ADVANTAGE ◀** [C usually singular] a situation in which you have an advantage over other people: *George was grateful to his parents for the start they'd given him.* | **a start in life** (=things that will help you to succeed in life) *Naturally we want to give our kids the best possible start in life.*
**6 ▶ IN A RACE/COMPETITION ◀** [C usually singular] the amount of time or space by which one person is ahead of another, especially in a race or competition: *They decided to give the younger boys a sixty metre start.* | [+ **on**] *The prisoners had a three hour start on their pursuers.*
**7 ▶ SUDDEN MOVEMENT ◀** [singular] a sudden movement of the body, usually caused by fear or surprise: **with a start** *Ted woke up with a start and felt for the light switch.* | **give you a start** (=frighten or surprise you) *The sound of footsteps gave me quite a start.*

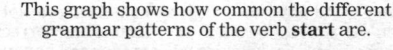

**8 for a start** used to emphasize the first of a list of facts or opinions you are stating: *Vincent should never have been picked for the team; for a start he has not had enough experience.* —see also FALSE START, **in/by fits and starts** (FIT³ (6))

**start·er** /ˈstɑːtə‖ˈstɑːrtər/ *n* [C] **1** a person, horse, car etc that is in a race when it starts: *Of the eight starters, only three finished the race.* **2 for starters** *informal* a phrase meaning to begin with, used to tell someone what should be done or said first: *Well, for starters, you'd better get an application form.* **3** someone who gives the signal for a race to begin: *The starter fired his gun.* | **under starter's orders** (=about to begin the race) **4** a piece of equipment for starting a machine, especially an electric motor for starting an engine **5** *BrE* the first part of a meal; APPETIZER: *Would you like soup or melon as a starter?* —see also NONSTARTER, SELF-STARTER

**starter home** /ˈ·· ·/ *n* [C] *BrE* a small house or apartment bought by people who are buying their first home

**starter mo·tor** /ˈ·· ˌ··/ *n* [C] a STARTER (4) —see picture at ENGINE

**starter pack** /ˈ·· ·/ *n* [C] the basic equipment and instructions that you need to start working, especially on a computer

**start·ing block** /ˈ·· ·/ *n* [C] one of a pair of blocks fixed to the ground that a runner pushes their feet against at the start of a race

**starting gate** /ˈ·· ·/ *n* [C] a gate or pair of gates that open to allow a horse or dog through at the start of a race

**starting price** /ˈ·· ·/ *n* [C] the last PRICE (=amount of money that is returned for money risked) that is offered just before a horse or dog race begins

**start·le** /ˈstɑːtl‖ˈstɑːrtl/ *v* [T] to make someone suddenly surprised or slightly shocked: *You startled me! I didn't hear you come in.* | **startled to see/hear/learn etc** *I was startled to see Amanda there.*

**start·ling** /ˈstɑːtlɪŋ‖ˈstɑːrt-/ *adj* very unusual or surprising: *Paddy's words had a startling effect on the children.* —**startlingly** *adv*: *startlingly pale*

**start-up** /ˈ· ·/ *adj* start-up costs are connected with beginning and developing a new business: *a start-up budget of $90,000*

**starv·a·tion** /stɑːˈveɪʃən‖stɑːr-/ *n* **1** [U] suffering or death caused by lack of food: *people dying of starvation in the famine* **2 starvation diet** *informal* very little food **3 starvation wages** extremely low wages

3 **starve** /stɑːv‖stɑːrv/ *v* [I,T] **1** to suffer or die because you do not have enough to eat, or to make someone else do this: *Thousands of people will starve if food doesn't reach the stricken city.* | **starve sth** *The dog looked like it had been starved.* | **starve to death** (=die from lack of food) *They'll either die from the cold or starve to death.* **2** to not give or not be given something very important, for example love or money, with harmful results: [+ **of**] *The schools are understaffed and starved of funds.* | **be starved for sth** *AmE* (=not get any at all) *That poor kid's just starved for attention.* **3 be starving** also **be starved** *especially AmE spoken* to be very hungry: *You must be starving! Come and eat lunch.*

**starve** sb **into** *phr v* [T] to force someone to do something, by preventing them from getting food or money: *The miners were starved into submission.*

**starve** sb **out** *phr v* [T] to force someone to leave a place by preventing them from getting food: *If we can't blast them out, we'll starve them out.*

**starve·ling** /ˈstɑːvlɪŋ‖ˈstɑːrv-/ *n* [C] *literary* a person or animal that is thin and unhealthy from lack of food

**starving** /ˈstɑːvɪŋ‖ˈstɑːr-/ *adj* **1** so hungry that you will die soon if you do not eat: *pictures of starving children* | **the starving** (=people who are starving) **2** [not before noun] *spoken* very hungry: *Can we get something to eat – I'm absolutely starving.*

**stash¹** /stæʃ/ *v* [T always + adv/prep] *informal* to store something in a safe, often secret, place: **stash sth away** *He has money stashed away in the Bahamas.* | [+ **in/under**] *You can stash your gear in here.*

**stash²** *n* [C] *informal* an amount of something that is kept in a secret place: [+ **of**] *a stash of drugs*

**state¹** /steɪt/ *n* S2 W2

**1 ▶ CONDITION ◀** [C] the mental, emotional, or physical condition that someone or something is in at a particular time: *Frankly I wouldn't trust his emotional state right now.* | *Water exists in three states: liquid, gaseous, and solid.* | **in a bad/good etc state** *The roads are in a terrible state after the severe winter weather.* | [+ **of**] *The driver was in a state of shock.* | **not in a fit state to do sth** (=not healthy enough or in a good enough condition) *David's in no fit state to go out yet.* | **state of mind** (=the way you feel) *Ames' dismissal had left him in a distressed state of mind.* | **be in a good/bad state of repair** (=not need repairing, or need repairing) *The house we're buying is in a good state of repair.* | **a state of war** (=officially fighting another country) —see also STATE OF EMERGENCY

**2 ▶ GOVERNMENT ◀** also **State** [singular, U] the government or political organization of a country: *If elected, they want to cut back the powers of the state.* | *The State has allocated special funds for the emergency.* | **state employees/property/regulations etc** *limits on salary increases for state workers* | **state-owned/state-funded/state-subsidized etc** (=owned, paid for etc by the government) *a state-funded community housing project* | **matters of state** (=the business of the government) —see also POLICE STATE, WELFARE STATE —see RACE¹ (USAGE)

**3 ▶ A COUNTRY ◀** [C] a country considered as a political organization: **democratic/totalitarian/one-party state** (=with that type of government) | **member state** (=a country belonging to an international organization) *NATO's member states* —see RACE¹ (USAGE)

**4 ▶ PART OF A COUNTRY ◀** also **State** [C] one of the areas with limited law-making powers that together make up a country controlled by a central government: *Queensland is one of the states of Australia.*

**5 ▶ CEREMONY ◀** [U] the grand, official ceremonies and events connected with governments and rulers: **state visit** (=official visit to another country) *the President's state visit to Moscow* | **state occasions** (=special public events) *Their band often plays at the White House on state occasions.* | **in state** (=with a lot of comfort and public attention) *The empress travelled in state with all her ladies.* —see also **lie in state** (LIE¹ (12))

**6 the States** *spoken* a word meaning the US, used especially by someone when they are outside the US: *Which part of the States would you suggest I should visit?*

**7 be in a state/get into a state** *spoken* to be or become very nervous, anxious, or excited: *Mom and Dad were in a state when I didn't come home until very late.*

**8 state of affairs** a situation: *I must say this is a very unsatisfactory state of affairs.*

**9 the state of play a)** the position reached in an activity or process that has not finished yet: *What is the state of play in the current negotiations?* **b)** the score points that have been gained at one time in a sports game

**state²** *v* [T] **1** to formally give a piece of information or your opinion, especially by saying it clearly: *Please state your name and address.* | *The Government needs to clearly state its policy on UN intervention.* | [+ **(that)**] *The witness stated that he had not seen the woman before.* | **state the obvious** (=say something that is completely unnecessary because it is already clear) **2** if a document, newspaper, ticket etc states information, it contains the information written clearly: *The price of the tickets is stated on them.* S3 W3

**state at·tor·ney** /ˌ· ·ˈ··/ *n* [C] *AmE* a lawyer who represents the state in court cases

**state ben·e·fit** /ˌ· ˈ···/ *n* [C,U] money given by the government in Britain to people who are poor, without a job, ill etc

**state court** /ˈ· ·/ *n* [C] a court in the US which deals with legal cases that are concerned with state laws or a state's CONSTITUTION (1)

**State De·part·ment** /ˈ· ˌ··/ *n* the American government department that deals with anything connected with foreign countries

**state·hood** /ˈsteɪthʊd/ *n* [U] **1** the condition of being an independent nation **2** the condition of being one of the states making up a nation, such as the US

**State·house** /ˈsteɪthaʊs/ *n* [C usually singular] the building where the lawyers in a US state do their work

**state·less** /ˈsteɪtləs/ *adj* not officially being a citizen of any country: *All stateless individuals were presumed to be lawless vagabonds.* —**statelessness** *n* [U]

**state line** /ˌ· ˈ·/ *n* [C] the line between two states in the US: *At the end of the trip we crossed the state line into California.*

**state·ly** /ˈsteɪtli/ *adj* **1** done slowly and with a lot of ceremony; formal: *the stately progress of the procession* **2** impressive in style and size; NOBLE[1] (2): *the stately trees of the pine forest*

**stately home** /ˌ·· ˈ·/ *n* [C] a large house in the countryside in Britain which has historical interest

S2 W1 **state·ment¹** /ˈsteɪtmənt/ *n* **1** [C] something you say or write publicly or officially to let people know your intentions or opinions, or to record facts: *False statements on your tax form could land you in jail.* | **make a statement (about)** *Before we begin, I'd like to make a statement about my involvement.* | **issue a statement** (=write something that can be read in public or given to newspapers) *The Congressman issued a statement to the press.* | **get/take a statement** (=officially write down what someone says) | **sworn statement** (=that you officially declare to be true) **2** [C] a list showing amounts of money paid, received, owing etc and their total: *the company's annual financial statement to shareholders* | **bank statement** (=sent regularly from your bank about your account) **3** [U] *formal* the act of expressing something in words: *The details of the agreement need more exact statement.*

S

**statement²** *v* [T] *BrE* if an education authority statements a child who has special educational needs, they give a school additional money to help teach that child —**statemented** *adj*

**state of e·mer·gen·cy** /ˌ· · ·ˈ···/ *n* [C] a situation that a government officially declares to be very dangerous, and in which it uses special laws so that it can react very quickly: *there has been a call for the lifting of the state of emergency*

**state-of-the-art** /ˌ· · · ˈ·◂/ *adj* using the most modern and recently developed methods, materials, or knowledge: *state-of-the-art technology*

**state park** /ˌ· ˈ·/ *n* [C] a large park owned and managed by a US state, often in an area of natural beauty

**state·room** /ˈsteɪtrʊm, -ruːm/ *n* [C] one of the large rooms in a palace

**State's at·tor·ney** /ˌ· ·ˈ··/ *n* [C] *AmE* STATE ATTORNEY

**state school** /ˈ· ˌ·/ *n* [C] a British school which receives money from the government and provides free education

**State's ev·i·dence** /ˌ· ˈ···/ *n AmE* **turn State's evidence** if a criminal turns State's evidence, they give information in a court of law about other criminals; QUEEN'S EVIDENCE *BrE*

**State·side** /ˈsteɪtsaɪd/ *adj, adv AmE informal* a word meaning in the US or connected with the US, used by people when they are not in the US: *When were you last Stateside?*

**states·man** /ˈsteɪtsmən/ *n* [C] a political or government leader, especially one who is respected as being wise, honourable, and fair —**statesmanlike** *adj*: *a statesmanlike performance in dealing with the crisis* —**statesmanship** *n* [U]

**state tax** /ˈ· ·/ *n* [C,U] *AmE* a tax in the US that is paid to the state rather than to the central government —compare FEDERAL TAX

**state troop·er** /ˌ· ˈ··/ *n* [C] *AmE* a member of a police force that is controlled by one of the US state governments who works anywhere in that state

**state u·ni·ver·si·ty** /ˌ· ··ˈ···/ *n* [C] *AmE* a university in the US which receives money from a state to help pay its costs

**state·wide** /ˈsteɪtwaɪd/ *adj AmE* affecting an entire US state: *Regulations will be local rather than statewide.*

**stat·ic¹** /ˈstætɪk/ *adj* not moving, changing, or developing, especially when movement or change would be good: *Economists predict that house prices will stay static for a long period.* —compare DYNAMIC[1] (2, 3)

**static²** *n* [U] **1** noise caused by electricity in the air that blocks or spoils the sound from radio or TV **2** static electricity **3** *AmE informal* complaints or opposition to a plan, situation, or action: *His promotion has caused a lot of static.* —**statically** /-kli/ *adv*

**static e·lec·tri·ci·ty** /ˌ·· ··ˈ···/ *n* [U] electricity that is not flowing in a current, but collects on the surface of an object and gives you a small ELECTRIC SHOCK

**stat·ics** /ˈstætɪks/ *n* [U] the science dealing with the forces that produce balance in objects that are not moving —compare **dynamics** (DYNAMIC[2] (16))

**sta·tion¹** /ˈsteɪʃən/ *n* 

**1** ▶ **TRAVEL** ◀ [C] **a)** a place where public vehicles regularly stop so that passengers can get on and off, goods can be loaded etc: *the city bus station* | **train station** *especially AmE*, **railway station** *especially BrE*: *It's time to meet Daddy at the train station.* | **subway station** *AmE*, **underground station** *BrE* (=for trains that run under the ground) **b)** the building or buildings at such a place: *Is there a waiting room in the station?* | *Grand Central Station*

**2** ▶ **ACTIVITY OR SERVICE** ◀ [C] a building or place that is a centre for a particular kind of service or activity: **(police/fire) station** *You'll have to go with the officer to the station.* | **petrol station** *BrE*, **gas station** *AmE* (=where petrol is sold) | **polling station** (=where you vote in an election) | **research station** *Frank spent six months at an arctic research station.* —compare ACTION STATIONS

**3** ▶ **BROADCASTING** ◀ [C] **a)** one of the many different signals you can receive on your radio or television, that a company broadcasts on: *Tom tuned the radio to a country music station.* | **get/pick up a station** *I can't get many stations on this thing.* **b)** an organization which makes television or radio broadcasts, or the building where this is done: *That woman from the local TV station is here for your interview.* —compare CHANNEL[1] (1, 2)

**4** ▶ **POSITION** ◀ [C] a place where someone stands or sits in order to be ready to do something quickly if needed: *You're not to leave your station unless told.*

**5** ▶ **FARMING** ◀ [C] a large sheep or cattle farm in Australia or New Zealand

**6** ▶ **SOCIAL RANK** ◀ [C] *old-fashioned* your position in society: **above your station** (=higher than your social rank) *Don't get ideas above your station.*

**7** ▶ **MILITARY** ◀ [C] a small military establishment

**8** ▶ **SHIPS** ◀ [U] *technical* a ship's position in relation to others in a group, especially a military ship

**station²** *v* [T usually passive] to put someone in a particular place in order to do a particular job or military duty: *He's still in the Army, stationed in Washington.* | *Two guards were stationed at the back of the room.*

**sta·tion·a·ry** /ˈsteɪʃənəri‖-neri/ *adj* standing still instead of moving: *How did you manage to drive into a stationary vehicle?*

**station break** /ˈ·· ·/ *n* [C] *AmE* a pause during a radio or television broadcast in the US, so that local stations can give their names

**sta·tion·er** /ˈsteɪʃənə‖-ər/ *n* [C] *BrE* **1** **stationer's** a shop that sells stationery **2** someone in charge of a shop that sells stationery

**sta·tion·e·ry** /ˈsteɪʃənəri‖-neri/ *n* [U] **1** materials that you use for writing, such as paper, pens, pencils etc **2** paper for writing letters on, usually with matching envelopes: *a letter on hotel stationery*

**sta·tion-house** /ˈ·· ˌ·/ *n* [C] *AmE old fashioned* the local office of the police in a town, part of a city etc; POLICE STATION

**station mas·ter** /ˈ·· ˌ··/ *n* [C] someone who is in charge of a train station

**station wag·on** /ˈ·· ˌ··/ *n* [C] *AmE* a large car with extra space at the back, with a door there for loading and unloading; ESTATE CAR *BrE*

S2 W3 **sta·tis·tic** /stəˈtɪstɪk/ *n* **1 a)** **statistics** [plural] a collection of numbers which represent facts or measurements: *Statistics on illness are used in planning health care.* | *Statistics show that 35% of new businesses fail in their first year.* **b)** [U] the science of dealing with and explaining such numbers: *Statistics is a branch of mathematics.* **2** [singular] a single number which represents a fact or measurement: *Is he aware of the statistic that women make up 40% of the work force?* —see also VITAL STATISTICS —**statistical** *adj*: *statistical evidence* —**statistically** /-kli/ *adv*: *The variation is not statistically significant.*

**stat·is·ti·cian** /ˌstætɪ̣ˈstɪʃən/ *n* [C] someone who works with statistics

**sta·tive** /ˈsteɪtɪv/ *adj technical* a stative verb describes a state rather than an action or event, and is not usually used in PROGRESSIVE[1] (3) forms, for example 'belong' in the sentence 'this book belongs to me'

**stats** /stæts/ *n* [plural] *informal* statistics

**stat·u·a·ry** /ˈstætʃuəri‖-tʃueri/ *n* [U] *technical* statues: *a fine collection of Greek statuary*

**stat·ue** /ˈstætʃuː/ *n* [C] an image of a person or animal that is made in solid material such as stone or metal and is usually large: *a bronze statue of a horse* | *The Communist Party had put up many statues of its leaders.* —compare SCULPTURE

**stat·u·esque** /ˌstætʃuˈesk/ *adj* large and beautiful in a formal way, like a statue: *a tall statuesque woman*

**stat·u·ette** /ˌstætʃuˈet/ *n* [C] a very small statue for putting on a table or shelf —compare BUST[2] (1)

**stat·ure** /ˈstætʃə‖-ər/ *n* [C,U] *formal* **1** the degree to which someone is admired or regarded as important: *Louis Armstrong was a musician of world stature.* **2** someone's height or size: *short in stature*

W2 **sta·tus** /ˈsteɪtəs‖ˈsteɪtəs, ˈstæ-/ *n* **1** [C,U] the legal position or condition of a person, group, country etc: *What is her immigration status?* | *Don't accept any money if it will effect your amateur status.* | **marital status** (=whether you are married or not) *Please state your name, age and marital status.* **2** [U] **a)** your social or professional rank or position, considered in relation to other people: **high/low status** *high status businessmen* **b)** high social position that makes people recognize and respect you: *Barnes has a great status in the community.* | **status symbol** (=something that you have or own that you think shows high social status) *a secretary is a boss's status symbol* **3** [C] a situation at a particular time, especially in an argument, discussion etc: *What's the status of the trade talks?*

**status quo** /ˌsteɪtəs ˈkwəʊ‖ˌsteɪtəs ˈkwoʊ, ˌstæ-/ *n* **the status quo** the state of a situation as it is: **maintain the status quo** (=not make any changes) *Managers want to maintain the status quo because they're afraid to take risks.*

**stat·ute** /ˈstætʃuːt/ *n* [C] **1** a law passed by a parliament, council etc and formally written down: **by statute** *Protection for the consumer is laid down by statute.* **2** a formal rule of an institution or organization: *College statutes forbid drinking on campus.*

**statute book** /ˈ·· ·/ *n not technical* **the statute book** a real or imaginary written collection of the laws in existence: **on the statute book** (=in operation) *The government would like to see this new law on the statute book as soon as possible.*

**statute law** /ˈ·· ·/ *n* [U] the whole group of written laws established by a parliament, council etc —compare COMMON LAW[2]

**statute of lim·i·ta·tions** /ˌ····ˈ··/ *n* [C] *AmE technical* a law which gives the period of time within which action may be taken on a legal question or crime

**stat·u·to·ry** /ˈstætʃʊ̣təri‖-tɔːri/ *adj* fixed or controlled by law: *statutory employment rights* | *She's below the statutory age for school attendance.* —**statutorily** *adv*

**statutory of·fence** /ˌ···· ·ˈ·/ *n* [C] *AmE technical* a crime that is described by a law and can be punished by a court

**statutory rape** /ˌ···· ˈ·/ *n* [C] *law* the act of having sex with someone who is not allowed by law to have sex

**staunch**[1] /stɔːntʃ‖stɒːntʃ, stɑːntʃ/ *adj* giving strong, loyal support to another person, organization, belief etc; STEADFAST: *They are staunch trade unionists.* | *a staunch friend and ally* —**staunchly** *adv* —**staunchness** *n* [U]

**staunch**[2] also **stanch** *AmE*— *v* [T] to stop the flow of liquid, especially of blood from a wound: *The blood seemed to pour from the wound and I thought I would never staunch the flow.*

**stave**[1] /steɪv/ *n* [C] **1** the set of five lines on which music is written **2** one of the thin curved pieces of wood fitted close together to form the sides of a BARREL[1] (1)

**stave**[2] *v*

**stave in** *phr v past tense and past participle* **staved** *or* **stove** [I,T] to break something inwards or be broken inwards by something: **stave sth ↔ in** *The ship's side was stove in when it went onto the rocks.*

**stave** sth ↔ **off** *phr v past tense and past participle* **staved** [T] to keep someone or something from reaching you or affecting you for a period of time: *She'd brought some fruit on the journey to stave off hunger.* | *Amazingly, the protestors have staved off the army for three nights running.*

**staves** /steɪvz/ the plural of STAFF

**stay**[1] /steɪ/ *v* S1 W1

**1 ► IN A PLACE ◄** [I] to stop and remain in a place rather than go or leave: **stay (for) an hour/a while etc** *Can't you stay a little longer?* | **stay late** *I had to stay later than planned at work.* | **stay here/there** *Stay right there! I'll be back in a minute.* | **stay to dinner/stay for lunch** *Can you stay for supper?* | **stay behind** (=remain after others have gone) *I stayed behind to help clean up after the party.* —see graph at REMAIN

**2 ► IN A POSITION ◄** [I, linking verb] to continue to be in a particular position, place, or state, without changing: **stay calm/quiet/warm etc** *It's going to stay cold for the next few days.* | *You'd think he could stay sober for once.* | **[+ away/back/on etc]** *Stay away from my daughter!* | *Get out of this house and stay out!* | *You stay on this road for one mile before turning off.* | **stay in/out** (=not leave your home, or remain away from home) *I won't have you staying out on a school night.* | **stay up** (=not go to bed) *I stayed up late to watch the film.* | **stay in a job** (=keep doing it) *I don't know whether to stay in teaching or not.* | **stay around** *informal* (=not leave someone) *How do you know he'll stay around?* | **stay up/down/the same etc** (=remain at the same level) *House prices have stayed down for a whole year.* | **stay out of** *spoken* (=not get involved) *Stay out of this, Ben, it's none of your business.*

**3 ► LIVE SOMEWHERE ◄** [I] to live in a place for a while as a visitor or guest: **[+ at/with]** *We stayed at the hotel for four nights.* | *My mother is staying with us this week.* | **stay the night/stay overnight/stay over** (=stay from one evening to the next day) *You can stay overnight if you don't want to drive home.*

**4 stay put** *spoken* to remain in one place and not move: *You stay put in the car while I run into the store!*

**5 be here to stay** to become accepted and used by most people: *Do you think computers are here to stay?*

**6 stay after school** to remain at school after the day's classes are finished, often as a punishment

**7 stay the course** *informal* to finish something in spite of difficulties: *Working in sales is very demanding and not many of our people stay the course.*

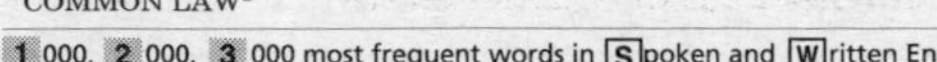

**8** ▶ **STOP** ◀ [I, T] *literary* to stop doing something, or stop someone from doing something
**9 stay!** used to tell a dog not to move
**stay on** *phr v* [I] to continue to do a job or to study after the usual or expected time for leaving: *"I thought your contract was done." "It is, but I'm staying on."*

**stay²** *n* **1** [C usually singular] a limited time of living in a place: *I met her towards the end of my stay in Los Angeles.* | *a short stay in the hospital* **2** [C,U] *law* the stopping or delay of an action because a judge has ordered it: **stay of execution** (=a delay of the punishment) **3** [C] a strong wire or rope used for supporting a ship's MAST (1) **4** [C] a short piece of plastic, bone, or wire used to keep a shirt COLLAR¹ (1) or a CORSET stiff **5 stays** [plural] a CORSET

**stay-at-home** /ˈ· · ˌ·/ *n* [C] *informal* someone who always stays at home and never does exciting things

**stay·er** /ˈsteɪə‖-ər/ *n* [C] *BrE* a horse or person who can keep going to the end of a long race, job etc

**stay·ing pow·er** /ˈ·· ˌ··/ *n* [U] the ability or energy to keep doing something difficult until it is finished: *They showed their staying power in the long-distance races.*

**St Ber·nard** /sənt ˈbɜːnəd‖ˌseɪnt bərˈnɑːrd/ *n* [C] a large strong Swiss dog that was trained in the past to help find people who were lost in the snow

**STD** /ˌes tiː ˈdiː/ *n* [U] **1** subscriber trunk dialling; the telephone system in Britain that allows people to connect their own LONG-DISTANCE calls **2** sexually transmitted disease; a disease that is passed on through having sex, such as AIDS, HERPES etc

**S**

**std** the written abbreviation of STANDARD

**stead** /sted/ *n* **do sth in sb's stead** *formal* to do something that someone else usually does or was going to do —see also **stand sb in good stead** (STAND¹ (43))

**stead·fast** /ˈstedfɑːst‖-fæst/ *adj literary* faithful and very loyal: [+ **in**] *Harold remained steadfast in his Christian faith throughout his life.* —**steadfastly** *adv* —**steadfastness** *n* [U]

W3 **stead·y¹** /ˈstedi/ *adj*
**1** ▶ **NOT MOVING** ◀ firmly held in a particular position and not moving or shaking: *Keep the camera steady while you take a picture.* | **a steady hand** *You need a steady hand for such a delicate job.*
**2** ▶ **CONTINUOUS** ◀ moving, happening, or developing in a continuous gradual way: *a steady decline in manufacturing output* | *Paul has made steady progress this year.* | **a steady stream of visitors/enquiries etc** *a steady stream of East Germans making their way through the new gap in the wall*
**3** ▶ **NOT CHANGING** ◀ a steady level, speed etc stays about the same: *We were driving at a steady 60 mph.*
**4** ▶ **PERSON** ◀ someone who is steady is sensible and you can depend on them: *a steady worker*
**5 steady job/work/income** a job or work that will definitely continue over a long period of time
**6 steady boyfriend/girlfriend** someone that you have been having a romantic relationship with
**7 steady relationship** a serious and strong relationship that continues for a long time —**steadily** *adv* —**steadiness** *n* [U]

**steady²** *v* **1** [T] to hold something steady or make it steady: **steady yourself** (=get back your balance in order to prevent yourself from falling) *He tried to steady himself by grabbing the tree.* **2** [I] to stop increasing or decreasing and remain about the same: *The dollar has steadied after early losses on the money markets.* **3 steady your nerves** to make yourself calm: *She had a brandy to steady her nerves.*

**steady³** *adv* **go steady (with sb)** to have a long regular romantic relationship with a BOYFRIEND or GIRLFRIEND

**steady⁴** *n* [C] *AmE informal* a BOYFRIEND or GIRLFRIEND that someone has been having a romantic relationship with: *Jill is Ray's steady.*

**steady⁵** *interjection BrE informal* **1** used when you want to tell someone to be careful or not to cause an accident: *Steady! You nearly knocked me over.* **2 Steady on!** used when you think that what someone is saying is too strong or extreme: *Steady on! Derek's not that bad.*

**steady state the·o·ry** /ˌ·· ˈ· ˌ···/ *n technical* the idea that things in space have always existed and have always been moving away from each other as new atoms begin to exist. —compare BIG BANG THEORY

**steak** /steɪk/ *n* **1** [C,U] good quality BEEF (=meat from a cow), or a large thick piece of any good quality red meat: *I like my steak rare.* **2** [U] *BrE* beef that is not of such good quality and is used in making CASSEROLES etc **3 cod/salmon/tuna etc steak** [C] a large thick piece of fish

**steak·house** /ˈsteɪkhaʊs/ *plural* **steakhouses** /-haʊzɪ̈z/ *n* [C] a restaurant that serves steak

**steak tar·tare** /ˌ· ·ˈ·/ *n* [U] steak that is cut into very small pieces and eaten raw, usually with a raw egg

**steal**

He stole her purse *BrE* / wallet *AmE*.
He robbed the woman (of her purse) *BrE* / wallet *AmE*.

**steal¹** /stiːl/ *v past tense* **stole** /stəʊl‖stoʊl/ *past participle* **stolen** /ˈstəʊlən‖ˈstoʊ-/ S3 W3
**1** ▶ **TAKE STH** ◀ [I,T] to take something that belongs to someone else: [+ **from**] *Some drug users steal from their own families to finance their habit.* | **steal sth** *Sean has a long history of stealing cars.* | **steal sth from sb** *He was accused of stealing ideas from a rival studio.*
**2** ▶ **MOVE SOMEWHERE** ◀ [I always + adv/prep] to move quietly without anyone noticing you: [+ **into/across etc**] *I tried to steal out of the room without waking Stefan.*
**3 steal the show/limelight/scene** to do something, especially when you are acting in a play, that makes people pay more attention to you than to other people
**4 steal a look/glance etc** to look at someone or something quickly and secretly
**5** ▶ **SPORT** ◀ [I,T] to run to the next BASE¹ (8) in the game of BASEBALL before someone hits the ball
**6 steal a kiss** to kiss someone quickly when they are not expecting it
**7 steal sb's thunder** to get the success and praise someone else should have got, by doing what they had intended to do
**8 steal a march on sb** to secretly or unexpectedly start something that someone else had planned to do, so that you gain an advantage over them
**9 steal sb's heart** *literary* to make someone fall in love with you

**USAGE NOTE: STEAL**

WORD CHOICE: **steal, take, rob, burgle, burglarize, pick sb's pocket**

People **steal** things (from people, cars, houses, shops, banks etc): *He's stolen my Walkman!* (NOT *stolen me* or *robbed my Walkman*) | *Someone stole his passport while he was asleep.*

**Take** is also often used in this sense: *Someone's taken my wallet.*

People **rob** other people (of things) especially in a public place: *A man was robbed by three youths as he walked home from work yesterday.*

People **rob** banks, or gas stations, but usually **burgle** (*BrE*) or **burglarize** (*AmE*) a house or office: *At least 10 houses in the area had been burgled during the night.*

If someone **picks your pocket**, they steal things from your pocket, usually when you are in a crowd of people.

**steal²** *n* [C] *informal* **1 be a steal** to be very cheap: *At 20 bucks the camera was a steal.* —see CHEAP² (USAGE) **2** the act of running to the next BASE¹ (8) in the game of BASEBALL before someone hits the ball

**stealth** /stelθ/ *n* [U] the action of doing something very quietly, slowly, or secretly so that no one notices you: *Cats rely on stealth to catch their prey.* | **by stealth** *They are trying to carry out their aims by stealth, after failing to impose them by law.*

**stealth bomb·er** /ˈ· ˌ··/ *n* [C] an American military aircraft that cannot be discovered by RADAR instruments

**stealth·y** /ˈstelθi/ *adj* moving or doing something quietly and secretly: *His eye caught a stealthy movement at the edge of the wood.* —**stealthily** *adv*

W3 **steam¹** /stiːm/ *n* [U]

**1 ▶GAS◀** the hot mist that water produces when it is boiled: *Be careful of the steam from the kettle.*

**2 ▶MIST ON A SURFACE◀** the mist that forms on windows, mirrors etc when warm wet air suddenly becomes cold

**3 ▶POWER◀** power that is produced by boiling water to make steam, in order to make things work or move: *The engines are driven by steam.* | **steam engine/train etc** (=an engine etc that works by the power produced by steam)

**4 let off steam** to get rid of your anger or excitement in a way that does not harm anyone by doing something active: *PE is a good time for the kids to let off steam!*

**5 run out of steam** to no longer have the energy or the desire to continue doing something, especially because you are tired: *The home team began to run out of steam in the last quarter.*

**6 get/pick up steam a)** if an engine gets up steam, it gradually starts to go faster **b)** if plans, beliefs etc get up steam, they gradually become more important and more people become interested in them

**7 under your own steam** if you go somewhere under your own steam, you get there without help from anyone else: *I'll get to the restaurant under my own steam.*

**8 go full steam ahead with** to do something with as much energy and eagerness as possible

**9 ▶RAILWAY◀** a railway system in which the trains use steam for power: *the age of steam*

**steam²** *v* **1** [I] if something steams, steam rises from it, especially because it is hot: *a mug of steaming coffee* **2** [T] to cook something in steam: *Steam the vegetables lightly.* **3** [I always + adv/prep] to travel somewhere in a boat or train that uses steam to produce power: [+ **into/from etc**] *During the next two weeks, we steamed from port to port.* **4 be steamed** *AmE spoken* to be very angry

**steam sth ↔ open/off** *phr v* [T] to use steam to open an envelope or to remove a stamp from an envelope

**steam up** *phr v* [I,T] to cover or become covered with steam: **steam sth ↔ up** *The warm room steamed up my glasses.* —see also STEAMED-UP

**steam·boat** /ˈstiːmbəʊt‖-boʊt/ *n* [C] a boat that uses steam to produce power and is used for sailing along rivers and coasts

**steam clean** /ˈ· ·/ *v* [T] to clean something made of cloth by using a machine that produces steam

**steam·ed-up** /ˌ· ˈ·/ *adj* [not before noun] *informal* excited and angry or worried: *Don't get so steamed-up about it – it's not really important.*

**steam·er** /ˈstiːmə‖-ər/ *n* [C] **1** a STEAMSHIP **2** a container used to cook food in steam

**steam·ing** /ˈstiːmɪŋ/ *adv* **1 steaming hot** very hot: *It was a steaming hot day.* **2** *ScotE* very drunk

**steam i·ron** /ˈ· ˌ··/ *n* [C] an electric iron that produces steam in order to make clothes easier to iron

**steam·roll** /ˈstiːmrəʊl‖-roʊl/ *v* [T] *AmE* to steamroller

**steam·roll·er¹** /ˈstiːmˌrəʊlə‖ˌroʊlər/ *n* [C] a heavy vehicle with very wide wheels that you drive over road surfaces to make them flat

**steamroller²** *v* [T] *informal* to force someone to do what you want them to do, or to make sure something happens by using all your power and influence; STEAMROLL *AmE*: *He steamrollered his bill through Parliament against fierce opposition.*

**steam·ship** /ˈstiːmˌʃɪp/ *n* [C] a large ship that uses steam to produce power

**steam shov·el** /ˈ· ˌ··/ *n* [C] *AmE* a large machine that digs and moves earth in a large bucket

**steam·y** /ˈstiːmi/ *adj* **1** full of steam or covered in steam: *steamy windows* **2** sexually exciting and slightly shocking: *a steamy love affair*

**steed** /stiːd/ *n* [C] *poetic* a strong fast horse

**steel¹** /stiːl/ *n* **1** [U] strong metal that can be shaped easily, consisting of iron and CARBON: *A bridge made of steel* | **stainless steel** *stainless steel cutlery* **2** [U] the industry that makes steel: *Sheffield is a major steel town.* **3 nerves of steel** the ability to be brave and calm in a dangerous or difficult situation: *You need nerves of steel to be a racing driver.* **4** [C] a thin bar of steel used to sharpen knives S2 W3

**steel²** *v* [T] **steel yourself** to prepare yourself to do something that you know will be unpleasant or upsetting: **steel yourself to do sth** *Bob steeled himself to tell her about her father's death.*

**steel band** /ˌ· ˈ·/ *n* [C] a group of people who play a type of music from the West Indies, in which you hit different areas on drums made from metal oil BARRELS to produce different musical sounds

**steel gui·tar** /ˌ· ·ˈ·/ *n* [C] a musical instrument with ten strings that is played using a steel bar and a PEDAL (=a bar you press with your foot)

**steel wool** /ˌ· ˈ·/ *n* [U] a rough material made of fine steel threads, that is used to make surfaces smooth, remove paint etc —compare WIRE WOOL

**steel·works** /ˈstiːlwɜːks‖-wɜːrks/ *n* [C] *plural* **steelworks** a factory where steel is made —**steelworker** *n* [C]

**steel·y** /ˈstiːli/ *adj* **1 steely determination/expression etc** an extremely strong and determined attitude, expression etc **2** having a grey colour like steel: *a steely sky*

**steep¹** /stiːp/ *adj* **1** a road, hill etc that is steep slopes at a high angle: *The road's too steep to ride up on a bike.* **2** steep prices, charges etc are unusually expensive: *landlords asking steep rents* **3** a steep increase or rise in something is a very big increase: *A steep increase in the number of car thefts in the area.* **4 that's/it's a bit steep** *BrE spoken* used to say that a request or action is unreasonable: *They want us to work on New Year's Day? That's a bit steep!* —**steeply** *adv* —**steepness** *n* [U] S3

**steep²** *v* [I,T] **1 be steeped in history/tradition etc** to have a lot of a particular quality such as history etc: *a town steeped in history* **2** to put food in a liquid and leave it there so that it becomes soft or has the same taste as the liquid: *Steep the raisins in sherry.*

**steep·en** /ˈstiːpən/ *v* [I,T] if a slope, road etc steepens or something steepens it, it becomes steeper

**stee·ple** /ˈstiːpəl/ *n* [C] a tall pointed tower on the roof of a church

**stee·ple·chase** /ˈstiːpəltʃeɪs/ *n* [C] **1** a long race in which horses jump over gates, water etc **2** a long race in which people run and jump over fences, water etc

**stee·ple·jack** /ˈstiːpəldʒæk/ *n* [C] someone whose work is repairing towers, tall CHIMNEYS etc

**steer[1]** /stɪə‖stɪr/ *v*

**1 ▶ CAR/BOAT ETC ◀** [I,T] to control the direction a vehicle is going, for example by turning a wheel: [+ **for/towards etc**] *I tried to steer around the bollard.*|*We turned about and steered for Port of Spain.*

**2 ▶ CHANGE SB/STH ◀** [T] to guide someone's behaviour or the way a situation develops without anyone noticing it: **steer sb towards/away from** *We steered Noel towards less expensive hobbies.*|**steer the conversation** *Helen tried to steer the conversation away from school.*

**3 ▶ BE IN CHARGE OF ◀** [T always + adv/prep] to be in charge of an organization, team etc and make decisions that help it be successful, especially during a difficult time: **steer sth through/to etc** *McKinney steered the company through the hard years of recession.*

**4 ▶ GUIDE SB TO A PLACE ◀** to guide someone to a place, especially by putting your hand on their back, shoulder etc and gently pushing them: **steer sb towards/to etc** *Joel steered the visitors towards the backyard.*

**5 steer clear (of)** *informal* to try to avoid someone or something unpleasant or difficult: *Paul's in a bad mood, so I'd steer well clear if I were you.*

**6 steer a middle course** to choose a course of action that is not extreme

**steer[2]** *n* [C] a young male cow that has had its sex organs removed —compare BULLOCK, HEIFER

**steer·age** /ˈstɪərɪdʒ‖ˈstɪr-/ *n* [U] the part of a passenger ship where people who had the cheapest tickets used to travel in the past

**steer·ing** /ˈstɪərɪŋ‖ˈstɪr-/ *n* [U] the parts of a car, boat etc that allow you to control its direction: *power steering*|*The steering on this car is lighter.*

**steering com·mit·tee** /ˈ.. .,../ *n* a committee that guides or directs a particular activity

**steering wheel** /ˈ.. ./ *n* [C] a wheel that you turn to control the direction of a car —see picture on page 409

**steers·man** /ˈstɪəzmən‖ˈstɪrz-/ *n* [C] someone who steers a ship

**stein** /staɪn/ *n* [C] a tall cup for drinking beer, often decorated and with a lid —see picture at CUP

**stel·lar** /ˈstelə‖-lər/ *adj* [only before noun] **1** *technical* connected with the stars —see also INTERSTELLAR **2** *AmE* done extremely well: **stellar performance** *Well, it wasn't exactly a stellar performance, was it Mike?*

**stem[1]** /stem/ *n* [C] **1** the long thin central part of a plant above the ground or the smaller parts that grow from it, from which leaves grow; STALK[1] (1) **2** the long thin part of a wine glass, VASE etc, between the base and the wide top **3** the narrow tube of a pipe used to smoke tobacco **4** the part of a word that stays the same when different endings are added to it, for example 'driv-' in 'driving' and 'driven' **5 from stem to stern** all the way from the front to the back, especially of a ship

**stem[2]** *v* **stemmed, stemming** [T] **1 stem the tide/flow of** to stop something from spreading or developing: *The public apology was intended to stem the tide of complaints from viewers.* **2** *formal* to stop the flow of a liquid: *stem the bleeding* **3 long-stemmed/short-stemmed etc** having a long stem, a short stem etc: *long-stemmed wine glasses*

**stem from** sth *phr v* [T not in progressive] to develop as a result of something else: *Most of the difficulties stemmed from poor workmanship.*

**stench** /stentʃ/ *n* [C usually singular] **1** a very strong unpleasant smell: *the stench of urine* **2** something unpleasant that makes you believe that something very bad and dishonest is happening: **the stench of privilege/injustice etc** *The stench of corruption hangs over this whole affair.*

**sten·cil[1]** /ˈstensəl/ *n* [C] a piece of plastic etc in which patterns or letters have been cut, or the decorative pattern or words made by putting paint or ink over this

**stencil[2]** *v* [T] to make a pattern, letters etc using a stencil

**Sten gun** /ˈsten ˌgʌn/ *n* [C] a small British SUBMACHINE GUN

**sten·o** /ˈstenəʊ‖-noʊ/ *n* [C] *informal* **1** [C] a stenographer **2** [U] stenography

**ste·nog·ra·pher** /stəˈnɒgrəfə‖-ˈnɑːgrəfər/ *n* [C] *AmE or BrE old-fashioned* someone whose job is to write down what someone else is saying, using stenography, and then type a copy of it; SHORTHAND TYPIST *BrE*

**ste·nog·ra·phy** /stəˈnɒgrəfi‖-ˈnɑː-/ *n* [U] *AmE or BrE old-fashioned* a system of writing quickly by using signs or shorter forms for letters, words, and phrases; SHORTHAND

**sten·to·ri·an** /stenˈtɔːriən/ *adj literary* a stentorian voice is very loud and powerful

**step[1]** /step/ *n* S2 W2

**1 ▶ MOVEMENT ◀** [C] the movement you make when you put one foot in front of the other when walking: *With every step my bags seemed heavier.*|**take a step** *Take two steps forward and one step back.*|**retrace your steps** (=go back the way you came)|**direct/bend your steps** *literary* (=walk in a particular direction) *The sun was setting as he bent his steps towards home.*

**2 ▶ ACTION ◀** [C] one of a series of things that you do in order to deal with a problem or to succeed: *Dole's first step will be to unite the party.*|[+ **towards**] *The talks are an important step towards reconciliation.*|**take steps** (=take action) *We must take steps to make sure such an accident can never happen again.*|**a step forward** *The discovery of penicillin was a major step forward in the treatment of infections.*|**a step in the right direction** (=an action that is not complete, but is good as a beginning)|**step backward** (=something you do that makes a situation worse) *Many teachers see an emphasis on written tests as a step backwards in education.*

**3 ▶ STAIR ◀** [C] a flat narrow piece of wood or stone, especially one in a series, that you put your foot on when you are going up or down in a building: *Jenny waited on the church steps.*|**flight of steps** (=set of steps) —see also DOORSTEP[1] (1)

**4 ▶ IN A PROCESS ◀** [C] a stage in a process or a position on a scale: *Every year you go up one step on the salary scale.*|**every step of the way** (=continuously during every stage of something) *Pam's husband has supported her every step of the way.*|**a step up** *Nina's promotion is quite a step up for one so young.* —compare STAGE[1] (1)

**5 ▶ DANCING ◀** [C] a movement of your feet in dancing: *Wayne's learning the steps for the new routine.*

**6 mind** *BrE*/**watch your step a)** to be careful about what you say or how you behave: *You'll get into trouble if you don't watch your step.* **b)** to be careful when you are walking: *Mind your step – the railing's loose.*

**7 be/keep in step a)** if people or their ideas are in step, they agree with each other or with what is usual, acceptable etc: *Suzie tries to keep in step with fashion.* **b)** to march with a group of people so that your right feet all go forward at the same time

**8 be out of step a)** if people or their ideas are out of step, they are different from the other people in a group: *Joshua's out of step with modern life.* **b)** if someone marching with a group is out of step, they are marching with their right foot going forward at a different time than everyone else

**9 ▶ SOUND ◀** [C] the sound you make when you set your foot down while walking: *I heard a step in the corridor.* —compare FOOTSTEP

**10 ▶ DISTANCE ◀** [C] the short distance you move when you take a step while walking: *There's a pub just a few steps down the road.* —compare PACE[1] (3)

**11 fall into step** to walk so that you are putting your

right foot forward at the same time as the people you are walking with: *Mr. Jones soon fell into step beside her.*
**12 step by step** slowly and gradually from one stage to the next: *Adam's learning the rules of chess step by step.*
**13 be one step ahead** to be better prepared for something or know more about something: *A good teacher should always be one step ahead of his students.*
**14 ▶ WAY SB WALKS ◀** [C usually singular] the way someone walks, which often tells you how they are feeling: *Gianni's usual bouncy step*
**15 steps** [plural] *BrE* a STEPLADDER
**16 ▶ EXERCISE ◀** [C,U] a type of exercise you do by walking onto and off a flat piece of equipment several inches high, of that piece of equipment itself: *Beginners' step class 7 pm.*
**17 ▶ MUSIC ◀** [C] *AmE* the difference in pitch (PITCH[2] (3)) between two musical notes that are separated by one key (KEY[1] (3)) on the piano; TONE[1] (8) *BrE*

W3 **step**[2] *v* **stepped, stepping** [I always + adv/prep]
**1 ▶ TAKE ONE STEP ◀** to raise one foot and put it down in front of the other one: [+ **forward/back/down etc**] *Step aside, let the doctor through.*
**2 ▶ WALK ◀** to walk a short distance: [+ **inside/outside etc**] *I stepped into the hall to wait.* | **step this way** (=come the way I am showing you)
**3 ▶ STAND ON STH ◀** to bring your foot down on something; TREAD[1] (1) *BrE*: [+ **in/on etc**] *I stepped in a puddle and got my shoes wet.*
**4 step forward** to come and offer help: *Police are appealing for witnesses to step forward.*
**5 step out of line** to behave badly by breaking rules or disobeying orders
**6 step on it/step on the gas** *AmE spoken* to drive faster: *If you don't step on it we'll miss the plane.*
**7 step lively!** *BrE spoken* used to tell someone to hurry —see also **step into the breach** (BREACH[1] (5))
**step down** also **step aside** *phr v* [I] to leave your job or official position: **step down as sth** *Eve has stepped down as chairperson.* | **step in favour of sb/sth** *Lister is stepping down in favor of a younger man.*
**step in** *phr v* [I] to become involved in a discussion or disagreement, especially in order to stop the trouble; INTERVENE: *If the dispute continues, the government will have to step in.*
**step out** *phr v* [I] **1** *AmE* to go out for a short time *BrE*: *Molly just stepped out but she'll be back soon.* —see also POP[1] (1) **2** *old-fashioned* to start walking fast
**step** sth ↔ **up** *phr v* [T] to increase the amount of an activity or the speed of a process in order to improve a situation: *We will be stepping up production to meet the increased demand.*

**step-** /step/ *prefix* related not by birth but because a parent has remarried: *my stepfather* (=not my real father, but a man who has married my mother) | *her stepchildren*

**step·broth·er** /ˈstepbrʌðə‖-ər/ *n* [C] a boy or man whose father or mother has married your father or mother

**step-by-step** /ˌ· · ˈ·◂/ *adj* [only before noun] a step-by-step plan, method etc does things carefully and in a particular order

**step·child** /ˈsteptʃaɪld/ *n* [C] a stepdaughter or stepson

**step·daugh·ter** /ˈstepdɔːtə‖-dɒːtər/ *n* [C] a daughter that your husband or wife has from being married to someone else before

**step·fa·ther** /ˈstepfɑːðə‖-ər/ *n* [C] the man who is married to your mother but who is not your father

**step·lad·der** /ˈstepˌlædə‖-ər/ *n* [C] a LADDER with two sloping parts that are joined at the top and that can be folded flat

**step·moth·er** /ˈstepmʌðə‖-ər/ *n* [C] a woman who is married to your father but who is not your mother

**step·par·ent** /ˈstepˌpeərənt‖-ˌper-/ *n* [C] a stepfather or stepmother

**steppes** /steps/ *n* **the steppes** a large area of land without trees, especially an area in Russia, parts of Asia, and southeast Europe

**step·ping-stone** /ˈ·· ·/ *n* [C] **1** something that helps you to progress towards achieving something especially in your work: *Think of this job as a stepping-stone to something better.* **2** one of a row of large flat stones that you walk on to get across a stream

**step·sis·ter** /ˈstepsɪstə‖-ər/ *n* [C] a girl or woman whose father or mother has married your mother or father

**step·son** /ˈstepsʌn/ *n* [C] a son that your husband or wife has from being married to someone else before

**-ster** /stə‖stər/ *suffix (in nouns)* **1** someone who has a particular quality: *a youngster* (=a young person) **2** someone who is connected with, deals with, or uses a particular thing: *a trickster* (=someone who plays deceiving tricks) | *a gangster* (=a member of a GANG) | *a pollster* (=someone who carries out POLLS)

**ster·e·o**[1] /ˈsteriəʊ, ˈstɪər-‖ˈsterioʊ, ˈstɪr-/ *n* **1** [C] a machine for playing records, CDS etc that produces sound from two speakers (SPEAKER (3)) **2 in stereo** if music, a radio programme etc is in stereo, it is being played or broadcast using a system in which sound is directed through two speakers: *This programme is being broadcast in stereo.* S3

**stereo**[2] also **ster·e·o·phon·ic** /ˌsteriəˈfɒnɪk◂, ˌstɪər-‖steriəˈfɑːnɪk◂, ˌstɪr-/ *adj* using a system of sound recording or broadcasting in which the sound is directed through two speakers (SPEAKER (3)) to make it seem more real: *stereo recording* —compare MONO[2], QUADRAPHONIC

**ster·e·o·gram** /ˈsteriəgræm, ˈstɪər-‖ˈster-, ˈstɪr-/ *n* [C] a picture that looks like a repeating pattern, but in which some people can see THREE-DIMENSIONAL objects

**ster·e·o·scop·ic** /ˌsteriəˈskɒpɪk◂, ˌstɪər-‖ˌsteriəˈskɑː-, ˌstɪr-/ *adj* a stereoscopic photograph, picture etc is made so that when you look at it through a special machine it looks solid

**stereo sys·tem** /ˈ··· ˌ··/ *n* [C] a set of equipment for playing music on, usually including a record player, CASSETTE PLAYER, and radio

**ster·e·o·type**[1] /ˈsteriətaɪp, ˈstɪər-‖ˈster-, ˈstɪr-/ *n* [C] a fixed idea or image of what a particular type of person or thing is like: *racial stereotypes* | [+ **of**] *the stereotype of a woman who stays at home with the children* —**stereotypical** /ˌsteriəˈtɪpɪkəl◂, ˌstɪər-‖ˌster-, ˌstɪr-/ *adj*

**stereotype**[2] *v* [T usually passive] to decide, usually unfairly, that certain people have particular qualities or abilities because they belong to a particular race, sex, or social class: [+ **as**] *Homeless people are often stereotyped as a bunch of alcoholics.* —**stereotyping** *n* [U]: *sexual stereotyping* —**stereotyped** *adj*

**ster·ile** /ˈsteraɪl‖-rəl/ *adj* **1** not able to have babies: *She became sterile because of exposure to radiation.* —compare FERTILE (2) **2** completely clean and not containing any BACTERIA: *Operations must be carried out in a sterile environment.* **3** land that is sterile cannot be used for growing crops **4** lacking new ideas or imagination: *sterile thought* —**sterility** /stəˈrɪləti/ *n* [U]

**ster·il·ize** also **-ise** *BrE* /ˈsterəlaɪz/ *v* [T usually passive] **1** to make something completely clean and kill any BACTERIA in it: *sterilized milk* | *Sterilize the bottles with boiling water.* **2** to perform an operation that makes a person or animal unable to have babies —**sterilizer** *n* [C] —**sterilization** /ˌsterəlaɪˈzeɪʃən‖-lə-/ *n* [C,U]

**ster·ling**[1] /ˈstɜːlɪŋ‖ˈstɜːr-/ *n* [U] the standard unit of money in the United Kingdom, based on the pound

**sterling²** *adj* **1 sterling silver/gold** silver or gold of a particular standard or pureness **2 sterling qualities/effort/character etc** *especially BrE* qualities etc that are excellent and dependable

**stern¹** /stɜːn‖stɜːrn/ *adj* **1** strict in a very serious and often unpleasant way: *a stern teacher|groups calling for sterner penalties for drug offences* **2 stern look/expression/rebuke** something that someone says or does that expresses disapproval —**sternly** *adv* —**sternness** *n* [U]

**stern²** *n* [C usually singular] the back part of a ship —compare BOW² (2) —see picture at YACHT

**ster·num** /ˈstɜːnəm‖ˈstɜːr-/ *n* [C] *plural* **sternums** or **sterna** /-nə/ *technical* a BREASTBONE —see picture at SKELETON

**ste·roid** /ˈstɪərɔɪd, ˈste-‖ˈstɪr-/ *n* [C] a chemical compound produced in the body, but also given as a drug by doctors for injuries and used illegally by people doing sports to improve their performance

**ster·to·rous** /ˈstɜːtərəs‖ˈstɜːr-/ *adj* stertorous breathing makes a noisy sound: *His breathing was stertorous but regular.*

**steth·o·scope** /ˈsteθəskəʊp‖-skoʊp/ *n* [C] an instrument used by doctors to listen to someone's heart or breathing

**stet·son** /ˈstetsən/ *n* [C] *trademark* a tall hat with a wide BRIM (=edge), worn especially in the American West —see picture at HAT

**ste·ve·dore** /ˈstiːvədɔː‖-dɔːr/ *n* [C] *AmE* someone whose job is loading and unloading ships; DOCKER *BrE*

**stew¹** /stjuː‖stuː/ *n* **1** [C] a cooked dish, made of meat and vegetables that are cooked slowly together in liquid: *beef stew* **2 in a stew** *informal* to be confused or anxious, especially because you are in a difficult situation: *You're in a real stew about this interview, aren't you?*

**stew²** *v* **1** [T] to cook something slowly in liquid: *stewed apples* **2 stew (in your own juice)** *informal* to worry because of something bad that has happened or a mistake you have made

**stew·ard** /ˈstjuːəd‖ˈstuːərd/ *n* [C] **1** a man who serves food and drinks to the passengers on a plane or ship **2** a man whose job is to look after a house and its lands, such as a farm **3** a man who arranges the supply and serving of food in a club, college etc **4** *BrE* someone who is in charge of a horse race, meeting, or other public event —see also SHOP STEWARD

**stew·ard·ess** /ˈstjuːədɪs‖ˈstuːərd-/ *n* [C] a woman who serves food and drinks to the passengers on a plane or ship

**stew·ard·ship** /ˈstjuːədʃɪp‖ˈstuːərd-/ *n* [U] the way in which someone controls and looks after an event or organization

**stewed** /stjuːd‖stuːd/ *adj* **1** [not before noun] *informal* drunk **2** *BrE* tea that is stewed tastes too strong and bitter because it has been left too long before being drunk

**stick out**

Peter's ears stick out. Lucy stuck her tongue out.

**stick¹** /stɪk/ *v past tense and past participle* **stuck** /stʌk/ S2 W3

**1 ▶ PUSH ◀** [T always + adv/prep, I always + adv/prep] if a pointed object sticks into something or you stick it into something, it is pushed into it: **stick sth in/into/through etc** *They stuck pins in the map to mark enemy positions.*|**stick in/through etc** *Joe had cactus spines sticking in his finger.*

**stick up**

Dad's hair sticks up.

**2 ▶ FIX ◀** [I,T] to fix something to something else with a sticky substance, or to become fixed to a surface: *I can't get this stamp to stick.*|**stick sth to/in/on etc** *It took hours to stick all these photos in my album.*|[+ **to**] *It was so hot his shirt was sticking to his back.*

**3 ▶ PUT ◀** [T always + adv/prep] *informal* to put something somewhere quickly and without thinking carefully; SHOVE¹ (2): **stick sth in/on/there etc** *Just stick your coat on that chair.*

**4 ▶ DIFFICULT TO MOVE ◀** [I] if something sticks it becomes fixed in one position so that it is difficult to move: *This cupboard door keeps sticking.*

**5 stick in sb's mind** if something sticks in your mind, you remember it very well, especially because it is unusual or interesting: *What really sticks in my mind is how sad the woman looked.*

**6 stick it** [T usually in negatives] to continue to deal with a difficult or unpleasant situation: *College is harder than I thought, I don't think I can stick it much longer.*

**7 make sth stick** *informal* to prove that someone is guilty: *The police won't bring the case to court because they don't think they can make the charges stick.*

**8 you/they can stick sth** *spoken* used to say angrily that you do not want what someone is offering you: *You can stick your job if you won't pay me more than that!*

**9 be stuck fast** to be fixed in one position and unable to move: *His arm was stuck fast in the drainpipe.*

**10 stick fast to a belief/idea etc** to continue to believe something although it may be difficult: *Through it all Stella has stuck fast to her belief in the Communist system.*

**11 be stuck for** *spoken* to be unable to think or to find something that you need to have: *If you're stuck for a babysitter, Alison's always free.*

**12 stick in your throat** *BrE*/**stick in your craw** *AmE* **a)** if a situation or someone's behaviour sticks in your throat, it is so annoying that you cannot accept it **b)** if words stick in your throat, you are unable to say what you want

**13 ▶ NAME ◀** [I] if a name that someone has invented sticks, people continue to use it: *One newspaper dubbed him 'Eddie the Eagle' and the name stuck.*

**14 ▶ CARD GAME ◀** [I] to decide not to take any more cards in some card games: *I'm sticking.*

**15 can't stick** *BrE spoken* to dislike someone or something very much: *I can't stick her husband, he's always so rude.*|**can't stick sb doing sth** *Lena can't stick anybody reading over her shoulder.* —see also **stick/poke your nose into** (NOSE¹ (4))

**stick around** *phr v* [I] *informal* to stay in the same place for a little longer, especially in order to wait for something that you expect to happen: *Stick around, there'll be dancing later.*

**stick at** sth *phr v* [T] *BrE* **1** to continue to study or work hard at something in a very determined way: **stick at it** *Just stick at it and you'll pass your exams easily.* **2 stick at nothing** *informal* to be willing to do anything, even if it is illegal, in order to achieve something: *Des'll stick at nothing to make money.*

**stick by** sb/sth *phr v* [T] **1** to continue to give your support to a friend who has problems: *Samuel promised to stick by her, whatever happened.* **2** to do what you said you would do or what you think you should do: **stick by a decision/promise etc**

**stick sth on sb** *phr v* [T] *informal* to prove or make it seem that someone is guilty of a crime: *They can't stick it on me – I wasn't even in the country at the time.*

**stick out** *phr v*

**1 ► COME UP OR FORWARD ◄** [I] if a part of something sticks out, it comes out further than the rest of a surface or comes out through a hole: *Francis wore glasses and his front teeth stuck out.* | **stick out of/from/through** *Careful – there's a nail sticking out of that board.*

**2 ► PUT STH OUT ◄** [T **stick** sth ↔ **out**] to deliberately make part of your body come forward or out from the rest of your body: *Carl stuck his leg out and tripped the man up.* | **stick your tongue out** (=show your tongue in order to be rude to someone)

**3 stick it out** to continue to the end of an activity that is difficult, painful, or boring: *The movie was really boring but we stuck it out.*

**4 stick out like a sore thumb** *informal* to look very unsuitable and different from everyone or everything around: *I'm not going to the party dressed like this, I'd stick out like a sore thumb.*

**5 it sticks out a mile** *informal* used to say that a fact about someone's character or feelings is very clear and easily noticed: *It always sticks out a mile when Jenny doesn't like someone, she just can't hide her feelings.*

**6 stick your neck out** *informal* to give your opinion about something when you know there is a risk that you may be wrong or that people may disagree with you

**stick out for** sth *phr v* [T] *informal* to refuse to accept less than what you asked for: *The unions are sticking out for a higher pay offer.*

**stick to** sth *phr v* [T]

**1 ► PROMISE/BELIEF ◄** to do or keep doing what you said you would do or what you believe in: *Just make a decision and stick to it.* | **stick to your decision/principles etc** *We have stuck to our election promises.*

**2 ► CONTINUE WITH SAME THING ◄** to keep using or doing one particular thing and not change to anything else: *If you're driving, stick to soft drinks.* | *Reporters should stick to investigating the facts.*

**3 stick to it** to continue to work or study in a very determined way in order to achieve something: *I hated practicing, but I stuck to it and now I can play pretty well.*

**4 stick to the point/subject/facts** to talk only about what you are supposed to be talking about or what is certain: *We'll never finish this meeting if people don't stick to the point.*

**5 stick to the path/road etc** to stay on a marked path or road so that you do not get lost

**6 stick to the rules** *informal* to do something exactly according to the rules

**7 stick to your guns** *informal* to refuse to change your mind about something even though other people are trying to persuade you that you are wrong

**8 That's my story and I'm sticking to it.** *spoken* used to say that you are not going to change any part of what you have already said

**stick together** *phr v* [I] *informal* if people stick together, they continue to support one another even when they have problems: *If we stick together we've got a better chance.*

**stick up** *phr v* **1** [I] if a part of something sticks up, it is raised up or points upward above a surface: *His hair stuck up as though he hadn't had time to comb it.* | [+ **from/out of/through etc**] *We could just see part of the boat sticking up out of the water.* **2 stick 'em up** *slang* used to tell someone to raise their hands when threatening them with a gun

**stick up for** sb *phr v* [T] *informal* to defend someone who is being criticized, especially when no one else will defend them: *At least my friends stuck up for me.* | **stick up for yourself** *She's always known how to stick up for herself.*

**stick with** sb/sth *phr v* [T] *informal* **1** to stay close to someone: *If you don't want to get lost, you'd better stick with me.* **2** to continue doing or using something the way you did or planned to do before: *Let's stick with the original arrangements.* **3** to continue doing something, especially something difficult: **stick with it** *Stick with it and you'll win through in the end.* **4** *informal* to remain in someone's memory: *One thing he said then has stuck with me ever since.*

**sticks**

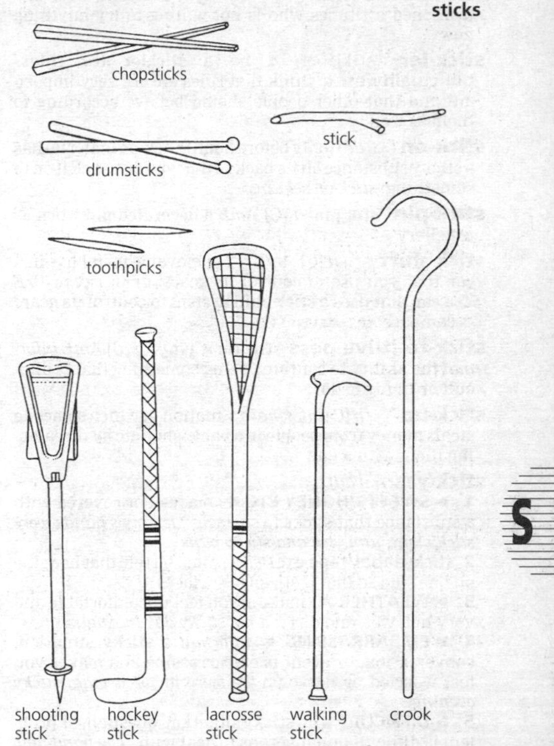


**stick²** *n* S3 W3

**1 ► FROM A TREE ◄** [C] a long thin piece of wood that has fallen or been cut from a tree

**2 ► FOR WALKING ◄** a long thin piece of wood or metal that you use to help you walk —see also CANE¹ (1)

**3 ► SPORT ◄** a long thin piece of wood that you use for hitting the ball in sports such as HOCKEY

**4 ► FOR HITTING SB ◄** a long thin piece of wood that you use to hit someone or something

**5 stick of celery/dynamite etc** a long thin piece of CELERY etc

**6 get (hold of) the wrong end of the stick** *spoken* to misunderstand one small thing that makes you misunderstand everything about a particular situation

**7 give sb stick** *BrE spoken* to criticize someone for something they have done, sometimes in a humorous way

**8 (out) in the sticks** very far from a town or city: *They live somewhere out in the sticks.*

**9 ► CAR ◄** *AmE informal* a STICK SHIFT

**10 up sticks** *BrE spoken* if you up sticks, you move to a different area or house: *He'd upped sticks and moved to London.*

**11 old stick** *BrE old-fashioned* used to describe someone in a friendly way: *Ned's a good old stick.*

**stick·ball** /ˈstɪkbɔːl‖-bɒːl/ *n* [U] a game like BASEBALL that is played in the street by children in the US, using a small ball and a stick

**stick·er** /ˈstɪkə‖-ər/ *n* [C]  S3 **1** a small piece of paper or plastic with a picture or writing on it that you can stick on to something —compare LABEL¹ (1) —see picture at SIGN¹ **2** *BrE informal* someone who keeps trying to do something even when it becomes very difficult

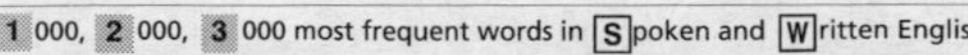

**stick·ing point** /ˈ·· ˌ·/ *n* [singular] the thing that prevents an agreement being made in a discussion: *The question of equal pay is likely to be the sticking point.*

**stick in·sect** /ˈ· ˌ··/ *n* [C] an insect with a long thin body that looks very like a small stick

**stick-in-the-mud** /ˈ· · · ˌ·/ *n* [C] someone with old-fashioned attitudes who is not willing to try anything new

**stick·ler** /ˈstɪklə‖-ər/ *n* **be a stickler for rules/punctuality etc** to think that rules etc are very important and that other people should behave according to them as well

**stick-on** /ˈ· ·/ *adj* [only before noun] stick-on material has a sticky substance on its back so that you can stick it on to something: *stick-on sequins*

**stick·pin** /ˈstɪkˌpɪn/ *n* [C] *AmE* a decorated pin worn as jewellery

**stick shift** /ˈ· ·/ *n* [C] *AmE* **1** a movable metal bar in a car that you use to control its gears; GEAR LEVER *BrE* **2** a car that uses a stick shift system to control its gears —compare AUTOMATIC[2] (2)

**stick-to-it-ive·ness** /stɪk ˈtuː ɪt ɨvnɨs/ *n* [U] *AmE informal* the ability to continue doing something that is difficult or tiring to do

**stick-up** /ˈ· ·/ *n* [C] *informal* a situation in which someone steals money from people in a bank, shop etc by threatening them with a gun

**stick·y** /ˈstɪki/ *adj*

**1** ▶ **SWEETS/HONEY ETC** ◀ made of or covered with a substance that sticks to surfaces: *Jeremy's hands were sticky with jam.* | *tea and sticky buns*

**2 sticky label/tape etc** *BrE* a LABEL[1] (1) etc that has glue on one side so that it sticks to surfaces

**3** ▶ **WEATHER** ◀ making you feel uncomfortable and very hot, wet, and dirty: *a hot sticky day in August*

**4** ▶ **EMBARRASSING** ◀ *informal* a sticky situation, conversation, or event is embarrassing and makes you feel worried or nervous: *We were in for a long, sticky evening.*

**5** ▶ **DIFFICULT** ◀ a sticky situation, question, or problem is difficult or dangerous to deal with: *The band now have a minder to get them out of sticky situations.*

**6** ▶ **NOT HELPFUL** ◀ *BrE* not willing to help you or do what you want: *I asked him to lend me some money, but he was rather sticky about it.*

**7 have sticky fingers** *informal* to be likely to steal something

**8 come to/meet a sticky end** *BrE informal* to die violently especially because you have been doing something bad: *The gangsters in his novels always come to a sticky end.*

**9 be on a sticky wicket** *BrE informal* to be in a situation that is difficult or that may become difficult —**stickiness** *n* [U]

S3 **stiff**[1] /stɪf/ *adj*

**1** ▶ **BODY** ◀ if a part of your body is stiff or you are stiff, your muscles hurt and it is difficult to move: *Arthritis makes your joints stiff and sore.* | **stiff neck/back/joint** *Alastair woke up with a stiff neck.* | **feel stiff** *I felt really stiff after playing basketball last week.*

**2** ▶ **DOOR/DRAWER ETC** ◀ difficult to move; bend or turn: *Pull hard – that drawer's very stiff.*

**3** ▶ **PAPER/MATERIAL** ◀ hard and difficult to bend: *a sheet of stiff cardboard*

**4** ▶ **MIXTURE** ◀ thick and almost solid, so that it is not easy to stir: *Beat the egg whites until stiff.* | *stiff dough*

**5** ▶ **UNFRIENDLY** ◀ unfriendly or very formal, so that other people feel uncomfortable: *He replied in a stiff, ironic voice.*

**6** ▶ **VERY HARD** ◀ more difficult, strict, or severe than usual: **stiff sentence/penalty/fine** *There's a stiff fine for speeding.* | **stiff competition** *He'll be facing stiff competition for that job.*

**7 a stiff wind/breeze** a fairly strong wind etc

**8 a stiff drink/whisky etc** a very strong alcoholic drink

**9 keep a stiff upper lip** to try to keep calm and not show your feelings in a situation when most people would become upset —**stiffly** *adv* —**stiffness** *n* [U]

**stiff**[2] *adv* **1 bored/scared/worried stiff** *informal* extremely bored etc: *As a child I was scared stiff of going down to the cellar.* **2 frozen stiff a)** extremely cold: *Joey was frozen stiff after walking through the snow.* **b)** cloth that has frozen stiff is hard because the water in it has become ice

**stiff**[3] *n* [C] *slang* **1** the body of a dead person **2 working stiff** *AmE informal* an ordinary person who works to earn enough money to live

**stiff**[4] *v* [T] *AmE informal* to not pay someone money that you owe them or that they expect to be given, especially by not leaving a tip (TIP[1] (2)) in a restaurant

**stiff·en** /ˈstɪfən/ *v* **1** [I] to suddenly become unfriendly, angry, or anxious: *Francesca stiffened at his suggestion that it was her fault.* **2** [I,T] to become stronger and more determined: *The advancing army met stiffening resistance.* | **stiffen sb's resolve** *His emotional speech was sure to stiffen their resolve.* **3** [T] to make material stiff so that it will not bend easily: *a spray to stiffen shirt collars* **4** [I] to become painful and difficult to move: *His joints had stiffened.*

**stiff-necked** /ˌ· ˈ·◂/ *adj* proud and refusing to change or obey; OBSTINATE (1)

**sti·fle** /ˈstaɪfəl/ *v* [T] **1** [I,T] to stop someone from breathing or be unable to breathe comfortably, especially because the air is too hot or not fresh: *He was almost stifled by the fumes.* **2** [T] to stop something from happening or developing: *rules and regulations that stifle initiative* **3** [T] to stop a feeling from being expressed: *He stifled an urge to hit her.* | **stifle a yawn/smile/laughter etc** *Nancy stifled a yawn as the teacher's voice droned on.*

**sti·fling** /ˈstaɪflɪŋ/ *adj* **1** a room or weather that is stifling is very hot and difficult to breathe in: *a stifling, crowded carriage* **2** a situation that is stifling stops you from developing your own ideas and character: *the stifling atmosphere of the court*

**stig·ma** /ˈstɪgmə/ *n* **1** [singular, U] a strong feeling in society that a type of behaviour is shameful: *There is a strong stigma attached to suicide.* | **the stigma of alcoholism/abortion etc** *The stigma of alcoholism makes it a more difficult problem to treat.* **2** [C] *technical* the top of the centre part of a flower that receives the POLLEN that allows it to form new seeds

**stig·ma·ta** /ˈstɪgmətə, stɪgˈmɑːtə/ *n* [plural] the marks on Christ's body caused by nails, or similar marks on the bodies of some holy people

**stig·ma·tize** also **-ise** *BrE* /ˈstɪgmətaɪz/ *v* [T] **be stigmatized** to be treated by society as if you should be ashamed of your situation or actions: *People with handicaps shouldn't be stigmatized.* —**stigmatization** /ˌstɪgmətaɪˈzeɪʃən‖-tə-/ *n* [U]

**stile** /staɪl/ *n* [C] a set of steps placed on either side of a fence so that people can climb over it

**sti·let·to** /stɨˈletəʊ‖-toʊ/ *plural* **stilettos** or **stilettoes** *n* [C] **1** also **stiletto heel** /ˌ·ˌ·· ˈ·/ a high thin heel of a woman's shoe **2** a shoe that has this kind of heel —see picture at SHOE[1]

**still**[1] /stɪl/ *adv* **1** up to a particular point in time and continuing at that moment: *Do you still play tennis?* | *With 30 minutes still to go, neither team had scored.* **2** in spite of what has just been said or done: *Clare didn't do much work, but she still passed the exam.* | [sentence adverb] *The hotel was terrible. Still, we were lucky with the* S1 W1 *weather.* | **still and all** (=all the same) *Still and all, you have to admire her.* **3** even more extreme than the situation or thing that you have just described: *It's cold today, but it'll be still colder tonight.* | *The first question is very difficult, and the second is more difficult still.* **4 still more/another/other etc** even more in amount: *There were still more reasons why the programme shouldn't go ahead.*

**USAGE NOTE: STILL**

WORD CHOICE: **still, already, yet**

**Still** suggests surprise that something has continued for longer than you might expect: *After fifty lessons I still can't drive very well.*

**Already** is usually used in positive sentences to express surprise that something has happened earlier than you thought it would: *Are they here already*?

**Yet** is used in negatives and questions to talk about things that you expect to happen, but have not happened or might not have happened: *I haven't had breakfast yet.*|*Has Bill arrived yet?*

Compare **yet** with **already** in a question. *Have you had lunch yet?* asks for information, while *Have you had your lunch already?* expresses surprise that lunch has already been eaten.

**Yet** used instead of **still** in a positive sentence is rare and a little formal: *We have yet to hear the truth.*|*The Council may yet surprise us.* In conversation, however, you are more likely to say something like: *We don't know the truth yet.*

GRAMMAR

**Still** usually comes immediately before any negative word: *She still isn't ready.*|*They still don't know.*|*A solution has still not been found* (or *...still hasn't,* NOT *...has not still*).

**Still** usually comes immediately after a positive modal verb: *I can still remember* (NOT *still can remember*). | *He may still be there* (or *...be still there...*).

Otherwise **still** comes after the verb **to be** and immediately before any main verb: *He's still eating* (NOT *still is eating*).|*It's still wet outside.*|*We still have time* (NOT *have still time*).|*I still love her.*

**still²** *adj* **1** not moving: *a still pool* | **keep/stand/lie etc still** *Keep still while I tie your shoe.* **2** not windy: *a hot, still, airless day* **3** quiet, calm, and without any activity: *It was so still you could have heard a pin drop.* **4** *BrE* a still drink does not contain gas **5 still waters run deep** used to say that someone who is quiet may have very strong feelings or a lot of knowledge —**stillness** *n* [U]

**still³** *n* [C] **1** a photograph of a scene from a cinema film **2** a piece of equipment for making alcoholic drinks out of grain or potatoes **3 the still of the night/evening etc** *literary* the calm and quiet of the night etc

**still⁴** *v* [T] *literary* **1** to make someone or something become quiet or calm: *The food stilled the baby's cries.* **2** if a doubt or fear is stilled, it becomes weaker or goes away

**still·birth** /ˈstɪlbɜːθ, ˌstɪlˈbɜːθ‖-ɜːrθ/ *n* [C,U] a birth in which the baby is born dead —compare ABORTION, MISCARRIAGE

**still·born** /ˈstɪlbɔːn, ˌstɪlˈbɔːn‖-ɔːrn/ *adj* **1** born dead: *a stillborn baby* **2** ending before having had a chance to start: *a stillborn romance*

**still life** /ˌ· ˈ·◂/ *plural* **still lifes** *n* [C,U] a picture of an arrangement of objects, especially flowers and fruit

**stilt** /stɪlt/ *n* [C usually plural] **1** one of two poles on which you can stand and walk high above the ground: *A clown crossed the ring on stilts.* **2** one of a set of poles that support a building so it is raised above ground or water level

**stilt·ed** /ˈstɪltɪ̍d/ *adj* a stilted style of writing or speaking is formal, and unnatural: *a stilted conversation* —**stiltedly** *adv*

**Stil·ton** /ˈstɪltən/ *n* [U] a kind of English cheese that is white with grey-blue marks and has a strong taste

**stim·u·lant** /ˈstɪmjɡ̍lənt/ *n* [C] **1** a drug or substance that makes you feel more active and full of energy: *Caffeine is a stimulant.* | [+ **to**] *a stimulant to appetite* | **stimulant effects/properties etc** *a drug with stimulant properties* **2** something that encourages more of a particular activity; STIMULUS: *economic stimulants* | [+ **to**] *Travel can be a stimulant to learning.*

**stim·u·late** /ˈstɪmjɡ̍leɪt/ *v* [T] **1** to encourage an activity to begin or develop further: *The discussions stimulated a free exchange of ideas.* | **stimulate growth/demand/the economy etc** (=make economic growth etc start or become stronger) **2** to encourage someone by making them excited about and interested in something: **stimulate sb to do sth** *An inspiring teacher can stimulate students to succeed.* **3** to make a plant or part of the body become active or stronger: *Light stimulates plant growth.* —**stimulative** /-lətɪv‖-leɪtɪv/ *adj* —**stimulation** /ˌstɪmjɡ̍ˈleɪʃən/ *n* [U]

**stim·u·lat·ing** /ˈstɪmjɡ̍leɪtɪŋ/ *adj* **1** exciting or full of new ideas: *We had a most stimulating conversation.* **2** making you feel more active and healthy: *I find mountain air much more stimulating.*

**stim·u·lus** /ˈstɪmjɡ̍ləs/ *plural* **stimuli** /-laɪ/ *n* **1** [singular, U] something that helps a process to develop more quickly or more strongly: [+ **to**] *The discovery of oil acted as a stimulus to the local economy.* **2** [C] something that causes a reaction in a plant or part of the body: *A reflex action is a response to a stimulus.*

**sting¹** /stɪŋ/ *v past tense and past participle* **stung** /stʌŋ/ **1** [I,T] if an insect or a plant stings you, it causes a sharp pain and that part of your body swells: *Henry was stung by a bee at the picnic.* **2** [I,T] to hurt or to make something hurt with a sudden sharp pain for a short time: *The antiseptic might sting a little.* | *Chopping onions makes my eyes sting.* **3** [T usually passive] if a remark or criticism stings, it makes you feel upset and embarrassed: *Days later she was still stung by the accusations.* | **sting sb into (doing) sth** *Her harsh words stung him into action.* | **stinging rebuke/sarcasm etc** (=severe and strongly expressed criticism etc)

**sting** sb **for** sth *informal* **1** *especially BrE* to charge someone too much for something: *The garage stung him for £300.* **2** *BrE* to borrow money from someone: *Can I sting you for a fiver?*

**sting²** *n*

**1** ▶ **INSECT/ANIMAL** ◀ [C] *BrE* a sharp needle-like part of an animal or insect's body that can be pushed through the skin of a person or animal, often leaving poison; STINGER *AmE*

**2** ▶ **WOUND** ◀ [C] a wound or mark made when an insect or plant stings you: *Rub ointment on to the wasp sting.*

**3** ▶ **PAIN** ◀ [singular] a sharp pain in your eyes or skin, caused by being hit, smoke etc: *the sting of salt in a wound*

**4 a sting in the tail** an unexpected end to a story, suggestion etc, that makes the whole thing less pleasant for the person listening

**5 take the sting out of** to make something unpleasant easier to deal with: *She smiled to take the sting out of her words.*

**6** ▶ **CRIME** ◀ [C] *AmE* **a)** a situation in which criminals obtain a large amount of money by cheating someone; SWINDLE² **b)** a situation in which the police catch criminals by pretending to be involved in criminal activity themselves

**sting·er** /ˈstɪŋə‖-ər/ *n* [C] *AmE* the sharp needle-like part of an animal or insect's body that can be pushed through the skin of a person or animal, often leaving poison; STING² (1) *BrE*

**stinging net·tle** /ˈ·· ˌ··/ *n* [C] a wild plant with leaves that sting and leave red marks on the skin

**sting·ray** /ˈstɪŋreɪ/ *n* [C] a large fish with a flat body and several sharp points on its back near its tail

**stin·gy** /ˈstɪndʒi/ *adj* **1** *informal* not generous, especially with money, when you can easily afford to be: *Jim's too stingy to give money to charity.* **2** a stingy amount of something, especially food, is too small to be enough: *The helpings here are pretty stingy.* **—stingily** *adv* **—stinginess** *n* [U]

S 3 **stink¹** /stɪŋk/ *past tense* **stank** /stæŋk/ *past participle* **stunk** /stʌŋk/ *v* [I] **1** to have a strong and very unpleasant smell: *That paint stinks!* | [+ **of**] *The place stank of old fish.* | **it stinks** *It stinks of smoke in here.* | **stink to high heaven** (=stink very much) **2 it stinks!** *spoken* used to say that you do not like something: *"What did you think of the show?" "It stank!"* **3** to make you think that something dishonest has been done secretly: *The whole business really stinks.*

**stink** sth **out** *BrE*, **stink** sth **up** *AmE phr v* [T] to fill a place with a very unpleasant smell: *Those onions are stinking the whole house out.*

**stink²** *n* [C] **1** a terrible smell: *What a stink!* | [+ **of**] *a stink of rotten eggs* **2 make/raise/cause etc a stink** to complain very strongly because you are annoyed about something: *I'm going to kick up a stink if they don't get us onto a flight soon.* **3 work/run/go like stink** *BrE* to work etc as fast and as well as you can: *We had to work like stink to meet the deadline.*

**stink bomb** /ˈ· ·/ *n* [C] a small container that produces an extremely bad smell when it is broken

**stink·er** /ˈstɪŋkə‖-ər/ *n* [C] *informal* **1** something that is very difficult or unpleasant: *This cold I've got is a real stinker.* **2** someone who behaves badly: *That son of theirs is a little stinker!*

**stink·ing** /ˈstɪŋkɪŋ/ *adj* **1** having a very strong unpleasant smell: *an alley full of stinking garbage cans* **2** *spoken* used to emphasize what you are saying when you are angry: *Just keep your stinking money then.* **3** [only before noun] *informal, especially BrE* very unpleasant: *Stinking weather we've had lately!* | **a stinking cold** *I've got an absolutely stinking cold.* **4 stinking rich** *informal* an expression meaning extremely rich, used especially when you think this is unfair **5 a stinking letter** *BrE* an angry letter in which you complain very strongly about something

**stink·y** /ˈstɪŋki/ *adj informal* smelling unpleasant; SMELLY: *stinky socks*

**stint¹** /stɪnt/ *n* [C usually singular] **1** a limited or fixed period of work or effort: [+ **as**] *the beginning of her stint as waitress* | **do a stint** *Mark did a two-year stint in the army.* | **do your stint** (=do some work that other people also have to do and that you do not expect to enjoy much) *Has he done his stint at the bar yet?* **2 without stint** *formal* very generously: *Sarah gave of her time and money without stint.*

**stint²** *v* [I usually in negatives] to give or use too little of something: **stint on sth** *You can't stint on the butter with that recipe.*

**sti·pend** /ˈstaɪpend/ *n* [C] an amount of money paid regularly to someone such as a priest or student as wages or money to live on

**sti·pen·di·a·ry¹** /staɪˈpendiəri‖-dieri/ *adj* receiving a stipend

**stipendiary²** also **stipendiary ma·gis·trate** /·,···· ˈ···/ *n* [C] a MAGISTRATE in Britain who is paid by the state

**stip·ple** /ˈstɪpəl/ *v* [T] to draw or paint a picture or pattern using short STROKES or spots instead of lines **—stippled** *adj* **— stippling** *n* [U]

**stip·u·late** /ˈstɪpjəleɪt/ *v* [T] to say that something must be done, when you are making an agreement or offer: *Vanessa clearly stipulated payment in advance.* | **stipulate that sth be done** *Tony stipulated that all expenses be refunded.*

**stip·u·la·tion** /ˌstɪpjəˈleɪʃən/ *n* [C,U] a specific condition that is stated as part of an agreement: [+ **that**] *Kay signed, with the stipulation that she would take 10% of the profits.*

**stir¹** /stɜː‖stɜːr/ *v* S W

**1 ▶ MIX ◀** [T] to move a liquid or substance around with a spoon or stick in order to mix it together: *Stir the paint to make sure it is smooth.* | **stir sth in/into** *When the sauce has cooled, add the grated cheese and stir it in.*

**2 ▶ FEELINGS ◀ a)** [T] to make someone have a strong feeling or reaction: *He was stirred by the man's enthusiasm.* | **stir sb's memory/imagination etc** *Her imagination was stirred by the scene.* | **stir memories/emotions etc** *The news stirred memories of their own persecution.* **b)** [I] a feeling stirs in you, you begin to feel it: *Excitement stirred inside her.*

**3 ▶ MOVE SLIGHTLY ◀** [I] **a)** to move slightly or change your position because you are uncomfortable or just before you wake up: *I never stirred all night long.* **b)** to move slightly: *Something stirred in the long grass.*

**4 ▶ DO STH ◀** [T] to make someone feel they must do something: *The incident stirred them to action.* | **stir yourself!** *especially BrE*: *He stirred himself to answer the door.*

**5 ▶ CAUSE TROUBLE ◀** [I] *BrE informal* to cause trouble between people by spreading false or secret information: *Ben's always stirring!*

**6 ▶ MAKE STH MOVE ◀** [T] to make something move slightly: *The wind stirred the fallen leaves*

**stir** sth ↔ **up** *phr v* [T] **1** to deliberately try to cause arguments or problems between people: *The new leader was accused of stirring up trouble.* | **stir things up** *Dave's just trying to stir things up because he's jealous.* **2** to make something move around in the air or in water: *The horse's hooves stirred up a lot of dust.*

**stir²** *n* **1** [C usually singular] an act of stirring something: **give sth a stir** *Give that pan a stir, will you?* **2** [C usually singular] a feeling of excitement or annoyance: [+ **of**] *a stir of disapproval* | **create/cause a stir** *Plans for the motorway caused quite a stir among local residents.*

**stir-cra·zy** /ˌ· ˈ··◂/ *adj informal* extremely nervous and upset, especially because you feel trapped in a place

**stir-fry** /ˈ· ·/ *v* [T] to cook something by mixing it in hot oil for a short time: *stir-fried vegetables* **—stir-fry** *n* [C]

**stir·rer** /ˈstɜːrə‖-ər/ *n* [C] *BrE informal* someone who likes to cause trouble between people by spreading false or secret information

**stir·ring** /ˈstɜːrɪŋ/ *adj* producing strong feelings or excitement in someone; ROUSING: *stirring music* | *a stirring speech* **—stirringly** *adv*

**stir·rings** /ˈstɜːrɪŋz/ *n* **stirrings of love/doubt/rebellion etc** early signs that love etc is starting

**stir·rup** /ˈstɪrəp‖ˈstɜː-/ *n* [C] a ring of metal that hangs from each side of a horse's SADDLE¹ (1) for someone to put their foot in —see picture at HORSE¹

**stitch¹** /stɪtʃ/ *n*

**1 ▶ SEWING ◀** [C] one of the short pieces of thread that you can see in a piece of cloth where it has been sewn: *Some of the stitches have come out of this shirt sleeve.*

**2 ▶ WITH WOOL ◀** [C] one of the small circles that join together to make a SWEATER etc, formed when you are knitting (KNIT¹ (1)) with wool: **drop a stitch** (=lose a stitch because the wool has come off the needle)

**3 ▶ STYLE ◀** [C,U] a particular way of sewing or knitting (KNIT¹ (2)) that makes a particular pattern: *Purl and plain are the two main stitches in knitting.*

**4 ▶ FOR WOUND ◀** [C] a piece of thread that fastens the edges of a wound together: *The cut needed 15 stitches.* | *He had three stitches in it.*

**5 ▶ PAIN ◀** [singular] a sharp pain in the side of your body, that you can get by running or laughing very hard: *I can't go any faster – I have a stitch.*
**6 in stitches** laughing uncontrollably: **have sb in stitches** (=make sb laugh) *Her jokes had us all in stitches.*
**7 not have a stitch on** *informal* to be wearing no clothes
**8 not have a stitch to wear** to not have any clothing that is suitable for a particular occasion
**9 a stitch in time (saves nine)** *spoken* used to say that it is better to deal with problems early than to wait until they get worse

**stitch²** *v* [T] to SEW two pieces of cloth together, or to sew a decoration onto a piece of cloth: *She stitches the pieces together to make a quilt.* | **stitch sth onto** *Nina stitched a flower onto the skirt.*

**stitch up** *phr v* [T] **1** [**stitch** sth ↔ **up**] to put stitches in cloth or a wound in order to fasten parts of it together: *She stitched up the cut and left it to heal.* **2** [**stitch** sth ↔ **up**] to get a deal or agreement completed satisfactorily so that it cannot be changed: *The deal was stitched up in minutes.* **3** [**stitch** sb ↔ **up**] *BrE informal* to make someone seem guilty of a crime by providing false information; FRAME² (3): *George said he'd been stitched up.*

**stitch·ing** /ˈstɪtʃɪŋ/ *n* [U] a line of stitches in a piece of material

**stoat** /stəʊt‖stoʊt/ *n* [C] a small thin animal with brown fur that is similar to a WEASEL, and kills other animals

**stocks**

S3 W3 **stock¹** /stɒk‖stɑːk/ *n*
**1 ▶ SUPPLIES ◀** [C] also **stocks** *plural* a supply of something that you keep and can use when you need to: *stocks of flour and sugar* | **build up a stock** *The country has been building up its stock of weapons.*
**2 ▶ IN A SHOP ◀** [C,U] a supply of a particular type of thing that a shop has to sell: *Buy now while stocks last!* | **out of/in stock** (=unavailable or available in a particular shop) *I'm sorry, that swimsuit is completely out of stock in your size.* | **take stock** (=check and count the goods in a shop)
**3 ▶ FINANCE ◀ a)** [C] *technical* a SHARE² (5) in a company **b)** [U] the total value of a company's shares (SHARE² (5))
**4 ▶ COOKING ◀** [C,U] a liquid made by boiling meat or bones and vegetables, which is used to make soups etc: *chicken stock*
**5 ▶ AMOUNT AVAILABLE ◀** [singular] also **stocks** *plural* the total amount of something that is available to be used in a particular area: *Cod stocks in the North Atlantic have dropped radically.*
**6 ▶ ANIMALS ◀** [U] farm animals, especially cattle; LIVESTOCK
**7 take stock (of sth)** to think carefully about the things that have happened in a situation in order to decide what to do next: *Turning 40 is a time to take stock of your life.*
**8 be of peasant/Protestant/Scottish stock etc** to be related to a particular type of family in the past
**9 sb's stock is high/low** if someone's stock is high or low, they are very popular or very unpopular: *The government's stock was high just before the election.*
**10 ▶ FLOWER ◀** [C] a plant with pink, white, or light purple flowers and a sweet smell
**11 ▶ PLANT ◀ a)** a plant that you can cut stems off to make new plants grow **b)** a thick part of a stem onto which another plant can be added so that the two plants grow together
**12 ▶ DOCUMENT ◀** [C] an official document promising that a government will pay back the money it has borrowed with a fixed amount of INTEREST¹ (4)
**13 a stock of jokes/knowledge/courage etc** the jokes, knowledge etc that someone knows or has: *John seems to have an inexhaustible stock of funny stories.*
**14 the stocks a)** a wooden structure in a public place to which criminals were fastened by their feet or hands in former times **b)** a wooden structure in which a ship is held while it is being built
**15 ▶ ACTORS ◀** [C] *AmE* a STOCK COMPANY (2) | **summer stock** (=a group of actors who work together on several plays during the summer) | **do stock** (=work as an actor in this group) *Jim's doing stock in Northern California.*
**16 ▶ CLOTHING ◀** [C] a wide band of cloth worn around the neck so that the ends hang in front of your chest, especially by some priests —see also **laughing stock** (LAUGH¹ (9)), **lock, stock, and barrel** (LOCK² (3)), ROLLING STOCK

**stock²** *v* [T] **1** if a shop stocks a particular product, it keeps a supply of it to be sold: *Do you stock English wines?* **2** to provide a supply of something so that it is ready to use: *The fridge was stocked with all the butter and eggs needed for the Christmas baking.* **3** to put fish in a lake or river: [+ **with**] *rivers stocked with trout* —see also WELL-STOCKED

**stock up** *phr v* [I] to buy a lot of something to use when you need to: [+ **on**] *We stocked up on wine when we went to Paris.*

**stock³** *adj* **1 stock excuse/question/remark etc** an excuse etc that people often say or use, especially when they cannot think of anything more interesting or original **2** [only before noun] kept in a shop as goods to be sold: *shoes in all the stock sizes*

**stock·ade¹** /stɒˈkeɪd‖stɑː-/ *n* [C usually singular] a wall or fence made of large upright pieces of wood, built to defend a place

**stockade²** *v* [T] to put a stockade around a place in order to defend it

**stock·breed·er** /ˈstɒkˌbriːdə‖ˈstɑːkˌbriːdər/ *n* [C] a farmer who breeds cattle

**stock·brok·er** /ˈstɒkˌbrəʊkə‖ˈstɑːkˌbroʊkər/ *n* [C] someone whose job is to buy and sell stocks (STOCK¹ (3)), bonds, (BOND¹ (1)) and shares (SHARE² (5)) for other people —**stockbroking** *n* [U]

**stock car** /ˈ· ·/ *n* [C] **1** a car that has been made stronger so that it can compete in a race where cars often crash into each other **2** *AmE* a railway carriage for cattle

**stock cer·tif·i·cate** /ˈ· ·ˌ···/ *n* [C] *AmE* an official document that shows that you own shares (SHARE² (5)) in a company

**stock com·pa·ny** /ˈ· ˌ···/ *n* [C] *AmE* **1** a company whose money is divided into shares (SHARE² (5)) so that many people own a small part of it; JOINT-STOCK COMPANY **2** a group of actors who work together doing several different plays

**stock cube** /ˈ· ·/ *n* [C] a small piece of solid substance made of dried juices from meat and vegetables, that is mixed with water to make STOCK¹ (4)

**stock ex·change** /ˈ· ·ˌ·/ *n* [C usually singular] **1** the business of buying stocks STOCK¹ (3) and shares SHARE² (5): *She made a fortune on the stock exchange.* **2** a place where stocks and shares are bought and sold

**stock·hold·er** /ˈstɒkˌhəʊldə‖ˈstɑːkˌhoʊldər/ *n* [C] *especially AmE* someone who owns stocks (STOCK¹ (3)) in a business; SHAREHOLDER *BrE*

**stock·i·nette** /ˌstɒkɪˈnet‖ˌstɑː-/ *n* [U] *especially BrE* a soft cotton material that stretches, used especially for BANDAGES

**stock·ing** /ˈstɒkɪŋ‖ˈstɑː-/ *n* [C usually plural] **1** a thin close-fitting piece of clothing that covers a woman's leg and foot —compare PANTYHOSE, TIGHTS **2** *old-fashioned* a man's sock **3 in your stockinged feet** not wearing any shoes —see also BODY STOCKING, CHRISTMAS STOCKING

**stock-in-trade** /ˌ. . ˈ./ *n* [U] **1** words or behaviour that a particular type of person often uses: *A pleasant manner is part of a politician's stock-in-trade.* **2** *old-fashioned* the things you need to do your job

**stock·ist** /ˈstɒkɪ̵st‖ˈstɑː-/ *n* [C] *BrE* a person, shop, or company that keeps a particular product or particular goods to sell

**stock·man** /ˈstɒkmən‖ˈstɑːk-/ *n* [C] a man whose job it is to look after farm animals

**stock mar·ket** /ˈ. ˌ../ *n* [C usually singular] the STOCK EXCHANGE

**stock·pile[1]** /ˈstɒkpaɪl‖ˈstɑːk-/ *n* [C + of] a large supply of goods, weapons etc that are kept ready to be used in the future, especially when they may become difficult to obtain

**stockpile[2]** *v* [T] to keep adding to a supply of goods, weapons etc that you are keeping ready to use if you need them in the future: *The Superpowers are stockpiling nuclear arms.*

**stock·pot** /ˈstɒkpɒt‖ˈstɑːkpɑːt/ *n* [C] a pot in which you make STOCK[1] (4)

**stock·room** /ˈstɒkrʊm, -ruːm‖ˈstɑːk-/ *n* [C] a room for storing things in a shop or office

**stock-still** /ˌ. ˈ./ *adv* not moving at all: *Oscar stood stock-still and listened.*

**stock·tak·ing** /ˈstɒkˌteɪkɪŋ‖ˈstɑːk-/ *n* [U] *BrE* an occasion when you make a list of all the goods that you have a supply of at a particular time, especially in a shop; INVENTORY (2) *AmE*

**stock·y** /ˈstɒki‖ˈstɑː-/ *adj* a stocky person is short and heavy and looks strong —**stockily** *adv* —**stockiness** *n* [U]

**stock·yard** /ˈstɒkjɑːd‖ˈstɑːkjɑːrd/ *n* [C] a place where cattle, sheep etc are kept before being taken to a market and sold

**stodge** /stɒdʒ‖stɑːdʒ/ *n* [U] **1** heavy food that makes you feel full very quickly **2** *BrE informal* something written that is very dull and difficult to read

**stodg·y** /ˈstɒdʒi‖ˈstɑː-/ *adj* **1** stodgy food is heavy and makes you feel full very quickly **2** *BrE informal* stodgy writing is dull and difficult to read **3** a stodgy person is dull and behaves rather formally —**stodginess** *n* [U]

**sto·gie** /ˈstəʊgi‖ˈstoʊ-/ *n* [C] *AmE informal* a CIGAR, especially a thick cheap one

**sto·ic** /ˈstəʊɪk‖ˈstoʊ-/ *n* [C] someone who does not show their emotions and does not complain when something unpleasant happens to them

**sto·ic·al** /ˈstəʊɪkəl‖ˈstoʊ-/ *adj* also **stoic** not complaining or feeling unhappy when bad things happen to you —**stoically** /-kli/ *adv*

**sto·i·cis·m** /ˈstəʊɪ̵sɪzəm‖ˈstoʊ-/ *n* [U] patience and calmness when bad things happen to you

**stoke** /stəʊk‖stoʊk/ also **stoke up** *v* [I,T] to add more coal or wood to a fire used for cooking or heating: **stoke sth with sth** *Stoke the furnace with wood.*

**stoke up** *phr v* [T] **1** to add more coal or wood to a fire: **stoke sth ↔ up** *Get the fire stoked up.* **2 to stoke up fear/anger etc** to make a lot of people feel frightened etc about something: *The leaflets stoked up a lot of fears of an invasion.* **3 stoke up on/with a)** to eat a lot of food, for example because you will not eat again for a long time: *We stoked up on hot soup before going out in the snow.* **b)** to buy a lot of something that you need: *stoking up on warm clothing*

**stoked** /stəʊkt‖stoʊkt/ *adj AmE spoken* very excited about something good that is happening and that you did not expect

**stok·er** /ˈstəʊkə‖ˈstoʊkər/ *n* [C] someone whose job is to put coal or other FUEL[1] (1) into a FURNACE

**stole[1]** /stəʊl‖stoʊl/ the past tense of STEAL

**stole[2]** *n* [C] a long straight piece of cloth or fur that a woman wears across her shoulders

**sto·len** /ˈstəʊlən‖ˈstoʊ-/ the past participle of STEAL: *stolen cars | books stolen from libraries*

**stol·id** /ˈstɒlɪ̵d‖ˈstɑː-/ *adj* someone who is stolid does not react to situations or seem excited by them when most people would react; IMPASSIVE —**stolidly** *adv* —**stolidness** also **stolidity** /stəˈlɪdɪ̵ti/ *n* [U]

**stom·ach[1]** /ˈstʌmək/ *n* [C] **1** the organ inside your body where food begins to be digested (DIGEST[1] (1)) —see picture at DIGESTIVE SYSTEM **2** the front part of your body, below your chest: *Andrew was lying on his stomach.* **3 do sth on an empty stomach** to do something when you have not eaten: *Don't go to work on an empty stomach.* **4 have a strong stomach** to be able to see or do things that are unpleasant without feeling sick or upset: *Don't watch that film unless you have a strong stomach.* **5 turn your stomach** to make you feel sick or upset: *The sight of the slaughtered cow turned my stomach.* **6 have no stomach for a fight/task etc** to have no desire to do something because you do not like doing it etc 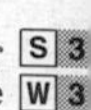

**stomach[2]** *v* [T usually in questions and negatives] **1** to be able to accept something, especially something unpleasant; ENDURE | **can't stomach** *Tracy couldn't stomach the idea of moving to Glasgow.* | **hard/difficult to stomach** *Rob found Cathy's attitude hard to stomach.* **2** to eat something without becoming ill: *I can't stomach fried food.*

**stom·ach·ache** /ˈstʌmək-eɪk/ *n* [C,U] pain in your stomach or near your stomach

**stomach pump** /ˈ.. ./ *n* [C] a machine with a tube that doctors use to suck out the food etc inside someone's stomach, especially after they have swallowed poison

**stomp** /stɒmp‖stɑːmp/ *v* [I always + adv/prep] **1** to walk with heavy steps, especially because you are angry: *Alex stomped angrily up the stairs.* **2 sb's stomping ground** a favourite place where someone often goes

**stone[1]** /stəʊn‖stoʊn/ *n* S2 W1

**1 ▶ ON THE GROUND ◀** [C] a small piece of rock of any shape, found on the ground: *Round, flat stones are the best for skimming across water.*

**2 ▶ ROCK ◀** [U] a hard mineral substance or rock: *honey colored stone | stone statues*

**3 ▶ JEWELLERY ◀** [C] a jewel: *gem stones*

**4 ▶ FRUIT ◀** [C] *BrE* a large hard single seed at the centre of some fruits; PIT[1] (9) *AmE* —compare PIP[1] (1)

**5 ▶ MEDICAL ◀** [C] a ball of hard material that can form in organs such as your BLADDER or KIDNEYS

**6 ▶ WEIGHT ◀** [C] *plural* **stone** or **stones** a measurement of weight used in Britain that is equal to 6.35kg —see table on page B2

**7 a stone's throw (away)** very close to something: *The villa was only a stone's throw from the beach.*

**8 be made of stone** also **have a heart of stone** to not show any emotions or pity for someone —see also FOUNDATION STONE, PAVING STONE, STEPPING-STONE

**stone[2]** *v* [T] **1** to throw stones at someone or something: **stone sb to death** (=kill someone with stones, especially as a punishment in the past) **2** *BrE* to take the stone out of fruit; PIT[2] (2) *AmE*: *stoned dates* **3 stone the crows!** also **stone me!** *BrE old-fashioned* used to express surprise or shock

**Stone Age** /ˈ. ./ *n* the earliest known time in human history, when only stone was used for making tools, weapons etc —compare BRONZE AGE, IRON AGE

**stone-cold** /ˌ. ˈ.◂/ *adj* **1** completely and unpleasantly cold: *The body's stone-cold.* **2 stone-cold sober** having drunk no alcohol at all

**stoned** /stəʊnd‖stoʊnd/ *adj* [not before noun] **1** *informal* feeling very excited or extremely relaxed because you have taken an illegal drug **2** very drunk

**stone dead** /ˌ· ˈ·◂/ *adj* completely dead

**stone deaf** /ˌ· ˈ·◂/ *adj* completely unable to hear

**stone-ground** /ˈ· ·/ *adj* stone-ground flour is made by crushing grain between two MILLSTONES

**stone·ma·son** /ˈstəʊnˌmeɪsən‖ˈstoʊn-/ *n* [C] someone whose job is cutting stone into pieces to be used in buildings

**stone·wall** /ˌstəʊnˈwɔːl‖ˌstoʊnˈwɒːl/ *v* [I] to delay a discussion, decision etc by talking a lot and refusing to answer questions

**stone·ware** /ˈstəʊnweə‖ˈstoʊnwer/ *n* [U] pots etc that are made from a special hard clay

**stone-washed** /ˌ· ˈ·◂/ *adj* stonewashed JEANS etc have been made softer by a washing process in which they are beaten with stones

**stone·work** /ˈstəʊnwɜːk‖ˈstoʊnwɜːrk/ *n* [U] the parts of a building that are made of stone, especially when they are decorative

**stonk·ered** /ˈstɒŋkəd‖ˈstɑːŋkərd/ *adj AustrE informal* very tired

**stonk·ing** /ˈstɒŋkɪŋ‖ˈstɑːŋ-/ *adj BrE informal* surprisingly good: *He scored a stonking goal.*

**ston·y** /ˈstəʊni‖ˈstoʊ-/ *adj* **1** covered by stones or containing stones: *stony soil* **2** without emotion or pity: *stony faces | a stony silence* **3 fall on stony ground** if a request, suggestion, joke etc falls on stony ground, it is ignored or people do not like it —**stonily** *adv*

**stony-faced** /ˌ·· ˈ·◂/ *adj* showing no emotion or friendliness

**stood** /stʊd/ the past tense and past participle of STAND[1]

**stooge** /stuːdʒ/ *n* [C] **1** one of two performers who is the subject of the jokes made by the other performer **2** *informal* someone who always does what someone else wants them to

**stook·ie** /ˈstʊki/ *n* [C] *ScotE* a PLASTER CAST

**stool** /stuːl/ *n* [C] **1** a seat without any supporting part for your back or arms: *a bar stool* —see picture at CHAIR[1] **2** *technical* a piece of solid waste from your body

**stool·pi·geon** /ˈstuːlˌpɪdʒɪn/ *n AmE informal* [C] someone, especially a criminal, who helps the police to catch another criminal; INFORMER

**stoop**[1] /stuːp/ *v* [I] **1** also **stoop down** to bend your body forwards and down: *The doorway was so low that Martin had to stoop to go in.* **2** to stand with your back and shoulders bent forwards

**stoop to** sth *phr v* [T] to do something, even though you know it is morally wrong, because you think it will help you achieve something: *Ray would stoop to anything to get what he wants.* | **stoop to doing sth** *I didn't expect you to stoop to lying.*

**stoop**[2] *n* **1** [singular] if you have a stoop. your shoulders slope forward or seem too round: *Jeff's developed a stoop.* **2** [C] *AmE* a raised area at the door of a house, usually big enough to sit on

**stooped** /stuːpt/ *adj* having a stoop: *a stooped old man*

**stoop·ing** /ˈstuːpɪŋ/ *adj* stooping shoulders are bent forwards or have become too round

S1 W1 **stop**[1] /stɒp‖stɑːp/ *v* **stopped, stopping**

**1 ▶NOT MOVE OR CONTINUE◀** [I,T] to no longer move or continue to do something, or to make someone or something do this: *Stop, thief!* | **stop sth** *Apply pressure to stop the bleeding.* | *You'll have to stop the generator, it's overheating.* | **stop doing sth** *Lena's trying to stop smoking.* | **stop that/it** *spoken*: *Stop it! You're hurting me.* | **stop short** (=stop walking suddenly) | **stop and do sth** *People stopped and stared as she screamed at him.* | **stop (dead)/stop in your tracks** (=stop walking or running very suddenly) | **stop (sth) at/outside/in etc** *Jill stopped the car outside the post office.* | **stop on a dime** *AmE* (=stop very quickly)

**2 ▶PREVENT◀** [T] to prevent someone from doing something or something from happening: *I'm leaving home and you can't stop me.* | **stop sb (from) doing sth** *Lynn's parents tried to stop her seeing him.* | **there's nothing to stop sb** *There's nothing to stop you calling her to say you're sorry.*

**3 ▶END◀** [I,T] to end or make something end: *We'll go out when the rain stops.* | **stop sth** *The referee stopped the fight.* | [+ **at**] *The road stops at the farm.*

**4 ▶PAUSE◀** [I] to pause in an activity, journey etc in order to do something before continuing: **stop for sth** *We stopped for a drink on the way home.* | **stop to do sth** *Maya stopped to tie her shoelace.* | **stop to think/consider etc** *It's time we stopped to think about our next move.*

**5 stop at nothing (to do sth)** to be ready to do anything, even if it is cruel, dishonest, or illegal, to get what you want: *Franca will stop at nothing to get a part in the film.*

**6 stop short of (doing) sth** to decide that you are not willing to do something wrong or dangerous, though you will do something similar that is less dangerous: *The US government supported sanctions but stopped short of military action.*

**7 ▶STAY◀** [I] *BrE informal* to stay somewhere for a short time, especially at someone's house: *I won't sit down – I'm not stopping.* | [+ **for**] *Can you stop for a chat?*

**8 ▶WALKING/TRAVELLING◀** [T] to go to someone and speak to them or make them stop when they are walking or travelling somewhere: *Someone stopped me in the street and asked the way.* | *if they try to get away, they'll be stopped at the border.*

**9 ▶MONEY◀** to prevent money from being paid after you agreed to pay it: **stop sth from sth** *Money for breakages will be stopped from your wages.* | **stop a cheque** (=tell your bank not to pay the money)

**10 ▶BLOCK◀** [T] also **stop up** to block something such as a pipe so that water, smoke etc cannot go through it

**stop back** *phr v* [I] *AmE* to go back to a place you have been to earlier: *Can you stop back later? I'm real busy right now.*

**stop by** *phr v* [I,T] to make a short visit to a place or person, especially when you are on your way to somewhere else: *Daniel stopped by the newsagent's on his way home.*

**stop** sth ↔ **down** *phr v* [T] to make the hole in a camera LENS (2) smaller so that less light gets in when you take a photograph

**stop in** *phr v* [I] *informal* **1** to make a short visit to a place or person, especially when you are on your way to somewhere else: [+ **at**] *Let's stop in at Vera's on our way.* **2** *BrE* to stay at home: *I'm stopping in to wash my hair tonight.*

**stop off** *phr v* [I] to make a short visit to a place during a journey, especially to rest or to see someone: *Shall we stop off somewhere on the way to Cornwall?* | [+ **in/at etc**] *We stopped off in Santa Rosa for a day.*

**stop out** *phr v* [I] *BrE informal* to stay out later than usual: *Lizzie stopped out all night on Saturday.*

**stop over** *phr v* [I] to make a short stay somewhere before continuing a long journey: *The plane stops over in Dubai on the way to India.*

**stop up** *phr v* [I] *BrE informal* to stay up late: *Joe stopped up till 3 o'clock to watch the boxing.*

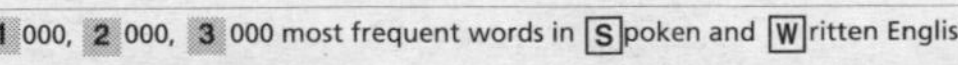

This graph shows how common the different grammar patterns of the verb **stop** are.

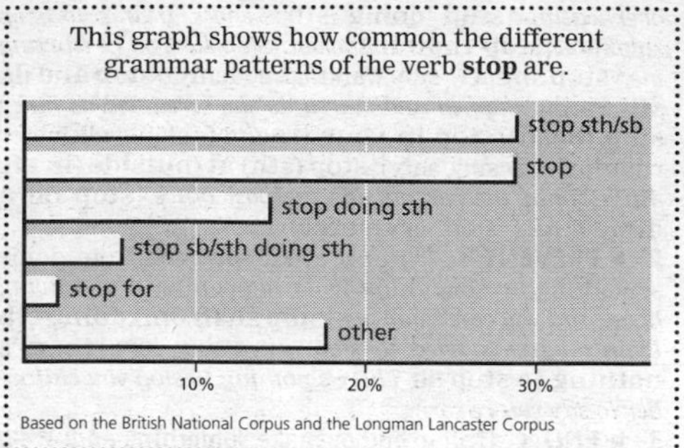


Based on the British National Corpus and the Longman Lancaster Corpus

S3 W3 **stop²** *n* [C]
**1 bring sth to a stop** to stop something moving or happening: *David brought the truck to a shuddering stop.*
**2 come/roll to a stop** if a vehicle, an activity etc comes to a stop, it stops moving or happening: *Work on the project has come to a stop because of lack of funding.*
**3 ▶ DURING JOURNEY ◀** a time or place when you stop during a journey for a short time: *Our first stop was Paris, and then we traveled on to Marseilles.* | **make a stop** (=stop somewhere while travelling) *We only made two stops on the long drive down through France.*
**4 ▶ BUS/TRAIN ◀** a place where a bus or train regularly stops for people to get on and off: *This is your stop, isn't it?*

**5 put a stop to sth** to prevent something from continuing or happening: *The new law should put a stop to this tax evasion.*
**6 pull out all the stops** to do everything you possibly can to make something happen and succeed: *The Bianchis had pulled out all the stops for their daughter's wedding.*
**7 ▶ MUSIC ◀ a)** a set of pipes on an ORGAN (2) that produce sound **b)** a set of handles that you push in or out in an organ to control the amount of sound it produces
**8 ▶ CONSONANT ◀** a consonant sound, like /p/ or /k/, made by stopping the flow of air completely and then suddenly letting it out of your mouth; PLOSIVE —see also FULLSTOP

**stop·cock** /ˈstɒpkɒk‖ˈstɑːpkɑːk/ *n* [C] a VALVE (1) that can be opened or closed with a TAP (=object you turn) to control the flow of a liquid in a pipe; TURNCOCK *BrE*

**stop·gap** /ˈstɒpgæp‖ˈstɑːp-/ *n* [C] something or someone that you use for a short time until you can replace it with something better: *a stopgap measure*

**stop-go** /ˌ· ˈ·◂/ *adj* **stop-go approach/policies etc** *BrE* a way of controlling the economy by restricting government spending for a period of time and then not restricting it so severely for a time

**stop·light** /ˈstɒplaɪt‖ˈstɑːp-/ *n* [C] also **stoplights** *plural AmE* a set of coloured lights used to control and direct traffic; TRAFFIC LIGHTS

**stop·o·ver** /ˈstɒpˌəʊvə‖ˈstɑːpˌoʊvər/ *n* [C] a short stay somewhere between parts of a journey, especially on a long plane journey: *a two-day stopover in Hong Kong*

**stop·page** /ˈstɒpɪdʒ‖ˈstɑː-/ *n* **1** [C] a situation in which workers stop working for a short time as a protest: *time lost in disputes and stoppages* **2** [C] something that blocks a tube or container: *an intestinal stoppage* **3** [C,U] *BrE* the act of stopping something from moving or happening: *complete stoppages of production* | *stoppages due to injury* **4 stoppages** [plural] *BrE* money kept back from your wages by your employer in order to pay your tax, for your PENSION etc

**stop·per** /ˈstɒpə‖ˈstɑːpər/ *n* [C] the thing that you put in the top part of a bottle to close it —**stopper** *v* [T] —see picture at LABORATORY

**stopping dis·tance** /ˈ·· ˌ··/ *n* [C,U] the distance that a driver is supposed to leave between their car and the one in front in order to be able to stop safely

**stop press** /ˌ· ˈ·◂/ *n* [singular] late news added to a newspaper after the main part has been printed

**stop·watch** /ˈstɒpwɒtʃ‖ˈstɑːpwɑːtʃ, -wɒːtʃ/ *n* [C] a watch used for measuring the exact time it takes to do something, especially to finish a race

**stor·age** /ˈstɔːrɪdʒ/ *n* [U] **1** the act of keeping or putting something in a special place while it is not being used: *the storage of radioactive material* | **storage space/capacity** (=space etc for storing things) **2 in storage** if furniture or other goods are in storage, they are being kept in a special place until you need to use them **3** the price you pay for having goods or furniture stored W3

**storage heat·er** /ˈ·· ˌ··/ *n* [C] *BrE* a HEATER that stores heat at times when electricity is cheaper

**store¹** /stɔː‖stɔːr/ *n* [C] S1 W1
**1 ▶ LARGE SHOP ◀** a large place that sells many different kinds of goods: *At Christmas the stores stay open late.* —see also CHAIN STORE, DEPARTMENT STORE, GENERAL STORE
**2 ▶ SHOP ◀** *AmE* a place where goods are sold to the public; SHOP¹ (1): *There are about 60 different stores in the Fallbrook Mall.* | **a shoe/clothing/grocery etc store** (=one that sells one type of goods) *She worked in a book store during college.* | **go to the store** *I need to go to the store for some milk.* —see graph at SHOP¹
**3 ▶ SUPPLY ◀** a supply of something that you keep to use later: [+ **of**] *Granny always had a special store of chocolate for us.*
**4 ▶ PLACE TO KEEP THINGS ◀** a large building in which goods are stored so they can be used or sold later WAREHOUSE: *a grain store*
**5 be in store** if something unexpected such as a surprise or problem is in store for someone, it is about to happen to them: *He's got a few surprises in store if he thinks he can order us around.*
**6 stores** [plural] **a)** supplies of food and equipment that are used by an army, navy etc **b)** the building or room in an army camp, ship etc where these are kept
**7 set great store by sth** to consider something to be very important: *Anne sets great store by that training course.*

**store²** *v* [T] **1** also **store away** to put things away and keep them until you need them: *Squirrels are storing up nuts for the winter.* **2** to keep facts or information in your brain or a computer: *A mass of data is stored in the computer.* **3 store up trouble/problems etc** to behave in a way that will cause trouble for you later: *Sarah is storing up problems for herself by lying to him.* S3 W3

**store brand** /ˈ· ·/ *n* [C] *especially AmE* a type of goods that are produced for a particular shop and have the shop's name on them

**store de·tec·tive** /ˈ· ·ˌ··/ *n* [C] someone who is employed in a large shop to watch the customers and to stop them stealing

**store·front** /ˈstɔːfrʌnt‖ˈstɔːr-/ *n* [C] *AmE* **1** the part of a store that faces the street **2 storefront law office/church/school** a small law office etc in a shopping area

**store·house** /ˈstɔːhaʊs‖ˈstɔːr-/ *n* [C] **1 a storehouse of information/memories etc** something that contains a lot of information etc **2** *old-fashioned* a building where things are stored: WAREHOUSE

**store·keep·er** /ˈstɔːˌkiːpə‖ˈstɔːrˌkiːpər/ *n* [C] *AmE* someone who owns or manages a shop; SHOPKEEPER *BrE*

**store·room** /ˈstɔːrʊm, -ruːm/ *n* [C] a room where goods are stored

**sto·rey** *BrE*, **story** *AmE* /ˈstɔːri/ *n* [C] **1** a floor or level of a building **2 two-storey/five-storey etc** having two etc storeys

**stor·ied** /ˈstɔːrid/ *adj* **1 two-storied/five storied etc** *AmE* having two etc storeys **2** [only before noun] *literary* being the subject of many stories; FAMOUS

**stork** /stɔːk‖stɔːrk/ *n* [C] a tall white bird with long legs and a long beak

W3 **storm¹** /stɔːm‖stɔːrm/ *n* **1** [C] a period of very bad weather when there is a lot of rain, strong winds, and often lightning: *crops damaged by recent heavy storms*| **the storm broke** (=suddenly started) —see picture on page 836 **2** [C usually singular] a situation in which people suddenly express very strong feelings about something that someone has said or done: *The governor found himself at the centre of a political storm.*| **a storm of protest/abuse/laughter etc** *Government plans for hospital closures provoked a storm of protest.* **3 take somewhere by storm a)** to be very successful in a particular place: *The new show took London by storm.* **b)** to attack a place using large numbers of soldiers and succeed in getting possession of it **4 a storm in a teacup** an unnecessary expression of strong feelings about something that is very unimportant **5 dance/sing/party up a storm** *AmE* to do something with all your energy: *They're dancing up a storm in there.*

**storm²** *v* **1** [T] to suddenly attack and enter a place using a lot of force: *An angry crowd stormed the embassy.* **2** [I always + adv/prep] to go somewhere in a noisy fast way that shows you are extremely angry: [+ **out of/into/off etc**] *Alan stormed out of the room.* **3** [I,T] *literary* to shout something because you feel extremely angry: *"What difference does it make?" she stormed.*

**storm cel·lar** /ˈ· ˌ··/ *n* [C] *AmE* a place under a house where you can go to be safe during violent storms

**storm cloud** /ˈ· ·/ *n* [C] **1** a dark cloud which you see before a storm **2** [usually plural] a sign that something very bad is going to happen: *Storm clouds are gathering over the East-West trade negotiations.*

**storm door** /ˈ· ·/ *n* [C] a second door that is fitted to the outside of a door in winter in the US to give protection against rain, snow etc

**storm lan·tern** /ˈ· ˌ··/ *n* [C] a lamp which has a cover to protect the flame against the wind

**storm·troop·er** /ˈstɔːmˌtruːpə‖ˈstɔːrmˌtruːpər/ *n* [C] a member of a special group of German soldiers in the Second World War who were trained to be particularly violent

**storm win·dow** /ˈ· ˌ··/ *n* [C] a second window fitted to the outside of a window in winter in the US to give more protection against rain, snow etc

**storm·y** /ˈstɔːmi‖ˈstɔːr-/ *adj* **1** stormy weather, sky etc is full of strong winds, heavy rain, and dark clouds: *The sky was starting to look rather stormy.* **2** a stormy relationship, meeting etc is full of strong and often angry feelings: *a stormy meeting*| *a stormy affair*

S2 W2 **sto·ry** /ˈstɔːri/ *n* [C]

**1** ▶ **FOR ENTERTAINMENT** ◀ a description of how something happened, that is intended to entertain people, and may be true or imaginary: *the story of Cinderella*| *Don't be frightened, Connie – it's only a story.* (=it is imaginary) [+ **about**] *a story about gangsters*| **fairy/ghost/love story** *a true-life love story*| **tell/read sb a story** *Mommy, will you read me a story?*

**2** ▶ **EVENTS** ◀ a description of the most important events in someone's life or in the development of something: *the story of the railways*| *the Tina Turner Story*| **sb's life story** *Nobody wants to hear your life story the first time you meet them.*

**3** ▶ **NEWS** ◀ a report in a newspaper or news broadcast about a recent event: *a front-page story in 'The Times'*| **run a story** (=report an event) *'The Observer' ran a big story about the scandal.*| **cover story** (=the main story in a magazine that is about the picture on the cover)| **success story** *Calvin's life was a success story – from farm boy to business tycoon.* —see graph at NEWS

**4** ▶ **OF A FILM/PLAY ETC** ◀ what happens in a film, play, or book; PLOT¹ (1): *Tom Hanks was brilliant, but the story was boring.*

**5** ▶ **EXCUSE** ◀ an excuse or explanation, especially one that you have invented: *Where were you? And don't give me any story about working late!*| *Well that's my story* (=that is what I say happened), *and I'm sticking to it.*

**6 my/your side of the story** the way that a particular person describes what happened: *Before we decide who is to blame, we want to hear your side of the story.*

**7** ▶ **WHAT PEOPLE SAY** ◀ information which people tell each other, but which may be untrue; RUMOUR: *There are a lot of wild stories going around.*| **so the story goes** (=people are saying this) *He was having an affair with Julie, or so the story goes.*

**8 it's a long story** *spoken* used to tell someone that you do not want to give them all the details that a full answer to their question would need

**9 it's the same story in/here/there etc** used to say the same thing is happening in another place: *Unemployment is falling in the US and it's the same story in Europe.*

**10 it's the same old story** *spoken* used to say that the present bad situation has often happened before: *It's the same old story – too much work and not enough time.*

**11 to cut a long story short** *BrE spoken,* **to make a long story short** *AmE spoken* used when you want to finish a story quickly

**12 but that's another story** *spoken* used when you have mentioned something that you are not going to talk about on this occasion

**13 that's not the whole story** *spoken* used to say that there are more details which people need to know in order to understand the situation

**14 that's the story of my life** *spoken* used after a disappointing experience to mean that similar disappointing things always seem to happen to you

**15 end of story** *BrE spoken* used to mean that there is nothing more to say about a particular subject: *As far as I'm concerned Terry is still a friend, end of story.*

**16** ▶ **A LIE** ◀ a word used by or to children meaning a lie: **tell stories** *Have you been telling stories again?*

**17** the American spelling of STOREY —see also SHORT STORY, **cock and bull story** (COCK¹ (3)), **hard luck story** (HARD¹ (23)), SOB STORY

**sto·ry·book¹** /ˈstɔːribʊk/ *n* [C] a book of stories for children: *a creature standing in front of us like something out of a storybook*

**storybook²** *adj* **a storybook ending/romance etc** an ending etc that is so happy or perfect that it is like one in a children's story: *I walked up the path in front of a lopsided storybook cottage.*

**story line** /ˈ·· ·/ *n* [C] the main set of connected events in a story; PLOT¹ (1)

**sto·ry·tell·er** /ˈstɔːriˌtelə‖-ər/ *n* [C] someone who tells stories, especially to children

**stoup** /stuːp/ *n* [C] **1** a container for holy water near the entrance to a church **2** a glass or MUG¹ (1,2) used for drinking in former times

**stout¹** /staʊt/ *adj* **1** fairly fat and heavy or having a thick body: *a short, stout man*| *She's gotten pretty stout since you last saw her.* —see FAT¹ (USAGE) **2** *literary* strong and thick: *a stout stick*| *a stout pair of shoes* **3** *literary* brave and determined: **stout defence/support/resistance** *Michael offered his usual stout support.* —**stoutly** *adv*: *He stoutly maintained his innocence.* —**stoutness** *n* [U]

**stout²** *n* [U] a strong dark beer

**stout·heart·ed** /ˌstaʊtˈhɑːtɪd◂‖-ɑːr-/ *adj literary* brave and determined

**stove¹** /stəʊv‖stoʊv/ *n* [C] **1** a thing used for heating a room or for cooking, which works by burning wood, coal, oil or gas: *a wood-burning stove*| *a camp stove* —compare COOKER (1) **2** *AmE* the top of a COOKER

**stove²** *v* the past tense and past participle of STAVE²

**stove·pipe hat** /ˌstəʊvpaɪp ˈhæt‖ˌstoʊv-/ *n* [C] *AmE* a tall black silk hat worn by men in the past

**stow** /stəʊ‖stoʊ/ also **stow away** *v* [T always + adv/prep] to put or pack something tidily away in a space until you need it again: *You can stow your gear under the bed.*

**stow away** *phr v* **1** [I] to hide on a ship or plane in order to travel secretly or without paying: *The boy was caught trying to stow away on a plane bound for India.* **2** [T **stow** sth ↔ **away**] to stow something —see also STOWAWAY

**stow·age** /ˈstəʊɪdʒ‖ˈstoʊ-/ *n* [C] space available on a boat for storing things

**stow·a·way** /ˈstəʊəweɪ‖ˈstoʊ-/ *n* [C] someone who hides on a ship or plane in order to avoid paying or to travel secretly

**strad·dle** /ˈstrædl/ *v* [T] **1** to sit or stand with your legs on either side of someone or something: *Joe sat straddling the beam.* **2** if something straddles a line, road, or river, part of it is on one side and part on the other side: *a little town straddling the frontier between France and Germany* **3** to include different areas of activity: *Her job straddled marketing and public relations.*

**strafe** /streɪf, strɑːf‖streɪf/ *v* [T] to attack a place by flying low and firing many bullets

**strag·gle** /ˈstræɡəl/ *v* [I] **1** to move at a slower speed than the group you are with so that you remain at a distance behind them: [+ **in**] *runners straggling in two hours after the leaders* **2** to move, grow, or spread out untidily in different directions: *thin, black, straggling hair* | *Her handwriting straggled over the page.*

**strag·gler** /ˈstræɡlə‖-ər/ *n* [C] someone who is too slow to stay with the others in a group so that they move along some distance behind: *Wait for the stragglers to catch up.*

**strag·gly** /ˈstræɡəli/ *adj* growing untidily and spreading out in different directions: *a straggly moustache* —see picture on page 412

S1 **straight**[1] /streɪt/ *adv*
W2 **1** ▶ **IN A STRAIGHT LINE** ◀ moving in a straight line: **straight ahead/at/down/in front of etc** *The book is on the table straight in front of you.* | *She was looking straight at me.* | *We're stuck in the middle of the road with this truck heading straight towards us.* | *She walked straight past me.* | *Terry was so tired he couldn't walk straight.* | *The cat sat in front of him, its tail stretched out straight.*

**2** ▶ **IMMEDIATELY** ◀ [+ adj/adv] immediately or without delay: **straight to/after/down/back etc** *Let's get straight down to business.* | *Go straight home and tell your mother.* | *We can meet straight after lunch.*

**3** ▶ **ONE AFTER THE OTHER** ◀ happening one after the other in a series, especially an unusually long series: *He's been without sleep now for three days straight.*

**4** ▶ **SEE/THINK** ◀ if you cannot think or see straight, you cannot think or see clearly: *Turn the radio down, I can't think straight.*

**5 tell sb straight/straight out** *spoken* to tell someone something clearly without trying to hide your meaning: *She told him straight out that she wouldn't work on Saturday.* | **straight to his/her face** *I'll tell him straight to his face what I think of him.*

**6 go straight** *informal* to stop being a criminal and live an honest life: *Tony's been trying to go straight for about six months.*

**7 straight off** also **straight away** *BrE spoken* immediately or at once: *I guessed it was you straight off.*

**8 straight up** *BrE spoken* **a)** used to ask someone if they are telling the truth: *"The shoes cost £250." "Straight up?"* **b)** used to emphasize that what you are saying is true: *I don't know where she is, straight up.*

**9 straight from the shoulder** *AmE informal* expressed plainly and directly, without trying to avoid unpleasantness

**10 damn straight** *AmE spoken* used to explain that something is completely true or right: *Damn straight that's good.*

S2 **straight**[2] *adj*
W3 **1** ▶ **NOT BENDING OR CURVING** ◀ something such as a line or road that is straight goes in one direction and does not bend or curve: *Anne loved Rome with its open spaces and long straight avenues.* | **in a straight line** *After five beers I was incapable of walking in a straight line* | **straight hair** (=hair without curls) —see picture on page 412

**2** ▶ **LEVEL/UPRIGHT** ◀ level, upright, or flat in position or shape: *Stand up straight.* | *Is my tie straight?*

**3** ▶ **ONE AFTER ANOTHER** ◀ immediately one after another in a series, especially in an unusually long series: *an amazing record of 43 straight wins*

**4** ▶ **TIDY** ◀ [not before noun] a room that is straight is clean and tidy and everything is in its proper place: *I'm trying to get the room straight before your parents get here.*

**5** ▶ **TRUTHFUL** ◀ honest and truthful: **be straight with sb** *Are you going to be straight with me or not?* | **a straight answer** *It's difficult to get a straight answer out of him.* | **straight talk/honesty** *No more of this fancy playing with words – I want some straight talk here.*

**6 get this/it straight** *spoken* to understand the true facts about a situation: *Let me get this straight – Tom sold the car and gave you the money?*

**7 set/put sb sth straight (about)** to make someone understand the true facts about a situation: *Tell him to ask Ruth – she'll put him straight.* | **set/put the record straight** *I'd like to put the record straight about Bill's resignation.*

**8 get/put/set things straight (between)** *spoken* to deal with the small problems you have in your relationship with someone: *I think it's best to get things straight from the start. This job is not easy.*

**9** ▶ **CHOICE/FIGHT** ◀ a straight choice or contest involves only two possible choices or opponents: *The election is seen as a straight fight between the Socialists and the ruling coalition.* | *How about a straight swap, my U2 album for this one?* —see also STRAIGHTFORWARD (2)

**10** ▶ **NOT LIMITED** ◀ simple and not limited by any conditions; STRAIGHTFORWARD (3): *Did you do it? Just give me a straight yes or no.*

**11 a straight face** someone who has a straight face looks serious although they really want to smile or laugh: **keep a straight face** *She looked so ridiculous it was hard to keep a straight face.*

**12** ▶ **ALCOHOLIC DRINKS** ◀ alcoholic drinks that are straight have no water or ice or any other liquid added; NEAT (4): *I like my vodka straight.*

**13** ▶ **NORMAL** ◀ *slang* someone who is straight behaves in a way that is accepted as normal by many people but which you think is dull and boring: *Dave's OK, but his wife is really straight.*

**14** ▶ **NOT OWING SB MONEY** ◀ [not before noun] no longer owing money to someone or being owed money by someone: *If you give me £10 then we're straight.*

**15** ▶ **SEX** ◀ *slang* HETEROSEXUAL

**16** ▶ **DRUGS** ◀ *slang* not using drugs

**straight**[3] *n* **1** [C] *slang* someone who is attracted to people of the opposite sex **2** [C] *slang* someone who is not a drug user **3** [singular] *especially BrE* the straight part of a RACETRACK; STRAIGHTAWAY *AmE* **4 keep to/stray from the straight and narrow** *humorous* to live in an honest and moral way, or to fail to do this

**straight ar·row** /ˌ· ˈ··/ *n* [C] *AmE informal* someone who never does anything illegal or unusual and exciting

**straight·a·way**[1] /ˌstreɪtəˈweɪ/ *adv* at once; immediately: *Let's start work straightaway.*

**straight·a·way**[2] /ˈtreɪtəweɪ/ *n* [singular] *AmE* the straight part of a RACETRACK ; STRAIGHT[3] (3) *BrE*

**straight·en** /ˈstreɪtn/ *v* **1** also **straighten out** [I, T] to become straight or make something straight: *Straighten your tie.* | *The road twisted and turned and then straightened out.* **2** also **straighten up** [I] to make your back straight, or to stand up straight after bending down **3** also **straighten up** to make something tidy: *You can't go out till you straighten your room.*

**straighten** sb/sth ↔ **out** *phr v* [T] **1** to settle a difficult situation by dealing with the things that are causing problems or confusion: *There are a few things that need* *straightening out between us.* **2** to deal with someone's bad behaviour or personal problems: *We try to help these kids straighten themselves out and get back into school.*

**straighten up** *phr v* [I] *AmE* to begin to behave well after behaving badly: *You'd better straighten up, young lady!*

**straight·faced** /ˌstreɪtˈfeɪst◂/ *adj* not showing by the expression on your face that you are really joking or doing something funny: *"I've never been so serious in all my life," Bart said straightfaced.* —**straightfacedly** /-ˈfeɪsɪ̵dli◂/ *adv*

S3 **straight·for·ward** /ˌstreɪtˈfɔːwəd◂‖-ˈfɔːrwərd◂/ *adj* **1** honest about your feelings or opinions and not hiding anything: *Jack is tough, but always straightforward and fair.* **2** simple and easy to understand: *The system itself is perfectly straightforward.* **3** [only before noun] not limited by any conditions: *a straightforward cash settlement* —**straightforwardly** *adv* —**straightforwardness** *n* [U]

**straight·jack·et** /ˈstreɪtˌdʒækɪ̵t/ *n* [C] another spelling of STRAITJACKET

**straight man** /ˈ· ·/ *n* [C] a male entertainer who works with a COMEDIAN, providing him or her with opportunities to make jokes

**straight shoot·er** /ˈ· ˌ··/ *n* [C] *AmE informal* an honest person who you can trust

**straight tick·et** /ˌ· ˈ··/ *n* [C] a vote in which someone chooses all the candidates of a particular political party in the US

**straight·way** /ˈstreɪt-weɪ/ *adv old use* STRAIGHTAWAY

**strain¹** /streɪn/ *n*

**1** ▶ **WORRY** ◀ [C,U] worry caused by having to deal with a problem or work too hard over a long period of time: *The trial has been a terrible strain for both of us.* | **put a strain on sb/sth** *Nick's frequent trips were putting a strain on their marriage.* | **be under (a) strain** *I know you've been under a lot of strain lately.* | **stresses and strains** (=problems and worries) *the stresses and strains of everyday working life*

**2** ▶ **DIFFICULTY** ◀ [C] a problem or difficulty that is caused when something is used more than is normal or acceptable: *The drought has put a heavy strain on our water resources.*

**3** ▶ **FORCE** ◀ [U] a force that pulls, stretches or pushes something: [+ **on**] *The strain on the cables supporting the bridge is enormous.* | **under the strain** (=because of the force) *The rope snapped under the strain.*

**4** ▶ **INJURY** ◀ [C,U] an injury to a muscle or part of your body caused by using it too much: *a back strain* —compare SPRAIN

**5** ▶ **DISTRUST** ◀ [C,U] a situation in which two people, groups etc have stopped being friendly or trusting each other; TENSION (2): *the current strain in relations between the two countries*

**6** ▶ **PLANT/ANIMAL** ◀ [C] a breed or type of animal, plant etc: [+ **of**] *trying to develop a new strain of wheat*

**7 the strains of sth** *literary* the sound of music being played: [+ **of**] *the strains of the Blue Danube Waltz*

**8** ▶ **QUALITY** ◀ [singular] a particular quality which people have, especially one that is passed from parents to children: [+ **of**] *There's a strain of madness in his family.*

**9 take the strain** to pull on something such as a rope until it is tight, then keep it in that position

**10** ▶ **WAY OF SAYING STH** ◀ [singular] *formal* the meaning of what you are saying or writing, or the way it is expressed: *a strain of bitterness in Young's later work*

**strain²** *v*

**1** ▶ **PART OF BODY** ◀ [T] to injure a muscle or part of your body by making it work too hard: *strain a muscle in your leg* | *You'll strain your eyes trying to read in this light.*

**2** ▶ **EFFORT** ◀ [I,T] to try very hard to do something using all your physical or mental strength: **strain to do sth** *The singer had to strain to reach the high notes.* | **strain for sth** *Bill choked and gasped, straining for air.* | **strain your ears/eyes** (=try very hard to hear or see) *I strained my ears, listening for any sound in the silence of the cave.* | **strain yourself** (=try too hard) *Don't strain yourself! You need to rest more.*

**3** ▶ **LIQUID** ◀ [T] to separate solid things from a liquid by pouring the mixture through something with very small holes in it —see picture on page 834

**4** ▶ **BEYOND A LIMIT** ◀ [T] to force something to be used to a degree that is beyond a normal or acceptable limit: *The influx of refugees is straining our limited facilities.* | **strain sth to the limit** *I tell you, my patience has been strained to the limit!*

**5 strain a friendship/relationship etc** to behave in a way that causes problems in a friendship etc: *Too many arguments about money can strain a relationship.*

**6** ▶ **PULL/PUSH** ◀ [I] to pull hard at something or push hard against something: [+ **against**] *Buddy's huge gut strained against the buttons on his shirt.* | [+ **at**] *a ship straining at its moorings*

**7 strain every nerve** to try as hard as possible to do something: *a comedian straining every nerve to get a laugh*

**8 straining at the leash** eager to be allowed to do what you want: *30,000 troops straining at the leash and the generals locked in indecision*

**strained** /streɪnd/ *adj* **1** a situation or behaviour that is strained makes people feel nervous and uncomfortable, and unable to behave naturally; TENSE¹ (1): *I couldn't stand the strained atmosphere at dinner anymore.* **2** showing the effects of worry or too much work: *Dinah's face looked white and strained.*

**strain·er** /ˈstreɪnə‖-ər/ *n* [C] a kitchen tool for separating solids from liquids: *a tea strainer*

**strait¹** /streɪt/ *n* [C] **1** also **straits** [plural] a narrow passage of water between two areas of land, usually connecting two seas: *the Strait of Gibraltar* **2 be in dire straits** to be in a difficult situation, especially a financial one, that could have very bad or dangerous results: *If one of the family is in dire straits, we try to help each other out.*

**strait²** *adj biblical* narrow and therefore usually difficult to pass through

**strait·ened** /ˈstreɪtnd/ *adj formal* **in straitened circumstances** in a difficult situation because of a lack of money: *an elderly spinster living in straitened circumstances*

**strait·jack·et, straightjacket** /ˈstreɪtˌdʒækɪ̵t/ *n* [C] **1** a special piece of clothing that is used to control the movements of someone who is mentally ill and violent **2** something such as a law or set of ideas that puts unfair limits on someone: *the straitjacket of censorship*

**strait·laced** /ˌstreɪtˈleɪst◂/ *adj* having strict, old-fashioned ideas about moral behaviour: *So then Sally and her straitlaced friend showed up and we all had to shut up.*

**strand**

**strand** /strænd/ *n* [C] **1** a single thin piece of thread, wire, hair etc: *a strand of yarn* **2** one of the parts of a story, problem etc: *Plato draws all the strands of the argument together at the end.*

**strand·ed** /ˈstrændɪ̵d/ *adj* a person or vehicle that is stranded is unable to move from the place where they are: **leave sb/sth stranded** *The tide had gone out, leaving the boat stranded on the rocks.* | [+ **in/on/at**] *There I was, stranded in Rome with no passport and no money.*

**strange¹** /streɪndʒ/ *adj* **1** unusual or surprising, especially in a way that is difficult to explain or understand: *a strange noise* | *Does Geoff's behaviour seem strange to you?* | **that's strange** *spoken*: *That's strange. I was sure Jude was right here a second ago.* | **it's strange that/how** *It's strange that you've never met him.* |

**there's something strange about** *There's something strange about that house.* | **strange to say** *BrE* (=strangely) *Strange to say, I was just thinking that myself.* **2** someone or something that is strange is not familiar because you have not seen or met them before: *all alone in a strange city* **3 feel strange** to feel unpleasant physically or emotionally: *Can you get me a glass of water? I feel a bit strange.* —**strangeness** *n* [U]

**strange²** *adv AmE* [only after verb] in a way that is different from what is normal: *The cat's been acting really strange – I wonder if it's sick.*

**strange·ly** /ˈstreɪndʒli/ *adv* **1** in an unusual way: *Mick's been acting very strangely lately.* | *a strangely shaped shell* **2 strangely enough** [sentence adverb] used to say that although something seems unlikely, it is true: *Strangely enough, I wasn't really that disappointed.* **3** in a way that is surprising or unexpected: *Her voice was strangely familiar.*

**strang·er** /ˈstreɪndʒə‖-ər/ *n* [C] **1** someone whom you do not know: *Children must not talk to strangers.* | **perfect/complete/total stranger** (=used to emphasize that you do not know them) *A perfect stranger waved to me in the street this morning.* **2 be no stranger to sth** to have had a lot of a particular kind of experience: *My sister is no stranger to hard times.* **3** someone in a new and unfamiliar place: *"Where's the station?" "Sorry, I'm a stranger here myself."* **4 Hello, stranger!** *spoken humorous* used to greet someone you have not seen for a long time

**stran·gle** /ˈstræŋgəl/ *v* [T] **1** to kill someone by pressing on their throat with your hands, a rope etc: *The victim had been strangled with a nylon stocking.* **2** to limit or prevent the growth or development of something: *UN sanctions are slowly strangling the economy.* —**strangler** *n* [C]

**stran·gled** /ˈstræŋgəld/ *adj* **strangled cry/gasp/sound etc** a cry etc that is suddenly stopped before it is finished

**stran·gle·hold** /ˈstræŋgəlhəʊld‖-hoʊld/ *n* **1** [C usually singular] complete control over a situation, organization etc: **have a stranglehold on** *firms have a stranglehold on the production of CDs.* | **break the stranglehold of sb** (=stop someone having complete control) **2** [C] a strong hold around someone's neck that is meant to stop them from breathing

**stran·gu·late** /ˈstræŋgjȳleɪt/ *v* [I,T] if a part of your body strangulates or is strangulated, it becomes tightly pressed so that the flow of blood stops

**stran·gu·la·tion** /ˌstræŋgjȳˈleɪʃən/ *n* [U] the act of killing someone by strangling them STRANGLE (1), or the fact of being killed in this way

**strap¹** /stræp/ *n* [C] a narrow band of strong material that is used to fasten, hang, or hold onto something: *a leather watch strap* | *a backpack with adjustable straps* —see also CHINSTRAP, SHOULDER STRAP

**strap²** *v* **strapped, strapping** [T] **1** [always + adv/prep] to fasten something or somebody in place with one or more straps: **strap sb/sth in/on/down etc** *Strap that saddle on good and tight.* | **be strapped in** (=have a belt fastened around you in a car) *Are the kids strapped in?* **2** *BrE* also **strap up** [often passive] to tie BANDAGES firmly round a part of your body that has been hurt; TAPE² (4) *AmE*

**strap·hang·ing** /ˈstræpˌhæŋɪŋ/ *n* [U] *BrE informal* supporting yourself while standing in a moving bus, train etc by holding onto a strap that hangs from the roof —**straphanger** *n* [C]

**strap·less** /ˈstræpləs/ *adj* **strapless dress/gown** a dress that leaves your shoulders completely bare

**strapped** /stræpt/ *adj* **strapped (for cash)** *informal* having little or no money at the moment: *Can you lend me ten dollars? I'm a little strapped for cash.*

**strap·ping** /ˈstræpɪŋ/ *adj* [only before noun] a strapping young man or woman is strong, tall, and looks healthy and active: *a strapping young man of 15 or so*

**stra·ta** /ˈstrɑːtə‖ˈstreɪtə/ *n* **1** the plural of STRATUM **2** a plural form often used instead of STRATUM

**strat·a·gem** /ˈstrætədʒəm/ *n* [C] *formal* a trick or plan to deceive an enemy or gain an advantage

**stra·te·gic** /strəˈtiːdʒɪk/ also **stra·te·gic·al** /-dʒɪkəl/ W3 *adj* **1** done as part of a plan, especially in a military, business, or political situation: *UN forces have made a strategic withdrawal to regroup.* | *strategic bombing* **2** useful or right for a particular purpose: *Marksmen were placed at strategic points along the president's route.* **3** used in fighting wars: *secret purchases of strategic materials* | **strategic arms/weapons** (=weapons designed to reach an enemy country from your own) —**strategically** /-kli/ *adv*

**strat·e·gist** /ˈstrætȷ̇dʒȷ̇st/ *n* [C] someone who is good at planning, especially military movements

**strat·e·gy** /ˈstrætȷ̇dʒi/ *n* **1** [U] the skill of planning in W2 advance the movements of armies or equipment in a war **2** [C] a well-planned series of actions for achieving an aim, especially success against an opponent: *Our strategy was to defend and then counterattack.* | [+ **for**] *a strategy for dealing with unemployment* **3** [U] skilful planning in general: *the need to focus on strategy for the entire company*

**strat·i·fi·ca·tion** /ˌstrætȷ̇fȷ̇ˈkeɪʃən/ *n* **1** [C,U + **of**] the way that a society develops into different social classes **2** [C,U] the way that different layers of earth, rock etc develop over time **3** [C, U] the position that different layers of something have in relation to each other

**strat·i·fied** /ˈstrætȷ̇faɪd/ *adj* **1** having different social classes: *a stratified society.* **2** having several layers of earth, rock etc: *stratified rock*

**strat·o·sphere** /ˈstrætəsfɪə‖-sfɪr/ *n* **1 the stratosphere** the outer part of the air surrounding the Earth, starting at about ten kilometres above the Earth **2 the fashion/pop music etc stratosphere** a very high position in fashion etc that makes you famous

**stra·tum** /ˈstrɑːtəm‖ˈstreɪ-/ *n plural* **strata** /-tə/ [C] **1** a layer of rock of a particular kind, especially one with different layers above and below it **2** a layer of earth, such as one where tools, bones etc from an ancient civilization are found by digging **3** a social class in a society

**straw** /strɔː‖strɒː/ *n* **1 a)** [U] the dried stems of wheat S3 or similar plants that are used for animals to sleep on, and for making things such as baskets, mats etc: *a straw hat* **b)** [C] a single dried stem of wheat etc: *Some straws were sticking to his jacket.* **2** [C] a thin tube of paper or plastic for sucking up liquid: *a boy happily drinking a chocolate milkshake through a straw* **3 the last straw/the straw that breaks the camel's back** the last problem in a series of problems that finally makes you give up, get angry etc **4 a straw in the wind** *BrE* a sign of what might happen in the future: *These stories of food riots may well be straws in the wind.* **5 straw man** *AmE* a weak opponent or imaginary argument that can easily be defeated —see also **you can't make bricks without straw** (BRICK¹ (4)), **clutch at straws** (CLUTCH¹), **draw the short straw** (DRAW¹ (26))

**straw·ber·ry** /ˈstrɔːbəri‖ˈstrɒːberi, -bəri/ *n* **1** [C] a soft S3 red juicy fruit with small pale seeds on its surface, or the plant that grows this fruit: *strawberries and cream* | *strawberry jam* **2** [U] a dark pink colour —see picture on page 413

**strawberry blonde** /ˌ··· ˈ·/ *n* [C] a woman with light reddish yellow hair —**strawberry blonde** *adj*

**strawberry mark** /ˈ··· ·/ *n* [C] a reddish mark on your skin at birth that never goes away; BIRTHMARK

**straw boat·er** /ˌ· ˈ··/ *n* [C] *BrE* a stiff hat made of straw that is usually worn in summer

**straw-col·oured** /ˈ· ˌ··/ *adj* light yellow

**straw poll** /ˌ· ˈ·/ also **straw vote** *n* [C] an unofficial test of people's opinions before an election, to see what the result is likely to be

**stray¹** /streɪ/ *v* [I] **1** to leave the place where you should be without intending to: *a warship that had strayed into enemy waters* **2** to begin to deal with a different subject than the main one, without intending to: **stray into/onto sth** *We're straying into ethnic issues here.*|**stray from the subject/point/question** *Try not to stray from the point in your answers.*

**stray²** *adj* [only before noun] **1** a stray animal walks around because it is lost or has no home **2** accidentally separated from other things of the same kind: *A stray spark must have started the blaze.*|*a few stray wisps of hair*

**stray³** *n* [C] **1** an animal that is lost and cannot find its home or has no home **2** *informal* someone or something that has become separated from others of the same kind —see also **waifs and strays** (WAIF (2))

**streak¹** /striːk/ *n* [C] **1** a coloured line, especially one that is not straight or has been made accidentally: *Sue has blonde streaks in her hair.* **2** a part of someone's character that is different from the rest of their character: *Mel has a romantic streak in him.*|*a sadistic streak* **3** a period of time during which you continue to be successful or to fail: *a streak of good luck*|**be on a winning/losing streak** (=have a period of time when you continue to win or lose) *After a month-long losing streak we finally won a game.* **4 a streak of lightning** a long straight burst of LIGHTNING|**like a streak of lightning** (=very fast) *The cat shot out the door like a streak of lightning.*

**streak²** *v* **1** [I always + adv/prep] to run or fly somewhere so fast you can hardly be seen: [+ **across/along/down etc**] *Two jets streaked across the sky.* **2** [T usually passive] to cover something with streaks: [+ **with**] *Colin's face was streaked with tears.* **3** [I] to run across a public place with no clothes on to shock people

**streak·er** /ˈstriːkə‖-ər/ *n* [C] someone who runs across a public place with no clothes on to shock people

**streak·y** /ˈstriːki/ *adj* marked with streaks: *When I washed the shirt it went all streaky.*

**streaky ba·con** /ˌ·· ˈ··/ *n* [U] *BrE* smoked or salted pig meat that has lines of fat between the meat; BACON *AmE*

W3 **stream¹** /striːm/ *n* [C]

**1 ▶SMALL RIVER◀** a natural flow of water that moves across the land and is narrower than a river: *a mountain stream* —see also DOWNSTREAM, UPSTREAM

**2 ▶CONTINUOUS SERIES◀** a long and almost continuous series of events, people, objects, etc: [+ **of**] *a stream of traffic*|*A steady stream of visitors came to the house.*|*a stream of abuse*

**3 ▶AIR/WATER◀** a current of water or air, or the direction in which it is flowing: *A stream of cold air rushed through the open door.* —see also GULF STREAM, JET STREAM

**4 come on stream** *technical* to start producing something such as oil, electricity, goods etc: *The new plant will come on stream at the end of the year.*

**5 go/swim against the stream** to do or think something differently from what people in general do or think

**6 ▶SCHOOL◀** *especially BrE* a level of ability within a group of students of the same age; TRACK *AmE*: *Caroline's in the top stream.* —see also BLOODSTREAM, STREAM OF CONSCIOUSNESS

**stream²** *v*

**1 ▶POUR◀** [I always + adv/prep,T] to flow quickly and in great amounts, or to make something flow in this way; pour: [+ **out/in/onto etc**] *Water came streaming out of the burst pipe.*|*Tears streamed down her cheeks.*

**2 ▶FLOW◀** [I always + adv/prep] to move in a continuous flow in the same direction: [+ **out/across/past etc**] *The crowd streamed out of the football ground.*

**3 ▶MOVE FREELY◀** [I always + adv/prep, usually in progressive] to move freely in a current of wind or water: [+ **in/out/behind etc**] *Elise ran, her hair streaming out behind her.*

**4 ▶GIVE OUT LIQUID◀** [I,T] to produce a continuous flow of liquid: [+ **with**] *The onions made my eyes stream.*

**5 ▶SCHOOL◀** [T] *especially BrE* to put school children in groups according to their ability; TRACK² (5) *AmE*

**6 a streaming cold** *BrE* a very bad cold, with liquid flowing from your nose

**stream·er** /ˈstriːmə‖-ər/ *n* [C] **1** a long narrow piece of coloured paper, used for decoration at special occasions **2** a long narrow flag

**stream·line** /ˈstriːmlaɪn/ *v* [T] **1** to form something into a smooth shape so that it moves easily through the air or water: *All these new cars have been aerodynamically streamlined.* **2** to make something such as a business, organization etc work more simply and effectively: *efforts to streamline the production process* —**streamlined** *adj*

**stream of con·scious·ness** /ˌ· · ˈ···/ *n* [U] the expression of thoughts and feelings in writing exactly as they pass through your mind, without the usual ordered structure they have in formal writing

**street** /striːt/ *n* [C] **1** a public road in a city or town that has houses, shops etc on one or both sides: *101 Oxford Street, London*|**street map** (=showing the names and positions of all the roads)|**street musicians** (=performing outdoors in towns) —see also HIGH STREET **2 the streets** a phrase meaning the roads of a city, used to mean a place where people live who have no home and where it is difficult to survive: **on the streets** *young people living on the streets* **3 the man/woman in the street** the average person, who represents the general opinion about things: *The man in the street wouldn't have a clue what a dongle is.* **4 (right) up your street** a job or course that is up your street is exactly right for you because you have the right skills and are interested in it **5 one-way/two-way street** a process that fully involves the opinions and feelings of only one person or group, or of both people or groups: *Trust is not a one-way street.* **6 walk the streets** *old-fashioned* an expression meaning to be a PROSTITUTE **7 streets ahead (of)** *BrE informal* much better than someone or something else: *James is streets ahead of the rest of the class at reading.* —see also BACK STREET, **be on easy street** (EASY¹ (11)), SIDE STREET, STREET SMARTS S1 W1

**USAGE NOTE: STREET**

WORD CHOICE: **street, road**

A **street** is in the middle of a town, and usually has shops and other buildings and pavements (*BrE*)/sidewalks (*AmE*): *a street corner* (NOT *road corner*)

A **road** can be in the town or in the country, and usually leads to another town, or to another part of a town: *the road to Birmingham* (NOT *street*)

BRE-AME DIFFERENCES

British speakers often say **in a street or road** where American speakers say **on a street or road**: *the shops in the High Street* (*BrE*)|*the stores on Main Street* (*AmE*)|*a house in Bristol Road* (*BrE*)|*a house on Boston Road* (*AmE*).

In spoken American English words like **street** are often left out especially when giving directions to numbered streets: *Where's the Empire State Building? At 34th and 5th.* In British English this would be: *At the junction of 34th Street and 5th Avenue.*

**street·car** /ˈstriːtkɑː‖-kɑːr/ *n* [C] *AmE* a type of bus that runs on electricity along metal tracks in the road; TRAM *BrE*

**street-cred** /ˈstriːt kred/ also **street cred·i·bil·i·ty** /ˌ· ··ˈ···/ *n* [U] popular acceptance and approval among young people, especially because you know how to survive in a city: *It'll wreck your street cred if you're seen helping the police.* —**street-credible** /ˈ· ˌ···/ *adj*

**street·lamp** /ˈstriːtlæmp/ *n* [C] a streetlight

**street·light** /ˈstriːtlaɪt/ *n* [C] a light at the top of a tall post in the street —see picture on page 410

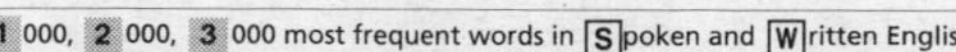

**street peo·ple** /ˈ· ˌ··/ *n* [plural] people who have no home and live on the streets

**street smarts** /ˈ· ·/ *n* [U] *AmE* the ability to deal with difficult situations on the streets of a big city: *unsuspecting tourists with no street smarts whatsoever*

**street style** /ˈ· ·/ *n* [U] style connected with the clothes, music etc of ordinary young people

**street val·ue** /ˈ· ˌ··/ *n* [C, U] the price for which a drug can be sold illegally to people: *The drugs haul had a street value of £100,000.*

**street·walk·er** /ˈstriːtˌwɔːkə‖-ˌwɒːkər/ *n* [C] *old-fashioned* a PROSTITUTE who stands on the street to attract customers

**street·wise** /ˈstriːtwaɪz/ *adj informal* clever and experienced enough to deal with difficult situations on the streets of a big city: *streetwise drug dealers overtaking the neighborhood*

S2 W2 **strength** /streŋθ, strenθ/ *n*
1 ▶ **PHYSICAL STRENGTH** ◀ [U] the physical power and energy that makes someone strong: *It took Susan weeks to regain her strength after the illness.* | **the strength to do sth** *I don't have the strength to climb any further.* | **with all your strength** *Diana pulled on the rope with all her strength.* | **not know your own strength** (=not realize how strong you are) —see also **outgrow your strength** (OUTGROW (4))
2 ▶ **OF AN OBJECT** ◀ [U] how strong an object or structure is, especially its ability to last for a long time without breaking: **[+ of]** *I have doubts about the strength of that beam in the ceiling.*
3 ▶ **OF CHARACTER** ◀ [U] the ability to deal with difficult or unpleasant situations in a brave or determined way: *moral strength* | **strength to do sth** *Where did you find the strength to keep trying?* | **strength of character** (=strong ability to deal with difficult situations) *the underlying strength of character behind Roosevelt's easy charm* | **inner strength** (=strength of spirit) *His troubles have bred in him an inner strength he'll never lose.* —see also **tower of strength** (TOWER[1] (3))
4 ▶ **OF FEELING/BELIEF/RELATIONSHIP** ◀ [U] how strong a feeling, belief, or relationship is: **[+ of]** *We can't ignore the strength of public opinion.* | *the strength of family bonds* | **strength of feeling** *Don't underestimate the strength of feeling that the abortion issue will generate.* | **strength of purpose** (=determination) *I began to feel my strength of purpose failing me.*
5 ▶ **POLITICAL/MILITARY/ECONOMIC** ◀ [U] political, military or economic power: **[+ of]** *the strength of the US economy* | **a show of strength** (=an occasion when a country shows how powerful its army etc is)
6 ▶ **OF A SUBSTANCE/MIXTURE** ◀ [C,U] how strong a substance or mixture is: *The drug is available in two strengths.* | **full-strength/half-strength/double-strength etc** *acid diluted to half-strength*
7 ▶ **USEFUL QUALITY OR ABILITY** ◀ [C] a particular quality or ability that gives someone or something an advantage: *The great strength of our plan lies in its simplicity.*
8 **position of strength** a position where you have an advantage over someone, especially in discussions: *If we keep our nuclear weapons, we can negotiate from a position of strength.*
9 ▶ **OF A TEAM/ARMY ETC** ◀ [U] the number of people in a team, army etc: **below strength** *The police force is below strength at the moment.* | **in strength** (=in large numbers)
10 ▶ **OF MONEY** ◀ [U] the value of a country's money: **[+ of]** *the strength of the dollar on the international money markets*
11 ▶ **COLOUR/LIGHT** ◀ [U] how strong a light or colour is: *the strength of the beam of light*
12 ▶ **OF A WIND/CURRENT** ◀ [U] how strong a wind or current of water is
13 **go from strength to strength** to have one success after another: *Since the advent of the personal computer, the software industry has gone from strength to strength.*
14 **on the strength of sth** because of something that persuaded you: *I bought the book on the strength of your recommendation.*
15 **give me strength** *spoken* used when you are annoyed or angry about something

**strength·en** /ˈstreŋθən, ˈstrenθən/ *v* 
1 ▶ **FEELING/BELIEF/RELATIONSHIP** ◀ [I,T] to become stronger or make something stronger: *Our friendship has steadily strengthened over the years.* | **strengthen sth** *Steve's opposition only strengthened her resolve to go ahead.*
2 ▶ **TEAM/ARMY ETC** ◀ [T] to make an organization, army etc more powerful, especially by increasing the number or quality of the people in it: *The team has been strengthened by the arrival of two Brazilian players.*
3 ▶ **MONEY** ◀ [I, T] to increase in value or to increase the value of money: *The pound has strengthened against other currencies.*
4 ▶ **FINANCIAL SITUATION** ◀ [T] to improve the financial situation of a country or company: *measures to strengthen the economy*
5 ▶ **STRUCTURE** ◀ [T] to make something physically or structurally stronger: *Metal supports were added to strengthen the outer walls.*
6 ▶ **PROOF/REASON** ◀ [T] to give support to a reason or an attempt to prove something: *Evidence from independent witnesses would greatly strengthen your case.*
7 ▶ **WIND/CURRENT** ◀ [I] to increase in force: *The wind had strengthened during the night.*

**stren·u·ous** /ˈstrenjuəs/ *adj* **1** needing great effort or strength: *a strenuous climb* | *The doctor advised Ken to avoid strenuous exercise.* **2** active and determined: **make strenuous efforts** *the strenuous efforts the council is making to improve security* —**strenuously** *adv*: *She strenuously denied the accusations.*

**strep throat** /ˌstrep ˈθrəʊt‖-ˈθroʊt/ *n* [C,U] *informal* an illness in which your throat is very painful

**strep·to·coc·cus** /ˌstreptəˈkɒkəs‖-ˈkɑː-/ *n plural* **streptococci** /-kaɪ/ [C] a BACTERIA causes infections, especially in your throat —**streptococcal** *adj*

**strep·to·my·cin** /ˌstreptəʊˈmaɪsɪ̣n, -tə-‖-toʊ-,tə-/ *n* [U] a strong drug used in medicines to kill BACTERIA

**stress**[1] /stres/ *n* **1** [C,U] continuous feelings of worry about your work or personal life, that prevent you from relaxing: *Your headaches are due to stress.* | **under stress** *Janet's been under a lot of stress since her mother's illness.* | **stresses and strains** (=problems and worries) | **stress-related** (=caused by stress) *a stress-related illness* **2** [C,U] the physical force or pressure on an object: *the stress exerted on an aircraft's wing* **3** [U] the special attention or importance given to a particular idea, fact, or activity; EMPHASIS | **put/lay stress on** *Pugh laid particular stress on the need for discipline.* **4** [C,U] the degree of force or loudness with which a part of a word is pronounced or a note in music is played, which makes it sound stronger than other parts or notes 

**stress**[2] *v* [T] **1** to emphasize a statement, fact, or idea: *I can't stress enough the need for cooperation.* **2** to pronounce a word or part of a word more forcefully or loudly: *The word 'machine' is stressed on the second syllable.*

**stressed** /strest/ *adj* **1** [not before noun] so worried and tired that you cannot relax **2** *technical* an object, especially a metal object, that is stressed has had a lot of pressure or force put on it

**stressed out** /ˌ· ˈ·◂/ *adj informal* so worried and tired that you cannot relax: *Rob looks so stressed out since he started this new job.*

**stress·ful** /ˈstresfəl/ *adj* a job, experience, or situation that is stressful makes you worry a lot: *Moving to a new house is a very stressful experience.*

**stress mark** /ˈ· ·/ *n* [C] a mark that shows which part of a word is pronounced more forcefully

**stretch**[1] /stretʃ/ *v* 
1 ▶ **MAKE STH BIGGER/LOOSER** ◀ **a)** [I,T] to make something bigger or looser by pulling it, or to become

bigger or looser as a result of being pulled: *My big, blue sweater has stretched completely out of shape.* **b)** [I not in progressive] if material stretches, it can become bigger or longer when you pull it and then return to its original shape when you stop: *Lycra shorts will stretch to fit you perfectly.*
**2 ▶ARM/BODY◀** [I,T] to straighten your arms, legs, or body to full length: *Carl sat up in bed, yawned and stretched.*
**3 ▶MAKE STH TIGHT◀** [T] to pull something so that it is tight: *a rope stretched between two poles* | **stretch sth tight** *Stretch the canvas tight over the frame.*
**4 ▶IN SPACE◀** [I always + adv/prep] to spread out or cover a large area of land: [+ **to/into/away**] *The desert stretched away as far as the eye could see.* | *a line stretching around the block*
**5 ▶IN TIME◀** [I always + adv/prep] to continue over a period of time: [+ **into/on/over**] *a research program stretching over several years*
**6 ▶RULE/LIMIT◀** [T] to allow something that would not normally be allowed by a rule or limit: *This once I'll stretch the rules and let you leave work early.* | **stretch a point** (=allow a rule to be broken) *We'll stretch a point and let the baby travel free this time.*
**7 stretch sb's patience/credulity etc** to be almost beyond the limits of what someone can accept, believe etc: **stretch sth to the limit** *Barry's behaviour has stretched my patience to the limit.*
**8 ▶ABILITIES◀** [T] to make someone use all of their skill, abilities or intelligence: *The work's too easy. The students aren't being stretched enough.*
**9 be stretched (to the limit)** to have hardly enough money or supplies for your needs: *We're stretched at the moment, otherwise I'd offer to lend you some money.*
**10 stretch the truth** to make something seem more important, bigger etc than it really is: **be stretching it** *He's a good player, but "world class" is stretching it.*
**11 not stretch to sth** if someone's money will not stretch to something, they cannot afford it: *Our savings don't stretch to a vacation this year.*
**12 stretch your legs** *informal* to go for a walk, especially after sitting for a long time —**stretchable** *adj*

**stretch out** *phr v* **1** [I always + adv/prep] *informal* to lie down, usually in order to sleep or rest: *I'm just going to stretch out on the couch for ten minutes.* **2** [T **stretch** sth ↔ **out**] to put out your hand, foot etc in order to reach something: *Jimmy stretched out his hand to take the candy.*

**stretch²** *n*
**1 ▶LENGTH OF LAND/WATER◀** [C] an area of land or water, especially one that is long and narrow: [+ **of**] *The boat rocked as it entered the stretch of rough water.* | *a beautiful stretch of countryside* | **home/final/finishing stretch** (=the last part of a track before the end of a race)
**2 ▶TIME◀** [C] a continuous period of time: [+ **of**] *a stretch of three weeks without sunshine.* | **at a stretch** (=without stopping) *I couldn't stand for hours at a stretch.*
**3 ▶BODY◀** [C] the action of stretching a part of your body out to its full length, or a particular way of doing this: *The ski instructor showed us some special stretches.*
**4 ▶MATERIAL◀** [U] the ability a material has to increase in length or width without tearing: *This elastic has lost its stretch.* —compare STRETCHY
**5 not by any stretch of the imagination** used to say that something cannot be true, even if you try very hard to imagine or believe it: *You wouldn't call him smart by any stretch of the imagination, but he did ok for himself.*
**6 ▶JAIL◀** [C usually singular] *informal* a period of time spent in prison
**7 at full stretch** *BrE* **a)** using everything that is available: *The emergency services were at full stretch after the motorway pile-up.* **b)** with your body or part of your body stretched as far as possible: *He dived and caught the ball at full stretch.*

**stretch·er¹** /ˈstretʃə‖-ər/ *n* [C] a covered frame for carrying someone who is too injured or ill to walk

**stretcher²** *v* [T always + adv/prep] to carry someone on a stretcher: **stretcher sb off/into etc** *Ward was stretchered off early in the game after a tackle by Townley.*

**stretcher-bear·er** /ˈ·· ˌ··/ *n* [C] someone, usually a soldier, who carries one end of a stretcher

**stretch lim·o** /ˈstretʃ ˌɪməʊ‖-moʊ/ also **stretch lim·ou·sine** /ˈ· ˌ···,ˈ· ··ˌ·/ *n* [C] a very large comfortable car that has been made longer than usual

**stretch·mark** /ˈstretʃmɑːk‖-mɑːrk/ *n* [C usually plural] a mark left on a your skin as a result of it stretching too much, especially during PREGNANCY

**stretch·y** /ˈstretʃi/ *adj* material that is stretchy can stretch when you pull it and then return to its original shape: *stretchy cotton leggings*

**strew** /struː/ *v past participle* **strewn** /struːn/ or **strewed** [T usually passive] **1** to scatter things around a large area: [+ **around/about/over**] *I found papers strewn all over the room.* | **be strewn with** *The yard was strewn with garbage.* **2** *literary* to lie scattered over something: *Flowers strewed the path.* **3 strewn with** containing a lot of something: *conversation liberally strewn with swear words*

**strewth** /struːθ/ *interjection BrE and AustrE* used to express surprise, annoyance etc

**stri·at·ed** /straɪˈeɪtɪ̣d‖ˈstraɪeɪtɪ̣d/ *adj technical* having narrow lines or bands of colour; STRIPED

**stri·a·tion** /straɪˈeɪʃən/ *n technical* [C usually plural] one of a number of narrow lines or bands of colour; STRIPE (1)

**strick·en** /ˈstrɪkən/ *adj formal* very badly affected by trouble, illness, unhappiness etc: *Supplies of medicine were rushed to the stricken city.* | [+ **by/with**] *stricken with a fatal disease* | **poverty stricken** (=very poor) *poverty stricken areas riddled with disease* | **panic stricken** (=filled with sudden terror) *Panic stricken crowds swarmed into the square.* | **grief stricken** *A grief stricken mother from Kansas wrote in to tell me of her tragedy.*

**strict** /strɪkt/ *adj* **1** someone who is strict demands that rules should always be obeyed: *a strict teacher* | [+ **with**] *The Stuarts are very strict with their children.* | [+ **about**] *This company is very strict about punctuality.* **2** a strict order or rule is one that must be obeyed: *You had strict instructions not to tell anybody.* | **in the strictest confidence** (=it must be kept completely secret) *I'm telling you this in the strictest confidence.* **3** [usually before noun] exact and correct, but often unreasonably exact: *He's using 'trust' in the strict legal sense.* **4 strict Muslim/vegetarian etc** someone who obeys all the rules of a particular religion, belief etc —**strictness** *n* [U] S3

**strict·ly** /ˈstrɪktli/ *adv* **1** exactly and completely: *That isn't strictly true.* **2 strictly speaking** used when you are using words or explaining rules in an exact and correct way: *Strictly speaking, spiders are not insects, although most people think they are.* **3** only for a particular person or thing and no one else: *This is strictly between us. Nobody else must know.* **4** in a way that must be obeyed: *Discipline will be strictly enforced.*

**stric·ture** /ˈstrɪktʃə‖-ər/ *n* [C often plural] *formal* **1** a severe criticism **2** [+ **on/against**] a rule that strictly limits you morally or physically

**stride¹** /straɪd/ *v past tense* **strode** /strəʊd‖stroʊd/ *past participle* **stridden** /ˈstrɪdn/ [I always + adv/prep] to walk quickly with long steps: [+ **across/into/down**] *Clarice jumped off the porch and strode across the lawn.*

**stride²** *n*
**1 ▶WALKING◀** [C] a long step: *Paco reached the door in only three strides.*
**2 ▶PATTERN OF STEPS◀** [U] the pattern of your steps or the way you walk or run; GAIT: *the runner's long, loping stride*
**3 ▶IMPROVEMENT◀** [C] an improvement in a situation or in the development of something: **make great/big/giant strides** *We've made great strides in medical technology this century.*
**4 get into your stride** *BrE*, **hit your stride** *AmE* to become comfortable with a job so you can do it

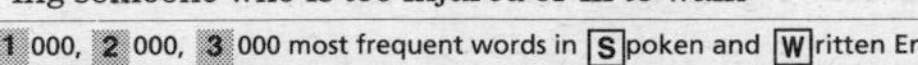

continuously and well: *Once I get into my stride I can finish the essay in a few hours.*
**5 take sth in your stride** to not allow something to annoy, embarrass, or upset you in any way: *Eva took all the setbacks in her stride.*
**6 put sb off their stride** to make someone stop giving all their attention to what they are doing: *Knowing that Bob was watching the game really put me off my stride.*
**7 (match sb) stride for stride** to manage to be just as fast, strong, skilled etc as someone else even if they keep making it harder for you
**8 without breaking stride** *especially AmE* without allowing something to interrupt or annoy you: *Zeke dealt with the reporters' questions without breaking stride.*
**9 strides** [plural] *AustrE informal* trousers

**stri·dent** /ˈstraɪdənt/ *adj* **1** a sound or voice that is strident is too loud and high and sounds unpleasant: *the strident blaring of a military band* **2** forceful and determined: *the strident demands of the American media* —**stridently** *adv* —**stridency** *n* [U]

**strife** /straɪf/ *n* [U] *formal* trouble between two people or groups; CONFLICT[1]: *a time of political strife*

## strike¹ /straɪk/ *v past tense and past participle* struck /strʌk/

① THINK/NOTICE
② STOP WORK
③ HIT
④ LIGHTNING
⑤ ATTACK/HARM
⑥ EXPRESS AN OPINION/FEELING
⑦ CLOCKS
⑧ STRONG FEELINGS
⑨ FIND
⑩ DO STH
⑪ OTHER MEANINGS

### ① THINK/NOTICE

**1** [T not in progressive] if a thought or idea strikes you, you suddenly realize that it is important, interesting, surprising, bad etc: *The funny side of the affair suddenly struck her.* | **it strikes sb that** *It struck Carol that what he'd said about Helen applied to her too.* | **be struck by** *We were struck by the generosity of even the poorest citizens.* —see OCCUR (USAGE)
**2 strike sb as sth** to seem to have a particular quality or feature: *His jokes didn't strike Jack as being very funny.* | *How did he strike you?* (=how did he seem to you?) **it strikes sb as** *It strikes me as a great idea.* | **strike sb as strange/odd/funny etc** *It struck me as odd at the time.*
**3 strike the eye** to be particularly noticeable: *What strikes your eye at once is her gorgeous red hair.*

### ② STOP WORK

**4** [I] to deliberately stop working for a time because of a disagreement about pay, working conditions etc: *The police are forbidden to strike.* | **strike for** *We're striking for another two dollars an hour.*

### ③ HIT

**5** [I always + adv/prep, T] *formal* to hit or knock hard against something: **strike (sth) against** *Then my shovel struck against something metallic.* | **strike sb/sth on** *A snowball struck him on the back of the head.* | **strike sth** *My foot struck a rock.* | **be struck by sth** *The car had been struck by a falling tree.*
**6 ▶WITH YOUR HAND◀** [T] *formal* to deliberately hit someone or something hard, especially with your hand: *I wouldn't dream of striking a woman.* | *strike the bass drum* | **strike sth with** *He struck the table with his fist.* | **strike a blow** *The blow was almost certainly struck with the left hand.* | **strike home** (=hit something exactly where you were aiming to hit it) *His sword struck home deep into the bull's neck.*
**7 strike a match/light** to light a match by hitting it against a hard surface

### ④ LIGHTNING

**8** [I,T] when LIGHTNING strikes something, it hits and damages it: *That old forked tree was once struck by lightning.*

### ⑤ ATTACK/HARM

**9** [I] to attack quickly and suddenly: *When the snake strikes, its mouth opens wide.* | *Police fear that the killer will strike again.* | **strike at** *This law strikes at the most vulnerable groups in our society.* | **strike at the heart of** *spending cuts that strike at the heart of socialized medicine*
**10** [I] if something unpleasant strikes, it suddenly happens: *Tragedy struck two days later when Tammy was in a serious car accident.*
**11** [I] to do something that gives you an advantage or harms your opponent in a fight, competition etc: *Brazil struck first with a goal in the third minute.* | **strike the first blow** (=gain the first advantage)
**12 strike a blow for** to do something to help an idea, belief, or organization: *It's time we struck a blow for women's rights.*
**13 strike a blow at** to have a harmful effect on people's behaviour or beliefs: *This latest research strikes a blow at the foundations of psychiatry.*

### ⑥ EXPRESS AN OPINION/FEELING

**14 strike a chord** to express an opinion or idea that other people agree with or have sympathy with: *Powell's angry speech struck a deep chord with his audience.*
**15 strike a happy/cheerful/cautious etc note** to express a particular feeling or attitude: *The article struck a conciliatory note.* | **strike the right note/a discordant note** (=express or fail to express what people are feeling) *Her speech appeared to strike exactly the right note.*
**16 strike home** if something that you say strikes home, it has exactly the effect on someone that you intended: *Anna's criticism of his laziness really struck home.*

### ⑦ CLOCKS

**17** [I,T] when a clock strikes or strikes one, six etc, its bell sounds a certain number of times to show what the time is: *The church clock began to strike twelve.* | **strike the hour** (=strike when it is exactly one o'clock, two o'clock etc)

### ⑧ STRONG FEELINGS

**18 strike terror/fear/a chill into sb's heart** to make someone feel afraid: *The word 'cancer' still strikes terror into many hearts.*
**19 be struck dumb** to be unable to speak, usually because you are very surprised: *When the Queen shook my hand, I was struck dumb.*

### ⑨ FIND

**20 strike gold/oil etc** to suddenly find gold, oil etc,

especially after you have been looking for it: *They finally struck gold in 1886.*
**21 strike it rich/lucky** to suddenly make a lot of money or have good luck: *With her last book she's really struck it rich.*

**⑩ DO STH**
**22 strike a balance** to give the correct amount of importance or attention to two opposing things: **strike the right balance** *The speech strikes the right balance between humour and seriousness.*
**23 strike a bargain/deal** to agree to do something if someone else does something for you: *The US and China have recently struck a deal over trade.*
**24 strike while the iron is hot** [usually imperative] to do something immediately rather than waiting until a later time when you are less likely to succeed

**⑪ OTHER MEANINGS**
**25 ▶ LIGHT ◀** [T] to fall on a surface: *What happens when light strikes a glass lens?*
**26 be within striking distance** to be very close to something or very near to achieving something
**27 strike a pose/attitude** to stand or sit with your body in a particular position: *Eva walked to the middle of the room, turned, and struck a pose with her head to one side.*
**28 strike sb/sth off/from** to remove a name or a thing from a written list: *We had to strike him off the short list.*
**29 ▶ TENT/SAIL ◀** [T] to take down a tent or sail: **strike camp** (=take down tents when leaving a camping place)

**strike back** *phr v* [I] to attack someone who has attacked you first: *The rebels struck back within hours.*

**strike** sb ↔ **down** *phr v* [T] **1** to hit someone so hard that they fall down **2** [usually passive] to make someone die or become seriously ill: *Hundreds died that winter, struck down by pneumonia.*

**strike off** *phr v* **be struck off** *BrE* if a doctor, lawyer etc is struck off, their name is removed from the official list of people who are allowed to work as doctors etc

**strike on/upon** sth *phr v* [T] **1** to discover something or have a good idea about something: *At last I've struck on a plan that might work.* **2 be struck on** *BrE informal* to think that something is good or well made: *I'm not very struck on these chocolates.*

**strike out** *phr v*
**1 ▶ NAME ◀** [T **strike** sth ↔ **out**] to draw a line through something written on a piece of paper
**2 ▶ WALK/SWIM ◀** [I always + adv/prep] to start walking or swimming in a particular direction, especially in a determined way: *He decided to follow her, striking out in the same direction.*
**3 strike out on your/his/their own** to start doing something new or living by yourself, without other people's help: *Eric left the family business and struck out on his own.*
**4 ▶ NOT SUCCEED ◀** [I] *informal especially AmE* to be unsuccessful at something: *"Did she say she'd go out with you?" "No, I struck out."*
**5 ▶ BASEBALL ◀ a)** [I] to be unable to continue trying to hit the ball in BASEBALL, because you have already missed it three times **b)** [T **strike** sb ↔ **out**] to put a player out in BASEBALL by making them fail to hit the ball three times

**strike up** *phr v* **1** [I,T] to begin playing a piece of music: **strike up the band** (=tell it to begin playing) **2 strike up a friendship/relationship/conversation** to start to become friendly with someone

S3 W3 **strike²** *n* [C]
**1 ▶ STOP WORK ◀** a period of time when a group of workers deliberately stop working because of a disagreement about pay, working conditions etc: **miners'/train/electricity etc strike** *During the teachers' strike, all the schools were closed.* | **go on strike/on strike** *The Boston police went on strike in 1919.* | **be (out) on strike** *Within half an hour, all the drivers were out on strike.* | **come out/go out on strike** (=start one) | **call a strike** (=ask people to stop working) | **call off a strike** (=decide not to continue it) | **strike action** *The mineworkers were solidly in favour of strike action.* | **general strike** (=involving most workers in the country)
**2 hunger/rent strike** a time when someone refuses to eat or pay rent as a protest about something: *a hunger strike by political prisoners*
**3 ▶ ATTACK ◀** a military attack, especially by aircraft dropping bombs: [+ **against/on**] *nuclear strikes on several targets* | **launch a strike** *American aircraft carriers have launched several strikes.* —see also FIRST STRIKE
**4 oil strike** the discovery of oil under the ground
**5 ▶ SPORT ◀ a)** a situation in BOWLING (1) in which you knock down all the PINS (=bottle shaped objects) with one or two balls **b)** an attempt to hit the ball in BASEBALL in which you miss hitting the ball

**strike·bound** /ˈstraɪkbaʊnd/ *adj* unable to move, travel, or happen because of a STRIKE² (1): *a strikebound port*

**strike·break·er** /ˈstraɪkˌbreɪkə‖-ər/ *n* [C] someone who takes the job of someone who is striking (STRIKE¹ (4)) —compare BLACKLEG, SCAB (2) —**strikebreaking** *n* [U]

**strike·out** /ˈstraɪkaʊt/ *n* [C] if the PITCHER (3) in BASEBALL throws a strikeout, he puts the player out by throwing three strikes (STRIKE² (5)) —see also **strike out** (STRIKE¹)

**strike pay** /ˈ· ·/ *n* [U] money paid to workers who are striking (STRIKE¹ (4)) by their union

**strik·er** /ˈstraɪkə‖-ər/ *n* [C] **1** someone who is striking (STRIKE¹ (4)) **2** a player in football whose main job is to kick a GOAL (2)

**strik·ing** /ˈstraɪkɪŋ/ *adj* **1** unusual or interesting enough to be noticed: **a striking contrast** *a striking contrast between the luxury hotels and the ghettos just a block away* **2** someone who is striking is very attractive, often in an unusual way: *a dark man with striking features* —see also **be within striking distance** (STRIKE¹ (27)), —**strikingly** *adv*

**string¹** /strɪŋ/ *n* S3 W2
**1 ▶ THREAD ◀** [C,U] a strong thread made of several threads twisted together, used for tying or fastening things: *Can you find me some string to tie up this package?* | *Puppets are worked by strings.* | *a piece of string*
**2 ▶ GROUP/SERIES ◀** [C] **a)** a number of similar things or events coming one after another: [+ **of**] *a string of hit albums* **b)** a group of similar things: [+ **of**] *She owns a string of health clubs.* **c)** *technical* a group of letters, words, or numbers, especially in a computer PROGRAM
**3 a string of pearls/beads/onions** several objects of the same kind connected with a thread
**4 ▶ MUSIC ◀ a)** [C] one of the long thin pieces of wire, NYLON etc that is stretched across a musical instrument and produces sound **b) strings** [plural] the people in an ORCHESTRA who play the instruments that have strings, such as VIOLINS
**5 have sb on a string** *informal* to be able to make someone do whatever you want: *Susie has her mother on a string.*
**6 no strings (attached)** if an agreement or relationship has no strings, there are no special conditions or limits: *The policy offers 15% interest with no strings attached.*
**7 pull strings** to secretly use your influence with important people in order to get what you want or help someone else: *Phil had to pull a few strings to get them to give me the job.* | **pull sb's strings** (=control them)
**8 have more than one string to your bow** to have more than one skill, idea, plan etc that you can use if you

need to —see also G-STRING, **hold/control the purse strings** (PURSE[1] (6))

**string²** *v past tense and past participle* **strung** /strʌŋ/ [T] **1** to put things together onto a thread, chain etc: *beads strung on a silver chain* **2** [always + adv/prep] to hang things in a line, high up, especially for decoration: [+ **string sth up/along/across etc**] *Dad had strung brightly-colored lights up in the back yard.* **3** to put a string or a set of strings onto a musical instrument

**string along** *phr v informal* **1** [T] to deceive someone for a long time by making them believe that you will help them, that you love them etc: *Timms will never pay you back; he's just stringing you along.* **2** [I] *BrE* to go somewhere with someone for a short time, especially because you do not have anything else to do: [+ **with**] *If you're going into town, I'll string along with you.*

**string** sth ↔ **out** *phr v* [T] **1** [usually passive] to spread something out in a long line: *The islands were strung out along the coastline.* —see also STRUNG-OUT **2** *informal* to make something last longer: *The whole deal was strung out for a lot longer than necessary.*

**string** sth ↔ **together** *phr v* [T] **string two words/sentences together** to say something that makes sense to other people: *He was so drunk he could hardly string two words together.*

**string** sth/sb ↔ **up** *phr v* [T] *informal* to kill someone by hanging them: *He should be strung up for what he did to that girl.* —see also STRUNG-UP

**string bean** /ˌ· ˈ·/ *n* [C] *especially AmE* a green bean with long thin pods (POD[1] (1)) that are eaten as food; RUNNER BEAN *BrE* —see picture on page 414

**stringed in·stru·ment** /ˌ· ˈ···/ *n* [C] a musical instrument that produces sound from a set of strings (STRING[1] (4)), such as a VIOLIN

**strin·gent** /ˈstrɪndʒənt/ *adj* **1 stringent rule/test/condition** very strict and must be obeyed: *stringent anti-noise regulations* **2** stringent economic conditions exist when there is a severe lack of money and strict controls on the supply of money —**stringently** *adv* —**stringency** *n* [U]

**string·er** /ˈstrɪŋə‖-ər/ *n* [C] someone who regularly sends in news stories to a newspaper, but who is not employed by that newspaper

**string tie** /ˌ· ˈ·/ *n* [C] a thick string worn around your neck and held in place by a decorative object, worn by men in the western US

**string·y** /ˈstrɪŋi/ *adj* **1** meat, fruit, or vegetables that are stringy are full of thin pieces that are difficult to eat: *Scoop out the pumpkin's stringy fibres.* **2** hair that is stringy is very thin and looks like string, especially because it is dirty: *old men with stringy beards leaning on walking sticks* **3** someone or a part of their body that is stringy is very thin so that their muscles show through their skin; WIRY: *I'd like to wring his stringy little neck!*

**strip¹** /strɪp/ *v* **stripped, stripping**

**1 ▶ TAKE OFF CLOTHES ◀** also **strip off** [I,T] to take off your clothes or take off someone else's clothes: *Jack stripped off and jumped into the shower.* | **strip sb** *The police stripped us all, looking for drugs.* | **stripped to the waist** (=not wearing any clothes on the top half of your body) | **strip down to your pants/socks etc** (=take off all your clothes except your pants etc) | **strip naked** (=remove all your clothes)

**2 ▶ REMOVE A LAYER ◀** [T] to remove something that is covering the surface of something else: **strip sth off/from** *We need to strip the wallpaper off the walls first.* | **strip sth of** *a branch stripped of its bark*

**3 strip sb of sth** to take away something important from someone as a punishment, for example their title, property, or power: *Captain Evans was found guilty and stripped of his rank.*

**4 ▶ ENGINES/EQUIPMENT ◀** also **strip down** [T] to separate an engine or piece of equipment into pieces in order to clean or repair it; DISMANTLE

**5 ▶ BUILDING/SHIP ◀** [T] to remove everything that is inside a building, ship, car etc so that it is completely empty: *The house was stripped by thieves.* —see also ASSET STRIPPING

**strip** sth ↔ **away** *phr v* [T] to gradually get rid of habits, customs etc: *Changes in society have stripped away men's role as protector and breadwinner.*

**strip²** *n* [C] **1** a long narrow piece of paper, cloth etc: *a* W3
*strip of paper* **2** a long narrow area of land: *A strip of sand between the cliffs and the sea.* **3 do a strip** to take your clothes off, especially in a sexually exciting way as a form of entertainment **4** *AmE* a road with a lot of shops, restaurants etc along it: *I could see the outline of the neon lights of the strip through the haze.* **5** *BrE* the clothes of a particular colour worn by a team: *Liverpool's famous red strip.* **6** a STRIP CARTOON —see also COMIC STRIP, LANDING STRIP, **tear sb off a strip** (TEAR[2] (9))

**strip car·toon** /ˌ· ·ˈ·/ *n* [C] *BrE* a series of drawings inside a row of small boxes that tells a short story COMIC STRIP *AmE* —compare CARTOON (1)

**strip club** /ˈ· ·/ *n* [C] a place where people go to see performers who take off their clothes to music

**stripe** /straɪp/ *n* [C] **1** a line of colour, especially one of several lines of colour all close together: *a shirt with black and white stripes* **2** a narrow piece of material worn on the arm of a uniform as a sign of rank: *A sergeant has three stripes.* **3 earn your stripes** *informal* to do something to deserve a particular rank or position

**striped** /straɪpt/ *adj* having lines or bands of colour: *a blue and white striped T-shirt* —see picture on page 839

**strip joint** /ˈ· ·/ *n* [C] *informal* a strip club

**strip light·ing** /ˈ· ˌ··, ˌ· ˈ··/ *n* [U] lighting provided by long, white FLUORESCENT tubes, usually in public buildings rather than in houses —see picture at LIGHT[1]

**strip·ling** /ˈstrɪplɪŋ/ *n* [C] *literary* a boy who is almost a young man

**strip mall** /ˈ· ·/ *n* [C] *AmE* a small shopping centre that consists of a single row of shops with parking spaces in front of them

**strip min·ing** /ˈ· ˌ··/ *n* [U] *especially AmE* a method of getting metal, coal etc by removing the earth from the surface of the ground, rather than by digging a passage under the ground —compare OPENCAST

**strip·per** /ˈstrɪpə‖-ər/ *n* [C] **1** someone, especially a woman, who takes off their clothes in a sexually exciting way in order to entertain people **2** a tool or liquid used to remove something from a surface: *paint stripper*

**strip pok·er** /ˌ· ˈ··/ *n* [C] a game of POKER (=card game) in which players that lose take off pieces of their clothing

**strip search** /ˈ· ·/ *n* [C] a process in which you have to remove your clothes so that your body can be checked, usually for hidden drugs

**strip show** /ˈ· ·/ *n* [C] a form of entertainment where people, especially women, take off their clothes in a sexually exciting way

**strip·tease** /ˈstrɪptiːz, ˌstrɪpˈtiːz/ *n* [C,U] a performance in which someone, especially a woman, takes off their clothes in a sexually exciting way —**striptease** *v* [I]

**strip·y** /ˈstraɪpi/ *adj BrE* STRIPED

**strive** /straɪv/ *v past tense* **strove** /strəʊv‖stroʊv/ *past participle* **striven** /ˈstrɪvən/ [I] *formal* to make a great effort to achieve something: [+ **for/after**] *We must continue to strive for greater efficiency.* | **strive to do sth** *The film studio is striving to improve its public image.*

**strobe light** /ˈstrəʊb ˌlaɪt‖ˈstroʊb-/ also **strobe** *n* [C] a light that flashes on and off very quickly, often used in places where you can dance

**strode** /strəʊd‖stroʊd/ the past tense of STRIDE

**stroke¹** /strəʊk‖stroʊk/ *n* [C] S3

**1 ▶ ILLNESS ◀** an occasion when a blood tube in your brain suddenly bursts or is blocked: *He was paralyzed by a severe stroke* | **have/suffer a stroke** *I'm afraid your aunt has had a slight stroke.*

**2 ▶ SWIMMING/ROWING ◀ a)** one of a set of movements in swimming or rowing in which you move your arms or the OAR forward and then back repeatedly: *She*

*swam with strong steady strokes.* **b)** a style of swimming or rowing: *the back stroke* **c)** the person who sets the speed at which everyone in the boat rows
**3 a) at a/one stroke** with a single sudden action: *Brian saw a chance of solving all his problems at one stroke.* **b) a bold stroke** something that someone does to achieve something that seems very brave
**4 ► A HIT ◄** an action in which you hit someone with something such as a whip or thin stick: *He cried out at each stroke of the whip.*
**5 on the stroke of seven/nine etc** at exactly seven o'clock etc: *She arrived punctually on the stroke of five.*
**6 ► CLOCK/BELL ◄** a single sound made by a clock giving the hours, or by a bell, GONG etc: *Maria appeared on the final stroke of the dinner gong.*
**7 a stroke of luck/fortune** something lucky that happens to you unexpectedly: *By an amazing stroke of luck, I ran into her that very evening.*
**8 a stroke of lightning** a bright flash of lightning, especially one that hits something
**9 a stroke of genius/inspiration etc** a very good idea about what to do to solve a problem: *It was a stroke of genius to make her the party chairman.*
**10 ► SPORT ◄** a hitting of the ball in games such as tennis, golf and cricket: *learn to play the basic backhand strokes*
**11 ► A MOVEMENT OF YOUR HAND ◄** a gentle movement of your hand over something: **give sth a stroke** *She gave the dog a stroke.*
**12 ► PEN/BRUSH ◄ a)** a single movement of a pen or brush when you are writing or painting: *Max made a few quick decisive strokes with his brush.* **b)** a line made by doing this: *the thick downward strokes of the characters*
**13 with/at a stroke of the pen** if you do something with a stroke of the pen, you do it by signing a piece of paper: *You cannot wipe out a thousand years of history at the stroke of a pen.*
**14 not do a stroke (of work)** *informal* to not do any work at all
**15 put sb off their stroke** *informal* to make someone stop giving all their attention to what they are doing: *Seeing Frank watching me put me off my stroke.*
**16 ► IN NUMBERS ◄** *BrE* used when you are saying a number written with the mark (/) in it: *The serial number is seventeen stroke one.* (=17/1)

**stroke²** *v* [T] **1** to move your hand gently over something: *He reached out and stroked her cheek tenderly.* —see picture on page 1260 **2** [always + adv/prep] to move something somewhere with gentle movements of your hand

**stroll** /strəʊl‖stroʊl/ *v* [I] to walk somewhere in a slow relaxed way: [+ **along/across/around**] *We strolled around the park for an hour or so.* —**stroll** *n* [C] —see picture on page 1262

**stroll·er** /ˈstrəʊlə‖ˈstroʊlər/ *n* [C] *AmE* a small chair on wheels in which a small child sits and is pushed along; PUSHCHAIR *BrE* —see picture at PRAM

**stroll·ing** /ˈstrəʊlɪŋ‖ˈstroʊ-/ *adj* [only before noun] a strolling entertainer travels around the country giving informal performances on the way

S1 W1 **strong** /strɒŋ‖strɔːŋ/ *adj*
**1 ► PHYSICAL STRENGTH ◄** having a lot of physical power so that, for example, you can lift heavy things: *He was a very strong man.* | *her strong hands*
**2 ► THINGS ◄** not easily broken or destroyed: *a tall, strong tree* | *a pair of strong scissors*
**3 ► ABLE TO DEAL WITH DIFFICULTY ◄** determined and able to deal with a difficult or upsetting situation: *I wasn't sure whether I was strong enough to go to the funeral.* | *My grandmother was a strong woman.*
**4 ► POWER ◄** having a lot of power or influence: *Margaret Thatcher was certainly a strong leader.* | *a strong navy*
**5 ► HEALTHY ◄** healthy, especially after you have been ill: *I don't think her heart is very strong.* | **have a strong constitution** (=be healthy and not easily become ill)
**6 ► FEELINGS/OPINIONS ◄** strong emotions, opinions, beliefs etc are ones that you feel or believe a lot and are very serious about: *The subject of abortion always arouses strong emotions.* | *Harris has received strong support from her colleagues.* | **strong sense of sth** *He has always had a strong sense of duty.*
**7 ► AFFECT/INFLUENCE ◄** a strong desire, influence etc affects you very much: *I was overcome by a strong desire to speak to her.* | *The temptation is very strong.*
**8 ► RELATIONSHIP ◄** a strong relationship, friendship etc is very loyal and likely to last a long time: *There is a very strong bond between the two of us.* | *He has strong links with the drugs trade.*
**9 ► ARGUMENT/REASON ETC ◄** a set of reasons that are likely to persuade other people that something is true or the correct thing to do: *There is strong evidence to support Evan's discrimination claim.*
**10 ► LIKELY ◄** likely to succeed or happen: *She's a strong candidate for the party leadership.* | **strong possibility/probability/chance** *I think there's a strong possibility that the Cowboys will win.*
**11 ► GROUP OF PEOPLE ◄** a strong team or other group of people is very good at doing something: *A strong cast was led by Leo McKern.* | *Germany has one of the strongest teams in the tournament.*
**12 ► GOOD AT ◄** something that someone is strong on is the thing that they do well: *Offence is where she's strong – her defensive play isn't good.* | **be sb's strong point/suit** *Tact never was my strong point.* | **be strong on** (=be good at doing something) *My family has always been strong on science.* | **strong subject** (=something you are studying that you are good at) *French was always my strong subject.*

**13 be in a strong position** to be in a situation where you have power over other people or are likely to get what you want: *The party has never been more popular and is in a strong position to win the election.*
**14 ► FOOD/DRINK ◄** having a lot of taste or a lot of the substance that gives something its effect: *strong coffee* | *a strong curry* | **strong drink** (=alcoholic drinks) *He hasn't touched strong drink for years.*
**15 ► TASTE/SMELL ◄** having a taste etc that you notice easily: *This cheese has a very strong flavour.* | *a strong smell of bonfires*
**16 ► LIGHT/COLOUR ◄** bright and easy to see: *The light was not very strong.*
**17 strong wind/current/tide** a wind etc that moves with great force: *strong spring tides*
**18 strong language** speech or writing that contains a lot of swearing: *This film is not suitable for children under 12 as it contains strong language.*
**19 strong accent** the way that someone pronounces words that shows clearly that they come from a particular area or country: *a strong German accent*
**20 strong nose/chin/features** a nose etc that is large and noticeable, especially in an attractive way: *She has the same strong features as her mother.*
**21 a strong pound/dollar/mark etc** a CURRENCY (=the type of money used in a country) that does not easily lose its value compared with other currencies
**22 600/10,000 etc strong** [only after number] used to give the number of people in a crowd or organization: *the 70,000 strong South African Domestic Workers Union*
**23 strong verb** *technical* a verb that does not add a regular ending in the past tense, but may change a vowel
**24 have a strong stomach** to be able to watch something unpleasant without feeling sick or upset: *It's a very violent film. You'll need a strong stomach to sit through it.*
**25 be still going strong** to continue to be active or successful, even after a long time: *I'm glad to see that the printing classes are still going strong.*
**26 be a bit strong** *especially BrE informal* to be too severe or extreme: *Describing him as "evil" was a bit strong, I thought.* —see also **come on strong** (COME¹) —**strongly** *adv*

**strong-arm** /ˈ· ·/ *adj* [only before noun] *informal* **strong-arm methods/tactics etc** methods etc that use force or violence, especially when this is not necessary —**strong-arm** *v* [T]

**strong·box** /ˈstrɒŋbɒks‖ˈstrɒːŋbɑːks/ *n* [C] a box, usually made of metal, that can be locked and is used for keeping valuable things in

**strong·hold** /ˈstrɒŋhəʊld‖ˈstrɒːŋhoʊld/ *n* [C] **1** an area where there is a lot of support for a particular way of life, political party etc: *The area is a Republican stronghold.* **2** *old-fashioned* a FORTRESS

**strong-mind·ed** /ˌ· ˈ··◂/ *adj* not easily influenced by other people to change what you believe or want: *You have to be pretty strong-minded to say "no" to him.* —**strong-mindedly** *adv* —**strong-mindedness** *n* [U]

**strong room** /ˈ· ·/ *n* [C] a special room in a bank, shop etc where valuable objects can be kept safely

**strong-willed** /ˌ· ˈ·◂/ *adj* knowing exactly what you want to do and being determined to achieve it, even if other people advise you against it

**stron·ti·um** /ˈstrɒntiəm‖ˈstrɑːntʃiəm, -tiəm/ *n* [U] a soft metal that is one of the chemical elements (ELEMENT (1))

**strop** /strɒp‖strɑːp/ *n* [C] **1** a narrow piece of leather used for sharpening a RAZOR **2 be in a strop** *BrE informal* to be annoyed about something

**strop·py** /ˈstrɒpi‖ˈstrɑːpi/ *adj BrE informal* bad-tempered and easily offended or annoyed: *Aaron, we won't go anywhere if you're going to be stroppy!* —**stroppily** *adv* —**stroppiness** *n* [U]

**strove** /strəʊv‖stroʊv/ the past tense of STRIVE

**struck** /strʌk/ the past tense of STRIKE

**struc·tur·al** /ˈstrʌktʃərəl/ *adj* connected with the structure of something: *structural damage* | *structural changes in the economy* —**structurally** *adv*

**structural en·gi·neer** /ˌ··· ··ˈ·/ *n* [C] an engineer skilled in planning the building of large structures such as bridges —**structural engineering** *n* [U]

**struc·tur·alism** /ˈstrʌktʃərəlɪzəm/ *n* [U] a method of studying language, literature, society etc in which you examine the different parts or ideas in a subject to find a common pattern —**structuralist** *adj n*

S3 W2 **struc·ture¹** /ˈstrʌktʃə‖-ər/ *n*

**1** ▶ **PARTS FORMING A WHOLE** ◀ [U] the way in which the parts of something are connected with each other and form a whole: *the structure of the brain* | *sentence structure*

**2** ▶ **BUILDING/BRIDGE ETC** ◀ [C] a large building, bridge etc, especially one that has many parts: *a six-story concrete structure*

**3** ▶ **PEOPLE/ORGANIZATIONS ETC** ◀ [C] the way in which relationships between people or groups are organized in a society or in an organization: *the power structure of world politics*

**4** ▶ **ORGANIZED ACTIVITY** ◀ [C, U] an activity that is carefully organized and planned: *Children need some sort of structure to their day.* —see also **career structure** (CAREER¹ (1))

**structure²** *v* [T] to arrange the different parts of something into a pattern or system in which each part is connected to the others: *You need to structure your arguments more carefully.*

**stru·del** /ˈstruːdl/ *n* [C,U] a type of Austrian or German cake, made of PASTRY with fruit inside: *apple strudel*

**strug·gle¹** /ˈstrʌgəl/ *v* [I] **1** to try extremely hard to achieve something, even though it is very difficult and you have a lot of problems: **struggle to do sth** *She's struggling to bring up a family on a very low income.* | [+ **for**] *a young artist struggling for recognition* **2** to fight someone who is attacking you or holding you, especially so that you can escape: [+ **with**] *Liz struggled fiercely with her attacker.* **3** if two people struggle, they fight each other for something, especially something one of them is holding: *They struggled briefly, then Ray grabbed the bag and ran.* **4** to move somewhere with great difficulty: [+ **towards/into etc**] *Kim struggled out of the wreckage, her head bleeding badly.*

**struggle on** *phr v* [I] to continue doing something that you find difficult, tiring etc: *We've lost two of our best players, but we're struggling on.*

**struggle²** *n* [C] **1** a long hard fight to get freedom, political rights etc: *the nation's struggle for independence* | **power struggle** (=a fight to get power in a country or organization) **2** a fight between two people for something, especially something one of them is holding: *After a short struggle I got the knife off him.* **3** an attempt to fight or escape from someone who is attacking you or holding on to you: *Police examined the body but found no signs of a struggle.* **4 be a struggle** if an activity, job etc is a struggle for someone, they find it very difficult to do: [+ **for**] *Reading is a struggle for Tim.* W3

**strum** /strʌm/ *v* **strummed, strumming** [I,T] to play an instrument such as a GUITAR by moving your fingers up and down across its strings

**strum·pet** /ˈstrʌmpɪt/ *n* [C] *old use* an insulting word meaning a woman who has sex for money

**strung** /strʌŋ/ the past tense and past participle of STRING²

**strung-out** /ˌ· ˈ·◂/ *adj* [not before noun] *informal* **1** if you are strung-out on a drug, that drug is affecting you a lot, so that you cannot react normally: [+ **on**] *strung-out on heroin* **2** extremely tired and worried

**strung-up** /ˌ· ˈ·◂/ *adj BrE informal* very nervous, worried, or excited

**strut¹** /strʌt/ *v* **strutted, strutting** [I] **1** to walk proudly with your head high and your chest pushed forwards, showing that you think you are important: [+ **about/across etc**] *Ryan was strutting around the office, issuing orders.* **2 strut your stuff** *informal* to show your skill at doing something: *Look at Dave strutting his stuff on the dance floor.*

**strut²** *n* **1** [C] a long thin piece of metal or wood used to support a part of a building, the wing of an aircraft etc **2** [singular] a proud way of walking, with your head high and your chest pushed forwards

**strych·nine** /ˈstrɪkniːn‖-naɪn, -niːn/ *n* [U] a very poisonous substance sometimes used in small amounts as a medicine

**stub¹** /stʌb/ *n* [C] **1** the short part that is left when the rest of something long and thin, such as a cigarette or pencil, has been used **2** the part of a ticket that is returned to you after it has been torn, as proof that you have paid **3** a piece of a cheque left in a cheque book as a record after the main part has been torn out

**stub²** *v* [T] **stub your toe** to hurt your toe by hitting it against something

**stub** sth ↔ **out** *phr v* [T] to stop a cigarette burning by pressing the end of it against something —see picture at PUT

**stub·ble** /ˈstʌbəl/ *n* [U] **1** short stiff hairs that grow on a man's face if he does not SHAVE¹ (1) | **designer stubble** (=stubble that a man has to look fashionable) **2** short stiff pieces left in the fields after wheat, corn etc has been cut —**stubbly** *adj*

**stub·born** /ˈstʌbən‖-ərn/ *adj* **1** determined not to change your mind, even when people think you are being unreasonable: **a stubborn streak** (=a stubborn part of your character) *I knew you'd be too stubborn to listen!* | **stubborn as a mule** (=very stubborn) **2 stubborn opposition/persistence etc** very strong and determined opposition etc: *The Broncos provided stubborn opposition throughout the whole game.* **3** difficult to remove, deal with, or use: *stubborn stains* —**stubbornly** *adv* —**stubbornness** *n* [U]

**stub·by** /ˈstʌbi/ *adj* short and thick or fat: *stubby little fingers*

**stuc·co** /ˈstʌkəʊ‖-koʊ/ *n* [U] a type of PLASTER¹ (1) surface on the outside walls of buildings

**stuck¹** /stʌk/ the past tense and past participle of STICK¹

**stuck²** *adj* [not before noun]
**1 ▶ FIXED ◀** fixed in a particular position and impossible to move: *Sheila tried to open the window but it was stuck.* | **get stuck** *The bus got stuck in the snow and we had to walk the rest of the way.* | **get sth stuck** *Tommy got his head stuck between the railings.*
**2 ▶ DIFFICULTY ◀** unable to do any more of something that you are working on because it is too difficult: *Can you help me with my homework Dad? I'm stuck.*
**3 ▶ SITUATION ◀** unable to escape from an unpleasant or boring situation: **[+ in/at]** *I wouldn't be able to stand being stuck in an office all day.* | **[+ with]** *I was stuck with my aunt all afternoon.*
**4 be stuck with sth** to have something you do not want because you cannot get rid of it: *We're renting the house, so we're stuck with this ugly wallpaper.*
**5 be stuck on sb** *informal* to be attracted to someone: *Jane's really stuck on the new boy in her class.*
**6 get stuck in** *BrE spoken* to start doing something eagerly and with a lot of energy: *Let's get stuck in and see if we can finish this by lunchtime.*

**stuck³** *n* [U] **be in stuck** *BrE informal* to be in trouble

**stuck-up** /ˌ· ˈ·◂/ *adj informal* proud and unfriendly because you think you are better and more important than other people: *a stuck-up officious little man*

**stud**

spike

stud *BrE* / cleat *AmE*

**stud¹** /stʌd/ *n*
**1 ▶ ON SHOES ◀** [C] one of a set of small pointed pieces of metal or plastic that are fixed onto the bottom of a running shoe, football boot etc to stop you from slipping
**2 ▶ IN YOUR EAR ◀** [C] a small, round EARRING —see picture at JEWELLERY
**3 ▶ DECORATION ◀** [C] a round piece of metal that is stuck into a surface for decoration: *a leather jacket with studs around the collar and cuffs*
**4 ▶ FOR A SHIRT ◀** [C] a small thing for fastening a shirt or collar that consists of two round, flat pieces of metal joined together by a bar —see also PRESS-STUD
**5 ▶ ANIMAL ◀** [C,U] animals such as horses that are kept for breeding: *a stud farm* | **put an animal out to stud** (=use the animal for breeding)
**6 ▶ MAN ◀** [C] *informal* an insulting word for a man who has a lot of sexual partners and who is very proud of his sexual ability
**7 ▶ BOARD ◀** [C] *AmE* the kind of board that is used to make the frame of a house

**stud²** *v* [T usually passive] *literary* to cover a surface or area with many small things: *field studded with daisies*

**stud·book** /ˈstʌdbʊk/ *n* [C] a list of names of race horses from which other race horses have been bred

**stud·ded** /ˈstʌdɪ̣d/ *adj* decorated with a lot of studs or small jewels etc: *a studded leather belt*

S1 W1 **stu·dent** /ˈstjuːdənt‖ˈstuː-/ *n* [C] **1** someone who is studying at a school, university etc: *a first year student at the University of Oslo* | **law/medical/engineering etc student** *A lot of art students live in this dorm.* | **student teacher/nurse** (=someone who is learning to be a teacher or nurse) | **A/B/C etc student** *AmE* (=someone who always earns A's etc for their work) —see also MATURE STUDENT **2 be a student of sth** to be very interested in a particular subject: *Myles was a profound student of human nature.*

**student bod·y** /ˌ·· ˈ··/ *n* [C] *AmE* all of the students in a HIGH SCHOOL, college, or university, considered as a group

**student gov·ern·ment** /ˌ·· ˈ···/ also **student council** /ˌ·· ˈ··/ *n* [C] *AmE* an elected group of students in a HIGH SCHOOL, college, or university who represent the students in meetings and who organize school activities

**student loan** /ˌ·· ˈ·/ *n* [C] a method of paying for your education in which students at a college or university borrow money from a bank or the government and repay it when they start working

**students' u·nion** /ˌ·· ˈ··/ also **student union** *n* [C] **1** a building where students go to meet socially **2** *BrE* an association of students in a particular college or university

**student teach·ing** /ˌ·· ˈ··/ *n* [U] *AmE* the period of time during which students who are learning to be teachers practise teaching in a school; TEACHING PRACTICE *BrE*

**stud·ied** /ˈstʌdid/ *adj* a studied way of behaving is deliberate and often insincere because you have planned your behaviour carefully: *She spoke with studied politeness.*

**stu·di·o** /ˈstjuːdiəʊ‖ˈstuːdioʊ/ *n* [C] W3
**1 ▶ FOR TELEVISION/RECORDS ◀** a room where television and radio programmes are made and broadcast or where music is recorded: *a TV studio*
**2 ▶ FILMS ◀** also **studios** a film company or the buildings it owns and uses to make its films: *Depardieu is making a film with one of the big Hollywood studios.*
**3 ▶ FOR PAINTING/PHOTOGRAPHY ◀ a)** a room where a painter or photographer regularly works **b)** a company that produces pictures or photographs
**4 ▶ FOR DANCING ◀** a room where dancing lessons are given or that dancers use to practise in
**5 ▶ APARTMENT ◀** also **studio apartment** *AmE*, **studio flat** *BrE* a small apartment with one main room

**studio au·di·ence** /ˌ··· ˈ···/ *n* [C] a group of people who watch and are sometimes involved in a radio or television programme while it is being made

**stu·di·ous** /ˈstjuːdiəs‖ˈstuː-/ *adj* **1** spending a lot of time studying and reading: *a quiet studious young man* **2** careful in your work: *studious attention to detail* —**studiously** *adv* —**studiousness** *n* [U]

**stud·y¹** /ˈstʌdi/ *n* S3 W2
**1 ▶ PIECE OF WORK ◀** [C] a piece of work that is done to find out more about a particular subject or problem, and usually includes a written report: **[+ of/into]** *We're doing a study into how much time people spend watching television.* | *a study of Australian wild birds* | **make/carry out/conduct a study** *a study of children's eating habits carried out in 1976*
**2 ▶ ROOM ◀** [C] a room in a house that is used for work or study
**3 ▶ SCHOOL WORK ◀** [U] the activity of studying: *Set aside a period of time specifically for study.*
**4 studies** [plural] subjects that people study, especially several related subjects: *the Department of Russian Studies*
**5 ▶ ART ◀** [C] a small detailed drawing, especially one that is done to prepare for a large painting: *Renoir's studies of small plants and flowers*
**6 ▶ MUSIC ◀** [C] a piece of music, usually for piano, that is often intended for practice
**7 be a study in sth** to be a perfect example of something: *His face was a study in incredulity.*
**8 be in a brown study** *old-fashioned* to be thinking deeply about something

**study²** **studied, studying** *v* **1** [I,T] to spend time reading, going to classes etc in order to learn about a subject: *I've been studying English for 6 years.* | *I can't study with that music playing all the time.* | **study to be a doctor/lawyer etc** *My brother's studying to be an*  S3 W3

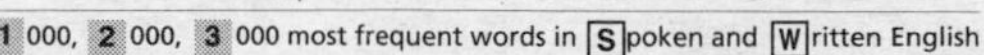

*accountant.* | **study for an exam/diploma etc** *I've only got three weeks left to study for my exams.* | **study under sb** (=be trained by a famous teacher) *a psychologist who studied under Jung in Zurich* —see KNOW[1] (USAGE) **2** [T] to watch and examine something carefully over a period of time in order to find out more about it: *Goodall was studying the behavior of gorillas in the wild.* | **study how/why/when etc** *studying how stress affects body chemistry* **3** [T] to spend a lot of time carefully examining a plan, document, problem etc: *I haven't had time to study the proposals yet.*

**study hall** /ˈ·· ·/ *n* [U] *AmE* a period of time during a school day in which a student does not have a class and usually goes somewhere to study

S1 W3 **stuff[1]** /stʌf/ *n* [U]
**1** ▶ **SUBSTANCE** ◀ *informal* a kind of substance or material: *What's that stuff you're drinking?* | *The dress was made of silky stuff.*
**2** ▶ **THINGS** ◀ *informal* a number of different things: *How do you think you're going to fit all that stuff into a car?*
**3** ▶ **SUBJECT** ◀ *informal* the subject of something such as a book, television programme, lesson etc: *What kind of stuff do you like to read?*
**4** ▶ **ACTIVITIES** ◀ all the activities that someone does: *I've got so much stuff to do this weekend.*
**5 sb's stuff** *informal* things that belong to someone: *I'm leaving in an hour and I still haven't packed my stuff.*
**6** ▶ **EQUIPMENT** ◀ *informal* the equipment you need for a particular activity: *Where's the camping stuff?*
**7 the stuff of dreams/life/politics** exactly the kind of thing that dreams etc consist of: *an enchanting place – the very stuff of dreams*
**8** ▶ **CHARACTER** ◀ the qualities of someone's character: **the right stuff** (=qualities that make you able to deal with difficulties) | **be made of sterner stuff** (=be more determined) *I thought you were made of sterner stuff – don't just give up.*
**9 do/show your stuff** to do what you are good at when everyone wants you to do it: *Come on Gina, get on the dance floor and do your stuff!*
**10 that's the stuff!** *spoken* used to express approval of what someone is doing or saying
**11 stuff and nonsense** *spoken* used to say that you think something is stupid or untrue —see also **bit of stuff** (BIT[1] (19)), **hot stuff** (HOT[1] (18)), **kid's stuff** (KID[1] (4)), **know your stuff** (KNOW[1] (13)), **strut your stuff** (STRUT[1] (2))

**stuff[2]** *v* [T]
**1** ▶ **PUSH** ◀ [always + adv/prep] to push something soft into a small space in a careless hurried way: **stuff sth into/in/up** *She stuffed two more sweaters into her bag.* | **be stuffed with** *a huge picnic basket stuffed with delicacies* | **stuffed full of** *a briefcase stuffed full of papers*
**2** ▶ **FILL** ◀ to fill something tightly with soft material, so that it becomes firm: *a pillow stuffed with feathers*
**3** ▶ **FOOD** ◀ to fill a chicken or another type of food, such as a TOMATO, with a mixture of bread, rice etc
**4** ▶ **DEAD ANIMAL** ◀ to fill the skin of a dead animal in order to make the animal look real: *a stuffed parrot*
**5 stuff yourself** also **stuff your face** *informal* to eat so much food that you cannot eat anything else: [+ **with**] *The kids have been stuffing themselves with candy.*
**6 get stuffed** *spoken* used to tell someone very rudely and angrily that you do not want to talk to them or accept their offer: *He only offered me £10 for it, so I told him to get stuffed.*
**7 you/they can stuff sth** *spoken* used to say very angrily or rudely that you do not want what someone is offering: *Yeah? Well you can stuff your damn contract!*
**8** ▶ **GAME** ◀ to defeat an opposing team easily: *We stuffed them, 15-2, 15-4, 15-3.*

**stuffed** /stʌft/ *adj* completely full, so that you cannot eat any more: *No, no dessert, I'm stuffed.*

**stuffed an·i·mal** /ˌ· ˈ···/ *n* [C] *AmE* a toy animal covered and filled with soft material; SOFT TOY *BrE*

**stuffed shirt** /ˌ· ˈ·, ˈ· ·/ *n* [C] someone who behaves in a very formal way and thinks that they are important

**stuffed-up** /ˌ· ˈ·◂/ *adj* unable to breathe properly through your nose because you have a cold

**stuff·ing** /ˈstʌfɪŋ/ *n* [U] **1** a mixture of bread, onion, egg and HERBS that you put inside meat before cooking it; DRESSING (2) *AmE*: *sage and onion stuffing* **2** soft material that is used to fill something such as a CUSHION — see also **knock the stuffing out of sb** (KNOCK[1] (10))

**stuff·y** /ˈstʌfi/ *adj* **1** a room or building that is stuffy does not have enough fresh air in it: *It's getting stuffy in here – do you mind if I open the window?* **2** someone who is stuffy is too formal and has old-fashioned ideas —**stuffily** *adv* —**stuffiness** *n* [U]

**stul·ti·fy·ing** /ˈstʌltɪ̣faɪ-ɪŋ/ *adj* so boring that you feel as though you are losing your ability to think: *a stultifying exercise* —**stultify** *v* [T] —**stultification** /ˌstʌltɪ̣fɪ̣ˈkeɪʃən/ *n* [U]

**stum·ble** /ˈstʌmbəl/ *v* [I] **1** to hit your foot against something or put your foot down awkwardly while you are walking or running, so that you almost fall: *In her hurry she stumbled and spilled the milk all over the floor.* | [+ **over/on**] *Vic stumbled over the step as he came in.* **2** to walk unsteadily and often almost fall: [+ **in/out/across etc**] *I finished the whisky and then stumbled upstairs and into bed.* **3** to stop or make a mistake when you are reading to people or speaking: [+ **over/at/through**] *I hope I don't stumble over any of the long words.* **4 stumbling block** a problem or difficulty that prevents you from achieving something: [+ **to**] *a territorial dispute which is the main stumbling block to a peace settlement* —**stumble** *n* [C]

**stumble on/across** sth *phr v* [T] to discover something or meet someone by chance and unexpectedly: *Boyce was killed because he stumbled across something he shouldn't have seen.*

**stump[1]** /stʌmp/ *n* [C]
**1** ▶ **TREE** ◀ the bottom part of a tree that is left in the ground after the rest of it has been cut down; TREE STUMP
**2** ▶ **SOMETHING BROKEN** ◀ the small useless part of something that remains after most of it has broken off or worn away: *the stump of a broken tooth*
**3** ▶ **ARM/LEG** ◀ the short part of someone's leg, arm etc that remains after the rest of it has been cut off
**4** ▶ **IN SPORT** ◀ one of the three upright sticks in CRICKET (2) that you throw the ball at
**5 stump speech** *AmE* a speech made while travelling around to get political support

**stump[2]** *v* **1** [T] to ask someone such a difficult question that they are completely unable to think of an answer: *trying to stump the teacher* | **be stumped** *Nobody knows – even the experts are stumped.* | **get/have sb stumped** *This question'll have them all stumped.* **2** [I + **up/along/across**] to walk with heavy steps; STOMP **3** [T] to put a BATSMAN out of the game in CRICKET (2) by touching the stumps with the ball when he is out of the hitting area **4** [I,T] *AmE* to travel around an area, meeting people and making speeches in order to gain political support: *I'm too old to keep stumping around the state.*

**stump up** *phr v* [I T] *BrE informal* to pay money, even if it is difficult: *That's ten quid you owe me. Come on, stump up.*

**stump·y** /ˈstʌmpi/ *adj BrE* stumpy legs, fingers etc are short and thick in an unattractive way: STUBBY

**stun** /stʌn/ *v* **stunned, stunning** [T not in progressive] **1** to surprise or upset someone so much that they do not react immediately: *Sacha was too stunned by what had happened to say anything.* | **stunned silence** (=silence because everyone is too surprised to speak) **2** to make someone unconscious for a short time: *Thank God that punch only stunned you!*

**stung** /stʌŋ/ the past tense and past participle of STING[1]

**stun gun** /ˈ· ·/ *n* [C] a weapon that produces a very strong electric current and can be used to make animals or people unconscious

**stunk** /stʌŋk/ a past tense and the past participle of STINK[1]

**stun·ner** /ˈstʌnə‖-ər/ *n* [C] *old-fashioned* someone or something that is very attractive, especially a woman

**stun·ning** /ˈstʌnɪŋ/ *adj* **1** extremely attractive or beautiful: *You look absolutely stunning in that dress.* | *a stunning view* **2** very surprising or shocking: *stunning news* —**stunningly** *adv*

**stunt[1]** /stʌnt/ *n* [C] **1** a dangerous action that is done to entertain people, especially in a film: *Not many actors do their own stunts.* **2** something that is done to attract people's attention, especially in advertising or politics: **publicity stunt** *Todd flew over the city in a hot air balloon as a publicity stunt.* **3 pull a stunt** to do something that is silly or that is slightly dangerous: *Next time you pull a stunt like that don't expect me to get you out of trouble.*

**stunt[2]** *v* [T] to stop something or someone from growing to their full size or developing properly: *Lack of sunlight will stunt the plant's growth.*

**stunt man** /ˈ· ·/ *n* [C] a man who is employed to take the place of an actor when something dangerous has to be done in a film

**stunt wom·an** /ˈ· ˌ··/ *n* [C] a woman who is employed to take the place of an actress when something dangerous has to be done in a film

**stu·pe·fied** /ˈstjuːpɪ̈faɪd‖ˈstuː-/ *adj* so surprised, tired, or bored that you cannot think clearly: *a stupefied expression* —**stupefaction** /ˌstjuːpɪ̈ˈfækʃən‖ˌstuː-/ *n* [U]

**stu·pe·fy·ing** /ˈstjuːpɪ̈faɪ-ɪŋ‖ˈstuː-/ *adj* making you feel extremely surprised, tired, or bored: *stupefying inefficiency* —**stupefy** *v* [T]

**stu·pen·dous** /stjuːˈpendəs‖stuː-/ *adj* surprisingly large or impressive: *a stupendous achievement* —**stupendously** *adv*

S1 W3 **stu·pid** /ˈstjuːpɪ̈d‖ˈstuː-/ *adj* **1** showing a lack of good sense or good judgment; silly: *stupid mistakes* | *I was very drunk last night – I hope I didn't do anything stupid.* | **it is stupid (of sb) to do sth** *It was stupid of me to lose my temper.* **2** having a low level of intelligence, so that you have difficulty learning or understanding things: *Charlie understands perfectly well what you mean. He's not stupid.* **3** *informal* used when you are talking about something that makes you annoyed or impatient: *I can't get this stupid radio to work.* **4** [singular] an insulting way of talking to someone who you think is being stupid: *No, stupid, don't do it like that!* **5 stupid with cold/sleep/shock etc** unable to think clearly because you are extremely tired, cold etc —**stupidly** *adv*: *Stupidly I forgot my umbrella and ended up getting soaked.*

**stu·pid·i·ty** /stjuːˈpɪdɪ̈ti‖stuː-/ *n* **1** [C usually plural, U] behaviour or actions that show a lack of good sense or good judgment: *all the horrors and stupidities of war* **2** [U] the quality of being stupid or unintelligent

**stu·por** /ˈstjuːpə‖ˈstuːpər/ *n* [C,U] a state in which you cannot think, speak, see or hear clearly, usually because you have drunk too much alcohol or taken drugs: **drunken stupor** *We found him lying at the bottom of the stairs in a drunken stupor.*

**stur·dy** /ˈstɜːdi‖ˈstɜːr-/ *adj* **1** someone who is sturdy is strong, short, and healthy looking: *a sturdy young man* | *sturdy legs* **2** an object that is sturdy is strong, well-made, and not easily broken: *a sturdy wall* **3** determined and not easily persuaded to change your opinions: *They kept up a sturdy opposition to the plan.* —**sturdily** *adv* —**sturdiness** *n* [U]

**stur·geon** /ˈstɜːdʒən‖ˈstɜːr-/ *n* [C,U] a large fish, from which CAVIAR is obtained, or the flesh of this fish which can be eaten

**stut·ter[1]** /ˈstʌtə‖-ər/ *v* **1** [I,T] to speak with difficulty because you cannot stop yourself from repeating the first CONSONANT of some words; STAMMER[1]: *"I'm D-d-david," he stuttered.* **2** [I] if a machine stutters, it keeps making little exploding noises and does not work smoothly

**stutter[2]** *n* [singular] an inability to speak normally because you stutter: *a nervous stutter*

**sty** /staɪ/ *n* [C] **1** a place where pigs are kept; PIGSTY[2] **2** also **stye** an infected place on the edge of your EYELID, which becomes red and swollen

**Sty·gi·an** /ˈstɪdʒiən/ *adj literary* unpleasantly dark: *the Stygian gloom*

**style[1]** /staɪl/ *n* S2 W1

**1 ▶ WAY OF DOING/MAKING ◀** [C] a particular way of doing something, designing something, or producing something, especially one that is typical of a particular period of time or of a particular group of people: *Styles of architecture* | *The Dutch created a completely new style of football.* | **Swedish/new/country etc style** (=done or made in a way that is typical of Sweden etc) *a gangland-style killing* | *The cathedral is one of the earliest examples of the gothic style.*

**2 ▶ WAY OF BEHAVING/WORKING ◀** [C] the particular way that someone does something or deals with other people: [+ **of**] *an authoritarian style of leadership* | **management/teaching etc style** *an attempt to use Japanese management style in a European business* | **it's not his/her style** (=it is not the way someone usually behaves) *I can't ask a man out – it's just not my style.* | **like sb's style** (=approve of the way someone does things, used especially by someone in authority) *I like your style, Simpson. I think you'll do well here.* | **be more sb's style** *spoken* (=used as a joking way of saying that you prefer something that does not need as much skill or bravery as something that has been mentioned) *I don't think the parachuting weekend is for me – the art class is more my style.* | **in true British/student etc style** (=in a way that is very typical of the behaviour of a particular type of person) *Then the sailors, in true navy style, drank a bottle of rum each.*

**3 ▶ DESIGN ◀** [C] the design of something, which decides what shape or appearance it will have: *Car styles have changed radically in the past 20 years*

**4 ▶ FASHION ◀** [C,U] a fashion in clothes or hair: *70's styles look very odd today.*

**5 ▶ WRITING/LITERATURE ◀** [C,U] the particular way someone uses words to express ideas, tell stories etc: *The stories are typical of Kelman's robust prose style.* —see also STYLISTIC

**6 ▶ ART/MUSIC/FILM ◀** [C,U] the typical way that someone paints, writes music etc, or a typical way of painting etc from a particular period of time: *A modern musician who composes in the style of Bach.*

**7 ▶ SPECIAL QUALITY ◀** [U] a confident and attractive quality that makes people admire you, and that is shown in your appearance, or the way you do things: **have style** *You may not like her, but she certainly has style!* —see also STYLISH

**8 in style** done in a way that people admire, especially because it is unusual, shows great determination, or involves spending a lot of money: **in great/grand/fine etc style** *Sampras won the title in fine style, not losing a single game.* —see also **cramp sb's style** (CRAMP[2] (2))

**style[2]** *v* [T] **1** to design clothing, furniture, or the shape of someone's hair in a particular way: *These shoes have been styled for maximum comfort.* | **have sth styled** *She has her hair styled by Giorgio.* **2 style yourself Lord/Dr etc** *formal* to give yourself a particular title or name: *They style themselves 'the terrible twins'.* —see also SELF-STYLED

**styling brush** /ˈ··· ·/ *n* [C] a heated brush used, especially by women, to make their hair a particular shape

**styl·ish** /ˈstaɪlɪʃ/ *adj* attractive in a fashionable way: *a stylish dresser* —**stylishly** *adv* —**stylishness** *n* [U]

**styl·ist** /ˈstaɪlɪ̈st/ *n* [C] **1** someone who cuts or arranges people's hair as their job **2** someone who has carefully developed a good style of writing

**styl·is·tic** /staɪˈlɪstɪk/ *adj* related to the style of a piece of writing or art —**stylistically** /-kli/ *adv*

**styl·is·tics** /staɪˈlɪstɪks/ *n* [U] the study of style in written or spoken language

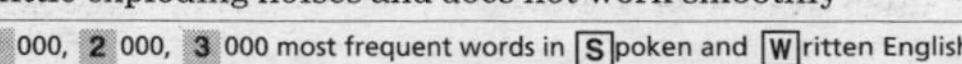

**sty·lized** also **-ised** *BrE* /ˈstaɪlaɪzd/ *adj* drawn or written in an artificial style, that does not include natural detail: *a stylised picture of a car* —**stylize** *v* [T]

**sty·lus** /ˈstaɪləs/ *n* [C] **1** the small pointed part of a RECORD PLAYER, that touches the record **2** a pointed instrument used in the past for writing on WAX[1] (1)

**sty·mie** /ˈstaɪmi/ *v* [T] *informal* to prevent someone from doing what they have planned or want to do; THWART: *He desperately wanted to save his marriage, but felt stymied and doomed to fail.*

**Sty·ro·foam** /ˈstaɪərəˌfəʊm‖ˈstaɪrəˌfoʊm/ *n* [U] *AmE trademark* a soft light plastic material that prevents heat or cold from passing through it, used especially to make containers; POLYSTYRENE *especially BrE*: *a styrofoam cup*

**suave** /swɑːv/ *adj* someone who is suave is polite, confident, and relaxed, especially in an insincere way: *a suave and sophisticated gentleman* —**suavely** *adv* —**suavity, suaveness** *n* [U]

**sub-** /sʌb/ *prefix* **1** under; below: *subzero temperatures* | *subsoil* (=beneath the surface) **2** less important or powerful than someone or something, or of lower rank than someone: *a subcommittee* | *a sublieutenant* **3** part of a bigger whole: *a subsection* **4** used to say that something is like something else, but not as good or not real: *dreary rows of sub-Victorian villas* **5** *technical* almost: *subtropical heat*

S3 **sub**[1] /sʌb/ *n* [C] *informal* **1** a SUBMARINE **2** a SUBSTITUTE in sports such as football **3** a SUBSCRIPTION **4** *BrE* part of your wages that you receive earlier than usual because you need money; ADVANCE[2] (4) *AmE* **5** *AmE* a long bread roll split open and filled with meat, cheese etc **6** *AmE* a SUBSTITUTE TEACHER **7** *BrE* a SUBEDITOR

**sub**[2] *v* **subbed, subbing** *informal* **1** [I + **for**] to act as a SUBSTITUTE for someone **2** [T] *BrE* to give someone part of their wages earlier than usual or lend them money: *I subbed Fenella a tenner to get a decent bunch of flowers.* **3** [T] *BrE* to SUBEDIT something

**sub·al·tern** /ˈsʌbəltən‖səˈbɒːltərn/ *n* [C] a middle rank in the British army, or someone who has this rank

**sub-aq·ua** /sʌb ˈækwə/ *adj* [only before noun] *BrE* related to sports that take place under water: *sub-aqua diving*

**sub·arc·tic** /ˌsʌbˈɑːktɪk◂‖-ˈɑːrk-/ *adj* near or typical of the Arctic Circle

**sub·a·tom·ic** /ˌsʌbəˈtɒmɪk◂‖-ˈtɑː-/ *adj* smaller than an atom or existing within an atom

**sub·com·mit·tee** /ˈsʌbkəˌmɪti/ *n* [C] a small group formed from a committee to deal with a particular subject in more detail

**sub·con·scious**[1] /sʌbˈkɒnʃəs‖-ˈkɑːn-/ *adj* subconscious feelings, desires etc are hidden in your mind and you do not know that you have them: *a subconscious fear of failure* —**subconsciously** *adv*

**subconscious**[2] *n* [singular] the part of your mind that has thoughts and feelings you do not know about; UNCONSCIOUS[2]

**sub·con·ti·nent** /ˌsʌbˈkɒntɪ̌nənt‖-ˈkɑːn-/ *n* [C] **1** a very large area of land that is part of a CONTINENT **2 the subcontinent** *especially BrE* the area of land that includes India, Pakistan, and Bangladesh

**sub·con·ti·nen·tal** /ˌsʌbkɒntɪ̌ˈnentl◂‖-kɑːn-/ *adj AmE* related to a subcontinent

**sub·con·tract** /ˌsʌbkənˈtrækt‖-ˈkɑːntrækt/ *v* [T] if a company subcontracts work, they pay other people to do part of their work for them: *We will be subcontracting most of the electrical work.* —**subcontract** /sʌbˈkɒntrækt‖-ˈkɑːn-/ *n* [C]

**sub·con·trac·tor** /ˌsʌbkənˈtræktər‖-ˈkɑːntræk‖-ər/ *n* [C] someone who does part of the work of another person or firm

**sub·cul·ture** /ˈsʌbˌkʌltʃər/ *n* [C] a particular group of people within a society and their behaviour, beliefs, and activities, which many people disapprove of: *the drug subculture of the inner city*

**sub·cu·ta·ne·ous** /ˌsʌbkjuːˈteɪniəs◂/ *adj technical* beneath your skin: *subcutaneous fat* —**subcutaneously** *adv*

**sub·di·vide** /ˌsʌbdɪ̌ˈvaɪd/ *v* [T] to divide into smaller parts something that is already divided: *The house was subdivided into apartments about ten years ago.*

**sub·di·vi·sion** /ˌsʌbdɪ̌ˈvɪʒən/ *n* **1** [C,U] the act of dividing something that has already been divided, or the parts that result from doing this **2** [C] *AmE* an area of land that has been subdivided for building houses on

**sub·due** /səbˈdjuː‖-ˈduː/ *v* [T] **1** to stop a person or group from behaving violently, especially by using force: *Police managed to subdue the angry crowd.* **2** *formal* to prevent your emotions from showing: *Frank subdued his grief in order to comfort Cathy.* **3** *formal* to take control of a place by defeating the people who live there: *Napoleon subdued much of Europe.*

**sub·dued** /səbˈdjuːd‖-ˈduːd/ *adj* **1** subdued lighting, colours etc are less bright than usual **2** a person or sound that is subdued is unusually quiet: *Richard seems very subdued tonight.* **3** an event or business activity that is subdued, does not have as much excitement or interest as you would expect: *The housing market is fairly subdued.*

**sub·ed·it** /ˌsʌbˈedɪ̌t/ *v* [T] *BrE* to examine other people's writing for mistakes and make them correct: COPYEDIT *AmE*

**sub·ed·i·tor** /ˌsʌbˈedɪ̌tə‖-ər/ *n* [C] *BrE* someone whose job is to examine other people's writing, such as a newspaper article, and to change mistakes

**sub·group** /ˈsʌbgruːp/ *n* [C] a separate, smaller, and sometimes less important part of a group

**sub·head·ing** /ˈsʌbˌhedɪŋ/ *n* [C] a short phrase used as a title for a small part within a longer piece of writing

**sub·hu·man** /sʌbˈhjuːmən‖-ˈhjuː-, -ˈjuː-/ *adj* behaving or thinking in a way that you do not expect from people, especially when this is very bad: *subhuman intelligence*

**sub·ject**[1] /ˈsʌbdʒɪkt/ *n* [C] S2 W2

**1** ▶ **THING TALKED ABOUT** ◀ the thing you are talking about or considering in a conversation, discussion, book, film etc: *Subjects covered in this chapter are exercise and nutrition.* | *Paul has strong opinions on most subjects.* | **change the subject** (=start talking about something different) *Stop trying to change the subject!* | **get onto the subject (of)** (=start talking about it) *How did we get onto the subject of drugs?* | **get off the subject (of)** (=start talking about something else instead of what you were supposed to be talking about) *Somehow we got off the subject of homework altogether.* | **be on the subject (of)** (=be talking about) *While we're on the subject of money, have you got the £10 you owe me?* | **be the subject of** (=be what is dealt with) *Truffaut's childhood memories were the subject of his first film.* | **be a subject of/for debate/discussion etc** *Genetic engineering is very much a subject for debate.*

**2** ▶ **ART** ◀ the thing you are dealing with when you paint a picture, take a photograph etc: *Monet loved to use gardens as his subjects.*

**3** ▶ **SCHOOL** ◀ an area of knowledge that you study at a school or university: *My favourite subject at school was English.*

**4** ▶ **TEST** ◀ a person or animal that is used in a test: *The subjects of this experiment were all men aged 18-35.*

**5** ▶ **GRAMMAR** ◀ a noun, noun phrase, or PRONOUN that usually comes before a main verb and represents the person or thing that performs the action of the verb, or about which something is stated, such as 'She' in 'She hit John' or 'elephants' in 'Elephants are big' —compare OBJECT[1] (6)

**6** ▶ **COUNTRY** ◀ someone who was born in a country that has a king or queen, or someone who has a right to live there: *a British subject* —compare CITIZEN (2), NATIONAL[2]

**subject²** *adj* **1** [not before noun] likely to be affected by something, especially something unpleasant: [+ **to**] *areas subject to strong winds|Kieran is subject to fits of depression.* **2 subject to** dependent on something else: *Your planning application is subject to review by the local council.* **3** *formal* [only before noun] a subject country, state, people etc are strictly governed by another country

**subject³** /səbˈdʒekt/ *v* [T] *formal* to force a country or group of people to be ruled by you and control them very strictly

**subject** sb/sth **to** sth *phr v* [T often passive] to force someone or something to experience something very unpleasant or difficult, especially over a long time: *Barker subjected his victim to a terrifying ordeal.*|**be subjected to** *All our products are subjected to rigorous testing.*

**sub·jec·tion** /səbˈdʒekʃən/ *n* [U] *formal* **1** the act of forcing a country or group of people to be ruled by you: *Rome was intent on the subjection of the world.* **2 in subjection (to)** strictly controlled by someone: *Grandfather kept the whole household in subjection to his wishes.*

**sub·jec·tive** /səbˈdʒektɪv/ *adj* **1** a statement, report, attitude etc that is subjective is influenced by personal opinion and can therefore be unfair: *As a critic, his writing is far too subjective.* —opposite OBJECTIVE² (1) **2** [no comparative] existing only in your mind or imagination: *our subjective perception of colours* **3** *technical* related to the subject in grammar —**subjectively** *adv* —**subjectivity** /ˌsʌbdʒekˈtɪvɪ̣ti/ *n* [U]

**subject mat·ter** /ˈ·· ˌ··/ *n* [U] what is being talked about in speech or writing, or represented in art: *The movie has been rated 'R' due to adult subject matter.*

**sub·join** /ˌsʌbˈdʒɔɪn/ *v* [T + **to**] *technical* to add a sentence or phrase at the end of a statement

**sub ju·di·ce** /ˌsʌb ˈdʒuːdɪsi‖ˌsʊb ˈjuːdɪkeɪ/ *adv* [only after verb] *law* a legal case being considered sub judice is now being dealt with by a court, and therefore is not allowed to be publicly discussed, for example in a newspaper

**sub·ju·gate** /ˈsʌbdʒʊ̣geɪt/ *v* [T] to defeat a person or group and make them obey you: *a subjugated people* —**subjugation** /ˌsʌbdʒʊ̣ˈgeɪʃən/ *n* [U]

**sub·junc·tive** /səbˈdʒʌŋktɪv/ *n* [C] a verb form or a set of verb forms in grammar, used in some languages to express doubt, wishes: *In 'if I were you' the verb 'to be' is in the subjunctive.* —compare IMPERATIVE¹ (3) INDICATIVE² —**subjunctive** *adj*

**sub·lease** /ˈsʌb-liːs‖sʌbˈliːs/ *n* [C] an agreement in which someone who rents property from its owner then rents that property to someone else —**sublease** /sʌbˈliːs/ *v* [I,T]

**sub·let** /sʌbˈlet/ *v* **subletted, subletting** [I,T] to rent to someone else a property that you rent from its owner —**sublet** /ˈsʌblet/ *n* [C]

**sub·lieu·ten·ant** /ˌsʌb-ləˈtenənt, -lef-‖-luː-/ *n* [C] a middle rank in the Royal Navy, or someone who has this rank —see table on page B4

**sub·li·mate¹** /ˈsʌblɪ̣meɪt/ *v* [I,T] *technical* to use the energy that comes from sexual feelings to do something, such as work or art, that is more acceptable to your society

**sub·li·mation** /ˌsʌblɪ̣ˈmeɪʃən/ *n* [U] **1** the process of sublimating (SUBLIMATE) **2** *technical* the process of changing a solid substance to a gas by heating it and then changing it back to a solid in order to make it pure

**sub·lime¹** /səˈblaɪm/ *adj* **1** excellent in a way that makes you feel extremely happy: *We had a sublime view over the Mediterranean.* **2** not caring or thinking at all about the result of your actions: *sublime insensitivity to other people's feelings* —**sublimely** *adv* —**sublimeness** *n* [U] —**sublimity** /səˈblɪmɪ̣ti/ *n* [U]

**sublime²** *n* **the sublime** **1** something that is excellent and makes you feel extremely happy: *The sublime, unlike beauty, can inspire awe.* **2 from the sublime to the ridiculous** used to say that a serious and important thing or event is being followed by a silly thing or event: *First Hamlet, now pantomime? That's going from the sublime to the ridiculous.*

**sub·lim·i·nal** /sʌbˈlɪmɪ̣nəl/ *adj* at a level of your mind that you are not conscious of: **subliminal messages** *Reverend Jones claims there are subliminal Satanic messages on that album.*|**subliminal advertising** (=with hidden messages and pictures in it)

**sub·ma·chine gun** /ˌsʌbməˈʃiːn gʌn/ *n* [C] a type of MACHINE GUN that is light and easily moved

**submarine**

**sub·ma·rine¹** /ˈsʌbməriːn, ˌsʌbməˈriːn/ *n* [C] a ship, especially a military one, that can stay under water: *a nuclear submarine*

**submarine²** *adj technical* growing or used under the sea: *submarine plant life*

**sub·mar·i·ner** /sʌbˈmærɪnə‖ˈsʌbməriːnər/ *n* [C] a sailor living and working in a submarine

**submarine sand·wich** /ˌ·· ˈ··/ *n* [C] *AmE* a SUB¹ (5)

**sub·merge** /səbˈmɜːdʒ‖-ˈmɜːrdʒ/ *v* **1** [I,T] to go under the surface of water, or to put something under water or another liquid: *The tunnel entrance was submerged by rising sea water.* **2** [T] to cover or completely hide something: *Feelings she thought she'd submerged were surfacing again.* **3 submerge yourself in sth** to make yourself very busy doing something: *Alice submerged herself in work to try and forget about Tom.* —**submergence** *n* [U]

**sub·merged** /səbˈmɜːdʒd‖-ˈmɜːrdʒd/ *adj* just under the surface of water or another liquid: *submerged rocks*

**sub·mersed** /səbˈmɜːst‖-ˈmɜːrst/ *adj* submersed plants etc live under the water

**sub·mer·si·ble** /səbˈmɜːsɪ̣bəl‖-ˈmɜːr-/ *n* [C] a vehicle that can travel under water

**sub·mer·sion** /səbˈmɜːʃən‖-ˈmɜːrʒən/ *n* [U] the act of going under water, or the state of being completely covered in liquid

**sub·mis·sion** /səbˈmɪʃən/ *n* **1** [U] the state of being completely controlled by a person or group, and accepting that you have to obey them: **force/frighten etc sb into submission** *The prisoners were eventually starved into submission.*|**in submission to** (=in obedience to) *I offer my resignation in submission to your request.* **2** [C,U] the act of giving a plan, piece of writing etc to someone in authority for them to consider or approve, or the plan, piece of writing etc itself: *The deadline for the submission of proposals is May 1st.* **3** [U] *formal* an opinion or thought that you state: **in my submission** *It is important, in my submission, that a wider view be taken.* **4** [C] *law* a request or suggestion that is given to a judge for them to consider S2

**sub·mis·sive** /səbˈmɪsɪv/ *adj* always willing to obey someone even if they are unkind to you: *Martin expects his wife to be meek and submissive.* —**submissively** *adv* —**submissiveness** *n* [U]

S2 W3 **sub·mit** /səbˈmɪt/ *v* **submitted, submitting** **1** [I,T] to obey someone when you have no choice about it because they have power over you: [**+ to**] *I will not submit to your bullying.* | **submit yourself to sb/sth** *Derek agreed to submit himself to questioning.* **2** [T] to give a plan, piece of writing etc to someone in authority for them to consider or approve: *All applications must be submitted by Monday.* **3** [T] *formal* to agree to obey a person, group, or set of rules: **submit sth to** *We are willing to submit to arbitration.* **4** [T] *formal* to suggest or say something: **submit that** *I submit that the jury has been influenced by the publicity in this case.*

**sub·nor·mal** /ˌsʌbˈnɔːməl◂‖-ˈnɔːr-/ *adj* less or lower than normal: *subnormal temperatures*

**sub·or·bit·al** /sʌbˈɔːbɪtl‖-ˈɔːr-/ *adj technical* making less than one complete ORBIT (=journey around the Earth) *a suborbital space flight*

**sub·or·di·nate¹** /səˈbɔːdɪnət‖-ˈbɔːr-/ *adj* less important than something else, or in a lower position with less authority: *a subordinate role on the committee* | [**+ to**] *a commission that is subordinate to the Security Council* —compare SUBSERVIENT

**subordinate²** *n* [C] someone who has a lower position and less authority than someone else in an organization

**sub·or·di·nate³** /səˈbɔːdɪneɪt‖-ˈbɔːr-/ *v* [T] to put someone or something in a less important position: **subordinate sth to sb/sth** *Joe subordinated his wishes to those of the group.* —**subordination** /səˌbɔːdɪˈneɪʃən‖-ˌbɔːr-/ *n* [U]

**subordinate clause** /·ˌ··· ˈ·/ *n* [C] a DEPENDENT CLAUSE

**sub·orn** /səˈbɔːn‖-ˈbɔːrn/ *v* [T] *law* to persuade someone to tell lies in a court of law or to do something else that is illegal, especially for money —**subornation** /ˌsʌbɔːˈneɪʃən‖-bɔːr-/ *n* [U]

**sub·plot** /ˈsʌbplɒt‖-plɑːt/ *n* [C] a PLOT (=set of events) that is less important than and separate from the main plot in a story, play etc

**sub·poe·na¹** /səˈpiːnə, səb-/ *n* [C] *law* a written order that you must come to a court of law and be a witness

**subpoena²** *v past tense* **subpoenaed** [T] *law* to order someone to come to a court of law and be a witness

**sub-post of·fice** /ˌ· ˈ· ˌ··/ *n* [C] a small British post office that has fewer services than a main post office

**sub·rou·tine** /ˌsʌbruːˈtiːn/ *n* [C] a part of a computer PROGRAM containing a set of instructions for doing a small job that is part of a larger job

**sub·scribe** /səbˈskraɪb/ *v* **1** [I] to pay money regularly to have copies of a newspaper or magazine sent to you: [**+ to**] *What newspaper do you subscribe to?* **2** [I] *BrE* to pay money regularly to be a member of an organization or to help its work: [**+ to**] *Chris subscribes to an environmental action group.* **3** [T] *BrE* to give money regularly for a service: *People in the office subscribe £1 a week for coffee.* **4** [T] *formal* to sign your name: *Please subscribe your name to the document.*

**subscribe for** sth *phr v* [T] to agree to buy or pay for shares (SHARE² (5)): *Each employee may subscribe for up to £2,000 worth of shares.*

**subscribe to** sth *phr v* [T usually in questions and negatives] if you subscribe to an idea, view etc, you agree with it or support it: *American administrations all subscribed to the belief that Communism was dangerous.*

**sub·scrib·er** /səbˈskraɪbə‖-ər/ *n* [C] **1** someone who pays money regularly to receive copies of a newspaper or magazine **2** *BrE* someone who pays money to be part of an organization or to help its work **3** *BrE* someone who gives money regularly for a service **4** someone who signs their name on a document

**sub·scrip·tion** /səbˈskrɪpʃən/ *n* [C] **1** an amount of money you pay regularly, especially once a year, to receive copies of a newspaper or magazine **2** *BrE* an amount of money you pay regularly to be a member of an organization or to help its work

**sub·sec·tion** /ˈsʌbsekʃən/ *n* [C] a part of a SECTION

W2 **sub·se·quent** /ˈsʌbsɪkwənt/ *adj formal* coming after or following something else: *These skills were then passed on to subsequent generations.* | **subsequent to** (=after) *events that happened subsequent to the accident* —compare CONSEQUENT

W3 **sub·se·quent·ly** /ˈsʌbsɪkwəntli/ *adv formal* after an event in the past: *The book was subsequently translated into 15 languages.*

**sub·ser·vi·ent** /səbˈsɜːviənt‖-ˈsɜːr-/ *adj* **1** someone who is subservient is too willing to do what other people want them to do **2** *formal* less important than something else; SUBORDINATE [**+ to**] *Your own needs must be subservient to those of the group.* —**subserviently** *adv* —**subservience** *n* [U]

**sub·set** /ˈsʌbset/ *n* [C] a set that is part of a larger set

**sub·side** /səbˈsaɪd/ *v* [I] **1** if a feeling or noise subsides, it gradually decreases: *Simon waited until the laughter subsided.* **2** if a building subsides, it gradually sinks further into the ground **3** if land subsides, its surface sinks to a lower level: *After the heavy rains, part of the road subsided.* **4** if bad weather conditions subside, they gradually return to a normal state: *Then the wind subsided, and all was quiet.*

**sub·si·dence** /səbˈsaɪdəns, ˈsʌbsɪdəns/ *n* [C,U] the process by which land sinks to a lower level, or the state of land or buildings that have sunk: *Is your house insured against subsidence?*

**sub·sid·i·ar·i·ty** /səbˌsɪdiˈærɪti/ *n* [U] a word meaning a political POLICY (1) in which more power, for example to make decisions, is given to a smaller group of people, used especially about the European Community giving power to its member countries

**sub·sid·i·a·ry¹** /səbˈsɪdiəri‖-dieri/ *n* [C] a company that is owned or controlled by another company: *a subsidiary of a US parent company*

**subsidiary²** *adj* connected with, but less important than, the main plan, subject, event etc: [**+ to**] *The smaller workshops are subsidiary to the main conference.*

**sub·si·dize** also **-ise** *BrE* /ˈsʌbsɪdaɪz/ *v* [T] to pay part of the cost of something so that the buyer can pay less for it: *Farming is partly subsidized by the government.* —**subsidizer** *n* [C] —**subsidization** /ˌsʌbsɪdaɪˈzeɪʃən/ *n* [U]

**sub·si·dy** /ˈsʌbsɪdi/ *n* [C] money that is paid by a government or organization to make prices lower, reduce the cost of producing goods etc: *international disagreement over trade subsidies*

**sub·sist** /səbˈsɪst/ *v* [I] to stay alive on only small amounts of food or money: [**+ on**] *We had to subsist on bread and water.*

**sub·sis·tence** /səbˈsɪstəns/ *n* [U] **1** the ability to live with very little money or food: *Not even subsistence is possible in such conditions.* **2** a small amount of money or food that is just enough to survive: **subsistence allowance** (=money given to you to live on) | **subsistence diet** (=only enough food to keep living) | **subsistence farmers** (=who produce just enough food to live on)

**subsistence crop** /·ˈ··· ·/ *n* [C] a crop that is grown to be used by the farmer rather than to be sold —compare CASH CROP

**subsistence lev·el** /·ˈ··· ˌ··/ *n* [singular] a very poor standard of living, which only provides the things that are completely necessary and nothing more: *Many of the poorer farmers live at subsistence level.*

**sub·soil** /ˈsʌbsɔɪl/ *n* [U] the layer of soil between the surface and the lower layer of hard rock

**sub·son·ic** /ˌsʌbˈsɒnɪk◂‖-ˈsɑː-/ *adj* slower than the speed of sound: *subsonic flight*

**sub·spe·cies** /ˈsʌbˌspiːʃiːz/ *n* [C] a group of similar plants or animals that is smaller than a SPECIES

W3 **sub·stance** /ˈsʌbstəns/ *n*

**1** ▶**MATERIAL**◀ [C] a type of solid or liquid that has particular characteristics: *a sticky substance* | *radioactive substances* | *Heroin is an illegal substance.*

**2** ▶**IDEAS**◀ [singular, U] *formal* the most important

ideas contained in an argument or piece of writing; ESSENCE (1) | **the substance of** *The substance of his argument was that too many people live below the poverty line.* | **in substance** *What she said in substance was that the mayor must resign.*
**3 ▶ IMPORTANCE ◀** [U] *formal* importance, especially because of dealing with things that are necessary; SIGNIFICANCE: *It was an entertaining speech, but without much substance.* (=without many important or serious ideas) | **matters/issues of substance** *Instead of debating points of procedure, we should be discussing matters of substance.*
**4 ▶ TRUTH ◀** [U usually in questions and negatives] *formal* basic facts that are true: [+ **to**] *There is no substance to the rumour that the princess is pregnant.* | **without substance** (=untrue)
**5 substance abuse** *technical* the habit of taking too many drugs so that you are harmed by them
**6 a man/woman of substance** *literary* a rich man or woman
**7 ▶ REAL ◀** [U] something that really exists that you can feel: *phantoms without substance*

**sub·stan·dard** /ˌsʌbˈstændəd◂‖-ərd◂/ *adj* not as good as the average, and not acceptable: *substandard housing* —compare NON-STANDARD, STANDARD[1]

S2 W2 **sub·stan·tial** /səbˈstænʃəl/ *adj* **1** large enough in amount or number to be noticeable or to have an important effect: *The document requires substantial changes.* | *We have the support of a substantial number of parents.* **2** large enough to be satisfactory: *a substantial salary* | *a substantial breakfast* **3** large and strongly made: *a substantial mahogany desk* **4** *formal* having a lot of influence or power, usually because of wealth: *a very substantial family in the wool trade*

**sub·stan·tial·ly** /səbˈstænʃəli/ *adv* **1** when considering the most important parts: *There are one or two minor differences, but they're substantially the same text.* **2** very much: *substantially higher prices*

**sub·stan·ti·ate** /səbˈstænʃieɪt/ *v* [T] *formal* to prove the truth of something that someone has said, claimed etc: *Can you substantiate your claim in a court of law?* —**substantiation** /səbˌstænʃiˈeɪʃən/ *n* [U]

**sub·stan·tive**[1] /səbˈstæntɪv, ˈsʌbstəntɪv/ *adj formal* **1** *formal* dealing with things that are important or real: **substantive discussions** (=in which important matters are discussed) **2** *technical* expressing existence, in grammar: *The substantive verb is 'to be'.* **3** [only before noun] *formal* real and continuing, rather than being only for a limited time: *the substantive rank of colonel* —**substantively** *adv*

**sub·stan·tive**[2] /ˈsʌbstəntɪv/ *n* [C] *technical* a noun —**substantival** /ˌsʌbstənˈtaɪvəl◂/ *adj*

**sub·sta·tion** /ˈsʌbˌsteɪʃən/ *n* [C] a place where electricity is passed on from the place that produces it into the main system

**sub·sti·tute**[1] /ˈsʌbstɪtjuːt‖-tuːt/ *n* [C] **1** someone who does someone else's job for a limited period of time especially in a sports team or performance: *The lead singer was ill and her substitute wasn't nearly as good.* **2** something new or different that you use instead of something else that you used previously: *a sugar substitute* **3 be no substitute for sth** to not have the same good or desirable qualities as something or someone else: *Vitamin pills are no substitute for healthy eating.*

**substitute**[2] *v* **1** [T] to use something new or different instead of something else: **substitute sth for/with sth** *You can substitute yogurt for the sour cream.* **2** [I,T] to do someone's job until the person who usually does it is able to do it again: [+ **for**] *Bill substituted for Larry who was off sick.*

**substitute teach·er** /ˌ··· ˈ··/ *n* [C] *AmE* a teacher who teaches a class when the usual teacher is ill; SUPPLY TEACHER *BrE*

**sub·sti·tu·tion** /ˌsʌbstɪˈtjuːʃən‖-ˈtuː-/ *n* [C,U] someone or something that you use instead of the person or thing you would usually use, or the act of using them: *Coach Packard made two substitutions in the second half.*

**sub·stra·tum** /ˌsʌbˈstrɑːtəm‖-ˈstreɪ-/ *n plural* **substrata** /-tə/ [C] **1** a layer that lies beneath another layer, especially in the earth: *a substratum of rock* **2** *formal* a quality that is hidden: *a substratum of truth in the argument*

**sub·struc·ture** /ˈsʌbˌstrʌktʃə‖-ər/ *n* [C] **1** one of the structures (STRUCTURE[1] (3)) within a society or organization that combines with others to form a whole **2** a solid base under the ground that supports a building above the ground

**sub·sume** /səbˈsjuːm‖-ˈsuːm/ *v* [T] *formal* to include someone or something as a member of a group or type, rather than considering it separately: **subsume sb/sth under sth** *For the purpose of the survey, typists are subsumed under office workers.*

**sub·ten·ant** /ˌsʌbˈtenənt/ *n* [C] someone who pays rent for an apartment, office etc to the person who is renting it from the owner —**subtenancy** *n* [C,U]

**sub·tend** /səbˈtend/ *v* [T] *technical* to be opposite to a particular angle or ARC, and form the limits of it in GEOMETRY

**sub·ter·fuge** /ˈsʌbtəfjuːdʒ‖-ər-/ *n* [C,U] *formal* a secret trick or slightly dishonest way of doing something, or the use of this: *Sereni was lured to Moscow by subterfuge.*

**sub·ter·ra·ne·an** /ˌsʌbtəˈreɪniən◂/ *adj* beneath the surface of the Earth: *subterranean passages*

**sub·text** /ˈsʌbtekst/ *n* [C] a hidden or second meaning in something that someone says or writes: *Whatever their text, the subtext is always this: political repression.*

**sub·ti·tle** /ˈsʌbˌtaɪtl/ *n* [C] **1 subtitles** [plural] the words printed over a film in a foreign language to translate what is being said by the actors: *a French film with English subtitles* **2** a less important title below the main title in a book —**subtitle** *v* [I,T]

**sub·ti·tled** /ˈsʌbˌtaɪtld/ *adj* having subtitles or a particular subtitle

**sub·tle** /ˈsʌtl/ *adj* **1** not easy to notice or understand unless you pay careful attention: *a subtle flavor of oranges* | *The pictures are similar, but there are subtle differences between them.* **2** someone who is subtle uses indirect methods to hide what they really want or intend to do: *Hugo didn't even try to be subtle about it – he stared right at her.* **3** clever, especially in order to deceive people: *a subtle plan* **4** very clever in noticing and understanding things; SENSITIVE (1): *a subtle mind* —**subtly** *adv*

**sub·tle·ty** /ˈsʌtlti/ *n* **1** [U] the quality of being subtle: *She argued her case with considerable subtlety.* **2** [C usually plural] a thought, idea, or detail that is important but difficult to notice or understand: [+ **of**] *Some of the subtleties of the language are lost in translation.*

**sub·to·tal** /ˈsʌbˌtəʊtl‖-ˌtoʊtl/ *n* [C] the total of a set of numbers, especially on a bill, that is added to other numbers to form a complete total

**sub·tract** /səbˈtrækt/ *v* [T] to take a number or an amount from something larger: **subtract sth from sth** *If you subtract 10 from 30 you get 20.* —compare ADD (2), DEDUCT, MINUS[1] (1)

**sub·trac·tion** /səbˈtrækʃən/ *n* [C] the act of subtracting —compare ADDITION (4)

**sub·trop·i·cal** /ˌsʌbˈtrɒpɪkəl◂‖-ˈtrɑː-/ *adj* related to an area near to a tropical area, or typical of that area: *subtropical vegetation*

**sub·urb** /ˈsʌbɜːb‖-ɜːrb/ *n* [C] an area away from the centre of a town or city, where a lot of people live: [+ **of**] *Blackheath is a suburb of London.* | **the suburbs** (=this type of area) *a naive kid from the suburbs*

**sub·ur·ban** /səˈbɜːbən‖-ˈbɜːr-/ *adj* **1** related to a suburb, or in a suburb: *suburban life* | *suburban streets with houses that all look the same* **2** boring and having very traditional beliefs and interests: *suburban attitudes*

**sub·ur·ban·ite** /səˈbɜːbənaɪt‖-ˈbɜːr-/ *n* [C] someone who lives in a suburb

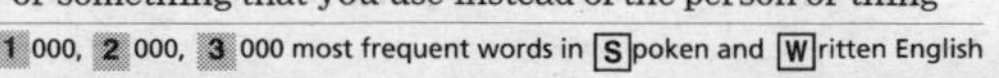

**sub·ur·bi·a** /səˈbɜːbiə‖-ˈbɜːr-/ *n* [U] **1** the behaviour, opinions, and ways of living that are typical of people who live in a suburb: *middle-class suburbia* **2** suburban areas in general

**sub·ven·tion** /səbˈvenʃən/ *n* [C] *formal* a gift of money for a special use

**sub·ver·sion** /səbˈvɜːʃən‖-ˈvɜːrʒən/ *n* [U] secret activities that are intended to encourage people to oppose the government

**sub·ver·sive¹** /səbˈvɜːsɪv‖-ˈvɜːr-/ *adj* ideas, activities etc that are subversive are often secret and intended to encourage people to oppose a government, religion etc: *subversive political activities* —**subversively** *adv* —**subversiveness** *n* [U]

**subversive²** *n* [C] someone who is subversive

**sub·vert** /səbˈvɜːt‖-ˈvɜːrt/ *v* [T] *formal* **1** to try to destroy the power and influence of a government or established system etc: *attempts to subvert the democratic process* **2** to destroy someone's beliefs or loyalty

**sub·way** /ˈsʌbweɪ/ *n* [C] **1** *BrE* a path for people to walk under a road or railway; UNDERPASS *AmE* **2** *AmE* a railway that runs under the ground; UNDERGROUND³ *BrE*

**sub-ze·ro** /ˌ· ˈ··◂/ *adj* below zero in temperature

S3 W2 **suc·ceed** /səkˈsiːd/ *v*

**1 ▶ NOT FAIL ◀** [I] to do what you have tried or wanted to do: *I'm sure you'll succeed if you work hard.* | **succeed in doing sth** *Negotiators have not yet succeeded in establishing a cease-fire.* | **succeed only in doing sth** (=fail and do the opposite of what you had wanted) *You've only succeeded in upsetting your mother.*

**2 ▶ HAVE A GOOD RESULT ◀** [I] to have the result or effect something was intended to have: *The anti-smoking campaign has only partly succeeded.*

**3 ▶ REACH A HIGH POSITION ◀** [I] to do well in your job, especially because you have worked hard at it for a long time: [+ **as**] *I'm not sure he has the determination to succeed as an actor.* | [+ **in**] *Women need to be tough to succeed in the male-dominated world of business.*

**4 ▶ FOLLOW IN A POSITION ◀** [I,T] to be the next person to take a position or rank after someone else: **succeed sb as sth** *Gingrich will succeed Foley as speaker of the house.*

**5 ▶ REPLACE ◀** [T] *formal* to come after and replace something else: *a new generation of computers designed to succeed their existing range*

**6 nothing succeeds like success** used to say that success often leads to even greater success

**suc·ceed·ing** /səkˈsiːdɪŋ/ *adj* coming after something else: *Over the succeeding weeks things went from bad to worse.*

S1 W1 **suc·cess** /səkˈses/ *n* **1** [U] the achieving of something you have been trying to do, with a good result: *success in a highly competitive market* | *She puts her success down to hard work and good luck.* | **have success in doing sth** *Did you have any success in persuading Adam to come?* **2** [C] something that has a good result or effect: *The play was an overnight success.* | **a great/huge/big success** *Kathy's wedding shower was a great success.* | **make a success of sth** *Dick's taken over a pub, I bet he makes a success of it.* | **prove a success** (=become successful) **3** [C] someone who does very well in their job: [+ **in**] *Janet is determined to be a success in whatever field she chooses.* | [+ **as**] *Tony's been a great success as our new coach.* **4 success story** someone or something that becomes successful in spite of difficulties: *Ewing has turned the business into a success story.*

S2 W1 **suc·cess·ful** /səkˈsesfəl/ *adj* **1** having the effect or result you intended: *Well, it wasn't a very successful meeting.* | **successful in doing sth** *Were you successful in persuading him to change his mind?* **2** a successful business, film etc makes a lot of money: *The show's had a pretty successful run.* **3** a successful person earns a lot of money or is very well known and respected: *luxury apartments for the successful young executive* | [+ **in**] *successful in politics* —opposite UNSUCCESSFUL —**successfully** *adv*

**suc·ces·sion** /səkˈseʃən/ *n* **1 in succession** happening one after the other without anything different happening in between: *She won the championship four times in succession.* | **in close/quick succession** (=quickly one after the other) **2 a succession of** a number of people or things of the same kind following, coming or happening one after the other: *A succession of visitors came to the door.* **3** [U] the act of taking over an office or position, or the right to be the next to take it: *If Prince Charles dies, the succession passes to his son.* | **succession to sth** *the queen's succession to the throne* —compare ACCESSION (1) W3

**suc·ces·sive** /səkˈsesɪv/ *adj* coming or following one after the other: *The hockey team has had five successive victories.* —**successively** *adv*

**suc·ces·sor** /səkˈsesə‖-ər/ *n* [C] **1** someone who takes a position previously held by someone else: [+ **as**] *His successor as chairman takes over next week.* **2** *formal* a machine, system etc that exists after another one in a process of development: *the transistor's successor, the microchip* — opposite PREDECESSOR

**suc·cinct** /səkˈsɪŋkt/ *adj approving* clearly expressed in a few words: *a very succinct explanation* —**succinctly** *adv* —**succinctness** *n* [U]

**suc·cor** /ˈsʌkə‖-ər/ *n* [U] the American spelling of SUCCOUR —**succor** *v* [T]

**suc·co·tash** /ˈsʌkətæʃ/ *n* [U] *AmE* a dish made from corn, beans, and TOMATO*es* cooked together

**suc·cour¹** *BrE*, **succor** *AmE* /ˈsʌkə‖-ər/ *n* [U] *literary* help that is given to someone who is having problems

**succour²** *BrE*, **succor** *AmE*— *v* [T] *literary* to help someone who has problems: *succouring the needy*

**suc·cu·bus** /ˈsʌkjʊ̈bəs/ *n plural* **succubi** /-baɪ/ [C] *literary* a female DEVIL that has sex with a sleeping man —compare INCUBUS (2)

**suc·cu·lent¹** /ˈsʌkjʊ̈lənt/ *adj* **1** juicy and delicious: *a succulent steak* **2** *technical* a succulent plant has thick soft leaves or stems that can hold a lot of liquid —**succulence** *n* [U]

**succulent²** *n* [C] *technical* a succulent plant such as a CACTUS

**suc·cumb** /səˈkʌm/ *v* [I] *formal* **1** to stop opposing someone or something that is stronger than you, and allow them to take control: *After an intense artillery bombardment the town finally succumbed.* | **succumb to temptation** *Gina finally succumbed to temptation and had some ice cream.* **2** if you succumb to an illness you become very ill or die of it

**such¹** /sʌtʃ/ *predeterminer, determiner* **1** used to talk about a person, thing etc which is of the same kind as that which has already been mentioned: *Such behavior is just not acceptable in this school.* | *The rules make it quite clear what should be done in such a situation.* | [+ **as**] *It was against such a background as this that the President made his speech.* **2 such as** used when giving an example of something: *The local community is still reliant on traditional industries such as farming and mining.* | *"There are lots of ways to increase productivity." "Such as?"* | **people/things etc such as** *professional people such as bank managers and solicitors* **3 such a kind man/such tall women etc** used to emphasize how kind a man is, how tall particular women are etc: *Did you have to buy such an expensive coat?* | *You haven't invited Ron have you? He's such a bore.* | *I've seen an eagle before, but never at such close quarters.* | [+ **(that)**] *It's such a tiny kitchen that I don't have to do much to keep it clean.* | *He's such an idiot, I don't even ask him to help any more.* **4 or some such person/thing etc** a person, thing etc like the one just mentioned: *He said she looked scruffy, or made some such helpful comment.* **5 such as it is/such as they are etc** *especially spoken* used when you do not think that something is good enough or impressive enough: *You're welcome to borrow my car such as it is.* **6 there's/no** S1 W1

**such person/thing as etc** used to say that a particular person or thing does not exist: *These days there's no such thing as a job for life.* **7 such...as** *formal or literary* used to emphasize that there is a small amount of something or that it is of poor quality: *Such food as they gave us was warm and nutritious.*

**such²** *pron* **1** used to talk about a person, thing, etc that is of the same kind as that which has already been mentioned: *A Welsh victory had been predicted and such indeed was the result.* **2 such...as/that** *formal or literary* used to give a reason or explanation for something: *The nature of the job was such that he felt obliged to tell no one about it.* | *His manner was such as to offend everyone who he met.* **3 and such** *spoken* and people or things like that: *It won't be anything special, just a few cakes and sandwiches and such.* **4 not...as such** *spoken* used to say that something is not really what you are calling it: *There isn't a garden as such, just a little vegetable patch.* **5 such...as** *formal* those people or things of a particular group or kind: *Such of you as wish to leave may do so now.*

**such and such** /ˈ· · ˌ·/ *predeterminer spoken* a certain time, amount etc that is not named: *If they tell you to come on such and such a day, don't agree unless it's convenient.*

**such·like¹** /ˈsʌtʃlaɪk/ *pron spoken* things of that kind: *Do you enjoy plays, films and suchlike?*

**suchlike²** *adj* [only before noun] *spoken* of that kind; SIMILAR: *tennis and baseball and suchlike summer sports*

S3 **suck¹** /sʌk/ *v* [I,T]

**1 ▶ DRINK ◀** to take liquid into your mouth by tightening your lips into a small hole and using the muscles of your mouth to pull the liquid in: **suck at sth** *a baby sucking at its mother's breast* | **suck sth up** *Jennie sucked up the last bit of milkshake with her straw.*

**2 ▶ PUT IN MOUTH ◀** to hold something in your mouth and pull on it with your tongue and lips: *Don't suck your thumb, dear!* | **suck on sth** *Lara's been sucking on that jawbreaker for half an hour.*

**3 ▶ PULL ◀** to pull someone or something with great power and force to a particular place: [+ **down/into**] *Something got sucked down into the boiler and clogged it.* | **suck sb under/along** *Be careful of rip tides! They'll suck you right under.*

**4 suck sb into sth** to make someone become involved in a particular situation, event etc, especially a bad one: *Gullible people can easily get sucked into religious cults.*

**5 sth sucks** *informal especially AmE* an impolite expression meaning that something is very bad in quality or that a situation is very bad: *Her acting sucks.*

**suck up** *phr v* [I] *informal* to say or do nice things in order to make someone like you or to get what you want: **suck up to sb** *He's always sucking up to the boss.*

**suck²** *n* [C] an act of sucking

**suck·er¹** /ˈsʌkə‖-ər/ *n* [C]

**1 ▶ PERSON ◀** *informal* someone who is easily deceived, tricked, or persuaded to do something they do not want to do: *You fell for that old line? Sucker!*

**2 be a sucker for sth** to like something so much that you cannot refuse it: *She's a real sucker for old movies.*

**3 ▶ PART OF AN ANIMAL ◀** *not technical* a part of an insect or of an animal's body that it uses to hold on to a surface: *Tree frogs have suckers on their feet.*

**4 ▶ SWEET ◀** *AmE* a LOLLIPOP (2)

**5 ▶ PLANT ◀** a part of a plant that grows from the root or lower stem of a plant to become a new plant

**6 ▶ RUBBER ◀** a flat piece of rubber that sticks to a surface by SUCTION

**sucker²** *v*

**sucker** sb **into** sth *phr v* [T] *AmE* to persuade someone to do something they do not want to do, especially by tricking them or lying to them: **sucker sb into doing sth** *Laurie got suckered into babysitting her little sister.*

**suck·le** /ˈsʌkəl/ *v* **1** [T] to feed a baby or young animal with milk from the breast: *a sheep suckling her lamb* **2** [I] if a baby or young animal suckles, it sucks milk from a breast —compare BREASTFEED, NURSE² (6)

**suck·ling** /ˈsʌklɪŋ/ *n* [C] *literary* a young human or animal still taking milk from its mother

**suckling pig** /ˈ·· ·/ *n* [C] a young pig still taking milk from its mother, which is often cooked and eaten on special occasions

**su·crose** /ˈsuːkrəʊz, ˈsjuː-‖ˈsuːkroʊz/ *n* [U] *technical* the common form of sugar —compare FRUCTOSE, LACTOSE

**suc·tion** /ˈsʌkʃən/ *n* [U] the process of removing air or liquid from an enclosed space so that another substance is sucked in, or so that two surfaces stick together

**suction cap** /ˈ·· ·/ *BrE*, **suction cup** *AmE* *n* [C] a small round piece of rubber or plastic that sticks to a surface by suction

**suction pump** /ˈ·· ·/ *n* [C] a pump that works by removing air from an enclosed space, so that the substance to be pumped is sucked in

**sud·den** /ˈsʌdn/ *adj* **1** happening, coming, or done quickly and unexpectedly: *I keep having sudden bouts of dizziness.* | *a sudden change in temperature* | *Marry you? Why, George, this is all so sudden!* **2 (all) of a sudden** suddenly: *We were driving along, when all of a sudden a car pulled straight out in front of us.* —**suddenness** *n* [U] S2 W3

**sudden death** /ˌ·· ˈ·/ *n* [U] if a game goes into sudden death, it continues after its usual ending time until one player or team gains the lead and wins

**sud·den·ly** /ˈsʌdnli/ *adv* quickly and unexpectedly: *Suddenly there was a huge bang.* | *George died very suddenly.* S2 W1

**suds** /sʌdz/ *n* [plural] **1** the mass of BUBBLES (BUBBLE¹ (1)) formed on the top of water with soap in it **2** *AmE informal* beer —**sudsy** *adj*

**sue** /sjuː‖suː/ *v* [I,T] to make a legal claim against someone, especially for an amount of money, because you have been harmed in some way: *If the builders don't fulfil their side of the contract, we'll sue.* | **sue sb for libel/negligence/malpractice etc** (=because of something they have done wrong) *Elton John sued a newspaper for libel.* | **sue sb for £100,000/damages** (=in order to get money) *I'll sue them for every penny they've got.* | **sue sb for divorce** (=in order to end a marriage)

**sue for** sth *phr v* [T] *formal* to BEG or ask for something: **sue for peace** *The rebels were forced to sue for peace.*

**suede** /sweɪd/ *n* [U] soft leather with a slightly rough surface: *suede shoes* —see picture on page 839

**su·et** /ˈsuːɪ̯t, ˈsjuːɪ̯t‖ˈsuː-/ *n* [U] hard fat from around an animal's KIDNEYS, used in cooking —**suety** *adj*

**suf·fer** /ˈsʌfə‖-ər/ *v* S1 W1

**1 ▶ PAIN ◀** [I,T] to experience physical or mental pain: *At least he died suddenly and didn't suffer.* | **I/you/she will suffer for it** (=will feel very ill or sore) *I know I'll suffer for it in the morning, but give me another gin.*

**2 ▶ BAD SITUATION ◀** [I,T] to be in a very bad situation that makes things very difficult for you: *Small businesses have suffered financially during the recession.* | **suffer the consequences** (=be punished) *If you break the law, you must be prepared to suffer the consequences.*

**3 ▶ EXPERIENCE ◀** [T] if someone suffers an unpleasant or difficult experience, it happens to them: **suffer a defeat** *The Democrats have just suffered a huge defeat in the polls.* | **suffer damage/injury/loss** *The car suffered severe damage in the accident.*

**4 ▶ WORSE ◀** [I] to become worse in quality because a bad situation is affecting something or because nobody is taking care of it: *The ferry operators denied that safety would suffer if costs were cut.*

**5 not suffer fools gladly** to not be patient with people you think are stupid

**6 suffer sb to do sth** *old use* to allow someone to do something

**suffer from** sth *phr v* [T] **1** to have an illness or a medical problem, especially one that is serious and affects you over a long period of time: *One in three women suffer from depression.* | *He was taken to hospital suffering from shock.* **2** to have a problem that prevents you from being successful: *British industry suffers from chronic under-investment.*

**suf·fer·ance** /ˈsʌfərəns/ *n* **on sufferance** *formal* if you live or work somewhere on sufferance, you are allowed to do it by someone who would rather you did not do it: *Martha made it clear I was only staying with them on sufferance.*



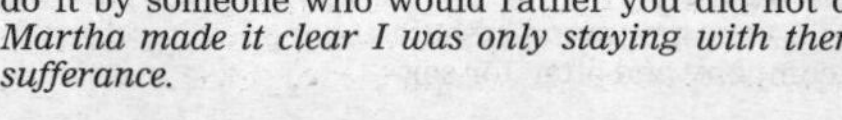

**suf·fer·er** /ˈsʌfərə‖-ər/ *n* [C] someone who suffers, especially from a particular illness: *a huge increase in the number of asthma sufferers*

**suf·fer·ing** /ˈsʌfərɪŋ/ *n* [C,U] physical or mental pain and difficulty, or an experience of this: *the suffering of innocent people during a war*

**suf·fice** /səˈfaɪs/ *v* [not in progressive] **1** [I] *formal* to be enough: *A light lunch will suffice.* | **suffice to do sth** *Two examples should suffice to illustrate my point.* **2 suffice (it) to say (that)** used to say that the statement that follows is enough to explain what you mean, even though you could say more: *Suffice to say it was a local person who called the police.* **3** [T] *formal* to be enough to satisfy someone: *Just some bread and soup will suffice me.*

**suf·fi·cien·cy** /səˈfɪʃənsi/ *n formal* **1** [U] the state of being or having enough **2 a sufficiency of** a supply that is enough: *Eating fruit should ensure a sufficiency of Vitamin C.*

S2 W2 **suf·fi·cient** /səˈfɪʃənt/ *adj formal* as much as is needed for a particular purpose; enough: *We can only prosecute if there is sufficient evidence.* | **sufficient to do sth** *His income is sufficient to keep him comfortable.* | **[+ for]** *There is sufficient food for everyone.* —opposite INSUFFICIENT —see ADEQUATE (USAGE)

**suf·fix** /ˈsʌfɪks/ *n* [C] a letter or letters added to the end of a word to form a new word: *You can add the suffix 'ness' to the word 'kind' to form 'kindness'.* —see also AFFIX —compare PREFIX[1] (1)

**suf·fo·cate** /ˈsʌfəkeɪt/ *v* **1** [I,T] to die or make someone die by preventing them from breathing: *She rolled onto her baby and actually sufffocated it!* **2 be suffocating** to feel uncomfortable because there is not enough fresh air: *Can you open a window? I'm suffocating.* **3** [T] to prevent a relationship, plan, business etc from developing well or being successful: *Jealousy can suffocate any relationship.* —**suffocation** /ˌsʌfəˈkeɪʃən/ *n* [U]

**suf·fra·gan** /ˈsʌfrəgən/ *adj* [only before noun] a suffragan BISHOP (1) helps another bishop of higher rank in their work —**suffragan** *n* [C]

**suf·frage** /ˈsʌfrɪdʒ/ *n* [U] the right to vote in national elections

**suf·fra·gette** /ˌsʌfrəˈdʒet/ *n* [C] a woman who tried to gain the right to vote for women especially as a member of a group in Britain or the US in the early 20th century

**suf·fuse** /səˈfjuːz/ *v* [T] *especially literary* if warmth, colour, liquid etc suffuses something or someone, it covers or spreads through them: *The light of the setting sun suffused the clouds.* —**suffusion** /səˈfjuːʒən/ *n* [U]

S2 W3 **sug·ar**[1] /ˈʃʊgə‖-ər/ *n* **1** [U] a sweet white or brown substance that is obtained from plants and used to sweeten food and drinks: *Do you take sugar in your coffee?* **2** [C] the amount of sugar that a small spoon can hold: *How many sugars do you want in your tea?* **3** *technical* one of several sweet substances formed in plants —compare GLUCOSE **4** *BrE spoken* used to address someone you like very much **5 (oh) sugar!** *spoken especially BrE* used when you are very annoyed about something stupid that you have just done, or when something goes wrong

**sugar**[2] *v* [T] **1** to add sugar or cover something with sugar; SWEETEN (1): *Did you sugar my coffee?* **2 sugar the pill** *especially BrE* to do something that makes an order, activity etc less unpleasant —**sugared** *adj*: *sugared almonds*

**sugar beet** /ˈ·· ·/ *n* [U] a vegetable that grows under the ground from which sugar is obtained; BEET (1)

**sug·ar·cane** /ˈʃʊgəkeɪn‖-ər-/ *n* [U] a tall tropical plant from whose stems sugar is obtained

**sugar-coat·ed** /ˌ·· ˈ··◂/ *adj* **1** covered with sugar **2** made to seem better than something really is: *I'm tired of hearing Fred's sugar-coated promises.*

**sugar cube** /ˈ·· ·/ *n* [C] a sugar lump

**sugar dad·dy** /ˈ·· ˌ··/ *n* [C] *informal* an older man who gives a young woman presents and money in return for her company and often for sex

**sugar lump** /ˈ·· ·/ *n* [C] *especially BrE* a square piece of solid sugar

**sugar ma·ple** /ˈ·· ˌ··/ *n* [C] a kind of MAPLE tree that grows in North America whose SAP (=liquid from the tree) is used to make MAPLE SYRUP

**sug·ar·y** /ˈʃʊgəri/ *adj* **1** containing sugar or tasting like sugar: *sugary snacks* **2** language, emotions etc that are sugary are too nice and seem insincere: *songs full of sugary sentiments about love*

**sug·gest** /səˈdʒest‖səgˈdʒest/ *v* [T] **1** to tell someone your ideas about what they should do, where they should go etc: *If this is not convenient, please suggest another date.* | **suggest doing sth** *John suggested going together in one car.* | **suggest (that)** *She suggested that we write that into the contract.* | **can/may I suggest** (=used to politely suggest a different idea) *May I suggest that you see a financial advisor?* | **suggest how/where etc** *Can you suggest where to stay in Rio?* —see PROPOSE (USAGE) **2** to tell someone about a suitable person for a job: **suggest sb for** *Mr Roberts Guarino has been suggested for the post of director.* **3** to make someone think that a particular thing is true; INDICATE (1): *The actual number of rapes may be higher than the statistics suggest.* | **[+ (that)]** *There was nothing to suggest that she intended to kill herself.* **4** to make someone have a new idea: **suggest sth to sb** *It was a magazine article that suggested the idea to me.* **5 I'm not suggesting** *spoken* used to say that what you are going to say is not meant to criticize someone as much as it may seem: *I'm not suggesting that you are lying, but it is very misleading.* **6** to remind someone of something or help them to imagine it: *The stage was bare, with only the lighting to suggest a prison.* S1 W1

**sug·ges·ti·ble** /səˈdʒestɪ̈bəl‖səg-/ *adj* easily influenced by other people or by things you see and hear: **highly/very suggestible** *At that age, kids are highly suggestible.*

**sug·ges·tion** /səˈdʒestʃən‖səg-/ *n* **1** [C] an idea, plan, or possibility that someone mentions: **have a suggestion** *We've had several suggestions on a name for the baby.* | **make a suggestion** *Can I just make one suggestion about how we might do this?* | **[+ that]** *He rejected my suggestion that we appoint Roger.* —see PROPOSE (USAGE) **2 a suggestion of** a slight amount of something: *There was just a suggestion of a smile on her face.* **3** [U] the act of telling someone your idea about what they should do: **at sb's suggestion** (=because someone suggested something) *At her father's suggestion, she left Paris and returned home.* | **open to suggestions** (=willing to listen to ideas) **4 suggestion that/of** [usually in questions and negatives] a slight possibility: *There was never any suggestion of criminal involvement.* **5** [U] an indirect way of making you accept an idea, for example by HYPNOTISM S1 W2

**sug·ges·tive** /səˈdʒestɪv‖səg-/ *adj* **1** a remark, behaviour etc that is suggestive makes you think of sex **2** reminding you of something: **suggestive of sth** *an abstract painting suggestive of a desert landscape* —**suggestively** *adv* **suggestiveness** *n* [U]

**su·i·cid·al** /ˌsuːɪ̈ˈsaɪdl◂, ˌsjuː-‖ˌsuː-/ *adj* **1** wanting to kill yourself: *After his wife left him he was suicidal.* | **suicidal tendencies** *For many years before treatment, Clare had suicidal tendencies.* **2** likely to lead to death: *the suicidal challenge of jumping over 50 cars on a motorcycle* **3** likely to lead to a lot of damage or trouble: *It would be suicidal for the senator to oppose this policy.*

**su·i·cide** /ˈsuːɪ̈saɪd, ˈsjuː-‖ˈsuː-/ *n* [C,U] **1** the act of killing yourself | **attempt suicide** (=try to kill yourself) | **commit suicide** (=kill yourself) *Gill committed suicide last year after losing her job.* —see KILL[1] (USAGE) **2 political/social suicide** something you do that ruins your good position in politics or society

**suicide pact** /ˈ··· ˌ·/ *n* [C] an arrangement between two or more people to kill themselves at the same time

**suit**[1] /suːt, sjuːt‖suːt/ *n* [C] S2 

**1 ▶ CLOTHES ◀** a set of clothes made of the same material, usually including a JACKET (=short coat) with trousers or a skirt: *a cream linen suit* | *a grey winter suit* —see also MORNING SUIT

**2 jogging/swim suit** a piece or pieces of clothing used for a special purpose —see also BOILER SUIT, SHELL SUIT, WETSUIT
**3 ▶ CARDS ◀** one of the four types of cards in a set of playing cards
**4 ▶ LAW ◀** an argument brought to a court of law by a private person or company, not by the police or government; LAWSUIT | **file suit** (=bring an argument to a court of law)
**5 sb's strong suit** *especially AmE* something that you are good at: *Politeness is not his strong suit.*
**6 plead/press your suit** *old use* to ask a woman to marry you —see also **in your birthday suit** (BIRTHDAY (2)), **follow suit** (FOLLOW (15))

S2 W3 **suit²** *v* [T] **1** to be acceptable or CONVENIENT for a particular person or in a particular situation: *Finding a date that suits us all is very difficult.* | *Buy a database program to suit your needs.* | **suit sb (fine)** *spoken* (=be completely acceptable) *"Eight o'clock?" "That suits me fine."* | **suit sb down to the ground** (=be exactly right for someone) *Yup, this little car suits me down to the ground.* **2** [not in passive] to make someone look attractive: *That coat really suits Paul.* | *Red suits you.* —see FIT¹ (USAGE) **3 well/best/ideally suited** to have the right qualities to do something: *Dirk would be ideally suited to the job.* **4 suit yourself** *spoken* used to tell someone they can do whatever they want to, even though it annoys you: *"I don't really feel like going out after all." "Suit yourself."* **5 suit sb's book** *BrE informal* to fit well into someone's plans
**suit** sth **to** sth *phr v* [T] *formal* to make something exactly right for something else: *Suit the punishment to the crime, I say.*

**suit·a·bil·i·ty** /ˌsuːtəˈbɪlɪ̣ti, ˌsjuː-‖ˌsuː-/ *n* [U] the degree to which something or someone has the right qualities for a particular purpose: [+ **for**] *There's no doubt about Christine's suitability for the job.*

S2 W2 **suit·a·ble** /ˈsuːtəbəl, ˈsjuː-‖ˈsuː-/ *adj* having the right qualities for a particular person, purpose, or situation: *We are hoping to find a suitable school.* | [+ **for**] *The house is not really suitable for a large family.* | **suitable to do sth** *Would this be suitable to wear to Deb's wedding?* —opposite UNSUITABLE —**suitableness** *n* [U]

**suit·a·bly** /ˈsuːtəbli, ˈsjuː-‖ˈsuː-/ *adv* **1 suitably dressed/prepared/equipped etc** wearing the right clothes, having the right information, equipment etc for a particular situation: *We were relieved that Gordon had arrived at the wedding suitably dressed.* **2 suitably impressed/amazed** showing the amount of feeling you would expect in a particular situation: *The others were suitably impressed by the huge trout I caught.*

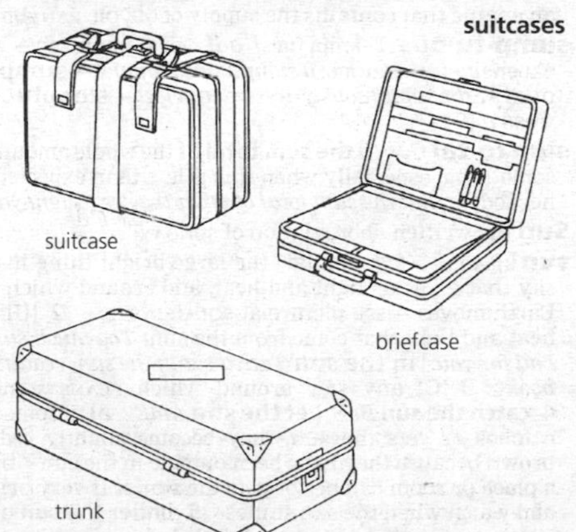


**suit·case** /ˈsuːtkeɪs, ˈsjuːt-‖ˈsuːt-/ *n* [C] a large case with a handle, used for carrying clothes and possessions when you travel

**suite** /swiːt/ *n* [C]
**1 ▶ ROOMS ◀** a set of rooms, especially expensive ones in a hotel: *a honeymoon suite* | **suite of rooms** *a suite of rooms for palace guests*
**2 ▶ FURNITURE ◀** *especially BrE* a set of matching furniture for a room: *a pink bathroom suite* | **three-piece suite** (=a large seat and two chairs)
**3 ▶ MUSIC ◀** a piece of music made up of several short parts: *the Nutcracker Suite*
**4 ▶ POLITICS ◀** the people who work for, advise, or help an important person; RETINUE
**5 ▶ COMPUTERS ◀** *technical* a group of related computer PROGRAMS that make a set

**suit·ing** /ˈsuːtɪŋ, ˈsjuː-‖ˈsuː-/ *n* [U] *technical* material used for making suits, especially woven wool

**sui·tor** /ˈsuːtə, ˈsjuː-‖ˈsuːtər/ *n* [C] *old use* a man who wants to marry a particular woman

**sul·fate** /ˈsʌlfeɪt/ *n* [C,I] the American spelling of SULPHATE

**sul·fide** /ˈsʌlfaɪd/ *n* [C,I] the American spelling of SULPHIDE

**sul·fur** /ˈsʌlfə‖-fər/ *n* [U] the American spelling of SULPHUR

**sulfur di·ox·ide** /ˌ·· ·ˈ··/ *n* [U] the American spelling of SULPHUR DIOXIDE

**sul·fu·ric a·cid** /sʌlˌfjʊərɪk ˈæsɪ̣d‖-ˌfjʊr-/ *n* [U] the American spelling of SULPHURIC ACID

**sul·fu·rous** /ˈsʌlfərəs/ *adj* the American spelling of SULPHUROUS

**sulk¹** /sʌlk/ *v* [I] to show that you are annoyed about something by being silent and having an unhappy expression on your face: *Stuart's sulking because I told him he couldn't go out and play.*

**sulk²** *n BrE* **in a sulk** angry and silent: *Neil's in a sulk because Paul won't play football with him.*

**sulk·y** /ˈsʌlki/ *adj* **1** showing that you are sulking: *a sulky frown* **2** tending to sulk: *a sulky child* —**sulkily** *adv* —**sulkiness** *n* [U]

**sul·len** /ˈsʌlən/ *adj* **1** silently showing anger or bad temper: *a look of sullen resentment* **2** *literary* sky or weather that is sullen is dark and unpleasant; GLOOMY (3) —**sullenly** *adv* —**sullenness** *n* [U]

**sul·ly** /ˈsʌli/ *v* [T] *formal or literary* to spoil or reduce the value of something that was perfect: *a scandal that sullied his reputation*

**sul·phate** *BrE*, **sulfate** *AmE* /ˈsʌlfeɪt/ *n* [C,U] a SALT¹ (4) formed from SULPHURIC ACID: *copper sulphate*

**sul·phide** *BrE*, **sulfide** *AmE* /ˈsʌlfaɪd/ *n* [C,U] a mixture of sulphur with another substance

**sul·phur** *BrE*, **sulfur** *AmE* /ˈsʌlfə‖-fər/ *n* [U] an ELEMENT (=simple substance) especially in the form of a light yellow powder, used in drugs, explosives, and industry

**sulphur di·ox·ide** *BrE*, **sulfur dioxide** *AmE* /ˌ·· ·ˈ··/ *n* [U] a poisonous gas that is a cause of air POLLUTION in industrial areas

**sul·phu·ric ac·id** *BrE*, **sulfuric acid** *AmE* /sʌlˌfjʊ-rɪk ˈæsɪ̣d‖-ˌfjʊr-/ *n* [U] a powerful acid

**sul·phu·rous** *BrE*, **sulfurous** *AmE* /ˈsʌlfərəs/ *adj* related to, full of, or used with sulphur

**sul·tan** /ˈsʌltən/ *n* [C] a ruler in some Muslim countries

**sul·ta·na** /sʌlˈtɑːnə‖-ˈtænə/ *n* [C] **1** a small pale RAISIN (=dried fruit) without seeds, used in baking; GOLDEN RAISIN *AmE* **2** also **Sultana** the wife, mother, or daughter of a sultan

**sul·tan·ate** /ˈsʌltəneɪt, -nɪ̣t/ *n* [C] **1** a country ruled by a sultan: *the sultanate of Oman* **2** the position of a sultan, or the period of time during which he rules

**sul·try** /ˈsʌltri/ *adj* **1** weather that is sultry is unpleasantly hot with no wind **2** a woman who is sultry makes other people feel strong sexual attraction to her: *a sultry look* —**sultriness** *n* [U]

S3 W2 **sum¹** /sʌm/ *n* **1 ▶ MONEY ◀** [C] an amount of money: **a large/small sum (of)** *Sid was left a large sum of money by his aunt.* | **for the sum of** *It was mine for the sum of £20.* —see also LUMP SUM **princely sum** (PRINCELY (1)) **2 the sum of** the total produced when you add two or more numbers together: *The sum of 6 and 4 is 10.* **3 greater/more than the sum of its parts** a group of things or people that is greater than the sum of its parts has a quality or effectiveness as a group that you would not expect from looking at each member **4 ▶ CALCULATION ◀** [C] *BrE* a simple calculation by adding, multiplying, dividing etc, especially one done by children at school **5 do your sums** *informal BrE* to calculate whether you have enough money to do something: *Well I've done my sums, and I think I can afford a holiday.* **6 in sum** *old-fashioned* used before a statement that gives the main information about something in a few simple words: *It was, in sum, a complete failure.* —see also SUM TOTAL

**sum²** *v*

**sum up, summed, summing** *phr v* **1** [I,T] to give the main information about a report, speech, TRIAL¹ (1) etc in a short statement at the end; SUMMARIZE | **to sum up** *So, to sum up, we need to concentrate on staff training.* | **sum** sth ↔ **up** *The last chapter sums up the arguments.* **2** [T **sum** sb/sth ↔ **up**] to form a judgment or opinion about someone or something: *Pat summed up the situation at a glance.* **3 that (about) sums it up** *spoken* used to say that you have said everything that is important about a subject —see also SUMMING-UP

**sum·ma cum lau·de** /ˌsʌmə kʌm ˈlɔːdi,-ˈlaʊdeɪ‖ˌsʊmə kʊm ˈlaʊdi/ *adj, adv AmE* the highest level of HONOURS given to American university or college students —compare CUM LAUDE

**sum·mar·ize** also **-ise** *BrE* /ˈsʌməraɪz/ *v* [I,T] to make a short statement giving only the main information and not the details of a plan, event, report etc: *Jack quickly summarized the main points of his plan.*

**sum·ma·ry¹** /ˈsʌməri/ *n* [C] a short statement that gives the main information about something, without giving all the details: *Please write a one-page summary of this report.* | *a news summary* | **in summary** *So, in summary, we've got to try to get further funding.*

**summary²** *adj* [only before noun] *formal* done immediately, without paying attention to the usual processes, rules etc: *a summary execution* —**summarily** *adv*: *Franklin was summarily dismissed.*

S2 **sum·mat** /ˈsʌmət/ *pron dialect* a spoken form of SOMETHING

**sum·ma·tion** /səˈmeɪʃən/ *n* [C] *formal* **1** a summary; SUMMING-UP **2** the total amount or number you get when two or more things are added together

S1 W1 **sum·mer¹** /ˈsʌmə‖-ər/ *n* **1** [C,U] the time of the year when the sun is hottest and the days are longest, between spring and autumn: *Are you going on vacation this summer?* | *the summer of 1940* | **be summer** *I'm so glad it's summer!* | **summer clothes/sports etc** (=used or done in summer) *a summer dress* | **high summer** (=the hottest part of summer) **2 summer rental** *AmE* [C] a house or apartment that you rent only during the summer **3 your 50/70 etc summers** *literary* a way of saying how old someone is: *looking younger than his 70 summers* —see also INDIAN SUMMER

**summer²** *v* [I] to spend the summer in a particular place

**summer camp** /ˈ·· ˌ·/ *n* [C,U] a place where children in the US can stay during the summer, and take part in various activities

**summer hol·i·days** /ˌ·· ˈ···/ *n* [plural] *BrE* the period of time during the summer when schools and universities are closed; SUMMER VACATION *AmE*

**sum·mer·house** /ˈsʌməhaʊs‖-ər-/ *n* [C] a building in your garden, where you can sit in warm weather

**summer pud·ding** /ˌ·· ˈ··/ *n* [C,U] a British sweet dish made from pieces of bread and fruit such as berries

**summer school** /ˈ·· ·/ *n* [C,U] courses you can take in the summer at a school, university, or college

**summer sol·stice** /ˌ·· ˈ··/ *n* [singular] the longest day in the northern HEMISPHERE (=top half of the earth), around June 22nd

**sum·mer·time** /ˈsʌmətaɪm‖-ər-/ *n* [U] the season when it is summer —see also BRITISH SUMMER TIME

**summer va·ca·tion** /ˌ·· ·ˈ··/ *n* [U] *AmE* the period of time during the summer when schools and universities are closed; SUMMER HOLIDAYS *BrE*

**sum·mer·y** /ˈsʌməri/ *adj* suitable for, or reminding you of the summer: *a light summery dress*

**summing-up** /ˌ·· ˈ·/ *n plural* **summings-up** [C] a statement giving the main facts but not the details of something, especially made by a judge at the end of a TRIAL¹ (1): *In his summing-up, the judge said it was dangerous to convict on this evidence alone.* —see also **sum up** (SUM²)

**sum·mit** /ˈsʌmɪ̈t/ *n* [C] **1** the top of a mountain: *The climbers reached the summit of Mount Everest yesterday.* —see picture on page 835 **2** a set of meetings between the leaders of several governments: *the recent Geneva summit* | **summit meeting** (=for a particular purpose) **3 the summit of** *formal* the greatest amount or highest level of something: *the summit of scientific achievement* W3

**sum·mon** /ˈsʌmən/ *v* [T] *formal* **1** to officially order someone to come to a meeting, a court of law etc: **summon sb to sth** *We were all summoned to a meeting with the principal.* | **summon sb to do sth** *They'll probably be summoning you to appear in court.* **2** also **summon** sth ↔ **up** to make a great effort use your strength, courage, energy etc: *Summoning all her strength, Julia gave one last pull.* | *I couldn't summon up the courage to ask you out until now.* **3 summon a meeting/conference etc** to arrange for a meeting to take place and order people to come to it; CONVENE

**sum·mons¹** /ˈsʌmənz/ *n plural* **summonses** [C] an official order to appear in a court of law: **serve a summons on sb** (=order someone to appear in court)

**summons²** *v* [T usually passive] to order someone to appear in a court of law: *I was summonsed to appear as a witness.*

**su·mo** /ˈsuːməʊ‖-moʊ/ also **sumo wrest·ling** /ˌ·· ˈ··/ *n* [U] a Japanese form of wrestling (WRESTLE (1)), done by men who are very large —**sumo wrestler** *n* [C]

**sump** /sʌmp/ *n* [C] **1** the lowest part of a DRAINAGE system where liquids or wastes remain **2** *BrE* the part of an engine that contains the supply of oil; OIL PAN *AmE*

**sump·tu·ous** /ˈsʌmptʃuəs/ *adj* very impressive and expensive; LUXURIOUS: *a sumptuous banquet* —**sumptuously** *adv*: *sumptuously dressed in velvet* —**sumptuousness** *n* [U]

**sum to·tal** /ˌ· ˈ··/ *n* **the sum total of** the whole amount of something, especially when this is less than expected or needed: *Is that the sum total of what they've taught you?*

**Sun** the written abbreviation of SUNDAY

**sun¹** /sʌn/ *n* **1** [singular] the large bright thing in the sky that gives us light and heat, and around which the Earth moves —see picture at SOLAR SYSTEM **2** [U] the heat and light that come from the sun: *Too much sun is bad for you.* | **in the sun** *Tanya sat in the sun, reading a book.* **3** [C] any star around which PLANETS move **4 catch the sun** *BrE*, **get the sun** *AmE* **a)** if someone catches or gets the sun, they become slightly red or brown because they have been outside in the sun **b)** if a place or room catches or gets the sun, it is very bright and warm when the sun shines **5 under the sun** used to emphasize that you are talking about something that includes very large numbers of ideas or things etc: *Santos could talk about any subject under the sun.* —see also **make hay while the sun shines** (HAY (3)) S2 W1

**sun²** *v* **sunned, sunning** [T] **sun yourself** to sit or lie outside when the sun is shining: *a cat sunning itself on the patio*

**sun-baked** /ˌ· ˈ·/ *adj* made very hard and dry by the sun: *the sun-baked earth of the western desert*

**sun·bathe** /ˈsʌnbeɪð/ *v* [I] to sit or lie outside in the sun, especially in order to become brown: *a good beach for sunbathing* —see BATH³ (USAGE)

**sun·beam** /ˈsʌnbiːm/ *n* [C] a beam of light from the sun that you can see because it is shining through a cloud

**sun·bed** /ˈsʌnbed/ *n* [C] **1** a metal structure the size of a bed that you lie on to make your skin brown using light from special lamps **2** a SUN LOUNGER —see also SUNLAMP

**sun·belt** /ˈsʌnbelt/ *n* [singular] the southern or south-western parts of the US, from Virginia to California

**sun blind** /ˈ· ·/ *n* [C] *BrE* the thing you pull down over a window to keep the sun out of a room

**sun·block** /ˈsʌnblɒk‖-blɑːk/ *n* [C,U] cream or oil that you rub into your skin, in order to completely stop the sun's light from burning you —compare SUNSCREEN

**sun·bon·net** /ˈsʌnbɒnɪ̣t‖-bɑː-/ *n* [C] a hat worn in the past by women as protection from the sun

**sun·burn** /ˈsʌnbɜːn‖-ɜːrn/ *n* [U] the condition of having skin that is red and painful, as a result of spending too much time in the sun —**sunburned** also **sunburnt** *adj* —compare SUNTAN

**sun cream** /ˈ· ·/ *n* [C,U] *BrE* a cream or oil that you rub into your skin to stop the sun from burning you too much; SUNTAN LOTION

**sun·dae** /ˈsʌndeɪ‖-di/ *n* [C] a dish made from ICE CREAM, fruit, sweet SAUCE, nuts etc: *a chocolate sundae*

**Sun·day** /ˈsʌndi/ written abbreviation **Sun.** *n* [C,U] **1** the day between Saturday and Monday. In Britain, Sunday is considered the last day of the week, and in the US it is considered the first day of the week: *I went to a concert last Sunday.* | *We're going to a match on Sunday.* | *Sunday nights are usually pretty quiet.* | **on Sundays** (=each Sunday) *Do you go to church on Sundays?* | **a Sunday** (=one of the Sundays in the year) *My birthday is on a Sunday this year.* | **the Sunday** *BrE* (=the Sunday of the week being mentioned) *Nan came on the Monday and left on the Sunday.* **2 Sunday best** your best clothes, worn only for special occasions or for church **3 Sunday driver** an insulting word meaning someone who annoys other people by driving too slowly —see also **never in a month of Sundays** (MONTH (7))

**Sunday school** /ˈ·· ·/ *n* [C,U] a place where children are taught about Christianity on Sundays

**sun·deck** /ˈsʌndek/ *n* [C] a part of a ship where people can sit in the sun

**sun·der** /ˈsʌndə‖-ər/ *v* [T] *literary* to break something into parts, especially violently —see also ASUNDER

**sun·dial** /ˈsʌndaɪəl/ *n* [C] an object used in the past for telling the time, by looking at the position of a shadow made on a stone circle by a pointed piece of metal

**sun·down** /ˈsʌndaʊn/ *n* [U] *old-fashioned* SUNSET (1)

**sun·down·er** /ˈsʌnˌdaʊnə‖-ər/ *n* [C] *informal especially BrE* an alcoholic drink drunk in the evening

**sun-drenched** /ˈ· ·/ *adj* a sun-drenched place is one where the sun shines most of the time: *sun-drenched tropical islands*

**sun·dress** /ˈsʌndres/ *n* [C] a dress that you wear in hot weather, that does not cover your arms, neck, or shoulders

**sun-dried** /ˈ· ·/ *adj* [only before noun] sun-dried food has been left in the sun to dry in order to give it a particular taste: *sun-dried tomatoes*

**sun·dries** /ˈsʌndriz/ *n* [plural] *formal* small objects that are not important enough to be named separately —see also SUNDRY

**sun·dry** /ˈsʌndri/ *adj* [only before noun] *formal* **1 all and sundry** everyone, not just a few carefully chosen people: *In the 80s the economy was booming and banks dished out loans to all and sundry.* **2** not similar enough to form a group; various: *pens, books, and other sundry articles*

**sun·fish** /ˈsʌnfɪʃ/ *n* [C,U] a fish that lives in the sea and has a large round body

**sun·flow·er** /ˈsʌnˌflaʊə‖-flaʊr/ *n* [C] a very tall plant with a large yellow flower and seeds that can be eaten

**sung** /sʌŋ/ the past participle of SING

**sun·glass·es** /ˈsʌnˌglɑːsɪ̣z‖-ˌglæ-/ *n* [plural] dark glasses that you wear to protect your eyes when the sun is very bright

**sun god** /ˈ· ·/ *n* [C] a god in some ancient religions who represents the sun or has power over it

**sun hat** /ˈ· ·/ *n* [C] a hat that you wear to protect your head from the sun —see picture at HAT

**sunk** /sʌŋk/ the past tense and past participle of SINK¹

**sunk·en** /ˈsʌŋkən/ *adj* **1** [only before noun] having fallen to the bottom of the sea: *a sunken ship* | *sunken treasure* **2** [only before noun] built or placed at a lower level than the surrounding floor, ground etc: *a sunken bath* | *a sunken garden* **3 sunken cheeks/eyes etc** cheeks or eyes that have fallen inwards, especially because you are old, or ill

**sun·lamp** /ˈsʌnlæmp/ *n* [C] a lamp that produces a special light used for making your skin brown

**sun·less** /ˈsʌnləs/ *adj* having no light from the sun: *the sunless depths of the ocean*

**sun·light** /ˈsʌnlaɪt/ *n* [U] natural light that comes from the sun: *bright sunlight* | *plants that need a lot of sunlight*

**sun·lit** /ˈsʌnlɪt/ *adj* made brighter by light from the sun: *a sunlit garden*

**sun lounge** /ˈ· ·/ *BrE n* [C] a room with large windows and often a glass roof, designed to let in lots of light; SUN PORCH *AmE*

**sun loun·ger** /ˈ· ˌ··/ *n* [C] a light chair like a folding bed, that you can sit or lie on outside

**Sun·na, Sun·nah** /ˈsʊnə, ˈsʌnə/ *n* **the Sunna** a set of Muslim customs and rules based on the words and acts of Muhammad

**Sun·ni** /ˈsʊni, ˈsʌni/ *n* [C] a Muslim who follows one of the two main branches of the Muslim religion —compare SHIITE

**sun·ny** /ˈsʌni/ *adj* **1** full of light from the sun: *a sunny day* | *a sunny room* **2** *informal* cheerful and happy: *a sunny smile*

**sunny-side up** /ˌ··· ˈ·/ *adj* [not before noun] *AmE* an egg that is cooked sunny-side up is cooked in hot fat on one side only, and not turned over in the pan

**sun porch** /ˈ· ·/ *AmE n* [C] a room with large windows and often a glass roof, designed to let in lots of light; SUN LOUNGE *BrE*

**sun·rise** /ˈsʌnraɪz/ *n* [U] **1** the time when the sun first appears in the morning: *We got up at sunrise.* **2** the part of the sky where the sun first appears in the morning: *sunrise over Mount Fuji*

**sunrise in·dus·try** /ˈ·· ˌ···/ *n* [C] an industry, such as ELECTRONICS or making computers, that uses modern processes and takes the place of older industries —compare HEAVY INDUSTRY

**sun·roof** /ˈsʌnruːf/ *n* [C] **1** a part of the roof of a car that you can open to let in air and light —see picture on page 409 **2** a flat roof of a building where you can sit when the sun is shining

**sun·screen** /ˈsʌnskriːn/ *n* [C,U] a cream or oil that you rub into your skin to stop the sun from burning you —see also SUNBLOCK

**sun·set** /ˈsʌnset/ *n* **1** [U] the time of day when the sun disappears and night begins: **at sunset** *The builders stop work at sunset.* **2** [C,U] the part of the sky where the sun gradually disappears at the end of the day: *We sat on the beach and watched the sunset.*

**sun·shade** /ˈsʌnʃeɪd/ *n* [C] an object shaped like an UMBRELLA, used especially in the past as protection from the sun; PARASOL

S3 **sun·shine** /ˈsʌnʃaɪn/ *n* [U] **1** a word meaning the light and heat that come from the sun, used when you want to say that this is pleasant: *Northern Ireland will start dry with some sunshine.* **2** *informal* happiness: **ray of sunshine** *Zoe was the only ray of sunshine during those depressing months.*

**sun·spot** /ˈsʌnspɒt‖-spɑːt/ *n* [C] **1** *technical* a small dark area on the sun's surface **2** *informal* a place where the sun shines a lot, that many people go to on holiday

**sun·stroke** /ˈsʌnstrəʊk‖-stroʊk/ *n* [U] fever, weakness etc caused by being outside in the sun for too long

**sun·tan** /ˈsʌntæn/ *n* [C] attractively brown skin which you get when you spend a lot of time in bright sunlight TAN² (2) —**suntanned** *adj* —compare SUNBURN

**suntan lo·tion** /ˈ·· ˌ··/ also **suntan oil** /ˈ·· ˌ·/ *n* [C,U] a cream or oil that you rub into your skin to stop the sun from burning you too much

**sun·trap** /ˈsʌntræp/ *n* [C] a place that is sheltered and gets a lot of heat and light from the sun: *Our terrace is a real suntrap.*

**sun-up** /ˈ· ·/ *n* [U] *old-fashioned* SUNRISE

**sun-wor·ship·per** /ˈ· ˌ···/ *n* [C] *informal* someone who likes to lie in the sun to get a SUNTAN

**sup** /sʌp/ *v* **1** [T] to drink something, especially slowly in small amounts: *Mrs Holliday was supping porridge in the back kitchen.* **2** *old use* to eat supper —**sup** *n* [C]

**super-** /suːpə, sjuː-‖suːpər/ *prefix* more, larger, greater, or more powerful than usual: *a supertanker* (=a ship that can carry extremely large loads)|*superglue*|*super-rich film stars*|*superheated steam*

S2 **su·per¹** /ˈsuːpə, ˈsjuː-‖ˈsuːpər/ *adj informal* extremely good; WONDERFUL: *It's a super place for a holiday.*|*That sounds super.*|*What a super idea!*

**super²** *n* [C] *informal* a SUPERINTENDENT (3)

**super³** *adv AmE spoken* extremely: *Sorry, I'm super tired, I have to turn in.*

**su·per·a·bun·dance** /ˌsuːpərəˈbʌndəns, ˌsjuː-‖ˌsuː-/ *n formal* **a superabundance of** more than enough of something —**superabundant** *adj*

**su·per·an·nu·at·ed** /ˌsuːpərˈænjueɪtɪ̬d, ˌsjuː-‖ˌsuː-/ *adj formal* old and no longer useful or no longer able: *a load of superannuated computer equipment*|*superannuated Tory politicians*

**su·per·an·nu·a·tion** /ˌsuːpərænjuˈeɪʃən, ˌsjuː-‖ˌsuː-/ *n* [U] *technical especially BrE* money paid as a PENSION¹, especially from your former employer

**superannuation scheme** /ˌ····ˈ·· ·/ *n* [C] *BrE* a type of PENSION PLAN that is paid for by your employer

**su·perb** /sjuːˈpɜːb, suː-‖sʊˈpɜːrb/ *adj* [no comparative] extremely good; excellent: *The food was superb.*|*a superb performance* —**superbly** *adv*

**su·per·bug** /ˈsuːpəbʌg, ˈsjuː-‖ˈsuːpər-/ *n* [C] *not technical* a type of BACTERIA that cannot be killed by traditional drugs

**su·per·charg·er** /ˈsuːpəˌtʃɑːdʒə, ˈsjuː-‖ˈsuːpərˌtʃɑːrdʒər/ *n* [C] *technical* a piece of equipment that increases the power of an engine by supplying air or FUEL¹ (1) at a pressure that is higher than normal —**supercharged** *adj*

**su·per·cil·i·ous** /ˌsuːpəˈsɪliəs◂, ˌsjuː-‖ˌsuːpər-/ *adj* behaving as if you think that other people are less important than you; HAUGHTY: *She's got a supercilious way of speaking that makes me want to scream!*|*a supercilious smile* —**superciliously** *adv* —**superciliousness** *n* [U]

**su·per·con·duc·tiv·i·ty** /ˌsuːpəkɒndʌkˈtɪvɪ̬ti, ˌsjuː-‖ˌsuːpərkɑːn-/ *n* [U] the ability of some substances to allow electricity to flow through them very easily, especially at very low temperatures

**su·per·con·duc·tor** /ˌsuːpəkənˈdʌktə, ˌsjuː-‖ˌsuːpərkənˈdʌktər/ *n* [C] a substance that allows electricity to flow through it very easily, especially at very low temperatures

**su·per·du·per** /ˌsuːpəˈduːpə◂, ˌsjuː-‖ˌsuːpərˈduːpər◂/ *adj old-fashioned* extremely good; SUPER¹

**su·per·e·go** /ˌsuːpərˈiːgəʊ, -ˈegəʊ, ˌsjuː-‖ˌsuːpərˈiːgoʊ, -egoʊ/ *n* [C] *technical* a word meaning your conscience, used in Freudian PSYCHOLOGY —compare EGO (3), ID

**su·per·fi·cial** /ˌsuːpəˈfɪʃəl◂, ˌsjuː-‖ˌsuːpər-/ *adj*
**1** ▶ **APPEARANCE** ◀ seeming to have a particular appearance at first, although this is not true or real: *Despite their superficial similarities, the two novels are in fact very different.*|*a superficial air of tranquility*
**2** ▶ **NOT LOOKING/STUDYING CAREFULLY** ◀ not studying or looking at something carefully and only noticing the most obvious things: *theories based on a superficial knowledge of Japanese business methods*
**3** ▶ **WOUND/DAMAGE** ◀ affecting only the surface of your skin or the outside part of something, and therefore not serious: *She escaped with only superficial cuts and bruises.*|**superficial examination/study etc** *Even a superficial inspection revealed grave flaws.*
**4** ▶ **PERSON** ◀ someone who is superficial does not think about things that are serious or important; SHALLOW¹ (2): *a weak-minded and superficial husband who seemed only interested in football*
**5** ▶ **NOT IMPORTANT** ◀ superficial changes, difficulties etc are not important and do not have a big effect: *superficial changes in government policies on the environment*
**6** ▶ **TOP LAYER** ◀ existing in or connected with the top layer of something, especially soil, rock etc —**superficially** *adv* —**superficiality** /ˌsuːpəfɪʃiˈælɪ̬ti, ˌsjuː-‖ˌsuːpər-/ *n* [U]

**su·per·flu·i·ty** /ˌsuːpəˈfluːɪ̬ti, ˌsjuː-‖ˌsuːpər-/ *n formal* **a superfluity of** a larger amount of something than is necessary

**su·per·flu·ous** /suːˈpɜːfluəs, sjuː-‖suːˈpɜːr-/ *adj formal* more than is needed or wanted; unnecessary: *We could all see what was going on, so the commentary was superfluous.* —**superfluously** *adv* —**superfluousness** *n* [U]

**su·per·glue** /ˈsuːpəgluː, ˈsjuː-‖ˈsuːpər-/ *n* [U] *trademark* a very strong glue that sticks very quickly and is difficult to remove —**superglue** *v* [T]

**su·per·grass** /ˈsuːpəgrɑːs, ˈsjuː-‖ˈsuːpərgræs/ *n* [C] *BrE* a criminal who gives the police information about many other criminals, in order to get a less severe punishment

**su·per·he·ro** /ˈsuːpəˌhɪərəʊ, ˈsjuː-‖ˈsuːpərˌhɪroʊ/ *n* [C] a character in stories who uses special powers, such as great strength or the ability to fly, to help people

**su·per·high·way** /ˈsuːpəˌhaɪweɪ, ˈsjuː-‖ˈsuːpər-/ *n* [C] *AmE* a very large road on which you can drive distances quickly —see also INFORMATION SUPERHIGHWAY

**su·per·hu·man** /ˌsuːpəˈhjuːmən◂, ˌsjuː-‖ˌsuːpərˈhjuː-, -ˈjuː-/ *adj* much greater than ordinary human powers or abilities: **superhuman effort/strength** *It will require a superhuman effort to get the job done on time.*

**su·per·im·pose** /ˌsuːpərɪmˈpəʊz, ˌsjuː-‖ˌsuːpərɪmˈpoʊz/ *v* [T] **1** to put one picture, image, or photograph on top of another so that both can be partly seen: **superimpose sth on/onto sth** *His face had been superimposed onto a different background.* **2** to combine two systems, ideas, opinions etc so that one influences the other: *Eastern themes superimposed onto Western architecture* —**superimposition** /ˌsuːpərɪmpəˈzɪʃən, ˌsjuː-‖ˌsuː-/ *n* [U]

**su·per·in·tend** /ˌsuːpərɪnˈtend, ˌsjuː-‖ˌsuː-/ *v* [T] *formal* to be in charge of something, and control how it is done —**superintendence** *n* [U]

**su·per·in·tend·ent** /ˌsuːpərɪnˈtendənt, ˌsjuː-‖ˌsuː-/ *n* [C] **1** someone who is officially in charge of a place, job, activity etc **2** a middle rank in the British police, or someone who has this rank **3** *AmE* someone who is in charge of an apartment building; CARETAKER (1) *BrE*

**4** also **superintendent of schools** someone who is in charge of all the schools in a particular area in the US

**su·pe·ri·or¹** /suːˈpɪəriə, sjuː-‖sʊˈpɪriər/ *adj* **1** having a higher position or rank than someone else: *I'll report you to your superior officer.* | **a superior court** **2** better, more powerful, more effective etc than a similar person or thing, especially one that you are competing against: *Fletcher's fitness and superior technique brought him victory.* | [+ **to**] *The new mark IV engine is superior to its rivals.* | **vastly superior** (=very much better than others) **3** a word meaning of very good quality, used especially in advertising: *a superior wine* | *superior craftsmanship* **4** thinking that you are better than other people: *He has such a superior attitude, I feel like spitting at him.* **5** *technical* higher in position; upper: *the superior limbs* (=arms) **6 Mother Superior** a title for the woman in charge of a group of NUNS —compare INFERIOR¹

**superior²** *n* [C] someone who has a higher rank or position than you, especially in a job: **sb's immediate superior** (=the person in a position directly above you) —compare INFERIOR

**su·per·i·or·i·ty** /suːˌpɪəriˈɒrɪ̈ti, sjuː-‖sʊˌpɪriˈɔːrɪ̈ti, -ˈɑː-/ *n* [U] **1** the quality of being better, more skilful, more powerful etc than other things: [+ **over**] *the intellectual superiority of humans over other animals* | [+ **in**] *US superiority in air power* **2** an attitude that shows you think you are better than other people: *Janet always spoke with an air of superiority.*

**su·per·la·tive¹** /suːˈpɜːlətɪv, sjuː-‖sʊˈpɜːr-/ *adj* **1** excellent: *a superlative performance* **2** a superlative adjective or adverb expresses the highest degree of a particular quality: *The superlative form of 'good' is 'best'.* —compare COMPARATIVE¹ (4)

**superlative²** *n* **1 the superlative** the superlative form of an adjective or adverb: *'Biggest' is the superlative of 'big'.* **2** [C] a word in this form, used especially when expressing great praise or admiration: **a string of superlatives** (=several superlative adjectives praising someone or something)

**su·per·la·tive·ly** /suːˈpɜːlətɪvli, sjuː-‖sʊˈpɜːr-/ *adv* extremely: *superlatively happy*

**su·per·man** /ˈsuːpəmæn, ˈsjuː-‖ˈsuːpər-/ *plural* **supermen** /-men/ *n* [C] a man of unusually great ability or strength

3 **su·per·mar·ket** /ˈsuːpəˌmɑːkɪ̈t, ˈsjuː-‖ˈsuːpərˌmɑːr-/ *n* [C] a very large shop where customers can choose from a large number of different kinds of food and other regularly needed goods

**su·per·nal** /suːˈpɜːnl, sjuː-‖sʊˈpɜːr-/ *adj formal* connected with the sky or heaven

**su·per·nat·u·ral¹** /ˌsuːpəˈnætʃərəl◂, ˌsjuː-‖ˌsuːpər-/ *adj* impossible to explain by natural causes, and therefore seeming to involve the powers of gods or magic: *supernatural forces* —**supernaturally** *adv*

**supernatural²** *n* **the supernatural** supernatural events, powers, and creatures: *belief in the supernatural*

**su·per·no·va** /ˌsuːpəˈnəʊvə, ˌsjuː-‖ˌsuːpərˈnoʊ-/ *n* [C] a very large exploding star —compare NOVA

**su·per·nu·me·ra·ry** /ˌsuːpəˈnjuːmərəri, ˌsjuː-‖ˌsuːpərˈnuːməreri/ *n* [C] *formal* someone or something that is additional to the number of people or things that are needed —**supernumerary** *adj*

**su·per·pow·er** /ˈsuːpəˌpaʊə, ˈsjuː-‖ˈsuːpərˌpaʊər/ *n* [C] a nation that has very great military and political power

**su·per·script** /ˈsuːpəskrɪpt, ˈsjuː-‖ˈsuːpər-/ *adj* written or printed above a number, letter etc —**superscript** *n* [C,U]

**su·per·sede** /ˌsuːpəˈsiːd, ˌsjuː-‖ˌsuːpər-/ *v* [T often passive] if a new idea, product, or method supersedes another one, it becomes used instead because it is more modern or effective: *Television superseded radio in the Fifties.*

**su·per·ser·ver** /ˈsuːpəˌsɜːvə, ˈsjuː-‖ˈsuːpərˌsɜːrvər/ *n* [C] a very powerful computer that controls other computers

**su·per·son·ic** /ˌsuːpəˈsɒnɪk◂, ˌsjuː-‖ˌsuːpərˈsɑː-/ *adj* faster than the speed of sound: *supersonic aircraft* —compare SUBSONIC

**su·per·star** /ˈsuːpəstɑː, ˈsjuː-‖ˈsuːpərstɑːr/ *n* [C] an extremely famous performer, especially a musician or film actor

**su·per·sti·tion** /ˌsuːpəˈstɪʃən, ˌsjuː-‖ˌsuːpər-/ *n* [C,U] a belief that some objects or actions are lucky and some are unlucky, based on old ideas of magic: *the old superstition that walking under a ladder is unlucky*

**su·per·sti·tious** /ˌsuːpəˈstɪʃəs◂, ˌsjuː-‖ˌsuːpər-/ *adj* influenced by old-fashioned beliefs about luck and magic —**superstitiously** *adv*

**su·per·store** /ˈsuːpəstɔː, ˈsjuː-‖ˈsuːpərstɔːr/ *n* [C] *BrE* a very large shop that sells many different types of goods, usually just outside a town

**su·per·struc·ture** /ˈsuːpəˌstrʌktʃə, ˈsjuː-‖ˈsuːpərˌstrʌktʃər/ *n* [singular, U] **1** a structure that is built on top of the main part of something such as a ship or building **2** *formal* political and social systems that are based on a simpler system: *a superstructure of religion based on nature worship*

**su·per·tank·er** /ˈsuːpəˌtæŋkə, ˈsjuː-‖ˈsuːpərˌtæŋkər/ *n* [C] an extremely large ship that can carry large quantities of oil or other liquids

**su·per·vene** /ˌsuːpəˈviːn, ˌsjuː-‖ˌsuːpər-/ *v* [I] *formal* to happen unexpectedly, especially in a way that stops or interrupts an event or situation

**su·per·vise** /ˈsuːpəvaɪz, ˈsjuː-‖ˈsuːpər-/ *v* [I,T] to be in charge of a group of workers or students and be responsible for making sure that they do their work properly —**supervisor** *n* [C] —**supervisory** /ˌsuːpəˈvaɪzəri◂, ˌsjuː-‖ˌsuːpər-/ *adj*: *She works there in a supervisory capacity.*

**su·per·vi·sion** /ˌsuːpəˈvɪʒən, ˌsjuː-‖ˌsuːpər-/ *n* [U] the act of supervising someone or something: *The patient is improving, but still needs constant supervision.* | **under sb's supervision** *We work under the Chief Engineer's supervision.*

**su·pine** /ˈsuːpaɪn, ˈsjuː-‖suːˈpaɪn/ *adj formal* **1** lying on your back —opposite PRONE (2) **2** allowing other people to make decisions instead of you in a way that seems very weak-minded: *a supine and cowardly press, scared by government threats of censorship* —**supinely** *adv*

**sup·per** /ˈsʌpə‖-ər/ *n* [C,U] the last meal of the evening

**sup·plant** /səˈplɑːnt‖səˈplænt/ *v* [T] to take the place of a person or thing so that they are no longer used, no longer in a position of power etc: *Barker was soon supplanted as party leader.*

**sup·ple** /ˈsʌpəl/ *adj* **1** someone who is supple bends and moves easily and gracefully: *She exercises every day to keep herself supple.* **2** leather, skin, wood etc that is supple is soft and bends easily —**suppleness** *n* [U]

**sup·ple·ment¹** /ˈsʌplɪ̈mənt/ *n* [C] **1** something that you add to something else to improve it or make it complete: *a dietary supplement* **2** an additional part at the end of a book, or a separate part of a newspaper, magazine etc: *the Sunday supplements* **3** an amount of money that is added to the price of a service, hotel room etc: *There is a £5 supplement for extra sheets and towels.*

**sup·ple·ment²** /ˈsʌplɪ̈ment/ *v* [T always + adv/prep] to add something, especially to what you earn or eat, in order to increase it to an acceptable level: **supplement sth by/with** *Kia supplements her regular salary by tutoring in the evenings.* —**supplementation** /ˌsʌplɪ̈menˈteɪʃən/ *n* [U]

**sup·ple·men·ta·ry** /ˌsʌplɪ̈ˈmentəri◂/ *adj* provided in addition to what already exists: *There is a supplementary water supply in case the main supply fails.*

**sup·pli·ant** /ˈsʌpliənt/ *n* [C] *literary* a supplicant —**suppliant** *adj*

**sup·pli·cant** /ˈsʌplɪkənt/ *n* [C] *literary* someone who asks for something, especially from someone in a position of power or from God

**sup·pli·cate** /ˈsʌplɪ̣keɪt/ *v* [I,T] *literary* to ask or pray for help from someone in power or from God —**supplication** /ˌsʌplɪ̣ˈkeɪʃən/ *n* [U] *Paolo knelt and bowed his head in supplication.*

**sup·pli·er** /səˈplaɪə‖-ər/ *n* [C] also **suppliers** a company that provides a particular product: *Continental is one of the world's biggest supplies of grain.*

S3 W2 **sup·ply¹** /səˈplaɪ/ *n*
**1** ► **AMOUNT AVAILABLE** ◄ [C] an amount of something that is available to be used: [+ **of**] *a regular supply of fresh vegetables | More donors are needed as blood supplies are running low.*
**2 be in short supply** if something is in short supply, there is very little of it available and it is difficult to get: *Chocolate was in short supply during the war.*
**3 gas/electricity/water supply** a system that is used to supply gas etc: **cut off a supply** (=stop the supply) *During the drought some households had their water supply cut off.*
**4** ► **NECESSARY THINGS** ◄ **supplies** [plural] food, clothes and things necessary for daily life, especially for a group of people over a period of time: *A convoy of trucks packed with vital medical supplies succeeded in reaching the town.*
**5 supply and demand** [U] the relationship between the amount of goods for sale and the amount that people want to buy, especially the way it influences prices
**6** ► **ACT OF SUPPLYING** ◄ [U] the act or process of supplying something: *The military government is trying to stop the supply of guns to the rebels. | supply of oxygen to the brain*
**7 supply ship/convoy/route etc** a ship etc used for bringing or storing supplies —see also MONEY SUPPLY

S3 W3 **supply²** *v* [T] to provide people with something that they need or want, especially regularly over a long period of time: **supply sb with sth** *US forces mounted a massive air operation to keep the city supplied with food. | An informer supplied the police with the names of those involved in the crime.* | **supply sth to sb** *They were arrested for supplying drugs to street dealers.*

**supply-side e·co·nom·ics** /ˌ·ˈ· · ··ˌ··/ *n* [U] *technical* the idea that if the government reduces taxes, producers will be able to make more goods and this will improve a country's economic situation

**supply teach·er** /ˌ·ˈ· ˌ··/ *n* [C] *BrE* a teacher who does the work of another teacher who is ill, on a course etc; SUBSTITUTE TEACHER *AmE*

S2 W2 **sup·port¹** /səˈpɔːt‖-ɔːrt/ *v* [T]
**1** ► **AGREE WITH SB/STH** ◄ to say that you agree with an idea, group, person etc and want them to succeed: *The bill was supported by a large majority in the Senate.* | **support sb in sth** *the peasants who supported Castro in his bid for power* | **strongly support** (=support something very much)
**2** ► **HOLD STH UP** ◄ to hold the weight of something, keep it in place, or prevent it from falling: *The middle part of the bridge is supported by two huge towers. | I grabbed the rail to support myself.*
**3** ► **PROVIDE MONEY TO LIVE** ◄ to provide enough money for someone to pay for all the things they need: *She needs a high income to support such a large family. | It's difficult to support yourself on this salary.*
**4** ► **GIVE MONEY TO STH** ◄ to encourage a group, organization or event etc by giving it money: *Please support your local theatre, buy some tickets today!*
**5** ► **HELP SB** ◄ to help someone by being sympathetic and kind to them during a difficult time in their life: *My wife supported me enormously when my mother died.*
**6** ► **LAND** ◄ if land can support people or animals, it is of good enough quality to grow enough food for them to live: *This land isn't fertile enough to support many cattle.*
**7** ► **A BAD HABIT** ◄ to get money in order to pay for a bad habit such as taking drugs: *He stole from his mother's savings to support his drug habit.*
**8** ► **PROVE STH** ◄ to show or prove that something is true or correct: *The results support our original theory.*
**9** ► **SPORTS TEAM** ◄ *especially BrE* to like a particular sports team and go to watch the games they play: *Trev supports Arsenal, but I like Spurs.*
**10** ► **BEAR STH** ◄ [usually in negatives] *formal* to be able to bear something; ENDURE: *She could not support the heat any longer.* —see also INSUPPORTABLE

**support²** *n* S W
**1** ► **APPROVAL** ◄ [U] approval and encouragement for an idea, plan etc: *Local people have given us a lot of support in our campaign.* | **in support of** *They signed a petition in support of the pay claim.* | **drum up support** (=get many people's approval) *The Americans used the story to drum up support for stronger measures against Libya.*
**2** ► **SYMPATHY/HELP** ◄ [U] sympathetic encouragement and help that you give to someone: *Thanks for all your support at this difficult time.* —see also **moral support** (MORAL¹ (3))
**3** ► **HOLD STH UP** ◄ [C,U] something such as a piece of wood that presses up on something else to hold it up or in position: *The roof may need extra support. | the supports of a bridge*
**4** ► **INJURED PART OF BODY** ◄ [C] something that you wear to hold a weak or damaged part of your body in the right place
**5** ► **PEOPLE WHO SUPPORT STH** ◄ [U] the people who support a political party, an idea, a team etc: *There isn't much local support for the new candidate.*

**sup·por·ta·ble** /səˈpɔːtəbəl‖-ɔːr-/ *adj* [usually in negatives] *formal* possible to bear; TOLERABLE

**sup·port·er** /səˈpɔːtə‖-ɔːrtər/ *n* [C] **1** someone who supports a particular person, group, or plan: **strong/firm/staunch supporter** *one of Clinton's stauchest supporters | supporters of animal rights legislation* **2** *especially BrE* someone who supports a sports team, especially by regularly going to watch them play; FAN¹ (1): *Manchester United supporters* S W

**support group** /·ˈ· ·/ *n* [C] a group of people who meet to help each other with a particular problem, for example ALCOHOLISM

**sup·port·ing** /səˈpɔtɪŋ‖-ɔːr-/ *adj* **1 supporting part/role/actor etc** a small part in a play or film, or the actor who plays such a part **2 supporting wall/beam etc** a wall etc that supports the weight of something

**sup·por·tive** /səˈpɔːtɪv‖-ɔːr-/ *adj approving* giving help or encouragement, especially to someone who is in a difficult situation: *I can always count on Gail to be supportive when things go wrong.*

**sup·pose¹** /səˈpəuz‖-ˈpouz/ *v* [T] **1 be supposed to do sth a)** used when saying what someone should or should not do, especially because of rules or what someone in authority has said: *You're supposed to ask the teacher if you want to leave the classroom. | We're not supposed to smoke here.* **b)** used when saying what people intended should happen, especially when it failed to happen: *The new laws are supposed to prevent crime. | The meeting was supposed to take place on Tuesday, but we've had to postpone it.* **2 be supposed to be sth** to be believed to be something by many people: *The castle is supposed to be haunted. | 'Dirty Harry' is supposed to be one of Eastwood's best films.* **3** to think that something is probably true, based on what you know: *There were many more deaths than was first supposed.* | **suppose (that)** *What makes you suppose we're going to sell the house?* | **be generally supposed** (=most people think that something was probably fine) *Mr Tyke was generally supposed to have left the country.* | **There is no reason to suppose (that)** (=used to say that you think something is unlikely) *There's no reason to suppose her new book will be any better than her last one.* **4** *formal* to expect that something will happen and base your plans on it: *The company's plan supposes a steady increase in orders.* S W

Frequencies of the verb **suppose** in spoken and written English.

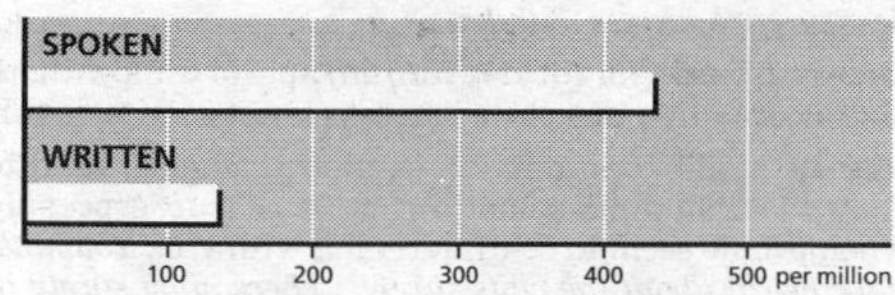


Based on the British National Corpus and the Longman Lancaster Corpus

This graph shows that the verb **suppose** is much more common in spoken English than in written English. This is because it is used in some common spoken phrases.

**suppose** (*v*) **SPOKEN PHRASES**

**5 I suppose** *especially BrE* **a)** used to say you think something is true, although you are uncertain about it: **I suppose (that)** *I suppose he could have shot himself, but where would he have got the gun?|I suppose Philip will be late, as usual.* **b)** used when agreeing to let someone do something, especially unwillingly: **I suppose so** *"Can we come with you?" "Oh, I suppose so."* **c)** used when guessing that something is true: *She looked about 50, I suppose.* **d)** used when saying in an angry way that you expect something is true: **I suppose (that)** *I suppose you thought you were being smart!* **e)** used to say that you think that something is probably true, although you wish it was not and hope someone will tell you it is not: **I suppose (that)** *I suppose it's too late to apply for that job now.* **6 suppose/supposing** used to ask someone to imagine what would happen if a particular situation existed: *Look, suppose you lost your job tomorrow, what would you do?* **7 I don't suppose (that)** *especially BrE* **a)** used to ask for something in a very polite way: *I don't suppose you'd give me a lift to the station?* **b)** used to say that you think it is unlikely something will happen: *I don't suppose I'll ever see her again.* **8 who/what etc do you suppose** used to ask someone who, what etc they think did something, is something etc: *Who on earth do you suppose could have done this?* **9 what's that supposed to mean?** used when you are annoyed by what someone has just said: *"I'll bear your offer in mind." "Bear it in mind! What's that supposed to mean?"*

**suppose²** *conjunction especially spoken* **1** used when imagining what the result would be if something happened; SUPPOSING **suppose (that)** *It's not worth the risk, suppose your mother found out?* **2** *informal* used to suggest something; SUPPOSING: *Suppose we try to sort this out before we go.*

**sup·posed** /sə'pəʊzd, sə'pəʊzɪ̈d‖-'poʊzd,-'poʊzɪ̈d/ *adj* [only before noun] claimed by other people to be true or real, although you do not think they are right: *the supposed benefits and advantages of privatizing state industries*

**sup·pos·ed·ly** /sə'pəʊzɪ̈dli‖-'poʊ-/ *adv* used when saying what many people say or believe is true, especially when you disagree with them: *In April 1912 this supposedly unsinkable slip hit an iceberg.* [sentence adverb] *Supposedly, she's a rich woman.*

**sup·pos·ing** /sə'pəʊzɪŋ‖-'poʊ-/ *conjunction* SUPPOSE²

**sup·po·si·tion** /ˌsʌpə'zɪʃən/ *n* [C,U] something that you think is true even though you are not certain and cannot prove it: *His version of events is pure supposition.*| **supposition (that)** *The police are acting on the supposition that she took the money.*

**sup·pos·i·to·ry** /sə'pɒzɪ̈təri‖sə'pɑːzɪ̈tɔːri/ *n* [C] a small piece of solid medicine that is placed in someone's RECTUM or VAGINA —compare PESSARY (1)

**sup·press** /sə'pres/ *v* [T] **1** to stop people from opposing the government, especially by using force: *The Hungarian uprising was ruthlessly suppressed by the Red Army.* **2** to prevent important information or opinions from becoming known, especially from people who have a right to know: *attempts by the Pentagon to suppress documents connected with the case* **3** to stop yourself from showing your feelings: *Susan could hardly suppress a giggle.|suppressed anger* **4** to prevent something from growing or developing, or from working effectively: *The virus suppresses the body's immune system.* **—suppressible** *adj* **—suppression** /-preʃən/ *n* [U]|*the suppression of free speech*

**sup·pu·rate** /'sʌpjɪ̈reɪt/ *v* [I] *technical* if a wound suppurates it produces or gives out PUS (=infected liquid) **—suppuration** /ˌsʌpjɪ̈'reɪʃən/ *n* [U]

**su·pra·na·tion·al** /ˌsuːprə'næʃənəl, ˌsjuː-‖ˌsuː-/ *adj* involving more than one country: *a supranational organization*

**su·prem·a·cist** /sə'preməsɪ̈st/ *n* [C] someone who believes that their own particular group or race is better than any other: *a white supremacist group*

**su·prem·a·cy** /sə'preməsi/ *n* [U] the position in which you are more powerful or advanced than anyone else: *Japan's unchallenged supremacy in the field of electronics.*

**su·preme** /suː'priːm, sjuː-, sə-‖sʊ-, suː-/ *adj* **1** having the highest position of power, importance, or influence: *the Supreme Allied Commander in Europe*|**reign supreme** *where justice reigns supreme* **2** [only before noun] the greatest possible: *supreme courage in the face of terrible danger*|**supreme effort** *It required a supreme effort to stop myself from giving up.*|**of supreme importance** *a matter of supreme importance* **3 make the supreme sacrifice** to die for your country, for a principle etc

**Supreme Be·ing** /ˌ·ˌ· '··/ *n* [singular] *literary* God

**Supreme Court** /·ˌ· '·/ *n* [singular] the most important court of law in some countries or some states of the US

**su·preme·ly** /suː'priːmli, sjuː-, sə-‖sʊ-, suː-/ *adv* [+ adj/adv] extremely or to the greatest possible degree: *a supremely talented player*

**su·prem·o** /suː'priːməʊ, sjuː-‖sʊ'priːmoʊ-, suː-/ *n* [C] *BrE informal* someone who controls a particular activity, organization, or industry, and has unlimited powers

**Supt.** the written abbreviation of SUPERINTENDENT

**sur·charge¹** /'sɜːtʃɑːdʒ‖'sɜːrtʃɑːrdʒ/ *n* [C] money that you have to pay in addition to the basic price of something: [+ **on**] *a 10% surcharge on airline tickets*

**surcharge²** *v* [T] to make someone pay an additional amount of money

**sur·coat** /'sɜːkəʊt‖'sɜːrkoʊt/ *n* [C] a piece of clothing with no arms which was worn over ARMOUR (1) in the past

**sure¹** /ʃɔː‖ʃʊr/ *adj* S1 W1

**1 ▶ CERTAIN YOU KNOW STH ◀** [not before noun] confident that you know something or that something is true or correct: *"What time does the show start?" "I'm not sure."*|**sure (that)** *I'm sure there's a logical explanation for all this.|Are you sure you know how to get there?*|[+ **of**] *You need to be sure of your facts before making any accusations.*|[+ **about**] *"That's the man I saw in the building last night." "Are you quite sure about that ?"*| **not sure how/where/whether etc** *I'm not sure where Michael is, to be honest.|"What time does the show start?" "I'm not sure."*|**not sure if** *Mr Watkins isn't sure if he'll be able to come.*|**pretty sure** (=almost certain) *I'm pretty sure Barbara still works there.*

**2 ▶ CERTAIN ABOUT YOUR FEELINGS ◀** [not before noun] certain about what you feel, want, like etc: *"Are you sure you really want a divorce?"*

**3 make sure a)** to find out if something is true or to check that something has been done: *"Did you lock the front door?" "I think so, but I'd better make sure."*|**make sure (that)** *Emma peered into the room to make sure that Ruth was asleep.* **b)** to do something so that you can be certain of the result: **make sure (that)** *I made sure that the rope was firmly fastened around his waist.*|**make sure of sth** *Ben made sure of winning by betting on all the horses.*

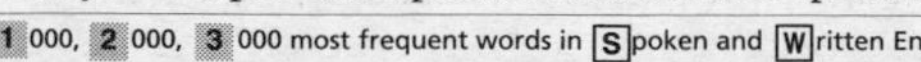

**4 ▶ CERTAIN TO BE TRUE ◀** certain to be true: **one thing is (for) sure** *One thing's for sure, we'll never be able to move this furniture on our own.* | **sure sign/indication** (=a sign that something is certainly going to happen) *Those black clouds are a sure sign of rain.*
**5 ▶ CERTAIN TO SUCCEED ◀** certain to succeed: **sure way/means** (=a way of doing something that will certainly achieve a particular result) *Arriving at work in pyjamas is a sure way of attracting attention to yourself!* | **a sure bet** *AmE* (=something that is certain to succeed) | **a sure thing** *AmE* (=something that will definitely happen, win, succeed etc)
**6 be sure of** to be certain to get something or be certain that something will happen: *United must beat Liverpool to be sure of winning the championship.* | *You can be sure of one thing – there'll be a lot of laughs.*
**7 sure of yourself** confident in your own abilities and opinions, sometimes in a way that annoys other people: *Kids nowadays seem very sure of themselves.*
**8 be sure to do sth** *spoken* used to tell someone to remember to do something: *Be sure to ring and let us know you've got back safely.*
**9 sure to do sth** certain to happen or to do something: *He's sure to get nervous and say something stupid.*
**10 (as) sure as hell** *spoken especially AmE* used to emphasize a statement: *I'm sure as hell not gonna do it.*
**11 to be sure** *BrE spoken* used to admit that something is true, before saying something that is the opposite: *Jamie's had his problems to be sure, but he's got potential.*
**12 sure thing** *AmE spoken* used to agree to something: *"See you next week?" "Sure thing."*
**13 have/get a sure hold/footing** if you have a sure hold or footing your hands or feet are placed firmly so they cannot slip —see also SURELY
**14 sure as eggs are eggs** *BrE old-fashioned* used to say that something is definitely true —**sureness** *n* [U]

Frequencies of the word **sure** in spoken and written English.

SPOKEN

WRITTEN

100 200 300 400 500 per million

Based on the British National Corpus and the Longman Lancaster Corpus

This graph shows that the word **sure** is much more common in spoken English than in written English. This is because it has special uses in spoken English and is used in some common spoken phrases.

**sure²** *adv*
**1 for sure** *spoken* **a)** certainly: *No one knows for sure what really happened.* **b)** used to emphasize that something is true: *I know one person who won't be happy with the decision, that's for sure.* **c)** [C] *AmE* used to agree with someone
**2 sure enough** used to say that something did actually happen in the way that you said it would: *Sure enough Mike managed to get lost.*
**3 ▶ USED TO SAY 'YES' ◀** *spoken especially AmE* used to say 'yes' to someone: *"Can you give me a ride to work tomorrow?" "Sure."*
**4 ▶ USED AS A REPLY ◀** *AmE spoken* used as a way of replying to someone when they thank you: *"Thanks for your help Karen." "Sure."*
**5 ▶ USED TO EMPHASIZE STH ◀** *AmE informal* used to emphasize a statement: *Mom's sure gonna be mad when she gets home.*
**6 ▶ USED BEFORE STATEMENT ◀** *AmE spoken* used at the beginning of a statement admitting that something is true, especially before adding something very different: *Sure Joey's happy now, but will it last?*

**sure·fire** /ˈʃɔːfaɪə‖ˈʃʊrfaɪr/ *adj* [only before noun] *informal* certain to succeed: *There's no surefire way to get rid of cockroaches.* | **surefire success** *I think the new show will be a surefire success with kids.*

**sure·foot·ed** /ˌʃɔːˈfʊtɪ̆d◂‖ˌʃʊr-/ *adj* able to walk without sliding or falling in a place where it is not easy to do this

**sure·ly** /ˈʃɔːli‖ˈʃʊrli/ *adv* **1** [sentence adverb] used to show that you think something must be true, especially when people seem to be disagreeing with you: *You must have heard about the riots surely?* | *There must surely be some explanation.* | *Surely we can't just stand back and let this happen?* **2 surely not** *spoken* used to show you cannot believe that something is true: *"The chairman's just handed in his resignation." "Surely not."* **3** *old-fashioned* certainly: *Such sinners will surely be punished.* **4** *AmE old-fashioned* used to say 'yes' to someone or to express agreement with them S W

**USAGE NOTE: SURELY**

WORD CHOICE: **surely, certainly, sure, definitely, of course, naturally, obviously**

**Surely** is usually used to show that you believe something, and would be surprised if others did not agree: *Surely they must realize that* (=I think they should realize that, and don't you agree?)|*They've gone home, surely* (=you seem to be still expecting to see them, but I'm sure they have gone).|*He surely doesn't expect me to pay him immediately* (=I hope he doesn't expect this and I don't think he ought to).

A sentence with **surely**, especially near the beginning, usually sounds like a question, even if nobody actually answers, and could easily be followed by a question tag: *Surely they know, don't they?*

**Certainly** is four times as frequent as **surely** in spoken English and shows that you strongly believe something, in spite of what others think: *He certainly doesn't expect me to pay him immediately* (=I know he doesn't expect the money now).|*She was amazed and I was certainly surprised too* (NOT *surely* because it would be strange to expect others to know how you feel).

**Certainly** often suggests that there may also be a slight doubt or condition, even if it is not actually followed by **but**: *It's certainly very beautiful, but it's far too expensive.*|*"He's a brilliant student, isn't he?" "Well, he certainly works very hard"* (=but I do not agree that he is brilliant).

In informal spoken American English **sure** is often used, especially just before the verb, with a similar meaning to **certainly**, but is often stronger and may show annoyance or impatience: *They sure are late!* (=they're late and isn't that surprising/annoying?).

**Definitely** shows that you believe something so strongly that there is no doubt or question about it at all: *He's definitely the best player in the team.*

**Of course**, **naturally**, and **obviously** show that you not only think something is true but also that it is not surprising: *They broke down on the way so of course they were late.*|*Naturally my mother loved me.*|*A vacation in Switzerland would obviously be expensive.*

For information about using these words in answer to questions see **of course** (WORD CHOICE).

**sur·e·ty** /ˈʃɔːrɪ̆ti‖ˈʃʊr-/ *n* [C,U] *law* **1** someone who will pay a debt, appear in court etc if someone else fails to do so **2 stand surety (for sb)** be responsible for paying a debt, appearing in court etc if someone else fails to do so **3** money someone gives to make sure that someone will appear in court

**surf¹** /sɜːf‖sɜːrf/ *v* [I] **1** to ride on waves standing on a special board: **go surfing** *When we were in Hawaii we went surfing every day.* **2 surf the net** to look quickly through information on the computer INTERNET for anything that interests you: *surfing the net with a high-speed modem* —**surfer** *n* [C]

**surf²** *n* [U] the white substance that forms on top of waves as they move towards the shore

**sur·face¹** /ˈsɜːfɪ̈s‖ˈsɜːr-/ *adj* [only before noun] appearing to be true or real, but not representing what someone really feels or what something is really like; SUPERFICIAL: *The surface calm of the city was shattered by a massive explosion.* | *surface resemblance*

S2 **surface²** *n* [C]
W1 **1** ►**WATER/LAND**◄ the top layer of an area of water or land: *the Earth's surface* | *Pieces of trash were floating on the surface of the river.* | *the surface of the road*
**2** ►**TOP LAYER**◄ the outside or top layer of an object: *a frying pan with a non-stick surface*
**3 on the surface** if someone or something is calm, nice etc on the surface, they seem that way until you know them better: *On the surface Mrs Lewis seemed nice enough but she had a nasty temper at times.*
**4 below/beneath/under the surface** if an emotion or quality is below, beneath, under the surface, it is not easy to notice at first: *I sensed a lot of tension and jealousy beneath the surface.*
**5 come/rise to the surface** if unpleasant feelings or attitudes come or rise to the surface they become noticeable after being hidden: *Violence and prejudice have risen to the surface in a lot of inner-city areas.*
**6** ►**FOR WORKING ON**◄ an area on a desk, table etc used for working: *Make sure all kitchen surfaces are clean and tidy.*
**7** ►**SIDE OF AN OBJECT**◄ *technical* one of the sides of an object: *How many surfaces does a cube have?* —see also **scratch the surface** (SCRATCH¹ (7))

**surface³** *v* **1** [I] to rise to the surface of water: *The bird dived and didn't surface for at least a minute.* **2** [I] if information or feelings surface, they become known after being hidden: *A few personality clashes have surfaced within the department.* **3** [I] *humorous* to get up, especially after being in bed for a long time: *Joe never surfaces before midday on Sunday.* **4** [T] to put a surface on a road

**surface a·re·a** /ˈ‥ ˌ‥‥/ *n* [C] the area of the outside of an object that can be measured

**surface mail** /ˈ‥ ˌ‥/ *n* [U] the system of sending letters or packages by land or sea

**surface ten·sion** /ˌ‥ ˈ‥/ *n* [U] the way the MOLECULES in the surface of a liquid stick together so that the surface is held together

**surface-to-air** /ˌ‥ · ˈ·◂/ *adj* **surface-to-air-missile** a MISSILE (1) that is fired at planes from the land or from a ship

**surface-to-surface** /ˌ‥ · ˈ‥◂/ *adj* **surface-to-surface missile** a MISSILE (1) that is fired from land or a ship at another point on land or at another ship

**surf·board** /ˈsɜːfbɔːd‖ˈsɜːrfbɔːrd/ *n* [C] a long piece of plastic, wood etc that you stand on to ride the waves —see picture at SURF

**sur·feit** /ˈsɜːfɪ̈t‖ˈsɜːr-/ *n formal* **a surfeit of sth** an amount of something that is too large or that is more than you need: *a surfeit of food and drink*

**surf·ing** /ˈsɜːfɪŋ‖ˈsɜːr-/ *n* [U] **1** the activity or sport of riding over the waves on a special board **2 channel/cyber surfing** looking quickly from one television programme to another, or looking through the computer INTERNET for something that interests you

**surge¹** /sɜːdʒ‖sɜːrdʒ/ *v* **1** [I always + adv/prep] if a crowd of people surges, they suddenly move forward together very quickly: [+ **forward/through etc**] *The crowd surged through the gates.* **2** also **surge up** [I] if a feeling surges or surges up you begin to feel it very strongly: *Helpless rage surged up within me.* **3** [I always + adv/prep] if a large amount of water surges, it moves very quickly and suddenly

**surge²** *n* [C usually singular] **1 a surge of** a sudden, large increase in a feeling: *a surge of excitement* **2** a sudden increase in something such as demand, profit, interest etc: [+ **in**] *stores expecting the usual surge in demand as Christmas approaches* **3** a sudden movement of a lot of people: [+ **of**] *a surge of refugees into the country*

**sur·geon** /ˈsɜːdʒən‖ˈsɜːr-/ *n* [C] a doctor who does operations in hospital —see also DENTAL SURGEON

**sur·ge·ry** /ˈsɜːdʒəri‖ˈsɜːr-/ *n* **1** [U] medical treatment in which a surgeon cuts open your body to repair or remove something inside: *major heart surgery* —see also COSMETIC SURGERY, PLASTIC SURGERY **2** [C,U] *especially AmE* the place where operations are done in a hospital; THEATRE (3) *BrE* **3** [C] *BrE* a place where a doctor or DENTIST gives treatment; OFFICE *AmE* **4** [U] *BrE* a regular period each day when people can see a doctor or DENTIST; **office hours** (OFFICE (3)) *AmE*: *Surgery is from 9am – 1pm on weekdays.* **5** [C] *BrE* a special period of time when people can see a MEMBER OF PARLIAMENT to discuss problems S2 W3

**sur·gi·cal** /ˈsɜːdʒɪkəl‖ˈsɜːr-/ *adj* [only before noun] **1** connected with or used for medical operations: *surgical techniques* **2 surgical stocking/collar etc** a STOCKING etc that someone wears to support a part of their body that is injured or weak —**surgically** /-kli/ *adv*: *The growth was surgically removed.*

**surgical spir·it** /ˌ‥ ˈ‥/ *n* [U] *BrE* a type of alcohol used for cleaning wounds or skin; RUBBING ALCOHOL *AmE*

**surgical strike** /ˌ‥ ˈ·/ *n* [C] a carefully planned quick military attack intended to destroy something in a particular place without damaging the surrounding area

**sur·ly** /ˈsɜːli‖ˈsɜːrli/ *adj* **surlier, surliest** bad-tempered, unfriendly, and often rude: *Passengers complain of frequent delays and surly staff.* —**surliness** *n* [U]

**sur·mise** /səˈmaɪz‖sər-/ *v* [T] *formal* to guess that something is true using the information you know already —**surmise** *n* [C,U]

**sur·mount** /səˈmaʊnt‖sər-/ *v* [T] *formal* **1** to succeed in dealing with a problem or difficulty; OVERCOME: *a program designed to help couples surmount marital difficulties* **2** [usually passive] to be above or on top of something: *a stone tower surmounted by a tall spire* —**surmountable** *adj*

**sur·name** /ˈsɜːneɪm‖ˈsɜːr-/ *n* [C] the name that you share with your parents, or often with your husband if you are a married woman, and which in English comes at the end of your full name; LAST NAME

**sur·pass** /səˈpɑːs‖sərˈpæs/ *v* [T] **1** to be even better or greater than someone or something else: *Gower became England's highest run scorer, surpassing Geoff Boycott's old record.* | **surpass expectations/hopes/dreams** (=be better than you had expected, hoped etc) **2 surpass yourself** (=an expression meaning to do something even better than you have ever done before, often used jokingly when someone has done something badly) *You've really surpassed yourself this time!*

**sur·pass·ing** /sə'pɑːsɪŋ‖sər'pæ-/ *adj* [only before noun] *literary* much better than that of other people or things: *a picture of surpassing beauty*

**sur·plice** /'sɜːplɪ̣s‖'sɜːr-/ *n* [C] a piece of clothing made of white material worn over other clothes by priests or singers in church

**sur·plus¹** /'sɜːpləs‖'sɜːr-/ *n* [C,U] **1** an amount of something that is more than what is needed or used: *Apply paste thinly to the back of the wallpaper taking care to remove any surplus.* | [+ **of**] *an enormous surplus of crude oil* **2** the amount of money that a country or company has left after it has paid for all the things it needs —see also TRADE SURPLUS

**surplus²** *adj* **1** more than what is needed or used: *Companies are likely to continue laying off surplus staff well into the recovery.* **2 be surplus to requirements** *formal* be no longer necessary: *Most of this furniture is now surplus to requirements.*

S3 W2 **sur·prise¹** /sə'praɪz‖sər-/ *n*
**1** ▶ **EVENT** ◀ [C] an unexpected or unusual event: *Joan! What a lovely surprise to see you again!* | **surprise visit/announcement/attack etc** *Let's pay grandma a surprise visit.* | *US forces launched a surprise attack on the Panamanian capital.* | **come as a surprise (to sb)** (=happen unexpectedly) *The news that George was leaving came as a surprise to everyone.* | **it came as no surprise** (=you expected it would happen) *It came as no surprise when Sarah announced she was pregnant.* | **there is a surprise in store for sb** (=something unexpected is going to happen to them)

**2** ▶ **FEELING** ◀ [U] the feeling you have when something unexpected or unusual happens: *Imagine my surprise when she told me she'd been married twice already.* | **get/have a surprise** *Harwich police got a nasty surprise yesterday when someone left a suspected unexploded bomb inside the police station.* | **in/with surprise** *She noticed with surprise the change in his appearance.* | **much to my surprise** (=in a way that surprises you) *Much to my surprise they offered me the job.*
**3 take sb by surprise** to happen unexpectedly: *The heavy snowfall had taken us all by surprise.*
**4 take sb/sth by surprise** to suddenly attack a place or an opponent when they are not ready: *Rebel forces took the town by surprise.*
**5** ▶ **GIFT/PARTY ETC** ◀ [C usually singular] an unexpected present, trip etc which you give to someone or organize for them, often on a special occasion: *I've got a little surprise waiting for you at home.* | *Jim's organized a trip to the opera as a surprise for his mum.*
**6 surprise guest/visitor etc** someone who arrives somewhere unexpectedly
**7 surprise!** *spoken* used when you are just about to show someone something that you know will surprise them
**8 a) surprise, surprise** used when saying in a joking way that you expected something to happen or be true: *The American TV networks are – surprise, surprise, full of stories about the royal divorce.* **b)** *spoken* used when you suddenly appear in front of someone who you know is not expecting to see you
**9** ▶ **METHOD** ◀ [U] the use of methods which are intended to cause surprise: **an element of surprise** *An element of surprise is important to any attack.*

**surprise²** *v* [T] **1** to make someone feel surprised: *Paul's news surprised her.* | **it surprises sb to see/find/know etc** *It surprised them to see Jane up so early.* | **it doesn't surprise me** *"Howard and Shari have split up." "I have to say it doesn't surprise me."* | **what surprises sb is** *What surprised me most was that she didn't seem to care.* —see SHOCK¹ (USAGE) **2** to find, catch, or attack someone when they are not expecting it, especially when they are doing something they should not be doing: **surprise sb doing sth** *A security guard surprised the burglars in the store room.*

**sur·prised** /sə'praɪzd‖sər-/ *adj* having a feeling of surprise: *Mr Benson looked surprised when I told him I was leaving.* | [+ **at/by**] *We were all surprised at Sue's outburst.* | **surprised (that)** *Harry was surprised that Carl didn't say anything to defend himself.* | **surprised to see/hear/learn etc** *I was pleasantly surprised to learn that I had passed.* | **surprised look/expression** *She just sat there with a surprised expression on her face.* | **don't be surprised if...** *spoken* (=used when saying that something is likely to happen) *Don't be surprised if they ask a lot of difficult questions.* | **I wouldn't be surprised** *spoken* (=used when saying that you expect something will happen) *"Do you think they'll get married?" "I wouldn't be at all surprised."* S W

**sur·pris·ing** /sə'praɪzɪŋ‖sər-/ *adj* unusual or unexpected: *a surprising lack of communication between management and staff* | **it is surprising (that)** *It's not really surprising that only a few people came tonight.* | **it is surprising how/what etc** *It's surprising how quickly those in the public eye fade.* | **it is hardly/scarcely surprising** *It's hardly surprising that she won't talk to you after what you said to her.* S W

**sur·pris·ing·ly** /sə'praɪzɪŋli‖sər-/ *adv* unusually or unexpectedly [+ adj/adv] *The exam was surprisingly easy.* | **not surprisingly** [sentence adverb] | *Not surprisingly, the UK has the highest divorce rate in the Community.* W

**sur·real** /sə'rɪəl/ *adj* a situation or experience that is surreal is very strange, like something from a dream: *American politics has always been more surreal than any satire.*

**sur·real·is·m** /sə'rɪəlɪzəm/ *n* [U] 20th century art or literature in which the artist or writer connects unrelated images and objects in a strange way —**surrealist** *adj*: *a surrealist painting* **surrealist** *n* [C]

**sur·real·is·tic** /səˌrɪə'lɪstɪk◂/ *adj* **1** seeming very strange because of a combination of many unusual, unrelated events, images etc **2** connected with surrealism —**surrealistically** /-kli/ *adv*

**sur·ren·der¹** /sə'rendə‖-ər/ *v* **1** [I] to say officially that you want to stop fighting because you realize that you cannot win: *The terrorists were given ten minutes to surrender.* | **surrender to sb** *The unit was forced to surrender to the enemy.* **2 surrender to sth** to allow yourself to be controlled or influenced by something: *Colette surrendered to temptation and took out a cigarette.* **3** [T] to give your soldiers or land to an enemy after they have beaten you in a battle: *The General had to surrender his troops.* **4** [T] to give up something that is important or necessary, often because you feel forced to: *Critics feel that Boyer has surrendered his artistic identity in his later films.* **5** [T] *formal* to give something such as a ticket or a PASSPORT to an official: **surrender sth to sb** *The court ordered Bond to surrender his passport to the authorities.*

**surrender²** *n* [singular, U] **1** the act of saying officially that you want to stop fighting because you realize that you cannot win: **unconditional surrender** (=act of accepting total defeat) **2** the act of allowing yourself to be controlled or influenced by something: *a surrender to the forces of evil*

**sur·rep·ti·tious** /ˌsʌrəp'tɪʃəs◂‖ˌsɜː-/ *adj* done secretly or quickly because you do not want other people to notice: *Robert stole a surreptitious glance at Myrna to see her reaction.* —**surreptitiously** *adv* —**surreptitiousness** *n* [U]

**sur·rey** /'sʌri‖'sɜː-/ *n* [C] *AmE* a light carriage with two seats, which was pulled by a horse and was used in the past

**sur·ro·gate** /'sʌrəgeɪt, -gɪ̣t‖'sɜːr-/ *adj* [only before noun] a surrogate person or thing is one that takes the place of someone or something else: *Uncle Giles became a sort of surrogate father to them after the accident.* —**surrogate** *n* [C]

**surrogate moth·er** /ˌ··· '··/ *n* [C] a woman who has a baby for another woman who cannot have one

**sur·round¹** /sə'raʊnd/ *v* [T] **1** [usually passive] to be W all around someone or something on every side: *The city is surrounded on all sides by hills.* | **be surrounded by sth** *Jill was sitting on the floor surrounded by boxes.* **2 be surrounded by sb/sth** to have a lot of a particular kind of people or things near you: *How can I work when I'm surrounded by idiots.* **3** if police or soldiers surround a place they arrange themselves in positions all the way around it: *We've got the place surrounded. Come out with your hands up.* **4** to be closely connected with a situation or event: *the controversy surrounding the group's "Cop Killer" track* **5 surround yourself with** to choose to have certain people or things near you all the time: *David loved to surround himself with young people.*

**surround²** *n* [C] an area around the edge of something, especially one that is decorated or made of a different material

**sur·round·ing** /səˈraʊndɪŋ/ *adj* [only before noun] near or around a particular place: *the surrounding towns* | *After the explosion the army sealed off the surrounding area.*

**sur·round·ings** /səˈraʊndɪŋz/ *n* [plural] the objects, buildings, natural things etc that are around a person or thng at a particular time: *It took me a few weeks to get used to my new surroundings.*

**sur·tax** /ˈsɜːtæks‖ˈsɜːr-/ *n* [U] an additional tax on money you earn if it is higher than a particular amount

**sur·veil·lance** /səˈveɪləns‖sər-/ *n* [U] the act of carefully watching a person or place because they may be connected with criminal activities: **keep sb/sth under surveillance** *Police are keeping the area under constant surveillance.*

3 **sur·vey¹** /ˈsɜːveɪ‖ˈsɜːr-/ *n* [C] **1** a set of questions that
3 you ask a large number of people in order to find out about their opinions or behaviour: **to carry out/conduct a survey** (=do a survey) *a recent survey conducted by Manchester university into children's attitudes to violence on television* **2** an examination of a house or other building done especially for someone who wants to buy it **3** an examination of an area of land in order to make a map of it **4** a general description or report about a particular subject or situation: *a survey of modern English literature*

**sur·vey²** /səˈveɪ‖sər-/ *v* [T] **1** [often passive] to ask a large number of people questions in order to find out their attitudes or opinions: *Almost 60% of those surveyed said they supported the President's action.* **2** to look at or consider someone or something carefully, especially in order to form an opinion about them: *He leaned back in his chair and surveyed her critically for a moment.* **3** to examine the condition of a house or other building and make a report on it, especially for people who want to buy it **4** to examine and measure an area of land and record the details on a map: *a surveying expedition*

**survey course** /ˈ·· ˌ·/ *n* [C] *AmE* a university course that gives an introduction to a subject for people who have not studied it before

**sur·vey·or** /səˈveɪə‖sərˈveɪər/ *n* [C] someone whose job is to examine the condition of a building, or to measure and record the details of an area of land —see also QUANTITY SURVEYOR

3 **sur·viv·al** /səˈvaɪvəl‖sər-/ [U] *n* **1** the state of continuing to live or exist: *His doctors said he had a 50-50 chance or survival.* | *Our disregard for the environment threatens the long-term survival of the planet.* | **fight for survival** (=struggle or work hard in order to continue to exist) *A lot of small companies are having to fight for survival.* **2 survival of the fittest** a situation in which only the strongest and most successful people or things continue to exist **3 a survival from** *especially BrE* something that has continued to exist from a much earlier period, especially when similar things have disappeared; RELIC

**survival kit** /ˈ·· ·/ *n* [C] a collection of things that you need to help you stay alive if you get hurt or lost

2 **sur·vive** /səˈvaɪv‖sər-/ *v* **1** [I,T] to not die in an accident
2 or war or from an illness: *Only 12 of the 140 passengers survived.* | **survive sth** *There are concerns that the refugees may not survive the winter.* **2** [I,T] to continue to exist in spite of many difficulties and dangers: *A few pages of the original manuscript still survive.* **3** *often spoken* [I,T] to continue to live normally and not be too upset by your problems: *I don't think I could survive another year as a teacher; it's just too stressful.* | *"How are you?" "Oh, surviving!"* **4 survive on** to continue to live a normal life even though you have very little money: *I don't know how you all manage to survive on Jeremy's salary.* **5** [T] to live longer than someone else, usually someone closely related to you: *Harry survived his wife by three months.*

**sur·vi·vor** /səˈvaɪvə‖sərˈvaɪvər/ *n* [C] **1** someone or something that still exists in spite of having been nearly destroyed or almost dead: **sole/lone survivor** (=only person who survives) *Major Hawkins was the lone survivor of the crash.* **2** someone who manages to live their life without being too upset by problems: *Don't worry about Kurt; he's a survivor.*

**sus·cep·ti·bil·i·ty** /səˌseptəˈbɪləti/ *n* **1** [U] the condition of being easily affected or influenced by something: *susceptibility to disease* **2 sb's susceptibilities** someone's feelings, especially when they are easily offended or upset: *The policy has no regard for the susceptibilities of minority groups.*

**sus·cep·ti·ble** /səˈseptəbəl/ *adj* **1 susceptible to sth a)** likely to suffer from a particular illness or be affected by a particular problem: *Certain people are more susceptible to stress than others.* **b)** easily influenced or affected by something: *Men are supposedly easily susceptible to feminine charms.* **2** *literary* tending to experience strong feelings easily and be easily influenced by other people IMPRESSIONABLE: *a susceptible young boy* **3 susceptible of change/interpretation/analysis etc** *formal* able to be changed etc

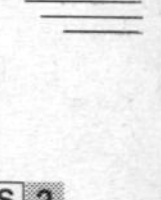

**su·shi** /ˈsuːʃi/ *n* [U] a Japanese dish consisting of pieces of raw fish on top of cooked rice

**sus·pect¹** /səˈspekt/ *v* [T not in progressive] **1** to think S 2
that something is probably true or likely, especially W 3
something bad: **suspect (that)** *She strongly suspected her husband had been lying.* | **suspect murder/foul play** (=suspect that someone has been murdered) | **suspect** *spoken*: *It was a decision, I suspect, that he will later regret.* **2** to think that someone is probably guilty: *Who do you suspect?* | **suspect sb of sth** *He's suspected of murder.* | **suspect sb of doing sth** *Pilcher was suspected of being a spy.* **3** to distrust someone or doubt the truth of something: *I began to suspect his motives when he asked to borrow more.*

**sus·pect²** /ˈsʌspekt/ *n* [C] someone who is thought to be guilty of a crime: *Two suspects were arrested today in connection with the robbery.*

**suspect³** *adj* **1** something that is suspect seems likely to have something wrong with it and should not be trusted, believed, or depended on: *The evidence against the four Irishmen was highly suspect.* | **highly suspect** **2** [only before noun] suspect packages, goods etc look as if they contain something illegal or dangerous: *Customs officers impounded the suspect crates.*

**sus·pect·ed** /səˈspektəd/ *adj* **1 suspected terrorist/spy etc** someone the police believe is a TERRORIST etc **2 a suspected broken knee/heart attack etc** if you have a suspected broken knee etc, doctors think that you may have a broken knee etc

**sus·pend** /səˈspend/ *v* [T] **1** to officially stop something from continuing, especially for a short time: *Sales of the drug will be suspended until more tests are completed.* **2** to make someone leave school, a job, or an organization temporarily, especially because they have broken the rules: **suspend sb from sth** *Dave was suspended from school for a week.* **3** *formal* to hang something from something else: **suspend sth from sth** *The long fluorescent tubes were suspended from the ceiling.* | **suspend sth by sth** *a ball suspended by a rope from a* *branch* **4 suspend judgment** to decide not to make a firm judgment about something until you know more about it **5** *technical* **be suspended in** (=if something is suspended in a liquid or in air, it floats in it without moving) *an insect suspended in a piece of amber*

**suspended an·i·ma·tion** /ˌ.. ..ˈ../ *n* [U] **1** a state in which someone's body processes are slowed down to a state almost like death **2** a feeling that you cannot do anything because you have to wait for what happens next

**suspended sen·tence** /ˌ.. ˈ../ *n* [C] a punishment given by a court in which the criminal will only go to prison if they do something else illegal within a particular period of time: *a two-year suspended sentence*

**sus·pend·er** /səˈspendə‖-ər/ *n* [C] **1** *BrE* something that hangs down from a woman's underwear to hold STOCKINGS up; GARTER (2) *AmE* **2 suspenders** *AmE* two bands of cloth that go over your shoulders and fasten to your trousers to hold them up; braces (BRACE² (5)) *BrE*

**suspender belt** /.ˈ.. ./ *n* [C] *BrE* a piece of women's underwear with suspenders joined to it; GARTER BELT *AmE*

**sus·pense** /səˈspens/ *n* [U] a feeling of excitement or anxiety when you do not know what will happen next: **in suspense** *The children waited in suspense to hear the end of the story.* | **keep sb in suspense** *We were kept in suspense waiting for the results of the contest.* | **the suspense is killing me!** (=used when you are excited or anxious because you do not know what will happen)

**sus·pen·sion** /səˈspenʃən/ *n* **1** [U] the act of officially stopping something from continuing for a period of time: [+ **of**] *EC sanctions included suspension of the 1980 trade agreement and import limits on textiles.* **2** [C] the removal of someone from a team, job, school etc for a period of time, especially to punish them: *Sean McCarthy is set to return to football after a three match suspension.* **3** [U] equipment fixed to the wheels of a vehicle to make it more comfortable on roads that are not smooth **4** [C] *technical* a liquid mixture consisting of very small pieces of solid material that are contained in the liquid but have not combined with it —compare COLLOID **5** [U] the act of hanging something from something else: *suspension cables*

**suspension bridge** /.ˈ.. ./ *n* [C] a bridge that is hung from strong steel ropes fixed to towers

**sus·pi·cion** /səˈspɪʃən/ *n* **1** [C,U] a feeling that someone is probably guilty of doing something wrong or dishonest: **have your suspicions** (=think you probably know who did something wrong) *I'm not sure who took it, but I have my suspicions.* | **have a sneaking suspicion** (=have a slight feeling that someone has done something wrong without having any definite information) | **arouse sb's suspicions** *Neighbours' suspicions were aroused by the bruises on the child's arms.* **2 on suspicion of** because someone is thought to be guilty of a crime: *She was arrested on suspicion of killing her boyfriend.* **3 under suspicion** someone who is under suspicion of a crime is thought to be guilty of it: **come/fall under suspicion** *When Stalin was in power everyone came under suspicion, even Communist Party members.* **4 above/beyond suspicion** if someone is above or beyond suspicion, they definitely could not be guilty of a crime or have done something wrong: *Just because she knew and liked Dysart did not mean that the man was necessarily above suspicion.* **5** [C,U] a feeling that you do not trust someone: *She always treated us with suspicion.* | **look upon/regard sb with suspicion** *Anyone who expressed any kind of liberal opinion was regarded with deep suspicion.* **6** [C] a feeling that something has happened is true: *There is always a suspicion that the legal system is designed to suit lawyers rather than to protect the public.* | **suspicion (that)** *I had a suspicion she might be hurt.* **7 a suspicion of sth** a very small amount of something seen, heard, tasted etc: *I could see the faintest suspicion of a tear in her eyes.*

S3 **sus·pi·cious** /səˈspɪʃəs/ *adj* **1** thinking that someone might be guilty of doing something wrong or dishonest, without being sure: *His behaviour that day made the police suspicious.* | [+ **of/about**] *I'm suspicious of Jen's intentions.* **2** making you think that something bad or illegal is happening: *Anyone who saw anything suspicious is asked to contact the police immediately.* | *They found a suspicious package under the seat.* | *a suspicious-looking character* | **in suspicious circumstances** *Her mother had died in suspicious circumstances.* —see also SUSPECT³ **3** feeling that you do not trust someone or that there is something wrong: [+ **of**] *Both parents and pupils are deeply suspicious of the new exams.*

**sus·pi·cious·ly** /səˈspɪʃəsli/ *adv* **1** in a way that shows you think someone has done something wrong or dishonest: *Meg looked at me very suspiciously.* **2** in a way that makes people think that something bad or illegal is happening: *He saw two youths acting suspiciously outside the pub.* **3** in a way that shows you think there is probably something wrong with something: *They sat in silence, eyeing the food suspiciously.* **4 looks/sounds etc suspiciously like** *often humorous* used when saying that something is very like something else: *That pen looks suspiciously like the one I lost last week!*

**suss** /sʌs/ *v* [T] *BrE informal* to realize something: **suss (that)** *We soon sussed she wasn't telling the truth.*

**suss** sb/sth ↔ **out** *phr v* [T] *BrE informal* to understand the important things about someone or something, especially things they are trying to hide: *She's bound to suss out the truth sooner or later.*

**sussed** /sʌst/ *adj BrE informal* knowing all about someone or something: *These boys are too sussed to believe their own hype.* | **get sth sussed** *It's so annoying, you get something sussed and then they change the rules.*

**sus·tain** /səˈsteɪn/ *v* [T] W

**1** ▶ **MAKE STH CONTINUE** ◀ to make something continue to exist over a period of time; MAINTAIN (1): *The teacher tried hard to sustain the children's interest.* —see also SUSTAINED

**2** ▶ **GIVE STRENGTH** ◀ to make it possible for someone to stay strong or hopeful: *A good breakfast will sustain you all morning.* | *They were sustained by the knowledge that help would come soon.*

**3 sustain damage/an injury/defeat/heavy losses etc** *formal* to be damaged, hurt or defeated or lose a lot of soldiers, money etc: *Allied forces sustained heavy losses in the first few weeks of the campaign.*

**4** ▶ **WEIGHT** ◀ *formal* to hold up the weight of something: *The floor wouldn't sustain the weight of a piano.*

**5** ▶ **IDEA** ◀ *formal* to support an idea, argument etc: *There was no proof to sustain his views.*

**6** ▶ **LAW** ◀ *spoken* **objection sustained** (=used by a judge when saying that someone was right to object to another person's statement)

**sus·tain·a·ble** /səˈsteɪnəbəl/ *adj* an action or process that is sustainable can continue or last for a long time: *sustainable economic growth*

**sus·tained** /səˈsteɪnd/ *adj* something that is sustained continues for a long time: *Paula owes her success to sustained hard work.* | *sustained economic development*

**sus·te·nance** /ˈsʌstənəns/ *n* [U] **1** *formal* food that keeps people strong and healthy; NOURISHMENT: *The children were thin and badly in need of sustenance.* **2** *informal* food you feel you need because you are tired and hungry: *I need sustenance! Let's go get some food!* | *There's not much sustenance in a bag of crisps.* **3** the act of sustaining something

**su·tra** /ˈsuːtrə/ *n* [C] a piece of Hindu or Buddhist holy writing

**sut·tee** /ˈsʌtiː/ *n* [U] the ancient custom in the Hindu religion of burning a wife with her dead husband

**su·ture** /ˈsuːtʃə‖-ər/ *n* [C,U] the act of sewing a wound together, or a stitch used in this —**suture** *v* [T]

**su·ze·rainty** /ˈsuːzəreɪnti‖-rənti, -reɪnti/ *n* [U] the right of a country or leader to rule over another country —**suzerain** /-reɪn/ *n* [singular]

**svelte** /svelt/ *adj* someone, especially a woman, who is svelte is thin and graceful: *a svelte young lady*

**Sven·ga·li** /svenˈgɑːli/ *n* [C] a man who has the power to control people's minds and make them behave in a bad way

**SW** the written abbreviation of SOUTHWEST and SOUTHWESTERN

**swab¹** /swɒb‖swɑːb/ *n* [C] **1** a small piece of material used by a doctor or nurse to clean a wound or take liquid from someone's body: *a cotton swab* **2** a test using such a piece of material: *Take a swab of his throat, nurse.*

**swab²** *v* **swabbed, swabbing** [T] **1** also **swab down** to clean something, especially the floors of a ship **2** also **swab out** to clean a wound with a piece of material

**swad·dle** /ˈswɒdl‖ˈswɑːdl/ *v* [T] *old-fashioned* to wrap a baby tightly to protect it

**swaddling clothes** /ˈ··· ·/ *n* [plural] *old use* the pieces of cloth wrapped around babies to protect them

**swag** /swæg/ *n* **1** [U] *slang* the goods stolen when someone is robbed —compare LOOT¹ (1) **2** [C] a deep fold of material, especially in or above a curtain **3** [U] *AustrE* a set of clothes and possessions wrapped in a cloth and carried by someone who is travelling on foot

**swag·ger¹** /ˈswægə‖-ər/ *v* [I] **1** [always + adv/prep] to walk proudly, swinging your shoulders in a way that shows too much confidence: [+ **down/in/out etc**] *He swaggered down the street with a foolish grin on his face.* **2** *old-fashioned* to talk or behave in a very proud way; BOAST¹ (1) —**swaggerer** *n* [C] **swaggeringly** *adv*

**swagger²** *n* [singular, U] a way of behaving or walking that is too confident or unusually confident: *He combines the cocky swagger of Johnny Rotten with the animal sexuality of Prince.*

**swain** /sweɪn/ *n* [C] *poetic* a young man from the country who loves a girl

S3 **swal·low¹** /ˈswɒləʊ‖ˈswɑːloʊ/ *v*

**1** ▶ **FOOD** ◀ [T] to make food or drink go down your throat and towards your stomach: *He swallowed the last of his coffee and asked for the bill.*

**2** ▶ **NERVOUSLY** ◀ [I] to make this kind of movement with your throat, especially because you are nervous: *Leo swallowed hard and walked into the interview.*

**3** ▶ **BELIEVE/ACCEPT** ◀ [T] *informal* to immediately believe a story, explanation etc that is not actually true: **swallow sth whole** (=believe something without asking questions) *Her excuse was obviously a lie, but Eric swallowed it whole.* | **hard to swallow** (=difficult to believe) *I find those old superstitions hard to swallow.*

**4** ▶ **FEELINGS** ◀ [T] to stop yourself from showing your feelings: *Daisy tried hard to swallow her doubts.*

**5 swallow your pride** to ignore your feelings and do something that is very embarrassing for you because you have no choice: *When Ken lost his job he had to swallow his pride and borrow money.* —see also **a bitter pill (to swallow)** (BITTER¹ (7))

**swallow** sb/sth **up** *phr v* [T usually passive] **1** if something such as a company or a country is swallowed up by a large company, organization etc it becomes part of it and no longer exists on its own: *Their company was swallowed up by a multinational.* **2** if something such as an amount of money is swallowed up by something else, it is made to disappear completely: *I got a pay rise, but it was swallowed up by the increase in train fares.*

**swallow²** *n* [C] **1** a small bird with a tail that comes to northern countries in the summer **2** an act of making food go down your throat: *He downed his whisky in one swallow.*

**swallow dive** /ˈ··· ·/ *n* [C] *BrE* a DIVE² (1) into water, that starts with your arms stretched out from the sides of your body; SWAN DIVE *AmE*

**swam** /swæm/ the past tense of SWIM¹

**swa·mi** /ˈswɑːmi/ *n* [C] a Hindu religious teacher

**swamp¹** /swɒmp‖swɑːmp,/ *n* [C,U] land that is always very wet or slightly covered with water —compare MARSH —**swampy** *adj*: *swampy ground*

**swamp²** *v* [T] **1** [usually passive] to suddenly give someone a lot of work, problems etc to deal with: **swamp sb with sth** *We've been swamped with calls since we put the ad in the paper.* **2** to suddenly cover something with a lot of water, especially in a way that causes damage: *The shoreline was swamped by the high tides.*

**swan¹** /swɒn‖swɑːn/ *n* [C] a large white bird with a long graceful neck that lives on rivers and lakes

**swan²** *v* **swanned, swanning** [I always + adv/prep] *BrE informal* to do things in a relaxed way that is not very responsible: [+**off/around**] *You can't just swan off to the cinema when you're supposed to be working!*

**swan dive** /ˈ· ·/ *n* [C] *AmE* a DIVE² (1) into water, that starts with your arms stretched out from the sides of your body; SWALLOW DIVE *BrE*

**swank¹** /swæŋk/ *v* [I] *informal especially BrE* to behave or speak too confidently, especially to try and make other people admire you: *Stop swanking; you're not the only person who's got a flash car.*

**swank²** *n informal especially BrE* **1** [U] proud, confident behaviour that is intended to make people admire you, but is annoying **2** [C] someone who talks and behaves confidently in order to make people admire them

**swank³** *adj especially AmE* swanky

**swank·y** /ˈswæŋki/ *adj informal* **1** very fashionable or expensive; POSH: *a really swanky reception* **2** *especially BrE* tending to act too confidently to get attention

**swan·song** /ˈswɒnsɒŋ‖ˈswɑːnsɔːŋ/ *n* [C] the last piece of work or performance of a poet, painter etc: *The 1992 tour was a swansong for the two Irish players.*

**swap¹, swop** /swɒp‖swɑːp/ *v* **swapped, swapping** S3 [I,T] **1** to exchange something with someone, especially so that each of you get what you want; TRADE² (1): *I liked her coat and she liked mine, so we swapped.* | **swap sth for sth** *Adam swapped three of his stickers for three of Alex's.* | **swap sth with sb** *I swapped hats with Mandy.* | **swap sb sth for sth** *I'll swap you two of mine for one of yours.* **2 swap places** also **swap round** *BrE* to let someone sit or stand in your place, so that you can have their place: *I want to sit by Val; can we swap places?*

**swap², swop** *n* [C] *informal* **1** [usually singular] an exchange of one thing for another: *a swap of arms for hostages* | **do a swap** *I like your doll better; let's do a swap.* **2** something that has been or may be exchanged

**swap meet** /ˈ· ˌ·/ *n* [C] *AmE* an occasion when people meet to buy and sell used goods, or to exchange them

**sward** /swɔːd‖swɔːrd/ *n* [C] *literary* a piece of grassy land

**swarf** /swɔːf‖swɔːrf/ *n* [U] small bits of metal, plastic etc that are produced when you use a cutting tool

**swarm¹** /swɔːm‖swɔːrm/ *n* [C] **1** a large group of insects, especially BEES, or animals moving together **2** a crowd of people who are moving quickly: [+ **of**] *Swarms of tourists jostled through the square.*

**swarm** 

a swarm of bees

**swarm²** *v* [I] **1** [always + adv/prep] if people swarm somewhere, they go there as a large, uncontrolled crowd: [+ **through/over/out etc**] *photographers swarming around the princess* **2** if BEES swarm they leave a HIVE (=place where they live) in a large group to look for another home

**swarm with** sb/sth *phr v* **be swarming with** to be full of a moving crowd of people or animals: *The museum was swarming with tourists.*

**swar·thy** /ˈswɔːði‖-ɔːr-/ *adj* someone who is swarthy has dark skin that is considered unattractive

**swash·buck·ling** /ˈswɒʃˌbʌkəlɪŋ‖ˈswɑːʃ-, ˈswɒːʃ-/ *adj* enjoying adventures, sword fighting etc: *swash-buckling pirates* —**swashbuckler** *n* [C]

**swas·ti·ka** /ˈswɒstɪkə‖ˈswɑː-/ *n* [C] an ancient sign consisting of a cross with each end bent at 90°, used in the twentieth century as a sign for the Nazi Party

**swat** /swɒt‖swɑːt/ *v* **swatted, swatting** [T] to hit an insect to try to kill it —**swat** *n* [C]

**swatch** /swɒtʃ‖swɑːtʃ/ *n* [C] a piece of cloth that is used as an example of a type of material or its quality

**swathe¹** /sweɪð‖swɑːð, swɒːð, sweɪð/ also **swath** /swɒθ‖swɑːθ/ *n* [C] **1** a long band of cloth: *swathes of cotton* **2** a line or area of grass or crops that has been cut by a machine or a cutting tool **3** any large area of land that is different from the land on either side of it: *Acid rain is now affecting great swathes of Western Europe.* **4 cut a swath through** if a fire, severe storm etc cuts a swath through a place, it destroys almost everything around it

**swathe²** *v* [T usually passive] *literary* **be swathed in sth** to be wrapped or covered in something, especially cloth: *women swathed in expensive furs*

**sway¹** /sweɪ/ *v* **1** [I,T] to move slowly from one side to another: *trees swaying gently in the breeze* | **sway sth** *Melanie swayed her hips in time with the music.* **2** [T often passive] to influence someone who has not yet decided about something so that they change their opinion: *Don't allow yourself to be swayed by his promises.*

**sway²** *n* [U] **1** swinging movement from side to side: *the sway of the ship* **2** *literary* power to rule or influence people; control: **hold sway** (=have great power or influence) *In medieval times the Church held great sway politically.*

**sway·back** /ˈsweɪbæk/ *n* [C usually singular] *AmE* a condition in which your back curves inward too much

S2 **swear** /sweə‖swer/ *v past tense* **swore** /swɔː‖swɔːr/ *past participle* **sworn** /swɔːn‖swɔːrn/

**1 ▶ OFFENSIVE LANGUAGE ◀** [I] to use offensive language, especially because you are angry: *Don't swear in front of the children.* | [+ **at**] *Rich tripped over the dog and swore at it.* | **swear like a trooper** (=use very offensive language)

**2 ▶ SERIOUS PROMISE ◀** [T] to make a very serious promise: **swear to do sth** *Mona swore never to return home.* | **swear (that)** *Victor swore he would get his revenge.* | [+ **on/by**] *Do you swear on your honour never to tell anyone?*

**3 ▶ PUBLIC PROMISE ◀** [I,T] to make a public official promise, especially in a court of law: [+ **on**] *Witnesses have to swear on the Bible.* | **swear an oath** *Before giving evidence you have to swear an oath to tell the truth.* | **swear allegiance** *Presidents must swear allegiance to the US constitution.*

**4 ▶ STATE THE TRUTH ◀** [T not in progressive] *informal* to say that what you have said is the truth: **swear (that)** *He says he was there all the time, but I swear I never saw him.* | **swear blind (that)** *informal* (=used to empasize you are telling the truth) *She swore blind that she had never met the man.* | **I could have sworn (that)** *informal* (=I was almost certain) *I could have sworn I left the keys on that table.* | **swear to God** *I never touched her I swear to God.*

**5 swear sb to secrecy/silence** to make someone promise not to tell anyone what you have told them

**swear by** sth *phr v* [T not in progressive] *informal* to have great confidence in the effectiveness of something: *He swears by vitamin C pills, and says he never gets ill.*

**swear** sb ↔ **in** *phr v* [T usually passive] **1** to make someone promise publicly to be loyal to a country, official job etc: *The new governor was sworn in.* | *the swearing-in ceremony* **2** to make someone give an official promise in a court of law: *The jury had to be sworn in first.*

**swear off** sth *phr v* [T] to promise to stop doing something that is bad for you: *I'm swearing off alcohol after last night!*

**swear to** *phr v* [T] **not swear to (doing) sth** to be unwilling to say that something is true because you are not sure about it: *I think it was Sue I saw, but I wouldn't swear to it.*

**swear word** /ˈ· ·/ *n* [C] a word that is considered to be offensive or shocking by most people

**sweat¹** /swet/ *v*

**1 ▶ LIQUID FROM SKIN ◀** [I] to have liquid coming out through your skin, especially because you are hot or frightened: *I was sweating after the long climb.* | **sweat heavily/profusely** (=sweat a lot) | **sweat like a pig** *informal* (=sweat a lot) | **sweat buckets** *informal* (=sweat a lot)

**2 ▶ WORK ◀** [I] *informal* to work hard: *For years she had struggled and sweated to keep the family fed.* | [+ **over**] *Tim really sweated over that thesis.* | **sweat blood** (=work very hard)

**3 ▶ WORRY ◀** [I] *informal* to be anxious, nervous, or worried about something: *We were all really sweating as we waited for the results.* | *Don't tell them yet – let them sweat a bit first!*

**4 don't sweat it** *AmE spoken* used to tell someone not to worry about something: *Don't sweat it, I'll lend you the money.*

**5 don't sweat the small stuff** *AmE spoken* used to tell someone not to worry about unimportant things

**6 sweat bullets** *AmE informal* to be very worried, anxious, or frightened

**7 ▶ PRODUCE LIQUID ◀** [I] if something such as cheese sweats, liquid from inside appears on its surface

**8 ▶ COOK ◀** [T] *BrE* to heat food gently in a little water or fat: *Sweat the vegetables until the juices run out.*

**sweat** sth ↔ **out** *phr v* [T] **1 sweat it out a)** to continue doing something until it is finished, even though it is difficult: *You can't leave the course now. Just sweat it out until the summer.* **b)** to do hard physical exercise: *They were sweating it out in the gym.* **2** to get rid of an illness by making yourself sweat a lot **3 sweat your guts out** *informal* to work very hard, especially using physical effort: *I've sweated my guts out trying to get this shed built on time.* **4 sweat sth out of sb** *AmE informal* to find out information from someone by asking lots of questions in a threatening way: *Finally they sweated the other names out of him.*

**sweat** sth ↔ **off** *phr v* [T] to lose weight by sweating a lot: *He sweated off two pounds in the sauna.*

**sweat²** *n*

**1 ▶ LIQUID ON SKIN ◀** [U] liquid that comes out through your skin when you are hot, frightened, or doing exercise: *Ian came off the squash court dripping with sweat.* | **work up a sweat** (=to do physical exercise or hard work that makes you sweat) | **break out in a sweat** (=start to sweat, especially because you are frightened) *I was ready to kill the guy, and he didn't even break out in a sweat!*

**2 get into a sweat about sth** *informal* to become nervous or frightened about something: *Don't get into such a sweat about it! It's only a test.*

**3 a cold sweat** a state of nervousness or fear, in which you start to sweat, even though you are not hot: *I woke up from the nightmare in a cold sweat.*

**4 no sweat** *spoken* used to say that you can do something easily: *"Are you sure you can do it on time?" "Yeah, no sweat!"*

**5 sweats** [plural] *AmE informal* **a)** clothes made of thick, soft cotton, worn especially for sport; SWEAT SUIT **b)** trousers of this type; SWEAT PANTS

**6 the sweat of sb's brow** *literary* the hard effort that someone has made in their work

**7 ▶ WORK ◀** [singular] *old-fashioned* hard work, especially when it is boring or unpleasant

**8 (old) sweat** *old-fashioned* someone who has a lot of experience, especially a soldier

**sweat·band** /ˈswetbænd/ *n* [C] **1** a narrow band of

cloth that you wear around your head or wrist to stop sweat running down when you are doing sport **2** a narrow piece of cloth that you wear sewn or stuck in the inside of a hat

**sweated la·bour** *BrE*, **sweated labor** *AmE* /ˌ·· ˈ··/ *n* [U] **1** hard work done for very low wages, especially in a factory **2** the people who do this work

**sweat·er** /ˈswetə‖-ər/ *n* [C] a piece of warm WOOLLEN or cotton clothing for the top half of your body that has long SLEEVES and no buttons; JUMPER (1) *BrE*

**sweat gland** /ˈ· ·/ *n* [C] a small organ under your skin that produces sweat

**sweat pants** /ˈ· ·/ *n* [plural] *AmE* thick cotton trousers, worn especially for sport

**sweat·shirt** /ˈswet-ʃɜːt‖-ʃɜːrt/ *n* [C] a piece of thick cotton clothing with long SLEEVES, worn on the top half of your body, especially for sport

**sweat·shop** /ˈswet-ʃɒp‖-ʃɑːp/ *n* [C] a small business, factory etc where people work hard in bad conditions for very little money: *Sweatshops often employ female or immigrant workers.*

**sweat suit** /ˈ· ·/ *n* [C] *AmE* a set of clothes made of thick soft cotton, worn especially for sport

**sweat·y** /ˈsweti/ *adj* **1** covered with SWEAT[2] (1): *We came home hot and sweaty after the day's work.*|*sweaty palms* **2** smelling unpleasantly of SWEAT[2]: *sweaty socks* **3** unpleasantly hot or difficult so that you SWEAT[1]: *a sweaty August day*|*a sweaty job* **4** cheese that is sweaty has drops of liquid on its surface

**Swede** /swiːd/ *n* [C] someone who comes from Sweden

**swede** *n* [C,U] *BrE* a round yellow vegetable that grows under the ground; RUTABAGA *AmE*

**Swe·dish[1]** /ˈswiːdɪʃ/ *n* [U] **1** the language spoken in Sweden **2 the Swedish** the people of Sweden

**Swedish[2]** *adj* from or connected with Sweden

S3 W3 **sweep[1]** /swiːp/ *v past tense and past participle* **swept** /swept/

**1 ► CLEAN STH ◄** [T] to clean the dust, dirt etc from the floor or ground using a special brush: *Bert swept the path in front of the house.*|*Sweep the floor clean for me please.* —see picture at CLEAN[2]

**2 ► PUSH STH SOMEWHERE ◄** [T always + adv/prep] **a)** to clean a surface by pushing something to a particular place or in a particular direction with a special brush: *Could you sweep the snow off the patio for me?* **b)** to move something to a particular place or in a particular direction with a brushing or swinging movement: *The wind swept the dead leaves away.*|*I swept the papers quickly into the drawer.*

**3 ► CROWD ◄** [I always + adv/prep] if a group of people sweep somewhere, they quickly move there together: [+ **through/along etc**] *The crowd swept through the gates of the stadium.*

**4 ► PERSON ◄** [I always + adv/prep] if someone sweeps somewhere, they move quickly and confidently, especially because they are impatient or like to seem important: [+ **into/through etc**] *Eva swept into the meeting and demanded to know what was going on*

**5 ► WIND/WAVES ETC ◄** [I always + adv/prep,T] if winds, waves, storms etc sweep a place or sweep through, across etc a place, they move quickly and with a lot of force: [+ **across/through etc**] *90 mile per hour winds swept across the plains.*|**sweep sth** *Thunderstorms swept the country.*

**6 ► IDEA/FEELING ◄** [I always + adv/prep,T] if an idea or feeling sweeps a group of people or sweeps across, over etc a group, it quickly becomes very popular with them: [+ **across/through etc**] *The new dance craze swept through the teenage population.*|**sweep sth** *a wave of nationalism sweeping the country*

**7 sweep sb along/away a)** if a crowd sweeps someone along or away it forces them to move in the same direction it is moving in: *I was swept away by the crowd and lost sight of Alyssa completely.* **b)** if a feeling or idea sweeps you along or away, you are so involved or interested in it that you forget about other things: *19th century scientists swept along on the tide of Darwin's theories.*

**8 sweep to victory/power** to win something easily and in an impressive way: *Nixon and Agnew swept to victory with 47 million votes.*

**9 sweep the board** to win everything that can be won, especially very easily

**10 ► FORM A CURVE ◄** [I always + adv/prep] to form a long curved shape: [+ **down/a long etc**] *The hills swept down to the sea.*

**11 ► LOOK ◄** [I always + adv/prep,T] to look quickly at all of something: *The General's eyes swept the horizon.*|[+ **over/across/around etc**] *Her eyes swept over Marcia appraisingly.*

**12 sweep sb off their feet** to make someone feel suddenly and strongly attracted to you in a romantic way: *Jill's been swept off her feet by an older man.*

**13 sweep sth under the carpet** also **sweep sth under the rug** *AmE* to try to keep something a secret, especially something you have done wrong

**sweep** sth ↔ **aside** *phr v* [T] to refuse to pay attention to something someone says

**sweep** sth ↔ **away** *phr v* [T] **1** to completely destroy something or make something disappear: *houses swept away by the floods*|*A sudden feeling of nostalgia swept all my anger away.* **2** to be so interested or involved in something that you forget about other things: **be swept away by** *We couldn't help being swept away by Bette's enthusiasm.*

**sweep** sth ↔ **back** *phr v* [T] if you sweep your hair back, you pull it back from your face, especially so that it stays in that style: [+ **in/into**] *Kerry swept her hair back into a bun.*

**sweep up** *phr v* **1** [I,T] to clean a place using a special brush, or to pick up dirt, dust etc in this way: *The janitor was just sweeping up as I left the building.* [**sweep** sth ↔ **up**]: *Jan was left to sweep up the bits of paper and broken glass.* **2** [T **sweep** sb ↔ **up**] to pick someone up in one quick movement: *Harriet swept the child up in her arms and stormed out.* **3 sweep sb's hair up** to pull someone's hair back away from their face, especially so that it stays in that style

**sweep[2]** *n* **1** [C] a long swinging movement of your arm, a weapon etc: *With one sweep of his sword, he cut through the rope.* **2** [C usually singular] *BrE* the act of sweeping something: *The kitchen needs a good sweep.* **3 the sweep of a)** a long curved line or area of land: [+ **of**] *the sweep of the hills in the distance* **b)** the quality that an idea, plan, piece of writing etc has of considering many different and important things: *the grand sweep of Whitman's poetic vision* **4** [C usually singular] a search or attack that moves over a large area **5 sweeps** [singular] *AmE informal* a SWEEPSTAKE **6** [C] a CHIMNEYSWEEP —see also **clean sweep** (CLEAN[1] (12))

**sweep·er** /ˈswiːpə‖-ər/ *n* [C] **1** someone or something that sweeps: *a road sweeper* **2** *BrE* a football player who plays in a position behind other defending players

**sweep·ing** /ˈswiːpɪŋ/ *adj* **1** affecting many things, or making a big difference to things: **sweeping changes/cuts etc** *sweeping changes that mean job cuts in every department*|*sweeping proposals* **2** lacking knowledge of or consideration for facts or details: *sweeping statements*|**sweeping generalization** *You shouldn't make sweeping generalizations about women drivers.*

**sweep·ings** /ˈswiːpɪŋz/ *n* [plural] dirt, dust etc that is left to be swept up: *a pile of sweepings*

**sweep·stake** /ˈswiːpsteɪk/ *n* [C] a type of betting (BET[1]), in which the winner gets all the money risked by everyone else: *a sweepstake on the horses*

**sweet[1]** /swiːt/ *adj*

**1 ► TASTE ◄** having a taste like sugar: *This tea is too sweet.*|*a sweet apple*|*sweet wine* —compare BITTER[1] (4), DRY[1] (9), SOUR[1] (1)

**2 ► CHARACTER ◄** kind, gentle, and friendly: *a sweet smile*|*How sweet of you to remember my birthday!* —see also SWEET-TEMPERED

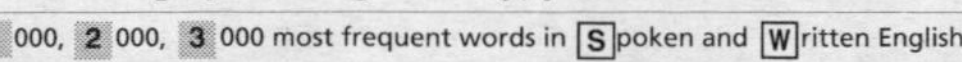

3 ▶ **CHILDREN/SMALL THINGS** ◀ *especially BrE* looking pretty and attractive; CUTE: *Your little boy looks very sweet in his new coat.*
4 ▶ **THOUGHTS/EMOTIONS** ◀ making you feel pleased, happy, and satisfied: *Revenge is sweet.*
5 ▶ **SMELLS** ◀ having a pleasant smell; FRAGRANT: *sweet-smelling flowers*
6 ▶ **SOUNDS** ◀ pleasant to listen to: *She had a very sweet singing voice.*
7 **have a sweet tooth** to like things that taste of sugar
8 **keep sb sweet** *informal* to behave in pleasant, friendly way towards someone, because you want them to help you later: *I'm trying to keep Angela sweet so that she'll lend me her notes.*
9 **in your own sweet way** if you do something in your own sweet way, you do it in exactly the way that you want to, without considering what other people say or think: *I'd rather carry on in my own sweet way, if you don't mind.*
10 **sweet deal** *AmE* a really good deal
11 **sweet FA** also **sweet Fanny Adams** *BrE informal* used to say FUCK ALL (=nothing at all) when you want to avoid using the word 'fuck': *"How much did they pay you for that job?" "Sweet FA!"*
12 **sweet nothings** things that lovers say to each other: *a couple whispering sweet nothings to each other*
13 **be sweet on sb** *old-fashioned* to be very attracted to or in love with someone —see also **home sweet home** (HOME[1] (16)), **short and sweet** (SHORT[1] (9)), SWEETNESS —**sweetly** *adv*

This graph shows how common the nouns **sweet** and **candy** are in British and American English.

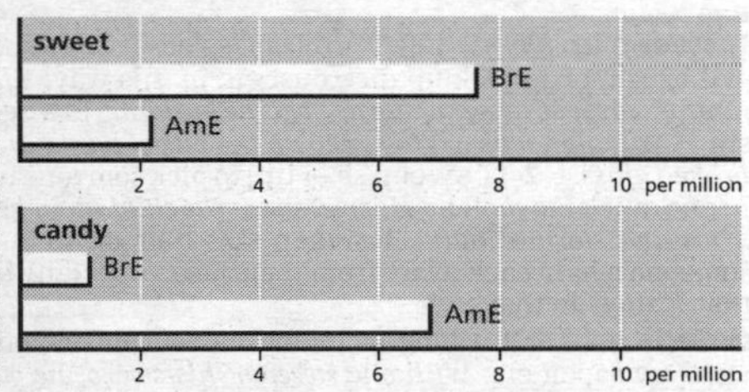


Based on the British National Corpus and the Longman Lancaster Corpus

In British English **sweet** is used to mean a small piece of sweet food made of sugar or chocolate. Americans use **candy** for this meaning. In British English **sweet** also means sweet food that is served at the end of a meal. Americans use **dessert** for this meaning.

S2 **sweet**[2] *n* 1 [C] *BrE* a small piece of sweet food made of sugar or chocolate; CANDY *AmE*: *Eating sweets is bad for your teeth.* 2 [C,U] *BrE* sweet food served at the end of a meal; DESSERT: *Would you like a sweet, or some cheese and biscuits?* 3 **(my) sweet** *old-fashioned* used when speaking to someone you love: *Don't cry, my sweet.*

**sweet-and-sour** /ˌ· · ˈ·◂/ *adj* [only before noun] a sweet-and-sour dish in Chinese cooking has both sweet and sour tastes together: *sweet-and-sour pork*

**sweet·bread** /ˈswiːtbred/ *n* [C] *old-fashioned* a small organ from a sheep or young cow, used as food

**sweet·corn** /ˈswiːtkɔːn‖-kɔːrn/ *n* [U] *BrE* the soft yellow seeds from MAIZE that are cooked and eaten; CORN[2] (2) *AmE*

**sweet·en** /ˈswiːtn/ *v* 1 [I,T] to make something sweeter, or become sweeter: *Sweeten the mixture with a little honey.* 2 also **sweeten** sb ↔ **up** [T] *informal* to try to persuade someone to do what you want, by giving them presents or money: *We're going to have to sweeten them up if we want that contract.* —see also SWEETENER (2) 3 [T] *literary* to make someone kinder, gentler etc: *Old age had not sweetened her.*

**sweetened con·densed milk** /ˌ·· ˈ·· ·/ *n* [U] *especially AmE* milk that has been made thicker and sweeter, and is usually sold in cans; CONDENSED MILK *BrE*

**sweet·ener** /ˈswiːtnə‖-ər/ *n* 1 [C,U] a substance used to make something taste sweeter: *No artificial sweeteners are used in this product.* 2 [C] *informal* something that you give to someone to persuade them to do something: *These tax cuts are just a pre-election sweetener.*

**sweet gum** /ˌ· ˈ·‖ˈ· ·/ *n* [C] a tree with hard wood and groups of seeds like PRICKLY balls, common in North America

**sweet·heart** /ˈswiːthɑːt‖-hɑːrt/ *n* [C] 1 a way of addressing someone you love: *Come here, sweetheart.* 2 an informal way of addressing a woman you do not know, which some women find offensive 3 *old-fashioned* the person that you love —see also DARLING[2], LOVE[2] (9)

**sweet·ie** /ˈswiːti/ *n* [C] 1 *BrE informal* a word for a SWEET[2] (1), used by or to children 2 *BrE informal* something or someone that is small, pretty, and easy to love: *Look at that little dog —isn't he a sweetie!* 3 *informal* a way of addressing someone you love

**sweetie pie** /ˈ·· ·/ *n* [C] *AmE informal* a way of addressing someone you love

**sweet·meat** /ˈswiːtmiːt/ *n* [C] *BrE old-fashioned* a SWEET[2] (1), or any food made of or preserved in sugar

**sweet·ness** /ˈswiːtnɪ̮s/ *n* [U] 1 how sweet something is 2 **be all sweetness and light** to behave in a way that is very pleasant and friendly, especially when you do not normally behave like this: *She's all sweetness and light when Paul's around.*

**sweet pea** /ˌ· ˈ·‖ˈ· ·/ *n* [C] a climbing plant with sweet-smelling flowers in pale colours

**sweet pep·per** /ˌ· ˈ··/ *n* [C] a green, red, or yellow vegetable that is hollow with many seeds; BELL PEPPER *AmE*

**sweet po·ta·to** /ˌ· ·ˈ··, ˈ· ·ˌ··/ *n* [C] a vegetable that looks like a red potato, is yellow inside and tastes sweet —compare YAM (1) —see picture at page 414

**sweet roll** /ˈ· ·/ *n* [C] *AmE* a small sweet PASTRY

**sweet-talk** /ˈ· ·/ *v* [T] *informal* to try to persuade someone to do something by talking to them in a pleasant way: **sweet-talk sb into doing sth** *I managed to sweet-talk her into driving me home.* —**sweet talk** *n* [U]

**sweet-temp·ered** /ˌ· ˈ··◂/ *adj* having a character that is kind and gentle

**sweet wil·liam** /ˌswiːt ˈwɪljəm/ *n* [C,U] a plant with sweet-smelling flowers

**swell**[1] /swel/ *v past tense* **swelled** *past participle* **swol·len** /ˈswəʊlən‖ˈswoʊ-/
1 ▶ **PART OF YOUR BODY** ◀ [I] also **swell up** to gradually increase in size: *Her ankle was already starting to swell.*
2 ▶ **PEOPLE** ◀ [T] to gradually increase in amount or number: *We asked them to come to the meeting to swell the numbers.* | *the crowd swelled* | **swell the ranks of sth** (=increase the number of people in a particular situation) *School leavers are swelling the ranks of the unemployed.*
3 ▶ **SOUND** ◀ [I] *literary* to become louder: *Music swelled around us.*
4 ▶ **SHAPE** ◀ [I,T] also **swell** (sth ↔) **out** to get or give something a full round shape: *The wind swelled the sails.*
5 **swell with pride/anger etc** to feel very proud, angry etc: *His heart swelled with pride as he watched his daughter collect her prize.*
6 ▶ **SEA** ◀ [I] to move suddenly and powerfully upwards —see also GROUNDSWELL, SWOLLEN

**swell**[2] *n* 1 [singular] the way the sea moves up and down: **heavy swell** (=very strong swell) *We didn't go sailing that day, as there was a heavy swell.* 2 [singular] an increase in sound level, especially in music; CRESCENDO (1) 3 [singular] the roundness and fullness of something: *the firm swell of her breasts* 4 [C] *old-fashioned* a fashionable or important person

**swell**[3] *adj AmE old-fashioned* very good: *You look swell!*

**swell-head·ed** /ˌ· ˈ··◂/ *adj AmE informal* thinking that you are more important or clever than you really are

**swell·ing** /ˈswelɪŋ/ *n* **1** [C] an area of your body that has become larger than normal, because of illness or injury: *a nasty swelling on my neck* **2** [U] the condition of having swelled: *The spider's bite can cause pain and swelling.*

**swel·ter** /ˈsweltə‖-ər/ *v* [I] to feel unpleasantly hot: *sitting and sweltering in the classroom*

**swel·ter·ing** /ˈsweltərɪŋ/ *adj* unpleasantly hot: *Open a window; it's sweltering in here!*

**swept** /swept/ the past tense and past participle of SWEEP

**swept-back** /ˌ· ˈ··◂/ *adj* **1** hair that is swept-back is brushed backward from your face **2** swept-back wings on an aircraft look like the letter v

**swerve** /swɜːv‖swɜːrv/ *v* [I] **1** to make a sudden sideways movement while moving forwards, especially in order to avoid hitting something: *Jo swerved to avoid a dog.* | [**+ across/off etc**] *The car swerved across the road and crashed into a wall.* —see picture on page 415 **2** [usually in negatives] *formal* to change from an idea, course of action, purpose etc: [**+ from**] *He vowed he would not swerve from his declared aims.* —**swerve** *n* [C] | *a swerve to the left*

**swift¹** /swɪft/ *adj* **1** happening quickly and immediately: *My letter received a swift reply.* **2** [only before noun] moving, or able to move, very fast: *a swift runner* | **swift of foot** *literary* (=able to run fast) **3 be swift to do sth** to do something as soon as you can, without any delay: *They were swift to deny the accusations.* —**swiftly** *adv* —**swiftness** *n* [U]

**swift²** *n* [C] a small brown bird that has pointed wings, flies very fast, and is similar to a SWALLOW² (1)

**swig** /swɪg/ *v* **swigged, swigging** [T] *informal* to drink something in large mouthfuls, especially from a bottle: *They sat there, swigging beer.* —**swig** *n* [C] | *He took a large swig from the bottle.*

**swill¹** /swɪl/ *v* [T] **1** to wash an area by pouring a lot of water over it or into it: **swill sth ↔ down/out** *Get a bucket to swill the yard down.* **2** *informal* to drink something in large amounts: *He does nothing but swill beer all day.*

**swill²** *n* **1** [U] food for pigs, mostly made of unwanted bits of human food —see also PIGSWILL **2** [C] the act of washing something by pouring a lot of water over it

**swim¹** /swɪm/ *v past tense* **swam** /swæm/ *past participle* **swum** /swʌm/ *present participle* **swimming**
**1** ▶ **MOVE THROUGH WATER** ◀ [I] to move yourself through water using your arms, legs etc: *My dad taught me to swim.* | *Exotic fish swam around in the tank.* | **go swimming** (=swim for fun) —see BATH² (USAGE)
**2** ▶ **IN A PARTICULAR AREA OF WATER** ◀ [T] to get across a particular area of water by doing this: *She was the first woman to swim the Channel.*
**3** ▶ **A PARTICULAR STYLE** ◀ [T] to use a particular style of swimming: *She can swim breaststroke, backstroke, and crawl.*
**4** ▶ **NOT THINKING/SEEING PROPERLY** ◀ [I] **a)** if your head swims, you start to feel confused or DIZZY (1): *My head was swimming after looking at that screen all day.* **b)** if something you are looking at swims, it seems to move because you feel DIZZY (1): *The numbers swam before my eyes.*
**5 be swimming with sth** also **be swimming in sth** to be very full of liquid or completely surrounded by liquid: *potatoes swimming in thick gravy*
**6 swim with the tide** to do or say the same things as most other people want because you do not want to seem different
**7 swim against the tide** to do or say different things from what most people do, because you do not mind being different —see also **sink or swim** (SINK¹ (17))

**swim²** *n* [C] **1** a period of time that you spend swimming: *Let's go for a swim.* **2 in the swim** *informal* knowing about and involved in what is happening in modern life

**swimmer** /ˈswɪmə‖-ər/ *n* [C] **a)** someone who swims well, often as a competitor: **good/strong swimmer** (=someone who swims well) **b)** someone who is swimming: *We watched the swimmers heading out across the lake.*

**swim·ming** /ˈswɪmɪŋ/ *n* [U] the sport of swimming: *Swimming is great exercise.* | *a swimming club* S2

**swimming bath** /ˈ··· ·/ *n* [C] *BrE old-fashioned* a public swimming pool, usually indoors

**swimming cos·tume** /ˈ·· ˌ··/ *n* [C] *BrE* a piece of clothing worn for swimming, especially the kind worn by women

**swim·ming·ly** /ˈswɪmɪŋli/ *adv old-fashioned* **go swimmingly** if something you plan goes swimmingly, it happens without problems

**swimming pool** /ˈ··· ·/ *n* [C] a hole in the ground that has been built and filled with water for people to swim in; POOL¹ (1): *a house with a swimming pool*

**swimming suit** /ˈ··· ·/ *n* [C] *AmE* a SWIMSUIT

**swimming trunks** /ˈ··· ·/ *n* [plural] *BrE* a piece of clothing like trousers with very short legs, worn by men for swimming

**swim·suit** /ˈswɪmsuːt, -sjuːt‖-suːt/ *n* [C] a piece of clothing worn for swimming

**swimwear** /ˈswɪmweə‖-wer/ *n* [U] clothing used for swimming

**swin·dle¹** /ˈswɪndl/ *v* [T] to get money from someone by deceiving them: **swindle sb out of sth** *He made a fortune swindling old ladies out of their life savings.*

**swindle²** *n* [C] a situation where someone gets money by deceiving someone else: *a big tax swindle*

**swine** /swaɪn/ *n* [C] **1** *plural* **swine** *or* **swines** *informal* someone who behaves very unpleasantly: *Leave her alone you filthy swine!* **2** *old use* a pig

**swine·herd** /ˈswaɪnhɜːd‖-hɜːrd/ *n* [C] *old use* someone who looks after pigs

**swing¹** /swɪŋ/ *v past tense and past participle* **swung** /swʌŋ/ W3
**1** ▶ **MOVE BACKWARDS/FORWARDS** ◀ [I,T] to move backwards and forwards hanging from a fixed point, or to make something do this: *a sign swinging in the wind* | *The soldiers swung their arms as they marched.*
**2** ▶ **MOVE IN A CURVE** ◀ [I always + adv/prep, T always + adv/prep] to move quickly in a smooth curve, or to make something move like this: *The heavy gates swung shut.* | **swing sth through/into etc sth** *She swung the car into the drive.* | *Bradley swung himself up into the saddle.*
**3** ▶ **CHANGE** ◀ [I,T] if emotions or opinions swing or something swings them, they change quickly to the opposite of what they were: *His mood could swing suddenly from great joy to complete despair.*
**4** ▶ **SWING IT** ◀ *informal* to make special arrangements for something to happen, especially something that is not usually allowed: *I'll see if I can swing it so my wife can come on that business trip with me.*
**5** ▶ **PLAY** ◀ [I] to sit on a SWING² (1) and make it move backwards and forwards by bending and unbending your legs: *The girl swung higher and higher.*
**6 swing for sth** *old-fashioned* to be killed by hanging (HANG¹ (3)) as a punishment for a crime
**7 swing both ways** *informal* to be BISEXUAL
**8 the swinging sixties** the years 1960 to 1969, thought of as a time when there was an increase in social and sexual freedom
**9 swing the lead** *BrE old-fashioned* to avoid doing your work or duty, especially by pretending to be ill —see also **no room to swing a cat** (ROOM¹ (2))

**swing around/round** *phr v* **1** [I, T] to turn around quickly or make something turn around quickly, to face in the opposite direction: *He swung around and yelled "that's a damn lie!"* | **swing sth ↔ around/round** *In seconds they had swung the big gun around.* **2** [I] if a wind swings around it changed direction suddenly and quickly: *The wind swung round to the North-East.*

**swing by** *phr v* [I,T] *AmE informal* to visit a place or person for a short time, usually for a particular purpose: **swing by sth** *I'll swing by the grocery store on my way home.*

S3 **swing²** *n*
1 ► **SEAT WITH ROPES** ◄ [C] a seat hanging from ropes or chains, for children to play on: *kids playing on the swings in the park*
2 ► **MOVEMENT** ◄ [C] a swinging movement with your arm, leg etc especially made in order hit something: **take a swing at sth** *He took a swing at my head and missed.*
3 ► **GOLF** ◄ [singular] the swinging movement of your arms and body when you hit the ball in GOLF: *I spent months correcting my swing.*
4 ► **CHANGE** ◄ [C] a noticeable change, especially in opinions or ideas: *a big swing towards right-wing ideology*
5 ► **MUSIC** ◄ [U] JAZZ music of the 1930s and 1940s with a strong regular beat, usually played by a big band
6 **get into the swing of sth** *BrE* to become fully involved in an activity or situation: *As soon as you get into the swing of it, you'll find it's quite easy.*
7 **be in full swing** if an event or process is in full swing it has reached its highest level of activity: *The party was in full swing when the police burst in.*
8 **swings and roundabouts** *BrE informal* used to say that every situation or decision has advantages and disadvantages

9 **go with a swing** *BrE* **a)** if a party or activity goes with a swing it is lively, enjoyable and successful **b)** if music goes with a swing it has a strong beat and a clear tune that is easy to dance to

**swing-boat** /ˈ· ·/ *n* [C] a large SWING² (1) shaped like a boat that two people can sit in

**swing bridge** /ˌ· ˈ·/ *n* [C] *BrE* a bridge that can be pulled upwards when tall ships need to pass through

**swing door** /ˌ· ˈ·/ *n* [C] a door that can be pushed open from either side, and swings shut afterwards —see picture on page 838

**swinge·ing** /ˈswɪndʒɪŋ/ *adj BrE* **swingeing cuts** very severe reductions in spending, especially by a government or organization; SWEEPING (1): *swingeing cuts in public spending*

**swing·er** /ˈswɪŋə‖-ər/ *n* [C] *old-fashioned* **1** someone who is very active and fashionable, and goes to many parties, NIGHTCLUBS etc **2** someone who has sexual relationships with many people

**swing·ing** /ˈswɪŋɪŋ/ *adj informal* exciting, fun, and enjoyable: *a swinging party* —see also **the swinging sixties** (SWING¹ (8))

**swing·om·e·ter** /swɪŋˈɒmɪ̣tə‖-ˈɑːmɪ̣tər/ *n* [C] *BrE informal* a special machine, used on television programmes during elections to show how much support each political party is getting as results become known

**swing set** /ˈ· ·/ *n* [C] *AmE* a tall metal frame with swings (SWING² (1)) hanging from it, for children to play on

**swing shift** /ˈ· ·/ *n* [singular] *AmE informal* workers who work from 3 or 4 o'clock in the afternoon until 11 or 12 o'clock at night, or the system of working these times

**swin·ish** /ˈswaɪnɪʃ/ *adj BrE* extremely unpleasant or difficult to deal with: *a swinish problem | swinish behaviour*

**swipe¹** /swaɪp/ *v* **1** [I,T] to hit or to try to hit someone or something by swinging you arm very quickly: *Jim swiped Bob across the face.* | [+ **at**] *The woman swiped at the child.* **2** [T] *informal* to steal something: *Who's swiped my pen?* **3** [T] to pull a special plastic card through a machine to record information on a computer: *You need to swipe your card to get in the building.*

**swipe²** *n* [C] **1** an act of hitting someone or something by swinging your arm very quickly: **take a swipe at** *He took a wild swipe at the policeman.* **2 take a swipe at** to publicly criticize someone in a speech or in writing: *In her latest article she takes a swipe at her detractors.*

**swirl¹** /swɜːl‖swɜːrl/ *v* [I,T] to turn around quickly in a twisting circular movement, or make something do this: *He swirled the brandy around in his glass.* | *The river had become a swirling torrent.*

**swirl²** *n* [C] **1** a swirling movement: [+ **of**] *a swirl of dust* **2** a twisting circular pattern

**swish¹** /swɪʃ/ *v* [I,T] to move or make something move quickly through the air with a smooth quiet sound: *Her skirt swished as she walked.* | *The horse swished his tail.* —**swish** *n* [singular]

**swish²** *adj BrE* fashionable and expensive-looking: *a really swish apartment*

**Swiss** /swɪs/ *adj* coming from or related to Switzerland

**Swiss chard** /ˌ· ˈ·/ *n* [U] CHARD

**swiss roll** /ˌ· ˈ·/ *n* [C,U] *BrE* a long thin cake that is rolled up with JAM¹ (1) or cream inside

**swiss steak** /ˌ· ˈ·/ *n* [C,U] *AmE* a thick flat piece of BEEF covered in flour and cooked in a SAUCE

**switch off**

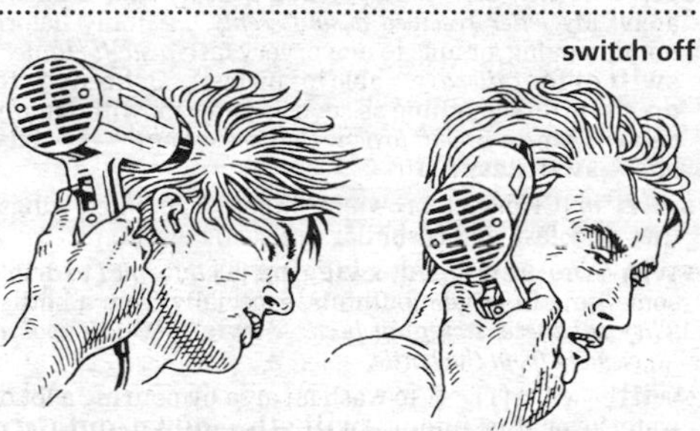

switch on / turn on switch off / turn off

**switch¹** /swɪtʃ/ *v* **1** [I,T] to change from one thing to another, usually suddenly: [+ **to**] *He used to play tennis, but now he's switched to golf.* | **switch sth to/from/away etc** *Duval switched easily and fluently from French to English.* | **switch jobs/positions etc** (=change from one job or position to another) **switch sth to/from/away etc** *We can switch the meeting to Tuesday if you like.* | **switch your attention** *Just switch your attention to the screen on your left.* **2** [T] to secretly remove one object and put another similar object in its place: *Someone must have switched suitcases at the airport.* **3** [I] to help someone you work with who needs time away from the job by agreeing to work certain hours for them if they do the same for you: **switch with sb** *Can you switch with me on Monday night?* **4** [T always + adv/prep] to change the way a machine operates by using a switch: *Switch the freezer to the 'extra cold' setting.* S2 W3

**switch off** *phr v* **1** [I,T] to turn off a machine, electric light, radio etc by using a switch: *Don't forget to switch off when you've finished.* | **switch sth ↔ off** *Can you switch the television off?* —see OPEN² (USAGE) **2** [I] *informal* to stop listening or paying attention: *He just switches off when you start talking to him.*

**switch on** *phr v* [I,T] to turn on a machine, electric light, radio etc by using a switch: **switch sth ↔ on** *Can you switch the light on?* —see OPEN² (USAGE)

**switch over** *phr v* **1** [I] to change completely from one method, product etc to another: [+ **from/to**] *A lot of banks are switching over to the new electronic system because it's more efficient.* **2** [I,T] *BrE* to change from one radio or television station to another: *Switch over if you don't like the programme.*

S 3 **switch**² *n* [C] **1** the part on a light, radio, machine etc that starts or stops the flow of electricity when you press it up or down: **light switch** *a light switch|the on/off switch*|**throw a switch** (=pull a large switch) *He threw a switch and all the lights in the theatre came on.* **2** a complete, and usually sudden, change from one thing to another: *The switch to a free market economy will not be easy.*|**that's a switch** *AmE* (=used to say that someone's behaviour is unusual for them) *"Mark's doing the dishes tonight." "That's a switch!"* **3 make the switch** to secretly remove one object and put another similar object in its place: *The original painting has been replaced by a fake, and no one knows when the switch was made.* **4** a thin stick that bends easily: *a willow switch*

**switch·back** /ˈswɪtʃbæk/ *n* [C] **1** a road or track that goes up and down steep slopes and around sharp bends **2** a ROLLERCOASTER

**switch·blade** /ˈswɪtʃbleɪd/ *n* [C] *AmE* a knife with a blade inside the handle which springs out when you press a button; FLICK KNIFE *BrE*

**switch·board** /ˈswɪtʃbɔːd‖-bɔːrd/ *n* [C] a central system used to connect telephone calls in an office building, hotel etc, or the people who operate the system: *Hello switchboard? Can I have an outside line?|switchboard operators*|**jam the switchboard** (=make too many calls for the switchboard to deal with)

**switch card** /ˈ· ·/ also **switch** *n* [C] *BrE trademark* a plastic card from your bank that you use to pay for things and that allows the money to be taken straight from your account

**switched-on** /ˌ· ˈ·◂/ *adj old-fashioned* quick to notice new ideas and fashions

**swiv·el**¹ /ˈswɪvəl/ **swivelled, swivelling** *BrE*, **swiveled, swiveling** *AmE* also **swivel around/round** *v* **1** [I,T] to turn something around that is fixed to a moving central point: *He swivelled the camera on the tripod to follow the riders.* **2** [I] to turn around quickly in this way

**swivel**² *n* [C] a thing that joins two parts of something in such a way that one or both parts can turn around freely

**swivel chair** /ˈ·· ·/ *n* [C] a chair that turns around on a swivel —see picture at CHAIR¹

**swiz, swizz** /swɪz/ *n BrE spoken* **what a swizz!** used when something makes you feel cheated or disappointed

**swiz·zle stick** /ˈswɪzəl ˌstɪk/ *n* [C] a small stick for mixing drinks

**swol·len**¹ /ˈswəʊlən‖ˈswoʊ-/ the past participle of SWELL¹

**swollen**² *adj* **1** a part of your body that is swollen is bigger than usual because of illness or injury: *He bandaged his swollen ankle.* **2** a river that is swollen has more water in it than usual **3 have a swollen head/be swollen-headed** *BrE* to be too proud so that you think you are very clever or important

**swoon** /swuːn/ *v* [I] **1** to feel so much excitement, happiness, or admiration that you almost faint: *The audience was full of swooning girls.* **2** *old use* to become unconscious and fall down; FAINT² (1) —**swoon** *n* [singular]

**swoop**¹ /swuːp/ *v* [I] **1** if a bird or aircraft swoops it moves suddenly and steeply down through the air, especially to attack something: [+ **in/down etc**] *The hawk swooped and seized a rabbit.* **2** to make a sudden, surprise attack: [+ **in/on etc**] *Police swooped in on gang hideouts in a series of raids.*

**swoop**² *n* [C] **1** a swooping movement or action **2** a sudden surprise attack: *Police hunting the killer arrested a man in a swoop on his flat last night.* —see also **at/in one fell swoop** (FELL⁴)

**swoosh** /swuːʃ/ *v* [I] to make a sound by moving quickly through the air —**swoosh** *n* [C]

**swop** /swɒp‖swɑːp/ another spelling of SWAP

swords

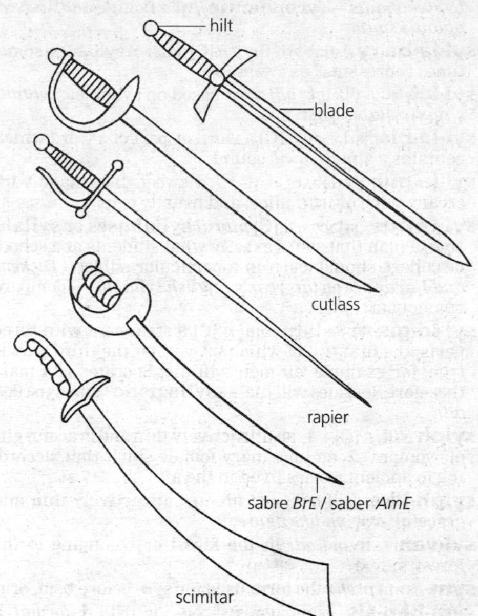


**sword** /sɔːd‖sɔːrd/ *n* [C] **1** a weapon with a long pointed blade and a handle **2 put sb to the sword** *old use* to kill someone with a sword **3 sword of Damocles** *literary* the possibility of something bad or dangerous happening at any time: *The treaty hung like a sword of Damocles over French politics.* —see also **cross swords (with)** (CROSS¹ (15))

**sword dance** /ˈ· ·/ *n* [C] a Scottish dance in which people dance between and around swords that are laid on the ground —**sword dancer** *n* [C] —**sword dancing** *n* [U]

**sword·fish** /ˈsɔːdˌfɪʃ‖ˈsɔːrd-/ *n* [C] a large fish with a very long pointed upper jaw like a sword

**swords·man** /ˈsɔːdzmən‖ˈsɔːrdz-/ *n* [C] someone who fights with a sword or someone who is skilled in this

**swords·man·ship** /ˈsɔːdzmənʃɪp‖ˈsɔːrdz-/ *n* [U] skill in fighting with a sword

**swore** /swɔː‖swɔːr/ the past tense of SWEAR

**sworn**¹ /swɔːn‖swɔːrn/ the past participle of SWEAR

**sworn**² *adj* **1 sworn enemies** two people or groups of people who will always hate each other **2 sworn statement/evidence/declaration** a statement etc that someone makes after officially promising to tell the truth

**swot**¹ /swɒt‖swɑːt/ *n* [C] *BrE informal* someone who spends too much time studying and seems to have no other interests —**swotty** *adj*

**swot**² *v* [I] *BrE informal* to study a lot in a short time, especially for an examination; CRAM (3) *AmE* [+ **for**] *I was busy swotting for my History exam.*

**swot up** *phr v* [I,T] *BrE* to study a subject a lot in a short time, especially to prepare for an examination: [+ **on**] *Jill's busy swotting up on German.*|**swot sth ↔ up** *I've got to swot up French irregular verbs.*

**swum** /swʌm/ the past participle of SWIM¹

**swung** /swʌŋ/ the past tense and past participle of SWING¹

**syb·a·rit·ic** /ˌsɪbəˈrɪtɪk◂/ *adj formal* wanting or enjoying expensive pleasures and comforts —**sybarite** /ˈsɪbəraɪt/ *n* [C]

**syc·a·more** /ˈsɪkəmɔː‖-mɔːr/ *n* [C] **1** a European tree that has leaves with five points and seeds with two parts like wings **2** an American PLANE TREE

**syc·o·phant** /ˈsɪkəfənt/ *n* [C] *formal* someone who

S

praises important or powerful people insincerely in order to get something from them: *a dictator surrounded by sycophants* —**sycophantic** /ˌsɪkəˈfæntɪk◂/ *adj* | *a sycophantic smile*

**syl·la·ba·ry** /ˈsɪləbəri‖-beri/ *n* [C] a list of syllables, sometimes represented as SYMBOLS

**syl·lab·ic** /səˈlæbɪk/ *adj* of or based on syllables: *syllabic stress* | *syllabic verse*

**syl·la·ble** /ˈsɪləbəl/ *n* [C] a word or part of a word which contains a single vowel sound

**syl·la·bub** /ˈsɪləbʌb/ *n* [C,U] a sweet dish made with cream, wine or fruit juice, and usually eggs

**syl·la·bus** /ˈsɪləbəs/ *n* [C] *plural* **syllabuses** or **syllabi** /-baɪ/ a plan that states exactly what students at a school or college should learn in a particular subject: *Dickens and Hardy are on this year's English syllabus.* —compare CURRICULUM

**syl·lo·gis·m** /ˈsɪlədʒɪzəm/ *n* [C] a statement with three parts, the first two of which prove that the third part is true, for example 'all men will die; Socrates is a man; therefore Socrates will die' —**syllogistic** /ˌsɪləˈdʒɪstɪk◂/ *adj*

**sylph** /sɪlf/ *n* [C] **1** an attractively thin and graceful girl or woman **2** an imaginary female spirit that, according to ancient stories lived in the air

**sylph·like** /ˈsɪlf-laɪk/ *adj literary* attractively thin and graceful: *a sylph-like figure*

**syl·van** /ˈsɪlvən/ *adj* in the forest or belonging to the forest; SILVAN

**sym-** /sɪm/ *prefix* the form used for SYN- before b, m, or p

**sym·bi·o·sis** /ˌsɪmbaɪˈəʊsəs‖-ˈoʊ-/ *n* [U] **1** *formal* a relationship between people or organizations that depend on each other equally **2** *technical* the relationship between two different living things that depend on each other for particular advantages —**symbiotic** /sɪmbaɪˈɒtɪk◂‖-ˈɑːt-/ *adj*: *a symbiotic relationship*

 **sym·bol** /ˈsɪmbəl/ *n* [C] **1** a picture or shape that has a particular meaning or represents an idea: [+ **of**] *The dove is a symbol of peace.* **2** a letter, number, or sign that represents a sound, an amount, a chemical substance etc: *'0' is the symbol for zero.* —see picture at SIGN[1] **3** someone or something that people think of as representing a particular quality or idea: *Space exploration provides a symbol of national pride.* —see also SEX SYMBOL

**sym·bol·ic** /sɪmˈbɒlɪk‖-ˈbɑː-/ also **sym·bol·i·cal** /-kəl/ *adj* used as a symbol, or containing symbols: *a symbolic painting* | **be symbolic of sth** *the snake is symbolic of evil* —**symbolically** /-kli/ *adv*

**sym·bol·is·m** /ˈsɪmbəlɪzəm/ *n* [U] the use of symbols to represent something: *religious symbolism*

**sym·bol·ize** also **-ise** *BrE* /ˈsɪmbəlaɪz/ *v* [T] **1** to be a symbol of something: *In Europe, the colour white symbolizes purity.* **2** to represent something with a symbol: *Peace is symbolised by a dove.* —**symbolization** /ˌsɪmbəlaɪˈzeɪʃən‖-lə-/ *n* [U]

symmetrical

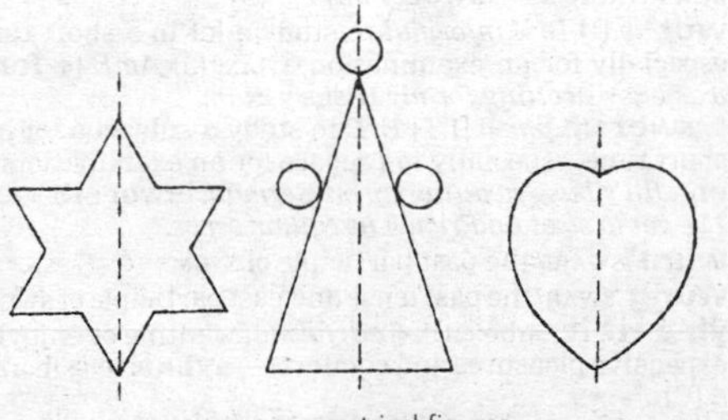

some symmetrical figures

**sym·met·ri·cal** /sɪˈmetrɪkəl/ also **sym·met·ric** /sɪˈmetrɪk/ *adj* a thing or design that is symmetrical has two halves that are exactly the same shape and size: *The leaves of most trees are symmetrical.* —opposite ASYMMETRICAL —**symmetrically** /-kli/ *adv*

**sym·me·try** /ˈsɪmətri/ *n* [U] exact likeness in size and shape between two sides of something: *the symmetry of the human body*

**sym·pa·thet·ic** /ˌsɪmpəˈθetɪk◂/ *adj* **1** willing to try to understand someone else's problems and give them any help they need: *You're not being very sympathetic, Joan.* | **a sympathetic ear** (=willingness to listen to someone else's problems) *Paul's great if you need a sympathetic ear or advice.* **2** [not before noun] willing to give approval and support to an aim or plan: [+ **to/towards**] *There is a group in the party sympathetic towards our aims.* **3** providing the right conditions to make the results you want to happen: *a sympathetic environment* **4 sympathetic figure/character** *literary* someone in a book, play etc who the author intends you to like —**sympathetically** /-kli/ *adv*

**sym·pa·thize** also **-ise** *BrE* /ˈsɪmpəθaɪz/ *v* [I] **1** to feel sorry for someone because you understand their problems: *I sympathize; you need to know exactly what caused the accident.* | [+ **with**] *I sympathize with the plight of the homeless.* **2** to support someone's ideas or actions: [+ **with**] *Many workers sympathized with the striking miners.*

**sym·pa·thiz·er** also **-iser** *BrE* /ˈsɪmpəθaɪzə‖-ər/ *n* [C] someone who supports the aims of an organization or political party but does not belong to it: *The anti-abortion rally attracted many sympathizers.*

**sym·pa·thy** /ˈsɪmpəθi/ *n* [U] **1** the feeling of being sorry for someone who is in a bad situation and understanding how they feel: *He wants your sympathy so he's pretending to be sick.* | **have/feel sympathy for sb** *I've a lot of sympathy for her; she brought up the children on her own.* | **have no sympathy for sb** (=feel that someone deserves something bad that is happening to them) | **play on sb's sympathy** (=make someone feel sorry for you in order to gain an advantage for yourself) | **you have my deepest sympathy** *formal* (=used in a letter to someone whose close relative has died) | **offer your sympathy** *formal*: *She wrote a letter offering her sympathy.* | **message/letter of sympathy** *The victim's parents have received thousands of messages of sympathy.* **2 be in sympathy with** also **have sympathy for** to agree with and support someone's aims and actions: *We have a lot of sympathy for your stand on lower taxes.* **3 come out in sympathy (with sb)** to STRIKE[1] (4) in order to give support to other people who are striking: *The miners were on strike and the railwaymen came out in sympathy.* **4 sympathies** [plural] **a)** feelings of support and approval: **sb's sympathies lie with** *Anne's sympathies lie firmly with the Conservative Party.* **b)** a message of comfort to someone who is very upset because someone has died —see also **tea and sympathy** (TEA (5)) **5** [U] a feeling that you understand someone because you are similar to them

**sym·pho·ny** /ˈsɪmfəni/ *n* [C] a long piece of music usually in four parts written for an ORCHESTRA : *Beethoven's Third Symphony*

**symphony or·ches·tra** /ˈ··· ˌ···/ *n* [C] a large ORCHESTRA (=group of musicians)

**sym·po·si·um** /sɪmˈpəʊziəm‖ˈpoʊ-/ *plural* **symposiums** *or* **symposia** /-ziə/ *n* [C] *formal* **1** a formal meeting in which people who know a lot about a particular subject have discussions about it: *a symposium on neurological science* **2** a group of articles on a particular subject collected together in a book

**symp·tom** /ˈsɪmptəm/ *n* [C] **1** a physical condition which shows that you have a particular illness: *Symptoms include headaches and vomiting.* | [+ **of**] *the first symptoms of malaria* **2** a sign that a serious problem exists: [+ **of**] *The crime rate is a symptom of social unrest.* —see also **withdrawal symptoms** (WITHDRAWAL (6)) W3

**symp·to·mat·ic** /ˌsɪmptəˈmætɪk◂/ *adj* **1 be symptomatic of sth** *formal* if a situation or kind of behaviour is symptomatic of something, it shows that a serious problem exists: *Her irritation seems symptomatic of something deeper.* **2** *technical* related to medical symptoms —**symptomatically** /-kli/ *adv*

**syn-** /sɪn/ *prefix* together; sharing: *a synthesis* (=combining of separate things)

**syn·a·gogue** /ˈsɪnəgɒg‖-gɑːg/ *n* [C] a building where Jewish people meet for religious worship

**sync, synch** /sɪŋk/ *n informal* **1 in sync** two or more parts of a machine, process etc that are in sync are working at the same rate **2 out of sync** two or more parts of a machine, process etc that are out of sync are not working at the same rate

**syn·chro·ni·city** /ˌsɪŋkrəˈnɪsɪ̇ti/ *n* [U] the fact of two or more events happening at the same time or place, when these events are believed to be connected in some way

**syn·chro·nize** also **-ise** *BrE* /ˈsɪŋkrənaɪz/ *v* **1** [T] to arrange for two or more actions to happen at exactly the same time: *If we synchronize our attacks they'll cause more disruption.* **2 synchronize your watches** to make two or more watches or clocks show exactly the same time **3** [I,T] if the sound and action of a film synchronize or if you synchronize them, they go at exactly the same speed —**synchronization** /ˌsɪŋkrənaɪˈzeɪʃən‖-nə-/ *n* [U]

**synchronized swim·ming** /ˌ··· ˈ··/ *n* [U] an activity in which swimmers move in patterns in the water to music

**syn·chro·nous** /ˈsɪŋkrənəs/ *adj* a synchronous signal on a computer is one in which the time between one BIT[1] (12) and the next is the same

**syn·co·pat·ion** /ˌsɪŋkəˈpeɪʃən/ *n* [U] a RHYTHM in a line of music in which the beats (BEAT[2] (3)) that are usually weak are emphasized

**syn·co·pe** /ˈsɪŋkəpi/ *n* [U] *technical* **1** the loss of consciousness when someone faints **2** a way of making a word shorter by leaving out of sounds or letters in the middle of it, for example changing 'cannot' to 'can't'

**syn·di·cal·is·m** /ˈsɪndɪkəlɪzəm/ *n* [U] a political system or belief whose aim is for workers to control industry —**syndicalist** *n* [C] —**syndicalist** *adj*

**syn·di·cate¹** /ˈsɪndɪ̇kɪ̇t/ *n* [C] a group of people or companies who join together in order to achieve a particular aim: *a syndicate of local industrialists*

**syn·di·cate²** /ˈsɪndɪ̇keɪt/ *v* **1** [T] to arrange for written work, photographs etc to be sold to a number of different newspapers, magazines etc: **be syndicated** *His column is syndicated throughout America.* **2** [I,T] to form into a syndicate —**syndication** /ˌsɪndɪ̇ˈkeɪʃən/ *n* [U]

**syn·drome** /ˈsɪndrəʊm‖-droʊm/ *n* [C] **1** *technical* a set of physical or mental effects that show that someone has a particular disease: *There is no satisfactory drug treatment for irritable bowel syndrome.* —see also DOWN'S SYNDROME **2** a set of qualities, events or behaviour that is typical of a particular kind of problem: *the syndrome of the bored middle-aged man*

**syn·er·gy** /ˈsɪnədʒi‖-ər-/ *n* [U] *technical* additional energy that is produced by two people combining their energy and ideas

**syn·od** /ˈsɪnəd/ *n* [C] an important meeting of church members to make decisions concerning the church

**syn·o·nym** /ˈsɪnənɪm/ *n* [C] a word with the same meaning or nearly the same meaning as another word in the same language, such as 'sad' and 'unhappy' —compare ANTONYM

**sy·non·y·mous** /sɪ̇ˈnɒnɪ̇məs‖-ˈnɑː-/ *adj* **1** a situation, quality, idea etc that is synonymous with something else is the same or nearly the same as another: [+ **with**] *She seems to think that being poor is synonymous with being lazy.* **2** two words that are synonymous have the same or nearly the same meaning —**synonymously** *adv*

**sy·nop·sis** /sɪ̇ˈnɒpsɪ̇s‖-ˈnɑːp-/ *n plural* **synopses** /-siːz/ [C + **of**] a short account of something longer, such as the story of a film, play, or book; SUMMARY[1]

**syn·tac·tic** /sɪnˈtæktɪk/ *adj technical* related to syntax: *The two sentences have the same syntactic structure.* —**syntactically** /-kli/ *adv*

**syn·tax** /ˈsɪntæks/ *n* [U] *technical* **1** the rules of grammar that are used for ordering and connecting words to form phrases or sentences **2** the rules that describe how words and phrases are used in a computer language —compare MORPHOLOGY (1)

**syn·the·sis** /ˈsɪnθɪ̇sɪ̇s/ *n* **1** [C] something such as a substance or an idea, made by combining different things: [+ **of**] *Their beliefs are a synthesis of Eastern and Western religions.* **2** [U] the act of combining separate things, ideas etc into a complete whole: *the synthesis of rubber from petroleum* **3** [C] the production of the sounds of speech or music by electronic means

**syn·the·size** also **-ise** *BrE* /ˈsɪnθɪ̇saɪz/ *v* [T] to produce something by combining different things, especially to make something similar to a natural product by combining chemicals: *Many minerals have been synthesized chemically.*

**syn·the·siz·er** also **synthesiser** *BrE* /ˈsɪnθɪ̇saɪzə‖-ər/ *n* [C] an electrical instrument that produces the sounds of various musical instruments —see also SPEECH SYNTHESIZER

**syn·thet·ic** /sɪnˈθetɪk/ *adj* produced by combining different artificial substances, rather than being naturally produced: *synthetic fabrics like nylon* —**synthetically** /-kli/ *adv*

**syph·i·lis** /ˈsɪfəlɪ̇s/ *n* [U] a very serious disease, passed on during sexual activity or from parent to child

**sy·phon** /ˈsaɪfən/ *n* [C] another spelling of SIPHON

**sy·ringe¹** /sɪ̇ˈrɪndʒ/ *n* [C] an instrument for taking blood from someone's body or putting liquid, drugs etc into it, consisting of a hollow plastic tube and a needle

**syringe²** *v* [T] to clean something with a syringe: *Get the doctor to syringe your ears.*

**syr·up** /ˈsɪrəp‖ˈsɜː-, ˈsɪ-/ *n* [U] **1** sweet liquid, especially sugar and water: *canned fruit in syrup* **2** thick sticky pale liquid made from sugar: *golden syrup* | *maple syrup* **3** medicine in the form of a thick sweet liquid: *cough syrup*

**syr·up·y** /ˈsɪrəpi‖ˈsɜː-, ˈsɪ-/ *adj* **1** thick and sticky like syrup or containing syrup: *syrupy drinks* **2** too sweet, nice or kind: *Her voice was syrupy.*

**sys·tem** /ˈsɪstɪ̇m/ *n* S1 W1

**1 ► RELATED PARTS ◄** [C] a group of related parts that work together as a whole for a particular purpose: *They have an alarm system in the house.* | *the body's immune system* | *the banking system in the US* | *the railway system*

**2 ► METHOD ◄** [C] an organized set of ideas, methods, or ways of working: [+ **of/for**] *What is the system for marking pronunciation in the dictionary?*

**3 ► THE BODY ◄** [C] your body considered as a set of working parts: *All this overeating is bad for my system.*

**4 ► COMPUTERS ◄** [C] the way in which a computer or set of computers works: *a fault in the system* | *What software does the system use?* —see also OPERATING SYSTEM

**5 the system** *informal* the combination of official rules and powerful groups or organizations that seem to govern your life and limit your freedom: *You can't beat the system in this company!*

**6 get sth out of your system** *informal* to do something that helps you get rid of unpleasant strong feelings: *I was furious, so I went for a run to get it out of my system.*

**7 ► ORDER ◄** [U] the use of sensible and organized methods: *We need a bit more system in the way we organize our files.*

**sys·te·mat·ic** /ˌsɪstɪ̇ˈmætɪk◂/ *adj* based on carefully organized methods; THOROUGH: *The way they've collected their data is not very systematic.* | *a systematic search of the building* —**systematically** /-kli/ *adv*

**sys·te·ma·tize** also **-ise** *BrE* /ˈsɪstɪ̇mətaɪz/ *v* [T] to put facts, numbers, ideas etc into a particular order —**systematization** /ˌsɪstɪ̇mətaɪˈzeɪʃən‖-tə-/ *n* [U]

**sys·te·mic** /sɪsˈtemɪk, -ˈtiːmɪk‖sɪsˈtemɪk/ *adj technical* having an effect on the whole of something, especially a living thing: *systemic injection* —**systemically** /-kli/ *adv*

**systems an·a·lyst** /ˈ·· ˌ···/ *n* [C] someone who studies business or industrial operations, and uses computers to plan them, improve them etc —**systems analysis** /ˌ·· ·ˈ···/ *n* [U]

**T, t** /tiː/ *plural* **T's** or **t's** **1** the 20th letter of the English alphabet **2 to a T** *informal* if something suits you to a T, it is exactly right for you: *That dress suits you to a T.*

**TA** /ˌtiː ˈeɪ/ *n* [singular] the abbreviation of TERRITORIAL ARMY

S3 **ta** /tɑː/ *interjection BrE informal* thank you

**tab** /tæb/ *n* [C]
**1** ▶ **SMALL PIECE OF PAPER/CLOTH** ◀ a small piece of paper, cloth etc that is fixed to the edge of something, especially giving information about it
**2** ▶ **ON A CAN** ◀ *AmE* a small piece of metal that you pull to open a can of drink
**3** ▶ **IN A BAR/RESTAURANT** ◀ a system used in some bars, restaurants etc in which they keep a record of what you have bought and you pay for it later: **put sth on a tab** *Don't worry about the meal. Put it on my tab.*
**4 keep tabs on sb** *informal* to watch someone carefully to check what they are doing: *The police have been keeping tabs on Rogers since he got out of prison.*
**5 pick up the tab** to pay for something, especially when it is not your responsibility to pay: *Taxpayers pick up the tab for government mismanagement of the economy.*
**6** ▶ **CIGARETTE** ◀ *slang* a cigarette
**7** ▶ **IN TYPING** ◀ a TAB STOP
**8** *slang* a solid form of the illegal drug LSD: *a tab of acid*

**Ta·bas·co** /təˈbæskəʊ‖-koʊ/ also **tabasco sauce** /-ˌ·· ˈ·-/ *n* [U] *trademark* a very hot-tasting red liquid made from CHILLI (2) peppers, used in cooking

**tab·by** /ˈtæbi/ *n* [C] a cat with grey, brown, or orange marks on its fur —**tabby** *adj*

**tab·er·nac·le** /ˈtæbənækəl‖-bər-/ *n* [C] **1 the tabernacle** the small tent in which the ancient Jews kept their most holy objects **2** a church or other building used by some Christian groups **3** a box used for keeping holy bread and wine in Roman Catholic churches

S1 W1 **ta·ble¹** /ˈteɪbəl/ *n*
**1** ▶ **FURNITURE** ◀ a piece of furniture with a flat top supported by legs: *a kitchen table* | **table lamp** (=made to be put on a small table) | **book a table** (=ask a restaurant to keep a table available for you) *I've booked a table for two for 8:00.* | **lay the table** *BrE* **set the table** *especially AmE* (=put knives, forks etc on a table before a meal) | **clear the table** (=take all the empty plates, dishes etc off a table after eating) | **at table** *BrE formal* (=sitting around a table having a meal) —see also COFFEE TABLE, HIGH TABLE
**2** ▶ **LIST** ◀ [C] a list of numbers, facts, or information arranged in rows across and down a page: **table of contents** *The table of contents at the front will tell you which page it's on.*
**3** ▶ **MATHS** ◀ a list that young children learn, in which all the numbers between 1 and 12 are multiplied by each other: **three/four etc times table** *He's 12 years old and still doesn't know his three times table.*
**4 on the table a)** an offer, idea etc that is on the table has been officially suggested and you are considering it: *The offer on the table at the moment is a 10% wage increase.* **b)** *AmE* an offer, idea etc that is on the table is no longer being considered at the moment but will be dealt with in the future
**5 turn the tables (on sb)** to suddenly become stronger than the opponent who used to be stronger than you: *Suddenly Harry felt that the tables had somehow been turned and that he was now the victim.*
**6 under the table** *informal* money that is paid under the table is paid secretly and illegally to get what you want: *payments made under the table to local officials*
**7** ▶ **GROUP** ◀ the group of people sitting around a table: *His stories kept the whole table amused.* —see also **drink sb under the table** (DRINK¹ (2))

**table²** *v* [T] **1** *BrE* **table a proposal/question/demand etc** to suggest a proposal etc for other people to consider **2** *AmE* **table a bill/measure/proposal etc** to leave an offer, idea etc to be dealt with in the future

**tab·leau** /ˈtæbləʊ‖ˈtæbloʊ, tæˈbloʊ/ *n* [C] a group of people who do not speak or move arranged on stage to show a famous event

**ta·ble·cloth** /ˈteɪbəlklɒθ‖-klɒːθ/ *n* [C] a cloth used for covering a table, —see picture on page 838

**table d'hôte** /ˌtɑːbəl ˈdəʊt‖-ˈdoʊt/ *n* [singular] a complete meal served at a fixed price in a hotel or restaurant

**ta·ble·land** /ˈteɪbəl-lænd/ also **tablelands** *n* [C] *technical* a large area of high flat land; PLATEAU (1)

**table lin·en** /ˈ·· ˌ··/ *n* [U] all the cloths used during the meal

**table man·ners** /ˈ·· ˌ··/ *n* [plural] the way in which someone eats their food, considered according to the usual rules of social behaviour about eating: *Piotr's got terrible table manners.*

**table mat** /ˈ·· ·/ *n* [C] a small mat that you put under a hot dish or plate —see picture on page 838

**ta·ble·spoon** /ˈteɪbəlspuːn/ *n* [C] **1** *BrE* a large spoon used for serving food, or the amount held in it: *three tablespoons of sugar* **2** *AmE* a medium-sized spoon which you use for eating **3** *AmE* a spoon that holds exactly 1/128 of a US pint of liquid —see picture at SPOON¹

**ta·ble·spoon·ful** /ˈteɪbəlspuːnfʊl/ *n plural* **tablespoonfuls, tablespoonsful** [C] the amount that a tablespoon holds: [+ **of**] *two tablespoonsful of flour*

**tab·let** /ˈtæblɪt/ *n* [C] **1** *especially BrE* a small round hard piece of medicine; PILL (1): *three tablets a day before meals* **2** a flat piece of soap **3** a flat piece of stone or metal with words cut into it

**table ten·nis** /ˈ·· ˌ··/ *n* [U] an indoor game played on a table by two or four players who hit a small plastic ball to each other across a net; PING-PONG

**ta·ble·ware** /ˈteɪbəlweə‖-wer/ *n* [U] the plates, glasses, knives etc used when eating a meal

**table wine** /ˈ·· ˌ·/ *n* [C,U] a fairly cheap wine intended for drinking with meals

**tab·loid** /ˈtæblɔɪd/ *n* [C] **1** *BrE* a newspaper that has a lot of stories about sex, famous people etc, and not much serious news: *The tabloids had the story splashed all over their front pages.* **2** a newspaper with a small page —compare BROADSHEET —**tabloid** *adj*: *the tabloid press*

**ta·boo¹** /təˈbuː, tæˈbuː/ *adj* **1 taboo subject/area/word** a subject etc that people avoid because they think it is offensive or embarrassing: *Death is still a taboo subject to some people.* **2** *technical* too holy or evil to be touched, or used

**taboo²** *n plural* **taboos** [C,U] **1** a social custom which means a particular activity or subject must be avoided: **about/on/against** *a strong taboo against fighting in public* **2** a religious custom that FORBIDS a particular activity because it may offend God

**ta·bor** /ˈteɪbə‖-ər/ *n* [C] a small DRUM¹ (1)

**tab stop** /ˈ· ·/ *n* [C] a button on a computer or TYPEWRITER that you push, in order to move forward to a particular place on a line of text

**tab·u·lar** /ˈtæbjʊlə‖-ər/ *adj* arranged in the form of a TABLE (=set of numbers arranged in rows across and down a page)

**tab·u·la ra·sa** /ˌtæbjʊlə ˈrɑːzə/ *n* [C usually singular] *Latin literary* your mind in its original state, before you have learned anything

**tab·u·late** /ˈtæbjʊleɪt/ *v* [T] to arrange figures or information together in a set or a list so that they can be easily compared —**tabulation** /ˌtæbjʊˈleɪʃən/ *n* [U]

**tach·o·graph** /ˈtækəgrɑːf‖-græf/ *n* [C] a piece of equipment for recording the speed of a vehicle, the distance it has travelled etc

**ta·chom·e·ter** /tæˈkɒmɪ̣tə‖-ˈkɑːmɪ̣tər/ *n* [C] a piece of equipment used to measure the speed, at which the engine of a vehicle turns

**ta·cit** /ˈtæsɪ̣t/ *adj* tacit agreement, support etc is accepted or understood without actually being stated or officially arranged: *a tacit agreement that no company would cut their prices* —**tacitly** *adv* —**tacitness** *n* [U]

**ta·ci·turn** /ˈtæsɪ̣tɜːn‖-ɜːrn/ *adj* speaking very little, so that you seem unfriendly —**taciturnly** *adv* —**taciturnity** /ˌtæsɪ̣ˈtɜːnɪ̣ti‖-ɜːr-/ *n* [U]

**tack¹** /tæk/ *n*
1 ▶ **NAIL** ◀ [C] a small nail with a sharp point and flat top
2 ▶ **PIN** ◀ [C] *AmE* a short pin with a large round flat top, for fixing notices to boards, walls etc; DRAWING PIN *BrE*, THUMBTACK *AmE*
3 **change tack/try a different tack etc** to do something completely different from what you were doing before, especially in order to achieve something: *Rudy changed tack, his tone suddenly becoming friendly.*
4 ▶ **SHIP** ◀ [C,U] the direction of a sailing ship, based on the direction of the wind and the position of its sails: *Ships on the starboard tack have right of way.*
5 ▶ **SEWING** ◀ [C] a long loose stitch used for fastening pieces of cloth together before SEWING them properly
6 ▶ **UGLY OBJECTS** ◀ [U] small objects that are very ugly and cheap, but are sold as decorations: *souvenir shops full of tack*
7 ▶ **HORSES** ◀ [U] all the equipment you need for horse riding

**tack²** *v* 1 [T always + adv/prep] to fasten something with a tack: [+ **up**] *tacking notices up on the board* 2 [T] to fasten pieces of cloth together with long loose stitches, before SEWING them properly 3 [I] to change the course of a sailing ship so that the wind blows against its sails from the opposite direction

**tack** sth ↔ **on** *phr v* [T] *informal* to add something to something that already exists or is complete, especially in a way that looks badly planned: *The environmental section of the bill was obviously tacked on afterwards.* | *a little porch tacked on to the front of the house*

S3 **tack·le¹** /ˈtækəl/ *v*
W3 1 [T] to make a determined effort to deal with a difficult problem: *It took twelve fire engines to tackle the blaze.*
2 [T] to talk to someone in order to deal with a difficult problem: **tackle sb about sth** *When I tackled Didi about it, she admitted he'd tried to do too much.*
3 [I, T] ▶ **SPORT** ◀ **a)** to try to take the ball away from an opponent in a game such as football or HOCKEY (1) —see picture on page 1264 **b)** to force someone to the ground so that they stop running, in a game such as American football or RUGBY
4 [T] to fight against another person, organization etc: *I certainly couldn't tackle both of them on my own.*

**tackle²** *n* 1 [C] **a)** the act of trying to take the ball from an opponent in a game of football or HOCKEY (1) **b)** [C] the act of stopping an opponent by forcing them to the ground, especially in American football or RUGBY 2 [C] a player in American football who stops other players by tackling them 3 [U] the equipment used in some sports, especially fishing 4 [U] *slang* a man's sexual organs 5 [C,U] ropes and PULLEYS (=wheels) used for moving a ship's sails, lifting heavy things etc

**tack·y** /ˈtæki/ *adj* 1 cheap looking and of very bad quality: *tacky ornaments* 2 slightly sticky: *The paint's still slightly tacky.* —**tackily** *adv* —**tackiness** *n* [U]

**ta·co** /ˈtɑːkəʊ‖-koʊ/ *n* [C] a type of Mexican food consisting of a flat circle made of CORN (2) flour folded and filled with BEEF¹ (1), beans etc

**tact** /tækt/ *n* [U] the ability to be polite and careful about what you say or do so that you do not upset or embarrass other people: *With great tact, Aunt Jo persuaded Theo to apologize.*

**tact·ful** /ˈtæktfəl/ *adj* careful not to say or do anything that will upset or embarrass other people: *Sam maintained a tactful silence as she ranted on.* —**tactfully** *adv*: *Everyone tactfully refrained from mentioning his argument with the boss.*

**tac·tic** /ˈtæktɪk/ *n* 1 [C] a method that you use to achieve something: *Salesmen employ all sorts of clever tactics to try and persuade you.* | **delaying tactic(s)** (=something you do in order to give yourself more time) | **strongarm tactics** (=the use of violence to achieve your aim) 2 [C usually plural] the way in which military forces are arranged in order to win a battle

**tac·tic·al** /ˈtæktɪkəl/ *adj* 1 done in order to achieve what you want at a later time, especially in a game or large plan: *a tactical move to avoid the threat of legal action* 2 **tactical error/mistake** a mistake that will harm your plans later: *Telling him your age was a tactical error.* 3 **tactical weapon/missile etc** a weapon etc that is only used over short distances: *tactical nuclear missiles* 4 connected with the organizing of military forces in order to win battles —**tactically** /-kli/ *adv*

**tactical vot·ing** /ˌ··· ˈ··/ *n* [U] the practice of voting for a political party that you do not support in order to prevent another party from winning an election

**tac·ti·cian** /tækˈtɪʃən/ *n* [C] someone who is very good at TACTICS

**tac·tile** /ˈtæktaɪl‖ˈtæktl/ *adj* connected with your sense of touch: *a tactile sensation*

**tact·less** /ˈtæktləs/ *adj* likely to upset or embarrass someone without intending to: *I wanted to know about the divorce, but thought it would be tactless to ask.* | *a tactless remark* —**tactlessly** *adv* —**tactlessness** *n* [U]

**tad** /tæd/ *n informal* **a tad** *BrE dialect* a small amount, or to a small degree: *"Would you like some milk?" "Just a tad."*

**tad·pole** /ˈtædpəʊl‖-poʊl/ *n* [C] a small creature that has a long tail, lives in water, and grows into a FROG (1) or TOAD

**taf·fe·ta** /ˈtæfɪ̣tə/ *n* [U] a shiny stiff cloth made from silk or NYLON

**Taf·fy** /ˈtæfi/ *n* [C usually singular] *BrE slang* a word for someone who is Welsh, often considered to be offensive

**taffy** *n* [U] *especially AmE* a soft sweet usually made from sugar boiled brown

**tag¹** /tæg/ *n* 1 [C] a small piece of paper, plastic etc, fixed to something to show what it is, who owns it, what it costs etc: **name/identification/price tag** *Where's the price tag on this dress?* 2 [U] a children's game in which one player chases and tries to touch the others 3 [C] a phrase such as 'isn't it?', 'won't it?', or 'does she?', added to the end of a sentence to make it a question or to ask you to agree with it 4 [C] a metal or plastic point at the end of a piece of string or SHOELACE that prevents it from splitting

**tag²** **tagged, tagging** *v* [T] 1 to fasten a tag onto something: *Tag the bottles now or we'll forget which one is which.* 2 **be tagged as stupid/a failure etc** to be thought of in a particular way that is difficult for you to change: *He quit after 4½ years because he didn't want to be tagged forever as a game show host.* 3 **Tag!** *spoken* used in a children's game when a player manages to touch someone they are chasing 4 *slang* to illegally paint your name or sign on a wall, vehicle etc

**tag along** *phr v* [I] *informal* go somewhere with someone, especially when they do not want you to: *Mom, I can't do anything with her tagging along all the time.*

**tag** sth ↔ **on** *phr v* [T] to add something to something that already exists or is complete, especially in a way that looks badly planned: *Why don't you just tag on a paragraph about the latest research*

**ta·glia·tel·le** /ˌtæljəˈteli‖ˌtɑː-/ *n* [U] a kind of PASTA that is cut in very long, thin, flat pieces —see picture at PASTA

**tai chi** /ˌtaɪ ˈtʃiː, -ˈdʒiː/ *n* [U] a Chinese form of physical exercise that trains your mind and body in balance and control

**tail¹** /teɪl/ *n* S2
1 ▶ **ANIMAL** ◀ [C] the movable part at the back of an animal's body: *The dog wagged its tail.* | *a fish's tail* —see picture at HORSE W3

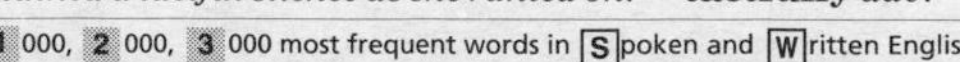

1 000, 2 000, 3 000 most frequent words in Spoken and Written English

2 ▶ **AIRCRAFT** ◀ [C] the back part of an aircraft —see picture at AIRCRAFT
3 ▶ **SHIRT** ◀ [C] the bottom part of your shirt at the back, that you put inside your trousers;
4 ▶ **BACK PART** ◀ [C usually singular] the back part of something, especially something that is moving away from you: *We saw the tail of the procession disappearing round the corner.*
5 **tails a)** [U] the side of a coin that does not have the head of the president, queen etc on it: *Which side do you want, heads or tails?* —opposite heads (HEAD[1] (36)) **b)** [plural] a man's formal JACKET (1) with two long parts that hang down at the back
6 ▶ **FOLLOW** ◀ [C] *informal* someone who is employed to watch and follow someone, especially a criminal: **put a tail on sb** (=order someone to follow another person)
7 **sit/be on sb's tail** *BrE informal* to follow another car too closely; TAILGATE[2] *AmE*
8 **turn tail** to run away because you are too frightened to fight or attack
9 **the tail end of a queue/meeting etc** the very last part of a QUEUE etc
10 **with your tail between your legs** embarrassed or unhappy because you have failed or been defeated
11 **the tail is wagging the dog** *informal* used to say that an unimportant thing is wrongly controlling a situation —see also **nose to tail** (NOSE[1] (19)), **a sting in the tail** (STING[2] (4))

**tail²** *v* [T] *informal* to follow someone and watch what they do, where they go etc —see also TOP AND TAIL
**tail away** *phr v* [I] to become quieter, thinner etc and then disappear: *The beach tailed away to nothing.*
**tail back** *phr v* [I] *especially BrE* to form a tailback
**tail off** *phr v* [I] to become gradually smaller or weaker, sometimes stopping completely: *Our profits tailed off towards the end of the year.*

T

**tail·back** /ˈteɪlbæk/ *n* [C] *BrE* a line of traffic that is moving very slowly or not moving at all: *a five mile tailback on the M25*

**tail·board** /ˈteɪlbɔːd‖-bɔːrd/ *n* [C] a TAILGATE[1]

**tail·bone** /ˈteɪlbəʊn‖-boʊn/ *n* [C] the bone at the very bottom of your back; COCCYX

**tail·coat** /teɪlˈkəʊt, ˈteɪlkəʊt‖-koʊt/ *n* [C] a coat worn by men to formal events such as weddings, that is short at the front and divides into two long pieces at the back

**tail·gate¹** /ˈteɪlgeɪt/ *n* [C] *AmE* a door at the back of a vehicle that opens outwards and downwards

**tailgate²** *v* [I,T] *especially AmE* to drive too closely behind another vehicle

**tailgate par·ty** /ˈ·· ˌ··/ also **tailgate** *n* [C] a party before an American football game where people eat and drink in the CARPARK of the place where the game is played

**tail-light** /ˈ· ·/ *n* [C] one of the two red lights at the back of a vehicle —see picture on page 409

**tai·lor¹** /ˈteɪlə‖-ər/ *n* [C] someone who makes men's clothes specially measured to fit each customer

**tailor²** *v* [T] **tailor sth to your needs/requirements** to make something so that it is exactly right for your particular needs: *We can tailor the insurance policy according to your family's needs.*

**tai·lored** /ˈteɪləd‖-ərd/ *adj* **1** a piece of clothing that is tailored is made to fit very well **2** made to fit a particular need or situation: *tailored financial advice*

**tai·lor·ing** /ˈteɪlərɪŋ/ *n* [U] the work of making men's clothes or the style in which they are made

**tailor-made** /ˌ·· ˈ·◂/ *adj* exactly right or suitable for someone or something: [+ **for**] *The job's tailor-made for John.*

**tail·piece** /ˈteɪlpiːs/ *n* [C] a part added at the end of a book, story etc

**tail pipe** /ˈ· ·/ *n* [C] *AmE* the pipe that takes unwanted gases out of a vehicle's engine; EXHAUST[2] (1) *BrE*

**tail·spin** /ˈteɪlˌspɪn/ *n* [C] an uncontrolled fall of a plane through the air, in which the back of the plane spins in a wider circle than the front

**tail·wind** /ˈteɪlˌwɪnd/ *n* [C] a wind blowing in the same direction that a vehicle is travelling

**taint¹** /teɪnt/ *v* [T usually passive] to make someone or something seem less pure and desirable by relating it to something unpleasant: **be tainted by/with** *a political reputation tainted by association with the Mafia*

**taint²** *n* [singular] the appearance of being related to something shameful or terrible: [+ **of**] *court officials free from the taint of corruption*

**taint·ed** /ˈteɪntɪ̈d/ *adj especially AmE* food or drink that is tainted is no longer safe because it has decayed or contains poison: *tainted milk*

S1 W1

## take¹ /teɪk/ *v past tense* took /tʊk/ *past participle* taken /ˈteɪkən/

① MOVE STH
② DO SOMETHING
③ NEED STH
④ SCHOOL/EXAMS
⑤ GET SOMETHING IN YOUR POSSESSION
⑥ TAKE PART
⑦ TAKE PLACE
⑧ ACCEPT SOMETHING
⑨ SPOKEN PHRASES
⑩ OTHER MEANINGS
⑪ PHRASAL VERBS

### ① MOVE STH

1 [T] to move someone or something from one place to another: *Don't forget to take your bag when you go.* | *Paul doesn't know the way – can you take him?* | **take sb/sth to** *We take the kids to school in the car.* | *Our neighbor was taken away in a police car.* | *Take the car to the garage to be repaired.* | **take sb sth** *Take your mother a cup of tea.* | **take sb/sth with you** *I'll take the dogs with me when I go to the lake.* —see BRING (USAGE)

### ② DO SOMETHING

2 [T] a word meaning to do something, used with many different nouns to form a phrase that means 'do the actions connected with the nouns': *take a walk* | *take a bath* | *take a breath* | *take a vacation*

### ③ NEED STH

3 **take (sb) 2 hours/6 months etc** to need a particular amount of time to do something or for something to happen: *The journey takes three hours.* | **take 2 hours/6 months etc to do sth** *It took three hours to fix the washing machine.* | *It took us half an hour to get there.*
4 ▶ **NEED MONEY/EFFORT/A QUALITY** ◀ [T] to need a particular quality, amount of money, or effort, in order for you to do something or for something to happen: *It takes strength and stamina to be a long-distance runner.* | **it takes sth to do sth** *It took a lot of courage to admit you were wrong*
5 ▶ **STH NEEDS STH** ◀ [T] if a machine, vehicle etc takes a particular kind of petrol, BATTERY (1) etc, you have to use that in it: *The car only takes unleaded.*

**6 have what it takes** *informal* to have the qualities needed to be successful: *Neil's got what it takes to be a great footballer.*

## ④ SCHOOL/EXAMS

**7 ▶ STUDY STH IN SCHOOL ◀** [T] to study a particular subject in a school or college, in order to do an examination: *I only had to take 6 credits my senior year*

**8 ▶ TEACH ◀** [T] *BrE* to teach a particular group of students in a school or college: **take sb for sth** *Who takes you for French?*

**9 take an exam/test** to do an examination or test: *I had to take my driving test three times before I passed.*

## ⑤ GET SOMETHING IN YOUR POSSESSION

**10 ▶ STEAL ◀** [T] to steal something, or borrow something without someone's permission: *The burglars took most of our jewellery.* | *She's taken my pen.* —see STEAL (USAGE)

**11 ▶ GET CONTROL ◀** [T] to get possession or control of something: *Enemy forces have taken the airport.* | **take control/charge** *Ann took control of the division last month.*

**12 ▶ GET STH ◀** [T] to get something for yourself: *Jim took all the credit, even though he hadn't done much of the work.*

**13 take a seat** to sit down

**14 take the lead** to take the leading position in a race, competition etc

**15 ▶ HOLD STH ◀** [T] to get hold of something in your hands: *Let me take your jacket.* | *She took my arm as we walked down the street.*

## ⑥ TAKE PART

**16 take part** to do an activity, sport etc with other people: *Greg was too sick to take part.* | **take part in sth** *She was invited to take part in a TV debate.*

## ⑦ TAKE PLACE

**17 take place** if an event takes place, it happens: *The contest takes place every four years.* | *We don't know exactly what took place, but they both looked furious afterward.* —see OCCUR (USAGE)

## ⑧ ACCEPT SOMETHING

**18 a)** [T] to accept something that someone offers you: *If I were you I'd take the job.* | **take it or leave it** *spoken* (=used to say that your offer will not change) *I'll give you £50 – take it or leave it.* | **take sb's advice** *I took your advice and went to the doctor's.* **b)** [T not in progressive] to be willing to accept that something is true and correct: *I refuse to take the blame.* | *Do they take credit cards in this shop?* | **take sb's word for it** (=accept that what someone says is true) *Don't take my word for it if you don't want – go back and see for yourself!*

**19 take sth as read** to accept that something is correct because you have no other choice: *We can take it as read that Judith will want to come*

**20 ▶ ACCEPT STH UNPLEASANT ◀** [T] *informal* to accept an unpleasant situation or someone's unpleasant behaviour without becoming upset: *I can't take any more of his lies and deceit.* | *Steve's tough – He can take it* | **hard to take** *All this uncertainty is really very hard to take.*

**21 ▶ SUFFER STH ◀** [T] to experience something unpleasant because you cannot avoid it: *Staff have agreed to take a 2% pay cut.*

## ⑨ SPOKEN PHRASES

**22 take sb/sth (for example)** used when you want to give an example of something you have just been talking about: *You don't need loads of qualifications – take me for example, I failed my exams, but still found a job.*

**23 I take it (that)** used to say that you expect someone will do something, know something etc: *I take it you've heard that Rick's resigned.*

**24 I take your point** used when you are accepting that what someone has said is true: *Mr Chairman, I take your point, but I also support Mr Baxter's view.*

**25 take it from me** used to persuade someone that what you are saying is true: *Ken won't last long in this job, take it from me.*

**26 take a hike** *especially AmE* used to tell someone to go away: *Look, Buddy, I'm tired of your mouth. Why don't you take a hike.*

**27 it takes all sorts (to make a world)** used to show that you think what someone is doing, likes etc is very strange

**28 what do you take me for?** used when someone has suggested you would do something and you want to say you would not do anything like that: *I won't tell her the secret – what do you take me for?*

## ⑩ OTHER MEANINGS

**29 ▶ NUMBERS ◀** [T] to subtract one number from another number: **take something from** *Take four from nine and what do you get?*

**30 ▶ HAVE SPACE FOR ◀** [T not in progressive or passive] to have only enough space to contain a particular amount of something, or a particular number of things: *The car takes five people.* | *The shelf won't take any more books.*

**31 ▶ MEDICINE/DRUG ◀** [T] to take a drug into your body: *Do you want to take an aspirin for your headache?* | **take drugs** (=take illegal drugs)

**32 take sides** to support one person more than another person in an argument: *You always take sides with Maggie without even listening to me!*

**33 be taken with/by** to be attracted by a particular idea, plan or person: *I'm quite taken by the idea of Christmas in Berlin.*

**34 be taken ill/sick etc** to suddenly become ill

**35 ▶ SEX ◀** [T] *literary* if a man takes a woman, he has sex with her

**36 ▶ EAT/DRINK ◀** [T] used in some phrases meaning to eat or drink something: **do you take sugar** (=do you take sugar in your tea or coffee)

**37 ▶ TAXI/BUS/TRAIN ETC ◀** [T] to go somewhere by taxi, bus, or train: *We were too exhausted to walk so we took the bus.*

**38 ▶ FEELINGS ◀** [T] to have or experience a particular feeling, used in some phrases: *Lin takes no interest in her work.* | **take pity on** (=help someone that you feel pity for) *that nice young man who took pity on me and helped me with my bags* | **take offence** (=feel offended by something) *Don't take offence. Roger says things like that to everybody.*

**39 take a picture/photograph** to photograph someone or something: [+ **of**] *I took several pictures of the cottage we stayed in.*

**40 ▶ WRITE ◀** [T] to write down information that you have just been given: *Don't let me forget to take your address before you leave.* | *It might be a good idea to take notes during the lecture.*

**41 take sth seriously/lightly** to consider someone or something in a particular way: *It's not the kind of comment you take lightly, is it?* | *I always take you seriously, don't I?*

**42 take sth well/badly** to react well or badly when you find something out: *"How did she take it when you told her?" "Er, not too well."*

[continued on next page]

Frequencies of the verb **take** in spoken and written English.

| | Frequency |
|---|---|
| SPOKEN | ~2000 per million |
| WRITTEN | ~1700 per million |



Based on the British National Corpus and the Longman Lancaster Corpus

This graph shows that the verb **take** is more common in spoken English than in written English. This is because it is used in some common spoken phrases. These are shown in the section marked SPOKEN PHRASES.

[continued from previous page]
**43 ▶ TEST/MEASURE STH ◀** [T] to test or measure something: *He took my temperature and blood pressure.*
**44 take sth to bits/pieces** to divide something into its separate parts: *We had to take the radio to pieces to find out what was wrong with it.*
**45 take a bend/fence/corner etc** [T] to try to get over or around something in a particular way: *We took the bend at over 60 and lost control.*
**46 ▶ SIZE ◀** [T] to wear a particular size of clothes or shoes: *I take size 6 shoes.*
**47 ▶ STH WORKS ◀** [I] if a DYE (=colouring substance) or INJECTION (=medicine) takes, it is successful

**⑪ PHRASAL VERBS**

**take aback** *phr v* [T] **be taken aback** to be very surprised about something: *He seemed quite taken aback by the news.*

**take after** sb *phr v* [T not in progressive] to look or behave like an older relative: *Jenni really takes after her mother.*

**take** sb/sth **apart** *phr v* [T] **1** to separate something into pieces; DISMANTLE **2 a)** to beat someone very easily in a game or sport **b)** to criticize someone very strongly

**take away from** sth *phr v* [T] to harm the good effect or success of something; DETRACT: *We won't allow a few troublemakers to take away from our enjoyment of the occasion*

**take back** *phr v* [T] **1** [**take** sth ↔ **back**] to admit that you were wrong to say something: *I'm sorry I was rude, I take it all back.* **2** [**take** sth ↔ **back**] to take something you have bought back to a shop because it is not suitable: *If the shirt doesn't fit, take it back.* **3** [**take** sb **back**] to make you remember a time in the past: *Seeing those old pictures really took me back.*

**take** sth ↔ **down** *phr v* [T] **1** to separate a large structure or machine into pieces: *They're taking the scaffolding down next week.* **2** to write something down: *Let me take down your name and number.* **3** to lower your trousers, shorts (SHORT[3] (2)) etc without actually removing them

**take in** *phr v* [T]
**1 ▶ PERSON ◀** [**take** sb ↔ **in**] to let someone stay in your house, especially because they have nowhere else to stay: *Brett's always taking in stray animals.*
**2 ▶ INCLUDE ◀** [**take** sth ↔ **in**] if a price or cost takes in something it includes it: *This price takes in the cost of all the accommodation and food.*
**3 take in a movie/show etc** *AmE* to go to see a film, play
**4 ▶ CLOTHES ◀** [**take** sth ↔ **in**] to make a piece of clothing narrower so that it fits you —opposite **let out** (LET[1] (4))
**5 ▶ UNDERSTAND/REMEMBER STH ◀** [**take** sth ↔ **in**] to understand and remember new facts and information: *I told Grandpa we were going away, but I don't think he took it in.*
**6 be taken in** to be completely deceived by someone so that you believe a lie: *Don't be taken in by products claiming to help you lose weight in a week.*

**take off** *phr v*
**1 ▶ REMOVE STH ◀** [T **take** sth↔ **off**] to remove something, especially a piece of clothing: *Take your coat off.* | *I forgot to take off my make-up last night.* —opposite **put on**
**2 ▶ AIRCRAFT/SPACECRAFT ◀** [I] to rise into the air at the beginning of a flight: *As the plane was taking off, I remembered I hadn't turned the iron off.*
**3 ▶ COPY SB ◀** [T **take** sb ↔ **off**] *informal* to copy the way someone speaks or behaves, in order to entertain people
**4 ▶ HOLIDAY ◀** [T **take** sth **off**] to have a holiday from work on a particular day, or for a particular length of time: *I'm taking Thursday off to do some Christmas shopping.*
**5 ▶ SUCCESS ◀** [I] to suddenly start being successful: *I hear the business is really taking off.*

**take off**

He took his coat off.

The plane took off.

**6 ▶ LEAVE A PLACE ◀** [I] *informal* to leave somewhere suddenly, especially without telling anyone: *Clare just took off without saying goodbye.*

**take on** *phr v* [T] **1** [**take** sb **on**] to start to employ someone: *We're taking on 50 new staff this year.* —see HIRE[1] (USAGE) **2** [**take on** sth] to begin to have a particular quality or appearance: *His face took on a worried look.* | *These insects can take on the colour of their surroundings.* **3** [**take** sb ↔ **on**] to start an argument or fight with someone **4** [**take** sth ↔ **on**] to agree to do some work or be responsible for something: *I'm worried about Doug, he's taking on too much work. He looks awful.*

**take out** *phr v* [T]
**1 ▶ PERSON ◀** [T **take** sb **out**] to take someone to a restaurant, cinema, club etc: *We're taking my folks out for a meal next week.*
**2 ▶ GET STH ◀** [**take** sth ↔ **out**] to arrange to get something officially, especially from an insurance company or a court of law: *I'm thinking of taking out a life insurance policy.* | *They've taken out an ad in the local paper.*
**3 take it out of sb** to make someone feel very tired: *Having the flu really takes it out of you!*
**4 ▶ KILL/DESTROY ◀** [**take** sb/sth ↔ **out**] *informal* to kill someone, or destroy something: *The building was completely taken out by a bomb.*
**5 take sb out of themselves** to make someone feel less worried about their problems

**take** sth **out on** sb *phr v* [T] **take it out on sb** to make someone suffer because you are feeling angry, tired etc: *Don't take it out on me, it's not my fault you've had a bad day.*

**take over** *phr v* [I,T] to take control of something: *Who will take over now that Ewing has resigned?* | **take** sth ↔ **over** *Will you take over the driving when we reach Madison.* —see also TAKEOVER

**take to** sb/sth *phr v* [T not inpassive] **1** to start to like someone or something: *I took to Paul as soon as I met him.* **2** to start doing something as a habit: *All this bad news is enough to make you take to drink.* | **take to doing sth** *Dee's taken to getting up at 6 and going jogging.* **3 take to your bed** to go to your bed and stay there

**take up** sth *phr v* [T]
**1 ▶ ACTIVITY/SUBJECT ◀** [T **take up** sth] to

become interested in a particular activity or subject and spend time doing it: *Glenn has taken up pottery.*
**2 ► JOB/RESPONSIBILITY ◄** [**take up** sth] to start a new job or have a new responsibility: *She took up her first teaching post in 1950.*
**3 ► POSITION ◄** [**take up** sth] to put yourself in a particular position ready for something to happen, or so that you can see better: *The runners took up their positions on the starting line.*
**4 ► IDEA/SUGGESTION/SUBJECT ◄** [**take** sth ↔ **up**] to do something about an idea or suggestion that you have been considering: *I'm going to take this matter up with my lawyer.*
**5 ► OFFER ◄** [**take** sth ↔ **up**] to accept an offer or CHALLENGE[2] (1) that someone has made: *Are you going to take up the challenge of lasting a whole week without arguing?*
**6 ► SPACE/TIME ◄** if something takes up a particular amount of time or space it fills it: *Writing the paper took up most of the weekend.* | *Your clutter takes up far too much space.*
**7 take up arms** to fight a battle using weapons
**8 take up residence** to start living somewhere
**9 ► CLOTHES ◄** [**take** sth ↔ **up**] to reduce the length of a skirt or pair of trousers
**10 ► CONTINUE AN ACTIVITY ◄** [**take** sth ↔ **up**] to continue a story or activity that someone else started, or that you have started but had to stop: *I'll take up the story where you left off.*

**take** sb **up on** sth *phr v* [T] to accept an invitation that someone has made: *I'll take you up on that offer of a drink, if it still stands!*

**take up with** sb/sth *phr v* [T] **1** to become friendly with someone, especially someone who may influence you badly: *Sean's taken up with a bunch of lazy hoods.* **2 be taken up with** to be very busy dealing with someone or something: *Jo's completely taken up with work at the moment.*

**take upon** *phr v* [T] **take it upon yourself to do sth** to decide to do something without permission or approval: *Stefan took it upon himself to sell the car while I was away.*

**take²** *n* [C] **1** the act of a scene for a film or television programme: *We had to do six takes for this particular scene.* **2** [usually singular] the amount of fish or animals caught at one particular time **3** [usually singular] *informal especially AmE* the amount of money earned by a shop or business in a particular period of time **4 be on the take** *informal* to be willing to do something wrong in return for money **5 sb's take on sth** *AmE informal* someone's opinion about a situation or idea: *What's your take on the Middle East issue?*

**take·a·way** /ˈteɪkəweɪ/ *n* [C] *BrE* **1** a meal that you buy at a shop or restaurant to eat at home; TAKE-OUT (1) *AmE*: *Let's have a takeaway tonight.* **2** a shop or restaurant that sells meals to be eaten somewhere else; TAKE-OUT (2) *AmE*

**take-home pay** /ˈ· · ˌ·/ *n* [U] the amount of money that you receive after you have paid tax etc

**tak·en** /ˈteɪkən/ the past participle of TAKE¹

**take-off** /ˈ· ·/ *n* **1** [C,U] the time when a plane or ROCKET rises into the air **2** [C] the act of leaving the ground as you make a jump **3** [C] an amusing performance that copies the way someone behaves: *Suzie did a brilliant take-off of the principal.* —see also **take off** (TAKE¹)

**take-out** /ˈ· ·/ *n* [C] *AmE* **1** a meal that you buy at a shop or restaurant to eat at home; TAKEAWAY (1) *BrE* **2** a shop or restaurant that sells cooked meals to be eaten somewhere else; TAKEAWAY (2) *BrE*

**take·o·ver** /ˈteɪkˌəʊvə‖-ˌoʊvər/ *n* [C] **1** the act of getting control of a company by buying most of its shares (SHARE² (6)) | **takeover bid** (=an attempt to get control) **2** an act of getting control of a country or political organization, especially by using force: *the communist takeover in Laos*

**ta·ker** /ˈteɪkə‖-ər/ *n* [C] **be no/few/not many takers** used to say that no-one accepted or wanted something that was offered: *There have been a few takers so far, but the price is a big obstacle*

**take-up** /ˈ· ·/ *n* [U] the rate at which people buy or accept something offered by a company, government etc: *Despite all the advertisements, the take-up has been slow.*

**tak·ings** /ˈteɪkɪŋz/ *n* [plural] the money that a shop gets from selling its goods: *Someone broke in and stole the day's takings from the safe.*

**talc** /tælk/ *n* [U] **1** talcum powder **2** a soft smooth mineral that feels like soap and is used for making paints, plastics, etc

**tal·cum pow·der** /ˈtælkəm ˌpaʊdə‖-dər/ *n* [U] a fine powder which you put on your skin after washing to make it dry or smell pleasant

**tale** /teɪl/ *n* [C] **1** a story of imaginary events, especially of an exciting kind: *tales of far-off lands* **2** a spoken description of an event or situation that is often not completely true: *tales of his life in post-war Berlin* **3 tell tales** *especially BrE* to tell someone in authority something untrue, unfair, or unpleasant, often because you want to harm someone else; TATTLE *AmE*: *Samantha's been telling tales to the teacher again.* **4 tale of misery/woe** a description of events that made you very unhappy **5 live/survive etc to tell the tale** *humorous* to still be alive after a dangerous or unpleasant event: *Yes. it's true. I've been to stay at my mother-in-law's and lived to tell the tale.* W3

**tal·ent** /ˈtælənt/ *n* **1** [C,U] a special natural ability or skill: *musical talent* | [+ **for**] *She showed a talent for acting at an early age.* | **a man/woman of many talents** (=someone who has the ability to do several things very well) | **talent contest/show/competition** (=a competition in which people show how well they can sing, dance, tell jokes etc) **2** [U] people who have a special natural ability or skill: **footballing/golfing etc talent** (=people who are good at football, GOLF etc) *Britain has lost a lot of its footballing talent to clubs abroad.* **3** [U] *BrE slang* sexually attractive people: *There's not much talent round here tonight.*

**tal·ent·ed** /ˈtæləntɪd/ *adj* very good at something such as singing, acting, or playing sports: *a talented actor*

**talent scout** /ˈ·· ·/ *n* [C] someone whose job is to find young people who are good at a sport or activity

**tal·is·man** /ˈtælɪzmən/ *n plural* **talismans** [C] an object that is believed to have magic powers of protection

**talk¹** /tɔːk‖tɒːk/ *v*
**1 ► CONVERSATION ◄** [I] to say things to someone, especially in a conversation: **talk to** *Who was that you were talking to at the party?* | **talk with** *Bob was talking with a pretty woman from the fire department.* | **talk about/of** *We were talking about our childhoods and realized we both went to the same school.* —see SAY¹ (USAGE) | **get talking** (=start having a conversation) *Once they got talking nothing could stop them.* | **talk sport/politics etc** (=have a conversation about sport etc) *I can't stand it when you talk politics.* —see SPEAK (USAGE)

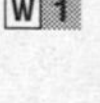

**2 ► SERIOUS SUBJECT ◄** [I] to discuss something with someone, especially an important or serious subject: *We need to talk before things get any worse.* | **talk about/of** *Jenny and I have talked about getting married some day.* | **talk to** *I think I'm going to have to talk to a solicitor.* —see also **talk shop** (SHOP¹ (6))
**3 ► SAY WORDS ◄** [I] to produce words in a language: *Most babies start to talk by 18 months.* | *Who would ever believed that computers would be able to talk?*
**4 people will talk/people are talking** *informal* used to emphasize that people will think you are doing something bad: *Don't leave your car outside my house; people will talk.*

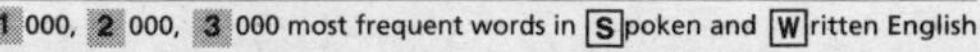

**5 ▸ SECRET INFORMATION ◂** [I] to give someone important secret information because they force you to: *Even after three days of interrogation, Maskell refused to talk.*
**6 not be talking** *informal* if two people are not talking they refuse to talk to each other because they have argued: *It's been 3 weeks and they're still not talking.*
**7 ▸ A SPEECH ◂** [I] to give a speech: **talk on/about** *This morning Mrs Elliott will be talking about the best way to cultivate roses.*
**8 talk sense** to give sensible opinions about things: *He's a little old-fashioned but he talks a lot of sense.*
**9 talk sense into** to persuade someone to behave in a sensible way: *Will you see if you can talk some sense into him – he says he wants to join the army.*
**10 talk your way out of** *informal* to escape from an unpleasant or embarrassing situation by giving explanations, excuses etc: *I'd like to see you talk your way out of this one!*
**11 talk the hind legs off a donkey** *informal* to talk a lot, especially about unimportant things
**12 talk nineteen to the dozen** *informal* **talk a blue streak** *AmE* to talk very quickly and without stopping
**13 talk turkey** *informal AmE* to talk seriously about important things, especially in order to agree on something: *"I'm ready to make a deal." "OK. Let's talk turkey."*
**14 talking point** a subject, problem, piece of news etc that many people are interested in
**15 talk dirty** *informal* to talk in a sexual way to someone in order to make them feel sexually excited
**16 talk tough** *informal* to tell people very strongly what you want from them
**17 be talking through your hat** *informal* to say silly or stupid things about something that you think you know a lot about

Frequencies of the verb **talk** in spoken and written English.

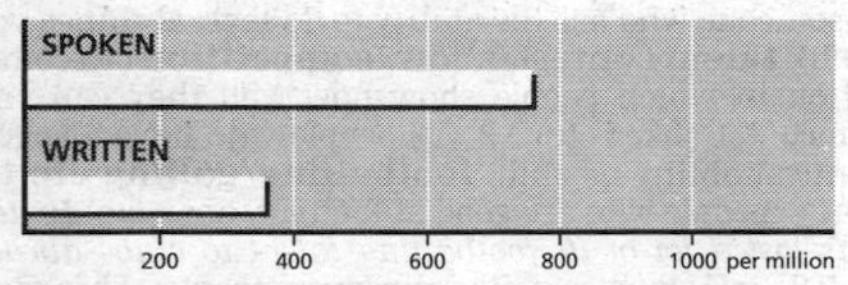


Based on the British National Corpus and the Longman Lancaster Corpus

This graph shows that the verb **talk** is much more common in spoken English than in written English. This is because it is used in a lot of common spoken phrases.

**talk** (*v*) **SPOKEN PHRASES**

**18 what are you talking about? a)** used when the person you are talking to has just said something stupid or annoying: *"I'm sorry – I didn't do the report because my cat hurt his paw." "What on earth are you taking about?"* **b)** used to ask someone what their conversation is about
**19 know what you are talking about** to know a lot about a particular subject: *I worked in hotels for years, so I know what I'm talking about.*
**20 talk about rich/funny/stupid etc** used to emphasize that the person or thing you are talking about is very rich, funny, stupid etc: *Talk about luck! That's the second competition he's won in a week!*
**21 talking of/about** used to say more about a subject that someone has just mentioned: *Talking of Venice, have you seen the masks I bought there last year?* —see SAY[1] (USAGE)
**22 now you're talking** used when you think someone's suggestion is a very good idea: *"We could go for a pizza instead." "Now you're talking."*
**23 look who's talking/you're a fine one to talk/you can talk** used to tell someone they should not criticize someone else because they are just as bad: *"Peggy shouldn't smoke so much." "Look who's talking!"*
**24 we're/you're talking (about) a)** used to tell someone what will be necessary in order to do or get what they are asking you about: *If you want the job done properly you're talking £10,000 at least.* **b)** used to explain something about a person or thing that is being discussed: *Don't forget, we're talking about a country where millions are starving.*
**25 don't talk rubbish/nonsense/crap etc** *especially BrE* used to tell someone that what they are saying is silly and completely wrong: *The best goalkeeper in England! Him? Oh, don't talk rubbish!*
**26 I'm talking to you!** used when you are angry because the person you are talking to is not paying attention to you: *Hey! I'm talking to you! Look at me!*

**talk around** *phr v* [T] **1** [**talk** sb ↔ **around**] to persuade someone to change their opinion and agree with you: *Leave Betty to me. I'll soon talk her around.* **2 talk around sth** to discuss a problem without really dealing with the important parts of it

**talk back** *phr v* [I] to answer someone rudely after they have criticized you or told you to do something: *I'd never let a child of mine talk back to me like that!*

**talk** sb/sth ↔ **down** *phr v* [T] **1** to give instructions on a radio to a PILOT[1] (1) so that they can bring an aircraft safely to the ground **2** to make something that is successful or good seem worse than it really is: *It's just like the Labour Party to talk down the achievements of the health service reforms.* **3** to persuade someone to come down from a high place when they are threatening to jump and kill themselves

**talk down to** sb *phr v* [T] to talk to someone as if they were stupid when in fact they are not; PATRONIZE: *You have to realize that kids aren't stupid; they know when they're being talked down to.*

**talk** sb **into** sth *phr v* [T] to persuade someone to do something: *She didn't want to come, but I talked her into it.* | **talk sb into doing sth** *Try to talk Liz into buying a ticket.*

**talk** sth ↔ **out** *phr v* [T] *informal* to talk about a problem in order to solve it: *We need to spend a little time talking it out.*

**talk** sb **out of** sth *phr v* [T] *informal* to persuade someone not to do something: *Stuart was threatening legal action but I think his sister talked him out of it.* | **talk sb out of doing sth** *Can't you talk them out of selling the house?*

**talk** sth ↔ **over** *phr v* [T] to discuss a problem or situation with someone before you decide what to do: *Don't worry, we have plenty of time to talk it over.* | [**+ with**] *Well obviously I wanted to talk it over with you first.*

**talk** sth ↔ **through** *phr v* [T] to discuss all of something so that you are sure you understand it: *I think we really need to talk this one through – there are so many things that could go wrong.*

**talk**[2] *n* S W
**1 ▸ CONVERSATION ◂** [C] a conversation: [**+ with/about**] *After a long talk , we decided to stop seeing each other.* | **have a talk** *Listen John, you're going to have to have a talk with Marty.*
**2 ▸ A SPEECH ◂** [C + about/on] a speech or LECTURE[1] (1): *a series of talks about literary theory* | **give a talk** *Dr. Howard is giving a talk on homeopathy today.*
**3 ▸ DISCUSSION ◂ talks** [plural] formally organized discussions between governments, organizations etc: *Peace talks* | *Talks with the rebels have failed yet again.*
**4 ▸ TYPE OF CONVERSATION ◂** [U] type of conversation: *Some people would say that kind of talk was treason!* | **girls' talk/football talk/fighting talk etc** *All this football talk bores me stiff!*
**5 be all talk** *spoken* to always be talking about what you have done or what you are going to do without ever actually doing anything: *Don't be scared of Jake. He's all talk!*
**6 be the talk of the town/company etc** to be the person or thing that everyone is talking about because they are very interested, excited, shocked etc: *Tim's been the talk of the department since his affair with Janice.*

**7 just talk/only talk** *informal* a story, claim etc that is just talk or only talk is very likely to be untrue: *Everyone says he was a spy but if you ask me it's just talk.*
**8 there's talk of** used to say that a lot of people are talking about something that might happen in the future: *There's talk of more factory closures in the area.* —see also SMALL TALK, SWEET TALK

**talk·a·tive** /ˈtɔːkətɪv‖ˈtɒːk-/ *adj* liking to talk a lot —**talkativeness** *n* [U]

**talk·er** /ˈtɔːkə‖ˈtɒːkər/ *n* [C] *informal* someone who talks a lot or talks in a particular way: *What a talker that man is!| We need a persuasive talker and a good organizer.*

**talk·ie** /ˈtɔːki‖ˈtɒːki/ *n* [C] *old-fashioned* a cinema film with sounds and words —compare SILENT FILM

**talking book** /ˌ·· ˈ·/ *n* [C] a book that has been recorded for blind people to listen to

**talking head** /ˌ·· ˈ·/ *n* [C] *informal* someone on television who talks directly to the camera, for example when reading the news

**talking-to** /ˈ·· ·/ *n* **give sb a talking-to** *informal* to talk to someone angrily because you are annoyed about something they have done: *If you ask me, what that girl needs is a good talking-to.*

**talk show** /ˈ· ·/ *n* [C] *AmE* a radio or television show on which famous people talk to each other and are asked questions; CHAT SHOW *BrE*

2 2 **tall** /tɔːl‖tɒːl/ *adj* **1** a person, building, tree etc that is tall has a greater than average height: **6 ft/2 metres etc tall** *I'm only five feet tall.* —see HIGH (USAGE) —see picture at HIGH **2** *AmE* a tall drink has a small amount of alcohol mixed with a large amount of a non-alcoholic drink and is served in a tall glass **3 be a tall order** *informal* if a request or piece of work is a tall order, it will be almost impossible for you to do: *Fixed by Monday? That's a tall order.* **4 tall story** *BrE*, **tall tale** *AmE* a story that is difficult to believe, because it makes events seem more exciting, dangerous etc than they really were: *Jim was full of tall stories about his travels.* —see also **stand tall** (STAND[1] (38)), **walk tall** (WALK[1] (9)) —**tallness** *n* [U]

**tall·boy** /ˈtɔːlbɔɪ‖ˈtɒːl-/ *n* [C] *BrE* a tall piece of wooden furniture containing several drawers; HIGHBOY *AmE*

**tal·low** /ˈtæləʊ‖-loʊ/ *n* [U] hard animal fat used for making CANDLES

**tal·ly[1]** /ˈtæli/ *n plural* **tallies** [C] **1** a record of how much you have spent, won, obtained etc so far: *England's tally at the moment is 15 points.* | **keep a tally** (=write down or remember) **2** a special stick that was used in the past to show an amount of money owed, a quantity of goods delivered etc

**tally[2]** *v* **tallied, tallying** **1** [I] if numbers or statements tally, they match each other exactly: *If the figures don't quite tally you might be missing an invoice.* | **tally with** *Your account of the accident doesn't tally with the facts.* **2** also **tally up** [T] to calculate the total number of points won, things done etc

**Tal·mud** /ˈtælmʊd/ *n* **the Talmud** the collection of writings that make up Jewish law about religious and non-religious life

**tal·on** /ˈtælən/ *n* [C] a sharp powerful curved nail on the feet of some birds that catch animals for food

**tam·a·rind** /ˈtæmərɪ̧nd/ *n* [C] a tropical tree, or the fruit of this tree

**tam·bour** /ˈtæmbʊə‖-bʊr/ *n* [C] a circular wooden frame used to hold cloth firmly in place while patterns are being sewn (SEW) on to it, EMBROIDERY HOOP

**tam·bou·rine** /ˌtæmbəˈriːn/ *n* [C] a circular musical instrument with small pieces of metal around the edge that makes a sound when you shake it

**tame[1]** /teɪm/ *adj* **1** *informal* boring or unexciting and disappointing: *After all that hype, the film was a bit tame.* **2** an animal that is tame has been trained to live with people —**tamely** *adv* —**tameness** *n* [U]

**tame[2]** *v* [T] **1** to reduce the power or strength of something and prevent it from causing trouble: *Over the years, a series of dams has tamed the might of the Colorado river.* **2** to train a wild animal to obey you and not to attack people —compare DOMESTICATE

**tam-o'-shan·ter** /ˌtæm ə ˈʃæntə‖-ər/ also **tam·my** /ˈtæmi/ *n* [C] a Scottish cap, usually made of wool, with a POMPOM (=small wool ball) in the centre

**tamp** /tæmp/ *v* [T always + adv/prep] also **tamp down** to press or push something down by lightly hitting it several times: *"Ah well," sighed Papa, absently tamping the tobacco down in his pipe.*

**Tam·pax** /ˈtæmpæks/ *n plural* **Tampax** [C] *trademark* the name of a very common type of TAMPON

**tam·per** /ˈtæmpə‖-ər/ *v*
**tamper with** sth *phr v* [T] to touch something or make changes to it without permission, especially in order to deliberately damage it: *How likely is it that the drugs could have been tampered with?| They just don't see the point in tampering with a system that's worked fine so far.*

**tamper-ev·i·dent** /ˈ·· ˌ···/ *adj BrE* a package or container that is tamper-evident is made so that you can see if someone has opened it before it is sold in the shops; TAMPER-RESISTANT *AmE*

**tamper-proof** /ˈ·· ·/ *adj* a package or container that is tamper-proof is made in a way that prevents someone opening it before it is sold

**tamper-re·sist·ant** /ˈ·· ·ˌ··/ *adj AmE* TAMPER-EVIDENT

**tam·pon** /ˈtæmpɒn‖-pɑːn/ *n* [C] a tube-shaped mass of cotton or similar material that a woman puts inside her VAGINA during her PERIOD

**tan[1]** /tæn/ *v* **tanned, tanning** **1** [I] if you tan, your skin becomes darker because you spend time in the sun: *People with fair skin usually don't tan very easily.* **2** [T] if the sun tans you, it makes your skin become darker **3** [T] to make animal skin into leather by treating it with TANNIN (=a kind of acid) **4 tan sb's hide** *old-fashioned* to hit someone a lot, as a punishment —**tan** *adj AmE*: *Did you see Lizzie? She's so tan!*

**tan[2]** *n* **1** [U] a light yellowish brown colour: *tan shoes* —see picture on page 411 **2** [C] the brown colour that someone with pale skin gets after they have been in the sun; SUNTAN: *I wish I could get a tan like that.* **3** [C] an abbreviation of TANGENT (2)

**tan·dem** /ˈtændəm/ *n* [C] **1** a bicycle built for two riders sitting one behind the other **2 in tandem with** happening at the same time: *Hastings' appointment in tandem with McDougan's should improve our sales expertise.* **3 work in tandem with** to work together with someone to get the best results

**tan·doo·ri** /tænˈdʊəri‖-ˈdʊri/ *n* [U] a northern Indian method of cooking in a large closed clay pot

**tang** /tæŋ/ *n* [singular] a strong sharp taste or smell: *the salty tang of the sea air* —**tangy** *adj*: *tangy oranges*

**tan·gent** /ˈtændʒənt/ *n* [C] **1 go/fly off at a tangent** *informal* to suddenly start thinking or talking about a completely new and different subject: *It's impossible to have a logical discussion with Rob because he keeps going off at a tangent.* **2** *technical* a straight line that touches the outside of a curve but does not cut across it **3** *technical* the FRACTION (2) calculated for an angle by dividing the length of the side that would be opposite it in a TRIANGLE with a RIGHT-ANGLE by the length of the side that would be next to it —compare COSINE, SINE

**tan·gen·tial** /tænˈdʒenʃəl/ *adj* **1** *formal* tangential information, comments etc are only indirectly related to a particular subject **2** *formal* tangential lines, roads etc move or go out in different directions; DIVERGENT **3** *technical* like a tangent —**tangentially** *adv*

**tan·ge·rine** /ˌtændʒəˈriːn‖ˈtændʒəriːn/ *n* [C] a small sweet fruit like an orange with a skin that comes off easily

**tan·gi·ble** /ˈtændʒəbəl/ *adj* **1 tangible proof/results/benefits etc** proof, results, advantages etc that are easy to see so that there is no doubt: *Welfare reform has not yet brought any tangible benefits.* —opposite INTANGIBLE **2** *formal* able to be felt by touch —**tangibly** *adv* —**tangibility** /ˌtændʒəˈbɪləti/ *n* [U]

**tan·gle¹** /ˈtæŋgəl/ *v* [I,T] to become twisted together or make something become twisted together in an untidy mass: *My hair tangles easily.* | **tangle sth** *Somebody's tangled all these cables under my computer.*

**tangle with** sb *phr v* [T] *informal* to argue or fight with someone: *I wouldn't tangle with him if I were you.*

**tangle²** *n* [C] **1** a twisted mass of something such as hair or thread: *Her hair was full of tangles after being out in the wind.* | **tangle of branches/weeds/threads etc** *We had to cut our way through a tangle of branches.* **2** a confused state: *My emotions were in a complete tangle.* **3** *informal* [+ **with**] a quarrel or fight

**tan·gled** /ˈtæŋgəld/ also **tangled up** *adj* **1** twisted together in an untidy mass: *The telephone cord is all tangled up.* **2** complicated or made up of many confusing parts: *What she needed was time to sort out her tangled feelings.*

**tan·go¹** /ˈtæŋgəʊ‖-goʊ/ *n plural* **tangos** [C] a lively dance from South America, or a piece of music for this dance

**tango²** *v* [I] **1** to dance the tango **2 it takes two to tango** *spoken* used to say that if a problem involves two people then both people are equally responsible

S2 W2 **tank¹** /tæŋk/ *n* [C] **1** a large container for storing liquid or gas: *The hot water tank is leaking.* | **fish tank** (=for keeping fish in) | **petrol tank** *BrE*/**gas tank** *AmE* (=part of a vehicle for holding petrol) **2** also **tankful** the amount of liquid or gas held in a tank: *I'll do over 400 miles on a full tank.* **3** a heavy military vehicle that has a large gun and runs on two metal belts fitted over its wheels **4** a large artificial pool for storing water —see also THINK-TANK, SEPTIC TANK

**tank²** *v*

**tank up** *phr v* [I] *especially AmE* to put petrol in your car so that the tank is full

**tan·kard** /ˈtæŋkəd‖-ərd/ *n* [C] a large metal cup, usually with a handle and lid, used for drinking beer —see picture at CUP

**tanked up** /ˌ· ˈ·/ also **tanked** /tæŋkt/ *AmE adj* [not before noun] *slang* drunk: *Jim gets really funny when he's tanked.*

**tank·er** /ˈtæŋkə‖-ər/ *n* [C] a vehicle or ship specially built to carry large quantities of gas or liquid, especially oil —see also OIL TANKER

**tank top** /ˈ· ·/ *n* [C] **1** *BrE* a piece of clothing like a SWEATER but with no sleeves (SLEEVE (1)) **2** *AmE* a piece of clothing like a shirt but with no sleeves (SLEEVE (1))

**tanned** /tænd/ *adj* having a darker skin colour because you have been in the sun —see picture on page 412

**tan·ner** /ˈtænə‖-ər/ *n* [C] **1** someone whose job is to make animal skin into leather by tanning (TAN¹ (3)) **2** *BrE old use* SIXPENCE (=a coin)

**tan·ne·ry** /ˈtænəri/ *n* [C] a place where animal skin is made into leather by tanning (TAN¹ (3))

**tan·nin** /ˈtænɪn/ also **tan·nic acid** /ˌtænɪk ˈæsɪd/ *n* [U] a reddish acid used in preparing leather, making ink etc

**tan·noy** /ˈtænɔɪ/ *n* [C] *BrE trademark* a system for giving out information in public places by means of LOUDSPEAKERS: **over the tannoy** *What were they saying about flight delays over the tannoy?*

**tan·ta·lize** also **-ise** *BrE* /ˈtæntəl-aɪz/ *v* [T usually passive] to show or promise something that someone really wants, but then not allow them to have it

**tan·ta·liz·ing** also **tantalising** *BrE* /ˈtæntəl-aɪzɪŋ/ *adj* making you feel a strong desire to have something that you cannot have: *The tantalizing smell of warm bread wafted out of the shop.* —**tantalizingly** *adv*

**tan·ta·lus** /ˈtæntəl-əs/ *n* [C] a case in which bottles of alcoholic drink can be locked up in such a way that they can be seen

**tan·ta·mount** /ˈtæntəmaʊnt/ *adj* **be tantamount to sth** if an action, suggestion, plan etc is tantamount to something, it is almost the same thing as it: *But that's tantamount to saying poor people are criminals!*

**tan·trum** /ˈtæntrəm/ *n* [C] a sudden moment of unreasonable bad temper and anger: **have/throw a tantrum** *Some kid thew a tantrum in the middle of the store.*

**Tao** /taʊ, daʊ/ *n* [U] the natural force that unites all things in the universe, according to Taoism

**Taoi·seach** /ˈtiːʃək, -ʃəx/ *n* **the Taoiseach** the title of the PRIME MINISTER of the Republic of Ireland

**Tao·is·m** /ˈtaʊɪzəm, ˈdaʊ-/ *n* [U] a way of thought developed in ancient China, based on the writings of Lao Tzu, emphasizing a natural and simple way of life

**tap¹** /tæp/ *n* S

**1 ▸ WATER/GAS ◂** [C] a piece of equipment for controlling the flow of water, gas etc from a pipe or container; FAUCET *AmE* | **turn on the tap** (=so that water comes out of it) *Carla, don't leave the taps running!* | **tap water** *In some countries, the tap water isn't safe enough to drink.* | **cold/hot tap** (=the tap that cold or hot water comes from) —see picture on page 833

**2 ▸ BARREL ◂** [C] a specially shaped object used for letting liquid out of a BARREL¹ (1)

**3 ▸ A LIGHT HIT ◂** [C] an act of hitting something lightly, especially to get someone's attention: **[+ at/on]** *There was a tap at the door.* | *Suddenly, I felt a tap on my shoulder and turned round to see Sheila there.*

**4 on tap a)** *informal* something that is on tap is ready to use when you need it: *We've got a lot of experts on tap to advise us.* **b)** beer that is on tap comes from a BARREL¹ (1)

**5 ▸ DANCING ◂** also **tap dancing** [U] dancing in which you wear special shoes with pieces of metal on the bottom which make a loud sharp sound on the floor

**6 ▸ TELEPHONE ◂** [C] an act of secretly listening to someone's telephone, using electronic equipment

**7 ▸ TUNE ◂ taps** a song or tune played on the BUGLE at night in an army camp, and at military funerals

**tap²** *v* **tapped, tapping** S

**1 ▸ HAND OR FOOT ◂** [I,T] to hit your hand or foot lightly against something, especially to get someone's attention or without thinking about it: *She tapped her feet in time to the music.* | **tap sth on/against etc** *He sat tapping his fingers on the arm of the chair.* | **[+ on]** *I went up and tapped on the window.* | **tap sb on the arm/shoulder etc** *"Hey Paul," she said, tapping him on the shoulder.* —compare KNOCK¹ —see picture on page 1259

**2 ▸ ENERGY ◂** also **tap into** [T] to use or take what is needed from an energy supply or power supply: *We have enormous reserves of oil still waiting to be tapped.*

**3 ▸ IDEAS ◂** [T] also **tap into** to make as much use as possible of the ideas, experience, knowledge etc that a group of people has: *Honestly, we have a vast pool of practical experience, just waiting to be tapped.*

**4 ▸ TELEPHONE ◂** [T] to listen secretly to someone's telephone by using a special piece of electronic equipment

**5 ▸ TREE ◂** [T] to get liquid from the TRUNK of a tree by making a hole in it: *tapping rubber trees*

**6 tap sb for sth** *BrE informal* to get money from someone: *Joey tapped me for a fiver.*

**tap** sth ↔ **in** *phr v* [T] to put information, numbers etc into a computer, telephone etc by pressing buttons or keys: *Tap in your password before you log on.*

**tap·as** /ˈtæpəs‖ˈtɑː-/ *n* [plural] small dishes of food eaten as part of the first course of a Spanish meal

**tap dan·cing** /ˈ· ˌ··/ *n* [U] dancing in which you wear

shoes with pieces of metal on the bottom, which make a sharp sound —**tap dance** *n* [C] —**tap dancer** *n* [C]

S3 W3 **tape¹** /teɪp/ *n*
**1 ▶ FOR RECORDING ◀ a)** [U] narrow plastic material covered with a special MAGNETIC substance, on which sounds, pictures, or computer information can be recorded and played: **on tape** (=recorded on tape) *We've got the film on tape.* | *I don't like the sound of my own voice on tape.* **b)** [C] a special plastic box containing a length of tape that you can record sound on; CASSETTE: *Turn the tape over when it's finished.* | *William lent me some of his Beatles tapes.* | **blank tape** (=with nothing recorded on it) **c)** [C] a special plastic box containing a length of tape that you can record sound and pictures on; VIDEOTAPE: *Police have seized a number of magazines and tapes.*
**2 ▶ PIECE OF MUSIC/FILM ◀** [C] a recording of a performance, piece of music, speech etc on tape: [+ **of**] *I'd like a tape of the concert.*
**3 ▶ STICKY MATERIAL ◀** [U] narrow length of sticky material used to stick things together; SELLOTAPE *BrE*; SCOTCH TAPE *AmE*: *a parcel fastened with tape*
**4 ▶ THIN PIECE OF MATERIAL ◀** [C,U] a long thin piece of material used for various purposes such as marking out an area of ground or to tie things together
**5 the tape** a string stretched out across the finishing line in a race and broken by the winner
**6 ▶ FOR MEASURING ◀** a TAPE MEASURE —see also RED TAPE

S3 **tape²** *v*
**1 ▶ RECORD STH ◀** also **tape record** [I,T] to record sound or pictures onto a TAPE¹ (1)
**2 ▶ FASTEN STH ◀** also **tape up** [T] to fasten a package, box etc with TAPE¹ (3)
**3 ▶ STICK STH ◀** [T] to stick something onto something else using TAPE¹ (3): *He had a picture of his girlfriend taped to the inside of his locker door.*
**4 ▶ INJURY ◀** also **tape up** [T usually passive] *especially AmE* to tie a BANDAGE¹ firmly around an injured part of someone's body; STRAP² (2) *BrE*: *We've got a nurse to tape that up for you.*
**5 have sth/sb taped** *BrE informal* to understand someone or something completely and have learned how to deal with them: *You can't fool Liz – she's got you taped.*

**tape deck** /'· ·/ *n* [C] the part of a TAPE RECORDER that winds the tape, and records and plays back sound

**tape drive** /'· ·/ *n* [C] a small machine attached to a computer that passes information from a computer to a tape or from a tape to a computer

**tape mea·sure** /'· ˌ··/ *n* [C] a long narrow band of cloth or steel, marked with centimetres, metres etc, used for measuring something

**ta·per¹** /'teɪpə‖-ər/ *v* [I,T] also **taper off** to become gradually narrower towards one end: *The jeans taper towards the ankle.*
**taper off** *phr v* [I] to decrease gradually: *Interest in the scandal seems to be tapering off.* —**tapering** *adj*: *long tapering fingers*

**taper²** *n* [C] **1** [usually singular] a gradual decrease in the width of a long object **2** a very thin CANDLE **3** a piece of string covered in WAX¹ (1), used for lighting lamps and CANDLES

**tape re·cord** /'· ·ˌ·/ *v* [T] to record sound using a tape recorder

**tape re·cord·er** /'· ·ˌ··/ *n* [C] a piece of electrical equipment that can record sound on tape and play it back

**tape re·cord·ing** /'· ·ˌ··/ *n* [C] something that has been recorded with a tape recorder: *The court heard secretly obtained tape recordings of the meeting.*

**ta·pered** /'teɪpəd‖-ərd/ *adj* having a shape that gets narrower towards one end: *tapered sleeves*

**tap·es·try** /'tæpəstri/ *n* [C,U] heavy cloth or a large piece of cloth on which coloured threads are woven to produce a picture, pattern etc: *the Bayeux Tapestry*

**tape·worm** /'teɪpwɜːm‖-wɜːrm/ *n* [C] a long flat PARASITE that lives in the bowels (BOWEL (1)) of humans and other animals

**tap·i·o·ca** /ˌtæpi'əʊkə‖-'oʊ-/ *n* [U] small hard white grains made from the crushed dried roots of CASSAVA, used especially for making sweet dishes

**ta·pir** /'teɪpə‖-ər/ *n* [C] an animal like a pig with thick legs, a short tail, and long nose, that lives in tropical America and Southeast Asia

**tap·pet** /'tæpət/ *n* [C] *technical* an engine part that moves up and down and makes another part of the engine move, open, close etc

**tap·root** /'tæpruːt/ *n* [C] the main root of a plant, that grows straight down and produces smaller side roots

**tar¹** /tɑː‖tɑːr/ *n* [U] **1** a black substance, thick and sticky when hot but hard when cold, used especially for making road surfaces —see also COAL TAR **2** a sticky substance that is formed by burning tobacco: **high/low/medium tar** *high tar cigarettes*

**tar²** *v* **tarred, tarring** [T] **1** to cover a surface with tar **2 be/get tarred with the same brush** to be blamed for someone else's faults or crimes **3 tar and feather** to cover someone in tar and feathers as a cruel unofficial punishment

**ta·ra·ma·sa·la·ta** /ˌtærəməsə'lɑːtə‖ˌtɑː-/ *n* [U] a Greek food consisting of a pink mixture made from fish eggs

**tar·an·tel·la** /ˌtærən'telə/ *n* [C] a fast Italian dance, or the music for this dance

**ta·ran·tu·la** /tə'ræntjələ‖-tʃələ/ *n* [C] a large poisonous SPIDER from Southern Europe and tropical America

**tar·dy** /'tɑːdi‖'tɑːrdi/ *adj formal* **1** done later than it should have been done: *We apologize for our tardy response to your letter.* **2** acting or moving slowly; SLUGGISH —**tardily** *adv* —**tardiness** *n* [U]

**tare** /teə‖ter/ *n* **1** [usually singular] *technical* the weight of wrapping material in which goods are packed **2** [usually singular] *technical* the weight of an unloaded goods vehicle, used to calculate the actual weight of its goods **3** [usually plural] *biblical* an unwanted plant growing in fields of grain; WEED¹ (1)

**tar·get¹** /'tɑːgət‖'tɑːr-/ *n* [C] S3 W2
**1 ▶ OBJECT OF ATTACK ◀** an object, person, or place that is deliberately chosen to be attacked: [+ **for/of**] *The docks are the main target for the bombing raids.* | **soft/easy target** *Cars without security devices are an easy target for the thief.* | **prime target** (=a very likely target)
**2 ▶ AN AIM ◀** a result, such as a total, an amount, or a time, which you aim to achieve; GOAL (1): *I've set myself a target of saving £20 a month.* | **meet targets** (=achieve targets) *Dealers are under pressure to meet sales targets.* | **on target** (=likely to achieve a target) *We're on target for 3% inflation by 1996.*
**3 ▶ SHOOTING ◀** something that you practise shooting at, especially a round board with circles on it: *A target 300 yards away* | **target practice** *The area is used by the army for target practice.*
**4 target group/area/audience etc** a limited group, area etc that a plan, idea etc is aimed at: *We need to clearly identify our target market.*
**5 be the target of criticism/complaints etc** to be criticized, blamed, etc for something: *She's become the target of much criticism since the affair became public.*

**target²** *v* [T] **1** to aim something at a target: **target sth on/at** *missiles targeted on American and European cities* **2** to make something have an effect on a particular limited group or area: [+ **on/at**] *We want to target more welfare on the poorest groups in society.* **3** to choose someone or something as your target: *It's clear that smaller, more vulnerable banks have been targeted.*

**tar·iff** /'tærəf/ *n* [C] **1** a tax on goods coming into a country or going out of a country —see TAX (USAGE) **2** *especially BrE* a list of fixed prices, such as the cost of meals or rooms, charged by a hotel or restaurant

**tar·mac¹** /'tɑːmæk‖'tɑːr-/ *n* **1** also **tar·ma·cad·am** /ˌtɑːmə'kædəm‖ˌtɑːr-/ [U] a mixture of TAR and very small stones, used for making the surface of roads; ASPHALT

**2 the tarmac** an area covered with tarmac, especially where planes take off or land

**tarmac²** *v* [T] to cover a road's surface with tarmac

**tar·nish¹** /ˈtɑːnɪʃ‖ˈtɑːr-/ *v* **1** [T] if an event or fact tarnishes someone's REPUTATION, record, image etc, it makes it worse: *a record tarnished by recent scandals* **2** [I,T] if metals such as silver, COPPER (1), or BRASS (1) tarnish, or if something tarnishes them, they become dull and lose their colour: *tarnished silver spoons*

**tarnish²** *n* [singular, U] dullness of colour, or loss of brightness

**ta·ro** /ˈtɑːrəʊ‖-roʊ/ *n* [C, U] a tropical plant grown for its thick root which is boiled and eaten

**tar·ot** /ˈtærəʊ‖-roʊ/ *n* [singular, U] a set of 78 cards, used for telling what will happen to someone in the future

**tar·pau·lin** /tɑːˈpɔːlɪn‖tɑːrˈpɒː-/ *n* [C,U] a heavy cloth prepared so that water will not pass through it, used to keep rain off things

**tar·ra·gon** /ˈtærəgən/ *n* [U] the leaves of a small European plant used as a HERB: *chicken with tarragon*

**tar·ry¹** /ˈtæri/ *v* [I] *literary* **1** to stay in a place, especially when you should leave; LINGER **2** to delay or be slow in going somewhere

**tar·ry²** /ˈtɑːri/ *adj* covered with TAR (=a thick black liquid)

**tar·sus** /ˈtɑːsəs‖ˈtɑːr-/ *n* [C] *technical* your ANKLE or one of the seven small bones in your ankle —**tarsal** *adj*

**tart¹** /tɑːt‖tɑːrt/ *n* **1** [C,U] a PIE (1) without a top on it, containing something sweet **2** [C] *informal* a woman whose appearance or behaviour makes you think that she is too willing to have sex **3** [C] *slang* a PROSTITUTE

**tart²** *adj* **1** food that is tart has a slightly sour taste that stings your tongue: *a tart apple* **2 tart reply/remark etc** a reply, remark etc that is sharp and unkind: *Her tart reply upset me.* —**tartly** *adv*: *Colin replied tartly that he hadn't invited me.* —**tartness** *n* [U]

**tart³** *v*

**tart** sth ↔ **up** *phr v* [T] *BrE informal* **1** to try to make something more attractive by decorating it, often in a way that other people think is cheap or ugly: *All they've done for the party is to tart up the old church hall.* **2 tart yourself up** *often humorous* if a woman tarts herself up she tries to make herself look attractive, by putting on jewellery MAKE-UP (1) etc

**tar·tan** /ˈtɑːtn‖ˈtɑːrtn/ *n* **1 a)** [U] woollen cloth, originally from Scotland woven with bands of different colours and widths that cross each other at right angles —see picture on page 839 **b)** [C] this pattern on other cloth: *Her skirt is a red and green tartan.* **2** [C] a special pattern of this type worn by a particular Scottish CLAN (=large family group) *the MacGregor tartan* —**tartan** *adj*: *a bright tartan shirt*

**tar·tar** /ˈtɑːtə‖ˈtɑːrtər/ *n* **1** [U] a hard substance that forms on your teeth **2** [U] a reddish-brown substance that forms on the inside of wine barrels **3** [U] a white powder used in baking and in medicine **4** [C] *informal* someone who has a violent temper or is difficult to deal with: *She's a real tartar.*

**tar·tare sauce** /ˌtɑːtə ˈsɔːs‖ˌtɑːrtər ˈsɒːs/ *n* [U] a cold white SAUCE often eaten with fish, made from egg, oil, GHERKINS and capers (CAPER² (1))

**tar·tar·ic ac·id** /tɑːˌtærɪk ˈæsɪd‖tɑːr-/ *n* [U] a strong acid that comes from a plant and is used in preparing some foods and medicines

**tart·y** /ˈtɑːti‖ˈtɑːrti/ *adj especially BrE* wearing the kind of clothes that people think a PROSTITUTE would wear

S2 W1 **task** /tɑːsk‖tæsk/ *n* [C] **1** a piece of work that must be done, especially one that is difficult or unpleasant or that must be done regularly: [+ **of**] *He was given the task of stacking the chairs in the auditorium.* | *the grim task of identifying the dead* | *daily tasks* | **thankless task** (=a boring task that no one wants to do) *Volunteers had the thankless task of distributing campaign leaflets.* **2** a piece of work that is difficult but very important: *Our main task is to improve the economy.* **3 take someone to task** to tell someone that you strongly disapprove of something they have done

**task force** /ˈ· ·/ *n* [C] **1** a group formed for a short time to deal with a particular problem: *a citizens' task force formed to rejuvenate the area* **2** a military force sent to a place for a special purpose

**task·mas·ter** /ˈtɑːskˌmɑːstə‖ˈtæskˌmæstər/ *n* **be a hard/stern/tough taskmaster** to force people to work very hard or use a lot of effort

**tas·sel** /ˈtæsəl/ *n* [C] a mass of threads tied together into a round ball at one end and hung as a decoration on clothes, curtains etc —**tasselled** *BrE* also **tasseled** *AmE adj*

**taste¹** /teɪst/ *n* 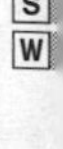

**1 ▶ FOOD ◀** [singular, U] the special feeling that is produced by a particular food or drink when you put it in your mouth: *Sugar has a sweet taste.* | *Has the milk gone sour? It's got a funny taste.* | *the strong taste of the coffee*

**2 ▶ JUDGEMENT ◀** [U] someone's judgement about what is good or suitable when they choose clothes, music etc: **have (good) taste** (=make good judgements) *She has instinctive good taste.* | **have bad/no taste** *Mick has really bad taste in clothes.*

**3 ▶ STH YOU LIKE ◀** [C,U] the type of thing that you tend to like: [+ **for/in**] *His tastes in films and books were very different from her own.* | **have a taste for** *I've always had a taste for jazz and blues music.* | **to sb's taste** (=in a way that someone likes) *She had the whole house redecorated to her taste.* | **have no taste for** (=not like something at all)

**4 ▶ SMALL AMOUNT ◀** [usually singular] a small amount of food or drink that you put in your mouth to try it: *Have a taste of this soup and see if it needs more salt.*

**5 ▶ WITH TONGUE ◀** [U] the sense by which you know one food from another: *You need a good sense of taste to be a chef.*

**6 be in bad/poor taste** jokes, remarks etc that are in bad taste are unacceptable, especially because they upset someone: *I thought your terrorist joke was in pretty bad taste.*

**7 a taste of fame/success etc** a short experience of something that you want more of

**8 leave a bad/nasty taste in your mouth** to feel angry or upset as a result of seeing or hearing something unpleasant: *The way he spoke to those children left a nasty taste in my mouth.*

**9 to taste** a phrase meaning as much as is needed to make something taste the way you like, used in instructions for cooking: *Add salt and pepper to taste.*

**10 an acquired taste** something that you like only after you have tried it several times: *Olives are something of an acquired taste.*

**11 there is no accounting for taste** used to say that you do not understand why someone has chosen something: *He's so nice – I don't see why you don't like him. But there's no accounting for taste.*

**taste²** *v* **1** [I not in progressive] to have a particular kind of taste: **taste delicious/sweet/fresh etc** *The mangoes tasted delicious.* | *This wine tastes too acidic.* | **taste like** *This chicken tastes more like turkey.* | *What does pumpkin taste like?* | **taste of** *over-ripe cheese tasting of ammonia* | **sweet-tasting/strong-tasting etc** (=having a sweet, strong etc taste) *strong-tasting coffee* **2** [T] to put a small amount of food or drink into your mouth to see what it is like: *You'd better taste the soup to see if I put enough salt in it.* | *Come on, just taste it!* **3** [T not in progressive] to experience the taste of food or drink: *I can hardly taste what I'm eating because of my cold.* **4 taste fame/freedom etc** to have a short experience of something that you want more of: *We had tasted success and wanted more.*

> **USAGE NOTE: TASTE**
>
> WORD CHOICE: **taste, try, sample, savour** (*BrE*)/**savor** (*AmE*)
>
> If you eat or drink a little of something just in order to find out its taste or flavour, you **taste** it: *Have you tasted this wine yet?* However, **taste** is much more often used in other meanings, where you receive the taste of something but do not actively search for it: *Can you taste the spices in this dish?*| *This wine tastes great* (NOT *This wine is very good taste*).
>
> In fact most often people use the word **try** for when they eat or drink something deliberately to see if they like it – not just what it tastes like, but also what it looks like, its smell etc: *You must try this wine/our local dishes/the salmon.*
>
> You may also **sample** food or drink, that is try just a little, perhaps not a full dish or meal: *You'll have a chance to sample all the cheeses of the region.*
>
> If you spend time enjoying the taste of something you **savour** it: *Here you can relax, chat and savour a variety of local dishes.*

**taste bud** /ˈ· ·/ *n* [C usually plural] one of the small parts of the surface of your tongue which can tell the difference between foods according to their taste

**taste·ful** /ˈteɪstfəl/ *adj* made, decorated, or chosen with good TASTE[1] (2): *a simple but tasteful arrangement of flowers* —compare TASTY —**tastefully** *adv*: *tastefully decorated* —**tastefulness** *n* [U]

**taste·less** /ˈteɪstləs/ *adj* **1** food or drink that is tasteless is unpleasant because it has no particular taste: *The vegetables were tasteless and soggy.* **2 tasteless joke/remark/comment etc** a joke etc that is unacceptable in a particular situation **3** made, decorated or chosen with bad TASTE[1] (2): *a tasteless outfit* —**tastelessly** *adv* —**tastelessness** *n* [U]

**tast·er** /ˈteɪstə‖-ər/ *n* [C] **1** someone whose job is to test the quality of foods, teas, wines etc by tasting them: *a wine taster* **2** *informal* a small example of something that is provided so that you can see if you like it: [+ **of**] *Here's just a taster of what will be in print next month.*

**tast·ing** /ˈteɪstɪŋ/ *n* [C] an event that is organized so that you can try different foods or drinks to see if you like them: *a wine and cheese tasting*

**tast·y** /ˈteɪsti/ *adj* **tastier, tastiest** **1** food that is tasty has a good taste: *a wide selection of tasty cold meats* —compare TASTEFUL **2** *informal* tasty news, GOSSIP etc is especially interesting and often connected with sex or surprising behaviour **3** *informal* a word meaning attractive, used especially by men about women: *She's well tasty.* —**tastiness** *n* [U]

**tat** /tæt/ *n* [U] *BrE* things that are cheap and badly made —see also TIT FOR TAT

S3 **ta-ta** /tæˈtɑː‖tɑːˈtɑː/ *interjection BrE informal* goodbye

**ta·ter** /ˈteɪtə‖-ər/ *n* [C] *informal* a potato

**tat·tered** /ˈtætəd‖-ərd/ *adj* **1** clothes, books etc that are tattered are old and torn: *an old man in a tattered brown coat* —see picture on page 1258 **2** dressed in old torn clothes

**tat·ters** /ˈtætəz‖-ərz/ *n* [plural] **1** clothing or pieces of cloth that are old and torn **2 in tatters a)** a plan, policy etc that is in tatters is ruined or badly damaged: *The government's income policy was in tatters.* **b)** clothes that are in tatters are old and torn

**tat·tie** /ˈtæti/ *n* [C] *ScotE* a potato: *neeps and tatties*

**tat·ting** /ˈtætɪŋ/ *n* [U] a kind of LACE that you make by hand, or the process of making it

**tat·tle** /ˈtætl/ *v* [I] **1** *old-fashioned* to talk about small unimportant things, or about other people's private affairs; GOSSIP **2** if a child tattles, they tell a parent or teacher that another child has done something bad —**tattler** *n* [C]

**tat·tle·tale** /ˈtætlteɪl/ *n* [C] *AmE informal* a word meaning someone who tattles, used by or to children; TELLTALE *BrE*

**tat·too**[1] /təˈtuː, tæˈtuː/ *n plural* **tattoos** **1** [C] a picture or message that is permanently marked on your skin with a needle and ink: *a tattoo of a snake* **2** [C] an outdoor military show with music, usually at night **3** [singular] a rapid continuous beating of drums, especially played as a military signal, or a sound like this

**tattoo**[2] *v* [T] **1** to make a permanent picture or message on someone's skin with a needle and ink DYES **2** to mark someone in this way —**tattooed** *adj*: *The Maori's face was heavily tattooed.*

**tat·too·ist** /təˈtuːɪ̥st, tæ-/ *n* [C] someone whose job is tattooing

**tat·ty** /ˈtæti/ *adj* **tattier, tattiest** *informal especially BrE* untidy or in a bad condition; SHABBY: *tatty jeans*| *a few tatty old chairs* —**tattily** *adv* —**tattiness** *n* [C]

**taught** /tɔːt‖tɒːt/ the past tense and past participle of TEACH: *She taught English in Prague.*

**taunt**[1] /tɔːnt‖tɒːnt/ *v* [T] to try to make someone angry or upset by saying unkind things or laughing at their faults or failures etc: [+ **about/over**] *The other children taunted him about his weight.* —**tauntingly** *adv*

**taunt**[2] *n* [C often plural] a remark or joke intended to make someone angry or upset: *The boy's taunts rang after her. 'Cry baby! Cry baby!'*

**taupe** /təʊp‖toʊp/ *n* [U] a brownish grey colour —**taupe** *adj*

**Tau·rus** /ˈtɔːrəs/ *n* **1** [singular] the second sign of the ZODIAC, represented by a BULL, and believed to affect the character and life of people born between April 21 and May 22 **2** [C] someone who was born between April 21 and May 22: *My husband's a Taurus.*

**taut** /tɔːt‖tɒːt/ *adj* **1** stretched tight: *the taut strings of the guitar*| *The runners were crouching, muscles taut.* —opposite SLACK[1] (4) **2** showing signs of worry or anxiety; TENSE[1] (1): *Catherine looked upset, her face taut.*

**taut·en** /ˈtɔːtn‖ˈtɒːtn/ *v* [I,T] to make something stretch tight, or to become stretched tight

**tau·tol·o·gy** /tɔːˈtɒlədʒi‖tɒːˈtɑː-/ *n* [C,U] a statement in which you unnecessarily say the same thing twice using different words, for example, 'He sat alone by himself.' —**tautological** /ˌtɔːtəˈlɒdʒɪkəl◂‖ˌtɒːtəˈlɑː-/ *adj* —**tautologically** /-kli/ *adv*

**tav·ern** /ˈtævən‖-ərn/ *n* [C] **1** *BrE old use* a PUB where you can also stay the night **2** word for a bar, often used in the name of a bar: *Murphy's Tavern*

**taw·dry** /ˈtɔːdri‖ˈtɒː-/ *adj* cheaply and badly made: *tawdry jewellery and fake furs* —**tawdriness** *n* [U]

**taw·ny** /ˈtɔːni‖ˈtɒː-/ *adj* brownish yellow in colour: *a lion's tawny fur*

**tax**[1] /tæks/ *n* **1** [C,U] an amount of money that you must pay to the government according to your income, property, goods etc that is used to pay for public services: *The government claimed it would lower taxes.*| [+ **on**] *If you cash in the investment early, then you have to pay tax on that.*| **before/after tax** (=before or after paying tax on something) *What are you earning before tax?*| **tax burden** (=the total amount of tax paid by an average person) **2** [singular] *formal* something that uses a lot of your strength, PATIENCE etc —see also CAPITAL GAINS TAX, **corporation tax** (CORPORATION (3)), INCOME TAX, PROPERTY TAX, SALES TAX, VAT S1 W1

**tax**[2] *v* [T] **1** to charge a tax on something: **heavily/lightly taxed** *Cigarettes are heavily taxed in Britain.* **2 tax a car/motorbike etc** *BrE* to pay the sum of money charged each year for using a vehicle on British roads **3 tax sb's patience/strength etc** to use almost all of someone's patience, strength etc: *The kids are really taxing my patience today.* —see also TAXING —**taxable** *adj*: *taxable income*

**tax** sb **with** sth *phr v* [T] *formal* to tell someone they have done something wrong, or blame them for it

**tax·a·tion** /tækˈseɪʃən/ *n* [U] **1** the system of charging taxes: *the reform of taxation*| **direct taxation** (=the taxing of income)| **indirect taxation** (=the taxing of the things people buy) **2** money collected from taxes: *We'll* 

*have to consider even higher taxation in the next year or two.*

**tax a·void·ance** /ˈ· ·ˌ··/ *n* [U] legal ways of paying less tax —compare TAX EVASION

**tax brack·et** /ˈ· ˌ··/ *n* [C] a particular range of income levels on which the same rate of tax is paid

**tax break** /ˈ· ·/ *n* [C] *AmE* a special reduction in taxes that the government allows for a particular purpose: *a tax break for insulating your home*

**tax-de·duc·ti·ble** /ˌ· ·ˈ···◂/ *adj* tax-deductible costs can be taken off your total income before it is taxed: *If you're self-employed, your travel expenses are tax-deductible.*

**tax-de·ferred** /ˌ· ·ˈ·◂/ *adj AmE* not taxed until a later time: *tax-deferred savings*

**tax disc** /ˈ· ·/ *n* [C] a small round piece of paper on a car WINDSCREEN in Britain that shows the driver has paid ROAD TAX

**tax dodge** /ˈ· ·/ *n* [C] a legal way of paying less tax

**tax e·va·sion** /ˈ· ·ˌ··/ *n* [U] illegal ways of paying less tax

**tax ex·empt** /ˌ· ·ˈ·◂/ *adj* tax exempt savings, income etc are not taxed

**tax ex·ile** /ˈ· ˌ··/ *n* [C] someone who lives abroad in order to avoid paying high taxes in their own country

**tax ha·ven** /ˈ· ˌ··/ *n* [C] a place where people go to live to avoid paying high taxes in their own country

**tax·i**[1] /ˈtæksi/ *n* [C] a car and driver that you pay to take you somewhere; CAB (1) | **flag (down)/hail a taxi** (=wave or shout at a taxi to make it stop)

**taxi**[2] *v* [I] if a plane taxis, it moves slowly along the ground before taking off or after landing

**taxi·cab** /ˈtæksikæb/ *n* [C] a taxi

**tax·i·der·mist** /ˈtæksɪ̵dɜːmɪ̵st‖-ɜːr-/ *n* [C] someone whose job is taxidermy

**tax·i·der·my** /ˈtæksɪ̵dɜːmi‖-ɜːr-/ *n* [U] the art of specially preparing the skins of dead animals, birds or fish then filling them with a special material so that they look as though they are alive

**tax·ing** /ˈtæksɪŋ/ *adj* needing a lot of effort; DEMANDING: *The job is taxing but enjoyable.*

**tax in·spect·or** /ˈ· ·ˌ··/ *n* [C] someone who works for the government, deciding how much tax a person or company should pay

**taxi rank** /ˈ·· ·/ also **taxi stand** *n* [C] *BrE* a place where taxis wait to be HIRED; CABSTAND *AmE*

**tax·man** /ˈtæksmæn/ *n* [C] **1** a tax collector or tax inspector **2 the taxman** the government department that collects taxes

**tax·on·o·my** /tækˈsɒnəmi‖-ˈsɑː-/ *n* [C,U] the process of organizing things such as plants or animals into different groups or sets that show their natural relationships

**tax·pay·er** /ˈtæks-peɪə‖-ər/ *n* [C] a person or organization that pays tax

**tax re·lief** /ˈ· ·ˌ·/ *n* [U] *BrE* the right to not have to pay tax on part of what you earn

**tax re·turn** /ˈ· ·ˌ·/ *n* [C] the form on which you have to give information so that your tax can be calculated

**tax shel·ter** /ˈ· ˌ··/ *n* [C] a plan or method that allows you to legally avoid paying tax

**tax year** /ˈ· ·/ *n* [C] the period of 12 months in which your income is calculated for paying taxes. The tax year begins on April 6th in Britain, and January 1st in the US

**TB** *BrE*, **Tb** *AmE* /ˌtiː ˈbiː/ *n* [U] tuberculosis; a serious infectious disease that affects your lungs and other parts of your body

**T-ball** /ˈtiː bɔːl‖-bɒːl/ *n* [U] *trademark* an easy form of BASEBALL for young children; TEE-BALL

**T-bone steak** /ˌtiː bəʊn ˈsteɪk‖-boʊn-/ *n* [C] a thinly cut piece of BEEF[1] (1) that has a T-shaped bone in it

**tbs, tbsp** *n* [C] the written abbreviation of TABLESPOON: *1 tbs sugar*

S1 W2 **tea** /tiː/ *n*

**1 ▶ DRINK ◀** [U] **a)** a hot brown drink made by pouring boiling water onto the dried leaves from a particular bush: *Do you take milk and sugar in your tea?* **b)** [C] *especially BrE* a cup of tea: *Three teas and a coffee, please.*

**2 mint/camomile etc tea** a hot drink made by pouring boiling water onto the leaves or flowers of a particular plant, sometimes used as a medicine

**3 ▶ LEAVES ◀** [U] the dried, finely cut leaves of a particular Asian bush, that is used for making tea: *China tea | Ceylon tea | tea plantations*

**4 ▶ MEAL ◀** [U] *BrE* **a)** a very small meal of cake or BISCUITS, eaten in the afternoon with a cup of tea **b)** a large meal that is eaten early in the evening in some parts of Britain —compare DINNER, SUPPER —see also HIGH TEA

**5 tea and sympathy** *BrE* kindness and attention that you give someone when they are upset

**6 (not) for all the tea in China** *informal* used to say that you would refuse to do something, whatever happened: *I wouldn't do his job, not for all the tea in China.* —see also **not be your cup of tea** (CUP[1] (8))

**tea·bag** /ˈtiːbæg/ *n* [C] a small paper bag with tea leaves inside, used for making tea

**tea break** /ˈ· ·/ *n* [C] *especially BrE* a short pause from work in the middle of the morning or afternoon for a drink, a rest etc; COFFEE BREAK

**tea cad·dy** /ˈ· ˌ··/ *n* [C] a small metal box that you keep tea in

**tea·cake** /ˈtiːkeɪk/ *n* [C] *BrE* a small flat round cake made of a bread-like mixture with RAISINS or CURRANTS in it

**teach** /tiːtʃ/ *past tense and past participle* **taught** /tɔːt‖tɒːt/ *v* S1 W2

**1 ▶ SCHOOL/COLLEGE ETC ◀** [I,T] to give lessons in a school, college, or university: *Guy's been teaching in France for 3 years now.* | **teach English/mathematics/history etc** *Janet teaches science at a local school.* | **teach sth to sb** *I'm teaching English to Italian students.* | **teach school/college etc** *AmE* (=teach in a school etc) *My Dad taught school in New York.*

**2 ▶ SHOW SB HOW ◀** [T] to show someone how to do something: **teach sb (how) to do sth** *My father taught me to swim.* | *Hamad is teaching me how to play the guitar.* | **teach sb sth** *Can you teach me one of your card tricks?*

**3 ▶ CHANGE SB'S IDEAS ◀** [T] to show or tell someone how they should behave or what they should think: **teach sb to do sth** *When I was young, children were taught to treat older people with respect.* | **teach sb sth** *The trouble is that parents don't teach their kids the difference between right and wrong.*

**4 ▶ EXPERIENCE SHOWS STH ◀** [T] if an experience or situation teaches you something, it helps you to understand something about life: **teach sb to do sth** *Poverty taught us to appreciate the little things in life.*

**5 that'll teach you!** *spoken* used when something unpleasant has just happened to someone because they ignored your warning: **that'll teach you to do sth** *That'll teach you to park your car in a restricted area!*

**6 teach sb a lesson** *informal* to punish someone to make sure that they will not behave badly again: *Next time he comes home drunk lock him out, that'll teach him a lesson.*

**7 you can't teach an old dog new tricks** used to say that older people often do not want to change the way they do things

**8 teach your grandmother (to suck eggs)** *BrE* to give someone advice about something that they already know

**USAGE NOTE: TEACH**

WORD CHOICE: **teach, instruct, coach, tutor, train, educate**

**Teach** is the general word for helping a person or group of people to learn something: *He teaches German at a local school.* | *Mom taught me to drive.*

If you **instruct** someone you usually teach them, especially in a practical way and about a practical skill: *First of all you'll be instructed in the use of the safety equipment.*

In British English you can **coach** a person, often outside the ordinary educational system, and often in a particular subject that they need additional help with: *She coaches kids in advanced Mathematics, usually in their homes.* In American English, you **tutor** someone when they need help learning a particular subject: *tutoring in reading and arithmetic.* People also may **coach** a person or team to become better in a sport: *Greg's coaching the football team this year.*

You can **train** a person or group of people, especially in particular skills and knowledge, up to a necessary level for a job: *It takes several years to train a doctor.* | *Soldiers are trained to kill.* You can also **train** an animal: *The dogs are trained to attack any stranger that comes near.*

**Educate** means to teach people over a long period of time, in all kinds of knowledge (not just school subjects). **Educating** someone is sometimes compared with **training** them in skills for jobs. *He was educated at Eton.* | *Parents should educate their children in how to behave.* | *The government's campaign aims to educate everyone about AIDS.*

GRAMMAR

**Teach** is not usually used with **about** except when it is transitive: *Children need to be taught about drugs.* | *She taught us about the new computer system* (but NOT *She taught about the new computer system*).

Remember the past tense and past participle forms are **taught**, never *teached*.

S1 W1 **teach·er** /ˈtiːtʃə‖-ər/ *n* [C] someone whose job is to teach: *Miss Tindale's my favourite teacher.*

**teacher's pet** /ˌ·· ˈ·/ *n* [singular] *informal* a child who everyone thinks is the teacher's favourite student and is therefore disliked by the other students

**tea chest** /ˈ· ·/ *n* [C] a large wooden box that used to have tea in it, often used afterwards for moving and storing things

S2 W2 **teach·ing** /ˈtiːtʃɪŋ/ *n* [U] **1** the work or profession of a teacher: *She's thinking of going into teaching.* (=becoming a teacher) | *a teaching career* | **teaching practice** *BrE*, **student teaching** *AmE* (=a period of teaching done by someone who is training to be a teacher) **2** *also* **teachings** [plural] the moral, religious, or political ideas spread by a particular person or group: *the teachings of Gandhi*

**teaching hos·pi·tal** /ˈ·· ˌ···/ *n* [C] a hospital where medical students receive practical training from experienced doctors

**tea cloth** /ˈ· ·/ *n* [C] *BrE* **1** a TEA TOWEL **2** a small piece of material used to cover a tea-table

**tea co·sy** /ˈ· ˌ··/ *n* [C] a thick cover that you put over a TEAPOT to keep the tea hot

**tea·cup** /ˈtiːkʌp/ *n* [C] a cup that you serve tea in —see also **storm in a teacup** (STORM[1] (4))

**tea gar·den** /ˈ· ˌ··/ *n* [C] a large area of land used for growing tea; tea PLANTATION (1)

**tea·house** /ˈtiːhaʊs/ *n* [C] a special house in China or Japan where tea is served, often as part of a ceremony

**teak** /tiːk/ *n* **1** [U] a very hard, yellowish brown wood that is used for making ships and good quality furniture **2** [C] the South Asian tree that this wood comes from

**teal** /tiːl/ *n* **1** [C] a small wild duck **2** [U] a greenish blue colour

**tea·leaf** /ˈtiːliːf/ *n* [C] **1** **tealeaves** [plural] the small, finely cut pieces of leaf used for making tea **2** *BrE slang* a thief

S1 W1 **team**[1] /tiːm/ *n* [C] **1** a group of people who play a game or sport together against another group: *There are nine players on a baseball team.* [also + plural verb *BrE*]: *Our team are winning.* | **play for a team** *Tim plays for the national volleyball team.* | **in a team** *BrE* | **on a team** *AmE*: *Is Mario going to be on the team this year?* | **make the team** *AmE* (=be chosen for a team) **2** a group of people who have been chosen to work together to do a particular job: [+ **of**] *a team of twelve scientists* **3** two or more animals that are used to pull a vehicle

**team**[2] *v*

**team up** *phr v* [I] to join with someone in order to work on something: [+ **with**] *You can team up with one other class member if you want.*

**team-mate** also **teammate** *especially AmE* /ˈ· ·/ *n* [C] someone who plays in the same team as you

**team spir·it** /ˌ· ˈ··/ *n* [U] willingness to work with other people as part of a team

**team·ster** /ˈtiːmstə‖-ər/ *n* [C] *AmE* someone whose job is to drive a TRUCK[1] (1)

**team·work** /ˈtiːmwɜːk‖-wɜːrk/ *n* [U] the ability of a group of people to work well together

**tea par·ty** /ˈ· ˌ··/ *n* [C] **1** a small party in the afternoon at which tea, cake etc is served **2** **be no tea party** *AmE informal* to be very difficult or unpleasant to do

**tea·pot** /ˈtiːpɒt‖-pɑːt/ *n* [C] a container for making and serving tea, which has a handle and a SPOUT[1] (1)

**tear**[1] /tɪə‖tɪr/ *n* **1** [C] a drop of salty liquid that flows from your eye when you are crying: *Tears just rolled down his face.* | *tear-stained cheeks* | **(be) in tears** (=crying) *My wife actually broke down in tears telling me.* | **burst into tears** (=suddenly start crying) *Bridget burst into tears and ran out.* | **be close to tears/be on the verge of tears** (=be almost crying) | **fight back tears** (=try very hard not to cry) | **bring tears to sb's eyes** (=make someone almost cry) *It's music that'll bring tears to the eyes of grown men.* | **reduce sb to tears** (=make someone cry, especially by being unkind to them) | **shed tears** (=cry because you are sad) *Few of us shed any tears when Miss Crabbe left.* | **tears of joy/laughter etc** *Tears of gratitude shone in his eyes.* **2** **it'll (all) end in tears** *BrE spoken* used to warn someone that what they are doing will have an unpleasant result and cause unhappiness —see also **bore sb to tears** (BORE[2] (1)), **shed crocodile tears** (CROCODILE (4)) S3 W3

**tear**[2] /teə‖ter/ *v past tense* **tore** /tɔː‖tɔːr/ *past participle* **torn** /tɔːn‖tɔːrn/ S2 W3

tear out

**1 a)** ► **PAPER CLOTH** ◄ [T] to damage something such as paper or cloth by pulling it too hard or letting it touch something sharp: *Oh no! I've torn my T-shirt.* | **tear sth on sth** *Be careful you don't tear your sleeve on that nail.* | **tear sth out/off/away etc** (=remove something by tearing it away from something else) *Someone's torn the last page out.* | **tear a hole in sth** *"Oh Rick, you've torn a hole in your best pants."* | **tear sth to shreds/pieces** (=tear something so much that it is in small pieces.) *The contract lay on the ground, torn to shreds.* | **tear sth open** (=to open something very quickly by tearing it) *Lister grabbed the envelope and tore it open to see if he'd got the job.* **b)** [I] if paper or cloth tears, a hole appears in it, or it splits, because it has been pulled too hard or has touched something sharp: *Careful, the paper is very old and tears easily.*

**2** ► **MOVE QUICKLY** ◄ [I always + adv/prep] to move somewhere very quickly, especially in a dangerous or careless way: [+ **away/up/past etc**] *The way the big kids tear around the garden on their bikes, it's dangerous for the little ones.*

**3** ► **REMOVE STH** ◄ [T always + adv/prep] to pull something violently from the place where it is fixed or held: **tear sth/from/away etc** *The wind tore the door from its hinges.*

**4 tear loose** to escape from something that is holding you by moving violently: *The dog tore loose and ran off.*
**5 be torn between** to be unable to decide between two people or things, because you want both: *I'm torn between getting a new car and going on vacation.*
**6 be torn by sth a)** to feel very worried, guilty, anxious etc because you are affected by a strong emotion or feeling: *I was torn by conflicting impulses.* **b)** if a country or family is torn by an argument, war etc, it is very badly affected by it: *a nation torn by war and riots*
**7 tear sb/sth to shreds/pieces** to criticize someone or something very severely: *In the end the prosecutor's case was torn to shreds by Russell's lawyer.*
**8 ▶ MUSCLE ◀** [T] to damage a muscle or LIGAMENT (=a strong band connected to your muscles)
**9 tear sb off a strip/tear a strip off sb** *BrE informal* to criticize someone angrily because they have done something wrong
**10 tear sb limb from limb** *humorous* to attack someone in a very violent way: *When I get hold of the person responsible, I'll tear them limb from limb.*
**11 tear your hair out** *informal* to be very anxious or angry about something: *I've been tearing my hair out sorting out these wedding arrangements.*
**12 be in a tearing hurry** *BrE* to be doing something very quickly, especially because you are late
**13 tear sb's heart out** to make someone feel extremely upset: *She's so lonely – it's tearing my heart out.*
**14 that's torn it!** *BrE spoken* used when something bad has happened that stops you from doing what you intended to do: *That's torn it! I've left my keys in the car!*

**tear** sb/sth **apart** *phr v* [T] **1** to make someone feel extremely unhappy or upset: *It tears me apart to see them argue.* **2** to cause serious arguments in an organization, group etc: *Scandal is tearing the government apart.* **3** to break something into many small pieces, especially in a violent way: *a carcass torn apart by wolves*

**tear at** sb/sth *phr v* [T] to pull violently at someone or something: *The children were screaming and tearing at each other's hair.*

**tear away** *phr v* **1** [I] to suddenly start moving very quickly: *The car tore away into the distance.* **2 tear yourself away (from)** to leave a place or person very unwillingly because you have to: *Could you please tear yourself away from the TV and help me for a minute.*

**tear** sth ↔ **down** *phr v* [T] to knock down a large building or part of a building: *It's time some of these old apartment blocks were torn down.*

**tear into** sb/sth *phr v* [T not in passive] **1** to attack someone by hitting them very hard: *boxers tearing into each other* **2** to criticize someone very strongly, especially unfairly: *All I said was that she could maybe try harder and she really tore into me.*

**tear off** *phr v* **1** [T **tear** sth ↔ **off**] to remove your clothes as quickly as you can: *Ben tore off his coat and dived in to rescue the child.* **2** [I] to suddenly start moving very quickly: *I must tear off to the store before it closes.* **3** [T **tear** sth ↔ **off**] *BrE informal* to write something in a short time: *I tore off a letter.*

**tear** sth ↔ **up** *phr v* [T]
**1** to destroy a piece of paper or cloth by breaking it into small pieces: *Crying, she tore up his letter.* **2** to damage or ruin a place, especially by behaving violently: *football fans tearing up the grounds* **3 tear up an agreement/contract etc** to suddenly decide to stop being restricted by a contract etc

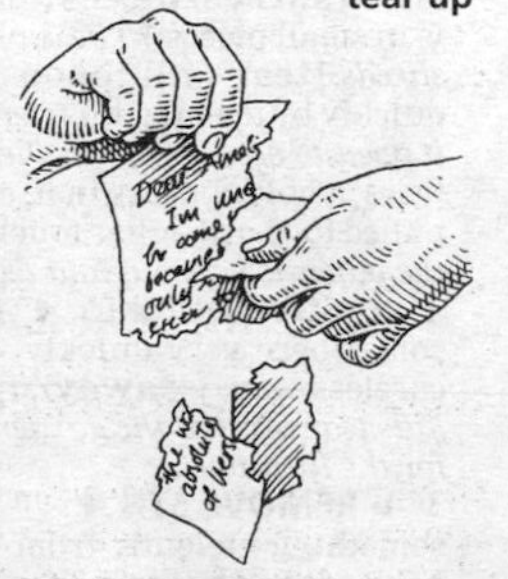
**tear up**

**tear³** /teə‖ter/ *n* [C] a hole in a piece of cloth, paper etc where it has been torn —see also **wear and tear** (WEAR² (4))

**tear·a·way** /ˈteərəweɪ‖ˈter-/ *n* [C] *informal* a young person who behaves badly and often gets into trouble: *One night some young tearaways set fire to the De Corizo house.*

**tear·drop** /ˈtɪədrɒp‖ˈtɪrdrɑːp/ *n* [C] *especially literary* a single drop of salty liquid from your eye

**tear·ful** /ˈtɪəfəl‖ˈtɪr-/ *adj* crying a little or almost crying: *a tearful reunion at the airport* —**tearfully** *adv*

**tear gas** /ˈtɪə gæs‖ˈtɪr-/ *n* [U] a gas that stings your eyes, used by the police to control crowds —**teargas** *v* [T]

**tear·jerk·er** /ˈtɪəˌdʒɜːkə‖ˈtɪrˌdʒɜːrkər/ *n* [C] *informal* a film, book, story etc that makes you feel very sad

**tea·room** /ˈtiːruːm, -rʊm/ *n* [C] a restaurant where tea and light meals are served

**tease¹** /tiːz/ *v* **1** [I,T] to make jokes and laugh at someone in order to have fun by embarrassing them, either in a friendly way or in an unkind way: *Don't get upset, I was only teasing.* | **tease sb** *Kids often tease each other.* | **tease sb about** *I was teased about my weight as a child.* **2** [T] to deliberately annoy an animal: *Stop teasing the cat!* **3** [I,T] to deliberately make someone sexually excited without intending to have sex with them **4** [T] *AmE* to comb your hair in the opposite direction to which it grows, so that it looks thicker; BACKCOMB *BrE*

**tease out** *phr v* [T] **1 tease sth out of sb** to persuade someone to tell you something that they do not want to tell you **2** [**tease** sth ↔ **out**] to gently loosen or straighten hairs or threads that are stuck together: *She teased out the knots in her hair.*

**tease²** *n* [C] *informal* **1** someone who enjoys making jokes at people, and embarrassing them, especially in a friendly way: *Don't take any notice of Joe – he's a big tease.* **2** someone who deliberately makes you sexually excited, but has no intention of having sex with you

**tea·sel** /ˈtiːzəl/ *n* [C] **1** a plant with PRICKLY leaves and flowers **2** a dried flower from this plant, used for brushing cloth to give it a soft surface

**teas·er** /ˈtiːzə‖-ər/ *n* [C] *informal* **1** a very difficult question, especially in a competition **2** a TEASE²

**tea ser·vice** /ˈ· ˌ··/ *n* [C] a matching set of cups, plates, teapot etc, used for serving tea

**tea shop** /ˈ· ·/ *n* [C] a TEAROOM

**tea·spoon** /ˈtiːspuːn/ *n* [C] **1** a small spoon used for mixing sugar into tea, coffee etc —see picture at SPOON¹ **2** also **tea·spoon·ful** /ˈtiːspuːnfʊl/ the amount a teaspoon can hold

**teat** /tiːt/ *n* [C] **1** *BrE* the rubber part on a baby's bottle that the baby sucks milk from; NIPPLE (3) *AmE* **2** one of the small parts on a female animal's body that her babies suck milk from

**tea tow·el** /ˈ· ˌ··/ *n* [C] *BrE* a cloth for drying cups, plates etc, after you have washed them; DISH TOWEL *AmE* —see picture on page 833

**tea trol·ley** /ˈ· ˌ··/ *n* [C] *BrE* a small table on wheels, that you serve food and drinks from

**tea urn** /ˈ· ·/ *n* [C] a large metal container with a TAP¹ (1) used for heating the water to make tea

**tea·zel, teazle** /ˈtiːzəl/ *n* [C] another spelling of TEASEL

**tech** /tek/ *n* [C] *BrE informal* a TECHNICAL COLLEGE

**tech·ie** /ˈteki/ *n* [C] *AmE informal* a TECHNICIAN (1)

**tech·ni·cal** /ˈteknɪkəl/ *adj* S2 W2
**1 ▶ INDUSTRY/SCIENCE ◀** connected with practical knowledge, skills, or methods, especially in industrial or scientific work: *technical experts* | *technical training* —see TECHNIQUE (USAGE)
**2 ▶ LANGUAGE ◀** using words in a special way that is difficult for most people to understand because it is connected with one particular subject: *technical terms*
**3 technical problem/hitch** a problem involving the way an engine or system works
**4 ▶ ACCORDING TO RULES ◀** according to the exact details in a set of rules: *a technical infringement of the rules*

5 ▶ **IN MUSIC/ART** ◀ concerning the special skill of doing something difficult, especially in music, art, sport etc: *Navratilova's technical mastery of the game*

**technical col·lege** /'··· ,··/ *n* [C] a college in Britain where students who have finished school study for further qualifications especially in practical subjects

**tech·ni·cal·i·ty** /,teknɪ̆'kælɪ̆ti/ *n* [C] **1 technicalities** [plural] details of a system or process that you need a special knowledge to understand: *Can you explain the technicalities of laser printing?* **2** a small detail in a law or a set of rules, especially one that forces you to make a decision that seems unfair: *A legal technicality meant Tollitt had to be released, although the evidence was against him.* | **on a technicality** (=only because of a technicality) *Wild lost the competition on a technicality.*

S3 **tech·ni·cally** /'teknɪkli/ *adv* **1** [sentence adverb] according to the exact details of rules, laws etc; STRICTLY (1): *Technically, I'm not supposed to do this, but we're short-staffed.* **2** [+ adj/adv] showing the special skills connected with a particular activity: *a technically brilliant pianist* **3 technically possible/impossible/difficult etc** possible etc using the scientific knowledge that is available now

**tech·ni·cian** /tek'nɪʃən/ *n* [C] **1** a skilled scientific or industrial worker: *a laboratory technician* —see TECHNIQUE (USAGE) **2** someone who is very good at the skills of a particular sport, art etc: *Whether he was a great artist or not, Dali was a superb technician.*

**Tech·ni·col·or** /'teknɪkʌlə‖-ər/ *n* [U] *trademark* a type of colour film process used for the cinema

**tech·ni·col·our** *BrE*, **technicolor** *AmE* /'teknɪkʌlə‖-ər/ *adj* [only before noun] *humorous* having many very bright colours, usually too bright

S3 W1 **tech·nique** /tek'ni:k/ *n* [C] **1** a special skill or way of doing something, especially one that has to be learned: *new techniques for producing special effects in movies* **2** [U] the level of skill or the set of skills that someone has: *a footballer with brilliant technique*

> **USAGE NOTE: TECHNIQUE**
>
> WORD CHOICE: **technique, technology, technical, technician, expert, high tech**
>
> A **technique** [C] is a specific way of doing something, usually involving some skill. It may or may not be scientific or involve machines: *a teaching/management/propaganda technique* | *a new technique that allows us to see inside the human body*
>
> **Technique** [U] is the way you do something practical or skilful: *She's a wonderful skater, her technique is superb.*
>
> **Technology** (usually [U]) is the general use of scientific knowledge for practical purposes, usually seen in actual machines or in industry: *high technology* (NOT *high techniques*) | *Computer/medical technology is changing the world* (NOT *the technology is changing the world*). | *An examination of the wrecked ship will tell us something about the technology of the past* (NOT *technique*).
>
> Something that is **technical** often relates to detailed practical knowledge of something involving science, technology, or machines: *a technical report on the plane crash* (= describing exactly what went wrong with the plane) | *The train is delayed due to a technical fault.* | *technical progress/subjects/information/help/expertise*
>
> More generally **technical** matters may involve knowledge about any job or subject that only someone specially trained would usually have: *a technical point of law* | *a technical grammatical term* | *a highly technical question*
>
> Someone who works with and mends scientific equipment or machines is a **technician**. Someone who knows all about a particular subject of any sort is an **expert** (NOT *a technical*).
>
> A machine, process or industry may be **high tech** (= using the latest scientific ideas, especially electronic) (but NOT *high technical*): *Surgeons now use the latest in high tech medical equipment.* | *high tech computer companies*
>
> SPELLING
>
> **Technique** is never spelt *technic* or *tecnique*.

**tech·no** /'teknəʊ‖-noʊ/ *n* [U] a type of popular electronic dance music with a fast, strong beat

**techno-** /teknə/ *prefix* **1** concerning TECHNOLOGY: *technocracy* (=rule by skilled specialists) | *technophobia* (=dislike of computers, machines etc) **2 techno-literacy/techno-babble/techno-theorist etc** connected with electronic equipment such as computers: *techno-literacy* (=skill in using computers)

**tech·noc·racy** /tek'nɒkrəsi‖-'nɑ:-/ *n* [C,U] a social system in which people with a lot of scientific or technical knowledge have a lot of power

**tech·no·crat** /'teknəkræt/ *n* [C] a highly skilled scientist who has a lot of power in industry or government

**tech·no·lo·gi·cal** /,teknə'lɒdʒɪkəl◂‖-'lɑ:-/ *adj* related to technology: *The steam engine was the greatest technological advance of the 19th century* —**technologically** /-kli/ *adv*: *technologically developed countries*

**tech·nol·o·gist** /tek'nɒlədʒɪ̆st‖-'nɑ:-/ *n* [C] someone who has special knowledge of technology

**tech·nol·o·gy** /tek'nɒlədʒi‖-'nɑ:-/ *n* **1** [C,U] knowledge about scientific or industrial methods or the use of these methods: *nuclear technology* | *the application of modern technologies to agriculture* —see TECHNIQUE (USAGE) **2** [U] machinery and equipment used or developed as a result of this knowledge: *The factory uses the very latest technology.* S2 W1

**tech·no·phobe** /'teknəfəʊb‖-foʊb/ *n* [C] someone who does not like modern machines, such as computers —**technophobia** /,teknə'fəʊbiə‖-'foʊ-/ *n* [U]

**ted·dy bear** /'tedi beə‖-ber/ *also* **teddy** *BrE n* [C] a soft toy in the shape of a bear

**teddy boy** /'·· ·/ *n* [C] a member of a group of young men in Britain in the 1950's who had their own special style of clothes and music

**te·di·ous** /'ti:diəs/ *adj* boring, tiring, and continuing for a long time: *a tedious lecture* —**tediously** *adv* —**tediousness** *n* [U]

**te·di·um** /'ti:diəm/ *n* [U] the quality of being tedious: *She hated the tedium of life in a small country village.*

**tee¹** /ti:/ *n* [C] **1** a small object, used in GOLF to hold the ball above the ground before you hit it —see picture on page 1263 **2** a flat, raised area from which you hit the ball in a game of GOLF

**tee²**

**tee off** *phr v* **1** [I] to hit the ball off the tee in a game of GOLF **2** [T **tee** sb **off**] *AmE informal* to make someone angry: *His attitude really tees me off.* **3** [T **tee off on** sb] *AmE informal* to be angry with someone or criticize them

**Tee-ball** /'· ·/ *n* [U] another spelling of T-BALL

**teed off** /,· '·/ *adj AmE slang* annoyed or angry; FED UP

**teem** /ti:m/ also **teem down** *v* [I] *BrE* to rain very heavily: *It's been teeming down all day.*

**teem with sth** *phr v* [T not in passive] to be full of people, animals etc: **be teeming with** *Times Square was teeming with theater-goers.*

**teem·ing** /'ti:mɪŋ/ *adj* full of people, animals, etc that are all moving around: **teeming city/streets/market etc** *the teeming streets of Cairo*

**teen¹** /ti:n/ *adj informal* [only before noun] teenage: *a teen magazine*

**teen²** *n* [C] *AmE informal* a teenager

**teen·age** /'ti:neɪdʒ/ also **teen·aged** /'ti:neɪdʒd/ *adj* [only before noun] aged between 13 and 19, or concerning someone of that age: *my teenage daughter*

**teen·ag·er** /ˈtiːneɪdʒə‖-ər/ *n* [C] also **teen** *AmE informal* someone who is between 13 and 19 years old: *a TV sex education series aimed at teenagers* —see CHILD (USAGE)

**teens** /tiːnz/ *n* [plural] the period of your life when you are between 13 and 19 years old: **be in your teens** *They were in their teens when they first met.*

**tee·ny** /ˈtiːni/ *adj informal* very small; TINY

**tee·ny·bop·per** /ˈtiːni,bɒpə‖-,bɑːpər/ *n* [C] *old-fashioned* a girl between the ages of about 9 and 14, who is very interested in popular music, teenage fashions etc

**tee·ny wee·ny** /,tiːni ˈwiːni◂/ *also* **teen·sy ween·sy** /,tiːnzi ˈwiːnzi◂/ *adj informal* a word meaning very small, used especially by or to children

**tee·pee** /ˈtiːpiː/ *n* [C] another spelling of TEPEE

**tee shirt** /ˈ· ,·/ *n* [C] another spelling of T-SHIRT

**tee·ter** /ˈtiːtə‖-ər/ *v* [I] **1** to stand or move unsteadily as if you are going to fall: **[+ on/along/across etc]** *She teetered along in her high-heeled shoes.* **2 be teetering on the brink/edge of** to be very close to an extreme and dangerous situation: *teetering on the brink of revolution*

**teeter-tot·ter** /ˈ·· ,··/ *n* [C] *AmE* a large toy like a board on which two children sit, one at each end; SEESAW[1]

**teeth**

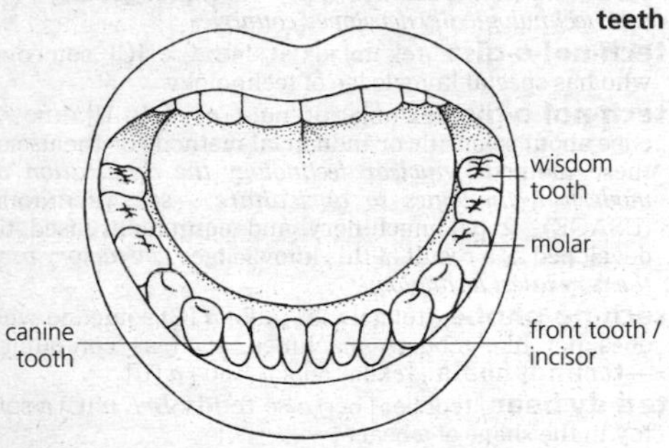


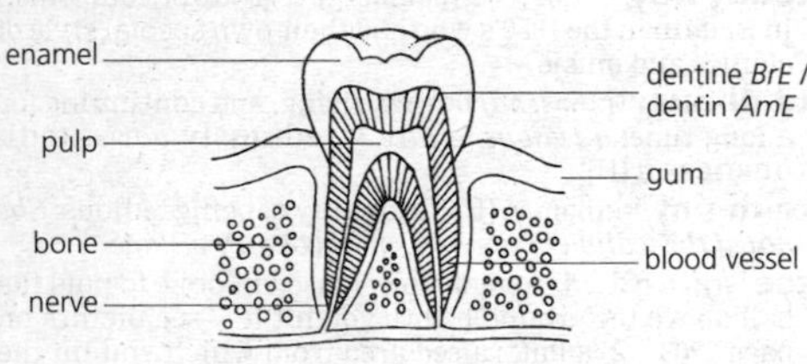


a cross-section of a tooth

**teeth** /tiːθ/ *n* the plural of TOOTH

**teethe** /tiːð/ *v* [I] **be teething** if a baby is teething, its first teeth are growing —**teething** *n* [U]

**teething troub·les** /ˈ·· ,··/ *n* [plural] small problems that a company, product, system etc has at the beginning: *a few teething troubles with the new computer system*

**tee·to·tal** /,tiːˈtəʊtl◂‖ˈtiː,toʊtl/ *adj* never drinking alcohol —**teetotalism** *n* [U]

**tee·to·tal·ler** *BrE*, **teetotaler** *AmE* /tiːˈtəʊtələ‖ˈtiː,toʊtələr/ *n* [C] someone who never drinks alcohol: *There was a time when no self-respecting pop star would admit to being a non-smoking teetotaller.*

**TEFL** /ˈtefəl/ *n* [U] the teaching of English as a foreign language —compare TESOL

**Tef·lon** /ˈteflɒn‖-lɑːn/ *n* [U] *trademark* a plastic that stops things from sticking to it, often used in making pans

**tel** the written abbreviation of TELEPHONE NUMBER

**tele-** /teli, telə̇/ *prefix* **1** at or over a long distance: *a telescope* (=for seeing a long way) | *telecommunications* | *telepathy* (=sending of thought messages) | *teleshopping* (=using a computer in your home to order goods) **2** by or for television: *a teleplay* | *a telerecording*

**tel·e·cast** /ˈtelikɑːst‖-kæst/ *n* [C] a broadcast on television

**tel·e·com·mu·ni·ca·tions** /,telikəmjuːnə̇ˈkeɪʃənz/ *n* [plural] the process or business of sending and receiving messages by telephone, radio, television etc: *a telecommunications satellite*

**tele·com·mut·er** /ˈtelikə,mjuːtə‖-tər/ *n* [C] someone who works for a company at home using a computer connected to the main office —**telecommuting** *n* [U]

**tel·e·gram** /ˈtelə̇græm/ *n* [C] a message sent by telegraph; WIRE[1] (3) *AmE*: *telegrams of congratulations*

**tel·e·graph[1]** /ˈtelə̇grɑːf‖-græf/ *n* **1** [U] an old-fashioned method of sending messages using radio or electrical signals **2** [C] a piece of equipment that receives or sends messages in this way —see also BUSH TELEGRAPH —**telegraphic** /,telə̇ˈgræfɪk◂/ *adj* —**telegraphically** /-kli/ *adv*

**telegraph[2]** *v* **1** [I,T] to send a message by telegraph: *Once he knew where we were, Lewis telegraphed every few hours.* **2** [T] *informal* to let people clearly see what you intend to do without saying anything: *Sampras rather telegraphed that shot.*

**te·leg·ra·pher** /tə̇ˈlegrəfə‖-ər/ *n* [C] someone whose job is to send and receive messages by telegraph

**tel·e·graph·ese** /,telə̇grəˈfiːz‖-græfˈiːz/ *n* [U] the style of language used in TELEGRAMS in which you only include the really necessary words

**te·leg·ra·phist** /tə̇ˈlegrəfə̇st/ *n* [C] a telegrapher

**telegraph line** /ˈ··· ,·/ *n* [C] a telegraph wire

**telegraph pole** /ˈ··· ,·/ *n* [C] *BrE* a tall wooden pole for supporting telephone wires; TELEPHONE POLE *AmE*

**telegraph post** /ˈ··· ,·/ *n* [C] *BrE* a telegraph pole

**telegraph wire** /ˈ··· ,·/ *n* [C] a wire for sending messages by TELEGRAPH[1]

**te·leg·ra·phy** /tə̇ˈlegrəfi/ *n* [U] *technical* the process of sending messages by TELEGRAPH[1]

**tel·e·ki·nes·is** /,telikɪˈniːsɪs, -kaɪ-/ *n* [U] the ability to move physical objects using only the power of your mind

**tel·e·mar·ket·ing** /,teliˈmɑːkə̇tɪŋ‖-ˈmɑːr-/ *n* [U] a method of selling things in which you telephone people to see if they want to buy something —compare TELESALES —**telemarketer** *n* [C]

**te·lem·e·try** /tə̇ˈlemə̇tri/ *n* [U] *technical* the use of special scientific equipment to measure something and send the results somewhere by radio

**tel·e·ol·o·gy** /,teliˈɒlədʒi‖,tiːliˈɑː-/ *n* [U] the belief that all natural things and events were specially planned for a particular purpose —**teleological** /,teliəˈlɒdʒɪkəl◂‖,tiːliəˈlɑː-/ *adj*

**tel·e·path·ic** /,telə̇ˈpæθɪk◂/ *adj* **1** having a mysterious ability to know what other people are thinking: *How did he know that? He must be telepathic.* **2** connected with or sent by telepathy: *telepathic messages*

**te·lep·a·thy** /tə̇ˈlepəθi/ *n* [U] the communication of thoughts directly from one person's mind to someone else's without speaking, writing, or signs —**telepathically** *adv* using telepathy

**tel·e·phone[1]** /ˈtelə̇fəʊn‖-foʊn/ *n* **1 the telephone** the system of communication that you use to have a conversation with someone in another place; PHONE[1] (1): *The telephone was invented by Alexander Graham Bell.* | *a telephone conversation* | **by telephone** *Reservations can be made by telephone.* **2** [C] the piece of equipment that you use when you are speaking to someone by telephone; PHONE[1] (2): *The telephone is ringing.* | *the cost of installing telephones* **3 be on the telephone a)** to be talking to someone using the telephone: *I was on the telephone when he came in.* **b)** to have a telephone in your home, office etc **4** [C] the part of a telephone that you hold close to your ear and mouth; RECEIVER (1) —**telephonic** /,telə̇ˈfɒnɪk◂‖-ˈfɑː-/ *adj* S W

**USAGE NOTE: TELEPHONE**

WORD CHOICE: words related to the telephone

**Telephone** can be used as a noun or a verb, as can the short form **phone**, which is four times more common in spoken English.

If someone phones you, you **have or receive a call** (NOT *a telephone*) from them.

If you want to **phone** a friend or **call** them (or **ring** them **(up)** (*BrE*), **give** them **a ring** (*BrE*)**/call**), you **dial** their **(phone) number**.

If you are phoning **long distance**, you will need to dial the **code** (*BrE*)**/area code** (*AmE*) (=number) for the region or country where they live, as well as their **local** number.

All these numbers are found in the **phone book** or **directory** (*BrE*), or by phoning **directory enquiries** (*BrE*)**/information** (*AmE*).

If you have a problem **getting through** to the person you are phoning, you may ring the **operator** for help.

When you phone someone, their phone will **ring**, and if they are at home they will answer by **picking up the phone** (or technically the **receiver**, or on cordless phones the **handset**).

If they are busy they may ask you to **phone/call/ring back** later or to **hold on**, or more officially and in American English **hold** (=wait).

If they do not want to speak to you, or have finished speaking to you, they may **hang up** (=replace the receiver or switch off the handset).

If someone is already **on the phone** when you call them, their number is **engaged** (*BrE*)**/busy** (*AmE*).

If someone does not want to receive any calls, they may **leave their phone off the hook** (=the receiver is not in its proper place) so that no calls will get through.

A telephone in a public place is a **public phone** or **payphone**, often placed in a **phone/call box** (*BrE*) or **phone booth** (*AmE*).

GRAMMAR

You **(tele)phone** a place or a person, NOT *to* them: *Please phone Mary/the hospital.* But you often speak of being **on the phone to** someone.

**telephone**[2] *v* [I,T] *BrE formal* to speak to someone by telephone; PHONE[2]: *Mr Dodd telephoned to say he was ill.*

Frequencies of the verbs **telephone**, **phone** and **call** in spoken and written English.

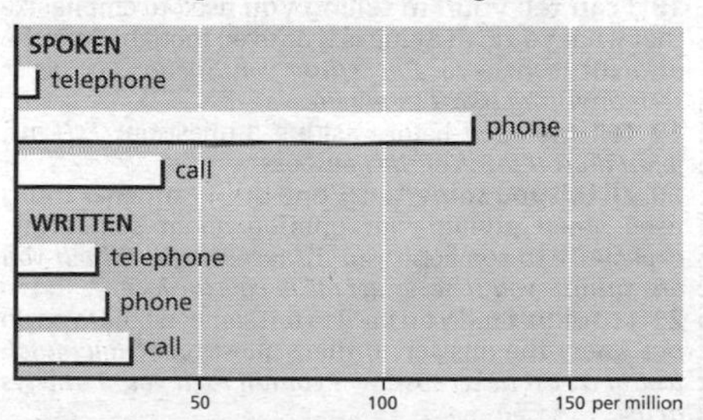


Based on the British National Corpus and the Longman Lancaster Corpus

This graph shows that it is much more usual in spoken English to use the verbs **phone** or **call** rather than **telephone**, which is formal and is therefore much more common in written English than in spoken English.

**telephone book** /ˈ··· ˌ·/ *n* [C] a TELEPHONE DIRECTORY

**telephone box** /ˈ··· ˌ·/ *BrE*, **telephone booth** *AmE n* [C] an enclosed structure containing a telephone that can be used by the public

**telephone call** /ˈ··· ˌ·/ *n* [C] an attempt to speak to someone by telephone: *There's a telephone call for you, Mr Baron.*

**telephone di·rec·to·ry** /ˈ··· ·ˌ···/ *n* [C] a book containing an alphabetical list of the names, addresses, and telephone numbers of all the people in a particular area

**telephone ex·change** /ˈ··· ·ˌ·/ *n* [C] a central building or office where telephone calls are connected to other telephones

**telephone num·ber** /ˈ··· ˌ··/ *n* [C] the number that you DIAL[2] to telephone a particular person or place

**telephone pole** /ˈ··· ˌ·/ *n* [C] *AmE* a tall wooden pole for supporting telephone wires; TELEGRAPH POLE *BrE*

**te·leph·o·nist** /təˈlefənəst/ *n* [C] *BrE* someone whose job is to connect telephone calls at a SWITCHBOARD or telephone exchange —compare OPERATOR (1)

**te·le·pho·to lens** /ˌteləfəutəu ˈlenz‖-foutou-/ *n* [C] a special camera LENS (2) used for taking clear photographs of things that are far away: *a time before the advent of chequebook journalism and telephoto lenses*

**tel·e·print·er** /ˈteləˌprɪntə‖-ər/ *n* [C] a machine for writing TELEX messages that you are sending, and for printing messages received; TELETYPEWRITER *AmE*

**Tel·e·prompt·er** /ˈteləˌprɒmptə‖-ˌprɑːmptər/ *n* [C] *trademark* a machine that helps someone speaking on television by showing them the words of their speech on a screen

**tel·e·sales** /ˈteliseɪlz/ *n* [U] the practice of telephoning people in order to try to sell them things —compare TELEMARKETING

**tel·e·scope**[1] /ˈteləskəup‖-skoup/ *n* [C] a piece of scientific equipment shaped like a tube, used for making distant objects look larger and closer: *the 250-ft Lovell telescope at Jodrell Bank* —see also RADIO TELESCOPE

**telescope**[2] *v* [T] to make a process or set of events seem to happen in a shorter time: *In the story the whole rebellion is telescoped into a few days.*

**tel·e·scop·ic** /ˌteləˈskɒpɪk◂‖-ˈskɑː-/ *adj* **1** made of parts that slide over each other so that the whole thing can be made longer or shorter: *a tripod with telescopic legs* **2** connected with a telescope: *a telescopic lens|a telescopic picture of Mars*

**tel·e·text, Teletext** /ˈtelitekst/ *n* [U] a system of broadcasting written information on television

**Tel·e·type** /ˈtelitaɪp/ *n* [C] *trademark* a TELEPRINTER

**tel·e·type·writ·er** /ˌteliˈtaɪpraɪtə‖-ər/ *n* [C] *AmE* a TELEPRINTER

**tel·e·vise** /ˈteləvaɪz/ *v* [T] to broadcast something on television: *The game will be televised live on ABC tonight.*

**tel·e·vi·sion** /ˈteləˌvɪʒən, ˌteləˈvɪʒən/ *n* **1** [C] also **television set** *formal* a thing shaped like a box with a screen, on which you can watch programmes; TV *a 16 inch colour television* **2** [U] a way of broadcasting pictures and sounds in the form of programmes that people can watch: *Who invented television?|television and radio journalism* **3** [U] the programmes broadcast in this way; TV|**watch television** *In the evenings I like to relax and watch television.*|**television programme/show/commercial etc** *the television news* **4 on (the) television** broadcast or being broadcast on television: *What's on television tonight?* **5** [U] the business of making and broadcasting programmes on television: *Jean works in television.*|**television producer/reporter/newsreader etc** *a television film-crew* S1 W1

**television li·cence** /ˈ···· ˌ··,··ˈ·· ˌ··/ *n* [C] an official piece of paper that you need to buy in Britain in order to legally use a television in your home

**tel·e·work·er** /ˈteliwɜːkə‖-wɜːrkər/ *n* [C] someone who works from home using a computer, FAX etc

**tel·ex**[1] /ˈteleks/ *n* **1** [U] the system of sending messages from one business to another on the telephone network, by SATELLITE (1) etc: **by telex** *We'll send you the reply by telex.* **2** [C] a message sent in this way

**telex²** *v* [I,T] to send a message, piece of information etc to someone using a telex

S1 W1 **tell** /tel/ *v past tense and past participle* **told** /təʊld‖toʊld/
**1 ► SAY/INFORMATION ◄** [T] to give someone facts or information about something: **tell sb (that)** *She wrote to tell me she couldn't come.* | *Don't tell me you've forgotten my birthday again.* | *Police will not name the body until the relatives have been told.* | **tell sb who/why/what etc** *There is a sign telling you where the emergency exits are.* | **tell sb about sth** *Harry's been telling me all about his last vacation.* | **tell sb sth** *Tell me your name and address.* | *Can you tell me the quickest way to Manchester?* | **tell a story/joke/secret/lie** *When I was young my father told me stories about the war.* | **tell the truth** *If Dan is telling the truth, the others are in danger.* | **tell sb straight** (=tell someone the true facts or your true feelings) *I told her straight I wasn't coming.* —see SAY¹ (USAGE)
**2 ► ORDER ◄** [T] to say that someone must do something; order: **tell sb to do sth** *The teacher told all the children to sit down quietly.* | **tell sb what/how etc** *Don't tell me how to behave in public!* | *Stop trying to tell me what to do all the time.* | **tell sb (that)** *All the hostages were told that they had to lie on the floor.* | **do as you are told** (=obey) *These kids will never do as they're told.*
**3 tell yourself** to remind yourself of the facts of a situation because it is difficult to accept or because it worries you: *I keep telling myself there is nothing I could have done to save him.*
**4 ► RECOGNIZE THE SIGNS ◄** [I,T not in progressive] to know something or be able to recognize something because of certain signs that show this: *Yes I do dye my hair. How can you tell?* | **tell (that)** *Even though it was so dark I could still tell it was you.* | **tell when/how etc** *It's hard to tell how long the job will take.* | **tell by/from** *You can tell by the way it walks that the dog has been injured.* | **tell a mile off** (=know very easily) *You could tell a mile off that he was lying.*
**5 ► RECOGNIZE DIFFERENCE ◄** [T not in progressive] to be able to see how one person or thing is different from another: **tell sth from sth** *Amateurs may be unable to tell the fake from the original painting.* | **tell sb and sb apart** *It's almost impossible to tell Jackie and Moira apart since they had their hair cut.* | **tell the difference** *Margarine and butter? I can't tell the difference.*
**6 ► WARN ◄** [T usually in past tense] to warn someone that something bad might happen: **tell sb (that)** *I told you it was a waste of time talking to him.* | **tell sb to do sth** *My mother told me not to trust Robert.*
**7 ► BE A SIGN OF STH ◄** [T not in progressive or passive] to give information in ways other than talking which helps you know or understand more about a situation: **tell sb (that)** *The bleeper tells you you've left your lights on.* | **tell sb what/why etc** *The red light tells you when the machine is ready to use.* | **tell sb about sth** *What do these fossils tells us about our ancestors?*
**8 tell the time** *BrE* **tell time** *AmE* to be able to know what time it is by looking at a clock
**9 ► AFFECT ◄** [I not in progressive] to have an effect on someone, especially a harmful one: *His years in the army certainly tell in his attitude to his work.* | **tell on sb** *These late nights are really beginning to tell on her.* | *The stress of work told on their marriage.* —see also TELLING
**10 ► BAD BEHAVIOUR ◄** [I] *informal* to tell someone in authority about something wrong that someone has done: *I'm going to tell, if you don't stop messing around.* | **tell on sb** *If you promise not to tell on me I'll put the money back where I found it.*
**11 tell tales** *BrE* to say something that is not true about someone else, especially to cause them trouble: *Have you been telling tales again?* | **tell tales on sb** *an unpopular child, always telling tales on the other children* —see also **tell tale** (TALE (3))
**12 tell sb where to get off** *informal* to tell someone angrily that you are not interested in them, what they want etc: *"Did you give him the money?" "No, I told him where to get off."*
**13 all told** altogether, when everyone or everything has been counted: *There must have been eight cars in the accident, all told.*
**14 ► VOTES ◄** [T] *technical* to count the votes in an election —see also SAY² (1)

Frequencies of the verb **tell** in spoken and written English.

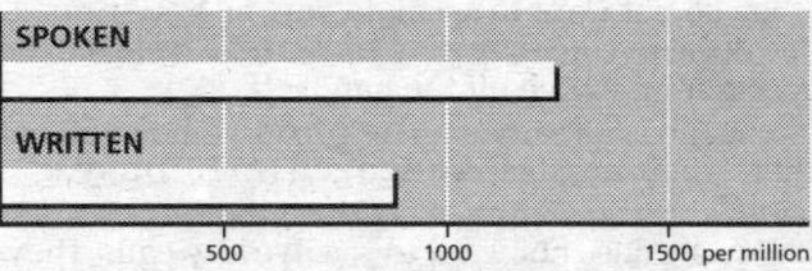


Based on the British National Corpus and the Longman Lancaster Corpus

This graph shows that the verb **tell** is more common in spoken English than in written English. This is because it is used in a lot of common spoken phrases.

**tell** (*v*) **SPOKEN PHRASES**

**15 I'll tell you what** used when you are suggesting or offering something: *I tell you what, we'll get you something to eat on the way.*
**16 I told you so** used when you have warned someone about a possible danger that has now happened and they have ignored your warning
**17 to tell (you) the truth** used to emphasize that you are being very honest: *I don't really want to go out, to tell the truth.*
**18 I can tell you/I'm telling you** used to emphasize that what you are saying is true even though it may be difficult to believe: *I'm telling you Sheila, I've never seen anything like it in my life.*
**19 tell me** used before asking a question: *Tell me, what do you think of the new boss?*
**20 I'll tell you something/one thing/another thing** used when giving your opinion about something, especially to someone you disagree with: *I'll tell you one thing – you'll never get me to vote for him.*
**21 I couldn't tell you** used to tell someone that you do not know the answer to their question: *"How much would a rail ticket cost?" "I couldn't tell you, I always drive."*
**22 I can't tell you a)** used to say that you cannot tell someone something because it is a secret: *"Where are you taking me?" "I can't tell you, it would spoil the surprise."* **b)** used to say that you cannot express your feelings or describe something properly: **I can't tell you how/what etc** *I just can't tell you how worried I've been.*
**23 don't tell me** used to interrupt someone because you know what they are going to say or because you want to guess: *"I'm sorry I'm late but..." "Don't tell me – the car broke down again?"*

**24 John/she etc tells me (that)** used to say what someone has told you: *Mike tells me you found a job.*
**25 I'm not telling (you)** used to say that you refuse to tell someone something
**26 that would be telling** used to say that you cannot tell someone something because it is a secret
**27 you're telling me** used to emphasize that you already know and agree with something that someone has just said: *"It's hot in here." "You're telling me!"*
**28 tell me about it** used to say that you already know how bad something is, especially because you have experienced it yourself: *"I've been so tired lately." "Yeah, tell me about it!"*
**29 you never can tell/you can never tell** used to say that you cannot be certain about what will happen in the future
**30 there's no telling what/how etc** used to say that it is impossible to know what has happened or what will happen next: *She's desperate. There's no telling what she'll try next.*
**31 tell me another** used when you do not believe what someone has told you

**tell against** sb *phr v* [T no passive] *BrE formal* if a bad quality or feature tells against you, it makes you unsuccessful in what you are trying to achieve: *She has the figure of a model but her height really tells against her.*

**tell** sb/sth **apart** *phr v* [T not in progressive] to be able to see which person or thing is which, even though they are very similar: *I've never been able to tell the twins apart.* | [+ **from**] *It's difficult to tell the forged stamp apart from the real one.*

**tell of** sb/sth *phr v* [T] *especially literary* to describe the details of an event or person: *The poem tells of the deeds of a famous warrior.*

**tell** sb↔ **off** *phr v* [T] **1** to talk angrily to someone because they have done something wrong: **be/get told off** *Do your homework or you'll get told off again.* | **tell sb off for doing sth** *My dad told me off for swearing.* **2** *formal* to separate a group of people from a larger group, in order to do special work or tasks: *Ten soldiers were told off to dig ditches.*

**tell·er** /ˈtelə‖-ər/ *n* [C] **1** someone whose job is to receive and pay out money in a bank **2** someone who counts votes

**tell·ing** /ˈtelɪŋ/ *adj* **1** having a great or important effect; SIGNIFICANT (1): *a telling argument* —see also TELL (12) **2** a remark that is telling shows what you really think although you may not intend it to —**tellingly** *adv*

**telling-off** /ˌ.. ˈ./ *n* **give sb a telling-off** to talk angrily to someone because they have done something wrong: *They gave the children a good telling-off.* —see also **tell off** (TELL)

**tell·tale¹** /ˈtelteɪl/ *adj* **telltale signs/marks etc** signs that clearly show something that is unpleasant or is supposed to be secret: *the telltale scars of injecting heroin*

**telltale²** *n* [C] *BrE* a word used by children, meaning a child who tells adults about other children's secrets or bad behaviour; TATTLETALE *AmE*

S3 **tel·ly** /ˈteli/ *n* [C,U] *BrE informal* television: **on telly** *Is there anything good on telly tonight?*

**te·me·ri·ty** /təˈmerəti/ *n* [U] *formal* unreasonable confidence that is likely to offend someone: **have the temerity to do sth** *I was amazed that you had the temerity to ask the question.*

**temp¹** /temp/ *n* [C] an office worker who is only employed temporarily

**temp²** *v* [I] to work as a temp: *Carol's temping until she can find another job.*

**tem·per¹** /ˈtempə‖-ər/ *n*
**1 ► TENDENCY TO BE ANGRY ◄** [C,U] a tendency to become angry suddenly: *That temper of hers will get her into trouble one of these days.* | *If he can't control his temper, he should give up teaching.* | **quick/fiery/violent temper** *Be careful, he's got a pretty voilent temper.* | **tempers become frayed** (=people become angry) *Tempers were becoming frayed as the day went on.*
**2 ► SHORT ANGRY FEELING ◄** [singular, U] an uncontrolled feeling of anger that lasts for a short time: **be in a temper** *It's no use talking to him when he's in a temper.* | **be in a foul/awful temper** (=be angry) | **a fit of temper** (=a quick expression of anger) *Pete hit his brother in a fit of temper.* | **fly into a temper** (=suddenly become very angry) | **temper tantrum** (=sudden angry behaviour like that of a small child)
**3 lose your temper** to suddenly become so angry that you cannot control yourself: *"Stop it," Helen shouted at the children, trying not to lose her temper.*
**4 keep your temper** to stay calm when it would be easy to get angry: *I was finding it increasingly difficult to keep my temper.*
**5 good-tempered/foul tempered etc** having a good, bad temper etc
**6 temper! temper!** *spoken* used humorously to tell someone not to get angry
**7 ► ATTITUDE ◄** [singular] *formal* the general attitude that people have in a particular place at one time: [+ **of**] *the temper of life in Renaissance Italy* —see also BAD-TEMPERED, EVEN-TEMPERED, ILL-TEMPERED

**temper²** *v* [T] **1** to make metal as hard as is needed by heating it and then putting it in cold water: *tempered steel* **2** *formal* to make something difficult or unpleasant more acceptable or pleasant

**tem·pe·ra** /ˈtempərə/ *n* [U] a method of painting in which the colour is mixed with a thick liquid such as egg

**tem·pe·ra·ment** /ˈtempərəmənt/ *n* [C,U] the emotional part of someone's character, especially how likely they are to be happy, angry etc; DISPOSITION (1): *a sunny temperament*

**tem·pe·ra·men·tal** /ˌtempərəˈmentl◂/ *adj* **1** likely to suddenly become upset, excited, or angry: *It's difficult to work for someone who's so temperamental.* **2** a machine, system etc that is temperamental does not always work properly **3** related to the emotional part of someone's character: *serious temperamental differences between the couple* —**temperamentally** *adv*

**tem·pe·rance** /ˈtempərəns/ *n* [U] **1** the practice of never drinking alcohol for moral or religious reasons: *the Victorian virtues of thrift, temperance, and hard work* **2** *formal* sensible control of the things you say and do, especially the amount of alcohol you drink

**tem·pe·rate** /ˈtempərət/ *adj* **1 temperate climate/region** a type of weather or a part of the world that is never very hot or very cold: *the temperate zone, north and south of the tropics* **2** *formal* behaviour that is temperate is calm and sensible —see also INTEMPERATE (1)

**tem·pe·ra·ture** /ˈtempərətʃə‖-ər/ *n* **1** [singular] a measure of how hot or cold a place or thing is: *The temperature of the water was just right for swimming.* | **a temperature of 20°/100° etc** *Water boils at a temperature of 100°C.* | **the temperature rises/goes up** (=it gets hotter) | **high/low temperatures** *a material that can withstand high temperatures* | **rise/fall etc in temperature** *a gradual rise in ocean temperatures* | **room temperature** (=normal, comfortable temperature of a room) *Let the mixture cool to room temperature.* | **air/water/body temperature** *You mustn't let the body temperature drop too low.* | **the temperature falls/drops etc** (=it gets colder) *The temperature in New York dropped to minus 10° last night.* | **temperature change** *a great temperature change from last week* | **constant temperature** (=a temperature that does not change) *The refrigerator keeps your food at a constant temperature.* **2 sb's temperature** the temperature of your blood: **take sb's temperature** (=measure their temperature) *The nurse took my temperature.* | **have/run a temperature** (=have a temperature that is higher than normal) *Susie has a temperature and has*

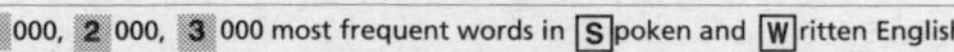

*gone to bed.* **3** [C] the temperature of a situation is the way people are reacting, for example whether they are behaving angrily or calmly: *Be careful what you say, the temperature's a bit hot in there.*

This graph shows some of the words most commonly used with the noun **temperature**.

| Phrase | Frequency (per million) |
|---|---|
| the temperature rises | ~7 |
| high temperature | ~5.7 |
| low temperature | ~4 |
| rise/fall etc in temperature | ~3.8 |
| room temperature | ~2.8 |
| air/water/body temperature | ~2.6 |
| the temperature falls/drops | ~2.5 |
| temperature change | ~1.8 |

2 4 6 8 10 per million

Based on the British National Corpus and the Longman Lancaster Corpus

**tem·pest** /ˈtempɪ̈st/ *n* [C] *literary* a violent storm

**tem·pes·tu·ous** /temˈpestʃuəs/ *adj* **1** a tempestuous relationship or period of time includes many strong emotions: *a tempestuous marriage* **2** *literary* a tempestuous sea or wind is very rough and violent; STORMY: *lost in the dark tempestuous night* —**tempestuously** *adv* **tempestuousness** *n* [U]

**tem·plate** /ˈtempleɪt, -plɪ̈t/ *n* [C] **1** a thin sheet of plastic or metal in a special shape or pattern used to help cut other materials in a similar shape **2** *technical* a system for arranging information on a computer screen

**tem·ple** /ˈtempəl/ *n* [C] **1** a building where people go to WORSHIP[1] (1), in the Hindu, Buddhist, Sikh, Mormon, or modern Jewish religions **2** [usually plural] one of the two fairly flat areas on each side of your forehead —see picture at HEAD[1]

**tem·po** /ˈtempəʊ‖-poʊ/ *n* [C] **1** the speed at which music is played or should be played **2** the speed at which something happens; PACE: *the easy tempo of island life*

**tem·po·ral** /ˈtempərəl/ *adj formal* **1** related to or limited by time: *the temporal character of human existence* **2** related to practical instead of religious affairs: *The Church has no temporal power in the modern state.*

S2 W3 **tem·po·ra·ry** /ˈtempərəri, -pəri‖-pəreri/ *adj* **1** lasting for only a limited period of time: *A lot of work now is temporary or part-time.* | *The accident caused a temporary disability.* **2** intended to be used for only a limited period of time: *The council have placed us in temporary accommodation.* —compare PERMANENT[1], PROVISIONAL[1] —**temporariness** *n* [U] —**temporarily** /ˈtempərərɪ̈li‖ˌtempəˈrerɪ̈li/ *adv* | *The library is temporarily closed for repairs.*

**tem·po·rize** also **-ise** *BrE* /ˈtempəraɪz/ *v* [I] *formal* to delay or avoid making a decision in order to gain time

S3 **tempt** /tempt/ *v* [T] **1** to make someone want to have or do something, even though they know they really should not: *If you leave valuables in your car it will tempt thieves.* | **be tempted** *I'm tempted to buy that dress even though it's expensive.* **2** to try to persuade someone to do something by making it seem attractive: **tempt sb into doing sth** *The ads hope to tempt people into buying their brand of coffee.* | **tempt sb to do sth** *free gifts to tempt people to join* **3 tempt fate/providence a)** to do something that involves unnecessary risk and may cause serious problems **b)** to say too confidently that something will have a good result, that there will be no problems etc

**temp·ta·tion** /tempˈteɪʃən/ *n* **1** [C,U] a strong desire to have or do something even though you know you should not: **temptation to do sth** *There might be a temptation to cheat if students sit too close together.* | **resist/overcome (the) temptation** (=not do something, even though you want to) | **give in to (the) temptation** (=do something although you know you should not) *I finally gave in to the temptation and had a cigarette.* **2** [C,U] something that makes you want to have or do something, even though you know you should not: *Having candy in the house is a great temptation!*

**temp·ting** /ˈtemptɪŋ/ *adj* something that is tempting seems very good and you would like to have it or do it: *a tempting job offer* | *That pie looks tempting!* | **it is tempting to do sth** *It's tempting to just ignore her when she's this upset.* —**temptingly** *adv*

**temp·tress** /ˈtemptrɪ̈s/ *n* [C] *old-fashioned* a woman who makes a man want to have sex with her

**tem·pus fu·git** /ˌtempəs ˈfjuːdʒɪ̈t/ *Latin* a phrase meaning 'time flies'; used to say that time passes very quickly

**ten** /ten/ *number* **1** 10 —see table on page B2 **2 ten to one** *informal* used to say that something is very likely: *Ten to one he'll have forgotten all about it tomorrow.* **3 be ten a penny** *BrE informal* to be very common and therefore not special or unusual —see also **a dime a dozen** (DIME (2)) **4 ten out of ten** *BrE* used in schools to give a perfect mark, or humorously to praise someone: *You get ten out of ten for effort, Simon.* —**tenth** *number*

**ten·a·ble** /ˈtenəbəl/ *adj* **1** a belief, argument etc that is tenable is reasonable and can be defended successfully —opposite UNTENABLE **2 be tenable for** a job or position that is tenable for a particular length of time will continue for that length of time

**te·na·cious** /tɪ̈ˈneɪʃəs/ *adj* determined to do something and unwilling to stop trying even when the situation becomes difficult —**tenaciously** *adv* —**tenaciousness or tenacity** /tɪ̈ˈnæsɪ̈ti/ *n* [U]

**ten·an·cy** /ˈtenənsi/ *n* **1** [C] the period of time that someone rents a house, land etc: *a six-month tenancy* **2** [C,U] the right to use a house, land etc that is rented

**ten·ant** /ˈtenənt/ *n* [C] someone who lives in a house, room etc and pays rent to the person who owns it S3 W2

**tenant farm·er** /ˌ·· ˈ··/ *n* [C] someone who farms land that is rented from someone else

**ten·ant·ry** /ˈtenəntri/ *n* **the tenantry** *old use* all the farmers who rent land from the same person in one place

**tend** /tend/ *v*

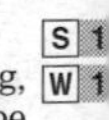

**1 tend to do sth** to often do a particular thing, especially something that is bad or annoying, and to be likely to do it again: *Sally tends to interfere in other people's business.* | *The car does tend to overheat.*

**2 tend towards sth** to have a particular quality or feature more than others: *Charles tends towards obesity.*

**3 tend bar** *especially AmE* to serve customers in a store, bar etc: *Theresa tends bar at the Irish Lion.*

**4 ▶ LOOK AFTER ◀** also **tend to** [T] *old-fashioned* to look after someone or something: *a shepherd tending sheep on the hillside*

**5 ▶ MOVE/DEVELOP ◀** [I always + adv/prep] *formal* to move or develop in a particular direction: [+ **upwards/downwards**] *Interest rates are tending upwards.*

**ten·den·cy** /ˈtendənsi/ *n* [C] **1** a PROBABILITY that you will develop, think or behave in a certain way: [+ **to/towards**] *Some people may inherit a tendency to alcoholism.* | **have a tendency to do sth** (=often do something and be more likely to do it than other people) *Jean's nice but she has a tendency to talk too much.* **2 artistic/alcoholic etc tendencies** particular skills, weaknesses or desires that make someone behave in a particular way: *kids with criminal tendencies* **3** a general change or development in a particular direction: [+ **for**] *We've noticed a growing tendency for people to work at*

*home instead of in offices.* | [+ **to/towards**] *There has been a general tendency towards conservation and recycling.* **4** [also + plural verb *BrE*] a group within a political party that supports ideas that are usually more extreme than those of the main party: *the growing fascist tendency*

**ten·den·tious** /tenˈdenʃəs/ *adj* a tendentious speech, remark, book etc expresses a strong opinion that is intended to influence people

**ten·der¹** /ˈtendə‖-ər/ *adj*
**1** ▶ **MEAT/VEGETABLES** ◀ easy to cut and eat, especially because they have been well cooked: *tender beef* —opposite TOUGH
**2** ▶ **PART OF YOUR BODY** ◀ a tender part of your body is painful if someone touches it: *My arm is still tender where I bruised it.*
**3** ▶ **GENTLE** ◀ gentle and careful in a way that shows love: *Sam's voice was full of tender concern.* | *a tender look*
**4 tender loving care** *usually spoken* sympathetic treatment and a lot of attention
**5 tender blossoms/plants etc** plants etc that are easily damaged
**6 tender age** *humorous or literary* the time when you are young or inexperienced: *I don't know that your jokes are suitable for someone of my tender age!* | **at the tender age of** *Nicholas was sent to boarding school at the tender age of seven.* —**tenderly** *adv* —**tenderness** *n* [U]

**tender²** *n* [C] **1** a formal statement of the price you would charge for doing a job or providing goods or services: **put sth out to tender** (=ask for statements of the price for doing a particular job) **2** a small boat that takes people or supplies between the shore and a larger boat **3** part of a steam train used for carrying coal and water for the train —see also BARTENDER, LEGAL TENDER

**tender³** *v* **1** [I] to make a formal offer to do a job or provide goods and services at a particular price: [+ **for**] *tendering for a road building contract* **2** [T] *formal* to give or show something to someone: *tender a proposal* | **tender your resignation** (=officially say that you are going to leave your job) **3** [T] *old-fashioned* to give money as a payment

**ten·der·foot** /ˈtendəfʊt‖-ər-/ *n* [C] *AmE informal* **1** someone who has just arrived at a place where life is much harder than they are used to **2** an inexperienced beginner: *a political tenderfoot*

**tender-heart·ed** /ˌ·· ˈ··◂/ *adj* very kind and gentle: *She was too tender-hearted to refuse.* —**tender-heartedly** *adv* —**tenderheartedness** *n* [U]

**ten·der·ize** also **-ise** *BrE* /ˈtendəraɪz/ *v* [T] to make meat softer and easier to eat by preparing it in a special way

**ten·der·loin** /ˈtendəlɔɪn‖-ər-/ *n* [U] meat that is soft and easy to eat, cut from each side of the backbone of cows or pigs: *pork tenderloin*

**ten·don** /ˈtendən/ *n* [C] a thick strong string-like part of your body that connects a muscle to a bone

**ten·dril** /ˈtendrɪl/ *n* [C] **1** a thin leafless curling stem by which a climbing plant fastens itself to a support **2** a thin curling piece of hair: *Ralph pushed the damp tendrils of hair out of his eyes.*

**ten·e·ment** /ˈtenɪmənt/ *n* [C] a large building divided into apartments, especially in the poorer areas of a city

**ten·et** /ˈtenɪt/ *n* [C] a principle or belief, especially one that is part of a larger system of beliefs: *the tenets of Buddhism*

**ten·fold** /ˈtenfəʊld‖-foʊld/ *adj, adv* ten times as much or as many of something: *Company turnover has risen tenfold to $550 million.*

**ten-gal·lon hat** /ˌ· ·· ˈ·/ *n* [C] a tall hat made of soft material with a wide BRIM, worn especially by COWBOYS

**ten·ner** /ˈtenə‖-ər/ *n* [C] *BrE informal* £10 or a ten-pound note: *Can you lend me a tenner?*

**tennis**

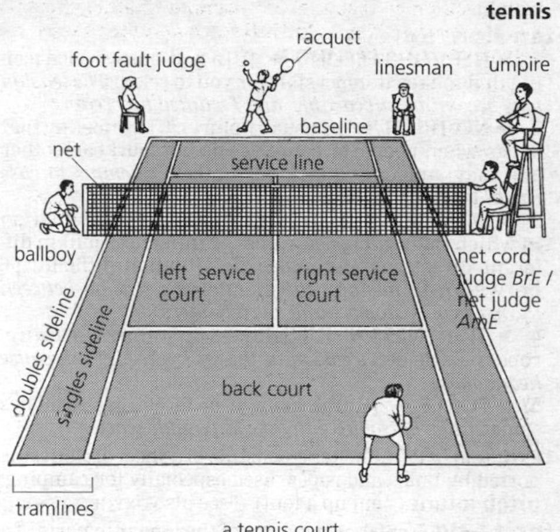


a tennis court

**ten·nis** /ˈtenɪs/ *n* [U] a game for two people or two pairs of people who use rackets (RACKET¹ (3)) to hit a small soft ball backwards and forwards over a net S3 W3

**tennis court** /ˈ·· ·/ *n* [C] the four-sided area that you play tennis on

**tennis el·bow** /ˌ·· ˈ··/ *n* [U] a medical problem in which your elbow is very painful

**tennis shoe** /ˈ·· ·/ *n* [C] a strong shoe used for sports

**ten·on** /ˈtenən/ *n* [C] an end of a piece of wood, that has been cut to fit exactly into a MORTISE in order to form a strong joint

**ten·or** /ˈtenə‖-ər/ *n* **1** [C] a man with a singing voice that can reach the range of notes just below the lowest woman's voice: *the famous tenor, Luciano Pavarotti* **2** [singular] the part of a piece of music this person sings: *Can you sing the tenor?* **3** [C] a musical instrument with the same range of notes as the singer **4 the tenor of a)** *formal* the general way in which an event or process takes place: *The general tenor of the debate was stressful.* **b)** the general meaning of something written or spoken: *the theological tenor of his speech*

**ten·pin** /ˈtenˌpɪn/ *n* [C] one of the ten bottle-shaped wooden objects that you try to knock down in BOWLING (1)

**tenpin bowl·ing** /ˌ·· ˈ··/ *n* [U] *BrE* an indoor sport in which you roll a heavy ball along a floor to knock down bottle-shaped wooden objects; BOWLING *AmE*

**tense¹** /tens/ *adj* **1** feeling very nervous and worried because of something bad that might happen: *The robbers were tense as they waited the long minutes for the van to arrive.* | **tense moment/atmosphere etc** *Marion spoke, eager to break the tense silence.* **2** unable to relax your body or part of your body because your muscles feel tight: *Massage is great if your neck and back are tense.* —see also TENSION —**tensely** *adv* —**tenseness** *n* [U]

**tense²** *v* [I,T] also **tense up** to make your muscles tight and stiff, or to become tight and stiff: *Relax, and try not to tense up so much.* | *She felt how his body tensed with anger.*

**tense³** *n* [C,U] any of the forms of a verb that show the time, continuance or completion of an action or state that is expressed by the verb. 'I am' is in the present tense, 'I was' is past tense, and 'I will be' is future tense

**tensed up** /ˌ· ˈ·/ *adj* [not before noun] *informal* feeling so nervous or worried that you cannot relax: *Why are you so tensed up?*

**ten·sile** /ˈtensaɪl‖ˈtensəl/ *adj* able to be stretched: *tensile rubber*

**tensile strength** /ˌ·· ˈ·/ *n* [U] *technical* the ability of a

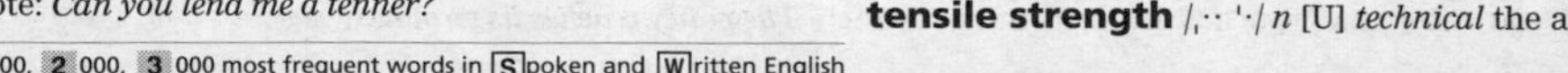

particular kind of steel, CONCRETE[1] etc to bear pressure or weight

S3 W2 **ten·sion** /ˈtenʃən/ *n*
**1 ▶ NERVOUS FEELING ◀** [U] a nervous worried feeling that makes it impossible for you to relax: *The tension was becoming unbearable, and I wanted to scream.*
**2 ▶ NO TRUST ◀** [C usually plural, U] the feeling that exists when people or countries do not trust each other and may suddenly attack each other: *attempts to ease racial tensions in inner cities*
**3 ▶ DIFFERENT INFLUENCES ◀** [singular] a situation in which different needs, forces or influences pull in different directions and make the situation difficult: [+ **between**] *In business there's always a tension between the needs of customers and shareholders.*
**4 ▶ TIGHTNESS ◀** [U] tightness or stiffness in a wire, rope, muscle etc: *Tension in the neck muscles can cause headaches.*
**5 ▶ FORCE ◀** [U] the amount of force that stretches something: *This wire will take 50 pounds tension.*

**tent** /tent/ *n* [C] a shelter consisting of a sheet of cloth supported by poles and ropes, used especially for camping: **pitch a tent** (=put up a tent) —see also OXYGEN TENT

**ten·ta·cle** /ˈtentɪkəl/ *n* [C] one of the long thin parts of a sea creature such as an OCTOPUS, which it uses for holding things —see picture at OCTOPUS

**ten·ta·tive** /ˈtentətɪv/ *adj* **1** not definite or certain, because you may want to change your mind: *We've fixed a tentative date for the meeting.* **2** done without confidence: *a tentative smile* —**tentatively** *adv*: *Albi knocked tentatively and entered.* —**tentativeness** *n* [U]

**ten·ter·hooks** /ˈtentəhʊks‖-ər-/ *n* **be on tenterhooks** to feel nervous and excited because you are waiting for something: *She had been on tenterhooks all night, expecting Joe to return at any moment.*

**tenth**[1] /tenθ/ *n* 10th

**tenth**[2] *n* [C] one of ten equal parts of something

**ten·u·ous** /ˈtenjuəs/ *adj* **1 tenuous link/relationship/evidence** a link etc that seems weak or doubtful: *a tenuous link with my past* **2** *literary* very thin and easily broken —**tenuously** *adv* —**tenuousness** *n* [U]

**ten·ure** /ˈtenjə, -juə‖-jər/ *n* [U] **1** the right to stay permanently in a teaching job at university **2** *formal* the period of time when someone has an important job: *throughout his tenure in office* **3** *law* the legal right to live in a house or use a piece of land for a period of time

**te·pee** /ˈtiːpiː/ *n* [C] a round tent used by Native Americans

**tep·id** /ˈtepɪd/ *adj* **1** tepid liquid is slightly warm, especially in a way that seems unpleasant: *I politely sipped my tepid coffee.* —see picture at HOT[1] **2** a feeling, reaction etc that is tepid shows a lack of excitement or interest: *The critics reaction to the play was tepid* —see also LUKEWARM —**tepidly** *adv* —**tepidness** or **tepidity** /teˈpɪdɪti/ *n* [U]

**te·qui·la** /tɪˈkiːlə/ *n* [C,U] a strong alcoholic drink made in Mexico from the CACTUS plant

**ter·cen·te·na·ry** /ˌtɜːsenˈtiːnəri‖ˌtɜːrsenˈtenəri, tɜːrˈsentneri/ *n* [C] the day or year exactly 300 years after a particular event

S1 W1 **term**[1] /tɜːm‖tɜːrm/ *n* [C]

① ONE WAY OF REGARDING SOMETHING
② WORDS/LANGUAGE
③ PERIOD OF TIME
④ CONDITIONS/AGREEMENT
⑤ RELATIONSHIP
⑥ OTHER SENSES

### ① ONE WAY OF REGARDING SOMETHING

**1 in financial/artistic/psychological etc terms** if you describe or consider something in financial etc terms, you are mainly interested in the financial etc side of it: *In artistic terms, the film was revolutionary.|the enormous cost of war, in human terms*
**2 in terms of** if you explain or judge something in terms of a particular fact or event, you are only interested in its connection with that fact or event: *US foreign policy tended to see everything in terms of the Vietnam war.|In terms of customer satisfaction, the policy cannot be criticized.*
**3 in sb's terms** according to one person's set of opinions: *In their terms, cutting government spending is the most important thing.*
**4 in real terms** a change of a price or cost in real terms has been calculated to include the effects of other changes such as price rises: *Our wages have gone down in real terms over the past year.*

### ② WORDS/LANGUAGE

**5 ▶ WORD/EXPRESSION ◀** [C] a word or expression that has a particular meaning, especially in a technical or scientific subject: **medical/legal/scientific term** *Contusion is the medical term for a bruise.*
**6 a term of abuse/endearment etc** a word or expression used to insult someone, say you love them etc: *To an islander, tourist was just about the worst term of abuse.*
**7 in glowing terms/in strong terms** if you describe something in glowing terms or say something in strong terms, you show that you admire something very much or that you are very angry: *I complained to the manager in the strongest possible terms.*
**8 in no uncertain terms** in a clear and usually angry way: *He told me in no uncertain terms not to park near his house.* —see also **a contradiction in terms** (CONTRADICTION (3))

### ③ PERIOD OF TIME

**9 ▶ SCHOOL/UNIVERSITY ◀** [C] *BrE* one of the three periods that the school or university year is divided into: **summer/autumn/spring term** *The main exams are at the end of the summer term*|**term time** (=during the term) *Teachers often feel overworked in term time.* —see also HALF-TERM —compare SEMESTER
**10 in the long/short/medium term** considered over a period from now until a long etc time in the future: *The company's prospects look good in the long term.*
**11 ▶ TIME IN A JOB ◀** [C] a period of time for which someone is elected to an important government job, or that a government has power: **term of office/term in office** *The president hopes to be elected to a second term of office.*
**12 prison/jail term etc** a period of time that someone must spend in prison: *The terrorists each received a 30 year prison term.*
**13 ▶ BUSINESS ◀** [singular] the period of time that a contract, LOAN[1] (1) etc continues for: *We're trying to extend the term on our mortgage.*
**14 ▶ END OF BUSINESS AGREEMENT ◀** [singular] *technical* the end of the period of a business agreement: *The policy reaches its term next year.*

**15 ▶ HAVING A BABY ◀** [U] *technical* the end of the period of time when a woman is PREGNANT —see also LONG-TERM, SHORT-TERM

### ④ CONDITIONS/AGREEMENT

**16 ▶ CONDITIONS ◀ terms** [plural] **a)** the conditions of an agreement, contract, or legal document: *Under the terms of the agreement, Hong Kong goes back to China in 1997.* **b)** the conditions under which you agree to buy or sell something: *I bought this car on very reasonable terms.* | **on easy terms** (=a way of paying for something gradually in small amounts)

**17 on your (own) terms** according to the conditions that you ask for: *If I agree to do this it will be on my own terms.*

**18 terms of reference** the agreed limits of what an official committee or report has been asked to study

### ⑤ RELATIONSHIP

**19 be on good/bad terms** to have a friendly relationship or bad relationship with someone: [+ **with**] *We're on good terms with all our neighbours.* | *He had been on bad terms with his father for years.*

**20 be on speaking terms** to be able to talk to someone and have a friendly relationship with them, especially after a quarrel: *They were barely on speaking terms.*

### ⑥ OTHER SENSES

**21 come to terms with sth** to accept an unpleasant situation or event and no longer feel upset or angry about it: *It's hard to come to terms with being unemployed.*

**22 on equal terms/on the same terms** having the same advantages, rights, or abilities as anyone else: *US companies want to be able to compete on equal terms with their overseas rivals.*

**23 be thinking/talking in terms of** to be considering doing something, buying something, arranging something etc: *She's talking in terms of resigning.* | *I was just thinking in terms of a small party.*

**24 ▶ NUMBER/SIGN ◀** [C] *technical* one of the numbers or signs used in a mathematical calculation

**term²** *v* [T usually passive] to use a particular word or expression to name or describe something: **be termed sth** *This condition is sometimes termed RSI, or repetitive strain injury.* | *The meeting could hardly be termed a success.*

**ter·ma·gant** /ˈtɜːməgənt‖ˈtɜːr-/ *n* [C] *literary* a noisy woman who often quarrels with people —**termagant** *adj*

**ter·mi·nal¹** /ˈtɜːmɪ̣nəl‖ˈtɜːr-/ *adj* **1** a terminal illness cannot be cured, and causes death: *terminal cancer* **2 terminal decline/decay** the state of becoming worse and worse and never getting better: *Britain's industrial base seems in a terminal decline.* **3 terminal boredom** *humorous* the feeling of being extremely bored **4** [only before noun] *technical* existing at the end of something: *terminal buds* —**terminally** *adv* | *terminally ill*

**terminal²** *n* [C] **1** a big building where people wait to get onto planes, buses, or ships, or where goods are loaded on: *Terminal 4 at Heathrow airport* **2** a piece of computer equipment consisting of at least a keyboard and a screen, that you use for putting in or taking out information from a large computer **3** one of the points at which you can connect wires in an electrical CIRCUIT

**ter·mi·nate** /ˈtɜːmɪ̣neɪt‖ˈtɜːr-/ *v* [I,T] *formal* if something terminates, or if you terminate it, it ends: *His contract was terminated immediately they found out who he was.*

**ter·mi·na·tion** /ˌtɜːmɪ̣ˈneɪʃən‖ˌtɜːr-/ *n* [C,U] **1** [C] *technical* a medical operation to end the life of a developing child before it is born; ABORTION **2** *formal* the act of ending something, or the end of something: *You may face a reduction or termination of benefits.*

**ter·mi·nol·o·gy** /ˌtɜːmɪ̣ˈnɒlədʒi‖ˌtɜːrmɪ̣ˈnɑː-/ *n* [C,U] the technical words or expressions that are used in a particular subject: *scientific terminology* —**terminological** /ˌtɜːmɪ̣nəˈlɒdʒɪkəl◂‖ˌtɜːmɪ̣nəˈlɑː-/ *adj*

**ter·mi·nus** /ˈtɜːmɪ̣nəs‖ˈtɜːr-/ *n* [C] the station or stop at the end of a railway line or bus service

**ter·mite** /ˈtɜːmaɪt‖ˈtɜːr-/ *n* [C] an insect that eats and destroys wood from trees and buildings

**term·ly** /ˈtɜːmli‖ˈtɜːrm-/ *adj BrE* happening each TERM (=one of the three periods in the school or university year)

**term pa·per** /ˈ· ˌ··/ *n* [C] *AmE* a long piece of written work by a US school or college student, that is the most important piece of work in their course

**tern** /tɜːn‖tɜːrn/ *n* [C] a black and white sea-bird that has long wings and a tail with two points

**ter·race** /ˈterɪ̣s/ *n* [C]
**1 ▶ HOUSES ◀** *especially BrE* a row of houses that are joined to each other, or a street with one of these rows in it: *21 Chestnut Terrace*
**2 ▶ PLACE YOU CAN SIT ◀** an area, especially next to a hotel or restaurant, where people can sit outside to eat or drink
**3 ▶ FOOTBALL ◀ the terraces** [plural] *BrE* the wide steps that the people watching a football match can stand on
**4 ▶ FLAT ROOF ◀** a flat roof used as an outdoor living area
**5 ▶ FLAT LAND ◀** a flat area cut out of a slope, usually one in a series that rise up the slope, that is often used to grow crops

**terraced house** /ˌ·· ˈ·/ *n* [C] *BrE* a house which is part of a row of houses that are joined together; ROW HOUSE *AmE* —see picture on page 410

**ter·ra·cot·ta** /ˌterəˈkɒtə◂‖-ˈkɑː-/ *n* [U] hard reddish-brown baked CLAY: *a terracotta pot*

**ter·ra fir·ma** /ˌterə ˈfɜːmə‖-ˈfɜːr-/ *n* [U] *Latin, usually humorous* land rather than sea or air: *We were glad to be back on terra firma again.*

**ter·rain** /teˈreɪn, tɪ̣-/ *n* [C,U] a word meaning a particular type of land, for example, hilly, rough etc: *rocky terrain*

**ter·ra·pin** /ˈterəpɪ̣n/ *n* [C] a small TURTLE (=animal with four legs and a hard shell) that lives in water in warm areas

**ter·rar·ium** /təˈreəriəm‖-ˈrer-/ *n* [C] a large glass container that you grow plants in as a decoration

**ter·res·tri·al** /tɪ̣ˈrestriəl/ *adj technical* **1** connected with the Earth rather than with the moon or other planets —see also EXTRATERRESTRIAL² **2** living on or connected with land rather than water **3 terrestrial TV/broadcasting/channels etc** TV etc that is broadcast from the earth rather than from SATELLITES (=special equipment in outer space) —**terrestrially** *adv*

**ter·ri·ble** /ˈterɪ̣bəl/ *adj* **1** extremely severe in a way that causes harm or damage: *a terrible accident* | *The poor lad took a terrible beating.* **2** making you feel afraid or shocked: *There was a terrible noise and the roof caved in.* **3** *informal* extremely bad; AWFUL¹ (1): *The hotel was absolutely terrible.* | *I'm a terrible cook.* S1 W3

**ter·ri·bly** /ˈterɪ̣bli/ *adv* **1** [+ adj/adv] *especially BrE* very; extremely: *We were terribly worried.* | *I'm terribly sorry to have kept you waiting.* **2** very badly; severely: *The little boy missed his mother terribly.* S2

**ter·ri·er** /ˈteriə‖-ər/ *n* [C] a small active type of dog that was originally used for hunting

**ter·rif·ic** /təˈrɪfɪk/ *adj* **1** *informal* very good, especially in a way that makes you feel happy and excited: *We had a terrific time on holiday.* | *I feel terrific!* **2** very large in size or degree: *Suddenly, there was a terrific bang!*

**ter·rif·i·cally** /təˈrɪfɪkli/ *adv* [+ adj/adv] *informal* very; extremely: *It's terrifically difficult for working parents to find adequate child care.*

T

**ter·ri·fied** /ˈterɪ̈faɪd/ *adj* very frightened: *a terrified animal* | [+ **of**] *I'm terrified of heights.* | [+ **at**] *Mark was terrified at the thought of parachuting.* | **terrified (that)** *We were both terrified that the bridge would collapse.*

**ter·ri·fy** /ˈterɪ̈faɪ/ *v* [T] to make someone extremely afraid: *Her husband's violence terrified her.*

**ter·ri·fy·ing** /ˈterɪ̈faɪ-ɪŋ/ *adj* extremely frightening: *The hostages suffered a terrifying ordeal.* —**terrifyingly** *adv*

**ter·rine** /teˈriːn,tə-/ *n* [C,U] a dish made of cooked meat, fish etc, formed into a LOAF shape and served cold; PÂTÉ

**ter·ri·to·ri·al¹** /ˌterɪ̈ˈtɔːriəl◂/ *adj* **1** [no comparative] related to land that is owned or controlled by a particular country **2** *technical* territorial animals, birds etc guard the area of land that they consider to be their own —**territoriality** /ˌterɪ̈tɔːriˈælɪ̈ti/ *n* [U]

**territorial²** often **Territorial** *n* [C] a member of the British Territorial Army

**Territorial Ar·my** /ˌ····· ˈ··/ *n* **the Territorial Army** a military force of people in Britain who train as soldiers in their free time; TA —compare NATIONAL GUARD

**territorial wa·ters** /ˌ····· ˈ··/ *n* [plural] the sea near a country's coast, which that country has legal control over

W2 **ter·ri·to·ry** /ˈterɪ̈təri‖-tɔːri/ *n*
**1** ▶ **GOVERNMENT LAND** ◀ [C,U] land that is owned or controlled by a particular government, ruler, or military force: *We crossed the river into enemy territory.*
**2** ▶ **TYPE OF LAND** ◀ [U] land of a particular type: *an expedition through previously unexplored territory*
**3 US Territory** land that belongs to the United States, but is not a state
**4** ▶ **EXPERIENCE** ◀ [U] a particular area of experience or knowledge: *The company is moving into unfamiliar territory with this new software.*
**5** ▶ **ANIMAL** ◀ [C,U] the area that an animal, bird etc regards as its own and will defend against other animals
**6** ▶ **BUSINESS** ◀ [C,U] an area of business, especially in selling, for which someone is responsible: *I'm in charge of the metropolitan Chicago territory.*
**7 come/go with the territory** to be a natural and accepted part of a particular job, situation, place etc: *I'm a cop – so I could get shot – it goes with the territory.*

**ter·ror** /ˈterə‖-ər/ *n*
**1** ▶ **FEAR** ◀ [U] a feeling of extreme fear: *Paul screamed, the terror bursting out of him.* | **in terror** (=very frightened) *The people fled in terror.* | **live in terror of** (=be very frightened of someone or something) *After being bullied, Steven lived in terror of going to school.* | **sheer terror** *There was a look of sheer terror on his face.* | **in terror of your life** (=very frightened that you will be killed)
**2** ▶ **VIOLENT ACTION** ◀ [U] violent action for political purposes; TERRORISM: *The resistance movement started a campaign of terror.*
**3** ▶ **FRIGHTENING SITUATION** ◀ [C] an event or situation that makes people feel extremely frightened, especially because they think they may die: *The hostages suffered untold terror.*
**4** ▶ **PERSON** ◀ [C] *informal* a very annoying person, especially a child: *That Johnson kid's a real terror!*
**5 hold no terrors for sb** *formal* to not frighten or worry someone: *Death held no terrors for me.* —see also **reign of terror** (REIGN¹ (2)), **a holy terror** (HOLY (4)), **strike terror into sb's heart** (STRIKE¹ (21))

**ter·ror·is·m** /ˈterərɪzəm/ *n* [U] the use of violence such as bombing, shooting or KIDNAPPING to obtain political demands: *The government is determined to combat international terrorism.*

**ter·ror·ist** /ˈterərɪ̈st/ *n* [C] someone who uses violence such as bombing, shooting etc to obtain political demands: *Two of the terrorists were shot dead.* | **terrorist attack/activity** *Twenty people were killed in the latest terrorist attack.* —compare GUERRILLA, PARTISAN² (2)

**ter·ror·ize** also **-ise** *BrE* /ˈterəraɪz/ *v* [T] to deliberately frighten people by threatening to harm them, especially so they will do what you want: *Many people have been terrorized into leaving their homes.*

**ter·ry·cloth** /ˈteriklɒθ‖-klɔːθ/ also **ter·ry** /ˈteri/ *n* [U] a type of thick cotton cloth with uncut threads on both sides, used to make TOWELS, bath mats etc —see picture on page 839

**terse** /tɜːs‖tɜːrs/ *adj* a terse reply, message etc uses very few words and often shows that you are annoyed: *Derek's terse reply ended the conversation.* —**tersely** *adv*: *"Continue!" he said tersely.* —**terseness** *n* [U]

**ter·tia·ry** /ˈtɜːʃəri‖ˈtɜːrʃieri, -ʃəri/ *adj technical* third in place, degree, or order

**tertiary ed·u·ca·tion** /ˌ··· ··ˈ··/ *n* [U] *formal* education at a college, university etc; HIGHER EDUCATION

**Te·ry·lene** /ˈterɪ̈liːn/ *n* [U] *BrE trademark* a light strong artificial cloth

**TESL** /ˈtesəl/ *n* [U] the teaching of English as a Second Language

**TESOL** /ˈtesɒl‖-sɑːl/ *n* [U] *especially AmE* the teaching of English to speakers of other languages

**tes·sel·la·ted** /ˈtesɪ̈leɪtɪ̈d/ *adj technical* made of small flat pieces in various shapes and colours that fit together to form a pattern

**test¹** /test/ *n* [C] S1 W1
**1** ▶ **EXAM** ◀ a set of questions, exercises or practical activities to measure someone's skill, ability, or knowledge: **spelling/driving/biology etc test** *How did you do on your maths test?* | **pass/fail a test** *She passed her driving test when she was 17.* | **do/take/sit a test** (=take part in it) *The thought of taking the test terrifies me.* | [+ **on**] *We have a test on irregular verbs tomorrow.* | **test result** *When do you get your test results back?*
**2** ▶ **MEDICAL** ◀ **a)** a short medical examination on a part of your body, or to find out what is wrong with you: *an eye test* | **run a test** (=do one quickly) *We'll just run some tests on your blood sample.* | **test results** *I'm still waiting for my test results from the hospital.* **b)** equipment for carrying out a medical test: *a pregnancy test*
**3** ▶ **FOR CHECKING STH** ◀ a process used to find out whether equipment works correctly, or whether something contains a particular substance: *nuclear weapons tests* | **a test for sth** (=a test to find sth) *a test for chemicals in the water* | **test site/equipment/procedure** *We went to the test site in Nevada.*
**4** ▶ **DIFFICULT SITUATION** ◀ a situation in which the qualities of someone or something are clearly shown: **a test of character/strength etc** *The problems she faced were a real test of character.* | **put sb/sth to the test** (=find out how good someone or something is) *Living together will soon put their relationship to the test.*
**5 stand the test of time** to be good enough, strong enough etc to last for a long time: *Our friendship has stood the test of time.*
**6** ▶ **STANDARD** ◀ something that is used as a standard to judge or examine something else: *It's difficult to know what's a good test of love.* —see also TEST CASE
**7** ▶ **SPORT** ◀ *BrE* the short form of TEST MATCH —see also BREATH TEST, MEANS TEST, SMEAR TEST

This graph shows some of the words most commonly used with the noun **test**.

test of
test for
pass/fail a test
do a test
test on
test result
take/sit a test
2 4 6 8 10 per million

Based on the British National Corpus and the Longman Lancaster Corpus

S3 W2 **test²** *v*
**1 ▶ EXAM ◀** [T] to ask someone spoken or written questions, or make them do a practical activity, to find out what they know about a subject: **test sb on** *We're being tested on grammar tomorrow.* | **test sth** *We'll have to test his knowledge of computers.*
**2 ▶ MEDICAL ◀ a)** [T] to give someone a short medical examination on a part of their body, or to find out what is wrong with them: *I must have my eyes tested.* | **test sb for sth** *I'm going to test you for diabetes.* **b)** to get a particular result when a medical test is done on you: *He tested positive for HIV.*
**3 ▶ MACHINE/PRODUCT ◀** [T] to use something for a short time to see if it works properly: *testing nuclear weapons* | **test sth on sb/sth** (=use something on someone or something to test it) *None of this range of cosmetics has been tested on animals.*
**4 ▶ FIND OUT ◀** [T] to examine something in order to find out something about it: *Test the cake to see if it's done.* | **test sth for sth** *testing ore samples for quality*
**5 ▶ BE DIFFICULT ◀** [T] to be so difficult that all of someone or something's good qualities will be needed to do it: *The next six months will test your powers of leadership.* —see also TESTING
**6 ▶ OIL/GAS ◀** [I,T] to search for oil, gas etc by carrying out tests: [+ **for**] *testing for oil*
**7 test the water** to check people's reaction to a plan before you decide to do anything: *We'll have to test the water before we ban smoking in the staffroom.* —see also **tried and tested** (TRIED²)

**tes·ta·ment** /ˈtestəmənt/ *n* [C] *formal* **1 a testament to sth** something that shows or proves something else very clearly: *The aircraft's safety record is an impressive testament to its designers' skill.* **2** a WILL² (2) —see also NEW TESTAMENT, OLD TESTAMENT —**testamentary** /ˌtestəˈmentəri◂/ *adj*

**test ban** /ˈ· ·/ *n* [C] an agreement between countries to stop testing NUCLEAR WEAPONS

**test card** /ˈ· ·/ *n* [C] a pattern or picture that is shown on television when there are no programmes

**test case** /ˈ· ·/ *n* [C] a legal case that establishes a particular principle and is then used as a standard which other similar cases can be judged against

**test cer·tif·i·cate** /ˈ· ·ˌ···/ *n* [C] *BrE* the official paper that proves that a car is legally safe enough to drive

**test drive** /ˈ· ·/ *n* [C] an occasion when you drive a car to see if it works correctly or if you like it so that you can decide if you want to buy it —**test-drive** *v* [T]

**test·er** /ˈtestə‖-ər/ *n* [C] a small bottle of PERFUME¹ (1) etc, in a shop, for customers to try

**tes·ti·cle** /ˈtestɪkəl/ *n* [C] one of the two round organs that produce SPERM in a male, that are enclosed in a bag of skin behind and below the PENIS

**tes·ti·fy** /ˈtestɪ̆faɪ/ *v* **1** [I,T] to make a formal statement of what is true, especially in a court of law: [+ **that**] *Can you testify that you saw the defendant at the scene of the crime?* | [+ **against**] *It would not be easy to testify against people you know.* | [+ **for**] *Vicky agreed to testify for the accused.* **2** [I,T] *formal* to be a clear sign that something is true: [+ **to**] *Mrs Parson's nervous behaviour testified to the strain she was under.* **3** [I] *AmE* to stand up and tell people about how God has helped you in your life

**tes·ti·mo·ni·al** /ˌtestɪ̆ˈməuniəl‖-ˈmou-/ *n* [C] **1** a formal written statement describing someone's character and abilities —see also REFERENCE (4) **2** something that is given or done to someone to show thanks, praise, or admiration: *a testimonial dinner*

**tes·ti·mo·ny** /ˈtestɪ̆məni‖-mouni/ *n* [C,U] **1** a formal statement that something is true, such as the one a WITNESS makes in a court of law: *Barker's testimony is crucial to the prosecution's case.* **2** a fact or situation that shows or proves something very clearly: [+ **to/of**] *These results are a testimony to your hard work.*

**test·ing** /ˈtestɪŋ/ *adj* a testing situation, experience etc is difficult to deal with: *a testing time in their relationship*

**testing ground** /ˈ··· ·/ *n* [C] **1** a place where machines, cars etc are tried to see if they work properly **2** a situation or problem in which you can try new ideas and methods to see if they work: *Eastern Europe has become a testing ground for high-speed privatization.*

**tes·tis** /ˈtestɪ̆s/ *n plural* **testes** /-tiːz/ [C] *technical* a TESTICLE

**test match** /ˈ· ·/ *n* [C] a CRICKET (2) or RUGBY match that is played between the teams of different countries

**tes·tos·ter·one** /teˈstɒstərəun‖-ˈstɑːstəroun/ *n* [U] the chemical in males that gives them their male qualities

**test pi·lot** /ˈ· ˌ··/ *n* [C] a pilot who flies new aircraft in order to test them

**test tube** /ˈ· ·/ *n* [C] a small glass container that is shaped like a tube and is used in chemistry —see picture at LABORATORY

**test-tube ba·by** /ˈ· · ˌ··/ *n* [C] *not technical* **1** a baby born as a result of ARTIFICIAL INSEMINATION **2** a baby that started to develop from an egg removed from a woman's body and was then put back inside the woman to continue developing

**tes·ty** /ˈtesti/ *adj* impatient and easily annoyed; IRRITABLE: *a testy old man* | *testy remarks* —**testily** *adv*: *"You can't!" Ralph interrupted him testily.* —**testiness** *n* [U]

**tet·a·nus** /ˈtetənəs/ *n* [U] a serious illness caused by BACTERIA that enter your body through cuts and wounds and make your muscles, especially your jaw, go stiff; LOCKJAW

**tetched** /tetʃt/ *adj AmE spoken* slightly crazy

**tetch·y** /ˈtetʃi/ *adj* likely to get angry or upset easily: *Jane's a bit tetchy this morning, watch what you say to her.* —**tetchily** *adv* —**tetchiness** *n* [U]

**tête-à-tête¹** /ˌteɪt ɑː ˈteɪt, ˌteɪt ə-/ *n* [C] *French* a private conversation between two people: *have a cosy tête-à-tête*

**tête-à-tête²** *adv* [only after verb] *French* if two people meet, speak, or eat tête-à-tête they are together in private

**teth·er¹** /ˈteðə‖-ər/ *n* [C] **1** a rope or chain that an animal is tied to so that it can only move around within a limited area **2 be at the end of your tether** to be so worried, tired etc, that you feel you can no longer deal with a difficult or upsetting situation: *Morel was at the end of his tether, too exasperated to answer.*

**tether²** *v* [T] to tie an animal to a post so that it can only move around within a limited area

**tetra-** /tetrə/ *prefix* having four of something: *a tetrahedron* (=solid shape with four sides)

**Teu·ton·ic** /tjuːˈtɒnɪk‖tuːˈtɑː-/ *adj* **1** *humorous* having qualities that are thought to be typical of German people: *Teutonic efficiency* **2** connected with the ancient German peoples of northwestern Europe

**Tex-mex** /ˈteks meks/ *adj AmE informal* connected with the music, cooking etc of Mexican-American people: *a Tex-Mex restaurant*

**text** /tekst/ *n* **1** [U] the writing that forms the main part of a book, magazine etc rather than the pictures or notes: *There ought not to be too much text in children's books.* **2** [U] any written material: *One disk can store the equivalent of 500 pages of text.* **3 the text of sth** the exact words of a speech, article etc: *Only 'The Times' printed the full text of the President's speech.* **4** [C] a book or other piece of writing that is connected with learning or intended for study: **a set text** (=a book that must be studied for an examination) *'Hamlet' is a set text for this year's English exam.* **5** [C] a short piece from the Bible that someone reads and talks about S2 W1

**text·book¹** /ˈtekstbuk/ *n* [C] a book that contains information about a subject that people study: *a biology textbook* —see also COURSEBOOK

T

**textbook²** *adj* [only before noun] done or happening exactly as something should be done or as it should happen: *That shot of Becker's was superb – textbook stuff.* | **textbook case/example** *The advertising campaign was a textbook example of how to sell a product.*

**tex·tile** /ˈtekstaɪl/ *n* [C] **1** a word used mainly in business for woven material that is made in large quantities: *Their main exports are textiles, especially silk and cotton.* | **textile industry/market etc** *a textile factory* **2 textiles** *plural* the industry involved in making cloth

**tex·tu·al** /ˈtekstʃuəl/ *adj* concerning the way that a book, magazine etc is written: *a detailed textual analysis*

**tex·ture** /ˈtekstʃə‖-ər/ *n* [C,U] **1** the way a surface, substance, or material feels when you touch it, especially how smooth or rough it is: *the smooth texture of silk* | *a soil with a loose sandy texture* **2** *literary* the way the different parts are combined in a piece of writing, music, art etc in order to make a particular impression on you; CHARACTER (2): *the rich texture of Shakespeare's English* —**textural** *adj* —**texturally** *adv*

**tex·tured** /ˈtekstʃəd‖-ərd/ *adj* **1** having a surface that is not smooth: *textured wallpaper* **2 coarse-textured/smooth-textured/fine-textured etc** having a texture that is smooth etc: *heart-shaped, rough-textured leaves*

**textured vege·ta·ble pro·tein** /ˌ‥ ˌ‥‥ ˈ‥/ *n* [U] a substance made from beans, used instead of meat; TVP

**-th** /θ/ *suffix* **1** forms ORDINAL numbers, except with 1, 2, or 3: *the 17th of June* | *a fifth of the total* —see also -ND, -RD, -ST **2** *old use or biblical* another form of the suffix -ETH: *he doth* (=does)

**Tha·lid·o·mide** /θəˈlɪdəmaɪd/ *n* [U] *trademark* a drug given to people to make them calm, until it was discovered that it harmed the development of the arms and legs of unborn babies

S1 W1 **than¹** /ðən; *strong* ðæn/ *conjunction* **1 higher than/cheaper than etc** used when comparing two things that are different to introduce the second thing: *The cost of the repairs was a lot cheaper than I thought.* **2 would rather/would sooner...than...** used to say that you prefer one thing to another: *If it's alright by you I'd rather walk than go by car.* **3 hardly/scarcely/no sooner etc ...than...** used to say that something had only just happened when something else happened: *No sooner had I mailed the letter than I realized she'd changed address.* **4** *informal* except: *They left me with no option other than to resign.*

S1 W1 **than²** *prep* **1 higher/more expensive than** used when comparing two things that are different to introduce the second thing: *Miranda has always been more intelligent than her two brothers.* | *Richard's marrying a woman who's older than his own mother.* | *The new tax system will definitely affect some people more than others.* **2 more/less/fewer etc than** used when comparing two different amounts, numbers etc to introduce the second amount or number: *The programme doesn't last any longer than an hour.* | *He's been unemployed for more than 18 months now.* | *It's a beautiful dress but it's much more than I can afford.*

**thane** /θeɪn/ *n* [C] a man who fought for the King but was below the rank of a KNIGHT¹ (1) in early English history

S1 W2 **thank** /θæŋk/ *v* [T] **1** to tell someone that you are pleased and grateful for something they have done, or to be polite about it: *Remember to thank Uncle Robin when you see him.* | **thank sb for** *Meg and Jo ran to thank their aunt for the presents.* | **thank sb for doing sth** *I must write and thank him for sending the cheque.* **2 thank God/goodness/heavens** used to show that you are very glad about something: *Thank God that's over! I've never been so nervous in my life!* | [+ **for**] *"Your son is safe!" "Thank heavens for that!"* —see GOD (USAGE) **3 have sb to thank (for sth)** used when saying who is responsible for something helpful or, humorously, who is responsible for something unhelpful: *I have Phil to thank for getting me my first job.* | *And who do I have to thank for that mess on my desk?* **4 only have yourself to thank (for sth)** *spoken* used to say that you are responsible for something bad that has happened to you: *She has only herself to thank if she doesn't have any friends.* **5 sb won't thank you (for doing something)** used to tell someone that another person will be annoyed because of what they have done: *I know you're just trying to help, but he won't thank you for telling him how to do it.* **6 thank your lucky stars** *spoken* used to tell someone that they are very lucky, especially because they have avoided an unpleasant or dangerous situation: *You should thank your lucky stars I got here when I did!* **7 you'll thank me** *spoken* used to tell someone not to be annoyed with you for doing or saying something, because it will be helpful to them later: *You'll thank me for this one day, Laura.* **8 I'll thank you to do sth** *spoken formal* used to tell someone in an angry way not to do something because it is annoying you: *I'll thank you to mind your own business.* —see also THANK YOU

**thank·ful** /ˈθæŋkfəl/ *adj* [not before noun] grateful and glad about something that has happened, especially because without it the situation would be much worse: [+ **for**] *I'll be thankful for a good night's sleep after the week I've had.* | **thankful (that)** *You should be thankful that you have me to look after you.* | **thankful to do sth** *I was thankful to make any sort of progress at all.* —see also **be thankful for small mercies** (MERCY (5)), —**thankfulness** *n* [U]

**thank·ful·ly** /ˈθæŋkfəli/ *adv* **1** [sentence adverb] used to say that you are glad that something has happened, especially because a difficult situation has ended or been avoided: *Thankfully, I managed to pay off all my debts before we got married.* **2** feeling grateful and glad about something, especially because a difficult situation has ended or been avoided: *We came in and collapsed thankfully onto our beds.*

**thank·less** /ˈθæŋkləs/ *adj* **1** a thankless job is difficult and you do not get any praise for doing it: **a thankless task** *Cooking for the family every day is a thankless task.* **2** *literary* a thankless person is not grateful: *a thankless child* —**thanklessly** *adv*

**thanks¹** /θæŋks/ *interjection* **1** used to tell someone that you are grateful for something they have given you or done for you; THANK YOU: *"Pass the salt, please ... thanks."* | **thanks for (doing) sth** *I'd love to go to the party. Thanks for asking me.* | *Thanks for the ride home – see you tomorrow!* | **thanks a lot** *informal*: *Thanks a lot for the drink.* | **many thanks** (=often used in a formal business letter) *Dear Mr Williams, Many thanks for the articles you sent me last week.* **2** used as a polite way of accepting something that someone has offered you: *"Do you want another cup of coffee?" "Oh, thanks."* **3 fine thanks** *spoken* used when politely answering someone's question: *"Hi, Bill, how are you?" "Fine, thanks."* **4 no thanks** used to say politely that you do not want something: *"How about some cake?" "Oh, no thanks, I'm on a diet."* S1 W2

**thanks²** *n* [plural] **1** the things you say or do to show that you are grateful to someone: *Joe got up and left without a word of thanks.* **2 thanks to a)** used to say that someone has done something very helpful or useful: *Thanks to Germaine's tireless efforts, the concert was a huge success.* —see OWING (USAGE) **b)** used to say, angrily or humorously that someone has caused a problem: *It was supposed to be a surprise, but thanks to your big mouth she knows all about it now.* **c)** used to say that something good is caused by something else: *Thanks to the warm Autumn, our fuel bills have been very low.* **3 no thanks to** *spoken* an expression meaning 'in spite of', used when someone should have helped you but did not: *It was no thanks to you that we managed to win the game.* —see also VOTE OF THANKS

**Thanks·giv·ing** /ˌθæŋksˈgɪvɪŋ◂/ *n* [U] a public holiday in the US in November, when families have a large meal together and celebrate the origins of their country

**thanksgiving** *n* [C,U] an expression of thanks to God

**thank you** /ˈ· ·/ *interjection* **1** used to tell someone that you are grateful for something they have given you or done for you; THANKS: *Margaret handed him the butter. "Thank you," said Samuel.* | *Thank you very much, Brian.* | **thank you for (doing) sth** *It's good to see you, Mr. Mathias. Thank you for coming.* | *Dear Grandma, thank you for the lovely shirt you sent for me Christmas.* **2** used as a polite way of saying that you would like something that someone has offered: *"Can I give you a lift into town?" "Oh, thank you."* **3** used when politely answering someone's question: *"How was your trip to Paris?" "Very pleasant, thank you."* **4 no thank you** used to say politely that you do not want something: *"Would you like some more coffee?" "No, thank you, I'm fine."* **5** used at the end of a sentence when telling someone firmly that you do not want their help or advice and are slightly annoyed by it: *I can manage quite well on my own, thank you!*

**thank-you**[1] *adj* **thank-you letter/note/card etc** a short letter etc in which you thank someone

**thank-you**[2] *n* [C] something you say or do in order to thank someone: *This present's a thank-you for helping me last week.*

S1 W1 **that**[1] /ðæt/ *determiner plural* **those** /ðəʊz‖ðoʊz/ **1** used to talk about a person, thing, idea etc that has already been mentioned or that the person you are talking to knows about already: *Who was that man I saw you with last night?* | *Those flowers that you gave me lasted over a week.* | *Later that day the news was being broadcast all over the world.* | *How much is that hat in the window?* | *The lawyer was expensive, but at that stage we wanted to make sure everything went smoothly.* **2** used to talk about the person or thing that is farthest from you, or the situation that is not happening at the moment: *That party of hers was great but this one will be even better.* | *So many cakes to choose from – I'll take that one over there.* | *Look at those men in that car. What on earth are they doing?*

S1 W1 **that**[2] *pron plural* **those** **1** used to talk about a person, thing, idea etc that has already been mentioned or that the person you are talking to already knows about: *Pregnant! Who told you that?* | *Where did you get those? I've been looking for some shoes just like that.* | *So that's why you don't like him.* | *I wish you wouldn't say things like that.* | **with that** (=after doing that) *She slammed the book on the table and with that ran out of the room.* **2** used to talk about the person or thing that is farthest from you, the situation that is not happening at the moment etc: *No, that's your desk, this one's mine.* | *Those were great years at college, but I think that I'm even happier now.* **3** *formal* used when talking about a particular person or thing, especially one which is a particular type or kind: *In my opinion the finest wines are those from France.* | **that of** *Rupert's manner was that of someone accustomed to mixing with aristocracy.* **4 that's life/men/politics etc** *spoken* used to say that someone's actions are typical of a particular group of people, situation etc: *"I washed all my clothes only to find I'd left a £20 note in the pocket." "That's life I suppose."* | *We go out for a romantic meal and all he wants to do is talk about football. That's men for you.* **5 at that** *especially spoken* used to give more information, about something mentioned before: *He'll have to buy a new car and a big one at that. There are 8 children in his family.* **6 and (all) that** *BrE spoken* and similar people or things: *There were lots of sandwiches and pies and that but I wasn't really hungry.* **7 that is (to say)** *spoken* used to correct something that you have just said or written: *I know how to operate a computer. That is, I thought I did until I saw this one.* **8 that's a clever dog/that's a good girl** *spoken* used to praise children or animals: *You've eaten all your supper – that's a good boy!* **9 that's it** *spoken* used when you are angry about a situation and you do not want it to continue: *That's it. I'm not taking any more. You can keep your rotten job.* **10 that's that** *spoken* used to say you will not change a decision: *I refuse to go and that's that!*

Frequencies of the pronoun **that** in spoken and written English.

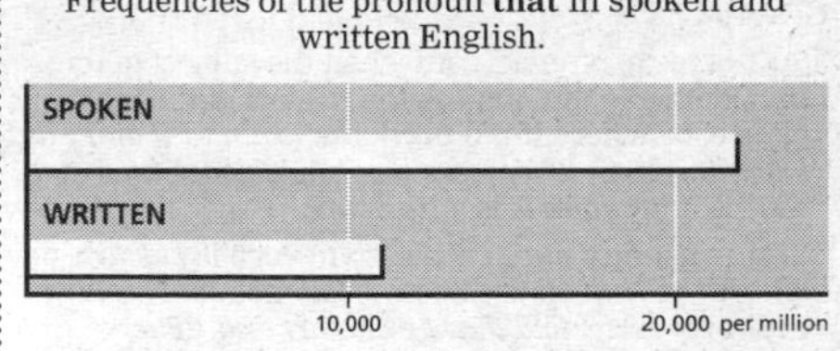


Based on the British National Corpus and the Longman Lancaster Corpus

This graph shows that the pronoun **that** is more common in spoken than in written English. This is because it is used a lot in conversation to refer to something that has already been mentioned, or when talking about the person or thing that is farthest from you, or a situation in the past. It is also used in some common spoken phrases.

**that**[3] /ðət; *strong* ðæt/ *conjunction* **1** used after verbs, nouns and adjectives to introduce a CLAUSE (2) which gives more information, a reason, an explanation etc: *If she said that she'd come, she'll come.* | *The rules state that only the goal keeper can handle the ball.* | *Is it true that the Robinsons are emigrating?* | *The fact that he is your brother-in-law should not affect your decision.* **2 a) so big/tall etc that ...** very big, very tall etc with the result that something happens or someone does something: *She's so tall that she has to have her clothes made for her.* **b) such a big man/such a tall house etc that** a very big man, a very tall house etc with the result that something happens or someone does something: *He's such a miserable so-and-so that none of the nurses like helping him.* **3** used as a RELATIVE PRONOUN like 'who', and 'which': *Did you know the man that bought the sportscar?* | *There are lots of things that I need to buy before the trip.* **4** used with objects of a PREPOSITION in a CLAUSE (2): *The police have found the gun that she was shot with.* | *There's Betty, my sister that I've been telling you about.* **5 the year/time etc that** the year, the time etc when something happened: *The day that my father died, I was on holiday in Greece.* **6** used to introduce a clause after a SUPERLATIVE (2): *Veronica is the most boring person that I've ever met.* | *He was the greatest boxer that ever lived.* **7** *formal* in order that, or so that something may happen or someone may do something: *We pray that he may recover soon.* **8** *literary* used when you wish that something would happen, that you could do something etc: *Oh, that I could fly.* —see also **so (that)** (SO[2] (2)) S1 W1

**USAGE NOTE: THAT**

SPOKEN-WRITTEN

In conversation it is not usual for **that** to actually be used in a *that* clause after a verb or adjective. This is especially true after the commonest verbs taking such clauses in spoken English –**think, say, know, see**, and after common adjectives like **sure, confident, afraid, sorry, aware, glad**: *I think Stuart's gone crazy.* | *I'm afraid it could be there for six months.*

In written English there are differences between different styles of writing. **That** is hardly ever left out in academic writing, where in any case the commonest verbs are not the same as in spoken English, but are words like **show, ensure**:

*Empirical data show that similar processes can be guided quite differently.* | *It is important that both groups are used in the experiment.*

In newspapers **that** is used at least twice as much as it is left out: *The police say that they don't have the time to worry about marijuana.* But in fiction it is left out more than it is kept in: *I'm sorry I hit you just now!*

GRAMMAR

**That** is more often left out when the subject of the *that* clause is the same as the subject of the main clause, or where it is a pronoun: *I think I'll make a shopping list.* | *They were glad she'd gone out.* But, *I suspect that John was a bit drunk.*

**That** is usually put in if the main verb is passive, or where the *that* clause does not immediately follow the verb: *I was told that he had arrived.* | *They warned him that it was dangerous.*

PUNCTUATION

**That** does not usually immediately follow a comma. *Who* and *which* may follow a comma in relative clauses that add information but do not restrict the meaning, but *that* is not used in these clauses. Look at this restrictive clause: *She visited her brother who/that lives in Detroit* (= she has more than one brother, and the relative clause with *who/that* tells us which one). Compare this non-restrictive clause: *She visited her brother, who lives in Detroit* (= she has only one brother, and the relative clause, which cannot begin with *that*, just adds further information about him).

**that**[4] /ðæt/ *adv* [+ adj/adv] **1 that long/many etc** *spoken* used to say how long or how many, especially because you are showing the size, number etc with your hands: *The fish was that long, give or take an inch or two.* | *He missed hitting the car in front by that much.* **2 not that long/many** *spoken* used when you mean fairly short, only a few etc: *Will's not that tall, considering he's 16 already.* | **not all that** *The film wasn't all that good really.* **3 that long/many etc (that)** *BrE spoken* so long, so many etc that something happens, someone does something etc: *She was that tired that she had to go upstairs and rest.* | *I've eaten that much, I think I'm going to be sick.*

**thatch**[1] /θætʃ/ *v* [I,T] to make the roof of a building with dried STRAW (=strong stems), REEDS etc —**thatched** *adj*: *a thatched cottage* —**thatcher** *n* [C]

**thatch**[2] *n* **1** [C] a roof made of dried STRAW, REEDS etc **2** [U] STRAW or REEDS used to make a roof **3** [singular] *humorous* a thick untidy pile of hair on someone's head

**thaw**[1] /θɔː‖θɒː/ *v* **1** [I,T] also **thaw out** if ice or snow thaws or is thawed, it becomes warmer and turns into water: *The lake thawed in March.* | **it thaws** (=ice and snow melt) *It thawed overnight.* **2** also **thaw out** [T] to let frozen food unfreeze until it is ready to cook: *Thaw frozen meat in its packet and then cook as soon as possible.* **3** [I] to become friendlier and less formal: *After a few glasses of wine Robert began to thaw a little.*

**thaw**[2] *n* **1** [singular] a period of warm weather during which snow and ice melt: *The thaw begins in March.* **2** [C] an improvement in relations between two countries after a period of unfriendliness

**the-** /θi/ *prefix* another form of the prefix THEO-

S1 W1 **the**[1] /ðə; *before vowels*, ði; *strong* ðiː/ *definite article, determiner* **1** used to refer to a particular thing or person when everyone knows which thing or person you are talking about, or because only one such person or thing exists: *I've got two cats now; the black and white one's called Rosie and the ginger one's called Joseph.* | *The audience clapped and cheered.* | *Take these letters to the post office will you.* | *The sky was gray and overcast.* | *They're holding an election later in the year.* | *the tallest building in the world* | **the United States/the Aegean Sea etc** (=used before the names of certain countries, seas etc) | **His Holiness the Pope/the Defense Minister etc** (=used as part of someone's title) | **the Smiths/the Kings/the Mitchells etc** *especially spoken* (=used before the name of a family to refer to all the members of that family) **2** used to refer to something that everyone knows because it happens in nature or is a part of daily life: *We drove through the night to get to New Orleans in time.* | *Ella's been complaining about the traffic keeping her awake at night.* | *We would ask tenants to switch off the water supply before vacating the property.* **3** used to refer to a part of the body or to someone or something that belongs to someone: *She hit him on the* (=his) *ear.* | *How's the* (=your) *arm?* | *The* (=my) *car broke down again today.* | **the wife** *spoken* (=used especially by men to refer to their own wife or to another man's wife and considered to be offensive by some women) **4** used before an adjective to make it into a noun when you are referring to all the people who that adjective describes: *We need more sheltered accommodation for the elderly.* | **the rich/the poor** *She devoted her life to helping the poor.* | **the wounded/the disabled/the physically handicapped etc** *parking facilities for the disabled* | **the Germans/the Japanese/the British** (=used to refer to all the people from a particular country) **5** *especially spoken* used before an adjective to make it into a noun when you are referring to a situation that that adjective describes: *Her behaviour is verging on the manic.* | **the impossible/the ridiculous/the insane** *Come on now, that's asking for the impossible.* **6** used before a singular noun to make it general: *The condor is in danger of extinction.* | *The computer has revolutionized office work.* **7** used before a plural noun to refer generally to a particular kind of thing: *I find it easier to get up when the mornings are lighter.* | *The shops are always packed just before Christmas.* **8** used before activities that people do, especially musical activities, but usually not including sports: *Fiona's learning the flute.* | *He plays the violin.* **9 the flu/the measles/the mumps** *spoken* used before the names of certain not very serious illnesses: *Amy's off school with the measles.* **10** *spoken* used before referring to a particular day, date, or month: *Tuesday the thirteenth of April* | *We moved house in the first week of July.* | *The meeting was scheduled for the Thursday.* **11** used to refer to a period of time that lasts ten or a hundred years: **the twenties/the thirties/the forties etc** *There was a severe recession in the mid-twenties.* | **the sixteen-hundreds/the seventeen-hundreds/the eighteen-hundreds** *the great novelists of the nineteen-hundreds* **12 by the metre/by the dozen/by the handful etc** used before the names of measurements when describing how something is calculated, sold, or used: *This cloth is sold by the metre.* (=it is measured in metres in order to calculate its price) | *We get paid by the hour.* **13** used before a noun, especially in negative sentences to show an amount or degree needed for a particular purpose: *I haven't the time to talk just now.* | *Eric didn't even have the common sense to send for a doctor.* **14** used before the name of a thing that represents a particular activity: *Rupert took to the bottle* (=began to drink a lot of alcohol) *after his wife died.* | *He's already been under the knife* (=had a medical operation) *twice this year.* **15** *spoken* used with strong pronunciation before a noun to show that it is the best, most famous etc person or thing of its kind: *"Apparently Paul McCartney's singing at the club tonight." "Not the Paul McCartney surely!"* **16** *spoken* used when describing someone or something when you are angry, jealous, surprised etc: *He's stolen my parking space, the bastard!* | *I can't get this drawing pin out, the stupid thing.* | *"Jamie's won a holiday in Hawaii." "The lucky devil!"* **17** *spoken* used in certain phrases that express anger, surprise etc: *What the hell are you doing here?* | *For the love of God what will the boy do next!*

**USAGE NOTE: THE**

GRAMMAR

**The** is not used with uncountable or plural nouns when you mean 'all' of something in general, or when what you are talking about is not already specifically known about by the reader or listener: *I love life/rock music/wine/ice cold beer/silk shirts/bananas.*|*We sat around eating cheese and crackers and listening to rock music.*

**The** is used if you are mentioning specific things that are already known to the reader or listener: *We drank the beer and the wine and watched the video* (=the beer etc that I just told you about or that you know about).

**The** is also used whenever you use an *of* phrase, relative clause, superlative etc, to say more specifically what kind of thing you mean: *I love the life of a writer/the food that you cook/the best things in life.*

**The** is not usually used at all in the following situations (though in a few specific cases it may be if the noun is restricted as just described):—

1. With many times of day and night and days, months etc, especially after **at, by,** and **on**: *at sunset/noon/by night/on Monday* (Compare *during the night/on the Monday after Christmas*). Compare also *Last week was awful* (=the one just before now) and *The last week was awful* (=the last week of my vacation etc some time ago).

2. When you give dates in speech you say: *June the third* (*BrE*)/*June third* (*AmE*) or *the third of June*, but you would write *June 3rd*.

3. When you are talking about meals, especially after **at, before, during, after, for,** and the verb **have**: *after/at/before/during breakfast*|*coffee for breakfast*|*When do you have breakfast?*|*Lunch is at one.* (compare *The breakfast she gave us was good.*)

4. In many fixed expressions such as: *by car/bus etc*|*at/to school/university etc*|*in/to bed/prison/church/*|*arm in arm*|*face to face*|*husband and wife*|*from beginning to end*

5. With names of languages and most diseases: *She speaks Greek.*|*He's got cancer/flu/mumps/a cold.* In informal spoken English, however, people often use **the** before the names of several common diseases: *He has got the flu/the mumps.*

6. With names of airports and railway stations: *I'm arriving at Heathrow airport/Grand Central Station.*

7. With many names of streets, places, countries, mountains etc: *Madison Avenue/Oxford Street/New York/Texas/Holland/Mount Fuji* (compare *This isn't the New York I remember*).

8. However, some such names always contain **the**: *The Strand, The Bronx, The Hague, The Sudan.* This includes especially the names of countries that are plural or contain the word *state, republic* etc: *The Netherlands, the USA, the UK, the Irish Republic.*

9. **The** is usually needed with names of hotels and restaurants if they do not end in *'s*: *The Hilton/The Grand Hotel/The Mandarin.* Also with names of rivers, seas, and groups of mountains: *The Ganges/The Atlantic/The Rockies*

**the²** *adv* **1** used in comparisons to show that two things happen together: *The more he eats the fatter he gets.*|*"When do you want this done?" "The sooner the better."* **2** used in comparisons to show that someone or something has more or less of a particular quality than before: **the better/the worse** *You'll feel all the better for having some time away from work.*|**none the wiser** (=not knowing more about something than before) *Her lengthy explanation left me none the wiser.* **3** used in front of adjectives and adverbs to emphasize that something is as big, good etc as it is possible to be: *He likes you the best.*|*I had the greatest difficulty understanding her.*

**theatre**

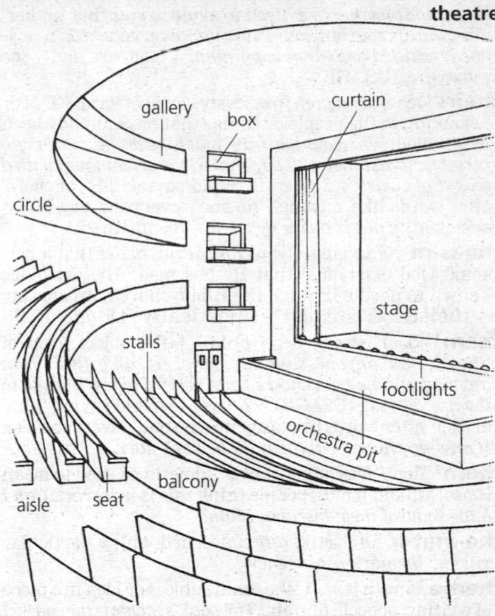


**thea·tre** *BrE*, **theater** *AmE* /ˈθɪətə‖-ər/ *n* S2 W2
**1** ▶ **BUILDING** ◀ [C] a building or place with a stage where plays are performed: *an open-air theatre*|*the Mercury Theater*
**2** ▶ **PLAYS** ◀ [U] **a)** plays as a form of entertainment: *I enjoy theater and swimming.*|**the theatre** *He's really interested in literature and the theatre.*|**good theatre** (=effective entertainment) *Yeats' plays are great poetry but they are not good theatre.* **b)** the work of acting in, writing, or organizing plays: *classes in theater and music*|*She's been working in the theatre for over thirty years.*
**3** ▶ **IN A HOSPITAL** ◀ [C,U] a special room in a hospital where medical operations are done; OPERATING THEATRE *BrE*
**4** ▶ **AREA** ◀ [C] a large area where a war is being fought: *the Pacific theater during World War II*
**5** ▶ **PLACE TO SEE A FILM** ◀ [C] *AmE AustrE* a building where films are shown; CINEMA (1) *BrE*, MOVIE THEATER *AmE*

**thea·tre·go·er** *BrE*, **theatergoer** *AmE* /ˈθɪətəˌgəʊə‖-tərˌgoʊər/ *n* [C] someone who regularly watches plays at the theatre: *Ken's a keen theatregoer.*

**theatre-in-the-round** /ˌ· · · · ˈ·/ *n* [U] the performance of a play on a central stage with the people watching sitting in a circle around it

**theatre weap·ons** /ˈ·· ˌ··/ *n* [plural] *technical* weapons, especially MISSILES that can only be fired a few hundred kilometres

**the·at·ri·cal** /θiˈætrɪkəl/ *adj* **1** connected with the performing of plays: *comic and theatrical skills* **2** behaving in a loud or very noticeable way that is intended to get people's attention: *He took her hand and kissed it in a theatrical gesture.* —**theatrically** /-kli/ *adv*

**the·at·ri·cals** /θiˈætrɪkəlz/ *n* [plural] **1** *BrE informal* deliberately emotional behaviour so that people will notice you: *We can do without all these theatricals, Andrew!* **2** performances of plays: *amateur theatricals*

**thee** /ðiː/ *pron old use* the object¹ (6) form of THOU; you

**theft** /θeft/ *n* **1** [U] the crime of stealing: *Car theft is on the increase.* **2** [C] an act of stealing something: *There have been a number of thefts in the area.*|[+ **of**] *the theft of £150 from the office*

**their** /ðə; *strong* ðeə‖ðər; *strong* ðer/ *determiner* [possessive form of *they*] **1** of or belonging to them: *They* S1 W1 *washed their faces and went to bed.* | *The twins spend all their time together.* **2** used to avoid saying 'his' or 'her' after words like 'anyone', 'no one', 'everyone' etc: *Everyone is entitled to their own opinion.* —compare HIS[1] —see EVERYONE (USAGE)

S3 **theirs** /ðeəz‖ðerz/ *pron* [possessive form of *they*] **1** of or belonging to the people or things that have already been mentioned: *When our washing machine broke, our neighbours let us use theirs.* | *They shared the prize money with a friend of theirs.* **2** used to avoid saying 'his' or 'hers' after words like 'anyone', 'no one', 'everyone' etc: *Everyone wants what is theirs by right.* —compare HIS[2]

**the·is·m** /ˈθiːɪzəm/ *n* [U] *technical* the belief that a personal God exists and that He has made His existence known to people through the Bible, church, dreams etc —**theistic** /θiˈɪstɪk/ *adj* —**theistically** /-kli/ *adv*

S1 W1 **them¹** /ðəm; *strong* ðem/ *pron* **1** the object form of 'they': *Has anyone seen my keys? I can't find them anywhere.* | *The police were very helpful when I spoke to them.* —see ME (USAGE) **2** used to avoid saying 'him' or 'her' after words like 'anyone', 'no one', 'everyone' etc: *If anyone phones, tell them I'll be back later.*

**them²** /ðem/ *determiner spoken* sometimes used to mean those, although most people think this is incorrect: *Can I have some of them biscuits, Mum?*

**the·mat·ic** /θɪˈmætɪk/ *adj* concerned with a particular THEME: *thematic consistency*

S2 W2 **theme** /θiːm/ *n* [C] **1** the main subject or idea in a piece of writing, speech, film etc: *The book's theme is the conflict between love and duty.* **2** a short simple tune that is repeated and developed in a piece of music: *Freia's theme in Wagner's opera* **3** *AmE* a short piece of writing on a particular subject that you do for school: *Your homework is to write a two-page theme on pollution.* **4 theme music/song/tune** music or a song that is often played during a film or musical play or at the beginning and end of a television or radio programme: *The kids were singing the theme song from 'The Brady Bunch'.*

**theme park** /ˈ· ·/ *n* [C] a type of park where you can have fun riding on big machines such as a ROLLER COASTER and the BIG WHEEL, but where the whole park is based on one subject such as water or space travel

**theme par·ty** /ˈ· ˌ··/ *n* [C] *BrE* a party where everyone has to dress in a particular way connected with a particular subject: *a wild West theme party*

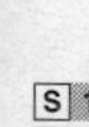

**them·selves** /ðəmˈselvz/ *pron* **1** the reflexive form of 'they': *The kids seem very pleased with themselves – what have they been doing?* | *Our neighbours have just bought themselves a jacuzzi.* **2** used to emphasize the pronoun 'they', a plural noun etc: *Doctors themselves are the first to admit the treatment has side effects.* **3** used after words like 'everyone', 'anyone', 'no one' etc when you talk about someone already mentioned and you do not know what sex they are or it is not important: *Someone told me they'd actually seen the accident happen themselves.* **4 in themselves** used to say that ideas or situations only become important, serious etc when you consider other related ideas or situations: *None of the witnesses' statements prove anything in themselves, but together they are quite conclusive.* **5 (all) by themselves a)** alone: *It is a sad fact that many pensioners now live by themselves.* **b)** without help: *Did the children make the model all by themselves?* **6 (all) to themselves** if people have something to themselves, they do not have to share it with anyone: *In the new house the children will have a room to themselves.* **7 not be/feel themselves** if people are not themselves, they do not feel or behave in the way they usually do because they are nervous, upset or ill —see YOURSELF (USAGE)

**then¹** /ðen/ *adv* **1** at a particular time in the past or future: *It was then that I realised she'd tricked me.* | *I used to go to school with Mavis Butterwick, or Mavis O'Brien as she then was.* | *The furniture is being delivered next week so until then we'll have to sit on the floor.* | **from then on** (=starting at that time) *They met in 1942 and from then on they were firm friends.* | **just then** *Silently she closed the door. Just then she heard a noise.* | **back then** (=a long time ago in the past, when things were different) *Back then we spent holidays in Blackpool.* | **then and only then** *Tidy your room, then and only then can you go out with Mike.* **2** next; after something has happened: *You're doing it all wrong. Mix the flour and butter and then add the eggs.* | *First the passengers and then the stewards jumped from the wreckage.* **3** used to say that because of what you know about the situation, something else is probably true: *Still in your pyjamas? Have you just got out of bed then?* | **if...then...** *If x = 3 and y = 5 then xy = 15* **4 but then (again)** *especially spoken* used to say that although something is true something else is also true which makes the first thing seem less important: *I don't spend much but then I don't really go out much.* **5** *spoken* used at the end of questions, statements etc, especially to agree with someone or to make people aware that you are speaking: *So, what do you do then?* | *Right then, shall we start?* | *"Mom, will you play tennis with me?" "Get the balls out then."* **6** *especially spoken* used when giving your opinion or advice about something: *If you're going to go then go.* | *"He's boring, rude and arrogant." "Then divorce him."* **7** so that something happens or so that someone does something: *Wear a big hat and dark glasses then no one will recognize you.* **8** used in a list of things when you have remembered something else you want to add: *I do all the washing and cleaning and then there's the ironing too.* **9 then and there** also **there and then** immediately: *I expected to have to wait a few days, but they issued the passport then and there.* —see also **now and then** (NOW¹ (6))

**then²** *adj* **the then President, Director etc** the President, Director etc at a particular time in the past: *secretary to the then Head of Light Entertainment*

**thence** /ðens/ *adv formal* **1** from there: *We went by boat to Trieste, and thence by train to Prague.* **2** for that reason

**thence·forth** /ðensˈfɔːθ‖ˈðensfɔːrθ/ also **thence·for·ward** /ðensˈfɔːwəd‖-ˈfɔːrwərd/ *adv formal* starting from that time: *Thenceforth he made his life in England.*

**theo-** /θɪə/ also **the-** *prefix* concerning God or gods: *theology* (=study of religion)

**the·oc·ra·cy** /θiˈɒkrəsi‖-ˈɑː-/ *n* [C] a social system or state controlled by religious leaders —**theocratic** /ˌθiːəˈkrætɪk◂/ *adj*: *the imposition of a theocratic State*

**the·od·o·lite** /θiˈɒdəlaɪt‖θiˈɑː-/ *n* [C] a piece of equipment used by a land SURVEYOR for measuring angles

**the·o·lo·gian** /ˌθiːəˈləʊdʒən‖-ˈloʊ-/ *n* [C] someone who has studied theology

**theological col·lege** /·ˌ··· ˌ··/ *BrE*, **theological sem·inary** /ˌ····· ˈ····/ *AmE* —*n* [C] a college for training people to become priests or church ministers

**the·ol·o·gy** /θiˈɒlədʒi‖θiˈɑː-/ *n* **1** [U] the study of religion and religious ideas and beliefs: *He studied theology at college.* **2** [C,U] a particular system of religious beliefs and ideas: *According to Muslim theology there is only one God.* —**theological** /ˌθiːəˈlɒdʒɪkəl◂‖-ˈlɑː-/ *adj*: *theological debate* —**theologically** /-kli/ *adv*

**theo·rem** /ˈθɪərəm‖ˈθiːə-/ *n* [C] *technical* a statement, especially in mathematics, that you can prove by reasoning

**theo·ret·i·cal** /θɪəˈretɪkəl‖ˌθiːə-/ also **theo·ret·ic** /θɪəˈretɪk‖ˌθiːə-/ *adj* **1** concerned with the study of scientific ideas rather than with practical uses of science or practical experience: *theoretical physics* —compare PRACTICAL¹ (1) **2** a theoretical situation or condition is supposed to exist but does not really exist: *Equality between men and women in our society is still only theoretical.* | *a theoretical risk of an explosion* W3

**theo·ret·i·cally** /θɪəˈretɪkli‖ˌθiːə-/ *adv* [sentence adverb] **1** used to say what is supposed to happen in a particular situation when the opposite is true: *Theoretically, Damian's the boss, but I co-ordinate the team on a day-to-day basis.* **2** according to a scientific idea that has not been proved to be true in a practical way: *It is theoretically possible for computers to be programmed to think like humans.*

**theo·rist** /ˈθɪərɪ̈st‖ˈθiːə-/ also **theo·re·ti·cian** /ˌθɪərəˈtɪʃən‖ˌθiːə-/ *n* [C] someone who develops ideas within a particular subject that explain why particular things happen or are true: *a leading economic theorist*

**theo·rize** also **-ise** *BrE* /ˈθɪəraɪz‖ˈθiːə-/ *v* [I + **about/on**, T + **that**] to think of a possible explanation for an event or fact

S2 W1 **theo·ry** /ˈθɪəri‖ˈθiːəri/ *n* **1** [C] an idea or set of ideas that is intended to explain something about life or the world, especially one that has not yet been proved to be true: *Darwin's theory of evolution* | **theory that** *the theory that light is made up of waves* **2** [U] the general principles or ideas of a subject, especially a scientific subject: *Freudian theory has had a great influence on psychology.* **3 in theory** something that is true in theory is not actually true although it is supposed to be: *In theory, a child could live on breast milk for ever, but this is hardly practical.* **4** [C] an idea that someone thinks is true but for which they have no proof: **theory that** *Detectives are working on a theory that his muderer was someone he knew.* **5** [U] the set of rules on which a practical subject or skill is based: *musical theory*

**ther·a·peu·tic** /ˌθerəˈpjuːtɪk◂/ *adj* **1** intended to help treat or cure an illness: *Nettles contain vitamins that have a therapeutic value.* **2** making you feel calm and relaxed: *I find swimming very therapeutic.* —**therapeutically** /-kli/ *adv*

**ther·a·peu·tics** /ˌθerəˈpjuːtɪks/ *n* [U] *technical* the part of medical science concerned with the treatment and cure of illness

**ther·a·pist** /ˈθerəpɪ̈st/ *n* [C] someone who has been trained to give a particular form of treatment for physical or mental illness: *a speech therapist*

**ther·a·py** /ˈθerəpi/ *n* [C,U] **1** the treatment of an illness or injury over a fairly long period of time, especially without using drugs or operations **2** the treatment or examination of someone's mental problems by talking to them for a long time about their feelings; PSYCHOANALYSIS: **be in therapy** (=be having therapy) *Rob was in therapy for several years.* —see also OCCUPATIONAL THERAPY, SPEECH THERAPY

S1 W1 **there¹** /ðeə,ðə‖ðer,ðər/ *pron* **1 there is/there are/there must be** used to say that something exists: *Is there life after death?* | *There's no special way of doing it – you just have to mix the dough slowly.* | *There must be some explanation for such outlandish behaviour.* | **there seems/appears to be** *There seems to be some mistake. I've never met you before in my life.* | **there exists/there remains etc** *formal*: *There remains the possibility that mistakes have been made.* **2 there was/there were etc** used to say that something happened: *Suddenly there was a loud crash as the clock fell to the floor.* | *There were several fights outside the stadium but no one was hurt.*

S1 W1 **there²** /ðeə‖ðer/ *adv* **1** in or to a particular place: *Sit there and wait until the teacher's finished.* | *Scotland? I've always wanted to go there.* | *Don't just stand there – do something!* | **out/in/under etc there** *I know there's a mouse under there somewhere.* | **over there** *How are you getting on over there in Paris?* —compare HERE¹ (1) **2** if something is there, it exists: *The chance was there, but I didn't take it.* | *All the food is there to be eaten so please enjoy it.* | *When asked why he climbed Everest, Mallory just said "Because it was there."* **3** *spoken* used to say which statement, idea or reason you agree with, you want to say something about etc: *"I believe we are all products of our environment." "I'm sorry but I disagree with you there."* **4** *spoken* used to get someone's attention when you are speaking to them or to make them notice someone or something: *Hey, you there! Watch out!* | *Hi there, I haven't seen you in ages.* | *There goes the phone again. It's not stopped ringing all morning.* **5 get there a)** to arrive in a particular place: *Most of the food had been eaten by the time I got there.* **b)** *spoken* to succeed in doing something: *It took me a lot of time and effort to qualify as a doctor but I got there in the end.* **6 be there (for sb)** *spoken* to be ready to help someone or be kind to them when they have problems: *That's what I loved about my father – he was always there for me.* **7 he's/she's not all there** *spoken* a phrase used to describe someone who is not very intelligent and seems slightly crazy, used when you want to avoid saying this directly **8 there and back** the distance, cost etc there and back is the total distance or cost of the journey to a place, added to the distance or cost of the return: *The journey's not too bad – only four hours there and back.* **9 there and then** also **then and there** immediately: *I thought I'd have to wait but they offered me the job there and then.* **10 there's a good boy/there's a clever dog etc** *spoken* used to praise a child or animal **11 there you are/go** *spoken* **a)** used to be polite when giving something to someone: *"Can I have two bottles of beer please?" "There you are, that'll be £3.20 please."* **b)** used when someone is upset, complains etc, to tell them that what has happened is typical or they should have expected it **12 that book there/those shoes there etc** *spoken* used when showing or pointing to where something is: *Can you pass me that wine glass there?* | **that there book/those there shoes etc** (=a form of this expression that is sometimes used although most people think it is incorrect) *It was those there holes in the road which made me fall down.*

**there³** /ðeə‖ðer/ *interjection* used to express success, satisfaction, sympathy etc: *There! I've done it! I've resigned.* | *It only lasted a week but there! What can you expect for £2 an hour.* | **there, there!** (=used to comfort someone who is crying) *There, there, don't get so upset!*

**there·a·bouts** /ˌðeərəˈbaʊts‖ˌðer-/ also **there·a·bout** /-ˈbaʊt/ *adv AmE* near a particular time, place, number etc, but not exactly: **or thereabouts** *These houses were built in 1930 or thereabouts.*

**there·af·ter** /ðeərˈɑːftə‖ðerˈæftər/ *adv formal* after a particular event or time; afterwards: *10,000 men had volunteered by the end of September; thereafter, approximately 1,000 men enlisted each month.*

**there·by** /ðeəˈbaɪ, ˈðeəbaɪ‖ðerˈbaɪ, ˈðer-/ *adv formal* with the result that something else happens: *He became a citizen in 1978, thereby gaining the right to vote.* W3

**there·fore** /ˈðeəfɔː‖ˈðerfɔːr/ *adv formal* as a result of something that has just been mentioned: *The dollar has gone down against the yen, therefore Japanese goods are more expensive for Americans.* —see THUS (USAGE) S2 W1

**there·in** /ðeərˈɪn‖ðer-/ *adv formal* **1** in that place, or in that piece of writing: *See Thompson, 1983, and the references cited therein.* **2 therein lies** used to say that something is caused by or comes from a particular situation: *The treaty was imposed by force, and therein lay the cause of its ineffectiveness.*

**there·in·af·ter** /ˌðeərɪnˈɑːftə‖ˌðerɪnˈæftər/ *adv law* later in the same official paper, statement etc

**there·of** /ðeərˈɒv‖ðerˈɑːv/ *adv formal* concerning something that has just been mentioned: *States differ in standards for products and the labelling thereof.*

**there·on** /ðeərˈɒn‖ðerˈɒːn,-ˈɑːn/ *adv formal* **1** on the thing that has just been mentioned **2** THEREUPON

**there·to** /ðeəˈtuː‖ðerˈtuː/ *adv formal* concerning an agreement or piece of writing that has just been mentioned: *the treaty and any conditions attaching thereto*

**there·un·der** /ðeərˈʌndə‖ðerˈʌndər/ *adv formal* **1** under something that has just been mentioned **2** according to a document, law, or part of an agreement that has just been mentioned

**there·up·on** /ˌðeərəˈpɒn, ˈðeərəpɒn‖ˌðerəˈpɒːn, -ˈpɑːn, ˈðerə-/ *adv formal* **1** immediately after something else has happened, and usually as a result of it; then: *Thereupon the whole audience stood up and began cheering.* **2** concerning a subject that has just been mentioned: *I have read your article, and wish to comment thereupon.*

**therm** /θɜːm‖θɜːrm/ *n* [C] a measurement of heat equal to

100,000 British Thermal Units, used in Britain for measuring how much gas someone has used

**therm-** /θɜːm‖θɜːrm/ *prefix* another form of the prefix THERMO-

**ther·mal¹** /ˈθɜːməl‖ˈθɜːr-/ *adj* [only before noun] **1** concerned with or caused by heat: *thermal energy | thermal conductivity* **2** thermal water is heated naturally under the earth: *thermal springs* **3** thermal clothing is made from special material to keep you warm in very cold weather: *thermal underwear*

**thermal²** *n* [C] **1** a rising current of warm air used by birds **2 thermals** [plural] *informal* special warm clothing, especially underwear

**ther·mi·on·ics** /ˌθɜːmiˈɒnɪks‖ˌθɜːrmiˈɑː-/ *n* [U] *technical* the part of science that deals with the flow of ELECTRONS from heated metal

**thermo-** /θɜːməʊ, -mə‖θɜːrmoʊ, -mə/ also **therm-** *technical prefix* concerning heat: *a thermostat* (=for controlling temperature) | *thermostable* (=not changing when heated)

**ther·mo·dy·nam·ics** /ˌθɜːməʊdaɪˈnæmɪks‖ˌθɜːrmoʊ-/ *n* [U] the science that deals with the relationship between heat and other forms of energy

**ther·mom·e·ter** /θəˈmɒmɪ̣tə‖θərˈmɑːmɪ̣tər/ *n* [C] a piece of equipment that measures the temperature of the air, of your body etc: *The thermometer was reading over 100°C.*

**ther·mo·nu·cle·ar** /ˌθɜːməʊˈnjuːkliə◂‖ˌθɜːrmoʊˈnuːkliər◂/ *adj* thermonuclear weapons use a NUCLEAR reaction, involving the splitting of atoms, to produce very high temperatures and a very powerful explosion: *a thermonuclear device*

**ther·mo·plas·tic** /ˌθɜːməʊˈplæstɪk◂‖ˌθɜːrmə-/ *n* [C,U] *technical* a plastic that is soft and bendable when heated but hard when cold

**ther·mos** /ˈθɜːməs‖ˈθɜːr-/ also **thermos flask** /ˈ··· ·/ *n* [C] *trademark* a special container like a bottle, that keeps drinks hot or cold —see picture at FLASK

**ther·mo·set·ting** /ˈθɜːməʊˌsetɪŋ‖ˈθɜːrmoʊ-/ *adj technical* thermosetting plastic becomes hard and unbendable after if has been heated

**ther·mo·stat** /ˈθɜːməstæt‖ˈθɜːr-/ *n* [C] an instrument used for keeping a room or a machine at a particular temperature —see picture at ENGINE

**the·sau·rus** /θɪˈsɔːrəs/ *n plural* **thesauruses** or **thesauri** /-raɪ/ [C] a book in which words are put into groups with other words that have similar meanings

**these** /ðiːz/ the plural of THIS

**the·sis** /ˈθiːsɪ̣s/ *n plural* **theses** /-siːz/ [C] **1** a long piece of writing about a particular subject that you do as part of an advanced university degree such as an MA or a PhD: *Writing a thesis on dance clubs is not as strange as it seems.* **2** *formal* an idea or theory that tries to explain why something happens: *Their main thesis is that inflation is caused by increases in the money supply.*

**thes·pi·an** /ˈθespiən/ *n* [C] *formal or humorous* an actor —**thespian** *adj*: *Aidan turns all his thespian charm on the beautiful Tara.*

S1 W1 **they** /ðeɪ/ *pron* [used as the subject of a verb] **1** used to talk about two or more people or things that have been mentioned already or that the person you are talking to already knows about: *Bob and Sue sold everything they owned and they now run a bar in Spain.* **2 they say/think etc** *especially spoken* used to say what people in general think or believe: *They say his wife ran off with a younger man.* **3** *especially spoken* **a)** the government, the police, the people who control an organization etc: *I see they're threatening to put up taxes again.* **b)** all the people in a group such as, all doctors, all scientists, all teachers etc: *Apparently she has something they call 'glue ear'.* **4** used to avoid saying 'he' or 'she' after words like 'anyone', 'no one', 'everyone' etc: *If anyone has any information related to the crime will they please contact the police.* —see EVERYONE (USAGE), HE (USAGE)

**they'd** /ðeɪd/ **1** the short form of 'they had': *If only they'd been there.* **2** the short form of 'they would': *It's a pity my parents didn't come, they'd have enjoyed it.*

**they'll** /ðeɪl/ the short form of 'they will': *They'll be tired after the long journey.*

**they're** /ðə; *strong* ðeə, ðeɪə‖ðr; *strong* ðer, ðeɪər/ the short form of 'they are': *They're going to Crete next week.*

**they've** /ðeɪv/ *especially BrE* the short form of 'they have', used especially in verb compounds: *They've had a lot of trouble with their car.* | *They really need the money, because they've a new baby to think of now.*

**thi·am·in** /ˈθaɪəmiːn,-mɪn/ also **thi·a·mine** /-miːn/ *n* [U] a natural chemical in some foods, that you need in order to prevent particular illnesses

**thick**

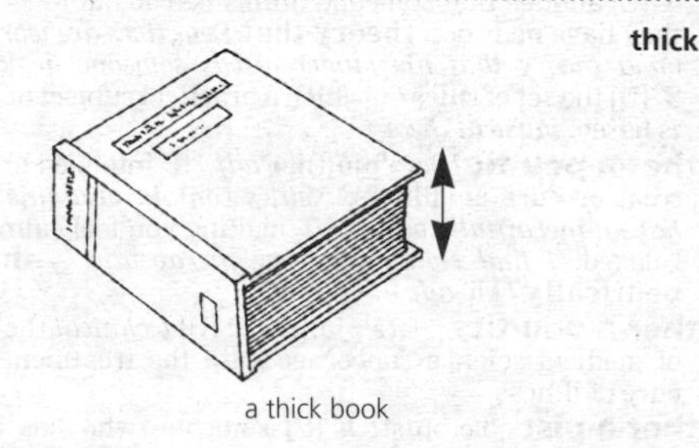

a thick book

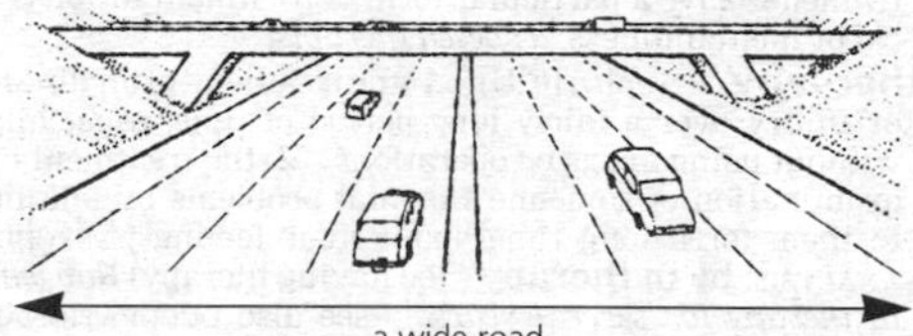

a wide road

**thick¹** /θɪk/ *adj* S2 W2

**1 ▶THINGS◀ a)** measuring a particular amount, especially more than usual, between two surfaces or sides: *a thick oak door* | *Wrap your baby in a thick towel or blanket.* | **3 feet/1cm/two inches etc thick** *In some places, the walls are over two meters thick.* | [+ **with**] (=forming a thick layer) *The staircase was crumbling, and thick with dust.* **b)** measuring more around the middle than usual: *Connect the battery using a thick cable.* —opposite THIN

**2 ▶PERSON◀** *BrE informal* stupid: *Don't think I can't see what's going on – I'm not that thick.* | *He's a nice guy, but he's a bit thick.* | **(as) thick as two short planks** (=very stupid)

**3 ▶LIQUID◀** not solid, but moving or flowing slowly: *For a thicker gravy, add more flour.* | *thick porridge*

**4 ▶SMOKE/CLOUD ETC◀** filling the air, and difficult to see through or breathe in: *At the scene of the riot, thick black smoke is still pouring from burning tires.* | *thick fog* | [+ **with**] *The air was thick with exhaust fumes.*

**5 be thick on the ground** to be present or available in large amounts or numbers: *Cheap houses aren't as thick on the ground as they used to be.* —opposite **thin on the ground** (THIN¹ (12))

**6 ▶VOICE◀ a)** clearly belonging to a particular place or part of the country: **a thick German/Yorkshire/Brazilian etc accent** *TV viewers will get just one more chance to hear his thick Scottish accent.* **b)** not as clear or high as usual, for example because someone has been crying: *Bill's voice was thick and gruff.*

7 ► **TREES/BUSHES ETC** ◄ growing very close together, or having a lot of leaves, so there is not much space in between: *The little animal tried to hide in the thick undergrowth.*|*a thick forest*
8 ► **HAIR/FUR ETC** ◄ forming a deep, soft covering: *She ran her fingers through her thick brown hair.*
9 **be (as) thick as thieves** if two people are as thick as thieves, they are very friendly with each other and seem to share a lot of secrets: *I don't trust those two. Lately they've been as thick as thieves.*
10 **give sb a thick ear/get a thick ear** *BrE spoken* to hit someone or be hit on the head, as a punishment: *Any more cheek from you and you'll get a thick ear.*
11 **have a thick skin** to not care if people criticize you or do not like you —see also THICK-SKINNED
12 **be thick with sb** to be very friendly with someone
13 **(it's) a bit thick** *BrE old-fashioned* used to say something is a little unfair or annoying —**thickly** *adv*

**thick**[2] *adv* 1 if you spread, cut etc something thick, you spread or cut it in a way that produces a thick layer or piece: *peanut butter spread thick* 2 **thick and fast** arriving or happening very frequently, in large amounts or numbers: *Competition entries have been coming in thick and fast.* —see also **lay it on thick** (LAY[2])

**thick**[3] *n* 1 **be in the thick of sth** to be involved in the busiest, most active, most dangerous etc part of a situation: *Following his recent operation, Governor Brown hopes to be back in the thick of the action as soon as possible.* 2 **through thick and thin** in spite of any difficulties or problems: **stick together through thick and thin** *As kids we promised to stick together through thick and thin.*

**thick·en** /ˈθɪkən/ *v* [I,T] to become thick, or make something thick: *The fog was beginning to thicken.*|**thicken sth** *You can thicken a sauce by adding cornstarch.* —see also **the plot thickens** (PLOT[1] (3))

**thick·en·er** /ˈθɪkənə, ˈθɪknə‖-ər/ also **thick·en·ing** /ˈθɪkənɪŋ,ˈθɪknɪŋ/ *n* [C,U] a substance used to thicken a liquid

**thick·et** /ˈθɪkɪ̣t/ *n* [C] a group of bushes and small trees

**thick-head·ed** /ˌ· ˈ··◂/ *adj informal* extremely stupid: *He's so thick-headed he can't understand the simplest instructions.*

**thick·ness** /ˈθɪknɪ̣s/ *n* 1 [C,U] how thick something is: *The length of nails you need depends on the thickness of the plank.* 2 [C] a layer of something: [+ **of**] *Wrap the cake in two thicknesses of greaseproof paper.*

**thick·o** /ˈθɪkəʊ‖-koʊ/ *n* [C] *informal* someone who is very stupid

**thick·set, thick-set** /ˌθɪkˈset◂/ *adj* having a wide strong body; STOCKY: *a short thickset man*

**thick-skinned** /ˌ· ˈ·◂/ *adj* not easily offended by other people's criticism or insults: *a thick-skinned insurance salesman*

**thief** /θiːf/ *n plural* **thieves** /θiːvz/ [C] someone who steals things, especially without using violence: *a car thief*|*Leaving ground floor windows open will encourage thieves.* —compare BURGLAR, ROBBER —see also **be (as) thick as thieves** (THICK[1] (9))

**thiev·e·ry** /ˈθiːvəri/ *n* [U] *formal* thieving

**thiev·ing** /ˈθiːvɪŋ/ *n* [U] *informal especially BrE* the practice of stealing things —**thieving** *adj*: *He's a nasty thieving good-for-nothing.*

**thiev·ish** /ˈθiːvɪʃ/ *adj literary* like a thief

**thigh** /θaɪ/ *n* [C] the top part of your leg, between your knee and your HIP[1] (1) —see picture at BODY

**thim·ble** /ˈθɪmbəl/ *n* [C] a small metal or plastic cap used to protect your finger when you are sewing

**thim·ble·ful** /ˈθɪmbəlfʊl/ *n* [C + **of**] *informal* a very small quantity of liquid

**thin**

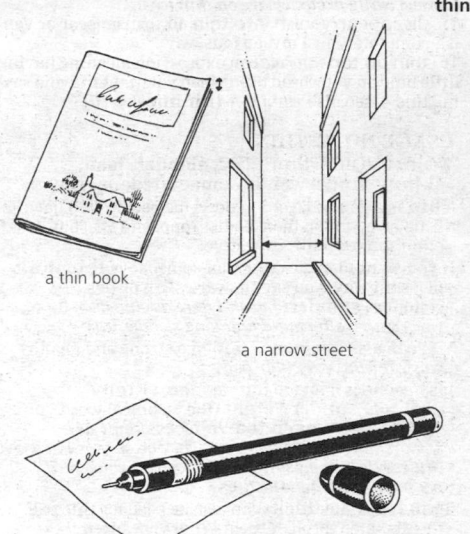

a thin book

a narrow street

a fine nib

**thin**[1] /θɪn/ *comparative* **thinner** *superlative* **thinnest** *adj* S2 W2
1 ► **NOT THICK** ◄ having a very small distance or a smaller distance than usual between two sides or two flat surfaces: *a thin nylon rope*|*She's only wearing a thin summer jacket.*|*two thin slices of bread*|*The road was covered with a thin layer of ice.*|**paper thin** (=very thin) *Keep your voice down, the walls are paper thin.* —opposite THICK[1] (1)
2 ► **NOT FAT** ◄ having little fat on your body: *Larry was tall and thin with dark brown hair.*|*I wish my legs were thinner.* —opposite FAT[1] (1)
3 ► **LIQUID** ◄ a liquid that is thin flows very easily because it has a lot of water in it: *thin paint*
4 ► **SMOKE/MIST** ◄ smoke or mist that is thin is easy to see through: *The fog is quite thin in places.* —opposite THICK[1] (4)
5 ► **AIR** ◄ air that is thin is more difficult to breathe than usual because it has less OXYGEN in it: *the thinner air high in the mountains*
6 ► **VOICE** ◄ a thin voice is high and unpleasant to listen to: *a thin cracked singing voice*
7 ► **SOUND** ◄ a thin sound is unpleasantly weak: *the thin mewing of a bedraggled kitten* —opposite FULL[1] (15)
8 ► **HAIR/PLANTS** ◄ hairs or plants that are thin have spaces between them: *a thin straggly beard*|*thin vegetation*
9 ► **EXCUSE/ARGUMENT/EXPLANATION** ◄ a thin excuse, argument, or explanation is not good or detailed enough to persuade you that it is true
10 ► **INFORMATION/DESCRIPTION** ◄ a piece of information or a description that is thin is not detailed enough to be useful or effective: *The evidence for Viking settlements in America is pretty thin.*
11 **the thin end of the wedge** *especially BrE spoken* an expression meaning something that you think is the beginning of a harmful development: *These job cuts are just the thin end of the wedge.*
12 **be thin on the ground** if a particular type of person or thing is thin on the ground, there are very few available: *Taxis seem to be thin on the ground.*
13 **be having a thin time (of it)** *spoken* to be in a difficult situation, especially one in which you do not have enough money
14 **be (skating) on thin ice** to be in a situation in which you are likely to upset someone or cause trouble: *I think*

T

*the people who argue that discoveries in genetics should be commercially protected are on thin ice.*
**15 disappear/vanish into thin air** to disappear or vanish completely in a mysterious way
**16 thin on top** *informal* an expression meaning having little hair on your head used when you want to avoid saying this —see also THINLY —**thinnness** *n* [U]

**USAGE NOTE: THIN**
WORD CHOICE: **thin, slim, slender, lean, skinny, underweight, emaciated, narrow**
**Thin** is a general word to describe people who have little or no fat on their bodies (opposite *fat*), but it often sounds a little negative.
If you want to make clear that someone is **thin** in a pleasant way, you say they are **slim** or (less common) **slender**: *I wish I were as slim as you.*|*with a slim build and long slender legs*
You can also say **lean** (=thin in a strong and healthy way): *a lean, muscular body*
If someone is a bit too thin they are **skinny** (informal), **underweight** (the technical word), or (worst of all) **emaciated**: *He looks skinny as a rake.*|*skinny fashion models*|*The doctor says I'm a little underweight since my illness.*|*the emaciated bodies of the famine victims*
**Thin** (opposite **thick**) can also be used for things if the distance through them is not very big: *a thin post/wire/dress/slice of cheese*
**Narrow** is usually used to describe something that is not very wide from side to side: *a narrow road/bed/gap.* However, in a few contexts, especially where something is both long and narrow, **thin** can be used in this sense too: *a thin stripe/strip of tape/a dress with very thin straps*

T

**thin²** *adv* so as to be thin: *Don't cut the bread so thin.*
**thin³** *v* **thinned, thinning** [T] **1** also **thin out** to make more room for plants to grow by removing the weaker ones: *thinning out the carrots* **2 thin the ranks** if something thins the ranks of a group of people, there are less of them as a result of it: *Illness had thinned our ranks.* **3** to make a liquid weaker by adding water or another liquid: *This paint needs thinning.*
**thin out** *phr v* [I] if a crowd thins out the people gradually separate and leave so there are fewer of them: *By midnight the crowd outside the theatre was starting to thin out.*
**thine¹** /ðaɪn/ *pron old use* yours
**thine²** *determiner old use* a word meaning your, used before a word beginning with a vowel or 'h'; THY
S1 W1 **thing** /θɪŋ/ *n*
**1 ▶IDEA/ACTION/FEELING/FACT◀** [C] anything that you can think of as a single item, for example an idea, an action, a feeling, or a fact: *The important thing is for us to tell the truth.*|*What a stupid thing to do.*|*A horrible thing happened yesterday.*|**do the right/decent/honourable etc thing** *I kept wondering if I was doing the right thing.*
**2 ▶OBJECT◀** [C] an object: *On top of the box there was a thing like a long handle.*|*I need to pop into the supermarket to get a few things.* —see MACHINE¹ (USAGE)
**3 ▶SITUATION◀ things** [plural] life in general and the way it is affecting people: *How are things with you?*|*Things could be worse.*|*Things are going really well at the moment.*
**4 there is no such thing** used to emphasize that something does not really exist or happen: *"There's no such thing as love," that's what she said.*
**5 not know a thing/not feel a thing/not see a thing etc** to know, feel etc nothing: *I can't feel a thing – my mouth is completely numb.*|*She doesn't do a thing to help around the house.*
**6 make a (big) thing out of sth** to make something seem more important than it really is, by getting angry, excited etc: *OK, so we disagree, but let's not make a big thing out of it.*
**7 the last thing sb wants/expects etc** something that someone does not want, expect etc at all: *The last thing I felt like doing was dancing.*
**8 ▶EQUIPMENT◀** [C] *especially BrE* the tools, equipment, clothes etc that you need for a particular job, sport etc: *I left my swimming things at home.*
**9 ▶AT THE END◀ last thing** at the end of a day, afternoon, evening etc: *He always polished his shoes last thing at night.*
**10 ▶AT THE BEGINNING◀ first thing** at the beginning of a day, morning, afternoon etc: *I'll phone you first thing Monday morning.*
**11 ▶CLOTHES/POSSESSIONS◀ things** [plural] *especially BrE* clothes and possessions: *Pack your things. We're leaving.*
**12 all things considered** having considered all the facts about something: *All things considered, the team didn't do too badly.*
**13 among other things** used when you are giving one fact, reason, effect etc but want to suggest that there are many others: *This led, among other things, to the resignation of the Director.*
**14 make things easy/difficult** to deliberately make it easy, difficult etc for someone to do something: [+ **for**] *He could make things difficult for you if he chooses.*
**15 be onto a good thing** *informal* to be in a situation that is very helpful, comfortable, or profitable for you: *When they offered to pay for her travel as well she realized she was onto a good thing.*
**16 the done thing** *informal* the way of behaving or doing something that is socially acceptable: *You can't serve beer with the meal. It's not the done thing.*
**17 poor thing/lovely little thing/funny little thing etc** a person or animal that is unlucky, attractive, funny etc: *You poor thing.*
**18 the (latest) thing** *informal* the thing that is popular or fashionable at the moment: *Platform heels are the thing at the moment.*
**19 be a thing of the past** to no longer exist or happen: *Good manners seem to be a thing of the past.*
**20 do your own thing** *informal* to do something in the way that you like instead of copying other people or following strict rules: *Do you prefer a structured exercise class, or do you like to do your own thing?*
**21 have a thing about** *informal* to have very strong and often unreasonable feelings about someone or something: *He's got a real thing about people smoking.*
**22 breakfast things/dinner things etc** *BrE* the plates, dishes etc used for a particular meal: *I'll just wash up the breakfast things.*
**23 taking one thing with another** *BrE* considering all the facts: *Taking one thing with another, I think it's a good scheme.*
**24 be all things to all men** to behave in a way that makes everyone like you: *You must stop trying to be all things to all men.*
**25 the shape of things to come** the way in which things will probably happen or develop in the future: *Perhaps shopping by computer is the shape of things to come.*
**26 in all things** in every situation: *She believes in being honest in all things.*

Frequencies of the noun **thing** in spoken and written English.

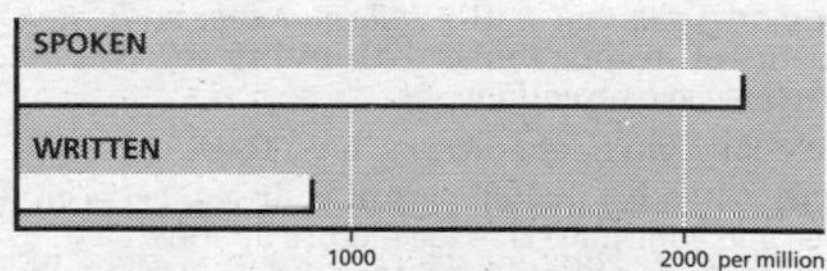


Based on the British National Corpus and the Longman Lancaster Corpus

This graph shows that the noun **thing** is much more common in spoken English than in written English. This is because it is used in a lot of common spoken phrases.

**thing** (*n*) **SPOKEN PHRASES**

**27 the thing is** used when explaining a problem or the reason for something: *The thing is, I can't afford to buy a car.*
**28 thing to do** something that someone does: *That was a really stupid thing to do.*
**29 thing to say** a remark: *What a strange thing to say!*
**30 light bulb thing/handle thing/switch thing etc** used when you do not know the correct name for something: *Is that it – that handle thing under the shelf?*
**31 for one thing** used to give one reason for something: *I wouldn't work abroad. I don't like travelling for one thing.*
**32 it is a good thing (that)** used to say that it is lucky or good that something has happened: *It's a good thing we brought some food with us.*
**33 that sort/kind of thing** used to mean 'other things of the same type', without giving more examples: *Oh, we spent the time reading, listening to the radio, that kind of thing.*
**34 and things** used to mean 'and other things', without giving more examples: *They sell jewellery and things, but it's all cheap stuff.*
**35 the thing with** used to say what the problem with someone or something is: *That's the thing with him, isn't it? You can't trust him.*
**36 just one of those things** used to say that something unpleasant or unlucky cannot be prevented: *It wasn't really the driver's fault, it was just one of those things.*
**37 it's (just) one thing after another** used to say that a lot of unpleasant or unlucky things keep happening to you: *Train strikes, computer problems, illness – it's just one thing after another!*
**38 just the thing/the very thing** exactly the thing that you want or that is necessary: *"Would this help?" "That's just the thing I was looking for."*
**39 what with one thing and another** used to explain that you have not done something because you have been too busy: *Well, what with one thing and another, we never got round to getting it fixed.*
**40 the way things are/stand** used to say that because of the present situation you must do or cannot do something: *The way things are we can't possibly afford a vacation this year.*
**41 it's no bad thing** used to say that even though an event seems to be unlucky it does actually help: *We had to sell the car, although it was no bad thing really because it was too expensive to run.*
**42 of all things** used to show that you are surprised or shocked by something that someone has done or said: *And for breakfast he had curry, of all things!*
**43 it's one thing to..., it's another thing to...,** used to say that doing one thing is very different from doing another thing: *It's one thing to play a computer game; it's quite another thing to write your own programs.*
**44 sb did/said etc no such thing** used to say angrily that someone did not do or say something: *"Jane says that you took the money out of the cash box." "I did no such thing!"*
**45 (do) the...thing** *AmE* used to talk about an activity and everything that is involved with it: *Jody tried the college thing but finally dropped out.*

**thing·a·ma·jig** /ˈθɪŋəmɪ̩dʒɪg/ also **thing·a·ma·bob** /ˈθɪŋəmɪ̩bɒb‖-bɑːb/ **thing·y** /ˈθɪŋi/ *n* [C] *spoken* used when you cannot remember or do not know the name of the person or thing you want to mention: *Have you got the thingamajig for opening the wine?* | *Is thingy coming tonight, you know, that bloke with the red hair?*

S1 W1 **think**[1] /θɪŋk/ *past tense and past participle* **thought** /θɔːt‖θɒːt/ *v*
**1 ▶ OPINION/BELIEF ◀** [T] to have an opinion or belief about something: **think (that)** *I think that she should have paid the money back.* | *Harry thought it was a lousy idea.* | *I didn't think anyone would believe me.* | *I remember thinking their behaviour was strange.* | *Well, Tom, what do you think?* | **think of sb/sth as sth** (=think that someone or something is something) *We now think of the car as being essential rather than a luxury.* | **think sb/sth (to be) sth** *We all thought her very intelligent.* | **think it right/important etc** *formal*: *Do you think it right for the government to cut funding in this way?* | **be thought to be (doing sth)** *formal*: *They are thought to be receiving arms from the Republic.*
**2 ▶ USE YOUR MIND ◀** [I] to use your mind to solve something, decide something etc: *We must think very carefully before we decide what to do.* | *Wait a minute, I'm thinking.* | [+ **about/of**] *She lay awake thinking about the money.* | *I tried not to think of Richard or what he was doing.* | **think deeply** (=think carefully, for a long time) *They clearly haven't thought very deeply about the possible consequences.*
**3 ▶ HAVE AN IDEA ◀** [T] to have an idea or thought in your mind, especially one that appears suddenly: *And then I thought: "Why the hell shouldn't I?"* | *"I certainly am in luck!" Katy thought.*
**4 think of/about doing sth** to consider the possibility of doing something: *I had never thought of becoming an actor.* | *We did think about buying a flat in London.*
**5 think better of it** to not do something that you had planned to do, because you realize that it is not a good idea: *He started to say something, then thought better of it.*
**6 think nothing of (doing sth)** to do something easily or without complaining, even though other people would find it difficult: *The people here think nothing of walking ten miles to collect firewood.*
**7 think for yourself** to have ideas and thoughts of your own rather than believing what other people say: *Parents have to teach their children to think for themselves.*
**8 think sth to yourself** to have a thought in your mind, but not tell it to anyone: *I thought to myself, when I'm 60, Patrick will still only be in high school.*
**9 think twice (before doing sth)** to think very carefully before deciding to do something, because you know about the dangers or problems: *I'll think twice before taking out such a large loan again.*
**10 think again** to think of a new idea or plan because you realize that you cannot use the first one that you thought of: *If we can't have the car we'll have to think again about how to get there.*
**11 think aloud/think out loud** to say what you are thinking, without talking to anyone in particular: *Oh, sorry; I guess I was thinking out loud.*
**12 think a lot of sb/think highly of sb** to admire or respect someone: *I can assure you, the management thinks very highly of you.*
**13 think the world of sb** to like or love someone very much: *He thinks the world of those children.*
**14 think badly of sb** to disapprove of someone or what they have done: *Please don't think badly of me. I had no choice.*
**15 not think much of** to think that someone or something is bad, useless etc: *I don't think much of that new restaurant.*
**16 think the best/worst of sb** to consider someone's actions in a way that makes them seem as good as possible or as bad as possible: *Ellie's the type of person that always thinks the best of people.*
**17 think big** *informal* to plan to do things that are difficult, but will be very impressive, make a lot of profit etc: *We had money, materials, and the opportunity to think big. It was up to us to do something with it.*
**18 think on your feet** to answer questions or think of ideas quickly, without preparing in advance: *A good teacher can think on her feet.*
**19 think to do sth** *literary* to try to do something: *They had thought to deceive me.*

Frequencies of the verb **think** in spoken and written English.

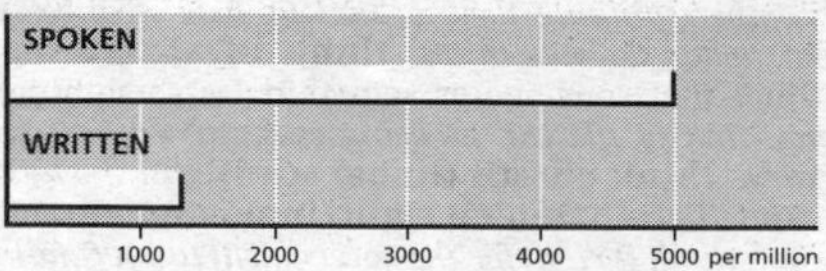


Based on the British National Corpus and the Longman Lancaster Corpus

This graph shows that the verb **think** is much more common in spoken English than in written English. This is because it is used in a lot of common spoken phrases.

**think** (*v*) **SPOKEN PHRASES**

**20 I think** used when you are saying that you believe something is true, although you are not sure: *Mary is in the garden, I think.* | *I don't think Ray will mind.*
**21 I think I'll** used when saying what you will probably do: *I think I'll go into town today.*
**22 I think so/I don't think so/I think not** used when answering a question, to say that you believe something is true or not true: *"Is Jenny still living in Manchester?" "I think so."*
**23 I thought (that) a)** used when you are politely suggesting something to do: *I thought we could meet for lunch.* | *I thought we'd go swimming tomorrow.* **b)** used to say what you thought or believed was true, although you were not sure: *I thought he was honest, but I was wrong.*
**24 I should/would think** used when you are saying that you believe something is probably true: *We'll need about six yards of material, I should think.*
**25 I can't think who/where/what** used to say that you cannot remember or understand something: *I can't think where I left my keys.* | *I can't think why she ever married him.*

**26 do you think (that)...? a)** used when you are asking someone politely to do something for you: *Do you think you could help me move these boxes?* **b)** used to ask someone's opinion: *Do you think I need to bring a jacket?*
**27 who/what etc do you think? a)** used to ask someone's opinion: *Who do you think will win?* **b)** used when asking someone angrily about something: *What do you think you're doing with that computer?* | *Where do you think you're going?*
**28 (now I) come to think of it** used when you are adding something more to what you have said, because you have just remembered it, or realized it: *My father looked worried and, now I come to think of it, so did my brother.*
**29 who would have thought?** used to say that something is very surprising: *Who would have thought she'd end up dancing for a living?*
**30 I thought as much** used to say that you are not surprised by what you have just found out: *"Andy failed his driving test." "I thought as much when I saw his face."*
**31 just think!** used to ask someone to imagine or consider something: *Just think – we could be millionaires!* | **[+of]** *It would be lovely, but just think of the expense!*
**32 you would have thought (that)/you would think (that)** used to say tnat you expect something to be true, although it is not: *You would have thought the school would do more to help a child like Craig.*
**33 anyone would think (that)** used to say that someone behaves as if a particular thing were true, although it is not: *Anyone would think he owns the place, the way he talks!*
**34 I wasn't thinking/I didn't think** used as a way of saying you are sorry because you have upset someone: *Sorry, I shouldn't have said that. I wasn't thinking.*
**35 to think (that)...!** used to show that you are very surprised about something: *To think that we lived next door to him and never realised what he was up to!*
**36 think nothing of it** used when someone has thanked you for doing something, to say politely that you did not mind doing it
**37 if you think...,you've got another think coming!** used to tell someone that if they think someone is going to do something, they are wrong: *If you think I'm going to wait around for you, you've got another think coming!*
**38 when you think about it** used to say that you realize something when you consider a fact or subject: *When you think about it, most of the things you worry about in life aren't that important.*
**39 that's what you/they etc think!** used to say that you strongly disagree with someone

**think back** *phr v* [I] to think about things that happened in the past: **[+on/to]** *When I think back to those nights, it is the crunch of snow and the warm lights from the windows that I remember.*

**think of** sb/sth *phr v* [T] **1** to produce a new idea, name, suggestion etc by thinking: *They're still trying to think of a name for the baby.* | *Can you think of anyone else who could do it?* **2** to remember a name or fact: *No, I can't think of the name of the hotel either.* **3** to behave in a way that shows that you want to treat other people well: *It was very good of you to think of me.* | *He never thinks of others, only of himself.* **4 what do you think of...?** used to ask what someone's opinion is about something: *So what do you think of this new manager then?*

**think** sth ↔ **out** *phr v* [T] to think about something carefully, considering all the possible problems, results etc: *He had spoken on the spur of the moment, without thinking things out first.*

**think** sth ↔ **over** *phr v* [T] to think about something carefully: *Why don't you think it over for a while, and give me a call in a couple of days.*

**think** sth ↔ **through** *phr v* [T] to think carefully about the possible results of doing something: *Having thought it through, I listed the pros and cons and made my decision.*

**think** sth ↔ **up** *phr v* [T] to produce a new idea, name etc by thinking hard about something: *We laugh at the absurdity of these laws and wonder how anyone ever thought them up.*

**think²** *n* **have a think** to think about a difficulty or question: *I don't know whether I'll go to the party, I'll have a think and let you know.*

**think·er** /ˈθɪŋkə‖-ər/ *n* [C] someone who is famous for their important work in a subject such as science or PHILOSOPHY: *Einstein was one of the world's great thinkers.*

**think·ing¹** /ˈθɪŋkɪŋ/ *n* [U] your opinion about something or your attitude towards it: *The Administration's thinking changed as the war progressed.* | **to my way of thinking** (=in my opinion) *Well, to my way of thinking, they should have done that years ago.* | **put on your thinking cap** *informal* (=think seriously about a problem, in order to try and solve it)

**thinking²** *adj* [only before noun] a thinking person is intelligent and tries to think carefully about important subjects: *No thinking person would seriously disagree with this point of view.*

**think-tank** /ˈ· ·/ *n* [C also + plural verb] a committee of people with experience in a particular subject that an organization or government establishes to produce ideas and give advice: *a right-wing political think-tank*

**thinly** *adv* **1** in a way that has a very small distance between two sides or two flat surfaces: *thinly sliced bread* **2** scattered or spread over a large area, with a lot of space in between: *Sow the raddish seeds thinly.* | **thinly populated/settled etc** *The mountain regions are more thinly populated than the lowlands.* **3 thinly**

**disguised/concealed etc** if something or someone is thinly disguised etc, you can easily see what it really is: *moralism thinly disguised as fiction*

**thin·ner** /ˈθɪnə‖-ər/ *n* [U] a liquid such as TURPENTINE that you add to paint to make it less thick

**thin-skinned** /ˌ· ˈ·◂/ *adj* too easily offended or upset by criticism

**third**[1] /θɜːd‖θɜːrd/ *number* 3rd: **third time lucky** *spoken* used when you have failed to do something twice and hope to be successful the third time

**third**[2] *n* [C] **1** one of three equal parts of something **2** the lowest type of degree that is given by a British university

**third class** /ˌ· ˈ·◂/ *n* [U] **1** a cheap class of mail in the US, usually used for sending advertisements **2** a THIRD[2] (2) **3** *old use* the cheapest and least comfortable part of a train or ship —**third-class** *adj, adv*: *We travelled third-class to Marseilles.*

**third de·gree** /ˌ· ·ˈ·◂/ *n* **give sb the third degree** *informal* to ask someone a lot of questions in order to get information from them: *I got home after midnight and Dad gave me the third degree.*

**third-degree burn** /ˌ· ·· ˈ·/ *n* [C] the most serious kind of burn, that goes right through your skin

**third par·ty** /ˌ· ˈ··◂/ *n* [C] *law* someone who is not one of the two main people involved in an agreement or legal case, but who is affected by it in some way: *third party insurance*

**third per·son** /ˌ· ˈ··◂/ *n* **1 the third person** a form of a verb or PRONOUN that is used for showing the person, thing or group that is being mentioned: *'He', 'she', 'it' and 'they' are third person pronouns.* **2 in the third person** a story in the third person is told as the experience of someone else, using the pronouns 'he' 'she', or 'they' —see also FIRST PERSON, SECOND PERSON

**third-rate** /ˌ· ˈ·◂/ *adj* of very bad quality: *a third-rate hotel*

**Third World** /ˌ· ˈ·◂/ *n* **the Third World** the poorer countries of the world that are not industrially developed —**Third World** *adj*: *Third World problems*

**thirst**[1] /θɜːst‖θɜːrst/ *n* **1** [singular] the feeling of wanting or needing a drink: **quench your thirst** (=get rid of your thirst by drinking something) *a thirst-quenching drink* | **work up a thirst** (=do work or exercise that makes you thirsty) *I really worked up a thirst during that game.* | **raging thirst** (=an extremely strong thirst) **2** [U] the state of not having enough to drink: *Half of the animals had died of thirst.* **3 a thirst for knowledge/excitement/power etc** *literary* a strong desire for knowledge etc: *These new immigrants had a thirst for education.*

**thirst**[2] *v* [I] *old use* to be thirsty

**thirst for/after** sth *phr v* [T] *literary* to want something very much: *young men thirsting for adventure*

**thirst·y** /ˈθɜːsti‖ˈθɜːr-/ *adj* **1** needing to drink or feeling that you want a drink: *Can I have a glass of water, I'm really thirsty.* | **thirsty work** (=work that makes you want a drink) *All this digging is thirsty work.* **2 thirsty for knowledge/power** *literary* having a strong desire for knowledge etc **3** *literary* fields or plants that are thirsty need water —**thirstily** *adv*

**thir·teen** /ˌθɜːˈtiːn◂‖ˌθɜːr-/ *number* 13

**thir·teenth**[1] /ˌθɜːˈtiːnθ‖ˌθɜr-/ *n* 13th

**thirteenth**[2] *n* [C] one of thirteen equal parts of something

**thir·ty** /ˈθɜːti‖ˈθɜːrti/ *number* **1** 30 **2 the thirties** the years from 1930 to 1939 **3 in your thirties** aged between 30 and 39: **in your early/late thirties** (=below or above 35) **4 in the thirties** if the temperature is in the thirties, it is between 30° and 39°: **in the high/low thirties** *a hot day, with temperatures in the low thirties* —**thirtieth** *adj*

**thir·ty·some·thing** /ˈθɜːtiˌsʌmθɪŋ‖ˈθɜːr-/ *n* [C] *informal* someone in their thirties who is well educated with a good job, plenty of money etc: *a glossy new magazine aimed at thirtysomethings* —**thirtysomething** *adj*: *a thirtysomething lawyer*

**this**[1] /ðɪs/ *determiner plural* **these** /ðiːz/ **1** used to talk about a person, thing, idea etc that has already been mentioned or that the person you are talking to already knows about: *Wait till you hear this joke.* | *What is the purpose of your visit to this country?* | *There will be another meeting later this week.* | *How can we help these poor children?* | *If we carry on at this rate we'll be bankrupt by the end of the week.* **2** used to talk about the person or thing nearest to you or the time that is soonest etc: *I'm going to visit my Mum this Wednesday.* | *I'll look in these rooms if you look in all the rest.* | *I'm surprised you like that photo – I prefer this one.* **3** *spoken* used in stories, jokes etc when you mean a person or thing, especially when you do not know their name: *When am I going to meet this boyfriend of yours?* | *I met this really weird guy tonight.* **4 this minute/second** immediately: *I want to see you in my office this minute!*

S1 W1

**this**[2] *pron plural* **these** **1** used to talk about a person, thing, idea etc that has already been mentioned or that the person you are talking to knows about already: *Where did you find these?* | *This is terrible. What on earth are we going to do?* | *If you think that's funny wait till you hear this.* **2** used to talk about the person or thing nearest to you, the time that is soonest etc: *These are your coats, aren't they?* | *That might be a much prettier dress but I feel more comfortable in this.* **3 a)** *informal* used to introduce someone to someone else: *Sam, this is my sister, Liz.* **b)** used when you have answered the telephone and you want to give your name: *"Can I speak to Joan please?" "This is Joan speaking."* **4** a particular time: *I thought he would have been back before this.* | *Well young lady, what time do you call this?* **5 this, that and the other** also **this and that** *especially spoken* various different things, subjects etc: *"What have you two been gossiping about all evening?" "Oh this, that and the other."* **6 what's (all) this?** *spoken* used to ask what is happening, what someone's problem is etc: *What's this? Crying again?*

S1 W1

**this**[3] *adv* [+ adj/adv] **this big/many etc** *spoken* used to say how big or how many, especially because you are showing the size, number etc with your hand: **this big/tall etc** *The table's about this high and this wide.* | **this much/many** *Do you know he cut this much off my fringe without even asking me!*

**this·tle** /ˈθɪsəl/ *n* [C,U] a wild plant with prickly leaves and purple or white furry flowers

thistle

**this·tle·down** /ˈθɪsəldaʊn/ *n* [U] the soft light feathery substance fastened to thistle seeds that helps them to float in the air

**thith·er** /ˈðɪðə‖ˈθɪðər/ *adv* *old use* in that direction

**tho'** /ðəʊ‖ðoʊ/ *adv* a short form of 'though'

**thong** /θɒŋ‖θɒːŋ/ *n* [C] **1** a long thin piece of leather used to fasten something or as part of a whip **2 thongs** [plural] *AmE* a type of shoe that you hold on with your toes; FLIPFLOPS *BrE* —see picture at SHOE[1] **3** a pair of KNICKERS or the bottom half of a BIKINI that has a single string instead of the back part

**tho·rax** /ˈθɔːræks/ *n plural* **thoraxes** *or* **thoraces** /-rəsiːz/ [C] **1** *technical* the part of your body between your neck and your waist **2** the part of an insect's body between its head and its ABDOMEN (2) —**thoracic** /θɔːˈræsɪk/ *adj*

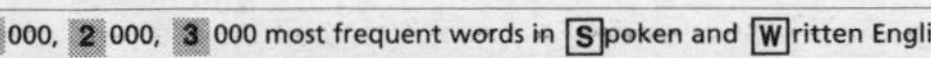

**thorn** /θɔːn‖θɔːrn/ *n* **1** [C] a sharp point that grows on the stem of a plant such as a rose **2** [C,U] a bush or tree that has thorns **3 a thorn in your side** someone or something that annoys you or causes problems for a long period of time: *He's been a thorn in the side of the party leadership for years.*

**thorn·y** /ˈθɔːni‖ˈθɔːrni/ *adj* **1 thorny question/problem/point/issue** a question etc that is complicated and difficult: *The thorny question of redundancies will have to be tackled sooner or later.* **2** a thorny bush, plant etc has thorns —**thorniness** *n* [U]

**thor·ough** /ˈθʌrə‖ˈθʌroʊ, ˈθʌrə/ *adj* **1** including every possible detail: *My doctor gave me a thorough check-up.* | *I made very thorough notes of the meeting.* **2** careful to do things properly so that you avoid mistakes: *Our mechanics will check everything, they're very thorough.* **3 a thorough pest/nuisance/mess** used to emphasize the bad qualities of someone or something —see also THOROUGHLY —**thoroughness** *n* [U]

**thor·ough·bred** /ˈθʌrəbred‖ˈθʌroʊ-, ˈθʌrə-/ *n* [C] **1** a horse that has parents of the same very good breed **2** someone who seems to do something naturally to a very high standard: *If we are talking about batsmen, Gower is a thoroughbred.*

**thor·ough·fare** /ˈθʌrəfeə‖ˈθʌroʊfer, ˈθʌrə-/ *n* **1** [C] the main road through a place such as a city or village: *The motel was off the main thoroughfare.* **2 no thoroughfare** a written sign used to tell people that they cannot go on a particular road or path

**thor·ough·go·ing** /ˌθʌrəˈgəʊɪŋ◂‖-ˈgoʊ-/ *adj* **1** very thorough and careful: *a thoroughgoing inspection of the site* **2** [only before noun] a thoroughgoing action or quality is complete: *the thoroughgoing materialism of this generation*

**thor·ough·ly** /ˈθʌrəli‖ˈθʌroʊli, ˈθʌrə-/ *adv* **1** completely: *She sat in her room feeling thoroughly miserable.* | *I thoroughly enjoyed the play this evening.* **2** carefully, so that nothing is forgotten: *to clean a room thoroughly*

**those** /ðəʊz‖ðoʊz/ the plural of THAT

**thou** /ðaʊ/ *pron old use* a word meaning you, used as the subject of a sentence —see also HOLIER-THAN-THOU

S1 W1 **though¹** /ðəʊ‖ðoʊ/ *conjunction* **1** used to introduce a statement that makes the other main statement seem surprising or unlikely: *Though he was only twelve he could run faster than any kid in the school.* | **though old/tired etc** *His childhood, though poverty stricken, had been a happy one.* | **old though it is/tired though he was etc** *Odd though it may seem, I actually like housework.* **2** used to add a fact or opinion which makes what you have just said seem less serious, less important etc: *These samosas are great, though there's not much meat in them.* | *The offenders were dealt with firmly though fairly.* **3 as though** as if: *The lights were on and cigarettes still burned in the ashtray, as though everyone had left in a hurry.* —see also ALTHOUGH, **even though** (EVEN¹ (6))

S1 **though²** *adv* [sentence adverb] *especially spoken* used at the end of a CLAUSE (2) to add a fact or opinion which makes what you have just said seem less important, or to add a very different fact or opinion etc: *Yeah, a Rolex for £150 is a great bargain. Is it real though?* | *Two heart attacks in a year. It hasn't stopped him smoking though.*

**thought¹** /θɔːt‖θɒːt/ past tense and past participle of THINK¹

S1 W1 **thought²** *n*
**1 ▶ STH YOU THINK ABOUT ◀** [C] something that you think of, remember, or realize; idea: *I was just going to pick up the phone when a sudden thought made me hesitate.* | [+ **of**] *a traveller's thoughts of home* | **the thought (that)** *I'm bothered by the thought that I might not have a job next year.* | **have a thought** (=suddenly think of something) *I've just had a thought – why don't we invite Judith?* | **the thought crossed my mind** (=I considered it) *"Do you think we should cancel the holiday?" "The thought had crossed my mind."* | **a/the thought occurs to sb** (=someone thinks of something) *The thought has just occurred to me, that we should get some insurance.* | **the very thought (of)** (=used when a thought produces strong feelings) *The very thought of moving to New York filled him with dread.* | **sobering thought** (=a serious and worrying thought) *It's a sobering thought that this country spends more on weapons than on education.* | **dark thoughts** (=evil or sad thoughts) *You must put such dark thoughts out of your mind.* | **cannot bear the thought of** (=be unable to accept an idea) *Louis could not bear the thought of being parted from her.*
**2 ▶ ACT OF THINKING ◀** [U] the act of thinking: **lost/deep in thought** (=thinking so much that you do not notice what is happening around you) *Derek was staring out of the window, lost in thought.* | **thought process** (=the way people's minds work) *Piaget helped teachers to understand children's thought processes.*
**3 ▶ CAREFUL CONSIDERATION ◀** [U] careful and serious consideration: *With more thought and care this would have been a first class essay.* | **give sth thought** (=think carefully about sth) *I've been giving your proposal a lot of thought.*
**4 that's a thought!** *spoken* used to say that someone has made a good suggestion: *"Why don't you ask Walter's advice?" "That's a thought! – I'll phone him right away."*
**5 it's just a thought** *spoken* used to say that what you have just said is only a suggestion and you have not thought about it very much: *I was wondering if your brother could help us – it was just a thought.*
**6 ▶ SUGGESTION ◀** [C] a suggestion or opinion about something: [+ **on**] *Do you have any thoughts on how we should spend the money?*
**7 ▶ INTENTION ◀** [C,U] intention or hope of doing something: [+ **of**] *I had no thought of gaining any personal advantage.*
**8 ▶ CARING ABOUT STH ◀** [C,U] a feeling of worrying or caring about something: [+ **for**] *Louis went back into the blazing building with no thought for his own safety.* | **you are always in my thoughts** (=used to tell someone that you think about them and care about them a lot)
**9 sb's thoughts turn to sth** if your thoughts turn to something, you start to think about it: *Debbie's thoughts had turned to more serious matters.*
**10 spare a thought for** used to tell someone that they should think about someone who is in a worse situation than they are: *Spare a thought for the homeless.*
**11 don't give it another thought** *spoken* used to tell someone politely not to worry after they have told you they are sorry
**12 it's the thought that counts** *spoken* used to say that someone's actions are very kind even if they have only done something small or unimportant
**13 ▶ WAY OF THINKING ◀** [U] a way of thinking that is typical of a particular group, period of history etc: *ancient Greek thought* —see also **perish the thought** (PERISH (3)), **second thoughts** (SECOND¹ (8)), **school of thought** (SCHOOL¹ (8))

**thought·ful** /ˈθɔːtfəl‖ˈθɒːt-/ *adj* **1** serious and quiet because you are thinking a lot: *a thoughtful expression* **2** always thinking of the things you can do to make people happy or comfortable: *You'll like Paul, he's very thoughtful.* | [+ **of**] *It was really thoughtful of you to remember my birthday.* —**thoughtfully** *adv* —**thoughtfulness** *n* [U]

**thought·less** /ˈθɔːtləs‖ˈθɒːt-/ *adj* forgetting about the needs and feelings of other people because you are thinking about what you want: *rash and thoughtless actions* | **it is thoughtless of sb to do sth** *It's so thoughtless of John to smoke when there's a baby around.* —**thoughtlessly** *adv* —**thoughtlessness** *n*

**thought-out** /ˌ· ˈ·◂/ *adj* **carefully/well/badly thought-out** planned and organized carefully, well etc: *a carefully thought-out speech*

**thou·sand** /ˈθaʊzənd/ *number* **1** 1000 —see HUNDRED (USAGE) **2 thousands** a lot: [+ **of**] *There were thousands of people at the concert.* —**thousandth** *adj*

**thral·dom** *BrE*, **thralldom** *AmE* /ˈθrɔːldəm‖ˈθrɒːl-/ *n* [U] *literary* the state of being a slave; SLAVERY

**thrall** /θrɔːl‖θrɒːl/ *n* **in sb's thrall** *literary* controlled or strongly influenced by someone or something: *The magic of the evening held them in thrall.*

**thrash¹** /θræʃ/ *n* **1** [singular] a violent movement from side to side **2** [C] *old-fashioned* a loud noisy party **3** [U] *informal* a type of ROCK¹ (2) music with very loud fast electric guitar playing

**thrash²** *v* **1** [T] to beat someone violently in order to punish them: *My poor brother used to get thrashed for all kinds of minor offences.* **2** [I always + adv/prep] to move or make something move from side to side in a violent or uncontrolled way: [+ **about/around**] *The fish were thrashing about in the bottom of the boat.* **3** [T] *informal* to defeat someone very easily in a game: *Brazil thrashed Italy 5 – 0.*

**thrash** sth ↔ **out** *phr v* [T] to discuss a problem thoroughly with someone until you find an answer: *We spent the whole day trying to thrash out a solution.*

**thrash·ing** /ˈθræʃɪŋ/ *n* [C] **give/get a thrashing a)** to beat someone or be beaten violently as a punishment: *If you speak to your mother like that again, you'll get a thrashing.* **b)** to defeat someone or be defeated easily in a game

**thread¹** /θred/ *n*
**1 ▶ COTTON/SILK ETC ◀** [C,U] a long thin string of cotton, silk etc used to SEW or weave cloth: *Have you got a needle and thread?*
**2 ▶ IDEAS ◀** [singular] the connection between the different parts of an explanation, story etc: *a common thread running through all the poems* | **lose the thread** (=stop understanding how ideas or events are connected) *I'm sorry, I've lost the thread of your argument.*
**3 pick up the threads** to begin something again after a long period, especially a relationship or way of life: *It's difficult to pick up the threads when you've been travelling for so long.*
**4 ▶ LIGHT/SMOKE ETC ◀** *literary* [C] a long thin line of something: [+ **of**] *The Colorado River is just a thread of silver, 4000 feet below.*
**5 ▶ ON A SCREW ◀** [C] a continuous raised line of metal that winds around the curved surface of a screw —see picture at SCREW¹
**6 threads** [plural] *old fashioned, especially AmE* clothes —see also **hang by a thread** (HANG¹ (5))

**thread²** *v* [T] **1** to put a thread or string through a hole: *Williams threaded the rope through the karabiner and attached it to the safety point.* | **thread a needle** (=push a thread through the hole in a needle) **2** to put a film, tape etc correctly through parts of a camera, PROJECTOR or TAPE RECORDER **3** to connect objects by pushing a string through a hole in them: *Thread the beads on a string and make a necklace.* **4 thread your way through/into etc** to move through a place by carefully going around things that are blocking your way: *She came towards me, threading her way through the traffic.*

**thread·bare** /ˈθredbeə‖-ber/ *adj* **1** clothes, carpets etc that are threadbare are very thin and in bad condition because they have been used a lot: *a threadbare old sofa* —see picture on page 1258 **2 threadbare excuse/argument/joke etc** an excuse etc that is no longer effective because it has been used too much

S2 W2 **threat** /θret/ *n* **1** [C,U] a statement that you will cause someone pain, unhappiness, or trouble: *Your threats don't scare me!* | [+ **of**] *the threat of strike action* | **make/issue a threat against** *Threats have been made against the book's author.* | **give in to threats** (=do what someone wants because they threaten you) *The government will not give in to terrorist threats.* | **carry out a threat** (=do what you threatened to do) | **empty threat** (=a threat to do something that you cannot really do) *Take no notice – they're empty threats.* | **death/bomb etc threat** *Police are investigating death threats made against the singer.* | **under threat of** *Mancini claims he was forced to carry out their orders under threat of death.* **2** [C usually singular] the possibility that something very bad will happen: [+ **of**] *There's a serious threat of famine.* | **be under threat of closure/attack etc** (=be likely to be closed, attacked etc) *The factory is still under threat of closure.* **3** [C usually singular] someone or something that is regarded as a possible danger: [+ **to**] *Automation presents the biggest threat to the workforce.* | **pose a threat** *Nuclear weapons continue to pose a threat.*

**threat·en** /ˈθretn/ *v* **1** [T] to say that you will cause someone pain, unhappiness, or trouble if they do not do what you want: **threaten to do sth** *Every time they quarrel, Jan threatens to leave.* | **threaten sb with sth** *We were threatened with the sack if we didn't co-operate.* | **threaten sb** *It's no use threatening me – I won't do it.* | **threaten sth** *The unions are threatening a one-day strike.* | **threaten that** *He's threatening that if he doesn't get his way, he'll resign.* **2** [T] to be likely to harm or destroy something: *Poaching threatens the survival of the rhino.* **3** [I,T] if something threatens to cause an unpleasant situation, it seems likely that it will cause it: **threaten sb/sth with** *Large areas of the jungle are now threatened with destruction.* | **threaten to do sth** *The incident threatens to ruin his chances in the election.* S2 W2 

**threat·en·ing** /ˈθretn-ɪŋ/ *adj* **1** talking or behaving in a way that is intended to threaten someone: *His voice sounded threatening.* **2** making threats: *a threatening letter* —**threateningly** *adv*

**three** /θriː/ *number* **1** 3 **2 the three R's** *old-fashioned* used when talking about children's education to mean reading, writing and ARITHMETIC S1 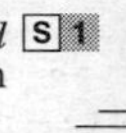

**three-cor·nered** /ˌ· ˈ··◂/ *adj* **1** having three corners **2 three-cornered contest/fight** a competition which involves three people or groups

**three-D, 3-D** /ˌθriː ˈdiː◂/ *adj* a three-D film or picture is made so that it appears to be three-dimensional —**three-D** *n* [U] *a film in 3-D*

**three-day e·vent** /ˌ· · ·ˈ·/ *n* [C] *BrE* a horse-riding competition that takes place for three days

**three-di·men·sion·al** /ˌ· ·ˈ···◂/ *adj* **1** having or seeming to have length, depth, and height: *a three-dimensional structure* **2** a three-dimensional character in a book, film etc, seems like a real person

**three·fold** /ˈθriːfəʊld‖-foʊld/ *adj* three times as much or as many —**threefold** *adv*

**three-half·pence** /·ˈ··/ *n* [U] *BrE old use* one and a half old pence

**three-leg·ged race** /ˌ· ˈ·· ·/ *n* [C] a race in which two people run together, and one person has their right leg tied to the other person's left leg

**three-line whip** /ˌ· · ˈ·/ *n* [C] an order from a leader of a British political party telling MPs in that party that they must vote in a particular way

**three·pence** /ˈθrepəns, ˈθrʌ-/ *n* [U] *BrE old use* three old pence

**three·pen·ny bit** /ˌθrepəni ˈbɪt, ˌθrʌ-/ *n* [C] a small coin used in Britain before 1971 that was worth three old pence

**three-piece suit** /ˌ· · ˈ·/ *n* [C] a suit that consists of a JACKET (1), WAISTCOAT, and trousers made from the same material

**three-piece suite** /ˌ· · ˈ·/ *n* [C] *especially BrE* two chairs and a SOFA covered in the same material

**three-ply** /ˈ· ·/ *adj* three-ply wood, wool, TISSUE (1) etc consists of three layers or threads

**three-point turn** /ˌ· · ˈ·/ *n* [C] a way of turning your car so that it faces the opposite way, by driving forwards, backwards, and then forwards again

**three-quar·ter** /ˌ· ˈ··◂/ *adj* [only before noun] three quarters of the full size, length etc of something: *a three-quarter violin* | **a three-quarter length coat** (=one that ends a little above your knees)

**three-quar·ters** /ˌ· ˈ··/ *n* [plural] an amount equal to three of the four equal parts that make up a whole: **[+ of]** *three-quarters of a hour*

**three-ring cir·cus** /ˌ· · ˈ··/ *n* [singular] *AmE informal* a place or situation that is confusing because there is too much activity: *I don't know how you can work in that office – it's like a three-ring circus.*

**three R's** /ˌθriː ˈɑːz‖-ˈɑrz/ *n* **the three R's** *old-fashioned* reading, writing, and ARITHMETIC (=working with numbers), considered as the basic things that children must learn

**three·score** /ˈθriːskɔː‖-skɔːr/ *number old use* 60 —see also SCORE[3] (1)

**three·some** /ˈθriːsəm/ *n* [C usually singular] *informal* a group of three people or things

**three-star** /ˈ· ·/ *adj* a three-star hotel, restaurant etc is officially judged to be of a good standard

**three-wheel·er** /ˌ· ˈ··◂/ *n* [C] a car that has three wheels

**thren·o·dy** /ˈθrenədi/ *n* [C] *literary* a funeral song for someone who has died

**thresh** /θreʃ/ *v* [I,T] to separate the grain from the rest of corn, wheat etc, by beating it with a special tool or machine —**thresher** *n* [C] —compare THRASH[2]

**threshing ma·chine** /ˈ·· ·ˌ·/ *n* [C] a machine used for separating the grain from the rest of corn, wheat etc

**thresh·old** /ˈθreʃhəʊld, -ʃəʊld‖-oʊld/ *n* [C] **1** the entrance to a room or building, or the area of floor at the entrance **2** the level at which something starts to happen or have an effect: *my boredom threshold* | **pain threshold** (=the amount of pain you can suffer before you react to it) | **have a high pain threshold** (=be able to suffer a lot of pain before you react) | **have a low pain threshold** (=not be able to suffer much pain before you react) **3 on the threshold of** at the beginning of a new and important event or development: *All Europe stands on the threshold of an era of prosperity.*

**threw** /θruː/ the past tense of THROW[1]

**thrice** /θraɪs/ *adv old use* three times

**thrift** /θrɪft/ *n* [U] *old-fashioned* wise and careful use of money, so that none is wasted —see also SPENDTHRIFT

**thrift shop** /ˈ· ·/ *n* [C] *AmE* a shop that sells used goods, especially clothes, often in order to get money for a CHARITY (2)

**thrift·y** /ˈθrɪfti/ *adj* using money carefully and wisely: *hard-working, thrifty folk* —**thriftily** *adv* —**thriftiness** *n* [U]

**thrill**[1] /θrɪl/ *n* **1** [C] a sudden strong feeling of excitement and pleasure, or the thing that makes you feel this: **get a thrill out of** *Even though I've been acting for years, I still get a thrill out of going on stage.* | **give sb a thrill** *Pete reckons that using guns gives him a thrill.* | **the thrill of (doing sth)** (=the excitement you get from something) *the thrill of travelling at speed* | **do sth for the thrill of it** (=do something for excitement and not for any serious reason) **2 thrills and spills** the excitement and danger involved in an activity, especially a sport —see also **cheap thrill** (CHEAP[1] (5))

**thrill**[2] *v* **1** [T] to make someone feel excited and happy: *The magic of his music continues to thrill audiences.* **2** [I] to feel excited: **[+ to]** *Thrill to the magic of the world's greatest guitarist.*

**thrilled** /θrɪld/ *adj* [not before noun] very excited, happy, and pleased: *We were so thrilled to hear about the baby.* | **thrilled to bits** (=very thrilled)

**thrill·er** /ˈθrɪlə‖-ər/ *n* [C] a book or film that tells an exciting story about murder or crime

**thril·ling** /ˈθrɪlɪŋ/ *adj* interesting and exciting: *a thrilling climax to the championship* —**thrillingly** *adv*

**thrive** /θraɪv/ *v past tense* **thrived** or **throve** /θrəʊv‖θroʊv/ [I] *formal* if something such as a company or plant thrives, it becomes very successful or very strong and healthy: *tree ferns that still thrive in tropical rainforests* | *a free-market economy in which businesses can thrive*

**thrive on** sth *phr v* [T] to enjoy or be successful in conditions that other people, businesses etc find difficult or unpleasant: *I wouldn't want that much pressure, but she seems to thrive on it.*

**thri·ving** /ˈθraɪvɪŋ/ *adj* a thriving company, business etc is very successful: *a thriving tourist industry*

**throat** /θrəʊt‖θroʊt/ *n* [C] S3 W3 **1** the passage from the back of your mouth to the top of the tubes that go down to your lungs and stomach —see picture at HEAD[1] **2** the front of your neck: *She fingered the pearls at her throat.* **3 clear your throat** to make a noise in your throat, especially before you speak, or in order to get someone's attention **4 force/ram sth down sb's throat** *informal* to force someone to accept or listen to your ideas and opinions **5 be at each other's throats** if two people are at each other's throats, they are fighting or arguing **6 cut your own throat** to behave in a way that is certain to harm you, especially because you are proud or angry —see also **bring a lump to sb's throat** (LUMP[1] (4)), **have a frog in your throat** (FROG (2)), **jump down sb's throat** (JUMP[1] (9)), **stick in your throat** (STICK[1] (11))

**throat·y** /ˈθrəʊti‖ˈθroʊ-/ *adj* making a low rough sound when you speak or sing —**throatily** *adv* —**throatiness** *n* [C,U]

**throb**[1] /θrɒb‖θrɑːb/ *v* [I] **throbbed, throbbing** **1** if a part of your body throbs, you get a regular feeling of pain in it: *Her foot was throbbing with pain.* **2** if music or a machine throbs it makes a sound with a strong regular beat **3** if your heart throbs, it beats faster or more strongly than usual

**throb**[2] *n* [C] a low, strong, regular beat or sensation: *the throb of distant drums* —see also HEARTTHROB

**throes** /θrəʊz‖θroʊz/ *n* [plural] **in the throes of** in the middle of a very difficult situation: *a country in the throes of a profound economic crisis* —see also DEATH THROES

**throm·bo·sis** /θrɒmˈbəʊsɪs‖θrɑːmˈboʊ-/ *n* [C,U] *technical* a serious medical problem caused by a CLOT[2] (1) forming in your blood, especially in your heart

**throne** /θrəʊn‖θroʊn/ *n* **1** [C] a special chair used by a king or queen at important ceremonies **2 the throne** the position and power of being a king or queen: **be on the throne** (=be ruling) *in 1913 when George V was on the throne* | **come to the throne** (=become king or queen) | **be next in line to the throne** (=be the person who will become king or queen when the present one dies)

**throng**[1] /θrɒŋ‖θrɒːŋ/ *n* [C] *literary* a large group of people in one place; crowd: *a milling throng of excited spectators* | **the throng** *She got lost in the throng.*

**throng**[2] *v* **1** [I always + adv/prep, T] if people throng a place, they go there in large numbers: *tourists still thronging the bars and restaurants* **2 be thronged with** if a place is thronged with people, it is very crowded with them: *streets thronged with Christmas shoppers*

**throt·tle**[1] /ˈθrɒtl‖ˈθrɑːtl/ *v* [T] **1** to hold someone's throat very tightly so that they cannot breathe; STRANGLE (1) **2** to make it difficult or impossible for something to succeed: *These policies are throttling individual initiative and effort.*

**throttle back** *phr v* [I,T] to reduce the amount of petrol or oil flowing into an engine, in order to reduce speed

**throttle**[2] *n* [C] *technical* **1** a piece of equipment that controls the amount of petrol, oil etc going into a vehicle's engine **2 at full throttle** as fast as possible in your car, boat etc

**through**[1] /θruː/ *prep* **1** entering something such as a door, passage, tube, or hole at one end or side and leaving it at the other: *They were suddenly plunged into darkness as the train went through the tunnel.* | *The ball went flying through the window.* | *As the water passes through the filter a lot of dirt is taken out.* **2** going into an area, group

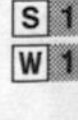

etc and moving across it or within it: *He had to push his way through the crowd to get to her.* | *The new ring road stops all the traffic driving through the centre of town.* | *gliding noiselessly through the air* —see picture on page 1257 **3** if you see something through glass, a window etc, you are on one side of the glass etc and it is on the other: *I could see her through the window.* | *Through the mist she could just make out his silhouette.* **4** passing a place where you are supposed to stop: *The driver had gone straight through the traffic lights and hit an oncoming car.* | *Once through passport control your luggage will be searched.* **5** cutting, breaking or making a hole from one side of something to the other: *Not only did the drill pierce the wood but it went straight through the table underneath too!* | *The goat had eaten right through the rope.* **6** during and to the end of a period of time: *Sometimes I go to bed at 5 a.m. and sleep right through the day.* | *I wouldn't worry about Joe, he's just going through a difficult period.* **7** if you get through a difficult situation or experience you deal with it successfully: *I've no idea how I managed to get through my exams last year.* | *He has lots of friends which really helped him through the divorce.* **8 look through/search through/go through etc** to do something from beginning to end and include all parts of it: *In the dress rehearsal he'll go through the play one final time.* | *I've searched through all my documents and I still can't find my passport.* **9** because of someone or something: *How many working days were lost through sickness last year?* | *Through your incompetence many of the hotel's regular guests have taken their business elsewhere.* **10 get through/go through** to use a lot of something: *You wouldn't believe how many packets of cigarettes she gets through.* **11** using a particular person, organization etc to help you achieve something: *I got my first job through an employment agency.* **12 May through June/Wednesday through Friday etc** *AmE* from May until June, from Wednesday until Friday etc: *The store is open Monday through Saturday.* —see INCLUSIVE (USAGE) **13** if you go through a country, you travel across it: *It was while we were travelling through Africa that we decided to settle over there.* **14** if a law passes through a parliament, it is agreed and accepted as a law: *The bill's passage through Congress was not a smooth one.* —see also THRU

S1 W2 **through²** *adv* **1** from one end or side of something to the other: *Let me through – I'm a doctor!* **2 read/think/talk etc sth through** to read, think etc about something very carefully from beginning to end: *If you think it through – we have no choice but to agree to his demands.* **3 get through/come through/pull through etc** to deal with a difficult situation or experience successfully: *I don't know why you worry about exams – you'll sail through as usual.* | *Doctors are unsure about whether she'll pull through.* **4 get through/make it through etc** to reach a person, place etc after a difficult journey: *It's snowing too heavily, you'll never get through.* | **[+ to]** *After days of effort, rescue teams have finally made it through to the survivors.* **5 wet through/cooked through etc** *informal* very wet, cooked completely etc: *You're wet through. What on earth have you been doing?* **6 get through/be through** *BrE* to be connected to someone by telephone: **[+ to]** *I managed to get through to her after several attempts.* | **put sb through** (=connect someone by telephone to someone else) *"Can I speak to Mr Henry please?" "I'm putting you through sir."* **7 go through to London/Paris etc** if something such as a train goes through to London it continues as far as London **8 through and through** if someone is a particular type of person through and through, they are completely that type of person: *I'll say one thing for Sandra – she's a professional through and through.*

**through³** *adj* **1 be through (with sb/sth)** *informal* **a)** to have finished doing something, using something etc: *I'm not through just yet – I should be finished in an hour.* **b)** to no longer be having a relationship with someone: *That's it! Simon and I are through.* **c)** to have stopped doing something or using something that is bad or that you do not like: *He says he's through with drugs but it's just not that easy.* **2 through train/road** a train or road by which you can reach a place, without having to use other trains or roads

**through·out¹** /θruːˈaʊt/ *prep* **1** in every part of a particular area, place etc: *a large international organization with offices throughout the world.* **2** during all of a particular period, from the beginning to the end: *He had misled the court throughout the trial.* S3 W1

**throughout²** *adv* [usually at the end of a sentence] **1** in every part of a particular area, place etc: *The house is in excellent condition with fitted carpets throughout.* **2** during all of a particular period, from the beginning to the end: *He managed to remain calm throughout.*

**through·put** /ˈθruːpʊt/ *n* [U] the amount of work, materials etc that can be dealt with in a particular period of time: *an airport with a weekly throughput of 100,000 passengers*

**through·way** /ˈθruːweɪ/ *n* [C] *AmE* a THRUWAY

**throve** /θrəʊv‖θroʊv/ *old-fashioned* the past tense of THRIVE

**throw¹** /θrəʊ‖θroʊ/ *v past* **threw** /θruː/ *past participle* **thrown** /θrəʊn‖θroʊn/ S1 W1

**1 ▶ THROW A BALL/STONE ETC ◀** [I,T] to make an object such as a ball move quickly through the air by moving your hand quickly: **throw sth at/to/towards etc** *Someone threw a stone at the car.* | *Cromartie throws the ball back to the pitcher.* | **throw sb sth** *Throw me that towel, would you.*

**2 ▶ PUT STH CARELESSLY ◀** [T always + adv/prep] to put something somewhere quickly and carelessly: **throw sth on/onto/down etc** *Don't just throw your clothes on the floor – pick them up!*

**3 ▶ PUSH ROUGHLY/VIOLENTLY ◀** [T always + adv/prep] to push someone or something roughly and violently in a particular direction or into a particular position: **throw sth ↔ open** *Smelling smoke, she threw open all the windows.* | **throw sb into the air** *Patrick was thrown into the air by the force of the explosion.* | **throw sb to the ground** *The guards threw Biko to the ground and started kicking him.*

**4 ▶ MAKE SB FALL ◀** [T] **a)** to make your opponent fall to the ground in WRESTLING or JUDO **b)** if a horse throws its rider it makes them fall onto the ground

**5 throw yourself at/on/into/down etc** to move or jump somewhere suddenly and with a lot of force: *I managed to open the door by throwing myself at it.*

**6 ▶ MOVE HANDS/HEAD ETC ◀** [T always + adv/prep] to suddenly and quickly move your hands, arms, head etc into a new position: **throw sth back/up/around etc** *I threw my arms around her and kissed her.*

**7 throw sb into prison/jail** to suddenly put someone in prison: *Anyone who opposes the regime is liable to be thrown in jail.*

**8 throw sb out of work/office etc** to suddenly take away someone's job or position in authority: *Nixon was thrown out of office, following the Watergate scandal.*

**9 throw sb into confusion/chaos/disarray etc** to suddenly make a group of people very confused and uncertain about what they should do: *Everyone was thrown into confusion by this news.*

**10 ▶ CONFUSE SB ◀** [T] to confuse or shock someone, especially by suddenly saying something: **throw sb completely** *This handsome young stranger said "Hello, Maria," – it threw me completely.*

**11 be thrown back on** to be forced to have to depend on your own skills, knowledge etc: *Once again we were thrown back on our own resources.*

**12 throw suspicion/doubt on** to make people think that someone is probably guilty or that something may not be true: *new discoveries that throw doubt on some basic scientific assumptions*

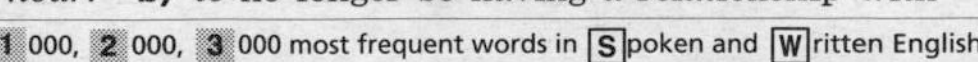

**13 throw sb a look/glance/smile etc** to quickly look at someone with a particular expression that shows how you are feeling
**14 throw a fit/scene/tantrum etc** to react in a very angry way: *I can't tell my parents – they'd throw a fit!*
**15 throw questions/a remark** to ask a lot of questions or suddenly say something: *They kept throwing awkward questions at me.*
**16 throw a switch/handle/lever** to make a large machine or piece of electrical equipment start or stop working by moving a SWITCH² (1)
**17 throw a party** to organize a party and invite people
**18 throw yourself into sth** to start doing an activity eagerly and using a lot of time and effort: *Since her husband died, she's thrown herself into her work.*
**19 throw dice/a six/a four etc** to roll DICE or to get a particular number by rolling dice: *You have to throw a six to start.*
**20 throw money at** *informal* to try to solve a problem by spending a lot of money but without really thinking about the problem
**21 throw good money after bad/throw money down the drain** to waste money by spending it on something that has already failed
**22 throw your weight around** to use your position of authority to tell people what to do in an unreasonable way: *He's the sort of insensitive bully who enjoys throwing his weight around.*
**23 throw your weight behind** to publicly support a plan, person etc and use your power to make sure they succeed: *The party leadership is throwing its weight behind the campaign.*
**24 throw cold water on** to say that a plan, suggestion etc is unlikely to succeed
**25 throw light on** to make something easier to understand by providing new information: *Startling revelations that throw new light on Elvis, the man.*

**26 throw a light/shadows/rays** [T] to make light, shadows etc fall on a particular place: *The trees threw long, dark shadows across the cornfield.*
**27 throw the book at** *informal* to punish someone as severely as possible or charge them with as many offences as possible
**28 throw caution to the wind(s)** to ignore the risks and deliberately behave in a way that may cause trouble or problems
**29 ▶ DELIBERATELY LOSE ◀** [T] to deliberately lose a fight or sports game that you could have won
**30 throw sth (back) in sb's face** to be unkind to someone after they have been kind to you or helped you
**31 throw a punch/a left/a right etc** to try to hit someone with your hand in a fight
**32 throw yourself at sb** *informal* to try very hard to attract someone's attention because you want to have a sexual relationship with them
**33 throw your hat into the ring** to officially announce that you will compete or take part in something
**34 throw the baby out with the bath water** to get rid of good useful parts of a system, organization etc when you are changing it in order to try and make it better
**35 ▶ POT ◀** [T] to make a clay object such as a bowl, using a POTTER'S WHEEL
**36 throw your voice** to use a special trick to make your voice seem to be coming from a different place from the place you are standing —see also **be thrown in at the deep end** (DEEP¹ (16))

**throw** sth ↔ **away** *phr v* [T] **1** to get rid of something that you do not want or need: *I shouldn't have thrown away the receipt.* **2** to lose or waste something good that you have, for example a skill or an opportunity: *This could be the best chance you'll ever have. Don't throw it away!*

**throw in** sth *phr v* [T] **1** [**throw** sth ↔ **in**] to add something to what you are selling, without increasing the price: *We paid $2000 for the boat, with the trailer and spares thrown in.* **2** [**throw** sth ↔ **in**] if you throw in a remark, you say it suddenly without thinking carefully **3 throw in the sponge/towel** *informal* to admit that you have been defeated

**throw** sb/sth ↔ **off** *phr v* [T] **1** [**throw** sth ↔ **off**] to take off a piece of clothing in a quick, careless way: *He threw off his sweater.* **2** [**throw** sth ↔ **off**] to get free from something that has been limiting your freedom: *In 1845 they finally threw off the yoke of foreign rule.* **3** [**throw** sth ↔ **off**] if you throw off a slight illness such as a COLD² (2), you succeed in getting better **4** [**throw** sb/sth ↔ **off**] to escape from someone or something that is chasing you: **throw sb off the scent** (=make someone who is following you unable to find where you have gone) *If we cross the stream it might throw them off the scent.* **5** [**throw** sth ↔ **off**] to produce large amounts of heat, light, RADIATION etc: *The engine was throwing off so much heat that the air above it shimmered with haze.*

**throw** sth ↔ **on** *phr v* [T] to put on a piece of clothing quickly and carelessly

**throw** sth ↔ **open** *phr v* [T] **1** to allow people to go into a place that is usually kept private: *plans to throw the Palace open to the public* **2** to allow anyone to take part in a competition or a discussion

**throw** sb/sth ↔ **out** *phr v* [T] **1** [**throw** sth ↔ **out**] to get rid of something that you do not want or need, especially when you are tidying: *We usually throw out all our old magazines.* **2** [**throw** sb ↔ **out**] to make someone leave a place, school, or organization etc quickly, especially because they have been behaving badly or made you angry: *Nick got thrown out of college in the second year for taking drugs.* | **throw sb out on the street** (=make someone leave their house immediately, even if they have nowhere else to live) **3** [**throw** sth ↔ **out**] if parliament or another official or political organization throws out a plan or suggestion, they refuse to accept it and make it legal, especially after voting: *The bill was thrown out by the Senate.* **4** [**throw** sth ↔ **out**] if something throws out smoke, heat, dust etc, it produces a lot of it and fills the air with it: *huge trucks throwing out noxious fumes from their exhausts*

**throw** sb **over** *phr v* [T] *old-fashioned* to end a romantic relationship with someone

**throw** sb/sth **together** *phr v* [T] **1** [**throw** sth ↔ **together**] to make something such as a meal quickly and not very carefully: *There's lots of food in the fridge – I'm sure I can throw something together.* **2** [**throw** sb ↔ **together**] if a situation throws people together, it makes them meet and know each other

**throw up** *phr v* **1** [I,T] to bring food or drink up from your stomach out through your mouth because you are ill or drunk etc; VOMIT¹: *Georgia was bent over the basin, throwing up.* —see SICK¹ (USAGE) **2** [T **throw** sth ↔ **up**] to produce new ideas, problems, or new people: *It wasn't a long meeting, but it did throw up some interesting suggestions.* **3** [T **throw** sth ↔ **up**] if a vehicle, runner etc throws up dust, water etc, they make it rise into the air as they move along **4** [T **throw** sth ↔ **up**] *informal* to suddenly leave your job, your home etc: *I can't just throw up everything and come and live with you.*

**throw²** *n* [C] **1** an act of throwing something such as a ball: *The throw went straight to Marinelli on first base.* **2** the distance which something is thrown: *a throw of over eighty metres* **3** the result of throwing something in a game such as darts (DART¹ (2)) or DICE¹ (1) **4 £5/£10/50p etc a throw** *BrE informal* £5, £10 etc each

**throw·a·way** /ˈθrəʊəweɪ‖ˈθroʊ-/ *adj* **1 throwaway remark/line/comment etc** a short remark etc that is said quickly and without careful thought: *a comedy act full of short throwaway lines* **2 throwaway cup/plate/razor etc** a cup, plate etc that has been produced cheaply so that it can be thrown away after it has been used; DISPOSABLE (1) **3 the throwaway society** used to show disapproval when talking about modern societies in which products are not made to last a long time

**throw·back** /ˈθrəʊbæk‖ˈθroʊ-/ *n* [C usually singular] something that is similar to or is a result of something that happened in the past: **be a throwback to** *This year's fashions are a throwback to the 1950s.*

**throw-in** /ˈ· ·/ *n* [C] the act of throwing the ball back onto the field in football, after it has gone over the line at the side of the field —see picture on page 1264

**thru** /θruː/ *adj, adv AmE informal* a short form of THROUGH —**thru** *prep*

**thrum** /θrʌm/ *v* **thrummed, thrumming** [I,T] to make a low sound like something beating or shaking: *the deep thrumming of the engine*

**thrush** /θrʌʃ/ *n* **1** [C] a brown bird with spots on its front **2** [U] an infectious disease that affects the VAGINA or mouth

**thrust¹** /θrʌst/ *v past tense and past participle* **thrust** [T] **1** to push something somewhere with a sudden or violent movement: **thrust sth into/back** *The man thrust a package into Jake's hand and ran away.* **2 have sth thrust upon you** to be forced to accept something that you did not expect or want **3** [I + **at**] to make a sudden movement forward with a sword or knife

**thrust** sth ↔ **aside** *phr v* [T] to refuse to think about something: *Our complaints were thrust aside and ignored.*

**thrust²** *n* **1** [C] a sudden strong movement that pushes forward: *the quick thrust of his sword* **2 the thrust** the main meaning or most important part of what someone says or does: *the main thrust of Clinton's healthcare reforms* **3** [U] *technical* the force of an engine that pushes something such as a plane forward

**thru·way**, **throughway** /ˈθruːweɪ/ *n* [C] *AmE* a wide road for fast traffic that you pay to use

**thud¹** /θʌd/ *n* [C] the low sound made by a heavy object hitting something else: *His head hit the wall with a dull thud.*

**thud²** *v* **thudded, thudding** [I] to hit or fall onto something with a low sound

**thug** /θʌg/ *n* [C] a violent man: *a bunch of thugs* —**thuggery** *n* [U]

**thumb¹** /θʌm/ *n* [C] **1** the part of your hand that is shaped like a thick short finger and helps you to hold things: *a baby sucking its thumb* **2** the part of a GLOVE that fits over your thumb **3 be all (fingers and) thumbs** *informal* to be unable to do things neatly and carefully with your hands: *Would you do up these buttons for me? I seem to be all thumbs today.* **4 give sth the thumbs up/down** *informal* to officially accept or reject a plan, suggestion etc: *The project had been given the thumbs up and we could now get started.* **5 be under sb's thumb** to be so strongly influenced by someone that they control you completely —see also **stick out like a sore thumb** (STICK¹), **rule of thumb** (RULE¹ (9))

**thumb²** *v* **1 thumb a lift** *BrE informal* **thumb a ride** *AmE informal* to persuade a driver of a passing car to stop and take you somewhere, by putting your hand out with your thumb raised **2 thumb your nose at** to show that you do not respect rules, laws etc or you do not care what someone thinks of you: *a chance to thumb his nose at authority*

**thumb through** sth *phr v* [I,T] to look through a book, magazine etc quickly: *thumbing through the pages of a gardening catalogue*

**thumb in·dex** /ˈ· ˌ··/ *n* [C] a series of U-shaped cuts in the edge of a large book, usually showing the letters of the alphabet, that help you find the part you want

**thumb·nail¹** /ˈθʌmneɪl/ *adj* **thumbnail sketch/description** a short description giving only the main facts about something

**thumbnail²** *n* [C] the nail on your thumb

**thumb·screw** /ˈθʌmskruː/ *n* [C] an instrument used in the past to punish or TORTURE² (1) people by crushing their thumbs

**thumb·tack** /ˈθʌmtæk/ *n* [C] *AmE* a short pin with a broad flat top used especially for fixing notices on walls; DRAWING PIN *BrE* —see picture at PIN¹

**thump¹** /θʌmp/ *v* **1** [T] *informal* to hit someone very hard with your hand closed: *If you don't shut up, I'm going to thump you!* —see picture on page 1259 **2** [I always + adv/prep, T] to make a dull loud sound by beating or falling against a surface: [+ **against/on/into**] *the dog's tail thumping against the floor* **3** [I] if your heart thumps, it beats very quickly because you are frightened or excited

**thump²** *n* **1** [C] the dull sound that is made when something hits a surface: *We heard a loud thump and then a scream from upstairs.* **2 give sb a thump on the back/head etc** *especially BrE* to hit someone on the back, head etc

**thump·ing** /ˈθʌmpɪŋ/ also **thumping great/big** *adj* [only before noun] *BrE informal* very big: *Mulroney swept to power with a thumping majority.*

**thun·der¹** /ˈθʌndə‖-ər/ *n* **1** [U] the loud noise that you hear during a storm, usually after a flash of LIGHTNING: **clap of thunder** (=one sudden noise of thunder) **2** [singular] a loud, deep noise like thunder: *the thunder of gunfire* **3 a face like thunder** looking very angry —see also BLOOD-AND-THUNDER, **steal sb's thunder** (STEAL¹ (7))

**thunder²** *v* **1 it thunders** if it thunders, there is a loud noise in the sky, usually after a flash of LIGHTNING **2** [I always + adv/prep] to move in a way that makes a very loud noise: *The children came thundering downstairs.* | [+ **against/onto**] *The sea thundered against the rocks.* **3** [T] to shout loudly and angrily

**thun·der·bolt** /ˈθʌndəbəʊlt‖-dərboʊlt/ *n* [C] **1** a flash of LIGHTNING and a noise of thunder together, which hits something **2** a sudden event or piece of news that shocks you **3** an imaginary weapon of thunder and lightning, used by gods to punish people

**thun·der·clap** /ˈθʌndəklæp‖-ər-/ *n* [C] a single loud noise of thunder

**thun·der·cloud** /ˈθʌndəklaʊd‖-ər-/ *n* [C] a large dark cloud that you see before or during a storm

**thun·der·ing** /ˈθʌndərɪŋ/ *adj, adv BrE old-fashioned* very bad, severe etc: *That's a thundering great lie!*

**thun·der·ous** /ˈθʌndərəs/ *adj* extremely loud: *thunderous applause* —**thunderously** *adv*

**thun·der·storm** /ˈθʌndəstɔːm‖-dərstɔːrm/ *n* [C] a storm with thunder and lightning

**thun·der·struck** /ˈθʌndəstrʌk‖-ər-/ *adj* [not before noun] extremely surprised or shocked: *Jeff was staring at me thunderstruck. "You mean it's been stolen?" he gasped.*

**thun·der·y** /ˈθʌndəri/ *adj* thundery weather is the type of weather that comes before a thunderstorm

**Thurs·day** /ˈθɜːzdi‖ˈθɜːr-/ written abbreviation **Thur.** or **Thurs.** *n* [C,U] the day between Wednesday and Friday. In Britain, Thursday is considered the fourth day of the week, and in the US it is considered the fifth day of the week: *We went to the theatre last Thursday.* | *I'll phone you on Thursday.* | *Christmas Day is on a Thursday this year.* | **Thursday morning/evening etc** *Shall we go to a film Thursday night?* | **on Thursdays** (=each Thursday) *I go to night school on Thursdays.* | **the Thursday** *BrE* (=the Thursday of the week being mentioned) *Angela's arriving on the Thursday and leaving on the Sunday.*

**thus** /ðʌs/ *adv formal* **1** [sentence adverb] as a result of something that you have just mentioned; HENCE: *Most of the evidence was destroyed in the fire. Thus it would be almost impossible to prove him guilty.* **2** in this manner or way: *He sold his car and used the money thus obtained to fly to Rio.* **3 thus far** until now: *Her political career thus far had remained unblemished.* W1

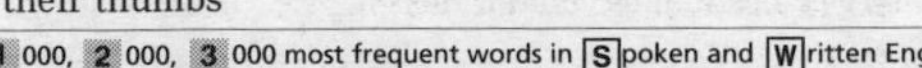

**USAGE NOTE: THUS**
WORD CHOICE: **thus, so, therefore, consequently, for this reason, as a result**
**Thus** is a little old-fashioned and only used in very formal English. In court you might hear: *They had no offer of finance, and thus were unable to achieve completion* (=they did not get the money so they could not buy the house).
In spoken English you usually use **so**: *I don't use the language much, so I tend to forget it* (NOT *thus*).
In formal speech and writing **therefore** will usually be used or, especially at the beginning of a sentence, **consequently**, **for this reason,** or **as a result**: *The country was beautiful. Consequently I decided to return the next year./I therefore decided to return the next year.*

**thwack**[1] /θwæk/ *n* [C] a short loud sound like something hitting a hard surface

**thwack**[2] *v* [T] to hit someone or something making a short loud sound

**thwart**[1] /θwɔːt‖θwɔːrt/ *v* [T] *formal* to prevent someone from doing what they are trying to do: *My plans were thwarted by the intervention of the police.*|*thwarted ambition*

**thwart**[2] *n* [C] *technical* a seat fixed across a ROWING BOAT

**thy** /ðaɪ/ *determiner old use* your: *We praise thy name, O Lord.*

**thyme** /taɪm/ *n* [U] a plant used for giving food a special taste

**thy·roid** /ˈθaɪrɔɪd/ also **thyroid gland** /ˈ·· ˌ·/ *n* [C] an organ in your neck that produces substances that affect the way you develop and behave

**thy·self** /ðaɪˈself/ *pron old use* yourself

**ti** /tiː/ *n* [singular] the seventh note in a musical SCALE[1] (8) according to the SOL-FA system

**ti·a·ra** /tiˈɑːrə/ *n* [C] a piece of jewellery like a small CROWN[1] (1a), that a woman wears on her head on formal occasions: *a diamond tiara*

**tib·i·a** /ˈtɪbiə/ *n plural* **tibiae** /-bi-iː/ *or* **tibias** [C] *technical* a bone in the front of your leg —see picture at SKELETON

**tic** /tɪk/ *n* [C] a sudden, uncontrolled movement of a muscle in your face, usually because of a nervous illness

**tick**[1] /tɪk/ *n* **1** [C] a mark (✓) written next to an answer, something on a list etc, to show that it is correct or has been dealt with; CHECK[2] (9) *AmE*: *Put a tick in the box if you agree with this statement.* **2** [C] a very small animal like an insect that lives under the skin of other animals and sucks their blood **3** [singular] the short repeated sound that a clock or watch makes every second —see picture on page 1261 **4** [singular] *spoken especially BrE* a very short time: **in a tick** (=soon) *I'll be with you in a tick.* **5 on tick** *informal old-fashioned* if you get something on tick, you arrange to take it now and pay later

**tick**[2] *v* **1** [I] if a clock or watch ticks, it makes a short sound every second **2** [T] *BrE* to mark a test, list of questions etc with a tick, usually to show that something is correct; CHECK[1] (5) *AmE*: *Tick the box next to the statement that best describes you.* **3 what makes sb tick** *informal* the thoughts, desires, opinions etc that give someone their character or make them behave in a particular way

**tick away/by** *phr v* **1** [I] if time ticks away or by, it passes, especially when you are waiting for something to happen: *We're going to have to make a decision – time's ticking away.* **2** [T **tick** sth ↔ **away**] if a clock or watch ticks away the hours, minutes etc, it shows them as they pass

**tick** sb/sth ↔ **off** *phr v* [T] **1** *BrE informal* to tell someone angrily that you are annoyed with them or disapprove of them: *The teacher ticked us off for talking in class.* **2** *BrE* to mark the things on a list with a tick to show that they are finished or have been dealt with: *She should have ticked off Miss Vine's name on her list.* **3** *AmE informal* to annoy someone

**tick over** *phr v* [I] *BrE* **1** if a vehicle's engine ticks over, it works slowly without moving the vehicle **2** if a system, business etc ticks over, it continues working but without producing very much or without much happening: *The business is just about ticking over.*

**tick·er** /ˈtɪkə‖-ər/ *n* [C] *informal* your heart

**ticker tape** /ˈ·· ·/ *n* **1** [U] long narrow paper on which information is printed by a special machine **2 ticker tape parade** *AmE* an occasion when someone important or famous arrives in an American city and pieces of paper are thrown from high buildings to welcome them

**tick·et**[1] /ˈtɪkɪ̣t/ *n* [C] S1 W2

**1** ▶ **CINEMA/BUS/TRAIN ETC** ◀ a printed piece of paper which shows that you have paid to enter a cinema, travel on a bus, plane etc: **theatre/train/airline ticket** *The plane ticket only cost $170.* —see also SEASON TICKET

**2** ▶ **DRIVING OFFENCE** ◀ a printed note ordering you to pay money because you have done something illegal while driving or parking your car: *a parking ticket*

**3** ▶ **IN SHOPS** ◀ a piece of paper fastened to something in a shop that shows its price, size etc

**4** ▶ **ELECTION** ◀ [singular] *especially AmE* **a)** a list of the people supported by a particular political party in an election: *He withdrew his name from the Democratic ticket.* **b)** the ideas that a political party supports in an election: *He fought the election on an openly racist ticket.*

**5 ticket to success/fame etc** *especially AmE* a way of getting success etc: *The part in the movie was his ticket to stardom.*

**6 be just the ticket** *old-fashioned* to be exactly what is needed —see also MEAL TICKET, DREAM TICKET

**ticket**[2] *v* [T] **1** to fasten a small piece of paper onto something to show its price, size etc **2** *AmE* to give someone a ticket for parking their car in the wrong place **3 be ticketed for** to be intended for a particular use, purpose, job etc: *These cars have been ticketed for sale abroad.*

**ticket tout** /ˈ·· ˌ·/ *n* [C] *BrE* someone who sells tickets outside a theatre or sports ground at a high price because there are not many available; SCALPER *AmE*

**tick·ing** /ˈtɪkɪŋ/ *n* [U] a thick strong cotton cloth used for making MATTRESS and PILLOW[1] (1) covers

**ticking off** /ˌ·· ˈ·/ *n* **give sb a ticking off** *BrE informal* to tell someone that you disapprove of something they have done —see also **tick off** (TICK[2])

**tick·le**[1] /ˈtɪkəl/ *v* **1** [T] to rub someone's body gently with your fingers in order to make them laugh —see picture on page 1259 **2** [I,T] if something touching your body tickles you, it makes you want to rub your body because it is uncomfortable: *Mommy, this blanket tickles.* **3** [T] if a situation, remark etc tickles you, it amuses or pleases you: *I was tickled by her description of the wedding.*|**be tickled pink** (=be very pleased or amused) *She was tickled pink to see you in the paper!* **4 tickle sb's fancy** *old-fashioned* if something tickles your fancy, it seems interesting and makes you want to do it: *The idea of appearing in a film rather tickled his fancy.* **5 tickle the ivories** *old-fashioned* to play the piano —see also **slap and tickle** (SLAP[2] (4))

**tickle**[2] *n* [singular] **1** a slight sore feeling which makes you want to cough or rub yourself; ITCH[2] (1): *I've got a tickle in my throat that won't go away.* **2 give sb a tickle** to rub someone lightly with your fingers in order to make them laugh

**tick·lish** /ˈtɪklɪʃ/ *adj* **1** someone who is ticklish is sensitive to tickling **2** *informal* a ticklish situation or problem must be dealt with very carefully, especially because you may offend or upset people: *You'll have the ticklish task of explaining to Rita why she hasn't been promoted.* —**ticklishly** *adv* —**ticklishness** *n* [U]

**tick-tack-toe** /ˌ· · ˈ·/ *n* [U] *AmE* a children's game in which two players draw X's or O's in a pattern of nine squares; NOUGHTS AND CROSSES *BrE*

**tick-tock** /ˌtɪk ˈtɒk‖-ˈtɑːk/ *n* [singular] the noise that a large clock makes when it ticks

**ticky-tacky** /ˌtɪki ˈtæki◂/ also **ticky-tack** /-ˈtæk/ *n* [U] *AmE informal* a material, especially for building, that is cheap and of low quality —**ticky-tacky** *adj*

**tid·al** /ˈtaɪdl/ *adj* connected with the regular rising and falling of the sea: *a tidal pool*

**tidal wave** /ˈ·· ˌ·/ *n* [C] **1** a very large ocean wave that flows over the land and destroys things **2** a very large amount of a particular kind of feeling or activity happening at one time: *a tidal wave of public condemnation*

**tid·bit** /ˈtɪdˌbɪt/ *n* [C] *AmE* **1** a small piece of food that tastes good; TITBIT *BrE* **2** a small piece of interesting information, news etc; TITBIT *BrE*: *tidbits of gossip*

**tid·dler** /ˈtɪdlə‖-ər/ *n* [C] *BrE informal* a very small fish

**tid·dly, tiddley** /ˈtɪdli/ *adj BrE informal* **1** slightly drunk **2** very small: *a tiddly little insect*

**tid·dly·winks** /ˈtɪdliwɪŋks/ *n* [U] a children's game in which you try to make small round pieces of plastic jump into a cup by pressing one edge with a larger piece

**tide¹** /taɪd/ *n* **1** [C usually singular] the regular rising and lowering of the level of the sea: *driftwood on the beach, brought in by the tide* | **the tide is in/out** (=the sea is at a high or low level) —see also HIGH TIDE, LOW TIDE **2** [C] a current of water caused by the tide: *Strong tides make swimming dangerous.* **3** [C usually singular] the way in which events, opinions etc are developing: **the tide turns against** (=people's opinions change so that they no longer approve of someone or something) *The tide of public opinion seems to be turning against the President.* | **swim with/against the tide** (=support or oppose what most people think) | **stem the tide** (=prevent something from developing and getting worse) *efforts to stem the tide of hysteria caused by the shootings* **4** [singular] a large number of people or things moving along together: *the tide of refugees crossing the border* | **stem the tide** (=stop this movement) **5 Christmastide/eveningtide/morningtide etc** *old use* a particular time of the year or day

**tide²**

**tide** sb **over** *phr v* [T] to help someone through a difficult period: *I can give you enough money to tide you over until next month.*

**tide-mark** /ˈ· ·/ *n* [C] **1** a mark left on the shore by the sea, that shows how high the water was **2** *BrE informal* a dirty mark left around the inside of a bath that shows how high the water was

**tide pool** /ˈ· ·/ *n* [C] *AmE* a small area of water left among rocks by the sea when the tide goes out; ROCK POOL *BrE*

**tide·wa·ter** /ˈtaɪdˌwɔːtə‖-ˌwɒːtər, -ˌwɑː-/ *n* **1** [U] water that flows onto the land when the tide rises to a very high level **2** [U] water in the parts of rivers that are affected by tides **3** [C] *AmE* an area of land at or near the sea coast

**tide·way** /ˈtaɪdweɪ/ *n* [C] *AmE* **1** a narrow area of water through which the tide flows **2** a strong current flowing through a tideway

**tid·ings** /ˈtaɪdɪŋz/ *n* [plural] *old use* news: **good/glad tidings** (=good news)

**ti·dy¹** /ˈtaɪdi/ *adj especially BrE* **1** a room, house, desk etc that is tidy is neatly arranged with everything in the right place: **neat and tidy** *Ellen's room always looks neat and tidy.* **2** someone who is tidy keeps their house, clothes etc neat and clean: *I've always been a naturally tidy person.* **3 a tidy sum/profit** *informal* a large amount of money: *We sold the house for a tidy sum and moved south.* —**tidily** *adv* —**tidiness** *n* [U]

**tidy²** also **tidy up** *v* [I,T] *especially BrE* to make a place look tidy: *You're not allowed to go out until you tidy up your room.* | **tidy up after** (=tidy a place after someone has made it untidy) *I'm tired of tidying up after you boys.*

**tidy** sth **away** *phr v* [T] *BrE* to put something back in the place where it should be: *Let's tidy these papers away.*

**tidy³** *n* [C] **desk/car/sink tidy** *BrE* a container for putting small objects in, used to keep your desk, car etc tidy

S2 W3 **tie¹** /taɪ/ *v*

**1 ▶ STRING/ROPE ◀ a)** [T] to fasten one thing to another with a piece of string, rope etc: **tie sth to/behind/onto etc** *Tie this label onto your suitcase.* | **tie sb to sth** *They tied him to a lamp-post and beat him up.* | **tie sb's hands/feet** (=tie them together) **b)** also **tie up** [T] to fasten a piece of string, rope etc around something to keep it closed or keep all its parts together: **tie sth with sth** *The package had been tied with strong green string.* | **[+ around/over/under etc]** *I'll just tie my hair back out of my eyes.* | **tie sth in bunches/bundles etc** *tie the sticks up in bundles* | **tie your hair back** (=fasten your hair to the back of your head so that it does not reach your face) **c)** [T] to make a knot in a piece of string, rope etc, for example to fasten shoes or other clothes: **tie sb's shoelaces** *Can you tie your shoelaces by yourself?* | **tie a knot/bow** *She pulled the ribbon tightly and tied a bow.* **d)** [I] to be fastened using pieces of string, RIBBON (1) etc: *The dress ties at the back.*

**2 ▶ GAME/COMPETITION ◀** also **be tied** [I] if two players, teams etc tie or are tied in a game or competition, they finish it with an equal number of points: **[+ with]** *At the end of the season, we were tied with the Tigers.* | **tie for first/second place** *Woosnam and Lyle tied for fourth place on 264.*

**3 be tied to a)** to be connected with something or dependent on it: *The flat is tied to the job.* **b)** to be unable to leave the situation, place, job etc that you are in: *a housewife tied to the kitchen all day*

**4 tie the knot** *informal* to get married

**5 tie yourself (up) in knots** *BrE informal* to become very confused when you are trying to explain something

**6 sb's hands are tied** if someone's hands are tied, they cannot do what they want because of particular conditions, rules etc: *Team manager, Ron Jones, would like to buy some new players, but his hands are tied at the moment.*

**7 tie one on** *AmE slang* to get drunk

**tie** sb **down** *phr v* [T] **1** to stop someone from being free to do the things they want to do: *He wouldn't marry her because he didn't want to feel tied down.* **2 tie yourself down (to sth)** to make a promise or agreement that restricts what you do: *I'm happy to do the job, but I don't want to tie myself down to a particular date.*

**tie in** *phr v* [I + **with**] **1** if one idea or statement ties in with another one, it helps to prove the same thing: *Marsden's conclusions tie in with our theory perfectly.* **2** to happen at the same time as something else: *We've planned the broadcast to tie in with the bicentenary celebrations.*

**tie up** *phr v*

**1 ▶ PERSON ◀** [T **tie** sb ↔ **up**] to tie someone's arms, legs etc so that they cannot move: *The intruders tied Kurt up and put him in the closet.*

**2 ▶ OBJECT ◀** [T **tie** sth ↔ **up**] to fasten something together by using string or rope

**3 ▶ BUSY ◀ be tied up** to be so busy that you cannot do anything else: *I can't see you tomorrow – I'm going to be tied up all day.*

**4 ▶ TRAFFIC ◀ be tied up** *especially AmE* if traffic is tied up, it is blocked and cannot move freely

**5 ▶ MONEY ◀ be tied up** if your money is tied up in something, it is all being used for that thing and you cannot use it for anything else: **[+ in]** *My money's all tied up in the house.*

**6 ▶ ARRANGEMENTS ◀** [T **tie** sth ↔ **up**] to finish arranging all the details of something such as an agreement or a plan: *We'd better tie up the details with a solicitor.*

**7 be tied up with** to be very closely connected with something: *Christianity in Africa is tied up with its colonial past.*

**8 tie up loose ends** to do the things that are necessary in order to finish a piece of work: *I just have to tie up a few loose ends before I go on vacation.*

**9 ▶ BOAT ◀** [I] to tie a boat to something: *We tied up alongside a barge.*

**tie²** *n* [C] S3 W3

**1 ▶ MEN'S CLOTHES ◀** a long narrow piece of cloth that you wear around your neck, tied in a special knot in front; —see also BLACK-TIE, BOW TIE

**2 ▶ CONNECTION/RELATIONSHIP ◀** a relationship

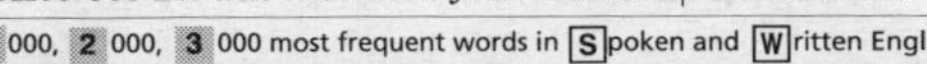

between two people, groups, or countries that connects them: *close economic ties between the two countries*
**3 ▶ FOR CLOSING STH ◀** a piece of string, wire etc used to fasten or close something such as a bag
**4 ▶ RESULT ◀** [usually singular] the result of a game, competition, or election in which two or more people get the same number of points, votes etc: **end in a tie** *The match ended in a tie.*
**5 ▶ GAME ◀** *BrE* one game, especially of football, that is part of a larger competition: *the fourth round tie of the FA cup*
**6 ▶ PREVENT YOU FROM DOING STH ◀** something that forces you to stay in one place, job etc or prevents you from being free to do what you want: *If you're the sort of person who enjoys travelling, young children can be a tie.*
**7 ▶ RAILWAY ◀** *AmE* a heavy piece of wood or metal supporting a railway track; SLEEPER (4) *BrE*

**tie·break·er** /ˈtaɪˌbreɪkə‖-ər/ also **tie·break** /ˈtaɪbreɪk/ *n* [C] **1** an additional question in a game or QUIZ, used to decide who will win when two people have the same number of points **2** the final game of a set (SET[3] (5)) in tennis when each player has won six games

**tied cot·tage** /ˌ· ˈ··/ *n* [C] *BrE* a house that a farm worker rents from a farmer while he is working in that farm

**tied house** /ˌ· ˈ·/ *n* [C] *BrE* a PUB that can only sell the beer made by a particular company

**tie-dye** /ˈ· ·/ *v* [T] to tie string around parts of a piece of material and colour it with DYE (=coloured liquid) in order to make a special pattern —see picture on page 839

**tie-in** /ˈ· ·/ *n* [C] a product such as a record, book, or toy that is connected with a new film, TV show etc

**tie-pin** /ˈ· ·/ *n* [C] a thing used for keeping a man's TIE[1] (1) fastened to his shirt or as a decoration

**tier** /tɪə‖tɪr/ *n* [C] **1** one of several rows of seats that rise one behind another **2** one of several levels in an organization or system: *The company has three tiers of management.* **3 two-tiered/three-tiered etc** having two, three etc layers: *a three-tiered wedding cake*

**tie-up** /ˈ· ·/ *n* [C] *informal* **1** an agreement to become business partners: [+ **with**] *IBM's tie-up with Auspex System Inc* **2** *BrE* a close connection between two or more things, especially when one causes the other: [+ **between**] the tie-up between class interests and politics **3** *AmE* a situation in which traffic is prevented from moving or there is a problem which prevents a system or plan from working —see also **tie up** (TIE[2])

**tiff** /tɪf/ *n* [C] a slight argument between two people who are in love: *Dave's had a tiff with his girlfriend.*

**tif·fin** /ˈtɪfɪ̣n/ *n* [U] *BrE old use or IndE* a light meal eaten in the morning or the middle of the day

**ti·ger** /ˈtaɪgə‖-ər/ *n* [C] a large strong animal that has yellow and black lines on its body and is a member of the cat family —see also **paper tiger** (PAPER[2] (4))

**tiger lil·y** /ˈ·· ˌ··/ *n* [C] a LILY (=flower) that has large orange flowers with black spots

**tiger moth** /ˈ·· ·/ *n* [C] a type of MOTH (=flying insect) with black stripes on its wings

S2 W3 **tight[1]** /taɪt/ *adj*
**1 ▶ CLOTHES ◀** fitting a part of your body very closely, especially in a way that is uncomfortable: *tight trousers | My shoes were far too tight and I was in agony by the time I got home.* | **be a tight fit** (=only just fits someone) *The top is rather a tight fit.* —see also SKIN-TIGHT, TIGHT-FITTING
**2 ▶ PULLED/STRETCHED ◀** string, wire, cloth etc that is tight has been pulled or stretched firmly so that it is straight or cannot move: **pull sth tight** *Pull the thread tight. | The bandage must be tight enough to stop the bleeding.*
**3 ▶ FIRMLY FIXED/FASTENED ◀** something such as a screw or lid that is tight is firmly fixed and is difficult to move: *Check that the screws are tight.*
**4 a tight hold/grip** a firm hold on something: *His mother kept a tight hold on his hand.*
**5 ▶ STRICT CONTROL ◀** controlled very strictly and firmly: *Spending is kept within very tight limits. | Security was very tight for the president's visit.* | **keep a tight rein on** (=control someone or something very strictly) | **run a tight ship** (=manage a company, organization etc very effectively by having strict rules)
**6 ▶ MONEY ◀** *informal* **a)** if money is tight, you do not have enough of it: **money is tight/things are tight** *Money was tight and he needed a job badly.* **b)** someone who is tight is not generous and tries very hard to avoid spending money; MEAN[2] (2) —see also TIGHT-FISTED
**7 ▶ LITTLE TIME ◀** if time is tight, it is difficult for you to do everything you need to do in the time available: **tight schedule/deadline** (=one that gives you very little time to do or finish something) *a tight deadline | It'll be a bit tight, but we should just get there and back in time.*
**8 ▶ LITTLE SPACE ◀** if space is tight, there is only just enough space to fit something into a place: **a tight squeeze/fit** (=a situation where there is only just enough space for things or people to fit) *It was a tight squeeze, but somehow we all got into the car.*
**9 ▶ CLOSE TOGETHER ◀** placed or standing very close together: *She wore her hair in a tight bun.*
**10 ▶ CLOSE RELATIONSHIP ◀** a tight group of people, countries etc have a close relationship with each other and are closely connected with each other
**11 ▶ CHEST/STOMACH ETC ◀** feeling painful or uncomfortable, because you are ill or worried: *He had been complaining of a tight chest and sore throat.*
**12 ▶ SMILE/EXPRESSION/VOICE ETC ◀** showing that you are annoyed, or upset: *Her mother gave a tight, forced smile.* —see also TIGHT-LIPPED
**13 ▶ BEND/TURN ◀** very curved so that it turns very quickly to another direction: *Careful now, there's a tight bend coming up.*
**14 in a tight corner/spot** *informal* in a difficult situation: *I'm always willing to help a friend in a tight spot.*
**15 ▶ PLAY/PERFORMANCE ◀** performed very exactly, with no unnecessary pauses: *a tight, well-rehearsed production*
**16 ▶ GAME/COMPETITION ◀** a tight game, competition etc is one in which the teams, competitors etc all play well and it is not easy to win: *It was a tight match, with the winning goal scored in the final minute.*
**17 ▶ DRUNK ◀** [never before noun] *old-fashioned informal* drunk —see also AIRTIGHT, WATERTIGHT
—**tightly** *adj*: *Marie held the baby tightly in her arms.*
—**tightness** *n* [U]

**tight[2]** *adv* very firmly or closely; tightly: **hold tight** *Hold tight to the safety rail.* | **keep sth tight shut** *I kept my eyes tight shut and hoped they would go away.* —see also **sit tight** (SIT (5)), **sleep tight** (SLEEP[2] (4))

**tight·en** /ˈtaɪtn/ also **tighten up** *v* **1** [T] to close or fasten something firmly by turning it: *Tighten up the screws. | You'll need to tighten the lid on the jar.* **2** [I,T] if you tighten a rope, wire etc, or if it tightens, it is stretched or pulled so that it becomes tight: *When you tighten guitar strings the note gets higher.* **3** to become stiff or make a part of your body become stiff: *I can feel my neck tightening up.* **4** [T] to make a rule, law, or system more strict: **tighten up on** *measures aimed at tightening up on security* **5 tighten your hold/grip on** to hold someone or something more firmly: *Sarah tightened her grip on my arm.* **6 tighten your belt** *informal* to try to spend less money than you used to: *When Maureen lost her job, we had to tighten our belts.*

**tight-fist·ed** /ˌtaɪt ˈfɪstɪ̣d◂/ *adj informal* not generous with money; STINGY —**tight-fistedness** *n* [U]

**tight-fit·ting** /ˌ· ˈ··◂/ *adj* fitting very closely or tightly: *a tight-fitting skirt | saucepan with a tight-fitting lid*

**tight-knit** /ˌ· ˈ·◂/ *adj* [only before noun] **1** a tight-knit group of people are closely connected with each other: *a tight-knit island community* **2** *AmE* a tight-knit plan is very carefully arranged so that nothing can go wrong

**tight-lipped** /ˌtaɪt ˈlɪpt◂/ *adj* **1** unwilling to talk about something: *Diplomats are remaining tight-lipped about the negotiations.* **2** with your lips tightly pressed together because you are angry

**tightly-knit** /ˌ·· ˈ·◂/ *adj* TIGHT-KNIT

**tight·rope** /ˈtaɪt-rəʊp‖-roʊp/ *n* [C] **1** a rope or wire high above the ground that someone walks along in a CIRCUS (1) **2 walk a tightrope** to be in a difficult situation in which you must be careful about what you say or do

3 **tights** /taɪts/ *n* [plural] **1** *BrE* a piece of women's clothing that fits closely around your feet and legs and up to your waist, made of very thin material; PANTYHOSE *AmE* —see picture on page 840 **2** a similar piece of clothing that is coloured and cannot be seen through, worn especially by dancers

**tight·wad** /ˈtaɪtwɒd‖-wɑːd/ *n* [C] *informal especially AmE* someone who hates to spend or give money: *My allowance is very small – Dad's a real tightwad.*

**ti·gress** /ˈtaɪgrɪ̣s/ *n* [C] a female tiger

**tike** /taɪk/ *n* [C] another spelling of TYKE

**til, 'til** /tɪl,tl/ a short form of TILL[1]

**til·de** /ˈtɪldə/ *n* [C] a mark (~) placed over the letter 'n' in Spanish to show that it is pronounced /nj/

3 **tile¹** /taɪl/ *n* **1** [C] a flat square piece of baked clay or other material, used for covering roofs, floors etc: *bathroom tiles* **2** [C] a thin curved piece of baked clay used for covering roofs **3 go out on the tiles** *BrE informal* to go out drinking, dancing etc for enjoyment

**tile²** *v* [T] to cover a roof, floor etc with tiles —**tiled** *adj*: *a tiled floor* —**tiler** *n* [C]

**til·ing** /ˈtaɪlɪŋ/ *n* [U] a set of tiles used to cover a roof, floor etc

1 **till¹** /tɪl, tl/ *prep, conjunction especially spoken* until: *I didn't learn to drive till I was thirty three.* | *The shop's open till nine o'clock most evenings.*

**till²** /tɪl/ *n* [C] *BrE* a machine used in shops, restaurants etc for calculating the amount of money you have to pay, and storing the money; REGISTER[1] (5) *AmE* —see also **be caught with your fingers in the till** (FINGER[1] (8))

**till³** *v* [T] *old use* to prepare land for growing crops

**till·age** /ˈtɪlɪdʒ/ *n* [U] *old use* the activity of preparing land for growing crops

**til·ler** /ˈtɪlə‖-ər/ *n* [C] a long handle fastened to the RUDDER (=part that controls the direction) of a boat —see picture at YACHT

**tilt¹** /tɪlt/ *v* **1** [I,T] to move or make something move into a position where one side is higher than the other: *The table tilted suddenly, spilling all the drinks.* **2** [T] to move your head or chin upwards or to the side: *Jodi tilted her head and looked thoughtful.* **3** [T] to influence an opinion or situation so that people prefer one person, belief etc: *This new evidence may tilt the balance of opinion in his favour.*

**tilt at** sb *phr v* [T] **1** to attack someone by what you say or write **2** *old use* to move quickly on a horse towards someone, in order to attack them with a LANCE

**tilt²** *n* **1 at full tilt** as fast as possible: *We rode down the hill at full tilt.* **2** [C,U] a movement or position in which one side of something is higher than the other **3** [C] a spoken or written attack on someone or something

**tim·ber** /ˈtɪmbə‖-ər/ *n* **1** [U] *especially BrE* wood used for building or making things, or the trees that produce this wood; LUMBER[2] (2) *AmE* **2** [C] a wooden beam, especially one that forms part of the main structure of a house **3 timber!** *spoken* used to warn people that a tree being cut down is about to fall —see also HALF-TIMBERED W3

**tim·ber·line** /ˈtɪmbəlaɪn‖-ər-/ *n* [singular] *technical* **1** the height above the level of the sea beyond which trees will not grow **2** the northern or southern limit in the world beyond which trees will not grow

**tim·bre** /ˈtæmbə, ˈtɪm-‖-ər/ *n* [C,U] the quality of the sound made by a particular instrument or voice

**tim·brel** /ˈtɪmbrəl/ *n* [C] *old use* a TAMBOURINE

## time¹ /taɪm/ *n*

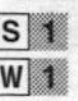

S1 W1

① TIME
② TIME SHOWN ON A CLOCK
③ OCCASION
④ HOW OFTEN
⑤ TIME WHEN STH HAPPENS
⑥ TIME WHEN STH SHOULD HAPPEN
⑦ SUITABLE TIME
⑧ PERIOD OF TIME
⑨ GOOD TIME/BAD TIME ETC
⑩ PERIOD IN HISTORY
⑪ TIME NEEDED TO DO STH
⑫ AVAILABLE TIME
⑬ SLOWLY/QUICKLY
⑭ MODERN
⑮ IN TIME
⑯ HOW MANY
⑰ COMPARISONS
⑱ GRADUALLY/EVENTUALLY
⑲ MUSIC
⑳ LIKE/DISLIKE
㉑ OTHER MEANINGS

### ① TIME

**1** [U] something that is measured in minutes, hours, years etc using clocks: *a machine that can travel through time*| *The basic unit of time, the second, was redefined in 1967.* **time passes/goes by**: *Time goes by so quickly these days.*

### ② TIME SHOWN ON A CLOCK

**2** [singular] a particular point in time shown on a clock in hours and minutes: *What time is it?*| **what time do you make it?** *BrE*/**what time do you have** *AmE* (=used to ask someone with a watch what time it is)| **have you got the time?** *BrE*/**do you have the time?** *AmE* (=used to ask someone if they know what time it is)| **tell the time** *BrE*/**tell time** *AmE* (=be able to know what time it is by looking at a clock): *He's ten years old and he still can't tell the time.* | **look at the time** *spoken* (=used when it is later than you thought it was) *Oh look at the time–we'd better get moving.*

**3 keep good/perfect etc time** if a clock or watch keeps good or perfect time, it works very well

**4 ► IN PART OF THE WORLD ◄** [U] the time in one particular part of the world, or the time used in one particular area: *Eastern Standard Time/British Summer Time* | **local time**: *We will be arriving in New York at 3 am local time.*

### ③ OCCASION

**5** [C] an occasion when something happens or someone does something | **every/each time**: *It was the*

[continued on next page]

[continued from previous page]
*only time I ever saw her lose her temper./Every time I meet her I always forget her name.*|**next time**: *Give us a call next time you're in town.*|**this time** *I won't report you this time but don't do it again.*|**the last time**: *When was the last time you were ill?*|**one time** (=once) *I came home one time and found that someone had smashed all the windows.*

### ④ HOW OFTEN

**6 three/four/ten etc times** used to say how often something happens: *I must have called you about five times.*|*How many times have you visited the US?*|*We visit him two or three times a month.*
**7 nine times out of ten/99 times out of 100** used to say that something is almost always true or almost always happens: *Nine times out of ten she's right.*
**8 all the time** continuously or very often: *It's a really useful book – I use it all the time.*
**9 most of the time** very often or almost always: *Most of the time they seem to just sit around watching TV.*
**10 the whole time** if something, happens the whole time, especially something annoying, it happens continuously: *The baby was crying the whole time.*
**11 time after time/time and time again** happening often over a long period, especially in a way that is annoying: *I've told her time after time not to bring that dog in here.*
**12 at times** sometimes but not usually: *At times I wonder if it's worth all the effort.*
**13 from time to time** sometimes, but not regularly or very often: *I still see her from time to time.*
**14 half the time** *especially spoken* if something happens half the time, especially something anoying, it happens quite often: *Half the time they don't even bother to answer my letters.*
**15 at no time** used to say strongly that something never happened or should never happen **at no time do/did etc** *At no time did I tell you that you could use my car.*

**16 at all times** used especially in official notices or announcements to say what always happens or should always happen: *Identification badges must be worn at all times.*

### ⑤ TIME WHEN STH HAPPENS

**17** [C,U] the particular minute, hour, day etc when something happens or someone does something: *What time did you get to bed?*|*Her note didn't give the time of the meeting.*|*We both left college at around the same time.*|**by the time**: *By the time you get this letter I'll be in Canada.*|**opening/closing time** (=the time when a shop, bar etc opens)|**arrival/departure time** (=the time when a train, plane etc leaves): *Departure times for all flights to Spain are subject to delay.*|**lunch/dinner/break etc time** (=the time when you usually have lunch etc)|**at any one time** (= at any particular time) *There are always at least two nurses on duty at any one time.*|**this time tomorrow/last week etc** *This time tomorrow I'll be getting on a plane to Dallas.*

### ⑥ TIME WHEN STH SHOULD HAPPEN

**18** [singular] the time when you should do something, when something should happen, or when something is expected to happen: **it's time to do sth** *Come on kids, it's time to go home.*|**it's time sb did sth/was doing sth** (=used when saying that someone should do something soon): *It's time we had a party.*|**it's time for** *The voters felt it was time for a change.*
**19 it's about time** *especially spoken* used to say strongly that you think something should happen soon or should already have happened: *It's about time he got himself a proper job.*
**20 and about time too/not before time** *spoken* used when you are annoyed because someone arrives late or something happens later than you expected or than was arranged: *"Here's Helen!" "And about time too – where has she been?"*
**21 on time** arriving or happening at the correct time or the time that was arranged: *These buses are never on time.*|**right/bang/dead on time** (=at exactly the right time): *Our train arrived bang on time.*
**22 ahead of/behind time** earlier or later than the time when a piece of work should be finished, someone should arrive somewhere etc: *The dam was completed two years ahead of time.*
**23 call time** *BrE* to tell the customers in a PUB that it is time to stop drinking

### ⑦ SUITABLE TIME

**24** [C,U] a suitable or convenient time for something to happen or someone to do something|**good/bad time** (=a convenient or inconvenient time): *I'm afraid you've caught me at a bad time – Can you call back later?*|**not be the time/be hardly the time**: *This is hardly the time to ask him for a loan.*|**come at the right/wrong time**: *The pay rise came at just the right time.*
**25 there's no time like the present** *especially spoken* used to say that now is a good time to do something: *If you're thinking of buying a house, there's no time like the present.*
**26 the time is ripe (for)** used to say that the conditions are suitable now for something to happen: *The time is ripe for a peace settlement.*
**27 when the time comes** when something that you expect to happen actually happens, or when something becomes necessary: *I'm sure she'll make the right choice when the time comes.*

### ⑧ PERIOD OF TIME

**28** [singular] a period of time during which something happens or someone does something: *I enjoyed my time as a student.* (=the period when I was a student)||**for a long time/for some time etc**: *The cheering went on for quite some time.*|**a long time ago/some time ago** *All this happened a very long time ago, before you were born.*|**time of year/day etc**: *It should be pretty out there at this time of the year.*
**29 at the time** at a particular moment or period in the past, especially when the situation is very different now: *It seemed like a good idea at the time.*|*I was living in Phoenix at the time.*
**30 at one time** at some time in the past but not now: *This used to be a very pretty valley at one time.*
**31 at this time** *AmE* at this particular moment: *I don't really want to start up any new relationships at this time.*
**32 for the time being** for a short period of time from now, but not permanently: *You can stay in the spare room for the time being.*
**33 for a time** for a fairly short time, until something happens to change the situation: *For a time we all lived together peacefully. Then the trouble started.*|*Peter lived in Italy for a time.*
**34 for some time** for a fairly long time: *I hadn't seen my family for some time.*
**35 for hours/months etc at a time** for a period that continues for several hours, months etc: *Alex is happy to read for hours at a time.*
**36 for any length of time** for more than just a short time: *He seemed unable to keep the same job for any length of time.*
**37 from time out of mind** *literary* for a very long time

### ⑨ GOOD TIME/BAD TIME ETC

**38** [C] a good time, bad time , difficult time, etc is a period or part of your life when you have good, bad, difficult etc experiences: *This was the happiest time of her life.*|**have a good/great/fantastic time** (=enjoy yourself a lot): *Thanks for the meal – we both had a really good time.*|**good/bad/hard etc times**: *It's best to forget the bad times and just remember the good ones.*

### ⑩ PERIOD IN HISTORY

**39** [C] also **times** [plural]— a particular period in history **Roman/Greek/ancient etc times** *a tradition that goes back to Medieval times*|*The film takes us back to the time of the American War of Independence.*|**our**

**time(s)** (=the present period in history) *peace in our time*

## ⑪ TIME NEEDED TO DO STH

**40** [C,U] the amount of time that it takes you to do something: *How much time will it take you to finish your essay?*| **journey time/travel time** *The Channel tunnel has cut the journey time from London to Paris by as much as 3 hours.*
**41 take time** if doing something takes time, it needs a long period of time: *Learning a language isn't easy – it takes time.*
**42 ► IN A RACE ◄** [C] the amount of time taken by a runner, swimmer etc in a race: *the fastest time in the world this year over 400 metres*
**43 have (the) time** to have enough time to do something [+ **for**] *Do you have time for a coffee?*| **have time to do sth** *I don't have time to talk to you right now.*| *She hung up before I had time to say sorry.*
**44 make/find time** to arrange your plans so that you have enough time to do something: *You should try and make time to see a doctor.*
**45 there is time** there is enough time for someone to do something: *We thought we'd do some shopping after lunch, if there's time.*| **there is time (for sb) to do sth** *We had to leave at once – there wasn't even time to pack.*

## ⑫ AVAILABLE TIME

**46** [U] the amount of time that is available for you to do something: *You'd better hurry up – we don't have much time.*| *Time is running out in the hostage crisis.*| **sb's time** (=the time they have available) *I seem to spend most of my time on the phone.*| **precious time** (=time that is valuable because there is not much available) *Hurry up—we're wasting precious time.*
**47 have all the time in the world** used to say that you have as much time as you want in which to do something
**48 time's up** *spoken* used in competitions and examinations to tell people that there is no more time left
**49 be out of time** an expression used on television and radio programmes when saying that there is no more time left: *Sorry, we're out of time – I'll have to stop you there.*

## ⑬ SLOWLY/QUICKLY

**50 take your time a)** to do something slowly or carefully without hurrying: *There's no need to rush back – just take your time.* **b)** to do something more slowly than seems reasonable: *The builders are certainly taking their time with our roof!*
**51 in no time at all/in next to no time** very quickly or soon, especially in a way that is surprising: *Jed got the car fixed in no time at all.*
**52 make good time** if you make good time on a journey, you travel quickly, especially more quickly than you expected: *There wasn't much traffic, so we made good time.*
**53 there's no time to lose** used to say that you must do something quickly because there is very little time
**54 with time to spare** sooner than expected or necessary: *There was very little traffic, and we got to the airport with time to spare.*
**55 time is of the essence** *formal* used to say that it is important that something is done quickly
**56 time is money** used to say that wasting time or delaying something costs money

## ⑭ MODERN

**57 ahead of your time** someone who is ahead of their time uses the newest ideas and methods, which are later used by many other people: *Matisse was well ahead of his time in his use of colour.*
**58 ahead of its time** a machine, system etc that is ahead of its time has a very modern and advanced design: **way ahead of its time** (=a long way ahead of its time) *The car, which featured a turbo-charged engine and disc-brakes, was way ahead of its time.*

## ⑮ IN TIME

**59 in 10 days/five years/a few minutes' etc time** ten days, five years etc from now: *Don't worry, we'll be at the hospital in a couple of minutes' time.*
**60 in time a)** early or soon enough to do something **in time to do sth** *Brian usually gets home in time to bath the children.*| **just in time**: *"Did you catch your plane?" "Yes – we got there just in time."*| **in good time/in plenty of time** (=early, so that you do not have to rush or you have enough time to get ready) *Let me know in good time if you need any help.* **b)** after a certain period of time, especially after a gradual process of change and development: *Don't worry – I'm sure things will get better in time.*

## ⑯ HOW MANY

**61 one/three/a few etc at a time** separately, or in groups of three, a few etc together at the same time: *We had to see the nurse one at a time.*| *He dragged himself along a few steps at a time.*

## ⑰ COMPARISONS

**62 five/ten/many etc times** used to say how much bigger, better etc one thing is than another: *Their garden is three times bigger than ours.*| *Sue earns five times as much as I do.*
**63 the best/biggest etc...of all time** the best, biggest etc of a particular kind of person or thing that has ever existed: *the most successful movie of all time*

## ⑱ GRADUALLY/EVENTUALLY

**64 all in good time** used to tell someone to be patient because something they are waiting for will certainly happen eventually, and probably quite soon
**65 it's (only) a matter/question of time** used to say that something will definitely happen at some time in the future, but you do not know when: *That road's dangerous – it's only a matter of time before someone gets killed.*
**66 (only) time will tell** used to say that it will eventually become clear whether or not something is true, right etc, at some time in the future: *I don't know if she's the best choice for the job – only time will tell.*
**67 over time** if something happens over time, it happens gradually during a long period: *Over time her husband's mood seemed to change.*
**68 with time/given time** after a certain period of time, especially after a gradual process of change and development: *I guess things will improve with time.*
**69 time heals all wounds** used to say that things you are worried or upset about will gradually disappear as time passes

## ⑲ MUSIC

**70 ► MUSIC ◄** [U] the number of beats BEAT² (4) in each bar (BAR² (6)) in a piece of music: *Waltzes are usually in three-four time*
**71 in time to** if you do something in time to a piece of music, you do it using the same RHYTHM and speed as the music: *She began moving her body in time to the music.*
**72 keep time** to play a piece of music using the right RHYTHM and speed
**73 keep/beat time** to show the RHYTHM and speed that a piece of music should be played at to a group of musicians, using your hands
**74 in/out of time (with)** if you are in or out of time with someone who is playing a piece of music, you are not following the same RHYTHM and speed as them

## ⑳ LIKE/DISLIKE

**75 have a lot of time for** *informal* to like or admire someone or something
**76 not have much time for/have no time for** *informal* to dislike and not want to waste your time on

[continued on next page]

[continued from previous page]
someone or something: *She's always complaining – I've got no time for people like that.*

### ㉑ OTHER MEANINGS

**77 before your time a)** something that is before your time happened before you were born, before you started working or living somewhere etc: *The Beatles were a bit before my time.* **b)** if you do something before your time, you do it before the time when most people usually do it in their lives: *She's growing old before her time.*
**78 in my/your etc time** during the period of time when you were living in a particular place or working in a particular company etc. *Of course in my time we didn't have all these computers.*
**79 in your own time** if you do work or studying in your own time, you do it outside normal school or work hours
**80 in your own good time** *informal* when you are ready: *I'll speak to him about it in my own good time.*
**81 (sb's) time is up** *spoken* used to say that someone has to stop doing something, because they have done it for long enough: *OK kids! Time's up – get out of the pool.*
**82 sb's time is up/sb's time is drawing near** someone is going to die soon
**83 be near her time** *old-fashioned* if a woman is near her time, she is going to have a baby soon
**84 time is on your side** used to say that someone is young enugh to be able to wait before doing something or until something happens
**85 against time** if you work against time to do something, you try to do it even though you have very little time
**86 time was (when)** used to say that there was a time when you used to be able to do something, when something used to happen etc: *Time was when you could buy a new car for less than $500.*
**87 pass the time of day (with sb)** to say hello to someone and have a short talk with them
**88 ► PRISON ◄ do time** to spend a period of time in prison
**89 time and a half** one and a half times the normal rate of pay —see also BIG-TIME, FULL-TIME, HALF TIME, LEAD TIME, PART-TIME, **at the best of times** (BEST[1] (13)), **it is high time** (HIGH[1] (20)), **bide your time** (BIDE (2)), **the fullness of time** (FULLNESS (1)), **kill time** (KILL[1] (9)), **lose time** (LOSE[1] (12)), **mark time** (MARK[1] (13)), **move with the times** (MOVE[1] (19)), **in the nick of time** (NICK[1] (1)), **for old times' sake** (OLD (18)), **once upon a time** (ONCE[1] (14)), **play for time** (PLAY[1] (15)), **at the same time** (SAME[1]) , **be a sign of the times** (SIGN[1] (10)), **a stitch in time (saves nine)** (STITCH[1] (9)), **have a whale of a time** (WHALE[1] (2))

**time[2]** *v* [T] **1** [usually passive] to arrange or choose that something should happen at a particular time: *You timed your arrival well; we're just going to eat.* | **be timed to do sth** *The bomb was timed to go off in the rush-hour.* | **be timed for sth** *The next show is timed for 8 o'clock.* **2** to measure how fast someone or something is going, how long it takes to do something etc: *We timed our journey: it took two and a half hours.* | **time sb/sth at** *Christie was timed at 10.02 seconds.* | **time how long** *Time how long it takes me to swim 4 lengths.* **3** to hit a ball or make a shot at a particular moment: *a perfectly timed smash* | **time sth well/badly etc** *Baggio timed that pass beautifully.* —see also ILL-TIMED, MISTIME, WELL-TIMED

**time and mo·tion stud·y** /ˌ· · ˈ·· ˌ··/ *n* [C] a study of working methods to find out how effective they are
**time bomb** /ˈ· ·/ *n* [C] **1** a bomb that is set to explode at a particular time **2** a situation that is likely to become a very serious problem: *the time bomb of youth unemployment*
**time cap·sule** /ˈ· ˌ··/ *n* [C] a container that is filled with objects from a particular time, so that people in the future will know what life was like then
**time card** /ˈ· ·/ *n* [C] a piece of card on which the hours you have worked are recorded by a special machine
**time clock** /ˈ· ·/ *n* [C] a special clock that records the exact time when someone arrives at and leaves work
**time-con·sum·ing** /ˈ· ·ˌ··/ *adj* taking a long time to do: *an expensive, complex, and time-consuming process*
**time-hon·oured** /ˈ· ˌ··/ *adj* a time-honoured method, custom etc is one that has existed for a long time: *the time-honoured patterns of sheep-grazing and cultivation*
**time·keep·er** /ˈtaɪmˌkiːpə‖-ər/ *n* [C] **1** someone who officially records the times taken to do something, especially at a sports event **2 good/bad timekeeper a)** someone who is good or bad at arriving at work at the right time **b)** a watch or clock that is good or bad at showing the right time —**timekeeping** *n* [U]
**time lag** /ˈ· ·/ also **time lapse** *n* [C] the period of time between two connected events: *There is a considerable time lag between the planning stage and the final product.*
**time-lapse** /ˈ· ·/ *adj* time-lapse photography makes a very slow process seem to happen much faster
**time·less** /ˈtaɪmləs/ *adj* **1** remaining beautiful, attractive etc and not becoming old-fashioned: *the timeless beauty of Venice* **2** *literary* continuing for ever: *the timeless universe* —**timelessly** *adv* —**timelessness** *n* [U]
**time lim·it** /ˈ· ˌ··/ *n* [C] the longest time that you are allowed in which to do something: *the legal time limit for abortions*
**time·ly** /ˈtaɪmli/ *adj* done or happening at exactly the right time: *a timely intervention* | **timely reminder** (=one that makes you remember something at the right time)
**time ma·chine** /ˈ· ·ˌ·/ *n* [C] an imaginary machine in which people can travel backwards or forwards in time
**time off** /ˌ· ˈ·/ *n* [U] time when you are officially allowed not to be at work or studying: **take/have etc time off** *If you're feeling tired you should take some time off.*
**time out** /ˌ· ˈ·/ *n* [C] **1 take time out** *informal* to rest or do something different from your usual job or activities **2** *technical* a short break during a sports match when the teams can rest, get instructions from their manager etc
**time·piece** /ˈtaɪmpiːs/ *n* [C] *old use* a clock or watch
**tim·er** /ˈtaɪmə‖-ər/ *n* [C] **1** an instrument that you use to measure time, when you are doing something such as cooking: *Set the timer on the cooker for three minutes.* —see also EGG-TIMER **2 part-timer/full-timer** someone who works part or all of a normal working week
**times** /taɪmz/ *prep* multiplied by: *two times two equals four (2 x 2 = 4)*
**time-sav·ing** /ˈ· ˌ··/ *adj* designed to reduce the time usually needed to do something: *a time-saving device* —**time-saver** *n* [C]
**time·scale** /ˈtaɪmskeɪl/ *n* [C] the period of time it takes for something to happen or be completed
**time·serv·er** /ˈtaɪmˌsɜːvə‖-ˌsɜːrvər/ *n* [C] *informal* someone who does the least amount of work possible —**time-serving** *adj n* [U]
**time·share** /ˈtaɪmʃeə‖-ʃer/ *n* [C] a holiday home that you buy with other people so that you can each spend a period of time there every year —**timeshare** *adj*
**time-shar·ing** /ˈ· ˌ··/ *n* [U] **1** *technical* the art of dealing with more than one computer PROGRAM at the same time **2** the practice of owning a timeshare
**time sheet** /ˈ· ·/ *n* [C] a piece of paper on which the hours you have worked are written or printed
**time sig·nal** /ˈ· ˌ··/ *n* [C] a sound on the radio that shows the exact time

**time sig·na·ture** /ˈ· ˌ···/ *n* [C] two numbers at the beginning of a line of music that tell you how many beats BEAT[2] (4) there are in a BAR[2] (6)

**time switch** /ˈ· ·/ *n* [C] an electronic control that can be set to start or stop a machine at a particular time

**time·ta·ble[1]** /ˈtaɪmˌteɪbəl/ *n* [C] *BrE* **1** a list of the times at which buses, trains, planes, etc arrive and leave; SCHEDULE *AmE* **2** a list of the times of classes in a school, college etc; SCHEDULE *AmE* **3** a plan of events and activities, with their dates and times; SCHEDULE

**timetable[2]** *v BrE* **1** [T usually passive] to plan that something will happen at a particular time in the future; SCHEDULE: **timetable sth for** *The meeting has been timetabled for 2 o'clock.* **2** [I,T] to arrange the times at which classes will take place in a school or college: *Timetabling is the responsibility of the deputy head.*

**time warp** /ˈ· ·/ *n* [C] **1 be (caught/stuck) in a time warp** to have not changed even though everyone or everything else has: *The whole college seems stuck in some 1960s time warp!* **2** an imaginary situation in which the past or future becomes the present

**time·worn** /ˈtaɪmwɔːn‖-wɔːrn/ *adj* something timeworn is old and has been used a lot: *time-worn phrases*

**time zone** /ˈ· ·/ *n* [C] one of the 24 areas that the world is divided into, each of which has its own time

**tim·id** /ˈtɪmɪ̈d/ *adj* not having courage or confidence: *a timid smile | a policy that is both timid and inadequate* —**timidly** *adv* —**timidity** /tɪ̈ˈmɪdɪ̈ti/ *n* [U]

**tim·ing** /ˈtaɪmɪŋ/ *n* [U] **1** a word meaning the time, day etc when someone does something or when something happens, especially when you are considering how suitable this is: **good/bad/perfect etc timing** *Ah good timing! I was just thinking I needed a coffee. | What perfect timing! I was just finishing my work as you arrived to pick me up.* **2** the way in which electricity is sent to the SPARK PLUGS in a car engine

**tim·o·rous** /ˈtɪmərəs/ *adj formal* lacking confidence and easily frightened: *She was no helpless, timorous female.* —**timorously** *adv* —**timorousness** *n* [U]

**tim·pa·ni** /ˈtɪmpəni/ *n* [U] a set of KETTLEDRUMS

**tim·pa·nist** /ˈtɪmpənɪ̈st/ *n* [C] someone who plays the timpani

3 **tin[1]** /tɪn/ *n* **1** [U] a soft white metal that is often used to cover and protect iron and steel: *a tin box* **2** [C] *BrE* a small metal container in which food or drink is sold; CAN *especially AmE*: *a sardine tin | a tin of beans* —see picture at CONTAINER **3** [C] a metal container with a lid in which food can be stored: *a biscuit tin* **4** [C] *BrE* a metal container in which food is cooked; PAN[1] (2) *AmE*: *a bread tin*

**tin[2]** *adj* **1** made of TIN: *a tin mug | a tin soldier* **2 have a tin ear** *AmE informal* to be unable to hear the difference between musical notes **3 tin god** *informal* someone gets much more admiration and respect than they really deserve

**tinc·ture** /ˈtɪŋktʃə‖-ər/ *n* [C,U] [+ **of**] *technical* a medical substance mixed with alcohol

**tin·der** /ˈtɪndə‖-ər/ *n* [U] dry material that burns easily and can be used for lighting fires

**tin·der·box** /ˈtɪndəbɒks‖-dərbɑːks/ *n* **1** [C usually singular] a place or situation that is dangerous and where there could suddenly be a lot of fighting or problems: *Racial tension was high, and the southern states were a real tinderbox.* **2** [C] a box containing things needed to make a flame, used in former times

**tinder-dry** /ˌ·· ˈ·◂/ *adj* extremely dry and likely to burn very easily: *The whole forest is tinder-dry.*

**tin·foil** /ˈtɪnfɔɪl/ *n* [U] thin shiny metal that bends like paper and is used for covering food etc

**ting** /tɪŋ/ *n* [C] a high clear ringing sound: *the ting of a bell* —**ting** *v* [I,T]

**ting-a-ling** /ˌ· · ˈ·◂/ *n* [C] *informal* the high clear ringing sound that is made by a small bell

**tinge[1]** /tɪndʒ/ *n* [C] a very small amount of a colour, emotion, or quality: [+ **of**] *a tinge of sadness in her voice*

**tinge[2]** *v* [T + **with**] to give something a small amount of a particular colour, emotion, or quality

**tinged** /tɪndʒd/ *adj* **tinged with** showing a small amount of a colour, emotion or quality: *black hair tinged with grey*

**tin·gle** /ˈtɪŋgəl/ *v* [I] **1** if a part of your body tingles, you feel a slight uncomfortable feeling, especially on your skin: [+ **with**] *My cheeks were tingling with the cold.* **2 tingle with excitement** to feel very excited —**tingle** *n* [C] *A nervous tingle ran down her spine.*

**tin hat** /ˌ· ˈ·/ *n* [C] a metal hat worn by soldiers

**tin·ker[1]** /ˈtɪŋkə‖-ər/ *n* [C] **1** someone who travels from place to place selling things or repairing metal pots, pans etc **2** *BrE old-fashioned* a disobedient or annoying young child **3 not give a tinker's curse/cuss** *BrE spoken* **not give a tinker's damn** *AmE spoken* to not care about something at all

**tinker[2]** *v* [I + **with**] to make small changes to something in order to repair it or make it work better: *It's no use just tinkering with the legislation.*

**tin·kle[1]** /ˈtɪŋkəl/ *n* [C usually singular] **1** a light ringing sound: *She could hear the tinkle of coffee cups.* —see picture on page 1261 **2 give sb a tinkle** *BrE informal* to call someone on the telephone: *I'll give you a tinkle tomorrow.* **3 have a tinkle** an expression meaning to URINATE (=pass water from your body), used especially by or to children

**tinkle[2]** *v* [I,T] to make light ringing sounds or to make something do this: *a tinkling bell*

**tinned** /tɪnd/ *adj BrE* tinned food is sold in a TIN[1] (2) and can be kept for a long time before it is opened: *tinned tomatoes*

**tin·ni·tus** /ˈtɪnɪtəs/ *n* [U] *technical* an illness in which you hear noises, especially ringing, in your ears

**tin·ny** /ˈtɪni/ *adj* **1** a tinny sound is unpleasant to listen to, like small pieces of metal hitting each other **2** a tinny metal object is badly or cheaply made

**tin o·pen·er** /ˈ· ˌ···/ *n* [C] *BrE* a tool for opening tins; CAN OPENER *especially AmE* —see picture on page 833

**Tin Pan Al·ley** /ˌ· · ˈ··/ *n* [U] *informal* the people who produce popular music and their way of life

**tin·plate** /ˈtɪnpleɪt/ *n* [U] very thin sheets of iron or steel covered with tin

**tin-pot** /ˈ· ·/ *adj* [only before noun] a tin-pot person, organization, etc is not very important, although they think that they are: *a tin-pot dictator*

**tin·sel** /ˈtɪnsəl/ *n* [U] **1** thin strings of shiny paper used as decorations, especially at Christmas **2** something that seems attractive but is not valuable or important: *the tinsel and glamour of Hollywood*

**tin shears** /ˈ· ·/ *n* [plural] *AmE* heavy scissors for cutting metal; snips (SNIP[2] (1)) *BrE*

**tint[1]** /tɪnt/ *n* [C] **1** a small amount of a particular colour: *autumn tints* **2** artificial colour, used to slightly change the colour of your hair: *She had put red tints in her hair.*

**tint[2]** *v* [T] **1** to slightly change the colour of someone's hair using artificial colour **2** to give hair an artificial colour

**tin·tack** /ˈtɪntæk/ *n* [C] a short nail made of iron and covered with tin

**tint·ed** /ˈtɪntɪ̈d/ *adj* [only before noun] tinted glass is coloured, rather than completely transparent

**tin·tin·nab·u·la·tion** /ˌtɪntɪ̈næbjʊ̈ˈleɪʃən/ *n* [C,U] *literary* the sound of bells

**ti·ny** /ˈtaɪni/ *adj* extremely small: *a tiny baby | The opium farmers receive only a tiny fraction of this sum.* S2 W2

**-tion** /ʃən/ *suffix (in nouns)* another form of the suffix -ION

**tip[1]** /tɪp/ *n* S2 W3

**1 ► END ◄** [C] the end of something, especially something pointed: *Use the tip of the brush to paint fine lines. | The tip of her nose was red.* —see also FINGERTIP

**2 ► MONEY ◄** [C] a small amount of additional

money that you give to someone, such as a WAITER or a taxi driver: *Did you leave a tip?|a 10% tip*
**3 ▶ ADVICE ◀** [C] a helpful piece of advice: [+ **on**] *Steve gave me some useful tips on how to take good pictures.*
**4 ▶ WASTE ◀** [C] *BrE* an area where unwanted waste is taken and left; DUMP² (1): *a rubbish tip*
**5 ▶ UNTIDY ◀** [singular] *BrE informal* an extremely dirty or untidy place: *Your room's a real tip! When are you going to clean it?*
**6 on the tip of your tongue** if a word, name etc is on the tip of your tongue, you know it but cannot remember it
**7 the tip of the iceberg** a small sign of a problem that is much larger: *The official statistics are probably only the tip of the iceberg.*
**8 ▶ HORSE RACE ◀** [C] *informal* special information about which horse will win a race

**tip²** *v* **tipped, tipping**
**1 ▶ FALL ◀** [I,T] also **tip over/up** to fall or turn over, or make something do this: *Careful you don't tip the milk jug over!|If you lean on the table, it'll tip up.*
**2 ▶ POUR ◀** [T] to pour something from one place or container into another: **tip sth out/into/onto etc** *She weighed out the flour and tipped it out into a bowl.* —see picture on page 838
**3 ▶ LEAN ◀** [I,T] to lean at an angle instead of being level or straight, or to make something do this: *Sit still and don't tip the chair back.*
**4 ▶ MONEY ◀** [I,T] to give an additional amount of money to someone such as a WAITER or taxi driver: *Did you remember to tip the waiter?*
**5 ▶ LIKELY TO SUCCEED ◀** [T usually passive] *especially BrE* to say who you think is most likely to be successful at something: **tip sb as/for** *She's been tipped for promotion.|* **tip sb/sth to do sth** *a horse that was tipped to win*

**6 ▶ COVER ◀ be tipped with** to have one end covered in something: *arrows tipped with poison*
**7 it's tipping down** *BrE spoken* it is raining
**8 tip the balance/scales** to give a slight advantage to someone or something: *Your support tipped the balance in our favour.*
**9 tip the scales at** to weigh a particular amount before a BOXING or WRESTLING match: *He tips the scales at 180 pounds.*
**10 tip sb the wink** *BrE informal* to give someone secret information
**11 tip your hat to** *AmE* to show that you think someone is very good, helpful, successful etc
**tip** sb ↔ **off** *phr v* [T] to give someone a secret warning or piece of information, especially to the police about illegal activities: *The police must have been tipped off.*

**tip-off** /ˈ· ·/ *n* [C] *informal* a warning that something is going to happen, especially to the police about illegal activities: *Acting on an anonymous tip-off, police raided the house.*

**Tipp-Ex** /ˈtɪp eks/ *n* [U] *BrE trademark* white liquid that is used to cover over mistakes in writing, typing etc; WHITE-OUT *AmE*

**tipp·ex** /ˈtɪpeks/ *v* [T + **out**] *BrE* to cover over a mistake in writing, typing etc, using white liquid

**tip·ple** /ˈtɪpəl/ *n informal especially BrE* **favourite tipple** someone's favourite alcoholic drink

**tip·pler** /ˈtɪplə‖-ər/ *n* [C] *informal especially BrE* someone who drinks alcohol

**tip·ster** /ˈtɪpstə‖-ər/ *n* [C] someone who gives information about which horse is likely to win a race

**tip·sy** /ˈtɪpsi/ *adj informal* slightly drunk —**tipsily** *adv* —**tipsiness** *n* [U]

**tip·toe¹** /ˈtɪptəʊ‖-toʊ/ *n* **on tiptoe(s)** if you stand on tiptoe you stand on your toes, in order to make yourself taller: *Anita stood on tiptoe and tried to see over the wall.*

**tiptoe²** *v* [I] to walk quietly and carefully on your toes [+ **across/down etc**] *He tiptoed across the hall and followed her into the kitchen.* —see picture on page 1262

**tip-top** /ˌ· ˈ·◂/ *adj informal* excellent: **in tip-top condition/shape etc** *The car's in tip-top condition.*

**ti·rade** /taɪˈreɪd, tɪ̇-‖ˈtaɪreɪd, tɪ̇ˈreɪd/ *n* [C] a long angry speech criticizing someone or something: *He launched into a tirade against the church.*

**tire¹** /taɪə‖taɪr/ *v* **1** [I,T] to start to feel tired or make someone feel tired: *As we neared the summit, we were tiring fast.* **2 tire of sth** to become bored with something: *Sooner or later he'll tire of politics.* **3 never tire of doing sth** to do something so much that it annoys other people: *She never tires of telling everyone how wonderful her new house is.*
**tire** sb ↔ **out** *phr v* [T] to make someone very tired

**tire²** *n* [C] the American spelling of TYRE

**tired** /taɪəd‖taɪrd/ *adj* **1** feeling that you want to sleep or rest: *I'm so tired I could sleep for a week.|She can't come tonight – she says she's too tired.* **2** bored with something because it is no longer interesting, or has become annoying: **tired of doing sth** *I'm tired of watching television, let's go for a walk.|*[+ **of**] *I was getting tired of all her negative remarks.* **3 tired out** very tired, especially after a lot of hard work, travelling etc **4 tired (old) subject/joke etc** a subject, joke etc that is boring because it is too familiar —see also DOG-TIRED, **be sick (and tired) of sth** (SICK¹ (7)), —**tiredness** *n* [U] —**tiredly** *adv* S W

**tire·less** /ˈtaɪələs‖ˈtaɪr-/ *adj* working very hard in a determined way without stopping: *the tireless efforts of the rescue workers* —**tirelessly** *adv*

**tire·some** /ˈtaɪəsəm‖ˈtaɪr-/ *adj* making you feel annoyed or impatient: *the whole tiresome business of filling out the forms*

**tir·ing** /ˈtaɪərɪŋ‖ˈtaɪr-/ *adj* making you feel that you want to sleep or rest: *We've all had a very tiring day – let's go to bed.*

**ti·ro** /ˈtaɪərəʊ‖ˈtaɪroʊ/ *n* [C] another spelling of TYRO

**'tis** /tɪz/ *poetical* the short form of 'it is'

**tis·sue** /ˈtɪʃuː, -sjuː‖-ʃuː/ *n* **1** [C] a piece of soft thin paper, used especially for blowing your nose on: *a box of tissues* **2** also **tissue paper** [U] light thin paper used for wrapping, packing etc **3** [U] the material forming animal or plant cells: **plant/lung/brain etc tissue** **4 a tissue of lies** a story or account that is completely untrue W

**tit** /tɪt/ *n* [C] **1** *informal* an offensive word for a woman's breast **2** *BrE slang* a stupid person **3 get on sb's tits** *BrE slang* to annoy someone a lot **4** a small European bird

**ti·tan, Titan** /ˈtaɪtn/ *n* [C] a very strong or important person; GIANT² (4)

**ti·tan·ic** /taɪˈtænɪk/ *adj* very big, strong, impressive etc: *a titanic struggle*

**ti·ta·ni·um** /taɪˈteɪniəm/ *n* [U] a strong, light, and very expensive metal

**tit·bit** /ˈtɪtˌbɪt/ *n* [C] *especially BrE* **1** a small piece of food; TIDBIT *AmE* **2 titbit of information/gossip/news etc** *plural* a small but interesting piece of information etc

**titch** /tɪtʃ/ *n* [singular] *BrE* a humorous or insulting way of addressing a small person

**titch·y** /ˈtɪtʃi/ *adj BrE informal* extremely small

**tit·fer** /ˈtɪtfə‖-ər/ *n* [C] *BrE old-fashioned slang* a hat

**tit for tat** /ˌ· · ˈ·/ *n* [U] *informal* something bad that you do to someone because they have done something bad to you

**tithe** /taɪð/ *n* [C usually plural] a tax paid to the church, in former times

**tit·il·late** /ˈtɪtɪ̇leɪt/ *v* [T] if a picture or a story titillates someone, it makes them feel sexually excited or interested: *the usual pin-ups to titillate the readers* —**titillating** *adj* —**titillation** /ˌtɪtɪ̇ˈleɪʃən/ *n* [U]

**tit·i·vate, tittivate** /ˈtɪtɪ̇veɪt/ *v* [I,T] *informal* to make yourself pretty or tidy —**titivation** /ˌtɪtɪ̇ˈveɪʃən/ *n* [U]

3 **ti·tle** /ˈtaɪtl/ *n* **1** [C] the name given to a particular book,
1 painting, play etc: *The title of this play is 'Othello'.* **2** [C] a book: *His novel was one of last year's best-selling titles.* **3** [C] **a)** a name such as 'Sir' or 'Professor', or letters such as 'Mrs' or 'Dr', that are used before someone's name to show their rank or profession, whether they are married etc **b)** a name that describes someone's job or position: *Her official title is editorial manager.* **4** [singular, U] *technical* the legal right to own something: [+ **to**] *He has title to the land.* **5** [C] the position of being the winner of an important sports competition: *Navratilova won a record number of Wimbledon titles.*

**ti·tled** /ˈtaɪtld/ *adj* having a title such as 'lord', DUKE, EARL etc

**title deed** /ˈ·· ·/ *n* [C] a piece of paper giving legal proof that someone owns a particular property

**title hold·er** /ˈ·· ˌ··/ *n* [C] **1** a person or team that is the winner of an important sports competition **2** someone who owns a title deed

**title page** /ˈ·· ·/ *n* [C] the page at the front of a book which shows the book's name, writer etc

**title role** /ˈ·· ·/ *n* [C] the main acting part in a play, which is the same as the name of the play

**tit·mouse** /ˈtɪtmaʊs/ *n* [C] a small European bird

**tit·ter** /ˈtɪtə‖-ər/ *v* [I] to laugh quietly in a high voice, especially because you are nervous: *At the word 'breast' some of the class tittered.* —**titter** *n* [C]

**tittle-tat·tle** /ˈtɪtl ˌtætl/ *n* [U] unimportant conversation about other people and what they are doing; GOSSIP¹ (1)

**tit·ty** /ˈtɪti/ *n* [C] *slang* a woman's breast; TIT

**tit·u·lar** /ˈtɪtʃʊ̆lə‖-ər/ *adj* [only before noun] **titular head/leader/monarch etc** someone who is the official leader or ruler of a country but who does not have real power or authority

**tiz·zy** /ˈtɪzi/ also **tizz** /tɪz/ *n* [singular] *informal* **in a tizzy** feeling worried, nervous, and confused

**T-junc·tion** /ˈtiː ˌdʒʌŋkʃən/ *n* [C] *BrE* a place where two roads meet and form the shape of the letter T

**TLC** /ˌtiː el ˈsiː/ *n* [U] *informal* tender loving care; kindness and love that you show someone to make them feel better and happier

**TM¹** a written abbreviation of TRADEMARK

**TM²** /ˌtiː ˈem/ an abbreviation of TRANSCENDENTAL MEDITATION

**TNT** /ˌtiː en ˈtiː/ *n* [U] a powerful explosive

1 **to¹** /tə, *before vowels* tʊ; *strong* tuː/ **1** [used before a verb
1 to show that it is the infinitive, but not before **can, could, may, might, will, would, shall, should, must,** or **ought** The following senses show the patterns in which **to** is used.] **2** used after verbs: *He lived to be 90.* | *I used to live in New York.* | *He wants to leave.* | *Let her leave if she wants to.* | *They allowed the hostages to go.* | *He told his men to shoot.* | *He told them not to.* **3** used after **how, where, who, whom, whose, which, when, what, or whether**: *I know where to go but I don't know how to get there.* | *She wondered whether or not to go.* | *She wondered whether to or not.* | *Would you tell me when to leave?* **4** used after nouns: *an attempt to make a joke* | *I haven't got the qualifications to apply.* | *There seemed to be no reason to stay.* **5** after adjectives: *That's very easy to say.* | *I'm glad to say she's making a good recovery.* | *We are sorry to announce the cancellation of the flight to Geneva.* **6** used to refer to, or to emphasize a particular verb: *'To find' takes a direct object.* | *It would be best to wear waterproof clothing.* | *What I really should have done was to say "no" straightaway.* **7** used to show that someone intends to do something: *They left early to catch the train.* | *She wore a large hat to keep the sun off her head.* | *I've taken some money out of the bank to buy Christmas presents.* **8** used after **too** + adjective: *It's too cold to go out.* | *Jim's too honest to play a trick like that.* **9** used after an adjective and **enough**: *I reckon it's warm enough to wear a T shirt.* | *It's cold enough to snow.* **10** used to introduce a statement: *To be quite honest, I've never even heard of him.* | *To put it another way, how are you going to get the cash to pay for it?* | *To begin with, let's look at Chapter 3.* **11** used after the pattern **There is** + noun: *There were plenty of things to eat.* | *There's also the cost to consider.*

**to²** /tuː/ *adv* **1** if you push a door to, or something moves a door to, it closes: *The wind blew the door to.* **2 come to** if someone comes to, they become awake or conscious after being asleep or unconscious: *John didn't come to for half-an-hour after falling and hitting his head.*

**to³** /tə, *before vowels* tʊ; *strong* tuː/ *prep* **1** in a direction S1
towards: *the road to London* | *a journey to China* | *She stood* W1
*up and walked to the window.* | *Sam threw the ball to his little sister.* **2** in a direction from a particular person or thing: *Chongqing is about 150 miles to the south of Chengdu.* | *I was sitting to the left of the President.* **3** in order to be in a particular place or area: *We're hoping to go to Istanbul for our holidays this year.* | *Don't forget; we're going to Eve's for supper tomorrow night.* | *I usually go to bed at 11p.m.* | *"Where's Emily?" "She's gone to the loo."* **4** in order to be in a particular situation, or in a particular physical or mental state: *After two difficult years the company is now on the road to recovery.* | *She sang the baby to sleep.* | *The mob stoned her to death.* | *Wait until the lights change to green.* **5** reaching as far as a particular thing: *The water came right up to our knees.* **6** in a position in which two things are touching: *The paper stuck firmly to the wall.* | **cheek to cheek** *They danced cheek to cheek.* **7** facing something or in front of it: *I sat with my back to the engine.* | **face to face** *We stood face to face.* | **back to back** *The two houses were back to back.* **8** until and including: *She can already count from one to twenty.* | *They stayed from Friday night to Sunday morning.* | *It's ten kilometres from here to Angers.* | **from beginning to end** *She read the novel from beginning to end.* | **a nine-to-five job** (=a typical job in which you begin work at nine o' clock and finish at five o'clock.) **9** used to show the person or thing to which actions or words are directed or to whom things belong: *This is a letter to Mildred from George.* | *Have you told all your news to John?* | *You have no right to this land.* | *Will they give you an office to yourself?* **10** used to show the person or thing that is affected by an action: *a danger to your health* | *She's very kind to animals.* | *What have you done to the radio? It's not working.* | *There's always an element of risk to starting up a new business.* **11** working for someone, or being a part of something that is necessary to make it work: *Have you seen the key to the back door?* | *Rona's secretary to the managing director.* **12** used when comparing two things, numbers etc: *I know he's successful but he's nothing to what he could have been.* | *England beat Scotland by two goals to one.* **13** used especially after verbs such as 'seem', 'feel', 'sound' to show how things affect, concern, or influence someone: *The whole thing sounds very suspicious to me.* | *Tickets cost £10 each and to some people that's a lot of money.* **14** according to a particular feeling or attitude: **to your liking/taste etc** *The decor wasn't really to our liking.* | **to your advantage** (=in a way that will help you or be good for you) *You could use this information to your advantage.* | **to your knowledge** (=according to what you know) *Brookner has not to my knowledge written any books since this one.* **15 to your surprise/annoyance/delight** in a way that makes you feel a particular emotion: *Much to her surprise she passed the exam with distinction.* | *To our amazement she climbed on the desk and started removing her clothes.* **16** *especially spoken* forming something or being one of the separate parts that makes something up: *We're only getting eight francs to the pound at the moment.* | *There are sixteen ounces to every pound.* | **there's more to sb/sth than meets the eye** (=used to say that a person or situation is more complicated than they seem to be) **17** used when adding one number to another or when thinking about two facts at the same time: *Add fifty to seventy-five.* | *In addition to all Ron's other problems his father died yesterday.* **18** used to show that there is a certain amount of time before an event or before a particular

time: *Only two weeks to Christmas.*|*How long is it to dinner?*|**ten to five/twenty to one etc** (=ten minutes, twenty minutes etc before a particular hour) **19** used between two numbers when you try to guess an exact number: *There must have been between eighteen to twenty thousand people at the concert.*|*He drowned in 10 to 12 feet of water.* **20** used when saying what the chances of something happening are or giving the ODDS in betting (BET[2] (1)): *It's 100-1 he'll lose.*|*Seagram is running at 11-8.*

**toad** /təʊd‖toʊd/ *n* [C] a small animal that looks like a large FROG and lives mostly on land

**toad-in-the-hole** /ˌ· · · ˈ·/ *n* [U] a British dish made of SAUSAGES cooked in a mixture of eggs, milk, and flour

**toad·stool** /ˈtəʊdstuːl‖ˈtoʊd-/ *n* [C] a wild plant like a MUSHROOM, that can be poisonous

**toad·y[1]** /ˈtəʊdi‖ˈtoʊ-/ *n* [C] *informal* someone who pretends to like an important person so that they will help you

**toady[2]** *v* [I] to pretend to like an important person so that they will help you: [**+ to**] *toadying to the boss*

**to and fro[1]** /ˌtuː ənd ˈfrəʊ‖-ˈfroʊ/ *adv* if someone or something moves to and fro, they move in one direction and then back again: *People walking to and fro on the promenade.* —**to-and-fro** *adj*

**to and fro[2]** *n* [U] *informal* continuous movement of people or things from place to place —see also TOING AND FROING

S 3 **toast[1]** /təʊst‖toʊst/ *n* **1** [U] bread that has been heated so that it is brown on both sides and no longer soft: *We had toast for breakfast.* **2** [C] an occasion when you ask people to all drink something in order to thank someone, wish someone luck etc: **propose a toast** (=ask people to drink a toast) **3 warm as toast** comfortably warm: *They sat near the fire, warm as toast.* **4 be the toast of Broadway/Hollywood etc** to be very popular and praised by many people for something you have done in a particular field of work —see also FRENCH TOAST

**toast[2]** *v* [T] **1** to drink a glass of wine, etc to thank someone, wish someone luck etc: *We toasted our success with champagne.* **2** to make bread or other food brown by placing it close to heat: *toasted cheese sandwiches* **3** to sit yourself near a fire to make yourself warm

**toast·er** /ˈtəʊstə‖ˈtoʊstər/ *n* [C] a machine you use for toasting bread —see picture on page 833

**toasting fork** /ˈ·· ·/ *n* [C] a long fork used to hold bread over a fire to toast it

**toast·mas·ter** /ˈtəʊstˌmɑːstə‖ˈtoʊstˌmæstər/ *n* [C] someone who introduces the speakers at a formal occasion such as a BANQUET (=large formal meal)

**toast·y** /ˈtəʊsti‖ˈtoʊs-/ *adj AmE informal* warm and comfortable

**to·bac·co** /təˈbækəʊ‖-koʊ/ *n* [U] the dried brown leaves that are smoked in cigarettes, pipes etc

**to·bac·co·nist** /təˈbækənɪst/ *n* [C] *BrE* **1** someone who has a shop that sells tobacco, cigarettes etc **2 tobacconist's** a shop that sells tobacco, cigarettes etc

**to·bog·gan[1]** /təˈbɒgən‖-ˈbɑː-/ *n* [C] a light wooden board with a curved front, used for sliding down hills covered in snow

**toboggan[2]** *v* [I] to slide down a hill on a toboggan

**to·by jug** /ˈtəʊbi dʒʌg‖ˈtoʊ-/ *n* [C] a container for drinking from, shaped like a fat man wearing a hat

**toc·ca·ta** /təˈkɑːtə/ *n* [C] a piece of music, usually for piano or organ, that is played very quickly

**toc·sin** /ˈtɒksɪn‖ˈtɑːk-/ *n* [C] *literary* a signal of danger that is made by ringing a bell

**tod** /tɒd‖tɑːd/ *n* **on your tod** *BrE slang* by yourself

S 1 W 1 **to·day[1]** /təˈdeɪ/ *adv* **1** on the day that is happening now: *I couldn't go shopping yesterday so I'll have to go today.*|*Ed has his music lesson today.*|**today week/a week today** *BrE* (=one week from today) *We're going on holiday today week.* —see picture at DAY **2** at the present time: *Students today seem to know very little about geography.*

**today[2]** *n* [U] **1** the day that is happening now —see picture at DAY: *Today is my birthday!*|*Have you read today's paper yet?* **2** the present period of time: *Today's computers are becoming much smaller and lighter.*|*The children of today have more choices than their parents.*

**tod·dle** /ˈtɒdl‖ˈtɑːdl/ *v* [I] if a small child toddles, it walks with short, unsteady steps

**tod·dler** /ˈtɒdlə‖ˈtɑːdlər/ *n* [C] a very young child who is just learning to walk —see CHILD (USAGE)

**tod·dy** /ˈtɒdi‖ˈtɑːdi/ *n* [C] a hot drink made with WHISKY, sugar, and hot water

**to-do** /tə ˈduː/ *n* [singular] *informal* unnecessary excitement or angry feelings about something; FUSS[1] (2): *What a to-do there was when I said I didn't want to be married in a church!*

**toe[1]** /təʊ‖toʊ/ *n* [C] **1** one of the five movable parts at the end of your foot: *He stubbed his toe on a rock.*|**big toe** (=the largest of your toes) **2** the part of a shoe or sock that covers the front part of your foot —see picture at SHOE[1] **3 step on sb's toes** *AmE* **tread on sb's toes** *BrE* to offend someone, especially by becoming involved in something that they are responsible for: *He's new in the department and will have to be careful not to step on anyone's toes.* **4 keep sb on their toes** to make sure that someone is ready for anything that might happen; ALERT[1] (1): *She certainly keeps the children on their toes!* **5 make sb's toes curl** to make someone feel very embarrassed or uncomfortable about something **6 touch your toes** to bend downwards so that your hands touch your toes —see also **from head to toe** (HEAD[1] (2)), **from top to toe** (TOP[1] (2)) S

**toe[2]** *v* [T] **toe the line** to do what other people in a job or organization say you should do, whether you agree with them or not: *You toe the line or you don't stay on the team!*

**toe·cap** /ˈtəʊkæp‖ˈtoʊ-/ *n* [C] a piece of metal or leather that covers the front part of a shoe

**toe·hold** /ˈtəʊhəʊld‖ˈtoʊhoʊld/ *n* **1** [singular] your first involvement in a particular activity, from which you can develop and become stronger: *The company has gained a toehold in the competitive computer market.* **2** [C] a small hole in a rock where you can put your foot when you are climbing

**toe·nail** /ˈtəʊneɪl‖ˈtoʊ-/ *n* [C] the hard part that covers the top of each of your toes —see picture at FOOT[1]

**toe·rag** /ˈtəʊræg‖ˈtoʊ-/ *n* [C] *BrE spoken* an offensive word for someone you dislike: *That toerag cheated me!*

**toff** /tɒf‖tɑːf/ *n* [C] *BrE old-fashioned* someone who is rich or has a high social position

**tof·fee** /ˈtɒfi‖ˈtɑːfi/ *n* [C,U] **1** a sticky sweet brown substance that you can eat, made by boiling sugar, water, and butter together, or a piece of this substance **2 can't do sth for toffee** *BrE informal* to be very bad at doing something: *He can't sing for toffee!*

**toffee ap·ple** /ˈ·· ˌ··/ *n* [C] an apple covered with toffee and put on a stick

**toffee-nosed** /ˈ·· ·/ *adj BrE informal* a toffee-nosed person thinks that they are better than other people because of their social position: *He's a toffee-nosed little creep!*

**to·fu** /ˈtəʊfuː‖ˈtoʊ-/ *n* [U] a soft white food like cheese, that is made from SOY BEANS

**tog[1]** /tɒg‖tɑːg, tɒːg/ *n* [C] **1 togs** [plural] *informal* clothes **2** *technical* a unit for measuring the warmth of QUILTS etc

**tog[2]** *v*

**tog** yourself **up/out** *phr v* [T] *informal* to put on clothes for a particular occasion or activity

**to·ga** /ˈtəʊgə‖ˈtoʊ-/ *n* [C] a long loose piece of clothing worn by people in ancient Rome

**to·geth·er[1]** /təˈgeðə‖-ər/ *adv* 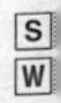
**1 ► MAKE ONE THING ◄** if you want to put two or more things together, you join them so that they form a single subject or group: *Mix the butter and sugar*

*together.* | *He added all the numbers together.* | *We stuck the pieces together again.* | *The model was held together with string.*
**2 ▶ IN ONE PLACE ◀** if you keep, collect etc things together, you keep or collect them all in one place: *I gathered all my favourite paintings together.*
**3 close/packed/crowded etc together** if people or objects are close together, packed together etc, they are placed very near to each other: *The climbers were sitting huddled together for warmth.* | *Her ornaments were all bunched together at one end of the shelf.*
**4 ▶ AGAINST EACH OTHER ◀** if you rub, bang etc things together, you rub or bang them against each other: *Max was rubbing his hands together with glee.* | *Knock the brushes together to clean them.*
**5 ▶ WITH EACH OTHER ◀** if two or more people are together or do something together, they are with each other or do something with each other: *We were at school together.* | *Let's all stay together or someone might get lost.* | *They've decided to spend more time together.* | *I hear George and his wife have got back together.* | **all together (now)** *spoken* (=used when you are asking a group of people to say or do something together) *Right, men. All together now...Push!*
**6 ▶ IN AGREEMENT ◀** if people are together, come together etc they are or become united and work with each other: *Together we can win.* | *We must work closely together on this one.* | *bring the two sides in the dispute together*
**7 ▶ AT THE SAME TIME ◀** at the same time: *Why do all the bills always come together?* | *You should have used both the tools together.*
**8 together with** in addition to; at the same time as: *Just bring it back to the store, together with your receipt.*
**9 ▶ WITHOUT STOPPING ◀** *old use* without interruption: *It rained for four days together.* —see also **get your act together** (ACT[2] (5)), **hold together** (HOLD[1]), **piece sth together** (PIECE[2]), **pull together** (PULL[1])

**together²** *adj spoken* someone who is together always thinks clearly and does things in a very sensible, organized way: *I admire Rosie – she's such a together person.*

**to·geth·er·ness** /tə'geðənɪ̵s‖-ðər-/ *n* [U] the feeling you have when you are part of a group of people who have a close relationship with each other: *I really miss the togetherness we felt at college.*

**tog·gle** /'tɒgəl‖'tɑː-/ *n* [C] **1** a small piece of wood or plastic that is used as a button on coats, bags etc —see picture at FASTENER **2** something on a computer that lets you change from one operation to another

**toggle switch** /'·· ·/ *n* [C] *technical* a small part on a machine that is used to turn electricity on and off by moving it up or down

**toil¹** /tɔɪl/ *v* [I always + adv/prep] **1** also **toil away** to work very hard for a long period of time: [+ **at/over**] *I've been toiling away at this essay all weekend.* **2** to move slowly and with great effort: [+ **up/through/against etc**] *They toiled slowly up the hill.*

**toil²** *n* [U] *formal* **1** hard unpleasant work done over a long period: *a life of toil* **2 the toils of** *literary* if you are caught in the toils of an unpleasant feeling or situation, you are trapped by it

2 **toi·let** /'tɔɪlɪ̵t/ *n* **1** [C] a large bowl that you sit on to get rid of waste liquid or waste matter from your body: *He flushed the toilet.* **2** [C] *especially BrE* a room or building containing a toilet; BATHROOM (2) *AmE*: *public toilets* **3 go to the toilet** *BrE* to pass waste liquid or waste matter from your body: *Mummy, I need to go to the toilet!* **4** [U] *old-fashioned* the act of washing and dressing yourself

**toilet bag** /'·· ·/ *n* [C] a bag in which you keep things such as soap, TOOTHPASTE etc when travelling; SPONGE BAG *BrE* —see picture at BAG[1]

**toilet pa·per** /'·· ,··/ *n* [U] soft thin paper used for cleaning yourself after you have used the toilet

**toi·let·ries** /'tɔɪlɪ̵triz/ *n* [plural] things such as soap and TOOTHPASTE that are used for washing yourself

**toilet roll** /'·· ·/ *n* [C] *BrE* toilet paper that is wound around a small tube

**toilet-train·ing** /'·· ,··/ *n* [U] the act of teaching a child to use a toilet —**toilet-train** *v* [T] —**toilet-trained** *adj*

**toilet wa·ter** /'·· ,··/ *n* [U] a kind of PERFUME (=pleasant smelling liquid) that does not have a very strong smell

**to·ing and fro·ing** /,tuːɪŋ ənd 'frəʊɪŋ‖-'froʊ-/ *n* [U] **1** movement backwards and forwards many times between two or more places **2** a lot of activity that does not help you to do something: *After much toing and froing they finally reached a decision.*

**to·ken¹** /'təʊkən‖'toʊ-/ *n* [C] **1** a round piece of metal that you use instead of money in some machines **2** *formal* something that represents a feeling, fact, event etc: **a token of your gratitude/respect/appreciation etc** *Please accept this gift as a small token of our appreciation.* —see also **by the same token** (SAME[1] (8)) **3 book/record/gift token** *BrE* a special piece of paper that you can exchange for a book, record etc in a shop; GIFT CERTIFICATE *AmE*: *a £10 book token*

**token²** *adj* [only before noun] **1** a token action, change etc is only done so that someone can pretend that they are dealing with a problem: *The government thinks it can get away with token gestures on environmental issues.* | **token black/woman etc** (=someone who is included in a group to make everyone think that it has all types of people in it, when this is not really true) **2** done as a first sign that an agreement, promise etc will be kept and that more will be done later: *A small token payment will keep the bank happy.*

**to·ken·ism** /'təʊkənɪzəm‖'toʊ-/ *n* [U] actions that are intended to make people think that an organization deals fairly with people or problems when in fact it does not

**told** /təʊld‖toʊld/ the past tense and past participle of TELL

**tol·e·ra·ble** /'tɒlərəbəl‖'tɑː-/ *adj* **1** a situation that is tolerable is not very good, but you are able to accept it: *The apartment is really too small, but it's tolerable for the time being.* **2** unpleasant or painful and only just able to be accepted: *The heat in this room is barely tolerable.*

**tol·e·ra·bly** /'tɒlərəbli‖'tɑː-/ *adv* [+ adj/adv] fairly, but not very much: *We were tolerably happy for the first year.*

**tol·e·rance** /'tɒlərəns‖'tɑː-/ *n* **1** [U] willingness to allow people to do, say, or believe what they want without criticizing them: [+ **of/towards**] *tolerance towards religious minorities* **2** [C,U] the degree to which someone can suffer pain, difficulty etc without being harmed or damaged: [+ **of/to**] *Many old people have a very limited tolerance to cold.* **3** [C,U] *technical* the amount by which the size, weight etc of something can change without causing problems

**tol·e·rant** /'tɒlərənt‖'tɑː-/ *adj* allowing people to do, say, or believe what they want without punishing or criticizing them: *Luckily, my parents were tolerant of my choice of music.*

**tol·e·rate** /'tɒləreɪt‖'tɑː-/ *v* [T] **1** to allow people to do, say, or believe something without criticizing or punishing them: *We simply will not tolerate vigilante groups on our streets.* **2** to be able to accept something unpleasant or difficult, even though you do not like it: *Many workers said they couldn't tolerate the long hours.*

**tol·e·ra·tion** /,tɒlə'reɪʃən‖,tɑː-/ *n* [U] willingness to allow people to believe what they want without being punished: *a long history of religious toleration*

**toll¹** /təʊl‖toʊl/ *n* [C] **1** the money you have to pay to use a particular road, bridge etc **2** [usually singular] the number of people killed or injured in a particular accident, by a particular illness etc: **death toll** *The death toll has risen to 83.* **3 take its toll (on)** to have a very bad effect on something or someone over a long period of time: *Years of smoking have taken their toll on his health.* **4** the sound of a large bell ringing slowly

**toll²** *v* [I,T] if a large bell tolls, or you toll it, it keeps ringing slowly, especially to show that someone has died

**toll·booth** /ˈtəʊlbuːθ‖ˈtoʊl-/ *n* [C] a place where you pay to drive on a road, bridge etc

**toll-bridge** /ˈ· ·/ *n* [C] a bridge that you pay to drive across

**toll-free** /ˌ· ˈ·◂/ *adv AmE* if you telephone a particular number toll-free, you do not have to pay for the call —**toll-free** *adj*: *Call this toll-free number for details!*

**toll·gate** /ˈtəʊlgeɪt‖ˈtoʊl-/ *n* [C] a gate across a road, at which you have to pay money before you can drive any further

**toll road** /ˈ· ·/ *n* [C] a road that you pay to use

**toll·way** /ˈtəʊlweɪ‖ˈtoʊl-/ *n AmE* a large long road that you pay to use

**tom** /tɒm‖tɑːm/ *n* [C] *informal* a TOMCAT

**tom·a·hawk** /ˈtɒməhɔːk‖ˈtɑːməhɒːk/ *n* [C] a light AXE¹ (1) used by Native Americans

S3 **to·ma·to** /təˈmɑːtəʊ‖-ˈmeɪtoʊ/ *n plural* **tomatoes** [C] a round soft red fruit eaten raw or cooked as a vegetable —see picture on page 414

**tomb** /tuːm/ *n* [C] a grave, especially a large one above ground: *the tomb of the Unknown Soldier*

**tom·bo·la** /tɒmˈbəʊlə‖tɑːmˈboʊ-/ *n* [U] *BrE* a game in which you buy a ticket with a number on it in order to try and win a prize

**tom·boy** /ˈtɒmbɔɪ‖ˈtɑːm-/ *n* [C] a girl who likes playing the same games as boys: *I was just coming out of my tomboy stage.*

**tomb·stone** /ˈtuːmstəʊn‖-stoʊn/ *n* [C] a stone that is put on a grave and shows the dead person's name, dates of birth and death etc; GRAVESTONE

**tom·cat** /ˈtɒmkæt‖ˈtɑːm-/ *n* [C] a male cat

**tome** /təʊm‖toʊm/ *n* [C] *literary* a large heavy book: *hefty leather-bound tomes of uncertain age*

**tom·fool** /ˌtɒmˈfuːl◂‖ˌtɑːm-/ *adj* very silly: *That was a tomfool thing to do!*

**tom·fool·e·ry** /tɒmˈfuːləri‖tɑːm-/ *n* [U] silly behaviour

**tom·my gun** /ˈtɒmi gʌn‖ˈtɑː-/ *n* [C] *informal* a small gun that can fire many bullets very quickly

S1 W2 **to·mor·row¹** /təˈmɒrəʊ‖-ˈmɔːroʊ,-ˈmɑː-/ *adv* on or during the day after today: *Our class is going to London tomorrow.* | **a week tomorrow** also **tomorrow week** *BrE* (=a week from tomorrow) *James's new job starts a week tomorrow.*

**tomorrow²** *n* **1** [U] the day after today: *I'll see you at tomorrow's meeting.* —see picture at DAY **2** the future, especially the near future: *The computers of tomorrow will be smaller and more powerful.* **3 do sth like there's no tomorrow** do something very quickly and carelessly, without worrying about the future: *Rita's spending money like there's no tomorrow.*

**tom-tom** /ˈ· ·/ *n* [C] a long narrow drum you play with your hands

S3 **ton** /tʌn/ *n* [C] **1** *plural* **tons** or **ton** a unit for measuring weight, equal to 2240 pounds or 1016 kilos in Britain, and 2000 pounds or 907.2 kilos in the US — compare TONNE —see table on page B2 **2 tons of** *informal* a lot of: *We've bought tons of beer for the party tonight.* **3 weigh a ton** *informal* to be very heavy: *Your bag weighs a ton!* **4 do a ton** *BrE informal* to drive at 100 miles an hour **5 come down on sb like a ton of bricks** *informal* to get very angry with someone about something they have done

**ton·al** /ˈtəʊnl‖ˈtoʊ-/ *adj* **1** connected with tones of colour or sound: *The tonal range she uses is wide and varied.* **2** *technical* a piece of music that is tonal is based on a particular KEY¹ (4) —opposite ATONAL

**ton·al·i·ty** /təʊˈnælɪ̈ti‖toʊ-/ *n* [C,U] *technical* the character of a piece of music that depends on the KEY¹ (4) of the music and the way in which the tunes and harmonies (HARMONY (1)) are combined

W **tone¹** /təʊn‖toʊn/ *n*

**1 ▶ VOICE SHOWING FEELING ◀** [C] [plural] the way your voice sounds that shows how you are feeling, or what you mean: *"Why would I lie?" Nora asked in an injured tone.* | *She spoke in warm tones about her family.* | **tone of voice** *spoken* (=used about someone's rude or angry way of speaking) *I don't like your tone of voice.* | **don't take that tone with me** *spoken* (=do not speak to me in that rude or unpleasant way)

**2 ▶ SOUND ◀** [C,U] the quality of a sound especially the sound of a musical instrument or someone's voice: *Your piano has a beautiful tone.* | **in tone** (=having a particular tone) *Margaret's voice was shrill in tone.* | **deep-toned/even-toned/shrill-toned etc** (=having a low, calm etc tone) *My father spoke in an even-toned voice.*

**3 ▶ GENERAL FEELING/ATTITUDE ◀** [singular, U] the general feeling or attitude expressed in a piece of writing, activity etc: *Sara had kept the tone of the meeting businesslike.* | **set the tone** (=establish the general attitude or feeling of an event, activity etc) *Unfortunately, their disagreement set the tone for the whole evening.*

**4 ▶ SOCIALLY ACCEPTABLE ◀** [U] the degree to which something is considered polite, interesting, socially acceptable etc: *The formal setting gave a certain tone to the evening.* | **lower/raise the tone** *That horrible building lowers the whole tone of the neighborhood.*

**5 ▶ COLOUR ◀** [C] one of the many types of a particular colour, each slightly darker, lighter, brighter etc than the next: *The entire painting was in tones of blue.* —see also TWO-TONE

**6 ▶ ELECTRONIC SOUND ◀** [C] a sound made by electronic equipment, such as a telephone: *Please leave a message after the tone.* | **dial/busy** *AmE* | **engaged** *BrE* | **tone** (=the sound you hear on a telephone that means you can dial, it is busy etc) —see also DIALLING TONE

**7 ▶ BODY ◀** [U] *technical* how firm and strong your muscles, skin etc are: *Swimming improves your muscle tone.*

**8 ▶ MUSIC ◀** [C] *technical* the difference in PITCH² (3) between two musical notes that are separated by one KEY¹ (4) on the piano; STEP¹ (18) *especially AmE*

**9 ▶ VOICE LEVEL ◀** [C] *technical* the PITCH² (3) of someone's voice as they speak: *The Chinese language has several tones.*

**tone²** *v* [T] to improve the strength and firmness of your skin, muscles etc: *It cleanses and tones your skin.*

**tone** sth ↔ **down** *phr v* [T] **1** to reduce the effect of a speech or piece or writing, so that people will not be offended: *His advisers told him to tone down his speech.* **2** to make a colour less bright

**tone** sth/sb ↔ **up** *phr v* [T] to make your body or part of your body feel healthier and stronger: *Aerobics really tones up your muscles.*

**tone-deaf** /ˌ· ˈ·◂‖ˈ· ·/ *adj* unable to tell the difference between different musical notes: *the tone-deaf morons in today's pop groups*

**tone lan·guage** /ˈ· ˌ··/ *n* [C] *technical* a language such as Chinese in which the way a sound goes up or down affects the meaning of the word

**tone·less** /ˈtəʊnləs‖ˈtoʊn-/ *adj* a toneless voice does not express any feelings: *"I'm sorry," he said, in a flat toneless voice.* —**tonelessly** *adv*

**tone po·em** /ˈ· ˌ··/ *n* [C] a piece of music written to represent an idea, scene, or story

**ton·er** /ˈtəʊnə‖ˈtoʊnər/ *n* [U] **1** a type of ink used in computer PRINTERS, PHOTOCOPIERS etc **2** a liquid that you put on your face to make your skin feel good

**tongs** /tɒŋz‖tɑːŋz, tɔːŋz/ *n* [plural] a tool that consists of two moveable bars joined at one end, used to pick up an object —see picture at LABORATORY

3 **tongue** /tʌŋ/ *n*
3 **1 ▶ MOUTH ◀** [C] the soft, moveable part inside your mouth that you use for tasting, eating, and speaking: *Joe ran his tongue over his dry lips.* | *The dog panted, his tongue hanging out in the heat.* | **stick your tongue out** (=put your tongue outside your mouth as a rude gesture) *Kim stuck her tongue out at the teacher.*
**2 sharp/eloquent/silver/acid etc tongue** if you have a sharp, silver etc tongue, you speak in a way that shows your anger, use beautiful language etc: *Gina's sharp tongue will get her into trouble one day.* | **rough-tongued/sharp-tongued/silver-tongued etc** (=speaking in a rough etc way) *He was clever and acid-tongued.*
**3 tongue in cheek** if you say something with your tongue in your cheek, you say it as a joke —see also TONGUE-IN-CHEEK
**4 slip of the tongue** a mistake in something you say: *Did I say $100? It must have been a slip of the tongue.*
**5 bite your tongue** to stop yourself saying something because it is better not to: *I wanted to argue but I had to bite my tongue.* | **bite your tongue!** (=used to tell someone angrily that they should not say the type of thing they have just said)
**6 Cat got your tongue?** also **Lost your tongue?** *spoken* used to ask someone why they are not talking
**7 get your tongue around** *informal* to be able to say a difficult word or phrase: *I can't get my tongue around the names of these Welsh towns.*
**8 ▶ LANGUAGE ◀** *literary* a language: *Anton lapsed into his own tongue when he was excited.* —see also MOTHER TONGUE **native tongue** (NATIVE[1] (3))
**9 watch your tongue!** *spoken* used to tell someone that they should not have said something rude
**10 ▶ FOOD ◀** [U] the tongue of a cow or sheep, cooked and eaten cold
**11 trip/roll off the tongue** *humorous* if a name, phrase etc trips or rolls off your tongue, it is easy or pleasant to say: *Agatha Boglewood: it doesn't exactly trip off the tongue does it?*
**12 ▶ SHAPE ◀** [C] something that has a long thin shape: [+ **of**] *tongues of fire*
**13 ▶ SHOE ◀** the part of a shoe that lies on top of your foot, under the part where you tie it —see picture at SHOE[1]
**14 loosen sb's tongue** if something, such as alcohol loosens your tongue, it makes you talk a lot: *Tongues loosened by drink, they told me what I needed to know.*
**15 find your tongue** to speak after being silent because you were afraid or shy: *Dana finally found his tongue and told them how he'd hated his first day at school.*
**16 hold your tongue!** *old-fashioned spoken* used to angrily tell someone to stop speaking
**17 wagging tongues** if you talk about tongues wagging, you mean that people are talking about someone in an unkind way: *Angela's divorce will certainly set tongues wagging.*
**18 keep a civil tongue in your head** *spoken* used when you think someone should speak politely
**19 speak with forked tongue** *humorous* to tell lies
**20 speak in tongues** to speak using strange words as part of a religious experience
**21 tongue and groove joint** *technical* a way of joining two pieces of wood —see also **on the tip of your tongue** (TIP[1] (6)), **give sb the rough side of your tongue** (ROUGH[1] (18))

**tongue de·press·or** /ˈ· ·ˌ··/ *n* [C] *AmE* a little flat piece of wood a doctor uses to hold down your tongue while examining your throat; SPATULA *BrE*

**tongue-in-cheek** /ˌ· · ˈ·◂/ *adj* a tongue-in-cheek remark, comment etc is said as a joke: *a splendidly tongue-in-cheek account of their first meeting* —**tongue-in-cheek** *adv*: *I believe he said this tongue-in-cheek.*

**tongue-tied** /ˈ· ·/ *adj* unable to speak easily to other people, especially because you feel embarrassed *He sat tongue-tied, like a shy schoolboy.*

**tongue twist·er** /ˈ· ˌ··/ *n* [C] a word or phrase that is difficult to say quickly and correctly

**ton·ic**[1] /ˈtɒnɪk‖ˈtɑː-/ *n* **1** [C,U] also **tonic water** a clear bitter tasting drink that is mixed with alcoholic drinks such as GIN or VODKA: *a gin and tonic* **2** [C usually singular] *BrE* something that improves your health, strength, or confidence: *The holiday was a real tonic.* **3** [C] a medicine that is designed to give you more energy or strength when you feel tired: *a herbal tonic* **4** [C usually singular] *technical* the first note in a musical SCALE[1] (4)

**tonic**[2] *adj formal* giving you energy and strength: *Sea air has a tonic quality.*

**to·night**[1] /təˈnaɪt/ *adv* on or during the night of today: S1 *I've been really tired all day so I think I'll go to bed early* W2 *tonight.* | *at 9 o'clock tonight*

**tonight**[2] *n* [U] the night of today: *Tonight is a very special occasion.* | *tonight's news bulletin*

**ton·nage** /ˈtʌnɪdʒ/ *n* [C,U] **1** the size of a ship or the amount of goods it can carry, shown in TONS **2** the total number of TONS that something weighs

**tonne** /tʌn/ *n plural* **tonnes** *or* **tonne** [C] a metric unit for measuring weight, equal to 1000 kilograms —see table on page B2

**tons** /tʌnz/ *adv informal* very much: *I feel tons better after a rest.* —see also **tons of** (TON (2))

**ton·sil** /ˈtɒnsəl‖ˈtɑːn-/ *n* [C] one of two small round pieces of flesh at the sides of the throat near the back of the tongue: *She had to have her tonsils out.* —see picture at RESPIRATORY

**ton·sil·li·tis** /ˌtɒnsɪ̵ˈlaɪtɪ̵s‖ˌtɑːn-/ *n* [U] a serious infection of the tonsils

**ton·so·ri·al** /tɒnˈsɔːriəl‖tɑːn-/ *adj humorous formal* connected with cutting hair: *a display of tonsorial perfection*

**ton·sure** /ˈtɒnʃə‖ˈtɑːnʃər/ *n* **1** [U] the act of removing all the hair from the top of your head to show that you are a MONK **2** [C] the top part of your head that has had the hair removed for this reason —**tonsured** *adj*

**ton-up** /ˈ· ·/ *adj BrE old fashioned* **ton-up driver/biker etc** someone who likes to drive very fast

**too** /tuː/ *adv* **1** [+ adj/adv] more than is reasonable, S1 possible, or necessary: *That music is too loud, turn the* W1 *radio down.* | **too much/little/many etc sth** *There's too much talking! Open your books and get down to work.* | **much/far/a little etc too** *Amanda is much too young to get married.* | **too tall/old etc for** *That crossword is too difficult for me.* | **too good/hot/big (a sth) to do sth** *My coffee is too hot to drink.* | *A free cruise to Acapulco – that's too good an opportunity to miss.* **2** [at the end of a sentence or clause] also: *It's a nutritious meal and cheap too!* | *Sheila wants to come too.* —compare EITHER **3** [+ adj/adv] very: *Dinner shouldn't be too long. Would you like a drink first?* | *You shouldn't have bought flowers. You're too kind.* **4 all too/only too** used to say that something is very easy to do, happens very often etc when it should not: *Sadly this kind of attack is becoming all too common these days.* **5** used to emphasize that you are angry, surprised, or agree with something: *"They've just built another car park next to the supermarket." "About time too."* **6 I am/he is/you are etc too** *informal especially AmE* used to emphasize that you disagree with what someone has said about you: *"You're not smart enough to use a computer." "I am too!"*

**took** /tʊk/ the past tense of TAKE

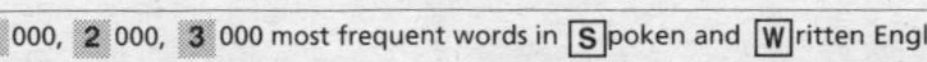
1 000, 2 000, 3 000 most frequent words in S poken and W ritten English

**tools**

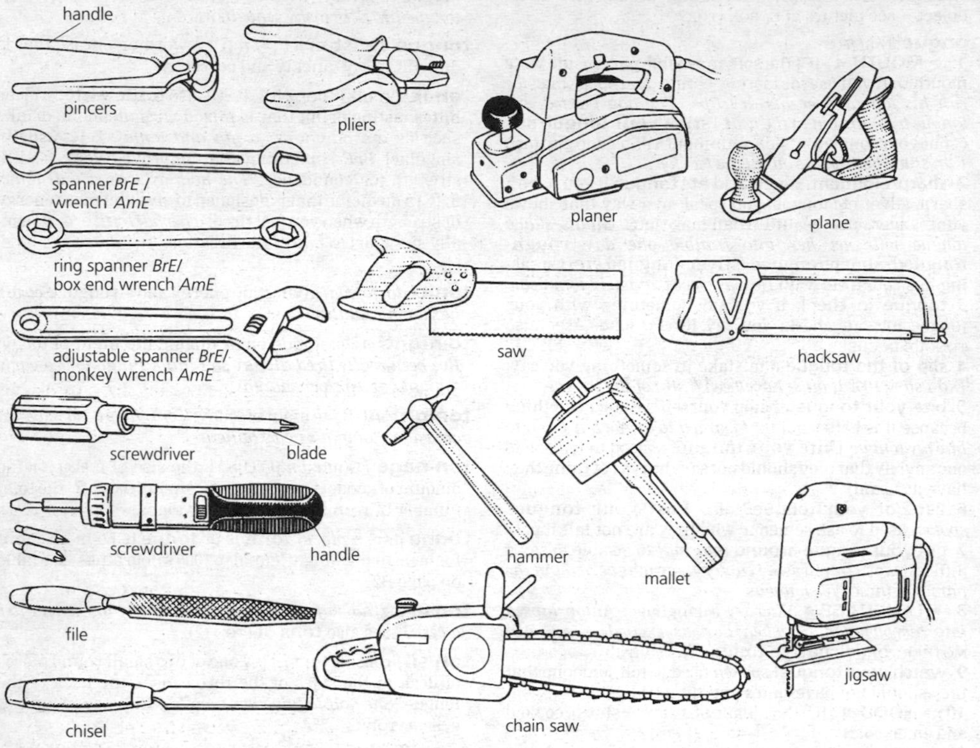

handle
pincers
pliers
spanner *BrE* / wrench *AmE*
ring spanner *BrE*/ box end wrench *AmE*
adjustable spanner *BrE*/ monkey wrench *AmE*
screwdriver
blade
screwdriver
handle
file
chisel
planer
plane
saw
hacksaw
hammer
mallet
jigsaw
chain saw

see also picture at **drill**

S2 W2 **tool[1]** /tuːl/ *n* [C] **1** something such as a hammer that you hold in your hand and use to do a particular job: *Rob didn't have the right tool to repair the engine.* **2** something such as a piece of equipment or skill that is useful for doing your job: *Television is an important tool for the modern teacher.* | **tools of the trade** *The poet is a craftsman and words are the tools of his trade.* **3** someone who is used unfairly by someone else: [+ **of**] *The king was merely a tool of the military government.* **4** *taboo slang* a PENIS (=the male sex organ) —see also **down tools** (DOWN[4] (3))

**tool[2]** *v* [I + **along/down**] *AmE informal* to drive along a street, especially for fun

**tool up** *phr v* [I,T **tool** sth ↔ **up**] to prepare a factory for production by providing the necessary tools and machinery: *tooled up to produce light weapons*

**tooled** /tuːld/ *adj* tooled leather has been decorated using a special tool

**tool kit** /ˈ· ·/ *n* [C] a set of various tools

**tool shed** /ˈ· ·/ *n* [C] a small wooden building in a garden, where tools are kept

**toot[1]** /tuːt/ *v* [I,T] **1** *especially BrE* if you toot your car horn, or if it toots, it makes a short, high sound: *The taxi driver was angrily tooting his horn.* **2** *AmE slang* to take COCAINE up through your nose

**toot[2]** *n* [C] a short high sound, made especially by a car horn

S2 W2 **tooth** /tuːθ/ *n plural* **teeth** /tiːθ/ [C]

**1** ▶ **IN MOUTH** ◀ one of the hard white objects in your mouth that you use to bite and CHEW your food: *Brush your teeth twice a day.* | *I'm going to the dentist to have a tooth out.* | **cut a tooth** (=grow a new tooth) *The baby's cutting a tooth.* | *The Doberman sank its teeth into his leg.*

**2** ▶ **ON A TOOL ETC** ◀ one of the pointed parts that sticks out from the edge of a comb, SAW[2] (1), COG (1), etc

**3 fight tooth and nail** to try with a lot of effort or determination to do something: *We fought tooth and nail to get our plans accepted.*

**4 get your teeth into** *informal* to start to do something with eagerness and energy: *I can't wait to get my teeth into the new course.*

**5 in the teeth of a)** in spite of opposition or danger from something: *The new law was passed in the teeth of public protest.* **b)** against a stormy wind: *sailing in the teeth of a storm*

**6 set sb's teeth on edge** if a sound, taste etc sets your teeth on edge, it makes you feel physically uncomfortable: *That scraping really sets my teeth on edge.*

**7** ▶ **LAW** ◀ **have teeth** if a law, regulation etc has teeth, or if you give it teeth, it has the power to force people to obey it: *The agreement works because it has teeth.*

**8 sharp-toothed/saw-toothed/fine-toothed etc** having sharp parts that stick out of the edge, etc: *a fine-toothed comb* —see also **armed to the teeth** (ARMED (1)), **cut your teeth on sth** (CUT[1] (16)), **by the skin of your teeth** (SKIN[1] (5)), **be a kick in the teeth** (KICK[2] (4)), **through your teeth** (LIE[3] (1)), **have a sweet tooth** (SWEET[1] (7)), **take the bit between your teeth** (BIT[1] (17))

**tooth·ache** /ˈtuːθ-eɪk/ *n* [C,U] a pain in a tooth

**tooth·brush** /ˈtuːθbrʌʃ/ *n* [C] a small brush for cleaning your teeth —see picture at BRUSH[1]

**tooth·less** /ˈtuːθləs/ *adj* **1** having no teeth: *a toothless smile* **2** a law that is toothless has no power to make someone obey it: *Without legal sanctions it is toothless.*

**tooth·paste** /ˈtuːθpeɪst/ *n* [U] a substance used to clean your teeth

**tooth·pick** /ˈtuːθˌpɪk/ *n* [C] a very small pointed stick for removing bits of food that are stuck between your teeth

**tooth pow·der** /ˈ· ˌ··/ *n* [U] a special powder used to clean your teeth

**tooth·some** /ˈtuːθsəm/ *adj humorous* tasting good; DELICIOUS: *the less toothsome corners of English cuisine*

**tooth·y** /ˈtuːθi/ *adj* **toothy smile/grin** a smile in which you show a lot of teeth

**toot·le** /ˈtuːtl/ *v* [I] *BrE* **1** *old-fashioned* to move slowly in a car **2** to play an instrument such as a FLUTE without producing any particular tune

**toots** /tʊts/ *n* [C] *AmE old-fashioned* a way of addressing a woman, sometimes considered offensive: *Hey toots! How're you doing?*

**toot·sie** /ˈtʊtsi/ *n* [C] **1** *AmE spoken* a way of addressing a woman, sometimes considered offensive **2 tootsies** [plural] *informal* a word meaning toes, used especially by or to children

1 **top[1]** /tɒp‖tɑːp/ *n* [C]
2 **1 ▶ THE HIGHEST PART ◀** the highest part of something: **the top of** *Place the mixture in the top of the oven.* | *The top of the mountain is covered with snow.* | *I filled the glass right to the top.* | *She could only just see over the tops of their heads.* | **at the top (of sth)** *Write your name at the top of the page.* | *I stood at the top of the stairs.* | **the very top** (=the highest part) *The book I wanted was at the very top of the stack.* | **up the top** *spoken* (=at or near the top of a tree, mountain etc) *You'll see it when you get up the top of the hill.* | **tree top/roof-top/hill-top etc** *the white cliff-tops in the distance* —opposite BOTTOM[1] (1)
**2 ▶ UPPER SURFACE ◀** the flat upper surface of an object: *papers spread all over the top of of piano* | *The table has a glass top.*
**3 ▶ BEST POSITION ◀ the top** the best, most successful, or most important position in an organization,company,group etc: *He started life at the bottom and worked his way up to the top.* | *the cult of secrecy at the top* | **the top of** *people who are near the top of the wages league* | **(at the) top of the class/division etc** (=the best in a list or in an order of things) *We came top of our group three years running.* | **top of the range** *informal* (=an expression meaning one of the best or most expensive, used especially in advertising) *a perfectly smooth ride, as you would expect from the top of the range product* | **the top of the tree** *informal* (=the highest position in a profession) *By now Vivien Westwood had reached the top of the fashion tree.* —opposite BOTTOM[1] (5)
**4 be (at the) top of the list/agenda** something that is at the top of the list etc will be dealt with or discussed first: *Defence, isn't always at the top of the political agenda!*
**5 on top a)** on the highest point or surface of something: *Sprinkle some Parmesan on top and grill.* | *a hat with a red pom-pom on top* | **on top of** *There's $10 on top of the refrigerator.* | **one on top of the other** also **on top of one another** (=in a pile) *The workmen were stacking the crates on top of one another;* opposite UNDERNEATH **b)** in the most successful or important position in business, a game etc: *The All Blacks stayed on top throughout the match.* **c)** on the highest part of your head: *Cut it short on top, please.*
**6 on top of** if something dangerous or threatening is on top of you, it is very near you: *The truck was almost on top of us.* **a)** if something bad happens to you on top of something else, it happens when you have other problems: *On top of everything else, I now owe my parents $10,000 for the fines!* **b)** in complete control of a job, situation etc: *Don't worry; I'm back on top of things now*
**7 come out on top** to win a difficult struggle or argument, especially one that has lasted for a long time: *It's very difficult to predict who will come out on top.*
**8 get on top of** if work, a problem etc gets on top of you, it begins to make you feel unhappy and upset: *Things are starting to get on top of him.*
**9 on top of the world** *informal* extremely happy: *When I heard she'd been released I felt on top of the world!*
**10 ▶ COVER ◀** something that you put on a pen, bottle etc to close it, especially something that you push or turn: *You've left the top off the toothpaste again!* | *Where's the top of this pen?* | **bottle/pen etc** *Milk bottle tops* —see also SCREW TOP
**11 ▶ CLOTHES ◀** a piece of clothing that you wear on the upper part of your body: *her stripy top* | *a skirt with a matching top* | *slip your pyjama top off*
**12 ▶ PLANT ◀** the part of a fruit or vegetable where it was attached to the plant, or the leaves of a plant whose root you can eat: *Cut the tops off the tomatoes.* | *carrot tops*
**13 the top of the milk** *BrE* the creamy part that rises to the top of a bottle of milk
**14 ▶ STREET/FIELD ETC ◀** the part of the street or of a piece of land that is the furthest away either from you or from the most important entrance to it: *I waited at the top of East Street.*
**15 the top of the table** the part of a long dinner table where the most important people sit —see also TOP TABLE
**16 off the top of your head** *informal* if you answer a question or provide information off the top of your head, you do it immediately without checking the facts: *Just off the top of my head I'd say there were about 50.*
**17 sing/shout at the top of your voice** to sing etc as loudly as you possibly can: *We yelled at the tops of our voices.*
**18 from the top** *spoken* an expression meaning from the beginning, used especially in the theatre: *Alright. Once more from the top. Action!*
**19 from top to bottom** if you clean or search somewhere from top to bottom, you do it very thoroughly
**20 from top to toe** if a person is dressed or covered in something from top to toe, they are completely dressed or covered in it: *expensive Parisian couture from top to toe*
**21 the top and bottom of** *BrE spoken* the general result or meaning of a situation, expressed in a few words: *He's trying to embarrass you, that's the top and bottom of it.*
**22 not have much up top** *BrE spoken* to be not very intelligent
**23 tops** *BrE spoken* used after a number to say that it is the highest possible amount of money you will get: *You'll make £200 from it, £250 tops.*
**24 be (the) tops** *old fashioned informal* to be the best
**25 ▶ TOY ◀** a child's toy that spins around on its point when the child twists it
**26 spin like a top** to spin or turn round very quickly: *The impact sent me spinning like a top.*
**27 sleep like a top** *BrE* to sleep very deeply and well

**top[2]** *adj* [only before noun] S1
**1 ▶ HIGHEST ◀** at the top; highest: *the top button of his shirt* | *I can dive off the top board.* | *Sprinkle cheese over the top layer of tomatoes.* | **top floor** *Andrew lives on the top floor.* | **top priority** *We are giving the matter top priority.* | **the top 50/third/20% etc** *She is among the top 5% of earners in this country.* | *We weren't even in the top 100 companies.* —opposite BOTTOM[2] (1) W1
**2 top left/right/centre** expressions meaning the picture at or nearest the top of the pages on the left or right or in the centre, used in magazines and newspapers: *Top right: Silk Blouse £95 from Harrods.*
**3 ▶ BEST ◀** best or most successful: *one of our top tennis players* | *a top New York salon* | *people in top jobs* | *top quality ingredients* | *She got top marks.* | **be on top form** (=to be doing something that you are good at especially well) *Our team's on top form at the moment.*
**4 top speed** the fastest speed a vehicle can move at: *We chased after them at top speed.*
**5 top copy** a piece of written material that is produced first and from which copies have been or can be made

**6 the top brass** *informal* people in positions of high rank, especially in the army, navy etc
**7 top dog** *informal* the person in the highest or most important position especially after a struggle or effort
**8 ▶ HIGH SOCIAL CLASS ◀** *old-fashioned informal* from the highest social class: *a top people's magazine*

**top³** *v* **topped, topping** [T]
**1 ▶ BE HIGHER ◀** to be higher or more than something: *Their profits have reportedly topped £1,000,000 this year.*
**2 top an offer/bid etc** to offer more money than someone else: *A rival company has topped our offer by $5 million.*
**3 ▶ BE BETTER ◀** if you top someone else's remarks or actions you say or do something better, funnier or more exciting: **top that** *And we also met Michael Jackson. Bet you can't top that!*
**4 top the bill/charts etc** to come first in a list or in an order of things: *Their party topped the poll in only 12 seats.* —see also CHART-TOPPING
**5 be topped by sth** if something, especially an article of clothing, a mountain, or a building, is topped by something else, it has that thing on its top: *Roofs topped by fat chimneys | trellis – topped brick walls*
**6 topped with cream/onions etc** with cream etc on the top: *spicy new pizzas topped with curry sauce* —see also TOPPING
**7 to top it all** *spoken* in addition to other bad things that have happened to you: *To top it all I lost my job.*
**8 top and tail** *BrE* to cut the top and bottom off a piece of fruit or a vegetable
**9 ▶ REACH THE TOP ◀** *literary* if you top a rising piece of ground, you reach the top of it: *Our wagon topped the crest of the hill and we gasped at the view before us.*
**10 top yourself** *BrE slang* to kill yourself deliberately

**top** sth ↔ **off** *phr v* [T] to complete something successfully by doing a last action or adding a last detail: *Let's top off the evening with a drink. | A cherry on each cake would top them off nicely.*

**top out** *phr v* [I] if something such as a price that is increasing tops out, it reaches its highest point and stops rising: *Do you think interest rates have topped out now?*

**top** sth/sb ↔ **up** *phr v* [T] *especially BrE* **1** to fill a partly empty container with liquid: *I'll just top up the coffee pot.* **2** to put more drink in someone's glass or cup: *Can I top you up?* **3** to increase the level of something slightly so as to bring it back to the level you want: *Top up your tan this winter!* —see also TOP-UP

**to·paz** /ˈtəʊpæz‖ˈtoʊ-/ *n* [C,U] a transparent yellow jewel or the mineral that it is cut from

**top-class** /ˌ· ˈ·◂/ *adj* being the best, most skilful etc: *top-class athletes such as Linford Christie | a top-class restaurant*

**top·coat** /ˈtɒpkəʊt‖ˈtɑːpkoʊt/ *n* **1** [C,U] the last layer of paint that is put on a surface **2** [C] *old-fashioned* a warm long coat

**top-down** /ˌ· ˈ·◂/ *adj BrE* a top-down plan etc is one in which you start with a general idea of what you want and then add the details later: *adopting a top-down managerial philosophy*

**top-drawer** /ˌ· ˈ·◂/ *adj informal* of the highest quality or social class: *top-drawer entertainment*

**top-dress·ing** /ˌtɒpˈdresɪŋ‖ˈtɑːpˌdresɪŋ/ *n* [C,U] *technical* a layer of FERTILIZER that is spread over land

**to·pee, topi** /ˈtəʊpiː‖toʊˈpiː/ *n* [C] a hard hat for protecting your head in tropical sunshine

**top-flight** /ˌ· ˈ·◂/ *adj* most successful, skilful, or important: *They've hired a really top-flight sales team.*

**top gear** /ˌ· ˈ·/ *n* [U] **1** the highest GEAR of a car, bus etc: **in top gear** *The car will cruise at 80 mph in top gear.* **2 be in top gear** to be at the highest level of activity: *The party's election campaign is now in top gear.*

**top-gross·ing** /ˈ· ˌ··/ *adj* a top-grossing film earns more money than any other film at a particular time

**top hat** /ˌ· ˈ·/ *n* [C] a man's tall black or grey hat, now worn only on formal occasions —see picture at HAT

**top-heav·y** /ˌ· ˈ··◂/ *adj* **1** too heavy at the top and therefore likely to fall over **2** an organization that is top heavy has too many managers compared to the number of ordinary workers: *burdened by a top-heavy bureaucracy*

**to·pi** /ˈtəʊpiː‖toʊˈpiː/ *n* [C] another spelling of TOPEE

**to·pi·a·ry** /ˈtəʊpiəri‖ˈtoʊpieri/ *n* [U] trees and bushes cut into the shapes of birds, animals etc, or the art of cutting them in this way

**top·ic** /ˈtɒpɪk‖ˈtɑː-/ *n* [C] a subject that people talk or write about: *The environment is a popular topic these days.* | **topic of conversation** *The wedding has been the only topic of conversation for weeks!* W

**top·ic·al** /ˈtɒpɪkəl‖ˈtɑː-/ *adj* a story, subject, problem etc that is topical is interesting because it deals with something that is important at the present time: *a new TV comedy dealing with topical issues* —**topically** /-kli/ *adv* —**topicality** /ˌtɒpɪˈkæləti‖ˌtɑː-/ *n* [U]

**top·knot** /ˈtɒpnɒt‖ˈtɑːpnɑːt/ *n* [C] a way of arranging your hair, often tied with RIBBONS, on top of your head

**top·less** /ˈtɒpləs‖ˈtɑːp-/ *adj* a woman who is topless is not wearing any clothes on the upper part of her body, so that her breasts are bare: *topless sunbathing* | **topless bar/show** (=one in which the women serving or performing are topless)

**top-lev·el** /ˌ· ˈ··◂/ *adj* [only before noun] involving the most powerful people in a country, organization etc: *Top-level talks are to be held between the heads of state.*

**top·most** /ˈtɒpməʊst‖ˈtɑːpmoʊst/ *adj* [only before noun] the topmost part of something is its highest part: *The topmost branches were still bathed in sunlight.*

**top-notch** /ˌ· ˈ·◂/ *adj informal* having the highest quality or standard: *I was lucky and got myself a job with a top-notch company.*

**to·pog·ra·phy** /təˈpɒɡrəfi‖-ˈpɑː-/ *n* [U] **1** the science of describing an area of land, or making maps of it **2** [+ **of**] the shape of an area of land, including its hills, valleys etc —**topographer** *n* [C] —**topographical** /ˌtɒpəˈɡræfɪkəl◂‖ˌtɑː-ˌˌtoʊ-/ *adj*

**top·per** /ˈtɒpə‖ˈtɑːpər/ *n* [C] *informal* a TOP HAT

**top·ping¹** /ˈtɒpɪŋ‖ˈtɑː-/ *n* [C,U] something you put on top of food to make it look nicer or taste better: *a pizza with extra cheese topping*

**topping²** *adj BrE old-fashioned* excellent

**top·ple** /ˈtɒpəl‖ˈtɑː-/ *v* **1** [I,T] to become unsteady and then fall over, or to make something do this: [+ **over**] *A stack of plates swayed, and began to topple over.* **2** [T] to take power away from a leader or government, especially by force; OVERTHROW¹ (1): *This scandal could topple the government.*

**top-rank·ing** /ˌ· ˈ··◂/ *adj* most powerful and important within an organization: *top-ranking diplomats*

**top-rat·ed** /ˌ· ˈ··◂/ *adj informal* very popular with the public: *a top-rated TV show*

**top round** /ˈ· ·/ *n* [U] *AmE* TOPSIDE *BrE*

**top-se·cret** /ˌ· ˈ··◂/ *adj* top-secret documents or information must be kept completely secret: *a top-secret military code*

**top·side¹** /ˈtɒpsaɪd‖ˈtɑːp-/ *n* [U] *BrE* high quality BEEF cut from the upper leg of the animal; TOP ROUND *AmE*

**topside²** also **top·sides** /-saɪdz/ *adv AmE* towards or onto the DECK (=upper surface) of a boat or ship

**top·soil** /ˈtɒpsɔɪl‖ˈtɑːp-/ *n* [U] the upper level of soil in which most plants have their roots

**top·spin** /ˈtɒpˌspɪn‖ˈtɑːp-/ *n* [U] the turning movement of a ball that has been hit or thrown in such a way that it spins forward

**top·sy-tur·vy** /ˌtɒpsi ˈtɜːvi◂‖ˌtɑːpsi ˈtɜːrvi◂/ *adj informal* in a state of complete disorder or confusion: *He left his room all topsy-turvy.*

**top tab·le** /ˌ· ˈ··/ *n* [C] *BrE* a table at a formal meal, for example at a wedding, where the most important people sit; HEAD TABLE *AmE*

**top-up** /ˈ· ·/ *n* [C] *BrE* an amount of liquid that you add to a glass, cup etc in order to make it full again: *Would you like a top-up?*

**tor** /tɔː‖tɔːr/ *n* [C] *BrE* a rocky hill

**Tor·ah** /ˈtɔːrə/ *n* [singular] all the writings and teachings concerned with Judaism, especially the first five books of the Jewish Bible

**torch¹** /tɔːtʃ‖tɔːrtʃ/ *n* [C] **1** *BrE* a small electric lamp that you carry in your hand; FLASHLIGHT *AmE*: *We shone our torches around the walls of the cavern.* **2** a long stick with burning material at one end that produces light: *the Olympic torch | a torch-light procession* **3 carry a torch for** *old-fashioned* to secretly love and admire someone

torch

**torch²** *v* [T] *informal* to deliberately make a building start to burn: *Rioters torched several abandoned cars.*

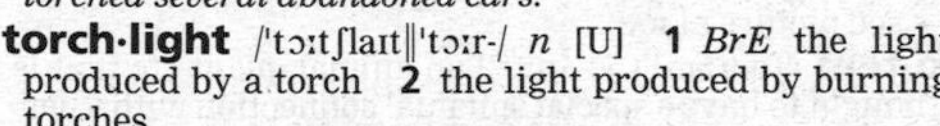

**torch·light** /ˈtɔːtʃlaɪt‖ˈtɔːr-/ *n* [U] **1** *BrE* the light produced by a torch **2** the light produced by burning torches

**tore** /tɔː‖tɔːr/ the past tense of TEAR²

**to·re·a·dor** /ˈtɒriədɔː‖ˈtɔːriədɔːr, ˈtɑː-/ *n* [U] the person who fights bulls (BULL¹ (1)) in a Spanish BULLFIGHT

**tor·ment¹** /ˈtɔːment‖ˈtɔːr-/ *n* **1** [U] severe mental or physical suffering, often lasting a long time: **in torment** *She lay awake all night in torment.* **2** [C] someone or something that makes you suffer

**tor·ment²** /tɔːˈment‖tɔːr-/ *v* [T] **1** to make someone suffer a lot, especially so that they feel guilty or very unhappy: *Seth was tormented by feelings of guilt. | tormented by hunger* **2** to deliberately treat someone cruelly by annoying them or hurting them: *The older boys would torment him whenever they had the chance.* —**tormentor** *n* [C]

**torn** /tɔːn‖tɔːrn/ the past participle of TEAR² —see picture on page 1258

**tor·na·do** /tɔːˈneɪdəʊ‖tɔːrˈneɪdoʊ/ *n plural* **tornadoes** *or* **tornados** [C] an extremely violent storm consisting of air that spins very quickly and causes a lot of damage — compare HURRICANE, CYCLONE

**tor·pe·do¹** /tɔːˈpiːdəʊ‖tɔːrˈpiːdoʊ/ *n plural* **torpedoes** [C] a long narrow weapon that is fired under the surface of the sea and explodes when it hits something

**torpedo²** *v* [T] **1** to attack or destroy a ship with a torpedo **2** to stop something such as a plan from succeeding: *New threats of violence have effectively torpedoed the peace talks.*

**tor·pid** /ˈtɔːpɪ̣d‖ˈtɔːr-/ *adj formal* not active because you are lazy or sleepy, or making you feel like this: *a torpid mind | the heavy torpid warmth of the evening air* —**torpidly** *adv*

**tor·por** /ˈtɔːpə‖ˈtɔːrpər/ *n* [singular, U] *formal* a state of being not active because you are lazy or sleepy: *stirring the wasps from their winter torpor* —**torpidity** /tɔːˈpɪdɪ̣ti‖tɔːr-/ *n* [U]

**torque** /tɔːk‖tɔːrk/ *n* [U] *technical* the force or power that makes something turn around a central point, especially in an engine

**tor·rent** /ˈtɒrənt‖ˈtɔː-, ˈtɑː-/ *n* [C] **1** a large amount of water moving very rapidly and strongly in a particular direction: **a raging torrent** (=a very violent torrent) *After five days of heavy rain the Telle river was a raging torrent.* **2 torrent of abuse/criticism/protest etc** a lot of insults, criticism etc that someone suddenly receives: *a torrent of protest over the proposed tax*

**tor·ren·tial** /tɒˈrenʃəl‖tɔː-/ *adj* **torrential rain** very heavy rain

**tor·rid** /ˈtɒrɪ̣d‖ˈtɔː-, ˈtɑː-/ *adj* **1** involving strong emotions, especially of sexual love: *a torrid love affair* **2** *literary* torrid weather is very hot: *the torrid desert sun*

**tor·sion** /ˈtɔːʃən‖ˈtɔːr-/ *n* [U] *technical* the twisting of a piece of metal

**tor·so** /ˈtɔːsəʊ‖ˈtɔːrsoʊ/ *n* [C] **1** your body, not including your head, arms, or legs: *Police have found the headless torso of a woman.* **2** a STATUE of a torso

**tort** /tɔːt‖tɔːrt/ *n* [C] *law* an action that is wrong but not criminal and can be dealt with in a CIVIL (3) court of law

**tor·til·la** /tɔːˈtiːjə‖tɔːr-/ *n* [C] a piece of thin flat bread made from corn or wheat flour from Mexico

**tor·toise** /ˈtɔːtəs‖ˈtɔːr-/ *n* [C] a slow-moving land animal that can pull its head and legs into the hard round shell that covers its body —compare TURTLE

**tor·toise·shell** /ˈtɔːtəsʃel, ˈtɔːtəʃel‖ˈtɔːr-/ *n* **1** [U] a hard, shiny brown and white material made from the shell of a tortoise **2** [C] a cat that has yellow, brown, and black marks on its fur **3** [C] a BUTTERFLY that has brown and orange wings

**tor·tu·ous** /ˈtɔːtʃuəs‖ˈtɔːr-/ *adj* **1** a tortuous path, stream, road etc has a lot of bends in it and is therefore difficult to travel along: *a tortuous path over the mountains to Kandahar* **2** complicated and long and therefore confusing: *The book begins with a long, tortuous introduction.* —**tortuously** *adv* —**tortuousness** *n* [U]

**tor·ture¹** /ˈtɔːtʃə‖ˈtɔːrtʃər/ *n* [C,U] **1** an act of deliberately hurting someone in order to force them to tell you something, to punish them, or to be cruel: *He died after five days of excruciating torture.* **2** severe physical or mental suffering: *Hearing her practice the violin is torture!*

**torture²** *v* [T] **1** to deliberately hurt someone to force them to give you information, to punish them, or to be cruel: *Political opponents of the regime may be tortured.* **2** if a feeling or knowledge tortures you, it makes you suffer mentally: *tortured by guilt* —**torturer** *n* [C]

**To·ry** /ˈtɔːri/ *n* [C] a member of the British Conservative Party: *a lifelong Tory | Tory principles*

**Tory Par·ty** /ˈ·· ˌ··/ *n* [singular] another name for the British Conservative Party

**toss¹** /tɒs‖tɔːs/ *v*

**1** ▶ **THROW** ◀ [T] to throw something, especially something light, with a quick gentle movement of your hand: **toss sth into/down/out of etc** *Toss that book over here, will you?* | **toss sth to sb** *"Catch!" said Sandra, tossing her bag to him.* | **toss sb sth** *Frank tossed her the newspaper.*

**2** ▶ **MOVE** ◀ [I,T] to move and turn around continuously in a violent or uncontrolled way, or make something do this: **toss sth about/around** *Our small boat was tossed about like a cork.* | **toss and turn** (=keep changing your position in bed because you cannot sleep) *I've been tossing and turning all night.*

**3** ▶ **THROW A FLAT OBJECT** ◀ [T] *BrE* to throw a flat object upwards so that it turns over in the air before it falls again; FLIP¹ (2) *AmE*: *tossing pancakes on Pancake Day*

**4** ▶ **A COIN** ◀ also **toss up** [I,T] *especially BrE* to make a coin go upwards and spin in the air, as a way of deciding something; FLIP¹ (2) *especially AmE*: *They tossed a coin to decide who would go first.* | **toss (up) for it** *Well we can't make up our minds; we'll just have to toss for it.*

**5** ▶ **IN COOKING** ◀ [T] to cover food in a liquid by shaking it around in the liquid: *Toss the carrots in some butter before serving.*

**6 toss your head** to move your head back suddenly, often with a shaking movement showing anger: *He tossed his head angrily and left the room.*

**7 toss your cookies** *AmE spoken* to VOMIT¹

**toss off** *phr v* **1** [T **toss** sth ↔ **off**] to produce something quickly and without much effort: *one of those painters who can toss off a couple of pictures before breakfast*

2 [T **toss** sth ↔ **off**] *old-fashioned* to drink something quickly: *He tossed off a few whiskies.* 3 [I,T **toss** sb ↔ **off**] *BrE taboo* to MASTURBATE

**toss²** *n* [C] 1 the act of throwing a coin in the air to decide something: *The toss of a coin decided who would serve first.* 2 a sudden backwards movement of your head, so that your hair moves: *"I'll see," the nurse said, with an officious toss of her head.* 3 **win/lose the toss** *especially BrE* to win or lose the right to make a choice at the beginning of a game or race, according to the result of tossing a coin 4 the act of gently throwing something: *Will distracted me and I missed the toss.* 5 **not give a toss** *BrE spoken* to not care about something at all: *I really couldn't give a toss what Dermot thinks.* —see also **argue the toss** (ARGUE (5))

**toss-up** /'· ·/ *n* 1 **it's a toss-up** *spoken* used when you do not know which of two things will happen, or which of two things to choose: *"I don't know who'll get the job – it's a toss-up between Carl and Steve."* 2 [C usually singular] *BrE* an act of tossing a coin in order to decide something

**tot¹** /tɒt‖tɑːt/ *n* [C] 1 *informal* a very small child 2 *especially BrE* a small amount of an alcoholic drink

**tot²** *v* **totted, totting**

**tot** sth ↔ **up** *phr v* [T] *informal* to add together numbers or amounts of money in order to find the total: *The waiter quickly totted up the bill.*

S1 W1 **to·tal¹** /'təʊtl‖'toʊ-/ *adj* 1 [only before noun] complete, and affecting or including everything: *The sales campaign was a total disaster.* | *a total ban on cigarette advertising* 2 **total number/amount/cost etc** the number, amount etc that is the total: *total sales of 200,000 per year*

S2 W2 **total²** *n* [C] 1 the final number or amount of things, people etc when everything has been counted: *If you add 30 and 45 the total is 75.* | **a total of** *They were jailed for a total of thirty years.* | **in total** *There were probably about 40 people there in total.* | **the sum total** (=the whole of an amount when everything is considered together) 2 **grand total** **a)** the final total, including all the totals added together **b)** *humorous* used when you think the final total is small: *I earned a grand total of $4.15.*

**total³** *v* **totalled, totalling** *BrE*, **totaled, totaling** *AmE* 1 [T, linking verb] to reach a particular total: *losses totalling $3 million* 2 [T] *AmE informal* to damage a car so badly that it cannot be repaired: *Chuck ran into a telephone pole and totaled his dad's new Toyota.*

**total** sth ↔ **up** *phr v* [T] to find the total number or total amount of something by adding: *At the end of the game total up everyone's score to see who has won.*

**to·tal·i·tar·i·an** /təʊˌtæləˈteəriən‖toʊˌtæləˈter-/ *adj* based on a political system in which ordinary people have no power and are completely controlled by the government: *a totalitarian régime* —**totalitarianism** *n* [U]

**to·tal·i·ty** /təʊ'tæləti‖toʊ-/ *n* [U] *formal* 1 the whole of something: **in its totality** (=as a complete thing) *It's essential that we look at the problem in its totality.* 2 a total amount

**to·tal·i·za·tor** also **-isator** /'təʊt əl-aɪˌzeɪtə‖ 'toʊt ələˌzeɪtər/ *n* [C] *BrE formal* a TOTE²

**tot·al·ly** /'təʊtli‖ˌtoʊ-/ *adv* completely: *That's a totally different matter.* | *It's like learning a totally new language.* | *a totally unexpected situation* S W

**tote¹** /təʊt‖toʊt/ also **tote around** *v* [T] *informal especially AmE* to carry something, especially regularly: *having to tote around heavy textbooks*

**tote²** *n* [C] a machine that adds together the amounts of money BET on a race and divides it among the winners

**tote bag** /'· ˌ·/ *n* [C] *AmE* a large bag for carrying things —see picture at BAG¹

**to·tem** /'təʊtəm‖'toʊ-/ *n* [C] an animal, plant etc that is thought to have a special spiritual connection with a particular tribe, especially in North America, or a figure made to look like the animal etc —**totemic** /təʊ'temɪk‖toʊ-/ *adj*

**totem pole** /'··· ·/ *n* [C] 1 a tall wooden pole with one or more totems cut or painted on it, made by the Native Americans of northwest North America 2 **low man on the totem pole** *AmE* someone of low rank in an organization or business

**to·to** /'təʊtəʊ‖'toʊtoʊ/ —see IN TOTO

**tot·ter** /'tɒtə‖'tɑːtər/ *v* [I] 1 to walk or move unsteadily from side to side as if you are going to fall over: *Lorrimer swayed a little, tottered, and fell.* —see picture on page 1262 2 if a political system or organization totters, it becomes less strong and is likely to stop working

**tou·can** /'tuːkən, -kæn/ *n* [C] a tropical American bird with bright feathers and a very large beak

S2 W2

## tou·ch¹ /tʌtʃ/ *v*

① FEEL SB/STH PHYSICALLY
② AFFECT SB'S FEELINGS
③ USE/HANDLE
④ DEAL/ATTEND TO
⑤ HAVE AN EFFECT ON
⑥ OTHER MEANINGS

### ① FEEL SB/STH PHYSICALLY

1 [T] to put your hand or another part of your body on something or someone so that you can feel them: *Small children are constantly moving and wanting to touch everything.* | *She couldn't bear the thought of touching a dead body.*

2 to put your hand or any part of your body on someone in a sexual way: *Ben hadn't touched her yet. Hadn't even kissed her.* | *She bent over me, touching me with her lips.*

3 [T] to put your hand on someone in order to show them kindness or affection: *He put his hand out to touch the young man's shoulder.* | *He was a remote man who hardly ever played with or even touched his children.*

4 [I,T] if two things are touching, they reach each other so that there is no space between them: *I sat facing him our knees touching.* | **touch sth** *The little boy's legs were too short to touch the ground.*

5 **not touch sb** to not hit someone or hurt them physically: *The older boys swore they hadn't touched the child.*

### ② AFFECT SB'S FEELINGS

6 [T] to make someone feel upset, sympathetic, interested etc: *His harsh words had obviously touched her although she tried not to show it.* | *Politics didn't touch me an awful lot those days.*

7 **touch a nerve** to mention a subject that makes someone feel upset, or angry: *I think you touched a nerve when you brought up the subject of divorce.*

8 **be touched by sth** to feel grateful for or pleased about something nice that someone does: *I was very touched by his kind letter.* —see also TOUCHING

### ③ USE/HANDLE

9 **a)** ▶ **OBJECT/POSSESSION** ◀ **not touch sth** to not use or handle something: *I've never touched a penny of that money.* | *He has a car but I'm sure he wouldn't let you touch it.* | **Don't touch (sth)** *spoken* (=used when

you are warning someone not to handle or touch something because it is dangerous or not allowed) *"Don't touch that switch!" his father shouted.* **b) ▶FOOD/DRINK◀** to not eat or drink the thing mentioned: *She went to school without touching her breakfast.* | *He rarely ever touches alcohol, except at Christmas.* | **not/never touch the stuff** (=not drink alcohol) *My grandfather was an alcoholic and as a result my father never touched the stuff.*

**④ DEAL/ATTEND TO**

**10 ▶PRACTICAL MATTER/SITUATION◀** [T] to deal with or become involved with a particular matter, situation or problem: *He was the only lawyer who would touch the case.* | *He's a walking disaster! Everything he touches goes wrong.*

**11 not touch sth** to not do any work on or give any time to something which needs work or attention: *The garden looks awful – I'm afraid I haven't touched it for weeks.*

**12 wouldn't touch sth/sb (with a bargepole)** *BrE* **ten-foot pole** *AmE* used as a way of saying that you think something or someone is bad in some way and you do not want to get or advise getting involved with them: *I wouldn't touch that house with a bargepole – it's almost falling down.*

**⑤ HAVE AN EFFECT ON**

**13** [T] to have an effect on someone or something so that it changes or influences them: *They had lived in such isolation that the outside world had barely touched them.*

**14 be touched by sth** to be affected by a particular quality: *All the family were touched by a common genius.* | *There was no denying that his motivation was touched by self interest.*

**15** [T] if an expression such as a smile touches your face, your face has that expression for a short time: *A rare frown touched his normally placid face.*

**⑥ OTHER MEANINGS**

**16** [T] to concern a particular subject, situation, or problem: *Though the question touched a new vein, Nelson answered promptly.*

**17 nothing/no one to touch sth/sb, nothing/no one that can touch sb/sth** nothing or no one that is as good as something or someone: *She's a brilliant tennis player – there's no one else here to touch her.* | *You can listen to a recording of a concert but nothing can touch actually being there.*

**18 touch bottom a)** to reach the ground at the bottom of a sea, river etc: *He swam down and down but could not touch bottom.* **b)** to reach the lowest level or worst condition: *After weeks of uncertainty, morale in the company has touched bottom.*

**19 touch wood** *especially BrE* used when you have just said that you have been lucky in some way in the past, because this expression is traditionally supposed to help your good luck to continue: *I haven't been ill yet this winter – touch wood.*

**touch down** *phr v* [I] if an aircraft touches down, it lands on the ground: *We all sighed with relief when the plane finally touched down safely.*

**touch** sb **for** sth *phr v* [T] *informal* to persuade someone to give or lend you something, especially money: *Can I touch you for a fiver until next week?*

**touch** sth ↔ **off** *phr v* [T] to cause a difficult situation or violent events to begin: *The government's actions touched off a storm of protest.*

**touch on/upon** sth *phr v* [T] to mention or deal with a particular subject briefly when talking or writing: *There is one factor we have not touched on, so far, in talking about personality.*

**touch** sth **up** *phr v* [T] to improve something by changing it or adding to it slightly: *The speech he finally gave had been touched up by his staff.* | *She quickly touched up her lipstick.*

**touch** sb **up** *phr v* [T] to touch someone in a sexual way when you should not: *He had a reputation for touching up his secretaries.*

2 **touch²** *n*
2 **1 ▶SENSE◀** [U] the sense that you use to discover what something feels like, by putting your hand or another part of your body on it: *Visually impaired people orient themselves by touch.* | **to the touch** *Natural fabrics feel much nicer to the touch.*

**2 ▶ACT OF TOUCHING◀** [C usually singular] what you do when you put your hand or another part of your body on or against something or someone either deliberately or not: *A smile, a friendly gesture, a touch – any of these can be of an enormous help.* | *I couldn't move. The slightest touch hurt.* | **at the touch of a button** (=used to emphasize how easily something practical can be done) *We can contact people on the other side of the world at the touch of a button nowadays.*

**3 ▶FEEL SB/STH◀** [C usually singular] the way that someone or something feels and the effect they have on your body: *She longed to see him again and feel his touch.* | *The child recoiled from the thought of the cold slimy touch of the snake's body.*

**4 be in touch** to speak especially on the telephone, or write to someone about something: *I'll be in touch when I get back from Paris.* | [+ **with**] *My officials have been in touch with the department concerning their comments.*

**5 get in touch** to write or speak to someone on the telephone in order to tell them something: *We'll get in touch as soon as we know the results of the test.* | [+ **with**] *You can get in touch with me at the office if necessary.*

**6 keep/stay in touch** to speak or write to someone when you can no longer see them as often as you used to: [+ **with**] *Our neighbours are moving away but I hope that we'll still keep in touch with each other.*

**7 lose touch** to no longer speak or write to someone because they do not live near you, work with you etc: [+ **with**] *I've lost touch with most of my friends from college.*

**8 put sb in touch with sb** to give someone the name, address, or telephone number of a person or organization they need: *Your doctor should be able to put you in touch with a specialist.*

**9 be/keep/stay in touch with sth** to have the latest information, knowledge, and understanding about a subject: *Through the media we are able to keep in touch with events on the other side of the world almost as they happen.*

**10 be out of touch with sth/lose touch with sth** to no longer have the correct information or a good understanding about a subject: *Government ministers are often being accused of being out of touch with real life.*

**11 ▶DETAIL/ADDITION◀** [C] a small detail that improves or completes something: *The flowers on every table were a very nice touch.* | *She was just adding the final touches to her speech.* | **finishing touch/touches** *The necklace was the finishing touch to her wedding outfit.*

**12 ▶WAY OF DOING STH◀** [C] a particular way of doing something: *A more sensitive touch is needed in our approach to this problem.* | *The room was decorated with a very artistic touch.*

**13 a touch of sth** a very small amount of something: *"I'm afraid I don't agree," said Hazel, with a touch of irritation.* | *She had a touch of fever in the night.*

**14 a touch cold/strange/unfair etc** slightly cold, strange etc: *He sounded a touch upset when I spoke to him on the phone.*

**15 lose your touch** to lose your ability to do something: *He's been playing so badly recently that it seems he's losing his touch.* —see also **the common touch** (COMMON¹ (8)), **a soft touch** (SOFT (11))

**touch-and-go** /,· · '·/ *adj informal* in a touch-and-go situation, there is a serious risk that something bad could happen: *It was touch-and-go whether the doctor would get there on time.*

**touch·down** /ˈtʌtʃdaʊn/ *n* [C] **1** the moment at which a plane or SPACECRAFT lands **2** an act of touching the ball down on the ground behind your opponent's GOAL (3) in RUGBY **3** an act of moving the ball across the opposing team's GOAL LINE in American football —see picture on page 1263

**tou·ché** /ˈtuːʃeɪ‖tuːˈʃeɪ/ *interjection* used when you want to emphasize in a humorous way that someone has made a very good point during an argument: *"You should be ashamed." "So should you." "Touché," he replied, not at all put out.*

**touched** /tʌtʃt/ *adj* [not before noun] **1** feeling happy and grateful because of someone's actions: *We were deeply touched by their present.* | **touched that** *Cathryn was touched that Sarah had come to see her off.* —see also TOUCH[1] (8) **2** *informal* slightly strange in your behaviour: *He seems a bit touched to me!*

**touch foot·ball** /ˈ· ˌ··/ *n* [U] *AmE* a type of American football in which you touch the person with the ball instead of tackling (TACKLE[1] (3)) them

**touch·ing[1]** /ˈtʌtʃɪŋ/ *adj* making you feel pity, sympathy, sadness etc: *a touching reunion of father and son* —see also TOUCH[1] (6) —**touchingly** *adv*

**touching[2]** *prep formal* concerning: *matters touching the conduct of diplomacy*

**touch·line** /ˈtʌtʃlaɪn/ *n* [C] a line along each of the two longer sides of a sports field, especially in football

**touch·pa·per** /ˈtʌtʃˌpeɪpə‖-ər/ *n* [C] a piece of slow-burning paper, that you light in order to start a FIREWORK burning: *Light the blue touchpaper, then retire to a safe distance.*

**touch·stone** /ˈtʌtʃstəʊn‖-stoʊn/ *n* [C] something used as a test or standard: **[+ of]** *Pupil behaviour was seen as 'the touchstone of quality' of the school system.*

**touch-tone phone** /ˈ· · ˌ·/ *n* [C] a telephone that produces different sounds when different numbers are pushed

T

**touch-type** /ˈ· ·/ *v* [I] to be able to use a TYPEWRITER without having to look at the letters while you are using it

**touch·y** /ˈtʌtʃi/ *adj* **1** easily becoming offended or annoyed: *Since his girlfriend left him, he's been very touchy.* **2 touchy subject/question etc** a subject etc that needs to be dealt with very carefully: *Asking about a reporter's sources can be a touchy business.* —**touchily** *adv* —**touchiness** *n* [U]

S2 W3 **tough[1]** /tʌf/ *adj*

**1 ▶ DIFFICULT ◀** difficult to do or deal with, and needing a lot of effort and determination: *Life as a single mother can be tough and depressing.* | *a tough decision* | *The reporters were asking a lot of tough questions.*

**2 ▶ STRONG PEOPLE ◀** able to live through difficult or severe conditions: *The men who work on the oil rigs are a tough bunch.* | **as tough as nails/as tough as old boots** (=very tough) *He's as tough as nails – a good man to have on the mountain rescue team.*

**3 ▶ STRONG THING ◀** not easily broken or made weaker: *a very tough, hard-wearing cloth*

**4 ▶ DETERMINED ◀** very determined or strict: *Congress is taking a tough anti-inflation line.* | **get tough with** (=punish or deal with someone in a determined and strict way) *It's time to get tough with drunk drivers.* | **be tough on** (=treat someone very strictly) *My mother was tougher on my older sister than she was on me.* | *It's time to get tough on crime.* | **tough nut/cookie/customer** *informal* (=someone who is very determined to do what they want and not what other people want)

**5 ▶ FOOD ◀** difficult to cut or eat: *The meat was tough and hard to chew.* | *the tough outer leaves of the cabbage* —opposite TENDER[1]

**6 ▶ ANGRY/NOT SORRY ◀** *spoken* used when you do not have any sympathy with someone: **tough!** *"I'm getting wet." "Tough! You should've brought your umbrella."* | *She didn't tell us she was coming, so if this screws up her plans that's just tough.*

**7 tough luck** *spoken* **a)** also **tough shit** *taboo* used when you do not have any sympathy for someone's problems: *Well, that's just their tough luck. It was their mistake.* **b)** *BrE* used when you feel sympathy about something bad that has happened to someone: *You didn't get the job? Oh, tough luck.*

**8 ▶ VIOLENT PERSON ◀** likely to behave violently and having no gentle qualities: *tough young thugs looking for trouble*

**9 ▶ VIOLENT AREA ◀** a tough part of a town has a lot of crime or violence: *tough areas of Chicago*

**10 ▶ UNFORTUNATE ◀** unfortunate in a way that seems unfair: **[+ on]** *It's really tough on him – his wife divorces him, then he has all these problems at work.*

**11 tough love** *AmE* love and strictness at the same time —**toughly** *adv* —**toughness** *n* [U]

**tough[2]** *n* [C] *old-fashioned* someone who often behaves in a violent way

**tough[3]** *v* **tough it out** to manage to stay in a difficult situation by being determined: *We toughed it out, knowing the boss would soon be leaving.*

**tough·en** /ˈtʌfən/ also **toughen up** *v* [I,T] to become tougher or make someone or something tougher: *toughened glass* | *Three years in the army toughened him up.*

**tou·pée** /ˈtuːpeɪ‖tuːˈpeɪ/ [C] a small artificial piece of hair that some men wear over a place on their heads where the hair no longer grows

**tour[1]** /tʊə‖tʊr/ *n* [C] **1** a journey for pleasure, during which you visit several different towns, areas etc: *a bicycle tour* | **[+ round/around/of]** *a 10-day tour of China* —see also PACKAGE TOUR **2** a short trip through a place to see it: **[+ of/round/around]** *a guided tour around the Kennedy Space Center* **3** a planned journey made by musicians, a sports team etc in order to perform or play in several places: **[+ of]** *the England cricket team's tour of India* | **on tour** *The Moscow Symphony Orchestra is here on tour.* | **a leg of a tour** (=one part of it) *the first leg of U2's European tour* **4** a period during which you go to live somewhere, usually abroad, to do your job, especially military work: *a two-year tour in Vietnam* **5 tour of inspection** an official visit to a place, institution, group etc in order to check its quality or performance W

**tour[2]** *v* [I,T] to visit somewhere on a tour: *We're touring the Greek islands this summer.*

**tour de force** /ˌtʊə də ˈfɔːs‖ˌtʊr də ˈfɔːrs/ *n* [singular] something that is done very skilfully and successfully, in a way that impresses people: *His speech to the Democratic Convention was a tour de force.*

**tour·is·m** /ˈtʊərɪzəm‖ˈtʊr-/ *n* [U] the business of providing things for people to do, places for them to stay etc while they are on holiday: *The country depends on tourism for most of its income.*

**tour·ist** /ˈtʊərɪst‖ˈtʊr-/ *n* [C] someone who is travelling or visiting a place for pleasure: *Cambridge is always full of tourists in the summer.* W

**tourist at·trac·tion** /ˈ·· ·ˌ··/ *n* [C] a place or event that a lot of tourists go to: *The Statue of Liberty is a major tourist attraction.*

**tourist class** /ˈ·· ·/ *n* [U] the cheapest standard of travelling conditions on a plane, ship etc

**tourist of·fice** /ˈ·· ˌ··/ also **tourist in·for·ma·tion of·fice** /ˌ·· ··ˈ·· ˌ··/ *n* [C] an office that gives information to tourists in an area

**tourist trap** /ˈ·· ˌ·/ *n* [C] a place that many tourists visit, but where drinks, hotels etc are more expensive

**tour·ist·y** /ˈtʊərɪsti‖ˈtʊr-/ *adj informal* **1** a place that is touristy is unpleasantly full of tourists and the things that attract tourists: *Benidorm is too touristy for me.* **2** a touristy activity is unpleasantly typical of the things that tourists do: *The boat trip was kind of touristy, but we did get to see a lot.*

**tour·na·ment** /ˈtʊənəmənt, ˈtɔː-‖ˈtɜːr-, ˈtʊr-/ *n* [C] **1 tennis/chess/badminton etc tournament** a competition in which players compete against each other in a series of games until there is one winner **2** a competition to show courage and fighting skill between soldiers in the Middle Ages

**tour·ni·quet** /ˈtʊənɪkeɪ, ˈtɔː-‖ˈtɜːrnɪkɪ̆t, ˈtʊr-/ *n* [C] a band of cloth that is twisted tightly around an injured arm or leg to stop it bleeding

**tour of du·ty** /ˌ· · ˈ··/ *n* [C] a period of time when you are working in a particular place or job, especially abroad while you are in the army etc

**tour op·e·rat·or** /ˈ· ˌ····/ *n* [C] *BrE* a company that arranges travel tours

**tou·sle** /ˈtaʊzəl/ *v* [T] to make someone's hair look untidy

**tou·sled** /ˈtaʊzəld/ *adj* tousled hair or a tousled appearance looks untidy: *She had just awakened, her eyes sleepy and her hair tousled.*

**tout¹** /taʊt/ *v* **1** [T] to praise something or someone in order to persuade people that they are important or worth a lot: *the much touted delights of England in the spring* | **be touted as sth** *Bates was widely touted as the next Olympic star.* **2** [I,T] *especially BrE* to try to persuade people to buy goods or services you are offering: **tout for business/custom** (=look for customers) **3** [I,T] *AmE* to give someone information about a horse in a race

**tout²** *n* [C] *BrE* **1** someone who buys tickets for a concert, sports match etc and sells them at a very high price; SCALPER *AmE* **2** someone who tries to sell goods or services to people passing on the street

**tow¹** /təʊ‖toʊ/ *v* [T] to pull a vehicle or ship along behind another vehicle using a rope or chain: *The ship had to be towed into the harbor.*

**tow²** *n* **1** [C] an act of pulling a vehicle behind another vehicle using a rope or chain: *Can you give us a tow?* **2 in tow** *informal* following closely behind someone or something: *Hannah arrived with her four kids in tow.* **3 take sth in tow** to connect a rope or a chain to a vehicle or ship so that it can be towed **4 on tow** *BrE* a vehicle that is on tow is being pulled along by another vehicle

1 **to·wards** /təˈwɔːdz‖tɔːrdz, twɔːrdz/ *especially BrE*,
1 **to·ward** /təˈwɔːd‖tɔːrd, twɔːrd/ *especially AmE prep* **1** moving, looking, or pointing in a particular direction: *He noticed two policemen coming towards him.* | *All the windows face toward the river.* | *He was standing with his back towards me.* —see picture on page 1257 **2** if you do something towards something, you do it in order to achieve it: *These negotiations are the first step toward reaching an agreement.* | *The council is constantly working towards racial and sexual equality.* **3** a feeling, attitude etc towards something is how you feel or what you think about it: *Brian's attitude towards his work has always been very positive.* **4** money put, saved, or given towards something is used to pay for it: *A lot of the donations will be put towards repairing the church roof.* **5 a)** just before a particular time: *Toward the end of the afternoon it began to rain.* **b)** near a particular place: *As you get towards the coast you notice more and more hotels and restaurants.*

**tow·a·way zone** /ˈtəʊəweɪ ˌzəʊn‖ˈtoʊəweɪ ˌzoʊn/ *n* [C] *AmE* an area where cars are not allowed to park, and from which they can be taken away by the police

**tow·bar** /ˈtəʊbɑː‖ˈtoʊbɑːr/ *n* [C] a metal bar on the back of a car for towing (TOW¹) a CARAVAN (1) or boat

**tow·el¹** /ˈtaʊəl/ *n* [C] a piece of cloth that you use for drying your skin or for drying things such as dishes: *a bath towel* —see also PAPER TOWEL, SANITARY TOWEL, TEA TOWEL, **throw in the towel** (THROW¹)

**towel²** *v* [T] *AmE* also **towel down** to dry yourself using a towel —see also TOWELLING

**tow·el·ette** /ˌtaʊəˈlet/ *n* [C] a small piece of soft wet paper that you use to clean your hands or face

**tow·el·ling** *BrE*, **toweling** *AmE* /ˈtaʊəlɪŋ/ *n* [U] thick soft cloth, used especially for making towels or BATHROBES —see picture on page 839

**towel rail** /ˈ··· ·/ also **towel rack** *n* [C] a bar or frame on which towels can be hung, especially in a bathroom

**tow·er¹** /ˈtaʊə‖-ər/ *n* [C] **1** a tall narrow building either built on its own or forming part of a castle, church etc: *They rebuilt the church tower in the 1870s.* **2** a tall structure, often made of metal, used for signalling, broadcasting etc: *an air traffic control tower* **3 tower of strength** someone who gives you a lot of help, sympathy, and support when you are in trouble: *Her father was a tower of strength to her when her marriage broke up.* —see also COOLING TOWER, **ivory tower** (IVORY (6)), WATER TOWER S3 W3

**tower²** *v* [I] **1** to be much taller than the people or things around you: [+ **about/over**] *Graham was 6 ft 5, and towered over the rest of us.* **2** to be much better than any other person or organization that does the same thing as you: [+ **about/over**] *Mozart towers over all other composers.*

**tower block** /ˈ··· ·/ *n* [C] *BrE* a tall building containing apartments or offices

**tower computer** /ˌ·· ·ˈ··/ *n* [C] a computer in the shape of a tall box —see picture on page 837

**tow·er·ing** /ˈtaʊərɪŋ/ *adj* [only before noun] **1** very tall: *great towering cliffs* **2** much better than other people of the same kind; OUTSTANDING (1): *a towering genius of his time* **3 in a towering rage** very angry

**tow·head** /ˈtəʊhed‖ˈtoʊ-/ *n* [C] someone with very light-coloured hair —**towheaded** *adj*

**tow·line** /ˈtəʊlaɪn‖ˈtoʊ-/ *n* [C] a TOWROPE

**town** /taʊn/ *n* S1 W1
**1 ▶ PLACE ◀** [C] a large area with houses, shops, offices etc where people live and work, that is smaller than a city and larger than a village: *an industrial town in the Midlands* | *the town of Norwalk, Connecticut*
**2 ▶ MAIN CENTRE ◀** [U] the business or shopping centre of a town: *We're going into town tonight to see a film.* | *They have a small apartment in town.*
**3 ▶ PEOPLE ◀** [singular] all the people who live in a particular town: *The whole town turned out to watch the procession.*
**4 ▶ WHERE YOU LIVE ◀** [U] *AmE* the town or city where you live: *Cam left town about an hour ago, he should be out at the farm by now.* | **out of town** *I'll be out of town for about a week.* | **in town** *Guess who's in town? Jodie's sister!* | **be from out of town** (=live in a different town than the one you are in) *Do you know of a good place to eat? I'm from out of town.*
**5 ▶ VILLAGE ◀** [C] *AmE* several houses forming a small group around a church, shops etc; VILLAGE *BrE*: *Rowayton is a small town of around 4000 people.*
**6 ▶ NOT COUNTRY ◀ the town** life in towns and cities in general: *Which do you prefer, the town or the country?*
**7 go to town (on)** *informal* to do something in a very eager or thorough way, often spending a lot of money: *Angela really went to town on buying things for her new house.*
**8 go/be out on the town** *informal* to go to restaurants, bars, theatres etc for entertainment in the evening
**9 town and gown** *BrE* used to describe the situation in which the people living in a town and the students in a town seem to be separate and opposing groups —see also GHOST TOWN, **blow town** (BLOW¹ (11)), MARKET TOWN, NEW TOWN, **paint the town (red)** (PAINT² (6))

**town cent·re** /ˌ· ˈ··/ *n* [C] *BrE* the main business area in the centre of a town; DOWNTOWN *AmE*

**town clerk** /ˌ· ˈ·/ *n* [C] an official who keeps records, advises on legal matters etc

**town coun·cil** /ˌ· ˈ··/ *n* [C] *BrE* a group of people who are responsible for public areas and services, such as roads, parks etc, in a particular town —**town councillor** *n* [C]

**town cri·er** /ˌ· ˈ··/ *n* [C] someone employed in former times to walk around the streets of a town, shouting news, warnings etc

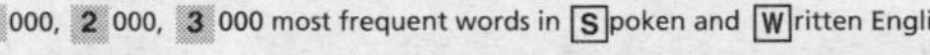

**town hall** /ˌ· ˈ·/ *n* [C] a public building used for a town's local government

**town house** /ˈ· ·/ *n* [C] **1** a house in a town or city, especially a fashionable one in a central area **2** a house in a town that belongs to someone who also owns a house in the countryside: *the Duke's townhouse in Mayfair* **3** *AmE* a house in a group of houses that share one or more walls

**town·ie** /ˈtaʊni/ *n* [C] *informal* someone who lives in a town or city and does not know anything about life in the countryside

**town meet·ing** /ˌ· ˈ··/ *n* [C] *AmE* a meeting at which the people who live in a town discuss subjects or problems that affect their town

**town plan·ning** /ˌ· ˈ··/ *n* [U] the study of the way towns work, so that roads, houses, services etc can be provided as effectively as possible

**town·ship** /ˈtaʊnʃɪp/ *n* [C] **1** a town in Canada or the US that has some local government **2** a town in South Africa where black citizens live: *the black township of Soweto*

**towns·peo·ple** /ˈtaʊnzˌpiːpəl/ also **towns·folk** /-fəʊk‖-foʊk/ *n* [plural] **1** all the people who live in a particular town: *the proud townspeople of Semer Water* **2** people who live in towns and not in the country

**tow·path** /ˈtəʊpɑːθ‖ˈtoʊpæθ/ *n* [C] a path along the side of a CANAL or river used especially in former times by horses pulling boats

**tow·rope** /ˈtəʊrəʊp‖ˈtoʊroʊp/ also **towline** *n* [C] a rope or chain used for pulling vehicles along

**tow·truck** /ˈtəʊtrʌk‖ˈtoʊ-/ *n* [C] *AmE* a strong vehicle that can pull cars behind it; BREAKDOWN TRUCK *BrE*

**tox·ae·mi·a** *BrE*, **toxemia** *AmE* /tɒkˈsiːmiə‖tɑːk-/ *n* [U] a medical condition in which your blood contains poisons

**tox·ic** /ˈtɒksɪk‖ˈtɑːk-/ *adj* containing poison, or caused by poisonous substances: *toxic fumes* | *a toxic waste dump* —**toxicity** /tɒkˈsɪsəti‖tɑːk-/ *n* [U]

**tox·i·col·o·gy** /ˌtɒksɪˈkɒlədʒi‖ˌtɑːksɪˈkɑː-/ *n* [U] the science and medical study of poisons and their effects

**toxic shock syn·drome** /ˌ·· ˈ· ˌ··/ *n* [U] a serious illness that causes a high temperature and is thought to be connected with the use of TAMPONS

**toxic waste** /ˌ·· ˈ·/ *n* [C,U] waste products from industry that are harmful to people, animals, or the environment

**tox·in** /ˈtɒksən‖ˈtɑːk-/ *n* [C] a poisonous substance, especially one that is produced by BACTERIA and causes a particular disease

**toy**[1] /tɔɪ/ *n* [C] **1** an object for children to play with: *some toys for the baby* | **toy boat/car/truck etc** *Davey wanted some toy soldiers for Christmas.* | **soft/cuddly toy** *BrE* (=a toy that looks like an animal and is covered in fur) **2** an object that you buy because it gives you pleasure and enjoyment: *The food mixer is her latest toy.*

**toy**[2] *v*

**toy with** sth *phr v* [T] **1** to think about an idea or possibility, usually for a short time and not very seriously: **toy with the idea of doing sth** *I've been toying with the idea of going to Japan to visit them.* **2** to play with an object, often while you are thinking about something else: *Elsa toyed with her coffee cup.*

**toy**[3] *adj* [only before noun] a toy animal or dog is a type of dog that is specially bred to be very small: *a toy poodle*

**toy boy** /ˈ· ·/ *n* [C] *informal* a young man who is having a sexual relationship with an older woman

**trace**[1] /treɪs/ *v* [T]

**1** ▶ **FIND SB/STH** ◀ to find someone or something that has disappeared by searching for them carefully: *She had given up all hope of tracing her missing daughter.*

**2** ▶ **ORIGINS** ◀ to find the origins of something, or where something came from: **trace sth (back) to** *The style of these paintings can be traced back to early medieval influences.*

**3** ▶ **HISTORY/DEVELOPMENT** ◀ to study or describe the history, development, or progress of something: *Sondheim's book traces the changing nature of the relationship between men and women.*

**4** ▶ **COPY** ◀ to copy a drawing, map etc by putting a piece of transparent paper over it and then drawing the lines you can see through the paper

**5** ▶ **DRAW** ◀ to draw real or imaginary lines on the surface of something, usually with your finger or toe: **trace sth on/in/across** *Rosie's fingers traced a delicate pattern in the sand.*

**6 trace a call** to use special electronic equipment to find out who made a telephone call —**traceable** *adj*

**trace**[2] *n*

**1** ▶ **SIGN OF STH** ◀ [C,U] a small sign that shows that someone or something was present or existed: **no trace** *There was no trace of anyone having entered the room since then.* | **all trace** *Petra's lost all trace of her German accent.* | **any trace** *Officers were unable to find any trace of drugs.* | **disappear/vanish/sink without trace** (=disappear completely, without leaving any sign of what happened) *The Roanoke colony vanished without trace.*

**2** ▶ **SMALL AMOUNT** ◀ [C] a very small amount of a quality, emotion, substance etc that is difficult to see or notice: [+ **of**] *I saw the faintest trace of a smile cross Sandra's face.* | *traces of poison*

**3** ▶ **TELEPHONE** ◀ [C] *technical* a search to find out where a telephone call came from, using special electronic equipment: *The police were able to put a trace on the call.*

**4** ▶ **INFORMATION RECORDED** ◀ [C] the mark or pattern made on a SCREEN or on paper by a machine that is recording an electrical signal: *This trace shows the heartbeat.*

**5 kick over the traces** to stop following the rules of a social group and do what you want

**6** ▶ **CART/CARRIAGE** ◀ [C] one of the two pieces of leather, rope etc by which a cart or carriage is fastened to the animal that is pulling it

**trac·er** /ˈtreɪsə‖-ər/ *n* [C] a bullet that leaves a line of smoke or flame behind it

**trac·e·ry** /ˈtreɪsəri/ *n* [C,U] **1** *technical* the curving and crossing lines of stone in the upper parts of some church windows **2** *literary* an attractive pattern of lines that cross each other: *the delicate tracery of the bare branches against the sky*

**tra·che·a** /trəˈkiːə‖ˈtreɪkiə/ *n* [C] *technical* the tube that takes air from your throat to your lungs —see picture at RESPIRATORY

**trach·e·ot·o·my** /ˌtrækiˈɒtəmi‖ˌtreɪkiˈɑːt-/ *n* [C] *technical* an operation to cut a hole in someone's throat so that they can breathe

**tra·cho·ma** /trəˈkəʊmə‖-ˈkoʊ-/ *n* [U] *technical* a painful illness that affects the transparent covering over your eyes

**trac·ing** /ˈtreɪsɪŋ/ *n* [C] a copy of a map, drawing etc made by tracing (TRACE[1] (4)) it

**tracing pa·per** /ˈ·· ˌ··/ *n* [U] strong transparent paper used for tracing (TRACE[1] (4))

**track**[1] /træk/ *n*

**1** ▶ **ROAD** ◀ [C] a narrow road with a rough uneven surface that cars can travel on: *The road leading to the farm was little more than a rough track.* | *a deeply-rutted cart track*

**2** ▶ **PATH** ◀ [C] a narrow path, especially one made by people or animals frequently walking in the same place: *a mountain track* | *The track led through dense forest.*

**3** ▶ **FOR RACING** ◀ [C] a circular course around which runners, cars etc race, often with a specially prepared surface: *To run a mile, you have to run four circuits of the track.* —see also DIRT TRACK

**4** ▶ **RAILWAY** ◀ [C] the two metal lines along which trains travel or the narrow strip of land to which they are fixed; RAILWAY LINE: *The track was damaged in several places.* —see picture at TUNNEL[1]

**5 tracks** [plural] a line of marks left on the ground by a

moving person, animal, or vehicle: *We followed the tyre tracks across a muddy field.* | *The tracks, which looked like a fox's, led into the woods.*
**6 be on the right/wrong track** to think in a way that is likely to lead to a correct or incorrect result: *He's not interested in her at all – you're on the wrong track there.*
**7 ▶ MUSIC/SONG ◀** [C] one of the songs or pieces of music on a record, CASSETTE, or CD: *There's a great Miles Davis track on side two.*
**8 keep/lose track of** to pay attention to someone or something so that you know where they are or what is happening to them, or to fail to do this: *It's difficult to keep track of all the new discoveries in genetics.*
**9 stop (dead) in your tracks** to suddenly stop, especially because something has frightened or surprised you: *Fay stopped in her tracks and pointed at the house.*
**10 cover/hide your tracks** to be careful not to leave any signs that could let people know where you have been or what you have done because you want to keep it a secret: *We don't know where Ford is, he's been very clever in covering his tracks.*
**11 be on the track of** to hunt or search for someone or something: *Police are on the track of a gang that has robbed five post offices in the last month.*
**12 ▶ SPORT ◀** [U] *AmE* **a)** sport that involves running on a track: *The next year he didn't run track or play football.* **b)** all the sports in an ATHLETICS competition such as running, jumping, or throwing the JAVELIN: *a famous track star* | *She went out for track in the spring.* (=she joined the school's track team)
**13 I'd better make tracks** *spoken* used to say you must leave a place, especially when you do not want to leave: *I'd love to stay, but it's time we started making tracks.*
**14 ▶ DIRECTION ◀** [C] the direction or line taken by something as it moves: [+ **of**] *islands that lie in the track of North Atlantic storms*
**15 ▶ ON A VEHICLE ◀** [C] an endless metal band driven by the wheels of a vehicle such as a BULLDOZER that allows it to move over uneven ground
**16 ▶ FOR RECORDING ◀** [C] a band on a TAPE[1] (1) on which music or information can be recorded: *Sergeant Pepper was recorded on eight tracks.*
**17 be on track** *spoken* to be likely to achieve the result you want: *We're still on track for 10% growth.*
**18 get off the track** *spoken* to begin to deal with a new subject rather than the main one which was being discussed: *Don't get off the track, we're looking at this year's figures not last year's.* —see also **off the beaten track** (BEATEN (3)), ONE-TRACK MIND **be from the wrong side of the tracks** (WRONG[1] (15))

**track²** *v*
**1 ▶ SEARCH ◀** [T] to search for a person or animal by following the marks they leave behind them on the ground, their smell etc: **track sb to sth** *The dogs tracked the wolf to its lair.*
**2 ▶ AIRCRAFT/SHIP ◀** [T] to follow the movements of an aircraft or ship by using RADAR: *a tracking station*
**3 ▶ CAMERA ◀** [I + **in/out**] to move a film or television camera away from or towards a scene in order to follow the action that you are recording
**4 ▶ RECORD ◀** [I] if a PICK-UP (4) tracks, it moves in the grooves (GROOVE[1] (1)) on a record
**5 ▶ SCHOOL ◀** [T] *AmE* to put school children in groups according to their ability; STREAM[1] (6) *BrE*
**6 ▶ MARK ◀** [T] *AmE* to leave behind a track of something such as mud or dirt when you walk: *Which of you boys tracked mud all over the kitchen floor?* —**tracker** *n* [C] *a police tracker dog*

**track** sb/sth ↔ **down** *phr v* [T] to find someone or something that is difficult to find by searching or making inquiries in several different places: *I finally managed to track down the book you wanted in a shop near the station.*

**track and field** /ˌ· ·ˈ·/ *n* [U] *AmE* sports such as running and jumping; ATHLETICS *BrE*

**track·ball** /ˈtrækbɔːl‖-bɒːl/ *n* [C] a small ball connected to a computer, that you turn in order to move the CURSOR

**tracker dog** /ˈ·· ·/ *n* [C] a dog that has been specially trained to follow and find people

**track e·vent** /ˈ· ·ˌ·/ *n* [C] *AmE* a running race

**tracking sta·tion** /ˈ·· ˌ··/ *n* [C] a place from which objects moving in space, such as SATELLITES and ROCKETS, can be recognized and followed

**track·lay·er** /ˈtrækˌleɪə‖-ər/ *n* [C] *AmE* a workman who builds or repairs railway tracks; PLATE-LAYER *BrE*

**track meet** /ˈ· ·/ *n* [C] *AmE* a sports event consisting of competitions in running, jumping etc

**track rec·ord** /ˈ· ˌ··/ *n* [singular] all the things that a person or organization has done in the past, which show how good they are at doing their job, dealing with problems etc: *We're looking for someone with a proven track record in selling advertising.*

**track·suit** /ˈtræksuːt, -sjuːt‖-suːt/ *n* [C] *BrE* loose clothes consisting of trousers and a JACKET (1), worn especially for sport

**tract** /trækt/ *n* [C] **1 digestive/reproductive/urinary etc tract** a system of connected organs that have one main purpose in a part of your body **2** a large area of land: *vast tracts of woodland* **3** *formal* a short piece of writing, especially about a moral or religious subject: *a tract on the dangers of drink*

**trac·ta·ble** /ˈtræktəbəl/ *adj formal* easy to control or deal with: *Separating a problem into separate chunks often makes it more tractable.* —opposite INTRACTABLE —**tractability** /ˌtræktəˈbɪlɪ̣ti/ *n* [U]

**trac·tion** /ˈtrækʃən/ *n* [U] **1** the process of treating a broken bone with special medical equipment that pulls it: **be in traction** (=be receiving this kind of treatment) *He was in traction for weeks after the accident.* **2** the force that prevents something such as a wheel sliding on a surface: *The tires were bald and lost traction on the wet road.* **3** the type of power needed to make a vehicle move, or to pull a heavy load

**trac·tor** /ˈtræktə‖-ər/ *n* [C] a strong vehicle with large wheels, used for pulling farm machinery

**trade¹** /treɪd/ *n* S3 W1
**1 ▶ BUYING/SELLING ◀** [U] the activity of buying, selling, or exchanging goods within a country or between countries: *There has been a marked increase in trade between East and West.* | **the arms trade** (=the buying and selling of weapons) —see also BALANCE OF TRADE, FREE TRADE, SLAVE TRADE
**2 the hotel/banking/tourist etc trade** the business done by banks, hotels etc: *My husband worked in the jewellery trade all his life.*
**3 ▶ AMOUNT OF BUSINESS ◀** [U] business activity, especially the amount of goods or products that are sold: *A lot of pubs nowadays do most of their trade at lunchtimes.* —see also **do a roaring trade** (ROARING (3))
**4 ▶ JOB/WORK ◀** [C] a particular job, especially one needing special skill with your hands: *In those days people would leave school at fourteen to learn a trade.* | **be sth by trade** (=be trained to do a particular job) *My grandfather was a plumber by trade.* | **tools of your trade** (=the things that you need to do your job) —see JOB (USAGE)
**5 the trade** a particular kind of business, and the people who are involved in it: *I could get Ron to look at your car for you; he works in the trade.*
**6 passing trade** people who go into a shop, restaurant etc because they see it, but are not regular customers: *Souvenir shops rely mainly on passing trade.* —see also STOCK-IN-TRADE, JACK-OF-ALL-TRADES, **tricks of the trade** (TRICK[1] (5))

**trade²** *v* **1** [I,T] to buy and sell goods, services etc: [+ **with**] *Britain built up her wealth by trading with other countries.* | [+ **in**] *These companies trade mainly in furs and animal skins.* | **trade sth** *Salesmen traded the new products all over the country.* | **trading partner** (=a country that buys your goods and sells their goods to

you) **2** [I] to exist and operate as a business: *The firm now trades under the name Lanski and Weber.*| **cease trading** (=stop being a business) **3** [T usually passive] *technical* to buy or sell something on the STOCK EXCHANGE: *Over a million shares were traded during the day.* **4 trade insults/blows etc** *informal* to insult or hit each other during an argument or fight **5** [I,T] *especially AmE* to exchange something you have for something someone else has: **trade sth for** *I'll trade my Roberto Clemente card for your Hank Aaron one.*| *We traded necklaces.*| **I'll trade you** *spoken* (=used to say you want to exchange something) *"I have peanut butter and jelly today." "Trade you. I have cream cheese."*

**trade** sth ↔ **down** *phr v* [T] *especially AmE* to sell something such as a car in order to buy one that costs less

**trade** sth ↔ **in** *phr v* [T] to give something such as a car to the person you are buying a new one from, so that you pay less: *He traded his old car in for a new model.* —see also TRADE-IN

**trade** sth ↔ **off** *phr v* [T] to balance one situation or quality against another, in order to produce an acceptable result: *We have to trade off the cost of research against the danger that our competitors will overtake us.* —see also TRADE-OFF

**trade on/upon** sth *phr v* [T] to use a situation or someone's kindness in order to get an advantage for yourself: *If you ask me they're just trading on Sam's good nature.*

**trade up** *phr v* [I,T] to give a used item, such as a car, for a similar item which is more expensive or valuable: **trade up sth** *Diego's traded up his old car for a more expensive model.*

**trade def·i·cit** /ˈ· ˌ···/ also **trade gap** *n* [C] the amount by which the value of what a country buys from abroad is more than the value of what it sells

**trade dis·count** /ˈ· ˌ··‖ˌ· ˈ··/ *n* [C] a special reduction in the price of goods sold to people who are going to sell the goods in their own shop or business

**trade fair** /ˈ· ·/ *n* [C] a large event when several companies show their goods or services in one place, to try to sell them

**trade gap** /ˈ· ·/ *n* [C] TRADE DEFICIT

**trade-in** /ˈ· ·/ *n* [C] *AmE* a used item, often a car, given to reduce the price of the new one that you are buying; PART-EXCHANGE *BrE* *Are you going to give your Ford as a trade-in?*| **trade-in price/value/figure** *The trade-in value of the car is roughly $3000.*

**trade·mark** /ˈtreɪdmɑːk‖-mɑːrk/ *n* [C] **1** a special name, sign, or word that is marked on a product to show that it is made by a particular company **2** a particular way of behaving, dressing etc by which someone or something can be easily recognized: *The striped T-shirt became the comedian's trademark.*

**trade name** /ˈ· ·/ *n* [C] a name given to a particular product, that helps you recognize it from other similar products; BRAND NAME

**trade-off** /ˈ· ·/ *n* [C] an acceptable balance between two opposing things that you want: *There has to be a trade-off between quality and quantity if we want to keep prices low.*

**trade price** /ˈ· ·/ *n* [C] the price at which goods are sold to shops by the companies that produce them

**trad·er** /ˈtreɪdə‖-ər/ *n* [C] someone who buys and sells goods

**trade route** /ˈ· ·/ *n* [C] a way across land or sea often used by traders' vehicles, ships etc

**trade school** /ˈ· ˌ·/ *n* [C] *especially AmE* a school where people go in order to learn a particular trade (TRADE[1] (4))

**trade se·cret** /ˌ· ˈ··/ *n* [C] **1** a piece of secret information about a particular business, that is only known by the people who work there: *The Coca-Cola formula is a well kept trade secret.* **2** *informal* a piece of information about how to do or make something, that you do not want other people to know: *Could you give me the recipe for that 'coq au vin' or is it a trade secret?*

**trades·man** /ˈtreɪdzmən/ *n* [C] **1** *especially BrE* someone who buys and sells goods, especially in a shop **2** *especially BrE* someone who goes to people's houses to sell or deliver goods **3** *especially AmE* someone who works at a job or trade (TRADE[1] (4)) that involves skill with your hands

**Trades U·nion Con·gress** /ˌ· ·· ˈ··/ *n* the TUC

**trade sur·plus** /ˌ· ˈ··/ *n* [C] *technical* the amount by which the value of the goods that a country sells to other countries is more than the value of what it buys from them

**trade u·nion** /ˌ· ˈ··/ also **trades union** *BrE* *n* [C] an organization, usually in a particular trade or profession, that represents workers, especially in meetings with employers; LABOR UNION *AmE* —**trade unionist** *n* [C]

**trade wind** /ˈ· ·/ *n* [C] a tropical wind that blows continually towards the EQUATOR from either the northeast or the southeast

**trading es·tate** /ˈ··· ˌ·/ *n* [C] *BrE* an area of land, often at the edge of a city, where there are small factories and businesses

**trading post** /ˈ·· ·/ *n* [C] a place where people can buy and exchange goods in a country area, especially in the US or Canada in the past: *a remote trading post in the Yukon*

**tra·di·tion** /trəˈdɪʃən/ *n* **1 a)** [C] a belief, custom, or way of doing something that has existed for a long time: *Christmas traditions*| [+ **of**] *a long tradition of wine-making*| **tradition that** *the tradition that the eldest son inherits the property* —see HABIT (USAGE) **b)** [U] beliefs or customs like this in general: *The British are lovers of tradition.*| **by tradition** *By tradition, it is the bride's parents who pay for the wedding.* **2** [C,U] the way in which things are done in a particular country, group of people etc: *the Western tradition in art*| *It had become a tradition in our house to stay up all night at New Year.*| **break with tradition** (=stop doing something in the way it has always been done) *Breaking with family tradition, they decided not to send Laura to boarding school.* **3 be in the tradition of** to have the same features as something that has been made or done in the past: *His paintings are very much in the tradition of Picasso and Matisse.* S W

**tra·di·tion·al** /trəˈdɪʃənəl/ *adj* **1** being part of the traditions of a country or group of people: *Kumar gave the traditional Hindu greeting.*| *traditional music*| **it is traditional (for sb) to do sth** *It is traditional for the bridegroom to make a speech.* **2** following ideas and methods that have existed for a long time, without being interested in anything new or different; CONVENTIONAL: *I went to a very traditional school.* —**traditionally** *adv* S W

**tra·di·tion·al·is·m** /trəˈdɪʃənəlɪzəm/ *n* [U] belief in the importance of TRADITIONS and customs

**tra·di·tion·al·ist** /trəˈdɪʃənəlɪst/ *n* [C] someone who respects TRADITION and does not like change —**traditionalist** *adj*

**tra·duce** /trəˈdjuːs‖-ˈduːs/ *v* [T] *formal* to deliberately say things that are untrue or unpleasant

**traf·fic[1]** /ˈtræfɪk/ *n* [U] **1** the vehicles moving along a road or street: *The noise of the traffic kept me awake.*| **heavy traffic** (=a large amount of traffic) *We were stuck in heavy traffic for more than an hour.* **2** the movement of aircraft, ships, trains etc from one place to another: *air traffic control* **3** *formal* the movement of people or goods by aircraft, ships, or trains: [+ **of**] *Most long-distance traffic of heavy goods is done by ships.* **4** the secret buying and selling of illegal goods: *drugs traffic*| [+ **in**] *traffic in firearms* S W

**traffic[2]** *v past tense and past participle* **trafficked**

**traffic in** sth *phr v* [T] to buy and sell illegal goods: *Lewis was found guilty of trafficking in drugs.*

**traffic calm·ing** /ˈ·· ˌ··/ *n* [U] *BrE* changes made to a road to stop people driving too fast along it

**traffic cir·cle** /ˈ·· ˌ··/ *n* [C] *AmE* a raised circular area that cars must drive around, where three or more roads join; ROUNDABOUT[1] (1) *BrE*

**traffic cone** /ˈ·· ˌ·/ *n* [C] a plastic marker in the shape of a CONE that is put on the road to show where repairs are being done

**traffic cop** /ˈ·· ˌ·/ *n* [C] *AmE informal* **1** a police officer who stands in the road and directs traffic **2** a police officer who stops drivers who drive in an illegal way

**traffic court** /ˈ·· ˌ·/ *n* [C] *AmE* a court in a town or city in the US that deals with people who have done something illegal while driving

**traffic is·land** /ˈ·· ˌ··/ *n* [C] a raised area in the middle of the road where people can wait for traffic to pass

**traffic jam** /ˈ·· ˌ·/ *n* [C] a long line of vehicles on a road that cannot move, or that can only move very slowly: *We were stuck in a traffic jam on the freeway for two hours.*

**traf·fick·er** /ˈtræfɪkə‖-ər/ *n* [C] someone who buys and sells illegal goods, especially drugs

**traf·fick·ing** /ˈtræfɪkɪŋ/ *n* [U] the buying and selling of illegal goods, especially drugs: *drug trafficking*

**traffic lights** /ˈ·· ˌ·/ *n* [C] special lights at a place where roads meet, that control the traffic by means of red, yellow, and green lights

**traffic school** /ˈ·· ˌ·/ *n* [C] *AmE* a class that teaches you about driving laws, that you can go to instead of paying money for something you have done wrong while driving

**traffic war·den** /ˈ·· ˌ··/ *n* [C] *BrE* someone whose job is to check that vehicles have not parked illegally on the streets

**tra·ge·di·an** /trəˈdʒiːdiən/ *n* [C] *formal* an actor or writer of tragedy

**tra·ge·dy** /ˈtrædʒədi/ *n* **1** [C,U] a very sad event, that shocks people because it involves death: *Tragedy struck the family when their two-year old son died of leukemia.* **2** [C] *informal* something that seems very sad and unnecessary because something will be wasted, lost, or harmed: *It's a tragedy to see so much talent going to waste.* **3 a)** [C] a serious play or book that ends sadly, especially with the death of the main character: *'Hamlet' is one of Shakespeare's best known tragedies.* **b)** [U] this type of plays or books: *an actor specializing in tragedy*

**tra·gic** /ˈtrædʒɪk/ *adj* **1** a tragic event or situation makes you feel very sad: *Lillian Board's death at 22 was a tragic loss for the world of British athletics.* **2** [only before noun] connected with tragedy in books or plays: *a great tragic actor* | **tragic hero** (=the main character in a tragedy) **3 tragic flaw** a weakness in the character of the main person in a tragedy that causes their own problems and usually death: *Jealousy is Othello's tragic flaw.*

**tra·gic·ally** /ˈtrædʒɪkli/ *adv* in a very sad or unfortunate way: [sentence adverb] *Tragically, her dancing career ended only six months later.* | [+ adj/adv] *Alan died tragically young.*

**tra·gi·com·e·dy** /ˌtrædʒɪˈkɒmədi‖-ˈkɑː-/ *n* [C,U] a play or a story that is both sad and funny —**tragicomic** /ˌtrædʒɪˈkɒmɪk◂‖-ˈkɑː-/ *adj*

**trail¹** /treɪl/ *v* **1** [I,T always + adv/prep] if something trails behind you, or if you trail it behind you, it gets pulled behind you as you move along: [+ **across/in/through**] *She walked slowly along the path, her skirt trailing in the mud.* | **trail sth in/on/through** *Rees was leaning out of the boat trailing his hand through the water.* **2** also **trail along** [I always + adv/prep] to walk slowly, especially because you are tired or bored, and often following other people: [+ **behind/around**] *Susie trailed along behind her parents.* **3** [I,T usually in progressive] to be losing in a game, competition, or election: *The Democrats are still trailing in the latest poll.* | **trail (sb) by** *At the end of the first half Bolton were trailing by two goals to nil.* **4** [T] to follow a person or animal by looking for signs that they have gone in a particular direction: *Police trailed the gang for several days.* —see also TRAILER

**trail away/off** *phr v* [I] if someone's voice trails away or off, it becomes gradually quieter and then stops: *She trailed off, silenced by the look Kris gave her.*

**trail²** *n* [C] **1 be on sb's trail** to be finding out where someone has gone in order to find or catch them: *Police believe they are on the trail of a dangerous killer.* | **be hard/hot on sb's trail** (=be close to finding someone you are trying to catch) **2 while the trail is still hot** if you chase someone while the trail is still hot, you follow them soon after they have left **3** the track or smell of a person or animal by which it can be hunted or followed: *The hunters lost the tiger's trail in the middle of the jungle.* **4** a rough path across open country or through a forest: *The trail led over Boulder Pass before descending to a lake.* **5 trail of blood/dust etc** a line or series of marks left by someone or something that is moving: *They left a trail of muddy footprints on the living room carpet.* | **trail of destruction** (=damage left by a moving storm or army) **6 a trail of broken hearts/unpaid bills etc** *humorous* a series of unhappy people or bad situations all caused by the same person: *He left a trail of broken hearts, of deserted women behind him.* see also **blaze a trail** (BLAZE¹ (4))

**trail·blaz·er** /ˈtreɪlˌbleɪzə‖-ər/ *n* [C] someone who is the first to discover or develop new methods of doing something: *a trailblazer in the field of medical research*

**trail·er** /ˈtreɪlə‖-ər/ *n* [C] **1** *AmE* a vehicle that can be pulled behind a car, used for living and sleeping in during a holiday; CARAVAN (1) *BrE* **2** a vehicle that can be pulled behind a vehicle, used for carrying something such as a boat or large piece of equipment **3** *especially BrE* an advertisement for a new film or television show, usually consisting of small scenes taken from it

**trailer park** /ˈ·· ·/ also **trailer court** *n* [C] *AmE* an area where TRAILERS are parked and used as people's homes

**trail·ing** /ˈtreɪlɪŋ/ *adj* a trailing plant grows along the ground or hangs down: *ivy and other trailing plants*

**train¹** /treɪn/ *n* [C] S1

**1 ▶ RAILWAY ◀** a number of connected carriages pulled by an engine along a railway line: *Jeff just missed the six o'clock train.* | [+ **to**] *I caught the early train to Bruges.* | **by train** *It's more relaxing to travel by train.* | **train driver/journey/service** *There's no train service between here and Wales.* —see also BOAT TRAIN W2

**2 ▶ SERIES ◀ train of** a series of connected events, actions etc: *That one incident sparked off a whole train of events.*

**3 train of thought** a connected series of thoughts developing in your mind: *The phone rang and interrupted my train of thought.*

**4 set sth in train** *formal* to make something start happening: *Plans to modernize have been set in train.*

**5 bring sth in its train** *formal* if an action or event brings something in its train, that thing happens as a result of it: *a decision that brought disaster in its train*

**6 ▶ PEOPLE/ANIMALS ◀** a long line of moving people, animals, or vehicles: *a camel train*

**7 ▶ DRESS ◀** a part of a long dress that spreads out over the ground behind the person who is wearing it: *a wedding dress with a long train*

**8 ▶ SERVANTS ◀** a group of servants or officers following an important person, especially in former times

**train²** *v* **1** [I,T] to teach someone or be taught the skills of a particular job or activity: [+ **as**] *Nadia trained as a singer under a famous professor of music.* | **train sb in** *Soldiers trained in hand-to-hand combat.* | **train to do sth** *Hugh's training to be a doctor.* —see TEACH (USAGE) **2** [T] to teach an animal to do something or to behave correctly: **train sth to do sth** *These dogs are trained to detect explosives.* | *a well-trained puppy* **3** [I,T] to prepare for a sporting event or tell someone how to prepare for it, especially by exercising: [+ **for**] *Brenda spends two hours a day training for the marathon.* **4** [T] to aim a gun, camera etc at someone or something: **train sth on/at** *The firemen trained their hoses on the burning building.* **5** [T] to make a plant grow in a particular direction by bending, cutting, or tying it —**trained** *adj*: *a highly trained technician* —**trainable** *adj* —see also TRAINING S1 W2

**train·bear·er** /ˈtreɪnˌbeərə‖-ˌberər/ *n* [C] someone who holds the train (TRAIN [1] (7)) of a dress, especially at a wedding

**train·ee** /ˌtreɪˈniː◂/ *n* [C] someone who is being trained for a job: *The new trainees will start next week.* | **trainee reporter/engineer/salesman etc** *a trainee hairdresser*

**train·er** /ˈtreɪnə‖-ər/ *n* [C] **1** someone who trains people or animals for sport, work etc: *a teacher trainer* **2** *BrE* a type of strong shoe that you wear for sport; SNEAKER *AmE* —see picture at SHOE[1]

S3 W1 **train·ing** /ˈtreɪnɪŋ/ *n* **1** [singular, U] the process of training or being trained: [+ **in**] *On the course we received training in every aspect of the job.* | *a training manual* **2** [U] special physical exercises that are part of a plan for keeping someone fit and healthy: *Lesley does weight training twice a week.* | **be in/out of training** (=be fit or not fit for a sport) *The champion is in training for his next fight.* —see also SPRING TRAINING

**training col·lege** /ˈ·· ˌ··/ *n* [C,U] *BrE* a college for adults that gives training for a particular profession: *a teacher training college* | *a training college for pilots*

**train set** /ˈ· ·/ *n* [C] a toy train with railway tracks

**train spot·ter** /ˈ· ˌ··/ *n* [C] *BrE* **1** someone who collects the numbers of railway engines and other information about them for fun **2** someone who you think is boring and only interested in unimportant details —**trainspotting** *n* [U]

**traipse** /treɪps/ *v* [I always + adv/prep] *informal* to walk somewhere slowly and unwillingly when you are tired: [+ **up/down/around etc**] *I've been traipsing round the shops all morning.*

**trait** /treɪ, treɪt‖treɪt/ *n* [C] *formal* a particular quality in someone's character: *Anne's generosity is one of her most pleasing traits.*

**trai·tor** /ˈtreɪtə‖-ər/ *n* [C] someone who is not loyal to their country or friends: *He was hanged as a traitor.* | *a traitor to the cause of women's rights*

**trai·tor·ous** /ˈtreɪt*ə*rəs/ *adj especially literary* not loyal to your country or friends —**traitorously** *adv*

**tra·jec·to·ry** /trəˈdʒekt*ə*ri/ *n* [C] *technical* the curved path of an object that is fired or thrown through the air

**tram** /træm/ also **tram·car** /ˈtræmkɑː‖-kɑːr/ *n* [C] *especially BrE* an electric vehicle for carrying passengers, which moves along the streets on metal tracks; STREETCAR *AmE*

**tram·lines** /ˈtræmlaɪnz/ *n* [plural] *BrE* **1** the metal tracks in the road that trams run along **2** *BrE informal* a pair of parallel lines at the edge of a tennis court —see picture at TENNIS

**tram·mels** /ˈtræm*ə*lz/ *n* [plural] *formal* something that limits or prevents free movement, activity, or development: *an urge to shake off the trammels of respectability* —see also UNTRAMMELLED

**tramp**[1] /træmp/ *n* [C] **1** someone who has no home or job and moves from place to place, often asking for food or money: *a group of tramps huddled around a fire* **2** a long or difficult walk: *It was a long tramp home through the snow.* **3** *old-fashioned especially AmE* a woman who has too many sexual partners **4 the tramp of** the sound of heavy walking: *the steady tramp of soldiers' feet on the road*

**tramp**[2] *v* [I always + adv/prep, T] to walk around or through somewhere with firm or heavy steps: **tramp sth** *I've tramped the streets all day looking for work.* | [+ **across/over/up etc**] *Who's been tramping all over the floor in muddy shoes?*

**tram·ple** /ˈtræmp*ə*l/ *v* [I always + adv/prep, T] **1** to step heavily on something so that you crush it with your feet: [+ **on/over/through etc**] *You trampled on my beautiful flowerbeds!* | **trample sb/sth underfoot** *She dropped her jacket and it was trampled underfoot.* | **trample sb to death** (=kill someone by stepping heavily on them) *Several people were nearly trampled to death in the rush to get out.* **2 trample on sth/trample sth underfoot** to behave in a way that shows that you do not care about someone's rights, hopes, ideas etc: *The colonial government had trampled on the rights of the native people.*

**tram·po·line** /ˈtræmpəliːn‖ˌtræmpəˈliːn/ *n* [C] a piece of equipment that you jump up and down on as a sport, made of a sheet of material tightly stretched across a metal frame —**trampoline** *v* [I] —**trampolining** *n* [U]

**trance** /trɑːns‖træns/ *n* [C] **1** a state in which you behave as if you were asleep but are still able to hear and understand what is said to you: *a hypnotic trance* **2** a situation in which you are thinking about something so much that you do not notice what is happening around you: **be in a trance** *What's the matter with you? You've been in a trance all day!*

**tran·quil** /ˈtræŋkwɪl/ *adj* pleasantly calm, quiet, and peaceful: *a tranquil village scene* —**tranquilly** *adv* —**tranquillity** *BrE*, **tranquility** *AmE* /træŋˈkwɪlɪti/ *n* [U] | *the tranquillity of the Tuscan countryside*

**tran·quil·lize** also **-ise** *BrE*, **tranquilize** *AmE* /ˈtræŋkwɪlaɪz/ *v* [T] to make a person or animal calm or unconscious by using a drug

**tran·quil·lizer** also **-iser** *BrE*, **tranquilizer** *AmE* /ˈtræŋkwɪlaɪzə‖-ər/ *n* [C] a drug used to reduce nervous anxiety and make you calm

**trans-** /træns, trænz/ *prefix* **1** on or to the far side of something; across: *transatlantic flights* | *the trans-Siberian railway* **2** between two things or groups; INTER-: *trans-racial fostering* **3** shows a change: *He's been transformed by the experience.* | *the transmutation of base metal into gold*

**trans·act** /trænˈzækt/ *v* [I,T] *formal* to do business: *Most deals are transacted over the phone.*

**trans·ac·tion** /trænˈzækʃ*ə*n/ *n formal* **1** [C] a business deal: *The bank charges a fixed rate for each transaction.* | *financial transactions* **2** [U] the process of doing business: *the transaction of his public duties* **3 transactions** [plural] discussions that take place at the meetings of a society, or a written record of these S W

**trans·at·lan·tic** /ˌtrænzətˈlæntɪk◂/ *adj* [only before noun] **1** crossing the Atlantic Ocean: *transatlantic flights* **2** involving countries on both sides of the Atlantic Ocean: *a transatlantic agreement* **3** on the other side of the Atlantic Ocean: *one of America's transatlantic military bases*

**trans·cei·ver** /trænˈsiːvə‖-ər/ *n* [C] a radio that can both send and receive messages

**tran·scend** /trænˈsend/ *v* [T] *formal* to go above or beyond the limits of something: *The desire for peace transcended political differences.*

**tran·scen·dent** /trænˈsendənt/ *adj formal* going far beyond ordinary limits: *the transcendent genius of Mozart* —**transcendently** *adv*

**tran·scen·den·tal** /ˌtrænsenˈdentl◂/ *adj* experiences or ideas going beyond human knowledge, understanding, and experience —**transcendentally** *adv*

**tran·scen·den·tal·is·m** /ˌtrænsenˈdent*ə*l-ɪz*ə*m/ *n* [U] the belief that knowledge can be obtained by studying thought and not necessarily by practical experience —**transcendentalist** *n* [C]

**transcendental med·i·ta·tion** /ˌ···· ··ˈ··/ *n* [U] a method of becoming calm by repeating special religious words in your mind

**trans·con·ti·nen·tal** /ˌtrænzkɒntɪˈnentl, ˌtræns-‖-kɑːn-/ *adj* crossing a CONTINENT: *a transcontinental railway*

**tran·scribe** /trænˈskraɪb/ *v* [T] *formal* **1** to write an exact copy of something: *transcribing an ancient manuscript* **2** to write down something exactly as it was said: *A secretary transcribed the witnesses' statements.* **3** *technical* to represent speech sounds with special PHONETIC letters **4** [+ **into**] *formal* to change a piece of writing into the alphabet of another language **5** to arrange a piece of music for a different instrument or voice: **transcribe sth for sth** *a piece transcribed for piano* **6** to copy recorded music, speech etc from one system to another, for example from TAPE[1] (1) to CD

**tran·script** /ˈtrænskrɪpt/ *n* [C] **1** an exact written or printed copy of something: **[+ of]** *A transcript of the tapes was presented in court as evidence.* **2** *AmE* an official document of a college or university that has a list of a student's classes and the results they received

**tran·scrip·tion** /trænˈskrɪpʃən/ *n* **1** [U] the act or process of transcribing something: *Pronunciation is shown by a system of phonetic transcription.* **2** [C] an exact written or printed copy of something; transcript

**tran·sept** /ˈtrænsept/ *n* [C] one of the two parts of a church that are built out from the main area of the church to form a cross shape

2 **trans·fer¹** /trænsˈfɜː‖-ˈfɜːr/ *v* **transferred, transferring**

**1 ▶ PERSON ◀** [I,T] to move or arrange for someone to move from one place or job to another, especially within the same organization: **transfer sb to** *They're transferring me to the Edinburgh office.*

**2 ▶ THING/ACTIVITY ◀** [T] *formal* to move something from one place or position to another: **transfer sth (from sth) to** *Transfer the cookies to a wire rack to cool.* | *We're transferring production to Detroit.*

**3 ▶ MONEY ◀** [T] to move money from the control of one account or institution to another: *I'd like to transfer £500 into my current account.* | *Will I be able to transfer my pension rights?*

**4 transfer your affection/loyalty etc** to change from loving or supporting one person to loving or supporting a different one: **[+ to]** *I immediately transferred my support to the other candidate.*

**5 ▶ PROPERTY ◀** [T] *law* to officially give property or money to someone else: *The assets were transferred into his wife's name.*

**6 transfer power/responsibility/control (to)** to officially give power etc to another person or organization: *transferring control of public land to the states*

**7 ▶ PLANE ◀** [I,T] to change from one plane to another during a journey, or arrange for someone to do this: *You'll have to transfer at Los Angeles.*

**8 ▶ RECORDING ◀** [T] to copy recorded information, music etc from one system to another, for example from TAPE[1] (1) to CD: *I decided to transfer the files onto floppy disk.* —**transferable** *adj* | *Airline tickets are not transferable.*

2 **trans·fer²** /ˈtrænsfɜː‖-fɜːr/ *n* **1 a)** [C,U] the process by which someone or something moves or is moved from one place, job etc to another: *Penny's applied for a transfer to another part of the company.* | *data transfer* **b)** [C] someone or something that has been moved in this way **2 transfer of power** a process by which the control of a country is taken from one person or group and given to another: *the peaceful transfer of power in South Africa* **3** [C] *especially BrE* a drawing, pattern etc that can be stuck or printed onto a surface; DECAL *especially AmE* **4** [C] *especially AmE* a ticket that allows a passenger to change from one bus, train etc to another without paying more money

**trans·fer·ence** /ˈtrænsfərəns‖trænsˈfɜːr-/ *n* [U] *formal* a process by which someone or something is moved from one place, position, job etc to another

**transfer fee** /ˈ··· ,/ *n* [C] *BrE* the money that is paid to one football club by another for the transfer of a player

**transfer list** /ˈ··· ,/ *n* [C] a list of the football players at one club who can transfer to other clubs

**trans·fig·ure** /trænsˈfɪɡə‖-ɡjər/ *v* [T] *literary* to change the way someone or something looks, especially so that they become more beautiful: *a face transfigured with joy* —**transfiguration** /træns,fɪɡəˈreɪʃən‖-ɡjə-/ *n* [C,U]

**trans·fix** /trænsˈfɪks/ *v* [T] *literary* to make a hole through something or someone with a sharp pointed weapon

**trans·fixed** /trænsˈfɪkst/ *adj* [not before noun] unable to move because you are very shocked, frightened etc: *Joe stood transfixed when I told him the terrible news.*

**trans·form** /trænsˈfɔːm‖-ˈfɔːrm/ *v* [T] to completely change the appearance, form, or character of something or someone, especially in a way that improves it: **transform sth into** *In the last 20 years Korea has been transformed into an advanced industrial power.* | **transform sb/sth** *Put yourself in the hands of our experts, who will transform your hair and makeup.* —**transformable** *adj* W3

**trans·for·ma·tion** /,trænsfəˈmeɪʃən‖-fər-/ *n* [U] a complete change in someone or something: *In recent years the film industry has undergone a complete transformation.*

**trans·form·er** /trænsˈfɔːmə‖-ˈfɔːrmər/ *n* [C] a piece of equipment for changing electricity from one VOLTAGE to another

**trans·fu·sion** /trænsˈfjuːʒən/ *n* [C,U] *formal* the process of putting blood from one person into another person's body: *A blood transfusion saved his life.*

**trans·gress** /trænzˈɡres‖træns-/ *v formal* [I,T] *formal* to do something that is against the rules of social behaviour or against a moral principle: *Those who have transgressed against custom must be punished.* —**transgressor** *n* [C] —**transgression** /-ˈɡreʃən/ *n* [C,U]

**tran·si·ent¹** /ˈtrænziənt‖ˈtrænʃənt/ *adj formal* **1** continuing only for a short time; TRANSITORY: *transient fashions* **2** passing quickly through a place or staying there for only a short time: *a transient population of gold prospectors* —**transience, transiency** *n* [U]

**transient²** *n* [C] *AmE* someone who has no home and moves around from place to place; TRAMP[1] (1)

**tran·sis·tor** /trænˈzɪstə, -ˈsɪstə‖-ər/ *n* [C] **1** a small piece of electronic equipment in radios, televisions etc that controls the flow of electricity **2** a transistor radio

**tran·sis·tor·ize** also **ise** *BrE* /trænˈzɪstəraɪz, -ˈsɪs-/ *v* [T] *technical* to put transistors into something so that it can be made smaller

**transistor ra·di·o** /·,·· ˈ···/ *n* [C] a small radio that has transistors in it instead of valves (VALVE (3))

**tran·sit** /ˈtrænsɪ̥t, -zɪ̥t/ *n* **1** [U] the process of moving goods or people from one place to another: **in transit** (=in the process of being moved) *goods damaged in transit* **2** [C,U] *technical* the movement of a PLANET or moon in front of a larger object in space, such as the sun

**transit camp** /ˈ·· ,·/ *n* [C] a place where REFUGEES stay before moving to somewhere more permanent

**tran·si·tion** /trænˈzɪʃən,-ˈsɪ-/ *n* [C,U] *formal* the act or process of changing from one form or state to another: *the band's gradual transition from hard rock hipsters to kings of pop* | **in transition** (=in the process of changing) *The book takes an interesting look at a marriage in transition.* W3

**tran·si·tion·al** /trænˈzɪʃənəl,-sɪ-/ *adj* **1 transitional stage/period etc** a period during which something is changing from one state or form into another: *maintaining law and order in the transitional period between governments* **2 transitional government** a government that is temporary during a period of change —**transitionally** *adv*

**tran·si·tive** /ˈtrænsɪ̥tɪv, -zɪ̥-/ *adj technical* a transitive verb must have an object, for example the verb 'break' in the sentence 'I broke the cup'. Transitive verbs are marked [T] in this dictionary. —compare DITRANSITIVE, INTRANSITIVE —**transitive** *n* [C] —**transitively** *adv*

**transit lounge** /ˈ·· ,·/ *n* [C] an area in an airport where passengers can wait

**tran·si·to·ry** /ˈtrænzɪ̥təri‖-tɔːri/ *adj* continuing or existing for only a short time; TRANSIENT

**transit vi·sa** /ˈ·· ,··/ *n* [C] a VISA (=special document) that allows someone to pass through one country on their way to another

**trans·late** /trænsˈleɪt, trænz-/ *v* **1** [I,T] to change speech or writing into another language: *Robin doesn't* *speak German so I'll have to translate.* | **translate sth (from sth) into** *We translated the text from Italian into English.* —compare INTERPRET (1) **2** [I] to be changed from one language into another: *Most poetry doesn't translate easily.* **3** [T] to change something from one form into another: **translate sth into** *We're hoping to translate our ideas into action.* —**translatable** *adj*

**trans·la·tion** /træns'leɪʃən,trænz-/ *n* **1** [C,U] the act of translating something or something that has been translated: *a translation of Aristotle's 'Ethics'* | **translation (from sth) into** *translatiion from Latin into English* | **in translation** *I've only read "Madame Bovary" in translation.* | **be lost in translation** (=be no longer effective when translated) *Much of the book's humour has been lost in translation.* **2** [U] *formal* the process of changing something into a different form: *the translation of ideas into deeds*

**trans·la·tor** /træns'leɪtə, trænz-‖-ər/ *n* [C] someone who changes speech or writing into a different language —compare INTERPRETER

**trans·lit·e·rate** /trænz'lɪtəreɪt‖træns-/ *v* [T] to write a word, sentence etc in the alphabet of a different language or writing system —**transliteration** /trænz,lɪtə'reɪʃən‖træns-/ *n* [C,U]

**trans·lu·cent** /trænz'luːsənt‖træns-/ *adj* not transparent, but clear enough to allow light to pass through: *translucent paper* —**translucence** *n* [U]

**trans·mi·gra·tion** /,trænzmaɪ'greɪʃən‖,træns-/ *n* [U] *technical* the time when the soul passes into another body after death, according to some religions

**trans·mis·sion** /trænz'mɪʃən‖træns-/ *n* **1** [U] the process of sending out of electrical signals, messages etc, by radio or similar equipment: *We apologize for the break in transmission earlier in the programme.* **2** [C] *formal* something that is broadcast on television, radio etc **3** [C] the parts of a vehicle that take power from the engine to the wheels: *My car has automatic transmission.* **4** [U] *formal* the process of sending or passing of something from one person, place, or thing to another: *the transmission of disease*

**trans·mit** /trænz'mɪt‖træns-/ *v* **transmitted, transmitting** **1** [I,T] to send out electric signals, messages etc by radio or other similar equipment; broadcast: *The US Open will be transmitted live via satellite.* **2** [T] to send or pass something from one person, place or thing to another: *an infection transmitted by mosquitoes* —see also SEXUALLY TRANSMITTED DISEASE **3** [T] *technical* if an object or substance transmits sound or light, it allows sound or light to travel through or along it

**trans·mit·ter** /trænz'mɪtə‖træns'mɪtər/ *n* [C] equipment that sends out radio or television signals

**trans·mog·ri·fy** /trænz'mɒgrɪ̈faɪ‖træns'mɑː-/ *v* [T] *humorous* to change the shape of something completely, as if by magic

**trans·mute** /trænz'mjuːt‖træns-/ *v* [T] *formal* to change one substance or type of thing into another: *Alchemists tried to transmute lead into gold.* —**transmutable** *adj* —**transmutation** /,trænzmjuː'teɪʃən‖,træns-/ *n* [C,U]

**tran·som** /'trænsəm/ *n* [C] **1** a bar of wood above a door, separating the door from a window above it **2** a bar of wood or stone across a window, dividing the window into two parts **3** *AmE* a small window over a door or over a larger window; FANLIGHT *BrE*

**trans·par·en·cy** /træn'spærənsi, -'speər-‖-'spær-,-'sper-/ *n* **1** [C] a piece of photographic film through which light can be shone to show a picture on a large screen; SLIDE² (4) **2** [U] the quality of glass, plastic etc that makes it possible for you to see through it

**trans·par·ent** /træn'spærənt, -'speər-‖-'spær-, -'sper-/ *adj* **1** something that is transparent allows light to pass through it, so that you can see the things through it: *Plain glass is transparent.* | *a transparent silk blouse* —compare OPAQUE, TRANSLUCENT **2** a lie, excuse etc that is transparent does not deceive people **3** *formal* speech or writing that is transparent is clear and easy to understand —**transparently** *adv*

**tran·spi·ra·tion** /,trænspɪ̈'reɪʃən/ *n* [U] *technical* the process of transpiring (TRANSPIRE (3))

**tran·spire** /træn'spaɪə‖-'spaɪr/ *v* **1 it transpires that** *formal* if it transpires that something is true, people find out that it is true: *It now transpires that he kept all the money for himself.* **2** [T] to happen: *Let's wait and see what transpires.* **3** [I,T] *technical* when a plant transpires, it gives off water from its surface

**trans·plant¹** /træns'plɑːnt‖-'plænt/ *v* [T] **1** to move a plant from one place and plant it in another **2** to move an organ, piece of skin etc from one person's body to another **3** *formal* to move something or someone from one place to another —**transplantation** /,trænsplɑːn'teɪʃən‖-plæn-/ *n* [U]

**trans·plant²** /'trænsplɑːnt‖-plænt/ *n* [C,U] **1** the operation of transplanting an organ, piece of skin etc: *heart transplant surgery* **2** the organ etc that is transplanted in this type of operation —compare IMPLANT

**trans·po·lar** /,trænz'pəʊlə◂‖,træns'poʊlər◂/ *adj* across the area around the North or South Pole

**trans·pond·er** /træn'spɒndə‖-'spɑːndər/ *n* [C] *technical* a piece of radio or RADAR equipment that sends out a particular signal when it receives a signal telling it to do this

**trans·port¹** /'trænspɔːt‖-ɔːrt/ *n* **1** [U] a system for carrying passengers or goods from one place to another; TRANSPORTATION (2) *AmE* | **public transport** (=buses, trains etc) *Public transport in Prague was excellent.* **2** [U] a method of travelling from one place to another: *It's easier to get to the college if you have your own transport* (=car, bicycle etc) . | **means of transport** *Horses provided the only means of transport.* **3** [U] the process or business of taking goods from one place to another; TRANSPORTATION (1) *AmE* [+ **of**] *The transport of freight by air is very expensive.* **4** [C] a ship or aircraft for carrying soldiers or supplies **5 be in a transport of delight/joy etc** *literary* to be feeling very strong emotions of pleasure, happiness etc S W

**trans·port²** /træn'spɔːt‖-ɔːrt/ *v* [T] **1** to take goods, people etc from one place to another in a vehicle: *Transporting goods by rail reduces pollution.* | **transport sb/sth to** *You will be transported to the resort by coach.* **2 be transported back/into etc** to imagine that you are in another place or time because of something that you see or hear: *Walking around the town, I was transported back to my youth.* **3** to send a criminal to a distant country as a punishment in former times **4 be transported with delight/joy etc** *literary* to feel very strong emotions of pleasure, happiness etc —**transportable** *adj*

**trans·por·ta·tion** /,trænspɔː'teɪʃən‖-spər-/ *n* [U] **1** the process or business of taking goods from one place to another: *the transportation of dangerous chemicals by road* **2** *AmE* a system for carrying passengers or goods from one place to another; TRANSPORT¹ (1) *BrE* **3** *old use* the punishment of sending a criminal to a distant country S W

**transport caf·e** /'·· ,··‖'·· ·,·/ *n* [C] *BrE* a cheap restaurant beside a main road, used mainly by drivers of heavy vehicles; TRUCK STOP *AmE*

**trans·port·er** /træn'spɔːtə‖-'spɔːrtər/ *n* [C] a long vehicle that can carry one or more other vehicles

**transport plane** /'·· ,·/ *n* [C] a plane that is used especially for carrying military equipment or soldiers

**transport ship** /'·· ,·/ *n* [C] a ship used especially for carrying soldiers

**trans·pose** /træn'spəʊz‖-'spoʊz/ *v* [T] *technical* **1** *formal* to change the order or position of two or more things **2** to write or perform a piece of music in a musical KEY¹ (4) that is different from the one that it was first written in —**transposition** /,trænspə'zɪʃən/ *n* [C,U]

**trans·put·er** /trænz'pjuːtə‖træns'pjuːtər/ *n* [C] *technical* a powerful computer MICROCHIP that can deal with very large amounts of information very fast

**trans·sex·u·al** /træn'sekʃuəl‖træns'sek-/ *n* [C] someone who wants to be or look like a member of the opposite sex, especially by having a medical operation —**transsexual** *adj* —**transsexualism** *n* [U]

**tran·sub·stan·ti·a·tion** /ˌtrænsəbstænʃiˈeɪʃən/ *n* [U] *technical* the belief of some Christians that the bread and wine in the MASS (=a religious ceremony) become the actual body and blood of Christ

**trans·verse** /trænzˈvɜːs‖trænsˈvɜːrs/ *adj* [no comparative] *technical* lying or placed across something: *a transverse beam*

**trans·ves·tite** /trænzˈvestaɪt‖træns-/ *n* [C] someone who enjoys dressing like a person of the opposite sex —**transvestite** *adj* —**transvestism** *n* [U]

**trap¹** /træp/ *n* [C]
**1** ▶ **FOR ANIMALS** ◀ a piece of equipment for catching animals: *a mouse caught in a trap* | **set a trap** (=prepare it) —see also MOUSETRAP
**2** ▶ **BAD SITUATION** ◀ an unpleasant or difficult situation that is difficult to escape from: *Amanda felt that marriage was a trap.*
**3** ▶ **CLEVER TRICK** ◀ a clever trick that is used to catch someone or to make them do or say something that they did not intend to: **fall/walk into a trap** *Hopefully, the thief will fall right into our trap.* | **lay a trap (for)** (=arrange a trap for someone)
**4 fall into the trap of doing sth** to do something that seems good at the time but is not sensible or wise: *Don't fall into the trap of investing all your money in one place.*
**5 keep your trap shut** *spoken* to not say anything about things that are secret: *Just keep your trap shut, and we won't get into trouble.*
**6 shut your trap!** *spoken* a rude way of telling someone to stop talking
**7** ▶ **VEHICLE** ◀ a light vehicle with two wheels, pulled by a horse: *a pony and trap*
**8** ▶ **SPORT** ◀ *AmE* a place on a GOLF COURSE where there is sand, and from which it is difficult to hit the ball; BUNKER (3) *BrE*
**9** ▶ **DOG RACE** ◀ a special gate from which a dog is set free at the beginning of a GREYHOUND race —see also BOOBY TRAP, DEATH TRAP, POVERTY TRAP, SPEED TRAP

3 **trap²** *v* [T]
**1** ▶ **IN A DANGEROUS PLACE** ◀ [usually passive] to prevent someone from escaping from a dangerous place: *Twenty miners were trapped underground.*
**2** ▶ **IN A BAD SITUATION** ◀ **be trapped** to be in a bad situation from which you cannot escape: *Julia felt trapped in a dead end job.*
**3** ▶ **ANIMAL** ◀ to catch an animal or bird using a trap
**4** ▶ **CATCH SB** ◀ to catch someone by forcing them into a place from which they cannot escape: *The police trapped the terrorists at a roadblock.*
**5** ▶ **TRICK SB** ◀ to trick someone so that you make them do or say something that they did not intend to: **trap sb into (doing) sth** *I was trapped into signing a confession.*
**6** ▶ **CRUSH** ◀ to get a part of your body crushed between two objects: *a four-year-old who had trapped his fingers in the door* | *pain from a trapped nerve in the back*
**7** ▶ **GAS/WATER ETC** ◀ to hold and keep gas, water etc so that it can be used later: *solar panels that trap the sun's heat*

**trap·door** /ˈtræpdɔː‖-dɔːr/ *n* [C] a small door that covers an opening in a roof or floor

**tra·peze** /trəˈpiːz‖træ-/ *n* [C] a short bar hanging from two ropes high above the ground, used by ACROBATS

**tra·pe·zi·um** /trəˈpiːziəm/ *n* [C] *technical* **1** *BrE* a shape with four sides, of which only two are parallel **2** *AmE* a shape with four sides of which none are parallel —see picture at SHAPE

**trap·e·zoid** /ˈtræpɪzɔɪd/ *n* [C] *technical* **1** a shape with four sides, of which none are parallel **2** *AmE* a shape with four sides of which only two are parallel —see picture at SHAPE

**trap·per** /ˈtræpə‖-ər/ *n* [C] someone who traps wild animals, especially for their fur

**trap·pings** /ˈtræpɪŋz/ *n* [plural] things such as clothes, possessions etc that show someone's rank, success, or position: [+ **of**] *all the trappings of fame*

**Trap·pist** /ˈtræpɪst/ *n* [C] a member of a Roman Catholic religious society whose members never speak

**trap·shoot·ing** /ˈtræpˌʃuːtɪŋ/ *n* [U] the sport of shooting at special clay objects fired into the air

**trash¹** /træʃ/ *n* [U] **1** *AmE* waste material that will be S3
thrown away; RUBBISH *BrE* —see graph at RUBBISH¹ **2** *informal* something that is of very poor quality: *There's a lot of trash on TV these days.* **3** *informal especially AmE* a very insulting word for people who you think do not deserve your respect

**trash²** *v* [T] *informal* to destroy something completely, either deliberately or by using it too much: *The place got trashed last time we had a party!*

**trash·can** /ˈtræʃkæn/ *n* [C] *AmE* **1** a large container with a lid for holding waste material from people's homes; DUSTBIN *BrE* **2** a container for waste paper etc in a public place; LITTER BIN *BrE*

**trash com·pac·tor** /ˈ· ·ˌ··/ *n* [C] *AmE* a machine that presses waste material together into a very small mass

**trashed** /træʃt/ *adj AmE spoken* **1** very drunk: *We went out and got trashed last night.* **2** completely destroyed: *We need a new map – this one's trashed.*

**trash·y** /ˈtræʃi/ *adj* of extremely bad quality: *trashy novels* —**trashiness** *n* [U]

**trau·ma** /ˈtrɔːmə, ˈtraʊmə‖ˈtraʊmə, ˈtrɒː-/ *n* **1** [C] a very unpleasant and upsetting experience: *the trauma of an attack or rape* **2** [U] a mental state of extreme shock caused by a very frightening or unpleasant experience: *compensation for the emotional trauma he had suffered since childhood* **3** [C,U] *technical* injury: *the hospital's trauma unit*

**trau·mat·ic** /trɔːˈmætɪk‖trɒː-/ *adj* a traumatic experience is so shocking and upsetting that it affects you for a long time: *The death of his son was the most traumatic event in Stan's life.* —**traumatically** /-kli/ *adv*

**trau·ma·tized** also **-ised** *BrE* /ˈtrɔːmətaɪzd,ˈtraʊ-‖ˈtraʊ-, ˈtrɒː-/ *adj* so shocked by something that you are unable to forget it or to continue your life as normal: *totally traumatized by his war experiences*

**trav·ail** /ˈtræveɪl/ *n* [U] *old use* **1** also **travails** [plural] very tiring work **2 in travail** a woman who is in travail is feeling the pain of giving birth

**trav·el¹** /ˈtrævəl/ *v* **travelled, travelling** *BrE*, **trav-** S2
**eled, travelling** *AmE* W2
**1** ▶ **JOURNEY** ◀ **a)** [I] to go from one place to another, or to several places, especially to distant places: *If I had a lot of money I'd travel.* | *They're travelling down from Edinburgh on Monday.* | **travel by train/car etc** *We travelled by train across Eastern Europe.* | **travel widely** (=go to many different places) | **travel around** (=go to different places over a period of time) *I met Tim while I was travelling around.* | **travel light** (=without taking many bags) **b) travel the world/country** to go to most parts of the world or most parts of a particular country
**2 well-travelled/widely travelled** having travelled to many different countries
**3** ▶ **DISTANCE** ◀ [I,T] to go a particular distance or at a particular speed: *The train was travelling at 100 mph.* | *They travelled 200 miles on the first day.*
**4** ▶ **FOOD/WINE** ◀ **travel well** to remain in good condition when taken long distances
**5** ▶ **LIGHT/SOUND** ◀ [I] to move at a particular speed or in a particular direction: *Light travels faster than sound.*
**6** ▶ **FOR BUSINESS** ◀ [I] to go from place to place to sell and take orders for your company's products: [+ **for**] *My wife travels for a London firm.*
**7** ▶ **MOVE QUICKLY** ◀ [I] *informal* to go very fast: *That motorbike was really travelling.*

**8 ▶ NEWS ◀** [I] to be passed quickly from one place to another: *News travels fast.*
**9 ▶ SPORT ◀** [I] *technical* to run while you are holding the ball in BASKETBALL

**USAGE NOTE: TRAVEL**

WORD CHOICE: **travel (*n,v*), sb's travels, journey, trip, voyage, flight**

**Travel** [U] is only used for the general activity of moving from place to place: *He came home after years of foreign travel.* The *-ing* form of the verb **travel** is also used widely with a similar meaning: *I do a bit of travelling abroad* (NOT *travel(s)*).| *travel/travelling expenses|air travel/travelling by air*

If someone moves from place to place over a period of time, you talk about **their travels**: *Did you go to Rome during your travels?|He's on his travels again.*

A particular time spent and distance covered when you go somewhere is a **journey**, especially if it is long or travelled regularly: *I get tired of the journey to work every day.|The journey to Darjeeling was awful — I was sick all the way* (NOT *travel*).

A journey to a place and back that is not made regularly, and is perhaps short, is a **trip**. *This is my first trip abroad.|The kids are going on a trip to the castle.|How long does the trip take?* (*travel* would not be used in any of these).

A journey by sea or in space is a **voyage**, and by plane a **flight**. You **take** a **flight** or **trip** and **make** or **go** on a **voyage** or **journey** (but NOT *a travel*).

GRAMMAR

**Travel** (*v*) is not often used transitively except when you are talking about: *travelling the country/the world.* Otherwise it is usually intransitive and a preposition is used with the place involved: *He travels a lot/all over the world.|We travelled to Paris/in India/ through many foreign countries* (NOT *travelled many countries*).

S2 W2 **travel²** *n* [U] **1** the act or activity of travelling: *Snow has disrupted travel in many parts of the country.* **2 travels** [plural] journeys, especially to places that are a long way away: *Tell us more about your travels.*|**be off on your travels** *informal* (=be travelling for pleasure) *Are you off on your travels again this summer?*

**travel a·gen·cy** /ˈ·· ˌ···/ *n* [C] an office or company that arranges travel and holidays for people

**travel a·gent** /ˈ·· ˌ··/ *n* [C] someone who owns or works in a travel agency

**trav·el·a·tor** /ˈtrævəleɪtə‖-ər/ *n* [C] another spelling of TRAVOLATOR

**travel bu·reau** /ˈ·· ˌ··/ *n* [C] a TRAVEL AGENCY

**trav·el·ler** *BrE*, **traveler** *AmE* /ˈtrævələ‖-ər/ *n* [C] **1** someone who is on a journey or someone who travels often: *Rail travellers will suffer as a result of fare increases.* **2** *BrE* someone who travels around from place to place in a CARAVAN as a way of life —compare GYPSY

**traveller's cheque** *BrE*, **traveler's check** *AmE* /ˈ··· ˌ·/ *n* [C] a special cheque that can be exchanged for the money of a foreign country

**trav·el·ling** *BrE*, **traveling** *AmE* /ˈtrævəlɪŋ/ *adj* **1 travelling musician/circus etc** a musician etc that goes from place to place in order to work or perform **2 travelling rug/clock etc** a clock etc designed to be used when you are travelling **3 travelling people/folk** travellers (TRAVELLER (2))

**travelling sales·man** *BrE*, **traveling salesman** *AmE* /ˌ··· ˈ··/ *n* [C] someone who goes from place to place, selling their company's products

**trav·el·ogue** also **travelog** *AmE* /ˈtrævəlɒg‖-lɔːg, -lɑːg/ *n* [C] a film or talk that describes travel in a particular country, or a particular person's travels

**travel-sick** /ˈ·· ·/ *adj* feeling ill because you are travelling in a vehicle: *Many children get travel-sick on long journeys.* —**travel sickness** *n* [U]

**tra·verse¹** /ˈtrævɜːs‖trəˈvɜːrs/ *v* [T] *formal* to move across, over, or through something: *They traversed the desert slowly.*

**trav·erse²** /ˈtrævɜːs‖-ɜːrs/ *n* [C] *technical* a sideways movement across a very steep slope in mountain-climbing: *the traverse of the mountain's north face*

**trav·es·ty** /ˈtrævɪ̣sti/ *n* [C] an extremely bad example of something; especially one that is very unfair or morally wrong and has the opposite result to the one it should have: *O'Brien described his trial as a travesty of justice.*

**trav·o·la·tor, travelator** /ˈtrævəleɪtə‖-ər/ *n* [C] *BrE formal* a flat moving band of material on the floor, that people can step onto so that they do not have to walk, especially in airports

**trawl¹** /trɔːl‖trɒːl/ *v* [I,T] **1** [I,T] to search through a lot of documents, lists, etc in order to find out information: [+ **through**] *I'll have to trawl through all my lecture notes again.* **2** to fish by dragging a special wide net behind a boat: *trawling the bay for herring*

**trawl²** *n* [C] **1** an act of searching through a lot of documents, lists etc in order to find something **2** a wide net that is pulled along the bottom of the sea to catch fish **3** a TRAWL LINE

**trawl·er** /ˈtrɔːlə‖ˈtrɒːlər/ *n* [C] a fishing boat that trawls

**traw·ler·man** /ˈtrɔːləmən‖ˈtrɒːlər-/ *n* [C] someone who works on a trawler

**trawl line** /ˈ· ·/ *n* [C] *AmE* a long fishing line to which many smaller lines are fastened

**trays**

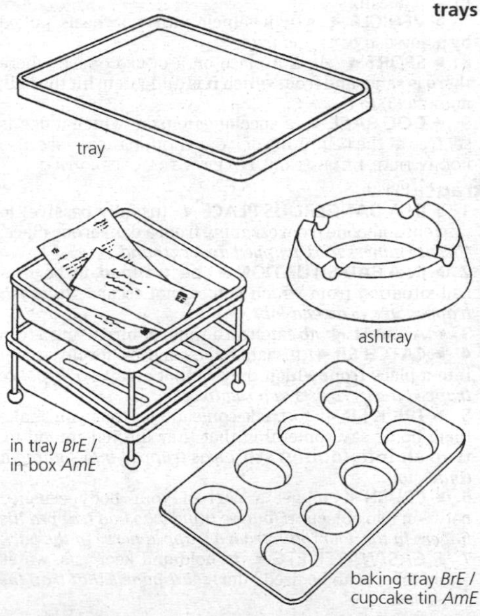


**tray** /treɪ/ *n* [C] **1** a flat piece of plastic, metal, or wood, with raised edges, used for carrying things such as plates, food etc: *The waiter brought drinks on a tray.* **2** *especially BrE* a flat open container with three sides used for holding papers, documents etc on a desk: **in tray** (=for holding documents you still have to deal with)|**out tray** (=for holding documents you have dealt with) —see also BAKING TRAY

**treach·e·rous** /ˈtretʃərəs/ *adj* **1** someone who is treacherous cannot be trusted because they are disloyal and secretly intend to harm you: *a treacherous plot to overthrow the leader* **2** ground or conditions that are treacherous are particularly dangerous because you cannot see the dangers: *There are treacherous currents in the bay.* —**treacherously** *adv*

**treach·e·ry** /ˈtretʃəri/ *n* **1** [U] behaviour that is not loyal to someone who trusts you, especially when this helps their enemies: *the treachery of those who plotted against the king* **2** [C usually plural] a disloyal action against someone who trusts you

**trea·cle** /ˈtriːkəl/ *n* [U] *BrE* **1** a thick sweet black sticky liquid that is obtained from the sugar plant and used in cooking; MOLASSES *AmE* **2** GOLDEN SYRUP: *a treacle tart*

**trea·cly** /ˈtriːkli/ *adj BrE* **1** thick and sticky, like treacle: *treacly black mud* **2** expressing feelings of love or fondness in a way that seems insincere

**tread¹** /tred/ *v past tense* **trod** /trɒd‖trɑːd/ *past participle* **trodden** /ˈtrɒdn‖ˈtrɑːdn/

**1** ▶ **STEP IN/ON** ◀ [I always + adv/prep] *BrE* to put your foot on or in something while you are walking; STEP [+ **in/on**] *Sorry – did I tread on your foot?* | *Be careful not to tread on that broken glass.*

**2** ▶ **CRUSH** ◀ **a)** [T] *BrE* to press or crush something into the floor or ground with your feet; TRACK² (6) *AmE*: **tread sth into/onto/over** *Stop treading mud all over my clean kitchen floor!* | *Bits of the broken vase got trodden into the carpet.* **b) tread grapes** to crush GRAPES with your feet in order to produce the juice from which wine is made

**3 tread carefully/warily/cautiously etc** to be very careful about what you say or do in a difficult situation: *We can't risk the talks breaking down – we'll have to tread carefully.*

**4 tread a path** *formal* to take a particular action or series of actions: *Anyone who makes such serious allegations is treading a very dangerous path.*

**5 tread water a)** to stay floating upright in deep water by moving your legs as if you were riding a bicycle **b)** to make no progress in a particular situation, especially because you are waiting for something to happen

**6 tread the boards** *humorous* to work as an actor

**7** ▶ **WALK** ◀ [I always + adv/prep,T] *literary especially BrE* to walk: *David trod wearily along behind the others.* —see also **step/tread on sb's toes** (TOE¹ (3))

**tread²** *n* **1** [C,U] the pattern of lines on the part of a tyre that touches the road **2** [C] the part of a stair that you put your foot on **3** [singular] the particular sound that someone makes when they walk: *I could hear our father's heavy tread outside the door.*

**trea·dle** /ˈtredl/ *n* [C] a flat piece of metal or wood that you move with your foot to turn a wheel in a machine

**tread·mill** /ˈtredˌmɪl/ *n* **1** [singular] work or a way of life that seems very boring because you always have to do the same things **2** [C] a MILL¹ (1) worked in the past by prisoners treading on steps fixed to a very large wheel

**trea·son** /ˈtriːzən/ *n* [U] the crime of being disloyal to your country or its government, especially by helping its enemies or trying to remove the government using violence: [+ **against**] *an act of treason against the state* | **commit treason** (=do something that is treason) | **high treason** (=treason of the worst kind)

**trea·son·a·ble** /ˈtriːzənəbəl/ also **trea·son·ous** /-zənəs/ *adj* a treasonable offence can be punished as treason: *a treasonable act against the head of state*

**trea·sure¹** /ˈtreʒə‖-ər/ *n* **1** [U] a store of gold, silver, jewels etc: *buried treasure* | **treasure chest** (=box containing treasure) **2** [C] a very valuable and important object such as a painting or ancient document: *the art treasures of the Louvre* **3** *informal old-fashioned* [singular] someone who is very useful or important to you: *Our housekeeper is a real treasure.*

**treasure²** *v* [T] to treat something as being very special, important, or valuable: *Thank you; I shall treasure this gift always.* | *treasured memories of happier days*

**treasure hunt** /ˈ·· ˌ·/ *n* [C] a game in which you have to find something that has been hidden by answering questions that are left in different places

**trea·sur·er** /ˈtreʒərə‖-ər/ *n* [C] someone who is in charge of the money for an organization, club, political party etc

**treasure trove** /ˈtreʒə trəʊv‖-ʒər troʊv/ *n* [U] *BrE law* valuable objects, coins etc that are found where they have been hidden or buried, which are not claimed by anyone

**trea·su·ry** /ˈtreʒəri/ *n* **1 the Treasury** a government department that controls the money that the country collects and spends: *a senior civil servant at the Treasury* **2** [C] a place where money or valuable objects are kept in a castle, church, PALACE etc

**treat¹** /triːt/ *v* [T] S2 W1

**1** ▶ **BEHAVE TOWARDS SB** ◀ [always + adv/prep] to behave towards someone in a particular way: **treat sb like/as** *She treats me like one of the family.* | *Even though they were much younger, we treated them as equals.* | **badly treated/well treated** *The prisoners were well treated by their guards.* | **treat sb with respect/contempt/kindness etc** *Despite her seniority, Margot was never treated with much respect.* | **treat sb like dirt/a dog** (=treat someone unkindly and without respect)

**2** ▶ **DEAL WITH STH** ◀ [always + adv/prep] to deal with or discuss something in a particular way: **treat sth as** *Please treat this information as completely confidential.* | **treat sth favourably/seriously/carefully etc** *Any complaint about safety standards must be treated very seriously.*

**3** ▶ **MEDICAL** ◀ to try to cure an illness or injury by using drugs, hospital care, operations etc: *Nowadays malaria can be treated with drugs.*

**4** ▶ **REGARD** ◀ [always + adv/prep] to regard an idea, subject, statement etc in a particular way: **treat sth as** *She treats everything I say as some kind of joke.*

**5** ▶ **BUY STH FOR SB** ◀ to buy something special for someone that you know they will enjoy: **treat sb to sth** *We treated Mom to lunch at the Savoy.* | **treat yourself to sth** (=buy yourself something special) *I treated myself to a new dress.*

**6** ▶ **PROTECT/CLEAN** ◀ to put a special substance on something or use a chemical process in order to protect, clean, or preserve it: *It is possible to treat sewage so that it can be used as fertilizer.* —see also TRICK OR TREAT

**treat with** sth *phr v* [T] *formal* to try to reach an official agreement with someone

**treat of** sth *phr v* [T] *formal* if a book, article etc treats of something, it is about that subject

**treat²** *n* **1** [C] something special that you give someone or do for them because you know they will enjoy it: *Steven took his son to the zoo as a birthday treat.* **2** [singular] an unexpected event that gives you a lot of pleasure: *I really miss everyone, and getting a letter from home is a big treat.* **3 my treat** *spoken* used to tell someone that you will pay for something such as a meal for them: *Let's go out for dinner – my treat this time.* **4 go down a treat** *BrE informal* if something goes down a treat, people like it very much: *Brightly coloured building blocks always go down a treat with toddlers.* **5 look/work a treat** *BrE informal* to look very good or work very well: *The sports ground looked a treat, with all the flags flying.*

**treat·a·ble** /ˈtriːtəbəl/ *adj* a treatable illness or injury can be helped with drugs or an operation

**trea·tise** /ˈtriːtɪ̈s, -tɪ̈z/ *n* [C + **on**] a serious book or article about a particular subject: *a treatise on medical ethics*

**treat·ment** /ˈtriːtmənt/ *n* S3

**1** ▶ **MEDICAL** ◀ [C,U] a method that is intended to cure an injury or illness: [+ **for**] *The best treatment for a cold is to rest and drink lots of fluids.* | **give sb treatment** *She was given emergency treatment by paramedics.* | **receive treatment** *receiving treatment for skin cancer* | **respond to treatment** (=get better when you are treated)

**2** ▶ **BEHAVIOUR TOWARDS SB** ◀ [U] a particular way of behaving towards someone or of dealing with them: [+ **of**] *Henchard's cruel treatment of his wife*| **special/preferential treatment** (=when one person is treated better than another) *The two young princes were not singled out for special treatment at school.*| **give sb the full treatment** *informal especially BrE* (=treat someone in a very special way and give them a lot of attention)

**3 ▶ OF A SUBJECT ◀** [C,U] a particular way of dealing with or talking about a subject: *I didn't think the film gave the issue serious enough treatment.*

**4 ▶ CLEAN/PROTECT ◀** [U] a process by which something is cleaned, protected etc: *the treatment of waste oils and solvents*

W2 **treat·y** /ˈtriːti/ *n* **1** [C] a formal agreement between two or more countries or governments: *the Treaty of Versailles*| **peace treaty** *A peace treaty was signed between the US and Vietnam.* **2** [U] *technical* formal agreement between two people, especially to buy a house

**treb·le¹** /ˈtrebəl/ *predeterminer* three times as big, as much, or as many as something else: *They sold the house for treble the amount they paid for it.*

**treble²** *v* [I,T] to become three times as big in amount, size, or number, or to make something increase in this way: *Their profits have trebled in the last two years.*

**treble³** *n* **1** [U] the upper half of the whole range of musical notes —compare BASS¹ (3) **2** [C] a boy with a high singing voice —**treble** *adj, adv: a clear treble voice*

**treble clef** /ˌ·· ˈ·/ *n* [C] *technical* a sign (𝄞) at the beginning of a line of written music which shows that the note written on the bottom line of the STAVE¹ (1) is an E above MIDDLE C —see picture at MUSIC

S1 W1 **tree** /triː/ *n* [C] **1** a very tall plant that has a wooden trunk, branches, and leaves, and lives for many years: *We planted an orange tree in the backyard.*| *Children love to climb trees.* **2** a drawing with many branching lines that shows how several things are related to each other —see also FAMILY TREE **3 be out of your tree** *informal* to not be thinking in a sensible or practical way —see also CHRISTMAS TREE **top of the tree** (TOP¹ (3)), **it doesn't grow on trees** (GROW (9)), **be up a gum tree** (GUM TREE (2))

**tree fern** /ˈ· ·/ *n* [C] a large tropical FERN

**tree·house** /ˈtriːhaʊs/ *n* [C] a wooden structure built in the branches of a tree for children to play in

**tree·less** /ˈtriːləs/ *adj* a treeless area has no trees in it

**tree line** /ˈ· ·/ *n* [singular] the TIMBERLINE

**tree-lined** /ˈ· ·/ *adj* a tree-lined road has trees on both sides

**tree sur·ge·ry** /ˈ· ˌ···/ *n* [U] the treatment of damaged trees, especially by cutting off branches

**tree·top** /ˈtriːtɒp‖-tɑːp/ *n* [C usually plural] the branches at the top of a tree: *looking out over the treetops*

**tree-trunk** /ˈ· ·/ *n* [C] the thick central part of a tree

**tre·foil** /ˈtriːfɔɪl, ˈtrefɔɪl/ *n* [C] **1** a type of small plant that has leaves which divide into three parts **2** a pattern in the shape of these leaves

**trek¹** /trek/ *v* **trekked, trekking** [I always + adv/prep] to make a long and difficult journey, especially on foot: [**+in/across etc**] *trekking in the Himalayas*

**trek²** *n* [C] **1** a long and difficult journey especially on foot: *the long trek to the Pole* **2** *informal* a distance that seems long when you walk it: *I'm afraid it's a bit of a trek to the station.*

**trel·lis** /ˈtreləs/ *n* [C] a frame made of long narrow pieces of wood that cross each other, used to support climbing plants

**trem·ble** /ˈtrembəl/ *v* [I] **1** to shake slightly in a way that you cannot control, especially because you are upset or frightened: *His lip started to tremble and then he started to cry.*| **tremble with anger/fear etc** *I stood there trembling with humiliation and rage.* **2** to shake slightly: *The whole house trembled as the train went by.* **3** if your voice trembles, it sounds nervous and unsteady **4** to be worried or frightened about something: **I tremble to think what/how** *I tremble to think what will happen when she finds out.* —**tremble** *n* [C] —**trembly** *adj*

**tre·men·dous** /trɪˈmendəs/ *adj* **1** very big, fast, powerful etc: *a tremendous explosion*| *I learned a tremendous amount in a short time.* **2** excellent: *She's got a tremendous voice, hasn't she?* S2

**trem·o·lo** /ˈtreməloʊ‖-loʊ/ *n* [C] rapidly repeated musical notes

**trem·or** /ˈtremə‖-ər/ *n* [C] **1** a small EARTHQUAKE in which the ground shakes slightly: *an earth tremor* **2** a slight shaking movement that you cannot control, especially because you are ill, weak, or upset: *He was left with a slight tremor in his hand after his stroke.*

**trem·u·lous** /ˈtremjələs/ *adj literary* shaking slightly, especially because you are nervous: *a tremulous voice* —**tremulously** *adv*

**trench** /trentʃ/ *n* [C] **1** a long narrow hole dug into the surface of the ground: *Plant your roses in a trench filled with manure.* **2** a deep trench dug in the ground as a protection for soldiers: *the trenches of World War I* **3** *technical* a long narrow valley in the ground beneath the sea: *the Marianas Trench in the Pacific Ocean*

**tren·chant** /ˈtrentʃənt/ *adj* expressed very strongly, effectively, and directly without worrying about offending people: *a trenchant attack on the principle of 'political correctness'* —**trenchantly** *adv* —**trenchancy** *n* [U]

**trench coat** /ˈ· ·/ *n* [C] a military style raincoat with a belt

**trench·er** /ˈtrentʃə‖-ər/ *n* [C] a wooden plate used in former times for serving food

**trench war·fare** /ˌ· ˈ··/ *n* [U] a method of fighting in which soldiers from opposing armies are in TRENCHES facing each other

**trend** /trend/ *n* [C] **1** a general tendency in the way a situation is changing or developing: [**+ in**] *recent trends in education*| [**+ towards**] *The current trend is towards more part-time employment.*| **reverse a trend** (=make a trend go in the opposite direction) *These figures reverse the trend of spending increases.*| **underlying trend** (=the trend over a long period of time) **2 set the trend** to start doing something that other people copy: *'Rambo' set the trend for a whole wave of violent action movies.* S2 W2

**trend·set·ter** /ˈtrendˌsetə‖-ər/ *n* [C] someone who starts a new fashion or makes it popular —**trendsetting** *adj*

**trend·y¹** /ˈtrendi/ *adj* influenced by the most fashionable styles and ideas: *He's a trendy photographer in Santa Monica.* —**trendily** *adv* —**trendiness** *n* [U]

**trendy²** *n* [C] *BrE informal* someone who is trendy because they want other people to think they are very modern: *young trendies with left-wing ideas*

**tre·pan** /trɪˈpæn/ *v* [T] to cut a round piece of bone out of your SKULL (=head) as part of a medical operation

**trep·i·da·tion** /ˌtrepəˈdeɪʃən/ *n* [U] a feeling of anxiety or fear about something that is going to happen: *With some trepidation, I opened the door.*

**tres·pass¹** /ˈtrespəs‖-pəs, -pæs/ *v* [I + **on**] **1** to go onto someone's private land without their permission **2** *old use* to do something wrong; SIN¹ —**trespasser** *n* [C]

**trespass on** sth *phr v* [T] to unfairly use more than you should of someone else's time, help etc, for your own advantage: *It would be trespassing on their hospitality to accept any more from them.*

**trespass²** *n* **1** [C,U] the offence of going onto someone's land without their permission: *prosecute him for trespass* **2** [C] *biblical* something you have done that is morally wrong; SIN

**tress·es** /ˈtresəz/ *n* [plural] *literary* a woman's beautiful long hair

**tres·tle** /ˈtresəl/ *n* [C] *especially BrE* an A-shaped frame used as one of the two supports for a temporary table

**trestle ta·ble** /ˈ·· ˌ··/ *n* [C] *especially BrE* a temporary table made of a long board supported on trestles

**trews** /truːz/ *n* [plural] a pair of trousers, especially with a TARTAN pattern

**trey** /treɪ/ *n* [C] *AmE* a playing card or the side of a DICE with three marks on it: *I have two pairs, treys and sevens.*

**tri-** /traɪ/ *prefix* three; three times: *trilingual* (=speaking three languages) | *triangle* (=a shape with three sides)

**tri·ad** /ˈtraɪæd/ *n* [C] **1** [singular] a Chinese secret criminal group **2** a group of three people or things that are related or similar to each other

S3 W2 **tri·al¹** /ˈtraɪəl/ *n*

**1 ▶ COURT ◀** [C,U] a legal process in which a court of law examines a case to decide whether someone is guilty of a crime: *a murder trial* | *The defendant has a right to a fair trial.* | **stand trial/be on trial (for)** (=be judged in a court of law) *Brady was on trial for assault.* | *a bank employee who is due to stand trial on embezzlement charges* | **come to trial** *formal* (=when a case is brought to a court of law) *By the time the case comes to trial he will have spent a year behind bars.* —see also SHOW TRIAL

**2 ▶ TEST ◀** [C,U] **a)** a process of testing to find out whether something works effectively and is safe: *a new drug that is undergoing clinical trials* **b)** a short period during which you use something or employ someone to find out whether they are satisfactory for a particular purpose or job: **take/have sth on trial** (=test something without having to buy it first) *Take the vacuum cleaner on trial for a week; if you don't like it you pay nothing.* | **trial period** *The security system will be reviewed after a three-month trial period.*

**3 by trial and error** if you do something by trial and error, you test many different methods of doing something in order to find the best: *You'll find out by trial and error which flowers grow best.*

**4 ▶ WORRY/ANNOY ◀ be a trial (to)** to be very worrying or annoying to someone: *My brothers and I were always a real trial to my parents.*

**5 trials and tribulations** difficulties and troubles: *After many trials and tribulations we reached our destination.*

**6 ▶ SPORTS ◀ trials** [plural] *BrE* a sports competition that tests a player's ability

**trial²** *v* [T] to thoroughly test something to see if it works correctly or is effective: *These techniques were trialled by teachers in 300 schools.*

**trial run** /ˌ·· ˈ·/ *n* [C] an occasion when you test a new method or system to see if it works well: *This year is something of a trial run for the new service.*

**trials bike** /ˈ·· ·/ *n* [C] *BrE* a type of MOTORCYCLE that you can ride on very rough ground

**tri·an·gle** /ˈtraɪæŋgəl/ *n* [C] **1** a flat shape with three straight sides and three angles —see picture at SHAPE¹ **2** something that is shaped like a triangle: *a triangle of land* **3** a musical instrument made of metal bent in the shape of a triangle, that you hit to make a ringing sound **4** *AmE* a flat plastic object with three sides that has one angle of 90° and is used for drawing angles; SET-SQUARE *BrE*

**tri·an·gu·lar** /traɪˈæŋgjʊlə‖-ər/ *adj* **1** shaped like a triangle **2** involving three people or teams: *a triangular sporting competition*

**tri·an·gu·la·tion** /traɪˌæŋgjʊˈleɪʃən/ *n* [U] a method of finding your position by measuring the lines and angles of a triangle on a map

**triangulation sta·tion** /·ˌ··ˈ·· ˌ··/ *n* [C] *formal* a TRIG POINT

**tri·ath·lon** /traɪˈæθlən/ *n* [C] a sports competition in which competitors run, swim, and cycle long distances

**trib·al** /ˈtraɪbəl/ *adj* connected with a tribe or tribes: *a tribal dance* | *tribal warfare*

**trib·al·is·m** /ˈtraɪbəl-ɪzəm/ *n* [U] **1** the state of being organized into tribes **2** behaviour and attitudes that are based on strong loyalty to your tribe

**tribe** /traɪb/ *n* [C] **1** a social group consisting of people of the same race who have the same beliefs, customs, language etc, and usually live in one particular area ruled by a chief: *the tribes living in the Amazonian jungle* —see RACE¹ (USAGE) **2** a group of related animals or plants: *the cat tribe* **3** *humorous* a large family: *We were only expecting Jack and his wife, but the whole tribe turned up.*

**tribes·man** /ˈtraɪbzmən/ *n* [C] a man who is a member of a tribe

**tribes·wom·an** /ˈtraɪbzˌwʊmən/ *n* [C] a woman who is a member of a tribe

**trib·u·la·tion** /ˌtrɪbjʊˈleɪʃən/ *n* [C,U] *formal* serious trouble or a serious problem: *the tribulations of his personal life* —see also **trials and tribulations** (TRIAL¹ (5))

**tri·bu·nal** /traɪˈbjuːnl/ *n* [C] a type of court that is given official authority to deal with a particular situation or problem: *The case of your redundancy will be heard by an independent tribunal.*

**trib·une** /ˈtrɪbjuːn/ *n* [C] an official in ancient Rome who was elected by the ordinary people to protect their rights

**trib·u·ta·ry¹** /ˈtrɪbjʊtəri‖-teri/ *n* [C] a stream or river that flows into a larger river

**tributary²** *adj formal* having a duty to pay TRIBUTE (3)

**trib·ute** /ˈtrɪbjuːt/ *n* **1** something that you say, do, or give in order to express your respect or admiration for someone: **pay tribute to** (=praise and thank someone publicly) *I'd like to pay tribute to the party workers for all their hard work.* **2 be a tribute to** to be a clear sign of the good qualities that someone or something has: *It was a tribute to her teaching methods that so many children passed the test.* **3** [C,U] a payment of goods or money by one ruler or country to another more powerful one **4 floral tribute** flowers sent to a funeral

**trice** /traɪs/ *n* **in a trice** *BrE literary* very quickly

**tri·ceps** /ˈtraɪseps/ *n* [C] the large muscle at the back of your upper arm

**trick¹** /trɪk/ *n* [C] S3

**1 ▶ DECEIVING SB ◀** something you do in order to deceive someone: *He pretended to be ill, but it was just a trick.* | *a clever trick to cheat the authorities*

**2 dirty/rotten/mean trick** an unkind or unfair thing to do: *He didn't turn up? What a rotten trick!*

**3 ▶ JOKE ◀** something you do to surprise someone and to make other people laugh: *I'm getting tired of your silly tricks.* | **play a trick on sb** *The girls were always playing tricks on their teacher.*

**4 do the trick** *spoken* if something does the trick it solves a problem or provides what is needed to get a good result: *A bit more flour should do the trick.*

**5 ▶ CLEVER METHOD ◀** a clever way of doing something that works very well: *The trick is to bend your knees as you catch the ball.* | **tricks of the trade** (=clever methods used in a particular job) *a salesman who knew all the tricks of the trade*

**6 use every trick in the book** to use every clever or dishonest method that you know to achieve what you want: *Ed used every trick in the book to get that contract.*

**7 sb can teach/show you a trick or two** *informal* used to say that someone knows a lot more than you

**8 be up to your (old) tricks** *informal* to be doing the same dishonest things that you have often done before: *Watch out for Joe, he's up to his old tricks again.*

**9 ▶ MAGIC ◀** a skilful set of actions that seem like magic, done to entertain people: *We spent the next hour performing card tricks.*

**10 a trick of the light** a strange effect of the light that changes the way things look or makes you see something that is not really there: *For a moment I thought you were Duncan, but it was just a trick of the light.*

**11 ▶ CARDS ◀** the cards played or won in one part of a game of cards: *He won the first three tricks easily.*

**12 ▶ HABIT ◀ have a trick of doing sth** to have a habit of using a particular expression or of moving your face or body in a particular way: *She had this trick of raising her eyebrows at the end of a question.*

**13 never miss a trick** *informal* to always know exactly what is happening even if it does not concern you: *Dave's found out. He never misses a trick, does he?*

**14 how's tricks?** *spoken* used to greet someone in a friendly way: *Hello Bill! How's tricks?*
**15 turn a trick** *AmE slang* to have sex with someone for money —see also CONFIDENCE TRICK, HAT-TRICK

**trick**[2] *v* **1** [T] to deceive someone in order to get something from them or to make them do something: *He knew he'd been tricked, but it was too late.* | **trick sb into doing sth** *Clients were tricked into believing their money was being invested.* | **trick sb out of** *The corporation was tricked out of $20 million.* **2 be tricked out with/in** *literary* to be decorated with something: *a hat tricked out with ribbons*

**trick**[3] *adj* **1 trick photography** photography that cleverly changes the way things look **2 trick question** a question which seems easy to answer but has a hidden difficulty **3 trick knee/ankle etc** *AmE* a joint that is weak and can suddenly cause you problems

**trick·e·ry** /'trɪkəri/ *n* [U] the use of tricks to deceive or cheat people

**trick·le**[1] /'trɪkəl/ *v* [I always + adv/prep] **1** if liquid trickles somewhere, it flows slowly in drops or in a thin stream: [+ **down/into/out**] *The tears trickled down her cheeks.* **2** if people, vehicles, goods etc trickle somewhere, they move there slowly in small groups or amounts: [+ **in/into/away**] *The first few fans started to trickle into the stadium.*

**trickle**[2] *n* [singular] **1** a thin slow flow of liquid: *The water in the stream had been reduced to a trickle.* **2** a movement of people, vehicles, goods etc into a place in very small numbers or amounts: *Recent legislation has reduced immigration to a trickle.*

**trickle charg·er** /'·· ,··/ *n* [C] a piece of equipment used to put electricity into a car BATTERY (1)

**trickle-down ef·fect** /,·· '· ,·/ *n* [singular] a belief that additional wealth gained by the richest people in society will have a good economic effect on the lives of everyone

**trick or treat** /,· · '·/ *v* **go trick or treating** if children go trick or treating, they go from house to house on HALLOWE'EN saying 'trick or treat' in order to get small presents

**trick·ster** /'trɪkstə‖-ər/ *n* [C] someone who deceives or cheats people: **confidence trickster** *a slick, fast-talking confidence trickster*

S3 **trick·y** /'trɪki/ *adj* **1** a tricky job is difficult to do because it is complicated and needs great care: *Finding the electrical fault was really tricky.* **2** a tricky situation is difficult to deal with and is full of problems: *I find myself in a very tricky situation.* **3** a tricky person is likely to deceive you; CRAFTY —**trickiness** *n* [U] —**trickily** *adv*

**tri·col·our** *BrE,* **tricolor** *AmE* /'trɪkələ‖'traɪ,kʌlər/ *n* [C] a flag with three equal bands of different colours, especially the national flags of France or Ireland

**tri·cy·cle** /'traɪsɪkəl/ *n* [C] a bicycle with three wheels, especially for young children

**tri·dent** /'traɪdənt/ *n* [C] **1** a weapon with three points that looks like a large fork **2 Trident** a type of NUCLEAR weapon sent from a SUBMARINE[1]

**tried**[1] /traɪd/ the past tense and past participle of TRY[1]

**tried**[2] *adj* **tried and tested/trusted** a tried and tested method has been used successfully many times: *tried and tested safety procedures* | *a tried and trusted formula*

**tri·en·ni·al** /traɪ'eniəl/ *adj* happening every three years

**tri·er** /'traɪə‖-ər/ *n* [C] *informal* someone who always makes a great effort, even if they do not often succeed

**trif·fid** /'trɪfɪ̣d/ *n* [C] an imaginary plant that grows very large, moves about, and attacks people

**tri·fle**[1] /'traɪfəl/ *n* **1 a trifle** *formal* slightly; rather: *You seem a trifle nervous.* **2** [C] *old-fashioned* something unimportant or not valuable: *I don't know why you waste your money on such trifles.* **3** [C,U] a cold sweet dish that consists of layers of cake, fruit, JELLY (1), CUSTARD (1), and cream

**trifle**[2] *v*
**trifle with** sb/sth *phr v* [T] to treat someone or something without proper respect or seriousness: *The boss is not a man to be trifled with.*

**tri·fling** /'traɪflɪŋ/ *adj* unimportant or of little value: *a trifling matter* | *a trifling sum*

**trig·ger**[1] /'trɪgə‖-ər/ *n* [C] **1** the part of a gun that you press with your finger to fire it | **pull/squeeze the trigger** *He aimed carefully and squeezed the trigger.* —see picture at GUN **2 be the trigger (for)** to be the thing that quickly causes a serious problem: *Even a minor incident could be the trigger for renewed fighting.*

**trigger**[2] also **trigger off** *v* [T] to make something happen very quickly, especially a series of violent events: *The assassination triggered off a wave of rioting.* | **trigger a feeling/memory** (=make you suddenly feel or remember something) *The song triggered many happy memories.*

**trigger-hap·py** /'·· ,··/ *adj informal* much too willing to shoot at people: *He nearly got shot by some trigger-happy cop.*

**trig·o·nom·e·try** /,trɪgə'nɒmɪ̣tri‖-'nɑː-/ *n* [U] the part of mathematics that is concerned with the relationship between the angles and sides of TRIANGLES —**trigonometrical** /,trɪgənə'metrɪkəl/ *adj*

**trig point** /'trɪg pɔɪnt/ *n* [C] *BrE* a point often marked by a stone block on top of a hill, used for measuring your position on a map

**trike** /traɪk/ *n* [C] *informal* a TRICYCLE

**tril·by** /'trɪlbi/ *n* [C] *especially BrE* a man's soft FELT[2] hat

**tri·lin·gual** /,traɪ'lɪŋgwəl◂/ *adj* able to speak or use three languages

**trill**[1] /trɪl/ *v* [I,T] **1** to sing with repeated short high notes: *birds trilling in the trees* **2** to say something in a pleasant high cheerful voice: *"Have a nice time, darling," she trilled.*

**trill**[2] *n* [C] **1** *technical* a musical sound made by quickly going up and down several times between two notes a SEMITONE apart **2** a sound like this, especially one made by a bird **3** *technical* a speech sound produced by quickly moving the end of your tongue against the top part of your mouth when you say 'r'

**tril·lion** /'trɪljən/ *number, quantifier* **1** one million million; 1,000,000,000,000 **2** also **trillions** *informal* a very large number of something

**tri·lo·bite** /'traɪləbaɪt/ *n* [C] a small simple sea creature that lived millions of years ago and is now a FOSSIL (1)

**tril·o·gy** /'trɪlədʒi/ *n* [C] a group of three connected plays, books, films etc about the same characters: *the second part of a trilogy*

**trim**[1] /trɪm/ **trimmed, trimming** *v* [T]
**1** ▶ **CUT** ◀ to make something look neater by cutting small pieces off it: *Your hair needs trimming.* | *Can you trim the hedge?*
**2** ▶ **REDUCE** ◀ to remove parts of a plan to reduce its cost: *We need to trim the Defence budget by a further £500m.*
**3** ▶ **DECORATE** ◀ [usually passive] to decorate the edges of clothes by adding a piece of different material: **trim sth with** *a dress trimmed with lace*
**4** ▶ **SAIL** ◀ to move the sails of a boat into a position that makes the boat go faster
**5 trim your sails** *informal* to spend less money
**trim** sth ↔ **off** *phr v* [T] to cut small pieces off something so that it looks neater: *Trim off the ragged edges.*

**trim**[2] *adj* **1** thin, attractive, and healthy looking: *I play tennis regularly to keep trim.* | *a trim figure* **2** neat and well looked after: *a trim suburban garden*

**trim**[3] *n* **1** [singular] an act of cutting something to make it look neater: *My beard needs a trim.* **2 be in (good) trim** *informal* to be in good physical condition: *The team is in good trim for the match.* **3** [U, singular] additional decoration on a car, piece of clothing etc: *1983 Ford Escort, metallic black with white trim* **4** [U] the degree to which an aircraft is level in relation to the horizon

**tri·ma·ran** /ˈtraɪməræn/ *n* [C] a sailing boat that has three separate but connected parts that float on the water

**tri·mes·ter** /trɪˈmestə‖traɪˈmestər/ *n* [C] **1** *AmE* one of three periods of equal length that the year is divided into in some schools; TERM[1] (9) *BrE* **2** one of the three-month periods of a PREGNANCY

**trim·mer** /ˈtrɪmə‖-ər/ *n* [C] a machine for cutting the edges of HEDGES, LAWNS etc

**trim·mings** /ˈtrɪmɪŋz/ *n* [plural] **1** pieces of material used to decorate clothes: *the fur trimmings on a hat* **2** the small pieces that are left after you have cut something larger: *hedge trimmings* **3 all the trimmings** *BrE informal* all the other types of food that are traditionally served with the main dish of a meal: *Christmas dinner with all the trimmings*

**trin·i·ty** /ˈtrɪnəti/ *n* **1 the Trinity** the union of Father, Son, and Holy Spirit in one God according to the Christian religion **2** [C] *literary* a group of three people or things

**trin·ket** /ˈtrɪŋkət/ *n* [C] a piece of jewellery or a small pretty object that is not worth much money: *a shop selling little trinkets and souvenirs*

**tri·o** /ˈtriːəʊ‖ˈtriːoʊ/ *n plural* **trios** [C] **1** a group of three people or three connected things: **[+ of]** *He was met by a trio of smiling executives.* **2** a group of three singers or musicians who perform together **3** a piece of music for three performers —compare DUET, QUARTET

S2 W2 **trip**[1] /trɪp/ *n* **1** [C] a journey to a place and back again: *Did you have a good trip?* | **make a trip** *I couldn't carry everything at once, so I had to make several trips.* | **go on/take a trip** *We're thinking of taking a trip to the mountains.* | **coach/boat trip** *a boat trip up the Thames* | **business/school/skiing etc** *a business trip to Japan* | **day trip** (=a pleasure trip done in one day) —see TRAVEL (USAGE) **2** [C] *slang* the experiences someone has while their mind is affected by a drug such as LSD: *a bad trip* **3** [C] an act of falling as a result of hitting something with your foot **4** [singular] *AmE slang* a person or experience that is amusing and very different from normal: *She's a real trip.* —see also EGO TRIP, ROUND TRIP

**trip**[2] *v*

**1** ▶ **FALL** ◀ also **trip up** [I] to hit something with your foot while you are walking or running so that you fall or almost fall: *I didn't push him, he tripped.* | **[+ over]** *Pick up that box or someone will trip over it.*

**2** ▶ **MAKE SB FALL** ◀ also **trip sb up** [T] to make someone fall by putting your foot in front of them when they are moving: *Baggio was clearly tripped inside the penalty area.*

**3** ▶ **WALK/DANCE** ◀ [I always + adv/prep] *literary* to walk or run with quick light steps as if you are dancing: **trip along/over/down etc** *a little girl tripping along the lane*

**4 trip off the tongue** to be easy to say or pronounce: *Monofluorophosphate! It doesn't exactly trip off the tongue, does it?*

**5 trip a switch/wire** to accidentally make an electrical system operate by moving part of it: *Alarm bells were ringing so I must have tripped a switch on my way in.*

**6** ▶ **DRUG** ◀ also **trip out** [I] *slang* to experience the effects of an illegal drug such as LSD

**7 trip the light fantastic** *humorous* to dance

**trip up** *phr v* **1** [T **trip** sb **up**] to trick someone into making a mistake: *The questions look simple, but they're designed to trip you up.* **2** [T **trip** sb **up**] to make someone fall by putting your foot in front of them when they are walking **3** [I] to hit something with your foot while you are walking so that you fall **4** [I] to make a mistake: **[+ over]** *It's easy to trip up over some of the regulations.*

**tri·par·tite** /traɪˈpɑːtaɪt‖-ˈpɑːr-/ *adj formal* **1 tripartite agreement/alliance etc** involving three groups or nations **2** having three parts: *a tripartite structure*

**tripe** /traɪp/ *n* [U] **1** the stomach of a cow or pig used for food **2** *informal* something that has been said or written which is stupid or untrue: *Why do you read such tripe?*

**trip·le**[1] /ˈtrɪpəl/ *adj* [only before noun] **1** having three parts or involving three members: *a triple alliance* **2 triple circle/line/coil etc** a set of three circles etc **3 triple murder/killing etc** the murder etc of three people

**triple**[2] *v* [I,T] to become three times as much or as many, or to make something do this: *The company has tripled in size in the last twenty years.* | **triple sth** *We should triple our profits next year.*

**triple**[3] *n* [C] a hit of the ball in BASEBALL that allows the BATTER[2] (3) to get to the third BASE[1] (8)

**triple jump** /ˈ·· ·/ *n* [singular] an ATHLETICS event in which you try to jump as far as you can by jumping with one foot, then onto the other foot, and finally with both feet

**trip·let** /ˈtrɪplət/ *n* [C] one of three children born at the same time to the same mother —compare COUPLET

**trip·lex** /ˈtrɪpleks‖ˈtrɪ-, ˈtraɪ-/ *n* [C] *AmE* an apartment which has rooms on three floors of a building

**Triplex** *n* [U] *BrE trademark* a special type of safety glass used in car windows

**trip·li·cate** /ˈtrɪplɪkət/ *n* **in triplicate** if a document is written in triplicate, there are three copies of it

**tri·pod** /ˈtraɪpɒd‖-pɑːd/ *n* [C] a support with three legs, used for a camera, TELESCOPE[1] etc —see picture at LABORATORY

**trip·per** /ˈtrɪpə‖-ər/ *n* [C] *BrE old-fashioned* someone visiting a place on a short pleasure trip for one day: **day tripper** *The beach was crowded with day trippers.*

**trip·tych** /ˈtrɪptɪk/ *n* [C] *technical* a picture, especially a religious one, painted on three pieces of wood that are joined together

**trip·wire** /ˈtrɪpˌwaɪə‖-waɪr/ *n* [C] a wire stretched across the ground as part of a trap

**tri·reme** /ˈtraɪriːm/ *n* [C] an ancient warship with three rows of OARS on each side

**tri·sect** /traɪˈsekt/ *v* [T] *technical* to divide a line, angle etc into three equal parts

**tri·state** /ˈtraɪsteɪt/ *adj AmE* related to a group of three states in the US

**trite** /traɪt/ *adj* a trite remark, idea etc has been used so often that it seems boring and not sincere: *a dull speech full of trite clichés* —**triteness** *n* [U]

**tri·umph**[1] /ˈtraɪəmf/ *n* **1** [C] an important victory or success, especially after a difficult struggle: *Winning the championship represents a personal triumph for the team's manager.* | **[+ over]** *a brave man's triumph over adversity* **2** a feeling of pleasure and satisfaction that you get from victory or success: *yells of triumph* **3** [C] a very successful example of something: *The gallery is a triumph of design.*

**triumph**[2] *v* [I] to gain a victory or success, especially after a difficult struggle: **[+ over]** *We know that in the end we shall triumph over evil.*

**tri·um·phal** /traɪˈʌmfəl/ *adj* [only before noun] done or made in order to celebrate a triumph: *a triumphal procession* | *a triumphal arch*

**tri·um·phal·is·m** /traɪˈʌmfəlɪzəm/ *n* [U] the expression of being too proud about a victory and too pleased about your opponent's defeat

**tri·um·phant** /traɪˈʌmfənt/ *adj* **1** having gained a victory or success: *the triumphant army* **2** expressing pleasure and pride because of your victory or success —**triumphantly** *adv*: *"I've done it!" he shouted triumphantly.*

**tri·um·vir·ate** /traɪˈʌmvərət/ *n* [C] *formal* a group of three very powerful people who share control over something

**triv·et** /ˈtrɪvət/ *n* [C] **1** a metal support, placed under a hot pot or dish to protect the surface of a table **2** a support for holding a pot over a fire

**triv·i·a** /ˈtrɪviə/ *n* [plural] **1** unimportant or useless details: *I'm not going to waste my time on such trivia.* **2** detailed facts about past events, famous people, sport etc used in QUIZ games

**triv·i·al** /ˈtrɪviəl/ *adj* **1** unimportant or of little value: *I'm sorry to bother you with what must seem a trivial problem.* | *a trivial sum* **2** ordinary: *trivial everyday duties* —**trivially** *adv*

**triv·i·al·i·ty** /ˌtrɪviˈæləti/ *n* **1** [U] the fact of being not at all important or serious **2** [C] something that is very unimportant: *Don't waste your time on trivialities.*

**triv·i·al·ize** also **-ise** *BrE* /ˈtrɪviəlaɪz/ *v* [T] to make an important subject seem less important than it really is: *The article trivializes the whole issue of equal rights.* —**trivialization** /ˌtrɪviəlaɪˈzeɪʃən‖-lə-/ *n* [U]

**Trivial Pur·suit** /ˌ··· ·ˈ·/ *n* [U] *trademark* a game in which people have to answer questions about many different subjects

**tro·chee** /ˈtrəʊkiː‖ˈtroʊ-/ *n* [C] *technical* a unit in poetry consisting of one strong or long beat followed by one weak or short beat, as in 'father'

**trod** /trɒd‖trɑːd/ the past tense of TREAD[1]

**trod·den** /ˈtrɒdn‖ˈtrɑːdn/ the past participle of TREAD[1]

**trog·lo·dyte** /ˈtrɒglədaɪt‖ˈtrɑːg-/ *n* [C] someone living in a CAVE[1], especially in very ancient times

**troi·ka** /ˈtrɔɪkə/ *n* [C] **1** a Russian carriage pulled by three horses side by side **2** a group of three people working together, especially in government

**Tro·jan** /ˈtrəʊdʒən‖ˈtroʊ-/ *n* **work like a Trojan** to work very hard

**troll** /trəʊl‖troʊl/ *n* [C] an imaginary creature in ancient Scandinavian stories, like a very large or very small ugly person

**trol·ley** /ˈtrɒli‖ˈtrɑːli/ *n* [C] **1** *especially BrE* a large metal basket or frame on wheels that you push along, used for carrying bags, shopping etc; CART[1] (2) *AmE*: *a supermarket trolley* **2** *BrE* a small table on very small wheels from which food and drinks are served: *a tea trolley;* CART[1] (3) *AmE* **3** *AmE* an electric vehicle for carrying passengers which moves along the street on metal tracks; TRAM *BrE* **4** a TROLLEYBUS **5** the part of an electric vehicle that connects it to the electric wires above **6 be off your trolley** *BrE humorous* to be crazy

**trol·ley·bus** /ˈtrɒlibʌs‖ˈtrɑː-/ *n* [C] a bus that gets its power from electric wires above the street

**trol·lop** /ˈtrɒləp‖ˈtrɑː-/ *n* [C] **1** *old-fashioned* an offensive word for a very untidy woman **2** an offensive word for a sexually immoral woman

**trom·bone** /trɒmˈbəʊn‖trɑːmˈboʊn/ *n* [C] a large musical instrument made of metal which you blow into and which has a long tube that you slide in and out to change the notes

**trom·bon·ist** /trɒmˈbəʊnɪst‖trɑːmˈboʊn-/ *n* [C] a musician who plays a trombone

S3 W2 **troop[1]** /truːp/ *n* **1 troops** [plural] soldiers, especially in organized groups: *Troops were sent in to stop the riots.* **2 troop movements/concentrations** movements or gatherings of troops **3** [C] a group of soldiers, especially on horses or in tanks (TANK[1] (3)) **4** [C] a group of people or wild animals, especially when they are moving **5** [C] a group of about 32 SCOUTS led by an adult —compare TROUPE

**troop[2]** *v* [I always + adv/prep] to move together in a group: [+ **into/along/out etc**] *We all trooped into the meeting.*

**troop car·ri·er** /ˈ· ˌ···/ *n* [C] a ship , aircraft, or vehicle used for carrying soldiers

**troop·er** /ˈtruːpə‖-ər/ *n* **1** [C] the lowest ranking soldier in the part of the army that uses tanks (TANK[1] (3)) or horses **2 swear like a trooper** to swear a lot **3** [C] a member of a state police force in the US

**troop·ship** /ˈtruːpˌʃɪp/ *n* [C] a ship used for carrying a large number of soldiers

**trope** /trəʊp‖troʊp/ *n* [C] *technical* a FIGURE OF SPEECH

**tro·phy** /ˈtrəʊfi‖ˈtroʊ-/ *n* [C] **1** a prize for winning a race or other competition, especially a silver cup or a PLAQUE (2): *the Football League Trophy* **2** something that you keep to show something successful that you have done, especially in war or hunting: *A lion's head was among the trophies of his African trip.*

**trop·ic** /ˈtrɒpɪk‖ˈtrɑː-/ *n* **1** [C] one of the two imaginary lines around the world, either the Tropic of Cancer which is $23\frac{1}{2}°$ north of the EQUATOR, or the Tropic of Capricorn which is $23\frac{1}{2}°$ south of the EQUATOR —see picture at EARTH[1] **2 the tropics** the hottest part of the world, which is between the two tropics

**trop·i·cal** /ˈtrɒpɪkəl‖ˈtrɑː-/ *adj* **1** coming from or existing in the hottest parts of the world: *the tropical rain forests* | **tropical medicine** (=study of diseases that are common in hot countries) **2** weather that is tropical is very hot and wet: *a steamy tropical night*

**trot[1]** /trɒt‖trɑːt/ *v* **trotted, trotting 1** [I] if a horse trots, it moves fairly quickly with each front leg moving at the same time as the opposite back leg **2** [I always + adv/prep] **a)** to run fairly slowly, taking short steps: *William trotted along happily beside his parents.* **b)** *spoken* to walk or go somewhere: *I'm just trotting down to the shops.*

**trot** sth ↔ **out** *phr v* [T] *informal* to give opinions, excuses, reasons etc that you have used too often to seem sincere: *Steve trotted out the same old excuses.*

**trot[2]** *n* **1** [singular] the movement of a horse at trotting (TROT[1]) speed: *We set off at a brisk trot.* **2** [C] a ride on a horse at trotting (TROT[1]) speed: *I'm going for a trot down the lane.* **3** [singular] a fairly slow way of running in which you take short steps: **break into a trot** (=increase your speed to a trot) **4 on the trot** *BrE informal* **a)** one after the other: *Sally's won three races on the trot.* **b)** busy doing something: *I've been on the trot all day.* **5** [C] *AmE* a book of translations or answers used by students; a CRIB[1] (4b) **6 the trots** *humorous* DIARRHOEA

**troth** /trəʊθ‖trɒːθ, trɑːθ, troʊθ/ *n old use* **1 by my troth** used when expressing an opinion strongly **2 in troth** truly; INDEED —see also **plight your troth** (PLIGHT[2])

**Trot·sky·ite** /ˈtrɒtskiaɪt‖ˈtrɑːt-/ also **Trot·sky·ist** /-skiɪst/ *n* [C] someone who believes in the political ideas of Leon Trotsky, especially that the working class should take control of the state —**Trotskyite** *adj*

**trot·ter** /ˈtrɒtə‖ˈtrɑːtər/ *n* [C] a pig's foot, cooked and used as food

**trou·ba·dour** /ˈtruːbədɔː, -dʊə‖-dɔːr, -dʊr/ *n* [C] a type of singer and poet who travelled around the PALACES and castles of Southern Europe in the 12th and 13th centuries

**troub·le[1]** /ˈtrʌbəl/ *n* S1 W2

**1 ▶ PROBLEMS ◀** [C,U] problems that make something difficult, spoil your plans, make you worry etc: *Every time there's trouble, I have to go along and sort it out.* | [+ **with**] *They're having a lot of trouble with the new baby.* | **trouble doing sth** *I never have any trouble getting to sleep.* | **what's the trouble?** *spoken* (=used to ask someone what is causing a particular problem) | **the trouble is** *spoken* (=used when explaining why something is impossible or difficult) *I'd like to give you the money now – the trouble is, I don't get paid till Friday.* | **sb's troubles** (=all the problems that you have in your life) *Because I'm a good listener people often come to me with their troubles.* | **teething troubles** (=small problems at the beginning) *After a few teething troubles, the new system worked perfectly.*

**2 ▶ FAULT ◀ the trouble with** *spoken* used when explaining what is unsatisfactory about something or someone: *The trouble with you is that you don't listen.* | *That's the trouble with lasagne – it takes so long to make.*

**3 ▶ HEALTH ◀** [U] a problem that you have with your health: [+ **with**] *He sometimes has trouble with his breathing.* | **heart/stomach/skin etc trouble** *Irene's at home today with stomach trouble.*

**4 ▶ MACHINE/SYSTEM ◀** [U] something that is

wrong with a machine, vehicle, or system: *engine trouble* | [+ **with**] *trouble with the central heating system*

**5 ▶ BAD SITUATION ◀** [U] a difficult or dangerous situation: **be in trouble** *an SOS from a ship in trouble* | **get/run into trouble** *The company ran into trouble when it tried to expand too quickly.* | **in serious/deep/big trouble** *If you connect the wrong wires to the power supply, you'll be in deep trouble.*

**6 be asking for trouble** *informal* to take risks or do something stupid that is likely to cause problems: *You're just asking for trouble if you don't get those brakes fixed.*

**7 ▶ EFFORT ◀** [U] an amount of effort and time that is needed to do something, especially when it is inconvenient for you to do it: **put sb to a lot of trouble** (=make someone use a lot of time and effort) *I'm sorry, I didn't mean to put you to so much trouble.* | **take the trouble to do sth** (=make a special effort to do something) *The teacher took the trouble to learn all our names on the first day.* | **go to/take a lot of trouble** (=use a lot of time and effort doing something carefully) | **save sb the trouble (of doing sth)** (=make it unnecessary for sb to do sth) *I thought if I phoned you, it would save you the trouble of writing a letter.* | **be more trouble than it's worth** *spoken* (=when something takes too much time and effort to do) *I find that making my own clothes is more trouble than it's worth.*

**8 no trouble/it's no trouble** *spoken* used to say that you are very willing to do something because it is not inconvenient for you

**9 be no trouble** *informal* if someone is no trouble, they do not annoy or worry you: *You can leave the children with me. They're no trouble.*

**10 ▶ ARGUMENT/VIOLENCE ◀** also **troubles** [plural] a situation in which people quarrel or fight with each other: *The trouble started when the police tried to break up the demonstration.* | *the recent troubles in Northern Ireland* | **cause/make trouble** (=deliberately cause trouble) *Don't give him another drink or he'll start causing trouble.*

**11 ▶ BLAME ◀** [U] a situation in which someone in authority is angry with you or is likely to punish you: *There'll be trouble when your father finds out what you've done.* | **be in trouble (with)** *My brother's in trouble with the police again.* | **get into trouble** *Don't copy my work or we'll both get into trouble.*

**12 get sb into trouble a)** to put someone into a situation in which they are likely to be punished: *Diane told a lie rather than get her friend into trouble.* **b)** *old-fashioned* to make a woman PREGNANT

Frequencies of the noun **trouble** in spoken and written English.

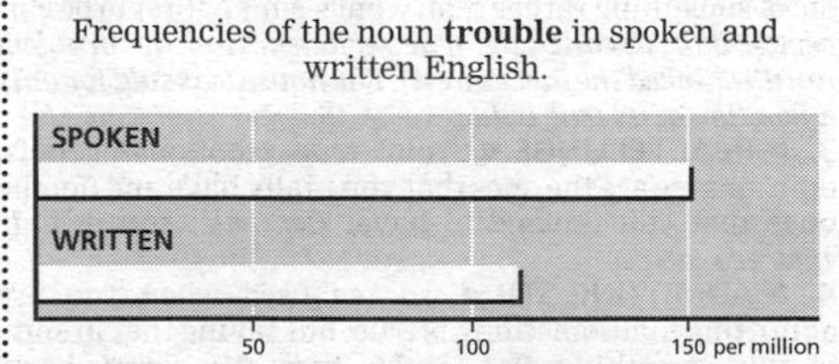


Based on the British National Corpus and the Longman Lancaster Corpus

This graph shows that the noun **trouble** is more common in spoken English than in written English. This is because it is used in some common spoken phrases. These are marked '*spoken*' in the entry.

**USAGE NOTE: TROUBLE**

WORD CHOICE. **trouble** (*n,v*), **problem, troubles, troubled, worried, bother**

**Trouble** [usually U] is usually used to talk about the worry etc that people have in some situations (especially when there is some specific difficulty): *Her back is giving her a lot of trouble* (=pain). | *Do you have much trouble with the kids? (= do they behave badly?)* | *Thanks for your trouble* (=effort).

When you speak of a **problem** [C], you are thinking more of a person, thing, or situation that is difficult (either for things or people): *Acid rain is an increasing environmental problem.* | *my biggest problem* (NOT *my best trouble*)

In many situations a **problem** is a source of **trouble**, so there are some contexts where both words may be used: *What's the trouble/problem?* | *I had a bit of trouble/a bit of a problem* | *the trouble/problem with my car*. However sometimes there is a clear difference in meaning: *There's trouble in the bar* (perhaps means people are fighting). But *There's a problem in the bar* (perhaps means there is no beer left).

In some contexts only **problem** can be used. You can *solve* problems but not trouble(s). Something may *pose* a problem but not trouble. In spoken English **trouble** is frequent only in certain phrases: *The (only) trouble is/was...* | *This/that is/was the trouble.* | *....Just don't cause any trouble ...* | *...have (no) trouble with...* | *be in (real/a lot of) trouble* | *...get into trouble...*

**Problem** is more common in technical or formal contexts, **trouble** in informal or conversational ones: *the nuclear problem* | *the problem with BCCI is more common* But you are more likely to say: *tummy trouble* | *The trouble with Paul is that he has no sense of humour*.

**Troubles** (plural) is used with a much more specific meaning either for all the things that worry a person, or all the difficulties of an organization or country: *money troubles* | *the troubles besetting the government* | *the troubles in Northern Ireland.* But you would say: *world/traffic problems* (NOT *troubles*)

**Trouble** (*v*) and **troubled** (*adj*) are not very common in ordinary spoken English: *I was worried about my work* (in writing you might perhaps use *troubled.*) | *Don't bother me while I'm watching TV.* | *My car had a problem* (NOT *was troubled.*)

GRAMMAR

Usually someone *has trouble* (NOT *troubles*) doing something (NOT *has trouble to do it*).

You may be *in trouble* (NOT *in a trouble/troubles*).

**trouble**[2] *v* **1** [T] if a problem troubles you, it makes you feel worried: *You must talk to your daughter and find out what's troubling her.* **2** [T] *formal* to ask someone to do something for you when it is inconvenient for them: *I promise not to trouble you again.* **3 may I trouble you?/sorry to trouble you** *spoken formal* used when politely asking someone to do something for you or give you something: *Sorry to trouble you, but could you tell me the way to the station, please.* | *May I trouble you for the salt?* | *Can I trouble you to close the door.* **4 not trouble to do sth** to not do something because it needs too much effort: *They never troubled to ask me what I would like.* **5** [T] if a medical problem troubles you, it causes you pain or makes you suffer: *Roy has been troubled by a stomach ulcer for months.*

**troub·led** /ˈtrʌbəld/ *adj* **1** feeling worried or anxious: *Benson looked troubled when he heard the news.* —see TROUBLE (USAGE) **2** having many problems: *These are troubled times for the coal industry.*

**trouble-free** /ˌ. ˈ.◂/ *adj* causing no difficulty or worry: *Since we changed our car we've had two years of trouble-free motoring.*

**troub·le·mak·er** /ˈtrʌbəlˌmeɪkə‖-ər/ *n* [C] someone who deliberately causes problems, especially by complaining or making people argue with each other: *a handful of trouble makers who are damaging the club's reputation*

**troub·le·shoot·er** /ˈtrʌbəlˌʃuːtə‖-ər/ *n* [C] someone who is employed by a company to deal with serious problems

**troub·le·some** /ˈtrʌbəlsəm/ *adj* causing you trouble or anxiety, over a long period of time: *a troublesome child*

**trouble spot** /ˈ·· ˌ·/ *n* [C] a place where trouble often happens, especially war or violence: *Extra police were drafted in to patrol late-night trouble spots.*

**trough** /trɒf‖trɒːf/ *n* [C] **1** a long narrow open container that holds water or food for animals **2** the hollow area between two waves in the sea or between two hills **3** a short period of low activity, low prices etc in something that is continuously measured over a longer period: *the peaks and troughs of economic cycles* **4** *technical* a long area of fairly low pressure on a weather map between two areas of high pressure

**trounce** /traʊns/ *v* [T] to defeat someone completely: *We were trounced 13-0.*

**troupe** /truːp/ *n* [C] a group of singers, actors, dancers etc who work together

**troup·er** /ˈtruːpə‖-ər/ *n* [C] *informal* someone who has a lot of experience of work in the entertainment business

**trouser press** /ˈ·· ·/ *n* [C] a piece of equipment that you can keep your trousers in to keep them flat and smooth

S 2 **trou·sers** /ˈtraʊzəz‖-ərz/ *n* [plural] a piece of clothing that covers the lower half of your body, with a separate part fitting over each leg: *I need a new pair of trousers for work.* | *short trousers* —**trouser** *adj* [only before noun] | *The tickets are in my trouser-pocket.* —see also **wear the trousers** (WEAR¹ (8)), **catch sb with their trousers down** (CATCH¹ (3)) —see picture on page 840

This graph shows how common the nouns **trousers** and **pants** are in British and American English.

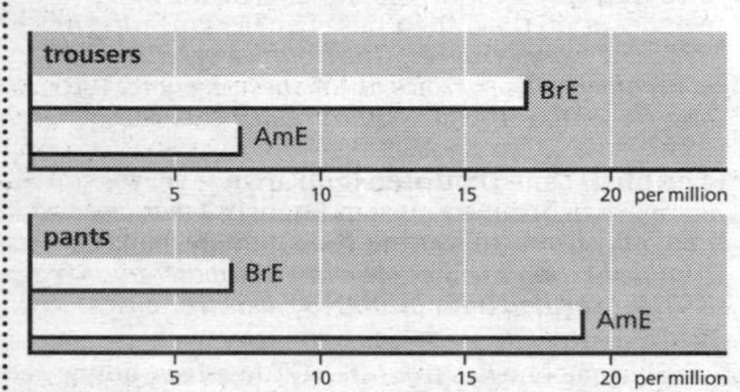


Based on the British National Corpus and the Longman Lancaster Corpus

In British English **trousers** is used to mean a piece of clothing that covers the lower half of your body, with a separate part fitting over each leg. In American English **pants** is used for this meaning. **Pants** is commonly used in British English to mean underwear, but Americans use the word **underwear**.

**trouser suit** /ˈ·· ·/ *n* [C] *BrE* a woman's suit consisting of a JACKET and matching trousers; PANTSUIT *AmE*

**trous·seau** /ˈtruːsəʊ, truːˈsəʊ‖-soʊ/ *n* [C] *old-fashioned* the personal possessions that a woman brings with her when she marries

**trout** /traʊt/ *n* **1** *plural* **trout** [C,U] a common river-fish, often used for food, or the flesh of this fish **2 old trout** *BrE spoken* an unpleasant or annoying old person, especially a woman

**trove** /trəʊv‖troʊv/ *n* —see TREASURE TROVE

**trow·el** /ˈtraʊəl/ *n* [C] **1** a garden tool like a very small SPADE **2** a small tool with a flat blade, used for spreading CEMENT on bricks etc

**troy weight** /ˈtrɔɪ weɪt/ *n* [U] a British weights system, used in former times for weighing gold, silver etc

**tru·an·cy** /ˈtruːənsi/ *n* [U] the practice of deliberately staying away from school without permission

**tru·ant** /ˈtruːənt/ *n* [C] **1** a student who stays away from school without permission **2 play truant** *BrE* to stay away from school without permission —**truant** *v* [I]

**truce** /truːs/ *n* [C] an agreement between enemies to stop fighting or arguing for a short time, or the period for which this is arranged: **call a truce** (=announce a truce) *The People's Liberation Army called a truce for the elections.*

**truck¹** /trʌk/ *n* **1** [C] a large road vehicle used to carry goods; LORRY *BrE*: *The trucks were loaded at the docks.* S 3 W 3
**2** [C] *BrE* a railway vehicle that is part of a train and carries goods; CAR¹ (3) *AmE*: *coal trucks* **3** [C] a simple piece of equipment on wheels used to move heavy objects **4 have no truck with sb** to avoid speaking or doing business with someone

**truck²** *v especially AmE* **1** [T] to take something somewhere by truck **2** [I always + adv/prep] *informal* to go, move, or travel: **truck along/down etc** *We were trucking on down to Jack's place.* **3 get trucking** *informal* to leave

**truck·er** /ˈtrʌkə‖-ər/ *n* [C] *AmE* a truck driver

**truck farm** /ˈ· ·/ *n* [C] *AmE* an area for growing vegetables and fruit for sale; MARKET GARDEN *BrE*

**truck·ing** /ˈtrʌkɪŋ/ *n AmE* **1** [U] the business of taking goods from place to place by road **2 keep on trucking** *spoken* used to encourage someone to continue what they are doing

**truck·le** /ˈtrʌkəl/ *v*
**truckle to** sb/sth *phr v* [T] *old-fashioned* to do what someone tells you in a way that seems weak

**truckle bed** /ˈ·· ˌ·/ *n* [C] *BrE* a low bed on small wheels, that you can slide under a larger bed; TRUNDLE BED *AmE*

**truck·load** /ˈtrʌkləʊd‖-loʊd/ *n* [C] the amount that fills a truck

**truck stop** /ˈ· ·/ *n* [C] *AmE* a cheap place to eat on a main road, used mainly by TRUCK¹ (1) drivers; TRANSPORT CAFE *BrE*

**truc·u·lent** /ˈtrʌkjɡ̊lənt/ *adj* bad-tempered and always willing to argue with people: *Most people resented his truculent manner.* —**truculently** *adv* —**truculence** *n* [U]

**trudge¹** /trʌdʒ/ *v* [I always + adv/prep] to walk with slow, heavy steps, especially because you are tired: **trudge home/along/through etc** *The old man trudged home through the snow.* —see picture on page 1262

**trudge²** *n* [singular] a long tiring walk

**true¹** /truː/ *adj* S 1
**1 ▶ NOT FALSE ◀** based on facts and not imagined or invented: *No, honestly, it's a true story.* | **it is true (that)** *Is it true that you're leaving?* | **be true of sb** *Babies need a lot of sleep and this is particularly true of newborns.* —opposite FALSE W 1
**2 the true value/seriousness/nature etc** the real value etc of something rather than what seems at first to be correct: *I didn't realize the true seriousness of the problem until I checked the fuel gauge.* | *The house was sold for only a fraction of its true value.*
**3 ▶ REAL FEELINGS ◀** your true emotions, beliefs, opinions etc are the ones that you really have and not the ones that you pretend to have: *Her true motives only emerged later.*
**4 ▶ ADMITTING STH ◀** *spoken* used when you are admitting that something is true, but saying that in spite of this something else is also true: *"He's very hard-working." "True, but I still don't think he's the right man for the job."*
**5 true love/courage/freedom etc** the type of love etc that is strong and has all the qualities that it should have: *True courage includes the recognition of your own fear.*
**6 come true** if wishes, dreams etc come true, they happen in the way that someone has said or hoped that they would: *By 1975 the worst economic predictions had come true.* —see also **a dream come true** (DREAM¹ (5))
**7 ▶ LOYAL ◀** faithful and loyal to someone, whatever happens: [+ **to**] *Throughout the whole ordeal, she remained true to her husband.*
**8 true friend/believer/sportsman etc** someone who behaves in the way that a good friend etc should behave: *You find out who your true friends are at times like this.*

**9 true to form/type** used to say that someone is behaving in the bad way that you expect them to: *True to form, Henry turned up late.*
**10 true to life** a book, play, description etc that is true to life seems very real and natural; REALISTIC
**11 true to your word** doing exactly what you have promised to do: *True to his word, John arrived promptly at 2 o'clock.*
**12 be true to your principles/beliefs etc** to behave according to the principles that you claim to believe in: *He remains true to the traditions of his profession.*
**13 only (too true)** used to say that you know something is true, especially when you do not like it: *It is only too true that people are judged by their accents.*
**14 true/mammal/fish/planet etc** having all the qualities of a particular class of object, animal, plant etc according to an exact description of it: *Despite its appearance, the whale is a true mammal.*
**15 ▶ STRAIGHT/LEVEL ◀** [not before noun] *technical* fitted, placed, or formed in a way that is perfectly flat, straight, correct etc: *If the door's not true, it won't close properly.*
**16 sb's aim is true** if your aim is true, you hit the thing that you were throwing or shooting at
**17 (there's) many a true word spoken in jest** used to say that when people are joking they sometimes say things that are true and important —see also **be too good to be true** (GOOD[1] (23)), **show yourself in your true colours** (COLOUR[1] (11)), **not ring true** (RING[2] (5)), TRULY, TRUTH

**true²** *adv* **1** in an exact straight line: *The arrow flew straight and true to its target.* **2** *old use* truthfully **3** *technical* if a type of animal breeds true, the young animals are exactly like their parents

**true³** *n* **out of true** not completely straight, level, or balanced: *The walls are slightly out of true.*

**true-blue** /ˌ· ˈ·◂/ *adj* **1** *BrE informal* believing completely in the ideas of the British CONSERVATIVE PARTY: *a true-blue Tory* **2** *AmE* completely loyal to a person or idea: *a true-blue friend*

**true-heart·ed** /ˌ· ˈ··◂/ *adj literary* faithful; loyal

**true-life** /ˌ· ˈ· ◂/ *adj* [only before noun] based on real facts and not invented: *a true-life adventure*

**true·love** /ˈtruːlʌv/ *n* [C] *poetic* the person that you love

**true north** /ˌ· ˈ·/ *n* [U] north as it appears on maps, calculated as a line through the centre of the earth rather than by using the MAGNETIC POLE

**truf·fle** /ˈtrʌfəl/ *n* [C] **1** a black or light brown FUNGUS that grows underground, and is a very expensive food **2** a soft creamy sweet made with chocolate: *a rum truffle*

**tru·is·m** /ˈtruːɪzəm/ *n* [C] a statement that is clearly true, so that there is no need to say it: *His speech was just a collection of clichés and truisms.*

W3 **tru·ly** /ˈtruːli/ *adv* [+ adj/adv] **1** used to emphasize that the way you are describing something is really true: *There was a truly beautiful view from the bedroom.* | *a truly amazing story* | *Truly, this is an honour.* **2** *formal* sincerely: *I am truly sorry.* **3** in an exact or correct way: *A spider cannot truly be described as an insect.* **4 well and truly** *especially spoken* completely; totally: *We were well and truly trapped.* **5 really and truly** *spoken* used to emphasize that something is definitely true: *I couldn't believe we were really and truly going at last.* **6 yours truly a)** used at the end of a business letter, before the signature —see also **yours faithfully, yours sincerely** (YOURS (3)) **b)** *informal humorous* used to mean yourself: *So, yours truly was left to clean up.*

**trump¹** /trʌmp/ *n* [C] **1** a card from the SUIT (=one of the four types of cards in a set) that has been chosen to have a higher value than the other suits in a particular game **2 trumps** [plural] also **trump** *AmE* the SUIT[1] (3) chosen to have a higher value than the other suits in a particular game: *Hearts are trumps.* **3 come up trumps/turn up trumps** to provide what is needed, especially unexpectedly and at the last moment: *Paul came up trumps and managed to borrow a car for us.*

**trump²** *v* [T] to play a trump that beats someone else's card in a game
**trump** sth ↔ **up** *phr v* [T] to use false information to make someone seem guilty of a crime: *They had trumped the whole thing up to get rid of him.* —see also TRUMPED-UP

**trumped-up** /ˌ· ˈ·◂/ *adj* **trumped-up charges/evidence etc** false information that has been used to make someone seem guilty of a crime: *Dissidents were routinely arrested on trumped-up charges.*

**trump·e·ry** /ˈtrʌmpəri/ *adj old use* not valuable

**trum·pet¹** /ˈtrʌmpɪt/ *n* **1** [C] a musical instrument that you blow into, which consists of a curved metal tube that is wide at the end with three buttons to change the note **2** [singular] the loud noise that an ELEPHANT makes —see also **blow your own trumpet** (BLOW[1] (21))

**trumpet²** *v* **1** [T] to tell everyone about something that you are proud of, in an annoying way: *She's always trumpeting her son's achievements.* **2** [I] if an ELEPHANT trumpets, it makes a loud noise

**trun·cate** /trʌŋˈkeɪt‖ˈtrʌŋkeɪt/ *v* [T] *formal* to make something shorter —**truncation** /trʌŋˈkeɪʃən/ *n* [U]

**trun·cat·ed** /trʌŋˈkeɪtɪd‖ˈtrʌŋkeɪtɪd/ *adj* made shorter than before, or shorter than usual

**trun·cheon** /ˈtrʌnʃən/ *n* [C] *especially BrE* a short thick stick that police officers carry as a weapon —compare NIGHTSTICK *AmE*

**trun·dle** /ˈtrʌndl/ *v* [I always + adv/prep, T] to move slowly along on wheels, or to make something do this by pushing or pulling it: *Two large wagons trundled by.*

**trundle bed** /ˈ·· ˌ·/ *n* [C] *AmE* a low bed on wheels that you can slide under a larger bed; TRUCKLE BED *BrE*

**trunk** /trʌŋk/ *n* [C] **1** the thick central wooden stem of a tree **2** *AmE* the part at the back of a car where you can put bags, tools etc; BOOT[1] (3) *BrE* **3** the very long nose of an ELEPHANT **4 trunks** [plural] a piece of clothing like very short trousers, worn by men for swimming **5** *technical* the main part of your body, not including your head, arms, or legs **6** a very large box made of wood or metal, in which clothes, books etc are stored or packed for travel —see picture at SUITCASE

**trunk call** /ˈ· ·/ *n* [C] *BrE old-fashioned* a telephone call between places that are a long distance apart

**trunk road** /ˈ· ·/ *n* [C] *BrE* a main road used for travelling long distances

**truss¹** /trʌs/ *v* [T] **1** also **truss up** to tie someone's arms, legs etc very firmly with rope so that they cannot move: *They trussed up their victim and left him for dead.* **2** to prepare a chicken, duck etc for cooking by tying its legs and wings into position

**truss²** *n* [C] **1** a special belt worn to support a HERNIA (=medical problem that affects the muscles below your stomach) **2** a frame supporting a roof or bridge

**trust¹** /trʌst/ *n* S1 W2
**1 ▶ BELIEF ◀** [U] a strong belief in the honesty, goodness etc of someone or something: *an agreement made on the basis of mutual trust* | **put your trust in** *You shouldn't put your trust in a man like that.* | **betray sb's trust** (=do something that shows someone should not have trusted you)
**2 take sth on trust** to believe that something is true without having any proof: *I just had to take it on trust that he would deliver the money.*
**3 ▶ FINANCIAL ARRANGEMENT ◀** [U] an arrangement by which someone has legal control of your money or property, especially until you are old enough to use it: **hold sth in trust** *The money your father left you will be held in trust until you are 21.*
**4 ▶ ORGANIZATION ◀** [C usually singular] an organization or group that has control over money that will be used to help someone else: *a charitable trust* —see also TRUST FUND

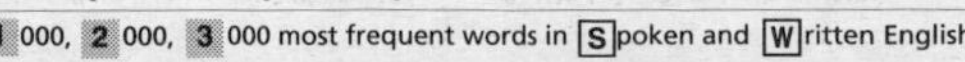

**5 a position of trust** a job or position in which you have been given the responsibility of making important decisions
**6 ► COMPANIES ◄** [C] *especially AmE* a group of companies that illegally work together to reduce competition and control prices: *anti-trust laws* —see also **breach of trust** (BREACH[1] (2)), UNIT TRUST

S2 **trust**[2] *v*
W3 **1 ► HONEST PEOPLE ◄** [T] to believe that someone is honest and will not harm you, cheat you etc: *I trusted Max, so I lent him the money.* | **trust sb to do sth** *Can they be trusted to look after the house?* | **trust sb completely/implicitly** *You must trust her implicitly and do everything she says.* | **not trust sb an inch** *BrE informal* (=not trust someone at all) —opposite DISTRUST
**2 ► DEPEND ON FACTS ◄** [T] to be sure that something is true or will happen: *I wouldn't trust any information I get from them.* | **trust sth to do sth** *You can't trust the trains to run on time.*
**3 trust sb's judgement** to think that someone is likely to make the right decisions
**4 trust you/him/them etc (to do sth)!** *spoken* used to say that someone has behaved in a bad way that is typical of them: *Trust you to be late!*
**5 I trust (that)** *spoken formal* used to say politely that you hope something is true: *I trust that your family is well.*
**6 trust sb with sth** to believe that someone would be careful with something valuable or dangerous if you gave it to them: *Would you trust that kid with a hammer?* —see also TRUSTING **tried and tested/trusted** (TRIED)
**trust in** sth/sb *phr v* [T] *formal* to believe in someone or something: *We trust in God.*
**trust to** sth *phr v* [T] **trust to luck/chance/fate etc** to hope that luck etc will help you, usually because there is nothing else you can do

S2 **trust·ee** /ˌtrʌsˈtiː◂/ *n* [C] **1** someone who has control of money or property that is in a TRUST[2] (3) for someone else **2** a member of a group that controls the money of a company, college, or other organization

**trust·ee·ship** /trʌsˈtiːʃɪp/ *n* **1** [C,U] the job of being a trustee **2** [U] government of an area by a country or countries that are given authority by the United Nations

**trust·ful** /ˈtrʌstfəl/ *adj* ready to trust other people —**trustfully** *adv* —**trustfulness** *n* [U]

**trust fund** /ˈ· ·/ *n* [C] money belonging to someone that is controlled for them by a trustee

**trust·ing** /ˈtrʌstɪŋ/ *adj* willing to believe that other people are good and honest: *Sara's trusting nature led her to believe Tony's lies.*

**trust·wor·thy** /ˈtrʌstˌwɜːði‖-ɜːr-/ *adj* someone who is trustworthy can be trusted and depended upon; DEPENDABLE —**trustworthiness** *n* [U]

**trust·y** /ˈtrʌsti/ *adj* [only before noun] *old use or humorous* a trusty weapon, vehicle, animal etc is one that you have had for a long time and can depend on: *his trusty sword* | *My trusty old car will get us home.*

S1 **truth** /truːθ/ *n*
W2 **1 ► TRUE FACTS ◄ the truth** the true facts about something, as opposed to what is untrue, imagined, or guessed: [+ **about**] *We never found out the truth about Mike's past.* | **tell the truth** *How can we be sure that she's telling the truth?* | **be the truth** *It's the truth. She really did it.* | **get to the truth** (=find out what really happened) *Only after several days of questioning did the police finally get to the truth.* | **the truth of the matter** *Reforms were promised, but the truth of the matter is that nothing has changed.*
**2 ► BEING TRUE ◄** [U] the state or quality of being true: *Do you think there's any truth in these rumours?* | **a grain of truth** (=a small amount of truth) *There wasn't a grain of truth in what he said.*
**3 ► IMPORTANT IDEAS ◄** [C usually plural] *formal* an important fact or idea that is accepted as being true: *the fundamental truths about mankind*
**4 to tell (you) the truth** *spoken* used when giving your personal opinion or admitting something: *Well, to tell you the truth, I've never really liked her.*
**5 if (the) truth be known** used when telling someone the real facts about a situation, or your real opinion: *If the truth be known, that was the main reason why we left.*
**6 nothing could be further from the truth** used to say that something is definitely not true
**7 the gospel truth** if you think something is the gospel truth, you believe completely that it is true: *I thought everything my teachers told me was the gospel truth.*
**8 in (all) truth** *old-fashioned* in fact; really: *In truth, I did not mind whether we went or not.*
**9 the truth will out** *old-fashioned* used to say that even if you try to stop people from knowing something, they will find out in the end —see also HALF-TRUTH, **home truths** (HOME[3] (6)), **the moment of truth** (MOMENT (11))

**truth drug** /ˈ· ·/ *BrE*, **truth serum** /ˈ· ˌ··/ *AmE* *n* [C,U] a drug that is supposed to make people tell the truth

**truth·ful** /ˈtruːθfəl/ *adj* **1** someone who is truthful does not usually tell lies: *a truthful child* **2** a truthful statement gives the true facts about something —**truthfully** *adv* —**truthfulness** *n* [U]

**try**[1] /traɪ/ *v* S1
**1 ► ATTEMPT ◄** [I,T] to attempt to do or get something: **try to do sth** *Don't shout at him; he's only trying to help.* | **try sth** *Roberts tried a shot at goal.* | **try and do sth** *You must try and control your temper.* | **try** *Tim may not be good at math but at least he tries.* | **try doing sth** (=try to do something) *I'm going to try cooking a paella this evening.* | **try hard/desperately** (=make a lot of effort to do something) *Sharon tried hard to keep a straight face.* | **try your best/hardest** (=make as much effort as possible to do something) *I'll try my best to finish the work for this evening.* | **try and try** (=keep making an effort to do something) *He tried and tried to make her stay but she refused.* | **try as you might** (=used to say that someone is making a lot of effort to do something) *Try as I might, I could not overcome my fear of heights.* | **it wasn't for lack/want of trying** (=used to say that if someone does not achieve something it is not because they have not tried) *If Simon doesn't get through his accountancy exams it won't be for lack of trying.* | **you couldn't do sth if you tried** *spoken* (=used to say that someone does not have the skill or ability to do something) *My Dad couldn't fix a car if he tried.* W1
**2 ► TEST/USE ◄** [T] to do or use something for a short while to discover if it is suitable, enjoyable etc: *It works really well – you should try it.* | **try doing sth** *Try taking deep, slow breaths.* | **try sth on sb/sth** *Scientists are trying the new drugs on rats.* | **try sb on sth** *Petra's trying the baby on solid foods.* | **try something new/different** (=do or use something that is different from what you usually do or use) *a different kind of holiday for those who are willing to try something new* | **try sth for size** (=put on a piece of clothing to find out whether it fits you)
**3 ► FOOD/DRINK ◄** [T] to taste food or drink to find out if you like it: *You must try that home-made apple pie.* —see TASTE (USAGE)
**4 ► TRY TO FIND SB/STH ◄** [I,T] to go to a place or person, or call them, in order to find something or someone: *"Where's the glue?" "Try Charles; maybe he knows."* | *We tried several hotels before finding one with two single rooms.* | *I'm sorry, but Ms Bouvier is out of the office. Could you try again later.*
**5 ► DOOR/WINDOW ◄** [T] to try to open a door, window etc in order to see if it is locked: *I tried the top drawer but it was locked.* | **try the lock/latch/handle** (=try to open a door, window etc by moving or pushing a lock etc)
**6 ► LAW ◄** [T usually passive] to examine and judge a legal case, or someone who is thought to be guilty of a crime in a court: *Lansman was tried for murder.*
**7 try sb's patience/temper/nerves etc** to make someone feel impatient, angry, nervous etc: *The constant noise from next door was trying my nerves to the utmost.* | **it's**

**enough to try the patience of a saint** *spoken* (=used to say that something or someone is very annoying) *These computer crashes are enough to try the patience of a saint.*
**8 try your hand at sth** to try a new activity in order to see whether it interests you or whether you are good at it: *You ought to try your hand at portrait painting.*
**9 try your luck** to try to achieve something or get something you want, usually by taking a risk: *After his singing career failed so miserably in England, he decided to try his luck abroad.*

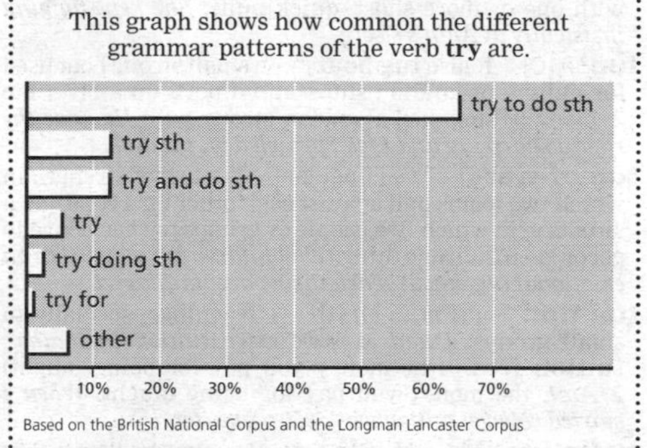

This graph shows how common the different grammar patterns of the verb **try** are.

Based on the British National Corpus and the Longman Lancaster Corpus

**try for** sth *phr v* [T] *BrE* to try to get something you really want such as a job, prize, or a chance to study somewhere: *Alison's trying for a job as a research assistant.*

**try** sth ↔ **on** *phr v* [T] **1** to put on a piece of clothing to see if it fits you or if it suits you: *She tried the shoes on but they were too small.* **2 try it on** *BrE spoken* to behave badly in order to find out how bad you can be before people become angry: *During your first few days' teaching the kids will probably try it on just to see how you react.*

**try** sth ↔ **out** *phr v* [T] **1** to test something such as a method or a piece of equipment to see if it is effective or works properly: *Jamie could hardly wait to try out his new bike.* **2** to practise a skill in order to improve it: **try sth out on sb/sth** *She enjoyed trying her French out on Jean-Pierre.*

**try out for** sth *phr v* [T] *AmE* to try to be chosen as a member of a team, for a part in a play etc: *Joan tried out for the school basketball team.*

S3 **try²** *n* [C] **1** [usually singular] an attempt to do something: *She didn't manage to break the record, but it was a good try.* | **have a try** *Let me have a try; I might be able to open it.* | **give it a try** *I'm not sure I can make him change his mind, but I'll give it a try.* | **worth a try** *My idea may not work, but it's worth a try.* **2 give sth/sb a try** to try using or doing something to see if it is suitable or successful, or to ask if someone can help you: *Shall we give that Tibetan restaurant a try?* **3** four points won by putting the ball on the ground behind the opponents' GOAL LINE in RUGBY

**try·ing** /ˈtraɪ-ɪŋ/ *adj* annoying or difficult in a way that makes you feel worried, tired etc: *That child is very trying.* —see also TRY¹

**try·out** /ˈtraɪaʊt/ *n* [singular] *AmE* a time when people who want to be in a sports team, activity etc are tested, so that the best can be chosen; TRIAL¹ (6) *BrE*: *Cheerleading tryouts will be held on Friday afternoon.*

**try-out** /ˈ· ·/ *n* [C] *BrE* a period of time spent trying a new method, tool, machine etc to see if it is useful

**tryst** /trɪst, traɪst/ *n* [C] *old use or humorous* **1** an arrangement between lovers to meet in a secret place or at a secret time **2** a place where lovers meet secretly

**tsar, tzar, czar** /zɑː, tsɑː‖zɑːr, tsɑːr/ *n* [C] a male ruler of Russia before 1917

**tsa·ri·na, tzarina, czarina** /zɑːˈriːnə, tsɑː-/ *n* [C] a female ruler of Russia before 1917, or the wife of a tsar

**tsar·ism, tzarism, czarism** /ˈzɑːrɪzəm, ˈtsɑː-/ *n* [U] a system of government controlled by a tsar, especially the system in Russia before 1917 —**tsarist** *n* [C] —**tsarist** *adj*

**tset·se fly, tzetze fly** /ˈtetsi flaɪ, ˈtsetsi-, ˈsetsi-/ *n* [C] an African fly that sucks the blood of people and animals and spreads serious diseases

**T-shirt, tee-shirt** /ˈtiː ʃɜːt‖-ʃɜːrt/ *n* [C] a soft, usually cotton shirt that stretches easily, has short SLEEVES and no collar: *She was wearing jeans and a T-shirt.*

**tsp** the written abbreviation of TEASPOON: *1 tsp of salt*

**T-square** /ˈtiː skweə‖-skwer/ *n* [C] a large T-shaped piece of wood or plastic used to draw exact plans or pictures

**tsu·na·mi** /tsʊˈnɑːmi/ *n* [C] *technical* a TIDAL WAVE

**tub** /tʌb/ *n* [C]
**1 ▶ CONTAINER ◀ a)** a small container made of paper or plastic with a lid, in which food is bought or stored: *a tub of margarine* **b)** a large round container without a lid, used for washing, storing things in etc: *There were roses in tubs on the balcony.*
**2 ▶ BATH ◀** *AmE* a large container in which you sit to wash yourself; BATHTUB
**3 ▶ AMOUNT ◀** also **tubful** the amount of liquid, food etc that a tub can contain: *We ate a whole tub of ice-cream.*
**4 ▶ BOAT ◀** *humorous* an old boat that travels slowly
**5 ▶ PERSON ◀** *AmE informal* someone who is short and fat: *Their children are all tubs.*

**tu·ba** /ˈtjuːbə‖ˈtuːbə/ *n* [C] a very large musical instrument, consisting of a curved metal tube, larger than a TRUMPET¹ (1) which you blow into and which produces a very deep sound

**tub·by** /ˈtʌbi/ *adj informal* short and slightly fat, with a round stomach; PLUMP¹ (1) —see FAT¹ (USAGE)

**tube** /tjuːb‖tuːb/ *n* S3 W3
**1 ▶ PIPE FOR LIQUID ◀** [C] a round pipe made of metal, glass, rubber etc, especially for liquids or gases to go through —see also INNER TUBE, TEST TUBE
**2 ▶ CONTAINER ◀** [C] a narrow container made of plastic or soft metal and closed at one end, that you press between your fingers in order to push out the soft substance that is inside: *a tube of toothpaste*
**3 ▶ IN YOUR BODY ◀** [C] a tube-shaped part inside your body: *the bronchial tubes*

**tubes**

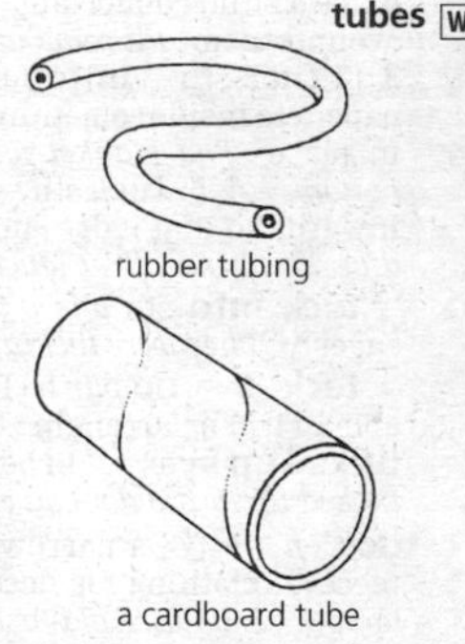
rubber tubing
a cardboard tube

**4 ▶ TRAINS ◀ the tube** *BrE* the system of trains that run under the ground in London: *Smoking is forbidden on the Tube.* | *a tube station* | **by tube** *It's quicker by tube.* —compare SUBWAY (2) —see also UNDERGROUND³
**5 go down the tubes** *informal* if a situation goes down the tubes, it quickly becomes ruined or spoiled: *I wasn't going to sit and watch my career go down the tubes.*
**6 ▶ TELEVISION ◀ the tube** *AmE informal* the television
**7 ▶ ELECTRICAL EQUIPMENT ◀** [C] *technical* the part of a television that creates the picture; CATHODE RAY TUBE

**tu·ber** /ˈtjuːbə‖ˈtuːbər/ *n* [C] a round swollen part that grows below the ground on the stem of certain plants such as the potato, from which new plants grow —**tuberous** *adj*

**tu·ber·cu·lar** /tjuːˈbɜːkjʊlə‖tʊˈbɜːrkjʊlər-/ also **tuberculous** /-kjʊləs/ *adj* connected with tuberculosis

**tu·ber·cu·lo·sis** /tjuːˌbɜːkjʊˈləʊsɪs‖tʊˌbɜːrkjʊˈloʊ-/ *n* [U] a serious infectious disease that affects many parts of your body, especially your lungs; TB

**tube top** /ˈ· ·/ *n* [C] *AmE informal* a piece of women's clothing that goes around your chest and back to cover your breasts but does not cover your shoulders or stomach; BOOB TUBE *BrE*

**tub·ing** /ˈtjuːbɪŋ‖ˈtuː-/ *n* [U] tubes in general, especially when connected together into a system: *rubber tubing*

**tub-thump·ing** /ˈ· ˌ··/ *adj* [only before noun] *BrE informal* trying to persuade people about your opinions in a loud and forceful way: *a tub-thumping speech* —**tub-thumping** *n* [U] —**tub-thumper** *n* [C]

**tu·bu·lar** /ˈtjuːbjələ‖ˈtuːbjələr/ *adj* **1** made of tubes or in the form of a tube: *tubular metal furniture* **2** *AmE* a word meaning very good or excellent, used especially by young people

**TUC** /ˌtiː juː ˈsiː/ *n* the abbreviation of Trades Union Congress; the association of British trade unions

**tuck¹** /tʌk/ *v* **1** [T always + adv/prep] to push the edge of a piece of cloth or paper into something so that it looks tidier or stays in place: **tuck sth into/under** *Nick was tucking his shirt into his trousers when she walked in.* **2** [T always + adv/prep] to put something into a small space, especially in order to protect or hide it: **tuck sth behind/under/into sth** *I tucked the letter into my bag.* **3** [T] to put a TUCK (=a special fold) in a piece of clothing

**tuck** sth ↔ **away** *phr v* [T] **1 be tucked (away) somewhere a)** if a place is tucked away it is in a quiet area: *The inn was tucked away in a remote mountain village.* **b)** if someone or something is tucked away they are hidden or difficult to find: *The key to the cellar was tucked away at the back of the shelf.* **2** *informal* to store something, especially money, in a safe place: *Over the years, she had tucked away over £2000.* **3** *informal* to eat a lot of food, usually quickly and with enjoyment: *I watched as he tucked away a huge plate of pie.*

**tuck in** *phr v* **1** [I] *informal especially BrE* to eat eagerly: *Come on everyone, tuck in!* **2** [T **tuck** sb ↔ **in**] to make a child comfortable in bed by arranging the sheets around them: *I'll come up and tuck you in in a minute.* **3** [T **tuck** sth ↔ **in**] to put the edge of a piece of clothing, paper etc inside something so that it looks tidier or stays in place: *The blanket was too short to tuck in at the bottom.* **4** [T **tuck** sth ↔ **in**] to move a part of your body inwards so that it does not stick out so much: *When you dive, keep your elbows tucked in.*

**tuck into** sth *phr v* [T] *informal* to eat something eagerly: *They were tucking into the Christmas turkey.*

**tuck** sb ↔ **up** *phr v* [T] **1** to make a child comfortable in bed by arranging the sheets around them **2 be tucked up** *informal* to be lying or sitting in bed: *He was tucked up in bed doing a crossword.*

**tuck²** *n* **1** [C] a narrow flat fold of cloth sewn into a piece of clothing for decoration or to give it a special shape **2** [U] *BrE old-fashioned* a word for cakes, sweets etc used especially by schoolchildren **3** [C] a small medical operation done to make your face or stomach look flatter and younger: *tiny tucks behind her ears*

**tuck·er¹** /ˈtʌkə‖-ər/ *v*

**tucker** sb **out** *phr v* [T] *AmE informal* to make someone very tired: *The kids were tuckered out after the walk.*

**tucker²** *n* [U] *AustrE, NZE informal* food —see also **your best bib and tucker** (BIB (3))

**-tude** /tjuːd‖tuːd/ *suffix (in nouns)* another form of the suffix -ITUDE: *disquietude* (=anxiety) | *desuetude*

**Tu·dor** /ˈtjuːdə‖ˈtuːdər/ *adj* connected with the period in British history between 1485 and 1603: **Tudor house/buildings/architecture etc** (=built in the style used in the Tudor period) *a rambling Tudor house overlooking the river*

**Tues·day** /ˈtjuːzdi‖ˈtuːz-/ written abbreviation **Tue.** or **Tues.** *n* [C,U] the day between Monday and Wednesday. In Britain, Tuesday is considered the second day of the week, and in the US it is considered the third day of the week: *We moved in last Tuesday.* | *The results come out on Tuesday.* | *His birthday is on a Tuesday this year.* | **Tuesday morning/evening etc** *Let's go out for a meal Tuesday night.* | **on Tuesdays** (=each Tuesday) *I usually stay in on Tuesdays.* | **the Tuesday** *BrE* (=the Tuesday of the particular week being mentioned) *We went out on the Tuesday.*

**tuft** /tʌft/ *n* [C] a bunch of hair, feathers, grass etc growing or held closely together at their base: *a few scrawny goats chewing at tufts of grass*

**tuft·ed** /ˈtʌftɪd/ *adj* with a tuft or tufts: *a tufted duck*

**tug¹** /tʌg/ *v* **tugged, tugging** [I,T] also **tug at** to pull with one or more short, quick pulls: *She kept tugging insistently at Alan's sleeve.*

**tug²** *n* [C] **1** also **tug boat** /ˈ· ·/ a small strong boat used for pulling or guiding ships into a port, up a river etc **2** [usually singular] a sudden strong pull: *He gave the rope a sharp tug and I fell sprawled on the deck.*

**tug-of-war** /ˌ· · ˈ·/ *n* [singular] **1** a test of strength in which two teams pull against each other on a rope **2** a situation in which two people or groups try very hard to get or keep the same thing: *The children are trapped in an emotional tug-of-war when their parents quarrel.*

**tu·i·tion** /tjuˈɪʃən‖tu-/ *n* [U] **1** teaching, especially in small groups: *I had to have extra tuition in maths.* | **tuition fees** (=the money you pay for being taught) **2** *AmE* the money you pay for being taught: *When I started college, tuition was $350 a quarter.*

**tu·lip** /ˈtjuːlɪp‖ˈtuː-/ *n* [C] a brightly coloured flower that is shaped like a cup and grows from a BULB (2) in spring

**tulle** /tjuːl‖tuːl/ *n* [U] a thin soft silk or NYLON material like a net

**tum·ble¹** /ˈtʌmbəl/ *v* [I] **1** [always + adv/prep] to fall quickly and suddenly downwards, especially with a rolling movement: [+ **over/backwards/down**] *She lost her balance and tumbled backwards.* **2** [always + adv/prep] to move in an uncontrolled way: [+ **into/through**] *The kids tumbled out of the car.* **3** if prices or figures tumble, they go down suddenly and by a large amount: *Stock market prices have tumbled over the past week.* **4** [always + adv/prep] if someone's hair tumbles down, it is long and thick and has curls: *Long blonde hair tumbled about her face.* **5** *AmE* to do TUMBLING

**tumble to** sth *phr v* [T] *informal* to suddenly understand or realize something: *It was a long time before she tumbled to what I meant.*

**tumble²** *n* [C] a fall, especially from a high place —see also ROUGH-AND-TUMBLE

**tum·ble·down** /ˈtʌmbəldaʊn/ *adj* [only before noun] **tumbledown building/house/cottage etc** old and beginning to fall down, often in a way that seems attractive: *a row of tumbledown labourer's cottages*

**tumble dry·er** /ˌ·· ˈ··/ *n* [C] *BrE* a machine that uses hot air to dry clothes after they have been washed; DRYER

**tum·bler** /ˈtʌmblə‖-ər/ *n* [C] **1** a glass with a flat bottom and no handle —see picture at GLASS¹ **2** also **tumblerful** /-fʊl/ the amount of liquid that this type of glass can contain: *Jack must have had about six tumblers of whisky last night.* **3** *old-fashioned* someone who performs special movements such as doing SOMERSAULTS (=a jump in which you turn over completely in the air); ACROBAT

**tum·ble·weed** /ˈtʌmbəlwiːd/ *n* [U] a plant that grows in the desert areas of North America and is blown from place to place by the wind

**tum·bling** /ˈtʌmblɪŋ/ *n* [U] a sport similar to GYMNASTICS but with all the exercises done on the floor

**tu·mes·cent** /tjuːˈmesənt‖tuː-/ *adj technical* swollen or swelling —**tumescence** *n* [U]

**tu·mid** /ˈtjuːmɪd‖ˈtuː-/ *adj technical* a tumid part of the body is swollen —**tumidity** /tjuːˈmɪdɪti‖tuː-/ *n* [U]

**tum·my** /ˈtʌmi/ *n* [C] a word for STOMACH, used especially by or to children: *Touch your head and pat your tummy.* | **tummy bug/upset** (=an illness of the stomach that makes you feel sick)

**tu·mour** *BrE*, **tumor** *AmE* /ˈtjuːmə‖ˈtuːmər/ a mass of diseased cells in your body that have divided and increased too quickly: *a brain tumour* | **malignant/benign tumour** (=dangerous/harmless tumour) —**tumourous** *adj*

**tu·mult** /ˈtjuːmʌlt‖ˈtuː-/ *n* [C,U] *formal* **1** a state of confusion, noise, and excitement, often caused by a large crowd: *His announcement was drowned in the tumult.* | **in tumult** (=in a state of confusion or change) *The whole country is in tumult.* **2** a state of mental confusion caused by strong emotions such as anger, sadness etc: **in tumult** (=anxious, confused, or unhappy) *His mind was in tumult.*

**tu·mul·tu·ous** /tjuːˈmʌltʃuəs‖tuː-/ *adj* **1** full of activity, confusion, or violence: *the tumultuous weeks leading up to the revolution* **2** very loud: *Tumultuous applause rang through the hall.* —**tumultuously** *adv*

**tu·mu·lus** /ˈtjuːmjʊləs‖ˈtuː-/ *n* [C] a very large pile of earth put over a grave by people in former times

**tu·na** /ˈtjuːnə‖ˈtuːnə/ *n* **1** [C] a large sea fish caught for food **2** [U] the flesh of this fish, usually sold cooked in tins

**tun·dra** /ˈtʌndrə/ *n* [U] the large flat areas of land in the north of Russia, Canada etc, where it is very cold and there are no trees

S 3 **tune[1]** /tjuːn‖tuːn/ *n* [C] **1** a series of musical notes that are played or sung one after the other to make a pattern of sound that is usually pleasant to listen to: *I recognize that tune but I can't remember the name of the song.* **2 in tune** playing or singing the correct musical note: *Sadie can't sing in tune.* **3 out of tune** playing or singing higher or lower than the correct musical note: *That old piano's completely out of tune.* **4 be in tune with/out of tune with** to be able or unable to realize, understand, or agree with what someone else thinks or wants: *Many politicians are totally out of tune with the needs of ordinary people.* **5 to the tune of $1000/£2 million etc** *informal* used to emphasize how large an amount or number is: *We're already in debt to the tune of £5000.* —see also **call the tune** (CALL[1] (25)), **change your tune** (CHANGE[1] (13)), **dance to sb's tune** (DANCE[1] (6))

**tune[2]** *v* [T] **1** to make a musical instrument play at the right PITCH[2] (3): *Someone's coming tomorrow to tune the piano.* **2** to make an engine work as well as possible **3** to make a radio or television receive broadcasts from a particular place: *The radio was tuned to a classical station.* | **stay tuned to (sth)** (=continue watching or listening to the same radio station or television programme) *Stay tuned for the latest news from Washington.* **4 finely tuned sense/perception/balance etc** a very careful and skilful way of judging something, understanding situations etc: *She had a finely tuned sense of right and wrong.*

**tune in** *phr v* [I,T] **1** to watch or listen to a broadcast on radio or television: *60 million people tuned in to watch the Royal Wedding.* | **tune sth ↔ in (to sth)** *Tune the radio in to KCRW.* **2 tuned in** able to realize or understand what is happening or what other people are thinking: *She doesn't seem very tuned in to these new developments.*

**tune out** *phr v* [I,T] *informal especially AmE* to ignore or stop listening to someone: *She tuned out after I said no extra money was involved.* | **tune sb/sth ↔ out** *I learned to tune out the background noise.*

**tune up** *phr v* **1** [I] when musicians tune up, they prepare their instruments to play at the same PITCH[2] (3) as each other **2** [T **tune** sth ↔ **up**] to make a musical instrument play at the right PITCH[2] (3)

**tune·ful** /ˈtjuːnfəl‖ˈtuːn-/ *adj* pleasant to listen to: *tuneful melodies from light opera* —**tunefully** *adv* —**tunefulness** *n* [U]

**tune·less** /ˈtjuːnləs‖ˈtuːn-/ *adj* not having a pleasant tune: *tuneless humming* —**tunelessly** *adv*

**tun·er** /ˈtjuːnə‖ˈtuːnər/ *n* [C] the part of a radio or television that you can change to receive different TV stations and radio stations

**tune-up** /ˈ· ·/ *n* [C] the process of making small changes to an engine so that it works as well as possible

**tung·sten** /ˈtʌŋstən/ *n* [U] a hard metal that is one of the ELEMENTS (=simple substances) used in making steel

**tu·nic** /ˈtjuːnɪk‖ˈtuː-/ *n* [C] **1** a long loose piece of clothing worn in former times, usually without sleeves (SLEEVE (1)) or a belt **2** *BrE* a specially shaped short coat worn by soldiers, police officers etc as part of a uniform

**tuning fork** /ˈ·· ·/ *n* [C] a small U-shaped steel instrument that makes a particular musical note when you hit it —see picture at FORK[1]

**tuning peg** /ˈ·· ·/ *n* [C] a wooden screw used for tightening the strings on a VIOLIN, GUITAR etc —see picture at PEG[1]

**tunnel**

**tun·nel[1]** /ˈtʌnl/ *n* [C] **1** a passage that has been dug under the ground for cars, trains etc to go through **2** a passage under the ground that animals have dug to live in W 3

**tunnel[2]** *v* **tunnelled, tunnelling** *BrE*, **tunneled, tunneling** *AmE* [I always + adv/prep T] to dig a long passage under the ground: [+ **under/through etc**] *tunneling through hard rock* | **tunnel your way into/through/under etc** (=move somewhere by digging a passage) *The prisoners tunneled their way under the fence.*

**tunnel vi·sion** /ˌ·· ˈ··/ *n* [U] **1** the tendency to only think about one part of something such as a problem or plan, instead of considering all the parts of it: *He had the paranoia and tunnel vision of the knee-jerk patriot.* **2** a condition in which someone's eyes are damaged so that they can only see things that are straight ahead

**tun·ny** /ˈtʌni/ *n* [C,U] a British form of the word TUNA

**tup·pence** /ˈtʌpəns/ *n* [C,U] a British spelling of TWOPENCE

**tup·penny** /ˈtʌpni/ *adj* [only before noun] a British spelling of TWOPENNY

**Tup·per·ware** /ˈtʌpəweə‖-pərwer/ *n* [U] *trademark* a type of plastic container that closes very tightly and is used to store food

**tur·ban** /ˈtɜːbən‖ˈtɜːr-/ *n* [C] a long piece of cloth that you wind tightly round your head, worn by men in parts of North Africa and Southern Asia and sometimes by women as a fashion

**tur·bid** /ˈtɜːbɪd‖ˈtɜːr-/ *adj formal* turbid water or liquid is dirty and muddy: *the silty, turbid waters of the Congo river* —**turbidity** /tɜːˈbɪdɪti‖tɜːr-/ *n* [U]

**tur·bine** /ˈtɜːbaɪn‖ˈtɜːrbɪn, -baɪn/ *n* [C] an engine or motor in which the pressure of a liquid or gas moves a special wheel around —see also GAS TURBINE, WIND TURBINE

**tur·bo·charg·er** /ˈtɜːbəʊˌtʃɑːdʒə‖ˈtɜːrboʊˌtʃɑːrdʒər/ *also* **turbo** *n* [C] a system that makes a vehicle more powerful by using a turbine to force air and petrol into the engine under increased pressure: *The 2.4 litre turbo diesel is the top-seller.* —**turbocharged** *adj*

**tur·bo·jet** /ˈtɜːbəʊdʒet‖ˈtɜːrboʊ-/ *n* [C] **1** a powerful engine that makes something, especially an aircraft, move forwards, by forcing out hot air and gases at the back **2** an aircraft that gets power from this type of engine

**tur·bo·prop** /ˈtɜːbəʊprɒp‖ˈtɜːrboʊprɑːp/ *n* [C] **1** a turbine engine that drives a PROPELLER **2** an aircraft that gets power from this type of engine

**tur·bot** /ˈtɜːbɒt, -bət‖ˈtɜːrbət/ *n* [C,U] a large flat European fish

**tur·bu·lence** /ˈtɜːbjᵊləns‖ˈtɜːr-/ *n* [U] **1** irregular and violent movements of air or water that are caused by the wind: *The flight was very uncomfortable because of turbulence.* **2** a political or emotional situation that is very confused: *A period of political turbulence followed the civil war.*

**tur·bu·lent** /ˈtɜːbjᵊlənt‖ˈtɜːr-/ *adj* **1** a turbulent situation or period of time is one in which there are a lot of sudden changes and often wars or violence: *The Reformation was one of the most turbulent periods in English history.* **2** turbulent air or water moves around a lot because of the wind: *turbulent weather conditions* **3** turbulent crowds or people are noisy and violent: *the turbulent populace of the city's teeming ghettos*

**turd** /tɜːd‖tɜːrd/ *n* [C] **1** *informal* a slightly rude word for a piece of the solid waste material you pass from your body **2** *taboo* an insulting word for an unpleasant person: *You stupid little turd!*

**tu·reen** /tjʊˈriːn‖təˈriːn/ *n* [C] a large dish with a lid used for serving soup or vegetables

**turf**[1] /tɜːf‖tɜːrf/ *n* **1** [U] a surface that is made up of soil and a thick covering of grass: *the springy turf of the lawn* **2** *plural* **turfs** *or* **turves** /tɜːvz‖tɜːrvz/ [C] *BrE* a square piece of turf cut out of the ground; SOD[1] (5) *AmE* **3 the turf** the sport of horse racing, or the track on which horses race: *devotees of the turf* **4** [U] *AmE informal* an area that you think of as being your own: *They resented these strangers invading their turf.* | **turf war** (=a fight or argument over the things you think belong to you) **5** [C,U] *AmE, IrishE* a soft brown substance like earth that is used for burning instead of coal, especially in Ireland; PEAT

**turf**[2] *v* [T] to cover an area of land with TURF[1] (1)

**turf** sb/sth ↔ **out** *phr v* [T] *BrE informal* to get rid of someone or something: *He's been turfed out of the golf club for bad behaviour.*

**turf ac·coun·tant** /ˈ· ·ˌ··/ *n* [C] *BrE* someone who has a business where people can BET[1] (1) on the results of horse races, football games etc; BOOKMAKER

**tur·gid** /ˈtɜːdʒᵻd‖ˈtɜːr-/ *adj* **1** turgid writing or speech is boring and difficult to understand: *The whole play is turgid, amateurish drivel.* **2** *formal* full and swollen with liquid or air —**turgidly** *adv* —**turgidity** /tɜːˈdʒɪdᵻti‖tɜːr-/ *n* [U]

**Turk** /tɜːk‖tɜːrk/ *n* [C] someone from Turkey

**tur·key** /ˈtɜːki‖ˈtɜːrki/ *n* **1** [C] a bird that looks like a large chicken and is often eaten at Christmas and at Thanksgiving **2** [U] the meat from a turkey eaten as food: *roast turkey* **3** [C] *AmE informal* someone who is silly or stupid: *That guy's a real turkey.* **4** *AmE informal* an unsuccessful film or play **5 talk turkey** *informal especially AmE* to talk seriously about details, especially in business —see also COLD TURKEY

**Turk·ish**[1] /ˈtɜːkɪʃ‖ˈtɜːr-/ *n* [U] the language of Turkey

**Turkish**[2] *adj* from or connected with Turkey

**Turkish bath** /ˌ·· ˈ·/ *n* [C] a health treatment that involves sitting in a very hot steamy room: *I walked into the club and it was like a Turkish bath!*

**Turkish cof·fee** /ˌ·· ˈ··/ *n* [C,U] very strong black coffee that you drink in small cups with sugar

**Turkish de·light** /ˌ·· ·ˈ·/ *n* [U] a type of sweet made from firm JELLY (1) that is cut into pieces and covered in sugar or chocolate

**tur·me·ric** /ˈtɜːmərɪk‖ˈtɜːr-/ *n* [U] yellow powder used to give a special colour or taste to food, especially CURRY[1]

**tur·moil** /ˈtɜːmɔɪl‖ˈtɜːr-/ *n* [U, singular] a state of confusion, excitement, and trouble: *The country is in complete turmoil.*

S1 W1

## turn[1] /tɜːn‖tɜːrn/ *v*

① CHANGE DIRECTION/POSITION
② COLOUR
③ AGE/TIME
④ CHANGE
⑤ PAGE
⑥ VEHICLE
⑦ OTHER MEANINGS

### ① CHANGE DIRECTION/POSITION

**1 a)** ► **YOUR BODY** ◄ [I] to move your body so that you are looking in a different direction: *Ricky turned and walked away.* | [+ **around/round/away etc**] *I turned around quickly to see if someone was following.* | *Dan turned away so Brody couldn't see the fear in his eyes.* | **turn to do sth** *She turned to look back at him as she got on the plane.* | *He turned to face Kim with tears in his eyes.* | **turn on your heel** (=turn away suddenly) *Brigitte glared at him, turned on her heel, and stomped out of the room.* **b)** ► **OBJECT** ◄ [I,T] to move something so that it is pointing or aiming in a different direction: *Turn the vase so the crack doesn't show.* | *The firemen turned the hose on the burning building.* | **turn sth to face sth** *I turned the chair to face him and began to talk.*

**2** ► **ROAD/RIVER/PATH ETC** ◄ [I] to curve in a particular direction: *The river turns east and flows down out of the mountains.* | *a small path twisting and turning through the woods*

**3** ► **MOVE AROUND CENTRAL POINT** ◄ [I,T] to move around a central or fixed point, or make something move in this way: *The wheel creaked as it turned.* | **turn sth** *Turn the handle as far as it will go to the right.*

### ② COLOUR

**4** ► **OBJECT** ◄ [linking verb] to become a different colour: *The clothes all turned pink in the wash.* | *The leaves turned red, orange, and yellow in the autumn air.*

**5** ► **PERSON** ◄ [linking verb] if a person turns a particular colour, their skin looks that colour because they feel ill, embarrassed etc: *Vy turned white when she saw all the blood on the floor.* | *Every time Inge speaks to Hans, he turns bright red.*

**6** ► **HAIR** ◄ [linking verb] if your hair turns grey or white, it becomes that colour because you are getting older: *Her face was lined and her hair was already turning grey.*

### ③ AGE/TIME

**7** ► **AGE** ◄ [linking verb] if someone turns a

particular age, they become that age: *"How old is Dennis?" "He's just turned 40."*
**8 ▶TIME◀** [linking verb] if it has turned a particular time, that time has just passed: *"What time is it?" "It's just turned 3:00."*

**④ CHANGE**

**9 turn nasty/mean/violent etc** to suddenly become angry, violent etc: *One day the dog just turned nasty and bit me.* | *The police are worried that the situation could turn violent.*
**10 turn cold/nasty** if the weather turns cold or nasty, it suddenly becomes cold, unpleasant etc: *The forecast says it's going to turn nasty.*
**11 ▶ACTIVITY◀** [I] to stop one activity and start something completely different: [+ **to**] *Our laughter turned to horror when we realized Jody really was hurt.* | *Many people here have turned to solar power as a source of electricity.*
**12 actor turned politician/football player turned author etc** someone who has done one job and then does something completely different
**13 turn traitor** to be disloyal to a person, group, or idea that you have strongly supported before: *Ramirez's lieutenant turned traitor and told the military where he was hiding.*

**⑤ PAGE**

**14** [T] if you turn a page in a book, you move it so that you can read the next page —see also **turn to** (TURN[1])

**⑥ VEHICLE**

**15** [I,T] if you turn a vehicle or it turns, it changes direction: [+ **into/off/left/right**] *Turn left at the next light.* | *The car in front of me turned into a driveway.* | **turn sth around/into** *Jason turned the car around while I brought the suitcases.*

**⑦ OTHER MEANINGS**

**16 ▶INJURY◀** [T] if you turn your ankle, you twist it in a way that injures it; SPRAIN: *Is it bad? No, I just turned my ankle on the step.*
**17 ▶MILK◀** [I] if milk turns, it becomes sour
**18 turn your back (on) a)** to refuse to help or give sympathy to someone when they need it: *How can you turn your back on your own mother?* **b)** to deliberately stop being involved in something that used to be very important for you: *Isn't it hard to turn your back on tennis after so many years at the top?* **c)** to turn so that your back is pointing towards someone or something: *He turned his back on her and spoke quietly into the phone.* | *As soon as you turn your back on these kids, they're acting like maniacs again!*
**19 turn sth inside out a)** to pull a piece of clothing, bag etc so that the inside is facing outwards: *Just turn the bag inside out to make sure there's nothing left in it.* **b)** also **turn sth upside down** to search everywhere for something, in a way that makes a place very untidy: *The thieves had turned the house upside down looking for the papers.*
**20 turn (people's) heads** if something turns people's heads, they are surprised by it: *Yes, it did turn a few heads when he moved back to the village.*
**21 turn sb's head** to be attractive in a romantic or sexual way to a particular person: *You mean that horrible old man actually managed to turn Jo's head?*
**22 have turned the corner** to have done the most difficult part of something, so that the rest looks fairly easy —see also **turn a blind eye** (BLIND[1] (26)), **turn the other cheek** (CHEEK[1] (6)), **sb would turn in their grave** (GRAVE[1] (3)), **not turn a hair** (HAIR (8)), **turn your hand to** (HAND[1] (10)), **turn over a new leaf** (LEAF[1] (3)), **turn your nose up (at)** (NOSE[1] (6)), **turn the tables (on sb)** (TABLE[1] (5)), **turn tail** (TAIL[1] (8))

**turn against** sb/sth *phr v* [T] to decide that you do not like someone or agree with something any more: *Public opinion in Panama turned against him.*

**turn** sb **against** sb/sth *phr v* [T] to make someone not to like someone any more or not agree with something any more: *After the divorce, Dave accused Christina of turning the kids against him.*

**turn around** also **turn round** *BrE phr v* **1** [T **turn sth ↔ round**] to complete the process of making a product or providing a service: *We can turn around a batch of 50 pressings in two hours.* **2** [T **turn** sth ↔ **round**] to manage an unsuccessful business so well that it becomes successful again: *In under three years she had completely turned the company around.* **3 turn around and say/tell** *spoken* to tell someone something that they think is unfair or unreasonable: *I complained about it but they just turned round and said it was my own fault.*

**turn away** *phr v* **1** [T **turn** sb ↔ **away**] to refuse to let someone into a place such as a theatre, cinema etc, because there is no more space: *They turned about 1000 people away at the Arena because all the tickets were gone.* **2** [I,T] to refuse to give someone sympathy, help, or support: *Europe cannot in good conscience turn away from these refugees.* | **turn sb ↔ away** *I can't turn her away. She's my brother's child.*

**turn back** *phr v* **1** [I] to go in the opposite direction: *It was late afternoon when we finally decided it was time to turn back.* | *One of the boats had to turn back because it was taking in water.* **2** [T **turn** sb ↔ **back**] to tell someone to go in the opposite direction, often because there is danger ahead: *We were turned back at the border because of the fighting.* **3 turn back the clock a)** if you want to turn back the clock, you wish you had the chance to do something again so you could do it better: *"I'd like to be able to turn back the clock and make things right with Brett," said Gloria.* **b)** to do something the way it was done at an earlier time, especially when that is worse than the way it is done now: *legislation that turns back the clock on human rights*

**turn down** *phr v* [T] **1** [**turn** sth ↔ **down**] to make a machine such as an oven, radio etc produce less heat, sound etc: *Can you please turn the TV down? I can't hear myself think!* **2** [**turn** sb/sth ↔ **down**] to refuse an offer, request, or invitation: *Pauline's turned down offers from several different law firms.* | *Jimmy offered to marry her again, but she'd already turned him down three times.* —see REFUSE[1] (USAGE)

**turn in** *phr v* **1** [T **turn** sth ↔ **in**] to give something back to the person that owns it, especially when it has been lost or borrowed: *Make sure to turn your security badge in before you leave the company.* | [+ **to**] *My wallet was turned in to the police two days after it was stolen.* **2** [T **turn** sth ↔ **in**] *especially AmE* to give a piece of work to a teacher, your boss etc: *Have you all turned in your homework from last night?* **3** [T **turn** sb ↔ **in**] to tell the police who or where a criminal is: *Margrove's wife finally turned him in after months of silence.* **4** [I] to go to bed: *Well, I think I'll turn in. I've got to get up early.*

**turn into** sth *phr v* **1** [T] to become something different, or make someone or something do this: **turn into sth** *In a few weeks, the caterpillar will turn into a butterfly.* | *The sofa turns into a bed.* | **turn sth into sth** *Lieutenant, do you have to turn everything into a question?* | **turn sb into sth** *You'll never turn me into a salesman, Dad. I'm not made for it.* **2** [T] to change by magic from one thing into another, or make something do this: **turn into sth** *In a flash of light, the prince turned into a frog.* | **turn sb/sth into sth** *The fairy godmother turned the pumpkin into a coach.* **3** [T] if one season turns into another season, it changes gradually from one to the next: *The snows melted, and winter turned into spring.* **4 days turned into weeks/months turned into years etc** used to say that time passed slowly while you waited for something to happen: *Weeks turned into months, and still there was no letter from Renata.* —see BECOME (USAGE)

**turn off** *phr v* **1** [T **turn** sth ↔ **off**] to stop the supply of water, gas etc from flowing by turning a handle or TAP as far as it will go: *Turn off the hot water.* | *They've turned the gas off for a couple of hours.* **2** [T **turn** sth ↔ **off**] to make a machine or piece of electrical equipment such as a television, car, light etc stop operating by pushing a button, turning a key etc: *Don't forget to turn off the lights when you leave.* | *Turn the TV off now.* **3** [I,T] to leave one road, especially a large one, and drive along another one: **turn off at/near**

[continued on next page]

[continued from previous page]
etc *I'm sure we should have turned off at the last exit.* | **turn off sth** *Gill turned off the A10 and started heading west.* —see also TURN-OFF **4** [T **turn** sb ↔ **off**] to do something that makes someone decide they do not like something: *Don't oversell the product. If your salespeople are pushy, they'll turn the customer off.* **5** [T **turn** sb ↔ **off**] to do something that makes someone feel that they are not attracted to you in a sexual way: *It really turns me off when Richard wears his smelly socks to bed.*

**turn on** *phr v* **1** [T **turn** sth ↔ **on**] to make the supply of water, gas etc start flowing from something by turning a handle or TAP[1] (1): *I turned the water on in the shower.* | *We'll be turning on the gas in about an hour.* **2** [T **turn** sth ↔ **on**] to make a machine or piece of electrical equipment such as a car, television, light etc start operating by pushing a button, turning a key etc: *Could you turn on the light, please?* | *When I turned the engine on it made a funny noise.* —see OPEN[2] (USAGE) **3** [T **turn on** sb] to suddenly attack someone or treat them badly, using physical violence or unpleasant words: *Peter turned on Rae with eyes blazing and screamed, "Get out of my sight!"* **4** [T **turn on** sth] if a situation, event, argument turns on a particular thing or idea, it depends on that thing in order to work: *The negotiations turned on getting the Italian delegation to agree.* **5** [T **turn** sb **on**] to make someone feel sexually excited: *A lot of guys are turned on by the idea of women in uniform.* —see also TURN-ON **6** [T **turn** sb **on to** sth] to make someone become interested in a product, idea etc: *Mark's that friend of mine who turned me on to classical music.*

**turn off**

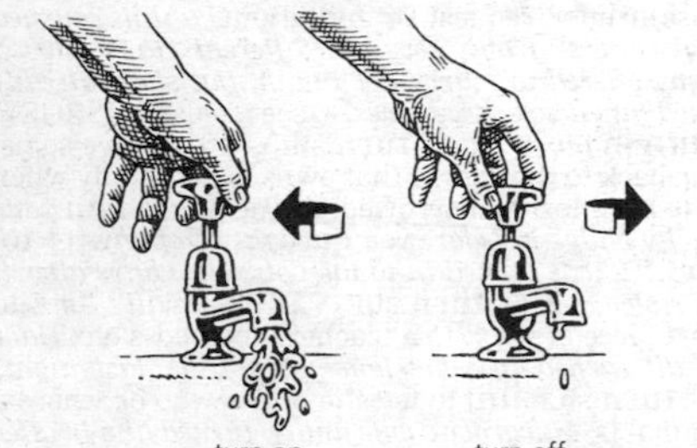

**turn out** *phr v* **1** [linking verb] to happen in a particular way, or to have a particular result, especially one that you did not expect: *I hate the way my hair turned out. The colour's all wrong.* | *Don't worry, I'm sure it will all turn out fine.* | **it turns out that** *It turned out that she didn't get the job in the end.* | **turn out to be** *That guy we met turned out to be Maria's second cousin.* | *His statement turned out to be false.* **2** [T **turn** sth ↔ **out**] if you turn out a light, you stop the flow of electricity to it by pushing a button, pulling a string etc: *Don't forget to turn out the lights when you go!* **3** [T **turn** sb ↔ **out**] to force someone to leave a place: *Benjamin turned his son out of the house without any money.* **4** [I] if people turn out for an event, they gather together to see it happen: *Crowds of people turned out to watch the filming of the final scene of Rocky.* —see also TURNOUT **5** [T **turn** sth ↔ **out**] to produce or make something: *The factory turns out 300 units a day.* **6 well/beautifully/badly turned out** to be dressed in good, beautiful etc clothes: *elegantly turned-out young ladies*

**turn over** *phr v* **1** [T **turn** sb ↔ **over to** sb] to bring a criminal to the police or other official organization: *The FBI caught Rostov and turned him over to the CIA.* **2** [T **turn** sth ↔ **over to** sb] to give someone the right to own or the responsibility for something such as a plan, business, piece of property etc: *I'm turning the shop over to my son when I retire.* | *When you leave, the project will be turned over to Mathias.* **3** [T **turn over** sth] if a business turns over a particular amount of money, it makes that amount in a particular period of time: *We were turning over $1500 a week when business was good.* **4** [I,T] *BrE* to turn a page in a book or a sheet of paper to the opposite side **5** [I] *BrE* to change the CHANNEL[1] (1) on a television: *I hate this programme. Can we please turn over?* **6 turn sth over in your mind** to think about something carefully, considering all the possibilities: *I turned Zeke's comments over in my mind for a long time that night.*

**turn to** *phr v* **1** [T **turn to** sb/sth] to try to get help, advice, or sympathy from someone or by doing something: *Nobody seems to understand. I don't know who to turn to.* | *Paul turned to drink* (=drinking alcohol) *to try to forget his problems at work.* **2** [T **turn to** sth] to look at a particular page in a book: *Turn to page 655 for more information on this subject.* **3 turn your attention/thoughts/efforts etc to sth** to begin to think about or do something different from what you have been doing **4** [I] *old-fashioned* to begin to work hard: *We'll really have to turn to in order to finish this on time.*

**turn up** *phr v* **1** [T **turn** sth ↔ **up**] to make a machine such as an oven, radio etc produce more heat, sound etc: *Turn the oven up to 220°C.* | *Turn up the radio!* **2** [I] to suddenly appear after having been lost or searched for: *I couldn't find my watch for ages, but then one day it turned up in a coat pocket.* **3** [I always + adv/prep] to arrive at a place: *Steven turned up late as usual.* **4** [I] if an opportunity or situation turns up, it happens, especially when you are not expecting it: *Don't worry, I'm sure a job will turn up soon.* **5** [T **turn** sth ↔ **up**] to find something by thoroughly searching for it: *The police investigation hasn't turned up any new evidence.* **6** [T **turn** sth ↔ **up**] *BrE* to shorten a skirt, trousers etc by folding up the bottom and SEWING it —see also **come up trumps/turn up trumps** (TRUMP[1] (3))

**turn upon** sb *phr v* [T] to suddenly attack someone or treat them badly, using physical violence or unpleasant words

S1 W1 **turn**[2] *n*

**1 it is sb's turn** if it is your turn to do something, it is the time when you can or should do it, because you are one of a number of people doing the same activity in a particular order: *It's your turn. Roll the dice.* | **sb's turn to do sth** *I think it's our turn to drive the kids to school this week.*

**2 take turns** also **take it in turns** *BrE* if many people take turns doing work or playing a game, they each do it one after the other in order to share work or play fairly: *You'll have to take turns being captain of the team.* | **take turns doing sth** *We took turns doing the driving on the way up to Canada.* | **take turns to do sth** *brainstorming sessions where we all took turns to throw in ideas*

**3 in turn a)** as a result of something: *Interest rates were cut, and in turn, share prices rose.* **b)** one after the other, especially in a particular order: *He asked each of us in turn to describe how alcohol had affected our lives.*

**4 ► VEHICLE ◄** [C] the act of changing direction in a vehicle, or making it do this: **make a left/right turn** *Make a left turn after the bank.*

**5 ► ACT OF TURNING STH ◄** [C] the act of turning something completely around a fixed point: *Tighten it another two or three turns.*

**6 ► ROAD ◄** [C] the place where one road goes in a different direction from another: *According to the map, we missed our turn back there at the light.*

**7 the turn of the century** the beginning of a century: *At the turn of the century, new technologies will already be in place.*

**8 take a turn for the worse/better** to suddenly become worse or better: *Paul's health took a turn for the worse on Tuesday.*

**9 turn of events** a change in what is happening, especially an unusual one: *The General's agreement to the peace talks is a welcome but unexpected turn of events.*

**10 turn of phrase a)** a particular way of saying something; expression: *I've never liked that turn of phrase – when people say 'I won't detain you any longer'.* **b)** the ability to say things in a clever or funny way: *Kate has a witty turn of phrase.*
**11 on the turn a)** if the TIDE is on the turn, it is starting to come in or go out **b)** starting to change, or in the process of changing: *I began to think that maybe my luck was on the turn.* **c)** *especially BrE* if milk, fish, or other food is on the turn, it is starting to become sour
**12 speak out of turn** to say something you should not say in a particular situation, especially because you do not have enough authority to say it: *I hope I'm not speaking out of turn, sir, but I don't think this is the best way to proceed.*
**13 do sb a good/bad turn** to do something that is helpful or unhelpful for someone: *You'll be doing me a good turn by driving Max home tonight.*
**14 at every turn** if something happens at every turn, it happens again and again: *We were frustrated at every turn in our efforts to get money for the project.*
**15 by turns** if someone shows different feelings or qualities by turns, they change from one to another: *That evening he was silly, witty, and mournful by turns.*
**16 turn of mind** *literary* the way that someone usually thinks or feels: *He was of a melancholoy turn of mind.*
**17 done/cooked to a turn** to be perfectly cooked
**18 one good turn deserves another** used to say that if someone does something nice for you, you should do something nice for them to thank them
**19 take a turn in/on etc** *old-fashioned* to walk somewhere just for pleasure: *I think they're out taking a turn in the gardens.*
**20 give sb a turn** *old-fashioned* to frighten someone
**21 have a turn** *BrE old-fashioned* to feel slightly ill or faint

**turn·a·bout** /ˈtɜːnəbaʊt‖ˈtɜːrn-/ *n BrE* [C usually singular] **1** a complete change in someone's opinions or ideas: *an extraordinary turnabout in public opinion* **2 turnabout is fair play** *AmE* used to say that because someone else has done something you can do it too

**turn·a·round** /ˈtɜːnəraʊnd‖ˈtɜːrn-/ *n* [C usually singular] *especially AmE* a TURNROUND

**turn·coat** /ˈtɜːnkəʊt‖ˈtɜːrnkoʊt/ *n* [C] someone who stops supporting a political party or group and joins the opposing side: *Casson was pilloried as a turncoat and a traitor.*

**turn·er** /ˈtɜːnə‖ˈtɜːrnər/ *n* [C] someone who uses a LATHE (=special tool) to make shapes out of wood or metal

**turn·ing** /ˈtɜːnɪŋ‖ˈtɜːr-/ *n* [C] *BrE* a road that connects with the one you are on; TURN[2] (6) *AmE*: *Take the first turning on the left.*

**turning cir·cle** /ˈ·· ˌ··/ *n* [C] the smallest space in which a vehicle can drive around in a circle

**turning point** /ˈ··· ·/ *n* [C] the time when an important change starts, especially one that improves the situation: *The Battle of El Alamein was a turning point in the war.*

**tur·nip** /ˈtɜːnɪ̥p‖ˈtɜːr-/ *n* [C,U] a large round pale yellow vegetable that grows under the ground, or the plant that produces it —see picture on page 414

**turn·key**[1] /ˈtɜːnkiː‖ˈtɜːrn-/ *n* [C] *old use* a JAILER

**turnkey**[2] *adj* [only before noun] ready to be used immediately: *low-cost turnkey systems for retail applications*

**turn-off** /ˈ· ·/ *n* **1** [C] a smaller road that leads off a main road **2** [singular] *informal* something that makes you lose interest in something, especially sex: *The music was a real turn-off so we left.* —see also **turn off** (TURN[1])

**turn-on** /ˈ· ·/ *n* [singular] *informal* something that makes you feel excited, especially sexually: *I found the whole thing a real turn-on.* —see also **turn on** (TURN[1])

**turn·out** /ˈtɜːnaʊt‖ˈtɜːrn-/ *n* **1** [singular] the number of people who go to a party, meeting, or other organized event: *Despite the rain, there was a good turnout.* **2** [singular] the number of people who vote in an election: **high turnout** (=a lot of people voting) *Feelings about the election were strong, which ensured a high turnout.* —see also **turn out** (TURN[1]) **3** [C] *AmE* a place at the side of a narrow road where cars can wait to let others pass

**turn·o·ver** /ˈtɜːnˌəʊvə‖ˈtɜːrnˌoʊvər/ *n* **1** [singular] the amount of business done in a particular period, measured by the amount of money earned: *an annual turnover of £5.6 million* **2** [singular] the rate at which people leave an organization and are replaced by others: *Low pay accounts for the high turnover of staff.* **3** [singular] the rate at which a particular type of goods is sold: *Supermarkets depend on a high turnover at low prices.* **4** [C] a small fruit PIE (1): *an apple turnover* **5** [C] *AmE* a situation in a game of American football or basketball in which something happens so that one team loses the ball and the other team gets it

**turn·pike** /ˈtɜːnpaɪk‖ˈtɜːrn-/ *n* [C] **1** *AmE* a large road for fast traffic, especially one that drivers have to pay to use: *the New Jersey Turnpike* **2** *BrE* a road in Britain in the 18th century that travellers had to pay to use

**turn·round** /ˈtɜːnraʊnd‖ˈtɜːrn-/ *BrE,* **turnaround** *especially AmE n* [C] **1** the time it takes to receive something, deal with it and send it back, especially on a plane, ship etc: *Some drivers are on a bonus for fast turnround and deliveries.* —see also **turn around** (TURN[1]) **2** [usually singular] a complete change from a bad situation to a good one: *This year's profits will confirm the company's remarkable turnaround.* **3** [usually singular] a complete change in someone's opinion or ideas; TURNABOUT *BrE*: *a turnround in government policy*

**turn sig·nal** /ˈ· ˌ··/ *n* [C] *AmE* one of the lights on a car that flash to show which way the car is turning; INDICATOR (3) *BrE*

**turn·stile** /ˈtɜːnstaɪl‖ˈtɜːrn-/ *n* [C] a small gate that spins around and only lets one person at a time go through an entrance: *We're getting far more spectators through the turnstiles than last year.*

**turn·ta·ble** /ˈtɜːnˌteɪbəl‖ˈtɜːrn-/ *n* [C] **1** the round flat surface on a RECORD PLAYER that you put records on **2** a large flat round surface on which railway engines are turned around

**turn-up** /ˈ· ·/ *n* **1** [C] *BrE* the bottom of a trouser leg that is folded up for decoration or to make it shorter; CUFF *AmE* —see picture on page 840 **2 a turn up for the book(s)** *BrE informal* an unexpected and surprising event: *Keith's buying the drinks – that's a turn up for the books!*

**tur·pen·tine** /ˈtɜːpəntaɪn‖ˈtɜːr-/ *n* [U] a type of oil used for making paint more liquid or removing it from clothes, brushes etc

**tur·pi·tude** /ˈtɜːpɪ̥tjuːd‖ˈtɜːrpɪ̥tuːd/ *n* [U] *formal* evil: *gross moral turpitude*

**turps** /tɜːps‖tɜːrps/ *n* [U] *BrE informal* turpentine

**tur·quoise** /ˈtɜːkwɔɪz, -kwɑːz‖ˈtɜːrkwɔɪz/ *n* **1** [C,U] a valuable greenish-blue stone or a jewel that is made from this **2** [U] a greenish-blue colour —**turquoise** *adj* —see picture on page 411

**tur·ret** /ˈtʌrɪ̥t/ *n* [C] **1** a small tower on a large building, especially a CASTLE (1) **2** the place on a TANK (=army vehicle) from which guns are fired —**turreted** *adj*

**tur·tle** /ˈtɜːtl‖ˈtɜːrtl/ *n* [C] **1** an animal that lives mainly in water and has a soft body covered by a hard shell **2 turn turtle** a ship or boat that turns turtle turns upside down

**tur·tle·dove** /ˈtɜːtldʌv‖ˈtɜːr-/ *n* [C] a type of bird that makes a pleasant soft sound and is sometimes used to represent love

**tur·tle·neck** /ˈtɜːtlnek‖ˈtɜːr-/ *n* [C] *AmE* a type of sweater with a high, close-fitting band that folds down as a collar; POLO NECK *BrE*: *wearing a tweed skirt and a turtleneck sweater* —**turtlenecked** *adj*

**turves** /tɜːvz‖tɜːrvz/ *n* [plural] the plural of TURF[1] (2)

**tush[1]** /tʌʃ/ *interjection old use* used to say that something is not worth considering

**tush[2]** /tʊʃ/ *n* [C] *AmE slang* the part of your body that you sit on; BOTTOM[1] (3)

**tusk** /tʌsk/ *n* [C] one of a pair of very long pointed teeth, that stick out of the mouth of animals such as ELEPHANTS

**tus·sle[1]** /ˈtʌsəl/ *n* [C] *informal* a struggle or fight using a lot of energy, especially one in which you pull or push someone rather than hit them: *After quite a tussle I finally wrenched the letter from him.*

**tussle[2]** *v* [I + **with**] *informal* to fight or struggle without using any weapons, by pulling or pushing someone rather than hitting them: *tussling with the other boys in the queue*

**tus·sock** /ˈtʌsək/ *n* [C] a small thick mass of grass

**tut[1]** *interjection* a sound that you make by touching the top of your mouth with your tongue in order to show disapproval —**tut** *n* [C]

**tut[2]** /tʌt/ *v* [I] to express disapproval by making a tut sound: *The nursed rushed in, tutting with irritation.*

**tu·te·lage** /ˈtjuːtǝlɪdʒ‖ˈtuː-/ *n* [U] *formal* **1** the state or period of being taught or looked after by someone: **under sb's tutelage** (=being taught by someone) *Under Sir Edward's meticulous tutelage, I soon developed a discriminating taste.* **2** regular teaching over many years or months **3** responsibility for someone's education, actions or property

**tu·tor[1]** /ˈtjuːtə‖ˈtuːtər/ *n* [C] **1** someone who teaches one pupil or a small group, and is paid directly by them: *a reading tutor* **2** a teacher in a British university or college: *She was my tutor at Durham.*

**tutor[2]** *v* [T + **in**] to teach someone as a tutor —see TEACH (USAGE)

**tu·to·ri·al[1]** /tjuːˈtɔːriəl‖tuː-/ *n* [C] a period of teaching and discussion with a tutor, especially in a British university: *the tutorial system*

**tutorial[2]** *adj* connected with a tutor or their work

**tut·ti frut·ti** /ˌtuːti ˈfruːti/ *n* [U] a type of ICE CREAM that has very small pieces of fruit and nuts in it

**tut-tut[1]** /ˌtʌt ˈtʌt/ *i* a sound made by touching the top of the mouth with the tongue twice, in order to show disapproval

**tut-tut[2]** *v* [I] to express disapproval by saying tut-tut

**tu·tu** /ˈtuːtuː/ *n* [C] a short skirt made of many folds of stiff material worn by BALLET dancers

**tu-whit tu-whoo** /tə ˌwɪt tə ˈwuː/ *n* [C] the sound made by an OWL

**tux** /tʌks/ *n* [C] *informal* a tuxedo

**tux·e·do** /tʌkˈsiːdəʊ‖-doʊ/ *n* [C] **1** a man's JACKET (1) that is usually black, worn on formal occasions **2** a man's suit that includes this type of jacket

S 2 **TV** /ˌtiː ˈviː◂/ *n* [C,U] television: **TV programme/series/drama/star etc** *a new TV series about exploration | Jonathan Ross, the TV personality* | **on TV** *Did you see it on TV? What a game! | a TV in every room*

**TV din·ner** /ˌ·· ˈ··/ *n* [C] a meal that is sold already prepared, so that you just need to heat it before eating

**TVP** /ˌtiː viː ˈpiː/ *n* [U] the abbreviation of TEXTURED VEGETABLE PROTEIN

**twad·dle** /ˈtwɒdl‖ˈtwɑːdl/ *n* [U] *informal* something that someone has said or written that you think is stupid; nonsense: *a load of self-indulgent twaddle*

**twain** /tweɪn/ *prep old use* **1** two **2 never the twain shall meet** used to say that two things are so different that they can never exist together

**twang[1]** /twæŋ/ *n* [C usually singular] **1** a quality in the way someone speaks, produced when the air used to speak passes through your nose as well as your mouth: *a rural twang* **2** a quick ringing sound like the one made by pulling a very tight wire and then suddenly letting it go

**twang[2]** *v* [I,T] if you twang something or if it twangs, it makes a quick ringing sound by being pulled and then suddenly let go: *She twanged the guitar strings.*

**twas** /twɒz‖twɑːz/ *poetical* it was

**twat** /twɒt, twæt‖twɑːt/ *n* [C] *BrE taboo* **1** a stupid or unpleasant person **2** the female sex organ

**tweak** /twiːk/ *v* [T] **1** to suddenly pull or twist something: *Matthew tweaked her nose.* **2** to make small changes to a machine, vehicle, or system in order to improve the way it works: *Of course the programme still needs tweaking to maximize efficiency.* —**tweak** *n* [C usually singular]

**twee** /twiː/ *adj BrE* something that is twee looks too pretty or perfect: *That picture of little cottages with lace curtains is rather twee.*

**tweed** /twiːd/ *n* [U] **1** rough WOOLLEN cloth woven from threads of different colours, used mostly to make jackets (JACKET (1)), suits, and coats —see picture on page 839 **2 tweeds** [plural] a suit of clothes made from this type of cloth

**tweed·y** /ˈtwiːdi/ *adj* **1** *BrE* wearing tweed clothes in a way that is thought to be typical of the British upper class: *the epitome of the tweedy country squire* **2** made of tweed or like tweed

**tween** /twiːn/ *prep poetic* between

**tweet** /twiːt/ *v* [I] to make the short high sound of a small bird —**tweet** *n* [C]

**tweet·er** /ˈtwiːtə‖-ər/ *n* [C] a SPEAKER (=piece of equipment) through which the high sounds from a STEREO etc are made louder —compare WOOFER

**twee·zers** /ˈtwiːzəz‖-ərz/ *n* [plural] a small tool that has two narrow pieces of metal joined at one end, used to pull or move very small objects: *plucking her eyebrows with a pair of tweezers*

tweezers

**twelfth** /twelfθ/ *n* [C] one of 12 equal parts of something

**twelve** /twelv/ *number* 12

**twelve-month** /ˈ· ·/ *n* [C] *old-fashioned* a year

**twen·ty** /ˈtwenti/ *number* **1** 20 **2 the twenties** also **the 20's** the years from 1920 to 1929: *a photo showing how the street looked in the early twenties* **3 be in your twenties** to be aged between twenty and twenty nine: *She met him when she was in her twenties.*

**twenty-first** /ˌ·· ˈ·◂/ *n* [C usually singular] your twenty-first BIRTHDAY or the celebration you have for it

**twenty-one** /ˌ·· ˈ·◂/ *n* [U] *AmE* a card game, usually played for money; PONTOON (1) *BrE*

**twenty-twenty vi·sion, 20/20 vision** /ˌ·· ·· ˈ··/ *n* [U] the ability to see perfectly: *To be a pilot you must have twenty-twenty vision.*

**twenty-two, .22** /ˌtwentiˈtuː/ *n* [C] a gun that fires small bullets, used for hunting small animals

**twerp** /twɜːp‖twɜːrp/ *n* [C] *informal* a stupid or annoying person

**twice** /twaɪs/ *pred* two times —see also **once bitten, twice shy** (ONCE[1] (17)), **once or twice** (ONCE[1] (7)), **think twice** (THINK[1] (9))

**twid·dle[1]** /ˈtwɪdl/ *v* [T] **1** also **twiddle with** to move or turn something around with your fingers many times, especially because you are bored **2 twiddle your thumbs** *informal* **a)** to do nothing while you are waiting for something to happen **b)** to join your fingers together and move your thumbs in a circle around each other, because you are bored —**twiddle** *n* [C]

**twiddle[2]** *n* [C] a small twist or turn, especially in a decorative pattern

**twiddly** /ˈtwɪdli/ *adj* **twiddly bit** *spoken* used to talk about a small part of an object without naming it: *Where's the twiddly bit for the top?*

**twig¹** /twɪg/ *n* [C] a small very thin stem of wood that grows from a branch on a tree —**twiggy** *adj*

**twig²** *v* [I,T] *BrE informal* to suddenly realize something about a situation: *Do you mean he still hasn't twigged?*

**twi·light** /ˈtwaɪlaɪt/ *n* **1** [U] the small amount of light in the sky as the day ends: *It appeared shadowy and insubstantial in the twilight.* **2** [U] the time when day is just starting to become night **3** [singular] the period just before the end of the most active part of someone's life: *the twilight of her acting career* | **twilight years** (=the last ones of your life) **4 twilight world** *literary* a strange situation involving mystery, dishonesty etc: *the twilight world of espionage*

**twi·lit** /ˈtwaɪlɪt/ *adj literary* lit by twilight: *the twilit gray of the sea*

**twill** /twɪl/ *n* [U] strong cloth woven to produce parallel sloping lines across its surface: *grey twill trousers*

**twin¹** /twɪn/ *n* [C] one of two children born at the same time to the same mother: *My brother and I look so alike that people often think we are twins.* | **twin sister/brother/daughters etc** *Meet my twin sister.* —see also IDENTICAL TWIN, SIAMESE TWIN

**twin²** *adj* [only before noun] **1 twin problems/goals etc** happening at the same time and related to each other: *a policy to combat the twin problems of poverty and unemployment* **2 twin beds/engines etc** two similar things that are intended to be used as a pair —see also TWIN SET, TWIN TOWN, TWIN TUB —see picture at BED

**twin³** *v* [T usually passive] *BrE* to form a relationship between two similar towns in different countries in order to encourage visits between them: [+ **with**] *Harlow in England is twinned with Stavanger in Norway.* —see also TWIN TOWN

**twin bed** /ˌ· ˈ·/ *n* [C] **1** [usually plural] one of a pair of beds in a room for two people **2** *AmE* a bed for one person —**twin-bedded** *adj*: *twin-bedded rooms*

**twine¹** /twaɪn/ *n* [U] strong string made by twisting together two or more threads or strings: *a bundle of papers tied up with twine*

**twine²** *v* [I,T] to wind or twist around something else: **twine sth around sth** *She twined her fingers round the empty cup.* | [+ **around**] *Ivy twined around the balcony.*

**twin-en·gined** /ˌtwɪn ˈendʒɨnd◂/ *adj* a twin-engined aircraft has two engines

**twinge** /twɪndʒ/ *n* [C] **1** a sudden feeling of slight pain: *I felt a twinge in my back.* **2 a twinge of guilt/jealousy/fear etc** a sudden slight feeling of guilt etc: *John felt a twinge of regret as he walked away.*

**twin·kle¹** /ˈtwɪŋkəl/ *v* [I] **1** if a star or light twinkles, it shines in the dark, quickly changing from bright to faint: *The lights of the town twinkled below us.* **2** if someone's eyes twinkle, they have a cheerful expression: [+ **with**] *Don's eyes twinkled with laughter.* **3 in the twinkling of an eye** *old-fashioned* very quickly

**twinkle²** *n* [C usually singular] **1 a twinkle in your eye** an expression in your eyes that shows you are happy or amused: *"I can get that at home!" she said with a twinkle in her eye.* **2 when you were just a twinkle in your father's eye** before you were born **3** a small bright shining light that becomes brighter and then fainter

**twin·set** /ˈtwɪnset/ *n* [C] *BrE* a woman's SWEATER and CARDIGAN that are meant to be worn together: *twinset and pearls*

**twin town** /ˌ· ˈ·/ *n* [C] *BrE* a town that has formed a relationship with a similar town in another country in order to encourage visits between them: *Oxford's twin town is Bonn.*

**twin tub** /ˌ· ˈ·/ *n* [C] *BrE* a type of WASHING MACHINE with one part for washing and one for spin-drying (SPIN-DRYER)

**twirl¹** /twɜːl‖twɜːrl/ *v* [I,T] to turn around and around or make something do this: [+ **around/round**] *twirling around the dance floor* | **twirl sth around/round** *He twirled the gun round in his hand.*

**twirl²** *n* [C] a sudden quick spinning movement —**twirly** *adj*

**twist¹** /twɪst/ *v* S3

**1 ▶BEND◀** [T] to bend and turn something several times, especially in order to make something or to tie it to something: **twist sth into/around etc** *She twisted the wire into the shape of a star.*

**2 ▶MOVE◀** [I] to turn a part of your body around or change your position by turning: *He twisted to try and get free of the ropes.*

**3 ▶TURN◀** [T] to turn something using your hand: **twist sth off** *Jack twisted the cap off the bottle.*

**4 ▶WIND◀** [T always + adv/prep] to wind something in a particular way: **twist sth round/around** *She twisted the streamers round the banisters.* | **twist sth together** *Twist the two ends of the wire together.*

**5 ▶ROAD/RIVER◀** [I] if a road, river etc twists, it changes direction in a series of curves: *The track twisted into the hills.*

**6 ▶WORDS◀** [T] to change the true or intended meaning of a statement, especially in order to get some advantage for yourself; distort; DISTORT: *Every time I try to discuss the situation, he twists what I say.*

**7 twist your wrist/ankle/knee** to hurt your wrist etc by pulling or turning it too suddenly while you are moving

**8 twist and turn a)** if a path, road, stream etc twists and turns, it has a lot of bends in it **b)** if a person or animal twists and turns, they make twisting movements: *The snake twisted and turned through the mud.*

**9 twist sb's arm a)** *informal* to persuade someone to do something they do not want to do: *I'm sure he'll come to the party if you twist his arm.* **b)** to bend someone's arm upwards behind their back in order to hurt them **c) twist my arm!** *spoken* used humorously to accept an invitation, a drink etc: *Oh, go on, twist my arm! I'll have a red wine.* —see also **twist/wrap sb around your little finger** (FINGER¹ (13)), **twist/turn the knife** (KNIFE¹ (4))

**twist²** *n* [C] **1** a twisting action or movement: *Give that lid a twist – it's coming loose.* **2** a bend in a river or road **3** an unexpected change in the meaning of a situation or in the progress of a series of events: *The story ends with a strange twist – the detective turns out to be the murderer.* | **a twist of fate/fortune** *By an amazing twist of fate, we met again in Madrid five years later.* **4** a small piece of something that is twisted into a particular shape: [+ **of**] *a twist of tobacco* | *a twist of lemon* **5 round the twist** *BrE* crazy: **drive sb round the twist** (=make someone angry by continuously doing something) **6 the twist** a popular fast dance in the 1960s in which you twist your body from side to side **7 round the twist** *BrE spoken* **a)** very angry: *You children are sending me round the twist!* **b)** crazy —**twisty** *adj*: *a twisty road* —see also **get your knickers in a twist** (KNICKERS¹ (3))

**twist·ed** /ˈtwɪstɨd/ *adj* **1** bent in many directions, so that it has lost its original shape: *a mass of twisted wreckage* **2** seeming to enjoy things that are cruel or shocking, in a way that is not normal: *Whoever sent those letters has a twisted mind.*

**twist·er** /ˈtwɪstə‖-ər/ *n* [C] **1** *BrE informal* someone who cheats other people **2** *AmE informal* a TORNADO

**twit** /twɪt/ *n* [C] *informal* a stupid or silly person

**twitch¹** /twɪtʃ/ *v* **1** [I,T] if a part of someone's body twitches, it makes a small, sudden, uncontrolled movement: *My eye won't stop twitching.* **2** [T] to move something quickly and suddenly: *Sarah twitched the reins, and we moved off.*

**twitch²** *n* [C] **1** a quick movement of a muscle that you cannot control: *a nervous twitch* **2** a sudden, quick movement: *A twitch of the line means you've caught a fish.*

**twitch·y** /ˈtwɪtʃi/ *adj* **1** behaving in a nervous way because you are anxious about something: *Why are you so*

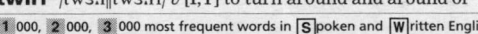

T

*twitchy today?* **2** repeatedly making sudden small movements: *a cat with a twitchy tail*

**twit·ter¹** /ˈtwɪtə‖-ər/ *v* [I] **1** if a bird twitters, it makes a lot of short high sounds: *the twittering of larks overhead* **2** if a woman twitters, she talks very quickly and nervously in a high voice

**twitter²** *n* **1** [singular] the short, high sounds that birds make **2 be all of a twitter** also **be in a twitter** to be excited and nervous: *She's been all of a twitter since her daughter's engagement.* —**twittery** *adj*

**twixt** /twɪkst/ *prep old use* between

**two** /tuː/ *number* **1** 2 **2 put two and two together** to guess the meaning of something you have heard or seen: *I didn't call to say I'd be late, but she put two and two together when she heard the weather reports.* **3 that makes two of us** *spoken* used to tell someone that you are in the same situation and feel the same way: *"Well, I don't want to be the one to tell him." "That makes two of us."* **4 two can play at that game** *spoken* used to tell someone that they will not have an advantage over you by doing something because you can do it too **5 two cents (worth)** [plural] *AmE informal* your opinion or what you want to say about a subject: *Everyone had to get in their two cents worth.* **6 for two cents** *AmE spoken* used when you are describing angrily what you would like to do to change a situation: *For two cents I'd kick him out.* **7 two bits** *AmE informal* twenty five CENTS, or a coin that is worth this amount of money **8 two's company, three's a crowd** used to say that it is better to leave two people alone to spend time with each other —see also **don't care two hoots** (HOOT¹ (5)), **be in two minds about** (MIND¹ (6)), **be two of a kind** (KIND¹ (8)), **be two a penny** (PENNY (11)), **it takes two to tango** (TANGO² (1))

**two-bit** /ˈ· ·/ *adj informal* not at all good or important: *She's just a two-bit movie star.*

**two-di·men·sion·al** /ˌ· ·ˈ···◂/ *adj* **1** a two-dimensional character in a book, play etc does not seem like a real person **2** flat: *a two-dimensional shape*

**two-edged** /ˌ· ˈ·◂/ *adj* **1** having disadvantages or bad effects that are less easy to see than the good effects: *the two-edged triumphs of technology* | **a two-edged sword** (=with as many bad results as good ones) *Strong leadership is a two-edged sword.* **2** having two edges that can cut

**two-faced** /ˌ· ˈ·◂/ *adj informal* changing what you say according to who you are talking to, in a way that is insincere and unpleasant: *He came out of the affair as a two-faced hypocrite.*

**two·fold** /ˈtuːfəʊld‖-foʊld/ *adj* **1** two times as much or as many of something: *a twofold increase in the incidence of TB* **2** having two important parts: *The reasons for the collapse are twofold.* —**twofold** *adv*

**two-hand·ed** /ˌ· ˈ··◂/ *adj* **1** using both hands to do something: *the tennis star's famous two-handed backhand* **2** a two-handed tool is used by two people together

**two-line whip** /ˌ· · ˈ·/ *n* [C] a written order given to members of the British Parliament about how they should vote on a particular subject

**two-man** /ˈ· ·/ *adj* designed to be used by two people: *a two-man tent*

**two-one, 2-1** /ˌtuː ˈwʌn/ *n* [C] the higher of two levels of a second-class university degree in Britain

**two·pence, tuppence** /ˈtʌpəns‖ˈtʌpəns, ˈtuːpens/ *n BrE* **1** [U] an amount of money worth two pence **2** [C] a British coin in former times that was worth two pence **3 not care twopence** *old-fashioned* to not care at all about something or someone

**two·pen·ny** /ˈtʌpəni‖ˈtʌpəni, ˈtuːpeni/ *adj BrE old-fashioned* **1** [only before noun] costing two pence; TUPPENNY **2 twopenny-halfpenny** worth almost nothing

**two-per·cent milk** /ˌ· ·ˈ·/ *n* [U] *AmE* milk that has had about half the fat removed; SEMI-SKIMMED *BrE*

**two-piece** /ˌ· ˈ·◂/ *adj* [only before noun] a two-piece suit consists of a matching JACKET (1) and trousers

**two-ply** /ˈ· ˌ·/ *adj* consisting of two threads or layers: *two-ply wool* | *two-ply tissues*

**two seat·er** /ˌ· ˈ··◂/ *n* [C] a car, aircraft etc with seats for two people

**two-sid·ed** /ˌ· ˈ··◂/ *adj* having two different parts: *a two-sided problem* —see also ONE-SIDED, MANY-SIDED

**two·some** /ˈtuːsəm/ *n* [C usually singular] two people who work together or spend a lot of time together: *the talented comedy twosome, French and Saunders*

**two-star** /ˈ· ·/ *adj* [only before noun] a level of quality used to judge hotels, restaurants etc, that shows they are of a medium standard

**two-step** /ˈ· ·/ *n* [singular] a dance with long sliding steps or the music for this type of dance

**two-stroke** /ˈ· ·/ *adj* a two-stroke engine is one in which there is a single up-and-down movement of a PISTON

**two-time** /ˈ· ·/ *v* [T] *informal* to have a secret relationship with someone who is not your regular partner: *If you're two-timing me, I'll kill you I swear!* —**two-timer** *n* [C]

**two-tone** /ˈ· ·/ *adj* **1** two-tone furniture, clothes etc are made of material in two colours: *two-tone shoes* **2** making two different sounds

**two-two, 2-2** /ˌ· ˈ·/ *n* [C] the lower of two levels of a second-class university degree in Britain: *She got a 2-2 in French.*

**two-way** /ˌ· ˈ·◂/ *adj* **1** moving or allowing movement in both directions: *two-way traffic* | *two-way trade* **2** two-way radio both sends and receives messages

**two-way mir·ror** /ˌ· · ˈ··/ *n* [C] glass that looks like a mirror from one side, but that you can see through from the other

**two-way street** /ˌ· · ˈ·/ *n* [C usually singular] *AmE informal* a situation that depends on two people working well together: *Marriage has to be a two-way street.*

**-ty** /ti/ *suffix (in nouns)* another form of the suffix -ITY: *certainty* (=being certain)

**ty·coon** /taɪˈkuːn/ *n* [C] someone who is successful in business or industry and has a lot of money and power: *Millionaire computer tycoon, Alan Sugar.*

**ty·ing** /ˈtaɪ-ɪŋ/ the present participle of TIE

**tyke** /taɪk/ *n* [C] **1** *spoken BrE* a child who is behaving badly **2** *AmE* a small child **3** *BrE informal* someone from Yorkshire

**tym·pa·num** /ˈtɪmpənəm/ *n* [C] *technical* an EAR DRUM

**type¹** /taɪp/ *n* **1** [C] one member of a group of people or things that have similar features or qualities: *There have been several incidents of this type in recent weeks.* | *Buy the right shampoo for your hair type.* | [+ **of**] *She's the type of person I admire.* **2** [U] printed letters: *italic type* **3** [C,U] a small block with a raised letter on it that is used to print with, or a set of these **4** [C] someone with particular qualities or interests: *the sporty type* **5 be sb's type** *especially spoken* to be the kind of person someone is sexually attracted to: *He wasn't my type really.* S1 W1

**type²** *v* **1** [T] to print a document on a piece of paper using a TYPEWRITER: *Does the report need to be typed?* **2** [I] to write using a TYPEWRITER or a computer: *He types with two fingers.* **3** [T] *technical* to find out what type a plant, disease etc is

**type·cast** /ˈtaɪpkɑːst‖-kæst/ *v* [T] **1** to always give an actor the same type of character to play: *He always gets typecast as the villain.* **2** to give someone a particular type of job, activity etc to do, because you think it suits their character

**type·face** /ˈtaɪpfeɪs/ *n* [C] a group of letters, numbers etc of the same style and size, used in printing

**type·script** /ˈtaɪpˌskrɪpt/ *n* [C] a copy of a document, made using a TYPEWRITER

**type·set·ter** /ˈtaɪpˌsetə‖-ər/ *n* [C] a person or machine that arranges the letters, words etc on a page or SCREEN[1] (1) for printing

**type·set·ting** /ˈtaɪpˌsetɪŋ/ *n* [U] the job or activity of arranging TYPE[1] (3) for printing —**typeset** *v* [T]

**type·writ·er** /ˈtaɪpˌraɪtə‖-ər/ *n* [C] a machine that prints letters of the alphabet onto paper

**type·writ·ten** /ˈtaɪpˌrɪtn/ *adj* written using a TYPEWRITER: *three sides of typewritten notes*

**ty·phoid** /ˈtaɪfɔɪd/ also **typhoid fe·ver** /ˌ·· ˈ··/ *n* [U] a serious infectious disease that is caused by dirty food or drink: *a sudden outbreak of typhoid*

**ty·phoon** /ˌtaɪˈfuːn◂/ *n* [C] a very violent storm in tropical areas in which the wind moves in circles

**ty·phus** /ˈtaɪfəs/ *n* [U] a serious infectious disease carried by insects that live on the bodies of people and animals

S2 W2 **typ·i·cal** /ˈtɪpɪkəl/ *adj* **1** having the usual features or qualities of a particular group or thing: *a typical British summer* | [+ **of**] *This painting is fairly typical of his early work.* **2** behaving or happening in the usual way: [+ **of**] *It was typical of him to get angry about it.* **3 typical!** *spoken* used to show that you are annoyed when something bad happens again

**typ·i·cally** /ˈtɪpɪkli/ *adv* **1** in a way that a person or group is generally believed to behave: *It's a typically British bureaucratic response.* **2** in the way that a particular type of thing usually happens: *The disease typically takes several weeks to appear.*

**typ·i·fy** /ˈtɪpɪ̈faɪ/ *v* [T not in progressive] **1** to be a typical example of something: *the arrogance that typifies this government's approach* **2** to be a typical part or feature of something: *the long complicated sentences that typify legal documents*

**typ·ing** /ˈtaɪpɪŋ/ *n* [U] the activity of using a TYPEWRITER to write something: *I've got a lot of typing to do today.*

**typing pool** /ˈ·· ·/ *n* [C] a group of typists in a large office who type letters for other people

**typ·ist** /ˈtaɪpɪ̈st/ *n* [C] **1** a secretary whose main job is to TYPE letters **2** someone who uses a TYPEWRITER: *I'm a slow typist.*

**ty·po** /ˈtaɪpəʊ‖-poʊ/ *n* [C] *informal* a small mistake in the way something has been typed (TYPE[2] (2)) or printed

**ty·pog·ra·pher** /taɪˈpɒgrəfə‖-ˈpɑːgrəfər/ *n* [C] **1** someone who designs TYPEFACES **2** a COMPOSITOR

**ty·po·graph·ic** /ˌtaɪpəˈgræfɪk◂/ also **ty·pograph·i·cal** /-fɪkəl/ *adj* connected with typography —**typographically** /-kli/ *adv*

**ty·pog·ra·phy** /taɪˈpɒgrəfi‖-ˈpɑː-/ *n* [U] **1** the work of preparing written material for printing **2** the arrangement, style and appearance of printed words

**ty·ran·ni·cal** /tɪ̈ˈrænɪkəl/ *adj* **1** behaving in a cruel and unfair way towards someone you have power over: *a tyrannical father* **2** tyrannical rules or laws etc are based on a system in which a single ruler uses their power unfairly: *the tyrannical laws relating to debtors*

**tyr·an·nize** also **-ise** *BrE* /ˈtɪrənaɪz/ *v* [T] to use power over someone cruelly or unfairly: *a family tyrannized by their grandfather*

**ty·ran·no·sau·rus** /tɪ̈ˌrænəˈsɔːrəs◂/ also **tyrannosaurus rex** /ˌ···· ˈ·/ *n* [C] a very large, flesh-eating DINOSAUR

**tyr·an·nous** /ˈtɪrənəs/ *adj old-fashioned* TYRANNICAL

**tyr·an·ny** /ˈtɪrəni/ *n* **1** [U] unfair and strict control over someone: *He longed to escape from the tyranny of his aunt.* **2** [C,U] government by one person or a small group that has gained power unfairly and uses it cruelly **3 the tyranny of fashion/the clock etc** the way that fashion etc limits people's freedom to do things the way they want to do **4** [C often plural] a cruel or unfair action that limits someone's freedom: *the tyrannies of Louis XVI's court*

**ty·rant** /ˈtaɪərənt‖ˈtaɪr-/ *n* [C] **1** a ruler who has complete power and uses it it in a cruel and unfair way: *Caligula and Nero, the two great tyrants* **2** someone who has power over other people, and uses it cruelly or unfairly

**tyre** *BrE*, **tire** *AmE* /taɪə‖taɪr/ *n* [C] **1** a thick, round band of rubber that fits around the wheel of a car, bicycle etc | **a flat tyre** (=one that has lost all its air) —see also SPARE TYRE —see picture on page 409 **2** a round band of metal that fits around the outside of a wooden wheel S3

**tzar** /zɑː, tsɑː‖zɑːr,tsɑːr/ *n* [C] another spelling of TSAR —**tzarist** *adj*

**tza·ri·na,** /zɑːˈriːnə, tsɑː-/ *n* [C] another spelling of TSARINA

**tzar·is·m** /ˈzɑːrɪzəm,ˈtsɑː-/ *n* [U] another spelling of TSARISM

**tze·tze fly** /ˈtetsi flaɪ, ˈtsetsi-, ˈsetsi-/ *n* [C] another spelling of TSETSE FLY

T

# U,u

**U, u** /juː/ *plural* **U's, u's** *n* [C] the 21st letter of the English alphabet

**U** /juː/ *n* **1** [C] a letter used in Britain to officially show that a film is suitable for people of any age **2** [C] a mark used in schools and examinations to show that your work or behaviour is extremely bad **3** [C] *BrE* a GRADE[1] (5) given in an examination to show that the work is too bad to be marked at all **4** [singular] *AmE old-fashioned* an abbreviation for university: *Indiana U*

**u·biq·ui·tous** /juːˈbɪkwɪ̈təs/ *adj formal or humorous* seeming to be everywhere: *We were tormented in the outback by the ubiquitous Australian fly.* —**ubiquitously** *adv* —**ubiquity** *n* [U]

**U-boat** /ˈjuː bəʊt‖-boʊt/ *n* [C] a German SUBMARINE, especially one that was used in the Second World War

**ud·der** /ˈʌdə‖-ər/ *n* [C] the part of a female cow, goat etc that hangs down between its back legs and that produces milk

**UFO** /ˈjuːfəʊ, ˌjuː ef ˈəʊ‖-foʊ, -ˈoʊ/ *n* [C] Unidentified Flying Object; a strange object in the sky, sometimes thought to be a SPACESHIP from another world

**ugh** /ʊx, ʌg/ *interjection* used to show strong dislike: *Ugh! This medicine tastes awful!*

**ug·ly** /ˈʌgli/ *adj* **1** extremely unattractive and unpleasant to look at: *He's just so ugly!|heavy, ugly furniture*|**ugly as sin** (=very ugly) **2** making you feel frightened, nervous, or threatened: *There were ugly scenes as rival gangs started attacking each other.* **3 rear its ugly head** to appear and start to cause problems: *Scandal has reared its ugly head yet again.* **4 ugly duckling** [C] someone who is less attractive, skilful etc than other people when they are young, but who becomes beautiful and successful later —**ugliness** *n* [U]



**UHF** /ˌjuː eɪtʃ ˈef/ *n* [U] ultra-high frequency; a range of radio waves (WAVE[1](3)) that produces a very good quality of sound

**uh huh** /ʌ ˈhʌ,ˈʌ hʌ/ *interjection informal* used to show that you understand or agree with what someone is saying to you: *"He's what, six years old?" "Uh huh."*

**UHT milk** /ˌjuː eɪtʃ tiː ˈmɪlk/ *n* [U] *BrE* milk that has been heated to a very high temperature to preserve it

**uh-uh** /ˈʌ ʌ/ *interjection informal* used to say no

**UK** /ˌjuː ˈkeɪ◂/ *n* the abbreviation of United Kingdom

**u·ke·le·le** /ˌjuːkəˈleɪli/ *n* [C] a musical instrument with four strings, like a small GUITAR

**-ular** /jʊ̈lə‖-ər/ *suffix* [in adjectives] of or concerning something: *glandular fever|tubular steel*

**ul·cer** /ˈʌlsə‖-ər/ *n* [C] a sore area on your skin or inside your body that may BLEED or produce poisonous substances: *stomach ulcers* —**ulcerous** *adj*

**ul·cer·ate** /ˈʌlsəreɪt/ *v* [I,T] to form an ulcer, or become covered with ulcers —**ulcerated** *adj* —**ulceration** /ˌʌlsəˈreɪʃən/ *n* [U]

**-ule** /juːl/ *suffix* [in nouns] *technical* a small type of something: *a granule* (=small grain)

**ul·na** /ˈʌlnə/ *n* [C] *technical* the inner bone of your lower arm, on the side opposite to your thumb —see picture at SKELETON

**ul·te·ri·or** /ʌlˈtɪəriə‖-ˈtɪriər/ *adj* **ulterior motives/purpose etc** reasons for doing something that you deliberately hide in order to get an advantage for yourself: *In some countries, Peace Corps volunteers were suspected of having ulterior motives, such as spying for the CIA.*

W 3 **ul·ti·mate¹** /ˈʌltɪ̈mɪ̈t/ *adj* [only before noun] **1** better, bigger, worse etc than all other objects of the same kind: *the ultimate sports car* **2** an ultimate aim, purpose etc is the final and most important one: *Complete disarmament was the ultimate goal of the conference.* **3** an ultimate decision, responsibility etc is one that you cannot pass on to someone else: *Ultimate responsibility lies with the President.*

**ultimate²** *n* **the ultimate in stupidity/luxury/technology etc** something that shows the highest possible level of stupidity etc: *This video-sound system is the ultimate in home entertainment technology.*

**ul·ti·mate·ly** /ˈʌltɪ̈mɪ̈tli/ *adv* after everything or everyone else has been done or considered [sentence adverb] *Ultimately the decision rests with the child's parents.* W 3

**ul·ti·ma·tum** /ˌʌltɪ̈ˈmeɪtəm/ *n* [C] a threat saying that if someone does not do what you want by a particular time, you will do something to punish them: **give sb an ultimatum** *Well, give him an ultimatum: either he pays by Friday or he finds somewhere else to live.*

**ultra-** /ʌltrə/ *prefix* **1** *technical* above in a range; beyond: *ultrasound* (=too high to hear) —compare INFRA- **2** extremely: *an ultramodern building|an ultracautious approach*

**ul·tra-high fre·quen·cy** /ˌ‥ ˈ‥/ *n* [U] UHF

**ul·tra·ma·rine** /ˌʌltrəməˈriːn◂/ *n* [C,U] a very bright blue colour —**ultramarine** *adj*

**ul·tra·son·ic** /ˌʌltrəˈsɒnɪk◂‖-ˈsɑː-/ *adj* ultrasonic sound waves are too high for humans to hear

**ultra·sound** /ˈʌltrəsaʊnd/ *n* **1** [U] sound that is too high for humans to hear, and is often used in medical processes **2** [C] a medical process using this type of sound that produces an image of something inside your body, especially a baby

**ul·tra·vi·o·let** /ˌʌltrəˈvaɪəlɪ̈t◂/ *adj* **1** ultraviolet light is beyond the purple end of the range of colours that people can see **2** [only before noun] an ultraviolet lamp, treatment etc uses this light to treat skin diseases or make your skin darker

**u·lu·la·tion** /ˌjuːljʊ̈ˈleɪʃən/ *n* [C] *literary* a long low sound made with your voice —**ululate** /ˈjuːljʊ̈leɪt/ *v* [I]

**um** /ʌm, əm/ *interjection* used when you cannot immediately decide what to say next: *Um, yeah, I guess so.*

**um·ber** /ˈʌmbə‖-ər/ *n* [C,U] a brown colour like earth —**umber** *adj*

**um·bil·i·cal cord** /ʌmˈbɪlɪkəl ˌkɔːd‖-ˌkɔːrd/ *n* [C] a long narrow tube of flesh that joins an unborn baby to its mother

**um·bil·i·cus** /ʌmˈbɪlɪkəs/ *n* [C] *technical* the small hollow place on your stomach; NAVEL

**um·brage** /ˈʌmbrɪdʒ/ *n* **take umbrage (at)** to be offended by something that someone has done or said: *James took umbrage at Mrs Dubose's remarks.*

**um·brel·la** /ʌmˈbrelə/ *n* [C] **1** a circular folding frame covered in cloth that you hold above you when it is raining —compare SUNSHADE, PARASOL **2 umbrella organization** an organization that includes many smaller groups **3 umbrella term/word** a word whose meaning includes many different types of a particular object **4** the protection given by a powerful country, army, a weapons system etc: *the political umbrella of the United Nations*

**umbrella**

**um·laut** /ˈʊmlaʊt/ *n* [C] a sign (¨) written over a German vowel to show how it is pronounced

**ump** /ʌmp/ *n* [C] *AmE spoken* an umpire

**um·pire¹** /ˈʌmpaɪə‖-paɪr/ *n* [C] the person in some sports who makes sure that the players obey the rules —see picture at TENNIS

**umpire²** *v* [I,T] to be the umpire for a game or competition

**ump·teen** /ˌʌmpˈtiːn◂/ *determiner informal* a large number of: *There seemed to be umpteen rules and regulations to learn.* —**umpteenth** *number*

**un** /ən/ *pron BrE spoken* **good 'un/bad 'un etc** a short form of one, used to say that someone or something is bad, good etc: *He's a bad 'un.* | *Those apples are little 'uns.*

**UN** /ˌjuː ˈen/ *n* [singular] the United Nations; an international organization that tries to find peaceful solutions to world problems

**un-** /ʌn/ *prefix* [especially in adjectives and adverbs] **1** shows a negative, a lack, or an opposite; not: *unfair* | *unhappy* | *unfortunately* **2** [especially in verbs] shows an opposite: *to undress* (=take your clothes off)

**un·a·bashed** /ˌʌnəˈbæʃt◂/ *adj* not ashamed or embarrassed, especially when doing something unusual or rude: *She stared at him with unabashed curiosity.*

**un·a·bat·ed** /ˌʌnəˈbeɪtɪ̬d◂/ *adj, adv* continuing without becoming any weaker or less violent: *The storm continued unabated throughout the night.* | *his unabated ambition*

S3 W2 **un·a·ble** /ʌnˈeɪbəl/ *adj* not able to do something **be unable to do sth**: *Many passengers were unable to reach the lifeboats.*

**un·a·bridged** /ˌʌnəˈbrɪdʒd◂/ *adj* a piece of writing, speech etc that is unabridged is in its full form without being made shorter: *the complete and unabridged works of Dickens*

**un·ac·cept·a·ble** /ˌʌnəkˈseptəbəl◂/ *adj* **1** something that is unacceptable is so wrong or bad that you think it should not be allowed: *unacceptable levels of unemployment* **2 the unacceptable face of** the bad or unfair part of a system, activity etc: *property speculation, the unacceptable face of capitalism* —**unacceptably** *adv*

**un·ac·com·pa·nied** /ˌʌnəˈkʌmpənid◂/ *adj* **1** someone who is unaccompanied has no one with them: *Unaccompanied children are not allowed on the premises.* **2** an unaccompanied singer or musician sings or plays alone: *a piece for unaccompanied voices* **3 unaccompanied bags/luggage etc** bags, cases etc that are sent on a plane, train etc without their owner

**un·ac·count·a·ble** /ˌʌnəˈkaʊntəbəl◂/ *adj formal* **1** very surprising and difficult to explain: *Patrick's disappearance was quite unaccountable.* **2** not having to explain your actions or decisions to anyone else: *It is not acceptable that the governors of this institution should be largely unaccountable.* —**unaccountably** *adv*

**un·ac·count·ed** /ˌʌnəˈkaʊntɪd◂/ *adj* something or someone that is unaccounted for cannot be found or their absence cannot be explained: *Two people are still unaccounted for after the floods.*

**un·ac·cus·tomed** /ˌʌnəˈkʌstəmd◂/ *adj formal* **1 unaccustomed to** not used to something: *a country boy, unaccustomed to city ways* **2** [only before noun] not usual, typical, or familiar: *unaccustomed physical exertion* **3 unaccustomed as I am (to)** *spoken formal* used before saying something in front of a lot of people

**un·ac·knowl·edged** /ˌʌnəkˈnɒlɪdʒd◂‖-ˈnɑː-/ *adj* **1** not generally or publicly known for something that should be rewarded, thanked, or praised: *Women's work in the home tends to be both unpaid and unacknowledged.* **2 the unacknowledged leader/authority etc** a leader etc who is not officially or publicly recognised: *Grandma was the unacknowledged boss of the family.* **3** ignored or not noticed: *The tap on the door went unacknowledged for some time.*

**un·a·dopt·ed** /ˌʌnəˈdɒptɪ̬d◂‖-ˈdɑːp-/ *adj BrE* an unadopted road must be repaired by the people who live along it and not by a town council

**un·a·dul·te·rat·ed** /ˌʌnəˈdʌltəreɪtɪ̬d◂/ *adj* **1** not mixed with other less pure substances **2** [only before noun] complete or total: *What unadulterated nonsense!*

**un·af·fect·ed** /ˌʌnəˈfektɪ̬d◂/ *adj* **1** not changed or influenced by something: [+ **by**] *The north west was unaffected by the drought.* **2** *approving* natural in the way you behave: *her easy, unaffected manner* —**unaffectedly** *adv*

**un·aid·ed** /ʌnˈeɪdɪ̬d/ *adj, adv* without help: *It was the first time she had walked unaided since her illness.*

**un·al·loyed** /ˌʌnəˈlɔɪd◂/ *adj literary* not mixed with anything else: *unalloyed happiness*

**un·al·ter·a·ble** /ʌnˈɔːltərəbəl/ *adj formal* not possible to change: *an unalterable fact* —**unalterably** *adv*

**un·am·big·u·ous** /ˌʌnæmˈbɪgjuəs◂/ *adj* a statement, instruction etc that is unambiguous is clear and easy to understand because it can only mean one thing: *a brief, unambiguous description of the problem* —**unambiguously** *adv*

**un·A·mer·i·can** /ˌ· ·ˈ···◂/ *adj* not loyal to generally accepted American customs and ways of thinking: **un-American activities** (=political activity believed to be harmful to the US)

**u·na·nim·i·ty** /ˌjuːnəˈnɪmɪ̬ti/ *n* [U] *formal* a state or situation of complete agreement among a group of people

**u·nan·i·mous** /juːˈnænɪ̬məs/ *adj* **1** a unanimous decision, statement etc is one that everyone agrees with **2** agreeing completely about something: **unanimous that** *The jury was unanimous that the defendant was guilty.* —**unanimously** *adv*

**un·an·nounced** /ˌʌnəˈnaʊnst◂/ *adj, adv* happening without anyone expecting or knowing about it: *We arrived unannounced.*

**un·an·swer·a·ble** /ʌnˈɑːnsərəbəl‖ʌnˈæn-/ *adj* **1** definitely true and therefore impossible to argue against: *an unanswerable case in law* **2** an unanswerable question is one that seems to have no possible answer or solution

**un·ap·peal·ing** /ˌʌnəˈpiːlɪŋ◂/ *adj* not pleasant or attractive: *an unappealing bowl of watery soup*

**un·ap·proach·a·ble** /ˌʌnəˈprəʊtʃəbəl◂‖-ˈproʊ-/ *adj* seeming unfriendly and therefore difficult to talk to: *Jo appeared, looking grim and unapproachable.*

**un·ar·gu·a·ble** /ʌnˈɑːgjuəbəl‖-ˈɑːr-/ *adj* something that is unarguable is definitely true or correct —**unarguably** *adv*

**un·armed** /ˌʌnˈɑːmd◂‖-ˈɑːrmd◂/ *adj* not carrying any weapons: **unarmed combat** (=fighting without weapons)

**un·a·shamed** /ˌʌnəˈʃeɪmd◂/ *adj* not feeling embarrassed or ashamed about something that people might disapprove of: *the unashamed luxury of our marble bath* —**unashamedly** *adv*

**un·asked** /ʌnˈɑːskt‖-ˈæskt/ *adj, adv* **1** if a question is unasked, no one asks it, often because they are embarrassed **2** if you do something unasked, you do it without anyone asking or inviting you to: *Jerry entered unasked, and stood by the fire.* | **unasked for** *hundreds of pounds in unasked for donations*

**un·as·sail·able** /ˌʌnəˈseɪləbəl◂/ *adj formal* not able to be criticized, attacked, or made weaker: *an unassailable argument*

**un·as·sum·ing** /ˌʌnəˈsjuːmɪŋ◂, -ˈsuː-‖-ˈsuː-/ *adj* showing no desire to be noticed or given special treatment; MODEST: *an unassuming middle-class family*

**un·at·tached** /ˌʌnəˈtætʃt◂/ *adj* **1** not involved in a romantic relationship; SINGLE[1] (4): *Sure, he's handsome, but is he unattached?* **2** not connected or fastened to anything

**un·at·tain·a·ble** /ˌʌnəˈteɪnəbəl◂/ *adj* impossible to achieve: *an unattainable goal*

**un·at·tend·ed** /ˌʌnəˈtendɪ̬d◂/ *adj* left alone without anyone in charge: *unattended luggage* | **leave sb/sth unattended** *Children should not be left unattended in the playground.*

**un·at·trac·tive** /ˌʌnəˈtræktɪv◂/ *adj* **1** not attractive, pretty, or pleasant to look at: *an unattractive man* **2** not good or desirable: *the unattractive aspects of nationalism* —**unattractively** *adv*

**un·au·tho·rized** /ʌn'ɔːθəraɪzd‖-'ɒː-/ also **-ised** *BrE adj* without official approval or permission: *laws to prevent unauthorized photocopying*

**un·a·vail·a·ble** /ˌʌnə'veɪləbəl/ *adj* [not before noun] **1** not able to be obtained: *Funding for the new school is unavailable.* **2** not able or willing to meet someone: *I'm sorry, the principal is unavailable just now.*

**un·a·vail·ing** /ˌʌnə'veɪlɪŋ◂/ *adj literary* not successful or effective: *unavailing efforts*

**un·a·void·a·ble** /ˌʌnə'vɔɪdəbəl/ *adj* impossible to prevent: *There are now fears that war is unavoidable* —**unavoidably** *adv*: *Molly was unavoidably delayed.*

**un·a·ware** /ˌʌnə'weə‖-'wer/ *adj* not noticing or realizing what is happening: [+ **of**] *Mike seems unaware of the trouble he's causing.* | **unaware that** *She remained unaware that she was being watched.* —**unawareness** *n* [U]

**un·a·wares** /ˌʌnə'weəz‖-'werz/ *adv* **1 take/catch sb unawares** to happen or to do something in a way that someone was not expecting and so was not prepared for: *Caught unawares like that, I was unable to think of an excuse.* **2** *formal* without noticing: *We had walked unawares over the border.*

**un·bal·anced** /ˌʌn'bælənst/ *adj* **1** someone who is unbalanced seems slightly crazy **2** a report, argument etc that is unbalanced is unfair because it emphasizes one opinion too much **3** a relationship that is unbalanced is not equal because one person has more influence, power etc

**un·bear·a·ble** /ʌn'beərəbəl‖-'ber-/ *adj* too unpleasant, painful, or annoying to bear; INTOLERABLE: *Their constant arguments were unbearable.* —**unbearably** *adj*: *an unbearably hot day*

**un·beat·a·ble** /ʌn'biːtəbəl/ *adj* **1** something that is unbeatable is the best of its kind: *unbeatable prices* **2** a team, player etc that is unbeatable cannot be defeated

**un·be·com·ing** /ˌʌnbɪ'kʌmɪŋ◂/ *adj old-fashioned* **1** clothes that are unbecoming do not make you look attractive: *a blouse in an unbecoming green color* **2** behaviour that is unbecoming is shocking or unsuitable: [+ **to**] *conduct unbecoming to a teacher*

**un·be·known** /ˌʌnbɪ'nəʊn‖-'noʊn/ also **unbeknownst** [sentence adverb] **unbeknown to sb** without that person knowing about it: *Unbeknown to him, his wife had been trying to phone him all morning.*

**un·be·lief** /ˌʌnbɪ̆'liːf/ *n* [U] *formal* a lack of belief or a refusal to believe in a religious faith —compare DISBELIEF

S3 **un·be·lie·va·ble** /ˌʌnbɪ̆'liːvəbəl◂/ *adj* **1** extremely surprising: *Dealers were paying unbelievable prices for her paintings.* **2** very difficult to believe and therefore probably untrue: *Yvonne's excuse for being late was totally unbelievable.* —**unbelievably** *adv*: *an unbelievably bad movie*

**un·be·liev·er** /ˌʌnbɪ̆'liːvə‖-ər/ *n* [C] someone who does not believe in a particular religion

**un·bend** /ʌn'bend/ *v* **1** [I,T] to become straight or make something straight **2** [I] to relax and start behaving in a less formal way: *She'd be a lot more likeable if she'd unbend a little.*

**un·bend·ing** /ʌn'bendɪŋ/ *adj* unwilling to change your opinions, decisions etc: *a stern, unbending man*

**un·bi·ased** /ʌn'baɪəst/ *adj* able to make a fair judgment, especially because you are not influenced by your own or other people's opinions: *With all the publicity surrounding the case, it's going to be hard to find an unbiased jury.*

**un·bid·den** /ˌʌn'bɪdn/ *adv literary* without being asked for, expected, or invited

**un·blem·ished** /ˌʌn'blemɪʃt/ *adj* not spoiled by any mistake or bad behaviour: *an unblemished reputation*

**un·born** /ˌʌn'bɔːn◂‖-ɔːrn◂/ *adj* not yet born: *an unborn child*

**un·bos·om** /ˌʌn'bʊzəm/ *v* [T] *literary* **unbosom yourself to** to tell someone about the things that are worrying you

**un·bound·ed** /ʌn'baʊndɪ̆d/ *adj formal* extreme or without any limit: *unbounded energy*

**un·bri·dled** /ʌn'braɪdld/ *adj literary* not controlled and too extreme or violent: *unbridled passion*

**un·bro·ken** /ʌn'brəʊkən‖-'broʊ-/ *adj* continuing without being broken or interrupted: *an unbroken silence* | *the unbroken prosperity of the last 25 years*

**un·buck·le** /ˌʌn'bʌkəl/ *v* [T] to unfasten the BUCKLE on something: *He unbuckled his belt.*

**un·bur·den** /ˌʌn'bɜːdn‖-ɜːr-/ *v* [T] **1 unburden yourself/your heart** to tell someone your problems, secrets etc so that you feel better: *Jane unburdened herself of a terrible secret.* | [+ **to**] *He felt an urge to unburden his heart to this stranger.* **2** *literary* to take a heavy load away from someone

**un·called-for** /ʌn'kɔːld fɔː‖-'kɒːld fɔːr/ *adj informal* behaviour or remarks that are uncalled-for are unfair or unsuitable: *That comment was totally uncalled-for.*

**un·can·ny** /ʌn'kæni/ *adj* very strange and difficult to explain: *an uncanny coincidence* —**uncannily** *adv*

**un·cared for** /ʌn'keəd fɔː‖-'kerd fɔːr/ *adj* not looked after or not looked after properly: *The dogs looked hungry and uncared for.*

**un·ceas·ing** /ʌn'siːsɪŋ/ *adj* never stopping: *an unceasing barrage of questions* —**unceasingly** *adv*

**un·ce·re·mo·ni·ous** /ˌʌnserɪ̆'məʊniəs◂‖-'moʊ-/ *adj* without paying any attention to politeness or good manners: *Philippa finished her meal with unceremonious haste.* —**unceremoniously** *adv* —**unceremoniousness** *n* [U]

**un·cer·tain** /ʌn'sɜːtn‖-ɜːr-/ *adj* **1** [not before noun] not sure or feeling doubt: *Lee moved awkwardly and looked uncertain.* | [+ **how/what/where etc**] *She hesitated, uncertain what to do next.* **2** likely to change, often in a way that is bad: *My whole future now seemed uncertain.* **3** [not before noun] not definite or decided: *Our holiday plans are still uncertain.* **4 in no uncertain terms** if you tell someone something in no uncertain terms, you tell them very clearly without trying to be polite: *I told Colin in no uncertain terms what I thought of him.* —**uncertainly** *adv* —**uncertainty** *n* [C,U]

**un·chal·lenged** /ʌn'tʃælɪ̆ndʒd/ *adj* **1** accepted and believed by everyone and not doubted: *Roy's authority was unchallenged.* **2** someone who goes somewhere unchallenged is not stopped and asked who they are or what they are doing: *How did the prisoners manage to get to the outer fence unchallenged?*

**un·chang·ing** /ʌn'tʃeɪndʒɪŋ/ *adj* always staying the same

**un·char·ac·ter·is·tic** /ʌnˌkærɪ̆ktə'rɪstɪk◂/ *adj* not typical of someone or something and therefore surprising: [+ **of**] *It's uncharacteristic of her to be late.* —**uncharacteristically** /-kli/ *adv*

**un·char·i·ta·ble** /ʌn'tʃærɪ̆təbəl/ *adj* unkind or unfair in the way you judge people: *It's very uncharitable to say Phillip's problems are all his own fault.*

**un·chart·ed** /ʌn'tʃɑːtɪ̆d‖-ɑːr-/ *adj literary* **1** not marked on any maps: *The ship arrived at a previously uncharted island.* **2 uncharted waters/territory** a situation or activity that you have never experienced or tried before: *This new operation was uncharted territory for the surgeons.*

**un·checked** /ˌʌn'tʃekt◂/ *adj* **1** an unchecked activity, illness etc develops and gets worse because it is not controlled or stopped: *We cannot allow such behaviour to continue unchecked.* **2** not tested for quality, safety etc: *The goods should not have left the factory unchecked.* —see also CHECK

**un·civ·i·lized** also **-ised** *BrE* /ʌn'sɪvɪ̆laɪzd/ *adj* **1** uncivilized behaviour is rude or socially unacceptable: *uncivilized incidents of racial violence* **2 an uncivilized hour** *informal* extremely early in the morning

**un·cle** /ˈʌŋkəl/ *n* [C] **1** the brother of your mother or father, or the husband of your aunt —see picture at FAMILY **2** a man whose brother or sister has a child: *Enrique was very excited about becoming an uncle.* **3** used as a name for a man who is a close friend of your parents **4 say uncle** *AmE spoken* used by children to tell someone to admit they have been defeated —see also **talk like a dutch uncle** (DUTCH² (3))

**un·clean** /ˌʌnˈkliːn◂/ *adj* **1** *biblical* morally or spiritually bad: *an unclean spirit* **2** unclean food, animals etc are those that must not be eaten, touched etc in a particular religion —**uncleanness** *n* [U]

**un·clear** /ˌʌnˈklɪə◂‖-ˈklɪr◂/ *adj* **1** difficult to understand or be sure about, so that there is doubt or confusion: *The terms of the contract are very unclear.* **2 be unclear about** to not understand something clearly: *I'm rather unclear about what I'm supposed to be doing here.*

**Uncle Sam** /ˌʌŋkəl ˈsæm/ *n* [singular] *informal* the US, or the US government, sometimes represented by the figure of a man with a white BEARD and tall hat

**Uncle Tom** /ˌʌŋkəl ˈtɒm‖-ˈtɑːm/ *n* [C] *AmE* a black person who is too friendly or respectful to white people, used in a disapproving way by other black people

**un·clothed** /ʌnˈkləʊðd‖-ˈkloʊðd/ *adj formal* not wearing clothes or not covered by clothes; NAKED

**un·coil** /ˌʌnˈkɔɪl/ *v* [I,T] if you uncoil something, or if it uncoils, it stretches out straight, after being wound around in a circle: *Slowly the snake uncoiled.*

**un·com·fort·a·ble** /ʌnˈkʌmftəbəl, -ˈkʌmfət-‖-ˈkʌmfərt-, -ˈkʌmft-/ *adj* **1** not feeling physically comfortable, or not making you feel comfortable: *This sofa is so uncomfortable.* **2** unable to relax because you are embarrassed: *an uncomfortable silence* —**uncomfortably** *adv*

**un·com·mit·ted** /ˌʌnkəˈmɪtɪ̣d◂/ *adj* not having decided or promised to support a particular group, political belief etc: *A large proportion of voters remain uncommitted.*

**un·com·mon** /ʌnˈkɒmən‖-ˈkɑː-/ *adj* rare or unusual: *Violent crimes against the elderly are fortunately very uncommon.* | **it is not uncommon for sb to do sth** *It is not uncommon nowadays for students to have bank loans.* —see RARE (USAGE)

**un·com·mon·ly** /ʌnˈkɒmənli‖-ˈkɑː-/ *adv* [+ adj/adv] *old-fashioned* very: *That's uncommonly kind of you.*

**un·com·plain·ing** /ˌʌnkəmˈpleɪnɪŋ◂/ *adj* willing to accept a difficult or unpleasant situation without complaining: *A dog can make a wonderful, uncomplaining walking companion.* —**uncomplainingly** *adv*

**un·com·pre·hen·ding** /ˌʌnkɒmprɪˈhendɪŋ‖-kɑːm-/ *adj* not understanding what is happening —**uncomprehendingly** *adv*

**un·com·pro·mis·ing** /ʌnˈkɒmprəmaɪzɪŋ‖-ˈkɑːm-/ *adj* unwilling to change your opinions or intentions: *an uncompromising opponent of democratic reform* —**uncompromisingly** *adv*

**un·con·cern** /ˌʌnkənˈsɜːn‖-ɜːrn/ *n* [U] an attitude of not caring about something that other people worry about: *In view of the deepening crisis, we are surprised at the government's apparent unconcern.*

**un·con·cerned** /ˌʌnkənˈsɜːnd‖-ɜːrnd/ *adj* **1** not worried about something because you think it does not affect you: [+ **about**] *Many large companies seem totally unconcerned about the environment.* **2** not interested in a particular aim or activity: [+ **with**] *unconcerned with making a profit* —**unconcernedly** /-nɪ̣dli/ *adv*

**un·con·di·tion·al** /ˌʌnkənˈdɪʃənəl◂/ *adj* not limited by or depending on any conditions: *the unconditional release of all political prisoners* | **unconditional surrender** *The Allies declared they would accept nothing less than unconditional surrender.* —**unconditionally** *adv*

**un·con·firmed** /ˌʌnkənˈfɜːmd◂‖-ˈfɜːrmd◂/ *adj* **unconfirmed report/story/rumour etc** a report etc that has not been proved or supported by official information: *We've received unconfirmed reports of an explosion in central London.*

**un·con·scion·a·ble** /ʌnˈkɒnʃənəbəl‖-ˈkɑːn-/ *adj formal* much more than is reasonable or acceptable: *an unconscionable amount of suffering* —**unconscionably** *adv*

**un·con·scious¹** /ʌnˈkɒnʃəs‖-ˈkɑːn-/ *adj* **1** unable to see, move, feel etc in the normal way because you are not conscious: *She was found alive but unconscious.* | **knock/beat sb unconscious** *Murphy was attacked and beaten unconscious.* **2** a feeling or thought that is unconscious is one that you have without realizing it: *an unconscious need to be loved* —compare SUBCONSCIOUS¹ **3 be unconscious of** to not realize the effect of something you have said or done: *Doreen appeared to be unconscious of the amusement she had caused.* **4** an action that is unconscious is not deliberate —**unconsciously** *adv* —**unconsciousness** *n* [U]

**unconscious²** *n* **the/sb's unconscious** the part of your mind in which there are thoughts and feelings that you do not realize you have; SUBCONSCIOUS²

**un·con·sid·ered** /ˌʌnkənˈsɪdəd◂‖-ərd/ *adj* **1** unconsidered remarks or actions are made without thinking about the possible results **2** *formal* not important or not noticed: *unconsidered trifles*

**un·con·sti·tu·tion·al** /ˌʌnkɒnstɪ̣ˈtjuːʃənəl‖-kɑːnstɪ̣ˈtuː-/ *adj* not allowed by the CONSTITUTION (=set of rules or principles by which a country or organization is governed) *the debate over whether flag-burning is an unconstitutional form of protest* —**unconstitutionality** /ˌʌnkɒnstɪ̣tjuːʃəˈnælɪ̣ti‖-kɑːnstɪ̣tuː-/ *n* [U]

**un·con·trol·lable** /ˌʌnkənˈtrəʊləbəl◂‖-ˈtroʊl-/ *adj* **1** uncontrollable emotions, desires or actions are ones that you cannot control or stop: *I felt an uncontrollable urge to scream.* **2** someone who is uncontrollable behaves badly and will not obey anyone **3** situations or conditions that are uncontrollable cannot be changed

**un·con·trolled** /ˌʌnkənˈtrəʊld◂‖-ˈtroʊld◂/ *adj* uncontrolled emotions or behaviour continue because you are not trying to stop or control them: *uncontrolled weeping*

**un·con·ven·tion·al** /ˌʌnkənˈvenʃənəl◂/ *adj* very different from the way people usually behave, think, dress etc: *unconventional political views*

**un·co·op·er·a·tive** /ˌʌnkəʊˈɒpərətɪv◂‖-koʊˈɑːp-/ *adj* not willing to work with or help someone: *The immigration authorities were brusque and uncooperative.*

**un·co·or·di·nat·ed** /ˌʌnkəʊˈɔːdɪ̣neɪtɪ̣d◂‖-koʊˈɔːr-/ *adj* **1** someone who is uncoordinated is not good at physical activities because they cannot control their movements effectively; CLUMSY: *I was always too uncoordinated to be good at tennis.* **2** a plan or operation that is uncoordinated is not well organized with the result that the different parts of it do not work together effectively

**un·cork** /ʌnˈkɔːk‖-ˈkɔːrk/ *v* [T] to open a bottle by removing its CORK¹ (2) —see picture on page 838

**un·count·a·ble** /ʌnˈkaʊntəbəl/ *adj* a noun that is uncountable has no plural form and means something which cannot be counted or regarded as either singular or plural, for example 'water', or 'beauty'. In this dictionary uncountable nouns are marked [U]; MASS NOUN

**un·couth** /ʌnˈkuːθ/ *adj* behaving and speaking in a way that is rude or socially unacceptable: *rough, uncouth men* —**uncouthly** *adv* —**uncouthness** *n* [U]

**un·cov·er** /ʌnˈkʌvə‖-ər/ *v* [T] **1** to find out about something that has been kept secret: *Customs officials uncovered a plot to smuggle weapons into the country.* **2** to remove the cover from something

**un·crit·i·cal** /ʌnˈkrɪtɪkəl/ *adj* unable or unwilling to see faults in something or someone: [+ **of**] *John's mother is totally uncritical of his behaviour.* —**uncritically** /-kli/ *adv*

**un·crowned** /ˌʌnˈkraʊnd◂/ *adj* **the uncrowned king/queen of** the person who is thought to be the best or most famous in a particular activity: *Martina Navratilova, the uncrowned queen of women's tennis*

**un·crush·a·ble** /ʌnˈkrʌʃəbəl/ *adj* 1 material or cloth that is uncrushable is easy to keep smooth 2 very determined and not easily discouraged: *her uncrushable will to survive*

**unc·tu·ous** /ˈʌŋktʃuəs/ *adj formal* too friendly and praising people too much in a way that seems very insincere: *There is something smug and unctuous about him.* —**unctuously** *adv* —**unctuousness** *n* [U]

**un·curl** /ˌʌnˈkɜː‖-ˈkɜːrl/ *v* [I,T] to stretch out straight from a curled position, or to make something do this

**un·cut** /ˌʌnˈkʌt◂/ *adj* 1 a film, book etc that is uncut has not been made shorter, for example by having violent or sexual scenes removed: *the uncut version of 'Lady Chatterley's Lover'* 2 an uncut jewel that is still in its natural form has not been cut into a particular shape: *uncut gem stones*

**un·daunt·ed** /ʌnˈdɔːntɪ̣d‖-ˈdɒːn-/ *adj* not afraid of continuing to try to do something in spite of difficulties or danger: [+ **by**] *Undaunted by the enormity of the task, they began rebuilding the village.*

**un·de·ceive** /ˌʌndɪˈsiːv/ *v* [T] *formal* to tell someone what the real facts are when they have previously believed something that was untrue

**un·de·cid·ed** /ˌʌndɪˈsaɪdɪ̣d/ *adj* 1 [not before noun] not having made a decision about something important: [+ **about**] *A third of the electorate remain undecided about how they will vote.* | [+ **what/which/whether etc**] *Nadine was undecided whether or not to go to college.* 2 a game or competition that is undecided has no definite winner —**undecidedly** *adv*

**un·de·mon·stra·tive** /ˌʌndɪˈmɒnstrətɪv‖-ˈmɑːn-/ *adj* not showing your feelings of love or friendliness, especially by not touching or kissing people

**un·de·ni·a·ble** /ˌʌndɪˈnaɪəbəl◂/ *adj* definitely true or certain: *undeniable proof* —**undeniably** *adv*

**under-** /ʌndə‖-dər/ *prefix* 1 too little: *underdevelopment | undercooked cabbage* 2 going underneath something: *an underpass* 3 inner; beneath others: *undergarments* 4 less important or lower in rank: *a head gardener and three under-gardeners*

S1 W1 **un·der¹** /ˈʌndə‖ər/ *prep*

1 ▶ **BELOW** ◀ directly below something, or covered by it: *Write your name under your picture.* | *She was carrying her handbag under her arm.* | *I could see something glittering under the water.*

2 ▶ **LESS THAN** ◀ less than a particular number, amount, age, or price: *gifts for under ten dollars* | *nursery education for children under five* | *I spend just under four hours a day seeing customers.* | **be under age** (=not be old enough to drink, have sex etc legally) *You're not allowed in the bar if you're under age.*

3 **be under construction/discussion/attack etc** to be in the process of being constructed, discussed etc: *The possibility of replacing the computers remains under consideration.* | *The National Health Service is very much under attack from the Tory government.*

4 ▶ **CONTROLLED** ◀ being controlled by a particular leader, government, system etc: *foreign policy under Kohl* | *The Los Angeles Philharmonic is under the baton of Esa-Pekka Salonen.*

5 ▶ **LAW/AGREEMENT** ◀ according to a particular agreement, law etc: *an exemption under Article 85*

6 ▶ **AFFECTED BY** ◀ being affected by particular conditions or situations: *She's been under a lot of pressure at work.* | *driving under the influence of alcohol* | *The solicitor has said that under no circumstances must I pay it.*

7 **be under (sb's) control/influence/spell etc** if someone or something is under someone's control etc, they control or influence it: *I'm glad to see that you have everything under control.* | *She seems to be coming under Gina's influence.*

8 ▶ **CLASS/GROUP** ◀ if an object, book, name etc is under a particular letter, list, system etc, that is where you can find it or that is the group it belongs to: *The baby's records are filed under the mother's last name.*

9 ▶ **POSITION AT WORK** ◀ if people are under someone in authority, they work for that person and have a lower position: *Guerrero works under him directly.*

10 **be under an impression/delusion** to believe something is true, especially when you are wrong in believing it: *I was under the impression that he was going on vacation that week.*

11 **be under anaesthesia/sedation/treatment etc** to be treated by a doctor using a particular drug or method

12 ▶ **DIFFERENT NAME** ◀ if you write something under another name, you write it using a name that is not your real name: *Eric Blair wrote under the name of George Orwell.*

**USAGE NOTE: UNDER**

WORD CHOICE: **under, underneath, below, beneath**

**Under** is the most common word used to talk about one thing being placed or moving directly under another, or being covered by it: *I found it under the table/cushion.* | *The railway runs directly under the main street.* | *Just push the note under the door.* | *The police all wear bullet-proof vests under their shirts.*

**Underneath** is often used instead of **under** to slightly emphasize the idea of covering, touching, or hiding: *He keeps his money in a secret safe underneath the floorboards.* | *I wonder what's underneath that cover?* | *a creature that makes its nest underneath desert rocks*

You use **under** to talk about something that is covered by something that is also all around it, but you would not use **underneath** so often in this way: *Sea lions can travel much faster under water.*

**Beneath** can also be used in all these ways, but is a little old-fashioned or literary. In a romantic story, for example, you might read: *They strolled hand in hand beneath the summer moon.*

**Below** suggests that one thing is in a lower position than another, perhaps a little to one side or in front: *Jed and Jackie live in the apartment below us.* | *There was a lake below the village, further down the valley.*

**under²** *adv* 1 in or to a place below something or covered by it: *He crawled under the blankets.* 2 less in age, number, amount etc than the age etc mentioned: *Children twelve and under must be accompanied by an adult.* S2 W2

**un·der·a·chiev·er** /ˌʌndərəˈtʃiːvə‖-ər/ *n* [C] someone who does not do as well as they could do, especially at school —**underachieve** *v* [I] —**underachievement** *n* [U]

**un·der·age** /ˌʌndərˈeɪdʒ◂/ *adj* too young to legally buy alcohol, drive a car, vote etc: *underage drinking*

**un·der·arm¹** /ˈʌndərɑːm‖-ɑːrm/ *adv* if you throw a ball underarm, you throw it without moving your arm above your shoulder; UNDERHAND² *AmE* —see picture on page 1264

**underarm²** *adj* **underarm deodorant/antiperspirant** a substance which smells pleasant that you put under your arms

**un·der·bel·ly** /ˈʌndəˌbeli‖-ər-/ *n literary* 1 the weakest or most easily damaged part of a country, plan etc: *regional warfare tearing at the country's underbelly* 2 the stomach of an animal such as a fish

**un·der·brush** /ˈʌndəbrʌʃ‖-ər-/ *n* [U] *especially AmE* bushes, small trees etc growing under and around larger trees in a forest; UNDERGROWTH

**un·der·cap·i·tal·ize** also **-ise** *BrE* /ˌʌndəˈkæpɪ̣tl-aɪz‖-dər-/ *v* [T usually passive] to not give a business enough money with the result that it cannot operate effectively

**un·der·car·riage** /ˈʌndəˌkærɪdʒ‖-ər-/ *n* [C] the wheels of an aircraft and the structure that holds them —see picture at AIRCRAFT

**und·er·charge** /ˌʌndəˈtʃɑːdʒ‖ˌʌndərˈtʃɑːrdʒ/ *v* [I,T] to charge too little or less than the correct amount of money for something: **undercharge sb by £1/$2 etc** *They undercharged me by about two dollars.* —opposite OVERCHARGE (1)

**un·der·class** /ˈʌndəklɑːs‖-dərklæs/ *n* [singular] the lowest social class, consisting of people who are very poor

**un·der·class·man** /ˌʌndəˈklɑːsmən‖-dərˈklæs-/ *n* [C] *AmE* a student in the first two years of school or college

**un·der·clothes** /ˈʌndəkləʊðz, -kləʊz‖-dər-kloʊðz, -kloʊz-/ also **un·der·clo·thing** /ˌkləʊðɪŋ‖-ˌkloʊ-/ *n* [plural] clothes that you wear next to your body under your other clothes; UNDERWEAR

**un·der·coat** /ˈʌndəkəʊt‖-dər-/ *n* [C] a layer of paint that you put onto a surface before you put the final layer on

**un·der·cov·er** /ˌʌndəˈkʌvə◂‖-dərˈkʌvər◂/ *adj* [only before noun] used or employed secretly, in order to catch criminals or find out information: *an undercover operation*

**un·der·cur·rent** /ˈʌndəˌkʌrənt‖-dərˌkɜːr-/ *n* [C] **1** a feeling, especially of anger or dissatisfaction, that people do not express openly: **[+ of]** *He sensed an undercurrent of resentment among the crowd.* **2** a hidden and often dangerous current of water that flows under the surface of the sea or a river

**un·der·cut** /ˌʌndəˈkʌt‖-ər-/ *v* [T] to sell goods or services more cheaply than another company

**un·der·de·vel·oped** /ˌʌndədɪˈveləpt◂‖-dər-/ *adj* **1 underdeveloped country/region etc** a country, region etc that is poor and where there is not much modern industry —compare **developing country** (DEVELOPING) **2** not having grown or developed as much as is usual or necessary: *a skinny, underdeveloped child*

**un·der·dog** /ˈʌndədɒg‖ˈʌndərdɒːg/ *n* [C] **1 the underdog** the person or team in a competition that is expected to lose **2** a person, country etc that is weak and is always treated badly

**un·der·done** /ˌʌndəˈdʌn◂‖-ər-/ *adj* meat that is underdone is not completely cooked —compare OVERDONE

**un·der·dressed** /ˌʌndəˈdrest◂‖-ər-/ *adj* wearing clothes that are too informal for a particular occasion

**un·der·em·ployed** /ˌʌndərɪmˈplɔɪd◂/ *adj* working in a job where you cannot use all your skills or where there is not enough work for you to do

**un·der·es·ti·mate¹** /ˌʌndərˈestɪmeɪt/ *v* **1** [I,T] to think that something is smaller, cheaper, less important etc than it really is: *People often underestimate the importance of training.* **2** [T] to think that someone is not as good, clever, or skilful, as they really are: *Don't underestimate Manville – he's a skilful campaigner.*

**un·der·es·ti·mate²** /ˌʌndərˈestɪmɪt/ *n* [C] a guessed amount or number that is too low: *14% may be an underestimate.*

**un·der·ex·pose** /ˌʌndərɪkˈspəʊz‖-ˈspoʊz/ *v* [T] to not let enough light reach the film when you are taking a photograph

**un·der·fed** /ˌʌndəˈfed‖-ər-/ *adj* not given enough food to eat

**un·der·felt** /ˈʌndəfelt‖-ər-/ *n* [U] *BrE* soft material that you put between a CARPET¹ (1) and the floor

**un·der·foot** /ˌʌndəˈfʊt‖-ər-/ *adv* **1** under your feet where you are walking: **wet/dry/firm etc underfoot** *The wet wood is very slippery underfoot.* **2 trample sb/sth underfoot a)** to crush someone or something on the ground by stepping heavily on them **b)** to completely destroy someone or something

**un·der·fund** /ˌʌndəˈfʌnd‖-ər-/ *v* [T] **be underfunded** to not be provided with enough money: *The childcare program is seriously underfunded.* —**underfunding** *n* [U]

**un·der·gar·ment** /ˈʌndəˌgɑːmənt‖ˈʌndərˌgɑːr-/ *n* [C] *old-fashioned* a piece of underwear

**un·der·go** /ˌʌndəˈgəʊ‖-dərˈgoʊ/ *v past tense* **underwent** /-ˈwent/ *past participle* **undergone** /-ˈgɒn‖-ˈgɒːn/ [T not in passive] if you undergo a change, an unpleasant experience etc, it happens to you, or is done to you: *She's undergoing surgery.*|*The company underwent several major changes.*

**un·der·grad·u·ate** /ˌʌndəˈgrædʒʊɪt◂‖-ər-/ *n* [C] *especially BrE* a student who is doing a university course for a first degree —compare GRADUATE¹ (1)

**un·der·ground¹** /ˈʌndəgraʊnd‖-ər-/ *adj* **1** below the surface of the earth: *an underground passage* **2** [only before noun] an underground group, organization etc is secret and illegal: *an underground terrorist organization*

**un·der·ground²** /ˌʌndəˈgraʊnd‖-ər-/ *adv* **1** under the earth's surface: *nuclear waste buried deep underground*|*The prairie dog burrows underground.* **2 go underground** to start doing something secretly, or hide in a secret place: *The ANC was forced to go underground when the government arrested its leaders.*

**un·der·ground³** /ˈʌndəgraʊnd‖-ər-/ *n* **the Underground a)** *BrE* a railway system under the ground; SUBWAY (2) *AmE*: *a map of the London Underground* **b)** an illegal group working in secret against the rulers of a country

**un·der·growth** /ˈʌndəgrəʊθ‖-dərgroʊθ-/ *n* [U] bushes, small trees, and other plants growing around and under bigger trees: *Something rustled in the undergrowth.*

**un·der·hand¹** /ˌʌndəˈhænd◂‖ˈʌndərhænd/ also **un·der·hand·ed** /ˌʌndəˈhændɪd◂‖ˈʌndərhændɪd/ *adj* dishonest and done secretly: *underhand dealings* —**underhandedly** *adv* —**underhandedness** *n* [U]

**underhand²** *adv AmE* if you throw a ball underhand, you throw it without moving your arm above your shoulder; UNDERARM¹

**un·der·lay** /ˈʌndəleɪ‖-ər-/ *n* [C,U] a large piece of material put under a CARPET¹ (1)

**un·der·lie** /ˌʌndəˈlaɪ‖-ər-/ *v past tense* **underlay** /-ˈleɪ/ *past participle* **underlaid** /-ˈleɪd/ [T] *formal* to be the real cause of or reason for something: *Social problems and poverty underlie much of the crime in today's big cities.*

**un·der·line** /ˌʌndəˈlaɪn‖ˈʌndərlaɪn-/ *v* [T] **1** to draw a line under a word to show that it is important **2** to show that something is important: *This tragic incident underlines the need for immediate action.*

**un·der·ling** /ˈʌndəlɪŋ‖-ər-/ *n* [C] an insulting word for someone who has a low rank

**un·der·ly·ing** /ˌʌndəˈlaɪ-ɪŋ◂‖-ər-/ *adj* **underlying reason/cause/aim etc** the reason, cause etc that is the most important, although it is not easily noticed: *the underlying causes of her depression* W3

**un·der·manned** /ˌʌndəˈmænd◂‖-ər-/ *adj* not having enough workers

**un·der·men·tioned** /ˌʌndəˈmenʃənd◂‖-ər-/ *adj formal* **1** mentioned later in the same piece of writing: *Please supply me with the undermentioned goods.* **2 the undermentioned** the people or things that are mentioned in the list that is written immediately below: *The undermentioned will report for duty.*

**un·der·mine** /ˌʌndəˈmaɪn‖-ər-/ *v* [T] **1** to gradually make someone or something less strong or effective: *She tried to undermine his authority at every opportunity.*|*economic policies that threaten to undermine the health care system* **2** to gradually take away the earth from under something

**un·der·neath¹** /ˌʌndəˈniːθ‖-ər-/ *prep, adv* **1** directly under or below another object, used especially when one thing is covering or hiding another: *It's near where the railway goes underneath the road.*|*A translation was written underneath.* —see UNDER¹ (USAGE) —see picture on page 1257 **2** if someone is nice, shy, etc underneath, they really are nice, etc even though their behaviour shows a different character: *She seems aggressive, but underneath she's pretty shy.* S2

**underneath²** *n BrE* **the underneath** the bottom surface of something, or the part of something that is below or under something else: *We need to paint the underneath with a rust preventer.*

**un·der·nour·ished** /ˌʌndəˈnʌrɪʃt◂‖ˌʌndərˈnɜː-, -ˈnʌ-/ *adj* unhealthy and weak because you have not had enough food —**undernourishment** *n* [U]

**un·der·paid** /ˌʌndəˈpeɪd◂‖-ər-/ *adj* earning less money than you deserve for your work: *Teachers are generally overworked and underpaid.* —**underpay** *v* [T]

**un·der·pants** /ˈʌndəpænts‖-ər-/ *n* [plural] **1** *BrE* a short piece of underwear worn by men under their trousers —see picture at UNDERWEAR **2** *AmE* a short piece of underwear of this type, worn by men or women

**un·der·pass** /ˈʌndəpɑːs‖ˈʌndərpæs/ *n* [C] a road or path that goes under another road or a railway

**un·der·pay** /ˌʌndəˈpeɪ‖-ər-/ *v past tense and past participle* **underpaid** /-ˈpeɪd/ [T] to pay someone too little for their work

**un·der·pin** /ˌʌndəˈpɪn‖ˈʌndərpɪn/ *v* [T] **1** to give strength or support to an idea, belief etc: *A solid basis of evidence underpins their theory.* **2** to put a solid piece of metal under something such as a wall in order to make it stronger —**underpinning** *n* [C,U]

**un·der·play** /ˌʌndəˈpleɪ‖-ər-/ *v* [T] **1** to make something seem less important than it really is **2 underplay your hand** to discuss something with someone without telling them everything about your plans, abilities etc

**un·der·priv·i·leged** /ˌʌndəˈprɪvəlɪdʒd◂‖-dər-/ *adj* very poor, with worse living conditions, educational opportunities etc than most people in society

**un·der·rate** /ˌʌndəˈreɪt/ *v* [T] to think that someone or something is less good, effective, skilful etc than they really are: *a much underrated novel*

**un·der·re·sourced** /ˌʌndərɪˈzɔːst, -ˈsɔːst‖-ɔːr-/ *adj* not provided with enough money, equipment etc

**un·der·score** /ˌʌndəˈskɔː‖ˈʌndərˌskɔːr/ *v* [T] *especially AmE* **1** to emphasize something so that people pay attention to it **2** to draw a line under a word or phrase to show that it is important; UNDERLINE

**un·der·sea** /ˈʌndəsiː‖-ər-/ *adj* [only before noun] happening or existing below the surface of the sea: *undersea exploration*

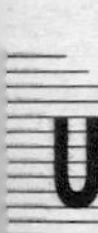

**un·der·sec·re·ta·ry** /ˌʌndəˈsekrətəri‖ˈʌndərˌsekrəteri/ *n* [C] **1** someone who is in charge of the daily work of a British government department **2** *AmE* a very important official in a government department who is one position in rank below the SECRETARY

**un·der·sell** /ˌʌndəˈsel‖-ər-/ *v past tense and past participle* **undersold** /-ˈsəʊld‖-ˈsoʊld/ [T] **1** to sell goods at a lower price than someone else **2** to make other people think that someone or something is less good, effective, skilful etc than they really are: *I think he undersold himself at the interview.*

**under-served** /ˌ·· ˈ·◂/ *adj AmE* not getting enough care and help from the government: *the under-served communities of the inner city*

**un·der·sexed** /ˌʌndəˈsekst◂‖-ər-/ *adj* having less desire to have sex than is normal

**un·der·shirt** /ˈʌndəʃɜːt‖ˈʌndərʃɜːrt/ *n* [C] *AmE* a piece of underwear with or without arms, worn under a shirt; VEST[1] (1) *BrE*

**un·der·side** /ˈʌndəsaɪd‖-ər-/ *n* [singular] **the underside** the bottom side or surface of something

**un·der·signed** /ˈʌndəsaɪnd‖-ər-/ *adj formal* **the undersigned** the person or people who have signed a piece of writing, used especially in formal letters

**un·der·sized** /ˌʌndəˈsaɪzd◂‖-ər-/ also **un·der·size** /-ˈsaɪz◂/ *adj* smaller than usual, or too small

**un·der·staffed** /ˌʌndəˈstɑːft◂‖ˌʌndərˈstæft◂/ *adj* not having enough workers, or fewer workers than usual

S1 W1 **un·der·stand** /ˌʌndəˈstænd‖-ər-/ *v past tense and past participle* **understood** /-ˈstʊd/ [not in progressive]
**1 ► MEANING ◄** [I,T] to know the meaning of what someone is telling you, or the language that they speak: *She doesn't understand English – try Spanish.* | *I'm sorry, I don't understand. Can you explain that again?* | **understand perfectly** *I understand perfectly, the children must be in bed by 8 o'clock.*
**2 ► FACT/IDEA ◄** [I,T] to know or realize how a fact, process, situation etc works, especially through learning or experience: *I don't really understand the political situation in Northern Ireland.* | **understand how/why/where etc** *You don't need to understand how computers work to be able to use them.* | **fully understand** *How the drug actually works isn't fully understood.*
**3 ► PERSON ◄** [I,T] to know and sympathize with how someone feels, and why they behave the way they do: *My parents just don't understand me.* | *Don tried to understand.* | **understand how/what etc** *I understand how you feel, but I think you're over-reacting.* | **understand sb doing sth** *I can understand her wanting to live alone and be independent.*
**4 I understand (that)** *spoken formal* used to say that someone has told you that something is true: *I understand that you'll be coming to work here soon.*
**5 make yourself understood** to be able to express simple things in another language: *I'm not very good at German, but I can make myself understood.*
**6 do you understand?** *spoken* used when you are telling someone what they should or should not do, especially when you are angry with them: *Never speak to me like that again! Do you understand?*
**7 be understood** *formal* used to say that something has been agreed and there is no need to discuss it: **be understood that** *I thought it was understood that if we worked late we'd get paid double.*
**8 understand sth/sb to mean sth** accept something as having a particular meaning: *In this document, 'children' is understood to mean people under 14.*
**9 give sb to understand sth** *formal* to make someone believe that something is true, something is going to happen etc, without telling them this directly: *I was given to understand that the property was in good condition.*

This graph shows how common the different grammar patterns of the verb **understand** are.

understand sth
understand how/why/where etc
understand (that)
understand
understand sth/sb to mean sth
understand sb doing sth
other

10% 20% 30% 40% 50%

Based on the British National Corpus and the Longman Lancaster Corpus

**un·der·stand·a·ble** /ˌʌndəˈstændəbəl‖ˌʌndər-/ *adj* **1** able to be understood; COMPREHENSIBLE: *The announcement was barely understandable.* **2** understandable behaviour, reactions etc seem normal and reasonable because of the situation you are in: *Her anger was entirely understandable in the circumstances.* —**understandably** *adv*

**un·der·stand·ing[1]** /ˌʌndəˈstændɪŋ‖-ər-/ *n* **1** [C usually singular] a private, unofficial agreement: **come to/reach an understanding** *I thought we had come to an understanding on this matter.* | **on the understanding that** (=on the condition that) *I lent him the money on the strict understanding that he paid it back next month.* W3 **2** [singular, U] knowlege about something, based on learning or experience: **have an understanding of** *The present Industry Secretary has only a limited understanding of economics.* **3** [singular, U] sympathy towards someone's character and behaviour: *Mutual understanding is important in all relationships.* **4** [U] the way in which you judge the meaning of something: [+ **of**] *According to my understanding of the letter, it means* *something quite different.* **5** [U] the ability to know and learn; INTELLIGENCE (1): *beyond a child's understanding*

**understanding²** *adj* sympathetic and kind about other people's problems: *Luckily, I have a very understanding boss.*

**un·der·state** /ˌʌndəˈsteɪt‖ˈʌbdərsteɪt/ *v* [T] to describe something in a way that makes it seem less important than it really is: *This report understates the seriousness of the situation.*

**un·der·state·ment** /ˌʌndəˈsteɪtmənt‖-dər-/ *n* **1** [C] a statement that is not strong enough to express how good, bad, impressive etc something really is: *To say the movie was bad is an understatement.* **2** [U] a way of describing things as being less good, bad, important etc than they really are

**un·der·stood** /ˌʌndəˈstʊd‖-ər-/ the past tense and past participle of UNDERSTAND

**un·der·stud·y¹** /ˈʌndəˌstʌdi‖-ər-/ *n* [C] an actor who learns a part in a play so that they can act if the usual actor is ill

**understudy²** *v* [T] to be an understudy for a particular actor in a play

**un·der·sub·scribe** /ˌʌndəsəbˈskraɪb/ *v* [T] **be undersubscribed** if an activity, sale, service etc is undersubscribed, not many people want it

W 3 **un·der·take** /ˌʌndəˈteɪk‖-ər-/ *v past tense* **undertook** /-ˈtʊk/ *past participle* **undertaken** /-ˈteɪkən/ [T] *formal* **1** to accept that you are responsible for a piece of work, and start to do it: *She undertook full responsibility for the new changes.* **2 undertake to do sth** to promise or agree to do something: *He undertook to pay the money back in six months.*

**un·der·tak·er** /ˈʌndəteɪkə‖-dərteɪkər/ *n* [C] *BrE* someone whose job is to arrange funerals; FUNERAL DIRECTOR

**un·der·tak·ing** /ˌʌndəˈteɪkɪŋ‖ˈʌndərteɪ-/ *n* **1** [C usually singular] an important job, piece of work, or activity that you are responsible for: *Starting a new business can be a risky undertaking.* **2** [C] *formal* a promise to do something: *an undertaking to respect people's privacy* **3** [U] the business of an undertaker

**under-the-coun·ter** /ˌ·· ·ˈ··◂/ *adj informal* under-the-counter goods are bought or sold secretly, especially because they are illegal

**un·der·tone** /ˈʌndətəʊn‖-dərtoʊn/ *n* **1** a feeling or quality that is not directly expressed but can still be recognized: [+ **of**] *There was an undertone of sadness in her letter.* **2** [C] a quiet voice or sound —see also OVERTONE

**un·der·tow** /ˈʌndətəʊ‖-dərtoʊ/ *n* [singular] the water current under the surface that pulls back towards the sea when a wave comes onto the shore

**un·der·used** /ˌʌndəˈjuːzd◂‖-ər-/ *adj* something that is underused is not used as much as it could be

**un·der·val·ue** /ˌʌndəˈvæljuː‖-ər-/ *v* [T] to think that someone or something is less important or valuable than they really are: *She felt that the company undervalued her work.*

**un·der·wa·ter** /ˌʌndəˈwɔːtə◂‖ˌʌndərˈwɒːtər◂, -ˈwɑː-/ *adj* [only before noun] below the surface of an area of water, or able to be used there: *underwater cameras* —**underwater** *adv*

**un·der·way** /ˌʌndəˈweɪ‖-ər-/ *adj* [not before noun] **1** happening now: *Plans to merge the two companies are already underway.* | **get underway** (=start happening) **2** something such as a boat or train that is underway is moving —see also **under way** (WAY¹ (67))

**underwater**

swimming underwater

**underwear**

camisole

body *BrE* / leotard *AmE*

vest *BrE* / undershirt *AmE*

boxer shorts

underpants /pants *BrE*

knickers *BrE* / panties *AmE*

bra

**un·der·wear** /ˈʌndəweə‖-dərwer/ *n* [U] clothes that you wear next to your body under your other clothes

**un·der·weight** /ˌʌndəˈweɪt‖-ər-/ *adj* weighing less than is expected or usual —opposite OVERWEIGHT —see THIN (USAGE)

**un·der·went** /ˌʌndəˈwent‖-ər-/ the past tense of UNDERGO

**un·der·whelm** /ˌʌndəˈwelm‖-ər-/ *v* [T] *humorous* to not be very impressive

**un·der·world** /ˈʌndəwɜːld‖ˈʌndərwɜːrld/ *n* [singular] **1** the criminals in a particular place and the criminal activities they are involved in **2** the place where the spirits of the dead are believed to live, especially in Ancient Greek stories

**un·der·write** /ˌʌndəˈraɪt/ *v past tense* **underwrote** /-ˈrəʊt‖-ˈroʊt/ *past participle* **underwritten** /-ˈrɪtn/ [T] **1** *formal* to support an activity, business plan etc with money, so that you are financially responsible for it: *The government has agreed to underwrite the project with a grant of £5 million.* **2** *technical* to be responsible for an insurance agreement

**un·der·writ·er** /ˈʌndəˌraɪtə‖-dərˌraɪtər/ *n* [C] someone who makes insurance contracts

**un·de·served** /ˌʌndɪˈzɜːvd◂‖-ˈzɜːrvd◂/ *adj* undeserved criticism, praise etc is unfair because you do not deserve it: *She had an undeserved reputation for making trouble.*

**un·de·sir·a·ble** /ˌʌndɪˈzaɪərəbəl◂‖-ˈzaɪr-/ *adj formal* something or someone that is undesirable is not welcome or wanted because they may affect a situation or person in a bad way: *The incident could have undesirable consequences for the government.*

**un·de·sir·a·bles** /ˌʌndɪˈzaɪərəbəlz‖-ˈzaɪr-/ *n* [plural] people who are considered to be immoral, criminal, or socially unacceptable

**un·de·vel·oped** /ˌʌndɪˈveləpt◂/ *adj* not yet developed —compare UNDERDEVELOPED

**un·did** /ʌnˈdɪd/ the past tense of UNDO

**un·dies** /ˈʌndiːz/ *n* [plural] *informal* underwear

**un·dig·ni·fied** /ʌnˈdɪgnɪ̣faɪd/ *adj* behaving in a way that is embarrassing or makes you look silly: *Sally made an undignified exit with her bathrobe clutched about her.*

**un·di·lut·ed** /ˌʌndaɪˈluːtɪ̣d◂/ *adj literary* an undiluted feeling is very strong and not mixed with any other feelings: *undiluted joy*

**un·dis·charged** /ˌʌndɪsˈtʃɑːdʒd◂‖-ɑːr-/ *adj technical* **1** an undischarged debt is one that has not been paid **2 an undischarged bankrupt** someone who still owes money and is not legally allowed to stop repaying their debt

**un·dis·crim·i·nat·ing** /ˌʌndɪˈskrɪmɪ̣neɪtɪŋ/ *adj* not having the ability to see a difference in value between two people or things, and therefore unable to make judgments about them

**un·dis·guised** /ˌʌndɪsˈgaɪzd◂/ *adj* clearly shown and not hidden: *undisguised contempt*

**un·di·sput·ed** /ˌʌndɪˈspjuːtɪ̣d◂/ *adj* **1** known to be definitely true: *They talk about an after-life as if it were an undisputed truth.* **2** accepted by everyone: *The brand has now become the undisputed market leader.*

**un·dis·turbed** /ˌʌndɪˈstɜːbd◂‖-ɜːr-/ *adj* not interrupted or moved: *At last I was able to work undisturbed.* | *The documents lay undisturbed for years.*

**un·di·vid·ed** /ˌʌndɪˈvaɪdɪ̣d◂/ *adj* complete: **undivided attention** *Please give the matter your undivided attention.*

**un·do** /ʌnˈduː/ *v past tense* **undid** /-ˈdɪd/ *past participle* **undone** /-ˈdʌn/ [T] **1** to unfasten something that is tied or wrapped: *She carefully undid the parcel.* —see OPEN[2] (USAGE) **2** to try to remove the bad effects of something you have done: *Well, the mistake has been made now and can't be undone.*

**un·do·ing** /ʌnˈduːɪŋ/ *n* **be sb's undoing** to cause someone's shame, failure etc: *In the end gambling was his undoing.*

**un·done** /ˌʌnˈdʌn◂/ *adj* [not before noun] **1** not fastened: *One of your buttons is coming undone.* | **come undone** (=become unfastened) **2 leave sth undone** not finish something **3** *old use* destroyed and without hope: *I am undone! My secret has been discovered!*

 **un·doubt·ed** /ʌnˈdaʊtɪ̣d/ *adj* definitely true or known to exist: *her undoubted talent* —**undoubtedly** *adv*: *That is undoubtedly true.*

**un·dreamed-of** /ʌnˈdriːmd -ɒv‖ -ɑːv/ also **undreamt-of** /ʌnˈdremt-/ *adj* much more or much better than you could imagine: *undreamed-of wealth* | *These technological advances were undreamt-of even 20 years ago.*

**un·dress**[1] /ʌnˈdres/ *v* [I,T] to take your clothes off, or take someone else's clothes off

**undress**[2] *n* [U] *formal* a state in which you are wearing few or no clothes: *The dancers walked around in various stages of undress.*

**un·dressed** /ˌʌnˈdrest◂/ *adj* **1** [not before noun] not wearing any clothes: **get undressed** (=take your clothes off) **2** an undressed wound has not been covered to protect it

**un·due** /ˌʌnˈdjuː◂‖-ˈduː◂/ *adj* [only before noun] *formal* more than is reasonable, suitable, or necessary: *We managed to get through Customs without undue difficulty.*

**un·du·late** /ˈʌndjɡ̈leɪt‖-dʒə-/ *v* [I] *formal* to move or be shaped like waves that are rising and falling: *undulating hills* —**undulation** /ˌʌndjɡ̈ˈleɪʃən‖-dʒə-/ *n* [C,U]

**un·du·ly** /ʌnˈdjuːli‖-ˈduː-/ *adv formal* too extreme or too much: *Perhaps I have been unduly severe in my judgment of him.*

**un·dy·ing** /ʌnˈdaɪ-ɪŋ/ *adj* [only before noun] continuing for ever: *They declared their undying love for each other.*

**un·earth** /ʌnˈɜːθ‖-ˈɜːrθ/ *v* [T] **1** to find out the truth about something: *The reporter had unearthed some important secrets about her.* **2** to find something after searching for it, especially something that has been buried in the ground

**un·earth·ly** /ʌnˈɜːθli‖-ˈɜːr-/ *adj* **1** very strange and unnatural: *I felt an unearthly presence in the room.* **2 unearthly hour/time etc** *informal* very early or very late and therefore extremely inconvenient: *We had to set off at some unearthly hour of the morning.* —**unearthliness** *n* [U]

**un·ease** /ʌnˈiːz/ *n* [U] a feeling of nervousness and anxiety that makes you unable to relax

**un·eas·y** /ʌnˈiːzi/ *adj* **1** nervous, anxious, and unable to relax because you think something bad might happen: *Katie felt uneasy about what she had done.* —see NERVOUS (USAGE) **2** an uneasy period of time is one when people have agreed to stop fighting or arguing, but which is not really calm: *An uneasy peace descended on the area.* **3** not comfortable, peaceful, or relaxed: *She eventually fell into an uneasy sleep.* | *an uneasy conscience* —**uneasily** *adv* **uneasiness** *n* [U]

**un·eat·able** /ʌnˈiːtəbəl/ *adj* a word meaning unpleasant or unsuitable to eat, that some people think is incorrect; INEDIBLE

**un·e·co·nom·ic** /ˌʌniːkəˈnɒmɪk◂, ˌʌnekə-‖-ˈnɑː-/ *adj* **1** not making enough money or profit: *Uneconomic mines will have to be closed.* **2** uneconomical

**un·e·co·nom·ic·al** /ˌʌniːkəˈnɒmɪkəl, ˌʌnekə-‖-ˈnɑː-/ *adj* using too much effort, money or materials: *The project was considered uneconomical and shelved.* —**uneconomically** /-kli/ *adv*

**un·ed·u·cat·ed** /ʌnˈedjɡ̈keɪtɪ̣d‖-dʒə-/ *adj* not educated to the usual level, or showing that someone is not well educated: *ignorant and uneducated opinions*

**un·e·mo·tion·al** /ˌʌnɪˈməʊʃənəl◂‖-ˈmoʊ-/ *adj* not showing your feelings: *He remained completely unemotional as the judge read out the sentence.*

**un·em·ploy·able** /ˌʌnɪmˈplɔɪəbəl◂/ *adj* not having the skills or qualities needed to get a job

**un·em·ployed**[1] /ˌʌnɪmˈplɔɪd◂/ *adj* without a job S2

**unemployed**[2] *n* **the unemployed** [plural] people who have no job: **the long-term unemployed** (=people who have not had a job for a long time) W3

**un·em·ploy·ment** /ˌʌnɪmˈplɔɪmənt/ *n* [U] **1** the number of people in a country who do not have a job: *levels of unemployment* | **high unemployment** (=lots of people without a job) **2** the fact of having no job: *Closure of the plant will mean unemployment for 500 workers.* **3** *AmE informal* money paid regularly by the government to people who have no job S2 W2

**unemployment ben·e·fit** /ˈ···ˌ···/ *BrE*, **unemployment com·pen·sa·tion** /ˈ·····ˌ··/ *AmE* — *n* [U] money paid regularly by the government to people who do not have a job

**un·end·ing** /ʌnˈendɪŋ/ *adj* something unpleasant or tiring that is unending seems as if it will continue for ever: *an unending struggle to survive*

**un·en·du·ra·ble** /ˌʌnɪnˈdjʊərəbəl◂‖-ˈdʊr-/ *adj formal* too unpleasant, painful etc to bear: *The pain was unendurable.*

**un·en·vi·a·ble** /ʌnˈenviəbəl/ *adj* difficult and unpleasant: **unenviable task** *the unenviable task of informing the victim's relations*

**un·e·qual** /ʌnˈiːkwəl/ *adj* **1** not equal in number, amount, or level: **of unequal size/length etc** *two posts of unequal length* | **be/unequal in size/weight etc** *the baskets were unequal in weight and looked likely to topple* **2** unfairly treating different people or groups in different ways: *an unequal contest* | *the unequal distribution of wealth* **3 be unequal to the task/job etc** to not have enough strength, ability etc to do something —**unequally** *adv*

**un·e·qualled** *BrE*, **unequaled** *AmE* /ʌnˈiːkwəld/ *adj* better than any other: *The school's success rate is unequalled in the area.*

**un·e·quiv·o·cal** /ˌʌnɪˈkwɪvəkəl◂/ *adj formal* completely clear and without any possibility of doubt: *His answer was an unequivocal "No".* —**unequivocally** /-kli/ *adv*

**un·er·ring** /ʌnˈɜːrɪŋ/ *adj* always exactly right: **unerring accuracy/judgement etc** *Max hit the target with unerring accuracy.* —**unerringly** *adv*

**un·eth·i·cal** /ʌnˈeθɪkəl/ *adj* not obeying rules of moral behaviour, especially those concerning a profession: *It is considered highly unethical for a psychiatrist to have a relationship with a patient.* —**unethically** /-kli/ *adv*

**un·e·ven** /ʌnˈiːvən/ *adj* **1** not smooth, flat, or level: *The ground was very uneven in places.* **2** not regular: *His breathing had become uneven.* **3** not equal or equally balanced: *an uneven contest* **4** good in some parts and bad in others: *a rather uneven performance* —**unevenly** *adv* —**unevenness** *n* [U]

**un·e·vent·ful** /ˌʌnɪˈventfəl◂/ *adj* with nothing exciting or unusual happening: *a quiet, uneventful life in a small town* —**uneventfully** *adv* —**uneventfulness** *n* [U]

**un·ex·am·pled** /ˌʌnɪgˈzɑːmpəld◂‖-ˈzæm-/ *adj formal* better than anything else of the same type; EXCEPTIONAL (1)

**un·ex·ci·ting** /ˌʌnɪkˈsaɪtɪŋ◂/ *adj* ordinary and slightly boring: *a good quality but unexciting wine*

**un·ex·pect·ed** /ˌʌnɪkˈspektɪ̈d◂/ *adj* an unexpected event, remark etc is one that is surprising because you were not expecting it: *Her angry outburst was totally unexpected.* —**unexpectedly** *adv* —**unexpectedness** *n* [U]

**un·ex·plained** /ˌʌnɪkˈspleɪnd◂/ *adj* something that is unexplained is something you cannot understand because you do not know the reason for it: *her unexplained death*

**un·ex·pur·gat·ed** /ʌnˈekspəgeɪtɪ̈d‖-pər-/ *adj* an unexpurgated book, play etc is complete and has not had parts that might offend people removed

**un·fail·ing** /ʌnˈfeɪlɪŋ/ *adj* always there, even in times of difficulty or trouble: *His unfailing good humour made him popular with everyone.* —**unfailingly** *adv*

S3 W3 **un·fair** /ˌʌnˈfeə◂‖-ˈfer◂/ *adj* **1** not right or fair: *It's so unfair – Mary gets more money for less work!* **2** not giving a fair or equal opportunity to everyone: *an unfair advantage | American workers feel threatened by unfair competition from abroad.* **3 unfair dismissal** a situation in which someone is illegally dismissed from their job —**unfairly** *adv* —**unfairness** *n* [U]

**un·faith·ful** /ʌnˈfeɪθfəl/ *adj* **1** someone who is unfaithful has sex with someone who is not their wife, husband, or usual partner: [+ **to**] *Edward discovered that Leonie had been unfaithful to him.* **2** not loyal to a principle, person etc —**unfaithfully** *adv* —**unfaithfulness** *n* [U]

**un·fal·ter·ing** /ʌnˈfɔːltərɪŋ‖-ˈfɒːl-/ *adj formal* strong, determined, and not becoming weaker: *his gaze was direct and unfaltering* —**unfalteringly** *adv*

**un·fa·mil·i·ar** /ˌʌnfəˈmɪliə◂‖-ər/ *adj* not known to you: [+ **to**] *The name was unfamiliar to me.* | [+ **with**] *Voters are unfamiliar with the real issues.* —**unfamiliarity** /ˌʌnfəmɪliˈærɪ̈ti/ *n*

**un·fash·ion·a·ble** /ʌnˈfæʃənəbəl/ *adj* not popular or fashionable at the present time: *an unfashionable old dress | His ideas have been unfashionable for some time.*

**un·fas·ten** /ʌnˈfɑːsn‖-ˈfæsn/ *v* [T] to undo something such as a button, belt, rope etc: *She unfastened her blouse.*

**un·fath·om·a·ble** /ʌnˈfæðəməbəl/ *adj literary* too strange or mysterious to be understood: *the unfathomable mysteries of human nature* —**unfathomably** *adv*

**un·fa·vou·ra·ble** *BrE*, **unfavorable** *AmE* /ʌnˈfeɪvərəbəl/ *adj* **1** unfavourable conditions, situations etc are not as good as they should be or usually are: *unfavourable weather* **2** expressing disapproval: *That new television series has had unfavourable reviews.* —**unfavourably** *adv*

**un·feel·ing** /ʌnˈfiːlɪŋ/ *adj* not sympathetic towards other people's feelings: *an unfeeling college bureaucracy* —**unfeelingly** *adv*

**un·fet·tered** /ʌnˈfetəd‖-ard/ *adj formal* not restricted by laws or rules: *free and unfettered trade*

**un·fin·ished** /ʌnˈfɪnɪʃt/ *adj* not completed: *She looked away, leaving her sentence unfinished.* | **unfinished business** (=something that has to be done or dealt with that you have not yet done)

**un·fit** /ʌnˈfɪt/ *adj* **1** not in a good physical condition: *She never gets any excercise – she must be really unfit.* | [+ **for**] *He was found to be medically unfit for overseas duty.* **2** not good enough for a particular purpose: [+ **for**] *unfit for public office* | **unfit for human habitation/consumption** *dwellings unfit for human habitation*

**un·flag·ging** /ʌnˈflægɪŋ/ *adj* continuing strongly and never becoming tired or weak: **unflagging energy/interest etc** *We couldn't have done it without your unflagging enthusiasm.* —**unflaggingly** *adv*

**un·flap·pa·ble** /ʌnˈflæpəbəl/ *adj informal* having the ability to stay calm and not get upset, even in difficult situations: *My unflappable assistant worked steadily on as the argument raged around her.* —**unflappably** *adv*

**un·flinch·ing** /ʌnˈflɪntʃɪŋ/ *adj* not changing or becoming weaker, even in a very difficult or dangerous situation: *unflinching courage* —**unflinchingly** *adv*

**un·fo·cused**, **unfocussed** /ʌnˈfəʊkəst‖-ˈfoʊ-/ *adj* **1** not dealing with or paying attention to the important ideas, causes etc: *The discussion was becoming unfocused.* **2** eyes that are unfocused are open, but are not looking at anything

**un·fold** /ʌnˈfəʊld‖-ˈfoʊld/ *v* [I,T] **1** to open something that was folded: *Chiara unfolded the map and spread it on the table.* **2** if a story, plan etc unfolds, it becomes clearer as you hear or learn more about it: *As the tale unfolds we learn more about Max's childhood.*

**un·fore·see·a·ble** /ˌʌnfɔːˈsiːəbəl◂‖-fɔːr-/ *adj* an unforeseeable event, situation etc could not have been expected

**un·fore·seen** /ˌʌnfɔːˈsiːn◂‖-fɔːr-/ *adj* an unforeseen situation is one that you did not expect to happen: *unforeseen delays* | **unforeseen circumstances** *Due to unforeseen circumstances, the play has been cancelled.*

**un·for·get·ta·ble** /ˌʌnfəˈgetəbəl◂‖-fər-/ *adj* an unforgettable experience, sight, etc affects you so strongly that you will never forget it, especially because it is particularly good or beautiful: *The colors of New England in the fall are unforgettable.* —**unforgettably** *adv*

**un·for·giv·a·ble** /ˌʌnfəˈgɪvəbəl◂‖-fər-/ *adj* an unforgivable action is so bad or cruel that you cannot forgive the person who did it: *Her husband had deceived her, and this was unforgivable.* —**unforgivably** *adv*

**un·for·giv·ing** /ˌʌnfəˈgɪvɪŋ◂‖-fər-/ *adj* someone who is unforgiving does not forgive people easily

**un·formed** /ˌʌnˈfɔːmd◂‖-ɔːr-/ *adj* not yet completely developed: *The foetus's fingers and toes are as yet unformed.*

**un·for·tu·nate¹** /ʌnˈfɔːtʃənɪt‖-ˈfɔːr-/ *adj* **1** happening because of bad luck and often having serious or dangerous results: *an unfortunate accident | his unfortunate death at the height of his career* **2** an unfortunate situation is one that you wish was different or had never happened: *an unfortunate turn of events* | **most unfortunate** *formal* (=very unfortunate) *It's most unfortunate that your father can't come to the wedding.* **3** *formal* unfortunate behaviour, remarks etc make people feel embarrassed or offended: *I thought his choice of music was a little unfortunate.* S3

**unfortunate²** *n* [C] *literary* someone who has no money, home, job etc

**un·for·tu·nate·ly** /ʌnˈfɔːtʃənɪ̈tli‖-ˈfɔːr-/ *adv* [sentence adverb] used when you are mentioning a fact that you wish were not true: *Unfortunately, you were out when we called.* S1 W3

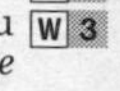

**un·found·ed** /ʌnˈfaʊndɪ̈d/ *adj* statements, feelings, opinions etc that are unfounded are wrong because they are not based on true facts: *Fears about the side-effects are largely unfounded.*

**un·fre·quent·ed** /ˌʌnfrɪˈkwentɪ̈d◂/ *adj formal* not often visited by many people: *an unfrequented spot*

**un·frock** /ʌnˈfrɒk‖ʌnˈfrɑːk/ *v* [T usually passive] to remove someone from their position as a priest as a punishment for behaviour or beliefs that the church does not approve of —**unfrocked** *adj*

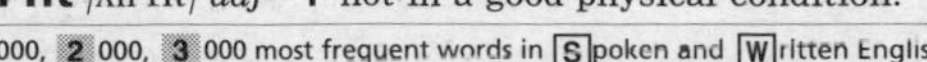

**un·ful·filled** /ˌʌnfʊlˈfɪld◂/ *adj* **1** a wish, desire, hope etc that is unfulfilled has not been achieved: *All her own dreams and ambitions remained unfulfilled.* **2** someone who is unfulfilled feels they could be achieving more in their job, relationship etc: *Her job left her feeling unfulfilled and unappreciated.*

**un·furl** /ʌnˈfɜːl‖-ɜːrl/ *v* [T] to unroll and open a flag, sail etc

**un·fur·nished** /ʌnˈfɜːnɪʃt‖-ɜːr-/ *adj* an unfurnished room, house etc has no furniture in it

**un·gain·ly** /ʌnˈgeɪnli/ *adj* moving in a way that does not look graceful: *I had been a tall, ungainly teenager with a bad haircut and National Health glasses.* —**ungainliness** *n* [U]

**un·glued** /ʌnˈgluːd/ *adj* **come unglued** *AmE informal* **a)** to become extremely upset or angry about something: *Pat came unglued when I told him about the accident.* **b)** if your plans come unglued, they do not work well

**un·god·ly** /ʌnˈgɒdli‖-ˈgɑːd-/ *adj* **1** [only before noun] *informal* an ungodly time or noise is unreasonable and annoying: *Why did you wake me up at such an ungodly hour?* **2** *literary* showing a lack of respect for God

**un·gov·er·na·ble** /ʌnˈgʌvənəbəl‖-vər-/ *adj* **1** *formal* feelings that are ungovernable are impossible to control: **ungovernable temper** (=extreme anger that cannot be controlled) **2** a country or area that is ungovernable is one in which the people cannot be controlled by the government, the police etc

**un·gra·cious** /ʌnˈgreɪʃəs/ *adj* not polite or friendly, especially towards someone who has said they are sorry to you or are being friendly to you —**ungraciously** *adv*

**un·grate·ful** /ʌnˈgreɪtfəl/ *adj* not expressing thanks for something that someone has given to you or done for you: *Don't be so ungrateful!* —**ungratefully** *adv* —**ungratefulness** *n* [U]

**un·guard·ed** /ʌnˈgɑːdɪ̣d‖-ɑːr-/ *adj* **1** an unguarded remark, statement etc is one that you make carelessly without thinking of the possible effects **2 in an unguarded moment** at a time when you are not paying attention to what you are doing or saying: *In an unguarded moment, I told her I was leaving.*

**un·guent** /ˈʌŋgwənt/ *n* [C] *literary* an oily substance used on your skin; OINTMENT

**un·hand** /ʌnˈhænd/ *v* [T] *old use* to stop holding someone you have caught: *Unhand me, sir!*

**un·hap·pi·ly** /ʌnˈhæpɪ̣li/ *adv* **1** in a way that shows you are not happy: *Zack looked at her unhappily.* **2** [sentence adverb] *old-fashioned* used when you are mentioning a fact that you wish were not true; UNFORTUNATELY: *Unhappily, she was not able to complete the course.*

S3 W3 **un·hap·py** /ʌnˈhæpi/ *adj* **unhappier, unhappiest** **1** not happy: *If you're so unhappy, why don't you change jobs?* **2** feeling worried or annoyed because you do not like what is happening in a situation: [+ **about**] *We were unhappy about the press reports of the demonstration* | [+ **with**] *If you're unhappy with your results, you can always take the exam again.* **3** *formal* an unhappy remark, situation etc is unsuitable or unlucky: *an unhappy turn of phrase* | *an unhappy coincidence* —**unhappily** *adv* —**unhappiness** *n* [U]

**un·harmed** /ʌnˈhɑːmd‖-ɑːr-/ *adj* [not before noun] not hurt or harmed: *They managed to escape unharmed.*

**un·health·y** /ʌnˈhelθi/ *adj* **1** likely to make you ill: *unhealthy living conditions* **2** not healthy: *unhealthy children who don't get enough exercise* **3** unhealthy skin, hair etc shows that you are ill or not healthy: *an unhealthy pale complexion* **4** behaviour that is unhealthy is not normal and may be harmful: **an unhealthy interest in** *Gareth had an unhealthy interest in death.* —**unhealthily** *adv* —**unhealthiness** *n* [U]

**un·heard** /ˌʌnˈhɜːd‖-ɜːrd/ *adj* [not before noun] not listened to: **go unheard** *Her cries for help went unheard.*

**unheard-of** /-ˈ· ·/ *adj* something that is unheard-of is so unusual that it has not happened or been known before: *It's unheard-of for anyone to pass the exam so young.*

**un·heed·ed** /ʌnˈhiːdɪ̣d/ *adj literary* noticed but not listened to, accepted, or believed: **go unheeded** *Her prayers went unheeded.*

**un·help·ful** /ʌnˈhelpfəl/ *adj* not willing or able to help in a situation and sometimes making it worse: *The authorities are being particularly unhelpful.* —**unhelpfully** *adv* —**unhelpfulness** *n* [U]

**un·her·ald·ed** /ʌnˈherəldɪ̣d/ *adj formal* not previously announced or mentioned

**un·hinge** /ʌnˈhɪndʒ/ *v* [T] to make someone become mentally ill: *The terrible experience seemed to have unhinged him slightly.* —**unhinged** *adj*

**un·hip** /ʌnˈhɪp/ *adj slang* unfashionable

**un·hitch** /ʌnˈhɪtʃ/ *v* [T] **1** to unfasten something that is joined to something else **2 get unhitched** *AmE informal* to get divorced (DIVORCE[1] (1))

**un·ho·ly** /ʌnˈhəʊli‖-ˈhoʊ-/ *adj* **1** [only before noun] *informal* unreasonable and annoying: *The kids were making an unholy noise in the playroom.* **2** not holy or not respecting what is holy **3 unholy alliance** an unusual agreement between two people or organizations who would not normally work together, usually for a bad purpose

**un·hoped-for** /ʌnˈhəʊpt fɔː‖-ˈhoʊpt fɔːr/ *adj* much better than had been expected: *unhoped-for success*

**un·hur·ried** /ʌnˈhʌrid‖-ˈhɜː-/ *adj* done slowly and calmly: *He began to sketch with precise, unhurried strokes.* —**unhurriedly** *adv*

**un·hurt** /ʌnˈhɜːt‖-ɜːrt/ *adj* [not before noun] not hurt: *He was shaken and frightened, but unhurt.*

**u·ni** /ˈjuːni/ *n* [C] *BrE, AustrE spoken* university

**uni-** /juːnɪ̣/ *prefix* one; single: *unidirectional*

**UNICEF** /ˈjuːnɪ̣sef/ *n* United Nations International Children's Fund; an organization that helps children in the world suffering from disease, HUNGER etc

**u·ni·corn** /ˈjuːnɪ̣kɔːn‖-ɔːrn/ *n* [C] an imaginary animal like a white horse with a long straight horn growing on its head

**u·ni·cy·cle** /ˈjuːniˌsaɪkəl/ *n* [C] a vehicle that is like a bicycle but has only one wheel

**un·i·den·ti·fied** /ˌʌnaɪˈdentɪ̣faɪd◂/ *adj* an unidentified person or thing is one that you do not recognize, do not know the name of etc: *An unidentified man was spotted near the scene of the crime.*

**u·ni·fi·ca·tion** /ˌjuːnɪ̣fɪ̣ˈkeɪʃən/ *n* [U] the act of combining separate countries to make a single country with one government: *the unification of Germany*

**u·ni·form**[1] /ˈjuːnɪ̣fɔːm‖-ɔːrm/ *n* [C,U] **1** a particular type of clothing worn by all the members of a group or organization such as the police, the army etc: *school uniform* **2 be in uniform a)** to be wearing a uniform **b)** to be a member of the army, navy etc S3

**uniform**[2] *adj* being the same in all its parts or among all its members: *a plank of uniform width* —**uniformly** *adv*

**u·ni·formed** /ˈjuːnɪ̣fɔːmd‖-ɔːr-/ *adj* wearing a uniform: *uniformed police officers*

**u·ni·form·i·ty** /ˌjuːmɪ̣ˈfɔːmɪ̣ti‖-ɔːr-/ *n* [U] the quality of being or looking the same as all other members of a group: *the dull uniformity of the houses in the area*

**u·ni·fy** /ˈjuːnɪ̣faɪ/ *v* [T] **1** to combine the parts of a country, organization etc to make a single unit: *Spain was unified in the 16th century.* **2** to change a group of things so that they are all the same

**u·ni·lat·e·ral** /ˌjuːnɪ̣ˈlætərəl◂/ *adj formal* a unilateral action or decision is done by only one of the groups involved in a situation: *a unilateral declaration of independence* | **unilateral disarmament** (=the process of a country getting rid of its own NUCLEAR weapons without waiting for other countries to do the same) —compare BILATERAL, MULTILATERAL —**unilateralism** *n* —**unilaterally** *adv*

**un·i·ma·gin·a·ble** /ˌʌnɪˈmædʒɪ̈nəbəl◂/ *adj* not possible to imagine: *an unimaginable amount of money*

**un·i·ma·gin·a·tive** /ˌʌnɪˈmædʒɪ̈nətɪv◂/ *adj* **1** lacking the ability to think of new or unusual ideas **2** too ordinary and boring: *an unimaginative shop window display* **3** an unimaginative solution to a problem does not work very well because it does not involve any new or intelligent ideas: *unimaginative housing policies*

**un·im·paired** /ˌʌnɪmˈpeəd◂‖-ˈperd◂/ *adj* not damaged by an unpleasant or unlucky experience: *She survived the accident with her sight unimpaired.*

**un·im·pea·cha·ble** /ˌʌnɪmˈpiːtʃəbəl◂/ *adj formal* so good or definite that criticism or doubt is impossible: *unimpeachable moral principles* —**unimpeachably** *adv*

**un·im·por·tant** /ˌʌnɪmˈpɔːtənt◂‖-ɔːr-/ *adj* not important: *Women's issues were assumed to be unimportant, especially in the political arena.*

**un·im·pressed** /ˌʌnɪmˈprest/ *adj* not thinking that someone or something is good, interesting, unusual etc: *Jay seemed unimpressed by the array of finery.*

**un·im·pres·sive** /ˌʌnɪmˈpresɪv◂/ *adj* someone or something that is unimpressive is not as good, large, important, skilful etc as you expected or as they are supposed to be: *The new building is singularly unimpressive.*

**un·in·formed** /ˌʌnɪnˈfɔːmd◂‖-ɔːr-/ *adj* not having enough knowledge or information: *uninformed criticism* —see also INFORMED

**un·in·hab·it·a·ble** /ˌʌnɪnˈhæbɪ̈təbəl◂/ *adj* **1** an uninhabitable place is impossible to live in **2** an uninhabitable house or apartment is too dirty, cold etc to live in —opposite HABITABLE

**un·in·hab·it·ed** /ˌʌnɪnˈhæbɪ̈tɪ̈d◂/ *adj* an uninhabited place does not have anyone living there: *an uninhabited island*

**un·in·hib·it·ed** /ˌʌnɪnˈhɪbɪ̈tɪ̈d◂/ *adj* expressing your feelings easily without feeling embarrassed: *uninhibited laughter* —**uninhibitedly** *adv*

**un·i·ni·ti·at·ed** /ˌʌnɪˈnɪʃieɪtɪ̈d◂/ *n* **the uninitiated** [plural] people who do not have special knowledge or experience of something: *To the uninitiated, this will make little sense.* —**uninitiated** *adj*

**un·in·spired** /ˌʌnɪnˈspaɪəd◂‖-ˈspaɪrd◂/ *adj* not showing any imagination: *an uninspired performance*

**un·in·spir·ing** /ˌʌnɪnˈspaɪərɪŋ‖-ˈspaɪr-/ *adj* not at all interesting or exciting: *an uninspiring piece of architecture*

**un·in·tel·li·gi·ble** /ˌʌnɪnˈtelɪ̈dʒɪ̈bəl◂/ *adj* impossible to understand: *Eva muttered something unintelligible.* —**unintelligibly** *adv*

**un·in·ten·tion·al** /ˌʌnɪnˈtenʃənəl◂/ *adj* not said or done deliberately: *I know she upset you, but I'm sure it was unintentional.* —**unintentionally** *adv*

**un·in·terest·ed** /ʌnˈɪntrɪ̈stɪ̈d/ *adj* not interested: [+ **in**] *Kevin seems uninterested in learning anything.* —compare DISINTERESTED

**un·in·ter·rupt·ed** /ˌʌnɪntəˈrʌptɪ̈d◂/ *adj* continuous: *a long, uninterrupted sleep* —**uninterruptedly** *adv*

**un·in·vit·ed** /ˌʌnɪnˈvaɪtɪ̈d◂/ *adj* not having been asked for: *uninvited guests*

**un·in·vit·ing** /ˌʌnɪnˈvaɪtɪŋ◂/ *adj* an uninviting place seems unattractive or unpleasant: *an uninviting, desolate landscape*

S1 W1 **u·nion** /ˈjuːnjən/ *n* **1** [C] an organization formed by workers to protect their rights; TRADE UNION: *the air traffic controllers' union* **2** a group of countries or states with the same central government: *the Soviet Union* **3** [singular, U] *formal* the act of joining two or more things together or the state of being joined together: *The artist's work shows the perfect union of craftsmanship and imagination.* | [+ **with**] *Scotland's union with England in 1603* **4** [singular, U] *formal* marriage

**u·nion·is·m** /ˈjuːnjənɪzəm/ *n* [U] belief in the principles of TRADE UNIONS

**U·nion·ist** /ˈjuːnjənɪ̈st/ *n* [C] a member of a political party that wants Northern Ireland to remain part of the United Kingdom —**Unionism** *n* [U]

**u·nion·ize** also **-ise** *BrE* /ˈjuːnjənaɪz/ *v* [I,T] if workers unionize or are unionized, they become members of a TRADE UNION —**unionization** /ˌjuːnjənaɪˈzeɪʃən‖ˌjuːnjənə-/ *n* [U]

**Union Jack** /ˌ·· ˈ·/ *n* [C] the national flag of Great Britain and Northern Ireland

**u·nion suit** /ˈ·· ˌ·/ *n* [C] *AmE* woollen underwear that covers the whole body; COMBINATIONS *BrE*

**u·nique** /juːˈniːk/ *adj* **1** [no comparative] being the only one of its kind: *Each person's fingerprints are unique* **2** *informal* unusually good and special: *a unique opportunity to travel* —**uniquely** *adv*: *an actor uniquely suited to the part* —**uniqueness** *n* [U] S3 W2

**USAGE NOTE: UNIQUE**

WORD CHOICE: **unique, only**

If you want to say that something has features or qualities that make it different from anything else, especially when this makes it better, you say it is **unique**: *His interpretation of the original screenplay is quite unique.*|*a style of folk art unique to these tribespeople* (=they are the only people who do it)

If you want to say that there is just one of something available in a particular place at a particular time out of all the others that may exist, you say it is the **only** one: *She was the only woman doctor in the district.*|*After the attack, only one building was left standing.*

GRAMMAR

Before a singular noun **unique** usually follows *a*, **only** often follows *the*: *This is a unique opportunity/the only opportunity I'll get.*

Many people think it is not correct to say something is *fairly* or *rather unique*, or *very unique*, as if **unique** can only be used in sense one. However, native speakers will often say this, because they are using **unique** in sense two to mean **unusual** or **special**.

**u·ni·sex** /ˈjuːnɪseks/ *adj* intended for both men and women: *a unisex hairdressing salon*

**u·ni·son** /ˈjuːnɪ̈sən, -zən/ *n* **1 in unison a)** if people speak in unison, they say the same words at the same time: *"No way!" the twins replied in unison.* **b)** if two groups, governments etc do something in unison they do it together because they agree with each other: *Management and workers must act in unison to compete with foreign business.* **2** [C] a way of singing or playing music in which everyone plays or sings the same tune

**u·nit** /ˈjuːnɪ̈t/ *n* [C] W3

**1** ▶ **PART** ◀ a thing, person or group that is regarded as one single whole part of something larger: *The family is the smallest social unit.*

**2** ▶ **GROUP** ◀ a group of people working together as part of the structure of a larger group, organization, company etc: *She works in the emergency unit at the hospital.*

**3** ▶ **FOR MEASURING** ◀ an amount or quantity of something used as a standard of measurement: [+ **of**] *The dollar is the basic unit of currency in the US.* | *The patient was given 2 units of blood.*

**4** ▶ **FURNITURE** ◀ a piece of furniture such as a cupboard, especially one that can be fitted to others of the same type: **kitchen/office/storage unit** (=a unit designed for the kitchen etc)

**5** ▶ **PART OF A MACHINE** ◀ a piece of machinery which is part of a larger machine: **control/filter/cooling unit** *The cooling unit must be replaced.*

**6** ▶ **PART OF A BOOK** ◀ one of the numbered parts into which a TEXTBOOK (=a book used in schools) is divided

**7** ▶ **PRODUCT** ◀ *technical* a single complete product

made by a company: *The factory's output is now up to 150,000 units each month.*
**8 ▶ SCHOOL/UNIVERSITY ◀** *AmE* an amount of work that a student needs to do in a particular course
**9 ▶ APARTMENT ◀** *AmE* a single apartment in a larger building
**10 ▶ NUMBER ◀ a)** *technical* the smallest whole number; the number 1 **b)** any whole number less than ten: *hundreds, tens, and units*

**U·ni·ta·ri·an** /ˌjuːnɪ̈ˈteəriən◂‖-ˈter-/ *adj* connected with a Christian group that believes its members should be free to believe what they want —**unitarian** *n* [C]

**u·nite** /juːˈnaɪt/ *v* [I,T] to join together with other people, organizations to achieve something: *two nations that are united by a bond of friendship* | [+ **in/against/behind**] *In a crisis, party members will always unite behind their leader.* | **unite to do sth** *We must unite to fight against racism.*

W3 **u·nit·ed** /juːˈnaɪtɪ̈d/ *adj* **1** joined or closely connected by feelings, aims etc: *working for a united Europe* **2** involving or done by everyone: *a united effort to clean up the environment* —**unitedly** *adv*

**United Na·tions** /ˌ·,·· ˈ··/ *n* [singular] an international organization that tries to find peaceful solutions to world problems

**unit price** /ˈ·· ˌ·/ *n* [C] the price that is charged for each single thing or quantity that is sold

**unit trust** /ˌ·· ˈ·/ *n* [C] *BrE* a company through which you can buy shares (SHARE[2] (6)) in many different businesses; MUTUAL FUND *AmE*

W3 **u·ni·ty** /ˈjuːnɪ̈ti/ *n* **1** [singular, U] a situation in which a group of people or countries work together for a particular purpose: *European unity* **2** [U] the quality of being complete: *The design has a pleasing unity and appearance.* **3** [U] *technical* the number 1

**Univ** *n* a written abbreviation of university

W3 **u·ni·ver·sal** /ˌjuːnɪ̈ˈvɜːsəl◂‖-ɜːr-/ *adj* **1** done by all the members of a group: *There was universal agreement on the issue of sex education.* **2** involving or understood by everyone in the world: *a topic of universal interest* **3** true or suitable in every situation: *a universal truth* —**universally** *adv* —**universality** /ˌjuːnɪ̈vɜːˈsælɪ̈ti‖-ɜːr-/ *n* [U]

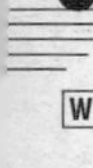

**universal joint** /ˌ···· ˈ·/ *n* [C] a part in a machine, at the point where two other parts join together, that can turn in all directions

W3 **u·ni·verse** /ˈjuːnɪ̈vɜːs‖-ɜːrs/ *n* [singular] **1 the universe** all space, including all the stars and PLANETS **2** the place where a particular person lives or works, including the people they know: **be the centre of sb's universe** (=be the most important thing to someone)

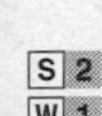
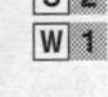

S2 W1 **u·ni·ver·si·ty** /ˌjuːnɪ̈ˈvɜːsɪ̈ti◂‖-ɜːr-/ *n* [C,U] an educational institution at the highest level, where you study for a DEGREE: **go to university** (=study at a university)

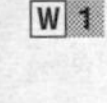

**un·just** /ˌʌnˈdʒʌst◂/ *adj* not fair or reasonable: *unjust laws* —**unjustly** *adv*

**un·just·i·fi·a·ble** /ʌnˈdʒʌstɪ̈faɪəbəl/ *adj* completely wrong and unacceptable: *Poisoning the earth's atmosphere is ecologically and morally unjustifiable.* —**unjustifiably** *adv*

**un·just·i·fied** /ʌnˈdʒʌstɪ̈faɪd/ *adj* criticism, bad treatment etc that is unjustified is unfair: *I think your criticisms of Mr Ward are completely unjustified.*

**un·kempt** /ˌʌnˈkempt◂/ *adj* not neat or tidy: *an unkempt garden*

**un·kind** /ˌʌnˈkaɪnd◂/ *adj* nasty, unpleasant, or cruel: *an unkind remark* | [+ **to**] *Her husband is very unkind to her.* —**unkindly** *adv* —**unkindness** *n* [U]

**un·know·ing** /ʌnˈnəʊɪŋ‖-ˈnoʊ-/ *adj* [only before noun] *formal* not realizing what you are doing or what is happening; UNAWARE: *Buying the stolen property made her an unknowing accomplice to the crime.* —**unknowingly** *adv*

W2 **un·known**[1] /ˌʌnˈnəʊn◂‖-ˈnoʊn◂/ *adj, adv* **1** not known about: *a voyage through unknown territory* | *The murderer's identity remains unknown.* **2** not famous: *an unknown artist* **3 unknown to sb** without someone knowing: *Unknown to the general public, peace negotiations were already taking place.* —see also UNBEKNOWN **4 be an unknown quantity** if someone or something is an unknown quantity, you do not know what their abilities are or how they are likely to behave

**unknown**[2] *n* **1** [C] someone who is not famous: *At that point in her career she was still an unknown.* **2 the unknown a)** a place that is not known about or that has not been visited by humans: *The astronauts began their journey into the unknown.* **b)** things that you do not know or understand: *a fear of the unknown*

**un·law·ful** /ʌnˈlɔːfəl/ *adj law* not legal —**unlawfully** *adv*

**un·lead·ed** /ʌnˈledɪ̈d/ *adj* unleaded petrol does not contain any LEAD[3] (1) so is less harmful to the environment

**un·learn** /ˌʌnˈlɜːn‖-ɜːrn/ *v* [T] *informal* to deliberately forget something you have learned: *It's difficult to unlearn bad driving habits.*

**un·leash** /ʌnˈliːʃ/ *v* [T] **1** to suddenly let a strong force, feeling etc have its full effect: *forces of change unleashed by the war* **2** to let a dog run free after it has been held on a LEASH[1] (1)

**un·leav·ened** /ʌnˈlevənd/ *adj* unleavened bread is flat because it is not made with YEAST

**un·less** /ʌnˈles, ən-/ *conjunction* used when one thing will only happen or be true as long as another thing happens or is true: *Milk quickly turns sour unless it's refrigerated.* | *Unless some extra money is found, the theatre will close.* S1 W1

**USAGE NOTE: UNLESS**

WORD CHOICE: **unless, if...not, if, provided/providing that**

You do not use **unless** about something that did not happen or you know is not true, but you can use **if...not** in this way. For example, you could not use **unless** in these sentences: *She would have died if the doctors hadn't operated immediately* (=but they did).|*If he wasn't such an idiot* (=but he is), *he would understand.*

You use **unless** about something that *could* happen if something else does not happen or is not done, or if something *could* be true: *Unless the doctors operate immediately, she'll die./She'll die unless the doctors operate immediately* (=the doctors have not operated yet, and may or may not do).|*Unless he's a complete idiot, he'll understand* (=he may or may not be a complete idiot).

**Unless** and **if...not** can both be used to say that what you will do depends on something else happening: *Unless he comes soon, I'm going without him.*|*If he doesn't come soon, I'm going without him.*

You use **provided (that)** or **providing (that)** when the condition is that something definitely happens or is definitely true: *Providing the weather's OK, we'll make the trip next Saturday.*

You often use **unless** to add a condition that you think of after you have finished speaking: *We'll go there next Saturday - unless it's raining of course.*

**un·let·tered** /ʌnˈletəd‖-ərd/ *adj formal* unable to read or uneducated

**un·li·censed** /ʌnˈlaɪsənst/ *adj* without a LICENSE (=official document that gives you permission to do or have something) *unlicensed firearms* | *unlicensed traders*

**un·like**[1] /ˌʌnˈlaɪk◂/ *prep* **1** completely different from a particular person or thing: *In his jeans and T-shirt, Charles looked most unlike a lawyer.* **2** not at all typical of something or someone: *It's unlike Beth to drink so much, I wonder if she's all right.* W3

**unlike**[2] *adj literary* not alike; different

S2 W2 **un·like·ly** /ʌnˈlaɪkli/ *adj* **1** not likely to happen: *Donna might come, but it's very unlikely.* | **it is unlikely that** *It's unlikely that the thieves will be caught.* | **in the unlikely event of** (=if something which is unlikely happens) *In the unlikely event of a fire, passengers should move to the top deck.* **2** not likely to be true: *an unlikely story* **3 unlikely couple** two people who are having a relationship but do not seem suitable for each other

**un·lim·i·ted** /ʌnˈlɪmɪ̈tɪ̈d/ *adj* **1** without a fixed limit: *unlimited credit* **2** very large amount: *an unlimited variety of cookies*

**un·list·ed** /ʌnˈlɪstɪ̈d/ *adj* **1** not shown on an official STOCK EXCHANGE list **2** *AmE* not in the list of numbers in the telephone DIRECTORY; EX-DIRECTORY *BrE*

**un·lit** /ˌʌnˈlɪt◂/ *adj* dark because there are no lights: *an unlit stairway*

**un·load** /ʌnˈləʊd‖-ˈloʊd/ *v*
**1** ▶ **VEHICLE/SHIP** ◀ **a)** to remove a load from a vehicle, ship etc: **unload sth from sth** *The driver unloaded some boxes from the back of the truck.* **b)** [I,T] if a vehicle, ship etc unloads, the goods that it carries are removed from it: *The ship is unloading at the dock right now.*
**2** ▶ **GUN** ◀ [I,T] to remove the bullets or shells (SHELL[1] (2, 3)) from a gun
**3** ▶ **CAMERA** ◀ to remove the film from a camera
**4** ▶ **GET RID OF** ◀ [T] *informal* **a)** to get rid of something illegal or not very good by selling it quickly: **unload sth on/onto** *Hundreds of cheap videos were unloaded on the British market.* **b)** to get rid of work or responsibility by giving it to someone else: **unload sth on/onto sb** *Don't let him unload his problems onto you.*

**un·lock** /ʌnˈlɒk‖-ˈlɑːk/ *v* [T] **1** to unfasten the lock on a door, box etc **2 unlock the secret of** to discover the most important facts about something

**un·looked-for** /ʌnˈlʊkt fɔː‖-fɔːr/ *adj informal* not expected

**un·loose** /ʌnˈluːs/ *v* [T] *formal* to untie or unfasten something: *She unloosed her hair.*

**un·loved** /ʌnˈlʌvd/ *adj* not loved by anyone

**un·love·ly** /ʌnˈlʌvli/ *adj literary* ugly

**un·luck·y** /ʌnˈlʌki/ *adj* **1** having bad luck: *He gambled frequently, but was usually unlucky.* | **[+ with]** *We were unlucky with the weather this weekend. It rained constantly.* **2** happening as a result of bad luck: **it is unlucky (for sb) that** *It was unlucky for Stephen that the boss happened to walk in just at that moment.* **3** causing bad luck —**unluckily** *adv*

**un·made** /ˌʌnˈmeɪd◂/ *adj* an unmade bed is not tidy because the sheets, BLANKETS etc have not been arranged since someone slept in it

**un·man·age·a·ble** /ʌnˈmænɪdʒəbəl/ *adj* difficult to control or deal with

**un·man·ly** /ʌnˈmænli/ *adj* not thought to be suitable for or typical of a man

**un·manned** /ˌʌnˈmænd◂/ *adj* a machine, vehicle etc that is unmanned does not have a person operating or controlling it: *an unmanned space craft*

**un·man·ner·ly** /ʌnˈmænəli‖-ər-/ *adj formal* not polite; rude: *a rough, unmannerly security guard*

**un·marked** /ˌʌnˈmɑːkt◂‖-ˈmɑːrkt◂/ *adj* something that is unmarked has no words or sign on it to show where or what it is: *an unmarked grave* | *an unmarked police car*

**un·mar·ried** /ˌʌnˈmærid◂/ *adj* not married; SINGLE[1] (4): *unmarried mothers*

**un·mask** /ʌnˈmɑːsk‖-ˈmæsk/ *v* [T] to make known the hidden truth about someone: *Sherlock Holmes once again unmasked the murderer.*

**un·matched** /ˌʌnˈmætʃt◂/ *adj literary* better than any other: *a woman of unmatched beauty*

**un·men·tion·a·ble** /ʌnˈmenʃənəbəl/ *adj* too shocking or embarrassing to talk about

**un·men·tion·a·bles** /ʌnˈmenʃənəbəlz/ *n* [plural] *old-fashioned* underwear

**un·mis·tak·a·ble, unmistakeable** /ˌʌnmɪ̈ˈsteɪkəbəl◂/ *adj* familiar and easy to recognize: *the unmistakable smell of rotting eggs* —**unmistakably** *adv*

**un·mit·i·gat·ed** /ʌnˈmɪtɪ̈geɪtɪ̈d/ *adj* [only before noun] **unmitigated disaster/failure etc** something that is completely bad: *The tour was an unmitigated disaster.*

**un·moved** /ʌnˈmuːvd/ *adj* [not before noun] feeling no pity, sympathy, or sadness, especially in a situation where most people would feel this: *Richard remained unmoved throughout the funeral.*

**un·named** /ˌʌnˈneɪmd◂/ *adj* an unnamed person, place, or thing is one whose name is not known publicly: *The journalist cited an unnamed source in parliament.*

**un·nat·u·ral** /ʌnˈnætʃərəl/ *adj* **1** different from what you would normally expect: *It seems unnatural for a child to prefer the company of adults.* **2** different from anything produced by nature: *Her hair was an unnatural orange colour.* **3** different from normal human behaviour in a way that seems morally wrong: *unnatural sexual practices* —**unnaturally** *adv*

**un·ne·ces·sa·ry** /ʌnˈnesəsəri‖-seri/ *adj* **1** not needed or more than is needed: *I'm trying to cut down on all my unnecessary spending.* **2** a remark or action that is unnecessary, is unkind or unreasonable —**unnecessarily** /ʌnˈnesəsərəli‖ˌʌn-nesəˈserɪ̈li/ *adv*: *I don't want to worry you unnecessarily.*

**un·nerve** /ˌʌnˈnɜːv‖-ɜːrv/ *v* [T] to upset or frighten someone so that they lose their confidence or their ability to think clearly: *Her first encounter with the boss unnerved her.* —**unnerving** *adj*

**un·no·ticed** /ʌnˈnəʊtɪ̈st‖-ˈnoʊ-/ *adj, adv* without being noticed: *Elsa stood unnoticed at the edge of the crowd.* | **go/pass unnoticed** *His remark went unnoticed by everyone except me.*

**un·num·bered** /ˌʌnˈnʌmbəd◂‖-ərd◂/ *adj* **1** not having a number: *an unnumbered Swiss bank account* **2** *literary* too many to be counted

**un·ob·served** /ˌʌnəbˈzɜːvd‖-ɜːrvd/ *adj, adv* not noticed: *Ruth slipped out of the meeting unobserved.*

**un·ob·tain·a·ble** /ˌʌnəbˈteɪnəbəl◂/ *adj* impossible to get: *Fresh fruit was unobtainable in the winter.*

**un·ob·tru·sive** /ˌʌnəbˈtruːsɪv◂/ *adj* not attracting attention and therefore not likely to be noticed: *a quiet unobtrusive student* —**unobtrusively** *adv*

**un·oc·cu·pied** /ʌnˈɒkjʊ̈paɪd‖-ˈɑːk-/ *adj* **1** a seat, house, room etc that is unoccupied has no one in it: *We moved in right away, as the flat was unoccupied.* **2** an unoccupied country or area is not controlled by the enemy during a war: *The family fled to unoccupied France.*

**un·of·fi·cial** /ˌʌnəˈfɪʃəl◂/ *adj* **1** without formal approval and permission from the organization or person in authority: *unofficial experiments carried out in secret laboratories* **2** not made publicly known as part of an official plan: *The President made an unofficial visit to the Senator's house on Cape Cod.* —**unofficially** *adv*

**un·or·ga·nized** also **-ised** *BrE* /ʌnˈɔːgənaɪzd‖-ˈɔːr-/ *adj* people who are unorganized do not have an organization, TRADE UNION, group etc to help or support them — compare DISORGANIZED

**un·or·tho·dox** /ʌnˈɔːθədɒks‖ʌnˈɔːrθədɑːks/ *adj* unorthodox beliefs or methods are different from what is usual or accepted by most people: *a tennis player with an unorthodox style*

**un·pack** /ʌnˈpæk/ *v* **1** [I,T] to take everything out of a box or SUITCASE: *Let's go upstairs and unpack.* **2** [T] *technical* to change information in a computer so that it is easier to understand but takes up more space

**un·paid** /ˌʌnˈpeɪd◂/ *adj* **1** an unpaid bill or debt has not been paid **2** done without receiving payment: *unpaid voluntary work*

**un·pal·at·a·ble** /ʌnˈpælətəbəl/ *adj formal* **1** an unpalatable fact or idea is very unpleasant and difficult to accept: *We were trying to avoid the unpalatable truth –*

*that the whole plan had failed.* **2** unpalatable food tastes unpleasant —**unpalatably** *adv*

**un·par·al·leled** /ʌnˈpærəleld/ *adj formal* greater or better than all others: *a period of unparalleled economic prosperity*

**un·par·don·a·ble** /ʌnˈpɑːdnəbəl‖-ˈpɑːr-/ *adj formal* unpardonable behaviour is completely unacceptable: *Your behaviour was unpardonable!* —**unpardonably** *adv*

**un·pick** /ʌnˈpɪk/ *v* [T] to take out stitches from a piece of cloth or KNITTING

**un·placed** /ˌʌnˈpleɪst◂/ *adj BrE* not one of the first three to finish in a race or competition

**un·pleas·ant** /ʌnˈplezənt/ *adj* **1** not pleasant or enjoyable: *the unpleasant side-effects of the drug|an unpleasant surprise* **2** not kind and friendly: *Our neighbours are extremely unpleasant.* —**unpleasantly** *adv*

**un·pleas·ant·ness** /ʌnˈplezəntnɪ̮s/ *n* [U] trouble or arguments: *I hate all this unpleasantness.*

**un·plug** /ʌnˈplʌg/ *v* [T] to disconnect a piece of electrical equipment by taking its PLUG[1] (1a,c) out of a SOCKET (1): *Unplug the TV before you go to bed.* —see picture at PLUG[2]

**un·plumbed** /ˌʌnˈplʌmd◂/ *adj* **the unplumbed depths of** something that is not known about because it has never been examined or explored: *the unplumbed depths of the ocean*

**un·pop·u·lar** /ʌnˈpɒpjələ‖-ˈpɑːpjələr/ *adj* not liked by most people: *an unpopular decision|He was very unpopular at school.* —**unpopularity** /ʌnˌpɒpjəˈlærɪ̮ti‖-ˌpɑːp-/ *n* [U]

**un·pre·ce·dent·ed** /ʌnˈpresɪ̮dentɪ̮d/ *adj* never having happened before, or never having happened so much: *unprecedented price increases* —**unprecedentedly** *adv*

**un·pre·dict·a·ble** /ˌʌnprɪˈdɪktəbəl◂/ *adj* **1** something that is unpredictable changes a lot so it is impossible to know what will happen: *The weather in Britain is very unpredictable.* **2** someone who is unpredictable tends to change their behaviour or ideas suddenly so that you never know what they are going to do or think

**un·pre·ju·diced** /ʌnˈpredʒədɪ̮st/ *adj* willing to consider different ideas and opinions

**un·pre·pared** /ˌʌnprɪˈpeəd◂‖-ˈperd◂/ *adj* not ready to deal with something: [+ **for**] *Doug was unprepared for the boredom that followed his retirement.*

**un·pre·pos·sess·ing** /ˌʌnpriːpəˈzesɪŋ/ *adj formal* not very attractive or noticeable

**un·pre·ten·tious** /ˌʌnprɪˈtenʃəs◂/ *adj approving* not trying to seem better, more important etc than you really are: *an unpretentious restaurant* —**unpretentiously** *adv* —**unpretentiousness** *n* [U]

**un·prin·ci·pled** /ʌnˈprɪnsɪ̮pəld/ *adj formal* not caring about whether what you do is morally right; UNSCRUPULOUS

**un·print·a·ble** /ʌnˈprɪntəbəl/ *adj* words that are unprintable are very rude or shocking

**un·pro·duct·ive** /ˌʌnprəˈdʌktɪv◂/ *adj* not producing any good results: *I've had a very unproductive week.*

**un·pro·fes·sion·al** /ˌʌnprəˈfeʃənəl◂/ *adj* someone who is unprofessional does not behave according to the standard that is expected in a particular profession or activity: *Johnson was fired for unprofessional conduct.* —**unprofessionally** *adv*

**un·prof·it·a·ble** /ʌnˈprɒfɪ̮təbəl‖-ˈprɑː-/ *adj* **1** making no profit: *unprofitable businesses* **2** *formal* bringing no advantage or gain: *It would be unprofitable to commit yourself to any firm plans at the moment.*

**un·prompt·ed** /ʌnˈprɒmptɪ̮d‖ʌnˈprɑːmp-/ *adj formal* unprompted actions are things that you do without anyone asking you to

**un·pro·nounce·a·ble** /ˌʌnprəˈnaʊnsəbəl◂/ *adj* an unpronounceable word or name is very difficult to say

**un·pro·tect·ed** /ˌʌnprəˈtektɪ̮d◂/ *adj* **1** something that is unprotected could hurt someone or be damaged: *Unprotected machinery can be dangerous.* **2 unprotected sex** sex without a CONDOM

**un·pro·ven** /ˌʌnˈpruːvən, *ScotE* -ˈprəvən/ *adj* not tested, and not shown to be definitely true: *unproven allegations*

**un·pro·voked** /ˌʌnprəˈvəʊkt◂‖-ˈvoʊkt◂/ *adj* unprovoked anger, attacks etc are directed at someone who has not done anything to deserve them: *The assault was completely unprovoked.*

**un·qual·i·fied** /ʌnˈkwɒlɪ̮faɪd‖-ˈkwɑː-/ *adj* **1** not having the right knowledge, experience, or education to do something: **unqualified to do sth** *I feel unqualified to advise you.* **2 unqualified success/approval etc** success etc that is complete and without any criticism: *The play was an unqualified success.*

**un·ques·tion·a·ble** /ʌnˈkwestʃənəbəl/ *adj* impossible to doubt; certain —**unquestionably** *adv*

**un·ques·tioned** /ʌnˈkwestʃənd/ *adj* something that is unquestioned is accepted or believed by everyone: *the monarch's unquestioned right to rule*

**un·ques·tion·ing** /ʌnˈkwestʃənɪŋ/ *adj* an unquestioning faith, attitude etc is very certain and without doubts: *an unquestioning belief in God|unquestioning loyalty* —**unquestioningly** *adv*

**un·qui·et** /ʌnˈkwaɪɪ̮t/ *adj literary* tending to make you feel nervous: *His unquiet gaze moved away from her.*

**un·quote** /ˌʌnˈkwəʊt‖-ˈkwoʊt/ *adv* see **quote...unquote** (QUOTE[1] (4))

**un·rav·el** /ʌnˈrævəl/ *v* **unravelled, unravelling** *BrE*, **unraveled, unraveling** *AmE* **1** [I,T] if you unravel threads or if they unravel, they become separated **2** [T] to understand or explain something that is very complicated: *It is difficult to unravel complex human emotions.*

**un·rea·da·ble** /ʌnˈriːdəbəl/ *adj* **1** an unreadable book or piece of writing is difficult to read because it is boring or complicated **2** unreadable writing is so untidy that you cannot read it; ILLEGIBLE

**un·real** /ˌʌnˈrɪəl◂/ *adj* **1** [not before noun] an experience, situation etc that is unreal seems so strange that you think you must be imagining or dreaming it: *The evening was so bizarre that it was beginning to seem unreal.* **2** not related to real things that happen: *Exam questions often deal with unreal situations.* **3** *spoken* very exciting; excellent: *Our trip to Disneyland was unreal.* —**unreality** /ˌʌnriˈælɪ̮ti/ *n* [U]

**un·rea·lis·tic** /ˌʌnrɪəˈlɪstɪk◂/ *adj* unrealistic ideas, hopes are not based on facts: *Predictions that Labour would win the election began to look unrealistic.*|**it is unrealistic to do sth** *It is unrealistic to expect children to sit still for hours.*|**be being unrealistic** *John, I think you're being totally unrealistic – we'll never be ready by then.* —**unrealistically** /-kli/ *adv*

**un·rea·son·a·ble** /ʌnˈriːzənəbəl/ *adj* **1** behaving in an unfair, unpleasant, or stupid way: *Will thinks I'm being unreasonable in not lending him the car.* **2** an unreasonable belief, request, action etc is wrong or unfair: **it is unreasonable to do sth** *I think it's unreasonable to expect you to work Sundays.*|**make unreasonable demands** *Get assertive if your boss makes unreasonable demands.* **3** unreasonable prices, costs etc are too high —opposite REASONABLE —**unreasonably** *adv* —**unreasonableness** *n* [U]

**un·rea·son·ing** /ʌnˈriːzənɪŋ/ *adj formal* an unreasoning feeling is one that is not based on fact or reason

**un·rec·og·niz·a·ble** also **-isable** *BrE* /ʌnˈrekəgnaɪzəbəl, -ˈrekə-/ *adj* someone or something that is unrecognizable has changed or been damaged so much that you do not recognize them: *They've built so many new buildings that the town centre was unrecognisable.*

**un·rec·og·nized** also **-ised** *BrE* /ʌnˈrekəgnaɪzd, -ˈrekə-/ *adj* **1** someone who is unrecognized for something they have done has not received the admiration or respect they deserve: *one of the great unrecognized jazzmen of the 1930s* **2** not noticed or not thought to be important: **go unrecognized** *Domestic violence went unrecognized for years.*

**un·re·cord·ed** /ˌʌnrɪˈkɔːdɪ̈d◂‖-ɔːr-/ *adj* not written down or recorded: **go unrecorded** *Many of the complaints have gone unrecorded.*

**un·re·fined** /ˌʌnrɪˈfaɪnd◂/ *adj* **1** [no comparative] an unrefined substance has not been separated from the other substances that it is combined with in its natural form: *unrefined oil | unrefined sugar* **2** *formal* not polite or educated —opposite REFINED

**un·re·gen·e·rate** /ˌʌnrɪˈdʒenərɪ̈t◂/ *adj formal* making no attempt to change your bad habits or bad behaviour: *an unregenerate liar*

**un·re·lat·ed** /ˌʌnrɪˈleɪtɪ̈d◂/ *adj* **1** not connected to each other in any way: *The police think that the two incidents are unrelated.* **2** people who are unrelated are not members of the same family

**un·re·lent·ing** /ˌʌnrɪˈlentɪŋ◂/ *adj formal* an unpleasant situation that is unrelenting continues for a long time without stopping: *the unrelenting pressures of the job | two days of unrelenting rain* —see also RELENT, RELENTLESS —**unrelentingly** *adv*

**un·re·li·a·ble** /ˌʌnrɪˈlaɪəbəl◂/ *adj* unable to be trusted or depended on: *The car's becoming very unreliable.* | **unreliable witness** (=someone who may not tell the truth in a court) —opposite RELIABLE

**un·re·lieved** /ˌʌnrɪˈliːvd◂/ *adj* an unpleasant situation that is unrelieved continues for a long time because nothing happens to change it: *unrelieved pain* —see also RELIEVE —**unrelievedly** /-ˈliːvɪ̈dli/ *adv*

**un·re·mark·a·ble** /ˌʌnrɪˈmɑːkəbəl◂‖-ɑːr-/ *adj formal* not especially beautiful or interesting: *unremarkable buildings*

**un·re·mit·ting** /ˌʌnrɪˈmɪtɪŋ◂/ *adj formal* an action or effort that is unremitting continues for a long time and probably will not stop: *lives of unremitting drudgery* —**unremittingly** *adv*

**un·re·peat·a·ble** /ˌʌnrɪˈpiːtəbəl◂/ *adj* **1** something that someone says that is unrepeatable is too rude or offensive for you to want to say it again: *Tim's comment was unrepeatable.* **2** unable to be done again

**un·re·pent·ant** /ˌʌnrɪˈpentənt◂/ *adj* not feeling ashamed of behaviour, or beliefs that other people may disapprove of: *an unrepentant right-winger*

**un·rep·re·sen·ta·tive** /ˌʌnreprɪˈzentətɪv/ *adj* **1** not typical of a group or type, and therefore not giving you any information about the other members of the same group or type: **[+ of]** *This painting is unrepresentative of the rest of her work.* **2** an unrepresentative government only has a few members from a variety of social groups, so that the opinions of many people are ignored

**un·re·quit·ed** /ˌʌnrɪˈkwaɪtɪ̈d◂/ *adj* **unrequited love** romantic love that you feel for someone, but that they do not feel for you

**un·re·served** /ˌʌnrɪˈzɜːvd◂‖-ɜːr-/ *adj* complete and without any doubts —**unreservedly** /-ˈzɜːvɪ̈dli‖-ɜːr-/ *adv*: *The company apologized unreservedly for its mistake.*

**un·re·solved** /ˌʌnrɪˈzɒlvd◂‖ˈzɑːlvd◂, -ˈzɒːlvd◂/ *adj* an unresolved problem or question has not been answered or solved

**un·res·pon·sive** /ˌʌnrɪˈspɒnsɪv‖-rɪˈspɑːn-/ *adj* **1** not reacting to something or affected by it: **[+ to]** *The disease is unresponsive to conventional treatment.* **2** not reacting to what people say to you: *She remained still and unresponsive.*

**un·rest** /ʌnˈrest/ *n* [U] a social or political situation in which people protest and tend to behave violently: *The country was in a state of unrest.* | **social/civil/political etc unrest** *These drastic measures were necessary to prevent further social unrest.*

**un·re·strained** /ˌʌnrɪˈstreɪnd◂/ *adj* not controlled or limited: *unrestrained laughter* —**unrestrainedly** *adv*

**un·ripe** /ˌʌnˈraɪp/ *adj* unripe fruit, grain etc is not fully developed or ready to be eaten: *green, unripe peaches*

**un·ri·valled** *BrE*, **unrivaled** *AmE* /ʌnˈraɪvəld/ *adj formal* better than any other: *an unrivalled collection of Chinese art*

**un·ruf·fled** /ʌnˈrʌfəld/ *adj approving* calm and not upset by a difficult situation: *The Under-Secretary remained completely unruffled.*

**un·ru·ly** /ʌnˈruːli/ *adj* **1** behaving in an uncontrolled or violent way: *unruly children* **2** unruly hair is untidy —**unruliness** *n* [U]

**un·sad·dle** /ʌnˈsædl/ *v* [T] **1** to remove the SADDLE (=leather seat) from a horse **2** if a horse unsaddles someone, it throws them off its back; UNSEAT

**un·said** /ʌnˈsed/ **be left unsaid** if something is left unsaid, you do not say it although you might be thinking it: *Some things are better left unsaid.* —**unsay** /ʌnˈseɪ/ *v* [T]

**un·san·i·ta·ry** /ˌʌnˈsænɪ̈təri‖-teri/ *adj especially AmE* conditions or places that are unsanitary are very dirty and likely to cause disease; INSANITARY

**un·sa·vour·y** *BrE*, **unsavory** *AmE* /ʌnˈseɪvəri/ *adj* unpleasant or morally unacceptable: *I hope that ends the whole unsavoury business.* | **unsavoury light** *The latest revelations show the actor in a very unsavoury light.* | **unsavoury character** (=an unpleasant and dishonest person)

**un·scathed** /ʌnˈskeɪðd/ *adj* [not before noun] not hurt by a bad or dangerous situation: *Faye walked away from the accident completely unscathed.*

**un·scram·ble** /ʌnˈskræmbəl/ *v* [T] to change a television SIGNAL or a message that has been sent in CODE (=a deliberately confusing way) so that it can be seen or read

**unscrew**

He tried to unscrew the lid.

**un·screw** /ʌnˈskruː/ *v* [T] **1** to undo something by twisting it **2** to take the screws out of something

**un·script·ed** /ˌʌnˈskrɪptɪ̈d◂/ *adj* an unscripted broadcast, speech etc is not written or planned before it is actually made

**un·scru·pu·lous** /ʌnˈskruːpjɪ̈ləs/ *adj* behaving in an unfair or dishonest way: *a cunning and unscrupulous politician* —**unscrupulously** *adv* —**unscrupulousness** *n* [U]

**un·sea·son·a·ble** /ʌnˈsiːzənəbəl/ *adj* unseasonable weather is unusual for the time of year

**un·seat** /ʌnˈsiːt/ *v* [T] **1** to remove someone from a position of power or strength: *You'll see – we'll unseat the President at the next election.* **2** if a horse unseats someone, it throws them off its back

**un·seed·ed** /ˌʌnˈsiːdɪ̈d◂/ *adj* not chosen as a SEED (=someone with a numbered rank in a competition), especially in a tennis competition

**un·see·ing** /ˌʌnˈsiːɪŋ◂/ *adj especially literary* not noticing anything even though your eyes are open: *Jack gazed unseeing out of the window.* —**unseeingly** *adv*

**un·seem·ly** /ʌnˈsiːmli/ *adj formal* unseemly behaviour is not polite or not suitable for a particular occasion: *Ann thought it unseemly to kiss her husband in public.* —**unseemliness** *n* [U]

**un·seen¹** /ˌʌnˈsiːn◂/ *adj formal* not noticed or seen —**unseen** *adv*: *She crept out of the building unseen.*

**unseen²** *n* [C] *BrE* a piece of writing in a foreign language that you have not seen before and that you must translate into your own language in an examination —see also **sight unseen** (SIGHT¹ (18))

**un·set·tle** /ʌnˈsetl/ *v* [T] to make someone feel upset or nervous: *The sudden changes unsettled Judy.* —**unsettling** *adj*

**un·set·tled** /ʌnˈsetld/ *adj*
**1** ▶**SITUATION**◀ making people feel uncertain about what will happen: *the unsettled times during the war*
**2** ▶**FEELING**◀ worried or excited about something so that you feel upset or nervous: *Children feel unsettled if their parents divorce.*
**3** ▶**ARGUMENT OR DISAGREEMENT**◀ still continuing without reaching any agreement: *The dispute between teachers and governors remains unsettled.*
**4** ▶**WEATHER**◀ changing a lot in a short period of time
**5** ▶**STOMACH**◀ making you feel uncomfortable and a little sick: *My stomach's a bit unsettled after all that rich food.*

**un·sha·kea·ble, unshakable** /ʌnˈʃeɪkəbəl/ *adj* unshakable faith, beliefs etc are very strong and cannot be destroyed or changed

**un·shav·en** /ʌnˈʃeɪvən/ *adj* a man who is unshaven has very short hairs growing on his face because he has not shaved (SHAVE¹ (1))

**un·sight·ly** /ʌnˈsaɪtli/ *adj* unpleasant to look at: *unsightly power stations ruining the landscape* —**unsightliness** *n* [U]

**un·skilled** /ˌʌnˈskɪld◂/ *adj* **1** an unskilled worker has not been trained for a particular type of job: **unskilled labour** (=people who have no special training) **2** unskilled work, jobs etc do not need people with special skills —compare SKILLED

**un·so·cia·ble** /ʌnˈsəʊʃəbəl‖-ˈsoʊ-/ *adj* not liking to be with people or to go to social events —see also UNSOCIAL

**un·so·cial** /ˌʌnˈsəʊʃəl◂‖ˈsoʊ-/ *adj* **work unsocial hours** also **work unsociable hours** to work very early in the morning, during the night, etc when most people do not work

**un·solved** /ˌʌnˈsɒlvd◂‖-ˈsɑːlvd◂, -ˈsɒːlvd◂/ *adj* a problem, mystery, or crime that is unsolved has never been solved

**un·so·phis·ti·cat·ed** /ˌʌnsəˈfɪstɪkeɪtɪd◂/ *adj* **1** having little knowledge or experience of modern fashionable things, and showing this by the way you talk or behave: *an unsophisticated boy from the provinces* **2** unsophisticated tools, methods, or processes are simple, without many of the features of more modern ones

**un·sound** /ˌʌnˈsaʊnd◂/ *adj* **1** unsound arguments, methods etc are not based on fact or reason: *ideologically unsound* **2** an unsound building or structure is in bad condition **3 of unsound mind** *formal* mentally ill and not responsible for your actions

**un·speak·a·ble** /ʌnˈspiːkəbəl/ *adj* **1** unspeakable actions or people are extremely bad: *the unspeakable atrocities in Bosnia* **2** *literary* unspeakable feelings are so extreme that it is impossible to describe them: *unspeakable terror* —**unspeakably** *adv*

**un·spoiled** /ˌʌnˈspɔɪld◂/ also **un·spoilt** /-ˈspɔɪlt◂/ *adj especially BrE* **1** *approving* an unspoiled place has not been changed for a long time, especially by new roads, buildings etc **2** someone who is unspoiled has not changed in spite of the good or bad things that have happened to them: *She remained unspoilt by her success.*

**un·sta·ble** /ʌnˈsteɪbəl/ *adj* **1** dangerous and likely to fall over because not balanced or properly supported **2** likely to change suddenly and perhaps become worse: *an unstable economy* **3** someone who is unstable changes very suddenly so that you do not know how they will react or behave **4** an unstable chemical is likely to separate into simpler compounds

**un·stint·ing** /ʌnˈstɪntɪŋ/ *adj* unstinting support, help, agreement etc is complete and given willingly —**unstintingly** *adv*

**un·stop** /ˌʌnˈstɒp‖ˌʌnˈstɑːp/ *v* [T] if you unstop a pipe, DRAIN² (1) etc, you remove something that is blocking it

**un·stop·pa·ble** /ʌnˈstɒpəbəl‖-ˈstɑːp-/ *adj* unable to be stopped: *Once Janet gets an idea, she's unstoppable.*

**un·stuck** /ˌʌnˈstʌk◂/ *adj* **come unstuck a)** if something comes unstuck, it becomes separated from something that it was stuck to **b)** *BrE informal* if someone comes unstuck, something that they are doing starts to go wrong

**un·stud·ied** /ˌʌnˈstʌdid/ *adj formal* an unstudied quality seems natural and is not a result of effort or practice: *unstudied grace*

**un·suit·able** /ˌʌnˈsuːtəbəl, ˌʌnsjuː-‖/ *adj* not having the right qualities for a particular person, purpose, or situation: **[+ for]** *Those books are quite unsuitable for children.* | *beaches judged unsuitable for swimming*

**un·sul·lied** /ʌnˈsʌlid/ *adj literary* not spoiled: *unsullied lush vegetation and wide open spaces*

**un·sung** /ˌʌnˈsʌŋ◂/ *adj* not praised or famous for something you have done although you deserve to be: **unsung hero** *Liam was an unsung hero during the crisis.*

**un·sure** /ˌʌnˈʃʊə◂‖-ˈʃʊr◂/ *adj* **1** not certain about something or about what you have to do: *If you are unsure about the operation, ask your doctor to explain it.* **2 unsure of yourself** to lack confidence: *Chris seemed nervous and unsure of herself.*

**un·sur·passed** /ˌʌnsəˈpɑːst◂‖-sərˈpæst◂/ *adj* a skill, quality, or achievement that is unsurpassed is better than all the others: *Her knowledge of the subject is unsurpassed.*

**un·sus·pect·ing** /ˌʌnsəˈspektɪŋ◂/ *adj* not knowing that something bad is about to happen: *unsuspecting victims*

**un·swerv·ing** /ʌnˈswɜːvɪŋ‖-ɜːr-/ *adj* an unswerving belief or attitude is one that is very strong and never changes: **unswerving in sth** *Liz was unswerving in her determination to be a journalist.* | **unswerving loyalty/admiration** *Nina has always shown unswerving loyalty to the family.*

**un·tan·gle** /ˌʌnˈtæŋgəl/ *v* [T] **1** to undo pieces of string etc that are twisted together: *fishermen untangling their nets* **2** to make something less complicated

**un·tapped** /ˌʌnˈtæpt◂/ *adj* an untapped RESOURCE¹, market etc has not yet been used

**un·ten·a·ble** /ʌnˈtenəbəl/ *adj* an untenable THEORY, argument etc is impossible to defend against criticism: **untenable position** *The scandal left the President in an untenable position.*

**un·thin·ka·ble** /ʌnˈθɪŋkəbəl/ *adj* impossible to accept or imagine: *It would have been unthinkable ten years earlier to choose a woman as party leader.*

**un·think·ing** /ʌnˈθɪŋkɪŋ/ *adj* not thinking about the effects of something you say or do —**unthinkingly** *adv*

**un·ti·dy** /ʌnˈtaɪdi/ *adj especially BrE* **1** not neat; MESSY (1): *an untidy room* **2** someone who is untidy does not keep their house, possessions etc neat —**untidily** *adv* —**untidiness** *n* [U]

**un·tie** /ʌnˈtaɪ/ *v* [T] to undo the knots in something or undo something that has been tied —**untied** *adj*: *walking about with shoelaces untied*

**un·til** /ʌnˈtɪl, ən-/ *prep, conjunction* **1** used to say that something stops happening or someone stops doing something at a particular time or when something else happens; TILL¹: *Gary was working for IBM until 1969, when he got a job at Sperry.* | *Black people were denied the vote in the US until well into the 1950s.* | **up until** *This ticket is valid up until the 12th of March.* **2** used to say that you should stop travelling at a particular place: *Stay on the train until Birmingham, and then change for Peterborough.* S1 W1

**un·time·ly** /ʌnˈtaɪmli/ *adj* **1 untimely death/end etc** a death etc that is much earlier than usual or expected

2 not suitable for a particular occasion or time —**untimeliness** *n* [U]

**un·tir·ing** /ʌn'taɪərɪŋ‖-'taɪr-/ *adj approving* never stopping while working hard or trying to do something: *untiring efforts to help the homeless* —**untiringly** *adv*

**un·to** /'ʌntuː/ *prep old use* to: *Thanks be unto God.*

**un·told** /ˌʌn'təʊld◂‖-'toʊld◂/ *adj* too much or too many to be measured: **untold misery** *The floods have caused untold misery to hundreds of homeowners.* | **untold damage** *The scandal has done untold damage to his reputation.*

**un·touch·a·ble** /ʌn'tʌtʃəbəl/ *adj* **1** someone who is untouchable is in such a strong position that they cannot be affected by, or punished for, anything: *He was the boss's husband and therefore untouchable.* **2** belonging to the lowest social group, especially in the Hindu CASTE system —**untouchable** *n* [C]

**un·touched** /ˌʌn'tʌtʃt◂/ *adj* untouched food has not been eaten: *The food looked so awful that it was left untouched.*

**un·to·ward** /ˌʌntə'wɔːd‖ˌʌn'tɔːrd/ *adj* **anything/nothing untoward** *formal* something or nothing that is unexpected, unusual, or not wanted: *We walked past the house but didn't notice anything untoward.*

**un·tram·melled** *BrE,* **untrameled** *AmE* /ʌn'træməld/ *adj formal* without any limits

**un·treat·ed** /ʌn'triːtɪ̥d/ *adj* **1** an untreated illness or injury has not had medical attention **2** harmful substances that are untreated have not been made safe: *untreated sewage*

**un·tried** /ˌʌn'traɪd◂/ *adj* **1** not having any experience of doing a particular job: *a young and untried minister* **2** not yet tested to see whether it is successful: *a relatively new and untried method*

**un·true** /ʌn'truː/ *adj* **1** a statement that is untrue does not give the right facts; false **2** *literary* someone who is untrue to their husband, wife etc is not faithful to them

**un·truth** /ʌn'truːθ, 'ʌntruːθ/ *n* [C] *formal* a word meaning a lie, used because you want to avoid saying this directly

**un·truth·ful** /ʌn'truːθfəl/ *adj* dishonest or not true —**untruthfully** *adv*

**un·used**[1] /ˌʌn'juːzd◂/ *adj* not being used, or never used: *unused office blocks*

**un·used**[2] /ʌn'juːst/ *adj* **unused to** not experienced in dealing with something: *a sensitive man unused to publicity* | **unused to doing sth** *Maggie was unused to being told what to do.*

S2 W3 **un·u·su·al** /ʌn'juːʒuəl, -ʒəl/ *adj* **1** different from what is usual or ordinary: *The cake has a very unusual flavor.* | **it is unusual to do sth** *It is unusual to find diamonds of this size.* | **it is unusual for sb to do sth** *Earlier this century, it was unusual for women to have a career.* —see RARE (USAGE) **2** interesting or attractive because of being different: *Alan's artwork is very unusual.*

**un·u·su·al·ly** /ʌn'juːʒuəli, -ʒəli/ *adv* **1** **unusually hot/difficult etc** more hot etc than is usual **2** in an unusual way: *The house was unusually quiet.*

**un·ut·ter·a·ble** /ʌn'ʌtərəbəl/ *adj formal* an unutterable feeling is too extreme to be expressed in words: *unutterable sadness* —**unutterably** *adv*

**un·var·nished** /ʌn'vɑːnɪʃt‖-ɑːr-/ *adj* [only before noun] **1** plain and without additional decoration or description: *the unvarnished truth* **2** without any VARNISH (=a transparent substance like paint, used to protect the surface of wood etc)

**un·veil** /ˌʌn'veɪl/ *v* [T] **1** to show or tell people something that was previously kept secret: *Reagan unveiled a series of budget cuts totaling $44 billion.* **2** to remove the cover from something, especially as part of a formal ceremony: *The Queen unveiled a statue of Prince Albert.* —**unveiling** *n* [C]

**un·versed** /ˌʌn'vɜːst‖-ɜːrst/ *adj formal* **unversed in sth** without any knowledge or experience of something: *unversed in city ways*

**un·voiced** /ˌʌn'vɔɪst◂/ *adj* **1** not expressed in words: *unvoiced fears* **2** *technical* unvoiced CONSONANTS are produced without moving the VOCAL CORDS: */d/ and /g/ are voiced consonants, and /t/ and /k/ are unvoiced*

**un·waged** /ˌʌn'weɪdʒd◂/ *adj BrE* not having a paid job; UNEMPLOYED

**un·want·ed** /ʌn'wɒntɪ̥d‖-'wɒːnt-, -'wɑːnt-/ *adj* not wanted or needed: *an unwanted pregnancy*

**un·war·rant·ed** /ʌn'wɒrəntɪ̥d‖-'wɔː-, -'wɑː-/ **unwarrantable** *adj* done without good reason, and therefore annoying: *unwarranted interference in our affairs*

**un·wa·ry** /ʌn'weəri‖-'weri/ *adj* not knowing about possible problems or dangers, and therefore easily harmed or deceived: **the unwary** (=people who are unwary) —**unwarily** *adv* —**unwariness** *n* [U]

**un·wel·come** /ʌn'welkəm/ *adj* **1** something that is unwelcome is not wanted, especially because it might cause embarrassment or problems: *unwelcome publicity* **2** unwelcome guests, visitors etc are people that you do not want in your home

**un·well** /ʌn'wel/ *adj* [not before noun] *formal* ill, especially for a short time —see SICK[1] (USAGE)

**un·wield·y** /ʌn'wiːldi/ *adj* **1** an unwieldy object is big and heavy and difficult to carry **2** an unwieldy system, argument, or plan is difficult to control or manage because it is too complicated: *unwieldy bureaucracy* —**unwieldiness** *n* [U]

**un·will·ing** /ʌn'wɪlɪŋ/ *adj* **1** [not before noun] not wanting to do something and refusing to do it: **unwilling to do sth** *They were unwilling to fund a project that had little chance of success.* **2** [only before noun] not wanting to do something but doing it: *an unwilling helper* —**unwillingly** *adv*

**un·wind** /ʌn'waɪnd/ *v past tense and past participle* **unwound** /-'waʊnd/ **1** [I] to relax and stop feeling anxious: *I love cooking. It helps me unwind.* **2** [I,T] to undo something that has been wrapped around something else

**un·wit·ting·ly** /ʌn'wɪtɪŋli/ *adv* in a way that shows you do not know or realize something: *Friedmann had unwittingly stumbled upon a vital piece of evidence.* —**unwitting** *adj* [only before noun]: *an unwitting accomplice*

**un·wont·ed** /ʌn'wəʊntɪ̥d‖-'woʊn-/ *adj* [only before noun] *formal* unusual and not what you expect to happen: *"Good day" he cried with unwonted good humour.*

**un·world·ly** /ʌn'wɜːldli‖-ɜːr-/ *adj* not interested in money or possessions

**un·wound** /ʌn'waʊnd/ the past tense and past participle of UNWIND

**un·writ·ten** /ʌn'rɪtn/ *adj* known about and understood by everyone but not formally written down: **unwritten rule/law** *It was an unwritten law among my friends that we never told our mothers what we did.*

**un·zip** /ˌʌn'zɪp/ *v* [T] to unfasten the ZIP on a piece of clothing, bag etc

**up-** /ʌp/ *prefix* **1** making something higher: *to upgrade a job* (=make it higher in importance) **2** [especially in adverbs and adjectives] at or towards the top or beginning of something: *uphill* | *upriver* (=nearer to where the river starts) **3** [especially in verbs] taking something from its place or turning it upside down: *an uprooted tree* | *She upended the bucket.* **4** [especially in adjectives and adverbs] at or towards the higher or better part of something: *up-market* (=suitable for the higher social groups) —compare DOWN-

**up**[1] /ʌp/ *adv* **1** towards a higher position from the floor, ground, or bottom of something: *She picked her pen up off the floor.* | *Can you lift that box up onto the shelf for me?* | *After swimming for several seconds underwater he came up for air.* | **up you come** *spoken* (=used especially to children when lifting them) **2** at or in a high position: *John's up in his bedroom.* | *The plane was flying 30,000 feet up.* **3** into an upright or raised position: *Everyone stood up for the National Anthem.* | *Mick turned his collar up against the biting winds.* **4** in or towards the North: *We're going to fly up to Scotland from London.* | *They live* 

*up North.* **5** towards someone so that you are near, or in the place where they are: *He came right up and asked my name.*|*A man sidled up to her and asked for money.* **6** increasing in loudness, strength, level of activity etc: *Can you turn the telly up a bit?*|*Competition between these two companies is really hotting up.* **7** so as to be completely finished or used so that there is nothing left: *Our savings are all used up.*|*She won't eat up her vegetables.* **8** so as to be in small pieces or divided into equal parts: *They divided up the money.*|*The plane hit the mountainside and broke up on impact.* **9** so as to be firmly fastened, covered, or joined: *Mr Cain was boarding up the windows.* **10** so as to be brought or gathered together: *Let's just add up these figures quickly.*|*Could you collect up the pens?* **11** if a surface or part of something is a particular way up, it is on top: **right side up/right way up** (=with the part that is going to be used, or that has words or pictures on it on top) *Put the playing cards right side up on the table.* **12** so as to receive attention: *The question of a pay rise came up again during the meeting.* **13** above and including a certain amount or level: *Power was lost from the tenth floor up.*|*Children of twelve up must pay full fare.* **14 up and down a)** higher and lower: *The crowd were jumping up and down and screaming excitedly.*|**look sb up and down** (=look at someone in order to judge their appearance or character) *Maisie looked her rival critically up and down.* **b)** backwards and forwards: *Ralph paced up and down the room looking agitated.* **15 up to a)** up to and including a certain amount or level: *Up to six people* (=any number between one and six) *can sleep in the caravan.* **b)** *also* **up till** if something happens up to a certain time, date etc it happens until that time: *She continued to care for her father up to the time of his death.* **c)** clever, good, or well enough for a particular purpose or in order to do something: *I'm afraid Tim just isn't up to the job* (=not good enough to do it properly).|*Gemma isn't really up to long walks at the moment* (=too ill to do them).|**up to doing** *My German isn't up to translating that letter.* **d)** if something is up to a particular standard it is good enough to reach that standard: *The new CD is not up to the group's usual standard.* **e)** doing something secret or something that you shouldn't be doing: *The children are very quiet; I wonder what they're up to.*|**up to no good** (=doing something wrong or illegal) *I'll bet that Joe and his mates are up to no good as usual.* **16 it's up to you** *spoken* used to tell someone that they must make a decision themselves: *"Shall we have red wine or white?" "It's up to you."* **17 up to your ears/eyes/neck in** *informal* deeply involved in a difficult or illegal situation: *Rona and Colin are up to their ears in debt* (=they owe a lot of money). **18 up the workers!/up the reds! etc** *spoken* used to express support and encouragement for a particular group of people or for a sports team

S1 W1 **up**[2] *prep* **1** towards or in a higher place: *We climbed slowly up the hill.*|*The water was getting up my nose.* **2** towards or at the top or far end of: *Her office is up those stairs.*|*They live just up the road* (=further along the road from here). **3** if you sail or go up a river you go towards its SOURCE[1] (4): *a boat trip up the Bosphorus* **4** *BrE spoken* used to mean to or at a particular place, although most people think this is incorrect: *Do you fancy going up the town?* **5 up yours!** *spoken taboo* used to insult someone when they have done or said something that annoys you: *"You'll never get promoted, you're not good enough." "Up yours!"*

**up**[3] *adj* **1** [not before noun] not in bed: *Are the kids still up?* **2** [not before noun] if a road is up, its surface is being repaired **3** [not before noun] if a computer system is up, it is working —opposite DOWN[2] (5) **4** [not before noun] if a number, level, or amount is up, it is higher than before: *Inflation is up by 2%.*|[+ **on**] *Profits are up on last year.*|**two goals up/three points up** (=having two goals, three points etc more than your opponents) *United were a goal up at half time.* **5** [not before noun] if a ball is up in tennis or similar sports, it has only hit the ground once and therefore can be hit back by the opponent **6 be up and about** *informal* to be well enough to walk about and have a normal life after you have been in bed because of an illness or accident **7 be up to here (with)** *spoken* to be very upset and angry because of a particular situation or person: *I'm up to here with this job; I'm resigning!* **8 be up and down** if someone is up and down, they sometimes feel well or happy and sometimes do not: *Jason's been very up and down since his girlfriend left him.* **9 be up against** to have to deal with a difficult situation or fight an opponent: *He came up against a lot of problems with his previous boss.*|**be up against it** *Murphy will be really up against it when he faces the reigning champion this afternoon.* **10 be up before** *informal* to appear in a court of law because you have been accused of a crime: *He was up before the Magistrates court charged with grievous bodily harm.* **11 be up for a)** to be intended for a particular purpose: *The house is up for sale.*|*Even the most taboo subjects were up for discussion.* **b)** to appear in a court of law because you have been accused of a crime: *Ron's up for drinking and driving next week.* **12 be (well) up on/in/with** *informal* to know a lot about something **13** *spoken* if something is up, someone is feeling unhappy because they have problems, or there is something wrong in a situation: *I could tell by the look on Joan's face that something was up.*|[+ **with**] *Is something up with Julie? She looks really miserable.*|**what's up?** *What's up? Why are you crying?* **14 not be up to much** *spoken* to not be of a very good quality or standard: *The food in that restaurant isn't up to much.* **15** [not before noun] *informal* if a period of time is up, it is finished: *The President may be asked to resign before his four-year term is up.* **16** [not before noun] *informal* when food or drink is up it is ready to be eaten or drunk: *Dinner's up!* **17 be up and running** if a new system or process is up and running, it is working properly: *The New York office was up and running in about half the time it took us in Paris.* **18 up to speed** knowing the necessary latest information or situation: *getting top-level managers up to speed on developments in on-line services*

**up**[4] *n* **1 be on an up** *spoken* to feel happy, especially after being upset and unhappy: *Kevin seems to be on an up at the moment; I hope it lasts.* **2 ups and downs** *informal* the mixture of good and bad experiences that happen in any situation or relationship: *We have our ups and downs like all couples.* **3 on the up and up** *informal* **a)** *BrE* improving and becoming more successful, especially financially **b)** *AmE* not hiding anything; HONEST

**up**[5] *v* **1** [T] to increase the amount or level of something: *They've upped their offer by a further 5%.* **2 up and ...** if you up and do something, you suddenly start to do something different or surprising: **up and leave** *Without saying another word, he upped and left.*

**up-and-com·ing** /ˌ· · ˈ··◂/ *adj* [only before noun] likely to be successful or popular: *an up-and-coming band from Manchester*

**up-and-un·der** /ˌ· · ˈ··/ *n* [C] a situation in RUGBY when the ball is kicked forwards high into the air, and the players all rush towards the place where the ball lands

**up·beat** /ˈʌpbiːt/ *adj* cheerful and making you feel that good things will happen: *a comedy film with an upbeat ending*

**up·braid** /ˌʌpˈbreɪd/ *v* [T] *formal* to tell someone angrily that they have done something wrong

**up·bring·ing** /ˈʌpˌbrɪŋɪŋ/ *n* [singular] the care and training that parents give their children when they are growing up: *Mike had had a strict upbringing.*

**up·chuck** /ˈʌptʃʌk/ *v* [I] *AmE informal* to bring food or drink up from your stomach and out through your mouth because you are ill or drunk; VOMIT[1]

**up·com·ing** /ˈʌpˌkʌmɪŋ/ *adj* [only before noun] happening soon: *the upcoming elections*

**up·coun·try** /ˌʌpˈkʌntri◂/ *adj* from an area of land

without many people or towns, especially in the middle of a country: *upcountry people* —**upcountry** *adv*

**up·date¹** /ʌp'deɪt/ *v* [T] **1** to add the most recent information to something: *The files need updating.* **2** to make something more modern in the way it looks or operates

**up·date²** /'ʌpdeɪt/ *n* [C] the most recent news about something: [+ **on**] *the latest update on the Whitewater affair*

**up·end** /ʌp'end/ *v* [T] to turn something over so that it is standing upside down

**up·front** /ˌʌp'frʌnt/ *adj* [not before noun] behaving or talking in a direct and honest way: *Mo's very upfront with him about their relationship.* —see also **up front** (FRONT¹ (15))

**up·grade** /ˌʌp'greɪd/ *v* **1** [I,T] to make a computer or other machine better and able to do more things **2** [T] to give someone a more important job **3** [T] to be given a better seat on a plane than the one you paid for —opposite DOWNGRADE —**upgrade** /'ʌpgreɪd/ *n* [C]

**up·heav·al** /ʌp'hiːvəl/ *n* [C,U] **1** a very big change that often causes problems: *political upheaval* **2** a very strong movement upwards, especially of the earth

**up·hill¹** /ˌʌp'hɪl◂/ *adj* **1** towards the top of a hill: *an uphill climb* **2** an uphill battle, struggle, job etc is very difficult and needs a lot of effort

**uphill²** *adv* towards the top of a hill

**up·hold** /ˌʌp'həʊld‖-'hoʊld/ *v past tense and past participle* **upheld** /-'held/ [T] **1** to defend or support a law, system, or principle so that it is not made weaker: *They want to uphold traditional family values.* **2** if a court upholds a decision made by another court, it states that the decision was correct —**upholder** *n* [C]

**up·hol·ster** /ʌp'həʊlstə‖ʌ'poʊlstər/ *v* [T] to cover a chair with material —**upholstered** *adj* —**upholsterer** *n* [C]

**up·hol·ster·y** /ʌp'həʊlstəri‖ʌ'poʊl-/ *n* [U] **1** material used to cover chairs **2** the process of covering chairs with material

**up·keep** /'ʌpkiːp/ *n* [U + **of**] the care needed to keep something in good condition

**up·lands** /'ʌpləndz/ *n plural* the parts of a country that are away from the sea and are higher than other areas —**upland** *adj*: *upland forests*

**up·lift¹** /'ʌplɪft/ *n* [U] a sudden happy feeling

**up·lift²** /ʌp'lɪft/ *v* [T] *formal* **1** to make someone feel more cheerful **2** to make something higher

**up·lift·ed** /ʌp'lɪftɪ̣d/ *adj* **1** feeling happier **2** *literary* raised upwards

**up·lift·ing** /ʌp'lɪftɪŋ/ *adj* making you feel more cheerful

**up·mar·ket** /ˌʌp'mɑːkɪ̣t◂‖'ʌpmɑːrkɪ̣t/ *adj* connected with people who belong to a high social class or who have a lot of money; UPSCALE *AmE*: *an upmarket fashion retailer* —compare DOWNMARKET

S3 W1 **up·on** /ə'pɒn‖ə'pɒːn, ə'pɑːn/ *prep formal* on: *an honour bestowed upon the association | We are completely dependent upon your help.* —see also **once upon a time** (ONCE¹ (14)) —see picture on page 1257

W2 **up·per¹** /'ʌpə‖-ər/ *adj* [only before noun] **1** in a higher position than something else: *the upper lip* **2** near or at the top of something: *The monkeys live in the upper branches.* **3 have/gain the upper hand** to have more power than someone else, so that you are able to control a situation: *Police have gained the upper hand over the drug dealers in the area.* **4** more important than other parts or ranks in an organization, system etc: **the upper echelons** (=the most important and most senior members of an organization) **5 the upper limit** the highest limit: *sounds that are at the upper limit of our hearing capability* **6** further from the sea or further north than other parts of an area: **the upper reaches** (=the parts of a river that are the furthest from the sea) *the upper reaches of the Nile* —see also **keep a stiff upper lip** (STIFF¹ (9))

**upper²** *n* [C] **1** the top part of a shoe that covers your foot: *leather uppers* —see picture at SHOE¹ **2 uppers** [plural] *slang* illegal drugs that make you feel happy and give you a lot of energy; AMPHETAMINE (1) **3 be on your uppers** *BrE old-fashioned* to have very little money

**upper case** /ˌ·· '·◂/ *n* [U] *technical* letters written in capitals (A, B, C) rather than in small form (a, b, c)

**upper class** /ˌ·· '·◂/ *n* [C] **the upper class** the group of people who belong to the highest social class: *upper class families* —**upper class** *adj*

**up·per·class·man** /ˌʌpə'klɑːsmən‖-pər'klæs-/ *n* [C] *AmE* a student in the last two years at a school or university —compare UNDERCLASSMAN

**up·per·class·wom·an** /ˌʌpə'klɑːswʊmən‖-pər'klæs-/ *n* [C] *AmE* a female student in the last two years of school or university

**up·per crust** /ˌ·· '·◂/ *n* [singular] *informal* the group of people who belong to the highest social class —**upper-crust** *adj*

**up·per·cut** /'ʌpəkʌt‖-ər-/ *n* [C] a way of hitting someone in which you swing your hand upwards into their chin

**Up·per House** /ˌ··'·/ *n* [singular] a group of elected representatives in a country, that is smaller and less powerful than the country's LOWER HOUSE

**up·per·most** /'ʌpəməʊst‖-pərmoʊst/ *adj* **1 uppermost in your mind** if something is uppermost in your mind, you think about it a lot because it is very important to you: *It is Tom's safety that is uppermost in our minds.* **2** more important than other things: *As he looked at her, curiosity was his uppermost feeling.* **3** higher than anything else: *the uppermost leaves on the tree*

**upper school** /'·· ·/ *n* [C] the classes of a school in Britain that are for older pupils, usually aged 14 to 18

**up·pi·ty** /'ʌpɪ̣ti/ also **up·pish** /'ʌpɪʃ/ *BrE adj informal* behaving as if you are more important than you really are: *Now, don't start getting uppity with me, young man.*

**up·right¹** /'ʌp-raɪt/ *adj* **1** standing straight up **2** always behaving in an honest way: *decent, upright citizens* —**uprightness** *n* [U]

**upright²** *adv* **1** sitting or standing with your back straight: **sit/stand bolt upright** *He sat bolt upright, startled by the scream.* **2** if something is pulled, held etc upright, it is put into a position in which it is standing straight up

**upright³** *n* [C] a long piece of wood or metal that stands straight up and supports something

**upright pi·an·o** /ˌ·· ·'··/ *n* [C] a piano with strings that are set in an up and down direction

**up·ris·ing** /'ʌpˌraɪzɪŋ/ *n* [C] an occasion when a group of people use violence to try to change the rules, laws etc in an institution or country: *the 1956 Hungarian uprising*

**up·riv·er** /ˌʌp'rɪvə‖-ər/ *adv* away from the sea towards the place where a river begins

**up·roar** /'ʌp-rɔː‖-rɔːr/ *n* [singular, U] a lot of noise or angry protest about something: **be in an uproar** *The house was in an uproar, with babies crying and people shouting.*

**up·roar·i·ous** /ʌp'rɔːriəs/ *adj* very noisy, because a lot of people are laughing or shouting —**uproariously** *adv*

**up·root** /ˌʌp'ruːt/ *v* [T] **1** to pull a plant and its roots out of the ground **2** to make someone leave their home for a new place, especially when this is difficult or upsetting: *My father was in the army, so every two years we were uprooted and moved again.*

**ups-a-dai·sy** /'ʌps ə ˌdeɪzi/ *interjection* another spelling of OOPS-A-DAISY

**up·scale** /'ʌpskeɪl/ *adj AmE* connected with people from a high social class who have a lot of money; UPMARKET

**up·set¹** /ʌp'set/ *v past tense and past participle* **upset**  [T] **1** to make someone feel unhappy or worried: *I'm sorry, I didn't mean to upset you.* **2** to change a plan or situation in a way that causes problems: *The delicate ecological balance of the area was upset.* **3** to push something over without intending to: *He upset a bottle of ink over the map.* **4 upset sb's stomach** to make someone feel sick **5 upset the apple cart** completely spoil someone's plans **—upsetting** *adj*

**up·set²** /ˈʌpset/ *n* **1** [C] an unexpected problem or difficulty: *Despite this upset, the General decided to go ahead with the attack.* **2** an occasion when a person or team surprisingly beats a stronger opponent in a competition, election etc: *It was a major upset when the young skater took the gold medal.* **3 stomach/tummy upset** an illness that affects the stomach and makes you feel sick **4** [C,U] worry and unhappiness caused by an unexpected problem

**up·set³** /ˌʌpˈset◂/ *adj* **1** [not before noun] unhappy and worried because something unpleasant or disappointing has happened: [+ **about/by/over etc**] *She was still upset about the argument she'd had with Harry.* | **upset that** *Dad was very upset that you didn't phone.* **2 an upset stomach/tummy** an illness that affects the stomach and makes you feel sick

**up·shot** /ˈʌpʃɒt‖ˈʌpʃɑːt/ *n* **the upshot (of)** the final result of a situation: *The upshot was that Jane decided to leave home.*

**up·side¹** /ˈʌpsaɪd/ *n* [singular] *especially AmE* the positive part of a situation that is generally bad: *The upside of the whole thing is that we got a free trip to Jamaica.*

**upside²** *prep* **upside the head/face etc** *AmE informal* on the side of someone's head etc

**up·side down** /ˌ·· ˈ·/ *adv* **1** with the top at the bottom and the bottom at the top: *You've hung that picture upside down!* **2** disorganized or untidy —see also **turn sth upside down** (TURN¹ (19b))

**up·stage¹** /ˌʌpˈsteɪdʒ◂/ *v* [T] to do something that takes people's attention away from someone else who is more important: *All the big name stars were upstaged by twelve year old Katy Rochford.*

**upstage²** *adv* towards the back of the stage in a theatre **—upstage** *adj*

S 2 **up·stairs¹** /ˌʌpˈsteəz◂‖-ˈsterz◂/ *adv* **1** towards a higher floor in a building, using the stairs: *Lucy came rushing upstairs after her sister.* —opposite DOWNSTAIRS (1) **2** on an upper floor in a building, especially a house: *My office is upstairs on the right.* —compare DOWNSTAIRS (2) —see also **kick sb upstairs** (KICK¹ (10)) **—upstairs** *adj*: *an upstairs window*

**upstairs²** *n* [singular] **1 the upstairs** one or all of the upper floors in a building —see picture on page 410 **2 not have much upstairs** to not be very intelligent **3 the man upstairs** *informal* God

**up·stand·ing** /ˌʌpˈstændɪŋ/ *adj formal* **1** honest and responsible: *an upstanding citizen* **2** tall and strong

**up·start** /ˈʌpstɑːt‖-ɑːrt/ *n* [C] someone who is new in their job and behaves as if they are more important than they really are: *an impudent young upstart* **—upstart** *adj*

**up·state** /ˈʌpsteɪt/ *adj AmE* [only before noun] in the northern part of a particular state: *upstate New York* **—upstate** *adv*

**up·stream** /ˌʌpˈstriːm◂/ *adv* along a river, in the opposite direction from the way the water is flowing **—upstream** *adj* —opposite DOWNSTREAM

**up·surge** /ˈʌpsɜːdʒ‖-ɜːr-/ *n* [C] **1** a sudden increase: [+ **in**] *There's been an upsurge in complaints about the police.* **2** sudden strong feelings: [+ **of**] *Adolescence is marked by an upsurge of sexual feeling.*

**up·swing** /ˈʌpˌswɪŋ/ *n* [C] an improvement or increase in the level of something: *an upswing in the economy*

**up·take** /ˈʌpteɪk/ *n* **1 be slow/quick on the uptake** *informal* to be slow or fast at learning or understanding things **2** [C,U] *technical* the rate at which a substance is taken into a system, machine etc: *the uptake of food and oxygen into an organism*

**up·tem·po** /ˌ· ˈ··◂/ *adj* moving or happening at a fast rate: *Music with an up-tempo beat.*

**up·tight** /ˈʌptaɪt, ʌpˈtaɪt/ *adj informal* behaving in an angry way because you are feeling nervous and worried

**up-to-date** /ˌ· · ˈ·◂/ *adj* **1** modern or fashionable: *up-to-date ideas on education* | **bring sth up-to-date** (=make something more modern) **2** including all the newest information: *up-to-date news* | *an up-to-date map* | **keep/bring sb up-to-date** (=give someone all the newest information about something)

**up-to-the-min·ute** /ˌ· · · ˈ··◂/ *adj* **1** including all the newest information: *up-to-the-minute financial information* **2** very modern or fashionable

**up·town** /ˌʌpˈtaʊn◂/ *adv AmE* towards the northern areas of a city, especially the areas where people have more money **—uptown** *adj*: *an uptown bar* **—uptown** *n* [U]

**up·trend** /ˈʌptrend/ *n* [C] a period of time when business or economic activity increases

**up·turn** /ˈʌptɜːn‖-ɜːrn/ *n* [C] an increase in the level of something: [+ **in**] *an upturn in the housing market*

**up·turned** /ˌʌpˈtɜːnd◂‖-ɜːr-/ *adj* **1** turning upwards at the end: *an upturned nose* **2** turned upside down: *upturned tables*

**up·ward** /ˈʌpwəd‖-wərd/ *adj* [only before noun] **1** moving or pointing towards a higher position: *an upward movement of the hand* **2** increasing to a higher level: *the upward trend in house prices* —opposite DOWNWARD

**upwardly mo·bile** /ˌ··· ˈ··/ *adj* moving up through the social classes and becoming richer **—upward mobility** *n* [U]

**up·wards** /ˈʌpwədz‖-wərdz-/ also **upward** *adv AmE* **1** moving or pointing towards a higher position: *Hold the gun so that it points upwards.* —opposite DOWNWARDS **2** increasing to a higher level: *Salary scales have been moving steadily upwards.* —opposite DOWNWARDS **3** more than a particular amount, time etc: *children of 14 and upwards* | **upwards of** *informal*: *The waiting time for an operation can be upwards of two years.*

**u·ra·ni·um** /jʊˈreɪniəm/ *n* [U] a heavy white metal that is an ELEMENT (=simple substance), is RADIOACTIVE, and is used to produce NUCLEAR power and weapons

**U·ra·nus** /ˈjʊərənəs, jʊˈreɪnəs‖ˈjʊr-, jʊˈreɪ-/ *n* [singular] **1** the PLANET seventh in order from the sun —see picture at SOLAR SYSTEM **2** the ruler of the universe, in ancient Greek stories

**ur·ban** /ˈɜːbən‖ˈɜːr-/ *adj* [only before noun] connected with a town or city: *urban crime* | *the urban population* W 2

**ur·bane** /ɜːˈbeɪn‖ɜːr-/ *adj* behaving in a relaxed and confident way in social situations: *Garroway's easy, urbane charm* **—urbanely** *adv* **—urbanity** *n* [U]

**ur·ban·ize** also **-ise** *BrE* /ˈɜːbənaɪz‖ˈɜːr-/ *v* [T] to build houses, towns etc in the countryside **—urbanization** /ˌɜːbənaɪˈzeɪ‖ˌɜːrbənə-/ *n* [U]

**urban myth** /ˌ·· ˈ·/ *n* [C] a well-known story that many people believe, about an unusual or terrible event that has happened to an ordinary person

**urban re·new·al** /ˌ·· ·ˈ··/ *n* [U] the process of improving poor city areas by building new houses, shops etc

**urban sprawl** /ˌ·· ˈ·/ *n* [U] the spread of city buildings and houses into an area that was countryside

**ur·chin** /ˈɜːtʃɪn‖ˈɜːr-/ *n* [C] *old-fashioned* a small dirty untidy child —see also SEA URCHIN

**Ur·du** /ˈʊəduː, ˈɜːduː‖ˈɜːrduː/ *n* [U] the official language of Pakistan, also used in India

**-ure** /jə‖jər/ *suffix* [in nouns] the action of doing something, or condition of being treated in a particular way: *the closure* (=closing) *of the factory* | *exposure*

**u·re·thra** /jʊˈriːθrə/ *n* [C] *technical* the tube through which waste liquid flows from your BLADDER and through which the SEMEN of males flows

**urge¹** /ɜːdʒ‖ɜːrdʒ/ *v* [T] **1** to strongly advise someone to do something: **urge sb to do sth** *Brown urged her to reconsider her decision.* | **urge that** *I urge that you read this report carefully.* **2** *formal* to strongly suggest that something should be done: *The UN has urged restraint in the current crisis.* | **urge sth on/upon sb** *This course of action was urged upon us by all parties.* **3** [always + adv/prep] to make someone or something move W 3 by shouting, pushing them etc: **urge sb/sth into/forward** *Daniel urged the horses forward with a whip.*

**urge** sb ↔ **on** *phr v* [T] to encourage a person or animal to work harder, go faster etc: *Urged on by the crowd, the Italian team scored two more goals.*

**urge²** *n* [C] a strong wish or need: *sexual urges* | **urge to do sth** *I felt a sudden urge to scream.*

S3 **ur·gent** /ˈɜːdʒənt‖ˈɜːr-/ *adj* **1** very important and needing to be dealt with immediately: *an urgent message* | **be in urgent need of** *in urgent need of medical attention* **2** *formal* done or said in a way that shows that you want something to be dealt with immediately: *an urgent whisper* —**urgency** *n* [U]: *a matter of great urgency* —**urgently** *adv*

**u·ric** /ˈjʊərɪk‖ˈjʊr-/ *adj* related to URINE

**u·ri·nal** /ˈjʊərɪ̇nəl, jʊˈraɪ-‖ˈjʊrɪ̇-/ *n* [C] **1** a type of toilet that men use that is fixed onto the wall **2** a building or room containing urinals

**u·ri·na·ry** /ˈjʊərɪ̇nəri‖ˈjʊrɪ̇neri/ *adj technical* connected with urine or the parts of your body through which urine passes

**u·ri·nate** /ˈjʊərɪ̇neɪt‖ˈjʊr-/ *v* [I] *technical* to make urine flow out of your body —**urination** /ˌjʊərɪ̇ˈneɪʃən‖ˌjʊr-/ *n* [U]

**u·rine** /ˈjʊərɪ̇n‖ˈjʊr-/ *n* [U] the liquid waste that comes out of your body when you go to the toilet

**urn** /ɜːn‖ɜːrn/ *n* [C] **1** a decorated container, especially one that is used for holding the ashes (ASH) of a dead body **2** a metal container that holds a large amount of tea or coffee

**US** /ˌjuː ˈes◂/ *n* also **USA** /ˌjuː es ˈeɪ◂/ the United States of America —**US** *adj*: *the US Navy*

S1 W1 **us** /əs, s; *strong* ʌs/ *pron* **1** the object form of 'we': *Do you think Dave saw us?* | *The house is too small for us now.* | *Emilio bought us a drink.* **2** *BrE spoken* used instead of 'me', although most people think this incorrect: *Give us a kiss.* | *Lend us a pound, will you?* —see ME (USAGE)

**us·a·ble** /ˈjuːzəbəl/ *adj* something that is usable is in a suitable state to be used

**us·age** /ˈjuːsɪdʒ, ˈjuːzɪdʒ/ *n* **1** [C,U] the way that words are used in a language: *a book on modern English usage* **2** [U] the way in which something is used, or the amount of it that is used

S1 W1 **use¹** /juːz/ *v* [T]

**1 ▶ USE STH ◀** if you use a particular tool, method, service, ability etc, you do something with that tool, by means of that method etc, for a particular purpose: *Can I use your phone?* | *More people are using the library than ever before.* | *I can't tell you what to do – you must use your own discretion.* | **use sth for doing sth** *We use this room for keeping all our junk in.* | **use sth as** *My mother uses old socks as dusters.* | **use force** (=use violent methods)

**2 ▶ AMOUNT OF STH ◀** to take something from a supply of food, gas, money etc with the result that there is less left: *We use about £40 worth of electricity a month.*

**3 ▶ USE A PERSON ◀** to make someone do something for you in order to get something you want: **use sb to do sth** *Smugglers use innocent people to carry drugs through customs.* | **use sb for your own ends** *Gerald had been using her for his own ends.*

**4 ▶ AN ADVANTAGE ◀** to take advantage of a situation: **use sth for** *Gordon used his family's wealth for his own publicity.* | **use sth to do sth** *She used her position as manager to get jobs for her friends.*

**5 could use** *spoken* if you say you could use something, you mean you would really like to have it: *I could use a drink.*

**6 ▶ PRODUCT ◀** to buy a particular product regularly: *I always use the same deodorant.*

**7 ▶ WORD ◀** to say or write a particular word or phrase: *an expression that would never be used in polite conversation*

**8 ▶ DRUGS ◀** to regularly take illegal drugs

**9 ▶ NAME ◀** to call yourself by a name that is not yours in order to keep your name secret: *Grant had checked into a Miami hotel using a false name.*

**use** sth ↔ **up** *phr v* [T] to use all of something: *Don't use up all the hot water.*

**use²** /juːs/ *n* **1** [C] a way in which something can be used, or a purpose for which it can be used: *Robots have many different uses in modern industry.* **2** [singular, U] the act of using something or the amount that is used: [+ **of**] *the increasing use of computers in education* | *the poet's use of metaphor* **3 make use of** to use something that is available in order to achieve something or get an advantage for yourself: *Not enough people are making use of the children's play scheme.* | *The artist makes use of scrap iron in her sculpture.* | **make good use of** (=get as much advantage as possible from something) *We must make the best possible use of the resources we have.* **4 put sth to (good) use** to use knowledge, skills etc for a particular purpose: *an opportunity to put her medical training to good use* **5** [U] the ability or right to use something: *Joe's given me the use of his office till he gets back.* | *He lost the use of both legs as a result of the accident.* **6 be no use** also **be of no use** *formal* to be completely useless: *This map's no use – it doesn't show the minor roads.* | **be (of) no use to sb** *Have this sweater – it's of no use to me any more.* **7 it's no use doing sth** *spoken* used to tell someone not to do something because it will have no effect: *It's no use arguing with her – she won't listen.* **8 it's no use!** *spoken* used to say that you are going to stop doing something because you do not think it will be successful: *Oh, it's no use! I can't fix it.* **9 what's the use (of)?** *spoken* used to say that something seems to be a waste of time: *What's the use of getting so angry?* **10 be in use** a machine, place etc that is in use is being used: *All the machines are in use at the moment.* **11 for the use of** provided for a particular person or group of people to use: *This parking lot is for the use of employees only.* **12 come into use/go out of use** to start or stop being used: *New printing techniques have recently come into use.* **13 out of use** a machine, place etc that is out of use is not being used **14 be of use** *formal* to be useful: *I wondered if this book might be of use to you.* **15 have no use for** to have no respect for someone or something: *She has no use for people who are always complaining.* **16 he/she/it has its uses** *spoken often humorous* used to say that something or someone can sometimes be useful **17** [C] one of the meanings of a word, or the way that a particular word is used

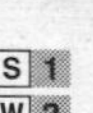

**use³** *v negative form of* **usedn't, usen't** *old-fashioned BrE* **used to do sth** if something used to happen, it happened regularly or all the time in the past, but does not happen now: *I used to go to the cinema a lot, but I never get the time now.* | *Beth used to like rock 'n' roll when she was young.* | **used to** *"Do you play golf?" "No, but I used to."* | **did not use to**, also **used not to** *BrE old-fashioned*: *I'm surprised to see you smoking. You didn't use to.* | *The shops usedn't to open on Sundays.* | **used to be** (=something was true in the past but is not true now) *She used to be such a happy lively girl.* | **did there use to be?** also **used there to be?** *formal*: *Did there use to be a hotel on that corner?*

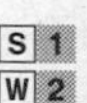

**used** /juːst/ *adj* **be used to** to have experienced something so that it no longer seems surprising, difficult, strange etc: *Lady Whitton wasn't used to people disagreeing with her.* | **get used to** *I'm sure I'll get used to the hard work.*

**used** /juːzd/ *adj* **1 used cars/clothes etc** cars, clothes etc that have already had an owner; SECOND-HAND: *a used car salesman* **2** dirty as a result of use: *a used tissue*

**use·ful** /ˈjuːsfəl/ *adj* **1** helping you to do or get what you want: *useful information* | *Dean's a really useful person to have around when things go wrong.* | **useful to sb** *information that may be useful to the enemy* | **useful for sth** *These yellow stickers are useful for leaving messages.* | **prove useful** (=be useful in a particular situation) *Clive's experience in the building trade proved useful for re-roofing the garage.* | **make yourself useful** (=help someone) *Can I do anything to make myself useful?* | **come**

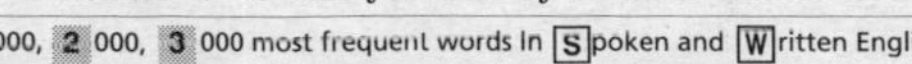

**in useful** (=be useful in a particular situation) *Keep that, it might come in useful later.* **2** *BrE informal* satisfactory: *The England cricket team scored quite a useful total.* —**usefully** *adv*

**use·ful·ness** /ˈjuːsfəlnɪ̈s/ *n* [U] the state of being useful: **outlive its usefulness** (=not be useful any more)

**use·less** /ˈjuːsləs/ *adj* **1** not useful or effective in any way: *This bag is useless – it has a hole in it.* | *a useless piece of information* | **completely/totally/utterly useless** *At that time, art was considered a completely useless activity.* | **useless for** *It's a nice watch, but it's useless for scuba diving.* | **it is useless to do sth** *It was useless to complain.* **2** *informal* unable or unwilling to do anything properly: *Don't ask Tim to fix it. He's completely useless.* —**uselessly** *adv* —**uselessness** *n* [U]

**us·er** /ˈjuːzə‖-ər/ *n* [C] someone or something that uses a product, service etc: *road users* —see also END USER

**user fee** /ˈ·· ·/ *n* [C] *AmE* a tax on a service provided for the public

**user friend·ly** /ˌ·· ˈ··◂/ *adj* easy to use or operate: *a user friendly guide to computing* —**user-friendliness** *n* [U]

**user in·ter·face** /ˌ·· ˈ···/ *n* [C] the part of a computer PROGRAM or SOFTWARE package that contains the commands and operations for the person using the computer

**ush·er**[1] /ˈʌʃə‖-ər/ *n* [C] **1** someone who shows people to their seats at a theatre, cinema, wedding etc **2** *BrE* someone who works in a law court whose job is to make sure there is no trouble

**usher**[2] *v* [T] to help someone to get from one place to another, especially by showing them the way: **usher sb into/to** *The guard ushered him into the room.*

**usher in** sth *phr v* [T] to be the start of something new: *The Stockholm Conference ushered in a new era of international co-operation.*

**ush·er·ette** /ˌʌʃəˈret/ *n* [C] *especially BrE* a woman who works in a cinema, showing people to their seats

**usu** the written abbreviation of USUALLY

**u·su·al** /ˈjuːʒuəl, ˈjuːʒəl/ *adj* **1** the same as what happens most of the time or in most situations: *I'll meet you at the usual time.* | *Gina was her usual cheerful self.* | **it is usual for sb to do sth** *Is it usual for lectures to start so early?* | **better/more etc than usual** *It seemed colder than usual in the house.* **2 as usual** in the way that happens or exists most of the time: *As usual, they'd left the children at home with Susan.* **3 as per usual** *spoken* used to say that something bad that often happens has just happened again: *Matthew was drunk as per usual.* **4 the usual** *spoken* the drink that you usually have

**u·su·al·ly** /ˈjuːʒuəli, ˈjuːʒəli/ *adv* used when describing what happens on most occasions or in most situations: *I'm usually in bed by 11.30.* | *Women usually live longer than men.* —see picture at FREQUENCY

**u·sur·er** /ˈjuːʒərə‖-ər/ *n* [C] *formal* someone who lends money to people and makes them pay too high a rate of INTEREST[1] (4)

**u·su·ri·ous** /juːˈzjʊəriəs‖juːˈʒʊr-/ *adj formal* a usurious price or rate of INTEREST[1] (4) is unfairly high

**u·surp** /juːˈzɜːp‖-sɜːrp/ *v* [T] *formal* to take someone else's power, position, job etc when you do not have the right to: *his deep jealousy at the thought of another man usurping his role as father* —**usurper** *n* [C] —**usurpation** /ˌjuːzɜːˈpeɪʃən‖-sɜːr-/ *n* [U]

**u·su·ry** /ˈjuːʒəri/ *n* [U] *formal* the practice of lending money to people and making them pay unfairly high rates of INTEREST[1] (4)

**u·ten·sil** /juːˈtensəl/ *n* [C] a tool or object with a particular use, especially in cooking: *kitchen utensils*

**u·te·rus** /ˈjuːtərəs/ *n plural* **uteri** /-raɪ/ or **uteruses** [C] *technical* the organ in a woman or female MAMMAL where babies develop; WOMB —**uterine** /-raɪn/ *adj*

**u·til·i·tar·i·an** /juːˌtɪlɪ̈ˈteəriən‖-ˈter-/ *adj* **1** *formal* useful and practical rather than being used for decoration: *ugly utilitarian buildings* **2** *technical* based on a belief in utilitarianism —compare MATERIALISTIC

**u·til·i·tar·i·an·is·m** /juːˌtɪlɪ̈ˈteəriənɪzəm‖-ˈter-/ *n* [U] *technical* the belief that an action is good if it helps the greatest possible number of people

**u·til·i·ty** /juːˈtɪlɪ̈ti/ *n* **1** [usually plural] *especially AmE* a service such as gas or electricity provided for people to use: *Does your rent include utilities?* **2** [U] *formal* the amount of usefulness that something has

**utility pole** /·ˈ··· ˌ·/ *n* [C] *AmE* a tall wooden pole for supporting telephone and electric wires

**utility room** /·ˈ··· ˌ·/ *n* [C] a room in a house where washing machines, FREEZERS etc are kept

**u·til·ize** also **-ise** *BrE* /ˈjuːtɪ̈laɪz/ *v* [T] *formal* to use something effectively: *a heating system that utilizes solar energy* —**utilizable** *adj* —**utilization** /ˌjuːtɪ̈laɪˈzeɪʃən‖-lə-/ *n* [U]

**ut·most**[1] /ˈʌtməʊst‖-moʊst/ *adj* **the utmost importance/respect/care etc** the greatest possible importance etc: *a matter of the utmost importance*

**utmost**[2] *n* [singular] **1** the most that can be done: *Both runners had pushed themselves to the utmost.* **2 do your utmost** to try as hard as you can to achieve something: *We've done our utmost to make the process as simple as possible.*

**u·to·pi·a** /juːˈtəʊpiə‖-ˈtoʊ-/ *n* [C,U] an imaginary perfect world where everyone is happy —**utopian** *adj*

**ut·ter**[1] /ˈʌtə‖-ər/ *adj* [only before noun] **utter failure/rubbish/fool etc** a complete failure etc: *What an utter waste of time!* | *We all watched in utter amazement.*

**utter**[2] *v* [T] *formal or literary* **1** to make a sound with your voice, especially with difficulty: *The wounded prisoner uttered a groan.* **2** to say things: *Uttering a stream of filthy curses, Medlock stomped away.*

**ut·ter·ance** /ˈʌtərəns/ *n formal* **1** [C] something you say: *Politicians are judged by their public utterances.* **2 give utterance to** to express something in words **3** [U] the action of saying something

**ut·ter·ly** /ˈʌtəli‖-ər-/ *adv* completely or totally: *You look utterly miserable.*

**ut·ter·most** /ˈʌtəməʊst‖-tərmoʊst/ *adj literary or formal* UTMOST[1]

**U-turn** /ˈjuː tɜːn‖ˌjuː ˈtɜːrn/ *n* [C] **1** a turn that you make in a car, on a bicycle etc, so that you go back in the direction you came from **2** *informal* a complete change of ideas, plans etc: *a government U-turn on economic policy*

**u·vu·la** /ˈjuːvjɪ̈lə/ *n* [C] *technical* a small soft piece of flesh which hangs down from the top of your mouth at the back

**u·vu·lar** /ˈjuːvjɪ̈lə‖-ər/ *n* [C] a CONSONANT sound that you make with the back of your tongue touching, or nearly touching, your uvula —**uvular** *adj*

**V, v** /viː/ **1** *plural* **V's, v's** the 22nd letter of the English alphabet **2** the number 5 in the system of ROMAN NUMERALS

**V** *n* [C usually singular] something that has a shape like the letter V: *She cut the material into a V.*

**v 1** the written abbreviation of VERB **2** *informal* the written abbreviation of VERY

**v.** the British abbreviation of VERSUS, used when talking about games in which two teams or players play against each other, or in the names of legal trials (TRIAL[1] (1)); VS *AmE*: *the England v. Australia cricket match*

**vac** /væk/ *n* [C usually singular] *BrE informal* a university VACATION[1] (2)

3 **va·can·cy** /ˈveɪkənsi/ *n* **1** [C] a room that is not being used in a hotel and is available for someone to stay in: *'No vacancies', the sign read.* **2** [C] a job that is available for someone to start doing: *Judge Ginsburg is to fill the vacancy on the US supreme court.* | [+ **for**] *vacancies for drivers* **3** [U] lack of interest or thought: *His mouth fell open and the look of vacancy returned.*

**va·cant** /ˈveɪkənt/ *adj* **1** a vacant seat, room etc is empty and available for someone to use: *Only a few apartments were still vacant.* **2** *formal* a vacant job or position in an organization is available for someone to start doing: **fall vacant** (=become vacant) **3 vacant expression/smile/stare etc** an expression that shows that someone is not thinking about anything **4 situations vacant** the part of a newspaper where jobs are advertised —**vacantly** *adv*: *Cindy was staring vacantly into space.*

**vacant lot** /ˌ·· ˈ·/ *n* [C] *especially AmE* an area of land that is not being used and on which nothing has been built, especially in a city

**vacant pos·ses·sion** /ˌ·· ·ˈ··/ *n* [U] *BrE technical* **house/flat with vacant possession** a home or other building whose previous owner has left, so that the new owner can move into it immediately

**va·cate** /vəˈkeɪt, veɪ-‖ˈveɪkeɪt/ *v* [T] *formal* **1** to leave a job or position so that it is available for someone else to do **2** to leave a seat, room etc so that someone else can use it: *Guests must vacate their rooms by 11 o'clock.*

2 3 **va·ca·tion[1]** /vəˈkeɪʃən‖veɪ-/ *n* **1** [C] *especially AmE* a holiday, or time spent not working: **on vacation** *They're on vacation for the next two weeks.* —see graph at HOLIDAY[1] **2** [C] one of the periods of time when universities are closed —see also LONG VACATION **3** [U] *formal* the act of leaving a place

**vacation[2]** *v* [I] *AmE* to go somewhere for a holiday: [+ **in/at**] *The Bernsteins are vacationing in Europe.*

**va·ca·tion·er** /vəˈkeɪʃənə‖veɪˈkeɪʃənər/ *n* [C] *AmE* someone who has gone somewhere for a holiday; HOLIDAYMAKER *BrE*

**vac·cin·ate** /ˈvæksɪneɪt/ *v* [T] to protect someone from a disease by putting a small amount of a substance containing that disease into their body: **vaccinate sb against sth** *All children should be vaccinated against measles.* —see also IMMUNIZE, INOCULATE —**vaccination** /ˌvæksɪˈneɪʃən/ *n* [C,U]

**vac·cine** /ˈvæksiːn‖vækˈsiːn/ *n* [C,U] a substance which contains the VIRUS that causes a disease and is used to protect people from that disease: *a polio vaccine* —compare SERUM (1)

**vac·il·late** /ˈvæsɪleɪt/ *v* [I] to continue to change your opinions, ideas etc; WAVER (2): *The administration is still vacillating over the Health Care issue.* —**vacillation** /ˌvæsɪˈleɪʃən/ *n* [C,U]

**va·cu·i·ty** /vəˈkjuːɪti, væ-‖væ-/ *n* [U] *formal* a lack of intelligent, interesting, or serious thought

**vac·u·ous** /ˈvækjuəs/ *adj formal* **1** a vacuous look or expression shows no sign of any feelings or intelligence **2** a vacuous life or existence seems to have no useful purpose —**vacuously** *adv* —**vacuousness** *n* [U]

**vac·u·um[1]** /ˈvækjuəm, -kjʊm/ *n* **1** [C] a space that is completely empty of all gas, especially one from which all the air has been taken away **2** [singular] a situation in which someone or something is missing or lacking, especially one that causes problems or makes you feel unhappy: *Her husband's death left a vacuum in her life.* | **power/political etc vacuum** *Nixon's departure from office created a political vacuum.* **3 in a vacuum** existing completely separately from other people or things and having no connection with them **4** [C] *old-fashioned* a vacuum cleaner

**vacuum[2]** *v* [I,T] to clean a place using a vacuum cleaner —see picture at CLEAN[2]

**vacuum clean·er** /ˈ··· ˌ··/ *n* [C] a machine that cleans floors by sucking up the dirt from them; HOOVER *BrE trademark*

**vacuum flask** /ˈ··· ˌ·/ *BrE old-fashioned n* [C] a special container that keeps liquids hot or cold; THERMOS

**vacuum-packed** /ˈ··· ˌ·‖ˌ··· ˈ·◂/ *adj* vacuum-packed food is surrounded by plastic from which most of the air has been removed, so that the food will stay fresh for longer

**vacuum pump** /ˈ··· ˌ·/ *n* [C] a pump for removing gas or air from an enclosed space

**vacuum tube** /ˈ··· ˌ·/ *n* [C] *AmE* a VALVE (3)

**vag·a·bond** /ˈvægəbɒnd‖-bɑːnd/ *n* [C] *especially literary* someone who has no home but travels from place to place —compare VAGRANT

**va·ga·ries** /ˈveɪgəriz/ *n* [plural] *formal* unusual or unexpected events, changes, ideas etc, that have an effect on your life: *the vagaries of the English weather*

**va·gi·na** /vəˈdʒaɪnə/ *n* [C] the passage from a woman's outer sexual organs to her WOMB —**vaginal** *adj*

**va·gran·cy** /ˈveɪgrənsi/ *n* [U] the criminal offence of living on the street and BEGGING from people

**va·grant** /ˈveɪgrənt/ *n* [C] *formal* someone who has no home or work, especially someone who begs

**vague** /veɪg/ *adj* **1** unclear because someone does not give enough details or does not say exactly what they S 3
mean: *vague promises of support* | [+ **about**] *Maria was very vague about her plans for the future.* **2 have a vague idea/feeling/recollection etc that** to think that something might be true or that you remember something, although you cannot be sure **3** not having a clear shape or form; INDISTINCT: *The vague shape of a figure loomed through the mist.* —**vagueness** *n* [U]

**vague·ly** /ˈveɪgli/ *adv* **1** slightly: *There was something vaguely familiar about him.* **2** in a way that shows you are not thinking about what you are doing: *He smiled vaguely at the ceiling.* **3** not exactly: *vaguely round*

**vain** /veɪn/ *adj* **1** someone who is vain is very proud of their good looks, abilities, or position; CONCEITED **2 in vain** without success in spite of your efforts: *I tried in vain to get Sue to come with us.* **3 vain attempt/hope/effort etc** an attempt, hope etc that fails to achieve the result you wanted **4 vain threat/promise etc** *literary* a threat, promise etc that is not worrying because the person cannot do what they say they will **5 take sb's name in vain** *humorous* to talk about someone, while they are not there, especially in a way that shows a lack of respect for them **6 take the Lord's name in vain** *old use* to swear using the words 'God', 'Jesus' etc —**vainly** *adv*: *The instructor struggled vainly to open his parachute.* —see also VANITY

**vain·glo·ri·ous** /veɪnˈglɔːriəs/ *adj literary* too proud of your own abilities, importance etc —**vaingloriously** *adv* —**vainglory** *n* [U]

**val·ance** /ˈvæləns/, **valence** *n* [C] **1** a narrow piece of cloth that hangs from the edge of a shelf or from the frame of a bed to the floor **2** *especially AmE* a narrow piece of cloth above a window, covering the RAIL the curtains hang on; PELMET *BrE*

**vale** /veɪl/ *n* [C] **1** *especially literary* a broad low valley **2 the vale of tears/misery etc** *literary* used to mean the difficulties of life

**val·e·dic·tion** /ˌvælɪ̌ˈdɪkʃən/ *n* [C,U] *formal* the act of saying goodbye, especially in a formal speech

**val·e·dic·to·ri·an** /ˌvælɪ̌dɪkˈtɔːriən/ *n* [C] *AmE* the student who has received the best marks all the way through school, and usually makes a speech

**val·e·dic·to·ry** /ˌvælɪ̌ˈdɪktəri◂/ *adj formal* connected with saying goodbye, especially on a formal occasion: *a valedictory speech*

**va·lence¹** /ˈveɪləns/ *n* [C] *especially AmE* valency

**va·lence²** /ˈvæləns/ *n* [C] another spelling of VALANCE

**va·len·cy** /ˈveɪlənsi/ *n* [C] *technical especially BrE* a measure of the power of atoms to combine together to form compounds

**valentine** /vaeləntaɪn/ *n* [C] **1** someone you love or think is attractive, that you send a card to on St Valentine's Day (February 14th): *Be my valentine.* **2** a card you send to someone on St Valentine's Day

**valet¹** /ˈvælɪ̌t, væleɪ‖væˈleɪ/ *n* [C] **1** a male servant who looks after a man's clothes, serves his meals etc **2** *BrE* someone who cleans the clothes of people staying in a hotel **3** *AmE* someone who parks your car for you at a hotel or restaurant: *valet service*

**valet²** *v* [T] *BrE* to clean someone's car: *a valeting service*

**valiant** /ˈvæliant/ *adj* very brave, especially in a difficult situation: *a valiant attempt to break the world record*

**val·id** /ˈvælɪ̌d/ *adj* **1** a valid ticket, document, or agreement can be used legally or is officially acceptable, especially for a fixed period of time or according to certain conditions: *a valid passport|Your return ticket is valid for three months.* **2 valid reason/argument/criticism etc** a reason, argument etc that is based on what is true or sensible, and so should be accepted or treated in a serious way: *His point about staff shortages was a valid one.* —**validity** /vəˈlɪdɪ̌ti/ *n* [U]: *I would question the validity of that statement.*

**val·i·date** /ˈvælɪ̌deɪt/ *v* [T] *formal* to prove that something is true or correct, or to make a document or agreement officially and legally acceptable —**validation** /ˌvælɪ̌ˈdeɪʃən/ *n* [C,U]

**va·lise** /vəˈliːz‖vəˈliːs/ *n* [C] *old-fashioned* a small SUITCASE

**Val·i·um** /ˈvæliəm/ *n* [U] a drug to make people feel calmer and less anxious

S3 W3 **val·ley** /ˈvæli/ *n* [C] an area of land between two lines of hills or mountains, usually with a river flowing through it: *the San Fernando valley*

**val·our** *BrE*, **valor** *AmE* /ˈvælə‖-ər/ *n* [U] *literary* great courage, especially in war —see also **discretion is the better part of valour** (DISCRETION (3))

W3 **val·u·a·ble** /ˈvæljuəbəl, -jɪ̌bəl‖ˈvæljɪ̌bəl/ *adj* **1** worth a lot of money: *a valuable painting* **2** valuable help, advice etc is very useful because it helps you to do something **3** important because there is only a limited amount available: *I won't waste any more of your valuable time.*

**val·u·a·bles** /ˈvæljuəbəlz, -jɪ̌bəlz‖-jɪ̌bəlz/ *n* [plural] things that you own that are worth a lot of money, such as jewellery, cameras etc: *Guests should leave their valuables in the hotel safe.*

**val·u·a·tion** /ˌvæljuˈeɪʃən/ *n* [C,U] a judgment about how much something is worth, how effective or useful a particular idea or plan will be etc: **put a valuation on** *The valuation they put on the house was far too high.*

S3 W1 **val·ue¹** /ˈvæljuː/ *n* [U]
**1 ▶ MONEY ◀** [C,U] the amount of money that something is worth: *The alterations doubled the value of the house.*|**increase/go down etc in value** *Shares can go down as well as go up in value.*|**market value** (=the amount of money that something can usually be sold for) *We paid a price that was well above the market value.*|**of value** (=worth a lot of money) *The thieves took nothing of value.*|**street value** (=the value of drugs when they are sold illegally)|**hold its value** (=continue to be worth the same amount of money) *It's a beautiful carpet – it should hold its value.* —see WORTH (USAGE)
**2 be good/excellent etc value** *BrE* also **be (good) value for money** used to say that you get a lot of something or that its quality is good, considering the price you pay for it —see CHEAP² (USAGE)
**3 be bad/poor etc value** *BrE* used to say that you do not get much of something or its quality is not very good, considering the price you pay for it: *I thought £10 for a record that only lasts 14 minutes was incredibly poor value.*
**4 ▶ IMPORTANCE/USEFULNESS ◀** [U] the importance or usefulness of something: **of great/little value** *His research has been of little practical value.*|**sentimental value** (=importance that something has for you because someone you like gave it to you, because it reminds you of the past etc)
**5 ▶ PRINCIPLES ◀ values** [plural] your principles about what is right and wrong, or your ideas about what is important in life: *Western liberal values*
**6 ▶ AMOUNT ◀** [C] *technical* a mathematical quantity shown by a letter of the alphabet or sign: *Let x have the value 25.*
**7 ▶ MUSIC ◀** [C] the length of a musical note
**8 curiosity/novelty/snob etc value** a quality something has that makes it seem interesting or desirable because it is different, new, or typical of high class people
**9 family values** an expression meaning the belief that the family is very important, used especially by politicians —see also FACE VALUE

**value²** *v* [T] **1** to think that something is important to you: *I value your advice.|a valued friend* **2** [usually passive] to decide how much money something is worth, by comparing it with similar things: **value sth at** *We decided to get the house valued.|Paintings valued at over $200,000 were stolen from her home.*

**value-ad·ded tax** /ˌ·· ·· ˈ·/ *n* [U] VAT

**value judg·ment** /ˈ·· ˌ··/ *n* [C] a decision or judgment about how good something is, based on opinions not facts

**val·u·er** /ˈvæljuə‖-ər/ *n* [C] someone whose job is to decide how much money things are worth

**valve** /vælv/ *n* [C] **1** a part of a tube or pipe that opens and shuts like a door to control the flow of liquid, gas, air etc passing through it: *the valves of the heart* —see picture at BICYCLE¹ **2** the part on a TRUMPET¹ (1) or similar musical instrument that you press to change the sound of the note **3** *BrE* a closed glass tube used to control the flow of electricity in old radios, televisions etc; VACUUM TUBE *AmE* —see also BIVALVE, SAFETY VALVE

**vamoose** /væˈmuːs, və-/ *interjection AmE old-fashioned* used to tell someone to go away

**vamp¹** /væmp/ *n* [C] *old-fashioned* a woman who uses her sexual attractiveness to make men do things for her

**vamp²** *v*
**vamp** sth ↔ **up** *phr v* [T] *informal* to make a story, music etc seem more exciting by adding things to it

**vam·pire** /ˈvæmpaɪə‖-paɪr/ *n* [C] an evil spirit that is believed to suck people's blood by biting their necks

**vampire bat** /ˈ·· ·/ *n* [C] a south American BAT that sucks the blood of other animals

**van** /væn/ *n* [C] **1** a vehicle used especially for carrying goods, which is smaller than a TRUCK and has a roof and usually no windows at the sides: *a delivery van|a van driver* **2** *especially BrE* a railway carriage with a roof and sides, used especially for carrying goods: *a luggage van* —see also GUARD'S VAN 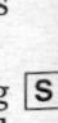 

**van·dal** /ˈvændl/ *n* [C] someone who deliberately damages things, especially public property

**van·dal·is·m** /ˈvændəl-ɪzəm/ *n* [U] the crime of deliberately damaging things, especially public property

**van·dal·ize** also **-ise** *BrE* /ˈvændəl-aɪz/ *v* [T] to damage or destroy things deliberately, especially public property

**vane** /veɪn/ *n* [C] a flat blade that is moved by wind or water to produce power to drive a machine: *the vanes of a propellor* —see also WEATHER VANE

**van·guard** /ˈvænɡɑːd‖-ɡɑːrd/ *n* **1 in the vanguard** in the most advanced position of development: *In the 19th century, Britain was in the vanguard of industrial progress.* **2 the vanguard** [singular] the leading position at the front of an army or group of ships moving into battle, or the soldiers who are in this position

**va·nil·la¹** /vəˈnɪlə/ *n* [U] a substance used to give a special taste to ICE CREAM, cakes etc, made from the beans of a tropical plant

**vanilla²** *adj* having the taste of vanilla: *vanilla ice-cream* | *vanilla essence*

**van·ish** /ˈvænɪʃ/ *v* [I] **1** to disappear suddenly, especially in a way that cannot easily be explained: *When I turned round again, the boy had vanished.* | **vanish into thin air** (=disappear completely in a very mysterious way) | **vanish without trace/vanish off the face of the earth** (=disappear so that no sign remains) **2** to suddenly stop existing: *Many species in South America have vanished completely.* **3 do a vanishing act** *informal* to suddenly disappear, especially when someone is looking for you

**vanishing point** /ˈ··· ˌ·/ *n* [singular] *technical* the point in the distance, especially on a picture, where parallel lines seem to meet

**van·i·ty** /ˈvænɨti/ *n* [U] **1** too much PRIDE in yourself, so that you are always thinking about yourself and your appearance **2 the vanity of sth** *literary* the lack of importance of something compared to other things that are much more important: *The poem warns of the vanity of mental ambition.*

**vanity case** /ˈ··· ˌ·/ *n* [C] a small bag used by a woman for carrying MAKE-UP etc

**vanity plate** /ˈ··· ˌ·/ *n* [C] *AmE* a car NUMBERPLATE that has a special combination of numbers or letters, for example the first letters of the driver's names

**vanity press** /ˈ··· ˌ·/ also **vanity pub·lish·er** /ˈ··· ˌ···/ *n* [C usually singular] a company that writers pay to print their books

**vanity ta·ble** /ˈ··· ˌ··/ *n* [C] *AmE* a DRESSING TABLE *BrE*

**van·quish** /ˈvæŋkwɪʃ/ *v* [T] *literary* to defeat someone or something completely

**van·tage point** /ˈvɑːntɪdʒ pɔɪnt‖ˈvæn-/ *n* [C] **1** a good position from which you can see something: *From my vantage point on the hill, I could see the whole procession.* **2** a way of thinking about things that comes from your own particular situation; POINT OF VIEW: *speaking from his vantage point as a major developer*

**vap·id** /ˈvæpɨd/ *adj formal* lacking intelligence, interest, or imagination: *vapid piped music* —**vapidly** *adv* —**vapidness** *n* [U] —**vapidity** /vəˈpɪdɨti/ *n* [U]

**va·por** /ˈveɪpə‖-ər/ *n* [C,U] the American spelling of vapour

**va·por·ize** also **-ise** *BrE* /ˈveɪpəraɪz/ *v* [I,T] to change into a vapour, or to make something do this: *Water vaporizes when it boils.* —**vaporization** /ˌveɪpəraɪˈzeɪʃən‖-rə-/ *n* [U]

**va·pour** *BrE*, **vapor** *AmE* /ˈveɪpə‖-ər/ *n* **1** [C,U] a mass of small drops of a liquid which float in the air, for example because the liquid has been heated: *water vapour* **2 the vapours** [plural] *old use* a condition when you suddenly feel faint —**vaporous** *adj*

**vapour trail** *BrE*, **vapor trail** *AmE* /ˈ·· ·/ *n* [C] the white line that is left in the sky by a plane

**var·i·a·ble¹** /ˈveəriəbəl‖ˈver-/ *n* [C] **1** something that may be different in different situations, so that you cannot be sure what will happen: *There are too many variables in the experiment to predict the result accurately.* **2** *technical* a mathematical quantity which can represent several different amounts —compare CONSTANT²

**variable²** *adj* **1** likely to change often: *the variable nature of the English climate* | *Consumer preferences are so variable that planning is almost impossible.* **2** sometimes good and sometimes bad; UNEVEN: *The team's performance has been very variable lately.* **3** able to be changed: *The machine has variable temperature settings.* —**variably** *adv* —**variability** /ˌveəriəˈbɪlɨti‖ˌver-/ *n* [U]

**var·i·ance** /ˈveəriəns‖ˈver-/ *n* [U] *formal* **1 be at variance with** if two people or things are at variance with each other, they do not agree or are very different: *Tradition and culture are often at variance with the needs of modern living.* **2** the amount by which two or more things are different or by which they change

**var·i·ant** /ˈveəriənt‖ˈver-/ *n* [C] **1** something that is slightly different from the usual form of something: [+ **on**] *a variant on the archetypal Hollywood hero* **2** *technical* a slightly different form of a word or phrase: *regional spelling variants in British and American English* —**variant** *adj*: *a variant form of the word*

**var·i·a·tion** /ˌveəriˈeɪʃən‖ˌver-/ *n*  **1** [C,U] a difference or change from the usual amount or form of something: [+ **in**] *There are wide regional variations in house prices.* **2** [C] something that is done in a way that is different from the way it is usually done: [+ **on**] *an interesting variation on the theme of betrayal and revenge* **3** [C] one of a set of short pieces of music, each based on the same simple tune: *Bach's Goldberg Variations*

**var·i·cose veins** /ˌværɨkəʊs ˈveɪnz‖-koʊs-/ *n* [plural] a medical condition in which the VEINS in your leg become swollen and painful

**var·ied** /ˈveərid‖ˈver-/ *adj* consisting of or including many different kinds of things or people, especially in a way that seems interesting: *The work's very varied.* | *human nature, in all its many and varied forms* | *products as varied as car bumpers and cigarette filters*

**var·ie·gat·ed** /ˈveərɪgeɪtɨd‖ˈver-/ *adj* **1** a variegated plant, leaf etc has different coloured marks on it: *variegated ivies* **2** *formal* consisting of a lot of different types of thing

**var·ie·ga·tion** /ˌveərɨˈgeɪʃən‖ˌver-/ *n* [U] marks of varied colours, especially in plants

**va·ri·e·ty** /vəˈraɪəti/ *n* 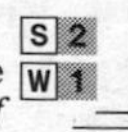

**1 a variety of** a lot of a particular type of things that are different from each other: *The girls come from a variety of different backgrounds.* | **a wide variety of** *The T-shirts are available in a wide variety of colors.*

**2 ▸DIFFERENCES◂** [U] the differences within a group, set of actions etc that make it interesting: **add variety to** (=make something more interesting) *There was little she could do to add variety to her daily routine.*

**3 ▸PLANT/ANIMAL◂** [C] a type of plant or animal that is different from others in the same group: [+ **of**] *a new variety of apple*

**4 ▸TYPE OF PERSON/THING◂** [C usually singular] *often humorous* a particular type of person or thing: **of the...variety** *The men are mostly of the noble, long-suffering husband variety!*

**5 variety is the spice of life** used to say that doing a lot of different things, meeting different people etc is what makes life interesting

**6 ▸ENTERTAINMENT◂** [U] a type of entertainment for theatre or television that includes a lot of different short performances

**variety store** /-ˈ··· ˌ·/ *n* [C] *AmE* a shop that sells many different kinds of goods, often at low prices

**var·i·ous** /ˈveəriəs‖ˈver-/ *adj* [usually before noun] 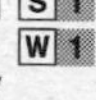 several different: *available in various colours*

**var·i·ous·ly** /ˈveəriəsli‖ˈver-/ *adv* **variously described/estimated etc** used to introduce a number of different descriptions, amounts etc, that people have made or used about something: *His fortune has been variously estimated at between $1 and $2 billion.*

V

**var·let** /ˈvɑːlɪ̣t‖ˈvɑːr-/ *n* [C] *old use* a bad man

**var·mint** /ˈvɑːmɪ̣nt‖ˈvɑːr-/ *n* [C] *old-fashioned* someone, especially a child, who causes a lot of trouble

**var·nish¹** /ˈvɑːnɪʃ‖ˈvɑːr-/ *n* [C,U] **1** a clear liquid that is painted onto things, especially things made of wood, to protect them and give them a hard shiny surface **2 the varnish** the clear shiny surface of something that has been covered in this liquid —compare LACQUER¹ (1)

**varnish²** *v* [T] to cover something with varnish

**var·si·ty** /ˈvɑːsɪ̣ti‖ˈvɑːr-/ *n* [C,U] **1** *AmE* the main team that represents a university, college, or school in a sport: *the varsity football team* —compare JUNIOR VARSITY **2** *BrE old-fashioned* a university, especially Oxford or Cambridge

S2 W2 **var·y** /ˈveəri‖ˈveri/ *v* **1** [I] if several things of the same type vary, they are all different from each other: **vary greatly/considerably/enormously** *Teaching methods vary greatly from school to school.* | **vary in price/quality/size** *flowers that vary in color and size* | **varying degrees of** *varying degrees of success* **2** [I] to change often: *Quentin's mood seems to vary according to the weather.* | **it varies** *"What do you normally have for lunch?" "Well, it varies from day to day."* **3** [T] to regularly change what you do or the way that you do it: *My doctor said I should vary my diet more.* —see also VARIED

**vas·cu·lar** /ˈvæskjʊ̣lə‖-ər/ *adj technical* connected with the tubes through which liquids flow in the bodies of animals or in plants: *the vascular system*

**vase** /vɑːz‖veɪs, veɪz/ *n* [C] a glass or baked clay container used to put flowers in or for decoration

**va·sec·to·my** /vəˈsektəmi/ *n* [C,U] a medical operation to cut the small tube that carries a man's SPERM so that he is unable to produce children

**Vas·e·line** /ˈvæsɪ̣liːn/ *n* [U] *trademark* a soft clear substance used for various medical and other purposes

**vas·sal** /ˈvæsəl/ *n* [C] **1** a man in the MIDDLE AGES who was given land to live on by a lord in return for promising to work or fight for him **2** *formal* a country that is controlled by another country: *a vassal state*

S2 W2 **vast** /vɑːst‖væst/ *adj* **1** extremely large: *vast areas of rainforest* | **vast expense** *A huge palace was constructed at vast public expense.* | **in vast numbers** *The refugees came across the border in vast numbers.* **2 the vast majority/bulk of** used when you want to emphasize that something is true about almost all of a group of people or things: *The vast majority of young people don't take drugs.* —**vastness** *n* [U]

**vast·ly** /ˈvɑːstli‖ˈvæstli/ *adv* very much: *This film is vastly superior to his last one.*

**VAT** /ˌviː eɪ ˈtiː, væt/ *n* [U] value added tax; a tax added to the price of goods and services in Britain and the EU

W3 **vat** /væt/ *n* [C] a very large container for storing liquids such as WHISKY or DYE, when they are being made

**Vat·i·can** /ˈvætɪkən/ *n* **the Vatican a)** the large PALACE in Rome where the Pope (=head of the Roman Catholic Church) lives and works **b)** the government of the Pope: *The Vatican is taking a hard line on birth control.*

**vau·de·ville** /ˈvɔːdəvɪl, ˈvəʊ-‖ˈvɒː-, ˈvoʊ-/ *n* [U] *AmE* a type of theatre entertainment, popular from 1880 to 1950, in which there were many short performances of different kinds, including singing, dancing, jokes etc

**vault¹** /vɔːlt‖vɒːlt/ *n* [C] **1** also **vaults** [plural] a room with thick walls and a strong door where money, jewels etc are kept to prevent them from being stolen or damaged **2** also **vaults** [plural] a room where people from the same family are buried, often under the floor of a church **3** a jump over something —see also POLE VAULT **4** a roof or CEILING (1) that consists of several ARCH*es* that are joined together, especially in a church

**vault²** also **vault over** *v* [T] to jump over something in one movement, using your hands or a pole to help you: *He vaulted over the fence and ran off into the night.* —**vaulter** *n* [C]

**vault·ed** /ˈvɔːltɪ̣d‖ˈvɒːl-/ *adj* **vaulted roof/ceiling etc** a roof, ceiling etc that consists of several ARCH*es* which are joined together

**vault·ing¹** /ˈvɔːltɪŋ‖ˈvɒːl-/ *n* [U] arches in a roof

**vaulting²** *adj* **vaulting ambition** *literary* the desire to achieve as much as possible

**vaulting horse** /ˈ·· ·/ *n* [C] *BrE* a large wooden box used for jumping over in GYMNASTICS

**vaunt** /vɔːnt‖vɒːnt/ *v* **much-vaunted** a much-vaunted achievement is one that people often say is very good, important etc, especially with too much pride: *Reagan's much vaunted economic miracle*

**VCR** /ˌviː siː ˈɑː‖-ˈɑːr/ *n* [C] *especially AmE* video cassette recorder; a machine which is used to record television programmes or to play VIDEOTAPES; VIDEO¹ (3) *BrE*

**VD** /ˌviː ˈdiː/ *n* [U] venereal disease; a disease that is passed from one person to another during sex

**VDU** /ˌviː diː ˈjuː/ *n* [C] visual display unit; a machine like a television that shows the information from a computer or WORD PROCESSOR

**'ve** /v, əv/ the short form of 'have': *We've finished*

**veal** /viːl/ *n* [U] meat from a CALF (=a young cow)

**vec·tor** /ˈvektə‖-ər/ *n* [C] *technical* **1** a quantity that has a direction as well as a size, usually represented by an ARROW (2) —compare SCALAR **2** the course taken by a plane

**Ve·da** /ˈveɪdə/ *n* [plural] the oldest writings of the Hindu religion

**vee·jay** /ˌviːˈdʒeɪ/ *n* [C] a VIDEO JOCKEY

**veep** /viːp/ *n* [C] *AmE informal* VICE PRESIDENT

**veer** /vɪə‖vɪr/ *v* [I] **1** [always + adv/prep] to change direction suddenly: **[+ off/away/across etc]** *The car veered sharply to the right and crashed.* **2** [always + adv/prep] to change suddenly to a very different belief, opinion, or subject: **[+ towards/away from etc]** *The country's leaders seemed to veer towards nationalism.* **3** *technical* if the wind veers in a particular direction, it changes round to that direction

**veg¹** /vedʒ/ *n* [plural] *BrE informal* vegetables: *fruit and veg*

**veg²** *v*

**veg out** *phr v* [I] *informal* to relax by doing something that needs very little effort, such as watching television

**ve·gan** /ˈviːgən‖ˈveɪgən, ˈviː-/ *n* [C] someone who does not eat meat, fish, eggs, cheese, or milk —**vegan** *adj*: *a vegan diet*

**ve·ge·bur·ger** /ˈvedʒiˌbɜːgə‖-ˌbɜːrgər/ *n* [C] *BrE* a BURGER made with vegetables, beans etc, but no meat

**vege·ta·ble** /ˈvedʒtəbəl/ *n* **1** [C,U] a plant such as a CABBAGE, CARROT, or potato which is eaten raw or cooked and is usually not sweet: *vegetable oil* | **green vegetables** *citrus fruits and fresh green vegetables* —see picture on page 414 **2** [C] *informal* someone who cannot think or move because their brain has been damaged in an accident S W

**vegetable mar·row** /ˌ··· ˈ··/ *n* [C] a MARROW (2)

**veg·e·tar·i·an** /ˌvedʒɪ̣ˈteəriən◂‖-ˈter-/ *n* [C] someone who eats only vegetables, bread, fruit, eggs etc and does not eat meat or fish —compare VEGAN —**vegetarian** *adj*: *a vegetarian restaurant*

**veg·e·tar·i·an·is·m** /ˌvedʒɪ̣ˈteəriənɪzəm‖-ˈter-/ *n* [U] the practice of not eating meat or fish

**veg·e·tate** /ˈvedʒɪ̣teɪt/ *v* [I] not to do anything and feel bored because there is nothing interesting for you to do: *I got fed up with vegetating at home.*

**veg·e·ta·tion** /ˌvedʒɪ̣ˈteɪʃən/ *n* [U] plants in general, especially in one particular area: *There was little vegetation on the island.*

**veg·gie** /ˈvedʒi/ *n* [C] *informal* **1** *BrE* a VEGETARIAN **2** *AmE* a VEGETABLE (1)

**vehe·ment** /ˈvɪəmənt/ *adj* showing very strong feelings or opinions: *a vehement attack on the President's budget proposals* —**vehemently** *adv*: *Dan vehemently denies the charges.* —**vehemence** *n* [U]

S2 W2 **ve·hi·cle** /ˈviːɪkəl/ *n* [C] **1** *especially formal* a thing such as a car, bus etc that is used for carrying people or things from one place to another: *"Is this your vehicle, sir?" asked the policeman.*|*a heavy goods vehicle* **2 vehicle for (doing) sth** something that you use in order to achieve something or as a way of spreading your ideas, expressing your opinions etc: *The government used the press as a vehicle for its propaganda.*

**ve·hic·u·lar** /viːˈhɪkjᵊlə‖-ər/ *adj formal* connected with road vehicles: *vehicular traffic*

**veil¹** /veɪl/ *n* [C] **1** a thin piece of material worn by women to cover their faces at formal occasions such as weddings, or for religious reasons **2 the veil** the system in Islamic countries in which women must keep their faces covered in public places **3 draw a veil over** deliberately not to talk about something that happened in the past because it is unpleasant or embarrassing: *I think it's better if we draw a veil over the whole sorry affair.*

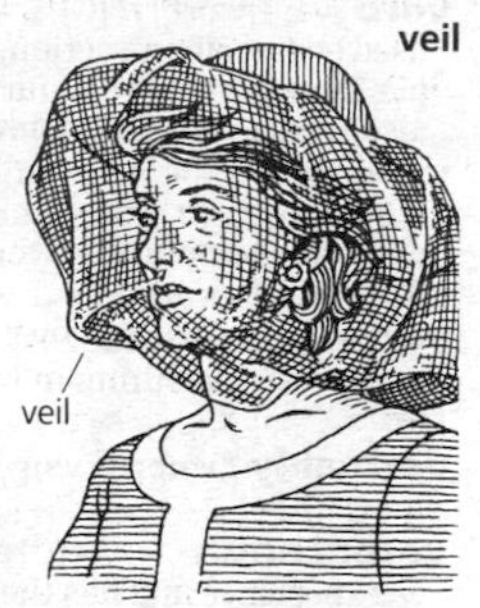


**4 veil of secrecy/deceit/silence etc** something that stops you knowing the full truth about a situation: *A veil of mystery surrounds Kelly's death.* **5 veil of mist/cloud etc** a thin layer of mist, cloud etc that covers something so that you cannot see it clearly **6 take the veil** *old-fashioned* to become a NUN

**veil²** *v* [T] **1 be veiled in mystery/secrecy** if something is veiled in mystery etc, very little is known about it and it seems mysterious **2** to cover something with a veil

**veiled** /veɪld/ *adj* **veiled criticism/threats/hints etc** criticisms, threats etc that are hidden because you do not say directly what you think or mean: **thinly veiled** (=only slightly hidden) *thinly veiled threats of retaliation*

**vein** /veɪn/ *n* **1** [C] one of the tubes through which blood flows to your heart from other parts of your body —compare ARTERY (1) **2** [C] **a)** one of the thin lines on a leaf or on the wing of an insect **b)** one of the thin lines on a piece of wood, cheese, MARBLE (1) etc **3** [C] a thin layer of a valuable metal or mineral which is contained in rock: *a rich vein of silver* **4** [singular] a particular style or way, especially when speaking or writing about something: **in the same vein/in a similar vein** *His second novel is in very much the same vein as the first.*|**in a serious/light-hearted vein** *The rest of the speech was in a more light-hearted vein.* **5 a vein of humour/malice etc** a small amount of a particular quality: **a rich vein** *There's a rich vein of humour running through her stories.*

**veined** /veɪnd/ *adj* having a pattern of thin lines on its surface that looks like veins: *black-veined marble*

**ve·lar** /ˈviːlə‖-ər/ *adj* a velar CONSONANT such as /k/ or /g/ is pronounced with the back of your tongue close to the soft part at the top of your mouth —**velar** *n* [C]

**Vel·cro** /ˈvelkrəʊ‖-kroʊ/ *n* [U] *trademark* a material used for fastening clothes, which sticks together when you press a piece with a rough surface against a piece with a soft surface —see picture at FASTENER

**veldt, veld** /velt/ *n* **the veldt** the high flat area of land in South Africa that is covered in grass and has few trees

**vel·lum** /ˈveləm/ *n* [U] a material used for making book covers, and in the past for writing on, made from the skins of young cows, sheep, or goats

**ve·lo·ci·pede** /vᵻˈlɒsᵻpiːd‖vᵻˈlɑː-/ *n* [C] a kind of bicycle, used in former times

**ve·lo·ci·ty** /vᵻˈlɒsᵻti‖vᵻˈlɑː-/ *n* **1** [C,U] *technical* the speed at which something moves in a particular direction: *the velocity of light*|*a high velocity bullet* **2** [U] *formal* a high speed

**vel·o·drome** /ˈvelədrəʊm‖-droʊm/ *n* [C] a circular track for bicycle racing

**ve·lour, velours** /vəˈlʊə‖-ˈlʊr/ *n* [U] heavy cloth which has a soft surface like velvet

**vel·vet** /ˈvelvᵻt/ *n* [U] cloth with a soft surface on one side which is used for making clothes, curtains etc —see picture on page 839

**vel·ve·teen** /ˌvelvᵻˈtiːn◂/ *n* [U] cheap material which looks like velvet

**vel·vet·y** /ˈvelvᵻti/ *adj* looking, feeling, tasting or sounding smooth and soft: *His voice had a wonderful velvety sound.*

**ve·nal** /ˈviːnl/ *adj formal* using power in a dishonest or unfair way and accepting money as a reward for doing this —compare VENIAL —**venally** *adv* —**venality** /viːˈnælᵻti/ *n* [U]

**vend** /vend/ *v* [T] *formal or law* to sell something

**ven·det·ta** /venˈdetə/ *n* [C] **1** a quarrel which continues for a long time in which one group or person tries to harm another because they feel angry about something that happened in the past: *The two sides have been engaged in a bitter private vendetta against each other.* **2** a quarrel that has continued for a long time between two families who try to kill each other because of murders in the past; a FEUD

**vending ma·chine** /ˈ·· ·ˌ·/ *n* [C] a machine that you can get cigarettes, chocolate, drinks etc from by putting in a coin

**vend·or** /ˈvendə‖-ər/ *n* [C] **1** someone who sells things: **news-vendor/ice-cream vendor etc** (=someone who sells ice-creams, newspapers etc in the street)|**street vendor** *I could hear the shouts of the street vendors.* **2** *law* someone who is selling something such as a house or an area of land

**ve·neer¹** /vᵻˈnɪə‖-ˈnɪr/ *n* **1** [C,U] a thin layer of good quality wood that covers the outside of a piece of furniture which is made of a cheaper material: *walnut veneer* **2 a veneer of** *formal* behaviour that hides someone's real character or feelings: *a veneer of self-confidence*

**veneer²** *v* [T + **with/in**] to cover something with a veneer

**ven·e·ra·ble** /ˈvenərəbəl/ *adj* **1** *formal or humorous* a venerable person or thing is very old and respected because of their age, experience, historical importance etc: *venerable financial institutions such as the Bank of England* **2 the Venerable...** **a)** the title given to a priest with the rank of ARCHDEACON in the Church of England **b)** the title given by the Roman Catholic Church to a dead person who is very holy but not yet a SAINT (1)

**ven·e·rate** /ˈvenəreɪt/ *v* [T] *formal* to treat someone or something with great respect, especially because they are old or connected with the past: *The Chinese venerate their ancestors.* —**veneration** /ˌvenəˈreɪʃən/ *n* [U]

**ve·ne·re·al dis·ease** /vᵻˈnɪəriəl dɪˌziːz‖-ˈnɪr-/ *n* [C,U] VD

**Ve·ne·tian blind** /vəˌniːʃən ˈblaɪnd/ *n* [C] a set of long flat bars of plastic or metal which can be raised or lowered to cover a window —see picture at BLIND³

**ven·geance** /ˈvendʒəns/ *n* **1** [U] something violent or harmful that you do to someone in order to punish them for harming you, your family etc: *Hamlet is driven by a desire for vengeance after his father is killed.* **2 with a vengeance** if something is done with a vengeance, it is done much more than is expected or normal: *The music started up again with a vengeance.*

**venge·ful** /ˈvendʒfəl/ *adj literary* very eager to punish someone who has harmed you: *a vengeful God* —**vengefully** *adv*

**ve·ni·al** /ˈviːniəl/ *adj formal* a venial fault, mistake etc is not very serious and can therefore be forgiven: *a venial sin* —compare VENAL

**ven·i·son** /ˈvenᵻzən, -sən/ *n* [U] the meat of a DEER

**Venn di·a·gram** /ˈven ˌdaɪəgræm/ *n* [C] a picture that shows the relationship between a number of things by using circles that OVERLAP each other

**ven·om** /ˈvenəm/ *n* [U] **1** a liquid poison that some snakes, insects etc produce and that they use when biting or stinging another animal or insect **2** extreme anger or hatred: *There was real venom in her voice.*

**ven·om·ous** /ˈvenəməs/ *adj* **1** full of extreme hatred or anger: *a venomous look* **2** a venomous snake, insect etc produces poison to attack its enemies —**venomously** *adv*

**ve·nous** /ˈviːnəs/ *adj* related to the VEINS (=tubes that carry the blood) in your body

**vent¹** /vent/ *n* [C] **1** a hole or pipe through which gases, smoke, liquid etc can enter or escape from an enclosed space or a container: *an air vent* **2 give vent to** *formal* to do something to express a strong feeling, especially of anger: *Joshua gave vent to his anger by kicking the chair.* **3** *technical* the small hole through which small animals, birds, fish, and snakes get rid of waste matter from their bodies **4** *technical* a narrow straight opening at the bottom of a jacket or coat, at the sides or back

**vent²** *v* [T] to do something to express your feelings, especially anger, often in a way that is unfair: **vent sth on sb** *Paul had a bad day at work and vented his anger on his family.*

**ven·ti·late** /ˈventɪleɪt‖-tl-eɪt/ *v* [T] **1** to let fresh air into a room, building etc: **well-ventilated/poorly ventilated etc** *a well-ventilated kitchen* **2** *formal* to express your opinions or feelings about something: *Doctrinal issues were never ventilated.* —**ventilation** /ˌventɪˈleɪʃən/ *n* [U]: *Workers complained about the factory's lack of ventilation.|a ventilation system*

**ven·ti·la·tor** /ˈventɪleɪtə‖-tl-eɪtər/ *n* [C] **1** a thing designed to let fresh air into a room, building etc **2** a piece of equipment that pumps air into and out of someone's lungs when they cannot breathe without help

**ven·tri·cle** /ˈventrɪkəl/ *n* [C] *technical* **1** one of the two spaces in the bottom of your heart that pump blood out into your body —compare ATRIUM (1) **2** a small hollow place in your body or in your brain

**ven·tril·o·quis·m** /venˈtrɪləkwɪzəm/ *n* [U] the art of speaking without moving your lips, so that the sound seems to come from someone else —**ventriloquist** *n* [C]

**ven·ture¹** /ˈventʃə‖-ər/ *n* [C] a new business activity that involves taking risks: *a commercial venture*|**joint venture** (=an agreement between two companies to do something together)

**venture²** *v formal* **1** [I always + adv/prep] to risk going somewhere when it could be dangerous: [+ **out/through/into etc**] *Today's the first time I've ventured out of doors since my illness.* **2** [T] to say something although you are afraid of how someone may react to it: **venture to do sth** *Nobody ventured to say a word.*|**venture an opinion** (=say what you think) *If I may venture an opinion, I'd say the plan needs more thought.* **3** [T] to take the risk of losing something; GAMBLE¹ (1): **venture sth on sth** *Jeff ventured his whole fortune on one throw of the dice.* **4 nothing ventured, nothing gained** used to say that you cannot achieve anything unless you take a risk

**venture on/upon** sth *phr v* [T] to try to do something that involves risks: *Now is not the time to venture on such an ambitious project.*

**venture cap·i·tal** /ˈ‥ ˌ‥‥/ *n* [U] money that is lent to someone so that they can start a new business

**ven·ture·some** /ˈventʃəsəm‖-tʃər-/ *adj especially literary* **1** a venturesome person is always ready to take risks **2** a venturesome action involves taking risks —**venturesomeness** *n* [U]

**ven·ue** /ˈvenjuː/ *n* [C] a place where something such as a concert or a meeting is arranged to take place: *the venue for the latest round of talks*

**Ve·nus** /ˈviːnəs/ *n* [singular] the PLANET second in order from the sun and nearest to the Earth —see picture at SOLAR SYSTEM

**Venus fly·trap** /ˌviːnəs ˈflaɪtræp/ *n* [C] a plant that catches and eats insects

**ve·ra·ci·ty** /vəˈræsɪti/ *n* [U] *formal* the quality of being true or of telling the truth —**veracious** *adj*

**ve·ran·da, verandah** /vəˈrændə/ *n* [C] an open area with a floor and a roof that is built on the side of a house on the ground floor: *Hannah sat sewing in the shade on the veranda.*

**verb** /vɜːb‖vɜːrb/ *n* [C] a word or group of words that is used to describe an action, experience, or state, for example 'come', 'see', 'be', 'put on': *to conjugate a verb* —see also AUXILIARY VERB, PHRASAL VERB

**verb·al** /ˈvɜːbəl‖ˈvɜːr-/ *adj* **1** spoken, not written: *a verbal agreement* —opposite NONVERBAL **2** connected with words or using words: *verbal skill|verbal abuse* **3** related to a verb

**verb·al·ize** also **-ise** *BrE* /ˈvɜːbəlaɪz‖ˈvɜːr-/ *v* [I,T] *formal* to express something in words: *He couldn't verbalize his fears.*

**verb·al·ly** /ˈvɜːbəli‖ˈvɜːr-/ *adv* in spoken words and not in writing

**verbal noun** /ˌ‥ ˈ‥/ *n* [C] a noun that describes an action or experience and has the form of a PRESENT PARTICIPLE. For example 'building' is a verbal noun in 'The building of the bridge was slow work', but simply a noun in 'The bank was a tall building'; GERUND —see also NOUN

**ver·ba·tim** /vɜːˈbeɪtɪm‖vɜːr-/ *adj, adv* repeating the actual words that were spoken or written: *a verbatim account of our conversation*

**ver·bi·age** /ˈvɜːbi-ɪdʒ‖ˈvɜːr-/ *n* [U] *formal* too many unnecessary words in speech or writing: *eliminate irrelevant verbiage*

**ver·bose** /vɜːˈbəʊs‖vɜːrˈboʊs/ *adj formal* using or containing too many words: *a verbose sermon* —compare VERBAL —**verbosely** *adv* —**verboseness** or **verbosity** /vɜːˈbɒsɪti‖vɜːrˈbɑː-/ *n* [U]

**ver·bo·ten** /vəˈbəʊtən‖vərˈboʊ-/ *adj German* not allowed; forbidden: *Being impolite to grown-ups was absolutely verboten in our household.*

**ver·dant** /ˈvɜːdənt‖ˈvɜːr-/ *adj literary* verdant land is covered with freshly growing green grass and plants: *verdant fields*

**ver·dict** /ˈvɜːdɪkt‖ˈvɜːr-/ *n* [C] **1** an official decision made by a JURY in a court of law about whether someone is guilty or not guilty of a crime: *a majority verdict of 10 to 2*|**return a verdict** *formal* (=give a verdict)|**reach a verdict** (=make a decision) *After a week the jury had still not reached a verdict.* **2** an official decision or opinion made by a person or group that has authority: *The panel will be giving their verdict tomorrow.* —see also OPEN VERDICT **3** *informal* an opinion or decision about something: [+ **on**] *What's your verdict on the movie?*

**ver·di·gris** /ˈvɜːdɪgriː,-griːs‖ˈvɜːr-/ *n* [U] a greenish-blue substance that forms a thin layer on COPPER (1) or BRASS (1) that is kept in wet conditions

**ver·dure** /ˈvɜːdʒə‖ˈvɜːrdʒər/ *n* [U] *literary* the bright green colour of grass, plants, trees etc, or the plants themselves

**verge¹** /vɜːdʒ‖vɜːrdʒ/ *n* [C] **1** *especially BrE* the edge or border of a road or path etc: *the grass verge* **2 be on the verge of** to be about to do something: *Jessica was on the verge of tears.|scientists on the verge of a major breakthrough*

**verge²** *v*

**verge on/upon** sth *phr v* [T] to be very close to a harmful or extreme state: **verge on madness/panic/chaos etc** *Daniela's strange behaviour sometimes verges on madness.*|**verging on the impossible/ridiculous** (=almost impossible etc)

**ver·ger** /ˈvɜːdʒə‖ˈvɜːrdʒər/ *n* [C] *especially BrE* someone whose job is to look after the contents of a church and perform small duties like showing people where to sit

**ver·i·fy** /ˈverɨ̥faɪ/ *v* **verified**, **verifying** [T] **1** to find out if a fact, statement etc is correct or true; check: **verify sth with sb** *These details must be verified with the Home Office.* | **verify that** *The bank will have to verify that you are the owner of the property.* **2** to state that something is true; CONFIRM: *The prisoner's statement was verified by several witnesses.* —**verifiable** *adj* —**verification** /ˌverɨ̥fɨ̥ˈkeɪʃən/ *n* [C,U]: *the verification of scientific laws*

**ver·i·ly** /ˈverɨ̥li/ *adv biblical* really

**ver·i·sim·il·i·tude** /ˌverɨ̥sɨ̥ˈmɪlɨ̥tjuːd‖-tuːd/ *n* [U] *formal* the quality of a piece of art, a performance etc that makes it seem like something real

**ver·i·ta·ble** /ˈverɨ̥təbəl/ *adj formal* a word used to emphasize a comparison that you think is correct: *The male bird is a veritable rainbow of colors.* —**veritably** *adv*

**ver·i·ty** /ˈverɨ̥ti/ *n* [C usually plural] *formal* an important principle or fact about life, the world etc, that is true in all situations: *one of the eternal verities*

**ver·mi·cel·li** /ˌvɜːmɨ̥ˈseli, -ˈtʃeli‖ˌvɜːr-/ *n* [U] Italian PASTA (=food that is made from a mixture of flour, eggs, and water) that is shaped into very thin strings and cooked in boiling water —see picture at PASTA

**ver·mil·lion** /vəˈmɪljən‖vər-/ *n* [U] a bright reddish-orange colour —**vermillion** *adj*

**ver·min** /ˈvɜːmɨ̥n‖ˈvɜːr-/ *n* [plural] **1** small animals or birds that destroy crops, spoil food etc, and are difficult to control: *a barn infested with vermin* —compare PEST **2** insects that live on people's or animals' bodies, bite them, and drink their blood: *a bed alive with vermin* **3** unpleasant people who cause problems for society: *He thinks all beggars are vermin.*

**ver·min·ous** /ˈvɜːmɨ̥nəs‖ˈvɜːr-/ *adj* **1** full of insects that bite you: *the tramp's verminous old coat* **2** very unpleasant or nasty: *verminous blackmail letters*

**ver·mouth** /ˈvɜːməθ‖vərˈmuːθ/ *n* [U] a drink made from wine that has strong-tasting substances added to it, usually drunk before a meal

**ver·nac·u·lar** /vəˈnækjʊ̈lə‖vərˈnækjʊ̈lər/ *n* [C usually singular] the language spoken in a country or area, especially when it is not the official language —**vernacular** *adj*

**ver·nal** /ˈvɜːnl‖ˈvɜːrnl/ *adj* [only before noun] *literary or technical* connected with the spring season

**ver·ru·ca** /vəˈruːkə/ *n* [C] a small hard infectious thing that can be painful and grows on the skin on the bottom of your foot; WART *AmE*

**versa** —see VICE VERSA

**ver·sa·tile** /ˈvɜːsətaɪl‖ˈvɜːrsətl/ *adj approving* **1** good at doing a lot of different things and able to learn new skills quickly and easily: *a very versatile performer* **2** having many different uses: *Nylon is a versatile material.* —**versatility** /ˌvɜːsəˈtɪlɨ̥ti‖ˌvɜːr-/ *n* [U]

**verse** /vɜːs‖vɜːrs/ *n* **1** [C] a set of lines that forms one part of a song: *Let's sing the last verse again.* —compare CHORUS¹ (1) **2** [C] a set of lines of poetry that forms one part of a poem, and that usually has a pattern that is repeated in the other parts: *Learn the first two verses of the poem.* **3** [U] words arranged in the form of poetry: *a book of comic verse* —compare PROSE —see also BLANK VERSE, FREE VERSE **4** [C] one of the numbered groups of sentences that make up each CHAPTER (=numbered part) of a book of the Bible —see also **give/quote chapter and verse** (CHAPTER (5))

**versed** /vɜːst‖vɜːrst/ *adj* **be (well) versed in** to know a lot about a subject or to be skilled in doing something: *a woman well versed in the art of diplomacy*

**ver·si·fi·ca·tion** /ˌvɜːsɨ̥fɨ̥ˈkeɪʃən‖ˌvɜːr-/ *n* [U] *technical* the particular pattern that a poem is written in

1 **ver·sion** /ˈvɜːʃən‖ˈvɜːrʒən/ *n* [C] **1** a copy of something that has been changed slightly so that it is different from the thing being copied: [+ **of**] *The dress is a cheaper version of one seen at the Paris fashion shows.* | **old/first/later etc version of** *This is a sophisticated version of the old tripod camera.* **2** a description of an event given by one person, especially when it is compared with someone else's description of the same thing: [+ **of**] *The two newspapers gave different versions of what happened.* **3** a play, film, piece of music etc that is slightly different from the book, piece of music etc on which it is based: [+ **of**] *an abridged version of the play* **4 an English/Japanese/Spanish version** an English etc translation of a book, poem, or other piece of writing: [+ **of**] *an English version of a German play*

**ver·so** /ˈvɜːsəʊ‖ˈvɜːrsoʊ/ *n* [C] *technical* a page on the left-hand side of a book —compare RECTO —**verso** *adj*

**ver·sus** /ˈvɜːsəs‖ˈvɜːr-/ written abbreviation **v** *or* **vs** *prep* **1** used to show that two people or teams are against each other in a game or court case: *the New York Knicks versus the Los Angeles Lakers* | *the Supreme Court decision in Roe versus Wade* **2** used when comparing the advantages of two different things, ideas etc: *The Finance Minister must weigh up the benefits of a tax cut versus those of increased public spending.*

**ver·te·bra** /ˈvɜːtɨ̥brə‖ˈvɜːr-/ *n plural* **vertebrae** /-bri, -breɪ/ [C] one of the small hollow bones down the centre of your back —**vertebral** *adj*

**ver·te·brate** /ˈvɜːtɨ̥brɨ̥t, -breɪt‖ˈvɜːr-/ *n* [C] a living creature that has a BACKBONE (1) —compare INVERTEBRATE —**vertebrate** *adj*

**ver·tex** /ˈvɜːteks‖ˈvɜːr-/ *n plural* **vertices** /-tɨ̥siːz/ *or* **vertexes** [C + **of**] *technical* **1** the angle opposite the base of a shape such as a PYRAMID, CONE, TRIANGLE etc **2** the point where the two lines of an angle meet **3** the highest point: *the vertex of an arch*

**ver·ti·cal¹** /ˈvɜːtɪkəl‖ˈvɜːr-/ *adj* **1** pointing straight up and down in a line and forming an angle of 90 degrees with the ground or with another straight line: *a vertical line* | *blue and green vertical stripes* | *a sheer, vertical cliff* **2** having a structure in which there are top, middle, and bottom levels: *a vertical power relationship between top decision makers and the rest of the organization* —compare HORIZONTAL —**vertically** /-kli/ *adv*

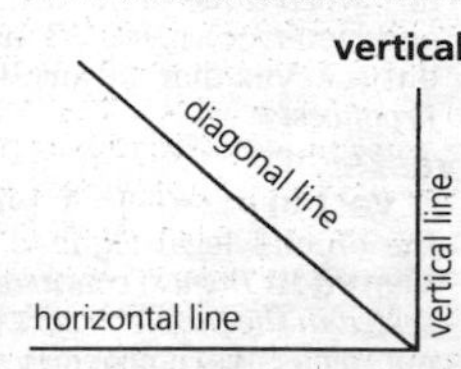


**vertical²** *n* **the vertical** the direction of something that is vertical: *an angle of about 30 degrees off the vertical*

**ver·tig·i·nous** /vɜːˈtɪdʒɨ̥nəs‖vɜːr-/ *adj formal* a vertiginous place or position makes you feel ill because it is so high: *a vertiginous drop to the valley below*

**ver·ti·go** /ˈvɜːtɪgəʊ‖ˈvɜːrtɪgoʊ/ *n* [U] a sick DIZZY (1) feeling caused by looking down from a very high place

**verve** /vɜːv‖vɜːrv/ *n* [U] the quality of being cheerful and exciting which is shown in the way someone does something: *Cziffra played the Hungarian dances with great verve.*

**ve·ry¹** /ˈveri/ *adv* **1** [+ adj/adv] used to emphasize an adjective or adverb or to add force to an expression: *"Can I help you with those bags?" "Thanks, that's very nice of you."* | *It feels very cold up in the bedrooms.* | *I feel a lot better today thanks very much.* | *We must be aware of the very real problems that these people face.* | *The traffic's moving very slowly this morning.* | *James was very much hoping you'd be able to come to the wedding.* | **the very same** (=used to emphasize the fact that one thing is exactly the same as something else) *She was wearing the very same shoes as me.* **2** [+ adj] used to emphasize superlative adjectives: *We only use the very best ingredients.* | *He might have told you he wasn't coming at the very least.* | *This is the very last time I lend you money.* **3 your very own** used to emphasize the fact that something belongs to one particular person and to no one else: *She was thrilled at the idea of having her very own toys to play with.* **4 not** S1 W1

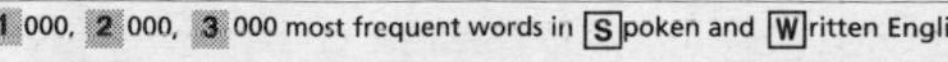

**very** **a)** used before a quality to mean exactly the opposite of that quality: *The teacher wasn't very pleased* (=was angry) *when she saw a dead mouse on the desk.* **b)** only slightly: *"Was the play interesting?" "Not very."*

S2 W1 **very²** *adj* [only before noun] used to emphasize a noun: *He died in this very room.* | **this very minute** (=now) *You'd better start doing some work this very minute.* | **the very thought** (=just thinking about something) *The very thought of food makes me feel ill.* | **the very idea!** (=used to express shock at what someone says or suggests) *Of course you shouldn't travel on your own at that time of night. The very idea!* | **the very thing** (=used to describe an object or idea that is exactly right for a particular purpose) *This gadget is the very thing for turning stiff taps.*

**very high fre·quen·cy** /ˌ·· ˈ···/ *n* [U] VHF

**Ver·y light** /ˈvɪəri laɪt‖ˌveri ˈlaɪt, ˌvɪri-/ *n* [C] *trademark* a bright light produced by a kind of burning bullet that is fired into the air as a signal that a ship needs help

**Very pis·tol** /ˌ·· ˈ··/ *n* [C] the gun from which a Very light is shot

**ves·pers** /ˈvespəz‖-ərz/ *n* [U] the evening service in some types of Christian church

**ves·sel** /ˈvesəl/ *n* [C] **1** *formal* a ship or large boat: *a fishing vessel* **2** *old use or formal* a container for holding liquids **3** *technical* a tube that carries blood through your body, such as a VEIN, or that carries liquid through a plant

**vest¹** /vest/ *n* [C] **1** *BrE* a piece of underwear without SLEEVES that you wear under a shirt; UNDERSHIRT *AmE* —see picture at UNDERWEAR **2** *AmE* a piece of clothing without arms that has buttons down the front and is usually worn under a JACKET, especially by men as part of a suit; WAISTCOAT *BrE* **3** a piece of special clothing without SLEEVES that is worn to protect your body: *a bulletproof vest*

**vest²** *v*

**vest in** *phr v* [T] **1** [**vest** sth **in** sb] to give someone the official legal right to use power, property etc: **be vested in** *In most countries the right to make new laws is vested in the people's representatives.* **2** [**vest in** sb/sth not in passive] if property, power etc vests in someone, it belongs to them legally or officially: *In former times this power vested in the Church.*

**vest** sb **with** sth *phr v* [T] *formal* to give someone the official or legal right to use power, property etc

**ves·tal vir·gin** /ˌvestl ˈvɜːdʒɪn‖-ɜːr-/ *n* [C] a young unmarried woman who had duties in one of the ancient Roman temples

**vested in·terest** /ˌ·· ˈ··/ *n* [C] **1** if you have a vested interest in something happening, you have a strong reason for wanting it to happen because you will get an advantage from it: *The tobacco companies have a vested interest in claiming that smoking isn't harmful.* **2 vested interests** [plural] the groups of people who have a vested interest in something: *The new reforms were opposed by both vested interests and welfare groups.*

**ves·ti·bule** /ˈvestɪbjuːl/ *n* [C] *formal* **1** a wide passage or small room inside the front door of a public building **2** *AmE* the enclosed passage at each end of a railway carriage that connects it with the next carriage

**ves·tige** /ˈvestɪdʒ/ *n* [C] *formal* **1** a small part or amount of something that still remains when most of it no longer exists: [**+ of**] *The new law removed the last vestiges of royal power.* **2** the smallest possible amount of a quality or feeling: [**+ of**] *There's not a vestige of truth in the story.*

**ves·ti·gi·al** /veˈstɪdʒiəl, -dʒəl/ *adj* **1** *technical* a vestigial part of the body has never developed completely or has almost disappeared because it is no longer used: *Some snakes have vestigial legs.* **2** *formal* remaining as a sign that something existed after most of it has disappeared: *vestigial traces of a past civilization* —**vestigially** *adv*

**vest·ment** /ˈvestmənt/ *n* [C often plural] a piece of clothing worn by priests during church services

**ves·try** /ˈvestri/ *n* [C] a small room in a church where the priest and CHOIR change into their vestments and where holy plates, cups etc are stored

**vet¹** /vet/ *n* [C] **1** someone who is trained to give medical care and treatment to sick animals; VETERINARIAN *AmE* **2** *AmE informal* a VETERAN¹: *a Vietnam vet* S

**vet²** *v* [T] **1** *BrE* to check someone's past activities, relationships etc in order to make sure they are suitable for a particular job, especially one that involves dealing with secret information: *The candidates are vetted by Central Office.* **2** to check a report or speech carefully to make sure it is acceptable

**vetch** /vetʃ/ *n* [C] a plant with small flowers, often used to feed farm animals

**vet·e·ran** /ˈvetərən/ *n* [C] **1** someone who has been a soldier, sailor etc in a war: *D Day veterans* | *a veteran of the Second World War* **2** someone who has had a lot of experience of a particular activity: *a veteran traveller* | [**+ of**] *a veteran of the anti-apartheid movement* | **veteran politician/campaigner/statesman etc** (=someone who has been a politician etc for a long time) *veteran Soviet politician Andrei Gromyko*

**veteran car** /ˌ··· ˈ·/ *n* [C] *BrE* a car built before 1905

**vet·e·ri·na·ri·an** /ˌvetərɪˈneəriən‖-ˈner-/ *n* [C] *AmE* someone who is trained to give medical care and treatment to sick animals; VET¹ (1)

**vet·e·ri·na·ry** /ˈvetərɪnəri‖-neri/ *adj* [only before noun] *technical* connected with the medical care and treatment of sick animals: *veterinary science*

**veterinary sur·geon** /ˈ···· ˌ··/ *n* [C] *BrE formal* a VET¹ (1)

**ve·to¹** /ˈviːtəʊ‖-toʊ/ *v* **vetoed, vetoing** [T] **1** to officially refuse to allow something to happen, especially something that other people or organizations have agreed: *The president vetoed a tax increase on gasoline last week.* **2** to refuse to accept a particular plan or suggestion: *Jenny wanted to invite all her friends, but I quickly vetoed that idea.*

**veto²** *n plural* **vetos** [C,U] a refusal to give official permission for something, or the right to refuse to give such permission: [**+ on**] *There is the threat of a presidential veto on this legislation.* | **power/right of veto** *They exercised their right of veto in the Security Council to prevent the resolution being passed.*

**vex** /veks/ *v* [T] *old-fashioned* to make someone feel annoyed or worried

**vex·a·tion** /vekˈseɪʃən/ *n* **1** [U] *formal* the feeling of being worried or annoyed by something **2** [C] *old-fashioned* something that worries or annoys you

**vex·a·tious** /vekˈseɪʃəs/ *adj old-fashioned* making you feel annoyed or worried —**vexatiously** *adv*

**vexed** /vekst/ *adj* **1** [**+ at/with**] *old-fashioned* annoyed or worried **2 vexed question/issue** a complicated problem that has caused a lot of arguments and is difficult to solve: *the vexed question of how to deal with hunger-strikers*

**V-for·ma·tion** /ˈviː fɔːˌmeɪʃən‖-fɔːr-/ *n* [C] if birds or planes fly in a V-formation, they form the shape of the letter V as they fly

**VGA** /ˌviː dʒiː ˈeɪ/ *n* [singular] Video Graphics Array; a standard of GRAPHICS (=pictures and letters) on a computer screen that has many different colours and is of a high quality

**VHF** /ˌviː eɪtʃ ˈef/ *n* [U] *technical* very high frequency; radio waves that move very quickly and produce good sound quality

**vi·a** /ˈvaɪə, ˈviːə/ *prep* **1** travelling through a place on the way to another place: *We flew to Athens via Paris.* **2** using a particular person, machine etc to send something: *I sent a message to Kitty via her sister.* W

**vi·a·ble** /ˈvaɪəbəl/ *adj* **1** a viable plan or system can work successfully: **a viable proposition/alternative/method etc** *Nuclear energy is only one viable alternative to coal or gas.* | **economically/commercially viable** *The project is not economically viable.* **2** *technical* able to continue to live or to develop into a living thing —**viably** *adv* —**viability** /ˌvaɪəˈbɪlɪ̈ti/ *n* [U]: *the long term viability of the company*

**vi·a·duct** /ˈvaɪədʌkt/ *n* [C] a long high bridge across a valley that has a road or railway on it

**vi·al** /ˈvaɪəl/ *n* [C] a PHIAL

**vi·ands** /ˈvaɪəndz/ *n* [plural] *old use* food

**vibes** /vaɪbz/ *n* [plural] *informal* **1** the good or bad feelings that a particular person, group of people, or situation seems to produce and that you react to: **good/bad/strange vibes** *I'm getting strange vibes from this guy, I think he's maybe lying to us.* **2** a VIBRAPHONE

**vi·brant** /ˈvaɪbrənt/ *adj* **1** exciting and full of activity and energy: *Hong Kong is a vibrant, fascinating city.* **2** a vibrant light or colour is bright and strong: *vibrant paintings of bullfights* —**vibrancy** *n* [U] —**vibrantly** *adv*

**vi·bra·phone** /ˈvaɪbrəfəʊn‖-foʊn/ *n* [C] an electronic musical instrument that consists of metal bars that you hit to produce a sound

**vi·brate** /vaɪˈbreɪt‖ˈvaɪbreɪt/ *v* [I,T] to shake or make something shake continuously with small fast movements: *We could feel the floor vibrating to the beat of the music.* | *The vocal cords vibrate as air passes over them.*

**vi·bra·tion** /vaɪˈbreɪʃən/ *n* [C,U] **1** a continuous slight shaking movement: *You can feel the vibrations of the ship's engine.* **2 vibrations** [plural] VIBES (1)

**vi·bra·to** /vɪˈbrɑːtəʊ‖-toʊ/ *n* [U] a way of singing or playing a musical note so that it goes up and down very slightly in PITCH[2] (3)

**vi·brat·or** /vaɪˈbreɪtə‖ˈvaɪbreɪtər/ *n* [C] a piece of electrical equipment that produces a small shaking movement, used especially in MASSAGE or to get sexual pleasure

**vic·ar** /ˈvɪkə‖-ər/ *n* [C] a priest in the Church of England who is in charge of a church in a particular area

**vic·ar·age** /ˈvɪkərɪdʒ/ *n* [C] a house where a vicar lives

**vi·car·i·ous** /vɪˈkeəriəs‖vaɪˈker-/ *adj* [only before noun] experienced by watching or reading about someone else doing something, rather than by doing it yourself: **vicarious pleasure/satisfaction/excitement etc** *the vicarious pleasure that parents get from their children's success* —**vicariously** *adv*

3 **vice** /vaɪs/ *n* **1** [U] evil or criminal activities that involve sex or drugs: **vice ring** (=a group of criminals involved in vice) *The police have smashed a vice ring in Chicago.* **2** [C] a bad habit: *Smoking is my only vice.* **3** [C] a bad or immoral quality in someone's character: *the vice of greed* —opposite VIRTUE **4** usually **vise** *AmE* [C] a tool that holds an object firmly so that you can work on it using both your hands

**vice-** /vaɪs/ *prefix* the person next in official rank below someone, who can represent them or act instead of them: *the Vice-President of the USA* | *the vice-captain of the cricket team*

**vice-ad·mi·ral** /ˌ· ˈ···◂/ *n* [C] a high rank in the British or US navy, or someone who has this rank —see table on page B4

**vice-chan·cel·lor** /ˌ· ˈ···/ *n* [C] **1** someone who is in charge of a British university —compare CHANCELLOR (2) **2** someone who is next in rank to the CHANCELLOR (=person in charge) of a university in the US

**vice·like** /ˈvaɪslaɪk/ *adj* **a vicelike grip** a very firm hold

**vice pres·i·dent** /ˌ· ˈ···/ *n* [C] **1** the person who is next in rank to the president of a country and who is responsible for the president's duties if he or she is ill **2** *AmE* someone who is responsible for a particular part of a company: *our executive vice president for marketing*

**vice·roy** /ˈvaɪsrɔɪ/ *n* [C] a man who was sent by the king or queen to rule another country, especially in the British Empire: *the viceroy of India*

**vice squad** /ˈ· ·/ *n* [C usually singular] the part of the police force that deals with crimes involving sex or drugs

**vice ver·sa** /ˌvaɪs ˈvɜːsə, ˌvaɪsi-‖-ɜːr-/ *adv* used when the opposite of a situation you have just described is also true: *Anything the men wanted the women didn't, and vice versa.*

**vi·cin·i·ty** /vɪ̈ˈsɪnɪ̈ti/ *n* **1 in the vicinity (of)** in the area around a particular place: *The car was found abandoned in the vicinity of Waterloo Station.* **2 in the vicinity of** *formal* close to a particular amount or measurement: *a price somewhere in the vicinity of £25,000*

**vi·cious** /ˈvɪʃəs/ *adj* **1** violent and dangerous, and likely to hurt someone: *a vicious attack* | *a vicious criminal* | *Keep away from that dog, he can be vicious.* **2** cruel and deliberately trying to hurt someone's feelings or make their character seem bad: *Sarah can be quite vicious at times.* | **vicious attack/campaign/rumour etc** *Senator Logan launched a vicious attack on the president and his advisors.* **3** unpleasantly strong or severe: *a vicious gust of wind* | *a vicious headache* —**viciously** *adv*: *He twisted her arm viciously.* —**viciousness** *n* [U]

**vicious cir·cle** /ˌ·· ˈ··/ *n* [singular] a situation in which one problem causes another problem that then causes the first problem again, so that the whole process continues to be repeated

**vi·cis·si·tudes** /vɪ̈ˈsɪsɪ̈tjuːdz‖-tuːdz/ *n* [plural] *formal* the continuous changes and problems that affect a situation or someone's life: *the vicissitudes of married life*

**vic·tim** /ˈvɪktɪ̈m/ *n* [C] **1** someone who has been attacked, robbed, or murdered: *In most sexual offences the attacker is known to the victim.* | **rape/murder etc victim** *Most homicide victims are under 30.* **2** someone who suffers because they are affected by a bad situation or by an illness: *a victim of circumstances* | **famine/earthquake/flood victims** *a massive aid program for the famine victims* | **polio/cholera/AIDS victim** *Many cholera victims were being left to die.* **3** something that is badly affected or destroyed by a situation or action: **fall victim to** (=become a victim of something) *Vital public services have fallen victim to budget cuts.* **4 be a victim of its own success** to be badly affected by some unexpected results of being very successful: *The once-peaceful village has attracted so many tourists that it has become a victim of its own success.* **5 sacrificial victim** a person or animal that is killed and offered as a SACRIFICE[1] (3) (=gift) to a god **6 fashion/style victim** *informal* someone who always wears the newest fashions whether it suits them or not S 2 W 2

**vic·tim·ize** also **-ise** *BrE* /ˈvɪktɪ̈maɪz/ *v* [T] to treat someone unfairly, especially because you dislike their beliefs or the race they belong to: *The sacked men claim they have been victimized because of their political activity.* —**victimization** /ˌvɪktɪ̈maɪˈzeɪʃən‖-mə-/ *n* [U]

**vic·tor** /ˈvɪktə‖-ər/ *n* [C] *formal* the winner of a battle, game, competition etc: *After the game the victors returned in triumph.*

**Vic·to·ri·an¹** /vɪkˈtɔːriən/ *adj* **1** connected with the period from 1837-1901 when Victoria was Queen of England **2** having the strict moral attitudes typical of the society of this period: *Victorian prudery*

**Victorian²** *n* [C] an English person living in the period when Queen Victoria ruled

**vic·to·ri·ous** /vɪkˈtɔːriəs/ *adj* having won a victory: *The victorious team held the trophy aloft.* | *We were confident that the Allies would emerge victorious.* (=finally win) —**victoriously** *adv*

**vic·to·ry** /ˈvɪktəri/ *n* [C,U] **1** the success you achieve by winning a battle, game, race etc: *The streets were full of crowds, all celebrating an Italian victory.* | [+ **over**] *A great shot by Johnson gave the Lakers victory over the Celtics.* | **win a victory** *The Republicans won three election victories in a row.* | **sweep to victory** (=win easily and impressively) *Olson scored four times as the Rams* W 2 *swept to victory.* | **resounding victory** (=a very great victory) —opposite DEFEAT² (1) **2 be a victory for common sense** to be the most sensible way of settling a quarrel, which is not regarded as favourable to either side —see also PYRRHIC VICTORY

**vict·ual** /ˈvɪtl/ *v* [T] to supply a large number of people with food

**vict·uals** /ˈvɪtlz/ *n* [plural] *old use* food and drink

**vi·cu·ña** /vɪˈkjuːnə‖-ˈkuːnjə, vaɪˈkuːnə/ *n* **1** [C] a large South American animal related to the LLAMA, from which soft wool is obtained **2** [U] the cloth made from this wool

**vi·de·li·cet** /vɪ̆ˈdiːlɪ̆set, -ket‖-ˈde-/ *adv Latin formal* VIZ

S1 W2 **vid·e·o¹** /ˈvɪdiəʊ‖-dioʊ/ *n* **1** [C] a copy of a film or television programme recorded on VIDEOTAPE: *I've borrowed the video of 'Gone with the Wind'.* | *a video shop* **2** [C,U] a VIDEOTAPE: *Have we got a blank video anywhere?* | **on video** *'Jurassic Park' is now available on video.* **3** [C] *BrE* a VIDEO CASSETTE RECORDER —see picture on page 837 **4** [U] the process of recording and showing television programmes, films, real events etc using video equipment: *Interactive learning has been greatly advanced by the introduction of video.*

**video²** *v* [T] to record a television programme, film, or a real event on a VIDEOTAPE; TAPE¹ (1a): *Could you video 'The Elvis Presley Story' for me at 8.00?* | *They got a friend to video the wedding.*

**video³** *adj* **1** [only before noun] related to or used in the process of recording and showing pictures on television: **video equipment/recording/system etc** *The VHS and Beta video systems are not compatible.* —compare AUDIO **2** using VIDEOTAPE: *a video recording*

**video ar·cade** /ˈ··· ·ˌ·/ *n* [C] *AmE* a public place where there are a lot of VIDEO GAMES that you play by putting money in the machines

**video cam·e·ra** /ˈ··· ˌ···/ *n* [C] a special camera that can be used to film events using VIDEOTAPE

**video cas·sette** /ˌ··· ·ˈ·/ *n* [C] a VIDEOTAPE

**video cas·sette re·cord·er** /ˌ··· ·ˈ· ·ˌ·/ *n* [C] a machine used to record television programmes or show videos (VIDEO¹ (1)); VCR *especially AmE*, VIDEO¹ (3) *BrE*

**video con·fe·ren·cing** /ˈ··· ˌ····/ *n* [U] a system that allows people to communicate with each other by sending pictures and sounds electronically

**vid·e·o·disc** /ˈvɪdiəʊˌdɪsk‖-dioʊ-/ *n* [C] a round flat piece of plastic from which films can be played in the same way as from a VIDEOTAPE

**video game** /ˈ··· ˌ·/ *n* [C] a game in which you move images on a screen by pressing electronic controls

**vid·e·og·ra·phy** /ˌvɪdiˈɒgrəfi‖-ˈɑːg-/ *n* [U] *formal* the art of recording events with a VIDEO CAMERA —**videographer** *n* [C]

**video jock·ey** /ˈ··· ˌ··/ *n* [C] someone who introduces short VIDEO films on television, especially those showing performances of popular music; VJ

**vid·e·o nas·ty** /ˌ··· ˈ··/ *n* [C] *BrE informal* a VIDEO that includes very violent scenes

**vid·e·o·phone** /ˈvɪdiəʊfəʊn‖-dioʊfoʊn/ *n* [C] a type of telephone that allows you to see the person you are talking to on a machine like a television

**video re·cord·er** /ˈ··· ·ˌ··/ *n* [C] a VIDEO CASSETTE RECORDER

**vid·e·o·tape¹** /ˈvɪdiəʊteɪp‖-dioʊ-/ *n* [C,U] a long narrow band of MAGNETIC material in a flat plastic container, on which films, television programmes etc can be recorded

**videotape²** *v* [T] to record a television programme, film etc on a videotape; VIDEO²

**Vid·e·o·tex** /ˈvɪdiəʊˌteks‖-dioʊ-/ *n* [U] *trademark* a form of communication that allows information to be exchanged using a television system

**vie** /vaɪ/ *v* **vied, vying** [I] to compete very hard with someone in order to get something: [+ **for**] *Simon and Julian were vying for her attention all through dinner.* | **vie with sb to do sth** *The major record companies are vying with each other to sign the group.*

She had a wonderful view from her hotel window.

**view¹** /vjuː/ *n*

**1 ▶ OPINION ◀** [C] what you think or believe about something: [+ **on/about**] *We'd like to find out young people's views on religion.* | **in my/your etc view** (=I, you etc think) *In my view, what this country needs is a change of government.* | **point of view** (=opinion) *No one seemed to want to listen to my point of view.* | **express the view that** (=say you think that) *The chairman expressed the view that it would be better not to increase investments.* | **take the view that** (=have the opinion that) *The judge took the view that a prison sentence would not be appropriate in this case.*

**2 ▶ WAY OF CONSIDERING ◀** [C usually singular] a way of considering or understanding something: [+ **of**] *Has your view of the role of women changed since you got married?* | *James always did have a rather romantic view of life.* | **an inside view** (=based on actual experience in an organization, group etc) *Healey's autobiography gives the reader an inside view of the Labour party.* | **clear view** (=a definite and specific idea about something) *Before doing anything you need to have a clear view of the kind of book you want to write.* | **take a dim/poor view of** (=disapprove) *She takes a pretty dim view of her son's recent behaviour.*

**3 ▶ SIGHT ◀** [C,U] what you are able to see or the possibility of seeing it: **have a good/bad/wonderful etc view (of)** (=be able to see a lot, very little etc) *We had a really good view of the whole stage from where we were sitting.* | **be in view** (=can be seen from where you are) *She waited until the whole island was in view and then took a photograph.* | **come into view** (=begin to be seen) *As we rounded the bend in the river the castle came into view.* | **in full view of** (=happening where people can see it clearly) *Francine screamed and slapped her husband in full view of all the guests.* | **block sb's view** (=stop someone from seeing something) *There was a tall guy sitting in front of me, blocking my view completely.* | **bird's eye view** (=a view seen from above) *We've got a bird's eye view of the football stadium from our office window.*

**4 ▶ SCENERY ◀** [C] the whole area, especially a beautiful place, that you can see from somewhere: *a spectacular view across the valley* | **spoil the view** (=make a view look less beautiful) *A huge nuclear reactor now spoils the view of the coastline.*

**5 ▶ PICTURE ◀** [C] a photograph or picture showing a beautiful or interesting place: *The book contains over fifty scenic views of Cambridge.*

**6 be on view** if paintings, photographs etc are on view, they are in a public place where people can go to look at them: *The Toulouse Lautrec posters are currently on view at the Hayward gallery.*

**7 in view of** used to introduce the reason for your decision or action: *In view of Sutton's recent conduct the club has decided to suspend him until further notice.*

**8 with a view to doing sth** because you are planning to do something in the future: *We bought the cottage with a view to moving there when we retired.*
**9 have sth in view** to have something in your mind as an aim: *He wants to find work, but he has nothing particular in view.*
**10 take the long view (of)** to think about the effect that something will have in the future rather than what happens now

**view²** *v* **1** [T] *formal* to look at something, especially because you are interested: **view sth from** *The buildings are much more impressive when viewed from the other side of the river.* | **view a house/apartment/property** (=go to see the inside of a house etc which you are interested in buying) | **view an exhibition/a garden etc** (=walk around it and look at it) *Thousands of tourists came to view the gardens every year.* **2** [T always + adv/prep] to regard something in a particular way: *Viewed from a financial standpoint, the show was a failure.* | **view sth as** *Conflict is viewed as an inevitable part of the child-parent relationship.* | **view sth with caution/enthusiasm/horror etc** *Offers of rides from strangers should always be viewed with suspicion.* **3** [I,T] *formal* to watch a television programme, film etc: *an opportunity to view the film before it goes on general release*

**view·er** /ˈvjuːə‖-ər/ *n* [C] **1** someone who watches television: *The new series has gone down well with viewers.* **2** a small box with a light in it used to look at SLIDES (=colour photographs on special film)

**view·find·er** /ˈvjuːˌfaɪndə‖-ər/ *n* [C] the small square of glass on a camera that you look through to see exactly what you are photographing —see picture at CAMERA

**view·point** /ˈvjuːpɔɪnt/ *n* [C] **1** a particular way of thinking about a problem or subject: **from a different/practical/religious etc viewpoint** *From an ecological viewpoint, the new motorway has been a disaster.* **2** a place from which you can see something

**vig·il** /ˈvɪdʒɪ̆l/ *n* [C,U] **1** a period of time, especially during the night, when you stay awake in order to pray or remain with someone who is ill: **keep (a) vigil** *For three weeks Jeff kept a vigil while his son lay in a coma.* **2** a silent political protest in which people wait outside a building, especially during the night: **hold a vigil** *Over 2000 demonstrators held a candlelit peace vigil in front of the US embassy.*

**vig·i·lance** /ˈvɪdʒɪ̆ləns/ *n* [U] careful attention that you give to what is happening, so that you will notice any danger or illegal activity: *Constant vigilance is essential to combat drug-smuggling.*

**vig·i·lant** /ˈvɪdʒɪ̆lənt/ *adj* giving careful attention to what is happening, so that you will notice any danger or illegal activity: *Please remain vigilant at all times and report anything suspicious.* —**vigilantly** *adv*

**vig·i·lan·te** /ˌvɪdʒɪ̆ˈlænti/ *n* [C] a member of an official group of people who join together to catch or punish criminals, usually because they think the police are ineffective

**vi·gnette** /vɪˈnjet/ *n* [C] **1** a short description in a book or play showing the typical features of a person or situation **2** a small drawing or pattern placed at the beginning of a book or CHAPTER (1)

**vig·or** /ˈvɪgə‖-ər/ *n* [U] the American spelling of VIGOUR

**vig·o·rous** /ˈvɪgərəs/ *adj* **1** using a lot of energy and strength or determination: *Vigorous efforts will be made to find alternative employment for those made redundant.* | *Your dog needs at least 20 minutes of vigorous exercise every day.* **2 a vigorous opponent/defender etc** someone who opposes or defends something strongly: *a vigorous campaigner for human rights* **3** strong and very healthy: *a vigorous man in the prime of life* —**vigorously** *adv*: *Boil vigorously for five minutes.*

**vig·our** *BrE*, **vigor** *AmE* /ˈvɪgə‖-ər/ *n* [U] physical and mental energy and determination: *He set about his task with renewed vigour.*

**Vi·king** /ˈvaɪkɪŋ/ *n* [C] one of a race of Scandinavian people in the 8th to 10th centuries who sailed in ships to attack areas along the coasts of northern and western Europe

**vile** /vaɪl/ *adj* **1** *informal* very unpleasant or nasty: *This soup is vile.* | *She has a vile temper.* **2** evil: *a vile slander* —**vilely** *adv* —**vileness** *n* [U]

**vil·i·fy** /ˈvɪlɪ̆faɪ/ *v* [T] *formal* to say bad things about someone, especially things that are not true, in order to influence other people against them —**vilification** /ˌvɪlɪ̆fɪ̆ˈkeɪʃən/ *n* [C]: *his vilification by the popular press*

**vil·la** /ˈvɪlə/ *n* [C] **1** a big country house with large gardens **2** *BrE* a house in another country that you can rent for your holidays: *a holiday villa* **3** an ancient Roman house with its own farm

**vil·lage** /ˈvɪlɪdʒ/ *n* [C] **1** *BrE* a very small town in the countryside: **village school/sports/life** *The village fête happens every year in May.* **2 the village** the people who live in a village: *The whole village came to the wedding.* S1 W1

**village green** /ˌ·· ˈ·/ *n* [C] an area of grass in the middle of an English village

**village id·i·ot** /ˌ·· ˈ···/ *n* [C] someone living in a village who is very stupid and does not understand the modern world

**vil·lag·er** /ˈvɪlɪdʒə‖-ər/ *n* [C] someone who lives in a village

**vil·lain** /ˈvɪlən/ *n* [C] **1** the main bad character in a film, play, or story **2** *BrE informal* a bad person or criminal: *Watch him – he's a bit of a villain!* **3 the villain of the piece** *often humorous* the person or thing that has caused all the trouble in a particular situation: *The CIA is commonly regarded as the villain of the piece.*

**vil·lain·ous** /ˈvɪlənəs/ *adj* **1** *literary* evil: *He gave a villainous leer.* **2** *informal* unpleasant or nasty: *a villainous smell*

**vil·lain·y** /ˈvɪləni/ *n* [U] evil or criminal behaviour

**-ville** /vɪl/ *suffix old-fashioned slang, especially AmE* **dullsville/squaresville etc** a place or thing that is dull etc: *This party is really dullsville.*

**vil·lein** /ˈvɪlɪ̆n, ˈvɪleɪn/ *n* [C] a poor farm worker in the Middle Ages who was given a small piece of land in return for working on the land of a rich lord —compare PEASANT (1)

**vim** /vɪm/ *n* [U] *old-fashioned* energy: *bursting with vim and vigour*

**vin·ai·grette** /ˌvɪnɪ̆ˈgret, ˌvɪneɪ-/ *n* [U] a mixture of oil, VINEGAR, salt, and pepper that you put on a SALAD

**vin·di·cate** /ˈvɪndɪ̆keɪt/ *v* [T] *formal* **1** to prove that someone or something is right or true; JUSTIFY: **vindicate an idea/method/decision** *Your decision not to resign has been fully vindicated.* **2** to prove that someone who was blamed for something is in fact not guilty: *The outcome of the trial vindicates Howells completely.* —**vindication** /ˌvɪndɪ̆ˈkeɪʃən/ *n* [singular, U] *Improved economic growth is seen as a vindication of government policies.*

**vin·dic·tive** /vɪnˈdɪktɪv/ *adj* deliberately cruel and unfair, especially to someone who has harmed you: *After the divorce Joan's ex-husband became increasingly vindictive.* —**vindictively** *adv*: *"That'll teach her," he thought vindictively.* —**vindictiveness** *n* [U]

**vine** /vaɪn/ *n* [C] **1** a plant that produces GRAPES **2** *technical* any plant that has thin twisting stems and grows up walls or posts or along the ground

**vin·e·gar** /ˈvɪnɪgə‖-ər/ *n* [U] an acid tasting liquid made from MALT or wine that is used to improve the taste of food or to preserve it

**vin·e·gar·y** /ˈvɪnɪgəri/ *adj* **1** tasting of vinegar **2** bad-tempered and always ready to say unkind things

**vine·yard** /ˈvɪnjəd‖-jərd/ *n* [C] a piece of land where VINES are grown in order to produce wine

**vi·no** /ˈviːnəʊ‖-noʊ/ *n* [U] *informal* wine

**vi·nous** /ˈvaɪnəs/ *adj formal* **1** connected with wine **2** having the colour of red wine

**vin·tage¹** /ˈvɪntɪdʒ/ *adj* **1** vintage wine is good quality wine made in a particular year **2** showing all the best or most typical qualities of something: *His latest film is vintage Spielberg.* **3** *often humorous* old: *Our plane was a vintage Cessna.* **4 vintage year a)** a year when a good quality wine was produced **b)** a year when something of very good quality was produced: *1963 was not a vintage year for movies.*

**vintage²** *n* [C] a particular year in which a wine is made: *1961 was a very good vintage.*

**vintage car** /ˌ·· ˈ·/ *n* [C] *BrE* a car made between 1919 and 1930

**vint·ner** /ˈvɪntnə‖-ər/ *n* [C] someone who buys and sells wines

**vi·nyl** /ˈvaɪnl̩/ *n* [U] **1** a type of strong plastic: *a vinyl chair|vinyl flooring* **2** a word for records that are played on a RECORD PLAYER, used when comparing them to CDS or TAPES: *This album is no longer available on vinyl.*

**vi·o·la** /viˈəʊlə‖-ˈoʊ-/ *n* [C] a musical instrument like a VIOLIN but larger and with a lower sound

**vi·o·late** /ˈvaɪəleɪt/ *v* [T] **1** to disobey or do something against an official agreement, law, principle etc: *practices that violate health and safety regulations|The arrest and detention of the protestors violated their civil liberties.* **2** *formal* to break open a grave, or force your way into a holy place without showing any respect: *The thieves violated the graves searching for gold.* **3 violate the peace/privacy of** *literary* to suddenly spoil a place or situation so that it is no longer peaceful or private **4** *literary* to force a woman to have sex; RAPE —**violator** *n* [C]

**vi·o·la·tion** /ˌvaɪəˈleɪʃən/ *n* [C,U] **1** an action that breaks a law, agreement, principle etc: *human rights violations|*[**+ of**] *violations of the ceasefire|***in violation of** *The court's ruling is in violation of the UN Charter.|a violation of the 3-second rule in basketball* **2** [C,U] *formal* an action that causes harm or damage by treating someone or their possessions without respect: [**+ of**] *I felt her visits were a violation of my privacy.|He regarded the burglary as a violation of his home.*

S2 W2 **vi·o·lence** /ˈvaɪələns/ *n* [U] **1** behaviour that is intended to hurt other people physically: *There is too much sex and violence shown on television.|sporadic outbreaks of violence|robbery with violence|***domestic violence** (=violence between family members)|**act of violence** *acts of violence against the new immigrants|* **resort to violence** (=use violence when nothing else is effective) **2** an angry way of speaking or reacting: *She spoke with a violence that surprised them both.* **3** extreme force: *the violence of the wind* **4 do violence to** *formal* to spoil something

S3 W3 **vi·o·lent** /ˈvaɪələnt/ *adj*
**1 ▶ ACTION ◀** involving actions that are intended to injure or kill people, by hitting them, shooting them etc: *violent crimes such as murder or rape|violent clashes between the police and demonstrators|***violent death** (=murder) *He met a violent death at the hands of the mob.*
**2 ▶ PERSON ◀** likely to attack, hurt, or kill other people: *My father was a violent and dangerous man.|***turn/get violent** (=suddenly become violent) *Keep the handcuffs on the prisoner in case he turns violent.*
**3 ▶ ARGUMENT/WORDS ◀** showing very strong angry emotions or opinions: *They had a violent quarrel over Dave's drinking.|His speech was full of violent denunciations of the government's promises.*
**4 ▶ EMOTIONS ◀** strong and very difficult to control: *She has a violent temper/|They took a violent dislike to each other.*
**5 violent film/play/drama** a film etc that shows a lot of violent actions
**6 violent storm/earthquake/explosion etc** a storm etc that happens with a lot of force
**7 a violent headache/fit/coughing etc** a physical feeling or reaction that is very painful or difficult to control
**8 ▶ COLOUR ◀** extremely bright: *Her cheeks turned a violent red colour.* —**violently** *adv*: *She became violently aggressive.|Matthew trembled violently.*

**vi·o·let** /ˈvaɪəlɪt/ *n* [C] **1** a small plant with sweet-smelling dark purple flowers —see also SHRINKING VIOLET **2** [C,U] a colour between purple and blue —**violet** *adj* —see picture on page 411

**vi·o·lin** /ˌvaɪəˈlɪn/ *n* [C] the smallest instrument in the group of wooden musical instruments that are played by pulling a special stick across wire strings —**violinist** *n* [C]

**vi·o·lin·cel·lo** /ˌvaɪəlɪnˈtʃeləʊ‖-loʊ/ *n* [C] a CELLO

**VIP** /ˌviː aɪ ˈpiː/ *n* [C] a very important person; someone who is very famous or powerful and is treated with special care and respect: *the VIP lounge at the airport*

**vi·per** /ˈvaɪpə‖-ər/ *n* [C] **1** a small poisonous snake **2** *literary* someone who behaves in a nasty way and harms other people

**vi·ra·go** /vɪˈrɑːgəʊ‖-goʊ/ *n* [C] *formal* a BAD-TEMPERED woman with a loud voice

**vi·ral** /ˈvaɪərəl‖ˈvaɪrəl/ *adj* connected with or caused by a VIRUS: *viral pneumonia*

**vir·gin¹** /ˈvɜːdʒɪn‖ˈvɜːr-/ *n* [C] **1** someone who has never had sex **2 the Virgin Mary**, the mother of Jesus

**virgin²** *adj* **1 virgin land/forest/soil etc** land etc that is still in its natural state and has not been used or changed by people: **virgin snow** (=fresh and not spoiled) **2** [only before noun] without sexual experience: *a virgin bride*

**vir·gin·al** /ˈvɜːdʒɪnəl‖ˈvɜːr-/ *adj* like a virgin

**vir·gin·als** /ˈvɜːdʒɪnəlz‖ˈvɜːr-/ *n* [plural] a small square musical instrument like a piano with no legs, popular in the 16th and 17th centuries

**virgin birth** /ˌ·· ˈ·/ *n* [singular] the birth of Jesus, which Christians believe was caused by God, not by sex between a man and a woman

**vir·gin·i·a creep·er** /vɜːˌdʒɪniə ˈkriːpə‖vɜːrˌdʒɪniə ˈkriːpər/ *n* [C,U] a garden plant that grows up walls and has large leaves that turn deep red in autumn; WOODBINE *AmE*

**vir·gin·i·ty** /vɜːˈdʒɪnɪti‖vɜːr-/ *n* [U] the condition of never having had sex: **lose your virginity** (=have sex for the first time) *She was 17 when she lost her virginity* —compare CHASTITY

**Vir·go** /ˈvɜːgəʊ‖ˈvɜːrgoʊ/ *n* **1** [singular] the sixth sign of the ZODIAC, represented by a young woman, and believed to affect the character and life of people born between August 23 and September 22 **2** [C] someone who was born between August 23 and September 22

**vir·ile** /ˈvɪraɪl‖ˈvɪrəl/ *adj* **1** looking or behaving in a way that is typical of a man by being strong, brave, full of energy etc and therefore sexually attractive: *He had a muscular and virile body.* **2** virile qualities and actions show typically male strength and energy: *virile sports such as rugby*

**vi·ril·i·ty** /vɪˈrɪlɪti/ *n* [U] **1** the typically male quality of being strong, brave, and full of energy, in a way that is sexually attractive **2** the ability of a man to have sex; POTENCY

**vi·rol·o·gy** /vaɪəˈrɒlədʒi‖vaɪˈrɑː-/ *n* [U] the scientific study of VIRUSes or of the diseases caused by them

**vir·tu·al** /ˈvɜːtʃuəl‖ˈvɜːr-/ *adj* **1 virtual peace/darkness/destruction etc** something that is so nearly complete peace etc that any difference is unimportant: *We have achieved virtual perfection in sound reproduction.|* **be a virtual certainty/impossibility etc** (=be almost certain, impossible etc) *Car ownership is a virtual necessity when you live in the country.* **2 virtual leader/prisoner etc** someone who is in fact a leader, prisoner etc but not officially one: *The president was so much under his wife's influence that she was the virtual ruler of the country.*

**vir·tu·al·ly** /ˈvɜːtʃuəli‖ˈvɜːr-/ *adv* so nearly that any difference is not important; ALMOST: *Communism has virtually disappeared from Western Europe.|Virtually all the children come to school by bus.*

**virtual re·al·i·ty** /ˌ··· ·'···/ *n* [U] an image produced by a computer that surrounds the person looking at it and seems almost real

3 **vir·tue** /'vɜːtʃuː‖'vɜːr-/ *n* **1** [U] *formal* moral goodness of character and behaviour: *a man of the highest virtue* —opposite VICE **2** [C] a particular good quality in someone's character: *Among her many virtues are loyalty, courage and truthfulness.* **3** [C,U] an advantage that makes something better or more useful than something else: *Free trade has a number of virtues.* | **the virtue of** *The Johnson plan has the virtue of flexibility.* **4 by/in virtue of** *formal* by means of or as a result of something: *She became a British citizen by virtue of her marriage.* **5 make a virtue of necessity** to get an advantage out of doing something that you have to do

**vir·tu·os·i·ty** /ˌvɜːtʃu'ɒsɪ̈ti‖ˌvɜːrtʃu'ɑː-/ *n* [U] *formal* a very high degree of skill in performing: *the violinist's incredible virtuosity*

**vir·tu·o·so** /ˌvɜːtʃu'əʊsəʊ‖ˌvɜːrtʃu'oʊsoʊ/ *n* [C] someone who is a very skilful performer, especially in music: *a virtuoso performance*

**vir·tu·ous** /'vɜːtʃuəs‖'vɜːr-/ *adj* **1** *formal* behaving in a very honest and moral way: *Thomas Dunlop was a virtuous man and a leader in the community.* **2** too satisfied with your own good behaviour and showing this in a way that annoys other people: *She threw up her hands in virtuous indignation.* —**virtuously** *adv* —**virtuousness** *n* [U]

**vir·u·lent** /'vɪrɪ̈lənt/ *adj* **1** *formal* virulent emotions or speeches are full of hatred and very strongly expressed: *virulent anti-Semitism* **2** a poison, disease etc that is virulent is very dangerous and affects people very quickly: *a virulent form of malaria* —**virulence** *n* [U]: *the virulence of an epidemic* —**virulently** *adv*

**vi·rus** /'vaɪərəs‖'vaɪrəs/ *n* **1** [C] a very small living thing, smaller than BACTERIA, that causes infectious illnesses: *the common cold virus* | *virus infections* **2** [C] the illness caused by a virus: *She's got some virus.* **3** [C,U] a set of instructions secretly put into a computer, that can destroy information stored in the computer

**vi·sa** /'viːzə/ *n* [C] an official mark put on your passport by the representative of a foreign country, that gives you permission to enter, pass through, or leave that country: **tourist/exit/entry visa** *She came here on a tourist visa, but it has expired.* —**visa** *v* [T]

**vis·age** /'vɪzɪdʒ/ *n* [C] *literary* a face

**vis-à-vis** /ˌviːz ɑː 'viː, ˌviːz ə 'viː/ *prep formal* in relation to or in comparison with something or someone: *the bargaining position of the worker vis-à-vis the employer*

**vis·ce·ra** /'vɪsərə/ *n* [plural] *technical* the large organs inside your body, such as your heart, lungs, stomach etc

**vis·ce·ral** /'vɪsərəl/ *adj* **1** *literary* visceral beliefs and attitudes are the result of strong feelings rather than careful thought: *a visceral hostility to communism* **2** *technical* connected with the viscera

**vis·cid** /'vɪsɪd/ *adj* VISCOUS

**vis·count** /'vaɪkaʊnt/ *n* [C] a British NOBLEMAN with a rank between that of an EARL and a BARON

**vis·count·cy** /'vaɪkaʊntsi/ *n* [C] the rank or title of a viscount

**vis·count·ess** /'vaɪkaʊntɪ̈s/ *n* [C] the wife of a viscount, or a woman who has the rank of a viscount

**vis·cous** /'vɪskəs/ *adj technical* a viscous liquid is thick and sticky and does not flow easily —**viscosity** /vɪ'skɒsɪ̈ti‖-'skɑː-/ *n* [U]

**vise** /vaɪs/ *n* [C] the usual American spelling of VICE (4)

**vis·i·bil·i·ty** /ˌvɪzɪ̈'bɪlɪ̈ti/ *n* [U] **1** how far it is possible to see, especially when this is affected by weather conditions: *Visibility is down to 20 metres due to heavy fog.* | **good/poor visibility** *The search for survivors was abandoned because of poor visibility.* **2** the fact of something being easy to see

3 **vis·i·ble** /'vɪzɪ̈bəl/ *adj* **1** something that is visible can be seen: *The outline of the mountains was clearly visible.* **2** an effect that is visible is strong enough to be noticed: *There is a visible change in attitudes to working women.* | *She showed visible signs of annoyance.* **3** someone who is visible is always on television, in the newspapers etc: *highly visible politicians*

**vis·i·bly** /'vɪzɪ̈bli/ *adv* in a way that is easy to see or notice: *He was visibly shaken by her accusation.*

**vi·sion** /'vɪʒən/ *n* 

**1 ▶ SIGHT ◀** [U] your ability to see: *With my new glasses my vision is perfect!* | *Tears blurred her vision.* | **field of vision** (=the area in which you are able to see things) *As the cars overtake you, they are temporarily outside your field of vision.* | **20-20 vision** (=perfect vision)

**2 ▶ IDEA ◀** [C] a picture in your mind of a possible situation or scene: [+ **of**] *He conjured up a vision of a world without national divisons.* | **have visions of** (=think a situation is likely to happen) *The airport bus broke down and Tim had visions of missing his plane.*

**3 ▶ IN A DREAM ◀** [C] something that you seem to see, especially in a dream, as part of a powerful religious experience: *She had a vision in which Jesus appeared before her.*

**4 ▶ FUTURE PLANS ◀** [U] the knowledge and imagination that are needed in planning for the future with a clear purpose: *At last we have a leader with vision and strong principles*

**5 a vision of innocence/beauty etc** *literary* something you see which shows a particular quality or attitude

**6 ▶ TELEVISION ◀** [U] the quality of a picture that you can see on a television: *interference affecting sound and vision*

**vi·sion·a·ry**[1] /'vɪʒənəri‖-neri/ *adj* **1** having clear ideas of what the world should be like in the future: *Le Corbusier was a great visionary architect.* **2** existing only in someone's mind and unlikely to ever exist in the real world

**visionary**[2] *n* [C] **1** someone who has clear ideas and strong feelings about the way something should be in the future: *a visionary with a passionate belief in liberty* **2** a holy person who has visions (VISION (3))

**vis·it**[1] /'vɪzɪ̈t/ *v* **1** [I,T] to go and spend time in a place or with someone, especially for pleasure or interest: *"Do you live here?" "No, we're just visiting".* | **visit sth** *We hope to visit the Grand Canyon on our trip.* | **visit sb** *Aunt Jane usually visits us for two or three weeks in the spring.* | [+ **in/on/at/with**] *AmE*: *When you are visiting in Washington, be sure to see the Air and Space Museum.* **2** [T] to go to see a doctor, lawyer etc in order to get treatment or advice **3** [T] to go to a place in order to examine it officially: *The building inspector is visiting the new housing project.* **4** [I] *AmE* to talk socially with someone: [+ **with**] *While Mom visited with Phyllis we played in the yard.* 

**visit** sth **on** sb/sth *phr v* [T] *especially biblical* to do something to punish someone or show them that you are angry: *God's wrath will be visited on sinners.*

**USAGE NOTE: VISIT**

WORD CHOICE: **visit, go to, go and see, have been to, come and see**

**Visit** is slightly formal. More often you would say you **go to** a place or **go and see/go to see** a place or a person. You might write: *We visited the Grand Canyon* or *I visited my mother* but in spoken English you are more likely to say: *We went to the Grand Canyon* or *I went to see my mother.* Note that you would also say: *I've been to Hong Kong several times* and *When you are in Tokyo you must come and see me.*

**visit**[2] *n* [C] W3 **1** an occasion when someone visits a place or person: [+ **to**] *a visit to New York* | **on a visit** *We're just here on a short visit.* | **pay sb a visit** *I must pay our new neighbors a visit.* | **have a visit from** *I've just had a visit from the police.* | **flying visit** (=a very short visit) *We made a flying visit to my mother's to pick up the wedding presents.* **2** an occasion when you see a doctor, lawyer etc for treatment or advice: **pay a visit** *I must pay a visit* *to the dentist.* | **home visit** (=when a doctor comes to your home) **3** *AmE* an occasion when you talk socially with someone, or the time you spend doing this: *Barbara and I had a nice long visit.*

**vis·i·ta·tion** /ˌvɪzəˈteɪʃən/ *n* [C] **1** *formal* an official visit, usually made in order to examine something or someone: *a parental visitation of the school* **2** *literary* an event that is believed to be God's punishment for something: [+ **of**] *visitations of plague, famine, and war* **3** *humorous* a long visit from someone that you do not want to see

**visiting card** /ˈ··· ·/ *n* [C] a small card with your name printed on it that people used to give to the people they visited

**visiting fire·man** /ˌ··· ˈ··/ *n* [C] *especially AmE* an important visitor that you need to entertain in a special way

**visiting hours** /ˈ··· ·/ *n* [plural] the times during which you can visit people who are ill in hospital

**visiting pro·fes·sor** /ˌ··· ·ˈ··/ *n* [C] a university teacher who has come from another university to teach for a period of time

S2 W2 **vis·it·or** /ˈvɪzətə‖-ər/ *n* [C] someone who comes to visit a place or a person: *They were expecting visitors and had cleaned the house.* | *travel tips for visitors to the USA* —see also HEALTH VISITOR

**visitors' book** /ˈ··· ·/ *n* [C] a book, especially in a church or other important building, in which visitors write their names and addresses

**vi·sor** /ˈvaɪzə‖-ər/ *n* [C] **1** the part of a HELMET (=protective hard hat) that can be lowered to protect your face **2** *AmE* the curved part of a cap that sticks out in front above your eyes; PEAK[1] (4) *BrE* —see picture at CAP[1] **3** a flat piece of material above the front window inside a car that can be pulled down to keep the sun out of your eyes; SUN VISOR **4** a curved piece of plastic that you wear on your head so that it sticks out above your eyes and protects them from the sun

**vis·ta** /ˈvɪstə/ *n* [C] **1** *literary* a far view of beautiful scenery, especially looking between rows of trees, buildings etc: *The balcony commanded a vista of the harbour.* **2** the possibility of new experiences, ideas, events etc: *Exchange programs open up new vistas for students.*

W3 **vi·su·al** /ˈvɪʒuəl/ *adj* connected with seeing: *visual identification of the subject by a witness* | *a powerful visual impact*

**visual aid** /ˌ··· ˈ·/ *n* [C] something such as a map, picture, film etc that helps people understand, learn, or remember information

**visual arts** /ˌ··· ˈ·/ *n* [plural] art such as painting, SCULPTURE, etc that you look at, as opposed to literature or music that you read or hear

**visual dis·play u·nit** /ˌ··· ·ˈ· ˌ··/ *n* [C] VDU

**vi·su·al·ize** also **-ise** *BrE* /ˈvɪʒuəlaɪz/ *v* [T] to form a picture of someone or something in your mind; IMAGINE: *Try to visualize a successful future.* | **visualize sb doing sth** *Somehow I can't visualize myself teaching adults.* | **visualize how/what etc** *It's hard to visualize how these tiles will look in our bathroom.* —**visualization** /ˌvɪʒuəlaɪˈzeɪʃən‖-lə-/ *n* [U]

**vi·su·al·ly** /ˈvɪʒuəli/ *adv* **1** in appearance: *a visually stunning production* **2** **visually impaired/handicapped** unable to see normally: *She teaches visually impaired children.* **3** if you explain something visually, you let people see it by using pictures or films, or by showing real things: *The process is easy to understand when it is demonstrated visually.*

W2 **vi·tal** /ˈvaɪtl/ *adj* **1** extremely important and necessary for something to succeed or exist: *Choosing the right equipment is vital.* | [+ **to**] *Such measures are vital to national security.* | [+ **for**] *Regular exercise is vital for your health.* | **it is vital that** *It is vital that you keep accurate records.* | **vital importance** *The industry is of vital importance to the national economy.* | **play a vital role** *Richardson played a vital role in the team's success.* **2** full of energy in a way that is exciting and attractive: *The drawings were crude but wonderfully vital.* | *a strong, vital man* **3** [only before noun] necessary in order to keep you alive: *the body's vital processes* | *the vital organs* (=heart, brain etc)

**vi·tal·i·ty** /vaɪˈtæləti/ *n* [U] **1** great energy and cheerfulness: *Despite her eighty years Elsie was full of vitality.* **2** the ability of an organization, country etc to continue working effectively: *The process of restructuring has injected some much-needed vitality into the company.*

**vi·tal·ly** /ˈvaɪtl-i/ *adv* in a very important or necessary way: *The way we treat our planet now will vitally affect the future of the human race.* | **vitally important** (=extremely important) *It's vitally important that you all attend the meeting.*

**vi·tals** /ˈvaɪtlz/ *n* [plural] *old use* the parts of your body that are necessary to keep you alive, such as your heart and lungs

**vital sta·tis·tics** /ˌ·· ·ˈ··/ *n* [plural] **1** *BrE humorous* a woman's chest, waist, and HIP measurements **2** figures that show the number of births, deaths, marriages etc within a population

**vit·a·min** /ˈvɪtəmən, ˈvaɪ-‖ˈvaɪ-/ *n* [C] a natural substance found in food that is necessary for good health: *Milk is rich in vitamins.* | *vitamin pills* | **vitamin A/B/C etc** (=a particular type of vitamin) *Lack of vitamin A can cause blindness.*

**vi·ti·ate** /ˈvɪʃieɪt/ *v* [T usually passive] *formal* to make something less effective or spoil it: *The conclusions were vitiated by doubts concerning the scientific evidence.* —**vitiation** /ˌvɪʃiˈeɪʃən/ *n* [U]

**vit·i·cul·ture** /ˈvɪtəkʌltʃə‖-ər/ *n* [U] the study or practice of growing GRAPES for making wine

**vit·re·ous** /ˈvɪtriəs/ *adj* made of or looking like glass

**vit·ri·fy** /ˈvɪtrəfaɪ/ *v* [I,T] *technical* if a substance vitrifies or is vitrified, it changes into glass —**vitrification** /ˌvɪtrəfəˈkeɪʃən/ *n* [U]

**vit·ri·ol** /ˈvɪtriəl/ *n* [U] **1** *literary* very cruel remarks that are intended to hurt someone's feelings **2** *old-fashioned* SULPHURIC ACID

**vit·ri·ol·ic** /ˌvɪtriˈɒlɪk◂‖-ˈɑːlɪk◂/ *adj* vitriolic language is very cruel and intended to hurt someone's feelings: *a vitriolic attack on homosexuals* —**vitriolically** /-kli/ *adv*

**vitro** *n* —see IN VITRO

**vi·tu·pe·ra·tion** /vɪˌtjuːpəˈreɪʃən‖vaɪˌtuː-/ *n* [U] *formal* angry and cruel criticism: *the subject of daily vituperation and abuse*

**vi·tu·pe·ra·tive** /vɪˈtjuːpərətɪv‖vaɪˈtuː-/ *adj formal* full of angry and cruel criticism

**vi·va**[1] /ˈvaɪvə/ *n* [C] *BrE informal* a spoken examination taken at the end of a university course; VIVA VOCE

**viva**[2] *interjection* used to show that you approve of someone and want them to continue to exist or be successful: *Viva Eliot!*

**vi·va·ce** /vɪˈvɑːtʃi, -tʃeɪ/ *adj, adv* music that is vivace is played quickly and with a lot of energy

**vi·va·cious** /vəˈveɪʃəs‖və-, vaɪ-/ *adj* a woman who is vivacious has a lot of energy and a happy attractive manner: *a vivacious and outgoing personality* —**vivaciously** *adv* —**vivaciousness** *n* [U] —**vivacity** /vəˈvæsəti‖və-, vaɪ-/ *n* [U]

**vi·var·i·um** /vaɪˈveəriəm‖-ˈver-/ *n* [C] a place indoors where animals are kept in conditions that are as similar as possible to their natural environment

**viv·a voc·e** /ˌvaɪvə ˈvəʊsi, -ˈvəʊtʃi‖ˌvaɪvə ˈvoʊsi, ˌviːvə ˈvoʊtʃeɪ/ *n* [C] *BrE formal* a VIVA[1]

**viv·id** /ˈvɪvəd/ *adj* **1** vivid memories, dreams, descriptions etc are so clear that they seem real: *a vivid account of their journey across the desert* **2** **vivid imagination** an ability to imagine unlikely situations very clearly **3** vivid colours or patterns are very bright: *The lake was a vivid blue.* —**vividly** *adv*: *I can vividly remember the day we met.* —**vividness** *n* [U]

**viv·i·sec·tion** /ˌvɪvɪ̈ˈsekʃən/ *n* [U] the practice of cutting open the bodies of living animals in order to do medical or scientific tests on them —**vivisectionist** *n* [C]

**vix·en** /ˈvɪksən/ *n* [C] **1** a female FOX¹ (1) **2** *old-fashioned* a BAD-TEMPERED woman —**vixenish** *adj*

**viz** /vɪz/ *adv formal* used to introduce specific details that make your meaning clearer; NAMELY

**vi·zier** /vɪ̈ˈzɪə‖-ˈzɪr/ *n* [C] an important politician in certain Muslim countries in the past

**VJ** /ˌviː ˈdʒeɪ/ *n* [C] a VIDEO JOCKEY

**V-neck** /ˈviː nek/ *n* [C] an opening for the neck shaped like the letter V, in a piece of clothing —**V-necked** *adj*: *a V-necked sweater* —see picture on page 840

**vo·cab** /ˈvəʊkæb‖ˈvoʊ-/ *n* [U] *informal* VOCABULARY (5)

**vo·cab·u·la·ry** /vəˈkæbjɵləri, vəʊ-‖-leri, voʊ-/ *n* **1** [C,U] all the words that someone knows, learns, or uses: *Considering he's only six, he has an excellent vocabulary.* | **wide/limited vocabulary** (=a large or small vocabulary) | **increase/extend/build up/enrich your vocabulary** *You should read more literature to enrich your vocabulary.* **2** [C,U] the words that are typically used when talking about a particular subject: *Most technical jobs use a specialized vocabulary.* | [+ **of**] *the vocabulary of politics* **3** [C] all the words in a particular language **4 the word failure/compromise etc is not in sb's vocabulary** used to say that someone never thinks of accepting failure etc **5** [C] a list of words with explanations of their meanings, in a book for learning foreign languages **6** [C,U] a list of the codes (CODE¹ (7)) or terms (TERM¹ (5)) used in a computer system

**vo·cal¹** /ˈvəʊkəl‖ˈvoʊ-/ *adj* **1** protesting or complaining strongly and loudly about something: *a vocal critic of the government* **2** [only before noun] connected with the voice: *The song suited the singer's vocal range.* —**vocally** *adv*

**vocal²** *n* [C usually plural] the part of a piece of music that is sung rather than played on an instrument: *vocals by John Lennon and Paul McCartney*

**vocal cords, vocal chords** /ˈ·· ·, ˌ·· ˈ·/ *n* [plural] thin pieces of muscle in your throat that produce sounds when you are speaking —see picture at BODY

**vo·cal·ist** /ˈvəʊkəlɪ̈st‖ˈvoʊ-/ *n* [C] someone who sings popular songs, especially with a band —compare INSTRUMENTALIST

**vo·ca·tion** /vəʊˈkeɪʃən‖voʊ-/ *n* **1** [C] a job that you do because you have a very strong feeling that doing this job is the purpose of your life, and especially because you want to help other people: *Teaching isn't just a job – it's a vocation.* | **find your vocation** *She felt that she had found her vocation when she began writing children's books.*—see JOB (USAGE) **2** [C,U] a special ability to do a particular job or activity, especially one that gives service to other people: [+ **for**] *He has a vocation for teaching.* **3** [C,U] a strong belief that you have been chosen by God to be a priest or a NUN: *a vocation for the priesthood*; CALLING

**vo·ca·tion·al** /vəʊˈkeɪʃənəl‖voʊ-/ *adj* **vocational training/guidance/course etc** training etc that teaches you the skills you need to do a particular job

**voc·a·tive** /ˈvɒkətɪv‖ˈvɑː-/ *n* [C] *technical* a particular form of a noun in certain languages, used when speaking or writing to someone —**vocative** *adj*

**vo·cif·er·ate** /vəˈsɪfəreɪt, vəʊ-‖voʊ-/ *v* [I] *formal* to shout loudly, especially when complaining —**vociferation** /vəˌsɪfəˈreɪʃən, vəʊ-‖voʊ-/ *n* [C, U]

**vo·cif·er·ous** /vəˈsɪfərəs, vəʊ-‖voʊ-/ *adj formal* **1** expressing your opinions loudly and strongly: *vociferous protesters* **2** vociferous opinions are loudly and strongly expressed: *a vociferous debate* —**vociferously** *adv* —**vociferousness** *n* [U]

**vod·ka** /ˈvɒdkə‖ˈvɑːdkə/ *n* [U] a strong clear alcoholic drink from Russia

**vogue** /vəʊg‖voʊg/ *n* [singular, U] if something is the vogue, it is popular or fashionable for a period of time: [+ **for**] *the vogue for childbirth at home* | **be in vogue/be the vogue** *Short skirts are very much in vogue just now.*

**vogue word** /ˌ· ˈ·/ *n* [C] a word that is fashionable for a short period of time

**voice¹** /vɔɪs/ *n* S2 W1

**1 ▶ SPEAKING ◀** [C,U] the sounds that you make when you speak: *He recognized her voice instantly.* | *I could hear voices in the next room.* | **a loud/deep/soft/husky etc voice** *a child with a squeaky voice* | **angry/excited/worried etc voice** *the angry voices of disgruntled passengers* | **in a deep/angry etc voice** *He spoke in a pleasantly deep voice.* | **a small voice** (=a quiet and shy voice) | **sb's tone of voice** (=the quality of someone's voice which expresses their attitude) *I could tell from his tone of voice that he was not impressed.* | **raise your voice** (=speak more loudly, especially in an angry way) *I know what you're saying – there's no need to raise your voice.* | **lower/drop your voice** (=speak more quietly) *She moved closer and lowered her voice so Alex wouldn't hear.* | **keep your voice down** *spoken* (=used to tell someone to speak more quietly) | **at the top of your voice** (=shouting as loudly as you can) *I could hear him screaming and yelling at the top of his voice.* | **sb's voice breaks** (=when a boy's voice becomes deeper like a man's) *He was 13 and his voice was already starting to break.* —see NOISE¹ (USAGE)

**2 deep-voiced/husky-voiced etc** having a voice that is deep etc

**3 ▶ ABILITY TO SPEAK ◀** [U] the ability to use your voice: *You won't have any voice left if you keep shouting like that.* | **close your voice** (=be unable to speak because you have a sore throat)

**4 ▶ SINGING ◀ a)** [C,U] the quality of sound you produce when you sing: *a young man with a fine singing voice* | **be in good voice** (=be singing well) **b)** [C] a person singing: *a piece written for six voices and piano*

**5 ▶ OPINION ◀ a)** [singular, U] the right or ability to express an opinion, to vote, or to influence decisions: **have a voice (in)** *It is important that parents should have a voice in deciding how their children are educated.* | **give voice to** (=express opinions or feelings openly) *Only Hartman dared to give voice to their discontent.* **b)** [C] an opinion or wish that is expressed: *The government should listen to the voice of the black community.* | **dissenting voices** (=people expressing disagreement) | **add/lend your voice etc** (=express your support for something) *Carter lent his powerful voice to the call for disarmament.* | **raise your voice against** (=oppose something publicly) *Not a voice was raised against the plan.* | **make your voice heard** (=express your opinion so that people notice it)

**6 speak with one voice** if a group of people speak with one voice, they all express the same opinion

**7 ▶ REPRESENTATIVE ◀** [singular] a person, organization, newspaper etc that expresses the opinions or wishes of a group of people: *Martin Luther King had become the voice of the Civil Rights Movement.*

**8 the voice of reason/sanity/experience etc** opinions or ideas that are reasonable, sensible, based on experience etc: *"Marriage is a very risky business." "Ah, there speaks the voice of experience!"*

**9 inner voice** thoughts or feelings which you do not express but which seem to warn you or advise you: *My inner voice told me to be cautious.*

**10 active/passive voice** *technical* the form of a verb that shows whether the subject of a sentence does an action or has an action done to it

**voice²** *v* [T] **1** to tell people your opinions or feelings about a particular subject: **voice opinions/doubts etc** *He voiced several objections to the plan.* **2** *technical* to produce a sound with a movement of the VOCAL CORDS as well as the breath

**voice box** /ˈ· ·/ *n* [C] *not technical* the part of your throat that you use to produce sounds when you speak; LARYNX

**voiced** /vɔɪst/ *adj technical* voiced sounds are made using the VOCAL CORDS. For example /d/ and /g/ are voiced consonants

**voice·less** /ˈvɔɪsləs/ *adj technical* voiceless sounds are made without using the VOCAL CORDS. For example /p/ and /k/ are voiceless consonants

**voice mail** /ˈ· ·/ *n* [U] a system in which spoken messages are recorded onto a computer so that someone can listen to them later

**voice-o·ver** /ˈ· ··/ *n* [C] an explanation or remarks that are spoken on a television advertisement or film by someone who cannot be seen

**voice print** /ˈ· ·/ *n* [C] the sound of a particular person's voice recorded on a machine, which can be used to check who that person is

**void[1]** /vɔɪd/ *adj* **1** *law* a contract or official agreement that is void is not legal and has no effect; NULL AND VOID **2 be void of** *formal* to completely lack something: *Her eyes were void of all expression.*

**void[2]** *n* [C usually singular] **1** a feeling of great sadness that you have when someone you love dies or when something is taken from you: *Their son's death left a painful void in their lives.* **2** an empty area of space where nothing exists: *the void between atoms* | *She looked over the cliff into the void.* **3** a situation in which something important or interesting that previously existed is no longer present: *Many women re-enter the workforce after raising a family to fill a void in their lives.*

**void[3]** *v* [T] **1** *law* to make a contract or agreement void so that it has no legal effect **2 void the bladder/bowels** *formal* to pass waste liquid or solid matter from your body

**voi·là** /vwɑːˈlɑː/ *interjection French* used when suddenly showing something to someone: *Voilà! Your birthday cake!*

**voile** /vɔɪl/ *n* [U] a very light almost transparent cloth made of cotton, wool, or silk

**vol.** the written abbreviation for VOLUME

**vol·a·tile** /ˈvɒlətaɪl‖ˈvɑːlətl/ *adj* **1** a volatile situation is likely to change suddenly and without much warning: *a volatile economic environment* **2** someone who is volatile can suddenly become angry or violent **3** a volatile liquid or substance changes easily into a gas —**volatility** /ˌvɒləˈtɪləti‖ˌvɑː-/ *n* [U]

**vol-au-vent** /ˌvɒl əʊ ˈvɒn‖ˌvɔːləˈvɑːn/ *n* [C] *French* a small round piece of PASTRY that is filled with chicken, vegetables etc

**vol·can·ic** /vɒlˈkænɪk‖vɑːl-/ *adj* **1** connected with or caused by a volcano: *black volcanic sand* **2** happening or reacting suddenly and violently: *a man of volcanic passions*

**vol·ca·no** /vɒlˈkeɪnəʊ‖vɑːlˈkeɪnoʊ/ *n plural* **volcanoes** *or* **volcanos** [C] a mountain with a large hole at the top, through which hot rocks, LAVA, and ash sometimes rise into the air from inside the earth: *Pompeii was destroyed when the volcano erupted in 79AD.* | **active volcano** (=a volcano that may explode at any time) | **dormant volcano** (=a volcano that is not active at present) | **extinct volcano** (=a volcano that is no longer active)

**vole** /vəʊl‖voʊl/ *n* [C] a small animal like a mouse with a short tail that lives in fields and woods and near rivers

**vo·li·tion** /vəˈlɪʃən‖voʊ-, və-/ *n* [U] *formal* the power to choose or decide something without being forced to do it: **of your own volition** (=because you want to do something, not because you are forced to do it) *Helena left the company of her own volition.*

**vol·ley[1]** /ˈvɒli‖ˈvɑːli/ *n* [C] **1** a large number of shots fired from a gun at the same time: [+ **of**] *a volley of bullets* **2** a lot of questions, insults, attacks etc that are all said or made at the same time: [+ **of**] *a volley of abuse* | *a volley of blows* **3** a hit in TENNIS, a kick in football etc when the player hits or kicks the ball before it touches the ground —see picture on page 1264 **4** a lot of objects that are thrown through the air at the same time: [+ **of**] *a volley of stones*

**volley[2]** *v* **1** [I,T] to hit or kick a ball before it touches the ground, especially in TENNIS or football: *Ince volleyed the ball over the net.* **2** [I] if a large number of guns volley, they are all fired at the same time

**vol·ley·ball** /ˈvɒlibɔːl‖ˈvɑːlibɒːl/ *n* **1** [U] a game in which two teams hit a ball backwards and forwards over a high net with their hands and do not allow it to touch the ground **2** [C] the ball used in this game

**volt** /vəʊlt‖voʊlt/ *n* [C] *technical* a unit for measuring the force of an electric current

**volt·age** /ˈvəʊltɪdʒ‖ˈvoʊl-/ *n* [C,U] *technical* electrical force measured in volts: *a high voltage fence*

**volte-face** /ˌvɒlt ˈfæs, -ˈfɑːs‖ˌvɒːlt ˈfɑːs/ *n* [C usually singular] *formal* a change to a completely opposite opinion or plan of action

**volt·me·ter** /ˈvəʊltˌmiːtə‖ˈvoʊltˌmiːtər/ *n* [C] an instrument for measuring voltage

**vol·u·ble** /ˈvɒljəbəl‖ˈvɑː-/ *adj formal* **1** talking a lot: *a voluble spokesman* **2** a voluble speech, explanation etc uses a lot of words and is spoken quickly: *She broke into voluble and perfect Italian.* —**volubly** *adv* —**volubility** /ˌvɒljəˈbɪləti‖ˌvɑːl-/ *n* [U]

**vol·ume** /ˈvɒljuːm‖ˈvɑːljəm/ *n*

**1** ▶ **SPACE FILLED** ◀ [C,U] the amount of space that a substance or object contains or fills: *The volume of the container measures 100,000 cubic metres.* | *an instrument for measuring the volume of a gas*

**2** ▶ **AMOUNT** ◀ [C,U] the total amount of something, especially when it is large or increasing: *The volume of traffic on the roads has increased dramatically in recent years.* | *the volume of trade*

**3** ▶ **SOUND** ◀ [U] the amount of sound produced by a television, radio etc: *Can you turn the volume down on the stereo.*

**4** ▶ **BOOK** ◀ **a)** [C] one of the books into which a very long book is divided **b)** [C] *formal* a book: *the M–Mon volume of the encyclopedia* | *a volume of poetry* —see also **speak volumes** (SPEAK (11))

**vo·lu·mi·nous** /vəˈluːmɪnəs, vəˈljuː-‖vəˈluː-/ *adj formal* **1** a voluminous piece of clothing is very large and loose: *a voluminous cloak* **2** voluminous books, documents etc are very long and contain a lot of detail: *He took voluminous notes during the lecture.* **3** a voluminous container is very large and can hold a lot of things: *a voluminous suitcase*

**vol·un·ta·ry[1]** /ˈvɒləntəri‖ˈvɑːlənteri/ *adj* **1 voluntary work/service etc** work etc that is done by people who do it because they want to, and without expecting any money for it: *When she retired she did a lot of voluntary work for the Red Cross.* | **on a voluntary basis** *Participants in the experiment took part on a voluntary basis.* **2 voluntary organization/society/institution etc** an organization etc that is organized or supported by people who give their money, services etc because they want to and without expecting reward: *a voluntary organization providing help for the elderly* **3 voluntary worker/helper/assistant etc** someone who works without expecting or receiving payment **4** done willingly and without being forced: *The suspect has given the police his voluntary cooperation.* | *Workers are being encouraged to take voluntary redundancy.* —compare COMPULSORY **5** *technical* voluntary movements of your body are controlled by you —opposite INVOLUNTARY —**voluntarily** /ˈvɒləntərəli, ˌvɒlənˈterəli‖ˌvɑːlənˈterəli/ *adv*: *She wasn't fired – she left voluntarily.*

**voluntary[2]** *n* [C] a piece of music, usually for the ORGAN (2), written to be played in church

**vol·un·teer[1]** /ˌvɒlənˈtɪə‖ˌvɑːlənˈtɪr/ *n* [C] **1** someone who does something without being paid, or who is willing to offer to help someone: *Most of the relief work was done by volunteers.* | *I need some volunteers to clean up the kitchen.* **2** someone who offers to join the army, navy, or air force

**volunteer[2]** *v* **1** [I,T] to offer to do something without expecting any reward, usually something that other people do not want to do: **volunteer to do sth** *The company volunteered to donate fifty trucks to help the war effort.* | [+ **for**] *Sidcup volunteered for guard duty.* |

**volunteer your services/help/advice** *I volunteered my services as a teacher.* **2** [T] to tell someone something without being asked: *Michael volunteered the information before I had a chance to ask.* **3** [I] to offer to join the army, navy, or airforce: *When war broke out, my father volunteered immediately.* **4** [T] to say that someone else will do a job even though they may not want to: **volunteer sb for sth** *Mum volunteered Dave for washing-up duties.*

**vo·lup·tu·a·ry** /vəˈlʌptʃuəri‖-tʃueri/ *n* [C] *literary* someone who enjoys physical, especially sexual, pleasure and having expensive possessions

**vo·lup·tu·ous** /vəˈlʌptʃuəs/ *adj* **1** a woman who is voluptuous has large breasts and a soft curved body **2** expressing strong sexual feeling or sexual pleasure: *a voluptuous gesture* **3** *literary* something that is voluptuous gives you pleasure because it looks, smells, or tastes good: *the voluptuous fragrance of a summer garden* —**voluptuously** *adv* —**voluptuousness** *n* [U]

**vom·it¹** /ˈvɒmɪ̣t‖ˈvɑː-/ *v* [I,T] to bring food or drink up from your stomach out through your mouth, because you are ill —see SICK¹ (USAGE)

**vomit²** *n* [U] food or other substances that come up from your stomach and through your mouth when you vomit

**voo·doo** /ˈvuːduː/ *n* [U] magical beliefs and practices used as a form of religion, especially by people in Haiti

**voodoo e·co·nom·ics** /ˌ·· ··ˈ··/ *n* [U] *AmE* economic ideas that seem attractive but that do not work effectively over a period of time

**vo·ra·cious** /vəˈreɪʃəs, vɒ-‖vɔː-, və-/ *adj* **1** eating or wanting large quantities of food: *Pigs are voracious feeders.* | **a voracious appetite** *Kids can have voracious appetites.* **2** extremely eager to read books, gain knowledge etc: *a voracious reader* —**voraciously** *adv* —**voraciousness** *n* [U] —**voracity** /-ˈræsɪ̣ti/ *n* [U]

**vor·tex** /ˈvɔːteks‖ˈvɔːr-/ *n* [C] *literary* **1** a mass of wind or water that spins rapidly and pulls things into its centre **2** [usually singular] a situation that has a powerful effect on people's lives and that influences their behaviour, even if they did not intend it to: [+ **of**] *a black vortex of paranoia*

**vo·ta·ry** /ˈvəʊtəri‖ˈvoʊ-/ *n* [C] *formal* someone who regularly practises a particular religion

W3 **vote¹** /vəʊt‖voʊt/ *n*

**1** ▶ **CHOICE** ◀ [C] a choice or decision that you make by voting in an election or meeting: *The Democratic Party is counting on your vote.* | [+ **for/against**] *There were 402 votes for Mr Williams, and 372 against.* | **cast your vote** (=vote in a political election) —see also CASTING VOTE

**2** ▶ **ELECTION** ◀ [C] an act of voting, when a group of people vote in order to decide or choose something: *The results of the vote were surprising – 80% of workers favoured strike action.* | **take/have a vote (on)** *We couldn't decide who to give the prize to so we took a vote on it.* | **put sth to the vote** (=decide something by voting) *Let's put it to the vote. All those in favor raise your hands.*

**3** ▶ **RESULT** ◀ [singular] the result of a vote: *a very close vote* | *The motion was passed by a vote of 215 to 84.*

**4** ▶ **PAPER** ◀ [C] the piece of paper which you use to make your vote: *Party members were up all night counting the votes.*

**5** ▶ **NUMBER OF VOTES** ◀ [singular] the total number of votes made in an election or the total number of people who vote: *The Republicans increased their share of the vote.* | *policies designed to win the African-American vote* (=all the votes of African-Americans)

**6 the vote** the right to vote in political elections: *In France women didn't get the vote until 1945.*

**7 sth gets my vote** *spoken* used to say that you are ready to support something: *Anything that will mean a better deal for our children gets my vote.*

W3 **vote²** *v*

S3 **1** ▶ **MAKE A CHOICE** ◀ [I,T] to show by marking a paper or raising your hand which person you want to elect or whether you support a particular plan: *In 1918 British women got the right to vote.* | **vote for sb** *I voted for the Labour candidate in the last election.* | [+ **on**] *If we can't agree, we'll have to vote on it.* | **vote to do sth** *Congress voted to increase foreign aid by 10%.* | **vote for/in favour of/against sth** *53% of Danes voted in favour of the Maastricht treaty.* | **vote sth ↔ down** (=defeat a plan, law etc by voting) | **vote sth ↔ through** (=approve a plan, law etc by voting) | **vote Democrat/Socialist/Republican etc** *I've voted Democrat all my life.*

**2** ▶ **ELECT** ◀ [T] to elect or dismiss someone by voting: **vote sb in/out** (=elect or dismiss someone from a position of power) *With policies like that he'll be voted out in the next election.* | **vote sb into power/office/parliament etc** *Callaghan had been voted into office.*

**3** ▶ **PRIZE** ◀ [T] to choose someone or something for a particular prize by voting for them: *'Schindler's List' was voted 'Film of the Year'.*

**4** ▶ **MONEY** ◀ [T] if a parliament, committee etc votes a sum of money for something, they decide by voting to provide money for that particular purpose: *Parliament has voted £20 million extra funding for road improvements.*

**5 vote sth a success/the best etc** if people vote something a success etc, they all agree that it is a success: *Tom's party was voted a great success by everyone there.*

**6** ▶ **SUGGEST** ◀ [T] *informal* to suggest something: [+ **that**] *I vote that we go to the movies.*

**7 vote with your feet** to show that you do not support a decision or action by leaving a place or organization

**vote of cen·sure** /ˌ· · ˈ··/ *n* [C] a process in which members of parliament vote in order to blame the government for something

**vote of con·fi·dence** /ˌ· · ˈ···/ *n* [C] **1** a formal process in which people vote in order to show that they support someone or something, especially the government: *a unanimous vote of confidence* **2** something that you do or say that shows you support someone and approve of their actions

**vote of no con·fi·dence** /ˌ· · · ˈ···/ *n* [C] **1** a formal process in which people vote in order to show that they do not support someone or something, especially the government **2** something that you do or say that shows that you do not support someone

**vote of thanks** /ˌ· · ˈ·/ *n* **propose a vote of thanks** *especially BrE* to make a short formal speech in which you thank someone, especially at a public meeting or a formal dinner

**vot·er** /ˈvəʊtə‖ˈvoʊtər/ *n* [C] someone who votes or has the right to vote, especially in a political election: *The party's policies do not appeal to the voters.* | *Tory voters* —see also FLOATING VOTER

**voting booth** /ˈ·· ·/ *n* [C] *AmE* an enclosed place where you can make your vote secretly; POLLING BOOTH *BrE*

**voting ma·chine** /ˈ·· ·ˌ·/ *n* [C] a machine that records votes as they are made

**vo·tive** /ˈvəʊtɪv‖ˈvoʊ-/ *adj technical* given or done to a promise made to God or to a SAINT: *votive offerings*

**vouch** /vaʊtʃ/ *v*

**vouch for** sb/sth *phr v* [T] **1** to say that you believe that someone will behave well and that you will be responsible for their behaviour, actions etc: *I can vouch for my son, officer.* **2** to say that you firmly believe that something is true or good because of your experience or knowledge of it: *I'll vouch for the quality of the report. I read it last night.*

**vouch·er** /ˈvaʊtʃə‖-ər/ *n* [C] **1** a kind of ticket that can S3 be used instead of money for a particular purpose: *a travel voucher* —see also LUNCHEON VOUCHER **2** an official statement or RECEIPT that is given to someone to prove that their accounts are correct or that money has been paid

**vouch·safe** /vaʊtʃˈseɪf/ *v* [T] *formal* **1** to offer, give, or tell something to someone in a way that shows you trust them: *insights into the future vouchsafed by God* **2** to make it certain that something will be safe: *political arrangements that vouchsafe peace*

**vow**[1] /vaʊ/ *n* [C] a serious promise: *marriage vows* | **vow to do sth** *a vow to avenge his brother's death* | **take/make a vow** *She made a vow never to tell anybody what she had heard.* | **keep/break a vow** (=do or not do what you promised) | **vow of silence** (=a promise made to God that you will never speak again) *monks who take the vow of silence* | **under a vow of** (=having promised to do something) *nuns under the vow of chastity*

**vow**[2] *v* [T] **1** *especially literary* to make a serious promise to yourself or someone else: **vow to do sth** *He vowed to kill his wife's lover.* | **vow (that)** *I vowed that I would never drink again.* **2** *formal* to make a religious promise that you will give something to God, the church etc

**vow·el** /ˈvaʊəl/ *n* [C] **1** one of the human speech sounds that you make by letting your breath flow out without closing any part of your mouth or throat **2** a letter of the alphabet used to represent a vowel. In English the vowels are a, e, i, o, u, and sometimes y.

**vox pop** /ˌvɒks ˈpɒp‖ˌvɑːks ˈpɑːp/ *n* [U] *BrE informal* opinions expressed by ordinary people when they are asked questions about a particular subject during a television, radio, or newspaper report

**voy·age**[1] /ˈvɔɪ-ɪdʒ/ *n* [C] a long journey in a ship: *The voyage from England to India used to take six months.*

**voyage**[2] *v* [I] *literary* to make a long journey in a ship —see TRAVEL (USAGE)

**voy·ag·er** /ˈvɔɪ-ɪdʒə‖-ər/ *n* [C] *literary* someone who makes long and often dangerous journeys on the sea

**voy·eur** /vwɑːˈjɜː‖-ˈjɜːr/ *n* [C] **1** someone who gets sexual pleasure from secretly watching other people's sexual activities **2** someone who enjoys watching other people's private behaviour or suffering —**voyeurism** *n* [U] —**voyeuristic** /ˌvwɑːjəˈrɪstɪk◂/ *adj* —**voyeuristically** /-kli/ *adv*

**VP** /ˌviː ˈpiː/ the abbreviation of Vice President

**vs** /ˈvɜːsəs‖ˈvɜːr-/ a written abbreviation of VERSUS

**V sign** /ˈviː saɪn/ *n* [C] **1** a sign meaning peace or victory made by holding up the first two fingers of your hand with the front of the hand facing forwards **2** *BrE* a rude sign made by holding up the first two fingers of your hand with the back of your hand facing towards another person

**vul·can·ize** also **-ise** *BrE* /ˈvʌlkənaɪz/ *v* [T] to make rubber stronger using a special chemical treatment —**vulcanization** /ˌvʌlkənaɪˈzeɪʃən‖-nə-/ *n* [U]

**vul·gar** /ˈvʌlgə‖-ər/ *adj* **1** remarks, jokes etc that are vulgar deal with sex in a very rude and offensive way **2** impolite and showing bad manners: *vulgar habits* **3** *especially BrE* not showing good judgment about what is beautiful or suitable: *a vulgar display of wealth* —**vulgarly** *adv*

**vulgar frac·tion** /ˌ‥ˈ‥/ *n* [C] *BrE old-fashioned* a FRACTION that is written as one number above a line and one number below it, and not as a DECIMAL; COMMON FRACTION *AmE*

**vul·gar·i·ty** /vʌlˈgærɪti/ *n* **1** [U] the state or quality of being vulgar **2** **vulgarities** [plural] vulgar remarks, jokes etc

**vul·gar·ize** also **-ise** *BrE* /ˈvʌlgəraɪz/ *v* [T] *formal* to spoil the quality or lower the standard of something that is good —**vulgarization** /ˌvʌlgəraɪˈzeɪʃən‖-rə-/ *n* [U]

**Vul·gate** /ˈvʌlgeɪt, -gɪt/ *n* **the Vulgate** the Latin Bible commonly used in the Roman Catholic Church

**vul·ne·ra·ble** /ˈvʌlnərəbəl/ *adj* **W** **1** someone who is vulnerable is easily harmed or hurt emotionally, physically, or morally: *a vulnerable young child* **2** a place, thing, or idea that is vulnerable is easy to attack: [+ **to**] *The fort was vulnerable to attack from the north.* | *a theory vulnerable to criticism* —**vulnerably** *adv* —**vulnerability** /ˌvʌlnərəˈbɪlɪti/ *n* [U]: *the vulnerability of airports to terrorist activity*

**vul·ture** /ˈvʌltʃə‖-ər/ *n* [C] **1** a large bird that eats dead animals **2** someone who uses other people's troubles for their own advantage

**vul·va** /ˈvʌlvə/ *n* [C] the outer part of a woman's sexual organs

**vy·ing** /ˈvaɪ-ɪŋ/ the present participle of VIE

# W, w

**W, w** /ˈdʌbəljuː/ *plural* **W's, w's** *n* [C] **1** the 23rd letter of the English alphabet **2** the written abbreviation of WEST OR WESTERN **3** the written abbreviation of WATT

**wack·y** /ˈwæki/ *adj informal* silly in an exciting or amusing way —**wackiness** *n* [U]

**wad**[1] /wɒd‖wɑːd/ *n* [C] **1** a thick pile of pieces of paper or thin material: *a wad of dollar bills* —see picture on page 416 **2** a thick soft mass of material that has been pressed together: *a wad of gauze* **3** a piece of tobacco that you hold in your mouth

**wad**[2] *v*

**wad** sth ↔ **up** *phr v* [T] *AmE* to press something such as a piece of paper or cloth into a small tight ball

**wad·ding** /ˈwɒdɪŋ‖ˈwɑː-/ *n* [U] soft material used for packing or to protect a wound

**wad·dle** /ˈwɒdl‖ˈwɑːdl/ *v* [I] to walk with short steps, swinging from one side to another like a duck: [+ **along/around etc**] *Julie came waddling up the path, eight months pregnant.* —**waddle** *n* [singular]

**wade** /weɪd/ *v* [I + **across/through**] [T] to walk through water that is not deep

**wade in** *phr v* [I] *BrE informal* to interrupt someone or become involved in something in an annoying way: *I wish you wouldn't always wade in with your opinion.*

**wade through** sth *phr v* [T] to read or deal with a lot of boring papers or written work: *Look at this pile of paperwork I have to wade through!* —see picture on page 1262

**wad·er** /ˈweɪdə‖-ər/ *n* [C] **1** a bird that walks around in water to find its food and has long legs and a long neck **2 waders** [plural] high rubber boots that you wear for walking in water

**wading bird** /ˈ·· ˌ·/ *n* [C] a WADER (1)

**wad·ing pool** /ˈ·· ·/ *n* [C] *AmE* a PADDLING POOL

**wa·fer** /ˈweɪfə‖-ər/ *n* [C] **1** a very thin BISCUIT (1) **2** a thin round piece of bread eaten with wine in the Christian religious ceremony of COMMUNION (2)

**wafer-thin** /ˌ·· ˈ·◂/ *adj* extremely thin: *wafer-thin chocolates*

**waf·fle**[1] /ˈwɒfəl‖ˈwɑː-/ *n* [C] **1** a thin flat cake, marked with a pattern of deep squares **2** [U] *informal especially BrE* talk or writing that uses a lot of words but says nothing important: *His exam answer was a load of old waffle.*

**waffle**[2] *v* [I] *informal* **1** also **waffle on** *especially BrE* to talk or write using a lot of words but without saying anything important: *Stop waffling and get to the point.* **2** *AmE informal* to be unable to decide what action to take: [+ **over**] *Karl waffles over every darn decision!*

**waffle i·ron** /ˈ·· ˌ··/ *n* [C] a piece of kitchen equipment used to cook waffles

**waf·fle·stomp·er** /ˈwɒfəlˌstɒmpə‖ˈwɑːfəlˌstɑːmpər/ *n* [C usually plural] *AmE* a type of very heavy walking boot

**waft** /wɑːft, wɒft‖wɑːft, wæft/ *v* [I always + adv/prep] to move gently through the air: + **up/along/off etc** *Cooking smells wafted up from downstairs.*

**wag**[1] /wæg/ *v* [I,T] **1** to shake your finger or head repeatedly, especially to show disapproval: **wag your finger** *"You naughty girl!" Mom said, wagging her finger at me.* **2** if a dog wags its tail, it moves it repeatedly from one side to the other **3 tongues wag** *informal* used to say that people are talking in a disapproving way about someone else's behaviour: *You'll have to stop visiting that woman – tongues are starting to wag.*

**wag**[2] *n* **1** [C usually singular] a wagging movement **2** [C] *old-fashioned* someone who talks or does something in a clever and amusing way: *Some wag had drawn a face on the wall.* —see also CHINWAG, WAGGISH

**wage**[1] /weɪdʒ/ *n* **1** [singular] also **wages** [plural] W3 money you earn that is paid according to the number of hours, days, or weeks that you work: *The job's not very exciting, but he earns a good wage.* | **wage increase** also **wage rise** *BrE*: *The wage increases will come into effect in June.* | **daily/weekly etc wage** *a weekly wage of $250* | **wage levels/rates** (=fixed amounts of money paid for particular jobs) —compare SALARY —see PAY[1] (USAGE) **2 a living wage** money you earn for work that is enough to pay for the basic things that you need to live **3 wage freeze** an action taken by a company, government etc to stop wages increasing **4 wage claim** the amount of money demanded by workers as an increase in wages

**wage**[2] *v* [T] to be involved in a war against someone, or a fight against something: **wage war (on)** *The police are waging war on drug pushers in the city.* | **wage a campaign/struggle/fight etc** *The struggle for political liberty waged throughout the 18th century.*

**wage-earn·er** /ˈ· ˌ··/ *n* [C] **1** someone who works for wages, often someone who works with their hands: *Both wage-earners and salaried officials were protected by the new regulations.* **2** someone in a family who earns money for the rest of the family

**wage-pack·et** /ˈ· ˌ··/ *n* [C] *BrE* an envelope that contains your wages

**wa·ger**[1] /ˈweɪdʒə‖-ər/ *n* [C] *old-fashioned* an agreement in which you win or lose money according to the result of something such as a race; BET[2] (1)

**wager**[2] *v* [T] *old-fashioned* **1** to agree to win or lose an amount of money on the result of something such as a race: **wager sth on** *Stipes wagered all his money on an unknown horse.* **2 I'll wager** used to say that you are so sure that something is true that you are willing to risk money on it: *I'll wager that boy's never worked in his life!*

**wag·gish** /ˈwægɪʃ/ *adj* a waggish person makes clever and amusing jokes, remarks etc —**waggishly** *adv* —**waggishness** *n* [U]

**wag·gle** /ˈwægəl/ *v* [I,T] to move something up and down or from side to side with short quick movements: *Can you waggle your ears?* —**waggle** *n* [C]

**wag·on** also **waggon** *BrE* /ˈwægən/ *n* [C] **1** a strong vehicle with four wheels, used for carrying heavy loads and usually pulled by horses **2** *BrE* a large open container pulled by a train, used for carrying goods **3 be on the wagon** *informal* to not drink alcohol any more **4 fall off the wagon** *informal* to start drinking alcohol again after you have decided to stop —see also PADDY WAGON

**wagon train** /ˈ·· ·/ *n* [C] a long line of wagons and horses used by the people who moved to the West of America in the 19th century

**wag·tail** /ˈwægteɪl/ *n* [C] a small European bird that moves its tail quickly up and down when it walks

**waif** /weɪf/ *n* [C] **1** someone who is pale and thin, especially a child, and looks as if they do not have a home: *a grubby little waif huddled by the door* | **waif-like** (=very thin) *teenage girls trying to emulate waif-like fashion models* **2 waifs and strays** children or animals, who do not have a home: *She loved cats, and would take any waifs and strays into her home.*

**wail** /weɪl/ *v* **1** [T] to say something in a loud, sad, and complaining way: *"But what shall I do?" Bernard wailed.* **2** [I] to cry out with a long, high sound, especially because you are very sad or in pain: **weeping and wailing** *weeping and wailing with grief* **3** [I] to make a long, high sound: *The wind wailed in the chimney.* —**wail** *n* [C]: *the wail of police sirens*

**wain·scot** /ˈweɪnskət, -skɒt‖-skət, -skɑːt/ *n* [C] **1** a SKIRTING BOARD; BASEBOARD *AmE* **2** also **wainscotting** a wooden covering, especially on the lower half of the walls of an old house —**wainscotted** *adj*

**waist** /weɪst/ *n* [C] **1** the narrow part in the middle of the human body: *wearing a belt around his waist* | **from**

**the waist up/down** (=in the top or bottom half of your body) *Lota was paralysed from the waist down.* | **stripped to the waist** (=not wearing any clothes on the top half of your body) | **slim-waisted/narrow-waisted/thick-waisted etc** (=having a thin, thick etc waist) —see picture at BODY **2** the part of a piece of clothing that goes around this part of your body **3** *technical* the middle part of a ship

**waist·band** /ˈweɪstbænd/ *n* [C] the part of a skirt, trousers etc that fastens around your waist —see picture on page 840

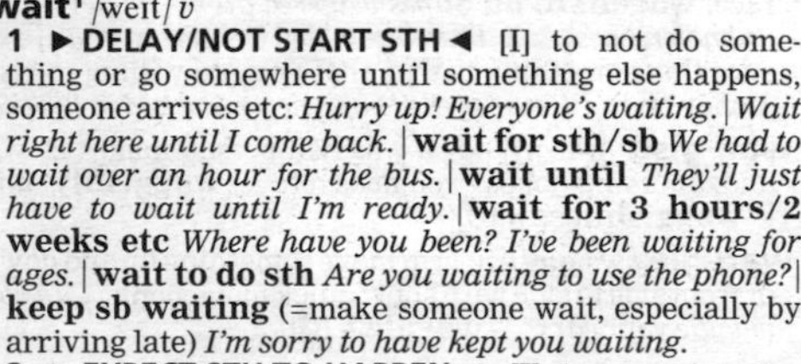


**waist·coat** /ˈweɪskəʊt, ˈweskət‖ˈweskət/ *n* [C] *BrE* a piece of clothing without arms that you wear over a shirt; VEST[1] (2) *AmE*

**waist-deep** /ˌ· ˈ·◂/ *adj, adv* deep enough to reach your waist: *waist-deep in muddy water*

**waist-high** /ˌ· ˈ·◂/ *adj, adv* high enough to reach your waist: *waist-high grass*

**waist·line** /ˈweɪstlaɪn/ *n* **1** [singular] the amount you measure around the waist, especially used to judge how fat or thin you are: *a trim waistline* | **watch your waistline** (=to be careful about what you eat so you do not get fat) **2** the position of the waist of a piece of clothing

S1 W1 **wait[1]** /weɪt/ *v*

**1 ▶ DELAY/NOT START STH ◀** [I] to not do something or go somewhere until something else happens, someone arrives etc: *Hurry up! Everyone's waiting.* | *Wait right here until I come back.* | **wait for sth/sb** *We had to wait over an hour for the bus.* | **wait until** *They'll just have to wait until I'm ready.* | **wait for 3 hours/2 weeks etc** *Where have you been? I've been waiting for ages.* | **wait to do sth** *Are you waiting to use the phone?* | **keep sb waiting** (=make someone wait, especially by arriving late) *I'm sorry to have kept you waiting.*

**2 ▶ EXPECT STH TO HAPPEN ◀** [I] to expect something to happen that has not happened yet: *"Have you heard about the job?" "No, I'm still waiting."* | **wait for sth** *I'm still waiting for my test results.* | **wait for sb to do sth/wait for sth to happen** *I'm just waiting for him to realize how stupid he's been.*

**3 wait a minute/second/moment etc** *spoken* **a)** used to stop someone for a short time when they are leaving or starting to do something: *Wait a second, I'll get my coat and come with you.* **b)** used to interrupt someone, especially because you do not agree with what they are saying: *Wait a minute! That's not what we agreed!* **c)** used when you suddenly remember or notice something: *Wait a moment, I'm sure I know her name.*

**4 I can't wait/I can hardly wait** *informal* **a)** used when you feel excited and impatient about something that is going to happen soon: *We're going to Australia on Saturday – I can't wait!* | **sb can't wait to do sth** *Tina can't wait to get home.* | [+ **for**] *I can't wait for my vacation.* **b)** *spoken humorous* used to say that something seems likely to be very boring: *A lecture on transformational grammar? I can hardly wait.*

**5 sth can/can't wait** used to say that something is not, or is very urgent: *"What's so important? Can't it wait till tomorrow?" "No, it can't."*

**6 wait and see** *especially spoken* used to say that someone should be patient because they will find out about something later: **sb will have to wait and see** *You'll have to wait and see what Father Christmas brings you.*

**7 wait until/till** *spoken* used when you are excited about telling or showing someone something: *Wait till you see Gaby's new house!*

**8 be waiting** if something is waiting for you, it is ready for you to use, collect etc: *The report was typed up and waiting when they came back from coffee.*

**9 wait your turn** to stay calm until it is your turn to do something, instead of trying to move ahead of other people

**10 sth is (well) worth waiting for** *spoken* used to say that something is very good, even though it takes a long time to come: *Their new album was well worth waiting for.*

**11 (just) you wait** *spoken* used to warn or threaten someone: *I'll get you back for what you've done, just you wait.*

**12 what are you waiting for?** *spoken* used to tell someone to do something immediately: *Well, what are you waiting for? Go and apologize.*

**13 what are we waiting for?** *spoken* used to say in a cheerful way that you think everyone should start doing something immediately

**14 wait for it** *spoken* **a)** used just before you tell someone something that is funny or surprising: *Guess how much he won? Wait for it – $400,000!* **b)** used to tell someone not to do something until the correct time because they seem very impatient to do it now

**15 wait your chance/opportunity (to do sth)** to wait until you have the best conditions to succeed in doing something: *Wilson was merely waiting his chance to get revenge.*

**16 be waiting in the wings** to be ready to do something if it is necessary or if a suitable time comes

**17 wait on tables/wait at table** *BrE formal* **wait tables** *AmE* to serve food to people at their table in a restaurant

**18 wait dinner/lunch etc (for sb)** *AmE* to delay a meal until someone arrives: *Don't wait dinner for me, I'll be home late.*

**19 (play) a waiting game** to do nothing deliberately and wait to see what other people do, in order to get an advantage for yourself

**wait around** also **wait about** *BrE phr v* [I] to stay in the same place and do nothing while you are waiting for something to happen, someone to arrive etc: *We waited around at the stage door to try and see the stars.*

**wait behind** *phr v* [I] to stay somewhere after other people have left: *Paolo waited behind to speak to her alone.*

**wait in** *phr v* [I] *BrE* to stay at home and wait there for someone to arrive: *I have to wait in for the repair man.*

**wait on** sb/sth *phr v* [T] **1** to serve food to someone at their table, especially in a restaurant **2** to wait for a particular event, piece of information etc, especially before doing something or making a decision: *We're waiting on the blood test results.* **3 wait on sb hand and foot** *often humorous* to do everything for someone while they do nothing: *His wife waits on him hand and foot.*

**wait** sth ↔ **out** *phr v* [T] if you wait out an event or period or time, especially an unpleasant one, you wait for it to finish: *Let's find a place where we can wait out the storm.*

**wait up** *phr v* [I] **1** to wait for someone to return before you go to bed: [+ **for**] *Don't wait up for me – I'll be very late.* **2 Wait up!** *AmE* used to tell someone to stop, so that you can talk to them or go with them

This graph shows how common the different grammar patterns of the verb **wait** are.

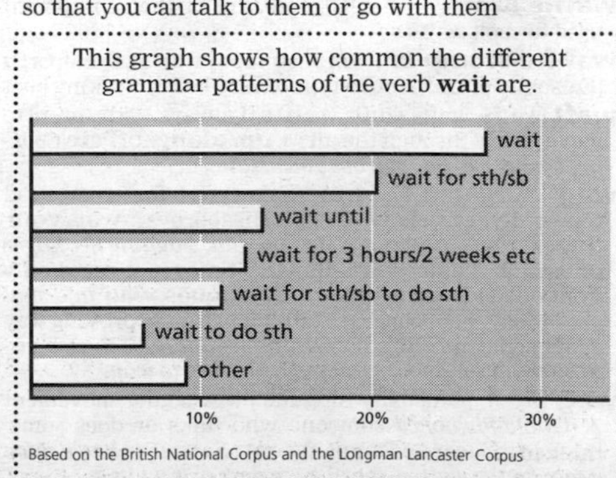


Based on the British National Corpus and the Longman Lancaster Corpus

**USAGE NOTE: WAIT**

WORD CHOICE: **wait for, await, wait, expect, look forward to**

If you **wait for** someone to come or for something to happen, you delay doing something or change what you are doing until they come or it happens. Often you do not do other things because you are **waiting:** *Why are you standing there? I'm waiting for John (to come).* | *I'm waiting to use that machine.* **Await** is a much more formal word for **wait for**.

If you **expect** someone or something, you are sure that the person will come or that the event will happen, but you do not necessarily change what you are doing now because of this: *We're expecting a cold winter.* | *What kind of result are you expecting?* **Waiting** is something you do; **expecting** is a state of mind.

If you are expecting something good to happen and feel happy about it, you **look forward to** it: *I'm looking forward to seeing him again.*

GRAMMAR

You **wait for** something (NOT *wait it*). But you **await** something (NOT *await for it*).

**wait²** *n* [singular] a period of time in which you wait for something to happen, someone to arrive etc: [+ **for**] *We then faced a six-month wait for the results to arrive.* —see also **lie in wait** (LIE¹ (6))

**wait·er** /ˈweɪtə‖-ər/ *n* [C] a man who serves food and drink at the tables in a restaurant —see picture on page 838

**wait·ing list** /ˈ·· ·/ *n* [C] a list of people who have asked for something but who must wait before they can have it: *a two-year waiting list*

**waiting room** /ˈ·· ·/ *n* [C] a room for people to wait in, for example to see a doctor, take a train etc

**wait·ress** /ˈweɪtrɪ̈s/ *n* [C] a woman who serves food and drink at the tables in a restaurant —see picture on page 838

**waive** /weɪv/ *v* [T] to state officially that a right, rule etc can be ignored, because at this time it is not useful or important: *She waived her right to a lawyer.*

**waiv·er** /ˈweɪvə‖-ər/ *n* [C] *technical* an official written statement saying that a right, claim etc can be waived

S2 W3 **wake¹** /weɪk/ *v past tense* **woke** /wəʊk‖woʊk/ *or* **waked** *AmE past participle* **woken** /ˈwəʊkən‖ˈwoʊ-/ *or* **waked** *AmE* [I,T] also **wake up** to stop sleeping, or to make someone stop sleeping: *James usually wakes up early.* | *I'll wake you up when it's time to leave.* | *Try not to wake the baby.*

**wake up** *phr v* [I,T] **1** to start to listen or pay attention to something: **Wake up!** (=give me your attention) *Wake up at the back there!* **2 wake up and smell the coffee** *AmE spoken* used to tell someone to recognize the truth or reality of something

**wake (up) to** *phr v* [T] **1** to experience something as you are waking up: *Nancy woke to the sound of birds outside her window.* **2** to start to realize and understand a danger, an idea etc: *It's time you woke up to the fact that it's a tough world out there.*

**wake²** *n* [C] **1 in the wake of** if something, especially something bad, happens in the wake of an event, it happens afterwards and usually as a result of it: *Famine followed in the wake of the drought.* **2 in sb's/sth's wake** behind or after someone or something: *The car left clouds of dust in its wake.* **3** the time before a funeral when friends and relatives meet to remember the dead person **4** the track made behind a boat as it moves through the water

**wake·ful** /ˈweɪkfəl/ *adj* **1 a)** unable to sleep: *lying wakeful in the hot night* **b)** a wakeful period of time is one when you cannot sleep **2** *formal* ready to do whatever is necessary —**wakefulness** *n* [U]

**wak·en** /ˈweɪkən/ also **waken up** *v* [I,T] *formal* to wake, or to wake someone: *She gently wakened the sleeping child.*

**wak·ey-wak·ey** /ˌweɪki ˈweɪki/ *interjection BrE spoken* used to tell someone in a joking way to wake up

**wak·ing** /ˈweɪkɪŋ/ *adj* **waking hours/life/day etc** all the time when you are awake: *How his face haunted her every waking moment!*

**walk¹** /wɔːk‖wɒːk/ *v* S1 W1

**1** ▶ **MOVE ALONG** ◀ [I] to move along putting one foot in front of the other: *We must have walked ten miles today.* | [+ **along/around/up etc**] *How long does it take to walk into town?* | *walk down the street* | **walk back/home** *Marcus and I walked back through the park.* | **walk up to/walk over to** (=to go towards someone or something) *She just walked up to him and slapped his face.* —see picture on page 1262

**2** ▶ **WALK ACROSS A PLACE** ◀ [T] to walk in order to get somewhere, across a particular area or distance: *I parked the car and walked the rest of the way.*

**3 walk the dog** to take a dog for a walk: *Grandma's out walking the dog.*

**4 walk sb home/to school etc** to walk somewhere with someone to make sure that they are safe: *It's late – I'll walk you home.*

**5 go walking** to walk for pleasure and exercise, especially in the countryside: *Rhys and I went walking in Snowdonia last summer.*

**6 walk it** *spoken* **a)** to make a journey by walking: *If the last bus has gone, we'll have to walk it.* **b)** *BrE* to succeed or win something easily: *We thought it would be a tough match but in fact we walked it, winning 5–0.*

**7 walk free** to leave a court of law without being punished or sent to prison: *the case of a teenage vandal who walked free from court*

**8 walking pace** the speed that you normally walk at

**9 walk tall** to be proud and confident because you know that you have not done anything wrong

**10 walk on eggs/eggshells** to treat someone very carefully because they easily become very angry

**11** ▶ **HEAVY OBJECT** ◀ [T] to move a heavy object slowly by moving first one side and then the other

**12 walk the plank a)** to be forced to walk along a board laid over the side of the ship until you fall off into the sea **b)** *AmE informal* to be dismissed from your job

**13 walk on air** to feel extremely happy

**14 walk sb off their feet** *BrE* to make someone tired by making them walk too far

**walk away** *phr v* [I + **from**] **1** to leave a bad situation, instead of trying to make it better: *You can't just walk away from 15 years of marriage!* **2** to come out of an accident or very bad situation without being harmed: *Miraculously both drivers walked away unscathed.*

**walk away with** sth *phr v* to win something easily: *She knew all the answers and walked away with the prize.*

**walk in** *phr v* [I,T] **1** to enter a building or room especially unexpectedly or without being invited: *You can't just walk in here whenever you feel like it!* | **walk in the door** *I walked in the door and caught him at it.* | **walk in off the street** (=visit someone such as a doctor without having previously arranged to see them) *People can walk in off the street and get confidential pregnancy counselling.* **2 walk in dirt/leaves etc** to make mud, leaves etc stick to the floor by walking over it when you have mud, leaves etc on your shoes

**walk in on** sb *phr v* [T] to go into a place and interrupt someone who you did not expect to be there: *Arriving home early one day, she walked in on her husband and his mistress.*

**walk into** sth *phr v* [T] **1** to hit an object accidentally as you are walking along: **walk straight/right/bang etc into** *Zeke wasn't looking where he was going* *and walked straight into a tree.* **2** if you walk into an unpleasant situation, you become involved in it without intending to **3** if you walk into a job, you get it very easily: *Nowadays you can't expect to leave university and walk into a job.* **4** to make yourself look stupid when you could easily have avoided it if you had been more careful: **walk straight/right into** *You walked right into that one!*

**walk off** *phr v* [I] **1** to leave someone by walking away from them, especially in a rude or angry way: *Don't just walk off when I'm trying to talk to you!* **2** [**walk** sth ↔ **off**] [T] if you walk off an illness or unpleasant feeling, you go for a walk to make it go away: *Let's go out – maybe I can walk off this headache.* | **walk off dinner/a meal etc** (=go for a walk so that your stomach feels less full)

**walk off with** sth *phr v* [T] to take or steal something, especially in a relaxed or confident way: *Thieves walked off with two million dollars' worth of jewellery.* | *Lottery winners can walk off with a cool £18 million.*

**walk over** sb *phr v* [T] to treat someone badly by always making them do what you want them to do: **walk all over sb** *It's terrible – she lets her kids just walk all over her.*

**walk out** *phr v* [I] **1** to go outside: [+ **into**] *Payton walked out into the cold morning air.* **2** to leave a place suddenly, especially because you disapprove of something: *Mike walked out after a row with one of his colleagues.* **3** to stop working as a protest: *The electricians have walked out, and will stay out until their demands are met.* **4 walk out (with)** *old use* to have a romantic relationship with someone

**walk out on** sb/sth *phr v* [T] **1** to leave your husband, wife etc suddenly: *When she was three months pregnant, Pete walked out on her.* **2** to stop doing something you have agreed to do or that you are responsible for: *"I never walk out on a deal," Dee said.*

**walk** sth ↔ **through** *phr v* [T] to practise something: *Let's walk through scene two to see how long it takes.* | **walk sb through sth** *I'll walk you through the procedure before you do it on your own.*

S2 W2 **walk²** *n* **1** [C] a journey that you make by walking, especially for exercise or enjoyment: *It's a long walk. Maybe we should get the bus.* | **go for a walk** *"What did you do yesterday?" "Nothing much – I went for a walk in the park."* | **take/have a walk** *She takes a short walk every day before breakfast.* | **take sb for a walk** *Why don't we take the kids for a walk?* | **walk to/through/across etc** *a short walk through the castle grounds* | **long/short/five-mile/ten-minute etc walk** *I would put on heavy boots and go for long walks.* **2** [C] a fixed ROUTE¹ (1) that you walk, especially through an attractive or interesting area: *There are some particularly interesting walks to the north of the city.* **3** [U] the way someone walks: *You can often recognize people by their walk.* **4 take a walk** *especially AmE spoken* used to rudely tell someone to go away or to stop talking nonsense: *"Harry's here to see you." "Well, tell him to take a walk."* — see also WALK OF LIFE, **sponsored walk** (SPONSORED)

**walk·a·bout** /ˈwɔːkəbaʊt‖ˈwɒːk-/ *n* [C] **1** *BrE informal* an occasion when an important person walks through a crowd, talking informally to people: **go on a walkabout** *The Prince went on a walkabout near the war memorial.* **2 go walkabout** *BrE spoken humorous* to disappear: *My watch seems to have gone walkabout again.*

**walk·a·way** /ˈwɔːkəweɪ‖ˈwɒːk-/ *n* [C] *AmE informal* an easy victory; WALKOVER *BrE*

**walk·er** /ˈwɔːkə‖ˈwɒːkər/ *n* [C] **1** *especially BrE* someone who walks for pleasure or exercise; HIKER: *a keen hillwalker* **2 a fast/slow etc walker** someone who walks fast, slowly etc **3** a piece of equipment for helping someone to walk; ZIMMER FRAME

**walk·ies** /ˈwɔːkiz‖ˈwɒːk-/ *n* [plural] *BrE spoken* used to tell a dog that you are going to take it for a walk: *Come on, Shep! Walkies!*

**walk·ie-talk·ie** /ˌwɔːki ˈtɔːki‖ˌwɒːki ˈtɒːki/ *n* [C] one of a pair of radios that you can carry with you, and use to speak to the person who has the other radio

**walk-in** /ˈ· ·/ *adj* [only before noun] big enough for a person to walk inside: *a walk-in closet*

**walk·ing¹** /ˈwɔːkɪŋ‖ˈwɒːk-/ *n* [U] **1** *especially BrE* the activity or sport of going for walks, especially in the countryside; go hiking (HIKE² (1)): **go walking** *We went walking near Cambridge last weekend.* **2** the sport of walking long distances as fast as you can without actually running

**walking²** *adj* [only before noun] **1 walking shoes/boots** shoes or boots that are strong and comfortable, because they are intended for walking long distances —see picture at BOOT¹ **2 walking holiday/tour etc** *especially BrE* a holiday etc in which you walk a lot, especially in the countryside; hiking trip (HIKING) **3 walking dictionary/encyclopaedia** *humorous* someone who knows a lot, and always has the information that you want **4 walking disaster (area)** *humorous* someone who always drops things, has accidents, makes mistakes etc

**walking pa·pers** /ˈ·· ˌ··/ *n* [plural] **give sb their walking papers** *AmE* to tell someone that they must leave a place or a job —see also **be given/get your marching orders** (MARCH¹ (5))

**walking stick** /ˈ·· ·/ *n* [C] **1** a stick that is used to support someone, especially an old person, while they walk —see picture at STICK² **2** *AmE* a STICK INSECT

**Walk·man** /ˈwɔːkmən‖ˈwɒːk-/ *n* [C] *trademark* a small CASSETTE PLAYER with HEADPHONES, that you carry with you so that you can listen to music; PERSONAL STEREO

**walk of life** /ˌ· · ˈ·/ *n* [C] the position in society someone has, especially the type of job they have: **from every walk of life/from all walks of life** *The club has members from every walk of life, from plumbers to doctors.*

**walk-on** /ˈ· ·/ also **walk-on part** /ˈ· · ˌ·/ *n* [C] a small acting part with no words to say in a play or film, or an actor who has a part like this

**walk·out** /ˈwɔːk-aʊt‖ˈwɒːk-/ *n* [C] an occasion when people stop working or leave somewhere as a protest: **stage a walk-out** *The Irish delegation staged a walk-out in protest.* —see also **walk out** (WALK¹)

**walk·o·ver** /ˈwɔːkˌəʊvə‖ˈwɒːkˌoʊvər/ *n* [C] *informal* a very easy victory; WALKAWAY *AmE* —see also **walk over** (WALK¹)

**walk-up** /ˈ· ·/ *n* [C] *AmE informal* **1** a tall building with apartments in it that does not have an ELEVATOR (1) **2** an apartment, office etc in a building like this

**walk·way** /ˈwɔːkweɪ‖ˈwɒːk-/ *n* [C] an outside path, often above the ground, built to connect two parts of a building or two buildings: *a covered walkway*

**wall¹** /wɔːl‖wɒːl/ *n* [C] S1 W1

**1** ► **AROUND AN AREA** ◄ an upright flat structure made of stone or brick, that divides one area from another: *The garden was surrounded by a high brick wall.*

**2** ► **IN A BUILDING** ◄ one of the sides of a room or building: *We decided to paint the walls blue.*

**3** ► **TUBE/CONTAINER** ◄ the side of something hollow, such as a pipe or tube: *The walls of the blood vessels had been damaged.*

**4 wall of fire/water etc** a tall mass of something such as fire or water, that prevents anything getting through: *A wall of fire was advancing through the forest.*

**5 wall of silence** a situation in which nobody will tell you what you want to know: *The police investigation was met with a wall of silence.*

**6 go up the wall** *BrE spoken* to become very angry: *My mum went up the wall when I told her I wanted to leave school.*

**7 drive sb up the wall** *spoken* to annoy someone very much: *I wish she'd stop muttering – it drives me up the wall!*

**8 go to the wall** *informal* if a company goes to the wall, it fails, especially because of financial difficulties
**9 these four walls** *spoken* the room that you are in, especially considered as a private place: *I don't want anything that I have said repeated outside these four walls.*
**10 be climbing/crawling up the wall** *informal* to be feeling extremely anxious, dissatisfied, and impatient, especially because you are waiting for something or cannot do something you want to do: *Last time I gave up smoking I was crawling up the wall within a few hours.*
**11 walls have ears** used to warn people to be careful what they say, because other people, especially enemies, could be listening
**12 hit the wall** *informal* to reach the point of greatest physical tiredness when doing a sport —see also **have your back to the wall** (BACK[1] (20)), **bang your head against a brick wall** (BANG[1] (5)), **like talking to a brick wall** (TALK), **the writing is on the wall** (WRITING (7)), OFF-THE-WALL

**wall**[2] *v*
**wall** sth ↔ **in** *phr v* [T] to surround an open area with walls: *They decided to wall the garden in.*
**wall** sth ↔ **off** *phr v* [T] to keep one area or room separate from another, by building a wall: *The control room is walled off by soundproof glass.*
**wall** sb/sth ↔ **up** *phr v* [T] **1** to fill in a doorway, window etc with bricks or stone: *The entrance had long since been walled up.* **2** used to say that someone is a prisoner: *I can't bear the thought of her walled up in a cell.*

**wal·la·by** /ˈwɒləbi‖ˈwɑː-/ *n* [C] an Australian animal like a small KANGAROO

**wal·lah, walla** /ˈwɒlə‖ˈwɑːlə/ *n* [C] *IndE, PakE* someone who does a particular kind of job or duty: *the medical wallahs*

**wall·chart** /ˈwɔːltʃɑːt‖ˈwɒːltʃɑːrt/ *n* [C] a large piece of paper with information on it that is fastened to a wall

**walled** /wɔːld‖wɒːld/ *adj* [only before noun] **walled garden/city/town etc** a garden etc that has a wall around it

**wal·let** /ˈwɒlɪ̣t‖ˈwɑː-/ *n* [C] **1** a small flat leather case that you carry in your pocket, for holding paper money etc; BILLFOLD *AmE* —compare PURSE[1] (2) —see picture at PURSE[1] **2** a long leather case for official documents

**wall-eyed** /ˌ· ˈ·◂‖ˈ· ·/ *adj AmE* having eyes that seem to point to the side, rather than straight forwards

**wall·flow·er** /ˈwɔːlˌflaʊə‖ˈwɒːlˌflaʊər/ *n* [C] **1** *informal* someone at a party, dance etc who is not asked to dance or take part in the activities **2** a sweet-smelling garden plant with yellow and red flowers

**wal·lop**[1] /ˈwɒləp‖ˈwɑː-/ *v* [T] *informal* to hit someone or something very hard

**wallop**[2] *n* [C] *informal* a hard hit, especially with your hand

**wal·lop·ing**[1] /ˈwɒləpɪŋ‖ˈwɑː-/ *n spoken* **give sb/get a walloping** to hit someone repeatedly as a punishment

**walloping**[2] *adj* [only before noun] **walloping great/big** *spoken* very big: *a walloping great house in the country*

**wal·low**[1] /ˈwɒləʊ‖ˈwɑːloʊ/ *v* [I] **1 wallow in self-pity/despair/defeat etc** to seem to enjoy being sad etc, especially because you get sympathy from other people: *Stop wallowing in self-pity, and do something positive.* **2** if an animal wallows, it rolls around in mud, water etc for pleasure: *hippos wallowing in the mud* **3** if a ship or boat wallows, it moves with difficulty through a rough sea

**wallow**[2] *n* **1 a wallow in sth** an act of wallowing in something: *She indulged in a wallow in self-pity.* **2** [C] a place where animals go to wallow, especially in mud

**wall paint·ing** /ˈ· ˌ··/ *n* [C] a picture that has been painted directly onto a wall, especially a FRESCO

**wall·pa·per**[1] /ˈwɔːlˌpeɪpə‖ˈwɒːlˌpeɪpər/ *n* [C,U] paper that you stick onto the walls of a room in order to decorate it

**wallpaper**[2] *v* [T] to put wallpaper onto the walls of a room

**Wall Street** /ˈ· ·/ *n* **1** a street in New York which is the most important financial centre in America: *Wall Street jitters caused by the Gulf War* **2** the American STOCK MARKET

**wall-to-wall** /ˌ· · ˈ·◂/ *adj* **1** [only before noun] covering the whole floor: *wall-to-wall carpeting* **2** *informal* filling all the space or time available, especially in a way you do not like: *wall-to-wall advertising on TV*

**wal·ly** /ˈwɒli‖ˈwɑː-/ *n* [C] *BrE informal* someone who behaves in a silly way: *Stop being such a wally!*

**wal·nut** /ˈwɔːlnʌt‖ˈwɒːl-/ *n* **1** [C] a nut that you can eat, shaped like a human brain: *coffee and walnut cake* **2** [C] also **walnut tree** a tree that produces this type of nut **3** [U] the wood from a walnut tree, often used to make furniture

**wal·rus** /ˈwɔːlrəs‖ˈwɒːl-, ˈwɑːl-/ *n* [C] a large sea animal with two long TUSKS (=like teeth) coming down from its head

**waltz**[1] /wɔːls‖wɒːlts/ *n* [C] **1** a fairly slow dance with a strong regular beat **2** a piece of music intended for this type of dance: *a Strauss waltz*

**waltz**[2] *v* **1** [I] to dance a waltz **2** [I + adv/prep always] *informal* to walk somewhere calmly and confidently: [+ **in/into/up to**] *Jeff just waltzed up to the bar and helped himself to a drink.*
**waltz off with** sth *phr v* [T] *informal* to take something without permission or without realizing that you have done this: *Joe must have waltzed off with my jacket!*
**waltz through** sth *phr v* [T] *informal* **waltz through an exam/test etc** to do an exam, test etc very well without any difficulty

**wam·pum** /ˈwɒmpəm‖ˈwɑːm-/ *n* [U] **1** shells put into strings, belts etc, used in the past as money by Native Americans **2** *AmE informal* money

**wan** /wɒn‖wɑːn/ *adj especially literary* looking pale, weak, or tired: *She gave a wan smile.* —**wanly** *adv*

**wand** /wɒnd‖wɑːnd/ *n* [C] **1** a thin stick you hold in your hand to do magic tricks **2** a tool that looks like a thin stick: *a mascara wand*

**wan·der**[1] /ˈwɒndə‖ˈwɑːndər/ *v* S3
**1 ▶ MOVE WITHOUT A DIRECTION ◀** [I,T] to move slowly across or around an area, without a clear direction or purpose: **wander in/through/around etc** *I'll just wander around the mall for half an hour.* | **wander sth** *Nomadic tribes wander these deserts.*
**2 ▶ MOVE AWAY ◀** also **wander off** [I] to move away from where you are supposed to stay: *Don't let any of the kids wander off.*
**3 ▶ CHANGE THE SUBJECT ◀** [I] to start to talk about something not connected with the main subject that you were talking about before: [+ **from/off**] *Pastor Riker started to wander from the point.*
**4 ▶ MIND/THOUGHTS ◀** [I] if your mind, thoughts etc wander, you no longer pay attention to something, especially because you are bored or worried: *I'm sorry, my mind was wandering. What did you say?*
**5 sb's mind is wandering** used to say that someone has become unable to think clearly, especially because they are old
**6 ▶ ROAD/RIVER ◀** [I] if a road or a river wanders somewhere, it does not go straight but in curves: [+ **through/across/along**] *The Missouri river wanders across several states.* —**wanderer** *n* [C]

**wander**[2] *n* [singular] a short relaxed walk: **go for/take a wander** *Let's take a wander down to the shops.*

**wan·der·ings** /ˈwɒndərɪŋz‖ˈwɑːn-/ *n* [plural] *literary* journeys to places where you do not stay for very long: *his wanderings through the Australian outback*

**wan·der·lust** /ˈwɒndəlʌst‖ˈwɑːndər-/ *n* [singular, U] a strong desire to travel to different places

**wane**[1] /weɪn/ *v* [I] **1** if something such as power, influence, or a feeling wanes, it becomes gradually less strong or less important: *My enthusiasm for the project was* *waning.* **2** when the moon wanes, you gradually see less of it —compare WAX² (4)

**wane²** *n* **on the wane** becoming smaller, weaker, or less important: *By the 5th century, the power of the Roman Empire was on the wane.*

**wan·gle** /ˈwæŋgəl/ *v* [T] *informal* to get something, or arrange for something to happen, by cleverly persuading or tricking someone: **wangle sth out of sb** *In the end she wangled an invitation out of them.* | **wangle it for sth to happen** *I managed to wangle it for us all to go.* | **wangle your way out of sth** (=get out of a difficult or unpleasant situation in this way) —**wangle** *n* [singular]

**wank¹** /wæŋk/ *v* [I] *BrE taboo* to MASTURBATE

**wank²** *n* [singular] *BrE taboo* an act of MASTURBATION

**wank·er** /ˈwæŋkə‖-ər/ *n* [C] *BrE taboo* someone who you think is stupid or unpleasant

**wan·na** /ˈwɒnə‖ˈwɑː-/ *spoken* **1** a short form of 'want to' **2** a short form of 'want a'

**wan·na·be** /ˈwɒnəbi‖ˈwɑː-/ *n* [C] *informal* someone who wants to be like someone famous or have money and power —compare **would-be**

S1 W1 **want¹** /wɒnt‖wɒːnt, wɑːnt/ *v* [not usually in progressive]
**1** ▶ **DESIRE** ◀ [T] to have a desire for something: *I want a drink.* | *What do you want for your birthday?* | **want to do sth** *Do you want to go to Kay's party?* | **want sb to do sth** *I don't want Linda to hear about this.* | **want sth of sb** *formal* (=want someone to do something) *I wish I knew what he wanted of me.*
**2** ▶ **NEED** ◀ [T] to need something: *Do you still want these magazines, or can I throw them out?* | **want to do sth** *You only want to use a little glue.* | **want sth done** *I want that letter typed today.* | **what sb wants with sth** (=what someone needs something for) *What do you want with a tool kit?* | **want doing** *especially BrE informal* (=need to be done) *The carpet really wants cleaning.*
**3** ▶ **ASK FOR SB** ◀ [T] to ask for someone to come and talk to you, or to come to a particular place: *You're wanted on the phone.*
**4** ▶ **SHOULD** ◀ [T] *spoken especially BrE* ought or should: **want to do sth** *You want to see a doctor about that cough.*
**5** ▶ **LACK** ◀ [I,T] *formal* to suffer because you do not have something: *In many poorer countries, people still want basic food and shelter.*
**6 want in/out** *informal* **a)** *especially AmE* to want to go in to or out of a place: *The cat wants out.* **b)** to want to take part in a plan or stop being involved: *If you want out, say so now.* —see also WANTED, WANTING, **waste not, want not** (WASTE² (7))

Frequencies of the verb **want** in spoken and written English.

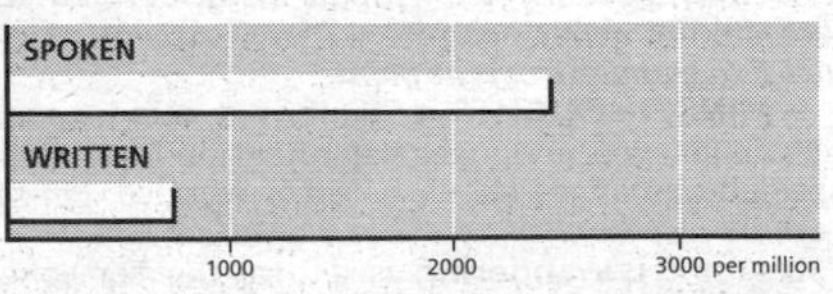


Based on the British National Corpus and the Longman Lancaster Corpus

This graph shows that the verb **want** is much more common in spoken English than in written English. This is because it is used in a lot of common spoken phrases.

**want** (*v*) **SPOKEN PHRASES**

**7 I want/I don't want**: *I want a new coat.* | *I don't want to go out tonight.* **8 what do you want?** used to ask, often in a slightly rude way, what someone wants you to give them, do for them etc: *What do you want now? I'm busy.* | *What do you want – chocolate or vanilla?* **9 do you want...?** used when offering something to someone: *Do you want a drink?* | *Do you want me to come with you?* **10 who wants...? a)** used to say that you do not like something, do not think that it is worth doing etc: *Who wants to go to a noisy disco anyway?* **b)** used when offering something to a group of people: *Who wants a cup of coffee?* **11 if you want** used when someone suggests doing something, to say that you will do it, although you do not especially want to: *"Hey, shall we go to the beach?" "If you want."* **12 I want you to do something** used to tell someone to do something: *I want you to go and get me a newspaper.* **13 want...?** used when offering something to someone: *Want a game of chess?* **14 what I want** used to explain or say exactly what it is that you want: *What I want is a car that's cheap and reliable.* **15 all I want** used to say that you only want something simple or small, and you think it is fair to ask for it: *Look, all I want is a decent job. It's not much to ask for, is it?* **16 you don't want** used to advise someone not to do something: *You don't want to go there, it's much too crowded.* **17 I just wanted to say/know etc** used to politely say something, ask about something etc: *I just wanted to check that the meeting is still on next week.* **18 it's/that's just what I (always) wanted** used to say that you like a present you have just been given very much

**want for** sth *phr v* [T] **1** to not have something that you need: *Say what you like, my kids never wanted for anything.*

**want²** *n*
**1** ▶ **LACK** ◀ [C,U] *formal* something that you need but do not have: **for want of sth** (=because of a lack of something) *People often take casual jobs in catering for want of any alternative.* | **satisfy a want** (=give someone what they need)
**2** ▶ **SITUATION WITHOUT FOOD/MONEY** ◀ [U] a situation in which you do not have enough food, money, clothes etc: *They had lived all their lives in want.*
**3 for want of a better word/term/phrase** used to say that there is no exact word to describe what you are talking about: *a feeling that, for want of a better word, we call love*
**4 for want of anything better (to do)** if you do something for want of anything better, you do it only because there is nothing else you want to do
**5 not for want of trying/asking etc** used to say that you should have got what you wanted because you tried very hard or asked for it many times: *Well, if he doesn't get the job it won't be for want of trying!*
**6 be in want of sth** *formal* to need something: *a creaking house, in want of repair*

**want ad** /ˈ· ·/ *n* [C] *AmE* CLASSIFIED AD

**want·ed** /ˈwɒntɪ̀d‖ˈwɒːn-,ˈwɑːn-/ *adj* someone who is wanted is being looked for by the police: *He is wanted in connection with the murder of a teenage girl.*

**want·ing** /ˈwɒntɪŋ‖ˈwɒːn-, ˈwɑːn-/ *adj* [not before noun] **1 be found wanting** proven not to be good enough for a particular purpose: *Traditional solutions had been tried and found wanting.* **2 wanting in sth** *formal* not having enough of something: *wanting in grace and tact* **3** *formal* lacking or missing: *A certain humanity is wanting in big cities.*

**wan·ton** /ˈwɒntən‖ˈwɒːn-, ˈwɑːn-/ *adj* **1** wanton cruelty, destruction etc deliberately harms someone or damages something for no reason: *an act of wanton aggression* **2** *old-fashioned* a wanton woman is considered immoral because she has sex with a lot of men **3** *formal* uncontrolled: *wanton jungle growth* —**wantonly** *adv* —**wantonness** *n* [U]

**war** /wɔː‖wɔːr/ *n* S3 W1
**1** ▶ **WAR IN GENERAL** ◀ [U] fighting between two or more countries or opposing groups within a country, involving large numbers of soldiers and weapons: *Cambodia has been ravaged by war for the past 20 years.* | **war breaks out** (=war begins) *War broke out in September of 1939.* | **be at war (with)** *In 1920 Poland and Russia were still at war.* | **declare war (on sb)** (=announce publicly and officially that you are going to fight a war) | **go to war (with)** (=start to fight a war with another country) |

**wage war (on/against)** (=start and continue a war, especially for a long period)|**the outbreak of war** (=the start of fighting in a war)
**2** ▶ **A PARTICULAR WAR** ◀ [C] a particular period of time when countries fight with soldiers and weapons: *Do you remember the last war?*|**the Vietnam/Seven Years/First World etc War** *America's defeat in the Vietnam War*|[+ **with/against**] *Iran's seven year war with Iraq*|**win/lose a war** *tactical errors that made France lose the war*|**fight a war** *Britain has fought two wars in Europe this century.*|**war between** *The war between England and France was to last another 50 years.*|**a nuclear war** *Both countries wanted to avoid a nuclear war.*|**a war hero** (=a brave soldier)|**a war veteran** (=a former soldier)
**3** ▶ **AGAINST CRIME/DISEASE ETC** ◀ [C,U] a struggle over a long period of time to control something harmful: [+ **against/on**] *the State's war on drugs*
**4** ▶ **FOR POWER/CONTROL** ◀ [C,U] a situation in which a person or group is fighting for power, influence, or control: *No one wants to start a trade war here.*
**5 This means war!** *spoken humorous* used to say that you are ready to fight about something
**6 the war** *especially BrE* the Second World War
**7 between the wars** the period between the First and Second World Wars
**8 look like you have been in the wars** *BrE spoken* to look injured or damaged —see also CIVIL WAR, COLD WAR, PRICE WAR, PRISONER OF WAR, WAR OF ATTRITION, WAR OF NERVES, WAR OF WORDS, WARRING

This graph shows some of the words most commonly used with the noun **war**.

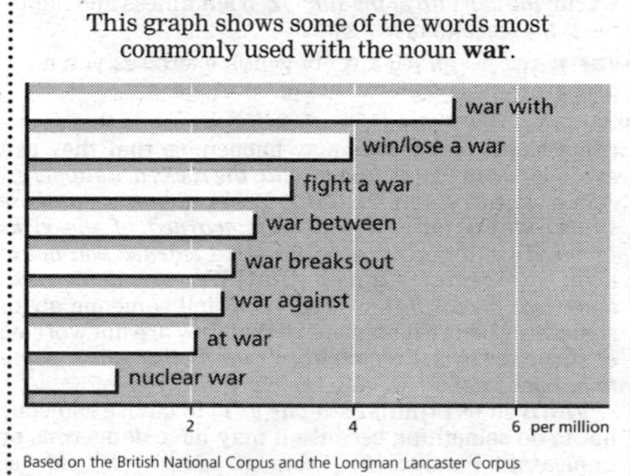


Based on the British National Corpus and the Longman Lancaster Corpus

**war·ble** /ˈwɔːbəl‖ˈwɔːr-/ *v* **1** [I] to sing with a high continuous but rapidly changing sound, the way a bird does **2** [I, T] *humorous* to sing: *Ned warbled a serenade.*

**war·bler** /ˈwɔːblə‖ˈwɔːrblər/ *n* [C] **1** a bird that can make musical sounds **2** *humorous* a singer, especially one who does not sing very well

**war bride** /ˈ· ·/ *n* [C] a woman who marries a foreign soldier who is in her country because there is a war

**war cab·i·net** /ˌ· ˈ···/ *n* [C] a group of important British politicians who meet to make decisions during a war

**war chest** /ˈ· ·/ *n* [C] *informal* the money that a government has available to spend on war

**war crime** /ˈ· ·/ *n* [C] an illegal and cruel act done during a war —**war criminal** *n* [C]

**war cry** /ˈ· ·/ *n* [C] a shout used by people fighting in a battle to show their courage and frighten the enemy —see also BATTLE CRY

**-ward** /wəd‖wərd/ *suffix* [in adjectives] towards a particular direction or place: *our homeward journey*|*a downward movement*

W3 **ward¹** /wɔːd‖wɔːrd/ *n* [C] **1** a large room in a hospital where people who need medical treatment stay: *She's in charge of three different wards.*|**maternity/general/geriatric etc ward** (=a ward for people with a particular medical condition) **2** *BrE* one of the small areas that a city has been divided into for the purpose of local elections —compare CONSTITUENCY (2) **3** *law* someone, especially a child, who is under the legal protection of another person or of a law court: *a ward of court*

**ward²** *v*
**ward** sth **off** *phr v* [T] to do something to prevent something such as an illness, danger, or attack from harming you: *a spell to ward off evil spirits*

**war dance** /ˈ· ·/ *n* [C] a dance performed by tribes in preparation for battle or to celebrate a victory

**war·den** /ˈwɔːdn‖ˈwɔːrdn/ *n* [C] **1** an official whose job is to make sure that rules are obeyed **2** *AmE* the person in charge of a prison; GOVERNOR (3) *BrE* **3** *BrE* someone who takes care of a building and the people in it, for example a place such as a home for old people —see also CHURCHWARDEN, GAME WARDEN, TRAFFIC WARDEN

**ward·er** /ˈwɔːdə‖ˈwɔːrdər/ *n* [C] *BrE* someone who works in a prison guarding the prisoners

**ward·ress** /ˈwɔːdrɪs‖ˈwɔːr-/ *n* [C] *BrE* a woman who works in a prison guarding prisoners

**war·drobe** /ˈwɔːdrəʊb‖ˈwɔːrdroʊb/ *n* **1** [C] *BrE* a piece of furniture like a large cupboard that you hang clothes in; CLOSET[1] (2) *AmE* **2** [C] the clothes that someone has: *Princess Diana requires an extensive wardrobe.* **3** [singular] a department in a theatre, television company etc that deals with the clothes worn by actors on stage: **a wardrobe mistress** (=woman in charge of this department)

**ward·room** /ˈwɔːdrʊm, -ruːm‖ˈwɔːrd-/ *n* [C] the space in a WARSHIP where the officers live and eat, except for the captain

**-wards** /wədz‖wərdz/ also **-ward** *especially AmE suffix* [in adverbs] towards a particular direction or place: *We're travelling northwards.*|*The plane plunged earthwards.*

**-ware** /weə‖wer/ *suffix* [in U nouns] **1** articles made of a particular material, especially for use in the home: *glassware* (=glass bowls, glasses, etc)|*silverware* (=silver dishes, knives, etc) **2** articles used in a particular place for the preparation or serving of food: *ovenware* (=dishes for use in the OVEN)|*tableware* (=plates, glasses, knives, etc) **3** things used in operating a computer: *software* (=PROGRAMS)|*liveware* (=people who operate computers)

**war ef·fort** /ˈ· ˌ··/ *n* [singular] things done by all the people in a country to help when that country is at war

**ware·house** /ˈweəhaʊs‖ˈwer-/ *n* [C] a large building for storing large quantities of goods

**wares** /weəz‖werz/ *n* [plural] things that are for sale, usually not in a shop: *the market trader's wares*

**war·fare** /ˈwɔːfeə‖ˈwɔːrfer/ *n* [U] **1** a word meaning the activity of fighting in a war, used especially when talking about particular methods of fighting: **nuclear/chemical/trench warfare** *the terrible prospect of large-scale nuclear warfare*|**guerrilla warfare** (=warfare by small groups of fighters in mountains, forests etc) **2** a continous struggle between groups, countries etc: *political warfare* —see also **psychological warfare** (PSYCHOLOGICAL (3))

**war game** /ˈ· ˌ·/ *n* [C] **1** an activity in which soldiers fight an imaginary battle in order to test military plans **2** a game played by adults in which models of soldiers, guns, horses etc are moved around a table

**war·head** /ˈwɔːhed‖ˈwɔːr-/ *n* [C] the explosive part at the front of a MISSILE (1)

**war·horse** /ˈwɔːhɔːs‖ˈwɔːrhɔːrs/ *n* [C] **1** *informal* a soldier or politician who has been in their job a long time, and enjoys dealing with all the difficulties involved in it **2** a horse used in battle

**war·like** /ˈwɔːlaɪk‖ˈwɔːr-/ *adj* **1** liking war and being skilful in it: *a warlike nation* **2** threatening war or attack: *a warlike stance*

**war·lock** /ˈwɔːlɒk‖ˈwɔːrlɑːk/ *n* [C] a man who has magical powers, especially evil powers

**war·lord** /ˈwɔːlɔːd‖ˈwɔːrlɔːrd/ *n* [C] a military leader, especially an unofficial one fighting against a government or king

S2 W2 **warm¹** /wɔːm‖wɔːrm/ *adj*
1 ▶ **BE WARM** ◀ slightly hot, especially pleasantly: *a warm bath*|*I hope we get some warmer weather soon.*| **keep sth warm** (=stop something from becoming cold) *I've put your dinner in the oven to keep it warm.* —see picture at HOT¹
2 ▶ **FEEL WARM** ◀ feeling slightly hot, or making you feel this way: *Are you warm enough?*|**keep warm** (=wear enough clothes not to feel cold) *Make sure you keep warm!*
3 ▶ **CLOTHES/BUILDINGS** ◀ clothes or buildings that are warm can keep in heat or keep out cold: *Here, put on your nice warm coat.*
4 ▶ **FRIENDLY** ◀ friendly in a way that makes you feel comfortable: *a warm, reassuring smile*|**a warm welcome** *Please give a warm welcome to our special guest!*
5 ▶ **COLOUR** ◀ colours that are warm are red, yellow, orange, and similar colours
6 **as warm as toast** pleasantly warm
7 ▶ **CORRECT** ◀ used especially in games to say that someone is near to guessing the correct answer or finding a hidden object: *You're getting warmer.* —opposite COLD¹ (13)
8 **make it/make things warm for sb** *informal* to cause problems for someone in order to punish them
9 **warm scent/trail** a smell or path that has been made recently, which a hunter can easily follow
10 ▶ **ANGRY/EXCITED** ◀ *AmE* fairly angry or excited: *The atmosphere in the meeting grew warm.* —see also **keep sb's seat warm** (KEEP) —**warmness** *n* [U]

**warm²** *v* also **warm up**
1 [T] to make someone or something warm or warmer: *Here, warm yourself by the fire.* **2** [I] to be heated: [+ **in/by/on**] *There's some soup warming in the pot.*

**warm to** sb/sth *phr v* [T] **1** to begin to like something, or someone you have just met: *Bruce didn't warm to him as he had to Casey.* **2** to become more eager or excited about something: **warm to a theme/subject/topic etc** *The more she spoke, the more she warmed to her subject.*

**warm up** *phr v*
1 ▶ **MAKE WARM** ◀ [I,T] to become warm or to make someone or something warm: **warm sb/sth ↔ up** *A brandy should warm you up.*|*If you're ready for your dinner I'll warm it up.*
2 ▶ **DO EXERCISES** ◀ [I] to do gentle physical exercises to prepare your body for dancing, sport etc: *The athletes are warming up before the race.*
3 ▶ **MACHINE/ENGINE** ◀ [I,T] if you warm up a machine or engine or it warms up, it becomes ready to work properly
4 ▶ **PARTY** ◀ [I,T] if a party warms up, it starts to become enjoyable: *Don't go, things are just starting to warm up.*
5 ▶ **BECOME CHEERFUL** ◀ [I,T] to become cheerful, eager, and excited, or to make someone feel this way: **warm sb ↔ up** *He warmed up the audience by telling them a few jokes.* —see also **like death warmed up/over** (DEATH (9))

**warm up to** sth *phr v* [T] *AmE* to warm to someone or something

**warm³** *n* **the warm** *especially BrE* a place that is warm: *Come into the warm!*

**warm⁴** *adv* **wrap up warm** to put on enough clothes so that you do not feel cold

**warm-blood·ed** /ˌ· ˈ··◂/ *adj* animals that are warm-blooded have a body temperature that remains fairly high whether the temperature around them is hot or cold —compare COLD-BLOODED

**warmed o·ver** /ˌ· ˈ··◂/ *adj AmE* **1** food that is warmed over has been cooked before and then heated again for eating **2** an idea or argument that is warmed over has been used before and is not interesting or useful any more —see also **like death warmed up/over** (DEATH (9))

**war me·mo·ri·al** /ˈ· ·ˌ···/ *n* [C] a MONUMENT (1) put up to remind people of those killed in a war

**warm front** /ˌ· ˈ·/ *n* [C] *technical* an expression used especially in weather reports meaning the front edge of a mass of warm air coming towards a place

**warm-heart·ed** /ˌ· ˈ··◂/ *adj* friendly, kind, and always willing to help: *a warm-hearted landlady* —compare COLD-HEARTED —**warm-heartedly** *adv* —**warm-heartedness** *n* [U]

**warm·ing¹** /ˈwɔːmɪŋ‖ˈwɔːr-/ *adj* making you feel pleasantly warm: *a warming cup of cocoa*

**warming²** *n* [U] an act of making something warm or warmer: **global warming** (=the increase in the temperature of the Earth's air) *global warming caused by pollution*

**warming pan** /ˈ·· ·/ *n* [C] a metal container with a long handle, used in the past to hold hot coals for warming beds

**warm·ly** /ˈwɔːmli‖ˈwɔːrm-/ *adv* **1** in a friendly way: *Teri greeted the visitor warmly.* **2** in a way that makes something or someone warm: *Pat wrapped the baby up warmly.*|**dress warmly** (=so you do not become cold) **3** eagerly: *"Do you like dancing?" "Love it," said Mary warmly.* **4** *AmE* slightly angrily: *I may have spoken too warmly.*

**war·mon·ger** /ˈwɔːˌmʌŋgə‖ˈwɔːrˌmɑːŋgər, -ˌmʌŋ-/ *n* [C] someone, especially a politician, who is eager to start a war to achieve an aim —**warmongering** *adj* —**warmongering** *n* [U]

**warmth** /wɔːmθ‖wɔːrmθ/ *n* [U] **1** a feeling of being warm: *the warmth of the sun* **2** friendliness and happiness: *the warmth of her smile*

**warm-up** /ˈ· ·/ *n* [C] a set of gentle exercises you do to prepare your body for dancing, sport etc

**warn** /wɔːn‖wɔːrn/ *v* [I,T] **1** to tell someone that something bad or dangerous may happen, so that they can avoid it or prevent it: *"Be careful, the rocks are slippery," Alex warned.*|**warn sb about** *I warned him about those stairs.*|**warn (sb) of** *You were warned of the risks involved.*|**warn sb not to do sth** *I warned you not to walk home alone.*|**warn sb (that)** *We warned them that there was a bull in the field.* **2** to tell someone about something before it happens so that they are not worried or surprised by it: *Can you warn your mother you're going to be back late?* S W

**warn** sb ↔ **against** sth *phr v* [T] to advise someone not to do something because it may have dangerous or unpleasant results: *Her financial adviser warned her against such a risky investment.*|**warn sb against doing sth** *The police have warned tourists against going to remoter regions.*

**warn** sb **off** *phr v* [T] **1** to tell someone to go away or not come near something, using threats: *The farmer waved his stick in the air to warn us off his land.* **2** to advise someone to go away or to avoid something: **warn sb off doing sth** *I tried to warn her off going out with him.*

**warn·ing** /ˈwɔːnɪŋ‖ˈwɔːrn-/ *n* **1** [C,U] something, especially a statement, that tells you that something bad, annoying, or dangerous might happen: *the government health warning on packs of cigarettes*|**warning against** *The police issued a warning against speeding.*|**warning of** *a warning of floods*|**warning to sb** *a warning to pregnant women not to drink alcohol*|**give a warning** *We were given no warning of possible delays at the airport.*|**a warning cry/sign/look etc** *Do not ignore warning signs such as tiredness and headaches.*|**without warning** *Without warning, the soldiers started firing into the crowd.*|**advance warning** (=warning before something happens) **2** [C] a statement telling someone that if they continue to behave in an unsatisfactory way, they will be punished: **give a warning** *I'm giving you a final warning – don't be late again.* **3** **give fair warning** to tell someone about something long enough before it happens so that they can be ready S W

**war of at·tri·tion** /ˌ· · ·ˈ··/ *n* [C] a struggle in which you harm your opponent in a lot of small ways, so that they become gradually weaker

**war of nerves** /ˌ· · ˈ·/ *n* [C] an attempt to make an enemy worried, and to destroy their courage by threatening them, spreading false information etc

**war of words** /ˌ· · ˈ·/ *n* [C] a public argument between politicians etc

**warp¹** /wɔːp‖wɔːrp/ *v* **1** [I,T] to bend or twist and to be no longer in the correct shape, or to make something do this: *The door's been warped or something, it won't close properly.* **2** to have a bad effect on someone so that they think strangely about things: *Henry's view of women had been warped by a painful divorce.*

**warp²** *n* **1 the warp** *technical* the threads used in weaving cloth that go from the top to the bottom —compare WEFT **2** [singular] a part of something that is not straight or in the right shape —see also TIME WARP

**war paint** /ˈ· ·/ *n* [U] **1** paint that some tribes put on their bodies and faces before going to war **2** *humorous* MAKE-UP (1): *Josie's just putting on her war paint.*

**war·path** /ˈwɔːpɑːθ‖ˈwɔːrpæθ/ *n informal* **be on the warpath** to be angry and looking for someone to fight or punish

**warped** /wɔːpt‖wɔːrpt/ *adj* **1** someone who is warped has ideas or thoughts that most people think are unpleasant or not normal: *a warped mind*|**have a warped sense of humour** (=think strange and unpleasant things are funny) **2** something that is warped is bent or twisted so that it is not in the correct shape

**war·rant¹** /ˈwɒrənt‖ˈwɔː-, ˈwɑː-/ *n* **1** [C] written permission from a court of law allowing the police to take a particular action: [+ **for**] *The magistrate issued a warrant for his arrest.*|**search warrant** (=permission to go into someone's house to look for something) —see also DEATH WARRANT **2** [U] *formal* good enough reason for doing something; JUSTIFICATION —see also UNWARRANTED

**warrant²** *v* **1** [T] to be a good enough reason for something: *This tiny crowd does not warrant such a large police presence.* **2** to promise that something is true; GUARANTEE¹ (1) **3** [I,T] *old-fashioned* used to say that you are sure about something: *I'll warrant we won't see him again.*

**warrant of·fic·er** /ˈ·· ˌ···/ *n* [C] a middle rank in the army, air force, or US Navy —see table on page B4

**war·ran·ty** /ˈwɒrənti‖ˈwɔː-, ˈwɑː-/ *n* [C] a written promise that a company makes to replace or fix a product if it breaks or does not work properly: *a five-year anti-corrosion warranty* —compare GUARANTEE² (3), SECURITY (4)

**war·ren** /ˈwɒrən‖ˈwɔː-, ˈwɑː-/ *n* [C] **1** the underground home of rabbits **2** a place with so many streets, rooms etc that it is difficult to know the correct way around it: *a warren of alleyways*

**war·ring** /ˈwɔːrɪŋ/ *adj* [only before noun] at war or fighting each other: **warring factions** (=groups of people fighting each other)

**war·ri·or** /ˈwɒriə‖ˈwɔːriər, ˈwɑː-/ *n* [C] a soldier or man experienced in fighting, especially in the past: *a noble warrior*

**war·ship** /ˈwɔːˌʃɪp‖ˈwɔːr-/ *n* [C] a ship with guns that is used in a war

**wart** /wɔːt‖wɔːrt/ *n* [C] **1** a small hard raised part on someone's skin —see also VERRUCA **2 warts and all** *informal* including all the faults or unpleasant things: *Well, you married him – warts and all.* —**warty** *adj*

**wart·hog** /ˈwɔːthɒg‖ˈwɔːrthɔːg, -hɑːg/ *n* [C] an African wild pig with long front teeth that stick out of its mouth

**war·time** /ˈwɔːtaɪm‖ˈwɔːr-/ *adj* happening or existing during the time when a country is at war: *a film set in wartime France* —**wartime** *n* [U] —opposite PEACETIME

**war-torn** /ˈ· ·/ *adj* [only before noun] a war-torn country, city etc is being destroyed by war, especially war between opposing groups from the same country

**war wid·ow** /ˈ· ˌ··/ *n* [C] a woman whose husband has been killed in a war

**war·y** /ˈweəri‖ˈweri/ *adj* someone who is wary is careful because they think something might be dangerous or harmful: **be wary of (doing) sth** *I'm a bit wary of driving in this fog.* —**wariness** *n* [U] —**warily** *adv*: *"I want to ask you a favour." "What is it?" Mike said warily.*

**war zone** /ˈ· ·/ *n* [C] an area where a war is being fought

**was** /wəz; *strong* wɒz‖wəz; *strong* wɑːz/ the first and third person singular of the past tense of BE

**wash¹** /wɒʃ‖wɒːʃ, wɑːʃ/ *v* 

**1 ► WASH SOMETHING ◄** [T] to clean something using soap and water: *I'm just going to wash my hands.*|*This shirt needs washing.*|**wash the dishes** *It's your turn to wash the dishes.*

**2 ► WASH YOURSELF ◄** [I] to clean yourself with soap and water: *Amy washed and went to bed.*

**3 ► FLOW ◄** [I always + adv/prep, T always + adv/prep] if a liquid or something carried by a liquid washes or is washed in a particular direction, it flows there: [+ **against/away etc**] *The waves washed against the shore.*|**wash sth away/against/down etc** *Floods had washed away the topsoil.*|**wash ashore** (=be brought to the shore by waves) *debris washed ashore by the tide*

**4 sth doesn't/won't wash** *spoken* used to say that you do not believe or accept someone's explanation, reason, attitude etc: *I'm sorry but all his charm just doesn't wash with me.*

**5 wash your hands of sth** to refuse to be responsible for something anymore: *I've washed my hands of the whole affair.*

**6 wash your dirty linen in public** to discuss something unpleasant or embarrassing in public

**7 wash your mouth out!** *spoken* used when someone has just sworn or said something rude, to tell them they should not have spoken that way

**8 wash well/badly** to be easy or difficult to clean using soap and water: *Silk doesn't wash well.* —see also **wash up**

**wash** sth ↔ **down** *phr v* [T] **1** to clean something large using a lot of water: *Can you wash down the driveway?* **2** to drink something to help you swallow food or medicine: **wash sth down with sth** *steak and chips washed down with red wine*

**wash** sth ↔ **off** *phr v* **1** [T] to clean dirt, dust etc from the surface of something with water **2** [I] if a substance washes off, you can remove it from the surface of something by washing: *Will this paint wash off?*

**wash** sth ↔ **out** *phr v* **1** [T] to wash something quickly to get rid of the dirt in it: *I'll just wash out my paint rags first.* **2** [I] if a substance washes out, you can remove it from a material by washing it **3 be washed out** if an event is washed out, it cannot continue because of rain: *The summer fair was washed out by the English weather.* —see also WASHED-OUT, WASHOUT

**wash over** sb *phr v* [T] if a feeling washes over you, you suddenly feel it very strongly: *A feeling of relief washed over her as the plane landed.*

**wash up** *phr v* **1** [I,T] *especially BrE* to wash plates, dishes, knives etc —see also WASHING-UP —see picture at CLEAN² **2** [I] *AmE* to wash your hands: *Go wash up before dinner.* **3** [T **wash** sth ↔ **up**] if waves wash something up, they bring it to the shore: *His body was washed up the next morning.* —see also **wash ashore** (WASH¹ (3)), WASHED UP

**USAGE NOTE: WASH**

GRAMMAR

You do not usually use the expression **wash yourself** unless a special effort is needed: *He washed/had a wash, dressed, and fixed breakfast.*|*Several children in the class still can't wash themselves.*

**wash²** *n*

**1 ► ACT OF CLEANING ◄** [C] an act of cleaning

W

something using soap and water: *Those drapes need a wash.* | **have a wash** *I'll just have a quick wash before we go.*
**2 in the wash** waiting to be washed, being washed, or drying: *Your blue shirt's in the wash – you'll have to wear another one.* | **shrink/fade/get damaged etc in the wash** *I'm afraid your black sweater shrank in the wash.*
**3 it'll all come out in the wash** *spoken* used to tell someone not to worry about a problem because it will be solved in the future
**4 ▶ BOAT ◀** [singular, U] the movement of water caused by a passing boat
**5 ▶ SEA/RIVER ◀ the wash of** the movement or sound made by flowing water: *the wash of the waves against the rocks*
**6 ▶ SKIN ◀** [C] a liquid used to clean your skin: *an anti-bacterial face wash*
**7 ▶ COLOUR ◀** [C] a very thin transparent layer of paint or colour
**8 ▶ CLOTHES ◀** [singular, U] *AmE* clothes that need to be washed, are being washed, or have just been washed; WASHING *BrE:* **do the wash** (=wash dirty clothes) | **hang the wash out** (=put it on the washing line)
**9 ▶ RIVER ◀** also **dry wash** [C] *AmE* a river in a desert that usually has no water in it
**10** *n* [singular] the area of land that is sometimes covered by the sea —see picture on page 835

**wash·a·ble** /ˈwɒʃəbəl‖ˈwɒː-, ˈwɑː-/ *adj* **1** something that is washable can be washed without being damaged: *washable cushion covers* | **machine washable** *machine washable wool* **2** paint, ink etc that is washable will come out of cloth when you wash it

**wash·ba·sin** /ˈwɒʃˌbeɪsən‖ˈwɒːʃ-, ˈwɑːʃ-/ *n* [C] *BrE* a container like a small SINK[2] used for washing your hands and face

**wash·board** /ˈwɒʃbɔːd‖ˈwɒːʃbɔːrd, ˈwɑːʃ-/ *n* [C] a piece of metal with a slightly rough surface, used in the past for rubbing clothes on when you are washing them

**wash·cloth** /ˈwɒʃklɒθ‖ˈwɒːʃklɒːθ, ˈwɑːʃ-/ *n* [C] *AmE* a small square cloth used for washing your hands and face; FACECLOTH *BrE*

**wash·day** /ˈwɒʃdeɪ‖ˈwɒːʃ-, ˈwɑːʃ-/ *n* [C,U] *old-fashioned* the day each week when you wash your clothes

**washed-out** /ˌ· ˈ·◂/ *adj* **1** not brightly coloured any more usually as a result of being washed many times: *a washed-out shade of blue* **2** feeling weak and looking unhealthy because you are very tired: *Debbie's looking a bit washed-out.* —see also **wash out** (WASH[1])

**washed-up** /ˌ· ˈ·◂/ *adj* if a person or an organization is washed-up, they will never be successful again: *washed-up ex-members of the Board* —see also **wash up** (WASH[1])

**wash·er** /ˈwɒʃə‖ˈwɒːʃər, ˈwɑː-/ *n* [C] **1** a thin flat ring of plastic, metal, rubber etc that is put over a BOLT[1] (2) before the NUT[1] (2) is put on, or between two pipes, to make a tighter joint **2** *informal* a WASHING MACHINE

**washer-dr·yer** also **washer-drier** *BrE* /ˌ·· ˈ··/ *n* [C] a machine that washes and dries clothes

**wash·er·wom·an** /ˈwɒʃəˌwʊmən‖ˈwɒːʃər-, ˈwɑː-/ *n* [C] a woman in the past whose job was to wash other people's clothes

**wash·ing** /ˈwɒʃɪŋ‖ˈwɒː-, ˈwɑː-/ *n* [singular, U] *BrE* clothes that need to be washed, are being washed, or have just been washed; WASH[2] (8) *AmE:* **do the washing** (=wash dirty clothes) | **put the washing out** (=hang it on a washing line)

**washing day** /ˈ·· ·/ *n* [C] WASHDAY

**washing line** /ˈ·· ·/ *n* [C,U] *BrE* a piece of string stretched between two poles that you hang wet clothes on so that they become dry; CLOTHESLINE

**washing liq·uid** /ˈ·· ˌ··/ *n* [C,U] soap in the form of a liquid used for washing clothes

**washing ma·chine** /ˈ·· ·ˌ·/ *n* [C] a machine for washing clothes —see picture on page 833

**washing pow·der** /ˈ·· ˌ··/ *n* [C,U] *BrE* soap in the form of a powder used for washing clothes

**washing so·da** /ˈ·· ˌ··/ *n* [U] a chemical that is added to water to clean very dirty things

**washing-up** /ˌ·· ˈ·/ *n* [U] *BrE* **1** the washing of plates, dishes, knives etc; dishes *AmE:* **do the washing-up** *It's your turn to do the washing-up, Conrad.* **2** the dirty pans, plates, dishes, knives etc that have to be washed; dishes *AmE*: *a pile of washing-up*

**washing-up liq·uid** /ˌ·· ˈ· ˌ··/ *n* [U] *BrE* a liquid soap for washing plates, knives etc; DISHWASHING LIQUID *AmE* —see picture on page 833

**wash·out** /ˈwɒʃ-aʊt‖ˈwɒːʃ-, ˈwɑːʃ-/ *n* [C] *informal* **1** a failure: *The picnic was a total washout – nobody turned up!* **2** an occasion when heavy rain washes the soil away from a place —see also **wash out** (WASH[1])

**wash·room** /ˈwɒʃrʊm, -ruːm‖ˈwɒːʃ-, ˈwɑːʃ-/ *n* [C] *AmE* a word meaning a room where you use the toilet, used to avoid saying this directly

**wash·stand** /ˈwɒʃstænd‖ˈwɒːʃ-, ˈwɑːʃ-/ *n* [C] a table in a bedroom used in the past for holding the things needed for washing your face

**wash·tub** /ˈwɒʃtʌb‖ˈwɒːʃ-, ˈwɑːʃ-/ *n* [C] a large bowl used in the past for washing clothes in

**was·n't** /ˈwɒzənt‖ˈwɑː-/ the short form of 'was not': *Jason wasn't at the party.*

**WASP** /wɒsp‖wɑːsp, wɒːsp/ *n* [C] *especially AmE* White Anglo-Saxon Protestant; an American whose family was originally from northern Europe and who is therefore considered to be part of the most powerful group in society

**wasp** /wɒsp‖wɑːsp, wɒːsp/ *n* [C] a thin black and yellow flying insect that can sting you

**wasp·ish** /ˈwɒspɪʃ‖ˈwɑː-, ˈwɒː-/ *adj* bad-tempered and cruel in the things that you say: *waspish remarks* —**waspishly** *adv* —**waspishness** *n* [U]

**was·sail** /ˈwɒseɪl‖ˈwɑː-/ *v* [I] *old use* to enjoy yourself eating and drinking at Christmas —**wassail** *n* [U]

**wast** /wəst; *strong* wɒst‖wəst; *strong* wɑːst/ *v* **thou wast** *old use* you were

**wast·age** /ˈweɪstɪdʒ/ *n* [U] **1 a)** the loss or destruction of something, especially in a way that is not useful or sensible **b)** the amount that is lost or destroyed: *high levels of wastage in the fast-food industry* **2 natural wastage** *BrE* a reduction in the number of workers because of people leaving, retiring (RETIRE (1)) etc and not because they have lost their jobs

**waste[1]** /weɪst/ *n* S W
**1 ▶ BAD USE ◀** [singular, U] things such as money or skills that should be used and are not, or that are not used effectively: *waste in government departments* | **[+ of]** *Being unemployed is such a waste of your talents.*
**2 be a waste of time/money/effort etc** to be not worth the time, money etc that you use because there is little or no result: *We should never have gone – it was a total waste of time.*
**3 go to waste** to be wasted: *Don't let all this food go to waste.*
**4 ▶ UNWANTED MATERIALS ◀** [U] unwanted materials or substances that are left after you have used something: *It's a good idea to recycle household waste.* | **industrial/chemical etc waste** *Industrial waste has found its way into the water supply.*
**5 a waste of space** *spoken* someone who has no good qualities: *That woman is a complete waste of space!*
**6 ▶ LAND ◀** [C usually plural] *especially literary* a large empty or useless area of land: *the icy wastes of Antarctica* —see also WASTELAND

**waste[2]** *v* [T] S W
**1 ▶ NOT USE SENSIBLY ◀** to use more money, time, energy etc than you should, or use it in a way that is not useful or sensible: *Leaving the heating on all the time wastes electricity.* | **waste sth on** *Don't waste your money on that junk!*
**2 waste your breath** *spoken* to say something that has no effect: *Don't try to reason with Paul – you're wasting your breath.*

**3 waste no time (in) doing sth** to do something as quickly as you can because it will help you: *Sandy wasted no time in getting to know the boss's daughter.*
**4 be wasted on sb** if something is wasted on someone they are too stupid or unsuitable to be able to use or enjoy it: *Her words of advice were wasted on me.*
**5 be wasted in sth** if someone is wasted in a job etc, they are not using all of their abilities: *Hannah's wasted in that clerical job.*
**6 ▶ BECAUSE OF ILLNESS ◀** if an illness wastes someone, they become thinner and weaker —see also WASTED (3), WASTING
**7 waste not, want not** *spoken* used to say that if you use what you have carefully, you will not be left with nothing later
**8 ▶ HARM SB ◀** *slang especially AmE* to kill someone, severely injure them, or defeat them
**waste away** *phr v* [I] to gradually become thinner and weaker, usually because you are ill

W3 **waste³** *adj* **1** waste materials, substances etc are unwanted because the good part of them has been removed **2** used for holding or carrying away materials and substances that are no longer wanted: *a waste pipe | a waste tank* **3** waste land is empty or not fit to be used —see also WASTE¹ (6), WASTELAND, **lay waste** (LAY¹)

**waste·bas·ket** /ˈweɪstˌbɑːskɪt‖-ˌbæs-/ *n* [C] *especially AmE* a small container, usually indoors, into which you put unwanted paper etc —see picture at BASKET

**wast·ed** /ˈweɪstɪd/ *adj* **1 a wasted journey/trip/phone-call etc** an action that is unsuccessful because it has no helpful result: *I'm sorry, you've had a wasted journey; Mr. Newton isn't here.* **2** *slang* very drunk or affected by drugs **3** very tired and weak-looking

**waste dis·pos·al** /ˈ· ·ˌ··/ *n especially BrE* **1** also **waste disposal un·it** /ˈ· ··· ˌ··/ [C] a machine connected to the waste pipe of a kitchen SINK that cuts solid waste into small pieces; GARBAGE DISPOSAL *AmE* **2** [U] the process or system of getting rid of unwanted materials or substances; DISPOSAL (1) *AmE*: *the waste disposal plant*

**waste·ful** /ˈweɪstfəl/ *adj* using things such as money, energy, or work in a way that wastes them: *It's wasteful to throw so much away.* —**wastefully** *adv*: *Half the wood's energy is wastefully burned.* —**wastefulness** *n* [U]

**waste·land** /ˈweɪstlænd, -lənd/ *n* [C,U] land that is empty, ugly, and not used for anything: **an industrial wasteland** (=with empty, ruined old factories)

**waste pa·per** /ˌ· ˈ··◂/ *n* [U] paper that has been thrown away, especially because it has already been used

**waste·pa·per bas·ket** /ˌweɪstˈpeɪpə ˌbɑːskɪt, ˈweɪst-ˌpeɪpə-‖ˈweɪstˌpeɪpərˌ bæ-/ *n* [C] a small container, usually indoors, into which you put unwanted paper etc —see picture at BASKET

**waste prod·uct** /ˈ· ˌ··/ *n* [C] something useless, such as ASH or gas, that is produced in a process that produces something useful: *The waste products of combustion are fed into the car's exhaust.*

**wast·er** /ˈweɪstə‖-ər/ *n* [C] **1** someone who wastes their time, money etc in a stupid way **2 time-waster** someone or something that uses up too much time: *Waiting in lines is such a time-waster.*

**wast·ing** /ˈweɪstɪŋ/ *adj* **wasting disease** a wasting disease is one that gradually makes you become thinner and weaker

**was·trel** /ˈweɪstrəl/ *n* [C] *literary* someone who wastes their time, money etc

S1 **watch¹** /wɒtʃ‖wɑːtʃ, wɔːtʃ/ *v*
W1 **1 ▶ LOOK AT ◀** [I,T] to look at and pay attention to something that is happening: *Do you want to join in or just sit and watch?* | **watch sb/sth** *Harriet watched the man with interest as he walked in.* | **watch sb do/doing sth** *Jack watched them slowly climb the wall.* | **watch television/a video/a film etc** *The Presidential debate was watched by over 10 million people.* | **watch what/how/when etc** *Watch how I do it.* —see picture at SEE¹
**2 ▶ BE CAREFUL ◀** [T] to be careful with something: **watch (that)** *Watch the milk doesn't boil over.* | **watch what/how/where etc** *Watch what you're doing with that knife!* | **watch your weight** (=be careful not to get fat)
**3 ▶ LOOK AFTER ◀** [T] to look after someone or something so that nothing bad happens to them: *Can you watch the kids for a couple of hours tonight?*
**4 ▶ SECRETLY ◀** [T] to secretly watch a person or place: *I feel like I'm being watched.*
**5 watch yourself** to control how you behave or what you do: *I have to watch myself when it comes to eating chocolate.*
**6 watch your step** *informal* used to warn someone to be careful, especially about making someone angry: *You'd better watch your step or you'll be in trouble again.*
**7 watch the clock** *informal* to keep checking to see if it is time to stop what you are doing, instead of doing it
**8 watch this space** *informal* an expression used especially in newspapers to tell people to wait because things are going to develop further
**9 watch the world go by** to spend time looking at what is happening around you: *Bill likes to sit in the park and watch the world go by.*
**10 watch the time** to make sure you know what time it is to avoid being late for something

Frequencies of the verb **watch** in spoken and written English.

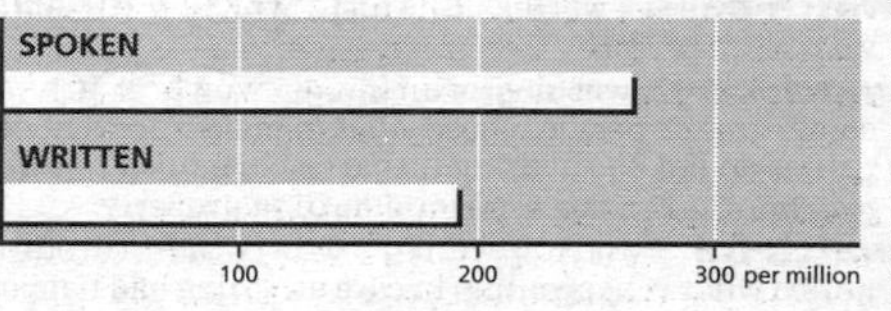


Based on the British National Corpus and the Longman Lancaster Corpus

This graph shows that the verb **watch** is more common in spoken English than in written English. This is because it is used in some common spoken phrases.

**watch** (*v*) **SPOKEN PHRASES**

**11 watch it! a)** used to tell someone to be more careful, especially in a dangerous situation: *Watch it! You nearly knocked my head off with that ladder!* **b)** used to threaten someone: *Just watch it, right, or I'll get you!* **12 watch yourself** used to warn someone to be careful not to hurt themselves, get into danger etc: *Hey, watch yourself, that's very hot!* **13 watch this/just watch** used to make someone watch you while you do something: *Watch this! I'm going to balance this bottle on my nose.* **14 you watch** used to tell someone to watch something because you know what is going to happen: *You watch. Every time she goes out he follows her.* **15 watch what you're doing** used to tell someone to do something more carefully: *Watch what you're doing! You're spilling it everywhere.* **16 watch your mouth** used to tell someone rudely or angrily to be careful what they say: *You'd better watch your mouth, young man!*

**watch for** *phr v* [T] to wait and be ready for something: *The prisoners watched for a chance to escape.*
**watch out** *phr v* [I usually in imperative] *spoken* used to tell someone to be careful: *Watch out! There's a car coming.*
**watch out for** sth/sb *phr v* [T] **1** to keep looking and waiting for someone or something: *Watch out for a tall man in a black hat.* **2** to be careful of something: *You have to watch out for fast traffic along here.*
**watch over** sb/sth *phr v* [T] to guard or take care of someone or something: *a shepherd watching over his sheep*

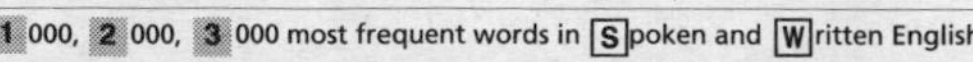

S3 W3 **watch²** *n*
**1 ▶ CLOCK ◀** [C] a small clock that you wear on your wrist or carry in your pocket: *My watch has stopped.*
**2 ▶ ACT OF WATCHING ◀** [singular, U] the act of watching something carefully in order to warn people of any danger: **keep watch** *I kept watch while the others slept.*
**3 keep a (close) watch on** **a)** to check a situation carefully so that you always know what is happening and are ready to deal with it: *UN forces are keeping a close watch on the area.* **b)** to watch someone carefully, either because you think they may be doing something illegal, or in order to make sure they are safe: *Police kept a 24-hour watch on the house.*
**4 keep a watch out for** to look carefully in order to try and find someone or something, while you are doing other things
**5 be on the watch (for)** to be looking and waiting for something that might happen or someone you might see: *You should always be on the watch for pickpockets.*
**6 ▶ PEOPLE ◀** [C] a group of people employed to guard or protect someone or something
**7 ▶ GUARDING STH ◀** [C,U] a fixed period of the day or night when a group of people must look carefully for any signs of danger or attack: *the first watch* | **be on watch** *Who's on watch tonight?*
**8 the watches of the night** *poetical* a period of the night when you are awake
**9 the (night) watch** the group of policemen in former times who were responsible for keeping a town or city safe at night —see also NEIGHBOURHOOD WATCH

**watch·band** /ˈwɒtʃbænd‖ˈwɑːtʃ-,ˈwɒːtʃ-/ *n* [C] *AmE* a WATCHSTRAP *BrE*

**watch·dog** /ˈwɒtʃdɒg‖ˈwɑːtʃdɒːg, ˈwɒːtʃ-/ *n* [C] **1** a committee or person whose job is to make sure that companies do not do anything illegal or harmful: *a consumer watchdog* **2** a dog used for guarding property

**watch·ful** /ˈwɒtʃfəl‖ˈwɑːtʃ-, ˈwɒːtʃ-/ *adj* careful to notice what is happening, in case anything bad happens: *watchful for any signs of activity* | **keep a watchful eye on** *Pam kept a watchful eye on the time.* —**watchfully** *adv* —**watchfulness** *n* [U]

**watch·ing brief** /ˈ·· ˌ·/ *n* [C] *law* instructions to a lawyer to watch a case that their client is not directly involved in

**watch·mak·er** /ˈwɒtʃˌmeɪkə‖ˈwɑːtʃˌmeɪkər, ˈwɒːtʃ-/ *n* [C] someone who makes or repairs watches (WATCH² (1)) and clocks

**watch·man** /ˈwɒtʃmən‖ˈwɑːtʃ-, ˈwɒːtʃ-/ *n* [C] *old-fashioned* someone whose job is to guard a building or place; SECURITY GUARD

**watch·strap** /ˈwɒtʃstræp‖ˈwɑːtʃ-, ˈwɒːtʃ-/ *n* [C] *BrE* a piece of leather or metal for fastening your watch to your wrist; WATCHBAND *AmE*

**watch·tow·er** /ˈwɒtʃˌtaʊə‖ˈwɑːtʃˌtaʊər,ˈwɒːtʃ-/ *n* [C] a high tower used for guarding a place, from which you can see things that are happening

**watch·word** /ˈwɒtʃwɜːd‖ˈwɑːtʃwɜːrd, ˈwɒːtʃ-/ *n* [singular] a word or phrase that explains what people should do in a particular situation: *The watchword is caution.*

S3 W1 **wa·ter¹** /ˈwɔːtə‖ˈwɒːtər, ˈwɑː-/ *n* [U]
**1 ▶ LIQUID ◀** **a)** the clear colourless liquid that falls as rain, fills lakes and rivers, and is necessary for life to exist: *This reservoir supplies the whole city with water.* | *The prisoners were given only bread and water.* | **seawater/bathwater/rainwater** (=a particular type of water) —see also FRESHWATER, SALTWATER **b)** the supply of water to homes, factories etc through pipes and TAPS: **running water** (=water that flows, not kept in a container or pool) *All rooms have hot and cold running water.* | **water shortage** (=a situation when there is not much water available)
**2 ▶ AREA OF WATER ◀** **a)** an area of water such as a lake, river etc: *the water's edge* | *Denzel dived into the water and swam towards her.* | **by water** (=by boat) *We can transport the goods by water.* **b)** the surface of a lake, river etc: *What's that floating on the water?* | **underwater/under water** *a camera designed for use under water*
**3 waters** [plural] **a)** the water in a particular lake, river etc: *the waters of the Amazon* **b)** an area of sea near or belonging to a particular country: *the coastal waters of Alaska* **c)** water containing minerals from a natural spring: **take the waters** (=drink the waters because you think it is good for your health)
**4 keep your head above water** *informal* to avoid trouble, especially because of lack of money: *The firm is barely keeping its head above water.*
**5 be (like) water off a duck's back** *informal* if advice, warnings, or rude remarks are like water off a duck's back to someone, they have no effect on them
**6 be (all) water under the bridge** *especially spoken* in the past, forgotten, and not worth worrying about: *Look, it's all water under the bridge now. Let's leave it behind us.*
**7 be all water under the bridge** used to say that a situation has changed, especially over a long period of time or since a particular event
**8 deep/murky/unknown etc waters** a situation that is unfamiliar or dangerous
**9 waters break** when a PREGNANT woman's waters break, liquid flows out of her body just before the baby is ready to be born
**10 high/low water** the highest or lowest level of the sea and some rivers; TIDE
**11 water on the brain/knee etc** liquid that collects around the brain, knee etc as the result of a disease
**12 make/pass water** *formal* to URINATE
**13 make water** if a ship makes water, water gets inside it because of a LEAK² (1) —see also HEAVY WATER, HOT WATER, SODA WATER, TOILET WATER, **in deep water** (DEEP¹ (13)), **take to sth like a duck to water** (DUCK¹ (4)), **of the first water** (FIRST (30)), **like a fish out of water** (FISH¹ (3)), **not hold water** (HOLD¹ (41)), **get into hot water** (HOT¹ (8)), **muddy the waters** (MUDDY² (2)), **pour cold water on** (POUR (7)), **still waters run deep** (STILL² (5)), **test the water** (TEST² (7)), **tread water** (TREAD¹ (4))

**water²** *v* S3
**1 ▶ PLANT/LAND ◀** [T] to pour water on an area of land, a plant etc, especially in order to make things grow: *You must water the garden, it's very dry.*
**2 eyes water** if your eyes water, tears (TEAR¹ (1)) come out of them because of cold weather, pain etc: *Chopping onions always makes my eyes water.* —see also MOUTH-WATERING, **make your mouth water** (MOUTH¹ (10))
**3 ▶ ANIMAL ◀** [T] to give an animal water to drink
**4 ▶ BY RIVER ◀** [T usually passive] *technical* if an area is watered by a river, the river flows through it and provides it with water: *Colombia is watered by several rivers.*
**5 ▶ WEAKEN LIQUID ◀** [T] to add water to a drink in order to make it weaker than it should be: *Someone had been watering the beer.*
**water** sth ↔ **down** *phr v* [T usually passive] **1** to make a statement, report etc less forceful by removing parts that may offend people —see also WATERED-DOWN **2** to add water to a liquid, especially for dishonest reasons; DILUTE¹ (1)

**wa·ter·bed** /ˈwɔːtəbed‖ˈwɒːtər-,ˈwɑː-/ *n* [C] a bed made of rubber and filled with water

**water bird** /ˈ·· ·/ *n* [C] a bird that swims or walks in water

**water bis·cuit** /ˈ·· ˌ··/ *n* [C] a hard BISCUIT (1) made from flour and water

**wa·ter·borne** /ˈwɔːtəbɔːn‖ˈwɒːtərbɔːrn, ˈwɑː-/ *adj* spread or carried by water: *waterborne diseases such as cholera*

**water bot·tle** /ˈ·· ˌ··/ *n* [C] **1** a bottle used for carrying drinking water **2** a HOT-WATER BOTTLE

**water buf·fa·lo** /ˈ·· ˌ···/ *n* [C] a large black animal like a cow with long horns, used for pulling vehicles and farm equipment in Asia

**water bug** /ˈ··· ·/ *n* [C] *AmE informal* a small insect that lives in or on water

**water butt** /ˈ·· ·/ *n* [C] *especially BrE* a BARREL[1] (1) used for collecting rainwater

**water can·non** /ˈ·· ˌ··/ *n* [C] a machine that sends out water at high pressure, used by police against crowds of people

**water chest·nut** /ˈ·· ˌ··/ *n* [C] a white fruit like a nut from a plant grown in water, used in Chinese cooking

**water clos·et** /ˈ·· ˌ··/ *n* [C] *old-fashioned* a WC (=a toilet)

**wa·ter·col·our** /ˈwɔːtəˌkʌlə‖ˈwɔːtərˌkʌlər, ˈwɑː-/ *n* **1** [C usually plural, U] paint that you mix with water and use for painting pictures **2** [C] a picture painted with watercolours

**wa·ter·course** /ˈwɔːtəkɔːs‖ˈwɒːtərkɔːrs, ˈwɑː-/ *n* [C] **1** a passage with water flowing through it, that can be natural or built **2** a flow of water such as a river or underground stream

**wa·ter·cress** /ˈwɔːtəkres‖ˈwɒːtər-, ˈwɑː-/ *n* [U] a small plant with strong tasting green leaves that grows in water

**wa·tered-down** /ˌ·· ˈ·◂/ *adj* **1** a watered-down statement, plan etc is much weaker and less effective than a previous plan etc: *a watered-down version of the original* **2** a watered-down drink, especially an alcholic drink, has had water added to it, especially in order to cheat people

**watered silk** /ˌ·· ˈ·/ *n* [U] a silk that looks as if it is covered with shiny waves

**wa·ter·fall** /ˈwɔːtəfɔːl‖ˈwɒːtərfɒːl, ˈwɑː-/ *n* [C] water that falls straight down over a cliff or big rock —see picture on page 835

**water foun·tain** /ˈ·· ˌ··/ *n* [C] a DRINKING FOUNTAIN

**wa·ter·fowl** /ˈwɔːtəfaʊl‖ˈwɒːtər-, ˈwɑː-/ *n plural* **waterfowl** [C,U] a bird that swims in water, such as a duck, GOOSE[1] (1) etc

**wa·ter·front** /ˈwɔːtəfrʌnt‖ˈwɒːtər-, ˈwɑː-/ *n* [C usually singular] a part of a town or an area of land that is next to the sea, a river etc

**wa·ter·hole** /ˈwɔːtəhəʊl‖ˈwɒːtərhoʊl, ˈwɑː-/ *n* [C] a small area of water in a dry country, where wild animals go to drink

**water ice** /ˈ·· ·/ *n* [C,U] *BrE* a SORBET

**water·ing can** /ˈ··· ·/ *n* [C] a container used for pouring water on garden plants, with a long tube at the front

**watering hole** /ˈ··· ·/ *n* [C] *humorous* a bar or other place where people go to drink alcohol: *a favorite watering-hole of Ernest Hemingway*

**watering place** /ˈ··· ·/ *n* [C] **1** a small area of water in a dry country, where wild animals go to drink **2** a place with a spring of MINERAL WATER where people went in the past to be cured of various diseases; a SPA (1)

**watering pot** /ˈ··· ·/ *n* [C] *AmE* a watering can

**water jump** /ˈ·· ·/ *n* [C] an area of water that horses or runners have to jump over during a race or competition

**wa·ter·less** /ˈwɔːtələs‖ˈwɒːtər-, ˈwɑː-/ *adj* with no water for people or animals to drink

**water lev·el** /ˈ·· ˌ··/ *n* [U] the height to which water has risen or fallen

**water lil·y** /ˈ·· ˌ··/ *n* [C] a plant that floats on the surface of water and has large white, yellow, or pink flowers

**wa·ter·line** /ˈwɔːtəlaɪn‖ˈwɒːtər-, ˈwɑː-/ *n* **the waterline** the level that water reaches on the side of a ship

**wa·ter·logged** /ˈwɔːtəlɒgd‖ˈwɒːtərlɒːgd, ˈwɑː-, -lɑːgd/ *adj* **1** an area that is waterlogged is flooded with water and cannot be used **2** a boat that is waterlogged is full of water and could soon sink

**water main** /ˈ·· ·/ *n* [C] a large underground pipe that carries the public supply of water to houses and other buildings

**wa·ter·mark** /ˈwɔːtəmɑːk‖ˈwɒːtərmɑːrk, ˈwɑː-/ *n* [C] **1** a design that is put into paper and can only be seen when you hold it up to the light: *Banknotes have a watermark to prevent forgery.* **2 high/low watermark a)** a line showing the highest or lowest levels of the sea or a river **b)** a period of great success or failure: *the high watermark of the Roman Empire*

**water mead·ow** /ˈ·· ˌ··/ *n* [C] a field near a river, which is often flooded

**wa·ter·mel·on** /ˈwɔːtəˌmelən‖ˈwɒːtər-, ˈwɑː-/ *n* [C,U] **1** a large round fruit with hard green skin, juicy red flesh, and a lot of black seeds —see picture on page 413 **2 swallow a watermelon seed** *AmE informal* to become PREGNANT

**water me·ter** /ˈ·· ˌ··/ *n* [C] a piece of equipment that measures how much water is used

**wa·ter·mill** /ˈwɔːtəˌmɪl‖ˈwɒːtər-, ˈwɑː-/ *n* [C] a MILL[1] (1) that has a big wheel that is turned by the flow of water

**water moc·ca·sin** /ˈ·· ˌ···/ *n* [C] a poisonous North American snake that lives in water

**water pipe** /ˈ·· ˌ·/ *n* [C] a pipe used for smoking tobacco, that consists of a long tube and a container of water; HOOKAH

**water pis·tol** /ˈ·· ˌ··/ *n* [C] a toy gun that shoots water

**water po·lo** /ˈ·· ˌ··/ *n* [U] a game played by two teams of swimmers with a ball

**water pow·er** /ˈ·· ˌ··/ *n* [U] power obtained from moving water, used to produce electricity or to make a machine work

**wa·ter·proof**[1] /ˈwɔːtəpruːf‖ˈwɒːtər-, ˈwɑː-/ *adj* waterproof clothing or material does not allow water to go through it

**waterproof**[2] *n* [C usually plural] *BrE* a piece of clothing such as a coat, that prevents you from getting wet

**water rat** /ˈ·· ·/ *n* [C] a small animal like a large mouse that lives in holes near water and can swim

**water-re·pel·lent** /ˈ·· ·ˌ··/ *adj* cloth or clothes that are water-repellent are specially treated with chemicals so that water runs off them

**water re·sis·tant** /ˈ·· ·ˌ··/ *adj* something that is water-resistant does not allow water to go through easily, but does not keep all water out: *a watch that is water resistant to a depth of 50 metres*

**wa·ter·shed** /ˈwɔːtəʃed‖ˈwɒːtər-, ˈwɑː-/ *n* [C] **1** an event or period when important changes or improvements happen in history or in someone's life: [**+ in**] *The 1932 election represented a watershed in American politics.* —compare TURNING POINT **2 the (9 o'clock) watershed** *BrE* the time in the evening after which television programmes that are not suitable for children may be shown **3** the high land separating two river systems

**wa·ter·side** /ˈwɔːtəsaɪd‖ˈwɒːtər-, ˈwɑː-/ *n* [singular] the edge of a lake, river etc —**waterside** *adj*: *a waterside restaurant*

**water ski·ing** /ˈ·· ˌ··/ *n* [U] a sport in which you SKI over water while being pulled by a boat —**water ski** *v* [I] —**water skier** *n* [C]

**water sof·ten·er** /ˈ·· ˌ···/ *n* **1** [U] a chemical used for removing unwanted minerals from water **2** [C] a piece of equipment used to do this

**water-sol·u·ble** /ˈ·· ˌ···/ *adj* a water-soluble substance becomes part of a liquid when mixed with water

**water sports** /ˈ·· ˌ·/ *n* [plural] sports played on or in water

**wa·ter·spout** /ˈwɔːtəspaʊt‖ˈwɒːtər-, ˈwɑː-/ *n* [C] **1** a pipe that water flows through **2** a type of storm over the sea in which a violent circular wind pulls water into a tall twisting mass —compare TORNADO

**water sup·ply** /ˈ·· ·ˌ·/ *n* [U] the water provided for a building or area, or the system of lakes, pipes etc through which it flows

**water ta·ble** /ˈ·· ˌ··/ *n* [C] the level below the surface of the ground where there is water

**wa·ter·tight** /ˈwɔːtətaɪt‖ˈwɒːtər-, ˈwɑː-/ *adj* **1** something that is watertight does not allow water to pass through it: *watertight boxes* **2 watertight plan/case/**

**argument etc** a plan etc that is made so carefully that there is no chance of any mistakes or problems: *The police can't do anything, he's got a watertight alibi.*

**water tow·er** /ˈ·· ˌ··/ *n* [C] a very tall structure supporting a large container into which water is pumped in order to supply water to surrounding buildings

**water va·pour** *BrE*, **water vapor** *AmE* /ˈ·· ˌ··/ *n* [U] water in the form of gas in the air

**water vole** /ˈ·· ·/ *n* [C] *BrE* a small animal like a large mouse that lives in holes near water and can swim; WATER RAT

**wa·ter·way** /ˈwɔːtəweɪ‖ˈwɒːtər-, ˈwɑː-/ *n* [C] a river or CANAL (1) that boats travel on: *inland waterways*

**wa·ter·wings** /ˈwɔːtəˌwɪŋz‖ˈwɒːtər-, ˈwɑː-/ *n* [plural] two bags filled with air that are attached to your arms when you learn to swim

**wa·ter·works** /ˈwɔːtəwɜːks‖ˈwɒːtərwɜːrks, ˈwɑː-/ *n* [plural] **1** the system of pipes and artificial lakes used to clean and store water before it is supplied to a town **2 turn on the waterworks** *spoken* to start crying in order to get someone's sympathy **3** *informal or humorous* the system of organs and tubes inside your body that remove URINE (=liquid waste) from it

**wa·ter·y** /ˈwɔːtəri‖ˈwɒː-, ˈwɑː-/ *adj* **1** weak and pale in colour: *a watery sun* **2** full of water: *a watery fluid* **3** related to water: *Watery gurgles came from the tank.* **4** watery food or drink contains too much water and does not taste good: *watery soup* **5 a watery grave** *literary* if someone comes to a watery grave, they drown

**watt** /wɒt‖wɑːt/ *n* [C] a measure of electrical power

**watt·age** /ˈwɒtɪdʒ‖ˈwɑː-/ *n* [singular, U] the power of a piece of electrical equipment measured in watts

**wat·tle** /ˈwɒtl‖ˈwɑːtl/ *n* [U] **1** a material used for making fences consisting of small sticks on a frame of rods **2 wattle and daub** a mixture of this material and mud or clay used in the past to make the walls of houses **3** a piece of red flesh that grows from the head or neck of a bird like the TURKEY (1) **4** an Australian tree with small yellow flowers; ACACIA

**Wave** /weɪv/ *n* [C] *AmE informal* a woman who is a member of a US navy VOLUNTEER[2] (2) group

S3 W2 **wave¹** /weɪv/ *n*
**1 ▶ON THE SEA◀** [C] a line of raised water that moves across the surface of the sea: *Dee watched the waves breaking on the rocks.*
**2 ▶OF YOUR HAND◀** [C usually singular] a movement of your hand or arm from side to side
**3 ▶OF LIGHT/SOUND◀** [C] the form in which some types of energy such as light and sound move: *radio waves* —see also LONG WAVE, MEDIUM WAVE, SHORT WAVE
**4 ▶SUDDEN INCREASE◀** [C] **a)** a sudden increase in a particular type of behaviour or activity, especially an unpleasant one: [+ **of**] *a new wave of terrorist bombings* | **crime wave** (=a sudden increase in crime) **b)** a sudden increase in the number of people or things arriving at the same time: [+ **of**] *a new wave of immigrants* **c)** a group of soldiers, aircraft etc that attack together: [+ **of**] *The next wave of troops went over the ridge.* **d)** a sudden strong feeling that spreads from one person to another: [+ **of**] *A wave of panic swept through the crowd.*
**5 in waves** if something happens in waves, a short period of activity is followed by a pause: *The pain swept over him in waves.*
**6 ▶OF HAIR◀** [C] a part of your hair that has an even curved shape
**7 make waves** *informal* to cause problems: *With so many jobs being cut, Parker didn't want to make waves.*
**8 the waves** *literary* the ocean

S3 W3 **wave²** *v*
**1 ▶HAND◀** [I,T] to move your hand or arm from side to side in order to greet someone or attract their attention: *Toyah waved her hand regally.* | **wave to/at sb** *Tommy waved to us as he came across the field.* | **wave sth at sb** *Lee waved his fist at me angrily.* | **wave sth around/about** *BrE*: *Stop waving your arms about.* | **wave sb goodbye/wave goodbye to sb** (=to say goodbye to someone by waving to them) *Wave bye-bye to Granny.*
**2 ▶SIGNAL◀** [T always + adv/prep] to show someone where to go by waving your hand in that direction: **wave sb through/on/away** *A guard waved me away from the fence.*
**3 ▶MAKE STH MOVE◀** [T] to hold something and move it from side to side: *The magician waved his wand and the door opened.* | **wave sth under/about/at etc** *Trudie waved a $50 bill under his nose.*
**4 ▶MOVE SMOOTHLY◀** [I] to move smoothly up and down, or from side to side: *flags waving in the wind*
**5 wave sth goodbye** *informal* to be forced to accept that something you want will not happen: *A 3–0 defeat means United have waved their promotion chances goodbye.*
**6 ▶HAIR◀** [I,T] if hair waves or is waved, it grows in loose curls

**wave** sth ↔ **aside** *phr v* [T] to refuse to accept someone's opinion or idea because you do not think it is important: *Nancy waved aside our objections.*

**wave** sb/sth ↔ **down** *phr v* [T] to signal to the driver of a car to stop by waving your arm at them

**wave** sb **off** *phr v* [T] to wave goodbye to someone as they leave

**wave·band** /ˈweɪvbænd/ *n* [C] a set of radio waves of similar length which are used to broadcast radio programmes

**wave·length** /ˈweɪvleŋθ/ *n* [C] **1** the size of a radio wave used to broadcast a radio signal **2** the distance between two waves of energy such as sound or light **3 be on the same wavelength/on a different wavelength** *informal* to have the same or different opinions and feelings as someone else: *We just aren't on the same wavelength when it comes to politics.*

**wa·ver** /ˈweɪvə‖-ər/ *v* [I] **1** to be or become weak and uncertain: *His voice wavered.* | **waver in sth** *Harris never wavered in his loyalty to the cause.* **2** to not make a decision because you have doubts: *wavering voters* | **waver between (doing)** *Maya wavered between accepting and refusing his offer.* **3** to move unsteadily first in one direction then in another: *reflections wavering in the water of the lake* —**waverer** *n* [C] *We must persuade the waverers to vote with us.* —**waveringly** *adv*

**wav·y** /ˈweɪvi/ *adj* **1** wavy hair grows in waves —see picture on page 412 **2** a wavy line or edge has smooth curves in it —**waviness** *n* [U]

**wax¹** /wæks/ *n* [U] **1** a solid material made out of fats or oils used to make CANDLES, polish etc: *wax crayon* **2** a natural sticky substance in your ears —see also BEESWAX

**wax²** *v*
**1 ▶FLOOR/FURNITURE◀** [T] to put a thin layer of wax on a floor or surface etc in order to polish it
**2 ▶MOON◀** [I] when the moon waxes, it grows larger
**3 wax romantic/eloquent/lyrical etc** *literary* to speak in a romantic way: *Mitch would wax eloquent on the subject of cars.*
**4 wax and wane** *literary* to increase and then decrease
**5 ▶LEGS◀** [T] to put a thin layer of wax on your arms or legs in order to remove hairs

**waxed pa·per** /ˌ· ˈ··/ also **wax·pa·per** /ˈwæksˌpeɪpə‖-ər/ *n AmE* [U] paper with a thin layer of wax on used to wrap food; GREASEPROOF PAPER *BrE*

**wax·en** /ˈwæksən/ *adj literary* **1** pale and shiny like wax **2** made of or covered in wax

**wax·work** /ˈwækswɜːk‖-wɜːrk/ *n* [C] **1 waxworks** *BrE* **wax museum** *AmE* a place where you pay to see models of famous people made of wax **2** a model of a person made of wax

**wax·y** /ˈwæksi/ *adj* **1** made of or covered in wax **2** looking or feeling like wax: *waxy petals* —**waxiness** *n* [U]

# **way¹** /weɪ/ *n*

① METHOD
② MANNER
③ ROAD/PATH
④ DIRECTION
⑤ DISTANCE
⑥ TIME
⑦ BEHAVIOUR
⑧ ATTITUDE TO A SITUATION
⑨ WHAT YOU WANT
⑩ PREVENT/BLOCK STH
⑪ DEVELOPMENT/PROGRESS
⑫ SITUATION/CONDITION
⑬ MAKE WAY
⑭ GIVE WAY
⑮ ON THE WAY
⑯ EITHER WAY
⑰ SPOKEN PHRASES
⑱ OTHER MEANINGS

## ① METHOD

**1** [C] a method of doing something: *These vegetables can be cooked in several different ways.* | *At that time, the Pill was the easiest way of ensuring effective contraception.* | *I've altered the way I teach science.* | *I'll tell her in my own time and in my own way.* | **way of doing sth** *I've got no way of contacting him at all.* | **way to do sth** *What's the right way to say this in English?* | **way to go about sth** *I think you're going about this the wrong way.*

**2 one way or another** *spoken* using one of several possible methods, although you do not yet know which one: *We'll find the money, one way or another.*

**3 ways and means** special methods for doing something, especially something secret or illegal: *There are ways and means of getting drugs in prison.* —see also WAYS AND MEANS COMMITTEE

**4 way out/around** a possible method of solving a problem or difficult situation: *I just can't see any way out of this mess.* | *There's no way around it – we'll have to tell Mom.* —see also WAY OUT, **take the easy way out** (EASY¹ (6))

**5 way into television/publishing etc** a possible method of getting a job in television etc, especially when this is difficult: *She thought that working in the box office might be a way into the theatre.*

## ② MANNER

**6** [C] a manner in which something can happen or be done, especially when there are several: *I don't see it that way at all.* | *Look at the way he's dressed!* | *Not all birds of prey suffered in this way (by eating insecticide), but many did.* | **in more ways than one** *spoken* (=in several ways) *This will benefit the company in more ways than one.*

**7 that's no way to do sth** *spoken* used to tell someone that they should not be doing something in a particular manner: *That's no way to speak to your father!*

## ③ ROAD/PATH

**8** [C] the road, path etc that you must follow in order to get to a particular place: [+ **to**] *Is this the way to Crouch End?* | **lose your way** *We lost our way in the forest.* | **know the way** *I hope Eric knows the way.*

## ④ DIRECTION

**9** [C] a particular direction from where you are now: *Which way is north?* | *Walk this way.* | *"Where's the lift?" "It's this way."* | **show sb/lead the way** *Could you just show me the way?*

**10 on sb's way** in the direction that someone is going: *I'll give you a lift – it's on my way.*

**11 out of sb's way** not in the direction that someone is going: *You can't take me home – it's miles out of your way.* —see also OUT-OF-THE-WAY (1)

## ⑤ DISTANCE

**12** [singular] also **ways** *AmE informal* a distance, especially a long one: *We have a ways to go yet.* | **a long way** *I was still a long way from home.* | **all this way** *It would be too bad to come all this way and not see them.* | **all the way down/across/through etc** (=continuing for the full distance or length of something) *Did you really swim all the way across?* | **way beyond** (=much further) *This achieves temperatures way beyond what is necessary.*

## ⑥ TIME

**13** [singular] a length of time, especially a long one: *The two events were a long way apart.*

## ⑦ BEHAVIOUR

**14** [C] a particular manner or style of behaving: *He had an annoying way of picking his nails.* | *We all have our funny little ways.* | **be (just) sb's way** *informal* (=be the way in which someone usually behaves, especially when this is unusual) *Oh, don't worry, that's just her way.* | **change/mend your ways** (=stop behaving badly) *Jamieson resolved to change his ways.* —see also **see the error of your ways** (ERROR (3))

## ⑧ ATTITUDE TO A SITUATION

**15** [C] one of the possible ways of thinking about a situation, or one of many parts of it: **in a way** *In a way, it's kind of nice to be working alone.* | **in one way** *Well, in one way you're right, but it's not as simple as that.* | **in some ways** *In some ways, I'd rather he wasn't involved at all.* | **in no way** (=used to say that you should definitely not think about a situation in this way) *This should in no way be seen as a defeat.*

## ⑨ WHAT YOU WANT

**16 get your (own) way** to do what you want to, even though someone else wants something different: *You shouldn't let the children always get their own way.*

**17 if I had my way** *spoken* used before telling someone how you think something should be done: *Of course, if I had my way, they'd all be shot!*

**18 have it your own way!** *spoken* used to tell someone in an annoyed way that you agree to what they want

**19 go your own way** to do what you want to do, make your own decisions etc

**20 have your (wicked) way with sb** *old-fashioned* to persuade someone to have sex with you

## ⑩ PREVENT/BLOCK STH

**21 be in the way/in sb's way** to be in a place or position that prevents someone or something else from moving freely: *There was a large truck blocking the way.* | *Get out of my way!* | [+ **of**] *Can you move that box? It's in the way of the door.*

**22 get in the way of** to prevent someone from doing something, or prevent something from happening: *You mustn't let your social life get in the way of your studies.*

**23 not stand in sb's way** to not try to stop someone

[continued on next page]

[continued from previous page]
from doing something they want to do: *If you want to leave home, I'm not going to stand in your way.*

### ⑪ DEVELOPMENT/PROGRESS

**24 have come a long way** to have developed or changed a lot: *Psychiatry has come a long way since the 1920s.*
**25 have a long way to go** to need to develop or change a lot in order to reach a particular standard: *Mac's still got a long way to go before he'll make a manager.*

### ⑫ SITUATION/CONDITION

**26 the way things are** *spoken* used to describe the situation that you are in now: *The way things are at the moment, I don't think we're going to be able to go on vacation at all.*
**27 be in a bad way** *BrE informal* to be very ill, injured, or upset

### ⑬ MAKE WAY

**28 make way a)** to move to one side so that someone or something can pass: [+ **for**] *The crowd stepped aside to make way for the riders.* **b)** to be removed so that something newer or better can take your place: [+ **for**] *Several houses were demolished to make way for the rail link.*
**29 make your way a)** to move towards something, especially when this takes a long time: *We made our way down the hill towards the town.* **b)** to slowly become successful in a particular job, activity, profession etc: *Gradually, Henderson began to make his way in politics.*
**30 make/find your own way** *informal* to go somewhere without the other people in your group: *You'll have to make your own way to the pub.*

### ⑭ GIVE WAY

**31** to break because of too much weight or pressure: *The floor eventually gave way.*
**32** to have your place taken by something newer, better, or different: [+ **to**] *Steam trains finally gave way to electricity.*|*After a while my anger gave way to depression.*
**33** to agree to do what someone else wants to do, instead of what you wanted to do: *Alison's too stubborn to give way.*
**34** *BrE* to allow vehicles to pass in front of you when you are driving; YIELD[1] (5) *AmE*: *You must give way to traffic coming from the right.*

### ⑮ ON THE WAY

**35 on your/the way (to)** while travelling from one place to another: *Why don't you stop by our place on your way to Boston?*| **on your way in/out/home etc** *Could you mail these letters on your way downtown?*

**36 be on the/its way** to be arriving soon: *There's a letter on its way to you.*|*More changes are on the way.*
**37 be on your way** *spoken* to be leaving one place in order to go somewhere else
**38 be well on the way to** to have almost finished changing from one state or situation to another, especially a better one: *The new building is well on the way to being finished.*|*Jen is now well on the way to recovery.*
**39 on/along the way** while developing from one situation or part of your life to another: *She had progressed smoothly through school and university, picking up several academic awards on the way.*
**40 have a baby on the way** *informal* to be PREGNANT

### ⑯ EITHER WAY

**41 either way** *spoken* used to say that something will be the same, whichever of two possible choices you make: *Either way, it's going to be expensive.*
**42 within two feet/ten years/one hour etc either way** if a measurement is within two feet, ten years etc either way, it may be two feet etc more or less than the correct amount: *Your answer must be within a centimetre either way.*
**43 could go either way** if a situation could go either way, both results are equally possible: *The election could go either way.*

### ⑰ SPOKEN PHRASES

**44 by the way** used before saying something that is not connected with the main subject you were talking about before: *By the way, have you seen my umbrella anywhere?*
**45 no way! a)** used to say that you will definitely not do something: *"Can I borrow your car?" "No way!"*|*No way am I going to help him.*| **no way José!** (=used to emphasize that you will not do something) **b)** *especially AmE* used to say that you do not believe something or are very surprised by it: *She's 45? No way!* **c)** used to say that something is not possible or cannot be done: *There's no way we're going to get this finished on time.*
**46 way out/over/across etc** *AmE* a long distance out, over etc: *"Where's the meter?" "It's way the hell over there."*
**47 in a big way** very much: *My little brother's into cars in a big way.*
**48 by a long way** by a large amount or difference: *He was the best in the group, by a long way.*
**49 no two ways about it** used to say that something is definitely true, especially something unpleasant
**50 you can't have it both ways** used to say that you cannot have the advantages from both of two different possible decisions or actions: *You're either going to have to work harder or settle for lower grades – you can't have it both ways!*
**51 be with sb all the way** to agree with someone completely: *I'm with you all the way on this salary issue, Joe.*
**52 to my way of thinking** used before telling someone your opinion: *To my way of thinking, it ought to be banned altogether.*
**53 have sth in the way of** to have particular amounts or types of something: *They don't have much in the way of leisure facilities.*
**54 have a way of doing sth** used to say that something usually happens in a particular way, especially when this is unpleasant or inconvenient: *These things have a way of turning up when you least expect them.*
**55 get sth out of the way** to finish, or deal with something, especially something difficult or unpleasant: *I'd rather have the interview in the morning and get it out of the way!*
**56 every which way a)** *BrE* every possible method: *We tried every which way we could think of, but it couldn't be done.* **b)** *AmE* in all directions: *When I came back there was popcorn flying every which way!*
**57 that's the way** used to tell someone that they are doing something correctly or well, especially when you are showing them how: *Now bring your foot gently off the clutch – that's the way.*
**58 come sb's way** if something comes your way, you get or experience it, especially unexpectedly or by chance: *You must make the most of the opportunities that come your way.*
**59 way to go!** *AmE* used to tell someone that they have done something very well, or achieved something special
**60 (that's/it's) always the way!** used to say that things always happen in the way that is least convenient: *The train was delayed – always the way when you're in a hurry!*
**61 across/over the way** on the opposite side of the street: *They live across the way from us at number 23.*
**62 down your/London etc way** in your area, the area of London etc
**63 way out!** *AmE* an expression meaning that something is very good or exciting, used especially in the 1970s
**64 get into the way of doing sth** *BrE* to start to do

something regularly: *I never got into the way of carrying my passport around with me.*
**65 go all the way (with sb)** to have sex with someone

**⑱ OTHER MEANINGS**

**66 lead the way** **a)** to walk at the front of a group of people: *We set off in single file with Lawrence leading the way.* **b)** to develop or discover something before other people: *a group that is leading the way in cancer research*
**67 be under way** **a)** to be happening or being done: *Plans are under way for a new link road.*| **get under way** (=start happening) *I'll wait till the campaign gets under way properly.*| **be well under way** (=be definitely happening, and too late to stop or change) *By the mid-sixties, the process of change was well under way.* **b)** to be moving forwards: *The boat gave a lurch, and we were under way.*
**68 split sth two/three etc ways** also **divide sth two/three etc ways** to divide something into two, three etc equal parts: *We'll split the cost between us five ways.*
**69 by way of** **a)** as a form of something, or instead of something: *We had sandwiches by way of a meal.*| *I'd just like to make a few comments by way of introduction.* **b)** if you travel by way of a place, you go through it: *We went by way of London.*
**70 way around/round** a particular order or position that something should be in: *Which way round does this skirt go?*| **right/wrong way around** *Make sure you get the slides the right way around.*
**71 know your way around** to be familiar with a place, system, or organization
**72 have a way with** to have a special ability to do something: *David seemed to have a way with children.*
**73 go out of your way to do sth** to do something that you do not have to do and that involves making an effort: *She went out of her way to be kind to the newcomer.*
**74 go some way towards doing sth** to help something to happen: *These donations will go some way towards repairing the damage.*
**75 go your separate ways** **a)** to start doing different things, having different interests etc, from someone you used to be friends with: *After leaving college, we went our separate ways.* **b)** to end a marriage or relationship: *John and I have gone our separate ways now.*
**76 keep out of sb's way** to avoid someone
**77 in sb's own way** used when you want to say that someone thinks, feels, or does something, although other people might think that they do not: *He seems harsh, I know, but in his own way he's quite caring.*
**78 Way** used in the names of roads: *Abercrombie Way*
**79 put sb in the way of (doing) sth** *old-fashioned BrE* to give someone the opportunity to do or get something —see also **in the family way** (FAMILY (6)), **go the way of all flesh** (FLESH[1] (10)), HALFWAY, **out of harm's way** (HARM[1] (6)), ONE-WAY, **the parting of the ways** (PARTING[1] (3)), **pave the way for** (PAVE (2)), **pay your way** (PAY[1] (12)), RIGHT OF WAY, **rub sb up the wrong way** (RUB[1] (9)), **see your way (clear) to** (SEE[1] (48)), TWO-WAY, **where there's a will there's a way** (WILL[2] (5))

S2 **way²** *adv* **1** by a large amount: **way above/below/out etc** *Her IQ is way above average.*| *Your guess was way out, he's actually thirty-eight.*| **way back** (=a long time ago) *We first met way back in the 70s.* **2** very far: **way ahead/behind/back** *American companies are way ahead when it comes to biotechnology.*| **way off/a ways off** *AmE* (=far from where you are) *Way off in the distance I could see snowcapped mountains.*| **way out in/past/beyond** (=far from the nearest town or from the point you mention) *O'Connell lives way out in the desert.* **3** *AmE informal* very: *"Hey, check out my new bike." "Way cool!"*

**way·far·er** /ˈweɪˌfeərə‖-ˌferər/ *n* [C] *literary* a traveller who walks from one place to another —**wayfaring** *adj* [only before noun]

**way·lay** /weɪˈleɪ/ *v past tense and past participle* **waylaid** /-ˈleɪd/ [T] to stop someone so that you can talk to them, rob them, or attack them

**way of life** /ˌ· · ˈ·/ *n plural* **ways of life** [C] **1** the way someone lives, or the way people in a society usually live: *The tribesmen's traditional way of life is under threat.*| **the American/British/etc way of life** (=the life typical of Americans, British people etc) **2** a job or interest that is so important that it affects everything you do: *Nursing isn't just a job; it's a whole way of life.*

**way out** /ˌ· ˈ·/ *n* [C] *BrE* **1** a door or a passage through which you can leave a building; EXIT **2** a way of getting away from a difficult or unpleasant situation —see also **take the easy way out** (EASY[1] (6)), **way out** (WAY[1] (4))

**way-out** /ˌ· ˈ·◂/ *adj informal* very modern, and unusual or strange: *I like jazz, but not the way-out stuff.*

**-ways** /weɪz/ *suffix* [in adverbs] in a particular direction: *leaning sideways* (=leaning to the side)

**Ways and Means Com·mit·tee** /ˌ· · ˈ· ·ˌ··/ *n* [C] *AmE* a group of representatives in the government of a US state or in Congress who must find money for the government to spend

**way·side** /ˈweɪsaɪd/ *n* [singular] *literary* the side of a road or path —see also **fall by the wayside** (FALL[1] (24))

**way sta·tion** /ˈ· ˌ··/ *n* [C] *AmE* a place between the main stations of a railway where a train stops

**way·ward** /ˈweɪwəd‖-wərd/ *adj* behaving in a way that is different from other people and that causes problems: *a wayward teenager* —**waywardly** *adv* —**waywardness** *n* [U]

**wa·zoo** /wəˈzuː/ *n* [C] *AmE informal* your bottom

**WC** /ˌdʌbəljuː ˈsiː/ *n* [C] water closet; a word for toilet used especially on signs in public places

**we** /wi; *strong* wiː/ *pron* [used as the subject of a sentence] **1** I and one or more others: *We were all amazed when we heard the news.*| *Shall we* (=you and I) *have a coffee, Ted?*| *Can we* (=I and the others) *go now, sir?* **2** *formal* used by a king or queen in official language to mean I: *We are not amused.* **3** used by a writer or a speaker to mean you (the reader or listener) and them: *We saw in the previous chapter how this situation had arisen.* **4** used especially to children and people who are ill to mean you: *And how are we feeling today, Mr. Robson?* **5** *formal* people in general: *Do we have the right to destroy the planet?* S1 W1

**weak** /wiːk/ *adj* S3 W2
**1** ▸ **PHYSICALLY** ◂ not physically strong: *The illness had left her feeling tired and weak.*| [+ **with**] *Nina was weak with hunger.*| **weak heart/bladder/eyes etc** (=that do not work properly)
**2** ▸ **CHARACTER** ◂ easily influenced by other people because you cannot make decisions by yourself: *a weak and indecisive man*
**3** ▸ **NOT GOOD AT** ◂ not having much ability or skill in a particular activity or subject: *a weak backhand*| [+ **at/in**] *Julie's always been weak in science.*
**4** ▸ **LEADERS/COUNTRIES/ORGANIZATIONS ETC** ◂ not having much power or influence: *weak trade unions*| *a weak leader*
**5** ▸ **ARGUMENT/EXPLANATION/STORY ETC** ◂ not having the power to persuade or interest people: *The play was well-acted but the plot was weak.*
**6** ▸ **INDUSTRY/COMPANY ETC** ◂ not successful financially: *a weak economy*| *The pound was weak against the dollar.*
**7** ▸ **BUILDINGS/OBJECTS** ◂ unable to support a lot of weight: *a weak bridge*

**8 ▶ DRINK/LIQUID ◀** containing a lot of water or having little taste: *weak tea*
**9 ▶ LIGHT/SOUND ◀** difficult to see or hear: *a weak radio signal*
**10 weak point/spot** a part of something or of someone's character that can easily be attacked or criticized: [+ **in**] *Agassi soon found the weak spots in Stich's game.*
**11 weak at the knees** not feeling well or strong, especially because you have had a sudden surprise or because you have seen someone you love: *His quick smile sent her weak at the knees.*
**12 weak smile** a slight smile, especially because you are not very happy
**13 a weak moment** a time when you can be persuaded more easily than usual: *David caught me at a weak moment and I lent him £10.*
**14 weak in the head** *informal* stupid or silly
**15 weak chin/jaw** a weak chin or jaw is not very well developed and people often think it suggests a weak character
**16 weak verb** *technical* a verb that forms the past tense and past participle in a regular way
**17 weak consonant/syllable** a weak CONSONANT or syllable is not emphasized —see also WEAKER SEX —**weakly** *adv*: *"I'm sorry," she said, smiling weakly.* | *He sank down weakly on the sofa.*

**weak·en** /ˈwiːkən/ *v*
**1 ▶ MAKE LESS POWERFUL ◀** [I,T] to make someone or something less powerful or less important, or to become less powerful: *Russia's influence on African affairs has weakened.*
**2 ▶ PHYSICALLY ◀** [I,T often passive] to make someone lose their physical strength, or to become physically weak: *Julia was weakened by her long illness.*
**3 ▶ BUILDING/OBJECT ◀** [T] to become less strong and less able to support a lot of weight: *The explosion severely weakened the foundations of the house.*
**4 weaken sb's determination/resolve** to make someone less determined: *The opposition she encountered did nothing to weaken her resolve.*
**5 ▶ BECOME LESS CERTAIN ◀** [I] to become less determined, especially so that you change your opinion and accept someone else's: *I think Mum's weakening about us going to that party.*
**6 ▶ MONEY ◀** [I,T] if a particular country's money or a company's SHARE[2] (5) prices weaken or are weakened, their value is reduced

**weak·er sex** /ˈ·· ˌ·/ *n* **the weaker sex** an expression meaning women, that is now usually considered offensive

**weak-kneed** /ˌ· ˈ·◂/ *adj informal* lacking courage and unable to make your own decisions

**weak·ling** /ˈwiːk-lɪŋ/ *n* [C] someone who is not physically strong

W3 **weak·ness** /ˈwiːknɪ̇s/ *n*
**1 ▶ PHYSICAL ◀** [U] the state of being physically weak: *weakness in the muscles*
**2 ▶ LACK OF DETERMINATION ◀** [U] lack of determination shown in someone's behaviour: **sign of weakness** *Most people saw her sensitivity as a sign of weakness.*
**3 ▶ LACK OF POWER ◀** [U] lack of power and influence: *the weakness of the Trade Union movement in post-Thatcher Britain*
**4 ▶ CHARACTER/DESIGN ETC ◀** [U] a fault in someone's character or in a system, organization, design etc: *We spent two hours analyzing the team's strengths and weaknesses.* | *a structural weakness in the aircraft*
**5 ▶ IDEA, PLAN ETC ◀** [C] a part of something that can easily be attacked or criticized: [+ **in**] *We finally found a weakness in their case.*
**6 a weakness for sth** if you have a weakness for something, you like it very much even though it may not be good for you: *Ryan's always had a weakness for fast cars.*

**weak-willed** /ˌ· ˈ·◂/ *adj* someone who is weak-willed cannot make decisions easily

**weal** /wiːl/ *n* [C] a red swollen mark on the skin where someone has been hit

**wealth** /welθ/ *n* **1** [U] a large amount of money and possessions: *The country's wealth comes from its oil.* **2 a wealth of experience/knowledge/resources etc** a large number or amount of experience etc W3

**wealth·y** /ˈwelθi/ *adj* **1** having a lot of money, possessions etc, especially because your family has owned them for a long time: *wealthy landowners* **2 the wealthy** people who have a lot of money, possessions etc

**wean** /wiːn/ *v* [I,T] to gradually stop feeding a baby or young animal on its mother's milk and start giving it ordinary food: *Some infants are weaned at six months.*
**wean** sb **off** sth *phr v* [T] to make someone gradually stop doing something you disapprove of: *I'm still trying to wean my daughter off sugary snacks.*
**wean** sb **on** sth *phr v* [T] **be weaned on** to be influenced by something from a very early age: *Like many of his generation, he was weaned on the Bible.*

**weap·on** /ˈwepən/ *n* [C] **1** something that you use to fight with, such as a knife, bomb, or gun: *The crowd picked up sticks and bottles to use as weapons.* | **lethal weapon** (=one that can kill) **2** a type of behaviour, knowledge of a particular subject etc that you can use against someone when you are in a difficult situation: *The only weapon she could use against him was guilt.* S2 W2

**weap·on·ry** /ˈwepənri/ *n* [U] a word meaning weapons, used especially when talking about particular types of weapons: *nuclear weaponry*

**wear**[1] /weə‖wer/ *v past tense* **wore** /wɔː‖wɔːr/ *past participle* **worn** /wɔːn‖wɔːrn/ S1 W1
**1 ▶ ON YOUR BODY ◀** [T] to have something such as clothes, shoes, or jewellery on your body: *I'm going to wear a black dress and my diamond earrings.* | *Why aren't you wearing your glasses?* | **wear a seatbelt** (=put it around yourself) | **wear blue/black/red etc** *I rarely wear bright colors.* | **wear sth to a party/dance/interview etc** *You can't wear jeans to the opera.*
**2 ▶ HAIR ◀** [T] to have your hair or BEARD in a particular style or shape: *Fay wore her hair in a ponytail.*
**3 ▶ BECOME DAMAGED ◀** [I] to become thinner or weaker after continuous use: *The stair carpet has worn in places.*
**4 ▶ HOLE ◀** [T] to change the shape or condition of something by using it a lot or gradually damaging it: **wear a hole/groove/gap etc in sth** *You've worn a hole in these socks.*
**5 wear well** to remain in good condition without becoming broken or damaged after a period of time: *The concrete buildings of the 60s haven't worn well.*
**6 ▶ EXPRESSION ◀** [T] to have a particular expression on your face: **wear a frown/smile/grin** *Harry's face wore a broad grin.*
**7 sth is wearing thin** if an excuse, explanation, opinion etc is wearing thin, it has been used so often that you no longer believe or accept it: *Neil says he has to work late again – I think that excuse is wearing thin.*
**8 wear the trousers** *BrE*, **wear the pants** *AmE informal* to be the person in a family who makes the decisions
**9 not wear sth** *BrE spoken* used to say that you will not allow or accept something: *Jane came home after 2 a.m. – I'm not wearing that.*
**10 wear your heart on your sleeve** *informal* to show your true feelings openly —**wearable** *adj*
**wear away** *phr v* [I,T] to gradually damage something or make it get thinner or weaker by using it, rubbing it etc: **wear sth ↔ away** *The cliff face is being worn away by the sea.*
**wear down** *phr v* **1** [I,T] to gradually become smaller or make something smaller, for example by rubbing it or using it a lot: *My shoes have worn down at the heel.* **2** [T] to make someone physically weaker or less determined: **wear sb ↔ down** *Haig's bullying was wearing me down.*

**wear off** *phr v* [I] **1** if pain or the effect of something wears off, it gradually stops: *The effects of the anaesthetic were starting to wear off.* **2 the novelty wears off** used to say that you stop feeling interested or excited about something because it is no longer new

**wear on** *phr v* [I] if time wears on, it passes very slowly, especially when you are waiting for something to happen: *As the night wore on there was still no news of the missing plane.*

**wear out** *phr v* [I,T] **1** to cause a lot of damage to something by using it a lot or for a long time so that it can no longer be used: *Damn! My camera batteries have worn out.* | **wear sth ↔ out** *I've worn out the soles of my shoes.* **2** to make someone feel extremely tired; EXHAUST[1] (1): **wear sb ↔ out** *Two nights without sleep have worn me out.* | **wear yourself out** *The baby has stopped crying. I think he's worn himself out.* —see also WORN-OUT

**wear²** *n* **1** [U] damage caused by continuous use over a long period: *The carpet is showing signs of wear.* **2** [U] the amount of use an object, piece of clothing etc has had, or the use you can expect to get from it: *Considering the wear it's had, your coat's in good condition.* | **have/get a lot of wear out of sth** *You'll get a lot of wear out of a canvas tent.* | **a lot of wear is left in sth** (=it is still useful or can still be worn) **3 sportswear/evening wear/childrens' wear etc** the clothes worn for a particular occasion or activity, or by a particular group of people: *a new range of casual wear* | *the menswear department* | *footwear* (=shoes) **4 wear and tear** the amount of damage you expect to be caused to furniture, cars, equipment etc when they are used for a long period of time: **normal/everyday wear and tear** *The washer should last for ten years allowing for normal wear and tear.* —see also **the worse for wear** (WORSE[1] (8))

**wear·er** /ˈweərə‖ˈwerər/ *n* [C] someone who wears a particular type of clothing, jewellery, etc: *Contact lens wearers often get red eyes.*

**wear·ing** /ˈweərɪŋ‖ˈwer-/ *adj* making you feel tired or annoyed: *The constant arguments at home are very wearing.*

**wear·i·some** /ˈwɪərisəm‖ˈwɪr-/ *adj formal* making you feel bored, tired, or annoyed: *a wearisome task*

**wear·y¹** /ˈwɪəri‖ˈwɪr-/ *adj* **1** very tired, especially because you have been doing something for a long time: *I just feel weary – I wish I didn't have to work nights.* | *a weary smile* | **weary of doing sth** *I'm weary of arguing all the time.* **2** *especially literary* making you very tired: *a long and weary march* —**wearily** *adv*: *Alice signed wearily.* —**weariness** *n* [U]

**weary²** *v* [I,T] *formal* to become very tired or make someone very tired: *Amanda wouldn't admit how much the children wearied her.* | **weary of doing** *Smoking is bad for you, as experts never weary of reminding us.*

**wea·sel¹** /ˈwiːzəl/ *n* [C] a small thin furry animal that kills and eats rats and birds

**weasel²** *v*

**weasel out** *phr v* [I] *informal* to avoid doing something you should do by using clever or dishonest excuses: [+ **of**] *We made a deal and you can't weasel out of it.*

**weasel word** /ˈ·· ,·/ *n* [C] *informal* a word used instead of another word because it is less direct, honest, or clear

S1 W2 **weath·er¹** /ˈweðə‖-ər/ *n* **1** [singular, U] the temperature and other conditions such as sun, rain, and wind: **the weather** *What was the weather like on your vacation?* | **hot/wet/cold etc weather** *a spell of very dry weather* | **weather forecast** (=a report saying what the weather is expected to be like in the near future) | **weather permitting** (=if the weather is good enough) *I'm playing golf this afternoon – weather permitting.* | **weather pattern** (=the way the weather usually is or changes over a long period of time) | **weather map/chart** *The weather map shows a ridge of high pressure coming in from the Atlantic.* | **weather report** (=description of weather conditions on radio or television) —see picture on page 836 **2 the weather** *informal* the description of what the weather will be like in the near future, on radio, television, in newspapers etc: *I always watch the weather after the news.* **3 in all weathers** in all types of weather, even when it is very hot or cold: *There are homeless people sleeping on the streets in all weathers.* **4 under the weather** *informal* slightly ill: *You look a bit under the weather.* **5 keep a weather eye on** to watch a situation carefully so that you notice anything unusual or unpleasant —see also **make heavy weather of sth** (HEAVY[1] (12))

**weather²** *v* **1** [I,T] if rock, wood etc weathers, or if wind, sun, rain etc weathers them, they change colour or shape over a period of time: *a badly weathered statue* **2** [T] to come through a very difficult situation safely: **weather the storm** *Many small firms did not weather the storm of the recession.*

**weath·er·board** /ˈweðəbɔːd‖-ərbɔːrd/ *n* **1** [U] *BrE* boards covering the outer walls of a house; CLAPBOARD *AmE* **2** [C] a board or set of boards fixed across the bottom of a door, to prevent water from getting inside

**weath·er·bound** /ˈweðəbaʊnd‖-ər-/ *adj* unable to move or travel because of bad weather

**weather cen·tre** *BrE*, **weather bureau** *AmE* /ˈ·· ,··/ *n* [C] a place where information about the weather is collected and where reports are produced

**weath·er·cock** /ˈweðəkɒk‖-ərkɑːk/ *n* [C] a WEATHER VANE in the shape of a COCK[1] (1)

**weath·er·man** /ˈweðəmæn‖-ər-/ *n* [C] a man on television or radio who tells you what the weather will be like

**weath·er·per·son** /ˈweðəpɜːsən‖-ðərpɜːr-/ *n* [C] someone on television or radio who tells you what the weather will be like

**weath·er·proof** /ˈweðəpruːf‖-ər-/ *adj* weatherproof clothing or material can keep out wind and rain —**weatherproof** *v* [T]

**weather ship** /ˈ·· ·/ *n* [C] a ship at sea which reports on weather conditions

**weather sta·tion** /ˈ·· ,··/ *n* [C] a place or building used for studying and recording weather conditions

**weather strip** /ˈ·· ·/ *n* [C] a thin piece of plastic or other material put along the edge of a door or window to keep out cold air —**weather stripping** *n* [U]

**weather vane** /ˈ·· ·/ *n* [C] a metal thing fixed to the top of a building that blows around to show the direction the wind is coming from

**weave¹** /wiːv/ *v past tense* **wove** /wəʊv‖woʊv/ *past participle* **woven** /ˈwəʊvən‖ˈwoʊ-/

**1 ▶ CLOTH ◀** [I,T] to make threads into cloth by crossing them under and over each other on a LOOM[1], or to make cloth in this way: *hand-woven scarves*

**2 ▶ MAKE STH ◀** [T] to make something by twisting pieces of something together: *traditional basket weaving* | **weave sth together** *Fir branches were woven together to make garlands.*

**3 ▶ STORY ◀** [T] to invent a complicated story or plan: *What I like is how he weaves elaborate plots.*

**4 get weaving** *BrE spoken* used to tell someone to hurry up and start doing something

**5 ▶ MOVE ◀** *past tense and past participle* **weaved** [I always + adv/prep, T always + adv/prep] to move somewhere by turning and changing direction a lot: [+ **through/across etc**] *cyclists weaving in and out of the traffic* | **weave your way** *Cindy weaved her way through the crowd.*

**weave²** *n* [C] the way in which a material is woven, and the pattern formed by this: *a fine weave*

**weav·er** /ˈwiːvə‖-ər/ *n* [C] someone whose job is to weave cloth

**web** /web/ *n* [C] **1** a net of thin threads made by a SPIDER to catch insects: **spin a web** (=make a web) —see also COBWEB —see picture at SPIDER **2 a web of sth** a closely related set of things that can be very complicated: *a web of lies* **3** pieces of skin that connect the toes of ducks and some other birds, and help them to swim well

**webbed** /webd/ *adj* webbed feet or toes have skin between the toes

**web·bing** /ˈwebɪŋ/ *n* [U] strong woven material in narrow bands, used for supporting seats etc

**web-foot·ed** /ˌ· ˈ··◂/ *adj* having toes that are joined by pieces of skin

**web off·set** /ˌ· ˈ··/ *n* [U] a method of printing using one continuous roll of paper

**web-toed** /ˌ· ˈ·◂/ *adj* web-footed

**Wed** a written abbreviation of WEDNESDAY

**we'd** /wid; *strong* wiːd/ **1** the short form of 'we had': *We'd better go now.* **2** the short form of 'we would': *We'd rather stay.*

**wed** /wed/ *v past tense and past participle* **wedded** or **wed** [I,T not in progressive] a word meaning to marry, used especially in literature or newspapers

**wed·ded** /ˈwedɪ̣d/ *adj* **1 sb's (lawful) wedded husband/wife** *formal* someone's legal husband or wife **2 be wedded to** to believe strongly in a particular idea or way of doing things: *They're still very wedded to the idea of public ownership.*

S2 W3 **wed·ding** /ˈwedɪŋ/ *n* [C] **1** a marriage ceremony, especially one with a religious service: **wedding present/reception/cake etc** *Careful with that vase! It was a wedding present.* **2 (hear the sound of) wedding bells** *spoken* used to say that you think it is likely that two people will get married: *I reckon it's wedding bells for Tony and Jane.*

**wedding break·fast** /ˈ·· ˌ··/ *n* [C usually singular] *BrE* a special meal after a wedding ceremony

**wedding chap·el** /ˈ·· ˌ··/ *n* [C] a building used in the US for wedding ceremonies

**wedding dress** /ˈ·· ·/ also **wedding gown** *n* [C] a long white dress worn at a traditional wedding

**wedding ring** /ˈ·· ·/ *n* [C] a ring worn on the third finger of your left hand to show that you are married

**wedge¹** /wedʒ/ *n* [C] **1** a piece of wood, metal etc that has one thick edge and one pointed edge and is used especially for keeping a door open or for splitting wood **2** a piece of food shaped like this: *a wedge of chocolate cake | Garnish with lemon wedges.* **3 drive a wedge between** to make the relationship between two people or groups worse: *Their divorce has driven a wedge between the two families.* —see also **the thin end of the wedge** (THIN¹ (11))

**wedge²** *v* **1** [T always + adv/prep] to force something firmly into a narrow space: **wedge sth behind/under/in etc** *Cloth wedged in the cracks failed to block out the drafts.* | **wedged in** (=stuck in a small space) *I was wedged in between Tom and Amy on the back seat.* **2 wedge sth open/shut** to put something under a door, window etc to make it stay open or shut

**wed·lock** /ˈwedlɒk‖-lɑːk/ *n* [U] *old use* **1 born out of wedlock** if a child is born out of wedlock, its parents are not married when it is born **2** the state of being married

**Wednes·day** /ˈwenzdi/ written abbreviation **Wed** or **Weds** *n* [C,U] the day between Tuesday and Thursday. In Britain, Wednesday is considered the third day of the week, and in the US it is considered the fourth day of the week: *She'll arrive on Wednesday. | It happened Wednesday afternoon. | They left last Wednesday.* | **on Wednesdays** (=each Wednesday) *We play tennis on Wednesdays.* | **a Wednesday** (=one of the Wednesdays of the year) *My birthday's on a Wednesday this year.* | **the Wednesday** *BrE* (=the Wednesday of the week being mentioned) *They're arriving on the Wednesday, and leaving just after Christmas.*

**Weds** a written abbreviation of Wednesday

**wee¹** /wiː/ *adj* [usually before noun] **1** *ScotE or informal* very small: *a wee kitten* **2 a wee bit** *informal* to a small degree: *I'm a wee bit tired.* **3 the wee (small) hours** *ScotE and AmE* the early hours of the morning, just after midnight; SMALL HOURS *BrE*

**wee²** *v* [I] *BrE spoken* a word meaning to pass water from your body, used by or to children; URINATE; WEE-WEE —**wee** *n* [singular, U] *Do you want a wee?*

**weed¹** /wiːd/ *n* **1** [C] a wild plant growing where it is not wanted and that prevents crops or garden flowers from growing properly **2** [U] a plant without flowers that grows on water in a large green floating mass **3** [C] *BrE informal* someone who is weak: *Nigel's such a weed, isn't he?* **4 the weed** *informal* cigarettes or tobacco **5** [U] *old-fashioned* CANNABIS **6 (widow's) weeds** *old use* black clothes worn by a woman whose husband has died

**weed²** *v* [I,T] to remove unwanted plants from a garden or other place

**weed** sb/sth↔ **out** *phr v* [T] to get rid of people or things that are not very good: *Unsuitable recruits were soon weeded out.*

**weed·kil·ler** /ˈwiːdˌkɪlə‖-ər/ *n* [C,U] poison used to kill unwanted plants

**weed·y** /ˈwiːdi/ *adj informal* **1** full of unwanted wild plants **2** *BrE* physically weak or having a weak character: *a weedy little man with glasses*

**week** /wiːk/ *n* [C] **1** a period of seven days and nights, usually measured in Britain from Monday to Sunday and in the US from Sunday to Saturday: *The flight to Accra goes twice a week. | See you next week.* **2** any period of seven days and nights: *The training program lasts three weeks.* **3** the part of the week when you go to work, usually from Monday to Friday; WORKING WEEK: *a 35-hour week | I don't see her much during the week.* **4 Monday week/Tuesday week etc** *BrE* a week after the day that is mentioned: *We're off to Spain Sunday week.* **5 a week on Monday etc** *BrE*/**a week from Monday etc** *AmE* a week after the day that is mentioned: *The Reids are coming for dinner a week from Sunday. | Keith's coming home two weeks on Saturday.* **6 week after week** also **week in week out** *usually spoken* continuously for many weeks: *I just seem to do the same things week in week out.* S1 W1

**week·day** /ˈwiːkdeɪ/ *n* [C] any day of the week except Saturday and Sunday

**week·end¹** /ˌwiːkˈend◂ ˈwiːkend‖ˈwiːkend/ *n* [C] **1** Saturday and Sunday (and sometimes also Friday evening), especially when considered as time when you do not work: *Are you doing anything nice this weekend?* | **a long weekend** (=Saturday and Sunday, and also Friday or Monday, or both) *We're going for a long weekend to EuroDisney.* | **at the weekend/at weekends** *BrE*: *I never work at weekends.* | **on the weekend/on weekends** *AmE*: *What are you doing on the weekend?* | **weekend cottage/cabin etc** (=a place in the country where you spend your weekends) **2** a holiday from Friday evening until Sunday evening: *You've won a weekend for two in Paris!* —see also **dirty weekend** (DIRTY¹ (2)) S1 W2

**weekend²** *v* [I always + adv/prep] to spend the weekend somewhere: *We're weekending on the coast.*

**week·end·er** /ˌwiːkˈendə‖ˈwiːkendər/ *n* [C] someone who spends time in a place only at weekends

**week·long** /ˈwiːklɒŋ‖-lɒːŋ/ *adj* [only before noun] continuing for a week: *a weeklong seminar*

**week·ly¹** /ˈwiːkli/ *adj* happening once a week or every week: *a weekly current affairs programme | twice-weekly flights to Hong Kong* —**weekly** *adv*: *The magazine is published weekly.* S3

**weekly²** *n* [C] a magazine that appears once a week: *a popular news weekly*

**week·night** /ˈwiːknaɪt/ *n* [C] any night apart from Saturday or Sunday

**wee·nie** /ˈwiːni/ *n* [C] *AmE informal* **1** a type of SAUSAGE; a WIENER (1): *a weenie roast* **2** a word meaning someone who is weak, afraid, or stupid, used especially by children

**wee·ny** /'wiːni/ *BrE*, **weensie** /'wiːnzi/ *AmE spoken adj* extremely small —see also TEENY WEENY

**weep** /wiːp/ *v past tense and past participle* **wept** /wept/ **1** [I,T] *formal or literary* to cry, especially because you feel very sad: *James broke down and wept.* | **weep bitterly** (=cry a lot) **2 I could have wept** *spoken* used to say that you felt very disappointed about something: *I could have wept when we lost by one point.* **3** [I] if a wound weeps, liquid comes out of it —**weep** *n* [singular]

**weep·ie** /'wiːpi/ *n* [C] another spelling of WEEPY[2]

**weep·ing** /'wiːpɪŋ/ *adj* **weeping willow/birch etc** a tree with branches that hang down towards the ground

**weep·y[1]** /'wiːpi/ *adj informal* tending to cry a lot: *feeling emotionally exhausted and weepy*

**weepy[2], weepie** *n* [C] *informal* a film or story that seems to be deliberately intended to make you cry

**wee·vil** /'wiːvəl/ *n* [C] a small insect that spoils grain, flour etc by eating it

**wee-wee** /'· ·/ *v* [I] *spoken* a word meaning to pass water from your body, used by or to children; URINATE —**wee-wee** *n* [singular, U]

**weft** /weft/ *n* **the weft** *technical* the threads in a piece of cloth that are woven across the threads that go from top to bottom; WOOF[2] —compare WARP[2] (1)

S3 **weigh** /weɪ/ *v*

**1** ▶ **BE A PARTICULAR WEIGHT** ◀ [linking verb] to have a particular weight: *Our Christmas turkey weighed 16 pounds.* | *How much do you weigh?*

**2** ▶ **MEASURE THE WEIGHT** ◀ [T] to use a machine to find out what something or someone weighs: *Have you weighed yourself lately?*

**3 weigh a ton** to be very heavy: *These books weigh a ton!*

**4** ▶ **CONSIDER/COMPARE** ◀ [T] to consider something carefully so that you can make a decision about it: *Tim weighed the alternatives in his mind.* | **weigh sth against sth** *We have to weigh the costs of the new system against the benefits it will bring.* —see also **weigh up** (WEIGH)

**5 weigh your words** to think very carefully about what you say because you do not want to say the wrong thing

**6** ▶ **INFLUENCE** ◀ [I always + adv/prep] *formal* to influence a result or decision: [+ **with**] *Her evidence weighed quite strongly with the judge.* | **weigh against/in favour of** *a new argument that weighed heavily in Mark's favour*

**7 weigh anchor** to raise an ANCHOR and sail away

**weigh** sb/sth ↔ **down** *phr v* [T usually passive] **1** to make someone or something bend or feel heavy under a load: *Sally was weighed down with shopping bags.* **2** to feel worried about a problem or difficulty: *a family weighed down with grief*

**weigh in** *phr v* [I] **1** to have your weight tested before taking part in a fight or a horse race —see also WEIGH-IN **2 weigh in (with)** *informal* to add a remark to a discussion or an argument: *Each member weighed in with their own opinion.*

**weigh on** sb/sth *phr v* [T] to make someone worried or give them problems: *Yvonne's responsibilities were beginning to weigh on her.* | **weigh on sb's mind** *I'm sure there's something weighing on his mind.* | **weigh heavily** *responsibilities that weighed heavily on young shoulders*

**weigh** sth ↔ **out** *phr v* [T] to measure an amount of something by weight: *I watched as he weighed out half a pound of coffee beans and ground them up.*

**weigh** sb/sth **up** *phr v* [T] **1** to consider a choice carefully so that you can make a decision: *We're just weighing up the pros and cons of the two deals.* **2** to form an opinion about someone by watching them, talking to them etc: *I can't quite weigh Marilyn up.*

**weigh·bridge** /'weɪˌbrɪdʒ/ *n* [C] a machine for weighing vehicles and their loads, with a flat area that you drive the vehicle onto

**weigh-in** /'· ·/ *n* [C usually singular] a check on the weight of a BOXER (1) or a JOCKEY[1] before a fight or a horse-race —see also **weigh in** (WEIGH)

**weight[1]** /weɪt/ *n* S1 W2

**1** ▶ **WHAT SB/STH WEIGHS** ◀ [C,U] how heavy something is when measured by a particular system: *The average weight of a baby at birth is just over seven pounds.*

**2** ▶ **HOW FAT** ◀ [U] how heavy and especially how fat someone is: *A lot of teenage girls are obsessed about their weight.* | **put on weight** (=get fatter) | **lose weight** (=get thinner) | **watch your weight** (=be careful about what you eat so that you do not get fat) | **have a weight problem** (=be too fat) —see also OVERWEIGHT; UNDERWEIGHT

**3** ▶ **HEAVINESS** ◀ [U] the fact of being heavy: *The weight of her boots made it hard for Sue to run.* | **under the weight of** (=supporting something heavy) *Karen staggered along under the weight of her backpack.*

**4** ▶ **HEAVY THING** ◀ [C] something that is heavy: *Omar can't lift heavy weights because of his bad back.*

**5** ▶ **FOR MEASURING QUANTITIES** ◀ [C] a piece of metal weighing a particular amount that is balanced against something else to measure what it weighs

**6** ▶ **FOR EXERCISE** ◀ [C] a piece of metal that weighs a certain amount and is lifted by people who want bigger muscles or who are competing in lifting competitions —see also WEIGHTLIFTING

**7** ▶ **SYSTEM** ◀ [C,U] a system of standard measures of weight: *metric weight* | *weights and measures*

**8** ▶ **RESPONSIBILITY/WORRY** ◀ [C] something that causes you a lot of worry: [+ **on**] *Since Jane's been sick, I've had to carry the full weight of running the school.*

**9 a weight off your mind** something that solves a problem and makes you feel happier: *Selling the house was a great weight off my mind.*

**10** ▶ **IMPORTANCE** ◀ [U] the influence or importance that something has when you are forming a judgment or opinions: *The weight of evidence against her led to her conviction.* | **carry weight** (=have influence) *Una's opinion doesn't carry much weight around here.* | **add weight to** *His declining health added weight to the argument that the king should abdicate.* | **attach weight to** (=think that something is important)

**11 throw your weight about/around** *informal* to use your position of authority to tell people what to do in an unpleasant and unreasonable way

**12 throw your weight behind** to use all your power and influence to support someone: *The US has thrown its weight behind the new leader.*

**13 pull your weight** to do your full share of work: *Some people in the office hadn't been pulling their weight.*

**14 take the weight off your feet** *spoken* used to tell someone to sit down: *Come in, take the weight off your feet.*

**15 weight of numbers** the combined strength, influence etc of a large group: *They are likely to win this battle through sheer weight of numbers.*

**16 summer-weight/winter-weight** a piece of clothing that is summer-weight or winter-weight, is made of material that is suitable for summer or winter

**17** ▶ **SCIENCE** ◀ [C,U] *technical* the amount of force with which an object is pulled down by GRAVITY (1) —see also **dead weight** (DEAD[1] (29))

**weight[2]** *v* [T] to add something heavy to something or put a weight on it, especially in order to keep it in place: *fishing nets weighted with lead*

**weight·ed** /'weɪtɪ̱d/ *adj* **weighted in favour/against** producing conditions that are favourable or unfavourable to one particular group: [+ **against**] *The voting system is weighted against the smaller parties.* | **weighted in favour of** *a pay increase heavily weighted in favour of the lower paid staff*

**weight·ing** /'weɪtɪŋ/ *n* [singular, U] *BrE* additional money that you get paid because of the high cost of living in a particular area: *a London weighting*

**weight·less** /'weɪtləs/ *adj* having no weight, especially when you are floating in space or water —**weightlessly** *adv* —**weightlessness** *n* [U]

**weight·lift·ing** /'weɪtˌlɪftɪŋ/ *n* [U] **1** the sport of lifting specially shaped weights (WEIGHT[1] (6)) **2** also

**weight training** *BrE* the activity of lifting specially shaped weights as a form of exercise —**weightlifter** *n* [C]

**weight·y** /ˈweɪti/ *adj* **1** important and serious: *weighty reasons for change* **2** *especially literary* heavy —**weightily** *adv* —**weightiness** *n* [U]

**weir** /wɪə‖wɪr/ *n* [C] **1** a low structure built across a river or stream to control the flow of water **2** a wooden fence built across a stream to make a pool where you can catch fish

S2 **weird** /wɪəd‖wɪrd/ *adj* **1** *informal* unusual and different from anything you have seen or heard before; BIZARRE: *Mike's got a really weird sense of humour.* | **weird and wonderful** *Tom's full of weird and wonderful ideas.* **2** very strange, mysterious, or frightening: *A weird green glow lit the sky.* —**weirdly** *adv* —**weirdness** *n* [U]

**weird·o** /ˈwɪədəʊ‖ˈwɪrdoʊ/ also **weird·ie** /ˈwɪədi‖ˈwɪr-/ *n* [C] *informal* someone who behaves strangely, wears unusual clothes etc: *Jenny's going out with a real weirdo.*

**welch** /weltʃ‖weltʃ/ *v* [I] another spelling of WELSH[2]

S3 W2 **wel·come¹** /ˈwelkəm/ *v* [T] **1** to say hello in a friendly way to someone who has just arrived: *The Queen welcomed the President as he got off the plane.* **2** to accept an idea, suggestion etc happily: *Henri doesn't welcome intrusions into his privacy.* | *The college welcomes applications from people of all races.* **3 welcome sb/sth with open arms** **a)** to be very glad that someone has come **b)** to be very happy to accept something

S2 W3 **welcome²** *adj* **1** someone who is welcome is gladly accepted in a place: *I had the feeling I wasn't really welcome.* | **make sb welcome** (=make someone feel that you are pleased they have come) **2** something that is welcome is pleasant and enjoyable, especially because it is just what you need or want: *a welcome break from the pressures of work* | *A cup of tea would be very welcome.* **3 be welcome to** *spoken* used to say that someone can have something if they want it, because you certainly do not want it: *If Rob wants that job he's welcome to it!* **4 be welcome to do sth** *spoken* used to invite someone to do something if they would like to: *You're welcome to stay for lunch.* **5 you're welcome!** *spoken, especially AmE* a polite way of replying to someone who has just thanked you for something: *"Thanks for the coffee." "You're welcome."*

**welcome³** *n* [C] **1** a greeting you give to someone when they arrive: *Mandela got a tremendous welcome at the airport.* | **extend a welcome to** *formal* (=welcome someone) **2 give sb/sth a warm welcome** **a)** to welcome someone in a very friendly way **b)** to gladly accept an idea, suggestion etc **3 outstay/overstay your welcome** to stay at someone's house longer than they want you to

**welcome⁴** *interjection* **1** an expression of greeting to a guest or someone who has just arrived: [+ **to**] *Welcome to London!* | *Welcome back – it's good to see you again.* | **welcome home** (=used when someone has been away and returns home) **2 welcome to the club** *spoken* used to make someone feel better when they are in a bad situation, by telling them you are already in that situation

**welcome wag·on** /ˈ·· ˌ··/ *n* [C] *AmE* someone or something that welcomes someone who has just arrived in a new place: *The company is bringing out the welcome wagon for the new sales recruits.*

**wel·com·ing** /ˈwelkəmɪŋ/ *adj* a person or place that is welcoming makes you feel happy and relaxed when you meet them or arrive there: *a welcoming smile* | *The room was bright and welcoming.* | **welcoming committee/party** (=group of people who welcome someone)

**weld¹** /weld/ *v* **1** [I,T] to join metals by melting them and pressing them together when they are hot, or to be joined in this way **2** [T always + adv/prep] to join or unite people into a single, strong group: *A person of vision was needed to weld the various political factions together.* —compare FORGE¹ (3), SOLDER²

**weld²** *n* [C] a joint that is made by welding two pieces of metal

**weld·er** /ˈweldə‖-ər/ *n* [C] someone whose job is to weld things

**wel·fare** /ˈwelfeə‖-fer/ *n* [U] **1** health, comfort, and happiness; WELL-BEING: *Our only concern is the children's welfare.* **2** help that is provided, especially by government organizations for people with social or financial problems: *The company's welfare officer deals with employees' personal problems.* | *welfare services* **3** *especially AmE* money paid by the government to people who are very poor, unemployed etc: **on welfare** *Most of the people in this neighborhood are on welfare.* —compare SOCIAL SECURITY S3 W2

**welfare state** /ˌ·· ˈ·‖ˈ·· ·/ *n* **1 the welfare state** a system by which the government provides money, free medical care etc for people who are unemployed or too old to work **2** [C] a country with such a system

**wel·far·is·m** /ˈwelfeərɪzəm‖-fer-/ *n* [U] a way of life in which someone does not work, but accepts money from the government and makes no attempt to improve their situation

**wel·kin** /ˈwelkɪn/ *n poetical* the sky

**we'll** /wil; *strong* wiːl/ the short form of 'we will' or 'we shall'

**well¹** /wel/ *adv comparative* **better** *superlative* **best** S1 W1

**1 ► SATISFACTORILY ◄** in a successful or satisfactory way: *Did you sleep well?* | *James reads well for his age.* | **fairly/moderately/pretty well** (=quite well) | **go well** (=happen in the way you planned or hoped) *I was really pleased that the concert had gone so well.*

**2 well-organized/well-educated etc** organized, educated etc to a high standard

**3 do well** **a)** to be successful, especially in work or business: *Elizabeth's done well for herself – a well-paid job, a nice house and a sports car.* **b)** if someone who has been ill is doing well, they are becoming healthy again: *The operation was successful and the patient is doing well.*

**4 ► THOROUGHLY ◄** in a thorough way: *Mix the flour and butter well.*

**5 as well as** in addition to something else: *They own a house in Provence as well as a villa in Spain.* | **as well as doing sth** *The organization encourages members to meet on a regular basis, as well as providing them with financial support.*

**6 as well** in addition to something or someone else: *We're going to the cinema tonight, why don't you come along as well?*

**7 may/might/could well do/be sth** used to say that something is likely to happen or is likely to be true: *What you say may well be true.* | *You could try the drugstore, but it may well be closed by now.*

**8 may/might/could (just) as well do sth** **a)** *informal* used when you do not particularly want to do something but you decide to do it: *I suppose we may as well get started.* **b)** used to mean that another course of action would have an equally good result: *The taxi was so slow, we might just as well have gone on the bus.*

**9 ► EMPHASIZING STH ◄** **a) well before/behind/down etc** a long way or a long time before, behind etc: *It was well after 12 o'clock when they arrived.* | *Stand well back from the bonfire.* **b) well pleased/well aware etc** very pleased etc: *I'm well aware of the problems involved.* | *Pardoe was well pleased with his day's work.* | **well worth (doing) sth** *The amphitheatre is well worth a visit.* **c)** [+ adj] *BrE spoken* used to emphasize an adjective that describes how someone feels or what sort of situation they are in: *Our boss came out of the meeting looking well fed-up.* **d) well and truly** completely: *I went out and got well and truly drunk.*

**10 know full well** to know or realize something very well: *You know full well what I mean.*

**11 speak/think well of** to talk about someone in an approving way or to have a favourable opinion of them: *Sue has always spoken well of you.*

**12 well done!/well played!** used to praise someone when you think they have done something very well

**13 be well in with** *informal* to have a friendly relationship with someone, especially someone important: *Paul's well in with the boss these days.*

**14 be well out of** *BrE spoken* to be lucky to no longer be involved in a particular situation: *She's well out of that marriage, her husband was a brute!*
**15 be well up in/on** *informal especially BrE* to know a lot about a particular subject: *Geoff's well up on the latest technological developments.*
**16 as well sb might/may** used to say that there is a good reason for someone's feelings or reactions: *Marilyn looked guilty when she saw me, as well she might.*
**17 do well by** *informal* to treat someone generously

S1 W1 **well²** *interjection*
**1 ▶ EMPHASIZING STH ◀** used before a statement or question to emphasize it: *Well, I think it's a good idea, I don't care what anyone else says.* | *Well, all I can say is it's a bloody waste of taxpayer's money!* | **well then** *"James doesn't want to come to the cinema with us." "Well then, let's go on our own."*
**2 ▶ PAUSING ◀** used to pause or give yourself time to think before saying something: *Mary's been a bit depressed and, well, I was worried she might do something stupid.* | *Well, let's see now, I could book you in for an appointment next Thursday.* | **well I mean** *Well, I mean the whole idea just sounds crazy to me.*
**3 ▶ ACCEPTING A SITUATION ◀** also **oh well** used to show that you accept a situation even though you feel disappointed or annoyed about it: *Well, I did my best, I can't do any more than that.* | *Oh well, we'll just have to cancel the holiday I suppose.*
**4 ▶ SHOWING SURPRISE ◀** also **well, well (,well)** used to express surprise or amusement: *Well, so Steve's a senior manager now is he?* | *Well, well, well, I didn't think I'd see you here Sue.*
**5 ▶ SHOWING ANGER ◀** used to express anger or disapproval: *Well, you'd think at least she might have phoned to say she wasn't coming!* | **well honestly/well really** *"They were playing music next door until 4 a.m." "Well honestly, you'd think they'd show a bit more consideration."*
**6 ▶ FINAL REMARK ◀** used to show that you are about to finish speaking or stop doing an activity: *Well, that's all for today, I'll see you all tomorrow.*
**7 ▶ EXPRESSING DOUBT ◀** used to express doubt or the fact that you are not sure about something: *"I reckon Mike Whelan is worth a place in the England side." "Well, he's not a very consistent player is he?"*
**8 ▶ AGREEING ◀ very well** used to show that you agree with or accept a suggestion, invitation etc: *"I think plain wallpaper would look better in this room." "Very well then, if you insist."*
**9 ▶ CONTINUING A STORY ◀** used to connect two parts of a story that you are telling people especially in order to make it seem more interesting: *You know that couple I was telling you about the other day? Well, the police came round and arrested them both!*
**10 ▶ DEMANDING AN EXPLANATION ◀ Well?** used to demand an explanation or answer when you are angry with someone: *Mrs Hawkins says she saw you hanging around the town centre with some of your mates last night. Well?*

Frequencies of the word **well** in spoken and written English.

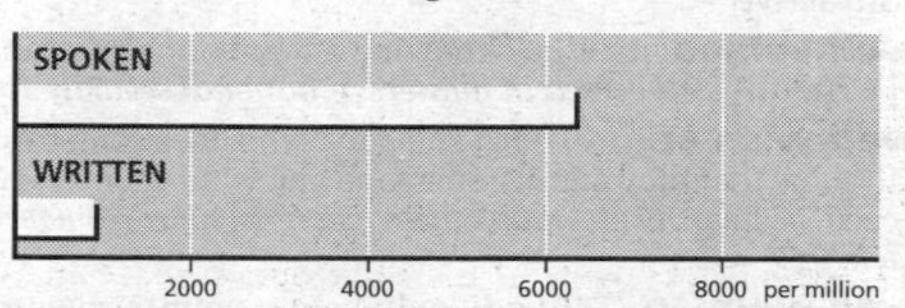


Based on the British National Corpus and the Longman Lancaster Corpus

This graph shows that **well** is much more common in spoken English than in written English. This is because it has several uses as an interjection in spoken English and is used in a lot of common spoken phrases.

**well³** *adj comparative* **better** /ˈbetə‖-ər/ *superlative* **best** /best/ S1 **1** healthy: *"How are you?" "Very well thanks."* | **look/feel well** *You're looking well, the vacation obviously did you good.* | **get well soon** (=used to say that you hope someone soon feels better) **2 it is just as well (that)** *spoken* used to say that things have happened in a way that is fortunate or desirable: *It's just as well I couldn't go to the funeral, I think I'd have found it too upsetting.* **3 it's/that's all very well but...** *spoken* used to say that you think something is not really satisfactory or acceptable, even if someone else thinks it is: *"They said Maria should go to bed and rest." "That's all very well but who's going to look after the children?"* **4 it might be as well** *spoken* used to give someone advice or make a helpful suggestion: *It might be as well to leave him on his own for a few hours.* **5 that's/it's all well and good** *spoken especially BrE* used to say that you accept or approve of one part of a situation or thing but not of another part: *Going off on foreign holidays is all well and good but you've got to get back to reality sometime.* **6 all is well/all is not well** *formal* used to say that a situation is satisfactory or not satisfactory: *All is not well with their marriage.* **7 all's well that ends well** used after a situation has ended in a satisfactory way **8** [not before noun] *literary* happy and comfortable: *We're very well where we are thank you.*

**well⁴** *n* [C] **1** a deep hole in the ground from which people take water: *She lowered her bucket into the well.* | **sink a well** (=dig a well) **2** an OIL WELL **3** an enclosed space in a building which goes straight up and down and surrounds a lift, stairs etc —see also STAIRWELL **4** *BrE* the space in front of a judge in a court of law

**well⁵** *v* also **well up** [I] *especially literary* **1** if liquids well or well up, they start to flow: *I felt tears well up in my eyes.* **2** if feelings well or well up, they start to get stronger: *Anger welled up within him.*

**well-ad·just·ed** /ˌ· ·ˈ··◂/ *adj* emotionally healthy and able to deal well with the problems of life

**well-ad·vised** /ˌ· ·ˈ·◂/ *adj* **you would be well-advised to do sth** used when you are strongly advising someone to do something that will help them avoid trouble: *You would be well-advised to accept this settlement rather than go to court.*

**well-ap·point·ed** /ˌ· ·ˈ··◂/ *adj formal* a well-appointed house, hotel etc has very good furniture and equipment

**well-bal·anced** /ˌ· ˈ··◂/ *adj* **1** a well-balanced meal or DIET¹ (1) contains all the things you need to keep you healthy **2** a well-balanced person is sensible and is not controlled by strong emotions; STABLE¹

**well-be·haved** /ˌ· ·ˈ·◂/ *adj* behaving in a polite or socially acceptable way: *a well-behaved child* | *The crowd was noisy but well-behaved.*

**well-be·ing** /ˌ· ˈ··, ˈ· ˌ··/ *n* [U] a feeling of being comfortable, healthy, and happy: [+ **of**] *We are responsible for the care and well-being of patients.* | **physical/social/economic etc well-being** *the economic well-being of the country* | **a sense of well-being** (=a feeling of being satisfied with your life)

**well-born** /ˌ· ˈ·◂/ *adj formal* born into a rich or UPPER CLASS family

**well-bred** /ˌ· ˈ·◂/ *adj old-fashioned* very polite, behaving or speaking as if you come from a family of high social class: *the epitome of a well-bred Englishwoman who never shows her feelings*

**well-brought-up** /ˌ· · ˈ·◂/ *adj* a child who is well-brought-up has been taught to be polite and to behave well

**well-built** /ˌ· ˈ·◂/ *adj* someone who is well-built is big and strong

**well-cho·sen** /ˌ· ˈ··◂/ *adj* carefully chosen: **well-chosen words** (=suitable for a particular situation)

**well-con·nect·ed** /ˌ· ·ˈ··◂/ *adj* knowing or being related to powerful and socially important people

**well-dis·posed** /ˌ· ·ˈ·◂/ *adj* feeling friendly towards a person or positive about an idea or plan: [+ **to/towards**] *The management is not well-disposed towards technical innovation.*

**well-doc·u·ment·ed** /ˌwel ˈdɒkjɡ̈mentɪ̈d/ *adj* well-documented events, behaviour etc definitely exist and people have written a lot about them: *the well-documented problems faced by prisoners' families*

**well-done** /ˌ· ˈ·◂/ *adj* food that is well-done, especially meat, has been cooked thoroughly —compare RARE (2) —see also **well done!** (WELL[1] (12))

**well-dressed** /ˌ· ˈ·◂/ *adj* wearing attractive, fashionable, and usually expensive clothes

**well-earned** /ˌ· ˈ·◂/ *adj* something that is well-earned is something you deserve because you have worked hard: *It's time for a well-earned rest.*

**well-en·dowed** /ˌ· ·ˈ·◂/ *adj informal or humorous* **1** a woman who is well-endowed has large breasts **2** a man who is well-endowed has a large PENIS (=sex organ)

**well-es·tab·lished** /ˌ· ·ˈ··◂/ *adj* established for a long time and respected: *a well-established law firm*

**well-fa·voured** /ˌ· ˈ··◂/ *adj old-fashioned* good-looking —compare ILL-FAVOURED

**well-fed** /ˌ· ˈ·◂/ *adj* regularly eating plenty of good healthy food, especially if this has made you a little fat

**well-found·ed** /ˌ· ˈ··◂/ *adj* a belief, feeling etc that is well-founded is based on facts or good judgment

**well-groomed** /ˌ· ˈ·◂/ *adj* having a very neat, clean appearance: *a well-groomed businesswoman*

**well-ground·ed** /ˌ· ˈ··◂/ *adj* **1 well-grounded in** fully trained in an activity or skill: *The soldiers were well-grounded in survival skills.* **2** WELL-FOUNDED: *well-grounded suspicions*

**well-heeled** /ˌ· ˈ·◂/ *adj informal* rich and usually of a high social class

**well-hung** /ˌ· ˈ·◂/ *adj informal or humorous* a man who is well-hung has a large PENIS (=sex organ)

**wel·lie** /ˈweli/ *n* [C] *BrE informal* a wellington —see also WELLY

**well-in·formed** /ˌ· ·ˈ·◂/ *adj* knowing a lot about a particular subject or about many subjects: [+ **about**] *They seemed to be remarkably well-informed about the royal family.*

**wel·ling·ton** /ˈwelɪŋtən/ also **wellington boot** /ˌ··· ˈ·/ *n* [C] *BrE* a long rubber boot that stops your feet getting wet; RUBBER BOOT —see picture at BOOT[1]

**well-in·ten·tioned** /ˌ· ·ˈ··◂/ *adj* trying to be helpful, but failing or actually making things worse: *well-intentioned grandparents who interfere between parents and children*

**well-kept** /ˌ· ˈ·◂/ *adj* **1** a well-kept building or garden is very well cared for and looks neat and clean **2** a well-kept secret is known only to a few people

**well-known** /ˌ· ˈ·◂/ *adj* known by a lot of people: *It's a well-known fact that smoking can cause lung cancer.* | *This is probably their best-known song.* | [+ **for**] *Mother Teresa is well-known for her work with the poor.* —see FAMOUS (USAGE)

**well-man·nered** /ˌ· ˈ··◂/ *adj* polite and having very good manners (MANNERS (3)): *the perfect well-mannered host* —opposite ILL-MANNERED

**well-mean·ing** /ˌ· ˈ··◂/ *adj* intending or intended to be helpful, but not succeeding: *a well-meaning but misguided attempt to reconcile the couple* —see also **he/she means well** (MEAN[1] (16))

**well-meant** /ˌ· ˈ·◂/ *adj* something you say or do that is well-meant is intended to be helpful, but does not have the result you intended: *His comments were well-meant but a little tactless.* —see also **he/she means well** (MEAN[1] (16))

**well·ness** /ˈwelnɪ̈s/ *n* [U] *AmE* the state of being healthy: *a wellness program to promote a healthy lifestyle*

**well-nigh** /ˈ· ·/ *adv BrE formal or AmE* almost, but not quite: *The company has existed for well-nigh 200 years.* | **well-nigh impossible** *Getting them to agree would be well-nigh impossible.*

**well-off** /ˌ· ˈ·◂/ *adj comparative* **better-off**, *superlative* **best-off** **1** having more money than many other people, or enough money to have a good standard of living: *The government claims that people are better off than they were five years ago.* **2 well-off for** having plenty of something, or as much of it as you need: *We're well-off for supermarkets in this area.* **3 you don't know when you're well-off** *spoken* used to tell someone that they are more fortunate than they realize —opposite BADLY-OFF

**well-oiled** /ˌ· ˈ·◂/ *adj* **1 a well-oiled machine** an organization or system that works very well **2** *informal* drunk

**well-paid** /ˌ· ˈ·◂/ *adj* providing or receiving good wages: *a well-paid job* | *well-paid managers*

**well-pre·served** /ˌ· ·ˈ·◂/ *adj humorous* someone who is well-preserved still looks fairly young although they are getting old

**well-read** /ˌwel ˈred◂/ *adj* having read many books and knowing a lot about different subjects

**well-round·ed** /ˌ· ˈ··◂/ *adj* **1** someone who is well-rounded has had a wide variety of experiences in life **2** well-rounded education or experience of life is complete and varied: *She has a well-rounded background in management.* **3** a woman who is well-rounded has a pleasantly curved figure; SHAPELY

**well-spok·en** /ˌ· ˈ··◂/ *adj* speaking in a clear and polite way, and with an ACCENT (=way of pronouncing words) that is socially approved of

**well·spring** /ˈwelˌsprɪŋ/ *n* [C + **of**] *literary* a never-ending supply of a personal quality: *There was a wellspring of courage within her which she could continually draw upon.*

**well-stacked** /ˌ· ˈ·◂/ *adj informal or humorous* a woman who is well-stacked has very large breasts

**well-stocked** /ˌ· ˈ·◂/ *adj* having a large supply and variety of things: *a well-stocked pantry*

**well-thought-of** /ˌ· ˈ· ·◂/ *adj* liked and admired by other people: *Her work is well-thought-of in academic circles.*

**well-thought-out** /ˌ· · ˈ·◂/ *adj* carefully and thoroughly planned: *a well-thought-out strategy*

**well-thumbed** /ˌ· ˈ·◂/ *adj* a well-thumbed book, magazine etc has been used a lot

**well-timed** /ˌ· ˈ·◂/ *adj* said or done at the most suitable moment: *My arrival wasn't very well-timed.*

**well-to-do** /ˌ· · ˈ·◂/ *adj* **1** rich and with a high social position: *well-to-do families* **2 the well-to-do** people who are rich

**well-tried** /ˌ· ˈ·◂/ *adj* **well-tried method/principle etc** a method or principle that has been used many times before and has always been successful

**well-turned** /ˌ· ˈ·◂/ *adj* a well-turned phrase or sentence is carefully expressed

**well-turned-out** /ˌ· · ˈ·◂/ *adj* someone who is well-turned-out wears fashionable clothes and looks attractive

**well-versed** /ˌ· ˈ·◂/ *adj* knowing a lot about something: [+ **in/on**] *well-versed in matters of national security*

**well-wish·er** /ˈ· ˌ··/ *n* [C] someone who does something to show that they admire someone and want them to succeed, be healthy etc: *many messages of support from well-wishers*

**well-wom·an** /ˌ· ˈ··/ *adj* [only before noun] providing medical care and advice for women, to make sure that they stay healthy: *a well-woman clinic*

**well-worn** /ˌ· ˈ·◂/ *adj* **1** worn or used for a long time: *a well-worn jacket* **2** a well-worn argument, phrase etc has been repeated so often that it is no longer interesting or effective: *well-worn excuses*

**wel·ly** /ˈweli/ *n* [C] *BrE informal* **1** a WELLINGTON (=kind of boot) **2 give it some welly!** *spoken* used to tell someone to put more effort into something they are doing

**Welsh** /welʃ/ *n* **1** [U] the original language of Wales **2 the Welsh** people from Wales —**Welsh** *adj*

**welsh, welch** /welʃ‖welʃ, weltʃ/ *v* [I + **on**] *informal* **1** to avoid paying money or your debts **2** to not do something you have promised to do for someone: *He gave us his solemn word and then he welshed on us.*

> **USAGE NOTE: WELSH**
> POLITENESS
> Some Welsh people consider this verb to be offensive.

**Welsh dres·ser** /ˌ· ˈ··/ *n* [C] *BrE* a piece of wooden furniture consisting of drawers and cupboards in the lower part and shelves on top; HUTCH (2) *AmE*

**Welsh rare·bit** /ˌwelʃ ˈreəbɪt‖-ˈrer-/ also **Welsh rabbit** /ˌ· ˈ··/ *n* [C,U] a dish of cheese melted on bread

**welt** /welt/ *n* [C] **1** a raised mark on someone's skin where they have been hit **2** a piece of leather around the edge of a shoe, to which the top and bottom of the shoe are stitched

**wel·ter** /ˈweltə‖-ər/ *n* **a welter of** a large and confusing number of different details, emotions etc: *The researchers were inundated with a welter of information.*

**wel·ter·weight** /ˈweltəweɪt‖-ər-/ *n* [C] a BOXER (1) who is heavier than a LIGHTWEIGHT[1] (2) but lighter than a MIDDLEWEIGHT

**wench** /wentʃ/ *n* [C] *old use or humorous* a girl or young woman, especially a servant

**wend** /wend/ *v* **wend your way** *especially literary* to move or travel slowly from one place to another: *The procession wended its way through the streets.*

**wen·dy house** /ˈwendi ˌhaʊs/ *n* [C] *BrE* a small house for children to play in; PLAY HOUSE *AmE*

**Wens·ley·dale** /ˈwenzlideɪl/ *n* [U] a white cheese that does not have a very strong taste, originally from Yorkshire

**went** /went/ the past tense of GO

**wept** /wept/ the past tense and past participle of WEEP

**we're** /wɪə‖wɪr/ the short form of 'we are'

**were** /wə; *strong* wɜː‖wər; *strong* wɜːr/ *negative short form* **weren't** /wɜːnt‖ˈwɜːrənt, wɜːrnt/ the past tense of BE

**were·wolf** /ˈweəwʊlf, ˈwɪə-‖ˈwer-, ˈwɪr-/ *n* [C] a person who, in some stories, sometimes changes into a WOLF

**wert** /wɜːt‖wɜːrt/ *v* **thou wert** *old use* you were

**West** /west/ *n* **the West** **1** the western part of the world and the people that live there, especially Western Europe and North America **2** the western part of the US —compare MIDWEST, WEST COAST, WILD WEST

**west**[1] *n* [singular, U] **1** the direction towards which the sun goes down, and which is on the left of someone who is facing north: **from/towards the west** *A strong wind was blowing from the west.* | **to the west of** *Birmingham is to the west of Leicester.* **2 the west** the western part of a country or area

S 2 W 2 **west**[2] *adj* [only before noun] **1** in the west or facing the west: *the west door of the church* | *West Africa* **2** a west wind comes from the west

**west**[3] *adv* **1** towards the west: *The room faces west.* **2 go west** *BrE old-fashioned humorous* **a)** to die **b)** to be damaged or ruined

**west·bound** /ˈwestbaʊnd/ *adj* travelling or leading towards the west

**West Coast** /ˈ· ·/ *n* **the West Coast** the western coastal states of the US

**West Coun·try** /ˈ· ˌ··/ *n* **the West Country** the south-west part of England

**West End** /ˌ· ˈ·◂/ *n* **the West End** the western part of central London where there are large shops, theatres, expensive hotels etc

**west·er·ly** /ˈwestəli‖-ərli/ *adj* **1** towards or in the west: *We set off in a westerly direction.* **2** a westerly wind comes from the west

**west·ern**[1], **Western** /ˈwestən‖-ərn/ *adj* from or connected with the west part of the world or of a country: *The Russian ballet is making a tour of Western Europe.* S 2 W 2

**western**[2] *n* [C] a film about life in the 19th century in the American West

**West·ern·er** /ˈwestənə‖-tərnər/ *n* [C] **1** someone who lives in or comes from the western part of the world **2** *AmE* someone who lives in or comes from the western part of the US

**west·ern·ize** also **-ise** *BrE* /ˈwestənaɪz‖-ər-/ *v* [T] to bring customs, business methods etc that are typical of Europe and the US to other countries —**westernization** /ˌwestənaɪˈzeɪʃən‖-tərnə-/ *n* [U]

**west·ern·ized** also **-ised** *BrE* /ˈwestənaɪzd‖-ər/ *adj* copying the customs, behaviour etc typical of the US or Europe

**western medi·cine** /ˌ·· ˈ··‖ˌ·· ˈ···/ *n* [U] the type of medical tratment that is standard in the WEST (1) —compare ALTERNATIVE MEDICINE

**west·ern·most** /ˈwestənməʊst‖-tərnmoʊst/ *adj* [no comparative] furthest west

**West In·di·an** /ˌ· ˈ···/ *adj* from or connected with the West Indies

**west·ward** /ˈwestwəd‖-wərd/ *adj* going towards the west —**westward, westwards** *adv*

**wet**[1] /wet/ *adj* 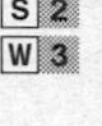
**1 ▶ WATER/LIQUID ◀** covered in or full of liquid: *wet grass* | *My shirt's all wet!* | [+ **with**] *His face was wet with sweat.* | **get (sth) wet** *Try not to get your feet wet.* | **wet through** (=completely wet) | **soaking/sopping/dripping wet** (=extremely wet) *soaking wet socks*
**2 ▶ WEATHER ◀** rainy: *wet weather* | *It's very wet outside.*
**3 the wet a)** rainy weather: *Come in out of the wet.* **b)** wet ground: *Don't trail your coat in the wet!*
**4 ▶ PAINT/INK ETC ◀** not yet dry: *Careful, the paint's still wet.*
**5 ▶ PERSON ◀ a)** *BrE informal* unable to make decisions or take firm actions: *Don't be so wet! Just tell them you don't want to go.* **b) be all wet** *AmE informal* to be completely wrong
**6 wet behind the ears** *informal* very young and without much experience of life —**wetly** *adv* —**wetness** *n* [U]

**wet**[2] *v past tense* **wet** *or* **wetted** [T] **1** to make something wet: *Wet your hair and apply the shampoo.* **2** to make yourself, your clothes, or your bed wet because you pass water from your body by accident: **wet yourself** *I nearly wet myself I was so scared.* **3 wet your whistle** *old-fashioned* to have an alcoholic drink

**wet·back** /ˈwetbæk/ *n* [C] *AmE* an offensive word for someone from Mexico who has come to the US illegally

**wet bar** /ˈ· ·/ *n* [C] *AmE* a small bar with equipment for making alcoholic drinks, in a house, hotel room etc

**wet blan·ket** /ˌ· ˈ··‖ˈ· ˌ··/ *n* [C] *informal* someone who tries to spoil other people's fun

**wet dream** /ˌ· ˈ·‖ˈ· ·/ *n* [C] a sexually exciting dream that a man has, resulting in an ORGASM

**wet fish** /ˌ· ˈ·/ *n* [U] *BrE* fresh uncooked fish that is on sale in a shop

**wet-look** /ˈ· ·/ *adj* [only before noun] wet-look clothes have a shiny surface so that they look as if they are wet

**wet nurse** /ˈ· ·/ *n* [C] *old use* a woman who is employed to give her breast milk to another woman's baby

**wet-nurse** *v* [T] to give someone too much care and attention as if they were a child

wet suit

**wet suit** /ˈ· ·/ *n* [C] a piece of clothing, usually made of rubber, that underwater swimmers wear to keep warm

**wet·ting a·gent** /ˈ·· ˌ··/ *n* [C] a chemical substance which, when spread on a solid surface, makes it hold liquid

**wetting so·lu·tion** /ˈ·· ·ˌ··/ *n* [C,U] a liquid used for storing contact lenses (CONTACT LENS) in, or for making them more comfortable to wear

**we've** /wiv; *strong* wiːv/ the short form of 'we have'

**whack¹** /wæk/ *v* [T] *informal* **1** to hit someone or something hard: *Ow! You whacked me with your elbow!* **2** *spoken* to put something somewhere: *Just whack it under the grill for a couple of minutes.*

**whack²** *n* [C] *especially spoken* **1** the act of hitting something hard or the noise this makes **2 have a whack at** to try to do something **3 do your whack** *BrE* to do a fair or equal share of a job or activity: *I've done more than my whack of the driving – it's your turn.* **4 (the) full whack** *BrE* the full amount: *You don't have to pay full whack if you're unemployed.* **5 at/in one whack** *AmE* all on one occasion: *Steve lost $500 at one whack.* **6 out of whack** *AmE* if a system, machine etc is out of whack, the parts are not working together correctly

**whacked** /wækt/ *adj* [not before noun] *informal* **1** also **whacked out** very tired **2 whacked out** *AmE* behaving strangely, especially because of having too much alcohol or drugs

**whack·ing** /ˈwækɪŋ/ *adj* **whacking great** *BrE spoken* very big; WHOPPING: *We got a whacking great gas bill this morning.*

**whack·y** /ˈwæki/ *adj* another spelling of WACKY

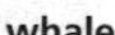

W

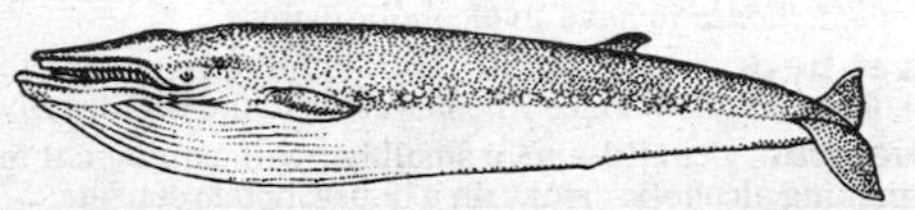

whale

**whale¹** /weɪl/ *n* [C] **1** a very large animal that lives in the sea and looks like a fish, but is actually a MAMMAL **2 have a whale of a time** *informal* to enjoy yourself very much

**whale²** *v* **whale into** *AmE* to start attacking someone

**whale·bone** /ˈweɪlbəʊn‖-boʊn/ *n* [U] a hard substance taken from the upper jaw of whales, used in the past for making women's clothes stiff

**whal·er** /ˈweɪlə‖-ər/ *n* [C] **1** someone who hunts whales **2** a boat which goes to hunt whales

**whal·ing** /ˈweɪlɪŋ/ *n* [U] the activity of hunting whales

**wham** /wæm/ *interjection* **1** used to describe the sound of something suddenly hitting something else very hard: *The car went wham into the wall.* **2** used to express the idea that something very unexpected suddenly happens: *Life is going along nicely and then, wham, you lose your job.*

**wham·my** /ˈwæmi/ *n* [C] **put the whammy on sb** to use magic powers to make someone have bad luck —see also DOUBLE WHAMMY

**wharf** /wɔːf‖wɔːrf/ *n* [C] *plural* **wharfs** or **wharves** a place built on the edge of a sea or river, where ships can be tied up to load and unload goods

**what¹** /wɒt‖wɑːt, wʌt/ *predeterminer, determiner, pron* **1** used when asking questions about a thing or person, or a kind of thing or person that you do not know anything about: *What are you doing?*| *What colour is the new carpet?*| *"What do you do?" "I'm a teacher."*| *What's your new boss like?*| *What do you mean, you want to spend Christmas alone?* **2** used especially in indirect questions to talk about things or information: *I believe what he told me.* | *Show me what you bought then.* | *They're discussing what to do next.* | *I don't know what you think but if you ask me it's a waste of time.* | *She gave him what money she had.* (=all the money she had, although she did not have much) **3** *spoken* used at the beginning of a statement to emphasize what you are going to say: *What that kid needs is some love and affection.* | *What we'll do is leave a note for Mum to tell her we won't be back till late.* **4 what?** *spoken* **a)** used to ask someone to repeat something they have just said because you didn't hear it properly: *"Have you got a pen I could borrow?" "What?"* **b)** used during conversations when you have heard someone talking to you and want to tell them to continue: *"Elaine!" "What?" "Are you coming?"* **c)** used to show that you are surprised by what someone has said: *"My wallet's missing." "What?"* **5** *spoken* used at the beginning of a sentence to show that you think something is very good, very bad etc: *What a lovely day!* (=the weather is good)| *What a horrible thing to do!* **6 what about...?** *spoken* **a)** used to make a suggestion: *What about Czechoslovakia for a holiday?*| **what about doing** *What about going to a movie this evening?* **b)** used to introduce a new person or thing into a conversation: *What about Patrick? What's he doing nowadays?*| *We've chosen the food, now, what about the wine?* **7 I tell you what** *spoken* used to make an offer or suggestion: *I tell you what, I'll give you £20 for it.* **8 guess what!** *spoken* used before telling someone some exciting or surprising news: *Guess what! Jane's getting married.* **9 what (...) for ?** *spoken* **a)** why?: *"She's decided to work part-time." "What for?"* **b)** used to ask what purpose something has: *What's this gadget for?* **10** *spoken* used to give yourself time to think before guessing a number or amount: *You're looking at, what, about £4000 for a decent second-hand car.* **11 what's his/her/its name** *also* **what d'you call him/her/it** *spoken* used when talking about a person or thing whose name you cannot immediately remember: *The hospital have just got a, what d'you call it, er.. a new scanner.* **12 (and) what's more** *spoken* used when adding something to what you have already said, especially when it is exciting or interesting: *These detergents are environmentally friendly, what's more, they're relatively cheap.* **13 what's what** *spoken* what a situation is really like as opposed to what people say it is like, or what they try and make you believe: *Shirley's been there before, she'll tell you what's what.* **14 what the hell/devil/blazes...?/what in God's name/heaven's name...?** *spoken* used to ask in an extremely angry or surprised way what is happening, what someone is doing etc: *What the hell do you think you're doing?*| *What in God's name will she think of next?* **15 what the hell!** *spoken* used to say that you have decided to do something even though it is very expensive, difficult etc: *Oh, what the hell! It's your birthday, let's have champagne!* **16 ...or what?** *spoken* used to show that you are impatient when asking a question or because you think there is only one possible answer to the question: *Are you coming then, or what?* | *Is that work going to be finished by Friday or what?* **17 so what?** *spoken* used to say that you do not care about something or to tell someone angrily that something does not concern them: *"Your room looks a real mess Tracey." "So what?"* **18 you what?** *spoken* **a)** used to ask someone to repeat something they have just said, in a way people think is not polite: *"Could you get the butter out of the fridge?" "You what?"* **b)** used to show that you are surprised: *"I got the job!" "You what?"* **19 what if...** *spoken* **a)** used to make a suggestion: *What if we go and see a film tomorrow night?* **b)** used to ask what will happen, usually if an unpleasant or frightening situation happens: *What if we get burgled while we're on holiday?* **20 ...and what have you** *spoken* used at the end of a list of things to mean other things of a similar kind: *The shelves were crammed with books, documents, and what have you.* **21 have what it takes** *spoken* to have the right qualities or skills in order to succeed: *I reckon Jordi's got what it takes to be an international footballer.* **22 what's with** **a)** *AmE spoken* used to ask a person or group of people who are behaving strangely or violently, why they are behaving in this way: *What's with you people?* **b)** used to ask the reason for something: *What's with the free sandwiches and beer?* **23 what of it?** *spoken* used to say that you do not care about something or to tell someone angrily that something does not concern them: *"I hear you've just got a new car." "Yes, what of it?"* **24 now what?** *spoken* used to ask what is going to happen next, what you should do etc

Frequencies of **what** in spoken and written English.

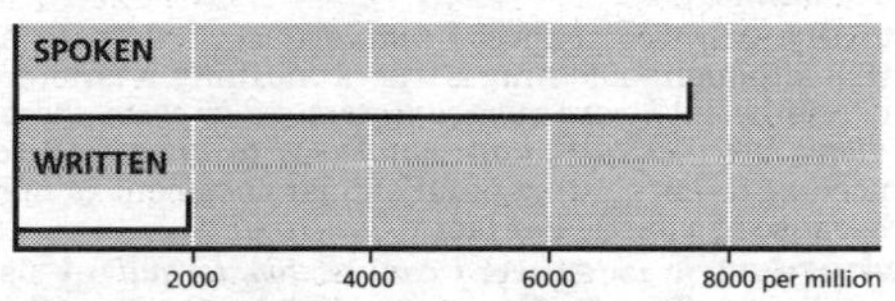


Based on the British National Corpus and the Longman Lancaster Corpus

This graph shows that **what** is much more common in spoken English than in written English. This is because it is used to ask questions, and it is used in a lot of common spoken phrases.

**what²** *adv* **1** used especially in questions to ask to what degree or in what way something matters: *What do you care about it?* (=I don't think you care at all) | *We may be a little late, but what does it matter?* **2 what with** *spoken* used to introduce a list of reasons that have made something happen or have made someone feel a particular way: *What with neighbours, relatives, and friends there, the house was overflowing with people.*

**what·cha·ma·call·it** /ˈwɒtʃəməˌkɔːlɪt‖ˈwɑːtʃəməˌkɒːl-, ˈwʌt-/ *n* [C] *spoken* a word you use when you cannot remember the name of something: *I've broken the whatchamacallit on my bag.*

**what·ev·er¹** /wɒtˈevə‖wɑːtˈevər, wʌt-/ *determiner, pron* **1** any or all of the things that are wanted, needed, or possible: *Help yourself to whatever you want.* | *Jake's dad told him he could have whatever he wanted for Christmas.* **2** used to say that it is not important what happens, what you do etc because it does not change the situation: *Whatever I suggest, he always disagrees.* | *The building must be saved whatever the cost.* | **whatever you do** *spoken*: *Don't, whatever you do, let anyone see that letter.* **3** *spoken* used to say that you do not know the exact meaning or name of someone or something: *Why don't you invite Steve, or whatever he's called, to supper?* **4 ... or whatever** *spoken* used after naming things on a list to mean other things of the same kind: *Anyone seen carrying boxes, bags, or whatever was stopped by the police.* | **...and whatever else** *Bring waterproof clothing, boots, and whatever else.* **5** *spoken* used to show that you are angry or surprised when making a statement or asking a question: *Whatever can he mean?* | **whatever next!** (=used to show surprise) *"Joan's learning Sanskrit." "Whatever next!"* **6** *spoken* used to tell someone that you do not care or are not interested when they ask you something: *"Shall I call you tonight or tomorrow?" "Whatever."* **7 whatever you say/whatever you think** *spoken* used to tell someone that you agree with them or will do what they want, often when you do not really agree or want to do it: *"I want to go camping, just for a change." "OK, whatever you say."*

Frequencies of **whatever** in spoken and written English.

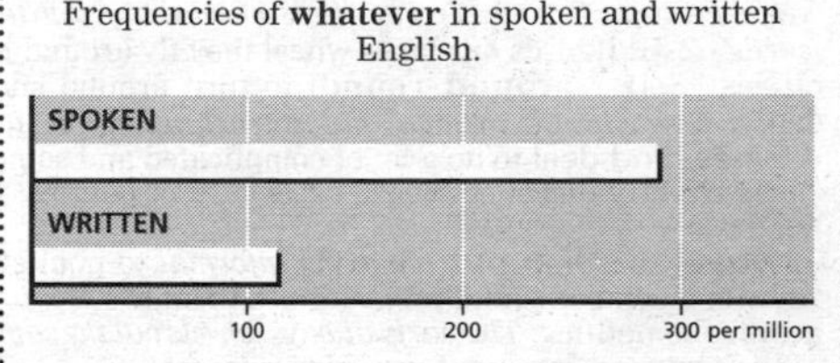


Based on the British National Corpus and the Longman Lancaster Corpus

This graph shows that **whatever** is more common in spoken English than in written English. This is because it is used in a lot of common spoken phrases.

**whatever²** *adv* used to emphasize a negative statement; WHATSOEVER: *She gave no sign whatever of what she was thinking.*

**whatever³** *adj* **1** of any possible kind: *I'll take whatever help I can get.* **2** of some kind, but you are not sure what: *Ellen's refusing to come, for whatever reason.*

**what·not** /ˈwɒtnɒt‖ˈwɑːtnɑːt, ˈwʌt-/ *n* **1 and whatnot** *spoken* an expression used at the end of a list of things when you do not want to give the names of everything: *Put your bags, cases and whatnot in the back of the car.* **2** [C] a piece of furniture with shelves used especially in the 19th century to show small pretty objects

**whats·it** /ˈwɒtsɪt‖ˈwɑːts-, ˈwʌts-/ *n* [C] *spoken* a word you use when you cannot think of the word you want: *Try and undo the screw to get the whatsit off.*

**what·so·ev·er** /ˌwɒtsəʊˈevə‖ˌwɑːtsoʊˈevər, ˌwʌt-/ *adv* used to emphasize a negative statement; WHATEVER: *Political factors played no part whatsoever in this decision.* S 2

**wheat** /wiːt/ *n* [U] **1** the grain that bread is made from **2** the plant that this grain grows on: *a field of wheat* **3 separate the wheat from the chaff** to choose the good and useful things or people and get rid of the others

**wheat·germ** /ˈwiːtdʒɜːm‖-dʒɜːrm/ *n* [U] the centre of a grain of wheat

**wheat·meal** /ˈwiːtmiːl/ *n* [U] *especially BrE* a brown flour made from whole grains of wheat

**whee** /wiː/ *interjection* used by children to express happiness or excitement

**whee·dle** /ˈwiːdl/ *v* [I,T] to try to persuade someone by saying pleasant things which you do not mean: *a wheedling voice* | **wheedle sb into doing sth** *He wheedled me into paying.* | **wheedle sth from/out of sb** *She managed to wheedle an extra day's pay out of him.*

**wheel¹** /wiːl/ *n* [C]

**1 ► ON A VEHICLE ◄** [C] one of the round things under a car, bus, bicycle etc that turn when it moves —see picture on page 409

**2 ► IN A MACHINE ◄** [C] a flat round part in a machine that turns round when the machine operates: *a gear wheel*

**3 ► FOR CONTROLLING A VEHICLE ◄** [C] the piece of equipment in the shape of a wheel that you turn to make a car, ship etc move in a particular direction: **at/behind the wheel** (=driving a car etc) | **take the wheel** (=drive instead of someone else) —see also STEERING WHEEL

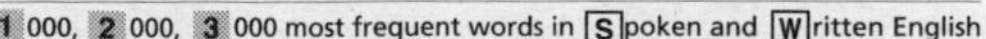

**4 on wheels** with wheels on the bottom: *a table on wheels*
**5 wheels/set of wheels** *spoken* a car: *Like my new wheels?*
**6 wheels within wheels** *spoken* used to say that a situation is complicated and difficult to understand because it involves processes and decisions that you know nothing about —see also **oil the wheels** (OIL² (2)), **put your shoulder to the wheel** (SHOULDER¹ (7)), **put a spoke in sb's wheel** (SPOKE² (2))

**wheel²** *v* **1** [T always + adv/prep] **a)** to push something that has wheels: **wheel sth out/down/into** *She wheeled her bike into the garage.* **b)** to move someone or something that is in an object with wheels, such as a WHEELCHAIR or a CART¹ (1): *The nurse wheeled him into the ward.* **2** [I] if birds or planes wheel they fly around in circles **3** [I + **around/round**] to turn around suddenly: *She wheeled around and started yelling at us.* **4 wheel and deal** to do a lot of complicated and sometimes slightly dishonest deals, especially in politics or business

**wheel** sb/sth ↔ **out** *phr v* [T] *informal* to publicly show someone or something, and use them to help you achieve something: *The party always wheels out the same old celebrities whenever they need to raise money.*

**wheel·bar·row** /ˈwiːlˌbærəʊ‖-roʊ/ *n* [C] a small CART¹ (1) that you use outdoors to carry things, with a single wheel and two handles

**wheel·base** /ˈwiːlbeɪs/ *n* [C] *technical* the distance between the front and back AXLES of a vehicle

**wheel·chair** /ˈwiːltʃeə‖-tʃer/ *n* [C] a chair with wheels used by people who cannot walk —see picture at CHAIR¹

**wheel clamp** /ˈ· ·/ *n* [C] a metal object that is fastened to the wheel of an illegally parked car; DENVER BOOT *AmE* —**wheel-clamp** *v* [T]

**wheeled** /wiːld/ *adj* having wheels

**wheeler-deal·er** /ˌ·· ˈ··/ *n* [C] someone who does a lot of complicated, often dishonest deals, especially in business or politics: *She was a real wheeler-dealer, sometimes loving the thrill of doing deals.*

**wheel·house** /ˈwiːlhaʊs/ *n* [C] the place on a ship where the CAPTAIN stands at the WHEEL¹ (3)

**wheel·ie** /ˈwiːli/ *n* [C] **do a wheelie** *informal* to balance on the back wheel of a bicycle that you are riding

**wheelie bin** /ˈ·· ·/ *n* [C] *BrE* a large container with wheels that you put household waste into

**wheel·ing and deal·ing** /ˌ·· · ˈ··/ *n* [U] activities that involve a lot of complicated and sometimes dishonest deals, especially in business or politics

**wheel·wright** /ˈwiːlraɪt/ *n* [C] someone who made and repaired the wooden wheels of vehicles pulled by horses in the past

**wheeze¹** /wiːz/ *v* [I] to breathe with difficulty, making a whistling sound in your throat and chest

**wheeze²** *n* [C] **1** the act or sound of wheezing **2** *old-fashioned or humorous* a clever and amusing idea or plan

**wheez·y** /ˈwiːzi/ *adj* wheezing or making a wheezing sound: *You sound wheezy.* | *a wheezy cough* —**wheezily** *adv* —**wheeziness** *n* [U]

**whelk** /welk/ *n* [C] a small sea animal that has a shell and can be eaten

**whelp¹** /welp/ *n* [C] a young animal, especially a dog or lion

**whelp²** *v* [I] *old-fashioned* if a dog or lion whelps, it gives birth

S1 W1 **when¹** /wen/ *adv, conjunction* **1** at what time: *When is Tara coming?* | *Do you know when she will arrive?* | *When did you hear about it?* **2** at the time that: *Things were different when I was young.* | *The dog jumped up when he whistled.* | *When I give the signal, turn off the light.* | *When completed the tunnel will be the longest in the world.* **3 day/time/afternoon when** the day, time etc on or at which: *There are times when I wonder what you're talking about.* **4** considering that: *Why do you want a new job when you've got such a good one already?* **5** even though or in spite of the fact that: *They kept digging when they must have known there was no hope.*

**when²** *pron* **1 since when** used in questions to mean since what time: *Since when has it been any of your business what I do?* **2** which time: *next May, by when the new house should be finished*

**whence** /wens/ *adv, pron old use* from where: *Whence came this man?* —compare WHITHER

**when·ev·er** /wenˈevə‖-ˈevər/ *adv, conjunction* **1** every time that a particular thing happens: *Whenever we come here we see someone we know.* | *If you feed a baby whenever he is hungry, you will have less difficulty with him later.* **2** at any time: *I'd like to see you whenever it's convenient.* **3** *spoken* used when it does not matter what time something happens, or when you do not know the exact time something happens: *"Should I come over around six?" "Whenever."* S2 W3

**where** /weə‖wer/ *adv, conjunction* **1** at, to, or from a particular place or position: *Where do you live?* | *I asked Lucy where she was going.* | *Where are you going to put it?* | *Sit where you like.* —see POSITION (USAGE) **2** in, towards, or from a particular situation or at a particular point in a speech, argument etc: *Now where was I? Oh yes, I was telling you about taking mother to the airport.* | *Where will all this fighting and bloodshed end?* **3** used at the beginning of a sentence in which the second part expresses the opposite, or something different from the first part: *Where most people saw nothing but a hardened criminal, Audrey saw a lonely and desperate man.* S1 W1

**where·a·bouts¹** /ˌweərəˈbaʊts◂‖ˈweərəbaʊts/ *adv spoken* used to ask in what general area something or someone is: *Whereabouts do you live?*

**where·a·bouts²** /ˈweərəbaʊts‖ˈwer-/ *n* [U] the place or area where someone or something is: **sb's whereabouts** *His family refused to reveal his whereabouts.* | **the whereabouts of** *the whereabouts of the missing documents*

**where·as** /weərˈæz‖wer-/ *conjunction* **1** used to say that although something is true of one thing, it is not true of another: *Why are some cancers cured by chemotherapy alone, whereas others are unaffected by drugs?* **2** *law* used at the beginning of an official document to mean because of a particular fact S2 W2

**where·at** /weərˈæt‖wer-/ *conjunction formal* **1** used when something happens immediately after something else, or as a result of something happening; WHEREUPON **2** at a particular place; WHERE (1)

**where·by** /weəˈbaɪ‖wer-/ *adv formal* by means of which or according to which: *a law whereby the wearing of seat belts becomes compulsory* S3

**where·fore** /ˈweəfɔː‖ˈwerfɔːr/ *adv, conjunction old use* **1** used to ask why something has happened: *Wherefore comest thou?* **2** for that reason: *Skills are the art of doing, wherefore they must be taught by practical example.* —see also **whys and wherefores** (WHY³)

**where·in** /weərˈɪn‖wer-/ *adv, conjunction literary* in which place or part: *The clay ovens wherein some farm wives still bake bread.* | *Wherein lies the difficulty?*

**where·of** /weərˈɒv‖werˈʌv, -ˈɑːv/ *adv, conjunction old use* of which: *Theirs are the houses whereof I speak.*

**where·on** /weərˈɒn‖weərˈɔːn, -ˈɑːn/ *adv, conjuction old use* on which: *The sparrow flitted to the statue, whereon it perched.*

**where·so·ever** /ˌweəsəʊˈevə‖ˈwersoʊˌevər/ *adv, conjunction literary* another word for WHEREVER

**where·to** /weəˈtuː‖wer-/ *adv, conjunction old use* to which place

**where·u·pon** /ˌweərəˈpɒn‖ˈwerəpɑːn, -pɔːn/ *conjunction* used when something happens immediately after something else, or as a result of something happening: *Molly banned her from the dining room, whereupon Bridget burst into tears.*

**wher·ev·er** /weərˈevə‖werˈevər/ *adv* **1** to or at whatever place, position, or situation: *If you could go wherever you wanted to in the world, where would you go?* | *Sleep wherever you like.* | **... or wherever** (=used to emphasize that you are talking about any place and not a specific place) *There has been an increase in crime whether it be in Britain, France, Germany, or wherever.* **2 wherever** S2

**possible** when it is possible to do something: *Wherever possible jobs are given to local people.* **3** used at the beginning of a question to show surprise: *Wherever did you get that idea?* **4 wherever that may be** used to say that you do not know where a place or town is or have never heard of it: *Rita lives in Horwich now, wherever that may be.*

**where·with·al** /ˈweəwɪðɔːl‖ˈwerwɪðɒːl/ *n* **the wherewithal to do sth** the money you need in order to do something: *We don't have the wherewithal to pay for a big wedding.*

**whet** /wet/ *v* [T] **1 whet sb's appetite (for sth)** if an experience whets your appetite for something, it increases your desire for it: *The trip to Paris has whetted my appetite for travel.* **2** *literary* to make the edge of a blade sharp

S1 W1 **wheth·er** /ˈweðə‖-ər/ *conj* **1** used when talking about a choice you have to make or about two different possibilities: *He asked me whether she was coming.* | *The decision whether to see her was mine alone.* | **whether or not** *I coudn't decide whether or not to go to the party.* **2** used to say that something definitely will or will not happen whatever the situation is: *I'm sure we'll see each other again soon whether here or in New York.* | **whether... or not** *Whether you like it or not, you're going to have to face him one day.*

**USAGE NOTE: WHETHER**

GRAMMAR

**Whether** and **if** are often used in similar contexts. However, **whether** is usually used for **if** when you also use the word **or** especially at the beginning of a sentence. People say: *Whether you see her or not, phone me later.* | *If you see her, phone me.*

**If** can usually be used instead of **whether** with clauses following some verbs and adjectives: *I wonder whether/if she can come.* | *He wasn't sure whether/if he could come* (NOT *...whether could he come*). But you use **whether** (NOT **if**) before infinitives: *The question is whether to go or stay.* **Whether** is also used after prepositions: *It depends on whether he's ready or not.* It is also used after nouns: *It's your decision whether you go or stay.*

You often use **whether** with **...or not** sentences, for example: *You're coming whether you like it or not.* | *We have to decide whether or not to support this proposal.*

SPELLING

Note the spelling is **whether** (NOT *wether*). *Weather* (=sunshine, snow etc) is a completely different word.

**whet·stone** /ˈwetstəʊn‖-stoʊn/ *n* [C] a stone used to make the blade of cutting tools sharp

**whew** /hjuː/ *interjection* used when you are surprised, very hot, or feeling glad that something bad did not happen; PHEW: *Whew, that man has some temper!*

**whey** /weɪ/ *n* [U] the watery liquid that is left after the solid part has been removed from sour milk

S1 W1 **which** /wɪtʃ/ *determiner, pron* **1** used to ask or state what people or things you mean when a choice has to be made: *Which of these books is yours?* | *Ask him which one he wants.* | *Karen comes from either Los Angeles or San Francisco, I can't remember which.* **2** used to show what specific thing or things you mean: *Did you see the letter which came today?* | *This is the book which I told you about.* **3** used especially in written language after a COMMA, to add more information about a specific thing or things, or about the first part of the sentence: *The train, which takes only two hours, is quicker than the bus, which takes three.* | *The police arrived, after which the situation became calmer.* | **in which case** (=used to talk about a situation that you have just mentioned) *She may have missed the train, in which case she won't arrive for another hour.* **4 which is which** used to say that you cannot tell the difference between two very similar people or things: *They look so alike it's difficult to tell which is which.*

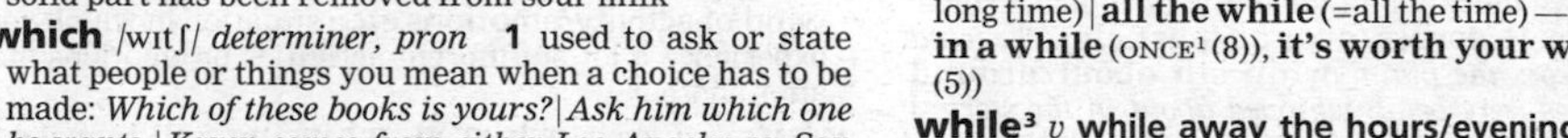

**USAGE NOTE: WHICH**

FORMALITY

As subject of a relative clause which restricts the meaning of a noun, **that** is used more often than **which** in informal English: *The street market which/that is held near my house.*

In informal or spoken English, you can often leave out **that** or **which**. For example, you are likely to say: *Did you get the things you wanted?* rather than: *Did you get the things that/which you wanted?*

The form **to which** is very formal: *He would lunch in one of the clubs to which be belonged.* You would more usually say: *...one of the clubs (that) he belonged to*

In relative clauses that add information but do not restrict the meaning of what comes before, you usually use **which**, especially after a comma: *He's always really rude, which is why people tend to avoid him.*

**which·ev·er** /wɪtʃˈevə‖-ˈevər/ *determiner, pron* **1** used to say that it does not matter what thing you choose, what you do etc because it does not change the situation or someone's intention: *You can have whichever you like best.* | *Whichever way you look at it this is disastrous news for the shipping industry.* **2** used to talk about a specific thing, method etc: *I'll use whichever remedy the vet recommends.*

**whiff** /wɪf/ *n* [C] **1** a very slight smell of something: [+ **of**] *a whiff of garlic* | **get/catch a whiff of** *As she walked past, I caught a whiff of her perfume.* **2 a whiff of danger/adventure/freedom etc** a slight sign that something dangerous, exciting etc might happen: *At the first whiff of trouble he was off like a shot.*

**whif·fy** /ˈwɪfi/ *adj BrE informal* having an unpleasant smell

**Whig** /wɪg/ *n* [C] a member of a British political party of the 18th and early 19th centuries which wanted to limit royal power, and later became the Liberal Party

**while**[1] /waɪl/ *conjunction* **1** during the time that something is happening: *They arrived while we were having dinner.* | *He got malaria while travelling in Africa.* **2** if something happens while something else is happening, it happens at the same time as it: *He was so tired he fell asleep while reading the newspaper.* **3** used to emphasize the difference between two situations, activities etc: *That region has plenty of natural resources while this one has none.* **4** used to show that you partly agree with, or accept something but not completely: *While she is a likeable girl she can be extremely difficult to work with.*  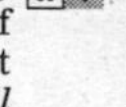

**while**[2] *n* **a while** a period of time, especially a short one: *Can you wait a while or do you have to leave right now?* | **a short/little while** *Bob's only been working here a short while.* | **for a while** *He sat for a while, thinking about what Janine had said to him.* | **quite a while** (=a fairly long time) | **all the while** (=all the time) —see also **once in a while** (ONCE[1] (8)), **it's worth your while** (WORTH[1] (5)) 

**while**[3] *v* **while away the hours/evening/days etc** to spend time in a pleasant and lazy way: *We whiled away the summer evenings talking and drinking wine.*

**whilst** /waɪlst/ *conjunction especially BrE formal* WHILE[2] 

**whim** /wɪm/ *n* [C] a sudden feeling that you would like to do something or have something, especially when there is no particularly important or good reason: **on a whim** (=because of a whim) *I went to visit her on a whim.* | **at the whim of** *The palace decor kept changing at the whim of the princess.* | **a passing whim** (=one that will soon be forgotten) | **sb's every whim** *I was spoiled. My every whim was catered to.*

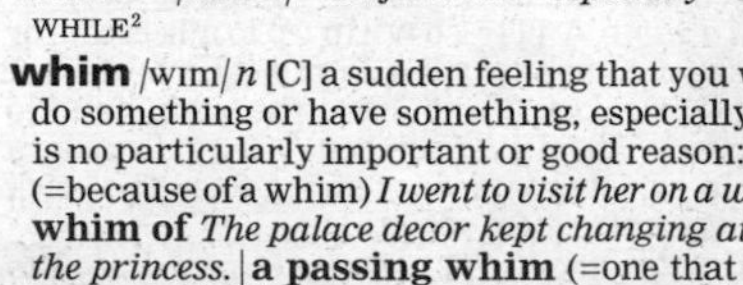

**whim·per** /ˈwɪmpə‖-ər/ *v* [I] to make low crying sounds, or to speak in this way: *The dog whimpered in the corner.* | *"Okay," he managed to whimper.* —**whimper** *n* [C]

**whim·si·cal** /ˈwɪmzɪkəl/ *adj* unusual or strange and often amusing: *a whimsical smile* —**whimsically** /-kli/ *adv* —**whimsicality** /ˌwɪmzɪˈkæləti/ *n* [U]

**whim·sy** /ˈwɪmzi/ *n* **1** [U] a way of thinking or behaving that is unusual, strange, and often amusing **2** [C] a strange idea or desire that does not seem to have any sensible purpose: *This room, by some architectural whimsy, completely unbalanced the house.*

**whine** /waɪn/ *v* [I] **1** to complain in a sad, annoying voice about something: *For goodness sake stop whining, it's not much further to go.* | [+ **about**] *Mark always seems to be whining about his job.* **2** to make a long high sound because you are in pain or unhappy: *a dog whining outside the door* **3** if a machine whines, it makes a continuous high sound —**whine** *n* [C] *the whine of the plane's engine* —**whiner** *n* [C]

**whinge** /wɪndʒ/ *v* [I] *BrE or AustrE* to keep complaining in an annoying way: *Stop whingeing and get on with it!* —**whinge** *n* [C] —**whinger** *n* [C] *People with genuine grievances are being dismissed as whingers.*

**whin·ny** /ˈwɪni/ *v* [I] if a horse whinnies, it NEIGHS (=makes the sound that horses makes) quietly —**whinny** *n* [C]

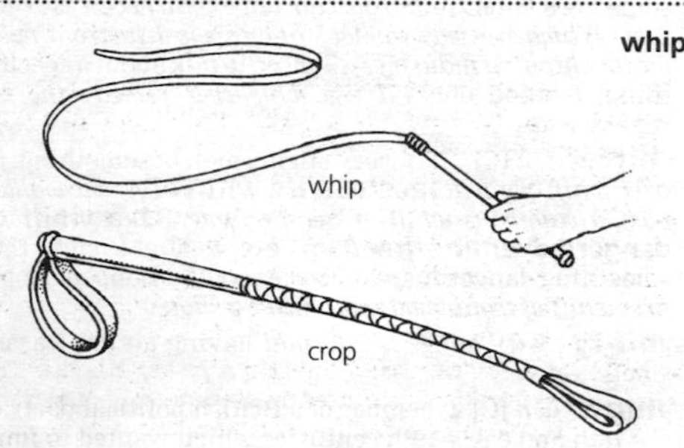


**whip¹** /wɪp/ *n* **1** [C] a long thin piece of rope or leather with a handle used for making animals move or punishing people: **crack a whip** (=make a loud noise with a whip) **2** [C] a member of the US Congress or the British Parliament who is responsible for making sure that the members of their party attend and vote —see also CHIEF WHIP **3** [C] a written order sent to members of the US Congress or the British Parliament telling them when and how to vote —see also TWO-LINE WHIP, THREE-LINE WHIP **4 chocolate whip/strawberry whip etc** [C,U] *BrE* a sweet dish made from the white part of eggs and chocolate or fruit, beaten together to make a smooth, light mixture —see also **crack of the whip** (CRACK¹ (20)), **give sb a fair crack of the whip** (FAIR¹ (11))

**whip², whipped, whipping** *v* **1** [T] to hit someone with a whip **2** [I always + adv/prep] [T always + adv/prep] to move quickly and violently, or to make something do this: [+ **across/around/past etc**] *The wind whipped across the plain.* | **whip sth about/around** *The branches were being whipped about in the storm.* | **whip around/round** (=turn around quickly) *Suddenly, he whipped around and glared at them.* **3** [T always + adv/prep] to move or remove something with a quick sudden movement: [+ **away/off/out etc**] *He whipped out a gun.* **4** [T] also **whip up** to mix cream or the clear part of an egg very hard until it becomes stiff —see also WHISK¹, BEAT¹ (7) **5 have the whip hand** to have power and control over someone **6** [T] to make a TOP¹ (25) spin by using a piece of string fixed to a stick **7** [T] *BrE informal* to steal something

**whip through** sth *phr v* [T] *informal especially BrE* to finish a job very quickly: *I can whip through all the cleaning in about half an hour.*

**whip up** *phr v* [T] **1 whip up support/anger/enthusiasm etc** to deliberately try to make people feel or react strongly: *The rally was organised to whip up support for the independence campaign.* | **whip up a crowd** *a speech designed to whip up the crowd* **2** [**whip** sth ↔ **up**] to quickly make something to eat: *I just had time to whip up a light salad before I went out again.*

**whip·cord** /ˈwɪpkɔːd‖-kɔːrd/ *n* [U] **1** a strong type of CORD¹ (1) **2** a strong woollen material

**whip·lash** /ˈwɪp-læʃ/ *n* [C,U] a neck injury caused when your head moves forward and back again suddenly and violently, especially in a car accident

**whipped cream** /ˌ· ˈ·/ *n* [U] cream that has been beaten until it is thick, eaten on sweet foods

**whip·per·snap·per** /ˈwɪpəˌsnæpə‖ˈwɪpərˌsnæpər/ *n* [C] *old-fashioned* a young person who is too confident and does not show enough respect to older people

**whip·pet** /ˈwɪpɪt/ *n* [C] a small thin racing dog like a GREYHOUND

**whip·ping** /ˈwɪpɪŋ/ *n* [C usually singular] a punishment given to someone by whipping them; WHIP² (1)

**whipping boy** /ˈ·· ·/ *n* [singular] someone or something that is blamed for someone else's mistakes; SCAPEGOAT

**whipping cream** /ˈ·· ˌ·/ *n* [U] a type of cream that becomes very stiff when you beat it

**whip·poor·will** /ˈwɪpʊəˌwɪl‖ˈwɪpər-/ *n* [C] a small North American bird which makes a noise that sounds like its name

**whip·py** /ˈwɪpi/ *adj* long, thin, and easy to bend

**whip-round** /ˈ· ·/ *n* **have a whip-round** *BrE informal* if a group of people have a whip-round, they all give some money so that they can buy something together: *We're having a whip-round to get Sandy something for her birthday.*

**whir** /wɜː‖wɜːr/ *v* [I] another spelling of WHIRR

**whirl¹** /wɜːl‖wɜːrl/ *v* **1** [I,T] to spin around very quickly, or to make something do this: [+ **about/around/toward etc**] *The snowflakes whirled around as they fell to the ground.* | **whirl sth about/around/away etc** *Jim whirled the bike around.* **2** [I] if your head is whirling, your mind is full of thoughts and ideas, and you feel very confused or excited

**whirl²** *n* [C usually singular] **1** a whirling movement: *a whirl of dust* **2 give sth a whirl** *informal* to try something that you are not sure you are going to like or be able to do **3** [singular] a lot of activity of a particular kind: *the mad social whirl around Christmas* **4 be in a whirl** to feel very excited or confused about something

**whir·li·gig** /ˈwɜːlɪˌgɪg‖ˈwɜːr-/ *n* [C] **1** a toy that spins; TOP¹ (25) **2** a MERRY-GO-ROUND (1)

**whirl·pool** /ˈwɜːlpuːl‖ˈwɜːrl-/ *n* [C] a powerful current of water that spins around and can pull things down into it

**whirl·wind** /ˈwɜːlˌwɪnd‖ˈwɜːrl-/ *n* [C] **1** an extremely strong wind that moves quickly with a circular movement, causing a lot of damage; TORNADO, TWISTER (2) *AmE* **2 a whirlwind romance/tour etc** something that happens much more quickly than usual **3 a whirlwind of activity/emotions etc** a situation in which you experience a lot of different activities or emotions one after another

**whirr** /wɜː‖wɜːr/ **whirred, whirring** *v* [I] to make a fairly quiet, regular sound, like the sound of a bird or insect moving its wings very fast: *Cameras whirred and reporters scribbled.* —**whirr** *n* [C usually singular] —see picture on page 1261

**whisk¹** /wɪsk/ *v* [T] to mix liquid or soft things very quickly so that air is mixed in, especially with a fork or a whisk

**whisk** sb/sth ↔ **away** *phr v* [T] **1** to take or remove something very quickly: *He whisked the letter away before I could read it.* **2** to take someone quickly away from a place: *At the end of the concert the band was whisked away to a secret location.*

**whisk** sb **off** *phr v* [T] to take someone quickly away from a place; whisk away

**whisk²** *n* [C] **1** a small kitchen tool made of curved pieces of wire used for beating eggs, cream etc —see picture on page 834 **2** [usually singular] a quick light sweeping movement: [+ **of**] *The cow brushed away the flies with a whisk of its tail.*

**whisk broom** /ˈ· ·/ *n* [C] *AmE* a small stiff BROOM (1) that you use to brush clothes

**whis·ker** /ˈwɪskə‖-ər/ *n* [C] **1** one of the long, stiff hairs that grow near the mouth of a cat, mouse etc **2 whiskers** [plural] the hair that grows on a man's face **3 do sth by a whisker/come within a whisker** *informal* to only just fail or just manage to do something: *We came within a whisker of defeat.* (=were almost defeated) —**whiskery** *adj*

**whis·key** /ˈwɪski/ *n* [C,U] a strong alcoholic drink made in Ireland or the US from grain, or a glass of this

S3 **whis·ky** /ˈwɪski/ *n* [C,U] a strong alcoholic drink made in Scotland from grain such as BARLEY, or a glass of this

W3 **whis·per¹** /ˈwɪspə‖-ər/ *v* **1** [I,T] to speak or say something very quietly, using your breath rather than your voice: *What are you two whispering about over there?* | **whisper sth to sb** *James leaned over to whisper something to Michael.* **2** [T + **that**] to say or suggest something privately or secretly: *Some White House staff were whispering that the President was no longer in control.*

**whisper²** *n* [C] **1** a very quiet voice, when you are whispering: **in a whisper** *"They're coming," he said in an excited whisper.* **2** a piece of news or information that has not been officially announced; RUMOUR: *The first whisper of the redundancies came from the newspapers.* | [+ **that**] *I've heard a whisper that he's going to resign.* **3 a whisper of wind/silk etc** *literary* a low soft sound made by wind etc

**whis·per·ing cam·paign** /ˈ··· ·,·/ *n* [C] an attack on someone that is made by privately spreading criticism about them

**whist** /wɪst/ *n* [U] a card game for four players in two pairs, in which each pair tries to win the most tricks (TRICK¹ (11))

**whist drive** /ˈ· ·/ *n* [C] a meeting to play whist between several pairs of partners who change opponents

**whis·tle¹** /ˈwɪsəl/ *v*

**1 ▶ HIGH SOUND ◀** [I,T] to make a high or musical sound by blowing air out through your lips: *Adam whistled happily as he walked along.* | **whistle a song/tune** *I heard this song on the radio and I've been whistling it all day.* | **whistle to sb** (=to get their attention) *Adrian whistled to them but they didn't seem to hear him.*

**2 ▶ USE A WHISTLE ◀** [I] to make a high sound by blowing into a whistle: *The referee whistled and the game began.*

**3 ▶ GO/MOVE FAST ◀** [I always + adv/prep] to move quickly with a whistling sound: *Bullets and shells were whistling overhead.*

**4 ▶ STEAM TRAIN/KETTLE ◀** [I] to make a high sound when air or steam is forced through a small hole

**5 ▶ BIRD ◀** [I] to make a high, often musical sound

**6 whistle in the dark** *informal* to try to show that you are brave when really you are afraid: *Her fine words had been so much whistling in the dark.*

**7 you can whistle for it** *BrE spoken* used to tell someone that there is no chance of them getting what they have asked for

**8 not be whistling Dixie** *AmE spoken* to be saying something because it is true, not just because you wish it was true: *Hey, this is good – and I'm not just whistling Dixie.*

**whistle²** *n* [C] **1** a small object that produces a high whistling sound when you blow into it: **blow a whistle** *Wait till the referee blows his whistle.* —see also PENNY WHISTLE **2** a high sound made by blowing a whistle, by blowing air out through your lips, or when air or steam is forced through a small opening —see also WOLF WHISTLE **3** the sound of something moving quickly through the air: *the whistle of the wind in the trees* —see also **blow the whistle on** (BLOW¹ (22)), **clean as a whistle** (CLEAN¹ (19)), **wet your whistle** (WET² (3))

**whistle-blow·er** /ˈ·· ,··/ *n* [C] someone who tells people in authority or the public about dishonest or illegal practices in business, government etc —see also **blow the whistle on** (BLOW¹ (22)) —**whistle-blowing** *n* [U]

**whistle-stop** /ˈ·· ·/ *n* [C] *AmE* a town where trains stop only if there are passengers who want to get on or off

**whistle-stop tour** /,·· · ˈ·/ *n* [C] a very quick trip around a place: *a whistle-stop tour of the United States*

**Whit** /wɪt/ *n* [C,U] *especially BrE* WHITSUN

**whit** *n* **not a whit** *old use* not at all

**white¹** /waɪt/ *adj* **1** having the colour of milk, salt or snow: *white paint* —see picture on page 411 **2** looking pale, because of illness, strong emotion etc: **white with anger/fear etc** *Her face was white with fear.* | **white as a sheet** (=extremely pale because you are frightened, ill etc) **3 a)** belonging to a race with pale skin **b)** of or for white people: *a white neighborhood* **4** white coffee has milk or cream in it —opposite BLACK¹ (3) **5** white wine is a very pale yellow or pale green colour —**whiteness** *n* [U] S1 W1

**white²** *n* **1** [U] the colour of milk, salt, and snow **2** [C] someone who belongs to a pale-skinned race: *The party got a lot of support from South Africa's whites.* **3** [C + **of**] the white part of your eye **4** [C,U] the transparent part of an egg that surrounds the YOLK (=yellow part) **5 whites** [plural] **a)** white clothes, sheets etc, which are separated from dark colours when they are washed **b)** *especially BrE* white clothes that are worn for some sports, such as TENNIS S3

**white ant** /,· ˈ·/ *n* [C] a TERMITE

**white·bait** /ˈwaɪtbeɪt/ *n* [U] very young fish of several types, used as food: *deep-fried whitebait*

**white blood cell** /,· ˈ· ·/ *n* [C] one of the cells in your blood which fights against infection; LEUCOCYTE —compare RED BLOOD CELL

**white·board** /ˈwaɪtbɔːd‖-bɔːrd/ *n* [C] a large board with a white, smooth surface used in classrooms for writing on —compare BLACKBOARD —see picture at BOARD¹

**white-bread** /ˈ· ·/ *adj AmE informal* ordinary and traditional in your opinions and way of life: *a white-bread family*

**white·caps** /ˈwaɪtkæps/ *n* [plural] *AmE* WHITE HORSES

**white-col·lar** /,· ˈ··◂/ *adj* **1** white-collar workers work in offices, banks etc as opposed to people who work in factories, mines etc **2 white-collar crime** crimes involving white-collar workers, for example when someone secretly steals money from the organization they work for —compare BLUE-COLLAR, PINK-COLLAR

**white cor·pus·cle** /,· ˈ···, ,· ·ˈ··‖,· ˈ···/ *n* [C] a WHITE BLOOD CELL

**white dwarf** /,· ˈ·/ *n* [C] *technical* a hot star, near the end of its life, that is more solid but less bright than the sun —compare RED GIANT

**white el·e·phant** /,· ˈ···/ *n* [C] something that is completely useless, although it may have cost a lot of money

**white flag** /,· ˈ·/ *n* [C] a sign that you accept that you have been defeated: **wave/show the white flag** (=accept defeat) *There was no question of the Republicans throwing in the towel or showing the white flag.*

**white flour** /,· ˈ·/ *n* [U] wheat flour from which the BRAN (=outer layer) and WHEATGERM (=inside seed) have been removed —compare WHOLEMEAL

**white goods** /ˈ· ·/ *n* [plural] a word used especially in business meaning large pieces of equipment used in the home, for example washing machines and REFRIGERATORS —compare BLACK GOODS

**White·hall** /ˈwaɪthɔːl, ˌwaɪtˈhɔːl‖-hɒːl/ *n* [U] **1** the British government, especially the government departments rather than parliament or the Prime Minister **2** the street in London where many of the government departments are

**white heat** /ˌ· ˈ·/ *n* [U] the very high temperature at which a metal turns white —see also WHITE-HOT

**white hors·es** /ˌ· ˈ··/ *n* [plural] *BrE* waves in the sea or on a lake that are white at the top; WHITECAPS *AmE*

**white-hot** /ˌ· ˈ·◂/ *adj* white-hot metal is so hot that it shines white

**White House** /ˈ· ·/ *n* **the White House** **1** the President of the US and the people who advise him **2** the official home in Washington DC of the President of the US

**white knight** /ˌ· ˈ·/ *n* [C] a person or company that puts money into a business in order to save it from being controlled by another company

**white-knuck·led** /ˌ· ˈ··◂/ *adj* anxious or afraid

**white lead** /ˌwaɪt ˈled/ *n* [U] a poisonous compound of lead with CARBON (1) and oxygen, used in the past in house paint

**white lie** /ˌ· ˈ·/ *n* [C] *informal* a lie that you tell in order to avoid hurting someone's feelings

**white light·ning** /ˌ· ˈ··/ *n* [U] *AmE slang* MOONSHINE (=illegal strong alcohol)

**white ma·gic** /ˌ· ˈ··/ *n* [U] magic used for good purposes —compare BLACK MAGIC

**white meat** /ˈ· ·/ *n* [U] **1** meat that is pale in colour, especially from some types of cooked bird, for example chicken **2** the pale meat from some types of cooked bird, for example chicken —compare RED MEAT

**whit·en** /ˈwaɪtn/ *v* [I,T] to become more white, or to make something do this

**whit·en·er** /ˈwaɪtnə‖-ər/ also **whit·en·ing** /ˈwaɪtnɪŋ/ *n* [C,U] a substance used to make something more white

**white noise** /ˌ· ˈ·/ *n* [U] noise coming from a radio or television which is turned on but not tuned (TUNE² (3)) to any programme

**white·out** /ˈwaɪtaʊt/ *n* **1** [C] weather conditions in which there is so much cloud or snow that you cannot see anything **2** [U] *AmE* TIPP-EX

**White Pag·es** /ˌ· ˈ··/ *n* **the White Pages** the white part of a telephone DIRECTORY in the US with the names, addresses, and phone numbers of people with telephones —compare YELLOW PAGES

**White Pa·per** /ˌ· ˈ··/ *n* [C] an official report from the British government, explaining their ideas and plans concerning a particular subject before a new law is introduced —compare GREEN PAPER

**white pep·per** /ˌ· ˈ··/ *n* [U] a white powder made from the crushed inside of a PEPPERCORN which gives a slightly hot taste to food

**white sale** /ˈ· ·/ *n* [C] *AmE* a period when sheets, TOWELS etc, are sold for a lower price

**white sauce** /ˌ· ˈ·‖ˈ· ·/ *n* [C,U] a thick white liquid made of flour, milk, and butter which is sometimes eaten with meat and vegetables

**white slav·e·ry** /ˌ· ˈ···/ *n* [U] *old-fashioned* the practice or business of taking girls to a foreign country and forcing them to be PROSTITUTES

**white space** /ˌ· ˈ·/ *n* [U] *AmE informal* free time

**white spir·it** /ˌ· ˈ··/ *n* [U] *BrE* a chemical liquid made from petrol, used for making paint thinner, removing marks on clothes etc; TURPENTINE

**white su·prem·a·cy** /ˌ· ·ˈ···/ *n* [U] the belief that white people are better than other races and that other races should be kept at a lower social level —**white supremacist** *n* [C]

**white-tailed deer** /ˌ· · ˈ·/ *n* [C] a common North American DEER with a long tail that is partly white

**white-tie** /ˌ· ˈ·◂/ *adj* a white-tie social occasion is a very formal one at which the men wear white BOW TIES and tails (TAIL¹ (5b) —compare BLACK-TIE

**white trash** /ˌ· ˈ·/ *n* [U] *AmE informal* an insulting expression meaning white people who are poor and uneducated

**white·wall** /ˈwaɪtwɔːl‖-wɒːl/ *n* [C] *AmE* a car tyre that has a wide white band on its side

**white·wash¹** /ˈwaɪtwɒʃ‖-wɒːʃ, -wɑːʃ/ *n* **1** [C,U] a report or examination of events that hides the true facts about something so that the person who is responsible will not be punished **2** [U] a white liquid mixture used especially for painting walls **3** [C] an easy win in sport

**whitewash²** *v* [T] **1** to hide the true facts about a serious accident or illegal action **2** to cover something with whitewash **3** to defeat an opponent in sport easily

**white·wa·ter** /ˌwaɪtˈwɔːtə◂‖-ˈwɒːtər◂,-ˈwɑː-/ *n* [U] a part of a river that looks white because the water is running very quickly over rocks; RAPIDS: *whitewater canoeing*

**white wed·ding** /ˌ· ˈ··/ *n* [C] a traditional wedding at which the woman being married wears a long white dress

**whit·ey** /ˈwaɪti/ *n* [C,U] *AmE slang* an insulting word for a white person or white people in general, used especially by black people

**whith·er** /ˈwɪðə‖-ər/ *adv old use* **1** a word meaning 'to which', used when talking about places: *the place whither he went* **2** a word meaning 'where' **3** *formal* a word used to ask what the future of something will be or how it will develop: *Whither socialism?* —compare WHENCE

**whit·ing** /ˈwaɪtɪŋ/ *n* [C] a black and silver fish that lives in the sea and can be eaten

**whit·ish** /ˈwaɪtɪʃ/ *adj* almost white in colour

**Whit·sun** /ˈwɪtsən/ *n* [C,U] **1** also **Whit Sun·day** /ˌ· ˈ··/ the seventh Sunday after Easter, when Christians celebrate the HOLY SPIRIT coming down from heaven; PENTECOST² **2** also **Whit·sun·tide** /ˈwɪtsəntaɪd/ the period around Whitsun

**whit·tle** /ˈwɪtl/ *v* [I,T] to cut a piece of wood into a particular shape by cutting off small pieces with a small knife

**whittle** sth ↔ **away** *phr v* [T] to gradually reduce the amount or value of something: *centralizing measures that had whittled away the powers of local government*

**whittle** sth ↔ **down** *phr v* [T] to gradually make something smaller by taking parts away: *I've whittled down the list of people from 30 to 16.*

**whizz¹** also **whiz** *especially AmE* /wɪz/ *v* [I] **1** [always + adv/prep] *informal* **a)** to move very quickly, often making a sound like something rushing through the air: [+ **by/around/past**] *Martin whizzed by us on his bicycle.* **b)** to do something very quickly: *Let's just whizz through it one more time.* **2** *AmE spoken* to URINATE —see also GEE WHIZ

**whizz²** also **whiz** *especially AmE*— *n* **1** [C] *informal* someone who is very fast, intelligent, or skilled in a particular activity: *a whiz on the computer* **2** *AmE spoken* [singular] an act of urinating (URINATE)

**whizz·bang, whizbang** /ˌwɪzˈbæŋ/ *n* [C] *AmE informal* something that is noticed a lot because it is very good, loud, or fast: *a whizzbang of a stereo*

**whizz·kid** also **whizkid** *especially AmE* /ˈwɪzkɪd/ *n* [C] *informal* a young person who is very skilled or successful at something: *financial whizzkids in the City*

**who** /huː/ *pron* **1** used in questions to ask what person or people: *Who's that woman over there?| Did they find out who stole the money?| Who did you stay with?* **2** used in a question or statement to show what person or people you are talking about: *Do you know the people who live over the road?| A postman is a man who delivers letters.* **3** used especially in written language after a COMMA, to add more information about a person or people: *I discussed it with my brother, who is a lawyer.* **4 who are you to...?** used to say that someone should not judge someone or something because they have faults themselves or do not have the necessary experience: *Who am I to say how you* S1 W1 *should bring up your kids; I don't have any.* **5 who's who** the people within a particular organization or group and how important each person is, what their job is etc: *I'm just getting to know who's who in the department.*

**USAGE NOTE: WHO**

FORMALITY

Except in very formal English, **who** is used instead of **whom** as an object in all kinds of questions: *Who did you see?* | *I wonder who she married in the end.* | *Who was she dancing with?* Compare the much more formal: *With whom was she dancing?*

The same is true when **who** is used in relative clauses that add information but do not restrict the meaning of the noun they follow, often after a comma: *This is Jed, who you haven't met before/who I work for* (=this is Jed, and I work for him).

In relative clauses that restrict the meaning of the noun, even **who** is rare as an object in informal or spoken English. Instead, **that** or nothing is used: *I'm the person (that) you need to see/speak to* (NOT *which*). It would be very formal to say: *...to whom you need to speak.* However, **whom** must be used immediately after a preposition, and you can avoid this by rephrasing your sentence. For example, instead of saying: *To whom are you sending that letter?* It is much more natural to say: *Who are you sending that letter to?*

You can also use **that** instead of **who** when it is the subject of a relative clause: *I hate people who/that can't stop talking.*

GRAMMAR

You can use **who** or **that** when a word for a group of people like **family** or **team** is followed by a plural word (N.B. this is only usual in British English): *a family who quarrel among themselves.* When such words are followed by a singular verb, you usually use **which** or **that**: *a team which/that has won most of its games*

**whoa** /wəʊ, həʊ‖woʊ, hoʊ/ *interjection* a command given to a horse to make it stop

**who·dun·it, whodunnit** /ˌhuːˈdʌnɪ̆t/ *n* [C] *informal* a book, film etc about a murder case, in which you do not find out who did the murder until the end

S2 **who·ev·er** /huːˈevə‖-ˈevər/ *pron* **1** used to say that it does not matter who does something, is in a particular place etc: *I'll take whoever wants to go.* | **...or whoever** (=used to emphasize that you are talking about anyone and not about a specific person) *You could ask Gary or Jane or whoever really.* **2** used to talk about a specific person or people: *Whoever is responsible for this will be punished.* **3** used at the beginning of a question to show surprise or anger: *Whoever would do a thing like that to an old woman?* **4 whoever she/he may be** used to say that you do not know who someone is: *You've got a message from someone called Tony Gower, whoever he may be.*

S1 W1 **whole¹** /həʊl‖hoʊl/ *adj* **1** all of something; ENTIRE: *You have your whole life ahead of you!* | *His whole attitude bugs me.* | **the whole school/country/village etc** (=all the people in a school, country etc) *The whole school meets together once a week.* | **the whole thing** (=everything about a situation) *The whole thing just makes me sick.* —see also **the whole of** **2 a whole variety/series/range etc** used to emphasize that there are a lot of things of the same type: *a whole series of embarrassing defeats* **3** complete and not divided or broken into parts: *Place a whole onion inside the chicken.* **4 the whole point (of)** an expression meaning the main idea or reason for something, used especially to emphasize this and make it completely clear: *I thought the whole point of the meeting was to decide which offer to accept.* **5 in the whole (wide) world** an expression meaning 'anywhere' or 'at all', used to emphasize a statement: *You're my best friend in the whole wide world!* **6 go the whole hog** *informal* to do something as completely or as well as you can, without any limits: *I'm gonna go the whole hog and have a live band at the barbecue.* **7 go the whole nine yards** *AmE spoken* to continue doing something until it is completely done and everything has been settled, even if this is difficult —see also WHOLLY, **a whole new ball game** (BALL GAME (3)), **the whole shebang** (SHEBANG), **the whole shooting match** (SHOOTING MATCH), **—wholeness** *n* [U]

**whole²** *n* **1 the whole of** all of something, especially something that is not a physical object: *The whole of the morning was wasted trying to find the documents.* **2 on the whole** used to say that something is generally true: *On the whole, life was much quieter after John left.* **3 as a whole** used to say that all the parts of something are being considered: *This rule does not only apply to seniors, but to the school as a whole.* **4** [C usually singular] something that consists of a number of parts, but is considered as a single unit: *Two halves make a whole.* S3 W2

**whole·food** /ˈhəʊlfuːd‖ˈhoʊl-/ *n* [C,U] food that is considered healthy because it is in a simple natural form

**whole-heart·ed** /ˌ· ˈ··◂/ *adj* **whole-hearted support/approval/effort etc** involving all your feelings, interest etc: *enjoying the whole-hearted support of both governments* **—whole-heartedly** *adv*

**whole·meal** /ˈhəʊlmiːl‖ˈhoʊl-/ *adj BrE* wholemeal flour or bread uses all of the grain, including the outer layer; WHOLE WHEAT *AmE*

**whole note** /ˈ· ·/ *n* [C] *AmE* a musical note which continues for as long as two HALF NOTES; SEMIBREVE *BrE* —see picture at MUSIC

**whole num·ber** /ˌ· ˈ··/ *n* [C] a number such as 0, 1, 2 etc or -1, -2 etc; INTEGER

**whole·sale¹** /ˈhəʊlseɪl‖ˈhoʊl-/ *n* [U] the business of selling goods in large quantities, especially at low prices —compare RETAIL¹

**wholesale²** *adj* **1** connected with the business of selling goods in large quantities, usually at low prices: *a wholesale price* **2** affecting almost everything or everyone, and often done without any concern for the results: *There will be no wholesale changes but a gradual modernization.* **—wholesale** *adv*: *I can get it for you wholesale.*

**whole·sal·er** /ˈhəʊlˌseɪlə‖ˈhoʊlˌseɪlər/ *n* [C] someone who sells goods wholesale: *This profit covers the wholesaler's overheads.*

**whole·some** /ˈhəʊlsəm‖ˈhoʊl-/ *adj* **1** likely to make you healthy: *well-balanced wholesome meals* **2** considered to have a good moral effect: *games that are just good clean wholesome fun* **—wholesomeness** *n* [U]

**whole wheat** /ˈ· ·/ *adj AmE* whole wheat flour etc uses all of the grain, including the outer layer; WHOLEMEAL *BrE*

**who'll** /huːl/ the short form of 'who will'

**whol·ly** /ˈhəʊl-li‖ˈhoʊl-/ *adv* [often with negatives] *formal* completely: *a wholly satisfactory solution* | *This seems to me a not wholly convincing argument.*

**whom** /huːm/ *pron* the object form of WHO, used especially in formal speech or writing: *a neighbour with whom I shared a garden* | *She brought with her three friends, none of whom I had ever met before.* W1

**whomp** /wɒmp‖wɑːmp, wɒːmp/ *v* [T] *spoken* **1** to hit someone very hard with your hand closed; PUNCH¹ (1) **2** to defeat another team easily

**whoop** /wuːp, huːp/ *v* [I] **1** to shout loudly and happily **2 whoop it up** *informal* to enjoy yourself very much, especially in a large group **—whoop** *n* [C] *whoops of victory*

**whoop-de-do** /ˌwuːp diː ˈduː, ˌhuːp-/ *n* [C] *AmE spoken* a noisy party or celebration

**whoo·pee[1]** /wʊˈpiː/ *interjection* a shout of happiness

**whoop·ee[2]** /ˈwʊpi/ *n* **make whoopee** a) *BrE old-fashioned* to go out and enjoy yourself b) *AmE old-fashioned* to have sex

**whoopee cush·ion** /ˈ·· ˌ··/ *n* [C] a rubber CUSHION[1] (1) filled with air that makes a funny noise when you sit on it

**whoop·ing cough** /ˈhuːpɪŋ kɒf‖-kɔːf/ *n* [U] an infectious disease that especially affects children, and makes them cough and have difficulty breathing

**whoops** /wʊps/ *interjection* **1** used when someone has fallen, dropped something, or made a small mistake: *Whoops! I nearly dropped it.* **2 whoops-a-daisy** used when someone, usually a child, falls down

**whoosh[1]** /wʊʃ‖wuːʃ/ *n* [C usually singular] a soft sound like air or water moving quickly: *a sudden whoosh of flame and then a big bang*

**whoosh[2]** *v* [I always + adv/prep] *informal* to move very fast with a soft rushing sound

**whop** /wɒp‖wɑːp/ *v* [T] *informal especially AmE* WHUP

**whop·per** /ˈwɒpə‖ˈwɑːpər/ *n* [C] *informal* **1** something unusually big: *The fish Mike caught was a real whopper!* **2** a lie

**whop·ping** /ˈwɒpɪŋ‖ˈwɑː-/ also **whopping great** /ˈ·· ·/ *adj* [only before noun] *spoken* very large: *a whopping fee*

**who're** /ˈhuːə‖-ər/ the short form of 'who are'

**whore** /hɔː‖hɔːr/ *n* [C] **1** an offensive word for a woman who has sex for money; PROSTITUTE **2** *taboo* an offensive word for a woman who has many sexual partners

**whore·house** /ˈhɔːhaʊs‖ˈhɔːr-/ *n* [C] *informal* a place where men can pay to have sex; BROTHEL

**whor·ing** /ˈhɔːrɪŋ/ *n* [U] *old-fashioned* the activity of having sex with a PROSTITUTE: *drinking, gambling and whoring*

**whorl** /wɜːl‖wɔːrl/ *n* [C] **1** a pattern made of a line that curls outwards in circles that get bigger and bigger **2** a circular pattern of leaves or flowers on a stem

**who's** /huːz/ the short form of 'who is' or 'who has'

S2 W1 **whose** /huːz/ *determiner, pron* **1** used to ask which person or people a particular thing belongs to: *Whose house is this?*| *Whose is this car?* **2** used to show the relationship between a person or thing and something that belongs to that person or thing: *That's the man whose house has burned down.*| *a new laptop computer whose low cost will make it attractive to students*

**who·so·ev·er** /ˌhuːsəʊˈevə‖-soʊˈevər/ *pron old use* WHOEVER (1)

**who've** /huːv/ the short form of 'who have'

**whup** /wʌp/ *v* [T] *informal especially AmE* to defeat someone easily in a sport or fight: *We whupped them!*

S1 W1 **why[1]** /waɪ/ *adv, conjunction* **1** for what reason: *Why do you say that?*| *Why should we bother waiting any longer?*| *I can't think why he would do such a thing.* | **why ever...?** (=used to add force to a question) *Why ever would he come specially to visit us?* **2 why not...?** a) used to make a suggestion: *Why not make your own Christmas cards instead of buying them?*| *Why don't you contact Eric – he may be able to help?* b) used to show that you agree with a suggestion or idea: *"It might be nice to see a film this afternoon." "Yes, why not?"* **3 why on earth...?** *spoken* used to ask in a surprised way why something has happened: *But why on earth didn't you ask me to help?* **4 why the hell...?** *spoken* used to ask in a very angry way why something has happened: *Why the hell did you buy it in the first place?* **5 why oh why...?** *spoken* used to show that you very much regret something you did: *Why oh why did I say those horrible things?* **6 why me/her?** *spoken* used to ask why something has been done, given etc to you or someone else: *Why me? Why can't someone else drive you?*

Frequencies of **why** in spoken and written English.

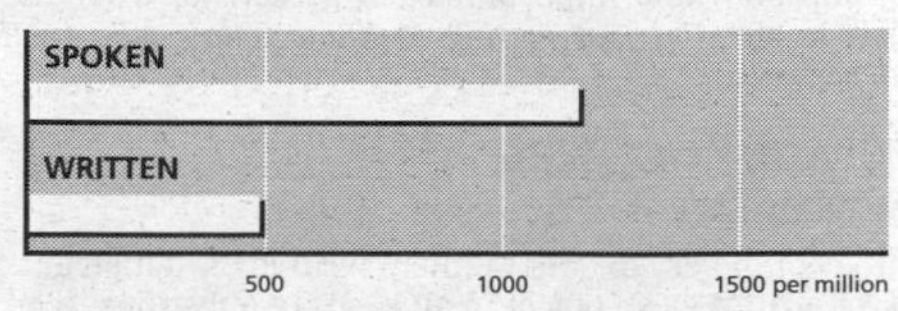


Based on the British National Corpus and the Longman Lancaster Corpus

This graph shows that **why** is much more common in spoken English than in written English. This is because it is used in questions and in some common spoken phrases.

**why[2]** *interjection especially AmE* used to show that you are surprised or annoyed: *Why, where on earth can Don have got to!*

**why[3]** *n* **the why(s) and the wherefore(s)** the reasons or explanations for something: *I'm not interested in the whys and the wherefores, just tell me what it will cost.*

**wick** /wɪk/ *n* [C] **1** the piece of thread in a candle that burns when you light it —see picture at CANDLE **2** a long piece of material in an oil lamp that sucks up oil so that the lamp can burn **3 get on sb's wick** *BrE spoken* to annoy someone

**wick·ed** /ˈwɪkɨd/ *adj* **1** behaving in a way that is morally wrong; evil: *the wicked stepmother in 'Hansel and Gretel'* **2** *informal* behaving badly in a way that is amusing; MISCHIEVOUS: *Carl had a wicked grin on his face as he crept up behind Ellen.* **3** *spoken* very good; excellent: *That's a wicked bike!* **—wickedly** *adv* **—wickedness** *n* [U]

**wick·er** /ˈwɪkə‖-ər/ *adj* [only before noun] made from thin dry branches or REEDS woven together: *a wicker basket*

**wick·er·work** /ˈwɪkəwɜːk‖ˈwɪkərwɜːrk/ *n* [U] objects made from wicker

**wick·et** /ˈwɪkɨt/ *n* [C] one of two sets of three wooden sticks that are stuck in the ground in a game of CRICKET (2), which the BOWLER tries to hit with the ball —see also **be on a sticky wicket** (STICKY (8))

**wicket gate** /ˈ·· ˌ·/ *n* [C] *old use* a small door or gate that is part of a larger one

**wicket keep·er** /ˈ·· ˌ··/ *n* [C] a player who stands behind the wicket in CRICKET (2)

**wide[1]** /waɪd/ *adj* S1 W1

**1 ▶ DISTANCE ◀** a) measuring a large distance from one side to the other: *a hat with a wide brim* —opposite NARROW[1] (1) b) **five metres/two miles etc wide** measuring five metres etc from one side to the other: *The door's three feet wide.* —see picture at THICK[1]

**2 ▶ VARIETY ◀** including or involving a large variety of different people, things, or situations: *a man with a wide experience of foreign affairs*| **wide range/variety/selection etc** *We stock a wide range of furnishing materials.*

**3 ▶ IN MANY PLACES ◀** [usually before noun] happening among many people or in many places: *The Whitewater scandal received wide publicity.*

**4 wide difference/gap/variation etc** a large and noticeable difference: *the ever-wider gap between the richest and poorest countries*

**5 the wider issues/view/context etc** the more general features of a situation, rather than the specific details: *We also have a wider aim: the restoration of democracy.*

**6 ▶ EYES ◀** *especially literary* wide eyes are fully open, especially when someone is very surprised, excited, or frightened: *Her eyes grew wide in anticipation.*

**7 give sb/sth a wide berth** *especially BrE* to avoid someone or something

**8 the big wide world** *especially spoken* places outside the small familiar place where you live: *Soon you'll leave school and go out into the big wide world.*

**9 nationwide/city-wide etc** happening or existing all

over the nation, city etc: *a country-wide problem* —see also WIDELY, WIDTH

**USAGE NOTE: WIDE**

WORD CHOICE: **wide, broad, big, large, wide-ranging**

**Wide** is the most usual word to describe something that measures a long distance from one side to another: *a wide road/lake/doorway/entrance/staircase* You also use **wide** to express how much something measures from side to side: *The gap was only a few inches wide.*

**Broad** is often used about parts of the body: *broad shoulders/hips | a broad nose/forehead.* **Broad** often suggests that something is wide in a good or attractive way: *a broad sunny avenue running through the middle of the town*

Sometimes you may need to think whether you really mean **wide** or **broad**, or just **big** or **large** (=wide in all directions): *a wide carpet/field* or *a large carpet/field*

**Wide-ranging** means covering a lot of different subjects or including a lot of different ideas: *a wide-ranging review/report/speech*

**wide²** *adv* **1 a)** a door or window that is wide open is open as fully as it can be **b)** if someone's eyes or mouth are wide open, they are open as far as possible, especially when they are surprised **c)** if a competition, election etc is wide open, it is possible for anyone to succeed: *After Milan's win the championship is wide open.* **2** opening or spreading as much as possible: *The door opened a little wider.* | **open/spread sth wide** *Spiro spread his arms wide in a welcoming gesture.* | **wide apart** *Sandy stood with his back to the fire, legs wide apart.* **3** not hitting the point you were aiming at: *One of the guards fired at us but the shot went wide.* **4 wide awake** completely awake —see also **far and wide** (FAR¹ (1)), **wide of the mark/off the mark** (MARK² (11))

**wide-an·gle lens** /ˌ· ··ˈ·/ *n* [C] a camera LENS (2) that lets you take photographs with a wider view than normal

**wide boy** /ˈ· ·/ *n* [C] *BrE informal* a man who makes money in dishonest ways and uses it to buy expensive clothes, cars etc: *Cockney wide boys trying to sell you something*

**wide-eyed** /ˌ· ˈ·◂/ *adj, adv* **1** with your eyes wide open, especially because you are surprised or frightened **2** too willing to believe, accept, or admire things because you do not have much experience of life; NAIVE

W2 **wide·ly** /ˈwaɪdli/ *adv* **1** in a lot of different places or by a lot of people: *widely publicized events* | *an author who had travelled widely in the Far East* **2** varying to a large degree: *The quality of the applicants varies widely.* **3 widely read a)** read by a lot of people: *a widely read magazine* **b)** having read many different books: *She's very widely read.*

**wid·en** /ˈwaɪdn/ *v* [I,T] **1** to become wider or make something wider: *They're widening the road.* **2** to become larger in degree or range, or make something do this: *The gap between income and expenditure has widened to 11%.* | *They are trying to widen the discussion to include environmental issues.* —opposite NARROW² (1)

**wide-rang·ing** /ˌ· ˈ··◂/ *adj* including a wide variety of subjects, things, or people: *a wide-ranging discussion* | *wide-ranging proposals to improve the rail network*

W3 **wide·spread** /ˈwaɪdspred/ *adj* existing or happening in many places or situations, or among many people: *the widespread use of chemicals in agriculture*

**wid·get** /ˈwɪdʒɪt/ *n* [C] **1** *spoken* a small piece of equipment that you do not know the name for **2** *informal* a word meaning an imaginary product that a company might produce: *Company A produces 6000 widgets a month at a unit price of $0.33.*

**wid·ow** /ˈwɪdəʊ‖-doʊ/ *n* [C] **1** a woman whose husband has died and who has not married again: *Mr Castle's widow, Anne, described the sentence as 'obscene'.* **2 football widow/golf etc widow** *humorous* a woman whose husband spends all his free time watching football, playing golf etc —see also GRASS WIDOW

**wid·owed** /ˈwɪdəʊd‖-doʊd/ *adj* having become a widow or widower: *She was widowed at the age of 25.*

**wid·ow·er** /ˈwɪdəʊə‖-doʊər/ *n* [C] a man whose wife has died and who has not married again

**wid·ow·hood** /ˈwɪdəʊhʊd‖-doʊ-/ *n* [U] the time when you are a widow

**width** /wɪdθ/ *n* **1** [C,U] the distance from one side of something to the other: *What's the width of the desk?* | **in width** *It's about 6 metres in width.* —compare BREADTH, LENGTH —see picture at LENGTH **2** [C] a piece of a material that has been measured and cut: *four widths of curtain material*

**wield** /wiːld/ *v* [T] **1 wield power/influence/authority etc** to have a lot of power or influence, and be ready to use it: *The Church wields immense power in Ireland.* **2** to hold a weapon or tool that you are going to use: *She had her car windows smashed by a gang wielding baseball bats.*

**wie·ner** /ˈwiːnə‖-ər/ also **wie·nie, weenie** /ˈwiːni/ *n* [C] *AmE* **1** a type of SAUSAGE **2** *informal* someone who does something stupid **3** a word used by children meaning a PENIS

**wife** /waɪf/ *plural* **wives** /waɪvz/ *n* [C] the woman that a man is married to: *Have you met his wife?* S1 W1

**wife·ly** /ˈwaɪfli/ *adj old-fashioned* connected with qualities that are supposed to be typical of a good wife

**wig** /wɪg/ *n* [C] artificial hair that you wear on your head

**wig·gle¹** /ˈwɪgəl/ *v* [I,T] to move with small movements from side to side or up and down, or make something move like this: *Henry wiggled his toes.*

**wiggle²** *n* [C] **1** a small movement from side to side or up and down: *a wiggle of the hips* **2 get a wiggle on!** *AmE spoken* used to tell someone to do something more quickly

**wig·gly** /ˈwɪgəli/ *adj informal* a wiggly line is one that has small curves in it; WAVY (2)

**wight** /waɪt/ *n* [C] *old use* a person

**wig·wam** /ˈwɪgwæm‖-wɑːm/ *n* [C] a tall tent in which some Native Americans used to live

**wild¹** /waɪld/ *adj* S3 W2

**1 ▶ PLANTS/ANIMALS ◀** living in a natural state, not changed or controlled by humans: *wild flowers* | *a wild rabbit* | **grow wild** *daffodils growing wild in the meadow*

**2 ▶ EMOTIONS ◀** feeling or expressing strong uncontrolled emotions, especially anger, happiness, or excitement: *wild laughter* | [+ **with**] *wild with excitement*

**3 go wild a)** to behave in a very excited way: *The crowd went wild as soon as Jackson stepped onto the stage.* **b)** to get very angry

**4 ▶ CRAZY ◀** behaving in an uncontrolled, sometimes violent way: *She's great fun, but a bit wild.* | *Jack had a wild look in his eyes.*

**5 ▶ ENJOYABLE ◀** *informal* very enjoyable and exciting: *That was a really wild party last night!*

**6 be wild about** to be very interested in or excited about something: *My son's wild about racing cars.*

**7 ▶ WITHOUT CAREFUL THOUGHT ◀** done or said without much thought or care, or without knowing all the facts: *wild accusations* | **a wild guess** *I just made a wild guess and it turned out to be right.*

**8 run wild a)** if a garden or plant runs wild, it grows uncontrollably because no one is looking after it **b)** if children run wild, they do what they like because they are not controlled by an adult

**9 beyond your wildest dreams** beyond anything you imagined or hoped for: *an invention that was to change our lives beyond our wildest dreams*

**10 ▶ WEATHER ◀** violent and strong: *wild winds*

**11 ▶ CARD GAMES ◀** a card that is wild can be used to represent any other card in a game —see also WILD CARD (1), **sow your wild oats** (SOW), —**wildly** *adv*: *The*

*crowd ran wildly through the streets.* | *wildly inaccurate statements* —**wildness** *n* [U]

**wild**[2] *n* **1 in the wild** in natural and free conditions, not kept or controlled by humans: *There are very few pandas living in the wild now.* **2 the wilds of Africa/Alaska etc** areas where there are no towns and not many people live

**wild boar** /ˌ· ˈ·/ *n* [C] a large wild pig with long hair

**wild card** /ˈ· ˌ·/ *n* [C] **1** a playing card that can represent any other card **2** *technical* a sign that can represent any letter in some computer commands **3** someone that you do not know well, so that you cannot guess how they will behave in certain situations

**wild·cat**[1] /ˈwaɪldkæt/ *n* [C] a type of cat that looks similar to a large pet cat and lives in mountains, forests etc

**wildcat**[2] *v* [I] *AmE* to look for oil in a place where nobody has found any yet —**wildcatter** *n* [C]

**wildcat strike** /ˌ·· ˈ·/ *n* [C] an occasion when people suddenly and unofficially stop working in order to protest about something

**wil·de·beest** /ˈwɪldəbiːst/ *n* [C] a large Southern African animal with a tail and curved horns; GNU

**wil·der·ness** /ˈwɪldənɪ̈s‖-dər-/ *n* [C usually singular] **1** a large area of land that has never been developed or farmed: *a bleak wilderness of undrained marshes* **2** any place where there is no sign of people or their effect: *That garden is a wilderness.* | *The south side of the city had become a lawless wilderness.* **3 in the wilderness** away from the centre of power and activity, especially political activity: *his return to office after several years in the wilderness*

**wilderness a·re·a** /ˈ··· ˌ···/ *n* [C] an area of public land in the US where no buildings or roads are allowed to be built

**wild·fire** /ˈwaɪldfaɪə‖-faɪr/ *n* [U] —see **spread like wildfire** (SPREAD[1] (3a))

**wild·fowl** /ˈwaɪldfaʊl/ *n* [plural] birds, especially ones that live near water

**wild-goose chase** /ˌ· ˈ· ˌ·/ *n* [C] a situation where you are looking for something that does not exist or that you are very unlikely to find, so that you waste a lot of time

**wild·life** /ˈwaɪldlaɪf/ *n* [U] animals and plants growing in natural conditions: *a wildlife park* | *studying the wildlife*

**wild rice** /ˌ· ˈ·/ *n* [U] the seed of a type of grass that grows in parts of North America and China

**wiles** /waɪlz/ *n* [plural] clever talk or tricks used to persuade someone to do what you want: *She used all her wiles to coax a young man to help her escape.*

**wil·ful** *BrE*, **willful** *AmE* /ˈwɪlfəl/ *adj* **1** continuing to do what you want, even after you have been told to stop: *a wilful child* **2 wilful damage/disobedience/exaggeration etc** deliberate damage etc, when you know that what you are doing is wrong —**wilfully** *adv* —**wilfulness** *n* [U]

**wi·li·ness** /ˈwaɪlinɪ̈s/ *n* [U] the quality of being WILY

S1 W1 **will**[1] /wɪl/ [modal verb] *v* **1** used to express the simple future tense: *A meeting will be held next Tuesday at 3 p.m.* | *What time will she arrive?* | *When will you be leaving for America?* **2** used to show that you are willing or ready to do something: *I will come up and help you clear the attic in a moment.* | *Alma won't come to the party I'm sure.* | *Dr Weir will see you now.* **3** used to ask someone to do something: *Will you phone me later?* | *Shut the door will you?* **4** used to say what always happens in a particular situation or what is generally true: *Oil will float on water.* | *Accidents will happen.* **5** used like 'can' to show what is possible: *This car will hold five people comfortably.* **6** used like 'must' to show what you think is likely to be true: *That will be Tim coming home now.* **7** used to order or tell someone angrily to do something: *Will you two shut up for God's sake!* **8** used to offer something to someone or to invite them to do something: *Will you be staying the night?* **9** used to describe someone's habits, especially when you find them strange or annoying: *Trish will keep asking damn silly questions.* **10 I will** *spoken* used during a wedding ceremony to show that you agree formally to marry

**will**[2] *n* S2 W2

**1 ► DETERMINATION ◄** [C,U] determination to do something that you have decided to do, even if this is difficult: *Children sometimes have very strong wills.* | **the will to live/fight/succeed etc** *The survivors never lost the will to live.* | **iron will** (=very strong determination) | **a battle/clash of wills** (=when two people who both have strong wills oppose each other) —see also FREE WILL, STRONG-WILLED, WEAK-WILLED

**2 ► LEGAL DOCUMENT ◄** [C] a legal document that says who you want your money and property to be given to after you die: **make a will** *Have you made a will yet?* | **in sb's will** *My grandmother left me these jewels in her will.*

**3 ► WHAT SB WANTS ◄** [singular] what someone wants to happen in a particular situation: *I wish he'd stop trying to impose his will on others.* | *obedience to God's will* | **against your will** *The prisoner was made to sign a confession against his will.*

**4 with the best will in the world** *spoken* used to say that something is not possible, however much you want to do it: *With the best will in the world, I don't see what more I can do.*

**5 where there's a will there's a way** *spoken* used to say that if you really want to do something, you will find a way to succeed

**6 at will** whenever you want and in whatever way you want: *a terrifying creature that could change its shape at will*

**7 with a will** in an eager and determined way

**will**[3] *v* **1** [T] to try to make something happen by thinking about it very hard: **will sb to do sth** *She was willing herself not to cry.* **2** [T] to officially give something that you own to someone else after you die **3** [I,T] *old use* to want something to happen: *The King wills it.*

**will·ful** /ˈwɪlfəl/ *adj* the American spelling of WILFUL

**wil·lie** /ˈwɪli/ *n informal* **1 get the willies** to feel nervous or frightened **2 give sb the willies** to make someone feel nervous or frightened: *It gives me the willies to even think about plastic surgery.* **3** [C] another spelling of WILLY

**will·ing** /ˈwɪlɪŋ/ *adj* **1 be willing (to do sth)** to be prepared to do something, or have no reason to not want to do it: *How much are they willing to pay?* | **quite/perfectly willing** *I told them I was perfectly willing to help.* **2 willing helper/worker etc** someone who is eager to help etc and does not have to be persuaded: *60% of voters said they would willingly pay higher taxes for better health care.* —**willingly** *adv* —**willingness** *n* [U]

**will o' the wisp** /ˌ· · · ˈ·/ *n* [C usually singular] **1** a blue moving light that can be seen over wet ground at night **2** someone that you can never completely depend on, or something that you can never achieve

**wil·low** /ˈwɪləʊ‖-loʊ/ *n* [C,U] a type of tree that has long thin branches and grows near water, or the wood from this tree

**wil·low·y** /ˈwɪləʊi‖-loʊi/ *adj* tall, thin, and graceful: *She was pale and willowy with the most amazing violet eyes.*

**will·pow·er** /ˈwɪlˌpaʊə‖-ˌpaʊər/ *n* [U] the ability to control your mind and body in order to achieve something that you want to do: *It took all his willpower to remain calm.*

**wil·ly, willie** /ˈwɪli/ *n* [C] *BrE informal* a PENIS

**willy-nil·ly** /ˌwɪli ˈnɪli/ *adv* if something happens willy-nilly, it happens whether you want it to or not: *The Church is being forced, willy-nilly, to make clear its position on homosexuality.*

**wilt**[1] /wɪlt/ *v* [I] **1** if a plant wilts, it bends over because it is too dry or old —see picture on page 1258 **2** *informal* to feel weak, tired, or upset, especially because you are too hot

**wilt**[2] *v old use* **thou wilt** you will

**wil·y** /ˈwaɪli/ *adj* clever at getting what you want,

especially by tricking people: *a wily politician* —**wiliness** *n* [U]

**wimp¹** /wɪmp/ *n* [C] *informal* **1** someone who has a weak character and is afraid to do something difficult or unpleasant: *Don't be such a wimp!* **2** a man who is thin and physically weak —**wimpish, wimpy** *adj*

**wimp²** *v*

**wimp out** *phr v* [I] *spoken* to not do something that you intended to do, because you do not feel brave enough, strong enough etc

**wim·ple** /ˈwɪmpəl/ *n* [C] a piece of cloth that a NUN wears over her head

S1 **win¹** /wɪn/ *v past tense and past participle* **won** /wʌn/
W1 *present participle* **winning**
**1 ▶ COMPETITION/RACE ◀** [I,T] to be the best or first in a competition, game, election etc: *Who do you think will win the next election?*| **win at sth** *I never win at cards.*| **win by a mile/10 points etc** *We won by just one point.*| **win hands down** (=win very easily)
**2 ▶ PRIZE ◀** [T] to get something as a prize for winning in a competition or game: *How does it feel to have won the gold medal?*| *She won £160 on the lottery.*
**3 ▶ GET/ACHIEVE ◀** [T] to get or achieve something that you want because of your efforts or abilities: *Do you think he will win the Republican nomination?*| **win sb sth** *Those tactics won't win them any votes.*| **win sb's approval/trust/love etc** *Proposals for an out-of-town shopping mall have won the approval of the city council.*| **win sb's heart** (=make them love you)
**4 you win** *spoken* used to agree to what someone wants after you have tried to persuade them to do something else: *OK, you win – we'll go to the movie.*
**5 you can't win** *spoken* used to say that there is no satisfactory way of dealing with a particular situation: *You can't win, can you? You either work late and upset Jenny, or go home and risk your job.*
**6 you can't win them all** *spoken* used to show sympathy when someone has had a disappointing experience
**7 win the day** to finally be successful in a discussion or argument; TRIUMPH²: *Common sense won the day, and the development plans were dropped.* —see also **win the toss** (TOSS² (3)), WINNER, WINNING

**win** sb ↔ **round/around** *phr v* [T] to win someone over

**win** sb/sth ↔ **back** *phr v* [T] to succeed in getting back something or someone that you had before: *How can I win back her trust?*

**win out** *phr v* [I] to win through

**win** sb ↔ **over** *phr v* [T] to get someone's support or friendship by persuading them or being nice to them: *We'll be working hard over the next ten days to win over the undecided voters.*

**win through** *phr v* [I] to eventually succeed in spite of problems: *As in most of his films, it's the good guys who win through in the end.*

**USAGE NOTE: WIN**

WORD CHOICE: **win, beat, defeat**

You can **win** a game, race, competition, election etc (NOT **gain**). After the event you can say *I've won!* A country can **win** a battle or war (NOT **gain**). As a result you can also **win** a victory, championship, prize, scholarship, or a seat in the Senate. (See also **gain** WORD CHOICE.)

When you win a game etc, you **beat** the other person or the other team or, more formally, you could say **defeat**: *We beat their team by ten points* (NOT won).| *He beat all his opponents/rivals for the seat.*

When a country wins a war it **defeats** its enemies. (**Beat** can be used informally): *The Americans defeated the British in 1781.*

W3 **win²** *n* [C] a success or victory, especially in sport: *We've had two wins so far this season.*| [+ **over**] *In the under-16 event England had their first win over Germany, by 2–1.* —see also NO-WIN SITUATION

**wince** /wɪns/ *v* [I] **1** to suddenly change the expression on your face as a reaction to something painful or upsetting: *Sandra winced as the dentist started to drill.* **2** to suddenly feel very uncomfortable or embarrassed because of something that happens, something you remember etc: **wince at the thought/idea/memory** *I still wince at the thought of that terrible evening.* —**wince** *n* [singular]

**win·cey·ette** /ˌwɪnsiˈet◂/ *n* [U] *BrE* light material with a soft surface, used especially for clothes you wear in bed; FLANNELETTE

**winch¹** /wɪntʃ/ *n* [C] a machine with a rope or chain for lifting heavy objects

**winch²** *v* [T always + adv/prep] to lift something or someone up using a winch: **winch sth out/from etc** *He was winched out of the sinking boat just in time.*

**wind¹** /wɪnd/ *n* S2
**1 ▶ AIR ◀** [C,U] moving air, especially when it moves W2
strongly or quickly in a current: *a 70-mile-an-hour wind*| *branches swaying in the wind*| **the wind blows** *A gentle wind was blowing through the trees.*| **strong/high winds** *The forecast is for strong winds and heavy rain.*| **a gust of wind** (=a short strong wind) *A sudden gust of wind blew the door shut.*| **east/west/north/south wind** (=coming from the east etc)| **a gentle/soft/light wind** *A soft wind teased a tendril of her hair.*| **a bitter/chill/biting wind** (=a very cold wind)| **the wind is up/gets up** (=blows more strongly)| **the wind drops** (=blows less strongly) *We'll wait till the wind drops before we put the tent up.* —see also HEADWIND —see picture on page 836
**2 get/have wind of** *informal* to hear or find out about something secret or private, especially if you learn it accidentally or unofficially: *Jeremy, I don't want that reporter getting wind of this.*
**3 ▶ BREATH ◀** [U] your ability to breathe without difficulty: **get your wind (back)** (=be able to breathe normally again, for example after running)| **knock the wind out of** (=hit someone in the stomach so that they cannot breathe for a moment) —see also SECOND WIND, WINDPIPE
**4 take the wind out of sb's sails** *informal* to make someone lose their confidence, especially by saying or doing something unexpected
**5 see which way the wind is blowing** to find out what the situation is before you do something or make a decision
**6 be in the wind** used to say that something is happening or going to happen, but not many people know what it is
**7 the winds of change/freedom/public opinion etc** events and changes that have started to happen and will have important effects, and that cannot be stopped
**8 get the wind up/put the wind up sb** *BrE informal* to become anxious or frightened, or to make someone feel this way: *The threat of legal action will be enough to put the wind up them.*
**9 ▶ IN YOUR STOMACH ◀** [U] *BrE* the condition of having air or gas in your stomach, or the air or gas itself; GAS *AmE*: *I can't drink beer, it gives me wind.*
**10 the winds/the wind section** all the musicians who play WIND INSTRUMENTS in a band
**11 ▶ TALK ◀** [U] *informal* useless talk that does not mean anything —see also WINDY, **break wind** (BREAK¹ (42)), **an ill wind (that blows no good)** (ILL¹ (5)), **sail close to the wind** (SAIL² (6)), **straw in the wind** (STRAW (4))

**wind²** /waɪnd/ *v past tense and past participle* **wound** /waʊnd/ **1** [I always + adv/prep, T always + adv/prep] to turn or twist something repeatedly, especially around something else: **wind sth around/round** *Wind the wires around those pins there.*| **wind sth forward/back** *Can you wind the video back a little way – I want to see that bit again.*| [+ **around/round**] *Make sure the thread winds evenly around the bobbin.* —see also REWIND **2** also **wind up** [T] to turn something such as a handle or part of a machine around and around, especially in order to make something move or start working: *What time is it? I forgot to wind my watch.* | *It was one of those old gramophones that you have to wind up.* | **wind sth down/up** *BrE*: *Would you mind winding down the window?* **3** [I always + adv/prep] if a road, track, river etc winds, it has many smooth bends and is usually very long: **wind (its way) through/along** *Highway 99 winds its way along the coast.* —see also WINDING

**wind down** *phr v* **1** [T **wind** sth ↔ **down**] to gradually reduce the work of a business or organization so that it can be closed down completely —compare **wind up** (2) (WIND) **2** [I] to rest and relax after a lot of hard work or excitement: *I find it difficult to wind down after a day at work.*

**wind up** *phr v* **1** [I, T **wind** sth ↔ **up**] bring an activity, meeting etc to an end: *OK, just to wind up, could I summarize what we've decided?* | *It's time to wind things up – I have a plane to catch.* **2** [T **wind** sth ↔ **up**] to close down a company or organization: *Our operations in Jamaica are being wound up.* —compare WIND DOWN[1] **3** [I, linking verb] *informal* to unintentionally get into an unpleasant situation or place as a result of something you have done: [+ **with/in/at etc**] *You know you're going to wind up in court over this.* | **wind up doing** *I wound up wishing I'd never come.* | **wind up drunk/dead/ill etc** *You keep driving like that and you'll wind up dead.* **4** [T **wind** sb ↔ **up**] *BrE* to deliberately say or do something in order to annoy someone, especially because you enjoy annoying them: *Stupid! They're only winding you up.* —see also WOUND-UP

**wind³** /waɪnd/ *n* [C] a bend or turn: **give sth a wind** *Give that crank another wind, will you?*

**wind⁴** /wɪnd/ *v* [T] to make someone have difficulty in breathing: **be winded** *"Is he OK?" "Yeah, I think he's just winded."*

**wind·bag** /ˈwɪndbæg/ *n* [C] *informal* someone who talks too much; GASBAG

**wind·break** /ˈwɪndbreɪk/ *n* [C] a fence, line of trees, or wall that is intended to protect a place from the wind

**wind break·er** /ˈwɪnd ˌbreɪkə‖-ər/ *AmE*, **windcheat·er** /ˈwɪndˌtʃiːtə‖-ər/ *BrE old-fashioned* *n* [C] a type of coat that is made specially to keep the wind out —see picture at COAT[1]

**wind chime** /ˈwɪnd tʃaɪm/ *n* [C] long thin pieces of metal or glass hanging together in a group that make musical sounds when the wind blows

**wind·ed** /ˈwɪndɪ̵d/ *adj* unable to breathe easily, because you have been running or you have been hit in the stomach

**wind·fall** /ˈwɪndfɔːl‖-fɒːl/ *n* [C] **1** an amount of money that you get unexpectedly: *Jackpot pools winner Salters toasted his £2 million windfall at his Edinburgh home.* | **windfall gain/profit etc** (=high profits that you did not expect to make) **2** a piece of fruit that has fallen off a tree

**wind·ing** /ˈwaɪndɪŋ/ *adj* having a twisting turning shape: *a winding path* —see also WIND² (3)

**winding sheet** /ˈwaɪndɪŋ ʃiːt/ *n* [C] *old use* a SHROUD[1] (1)

**wind in·stru·ment** /ˈwɪnd ˌɪnstrʊ̵mənt/ *n* [C] a musical instrument that you play by blowing through it

**wind·jam·mer** /ˈwɪndˌdʒæmə‖-ər/ *n* [C] a large sailing ship of the type that was used for trade in the 19th century

**wind·lass** /ˈwɪndləs/ *n* [C] a machine for pulling or lifting heavy objects

**wind·mill** /ˈwɪndˌmɪl/ *n* [C] **1** a building or structure with parts that turn around in the wind, used for producing electrical power or crushing grain **2** *BrE* a toy consisting of a stick with curved pieces of plastic at the end that turn around when they are blown; PINWHEEL *AmE*

S1 W1 **win·dow** /ˈwɪndəʊ‖-doʊ/ *n* [C] **1** an opening in the wall of a building, car etc that lets in light and air, and is usually covered with glass: *Do you mind if I open the window?* | *looking at the Christmas displays in the shop windows* —see picture on page 409 **2** one of the separate areas on a computer screen where different processes or PROGRAMS are operating **3** a short period of time that is available for a particular activity **4 go out (of) the window** *informal* to disappear completely or no longer have any effect: *One glass of wine, and all my good intentions went out the window.* **5 window of opportunity** a lucky opportunity to do something that you will not always be able to do

**window box** /ˈ·· ·/ *n* [C] a long narrow box in which you can grow plants outside your window

**window clean·er** /ˈ·· ˌ··/ *n* [C] someone whose job is to clean windows

**window dress·er** /ˈ·· ˌ··/ *n* [C] someone whose job is to arrange goods attractively in shop windows

**window dress·ing** /ˈ·· ˌ··/ *n* [U] **1** something that is intended to give people a favourable idea about your plans or activities, and to stop them seeing the true situation: *All these glossy pamphlets are just window dressing – the fact is that the new mall will ruin the environment.* **2** the art of arranging goods in a shop window so that they look attractive to customers

**win·dow·pane** /ˈwɪndəʊpeɪn‖-doʊ-/ *n* [U] a single whole piece of glass in a window

**Win·dows** /ˈwɪndəʊz‖-doʊz/ *n* [U] *trademark* a system produced by the Microsoft Corporation for organizing information on a personal computer, which can run several PROGRAMS in separate areas of the computer screen

**window seat** /ˈ·· ˌ·/ *n* [C] **1** a seat next to the window on a bus, plane etc **2** a seat directly below a window

**window shade** /ˈ·· ˌ·/ *n* [C] *AmE* BLIND³ (1)

**window-shopping** /ˈ·· ˌ··/ *n* [U] the activity of looking at goods in shop windows without intending to buy them —**window-shopper** *n* [C]

**win·dow·sill** /ˈwɪndəʊˌsɪl‖-doʊ-/ *n* [C] a shelf fixed along the bottom of a window —see picture on page 410

**wind·pipe** /ˈwɪndpaɪp/ *n* [C] the tube through which air passes from your mouth to your lungs

**wind·screen** /ˈwɪndskriːn/ *n* [C] *BrE* the large window at the front of a car, bus etc; WINDSHIELD *AmE* —see picture on page 409

**windscreen wip·er** /ˈ·· ˌ··/ *n* [C] *BrE* a long thin piece of metal with a rubber edge that moves across a windscreen to remove rain; WINDSHIELD WIPER *AmE* —see picture on page 409

**wind·shield** /ˈwɪndʃiːld/ *n* [C] **1** *AmE* a windscreen —see picture on page 409 **2** a piece of glass or clear plastic fixed at the front of a MOTORCYCLE

**windshield wip·er** /ˈ·· ˌ··/ *n* [C] *AmE* a windscreen wiper —see picture on page 409

**wind·sock** /ˈwɪndsɒk‖-sɑːk/ *n* [C] a tube of material fastened to a pole at airports to show the direction of the wind

**wind·storm** /ˈwɪndstɔːm‖-stɔːrm/ *n* [C] a period of bad weather when there are strong winds but not much rain

**wind-surf**

**wind·surf·ing** /ˈwɪnd ˌsɜːfɪŋ‖-ˌsɜːr-/ *n* [U] the sport of sailing across water by standing on a board and holding on to a large sail —**wind·surfer** *n* [C] —**wind·surf** *v* [I]

**wind·swept** /ˈwɪndswept/ *adj* **1** a place that is windswept is often windy because there are not many trees or buildings to protect it: *windswept moors* **2** hair, clothes etc that are windswept have been blown around by the wind

**wind tun·nel** /ˈwɪnd ˌtʌnl/ *n* [C] a large enclosed passage where aircraft are tested by forcing air past them

**wind tur·bine** /ˈwɪnd ˌtɜːbaɪn‖-ˌtɜːrbɪ̥n, -baɪn/ *n* [C] a modern WINDMILL (1) for providing electrical power

**wind-up** /ˈwaɪnd ʌp/ *n* [C] *BrE informal* something you say or do to deliberately make someone angry or worried

**wind·ward¹** /ˈwɪndwəd‖-wərd/ *adj, adv* **1** towards the direction from which the wind is blowing **2** pointing towards the wind: *the windward side of the boat* —opposite LEEWARD

**windward²** *n* [U] the place from which the wind is blowing: *We sailed to windward across Oyster Bay.*

S3 **wind·y** /ˈwɪndi/ *adj* **1** with a lot of wind blowing: *It's too windy for a picnic.* **2** getting a lot of wind: *a windy hillside* **3** windy talk is full of words that sound impressive but do not mean much: *the politician's windy generalizations* —**windily** *adv* —**windiness** *n* [U]

S2 W2 **wine¹** /waɪn/ *n* [C,U] **1** an alcoholic drink made from GRAPES, or a type of this drink: *a glass of white wine|a delicious Californian wine* **2** an alcoholic drink made from another fruit or plant: *elderflower wine* **3 wine, women and song** *old-fashioned* a pleasant, enjoyable life of dancing, drinking etc

**wine²** *v* [T] **wine and dine** to entertain someone well with a meal, wine etc: *Hawksworth wined and dined potential clients.*

**wine bar** /ˈ· ·/ *n* [C] *BrE* a place that serves mainly wine and light meals

**wine cool·er** /ˈ· ˌ··/ *n* [C] **1** *AmE* a drink made with wine, fruit juice, and water **2** a special container that you put a bottle of wine into to make it cool

**wine vin·e·gar** /ˌ· ˈ···/ *n* [U] a type of VINEGAR made from sour wine, used in cooking

S2 W2 **wing¹** /wɪŋ/ *n* [C]

**1** ► **BIRDS** ◄ **a)** one of the parts of a bird's or insect's body that it uses for flying: *a butterfly with beautiful markings on its wings*|**flap its wings** (=move them up and down) *vultures circling overhead, lazily flapping their wings.* **b)** the meat on the wing bone of a chicken, duck etc, used as food: *spicy chicken wings*

**2** ► **PLANE** ◄ one of the large flat parts that stick out from the side of a plane and help to keep it in the air —see picture at AIRCRAFT

**3** ► **BUILDING** ◄ one of the parts of a large building, especially one that sticks out from the main part: *the east wing of the palace|She works in the hospital's maternity wing.*

**4** ► **POLITICS** ◄ a group within a political party or similar organization, whose members share particular opinions and aims, especially when these are different from those of most people in the organization: *She's on the liberal wing of the Republican Party.* —see also LEFT WING, RIGHT WING

**5** ► **SPORT** ◄ **a)** someone who plays on the far left or far right of the field in games like football **b)** the far left or right part of the field

**6** ► **CAR** ◄ *BrE* the part of a car's body that covers the wheels; FENDER (2) *AmE* —see picture on page 409

**7 take sb under your wing** to give help and protection, especially to someone younger or less experienced

**8 (waiting) in the wings** ready to take action or ready to be used when the time is right: *There's a whole series of tax-cutting measures waiting in the wings.*

**9** ► **THEATRE** ◄ **the wings** [plural] the parts at either side of a stage where the actors are hidden from view

**10 be on the wing** *literary* if a bird is on the wing, it is flying

**11 take wing** *literary* to fly away

**12 get your wings** to pass the necessary flying exams and become a pilot

**wing²** *v* **1** [I always + adv/prep] *especially literary* to fly: *a flock of geese winging down the coast from Iceland* **2 wing its way a)** to fly: *planes winging their way to exotic destinations* **b)** to be sent quickly from one place to another: *Our special first prize will soon be winging its way towards you.* **3** [T] to wound a person or bird in the arm or wing **4 wing it** *AmE spoken* to do something without planning or preparation: *I didn't have time to prepare for the meeting – I'll just have to wing it.*

**wing chair** /ˈ· ·/ *n* [C] a comfortable chair that has a high back and pieces pointing forward on each side

**wing col·lar** /ˌ· ˈ··/ *n* [C] a type of shirt collar for men that is worn with very formal clothes

**wing com·mand·er** /ˈ· ·ˌ··/ *n* a rank in the Royal Air Force —see table on page B4

**wing·ding** /ˈwɪŋˌdɪŋ/ *n* [C] *AmE old-fashioned* a party

**winge** /wɪndʒ/ *v* another spelling of WHINGE

**winged** /wɪŋd/ *adj* having wings: *winged insects*

**wing·er** /ˈwɪŋə‖-ər/ *n* [C] **1** a player in games such as football, whose position is on the far left or far right of the field —see also WING¹ (5) **2 right-winger/left-winger** someone who belongs to the RIGHT WING or LEFT WING² of a political group

**wing mir·ror** /ˈ· ˌ··/ *n* [C] a mirror fixed to the side of a car —see picture on page 409

**wing nut** /ˈ· ·/ *n* [C] a NUT¹ (2) for fastening things, which has sides that stick out to make it easier to turn

**wing·span** /ˈwɪŋspæn/ *n* [C] the distance from the end of one wing to the end of the other

**wing·tip** /ˈwɪŋtɪp/ *n* [C] **1** the point at the end of a bird's or a plane's wing **2** *AmE* a type of man's shoe with a pattern of small holes on the toe

**wink¹** /wɪŋk/ *v* **1** [I,T] to close and open one eye quickly, usually to communicate amusement or a secret message: **[+ at]** *Joel winked at me, and I realized he was joking.* **2** [I] to shine with a light that flashes on and off: *the winking lights of buoys out to sea*

**wink at** sth *phr v* [T] to pretend not to notice something bad or illegal, in a way that suggests you approve of it

wink

**wink²** *n* **1** [C] a quick opening and closing of your eye, usually as a signal between people: *a conspiratorial wink* **2 not get a wink of sleep/not sleep a wink** not be able to sleep at all **3 tip sb the wink** to secretly warn someone about something or give them information **4 quick as a wink** *AmE* very quickly —see also FORTY WINKS, **a nod's as good as a wink** (NOD² (3))

**wink·ers** /ˈwɪŋkəz‖-ərz/ *n* [plural] *BrE informal* the small usually orange lights on a car that flash on the right or left to show that the car is turning; BLINKERS (3) *AmE*

**win·kle¹** /ˈwɪŋkəl/ *n* [C] a small sea animal that lives in a shell and is used for food

**winkle²** *v*

**winkle** sth/sb ↔ **out** *phr v* [T] **1** to make someone leave somewhere: *Government critics were winkled out of their positions of influence.* **2** to discover something such as information: *Candy was very good at winkling out secrets.*

**winkle pick·er** /ˈ·· ˌ··/ *n* [C usually plural] *BrE* a type of man's shoe with very pointed toes, popular in the 1950's

S3 W2 **win·ner** /ˈwɪnə‖-ər/ *n* [C] **1** a person or an animal that has won something: *a Nobel prize winner* | *Sid backed a winner at this year's Derby.* **2** *informal* someone or something that is likely to be very successful: *That idea's a real winner.* | **be onto a winner** (=be selling, producing etc something that is very likely to be successful)

**win·ning** /ˈwɪnɪŋ/ *adj* [only before noun] very pleasant and attractive in a way that makes everyone like you: *a winning smile*

**winning post** /ˈ·· ˌ·/ *n* [singular] *especially BrE* the place where a horse race ends

**win·nings** /ˈwɪnɪŋz/ *n* [plural] money that you win in a game or by betting (BET[1] (1))

**win·now** /ˈwɪnəʊ‖-noʊ/ *v* [T] to blow the CHAFF (=outer part) away from grain

**wi·no** /ˈwaɪnəʊ‖-noʊ/ *n* [C] *informal* someone who drinks a lot of cheap alcohol and lives on the streets: *accosted by winos asking for money*

**win·some** /ˈwɪnsəm/ *adj literary* pleasant and attractive, especially in a simple, direct way: *a winsome smile*

S2 W2 **win·ter¹** /ˈwɪntə‖-ər/ *n* [C,U] the season after autumn and before spring: *the cold Canadian winters* | *the winter of 1942* | **in (the) winter** *It usually snows here in winter.* | **winter coat/shoes etc** (=designed for cold weather)

**winter²** *v* [I always + adv/prep] to spend the winter somewhere: *Swallows winter in Africa or India.*

**win·ter·ize** /ˈwɪntəraɪz/ *v* [T] *AmE* to prepare your car, house etc for winter conditions

**winter sol·stice** /ˌ·· ˈ··/ *n* [singular] the shortest day of the year in the Northern Hemisphere, usually around December 22nd

**winter sports** /ˌ·· ˈ·/ *n* [plural] sports that take place on snow or ice, such as skiing (SKI²)

**win·ter·time** /ˈwɪntətaɪm‖-ər-/ *n* [U] the winter season when the weather is cold

**win·try** /ˈwɪntri/ also **win·ter·y** /ˈwɪntəri/ *adj* like winter, or typical of winter, especially because it is cold: *a wintry night*

S3 **wipe¹** /waɪp/ *v*

**1** ▶ **CLEAN/RUB** ◀ [T] **a)** to rub a surface with a cloth in order to remove dirt, liquid etc: *I wiped the table with a damp cloth.* | **wipe your eyes** (=stop crying or remove tears from your face) **b)** to clean something by rubbing it against a surface: *She wiped her hands on the back of her jeans.*

**2** ▶ **REMOVE DIRT** ◀ [T always + adv/prep] to remove liquid, dirt, or marks by wiping: *Wipe any dirt from round the cap before unscrewing it.* | **wipe sth off/away from** *I'll just wipe all these crumbs off the table.*

**3** ▶ **COMPUTER/TAPE** ◀ [T] to remove all the information that has been stored on a TAPE¹ (1a), VIDEO¹ (1, 2), or computer DISK

**4** ▶ **FORGET** ◀ [T] to try to forget an unhappy or upsetting experience: *I tried to wipe the whole experience from my mind.*

**5 wipe the floor with** *informal* to defeat someone completely in a competition or argument

**6 wipe the slate clean** to agree to forget about mistakes or arguments that happened in the past

**7 wipe the smile/grin off sb's face** *informal* to make someone less pleased or satisfied, especially because they are annoying you: *Tell him how much it'll cost – that should wipe the smile off his face!*

**8 wipe sth off the face of the earth/off the map** to destroy something completely so that it no longer exists: *Another few years and this species could be wiped off the face of the earth.*

**9** ▶ **PLATES/CUPS ETC** ◀ [I,T] *BrE* to dry plates, cups etc that have been washed: *You wash, I'll wipe.*

**wipe** sth ↔ **down** *phr v* [T] to completely clean a surface using a wet cloth

**wipe out** *phr v* **1** [T **wipe** sb/sth ↔ **out**] to destroy, remove, or get rid of something completely: *Half the population was wiped out by plague.* **2** [T **wipe** sb ↔ **out**] *informal* to make you feel extremely tired: *The heat had wiped us out.* —see also WIPED OUT **3** [I] *AmE* to fall or hit another object when driving a car, bicycle etc

**wipe** sth ↔ **up** *phr v* [T] to remove liquid from a surface using a cloth: *I hastily wiped up the milk I had spilled.* —see picture at CLEAN²

**wipe²** *n* [C] **1** a wiping movement with a cloth: *An occasional wipe with a soft cloth will keep the surface shiny.* | **give sth a wipe** *Give the baby's nose a wipe, would you?* **2** a special piece of wet material that you use to clean something and then throw away: *antiseptic wipes*

**wiped out** /ˌ· ˈ·/ *adj* [not before noun] *informal* extremely tired; EXHAUSTED (1)

**wip·er** /ˈwaɪpə‖-ər/ *n* [C] a WINDSCREEN WIPER or WINDSHIELD WIPER

**wire¹** /waɪə‖waɪr/ *n* **1** [U] thin metal in the form of a thread: *String wasn't strong enough, so we used wire.* | *a wire fence* **2** [C] a piece of metal like this, usually covered in plastic, used for taking electricity from one place to another **3 get your wires crossed** to become confused about what someone is saying because you think they are talking about something else **4 right down to the wire** *informal* with very little time left before something must be finished or completed **5** [C] *AmE* a piece of electronic recording equipment, usually worn secretly on someone's clothes **6** [C] *AmE* a TELEGRAM —see also LIVE WIRE, WIRY S3 W3

**wire²** *v* [T] **1** also **wire up** to connect wires to something, especially in an electrical system: *Check that the plug has been wired up properly.* **2** to fasten two or more things together using wire: *The poles had all been wired together.* **3** to send money electronically from one bank to another **4** *AmE* to send a TELEGRAM to someone —see also WIRING

**wire cut·ters** /ˈ· ˌ··/ *n* [plural] a special tool like very strong scissors, used for cutting wire

**wired** /waɪəd‖waɪrd/ *adj* **1** also **wired up** fitted with hidden electronic recording equipment for listening to people's conversations: *Careful what you say – the room could be wired.* **2** *AmE informal* very excited or nervous; TENSE¹ (1) **3** *AmE informal* very active and excited, because you have taken a drug

**wire-haired** /ˌ· ˈ·◂‖ˈ· ·/ *adj* a wire-haired dog has fur that is stiff not soft: *a wire-haired terrier*

**wire·less** /ˈwaɪələs‖ˈwaɪr-/ *n* [C,U] *old-fashioned especially BrE* a radio

**wire net·ting** /ˌ· ˈ··/ *n* [U] wires that have been woven together to form a net, used especially for fences

**wire·tap** /ˈwaɪətæp‖ˈwaɪr-/ *v* [T] to secretly listen to other people's telephone conversations, by fixing something to the wires of their phone —**wiretap** *n* [C] —**wiretapping** *n* [U]

**wire wool** /ˌ· ˈ·/ *n* [U] a mass of very thin pieces of wire, used for cleaning pans

**wir·ing** /ˈwaɪərɪŋ‖ˈwaɪr-/ *n* [singular] **1** the network of wires that form the electrical system in a building: *faulty wiring* | *The wiring needs to be replaced.* **2** a length of wire that is used for making a network for electricity: *copper wiring*

**wir·y** /ˈwaɪəri‖ˈwaɪri/ *adj* **1** someone who is wiry is thin but has strong muscles **2** hair that is wiry is stiff and curly —**wiriness** *n* [U]

**wis·dom** /ˈwɪzdəm/ *n* [U] **1** good sense and judgment, based especially on your experience of life: *a man of great wisdom* | **question the wisdom of** *formal* (=say that you think something is not sensible) *I would question the wisdom of lending him such a large sum of money.* **2** knowledge gained over a long period of time through learning or experience: *the collected wisdom of many centuries* **3 received/conventional wisdom** a belief that is generally thought to be true: *The received wisdom is that boys mature more slowly than girls.* **4 in his/her**

**(infinite) wisdom** used to say jokingly that you do not understand why someone has decided to do something: *The boss, in her infinite wisdom, has decided to reorganize the whole office yet again.*

**wisdom tooth** /'·· ·/ *n* [C] one of the four large teeth at the back of your mouth that do not grow until you are an adult —see picture at TEETH

S3 **wise[1]** /waɪz/ *adj*
**1 ▶DECISION/IDEA ETC◀** wise decisions and judgements are based on good sense and experience; sensible: *I think that would be a wise precaution.* | **be wise to do sth** *I think you were wise to leave when you did.*
**2 ▶PERSON◀** someone who is wise makes good decisions, gives good advice etc, especially because they have a lot of experience of life: *a wise old man* | **older and wiser** (=having learned from the experiences of life) | **wise in the ways of** *formal* (=knowing a lot about something)
**3 get wise to/be wise to** *informal* to realize that someone is being dishonest: *I've got wise to his little tricks now.* —see also **wise up** (WISE[2])
**4 be none the wiser** *informal* to not understand something, even after it has been explained: *Charlie explained how the system works, but I'm still none the wiser.*
**5 no-one will be any the wiser** *spoken* used to say that no-one will find out about something bad someone has done: *Just put it back on the shelf, and no-one will be any the wiser.*
**6 wise guy** *informal especially AmE* an annoying person who thinks they know more than they really do: *OK, wise guy, shut up and listen for a minute!*
**7 act wise** *AmE spoken* to speak or behave in a rude way
**8 be wise after the event** to know how a mistake could have been avoided, after it has been made —see also WISDOM, **sadder but wiser** (SAD (6)), **—wisely** *adv*: *Invest the money wisely.* | *He nodded wisely.*

**wise[2]** *v*
**wise up** *phr v informal* **1** [I] to realize the unpleasant truth about a situation: *Wise up, Vic – he's cheating you!* **2** [T **wise** sb **up (to)**] *especially AmE* to make someone realize the unpleasant truth about a situation

**wise[3]** *n* **1 price-wise/time-wise etc** *especially spoken* concerning or connected with prices etc: *Time-wise we're not doing too badly.* **2 crosswise/lengthwise etc** in a direction across something, along the length of something etc: *Cut the carrots lengthwise.* **3** [singular] *old use* a way or manner: *They are in no wise to blame.* —see also STREETWISE

**wise·a·cre** /'waɪzeɪkə‖-ər/ *n* [C] *informal especially AmE* an annoying person who thinks they know more than they really do

**wise·crack** /'waɪzkræk/ *n* [C] a clever funny remark or reply —**wisecrack** *v* [I]

S1 W1 **wish[1]** /wɪʃ/ *v*
**1 ▶WANT STH IMPOSSIBLE◀** [T] to want something to be true although you know it is either impossible or unlikely: **wish (that)** *I wish I didn't have to go to work today.* | **wish to goodness** *spoken* (=wish very much) *I wish to goodness they'd hurry up!*
**2 ▶WANT TO DO STH◀** [I,T] *formal* to want to do something: **wish to do sth** *I wish to make a complaint.* | **if you wish** *You may leave now, if you wish.* | **(just) as you wish** (=used to tell someone you will do what they want) *"I'd like it ready by six." "Just as you wish, sir."*
**3 ▶HAPPINESS/LUCK ETC◀** [T] to say that you hope someone will have good luck, a happy life etc: **wish sb sth** *We wish you a Merry Christmas and a Happy New Year!* | *Wish me luck!* | **wish sb well** (=hope that good things happen to someone) *They wished me well in my new job.*
**4 I don't wish to interfere/be nosy etc** *spoken* used to show you are sorry if what you are going to say upsets or annoys someone: *I don't wish to seem ungrateful, but it's not quite what I expected.*
**5 I (only) wish I knew** *spoken* used to emphasize that you do not know something, and you wish you did know: *"Where on earth have they gone?" "I wish I knew!"*
**6 I/you wish!** *spoken* used to say that something is not true, but you wish it was: *"Oh no, you're quite thin really." "I wish!"*
**7 wouldn't wish sth on/upon sb** *spoken* used to say that something is very unpleasant: *It's so painful, you wouldn't wish it on your worst enemy, honestly!*

**wish for** sth *phr v* [T] **1 the best/nicest etc that you would wish for** used to emphasize that something is as good, nice etc as it could possibly be: *It was as fine an afternoon as you could wish for.* | *He had everything a child could possibly wish for.* **2** [I] to ask silently for something you want and hope that it will happen: *Her only hope now was to wish for a miracle.*

**wish** sth ↔ **away** *phr v* [T] to want something unpleasant to disappear, without doing anything about it: *You can't just wish your problems away, you know!*

**USAGE NOTE: WISH**

WORD CHOICE: **wish, want**

In sentences where both can be used, **wish** sounds much more formal than **want**. In a conversation you might say: *I want to write to him but I don't know his address.* | *They want us to come to dinner.* But speaking officially you might say: *You may leave if you wish.* You are more likely to see **wish** on official forms and notices.

GRAMMAR

An infinitive after **wish**, **want**, or **hope** must always have *to* with it: *I want/hope to see you soon* (NOT *...want see you...*) | *I wish to speak* (NOT *wish speak*).

**Wish** and **hope**, unlike **want**, are not used with a direct object: *Everybody wants a happy life* (NOT *wishes* or *hopes*, but you could say: *Everybody wishes to have a happy life/hopes for a happy life*).

**Wish** and **hope** (but NOT **want**) are both used with *that* clauses, but the verbs in them usually have to be in different tenses: *I hope (that) you will be happy* (NOT *wish* or *want*). | *I wish (that) you could be happy.* (For the difference in meaning see **hope** WORD CHOICE). These are the main tenses used after **wish**:

If you wish a particular situation existed at this moment, you use the past tense: *I wish I knew/had my own house.* | *He wished it were Tuesday already.* In informal British English it is common to use *was* instead of *were* in sentences like the last, but in American English *was* would be considered incorrect here.

If you wish a situation would exist in the future, you use *could*: *I wish I could have my own house.* (NOT *I wish I'll have my own house* or *I wish I would...* or *I wish if I could...*).

If you wish a situation had existed or something had happened in the past, you use the past perfect: *I wish I had been alive in the twenties.* | *I wish I'd had a chance to talk to you before you left.*

If you wish something would happen at this moment or at some time in the future, you use **would** or **could**: *I wish you could/would come* (*could*=but something is stopping you; *would*=but you don't want to). | *He wished the problem could be solved* (NOT *...problem be solved*). | *I wish you wouldn't go out every night.*

**wish[2]** *n* [C] S3
**1 ▶DESIRE◀** a feeling of wanting to do something, or wanting something to happen: *It's important to respect the wishes of the patient.* | **a wish to do sth** *She had expressed a wish to see the children.*
**2 ▶THING YOU WANT◀** something that you want to have or to happen: *She wanted a new bike for Christmas, and she got her wish.* | *the wishes of the majority* |

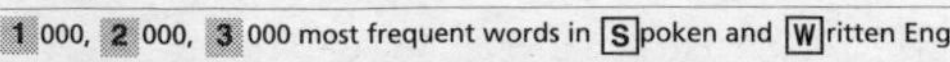

**dearest/greatest wish** (=what you want most of all) *His dearest wish was to become a father.* | **sb's wish is granted/fulfilled** (=they get what they want) | **sb's wish comes true** (=they get what they want, especially in a surprising and unexpected way) | **last wish/dying wish** (=something that you say you want just before you die)
**3 against sb's wishes** if you do something against someone's wishes, you do it even though you know they do not want you to: *She had left school against her mother's wishes.* | **go against sb's wishes** (=do something against their wishes)
**4 have no wish to do sth** *formal* used to emphasize that you do not want or intend to do something: *I have no wish to speak to her ever again.*
**5 best wishes** **a)** used in cards to say that you hope someone will be happy: *best wishes for your married life* **b)** used as a greeting at the end of a letter
**6 ► SILENT REQUEST ◄** a silent request for something to happen as if by magic: **make a wish** *I closed my eyes and made a wish.*
**7 your wish is my command** *especially humorous* used to say that you will do whatever someone asks you to do

**wish·bone** /ˈwɪʃbəʊn‖-boʊn/ *n* [C] the breast bone from a cooked chicken etc, which two people pull apart to decide who will make a wish

**wish·ful think·ing** /ˌ·· ˈ··/ *n* [U] the false belief that something will happen just because you want it to

**wish·ing well** /ˈ·· ·/ *n* [C] a WELL⁴ (1) or pool of water that people throw coins into while making a wish

**wish list** /ˈ· ·/ *n* [C] *informal, especially AmE* all the things that you want in a particular situation

**wish·y-wash·y** /ˈwɪʃi ˌwɒʃi‖-ˌwɔːʃi, -ˌwɑːʃi/ *adj informal* **1** a wishy-washy person does not have firm or clear ideas and seems unable to decide what they want: *a bunch of wishy-washy liberals* **2** colours that are wishy-washy are pale, not strong or dark

**wisp** /wɪsp/ *n* [C] **1 wisp of hair/hay/grass etc** a thin piece of hair etc that is separate from the rest: *A wisp of hair had escaped from under her hat.* —see picture on page 416 **2 wisp of smoke/cloud etc** a small thin line of smoke etc that rises upwards —see also WILL O' THE WISP —**wispy** *adj*

**wis·te·ri·a** /wɪˈstɪəriə‖-ˈstɪr-/ *n* [C,U] a climbing plant with purple or white flowers

**wist·ful** /ˈwɪstfəl/ *adj* feeling rather sad and thoughtful, especially because of something that you would like but can no longer have: *wistful memories of her lost youth* —**wistfully** *adv* —**wistfulness** *n* [U]

**wit** /wɪt/ *n*
**1 ► AMUSING ◄** [U] the ability to say things that are clever and amusing: *a woman of great wit and charm* | **quick/dry/sharp wit** *His sharp wit had them all smiling.*

**2 ► AMUSING PERSON ◄** [C] someone who is able to say clever and funny things: *Oscar Wilde was a famous wit.*
**3 wits** [plural] your ability to think quickly and make the right decisions: *It was a tricky situation – I had to use all my wits to extricate myself.* | **keep/have your wits about you** (=be ready to think quickly and do what is necessary in a difficult situation)
**4 have the wit to do sth** to be clever enough to know the right thing to do
**5 frighten/scare sb out of their wits** *informal* to frighten someone very much
**6 at your wits' end** very worried, because you have tried everything possible to solve a problem
**7 not beyond the wit of** *often humorous* not too difficult for someone to do: *It's surely not beyond the wit of man to come up with a solution.*
**8 to wit** *old use* that is to say; NAMELY —see also **battle of wits** (BATTLE¹ (5)), HALF-WIT, **live by your wits** (LIVE¹ (9)), OUTWIT, QUICK-WITTED, WITTY —**witless** *adj*

**witch** /wɪtʃ/ *n* [C] **1** a woman who is supposed to have magic powers, especially to do bad things **2** *informal* an insulting word for an old or unpleasant woman —see also BEWITCH

**witch·craft** /ˈwɪtʃkrɑːft‖-kræft/ *n* [U] the use of magic to make things happen

**witch-doc·tor** /ˈ· ˌ··/ *n* [C] a man who is believed to have magic powers and the ability to cure people of diseases, especially in some parts of Africa

**witch-ha·zel** /ˈ· ˌ··/ *n* [C,U] a substance used for treating small wounds on the skin, or the tree that produces it

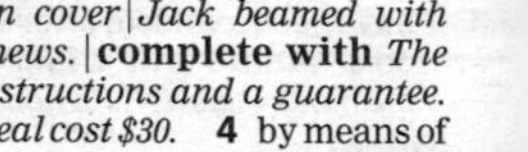

**witch-hunt** /ˈ· ·/ *n* [C] a deliberate attempt, often based on false information, to find and punish people in a society or organization whose opinions are regarded as wrong or dangerous: *McCarthy's Communist witch-hunts*

**witch·ing hour** /ˈ·· ˌ·/ *n* [singular] *literary* the time, especially in the middle of the night, when strange or magic things are believed to happen

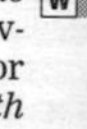

**with** /wɪð, wɪθ/ *prep* **1** near someone or something, or in someone's presence: *I saw Bob in town with his girlfriend.* | *Mix the powder with boiling water.* **2** having, possessing, or showing a particular thing, quality or feeling: *a book with a green cover* | *Jack beamed with pleasure when he heard the news.* | **complete with** *The mixer comes complete with instructions and a guarantee.* **3** including: *With a tip, the meal cost $30.* **4** by means of something or using it: *Eat your melon with a knife and fork.* | *What will you buy with the money?* **5** used to show the idea of filling, covering, or containing something: *Her boots were covered with mud.* | *Fill the bowl with sugar.* **6** concerning, or in the case of: *Be careful with that glass.* | *Britain's trade with Japan* | *He's in love with you.* **7** supporting or liking someone or something: *Some opposition MPs voted with the Government.* | *You're either with me or against me.* **8** against or opposing someone: *Stop fighting with your brother!* | *We're competing with foreign businesses.* **9** in the same direction as someone or something: *We sailed with the wind.* **10** at the same time or rate as something else: *This wine improves with age.* **11** used when comparing two things or considering the relationship between them: *Compared with other children of the same age, Robert's very tall.* **12** used in some expressions to show that one person or thing separates from another: *Joan doesn't want to part with the money.* | *a complete break with tradition* **13** in spite of: *With all his faults, I still like him.* **14** because of or considering the fact of: *They were trembling with fear.* | *With John away there's more room in the house.* **15** used to express a strong wish or command: *Down with school!* | *Off to bed with you!* **16 with it** *informal* **a)** dressing in fashionable clothes and knowing about new ideas: *I can't get over how with it your mother is.* **b)** lively and able to understand things: *I'm sorry I'm not feeling very with it today.* —see also WITH-IT **17 with you** *informal* **a)** understanding someone's explanation about something: *I'm sorry, I'm not really with you; could you repeat what you just said.* **b)** supporting someone by agreeing with what they say or do: *I'm with Harry all the way on this one.* **18 with that** *also* **at that** used to say that something happens immediately after something else: *He gave a little wave and with that he was gone.*

**with·al** /wɪðˈɔːl‖-ˈɒːl/ *adv old use* besides; together with this

**with·draw** /wɪðˈdrɔː, wɪθ-‖-ˈdrɒː/ *v past tense* **withdrew** /-ˈdruː/ *past participle* **withdrawn** /-ˈdrɔːn‖-ˈdrɒːn/ W2
**1 ► MONEY ◄** [T] to take money out of a bank

account: **withdraw sth from** *Liz withdrew $100 from her account.*
**2 ▶ TAKE AWAY ◀** [T] to remove something or take it away or take it back, often because of an official decision: *a government decision to withdraw funding* | *One of the minority parties had withdrawn its support for Chancellor Kohl.* | **withdraw sth from** *She withdrew a document from her briefcase.* | **withdraw sth from sale/from the market** (=stop selling it) *The drug has been withdrawn from the market for further tests.*
**3 withdraw a remark/accusation** to say that a remark that you made earlier was completely untrue; RETRACT: *The newspaper has agreed to withdraw its allegations.*
**4 ▶ NOT TAKE PART ◀ a)** [I] to no longer take part in or belong to an organization: [+ **from**] *Calls for Britain to withdraw from the European Union.* **b)** [I,T] to no longer take part in an activity, race etc, or to prevent someone from doing this: [+ **from**] *Injury forced Clare to withdraw from the event.* | **withdraw sth/sb from** *Ted withdrew his horse from the race.*
**5 ▶ LEAVE ◀ a)** [I] to leave a place, especially in order to be alone or go somewhere quiet: *We withdrew to the garden for a private talk.* **b)** [I,T] if an army withdraws or is withdrawn, it leaves a place, especially in order to avoid defeat
**6 ▶ STOP COMMUNICATING ◀** [I] to become quieter, less friendly, and more concerned about your own thoughts: [+ **into/from**] *The little girl seemed to withdraw into a private world.*

W3 **with·draw·al** /wɪð'drɔːəl, wɪθ-‖-'drɒːəl/ *n*
**1 ▶ MONEY ◀** [C,U] the act of taking money from a bank account, or the amount you take out
**2 ▶ ARMY ◀** [C,U] the act of moving an army, weapons etc away from the area where they were fighting: [+ **of/from**] *the withdrawal of all UN forces from the region*
**3 ▶ REMOVAL/ENDING ◀** [U] the removal or stopping of something such as support, an offer, or a service: [+ **of**] *withdrawal of government aid*
**4 ▶ STOP TAKING PART ◀** [U] the act of no longer taking part in an activity or being a member of an organization: [+ **from**] *Germany's withdrawal from the talks*
**5 ▶ DRUGS ◀** [U] the period after you have given up a drug that you were dependent on, and the mental and physical effects that this process involves: **withdrawal symptoms** (=the painful or unpleasant effects caused by withdrawal)
**6 ▶ STATEMENT ◀** [U] the act of saying that something you previously said was in fact untrue: [+ **of**] *the withdrawal of all allegations*

**with·drawn** /wɪð'drɔːn, wɪθ-‖-drɒːn/ *adj* very shy and quiet, and concerned only about your own thoughts

**with·er** /'wɪðə‖-ər/ *v* also **wither away** [I,T] if plants wither they become drier and smaller and start to die

**with·ered** /'wɪdəd‖-ərd/ *adj* **1** a withered plant has become drier and smaller and is dead or dying **2** a withered person looks thin and weak and old **3** a withered arm or leg has not developed properly and is thin and weak

**with·er·ing** /'wɪðərɪŋ/ *adj* **a withering look/remark etc** a look, remark etc that makes someone feel stupid, embarrassed, or lose confidence: *She gave him a withering glance.* —**witheringly** *adv*

**with·ers** /'wɪðəz‖-ərz/ *n* [plural] the highest part of a horse's back, above its shoulders —see picture at HORSE[1]

**with·hold** /wɪð'həʊld, wɪθ-‖-'hoʊld/ *v past tense and past participle* **withheld** /-'held/ [T] **1** to refuse to let someone have something, especially until something else is done: *I withheld payment until they had completed the work.* **2 withhold facts/evidence/information** to refuse to give information: *Ian was accused of withholding vital information from the police.*

**with·hold·ing tax** /·'·· ,·/ *n* [C,U] *AmE* money that is taken out of your wages as tax

**with·in** /wɪð'ɪn‖wɪð'ɪn, wɪθ'ɪn/ *adv, prep* **1 a)** before a certain period of time has passed: *Ray left suddenly promising to be back within the hour.* **b)** during a certain period of time: *Her car has been broken into three times within a month.* | **within the space of...** *Within the space of a year three of the town's biggest factories have closed down.* **2** inside a certain area and not beyond it: *Children must remain within the school grounds during the lunch break.* | **within 20 metres/50 kilometres/10 miles of etc** (=less than twenty metres, fifty kilometres etc from a particular place) *We are now within two kilometres of the centre of Istanbul.* | **apply/enquire within** (=used on notices and advertisements especially when someone is trying to sell something) *Baby rabbits for sale. Enquire within.* **3** inside a society, organization, or group of people: *There have been a lot of changes within the department since I joined.* | **from within** *an attempt to reform the system from within* **4** according to particular limits or rules: *We have to operate within a very tight budget.* | *This clause is no longer valid within the terms of the new settlement.* **5 within sight/earshot etc** if something is within sight, earshot etc you can see or hear it **6 within reach a)** near, so that people can get there without difficulty: *We live within easy reach of the shops.* **b)** near enough to be picked up or touched when you stretch out your hand: *The key was hanging from a hook on the wall, just within my reach.* **7 a play within a play/a university within a university etc** a small place, thing etc which exists inside a bigger place or thing of the same kind

**with-it** /'· ·/ *adj old-fashioned* fashionable and modern in the way that you dress, think etc —see also **with it** (WITH)

**with·out** /wɪð'aʊt‖wɪð'aʊt, wɪθ'aʊt/ *adv, prep* **1** lacking something, especially something that is basic or necessary: *We had to survive without light or heating for a whole month.* | **can't do without** (=unable to live or work without something) *We can't do without hot water for too long.* **2** not doing or having something, or not showing a particular feeling, especially when it is considered normal or polite: *He had gone out without his parents' permission.* | **without doing** *How dare you do such a thing without consulting me?* | **without so much as...** (=used to say that someone does not do something that they should do) *Without so much as a word of thanks Bowen turned and went back into the office.* **3** not being with someone, or not having them to help you, especially someone you like or need: *She found it hard to face up to the prospect of life without Ken.* **4** if something happens without something unpleasant happening, it happens in a way that is pleasant or easy: *I managed to get through the exam without too much trouble.* **5 without wanting to/without wishing to** used before a criticism, complaint, or other statement to make it less definite: *Without wanting to sound too boastful, I think we have the best television programmes in the world.* **6** *old use* outside S1 W1

**with·stand** /wɪð'stænd, wɪθ-/ *v past tense and past participle* **withstood** /-'stʊd/ [T] **1** to be strong enough to remain unharmed by something such as great heat or cold, great pressure etc: *a type of desert bush that can withstand extremes of temperature* | **withstand the test of time** (=still be important, effective etc after a long time) *theories that have withstood the test of time* **2** to defend yourself against attack, and successfully oppose someone or something: *withstanding a heroic doomed attack by six allied divisions*

**wit·less** /'wɪtləs/ *adj* **1** not very intelligent or sensible; silly: *if I catch the witless yobs who did this* **2 scare sb witless** to make someone very frightened —**witlessly** *adv* —**witlessness** *n* [U]

**wit·ness**[1] /'wɪtnɪ̥s/ *n* **1** [C] someone who sees a crime or an accident and can describe what happened: *Police have appealed for witnesses to come forward.* **2** [C] S2 W3

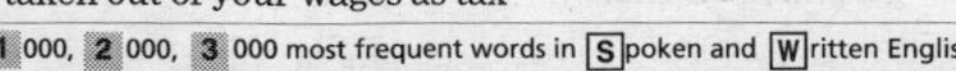

someone in a court of law who tells what they saw or what they know about a crime: *One witness claimed to have seen the gun.* **3 bear witness** *formal* to show or prove that something is true or that something happened in the past: *The temples and theatres all bear witness to the city's former greatness.* **4** [C] someone who is present when an official paper is signed and who signs it to prove this: **witness to** *a witness to a will* **5 be witness to** *formal* to be present when something happens, and watch it happening: *We were witness to the worst excesses of the military.* **6** [C,U] *AmE* a public statement of strong Christian belief, or someone who makes such a statement

**witness²** *v* **1** [T] to see something happen, especially a crime or accident, because you are present when it happens: *Police are appealing to any driver who may have witnessed the accident.* **2** [T] **a)** to experience important events or changes because you are there when they are happening: *We are now witnessing the break-up of the Soviet empire.* **b)** if a time or place witnesses an event, the event happens during that time or in that place: *The 1980s witnessed increasing unemployment throughout Europe.* **3** [T] to be present when someone signs an official document, and sign it yourself to show this: *Will you witness my signature?* **4** [T] **a)** to be a sign or proof of something: *the rise in crime, as witnessed by our overcrowded prisons* **b)** used to give an example that proves something you have just mentioned: *Poor school grades don't prove much – witness Dana's amazing success in business.* **5** [I] *AmE* to speak publicly about your strong Christian beliefs

**witness to** sth *phr v* [T] to formally state that something is true or happened: *Her principal was called to witness to her good character.* | **witness to doing sth** *The driver witnessed to having seen the man enter the building.*

**witness box** *BrE*, **witness stand** *AmE* /ˈ· · ·/ *n* [C] the place in a court of law where a witness stands to answer questions

**wit·ter** /ˈwɪtə‖-ər/ also **witter on** *v* [I] *informal* to talk a lot in a boring way or about something unimportant: [+ **about**] *I'm sick of her wittering on about New Men.*

**wit·ti·cis·m** /ˈwɪtɪsɪzəm/ *n* [C] a clever amusing remark

**wit·ty** /ˈwɪti/ *adj* using words in a clever and amusing way: *a witty speaker* | *witty remarks* —**wittily** *adv* —**wittiness** *n* [U]

**wives** /waɪvz/ the plural of WIFE

**wiz·ard** /ˈwɪzəd‖-ərd/ *n* [C] **1** a man who is supposed to have magic powers **2** someone who is very good at something: *a financial wizard* | [+ **at**] *Ben's a real wizard at chess.*

**wiz·ard·ry** /ˈwɪzədri‖-ər-/ *n* [U] impressive ability at something or an impressive achievement: *The best thing about the movie is the sheer wizardry of the special effects.*

**wiz·ened** /ˈwɪzənd/ *adj* a wizened person, fruit etc is small and thin and has skin with a lot of lines and WRINKLES: *wizened old Frenchmen playing boules in the square*

**wk** the written abbreviation of WEEK

**woad** /wəʊd‖woʊd/ *n* [U] a blue DYE (=colouring substance) used in ancient times to colour people's bodies

**wob·ble** /ˈwɒbəl‖ˈwɑː-/ *v* **1** [I,T] to move unsteadily from side to side, or make something do this: *The pile of bricks wobbled and fell.* | *His fat thighs wobbled as he ran along.* | **wobble sth** *Stop wobbling the table with your foot.* **2** [I always + adv/prep] to go in a particular direction while moving unsteadily from side to side: [+ **off/along/across etc**] *Cindy wobbled along the street on her bike.* **3** *AmE* to be unsure whether to do something: *The President appeared to wobble over sending the troops in.* —**wobble** *n* [C]

**wob·bly¹** /ˈwɒbli‖ˈwɑː-/ *adj* **1** moving unsteadily from side to side: *a wobbly table* **2** *informal* feeling weak and unable to keep your balance: *I've gone all wobbly – I think I'll sit down.* **3** a wobbly voice is weak and shakes, especially when you feel frightened or upset

**wobbly²** *n* [C] *BrE informal* **throw a wobbly** to suddenly become very angry or frightened

**wodge** /wɒdʒ‖wɑːdʒ/ *n* [C] *BrE informal* a thick, solid piece or large amount of something: *a wodge of ten pound notes*

**woe** /wəʊ‖woʊ/ *n* **1** *literary* [U] great sadness: *a tale of woe* **2 woes** [plural] *formal* the problems and troubles affecting someone: *They tend to blame all of Africa's woes on colonialism.* **3 woe betide** *especially humorous* used to warn someone that there will be trouble if they do something: *Woe betide anyone who smokes in our house!*

**woe·be·gone** /ˈwəʊbɪgɒn‖ˈwoʊbɪgɒːn, -gɑːn/ *adj especially literary* looking very sad: *Her woebegone expression made him feel protective.*

**woe·ful** /ˈwəʊfəl‖ˈwoʊ-/ *adj* **1** very bad or serious; DEPLORABLE: *a woeful lack of information* **2** *literary* very sad; PATHETIC: *The little girl looked up at him with woeful eyes.* —**woefully** *adv*: *woefully inadequate facilities*

**wog** /wɒg‖wɑːg/ *n* [C] *BrE taboo* a very offensive word for a black person

**wok** /wɒk‖wɑːk/ *n* [C] a wide pan shaped like a bowl, used in Chinese cooking —see picture at PAN¹

**woke** /wəʊk‖woʊk/ the past tense of WAKE¹

**wok·en** /ˈwəʊkən‖ˈwoʊ-/ the past participle of WAKE¹

**wolds** /wəʊldz‖woʊldz/ *n* [plural] *BrE* a word for an area of hilly countryside, especially used in the names of places: *the Yorkshire Wolds*

**wolf¹** /wʊlf/ *n plural* **wolves** /wʊlvz/ [C] **1** a wild animal that looks like a large dog and lives and hunts in groups: *a pack of wolves* **2 a wolf in sheep's clothing** someone who seems to be friendly but is in fact, unpleasant etc **3 cry wolf** to keep asking for help that you do not really need, with the result that when you do need help people do not believe you: *Jurgen's cried wolf one too many times. I'm sick of it!* **4 keep the wolf from the door** to earn just enough money to buy the basic things you need: *Between us, we earn just enough to keep the wolf from the door.* —see also LONE WOLF —**wolfish** *adj*: *a wolfish grin*

**wolf²** also **wolf down** *v* [T] *informal* to eat something very quickly, swallowing it in big pieces

**wolf·hound** /ˈwʊlfhaʊnd/ *n* [C] an extremely large dog

**wol·fram** /ˈwʊlfrəm/ *n* [U] TUNGSTEN

**wolf whis·tle** /ˈ· ˌ··/ *n* [C] a way of whistling that men sometimes use to show that they think a woman is attractive —**wolf-whistle** *v* [I]

**wolves** /wʊlvz/ the plural of WOLF

**wom·an** /ˈwʊmən/ *n plural* **women** /ˈwɪmɪn/ S W
**1** ▶ **FEMALE** ◀ [C] an adult female person: *I was talking to a woman I met on the flight.* | *married women* | **a woman priest/driver etc** *How long will it be until we have a woman President?* | **women's clothes/organization etc** *Kate works for a popular women's magazine.* —see MAN¹ (USAGE)
**2** ▶ **FORM OF ADDRESS** ◀ *spoken* a rude way of addressing a woman when you are angry, annoyed etc: *Pull yourself together, woman!*
**3 another woman/the other woman** *informal* a woman that a man is having a sexual relationship with, even though he is married to someone else: *I'm sure he's got another woman.*

**4 ▶ GENERAL TERM ◀** [singular] *formal* women in general: *A woman's work is never done.*

**5 ▶ PARTNER ◀** also **the old woman** [singular] *spoken* expressions meaning your girlfriend or wife, which many women find offensive: *Did he bring his woman with him?*

**6 businesswoman/spokeswoman etc** a woman who has a particular kind of job: *a spokeswoman for the charity*

**7 be your own woman** to make your own decisions and be in charge of your own life, without depending on anyone else

**8 woman of easy virtue/woman of the night** *old-fashioned* a PROSTITUTE[1] (1)

**9 ▶ SERVANT ◀** [C] a female servant or person who does works for you in your house —see also OLD WOMAN **make an honest woman of** (HONEST (8)), **man/woman of the world** (WORLD[1] (26)), **wine, women and song** (WINE[1] (3))

**wom·an·hood** /ˈwʊmənhʊd/ *n* [U] **1** the state of being a woman, not a man or a girl **2** *formal* women in general —compare MANHOOD

**wom·an·ish** /ˈwʊmənɪʃ/ *adj* a womanish man looks or behaves in a way that is supposed to be typical of women

**wom·an·izer** also **iser** *BrE* /ˈwʊmənaɪzə‖-ər/ *n* [C] a man who has sexual relationships with many different women —**womanize** *v* [I] —**womanizing** *n* [U]

**wom·an·kind** /ˈwʊmənkaɪnd/ *n* [U] women considered together as a group —compare MANKIND

**wom·an·ly** /ˈwʊmənli/ *adj approving* behaving, dressing etc in a way that is thought to be typical of or suitable for a woman: *her soft womanly curves* —**womanliness** *n* [U]

**womb** /wuːm/ *n* [C] the part of a female's body where her baby grows before it is born

**wom·bat** /ˈwɒmbæt‖ˈwɑːm-/ *n* [C] an Australian animal like a small bear whose babies live in a pocket of skin on its body

**wom·en** /ˈwɪmɪn/ the plural of WOMAN

**wom·en·folk** /ˈwɪmɪnfəʊk‖-foʊk/ *n* [plural] all the women in a particular family or society

**wom·en's lib** /ˌ·· ˈ·/ also **women's lib·e·ra·tion** /ˌ·· ··ˈ··/ *n* [U] *old-fashioned* all the ideas, actions, and politics connected with giving women the same rights and opportunities as men —**women's libber** *n* [C]

**women's move·ment** /ˈ·· ˌ··/ *n* **the women's movement** all the women who are involved in the aim of improving the social, economic, and political position of women and of ending sexual DISCRIMINATION (1)

**women's re·fuge** /ˌ·· ˈ··/ *n* [C] a special place where women and their children can go to escape being physically hurt by their husband, partner etc

**women's room** /ˈ·· ·/ *n* [C] *especially AmE* a public TOILET (2) for women

**won** /wʌn/ the past tense and past participle of WIN[1]

S1 W2 **won·der[1]** /ˈwʌndə‖-ər/ *v* [I,T] **1** to think about something that you are not sure about and try to guess what is true, what will happen etc: **wonder who/what/how etc** *I wonder how James is getting on.* | *What are they going to do now, I wonder?* | **wonder if/whether/why** *I wonder if I'll recognize Philip after all these years.* | **it makes you wonder** *especially spoken*: *Patrick's reaction made me wonder if he knew more than he'd told me.* **2 I wonder if/whether** *spoken* used to ask politely for something: *I wonder if I might have a glass of water?* **3 I was wondering if/whether a)** *spoken* used to politely ask someone to help you: *I was wondering if I could borrow your car?* **b)** used to ask someone politely if they would like to do something: *I was wondering if you'd like to come to dinner.* **4** [I,T] to feel surprised and unable to believe something: [+ **about/at**] *Sometimes I wonder about his behaviour.* | [+ **how**] *I wonder how he dares to show his face after last night!* | **I don't wonder** *BrE spoken* (=I am not surprised) *I don't wonder you're tired after the day you've had.* | **I shouldn't wonder** *BrE spoken* (=I would not be surprised about something) *He'll come back soon enough, I shouldn't wonder.* **5** [I,T] to doubt or question whether something is true: *"Is she serious?" "I wonder."* | **wonder if/whether** *Ken says such stupid things that I wonder if he's got any sense at all!*

**wonder[2]** *n*

**1 ▶ ADMIRATION ◀ a)** [U] a feeling of surprise and admiration for something very beautiful or new to you: *The sight of the Taj Mahal filled us with wonder.* **b)** [C] something that makes you feel surprise and admiration: *technological wonders* | *the Seven Wonders of the World*

**2 (it's) no wonder/small wonder/little wonder** *especially spoken* used to say that you are not surprised by something: *No wonder you've got a headache, the amount you drank last night.*

**3 ▶ SURPRISING ◀ it's a wonder (that)** *especially spoken* used to say that something is very surprising: *It's a wonder Louise remembered to come, she's so scatty.*

**4 do/work wonders** to be very effective in solving a problem

**5 ▶ CLEVER PERSON ◀** [singular] *BrE* someone who is clever at doing difficult things: *Philip's a wonder, the way he manages on his own.*

**6 wonders will never cease!** *spoken humorous* used to show you are surprised and pleased about something —see also **chinless wonder** (CHINLESS (3)), **nine days wonder** (NINE (3))

**wonder[3]** *adj* [only before noun] very good and effective: *a new wonder drug*

**won·der·ful** /ˈwʌndəfəl‖-dər-/ *adj* **1** making you feel very happy: *We had a wonderful time in Spain.* S1 W2
**2** making you admire someone or something very much: *It's wonderful what doctors can do nowadays.* —**wonderfully** *adv*

**won·der·ingly** /ˈwʌndərɪŋli/ *adv* in a way that shows admiration, surprise, and pleasure

**won·der·land** /ˈwʌndəlænd‖-ər-/ *n* [U] an imaginary place in stories

**won·der·ment** /ˈwʌndəmənt‖-dər-/ *n* [U] *literary* a feeling of pleasant surprise or admiration

**won·drous** /ˈwʌndrəs/ *adj poetical* good or impressive in a surprising way

**won·ga** /ˈwɒŋgə‖ˈwɑːŋ-/ *n* [U] *BrE slang* money

**wonk** /wɒŋk‖wɑːŋk/ *n* [C] *AmE informal* someone who works hard and is very serious: *policy wonks surrounding the President*

**won·ky** /ˈwɒŋki‖ˈwɑːŋki/ *adj BrE informal* unsteady or not straight or level: *a wonky table*

**won't** /wəʊnt‖woʊnt/ the short form of 'will not'

**wont[1]** /wəʊnt‖wɒːnt/ *n old-fashioned* **as is sb's wont** used to say that it is someone's habit to do something: *He spoke for too long, as is his wont.*

**wont[2]** *adj formal* **be wont to do sth** to be likely to do something

**wont·ed** /ˈwəʊntɪd‖ˈwɒːn-/ *adj* [only before noun] *old-fashioned* usual

**woo** /wuː/ *v* [T] **1** to try to persuade someone to buy something from you, vote for you etc: *The politicians will be wooing the voters before the election.* **2** *old-fashioned* to try to persuade a woman to love you and marry you —**wooer** *n* [C]

**wood** /wʊd/ *n* **1** [C,U] the material that trees are made of: *Put some more wood on the fire.* | *a polished wood floor* | S2 W2
**soft/hard wood** *Pine is a soft wood.* **2** [C] also **the woods** a small forest: *a walk in the woods.* **3** [C] one of a set of four GOLF CLUBS with wooden heads **4 not be out of the wood(s) yet** *informal* used to say that there are likely to be more difficulties before things improve: *It's been going well lately, but we're not totally out of the woods yet.* **5 not see the wood for the trees** to not notice what is important about something because you give too much of your attention to small details —see also **dead wood** (DEAD[1] (30))

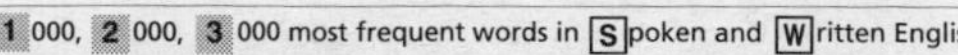

**wood·bine** /ˈwʊdbaɪn/ *n* [U] **1** *poetical* HONEYSUCKLE **2** *AmE* VIRGINIA CREEPER

**wood·block** /ˈwʊdblɒk‖-blɑːk/ *n* [C] **1** a piece of wood with a shape cut on it, used for printing **2** a block of wood used in making a floor

**wood·carv·ing** /ˈwʊdkɑːvɪŋ‖-kɑːr-/ *n* [C,U] the process of shaping wood with special tools, or a piece of art produced in this way

**wood·chuck** /ˈwʊdtʃʌk/ *n* [C] a GROUNDHOG

**wood·cock** /ˈwʊdkɒk‖-kɑːk/ *n* [C] a brown bird that lives in woods

**wood·craft** /ˈwʊdkrɑːft‖-kræft/ *n* [U] the practical knowledge of woods and forests

**wood·cut** /ˈwʊdkʌt/ *n* [C] **1** a picture that you make by pressing a shaped piece of wood and a colouring substance onto paper **2** a WOODBLOCK (1)

**wood·cut·ter** /ˈwʊdˌkʌtə‖-ər/ *n* [C] someone whose job is to cut down trees in a forest

**wood·ed** /ˈwʊdɪ̠d/ *adj* having woods or covered with trees: *densely wooded hills*

S3 W3 **wood·en** /ˈwʊdn/ *adj* **1** made of wood: *a wooden bench* **2** not showing enough expression, emotion, or movement, especially when performing in public: *a rather wooden performance* —**woodenly** *adv* —**woodenness** *n* [U]

**wooden-head·ed** /ˌ·· ˈ··◂/ *adj informal* stupid and slow to understand things

**wooden spoon** /ˌ·· ˈ·/ *n* [C] a large wooden spoon used in cooking —see picture at SPOON[1]

**wood·land** /ˈwʊdlənd, -lænd/ also **woodlands** *plural n* [U] an area of land covered with trees

**wood·louse** /ˈwʊdlaʊs/ *n plural* **woodlice** /-laɪs/ [C] a small grey insect that lives under wood, stones etc

**wood·peck·er** /ˈwʊdˌpekə‖-ər/ *n* [C] a bird with a long beak that it uses to make holes in trees

**wood·pile** /ˈwʊdpaɪl/ *n* [C] a pile of firewood

**wood pulp** /ˈ· ·/ *n* [U] wood crushed into a soft mass, used for making paper

**wood·shed** /ˈwʊdʃed/ *n* [C] a place for storing wood for burning

**woods·man** /ˈwʊdzmən/ *n plural* **woodsmen** /-mən/ [C] someone who works in a forest cutting down trees etc

**wood·sy** /ˈwʊdzi/ *n AmE informal* connected with the woods: *a woodsy smell*

**wood·wind** /ˈwʊdˌwɪnd/ also **the woodwind** *n* [C,U] the group of musical instruments that you play by blowing and pressing keys (KEY[1] (3)) —**woodwind** *adj*

**wood·work** /ˈwʊdwɜːk‖-wɜːrk/ *n* [U] **1** *BrE*, **wood·work·ing** /ˈwʊdwɜːkɪŋ‖-ɜːr-/ *AmE* the skill or activity of making wooden objects **2** the parts of a house or room that are made of wood: *The woodwork needs painting.* **3 crawl/come out of the woodwork** if people you don't like crawl out of the woodwork, there suddenly seems to be a lot of them: *When they heard about the funeral, suddenly all our weird relatives came crawling out of the woodwork.*

**wood·worm** /ˈwʊdwɜːm‖-wɜːrm/ *n* [C] **1** a small insect that makes holes in wood **2** [U] the damage that is caused to wood by this creature

**wood·y** /ˈwʊdi/ *adj* **1** a plant that is woody has a stem like wood **2** a woody area of land has a lot of trees growing on it

**woof**[1] /wʊf/ *interjection* a word used for describing the sound a dog makes —**woof** *v* [I] *informal*

**woof**[2] /wuːf‖wʊf, wuːf/ *n* [C] WEFT

**woof·er** /ˈwuːfə‖ˈwʊfər/ *n* [C] a LOUDSPEAKER (1) that produces deep sounds —compare TWEETER

**woof·ter** /ˈwʊftə‖-ər/ *n* [C] *BrE slang* an offensive word for a man who speaks or behaves in a way that is considered typical of HOMOSEXUALS

**wool** /wʊl/ *n* [U] **1** the soft thick hair that sheep and some goats have on their body **2** material made from wool: *Is this coat wool?* | **wool jacket/carpet/blanket etc** *a pure wool skirt* **3** thread made from wool that you use for knitting (KNIT[1] (1)) clothes **4 pull the wool over sb's eyes** to deceive someone by not telling the truth —see also COTTON WOOL, DYED-IN-THE-WOOL, WIRE WOOL

**wool·len** *BrE*, **woolen** *AmE* /ˈwʊlən/ *adj* [only before noun] made of wool —see picture on page 839

**wool·lens** *BrE*, **woolens** *AmE* /ˈwʊlənz/ *n* [plural] clothes made from wool, especially wool that has been knitted (KNIT[1] (1)) —see also WOOLLY[2]

**wool·ly**[1] *BrE*, **wooly** *AmE* /ˈwʊli/ *adj* **1** made of or feeling like wool: *a woolly hat* **2** not showing clear thinking: *a woolly argument.* —**wooliness** *n* [U]

**woolly**[2] *n* [C usually plural] *BrE* a piece of clothing made of wool, especially wool that has been knitted (KNIT[1] (1)): *winter woollies*

**woolly-head·ed** /ˌ·· ˈ··◂/ *adj* not able to think clearly

**woo·zy** /ˈwuːzi/ *adj informal* feeling weak and unsteady; DIZZY (1)

**wop** /wɒp‖wɑːp/ *n* [C] a very offensive word for someone who is Italian

S W

## word[1] /wɜːd‖wɜːrd/ *n*

① LANGUAGE/STH YOU SAY OR WRITE
② TALK/DISCUSSION
③ INFORMATION/NEWS
④ ORDER/DECISION
⑤ PROMISE
⑥ OTHER MEANINGS

### ① LANGUAGE/STH YOU SAY OR WRITE

**1** [C] the smallest unit of language that people can understand if it is said or written on its own: *Write an essay of about five hundred words.* | *There were a lot of words in the film I couldn't understand.* | *It's not a word I often use.* | *I know the tune, but not the words.* | **a word for** (=a word that means) *"Casa" is the Italian word for house.* | **sb's words** (=what someone says) *Those are the editor's words, not mine.* | **in your own words** *Tell us exactly what happened in your own words.*

**2 not believe/hear/understand a word** to not believe etc what someone says or writes: *He says he played in a jazz group, but I don't beleive a word of it.* | *Stuart didn't understand a word of that stuff on genetics either.* | *Can you speak up, we can't hear a word.*

**3 put your feelings into words** to express what you want to say clearly: *I'm not very good at putting my feelings into words, but I'll try to explain.*

**4 find the words** to choose the words that express your feelings or ideas clearly: *She only wished she could find the words to express her affection for the old man.*

### ② TALK/DISCUSSION

**5 have a word (with)** *especially spoken* to talk to someone quickly, especially because you need their advice about something or you want to tell them to do

something: *Could I have a word with you after the meeting.*|**have/exchange a few words** (=have a short conversation)|**have a quick/brief word (with)** (=have a short conversation) *We managed to have a quick word before the others arrived.*
**6 want a (little) word** *spoken* to want to speak to someone, especially in order to criticize or warn them: *The boss wants a little word with you.*
**7 a word/a few words** a short talk for a particular purpose: **a word of advice/warning/encouragement etc** *Could you give the boys a few words of encouragement?*
**8 not say/breathe a word** to not say anything about something to anyone because it is a secret: *Don't say a word about the party to Dad.*
**9 have/drop a word in sb's ear** to say something to someone privately especially in order to arrange something that would otherwise have been difficult: *Don't worry – I've dropped a word in his ear – everything's settled.*
**10 have/exchange words (with)** an expression meaning to quarrel, used to avoid saying this directly: *I saw Gwen after the meeting. We had words.*

### ③ INFORMATION/NEWS
**11** [singular, U] a piece of news or a message: **word gets out/around** (=people hear about something) *If word of the Royal visit gets out, we'll have the press here in force.*|**The word is (that)/word has it (that)** (=people are saying that) *The word is that Ben is leaving after Christmas.*|**no word from** *There's been no word from Susan since July.*|**send/bring word** (=send or bring a message) *The mayor sent word he'd be late.*|**spread/pass the word** (=tell other people the news)

### ④ ORDER/DECISION
**12 the last/final word a)** the power to decide whether or how to do something: *The final word rests with the board.*|**have the last/final word** *My boss has the final word on hiring staff.* **b)** the last statement or speech in a discussion or argument: **have the last/final word** *Why must you always have the last word in any argument?*
**13** [C usually singular] an order to do something: *On the word 'go' I want you to start running.*|**give the word** *Captain Rix gave the word and we moved forward.*

### ⑤ PROMISE
**14 my/sb's word** a sincere promise: **give sb your word** (=promise someone very sincerely that you will do something)|**keep your word** *Gail kept her word and returned all the money.*|**be as good as your word** (=do exactly what you have promised to do)|**a man of his word/woman of her word** (=a man or woman who does what they have promised to do)
**15 take sb at their word** to choose to believe what someone has said even though it is possible they do not mean it: *Geoff said we could call him any time, so let's take him at his word.*
**16 take my word for it** *spoken* used to say that someone should accept what you say as true: *The business is doing very well. You can take my word for it.*

### ⑥ OTHER MEANINGS
**17 in other words** used to introduce a simpler explanation or version of something you have said: *In other words, the objective is to avoid losing.*|*The woman has stopped going through her monthly cycle, in other words she is pregnant.*
**18 in a word** used to introduce a very simple answer or explanation: *"Did you enjoy the film?" "In a word – no."*
**19 in as many words/not in so many words** in a clear direct way or not in a clear direct way: *"Did Kathy say she liked him?" "Not in so many words."*|*Aunt Fay was angry and said so in as many words.*
**20 word for word a)** in exactly the same words: *The newspaper printed his speech more or less word for word.* **b)** also **word by word** if you translate a piece of writing from a foreign language word for word, you translate the meaning of each single word rather than the meaning of a whole phrase or sentence
**21 take the words (right) out of sb's mouth** *spoken* if someone takes the words out of your mouth, they have just said what you were going to say
**22 put words into sb's mouth** *spoken* to suggest falsely that someone has said a particular thing: *Will you stop putting words into my mouth – I never said I disliked the job.*
**23 too silly/ridiculous/stupid etc for words** *spoken* very silly, ridiculous etc
**24 put in a (good) word for sb** to praise someone or suggest them for a particular job: *Can you put in a good word for me with the Marketing Manager?*
**25 words fail me** *spoken* used to say that you are so surprised, angry, or shocked that you do not know what to say: *I ... words fail me.*
**26 (Upon) my word!** *old-fashioned spoken* used to say you are very surprised because something unusual has happened
**27 tired/angry/pleased isn't the word for it** *spoken* used to say you are extremely tired or angry etc
**28 the last word in comfort/luxury/elegance etc** the most comfortable or luxurious etc thing of its type: *a kitchen that is the last word in luxury*
**29 by word of mouth** if information or news comes to you by word of mouth, someone tells you instead of you reading about it or seeing an advertisement
**30 never have a good word to say for sb** *spoken* if you never have a good word to say for someone, you never praise them even if they do something well
**31 get a word in edgeways** also **edgewise** *AmE informal* to get a chance to speak: *Once Terry starts talking it's difficult to get a word in edgeways.*
**32 the Word (of God)** the religious teachings in the Bible
**33 from the word go** *spoken* from the beginning: *Lena was against me from the word go.* —see also **eat your words** (EAT (8)), FOUR-LETTER WORD, **mark my words** (MARK[1] (9)), **not mince your words** (MINCE[1] (3)), **play on words** (PLAY[2] (8)), **say the word** (SAY[1] (28))

**word**[2] *v* [T] to use words that are carefully chosen in order to express something: *The final version was worded in general terms.*

**word blind·ness** /ˈ· ˌ··/ *n* [U] DYSLEXIA

**word·ed** /ˈwɜːdʒd‖ˈwɜːr-/ *adj* **carefully/clearly/strongly etc worded** using words that express an idea carefully or clearly: *a carefully worded question*

**word·ing** /ˈwɜːdɪŋ‖ˈwɜːr-/ *n* [U] the words and phrases used to express something: *the exact wording of the contract*

**word·less** /ˈwɜːdləs‖ˈwɜːrd-/ *adj* without words; silent: *a wordless prayer*

**word-per·fect** /ˌ· ˈ··/ *BrE adj* able to remember and say every word of something correctly: *She rehearsed her speech until she was word-perfect.*

**word-play** /ˈ· ·/ *n* [U] making jokes by using words in a clever way

**word pro·cess·or** /ˈ· ˌ···/ *n* [C] a small computer used especially for writing letters or storing information —**word processing** *n* [U] —see picture on page 837

**word·y** /ˈwɜːdi‖ˈwɜːrdi/ *adj* using too many formal words: *a wordy explanation* —**wordily** *adv* —**wordiness** *n* [U]

**wore** /wɔː‖wɔːr/ the past tense of WEAR[1]

S1 W1

# work¹ /wɜːk‖wɜːrk/ *v*

① DO A JOB
② USE YOUR TIME AND ENERGY TO DO STH
③ MATERIAL/SUBSTANCE
④ MACHINE
⑤ PRODUCE RESULTS/BE SUCCESSFUL
⑥ MOVE
⑦ OTHER MEANINGS

## ① DO A JOB

**1** [I] to do a job that you are paid for: *Harry is 78, and still working.* | [+ **for**] *David works for the BBC.* | **work as a secretary/builder etc** *She works as a management consultant for a design company.* | **work long hours/nights etc** *There's no way I'm working Sundays.*
**2** [I,T] to do the activities and duties that are part of your job: *Sally isn't working tomorrow.* | *I'm tired of working ten-hour days.*
**3** ▶ **HELP** ◀ [I + **with**] if you work with someone or a group of people, your job involves trying to help them: *Jane works with deaf children.*
**4** ▶ **AREA** ◀ [T] to travel around a particular area as part of your job, especially in order to sell something: *Markowitz works the Tri-State area.*

## ② USE YOUR TIME AND ENERGY TO DO STH

**5** [I] to do an activity which needs time and effort, especially one that you want to do or that needs to be done: *Dad's been working all day in the garden.* | *We had to work non-stop to get everything ready for the party.* | [+ **on**] *Whenever I get the time we go out to the camp and work on it.* | [+ **at**] *Juan's English isn't very good, but he works at it.*
**6** ▶ **STUDY** ◀ [I] *BrE* to study a subject by reading books, doing exercises etc, especially in order to pass an exam: *You'll have to work really hard if you want to pass your exams.*
**7 work sb hard** [T] to make someone use a lot of time or effort when doing a job or activity: *The coach has been working us really hard this week.*
**8** [I] to try continuously and patiently to achieve a particular thing: [+ **for**] *a life spent working for peace and justice* | **work to do sth** *We worked hard to persuade the French to attend the meeting.* | **work tirelessly** (=work hard) *an organization that works tirelessly on behalf of the poor* | **work your passage** (=to work instead of paying for a journey)

## ③ MATERIAL/SUBSTANCE

**9** [T] if you work a material such as metal, leather, or clay you cut, SEW, or shape it in order to make something
**10** [I] to use a particular material or substance in order to make something such as a picture, design, jewellery etc: [+ **in/with**] *a sculptor who works in steel* | *a jeweller who works with silver*
**11** ▶ **LAND/SOIL** ◀ [T] if you work the land or the soil, you do all the work necessary to grow crops on it
**12** ▶ **MINE** ◀ [T] if you work a mine you remove a substance such as coal, gold, or oil from it

## ④ MACHINE

**13 a)** [I] if a machine or piece of equipment works, it does what it is supposed to do: *The remote control doesn't work.* | *Damn! The TV's not working again.* **b)** [T] to make a complicated machine or piece of equipment do what it is supposed to do: *Does anyone know how to work the microwave?*

## ⑤ PRODUCE RESULTS/BE SUCCESSFUL

**14** [I] if a method, plan, or system works, it produces the results you want: *What do you think of Jill's suggestion? Will it work?* | *The recipe works just as well if you use margarine instead of butter.* | *I told Mum I was too sick to go to school, but it didn't work.*
**15 work like magic/like a charm** if a plan, method, or trick works like magic or like a charm, it happens in exactly the way you planned it to happen
**16** ▶ **ART/LITERATURE** ◀ if a painting, film, piece of writing etc works, it is successful artistically because it has the effect on you that its maker intended: *I don't think the scene where the family is seated around the table really works, do you?*
**17** ▶ **MEDICINE/TREATMENT** ◀ [I] if a medicine or medical treatment works, it has the physical effect you want it to have: *The antibiotics will only work if you take them every day for ten days.*
**18** ▶ **HAVE AN EFFECT** ◀ [I always + adv/prep] if something such as a fact, situation, or system works in particular way, it has a particular effect on someone or something: **work in sb's favour** (=help someone) *The fact that you went to the same school should work in your favour.* | **work against sb** (=harm someone or cause them problems) *Tax laws tend to work against small organizations.*

## ⑥ MOVE

**19** [I always + adv/prep,T always + adv/prep] to move into a particular state or position very gradually, either in a series of small movements or after a long time: *Slowly he worked the screwdriver into the crack.* | **work (its way) loose** *One of the screws must have worked loose.*
**20** [I,T] if a part of your body works or you work it, it moves: **work sth** *He tried to work his face into a smile.*
**21 work your way** if you work your way somewhere, you go there slowly and with great effort: *Although exhausted, he managed to work his way up the last few feet of rock.*

## ⑦ OTHER MEANINGS

**22** [T] to operate a machine or piece of equipment: *How do you work the zoom lens on the camera?*
**23** ▶ **MIND/BRAIN** ◀ [I] if your mind or brain is working, you are thinking or trying to solve a problem
**24 work yourself into a state/rage/frenzy etc** to make yourself become very excited, upset or angry: *You could tell he was working himself into a panic about it.*
**25 work wonders** to be surprisingly effective in dealing with a difficult problem or situation: *Try rubbing salt on it. It can work wonders with stains.*
**26 work it/things** *spoken* to make arrangements for something to happen, especially by acting in a clever or skilful way: *We should try and work it so that we can all go together.*
**27 work your fingers to the bone** *informal* to work very hard
**28 beer/wine** [I] *technical* to FERMENT¹
**29** ▶ **CALCULATE** ◀ [T] *AmE formal* to calculate the answer to a mathematical problem
**30 work to rule** *BrE* to protest about a situation at work by doing your job slowly with the excuse that you must obey all the rules exactly

**work** sth ↔ **in** *phr v* [T] **1** to add one substance to another and mix them together in a very thorough way: **work sth into sth** *Work the butter into the flour with your fingers.* **2** to include something you want to say or do while you are doing or saying something else: *Do you think you can work in a reference to our project?* | **work sth into sth** *The minister will try and work a visit to hospital into his schedule.*

**work** sth ↔ **off** *phr v* [T] to try to get rid of a feeling such as anger, disappointment, or embarrassment, especially by being unpleasant to other people or behaving violently: *I'm sorry about all the yelling, it was Terry trying to work off his frustration.*

**work on** *phr v* [T] **1** [**work on** sth] to spend time making or fixing something: *Ken was working on some sets for an opera at the Met.* | *I worked all night on that article.* **2** to try continuously to influence someone or persuade them to do something: **work on sb to do sth** *My parents spent the weekend working on me to go on holiday with them.*

**work out** *phr v*

**1 ▶ CALCULATE ◀** [T **work** sth ↔ **out**] to calculate an answer, amount, price, or value: *You can work out the answer by adding all the numbers.* | *See if you can work this bill out.* | **work out how much/how many etc** *We'll have to work out how much food we'll need for the party.*

**2 ▶ UNDERSTAND ◀** *especially BrE* [T **work** sth ↔ **out**] to think about something and manage to understand it: *The plot is very complicated, it'll take you a while to work it out.* | **work sth out for yourself** *I'm not telling you the answer – work it out for yourself.*

**3** [I, linking verb + adj] if something works out at a particular amount, you calculate that it costs that amount: **work out at/to £10/$500 etc** *The bill works out at £15 each.* | **work out expensive/costly/cheap etc** (=be expensive or cheap) *If we go by taxi, it's going to work out very expensive.*

**4 ▶ PLAN ◀** [T **work** sth ↔ **out**] to think carefully about how you are going to do something and plan a good way of doing it: *UN negotiators have worked out a set of compromise proposal.* | **work out what/where/how etc** *I haven't worked out who's going to look after the kids tonight.* | **have it all worked out** (=have completely planned how you are going to do something) *Listen, I've got it all worked out. Here's what we should do.*

**5 ▶ GET BETTER ◀** [I,T] if a problem or complicated situation works out, it gradually gets better or gets solved: *Ken and Ella had loads of problems when they first got married, but things worked out in the end.* | *I hope it all works out between Gina and Andy.* | **work itself out** *I know you're not happy with things right now, but I'm sure everything will work itself out.*

**6 ▶ HAPPEN ◀** if a situation works out in a particular way, it happens in that way: **work out well/badly** *Financially, things have worked out very well for us.*

**7 I can't work sb out** *spoken* an expression meaning you cannot understand someone's behaviour: *I can't work Geoff out, one day he's friendly the next day he ignores me completely.*

**8 ▶ EXERCISE ◀** [I] to make your body fit and strong, especially by doing a programme of exercises regularly: *He works out with weights twice a week.*

**9 be worked out** if a mine is worked out, all the coal, gold etc has been removed from it

**work** sb **over** *phr v* [T] *informal* to hit someone hard and repeatedly all over their body

**work** sb/sth ↔ **up** *phr v* **1 work up enthusiasm/interest/courage etc** to become enthusiastic or interested etc: *I'm trying to work up enough courage to go to the dentist.* **2 work up an appetite/thirst** to make yourself hungry or THIRSTY, especially by doing physical exercise or waiting a long time before you eat or drink: *You can work up a really big thirst playing tennis.* **3** to make someone very angry, excited, or upset about something: **work yourself up** *Paula has worked herself up into a complete state about the exam.* **4** to develop and improve a skill or a piece of writing: *Jack took notes which he would work up into a report later.*

**work up to** sth *phr v* [T] to prepare yourself to do something that you do not want to do by gradually making yourself more and more determined to do it: *I haven't told Carmela I don't want to go, I'm still working up to it.*

S1 W1 **work²** *n*

**1** [U] a job you are paid to do or an activity that you do regularly to earn money: *My father started work when he was 14.* | *The work is interesting and well paid.* | *There isn't a lot of work at this time of the year.* | **be in work/out of work** (=have or not have a job) | **look for work/find work** *Anne left college a year ago and she's still looking for work.* | *He eventually found work on a construction site.* | **return to work** (=start work again after a long period of time) *Dawn didn't return to work until the kids had started school.* | **after/before work** (=after or before you start work each day) | **sb's line of work** (=the kind of work someone does) *In my line of work we use a lot of heavy equipment – back-hoes, things like that.* —see JOB (USAGE)

**2 ▶ PLACE ◀** [U] a place where you do your job, which is not your home: *He left work at the usual time.* | *I'll see you at work tomorrow.* | **be at work** (=be working at your job at a place which is not your home) *My Dad's at work.*

**3 ▶ DUTIES ◀** [U] the duties and activities that are part of your job: *What kind of work are you looking for?* | *A large part of the work we do involves using computers.* | **secretarial/legal/bar etc work** *I've been working in the field for 6 years, and would like a chance at some museum work.* | **voluntary work** (=work that you do not get paid for)

**4 ▶ RESULT ◀** [U] something that you produce as a result of doing your job or doing an activity: *Send a résumé and example of your work.* | **piece of work** *This report really is an excellent piece of work.*

**5 ▶ USEFUL ACTIVITY ◀** [U] the act of doing something that needs to be done or that you want to do, or the time and effort needed to do it: *Ted's done a lot of work on the car.* | *The house must have taken a lot of work.* | *Come on – hard work never hurt anyone.* | **get down to work** (=start doing work) | *We decided to watch TV for a while before getting down to work.*

**6 ▶ STUDY ◀** [U] study or RESEARCH, especially for a particular purpose: *He did his postgraduate work in Sociology.* | *Limited work was carried out on subjects between the ages of 16 and 20.*

**7 at work a)** doing your job or a particular activity: *Danger – men at work.* **b)** having a particular influence or effect: *Listen to her voice, you can hear her operatic training at work.*

**8 ▶ BOOK/PAINTING/MUSIC ◀** [C] something such as a book, play, painting, or piece of music produced by a writer, painter, or musician: *the Collected Works of Shakespeare* | *Thirty-five Old Master works will be on loan from the Met.*

**9 the (whole) works** *spoken* everything: *"What would you like – eggs, bacon, sausages, fries?" " The works."*

**10 nice work/quick work** *spoken* used to praise someone for doing something well or quickly: *The last image flickered on the screen and I turned to Herb and said 'Nice work!'*

**11 works a)** *old-fashioned* a building or group of buildings in which goods are produced in large quantities or an industrial process happens: **ironworks/gasworks/cement works** *The brick works closed last year.* **b)** the activity involved in building something on a large scale: **engineering works/irrrigaton works/roadworks** *the official in charge of the engineering works*

**12 it's all in a day's work** *spoken* used to say that you do not mind doing something even though it will give you more work than usual

**13 sb will have his/her work cut out** *informal* it will be very difficult for someone to do something: *Dad and Sam will have their work cut out for them trying to calm her down.*
**14 the works** the moving parts of a machine
**15** [U] *technical* force multiplied by distance —see also CLERK OF WORKS, **do sb's dirty work** (DIRTY¹ (7)), **make short work of sth** (SHORT¹ (6)), PUBLIC WORKS

**wor·ka·ble** /ˈwɜːkəbəl‖ˈwɜːr-/ *adj* **1** a workable system, idea etc can be used in a practical and efficient way: *a workable timetable* **2** a substance that is workable can be shaped with your hands: *workable clay for making pots*

**work·a·day** /ˈwɜːkədeɪ‖ˈwɜːr-/ *adj* [only before noun] ordinary and not interesting: *The views from the plateau are in stark contrast to the workaday cottages below.*

**work·a·hol·ic** /ˌwɜːkəˈhɒlɪk‖ˌwɜːrkəˌˈhɒː-/ *n* [C] *informal* someone who cannot stop working, and does not have time for anything else

**work·bas·ket** /ˈwɜːkˌbɑːskɪt‖ˈwɜːrkˌbæs-/ *n* [C] a container for SEWING equipment

**work·bench** /ˈwɜːkbentʃ‖ˈwɜːrk-/ *n* [C] a strong table with a hard surface for working on with tools

**work·book** /ˈwɜːkbʊk‖ˈwɜːrk-/ *n* [C] a school book containing questions and exercises

**work·day** /ˈwɜːkdeɪ‖ˈwɜːrk-/ *adj* the amount of time that you spend working in a day: *a 10 hour workday*

**worked up** /ˌ· ˈ·/ *adj* [not before noun] *informal* very upset or excited about something: [+ **about**] *Don't get worked up about it! It was only a suggestion.* —see also **work up** (WORK¹)

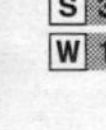

S3 W1 **work·er** /ˈwɜːkə‖ˈwɜːrkər/ *n* [C] **1** one of the people who work for an organization, business etc and are below the level of a manager: **factory/farm/office etc worker** *new health and safety regulations for factory workers* | **skilled/unskilled worker** (=someone who has or does not have special skills) | **manual worker** (=someone who does physical work) **2 research/rescue etc worker** someone who works to achieve a particular purpose: *Rescue workers worked all night to free the victims.* **3** someone who works very well or quickly: *Mavis is a real worker – she gets twice as much done as everyone else.* | **good/hard/quick etc worker** *Mike's always been a hard worker.* **4 the workers** the members of the WORKING CLASS: *the workers' revolution* —see also SOCIAL WORKER

**work eth·ic** /ˈ· ˌ··/ *n* [singular, U] a belief in the moral value of work: *the Protestant work ethic*

**work ex·pe·ri·ence** /ˈ· ·ˌ···/ *n* **1** the experience you have had of working in a particular type of job: *She's well qualified but has no relevant work experience.* **2** *BrE* a period of time that a young person spends working in a particular place, as a form of training

W

**work·fare** /ˈwɜːkfeə‖ˈwɜːrkfer/ *n* [U] a system that requires unemployed people to work before they are given money for food, rent etc by the government

**work·force** /ˈwɜːkfɔːs‖ˈwɜːrkfɔːrs/ *n* [singular] all the people who work in a particular country, industry, or factory: *a workforce of 3500 employees*

**work·horse** /ˈwɜːkhɔːs‖ˈwɜːrkhɔːrs/ *n* [C] **1** someone who does most of the work, especially when it is hard or boring **2** a machine or vehicle that can be used to do a lot of work: *a software program that is rapidly becoming the architect's workhorse*

**work·house** /ˈwɜːkhaʊs‖ˈwɜːrk-/ *n* [C] a building in Britain in the past where poor people lived

S1 W1 **work·ing¹** /ˈwɜːkɪŋ‖ˈwɜːr-/ *adj* [only before noun]
**1 ▶ HAVING A JOB ◀ a)** having a job that you are paid for: *a working mother* **b)** having a job that requires physical rather than intellectual skill: *an ordinary working man*
**2 ▶ CLOTHES ◀** working clothes are designed for people to work in rather than to look attractive
**3 ▶ CONDITIONS/PRACTICES ◀** working conditions or practices are the ones you have in your job: *recent improvements in working conditions*
**4 ▶ HOURS ◀** your working hours are the period of time during the day when you are doing your job
**5 have a working knowledge of** to have enough knowledge of a system, foreign language etc to be able to use it, although your knowledge is limited: *Gita has a working knowledge of Spanish and French.*
**6 ▶ RELATIONSHIP ◀** a working relationship is the kind of relationship that two people have who work well together: *The working relationship between Hodges and Bradley began to deteriorate.*
**7 ▶ MODEL ◀** a working model is one that has parts that move
**8 ▶ PARTS OF A MACHINE ◀** the working parts of a machine are the parts that move and operate the machine
**9 be in working order** to be working properly and not broken: **be in good/perfect working order** *The car was old, but the engine was still in good working order.* —see graph at ORDER¹
**10 ▶ THEORY/DEFINITION ◀** a working theory or definition is not complete in every detail, but is good enough for you to use as a basis for studying something or doing a job
**11 working breakfast/lunch/dinner** a breakfast, lunch etc which is also a business meeting

**working²** *n* **1** [singular] also **workings** the way something such as a system, piece of equipment, or organization works: [+ **of**] *the inside workings of the Reagan presidency* | *I shall never understand the workings of his mind.* **2** [C usually plural] a mine or part of a mine where soil has been dug out in order to remove metals or stone: *the workings of a long-disused quarry*

**working cap·i·tal** /ˌ·· ˈ···/ *n* [U] the money that is available to be used for the costs of a business —see also VENTURE CAPITAL

**working class** /ˌ·· ˈ·◂/ *n* [singular] *especially BrE* the group of people in society who traditionally do physical work and do not have much money or power —compare LOWER CLASS, MIDDLE CLASS, UPPER CLASS —**working class** *adj*

**working day** /ˌ·· ˈ·◂‖ˈ·· ·/ *n* [C] **1** the amount of time that you spend working in a day **2** a day when you have to work

**working girl** /ˈ·· ·/ *n* [C] *old-fashioned* **1** a word for a woman who has sex for money, used when you want to avoid saying this directly **2** a young woman who has a paid job

**working group** /ˈ·· ·/ *n* [C] a committee that is established to examine a particular situation or problem and suggest ways of dealing with it

**working life** /ˌ·· ˈ·/ *n* [C] the part of your adult life when you work: *Geoff spent all his working life in the same company.*

**working ma·jor·i·ty** /ˌ·· ·ˈ···/ *n* [singular] *BrE* enough support in parliament for a government to continue making laws and ruling a country

**working or·der** /ˈ·· ˌ··/ *n* [U] **in working order** a system, machine etc that is in working order is working well, with no problems

**working pa·pers** /ˈ·· ˌ··/ *n* [plural] an official document that you need in the US in order to get a job if you are young or were born in a different country

**working par·ty** /ˈ·· ˌ··/ *n* [C] *BrE* a WORKING GROUP

**working prac·tices** /ˈ·· ˌ···/ *n* [plural] the way in which things are usually done in your job: *The changes in working practices are designed to increase efficiency.*

**work·ings** /ˈwɜːkɪŋz‖ˈwɜːr-/ *n* [plural] **1** the way in which something works: *I shall never understand the workings of his mind.* **2** the parts of a mine that have been dug out

**working week** /ˌ·· ˈ·/ *n* [C] the days when you do your job, usually between Monday and Friday

**work·load** /ˈwɜːkləʊd‖ˈwɜːrkloʊd/ *n* [C] the amount of work that a person or machine is expected to do: *Paul has a heavy workload at the moment.*

**work·man** /ˈwɜːkmən‖ˈwɜːrk-/ *n* [C] someone who does physical work such as building, repairing things etc

**work·man·like** /ˈwɜːkmənlaɪk‖ˈwɜːrk-/ *adj* a workmanlike piece of work has been done well and looks good

**work·man·ship** /ˈwɜːkmənʃɪp‖ˈwɜːrk-/ *n* [U] *formal* skill in making things, especially in a way that makes them look good

**work·mate** /ˈwɜːkmeɪt‖ˈwɜːrk-/ *n* [C] someone you work with

**work of art** /ˌ· · ˈ·/ *n plural* **works of art** [C] **1** a painting, SCULPTURE etc of very high quality **2** *often humorous* something that is very attractive and skilfully made: *That cake's a real work of art!*

**workout**

**work·out** /ˈwɜːkaʊt‖ˈwɜːrk-/ *n* [C] a period of physical exercise, especially as training for a sport —see also **work out** (WORK¹)

**work per·mit** /ˈ· ˌ··/ *n* [C] an official document that you need if you want to work in a foreign country

**work·place** /ˈwɜːkpleɪs‖ˈwɜːrk-/ *n* [C] the room, building etc where you work

**work·room** /ˈwɜːkrʊm, -ruːm‖ˈwɜːrk-/ *n* [C] a room that you work in

**work·sheet** /ˈwɜːkʃiːt‖ˈwɜːrk-/ *n* [C] a piece of paper with questions, exercises etc for students

S3 W3 **work·shop** /ˈwɜːkʃɒp‖ˈwɜːrkʃɑːp/ *n* [C] **1** a room or building where tools and machines are used for making or repairing things **2** a meeting at which people try to improve their skills by discussing their experiences and doing practical exercises

**work-shy** /ˈ· ·/ *adj* someone who is work-shy tries to avoid working because they do not like it

**work·sta·tion** /ˈwɜːkˌsteɪʃən‖ˈwɜːrk-/ *n* [C] the part of an office where you work, where your desk, computer etc are —see picture on page 837

**work-sur·face** /ˈ· ˌ··/ also **work·top** /ˈwɜːktɒp‖ˈwɜːrktɑːp/ *n* [C] *especially BrE* a flat surface for working on, especially in a kitchen; COUNTER¹ (4) *AmE* —see picture on page 833

**work-to-rule** /ˌ· · ˈ·/ *n* [singular] a situation in which people in a particular job refuse to do any additional work as a protest —see also **work to rule** (WORK¹ (30))

**work·week** /ˈwɜːkwiːk‖ˈwɜːrk-/ *n* [C] *AmE* the total amount of time that you spend working during a week: *a 40 hour workweek*

S1 W1 **world¹** /wɜːld‖wɜːrld/ *n*

**1 ► OUR PLANET/EVERYONE ON IT ◄ the world** the planet we live on, and all the people, cities, and countries on it; the Earth: *the world's tallest building | Tuberculosis is still common in some parts of the world. | At that time China was the most powerful country in the world. | The Press Association flashed the news to the world.* | **all over the world** (=everywhere in the world) *Delegates from all over the world will be at the conference.*

**2 in the world** used to emphasize a statement you are making: **the happiest/most exciting etc ... in the world** *If she asked me to marry her I'd be the happiest man in the world.* | **not have a care in the world** (=not be worried at all about anything) | **nothing in the world** (=nothing at all) *Nothing in the world can save them now.* | **have all the time in the world** (=have a lot of time so that you do not have to hurry) *Don't worry, we've got all the time in the world.* | **What/Who/ Where/How etc in the world ...?** (=used after what or who etc to emphasize a question in order to show that you are very surprised, annoyed, or angry) *What in the world are you doing here at seven in the morning?*

**3 the outside world** the people who live outside a particular place, country etc; especially when the people living in that place or country cannot meet them or talk to them: *a jungle tribe who have no contact with the outside world*

**4 ► THE SOCIETY WE LIVE IN ◄** the society that we live in and the kind of life we have: *The world is being transformed by information technology. | Parents want a better world for their children.* —see LAND¹ (USAGE)

**5 ► GROUP OF COUNTRIES ◄ the Western World/ the industrialized world/the developing world etc** a particular group of countries: *The British are among the biggest sugar consumers in the developed world.* —see also THIRD WORLD

**6 ► PERIOD IN HISTORY ◄ the Roman world/the Medieval world, etc** a particular period in history and the society and people of that time: *the artistic, literary, and intellectual culture of the Roman World*

**7 ► AREA OF ACTIVITY/WORK ◄** [C usually singular] a particular area of activity or work, and the people who are involved in it: *the world of politics | an influential figure in the business world | The show-business world was out in force at the Oscar ceremony.*

**8 ► SB'S LIFE ◄** [C] the life a particular person or group of people lives, especially the things they do and the people they know: *the world of children | Dean's world was filled with music and laughter.*

**9 in a world of your own** *informal* if someone lives in a world of their own, they do not seem to notice what is happening around them and are more concerned with their own thoughts: *I can't get through to that girl – she seems to be in a world of her own.*

**10 ► KIND OF PLACE/SITUATION ◄** a particular kind of place or situation, especially one that someone describes or which you imagine: *the nightmare world of Orwell's novel 1984 | Italy's mountains and lakes are a stunning world of peace and tranquillity.*

**11 the animal/plant/insect world** animals etc considered as a group of living things with their own particular way of living or behaving

**12 ► PLACE LIKE THE EARTH ◄** [C] a place like the Earth in another part of the universe where other things may live: *strange creatures from another world*

**13 be out of this world** *informal* something that is out of this world is so good, enjoyable etc, it is unlike anything else you have ever experienced: *Tracy's new apartment is just out of this world.*

**14 do sb a world of good** *informal* if something does someone a world of good, it makes them feel much better: *Why don't you go for a walk, it'll do you a world of good.*

**15 be/feel on top of the world** *informal* to feel extremely happy

**16 be/mean all the world to** to be more important to you than anyone or anything else: *I'd hate to lose her – she means all the world to me.*

**17 think the world of sb** to love and respect someone very much: *Lee thinks the world of you – you know that.*

**18 see the world** to travel to many different countries so that you can get a lot of different experiences

**19 the world over** in every country or area of the world; everywhere: *It's the same the world over. | Her books have delighted adults and children the world over.*

**20 move up/go up in the world** to move into a higher social class: *He's gone up in the world now – he's far too posh to talk to me.*

**21 go down/come down in the world** to move down to a lower social class

**22 there's a world of difference between** used when saying that two things or situations are completely different and people should not expect them to be the same: *There's a world of difference between enjoying cooking and doing it for a living.*
**23 be worlds apart/be a world apart** people, beliefs, or ideas that are worlds apart are so completely different that there is almost nothing about them that is similar: *Their political views are just worlds apart.*
**24 for all the world as if/like** *literary* exactly as if or exactly like: *She sat reading her paper, looking for all the world as if nothing had happened.*
**25 not for the world** if someone would not do a particular thing for the world, they would never do it whatever happened: *I wouldn't hurt her for the world.*
**26 be a man/woman of the world** to be someone who has had many experiences and is not easily shocked: *Victor is a man of the world – I'm sure he'll understand.*
**27 set the world on fire/alight** *spoken* an expression meaning to have a big effect or be very successful, often used when you think someone or something has failed to do this: *His last film didn't exactly set the world on fire.*
**28 set/put the world to rights** to discuss or say how the world should be changed to make people's lives better: *We were having a few beers and generally putting the world to rights.*
**29 the next world/the world to come** *literary* the place where people's souls are believed to go after they die
**30 not be long for this world** to not be going to live much longer
**31 this world** *literary* the state of being alive: **depart/leave this world** (=die)
**32 bring a child into the world** *formal* **a)** if a woman brings a child into the world she gives birth to it **b)** if a doctor brings a child into the world he helps the mother give birth
**33 come into the world** *literary* to be born
**34 the Michael Jacksons/Paul Smiths etc of this world** *spoken* used when making a general comment about a particular kind of person: *The Frank Clarkes of this world are only interested in furthering their own careers.*
**35 the world is your oyster** used to tell someone that there is no limit to the opportunities that they have: *"If you've got a good education, the world is your oyster", my father used to say.*
**36 workers/women etc of the world** used when addressing all workers, women etc in a speech, book etc
**37 ► NOT RELIGIOUS ◄ the world** the way of life most people live rather than a spiritual way of life: *monks who renounce the world* —see also **best of both worlds** (BEST[3] (5)), **dead to the world** (DEAD[1] (9)), NEW WORLD, OLD WORLD

**world**[2] *adj* [only before noun] **1** existing in or affecting the whole world: *The prospects for world peace are improving.* | *the world recession of the early nineties* | **world champion/record etc** (=the best in the world, especially in a sport) *Hawthorn became Britain's first world champion.* **2** important or powerful enough to influence or affect the whole world: *Britain's attempts to remain a world power* | *a world figure on the international stage*

**world-beat·er** /ˈ· ˌ··/ *n* [C] someone or something that is the best at a particular activity —**world-beating** *adj*

**world-class** /ˌ· ˈ·◂/ *adj* among the best in the world: *a world-class tennis champion*

**world-fa·mous** /ˌ· ˈ··◂/ *adj* known about by people all over the world: *a world-famous singer*

**world·ly** /ˈwɜːldli‖ˈwɜːrld-/ *adj* [only before noun] **1 worldly goods** everything you own **2** having a lot of experience and knowledge about people and life: *Crystal was worldly but willing to take a risk.* —opposite UNWORLDLY **3** connected with ordinary daily life rather than spiritual or religious ideas; MUNDANE —**worldliness** *n* [U]

**worldly-wise** /ˌ·· ˈ·◂‖ˈ·· ·/ *adj* having a lot of experience and knowledge about life so that you are not easily shocked or deceived

**world pow·er** /ˌ· ˈ··/ *n* [C] a country that has a lot of power and influence in many parts of the world

**world-shak·ing** /ˈ· ˌ··/ *adj* extremely important and having a great effect: *a world-shaking announcement*

**world-wear·y** /ˌ· ˈ··◂/ *adj* no longer finding life interesting or exciting —**world-weariness** *n* [U]

**world·wide** /ˌwɜːldˈwaɪd◂‖ˌwɜːrld-/ *adj, adv* everywhere in the world: *cars with a worldwide reputation for reliability*

**worm**[1] /wɜːm‖wɜːrm/ *n* [C] **1** a long thin creature with no bones and no legs that lives in soil **2** someone who you do not like or respect **3 have worms** to have PARASITES (=small creature that eats your food or your blood) in your body **4 the worm turns** *literary* used to say that someone who is normally quiet and obedient will change if they really need to —see also **can of worms** (CAN[2] (4))

**worm**[2] *v* [T] **1 worm your way into/through etc** to move through a small place or a crowd slowly, carefully, or with difficulty: *They wormed their way through the crowd.* **2 worm your way into sb's affections/heart/confidence etc** to gradually make someone love or trust you, especially by being dishonest **3 worm sth out of sb** to get information from someone who does not want to give it **4 worm your way out of (doing) sth** to avoid doing something that you have been asked to do by making an excuse that is dishonest but clever: *Steve has managed to worm his way out of going to the meeting.* **5** to give an animal medicine in order to remove PARASITES (1) that live inside them

**worm-eat·en** /ˈ· ˌ··/ *adj* **1** worm-eaten wood or fruit has holes in it because it has been eaten by worms **2** old and damaged —see picture on page 1258

**worm·hole** /ˈwɜːmhəʊl‖ˈwɜːrmhoʊl/ *n* [C] a hole in a piece of wood etc made by a type of WORM[1] (1)

**worm·wood** /ˈwɜːmwʊd‖ˈwɜːrm-/ *n* [U] a plant with a bitter taste

**worm·y** /ˈwɜːmi‖ˈwɜːrmi/ *adj* full of worms (WORM[1] (1))

**worn**[1] /wɔːn‖wɔːrn/ the past participle of WEAR[1]

**worn**[2] *adj* **1** a worn object is old and damaged: *a worn patch on the carpet* **2** someone who looks worn seems tired

**worn out** /ˌ· ˈ·◂/ *adj* **1** very tired because you have been working hard: *You look worn-out!* **2** too old or damaged to be used: *a pair of old worn out walking boots*

**wor·ried** /ˈwʌrid‖ˈwɜːrid/ *adj* **1** unhappy because you keep thinking about a problem, or are anxious about something: *Don't look so worried – we'll find him.* | [+ **about**] *She's so worried about her exams.* | **worried that** *I was worried that we wouldn't have enough money.* | **get worried** *I got really worried when I saw a police car outside our house.* | **worried expression/look/frown etc** *Jim looked up with a slightly worried expression.* | **worried sick** *spoken* (=extremely worried) *Where on earth have you been? I was worried sick!* —see NERVOUS (USAGE) **2 you had me worried** *spoken* used to say that someone made you feel confused or anxious because you did not properly understand what they said, or did not realize that is was a joke: *You had me worried there for a minute – I thought the house really had burnt down!* **3 I'm not worried** *spoken* used to say that you do not mind what happens: *"Shall we go out or stay in?" "Oh, I'm not worried – whichever you want."* —**worriedly** *adv*

**wor·ri·er** /ˈwʌriə‖ˈwɜːriər/ *n* [C] someone who often worries about things: *Her mother was a born worrier.*

**wor·ri·some** /ˈwʌrisəm‖ˈwɜːri-/ *adj formal* making you anxious: *a worrisome problem*

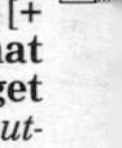

**wor·ry**[1] /ˈwʌri‖ˈwɜːri/ *v*
**1 ► BE ANXIOUS ◄** [I] to be anxious or unhappy about something so that you think about it a lot: [+ **about**] *You've really got no need to worry about your weight.* | **worry that** *He's worried that he might lose his job.* | [+ **over**] *Dad worries over the slightest thing.*
**2 don't worry** *spoken* **a)** used when you are trying to make someone feel less anxious: *Don't worry, darling, Daddy's here.* **b)** used to tell someone that they do not need to do something: *Don't worry about sorting them out – I'll do it later.* **c)** used to tell someone that you will

definitely do something: *Oh don't worry, I'll get my own back on him somehow!*
**3 ▶ MAKE SB ANXIOUS ◀** [T] to make someone feel anxious about something: *The recent changes in the Earth's climate are beginning to worry scientists.* | **worry sb that** *Doesn't it worry you that Sarah spends so much time away from home?* | **worry yourself** (=feel anxious, especially when there is no need to)
**4 not to worry** *BrE spoken* used to say that something is not important: *Not to worry, we can always go another time.*
**5 nothing to worry about** *spoken* used to tell someone that something is not as serious or difficult as they think: *It's just a routine check-up – nothing to worry about.*
**6 have enough to worry about** *spoken* used to say that someone already has a lot of problems or is very busy: *I don't think we should tell Mum about this – she's got enough to worry about as it is.*
**7 ▶ ANNOY ◀** [T] to annoy someone: **worry sb with sth** *Stop worrying your grandfather with all those questions.*
**8 ▶ ANIMAL ◀** [T] if a dog worries sheep, it tries to bite or kill them

**worry at** sth/sb *phr v* [T] **1** If an animal worries at a bone or piece of meat, it bites and shakes it **2** if you worry at a problem, you think about it a lot in order to try and find a solution: *Jez was never happy unless he was worrying at some problem.*

S3 **worry²** *n* **1** [C] a problem that you are anxious about or are not sure how to deal with: *My main worry is how the divorce will affect the kids.* | *financial worries* | [+ **about**] *We've got no more worries about the schedule at the moment.* | **be a worry to/for sb** *Money was always a big worry for us.* **2** [U] the feeling of being anxious about something: *The missing child's parents were frantic with worry.* **3 no worries** *spoken* used to agree to what someone wants and to say that it will be no problem: *Can you deliver on Thursday? Yeah, no worries, mate.*

**worry beads** /'·· ·/ *n* [plural] small stones or wooden balls on a string that you move and turn in order to keep yourself calm

S3 **wor·ry·ing** /'wʌri-ɪŋ‖'wɜː-/ *adj* **1** making you feel anxious: *a worrying development* **2 worrying time/week/year etc** a time etc when you have many problems: *It's been a worrying few weeks for us all.* —**worryingly** *adv*: *a worryingly high level of pollutants in the atmosphere*

**wor·ry·wart** /'wʌriwɔːt‖'wɜːriwɔːrt/ *n* [C] *AmE informal* someone who worries about unimportant things

**worse¹** /wɜːs‖wɜːrs/ *adj* **1** [the comparative of *bad*] not as good as someone or something else, or more unpleasant or of a lower standard: *The meal couldn't have been much worse.* | **worse than** *The weather was worse than last year.* | **there's nothing worse than** *spoken*: *There's nothing worse than being angry about something and knowing it's your own fault.* | **a lot/much worse** *The traffic is much worse after five.* | **get worse** *I didn't like the noise when I first came and it's got worse since then.* | **worse and worse** *Paul's manners seem to get worse and worse.* | **make matters/things/it worse** (=make a bad or difficult situation even worse) *I tried to help but I think I made things worse.* **2** [comparative of *ill*] more ill than before: *If she's worse in the morning, I'll call the doctor.* | **get worse** *After the operation he got worse instead of better.* **3 be none the worse for** to not have been harmed, or not be worse because of something: *The children were out in the rain all afternoon, but seem none the worse for it.* **4 worse luck** *spoken* used to say that you are disappointed or annoyed by something: *When we got there the car had already been sold, worse luck!* **5 sb can/could do worse than do sth** *spoken* used to say that you think it is a good idea if someone does a particular thing: *You could do worse than buy a few bottles of the local wine.* **6 it could have been worse** *spoken* used to say that a bad situation has something good about it **7 take a change/turn for the worse** to change and become worse **8 the worse for wear** *informal* in poor condition, or very tired: *The living room carpet is looking the worse for wear.* —compare BETTER¹ —see also **go from bad to worse** (BAD¹ (13))

> **USAGE NOTE: WORSE**
> GRAMMAR
> **More** and **most** are not used together with **worse** or **worst**: *Math is my worst subject* (NOT *my most worse/most worst subject*). | *The situation is much worse than it was last week* (NOT *much more worse*).
> Some people think that **worse** should not be used as an adverb meaning 'in a worse way'. But in spoken English you will often hear: *Because we're so short of time we're doing it worse than we should.* You can avoid this problem by saying for example: *...we're not doing it as well as we should.*
> Things *go/get bad*, but they *get worse*.
> SPELLING
> Remember the spellings: *even worse* is spelt with an 'e'; *the worst* with a 't'.

**worse²** *n* [U] something worse: *We thought the situation was bad, but worse was to follow.* | **a change for the worse** (=a bad change) —compare BETTER³

**worse³** *adv* [comparative of *badly*] **1** in a more severe or serious way than before: *My head aches much worse than before.* **2** to a lower standard or quality or less successfully: *Dick scored worse than you in the test.*

**wors·en** /'wɜːsən‖'wɜːr-/ *v* [I,T] to become worse or make something worse: *a worsening political situation*

**worse off** /,· '·◂/ *adj* [not before noun] **1** having less money than before or than someone else; poorer: *The tax increases will leave us worse off.* **2** in a worse situation than before or than someone else: *The factories on the east bank of the river were even worse off as they had no direct link to the motorway.*

**wor·ship¹** /'wɜːʃɪp‖'wɜːr-/ *v* **worshipped, worshipping** also **worshiped, worshiping** *AmE* **1** [I,T] to show respect and love for a god, especially by praying in a church, TEMPLE etc **2** [T] to admire and love someone very much: *She absolutely worships those children.* **3 worship the ground sb walks on** to admire or love someone so much that you cannot see their faults —**worshipper** *n* [C] *She was a regular worshipper at the Parish Church.*

**worship²** *n* [U] **1** a strong feeling of respect and love for a god: *They bowed their heads in worship.* **2** the activity of praying in a church, TEMPLE etc in order to show respect and love for a god: **act of worship** (=religious service) | **house/place of worship** (=a church, temple etc) **3** a strong feeling of love or admiration for someone or something, especially so that you cannot see their faults —see also HERO WORSHIP **4 Your/His Worship** *BrE formal* used to address or talk about a public official such as a MAYOR or MAGISTRATE

**wor·ship·ful** /'wɜːʃɪpfəl‖'wɜːr-/ *adj formal* showing respect or admiration for someone or something

**worst¹** /wɜːst‖wɜːrst/ *adj* [the superlative of *bad*] **1** [only before noun] worse than anything else of the same kind or worse than at any time before: *Ken is easily the worst player in the team.* | *What's the worst thing that could happen?* | **by far the worst** *This is by far the worst book she's written.* **2 be your own worst enemy** to continue to behave in a stupid or thoughtless way that harms you or stops you from becoming successful **3 come off worst** to lose a fight or argument

**worst²** *n* **1 the worst** the person, thing, situation, state, part etc that is worse than all others of the same kind or worse than at any time before: *None of them can play well, but Jane is the worst.* | **the worst of it** (=the worst part of something) *I think we've done the worst of it.* | *The worst of it is, I can't let her know what's happening.* | **get/have the worst of it** *spoken* (=lose a fight or argument) | **expect/fear the worst** (=expect the situation to have the worst possible result) *England play Brazil next week and I fear the worst.* | **at his/its etc worst** (=as bad as he or it can be) *You saw the garden at its worst, I'm afraid.* **2 at (the) worst** if things are as bad as they can be: *Choosing the right software can be time-consuming at best and confusing or frustrating at worst.* **3 sb/sth can do their worst** used to say that you are not worried by the power of someone or something to harm you: *All the wheat has been harvested, so the storm can do its worst.* **4 if the worst comes to the worst** if the situation develops in the worst possible way: *If the worst comes to the worst, we'll have to sell the car.*

**worst**[3] *adv* [the superlative of *badly*] most badly: *Aid is being sent to the worst affected areas.*|*the worst-dressed man in the office*

**worst**[4] *v* [T usually passive] *old-fashioned* to defeat someone in a fight, competition, or argument

**wor·sted** /ˈwʊstɪ̣d/ *n* [U] a type of cloth made from wool

S1 W2 **worth**[1] /wɜːθ‖wɜːrθ/ *prep* **1 be worth** to have a value in money: *How much is the ring worth?*|**be worth £10/$500 etc** *The picture is worth about two thousand pounds.*|**be worth a lot** *informal* (=be worth a lot of money)|**be worth nothing/not be worth anything** *I don't think my stereo is worth anything*|**be worth a fortune** *informal* (=be extremely valuable) *Now they've found oil the land must be worth a fortune.* **2 be worth millions/a fortune** *informal* to be extremely rich: *The man who founded CNN must be worth a fortune.* **3 be worth doing/reading/finding etc** to be something that will be useful and helpful if you do it or read it etc: *a film worth seeing*|*It may be worth putting an advertisement in the local paper.*|**be worth it** *I didn't write to Louise, because I didn't think it was worth it.* **4 it's worth doing sth** used to say that someone should give the time or money needed to do something, because they will gain something useful: *It's worth taking your time when you visit the cathedral.*|**it's worth the time/effort** *It's worth all the hard work you put in when you see so many happy children.*|**it's worth it** *Have a medical every year, it's worth it.*|**it's not worth it** *Don't get angry, it's not worth it.*|**it's well worth doing sth/it** *It's well worth getting there an hour early, if you want a good seat.* **5 it's worth your/sb's while** *spoken* used to say that someone should give the time or money needed to do something, because they will gain something useful: **it's worth your/sb's while to do sth** *It would be worth your while to talk to the editor.*|*I don't sell French books, it's not worth my while.* (=I would not make any money) **6 make it worth sb's while** *spoken* to offer someone money if they agree to do something for you, especially something dishonest: *Look, if you forget about the whole thing I'll make it worth your while.* **7 what's it worth?** *spoken humorous* used to ask someone how they will reward you if you do something for them **8 for what it's worth** *spoken* used to say that you are not sure of the value or usefulness of what you are saying: *My suggestion – for what it's worth – is that we buy a bigger car.* **9 for all you are/he is etc worth** with as much effort as possible: *Tom kept pulling away at the rope for all he was worth.* **10 worth his/her salt** doing their job well or deserving respect: *No translator worth his salt would rely on a bilingual dictionary.* **11 worth its/his/her weight in gold** very useful or valuable

**USAGE NOTE: WORTH**

WORD CHOICE: **worth, value**

**Worth** is common only after the verb **to be** and after words for amounts of something, as in: *$100 worth of damage*|*a week's worth of newspapers*. As a noun it means the same as **value** but is a little old-fashioned and literary: *the value of life* (NOT the *worth*). In an old story you might read: *a pearl of great worth*

GRAMMAR

**be worth** is often followed by the *-ing* form of a verb: *Is it worth running such a risk?* (NOT *...worth to run...*)|*Niagara Falls is worth seeing* (NOT *...to be seen*).

**be worth while** may also be followed by the *-ing* form of a verb, or the infinitive: *It'll be well worth while you coming/for you to come* (NOT *...worth while you come*).

**worth**[2] *n* **1** [U] value and importance, or value in money: *Eliot's poems are of more lasting worth than the plays.*|*The balance sheet will not show the current worth of the company.*|**ten pounds'/$500 etc worth of sth** (=an amount of something worth ten pounds or $500) *Dick cashed about a thousand pounds' worth of travellers cheques.*|*$4,000 worth of camera equipment* **2 ten minutes'/a week's etc worth of sth** something that takes ten minutes or a week to happen, do, or use: *a quarter of an hour's worth of music*|*There's about a week's worth of work left.* W3

**worth·less** /ˈwɜːθləs‖ˈwɜːrθ-/ *adj* **1** having no value, importance, or use: *a completely worthless exercise* **2** a worthless person has no good qualities or useful skills —**worthlessly** *adv* —**worthlessness** *n* [U]

**worth·while** /ˌwɜːθˈwaɪl◂‖ˌwɜːrθ-/ *adj* something worthwhile deserves the time, effort, or money you give to it: *I'd rather the money went to a worthwhile cause.* S3

**wor·thy**[1] /ˈwɜːði‖ˈwɜːrði/ *adj* **1** a worthy person, plan etc deserves respect or admiration because they have good qualities: *a worthy opponent* **2 be worthy of** to deserve to be thought about or treated in a particular way: [+ **of**] *The plan is only worthy of our contempt.* **3** having many good qualities but not very interesting or exciting

**worthy**[2] *n* [C] *formal* someone who is important and should be respected: *Victorian worthies such as Ruskin*

**wot**[1] /wɒt‖wɑːt/ *BrE* an informal spelling of WHAT

**wot**[2] *v* [I] *old use* to know

**wotch·a** /ˈwɒtʃə‖ˈwɑː-/ *interjection BrE slang* hello

**would** /wʊd/ *v* [modal verb] **1** used instead of 'will' to describe what someone has said, asked etc: *They said they would meet us at 10.30 at the station.* **2** used instead of 'will' with a past tense verb or to show what is likely or possible: *What would you do if you won a million pounds?*|*He said there had been a serious accident, but wouldn't give any details.* **3** used to describe what someone used to do a lot or what used to happen a lot: *When we worked in the same office, we would often have coffee together.* **4** used to show disapproval when talking about someone's annoying habits or behaviour: *You would go and spoil it, wouldn't you!* **5 would rather** used to say that you would prefer to do or have one thing rather than another thing: *Which would you rather do, go to the cinema or go for a meal?* **6 would you...? a)** used to express a polite request: *Would you shut the window please?* **b)** used to express a polite offer or invitation: *Would you like to have a meal with us tomorrow evening?* **7 I would...** *spoken* used to tell someone what you think they should do in a particular situation: *I would ring Joe and explain that you can't see him tomorrow.* **8** used before verbs that express what you think, feel, or suppose, to make your opinion or feeling less definite: *I would imagine that the kids will stay with their grandparents.* **9 would that...** *literary* used to express a strong wish or desire: *Would that we had seen her before she died.* S1 W1

**would-be** /ˈ· ·/ *adj* **would-be actor/murderer etc** someone who hopes to have a particular job or intends to do a particular thing

**would·n't** /ˈwʊdnt/ the short form of 'would not'

**wouldst** /wʊdst/ *old use* the second person singular of 'would'

**would've** /ˈwʊdəv/ the short form of 'would have'

**wound**[1] /waʊnd/ the past tense and past participle of WIND[2]

**wound**[2] /wuːnd/ *n* [C] **1** an injury, especially a cut or hole made in your skin by a weapon such as a knife or a bullet: *A nurse cleaned and bandaged the wound.*|*gunshot wounds*|**flesh wound** (=slight injury caused by a bullet touching your skin) **2** a feeling of emotional or mental pain that you get when someone says or does something unpleasant to you: *the mental wounds caused by parental abuse*|*a wound to my pride* **3 open old wounds** to remind someone of unpleasant things that happened in the past —see also **lick your wounds** (LICK[1] (6)), **rub salt into sb's wounds** (RUB[1] (7))

**wound³** *v* [T] **1** to injure someone, especially by making a cut or hole in their skin using a knife, gun etc: *Gunmen killed two people and wounded six others in an attack today.* **2** to make someone feel unhappy or upset: *a wounding remark*

**wound·ed** /ˈwuːndɪ̣d/ *adj* **1** injured by a weapon such as a gun or knife: *a wounded soldier*| **mortally wounded** (=injured so badly that you will die) **2** very upset because of something that someone has said or done: *wounded pride* **3 the wounded** people who have been injured, especially in a war

**wound up** /ˌwaʊnd ˈʌp/ *adj* [not before noun] anxious, worried, or excited: *I was too wound up to sleep.*

**wove** /wəʊv‖woʊv/ the past tense of WEAVE¹

**wov·en** /ˈwəʊvən‖ˈwoʊ-/ the past participle of WEAVE¹

**wow¹** /waʊ/ *interjection informal* used when you think something is impressive or surprising: *"Wow! Look at that car!"*

**wow²** *v* [T] *informal* to make people admire you very much: *Her performance wowed the critics.*

**wow³** *n* [singular] *informal* a great success

**wow·ser, wowzer** /ˈwaʊzə‖-ər/ *n* [C] *AusE, NZE informal* someone who seems to stop you from having fun

**WP** /ˌdʌbəljuː ˈpiː/ the abbreviation of WORD PROCESSOR

**WPC** /ˌdʌbəljuː piː ˈsiː◂/ *n* [C] *BrE* Woman Police Constable; a female police officer

**wpm** /ˌdʌbəljuː piː ˈem/ words per minute

**wrack** /ræk/ *n* [U] **1** a type of SEAWEED **2** another spelling of RACK²

**wraith** /reɪθ/ *n* [C] *literary* a GHOST¹ (1) especially of someone who has just died

**wran·gle¹** /ˈræŋgəl/ *n* [C] a long and complicated argument: *a damaging legal wrangle*|*a bitter wrangle over imports*

**wrangle²** *v* **1** [I] to argue with someone angrily for a long time **2** [T] *AmE informal* to gather together cows or horses from a large area

**wran·gler** /ˈræŋglə‖-ər/ *n* [C] *AmE informal* a COWBOY (1)

wrap

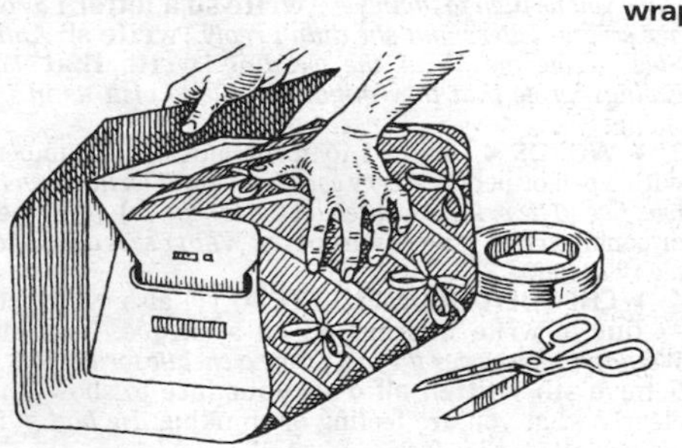

She wrapped the box in patterned paper.

3 **wrap¹** /ræp/ *v* [T] **1** to wind or fold cloth, paper etc around something: *a present wrapped in shiny paper*| **wrap sth around sth/sb** *Ella wrapped a thick coat around her shoulders.*| **wrap sth/sb in sth** *Wrap the cake in tin foil.* **2** if you wrap your arms, legs, fingers etc around something, you use them to hold it: *Chloe sat with her arms wrapped round her knees.* —see also **wrap sb in cotton wool** (COTTON WOOL (2))

**wrap up** *phr v* **1** [T **wrap** sth↔ **up**] to completely cover something by folding paper, cloth etc around it: *I haven't even wrapped my presents up yet!* **2** [I] to put on warm clothes: **wrap up warm/well** *Make sure you wrap up warm – it's freezing outside.* **3** [T **wrap** sth↔ **up**] to finish or complete a job, meeting etc: *The police will soon be wrapping up the investigation.* **4 be wrapped up in your children/work etc** to give so much of your attention to your children, your work etc that you do not have time for anything else —see also **twist/wrap sb around your little finger** (FINGER¹ (13))

**wrap²** *n* **1** [C] a piece of thick cloth that you wear around your shoulders **2** [U] *AmE* plastic used to cover food **3 keep sth under wraps** to keep something secret **4** [singular] the end of a day's filming: *OK everybody, it's a wrap!*

**wrap-a·round** /ˈ· · ˌ·/ *adj* a wrap-around skirt is wound around your body with a double layer of cloth at the front

**wrap·per** /ˈræpə‖-ər/ *n* [C] the piece of paper or plastic that covers something when it is sold: *a candy wrapper*

**wrap·ping** /ˈræpɪŋ/ also **wrappings** *n* [C,U] cloth, paper, or plastic that is wrapped around something to protect it: *Torn Christmas wrapping littered the floor.*

**wrapping pa·per** /ˈ·· ˌ··/ *n* [U] coloured paper that you use for wrapping presents

**wrap-up** /ˈ· ·/ *n* [C] *AmE informal* a short report at the end of something, giving the main points again: *And finally here's a wrap-up of the six o'clock news.*

**wrath** /rɒθ‖ræθ/ *n* [U] *formal* extreme anger: *fearing the wrath of God* —**wrathful** *adj* —**wrathfully** *adv*

**wreak** /riːk/ *v past tense and past participle* **wreaked** also **wrought** /rɔːt‖rɒːt/ **wreak havoc/revenge** to cause a lot of damage, problems, and suffering: *A major power failure wreaked havoc in New York last night.*

**wreath** /riːθ/ *n* [C] **1** a circle made from leaves or flowers that you put on a grave or hang on the door at Christmas **2** a circle made from leaves that was given to someone in past times as an honour: *a laurel wreath*

**wreathe** /riːð/ *v literary* **1 be wreathed in sth** to be surrounded by or covered in something: *The mountains were wreathed in mist.* **2 wreathed in smiles** looking very happy

**wreck¹** /rek/ *v* [T] **1** to completely spoil or destroy something such as a plan, relationship, or opportunity: *I just hope the weather doesn't wreck our plans!* **2** to damage something such as a building, vehicle etc so badly that it cannot be repaired: *Hundreds of old buildings were wrecked by the earthquake.* **3** [usually passive] to destroy a ship, especially by hitting rocks in a storm: *The ship was wrecked off the coast of Africa.*

**wreck²** *n* [C] **1** a ship that has sunk or is so badly damaged that it cannot sail: *the wreck of an old Spanish galleon* **2** something such as a car or plane that has been damaged very badly, especially in an accident: *a plane wreck off the coast* **3** [usually singular] *informal* someone who is very nervous, tired, or unhealthy: *Look at me – I'm a complete wreck!*| **nervous wreck** *Dean hated flying, and by the time we reached the airport he was a nervous wreck.* **4** *AmE* an accident involving cars or other vehicles: *The wreck caused a traffic jam three miles long.* **5** *informal* something, especially a car, that is in a very bad condition: *Jo drives an old wreck of a Ford.*

**wreck·age** /ˈrekɪdʒ/ *n* [singular, U] **1** the parts of something such as a plane, ship, or building that are left after it has been destroyed in an accident: *sifting through the wreckage for survivors* **2** the destruction of someone's relationships, hopes, plans etc

**wrecked** /rekt/ *adj* [not before noun] *informal* **1** *BrE* very drunk **2** extremely tired

**wreck·er** /ˈrekə‖-ər/ *n* [C] **1** someone who destroys a relationship, plan, opportunity etc: *a home wrecker* **2** *AmE* a vehicle used to move damaged cars or other vehicles **3** someone in past times who deliberately made ships hit rocks so that they could steal goods from them **4** someone whose job is to save goods from ships that have been damaged

**wren** /ren/ *n* [C] a very small brown bird

**wrench¹** /rentʃ/ *v* **1** [T always + adv/prep] to twist and pull something from its position using force: **wrench sth away/free/off etc** *I managed to wrench the knife away from him.* **2** [T always + adv/prep] to use your strength to pull yourself away from someone who is holding you: **wrench yourself away/free etc** *Tim struggled to wrench himself free from her grasp.* **3** [T] to twist a joint in your body suddenly and painfully: *I wrenched my knee playing soccer.*

**wrench**² *n* **1** [singular] a strong feeling of sadness that you get when you leave a person or place that you love: *Leaving Arizona for New York had been a terrible wrench.* **2** [C usually singular] a twisting movement that pulls something violently: *With one almighty wrench, the door opened.* **3** [C] **a)** *AmE* a metal tool with a round end that fits over and turns nuts (NUT¹ (2)); SPANNER *BrE* **b)** *especially AmE* also **monkey wrench** a tool that you can use to hold or turn nuts (NUT¹ (2) that are different sizes; adjustable spanner *BrE* —see picture at TOOL¹

**wrest** /rest/ *v* [T always + adv/prep] *formal* **1** to take power or influence away from someone, especially when this is difficult **2** to pull something away from someone violently: *I wrested the photograph from his grasp.*

**wres·tle** /ˈresəl/ *v* **1** [I,T] to fight someone by holding onto them and pulling or pushing them: [+ **with**] *The kids were wrestling with each other in the yard.* | **wrestle sb to the ground** (=make someone fall down by holding onto them and pushing them) **2** [I,T] to have difficulty controlling or holding something that is very large, heavy, or difficult to use: [+ **with**] *Daisy was wrestling with one of the larger boxes.* **3** [I] to try to deal with or find a solution to a difficult problem: [+ **with**] *I spent two hours wrestling with my maths homework.*

**wres·tler** /ˈreslə‖-ər/ *n* [C] someone who wrestles as a sport

**wres·tling** /ˈreslɪŋ/ *n* [U] a sport in which two people fight by holding onto each other and trying to make each other fall to the ground

**wretch** /retʃ/ *n* [C] **1** someone that you feel sorry for: *The poor wretch had really suffered.* **2** *often humorous* someone you are annoyed with: *You wretch! You've soaked my dress!* **3** *literary* an evil person

**wretch·ed** /ˈretʃɪ̣d/ *adj* **1** very unhappy or ill: *I lay in bed feeling thoroughly wretched.* **2** [only before noun] making you feel annoyed or angry: *What does the wretched woman want this time?* **3** *literary* extremely bad or of very poor quality: *wretched living conditions* —**wretchedly** *adv* —**wretchedness** *n* [U]

**wrig·gle**¹ /ˈrɪgəl/ *v* **1** [I] to twist from side to side with small quick movements: *Stop wriggling and let me put your T-shirt on.* | [+ **under/through/into**] *The hole was just deep enough for the dog to wriggle under the fence.* **2** [T] to make a part of your body move in this way —**wriggly** *adj*

**wriggle out of** sth *phr v* [T] to avoid doing something by using clever excuses

**wriggle**² *n* [C] a wriggling movement

**-wright** /raɪt/ *suffix* [in nouns] a maker of things of a particular kind: *wheelwright* (=someone who makes wheels) | *a playwright* (=someone who writes plays)

**wring** /rɪŋ/ *v past tense and past participle* **wrung** /rʌŋ/ [T] **1** [always + adv/prep] to succeed in getting money, information, an agreement etc from someone, but only after a lot of effort: **wring sth from sb/out of sb** *We finally succeeded in wringing a confession out of him.* **2** also **wring out** to tightly twist a wet cloth or wet clothes in order to force out the water **3 wring your hands** to rub and twist your hands together because you are worried and upset **4 wring sth's neck** to kill something such as a chicken by twisting its neck **5 I'll wring sb's neck** *spoken* used when someone has made you angry: *If you say that again I'll wring your neck!* **6 wringing wet** extremely wet **7 wring sb's hand** to shake hands very firmly with someone **8 wring your heart/soul** *literary* to make you feel very sorry for someone

**wring·er** /ˈrɪŋə‖-ər/ *n* [C] **1** a machine with two rollers (ROLLER (1)) that press the water from washed clothes when you turn a handle **2 go through the wringer** *AmE informal* to have an upsetting experience: *She's really been through the wringer since her husband died.*

**wrin·kle**¹ /ˈrɪŋkəl/ *n* [C] **1** a line on your face or skin that you get when you are old: *wrinkles around the eyes* **2** a small untidy fold in a piece of clothing or paper **3 iron out the wrinkles** to solve the small problems in something —**wrinkly** *adj*

**wrinkle**² *v* **1** [I,T] if you wrinkle a piece of clothing or if it wrinkles, it gets small untidy folds in it: *The trouble with linen is that it wrinkles so easily.* **2 wrinkle your nose/eyes/brow etc** to move part of your face so that there are wrinkles on or around it

**wrin·kled** /ˈrɪŋkəld/ *adj* skin, cloth, or paper that is wrinkled has lines or small untidy folds in it

**wrin·kly** /ˈrɪŋkli/ *n plural* **wrinklies** [C] *BrE informal* an impolite expression meaning someone who is old

**wrist** /rɪst/ *n* [C] the joint between your hand and the lower part of your arm —see picture at BODY **S**

**wrist·band** /ˈrɪstbænd/ *n* [C] **1** a band worn especially by tennis players around their wrists to keep their hands dry **2** a band worn around your wrist, for example in a hospital

**wrist·watch** /ˈrɪstwɒtʃ‖-wɑːtʃ, -wɒːtʃ/ *n* [C] a watch that you wear on your wrist

**writ**¹ /rɪt/ *n* [C] a document from a court that orders someone to do or not to do something —see also HOLY WRIT

**writ**² *adj* **writ large** *literary* **a)** made clearer and easier to notice **b)** in a clearer and stronger form: *The new evangelism is really old time religion writ large.*

**write** /raɪt/ *v past tense* **wrote** /rəʊt‖roʊt/ *past participle* **written** /ˈrɪtn/ **S** **W**

**1 ▶ BOOK/ARTICLE ETC ◀ a)** [I,T] to produce a new book, poem song etc: *I can't come with you – I have an essay to write.* | *a concerto written by Mozart* | **write about** (=describe something) *The children are writing about their summer holidays.* | **well/badly written** *The article's very well written.* | **write a program** (=produce it on a computer) *We're writing a program for a new spellchecker.* **b)** [I] to be a writer of books, plays, articles etc: *"What do you do?" "I write."* | [+ **for**] *Shaw started to write for the stage.* | [+ **on**] *She writes on gardening for 'The Daily Telegraph'.*

**2 ▶ LETTER ◀** [I,T] to write a letter to someone: [+ **to**] *Have you written to John yet?* | **write sb a letter** *I wrote her several letters, but she didn't reply.* | **write sb** *AmE*: *Steve wrote me about the wedding.* | **write that** *The Ewings wrote that they might be able to visit us in the spring.*

**3 ▶ WORDS ◀ a)** [I,T] to form letters or numbers with a pen or pencil: *Kerry could read and write when he was five.* | *The price is written on the label.* **b)** [I] if a pen or pencil writes, it works properly: *What use is a pen that won't write?*

**4 ▶ CHEQUE/DOCUMENT ETC ◀** [T] also **write** sth ↔ **out** to write information on a cheque, form etc: *Wouldn't it be easier if I just wrote a cheque for the lot?*

**5 have sth written all over your face** to show very clearly what you are feeling or thinking: *He had guilt written all over his face.*

**6 nothing to write home about** *informal* not particularly good or special: *The hotel was good, but the food was nothing to write home about.*

**7 sb wrote the book on it** *spoken* used to say that someone knows a lot about a subject: *Ask Harry about shark fishing, he wrote the book on it!*

**write away for** sth *phr v* [T] *AmE* to write to a company for something that has been advertised: *Write away for your free kitchen catalog today.*

**write back** *phr v* [I] to answer someone's letter by sending them a letter: *I sent them a card once, but they never wrote back.*

**write** sth ↔ **down** *phr v* [T] to write information, ideas etc on a piece of paper in order to remember them: *I wrote down the address in the back of my diary.*

**write in** *phr v* **1** [I] to write to an organization asking them for information or giving an opinion: *Hundreds of viewers have written in wanting to know the name of our signature tune.* **2** [T **write** sb/sth ↔ **in**] *AmE* **a)** to add someone's name to your BALLOT PAPER in order to vote for them —see also WRITE-IN

**write** sth **into** sth *phr v* [T] to include something such as a rule or condition in a document, agreement etc: *I have to attend regular training sessions – it's written into my contract.*

**write off** *phr v* **1** [T **write** sb/sth ↔ **off**] to decide that someone or something is useless, unimportant, or a failure: [+ **as**] *We've written the project off as a non-starter.* **2** [T **write** sth ↔ **off**] to officially say that someone does not have to pay a debt: *As part of the deal, all their debts were written off.* **3** [I] to write to a company asking them to send you information on one of their products: [+ **for**] *Are you going to write off for that free poster?* **4** [T **write** sth ↔ **off**] *BrE* to damage a vehicle so badly that it can never be used again —see also WRITE-OFF

**write** sb/sth ↔ **out** *phr v* [T] **1** to write a list, report etc including all the necessary details: *Write out exactly what happened and give it to your solicitor.* **2** to write information on a cheque or a form: *She calmly wrote out a check for $500 and handed it to Will.* **3** to write something again in a better or more complete way: *I'll write my essay out neatly and give it in tomorrow.* **4** to remove one of the characters from a regular radio or television programme

**write** sth ↔ **up** *phr v* [T] **1** to write a report, article etc using notes that you made earlier: *I have to write up my report before the meeting.* **2** to write your opinion about a new book, play, or product for a newspaper, magazine etc —see also WRITE-UP

**write-in** /ˈ· ·/ *n* [C] *AmE* a vote you give to someone by writing their name on your BALLOT PAPER

**write-off** /ˈ· ·/ *n* [C] **1** *BrE* a vehicle that has been so badly damaged that it can never be used again: *The car was a complete write-off.* —see also **write off** (4) (WRITE) **2** an official agreement that someone does not have to pay a debt

3 **writ·er** /ˈraɪtə‖-ər/ *n* [C] someone who writes books, sto-
2 ries etc, especially as a job: *a science-fiction writer* | [+ **on**] *a well-known writer on astrology* | [+ **of**] *a writer of children's stories*

**writer's block** /ˌ·· ˈ·/ *n* [U] the problem that a writer sometimes has of not being able to think of new ideas

**writer's cramp** /ˌ·· ˈ·/ *n* [U] a feeling of stiffness in your hand that you get after writing for a long time

**write-up** /ˈ· ·/ *n* [C] a written opinion about a new book, play, or product in a newspaper, magazine etc: *The play got a really good write-up in the press.* —opposite RIGHT[1] (6)

**writhe** /raɪð/ *v* [I] **1** to twist your body from side to side violently, especially because you are suffering pain: **writhe in pain/agony** *He lay on the floor writhing in pain.* **2 writhe with anger/hate/shame etc** *literary* to feel very violent emotions of anger etc

2 **writ·ing** /ˈraɪtɪŋ/ *n* [U] **1** words that have been written
3 or printed: *What does the writing on the back say?* **2 in writing** if you get something in writing, it is official proof of an agreement, promise etc: **put sth in writing** *Could you put that in writing please?* **3** books, poems etc in general, especially those by a particular writer or about a particular subject: *Some of his most powerful writing is based on his childhood experiences.* **4** the activity of writing books, stories etc: *In 1991 she retired from politics and took up writing as a career.* **5** the particular way that someone writes with a pen or pencil; HANDWRITING: *Your writing is very neat.* **6 writings** *plural* the books, stories etc that a particular person writes: *Darwin's scientific writings* **7 the writing is on the wall** used to say that it seems very likely that something will not exist much longer or someone will fail: *The writing is on the wall for the old manufacturing industries.*

**writing desk** /ˈ·· ·/ *n* [C] a desk with special places for pens, paper etc

**writing pa·per** /ˈ·· ˌ··/ *n* [U] good quality paper that you use for writing letters

**writ·ten¹** /ˈrɪtn/ the past participle of WRITE

**written²** *adj* [only before noun] **1** recorded in writing: **written agreement/reply etc** *You'll get a written report of my conclusions within ten days.* **2 written test/exam** a test etc in which you have to write the answers **3 the written word** *formal* writing as a way of expressing ideas, emotions etc

**wrong¹** /rɒŋ‖rɔːŋ/ *adj* 
**1** ▶ **NOT CORRECT** ◀ saying, believing, or depending  on something that is not correct: *Your calculations must be wrong.* | **be wrong to think/say** *I'm sorry; I was wrong to assume that you wanted to go.* | **prove sb wrong** *I wish you'd stop trying to prove me wrong all the time.*
**2** ▶ **NOT THE RIGHT ONE** ◀ not the one that you intended or the one that you should use: *The letter was delivered to the wrong address.* | *driving on the wrong side of the road*
**3** ▶ **TELEPHONE** ◀ **wrong number** used when you have telephoned the wrong person by mistake: *There's no-one called Julia here – I think you must have the wrong number.*
**4** ▶ **NOT MORAL** ◀ not morally right or acceptable: **it is wrong to do sth** *You must have known it was wrong to take the money.* | **it is wrong that** *It's wrong that people should have to sleep on the streets.* —opposite RIGHT[1] (6)
**5** ▶ **NOT SUITABLE** ◀ not suitable for a particular purpose, situation, or person: *It's the wrong time of year to be planning a holiday.* | [+ **for**] *This is the wrong climate for growing grapes.*
**6 be the wrong way round/around a)** to be in the wrong order: *These two paragraphs are the wrong way round.* **b)** to be pointing in the wrong direction: *You've got your T-shirt on the wrong way around.*
**7 be in the wrong place at the wrong time** *spoken* to get involved in trouble without intending to
**8 get on the wrong side of sb** to do something that gives someone a bad opinion of you, so that they do not like or respect you in the future
**9 get on the wrong side of the law** to get into trouble with the police
**10 get off on the wrong foot** to start a job, relationship etc badly by making a mistake that annoys people
**11 take sth the wrong way** to be offended by a remark because you have understood it wrongly
**12 get the wrong end of the stick** *informal* to understand a situation in completely the wrong way
**13 be on the wrong track/tack** to have the wrong idea about a situation so that you are unlikely to get the result you want
**14 be from the wrong side of the tracks** *AmE* to be from a poor part of a town or a poor part of society
**15 be on the wrong side of thirty/forty etc** *informal* to be older than thirty etc —see also **get out of bed on the wrong side** (BED[1] (9))

Frequencies of the adjective **wrong** in spoken written English.

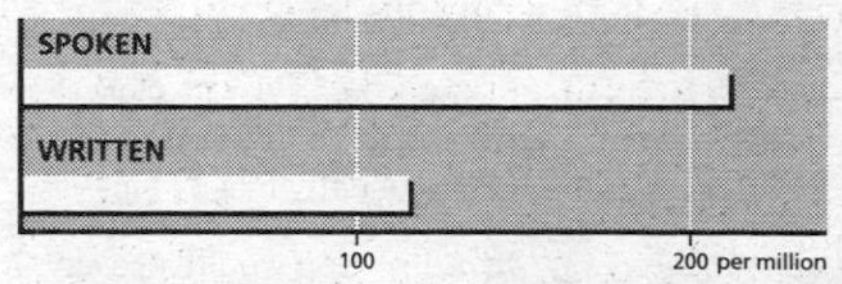


Based on the British National Corpus and the Longman Lancaster Corpus

This graph shows that the adjective **wrong** is much more common in spoken English than in written English. This is because it is used in some common spoken phrases.

**wrong** (*adj*) **SPOKEN PHRASES**

**16 what's wrong? a)** used to ask someone what problem they have, why they are unhappy etc: *"What's wrong?" "Oh, I'm just a bit worried about tomorrow."* **b)** used to ask why something doesn't work: [+ **with**] *What's wrong with this clock?* **c)** used to say that you think something is good, fair etc, and you do not

W

understand why other people think it is not: [+ with] *What's wrong with eating meat? I think it's natural.*
**17 there's something wrong** used to say that there is a fault or problem with something: *There's something wrong. The car won't start.* | [+ **with**] *There's something wrong with the phone, the line's dead.* | **have sth wrong with** *She had to go home early – she's got something wrong with her back.*
**18 there's nothing wrong a)** used to say that something has not got any faults or problems: *It's O.K. don't worry, there's nothing wrong.* | [+ **with**] *There's nothing wrong with the TV, it just wasn't plugged in.* **b)** used to say that you do not think that something is bad or immoral: [+ **with**] *There's nothing wrong with drinking, as long as you know when to stop.*
**19 correct me if I'm wrong** used as a polite way of saying that you think what you are going to say is correct: *Correct me if I'm wrong, but didn't you say you were going to do it?*
**20 you're not wrong** used to agree with someone: *"This government is ruining the country!" "You're not wrong!"*

S2 **wrong²** *adv* **1** not in the correct way: *You've spelt my name wrong.* | **do sth all wrong** (=in completely the wrong way) *I asked him to sort those files, but he's done it all wrong.* **2 go wrong a)** to stop working properly: *The television's gone wrong again.* | [+ **with**] *Something's gone wrong with my watch.* **b)** to make a mistake during a process so that you do not get the right result: **you can't go wrong** (=you are sure to succeed) *Follow these instructions and you can't go wrong.* **c)** to do something that makes a plan, relationship etc fail: *Thinking back on the marriage, I just don't know where we went wrong.* **3 get sth wrong** to make a mistake in the way you write, judge, or understand something: *This isn't it. We must have got the address wrong.* | **get/have it all wrong** (=understand a situation in completely the wrong way) *No, no – you've got it all wrong! We're just friends!* **4 don't get me wrong** *spoken* used when you think someone may understand your remarks wrongly, or be offended by them: *Don't get me wrong – I like Jenny.* **5 you can't go wrong (with sth)** *spoken* used to say that a particular object will always be suitable, satisfactory or work well: *You can't go wrong with a little black dress, can you?*

**USAGE NOTE: WRONG**
COLLOCATION/GRAMMAR
Many meanings of **wrong** only belong in particular phrases or structures that cannot be changed. For example, if someone's health is bad, you can say something **is wrong with** them but not: *They are wrong* (which means not correct).
You can **do something wrong** (=not in the correct way) but not **do a wrong thing** (though you can **do the wrong thing**). If you **do something wrong** that, does not mean there is something **wrong with you**: *He was angry with me but I hadn't done anything wrong.* Note ...**there was nothing wrong with me** (= I was not ill).
**Wrong** used before a noun usually means 'not correct', 'not correctly chosen' or 'not suitable': *the wrong answer/key/furniture.* You would also say: *I can't find what is wrong/has gone wrong* (NOT *I can't find the wrong thing*) if you mean that something is not working. **Wrong** also means 'morally wrong', and is used in this way: *What you did was completely wrong* (NOT *You did wrong things/action*).

Sometimes **bad** is a better word to use. You would call a day when everything **goes wrong** a *bad day* (NOT a *wrong day*). If you **get things wrong** you make a lot of mistakes, and may get a *bad record* but not *a wrong record* (which means not correct).

**wrong³** *n* **1** [U] behaviour that is not morally right: *He's too young to know right from wrong.* | **sb can do no wrong** (=they are perfect) *That man seems to think he can do no wrong.* **2** [C] an action, judgement, or situation that is unfair: *The black population suffered countless wrongs at the hands of a racist regime.* | **right a wrong** (=bring justice to an unfair situation) **3 be in the wrong** to make a mistake or deserve the blame for something: *Which driver was in the wrong?* **4 do sb wrong** *humorous* to treat someone badly and unfairly **5 two wrongs don't make a right** *spoken* used to say that punishing someone will not make a bad situation right or fair

**wrong⁴** *v* [T] *formal* to treat or judge someone unfairly: *I felt I had been grievously wronged.*

**wrong·do·ing** /ˈrɒŋˌduːɪŋ‖ˌrɔːŋˈduːɪŋ/ *n* [C,U] *formal* illegal or immoral behaviour —**wrongdoer** *n*

**wrong·foot** /ˌrɒŋˈfʊt‖ˌrɔːŋ-/ *v* [T] to surprise and embarrass someone, especially by asking a question they did not expect

**wrong·ful** /ˈrɒŋfəl‖ˈrɔːŋ-/ *adj* **wrongful arrest/conviction/dismissal etc** a wrongful arrest etc is unfair or illegal because you have done nothing wrong: *She's threatening to sue her employers for wrongful dismissal.* —**wrongfully** *adv*

**wrong·head·ed** /ˌrɒŋˈhedɪd◂‖ˌrɔːŋ-/ *adj* based on or influenced by wrong ideas that you are not willing to change —**wrongheadedly** *adv*

**wrong·ly** /ˈrɒŋli‖ˈrɔːŋ-/ *adv* **1** incorrectly or in a way that is not based on facts: *You're holding the racket wrongly.* | *Matthew was wrongly diagnosed as having a brain tumour.* **2** in a way that is unfair or immoral: **wrongly convicted/imprisoned/accused/blamed** *Human rights organizations maintain that the men have been wrongly convicted.* **3** in a way that is not suitable or socially acceptable: *I was wrongly dressed for a formal dinner.* —see also **rightly or wrongly** (RIGHTLY)

**wrote** /rəʊt‖roʊt/ the past tense of WRITE

**wroth** /rəʊθ‖rɔːθ/ *adj old use* angry

**wrought i·ron** /ˌrɔːt ˈaɪən◂‖ˌrɔːt ˈaɪərn◂/ *n* [U] long thin pieces of iron formed into shapes to make gates, fences etc

**wrought-up** /ˌ· ˈ·◂/ *adj* very nervous and excited

**wrung** /rʌŋ/ the past tense and past participle of WRING

**wry** /raɪ/ *adj* [only before noun] showing a mixture of amusement and displeasure or disbelief: *He took a gulp of his Scotch and gave a wry smile at the injustices of the world.*

**wt** the written abbreviation of WEIGHT

**wun·der·kind** /ˈwʌndəkɪnd‖-ər-/ *n* [C] *German* a young person who is very successful

**wuss** /wʌs/ *n* [C] *AmE slang* someone who you think is weak because they are afraid to do something difficult or unpleasant

**WYSIWYG** /ˈwɪziwɪg/ *n* [U] What You See Is What You Get; a word used in computing meaning what you see on the screen is exactly what will be printed

**wy·vern** /ˈwaɪvən‖-ərn/ *n* [C] an imaginary animal that has two legs and wings and looks like a DRAGON (1)

**X,x**[1] /eks/ *plural* **X's,x's** *n* [C] **1** the 24th letter of the English alphabet **2** the number 10 in the system of ROMAN NUMERALS **3** *technical* a letter used in mathematics to represent an unknown quantity or value: *if 3x=6, x=2* **4** a mark used to show that a written answer is wrong **5** a mark used to show that you have chosen something on an official piece of paper, for example when voting **6** a mark used instead of a signature by someone who cannot write **7** a mark used to show a kiss, especially at the end of a letter **8** a letter used to show that a film is not suitable for people under 18 **9** a letter used instead of someone or something's real name because you want to keep it secret or you do not know it: *At the trial, Ms X said that she had known the defendant for three years* **10 X number of** used to say that there are a certain number of people or things when the exact number is not important **11 X marks the spot** used on maps in adventure stories to show that something is buried in a particular place

**X**[2] *v*

**X out** sth *phr v* [T] *AmE* to mark or remove a mistake in a piece of writing using an X; **cross out** CROSS[1]

**X-cer·tif·i·cate** /ˈeks səˌtɪfɪkət‖-sər-/ *adj* an X-certificate film is one that people under 18 are not allowed to see in Britain because it includes sex or violence —compare PG, R[2] (4), U (1)

**X chro·mo·some** /ˈeks ˌkrəʊməsəʊm‖-ˌkrouməsoum/ *n* [C] a type of CHROMOSOME that exists in pairs in female cells, and with a Y CHROMOSOME in male cells

**xen·on** /ˈzenɒn‖ˈziːnɑːn, ˈze-/ *n* [U] a rare gas that is one of the chemical elements ELEMENT (1)

**xen·o·phò·bi·a** /ˌzenəˈfəʊbiə‖-ˈfou-/ *n* [U] extreme fear or dislike of people from other countries —**xenophobic** *adj*

**Xe·rox** /ˈzɪərɒks, ˈze-‖ˈzɪrɑːks, ˈziː-/ *n* [C] *trademark* a copy of a piece of paper with writing or printing on it, made using a special machine; a kind of PHOTOCOPY[1] —**Xerox** *v* [T]

**Xerox ma·chine** /ˈ·· ·ˌ·/ *n* [C] *trademark* a special electric machine used for making copies of written or printed material; a kind of PHOTOCOPIER —see picture on page 837

**X·mas** /ˈkrɪsməs, ˈeksməs/ *n* [C,U] *informal* a word that means Christmas, often written on signs or cards

**X-rated** /ˈeks ˌreɪtɪ̣d/ *adj* an X-rated film is one that people under 18 are not allowed to see because it includes sex or violence

**X-ray**[1] /ˈeks reɪ/ *n* [C] **1** a beam of RADIATION (1) that can go through solid objects and is used for photographing the inside of the body **2** a photograph of part of the body, taken in this way to see if anything is wrong: *The X-ray showed that her leg was not broken.*|*a chest X-ray* **3** a medical examination made using x-rays: *I had to go to hospital for an x-ray.*

**X-ray**[2] *v* [T] to photograph the inside of someone's body using X-rays: *The problem was only discovered when her lungs were X-rayed.*

**xy·lo·phone** /ˈzaɪləfəʊn‖-foun/ *n* [C] a musical instrument which consists of metal or wooden bars that you hit with a special stick to make sounds

**Y, y** /waɪ/ *plural* **Y's, y's** **1** the 25th letter of the English alphabet **2 the Y** *AmE informal* the YMCA or the YWCA

**-y¹, -ey** /i/ *suffix* [in adjectives] **1** full of or covered with something: *dirty hands* (=covered with dirt)| *a hairy chest* **2** tending to do something, or doing something: *curly hair* (=hair that curls)| *feeling sleepy* **3** like or typical of something: *a cold wintry day* (=typical of winter)| *his long, horsy face* (=he looks like a horse) **4** fond of or interested in something: *a horsy woman* (=who likes riding horses) —**-ily** [in adverbs] —**-iness** [in nouns]

**-y²** *suffix* [in nouns] **1** also **-ie** used, especially when speaking to children, to make a word or name less formal, and often to show fondness: *Where's little Johnny?* (=John)| *my daddy* (=father)| *What a nice doggy!* (=dog)| *wellies* (=WELLINGTONS) **2** the action of doing something: *the expiry date* (=date when something EXPIRES)

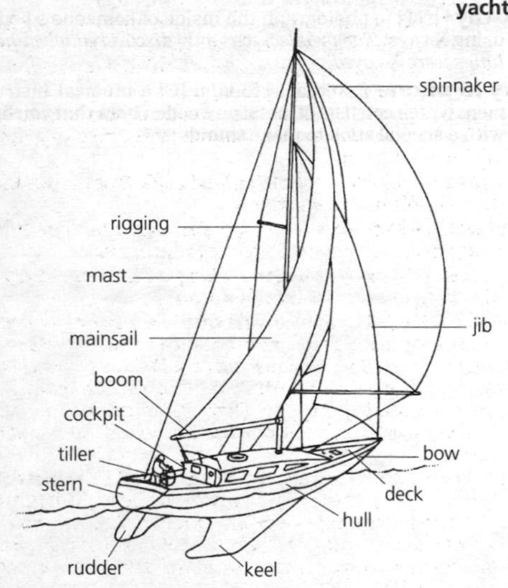


**yacht** /jɒt‖jɑːt/ *n* [C] a large sailing boat, especially one that you can sleep on —compare SAILING BOAT, SAIL BOAT

**yacht·ing** /ˈjɒtɪŋ‖ˈjɑːtɪŋ/ *n* [U] *especially BrE* sailing, travelling, or racing in a yacht —compare SAILING

**yachts·man** /ˈjɒtsmən‖ˈjɑːts-/ *n* [C] someone who owns or sails a yacht

**yachts·wom·an** /ˈjɒtswʊmən‖ˈjɑːts-/ *n* [C] a woman who owns or sails a yacht

**ya·hoo** /jɑːˈhuː/ *n* [C] *old-fashioned* someone who is rough, noisy, or bad-mannered

**Yah·weh** /ˈjɑːweɪ/ *n* [singular] a Hebrew name for God

**yak¹** /jæk/ *n* [C] an animal of central Asia that looks like a cow with long hair

**yak²** *v* **yakked, yakking** [I] *informal* to talk continuously about things that are not very serious; CHATTER¹ (1)

**y'all** /jɔːl‖jɒːl/ *pron AmE informal* a word meaning 'all of you,' used mainly in the southern US states when speaking to more than one person: *Are y'all coming over for lunch?*

**yam** /jæm/ *n* [C] **1** a tropical climbing plant grown for its root, which is eaten as a vegetable —see picture on page 414 **2** *AmE* a type of SWEET POTATO

**yam·mer** /ˈjæmə‖-ər/ also **yammer on** *v* [I] *BrE informal* to talk noisily and continuously: *a crowd of yammering aunts and cousins*

**yang** /jæŋ/ *n* [U] the male principle in Chinese PHILOSOPHY which is active, light, positive and which combines with YIN (=the female principle) to influence everything in the world

**Yank** /jæŋk/ *n* [C] *informal* **1** a word meaning someone from the US, sometimes used in an insulting way by someone who is not American **2** also **Yankee** *AmE* someone born or living in the northern, especially the northeastern, states of the US

**yank** *v* [I,T] *informal* to suddenly pull something quickly and forcefully: **yank (on) sth** *John keeps yanking on my ponytail!*| **yank sth out/back/open etc** *Keith yanked Robert out of his chair.*

**Yan·kee** /ˈjæŋki/ *n* [C] *informal* **1** *AmE* someone born or living in the northern, especially the northeastern, states of the US **2** *especially BrE* someone from the US

**yap¹** /jæp/ *v* **yapped, yapping** [I] **1** if a small dog yaps, it BARKS (=makes short loud sounds) in an excited way **2** to talk noisily without saying anything very important or serious: *Don't start yapping again.*

**yap²** *n* [C] the sound a small dog makes when it yaps

**yard** /jɑːd‖jɑːrd/ *n* [C] S W
**1** ▶ **ENCLOSED AREA** ◀ an enclosed area next to a building or group of buildings, used for a special purpose, activity, or business: *a cattle yard*| *Their house is next to a builder's yard.*
**2** ▶ **MEASURE** ◀ written abbreviation **yd** a unit for measuring length, equal to 3 feet or .9144 metres —see table on page B2
**3** ▶ **GARDEN** ◀ *AmE* the ground around a house, usually covered with grass; GARDEN¹ (1) *BrE*: *back yard*| *Their front yard was full of kids playing tag.* —see also BACKYARD
**4 prison/school yard** an area outside a prison or school where prisoners or students go to do activities outdoors
**5** ▶ **BACK OF HOUSE** ◀ *BrE* an enclosed area without grass at the back of a small house
**6** ▶ **SAILING** ◀ *technical* a long pole that supports a square sail —see also CHURCHYARD, FARMYARD, SHIPYARD

**yard·age** /ˈjɑːdɪdʒ‖ˈjɑːr-/ *n* [C,U] *technical* **1** the size of something measured in yards or square yards: *a large yardage of sail* **2** [U] the number of yards that a team or player moves forward in a game of American football

**yard·arm** /ˈjɑːd-ɑːm‖ˈjɑːrd-ɑːrm/ *n* [C] one of the ends of the pole that supports a square sail

**yard·bird** /ˈjɑːdbɜːd‖ˈjɑːrdbɜːrd/ *n* [C] *AmE slang* **1** someone who is in prison, especially for a long time **2** someone who has just joined the army and has outdoor duties

**yard sale** /ˈ· ·/ *n* [C] *AmE* a sale of used things from someone's house that takes place in their YARD (3) —compare GARAGE SALE

**yard·stick** /ˈjɑːdˌstɪk‖ˈjɑːrd-/ *n* [C] **1** something that you compare another thing with, in order to judge how good or successful they are: [+ **of/against**] *Is profit the only yardstick of success?* **2** a special stick for measuring things that is exactly one YARD (2) long

**yar·mul·ke** /ˈjɑːmʊlkə‖ˈjɑːr-/ *n* [C] a small circular cap worn by Jewish men

**yarn** /jɑːn‖jɑːrn/ *n* **1** [U] *especially AmE* long thick thread, made of cotton or wool used to KNIT or make cloth **2** [C] *informal* a story of adventures, travels etc, usually made more exciting and interesting by adding things that never really happened: **spin a yarn** (=tell a long and often not completely true story) *The old captain would often spin us a yarn about life aboard ship.*

**yash·mak** /ˈjæʃmæk/ *n* [C] a piece of cloth that Muslim women wear across their faces

**yaw** /jɔː‖jɒː/ *v* [I] *technical* if a ship, aircraft etc yaws it makes a turn away from its proper course —compare PITCH¹ (4), ROLL¹ (9) —**yaw** *n* [C,U]

**yawl** /jɔːl‖jɒːl/ *n* [C] **1** a sailing boat with a main MAST (=pole) and sails and another small mast and sail close to the back **2** a small boat carried on a ship

**yawn¹** /jɔːn‖jɒːn/ *v* [I] **1** to open your mouth wide and breathe in deeply, usually because you are tired, or bored: *The boy stretched and yawned.* **2** to be or become wide open: *a yawning hole*|[+ **open**] *The pit yawned open in front of them.*|**yawning gap/gulf** *the yawning gap between training needs and training resources*

yawn

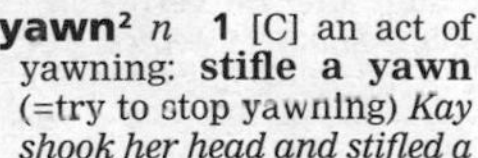

**yawn²** *n* **1** [C] an act of yawning: **stifle a yawn** (=try to stop yawning) *Kay shook her head and stifled a yawn.* **2** [singular] *informal* someone or something that is boring: *The party was a big yawn.*

**yaws** /jɔːz‖jɒːz/ *n* [U] a tropical skin disease

**Y chro·mo·some** /ˈwaɪ ˌkrəʊməsəʊm‖-ˌkroʊməsoʊm/ *n* [C] the part of a GENE that makes someone a male instead of a female —see also X CHROMOSOME

**yd** the written abbreviation of YARD² or yards

**ye¹** /jiː/ *pron old use* a word meaning 'you', used especially when speaking to more than one person

**ye²** *determiner* **1** a word meaning 'the', used especially in the names of shops and PUBS to make them seem old: *The sign said 'Ye Olde Dog and Duck'.* **2 ye gods** *spoken* used to show that you are very surprised, or shocked, by something: *Ye gods! I can't believe this.*

**yea¹** /jeɪ/ *adv old use* yes —opposite NAY¹ (2) —see also AYE²

**yea²** *n* [C] a vote or voter that supports an idea, plan, law etc —opposite NAY² —see also AYE¹ (1)

S1 **yeah** /jeə/ *adv spoken* yes

S1 W1 **year** /jɪə, jɜː‖jɪr/ *n* [C]

**1 ▶12 MONTHS◀** a period of about 365 days or 12 months, measured from any particular time: *I arrived here two years ago.*|*We've known each other for over a year.*|*15 years old*|*a three-year development*|*a four-year-old child*|**tax/fiscal/financial year** *The tax year begins in April.*|**school year** (=period during a year when students are in school, university etc)

**2 ▶JANUARY TO DECEMBER◀** also **calendar year** a period of 365 or 366 days divided into 12 months beginning on January 1st and ending on December 31st: *the year that Martin Luther King died*|*Their lease expires at the end of the year.*|*1995 was a profitable year.*|*the year 2000*|**all (the) year round** (=during the whole year)

**3 ▶MEASURE OF TIME◀** *technical* a measure of time equal to 365¼ days, which is the amount of time it takes for the Earth to travel once around the sun

**4 childhood/war/retirement etc years** a particular period of time in someone's life or in history: *He started writing poetry during his Harvard years.*|*the boom years of the 1980's*

**5 years a)** *informal* many years: **in/for years** *I haven't been there for years.*|*It's years since I rode a bike.* **b)** age, especially old age: *Gramps is very active for a man of his years.*|**getting on in years** (=no longer young)|**be 12/21 etc years of age** (=12/21 etc years old)

**6 year by year** as each year passes: *Year by year their business grew.*

**7 year after year** continuously for many years: *It's always the same, year after year.*

**8 never/not in a million years** *spoken* used to say strongly that you will never do something: *I won't forgive him – never in a million years.*

**9 first/second etc year** *BrE* someone who is in their first etc year at school or university

**10 put years on sb/take years off sb** to make someone look or feel older or younger: *Theresa's divorce has put years on her.* —see also **donkey's years** (DONKEY (3)), YEARLY

**11 the year dot** *BrE informal* a very long time ago: *Scientists have been involved in war since the year dot.*

**year·book** /ˈjɪəbʊk, ˈjɜː-‖ˈjɪr-/ *n* [C] *AmE* a book printed once a year, especially by a school or college, with information and pictures about what happened there in the year just past

**year·ling** /ˈjɪəlɪŋ, ˈjɜː-‖ˈjɪr-/ *n* [C] an animal, especially a young horse, between one and two years old

**year·long** /ˌjɪəˈlɒŋ◂, ˈjɜː-‖ˌjɪrˈlɒːŋ◂/ *adj* [only before noun] lasting for a year or all through the year: *We store the apples so we have a yearlong supply.*

**year·ly** /ˈjɪəli, ˈjɜː-‖ˈjɪrli/ *adj* happening or appearing every year or once a year: *a yearly pay award*|**3-yearly/5-yearly etc** (=every three years etc) *a check-up at five-yearly intervals* —**yearly** *adv*: *We pay the fee yearly.*

**yearn** /jɜːn‖jɜːrn/ *v* [I] *literary* to have a strong desire for something, especially something that is difficult or impossible to get: **yearn for sth** *Hannah yearned for a child*|**yearn to do sth** *yearning to go home*

**yearn·ing** /ˈjɜːnɪŋ‖ˈjɜːr-/ *n* [C,U] a strong desire or feeling of wanting something: [+ **for**] *an actor with a yearning for recognition*|**a yearning to do sth** *a yearning to travel*

**yeast** /jiːst/ *n* [U] a substance used for producing alcohol in beer and wine and for making bread rise —**yeasty** *adj*: *a yeasty taste*

**yeast ex·tract** /ˈ· ˌ··/ *n* [U] a food made from yeast, used to make things taste better

**yeast in·fec·tion** /ˈ· ·ˌ··/ *n* [C] an infectious condition that affects the VAGINA in adult women; THRUSH¹ (2)

**yecch** /jʌk/ *interjection AmE slang* used to say that you think something is very unpleasant; YUCK

**yell¹** /jel/ *v* [I,T] **1** also **yell out** to shout or say something very loudly, especially because you are frightened, angry, or excited: *The spectators yelled and cheered.*|[+ **at**] *Don't you yell at me like that!*|*"Go, go!" he yelled out.*|**yell at sb to do sth** *They yelled at him to stop.* **2** *spoken, especially AmE* to ask for help: *If you need me just yell.*

**yell²** *n* [C] **1** a loud shout: **let out a yell** *Frank let out a yell and jumped away.*|**a yell of delight/triumph/warning etc** *He gave a yell of delight as the election results came in.* **2** *AmE* words or phrases that students and CHEERLEADERS shout to show support for their school, college etc

**yel·low¹** /ˈjeləʊ‖-loʊ/ *adj* **1** having the colour of butter, gold, or the middle part of an egg —see picture on page 411 **2** an offensive way of describing the skin colour of people from parts of Asia **3** also **yellow-bellied** *informal* not brave; COWARDLY —**yellow** *n* [U] S2 W3

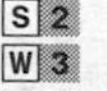

**yellow²** *v* [I,T] to become yellow or make something become yellow: *The paper was yellowed with age.*

**yellow card** /ˌ·· ˈ·/ *n* [C] a yellow card held up by a football REFEREE¹ (1) to show that a player has done something wrong

**yellow fe·ver** /ˌ·· ˈ··/ *n* [C] a dangerous tropical disease in which your skin turns slightly yellow

**yel·low·ham·mer** /ˈjeləʊˌhæmə‖-loʊˌhæmər/ *n* [C] a small European bird with a yellow head

**yellow line** /ˌ·· ˈ·/ *n* [C] a line of yellow paint along the edge of a street in Britain which means you can only park your car for a short time or at particular times: **double yellow line** (=two lines of paint that mean you cannot park there)

**Yellow Pag·es** /ˌ·· ˈ··/ *n* [singular] *trademark* the name of a book that contains the telephone numbers of

Y



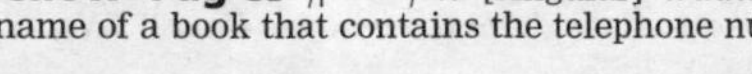

businesses and organizations in an area, arranged according to the type of business they do —compare WHITE PAGES

**yel·low·y** /ˈjeləʊi‖-loʊi/ *adj* having a slight yellow colour: *The cream was thick and yellowy.*

**yelp** /jelp/ *v* [I] to make a short sharp high cry because of excitement, pain etc: | *The dog ran up and down, yelping.* | *He yelped as his bare foot hit the box.* —**yelp** *n* [C] *Rose gave a yelp of dismay.*

**yen** /jen/ *n plural* **yen** **1** [C] the standard unit of money in Japan **2** [singular] a strong desire: [+ **to/for**] *a yen to travel*

**yeo·man** /ˈjəʊmən‖ˈjoʊ-/ *n plural* **yeomen** /-mən/ [C] **1** *BrE especially literary or for old use* a farmer who owned and worked on his own land in former times **2** an officer in the US navy who often has secretarial duties

**yeo·man·ry** /ˈjəʊmənri‖ˈjoʊ-/ *n* **the yeomanry** *BrE literary* the people who owned and farmed their own land in the past

**yeoman ser·vice** /ˌ·· ˈ··/ *n* [U] *BrE formal* long and loyal service, help and support

**yer** /jə‖jər/ *determiner* used in writing as an informal way of saying 'your'

S1 W1 **yes¹** /jes/ *adv spoken* **1** used as an answer to say that something is true, that you agree, that you want something, or that you are willing to do something: *"Is that real gold?" "Yes, it is."* | *"It was a great film." "Yes, it was."* | *"Would you like a sandwich?" "Yes, please."* | *"Can you help us on Saturday?" "Yes I think so."* —opposite NO **2** used as an answer to give permission: *"Can I have a glass of water?" "Yes, of course."* | **say yes to (doing) sth** *I hope my parents will say yes to the party.* **3** used to politely show that you do not agree with all or some of what someone has said: **yes but** *"We need a new car." "Yes, but where will we get the money?"* **4** used to show that you have heard a request, call, command etc: *"Can you close the door, please?" "Yes, in a minute."* | *"Michael!" "Yes?"* **5** used to ask someone what they want: *Yes? Can I help you find something, madam?* **6 yes, yes** used to show annoyance when someone is talking to you and you do not want to listen: *"And don't forget to lock the door!" "Yes, yes ok."* **7 yes and no** used to show that there is not one clear answer to a question: *"Did you have a good time?" "Well, yes and no. The lake was beautiful, but Craig and Jen fought the whole time."* **8 yes/no question** a question to which you only answer yes or no —see also YEAH

**yes²** *n* [C] a vote, voter, or reply that agrees with an idea, plan, law etc: *five yeses and three nos* —**yes** *adj*: *a yes vote*

**ye·shi·va, ye·sh·ivah** /jəˈʃiːvə/ *n* a school for Jewish students, where they can train to become RABBIS (=religious leaders)

**yes-man** /ˈjes mæn/ *n plural* **yes-men** /-men/ [C] someone who always agrees with and obeys their employer, leader, etc in order to gain some advantage

S1 W1 **yes·ter·day** /ˈjestədi‖-ər-/ *n* **1** [U] the day before today: *What did you do yesterday?* | *The day before yesterday was Monday.* | *He left yesterday afternoon.* | *I'm looking for yesterday's paper.* —see picture at DAY **2** [C] the recent past: **yesterday's news** (=not new or modern and therefore no longer of any interest) *The voters won't care about the scandal – that's yesterday's news.* **3 I wasn't born yesterday** used to say that you cannot be easily deceived: *Don't lie to me! Do you think I was born yesterday?*

**yes·ter·year** /ˈjestəjɪə, -jɜː‖ˈjestərjɪr/ *n* **of yesteryear** *literary* from a time in the past: *the familiar songs of yesteryear*

S1 W1 **yet¹** /jet/ *adv* **1** [in questions or negatives] until now or until a particular time: *Has Edmund arrived yet?* | *The potatoes aren't quite ready yet.* —see JUST (USAGE) **2 as yet** an expression meaning until this moment, used in questions and negatives: *We've had no luck as yet.* | *As yet, there's been no news.* **3 not yet** an expression meaning not at the present time, used especially in the answer to questions: *"Are you ready to leave?" "Not just yet."* **4** but or in spite of something: *a simple yet effective system* **5 months/weeks/ages yet** used to emphasize how long it will be before something happens or how long a situation will last: *"When's your holiday?" "Oh, not for ages yet."* **6** in the future, in spite of the way that things seem now: *We may win yet.* | *The plan could yet succeed.* **7** even or still: *yet another reason to be cautious* | *a yet worse mistake* | **yet again** (=one more time after many others) *I'm sorry to disturb you yet again.* **8** *formal* still: *I have yet to hear Ray's version of what happened.* (=I still have not heard it)

**USAGE NOTE: YET**

FORMALITY

**Yet** often comes either immediately after a negative word or at the end of a clause, but there is a difference of style. In a formal meeting you might hear: *We do not yet know the answer*. In informal conversation you might say: *I don't know the answer yet* (NOT *I don't know yet the answer*). Yet may also be placed immediately after the verb where a clause follows: *I don't know yet whether she'll come or not.*

**yet²** *conjunction* used to introduce a statement that is surprising after what you have just said: *It's only a little shop and yet it always has such lovely decorations.* | *She's a funny girl, yet you can't help liking her.*

**yet·i** /ˈjeti/ *n* [C] a large hairy animal like a human which is supposed to live in the Himalayan mountains but many people do not believe exists

**yew** /juː/ *n* [C,U] a tree with dark green leaves and red berries, or the wood of this tree

**y-fronts** /ˈwaɪ frʌnts/ *n* [plural] *BrE* men's underwear which has a part at the front shaped like an upside down Y

**yid** /jɪd/ *n* [C] *taboo* an extremely offensive word for a Jewish person

**Yid·dish** /ˈjɪdɪʃ/ *n* [U] a language based on German used by Jewish people, especially those who are from eastern Europe

**yield¹** /jiːld/ *v*

**1** ▶ **CROPS/PROFITS** ◀ [T] to produce crops, profits etc: *The land yielded a good wheat crop.* | *Mining shares often yield a high level of return.*

**2** ▶ **RESULT** ◀ [T] to produce a result, answer, or a piece of information: *Careful analysis yielded the following conclusions.*

**3** ▶ **AGREE** ◀ [I,T] to agree to do something you do not want to do because you have been forced or persuaded to: [+ **to**] *The hijackers refuse to yield to demands to release the passengers.*

**4 yield to your emotions/feelings** to finally decide to do something because you cannot control your feelings any longer

**5** ▶ **TRAFFIC** ◀ [I] *AmE* to allow other traffic on a bigger road to go first; GIVE WAY *BrE* WAY¹ (34)

**6** ▶ **GIVE UP FIGHTING** ◀ [I] *literary* to stop fighting and accept defeat

**7** ▶ **MOVE/BEND/BREAK** ◀ [I] to move, bend, or break because of physical force or pressure: *The door wouldn't yield despite all our efforts to move it.*

**8** ▶ **CHANGE** ◀ [I] *formal* if one thing yields to another thing, this other thing replaces it: [+ **to**] *Open spaces around town are yielding to huge hyper-stores.*

**yield** sth ↔ **up** *phr v* [T] *literary* to show or give someone something that has been hidden for a long time or is very difficult to obtain: *Little by little, the universe yields up its many secrets.*

**yield²** *n* [C] the amount of profits, crops etc that you get: *investments with high yields*

**yield·ing** /ˈjiːldɪŋ/ *adj* **1** a surface that is yielding is soft and will move or bend when you press it **2** willing to agree with other people's wishes and letting them decide instead of you: *She is too yielding when clients make demands on her time.* **3 high/low yielding** producing a large or small amount of something such as crops

**yin** /jɪn/ *n* [U] the female principle in Chinese PHILOSOPHY which is inactive, dark and negative, and which combines with YANG (=the male principle) to influence everything in the world

**yin and yang** /ˌ· · ˈ·/ *n* [U] the ancient Chinese PHILOSOPHY which is based on the idea that everything in the Universe is formed and influenced by the combination of two forces called YIN and YANG

**yip·pee** /jɪˈpiː‖ˈjɪpi/ *interjection* used when you are very pleased or excited about something

**YMCA** /ˌwaɪ em siː ˈeɪ/ *n* [singular] Young Men's Christian Association; an organization in many countries that provides places to stay and sports activities for young people

**yo** /jəʊ‖joʊ/ *interjection slang, especially AmE* used to greet someone or get their attention: *Yo dude! How's it goin'?*

**yob** /jɒb‖jɑːb/ also **yob·bo** /ˈjɒbəʊ‖ˈjɑːboʊ/ *n* [C] *BrE* **1** a rude, noisy, sometimes violent, young man **2 yob culture/uniform/element etc** behaviour, clothes etc connected with yobs —**yobbery** *n* [U]

**yo·del¹** /ˈjəʊdl‖ˈjoʊdl/ *v* **yodelled, yodelling** *BrE*, **yodeled, yodeling** *AmE* [I,T] to sing while changing between your natural voice and a very high voice, traditionally done in the mountains of countries such as Switzerland and Austria —**yodeller** *n* [C]

**yodel²** *n* [C] a song or sound made by yodelling

**yo·ga** /ˈjəʊgə‖ˈjoʊgə/ *n* [U] **1** a Hindu PHILOSOPHY in which you learn exercises to control your mind and body in order to try to achieve a union with God **2** a system of these exercises that helps you relax

3 **yog·hurt, yogurt** /ˈjɒgʊət‖ˈjoʊgərt/ *n* [C,U] a thick liquid food that tastes slightly sour and is made from milk, or an amount of this

**yo·gi** /ˈjəʊgi‖ˈjoʊgi/ *n* [C] someone who is very skilled at and has a lot of knowledge about yoga and who often teaches it to other people

**yog·urt** /ˈjɒgət‖ˈjoʊgərt/ *n* [C,U] another spelling of yoghurt

**yoke¹** /jəʊk‖joʊk/ *n* [C] **1** a wooden bar used for joining two animals, especially cattle, together in order to pull heavy loads **2** a frame fitted across someone's shoulders so that they can carry two equal loads **3 the yoke of sth** *literary* something that restricts your freedom, making life hard or unpleasant: *the yoke of tradition* **4** a part of a skirt or shirt just below the waist or collar, from which the main piece of material hangs in folds

**yoke²** *v* [T + **together/to**] **1** to join two animals with a yoke **2** *literary* to bring two ideas or people together so that they work well with each other: *The poet's choice of metaphor cleverly yokes together two dissimilar things.*

**yo·kel** /ˈjəʊkəl‖ˈjoʊ-/ *n* [C] *humorous* someone who comes from the countryside, seems to be a little stupid, and does not know much about modern life, ideas etc

**yolk** /jəʊk‖joʊk, jelk/ *n* [C,U] the yellow part in the centre of an egg

**Yom Kip·pur** /ˌjɒm ˈkɪpə, -kɪˈpʊə‖ˌjoʊm ˈkɪpər, -kɪˈpʊr/ *n* [singular] the religious holiday when Jewish people do not eat, but pray to be forgiven for the things they have done wrong

**yon·der** /ˈjɒndə‖ˈjɑːndər/ also **yon** *adv, determiner old use* used for telling someone which place or direction you mean: *the fresh blooms on yonder tree*

**yonks** /jɒŋks‖jɑːŋks/ *n* [U] *BrE spoken* a long time: *It's yonks since we had a good night out.* | **not do sth for yonks** *We haven't seen Tom and Jean for yonks.* | **yonks ago** *We went to Blackpool once, yonks ago.*

**yoo-hoo** /ˌjuː ˈhuː,ˈjuː huː/ *interjection informal* used to attract someone's attention when they are a long way from you

**yore** /jɔː‖jɔːr/ *n* **of yore** *literary* of a long time ago

**York·shire pud·ding** /ˌjɔːkʃə ˈpʊdɪŋ‖ˌjɔːrkʃər-/ *n* [C,U] a food made from flour, eggs and milk, eaten with meat in Britain

**Yorkshire ter·ri·er** /ˌjɔːkʃə ˈteriə‖ˌjɔːrkʃər ˈteriər/ *n* [C] a type of dog that is very small with long brown hair

**you** /jə, jʊ; *strong* juː/ *pron* [used as a subject or an object] **1** the person or people someone is speaking or writing to: *You look nice, Sally.* | *You must all listen carefully.* | *I can see you.* | *Did Robin give the money to you?* | *I told you this would happen.* | *Only you can make this decision.* **2** people in general: *You have to be careful with people you don't know.* | *You can't learn to ride a horse by reading books about it.* **3** used with nouns or phrases when you are talking to or calling someone: *You boys have got to learn to behave yourselves.* | *You twit!* | *Hey, you over there! Get out of the way!*

**you'd** /jəd, jʊd; *strong* juːd/ **1** the short form of 'you had' **2** the short form of 'you would'

**you'll** /jəl, jʊl; *strong* juːl/ **1** the short form of 'you will' **2** the short form of 'you shall'

**young¹** /jʌŋ/ *adj* **1** not having lived for very long: *a young child* | *young seedlings* | *You're too young to learn to drive.* | **in your younger days** (=when you were young) *John was a great footballer in his younger days.* **2** not having existed for a long time: *a young country* **3 young for your age** looking or behaving in a way that makes you seem as if you are younger than you really are **4 young at heart** *approving* thinking and behaving as if you are young even though you are old: *Arthur's 96, but he's still young at heart.* **5** seeming or looking younger than you are; YOUTHFUL: *Rosie has a very young face.* **6** designed or meant for young people: *That hat is too young for you.*

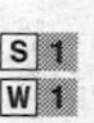

**young²** *n* **1 the young** young people considered as a group **2** [plural] a group of young animals that belong to a particular mother or type of animal: *The lioness fought to protect her young.*

**young·er** /ˈjʌŋgə‖-ər/ *adj* **sb the younger** *old-fashioned* someone who has the same name as their mother or father: *William Pitt the younger* —compare ELDER¹ (1)

**young la·dy** /ˌ· ˈ··/ *n* [C] *old-fashioned* **1** a way of speaking to a young girl when you are angry: *Now, listen to me, young lady!* **2** someone's GIRLFRIEND

**young man** /ˌ· ˈ·/ *n* [C] *old-fashioned* **1** a way of speaking to a young boy when you are angry: *You'd better do as I tell you, young man.* **2** someone's BOYFRIEND

**young mar·rieds** /ˌ· ˈ··/ *n* [plural] *especially AmE* young people who have recently got married

**young of·fend·er** /ˌ· ·ˈ··/ *n* [C] a criminal in Britain who is not an adult according to the law

**young·ster** /ˈjʌŋstə‖-ər/ *n* [C] *old-fashioned* a young person

**your** /jə; *strong* jɔː‖jər; *strong* jɔːr/ *determiner* **1** belonging to or connected with the person or people someone is speaking to: *Could you move your car?* | *That's your problem.* | *You must all come – and bring your husbands.* | *It's your own fault if you've lost them.* **2** belonging to any person: *If you are facing north, east is on your right.* **3** *informal* used when mentioning something that is a good example of a particular type of thing or quality: *Your typical 60s pop group had 3 guitarists and a drummer.* | *Where are your Georgie Bests in today's game?*

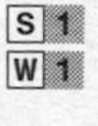

**you're** /jə; *strong* jɔː‖jər; *strong* jʊr, jɔːr/ the short form of 'you are'

**yours** /jɔːz‖jʊrz, jɔːrz/ *pron* **1** belonging to or connected with the person or people someone is speaking to: *This is our room, and yours (=your room) is just opposite.* | *My eyes are blue and yours are green.* | *Is Maria a friend of yours?* **2 be yours for the taking/asking** if something

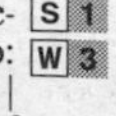

important, desirable etc is yours for the taking, you can easily obtain or achieve it: *If you want the job, it's yours for the taking.* **3 Yours faithfully/truly** used to end a formal letter that begins 'Dear Sir' or 'Dear Madam' **4 Yours sincerely/Yours** used to end a less formal letter that begins 'Dear Mr. Graves', 'Dear Miss Hope' etc **5 yours truly** *informal* used to mean 'I', 'me', or 'myself': *They all went out, leaving yours truly to clear up the mess.*

S1 W2 **your·self** /jə'self‖jər-/ *pron plural* **yourselves** /-'selvz/ **1** the REFLEXIVE form of 'you': *Mind you don't hurt yourself with those scissors.* | *Go and buy yourself an ice-cream.* **2** used as a stronger form of "you": *You yourself said he was a dead loss.* | *If you don't trust me you'd better go yourself.* **3 not be/feel yourself** *informal* to be slightly ill, tired, or upset: *Of course I'll forgive you; I know you weren't yourself yesterday.* | *Are you all right? You don't seem yourself this morning.* **4 (all) by yourself a)** without anyone helping you: *Can you put your shoes on all by yourself, Ben?* **b)** with no other people with you: *You can't go home by yourself in the dark.* —see ALONE[1] (USAGE) **5 to yourself** if you have a room, time etc to yourself, it is your own and you do not have to share it with anyone: *If you got there early you had the whole beach to yourself.* | *It's nice to have an evening to yourself now and then.* —see also DO-IT-YOURSELF, **keep sth to yourself** (KEEP[1])

S2 W2 **youth** /juːθ/ *n plural* **youths** /juːðz‖juːðz, juːθs/ **1** [U] the period of time when someone is young, especially the period between being a child and being fully grown: *Youth is a time when many people rebel against their parents.* | **in sb's youth** (=when they were young) *In his youth, Jimmy was an idealist and a rebel.* **2** [C] a word meaning boy or young man, especially a TEENAGER, used especially when you disapprove of them: *gangs of youths hanging about on street corners* —see CHILD (USAGE) **3** [also + plural verb *BrE*] young people considered as a group: *the courage of youth* | **the youth of** *The youth of the country are being ignored by politicians.* **4** [singular, U] the quality or state of being young: *a product that claims to restore youth and vitality to your skin*

**youth club** /'· ·/ *n* [C] a meeting place for young people where they can drink coffee, play games etc

**youth cul·ture** /'· ˌ··/ *n* [U] the interests and activities of young people, especially the music, films etc they enjoy

**youth·ful** /'juːθfəl/ *adj* **1** typical of or having qualities typical of youth: *youthful enthusiasm* | *She's over 50, but has a youthful complexion.* **2** young: *youthful soldiers* —**youthfully** *adv* —**youthfulness** *n* [U]

**youth hos·tel** /'· ˌ··/ *n* [C] a place where people, especially young people who are travelling, can stay very cheaply for a short time

**youth hos·tel·ling** /'· ˌ···/ *n* [U] *BrE* the activity of staying in youth hostels and walking or cycling between them: **go youth hostelling** *I went youth hostelling in the Peak District.*

**you've** /jəv; *strong* juːv/ the short form of 'you have'

**yowl** /jaʊl/ *v* [I] to make a long loud cry, especially because you are sad or in pain: *A tomcat was yowling out on the lawn.* —**yowl** *n* [C]

**yo-yo** /'jəʊ jəʊ‖'joʊ joʊ/ *n* [C] a toy you hold in your hand made of two circular parts joined together that go up and down a string as you lift your hand up and down

**yr** *plural* **yrs** the written abbreviation of YEAR

**yu·an** /jʊ'ɑːn/ *n* [C] the standard unit of money in China

**yuc·ca** /'jʌkə/ *n* [C] a desert plant with long pointed leaves on a thick straight stem

**yuck, yuk** /jʌk/ *interjection informal* used to show that you think something is very unpleasant

**yuck·y** /'jʌki/ *adj informal* extremely unpleasant: *a yucky colour* | *The food was yucky.*

**yuk** /jʌk/ *interjection* another spelling of yuck

**Yule** /juːl/ *n old use* Christmas

**yule log** /'· ·/ *n* [C] **1** a LOG of wood traditionally burnt on the evening before Christmas **2** a chocolate cake shaped like a LOG and eaten at Christmas

**Yule·tide** /'juːltaɪd/ *n* [U] *poetical* Christmas

**yum·my** /'jʌmi/ *adj informal* food that is yummy tastes very good

**yup·pie, yuppy** /'jʌpi/ *n* [C] a young person who seems to be only concerned with their job, making a lot of money, and spending it on expensive things: *The Docklands area has been converted into smart flats for yuppies.*

**YWCA** /ˌwaɪ dʌbəljuː siː 'eɪ/ *n* [singular] Young Women's Christian Association; an organization in many countries that provides places to stay and sports activities for young people

# Z,z

**Z, z** /zed‖ziː/ *plural* **Z's, z's** or **Zs, zs** **1** the last letter of the English alphabet **2 Z's** *AmE informal* sleep: **catch/get some Z's** (=to sleep) *I think I'll go catch some Z's.*

**za·ny** /ˈzeɪni/ *adj* crazy or unusual in a way that is amusing: *zany comedian Lenny Henry*

**zap¹** /zæp/ *v* **zapped, zapping** *informal* **1** [T] to quickly attack or destroy something, especially in a computer game: *You get 100 points for each plane you zap.* **2** [T always + adv/prep, I always + adv/prep] to do something very quickly or go somewhere very quickly: **zap sth in/into** *He zapped the car into fourth gear and screeched off.* | **[+ past/through/along etc]** *I'll have to zap through the work to make the deadline.* **3** [T] *AmE informal* to cook something in a MICROWAVE¹ (1)

**zap²** *n* [U] *BrE informal* interest and excitement; ENERGY¹: *The advert needs a bit more zap.*

**zap·per** /ˈzæpə‖-ər/ *n* [C] *AmE informal* **1** a thing you use for changing channels (CHANNEL¹ (1)) on a television from a distance; REMOTE CONTROL (1) **2** a piece of electrical equipment that attracts and kills insects

**zap·py** /ˈzæpi/ *adj BrE informal* interesting and exciting: *a zappy poster*

**zeal** /ziːl/ *n* [U] eagerness to do something, especially to achieve a particular religious or political aim: *revolutionary zeal*

**zeal·ot** /ˈzelət/ *n* [C] someone who has extremely strong beliefs, especially religious or political beliefs, and is too eager to make other people share them: *religious zealots* —**zeolotry** *n* [U]

**zeal·ous** /ˈzeləs/ *adj* extremely enthusiastic about something that you believe in very strongly and behaving in a way that shows this: *a zealous preacher* —**zealously** *adv* —**zealousness** *n* [U]

**ze·bra** /ˈziːbrə, ˈze-‖ˈziːbrə/ *n* [C] an animal that looks like a horse but has black and white lines all over its body

**zebra cross·ing** /ˌ·· ˈ··/ *n* [C] *BrE* a place marked with black and white lines where people who are walking can cross a road safely; CROSSWALK *AmE* —compare PELICAN CROSSING

**zed** /zed/ *BrE*, **zee** *AmE n* [C] a way of writing the letter 'z' that shows how you pronounce it

**zeit·geist** /ˈzaɪtgaɪst/ *n* [singular] *German* the general spirit or feeling of a period in history, as shown by people's ideas and beliefs at the time

**Zen** /zen/ *n* [U] a kind of Buddhism that is popular in Japan

**zen·ith** /ˈzenɪθ‖ˈziː-/ *n* [C usually singular] **1** the most successful point in the development of something: **reach its zenith/be at its zenith** *Opera reached its zenith at the turn of the century.* **2** the highest point that is reached by the sun or the moon in the sky

**zeph·yr** /ˈzefə‖-ər/ *n* [C] *poetical* a soft gentle wind

**zep·pe·lin** /ˈzepəlɪn/ *n* [C] a German AIRSHIP used in World War I

**ze·ro¹** /ˈzɪərəʊ‖ˈziːroʊ/ *n plural* **zeros** or **zeroes** *number*
**1 ▶NUMBER◀** 0
**2 ▶MEASUREMENT◀** the point between + and – on a scale for measuring something, or the lowest point on a scale that shows how much there is left of something: *The petrol gauge was already at zero.*
**3 ▶TEMPERATURE◀** the point on the Celsius scale at which water freezes: *It was five degrees below zero last night.* | *sub-zero temperatures* —see also ABSOLUTE ZERO
**4 ▶NOTHING◀** *informal* the lowest possible amount or level of something: *'Today?' I said, my spirits sinking to zero.* | *The kids showed zero interest in what I was saying.*
**5 zero growth/inflation/gravity** no growth, INFLATION (1) etc at all: *The country is aiming at zero growth in its population by the year 2010.*

**zero²** *v*
**zero in on** sb/sth *phr v* [T] **1** to direct all your attention towards a particular person or thing: *Hayley zeroed in on the toys, the minute she saw them.* **2** to aim a gun towards something or someone

**zero hour** /ˈ·· ·/ *n* [singular] the time when a military operation or an important event is planned to begin

**zero-sum game** /ˌ·· ˈ· ˌ·/ *n* [singular] *AmE* a situation in which you receive as much money or advantages as you give away: *Diplomatic negotiations often aim at a zero-sum game.*

**zest** /zest/ *n* **1** [U] eager interest and enjoyment: *zest for life* **2** [singular, U] the quality of being exciting and interesting: *The danger of being caught added a certain zest to the affair.* **3** [U] the outer skin of an orange or LEMON (1), used in cooking —**zestful** *adj* —**zestfully** *adv*

**zig·zag¹** /ˈzɪgzæg/ *n* [C] a pattern that looks like a line of z's joined together: *a zigzag path along the cliff* —see picture on page 839

**zigzag²** *v* **zigzagged, zigzagging** [I] to move forward in sharp angles, first to the left and then to the right etc: *The path zigzagged down the hillside.*

**zilch** /zɪltʃ/ *n* [U] *informal* nothing at all: *"How much money is left?" "Zilch."*

**zil·lion** /ˈzɪljən/ *n* [C] *informal* an extremely large number of something: **[+ of]** *zillions of mosquitoes*

**zim·mer frame** /ˈzɪmə freɪm‖-mər-/ *n* [C] *BrE trademark* a metal frame that old or ill people use to help them walk; WALKER (3) *AmE*

**zinc** /zɪŋk/ *n* [U] a bluish-white metal, used to make BRASS and to cover and protect objects made of iron

**zing¹** /zɪŋ/ *n* [U] *informal* the quality of being full of energy or taste: *Lemon juice adds zing to drinks and sorbets.* —**zingy** *adj*

**zing²** *v* [I always + adv/prep] *informal* to move quickly, making a whistling noise: **[+ past/off]** *The shots went zinging off the rocks.*

**Zi·on·is·m** /ˈzaɪənɪzəm/ *n* [U] support for the establishment and development of a state for the Jews in Israel —**Zionist** *n* [C]

**zip¹** /zɪp/ *n* **1** [C] *BrE* two lines of small metal or plastic pieces that slide together to fasten a piece of clothing; ZIPPER *especially AmE*: *The zip on my skirt had broken.* | **do up/undo your zip** (=close or open a piece of clothing using a zip) *Your zip's undone at the back.* —see picture at FASTENER **2** [U] *informal* if someone or something has zip, they can do something quickly and with a lot of energy: *This car goes with a bit more zip than my last one.* **3** [singular] *AmE informal* nothing at all or zero: *We beat them 10 to zip.* | *"How much money have you got left?" "Zip!"*

**zip²** *v* **zipped, zipping** **1** [T always + adv/prep] to open or shut something using a zip: **[+ in/inside]** *The money was safely zipped inside my jacket.* | **zip sth shut/open** *Olsen zipped the bag shut.* **2** [I always + adv/prep] *informal* to do something or go somewhere very quickly: **[+ through/past/along etc]** *We zipped through customs in no time.* **3 zip your lip** *AmE spoken* used to tell someone not to say anything about something, or to tell them to be quiet: *You'd better zip your lip or you'll be in trouble!*
**zip up** *phr v* [T] **1 zip** sth ↔ **up** to fasten a piece of clothing using a zip: *Zip your jacket up – you'll get cold.* —opposite UNZIP **2 [zip** sb **up]** to close the zip on a piece of clothing that someone else is wearing: *"Could you zip me up please? I can't reach."*

**zip code** /ˈ· ·/ *n* [C] *AmE* a number that you put below the address on an envelope to help the post office deliver the mail more quickly; POSTCODE *BrE*

**zip·per** /ˈzɪpə‖-ər/ *n* [C] *especially AmE* two lines of small

metal or plastic pieces that slide together to fasten a piece of clothing; ZIP[1] (1) *BrE* —see picture at FASTENER

**zip·po** /ˈzɪpəʊ‖-poʊ/ *n* [singular] *AmE informal* nothing at all or zero

**zit** /zɪt/ *n* [C] *informal* a spot on someone's skin; PIMPLE

**zith·er** /ˈzɪðə‖-ər/ *n* [C] a musical instrument from Eastern Europe, played by pulling its wire strings with your fingers

**zo·di·ac** /ˈzəʊdiæk‖ˈzoʊ-/ *n* **the zodiac** an imaginary area through which the sun, moon, and PLANETS appear to travel, which some people believe influences our lives: **sign of the zodiac** (=one of the twelve parts that this area is divided into) *"Which sign of the zodiac were you born under?" "Leo."* —see also HOROSCOPE —**zodiacal** /zəʊˈdaɪəkəl‖zoʊ-/ *adj*

**zom·bie** /ˈzɒmbi‖ˈzɑːm-/ *n* [C] **1** *informal* someone who moves very slowly and does not seem to be thinking about what they are doing, especially because they are very tired **2** a dead person whose body is made to move by magic, according to some African and Caribbean religions

**zon·al** /ˈzəʊnl‖ˈzoʊnl/ *adj technical* connected with or arranged in zones —**zonally** *adv*

W3 **zone** /zəʊn‖zoʊn/ *n* [C] a large area that is different from other areas around it in some way: *This is a no-parking zone.* | *a nuclear-free zone* | **danger zone** (=an area where it is dangerous to go) | **war/battle/combat zone** *The south side of the city has virtually become a war zone.* | **pedestrian zone** (=an area where no cars are allowed) | **residential/industrial/commercial etc zone** (=an area of a city that is used for a particular purpose, such as houses or shops) —see also **buffer zone** (BUFFER[1] (3)), EROGENOUS ZONE, **exclusion zone** (EXCLUSION (3)), TIME ZONE

**zoned** /zəʊnd‖zoʊnd/ also **zoned out** *adj* [not before noun] *AmE informal* unable to think clearly and quickly, especially because you are tired or ill

**zon·ing** /ˈzəʊnɪŋ‖ˈzoʊ-/ *n* [U] a system of choosing areas to be developed for particular purposes, such as houses or shops, when planning a town

**zonked** /zɒŋkt‖zɑːŋkt/ also **zonked out** *adj* [not before noun] *informal* extremely tired; EXHAUSTED (1): *Paul was zonked after the conference in Amsterdam.*

**zoo** /zuː/ *n* [C] a place, usually in a city, where animals of many kinds are kept so that people can go to look at them

**zoo·keep·er** /ˈ· ˌ··/ *n* [C] someone who looks after animals in a zoo

**zo·ol·o·gist** /zuːˈɒlədʒɪst, zəʊˈɒ-‖zoʊˈɑːl-/ *n* [C] a scientist who studies animals and their behaviour

**zo·ol·o·gy** /zuːˈɒlədʒi, zəʊˈɒ-‖zoʊˈɑːl-/ *n* [U] the scientific study of animals and their behaviour —**zoological** /ˌzuːəˈlɒdʒɪkəl◂, ˌzəʊ-‖ˌzoʊəˈlɑː-/ *adj* —**zoologically** /-kli/ *adv*

**zoom[1]** /zuːm/ *v* [I] *informal* **1** [always + adv/prep] to go somewhere or do something very quickly: [+ **past/through/off etc**] *Brenda zoomed past on her Honda.* | *The work was really easy and I was able to zoom through it in a couple of hours.* **2** to increase suddenly and quickly: [+ **to**] *Interest rates zoomed up to 20% in the late 80s.*

**zoom in/out** *phr v* [I] if a camera zooms in or out, it moves quickly between a picture that is close and detailed and one that is distant: **zoom in on sth/sb** *The camera zoomed in on the child's face.*

**zoom[2]** *n* [singular] *informal* a sound made by a vehicle that is travelling fast

**zoom lens** /ˈ· ˌ·/ *n* [C] a camera LENS (2) that can change from a distant to a close view —see picture at CAMERA

**zoot suit** /ˈzuːt suːt, -sjuːt‖-suːt/ *n* [C] a suit that consists of wide trousers and a JACKET with wide shoulders, worn especially in the 1940s and 1950s

**zuc·chi·ni** /zʊˈkiːni/ *n* [C] *AmE* a small vegetable with a dark green skin, shaped like a short stick; COURGETTE *BrE* —see picture on page 414

**Zu·lu** /ˈzuːluː/ *n* **1 the Zulu** a large tribe of people who live in South Africa **2** [C] a member of this tribe —**Zulu** *adj*

**zwie·back** /ˈzwiːbæk‖ˈzwaɪ-/ *n* [U] *AmE* a kind of hard dry bread, often given to babies —compare RUSK *BrE*

**zy·de·co** /ˈzaɪdəkəʊ‖-koʊ/ *n* [U] a kind of Cajun music

**zy·gote** /ˈzaɪgəʊt‖-goʊt/ *n* [C] a cell that is formed when an egg is fertilized (FERTILIZE (1))

# Tables

## 1 Numbers

### How numbers are spoken

Numbers over 20

| | |
|---|---|
| 21 | twenty-one |
| 22 | twenty-two |
| 32 | thirty-two |
| 99 | ninety-nine |

Numbers over 100

| | |
|---|---|
| 101 | a/one hundred (and) one |
| 121 | a/one hundred (and) twenty-one |
| 200 | two hundred |
| 232 | two hundred (and) thirty-two |
| 999 | nine hundred (and) ninety-nine |

Note: In British English the "and" is always used: *two hundred and thirty-two.* But in American English it is often left out: *two hundred thirty-two.*

Numbers over 1000

| | |
|---|---|
| 1001 | a/one thousand (and) one |
| 1121 | one thousand one hundred (and) twenty-one |
| 2000 | two thousand |
| 2232 | two thousand two hundred (and) thirty-two |
| 9999 | nine thousand nine hundred (and) ninety-nine |

Ordinal numbers

| | |
|---|---|
| 20th | twentieth |
| 21st | twenty-first |
| 25th | twenty-fifth |
| 90th | ninetieth |
| 99th | ninety-ninth |
| 100th | hundredth |
| 101st | hundred and first |
| 225th | two hundred (and) twenty-fifth |

Dates

| | |
|---|---|
| 1624 | sixteen twenty-four |
| 1903 | nineteen-oh-three |
| 1987 | nineteen eighty-seven |

### What numbers represent

Numbers are often used on their own to show:

| | |
|---|---|
| Price | *It cost eight seventy-five* (=8 pounds 75 pence or 8 dollars 75 cents: £8.75 or $8.75). |
| Time | *We left at two twenty-five* (=25 minutes after 2 o'clock). |
| Age | *She's forty-six* (= 46 years old).\|*He's in his sixties* (=between 60 and 69 years old). |
| Size | *This shirt is a thirty-eight* (=size 38). |
| Temperature | *The temperature fell to minus fourteen* (= –14°).\|*The temperature was in the mid-thirties* (= about 34–36°). |
| The score in a game | *Becker won the first set six-three* (= by six games to three: 6–3). |
| Something marked with the stated number | *She played two nines and an eight* (= playing cards marked with these numbers). |
| A set or group of the stated number | *The teacher divided us into fours* (= groups of 4).\|*You can buy cigarettes in tens or twenties* (= in packets containing 10 or 20). |

### Numbers and grammar

Numbers can be used as:

| | |
|---|---|
| Determiners | *Five people were hurt in the accident.\| the three largest companies in the US\|several hundred cars* |
| Pronouns | *We invited a lot of people but only twelve came/only twelve of them came.\|Do exercise five on page nine.* |
| Nouns | *Six can be divided by two and three.\|Three twos make six.* |

## 2 Weights and measures

The words in **dark type** are the ones that are most commonly used in general speech.

### METRIC

#### Units of length

| | | |
|---|---|---|
| | 1 **millimetre** | = 0.03937 inch |
| 10 mm | = 1 **centimetre** | = 0.3937 inch |
| 10 cm | = 1 decimetre | = 3.937 inches |
| 10 dm | = 1 **metre** | = 39.37 inches |
| 10 m | = 1 decemetre | = 10.94 yards |
| 10 dam | = 1 hectometre | = 109.4 yards |
| 10 hm | = 1 **kilometre** | = 0.6214 mile |

#### Units of weight

| | | |
|---|---|---|
| | 1 **milligram** | = 0.015 grain |
| 10 mg | = 1 centigram | = 0.154 grain |
| 10 cg | = 1 decigram | = 1.543 grains |
| 10 dg | = 1 **gram** | = 15.43 grains = 0.035 ounces |
| 10 g | = 1 decagram | = 0.353 ounce |
| 10 dag | = 1 hectogram | = 3.527 ounces |
| 10 hg | = 1 **kilogram** | = 2.205 pounds |
| 100 kg | = 1 **tonne** | = 0.984 (long) ton |
| | (metric ton) | = 2204.62 pounds |

#### Units of capacity

| | | |
|---|---|---|
| | 1 millilitre | = 0.00176 pint |
| 10 ml | = 1 centilitre | = 0.0176 pint |
| 10 cl | = 1 decilitre | = 0.176 pint |
| 10 dl | = 1 **litre** | = 1.76 pints = 0.22 UK gallon |
| 10 l | = 1 decalitre | = 2.20 gallons |
| 10 dal | = 1 hectolitre | = 22.0 gallons |
| 10 hl | = 1 kilolitre | = 220.0 gallons |

#### Square measure

1 square measure = 0.00155 square inch

| | | |
|---|---|---|
| 100 mm$^2$ | = 1 square centimetre | = 0.1550 square inch |
| 100 cm$^2$ | = 1 square metre | = 1.196 square yards |
| 100 m$^2$ | = 1 are | = 119.6 square yards |
| 100 ares | = 1 **hectare** | = 2.471 acres |
| 100 ha | = 1 square kilometre | = 247.1 acres |

#### cubic measure

| | | |
|---|---|---|
| | 1 cubic centimetre | = 0.06102 cubic inch |
| 1000 cm$^3$ | = 1 cubic decimetre | = 0.03532 cubic foot |
| 1000 dm$^3$ | = 1 cubic metre | = 1.308 cubic yards |

#### Circular measure

1 microradian = 0.206 seconds

1000 µrad = 1 milliradian = 3.437 minutes

1000 mrad = 1 radian = 57.296 degrees = 180/π degrees

#### Metric prefixes

| | *Abbreviation* | *Factor* |
|---|---|---|
| tera- | T | $10^{12}$ |
| giga- | G | $10^{9}$ |
| mega- | M | $10^{6}$ |
| kilo- | k | $10^{3}$ |
| hecto- | h | $10^{2}$ |
| deca- | da | $10^{1}$ |
| deci- | d | $10^{-1}$ |
| centi- | c | $10^{-2}$ |
| milli- | m | $10^{-3}$ |
| micro- | µ | $10^{-6}$ |
| nano- | n | $10^{-9}$ |
| pico- | p | $10^{-12}$ |
| femto- | f | $10^{-15}$ |
| atto- | a | $10^{-18}$ |

### BRITISH AND AMERICAN

#### Units of length

| | | |
|---|---|---|
| | 1 **inch** | = 2.54 cm |
| 12 inches | = 1 **foot** | = 0.3048 m |
| 3 feet | = 1 **yard** | = 0.9144 m |
| $5\frac{1}{2}$ yards | = 1 rod, pole, or perch | = 5.029 m |
| 22 yards | = 1 chain | = 20.12 m |
| 10 chains | = 1 furlong | = 0.2012 km |
| 8 furlongs | = 1 **mile** | = 1.609 km |
| 6076.12 feet | = 1 nautical mile | = 1852 m |

#### Units of weight

1 grain = 64.8 mg

1 dram = 1.772 g

| | | |
|---|---|---|
| 16 drams | = 1 **ounce** | = 28.35 g |
| 16 ounces | = 1 **pound** | = 0.4536 kg |
| 14 pounds | = 1 stone | = 6.350 kg |
| 2 stones | = 1 quarter | = 12.70 kg |
| 4 quarters | = 1 (long) **hundredweight** | = 50.80 kg |
| 20 hundredweight | = 1 (long) **ton** | = 1.016 tonnes |

**Units of weight** *(continued)*

| | | |
|---|---|---|
| 100 pounds | = 1 (short) **hundredweight** | = 45.36 kg |
| 2000 pounds | = 1 (short) **ton** | = 0.9072 tonnes |

The short hundredweight and ton are more common in the US.

**Units of capacity**

| | | |
|---|---|---|
| | 1 fluid ounce | = 28.41 $cm^3$ |
| 5 fluid ounces | = 1 gill | = 0.1421 $dm^3$ |
| 4 gills | = 1 **pint** | = 0.5683 $dm^3$ |
| 2 pints | = 1 **quart** | = 1.137 $dm^3$ |
| 4 quarts | = 1 (UK) **gallon** | = 4.546 $dm^3$ |
| 231 cubic inches | = 1 (US) **gallon** | = 3.785 $dm^3$ |
| 8 gallons | = 1 bushel | = 36.369 $dm^3$ |

**Square measure**

| | | |
|---|---|---|
| 1 square inch | = 645.16 $mm^2$ | |
| 144 square inches | = 1 square foot | = 0.0929 $m^2$ |
| 9 square feet | = 1 square yard | = 0.8361 $m^2$ |
| 4840 square yards | = 1 acre | = 4047 $m^2$ |
| 640 acres | = 1 square mile | = 259 ha |

**Cubic measure**

| | | |
|---|---|---|
| | = 1cubic inch | = 16.39 $cm^3$ |
| 1728 cubic inches | = 1 cubic foot | = 0.02832 $m^3$ = 28.32 $dm^3$ |
| 27 cubic feet | = 1 cubic yard | = 0.7646 $m^3$ = 764.6 $dm^3$ |

**Circular measure**

| | | |
|---|---|---|
| | 1 second | = 4.860 μrad |
| 60 seconds | = 1 minute | = 0.2909 μrad |
| 60 minutes | = 1 degree | = 17.45 μrad = π/180 rad |
| 45 degrees | = 1 oxtant | = π/4 rad |
| 60 degrees | = 1 sextant | = π/3 rad |
| 90 degrees | = 1 quadrant or 1 right angle | = π/2 rad |
| 360 degrees | = 1 circle or 1 circumference | = 2π rad |
| 1 grade or gon | = 1/100th of a right angle | = π/200 rad |

**US dry measure**

| | | |
|---|---|---|
| 1 pint | = 0.9689 UK pint | = 0.5506 $dm^3$ |
| 1 bushell | = 0.9689 UK bushell | = 35.238 $dm^3$ |

**US liquid measure**

| | |
|---|---|
| 1 fluid ounce | = 1.0408 UK fluid ounces = 0.0296 $dm^3$ |
| 16 fluid ounces | = 1 pint = 0.8327 UK pint = 0.4732 $dm^3$ |
| 8 pints | = 1 gallon = 0.8327 UK gallon = 3.7853 $dm^3$ |

**Temperature**

° *Fahrenheit* = $\left(\frac{9}{5} \times \chi°C\right) + 32$

° *Celsius* = $\frac{5}{9} \times (\chi°F - 32)$

## 3 Military ranks

| Royal Navy | US Navy |
|---|---|
| Admiral of the Fleet | Fleet Admiral |
| Admiral | Admiral |
| Vice-Admiral | Vice Admiral |
| Rear-Admiral | Rear Admiral |
| Commodore | Commodore |
| Captain | Captain |
| Commander | Commander |
| Lieutenant-Commander | Lieutenant Commander |
| Lieutenant | Lieutenant |
| Sub-Lieutenant | Lieutenant Junior Grade |
| Midshipman | Ensign |
| | Chief Warrant Officer |
| Fleet Chief Petty Officer | Warrant Officer |
| – | Master Chief Petty Officer |
| – | Senior Chief Petty Officer |
| Chief Petty Officer | Chief Petty Officer |
| Petty Officer | Petty Officer 1st Class |
| – | Petty Officer 2nd Class |
| Leading Seaman | Petty Officer 3rd Class |
| Able Seaman | Seaman |
| Ordinary Seaman | Seaman Apprentice |
| Junior Seaman | Seaman Recruit |

| British Army | US Army |
|---|---|
| Field-Marshal | General of the Army |
| General | General |
| Lieutenant-General | Lieutenant General |
| Major-General | Major General |
| Brigadier | Brigadier General |
| Colonel | Colonel |
| Lieutenant-Colonel | Lieutenant Colonel |
| Major | Major |
| Captain | Captain |
| Lieutenant | 1st Lieutenant |
| 2nd Lieutenant | 2nd Lieutenant |
| – | Chief Warrant Officer |
| Warrant Officer 1st Class | Warrant Officer |
| Warrant Officer 2nd Class | – |
| Staff Sergeant | Sergeant Major |
| Sergeant | Master Sergeant |
| – | 1st Sergeant |
| – | Sergeant 1st Class |
| – | Staff Sergeant |
| – | Sergeant |
| Corporal | Corporal |
| Lance Corporal | Private 1st Class |
| Private | Private |

| RAF | USAF |
|---|---|
| Marshal of the Royal Air Force | General of the Airforce |
| Air Chief Marshal | General |
| Air Marshal | Lieutenant General |
| Air Vice Marshal | Major General |
| Air Commodore | Brigadier General |
| Group Captain | Colonel |
| Wing-Commander | Lieutenant Colonel |
| Squadron Leader | Major |
| Flight Lieutenant | Captain |
| Flying Officer | First Lieutenant |
| Pilot Officer | Second Lieutenant |
| – | Chief Warrrant Officer |
| Warrant Officer | Chief Master Sergeant |
| – | Senior Master Sergeant |
| Flight Sergeant | Master Sergeant |
| Chief Technician | Technical Sergeant |
| Sergeant | Staff Sergeant |
| Corporal | Airman 1st Class |
| Junior Technician | – |
| Senior Aircraftman | Airman 2nd Class |
| Leading Aircraftman | Airman 3rd Class |
| Aircraftman | Airman Basic |

| Royal Marines | US Marine Corps |
|---|---|
| General | General |
| Lieutenant-General | Lieutenant General |
| Major-General | Major General |
| Brigadier | Brigadier General |
| Colonel | Colonel |
| Lieutenant-Colonel | Lieutenant Colonel |
| Major | Major |
| Captain | Captain |
| Lieutenant | 1st Lieutenant |
| 2nd Lieutenant | 2nd Lieutenant |
| – | Chief Warrant Officer |
| Warrant Officer 1st Class | Warrant Officer |
| Warrant Officer 2nd Class | – |
| Colour Sergeant | Sergeant Major |
| – | Master Gunnery Sergeant |
| Sergeant | Master Sergeant |
| – | 1st Sergeant |
| – | Gunnery Sergeant |
| – | Staff Sergeant |
| – | Sergeant |
| Corporal | Corporal |
| | Lance Corporal |
| Lance Corporal | Private 1st Class |
| Marine | Private |

# 4 Word formation

In English there are many word beginnings (prefixes) and word endings (suffixes) that can be added to a word to change its meaning or its word class. The most common ones are shown here, with examples of how they are used in the process of word formation. Many more are listed in the dictionary.

## Verb formation

The endings **-ize** and **-ify** can be added to many nouns and adjectives to form verbs, like this:

| | | |
|---|---|---|
| American | | Americanize |
| legal | **-ize** | legalize |
| modern | | modernize |
| popular | | popularize |

*They want to make the factory more* **modern**. *They want to* **modernize** *the factory.*

| | | |
|---|---|---|
| beauty | | beautify |
| liquid | **-fy** | liquefy |
| pure | | purify |
| simple | | simplify |

*These tablets make the water* **pure**. *They* **purify** *the water.*

## Adverb formation

The ending **-ly** can be added to most adjectives to form adverbs, like this:

| | | |
|---|---|---|
| easy | | easily |
| main | **-ly** | mainly |
| quick | | quickly |
| stupid | | stupidly |

*His behaviour was* **stupid**. *He behaved* **stupidly.**

## Noun formation

The endings **-er, -ment**, and **-ation** can be added to many verbs to form nouns, like this:

| | | |
|---|---|---|
| drive | | driver |
| fasten | **-er** | fastener |
| open | | opener |
| teach | | teacher |

*John* **drives** *a bus. He is a bus* **driver**.
*A can* **opener** *is a tool for* **opening** *cans.*

| | | |
|---|---|---|
| amaze | | amazement |
| develop | **-ment** | development |
| pay | | payment |
| retire | | retirement |

*Children* **develop** *very quickly. Their* **development** *is very quick.*

| | | |
|---|---|---|
| admire | | admiration |
| associate | **-ation** | association |
| examine | | examination |
| organize | | organization |

*The doctor* **examined** *me carefully. He gave me a careful* **examination**.

The endings **-ity** and **-ness** can be added to many adjectives to form nouns, like this:

| | | |
|---|---|---|
| cruel | | cruelty |
| odd | **-ity** | oddity |
| pure | **-ty** | purity |
| stupid | | stupidity |

*Don't be so* **cruel**. *I hate* **cruelty**

| | | |
|---|---|---|
| dark | | darkness |
| deaf | **-ness** | deafness |
| happy | | happiness |
| kind | | kindness |

*It was very* **dark**. *The* **darkness** *made it impossible to see.*

## Adjective formation

The endings **-y**, **-ic**, **-ical**, **-ful**, and **-less** can be added to many nouns to form adjectives like this.

| | | |
|---|---|---|
| bush | | bushy |
| dirt | **-y** | dirty |
| hair | | hairy |
| smell | | smelly |

*There was an awful* **smell** *in the room. The room was very* **smelly**.

| | | |
|---|---|---|
| atom | | atomic |
| biology | **-ic** | biological |
| grammar | **-ical** | grammatical |
| poetry | | poetic |

*This book contains exercises on* **grammar**. *It contains* **grammatical** *exercises.*

| | | |
|---|---|---|
| pain | | painful |
| hope | **-ful** | hopeful |
| care | | careful |

*His broken leg caused him a lot of* **pain**. *It was very* **painful**.

| | | |
|---|---|---|
| pain | | painless |
| hope | **-less** | hopeless |
| care | | careless |

*The operation didn't cause her any* **pain**. *It was* **painless**.

The ending **-able** can be added to many verbs to form adjectives, like this:

| | | |
|---|---|---|
| wash | | washable |
| love | **-able** | lovable |
| debate | | debatable |
| break | | breakable |

*You can* **wash** *this coat. It's* **washable**.

## Opposites

The following prefixes can be used in front of many words to produce an opposite meaning. Note, however, that the words formed in this way are not always EXACT opposites and may have a slightly different meaning.

| | | |
|---|---|---|
| | happy | unhappy |
| **un-** | fortunate | unfortunate |
| | wind | unwind |
| | block | unblock |

*I'm not very* **happy**. *In fact I'm very* **unhappy**.

| | | |
|---|---|---|
| **in-** | efficient | inefficient |
| **im-** | possible | impossible |
| **il-** | literate | illiterate |
| **ir-** | regular | irregular |

*It's just not* **possible** *to do that, it's* **impossible**.

| | | |
|---|---|---|
| | agree | disagree |
| **dis-** | approve | disapprove |
| | honest | dishonest |

*I don't* **agree** *with everything you said. I* **disagree** *with the last part.*

| | | |
|---|---|---|
| | centralize | decentralize |
| **de-** | increase | decrease |
| | ascend | descend |
| | inflate | deflate |

**Increase** *means to make or become larger in amount or number.* **Decrease** *means to make or become smaller in amount or number.*

| | | |
|---|---|---|
| | sense | nonsense |
| **non-** | payment | nonpayment |
| | resident | nonresident |
| | conformist | nonconformist |

*The hotel serves meals to* **residents** (= people who are staying in the hotel) *only.* **Nonresidents** *are not allowed in.*

## 5 The verb "be"

**present**

| | | *questions* | *negatives* |
|---|---|---|---|
| I | I am, I'm | am I? | I am not, I'm not, aren't I? |
| you | you are, you're | are you? | you are not, you're not, you aren't |
| she/he/it | she is, he's | is she/he/it? | it is not, he's not, she isn't |
| we/they | we are, they're | are we/they? | we are not, they're not, we aren't |

**present participle:** being

**past**

| | | *questions* | *negatives* |
|---|---|---|---|
| I | I was | was I? | I was not, I wasn't |
| you | you were | were you? | you were not, you weren't |
| she/he/it | he was | was she/he/it | she was not, it wasn't |
| we/they | we were | were we/they | they were not, we weren't |

**past participle:** been

## 6 Irregular verbs

| verb | past tense | past participle |
|---|---|---|
| abide | abided, abode | abided |
| arise | arose | arisen |
| awake | awoke, awakened | awoken |
| bear | bore | borne |
| beat | beat | beaten |
| become | became | become |
| befall | befell | befallen |
| beget | begot (also begat *bibl*) | begotten |
| begin | began | begun |
| behold | beheld | beheld |
| bend | bent | bent |
| bereave | bereft, bereaved | bereft, bereaved |
| beseech | besought, beseeched | besought, beseeched |
| beset | beset | beset |
| bestride | bestrode | bestridden |
| bet | bet,betted | bet, betted |
| betake | betook | betaken |
| bid | bade, bid | bid, bidden |
| bind | bound | bound |
| bite | bit | bitten |
| bleed | bled | bled |
| bless | blessed, blest | blessed, blest |
| blow | blew | blown |
| break | broke | broken |
| breed | bred | bred |
| bring | brought | brought |
| broadcast | broadcast | broadcast |
| browbeat | browbeat | browbeaten |
| build | built | built |
| burn | burned, burnt | burned, burnt |
| burst | burst | burst |
| bust | (*BrE*) bust, (esp *AmE*) busted | (*BrE*) bust, (esp *AmE*) busted |
| buy | bought | bought |
| can | (see dictionary entry) | |
| cast | cast | cast |
| catch | caught | caught |
| chide | chided, chid | chid, chidden |
| choose | chose | chosen |
| cleave | cleaved, cleft | clove, cleaved, cleft, cloven |
| cling | clung | clung |

| verb | past tense | past participle |
|---|---|---|
| come | came | come |
| cost | cost | cost |
| could | (see dictionary entry) | |
| creep | crept | crept |
| cut | cut | cut |
| deal | dealt/delt/ | dealt |
| dig | dug | dug |
| dive | dived, (*AmE*) dove | dived |
| do | did | done |
| draw | drew | drawn |
| dream | dreamed, dreamt | dreamed, dreamt |
| drink | drank | drunk |
| drive | drove | driven |
| dwell | dwelt, dwelled | dwelt, dwelled |
| eat | ate | eaten |
| fall | fell | fallen |
| feed | fed | fed |
| feel | felt | felt |
| fight | fought | fought |
| find | found | found |
| flee | fled | fled |
| fling | flung | flung |
| fly | flew | flown |
| forbid | forbade, forbad | forbidden |
| forecast | forecast | forecast |
| foresee | foresaw | foreseen |
| foretell | foretold | foretold |
| forget | forgot | forgotten |
| forgive | forgave | forgiven |
| forego | forewent | foregone |
| foresake | forsook | forsaken |
| forswear | forswore | forsworn |
| freeze | froze | frozen |
| gainsay | gainsaid | gainsaid |
| get | got | got (also gotten *AmE*) |
| gird | girded, girt | girded, girt |
| give | gave | given |
| go | went | gone |
| grind | ground | ground |
| grow | grew | grown |
| hamstring | hamstring, -strung | hamstringed, -strung |
| hang | hung, hanged | hung, hanged |
| have | had | had |
| hear | heard | heard |
| heave | heaved, hove | heaved, hove |
| hide | hid | hidden, hid |
| hit | hit | hit |
| hold | held | held |
| hurt | hurt | hurt |
| input | inputted, input | inputted, input |
| inset | inset, insetted | inset, insetted |
| interbreed | interbred | interbred |
| interweave | interwove | interwoven |
| keep | kept | kept |
| kneel | knelt, (esp *AmE*) kneeled | knelt, (esp *AmE*) kneeled |
| knit | knitted, knit | knitted, knit |
| know | knew | known |
| lay | laid | laid |
| lead | led | led |
| lean | leaned (also leant esp *Br E*) | leaned (also leant esp *BrE*) |
| leap | leapt, (esp *AmE*) leaped | leapt, (esp *AmE*) leaped |
| learn | learned, learnt | learned, learnt |
| leave | left | left |
| lend | lent | lent |
| let | let | let |
| lie | lay | lain |

| verb | past tense | past participle |
|---|---|---|
| light | lit, lighted | lit, lighted |
| lose | lost | lost |
| make | made | made |
| may | (see dictionary entry) | |
| mean | meant | meant |
| meet | met | met |
| might | (see dictionary entry) | |
| miscast | miscast | miscast |
| mishear | misheard | misheard |
| mislay | mislaid | mislaid |
| mislead | misled | misled |
| misread | misread | misread |
| misspell | misspelt, misspelled | misspelt, misspelled |
| misspend | misspent | misspent |
| mistake | mistook | mistaken |
| misunderstand | misunderstood | misunderstood |
| mow | mowed | mown, mowed |
| outbid | outbid | outbid |
| outdo | outdid | outdone |
| outgrow | outgrew | outgrown |
| outride | outrode | outridden |
| outrun | outran | outrun |
| outsell | outsold | outsold |
| outshine | outshone | outshone |
| overbear | overbore | overborne |
| overcast | overcast | overcast |
| overcome | overcame | overcome |
| overdo | overdid | overdone |
| overdraw | overdrew | overdrawn |
| overeat | overate | overeaten |
| overhang | overhung | overhung |
| overhear | overheard | overheard |
| overlay | overlaid | overlaid |
| overload | overloaded | overloaded, overladen |
| overpay | overpaid | overpaid |
| override | overrode | overridden |
| overun | overan | overun |
| oversee | oversaw | overseen |
| oversell | oversold | oversold |
| overshoot | overshot | overshot |
| oversleep | overslept | overslept |
| overtake | overtook | overtaken |
| overthrow | overthrew | overthrown |
| partake | partook | partaken |
| pay | paid | paid |
| plead | pleaded, (esp *AmE*) pled | pleaded, (esp *AmE*) pled |
| pre-set | pre-set | pre-set |
| proofread | proofread | proofread |
| prove | proved | proved (also proven *AmE*) |
| put | put | put |
| read | read/red/ | read/red/ |
| rebind | rebound | rebound |
| rebuild | rebuilt | rebuilt |
| recast | recast | recast |
| redo | redid | redone |
| relay | relaid | relaid |
| remake | remade | remade |
| rend | rent | rent |
| repay | repaid | repaid |
| rerun | reran | rerun |
| resell | resold | resold |
| reset | reset | reset |
| resit | resat | resat |
| rethink | rethought | rethought |
| rewind | rewound | rewound |
| rewrite | rewrote | rewritten |
| rid | rid, ridded | rid, ridded |

| verb | past tense | past participle |
|---|---|---|
| ride | rode | ridden |
| ring | rang | rung |
| rise | rose | risen |
| run | ran | run |
| saw | sawed | sawn, sawed |
| say | said | said |
| see | saw | seen |
| seek | sought | sought |
| sell | sold | sold |
| send | sent | sent |
| set | set | set |
| sew | sewed | sewn, sewed |
| shake | shook | shaken |
| shall | (see dictionary entry) | |
| shear | sheared | shorn, sheared |
| shed | shed | shed |
| shine | shone, shined | shone, shined |
| shit | shit, shat | shit, shat |
| shoe | shod | shod |
| shoot | shot | shot |
| should | (see dictionary entry) | |
| show | showed | shown, showed |
| shrink | shrank, shrunk | shrunk |
| shut | shut | shut |
| sing | sang | sung |
| sink | sank, sunk | sunk |
| sit | sat | sat |
| slay | slew | slain |
| sleep | slept | slept |
| slide | slid | slid |
| sling | slung | slung |
| slink | slunk | slunk |
| slit | slit | slit |
| smell | (esp *BrE*) smelt, (esp *AmE*) smelled | (esp *BrE*) smelt, (esp *AmE*) smelled |
| smite | smote | smitten |
| sow | sowed | sown, sowed |
| speak | spoke | spoken |
| speed | sped, speeded | sped, speeded |
| spell | (esp *BrE*) spelt, (esp *AmE*) spelled | (esp *BrE*) spelt, (esp *AmE*) spelled |
| spend | spent | spent |
| spill | (esp *BrE*) spilt, (esp *AmE*) spilled | (esp *BrE*) spilt, (esp *AmE*) spilled |
| spin | spun, span | spun |
| spit | spat (also spit *AmE*) | spat (also spit *AmE*) |
| split | split | split |
| spoil | spoiled, spoilt | spoiled, spoilt |
| spoon-feed | spoon-fed | spoon-fed |
| spotlight | spotlighted, spotlit | spotlighted, spotlit |
| spread | spread | spread |
| spring | sprang (also sprung *AmE*) | sprung |
| stand | stood | stood |
| steal | stole | stolen |
| stick | stuck | stuck |
| sting | stung | stung |
| stink | stank, stunk | stunk |
| strew | strewed | strewn, strewed |
| stride | strode | stridden |
| strike | struck | struck |
| string | strung | strung |
| strive | strove, strived | striven, strived |
| swear | swore | sworn |
| sweep | swept | swept |
| swell | swelled | swollen, swelled |
| swim | swam | swum |
| swing | swung | swung |
| take | took | taken |
| teach | taught | taught |
| tear | tore | torn |

| verb | past tense | past participle |
|---|---|---|
| tell | told | told |
| think | thought | thought |
| thrive | thrived, throve | thrived |
| throw | threw | thrown |
| thrust | thrust | thrust |
| tread | trod | trodden, trod |
| unbend | unbent | unbent |
| unbind | unbound | unbound |
| underlie | underlay | underlaid |
| undersell | undersold | undersold |
| understand | understood | understood |
| undertake | undertook | undertaken |
| underwrite | underwrote | underwritten |
| undo | undid | undone |
| unwind | unwound | unwound |
| uphold | upheld | upheld |
| upset | upset | upset |
| wake | woke, waked | woken, waked |
| wear | wore | worn |
| weave | wove | woven |
| wed | wedded, wed | wedded, wed |
| weep | wept | wept |
| wet | wetted, wet | wetted, wet |
| will | (see dictionary entry) | |
| win | won | won |
| wind/waind/ | wound | wound |
| withdraw | withdrew | withdrawn |
| withold | witheld | witheld |
| withstand | withstood | withstood |
| would | (see dictionary entry) | |
| wreak | wreaked, wrought | wreaked, wrought |
| wring | wrung | wrung |
| write | wrote | written |

## 7 Geographical names

This list of geographical names is included to help advanced students in their reading of contemporary newspapers and magazines.

<table>
<tr><th>Name</th><th>Adjective</th></tr>
<tr><td>Afghanistan /æf'gænᵻstɑːn || -stæn/</td><td>Afghan /'æfgæn/ *person:* Afghanistani /æfˌgænᵻ'stɑːni || -æni/, Afghan</td></tr>
<tr><td>Africa /'æfrɪkə/</td><td>African /'æfrɪkən/</td></tr>
<tr><td>Alaska /ə'læskə/</td><td>Alaskan /ə'læskən/</td></tr>
<tr><td>Albania /æl'beɪniə/</td><td>Albanian /æl'beɪniən/</td></tr>
<tr><td>Algeria /æl'dʒɪəriə || -'dʒɪr-/</td><td>Algerian /æl'dʒɪəriən || -'dʒɪr-/</td></tr>
<tr><td>America /ə'merᵻkə/</td><td>American /ə'merᵻkən/</td></tr>
<tr><td>Andorra /æn'dɔːrə/</td><td>Andorran /æn'dɔːrən/</td></tr>
<tr><td>Angola /æŋ'gəʊlə || -'goʊ-/</td><td>Angolan /æŋ'gəʊlən || -'goʊ-/</td></tr>
<tr><td>Antarctic /æn'tɑːktɪk || -ɑːr-/</td><td>Antarctic</td></tr>
<tr><td>Antigua /æn'tiːgə/</td><td>Antiguan /æn'tiːgən/</td></tr>
<tr><td>Arctic /'ɑːktɪk || 'ɑːrk-/</td><td>Arctic</td></tr>
<tr><td>Argentina /ˌɑːdʒən'tiːnə || ˌɑːr-/</td><td>Argentinian /ˌɑːdʒən'tɪniən || ˌɑːr-/</td></tr>
<tr><td>Armenia /ɑː'miːniə || ɑːr-/</td><td>Armenian /ɑː'miːniən || ɑːr-/</td></tr>
<tr><td>Asia /'eɪʃə, -ʒə || -ʒə, -ʃə/</td><td>Asian /'eɪʃən, -ʒən || -ʒən, -ʃən/</td></tr>
<tr><td>Atlantic /ət'læntɪk/</td><td>Atlantic</td></tr>
<tr><td>Australia /ɒ'streɪliə || ɒː-, ɑː-/</td><td>Australian /ɒ'streɪliən || ɒː-, ɑː-/</td></tr>
<tr><td>Austria /'ɒstriə || 'ɒː-, 'ɑː-/</td><td>Austrian /'ɒstriən || 'ɒː-, 'ɑː-/</td></tr>
<tr><td>Azerbaijan /ˌæzəbaɪ'dʒɑːn || -zər-/</td><td>Azerbaijani /ˌæzəbaɪ'dʒɑːni◂ || -zər-/</td></tr>
<tr><td>Bahamas /bə'hɑːməz/</td><td>Bahamian /bə'heɪmiən/</td></tr>
<tr><td>Bahrain /bɑː'reɪn/</td><td>Bahraini /bɑː'reɪni/</td></tr>
<tr><td>Baltic /'bɔːltɪk || 'bɒːl-/</td><td>Baltic</td></tr>
<tr><td>Bangladesh /ˌbæŋglə'deʃ/</td><td>Bangladesh *person:* Bangladeshi /ˌbæŋglə'deʃi/</td></tr>
<tr><td>Barbados /bɑː'beɪdɒs || bɑːr'beɪdəs,-dɑːs/</td><td>Barbadian /bɑː'beɪdiən || bɑːr-/</td></tr>
<tr><td>Belarus /ˌbelə'ruːs/ (Belorussia) /ˌbeləʊ'rʌʃə || -loʊ-/</td><td>Belorussian /ˌbeləʊ'rʌʃən || -loʊ-/</td></tr>
<tr><td>Belgium /'beldʒəm/</td><td>Belgian /'beldʒən/</td></tr>
<tr><td>Belize /bə'liːz/</td><td>Belizean /bə'liːziən/</td></tr>
<tr><td>Benin /be'niːn || bə'nɪn/</td><td>Beninese /ˌbenɪ'niːz◂/</td></tr>
<tr><td>Bermuda /bə'mjuːdə || bər-/</td><td>Bermudan /bə'mjuːdn || bər-/</td></tr>
<tr><td>Bhutan /buː'tɑːn/</td><td>Bhutanese /ˌbuːtə'niːz◂ || ˌbuːtn-'iːz◂/</td></tr>
<tr><td>Bolivia /bə'lɪviə/</td><td>Bolivian /bə'lɪviən/</td></tr>
<tr><td>Bosnia and Herzegovina /ˌbɒzniə ənd ˌhɜːtsəgəʊ'viːnə || ˌbɑːz-niə ənd ˌhertsəgoʊ-/</td><td>Bosnian /'bɒzniən || 'bɑːz-/</td></tr>
<tr><td>Botswana /bɒt'swɑːnə || bɑːt-/</td><td>Tswana /'tswɑːnə, 'swɑː-/ *person: sing.*= Motswana /mɒt'swɑːnə || mɑːt-/ *pl.* = Batswana /bæt'swɑːnə/</td></tr>
<tr><td>Burkina Faso /bɜːˌkiːnə 'fæsəʊ || bʊrˌkiːnə 'fɑːsoʊ/</td><td>Burkina *person:* Burkinabe /ˌbɜːkiːnæ'beɪ || ˌbʊr-/</td></tr>
<tr><td>Brazil /brə'zɪl/</td><td>Brazilian /brə'zɪliən/</td></tr>
<tr><td>Brunei /'bruːnaɪ/</td><td>Bruneian /bruː'naɪən/</td></tr>
<tr><td>Bulgaria /bʌl'geəriə || -'ger-/</td><td>Bulgarian /bʌl'geəriən || -'ger-/</td></tr>
<tr><td>Burma /'bɜːmə || 'bɜːr-/ former name of Myanmar</td><td></td></tr>
<tr><td>Burundi /bʊ'rʊndi || -'ruː-/</td><td>Burundian /bʊ'rʊndiən || -'ruː-/</td></tr>
<tr><td>Cambodia /kæm'bəʊdiə || -'boʊ-/</td><td>Cambodian /kæm'bəʊdiən || -'boʊ-/</td></tr>
<tr><td>Cameroon /ˌkæmə'ruːn/</td><td>Cameroonian /ˌkæmə'ruːniən◂/</td></tr>
<tr><td>Canada /'kænədə/</td><td>Canadian /kə'neɪdiən/</td></tr>
<tr><td>Cape Verde /keɪp 'vɜːd || -'vɜːrd/</td><td>Cape Verdean /keɪp 'vɜːdiən || -'vɜːr-/</td></tr>
<tr><td>Caribbean /ˌkærɪ'biːən◂ || kə'rɪbiən/</td><td>Caribbean</td></tr>
<tr><td>Cayman Islands /'keɪmən ˌaɪləndz/</td><td>Cayman Island /ˌkeɪmən 'aɪlənd◂/ *person:* Cayman Islander /ˌkeɪmən 'aɪləndə || -dər/</td></tr>
<tr><td>Central African Republic /ˌsentrəl ˌæfrɪkən rɪ'pʌblɪk/</td><td></td></tr>
<tr><td>Chad /tʃæd/</td><td>Chadian /'tʃædiən/</td></tr>
<tr><td>Chile /'tʃɪli/</td><td>Chilean /'tʃɪliən/</td></tr>
<tr><td>China /'tʃaɪnə/</td><td>Chinese /ˌtʃaɪ'niːz◂/</td></tr>
<tr><td>Colombia /kə'lʌmbiə/'</td><td>Colombian /kə'lʌmbiən/</td></tr>
<tr><td>Congo /'kɒŋgəʊ || 'kɑːŋgoʊ/</td><td>Congolese /ˌkɒŋgə'liːz◂ || ˌkɑːŋ-/</td></tr>
<tr><td>Costa Rica /ˌkɒstə 'riːkə || ˌkoʊ-/</td><td>Costa Rican /ˌkɒstə 'riːkən◂ || ˌkoʊ-/</td></tr>
<tr><td>Croatia /krəʊ'eɪʃə || kroʊ-/</td><td>Croatian /krəʊ'eɪʃən || kroʊ-/</td></tr>
<tr><td>Cuba /'kjuːbə/</td><td>Cuban /'kjuːbən/</td></tr>
<tr><td>Cyprus /'saɪprəs/</td><td>Cypriot /'sɪpriət/</td></tr>
<tr><td>Czech Republic /ˌtʃek rɪ'pʌblɪk/</td><td>Czech /tʃek/</td></tr>
<tr><td>Denmark /'denmɑːk || -mɑːrk/</td><td>Danish /'deɪnɪʃ/ *person:* Dane /deɪn/</td></tr>
<tr><td>Djibouti /dʒᵻ'buːti/</td><td>Djiboutian /dʒᵻ'buːtiən/</td></tr>
<tr><td>Dominica /ˌdɒmᵻ'niːkə || ˌdɑː-/</td><td>Dominican /ˌdɒmᵻ'niːkən◂ || ˌdɑː-/</td></tr>
<tr><td>Dominican Republic /dəˌmɪnɪkən rɪ'pʌblɪk/</td><td>Dominican /də'mɪnɪkən/</td></tr>
<tr><td>Ecuador /'ekwədɔː || -ɔːr/</td><td>Ecuadorian /ˌekwə'dɔːriən◂/</td></tr>
</table>

| Name | Adjective |
|---|---|
| Egypt /'iːdʒɪpt/ | Egyptian /ɪ'dʒɪpʃən/ |
| El Salvador /el 'sælvəˌdɔː ‖ -ɔːr/ | Salvadorian /ˌsælvə'dɔːriən◂/ |
| Equatorial Guinea /ˌekwətɔːriəl 'gɪni ‖ ˌiː-/ | Equatorial Guinean /ˌekwətɔːriəl 'gɪniən ‖ ˌiː-/ |
| Eritrea /ˌerɪ'treɪə/ | Eritrean /ˌerɪ'treɪən◂/ |
| Estonia /e'stəʊniə ‖ e'stoʊ-/ | Estonian /e'stəʊniən ‖ e'stoʊ-/ |
| Ethiopia /ˌiːθi'əʊpiə ‖ -'oʊ-/ | Ethiopian /ˌiːθi'əʊpiən◂ ‖ -'oʊ-/ |
| Europe /'jʊərəp ‖ 'jʊr-/ | European /ˌjʊərə'piːən◂ ‖ ˌjʊr-/ |
| Fiji /'fiːdʒiː/ | Fijian /fɪ'dʒiːən ‖ 'fiːdʒiən/ |
| Finland /'fɪnlənd/ | Finnish /'fɪnɪʃ/ *person:* Finn /fɪn/ |
| France /frɑːns ‖ fræns/ | French /frentʃ/ *person: sing.* = Frenchman /'frentʃmən/ (*fem.* -woman) /ˌwʊmən/: *pl.* = Frenchmen /'frentʃmən/, *people*: French |
| Gabon /gæ'bɒn ‖ -'boʊn/ | Gabonese /ˌgæbə'niːz◂/ |
| Gambia /'gæmbiə/ | Gambian /'gæmbiən/ |
| Georgia /'dʒɔːdʒə ‖ 'dʒɔːr-/ | Georgian /'dʒɔːdʒən ‖ 'dʒɔːr-/ |
| Germany /'dʒɜːməni ‖ -ɜːr-/ | German /'dʒɜːmən◂ ‖ -ɜːr-/ |
| Ghana /'gɑːnə/ | Ghanian /gɑː'neɪən/ |
| Gibraltar /dʒɪ'brɔːltə ‖ -'brɒːl-/ | Gibraltarian /ˌdʒɪbrɔːl'teəriən ‖ -brɒːl'ter-/ |
| Greece /griːs/ | Greek /griːk/ |
| Greenland /'griːnlənd, -lænd/ | Greenlandic /griːn'lændɪk/ *person:* Greenlander /'griːnləndə ‖ -dər/ |
| Grenada /grə'neɪdə/ | Grenadian /grə'neɪdiən/ |
| Guatemala /ˌgwɑːtə'mɑːlə/ | Guatemalan /ˌgwɑːtə'mɑːlən◂/ |
| Guiana /gi'ɑːnə ‖ gi'ænə, -'ɑːnə/ | Guianan /gi'ɑːnən ‖ gi'ænən, -'ɑːnən/ |
| Guinea /'gɪni/ | Guinean /'gɪniən/ |
| Guinea-Bissau /ˌgɪni bɪ'saʊ/ | Guinea-Bissauan /ˌgɪni bɪ'saʊən/ |
| Guyana /gaɪ'ænə/ | Guyanese /ˌgaɪə'niːz◂/ |
| Haiti /'heɪti/ | Haitian /'heɪʃən/ |
| Holland /'hɒlənd ‖ 'hɑː-/ another name for The Netherlands | Dutch /dʌtʃ/ |
| Honduras /hɒn'djʊərəs ‖ hɑːn-'djʊrəs, -'dʊ-/ | Honduran /hɒn'djʊərən ‖ hɑːn-'djʊrən, -'dʊ-/ |
| Hong Kong /ˌhɒŋ 'kɒŋ ‖ 'hɑːŋ ˌkɑːŋ/ | |
| Hungary /'hʌŋgəri/ | Hungarian /hʌŋ'geəriən ‖ -'ger-/ |
| Iceland /'aɪslənd/ | Icelandic /aɪs'lændɪk/ *person:* Icelander /'aɪsləndə ‖ -dər/ |

| Name | Adjective |
|---|---|
| India /'ɪndiə/ | Indian /'ɪndiən/ |
| Indonesia /ˌɪndə'niːʒə, -ziə ‖ -ʒə, -ʃə/ | Indonesian /ˌɪndə'niːʒən◂, -ziən◂ ‖ -ʒən, -ʃən◂/ |
| Iran /ɪ'rɑːn, -æn/ | Iranian /ɪ'reɪniən/ |
| Iraq /ɪ'rɑːk, -æk/ | Iraqi /ɪ'rɑːki, -æki/ |
| Irish Republic /ˌaɪərɪʃ rɪ'pʌblɪk ‖ ˌaɪr-/ | Irish /'aɪərɪʃ ‖ 'aɪr-/ *person:* sing. = Irishman /'aɪərɪʃmən ‖ 'aɪr-/ (*fem.* -woman) /ˌwʊmən/; *pl.* = Irishmen /'aɪərɪʃmən ‖ 'aɪr-/ *people:* Irish |
| Israel /'ɪzreɪl/ | Israeli /ɪz'reɪli/ |
| Italy /'ɪtəli/ | Italian /ɪ'tæliən/ |
| Ivory Coast /ˌaɪvəri 'kəʊst ‖ -'koʊst/ | Ivorian /aɪ'vɔːriən/ |
| Jamaica /dʒə'meɪkə/ | Jamaican /dʒə'meɪkən/ |
| Japan /dʒə'pæn/ | Japanese /ˌdʒæpə'niːz◂/ |
| Jordan /'dʒɔːdn ‖ 'dʒɔːr-/ | Jordanian /dʒɔː'deɪniən ‖ dʒɔːr-/ |
| Kazakhstan /ˌkæzæk'stɑːn ‖ ˌkɑːzɑːk-/ | Kazakh /kə'zæk, -'zɑːk/ |
| Kenya /'kenjə, 'kiː-/ | Kenyan /'kenjən, 'kiː-/ |
| Korea, North /ˌnɔːθ kə'rɪə ‖ ˌnɔːrθ-/ | North Korean /ˌnɔːθ kə'rɪən ‖ ˌnɔːrθ-/ |
| Korea, South /ˌsaʊθ kə'rɪə/ | South Korean /ˌsaʊθ kə'rɪən/ |
| Kuwait /kʊ'weɪt/ | Kuwaiti /kʊ'weɪti/ |
| Laos /'lɑːɒs, laʊs ‖ laʊs, 'leɪɑːs/ | Laotian /'laʊʃən/ |
| Latvia /'lætviə/ | Latvian /'lætviən/ |
| Lebanon /'lebənən/ | Lebanese /ˌlebə'niːz◂/ |
| Lesotho /lə'suːtuː ‖ -'soʊtoʊ/ | Sotho /'suːtuː ‖ 'soʊtoʊ/ *person: sing.* = Mosotho /mə'suːtuː ‖ -'soʊtoʊ/; *pl.* = Bosotho /bə'suːtuː ‖ -'soʊtoʊ/ |
| Liberia /laɪ'bɪəriə ‖ -'bɪr-/ | Liberian /laɪ'bɪəriən ‖ -'bɪr-/ |
| Libya /'lɪbiə/ | Libyan /'lɪbiən/ |
| Liechtenstein /'lɪktənstaɪn/ | Liechtenstein *person:* Liechtensteiner /'lɪktənstaɪnə ‖ -ər/ |
| Lithuania /ˌlɪθju'eɪniə ‖ -θu- | Lithuanian /ˌlɪθju'eɪniən◂ ‖ -θu-/ |
| Luxemburg /'lʌksəmbɜːg ‖ -bɜːrg/ | Luxemburg *person:* Luxemburger /'lʌksəmbɜːgə ‖ -bɜːrgər/ |
| Macedonia /ˌmæsɪ'dəʊniə ‖ -'doʊ-/ | Macedonian /ˌmæsə'dəʊniən◂ ‖ -'doʊ-/ |
| Madagascar /ˌmædə'gæskə ‖ -kər/ | Malagasy /ˌmælə'gæsi◂/ |
| Malawi /mə'lɑːwi/ | Malawian /mə'lɑːwiən/ |
| Malaysia /mə'leɪziə ‖ -ʒə, -ʃə/ | Malaysian /mə'leɪziən ‖ -ʒən, -ʃən/ |
| Maldives /'mɔːldiːvz ‖ 'mɒːl-/ | Maldivian /mɔːl'dɪviən ‖ mɒːl-/ |
| Mali /'mɑːli/ | Malian /'mɑːliən/ |
| Malta /'mɔːltə ‖ 'mɒːl-/ | Maltese /ˌmɔːl'tiːz◂ ‖ ˌmɒːl-/ |

| Name | Adjective |
|---|---|
| Marshall Islands /'mɑːʃəl ˌaɪləndz ‖ 'mɑːr-/ | Marshall Islander /ˌmɑːʃəl 'aɪləndə ‖ ˌmɑːrʃə 'aɪləndər/ |
| Mauritania /ˌmɒrɨ'teɪniə ‖ ˌmɔː-/ | Mauritanian /ˌmɒrɨ'teɪniən◂ ‖ ˌmɔː-/ |
| Mauritius /mə'rɪʃəs, mɔː-/ | Mauritian /mə'rɪʃən, mɔː-/ |
| Mediterranean /ˌmedɨtə'reɪniən◂/ | Mediterranean |
| Melanesia /ˌmelə'niːziə ‖ -ʒə, -ʃə/ | Melanesian /ˌmelə'niːziən◂ ‖ -ʒən◂, -ʃən◂/ |
| Mexico /'meksɪkəʊ ‖ -koʊ/ | Mexican /'meksɪkən/ |
| Micronesia /ˌmaɪkrəʊ'niːziə ‖ -kroʊ'niːʒə, -ʃə/ | Micronesian /ˌmaɪkrəʊ'niːziən, -ʒən ‖ -kroʊ'niːʒən, -ʃən/ |
| Moldova /mɒl'dəʊvə ‖ mɑː'ldoʊ-/ | Moldovian /mɒl'dəʊviən ‖ mɑːl'doʊ-/ |
| Monaco /'mɒnəkəʊ ‖ 'mɑːnəkoʊ/ | Monegasque /ˌmɒnɪ'gæsk◂ ‖ ˌmɑː-/ |
| Mongolia /mɒŋ'gəʊliə ‖ mɑːŋ'goʊ-/ | Mongolian /mɒŋ'gəʊliən ‖ mɑːŋ-'goʊ-/ *person:* Mongolian or Mongol /'mɒŋgɒl, -gəl ‖ 'mɑːŋgəl/ |
| Montserrat /ˌmɒntse'ræt ‖ ˌmɑː-/ | Montserratian /ˌmɒntse'reɪʃən◂ ‖ ˌmɑː-/ |
| Morocco /mə'rɒkəʊ ‖ -'rɑːkoʊ/ | Moroccan /mə'rɒkən ‖ -'rɑː-/ |
| Mozambique /ˌməʊzəm'biːk ‖ ˌmoʊ-/ | Mozambican /ˌməʊzəm'biːkən◂ ‖ ˌmoʊ-/ |
| Myanmar /'mjænmɑː ‖ 'mjɑːn-mɑːr/ | Burmese /ˌbɜː'miːz◂ ‖ ˌbɜːr-/ |
| Namibia /nə'mɪbiə/ | Namibian /nə'mɪbiən/ |
| Nauru /nɑː'uːruː, nɑː'ruː/ | Nauruan /nɑː'uːruən, nɑː'ruːən/ |
| Nepal /nɪ'pɔːl ‖ nə'pɒːl, -'pɑːl/ | Nepalese /ˌnepə'liːz◂/ |
| The Netherlands /ðə 'neðələndz ‖ -ðər-/ | Dutch /dʌtʃ/ *person: sing.* = Dutchman /'dʌtʃmən/ (*fem.* -woman) /ˌwʊmən/; *pl.* = Dutchmen /'dʌtʃmən/; *people:* Dutch |
| New Zealand /njuː 'ziːlənd ‖ nuː-/ | New Zealand, Maori /'maʊri/ *person:* New Zealander /njuː 'ziːləndə ‖ nuː 'ziːləndər/ |
| Nicaragua /ˌnɪkə'rægjuə ‖ -'rɑːgwə/ | Nicaraguan /ˌnɪkə'rægjuən◂ ‖ -'rɑːgwən◂/ |
| Niger /'naɪdʒə, niː'ʒeə ‖ 'niːʒər/ | Nigerien /niː'ʒeəriən ‖ -'ʒer-/ |
| Nigeria /naɪ'dʒɪəriə ‖ -'dʒɪr-/ | Nigerian /naɪ'dʒɪəriən ‖ -'dʒɪr-/ |
| Norway /'nɔːweɪ ‖ 'nɔːr-/ | Norwegian /nɔː'wiːdʒən ‖ nɔːr-/ |
| Oman /əʊ'mɑːn ‖ oʊ-/ | Omani /əʊ'mɑːni ‖ oʊ-/ |
| Pacific /pə'sɪfɪk/ | Pacific |
| Pakistan /ˌpɑːkɪ'stɑːn, ˌpækɪ'stæn/ | Pakistani /ˌpɑːkɪ'stɑːni◂, ˌpæk- ‖ -'stɑːni◂, -'stæni◂/ |
| Palestine /'pæləstaɪn/ | Palestinian /ˌpælə'stɪniən/ |
| Panama /ˌpænə'mɑː◂ ‖ 'pænə-mɑː/ | Panamanian /ˌpænə'meɪniən/ |
| Papua New Guinea /ˌpæpuə njuː 'gɪni ‖ ˌpæpjuə nuː-/ | Papuan /'pæpuən ‖ 'pæpjuən/ |
| Paraguay /'pærəgwaɪ/ | Paraguayan /ˌpærə'gwaɪən◂/ |
| Persia /'pɜːʃə, -ʒə ‖ 'pɜːrʒə/former name of Iran | |
| Peru /pə'ruː/ | Peruvian/pə'ruːviən/ |
| Philippines /'fɪlɨpiːnz ‖ ˌfɪlə'piːnz/ | Philippine /'fɪlɨpiːn ‖ ˌfɪlə'piːn/ *person:* Filipino /ˌfɪlɨ'piːnəʊ ‖ -noʊ/ |
| Poland /'pəʊlənd ‖ 'poʊ-/ | Polish /'pəʊlɪʃ ‖ 'poʊ-/ *person:* Pole /pəʊl ‖ poʊl/ |
| Polynesia /ˌpɒlɪ'niːziə ‖ ˌpɑːlə'niː-ʒə/ | Polynesian /ˌpɒlɪ'niːziən◂ ‖ ˌpɑːlə-'niːʒən◂/ |
| Portugal /'pɔːtʃʊgəl ‖ 'pɔːr-/ | Portuguese/ˌpɔːtʃʊ'giːz◂ ‖ ˌpɔːr-/ |
| Puerto Rico /ˌpwɜːtəʊ 'riːkəʊ ‖ ˌpɔːrtoʊ 'riːkoʊ/ | Puerto Rican /ˌpwɜːtəʊ 'riːkən ‖ ˌpɔːrtoʊ-/ |
| Qatar /kʌ'tɑː ‖ 'kɑːtər/ | Qatari /kʌ'tɑːri/ |
| Quebec /kwɪ'bek/ | Quebecois /ˌkebe'kwɑː/ |
| Romania /ruː'meɪniə ‖ roʊ-/ | Romanian /ruː'meɪniən ‖ roʊ-/ |
| Russia /'rʌʃə/ | Russian Federation, /ˌrʌʃən fedə'reɪʃən/ *person:* Russian /'rʌʃən/ |
| Rwanda /ru'ændə ‖ -'ɑːn-/ | Rwandan /ru'ændən ‖ -'ɑːn-/ |
| Saint Kitts & Nevis /sənt ˌkɪts ənd 'niːvɨs ‖ seɪnt-/ | Kittitian /kɨ'tɪʃən/ Nevisian /nɨ'vɪziən ‖ -ʒən/ |
| Saint Lucia /sənt 'luːʃə ‖ seɪnt-/ | Saint Lucian /sənt 'luːʃən ‖ seɪnt-/ |
| Samoa /sə'məʊə ‖ -'moʊə/ | Samoan /sə'məʊən ‖ -'moʊ-/ |
| San Marino /sæn mə'riːnəʊ ‖ -noʊ/ | Sanmarinese /ˌsænmærɨ'niːz/ |
| São Tomé & Principe /ˌsaʊn təˌmeɪ ənd 'prɪnsɨpeɪ ‖ -səpə/ | São Toméan /ˌsaʊn tə'meɪən/ |
| Saudi Arabia /ˌsaʊdi ə'reɪbiə/ | Saudi Arabian /ˌsaʊdi ə'reɪbiən/ *person:* Saudi or Saudi Arabian |
| Senegal /ˌsenɪ'gɔːl ‖ -'gɒːl/ | Senegalese /ˌsenɪgə'liːz◂/ |
| Seychelles /seɪ'ʃelz/ | Seychellois /ˌseɪʃel'wɑː◂/ |

| Name | Adjective |
|---|---|
| Sierre Leone /siˌerə liˈəʊn ‖ -ˈoʊn/ | Sierra Leonean /siˌerə liˈəʊniən ‖ -ˈoʊn-/ |
| Singapore /ˌsɪŋəˈpɔː ‖ ˈsɪŋəpɔːr/ | Singaporean /ˌsɪŋəˈpɔːriən◂/ |
| Slovak Republic /ˌsləʊvæk rɪˈpʌblɪk ‖ ˌsloʊvɑːk-/ | Slovak /ˈsləʊvæk ‖ ˈsloʊvɑːk/ |
| Slovenia /sləʊˈviːniə ‖ sloʊ-/ | Slovene /ˈsləʊviːn ‖ ˈsloʊ-/ *person:* Slovenian /sləʊˈviːniən ‖ sloʊ-/ |
| Solomon Islands /ˈsɒləmən ˌaɪləndz ‖ ˈsɑː-/ | Solomon Islander /ˌsɒləmən ˈaɪləndə ‖ ˌsɑːləmən ˈaɪləndər/ |
| Somalia /səʊˈmɑːliə ‖ soʊ-/ | Somali /səʊˈmɑːli ‖ soʊ-/ |
| South Africa /saʊθ ˈæfrɪkə/ | South African /saʊθ ˈæfrɪkən/ |
| Spain /speɪn/ | Spanish /ˈspænɪʃ/ *person:* Spaniard /ˈspænjəd ‖ -jərd/ |
| Sri Lanka/sriː ˈlæŋkə ‖ -ˈlɑːŋ-/ | Sri Lankan /sriː ˈlæŋkən ‖ -ˈlɑːŋ-/ |
| Sudan /suˈdæn, -ˈdɑːn/ | Sudanese /ˌsuːdəˈniːz◂/ |
| Surinam /ˌsʊərɪ̵ˈnæm ‖ ˌsʊrɪ̵ˈnɑːm/ | Surinamese /ˌsʊərɪ̵nəˈmiːz◂ ‖ ˌsʊr-/ *person:* Surinamer /ˌsʊərɪ̵ˈnɑːmə ‖ ˌsʊrɪ̵ˈnɑːmər/ |
| Swaziland /ˈswɑːzilænd/ | Swazi/ˈswɑːzi/ |
| Sweden /ˈswiːdn/ | Swedish /ˈswiːdɪʃ/ *person:* Swede /swiːd/ |
| Switzerland /ˈswɪtsələnd ‖ -sər-/ | Swiss /swɪs/ |
| Syria /ˈsɪriə/ | Syrian /ˈsɪriən/ |
| Tahiti /təˈhiːti/ | Tahitian /təˈhiːʃən/ |
| Taiwan /ˌtaɪˈwɑːn/ | Taiwanese /ˌtaɪwəˈniːz◂/ |
| Tajikistan /tɑːˌdʒiːkɪˈstɑːn/ | Tajik /tɑːˈdʒiːk ‖ -ˈdʒɪk, -ˈdʒiːk/ |
| Tanzania /ˌtænzəˈnɪə/ | Tanzanian /ˌtænzəˈnɪən◂/ |
| Thailand /ˈtaɪlænd, -lənd/ | Thai /taɪ/ |
| Tibet /tɪˈbet/ | Tibetan /tɪˈbetn/ |
| Timor, East /ˌiːst ˈtiːmɔː ‖ -mɔːr/ | Timorese /ˌtiːmɔːˈriːz◂/ |
| Togo /ˈtəʊgəʊ ‖ ˈtoʊgoʊ/ | Togolese /ˌtəʊgəˈliːz◂ ‖ ˌtoʊ-/ |
| Tonga /ˈtɒŋgə ‖ /ˈtɑːŋ-/ | Tongan /ˈtɒŋgən ‖ ˈtɑːŋ-/ |
| Trinidad & Tobago /ˌtrɪnɪdæd ən təˈbeɪgəʊ ‖ -goʊ/ | Trinidadian /ˌtrɪnɪ̵ˈdædiən◂/ Tobagonian/ˌtəʊbəˈgəʊniən ‖ ˌtoʊbəˈgoʊ-/ |
| Tunisia /tjʊˈnɪziə ‖ tuːˈniːʒə/ | Tunisian /tjuːˈnɪziən ‖ tuːˈniːʒən/ |
| Turkey /ˈtɜːki ‖ ˈtɜːr-/ | Turkish/ˈtɜːkɪʃ ‖ ˈtɜːr-/ *person:* Turk /tɜːk ‖ tɜːrk/ |
| Turkmenistan /ˌtɜːkmenɪ̵ˈstɑːn ‖ ˌtɜːrkmenɪ̵ˈstæn/ | Turkmen /ˈtɜːkmən ‖ ˈtɜːrk-/ |
| Uganda /juːˈgændə/ | Ugandan /juːˈgændən/ |
| Ukraine /juːˈkreɪn/ | Ukranian /juːˈkreɪniən/ |
| United Arab Emirates /juːˌnaɪtɪ̵d ˌærəb ˈemɪrɪ̵ts/ | Emirian /eˈmɪəriən ‖ eˈmɪr-/ |

| Name | Adjective |
|---|---|
| United Kingdom /juːˌnaɪtɪ̵d ˈkɪŋdəm/ of Great Britain /əv greɪt ˌbrɪtən/ and Northern Ireland / ənd ˌnɔːðən ˌaɪələnd ‖ -ˌnɔːrðərn ˈaɪrlənd/ | British /ˈbrɪtɪʃ/ *person:* Briton /ˈbrɪtən/, *AmE* Britisher /ˈbrɪtɪʃə ‖ -ər/ *people:* British |
| England / ˈɪŋglənd / | English /ˈɪŋglɪʃ/ *person: sing.*= Englishman /ˈɪŋglɪʃmən (*fem.* -woman) /ˌwʊmən/; *pl.* = Englishmen /ˈɪŋglɪʃmən/; *people:* English |
| Scotland /ˈskɒtlənd ‖ ˈskɑːt-/ | Scottish /ˈskɒtɪʃ ‖ ˈskɑː-/ or Scots /skɒts ‖ skɑːts/ *person: sing.* = Scot or Scotsman /ˈskɒtsmən ‖ ˈskɑː-/ (*fem.* -woman) /ˌwʊmən/; *pl.* = Scotsmen /ˈskɒtsmən ‖ ˈskɑː-/; *people:* Scots |
| Wales /weɪlz/ | Welsh /welʃ/ *person: sing.* = Welshman /ˈwelʃmən/ (*fem.* -woman) /ˌwʊmən/; *pl.* = Welshmen /ˈwelʃmən/; *people:* Welsh |
| United States /juːˌnaɪtɪ̵d ˈsteɪts/ | American /əˈmerɪ̵kən/ US, *person:* American /əˈmerɪ̵kən/ |
| Upper Volta /ˌʌpə ˈvɒltə ‖ ˌʌpər ˈvɑːl-/ former name of Burkina Faso | |
| Uruguay /ˈjʊərəgwaɪ ‖ ˈjʊr-/ | Uruguayan /ˌjʊərəˈgwaɪən◂ ‖ ˌjʊr-/ |
| Uzbekistan /ˌʊzbekɪ̵ˈstɑːn ‖ ʊzˌbekɪ̵ˈstæn/ | Uzbek /ˈʊzbek/ |
| Vanuatu /ˌvænuˈɑːtuː ‖ ˌvænwɑːˈtuː/ | Vanuatuan /ˌvænuˈɑːtuən ‖ ˌvænwɑːˈtuːən/ |
| Venezuela /ˌvenɪ̵ˈzweɪlə/ | Venezuelan /ˌvenɪ̵ˈzweɪlən◂/ |
| Vietnam /ˌvjetˈnæm ‖ -ˈnɑːm/ | Vietnamese /ˌvjetnəˈmiːz◂/ |
| West Samoa /ˌwest səˈməʊə ‖ -ˈmoʊə/ | Samoan /səˈməʊən ‖ -ˈmoʊ-/ |
| Yemen /ˈjemən/ | Yemeni /ˈjeməni/ |
| Yugoslavia /ˌjuːgəʊˈslɑːviə ‖ -goʊ-/ | Yugoslavia /ˌjuːgəʊˈslɑːviən◂ ‖ -goʊ-/ *person:* Yugoslav /ˈjuːgəʊslɑːv ‖ -goʊ-/ |
| Zaire /zaɪˈɪə ‖ zɑːˈɪr/ | Zairean /zaɪˈɪəriən ‖ zɑːˈɪr-/ |
| Zambia /ˈzæmbiə/ | Zambian /ˈzæmbiən/ |
| Zimbabwe /zɪmˈbɑːbweɪ/ | Zimbabwean /zɪmˈbɑːbweɪən/ |

# The Longman Defining Vocabulary

The Longman Defining Vocabulary of around 2000 common words has been used to write all the definitions in this dictionary. The words in the Defining Vocabulary have been carefully chosen to ensure that the definitions are clear and easy to understand, and that the words used in explanations are easier than the words being defined. Words in the Defining Vocabulary have been checked to make sure that they are frequent in the Longman Corpus Network, and that they are used correctly by learners in the Longman Learner's Corpus. Over 200 students took part in tests for this new dictionary, to check that they understood the definitions and could find the correct translation in their own language for words used.

We have also used a special computer program that checks every entry to make sure that words from outside the defining vocabulary have not been used.

The words listed below are the main forms which are used in definitions. However, there are other limits on which word forms and meanings may be used:

## Word meanings

The definitions only use the most common and 'central' meanings of the words in the list.

## Word classes

For some words in the list, a word class label such as *n* or *adj* is shown. This means that this particular word is used in definitions only in the word class shown. So **anger**, for example, is used only as a noun and not as a verb.

## Phrasal verbs

Phrasal verbs are not used in definitions, except for the ones included in the list. Other phrasal verbs which are common in English and could be formed from words in the defining vocabulary list (such as **put up with**) are not used.

## Prefixes and suffixes

Some words on the list may have prefixes (like **un-**) or suffixes (like **-ly**) added to them to make different word forms in the definition. The list of these affixes is included at the end of the Defining Vocabulary list. The forms which are common, or which change their meaning when a prefix or suffix is added, (such as **acceptable** and **agreement**) are included in the full list.

## Proper names

The Defining Vocabulary does not include the names of actual places, nationalities, religions, and so on, which are occasionally mentioned in definitions.

## Words not in the Defining Vocabulary

It is sometimes necessary or helpful to use a word that is not in the Defining Vocabulary. These are shown in SMALL CAPITAL LETTERS, and sometimes followed by an explanation in brackets.

**insider trading** /.....'.. / also **insider dealing** *n* [U] illegal buying and selling of a company's shares (SHARE[2] (5) involving the use of secret information known only by people connected with the company.

Sometimes a definition includes a word which has its own entry and definition very close by. This word is written in ordinary type, even if it is not in the defining vocabulary. For example:

**in·sin·u·a·tion** / ɪnˌsɪnjuˈeɪʃən/*n* **1** [C] something that someone insinuates: *the insinuation that they did not know how to run their own business* **2** [U] the act of insinuating something

The word **insinuate** is not in the special list of defining words, but its own definition is only one entry away, so it can be found very easily.

## Example sentences

The example sentences in this dictionary are not written using only the defining vocabulary. They are based on corpus evidence, and show the ways in which a word or phrase is used in a natural, typical context. However, care has been taken to make sure that these examples are helpful to the student. Where necessary, changes have been made to sentences foun on corpus, or new examples have been written, to show the uses found on corpus in a simpler form.

**A**

abbreviation
ability
able
about
above *adv, prep*
abroad
absence
absent *adj*
accept
acceptable
accident
accidental
according (to)
account *n*
achieve
achievement
acid
across
act
action
active
activity
actor, actress
actual
actually
add
addition
additional
address
adjective
admiration
admire
admit
adult
advanced
advantage
adventure *n*
adverb
advertise
advertisement
advice
advise
affair
affect
afford
afraid
after *adv, conj, prep*
afternoon
afterwards
again
against
age *n*
ago
agree
agreement
ahead
aim
air *n*
aircraft
airport
alcohol
alive
all *adv, pron, determiner, predeterminer*
allow
almost
alone
along
alphabet
already
also
although
always
among
amount *n*
amuse
amusement
amusing
an
ancient *adj*
and
anger *n*
angle *n*
angry
animal
announce
annoy
annoying
another
answer
anxiety
anxious
any
anyone
anything
anywhere
apart
apartment
appear
appearance
apple
approval
approve
area
argue
argument
arm *n*
army
around
arrange
arrangement
arrival
arrive
art
article
artificial
as
as opposed to
ashamed
ask
asleep
association
at
atom
attack
attempt
attend
attention
attitude
attract
attractive
authority
autumn
available
average *adj, n*
avoid
awake *adj*
away *adv*
awkward

**B**

baby
back *adj, adv, n*
background
backward(s) *adv*
bad
bag *n*
bake *v*
balance
ball *n*
band *n*
bank *n*
bar *n*
base *n, v*
basic
basket
bath *n*
battle *n*
be
beach *n*
beak
beam *n*
bean
bear
beat
beautiful
beauty
because
become
bed
beer
before
begin
beginning
behave
behaviour
behind *adv, prep*
belief
believe
bell
belong
below
belt *n*
bend
beneath
beside(s)
best
better *adj, adv*
between
beyond *adj, adv*
bicycle *n*
big *adj*
bill
bird
birth
bit
bite
bitter *adj*
black *adj, n*
blade
blame
blind *adj*
block
blood
blow
blue
board *n*
boat
body
boil
bomb
bone *n*
book *n*
boot *n*
border *n*
bored
boring
born
borrow
both
bottle *n*
bottom *n*
bowl *n*
box *n*
boy
brain *n*
branch *n*
brave *adj*
bread
break *v*
breakfast *n*
breast
breath
breathe
breed
brick
bridge *n*
bright
bring
broad *adj*
broadcast *v*
brother
brown *adj, n*
brush
build *v*
building
bullet
burn
burst *v*
bury
bus
bush
business
busy
but *conj*
butter *n*
button *n*
buy *v*
by *prep*

**C**

cake *n*
calculate
call *v*
calm *adj*
camera
camp *n, v*
can
cap
capital
car
card
care
careful
careless
carriage
carry
case *n*
castle
cat
catch *v*
cattle
cause
ceiling
celebrate
cell
central
centre *n*
century
ceremony
certain *adj, determiner*
chain *n*
chair *n*
chance *n*
change
character
charge
chase *v*
cheap
cheat *v*
check
cheek *n*
cheerful
cheese
chemical
chemistry
cheque
chest
chicken
chief
child
children
chin
chocolate
choice *n*
choose
church *n*
cigarette
cinema
circle *n*
circular *adj*
citizen
city
claim *v*
class *n*
clay
clean *adj, v*
clear *adj, v*
clever
cliff
climb *v*
clock *n*
close *adj, adv, v*
cloth
clothes
clothing
cloud *n*
club *n*
coal
coast *n*
coat *n*
coffee
coin *n*
cold *adj, n*
collar *n*
collect *v*
college
colour
comb
combination
combine *v*
come
comfort
comfortable
command
committee
common *adj*
communicate

communication
company
compare *v*
comparison
compete
competition
competitor
complain
complaint
complete
completely
complicated
compound *n*
computer
concern *v*
concerning
concert
condition *n*
confidence
confident
confuse
confusing
connect
connection
conscious
consider
consist
contain
container
continue
continuous
contract *n*
control
conversation
cook *n, v*
copy
corn
corner *n*
correct *adj, v*
cost
cotton
cough
could
council *n*
count *v*
country *n*
countryside
courage
course *n*
court *n*
cover
cow *n*
crack *n, v*
crash *n, v*
crazy
cream *n*
creature
crime
criminal
criticism
criticize
crop *n*
cross *n, v*
crowd
cruel
crush *v*
cry
cup *n*
cupboard
cure
curl
current *n*
curtain *n*
curve
custom *n*
customer
cut
cycle *v*

**D**

daily *adj, adv*
damage
dance
danger
dangerous
dark
date *n*
daughter
day
dead *adj*
deal *n*
deal with
death
debt
decay
deceive
decide
decision
decorate
decoration
decrease
deep *adj*
defeat
defence
defend
definite
definitely
degree
delay
deliberate *adj*
deliberately
delicate
deliver
demand
department
depend
dependent
depth
describe
description
desert *n*
deserve
design
desirable
desire
desk
destroy
destruction
detail *n*
determination
determined
develop
dictionary
die *v*
difference
different
difficult
difficulty
dig *v*
dinner
direct
direction
dirt
dirty *adj*
disappoint
disappointing
discover
discovery
discuss
discussion
disease *n*
dish *n*
dismiss
distance
distant
divide
do *v*
doctor *n*
document *n*
dog *n*
dollar
door
double *adj, v, predeterminer*
doubt
down *adv, prep*
draw *v*
drawer
dream
dress *n, v*
drink
drive *n, v*
drop
drug *n*
drum *n*
drunk *pastpart, adj*
dry
duck *n*
dull *adj*
during
dust *n*
duty

**E**

each
eager
ear
early
earn
earth *n*
east
eastern
easy *adj*
eat
economic
edge *n*
educate
educated
education
effect *n*
effective
effort
egg
eight
either
elbow
elect *v*
election
electric
electricity
electronic
else
embarrass
embarrassing
emotion
emphasize
employ *v*
employer
employment
empty *adj, v*
enclose
encourage
end
enemy
energy
engine
engineer *n*
enjoy
enjoyable
enjoyment
enough
enter
entertain
entertainment
entrance *n*
envelope
environment
equal *adj, n*
equipment
escape
especially
establish
even *adj, adv*
evening
event
ever
every
everyone
everything
everywhere
evil
exact *adj*
exactly
examination
examine
example
excellent
except *conj, prep*
exchange
excite
exciting
excuse
exercise
exist
existence
expect
expensive
experience
explain
explanation
explode
explosion
explosive
express *v*
expression
extreme *adj*
extremely
eye

**F**

face
fact
factory
fail *v*
failure
fair *adj*
fairly
faith
faithful *adj*
fall
false
familiar
family
famous
far
farm
farmer
fashion *n*
fashionable
fast *adj, adv*
fasten
fat
father *n*
fault *n*
favourable
favourite *adj*
fear *n*
feather *n*
feature *n*
feed *v*
feel *v*
feeling(s)
female
fence *n*
fever
few
field *n*
fifth
fight
figure *n*
fill *v*
film
final *adj*
finally
financial
find *v*
find out
fine *adj*
finger *n*
finish *v*
fire
firm *adj*
first *adj, determiner*
fish
fit *adj, v*
five
fix *v*
flag *n*
flame *n*
flash *n, v*
flat *adj*
flesh
flight
float *v*
flood
floor *n*
flour *n*
flow
flower *n*
fly *n, v*
fold
follow
fond
food
foot *n*
football
for *prep*
force
foreign
foreigner

forest *n*
forget
forgive
fork *n*
form
formal
former
fortunate
forward(s) *adv*
four(th)
frame *n*
free
freedom
freeze *v*
frequent *adj*
fresh
friend
friendly
frighten
frightening
from
front *adj*, *n*
fruit *n*
full *adj*
fun
funeral
funny
fur *n*
furniture
further *adj*, *adv*
future

**G**

gain *v*
game *n*
garage *n*
garden
gas *n*
gate
gather *v*
general *adj*
generally
generous
gentle
gentleman
get
gift
girl
give *v*
glad
glass *adj*, *n*
glue
go *v*
goat
god
gold
good
goodbye
goods
govern
government
graceful
gradual
grain
gram
grammar
grand *adj*
grandfather
grandmother
grandparent
grass *n*
grateful
grave *n*
great *adj*
green
greet
greeting
grey *adj*, *n*
ground *n*
group *n*
grow
growth
guard *v*
guess *v*
guest *n*
guide
guilty
gun *n*

**H**

habit
hair
half
hall
hammer *n*
hand *n*
handle
hang *v*
happen *v*
happy
hard
hardly
harm
harmful
hat
hate *v*
hatred
have
he
head *n*
health
healthy
hear
heart
heat
heaven
heavy *adj*
heel *n*
height
hello
help
helpful
her(s)
here
herself
hide *v*
high *adj*, *adv*
hill
him
himself
his
historical
history
hit
hold *v*
hole
holiday *n*
hollow *adj*
holy
home *adv*, *n*
honest
honour *n*
hook *n*
hope
hopeful
horn
horse *n*
hospital
hot *adj*
hotel
hour
house *n*
how *adv*
human
humorous
humour
hundred(th)
hungry
hunt *v*
hurry
hurt *v*
husband *n*

**I**

ice *n*
idea
if
ignore
ill *adj*
illegal
illness
image
imaginary
imagination
imagine
immediately
importance
important
impressive
improve
improvement
in *adv*, *prep*
include
including
income
increase
independent
indoor(s)
industrial
industry
infect
infection
infectious
influence *v*
inform
information
injure
injury
ink *n*
inner
insect
inside
instead
institution
instruction
instrument
insult *v*
insulting
insurance
insure
intelligence
intelligent
intend
intention
interest
interesting
international *adj*
interrupt
into
introduce
introduction
invent
invitation
invite *v*
involve
inwards
iron *adj*, *n*
island
it *pron*
its

**J**

jaw
jewel
jewellery
job
join
joint
joke
journey *n*
judge
judgement
juice
jump
just *adv*
justice

**K**

keen
keep *v*
key *n*
kick
kill *v*
kilo
kilogram
kilometre
kind
king
kiss
kitchen
knee *n*
kneel
knife *n*
knock *v*
knot
know *v*
knowledge

**L**

lack
lady
lake
lamb
lamp
land
language
large
last *adv*, *determiner*
late
lately
laugh
laughter
law
lawyer
lay *v*
layer *n*
lazy
lead *v*
leaf *n*
lean *v*
learn
least
leather
leave *v*
left
leg *n*
legal
lend
length *adv*, *pron*, *determiner*
less
lesson
let *v*
let go of
letter
level *adv*, *adj*, *n*
library
lid
lie
lie down
life
lift
light
like *prep*, *v*
likely
limit
line *n*
lion
lip
liquid
list *n*
listen *v*
literature
litre
little
live *v*
load
local *adj*
lock
lonely
long *adj*, *adv*
look
look
look after
look for
look sth up
loose *adj*
lord *n*
lose
loss
lot
loud
love
low *adj*
lower
loyal
loyalty
luck *n*
lucky
lung

**M**

machine *n*
machinery

magazine
magic
mail
main *adj*
make *v*
make into
make up *v*
male
man *n*
manage
manager
manner
many
map *n*
march *v*
mark
market *n*
marriage
married
marry
mass *n*
match
material *n*
mathematics
matter
may *v*
me
meal
mean *v*
meaning *n*
means
measure
measurement
meat
medical *adj*
medicine
meet *v*
meeting
melt
member
memory
mental
mention *v*
message
metal *n*
method
metre
middle
might *v*
mile
military *adj*
milk *n*
million(th)
mind
mine *n, pron*
mineral
minister *n*
minute *n*
mirror *n*
miss *v*
mist *n*
mistake *n*
mix *v*
mixture
model *n*
modern *adj*
moment
money
monkey *n*
month
moon *n*
moral *adj*
more
morning
most
mother *n*
motor *adj, n*
mountain
mouse
mouth *n*
move *v*
movement
much
mud
multiply
murder
muscle *n*
music
musician
must *v*
my
mysterious
mystery

## N

nail
name
narrow *adj*
nasty
nation
national *adj*
natural *adj*
nature
navy
near *adj, adv, prep*
nearly
neat
necessary
neck
need
needle *n*
negative *adj*
neither
nerve *n*
net *n*
network *n*
never
new
news
newspaper
next *adj, adv*
nice
night
nine
ninth
no *adv, determiner*
noise *n*
none *pron*
nonsense
no one
nor
normal
north
northern
nose *n*
not
note *n*
nothing
notice
noticeable
noun
now
nowhere
number *n*
nurse
nut

## O

obey
object *n*
obtain
occasion *n*
ocean
o'clock
of
off *adv, prep*
offence
offend
offensive *adj*
offer
office
officer
official
often
oil *n*
old
old-fashioned
on *adv, prep*
once *adv*
one
onion
only
only just
onto
open *adj, v*
operate
operation
opinion
opponent
opportunity
oppose
as opposed to
opposite
opposition
or
orange
order
ordinary
organ
organise
organization
origin
original
other
ought
our(s)
out *adj, adv*
outdoor(s)
outer
outside
over *adv, prep*
owe
own
owner
oxygen

## P

pack *v*
package
page *n*
pain *n*
painful
paint
painting
pair *n*
pale *adj*
pan *n*
paper *n*
parallel *adj, n*
parent
park
parliament
part *n*
participle
particular *adj*
partly
partner *n*
party *n*
pass *v*
passage
passenger
past
path
patient *adj*
pattern *n*
pause
pay
payment
peace
peaceful
pen *n*
pence
pencil *n*
people *n*
pepper *n*
per cent
perfect *adj*
perform
performance
perhaps
period *n*
permanent
permission
person
personal
persuade
pet *n*
petrol
photograph
phrase *n*
physical *adj*
piano *n*
pick *v*
pick up
picture *n*
piece *n*
pig *n*
pile *n*
pilot *n*
pin
pink *adj, n*
pipe *n*
pity
place
plain *adj, n*
plan
plane *n*
plant
plastic
plate *n*
play
pleasant
please
pleased
pleasure *n*
plenty *pron*
plural
pocket *n*
poem
poet
poetry
point
pointed
poison
poisonous
pole *n*
police *n*
polish *v*
polite
political
politician
politics
pool *n*
poor
popular
population
port *n*
position *n*
positive
possess
possession
possible *adj*
possibly
possibility
post
pot *n*
potato
pound *n*
pour
powder *n*
power *n*
powerful
practical
practice
practise
praise
pray
prayer
prefer
preparation
prepare
present *adj, n*
preserve *v*
president
press *v*
pressure *n*
pretend
pretty *adj*
prevent
previous
price *n*
priest
prince
principle
print
prison
prisoner
private *adj*
prize *n*
probably *adj*
problem
process *n*
produce *v*
product
production
profession
profit *n*
programme
progress *n*
promise

pronounce
pronunciation
proof *n*
proper
property
proposal
protect
protection
protective
protest
proud
prove
provide
public
pull
pump
punish
punishment
pupil
pure
purple
purpose *n*
push
put

**Q**
quality
quantity
quarrel
quarter *n*
queen *n*
question
quick *adj*
quiet *adj*, *n*
quite

**R**
rabbit *n*
race
radio *n*
railway
rain
raise *v*
range *n*
rank *n*
rapid *adj*
rare
rat *n*
rate *n*
rather
raw
reach *v*
react
reaction
read *v*
ready *adj*
real
realize
really
reason
reasonable
receive
recent
recently
recognize
record *n*, *v*
red
reduce
reduction
refusal
refuse *v*
regard *v*
regular *adj*
related
relative
relation
relationship
relax
relaxing
religion
religious
remain
remark *n*
remember
remind
remove *v*
rent
repair
repeat *v*
replace
reply
report
represent
representative *n*
request *n*
respect
responsible
rest
restaurant
restrict
result
return *n*, *v*
reward
rice
rich
rid
ride
right *adj*, *adv*, *n*
ring *n*
rise
risk
river
road
rob
rock *n*
roll *v*
romantic *adj*
roof *n*
room *n*
root *n*
rope *n*
rose
rough *adj*
round *adj*, *adv*, *prep*
row
royal *adj*
rub *v*
rubber
rude
ruin *v*
rule
ruler
run
rush *v*

**S**
sad
safe *adj*
safety
sail
sale
salt *n*
same
sand *n*
satisfaction
satisfactory
satisfy
save *v*
say *v*
scale *n*
scatter *v*
scene
school *n*
science
scientific
scientist
scissors
screen *n*
screw
sea
search
season *n*
seat
second *adv*, *n*, *determiner*
secret
secretary
see *v*
seed *n*
seem
sell *v*
send
sense *n*
sensible
sensitive
sentence *n*
separate *adv*, *v*
series
serious
servant
serve
service *n*
set *n*, *v*
settle *v*
seven(th)
several
severe
sex *n*
sexual
shade
shadow *n*
shake
shall
shame *n*
shape
share
sharp *adj*
she
sheep
sheet
shelf
shell *n*
shelter
shine *v*
shiny
ship *n*
shirt
shock *n*, *v*
shocking
shoe *n*
shoot *v*
shop
shore *n*
short *adj*
shot *n*
should
shoulder *n*
shout
show *n*, *v*
shut
shy
sick *adj*
side *n*
sideways
sight *n*
sign
signal
silence *n*
silent
silk
silly
silver
similar
simple
since
sincere *n*
sing
single *adj*
singular
sink *v*
sister
sit
situation
six(th)
size *n*
skilful
skill
skin *n*
skirt *n*
sky *n*
sleep
slide *v*
slight *adj*
slippery
slope
slow
small
smell
smile
smoke
smooth *adj*
snake *n*
snow
so
soap *n*
social *adj*
society
sock *n*
soft
soil *n*
soldier *n*
solid
solution
solve
some *pron*, *determiner*
somehow
someone
something
sometimes
somewhere
son
song
soon
sore *adj*
sorry
sort *n*
soul
sound *n*, *v*
soup
sour *adj*
south
southern
space *n*
speak
special *adj*
specific
speech
speed *n*
spell *v*
spend
spin *v*
spirit *n*
in spite of
split *v*
spoil *v*
spoon *n*
sport *n*
spot *n*
spread *v*
spring
square *adj*, *n*
stage *n*
stair
stamp
stand *v*
standard
star *n*
start
state
statement
station *n*
stay
steady *adj*
steal *v*
steam *n*
steel *n*
steep *adj*
stem *n*
step
stick
sticky
stiff *adj*
still *adj*, *adv*
sting
stitch
stomach *n*
stone *n*
stop
store
storm *n*
story
straight *adj*, *adv*
strange
stream *n*
street
strength
stretch *v*
strict
strike *v*
string *n*
strong
structure *n*
struggle
student
study
stupid
style *n*
subject *n*

substance
succeed
success
successful
such
suck *v*
sudden
suffer
sugar *n*
suggest
suit
suitable
sum *n*
summer
sun *n*
supply *n, v*
support *n, v*
suppose
sure *adj*
surface *n*
surprise
surprising
surround *v*
swallow *v*
swear
sweep *v*
sweet
swell *v*
swim
swing
sword
sympathetic
sympathy
system

**T**
table *n*
tail *n*
take *v*
talk
tall
taste
tax
taxi *n*
tea
teach
team *n*
tear
technical
telephone
television
tell
temper *n*
temperature
temporary
ten
tend
tendency
tennis
tense *n*
tent
terrible
test
than
thank
that *conj, pron, determiner*
the
theatre
their(s)
them
then *adv*
there
therefore
these
they
thick *adj*
thief
thin *adj*
thing
think *v*
third
this *pron, determiner*
thorough
those
though
thought
thousand(th)
thread *n*
threat
threaten
threatening
three
throat
through *adv, prep*
throw
thumb *n*
ticket *n*
tidy *adj, v*
tie
tight *adj*
time *n*
tired
tiring
title
to
tobacco
today
toe *n*
together
toilet
tomorrow
tongue
tonight
too
tool *n*
tooth
top *adj, n*
total *adj, n*
touch
tourist
towards
tower *n*
town
toy *n*
track *n*
trade *n*
traditional
traffic *n*
train
training
translate
transparent
trap
travel
treat *v*
treatment
tree
tribe
trick *n, v*
trip *n*
tropical
trouble
trousers
true *adj*
trust
truth
try *v*
tube
tune *n*
turn
twice
twist
two
type *n*
typical
tyre

**U**
ugly
under *prep*
understand
underwear
undo
unexpected
uniform *n*
union
unit
unite
universe
university
unless
until
unusual
up *adj, adv, prep*
upper
upright *adj, adv*
upset *v, adj*
upside down
upstairs *adj, adv*
urgent
us
use
useful
useless
usual

**V**
valley
valuable *adj*
value *n*
variety
various
vegetable
vehicle
verb
very *adv*
victory
view *n*
village
violence
violent
visit
voice *n*
vote
vowel

**W**
wages
waist
wait *v*
wake *v*
walk
wall *n*
want
war *n*
warm *adj, v*
warmth
warn
warning
wash
waste
watch
water
wave
way
we
weak
wealth
weapon
wear *v*
weather *n*
weave *v*
wedding
week
weekly *adj, adv*
weigh
weight *n*
welcome
well *adj, adv, n*
west
western *adj*
wet *adj*
what *predeterminer, determiner, pron*
whatever
wheat
wheel *n*
when *adv, conj*
whenever
where
whether
which
while *conj*
whip
whistle
white
who
whole
whose
why *adv, conj*
wide *adj, adv*
width
wife
wild *adj, adv*
will
willing
win *v*
wind
window
wine *n*
wing *n*
winter
wire *n*
wise *adj*
wish
with
within
without
woman
wood
wooden
wool
word *n*
work
world
worry
worse
worst
worth
would
wound
wrap *v*
wrist
write
wrong *adj, adv, n*

**Y**
year
yellow
yes
yet
you
young *adj*
your(s)

**Z**
zero

## Prefixes and suffixes that can be used with words in the Defining Vocabulary

-able
-al
-ance
-ation
dis-
-ed
-ence
-er
-ful
-ic
-ical
im-
in-
-ing
-ion
ir-
-ish
-ity
-ive
-ize
-less
-ly
-ment
-ness
non-
re-
self
-th
un-
-y